SCOTT

1999 Standard Postage Stamp Catalogue

ONE HUNDRED AND FIFTY-FIFTH EDITION IN SIX VOLUMES

VOLUME 5

COUNTRIES OF THE WORLD P-Sl

Released August 1998

Includes New Stamp Listings through the July, 1998 *Scott Stamp Monthly* Catalogue Update

Scott Publishing Co.

911 Vandemark Road, Sidney, OH 45365-0828

A division of AMOS PRESS, INC., publishers of *Linn's Stamp News, Coin World, Cars & Parts* magazine, *Moneycard Collector* and *The Sidney Daily News.*

Table of Contents

See Volume 1 for United States, United Nations and Countries of the World A-B.
See Volumes 2, 3, 4, 6 for Countries of the World C-O, So-Z.

Volume 2: C-F
Volume 3: G-I
Volume 4: J-O
Volume 6: So-Z

Scott Publishing Mission Statement

The Scott Publishing Team exists to serve the recreational, educational and commercial hobby needs of stamp collectors and dealers.

We strive to set the industry standard for philatelic information and products by developing and providing goods that help collectors identify, value, organize and present their collections.

Quality customer service is, and will continue to be, our highest priority. We aspire toward achieving total customer satisfaction.

Copyright Notice

Trademark Notice

ISBN 0-89487-244-3

Library of Congress Card No. 2-3301

Scott Publishing Co.

SCOTT 911 VANDEMARK ROAD, P. O. Box 828, SIDNEY, OHIO 45365-0828 937-498-0802

Dear Catalogue User,

Robust stamp buying activity continues with new levels of support arising from many quarters. Since the previous edition of this volume there has been increased competition at auctions, an ever-diminishing supply of good material coming to market and the emergence of a whole new world of philatelic commerce on the Internet.

More than 15,000 values have changed in Volume 5 of the *1999 Scott Standard Postage Stamp Catalogue*. Value changes appear across the board with many revisions in Russia, St. Pierre and Miquelon and Poland. This volume contains listings for countries of the world P-Slovenia.

As faithful readers of this letter page already know, I have the curious habit of asking myself questions. Here goes:

Does Russia rule value changes?

Russia is the czar of value changes with nearly 4,000 revisions. Scott 26-30, the 1875-79 Arms set on horizontally laid paper, jumps to $93 unused from the 1998 level of $76. Scott 39, the 3.50r Arms on vertically laid paper of 1884, zips to $475 unused and $400 used, from $425 unused and $300 used. Scott 739a, the unwatermarked version of the 1939 30k surcharge on the 4k farm worker stamp, flies to $100 hinged from $40. The 1948 Komsomol set, Scott 1289-1294, zips to $35 mint never hinged from $25. The 1951 Soviet-Czechoslovak Friendship set, Scott 1605-1609, shoots to $48 mint never hinged from $30.

What tune is Poland playing?

I'm not sure, but whatever it is, it certainly is upbeat (sorry to disappoint those who where waiting for a bad Polka joke).

Poland records many modest to strong increases. In the Cracow issues, Scott 58, the Austrian 25h stamp overprinted "Poczta Polska," rockets to $1,250 unused and $725 used, from $650 unused and used. The 1919 Gniezno provisionals, Scott 77-78, shoot to $375 unused and $260 used, from $275 unused and $210 used. In the Communist era issues the 1954 Return of Pomerania set, Scott 639-643, zooms to $10 mint never hinged from $3.

What about St. Pierre?

Most of the changes in St. Pierre & Miquelon are increases, with modest action in the classic issues, and robust jumps in recent issues. Scott 1, the 1885 05c on 40c, climbs to $75 unused and $32.50 used, from $60 unused and $30 used. The 1967 technological achievements set, Scott 374-376, rises to $20 mint never hinged from $14. The 1971 St. Pierre Museum set, Scott 415-416, zooms to $30 mint never hinged from $7.25.

What's not hot?

In Papua New Guinea, most of the changes are decreases, and some are down sharply. Scott 8, the 2sh6p high value of the 1901 Lakatoi set, slides to $525 unused from $575. The 1915 perf. 14 light red 1p Lakatoi, Scott 59 slips to $6 unused and $2 used, from $10 unused and $5.50 used. The 1958-60 definitives, Scott 139-146, drop to $70 mint never hinged from $82, and the 1962 South Pacific Conference set, Scott 167-169, drops to $7 mint never hinged from $12.

Anything else?

In Saudi Arabia, decreases which average about 10% are found throughout the country with the exception of issues of the past ten years.

What about editorial changes?

Stamps for the Palestinian Authority have been added for the first time. The August issue of the Scott Stamp Monthly contains two articles about these stamps.

In Poland, many values have been added for never-hinged stamps and sets found before the never-hinged breakpoint. These values can be found starting in postage with the 1924 Arms set, Scott 205-214, the 1925 semi-postals, Scott B15-B25, the 1925 Airmails, Scott C1-C9, the 1930 postage due, Scott J83, the 1933 Officials, Scott O17-O18, and the 1929-30 Polish offices abroad set, Scott 1K18-1K19. Also, the exile government issues and all Occupation stamps starting with those released in 1939 are now also valued in both unused and mint never-hinged condition.

Two new items have been added in Russia - Scott 35c, an example of the blue 7k of the 1883-88 series with a double impression of the frame and center, which is unvalued, and Scott 199b, a pelure paper variety of the 500r on 20r of 1922, valued at $5 unused and used.

Listings for se-tenant items have been added in Panama, Philippines, Romania, Russia, St. Vincent, Salvador and Senegal.

Saudi Arabia Scott 177 has been moved to the Postal Tax section as Scott RA4B. Renumbering also affects the 1992 and 1995 Palau airmails, the 1993-97 Philippines definitives, the 1963 Cosmonauts' Day issue of Russia, St. Lucia's 1985 Leaders of the World Locomotives set, St. Pierre & Miquelon's 1997-98 definitives, St. Thomas & Prince's 1991 Landmarks and Fauna sets, and the 1985 Leaders of the World Battleships set from Bequia in the St. Vincent Grenadines. Date varieties of the aforementioned Philippines set have been added to the footnote below the listings.

Anything big brewing for 1999?

Yes. IBRA 99, the international show to be held in Nuremberg, Germany from April 27 to May 4, 1999 promises to be a blockbuster. This is the first big international stamp show to be held in Germany since World War II. Attendance should be huge and the selection of material promises to be awe inspiring. Start making your travel plans now.

Are you still having your share of collecting fun?

If you've peaked in your specialty, have only the expensive stamps to buy in France, or if the mania surrounding gum condition is getting you down, maybe you need a new area to collect. Perhaps you're the type that just likes to dream. If so I would highly recommend the Scott Product Guide. There is no other wishbook like it in the hobby. The Product Guide is chockfull of collecting ideas and it is absolutely free. Just call 1-800-572-6885.

Happy collecting,

Stuart Morrissey

Stuart Morrissey/Publisher

Acknowledgments

Our appreciation and gratitude go to the following individuals who have assisted us in preparing information included in the 1999 Scott Catalogues. Some helpers prefer anonymity. These individuals have generously shared their stamp knowledge with others through the medium of the Scott Catalogue.

Those who follow provided information that is in addition to the hundreds of dealer price lists and advertisements and scores of auction catalogues and realizations which were used in producing the catalogue values. It is from those noted here that we have been able to obtain information on items not normally seen in published lists and advertisements. Support from these people goes beyond data leading to catalogue values, for they also are key to editorial changes.

A.R. Allison (Orange Free State Study Circle)
B. J. Ammel (The Nile Post)
Mike Armus
Robert Ausubel
Jack Hagop Barsoumian (International Stamp Co.)
Jules K. Beck
John Birkinbine II
John R. Boker, Jr.
Victor Bove
Jeff Brasor (Honduras Collectors Club, Associated Collectors of El Salvador)
George W. Brett
Roger S. Brody
Lawrence A. Bustillo
Nathan Carlin
Richard A. Champagne
Charlie Chesloe (Tribuna Stamp Co.)
Henry Chlanda
Laurie Conrad
Frank D. Correl
Andrew Cronin (Canadian Society of Russian Philately)
William T. Crowe
Bob Dumaine (Sam Houston Duck Company)
William S. Dunn
Leon Finik (Loral Stamps)
Henry Fisher
Geoffrey Flack
Joseph E. Foley (Eire Philatelic Association)
Marvin Frey
Huguette Gagnon (Ethiopian Philatelic Society)
Bob Genisol (Sultan Stamp Center)
Richard B. Graham
Gary Griffith
Harry Hagendorf
Calvet M. Hahn
Rudolf Hamar (Estonian Philatelic Society)
John B. Head
Robert R. Hegland
Erich E. Hamm (Philactica)
Dale S. Hendricks (Dale Enterprises, Inc.)
Clifford O. Herrick (Fidelity Trading Company)
Lee H. Hill, Jr.
Dr. Eugene H. Holmok (Tatra Stamps, Reg'd.)
Jack R. Hughes (Fellowship of Samoa Specialists)
Wilson Hulme (U.S. Philatelic Classics Society)
Eric Jackson
Peter C. Jeannopoulos
Clyde Jennings
Stanford M. Katz
Lewis Kaufman
Dr. James W. Kerr
Charles Kezbers
Ken Lawrence
Dr. Jay Levinson
Pedro Llach (Filatelia Llach S.L.)
David MacDonnell
F. Brian Marshall (Sarawak Specialists' Society)
Marilyn R. Mattke
Dr. Hector R. Mena (Society of Costa Rica Collectors)
Robert Meyersburg
Jack E. Molesworth (Jack E. Molesworth, Inc.)
William E. Mooz
Gary M. Morris (Pacific Midwest Co.)
Peter Mosiondz, Jr.
Bruce M. Moyer
Richard H. Muller (Richard's Stamps)
Victor Ostolaza
Souren V. Panirian
John E. Pearson (Pittwater Philatelic Service)
Otto Peetoom (Ormskirk Stamps)
Donald J. Peterson
Stanley Piller (Stanley M. Piller & Associates)
Stephen Radin (Albany Stamp Co.)
Siddique Mahmudur Rahman (Bangladesh Institute of Philatelic Studies)
Jon W. Rose
Frans H. A. Rummens (American Society for Netherlands Philately)
Richard H. Salz
Theodosios Sampson (Superior Stamp & Coin)
Jacques C. Schiff, Jr. (Jacques C. Schiff, Jr., Inc.)
Bernard Seckler (Fine Arts Philatelists)
F. Burton Sellers
Michael Shamilzadeh
Jeff Siddiqui (Pakistan Study Circle)
Richard Simchak
Sergio & Liane Sismondo (The Classic Collector)
Dr. Russell V. Skavaril (St. Helena, Ascension & Tristan da Cunha Philatelic Society)
Dr. Hubert C. Skinner
Roger D. Skinner
Jay Smith
Ekrem Spahich (Croatian Philatelic Society)
Richard Stambaugh
Glenn Tjia (Quality Philatelics)
Scott R. Trepel (Siegel Auction Galleries, Inc.)
Ming W. Tsang (Hong Kong Stamp Society)
Jerome S. Wagshal
Richard A. Washburn
Giana Wayman
Raymond H. Weill
Dr. Gary B. Weiss
Hans A. Westphal
John M. Wilson
Robert F. Yacano (K-Line Philippines)
Val Zabijaka

A special acknowledgment to Liane and Sergio Sismondo of The Classic Collector for their extraordinary assistance and knowledge sharing that has aided in the preparation of this year's Standard and Classic Specialized Catalogues.

Addresses, Telephone Numbers, Web Sites, E-Mail Addresses of General & Specialized Philatelic Societies

Collectors can contact the following groups for information about the philately of the areas within the scope of these societies, or inquire about membership in these groups. Aside from the general societies, we limit this list to groups that specialize in particular fields of philately, particular areas covered by the Scott Standard Postage Stamp Catalogue, and topical groups. Many more specialized philatelic societies exist than those listed below. These addresses were compiled in January 1998, and are, to the best of our knowledge, correct and current. Groups should inform the editors of address changes whenever they occur. The editors also want to hear from other such specialized groups not listed.

General "Umbrella" Societies

American Philatelic Society
PO Box 8000
State College PA 16803
Ph: (814) 237-3803
http://www.west.net/~stamps1/aps.html
E-mail: relamb@stamps.org

American Stamp Dealers' Association
Joseph Savarese
3 School St.
Glen Cove NY 11542
Ph: (516) 759-7000
http://www.amerstampdlrs.com
E-mail: asda@inx.net

International Society of Worldwide Stamp Collectors
Carol Cervenka
2502 Second St.
Caddo Mills TX 75135-9704
Ph: (903) 527-3957
http://www.frontiernet/~stamptmf/iswsc.html
E-mail: iswsc@webwide.net

Junior Philatelists of America
Ellie Chapman
PO Box 850
Boalsburg PA 16827-0850
http://www.jpastamps.org
E-mail: jpaellie@aol.com

Royal Philatelic Society
41 Devonshire Place
London, United Kingdom W1N 1PE

Royal Philatelic Society of Canada
PO Box 929, Station Q
Toronto, ON, Canada M4T 2P1
http://www.interlog.com/~rspc
E-mail: rpsc@interlog.com

Groups focusing on fields or aspects found in world-wide philately (some may cover U.S. area only)

American Air Mail Society
Stephen Reinhard
PO Box 110
Mineola NY 11501
http://ourworld.compuserve.com/homepages/aams/
E-mail: sr1501@aol.com

American First Day Cover Society
Douglas Kelsey
PO Box 65960
Tucson AZ 85728-5960
E-mail: afdcs@aol.com

American Revenue Association
Bruce Miller
Suite 332, 701 South First Ave.
Arcadia CA 91006

American Topical Association
Douglas Kelsey
PO Box 65749
Tucson AZ 85728
Ph: (520) 321-9292
E-mail: ataoffice@aol.com

Errors, Freaks and Oddities Collectors Club
Jim McDevitt
138 Lakemont Dr. East
Kingsland GA 31548
Ph: (912) 729-1573
E-mail: cwouscg@aol.com

National Duck Stamp Collectors Society
Anthony J. Monico
PO Box 43
Harleysville PA 19438-0043

No Value Identified Club
Albert Sauvanet
Le Clos Royal B, Boulevard des Pas Enchantes
St. Sebastien-sur Loire, France 44230
E-mail: alain.vailly@irin.univ_nantes.fr

The Perfins Club
Kurt Ottenheimer
462 West Walnut St.
Long Beach NY 11561

Post Mark Collectors Club
Larry Boing
2351 Grandview Road
Crest Hill IL 60435-1951

Postal History Society
Kalman V. Illyefalvi
8207 Daren Court
Pikesville MD 21208-2211
Ph: (410) 653-0665

Precancel Stamp Society
1750 Skippack Pk. #1603
Center Square PA 19422
Ph: (610) 279-6014

United Postal Stationery Society
Joann Thomas
PO Box 48
Redlands CA 92373
http://www.uh.edu/~lib19/upss.htm

Groups focusing on U.S. area philately as covered in the Standard Catalogue

Bureau Issues Association
David G. Lee
PO Box 2641
Reston VA 20195-0641

Canal Zone Study Group
Richard H. Salz
60 27th Ave.
San Francisco CA 94121

Carriers and Locals Society
Steven M. Roth
PO Box 57160
Washington DC 20036
Ph: (202) 293-6813
E-mail: smroth@wizard.net

Confederate Stamp Alliance
Richard L. Calhoun
PO Box 581
Mt. Prospect IL 60056-0581

Hawaiian Philatelic Society
Kay H. Hoke
PO Box 10115
Honolulu HI 96816-0115
Ph: (808) 521-5721
http://www.stampshows.com/hps.html

Plate Number Coil Collectors Club
Gene C. Trinks
3603 Bellows Court
Troy MI 48083
http://www.geocities.com/Heartland/Hills/6283
E-mail: gctrinks@tir.com

United Nations Philatelists
Alex Bereson
18 Portola Drive
San Francisco CA 94131-1518
E-mail: bereson@ix.netcom.com

U.S. Philatelic Classics Society
Mark D. Rogers
PO Box 80708
Austin TX 78708-0708
http://www.scruz.net/~eho/uspcs
E-mail: mdr3@swbell.net

U.S. Possessions Philatelic Society
David S. Durbin
1608 S. 22nd St.
Blue Springs MO 64015

Groups focusing on philately of foreign countries or regions

American Society of Polar Philatelists (Antarctic areas)
Richard Julian
1153 Fairview Dr.
York PA 17403
E-mail: rajulian@netrax.net

American Belgian Philatelic Society
Kenneth L. Costilow
621 Virginius Dr.
Virginia Beach VA 23452-4417
Ph: (757) 463-6081
E-mail: ken_costilow@prodigy.com

Bermuda Collectors Society
Thomas J. McMahon
364 Nash Road
North Salem NY 10560

Brazil Philatelic Association
Kurt Ottenheimer
462 West Walnut St.
Long Beach NY 11561

British Caribbean Philatelic Study Group
Gale J. Raymond
Bali-Hai, PO Box 228
Sugar Land TX 77478-0228

British North America Philatelic Society (Canada & Provinces)
Jerome C. Jarnick
108 Duncan Drive
Troy MI 48098
Ph: (248) 689-1966
http://www.compusmart.ab.ca/stalbert/bnaps.htm
E-mail: jarnick@compuserve.com

Burma Philatelic Study Circle
A. Meech
7208 91st Ave.
Edmonton, AB, Canada T6B 0R8
E-mail: alan.meech@ualberta.ca

China Stamp Society
Paul H. Gault
120 West 18th Ave.
Columbus OH 43210
http://www.azstarnet.com/~gersten/China.Stamp.Society.html
E-mail: gault.1@osu.edu

Colombia/Panama Philatelic Study Group
PO Box 2245
El Cajon CA 92021
E-mail: jimacross@juno.com

Society of Costa Rica Collectors
Dr. Hector R. Mena
PO Box 14831
Baton Rouge LA 70808
http://www.intersurf.com/~hrmena
E-mail: hrmena@intersurf.com

Croatian Philatelic Society (Croatia & other Balkan areas)
Ekrem Spahich
502 Romero, PO Box 696
Fritch TX 79036-0696
Ph: (806) 857-0129
http://www.hrnet.org/cps
E-mail: ou812@arn.net

Society for Czechoslovak Philately
Robert T. Cossaboom
PO Box 25332
Scott AFB IL 62225-0332
http://www.erols.com/sibpost
E-mail: klfck1@aol.com

Estonian Philatelic Society
Rudolf Hamar
1912 Nugget Drive
Felton CA 95018

Ethiopian Philatelic Society
Huguette Gagnon
PO Box 8110-45
Blaine WA 98231-8110
Ph: (604) 584-1701

Falkland Islands Philatelic Study Group
Carl J. Faulkner
Williams Inn, On-the-Green
Williamstown MA 01267-2620

France & Colonies Philatelic Society
Walter Parshall
103 Spruce St.
Bloomfield NJ 07003-3514

Germany Philatelic Society
PO Box 779
Arnold MD 21012-4779

Great Britain Collectors Club
Frank J. Koch
PO Box 309
Batavia OH 45103-0309
http://www.netxpress.com/users/winphins/gbcc/gbcc_hp.html
E-mail: koch.fj@pg.com

Hellenic Philatelic Society of America (Greece and related areas)
Dr. Nicholas Asimakopulos
541 Cedar Hill Ave.
Wyckoff NJ 07481
Ph: (201) 447-6262

International Society of Guatemala Collectors
Mrs. Mae Vignola
105 22nd Ave.
San Francisco CA 94121

Haiti Philatelic Society
Ubaldo Del Toro
5709 Marble Archway
Alexandria VA 22310

Honduras Collectors Club
Jeff Brasor
PO Box 173
Coconut Creek FL 33097

Hong Kong Stamp Society
Dr. An-Min Chung
120 Deerfield Rd.
Broomall PA 19008
Ph: (215) 576-6850

Hungary Philatelic Society
Thomas Phillips
PO Box 1162
Fairfield CT 06432-1162

India Study Circle
John Warren
PO Box 70775
Washington DC 20024
Ph: (202) 260-9464
E-mail: warren.john@epamail.epa.gov

Society of Indochina Philatelists
Paul Blake
1466 Hamilton Way
San Jose CA 95125

Iran Philatelic Study Circle
David J. Armacost
PO Box 33381
Phoenix AZ 85067

Eire Philatelic Association (Ireland)
Michael J. Conway
19 Pine Needle Drive
Shelton CT 06484
http://ourworld.compuserve.com/homepages/aranman/epa.htm
E-mail: brennan704@aol.com

Society of Israel Philatelists
Paul S. Aufrichtig
300 East 42nd St.
New York NY 10017

International Society for Japanese Philately
Kenneth Kamholz
PO Box 1283
Haddonfield NJ 08033
http://www.west.net/~lmevans/isjp.html
E-mail: kamholz@mosquito.com

Korea Stamp Society
William M. Collyer
PO Box 4158
Saticoy CA 93007-0158

Latin American Philatelic Society
Piet Steen
197 Pembina Ave.
Hinton, AB, Canada T7V 2B2

Cuyahoga Latvian Philatelist Club
Arturs Rubenis
1460 West Clifton Blvd.
Lakewood OH 44107-3309

Latvian Philatelic Society
J. Ronis
7 Lowes Ave.
Brampton, ON, Canada L6X 1R8

Liberian Philatelic Society
William Thomas Lockard
PO Box 267
Wellston OH 45692
Ph: (614) 384-2020

Liechtenstudy USA (Liechtenstein)
Ralph Schneider
PO Box 23049
Belleville IL 62223
Ph: (618) 277-8543
http://www.rschneiderstamps.com/info.html
E-mail: rschneider@aol.com

Lithuanian Philatelic Society
Fred Baumgartner
446 S. 6th Ave.
La Grange IL 60525
Ph: (708) 354-5909

Lithuanian Philatelic Society of New York
Vincent M. Alones
217 McKee St.
Floral Park NY 11001-1314

Mexico-Elmhurst Philatelic Society International
Juan Jose Cabuto-Vidrio
PO Box 435360
San Ysidro CA 92143-5360

Nepal & Tibet Philatelic Study Group
Roger D. Skinner
1020 Covington Road
Los Altos CA 94022-5003
Ph: (415) 968-4163

American Society of Netherlands Philately
Jan Enthoven
W6428 Riverview Drive
Onalaska WI 54650
Ph: (608) 781-8612
http://www.cs.cornell.edu/Info/People/aswin/NL/neth

Society of Australasian Specialists / Oceania
Henry Bateman
PO Box 4862
Monroe LA 71211
Ph: (800) 571-0293
E-mail: ck100@iamerica.net

Orange Free State Study Circle
J. R. Stroud
28 Oxford St.
Burnham-on-sea, Somerset,
United Kingdom TA8 1LQ

Pakistan Study Circle
Jeff Siddiqui
PO Box 7002
Lynnwood WA 98046
E-mail: jeffsiddiqui@msn.com

Papuan Philatelic Society
Steven Zirinsky
PO Box 49, Ansonia Station
New York NY 10023
Ph: (212) 665-0765
E-mail: szirinsky@compuserve.com

International Philippine Philatelic Society
Robert F. Yacano
PO Box 94
Eden NY 14057
Ph: (716) 992-9665

Pitcairn Islands Study Group
Nelson A. L. Weller
2940 Wesleyan Lane
Winston-Salem NC 27106
Ph: (910) 724-6398
E-mail: nalweller@juno.com

Plebiscite-Memel-Saar Study Group
Clay Wallace
100 Lark Court
Alamo CA 94507

Polonus Philatelic Society (Poland)
PO Box 458
Berwyn IL 60402

International Society for Portuguese Philately
Clyde Homen
1491 Bonnieview
Hollister CA 95023-5117
E-mail: cjh@hollinet.com

Rhodesian Study Circle
William R. Wallace
PO Box 16381
San Francisco CA 94116

Romanian Chapter of Croatian Philatelic Society
Dan Demetriade
PO Box 09700
Detroit MI 48209

Canadian Society of Russian Philately
Andrew Cronin
PO Box 5722, Station A
Toronto, ON, Canada M5W 1P2
Fax: (905) 764-8968

Rossica Society of Russian Philately
George G. Werbizky
409 Jones Rd.
Vestal NY 13850

Ryukyu Philatelic Specialist Society
Carmine J. DiVincenzo
PO Box 381
Clayton CA 94517-0381

St. Helena, Ascension & Tristan Da Cunha Philatelic Society
Dr. Russell V. Skavaril
222 East Torrance Road
Columbus OH 43214-3834
Ph: (614) 262-3046
http://ourworld.compuserve.com/homepages/st_helena_ascen_tdc

St. Pierre & Miquelon Study Group
David Salovey
PO Box 464
New York NY 10014-0464

Associated Collectors of El Salvador
Jeff Brasor
PO Box 173
Coconut Creek FL 33097

Fellowship of Samoa Specialists
Jack R. Hughes
1541 Wellington St.
Oakland CA 94602-1751

Sarawak Specialists' Society
Art Bunce
PO Box 2516
Escondido CA 92033

Arabian Philatelic Association (Saudi Arabia)
ARAMCO, Box 1929
Dhahran, Saudi Arabia 31311

Scandinavian Collectors Club
Donald B. Brent
PO Box 13196
El Cajon CA 92020
http://www.nb.net/~downs/scc/scc.htm
E-mail: dbrent47@sprynet.com

Slovakia Stamp Society
Jack Benchik
PO Box 555
Notre Dame IN 46556

Philatelic Society for Greater Southern Africa
William C. Brooks VI
PO Box 2698
San Bernardino CA 92406-2698

Spanish Philatelic Society
Robert H. Penn
3021 Valley View Dr.
Bangor PA 18013
Ph: (610) 588-5627

American Helvetia Philatelic Society (Switzerland, Liechtenstein)
Richard T. Hall
PO Box 666
Manhattan Beach CA 90267-0666
E-mail: rtavish@pacbell.net

Tannu Tuva Collectors Society
Ken Simon
513 Sixth Ave. So.
Lake Worth FL 33460-4507
Ph: (561) 588-5954
http://www.blarg.net/~brad/ttcs.htm
E-mail: p003115b@pb.seflin.org

Society for Thai Philately
H. R. Blakeney
PO Box 25644
Oklahoma City OK 73125

Tonga/Tin Can Mail Study Circle
Laurence L. Benson
1832 Jean Avenue
Tallahassee, FL 32308-5227
http://members.aol.com/tongajan/ttcmsc.html
E-mail: LLbenson@aol.com

Turkish and Ottoman Philatelic Society
Gary F. Paiste
4249 Berritt St.
Fairfax VA 22030

Ukrainian Philatelic & Numismatic Society
Bohdan O. Pauk
PO Box 11184
Chicago IL 60611-0184
Ph: (773) 276-0355

Yugoslavia Study Group
Michael Lenard
1514 North 3rd Ave.
Wausau WI 54401

Topical Groups

American Indian Philatelic Society
Charles Eson
128 Western Ave. Altamont NY 12009

Americana Unit
Dennis Dengel
17 Peckham Rd.
Poughkeepsie NY 12603-2018
http://www.philately.com/society_news/americana_unit.htm
E-mail: 70363.3621@compuserve.com

Astronomy Study Unit
George Young
PO Box 632
Tewksbury MA 01876-0632
Ph: (978) 851-8283
http://www.fandm.edu/departments/astronomy/miscell/astunit.html
E-mail: george-young@msn.com

Bicycle Stamp Club
Norman Batho
358 Iverson Place
East Windsor NJ 08520
Ph: (609) 448-9547
E-mail: normbatho@worldnet.att.net

Canadiana Study Unit
John Peebles
PO Box 3262, Station "A"
London, ON, Canada N6A 4K3
E-mail: john.peebles@odyssey.on.ca

Captain Cook Study Unit
Brian P. Sandford
173 Minuteman Dr.
Concord MA 01742-1923
http://freespace.virgin.net/chris.jones/index.htm
E-mail: borehami@wcg.co.uk

Casey Jones Railroad Unit
Oliver Atchison
PO Box 31631
San Francisco CA 94131-0631
Ph: (415) 648-8057
E-mail: casey_jones@gowebway.com

Cats on Stamps Study Unit
Mary Ann Brown
3006 Wade Rd.
Durham NC 27705

Chess on Stamps Study Unit
Anne Kasonic
7624 County Road #153
Interlaken NY 14847
http://www.iglobal.net/home/reott/stamps1.htm#cossu
E-mail: akasonic@epix.net

Christopher Columbus Philatelic Society
Donald R. Ager
PO Box 71
Hillsboro NH 03244
Ph: (603) 464-5379
E-mail: don_ager@conknet.com

Dogs on Stamps Study Unit
Morris Raskin
202A Newport Rd.
Cranbury NJ 08512
Ph: (609) 655-7411
E-mail: mraskin@worldnet.att.net

Earth's Physical Features Study Group
Fred Klein
515 Magdalena Ave.
Los Altos CA 94024
http://www.philately.com/society_news/earths_physical.htm

Embroidery, Stitchery, Textile Unit
Helen N. Cushman
1001 Genter St., Apt. 9H
La Jolla CA 92037
Ph: (619) 459-1194

Europa Study Unit
Hank Klos
PO Box 611
Bensenville IL 60106
E-mail: hank@bensenville.lib.il.us

Fine & Performing Arts
Ruth Richards
10393 Derby Dr.
Laurel MD 20723
E-mail: bersec@aol.com

Gay & Lesbian History Stamp Club
Joe Petronie
PO Box 515981
Dallas TX 75251-5981

Gems, Minerals & Jewelry Study Group
George Young
PO Box 632
Tewksbury MA 01876-0632
Ph: (978) 851-8283
http://www.rockhounds.com/rockshop/gmjsuapp.txt
E-mail: george-young@msn.com

Graphics Philately Association
Dulcie Apgar
PO Box 1513
Thousand Oaks CA 91358

Lighthouse Stamp Society
Dalene Thomas
8612 West Warren Lane
Lakewood CO 80227-2352
Ph: (303) 986-6620
http://www.nyx.net/~dathomas
E-mail: dathomas@nyx.net

Mask Study Unit
Carolyn Weber
PO Box 2542
Oxnard CA 93034
http://www.philately.com/society_news/masks.htm

Mathematical Study Unit
Estelle Buccino
5615 Glenwood Rd.
Bethesda MD 20817
Ph: (301) 718-8898

Medical Subjects Unit
Dr. Frederick C. Skvara
PO Box 6228
Bridgewater NJ 08807

Mesoamerican Archeology Study Unit
Chris Moser
PO Box 1442, Riverside CA 92502

Napoleonic Age Philatelists
Ken Berry
7513 Clayton Dr.
Oklahoma City OK 73132-5636
Ph: (405) 721-0044

Petroleum Philatelic Society International
Feitze Papa
922 Meander Dr.
Walnut Creek CA 94598-4239

Philatelic Music Circle
Cathleen Osborne
PO Box 1781
Sequim WA 98382

Rainbow Study Unit
Shirley Sutton
PO Box 37
Lone Pine, AB, Canada T0G 1M0
Ph: (304) 584-2268
E-mail: george-young@msn.com

Rotary on Stamps Unit
Donald Fiery
PO Box 333, Hanover PA 17331
Ph: (717) 632-8921

Scouts on Stamps Society International
Carl Schauer
PO Box 526
Belen NM 87002
Ph: (505) 864-0098

Ships on Stamps Unit
Robert Stuckert
2750 Highway 21 East
Paint Lick KY 40461
Ph: (606) 925-4901

Sports Philatelists International
Margaret Jones
5310 Lindenwood Ave.
St. Louis MO 63109-1758
http://www.concentric.net/~laimins/spi.html

Stamps on Stamps/Centenary Unit
William Critzer
13385 Country Way
Los Altos Hills CA 94022
Ph: (650) 941-1567
E-mail: willcrit@aol.com

Windmill Study Unit
Walter J. Hollien
PO Box 346
Long Valley NJ 07853-0346

Wine on Stamps Study Unit
James Crum
5132 Sepulveda
San Bernardino CA 92404-1134
Ph: (909) 886-3186

Women on Stamps Study Unit
Phebe Quattrucci
259 Middle Road
Falmouth ME 04105

Expertizing Services

The following organizations will, for a fee, provide expert opinions about stamps submitted to them. Collectors should contact these organizations to find out about their fees and requirements before submitting philatelic material to them. The listing of these groups here is not intended as an endorsement by Scott Publishing Co.

American Philatelic Expertizing Service
PO Box 8000
State College PA 16803

Philatelic Foundation
501 Fifth Ave., Rm. 1901
New York NY 10017

Professional Stamp Experts
1 Datran Center, Suite 1149
9100 South Dadeland Blvd.
Miami FL 33156

Confederate Stamp Alliance Authentication Service
522 Old State Road
Lincoln, DE 19960-9797

Ukrainian Philatelic & Numismatic Society Expertizing Service
30552 Dell Lane
Warren MI 48092-1862

Information on Catalogue Values, Grade and Condition

Catalogue Value

The Scott Catalogue value is a retail value; that is, an amount you could expect to pay for a stamp in the grade of Very Fine with no faults. Any exceptions to the grade valued will be noted in the text. The general introduction on the following pages and the individual section introductions further explain the type of material that is valued. The value listed for any given stamp is a reference that reflects recent actual dealer selling prices for that item.

Dealer retail price lists, public auction results, published prices in advertising and individual solicitation of retail prices from dealers, collectors and specialty organizations have been used in establishing the values found in this catalogue. Scott Publishing Co. values stamps, but Scott is not a company engaged in the business of buying and selling stamps as a dealer.

Use this catalogue as a guide for buying and selling. The actual price you pay for a stamp may be higher or lower than the catalogue value because of many different factors, including the amount of personal service a dealer offers, or increased or decreased interest in the country or topic represented by a stamp or set. An item may occasionally be offered at a lower price as a "loss leader," or as part of a special sale. You also may obtain an item inexpensively at public auction because of little interest at that time or as part of a large lot.

Stamps that are of a lesser grade than Very Fine, or those with condition problems, generally trade at lower prices than those given in this catalogue. Stamps of exceptional quality in both grade and condition often command higher prices than those listed.

Values for pre-1900 unused issues are for stamps with approximately half or more of their original gum. Stamps with most or all of their original gum may be expected to sell for more, and stamps with less than half of their original gum may be expected to sell for somewhat less than the values listed. On rarer stamps, it may be expected that the original gum will be somewhat more disturbed than it will be on more common issues. Post-1900 unused issues are assumed to have full original gum. From breakpoints in most countries' listings, stamps are valued as never hinged, due to the wide availability of stamps in that condition. These notations are prominently placed in the listings and in the country information preceding the listings. Some countries also feature listings with dual values for hinged and never-hinged stamps.

Grade

A stamp's grade and condition are crucial to its value. The accompanying illustrations show examples of Very Fine stamps from different time periods, along with examples of stamps in Fine to Very Fine and Extremely Fine grades as points of reference.

FINE stamps (illustrations not shown) have designs that are noticeably off center on two sides. Imperforate stamps may have small margins, and earlier issues may show the design touching one edge of the stamp design. For perforated stamps, perfs may barely clear the design on one side, and very early issues normally will have the perforations slightly cutting into the design. Used stamps may have heavier than usual cancellations.

FINE-VERY FINE stamps may be somewhat off center on one side, or slightly off center on two sides. Imperforate stamps will have two margins of at least normal size, and the design will not touch any edge. For perforated stamps, the perfs are well clear of the design, but are still noticeably off center. *However, early issues of a country may be printed in such a way that the design naturally is very close to the edges. In these cases, the perforations may cut into the design very slightly.* Used stamps will not have a cancellation that detracts from the design.

VERY FINE stamps may be slightly off center on one side, but the design will be well clear of the edge. The stamp will present a nice, balanced appearance. Imperforate stamps will have three normal-sized margins. *However, early issues of many countries may be printed in such a way that the perforations may touch the design on one or more sides. Where this is the case, a boxed note will be found defining the centering and margins of the stamps being valued.* Used stamps will have light or otherwise neat cancellations. This is the grade used to establish Scott Catalogue values.

EXTREMELY FINE stamps are close to being perfectly centered. Imperforate stamps will have even margins that are larger than normal. Even the earliest perforated issues will have perforations clear of the design on all sides.

Condition

Grade addresses only centering and (for used stamps) cancellation. *Condition* refers to factors other than grade that affect a stamp's desirability.

Factors that can increase the value of a stamp include exceptionally wide margins, particularly fresh color, the presence of selvage, and plate or die varieties. Unusual cancels on used stamps (particularly those of the 19th century) can greatly enhance their value as well.

Factors other than faults that decrease the value of a stamp include loss of original gum, regumming, a hinge remnant or foreign object adhering to the gum, natural inclusions, straight edges, and markings or notations applied by collectors or dealers.

Faults include missing pieces, tears, pin or other holes, surface scuffs, thin spots, creases, toning, short or pulled perforations, clipped perforations, oxidation or other forms of color changelings, soiling, stains, and such man-made changes as reperforations or the chemical removal or lightening of a cancellation.

Scott Publishing Co. recognizes that there is no formally enforced grading scheme for postage stamps, and that the final price you pay or obtain for a stamp will be determined by individual agreement at the time of transaction.

On the following two pages are illustrations of various stamps from countries appearing in this volume. These stamps are arranged by country, and they represent early or important issues that are often found in widely different grades in the marketplace. The editors believe the illustrations will prove useful in showing the margin size and centering that will be seen on the various issues.

In addition to the matters of margin size and centering, collectors are reminded that the very fine stamps valued in the Scott catalogues also will possess fresh color and intact perforations, and they will be free from defects.

Most examples shown are computer – manipulated images made from single digitized master illustrations.

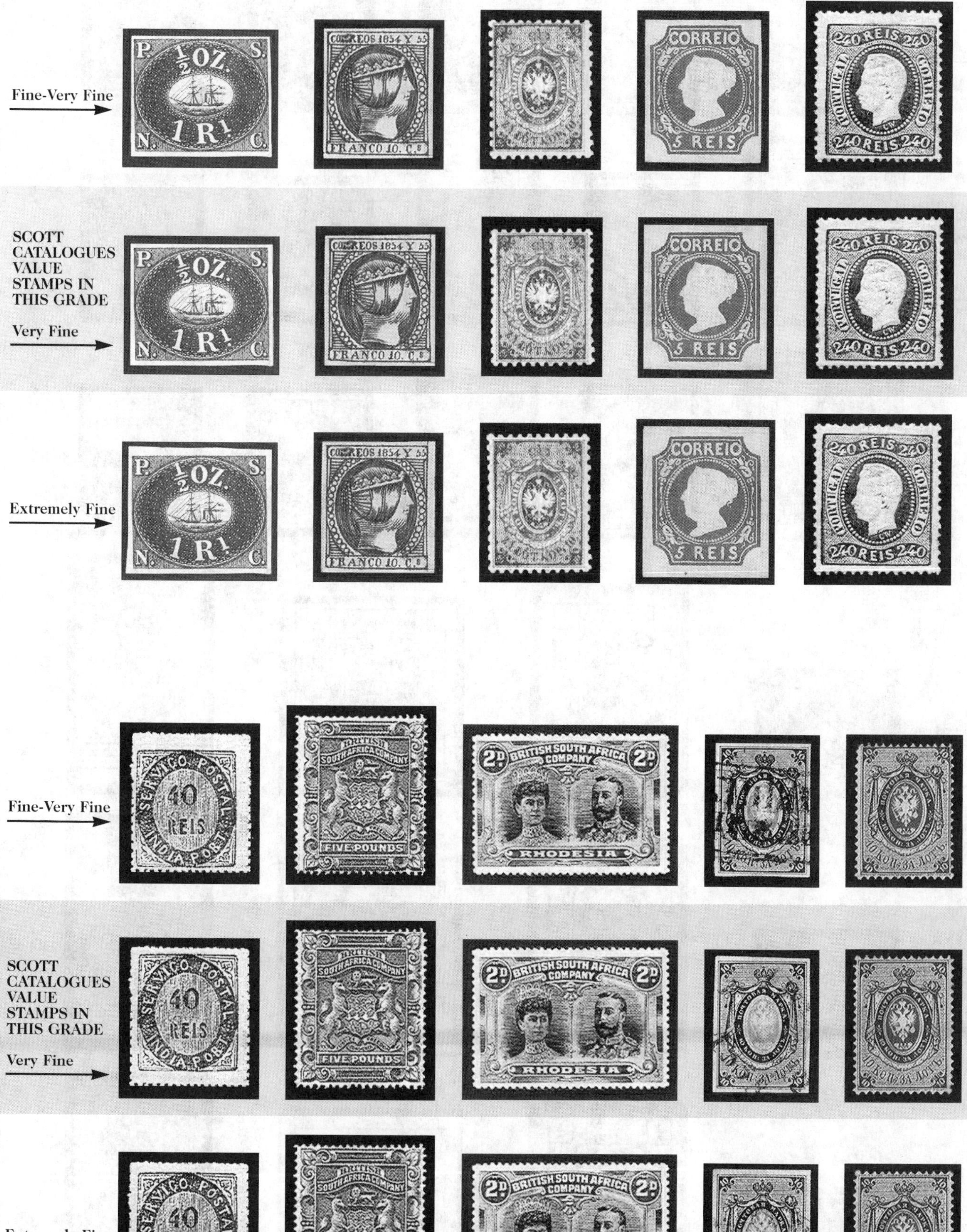
Fine-Very Fine
SCOTT CATALOGUES VALUE STAMPS IN THIS GRADE
Very Fine
Extremely Fine
Fine-Very Fine
SCOTT CATALOGUES VALUE STAMPS IN THIS GRADE
Very Fine
Extremely Fine

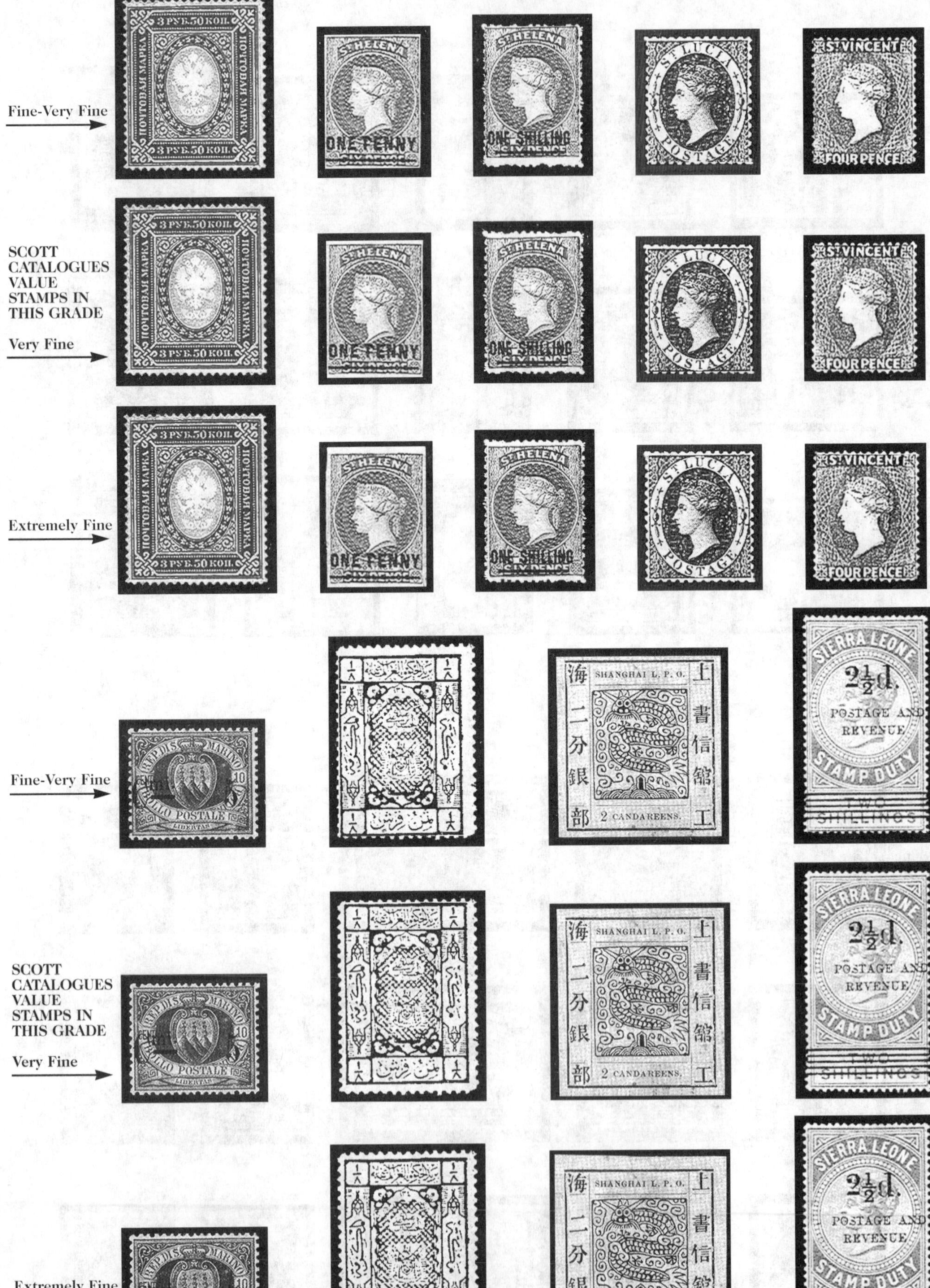
Fine-Very Fine
SCOTT CATALOGUES VALUE STAMPS IN THIS GRADE
Very Fine
Extremely Fine
Fine-Very Fine
SCOTT CATALOGUES VALUE STAMPS IN THIS GRADE
Very Fine
Extremely Fine

For purposes of helping to determine the gum condition and value of an unused stamp, Scott Publishing Co. presents the following chart which details different gum conditions and indicates how the conditions correlate with the Scott values for unused stamps. Used together, the Illustrated Grading Chart on the previous pages and this Illustrated Gum Chart should allow catalogue users to better understand the grade and gum condition of stamps valued in the Scott catalogues.

Gum Categories:	**MINT N.H.**	**ORIGINAL GUM (O.G.)**				**NO GUM**
	Mint Never Hinged *Free from any disturbance*	**Lightly Hinged** *Faint impression of a removed hinge over a small area*	**Hinge Mark or Remnant** *Prominent hinged spot with part or all of the hinge remaining*	**Large part o.g.** *Approximately half or more of the gum intact*	**Small part o.g.** *Approximately less than half of the gum intact*	**No gum** *Only if issued with gum*
Commonly Used Symbol:	★★	★	★	★	★	(★)
Pre-1900 Issues (Pre-1890 for U.S.)	*Very fine pre-1900 stamps in these categories trade at a premium over Scott value*			Scott Value for "Unused"		Scott "No Gum" listings for selected unused classic stamps
From 1900 to break-points for listings of never-hinged stamps	Scott "Never Hinged" listings for selected unused stamps	Scott Value for "Unused" (Actual value will be affected by the degree of hinging of the full o.g.)				
From breakpoints noted for many countries	Scott Value for "Unused"					

Never Hinged (NH; ★★): A never-hinged stamp will have full original gum that will have no hinge mark or disturbance. The presence of an expertizer's mark does not disqualify a stamp from this designation.

Original Gum (OG; ★): Pre-1900 stamps should have approximately half or more of their original gum. On rarer stamps, it may be expected that the original gum will be somewhat more disturbed that it will be on more common issues. Post-1900 stamps should have full original gum. Original gum will show some disturbance caused by a previous hinge(s) which may be present or entirely removed. The actual value of a post-1900 stamp will be affected by the degree of hinging of the full original gum.

Disturbed Original Gum: Gum showing noticeable effects of humidity, climate or hinging over more than half of the gum. The significance of gum disturbance in valuing a stamp in any of the Original Gum categories depends on the degree of disturbance, the rarity and normal gum condition of the issue and other variables affecting quality.

Regummed (RG; (★)): A regummed stamp is a stamp without gum that has had some type of gum privately applied at a time after it was issued. This normally is done to deceive collectors and/or dealers into thinking that the stamp has original gum and therefore has a higher value. A regummed stamp is considered the same as a stamp with none of its original gum for purposes of grading.

Catalogue Listing Policy

It is the intent of Scott Publishing Co. to list all postage stamps of the world in the *Scott Standard Postage Stamp Catalogue.* The only strict criteria for listing is that stamps be decreed legal for postage by the issuing country. Whether the primary intent of issuing a given stamp or set was for sale to postal patrons or to stamp collectors is not part of our listing criteria. Scott's role is to provide basic comprehensive postage stamp information. It is up to each stamp collector to choose which items to include in a collection.

It is Scott's objective to seek reasons why a stamp should be listed, rather than why it should not. Nevertheless, there are certain types of items that will not be listed. These include the following:

1. Unissued items that are not officially distributed or released by the issuing postal authority. Even if such a stamp is "accidentally" distributed to the philatelic or even postal market, it remains unissued. If such items are officially issued at a later date by the country, they will be listed. Unissued items consist of those that have been printed and then held from sale for reasons such as change in government, errors found on stamps or something deemed objectionable about a stamp subject or design.
2. Stamps "issued" by non-existent postal entities or fantasy countries, such as Nagaland, Occusi-Ambeno, Staffa, Sedang, Torres Straits and others.
3. Semi-official or unofficial items not required for postage. Examples include items issued by private agencies for their own express services. When such items are required for delivery, or are valid as prepayment of postage, they are listed.
4. Local stamps issued for local use only. Postage stamps issued by governments specifically for "domestic" use, such as Haiti Scott 219-228, or the United States non-denominated stamps, are not considered to be locals, since they are valid for postage throughout the country of origin.
5. Items not valid for postal use. For example, a few countries have issued souvenir sheets that are not valid for postage. This area also includes a number of worldwide charity labels (some denominated) that do not pay postage.
6. Intentional varieties, such as imperforate stamps that look like their perforated counterparts and are issued in very small quantities. These are often controlled issues intended for speculation.
7. Items distributed by the issuing government only to a limited group, such as a stamp club, philatelic exhibition or a single stamp dealer, and later brought to market at inflated prices. These items normally will be included in a footnote.

The fact that a stamp has been used successfully as postage, even on international mail, is not in itself sufficient proof that it was legitimately issued. Numerous examples of so-called stamps from non-existent countries are known to have been used to post letters that have successfully passed through the international mail system.

There are certain items that are subject to interpretation. When a stamp falls outside our specifications, it may be listed along with a cautionary footnote.

A number of factors are considered in our approach to analyzing how a stamp is listed. The following list of factors is presented to share with you, the catalogue user, the complexity of the listing process.

Additional printings — "Additional printings" of a previously issued stamp may range from an item that is totally different to cases where it is impossible to differentiate from the original. At least a minor number (a small-letter suffix) is assigned if there is a distinct change in stamp shade, noticeably redrawn design, or a significantly different perforation measurement. A major number (numeral or numeral and capital-letter combination) is assigned if the editors feel the "additional printing" is sufficiently different from the original that it constitutes a different issue.

Commemoratives — Where practical, commemoratives with the same theme are placed in a set. For example, the U.S. Civil War Centenniel set of 1961-65 and the Constitution Bicentennial series of 1989-90 appear as sets. Countries such as Japan and Korea issue such material on a regular basis, with an announced, or at least predictable, number of stamps known in advance. Occasionally, however, stamp sets that were released over a period of years have been separated. Appropriately placed footnotes will guide you to each set's continuation.

Definitive sets — Blocks of numbers generally have been reserved for definitive sets, based on previous experience with any given country. If a few more stamps were issued in a set than originally expected, they often have been inserted into the original set with a capital-letter suffix, such as U.S. Scott 1059A. If it appears that many more stamps than the originally allotted block will be released before the set is completed, a new block of numbers will be reserved, with the original one being closed off. In some cases, such as the British Machin Head series or the U.S. Transportation and Great Americans series, several blocks of numbers exist. Appropriately placed footnotes will guide you to each set's continuation.

New country — Membership in the Universal Postal Union is not a consideration for listing status or order of placement within the catalogue. The index will tell you in what volume or page number the listings begin.

"No release date" items — The amount of information available for any given stamp issue varies greatly from country to country and even from time to time. Extremely comprehensive information about new stamps is available from some countries well before the stamps are released. By contrast some countries do not provide information about stamps or release dates. Most countries, however, fall between these extremes. A country may provide denominations or subjects of stamps from upcoming issues that are not issued as planned. Sometimes, philatelic agencies, those private firms hired to represent countries, add these later-issued items to sets well after the formal release date. This time period can range from weeks to years. If these items were officially released by the country, they will be added to the appropriate spot in the set. In many cases, the specific release date of a stamp or set of stamps may never be known.

Overprints — The color of an overprint is always noted if it is other than black. Where more than one color of ink has been used on overprints of a single set, the color used is noted. Early overprint and surcharge illustrations were altered to prevent their use by forgers.

Se-tenants — Connected stamps of differing features (se-tenants) will be listed in the format most commonly collected. This includes pairs, blocks or larger multiples. Se-tenant units are not always symmetrical. An example is Australia Scott 508, which is a block of seven stamps. If the stamps are primarily collected as a unit, the major number may be assigned to the multiple, with minors going to each component stamp. In cases where continuous-design or other unit se-tenants will receive significant postal use, each stamp is given a major Scott number listing. This includes issues from the United States, Canada, Germany and Great Britain, for example.

Understanding the Listings

On the opposite page is an enlarged "typical" listing from this catalogue. Below are detailed explanations of each of the highlighted parts of the listing.

1 Scott number — Scott catalogue numbers are used to identify specific items when buying, selling or trading stamps. Each listed postage stamp from every country has a unique Scott catalogue number. Therefore, Germany Scott 99, for example, can only refer to a single stamp. Although the Scott catalogue usually lists stamps in chronological order by date of issue, there are exceptions. When a country has issued a set of stamps over a period of time, those stamps within the set are kept together without regard to date of issue. This follows the normal collecting approach of keeping stamps in their natural sets.

When a country issues a set of stamps over a period of time, a group of consecutive catalogue numbers is reserved for the stamps in that set, as issued. If that group of numbers proves to be too few, capital-letter suffixes, such as "A" or "B," may be added to existing numbers to create enough catalogue numbers to cover all items in the set. A capital-letter suffix indicates a major Scott catalogue number listing. Scott uses a suffix letter only once. Therefore, a catalogue number listing with a capital-letter prefix will not also be found with the same letter (lower case) used as a minor-letter listing. If there is a Scott 16A in a set, for example, there will not also be a Scott 16a.

Suffix letters are not cumulative. A minor variety of Scott 16A would be Scott 16b, not Scott 16Ab. Any exceptions, such as Great Britain Scott 358cp, are clearly indicated.

There are times when a reserved block of Scott catalogue numbers is too large for a set, leaving some numbers unused. Such gaps in the numbering sequence also occur when the catalogue editors move an item's listing elsewhere or have removed it entirely from the catalogue. Scott does not attempt to account for every possible number, but rather attempts to assure that each stamp is assigned its own number.

Scott numbers designating regular postage normally are only numerals. Scott numbers for other types of stamps, such as air post, semi-postal, postal tax, postage due, occupation and others have a prefix consisting of one or more capital letters or a combination of numerals and capital letters.

2 Illustration number — Illustration or design-type numbers are used to identify each catalogue illustration. For most sets, the lowest face-value stamp is shown. It then serves as an example of the basic design approach for other stamps not illustrated. Where more than one stamp use the same illustration number, but have differences in design, the design paragraph or the description line clearly indicates the design on each stamp not illustrated. Where there are both vertical and horizontal designs in a set, a single illustration may be used, with the exceptions noted in the design paragraph or description line.

When an illustration is followed by a lower-case letter in parentheses, such as "A2(b)," the trailing letter indicates which overprint or surcharge illustration applies.

Illustrations normally are 75 percent of the original size of the stamp. An effort has been made to note all illustrations not illustrated at that percentage. Virtually all souvenir sheet illustrations are reduced even more. Overprints and surcharges are shown at 100 percent of their original size, unless otherwise noted. In some cases, the illustration will be placed above the set, between listings or omitted completely. Overprint and surcharge illustrations are not placed in this catalogue for purposes of expertizing stamps.

3 Paper color — The color of a stamp's paper is noted in italic type when the paper used is not white.

4 Listing styles — There are two principal types of catalogue listings: major and minor.

Major listings are in a larger type style than minor listings. The catalogue number is a numeral that can be found with or without a capital-letter suffix, and with or without a prefix.

Minor listings are in a smaller type style and have a small-letter suffix or (if the listing immediately follows that of the major number) may show only the letter. These listings identify a variety of the major item. Examples include perforation, color, watermark or printing method differences, multiples (some souvenir sheets, booklet panes and se-tenant combinations), and singles of multiples.

Examples of major number listings include 16, 28A, B97, C13A, 10N5, and 10N6A. Examples of minor numbers are 16a and C13b.

5 Basic information about a stamp or set — Introducing each stamp issue is a small section (usually a line listing) of basic information about a stamp or set. This section normally includes the date of issue, method of printing, perforation, watermark and, sometimes, some additional information of note. *Printing method, perforation and watermark apply to the following sets until a change is noted.* Stamps created by overprinting or surcharging previous issues are assumed to have the same perforation, watermark and printing method as the original. Dates of issue are as precise as Scott is able to confirm and often reflect the dates on first-day covers, rather than the actual date of release.

6 Denomination — This normally refers to the face value of the stamp; that is, the cost of the unused stamp at the post office at the time of issue. When a denomination is shown in parentheses, it does not appear on the stamp. This includes the non-denominated stamps of the United States, Brazil and Great Britain, for example.

7 Color or other description — This area provides information to solidify identification of a stamp. In many recent cases, a description of the stamp design appears in this space, rather than a listing of colors.

8 Year of issue — In stamp sets that have been released in a period that spans more than a year, the number shown in parentheses is the year that stamp first appeared. Stamps without a date appeared during the first year of the issue. Dates are not always given for minor varieties.

9 Value unused and Value used — The Scott catalogue values are based on stamps that are in a grade of Very Fine unless stated otherwise. Unused values refer to items that have not seen postal, revenue or any other duty for which they were intended. Pre-1900 unused stamps that were issued with gum must have at least most of their original gum. Later issues are assumed to have full original gum. From breakpoints specified in most countries' listings, stamps are valued as never hinged. Stamps issued without gum are noted. Modern issues with PVA or other synthetic adhesives may appear ungummed. Self-adhesive stamps are valued as appearing undisturbed on their original backing paper. For a more detailed explanation of these values, please see the "Catalogue Value," "Condition" and "Understanding Valuing Notations" elsewhere in this introduction.

In some cases, where used stamps are more valuable than unused stamps, the value is for an example with a contemporaneous cancel, rather than a modern cancel or a smudge or other unclear marking. For those stamps that were released for postal and fiscal purposes, the used value represents a postally used stamp. Stamps with revenue cancels generally sell for less.

10 Changes in basic set information — Bold type is used to show any changes in the basic data given for a set of stamps. This includes perforation differences from one stamp to the next or a different paper, printing method or watermark.

11 Total value of a set — The total value of sets of three or more stamps issued after 1900 are shown. The set line also notes the range of Scott numbers and total number of stamps included in the grouping. *Set value* is the term used to indicate the value of a stamp set when its combined total is less than the sum of the individual stamps. This happens when some of the stamps in a set have the minimum catalogue value.

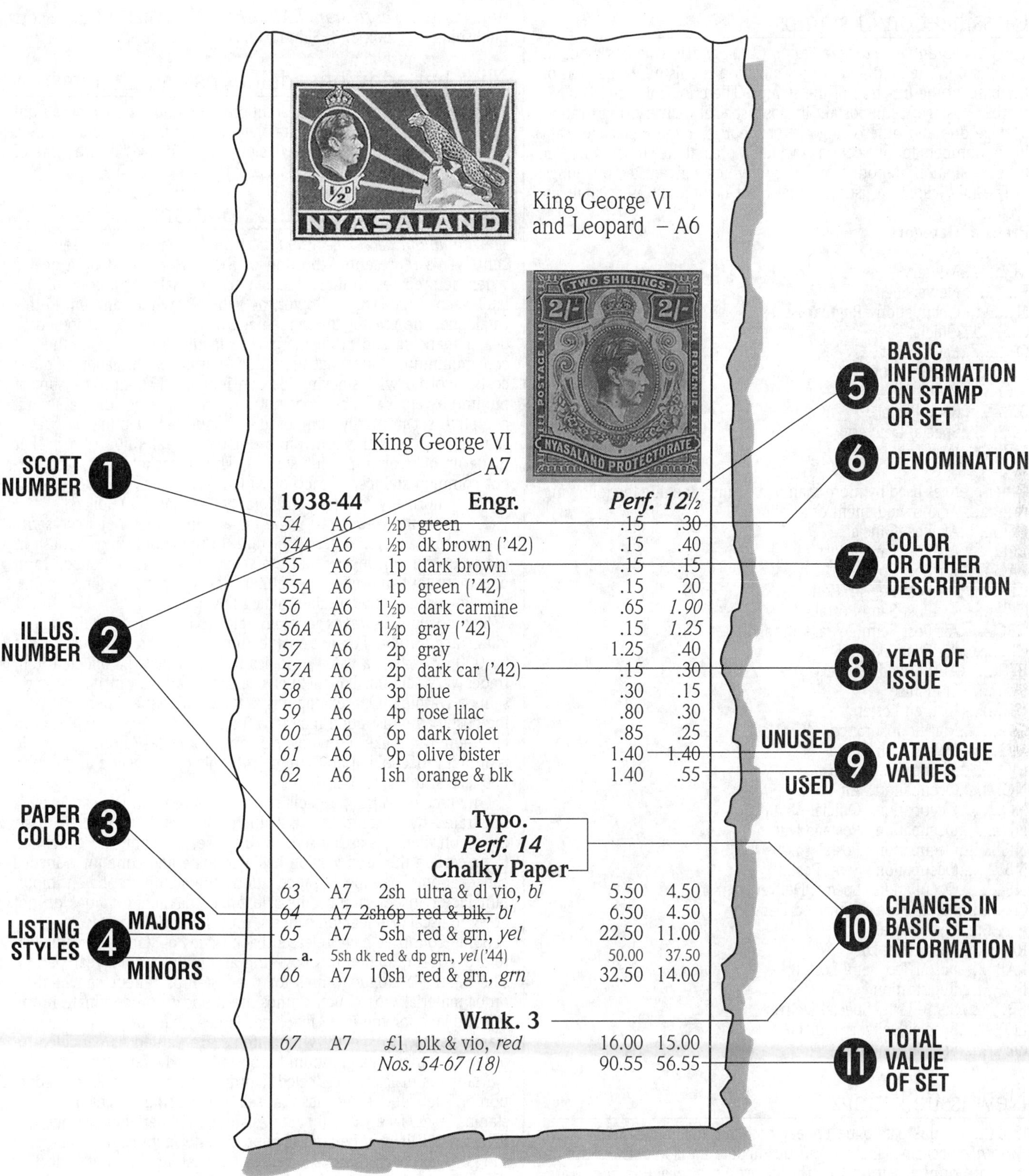
NYASALAND
King George VI and Leopard – A6
TWO SHILLINGS
2/-
POSTAGE
REVENUE
NYASALAND PROTECTORATE
King George VI A7
1938-44 Engr. Perf. 12½
54 A6 ½p green .15 .30
54A A6 ½p dk brown ('42) .15 .40
55 A6 1p dark brown .15 .15
55A A6 1p green ('42) .15 .20
56 A6 1½p dark carmine .65 1.90
56A A6 1½p gray ('42) .15 1.25
57 A6 2p gray 1.25 .40
57A A6 2p dark car ('42) .15 .30
58 A6 3p blue .30 .15
59 A6 4p rose lilac .80 .30
60 A6 6p dark violet .85 .25
61 A6 9p olive bister 1.40 1.40
62 A6 1sh orange & blk 1.40 .55
Typo.
Perf. 14
Chalky Paper
63 A7 2sh ultra & dl vio, bl 5.50 4.50
64 A7 2sh6p red & blk, bl 6.50 4.50
65 A7 5sh red & grn, yel 22.50 11.00
a. 5sh dk red & dp grn, yel ('44) 50.00 37.50
66 A7 10sh red & grn, grn 32.50 14.00
Wmk. 3
67 A7 £1 blk & vio, red 16.00 15.00
Nos. 54-67 (18) 90.55 56.55
1 SCOTT NUMBER
2 ILLUS. NUMBER
3 PAPER COLOR
4 LISTING STYLES
MAJORS
MINORS
5 BASIC INFORMATION ON STAMP OR SET
6 DENOMINATION
7 COLOR OR OTHER DESCRIPTION
8 YEAR OF ISSUE
UNUSED
USED
9 CATALOGUE VALUES
10 CHANGES IN BASIC SET INFORMATION
11 TOTAL VALUE OF SET

Special Notices

Classification of stamps

The *Scott Standard Postage Stamp Catalogue* lists stamps by country of issue. The next level of organization is a listing by section on the basis of the function of the stamps. The principal sections cover regular postage, semi-postal, air post, special delivery, registration, postage due and other categories. Except for regular postage, catalogue numbers for all sections include a prefix letter (or number-letter combination) denoting the class to which a given stamp belongs.

The following is a listing of the most commonly used catalogue prefixes.

Prefix....Category
C ....Air Post
M..........Military
P ....Newspaper
N ....Occupation - Regular Issues
O ....Official
Q ....Parcel Post
J............Postage Due
RA ....Postal Tax
B...........Semi-Postal
E...........Special Delivery
MR ....War Tax

Other prefixes used by more than one country include the following:
H ....Acknowledgment of Receipt
CO.........Air Post Official
CQ.........Air Post Parcel Post
RAC.......Air Post Postal Tax
CF.........Air Post Registration
CB ....Air Post Semi-Postal
CBO.......Air Post Semi-Postal Official
CE ....Air Post Special Delivery
EY.........Authorized Delivery
S ....Franchise
G ....Insured Letter
GY ....Marine Insurance
MC ....Military Air Post
MQ........Military Parcel Post
NC.........Occupation - Air Post
NO.........Occupation - Official
NJ ....Occupation - Postage Due
NRA.......Occupation - Postal Tax
NB ....Occupation - Semi-Postal
NE ....Occupation - Special Delivery
QY ....Parcel Post Authorized Delivery
AR ....Postal-fiscal
RAJ ....Postal Tax Due
RAB ....Postal Tax Semi-Postal
F ....Registration
EB..........Semi-Postal Special Delivery
EO ....Special Delivery Official
QE ....Special Handling

New issue listings

Updates to this catalogue appear each month in the *Scott Stamp Monthly* magazine. Included in this update are additions to the listings of countries found in the *Scott Standard Postage Stamp Catalogue* and the *Specialized Catalogue of United States Stamps*, as well as corrections and updates to current editions of this catalogue.

From time to time there will be changes in the final listings of stamps from the *Scott Stamp Monthly* to the next edition of the catalogue. This occurs as more information about certain stamps or sets becomes available.

The catalogue update section of the *Scott Stamp Monthly* is the most timely presentation of this material available. Annual subscriptions to the *Scott Stamp Monthly* are available from Scott Publishing Co., Box 828, Sidney, OH 45365-0828.

Number additions, deletions and changes

A listing of catalogue number additions, deletions and changes from the previous edition of the catalogue appears in each volume. See Catalogue Number Additions, Deletions & Changes in the table of contents for the location of this list.

Understanding valuing notations

The *minimum catalogue value* of an individual stamp or set is 15 cents. This represents a portion of the cost incurred by a dealer when he prepares an individual stamp for resale. As a point of philatelic-economic fact, the lower the value shown for an item in this catalogue, the greater the percentage of that value is attributed to dealer mark up and profit margin. In many cases, such as the 15-cent minimum value, that price does not cover the labor or other costs involved with stocking it as an individual stamp. The sum of minimum values in a set does not properly represent the value of a complete set primarily composed of a number of minimum-value stamps, nor does the sum represent the actual value of a packet made up of minimum-value stamps. Thus a packet of 1,000 different common stamps — each of which has a catalogue value of 15 cents — normally sells for considerably less than 150 dollars!

The *absence of a retail value* for a stamp does not necessarily suggest that a stamp is scarce or rare. In the U.S. listings, a dash in the value column means that the stamp is known in a stated form or variety, but information is either lacking or insufficient for purposes of establishing a usable catalogue value.

Stamp values in *italics* generally refer to items that are difficult to value accurately. For expensive items, such as those priced at $1,000 or higher, a value in italics indicates that the affected item trades very seldom. For inexpensive items, a value in italics represents a warning. One example is a "blocked" issue where the issuing postal administration may have controlled one stamp in a set in an attempt to make the whole set more valuable. Another example is an item that sold at an extreme multiple of face value in the marketplace at the time of its issue.

One type of warning to collectors that appears in the catalogue is illustrated by a stamp that is valued considerably higher in used condition than it is as unused. In this case, collectors are cautioned to be certain the used version has a genuine and contemporaneous cancellation. The type of cancellation on a stamp can be an important factor in determining its sale price. Catalogue values do not apply to fiscal or telegraph cancels, unless otherwise noted.

Some countries have released back issues of stamps in canceled-to-order form, sometimes covering as much as a 10-year period. The Scott Catalogue values for used stamps reflect canceled-to-order material when such stamps are found to predominate in the marketplace for the issue involved. Notes frequently appear in the stamp listings to specify which items are valued as canceled-to-order, or if there is a premium for postally used examples.

Many countries sell canceled-to-order stamps at a marked reduction of face value. Countries that sell or have sold canceled-to-order stamps at *full* face value include Australia, Netherlands, France and Switzerland. It may be almost impossible to identify such stamps if the gum has been removed, because official government canceling devices are used. Postally used copies of these items on cover, however, are usually worth more than the canceled-to-order stamps with original gum.

Abbreviations

Scott Publishing Co. uses a consistent set of abbreviations throughout this catalogue to conserve space, while still providing necessary information.

COLOR ABBREVIATIONS

amb.....amber
anil......aniline
ap........apple
aqua.....aquamarine
az........azure
bis........bister
bl.........blue
bld.......blood
blk.......black
bril.......brilliant
brn.......brown
brnsh...brownish
brnz.....bronze
brt.......bright
brnt.....burnt
car.......carmine
cer.......cerise
chlky....chalky
cham...chamois
chnt.....chestnut
choc.....chocolate
chr.......chrome
cit........citron
cl.........claret
cob......cobalt
cop......copper
crim.....crimson
cr.........cream
dk........dark
dl.........dull
dp........deep
db........drab
emer....emerald
gldn.....golden
grysh....grayish
grn.......green
grnsh...greenish
hel.......heliotrope
hn........henna
ind.......indigo
int........intense
lav.......lavender
lem......lemon
lil.........lilac
lt..........light
mag.....magenta
man.....manila
mar......maroon
mv.......mauve
multi....multicolored
mlky....milky
myr......myrtle
ol.........olive
olvn.....olivine
org.......orange
pck......peacock
pnksh...pinkish
Prus.....Prussian
pur.......purple
redsh...reddish
res.......reseda
ros.......rosine
ryl........royal
sal........salmon
saph.....sapphire
scar......scarlet
sep.......sepia
sien......sienna
sil........silver
sl.........slate
stl........steel
turq.....turquoise
ultra.....ultramarine
Ven......Venetian
ver.......vermilion
vio.......violet
yel.......yellow
yelsh....yellowish

When no color is given for an overprint or surcharge, black is the color used. Abbreviations for colors used for overprints and surcharges include: "(B)" or "(Blk)," black; "(Bl)," blue; "(R)," red; and "(G)," green.

Additional abbreviations in this catalogue are shown below:

Adm. ....Administration
AFL ....American Federation of Labor
Anniv. ....Anniversary
APS ....American Philatelic Society
Assoc. ....Association
ASSR. ....Autonomous Soviet Socialist Republic
b.......................Born
BEP ....Bureau of Engraving and Printing
Bicent. ....Bicentennial
Bklt...................Booklet
Brit. ....British
btwn..................Between
Bur. ....Bureau
c. or ca.............Circa
Cat. ....Catalogue
Cent. ....Centennial, century, centenary
CIO ....Congress of Industrial Organizations
Conf. ....Conference
Cong..................Congress
Cpl. ....Corporal
CTO ....Canceled to order
d.......................Died
Dbl. ....Double
EKU..................Earliest known use
Engr..................Engraved
Exhib................Exhibition
Expo.................Exposition
Fed. ....Federation
GB....................Great Britain
Gen. ....General
GPO ....General post office
Horiz. ....Horizontal
Imperf..............Imperforate
Impt. ....Imprint
Intl. ....International
Invtd.................Inverted
L........................Left
Lieut., lt. ....Lieutenant
Litho.................Lithographed
LL.....................Lower left
LR ....Lower right
mm...................Millimeter
Ms.....................Manuscript
Natl. ....National
No. ....Number
NY....................New York
NYC ....New York City
Ovpt. ....Overprint
Ovptd. ....Overprinted
P........................Plate number
Perf...................Perforated, perforation
Phil. ....Philatelic
Photo................Photogravure
PO ....Post office
Pr. ....Pair
P.R. ....Puerto Rico
Prec. ....Precancel, precanceled
Pres. ....President
PTT ....Post, Telephone and Telegraph
Rio....................Rio de Janeiro
Sgt. ....Sergeant
Soc. ....Society
Souv. ....Souvenir
SSR...................Soviet Socialist Republic, see ASSR
St.......................Saint, street
Surch. ....Surcharge
Typo. ....Typographed
UL ....Upper left
Unwmkd. ....Unwatermarked
UPU ....Universal Postal Union
UR....................Upper Right
US ....United States
USPOD.............United States Post Office Department
USSR ....Union of Soviet Socialist Republics
Vert. ....Vertical
VP ....Vice president
Wmk. ....Watermark
Wmkd. ....Watermarked
WWI ....World War I
WWII ....World War II

Examination

Scott Publishing Co. will not comment upon the genuineness, grade or condition of stamps, because of the time and responsibility involved. Rather, there are several expertizing groups that undertake this work for both collectors and dealers. Neither will Scott Publishing Co. appraise or identify philatelic material. The company cannot take responsibility for unsolicited stamps or covers sent by individuals.

How to order from your dealer

When ordering stamps from a dealer, it is not necessary to write the full description of a stamp as listed in this catalogue. All you need is the name of the country, the Scott catalogue number and whether the desired item is unused or used. For example, "Japan Scott 422 unused" is sufficient to identify the unused stamp of Japan listed as "422 A206 5y brown."

Basic Stamp Information

A stamp collector's knowledge of the combined elements that make a given stamp issue unique determines his or her ability to identify stamps. These elements include paper, watermark, method of separation, printing, design and gum. On the following pages each of these important areas is briefly described.

Paper

Paper is an organic material composed of a compacted weave of cellulose fibers and generally formed into sheets. Paper used to print stamps may be manufactured in sheets, or it may have been part of a large roll (called a web) before being cut to size. The fibers most often used to create paper on which stamps are printed include bark, wood, straw and certain grasses. In many cases, linen or cotton rags have been added for greater strength and durability. Grinding, bleaching, cooking and rinsing these raw fibers reduces them to a slushy pulp, referred to by paper makers as "stuff." Sizing and, sometimes, coloring matter is added to the pulp to make different types of finished paper.

After the stuff is prepared, it is poured onto sieve-like frames that allow the water to run off, while retaining the matted pulp. As fibers fall onto the screen and are held by gravity, they form a natural weave that will later hold the paper together. If the screen has metal bits that are formed into letters or images attached, it leaves slightly thinned areas on the paper. These are called watermarks.

When the stuff is almost dry, it is passed under pressure through smooth or engraved rollers - dandy rolls - or placed between cloth in a press to be flattened and dried.

Stamp paper falls broadly into two types: wove and laid. The nature of the surface of the frame onto which the pulp is first deposited causes the differences in appearance between the two. If the surface is smooth and even, the paper will be of fairly uniform texture throughout. This is known as *wove paper.* Early papermaking machines poured the pulp onto a continuously circulating web of felt, but modern machines feed the pulp onto a cloth-like screen made of closely interwoven fine wires. This paper, when held to a light, will show little dots or points very close together. The proper name for this is "wire wove," but the type is still considered wove. Any U.S. or British stamp printed after 1880 will serve as an example of wire wove paper.

Closely spaced parallel wires, with cross wires at wider intervals, make up the frames used for what is known as *laid paper.* A greater thickness of the pulp will settle between the wires. The paper, when held to a light, will show alternate light and dark lines. The spacing and the thickness of the lines may vary, but on any one sheet of paper they are all alike. See Russia Scott 31-38 for examples of laid paper.

Batonne, from the French word meaning "a staff," is a term used if the lines in the paper are spaced quite far apart, like the printed ruling on a writing tablet. Batonne paper may be either wove or laid. If laid, fine laid lines can be seen between the batons. The laid lines, which are a form of watermark, may be geometrical figures such as squares, diamonds, rectangles or wavy lines.

Quadrille is the term used when the lines in the paper form little squares. *Oblong quadrille* is the term used when rectangles, rather than squares, are formed. See Mexico-Guadalajara Scott 35-37 for examples of oblong quadrille paper.

Paper also is classified as thick or thin, hard or soft, and by color if dye is added during manufacture. Such colors may include yellowish, greenish, bluish and reddish.

Brief explanations of other types of paper used for printing stamps, as well as examples, follow.

Pelure — Pelure paper is a very thin, hard and often brittle paper that is sometimes bluish or grayish in appearance. See Serbia Scott 169-170.

Native — This is a term applied to handmade papers used to produce some of the early stamps of the Indian states. Stamps printed on native paper may be expected to display various natural inclusions that are normal and do not negatively affect value. Japanese paper, originally made of mulberry fibers and rice flour, is part of this group. See Japan Scott 1-18.

Manila — This type of paper is often used to make stamped envelopes and wrappers. It is a coarse-textured stock, usually smooth on one side and rough on the other. A variety of colors of manila paper exist, but the most common range is yellowish-brown.

Silk — Introduced by the British in 1847 as a safeguard against counterfeiting, silk paper contains bits of colored silk thread scattered throughout. The density of these fibers varies greatly and can include as few as one fiber per stamp or hundreds. U.S. revenue Scott R152 is a good example of an easy-to-identify silk paper stamp.

Silk-thread paper has uninterrupted threads of colored silk arranged so that one or more threads run through the stamp or postal stationery. See Great Britain Scott 5-6 and Switzerland Scott 14-19.

Granite — Filled with minute cloth or colored paper fibers of various colors and lengths, granite paper should not be confused with either type of silk paper. Austria Scott 172-175 and a number of Swiss stamps are examples of granite paper.

Chalky — A chalk-like substance coats the surface of chalky paper to discourage the cleaning and reuse of canceled stamps, as well as to provide a smoother, more acceptable printing surface. Because the designs of stamps printed on chalky paper are imprinted on what is often a water-soluble coating, any attempt to remove a cancellation will destroy the stamp. *Do not soak these stamps in any fluid.* To remove a stamp printed on chalky paper from an envelope, wet the paper from underneath the stamp until the gum dissolves enough to release the stamp from the paper. See St. Kitts-Nevis Scott 89-90 for examples of stamps printed on this type of chalky paper.

India — Another name for this paper, originally introduced from China about 1750, is "China Paper." It is a thin, opaque paper often used for plate and die proofs by many countries.

Double — In philately, the term double paper has two distinct meanings. The first is a two-ply paper, usually a combination of a thick and a thin sheet, joined during manufacture. This type was used experimentally as a means to discourage the reuse of stamps.

The design is printed on the thin paper. Any attempt to remove a cancellation would destroy the design. U.S. Scott 158 and other Banknote-era stamps exist on this form of double paper.

The second type of double paper occurs on a rotary press, when the end of one paper roll, or web, is affixed to the next roll to save time feeding the paper through the press. Stamp designs are printed over the joined paper and, if overlooked by inspectors, may get into post office stocks.

Goldbeater's Skin — This type of paper was used for the 1866 issue of Prussia, and was a tough, translucent paper. The design was printed in reverse on the back of the stamp, and the gum applied over the printing. It is impossible to remove stamps printed on this type of paper from the paper to which they are affixed without destroying the design.

Ribbed — Ribbed paper has an uneven, corrugated surface made by passing the paper through ridged rollers. This type exists on some copies of U.S. Scott 156-165.

Various other substances, or substrates, have been used for stamp manufacture, including wood, aluminum, copper, silver and gold foil, plastic, and silk and cotton fabrics.

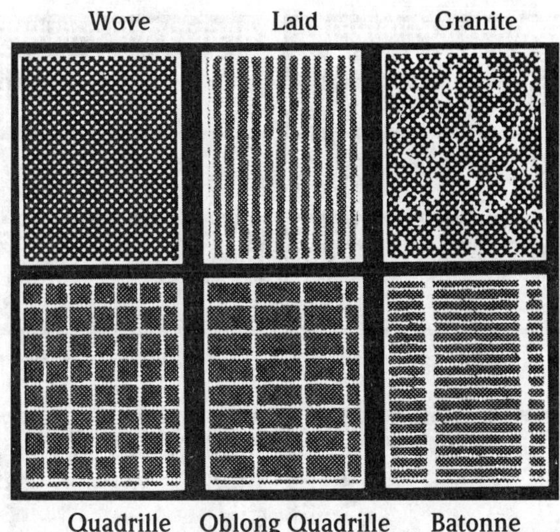

Watermarks

Watermarks are an integral part of some papers. They are formed in the process of paper manufacture. Watermarks consist of small designs, formed of wire or cut from metal and soldered to the surface of the mold or, sometimes, on the dandy roll. The designs may be in the form of crowns, stars, anchors, letters or other characters or symbols. These pieces of metal - known in the paper-making industry as "bits" - impress a design into the paper. The design sometimes may be seen by holding the stamp to the light. Some are more easily seen with a watermark detector. This important tool is a small black tray into which a stamp is placed face down and dampened with a fast-evaporating watermark detection fluid that brings up the watermark image in the form of dark lines against a lighter background. These dark lines are the thinner areas of the paper known as the watermark. Some watermarks are extremely difficult to locate, due to either a faint impression, watermark location or the color of the stamp. There also are electric watermark detectors that come with plastic filter disks of various colors. The disks neutralize the color of the stamp, permitting the watermark to be seen more easily.

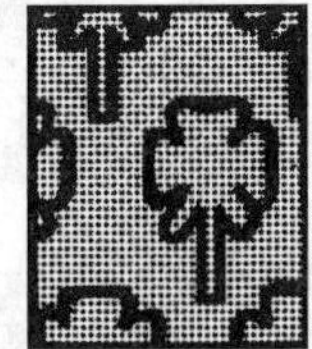

Multiple watermarks of Crown Agents and Burma

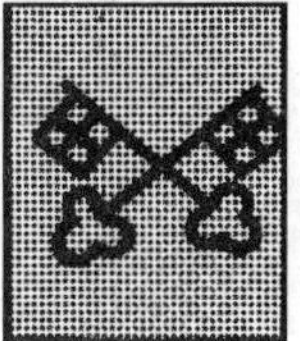

Watermarks of Uruguay, Vatican City and Jamaica

WARNING: Some inks used in the photogravure process dissolve in watermark fluids (Please see the section on Soluble Printing Inks). Also, see "chalky paper."

Watermarks may be found normal, reversed, inverted, reversed and inverted, sideways or diagonal, as seen from the back of the stamp. The relationship of watermark to stamp design depends on the position of the printing plates or how paper is fed through the press. On machine-made paper, watermarks normally are read from right to left. The design is repeated closely throughout the sheet in a "multiple-watermark design." In a "sheet watermark," the design appears only once on the sheet, but extends over many stamps. Individual stamps may carry only a small fraction or none of the watermark.

"Marginal watermarks" occur in the margins of sheets or panes of stamps. They occur on the outside border of paper (ostensibly outside the area where stamps are to be printed). A large row of letters may spell the name of the country or the manufacturer of the paper, or a border of lines may appear. Careless press feeding may cause parts of these letters and/or lines to show on stamps of the outer row of a pane.

Soluble Printing Inks

WARNING: Most stamp colors are permanent; that is, they are not seriously affected by short-term exposure to light or water. Many colors, especially of modern inks, fade from excessive exposure to light. There are stamps printed with inks that dissolve easily in water or in fluids used to detect watermarks. Use of these inks was intentional to prevent the removal of cancellations. Water affects all aniline inks, those on so-called safety paper and some photogravure printings - all such inks are known as *fugitive colors. Removal from paper of such stamps requires care and alternatives to traditional soaking.*

Separation

"Separation" is the general term used to describe methods used to separate stamps. The three standard forms currently in use are perforating, rouletting and die-cutting. These methods are done during the stamp production process, after printing. Sometimes these methods are done on-press or sometimes as a separate step. The earliest issues, such as the 1840 Penny Black of Great Britain (Scott 1), did not have any means provided for separation. It was expected the stamps would be cut apart with scissors or folded and torn. These are examples of imperforate stamps. Many stamps were first issued in imperforate formats and were later issued with perforations. Therefore, care must be observed in buying single imperforate stamps to be certain they were issued imperforate and are not perforated copies that have been altered by having the perforations trimmed away. Stamps issued imperforate usually are valued as singles. However, imperforate varieties of normally perforated stamps should be collected in pairs or larger pieces as indisputable evidence of their imperforate character.

PERFORATION

The chief style of separation of stamps, and the one that is in almost universal use today, is perforating. By this process, paper between the stamps is cut away in a line of holes, usually round, leaving little bridges of paper between the stamps to hold them together. Some types of perforation, such as hyphen-hole perfs, can be confused with roulettes, but a close visual inspection reveals that paper has been removed. The little perforation bridges, which project from the stamp when it is torn from the pane, are called the teeth of the perforation.

As the size of the perforation is sometimes the only way to differentiate between two otherwise identical stamps, it is necessary to be able to accurately measure and describe them. This is done with a perforation gauge, usually a ruler-like device that has dots or graduated lines to show how many perforations may be counted in the space of two centimeters. Two centimeters is the space universally adopted in which to measure perforations.

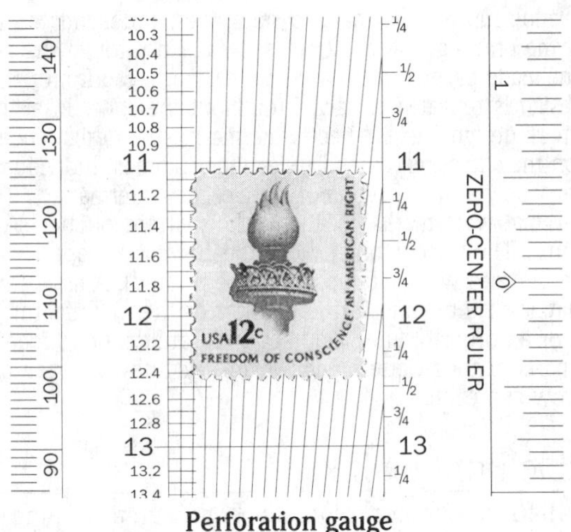

Perforation gauge

To measure a stamp, run it along the gauge until the dots on it fit exactly into the perforations of the stamp. If you are using a graduated-line perforation gauge, simply slide the stamp along the surface until the lines on the gauge perfectly project from the center of the bridges or holes. The number to the side of the line of dots or lines that fit the stamp's perforation is the measurement. For example, an "11" means that 11 perforations fit between two centimeters. The description of the stamp therefore is "perf. 11." If the gauge of the perforations on the top and bottom of a stamp differs from that on the sides, the result is what is known as *compound perforations.* In measuring compound perforations, the gauge at top and bottom is always given first, then the sides. Thus, a stamp that measures 11 at top and bottom and 10 1/2 at the sides is "perf. 11 x 10 1/2." See U.S. Scott 632-642 for examples of compound perforations.

Stamps also are known with perforations different on three or all four sides. Descriptions of such items are clockwise, beginning with the top of the stamp.

A perforation with small holes and teeth close together is a "fine perforation." One with large holes and teeth far apart is a "coarse perforation." Holes that are jagged, rather than clean-cut, are "rough perforations." *Blind perforations* are the slight impressions left by the perforating pins if they fail to puncture the paper. Multiples of stamps showing blind perforations may command a slight premium over normally perforated stamps.

The term *syncopated perfs* describes intentional irregularities in the perforations. The earliest form was used by the Netherlands from 1925-33, where holes were omitted to create distinctive patterns. Beginning in 1992, Great Britain has used an oval perforation to help prevent counterfeiting. Several other countries have started using the oval perfs.

A new type of perforation, still primarily used for postal stationery, is known as microperfs. Microperfs are tiny perforations (in some cases hundreds of holes per two centimeters) that allows items to be intentionally separated very easily, while not accidentally breaking apart as easily as standard perforations. These are not currently measured or differentiated by size, as are standard perforations.

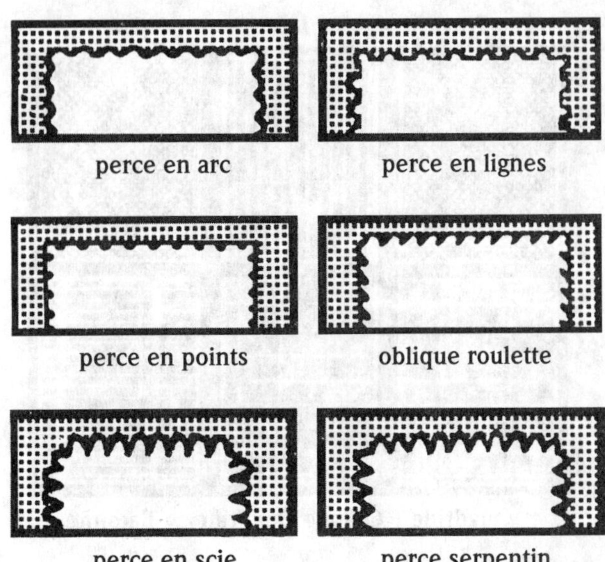
perce en arc — perce en lignes
perce en points — oblique roulette
perce en scie — perce serpentin

ROULETTING

In rouletting, the stamp paper is cut partly or wholly through, with no paper removed. In perforating, some paper is removed. Rouletting derives its name from the French roulette, a spur-like wheel. As the wheel is rolled over the paper, each point makes a small cut. The number of cuts made in a two-centimeter space determines the gauge of the roulette, just as the number of perforations in two centimeters determines the gauge of the perforation.

The shape and arrangement of the teeth on the wheels varies. Various roulette types generally carry French names:

Perce en lignes - rouletted in lines. The paper receives short, straight cuts in lines. This is the most common type of rouletting. See Mexico Scott 500.

Perce en points - pin-rouletted. This differs from a small perforation because no paper is removed, although round, equidistant holes are pricked through the paper. See Mexico Scott 242-256.

Perce en arc and *perce en scie* - pierced in an arc or saw-toothed designs, forming half circles or small triangles. See Hanover (German States) Scott 25-29.

Perce en serpentin - serpentine roulettes. The cuts form a serpentine or wavy line. See Brunswick (German States) Scott 13-18.

Once again, no paper is removed by these processes, leaving the stamps easily separated, but closely attached.

DIE-CUTTING

The third major form of stamp separation is die-cutting. This is a method where a die in the pattern of separation is created that later cuts the stamp paper in a stroke motion. Although some standard stamps bear die-cut perforations, this process is primarily used for self-adhesive postage stamps. Die-cutting can appear in straight lines, such as U.S. Scott 2522, shapes, such as U.S. Scott 1551, or imitating the appearance of perforations, such as New Zealand Scott 935A and 935B.

Printing Processes

ENGRAVING (Intaglio, Line-engraving, Etching)

Master die — The initial operation in the process of line engraving is making the master die. The die is a small, flat block of softened steel upon which the stamp design is recess engraved in reverse.

Master die

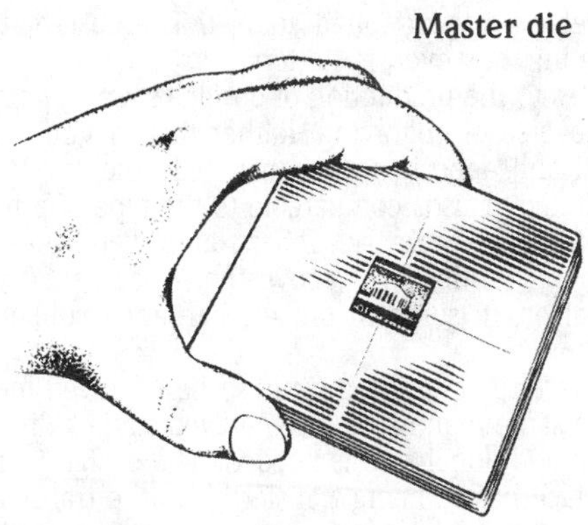

Photographic reduction of the original art is made to the appropriate size. It then serves as a tracing guide for the initial outline of the design. The engraver lightly traces the design on the steel with his graver, then slowly works the design until it is completed. At various points during the engraving process, the engraver hand-inks the die and makes an impression to check his progress. These are known as progressive die proofs. After completion of the engraving, the die is hardened to withstand the stress and pressures of later transfer operations.

Transfer roll

Transfer roll — Next is production of the transfer roll that, as the name implies, is the medium used to transfer the subject from the master die to the printing plate. A blank roll of soft steel, mounted on a mandrel, is placed under the bearers of the transfer press to allow it to roll freely on its axis. The hardened die is placed on the bed of the press and the face of the transfer roll is applied to the die, under pressure. The bed or the roll is then rocked back and forth under increasing pressure, until the soft steel of the roll is forced into every engraved line of the die. The resulting impression on the roll is known as a "relief" or a "relief transfer." The engraved image is now positive in appearance and stands out from the steel. After the required number of reliefs are "rocked in," the soft steel transfer roll is hardened.

Different flaws may occur during the relief process. A defective relief may occur during the rocking in process because of a minute piece of foreign material lodging on the die, or some other cause. Imperfections in the steel of the transfer roll may result in a breaking away of parts of the design. This is known as a relief break, which will show up on finished stamps as small, unprinted areas. If a damaged relief remains in use, it will transfer a repeating defect to the plate. Deliberate alterations of reliefs sometimes occur. "Altered reliefs" designate these changed conditions.

Plate — The final step in pre-printing production is the making of the printing plate. A flat piece of soft steel replaces the die on the bed of the transfer press. One of the reliefs on the transfer roll is positioned over this soft steel. Position, or layout, dots determine the correct position on the plate. The dots have been lightly marked on the plate in advance. After the correct position of the relief is determined, the design is rocked in by following the same method used in making the transfer roll. The difference is that this time the image is being transferred from the transfer roll, rather than to it. Once the design is entered on the plate, it appears in reverse and is recessed. There are as many transfers entered on the plate as there are subjects printed on the sheet of stamps. It is during this process that double and shifted transfers occur, as well as re-entries. These are the result of improperly entered images that have not been properly burnished out prior to rocking in a new image.

Modern siderography processes, such as those used by the U.S. Bureau of Engraving and Printing, involve an automated form of rocking designs in on preformed cylindrical printing sleeves. The same process also allows for easier removal and re-entry of worn images right on the sleeve.

Transferring the design to the plate

Following the entering of the required transfers on the plate, the position dots, layout dots and lines, scratches and other markings generally are burnished out. Added at this time by the siderographer are any required *guide lines, plate numbers* or other *marginal markings.* The plate is then hand-inked and a proof impression is taken. This is known as a plate proof. If the impression is approved, the plate is machined for fitting onto the press, is hardened and sent to the plate vault ready for use.

On press, the plate is inked and the surface is automatically wiped clean, leaving ink only in the recessed lines. Paper is then forced under pressure into the engraved recessed lines, thereby receiving the ink. Thus, the ink lines on engraved stamps are slightly raised, and slight depressions (debossing) occur on the back of the stamp. Prior to the advent of modern high-speed presses and more advanced ink formulations, paper had to be dampened before receiving the ink. This sometimes led to uneven shrinkage by the time the stamps were perforated, resulting in improperly perforated stamps, or misperfs. Newer presses use drier paper, thus both *wet* and *dry printings* exist on some stamps.

Rotary Press — Until 1914, only flat plates were used to print engraved stamps. Rotary press printing was introduced in 1914, and slowly spread. Some countries still use flat-plate printing.

After approval of the plate proof, older *rotary press plates* require additional machining. They are curved to fit the press cylinder. "Gripper slots" are cut into the back of each plate to receive the "grippers," which hold the plate securely on the press. The plate is then hardened. Stamps printed from these bent rotary press plates are longer or wider than the same stamps printed from flat-plate presses. The stretching of the plate during the curving process is what causes this distortion.

Re-entry — To execute a re-entry on a flat plate, the transfer roll is re-applied to the plate, often at some time after its first use on the press. Worn-out designs can be resharpened by carefully burnishing out the original image and re-entering it from the transfer roll. If the original impression has not been sufficiently removed and the transfer roll is not precisely in line with the remaining impression, the resulting double transfer will make the re-entry obvious. If the registration is true, a re-entry may be difficult or impossible to distinguish. Sometimes a stamp printed from a successful re-entry is identified by having a much sharper and clearer impression than its neighbors. With the advent of rotary presses, post-press re-entries were not possible. After a plate was curved for the rotary press, it was impossible to make a re-entry. This is because the plate had already been bent once (with the design distorted).

However, with the introduction of the previously mentioned modern-style siderography machines, entries are made to the preformed cylindrical printing sleeve. Such sleeves are dechromed and softened. This allows individual images to be burnished out and re-entered on the curved sleeve. The sleeve is then rechromed, resulting in longer press life.

Double Transfer — This is a description of the condition of a transfer on a plate that shows evidence of a duplication of all, or a portion of the design. It usually is the result of the changing of the registration between the transfer roll and the plate during the rocking in of the original entry. Double transfers also occur when only a portion of the design has been rocked in and improper positioning is noted. If the worker elected not to burnish out the partial or completed design, a strong double transfer will occur for part or all of the design.

It sometimes is necessary to remove the original transfer from a plate and repeat the process a second time. If the finished reworked image shows traces of the original impression, attributable to incomplete burnishing, the result is a partial double transfer.

With the modern automatic machines mentioned previously, double transfers are all but impossible to create. Those partially doubled images on stamps printed from such sleeves are more than likely re-entries, rather than true double transfers.

Re-engraved — Alterations to a stamp design are sometimes necessary after some stamps have been printed. In some cases, either the original die or the actual printing plate may have its "temper" drawn (softened), and the design will be re-cut. The resulting impressions from such a re-engraved die or plate may differ slightly from the original issue, and are known as "re-engraved." If the alteration was made to the master die, all future printings will be consistently different from the original. If alterations were made to the printing plate, each altered stamp on the plate will be slightly different from each other, allowing specialists to reconstruct a complete printing plate.

Dropped Transfers — If an impression from the transfer roll has not been properly placed, a dropped transfer may occur. The final stamp image will appear obviously out of line with its neighbors.

Short Transfer — Sometimes a transfer roll is not rocked its entire length when entering a transfer onto a plate. As a result, the finished transfer on the plate fails to show the complete design, and the finished stamp will have an incomplete design printed. This is known as a "short transfer." U.S. Scott No. 8 is a good example of a short transfer.

TYPOGRAPHY (Letterpress, Surface Printing, Flexography, Dry Offset, High Etch)

Although the word "Typography" is obsolete as a term describing a printing method, it was the accepted term throughout the first century of postage stamps. Therefore, appropriate Scott listings in this catalogue refer to typographed stamps. The current term for this form of printing, however, is "letterpress."

As it relates to the production of postage stamps, letterpress printing is the reverse of engraving. Rather than having recessed areas trap the ink and deposit it on paper, only the raised areas of the design are inked. This is comparable to the type of printing seen by inking and using an ordinary rubber stamp. Letterpress includes all printing where the design is above the surface area, whether it is wood, metal or, in some instances, hardened rubber or polymer plastic.

For most letterpress-printed stamps, the engraved master is made in much the same manner as for engraved stamps. In this instance, however, an additional step is needed. The design is transferred to another surface before being transferred to the transfer roll. In this way, the transfer roll has a recessed stamp design, rather than one done in relief. This makes the printing areas on the final plate raised, or relief areas.

For less-detailed stamps of the 19th century, the area on the die not used as a printing surface was cut away, leaving the surface area raised. The original die was then reproduced by stereotyping or electrotyping. The resulting electrotypes were assembled in the required number and format of the desired sheet of stamps. The plate used in printing the stamps was an electroplate of these assembled electrotypes.

Once the final letterpress plates are created, ink is applied to the raised surface and the pressure of the press transfers the ink impression to the paper. In contrast to engraving, the fine lines of letterpress are impressed on the surface of the stamp, leaving a debossed surface. When viewed from the back (as on a typewritten page), the corresponding line work on the stamp will be raised slightly (embossed) above the surface.

PHOTOGRAVURE (Gravure, Rotogravure, Heliogravure)

In this process, the basic principles of photography are applied to a chemically sensitized metal plate, rather than photographic paper. The design is transferred photographically to the plate through a halftone, or dot-matrix screen, breaking the reproduction into tiny dots. The plate is treated chemically and the dots form depressions, called cells, of varying depths and diameters, depending on the degrees of shade in the design. Then, like engraving, ink is applied to the plate and the surface is wiped clean. This leaves ink in the tiny cells that is lifted out and deposited on the paper when it is pressed against the plate.

Gravure is most often used for multicolored stamps, generally using the three primary colors (red, yellow and blue) and black. By varying the dot matrix pattern and density of these colors, virtually any color can be reproduced. A typical full-color gravure stamp will be created from four printing cylinders (one for each color). The original multicolored image will have been photographically separated into its component colors.

For examples of the first photogravure stamps printed (1914), see Bavaria Scott 94-114.

LITHOGRAPHY (Offset Lithography, Stone Lithography, Dilitho, Planography, Collotype)

The principle that oil and water do not mix is the basis for lithography. The stamp design is drawn by hand or transferred from engraving to the surface of a lithographic stone or metal plate in a greasy (oily) substance. This oily substance holds the ink, which will later be transferred to the paper. The stone (or plate) is wet with an acid fluid, causing it to repel the printing ink in all areas not covered by the greasy substance.

Transfer paper is used to transfer the design from the original stone or plate. A series of duplicate transfers are grouped and, in turn, transferred to the final printing plate.

Photolithography — The application of photographic processes to lithography. This process allows greater flexibility of design, related to use of halftone screens combined with line work. Unlike photogravure or engraving, this process can allow large, solid areas to be printed.

Offset — A refinement of the lithographic process. A rubber-covered blanket cylinder takes the impression from the inked lithographic plate. From the "blanket" the impression is *offset* or transferred to the paper. Greater flexibility and speed are the principal reasons offset printing has largely displaced lithography. The term "lithography" covers both processes, and results are almost identical.

EMBOSSED (Relief) Printing

Embossing, not considered one of the four main printing types, is a method in which the design first is sunk into the metal of the die. Printing is done against a yielding platen, such as leather or linoleum. The platen is forced into the depression of the die, thus forming the design on the paper in relief. This process is often used for metallic inks.

Embossing may be done without color (see Sardinia Scott 4-6); with color printed around the embossed area (see Great Britain Scott 5 and most U.S. envelopes); and with color in exact registration with the embossed subject (see Canada Scott 656-657).

COMBINATION PRINTINGS

Sometimes two or even three printing methods are combined in producing stamps. In these cases, such as Austria Scott 933, the stamp's dual printing technique can be determined by studying the individual characteristics of each printing type (intaglio and offset). A few stamps, such as Singapore Scott 684-684A, combine as many as three of the four major printing types (offset, intaglio and letterpress). When this is done it often indicates the incorporation of security devices against counterfeiting.

INK COLORS

Inks or colored papers used in stamp printing often are of mineral origin, although there are numerous examples of organic-based pigments. As a general rule, organic-based pigments are far more subject to varieties and change than those of mineral-based origin.

The appearance of any given color on a stamp may be affected by many aspects, including printing variations, light, color of paper, aging and chemical alterations.

Numerous printing variations may be observed. Heavier pressure or inking will cause a more intense color, while slight interruptions in the ink feed or lighter impressions will cause a lighter appearance. Stamps printed in the same color by water-based and solvent-based inks can differ significantly in appearance. This affects several stamps in the U.S. Prominent Americans series. Hand-mixed ink formulas (primarily from the 19th century) produced under different conditions (humidity and temperature) account for notable color variations in early printings of the same stamp (see U.S. Scott 248-250, 279B, for example). Different sources of pigment can also result in significant differences in color.

Light exposure and aging are closely related in the way they affect stamp color. Both eventually break down the ink and fade colors, so that a carefully kept stamp may differ significantly in color from an identical copy that has been exposed to light. If stamps are exposed to light either intentionally or accidentally, their colors can be faded or completely changed in some cases.

Papers of different quality and consistency used for the same stamp printing may affect color appearance. Most pelure papers, for example, show a richer color when compared with wove or laid papers. See Russia Scott 181a, for an example of this effect.

The very nature of the printing processes can cause a variety of differences in shades or hues of the same stamp. Some of these shades are scarcer than others, and are of particular interest to the advanced collector.

Luminescence

All forms of tagged stamps fall under the general category of luminescence. Within this broad category is fluorescence, dealing with forms of tagging visible under longwave ultraviolet light, and phosphorescence, which deals with tagging visible only under shortwave light. Phosphorescence leaves an afterglow and fluorescence does not. These treated stamps show up in a range of different colors when exposed to UV light. The differing wavelengths of the light activates the tagging material, making it glow in various colors that usually serve different mail processing purposes.

Intentional tagging is a post-World War II phenomenon, brought about by the increased literacy rate and rapidly growing mail volume. It was one of several answers to the problem of the need for more automated mail processes. Early tagged stamps served the purpose of triggering machines to separate different types of mail. A natural outgrowth was to also use the signal to trigger machines that faced all envelopes the same way and canceled them.

Tagged stamps come in many different forms. Some tagged stamps have luminescent shapes or images imprinted on them as a form of security device. Others have blocks (United States), stripes, frames (South Africa and Canada), overall coatings (United States), bars (Great Britain and Canada) and many other types. Some types of tagging are even mixed in with the pigmented printing ink (Australia Scott 366, Netherlands Scott 478 and U.S. Scott 1359 and 2443).

The means of applying taggant to stamps differs as much as the intended purposes for the stamps. The most common form of tagging is a coating applied to the surface of the printed stamp. Since the taggant ink is frequently invisible except under UV light, it does not interfere with the appearance of the stamp. Another common application is the use of phosphored papers. In this case the paper itself either has a coating of taggant applied before the stamp is printed or has taggant applied during the papermaking process, incorporating it into the fibers. This is currently in use in the United States. A similar form is the application of a fluorescent coating either to the finished paper or during the papermaking process. This type of tagging has been extensively used by Australia and Germany.

Many countries now use tagging in various forms to either expedite mail handling or to serve as a printing security device against counterfeiting. Following the introduction of tagged stamps for public use in 1959 by Great Britain, other countries have steadily joined the parade. Among those are Germany (1961); Canada and Denmark (1962); United States, Australia, France and Switzerland (1963); Belgium and Japan (1966); Sweden and Norway (1967); Italy (1968); and Russia (1969). Since then, many other countries have begun using forms of tagging, including Brazil, China, Czechoslovakia, Hong Kong, Guatemala, Indonesia, Israel, Lithuania, Luxembourg, Netherlands, Penrhyn Islands, Portugal, St. Vincent, Singapore, South Africa, Spain and Sweden to name a few.

In some cases, including United States, Canada, Great Britain and Switzerland, stamps were released both with and without tagging. Many of these were released during each country's experimental period. Tagged and untagged versions are listed for the aforementioned countries and are noted in some other countries' listings. For at least a few stamps, the experimentally tagged version is worth far more than its untagged counterpart, such as the 1963 experimental tagged version of France Scott 1024.

In some cases, luminescent varieties of stamps were inadvertently created. Several Russian stamps, for example, sport highly fluorescent ink that was not intended as a form of tagging. Older stamps, such as early U.S. postage dues, can be positively identified by the use of UV light, since the organic ink used has become slightly fluorescent over time. Other stamps, such as Austria Scott 70a-82a (varnish bars) and Obock Scott 46-64 (printed quadrille lines), have become fluorescent over time.

Various fluorescent substances have been added to paper to make it appear brighter. These optical brightners, as they are known, greatly affect the appearance of the stamp under UV light. The brightest of these is known as Hi-Brite paper. These paper varieties are beyond the scope of the Scott Catalogue.

Shortwave UV light also is used extensively in expertizing, since each form of paper has its own fluorescent characteristics that are impossible to perfectly match. It is therefore a simple matter to detect filled thins, added perforation teeth and other alterations that involve the addition of paper. UV light also is used to examine stamps that have had cancels chemically removed and for other purposes as well.

Gum

The Illustrated Gum Chart in the first part of this introduction shows and defines various types of gum condition. Because gum condition has an important impact on the value of unused stamps, we recommend studying this chart and the accompanying text carefully.

The gum on the back of a stamp may be shiny, dull, smooth, rough, dark, white, colored or tinted. Most stamp gumming adhesives use gum arabic or dextrine as a base. Certain polymers such as polyvinyl alcohol (PVA) have been used extensively since World War II.

The *Scott Standard Postage Stamp Catalogue* does not list items by types of gum. The *Scott Specialized Catalogue of United States Stamps* does differentiate among some types of gum for certain issues.

Reprints of stamps may have gum differing from the original issues. In addition, some countries have used different gum formulas for different seasons. These adhesives have different properties that may become more apparent over time.

Many stamps have been issued without gum, and the catalogue will note this fact. See United States Scott PR33-PR56. Sometimes, gum may have been removed to preserve the stamp. Germany Scott B68, for example, has a highly acidic gum that eventually destroys the stamps. This item is valued in the catalogue with gum removed.

Reprints and Reissues

These are impressions of stamps (usually obsolete) made from the original plates or stones. If they are valid for postage and reproduce obsolete issues (such as U.S. Scott 102-111), the stamps are *reissues.* If they are from current issues, they are designated as *second, third,* etc., *printing.* If designated for a particular purpose, they are called *special printings.*

When special printings are not valid for postage, but are made from original dies and plates by authorized persons, they are *official reprints. Private reprints* are made from the original plates and dies by private hands. An example of a private reprint is that of the 1871-1932 reprints made from the original die of the 1845 New Haven, Conn., postmaster's provisional. *Official reproductions* or imitations are made from new dies and plates by government authorization. Scott will list those reissues that are valid for postage if they differ significantly from the original printing.

The U.S. government made special printings of its first postage stamps in 1875. Produced were official imitations of the first two stamps (listed as Scott 3-4), reprints of the demonetized pre-1861 issues (Scott 40-47) and reissues of the 1861 stamps, the 1869 stamps and the then-current 1875 denominations. Even though the official imitations and the reprints were not valid for postage, Scott lists all of these U.S. special printings.

Most reprints or reissues differ slightly from the original stamp in some characteristic, such as gum, paper, perforation, color or watermark. Sometimes the details are followed so meticulously that only a student of that specific stamp is able to distinguish the reprint or reissue from the original.

Remainders and Canceled to Order

Some countries sell their stock of old stamps when a new issue replaces them. To avoid postal use, the *remainders* usually are canceled with a punch hole, a heavy line or bar, or a more-or-less regular-looking cancellation. The most famous merchant of remainders was Nicholas F. Seebeck. In the 1880s and 1890s, he arranged printing contracts between the Hamilton Bank Note Co., of which he was a director, and several Central and South American countries. The contracts provided that the plates and all remainders of the yearly issues became the property of Hamilton. Seebeck saw to it that ample stock remained. The "Seebecks," both remainders and reprints, were standard packet fillers for decades.

Some countries also issue stamps *canceled-to-order (CTO),* either in sheets with original gum or stuck onto pieces of paper or envelopes and canceled. Such CTO items generally are worth less than postally used stamps. In cases where the CTO material is far more prevalent in the marketplace than postally used examples, the catalogue value relates to the CTO examples, with postally used examples noted as premium items. Most CTOs can be detected by the presence of gum. However, as the CTO practice goes back at least to 1885, the gum inevitably has been soaked off some stamps so they could pass as postally used. The normally applied postmarks usually differ slightly from standard postmarks, and specialists are able to tell the difference. When applied individually to envelopes by philatelically minded persons, CTO material is known as *favor canceled* and generally sells at large discounts.

Cinderellas and Facsimiles

Cinderella is a catch-all term used by stamp collectors to describe phantoms, fantasies, bogus items, municipal issues, exhibition seals, local revenues, transportation stamps, labels, poster stamps and many other types of items. Some cinderella collectors include in their collections local postage issues, telegraph stamps, essays and proofs, forgeries and counterfeits.

A *fantasy* is an adhesive created for a nonexistent stamp-issuing authority. Fantasy items range from imaginary countries (Occusi-Ambeno, Kingdom of Sedang, Principality of Trinidad or Torres Straits), to non-existent locals (Winans City Post), or nonexistent transportation lines (McRobish & Co.'s Acapulco-San Francisco Line).

On the other hand, if the entity exists and could have issued stamps (but did not) or was known to have issued other stamps, the items are considered *bogus* stamps. These would include the Mormon postage stamps of Utah, S. Allan Taylor's Guatemala and Paraguay inventions, the propaganda issues for the South Moluccas and the adhesives of the Page & Keyes local post of Boston.

Phantoms is another term for both fantasy and bogus issues.

Facsimiles are copies or imitations made to represent original stamps, but which do not pretend to be originals. A catalogue illustration is such a facsimile. Illustrations from the Moens catalogue of the last century were occasionally colored and passed off as stamps. Since the beginning of stamp collecting, facsimiles have been made for collectors as space fillers or for reference. They often carry the word "facsimile," "falsch" (German), "sanko" or "mozo" (Japanese), or "faux" (French) overprinted on the face or stamped on the back. Unfortunately, over the years a number of these items have had fake cancels applied over the facsimile notation and have been passed off as genuine.

Forgeries and Counterfeits

Forgeries and counterfeits have been with philately virtually from the beginning of stamp production. Over time, the terminology for the two has been used interchangeably. Although both forgeries and counterfeits are reproductions of stamps, the purposes behind their creation differ considerably.

Among specialists there is an increasing movement to more specifically define such items. Although there is no universally accepted terminology, we feel the following definitions most closely mirror the items and their purposes as they are currently defined.

Forgeries (also often referred to as *Counterfeits*) are reproductions of genuine stamps that have been created to defraud collectors. Such spurious items first appeared on the market around 1860, and most old-time collections contain one or more. Many are crude and easily spotted, but some can deceive experts.

An important supplier of these early philatelic forgeries was the Hamburg printer Gebruder Spiro. Many others with reputations in this craft included S. Allan Taylor, George Hussey, James Chute, George Forune, Benjamin & Sarpy, Julius Goldner, E. Oneglia and L.H. Mercier. Among the noted 20th-century forgers were Francois Fournier, Jean Sperati and the prolific Raoul DeThuin.

Forgeries may be complete replications, or they may be genuine stamps altered to resemble a scarcer (and more valuable) type. Most forgeries, particularly those of rare stamps, are worth only a small fraction of the value of a genuine example, but a few types, created by some of the most notable forgers, such as Sperati, can be worth as much or more than the genuine. Fraudulently produced copies are known of most classic rarities and many medium-priced stamps.

In addition to rare stamps, large numbers of common 19th- and early 20th-century stamps were forged to supply stamps to the early packet trade. Many can still be easily found. Few new philatelic forgeries have appeared in recent decades. Successful imitation of well-engraved work is virtually impossible. It has proven far easier to produce a fake by altering a genuine stamp than to duplicate a stamp completely.

Counterfeit (also often referred to as *Postal Counterfeit* or *Postal Forgery*) is the term generally applied to reproductions of stamps that have been created to defraud the government of revenue. Such items usually are created at the time a stamp is current and, in some cases, are hard to detect. Because most counterfeits are seized when the perpetrator is captured, postal counterfeits, particularly used on cover, are usually worth much more than a genuine example to specialists. The first postal counterfeit was of Spain's 4-cuarto carmine of 1854 (the real one is Scott 25). Apparently, the counterfeiters were not satisfied with their first version, which is now very scarce, and they soon created an engraved counterfeit, which is common. Postal counterfeits quickly followed in Austria, Naples, Sardinia and the Roman States. They have since been created in many other countries as well, including the United States.

An infamous counterfeit to defraud the government is the 1-shilling Great Britain "Stock Exchange" forgery of 1872, used on telegraph forms at the exchange that year. The stamp escaped detection until a stamp dealer noticed it in 1898.

Fakes

Fakes are genuine stamps altered in some way to make them more desirable. One student of this part of stamp collecting has estimated that by the 1950s more than 30,000 varieties of fakes were known. That number has grown greatly since then. The widespread existence of fakes makes it important for stamp collectors to study their philatelic holdings and use relevant literature. Likewise, collectors should buy from reputable dealers who guarantee their stamps and make full and prompt refunds should a purchased item be declared faked or altered by some mutually agreed-upon authority. Because fakes always have some genuine characteristics, it is not always possible to obtain unanimous agreement among experts regarding specific items. These students may change their opinions as philatelic knowledge increases. More than 80 percent of all fakes on the philatelic market today are regummed, reperforated (or perforated for the first time), or bear forged overprints, surcharges or cancellations.

Stamps can be chemically treated to alter or eliminate colors. For example, a pale rose stamp can be re-colored to resemble a blue shade of high market value. In other cases, treated stamps can be made to resemble missing color varieties. Designs may be changed by painting, or a stroke or a dot added or bleached out to turn an ordinary variety into a seemingly scarcer stamp. Part of a stamp can be bleached and reprinted in a different version, achieving an inverted center or frame. Margins can be added or repairs done so deceptively that the stamps move from the "repaired" into the "fake" category.

Fakers have not left the backs of the stamps untouched either. They may create false watermarks, add fake grills or press out genuine grills. A thin India paper proof may be glued onto a thicker backing to create the appearance an issued stamp, or a proof printed on cardboard may be shaved down and perforated to resemble a stamp. Silk threads are impressed into paper and stamps have been split so that a rare paper variety is added to an otherwise inexpensive stamp. The most common treatment to the back of a stamp, however, is regumming.

Some in the business of faking stamps have openly advertised fool-proof application of "original gum" to stamps that lack it, although most publications now ban such ads from their pages. It is believed that very few early stamps have survived without being hinged. The large number of never-hinged examples of such earlier material offered for sale thus suggests the widespread extent of regumming activity. Regumming also may be used to hide repairs or thin spots. Dipping the stamp into watermark fluid, or examining it under longwave ultraviolet light often will reveal these flaws.

Fakers also tamper with separations. Ingenious ways to add margins are known. Perforated wide-margin stamps may be falsely represented as imperforate when trimmed. Reperforating is commonly done to create scarce coil or perforation varieties, and to eliminate the naturally occurring straight-edge stamps found in sheet margin positions of many earlier issues. Custom has made straight-edged stamps less desirable. Fakers have obliged by perforating straight-edged stamps so that many are now uncommon, if not rare.

Another fertile field for the faker is that of overprints, surcharges and cancellations. The forging of rare surcharges or overprints began in the 1880s or 1890s. These forgeries are sometimes difficult to detect, but experts have identified almost all. Occasionally, overprints or cancellations are removed to create non-overprinted stamps or seemingly unused items. This is most commonly done by removing a manuscript cancel to make a stamp resemble an unused example. "SPECIMEN" overprints may be removed by scraping and repainting to create non-overprinted varieties. Fakers use inexpensive revenues or pen-canceled stamps to generate unused stamps for further faking by adding other markings. The quartz lamp or UV lamp and a high-powered magnifying glass help to easily detect removed cancellations.

The bigger problem, however, is the addition of overprints, surcharges or cancellations - many with such precision that they are very difficult to ascertain. Plating of the stamps or the overprint can be an important method of detection.

Fake postmarks may range from many spurious fancy cancellations to a host of markings applied to transatlantic covers, to adding normally appearing postmarks to definitives of some countries with stamps that are valued far higher used than unused. With the increased popularity of cover collecting, and the widespread interest in postal history, a fertile new field for fakers has come about. Some have tried to create entire covers. Others specialize in adding stamps, tied by fake cancellations, to genuine stampless covers, or replacing less expensive or damaged stamps with more valuable ones. Detailed study of postal rates in effect at the time a cover in question was mailed, including the analysis of each handstamp used during the period, ink analysis and similar techniques, usually will unmask the fraud.

Restoration and Repairs

Scott Publishing Co. bases its catalogue values on stamps that are free of defects and otherwise meet the standards set forth earlier in this introduction. Most stamp collectors desire to have the finest copy of an item possible. Even within given grading categories there are variances. This leads to a controversial practice that is not defined in any universal manner: stamp *restoration.*

There are broad differences of opinion about what is permissible when it comes to restoration. Carefully applying a soft eraser to a stamp or cover to remove light soiling is one form of restoration, as is washing a stamp in mild soap and water to clean it. These are fairly accepted forms of restoration. More severe forms of restoration include pressing out creases or removing stains caused by tape. To what degree each of these is acceptable is dependent upon the individual situation. Further along the spectrum is the freshening of a stamp's color by removing oxide build-up or the effects of wax paper left next to stamps shipped to the tropics.

At some point in this spectrum the concept of *repair* replaces that of restoration. Repairs include filling thin spots, mending tears by reweaving or adding a missing perforation tooth. Regumming stamps may have been acceptable as a restoration or repair technique many decades ago, but today it is considered a form of fakery.

Restored stamps may or may not sell at a discount, and it is possible that the value of individual restored items may be enhanced over that of their pre-restoration state. Specific situations dictate the resultant value of such an item. Repaired stamps sell at substantial discounts from the value of sound stamps.

Terminology

Booklets — Many countries have issued stamps in small booklets for the convenience of users. This idea continues to become increasingly popular in many countries. Booklets have been issued in many sizes and forms, often with advertising on the covers, the panes of stamps or on the interleaving.

The panes used in booklets may be printed from special plates or made from regular sheets. All panes from booklets issued by the United States and many from those of other countries contain stamps that are straight edged on the sides, but perforated between. Others are distinguished by orientation of watermark or other identifying features. Any stamp-like unit in the pane, either printed or blank, that is not a postage stamp, is considered to be a *label* in the catalogue listings.

Scott lists and values booklet panes only. Complete booklets are listed and valued in only a few cases, such as Grenada Scott 1055 and some forms of British prestige booklets. Individual booklet panes are listed only when they are not fashioned from existing sheet stamps and, therefore, are identifiable from their sheet stamp counterparts.

Panes usually do not have a used value assigned to them because there is little market activity for used booklet panes, even though many exist used and there is some demand for them.

Cancellations — The marks or obliterations put on stamps by postal authorities to show that they have performed service and to prevent their reuse are known as cancellations. If the marking is made with a pen, it is considered a "pen cancel." When the location of the post office appears in the marking, it is a "town cancellation." A "postmark" is technically any postal marking, but in practice the term generally is applied to a town cancellation with a date. When calling attention to a cause or celebration, the marking is known as a "slogan cancellation." Many other types and styles of cancellations exist, such as duplex, numerals, targets, fancy and others. See also "precancels," below.

Coil Stamps — These are stamps that are issued in rolls for use in dispensers, affixing and vending machines. Those coils of the United States, Canada, Sweden and some other countries are perforated horizontally or vertically only, with the outer edges imperforate. Coil stamps of some countries, such as Great Britain and Germany, are perforated on all four sides and may in some cases be distinguished from their sheet stamp counterparts by watermarks, counting numbers on the reverse or other means.

Covers — Entire envelopes, with or without adhesive postage stamps, that have passed through the mail and bear postal or other markings of philatelic interest are known as covers. Before the introduction of envelopes in about 1840, people folded letters and wrote the address on the outside. Some people covered their letters with an extra sheet of paper on the outside for the address, producing the term "cover." Used airletter sheets, stamped envelopes and other items of postal stationery also are considered covers.

Errors — Stamps that have some major, consistent, unintentional deviation from the normal are considered errors. Errors include, but are not limited to, missing or wrong colors, wrong paper, wrong watermarks, inverted centers or frames on multicolor printing, inverted or missing surcharges or overprints, double impressions, missing perforations and others. Factually wrong or misspelled information, if it appears on all examples of a stamp, are not considered errors in the true sense of the word. They are errors of design. Inconsistent or randomly appearing items, such as misperfs or color shifts, are classified as freaks.

Overprints and Surcharges — Overprinting involves applying wording or design elements over an already existing stamp. Overprints can be used to alter the place of use (such as "Canal Zone" on U.S. stamps), to adapt them for a special purpose ("Porto" on Denmark's 1913-20 regular issues for use as postage due stamps, Scott J1-J7) or to commemorate a special occasion (United States Scott 647-648).

A *surcharge* is a form of overprint that changes or restates the face value of a stamp or piece of postal stationery.

Surcharges and overprints may be handstamped, typeset or, occasionally, lithographed or engraved. A few hand-written overprints and surcharges are known.

Precancels — Stamps that are canceled before they are placed in the mail are known as precancels. Precanceling usually is done to expedite the handling of large mailings and generally allow the affected mail pieces to skip certain phases of mail handling.

In the United States, precancellations generally identified the point of origin; that is, the city and state. This information appeared across the face of the stamp, usually centered between parallel lines. More recently, bureau precancels retained the parallel lines, but the city and state designations were dropped. Recent coils have a service inscription that is present on the original printing plate. These show the mail service paid for by the stamp. Since these stamps are not intended to receive further cancellations when used as intended, they are considered precancels. Such items often do not have parallel lines as part of the precancellation.

In France, the abbreviation *Affranchts* in a semicircle together with the word *Postes* is the general form of precancel in use. Belgian precancellations usually appear in a box in which the name of the city appears. Netherlands precancels have the name of the city enclosed between concentric circles, sometimes called a "lifesaver." Precancellations of other countries usually follow these patterns, but may be any arrangement of bars, boxes and city names.

Precancels are listed in the Scott catalogues only if the precancel changes the denomination (Belgium Scott 477-478); if the precanceled stamp is different from the non-precanceled version (such as untagged U.S. precancels); or if the stamp exists only precanceled (France Scott 1096-1099, U.S. Scott 2265).

Proofs and Essays — Proofs are impressions taken from an approved die, plate or stone in which the design and color are the same as the stamp issued to the public. Trial color proofs are impressions taken from approved dies, plates or stones in colors that vary from the final version. An essay is the impression of a design that differs in some way from the issued stamp. "Progressive die proofs" generally are considered to be essays.

Provisionals — These are stamps that are issued on short notice and intended for temporary use pending the arrival of regular issues. They usually are issued to meet such contingencies as changes in government or currency, shortage of necessary postage values or military occupation.

During the 1840s, postmasters in certain American cities issued stamps that were valid only at specific post offices. In 1861, postmasters of the Confederate States also issued stamps with limited validity. Both of these examples are known as "postmaster's provisionals."

Se-tenant — This term refers to an unsevered pair, strip or block of stamps that differ in design, denomination or overprint.

Unless the se-tenant item has a continuous design (see U.S. Scott 1451a, 1694a) the stamps do not have to be in the same order as shown in the catalogue (see U.S. Scott 2158a).

Specimens — The Universal Postal Union required member nations to send samples of all stamps they released into service to the International Bureau in Switzerland. Member nations of the UPU received these specimens as samples of what stamps were valid for postage. Many are overprinted, handstamped or initial-perforated "Specimen," "Canceled" or "Muestra." Some are marked with bars across the denominations (China-Taiwan), punched holes (Czechoslovakia) or back inscriptions (Mongolia).

Stamps distributed to government officials or for publicity purposes, and stamps submitted by private security printers for official approval, also may receive such defacements.

The previously described defacement markings prevent postal use, and all such items generally are known as "specimens."

Tete Beche — This term describes a pair of stamps in which one is upside down in relation to the other. Some of these are the result of intentional sheet arrangements, such as Morocco Scott B10-B11. Others occurred when one or more electrotypes accidentally were placed upside down on the plate, such as Colombia Scott 57a. Separation of the tete-beche stamps, of course, destroys the tete beche variety.

Currency Conversion

Country	Dollar	Pound	S Franc	Guilder	Yen	Lira	HK Dollar	D-Mark	Fr Franc	Cdn Dollar	Aust Dollar
Australia	1.5308	2.5927	1.0221	0.7543	0.0116	0.0009	0.1976	0.8493	0.2534	1.0686	....
Canada	1.4325	2.4262	0.9565	0.7059	0.0109	0.0008	0.1849	0.7947	0.2371	....	0.9358
France	6.0407	10.231	4.0333	2.9767	0.0459	0.0034	0.7798	3.3513	....	4.2169	3.9461
Germany	1.8025	3.0529	1.2035	0.8882	0.0137	0.0010	0.2327	....	0.2984	1.2583	1.1775
Hong Kong	7.7465	13.12	5.1723	3.8173	0.0589	0.0043	....	4.2976	1.2824	5.4077	5.0604
Italy	1780.95	3016.4	1189.12	877.62	13.544	....	229.9	988.04	294.83	1243.25	1163.41
Japan	131.49	222.7	87.795	64.796	....	0.0738	16.974	72.949	21.767	91.791	85.896
Netherlands	2.0293	3.437	1.3549	....	0.0154	0.0011	0.262	1.1258	0.3359	1.4166	1.3256
Switzerland	1.4977	2.5367	....	0.738	0.0114	0.0008	0.1933	0.8309	0.2479	1.0455	0.9784
U.K.	0.5904	....	0.3942	0.2909	0.0045	0.0003	0.0762	0.3276	0.0977	0.4122	0.3857
U.S.	....	1.6937	0.6677	0.4928	0.0076	0.0006	0.1291	0.5548	0.1655	0.6981	0.6533

Country	Currency	U.S. $ Equiv.
Pakistan	rupee	.0226
Palau	U.S. dollar	1.00
Panama	balboa	1.00
Papua New Guinea	kina	.50
Paraguay	guarani	.0004
Penrhyn Island	New Zealand dollar	.5585
Peru	new sol	.354
Philippines	peso	.0263
Pitcairn Islands	New Zealand dollar	.5585
Poland	zloty	.2937
Portugal	escudo	.0054
Qatar	riyal	.2747
Romania	leu	.0001
Russia	ruble	.1635
Rwanda	Franch franc	.1655
St. Helena	British pound	1.6937
St. Kitts	East Caribbean dollar	.3703
St. Lucia	East Caribbean dollar	.3703
St. Pierre & Miquelon	French franc	.1655
St. Thomas & Prince	dobra	.0004
St. Vincent	East Caribbean dollar	.3703
St. Vincent Grenadines	East Caribbean dollar	.3703
El Salvador	colon	.1142
Samoa	dollar	1.00
San Marino	lira	.0006
Saudi Arabia	riyal	.2666
Senegal	Community of French Africa (CFA) franc	.0017
Seychelles	rupee	.1952
Zil Elwannyen Sesel	rupee	.1952
Sierra Leone	leone	.0011
Singapore	dollar	.6254
Slovakia	koruna	.0287
Slovenia	tolar	.006

*Source: **Wall Street Journal** Apr. 13, 1998. Figures reflect values as of Apr. 10, 1998.*

Colonies, Former Colonies, Offices, Territories Controlled by Parent States

Belgium

Belgian Congo
Ruanda-Urundi

Denmark

Danish West Indies
Faroe Islands
Greenland
Iceland

Finland

Aland Islands

France

COLONIES PAST AND PRESENT, CONTROLLED TERRITORIES

Afars & Issas, Territory of
Alaouites
Alexandretta
Algeria
Alsace & Lorraine
Anjouan
Annam & Tonkin
Benin
Cambodia (Khmer)
Cameroun
Castellorizo
Chad
Cilicia
Cochin China
Comoro Islands
Dahomey
Diego Suarez
Djibouti (Somali Coast)
Fezzan
French Congo
French Equatorial Africa
French Guiana
French Guinea
French India
French Morocco
French Polynesia (Oceania)
French Southern & Antarctic Territories
French Sudan
French West Africa
Gabon
Germany
Ghadames
Grand Comoro
Guadeloupe
Indo-China
Inini
Ivory Coast
Laos
Latakia
Lebanon
Madagascar
Martinique
Mauritania
Mayotte
Memel
Middle Congo
Moheli
New Caledonia
New Hebrides
Niger Territory
Nossi-Be
Obock
Reunion
Rouad, Ile
Ste.-Marie de Madagascar
St. Pierre & Miquelon
Senegal
Senegambia & Niger
Somali Coast
Syria
Tahiti
Togo
Tunisia
Ubangi-Shari
Upper Senegal & Niger
Upper Volta
Viet Nam
Wallis & Futuna Islands

POST OFFICES IN FOREIGN COUNTRIES

China
Crete
Egypt
Turkish Empire
Zanzibar

Germany

EARLY STATES

Baden
Bavaria
Bergedorf
Bremen
Brunswick
Hamburg
Hanover
Lubeck
Mecklenburg-Schwerin
Mecklenburg-Strelitz
Oldenburg
Prussia
Saxony
Schleswig-Holstein
Wurttemberg

FORMER COLONIES

Cameroun (Kamerun)
Caroline Islands
German East Africa
German New Guinea
German South-West Africa
Kiauchau
Mariana Islands
Marshall Islands
Samoa
Togo

Italy

EARLY STATES

Modena
Parma
Romagna
Roman States
Sardinia
Tuscany
Two Sicilies
  Naples
  Neapolitan Provinces
  Sicily

FORMER COLONIES, CONTROLLED TERRITORIES, OCCUPATION AREAS

Aegean Islands
  Calimno (Calino)
  Caso
  Cos (Coo)
  Karki (Carchi)
  Leros (Lero)
  Lipso
  Nisiros (Nisiro)
  Patmos (Patmo)
  Piscopi
  Rodi (Rhodes)
  Scarpanto
  Simi
  Stampalia
Castellorizo
Corfu
Cyrenaica
Eritrea
Ethiopia (Abyssinia)
Fiume
Ionian Islands
  Cephalonia
  Ithaca
  Paxos
Italian East Africa
Libya
Oltre Giuba
Saseno
Somalia (Italian Somaliland)
Tripolitania

POST OFFICES IN FOREIGN COUNTRIES

"ESTERO"*
Austria
China
  Peking
  Tientsin
Crete
Tripoli
Turkish Empire
  Constantinople
  Durazzo
  Janina
Jerusalem
Salonika
Scutari
Smyrna
Valona

*Stamps overprinted "ESTERO" were used in various parts of the world.

Netherlands

Aruba
Netherlands Antilles (Curacao)
Netherlands Indies
Netherlands New Guinea
Surinam (Dutch Guiana)

Portugal

COLONIES PAST AND PRESENT, CONTROLLED TERRITORIES

Angola
Angra
Azores
Cape Verde
Funchal
Horta
Inhambane
Kionga
Lourenco Marques
Macao
Madeira
Mozambique
Mozambique Co.
Nyassa
Ponta Delgada
Portuguese Africa
Portuguese Congo
Portuguese Guinea
Portuguese India
Quelimane
St. Thomas & Prince Islands
Tete
Timor
Zambezia

Russia

ALLIED TERRITORIES AND REPUBLICS, OCCUPATION AREAS

Armenia
Aunus (Olonets)
Azerbaijan
Batum
Estonia
Far Eastern Republic
Georgia
Karelia
Latvia
Lithuania
North Ingermanland
Ostland
Russian Turkestan
Siberia
South Russia
Tannu Tuva
Transcaucasian Fed. Republics
Ukraine
Wenden (Livonia)
Western Ukraine

Spain

COLONIES PAST AND PRESENT, CONTROLLED TERRITORIES

Aguera, La
Cape Juby
Cuba
Elobey, Annobon & Corisco
Fernando Po
Ifni
Mariana Islands
Philippines
Puerto Rico
Rio de Oro
Rio Muni
Spanish Guinea
Spanish Morocco
Spanish Sahara
Spanish West Africa

POST OFFICES IN FOREIGN COUNTRIES

Morocco
Tangier
Tetuan

British Commonwealth of Nations

Dominions, Colonies, Territories, Offices and Independent Members

Comprising stamps of the British Commonwealth and associated nations.

A strict observance of technicalities would bar some or all of the stamps listed under Burma, Ireland, Kuwait, Nepal, New Republic, Orange Free State, Samoa, South Africa, South-West Africa, Stellaland, Sudan, Swaziland, the two Transvaal Republics and others but these are included for the convenience of collectors.

1. Great Britain

Great Britain: Including England, Scotland, Wales and Northern Ireland.

2. The Dominions, Present and Past

AUSTRALIA

The Commonwealth of Australia was proclaimed on January 1, 1901. It consists of six former colonies as follows:

New South Wales
Queensland
South Australia
Victoria
Tasmania
Western Australia

Territories belonging to, or administered by Australia: Australian Antarctic Territory, Christmas Island, Cocos (Keeling) Islands, Nauru, New Guinea, Norfolk Island, Papua New Guinea.

CANADA

The Dominion of Canada was created by the British North America Act in 1867. The following provinces were former separate colonies and issued postage stamps:

British Columbia and Vancouver Island
New Brunswick
Newfoundland
Nova Scotia
Prince Edward Island

FIJI

The colony of Fiji became an independent nation with dominion status on Oct. 10, 1970.

GHANA

This state came into existence Mar. 6, 1957, with dominion status. It consists of the former colony of the Gold Coast and the Trusteeship Territory of Togoland. Ghana became a republic July 1, 1960.

INDIA

The Republic of India was inaugurated on January 26, 1950. It succeeded the Dominion of India which was proclaimed August 15, 1947, when the former Empire of India was divided into Pakistan and the Union of India. The Republic is composed of about 40 predominantly Hindu states of three classes: governor's provinces, chief commissioner's provinces and princely states. India also has various territories, such as the Andaman and Nicobar Islands.

The old Empire of India was a federation of British India and the native states. The more important princely states were autonomous. Of the more than 700 Indian states, these 43 are familiar names to philatelists because of their postage stamps.

CONVENTION STATES

Chamba
Faridkot
Gwalior
Jhind
Nabha
Patiala

NATIVE FEUDATORY STATES

Alwar
Bahawalpur
Bamra
Barwani
Bhopal
Bhor
Bijawar
Bundi
Bussahir
Charkhari
Cochin
Dhar
Duttia
Faridkot (1879-85)
Hyderabad
Idar
Indore
Jaipur
Jammu
Jammu and Kashmir
Jasdan
Jhalawar
Jhind (1875-76)
Kashmir
Kishangarh
Las Bela
Morvi
Nandgaon
Nowanuggur
Orchha
Poonch
Rajpeepla
Sirmur
Soruth
Travancore
Wadhwan

NEW ZEALAND

Became a dominion on September 26, 1907. The following islands and territories are, or have been, administered by New Zealand:

Aitutaki
Cook Islands (Rarotonga)
Niue
Penrhyn
Ross Dependency
Samoa (Western Samoa)
Tokelau Islands

PAKISTAN

The Republic of Pakistan was proclaimed March 23, 1956. It succeeded the Dominion which was proclaimed August 15, 1947. It is made up of all or part of several Moslem provinces and various districts of the former Empire of India, including Bahawalpur and Las Bela. Pakistan withdrew from the Commonwealth in 1972.

SOUTH AFRICA

Under the terms of the South African Act (1909) the self-governing colonies of Cape of Good Hope, Natal, Orange River Colony and Transvaal united on May 31, 1910, to form the Union of South Africa. It became an independent republic May 3, 1961.

Under the terms of the Treaty of Versailles, South-West Africa, formerly German South-West Africa, was mandated to the Union of South Africa.

SRI LANKA (CEYLON)

The Dominion of Ceylon was proclaimed February 4, 1948. The island had been a Crown Colony from 1802 until then. On May 22, 1972, Ceylon became the Republic of Sri Lanka.

3. Colonies, Past and Present; ControlledTerritory and Independent Members of the Commonwealth

Aden
Aitutaki
Antigua
Ascension
Bahamas
Bahrain
Bangladesh
Barbados
Barbuda
Basutoland
Batum
Bechuanaland
Bechuanaland Prot.
Belize
Bermuda
Botswana
British Antarctic Territory
British Central Africa
British Columbia and Vancouver Island
British East Africa
British Guiana

British Honduras
British Indian Ocean Territory
British New Guinea
British Solomon Islands
British Somaliland
Brunei
Burma
Bushire
Cameroons
Cape of Good Hope
Cayman Islands
Christmas Island
Cocos (Keeling) Islands
Cook Islands
Crete,
British Administration
Cyprus
Dominica
East Africa & Uganda
Protectorates
Egypt
Falkland Islands
Fiji
Gambia
German East Africa
Gibraltar
Gilbert Islands
Gilbert & Ellice Islands
Gold Coast
Grenada
Griqualand West
Guernsey
Guyana
Heligoland
Hong Kong
Indian Native States
(see India)
Ionian Islands
Jamaica
Jersey
Kenya
Kenya, Uganda & Tanzania
Kuwait
Labuan
Lagos
Leeward Islands
Lesotho
Madagascar
Malawi
Malaya
Federated Malay States
Johore
Kedah
Kelantan
Malacca
Negri Sembilan
Pahang
Penang
Perak
Perlis
Selangor
Singapore
Sungei Ujong
Trengganu
Malaysia
Maldive Islands
Malta
Man, Isle of
Mauritius
Mesopotamia
Montserrat
Muscat
Namibia
Natal
Nauru
Nevis
New Britain
New Brunswick
Newfoundland
New Guinea
New Hebrides
New Republic
New South Wales
Niger Coast Protectorate
Nigeria
Niue
Norfolk Island
North Borneo
Northern Nigeria
Northern Rhodesia
North West Pacific Islands
Nova Scotia
Nyasaland Protectorate
Oman
Orange River Colony
Palestine
Papua New Guinea
Penrhyn Island
Pitcairn Islands
Prince Edward Island
Queensland
Rhodesia
Rhodesia & Nyasaland
Ross Dependency
Sabah
St. Christopher
St. Helena
St. Kitts
St. Kitts-Nevis-Anguilla
St. Lucia
St. Vincent
Samoa
Sarawak
Seychelles
Sierra Leone
Solomon Islands
Somaliland Protectorate
South Arabia
South Australia
South Georgia
Southern Nigeria
Southern Rhodesia
South-West Africa
Stellaland
Straits Settlements
Sudan
Swaziland
Tanganyika
Tanzania
Tasmania
Tobago
Togo
Tokelau Islands
Tonga
Transvaal
Trinidad
Trinidad and Tobago
Tristan da Cunha
Trucial States
Turks and Caicos
Turks Islands
Tuvalu
Uganda
United Arab Emirates
Victoria
Virgin Islands
Western Australia
Zambia
Zanzibar
Zululand

POST OFFICES IN FOREIGN COUNTRIES

Africa
East Africa Forces
Middle East Forces
Bangkok
China
Morocco
Turkish Empire

Common Design Types

Pictured in this section are issues where one illustration has been used for a number of countries in the Catalogue. Not included in this section are overprinted stamps or those issues which are illustrated in each country.

EUROPA

Europa Issue, 1956

The design symbolizing the cooperation among the six countries comprising the Coal and Steel Community is illustrated in each country.

Belgium	496-497
France	805-806
Germany	748-749
Italy	715-716
Luxembourg	318-320
Netherlands	368-369

Europa Issue, 1958

"E" and Dove CD1

European Postal Union at the service of European integration.

1958, Sept. 13

Belgium	527-528
France	889-890
Germany	790-791
Italy	750-751
Luxembourg	341-343
Netherlands	375-376
Saar	317-318

Europa Issue, 1959

6-Link Endless Chain – CD2

1959, Sept. 19

Belgium	536-537
France	929-930
Germany	805-806
Italy	791-792
Luxembourg	354-355
Netherlands	379-380

Europa Issue, 1960

19-Spoke Wheel – CD3

First anniverary of the establishment of C.E.P.T. (Conference Europeenne des Administrations des Postes et des Telecommunications.)

The spokes symbolize the 19 founding members of the Conference.

1960, Sept.

Belgium	553-554
Denmark	379
Finland	376-377
France	970-971
Germany	818-820
Great Britain	377-378
Greece	688
Iceland	327-328
Ireland	175-176
Italy	809-810
Luxembourg	374-375
Netherlands	385-386
Norway	387
Portugal	866-867
Spain	941-942
Sweden	562-563
Switzerland	400-401
Turkey	1493-1494

Europa Issue, 1961

19 Doves Flying as One – CD4

The 19 doves represent the 19 members of the Conference of European Postal and Telecommunications Administrations C.E.P.T.

1961-62

Belgium	572-573
Cyprus	201-203
France	1005-1006
Germany	844-845
Great Britain	383-384
Greece	718-719
Iceland	340-341
Italy	845-846
Luxembourg	382-383
Netherlands	387-388
Spain	1010-1011
Switzerland	410-411
Turkey	1518-1520

Europa Issue 1962

Young Tree with 19 Leaves CD5

The 19 leaves represent the 19 original members of C.E.P.T.

1962-63

Belgium	582-583
Cyprus	219-221
France	1045-1046
Germany	852-853
Greece	739-740
Iceland	348-349
Ireland	184-185
Italy	860-861
Luxembourg	386-387
Netherlands	394-395
Norway	414-415
Switzerland	416-417
Turkey	1553-1555

Europa Issue, 1963

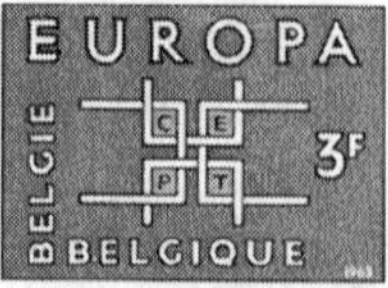

Stylized Links, Symbolizing Unity – CD6

1963, Sept.

Belgium	598-599
Cyprus	229-231
Finland	419
France	1074-1075
Germany	867-868
Greece	768-769
Iceland	357-358
Ireland	188-189
Italy	880-881
Luxembourg	403-404
Netherlands	416-417
Norway	441-442
Switzerland	429
Turkey	1602-1603

Europa Issue, 1964

Symbolic Daisy – CD7

5th anniversary of the establishment of C.E.P.T. The 22 petals of the flower symbolize the 22 members of the Conference.

1964, Sept.

Austria	738
Belgium	614-615
Cyprus	244-246
France	1109-1110
Germany	897-898
Greece	801-802
Iceland	367-368
Ireland	196-197
Italy	894-895
Luxembourg	411-412
Monaco	590-591
Netherlands	428-429
Norway	458
Portugal	931-933
Spain	1262-1263
Switzerland	438-439
Turkey	1628-1629

Europa Issue, 1965

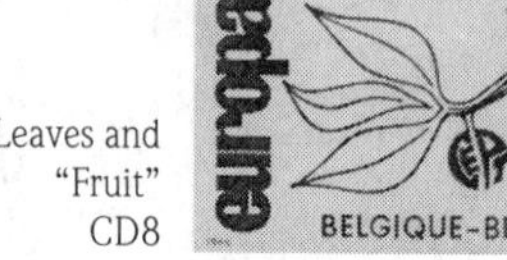

Leaves and "Fruit" CD8

1965

Belgium	636-637
Cyprus	262-264
Finland	437
France	1131-1132
Germany	934-935
Greece	833-834
Iceland	375-376
Ireland	204-205
Italy	915-916
Luxembourg	432-433
Monaco	616-617
Netherlands	438-439
Norway	475-476
Portugal	958-960
Switzerland	469
Turkey	1665-1666

Europa Issue, 1966

Symbolic Sailboat – CD9

1966, Sept.

Andorra, French	172
Belgium	675-676
Cyprus	275-277
France	1163-1164
Germany	963-964
Greece	862-863
Iceland	384-385
Ireland	216-217
Italy	942-943
Liechtenstein	415
Luxembourg	440-441
Monaco	639-640
Netherlands	441-442
Norway	496-497
Portugal	980-982
Switzerland	477-478
Turkey	1718-1719

Europa Issue, 1967

Cogwheels CD10

1967

Andorra, French	174-175
Belgium	688-689
Cyprus	297-299
France	1178-1179
Greece	891-892
Germany	969-970
Iceland	389-390
Ireland	232-233
Italy	951-952
Liechtenstein	420
Luxembourg	449-450
Monaco	669-670
Netherlands	444-447
Norway	504-505
Portugal	994-996
Spain	1465-1466
Switzerland	482
Turkey	B120-B121

Europa Issue, 1968

Golden Key with C.E.P.T. Emblem CD11

1968

Andorra, French	182-183
Belgium	705-706
Cyprus	314-316
France	1209-1210
Germany	983-984
Greece	916-917
Iceland	395-396
Ireland	242-243
Italy	979-980
Liechtenstein	442
Luxembourg	466-467
Monaco	689-691
Netherlands	452-453
Portugal	1019-1021
San Marino	687
Spain	1526
Turkey	1775-1776

Europa Issue, 1969

"EUROPA" and "CEPT" – CD12

Tenth anniversary of C.E.P.T.

1969

Andorra, French	188-189
Austria	837
Belgium	718-719
Cyprus	326-328
Denmark	458
Finland	483
France	1245-1246
Germany	996-997
Great Britain	585
Greece	947-948
Iceland	406-407
Ireland	270-271
Italy	1000-1001
Liechtenstein	453
Luxembourg	474-475
Monaco	722-724
Netherlands	475-476
Norway	533-534
Portugal	1038-1040
San Marino	701-702
Spain	1567

Sweden 814-816
Switzerland 500-501
Turkey.....................................1799-1800
Vatican....................................470-472
Yugoslavia 1003-1004

Europa Issue, 1970

Interwoven Threads CD13

1970
Andorra, French 196-197
Belgium....................................741-742
Cyprus.....................................340-342
France.....................................1271-1272
Germany....................................1018-1019
Greece.....................................985, 987
Iceland....................................420-421
Ireland....................................279-281
Italy......................................1013-1014
Liechtenstein..............................470
Luxembourg.................................489-490
Monaco.....................................768-770
Netherlands................................483-484
Portugal...................................1060-1062
San Marino.................................729-730
Spain......................................1607
Switzerland................................515-516
Turkey.....................................1848-1849
Yugoslavia.................................1024-1025

Europa Issue, 1971

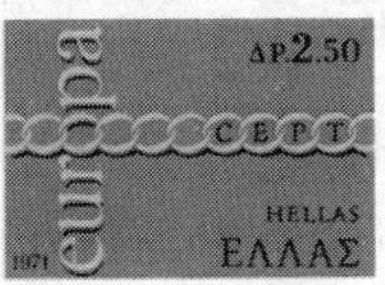

"Fraternity, Cooperation, Common Effort" – CD14

1971
Andorra, French 205-206
Belgium....................................803-804
Cyprus.....................................365-367
Finland....................................504
France.....................................1304
Germany....................................1064-1065
Greece.....................................1029-1030
Iceland....................................429-430
Ireland....................................305-306
Italy......................................1038-1039
Liechtenstein..............................485
Luxembourg.................................500-501
Malta......................................425-427
Monaco.....................................797-799
Netherlands................................488-489
Portugal...................................1094-1096
San Marino.................................749-750
Spain......................................1675-1676
Switzerland................................531-532
Turkey.....................................1876-1877
Yugoslavia.................................1052-1053

Europa Issue, 1972

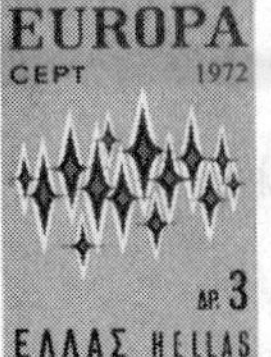

Sparkles, Symbolic of Communications CD15

1972
Andorra, French 210-211
Andorra, Spanish 62
Belgium....................................825-826
Cyprus.....................................380-382
Finland....................................512-513
France.....................................1341
Germany....................................1089-1090
Greece.....................................1049-1050
Iceland....................................439-440
Ireland....................................316-317
Italy......................................1065-1066
Liechtenstein..............................504
Luxembourg.................................512-513
Malta......................................450-453
Monaco.....................................831-832
Netherlands................................494-495
Portugal...................................1141-1143
San Marino.................................771-772
Spain......................................1718
Switzerland................................544-545
Turkey.....................................1907-1908
Yugoslavia.................................1100-1101

Europa Issue, 1973

Post Horn and Arrows CD16

1973
Andorra, French 319-320
Andorra, Spanish 76
Belgium....................................839-840
Cyprus.....................................396-398
Finland....................................526
France.....................................1367
Germany....................................1114-1115
Greece.....................................1090-1092
Iceland....................................447-448
Ireland....................................329-330
Italy......................................1108-1109
Liechtenstein..............................528-529
Luxembourg.................................523-524
Malta......................................469-471
Monaco.....................................866-867
Netherlands................................504-505
Norway.....................................604-605
Portugal...................................1170-1172
San Marino.................................802-803
Spain......................................1753
Switzerland................................580-581
Turkey.....................................1935-1936
Yugoslavia.................................1138-1139

PORTUGAL & COLONIES

Vasco da Gama Issue

Fleet Departing CD20

Fleet Arriving at Calicut CD21

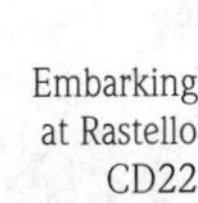

Embarking at Rastello CD22

Muse of History – CD23

San Gabriel, da Gama and Camoens – CD24

Archangel Gabriel, the Patron Saint CD25

Flagship San Gabriel CD26

Vasco da Gama CD27

Fourth centenary of Vasco da Gama's discovery of the route to India.

1898
Azores.....................................93-100
Macao......................................67-74
Madeira....................................37-44
Portugal...................................147-154
Port. Africa...............................1-8
Port. india................................189-196
Timor......................................45-52

Pombal Issue

POSTAL TAX

Marquis de Pombal CD28

Planning Reconstruction of Lisbon, 1755 CD29

Pombal Monument, Lisbon CD30

Sebastiao Jose de Carvalho e Mello, Marquis de Pombal (1699-1782), statesman, rebuilt Lisbon after earthquake of 1755. Tax was for the erection of Pombal monument. Obligatory on all mail on certain days throughout the year.

Postal Tax Dues are inscribed "Multa."

1925
Angola.....................RA1-RA3, RAJ1-RAJ3
Azores.....................RA9-RA11, RAJ2-RAJ4
Cape Verde.................RA1-RA3, RAJ1-RAJ3
Macao......................RA1-RA3, RAJ1-RAJ3
Madeira....................RA1-RA3, RAJ1-RAJ3
Mozambique.................RA1-RA3, RAJ1-RAJ3
Nyassa.....................RA1-RA3, RAJ1-RAJ3
Portugal...................RA11-RA13, RAJ2-RAJ4
Port. Guinea...............RA1-RA3, RAJ1-RAJ3
Port. India................RA1-RA3, RAJ1-RAJ3
St. Thomas & Prince Islands................RA1-RA3, RAJ1-RAJ3
Timor......................RA1-RA3, RAJ1-RAJ3

Vasco da Gama CD34

Mousinho de Albuquerque CD35

Dam CD36

Prince Henry the Navigator – CD37

Affonso de Albuquerque CD38

Plane over Globe CD39

1938-39
Angola.....................................274-291
Cape Verde.................................234-251
Macao......................................289-305
Mozambique.................................270-287
Port. Guinea...............................233-250
Port. India................................439-453
St. Thomas & Prince Islands................302-319, 323-340
Timor......................................223-239

1938-39
Angola.....................................C1-C9
Cape Verde.................................C1-C9
Macao......................................C7-C15
Mozambique.................................C1-C9
Port. Guinea...............................C1-C9
Port. India................................C1-C8
St. Thomas & Prince Islands................C1-C18
Timor......................................C1-C9

Lady of Fatima Issue

Our Lady of the Rosary, Fatima, Portugal CD40

1948-49
Angola.....................................315-318
Cape Verde.................................266
Macao......................................336
Mozambique.................................325-328
Port. Guinea...............................271
Port. India................................480
St. Thomas & Prince Islands................351
Timor......................................254

A souvenir sheet of 9 stamps was issued in 1951 to mark the extension of the 1950 Holy Year. The sheet contains: Angola No. 316, Cape Verde No. 266, Macao No. 336, Mozambique No. 325, Portuguese Guinea No. 271, Portugese India Nos. 480, 485, St. Thomas & Prince Islands No. 351, Timor No. 254.

The sheet also contains a portrait of Pope Pius XII and is inscribed "Encerramento do Ano Santo, Fatima 1951." It was sold for 11 escudos.

Holy Year Issue

Church Bells and Dove CD41 — Angel Holding Candelabra CD42

Holy Year, 1950.

1950-51

Angola	331-332
Cape Verde	268-269
Macao	339-340
Mozambique	330-331
Port. Guinea	273-274
Port. India	490-491, 496-503
St. Thomas & Prince Islands	353-354
Timor	258-259

A souvenir sheet of 8 stamps was issued in 1951 to mark the extension of the Holy Year. The sheet contains: Angola No. 331, Cape Verde No. 269, Macao No. 340, Mozambique No. 331, Portuguese Guinea No. 275, Portuguese India No. 490, St. Thomas & Prince Islands No. 354, Timor No. 258, some with colors changed. The sheet contains doves and is inscribed "Encerramento do Ano Santo, Fatima 1951." It was sold for 17 escudos.

Holy Year Conclusion Issue

Our Lady of Fatima CD43

Conclusion of Holy Year. Sheets contain alternate vertical rows of stamps and labels bearing quotation from Pope Pius XII, different for each colony.

1951

Angola	357
Cape Verde	270
Macao	352
Mozambique	356
Port. Guinea	275
Port. India	506
St. Thomas & Prince Islands	355
Timor	270

Medical Congress Issue

CD44

First National Congress of Tropical Medicine, Lisbon, 1952.

Each stamp has a different design.

1952

Angola	358
Cape Verde	287
Macao	364
Mozambique	359
Port. Guinea	276
Port. India	516
St. Thomas & Prince Islands	356
Timor	271

POSTAGE DUE STAMPS

CD45

1952

Angola	J37-J42
Cape Verde	J31-J36
Macao	J53-J58
Mozambique	J51-J56
Port. Guinea	J40-J45
Port. India	J47-J52
St. Thomas & Prince Islands	J52-J57
Timor	J31-J36

Sao Paulo Issue

Father Manuel de Nobrega and View of Sao Paulo CD46

Founding of Sao Paulo, Brazil, 400th anniv.

1954

Angola	385
Cape Verde	297
Macao	382
Mozambique	395
Port. Guinea	291
Port. India	530
St. Thomas & Prince Islands	369
Timor	279

Tropical Medicine Congress Issue

CD47

Sixth International Congress for Tropical Medicine and Malaria, Lisbon, Sept. 1958.

Each stamp shows a different plant.

1958

Angola	409
Cape Verde	303
Macao	392
Mozambique	404
Port. Guinea	295
Port. India	569
St. Thomas & Prince Islands	371
Timor	289

Sports Issue

CD48

Each stamp shows a different sport.

1962

Angola	433-438
Cape Verde	320-325
Macao	394-399
Mozambique	424-429
Port. Guinea	299-304
St. Thomas & Prince Islands	374-379
Timor	313-318

Anti-Malaria Issue

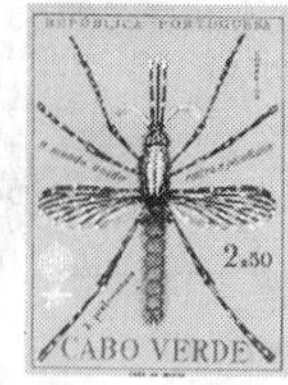

Anopheles Funestus and Malaria Eradication Symbol CD49

World Health Organization drive to eradicate malaria.

1962

Angola	439
Cape Verde	326
Macao	400
Mozambique	430
Port. Guinea	305
St. Thomas & Prince Islands	380
Timor	319

Airline Anniversary Issue

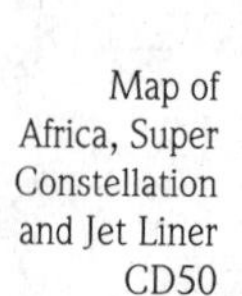

Map of Africa, Super Constellation and Jet Liner CD50

Tenth anniversary of Transportes Aereos Portugueses (TAP).

1963

Angola	490
Cape Verde	327
Mozambique	434
Port. Guinea	318
St. Thomas & Prince Islands	381

National Overseas Bank Issue

Antonio Teixeira de Sousa CD51

Centenary of the National Overseas Bank of Portugal.

1964, May 16

Angola	509
Cape Verde	328
Port. Guinea	319
St. Thomas & Prince Islands	382
Timor	320

ITU Issue

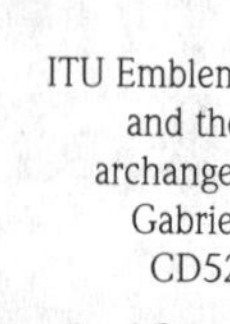

ITU Emblem and the archangel Gabriel CD52

International Communications Union, Cent.

1965, May 17

Angola	511
Cape Verde	329
Macao	402
Mozambique	464
Port. Guinea	320
St. Thomas & Prince Islands	383
Timor	321

National Revolution Issue

CD53

40th anniv. of the National Revolution.

Different buildings on each stamp.

1966, May 28

Angola	525
Cape Verde	338
Macao	403
Mozambique	465
Port. Guinea	329
St. Thomas & Prince Islands	392
Timor	322

Navy Club Issue

CD54

Centenary of Portugal's Navy Club.

Each stamp has a different design.

1967, Jan. 31

Angola	527-528
Cape Verde	339-340
Macao	412-413
Mozambique	478-479
Port. Guinea	330-331
St. Thomas & Prince Islands	393-394
Timor	323-324

Admiral Coutinho Issue

CD55

Centenary of the birth of Admiral Carlos Viegas Gago Coutinho (1869-1959), explorer and aviation pioneer.

Each stamp has a different design.

1969, Feb. 17

Angola	547
Cape Verde	355
Macao	417
Mozambique	484
Port. Guinea	335
St. Thomas & Prince Islands	397
Timor	335

Administration Reform Issue

Luiz Augusto Rebello da Silva – CD56

Centenary of the administration reforms of the overseas territories.

1969, Sept. 25

Angola	549
Cape Verde	357
Macao	419
Mozambique	491
Port. Guinea	337
St. Thomas & Prince Islands	399
Timor	338

Marshal Carmona Issue

CD57

Birth centenary of Marshal Antonio Oscar Carmona de Fragoso (1869-1951), President of Portugal.

Each stamp has a different design.

1970, Nov. 15

Angola....563
Cape Verde....359
Macao....422
Mozambique....493
Port. Guinea....340
St. Thomas & Prince Islands....403
Timor....341

Olympic Games Issue

CD59

20th Olympic Games, Munich, Aug. 26-Sept. 11.

Each stamp shows a different sport.

1972, June 20

Angola....569
Cape Verde....361
Macao....426
Mozambique....504
Port. Guinea....342
St. Thomas & Prince Islands....408
Timor....343

Lisbon-Rio de Janeiro Flight Issue

CD60

50th anniversary of the Lisbon to Rio de Janeiro flight by Arturo de Sacadura and Coutinho, March 30-June 5, 1922.

Each stamp shows a different stage of the flight.

1972, Sept. 20

Angola....570
Cape Verde....362
Macao....427
Mozambique....505
Port. Guinea....343
St. Thomas & Prince Islands....409
Timor....344

WMO Centenary Issue

WMO Emblem – CD61

Centenary of international meterological cooperation.

1973, Dec. 15

Angola....571
Cape Verde....363
Macao....429
Mozambique....509
Port. Guinea....344
St. Thomas & Prince Islands....410
Timor....345

FRENCH COMMUNITY

Upper Volta can be found under Burkina Faso in Vol. 1

Colonial Exposition Issue

People of French Empire CD70

Women's Heads CD71

France Showing Way to Civilization CD72

"Colonial Commerce" CD73

International Colonial Exposition, Paris.

1931

Cameroun....213-216
Chad....60-63
Dahomey....97-100
Fr. Guiana....152-155
Fr. Guinea....116-119
Fr. India....100-103
Fr. Polynesia....76-79
Fr. Sudan....102-105
Gabon....120-123
Guadeloupe....138-141
Indo-China....140-142
Ivory Coast....92-95
Madagascar....169-172
Martinique....129-132
Mauritania....65-68
Middle Congo....61-64
New Caledonia....176-179
Niger....73-76
Reunion....122-125
St. Pierre & Miquelon....132-135
Senegal....138-141
Somali Coast....135-138
Togo....254-257
Ubangi-Shari....82-85
Upper Volta....66-69
Wallis & Futuna Isls....85-88

Paris International Exposition Issue
Colonial Arts Exposition Issue

"Colonial Resources"
CD74 CD77

Overseas Commerce – CD75

Exposition Building and Women CD76

"France and the Empire" CD78

Cultural Treasures of the Colonies CD79

Souvenir sheets contain one imperf. stamp.

1937

Cameroun....217-222A
Dahomey....101-107
Fr. Equatorial Africa....27-32, 73
Fr. Guiana....162-168
Fr. Guinea....120-126
Fr. India....104-110
Fr. Polynesia....117-123
Fr. Sudan....106-112
Guadeloupe....148-154
Indo-China....193-199
Inini....41
Ivory Coast....152-158
Kwangchowan....132
Madagascar....191-197
Martinique....179-185
Mauritania....69-75
New Caledonia....208-214
Niger....72-83
Reunion....167-173
St. Pierre & Miquelon....165-171
Senegal....172-178
Somali Coast....139-145
Togo....258-264
Wallis & Futuna Isls....89

Curie Issue

Pierre and Marie Curie CD80

40th anniversary of the discovery of radium. The surtax was for the benefit of the Intl. Union for the Control of Cancer.

1938

Cameroun....B1
Cuba....B1-B2
Dahomey....B2
France....B76
Fr. Equatorial Africa....B1
Fr. Guiana....B3
Fr. Guinea....B2
Fr. India....B6
Fr. Polynesia....B5
Fr. Sudan....B1
Guadeloupe....B3
Indo-China....B14
Ivory Coast....B2
Madagascar....B2
Martinique....B2
Mauritania....B3
New Caledonia....B4
Niger....B1
Reunion....B4
St. Pierre & Miquelon....B3
Senegal....B3
Somali Coast....B2
Togo....B1

Caillie Issue

Rene Caille and Map of Northwestern Africa - CD81

Death centenary of Rene Caillie (1799-1838), French explorer.

All three denominations exist with colony name omitted.

1939

Dahomey....108-110
Fr. Guinea....161-163
Fr. Sudan....113-115
Ivory Coast....160-162
Mauritania....109-111
Niger....84-86
Senegal....188-190
Togo....265-267

New York World's Fair Issue

Natives and New York Skyline CD82

1939

Cameroun....223-224
Dahomey....111-112
Fr. Equatorial Africa....78-79
Fr. Guiana....169-170
Fr. Guinea....164-165
Fr. India....111-112
Fr. Polynesia....124-125
Fr. Sudan....116-117
Guadeloupe....155-156
Indo-China....203-204
Inini....42-43
Ivory Coast....163-164
Kwangchowan....121-122
Madagascar....209-210
Martinique....186-187
Mauritania....112-113
New Caledonia....215-216
Niger....87-88
Reunion....174-175
St. Pierre & Miquelon....205-206
Senegal....191-192
Somali Coast....179-180
Togo....268-269
Wallis & Futuna Isls....90-91

French Revolution Issue

Storming of the Bastille – CD83

French Revolution, 150th anniv. The surtax was for the defense of the colonies.

1939

Cameroun....B2-B6
Dahomey....B3-B7
Fr. Equatorial Africa....B4-B8, CB1
Fr. Guiana....B4-B8, CB1
Fr. Guinea....B3-B7
Fr. India....B7-B11
Fr. Polynesia....B6-B10, CB1
Fr. Sudan....B2-B6
Guadeloupe....B4-B8
Indo-China....B15-B19, CB1
Inini....B1-B5
Ivory Coast....B3-B7
Kwangchowan....B1-B5
Madagascar....B3-B7, CB1
Martinique....B3-B7
Mauritania....B4-B8
New Caledonia....B5-B9, CB1
Niger....B2-B6
Reunion....B5-B9, CB1
St. Pierre & Miquelon....B4-B8
Senegal....B4-B8, CB1
Somali Coast....B3-B7
Togo....B2-B6
Wallis & Futuna Isls....B1-B5

Plane over Coastal Area CD85

All five denominations exist with colony name omitted.

1940

Dahomey..........C1-C5
Fr. Guinea..........C1-C5
Fr. Sudan..........C1-C5
Ivory Coast..........C1-C5
Mauritania..........C1-C5
Niger..........C1-C5
Senegal..........C12-C16
Togo..........C1-C5

Colonial Infantryman CD86

1941

Cameroun..........B13B
Dahomey..........B13
Fr. Equatorial Africa..........B8B
Fr. Guiana..........B10
Fr. Guinea..........B13
Fr. India..........B13
Fr. Polynesia..........B12
Fr. Sudan..........B12
Guadeloupe..........B10
Indo-China..........B19B
Inini..........B7
Ivory Coast..........B13
Kwangchowan..........B7
Madagascar..........B9
Martinique..........B9
Mauritania..........B14
New Caledonia..........B11
Niger..........B12
Reunion..........B11
St. Pierre & Miquelon..........B8B
Senegal..........B14
Somali Coast..........B9
Togo..........B10B
Wallis & Futuna Isls...........B7

Cross of Lorraine & Four-motor Plane CD87

1941-5

Cameroun..........C1-C7
Fr. Equatorial Africa..........C17-C23
Fr. Guiana..........C9-C10
Fr. India..........C1-C6
Fr. Polynesia..........C3-C9
Fr. West Africa..........C1-C3
Guadeloupe..........C1-C2
Madagascar..........C37-C43
Martinique..........C1-C2
New Caledonia..........C7-C13
Reunion..........C18-C24
St. Pierre & Miquelon..........C1-C7
Somali Coast..........C1-C7

Transport Plane CD88

Caravan and Plane CD89

1942

Dahomey..........C6-C13
Fr. Guinea..........C6-C13
Fr. Sudan..........C6-C13
Ivory Coast..........C6-C13
Mauritania..........C6-C13
Niger..........C6-C13
Senegal..........C17-C25
Togo..........C6-C13

Red Cross Issue

Marianne CD90

The surtax was for the French Red Cross and national relief.

1944

Cameroun..........B28
Fr. Equatorial Africa..........B38
Fr. Guiana..........B12
Fr. India..........B14
Fr. Polynesia..........B13
Fr. West Africa..........B1
Guadeloupe..........B12
Madagascar..........B15
Martinique..........B11
New Caledonia..........B13
Reunion..........B15
St. Pierre & Miquelon..........B13
Somali Coast..........B13
Wallis & Futuna Isls...........B9

Eboue Issue

CD91

Felix Eboue, first French colonial administrator to proclaim resistance to Germany after French surrender in World War II.

1945

Cameroun..........296-297
Fr. Equatorial Africa..........156-157
Fr. Guiana..........171-172
Fr. India..........210-211
Fr. Polynesia..........150-151
Fr. West Africa..........15-16
Guadeloupe..........187-188
Madagascar..........259-260
Martinique..........196-197
New Caledonia..........274-275
Reunion..........238-239
St. Pierre & Miquelon..........322-323
Somali Coast..........238-239

Victory Issue

Victory – CD92

European victory of the Allied Nations in World War II.

1946, May 8

Cameroun..........C8
Fr. Equatorial Africa..........C24
Fr. Guiana..........C11
Fr. India..........C7
Fr. Polynesia..........C10
Fr. West Africa..........C4
Guadeloupe..........C3
Indo-China..........C19
Madagascar..........C44
Martinique..........C3
New Caledonia..........C14
Reunion..........C25
St. Pierre & Miquelon..........C8
Somali Coast..........C8
Wallis & Futuna Isls...........C1

Chad to Rhine Issue

Leclerc's Departure from Chad – CD93

Battle at Cufra Oasis – CD94

Tanks in Action, Mareth – CD95

Normandy Invasion – CD96

Entering Paris – CD97

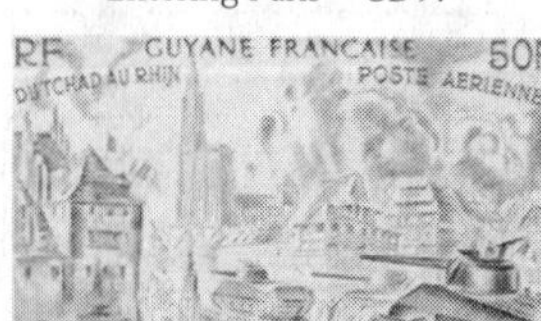

Liberation of Strasbourg – CD98

"Chad to the Rhine" march, 1942-44, by Gen. Jacques Leclerc's column, later French 2nd Armored Division.

1946, June 6

Cameroun..........C9-C14
Fr. Equatorial Africa..........C25-C30
Fr. Guiana..........C12-C17
Fr. India..........C8-C13
Fr. Polynesia..........C11-C16
Fr. West Africa..........C5-C10
Guadeloupe..........C4-C9
Indo-China..........C20-C25
Madagascar..........C45-C50
Martinique..........C4-C9
New Caledonia..........C15-C20
Reunion..........C26-C31
St. Pierre & Miquelon..........C9-C14
Somali Coast..........C9-C14
Wallis & Futuna Isls...........C2-C7

UPU Issue

French Colonials, Globe and Plane CD99

Universal Postal Union, 75th anniv.

1949, July 4

Cameroun..........C29
Fr. Equatorial Africa..........C34
Fr. India..........C17
Fr. Polynesia..........C20
Fr. West Africa..........C15
Indo-China..........C26
Madagascar..........C55
New Caledonia..........C24
St. Pierre & Miquelon..........C18
Somali Coast..........C18
Togo..........C18
Wallis & Futuna Isls...........C10

Tropical Medicine Issue

Doctor Treating Infant CD100

The surtax was for charitable work.

1950

Cameroun..........B29
Fr. Equatorial Africa..........B39
Fr. India..........B15
Fr. Polynesia..........B14
Fr. West Africa..........B3
Madagascar..........B17
New Caledonia..........B14
St. Pierre & Miquelon..........B14
Somali Coast..........B14
Togo..........B11

Military Medal Issue

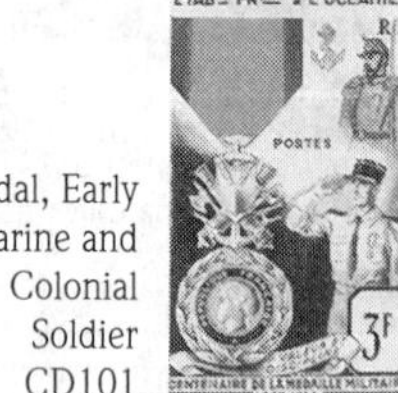

Medal, Early Marine and Colonial Soldier CD101

Centenary of the creation of the French Military Medal.

1952

Cameroun..........332
Comoro Isls...........39
Fr. Equatorial Africa..........186
Fr. India..........233
Fr. Polynesia..........179
Fr. West Africa..........57
Madagascar..........286
New Caledonia..........295
St. Pierre & Miquelon..........345
Somali Coast..........267
Togo..........327
Wallis & Futuna Isls...........149

Liberation Issue

Allied Landing, Victory Sign and Cross of Lorraine – CD102

Lberation of France, 10th anniv.

1954, June 6

Cameroun	C32
Comoro Isls.	C4
Fr. Equatorial Africa	C38
Fr. India	C18
Fr. Polynesia	C22
Fr. West Africa	C17
Madagascar	C57
New Caledonia	C25
St. Pierre & Miquelon	C19
Somali Coast	C19
Togo	C19
Wallis & Futuna Isls.	C11

FIDES Issue

Plowmen CD103

Efforts of FIDES, the Economic and Social Development Fund for Overseas Possessions (Fonds d' Investissement pour le Developpement Economique et Social).

Each stamp has a different design.

1956

Cameroun	326-329
Comoro Isls.	43
Fr. Polynesia	181
Madagascar	292-295
New Caledonia	303
Somali Coast	268
Togo	331

Flower Issue

CD104

Each stamp shows a different flower.

1958-9

Cameroun	333
Comoro Isls.	45
Fr. Equatorial Africa	200-201
Fr. Polynesia	192
Fr. So. & Antarctic Terr.	11
Fr. West Africa	79-83
Madagascar	301-302
New Caledonia	304-305
St. Pierre & Miquelon	357
Somali Coast	270
Togo	348-349
Wallis & Futuna Isls.	152

Human Rights Issue

Sun, Dove and U.N. Emblem – CD105

10th anniversary of the signing of the Universal Declaration of Human Rights.

1958

Comoro Isls.	44
Fr. Equatorial Africa	202
Fr. Polynesia	191
Fr. West Africa	85
Madagascar	300
New Caledonia	306
St. Pierre & Miquelon	356
Somali Coast	274
Wallis & Futuna Isls.	153

C.C.T.A. Issue

CD106

Commission for Technical Cooperation in Africa south of the Sahara, 10th anniv.

1960

Cameroun	335
Cent. African Rep.	3
Chad	66
Congo, P.R.	90
Dahomey	138
Gabon	150
Ivory Coast	180
Madagascar	317
Mali	9
Mauritania	117
Niger	104
Upper Volta	89

Air Afrique Issue, 1961

Modern and Ancient Africa, Map and Planes – CD107

Founding of Air Afrique (African Airlines).

1961-62

Cameroun	C37
Cent. African Rep.	C5
Chad	C7
Congo, P.R.	C5
Dahomey	C17
Gabon	C5
Ivory Coast	C18
Mauritania	C17
Niger	C22
Senegal	C31
Upper Volta	C4

Anti-Malaria Issue

CD108

World Health Organization drive to eradicate malaria.

1962, Apr. 7

Cameroun	B36
Cent. African Rep.	B1
Chad	B1
Comoro Isls.	B1
Congo, P.R.	B3
Dahomey	B15
Gabon	B4
Ivory Coast	B15
Madagascar	B19
Mali	B1
Mauritania	B16
Niger	B14
Senegal	B16
Somali Coast	B15
Upper Volta	B1

Abidjan Games Issue

CD109

Abidjan Games, Ivory Coast, Dec. 24-31, 1961. Each stamp shows a different sport.

1962

Chad	83-84
Cent. African Rep.	19-20
Congo, P.R.	103-104
Gabon	163-164, C6
Niger	109-111
Upper Volta	103-105

African and Malagasy Union Issue

Flag of Union CD110

First anniversary of the Union.

1962, Sept. 8

Cameroun	373
Cent. African Rep.	21
Chad	85
Congo, P.R.	105
Dahomey	155
Gabon	165
Ivory Coast	198
Madagascar	332
Mauritania	170
Niger	112
Senegal	211
Upper Volta	106

Telstar Issue

Telstar and Globe Showing Andover and Pleumeur-Bodou – CD111

First television connection of the United States and Europe through the Telstar satellite, July 11-12, 1962.

1962-63

Andorra, French	154
Comoro Isls.	C7
Fr. Polynesia	C29
Fr. So. & Antarctic Terr.	C5
New Caledonia	C33
Somali Coast	C31
St. Pierre & Miquelon	C26
Wallis & Futuna Isls.	C17

Freedom From Hunger Issue

World Map and Wheat Emblem CD112

U.N. Food and Agriculture Organization's "Freedom from Hunger" campaign.

1963, Mar. 21

Cameroun	B37-B38
Cent. African Rep.	B2
Chad	B2
Congo, P.R.	B4
Dahomey	B16
Gabon	B5
Ivory Coast	B16
Madagascar	B21
Mauritania	B17
Niger	B15
Senegal	B17
Upper Volta	B2

Red Cross Centenary Issue

CD113

Centenary of the International Red Cross.

1963, Sept. 2

Comoro Isls.	55
Fr. Polynesia	205
New Caledonia	328
St. Pierre & Miquelon	367
Somali Coast	297
Wallis & Futuna Isls.	165

African Postal Union Issue

UAMPT Emblem, Radio Masts, Plane and Mail CD114

Establishment of the African and Malagasy Posts and Telecommunications Union.

1963, Sept. 8

Cameroun	C47
Cent. African Rep.	C10
Chad	C9
Congo, P.R.	C13
Dahomey	C19
Gabon	C13
Ivory Coast	C25
Madagascar	C75
Mauritania	C22
Niger	C27
Rwanda	36
Senegal	C32
Upper Volta	C9

Air Afrique Issue, 1963

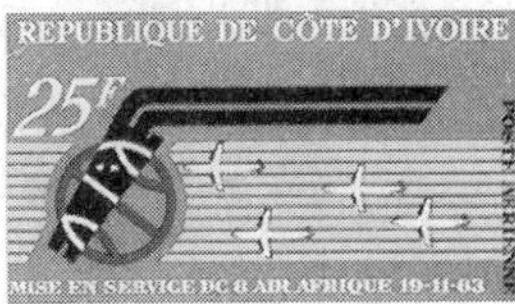

Symbols of Flight – CD115

First anniversary of Air Afrique and inauguration of DC-8 service.

1963, Nov. 19

Cameroun	C48
Chad	C10
Congo, P.R.	C14
Gabon	C18
Ivory Coast	C26
Mauritania	C26
Niger	C35
Senegal	C33

Europafrica Issue

Europe and Africa Linked CD116

Signing of an economic agreement between the European Economic Community and the African and Malagasy Union, Yaounde, Cameroun, July 20, 1963.

1963-64

Cameroun 402
Chad C11
Cent. African Rep. C12
Congo, P.R. C16
Gabon C19
Ivory Coast 217
Niger C43
Upper Volta C11

Human Rights Issue

Scales of Justice and Globe CD117

15th anniversary of the Universal Declaration of Human Rights.

1963, Dec. 10

Comoro Isls. 58
Fr. Polynesia 206
New Caledonia 329
St. Pierre & Miquelon 368
Somali Coast 300
Wallis & Futuna Isls. 166

PHILATEC Issue

Stamp Album, Champs Elysees Palace and Horses of Marly – CD118

Intl. Philatelic and Postal Techniques Exhibition, Paris, June 5-21, 1964.

1963-64

Comoro Isls. 60
France 1078
Fr. Polynesia 207
New Caledonia 341
St. Pierre & Miquelon 369
Somali Coast 301
Wallis & Futuna Isls. 167

Cooperation Issue

CD119

Cooperation between France and the French-speaking countries of Africa and Madagascar.

1964

Cameroun 409-410
Cent. African Rep. 39
Chad 103
Congo, P.R. 121
Dahomey 193
France 1111
Gabon 175
Ivory Coast 221
Madagascar 360
Mauritania 181
Niger 143
Senegal 236
Togo 495

ITU Issue

Telegraph, Syncom Satellite and ITU Emblem CD120

Intl. Telecommunication Union, Cent.

1965, May 17

Comoro Isls. C14
Fr. Polynesia C33
Fr. So. & Antarctic Terr. C8
New Caledonia C40
New Hebrides 124-125
St. Pierre & Miquelon C29
Somali Coast C36
Wallis & Futuna Isls. C20

French Satellite A-1 Issue

Diamant Rocket and Launching Installation – CD121

Launching of France's first satellite, Nov. 26, 1965.

1965-66

Comoro Isls. C15-C16
France 1137-1138
Fr. Polynesia C40-C41
Fr. So. & Antarctic Terr. C9-C10
New Caledonia C44-C45
St. Pierre & Miquelon C30-C31
Somali Coast C39-C40
Wallis & Futuna Isls. C22-C23

French Satellite D-1 Issue

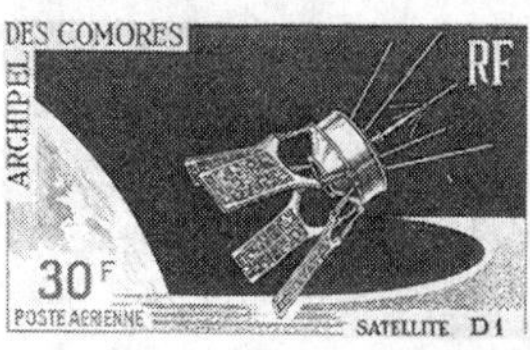

D-1 Satellite in Orbit – CD122

Launching of the D-1 satellite at Hammaguir, Algeria, Feb. 17, 1966.

1966

Comoro Isls. C17
France 1148
Fr. Polynesia C42
Fr. So. & Antarctic Terr. C11
New Caledonia C46
St. Pierre & Miquelon C32
Somali Coast C49
Wallis & Futuna Isls. C24

Air Afrique Issue, 1966

Planes and Air Afrique Emblem – CD123

Introduction of DC-8F planes by Air Afrique.

1966

Cameroun C79
Cent. African Rep. C35
Chad C26
Congo, P.R. C42
Dahomey C42
Gabon C47
Ivory Coast C32
Mauritania C57
Niger C63
Senegal C47
Togo C54
Upper Volta C31

African Postal Union, 1967

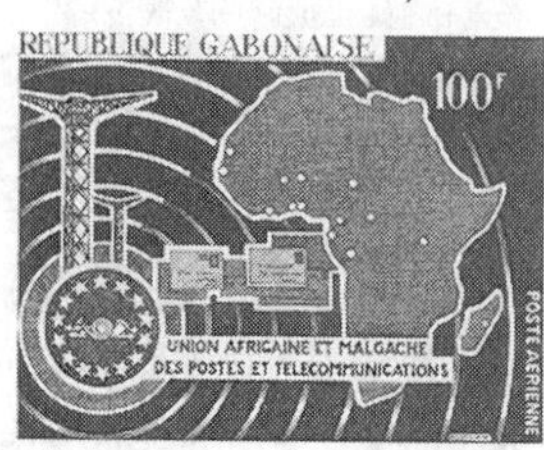

Telecommunications Symbols and Map of Africa – CD124

Fifth anniversary of the establishment of the African and Malagasy Union of Posts and Telecommunications, UAMPT.

1967

Cameroun C90
Cent. African Rep. C46
Chad C37
Congo, P.R. C57
Dahomey C61
Gabon C58
Ivory Coast C34
Madagascar C85
Mauritania C65
Niger C75
Rwanda C1-C3
Senegal C60
Togo C81
Upper Volta C50

Monetary Union Issue

Gold Token of the Ashantis, 17-18th Centuries – CD125

West African Monetary Union, 5th anniv.

1967, Nov. 4

Dahomey 244
Ivory Coast 259
Mauritania 238
Niger 204
Senegal 294
Togo 623
Upper Volta 181

WHO Anniversary Issue

Sun, Flowers and WHO Emblem CD126

World Health Organization, 20th anniv.

1968, May 4

Afars & Issas 317
Comoro Isls. 73
Fr. Polynesia 241-242
Fr. So. & Antarctic Terr. 31
New Caledonia 367
St. Pierre & Miquelon 377
Wallis & Futuna Isls. 169

Human Rights Year Issue

Human Rights Flame CD127

1968, Aug. 10

Afars & Issas 322-323
Comoro Isls. 76
Fr. Polynesia 243-244
Fr. So. & Antarctic Terr. 32
New Caledonia 369
St. Pierre & Miquelon 382
Wallis & Futuna Isls. 170

2nd PHILEXAFRIQUE Issue

CD128

Opening of PHILEXAFRIQUE, Abidjan, Feb. 14. Each stamp shows a local scene and stamp.

1969, Feb. 14

Cameroun C118
Cent. African Rep. C65
Chad C48
Congo, P.R. C77
Dahomey C94
Gabon C82
Ivory Coast C38-C40
Madagascar C92
Mali C65
Mauritania C80
Niger C104
Senegal C68
Togo C104
Upper Volta C62

Concorde Issue

Concorde in Flight CD129

First flight of the prototpye Concorde super-sonic plane at Toulouse, Mar. 1, 1969.

1969

Afars & Issas C56
Comoro Isls. C29
France C42
Fr. Polynesia C50
Fr. So. & Antarctic Terr. C18
New Caledonia C63
St. Pierre & Miquelon C40
Wallis & Futuna Isls. C30

Development Bank Issue

Bank Emblem CD130

African Development Bank, fifth anniv.

1969

Cameroun 499

Chad.....217
Congo, P.R.....181-182
Ivory Coast.....281
Mali.....127-128
Mauritania.....267
Niger.....220
Senegal.....317-318
Upper Volta.....201

ILO Issue

ILO Headquarters, Geneva, and Emblem – CD131

Intl. Labor Organization, 50th anniv.

1969-70

Afars & Issas.....337
Comoro Isls.....83
Fr. Polynesia.....251-252
Fr. So. & Antarctic Terr.....35
New Caledonia.....379
St. Pierre & Miquelon.....396
Wallis & Futuna Isls.....172

ASECNA Issue

Map of Africa, Plane and Airport – CD132

10th anniversary of the Agency for the Security of Aerial Navigation in Africa and Madagascar (ASECNA, Agence pour la Securite de la Navigation Aerienne en Afrique et a Madagascar).

1969-70

Cameroun.....500
Cent. African Rep.....119
Chad.....222
Congo, P.R.....197
Dahomey.....269
Gabon.....260
Ivory Coast.....287
Mali.....130
Niger.....221
Senegal.....321
Upper Volta.....204

U.P.U. Headquarters Issue

CD133

New Universal Postal Union headquarters, Bern, Switzerland.

1970

Afars & Issas.....342
Algeria.....443
Cameroun.....503-504
Cent. African Rep.....125
Chad.....225
Comoro Isls.....84
Congo, P.R.....216
Fr. Polynesia.....261-262
Fr. So. & Antarctic Terr.....36
Gabon.....258
Ivory Coast.....295
Madagascar.....444
Mali.....134-135
Mauritania.....283
New Caledonia.....382
Niger.....231-232
St. Pierre & Miquelon.....397-398
Senegal.....328-329
Tunisia.....535
Wallis & Futuna Isls.....173

De Gaulle Issue

CD134

First anniversary of the death of Charles de Gaulle, (1890-1970), President of France.

1971-72

Afars & Issas.....356-357
Comoro Isls.....104-105
France.....1322-1325
Fr. Polynesia.....270-271
Fr. So. & Antarctic Terr.....52-53
New Caledonia.....393-394
Reunion.....377, 380
St. Pierre & Miquelon.....417-418
Wallis & Futuna Isls.....177-178

African Postal Union Issue, 1971

UAMPT Building, Brazzaville, Congo – CD135

10th anniversary of the establishment of the African and Malagasy Posts and Telecommunications Union, UAMPT.

Each stamp has a different native design.

1971, Nov. 13

Cameroun.....C177
Cent. African Rep.....C89
Chad.....C94
Congo, P.R.....C136
Dahomey.....C146
Gabon.....C120
Ivory Coast.....C47
Mauritania.....C113
Niger.....C164
Rwanda.....C8
Senegal.....C105
Togo.....C166
Upper Volta.....C97

West African Monetary Union Issue

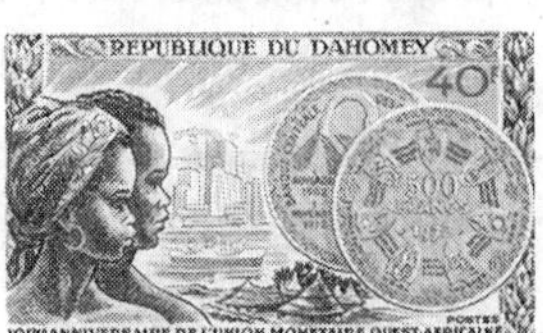

African Couple, City, Village and Commemorative Coin – CD136

West African Monetary Union, 10th anniv.

1972, Nov. 2

Dahomey.....300
Ivory Coast.....331
Mauritania.....299
Niger.....258
Senegal.....374
Togo.....825
Upper Volta.....280

African Postal Union Issue, 1973

Telecommunications Symbols and Map of Africa – CD137

11th anniversary of the African and Malagasy Posts and Telecommunications Union (UAMPT).

1973, Sept. 12

Cameroun.....574
Cent. African Rep.....194
Chad.....294
Congo, P.R.....289
Dahomey.....311
Gabon.....320
Ivory Coast.....361
Madagascar.....500
Mauritania.....304
Niger.....287
Rwanda.....540
Senegal.....393
Togo.....849
Upper Volta.....297

Philexafrique II — Essen Issue

CD138

CD139

Designs: Indigenous fauna, local and German stamps.

Types CD138-CD139 printed horizontally and vertically se-tenant in sheets of 10 (2x5). Label between horizontal pairs alternately commemoratives Philexafrique II, Libreville, Gabon, June 1978, and 2nd International Stamp Fair, Essen, Germany, Nov. 1-5.

1978-1979

Benin.....C285-C286
Central Africa.....C200-C201
Chad.....C238-C239
Congo Republic.....C245-C246
Djibouti.....C121-C122
Gabon.....C215-C216
Ivory Coast.....C64-C65
Mali.....C356-C357
Mauritania.....C185-C186
Niger.....C291-C292
Rwanda.....C12-C13
Senegal.....C146-C147
Togo.....C363-C364
Upper Volta.....C253-C254

BRITISH COMMONWEALTH OF NATIONS

The listings follow established trade practices when these issues are offered as units by dealers. The Peace issue, for example, includes only one stamp from the Indian state of Hyderabad. The U.P.U. issue includes the Egypt set. Pairs are included for those varieties issues with bilingual designs se-tenant.

Silver Jubilee Issue

Windsor Castle and King George V
CD301

Reign of King George V, 25th anniv.

1935

Antigua.....77-80
Ascension.....33-36
Bahamas.....92-95
Barbados.....186-189
Basutoland.....11-14
Bechuanaland Protectorate.....117-120
Bermuda.....100-103
British Guiana.....223-226
British Honduras.....108-111
Cayman Islands.....81-84
Ceylon.....260-263
Cyprus.....136-139
Dominica.....90-93
Falkland Islands.....77-80
Fiji.....110-113
Gambia.....125-128
Gibraltar.....100-103
Gilbert & Ellice Islands.....33-36
Gold Coast.....108-111
Grenada.....124-127
Hong Kong.....147-150
Jamaica.....109-112
Kenya, Uganda, Tanganyika.....42-45
Leeward Islands.....96-99
Malta.....184-187
Mauritius.....204-207
Montserrat.....85-88
Newfoundland.....226-229
Nigeria.....34-37
Northern Rhodesia.....18-21
Nyasaland Protectorate.....47-50
St. Helena.....111-114
St. Kitts-Nevis.....72-75
St. Lucia.....91-94
St. Vincent.....134-137
Seychelles.....118-121
Sierra Leone.....166-169
Solomon Islands.....60-63
Somaliland Protectorate.....77-80
Straits Settlements.....213-216
Swaziland.....20-23
Trinidad & Tobago.....43-46
Turks & Caicos Islands.....71-74
Virgin Islands.....69-72

The following have different designs but are included in the omnibus set:

Great Britain.....226-229
Offices in Morocco.....67-70, 226-229, 422-425, 508-510
Australia.....152-154
Canada.....211-216
Cook Islands.....98-100
India.....142-148
Nauru.....31-34
New Guinea.....46-47
New Zealand.....199-201
Niue.....67-69
Papua.....114-117
Samoa.....163-165
South Africa.....68-71
Southern Rhodesia.....33-36
South-West Africa.....121-124

249 stamps, Never Hinged $975.

Coronation Issue

Queen Elizabeth and King George VI
CD302

1937

Aden.....13-15
Antigua.....81-83
Ascension.....37-39
Bahamas.....97-99
Barbados.....190-192
Basutoland.....15-17
Bechuanaland Protectorate.....121-123

Bermuda..115-117
British Guiana................................227-229
British Honduras.............................112-114
Cayman Islands 97-99
Ceylon..275-277
Cyprus..140-142
Dominica..94-96
Falkland Islands 81-83
Fiji..114-116
Gambia...129-131
Gibraltar...104-106
Gilbert & Ellice Islands 37-39
Gold Coast 112-114
Grenada 128-130
Hong Kong......................................151-153
Jamaica...113-115
Kenya, Uganda, Tanganyika 60-62
Leeward Islands.............................100-102
Malta..188-190
Mauritius..208-210
Montserrat 89-91
Newfoundland................................230-232
Nigeria 50-52
Northern Rhodesia.............................22-24
Nyasaland Protectorate 51-53
St. Helena.......................................115-117
St. Kitts-Nevis 76-78
St. Lucia 107-109
St. Vincent......................................138-140
Seychelles.......................................122-124
Sierra Leone 170-172
Solomon Islands.................................64-66
Somaliland Protectorate 81-83
Straits Settlements 235-237
Swaziland 24-26
Trinidad & Tobago 47-49
Turks & Caicos Islands 75-77
Virgin Islands.....................................73-75

The following have different designs but are included in the omnibus set:
Great Britain..234
Offices in Morocco 82, 439, 514
Canada...237
Cook Islands...................................109-111
Nauru...35-38
Newfoundland.................................233-243
New Guinea 48-51
New Zealand 223-225
Niue...70-72
Papua...118-121
South Africa..74-78
Southern Rhodesia...............................38-41
South-West Africa............................125-132
202 stamps, Never Hinged $80.

Peace Issue

King George VI and Parliament Buildings, London – CD303

Return to peace at the close of World War II.

1945-46

Aden 28-29
Antigua 96-97
Ascension 50-51
Bahamas..130-131
Barbados...207-208
Bermuda..131-132
British Guiana.................................242-243
British Honduras..............................127-128
Cayman Islands 112-113
Ceylon...293-294
Cyprus...156-157
Dominica..112-113
Falkland Islands 97-98
Falkland Islands Dep. 1L9-1L10
Fiji..137-138
Gambia..144-145
Gibraltar..119-120
Gilbert & Ellice Islands 52-53
Gold Coast 128-129
Grenada 143-144
Jamaica..136-137
Kenya, Uganda, Tanganyika 90-91
Leeward Islands..............................116-117
Malta...206-207
Mauritius...223-224
Montserrat 104-105
Nigeria 71-72
Northern Rhodesia...............................46-47
Nyasaland Protectorate 82-83
Pitcairn Island..9-10
St. Helena..128-129
St. Kitts-Nevis 91-92
St. Lucia 127-128
St. Vincent.......................................152-153
Seychelles..149-150
Sierra Leone 186-187
Solomon Islands..................................80-81
Somaliland Protectorate 108-109
Trinidad & Tobago 62-63
Turks & Caicos Islands 90-91
Virgin Islands......................................88-89

The following have different designs but are included in the omnibus set:
Great Britain...................................264-265
Offices in Morocco.........................523-524
Aden
Kathiri State of Seiyun........................12-13
Qu'aiti State of Shihr and Mukalla...................................12-13
Australia 200-202
Basutoland..29-31
Bechuanaland Protectorate.............137-139
Burma 66-69
Cook Islands....................................127-130
Hong Kong......................................174-175
India..195-198
Hyderabad...51
New Zealand 247-257
Niue 90-93
Pakistan-Bahawalpur O16
Samoa 191-194
South Africa....................................100-102
Southern Rhodesia...............................67-70
South-West Africa............................153-155
Swaziland 38-40
Zanzibar 222-223
164 stamps, Never Hinged $42.50

Silver Wedding Issue

King George VI and Queen Elizabeth
CD304 CD305

1948-49

Aden 30-31
Kathiri State of Seiyun........................14-15
Qu'aiti State of Shihr and Mukalla....................................14-15
Antigua 98-99
Ascension 52-53
Bahamas..148-149
Barbados...210-211
Basutoland..39-40
Bechuanaland Protectorate.............147-148
Bermuda..133-134
British Guiana.................................244-245
British Honduras..............................129-130
Cayman Islands 116-117
Cyprus...158-159
Dominica..114-115
Falkland Islands 99-100
Falkland Islands Dep. 1L11-1L12
Fiji..139-140
Gambia..146-147
Gibraltar..121-122
Gilbert & Ellice Islands 54-55
Gold Coast 142-143
Grenada 145-146
Hong Kong......................................178-179
Jamaica..138-139
Kenya, Uganda, Tanganyika 92-93
Leeward Islands..............................118-119
Malaya
Johore 128-129
Kedah 55-56
Kelantan...44-45
Malacca...1-2
Negri Sembilan 36-37
Pahang 44-45
Penang 1-2
Perak..99-100
Perlis..1-2
Selangor 74-75
Trengganu 47-48
Malta...223-224
Mauritius...229-230
Montserrat 106-107
Nigeria 73-74
North Borneo 238-239
Northern Rhodesia...............................48-49
Nyasaland Protectorate 85-86
Pitcairn Island.......................................11-12
St. Helena..130-131
St. Kitts-Nevis 93-94
St. Lucia 129-130
St. Vincent.......................................154-155
Sarawak...174-175
Seychelles..151-152
Sierra Leone 188-189
Singapore 21-22
Solomon Islands..................................82-83
Somaliland Protectorate 110-111
Swaziland 48-49
Trinidad & Tobago 64-65
Turks & Caicos Islands 92-93
Virgin Islands......................................90-91
Zanzibar 224-225

The following have different designs but are included in the omnibus set:
Great Britain...................................267-268
Offices in Morocco............93-94, 525-526
Bahrain..62-63
Kuwait 82-83
Oman 25-26
South Africa...106
South-West Africa...................................159
138 stamps, Never Hinged $1,600.

U.P.U. Issue

Mercury and Symbols of Communications – CD306

Plane, Ship and Hemispheres – CD307

Mercury Scattering Letters over Globe CD308

U.P.U. Monument, Bern – CD309

Universal Postal Union, 75th anniversary.

1949

Aden 32-35
Kathiri State of Seiyun........................16-19
Qu'aiti State of Shihr and Mukalla....................................16-19
Antigua 100-103
Ascension 57-60
Bahamas..150-153
Barbados...212-215
Basutoland..41-44
Bechuanaland Protectorate.............149-152
Bermuda..138-141
British Guiana.................................246-249
British Honduras..............................137-140
Brunei 79-82
Cayman Islands 118-121
Cyprus...160-163
Dominica..116-119
Falkland Islands 103-106
Falkland Islands Dep. 1L14-1L17
Fiji..141-144
Gambia..148-151
Gibraltar..123-126
Gilbert & Ellice Islands 56-59
Gold Coast 144-147
Grenada 147-150
Hong Kong......................................180-183
Jamaica..142-145
Kenya, Uganda, Tanganyika 94-97
Leeward Islands..............................126-129
Malaya
Johore 151-154
Kedah 57-60
Kelantan...46-49
Malacca..18-21
Negri Sembilan 59-62
Pahang 46-49
Penang 23-26
Perak..101-104
Perlis..3-6
Selangor 76-79
Trengganu 49-52
Malta...225-228
Mauritius...231-234
Montserrat 108-111
New Hebrides......................................62-65
Nigeria 75-78
North Borneo 240-243
Northern Rhodesia...............................50-53
Nyasaland Protectorate 87-90
Pitcairn Islands 13-16
St. Helena..132-135
St. Kitts-Nevis 95-98
St. Lucia 131-134
St. Vincent.......................................170-173
Sarawak...176-179
Seychelles..153-156
Sierra Leone 190-193
Singapore 23-26
Solomon Islands..................................84-87
Somaliland Protectorate 112-115
Southern Rhodesia...............................71-72
Swaziland 50-53
Tonga 87-90
Trinidad & Tobago 66-69
Turks & Caicos Islands 101-104
Virgin Islands......................................92-95
Zanzibar 226-229

The following have different designs but are included in the omnibus set:
Great Britain...................................276-279
Offices in Morocco.........................546-549
Australia 223
Bahrain..68-71
Burma 116-121
Ceylon...304-306
Egypt...281-283
India..223-226
Kuwait 89-92
Oman 31-34
Pakistan-Bahawalpur 26-29, O25-O28
South Africa....................................109-111
South-West Africa............................160-162
315 stamps, Never Hinged $325.

University Issue

Arms of University College CD310 Alice, Princess of Athlone CD311

1948 opening of University College of the West Indies at Jamaica.

1951

Antigua 104-105
Barbados...228-229
British Guiana.................................250-251
British Honduras..............................141-142
Dominica..120-121
Grenada 164-165
Jamaica..146-147
Leeward Islands..............................130-131
Montserrat 112-113
St. Kitts-Nevis 105-106
St. Lucia 149-150
St. Vincent.......................................174-175

Trinidad & Tobago ... 70-71
Virgin Islands ... 96-97
28 stamps

Coronation Issue

Queen Elizabeth II CD312

1953

Aden ... 47
Kathiri State of Seiyun ... 28
Qu'aiti State of Shihr and Mukalla ... 28
Antigua ... 106
Ascension ... 61
Bahamas ... 157
Barbados ... 234
Basutoland ... 45
Bechuanaland Protectorate ... 153
Bermuda ... 142
British Guiana ... 252
British Honduras ... 143
Cayman Islands ... 150
Cyprus ... 167
Dominica ... 141
Falkland Islands ... 121
Falkland Islands Dependencies ... 1L18
Fiji ... 145
Gambia ... 152
Gibraltar ... 131
Gilbert & Ellice Islands ... 60
Gold Coast ... 160
Grenada ... 170
Hong Kong ... 184
Jamaica ... 153
Kenya, Uganda, Tanganyika ... 101
Leeward Islands ... 132
Malaya
Johore ... 155
Kedah ... 82
Kelantan ... 71
Malacca ... 27
Negri Sembilan ... 63
Pahang ... 71
Penang ... 27
Perak ... 126
Perlis ... 28
Selangor ... 101
Trengganu ... 74
Malta ... 241
Mauritius ... 250
Montserrat ... 127
New Hebrides ... 77
Nigeria ... 79
North Borneo ... 260
Northern Rhodesia ... 60
Nyasaland Protectorate ... 96
Pitcairn ... 19
St. Helena ... 139
St. Kitts-Nevis ... 119
St. Lucia ... 156
St. Vincent ... 185
Sarawak ... 196
Seychelles ... 172
Sierra Leone ... 194
Singapore ... 27
Solomon Islands ... 88
Somaliland Protectorate ... 127
Swaziland ... 54
Trinidad & Tobago ... 84
Tristan da Cunha ... 13
Turks & Caicos Islands ... 118
Virgin Islands ... 114

The following have different designs but are included in the omnibus set:

Great Britain ... 313-316
Offices in Morocco ... 579-582
Australia ... 259-261
Bahrain ... 92-95
Canada ... 330
Ceylon ... 317
Cook Islands ... 145-146
Kuwait ... 113-116
New Zealand ... 280-284
Niue ... 104-105
Oman ... 52-55
Samoa ... 214-215
South Africa ... 192
Southern Rhodesia ... 80
South-West Africa ... 244-248
Tokelau Islands ... 4
106 stamps, Never Hinged $70.

Royal Visit 1953

Separate designs for each country for the visit of Queen Elizabeth II and the Duke of Edinburgh.

1953

Aden ... 62
Australia ... 267-269
Bermuda ... 163
Ceylon ... 318
Fiji ... 146
Gibraltar ... 146
Jamaica ... 154
Kenya, Uganda, Tanganyika ... 102
Malta ... 242
New Zealand ... 286-287
13 stamps

West Indies Federation

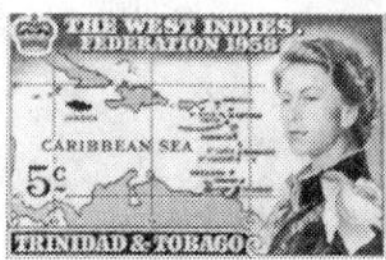

Map of the Caribbean – CD313

Federation of the West Indies, April 22, 1958.

1958

Antigua ... 122-124
Barbados ... 248-250
Dominica ... 161-163
Grenada ... 184-186
Jamaica ... 175-177
Montserrat ... 143-145
St. Kitts-Nevis ... 136-138
St. Lucia ... 170-172
St. Vincent ... 198-200
Trinidad & Tobago ... 86-88
30 stamps, Never Hinged $6.

Freedom from Hunger Issue

Protein Food CD314

U.N. Food and Agricultural Organization's "Freedom from Hunger" campaign.

1963

Aden ... 65
Antigua ... 133
Ascension ... 89
Bahamas ... 180
Basutoland ... 83
Bechuanaland Protectorate ... 194
Bermuda ... 192
British Guiana ... 271
British Honduras ... 179
Brunei ... 100
Cayman Islands ... 168
Dominica ... 181
Falkland Islands ... 146
Fiji ... 198
Gambia ... 172
Gibraltar ... 161
Gilbert & Ellice Islands ... 76
Grenada ... 190
Hong Kong ... 218
Malta ... 291
Mauritius ... 270
Montserrat ... 150
New Hebrides ... 93
North Borneo ... 296
Pitcairn ... 35
St. Helena ... 173
St. Lucia ... 179
St. Vincent ... 201
Sarawak ... 212
Seychelles ... 213
Solomon Islands ... 109
Swaziland ... 108
Tonga ... 127
Tristan da Cunha ... 68
Turks & Caicos Islands ... 138
Virgin Islands ... 140
Zanzibar ... 280
37 stamps

Red Cross Centenary Issue

Red Cross and Elizabeth II – CD315

1963

Antigua ... 134-135
Ascension ... 90-91
Bahamas ... 183-184
Basutoland ... 84-85
Bechuanaland Protectorate ... 195-196
Bermuda ... 193-194
British Guiana ... 272-273
British Honduras ... 180-181
Cayman Islands ... 169-170
Dominica ... 182-183
Falkland Islands ... 147-148
Fiji ... 203-204
Gambia ... 173-174
Gibraltar ... 162-163
Gilbert & Ellice Islands ... 77-78
Grenada ... 191-192
Hong Kong ... 219-220
Jamaica ... 203-204
Malta ... 292-293
Mauritius ... 271-272
Montserrat ... 151-152
New Hebrides ... 94-95
Pitcairn Islands ... 36-37
St. Helena ... 174-175
St. Kitts-Nevis ... 143-144
St. Lucia ... 180-181
St. Vincent ... 202-203
Seychelles ... 214-215
Solomon Islands ... 110-111
South Arabia ... 1-2
Swaziland ... 109-110
Tonga ... 134-135
Tristan da Cunha ... 69-70
Turks & Caicos Islands ... 139-140
Virgin Islands ... 141-142
70 stamps

Shakespeare Issue

Shakespeare Memorial Theatre, Stratford-on-Avon – CD316

400th anniversary of the birth of William Shakespeare.

1964

Antigua ... 151
Bahamas ... 201
Bechuanaland Protectorate ... 197
Cayman Islands ... 171
Dominica ... 184
Falkland Islands ... 149
Gambia ... 192
Gibraltar ... 164
Montserrat ... 153
St. Lucia ... 196
Turks & Caicos Islands ... 141
Virgin Islands ... 143
12 stamps

ITU ISSUE

ITU Emblem CD317

Intl. Telecommunication Union, cent.

1965

Antigua ... 153-154
Ascension ... 92-93
Bahamas ... 219-220
Barbados ... 265-266
Basutoland ... 101-102
Bechuanaland Protectorate ... 202-203
Bermuda ... 196-197
British Guiana ... 293-294
British Honduras ... 187-188
Brunei ... 116-117
Cayman Islands ... 172-173
Dominica ... 185-186
Falkland Islands ... 154-155
Fiji ... 211-212
Gibraltar ... 167-168
Gilbert & Ellice Islands ... 87-88
Grenada ... 205-206
Hong Kong ... 221-222
Mauritius ... 291-292
Montserrat ... 157-158
New Hebrides ... 108-109
Pitcairn Islands ... 52-53
St. Helena ... 180-181
St. Kitts-Nevis ... 163-164
St. Lucia ... 197-198
St. Vincent ... 224-225
Seychelles ... 218-219
Solomon Islands ... 126-127
Swaziland ... 115-116
Tristan da Cunha ... 85-86
Turks & Caicos Islands ... 142-143
Virgin Islands ... 159-160
64 stamps, Never Hinged $50.

Intl. Cooperation Year Issue

ICY Emblem – CD318

1965

Antigua ... 155-156
Ascension ... 94-95
Bahamas ... 222-223
Basutoland ... 103-104
Bechuanaland Protectorate ... 204-205
Bermuda ... 199-200
British Guiana ... 295-296
British Honduras ... 189-190
Brunei ... 118-119
Cayman Islands ... 174-175
Dominica ... 187-188
Falkland Islands ... 156-157
Fiji ... 213-214
Gibraltar ... 169-170
Gilbert & Ellice Islands ... 104-105
Grenada ... 207-208
Hong Kong ... 223-224
Mauritius ... 293-294
Montserrat ... 176-177
New Hebrides ... 110-111
Pitcairn Islands ... 54-55
St. Helena ... 182-183
St. Kitts-Nevis ... 165-166
St. Lucia ... 199-200
Seychelles ... 220-221
Solomon Islands ... 143-144
South Arabia ... 17-18
Swaziland ... 117-118
Tristan da Cunha ... 87-88
Turks & Caicos Islands ... 144-145
Virgin Islands ... 161-162
62 stamps

Churchill Memorial Issue

Winston Churchill and St. Paul's, London, During Air Attack – CD319

1966

Antigua ... 157-160
Ascension ... 96-99
Bahamas ... 224-227
Barbados ... 281-284
Basutoland ... 105-108
Bechuanaland Protectorate ... 206-209
Bermuda ... 201-204
British Antarctic Territory ... 16-19
British Honduras ... 191-194
Brunei ... 120-123
Cayman Islands ... 176-179
Dominica ... 189-192
Falkland Islands ... 158-161

Fiji.....215-218
Gibraltar.....171-174
Gilbert & Ellice Islands.....106-109
Grenada.....209-212
Hong Kong.....225-228
Mauritius.....295-298
Montserrat.....178-181
New Hebrides.....112-115
Pitcairn Islands.....56-59
St. Helena.....184-187
St. Kitts-Nevis.....167-170
St. Lucia.....201-204
St. Vincent.....241-244
Seychelles.....222-225
Solomon Islands.....145-148
South Arabia.....19-22
Swaziland.....119-122
Tristan da Cunha.....89-92
Turks & Caicos Islands.....146-149
Virgin Islands.....163-166
132 stamps

Royal Visit Issue, 1966

Queen Elizabeth II and Prince Philip CD320

Caribbean visit, Feb. 4 - Mar. 6, 1966.

1966

Antigua.....161-162
Bahamas.....228-229
Barbados.....285-286
British Guiana.....299-300
Cayman Islands.....180-181
Dominica.....193-194
Grenada.....213-214
Montserrat.....182-183
St. Kitts-Nevis.....171-172
St. Lucia.....205-206
St. Vincent.....245-246
Turks & Caicos Islands.....150-151
Virgin Islands.....167-168
26 stamps

World Cup Soccer Issue

Soccer Player and Jules Rimet Cup CD321

World Cup Soccer Championship, Wembley, England, July 11-30.

1966

Antigua.....163-164
Ascension.....100-101
Bahamas.....245-246
Bermuda.....205-206
Brunei.....124-125
Cayman Islands.....182-183
Dominica.....195-196
Fiji.....219-220
Gibraltar.....175-176
Gilbert & Ellice Islands.....125-126
Grenada.....230-231
New Hebrides.....116-117
Pitcairn Islands.....60-61
St. Helena.....188-189
St. Kitts-Nevis.....173-174
St. Lucia.....207-208
Seychelles.....226-227
Solomon Islands.....167-168
South Arabia.....23-24
Tristan da Cunha.....93-94
40 stamps

WHO Headquarters Issue

World Health Organization Headquarters, Geneva – CD322

1966

Antigua.....165-166
Ascension.....102-103
Bahamas.....247-248
Brunei.....126-127
Cayman Islands.....184-185
Dominica.....197-198
Fiji.....224-225
Gibraltar.....180-181
Gilbert & Ellice Islands.....127-128
Grenada.....232-233
Hong Kong.....229-230
Montserrat.....184-185
New Hebrides.....118-119
Pitcairn Islands.....62-63
St. Helena.....190-191
St. Kitts-Nevis.....177-178
St. Lucia.....209-210
St. Vincent.....247-248
Seychelles.....228-229
Solomon Islands.....169-170
South Arabia.....25-26
Tristan da Cunha.....99-100
44 stamps

UNESCO Anniversary Issue

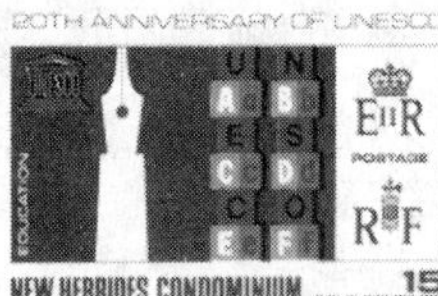

"Education" – CD323

"Science" (Wheat ears & flask enclosing globe). "Culture" (lyre & columns).
20th anniversary of the UNESCO.

1966-67

Antigua.....183-185
Ascension.....108-110
Bahamas.....249-251
Barbados.....287-289
Bermuda.....207-209
Brunei.....128-130
Cayman Islands.....186-188
Dominica.....199-201
Gibraltar.....183-185
Gilbert & Ellice Islands.....129-131
Grenada.....234-236
Hong Kong.....231-233
Mauritius.....299-301
Montserrat.....186-188
New Hebrides.....120-122
Pitcairn Islands.....64-66
St. Helena.....192-194
St. Kitts-Nevis.....179-181
St. Lucia.....211-213
St. Vincent.....249-251
Seychelles.....230-232
Solomon Islands.....171-173
South Arabia.....27-29
Swaziland.....123-125
Tristan da Cunha.....101-103
Turks & Caicos Islands.....155-157
Virgin Islands.....176-178
81 stamps

Silver Wedding Issue, 1972

Queen Elizabeth II and Prince Philip CD324

Designs: borders differ for each country.

1972

Anguilla.....161-162
Antigua.....295-296
Ascension.....164-165
Bahamas.....344-345
Bermuda.....296-297
British Antarctic Territory.....43-44
British Honduras.....306-307
British Indian Ocean Territory.....48-49
Brunei.....186-187
Cayman Islands.....304-305
Dominica.....352-353
Falkland Islands.....223-224
Fiji.....328-329
Gibraltar.....292-293
Gilbert & Ellice Islands.....206-207
Grenada.....466-467
Hong Kong.....271-272
Montserrat.....286-287
New Hebrides.....169-170
Pitcairn Islands.....127-128
St. Helena.....271-272
St. Kitts-Nevis.....257-258
St. Lucia.....328-329
St.Vincent.....344-345
Seychelles.....309-310
Solomon Islands.....248-249
South Georgia.....35-36
Tristan da Cunha.....178-179
Turks & Caicos Islands.....257-258
Virgin Islands.....241-242
60 stamps

Princess Anne's Wedding Issue

Princess Anne and Mark Phillips CD325

Wedding of Princess Anne and Mark Phillips, Nov. 14, 1973.

1973

Anguilla.....179-180
Ascension.....177-178
Belize.....325-326
Bermuda.....302-303
British Antarctic Territory.....60-61
Cayman Islands.....320-321
Falkland Islands.....225-226
Gibraltar.....305-306
Gilbert & Ellice Islands.....216-217
Hong Kong.....289-290
Montserrat.....300-301
Pitcairn Island.....135-136
St. Helena.....277-278
St. Kitts-Nevis.....274-275
St. Lucia.....349-350
St. Vincent.....358-359
St. Vincent Grenadines.....1-2
Seychelles.....311-312
Solomon Islands.....259-260
South Georgia.....37-38
Tristan da Cunha.....189-190
Turks & Caicos Islands.....286-287
Virgin Islands.....260-261
44 stamps

Elizabeth II Coronation Anniversary Issue

CD326

CD327

CD328

Designs: Royal and local beasts in heraldic form and simulated stonework. Portrait of Elizabeth II by Peter Grugeon.
25th anniversary of coronation of Queen Elizabeth II.

1978

Ascension.....229
Barbados.....474
Belize.....397
British Antarctic Territory.....71
Cayman Islands.....404
Christmas Island.....87
Falkland Islands.....275
Fiji.....384
Gambia.....380
Gilbert Islands.....312
Mauritius.....464
New Hebrides.....258
St. Helena.....317
St. Kitts-Nevis.....354
Samoa.....472
Solomon Islands.....368
South Georgia.....51
Swaziland.....302
Tristan da Cunha.....238
Virgin Islands.....337
20 sheets

Queen Mother Elizabeth's 80th Birthday

CD330

Designs: Photographs of Queen Mother Elizabeth. Falkland Islands issued in sheets of 50; others in sheets of 9.

1980

Ascension.....261
Bermuda.....401
Cayman Islands.....443
Falkland Islands.....305
Gambia.....412
Gibraltar.....393
Hong Kong.....364
Pitcairn Islands.....193
St. Helena.....341
Samoa.....532
Solomon Islands.....426
Tristan da Cunha.....277
12 stamps

Royal Wedding Issue, 1981

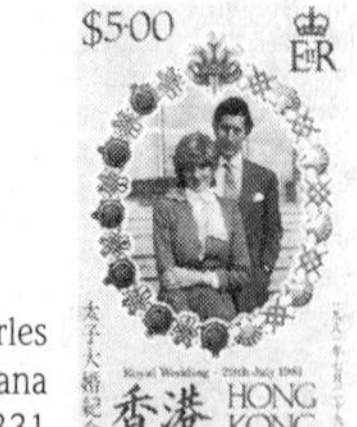

Prince Charles and Lady Diana CD331

Wedding of Charles, Prince of Wales, and Lady Diana Spencer, St. Paul's Cathedral, London, July 29, 1981.

1981

Antigua.....623-625
Ascension.....294-296
Barbados.....547-549
Barbuda.....497-499
Bermuda.....412-414
Brunei.....268-270
Cayman Islands.....471-473
Dominica.....701-703
Falkland Islands.....324-326
Falkland Islands Dep......1L59-1L61
Fiji.....442-444
Gambia.....426-428
Ghana.....759-761
Grenada.....1051-1053
Grenada Grenadines.....440-443
Hong Kong.....373-375
Jamaica.....500-503
Lesotho.....335-337
Maldive Islands.....906-908
Mauritius.....520-522
Norfolk Island.....280-282
Pitcairn Islands.....206-208
St. Helena.....353-355
St. Lucia.....543-545
Samoa.....558-560
Sierra Leone.....509-517
Solomon Islands.....450-452
Swaziland.....382-384

Tristan da Cunha...........................294-296
Turks & Caicos Islands...................486-488
Caicos Island..8-10
Uganda...314-316
Vanuatu...308-310
Virgin Islands.................................406-408

Princess Diana

CD332 CD333

Designs: Photographs and portrait of Princess Diana, wedding or honeymoon photographs, royal residences, arms of issuing country. Portrait photograph by Clive Friend. Souvenir sheet margins show family tree, various people related to the princess. 21st birthday of Princess Diana of Wales, July 1.

1982

Antigua...663-666
Ascension.......................................313-316
Bahamas...510-513
Barbados..585-588
Barbuda..544-546
British Antarctic Territory...................92-95
Cayman Islands..............................486-489
Dominica..773-776
Falkland Islands..............................348-351
Falkland Islands Dep.................1L72-1L75
Fiji..470-473
Gambia...447-450
Grenada.....................................1101A-1105
Grenada Grenadines........................485-491
Lesotho..372-375
Maldive Islands...............................952-955
Mauritius...548-551
Pitcairn Islands...............................213-216
St. Helena.......................................372-375
St. Lucia..591-594
Sierra Leone....................................531-534
Solomon Islands..............................471-474
Swaziland..406-409
Tristan da Cunha.............................310-313
Turks and Caicos Islands.............530A-534
Virgin Islands..................................430-433

250th anniv. of first edition of Lloyd's List (shipping news publication) and of Lloyd's marine insurance.

BAHAMAS 5c CD335

Designs: First page of early edition of the list; historical ships, modern transportation or harbor scenes.

1984

Ascension.......................................351-354
Bahamas...555-558
Barbados..627-630
Cayes of Belize....................................10-13
Cayman Islands..............................522-525
Falkland Islands..............................404-407
Fiji..509-512
Gambia...519-522
Mauritius...587-590
Nauru...280-283
St. Helena.......................................412-415
Samoa..624-627
Seychelles......................................538-541
Solomon Islands..............................521-524
Vanuatu...368-371
Virgin Islands..................................466-469

Queen Mother 85th Birthday

CD336

Designs: Photographs tracing the life of the Queen Mother, Elizabeth. The high value in each set pictures the same photograph taken of the Queen Mother holding the infant Prince Henry.

1985

Ascension.......................................372-376
Bahamas...580-584
Barbados..660-664
Bermuda...469-473
Falkland Islands..............................420-424
Falkland Islands Dep.................1L92-1L96
Fiji..531-535
Hong Kong......................................447-450
Jamaica..599-603
Mauritius...604-608
Norfolk Island..................................364-368
Pitcairn Islands...............................253-257
St. Helena.......................................428-432
Samoa..649-653
Seychelles......................................567-571
Solomon Islands..............................543-547
Swaziland..476-480
Tristan da Cunha.............................372-376
Vanuatu...392-396
Zil Elwannyen Sesel........................101-105

Queen Elizabeth II, 60th Birthday

CD337

1986, April 21

Ascension.......................................389-393
Bahamas...592-596
Barbados..675-679
Bermuda...499-503
Cayman Islands..............................555-559
Falkland Islands..............................441-445
Fiji..544-548
Hong Kong......................................465-469
Jamaica..620-624
Kiribati..470-474
Mauritius...629-633
Papua New Guinea..........................640-644
Pitcairn Islands...............................270-274
St. Helena.......................................451-455
Samoa..670-674
Seychelles......................................592-596
Solomon Islands..............................562-566
South Georgia..................................101-105
Swaziland..490-494
Tristan da Cunha.............................388-392
Vanuatu...414-418
Zambia..343-347
Zil Elwannyen Sesel........................114-118

Royal Wedding

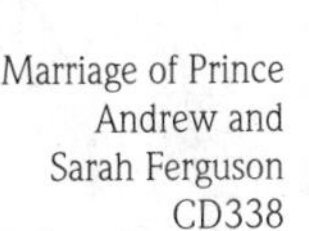

Marriage of Prince Andrew and Sarah Ferguson CD338

1986, July 23

Ascension.......................................399-400
Bahamas...602-603
Barbados..687-688
Cayman Islands..............................560-561
Jamaica..629-630
Pitcairn Islands...............................275-276
St. Helena.......................................460-461
St. Kitts...181-182
Seychelles......................................602-603
Solomon Islands..............................567-568
Tristan da Cunha.............................397-398
Zambia..348-349
Zil Elwannyen Sesel........................119-120

Queen Elizabeth II, 60th Birthday

Queen Elizabeth II Inspecting Guard, 1946 CD339

Designs: Photographs tracing the life of Queen Elizabeth II.

1986

Anguilla..674-677
Antigua...925-928
Barbuda..783-786
Dominica..950-953
Gambia...611-614
Grenada.......................................1371-1374
Grenada Grenadines........................749-752
Lesotho..531-534
Maldive Islands.............................1172-1175
Sierra Leone....................................760-763
Uganda...495-498

Royal Wedding Issue, 1986

CD340

Designs: Photographs of Prince Andrew and Sarah Ferguson during courtship, engagement and marriage.

1986

Antigua...939-942
Barbuda..809-812
Dominica..970-973
Gambia...635-638
Grenada.......................................1385-1388
Grenada Grenadines........................758-761
Lesotho..545-548
Maldive Islands.............................1181-1184
Sierra Leone....................................769-772
Uganda...510-513

Lloyds of London, 300th Anniv.

BAHAMAS CD341

Designs: 17th century aspects of Lloyds, representations of each country's individual connections with Lloyds and publicized disasters insured by the organization.

1986

Ascension.......................................454-457
Bahamas...655-658
Barbados..731-734
Bermuda...541-544
Falkland Islands..............................481-484
Liberia..1101-1104
Malawi..534-537
Nevis..571-574
St. Helena.......................................501-504
St. Lucia..923-926
Seychelles......................................649-652
Solomon Islands..............................627-630
South Georgia..................................131-134
Trinidad & Tobago...........................484-487
Tristan da Cunha.............................439-442
Vanuatu...485-488
Zil Elwannyen Sesel........................146-149

Moon Landing, 20th Anniv.

CD342

Designs: Equipment, crew photographs, spacecraft, official emblems and report profiles created for the Apollo Missions. Two stamps in each set are square in format rather than like the stamp shown; see individual country listings for more information.

1989

Ascension Is....................................468-472
Bahamas...674-678
Belize..916-920
Kiribati..517-521
Liberia..1125-1129
Nevis..586-590
St. Kitts...248-252
Samoa..760-764
Seychelles......................................676-680
Solomon Islands..............................643-647
Vanuatu...507-511
Zil Elwannyen Sesel........................154-158

Queen Mother, 90th Birthday

CD343 CD344

Designs: Portraits of Queen Elizabeth, the Queen Mother. See individual country listings for more information.

1990

Ascension Is....................................491-492
Bahamas...698-699
Barbados..782-783
British Antarctic Territory.................170-171
British Indian Ocean Territory..........106-107
Cayman Islands..............................622-623
Falkland Islands..............................524-525
Kenya...527-528
Kiribati..555-556
Liberia..1145-1146
Pitcairn Islands...............................336-337
St. Helena.......................................532-533
St. Lucia..969-970
Seychelles......................................710-711
Solomon Islands..............................671-672
South Georgia..................................143-144
Swaziland..565-566
Tristan da Cunha.............................480-481
Zil Elwannyen Sesel........................171-172

Queen Elizabeth II, 65th Birthday, and Prince Philip, 70th Birthday

CD345 CD346

Designs: Portraits of Queen Elizabeth II and Prince Philip differ for each country. Printed in sheets of 10 + 5 labels (3 different) between. Stamps alternate, producing 5 different triptychs.

1991

Ascension Is. 505-506
Bahamas 730-731
Belize 969-970
Bermuda 617-618
Kiribati 571-572
Mauritius 733-734
Pitcairn Islands 348-349
St. Helena 554-555
St. Kitts 318-319
Samoa 790-791
Seychelles 723-724
Solomon Islands 688-689
South Georgia 149-150
Swaziland 586-587
Vanuatu 540-541
Zil Elwannyen Sesel 177-178

Royal Family Birthday, Anniversary

CD347

Queen Elizabeth II, 65th birthday, Charles and Diana, 10th wedding anniversary: Various photographs of Queen Elizabeth II, Prince Philip, Prince Charles, Princess Diana and their sons William and Henry.

1991

Antigua 1446-1455
Barbuda 1229-1238
Dominica 1328-1337
Gambia 1080-1089
Grenada 2006-2015
Grenada Grenadines 1331-1340
Guyana 2440-2451
Lesotho 871-875
Maldive Islands 1533-1542
Nevis 666-675
St. Vincent 1485-1494
St. Vincent Grenadines 769-778
Sierra Leone 1387-1396
Turks & Caicos Islands 913-922
Uganda 918-927

Queen Elizabeth II's Accession to the Throne 40th Anniversary

CD348

CD349

Various photographs of Queen Elizabeth II with local Scenes.

1992 - CD348

Antigua 1513-1518
Barbuda 1306-1309
Dominica 1414-1419
Gambia 1172-1177
Grenada 2047-2052
Grenada Grenadines 1368-1373
Lesotho 881-885
Maldive Islands 1637-1642
Nevis 702-707
St. Vincent 1582-1587
St. Vincent Grenadines 829-834
Sierra Leone 1482-1487
Turks and Caicos Islands 978-987
Uganda 990-995
Virgin Islands 742-746

1992 - CD349

Ascension Islands 531-535
Bahamas 744-748
Bermuda 623-627
British Indian Ocean Territory 119-123
Cayman Islands 648-652
Falkland Islands 549-553
Gibraltar 605-609
Hong Kong 619-623
Kenya 563-567
Kiribati 582-586
Pitcairn Islands 362-366
St. Helena 570-574
St. Kitts 332-336
Samoa 805-809
Seychelles 734-738
Soloman Islands 708-712
South Georgia 157-161
Tristan da Cunha 508-512
Vanuatu 555-559
Zambia 561-565
Zil Elwannyen Sesel 183-187

Royal Air Force, 75th Anniversary

CD350

1993

Ascension 557-561
Bahamas 771-775
Barbados 842-846
Belize 1003-1008
Bermuda 648-651
British Indian Ocean Territory 136-140
Falkland Is. 573-577
Fiji 687-691
Montserrat 830-834
St. Kitts 351-355

End of World War II, 50th Anniv.

CD351

CD352

1995

Ascension 613-617
Bahamas 824-828
Barbados 891-895
Belize 1047-1050
British Indian Ocean Territory 163-167
Cayman Islands 704-708
Falkland Islands 634-638
Fiji 720-724
Kiribati 662-668
Liberia 1175-1179
Mauritius 803-805
St. Helena 646-654
St. Kitts 389-393
St. Lucia 1018-1022
Samoa 890-894
Solomon Islands 799-803
South Georgia & S. Sandwich Is. 198-200
Tristan da Cunha 562-566

UN, 50th Anniv.

CD353

1995

Bahamas 839-842
Barbados 901-904
Belize 1055-1058
Jamaica 847-851
Liberia 1187-1190
Mauritius 813-816
Pitcairn Islands 436-439
St. Kitts 398-401
St. Lucia 1023-1026
Samoa 900-903
Tristan da Cunha 568-571
Virgin Islands 807-810

Queen Elizabeth, 70th Birthday

CD354

1996

Ascension 632-635
British Antarctic Territory 240-243
British Indian Ocean Territory 176-180
Falkland Islands 653-657
Pitcairn Islands 446-449
St. Helena 672-676
Samoa 912-916
Tokelau 223-227
Tristan da Cunha 576-579
Virgin Islands 824-828

PAKISTAN

'pa–ki–ˌstan

LOCATION — In southern, central Asia
GOVT. — Republic
AREA — 307,293 sq. mi.
POP. — 88,000,000 (est. 1983)
CAPITAL — Islamabad

Pakistan was formed August 15, 1947, when India was divided into the Dominions of the Union of India and Pakistan, with some princely states remaining independent. Pakistan became a republic on March 23, 1956.

Pakistan had two areas made up of all or part of several predominantly Moslem provinces in the northwest and northeast corners of pre-1947 India. Western Pakistan consists of the entire provinces of Baluchistan, Sind (Scinde) and "Northwest Frontier," and 15 districts of the Punjab. Eastern, consisting of the Sylhet district in Assam and 14 districts in Bengal Province, became independent as Bangladesh in December 1971.

The state of Las Bela was incorporated into Pakistan.

12 Pies = 1 Anna
16 Annas = 1 Rupee
100 Paisa = 1 Rupee (1961)

Catalogue values for all unused stamps in this country are for Never Hinged items.

Watermarks

Wmk. 274

Wmk. 351-Crescent and Star Multiple

Stamps of India, 1937-43,
Overprinted in Black:

PAKISTAN Nos. 1-12 **PAKISTAN** Nos. 13-19

Perf. 13½x14

1947, Oct. 1 Wmk. 196

No.	Type	Denom.	Color	Unused	Used
1	A83	3p	slate	.15	.15
2	A83	½a	rose violet	.15	.15
3	A83	9p	lt green	.15	.15
4	A83	1a	carmine rose	.15	.15
4A	A84	1a3p	bister ('49)	3.00	5.00
5	A84	1½a	dk purple	.15	.15
6	A84	2a	scarlet	.15	.15
7	A84	3a	violet	.15	.15
8	A84	3½a	ultra	3.50	1.50
9	A85	4a	chocolate	.15	.15
10	A85	6a	peacock blue	.65	.50
11	A85	8a	blue violet	.25	.20
12	A85	12a	carmine lake	.80	.60
13	A81	14a	rose violet	1.90	1.40
14	A82	1r	brown & slate	1.50	1.10
a.			Inverted overprint	110.00	
b.			Pair, one without ovpt.	425.00	
15	A82	2r	dk brn & dk vio	1.50	1.10
16	A82	5r	dp ultra & dk grn	3.50	3.00
17	A82	10r	rose car & dk vio	3.50	2.50
18	A82	15r	dk grn & dk brn	40.00	40.00
19	A82	25r	dk vio & bl vio	47.50	40.00
			Nos. 1-19 (20)	108.80	98.10

The overprint on Nos. 14-19 is slightly smaller than the illustration.

Provisional use of stamps of India with handstamped or printed "PAKISTAN" was authorized in 1947-49. Nos. 4A, 14a 14b exist only as provisional issues.

Constituent Assembly Building, Karachi
A1

Crescent and Urdu Inscription — A2

Designs: 2½a, Karachi Airport entrance. 3a, Lahore Fort gateway.

1948, July 9 Unwmk. Engr. *Perf. 14*

No.	Type	Denom.	Color	Unused	Used
20	A1	1½a	bright ultra	.30	.15
21	A1	2½a	green	.30	.15
22	A1	3a	chocolate	.30	.15

Perf. 12

No.	Type	Denom.	Color	Unused	Used
23	A2	1r	red	1.65	.75
a.			Perf. 14	4.00	4.00
			Nos. 20-23 (4)	2.55	1.20

Pakistan's independence, Aug. 15, 1947.

Scales, Star and Crescent — A3

Star and Crescent — A4

Karachi Airport Building — A5

Karachi Port Authority Building — A6

Khyber Pass — A7

2½a, 3½a, 4a, Ghulan Muhammed Dam, Indus River, Sind. 1r, 2r, 5r, Salimullah Hostel.

Perf. 12½, 13½x14, 14x13½

1948-57 Unwmk.

No.	Type	Denom.	Color	Unused	Used
24	A3	3p	org red, perf. 13 ('54)	.15	.15
a.			Perf. 12½	.15	.15
25	A3	6p	pur, perf. 12½	.70	.15
a.			Perf. 13 ('54)	1.25	.30
26	A3	9p	dk grn, perf. 12½	.45	.15
a.			Perf. 13 ('54)	.50	.15
27	A4	1a	dark blue	.15	.15
28	A4	1½a	gray green	.15	.15
29	A4	2a	orange red	.15	.15
30	A6	2½a	green	2.25	2.50
31	A5	3a	olive green	4.75	.15
32	A6	3½a	violet blue	3.00	3.00
33	A6	4a	chocolate	.45	.15
34	A6	6a	deep blue	.45	.15
35	A6	8a	black	.45	.15
36	A5	10a	red	4.00	4.00
37	A6	12a	red	5.75	.40
38	A5	1r	ultra, perf. 13½x14	4.75	.15
a.			Perf. 13 ('54)	9.00	1.10
39	A5	2r	dark brown, perf. 13½x14	17.00	.20
a.			Perf. 13 ('54)	17.00	.50
40	A5	5r	car, perf. 13 ('54)	8.00	.15
a.			Perf. 13½x14	13.00	.15

Perf. 13½x13

No.	Type	Denom.	Color	Unused	Used
41	A7	10r	rose lilac ('51)	14.00	.20
a.			Perf. 14x13½	8.00	10.00
b.			Perf. 12	50.00	3.25
42	A7	15r	blue green ('57)	15.00	10.00
a.			Perf. 14x13½	11.00	22.50
b.			Perf. 12	14.00	7.00

Perf. 14x13½

No.	Type	Denom.	Color	Unused	Used
43	A7	25r	purple	27.50	15.00
a.			Perf. 13½x13 ('54)	47.50	50.00
b.			Perf. 12	22.50	25.00

See No. 259, types A9-A11. For surcharges and overprints see Nos. 124, O14-O26, O35-O37, O41-O43A, O52, O63, O68.

"Quaid-i-Azam" (Great Leader), "Mohammed Ali Jinnah" — A8

1949, Sept. 11 Engr. *Perf. 13½x14*

No.	Type	Denom.	Color	Unused	Used
44	A8	1½a	brown	.75	.20
45	A8	3a	dark green	1.00	.25
46	A8	10a	blk *(English inscriptions)*	4.75	1.50
			Nos. 44-46 (3)	6.50	1.95

1st anniv. of the death of Mohammed Ali Jinnah (1876-1948), Moslem lawyer, pres. of All-India Moslem League.

Re-engraved (Crescents Reversed)

A9

A10

A11

Perf. 12½, 13½x14 (3a, 10a), 14x13½ (6a, 12a)

1949-53

No.	Type	Denom.	Color	Unused	Used
47	A10	1a	dk blue ('50)	1.25	.15
a.			Perf. 13 ('52)	1.40	.15
48	A10	1½a	gray green	1.25	.15
a.			Perf. 13 ('53)	1.40	.15
49	A10	2a	orange red	1.25	.15
a.			Perf. 13 ('52)	1.40	.15
50	A9	3a	olive green	1.50	.15
51	A11	6a	deep blue ('50)	3.25	.15
52	A11	8a	black ('50)	1.40	.15
53	A9	10a	red	3.50	.15
54	A11	12a	red ('50)	6.50	.20
			Nos. 47-54 (8)	19.90	
			Set value		.60

For overprints see #O27-O31, O38-O40.

Vase and Plate — A12

Star and Crescent, Plane and Hour Glass — A13

Moslem Leaf Pattern — A14

Arch and Lamp of Learning — A15

1951, Aug. 14 Engr. *Perf. 13*

No.	Type	Denom.	Color	Unused	Used
55	A12	2½a	dark red	.15	.15
56	A13	3a	dk rose lake	.15	.15
57	A12	3½a	dp ultra (Urdu "½3")	.70	.45
57A	A12	3½a	dp ultra (Urdu "3½") ('56)	1.25	1.00
58	A14	4a	deep green	.25	.15
59	A14	6a	red orange	.35	.15
60	A15	8a	brown	4.00	.50
61	A15	10a	purple	.80	.35
62	A13	12a	dk slate blue	.50	.35
			Nos. 55-62 (9)	8.15	3.25

Fourth anniversary of independence.

On No. 57, the characters of the Urdu denomination at right appears as "½3." On the reengraved No. 57A, they read "3½."

Issue date: Dec. 1956.

See Nos. 88, O32-O34.

For surcharges see Nos. 255, 257.

Scinde District Stamp and Camel Train — A16

1952, Aug. 14

No.	Type	Denom.	Color	Unused	Used
63	A16	3a	olive green, *citron*	.80	.45
64	A16	12a	dark brown, *salmon*	2.25	1.25

5th anniv. of Pakistan's Independence and the cent. of the 1st postage stamps in the Indo-Pakistan sub-continent.

Peak K-2, Karakoram Mountains — A17

1954, Dec. 25

No.	Type	Denom.	Color	Unused	Used
65	A17	2a	violet	.30	.15

Conquest of K-2, world's 2nd highest mountain peak, in July 1954.

Kaghan Valley — A18

Gilgit Mountains — A19

Tea Garden, East Pakistan
A20

Designs: 1a, Badshahi Mosque, Lahore. 1½a, Emperor Jahangir's Mausoleum, Lahore. 1r, Cotton field. 2r, River craft and jute field.

1954, Aug. 14 Engr.

No.	Type	Denom.	Color	Unused	Used
66	A18	6p	rose violet	.30	.15
a.			Booklet pane of 4	1.25	
67	A19	9p	blue	.30	.15
68	A19	1a	carmine rose	.30	.15
69	A18	1½a	red	.30	.15
a.			Booklet pane of 4	1.25	
70	A20	14a	dark green	1.75	.15
71	A20	1r	yellow green	2.25	.15
72	A20	2r	orange	5.00	.15
			Nos. 66-72 (7)	10.20	
			Set value		.40

Seventh anniversary of independence.

For overprints & surcharges see #77, 101, 123, 126, O44-O50, O53-O56, O60-O62, O67, O69-O71.

Karnaphuli Paper Mill, East Pakistan (Urdu "½2") — A21

6a, Textile mill. 8a, Jute mill. 12a, Sui gas plant.

1955, Aug. 14 Unwmk. *Perf. 13*

No.	Type	Denom.	Color	Unused	Used
73	A21	2½a	dk car (Urdu "½2")	.90	.15
73A	A21	2½a	dk car (Urdu "2½") ('56)	1.00	.15
74	A21	6a	dark blue	1.10	.15

75 A21 8a violet 1.50 .15
76 A21 12a car lake & org 2.75 .15
Nos. 73-76 (5) 7.25
Set value .44

Eighth anniversary of independence.
On No. 73, the characters of the Urdu denomination at right appear as "1/2." On the reengraved No. 73A, they read "2 1/2."
Issue date: Dec. 1956.
See No. 87. For overprints and surcharges see Nos. 78, 102-103, 256, O51, O58-O59.

Nos. 69 and 76 Overprinted in Ultramarine

TENTH ANNIVERSARY UNITED NATIONS
24. 10. 55.

1955, Oct. 24
77 A18 1 1/2a red 1.75 1.75
78 A21 12a car lake & org 1.75 1.75

UN, 10th anniv.

Map of West Pakistan — A22

1955, Dec. 7 Unwmk. Perf. 13 1/2x13
79 A22 1 1/2a dark green .15 .15
80 A22 2a dark brown .18 .15
81 A22 12a deep carmine .75 .50
Nos. 79-81 (3) 1.08 .80

West Pakistan unification, Nov. 14, 1955.

National Assembly A23

1956, Mar. 23 Litho. Perf. 13x12 1/2
82 A23 2a green .15 .15

Proclamation of the Republic of Pakistan, Mar. 23, 1956.

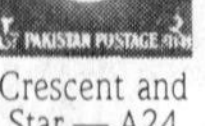

Crescent and Star — A24

Map of East Pakistan — A25

1956, Aug. 14 Engr. Perf. 13
83 A24 2a red .15 .15

Ninth anniversary of independence.
For surcharges and overprints see Nos. 127, O57, O72-O73.

1956, Oct. 15 Perf. 13 1/2x13
84 A25 1 1/2a dark green .20 .15
85 A25 2a dark brown .20 .15
86 A25 12a deep red .85 .50
Nos. 84-86 (3) 1.25 .80

1st Session at Dacca (East Pakistan) of the National Assembly of Pakistan.

Redrawn Types of 1951, 1955 and

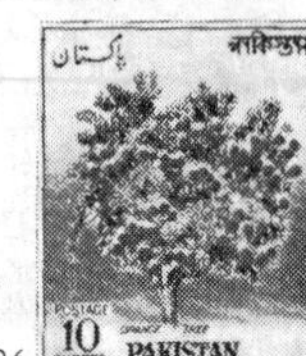

Orange Tree — A26

Perf. 13x13 1/2, 13 1/2x13
1957, Mar. 23 Engr.
87 A21 2 1/2a dark carmine .15 .15
88 A12 3 1/2a bright blue .15 .15
89 A26 10r dk green & orange 2.75 1.10
Nos. 87-89 (3) 3.05 1.40

Nos. 87-89 inscribed "Pakistan" in English, Urdu and Bengali. Denomination in English only.
Islamic Republic of Pakistan, 1st anniv.
See Nos. 95, 258, 475A. For surcharge and overprint see Nos. 159, O64.

Flag and Broken Chain — A27

1957, May 10 Litho. Perf. 13
90 A27 1 1/2a green .18 .15
91 A27 12a blue .40 .35

Cent. of the struggle for Independence (Indian Mutiny).

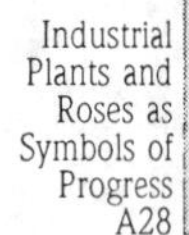

Industrial Plants and Roses as Symbols of Progress A28

1957, Aug. 14 Unwmk. Perf. 13 1/2
92 A28 1 1/2a light ultra .15 .15
93 A28 4a orange vermilion .25 .15
94 A28 12a red lilac .50 .50
Nos. 92-94 (3) .90 .80

Tenth anniversary of independence.

Type of 1957.

Design: 15r, Coconut Tree.

1958, Mar. 23 Engr. Perf. 13 1/2x13
95 A26 15r rose lilac & red 5.00 4.25

Issued to commemorate the second anniversary of the Islamic Republic of Pakistan.

Verse of Iqbal Poem — A29

1958, Apr. 21 Photo. Perf. 14 1/2x14
Black Inscriptions
96 A29 1 1/2a citron .15 .15
97 A29 2a orange brown .15 .15
98 A29 14a aqua .40 .30
Nos. 96-98 (3) .70
Set value .44

20th anniv. of the death of Mohammad Iqbal (1877-1938), Moslem poet and philosopher.

Globe and Book — A30

1958, Dec. 10 Litho. Perf. 13
99 A30 1 1/2a Prus blue .15 .15
100 A30 14a dark brown .40 .35
Set value .47 .41

10th anniv. of the signing of the Universal Declaration of Human Rights.

Nos. 66 and 75 Overprinted: "Pakistan Boy Scout 2nd National Jamboree Chittagong Dec. 58-Jan. 59"

1958, Dec. 28 Engr. Perf. 13
101 A18 6p rose violet .15 .15
102 A21 8a violet .40 .40

2nd National Boy Scout Jamboree held at Chittagong, Dec. 28-Jan. 4.

No. 74 Overprinted in Red: "Revolution Day, Oct. 27, 1959."

1959, Oct. 27
103 A21 6a dark blue .18 .15

First anniversary of the 1958 Revolution.

Red Cross — A31

Engr.; Cross Typo.
1959, Nov. 19 Unwmk. Perf. 13
104 A31 2a green & red .18 .15
105 A31 10a dk blue & red .85 .18
Set value .28

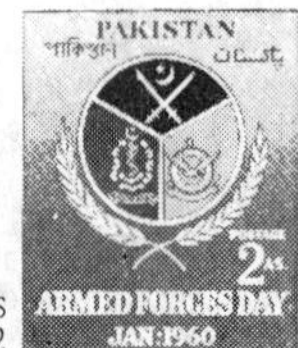

Armed Forces Emblem — A32

1960, Jan. 10 Litho. Perf. 13
106 A32 2a blue grn, red & ultra .15 .15
107 A32 14a ultra & red .35 .22
Set value .41 .27

Issued for Armed Forces Day.

Map Showing Disputed Areas A33

1960, Mar. 23 Engr. Unwmk.
108 A33 6p purple .15 .15
109 A33 2a copper red .15 .15
110 A33 8a green .18 .15
111 A33 1r blue .38 .28
Set value .67 .48

Publicizing the border dispute with India over Jammu and Kashmir, Junagarh and Manavadar.
For overprints and surcharges see Nos. 122, 125, 128, 178, O65-O66, O74-O75.

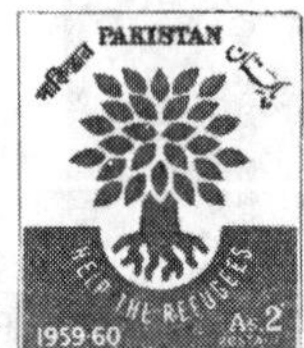

Uprooted Oak Emblem — A34

1960, Apr. 7
112 A34 2a carmine rose .15 .15
113 A34 10a green .28 .22
Set value .34 .27

Issued to publicize World Refugee Year, July 1, 1959-June 30, 1960.

House, Field and Column (Allegory of Democratic Development) A35

1960, Oct. 27 Photo. Perf. 13
114 A35 2a brown, pink & grn .15 .15
a. Green & pink omitted 13.50
115 A35 14a multicolored .35 .28
Set value .41 .33

Revolution Day, Oct. 27, 1960.
No. 114a is easily counterfeited.

Punjab Agricultural College, Lyallpur A36

Design: 8a, College shield.

1960, Oct. Engr. Perf. 12 1/2x14
116 A36 2a rose red & gray blue .15 .15
117 A36 8a lilac & green .35 .28
Set value .41 .33

50th anniv. of the Punjab Agricultural College, Lyallpur.

Caduceus, College Emblem — A37

1960, Nov. 16 Photo. Perf. 13 1/2x13
118 A37 2a blue, yel & blk .15 .15
119 A37 14a car rose, blk & emerald .35 .30
Set value .42 .37

King Edward Medical College, Lahore, cent.

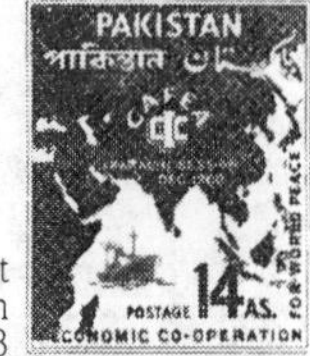

Map of South-East Asia and Commission Emblem — A38

1960, Dec. 5 Engr. Perf. 13
120 A38 14a red orange .40 .30

Conf. of the Commission on Asian and Far Eastern Affairs of the Intl. Chamber of Commerce, Karachi, Dec. 5-9.

"Kim's Gun" and Scout Badge A39

Perf. 12 1/2x14
1960, Dec. 24 Unwmk.
121 A39 2a dk green, car & yel .18 .15

3rd Natl. Boy Scout Jamboree, Lahore, Dec. 24-31.

No. 110 Overprinted in Red

LAHORE STAMP EXHIBITION 1961

1961, Feb. 12
122 A33 8a green .28 .20

10th Lahore Stamp Exhibition, Feb. 12.

New Currency

Nos. 24, 68-69, 83, 108-109 Surcharged with New Value in Paisa

1961 Perf. 13
123 A18 1p on 1 1/2a red .15 .15
124 A3 2p on 3p orange red .15 .15
125 A33 3p on 6p purple .15 .15
126 A19 7p on 1a car rose .15 .15
127 A24 13p on 2a red .16 .15
128 A33 13p on 2a copper red .22 .15
Set value .65 .40

Various violet handstamped surcharges were applied to a variety of regular-issue stamps. Most of these repeat the denomination of the basic stamp and add the new value. Example: "8 Annas (50 Paisa)" on No. 75. Many errors exist.
For overprints see Nos. O74-O75.

Khyber Pass — A40

Chota Sona Masjid Gate — A41

Design: 10p, 13p, 25p, 40p, 50p, 75p, 90p, Shalimar Gardens, Lahore.

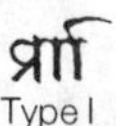
Type I

Type II

Two types of 1p, 2p and 5p:
I - First Bengali character beside "N" lacks appendage at left side of loop.
II - This character has a downward-pointing appendage at left side of loop.

1961-63 Engr. *Perf. 13½x14*

No.	Type	Value	Color	Unused	Used
129	A40	1p	violet (II)	.20	.20
a.			Type I	1.00	.15
130	A40	2p	rose red (II)	.25	.20
a.			Type I	1.00	.15
131	A40	3p	magenta	.15	.15
132	A40	5p	ultra (II)	.20	.20
a.			Type I	2.50	.15
133	A40	7p	emerald	.15	.15
134	A40	10p	brown	.15	.15
135	A40	13p	blue vio	.20	.15
136	A40	25p	dark blue ('62)	6.00	.15
137	A40	40p	dull purple ('62)	.30	.15
138	A40	50p	dull green ('62)	.50	.15
139	A40	75p	dk carmine ('62)	.75	.15
140	A40	90p	lt olive grn ('62)	.75	.15

Perf. 13½x13

No.	Type	Value	Color	Unused	Used
141	A41	1r	vermilion ('63)	.80	.15
142	A41	1.25r	purple	1.00	.50
143	A41	2r	orange ('63)	1.65	.15
144	A41	5r	green ('63)	5.25	2.00
			Nos. 129-144 (16)	18.30	
			Set value		4.00

See #200-203. For surcharge and overprints see Nos. 184, O76-O82, O85-O93A.

Designs Redrawn

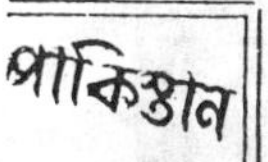

1961-62 Bengali Inscription

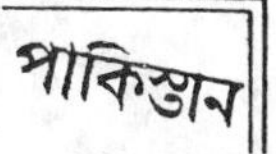
Redrawn Bengali Inscription

Bengali inscription redrawn with straight connecting line across top of characters. Shading of scenery differs, especially in Shalimar Gardens design where reflection is strengthened and trees at right are composed of horizontal lines instead of vertical lines and dots.

Designs as before; 15p, 20p, Shalimar Gardens.

1963-70 *Perf. 13½x14*

No.	Type	Value	Color	Unused	Used
129b	A40	1p	violet	.15	.15
130b	A40	2p	rose red ('64)	.15	.15
131a	A40	3p	magenta ('70)	.15	.15
132b	A40	5p	ultra	.15	.15
133a	A40	7p	emerald ('64)	.15	.15
134a	A40	10p	brown	.15	.15
135a	A40	13p	blue violet	.15	.15
135B	A40	15p	rose lilac ('64)	.15	.15
135C	A40	20p	dull green ('70)	.15	.15
136a	A40	25p	dark blue	.15	.15
137a	A40	40p	dull purple ('64)	.15	.15
138a	A40	50p	dull green ('64)	.28	.15
139a	A40	75p	dark carmine ('64)	.32	.15
140a	A40	90p	lt olive green ('64)	.75	.15
			Set value	2.15	1.00

For overprints see #174, O76b, O77b, O78a, O79b, O80a, O81a, O82a, O83-O84A, O85a, O86a.

Warsak Dam, Kabul River — A42

1961, July 1 Engr. *Perf. 12½x13½*
150 A42 40p black & lt ultra .20 .15

Dedication of hydroelectric Warsak Project.

Symbolic Flower — A43

1961, Oct. 2 Unwmk. *Perf. 14*
151 A43 13p greenish blue .15 .15
152 A43 90p red lilac .42 .28
Set value .34

Issued for Children's Day.

Roses — A44

1961, Nov. 4 *Perf. 13½x13*
153 A44 13p deep green & ver .15 .15
154 A44 90p blue & vermilion .62 .22
Set value .27

Cooperative Day.

Police Crest and Traffic Policeman's Hand — A45

1961, Nov. 30 Photo. *Perf. 13x12½*
155 A45 13p dk blue, sil & blk .15 .15
156 A45 40p red, silver & blk .55 .40
Set value .45

Centenary of the police force.

"Eagle Locomotive, 1861" A46

Design: 50pa, Diesel Engine, 1961.

1961, Dec. 31 *Perf. 13½x14*
157 A46 13p yellow, green & blk .25 .15
158 A46 50p green, blk & yellow .75 .35

Centenary of Pakistan railroads.

No. 87 Surcharged in Red with New Value, Boeing 720-B Jetliner and: "FIRST JET FLIGHT KARACHI-DACCA"

1962, Feb. 6 Engr. *Perf. 13*
159 A21 13p on 2½a dk carmine .20 .15

1st jet flight from Karachi to Dacca, Feb. 6, 1962.

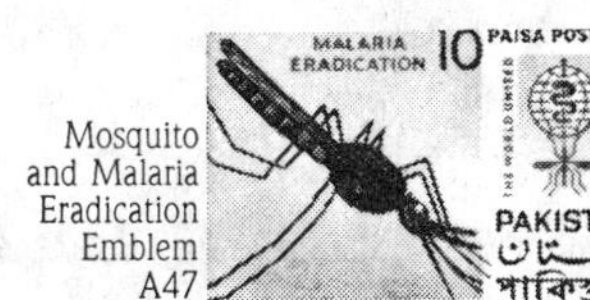
Mosquito and Malaria Eradication Emblem A47

13p, Dagger pointing at mosquito, and emblem.

1962, Apr. 7 Photo. *Perf. 13½x14*
160 A47 10p multicolored .15 .15
161 A47 13p multicolored .15 .15
Set value .15

WHO drive to eradicate malaria.

Map of Pakistan and Jasmine — A48

1962, June 8 Unwmk. *Perf. 12*
162 A48 40p grn, yel grn & gray .28 .18

Introduction of new Pakistan Constitution.

Soccer A49

13p, Hockey & Olympic gold medal. 25p, Squash rackets & British squash rackets championship cup. 40p, Cricket & Ayub challenge cup.

Perf. 12½x13½
1962, Aug. 14 Engr.
163 A49 7p blue & black .15 .15
164 A49 13p green & black .18 .15
165 A49 25p lilac & black .30 .15
166 A49 40p brown org & blk 1.10 .18
Nos. 163-166 (4) 1.73
Set value .36

Marble Fruit Dish and Clay Flask — A50

Designs: 13p, Sporting goods. 25p, Camel skin lamp and brass jug. 40p, Wooden powder bowl and cane basket. 50p, Inlaid box and brassware.

1962, Nov. 10 *Perf. 13½x13*
167 A50 7p dark red .15 .15
168 A50 13p dark green .15 .15
169 A50 25p bright purple .15 .15
170 A50 40p yellow green .45 .15
171 A50 50p dull red .48 .25
Nos. 167-171 (5) 1.38
Set value .58

Pakistan Intl. Industries Fair, Oct. 12-Nov. 20, publicizing Pakistan's small industries.

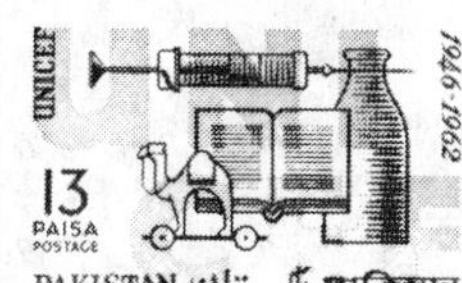
Children's Needs A51

1962, Dec. 11 Photo. *Perf. 13½x14*
172 A51 13p blue, plum & blk .15 .15
173 A51 40p multicolored .20 .18
Set value .26 .23

16th anniv. of UNICEF.

No. 135a Overprinted in Red: "U.N. FORCE W. IRIAN"

1963, Feb. 15 Engr. Unwmk.
174 A40 13p blue violet .15 .15

Issued to commemorate the dispatch of Pakistani troops to West New Guinea.

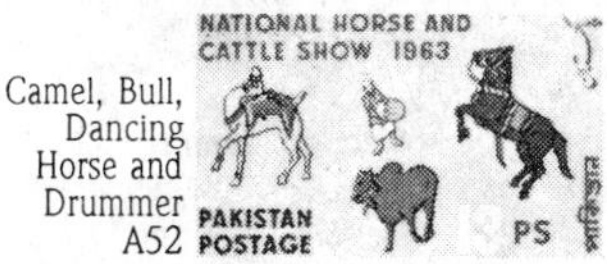
Camel, Bull, Dancing Horse and Drummer A52

1963, Mar. 13 Photo. *Perf. 12*
175 A52 13p multicolored .15 .15

National Horse and Cattle Show, 1963.

Wheat and Tractor A53

Design: 50p, Hands and heap of rice.

Perf. 12½x13½
1963, Mar. 21 Engr.
176 A53 13p brown orange .22 .15
177 A53 50p brown .85 .18
Set value .24

FAO "Freedom from Hunger" campaign.

No. 109 Surcharged with New Value and: "INTERNATIONAL/DACCA STAMP/EXHIBITION/1963"

1963, Mar. 23 *Perf. 13*
178 A33 13p on 2a copper red .25 .22

International Stamp Exhibition at Dacca.

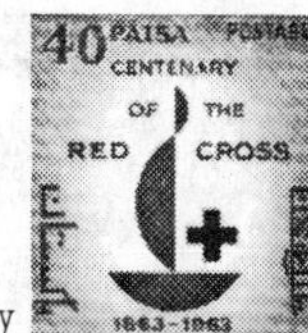
Centenary Emblem — A54

Perf. 13½x12½
1963, June 25 Engr. and Typo.
179 A54 40p dark gray & red .30 .15

International Red Cross, cent.

Paharpur Stupa A55

Designs: 13p, Cistern, Mohenjo-Daro, vert. 40p, Stupas, Taxila. 50pa, Stupas, Mainamati.

Perf. 12½x13½, 13½x12½
1963, Sept. 16 Engr. Unwmk.
180 A55 7p ultra .15 .15
181 A55 13p brown .15 .15
182 A55 40p carmine rose .22 .18
183 A55 50p dark violet .35 .20
Set value .71 .48

No. 131 Surcharged and Overprinted: "100 YEARS OF P.W.D. OCTOBER, 1963"

1963, Oct. 7 *Perf. 13½x14*
184 A40 13p on 3pa magenta .15 .15

Centenary of Public Works Department.

Atatürk Mausoleum, Ankara — A56

1963, Nov. 10 *Perf. 13x13½*
185 A56 50p red .22 .18

25th anniv. of the death of Kemal Atatürk, pres. of Turkey.

Globe and UNESCO Emblem A57

1963, Dec. 10 Photo. *Perf. 13½x14*
186 A57 50p dk brn, vio blue & red .15 .15

15th anniv. of the Universal Declaration of Human Rights.

Multan Thermal Power Station A58

Perf. 12½x13½
1963, Dec. 25 Engr.
187 A58 13p ultra .15 .15

Issued to mark the opening of the Multan Thermal Power Station.

Type of 1961-63
Perf. 13½x13

1963-65 Engr. Wmk. 351

No.	Type	Value	Color	Unused	Used
200	A41	1r	vermilion	.40	.15
201	A41	1.25r	purple ('64)	.50	.22
202	A41	2r	orange	.80	.15
203	A41	5r	green ('65)	2.25	.62
			Nos. 200-203 (4)	3.95	1.14

For overprints see Nos. O92-O93A.

A59

Designs: 13p, Temple of Thot, Dakka, and Queen Nefertari with Goddesses Hathor and Isis. 50p, Ramses II, Abu Simbel, and View of Nile.

Perf. 13x13½

1964, Mar. 30 **Unwmk.**

204	A59	13p brick red & turq blue	.15	.15
205	A59	50p black & rose lilac	.30	.22
		Set value	.38	.26

UNESCO world campaign to save historic monuments in Nubia.

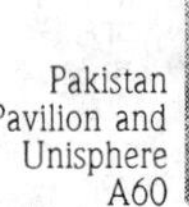

Pakistan Pavilion and Unisphere A60

1.25r, Pakistan pavilion and Unisphere, vert.

Perf. 12½x14, 14x12½

1964, Apr. 22 **Engr.** **Unwmk.**

206	A60	13p ultramarine	.15	.15
207	A60	1.25r dp orange & ultra	.60	.40

New York World's Fair, 1964-65.

Mausoleum of Shah Abdul Latif — A61 Mausoleum of Jinnah — A62

1964, June 25 *Perf. 13½x13*

208	A61	50p magenta & ultra	.25	.15

Bicentenary (?) of the death of Shah Abdul Latif of Bhit (1689-1752).

1964, Sept. 11 **Unwmk.** *Perf. 13*

Design: 15p, Mausoleum, horiz.

209	A62	15p green	.15	.15
210	A62	50p greenish gray	.22	.20
		Set value	.30	.26

16th anniv. of the death of Mohammed Ali Jinnah (1876-1948), the Quaid-i-Azam (Great Leader), founder and president of Pakistan.

Bengali Alphabet on Slate and Slab with Urdu Alphabet — A63

1964, Oct. 5 **Engr.**

211	A63	15p brown	.15	.15

Issued for Universal Children's Day.

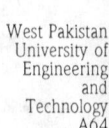

West Pakistan University of Engineering and Technology A64

1964, Dec. 21 *Perf. 12½x14*

212	A64	15p henna brown	.15	.15

1st convocation of the West Pakistan University of Engineering & Technology, Lahore, Dec. 1964.

Eyeglasses and Book — A65

Perf. 13x13½

1965, Feb. 28 **Litho.** **Unwmk.**

213	A65	15p yellow & ultra	.15	.15

Issued to publicize aid for the blind.

ITU Emblem, Telegraph Pole and Transmission Tower — A66

1965, May 17 **Engr.** *Perf. 12½x14*

214	A66	15p deep claret	.85	.15

Cent. of the ITU.

ICY Emblem A67

1965, June 26 **Litho.** *Perf. 13½*

215	A67	15p blue & black	.40	.15
216	A67	50p yellow & green	.70	.15
		Set value		.17

International Cooperation Year, 1965.

Hands Holding Book — A68

50p, Map & flags of Turkey, Iran & Pakistan.

Perf. 13½x13, 13x12½

1965, July 21 **Litho.** **Unwmk.**

Size: 46x35mm

217	A68	15p org brn, dk brn & buff	.15	.15

Size: 54x30½mm

218	A68	50p multicolored	.22	.20
		Set value		.26

1st anniv. of the signing of the Regional Cooperation for Development Pact by Turkey, Iran and Pakistan.

Tanks, Army Emblem and Soldier A69

Designs: 15p, Navy emblem, corvette No. O204 and officer. 50p, Air Force emblem, two F-104 Starfighters and pilot.

1965, Dec. 25 **Litho.** *Perf. 13½x13*

219	A69	7p multicolored	.15	.15
220	A69	15p multicolored	.18	.15
221	A69	50p multicolored	.60	.18
		Nos. 219-221 (3)	.93	
		Set value		.29

Issued to honor the Pakistani armed forces.

Emblems of Pakistan Armed Forces — A70

1966, Feb. 13 **Litho.** *Perf. 13½x13*

222	A70	15p buff, grn & dk bl	.15	.15

Issued for Armed Forces Day.

Atomic Reactor, Islamabad — A71

Unwmk.

1966, Apr. 30 **Engr.** *Perf. 13*

223	A71	15p black	.15	.15

Pakistan's first atomic reactor.

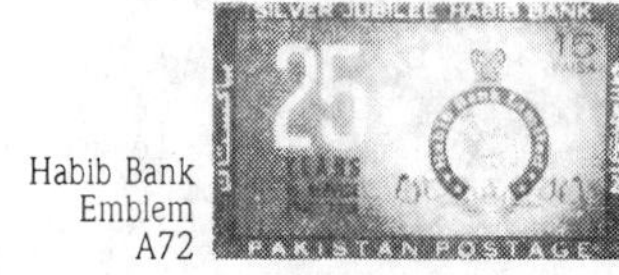

Habib Bank Emblem A72

Perf. 12½x13½

1966, Aug. 25 **Litho.** **Unwmk.**

224	A72	15p brown, org & dk grn	.15	.15

25th anniversary of the Habib Bank.

Boy and Girl — A73

1966, Oct. 3 **Litho.** *Perf. 13x13½*

225	A73	15p multicolored	.15	.15

Issued for Children's Day.

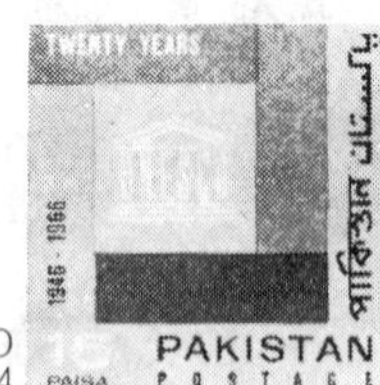

UNESCO Emblem — A74

1966, Nov. 24 **Unwmk.** *Perf. 14*

226	A74	15p multicolored	.15	.15

20th anniv. of UNESCO.

Secretariat Buildings, Islamabad, Flag and Pres. Mohammed Ayub Khan — A75

1966, Nov. 29 **Litho.** *Perf. 13*

227	A75	15p multicolored	.15	.15
228	A75	50p multicolored	.18	.15
		Set value	.25	.18

Issued to publicize the new capital, Islamabad.

Avicenna — A76 Mohammed Ali Jinnah — A77

1966, Dec. 3 *Perf. 13½*

229	A76	15p salmon pink & slate grn	.15	.15

Issued to publicize the Health Institute.

Lithographed and Engraved

1966, Dec. 25 **Unwmk.** *Perf. 13*

Design: 50p, Different frame.

230	A77	15p orange, blk & bl	.15	.15
231	A77	50p lilac, blk & vio bl	.18	.15
		Set value	.25	.18

90th anniv. of the birth of Mohammed Ali Jinnah (1876-1948), 1st Governor General of Pakistan.

ITY Emblem A78

1967, Jan. 1 **Litho.**

232	A78	15p bister brn, blue & blk	.15	.15

International Tourist Year, 1967.

Red Crescent Emblem — A79

1967, Jan. 10 **Litho.** *Perf. 13½*

233	A79	15p brn, brn org & red	.15	.15

Tuberculosis eradication campaign.

Scout Sign and Emblem A80

Perf. 12½x13½

1967, Jan. 29 **Photo.**

234	A80	15p dp plum & brn org	.18	.15

4th National Pakistan Jamboree.
"Faisa" is a plate flaw, not an error.

Justice Holding Scales — A81

Unwmk.

1967, Feb. 17 **Litho.** *Perf. 13*

235	A81	15p multicolored	.15	.15

Centenary of High Court of West Pakistan.

Mohammad Iqbal — A82

1967, Apr. 21 Litho. *Perf. 13*
236 A82 15p red & brown .15 .15
237 A82 1r dk green & brn .28 .22
Set value .35 .27

90th anniv. of the birth of Mohammad Iqbal (1877-1938), poet and philosopher.

Holy War Flag — A83

1967, May 15 Litho. *Perf. 13*
238 A83 15p multicolored .15 .15

Holy War Flag awarded for valor to the cities of Lahore, Sialkot and Sargodha.

Star and "20" — A84

1967, Aug. 14 Photo. Unwmk.
239 A84 15p red & slate green .15 .15

20th anniversary of independence.

Rice Plant and Globe — A85

Cotton Plant, Bale and Cloth — A86

Design: 50p, Raw jute, bale and cloth.

1967, Sept. 26 Photo. *Perf. 13x13½*
240 A85 10p dk blue & yellow .15 .15

Perf. 13
241 A86 15p orange, bl grn & yel .15 .15
242 A86 50p blue grn, brn & tan .18 .15
Set value .30 .22

Issued to publicize major export products.

Toys — A87

1967, Oct. 2 Litho. *Perf. 13*
243 A87 15p multicolored .15 .15

Issued for International Children's Day.

Shah and Empress Farah of Iran — A88

Lithographed and Engraved
1967, Oct. 26 *Perf. 13*
244 A88 50p yellow, blue & lilac .22 .20

Coronation of Shah Mohammed Riza Pahlavi and Empress Farah of Iran.

"Each for all, . . ." — A89

1967, Nov. 4 Litho. *Perf. 13*
245 A89 15p multicolored .15 .15

Cooperative Day, 1967.

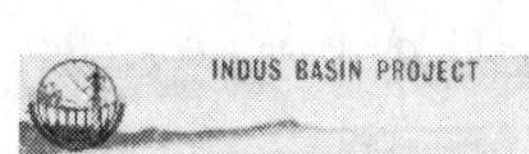

Mangla Dam — A90

1967, Nov. 23 Litho. *Perf. 13*
246 A90 15p multicolored .15 .15

Indus Basin Project, harnessing the Indus River for flood control and irrigation.

"Fight Against Cancer" — A91

Human Rights Flame — A92

1967, Dec. 26
247 A91 15p red & dk brown .15 .15

Issued to publicize the fight against cancer.

1968, Jan. 31 Photo. *Perf. 14x12½*
248 A92 15p Prus green & red .15 .15
249 A92 50p yellow, silver & red .28 .15
Set value .36 .20

International Human Rights Year 1968.

Agricultural University and Produce A93

1968, Mar. 28 Litho. *Perf. 13½*
250 A93 15p multicolored .15 .15

Issued to publicize the first convocation of the East Pakistan Agricultural University.

WHO Emblem — A94

Perf. 13½x12½
1968, Apr. 7 Photo.
251 A94 15p emerald & orange .15 .15
252 A94 50p orange & dk blue .28 .15
Set value .36 .18

20th anniv. of WHO. "Pais" is a plate flaw, not an error.

Kazi Nazrul Islam A95

Lithographed and Engraved
1968, June 25 Unwmk. *Perf. 13*
253 A95 15p dull yellow & brown .15 .15
254 A95 50p rose & brown .22 .15
Set value .30 .20

Kazi Nazrul Islam, poet and composer.

Nos. 56, 61 and 74 Surcharged with New Value and Bars in Black or Red

1968, Sept. Engr. *Perf. 13*
255 A13 4p on 3a dk rose lake .15 .15
256 A21 4p on 6a dk blue (R) .15 .15
257 A15 60p on 10a purple (R) .32 .20
a. Black surcharge .40 .30
Set value .42 .30

Types of 1948-57

1968 Wmk. 351 Engr. *Perf. 13*
258 A26 10r dk green & orange 1.00 .90
259 A7 25r purple 3.00 2.75

Children with Hoops A96

Unwmk.
1968, Oct. 7 Litho. *Perf. 13*
260 A96 15p buff & multi .15 .15

Issued for International Children's Day.

Symbolic of Political Reforms — A97

Designs: 15p, Agricultural and industrial development. 50p, Defense. 60p, Scientific and cultural advancement.

1968, Oct. 27 Litho. *Perf. 13*
261 A97 10p multicolored .15 .15
262 A97 15p multicolored .15 .15
263 A97 50p multicolored .20 .15
264 A97 60p multicolored .28 .18
Set value .60 .43

Development Decade, 1958-1968.

Chittagong Steel Mill — A98

1969, Jan. 7 Unwmk. *Perf. 13*
265 A98 15p lt gray grn, lt blue & blk .15 .15

Opening of Pakistan's first steel mill.

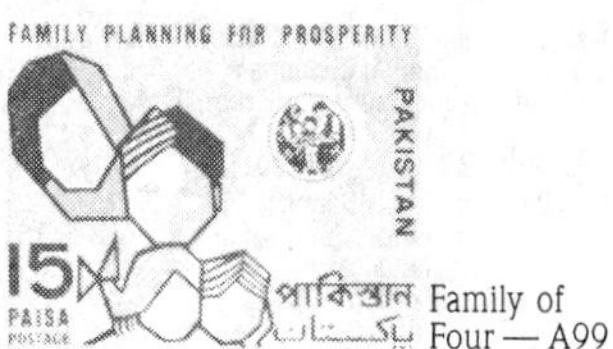

Family of Four — A99

1969, Jan. 14 Litho. *Perf. 13½*
266 A99 15p lt blue & plum .15 .15

Issued to publicize family planning.

Hockey Player and Medal — A100

1969, Jan. 30 Photo. *Perf. 13½*
267 A100 15p green, lt bl, blk & gold .15 .15
268 A100 1r grn, sal pink, blk & gold .60 .25
Set value .32

Pakistan's hockey victory at the 19th Olympic Games in Mexico.

Mirza Ghalib A101

1969, Feb. 15 Litho. *Perf. 13*
269 A101 15p blue & multi .15 .15
270 A101 50p multicolored .18 .15
Set value .25 .20

Mirza Ghalib (Asad Ullab Beg Khan, 1797-1869), poet who modernized the Urdu language.

Dacca Railroad Station A102

1969, Apr. 27 Litho. *Perf. 13*
271 A102 15p yel, grn, blk & dull bl .25 .15

Opening of the new railroad station in Kamalpur area of Dacca.

ILO Emblem and Ornamental Border A103

1969, May 15 Litho. *Perf. 13½*
272 A103 15p bright green & ocher .15 .15
273 A103 50p carmine rose & ocher .28 .18
Set value .35 .24

50th anniv. of the ILO.

Lady on Balcony, Mogul Miniature, Pakistan — A104

Designs: 50p, Lady Serving Wine, Safavi miniature, Iran. 1r, Sultan Suleiman Receiving Sheik Abdul Latif, 16th century miniature, Turkey.

1969, July 21 Litho. *Perf. 13*

274 A104 20p multicolored			.15	.15
275 A104 50p multicolored			.18	.15
276 A104 1r multicolored			.35	.28
	Nos. 274-276 (3)		.68	
	Set value			.48

5th anniv. of the signing of the Regional Cooperation for Development Pact by Turkey, Iran and Pakistan.

Eastern Refinery, Chittagong A105

1969, Sept. 14 Photo. *Perf. 13½*

277 A105 20p yel, blk & vio bl .15 .15

Opening of the 1st oil refinery in East Pakistan.

Children Playing — A106

1969, Oct. 6 *Perf. 13*

278 A106 20p blue & multi .15 .15

Issued for Universal Children's Day.

Japanese Doll, Map of Dacca-Tokyo Pearl Route A107

1969, Nov. 1 Litho. *Perf. 13½x13*

279 A107 20p multicolored		.15	.15
280 A107 50p ultra & multi		.24	.16
	Set value	.34	.24

Inauguration of the Pakistan International Airways' Dacca-Tokyo "Pearl Route."

Reflection of Light Diagram — A108

1969, Nov. 4 *Perf. 13*

281 A108 20p multicolored .16 .15

Alhazen (abu-Ali al Hasan ibn-al-Haytham, 965-1039), astronomer and optician.

Vickers Vimy and London-Darwin Route over Karachi — A109

1969, Dec. 2 Photo. *Perf. 13½x13*

282 A109 50p multicolored .40 .22

50th anniv. of the 1st England to Australia flight.

View of EXPO '70, Sun Tower, Flags of Pakistan, Iran and Turkey — A110

1970, Feb. 15 Litho. *Perf. 13*

283 A110 50p multicolored .22 .16

Issued to publicize EXPO '70 International Exhibition, Osaka, Japan, Mar. 15-Sept. 13.

UPU Headquarters, Bern — A111

1970, May 20 Litho. *Perf. 13½x13*

284 A111 20p multicolored		.15	.15
285 A111 50p multicolored		.30	.15
	Set value	.38	.20

Opening of new UPU headquarters in Bern.

A souvenir sheet of 2 exists, inscribed "U.P.U. Day 9th Oct. 1971". It contains stamps similar to Nos. 284-285, imperf.

UN Headquarters, New York — A112

Design: 50p, UN emblem.

1970, June 26

286 A112 20p green & multi		.15	.15
287 A112 50p violet & multi		.28	.15
	Set value	.36	.20

25th anniversary of the United Nations.

Education Year Emblem and Open Book A113

1970, July 6 Litho. *Perf. 13*

288 A113 20p blue & multi		.15	.15
289 A113 50p orange & multi		.22	.15
	Set value	.30	.15

International Education Year, 1970.

Saiful Malook Lake, Pakistan A114

Designs: 50p, Seeyo-Se-Pol Bridge, Esfahan, Iran. 1r, View, Fethiye, Turkey.

1970, July 21

290 A114 20p yellow & multi			.15	.15
291 A114 50p yellow & multi			.24	.15
292 A114 1r yellow & multi			.45	.24
	Nos. 290-292 (3)		.84	
	Set value			.39

6th anniv. of the signing of the Regional Cooperation for Development Pact by Pakistan, Iran and Turkey.

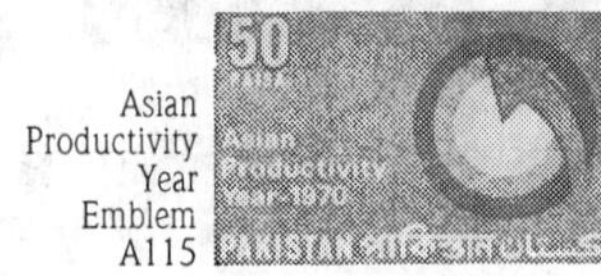

Asian Productivity Year Emblem A115

1970, Aug. 18 Photo. *Perf. 12½x14*

293 A115 50p black, yellow & green .18 .15

Asian Productivity Year, 1970.

Dr. Maria Montessori — A116

1970, Aug. 31 Litho. *Perf. 13*

294 A116 20p red & multi		.15	.15
295 A116 50p multicolored		.20	.15
	Set value	.28	.17

Maria Montessori (1870-1952) Italian educator and physician.

Tractor and Fertilizer Factory — A117

1970, Sept. 12

296 A117 20p yel grn & brn org .15 .15

10th Regional Food and Agricultural Organization Conf. for the Near East in Islamabad.

Boy, Girl, Open Book A118

Flag and Inscription A119

1970, Oct. 5 Photo. *Perf. 13*

297 A118 20p multicolored .15 .15

Issued for Children's Day.

1970, Dec. 7 Litho. *Perf. 13½x13*

298 A119 20p violet & green		.15	.15
299 A119 20p brt pink & green		.15	.15
	Set value	.16	.15

No. 298 inscribed "Elections for National Assembly 7th Dec. 1970," No. 299 inscribed "Elections for Provincial Assemblies 17th Dec. 1970."

Emblem and Burning of Al Aqsa Mosque — A120

1970, Dec. 26 *Perf. 13½x12½*

300 A120 20p multicolored .50 .25

Islamic Conference of Foreign Ministers, Karachi, Dec. 26-28.

Coastal Embankment — A121

1971, Feb. 25 Litho. *Perf. 13*

301 A121 20p multicolored .15 .15

Development of coastal embankments in East Pakistan.

Men of Different Races — A122

1971, Mar. 21 Litho. *Perf. 13*

302 A122 20p multicolored		.15	.15
303 A122 50p lilac & multi		.18	.15
	Set value	.25	.15

Intl. Year against Racial Discrimination.

Cement Factory, Daudkhel A123

1971, July 1 Litho. *Perf. 13*

304 A123 20p purple, blk & brn .15 .15

20th anniversary of Colombo Plan.

Badshahi Mosque, Lahore — A124

Designs: 10pa, Mosque of Selim, Edirne, Turkey. 50pa, Religious School, of Chaharbagh, Isfahan, Iran, vert.

1971, July 21 Litho. *Perf. 13*

305 A124 10p red & multi	.15	.15
306 A124 20p green & multi	.15	.15
307 A124 50p blue & multi	.28	.18
Set value	.45	.28

7th anniversary of Regional Cooperation among Pakistan, Iran and Turkey.

Electric Train and Boy with Toy Locomotive — A125

1971, Oct. 4 Litho. *Perf. 13*

308 A125 20p slate & multi .40 .22

Children's Day.

Messenger and Statue of Cyrus the Great — A126

1971, Oct. 15

309 A126 10p green & multi	.15	.15
310 A126 20p blue & multi	.15	.15
311 A126 50p red & multi	.38	.22
Set value	.40	.32

2500th anniversary of the founding of the Persian Empire by Cyrus the Great.

A souvenir sheet of 3 contains stamps similar to Nos. 309-311, imperf.

Hockey Player and Cup — A127

1971, Oct. 24

312 A127 20p red & multi .35 .15

First World Hockey Cup, Barcelona, Spain, Oct. 15-24.

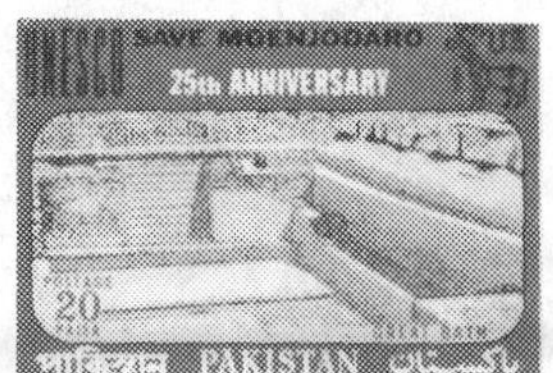

Great Bath at Mohenjo-Daro — A128

1971, Nov. 4

313 A128 20p dp org, dk brn & blk .15 .15

25th anniv. of UNESCO.

UNICEF Emblem A129

1971, Dec. 11 Litho. *Perf. 13*

314 A129 50p dull blue, org & grn .30 .15

25th anniv. of UNICEF.

King Hussein and Jordan Flag A130

1971, Dec. 25

315 A130 20p blue & multi .15 .15

50th anniversary of the Hashemite Kingdom of Jordan.

Pakistan Hockey Federation Emblem, and Cup A131

1971, Dec. 31

316 A131 20p yellow & multi .18 .15

Pakistan, world hockey champions, Barcelona, Oct. 1971.

Arab Scholars — A132

1972, Jan. 15 Litho. *Perf. 13½*

317 A132 20p brown, blk & blue .15 .15

International Book Year 1972.

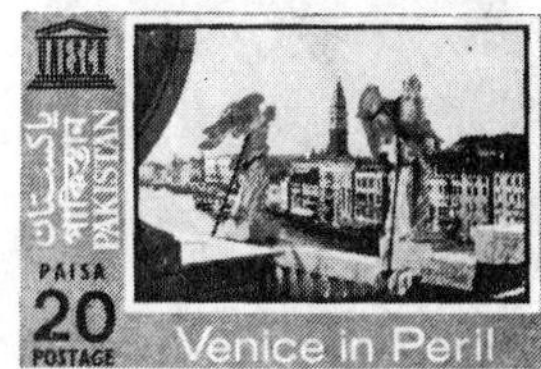

Angels and Grand Canal, Venice — A133

1972, Feb. 5 *Perf. 13*

318 A133 20p blue & multi .15 .15

UNESCO campaign to save Venice.

ECAFE Emblem A134

1972, Mar. 28 Litho. *Perf. 13*

319 A134 20p blue & multi .15 .15

Economic Commission for Asia and the Far East (ECAFE), 25th anniversary.

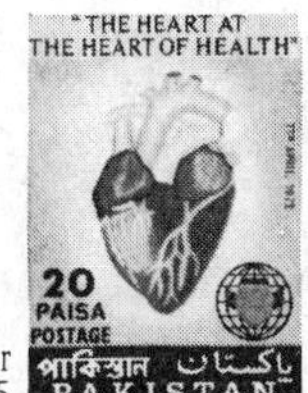

"Your Heart is your Health" — A135

1972, Apr. 7 *Perf. 13x13½*

320 A135 20p vio blue & multi .15 .15

World Health Day 1972.

"Only One Earth" — A136

1972, June 5 Litho. *Perf. 12½x14*

321 A136 20p ultra & multi .18 .15

UN Conference on Human Environment, Stockholm, June 5-16.

Young Man, by Abdur Rehman Chughtai — A137

Paintings: 10p, Fisherman, by Cevat Dereli (Turkey). 20p, Persian Woman, by Behzad.

1972, July 21 Litho. *Perf. 13*

322 A137 10p multicolored	.15	.15
323 A137 20p multicolored	.15	.15
324 A137 50p multicolored	.18	.15
Set value	.30	.20

Regional Cooperation for Development Pact among Pakistan, Turkey and Iran, 8th anniversary.

Jinnah and Independence Memorial — A138

"Land Reforms" — A139

Designs: Nos. 326-329, Principal reforms. 60pa, State Bank, Islamabad, meeting-place of National Assembly, horiz.

Perf. 13 (A138), 13½x12½ (A139)

1972, Aug. 14

325 A138 10p shown	.15	.15
326 A139 20p shown	.15	.15
327 A139 20p Labor reforms	.15	.15
328 A139 20p Education	.15	.15
329 A139 20p Health care	.15	.15
a. Vert. strip of 4, #326-329	.50	
330 A138 60p rose lilac & car	.22	.15
Set value	.80	.35

25th anniversary of independence. No. 329a has decorative labels adjoining.

Blood Donor, Society Emblem — A140

1972, Sept. 6 Litho. *Perf. 14x12½*

331 A140 20p multicolored .15 .15

Pakistan National Blood Transfusion Service.

Census Chart — A141

1972, Sept. 16 Litho. *Perf. 13½*

332 A141 20p multicolored .15 .15

Centenary of population census.

Children Leaving Slum for Modern City — A142

1972, Oct. 2 Litho. *Perf. 13*

333 A142 20p multicolored .15 .15

Children's Day.

Giant Book and Children A143

1972, Oct. 23

334 A143 20p purple & multi .15 .15

Education Week.

Nuclear Power Plant, Karachi A144

1972, Nov. 28 Litho. *Perf. 13*

335 A144 20p multicolored .15 .15

Pakistan's first nuclear power plant.

Copernicus in Observatory, by Jan Matejko — A145

1973, Feb. 19 Litho. *Perf. 13*

336 A145 20p multicolored .15 .15

500th anniversary of the birth of Nicolaus Copernicus (1473-1543), Polish astronomer.

Dancing Girl, Public Baths, Mohenjo-Daro — A146

1973, Feb. 23 *Perf. 13½x13*

337 A146 20p multicolored .15 .15

50th anniv. of the Mohenjo-Daro excavations.

Radar, Lightning, WMO Emblem — A147

1973, Mar. 23 **Litho.** *Perf. 13*

338 A147 20p multicolored .15 .15

Cent. of intl. meteorological cooperation.

Prisoners of War A148

1973, Apr. 18

339 A148 1.25r black & multi .18 .15

A plea for Pakistani prisoners of war in India.

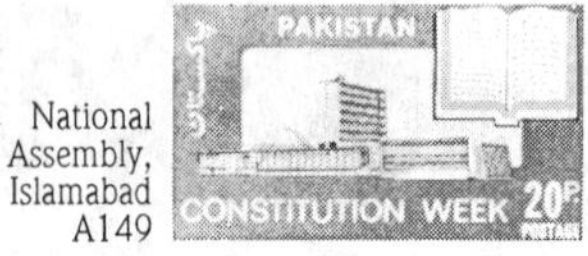

National Assembly, Islamabad A149

1973, Apr. 21 *Perf. 12½x13½*

340 A149 20p green & multi .15 .15

Constitution Week.

State Bank and Emblem A150

1973, July 1 **Litho.** *Perf. 13*

341 A150 20p multicolored .15 .15
342 A150 1r multicolored .25 .15
Set value .15

State Bank of Pakistan, 25th anniversary.

Street, Mohenjo-Daro, Pakistan — A151

Designs: 20p, Statue of man, Shahdad, Kerman, Persia, 4000 B.C. 1.25r, Head from mausoleum of King Antiochus I (69-34 B.C.), Turkey.

1973, July 21 *Perf. 13x13½*

343 A151 20p blue & multi .15 .15
344 A151 60p emerald & multi .16 .15
345 A151 1.25r red & multi .35 .25
Nos. 343-345 (3) .66
Set value .40

Regional Cooperation for Development Pact among Pakistan, Turkey and Iran, 9th anniversary.

Pakistani Flag and Constitution A152

1973, Aug. 14 **Litho.** *Perf. 13*

346 A152 20p blue & multi .15 .15

Independence Day.

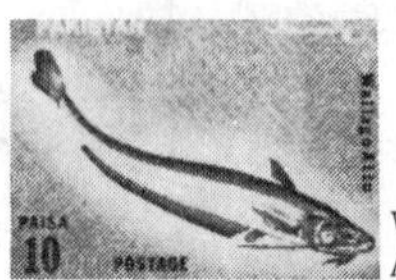

Mohammed Ali Jinnah — A153

1973, Sept. 11 **Litho.** *Perf. 13*

347 A153 20p emerald, yel & blk .15 .15

Mohammed Ali Jinnah (1876-1948), president of All-India Moslem League.

Wallago Attu — A154

Fish: 20p, Labeo rohita. 60p, Tilapia mossambica. 1r, Catla catla.

1973, Sept. 24 **Litho.** *Perf. 13½*

348 A154 10p multicolored .20 .15
349 A154 20p multicolored .25 .15
350 A154 60p multicolored .50 .20
351 A154 1r ultra & multi .85 .35
a. Strip of 4, #348-351 1.80 .75

Book, Torch, Child and School A155

1973, Oct. 1

352 A155 20p multicolored .15 .15

Universal Children's Day.

Kemal Ataturk and Ankara A157

1973, Oct. 29

354 A157 50p multicolored .15 .15

50th anniversary of Turkish Republic.

Scout Pointing to Planet and Stars — A158

Human Rights Flame, Sheltered Home — A159

Perf. 13½x12½

1973, Nov. 11 **Litho.**

355 A158 20p dull blue & multi .30 .15

25th anniversary of Pakistani Boy Scouts and Silver Jubilee Jamboree.

1973, Nov. 16

356 A159 20p multicolored .15 .15

25th anniversary of the Universal Declaration of Human Rights.

al-Biruni and Jhelum Observatory — A160

1973, Nov. 26 **Litho.** *Perf. 13*

357 A160 20p multicolored .15 .15
358 A160 1.25r multicolored .50 .35
Set value .40

International Congress on Millenary of abu-al-Rayhan al-Biruni, Nov. 26-Dec. 12.

Dr. A. G. Hansen — A161

1973, Dec. 29

359 A161 20p ultra & multi .15 .15

Centenary of the discovery by Dr. Armauer Gerhard Hansen of the Hansen bacillus, the cause of leprosy.

Family and WPY Emblem A162

1974, Jan. 1 **Litho.** *Perf. 13*

360 A162 20p yellow & multi .15 .15
361 A162 1.25r salmon & multi .35 .25
Set value .41 .30

World Population Year 1974.

Summit Emblem and Ornament — A163

Emblem, Crescent and Rays A164

1974, Feb. 22 *Perf. 14x12½, 13*

362 A163 20p multicolored .15 .15
363 A164 65p multicolored .18 .15
a. Souvenir sheet of 2 1.75 1.75
Set value .24 .19

Islamic Summit Meeting. No. 363a contains two stamps similar to Nos. 362-363 with simulated perforations.

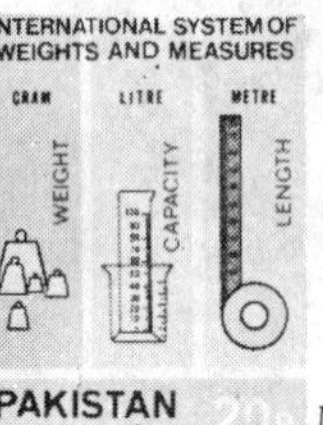

Metric Measures — A165

1974, July 1 **Litho.** *Perf. 13*

364 A165 20p multicolored .15 .15

Introduction of metric system.

Kashan Rug, Lahore — A166

Designs: 60p, Persian rug, late 16th century. 1.25r, Anatolian rug, 15th century.

1974, July 21

365 A166 20p multicolored .15 .15
366 A166 60p multicolored .16 .15
367 A166 1.25r multicolored .35 .25
Nos. 365-367 (3) .66
Set value .40

10th anniversary of the Regional Cooperation for Development Pact among Pakistan, Iran and Turkey.

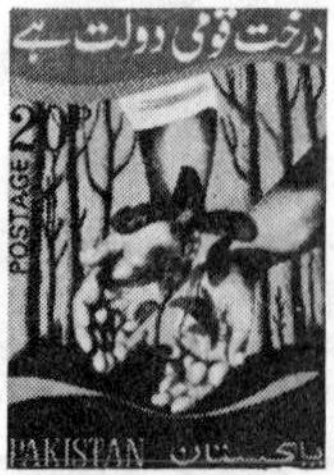

Hands Protecting Sapling — A167

1974, Aug. 9 **Litho.** *Perf. 13*

368 A167 20p multicolored .15 .15

Arbor Day.

Torch over Map of Africa with Namibia — A168

1974, Aug. 26

369	A168	60p green & multi	.20	.15

Namibia (South-West Africa) Day. See note after United Nations No. 241.

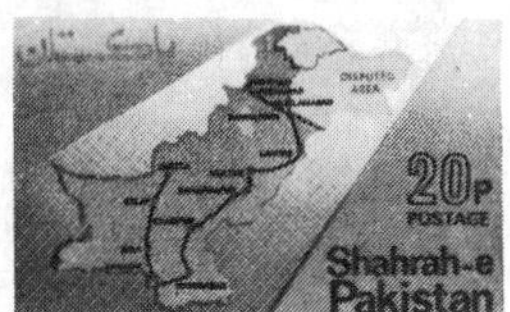

Map of Pakistan with Highways and Disputed Area — A169

1974, Sept. 23

370	A169	20p multicolored	.15	.15

Highway system under construction.

Child and Students — A170

1974, Oct. 7 Litho. *Perf. 13*

371	A170	20p multicolored	.15	.15

Universal Children's Day.

UPU Emblem — A171

Liaqat Ali Khan — A172

Design: 2.25r, Jet, UPU emblem, mail coach.

1974, Oct. 9

Size: 24x36mm

372	A171	20p multicolored	.15	.15

Size: 29x41mm

373	A171	2.25r multicolored	.60	.50
a.		Souv. sheet of 2, #372-373, imperf.	1.75	1.75

Centenary of Universal Postal Union.

1974, Oct. 16 Litho. *Perf. 13x13½*

374	A172	20p black & red	.15	.15

Liaqat Ali Khan, Prime Minister 1947-1951.

Mohammad Allama Iqbal — A173

1974, Nov. 9 Litho. *Perf. 13*

375	A173	20p multicolored	.15	.15

Mohammad Allama Iqbal (1877-1938), poet and philosopher.

Dr. Schweitzer on Ogowe River, 1915 A174

1975, Jan. 14 Litho. *Perf. 13*

376	A174	2.25r multicolored	.85	.50

Dr. Albert Schweitzer (1875-1965), medical missionary, birth centenary.

Tourism Year 75 Emblem — A175

1975, Jan. 15

377	A175	2.25r multicolored	.50	.40

South Asia Tourism Year, 1975.

Flags of Participants, Memorial and Prime Minister Bhutto — A176

1975, Feb. 22 Litho. *Perf. 13*

378	A176	20p lt blue & multi	.15	.15
379	A176	1r brt pink & multi	.28	.28
		Set value	.34	.32

2nd Lahore Islamic Summit, Feb. 22, 1st anniv.

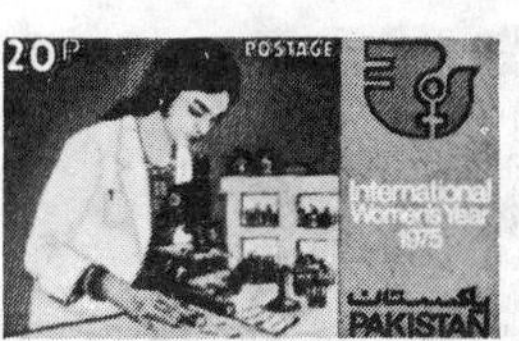

IWY Emblem and Woman Scientist — A177

Design: 2.25r, Old woman and girl learning to read and write.

1975, June 15 Litho. *Perf. 13*

380	A177	20p multicolored	.15	.15
381	A177	2.25r multicolored	.60	.50
		Set value		.55

International Women's Year 1975.

Globe with Dates, Arabic "X" — A178

Camel Leather Vase, Pakistan — A179

1975, July 14 Litho. *Perf. 13*

382	A178	20p multicolored	.15	.15

International Congress of Mathematical Sciences, Karachi, July 14-20.

1975, July 21

Designs: 60p, Ceramic plate and RCD emblem, Iran, horiz. 1.25r, Porcelain vase, Turkey.

383	A179	20p lilac & multi	.15	.15
384	A179	60p violet blk & multi	.16	.15
385	A179	1.25r blue & multi	.30	.18
		Set value	.53	.32

Regional Cooperation for Development Pact among Turkey, Iran and Pakistan.

Sapling, Trees and Ant — A180

Black Partridge — A181

1975, Aug. 9 Litho. *Perf. 13x13½*

386	A180	20p multicolored	.15	.15

Tree Planting Day.

1975, Sept. 30 Litho. *Perf. 13*

387	A181	20p blue & multi	.30	.15
388	A181	2.25r yellow & multi	1.40	.55

Wildlife Protection.

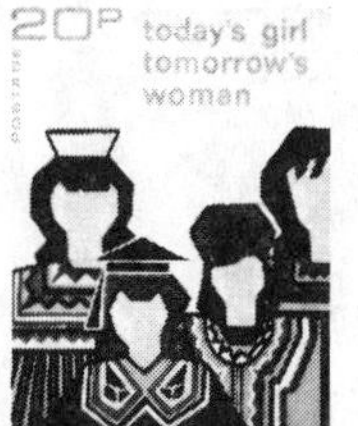

Girls — A182

1975, Oct. 6

389	A182	20p multicolored	.15	.15

Universal Children's Day.

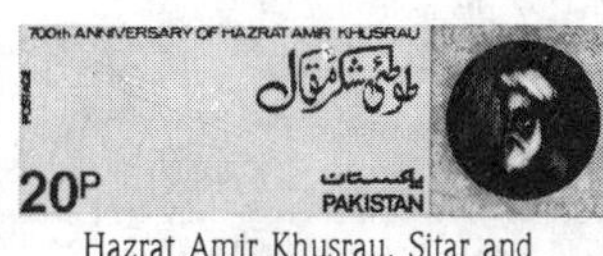

Hazrat Amir Khusrau, Sitar and Tabla — A183

1975, Oct. 24 Litho. *Perf. 14x12½*

390	A183	20p lt blue & multi	.15	.15
391	A183	2.25r pink & multi	.50	.40
		Set value		.45

700th anniversary of Hazrat Amir Khusrau (1253-1325), musician who invented the sitar and tabla instruments.

Mohammad Iqbal — A184

1975, Nov. 9 *Perf. 13*

392	A184	20p multicolored	.15	.15

Mohammad Allama Iqbal (1877-1938), poet and philosopher, birth centenary.

Wild Sheep of the Punjab — A185

1975, Dec. 31 Litho. *Perf. 13*

393	A185	20p multicolored	.45	.25
394	A185	3r multicolored	2.50	.75

Wildlife Protection. See Nos. 410-411.

Mohenjo-Daro and UNESCO Emblem A186

Designs: View of Mohenjo-Daro excavations.

1976, Feb. 29 Litho. *Perf. 13*

395	A186	10p multicolored	.15	.15
396	A186	20p multicolored	.15	.15
397	A186	65p multicolored	.15	.15
398	A186	3r multicolored	.70	.40
399	A186	4r multicolored	.85	.60
a.		Strip of 5, #395-399	1.40	1.40

UNESCO campaign to save Mohenjo-Daro excavations.

Dome and Minaret of Rauza-e-Mubarak Mausoleum A187

1976, Mar. 3 Photo. *Perf. 13½x14*

400	A187	20p blue & multi	.15	.15
401	A187	3r gray & multi	.50	.40
		Set value	.55	.45

International Congress on Seerat, the teachings of Mohammed, Mar. 3-15.

Alexander Graham Bell, 1876 Telephone and Dial — A188

1976, Mar. 10 *Perf. 13*

402	A188	3r blue & multi	.85	.85

Centenary of first telephone call by Alexander Graham Bell, Mar. 10, 1876.

College Emblem — A189

1976, Mar. 15 Litho. *Perf. 13*

403	A189	20p multicolored	.15	.15

Cent. of Natl. College of Arts, Lahore.

Peacock
A190

1976, Mar. 31 Litho. *Perf. 13*
404 A190 20p lt blue & multi .35 .18
405 A190 3r pink & multi 2.00 .65

Wildlife protection.

Eye and WHO Emblem — A191

1976, Apr. 7
406 A191 20p multicolored .15 .15

World Health Day: "Foresight prevents blindness."

Mohenjo-Daro, UNESCO Emblem, Bull (from Seal) — A192

1976, May 31 Litho. *Perf. 13*
407 A192 20p multicolored .15 .15

UNESCO campaign to save Mohenjo-Daro excavations.

Jefferson Memorial, US Bicentennial Emblem — A193

Declaration of Independence, by John Trumbull — A194

1976, July 4 *Perf. 13*
408 A193 90p multicolored .15 .15
Perf. 13½x13
409 A194 4r multicolored 1.10 1.10

American Bicentennial.

Wildlife Type of 1975

Wildlife protection: 20p, 3r, Ibex.

1976, July 12
410 A185 20p multicolored .35 .18
411 A185 3r multicolored 2.00 .65

Mohammed Ali Jinnah — A195

65p, Riza Shah Pahlavi. 90p, Kemal Ataturk.

1976, July 21 Litho. *Perf. 14*
412 A195 20p multicolored .15 .15
413 A195 65p multicolored .15 .15
414 A195 90p multicolored .18 .15
a. Strip of 3, #412-414 .35 .35

Regional Cooperation for Development Pact among Pakistan, Turkey and Iran, 12th anniversary.

Ornament
A196

Jinnah and Wazir Mansion
A197

Designs (Jinnah and): 40p, Sind Madressah (building). 50p, Minar Qarardad (minaret). 3r, Mausoleum.

1976, Aug. 14 Litho. *Perf. 13½*
415 A196 5p multicolored .15 .15
416 A196 10p multicolored .15 .15
417 A196 15p multicolored .15 .15
418 A197 20p multicolored .18 .15
419 A197 40p multicolored .20 .15
420 A197 50p multicolored .28 .15
421 A196 1r multicolored .35 .15
422 A197 3r multicolored .65 .50
a. Block of 8, #415-422 2.25 2.00
Set value 1.00

Mohammed Ali Jinnah (1876-1948), first Governor General of Pakistan, birth centenary. Horizontal rows of types A196 and A197 alternate in sheet.

Mohenjo-Daro and UNESCO Emblem — A198

1976, Aug. 31 *Perf. 14*
423 A198 65p multicolored .15 .15

UNESCO campaign to save Mohenjo-Daro excavations.

Racial Discrimination Emblem — A199

Perf. 12½x13½
1976, Sept. 15 Litho.
424 A199 65p multicolored .22 .18

Fight against racial discrimination.

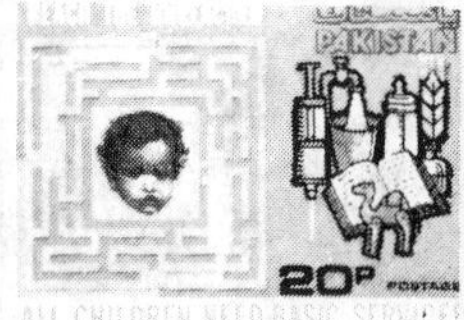

Child's Head, Symbols of Health, Education and Food
A200

1976, Oct. 4 *Perf. 13*
425 A200 20p blue & multi .15 .15

Universal Children's Day.

Verse by Allama Iqbal
A201

1976, Nov. 9 Litho. *Perf. 13*
426 A201 20p multicolored .15 .15

Mohammed Allama Iqbal (1877-1938), poet and philosopher, birth centenary.

Scout Emblem, Jinnah Giving Salute — A202

Children Reading — A203

1976, Nov. 20
427 A202 20p multicolored .15 .15

Quaid-I-Azam Centenary Jamboree, Nov. 1976.

1976, Dec. 15 Litho. *Perf. 13*
428 A203 20p multicolored .15 .15

Books for children.

Mohammed Ali Jinnah — A204

Lithographed and Embossed

1976, Dec. 25 *Perf. 12½*
429 A204 10r gold & green 1.25 1.25

Mohammed Ali Jinnah (1876-1948), 1st Governor General of Pakistan.

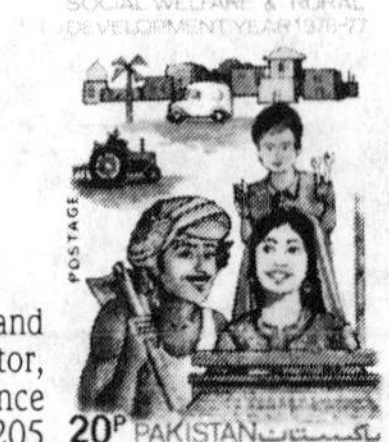

Farm Family and Village, Tractor, Ambulance
A205

1977, Apr. 14 Litho. *Perf. 13*
430 A205 20p multicolored .15 .15

Social Welfare and Rural Development Year, 1976-77.

Terracotta Bullock Cart, Pakistan
A206

Designs: 20p, Terra-cotta jug, Turkey. 90p, Decorated jug, Iran.

1977, July 21 Litho. *Perf. 13*
431 A206 20p ultra & multi .15 .15
432 A206 65p blue green & multi .20 .15
433 A206 90p lilac & multi .35 .18
Nos. 431-433 (3) .70
Set value .32

Regional Cooperation for Development Pact among Pakistan, Turkey and Iran, 13th anniversary.

Trees — A207

1977, Aug. 9 Litho. *Perf. 13*
434 A207 20p multicolored .15 .15

Tree planting program.

Desert
A208

1977, Sept. 5 Litho. *Perf. 13*
435 A208 65p multicolored .15 .15

UN Conference on Desertification, Nairobi, Kenya, Aug. 29-Sept. 9.

"Water for the Children" — A209

1977, Oct. 3 Litho. *Perf. 14x12½*
436 A209 50p multicolored .15 .15

Universal Children's Day.

Aga Khan III — A210

1977, Nov. 2 Litho. *Perf. 13*
437 A210 2r multicolored .35 .35

Aga Khan III (1877-1957), spiritual ruler of Ismaeli sect, statesman, birth centenary.

Mohammad Iqbal — A211

20p, Spirit appearing to Iqbal, painting by Behzad. 65p, Iqbal looking at Jamaluddin Afghani & Saeed Halim offering prayers, by Behzad. 1.25r, Verse in Urdu. 2.25r, Verse in Persian.

1977, Nov. 9

438 A211	20p	multicolored	.15	.15
439 A211	65p	multicolored	.15	.15
440 A211	1.25r	multicolored	.20	.18
441 A211	2.25r	multicolored	.40	.35
442 A211	3r	multicolored	.85	.65
a.		Strip of 5, #438-442	1.60	1.60

Mohammad Allama Iqbal (1877-1938), poet and philosopher, birth centenary.

Holy Kaaba, Mecca — A212

1977, Nov. 21 *Perf. 14*
443 A212 65p green & multi .15 .15

1977 pilgrimage to Mecca.

Healthy and Sick Bodies A213

Woman from Rawalpindi-Islamabad A214

1977, Dec. 19 Litho. *Perf. 13*
444 A213 65p blue green & multi .15 .15

World Rheumatism Year.

1978, Feb. 5 Litho. *Perf. 12½x13½*
445 A214 75p multicolored .20 .15

Indonesia-Pakistan Economic and Cultural Cooperation Organization.

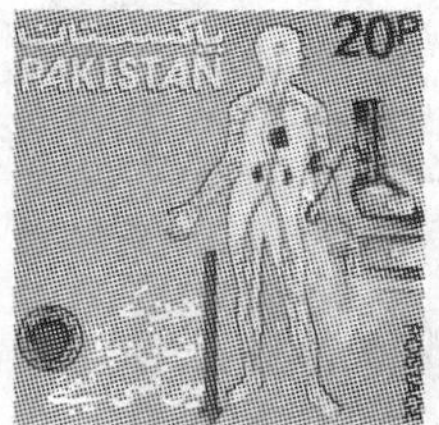

Blood Circulation and Pressure Gauge A215

1978, Apr. 20 Litho. *Perf. 13*

446 A215	20p	blue & multi	.15	.15
447 A215	2r	yellow & multi	.35	.35
		Set value	.40	.40

Campaign against hypertension.

Henri Dunant, Red Cross, Red Crescent A216

1978, May 8 *Perf. 14*
448 A216 1r multicolored .18 .18

Henri Dunant (1828-1910), founder of Red Cross, 150th birth anniversary.

Red Roses, Pakistan — A217

90p, Pink roses, Iran. 2r, Yellow rose, Turkey.

1978, July 21 Litho. *Perf. 13½*

449 A217	20p	multicolored	.15	.15
450 A217	90p	multicolored	.15	.15
451 A217	2r	multicolored	.35	.35
a.		Strip of 3, #449-451	.55	.55

Regional Cooperation for Development Pact among Turkey, Iran and Pakistan.

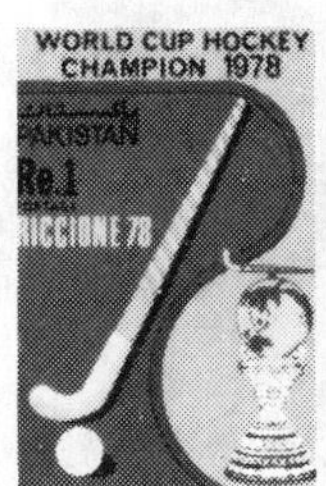

Hockey Stick and Ball, Championship Cup — A218

Fair Building, Fountain, Piazza Tourismo — A219

1978, Aug. 26 Litho. *Perf. 13*

452 A218	1r	multicolored	.18	.18
453 A219	2r	multicolored	.35	.35

Riccione '78, 30th International Stamp Fair, Riccione, Italy, Aug. 26-28. No. 452 also commemorates Pakistan as World Hockey Cup Champion.

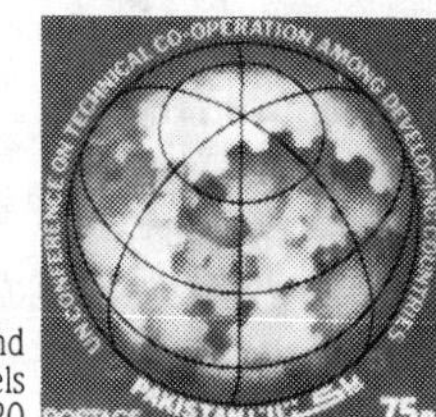

Globe and Cogwheels A220

1978, Sept. 3
454 A220 75p multicolored .15 .15

UN Conference on Technical Cooperation among Developing Countries, Buenos Aires, Argentina, Sept. 1978.

St. Patrick's Cathedral, Karachi — A221

Design: 2r, Stained-glass window.

1978, Sept. 29 Litho. *Perf. 13*

455 A221	1r	multicolored	.22	.18
456 A221	2r	multicolored	.50	.35

St. Patrick's Cathedral, Karachi, centenary.

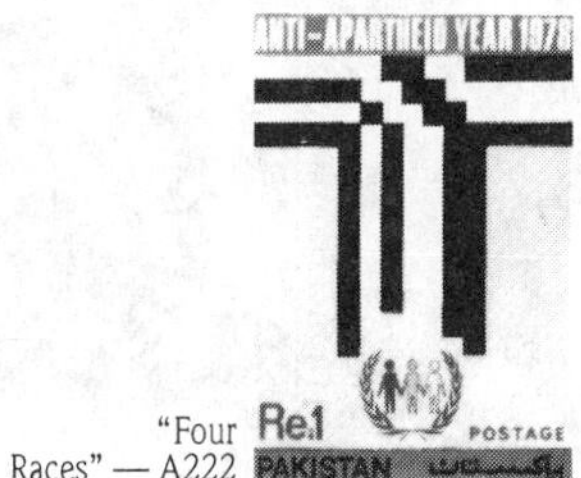

"Four Races" — A222

1978, Nov. 20 Litho. *Perf. 13*
457 A222 1r multicolored .18 .15

Anti-Apartheid Year.

Maulana Jauhar — A223

1978, Dec. 10 Litho. *Perf. 13*
458 A223 50p multicolored .15 .15

Maulana Muhammad Ali Jauhar, writer, journalist and patriot, birth centenary.

Type of 1957 and

Qarardad Monument A224

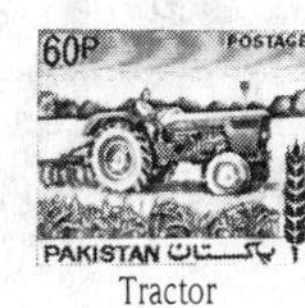

Tractor A225

Tomb of Ibrahim Khan Makli — A225a

Engr.; Litho. (10p, 25p, 40p, 50p, 90p)
1978-81 *Perf. 14*

459 A224	2p	dark green	.15	.15
460 A224	3p	black	.15	.15
461 A224	5p	violet blue	.15	.15
462 A225	10p	lt blue & blue ('79)	.15	.15
463 A225	20p	yel green ('79)	.15	.15
464 A225	25p	rose car & grn ('79)	.15	.15
465 A225	40p	carmine & blue	.15	.15
466 A225	50p	bl grn & vio ('79)	.15	.15
467 A225	60p	black	.18	.15
468 A225	75p	dull red	.20	.15
469 A225	90p	blue & carmine	.25	.15

Perf. 13½x13
Engr. Wmk. 351

470 A225a	1r	olive ('80)	.28	.15
471 A225a	1.50r	dp orange ('79)	.40	.15
472 A225a	2r	car rose ('79)	.55	.16
473 A225a	3r	indigo ('80)	.85	.22
474 A225a	4r	black ('81)	1.10	.35
475 A225a	5r	dk brown ('81)	1.40	.40
475A A26	15r	rose lil & red ('79)	5.00	4.00
		Nos. 459-475A (18)	11.41	
		Set value		5.75

Lithographed stamps, type A225, have bottom panel in solid color with colorless lettering and numerals 2mm high instead of 3mm.

For overprints see Nos. O94-O110.

Tornado Jet Fighter, de Havilland Rapide and Flyer A — A226

Wright Flyer A and: 1r, Phantom F4F jet fighter & Tristar airliner. 2r, Bell X15 fighter & TU-104 airliner. 2.25r, MiG fighter & Concorde.

Unwmk.
1978, Dec. 24 Litho. *Perf. 13*

476 A226	65p	multicolored	.15	.15
477 A226	1r	multicolored	.20	.15
478 A226	2r	multicolored	.50	.18
479 A226	2.25r	multicolored	.60	.20
a.		Block of 4, #476-479	1.10	
		Set value		.52

75th anniv. of 1st powered flight. Nos. 476-479 printed se-tenant in sheets of 40.

Koran Lighting the World and Mohammed's Tomb — A227

1979, Feb. 10 Litho. *Perf. 13*
480 A227 20p multicolored .15 .15

Mohammed's birth anniversary.

Mother and Children A228

1979, Feb. 25
481 A228 50p multicolored .15 .15

APWA Services, 30th anniversary.

Lophophorus Impejanus — A229

Pheasants: 25p, Lophura leucomelana. 40p, Pucrasia macrolopha. 1r, Catreus walichii.

1979, June 17 Litho. *Perf. 13*

482 A229	20p	multicolored	.15	.15
483 A229	25p	multicolored	.15	.15
484 A229	40p	multicolored	.15	.15
485 A229	1r	multicolored	.35	.15
		Set value	.55	.22

For overprint see No. 525.

The values of stamps in less than very fine condition generally are less than catalogue value.

15TH ANNIVERSARY RCD

At the Well, by Allah Baksh — A230

Paintings: 75p, Potters, by Kamalel Molk, Iran. 1.60r, Plowing, by Namik Ismail, Turkey.

1979, July 21 Litho. *Perf. 14x13*

486 A230 40p multicolored .15 .15
487 A230 75p multicolored .15 .15
488 A230 1.60r multicolored .22 .15
a. Strip of 3, #486-488 .38 .38
Set value .22

Regional Cooperation for Development Pact among Pakistan, Iran and Turkey, 15th anniversary.

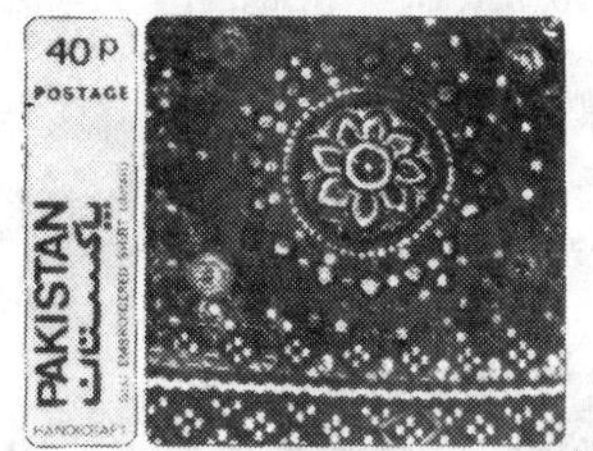

Guj Embroidery — A231

Handicrafts: 1r, Enamel inlay brass plate. 1.50r, Baskets. 2r, Peacock, embroidered rug.

1979, Aug. 23 Litho. *Perf. 14x13*

489 A231 40p multicolored .15 .15
490 A231 1r multicolored .15 .15
491 A231 1.50r multicolored .20 .15
492 A231 2r multicolored .28 .16
a. Block of 4, #489-492 .80 .80
Set value .40

Children, IYC and SOS Emblems A232

1979, Sept. 10 Litho. *Perf. 13*

493 A232 50p multicolored .15 .15

SOS Children's Village, Lahore, opening.

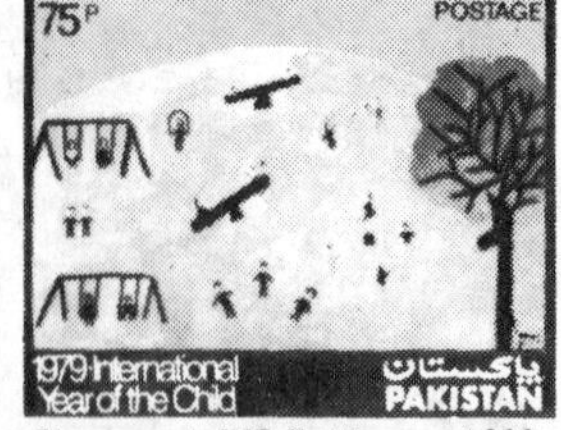

Playground, IYC Emblem — A233

IYC Emblem and: Children's drawings.

1979, Oct. 22 *Perf. 14x12½*

494 A233 40p multicolored .15 .15
495 A233 75p multicolored .15 .15
496 A233 1r multicolored .15 .15
497 A233 1.50r multicolored .20 .15
a. Block of 4, #494-497 .50 .50
Set value .28

Souvenir Sheet

Imperf

498 A233 2r multi, vert. 1.75 1.40

IYC. For overprints see #520-523.

Fight Against Cancer — A234

Unwmk.

1979, Nov. 12 Litho. *Perf. 14*

499 A234 40p multicolored .15 .15

Pakistan Customs Service Centenary — A235

1979, Dec. 10 *Perf. 13x13½*

500 A235 1r multicolored .15 .15

"1378" is a plate flaw, not an error.

Tippu Sultan Shaheed — A236

1979, Mar. 23 Wmk. 351 *Perf. 14*

501 A236 10r shown 1.75 1.25
502 A236 15r Syed Ahmad Khan 2.75 2.00
503 A236 25r Altaf Hussain Hali 4.75 3.25
a. Strip of 3, #501-503 10.00 10.00

See No. 699.

A237

A238

Ornament — A239

Perf. 12x11½, 11½x12

1980 Unwmk.

506 A237 10p dk grn & yel org .15 .15
507 A237 15p dk grn & apple grn .15 .15
508 A237 25p multicolored .15 .15
509 A237 35p multicolored .15 .15
510 A238 40p red & lt brown .15 .15
511 A239 50p olive & vio bl .15 .15
512 A239 80p black & yel grn .22 .15
Set value .76 .35

Issued: 25, 35, 50, 80p, Mar. 10; others, Jan. 15. See Nos. O111-O117.

Pakistan International Airline, 25th Anniversary — A240

1980, Jan. 10 Litho. *Perf. 13*

516 A240 1r multicolored .15 .15

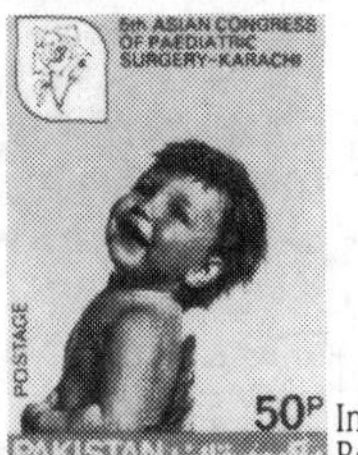

Infant, Rose — A241

1980, Feb. 16 *Perf. 13*

517 A241 50p multicolored .15 .15

5th Asian Congress of Pediatric Surgery, Karachi, Feb. 16-19.

Conference Emblem A242

1980, May 17 Litho. *Perf. 13*

518 A242 1r multicolored .20 .15

11th Islamic Conference of Foreign Ministers, Islamabad, May 17-21.

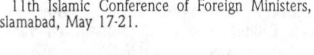

Lighthouse, Oil Terminal, Map Showing Karachi Harbor — A243

1980, July 15 *Perf. 13½*

519 A243 1r multicolored .20 .15

Karachi Port, cent. of independent management.

Nos. 494-497 Overprinted in Red: RICCIONE 80

1980, Aug. 30 Litho. *Perf. 14x12½*

520 A233 40p multicolored .15 .15
521 A233 75p multicolored .18 .15
522 A233 1r multicolored .35 .15
523 A233 1.50r multicolored .65 .15
Nos. 520-523 (4) 1.33
Set value .28

RICCIONE 80 International Stamp Exhibition, Riccione, Italy, Aug. 30-Sept. 2.

Quetta Command and Staff College, 75th Anniversary A244

1980, Sept. 18 Litho. *Perf. 13*

524 A244 1r multicolored .15 .15

No. 485 Overprinted: "World Tourism Conference/Manila 80"

1980, Sept. 27

525 A229 1r multicolored .15 .15

World Tourism Conf., Manila, Sept. 27.

Birth Centenary of Mohammed Shairani — A245

1980, Oct. 5 Litho. *Perf. 13*

526 A245 40p multicolored .15 .15

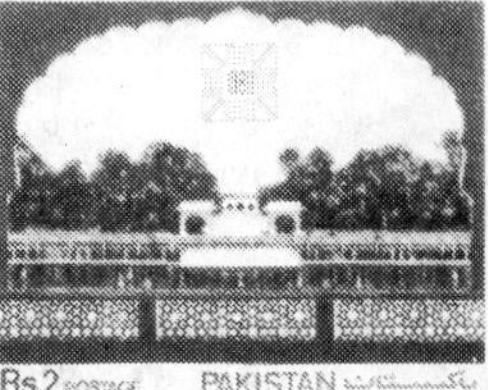

Aga Khan Architecture Award — A246

1980, Oct. 23 Litho. *Perf. 13½*

527 A246 2r multicolored .28 .15

Rising Sun A247

1981, Mar. 7 Litho. *Perf. 13*

Size: 30x41mm

528 A247 40p Hegira emblem .15 .15

1980, Nov. 6 Litho. *Perf. 13*

529 A247 40p shown .15 .15

Perf. 14

Size: 33x33mm

530 A247 2r Moslem symbols .28 .15

Perf. 13x13½

Size: 31x54mm

531 A247 3r Globe, hands holding Koran .40 .20
Nos. 528-531 (4) .98 .65

Souvenir Sheet

Imperf

532 A247 4r Candles 1.75 .65

Hegira (Pilgrimage Year).

Airmail Service, 50th Anniversary — A248

Postal History: No. 533, Postal card cent. No. 534, Money order service cent.

1980-81 *Perf. 13*

533 A248 40p multicolored .15 .15
534 A248 40p multicolored .15 .15
535 A248 1r multicolored .15 .15
Set value .26 .17

Issue dates: No. 533, Dec. 20; No. 534, Dec. 27; No. 535, Feb. 15, 1981.

Heinrich von Stephan, UPU Emblem A249

1981, Jan. 7 *Perf. 13½*

536 A249 1r multicolored .15 .15

Von Stephan (1831-97), founder of UPU.

Conference Emblem, Afghan Refugee A250

*3rd ISLAMIC SUMMIT CONFERENCE

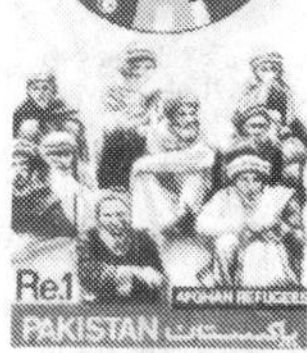

Conference Emblem, Flags of Participants, Men — A251

Conference Emblem, Map of Afghanistan — A252

1981, Mar. 29 **Litho.** *Perf. 13*

537 A250 40p multicolored .15 .15
538 A251 40p multicolored .15 .15
539 A250 1r multicolored .28 .15
540 A251 1r multicolored .28 .15
541 A252 2r multicolored .50 .35
Nos. 537-541 (5) 1.36
Set value .65

3rd Islamic Summit Conference, Makkah al-Mukarramah, Jan. 25-28.

Conference Emblem in Ornament A253

Conference Emblem, Flags of Participants — A254

1981, Mar. 29 **Litho.** *Perf. 13½*

542 A253 40p multicolored .15 .15
543 A254 40p multicolored .15 .15
544 A253 85p multicolored .22 .15
545 A254 85p multicolored .22 .15
Set value .58 .30

3rd Islamic Summit Conference, Makkah al-Mukarramah, Jan. 25-28.

Kemal Ataturk (1881-1938), First President of Turkey — A255

1981, May 19 **Litho.** *Perf. 13x13½*

546 A255 1r multicolored .20 .15

Green Turtle — A256

1981, June 20 **Litho.** *Perf. 12x11½*

547 A256 40p multicolored .30 .15

Palestinian Cooperation A257

1981, July 25 **Litho.** *Perf. 13*

548 A257 2r multicolored .65 .35

Mt. Haramosh
A258 A259

Designs: Mountain ranges and peaks.

1981, Aug. 20 *Perf. 14x13½*

549 A258 40p Malubiting West, range .15 .15
550 A259 40p Peak .15 .15
a. Pair, #549-550 .25
551 A258 1r shown .25 .15
552 A259 1r shown .25 .15
a. Pair, #551-552 .50
553 A258 1.50r K6, range .45 .15
554 A259 1.50r Peak .45 .15
a. Pair, #553-554 .90
555 A258 2r K2, range .70 .15
556 A259 2r Peak .70 .15
a. Pair, #555-556 1.40
Nos. 549-556 (8) 3.10
Set value .70

Inauguration of Pakistan Steel Furnace No. 1, Karachi — A260

1981, Aug. 31 *Perf. 13*

557 A260 40p multicolored .15 .15
558 A260 2r multicolored .28 .15
Set value .34 .18

Western Tragopan in Summer A261

1981, Sept. 15 **Litho.** *Perf. 14*

559 A261 40p shown .55 .15
560 A261 2r Winter 4.50 .30
Set value .35

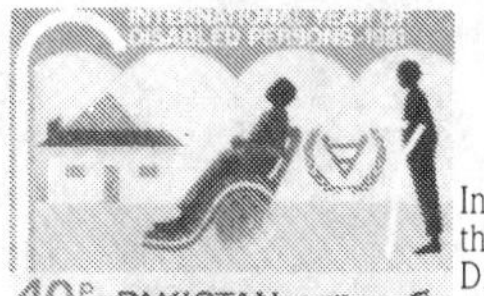

Intl. Year of the Disabled A262

1981, Dec. 12 **Litho.** *Perf. 13*

561 A262 40p multicolored .15 .15
562 A262 2r multicolored .28 .15
Set value .34 .18

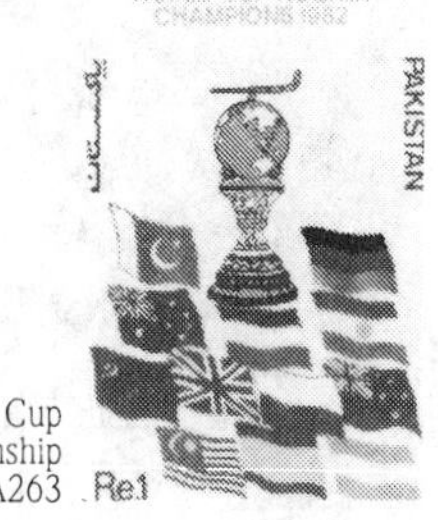

World Cup Championship A263

1982, Jan. 31 **Litho.** *Perf. 13½x13*

563 A263 1r Cup, flags in arc .15 .15
564 A263 1r shown .15 .15
a. Pair, #563-564 .30 .30
Set value .15

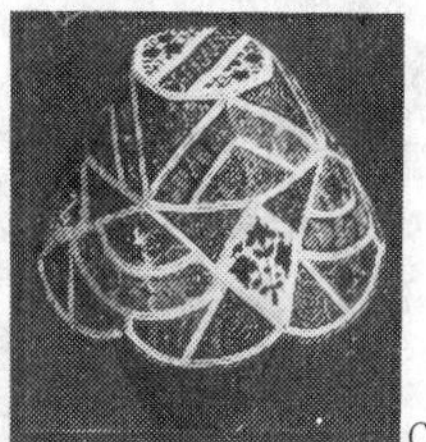

Camel Skin Lampshade A264

1982, Feb. 20 **Litho.** *Perf. 14*

565 A264 1r shown .15 .15
566 A264 1r Hala pottery .15 .15
Set value .15

See Nos. 582-583.

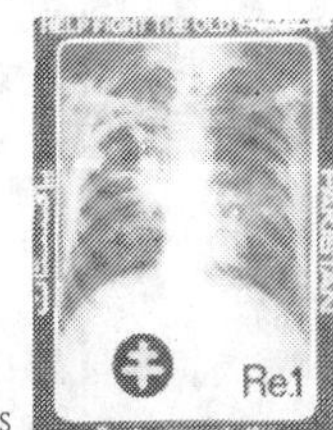

TB Bacillus Centenary — A265

1982, Mar. 24

567 A265 1r multicolored .20 .18

Blind Indus Dolphin A266

1982, Apr. 24 **Litho.** *Perf. 12x11½*

568 A266 40p Dolphin .30 .15
569 A266 1r Dolphin, diff. .80 .15
Set value .20

Peaceful Uses of Outer Space — A267

1982, June 7 **Litho.** *Perf. 13*

570 A267 1r multicolored .20 .15

50th Anniv. of Sukkur Barrage — A268

1982, July 17 **Litho.** *Perf. 13*

571 A268 1r multicolored .15 .15

For overprint see No. 574.

Independence Day — A269

1982, Aug. 14

572 A269 40p Flag .15 .15
573 A269 85p Map .15 .15
Set value .18 .15

No. 571 Overprinted: "RICCIONE-82/1932-1982"

1982, Aug. 28

574 A268 1r multicolored .35 .18

RICCIONE '82 Intl. Stamp Exhibition, Riccione, Italy, Aug. 28-30.

University of the Punjab Centenary — A270

1982, Oct. 14 **Litho.** *Perf. 13½*

575 A270 40p multicolored .15 .15

15-Cent Minimum Value
The minimum value for a single stamp is 15 cents. This value reflects the costs of handling inexpensive stamps.

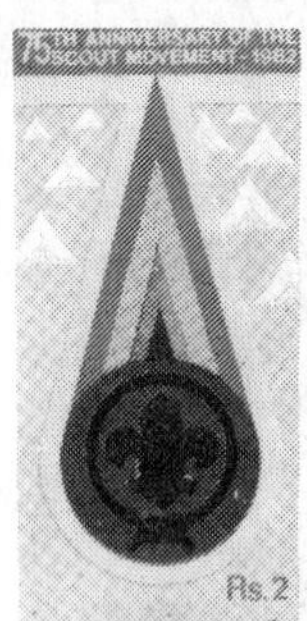

Scouting Year — A271

1982, Dec. 23 Litho. *Perf. 13*
576 A271 2r Emblem .50 .20

Quetta Natural Gas Pipeline Project A272

1983, Jan. 6 Litho. *Perf. 13*
577 A272 1r multicolored .20 .15

Common Peacock A273

1983, Feb. 15 Litho. *Perf. 14*
578 A273 40p shown .15 .15
579 A273 50p Common rose .15 .15
580 A273 60p Plain tiger .15 .15
581 A273 1.50r Lemon butterfly .28 .15
Set value .49 .28

Handicraft Type of 1982

1983, Mar. 9
582 A264 1r Straw mats .15 .15
583 A264 1r Five-flower cloth design .15 .15
Set value .15

Opening of Aga Khan University — A274

1983, Mar. 16 *Perf. 13½*
584 A274 2r multicolored .28 .15

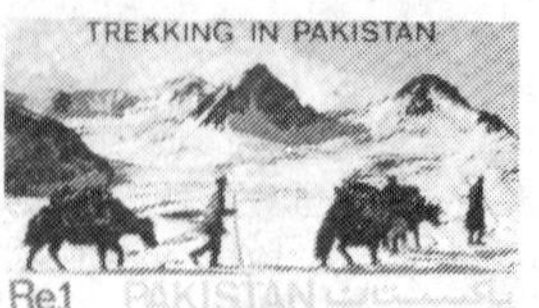

Yak Caravan, Zindiharam-Darkot Pass, Hindu Kush Mountains — A275

1983, Apr. 28 Litho. *Perf. 13*
585 A275 1r multicolored .20 .15

Marsh Crocodile A276

1983, May 19 *Perf. 13½x14*
586 A276 3r multicolored .55 .28

1983, June 20 Litho. *Perf. 14*
Size: 50x40mm
587 A276 1r Gazelle .28 .15

36th Anniv. of Independence A277

1983, Aug. 14 *Perf. 13*
588 A277 60p Star .15 .15
589 A277 4r Torch .55 .28
Set value .32

25th Anniv. of Indonesia-Pakistan Economic and Cultural Cooperation Org. — A278

Weavings.

1983, Aug. 19 Litho. *Perf. 13*
590 A278 2r Pakistani (geometric) .28 .15
591 A278 2r Indonesian (figures) .28 .15

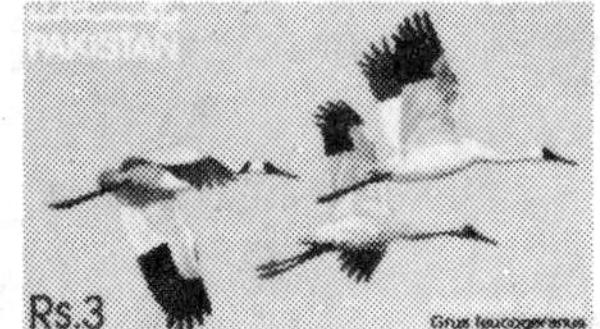

Siberian Cranes — A279

1983, Sept. 8 *Perf. 13½*
592 A279 3r multicolored .50 .20

World Communications Year — A280

1983, Oct. 9 Litho. *Perf. 13*
593 A280 2r multicolored .28 .15
Size: 33x33mm
594 A280 3r Symbol, diff. .40 .20

World Food Day — A281

1983, Oct. 24 Litho. *Perf. 13*
595 A281 3r Livestock .42 .20
596 A281 3r Fruit .42 .20
597 A281 3r Grain .42 .20
598 A281 3r Seafood .42 .20
a. Strip of 4, #595-598 1.75 1.75

A282 A283

1983, Oct. 24 Litho. *Perf. 13½*
599 A282 60p multicolored .15 .15

National Fertilizer Corp.

1983, Nov. 13 Litho. *Perf. 13*
600 Strip of 6, View of Lahore City, 1852 .85 .28
a.-f. A283 60p any single .15 .15

PAKPHILEX '83 Natl. Stamp Exhibition.

Yachting Victory in 9th Asian Games, 1982 — A284

1983, Dec. 31 Litho. *Perf. 13*
601 A284 60p OK Dinghy .15 .15
602 A284 60p Enterprise .15 .15
Set value .15

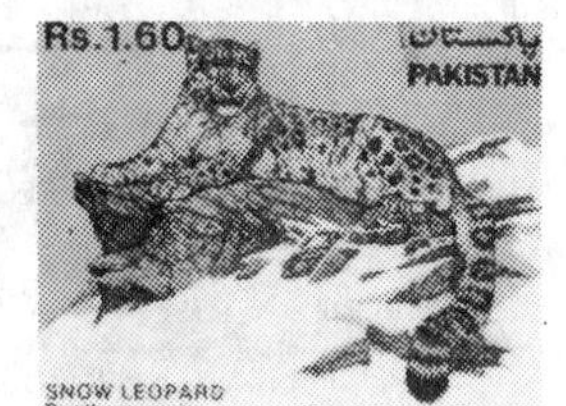

Snow Leopard — A285

1984, Jan. 21 *Perf. 14*
603 A285 40p lt green & multi .15 .15
604 A285 1.60r blue & multi .40 .15
Set value .15

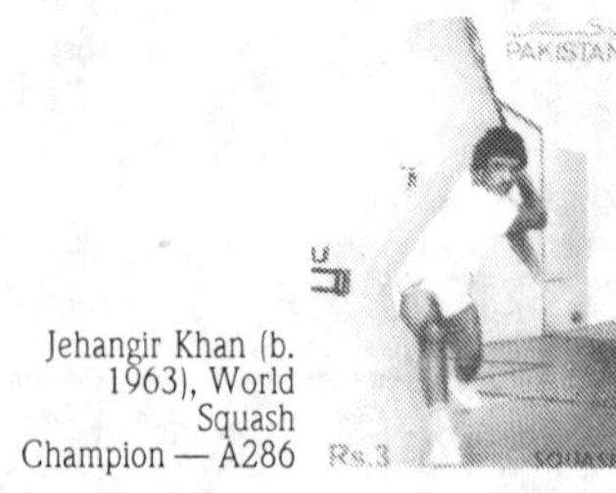

Jehangir Khan (b. 1963), World Squash Champion — A286

1984, Mar. 17 Litho. *Perf. 13*
605 A286 3r multicolored .30 .15

Pakistan Intl. Airway China Service, 20th Anniv. — A287

1984, Apr. 29 Litho. *Perf. 13*
606 A287 3r Jet .30 .15

Glass Work, Lahore Fort A288

Various glass panels.

1984, May 31 Litho. *Perf. 13*
607 A288 1r green & multi .15 .15
608 A288 1r purple & multi .15 .15
609 A288 1r vermilion & multi .15 .15
610 A288 1r brt blue & multi .15 .15
Set value .40 .24

Forts — A289

1984-88 Litho. *Perf. 11*
613 A289 5p Kot Diji .15 .15
614 A289 10p Rohtas .15 .15
615 A289 15p Bala Hissar ('86) .15 .15
616 A289 20p Attock .15 .15
617 A289 50p Hyderabad ('86) .15 .15
618 A289 60p Lahore .15 .15
619 A289 70p Sibi ('88) .16 .15
620 A289 80p Ranikot ('86) .19 .15
Set value .75 .32

Issued: 5p, Nov. 1; 10p, Sept. 25; 80p, July 1.
For overprints see Nos. O118-O124.

Shah Rukn-i-Alam Tomb, Multan — A290

1984, June 26 Litho. *Perf. 13*
624 A290 60p multicolored .15 .15

Aga Khan Award for Architecture.

Asia-Pacific Broadcasting Union, 20th Anniv. — A290a

1984, July 1 Litho. *Perf. 13*
625 A290a 3r multicolored .28 .15

1984 Summer Olympics, Los Angeles — A291

1984, July 31
626 A291 3r Athletics .50 .15
627 A291 3r Boxing .50 .15
628 A291 3r Hockey .50 .15
629 A291 3r Yachting .50 .15
630 A291 3r Wrestling .50 .15
Nos. 626-630 (5) 2.50 .75

Issued in sheets of 10.

Independence, 37th Anniv. — A292

1984, Aug. 14

631 A292	60p Jasmine	.15	.15
632 A292	4r Lighted torch	.65	.35
	Set value		.41

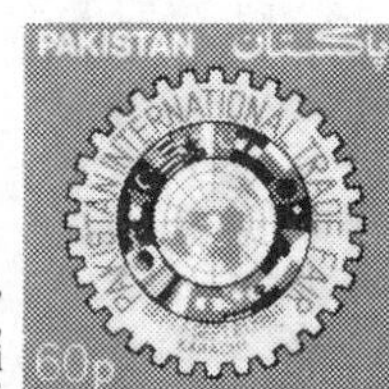

Intl. Trade Fair, Sept. 1-21, Karachi A293

1984, Sept. 1

633 A293	60p multicolored	.15	.15

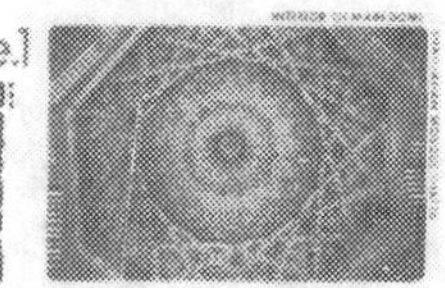

1984 Natl. Tourism Convention, Karachi, Nov. 5-8 — A293a

Shah Jahan Mosque: a, Main dome interior. b, Tile work. c, Entrance. d, Archways. e, Dome interior, diff.

1984, Nov. 5 Litho. *Perf. 13½*

634	Strip of 5	.50	.28
a.-e.	A293a 1r any single	.15	.15

United Bank Limited, 25th Anniv. A294

1984, Nov. 7

635 A294	60p multicolored	.15	.15

UNCTAD, UN Conference on Trade and Development, 20th Anniv. — A294a

1984, Dec. 24 *Perf. 14½x14*

636 A294a	60p multicolored	.15	.15

Postal Life Insurance, Cent. — A295

1984, Dec. 29 *Perf. 13½x14*

637 A295	60p multicolored	.15	.15
638 A295	1r multicolored	.15	.15
	Set value	.16	.15

UNESCO World Heritage Campaign — A296

1984, Dec. 31

639 A296	2r Unicorn, rock painting	.20	.15
640 A296	2r Unicorn seal, round	.20	.15
a.	Pair, #639-640	.40	.30
	Set value		.20

Restoration of Mohenjo-Daro.

IYY, Girl Guides 75th Anniv. — A297

1985, Jan. 5 *Perf. 13½*

641 A297	60p Emblems	.15	.15

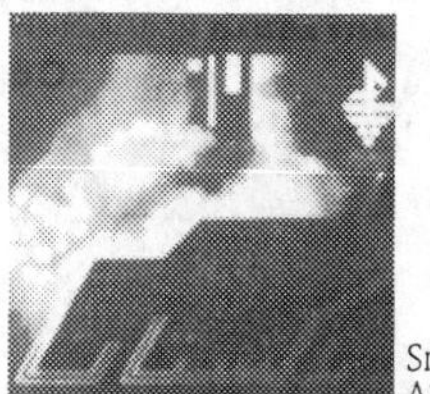
Smelting A298

Pouring Steel — A299

1985, Jan. 15 *Perf. 13*

642 A298	60p multicolored	.15	.15
643 A299	1r multicolored	.15	.15
	Set value	.16	.15

Referendum Reinstating Pres. Zia — A300

1985, Mar. 20 Litho. *Perf. 13*

644 A300	60p Map, sunburst	.15	.15

Minar-e-Qarardad-e-Pakistan Tower — A301

Ballot Box — A302

1985 Elections.

1985, Mar. 23

645 A301	1r multicolored	.15	.15
646 A302	1r multicolored	.15	.15
	Set value	.20	.15

Mountaineering — A303

1985, May 27 Litho. *Perf. 14*

647 A303	40p Mt. Rakaposhi, Karakoram	.15	.15
648 A303	2r Mt. Nangaparbat, Western Himalayas	.20	.15
	Set value	.25	.15

Championship Pakistani Men's Field Hockey Team — A304

Design: 1984 Olympic gold medal, 1985 Dhaka Asia Cup, 1982 Bombay World Cup.

1985, June 5 Litho. *Perf. 13*

649 A304	1r multicolored	.15	.15

King Edward Medical College, Lahore, 125th Anniv. — A305

1985, July 28 Litho. *Perf. 13*

650 A305	3r multicolored	.40	.20

Natl. Independence Day — A306

Designs: No. 651a, 37th Independence Day written in English. No. 651b, In Arabic.

1985, Aug. 14

651	Pair + 2 labels	.20	.15
a.-b.	A306 60p any single	.15	.15

Printed in sheets of 4 stamps + 4 labels.

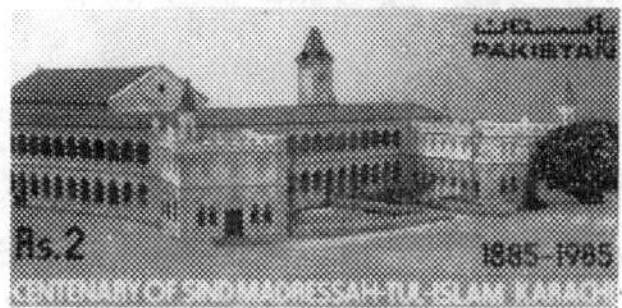

Sind Madressah-Tul-Islam, Karachi, Education Cent. — A307

1985, Sept. 1

652 A307	2r multicolored	.35	.18

Mosque, Jinnah Avenue, Karachi — A308

1985, Sept. 14

653 A308	1r Mosque by day	.18	.15
654 A308	1r At night	.18	.15
	Set value		.16

35th anniv. of the Jamia Masjid Pakistan Security Printing Corporation's miniature replica of the Badshahi Mosque, Lahore.

Lawrence College, Murree, 125th Anniv. — A309

1985, Sept. 21

655 A309	3r multicolored	.50	.25

UN, 40th Anniv. — A310

1985, Oct. 24 Litho. *Perf. 14x14½*

656 A310	1r UN building, sun	.15	.15
657 A310	2r Building emblem	.20	.15
	Set value	.30	.16

10th Natl. Scouting Jamboree, Lahore, Nov. 8-15 — A311

1985, Nov. 8 *Perf. 13*

658 A311	60p multicolored	.15	.15

Islamabad and Capital Development Authority Emblem — A312

1985, Nov. 30 *Perf. 14½*

659 A312 3r multicolored .50 .25

Islamabad, capital of Pakistan, 25th anniv.

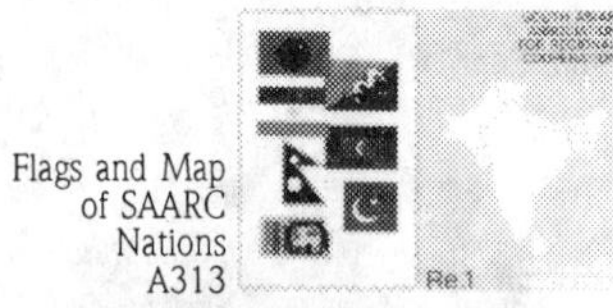

Flags and Map of SAARC Nations A313

Flags as Flower Petals A314

1985, Dec. 8 *Perf. 13½, 13*

660 A313 1r multicolored .15 .15
661 A314 2r multicolored .20 .15
Set value .30 .16

SAARC, South Asian Assoc. for Regional Cooperation.

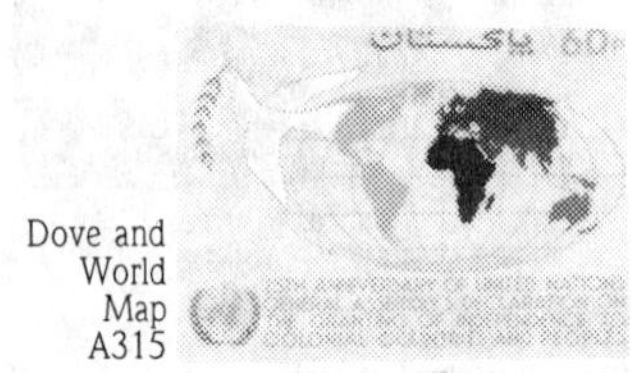

Dove and World Map A315

1985, Dec. 14 *Perf. 13*

662 A315 60p multicolored .15 .15

UN Declaration on the Granting of Independence to Colonial Countries and Peoples, 25th Anniv.

Shaheen Falcon — A316

1986, Jan. 20 *Perf. 13½x14*

663 A316 1.50r multicolored .35 .18

Agricultural Development Bank, 25th Anniv. — A317

1986, Feb. 18 **Litho.** *Perf. 13*

664 A317 60p multicolored .15 .15

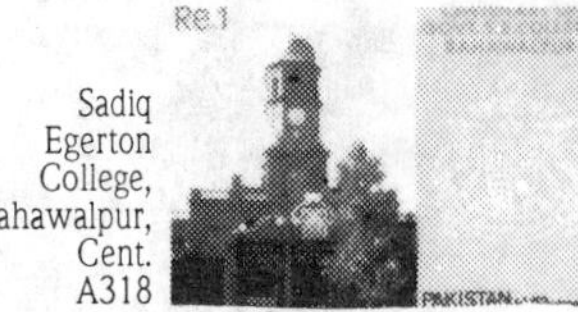

Sadiq Egerton College, Bahawalpur, Cent. A318

1986, Apr. 25

665 A318 1r multicolored .15 .15

A319 A320

1986, May 11 *Perf. 13½*

666 A319 1r multicolored .15 .15

Asian Productivity Organization, 25th anniv.

1986, Aug. 14 **Litho.** *Perf. 14½x14*

667 A320 80p "1947-1986" .15 .15
668 A320 1r Urdu text, fireworks .15 .15
Set value .20 .15

Independence Day, 39th anniv.

A321 A322

1986, Sept. 8 *Perf. 13*

669 A321 1r Teacher, students .15 .15

Intl. Literacy Day.

1986, Oct. 28 **Litho.** *Perf. 13½x13*

670 A322 80p multicolored .15 .15

UN Child Survival Campaign.

Aitchison College, Lahore, Cent. — A323

1986, Nov. 3 *Perf. 13½*

671 A323 2.50r multicolored .28 .15

Intl. Peace Year — A324

1986, Nov. 20 *Perf. 13*

672 A324 4r multicolored .42 .22

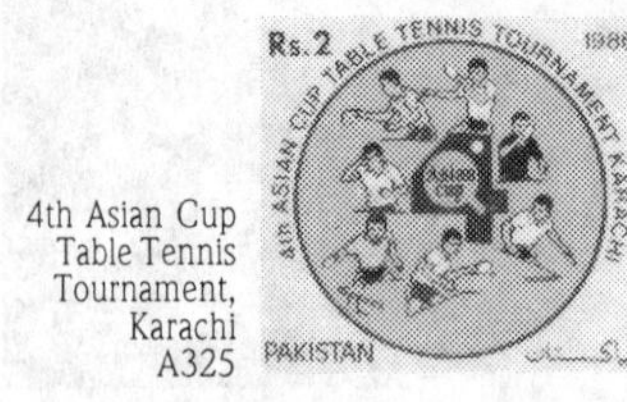

4th Asian Cup Table Tennis Tournament, Karachi A325

1986, Nov. 25 *Perf. 14½*

673 A325 2r multicolored .22 .15

Marcopolo Sheep — A326

1986, Dec. 4 **Litho.** *Perf. 14*

674 A326 2r multicolored .22 .15

See No. 698.

Eco Philex '86 — A327

Mosques: No. 675a, Selimiye, Turkey. No. 675b, Gawhar Shad, Iran. No. 675c, Grand Mosque, Pakistan.

1986, Dec. 20 *Perf. 13*

675 Strip of 3 1.00 .48
a.-c. A327 3r any single .32 .16

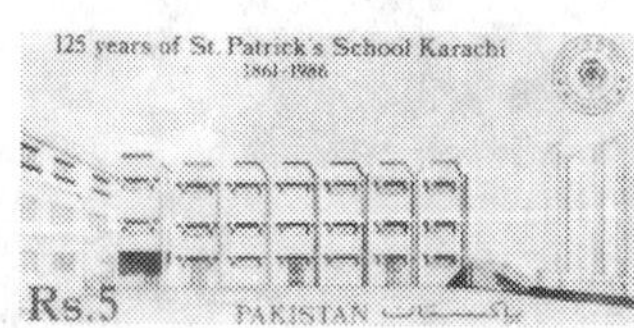

St. Patrick's School, Karachi, 125th Anniv. — A328

1987, Jan. 29 **Litho.** *Perf. 13*

676 A328 5r multicolored .55 .28

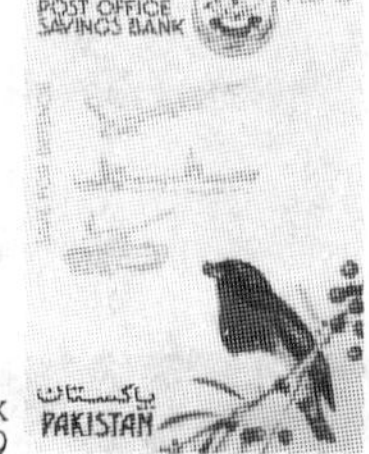

Savings Bank Week — A329

Birds, berries and: a, National defense. b, Education. c, Agriculture. d, Industry.

1987, Feb. 21 **Litho.** *Perf. 13*

677 Block of 4 + 2 labels 2.25 1.10
a.-d. A329 5r any single .55 .28

Parliament House Opening, Islamabad — A330

1987, Mar. 23

678 A330 3r multicolored .32 .16

Fight Against Drug Abuse — A331

1987, June 30 **Litho.** *Perf. 13*

679 A331 1r multicolored .15 .15

Natl. Independence, 40th Anniv. — A332

Natl. flag and: 80p, Natl. anthem, written in Urdu. 3r, Jinnah's first natl. address, the Minar-e-Qarardad-e-Pakistan and natl. coat of arms.

1987, Aug. 14 **Litho.** *Perf. 13*

680 A332 80p multicolored .15 .15
681 A332 3r multicolored .40 .20
Set value .26

Miniature Sheet

Air Force, 40th Anniv. — A333

Aircraft: a, Tempest II. b, Hawker Fury. c, Super Marine Attacker. d, F86 Sabre. e, F104 Star Fighter. f, C130 Hercules. g, F6. h, Mirage III. i, A5. j, F16 Fighting Falcon.

1987, Sept. 7 **Litho.** *Perf. 13½*

682 Sheet of 10 4.00 2.00
a.-j. A333 3r any single .40 .20

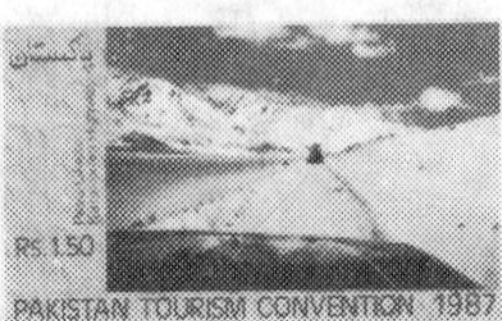

Tourism Convention 1987 — A334

Views along Karakoram Highway: a, Pasu Glacier. b, Apricot trees. c, Highway winding through hills. d, Khunjerab peak.

1987, Oct. 1 *Perf. 13*

683 Block of 4 .80 .40
a.-d. A334 1.50r any single .20 .15

Shah Abdul Latif Bhitai Mausoleum — A335

1987, Oct. 8 *Perf. 13*
684 A335 80p multicolored .15 .15

D.J. Sind Government Science College, Karachi, Cent. — A336

1987, Nov. 7
685 A336 80p multicolored .15 .15

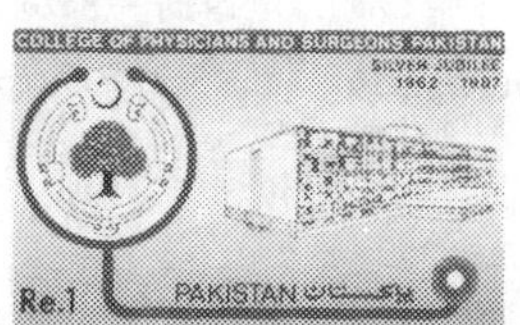

College of Physicians and Surgeons, 25th Anniv. — A337

1987, Dec. 9 **Litho.** *Perf. 13*
686 A337 1r multicolored .15 .15

Intl. Year of Shelter for the Homeless — A338

1987, Dec. 15
687 A338 3r multicolored .45 .22

Cathedral Church of the Resurrection, Lahore, Cent. — A339

1987, Dec. 20
688 A339 3r multicolored .45 .22

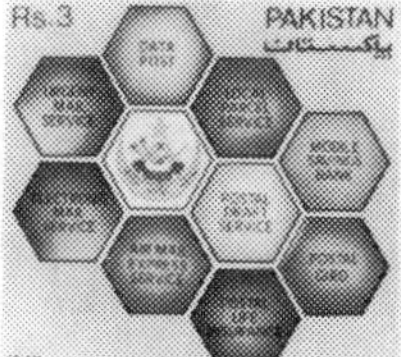

Natl. Postal Service, 40th Anniv. A340

1987, Dec. 28
689 A340 3r multicolored .45 .22

Radio Pakistan A341

1987, Dec. 31
690 A341 80p multicolored .15 .15

Jamshed Nusserwanjee Mehta (1886-1952), Mayor of Karachi, Member of the Sind Legislative Assembly — A342

1988, Jan. 7
691 A342 3r multicolored .45 .22

World Leprosy Day — A343

1988, Jan. 31
692 A343 3r multicolored .45 .22

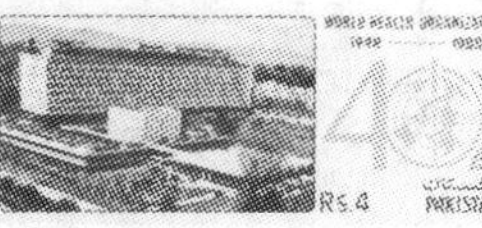

World Health Organization, 40th Anniv. — A344

1988, Apr. 7 **Litho.** *Perf. 13*
693 A344 4r multicolored .50 .25

Intl. Red Cross and Red Crescent Organizations, 125th Annivs. — A345

1988, May 8
694 A345 3r multicolored .45 .22

Independence Day, 41st Anniv. — A346

1988, Aug. 14 **Litho.** *Perf. 13½*
695 A346 80p multicolored .15 .15
696 A346 4r multicolored .50 .25
Set value .31

Miniature Sheet

1988 Summer Olympics, Seoul — A347

Events: a, Discus, shot put, hammer throw, javelin. b, Relay, hurdles, running, walking. c, High jump, long jump, triple jump, pole vault. d, Gymnastic floor exercises, rings, parallel bars. e, Table tennis, tennis, field hockey, baseball. f, Volleyball, soccer, basketball, team handball. g, Wrestling, judo, boxing, weight lifting. h, Sport pistol, fencing, rifle shooting, archery. i, Swimming, diving, yachting, quadruple-sculling, kayaking. j, Equestrian jumping, cycling, steeplechase.

1988, Sept. 17 **Litho.** *Perf. 13½x13*
697 Sheet of 10+32 labels 12.50 6.25
a.-j. A347 10r any single 1.25 .62

Labels contained in No. 697 picture the Seoul Games character trademark or emblem. Size of No. 697: 251x214mm.

Fauna Type of 1986

1988, Oct. 29 **Litho.** *Perf. 14*
698 A326 2r Suleman markhor, vert. .25 .15

Pioneers of Freedom Type of 1979

1989, Jan. 23 **Litho.** **Wmk. 351**
699 A236 3r Maulana Hasrat Mohani .38 .20

Islamia College, Peshawar, 75th Anniv. — A348

1988, Dec. 22 **Unwmk.** *Perf. 13½*
700 A348 3r multicolored .38 .20

SAARC Summit Conference, Islamabad — A349

Designs: 25r, Flags, symbols of commerce. 50r, Globe, communication and transportation. 75r, Bangladesh #69, Maldive Islands #1030, Bhutan #98, Pakistan #403, Ceylon #451, India #580, Nepal #437.

1988, Dec. 29 *Perf. 13*
701 A349 25r shown 2.50 1.25

Size: 33x33mm

Perf. 14
702 A349 50r multicolored 5.00 2.50

Size: 52x28mm

Perf. 13½x13
703 A349 75r multicolored 7.50 3.75
Nos. 701-703 (3) 15.00 7.50

Adasia '89, 16th Asian Advertising Congress, Lahore, Feb. 18-22 — A350

1989, Feb. 18 **Litho.** *Perf. 13*
704 Strip of 3 .38 .20
a. A350 1r deep rose lilac & multi .15 .15
b. A350 1r green & multi .15 .15
c. A350 1r bright vermilion & multi .15 .15

Printed in sheets of 9.

Pres. Zulfikar Ali Bhutto (1928-1979), Ousted by Military Coup and Executed A351

Portraits.

1989, Apr. 4 **Litho.** *Perf. 13*
705 A351 1r shown .15 .15
706 A351 2r multi, diff. .25 .15
Set value .18

Submarine Operations, 25th Anniv. — A352

Submarines: a, *Agosta*. b, *Daphne*. c, *Fleet Snorkel*. Illustration reduced.

1989, June 1 **Litho.** *Perf. 13½*
707 Strip of 3 .36 .18
a.-c. A352 1r any single .15 .15

Oath of the Tennis Court, by David — A353

1989, June 24 **Litho.** *Perf. 13½*
708 A353 7r multicolored .75 .38

French revolution, bicent.

Archaeological Heritage A354

Terra cotta vessels excavated in Baluchistan: a, Pirak, c. 2200 B.C. b, Nindo Damb, c. 2300 B.C. c, Mehrgarh, c. 3600 B.C. d, Naushiro, c. 2600 B.C.

1989, June 28 *Perf. 14½x14*
709 Block of 4 .45 .22
a.-d. A354 1r any single .15 .15

Asia-Pacific Telecommunity, 10th Anniv. — A355

1989, July 1 *Perf. 13½x14*
710 A355 3r multicolored .32 .16

Laying the Foundation Stone for the 1st Integrated Container Terminal, Port Qasim — A356

1989, Aug. 5 **Litho.** *Perf. 14*
711 A356 6r Ship in berth .65 .32

Mohammad Ali Jinnah — A357

Litho & Engr.

1989, Aug. 14 **Wmk. 351** *Perf. 13*

712	A357	1r multicolored	.15	.15
713	A357	1.50r multicolored	.16	.15
714	A357	2r multicolored	.22	.15
715	A357	3r multicolored	.33	.16
716	A357	4r multicolored	.45	.22
717	A357	5r multicolored	.55	.28
		Nos. 712-717 (6)	1.86	
		Set value		.90

Independence Day.

Abdul Latif Bhitai Memorial — A358

1989, Sept. 16 **Litho.** **Unwmk.**
718 A358 2r multicolored .22 .15

245th death and 300th birth annivs. of Shah Abdul Latif Bhitai.

World Wildlife Fund — A359

Himalayan black bears and WWF emblem: a, Bear on slope, emblem UR. b, Bear on slope, emblem UL. c, Bear on top of rock, emblem UR. d, Seated bear, emblem UL.

Perf. 14x13½

1989, Oct. 7 **Litho.** **Unwmk.**
719 Block of 4 1.80 .90
a.-d. A359 4r any single .45 .22

World Food Day — A360

1989, Oct. 16 *Perf. 14x12½*
720 A360 1r multicolored .15 .15

Quilt and Bahishiti Darwaza (Heavenly Gate) — A361

1989, Oct. 20 *Perf. 13*
721 A361 3r multicolored .35 .16

800th Birth anniv. of Baba Farid.

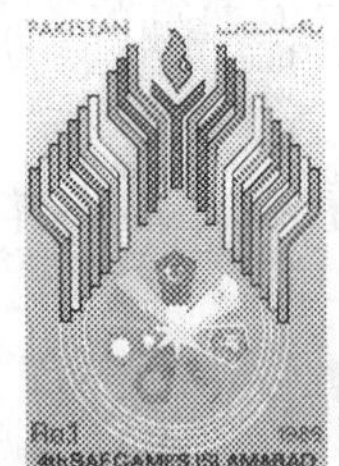

4th SAF Games, Islamabad — A362

1989, Oct. 20
722 A362 1r multicolored .15 .15

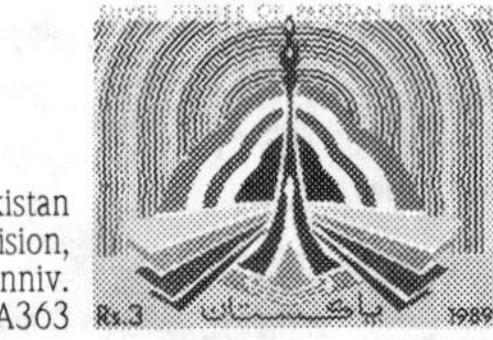

Pakistan Television, 25th Anniv. A363

1989, Nov. 26 **Litho.** *Perf. 13½*
723 A363 3r multicolored .35 .16

SAARC Year Against Drug Abuse and Drug Trafficking A364

1989, Dec. 8 *Perf. 13*
724 A364 7r multicolored .80 .40

Murray College, Sialkot, Cent. A365

1989, Dec. 18 *Perf. 14*
725 A365 6r multicolored .70 .35

Government College, Lahore, 125th Anniv. — A366

1989, Dec. 21 *Perf. 13*
726 A366 6r multicolored .70 .35

Center on Integrated Rural Development for Asia and the Pacific (CIRDAP), 10th Anniv. — A367

1989, Dec. 31
727 A367 3r multicolored .35 .16

Organization of the Islamic Conference (OIC), 20th Anniv. — A368

1990, Feb. 9 **Litho.** *Perf. 13*
728 A368 1r multicolored .15 .15

7th World Field Hockey Cup, Lahore, Feb. 12-23 — A369

Illustration reduced.

1990, Feb. 12 *Perf. 14x13½*
729 A369 2r multicolored .24 .15

A370

Pakistan Resolution, 50th Anniv. — A371

Designs: a, Allama Mohammad Iqbal addressing the Allahabad Session of the All-India Muslim League and swearing-in of Liat Ali Khan as league secretary-general. b, Freedom fighter Maulana Mohammad Ali Jauhar at Muslim rally and Mohammed Ali Jinnah at microphone. c, Muslim woman holding flag and swearing-in of Mohammed Ali Jinnah as governor-general of Pakistan, Aug. 14, 1947. 7r, English and Urdu translations of the resolution, natl. flag and Minar-e-Qarardade Pakistan.

1990, Mar. 23 **Litho.** *Perf. 13*
730 Strip of 3 .36 .18
a.-c. A370 1r any single .15 .15

Size: 90x45mm

Perf. 13½

731 A371 7r multicolored .85 .42

Safe Motherhood South Asia Conference, Lahore — A372

1990, Mar. 24 *Perf. 13½*
732 A372 5r multicolored .60 .30

Calligraphic Painting of a Ghalib Verse, by Shakir Ali (1916-1975) — A373

1990, Apr. 19 **Litho.** *Perf. 13½x13*
733 A373 1r multicolored .15 .15

See Nos. 757-758.

Badr-1 Satellite — A374

1990, July 26 **Litho.** *Perf. 13*
734 A374 3r multicolored .28 .15

Pioneers of Freedom — A375

No. 735: a, Allama Mohammad Iqbal (1877-1938). b, Mohammad Ali Jinnah (1876-1948). c, Sir Syed Ahmad Khan (1817-98). d, Nawab Salimullah (1884-1915). e, Mohtarma Fatima Jinnah (1893-1967). f, Aga Khan III (1877-1957). g, Nawab Mohammad Ismail Khan (1884-1958). h, Hussain Shaheed Suhrawardy (1893-1963). i, Syed Ameer Ali (1849-1928).

No. 736: a, Nawab Bahadur Yar Jung (1905-44). b, Khawaja Nazimuddin (1894-1964). c, Maulana Obaidullah Sindhi (1872-1944). d, Sahibzada Abdul Qaiyum Khan (c. 1863-1937). e, Begum Jahanara Shah Nawaz (1896-1979). f, Sir Shulam Hussain Hidayatullah (1879-1948). g, Qazi Mohammad Isa (1913-76). h, Sir M. Shahnawaz Khan Mamdot (1883-1942). i, Pir Shaib of Manki Sharif (1923-60).

No. 737: a, Liaquat Ali Khan (1895-1951). b, Maulvi A.K. Fazl-Ul-Haq (1873-1962). c, Allama Shabbir Ahmad Usmani (1885-1949). d, Sardar Abdur Rab Nishtar (1899-1958). e, Bi Amma (c. 1850-1924). f, Sir Abdullah Haroon (1872-1942). g, Chaudhry Rahmat Ali (1897-1951). h, Raja Sahib of Mahmudabad (1914-73). i, Hassanally Effendi (1830-1895).

No. 737J: k, Maulana Zafar Ali Khan (1873-1956). l, Maulana Mohamed Ali Jauhar (1878-1931). m, Chaudhry Khaliquzzaman (1889-1973). n, Hameed Nizami (1915-62). o, Begum Ra'ana

Liaquat Ali Khan (1905-90). p, Mirza Abol Hassan Ispahani (1902-81). q, Raja Ghazanfar Ali Khan (1895-1963). r, Malik Barkat Ali (1886-1946). s, Mir Jaffer Khan Jamali (c. 1911-67).

1990-91 Litho. *Perf. 13*

Miniature Sheets

735	Sheet of 9	.90	.90
a.-i.	A375 1r any single	.15	.15
736	Sheet of 9	.90	.90
a.-i.	A375 1r any single	.15	.15
737	Sheet of 9	.90	.90
a.-i.	A375 1r any single	.15	.15
737J	Sheet of 9 ('91)	.90	.90
k.-s.	A375 1r any single	.15	.15
	Nos. 735-737J (4)	3.60	3.60

Issued: #735-737, Aug. 19; #737J, 1991.

See Nos. 773, 792, 804859-860, 865, 875-876.

Indonesia Pakistan Economic and Cultural Cooperation Organization, 1968-1990 — A376

1990, Aug. 19

738 A376 7r multicolored .65 .32

Intl. Literacy Year — A377

1990, Sept. 8

739 A377 3r multicolored .28 .15

A378

1990, Sept. 22

740 A378 2r multicolored .18 .15

Joint meeting of Royal College of Physicians, Edinburgh and College of Physicians and Surgeons, Pakistan.

World Summit for Children — A379

1990, Sept. 19

741 A379 7r multicolored .65 .32

Year of the Girl Child A380

1990, Nov. 21 Litho. *Perf. 13½*

742 A380 2r multicolored .18 .15

Security Papers Ltd., 25th Anniv. — A381

1990, Dec. 8 *Perf. 13*

743 A381 3r multicolored .28 .15

Intl. Civil Defense Day — A382

1991, Mar. 1 Litho. *Perf. 13*

744 A382 7r multicolored .28 .15

South & West Asia Postal Union — A383

1991, Mar. 21

745 A383 5r multicolored .20 .15

World Population Day — A384

1991, July 11

746 A384 10r multicolored .40 .20

Intl. Special Olympics — A385

1991, July 19

747 A385 7r multicolored .28 .15

Habib Bank Limited, 50th Anniv. — A386

1991, Aug. 25 Litho. *Perf. 13*

748	A386 1r brt red & multi	.15	.15
749	A386 5r brt green & multi	.20	.15
	Set value	.30	.15

St. Joseph's Convent School, Karachi — A387

1991, Sept. 8

750 A387 5r multicolored .20 .15

Emperor Sher Shah Suri (c. 1472-1545) A388

1991, Oct. 5

751 A388 5r multicolored .20 .15

Souvenir Sheet

Size: 90x81mm

Imperf

752 A388 7r multicolored .90 .45

Pakistani Scientific Expedition to Antarctica — A389

1991, Oct. 28

753 A389 7r multicolored .28 .15

Houbara Bustard — A390

1991, Nov. 4

754 A390 7r multicolored .28 .15

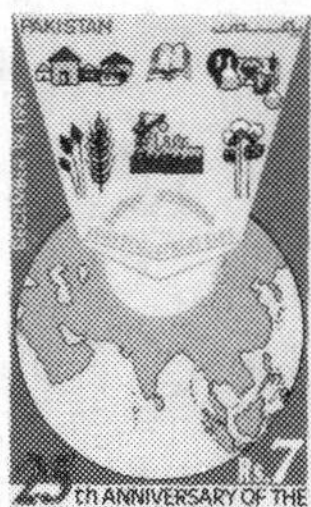

Asian Development Bank, 25th Anniv. — A391

1991, Dec. 19 Litho. *Perf. 13*

755 A391 7r multicolored .90 .45

Hazrat Sultan Bahoo, 300th Death Anniv. A392

1991, Dec. 22

756 A392 7r multicolored .90 .45

Painting Type of 1990

Paintings and artists: No. 757, Village Life, by Allah Ustad Bux (1892-1978). No. 758, Miniature of Royal Procession, by Muhammad Haji Sharif (1889-1978).

1991, Dec. 24

757	A373 1r multicolored	.15	.15
758	A373 1r multicolored	.15	.15

American Express Travelers Cheques, 100th Anniv. — A393

Illustration reduced.

1991, Dec. 26 *Perf. 13½*

759 A393 7r multicolored .90 .45

Muslim Commercial Bank, First Year of Private Operation — A394

7r, City skyline, worker, cogwheels, computer operators.

1992, Apr. 8 Litho. *Perf. 13*

760	A394 1r multicolored	.15	.15
761	A394 7r multicolored	.90	.45
	Set value		.52

Pakistan, 1992 World Cricket Champions — A395

World Cricket Cup and: 2r, Pakistani player, vert. 7r, Pakistan flag, fireworks, vert.

1992, Apr. 27

762	A395 2r multicolored	.25	.15
763	A395 5r multicolored	.65	.65
764	A395 7r multicolored	.90	.45
	Nos. 762-764 (3)	1.80	1.25

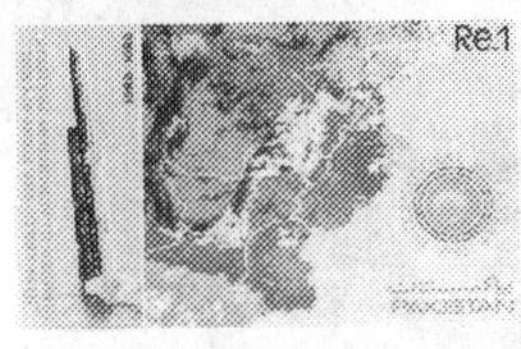

Intl. Space Year A396

Design: 2r, Globe, satellite.

1992, June 7 Litho. *Perf. 13*

771 A396 1r multicolored .15 .15
772 A396 2r multicolored .22 .22

30th anniv. of first Pakistani rocket (#771).

Pioneers of Freedom Type of 1990

Designs: a, Syed Suleman Nadvi (1884-1953). b, Nawab Iftikhar Hussain Khan Mamdot (1906-1969). c, Maulana Muhammad Shibli Naumani (1857-1914).

1992, Aug. 14 Litho. *Perf. 13*

773 A375 1r Strip of 3, #a.-c. .30 .30

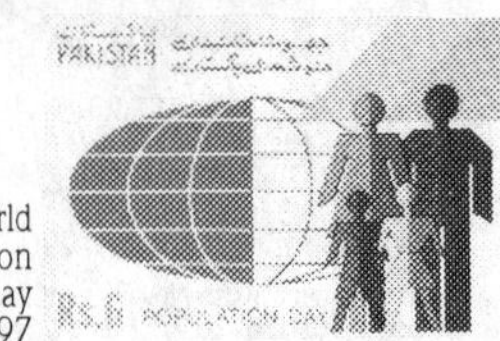

World Population Day A397

1992, July 25

774 A397 6r multicolored .65 .65

Medicinal Plants A398

1992, Nov. 22 Litho. *Perf. 13*

775 A398 6r multicolored .58 .58

See No. 791.

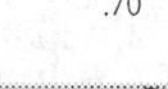

Extraordinary Session of Economic Cooperation Organization Council of Ministers, Islamabad — A399

1992, Nov. 28

776 A399 7r multicolored .70 .70

Intl. Conference on Nutrition, Rome — A400

1992, Dec. 5 *Perf. 14*

777 A400 7r multicolored .70 .70

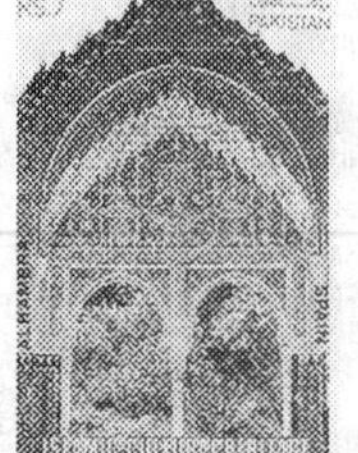

A401 A402

1992, Dec. 14 *Perf. 13*

778 A401 7r Alhambra, Spain .70 .70

Islamic cultural heritage.

1992, Aug. 23 *Perf. 14x12½*

779 A402 6r 6th Jamboree .58 .58
780 A402 6r 4th Conference .58 .58

Islamic Scouts, Islamabad.

Government Islamia College, Lahore, Cent. — A403

1992, Nov. 1 *Perf. 13*

781 A403 3r multicolored .35 .35

Industries A404

Designs: a, 10r, Surgical instruments. b, 15r, Leather goods. c, 25r, Sports equipment.

1992, July 5 Litho. *Perf. 13½x13*

782 A404 Strip of 3, #a.-c. 5.00 5.00

World Telecommunications Day — A405

1993, May 17 Litho. *Perf. 13*

783 A405 1r multicolored .15 .15

21st Islamic Foreign Ministers Conference A406

1993, Apr. 25

784 A406 1r buff & multi .15 .15
785 A406 6r green & multi .60 .60

A407 A408

Traditional costumes of provinces.

1993, Mar. 10

786 A407 6r Sindh .60 .60
787 A407 6r North West Frontier .60 .60
788 A407 6r Baluchistan .60 .60
789 A407 6r Punjab .60 .60
Nos. 786-789 (4) 2.40 2.40

1992, Dec. 31 *Perf. 14x13*

Birds: a, Gadwall. b, Common shelduck. c, Mallard. d, Greylag goose. The order of the birds is different on each row. Therefore the arc of the rainbow is different on each of the 4 Gadwalls, etc.

790 A408 5r Sheet of 16 10.00 10.00

Medicinal Plants Type

1993, June 20 Litho. *Perf. 13*

791 A398 6r Fennel, chemistry equipment .60 .60

Pioneers of Freedom Type of 1990

Designs: a, Rais Ghulam Mohammad Bhurgri (1878-1924). b, Mir Ahmed Yar Khan, Khan of Kalat (1902-1977). c, Mohammad Abdul Latif Pir Sahib Zakori Sharif (1914-1978).

1993, Aug. 14 Litho. *Perf. 13*

792 A375 1r Strip of 3, #a.-c. .30 .30

Gordon College, Rawalpindi, Cent. — A410

1993, Sept. 1

793 A410 2r multicolored .22 .22

Juniper Forests, Ziarat — A411

1993, Sept. 30

794 A411 7r multicolored .80 .80

See No. 827.

World Food Day — A412

1993, Oct. 16 *Perf. 14*

795 A412 6r multicolored .65 .65

A413 A414

Perf. 13½

1993, Dec. 25 Litho. Wmk. 351

796 A413 1r multicolored .15 .15

Wazir Mansion, birthplace of Muhammad Ali Jinnah.

Perf. 13x13½

1993, Oct. 28 Unwmk.

797 A414 7r multicolored .55 .55

Burn Hall Institutions, 50th anniv.

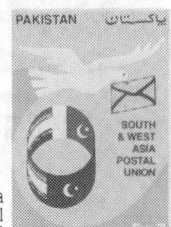

South & West Asia Postal Union — A415

1993, Nov. 18 *Perf. 13*

798 A415 7r multicolored .55 .55

Pakistani College of Physicians & Surgeons, Intl. Medical Congress — A416

1993, Dec. 10

799 A416 1r multicolored .15 .15

ILO, 75th Anniv. A417

1994, Apr. 11 Litho. *Perf. 13*

800 A417 7r multicolored .55 .55

Bio-diversity A418

Designs: a, Ratan jot, medicinal plant. b, Wetlands. c, Mahseer fish. d, Himalayan brown bear.

1994, Apr. 20 Litho. *Perf. 13½*

801 A418 6r Strip or block of 4, #a.-d. 1.90 1.90

Intl. Year of the Family — A419

1994, May 15 *Perf. 13*

802 A419 7r multicolored .52 .52

World Population Day — A420

1994, July 11 Litho. *Perf. 13*

803 A420 7r multicolored .52 .52

Pioneers of Freedom Type of 1990
Miniature Sheet of 8

Designs: a, Nawab Mohsin-Ul-Mulk (1837-1907). b, Sir Shahnawaz Bhutto (1888-1957). c, Nawab Viqar-Ul-Mulk (1841-1917). d, Pir Ilahi Bux (1890-1975). e, Sheikh Sir Abdul Qadir (1874-1950). f, Dr. Sir Ziauddin Ahmed (1878-1947). g,

Jam Mir Ghulam Qadir Khan (1920-88). h, Sardar Aurangzeb Khan (1899-1953).

1994, Aug. 14 Litho. *Perf. 13*
804 A375 1r #a.-h. + label .70 .70

A421 A422

1994, Oct. 2 *Perf. 13x13½*
805 A421 2r multicolored .22 .22

First Intl. Festival of Islamic Artisans.

1994, Sept. 8
806 A422 7r multicolored .55 .55

Intl. Literacy Day.

Hyoscyamus Niger — A423

1994 *Perf. 13*
807 A423 6r multicolored .50 .50

Mohammed Ali Jinnah A424

Litho. & Engr.
1994, Sept. 11 Wmk. 351 *Perf. 13*

808	A424	1r slate & multi	.15	.15
809	A424	2r claret & multi	.15	.15
810	A424	3r bright blue & multi	.22	.22
811	A424	4r emerald & multi	.30	.30
812	A424	5r lake & multi	.38	.38
813	A424	7r blue & multi	.50	.50
814	A424	10r green & multi	.75	.75
815	A424	12r orange & multi	.90	.90
816	A424	15r violet & multi	1.10	1.10
817	A424	20r rose & multi	1.50	1.50
818	A424	25r brown & multi	1.90	1.90
819	A424	30r olive brown & multi	2.25	2.25
		Nos. 808-819 (12)	10.10	10.10

2nd SAARC & 12th Natl. Scout Jamboree, Quetta — A425

1994, Sept. 22 Litho.
820 A425 7r multicolored .60 .60

Publication of Ferdowsi's Book of Kings, 1000th Anniv. — A426

1994, Oct. 27
821 A426 1r multicolored .15 .15

Indonesia-Pakistan Economic & Cultural Cooperation Organization A427

1994, Aug. 19
822 A427 10r Hala pottery .75 .75
823 A427 10r Lombok pottery .75 .75
a. Pair, #822-823 1.50 1.50

See Indonesia Nos. 1585-1586.

Lahore Museum, Cent. — A428

Wmk. 351
1994, Dec. 27 Litho. *Perf. 13*
824 A428 4r multicolored .25 .25

Pakistan, 1994 World Cup Field Hockey Champions A429

1994, Dec. 31
825 A429 5r multicolored .32 .32

World Tourism Organization, 20th Anniv. — A430

1995, Jan. 2
826 A430 4r multicolored .25 .25

Juniper Forests Type of 1993

1995, Feb. 14 Litho. *Perf. 13*
827 A411 1r like #794 .15 .15

Third Economic Cooperation Organization Summit, Islamabad A431

1995, Mar. 14 Litho. *Perf. 14*
828 A431 6r multicolored .48 .48

Khushall Khan Khatak (1613-89) — A432

1995, Feb. 28 *Perf. 13*
829 A432 7r multicolored .55 .55

Earth Day — A433

Wmk. 351
1995, Apr. 20 Litho. *Perf. 13*
830 A433 6r multicolored .60 .60

Snakes A434

Designs: a, Krait. b, Cobra. c, Python. d, Viper.

1995, Apr. 15 Unwmk. *Perf. 13½*
831 A434 6r Block of 4, #a.-d. 2.25 2.25

Traditional Means of Transportation — A435

Wmk. 351
1995, May 22 Litho. *Perf. 13*
832 A435 5r Horse-drawn carriage .40 .40

Louis Pasteur (1822-95) — A436

Wmk. 351
1995, Sept. 28 Litho. *Perf. 13*
833 A436 5r multicolored .40 .40

UN, FAO, 50th Anniv. A437

1995, Oct. 16
834 A437 1.25r multicolored .20 .20

Kinnaird College for Women, Lahore — A438

4th World Conference on Women, Beijing — A439

1995, Nov. 3 *Perf. 14x13*
835 A438 1.25r multicolored .20 .20

1995, Sept. 15 *Perf. 13*

Women in various activities: a, Playing golf, in armed forces, repairing technical device. b, Graduates, student, chemist, computer operator, reading gauge. c, At sewing machine, working with textiles. d, Making rugs, police woman, laborers.

836 A439 1.25r Strip of 4, #a.-d. .45 .45

Presentation Convent School, Rawalpindi, Cent. — A440

Perf. 13½
1995, Sept. 8 Litho. Wmk. 351
837 A440 1.25r multicolored .20 .20

Liaquat Ali Khan (1895-1951) — A441

1995, Oct. 1 *Perf. 13*
838 A441 1.25r multicolored .20 .20

1st Conference of Women Parliamentarians from Muslim Countries — A442

Designs: No. 839, Dr. Tansu Ciller, Prime Minister of Turkey. No. 840, Mohtarma Benazir Bhutto, Prime Minister of Pakistan.

1995, Aug. 1 Unwmk.
839 A442 5r multicolored .40 .40
840 A442 5r multicolored .40 .40
a. Pair, #839-840 .80 .80

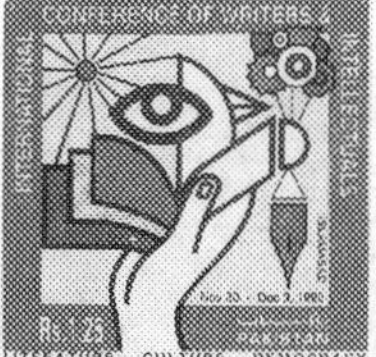

Intl. Conference of Writers and Intellectuals A443

Wmk. 351

1995, Nov. 30 Litho. *Perf. 14*

841 A443 1.25r multicolored .20 .20

Allama Iqbal Open University, 20th Anniv. — A444

1995, Dec. 16 *Perf. 13*

842 A444 1.25r multicolored .20 .20

Butterflies A445

Designs: a, Érasmie. b, Catogramme. c, Ixias. d, Héliconie.

Perf. 13½

1995, Sept. 1 Litho. Wmk. 351

843 A445 6r Strip of 4, #a.-d. 1.75 1.75

Fish — A446

Designs: a, Sardinella long. b, Tilapia mossambica. c, Salmo fario. d, Labeo rohita.

1995, Sept. 1

844 A446 6r Strip of 4, #a.-d. 1.75 1.75

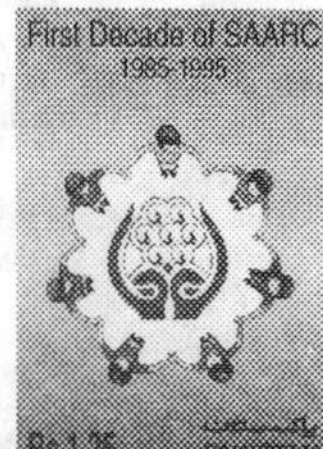

SAARC, 10th Anniv. — A447

1995, Dec. 8 *Perf. 13*

845 A447 1.25r multicolored .15 .15

UN, 50th Anniv. A448

Perf. 13½

1995, Oct. 24 Litho. Wmk. 351

846 A448 7r multicolored .50 .50

Karachi '95, Natl. Water Sports Gala — A449

Designs: a, Man on jet ski. b, Gondola race. c, Sailboard race. d, Man water skiing.

1995, Dec. 14 *Perf. 14x13*

847 A449 1.25r Block of 4, #a.-d. .40 .40

University of Baluchistan, Quetta, 25th Anniv. — A452

Wmk. 351

1995, Dec. 31 Litho. *Perf. 13*

850 A452 1.25r multicolored .15 .15

Zulfikar Ali Bhutto (1928-79), Politician, President — A455

Designs: 1.25r, Bhutto, flag, crowd of people, vert. 8r, like No. 855

Wmk. 351

1996, Apr. 4 Litho. *Perf. 13*

855 A455 1.25r multicolored .15 .15
856 A455 4r shown .30 .30

Size: 114x69mm

Imperf

857 A455 8r multicolored .60 .60

Raja Aziz Bhatti Shaheed (1928-65) A456

Wmk. 351

1995, Sept. 5 Litho. *Perf. 13*

858 A456 1.25r multicolored .20 .20

Pioneers of Freedom Type of 1990

#859, Maulana Shaukat Ali (1873-1938). #860, Chaudhry Ghulam Abbas (1904-67).

1995, Aug. 14 Unwmk. *Perf. 13*

859 A375 1r green & brown .15 .15
860 A375 1r green & brown .15 .15
a. Pair, #859-860 .20 .20

1996 Summer Olympic Games, Atlanta — A457

Design: 25r, #861-864 without denominations, simulated perfs, Olympic rings, "100," Atlanta '96 emblem. Illustration reduced.

1996 Litho. Wmk. 351 *Perf. 13*

861 A457 5r Wrestling .35 .35
862 A457 5r Boxing .35 .35
863 A457 5r Pierre de Coubertin .35 .35
864 A457 5r Field hockey .35 .35
Nos. 861-864 (4) 1.40 1.40

Imperf

Size: 111x101mm

864A A457 25r multicolored 1.75 1.75

Pioneers of Freedom Type of 1990

Allama Abdullah Yousuf Ali (1872-1953).

1996 Litho. Unwmk. *Perf. 13*

865 A375 1r green & brown .15 .15

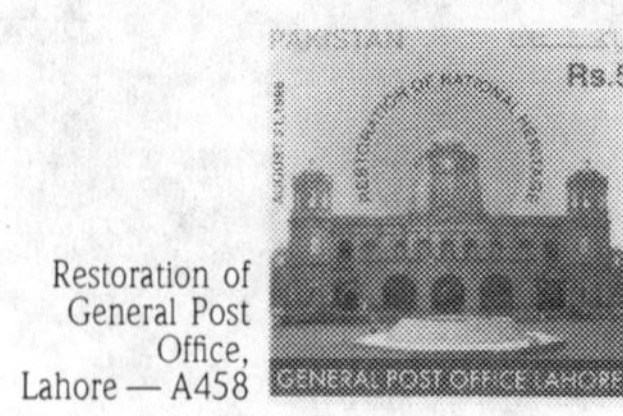

Restoration of General Post Office, Lahore — A458

1996, Aug. 21 Wmk. 351 *Perf. 14*

866 A458 5r multicolored .35 .35

Intl. Literacy Day — A459

1996, Sept. 8 Wmk. 351 *Perf. 13*

867 A459 2r multicolored .20 .20

Faiz Ahmed Faiz, Poet, 86th Birthday — A460

1997 Litho. Unwmk. *Perf. 13*

868 A460 3r multicolored .20 .20

Tamerlane (1336-1405) A461

Unwmk.

1997, Apr. 8 Litho. *Perf. 13*

869 A461 3r multicolored .20 .20

Famous Men — A462

Designs: No. 870, Allama Mohammad Iqbal. No. 871, Jalal-Al-Din Moulana Rumi.

1997, Apr. 21 *Perf. 13½*

870 A462 3r multicolored .20 .20
871 A462 3r multicolored .20 .20

Pakistani Independence, 50th Anniv. — A463

1997, Mar. 23 *Perf. 13*

872 A463 2r multicolored .15 .15

Special Summit of Organization of Islamic Countries, Islamabad.

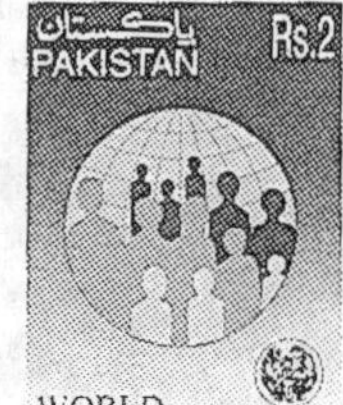

World Population Day — A464

Unwmk.

1997, July 11 Litho. *Perf. 13*

873 A464 2r multicolored .20 .20

Intl. Atomic Energy Agency-Pakistan Atomic Energy Commission Cooperation, 40th Anniv. — A465

1997, July 29 *Perf. 14*

874 A465 2r multicolored .20 .20

Pioneers of Freedom Type of 1990

#875, Begum Salma Tassaduq Hussain (1908-95). #876, Mohammad Ayub Khuhro (1901-80).

1997, Aug. 14 Litho. *Perf. 13*

875 A375 1r green & brown .15 .15
876 A375 1r green & brown .15 .15

Fruits of Pakistan — A466

1997, May 8

877 A466 2r Apples .20 .20

Independence, 50th Anniv. — A467

Designs: a, Allama Mohammad Iqbal. b, Mohammad Ali Jinnah. c, Liaquat Ali Khan. d, Mohtarma Fatima Jinnah.

1997, Aug. 14

Block of 4 + 2 Labels

878 A467 3r #a.-d. .75 .75

Lophophorus Impejanus — A468

1997 Litho. Wmk. 351 *Perf. 13*
879 A468 2r multicolored .20 .20

Lahore College for Women, 75th Anniv. — A469

1997, Sept. 23
880 A469 3r multicolored .20 .20

Intl. Day of the Disabled A470

1997 Litho. Unwmk. *Perf. 13*
881 A470 4r multicolored .25 .25

Protection of the Ozone Layer — A471

1997
882 A471 3r multicolored .20 .20

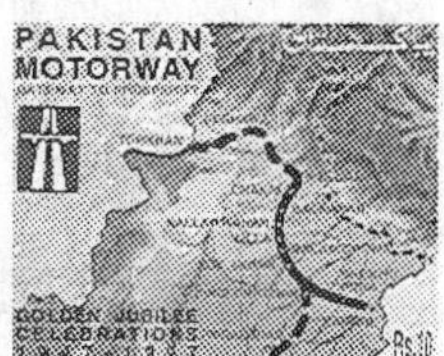

Pakistan Motorway, 50th Anniv. A472

1997 *Perf. 13½*
883 A472 10r multicolored .55 .55
a. Souvenir sheet of 1 .85 .85

No. 883a sold for 15r.

Karachi Grammar School, 150th Anniv. A473

1997 Litho. *Perf. 13½*
884 A473 2r multicolored .20 .20

Garlic A474

1997 *Perf. 13*
885 A474 2r multicolored .20 .20

Mirza Asad Ullah Khan Ghalib (1797-1869), Poet — A475

1997
886 A475 2r multicolored .20 .20

OFFICIAL STAMPS

Official Stamps of India, 1939-43, Overprinted in Black **PAKISTAN**

1947-49 Wmk. 196 *Perf. 13½x14*
O1 O8 3p slate .70 .15
O2 O8 ½a dk rose vio .25 .15
O3 O8 9p green 3.00 .15
O4 O8 1a carmine rose .25 .15
O4A O8 1a3p bister ('49) 3.75 3.75
O5 O8 1½a dull purple .25 .15
O6 O8 2a scarlet .25 .15
O7 O8 2½a purple 4.50 4.50
O8 O8 4a dk brown 1.10 .15
O9 O8 8a blue violet 1.40 .50
Nos. O1-O9 (10) 15.45 9.80

India Nos. O100-O103 Overprinted in Black **PAKISTAN**

O10 A82 1r brown & slate .70 .50
O11 A82 2r dk brn & dk vio 3.25 .25
O12 A82 5r dp ultra & dk grn 12.50 *30.00*
Telegraph cancel 7.50
O13 A82 10r rose car & dk vio 32.50 *40.00*
Telegraph cancel *20.00*

Regular Issue of 1948 Overprinted in Black or Carmine — a **SERVICE**

Perf. 12½, 13, 13½x14, 14x13½
1948, Aug. 14 Unwmk.
O14 A3 3p orange red .20 .15
O15 A3 6p purple (C) .20 .15
O16 A3 9p dk green (C) .20 .15
O17 A4 1a dk blue (C) 3.25 .15
O18 A4 1½a gray grn (C) 3.00 .15
O19 A4 2a orange red 1.25 .15
O20 A5 3a olive green 14.00 3.25
O21 A6 4a chocolate .70 .15
O22 A6 8a black (C) 1.10 *3.50*
O23 A5 1r ultra .90 .15
O24 A5 2r dark brown 11.00 3.75
O25 A5 5r carmine 16.00 3.75
O26 A7 10r rose lil, perf. 14x13½ 11.00 *25.00*
a. Perf. 12 13.00 *25.00*
b. Perf. 13 11.00 *32.50*
Nos. O14-O26 (13) 62.80 40.45

Issued: #O26a, Oct. 10, 1951; #O26b, 1954(?).

Nos. 47-50 and 52 Overprinted Type "a" in Black or Carmine

1949-50 *Perf. 12½, 13½x14*
O27 A10 1a dark blue (C) .80 .15
O28 A10 1½a gray green (C) .25 .15
a. Inverted ovpt. 75.00
O29 A10 2a orange red .80 .15
O30 A9 3a olive green ('49) 10.50 2.75
O31 A11 8a black (C) 19.00 9.00
Nos. O27-O31 (5) 31.35 12.20

Types of Regular Issue of 1951, "Pakistan" or "Pakistan Postage" Replaced by "SERVICE"

Unwmk.
1951, Aug. 14 Engr. *Perf. 13*
O32 A13 3a dark rose lake 3.25 *4.00*
O33 A14 4a deep green 1.25 .15
O34 A15 8a brown 4.50 1.75
Nos. O32-O34 (3) 9.00 *5.90*

Nos. 24-26, 47-49, 38-41 Overprinted in Black or Carmine

b **SERVICE**

1954
O35 A3 3p orange red .15 .15
O36 A3 6p purple (C) .15 .15
O37 A3 9p dk green (C) .15 .15
O38 A10 1a dk blue (C) .15 .15
O39 A10 1½a gray green (C) .15 .15
O40 A10 2a orange red .15 .15
O41 A5 1r ultra 1.75 .32
O42 A5 2r dark brown 1.50 .15
O43 A5 5r carmine 5.25 1.10
O43A A7 10r rose lilac 8.00 *16.00*
Nos. O35-O43A (10) 17.40 *18.47*

Nos. 66-72 Overprinted Type "b" in Carmine or Black

1954, Aug. 14
O44 A18 6p rose violet (C) .15 *.30*
O45 A19 9p blue (C) .15 *2.00*
O46 A19 1a carmine rose .15 *.25*
O47 A18 1½a red .15 *.25*
O48 A20 14a dk green (C) .60 *1.25*
O49 A20 1r yellow grn (C) .75 *.15*
O50 A20 2r orange 1.25 .20
Nos. O44-O50 (7) 3.20 *4.40*

No. 75 Overprinted in Carmine Type "b" Overprint: 13x2½mm

1955, Aug. 14 Unwmk. *Perf. 13*
O51 A21 8a violet .18 .15

Nos. 24, 40, 66-72, 74-75, 83, 89 Overprinted in Black or Carmine

c **SERVICE**

1957-61
O52 A3 3p orange red ('58) .15 .15
O53 A18 6p rose vio (C) .15 .15
O54 A19 9p blue (C) ('58) .15 *.25*
O55 A19 1a carmine rose .15 .15
O56 A18 1½a red .15 .15
O57 A24 2a red ('58) .15 .15
O58 A21 6a dk bl (C) ('60) .15 .15
O59 A21 8a vio (C) ('58) .15 .15
O60 A20 14a dk grn (C) ('58) .40 *1.00*
O61 A20 1r yel grn (C) ('58) .40 .15
O62 A20 2r orange ('58) 2.25 .15
O63 A5 5r carmine ('58) 3.00 .25
O64 A26 10r dk grn & org (C) ('61) 6.00 4.00
Nos. O52-O64 (13) 13.25
Set value 5.90

For surcharges see Nos. O67-O73.

Nos. 110-111 Overprinted Type "c"

1961, Apr.
O65 A33 8a green .18 .15
O66 A33 1r blue .25 .15
a. Inverted overprint 8.25
Set value .15

New Currency

Nos. O52, O55-O57 Surcharged with New Value in Paisa

1961
O67 A18 1p on 1½a red .15 .15
a. Overprinted type "b" 6.00 4.00
O68 A3 2p on 3p orange red .15 .15
a. Overprinted type "b" 6.00 4.00
O69 A19 6p on 1a car rose
O70 A19 7p on 1a car rose .15 .15
a. Overprinted type "b" 2.25 2.25
O71 A18 9p on 1½a red
O72 A24 13p on 2a red ("PAISA") .15 .15
O73 A24 13p on 2a red ("Paisa")

Nos. O69, O71, O73 were locally overprinted at Mastung. On these stamps "paisa" is in lower case.

Nos. 125, 128 Overprinted Type "c"

1961
O74 A33 3p on 6p purple .15 .15
O75 A33 13p on 2a copper red .15 .15
Set value .15 .15

Various violet handstamped surcharges were applied to several official stamps. Most of these repeat the denomination of the basic stamp and add the new value. Example: "4 ANNAS (25 Paisa)" on No. O33.

Nos. 129-135, 135B, 135C, 136a, 137-140a Overprinted in Carmine

d **SERVICE**

1961-78 *Perf. 13½x14*
O76 A40 1p violet (II) .15 .15
a. Type I .15 .15
O77 A40 2p rose red (II) .15 .15
a. Type I .15 .15
O78 A40 3p magenta .15 .15
O79 A40 5p ultra (II) .15 .15
a. Type I .15 .15
O80 A40 7p emerald .15 .15
O81 A40 10p brown .15 .15
O82 A40 13p blue violet .15 .15
O83 A40 15p rose lil (#135B) ('64) .15 .15
O84 A40 20p dl grn (#135C) ('70) .15 .15
O84A A40 25p dark blue (#136a) ('77) .15 .15
O85 A40 40p dull pur ('62) .15 .15
O86 A40 50p dull grn ('62) .18 .15
O87 A40 75p dk car ('62) .22 .15
O88 A40 90p lt ol grn ('78) .30 .15
Set value 1.35 .75

Designs Redrawn

1961-66
O76b A40 1p violet (#129b) ('63) .15 .15
O77b A40 2p rose red (#130b) ('64) .15 .15
O78a A40 3p magenta (#131a) ('66) .15 .15
O79b A40 5p ultra (#132b) ('63) .15 .15
O80a A40 7p emerald (#133a) 2.00 .15
O81a A40 10p brown (#134a) ('64) .15 .15
O82a A40 13p blue vio (#135a) ('63) .15 .15
O85a A40 40p dull purple (#137a) .35 .15
O86a A40 50p dull grn (#138a) ('64) .18 .15
O87a A40 75p dark carmine (#139a)
Set value, #O76b-O86a 2.75 .45

Nos. 141, 143-144 Overprinted Type "c" in Black or Carmine

1963, Jan. 7 Unwmk. *Perf. 13½x13*
O89 A41 1r vermilion .50 .15
O90 A41 2r orange 2.00 .30
O91 A41 5r green (C) 5.00 4.00
Nos. O89-O91 (3) 7.50 4.45

Nos. 200, 202-203 Overprinted Type "c"

1968-? Wmk. 351 *Perf. 13½x13*
O92 A41 1r vermilion .40 .15
O93 A41 2r orange 1.25 .25
O93A A41 5r green (C) 6.00 5.00
Nos. O92-O93A (3) 7.65 5.40

Nos. 459-468, 470-475 Overprinted Type "d" in Carmine or Black

1980-84
O94 A224 2p dark green .15 .15
O95 A224 3p black .15 .15
O96 A224 5p violet blue .15 .15
O97 A225 10p grnsh blue .15 .15
O98 A225 20p yel grn ('81) .15 .15
O99 A225 25p rose car & grn ('81) .15 .15
O100 A225 40p car & bl ('81) .15 .15
O101 A225 50p bl grn & vio .15 .15
O102 A225 60p black .15 .15
O103 A225 75p dp orange .15 .15
O105 A225a 1r olive ('81) .15 .15
O106 A225a 1.50r dp orange .20 .18
O107 A225a 2r car rose (B) .28 .15
O108 A225a 3r indigo ('81) .40 .35
O109 A225a 4r black ('84) .65 .50
O110 A225a 5r dk brown ('84) .85 .65
Set value 3.00 2.40

Types A237-A239 Inscribed "SERVICE POSTAGE"

1980 Litho. *Perf. 12x11½, 11½x12*
O111 A237 10p dk grn & yel org .15 .15
O112 A237 15p dk grn & ap grn .15 .15
O113 A237 25p dp vio & rose car .15 .15
O114 A237 35p rose pink & brt yel grn .15 .15
O115 A238 40p red & lt brn .15 .15
O116 A239 50p olive & vio bl .15 .15
O117 A239 80p blk & yel grn .15 .15
Set value .50 .35

Issued: 10p, 15p, 40p, Jan. 15, others, Mar. 10.

Nos. 613-614, 616-620 Ovptd. "SERVICE" in Red

1984-87 Litho. *Perf. 11*
O118 A289 5p Kot Diji .15 .15
O119 A289 10p Rohtas .15 .15
O120 A289 20p Attock Fort .15 .15
O121 A289 50p Hyderabad .15 .15
O122 A289 60p Lahore ('86) .15 .15
O123 A289 70p Sibi .16 .15
O124 A289 80p Ranikot .19 .15
Set value .60 .40

Issued: 10p, Sept. 25, 1984; 80p, Aug. 3, 1987.

No. 712 Ovptd. "SERVICE"

1989, Dec. 24 Litho. & Engr. *Perf. 13*
O124A A357 1r multicolored .15 .15

National Assembly, Islamabad O1

Perf. 13½

1991, Apr. 12 Litho. Wmk. 351

O125	O1	1r green & red	.20	.15
O126	O1	2r rose car & red	.40	.15
O127	O1	3r ultra & red	.60	.15
O128	O1	4r red brown & red	.80	.15
O129	O1	5r rose lilac & red	1.00	.15
		Nos. O125-O129 (5)	3.00	
		Set value		.25

BAHAWALPUR

LOCATION — A State of Pakistan.
AREA — 17,494 sq. mi.
POP. — 1,341,209 (1941)
CAPITAL — Bahawalpur

Bahawalpur was a State of India until 1947. These stamps had franking power solely within Bahawalpur.

Seventeen King George VI stamps of India exist overprinted with star, cresent and a line of Arabic. These are not considered to be legitimate stamps.

Used values are for c-t-o or favor cancels.

Amir Muhammad Bahawal Khan I Abbasi — A1

Perf. 12½x12

1947, Dec. 1 Wmk. 274 Engr.

1	A1	½a brt car rose & blk	.15	.15

Bicentenary of the ruling family.

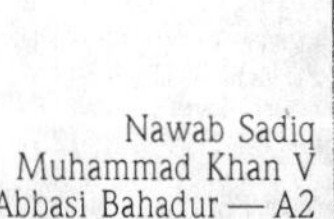

Nawab Sadiq Muhammad Khan V Abbasi Bahadur — A2

Tombs of the Amirs — A3

Mosque, Sadiq Garh — A4

Fort Dirawar — A5

Nur-Mahal Palace — A6

Palace, Sadiq Garh — A7

Nawab Sadiq Muhammad Khan V Abbasi Bahadur — A8

A9

Perf. 12½ (A2), 12x12½ (A3, A5, A6, A7), 12½x12 (A4, A8), 13x13½ (A9)

1948, Apr. 1 Engr. Wmk. 274

2	A2	3p dp blue & blk	.25	.15
3	A2	½a lake & blk	.25	.15
4	A2	9p dk green & blk	.25	.15
5	A2	1a dp car & blk	.25	.15
6	A2	1½a violet & blk	.25	.25
7	A3	2a car & dp grn	.45	.45
8	A4	4a brn & org red	.55	.55
9	A5	6a dp bl & vio brn	.60	.60
10	A6	8a brt pur & car	.65	.65
11	A7	12a dp car & dk bl grn	.70	.70
12	A8	1r chocolate & vio	12.50	12.50
13	A8	2r dp mag & dk grn	20.00	20.00
14	A8	5r purple & black	25.00	25.00
15	A9	10r black & carmine	25.00	25.00
		Nos. 2-15 (14)	86.70	86.30

See #18-21. For overprints see #O17-O24.

Soldiers of 1848 and 1948 — A10

1948, Oct. 15 Engr. *Perf. 11½*

16	A10	1½a dp car & blk	.15	.15

Centenary of the Multan Campaign.

Amir Khan V and Mohammed Ali Jinnah — A11

1948, Oct. 3 *Perf. 13x12½*

17	A11	1½a grn & car rose	.15	.15

1st anniv. of the union of Bahawalpur with Pakistan.

Types of 1948

1948 *Perf. 12x11½*

18	A8	1r orange & dp grn	.15	.15
19	A8	2r carmine & blk	.15	.20
20	A8	5r ultra & red brn	.30	.30

Perf. 13½

21	A9	10r green & red brn	.55	.55
		Nos. 18-21 (4)	1.15	1.20

Panjnad Weir — A12

1949, Mar. 3 *Perf. 14*

22	A12	3p shown	.15	.15
23	A12	½a Wheat	.15	.15
24	A12	9p Cotton	.15	.15
25	A12	1a Sahiwal Bull	.15	.15
		Set value	.20	.20

25th anniv. of the acquisition of full ruling powers by Amir Khan V.

UPU Monument, Bern — A13

1949, Oct. 10 *Perf. 13*

Center in Black

26	A13	9p green	.15	.15
27	A13	1a red violet	.15	.15
28	A13	1½a brown orange	.15	.15
29	A13	2½a blue	.45	.45
		Nos. 26-29 (4)	.90	.90

UPU, 75th anniv. Exist perf 17½x17. Exist imperf.

For overprints see Nos. O25-O28.

OFFICIAL STAMPS

Panjnad Weir — O1

Camel and Colt — O2

Antelopes — O3

Pelicans — O4

Juma Masjid Palace, Fort Derawar — O5

Temple at Pattan Munara — O6

Red Overprint

Wmk. 274

1945, Jan. 1 Engr. *Perf. 14*

O1	O1	½a brt grn & blk	2.00	2.00
O2	O2	1a carmine & blk	3.00	3.00
O3	O3	2a violet & blk	3.00	3.00
O4	O4	4a olive & blk	6.75	6.75
O5	O5	8a brown & blk	12.50	8.75
O6	O6	1r orange & blk	15.00	8.75
		Nos. O1-O6 (6)	42.25	32.25

For types overprinted see Nos. O7-O9, O11-O13.

Types of 1945, Without Red Overprint, Surcharged in Black

1945 Unwmk.

O7	O5	½a on 8a lake & blk	3.75	3.00
O8	O6	1½a on 1r org & blk	21.00	7.25
O9	O1	1½a on 2r ultra & blk	85.00	8.00
		Nos. O7-O9 (3)	109.75	18.25

Camels — O7

1945, Mar. 10 Red Overprint

O10	O7	1a brown & black	27.50	35.00

Types of 1945, Without Red Overprint, Overprinted in Black

1945

O11	O1	½a carmine & black	1.10	1.10
O12	O2	1a carmine & black	1.90	1.90
O13	O3	2a orange & black	3.00	3.00
		Nos. O11-O13 (3)	6.00	6.00

Nawab Sadiq Muhammad Khan V Abbasi Bahadur — O8

1945

O14	O8	3p dp blue & blk	1.75	1.75
O15	O8	1½a dp violet & blk	10.00	5.25

Flags of Allied Nations — O9

1946, May 1

O16	O9	1½a emerald & gray	1.65	1.65

Victory of Allied Nations in World War II.

Stamps of 1948 Overprinted in Carmine or Black

Perf. 12½, 12½x12, 12x11½, 13½

1948 Wmk. 274

O17	A2	3p dp bl & blk (C)	.45	.45
O18	A2	1a dp carmine & blk	.45	.45
O19	A3	2a car & dp grn	.45	.45
O20	A4	4a brown & org red	.45	.45
O21	A8	1r org & dp grn (C)	.45	.45
O22	A8	2r car & blk (C)	.45	.45
O23	A8	5r ultra & red brn (C)	.45	.45
O24	A9	10r grn & red brn (C)	.45	.45
		Nos. O17-O24 (8)	3.60	3.60

Same Ovpt. in Carmine on #26-29

1949 *Perf. 13, 18*

Center in Black

O25 A13 9p green .25 .25
O26 A13 1a red violet .25 .25
O27 A13 1½a brown orange .25 .25
O28 A13 2½a blue .25 .25
Nos. O25-O28 (4) 1.00 1.00

75th anniv. of the UPU. Exist perf 17½x17. Exist imperf.

PALAU

pə-'laú

LOCATION — Group of 100 islands in the West Pacific Ocean about 1,000 miles southeast of Manila
AREA — 179 sq. mi.
POP. — 16,000 (est. 1983)
CAPITAL — Koror (Headquarters)

Palau, the western section of the Caroline Islands (Micronesia), was part of the US Trust Territory of the Pacific, established in 1947. By agreement with the USPS, the republic began issuing its own stamps in 1984, with the USPS continuing to carry the mail to and from the islands.

On Jan. 10, 1986 Palau became a Federation as a Sovereign State in Compact of Free Association with the US.

100 Cents = 1 Dollar

Catalogue values for all unused stamps in this country are for Never Hinged items.

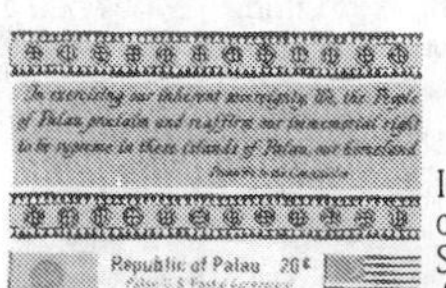

Inauguration of Postal Service A1

1983, Mar. 10 **Litho.** *Perf. 14*

1 A1 20c Constitution preamble .50 .50
2 A1 20c Hunters .50 .50
3 A1 20c Fish .50 .50
4 A1 20c Preamble, diff. .50 .50
a. Block of 4, #1-4 2.00 2.00

Palau Fruit Dove — A2

1983, May 16 *Perf. 15*

5 A2 20c shown .40 .40
6 A2 20c Palau morningbird .40 .40
7 A2 20c Giant white-eye .40 .40
8 A2 20c Palau fantail .40 .40
a. Block of 4, #5-8 1.65 1.65

Sea Fan — A3

1983-84 **Litho.** *Perf. 13½x14*

9 A3 1c shown .15 .15
10 A3 3c Map cowrie .15 .15
11 A3 5c Jellyfish .15 .15
12 A3 10c Hawksbill turtle .15 .15
13 A3 13c Giant Clam .20 .20
a. Booklet pane of 10 *9.00* —
b. Bklt. pane of 10 (5 #13, 5 #14) *9.00* —
14 A3 20c Parrotfish .35 .35
b. Booklet pane of 10 *10.00* —
15 A3 28c Chambered Nautilus .45 .45
16 A3 30c Dappled sea cucumber .50 .50
17 A3 37c Sea Urchin .55 .55
18 A3 50c Starfish .80 .80
19 A3 $1 Squid 1.50 1.50

Perf. 15x14

20 A3 $2 Dugong 4.25 4.25
21 A3 $5 Pink sponge 10.00 10.00
Nos. 9-21 (13) 19.20 19.20

See Nos. 75-85.

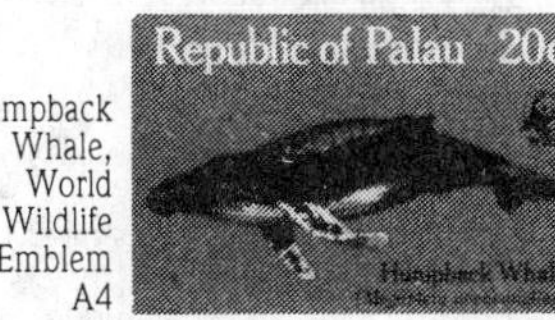

Humpback Whale, World Wildlife Emblem A4

1983, Sept. 21 *Perf. 14*

24 A4 20c shown .50 .50
25 A4 20c Blue whale .50 .50
26 A4 20c Fin whale .50 .50
27 A4 20c Great sperm whale .50 .50
a. Block of 4, #24-27 2.00 2.00

Christmas 1983 — A5

Paintings by Charlie Gibbons, 1971.

1983, Oct. **Litho.** *Perf. 14½*

28 A5 20c First Child ceremony .50 .50
29 A5 20c Spearfishing from Red Canoe .50 .50
30 A5 20c Traditional feast at the Bai .50 .50
31 A5 20c Taro gardening .50 .50
32 A5 20c Spearfishing at New Moon .50 .50
a. Strip of 5, #28-32 2.50 2.50

A6

Capt. Wilson's Voyage, Bicentennial — A7

1983, Dec. 14 *Perf. 14x15*

33 A6 20c Capt. Henry Wilson .50 .50
34 A7 20c Approaching Pelew .50 .50
35 A7 20c Englishman's Camp on Ulong .50 .50
36 A6 20c Prince Lee Boo .50 .50
37 A6 20c King Abba Thulle .50 .50
38 A7 20c Mooring in Koror .50 .50
39 A7 20c Village scene of Pelew Islands .50 .50
40 A6 20c Ludee .50 .50
a. Block or strip of 8, #33-40 4.00 4.00

Local Seashells — A8

Shell paintings (dorsal and ventral) by Deborah Dudley Max.

1984, Mar. 15 **Litho.** *Perf. 14*

41 A8 20c Triton trumpet, d. .40 .40
42 A8 20c Horned helmet, d. .40 .40
43 A8 20c Giant clam, d. .40 .40
44 A8 20c Laciniate conch, d. .40 .40
45 A8 20c Royal cloak scallop, d. .40 .40
46 A8 20c Triton trumpet, v. .40 .40
47 A8 20c Horned helmet, v. .40 .40
48 A8 20c Giant clam, v. .40 .40
49 A8 20c Laciniate conch, v. .40 .40
50 A8 20c Royal cloak scallop, v. .40 .40
a. Block of 10, #41-50 4.00 4.00

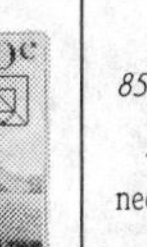

Explorer Ships — A9

1984, June 19 **Litho.** *Perf. 14*

51 A9 40c Oroolong, 1783 .85 .85
52 A9 40c Duff, 1797 .85 .85
53 A9 40c Peiho, 1908 .85 .85
54 A9 40c Albatross, 1885 .85 .85
a. Block of 4, #51-54 3.50 3.50

UPU Congress.

Ausipex '84 A10

Fishing Methods.

1984, Sept. 6 **Litho.** *Perf. 14*

55 A10 20c Throw spear fishing .45 .45
56 A10 20c Kite fishing .45 .45
57 A10 20c Underwater spear fishing .45 .45
58 A10 20c Net fishing .45 .45
a. Block of 4, #55-58 1.90 1.90

Christmas Flowers — A11

1984, Nov. 28 **Litho.** *Perf. 14*

59 A11 20c Mountain Apple .45 .45
60 A11 20c Beach Morning Glory .45 .45
61 A11 20c Turmeric .45 .45
62 A11 20c Plumeria .45 .45
a. Block of 4, #59-62 1.90 1.90

Audubon Bicentenary A12

1985, Feb. 6 **Litho.** *Perf. 14*

63 A12 22c Shearwater chick .60 .60
64 A12 22c Shearwater's head .60 .60
65 A12 22c Shearwater in flight .60 .60
66 A12 22c Swimming .60 .60
a. Block of 4, #63-66 2.50 2.50
Nos. 63-66,C5 (5) 3.20 3.20

Canoes and Rafts A13

1985, Mar. 27 **Litho.**

67 A13 22c Cargo canoe .55 .55
68 A13 22c War canoe .55 .55
69 A13 22c Bamboo raft .55 .55
70 A13 22c Racing/sailing canoe .55 .55
a. Block of 4, #67-70 2.25 2.25

Marine Life Type of 1983

1985, June 11 **Litho.** *Perf. 14½x14*

75 A3 14c Trumpet triton .20 .20
a. Booklet pane of 10 *6.00* —
76 A3 22c Bumphead parrotfish .35 .35
a. Booklet pane of 10 *10.00* —
b. Booklet pane, 5 14c, 5 22c *9.00* —
77 A3 25c Soft coral, damsel fish .40 .40
79 A3 33c Sea anemone, clownfish .55 .55
80 A3 39c Green sea turtle .65 .65
81 A3 44c Pacific sailfish .70 .70

Perf. 15x14

85 A3 $10 Spinner dolphins 15.00 15.00
Nos. 75-85 (7) 17.85 17.85

This is an expanding set. Numbers will change if necessary.

A14

A15

IYY emblem and children of all nationalities joined in a circle.

1985, July 15 **Litho.** *Perf. 14*

86 A14 44c multicolored .75 .75
87 A14 44c multicolored .75 .75
88 A14 44c multicolored .75 .75
89 A14 44c multicolored .75 .75
a. Block of 4, #86-89 3.00 3.00

No. 89a has a continuous design.

1985, Oct. 21 **Litho.** *Perf. 14*

Christmas: Island mothers and children.

90 A15 14c multicolored .35 .35
91 A15 22c multicolored .50 .50
92 A15 33c multicolored .80 .80
93 A15 44c multicolored 1.10 1.10
Nos. 90-93 (4) 2.75 2.75

Souvenir Sheet

Pan American Airways Martin M-130 China Clipper A16

1985, Nov. 21 **Litho.** *Perf. 14*

94 A16 $1 multicolored 2.50 2.50

1st Trans-Pacific Mail Flight, Nov. 22, 1935. See Nos. C10-C13.

Return of Halley's Comet A17

Fictitious local sightings.

1985, Dec. 21 **Litho.** *Perf. 14*

95 A17 44c Kaeb canoe, 1758 .75 .75
96 A17 44c U.S.S. Vincennes, 1835 .75 .75
97 A17 44c S.M.S. Scharnhorst, 1910 .75 .75
98 A17 44c Yacht, 1986 .75 .75
a. Block of 4, #95-98 3.00 3.00

Songbirds — A18

1986, Feb. 24 **Litho.** *Perf. 14*

99 A18 44c Mangrove flycatcher .75 .75
100 A18 44c Cardinal honeyeater .75 .75
101 A18 44c Blue-faced parrotfinch .75 .75
102 A18 44c Dusky and bridled white-eyes .75 .75
a. Block of 4, #99-102 3.00 3.00

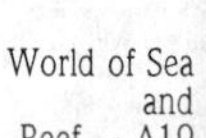

World of Sea and Reef — A19

1986, May 22 Litho. *Perf. 15x14*

103 Sheet of 40 *35.00*
a. A19 14c any single .25 .25

AMERIPEX '86, Chicago, May 22-June 1

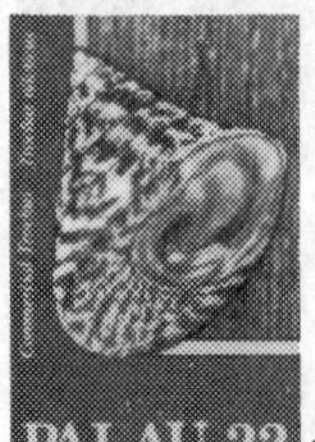

Seashells — A20

1986, Aug. 1 Litho. *Perf. 14*

104 A20 22c Commercial trochus .50 .50
105 A20 22c Marble cone .50 .50
106 A20 22c Fluted giant clam .50 .50
107 A20 22c Bullmouth helmet .50 .50
108 A20 22c Golden cowrie .50 .50
a. Strip of 5, #104-108 2.50 2.50

See Nos. 150-154, 191-195, 212-216.

Intl. Peace Year A21

1986, Sept. 19 Litho.

109 A21 22c Soldier's helmet .55 .55
110 A21 22c Plane wreckage .55 .55
111 A21 22c Woman playing guitar .55 .55
112 A21 22c Airai vista .55 .55
a. Block of 4, #109-112 2.20 2.20
Nos. 109-112,C17 (5) 3.10 3.10

Reptiles A22

1986, Oct. 28 Litho. *Perf. 14*

113 A22 22c Gecko .60 .60
114 A22 22c Emerald tree skink .60 .60
115 A22 22c Estuarine crocodile .60 .60
116 A22 22c Leatherback turtle .60 .60
a. Block of 4, #113-116 2.50 2.50

Christmas — A23 Butterflies — A23a

Joy to the World, carol by Isaac Watts and Handel: No. 117, Girl playing guitar, boys, goat. No. 118, Girl carrying bouquet, boys singing. No. 119, Palauan mother and child. No. 120, Children, baskets of fruit. No. 121, Girl, fairy tern. Nos. 117-121 printed in a continuous design.

1986, Nov. 26 Litho.

117 A23 22c multicolored .35 .35
118 A23 22c multicolored .35 .35
119 A23 22c multicolored .35 .35
120 A23 22c multicolored .35 .35
121 A23 22c multicolored .35 .35
a. Strip of 5, #117-121 1.75 1.75

1987, Jan. 5 Litho. *Perf. 14*

121B A23a 44c Tangadik, soursop .85 .85
121C A23a 44c Dira amartal, sweet orange .85 .85
121D A23a 44c Ilhuochel, swamp cabbage .85 .85
121E A23a 44c Bauosech, fig .85 .85
f. Block of 4, #121B-121E 3.40 3.40

See Nos. 183-186.

Fruit Bats — A24

1987, Feb. 23 Litho.

122 A24 44c In flight .80 .80
123 A24 44c Hanging .80 .80
124 A24 44c Eating .80 .80
125 A24 44c Head .80 .80
a. Block of 4, #122-125 3.25 3.25

Indigenous Flowers — A25

1987-88 Litho. *Perf. 14*

126 A25 1c Ixora casei .15 .15
127 A25 3c Lumnitzera littorea .15 .15
128 A25 5c Sonneratia alba .15 .15
129 A25 10c Tristellateria australasiae .15 .15
130 A25 14c Bikkia palauensis .20 .20
a. Booklet pane of 10 3.00 —
131 A25 15c Limnophila aromatica ('88) .20 .20
a. Booklet pane of 10 ('88) 2.25 —
132 A25 22c Bruguiera gymnorhiza .35 .35
a. Booklet pane of 10 4.00 —
b. Booklet pane, 5 each 14c, 22c 4.00 —
133 A25 25c Fagraea ksid ('88) .40 .40
a. Booklet pane of 10 ('88) 4.00 —
b. Booklet pane, 5 each 15c, 25c ('88) 4.00 —
134 A25 36c Ophiorrhiza palauensis ('88) .55 .55
135 A25 39c Cerbera manghas .60 .60
136 A25 44c Sandera indica .70 .70
137 A25 45c Maesa canfieldiae ('88) .70 .70
138 A25 50c Dolichandrone spathacea .85 .85
139 A25 $1 Barringtonia racemosa 1.60 1.60
140 A25 $2 Nepenthes mirabilis 3.25 3.25
141 A25 $5 Dendrobium palawense 8.00 8.00

Size: 49x28mm

142 A25 $10 Bouquet ('88) 13.00 13.00
Nos. 126-142 (17) 31.00 31.00

Issue dates: Mar. 12. $10, Mar. 17. 15c, 25c, 36c, 45c, July 1. Nos. 131a, 133a-133b, July 5.

CAPEX '87 A26

1987, June 15 Litho. *Perf. 14*

146 A26 22c Babeldaob Is. .45 .45
147 A26 22c Floating Garden Isls. .45 .45
148 A26 22c Rock Is. .45 .45
149 A26 22c Koror .45 .45
a. Block of 4, #146-149 1.80 1.80

Seashells Type of 1986

1987, Aug. 25 Litho. *Perf. 14*

150 A20 22c Black-striped triton .55 .55
151 A20 22c Tapestry turban .55 .55
152 A20 22c Adusta murex .55 .55
153 A20 22c Little fox miter .55 .55
154 A20 22c Cardinal miter .55 .55
a. Strip of 5, #150-154 2.75 2.75

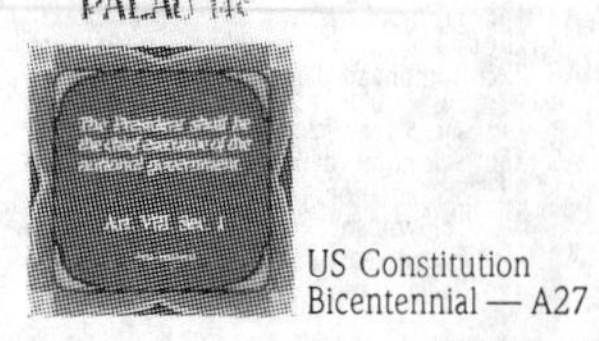

US Constitution Bicentennial — A27

Excerpts from Articles of the Palau and US Constitutions and Seals.

1987, Sept. 17 Litho. *Perf. 14*

155 A27 14c Art. VIII, Sec. 1, Palau .20 .20
156 A27 14c Presidential seals .20 .20
157 A27 14c Art. II, Sec. 1, US .20 .20
a. Triptych + label, #155-157 .60 .60
158 A27 22c Art. IX, Sec. 1, Palau .35 .35
159 A27 22c Legislative seals .35 .35
160 A27 22c Art. I, Sec. 1, US .35 .35
a. Triptych + label, #158-160 1.05 1.05
161 A27 44c Art X, Sec. 1, Palau .70 .70
162 A27 44c Supreme Court seals .70 .70
163 A27 44c Art. III, Sec. 1, US .70 .70
a. Triptych + label, #161-163 2.10 2.10
Nos. 155-163 (9) 3.75 3.75

Triptychs printed se-tenant with inscribed label picturing national flags.

Japanese Links to Palau — A28

Japanese stamps, period cancellations and installations: 14c, No. 257 and 1937 Datsun sedan used as mobile post office, near Ngerchelechuus Mountain. 22c, No. 347 and phosphate mine at Angaur. 33c, No. B1 and Japan Airways DC-2 over stone monuments at Badrulchau. 44c, No. 201 and Japanese post office, Koror. $1, Aviator's Grave, Japanese Cemetary, Peleliu, vert.

1987, Oct. 16 Litho. *Perf. 14x13½*

164 A28 14c multicolored .30 .30
165 A28 22c multicolored .45 .45
166 A28 33c multicolored .65 .65
167 A28 44c multicolored .85 .85
Nos. 164-167 (4) 2.25 2.25

Souvenir Sheet

Perf. 13½x14

168 A28 $1 multicolored 1.90 1.90

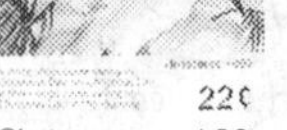

Christmas — A30 Symbiotic Marine Species — A31

Verses from carol "I Saw Three Ships," Biblical characters, landscape and Palauans in outrigger canoes.

1987, Nov. 24 Litho. *Perf. 14*

173 A30 22c I saw... .45 .45
174 A30 22c And what was... .45 .45
175 A30 22c 'Twas Joseph... .45 .45
176 A30 22c Saint Michael... .45 .45
177 A30 22c And all the bells... .45 .45
a. Strip of 5, #173-177 2.25 2.25

1987, Dec. 15

Designs: No. 178, Snapping shrimp, goby. No. 179, Mauve vase sponge, sponge crab. No. 180, Pope's damselfish, cleaner wrasse. No. 181, Clown anemone fish, sea anemone. No. 182, Four-color nudibranch, banded coral shrimp.

178 A31 22c multicolored .50 .50
179 A31 22c multicolored .50 .50
180 A31 22c multicolored .50 .50
181 A31 22c multicolored .50 .50
182 A31 22c multicolored .50 .50
a. Strip of 5, #178-182 2.50 2.50

Butterflies and Flowers Type of 1987

Designs: No. 183, Dannaus plexippus, Tournefotia argentia. No. 184, Papilio machaon, Citrus reticulata. No. 185, Captopsilia, Crataeva speciosa. No. 186, Colias philodice, Crataeva speciosa.

1988, Jan. 25

183 A23a 44c multicolored .75 .75
184 A23a 44c multicolored .75 .75
185 A23a 44c multicolored .75 .75
186 A23a 44c multicolored .75 .75
a. Block of 4, #183-186 3.00 3.00

Ground-dwelling Birds — A32

1988, Feb. 29 Litho. *Perf. 14*

187 A32 44c Whimbrel .75 .75
188 A32 44c Yellow bittern .75 .75
189 A32 44c Rufous night-heron .75 .75
190 A32 44c Banded rail .75 .75
a. Block of 4, #187-190 3.00 3.00

Seashells Type of 1986

1988, May 11 Litho. *Perf. 14*

191 A20 25c Striped engina .55 .55
192 A20 25c Ivory cone .55 .55
193 A20 25c Plaited miter .55 .55
194 A20 25c Episcopal miter .55 .55
195 A20 25c Isabelle cowrie .55 .55
a. Strip of 5, #191-195 2.75 2.75

Souvenir Sheet

Postal Independence, 5th Anniv. — A33

FINLANDIA '88: a, Kaep (pre-European outrigger sailboat). b, Spanish colonial cruiser. c, German colonial cruiser SMS Cormoran, c. 1885. d, Japanese mailbox, WWII machine gun, Koror Museum. e, US Trust Territory ship, Malakal Harbor. f, Koror post office.

1988, June 8 Litho. *Perf. 14*

196 Sheet of 6 2.50 2.50
a.-f. A33 25c multicolored .40 .40

Souvenir Sheet

US Possessions Phil. Soc., 10th Anniv. — A34

PRAGA '88: a, "Collect Palau Stamps," original artwork for No. 196f and head of a man. b, Soc. emblem. c, Nos. 1-4. d, China Clipper original artwork and covers. e, Man and boy studying covers. f, Girl at show cancel booth.

1988, Aug. 26 Litho. *Perf. 14*

197 A34 Sheet of 6 4.25 4.25
a.-f. 45c any single .70 .70

Christmas — A35

Hark! The Herald Angels Sing: No. 198, Angels playing the violin, singing and sitting. No. 199, 3 angels and 3 children. No. 200, Nativity. No. 201, 2 angels, birds. No. 202, 3 children and 2 angels playing horns. Se-tenant in a continuous design.

1988, Nov. 7 Litho. *Perf. 14*

198 A35 25c multicolored .45 .45
199 A35 25c multicolored .45 .45
200 A35 25c multicolored .45 .45
201 A35 25c multicolored .45 .45
202 A35 25c multicolored .45 .45
a. Strip of 5, #199-202 2.25 2.25

Miniature Sheet

Chambered Nautilus — A36

Designs: a, Fossil and cross section. b, Palauan *bai* symbols for the nautilus. c, Specimens trapped for scientific study. d, *Nautilus belauensis, pompilius, macromphalus, stenomphalus* and *scrobiculatus*. e, Release of a tagged nautilus.

1988, Dec. 23 Litho. *Perf. 14*
203 A36 Sheet of 5 2.75 2.75
a.-e. 25c multicolored .55 .55

Endangered Birds of Palau — A37

1989, Feb. 9 Litho. *Perf. 14*
204 A37 45c Nicobar pigeon .75 .75
205 A37 45c Ground dove .75 .75
206 A37 45c Micronesian megapode .75 .75
207 A37 45c Owl .75 .75
a. Block of 4, #204-207 3.00 3.00

Exotic Mushrooms — A38

1989, Mar. 16 Litho. *Perf. 14*
208 A38 45c Gilled auricularia .75 .75
209 A38 45c Rock mushroom .75 .75
210 A38 45c Polyporous .75 .75
211 A38 45c Veiled stinkhorn .75 .75
a. Block of 4, #208-211 3.00 3.00

Seashell Type of 1986

1989, Apr. 12 Litho. *Perf. 14x14½*
212 A20 25c Robin redbreast triton .50 .50
213 A20 25c Hebrew cone .50 .50
214 A20 25c Tadpole triton .50 .50
215 A20 25c Lettered cone .50 .50
216 A20 25c Rugose miter .50 .50
a. Strip of 5, #212-216 2.50 2.50

Palau stamps can be mounted in the Scott U.S. Trust Territories album.

Souvenir Sheet

A Little Bird, Amidst Chrysanthemums, 1830s, by Hiroshige (1797-1858) — A39

1989, May 17 Litho. *Perf. 14*
217 A39 $1 multicolored 1.90 1.90

Hirohito (1901-1989) and enthronement of Akihito as emperor of Japan.

Miniature Sheet

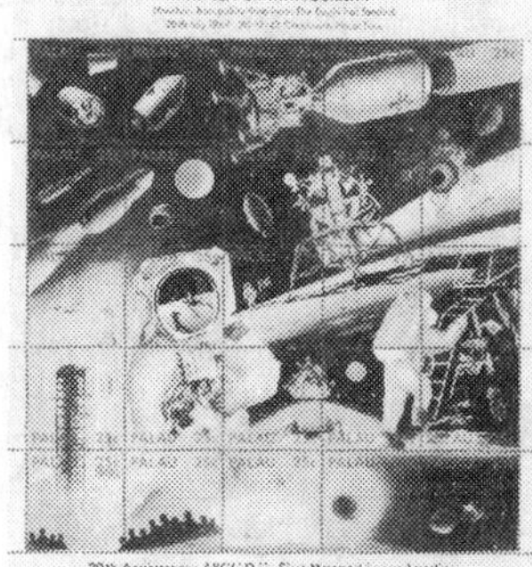

First Moon Landing, 20th Anniv. — A40

Apollo 11 mission: a, Third stage jettison. b, Lunar spacecraft. c, Module transposition *(Eagle)*. d, *Columbia* module transposition (command module). e, *Columbia* module transposition (service module). f, Third stage burn. g, Vehicle entering orbit, Moon. h, *Columbia* and *Eagle*. i, *Eagle* on the Moon. j, *Eagle* in space. k, Three birds, Saturn V third stage, lunar spacecraft and escape tower. l, Astronaut's protective visor, pure oxygen system. m, Astronaut, American flag. n, Footsteps on lunar plain Sea of Tranquillity, pure oxygen system. o, Armstrong descending from *Eagle*. p, Mobile launch tower, Saturn V second stage. q, Space suit remote control unit and oxygen hoses. r, *Eagle* lift-off from Moon. s, Armstrong's first step on the Moon. t, Armstrong descending ladder, module transposition *(Eagle* and *Columbia)*. u, Launch tower, spectators and Saturn V engines achieving thrust. v, Spectators, clouds of backwash. w, Parachute splashdown, U.S. Navy recovery ship and helicopter. x, Command module reentry. y, Jettison of service module prior to reentry.

1989, July 20 Litho. *Perf. 14*
218 A40 Sheet of 25 10.50 10.50
a.-y. 25c any single .40 .40

Buzz Aldrin Photographed on the Moon by Neil Armstrong A41

1989, July 20 *Perf. 13½x14*
219 A41 $2.40 multicolored 4.25 4.25

First Moon landing 20th anniv.

Literacy — A42

Imaginary characters and children reading: a, Youth astronaut. b, Boy riding dolphin. c, Cheshire cat in palm tree. d, Mother Goose. e, New York Yankee at bat. f, Girl reading. g, Boy reading. h, Mother reading to child. i, Girl holding flower and listening to story. j, Boy dressed in baseball uniform. Printed se-tenant in a continuous design.

1989, Oct. 13 Litho. *Perf. 14*
220 Block of 10 4.00 4.00
a.-j. A42 25c any single .40 .40

No. 220 printed in sheets containing two blocks of ten with strip of 5 labels between. Inscribed labels contain book, butterflies and "Give Them / Books / Give Them / Wings."

Miniature Sheet

Stilt Mangrove Fauna — A43

World Stamp Expo '89: a, Bridled tern. b, Sulphur butterfly. c, Mangrove flycatcher. d, Collared kingfisher. e, Fruit bat. f, Estuarine crocodile. g, Rufous night-heron. h, Stilt mangrove. i, Bird's nest fern. j, Beach hibiscus tree. k, Common eggfly. l, Dog-faced watersnake. m, Jingle shell. n, Palau bark cricket. o, Periwinkle, mangrove oyster. p, Jellyfish. q, Striped mullet. r, Mussels, sea anemones, algae. s, Cardinalfish. t, Snapper.

1989, Nov. 20 Litho. *Perf. 14½*
221 A43 Block of 20 9.00 9.00
a.-t. 25c any single .45 .45

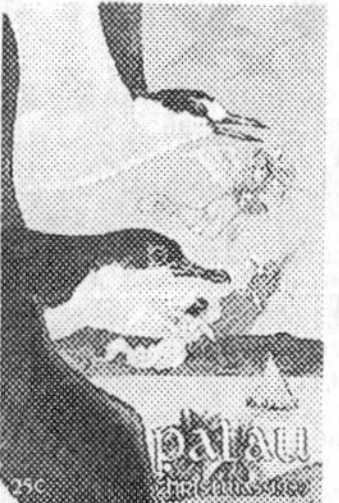

Christmas — A44 Soft Coral — A45

Whence Comes this Rush of Wings? a carol: No. 222, Dusky tern, Audubon's shearwater, angels, island. No. 223, Fruit pigeon, angel. No. 224, Madonna and Child, ground pigeons, fairy terns, rails, sandpipers. No. 225, Angel, blue-headed green finch, red flycatcher, honeyeater. No. 226, Angel, black-headed gulls. Printed se-tenant in a continuous design.

1989, Dec. 18 Litho. *Perf. 14*
222 A44 25c multicolored .50 .50
223 A44 25c multicolored .50 .50
224 A44 25c multicolored .50 .50
225 A44 25c multicolored .50 .50
226 A44 25c multicolored .50 .50
a. Strip of 5, #222-226 2.50 2.50

1990, Jan. 3
227 A45 25c Pink coral .50 .50
228 A45 25c Pink & violet coral .50 .50
229 A45 25c Yellow coral .50 .50
230 A45 25c Red coral .50 .50
a. Block of 4, #227-230 2.00 2.00

Birds of the Forest A46

1990, Mar. 16
231 A46 45c Siberian rubythroat .75 .75
232 A46 45c Palau bush-warbler .75 .75
233 A46 45c Micronesian starling .75 .75
234 A46 45c Cicadabird .75 .75
a. Block of 4, #231-234 3.00 3.00

Miniature Sheet

State Visit of Prince Lee Boo of Palau to England, 1784 A47

Prince Lee Boo, Capt. Henry Wilson and: a, HMS *Victory* docked at Portsmouth. b, St. James's Palace, London. c, Rotherhithe Docks, London. d, Capt. Wilson's residence, Devon. e, Lunardi's Grand English Air Balloon. f, St. Paul's and the Thames. g, Lee Boo's tomb, St. Mary's Churchyard, Rotherhithe. h, St. Mary's Church. i, Memorial tablet, St. Mary's Church.

1990, May 6 Litho. *Perf. 14*
235 Sheet of 9 3.50 3.50
a.-i. A47 25c any single .40 .40

Stamp World London '90.

Souvenir Sheet

Penny Black, 150th Anniv. — A48

1990, May 6
236 A48 $1 Great Britain #1 1.75 1.75

Orchids — A49

1990, June 7 *Perf. 14*
237 A49 45c *Corymborkis veratrifolia* .65 .65
238 A49 45c *Malaxis setipes* .65 .65
239 A49 45c *Dipodium freycinetianum* .65 .65
240 A49 45c *Bulbophyllum micronesiacum* .65 .65
241 A49 45c *Vanda teres* and *hookeriana* .65 .65
a. Strip of 5, #237-241 3.25 3.25

Butterflies and Flowers A50

1990, July 6 Litho. *Perf. 14*

242 A50 45c Wedelia strigulosa	.70	.70
243 A50 45c Erthrina variegata	.70	.70
244 A50 45c Clerodendrum inerme	.70	.70
245 A50 45c Vigna marina	.70	.70
a. Block of 4, #242-245	2.80	2.80

Miniature Sheet

Fairy Tern, Lesser Golden Plover, Sanderling A51

Lagoon life: b, Bidekill fisherman. c, Sailing yacht, insular halfbeaks. d, Palauan kaeps. e, White-tailed tropicbird. f, Spotted eagle ray. g, Great barracuda. h, Reef needlefish. i, Reef blacktip shark. j, Hawksbill turtle. k, Octopus. l, Batfish. m, Lionfish. n, Snowflake moray. o, Porcupine fish, sixfeeler threadfins. p, Blue sea star, regal angelfish, cleaner wrasse. q, Clown triggerfish. r, Spotted garden eel and orange fish. s, Blue-lined sea bream, bluegreen chromis, sapphire damselfish. t, Orangespine unicornfish, white-tipped soldierfish. u, Slatepencil sea urchin, leopard sea cucumber. v, Partridge tun shell. w, Mandarinfish. x, Tiger cowrie. y, Feather starfish, orange-fin anemonefish.

1990, Aug. 10 Litho. *Perf. 15x14½*

246 A51 25c Sheet of 25, #a.-y. 10.50 10.50

Nos. 246a-246y inscribed on reverse.

Pacifica — A52

1990, Aug. 24 Litho. *Perf. 14*

247 A52 45c Mailship, 1890	1.00	1.00
248 A52 45c US #803 on cover, forklift, plane	1.00	1.00
a. Pair, #247-248	2.00	2.00

Christmas — A53

Here We Come A-Caroling: No. 250, Girl with music, poinsettias, doves. No. 251, Boys playing guitar, flute. No. 252, Family. No. 253, Three girls singing.

1990, Nov. 28

249 A53 25c multicolored	.40	.40
250 A53 25c multicolored	.40	.40
251 A53 25c multicolored	.40	.40
252 A53 25c multicolored	.40	.40
253 A53 25c multicolored	.40	.40
a. Strip of 5, #249-253	2.00	2.00

US Forces in Palau, 1944 A54

Designs: No. 254, B-24s over Peleliu. No. 255, LCI launching rockets. No. 256, First Marine Division launching offensive. No. 257, Soldier, children. No. 258, USS *Peleliu*.

1990, Dec. 7

254 A54 45c multicolored	.80	.80
255 A54 45c multicolored	.80	.80
256 A54 45c multicolored	.80	.80
257 A54 45c multicolored	.80	.80
a. Block of 4, #254-257	3.25	3.25

Souvenir Sheet

Perf. 14x13½

258 A54 $1 multicolored 2.00 2.00

No. 258 contains one 51x38mm stamp.

See No. 339 for No. 258 with added inscription.

Coral — A55

1991, Mar. 4 Litho. *Perf. 14*

259 A55 30c Staghorn	.50	.50
260 A55 30c Velvet Leather	.50	.50
261 A55 30c Van Gogh's Cypress	.50	.50
262 A55 30c Violet Lace	.50	.50
a. Block of 4, #259-262	2.00	2.00

Miniature Sheet

Angaur, The Phosphate Island A56

Designs: a, Virgin Mary Statue, Nkulangelul Point. b, Angaur kaep, German colonial postmark. c, Swordfish, Caroline Islands No. 13. d, Phosphate mine locomotive. e, Copra ship off Lighthouse Hill. f, Dolphins. g, Estuarine crocodile. h, Workers cycling to phosphate plant. i, Ship loading phosphate. j, Hammerhead shark, German overseer. k, Marshall Islands No. 15. l, SMS Scharnhorst. m, SMS Emden. n, Crab-eating macaque monkey. o, Great sperm whale. p, HMAS Sydney.

1991, Mar. 14

263 A56 30c Sheet of 16, #a.-p. 7.75 7.75

Nos. 263b-263c, 263f-263g, 263j-263k, 263n-263o printed in continuous design showing map of island.

Birds — A57

Perf. 14½x15, 13x13½

1991-92 Litho.

266 A57	1c Palau bush-warbler	.15	.15
267 A57	4c Common moorhen	.15	.15
268 A57	6c Banded rail	.15	.15
269 A57	19c Palau fantail	.30	.30
b.	Booklet pane, 10 #269	3.00	—
	Complete booklet, #269b	3.00	
270 A57	20c Mangrove flycatcher	.30	.30
271 A57	23c Purple swamphen	.35	.35
272 A57	29c Palau fruit dove	.45	.45
a.	Booklet pane, 5 each #270, #272	4.00	—
	Complete booklet, #272a	4.00	
b.	Booklet pane, 10 #272	4.75	—
	Complete booklet, #272b	4.75	
273 A57	35c Great crested tern	.55	.55
274 A57	40c Pacific reef heron	.60	.60
275 A57	45c Micronesian pigeon	.70	.70
276 A57	50c Great frigatebird	.75	.75
277 A57	52c Little pied cormorant	.80	.80
278 A57	75c Jungle night jar	1.10	1.10
279 A57	95c Cattle egret	1.40	1.40
280 A57	$1.34 Great sulphur-crested cockatoo	2.00	2.00
281 A57	$2 Blue-faced parrotfinch	3.00	3.00
282 A57	$5 Eclectus parrot	7.75	7.75

Size: 52x30mm

283 A57	$10 Palau bush warbler	15.00	15.00
	Nos. 266-283 (18)	35.50	35.50

The 1, 6, 20, 52, 75c, $10 are perf. 14½x15.

Issued: 1, 6, 20, 52, 75c, $5, 4/6/92; $10, 9/10/92; #269b, 272a, 272b, 8/23/91; others, 4/18/91.

Miniature Sheet

Christianity in Palau, Cent. — A58

Designs: a, Pope Leo XIII, 1891. b, Ibedul Ilengelekei, High Chief of Koror, 1871-1911. c, Fr. Marino de la Hoz, Br. Emilio Villar, Fr. Elias Fernandez. d, Fr. Edwin G. McManus (1908-1969), compiler of Palauan-English dictionary. e, Sacred Heart Church, Koror. f, Pope John Paul II.

1991, Apr. 28 *Perf. 14½*

288 A58 29c Sheet of 6, #a.-f. 2.75 2.75

Miniature Sheet

Marine Life A59

Designs: a, Pacific white-sided dolphin. b, Common dolphin. c, Rough-toothed dolphin. d, Bottlenose dolphin. e, Harbor porpoise. f, Killer whale. g, Spinner dolphin, yellowfin tuna. h, Dall's porpoise. i, Finless porpoise. j, Map of Palau, dolphin. k, Dusky dolphin. l, Southern right-whale dolphin. m, Striped dolphin. n, Fraser's dolphin. o, Peale's dolphin. p, Spectacled porpoise. q, Spotted dolphin. r, Hourglass dolphin. s, Risso's dolphin. t, Hector's dolphin.

1991, May 24 Litho. *Perf. 14*

289 A59 29c Sheet of 20, #a.-t. 11.00 11.00

Miniature Sheet

Operations Desert Shield / Desert Storm A60

Designs: a, F-4G Wild Weasel fighter. b, F-117A Stealth fighter. c, AH-64A Apache helicopter. d, TOW missle launcher on M998 HMMWV. e, Pres. Bush. f, M2 Bradley fighting vehicle. g, Aircraft carrier USS Ranger. h, Corvette fast patrol boat. i, Battleship Wisconsin.

1991, July 2 Litho. *Perf. 14*

290 A60 20c Sheet of 9, #a.-i. 3.50 3.50

Size: 38x51mm

291 A60 $2.90 Fairy tern, yellow ribbon 3.75 3.75

Souvenir Sheet

292 A60 $2.90 like #291 4.00 4.00

No. 291 has a white border around design. No. 292 printed in continuous design.

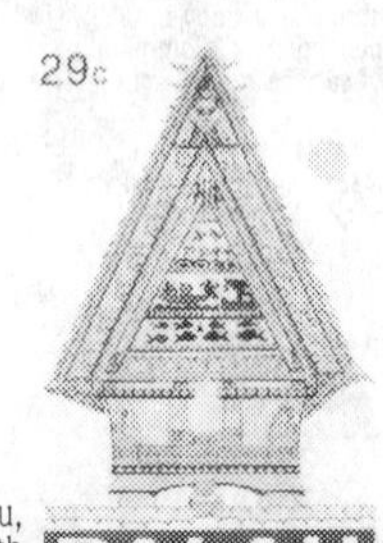

Republic of Palau, 10th Anniv. — A61

Designs: a, Palauan bai. b, Palauan bai interior, denomination UL. c, Same, denomination UR. d, Demi-god Chedechuul. e, Spider, denomination at UL. f, Money bird facing right. g, Money bird facing left. h, Spider, denomination at UR.

1991, July 9 *Perf. 14½*

293 A61 29c Sheet of 8, #a.-h. 4.00 4.00

See No. C21.

Miniature Sheet

Giant Clams A62

Designs: a, Tridacna squamosa, Hippopus hippopus, Hippopus porcellanus, and Tridacna derasa. b, Tridacna gigas. c, Hatchery and tank culture. d, Diver, bottom-based clam nursery. e, Micronesian Mariculture Demonstration Center.

1991, Sept. 17 Litho. *Perf. 14*

294 A62 50c Sheet of 5, #a.-e. 3.50 3.50

No. 294e is 109x17mm and imperf on 3 sides, perf 14 at top.

Miniature Sheet

Japanese Heritage in Palau A63

Designs: No. 295: a, Marine research. b, Traditional arts, carving story boards. c, Agricultural training. d, Archaeological research. e, Training in architecture and building. f, Air transportation. $1, Map, cancel from Japanese post office at Parao.

1991, Nov. 19

295 A63 29c Sheet of 6, #a.-f. 2.75 2.75

Souvenir Sheet

296 A63 $1 multicolored 1.50 1.50

Phila Nippon '91.

Miniature Sheet

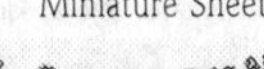

Peace Corps in Palau, 25th Anniv. A64

Children's drawings: No. 297a, Flag, doves, children, and islands. b, Airplane, people being greeted. c, Red Cross instruction. d, Fishing industry. e, Agricultural training. f, Classroom instruction.

1991, Dec. 6 Litho. *Perf. 13½*

297 A64 29c Sheet of 6, #a.-f. 3.00 3.00

Christmas — A65

Silent Night: No. 298: a, Silent night, holy night. b, All is calm, all is bright. c, Round yon virgin, mother and Child. d, Holy Infant, so tender and mild. e, Sleep in heavenly peace.

1991, Nov. 14 *Perf. 14*

298 A65 29c Strip of 5, #a.-e. 2.25 2.25

Miniature Sheet

World War II in the Pacific — A66

Designs: No. 299a, Pearl Harbor attack begins. b, Battleship Nevada gets under way. c, USS Shaw explodes. d, Japanese aircraft carrier Akagi sunk. e, USS Wasp sunk off Guadalcanal. f, Battle of the Philippine Sea. g, US landing craft approach Saipan.

h, US 1st Cavalry on Leyte. i, Battle of Bloody Nose Ridge, Peleliu. j, US troops land on Iwo Jima.

1991, Dec. 6 *Perf. 14½x15*
299 A66 29c Sheet of 10, #a.-j. 4.25 4.25

See No. C22.

A67 A68

Butterflies: a, Troides criton. b, Alcides zodiaca. c, Papillio poboroi. d, Vindula arsinoe.

1992, Jan. 20 Litho. *Perf. 14*
300 A67 50c Block of 4, #a.-d. 3.00 3.00

1992, Mar. 11

Shells: a, Common hairy triton. b, Eglantine cowrie. c, Sulcate swamp cerith. d, Black-spined murex. e, Black-mouth moon.

301 A68 29c Strip of 5, #a.-e. 2.50 2.50

Miniature Sheet

Age of Discovery — A69

Designs: a, Columbus. b, Magellan. c, Drake. d, Wind as shown on old maps.

Maps and: e, Compass rose. f, Dolphin, Drake's ship Golden Hinde. g, Corn, Santa Maria. h, Fish. i, Betel palm, cloves and black pepper. j, Victoria, shearwater and great crested tern. k, White-tailed tropicbird, bicolor parrotfish, pineapple and potatoes. l, Compass. m, Sea monster. n, Paddles and astrolabe. o, Parallel ruler, dividers and Inca gold treasures. p, Back staff.

Portraits: q, Wind, diff. r, Vespucci. s, Pizarro. t, Balboa.

1992, May 25 Litho. *Perf. 14*
302 A69 29c Sheet of 20, #a.-t. 9.50 9.50

Miniature Sheet

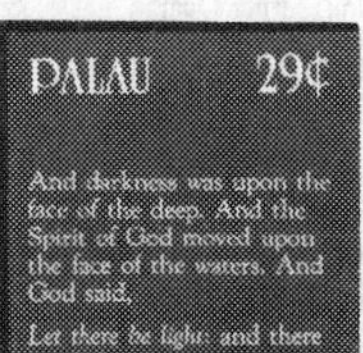

Biblical Creation of the World — A70

Designs: a, "And darkness was..." b, Sun's rays. c, Water, sun's rays. d, "...and it was good." e, "Let there be a..." f, Land forming. g, Water and land. h, "...and it was so." i, "Let the waters..." j, Tree branches. k, Shoreline. l, Shoreline, flowers, tree. m, "Let there be lights..." n, Comet, moon. o, Mountains. p, Sun, hillside. q, "Let the waters..." r, Birds. s, Fish, killer whale. t, Fish. u, "Let the earth..." v, Woman, man. w, Animals. x, "...and it was very good."

1992, June 5 *Perf. 14½*
303 A70 29c Sheet of 24, #a.-x. 10.50 10.50

Nos. 303a-303d, 303e-303h, 303i-303l, 303m-303p, 303q-303t, 303u-303x are blocks of 4.

Souvenir Sheets

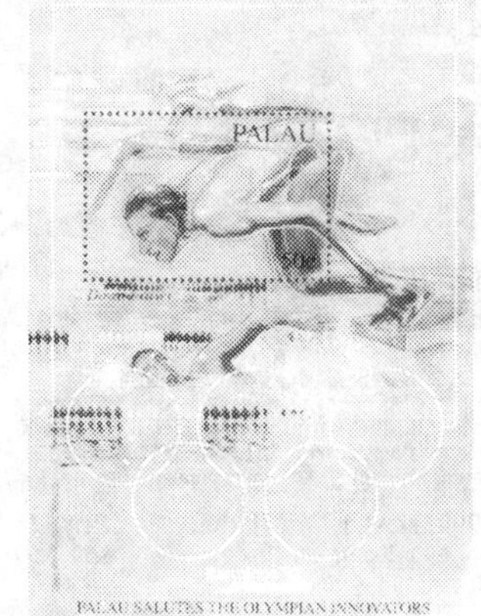

1992 Summer Olympics, Barcelona — A71

1992, July 10 *Perf. 14*

304	A71	50c	Dawn Fraser	.90	.90
305	A71	50c	Olga Korbut	.90	.90
306	A71	50c	Bob Beamon	.90	.90
307	A71	50c	Carl Lewis	.90	.90
308	A71	50c	Dick Fosbury	.90	.90
309	A71	50c	Greg Louganis	.90	.90
			Nos. 304-309 (6)	5.40	5.40

Miniature Sheet

Elvis Presley A72

Various portraits.

1992, Aug. 17 *Perf. 13½x14*
310 A72 29c Sheet of 9, #a.-i. 5.50 5.50

See No. 350.

Christmas — A73

The Friendly Beasts carol depicting animals in Nativity Scene: No. 312a, "Thus Every Beast." b, "By Some Good Spell." c, "In The Stable Dark Was Glad to Tell." d, "Of The Gift He Gave Emanuel." e, "The Gift He Gave Emanuel."

1992, Oct. 1 Litho. *Perf. 14*
312 A73 29c Strip of 5, #a.-e. 2.25 2.25

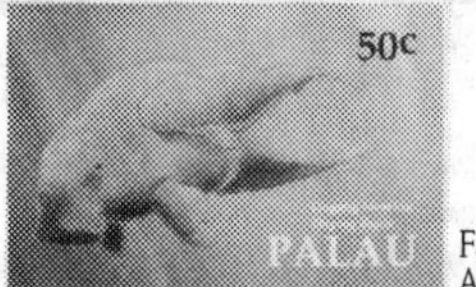

Fauna A74

Designs: a, Dugong. b, Masked booby. c, Macaque. d, New Guinean crocodile.

1993, July 9 Litho. *Perf. 14*
313 A74 50c Block of 4, #a.-d. 3.00 3.00

Seafood A75

Designs: a, Giant crab. b, Scarlet shrimp. c, Smooth nylon shrimp. d, Armed nylon shrimp.

1993, July 22
314 A75 29c Block of 4, #a.-d. 1.90 1.90

Sharks A76

Designs: a, Oceanic whitetip. b, Great hammerhead. c, Leopard. d, Reef black-tip.

1993, Aug. 11 Litho. *Perf. 14½*
315 A76 50c Block of 4, #a.-d. 3.00 3.00

Miniature Sheet

World War II in the Pacific — A77

Actions in 1943: a, US takes Guadalcanal, Feb. b, Hospital ship Tranquility supports action. c, New Guineans join Allies in battle. d, US landings in New Georgia, June. e, USS California participates in every naval landing. f, Dauntless dive bombers over Wake Island, Oct. 6. g, US flamethrowers on Tarawa, Nov. h, US landings on Makin, Nov. i, B-25s bomb Simpson Harbor, Rabaul, Oct. 23. j, B-24s over Kwajalein, Dec. 8.

1993, Sept. 23 Litho. *Perf. 14½x15*
316 A77 29c Sheet of 10, #a.-j. + label 5.75 5.75

See Nos. 325-326.

Christmas — A78

Christmas carol, "We Wish You a Merry Christmas," with Palauan customs: a, Girl, goat. b, Goats, children holding leis, prow of canoe. c, Santa Claus. d, Children singing. e, Family with fruit, fish.

1993, Oct. 22 Litho. *Perf. 14*
317 A78 29c Strip of 5, #a.-e. 2.25 2.25

Miniature Sheet

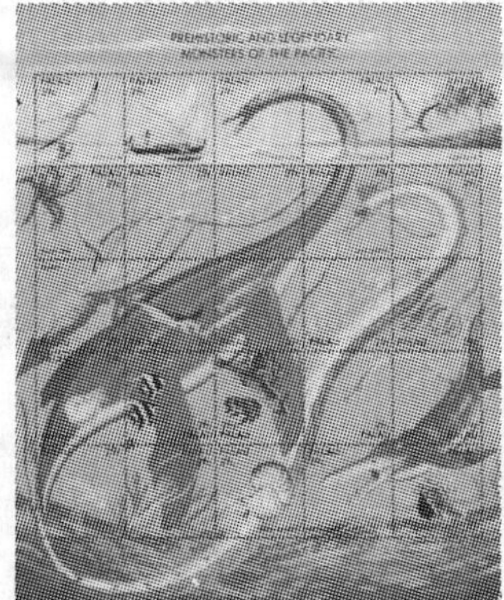

Prehistoric and Legendary Sea Creatures — A79

Illustration reduced.

1993, Nov. 26 Litho. *Perf. 14*
318 A79 29c Sheet of 25, #a.-y. 11.00 11.00

Miniature Sheet

Intl. Year of Indigenous People — A80

Paintings, by Charlie Gibbons: No. 319: a, After Child-birth Ceremony. b, Village in Early Palau.

Storyboard carving, by Ngiraibuuch: $2.90, Quarrying of Stone Money, vert.

1993, Dec. 8 *Perf. 14x13½*
319 A80 29c Sheet of 2 each, a.-b. 1.90 1.90

Souvenir Sheet

Perf. 13½x14

320 A80 $2.90 multicolored 5.00 5.00

Miniature Sheet

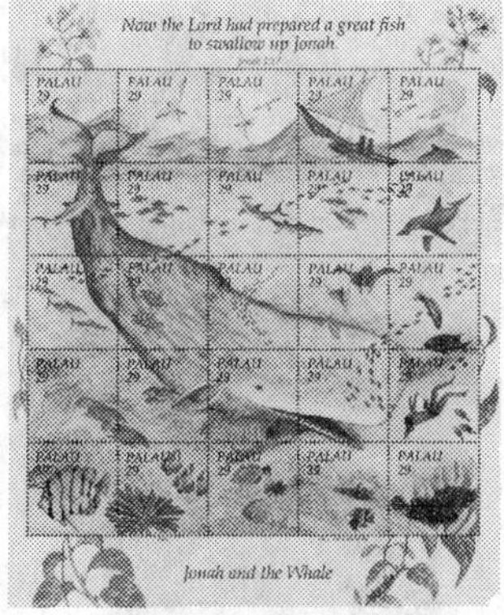

Jonah and the Whale — A81

Illustration reduced.

1993, Dec. 28 Litho. *Perf. 14*
321 A81 29c Sheet of 25, #a.-y. 12.00 12.00

Hong Kong '94 A82

Rays: a, Manta (b). b, Spotted eagle (a). c, Coachwhip (d). d, Black spotted.

1994, Feb. 18 Litho. *Perf. 14*
322 A82 40c Block of 4, #a.-d. 2.50 2.50

Estuarine Crocodile A83

Designs: a, With mouth open. b, Hatchling. c, Crawling on river bottom. d, Swimming.

1994, Mar. 14
323 A83 20c Block of 4, #a.-d. 1.90 1.90

World Wildlife Fund.

Large Seabirds — A84

Designs: a, Red-footed booby. b, Great frigatebird. c, Brown booby. d, Little pied cormorant.

1994, Apr. 22 Litho. *Perf. 14*

324 A84 50c Block of 4, #a.-d. 3.00 3.00

World War II Type of 1993

Miniature Sheets

Action in the Pacific, 1944: No. 325: a, US Marines capture Kwajalien, Feb. 1-7. b, Japanese enemy base at Truk destroyed, Feb. 17-18. c, SS-284 Tullibee participates in Operation Desecrate, March. d, US troops take Saipan, June 15-July 9. e, Great Marianas Turkey Shoot, June 19-20. f, Guam liberated, July-Aug. g, US troops take Peleliu, Sept. 15-Oct. 14. h, Angaur secured in fighting, Sept. 17-22. i, Gen. Douglas MacArthur returns to Philippines, Oct. 20. j, US Army Memorial, Palau, Nov. 27.

D-Day, Allied Invasion of Normandy, June 6, 1944: No. 326: a, C-47 transport aircraft dropping Allied paratroopers. b, Allied warships attack beach fortifications. c, Commandos attack from landing craft. d, Tanks land. e, Sherman flail tank beats path through minefields. f, Allied aircraft attack enemy reinforcements. g, Gliders deliver troops behind enemy lines. h, Pegasus Bridge, first French house liberated. i, Allied forces move inland to form bridgehead. j, View of beach at end of D-Day.

1994, May *Perf. 14½*

Sheets of 10

325 A77 29c #a.-j. + label 4.50 4.50
326 A77 50c #a.-j. + label 8.00 8.00

Pierre de Coubertin (1863-1937) — A85

Winter Olympic medalists: No. 328, Anne-Marie Moser, vert. No. 329, James Craig. No. 330, Katarina Witt. No. 331, Eric Heiden, vert. No. 332, Nancy Kerrigan. $2, Dan Jansen.

1994, July 20 Litho. *Perf. 14*

327 A85 29c multicolored .60 .60

Souvenir Sheets

328 A85 50c multicolored .85 .85
329 A85 50c multicolored .85 .85
330 A85 $1 multicolored 1.65 1.65
331 A85 $1 multicolored 1.65 1.65
332 A85 $1 multicolored 1.65 1.65
333 A85 $2 multicolored 3.25 3.25

Intl. Olympic Committee, cent.

Miniature Sheets of 8

PHILAKOREA '94 — A86

Wildlife carrying letters: No. 334: a, Sailfin goby. b, Sharpnose puffer. c, Lightning butterflyfish. d, Clown anemonefish. e, Parrotfish. f, Batfish. g, Clown triggerfish. h, twinspot wrasse.

No. 335a, Palau fruit bat. b, Crocodile. c, Dugong. d, Banded sea snake. e, Bottle-nosed dophin. f, Hawksbill turtle. g, Octopus. h, Manta ray.

No. 336: a, Palau fantail. b, Banded crake. c, Island swiftlet. d, Micronesian kingfisher. e. Red-footed booby. f, Great frigatebird. g, Palau owl. h, Palau fruit dove.

1994, Aug. 16 Litho. *Perf. 14*

334 A86 29c #a.-h. 4.75 4.75
335 A86 40c #a.-h. 6.50 6.50
336 A86 50c #a.-h. 8.00 8.00

No. 336 is airmail.

Miniature Sheet of 20

First Manned Moon Landing, 25th Anniv. — A87

Various scenes from Apollo moon missions.

1994, July 20

337 A87 29c #a.-t. 10.00 10.00

Independence Day — A88

Designs: No. 338: b, Natl. seal. c, Pres. Kuniwo Nakamura, Palau, US Pres. Clinton. d, Palau, US flags. e, Musical notes of natl. anthem.

1994, Oct. 1 *Perf. 14*

338 A88 29c Strip of 5, #a.-e. 2.50 2.50

No. 338c is 57x42mm.

No. 258 with added text "50th ANNIVERSARY / INVASION OF PELELIU / SEPTEMBER 15, 1944"

1994 Litho. *Perf. 14X13½*

339 A54 $1 multicolored 1.50 1.50

Miniature Sheet of 9

Disney Characters Visit Palau — A89

No. 340: a, Mickey, Minnie arriving. b, Goofy finding way to hotel. c, Donald enjoying beach. d, Minnie, Daisy learning the Ngloik. e, Minnie, Mickey sailing to Natural Bridge. f, Scrooge finding money in Babeldaob jungle. g, Goofy, Napoleon Wrasse. h, Minnie, Clam Garden. i, Grandma Duck weaving basket.

No. 341, Mickey exploring underwater shipwreck. No. 342, Donald visiting Airai Bai on Babeldaob. No. 343, Pluto, Mickey in boat, vert.

1994, Oct. 14 *Perf. 13½x14*

340 A89 29c #a.-i. 5.00 5.00

Souvenir Sheets

341-342 A89 $1 each 1.75 1.75

Perf. 14x13½

343 A89 $2.90 multicolored 5.25 5.25

Miniature Sheet of 12

Intl. Year of the Family — A90

Story of Tebruchel: a, With mother as infant. b, Father. c, As young man. d, Wife-to-be. e, Bringing home fish. f, Pregnant wife. g, Elderly mother. h, Elderly father. i, With first born. j, Wife seated. k, Caring for mother. l, Father, wife and baby.

1994, Nov. 1 Litho. *Perf. 14*

344 A90 20c #a.-l. 3.50 3.50

Christmas — A91

O Little Town of Bethlehem: a, Magi, cherubs. b, Angel, shepherds, sheep. c, Angels, nativity. d, Angels hovering over town, shepherd, sheep. e, Cherubs, doves.

1994, Nov. 23 Litho. *Perf. 14*

345 A91 29c Strip of 5 2.50 2.50

No. 345 is a continuous design and is printed in sheets containing three strips. The bottom strip is printed with se-tenant labels.

Miniature Sheets of 12

1994 World Cup Soccer Championships, US — A92

US coach, players: No. 346: a, Bora Milutinovic. b, Cle Kooiman. c, Ernie Stewart. d, Claudio Reyna. e, Thomas Dooley. f, Alexi Lalas. g, Dominic Kinnear. h, Frank Klopas. i, Paul Caligiuri. j, Marcelo Balboa. k, Cobi Jones. l, US flag, World Cup trohpy.

US players: No. 347a, Tony Meola. b, John Doyle. c, Eric Wynalda. d, Roy Wegerle. e, Fernando Clavijo. f, Hugo Perez. g, John Harkes. h, Mike Lapper. i, Mike Sorber. j, Brad Friedel. k, Tab Ramos. l, Joe-Max Moore.

No. 348: a, Babeto, Brazil. b, Romario, Brazil. c, Franco Baresi, Italy. d, Roberto Baggio, Italy. e, Andoni Zubizarreta, Spain. f, Oleg Salenko, Russia. g, Gheorghe Hagi, Romania. h, Dennis Bergkamp, Netherlands. i, Hristo Stoichkov, Bulgaria. j, Tomas Brolin, Sweden. k, Lothar Matthaus, Germany. l, Arrigo Sacchi, Italy, Carlos Alberto Parreira, Brazil, flags of Italy & Brazil, World Cup trophy.

1994, Dec. 23

346 A92 29c #a.-l. 5.50 5.50
347 A92 29c #a.-l. 5.50 5.50
348 A92 50c #a.-l. 9.50 9.50

Elvis Presley Type of 1992

Miniature Sheet

Various portraits.

1995, Feb. 28 Litho. *Perf. 14*

350 A72 32c Sheet of 9, #a.-i. 5.00 5.00

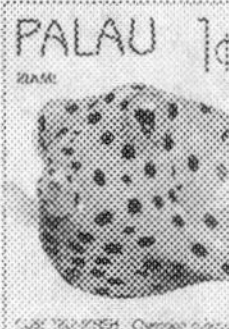

Fish — A93

Type A

A. On two longer sides, groups of eleven and two holes separated by an oval hole equal in width to three holes.

1c, Cube trunkfish. 2c, Lionfish. 3c, Long-jawed squirrelfish. 4c, Longnose filefish. 5c, Ornate butterflyfish. 10c, Yellow seahorse. 20c, Magenta dottyback. 32c, Reef lizardfish. 50c, Multibarred goatfish. 55c, Barred blenny. $1, Fingerprint sharpnose puffer. $2, Longnose hawkfish. $3, Mandarinfish. $5, Blue surgeonfish. $10, Coral grouper.

1995, Apr. 3 Litho. *Perf. 14½*

351 A93 1c multicolored .15 .15
352 A93 2c multicolored .15 .15
353 A93 3c multicolored .15 .15
354 A93 4c multicolored .15 .15
355 A93 5c multicolored .15 .15
356 A93 10c multicolored .15 .15
357 A93 20c multicolored .30 .30
358 A93 32c multicolored .45 .45
359 A93 50c multicolored .70 .70
360 A93 55c multicolored .80 .80
361 A93 $1 multicolored 1.40 1.40
362 A93 $2 multicolored 3.00 3.00
363 A93 $3 multicolored 4.25 4.25
364 A93 $5 multicolored 7.25 7.25

Size: 48x30mm

365 A93 $10 multicolored 15.00 15.00
Nos. 351-365 (15) 34.05 34.05

Booklet Stamps

Size: 18x21mm

Perf. 14x14½ Syncopated Type A

366 A93 20c multicolored .30 .30
a. Booklet pane of 10 3.00
Complete booklet, #366a 3.00
367 A93 32c multicolored .45 .45
a. Booklet pane of 10 4.50
Complete booklet, #367a 4.50
b. Booklet pane of 5 each, #366, 367 3.75
Complete booklet, #367b 3.75

Miniature Sheet of 18

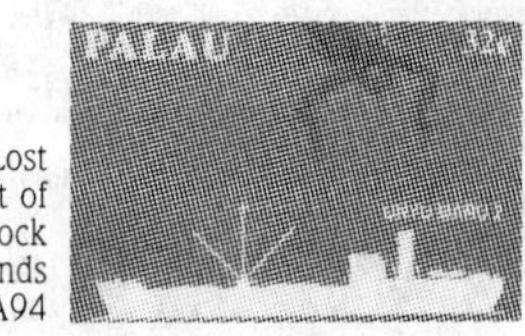

Lost Fleet of the Rock Islands A94

Underwater scenes, silhouettes of Japanese ships sunk during Operation Desecrate, 1944: a, Unyu Maru 2. b, Wakatake. c, Teshio Maru. d, Raizan Maru. e, Chuyo Maru. f, Shinsei Maru. g, Urakami Maru. h, Ose Maru. i, Iro. j, Shosei Maru. k, Patrol boat 31. l, Kibi Maru. m, Amatsu Maru. n, Gozan Maru. o, Matuei Maru. p, Nagisan Maru. q, Akashi. r, Kamikazi Maru.

1995, Mar. 30 Litho. *Perf. 14*

368 A94 32c #a.-r. 9.50 9.50

Miniature Sheet of 18

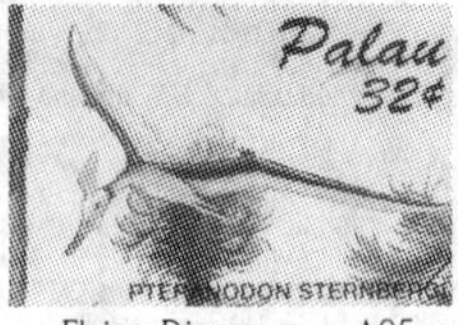

Flying Dinosaurs — A95

Designs: a, Pteranodon sternbergi. b, Pteranodon ingens (a, c). c, Pterodoctyls (b). d, Dorygnathus (e). e, Dimorphodon (f). f, Nyctosaurus (e, c). g, Pterodactylus kochi. h, Ornithodesmus (g, i). i, Diatryma (l). j, Archaeopteryx. k, Campylognathoides (l). l, Gallodactylus. m, Batrachognathus (j). n, Scaphognathus (j, k, m, o). o, Peteinosaurus (l). p, Ichthyorinis. q, Ctenochasma (m, p, r). r, Rhamphorhynchus (n, o, q).

1995 Litho. *Perf. 14*

369 A95 32c #a.-r. 9.50 9.50

Earth Day, 25th anniv.

Miniature Sheet

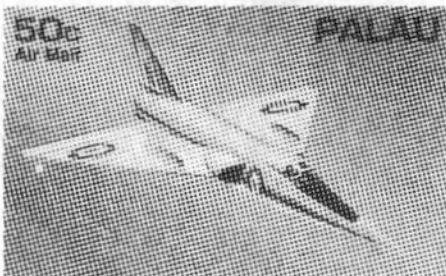

Research & Experimental Jet Aircraft — A96

Designs: a, Fairey Delta 2. b, B-70 "Valkyrie." c, Douglas X-3 "Stilletto." d, Northrop/NASA HL-10. e, Bell XS-1. f, Tupolev Tu-144. g, Bell X-1. h, Boulton Paul P.111. i, EWR VJ 101C. j, Handley Page HP-115. k, Rolls Royce TMR "Flying Bedstead." l, North American X-15.

$2, BAC/Aerospatiale Concorde SST.

1995 Litho. *Perf. 14*

370 A96 50c Sheet of 12, #a.-l. 10.00 10.00

Souvenir Sheet

371 A96 $2 multicolored 3.25 3.25

No. 370 is airmail. No. 371 contains one 85x29mm stamp.

Miniature Sheet of 18

Submersibles — A97

Designs: a, Scuba gear. b, Cousteau diving saucer. c, Jim suit. d, Beaver IV. e, Ben Franklin. f, USS Nautilus. g, Deep Rover. h, Beebe Bathysphere. i, Deep Star IV. j, DSRV. k, Aluminaut. l. Nautile. m, Cyana. n, FNRS Bathyscaphe. o, Alvin. p, Mir 1. q, Archimede. r, Trieste.

1995, July 21 Litho. *Perf. 14*

372 A97 32c #a.-r. 9.50 9.50

Singapore '95 — A98

Designs: a, Dolphins, diver snorkeling, marine life. b, Turtle, diver, seabirds above. c, Fish, coral, crab. d, Coral, fish, diff.

1995, Aug. 15 Litho. *Perf. 13½*

373 A98 32c Block of 4, #a.-d. 2.25 2.25

No. 373 is a continuous design and was issued in sheets of 24 stamps.

UN, FAO, 50th Anniv. A99

Designs: No. 374a, Outline of soldier's helmet, dove, peace. b, Outline of flame, Hedul Gibbons, human rights. c, Books, education. d, Outline of tractor, bananas, agriculture.

No. 375, Palau flag, bird, UN emblem. No. 376, Water being put on plants, UN emblem, vert.

1995, Sept. 15 Litho. *Perf. 14*

374 A99 60c Block of 4, #a.-d. 4.00 4.00

Souvenir Sheets

375 A99 $2 multicolored 3.00 3.00

376 A99 $2 multicolored 3.00 3.00

Independence, 1st Anniv. — A100

Palau flag and: a, Fruit doves. b, Rock Islands. c, Map of islands. d, Orchid, hibiscus.

32c, Marine life.

1995, Sept. 15 *Perf. 14½*

377 A100 20c Block of 4, #a.-d. 1.40 1.40

378 A100 32c multicolored .55 .55

No. 377 was issued in sheets of 16 stamps. See US No. 2999.

Miniature Sheets

A101

End of World War II, 50th Anniv. A102

Paintings by Wm. F. Draper: No. 379a, Preparing Tin-Fish. b, Hellcats Take-off into Palau's Rising Sun. c, Dauntless Dive Bombers over Malakai Harbor. d, Planes Return from Palau. e, Communion Before Battle. f, The Landing. g, First Task Ashore. h, Fire Fighters Save Flak-torn Pilot.

Paintings by Tom Lea: No. 379i, Young Marine Headed for Peleliu. j, Peleliu. k, Last Rites. l, The Thousand-Yard Stare.

Portraits by Albert Murray, vert.: No. 380a, Adm. Chester W. Nimitz. b, Adm. William F. Halsey. c, Adm. Raymond A. Spruance. d, Vice Adm. Marc A. Mitscher. e, Gen. Holland M. Smith, USMC.

$3, Nose art of B-29 Bock's Car.

1995, Oct. 18 *Perf. 14x13½*

379 A101 32c Sheet of 12, #a.-l 7.50 7.50

Perf. 13½x14

380 A101 60c Sheet of 5, #a.-e. 6.00 6.00

Souvenir Sheet

Perf. 14

381 A102 $3 multicolored 5.00 5.00

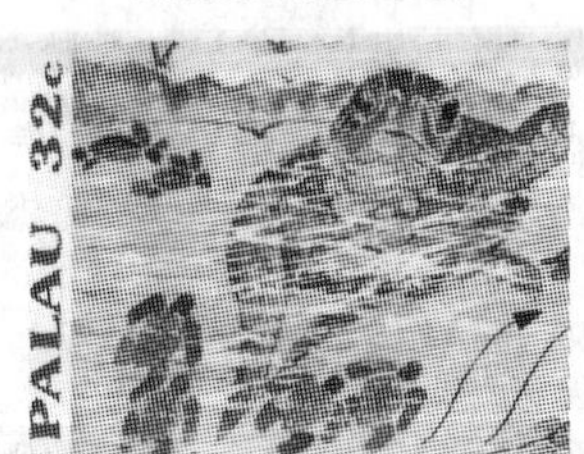

Christmas — A103

Native version of "We Three Kings of Orient Are:" a, Angel, animals. b, Two wise men. c, Joseph, Mary, Jesus in manger. d, Wise man, shepherd, animals. e, Girl with fruit, goat, shepherd.

1995, Oct. 31 Litho. *Perf. 14*

382 A103 32c Strip of 5, #a.-e. 2.75 2.75

No. 382 is a continuous design and was issued in sheets of 15 stamps + 5 labels se-tenant with bottom row of sheet.

Miniature Sheet of 12

Life Cycle of the Sea Turtle — A104

Small turtles, arrows representing routes during life cycle and: a, Large turtle. b, Upper half of turtle shell platter, Palau map. c, Rooster in tree, island scene. d, Native woman. e, Lower half of turtle shell platter, Palau map, island couple. f, Fossil, palm trees, native house

1995, Nov. 15 Litho. *Perf. 14*

383 A104 32c 2 each, #a.-f. 7.00 7.00

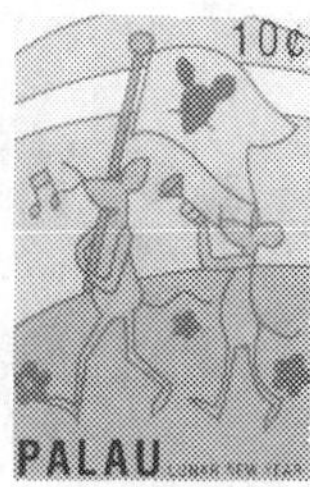

John Lennon (1940-80) — A105

1995, Dec. 8 Litho. *Perf. 14*

384 A105 32c multicolored .65 .65

No. 384 was issued in sheets of 16.

Miniature Sheet

New Year 1996 (Year of the Rat) — A106

Stylized rats in parade: No. 385: a, One carrying flag, one playing horn. b, Three playing musical instruments. c, Two playing instruments. d, Family in front of house.

Mirror images, diff. colors: No. 386: a, Like #385c-385d. b, Like #385a-385b.

1996, Feb. 2 Litho. *Perf. 14*

385 A106 10c Strip of 4, #a.-d. .80 .80

Miniature Sheet

386 A106 60c Sheet of 2, #a.-b. 2.50 2.50

No. 385 was issued in sheets of 2 + 4 labels like No. 386. Nos. 386a-386b are airmail and are each 56x43mm.

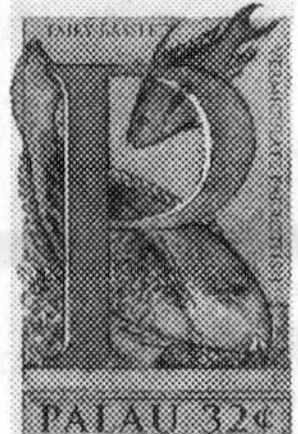

UNICEF, 50th Anniv. — A107

Three different children from Palau in traditional costumes, child in middle wearing: a, Red flowerd dress. b, Pink dress. c, Blue shorts. d, Red headpiece and shorts.

1996, Mar. 12 Litho. *Perf. 14*

387 A107 32c Block of 4, #a.-d. 2.50 2.50

No. 387 was issued in sheets of 4.

Marine Life — A108

Letter spelling "Palau," and: a, "P," fairy basslet, vermiculate parrotfish. b, "A," yellow cardinalfish. c, "L," Marten's butterflyfish. d, "A," starry moray, slate pencil sea urchin. e, "U," cleaner wrasse, coral grouper.

1996, Mar. 29 Litho. *Perf. 14*

388 A108 32c Strip of 5, #a.-e. 3.25 3.25

No. 388 was issued in miniature sheets of 3. China '96, Intl. Stamp Exhibition, Beijing.

Sheets of 9

Capex '96 A109

Circumnavigators of the earth: No. 389: a, Ferdinand Magellan, ship Victoria. b, Charles Wilkes, ship Vincennes. c, Joshua Slocum, oyster boat Spray. d, Ben Carlin, amphibious vehicle Half-Safe. e, Edward L. Beach, submarine USS Triton. f, Naomi James, yacht Express Crusader. g, Sir Ranulf Fiennes, polar vehicle. h, Rick Hansen, wheel chair. i, Robin Knox-Johnson, catamaran Enza New Zealand.

No. 390: a, Lowell Smith, Douglas World Cruisers. b, Ernst Lehmann, Graf Zeppelin. c, Wiley Post, Lockheed Vega Winnie Mae. d, Yuri Gagarin, spacecraft Vostok I. e, Jerrie Mock, Cessna 180 Spirit of Columbus. f, Ross Perot, Jr., Bell Longranger III, Spirit of Texas. g, Brooke Knapp, Gulfstream III, The American Dream. h, Jeana Yeager, Dick Rutan, airplane Voyager. i, Fred Lasby, piper Commanche.

No. 391, Bob Martin, Mark Sullivan, Troy Bradley, Odyssey Gondola. No. 392, Sir Francis Chichester, yacht Gipsy Moth IV.

1996, May 3 Litho. *Perf. 14*

389 A109 32c #a.-i. 5.75 5.75

390 A109 60c #a.-i. 11.00 11.00

Souvenir Sheets

391-392 A109 $3 each 6.00 6.00

No. 390 is airmail.

Miniature Sheet

Disney Sweethearts — A110

Designs: a, Simba, Nala, Timon. b, Bernard, Bianca, Mr. Chairman. c, Georgette, Tito, Oliver. d, Duchess, O'Malley, Marie. e, Bianca, Jake, Polly. f, Tod, Vixey, Copper. g, Robin Hood, Maiden Marian, Alan-a-Dale. h, Thumper, Flower, their sweethearts. i, Pongo, Perdita, puppies.

No. 394, Lady, vert. No. 395, Bambi, Faline.

1996, May 30 Litho. *Perf. 14x13½*

393 A110 60c Sheet of 9, #a.-i. 11.00 11.00

Souvenir Sheets

Perf. 13½x14, 14x13½

394-395 A110 $2 each 4.00 4.00

Jerusalem, 3000th Anniv. — A111

Biblical illustrations of the Old Testament appearing in "In Our Image," by Guy Rowe (1894-1969): Creation, Adam and Eve, Noah and his Wife, Abraham, Jacob's Blessing, Jacob Becomes Israel, Joseph and his Brethren, Moses and the Burning Bush, Moses and the Tablets, Balaam, Joshua, Gideon, Jephthah, Samson, Ruth and Naomi, Saul Anointed, Saul Denouced, David and Jonathan, David and Nathan, David Mourns, Solomon Praying, Solomon Judging, Elijah, Elisha, Job, Isaiah, Jeremiah, Ezekiel, Nebuchadnezzar's Dream, Amos.

1996, June 15 Litho. *Perf. 14*

396 A111 20c Sheet of 30 12.00 12.00

PALAU 60

1996 Summer Olympics, Atlanta A112

No. 397, Fanny Blankers Koen, gold medalist, 1948, vert. No. 398, Bob Mathias, gold medalist, 1948, 1952, vert. No. 399, Torchbearer entering Wembley Stadium, 1948. No. 400, Olympic flag, flags of Palau and U.K. before entrance to Stadium, Olympia, Greece.

Athletes: No. 401: a, Hakeem Olajuwan, US. b, Pat McCormick, US. c, Jim Thorpe, US. d, Jesse Owens, US. e, Tatyana Gutsu, Unified Team. f, Michael Jordan, US. g, Fu Mingxia, China. h, Robert Zmelik, Czechoslovakia. i, Ivan Pedroso, Cuba. j, Nadia Comaneci, Romania. k, Jackie Joyner-Kersee, US. l, Michael Johnson, US. m, Kristin Otto, E. Germany. n, Vitali Scherbo, Unified Team. o, Johnny Weissmuller, US. p, Babe Didrikson, US. q, Eddie Tolan, US. r, Krisztina Egerszegi, Hungary. s, Sawao Kato, Japan. t, Alexander Popov, Unified Team.

1996, June 17 Litho. *Perf. 14*

397 A112 40c multicolored .80 .80
398 A112 40c multicolored .80 .80
a. Pair, #397-398 1.60 1.60
399 A112 60c multicolored 1.20 1.20
400 A112 60c multicolored 1.20 1.20
a. Pair, #399-400 2.40 2.40
401 A112 32c Sheet of 20, #a.-t. 13.00 13.00

Nos. 398a, 400a were each issued in sheets of 20 stamps. No. 401 is a continuous design.

Birds Over Palau Lagoon A113

Designs: a, Lakkotsiang, female. b, Maladaob. c, Belochel (g). d, Lakkotsiang, male. e, Sechosech. f, Mechadelbedaoch (j). g, Laib. h, Cheloteachel. i, Deroech. j, Kerkirs. k, Dudek. l, Lakkotsiang. m, Bedaoch. n, Bedebedchaki. o, Sechou (gray Pacific reef-heron) (p). p, Kekereiderariik. q, Sechou (white Pacific reef-heron). r, Ochaieu. s, Oltirakladial. t, Omechederiibabad.

1996, July 10

402 A113 50c Sheet of 20, #a.-t. 20.00 20.00

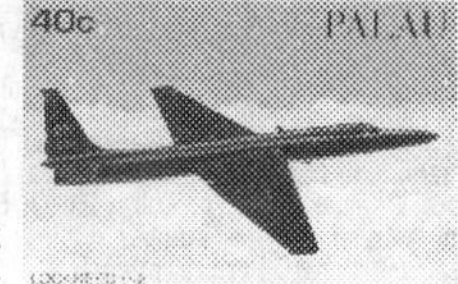

Aircraft A114

Stealth, surveillance, and electronic warfare: No. 403: a, Lockheed U-2. b, General Dynamics EF-111A. c, Lockheed YF-12A. d, Lockheed SR-71. e, Teledyne-Ryan-Tiere II Plus. f, Lockheed XST. g, Lockhood ER-2. h, Lockheed F-117A Nighthawk. i, Lockheed EC-130E. j, Ryan Firebee. k, Lockheed Martin/Boeing "Darkstar." l, Boeing E-3A Sentry.

No. 404: a, Northrop XB-35. b, Leduc O.21. c, Convair Model 118. d, Blohm Und Voss BV 141. e, Vought V-173. f, McDonnell XF-85 Goblin. g, North American F-82B Twin Mustang. h, Lockheed XFV-1. i, Northrop XP-79B. j, Saunders Roe SR/A1. k, Caspian Sea Monster. l, Grumman X-29.

No. 405, Northrop B-2A Stealth Bomber. No. 406, Martin Marietta X-24B.

1996, Sept. 9 Litho. *Perf. 14*

403 A114 40c Sheet of 12, #a.-l. 9.50 9.50
404 A114 60c Sheet of 12, #a.-l. 14.40 14.40

Souvenir Sheets

405 A114 $3 multicolored 6.00 6.00
406 A114 $3 multicolored 6.00 6.00

No. 404 is airmail. No. 406 contains one 85x28mm stamp.

Independence, 2nd Anniv. — A115

Paintings, by Koh Sekiguchi: No. 407, "In the Blue Shade of Trees-Palau (Kirie). No. 408 "The Birth of a New Nation (Kirie).

1996, Oct. 1 Litho. *Perf. 14½*

407 A115 20c multicolored .40 .40
408 A115 20c multicolored .40 .40
a. Pair, #407-408 .80 .80

No. 408a was issued in sheets of 16 stamps.

Christmas — A116

Christmas trees: a, Pandanus. b, Mangrove. c, Norfolk Island pine. d, Papaya. e, Casuarina.

1996, Oct. 8 *Perf. 14*

409 A116 32c Strip of 5, #a.-e. 3.25 3.25

No. 409 was issued in sheets of 3.

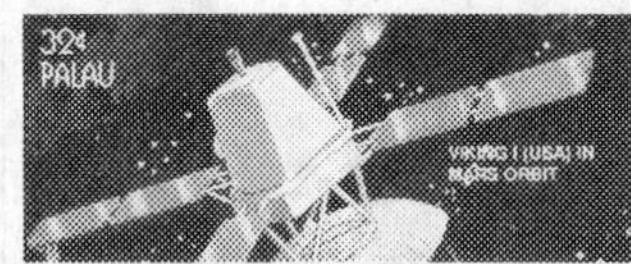

Voyage to Mars — A117

No. 410: a, Viking 1 (US) in Mars orbit. b, Mars Lander fires de-orbit engines. c, Viking 1 symbol (top). d, Viking 1 symbol (bottom). e, Martian moon phobos. f, Mariner 9 in Mars orbit. g, Viking lander enters Martian atmosphere. h, Parachute deploys for Mars landing, heat shield jettisons. i, Proposed manned mission to Mars, 21st cent., US-Russian spacecraft (top). j, US-Russian spacecraft (botton). k, Lander descent engines fire for Mars landing. l, Viking 1 lands on Mars, July 20, 1976.

No. 411, NASA Mars rover. No. 412, NASA water probe on Mars. Illustration reduced.

1996, Nov. 8 Litho. *Perf. 14x14½*

410 A117 32c Sheet of 12, #a.-l. 7.75 7.75

Souvenir Sheets

411-412 A117 $3 each 6.00 6.00

No. 411 contains one 38x30mm stamp.

Souvenir Sheet

South Pacific Commission, 50th Anniv. — A118

Illustration reduced.

1997, Feb. 6 Litho. *Perf. 14*

413 A118 $1 multicolored 2.00 2.00

Hong Kong '97 — A119

Flowers: 1c, Pemphis acidula. 2c, Sea lettuce. 3c, Tropical almond. 4c, Guettarda. 5c, Pacific coral bean. $3, Sea hibiscus.

No. 420: a, Black mangrove. b, Cordia. c, Lantern tree. d, Palau rock-island flower.

No. 421: a, Fish-poison tree. b, Indian mulberry. c, Pacific poison-apple. d, Ailanthus.

Perf. 14½, 13½ (#419)

1997, Feb. 12

414-419 A119 Set of 6 6.25 6.25
420 A119 32c Block of 4, #a.-d. 2.50 2.50
421 A119 50c Block of 4, #a.-d. 4.00 4.00

Size of No. 419 is 73x48mm.

Nos. 420-421 were each issued in sheets of 16 stamps.

Bicent. of the Parachute A120

Uses of parachute: No. 422: a, Apollo 15 Command Module landing safely. b, "Caterpillar Club" flyer ejecting safely over land. c. Skydiving team formation. d, Parasailing. e, Military parachute demonstration teams. f, Parachute behind dragster. g, Dropping cargo from C-130 aircraft. h, "Goldfish Club" flyer ejecting safely at sea.

No. 423: a, Demonstrating parachute control. b, A.J. Gernerin, first succussful parachute descent, 1797. c, Slowing down world land-speed record breaking cars. d, Dropping spies behind enemy lines. e, C-130E demonstrating "LAPES." f, Parachutes used to slow down high performance aircraft. g, ARD parachutes. g, US Army parachutist flying Parafoil.

No. 424 Training tower at Ft. Benning, Georgia. No. 425, "Funny Car" safety chute.

Perf. 14½x14, 14x14½

1997, Mar. 13 Litho.

422 A120 32c Sheet of 8, #a.-h. 5.25 5.25
423 A120 60c Sheet of 8, #a.-h. 9.75 9.75

Souvenir Sheets

Perf. 14

424-425 A120 $2 each 4.00 4.00

Nos. 422a-423a, 422b-423b, 422g-423g, 422h-423h are 20x48mm. No. 424 contains one 28x85mm, No. 425 one 57x42mm stamps.

No. 423 is airmail.

Postage Stamp Mega-Event, NYC, Mar. 1997 (#422-423).

Native Birds — A121

a, Gray duck, banana tree. b, Red junglefowl, calamondin. c, Nicobar pigeon, fruited parinari tree. d, Cardinal honeyeater, wax apple tree. e, Yellow bittern, purple swamphen, giant taro, taro. f, Eclectus parrot, pangi football fruit tree. g, Micronesian pigeon, Rambutan. h, Micronesian starling, mango tree. i, Fruit bat, breadfruit tree. j, Collared kingfisher, coconut palm. k, Palau fruit dove, sweet orange tree. l, Chestnut mannikin, sour-sop tree.

1997, Mar. 27 Litho. *Perf. 13½x14*

426 A121 20c Sheet of 12, #a.-l. 4.75 4.75

UNESCO, 50th Anniv. — A122

Sites in Japan, vert: Nos. 427: a, c-h, Himeji-jo. b, Kyoto.

Sites in Germany: Nos. 428: a-b, Augustusburg Castle. c, Falkenlust Castle. d, Roman ruins, Trier. e, Historic house, Trier.

No. 429, Forest, Shirakami-Sanchi, Japan. No. 430, Yakushima, Japan.

Perf. 13½x14, 14x13½

1997, Apr. 7 Litho.

Sheets of 8 or 5 + Label

427 A122 32c #a.-h. 5.25 5.25
428 A122 60c #a.-e. 6.00 6.00

Souvenir Sheets

429-430 A122 $2 each 4.00 4.00

A123 A124

Paintings by Hiroshige (1797-1858): No. 431: a, Swallows and Peach Blossoms under a Full Moon. b, A Parrot on a Flowering Branch. c, Crane and Rising Sun. d, Cock, Umbrella, and Morning Glories. e, A Titmouse Hanging Head Downward on a Camellia Branch.

No. 432, Falcon on a Pine Tree with the Rising Sun. No. 433, Kingfisher and Iris.

1997, June 2 Litho. *Perf. 14*

431 A123 32c Sheet of 5, #a.-e. 3.75 3.75

Souvenir Sheets

432-433 A123 $2 each 4.00 4.00

1997 Litho. *Perf. 14*

Volcano Goddesses of the Pacific: a, Darago, Philippines. b, Fuji, Japan. c, Pele, Hawaii. d, Pare, Maori. e, Dzalarhons, Haida. f, Chuginadak, Aleuts.

434 A124 32c Sheet of 6, #a.-f. 3.75 3.75

PACIFIC 97.

Independence, 3rd Anniv. — A125

1997, Oct. 1 Litho. *Perf. 14*

435 A125 32c multicolored .65 .65

No. 435 was issued in sheets of 12.

Oceanographic Research A126

Ships: No. 436: a, Albatross. b, Mabahiss. c, Atlantis II. d, Xarifa. e, Meteor. f, Egabras III. g, Discoverer. h, Kaiyo. i, Ocean Defender.

No. 437, Jacques-Yves Cousteau (1910-97). No. 438, Cousteau, diff., vert. No. 439, Pete Seeger, vert.

1997, Oct. 1 *Perf. 14x14½, 14½x14*

436 A126 32c Sheet of 9, #a.-i. 5.75 5.75

Souvenir Sheets

437-439 A126 $2 each 4.00 4.00

Diana, Princess of Wales (1961-97) A127

1997, Nov. 26 Litho. *Perf. 14*

440 A127 60c multicolored 1.20 1.20

No. 440 was issued in sheets of 6.

Disney's "Let's Read" — A128

Various Disney characters: No. 447: a, "Exercise your right to read." b, "Reading is the ultimate luxury." c, "Share your knowledge." d, "Start them Young." e, "Reading is fundamental." f, "The insatiable reader." g, "Reading time is anytime." h, "Real men read." i, "I can read by myself."

No. 448, Daisy, "The library is for everyone," vert. No. 449, Mickey, "Books are magical."

Perf. 13½x14, 14x13½

1997, Oct. 21

447 A128 32c Sheet of 9, #a.-i. 5.75 5.75

Souvenir Sheets

448 A128 $2 multicolored 4.00 4.00
449 A128 $3 multicolored 6.00 6.00

Christmas — A129

Children singing Christmas carol, "Some Children See Him:" No. 450: a, Girl, boy in striped shirt. b, Boy, girl in pigtails. c, Girl, boy, Madonna and Child. d, Girl, two children. e, Boy, girl with long black hair.

1997, Oct. 28 *Perf. 14*

450 A129 32c Strip of 5, #a.-e. 3.20 3.20

No. 450 was issued in sheets of 3 strips, bottom strip printed se-tenant with 5 labels containing lyrics.

Souvenir Sheets

New Year 1998 (Year of the Tiger) — A130

Chinese toys in shape of tiger: No. 451, White background. No. 452, Green background.
Illustration reduced.

1998, Jan. 2 Litho. *Perf. 14*

451 A130 50c multicolored 1.00 1.00
452 A130 50c multicolored 1.00 1.00

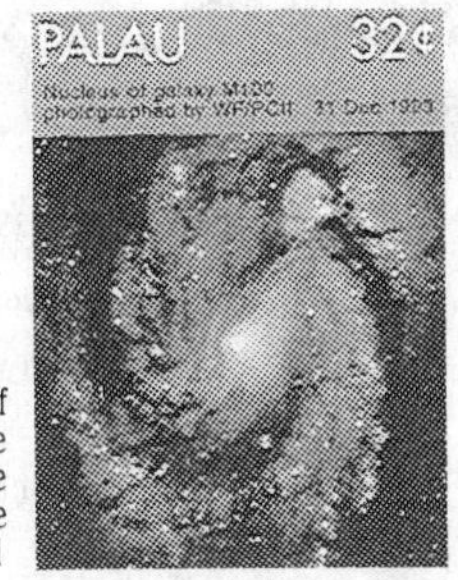

Repair of Hubble Space Telescope A131

No. 453: a, Photograph of nucleus of galaxy M100. b, Top of Hubble telescope with solar arrays folded. c, Astronaut riding robot arm. d, Astronaut anchored to robot arm. e, Astronaut in cargo space with Hubble mounted to shuttle Endeavor. f, Hubble released after repair.

No. 454, Hubble cutaway, based on NASA schematic drawing. No. 455, Edwin Hubble (1889-1953), astronomer who proved existence of star systems beyond Milky Way. No. 456, Hubble Mission STS-82/Discovery.

1998, Mar. 9 Litho. *Perf. 14*

453 A131 32c Sheet of 6, #a.-f. 3.75 3.75

Souvenir Sheets

454-456 A131 $2 each 4.00 4.00

Mother Teresa (1910-97) — A132

Various portraits.

1998, Mar. 12 Litho. *Perf. 14*

457 A132 60c Sheet of 4, #a.-d. 4.75 4.75

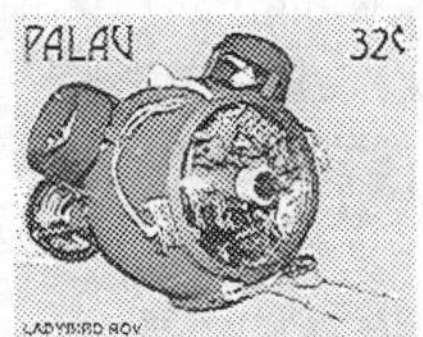

Deep Sea Robots A133

No. 458: a, Ladybird ROV. b, Slocum Glider. c, Hornet. d, Scorpio. e, Odyssey AUV. f, Jamstec Survey System Launcher. g, Scarab. h, USN Torpedo Finder/Salvager. i, Jamstec Survey System Vehicle. j, Cetus Tether. k, Deep Sea ROV. l, ABE. m, OBSS. n, RCV 225G Swimming Eyeball. o, Japanese UROV. p, Benthos RPV. q, CURV. r, Smartie.

No. 459, Jason Jr. inspecting Titanic. No. 460, Dolphin 3K.

1998, Apr. 21

458 A133 32c Sheet of 18, #a.-r. 11.50 11.50

Souvenir Sheets

459-460 A133 $2 each 4.00 4.00

UNESCO Intl. Year of the Ocean.

SEMI-POSTAL STAMPS

Olympic Sports SP1

1988, Aug. 8 Litho. *Perf. 14*

B1 SP1 25c +5c Baseball glove, player .50 .50
B2 SP1 25c +5c Running shoe, athlete .50 .50
a. Pair, #B1-B2 1.00 1.00
B3 SP1 45c +5c Goggles, swimmer 1.00 1.00
B4 SP1 45c +5c Gold medal, diver 1.00 1.00
a. Pair, #B3-B4 2.00 2.00

AIR POST STAMPS

White-tailed Tropicbird AP1

1984, June 12 Litho. *Perf. 14*

C1 AP1 40c shown .70 .70
C2 AP1 40c Fairy tern .70 .70
C3 AP1 40c Black noddy .70 .70
C4 AP1 40c Black-naped tern .70 .70
a. Block of 4, #C1-C4 2.80 2.80

Audubon Type of 1985

1985, Feb. 6 Litho. *Perf. 14*

C5 A12 44c Audubon's Shearwater .80 .80

Palau-Germany Political, Economic & Cultural Exchange Cent. — AP2

Germany Nos. 40, 65, Caroline Islands Nos. 19, 13 and: No. C6, German flag-raising at Palau, 1885. No. C7, Early German trading post in Angaur. No. C8, Abai architecture recorded by Prof. & Frau Kramer, 1908-1910. No. C9, S.M.S. Cormoran.

1985, Sept. 19 Litho. *Perf. 14x13½*

C6 AP2 44c multicolored .80 .80
C7 AP2 44c multicolored .80 .80
C8 AP2 44c multicolored .80 .80
C9 AP2 44c multicolored .80 .80
a. Block of 4, #C6-C9 3.25 3.25

Trans-Pacific Airmail Anniv. Type of 1985

Aircraft: No. C10, 1951 Trans-Ocean Airways PBY-5A Catalina Amphibian. No. C11, 1968 Air Micronesia DC-6B Super Cloudmaster. No. C12, 1960 Trust Territory Airline SA-16 Albatross. No. C13, 1967 Pan American Douglas DC-4.

1985, Nov. 21 Litho. *Perf. 14*

C10 A16 44c multicolored .75 .75
C11 A16 44c multicolored .75 .75
C12 A16 44c multicolored .75 .75
C13 A16 44c multicolored .75 .75
a. Block of 4, #C10-C13 3.00 3.00

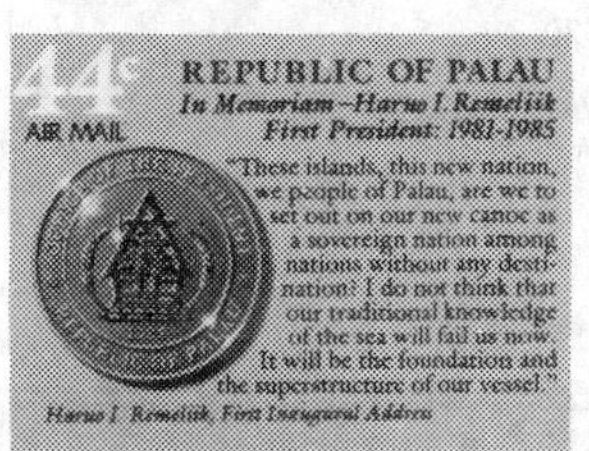

Haruo I. Remeliik (1933-1985), 1st President — AP3

Designs: No. C14, Presidential seal, excerpt from 1st inaugural address. No. C15, War canoe, address excerpt, diff. No. C16, Remeliik, US Pres. Reagan, excerpt from Reagan's speech, Pacific Basin Conference, Guam, 1984.

1986, June 30 Litho. *Perf. 14*

C14 AP3 44c multicolored 1.00 1.00
C15 AP3 44c multicolored 1.00 1.00
C16 AP3 44c multicolored 1.00 1.00
a. Strip of 3, #C14-C16 3.00 3.00

Intl. Peace Year, Statue of Liberty Cent. — AP4

1986, Sept. 19 Litho.

C17 AP4 44c multicolored .90 .90

Aircraft — AP5

Birds — AP6

1989, May 17 Litho. *Perf. 14x14½*

C18 AP5 36c Cessna 207 Skywagon .55 .55
a. Booklet pane of 10 5.75 —
C19 AP5 39c Embraer EMB-110 Bandeirante .65 .65
a. Booklet pane of 10 6.75 —
C20 AP5 45c Boeing 727 .75 .75
a. Booklet pane of 10 7.50 —
b. Booklet pane, 5 each 36c, 45c 6.75 —
Nos. C18-C20 (3) 1.95 1.95

Palauan Bai Type

1991, July 9 Litho. *Die Cut*

Self-Adhesive

C21 A61 50c like #293a .75 .75

World War II in the Pacific Type Miniature Sheet

Aircraft: No. C23: a, Grumman TBF Avenger, US Navy. b, Curtiss P-40C, Chinese Air Force "Flying Tigers." c, Mitsubishi A6M Zero-Sen, Japan. d, Hawker Hurricane, Royal Air Force. e, Consolidated PBY Catalina, Royal Netherlands Indies Air Force. f, Curtiss Hawk 75, Netherlands Indies. g, Boeing B-17E, US Army Air Force. h, Brewster Buffalo, Royal Australian Air Force. i, Supermarine Walrus, Royal Navy. j, Curtiss P-40E, Royal New Zealand Air Force.

1992, Sept. 10 Litho. *Perf. 14½x15*

C22 A66 50c Sheet of 10, #a.-j. 9.00 9.00

1994, Mar. 24 Litho. *Perf. 14*

Designs: a, Palau swiftlet. b, Barn swallow. c, Jungle nightjar. d, White-breasted woodswallow.

C23 AP6 50c Block of 4, #a.-d. 3.00 3.00

No. C23 is printed in sheets of 16 stamps.

PALESTINE

ˈpa–lə–ˌstin

LOCATION — Western Asia bordering on the Mediterranean Sea
GOVT. — Former British Mandate
AREA — 10,429 sq. mi.
POP. — 1,605,816 (estimated)
CAPITAL — Jerusalem

Formerly a part of Turkey, Palestine was occupied by the Egyptian Expeditionary Forces of the British Army in World War I and was mandated to Great Britain in 1923. Mandate ended May 14, 1948.

10 Milliemes = 1 Piaster
1000 Milliemes = 1 Egyptian Pound
1000 Mils = 1 Palestine Pound (1928)

Jordan stamps overprinted with "Palestine" in English and Arabic are listed under Jordan.

Watermark

Wmk. 33

Issued under British Military Occupation

For use in Palestine, Transjordan, Lebanon, Syria and in parts of Cilicia and northeastern Egypt

A1

Wmk. Crown and "GvR" (33)

1918, Feb. 10 Litho. ***Rouletted 20***

No.	Type	Description	Unused	Used
1	A1	1pi deep blue	200.00	125.00
2	A1	1pi ultra	3.00	2.00

No. 2 Surcharged in Black

5 MILLIEMES

1918, Feb. 16

No.	Type	Description	Unused	Used
3	A1	5m on 1pi ultra	6.00	5.00
a.		5m on 1pi gray blue	125.00	*700.00*

Nos. 1 and 3a were issued without gum. No. 3a is on paper with a surface sheen.

1918 Typo. ***Perf. 15x14***

No.	Type	Description	Unused	Used
4	A1	1m dark brown	.15	.15
5	A1	2m blue green	.20	.20
6	A1	3m light brown	.25	.30
7	A1	4m scarlet	.30	.35
8	A1	5m orange	.30	.30
9	A1	1pi indigo	.30	.20
10	A1	2pi olive green	.50	.40
11	A1	5pi plum	1.50	1.65
12	A1	9pi bister	2.50	3.50
13	A1	10pi ultramarine	2.50	3.50
14	A1	20pi gray	9.00	11.00
		Nos. 4-14 (11)	17.50	21.55

Many shades exist.

Nos. 4-11 exist with rough perforation.

Issued: 1m, 2m, 4m, 2pi, 5pi, July 16; 5m, Sept. 25; 1pi, Nov. 9; 3m, 9pi, 10pi, Dec. 17; 20pi, Dec. 27.

Nos. 4-11 with overprint "O. P. D. A." (Ottoman Public Debt Administration) or "H.J.Z." (Hejaz-Jemen Railway) are revenue stamps; they exist postally used.

For overprints on stamps and types see #15-62 & Jordan #1-63, 73-90, 92-102, 130-144, J12-J23.

Issued under British Administration

Overprinted at Jerusalem

فلسطين

Stamps and Type of 1918 Overprinted in Black or Silver

PALESTINE

פלשתינה א״י

1920, Sept. 1 Wmk. 33 ***Perf. 15x14***

Arabic Overprint 8mm long

No.	Type	Description	Unused	Used
15	A1	1m dark brown	1.25	1.25
16	A1	2m blue green, perf. 14	1.00	1.10
d.		Perf. 15x14	7.00	4.00
17	A1	3m lt brown	3.00	3.25
d.		Perf. 14	40.00	*45.00*
e.		Inverted overprint	375.00	*600.00*
18	A1	4m scarlet	1.25	1.50
19	A1	5m orange, perf. 14	1.25	.95
e.		Perf. 15x14	7.00	3.75
20	A1	1pi indigo (S)	1.00	.60
21	A1	2pi olive green	1.75	1.75
22	A1	5pi plum	9.00	13.00
23	A1	9pi bister	10.00	15.00
24	A1	10pi ultra	10.00	15.00
25	A1	20pi gray	20.00	32.50
		Nos. 15-25 (11)	59.50	85.90

Forgeries exist of No. 17e.

Similar Overprint, with Arabic Line 10mm Long, Arabic "S" and "T" Joined, ".." at Left Extends Above Other Letters

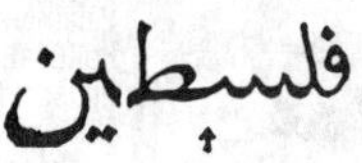

1920-21 ***Perf. 15x14***

No.	Type	Description	Unused	Used
15a	A1	1m dark brown	.50	.75
e.		Perf. 14	600.00	750.00
g.		As "a," invtd. ovpt.		
16a	A1	2m blue green	2.25	2.75
e.		"PALESTINE" omitted	*2,500.*	*1,500.*
f.		Perf. 14	2.25	2.75
17a	A1	3m light brown	.50	.75
18a	A1	4m scarlet	.85	1.10
b.		Perf. 14	60.00	80.00
19a	A1	5m orange	1.75	.60
f.		Perf. 14	1.50	1.00
20a	A1	1pi indigo, perf. 14 (S) ('21)	25.00	1.75
d.		Perf. 15x14	500.00	37.50
21a	A1	2pi olive green ('21)	65.00	30.00
22a	A1	5pi plum ('21)	20.00	8.00
d.		Perf. 14	190.00	*750.00*
		Nos. 15a-22a (8)	115.85	45.70

This overprint often looks grayish to grayish black. In the English line the letters are frequently uneven and damaged.

Similar Overprint, with Arabic Line 10mm Long, Arabic "S" and "T" Separated and 6mm Between English and Hebrew Lines

1920, Dec. 6

No.	Type	Description	Unused	Used
15b	A1	1m dk brown, perf. 14	22.50	30.00
17b	A1	3m lt brown, perf. 15x14	27.50	35.00
19b	A1	5m orange, perf. 14	400.00	30.00
d.		Perf. 15x14	*17,500.*	*15,000.*
		Nos. 15b-19b (3)	450.00	95.00

Overprinted as Before, 7½mm Between English and Hebrew Lines, ".." at Left Even With Other Letters

1921 ***Perf. 15x14***

No.	Type	Description	Unused	Used
15c	A1	1m dark brown	5.00	2.00
f.		1m dull brown, perf. 14		*2,500.*
16c	A1	2m blue green	6.00	3.25
17c	A1	3m light brown	15.00	1.50
18c	A1	4m scarlet	12.00	1.50
19c	A1	5m orange	15.00	.75
20c	A1	1pi indigo (S)	15.00	.70
21c	A1	2pi olive green	20.00	5.00
22c	A1	5pi plum	17.00	8.00
23c	A1	9pi bister	30.00	*100.00*
24c	A1	10pi ultra	30.00	15.00
25c	A1	20pi pale gray	90.00	60.00
d.		Perf. 14	*14,000.*	*2,000.*
		Nos. 15c-25c (11)	255.00	*197.70*

Overprinted at London

فلسطين

Stamps of 1918 Overprinted

PALESTINE

פלשתינה א״י

1921 ***Perf. 15x14***

No.	Type	Description	Unused	Used
37	A1	1m dark brown	.30	.22
38	A1	2m blue green	.30	.22
39	A1	3m light brown	.30	.22
40	A1	4m scarlet	1.00	.50
41	A1	5m orange	.30	.20
42	A1	1pi bright blue	.55	.20
43	A1	2pi olive green	1.10	.50
44	A1	5pi plum	4.50	5.50
45	A1	9pi bister	14.00	16.00
46	A1	10pi ultra	16.00	—
47	A1	20pi gray	45.00	—
		Nos. 37-47 (11)	83.35	
		Nos. 37-45 (9)		23.56

The " (2nd from left on bottom line) consists of long thin lines.

Deformed or damaged letters exist in all three lines of the overprint.

Similar Overprint on Type of 1921 Issue

1922 Wmk. 4 ***Perf. 14***

No.	Type	Description	Unused	Used
48	A1	1m dark brown	.20	.15
a.		Inverted overprint		*15,000.*
b.		Double overprint	225.00	400.00
49	A1	2m yellow	.40	.15
50	A1	3m Prus blue	.25	.15
51	A1	4m rose	.20	.15
52	A1	5m orange	.35	.15
53	A1	6m blue green	.50	.15
54	A1	7m yellow brown	.60	.20
55	A1	8m red	.55	.15
56	A1	1pi gray	.55	.15
57	A1	13m ultra	.60	.15
58	A1	2pi olive green	1.00	.25
a.		Inverted overprint	350.00	400.00
b.		2pi yellow bister	*125.00*	*6.00*
59	A1	5pi plum	5.00	1.00
a.		Perf. 15x14	30.00	3.25

Perf. 15x14

No.	Type	Description	Unused	Used
60	A1	9pi bister	10.00	9.00
a.		Perf. 14	1,200.	200.00
61	A1	10pi light blue	9.00	5.00
a.		Perf. 14	20.00	7.00
62	A1	20pi violet	7.50	4.00
a.		Perf. 14	175.00	80.00
		Nos. 48-62 (15)	36.70	20.80

The "" (2nd from left on bottom line) consists of short thick lines.

The "E. F. F." for "E. E. F." on No. 61 is caused by damaged type.

Rachel's Tomb — A3

Mosque of Omar (Dome of the Rock) — A4

Citadel at Jerusalem A5

Tiberias and Sea of Galilee A6

1927-42 Typo. ***Perf. 13½x14½***

No.	Type	Description	Unused	Used
63	A3	2m Prus blue	.15	.15
64	A3	3m yellow green	.15	.15
65	A4	4m rose red	1.10	.35
66	A4	4m violet brn ('32)	.15	.15
67	A5	5m brown org	.15	.15
c.		Perf. 14½x14 (coil stamp) ('36)	2.25	2.75
68	A4	6m deep green	.15	.15
69	A5	7m deep red	1.40	.25
70	A5	7m dk violet ('32)	.15	.15
71	A4	8m yellow brown	6.75	3.00
72	A4	8m scarlet ('32)	.25	.15
73	A3	10m deep gray	.15	.15
a.		Perf. 14½x14 (coil stamp) ('38)	2.50	3.00
74	A4	13m ultra	2.00	.20
75	A4	13m olive bister ('32)	.15	.15
76	A4	15m ultra ('32)	.15	.15
77	A5	20m olive green	.15	.15

Perf. 14

No.	Type	Description	Unused	Used
78	A6	50m violet brown	.50	.15
79	A6	90m bister	42.50	35.00
80	A6	100m bright blue	.60	.15
81	A6	200m dk violet	1.00	.55
82	A6	250m dp brown ('42)	.90	.80
83	A6	500m red ('42)	1.90	1.65
84	A6	£1 gray black ('42)	3.00	2.50
		Nos. 63-84 (22)	63.40	46.25

Issue dates: 3m, No. 74, June 1. 2m, 5m, 6m, 10m, Nos. 65, 69, 71, 77-81, Aug. 14. Nos. 70, 72, June 1, 1932. No. 75, 15m, Aug. 1, 1932. No. 66, Nov. 1, 1932. Nos. 82-84, Jan. 15, 1942.

POSTAGE DUE STAMPS

D1

1923 Unwmk. Typo. ***Perf. 11***

No.	Type	Description	Unused	Used
J1	D1	1m bister brown	11.00	15.00
b.		Horiz. pair, imperf. btwn.	1,300.	
J2	D1	2m green	6.00	6.00
J3	D1	4m red	7.00	8.00
J4	D1	8m violet	3.50	3.50
b.		Horiz. pair, imperf. btwn.		*2,750.*
J5	D1	13m dark blue	3.50	3.50
a.		Horiz. pair, imperf. btwn.	1,150.	
		Nos. J1-J5 (5)	31.00	36.00

Imperfs. of 1m, 2m, 8m, are from proof sheets.

Values for Nos. J1-J5 are for fine centered copies.

D2

D3

1924, Dec. 1 **Wmk. 4**

No.	Type	Description	Unused	Used
J6	D2	1m brown	.90	.90
J7	D2	2m yellow	1.00	1.00
J8	D2	4m green	1.10	.90
J9	D2	8m red	1.50	.50
J10	D2	13m ultramarine	3.50	2.25
J11	D2	5pi violet	8.00	1.50
		Nos. J6-J11 (6)	16.00	7.05

1928-45 ***Perf. 14***

No.	Type	Description	Unused	Used
J12	D3	1m lt brown	.35	.35
a.		Perf. 15x14 ('45)	21.00	37.50
J13	D3	2m yellow	.45	.50
J14	D3	4m green	.50	.65
a.		4m bluish grn, perf. 15x14 ('45)	35.00	50.00
J15	D3	6m brown org ('33)	6.00	5.50
J16	D3	8m red	.65	.60
J17	D3	10m light gray	.65	.45
J18	D3	13m ultra	1.50	1.00
J19	D3	20m olive green	1.40	1.00
J20	D3	50m violet	1.50	1.00
		Nos. J12-J20 (9)	13.00	11.05

The Hebrew word for "mil" appears below the numeral on all values but the 1m.

Issue dates: 6m, Oct. 1933, others, Feb. 1, 1928.

PALESTINIAN AUTHORITY

LOCATION — Areas of the West Bank and the Gaza Strip.

1000 Fils (Mils) = 10 New Israeli Shekels
1000 Fils = 1 Jordanian Dinar (Jan. 1, 1998)

Catalogue values for all unused stamps in this country are for Never Hinged items.

Hisham Palace, Jericho A1

5m, 10m, 20m, Hisham Palace. 30m, 40m, 50m, 75m, Mosque, Jerusalem. 125, 150m, 250m, 300m, 500m, Flag. 1000m, Dome of the Rock.

1994 Litho. *Perf. 14*

No.	Type	Denomination		Unused	Used
1	A1	5m	multicolored	.15	.15
2	A1	10m	multicolored	.15	.15
3	A1	20m	multicolored	.15	.15
4	A1	30m	multicolored	.15	.15
5	A1	40m	multicolored	.15	.15
6	A1	50m	multicolored	.20	.20
7	A1	75m	multicolored	.30	.30
8	A1	125m	multicolored	.50	.50
9	A1	150m	multicolored	.60	.60
10	A1	250m	multicolored	1.00	1.00
11	A1	300m	multicolored	1.20	1.20
			Size: 51x29mm		
12	A1	500m	multicolored	2.00	2.00
13	A1	1000m	multicolored	4.00	4.00
			Nos. 1-13 (13)	10.55	10.55

Issued: 125m, 150m, 250m, 300m, 500m, 8/15; others, 9/1.

Nos. 1-13 Surcharged "FILS" in English and Arabic in Black or Silver and with Black Bars Obliterating "Mils"

1995, Apr. 10 Litho. *Perf. 14*

No.	Type	Denomination		Unused	Used
14	A1	5f	multicolored	.15	.15
15	A1	10f	multicolored	.15	.15
16	A1	20f	multicolored	.15	.15
17	A1	30f	multicolored (S)	.15	.15
18	A1	40f	multicolored (S)	.15	.15
19	A1	50f	multicolored (S)	.25	.25
20	A1	75f	multicolored (S)	.35	.35
21	A1	125f	multicolored	.55	.55
22	A1	150f	multicolored	.65	.65
23	A1	250f	multicolored	1.10	1.10
24	A1	300f	multicolored	1.25	1.25
			Size: 51x29mm		
25	A1	500f	multicolored	2.25	2.25
26	A1	1000f	multicolored	4.75	4.75
			Nos. 14-26 (13)	11.90	11.90

Palestine No. 63 — A2

350f, Palestine #67. 500f, Palestine #72.

1995, May 17 Litho. *Perf. 14*

No.	Type	Denomination		Unused	Used
27	A2	150f	multicolored	.70	.70
28	A2	350f	multicolored	1.50	1.50
29	A2	500f	multicolored	2.25	2.25
			Nos. 27-29 (3)	4.45	4.45

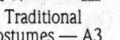

Traditional Costumes — A3

Christmas — A4

Women wearing various costumes.

1995, May 31

No.	Type	Denomination		Unused	Used
30	A3	250f	multicolored	1.10	1.10
31	A3	300f	multicolored	1.35	1.35
32	A3	550f	multicolored	2.50	2.50
33	A3	900f	multicolored	4.00	4.00
			Nos. 30-33 (4)	8.95	8.95

1995, Dec. 18

Designs: 10f, Ancient view of Bethlehem. 20f, Modern view of Bethlehem. 50f, Entrance to grotto, Church of the Nativity. 100f, Yasser Arafat, Pope John Paul II. 1000f, Star of the Nativity, Church of the Nativity, Bethlehem.
10f, 20f, 100f, 1000f are horiz.

No.	Type	Denomination		Unused	Used
34	A4	10f	multicolored	.15	.15
35	A4	20f	multicolored	.15	.15
36	A4	50f	multicolored	.25	.25
37	A4	100f	multicolored	.50	.50
38	A4	1000f	multicolored	5.00	5.00
			Nos. 34-38 (5)	6.05	6.05

Pres. Yasser Arafat — A5

1996, Mar. 20

No.	Type	Denomination		Unused	Used
39	A5	10f	red violet & bluish black	.15	.15
40	A5	20f	yellow & bluish black	.15	.15
41	A5	50f	blue & bluish black	.25	.25
42	A5	100f	apple grn & bluish blk	.50	.50
43	A5	1000f	orange & bluish black	5.00	5.00
			Nos. 39-43 (5)	6.05	6.05

1996 Intl. Philatelic Exhibitions — A6

Exhibition, site: 20f, CHINA '96, Summer Palace, Beijing. 50f, ISTANBUL '96, Hagia Sofia. 100f, ESSEN '96, Villa Hugel. 1000f, CAPEX '96, Toronto skyline.

1996, May 18

No.	Type	Denomination		Unused	Used
44	A6	20f	multicolored	.15	.15
45	A6	50f	multicolored	.30	.30
46	A6	100f	multicolored	.60	.60
47	A6	1000f	multicolored	6.00	6.00
a.			Sheet, 2 each #44-47 + 2 labels	14.50	

Souvenir Sheet

1st Palestinian Parliamentary & Presidential Elections — A7

Illustration reduced.

1996, May 20

No.	Type	Denomination		Unused	Used
48	A7	1250f	multicolored	6.50	6.50

1996 Summer Olympic Games, Atlanta — A8

Designs: 30f, Boxing. 40f, Medal, 1896. 50f, Runners. 150f, Olympic flame. 1000f, Palestinian Olympic Committee emblem.

1996, July 19 *Perf. 13½*

No.	Type	Denomination		Unused	Used
49	A8	30f	multicolored	.15	.15
50	A8	40f	multicolored	.20	.20
51	A8	50f	multicolored	.30	.30
52	A8	150f	multicolored	.90	.90
a.			Sheet of 3, #49, 51-52	*4.25*	
53	A8	1000f	multicolored	5.75	5.75
			Nos. 49-53 (5)	7.30	7.30

Flowers — A9

1996, Nov. 22

No.	Type	Denomination		Unused	Used
54	A9	10f	Poppy	.15	.15
55	A9	25f	Hibiscus	.15	.15
56	A9	100f	Thyme	.60	.60
57	A9	150f	Lemon	.85	.85
58	A9	750f	Orange	4.25	4.25
			Nos. 54-58 (5)	6.00	6.00
			Souvenir Sheet		
59	A9	1000f	Olive	5.50	5.50

Souvenir Sheet

Christmas A10

a, 150f, Magi. b, 350f, View of Bethlehem. c, 500f, Shepherds, sheep. d, 750f, Nativity scene.

1996, Dec. 14 *Perf. 14*

No.	Type		Unused	Used
60	A10	Sheet of 4, #a.-d.	8.50	8.50

Birds — A11

1997, May 29

No.	Type	Denomination		Unused	Used
61	A11	25f	Great tit	.15	.15
62	A11	75f	Blue rock thrush	.35	.35
63	A11	150f	Golden oriole	.75	.75
64	A11	350f	Hoopoe	1.75	1.75
65	A11	600f	Peregrine falcon	3.00	3.00
			Nos. 61-65 (5)	6.00	6.00

Historic Views — A12

1997, June 19

No.	Type	Denomination		Unused	Used
66	A12	350f	Gaza, 1839	1.75	1.75
67	A12	600f	Hebron, 1839	3.00	3.00

Souvenir Sheet

Return of Hong Kong to China — A13

Illustration reduced.

1997, July 1

No.	Type	Denomination		Unused	Used
68	A13	225f	multicolored	1.00	1.00

SEMI-POSTAL STAMPS

Souvenir Sheet

Gaza-Jericho Peace Agreement — SP1

Illustration reduced.

1994, Oct. 7 Litho. *Perf. 14*

No.	Type	Denomination		Unused	Used
B1	SP1	750m +250m	multi	4.50	4.50

For surcharge see No. B3.

Souvenir Sheet

Arab League, 50th Anniv. — SP2

Painting: View of Palestine, by Ibrahim Hazimeh. Illustration reduced.

1995, Mar. 22 *Perf. 13½*

No.	Type	Denomination		Unused	Used
B2	SP2	750f +250f	multi	5.00	5.00

No. B1 Surcharged "FILS" in English & Arabic

1995, Apr. 10 Litho. *Perf. 14*

No.	Type	Denomination		Unused	Used
B3	SP1	750f +250f	multi	4.75	4.75

OFFICIAL STAMPS

Natl. Arms — O1

1994, Aug. 15 Litho. *Perf. 14*

No.	Type	Denomination		Unused	Used
O1	O1	50m	yellow	.20	.20
O2	O1	100m	green blue	.40	.40
O3	O1	125m	blue	.50	.50
O4	O1	200m	orange	.80	.80
O5	O1	250m	olive	1.00	1.00
O6	O1	400m	maroon	1.60	1.60
			Nos. O1-O6 (6)	4.50	4.50

Nos. O1-O6 could also be used by the general public, and non-official-use covers are known.

PANAMA

'pa–nə–,mä

LOCATION — Central America between Costa Rica and Colombia
GOVT. — Republic
AREA — 30,134 sq. mi.
POP. — 1,970,000 (est. 1983)
CAPITAL — Panama

Formerly a department of the Republic of Colombia, Panama gained its independence in 1903. Dividing the country at its center is the Panama Canal.

100 Centavos = 1 Peso
100 Centesimos = 1 Balboa (1906)

Catalogue values for unused stamps in this country are for Never Hinged items, beginning with Scott 350 in the regular postage section, Scott C82 in the airpost section, Scott CB1 in the airpost semi-postal section, and Scott RA21 in the postal tax section.

Watermarks

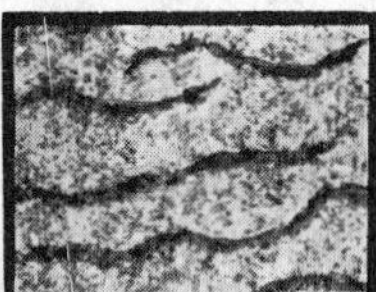
Wmk. 229- Wavy Lines

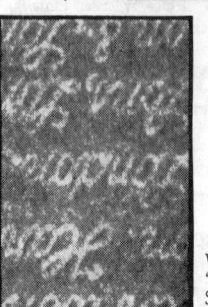
Wmk. 233- "Harrison & Sons, London." in Script

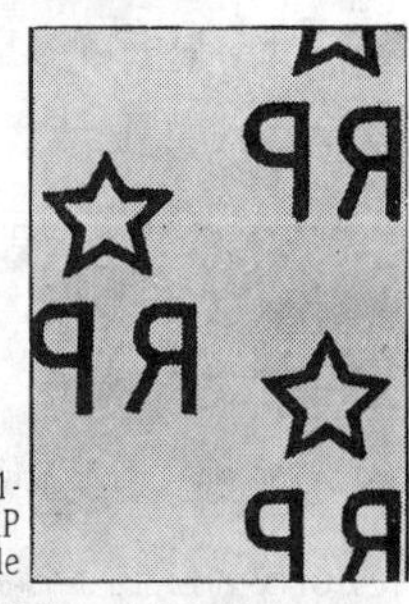
Wmk. 311- Star and RP Multiple

Wmk. 334- Rectangles

Wmk. 343- RP Multiple

Wmk. 365- Argentine Arms, Casa de Moneda de la Nacion & RA Multiple

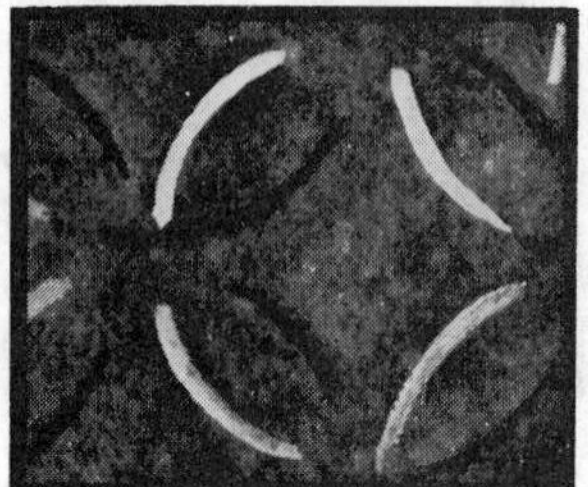
Wmk. 377- Interlocking Circles

Wmk. 382- Stars

Wmk. 382 may be a sheet watermark. It includes stars with rays, wings and "Panama R de P."

Issues of the Colombian State of Panama

Valid only for domestic mail.

Coat of Arms
A1 A2

1878 Unwmk. Litho. *Imperf.*

Thin Wove Paper

1 A1 5c gray green 25.00 30.00
a. 5c yellow green 25.00 30.00
2 A1 10c blue 65.00 75.00
3 A1 20c rose red 40.00
Nos. 1-3 (3) 130.00

Very Thin Wove Paper

4 A2 50c buff *1,500.*

All values of this issue are known rouletted unofficially.

Medium Thick Paper

5 A1 5c blue green 25.00 30.00
6 A1 10c blue 65.00 70.00
7 A2 50c orange 13.00
Nos. 5-7 (3) 103.00

Nos. 5-7 were printed before Nos. 1-4, according to Panamanian archives.

Values for used Nos. 1-5 are for handstamped postal cancellations.

These stamps have been reprinted in a number of shades, on thin to moderately thick, white or yellowish paper. They are without gum or with white, crackly gum. All values have been reprinted from new stones made from retouched dies. The marks of retouching are plainly to be seen in the sea and clouds. On the original 10c the shield in the upper left corner has two blank sections; on the reprints the design of this shield is completed. The impression of these reprints is frequently blurred.

Reprints of the 50c are rare. Beware of remainders of the 50c offered as reprints.

Issues of Colombia for use in the Department of Panama

Issued because of the use of different currency.

Map of Panama
A3 A4

1887-88 ***Perf. 13½***

8 A3 1c black, *green* .80 .80
9 A3 2c black, *pink* ('88) 1.65 1.25
a. 2c black, *salmon*
10 A3 5c black, *blue* .80 .35
11 A3 10c black, *yellow* .80 .40
a. Imperf., pair
12 A3 20c black, *lilac* .90 .52
13 A3 50c brown ('88) 2.00 1.00
a. Imperf.
Nos. 8-13 (6) 6.95 4.32

See No. 14. For surcharges and overprints see Nos. 24-30, 107-108, 115-116, 137-138.

1892 Pelure Paper

14 A3 50c brown 2.50 1.10

The stamps of this issue have been reprinted on papers of slightly different colors from those of the originals. These are: 1c yellow green, 2c deep rose, 5c bright blue, 10c straw, 20c violet. The 50c is printed from a very worn stone, in a lighter brown than the originals. The series includes a 10c on lilac paper. All these stamps are to be found perforated, imperforate, imperforate horizontally or imperforate vertically. At the same time that they were made, impressions were struck upon a variety of glazed and surface-colored papers.

Wove Paper

1892-96 Engr. ***Perf. 12***

15 A4 1c green .25 .22
16 A4 2c rose .40 .25
17 A4 5c blue 1.50 .50
18 A4 10c orange .35 .25
19 A4 20c violet ('95) .50 .35
20 A4 50c bister brn ('96) .50 .35
21 A4 1p lake ('96) 6.50 4.00
Nos. 15-21 (7) 10.00 5.92

In 1903 Nos. 15-21 were used in Cauca and three other southern Colombia towns. Stamps canceled in these towns are worth much more.

For surcharges and overprints see Nos. 22-23, 51-106, 109-114, 129-136, 139, 151-162, 181-184, F12-F15, H4-H5.

Nos. 16, 12-14 Surcharged:

HABILITADO. 1894 1 CENTAVO. — a

HABILITADO. 1894 1 CENTAVO. — b

HABILITADO. 1894 5 CENTAVOS. — c

HABILITADO. 1894 5 CENTAVOS. — d

HABILITADO. 1894 5 CENTAVOS. — e

HABILITADO. 1894 10 CENTAVOS. — f

HABILITADO. 1894 10 CENTAVOS, — g

1894 Black Surcharge

22 (a) 1c on 2c rose .50 .40
a. Inverted surcharge 2.50 2.50
b. Double surcharge
23 (b) 1c on 2c rose .40 .50
a. "CCNTAVO" 2.50 2.50
b. Inverted surcharge 2.50 2.50
c. Double surcharge

Red Surcharge

24 (c) 5c on 20c black, *lil* 2.50 1.50
a. Inverted surcharge 12.50 12.50
b. Double surcharge
c. Without "HABILITADO"
25 (d) 5c on 20c black, *lil* 3.50 3.00
a. "CCNTAVOS" 7.50 7.50
b. Inverted surcharge 12.50 12.50
c. Double surcharge
d. Without "HABILITADO"
26 (e) 5c on 20c black, *lil* 6.00 5.00
a. Inverted surcharge 12.50 12.50
b. Double surcharge
27 (f) 10c on 50c brown 3.00 3.00
a. "1894" omitted
b. Inverted surcharge
c. "CCNTAVOS" 15.00
28 (g) 10c on 50c brown 12.50 12.50
a. "CCNTAVOS" 32.50
b. Inverted surcharge

Pelure Paper

29 (f) 10c on 50c brown 4.00 3.00
a. "1894" omitted 7.50
b. Inverted surcharge 12.50 12.50
c. Double surcharge
30 (g) 10c on 50c brown 10.00 10.00
a. "CCNTAVOS"
b. Without "HABILITADO"
c. Inverted surcharge 25.00 25.00
d. Double surcharge
Nos. 22-30 (9) 42.40 38.90

There are several settings of these surcharges. Usually the surcharge is about 15½mm high, but in one setting, it is only 13mm. All the types are to be found with a comma after "CENTAVOS." Nos. 24, 25, 26, 29 and 30 exist with the surcharge printed sideways. Nos. 23, 24 and 29 may be found with an inverted "A" instead of "V" in "CENTAVOS." There are also varieties caused by dropped or broken letters.

Issues of the Republic Issued in the City of Panama

Stamps of 1892-96 Overprinted — REPUBLICA DE PANAMA

1903, Nov. 16

Rose Handstamp

51 A4 1c green 2.00 1.50
52 A4 2c rose 5.00 3.00
53 A4 5c blue 2.00 1.25
54 A4 10c yellow 2.00 2.00
55 A4 20c violet 4.00 3.50
56 A4 50c bister brn 10.00 7.00
57 A4 1p lake 50.00 40.00
Nos. 51-57 (7) 75.00 58.25

Blue Black Handstamp

58 A4 1c green 2.00 1.25
59 A4 2c rose 1.00 1.00
60 A4 5c blue 7.00 6.00
61 A4 10c yellow 5.00 3.50
62 A4 20c violet 10.00 7.50
63 A4 50c bister brn 10.00 7.50
64 A4 1p lake 50.00 42.50
Nos. 58-64 (7) 85.00 69.25

The stamps of this issue are to be found with the handstamp placed horizontally, vertically or diagonally; inverted; double; double, one inverted; double, both inverted; in pairs, one without handstamp; etc.

This handstamp is known in brown rose on the 1, 5, 20 and 50c, in purple on the 1, 2, 50c and 1p, and in magenta on the 5, 10, 20 and 50c.

Reprints were made in rose, black and other colors when the handstamp was nearly worn out, so that the "R" of "REPUBLICA" appears to be shorter than usual, and the bottom part of "LI" has been broken off. The "P" of "PANAMA" leans to the left and the tops of "NA" are broken. Many of these varieties are found inverted, double, etc.

Overprinted

PANAMA PANAMA

1903, Dec. 3

Bar in Similar Color to Stamp

Black Overprint

65 A4 2c rose 2.50 2.50
a. "PANAMA" 15mm long 3.50
b. Violet bar 5.00
66 A4 5c blue 100.00
a. "PANAMA" 15mm long 100.00
67 A4 10c yellow 2.50 2.50
a. "PANAMA" 15mm long 6.00
b. Horizontal overprint 17.50

Gray Black Overprint

68 A4 2c rose 2.00 2.00
a. "PANAMA" 15mm long 2.50

Carmine Overprint

69 A4 5c blue 2.50 2.50
a. "PANAMA" 15mm long 3.50
b. Bar only 75.00 75.00
c. Double overprint
70 A4 20c violet 7.50 6.50
a. "PANAMA" 15mm long 10.00
b. Double overprint, one in black 150.00
Nos. 65,67-70 (5) 17.00 16.00

This overprint was set up to cover fifty stamps. "PANAMA" is normally 13mm long and 1¾mm high but, in two rows in each sheet, it measures 15 to 16mm. This word may be found with one or more of the letters taller than usual; with one, two or three inverted "V's" instead of "A's"; with an inverted "Y" instead of "A"; an inverted "N"; an "A" with accent; and a fancy "P." Owing to misplaced impressions, stamps exist with "PANAMA" once only, twice on one side, or three times.

Overprinted in Red

PANAMA PANAMA

1903, Dec.

71 A4 1c green .75 .60
a. "PANAMA" 15mm long 1.25
b. "PANAMA" reading down 3.00 .75
c. "PANAMA" reading up and down 3.00
d. Double overprint 8.00
72 A4 2c rose .50 .40
a. "PANAMA" 15mm long 1.00
b. "PANAMA" reading down .75 .50
c. "PANAMA" reading up and down 4.00
d. Double overprint 8.00
73 A4 20c violet 1.50 1.00
a. "PANAMA" 15mm long 2.25
b. "PANAMA" reading down
c. "PANAMA" reading up and down 8.00 8.00
d. Double overprint 18.00 18.00
74 A4 50c bister brn 3.00 2.50
a. "PANAMA" 15mm long 5.00
b. "PANAMA" reading up and down 12.00 12.00
c. Double overprint 6.00 6.00
75 A4 1p lake 6.00 4.50
a. "PANAMA" 15mm long 6.25
b. "PANAMA" reading up and down 15.00 15.00
c. Double overprint 15.00
d. Inverted overprint 25.00
Nos. 71-75 (5) 11.75 9.00

This setting appears to be a re-arrangement (or two very similar re-arrangements) of the previous overprint. The overprint covers fifty stamps. "PANAMA" usually reads upward but sheets of the 1, 2 and 20c exist with the word reading upward on one half the sheet and downward on the other half.

In one re-arrangement one stamp in fifty has the word reading in both directions. Nearly all the varieties of the previous overprint are repeated in this setting excepting the inverted "Y" and fancy "P." There are also additional varieties of large letters and "PANAMA" occasionally has an "A" missing or inverted. There are misplaced impressions, as the previous setting.

Overprinted in Red

PANAMA PANAMA

1904-05

76 A4 1c green .20 .18
a. Both words reading up 1.50
b. Both words reading down 2.75
c. Double overprint
d. Pair, one without overprint 15.00
e. "PANAAM" 20.00
f. Inverted "M" in "PANAMA" 5.00
77 A4 2c rose .20 .18
a. Both words reading up 2.50
b. Both words reading down 2.50
c. Double overprint 10.00
d. Double overprint, one inverted 14.00
e. Inverted "M" in "PANAMA" 5.00
78 A4 5c blue .25 .20
a. Both words reading up 3.00
b. Both words reading down 4.25
c. Inverted overprint 12.50
d. "PANAAM" 25.00
e. "PANANA" 8.00
f. "PAMANA" 5.00
g. Inverted "M" in "PANAMA" 5.00
h. Double overprint 20.00
79 A4 10c yellow .25 .20
a. Both words reading up 5.00
b. Both words reading down 5.00
c. Double overprint 15.00
d. Inverted overprint 6.75
e. "PAMANA" 8.00
f. Inverted "M" in "PANAMA" 15.00
g. Red brown overprint 7.50 3.50
80 A4 20c violet 2.00 1.00
a. Both words reading up 5.00
b. Both words reading down 10.00
81 A4 50c bister brn 2.00 1.65
a. Both words reading up 10.50
b. Both words reading down 10.00
c. Double overprint
82 A4 1p lake 5.00 5.00
a. Both words reading up 12.50
b. Both words reading down 12.50
c. Double overprint
d. Double overprint, one inverted 20.00
e. Inverted "M" in "PANAMA" 45.00
Nos. 76-82 (7) 9.90 8.41

This overprint is also set up to cover fifty stamps. One stamp in each fifty has "PANAMA" reading upward at both sides. Another has the word reading downward at both sides, a third has an inverted "V" in place of the last "A" and a fourth has a small thick "N." In a resetting all these varieties are corrected except the inverted "V." There are misplaced overprints as before.

Later printings show other varieties and have the bar 2½mm instead of 2mm wide. The colors of the various printings of Nos. 76-82 range from carmine to almost pink.

Experts consider the black overprint on the 50c to be speculative.

The 20c violet and 50c bister brown exist with bar 2½mm wide, including the error "PAMANA," but are not known to have been issued. Some copies have been canceled "to oblige."

Issued in Colon

Handstamped in Magenta or Violet — REPUBLICA DE PANAMA

On Stamps of 1892-96

1903-04

101 A4 1c green .75 .75
102 A4 2c rose .75 .75
103 A4 5c blue 1.00 1.00
104 A4 10c yellow 3.50 3.00
105 A4 20c violet 8.00 6.50
106 A4 1p lake 80.00 70.00

On Stamps of 1887-92

Ordinary Wove Paper

107 A3 50c brown 25.00 20.00
Nos. 101-107 (7) 119.00 102.00

Pelure Paper

108 A3 50c brown 70.00

Handstamped in Magenta, Violet or Red — PANAMA

On Stamps of 1892-96

109 A4 1c green 5.50 5.00
110 A4 2c rose 5.50 5.00
111 A4 5c blue 5.50 5.00
112 A4 10c yellow 8.25 7.00
113 A4 20c violet 12.00 9.00
114 A4 1p lake 70.00 60.00

On Stamps of 1887-92

Ordinary Wove Paper

115 A3 5c brown 35.00 25.00
Nos. 109-115 (7) 141.75 116.00

Pelure Paper

116 A3 50c brown 50.00 37.50

The first note after No. 64 applies also to Nos. 101-116.

The handstamps on Nos. 109-116 have been counterfeited.

REPUBLICA DE PANAMA

Stamps with this overprint were a private speculation. They exist on cover. The overprint was to be used on postal cards.

Overprinted g — *República de Panamá*

On Stamps of 1892-96

Carmine Overprint

129 A4 1c green .40 .40
a. Inverted overprint 6.00
b. Double overprint 2.25
c. Double overprint, one inverted 6.00
130 A4 5c blue .50 .50

Brown Overprint

131 A4 1c green 12.00
a. Double overprint, one inverted

Black Overprint

132 A4 1c green 60.00 30.00
a. Vertical overprint 42.50
b. Inverted overprint 42.50
c. Double overprint, one inverted 42.50
133 A4 2c rose .50 .50
a. Inverted overprint
134 A4 10c yellow .50 .50
a. Inverted overprint 4.00
b. Double overprint 16.00
c. Double overprint, one inverted 6.00
135 A4 20c violet .50 .50
a. Inverted overprint 4.00
b. Double overprint 5.50
136 A4 1p lake 16.00 14.00

On Stamps of 1887-88

Blue Overprint

Ordinary Wove Paper

137 A3 50c brown 3.00 3.00

Pelure Paper

138 A3 50c brown 3.00 3.00
a. Double overprint 14.00

This overprint is set up to cover fifty stamps. In each fifty there are four stamps without accent on the last "a" of "Panama," one with accent on the "a" of "Republica" and one with a thick, upright "i."

Overprinted in Carmine — REPUBLICA DE PANAMA.

On Stamp of 1892-96

139 A4 20c violet *200.00*
a. Double overprint

Unknown with genuine cancels.

Issued in Bocas del Toro

Stamps of 1892-96 Overprinted

Handstamped in Violet — R DE PANAMA

1903-04

151 A4 1c green 20.00 14.00
152 A4 2c rose 20.00 14.00
153 A4 5c blue 25.00 16.00
154 A4 10c yellow 15.00 8.25
155 A4 20c violet 50.00 30.00
156 A4 50c bister brn 100.00 55.00
157 A4 1p lake 140.00 110.00
Nos. 151-157 (7) 370.00 247.25

The handstamp is known double and inverted. Counterfeits exist.

Handstamped in Violet — Panama

158 A4 1c green *100.00*
159 A4 2c rose *70.00*
160 A4 5c blue *80.00*
161 A4 10c yellow *100.00*
Nos. 158-161 (4) *350.00*

This handstamp was applied to these 4 stamps only by favor, experts state. Counterfeits are numerous. The 1p exists only as a counterfeit.

General Issues

A5

1905, Feb. 4 **Engr.** ***Perf. 12***

179 A5 1c green .60 .40
180 A5 2c rose .80 .50

Panama's Declaration of Independence from the Colombian Republic, Nov. 3, 1903.

Surcharged in Vermilion on Stamps of 1892-96 Issue:

Panamá Panamá 1 ct.

1906

181 A4 1c on 20c violet .25 .22
a. "Panrma" 2.25 2.25
b. "Pnnama" 2.25 2.25
c. "Pauama" 2.25 2.25
d. Inverted surcharge 4.00 4.00
e. Double surcharge 3.50 3.50
f. Double surcharge, one inverted

PANAMÁ PANAMÁ 2 cts.

182 A4 2c on 50c bister brn .25 .22
a. 3rd "A" of "PANAMA" inverted 2.25 2.25
b. Both "PANAMA" reading down 4.00 4.00
c. Double surcharge
d. Inverted surcharge 2.50

The 2c on 20c violet was never issued to the public. All copies are inverted. Value, 75c.

Carmine Surcharge

183 A4 5c on 1p lake .60 .40
a. Both "PANAMA" reading down 6.00 6.00
b. "5" omitted
c. Double surcharge
d. Inverted surcharge
e. 3rd "A" of "PANAMA" inverted 5.50 5.50

On Stamp of 1903-04, No. 75

184 A4 5c on 1p lake .60 .40
a. "PANAMA" 15mm long
b. "PANAMA" reading up and down
c. Both "PANAMA" reading down
d. Inverted surcharge
e. Double surcharge
f. 3rd "A" of "PANAMA" inverted
Nos. 181-184 (4) 1.70 1.24

National Flag — A6

Vasco Núñez de Balboa — A7

Fernández de Córdoba — A8

Coat of Arms — A9

Justo Arosemena A10

Manuel J. Hurtado A11

José de Obaldía — A12

Tomás Herrera — A13

José de Fábrega — A14

1906-07 **Engr.** ***Perf. 11½***

No.	Type	Description	Unused	Used
185	A6	½c orange & multi	.45	.35
186	A7	1c dk green & blk	.45	.35
187	A8	2c scarlet & blk	.60	.35
188	A9	2½c red orange	.75	.35
189	A10	5c blue & black	1.75	.35
a.		5c ultramarine & black	2.00	.50
190	A11	8c purple & blk	1.00	.65
191	A12	10c violet & blk	1.00	.50
192	A13	25c brown & blk	2.50	1.00
193	A14	50c black	6.50	3.50
		Nos. 185-193 (9)	15.00	7.40

Inverted centers exist of Nos. 185-187, 189, 189a, 190-193, Value, each $25. Nos. 185-193 exist imperf.

For surcharge see No. F29.

Map — A17

Balboa — A18

Córdoba — A19

Arms — A20

Arosemena A21

Obaldía A23

1909-15 ***Perf. 12***

No.	Type	Description	Unused	Used
195	A17	½c orange ('11)	.60	.32
a.		Booklet pane of 6		
196	A17	½c rose ('15)	.60	.60
197	A18	1c dk grn & blk	.80	.35
a.		Inverted center		
b.		Booklet pane of 6	*165.00*	
198	A19	2c red & blk	.60	.20
a.		Booklet pane of 6	*165.00*	
199	A20	2½c red orange	1.00	.20
a.		Booklet pane of 6		
200	A21	5c blue & blk	1.65	.20
a.		Booklet pane of 6	*165.00*	
201	A23	10c violet & blk	2.50	.80
a.		Booklet pane of 6		
		Nos. 195-201 (7)	7.75	2.67

For overprints and surcharges see #H23, I4-I7.

Balboa Sighting Pacific Ocean, His Dog "Leoncico" at His Feet — A24

1913, Sept.

No.	Type	Description	Unused	Used
202	A24	2½c dk grn & yel grn	.80	.65

400th anniv. of Balboa's discovery of the Pacific Ocean.

Panama Exposition Issue

Chorrera Falls — A25

Map of Panama Canal — A26

Balboa Taking Possession of the Pacific — A27

Ruins of Cathedral of Old Panama — A28

Palace of Arts — A29

Gatun Locks — A30

Culebra Cut — A31

Santo Domingo Monastery's Flat Arch — A32

1915-16 ***Perf. 12***

No.	Type	Description	Unused	Used
204	A25	½c ol grn & blk	.40	.32
205	A26	1c dk green & blk	.90	.32
206	A27	2c carmine & blk	.70	.32
a.		2c ver & blk ('16)	.70	.32
208	A28	2½c scarlet & blk	.90	.35
209	A29	3c violet & blk	1.50	.55
210	A30	5c blue & blk	2.00	.35
a.		Center inverted	750.00	650.00
211	A31	10c orange & blk	2.00	.70
212	A32	20c brown & blk	10.00	3.25
a.		Center inverted	275.00	
		Nos. 204-212 (8)	18.40	6.16

For surcharges and overprints see Nos. 217, 233, E1-E2.

Manuel J. Hurtado — A33

1916

No.	Type	Description	Unused	Used
213	A33	8c violet & blk	7.00	4.25

For surcharge see No. 30.

S. S. Panama in Culebra Cut Aug. 11, 1914 A34

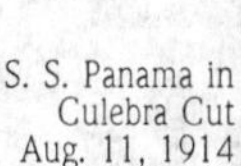

S. S. Panama in Culebra Cut Aug. 11, 1914 A35

S. S. Cristobal in Gatun Lock — A36

1918

No.	Type	Description	Unused	Used
214	A34	12c purple & blk	15.00	5.75
215	A35	15c brt blue & blk	10.00	3.50
216	A36	24c yellow brn & blk	15.00	3.50
		Nos. 214-216 (3)	40.00	12.75

No. 208 Surcharged in Dark Blue

1519 1919

2 CENTESIMOS 2

1919, Aug. 15

No.	Type	Description	Unused	Used
217	A28	2c on 2½c scar & blk	.30	.30
a.		Inverted surcharge	10.00	8.25
b.		Double surcharge	12.00	10.00

City of Panama, 400th anniversary.

Dry Dock at Balboa — A38

Ship in Pedro Miguel Lock — A39

1920 **Engr.**

No.	Type	Description	Unused	Used
218	A38	50c orange & blk	30.00	22.50
219	A39	1b dk violet & blk	40.00	27.50

For overprint and surcharge see Nos. C6, C37.

Arms of Panama City A40

José Vallarino A41

"Land Gate" — A42

Simón Bolivar — A43

Statue of Cervantes A44

Bolívar's Tribute A45

Carlos de Ycaza — A46

Municipal Building in 1821 and 1921 — A47

Statue of Balboa — A48

Villa de Los Santos Church — A49

Herrera — A50

Fábrega — A51

1921, Nov.

No.	Type	Description	Unused	Used
220	A40	½c orange	.45	.22
221	A41	1c green	.55	.18
222	A42	2c carmine	.60	.22
223	A43	2½c red	1.40	1.10
224	A44	3c dull violet	1.40	1.10
225	A45	5c blue	1.40	.35
226	A46	8c olive green	5.00	2.75
227	A47	10c violet	3.25	1.25
228	A48	15c lt blue	4.00	1.65
229	A49	20c olive brown	7.00	3.25
230	A50	24c black brown	7.00	4.00
231	A51	50c black	12.00	6.00
		Nos. 220-231 (12)	44.05	22.07

Centenary of independence.

For overprints and surcharges see Nos. 264, 275-276, 299, 304, 308-310, C35.

Hurtado — A52

Arms — A53

1921, Nov. 28

No.	Type	Description	Unused	Used
232	A52	2c dark green	.50	.50

Manuel José Hurtado (1821-1887), president and folklore writer.

For overprints see Nos. 258, 301.

No. 208 Surcharged in Black

1923

2 CENTESIMOS 2

1923

No.	Type	Description	Unused	Used
233	A28	2c on 2½c scar & blk	.35	.35

Surcharge varieties include wrong or omitted date, double surcharge and pair, one without surcharge. Value $2.50 each.

Two stamps in each sheet have a bar above "CENTESIMOS."

1924, May **Engr.**

No.	Type	Description	Unused	Used
234	A53	½c orange	.15	.15
235	A53	1c dark green	.15	.15
236	A53	2c carmine	.18	.15
237	A53	5c dark blue	.35	.15
238	A53	10c dark violet	.50	.15
239	A53	12c olive green	.60	.32
240	A53	15c ultra	.80	.32
241	A53	24c yellow brown	1.75	.80
242	A53	50c orange	3.50	.90
243	A53	1b black	5.25	2.00
		Nos. 234-243 (10)	13.23	5.09

For overprints & surcharges see #277, 321A, 331-338, 352, C19-C20, C68, RA5, RA10-RA22.

Bolívar — A54

Statue of Bolívar — A55

Bolívar Hall — A56

1926, June 10 *Perf. 12½*

244	A54	½c orange	.25	.22
245	A54	1c dark green	.25	.22
246	A54	2c scarlet	.35	.30
247	A54	4c gray	.45	.35
248	A54	5c dark blue	.70	.50
249	A55	8c lilac	1.10	.80
250	A55	10c dull violet	.80	.80
251	A55	12c olive green	1.25	1.00
252	A55	15c ultra	1.65	1.25
253	A55	20c brown	3.25	1.65
254	A56	24c black violet	4.00	2.00
255	A56	50c black	6.50	5.00
		Nos. 244-255 (12)	20.55	14.09

Bolivar Congress.

For surcharges and overprints see Nos. 259-263, 266-267, 274, 298, 300, 302-303, 305-307, C33-C34, C36, C38-C39.

Lindbergh's Airplane, "The Spirit of St. Louis" — A57

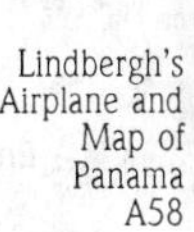

Lindbergh's Airplane and Map of Panama A58

1928, Jan. 9 **Typo.** *Rouletted 7*

256	A57	2c dk red & blk, *salmon*	.30	.25
257	A58	5c dk blue, *grn*	.45	.38

Visit of Colonel Charles A. Lindbergh to Central America by airplane.

No. 232 Overprinted in Red

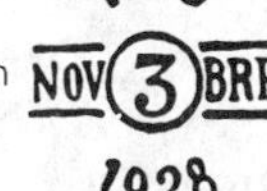

1928, Nov. 1 *Perf. 12*

258	A52	2c dark green	.25	.25

25th anniversary of the Republic.

No. 247 Surcharged in Black

1930, Dec. 17 *Perf. 12½, 13*

259	A54	1c on 4c gray	.22	.20

Centenary of the death of Simón Bolívar, the Liberator.

Nos. 244-246 Overprinted in Red or Blue — HABILITADA

1932 *Perf. 12½*

260	A54	½c orange (R)	.20	.20
261	A54	1c dark green (R)	.35	.20
a.		Double overprint	18.00	
262	A54	2c scarlet (Bl)	.35	.25

No. 252 Surcharged in Red — HABILITADA 10 c.

263	A55	10c on 15c ultra	1.00	.50
a.		Double surcharge	55.00	
		Nos. 260-263 (4)	1.90	1.15

No. 220 Overprinted as in 1932 in Black

1933 *Perf. 12*

Overprint 19mm Long

264	A40	½c orange	.35	.20
a.		Overprint 17mm long		

Dr. Manuel Amador Guerrero — A60

1933, July 3 **Engr.** *Perf. 12½*

265	A60	2c dark red	.50	.20

Centenary of the birth of Dr. Manuel Amador Guerrero, founder of the Republic of Panama and its first President.

No. 251 Surcharged in Red — HABILITADA 10 c.

1933

266	A55	10c on 12c olive grn	1.25	.65

No. 253 Overprinted in Red — HABILITADA

267	A55	20c brown	1.75	1.75

José Domingo de Obaldía — A61

Quotation from Emerson — A63

National Institute — A64

Designs: 2c, Eusebio A. Morales. 12c, Justo A. Facio. 15c, Pablo Arosemena.

1934, July **Engr.** *Perf. 14*

268	A61	1c dark green	.70	.50
269	A61	2c scarlet	.70	.45
270	A63	5c dark blue	1.00	.80
271	A64	10c brown	2.75	1.50
272	A61	12c yellow green	5.00	2.00
273	A61	15c Prus blue	6.75	2.50
		Nos. 268-273 (6)	16.90	7.75

25th anniv. of the First Natl. Institute.

Nos. 248, 227 Overprinted in Black or Red — HABILITADA

1935-36 *Perf. 12½, 12*

274	A54	5c dark blue	.70	.30
275	A47	10c violet (R) ('36)	1.00	.60

No. 225 Surcharged in Red — HABILITADA B. 0.01

1936 *Perf. 11½*

276	A45	1c on 5c blue	.40	.40
a.		Lines of surcharge 1½mm between	6.50	

No. 241 Surcharged in Blue

1936, Sept. 24 *Perf. 12*

277	A53	2c on 24c yellow brn	.60	.50
a.		Double surcharge	20.00	

Centenary of the birth of Pablo Arosemena, president of Panama in 1910-12. See Nos. C19-C20.

Ruins of Custom House, Portobelo A67

Designs: 1c, Panama Tree. 2c, "La Pollera." 5c, Simon Bolivar. 10c, Cathedral Tower Ruins. Old Panama. 15c, Francisco Garcia y Santos, 20c, Madden Dam, Panama Canal. 25c, Columbus. 50c, Gaillard Cut. 1b, Panama Cathedral.

1936, Dec. **Engr.** *Perf. 11½*

278	A67	½c yellow org	.40	.25
279	A67	1c blue green	.40	.20
280	A67	2c carmine rose	.40	.20
281	A67	5c blue	.70	.50
282	A67	10c dk violet	1.25	.75
283	A67	15c turq blue	1.25	.75
284	A67	20c red	1.60	1.50
285	A67	25c black brn	2.50	2.00
286	A67	50c orange	6.50	5.00
287	A67	1b black	15.00	12.00
		Nos. 278-287,C21-C26 (16)	50.65	39.90

4th Postal Congress of the Americas and Spain.

Stamps of 1936 Overprinted in Red or Blue

1937

288	A67	½c yellow org (R)	.30	.30
a.		Inverted overprint	18.00	
289	A67	1c blue green (R)	.35	.18
290	A67	2c car rose (Bl)	.35	.18
291	A67	5c blue (R)	.50	.22
292	A67	10c dk vio (R)	1.00	.35
293	A67	15c turq bl (R)	4.50	3.25
294	A67	20c red (Bl)	1.65	1.25
295	A67	25c black brn (R)	2.50	1.25
296	A67	50c orange (Bl)	6.75	6.00
297	A67	1b black (R)	12.00	10.00
		Nos. 288-297,C27-C32 (16)	64.30	54.03

Stamps of 1921-26 Overprinted in Red or Blue — 1937-38

1937, July *Perf. 12, 12½*

298	A54	½c orange (R)	.80	.80
a.		Inverted overprint	30.00	
299	A41	1c green (R)	.25	.25
a.		Inverted overprint	30.00	
300	A54	1c dk green (R)	.25	.25
301	A52	2c dk green (R)	.35	.35
302	A54	2c scarlet (Bl)	.35	.35

Stamps of 1921-26 Surcharged in Red — 1937-38 2¢

303	A54	2c on 4c gray	.60	.45
304	A46	2c on 8c ol grn	.60	.60
305	A55	2c on 8c lilac	.60	.45
306	A55	2c on 10c dl vio	.60	.50
307	A55	2c on 12c ol grn	.60	.45
308	A48	2c on 15c lt blue	.60	.60
309	A50	2c on 24c blk brn	.60	.75
310	A51	2c on 50c black	.60	.35
		Nos. 298-310 (13)	6.80	6.15

Ricardo Arango A77

Juan A. Guizado A78

La Concordia Fire — A79

Modern Fire Fighting Equipment A80

Firemen's Monument A81

David H. Brandon A82

Perf. 14x14½, 14½x14

1937, Nov. 25 **Photo.** **Wmk. 233**

311	A77	½c orange red	.40	.35
312	A78	1c green	.40	.35
313	A79	2c red	.40	.25
314	A80	5c brt blue	.80	.50
315	A81	10c purple	1.50	1.25
316	A82	12c yellow grn	2.50	2.00
		Nos. 311-316,C40-C42 (9)	9.25	7.05

50th anniversary of the Fire Department.

Old Panama Cathedral Tower and Statue of Liberty Enlightening the World, Flags of Panama and US — A83

Engr. & Litho.

1938, Dec. 7 **Unwmk.** *Perf. 12½*

Center in Black; Flags in Red and Ultramarine

317	A83	1c deep green	.30	.25
318	A83	2c carmine	.38	.18
319	A83	5c blue	.65	.30
320	A83	12c olive	1.25	.75
321	A83	15c brt ultra	1.50	1.25
		Nos. 317-321,C49-C53 (10)	15.13	13.54

150th anniv. of the US Constitution.

No. 236 Overprinted in Black — NORMAL DE SANTIAGO JUNIO 5 1938

1938, June 5 *Perf. 12*

321A	A53	2c carmine	.25	.25
b.		Inverted overprint	22.50	
		Nos. 321A,C53A-C53B (3)	1.05	1.05

Opening of the Normal School at Santiago, Veraguas Province, June 5, 1938.

Gatun Lake — A84

Liberty — A93

Designs: 1c, Pedro Miguel Locks. 2c, Allegory. 5c, Culebra Cut. 10c, Ferryboat. 12c, Aerial View of Canal. 15c, Gen. William C. Gorgas. 50c, Dr. Manuel A. Guerrero. 1b, Woodrow Wilson.

1939, Aug. 15 Engr. *Perf. 12½*

322 A84 ½c yellow .22 .15
323 A84 1c dp blue grn .40 .15
324 A84 2c dull rose .50 .15
325 A84 5c dull blue .80 .15
326 A84 10c dk violet 1.00 .35
327 A84 12c olive green 1.00 .50
328 A84 15c ultra 1.00 .80
329 A84 50c orange 2.50 1.65
330 A84 1b dk brown 5.00 3.00
Nos. 322-330,C54-C61 (17) 29.12 13.68

25th anniversary of the opening of the Panama Canal. For surcharges see Nos. C64, G2.

Stamps of 1924 Overprinted in Black or Red

1941, Jan. 2 *Perf. 12*

331 A53 ½c orange .25 .25
332 A53 1c dk grn (R) .30 .30
333 A53 2c carmine .30 .15
334 A53 5c dk bl (R) .40 .30
335 A53 10c dk vio (R) .65 .50
336 A53 15c ultra (R) 1.40 .65
337 A53 50c dp org 5.25 3.50
338 A53 1b blk (R) 12.00 6.00
Nos. 331-338,C67-C71 (13) 41.00 27.35

New Panama constitution, effective Jan. 2, 1941.

Black Overprint

1942, Feb. 19 Engr.

339 A93 10c purple 1.00 1.00

Surcharged with New Value

340 A93 2c on 5c dk bl 1.25 .50
Nos. 339-340,C72 (3) 5.25 4.00

Flags of Panama and Costa Rica A94

1942 Engraved and Lithographed

341 A94 2c rose red, dk bl & dp rose .30 .22

1st anniv. of the settlement of the Costa Rica-Panama border dispute. See No. C73.

National Emblems — A95

Farm Girl in Work Dress — A96

Cart Laden with Sugar Cane (Inscribed "ACARRERO DE CAÑA") A97

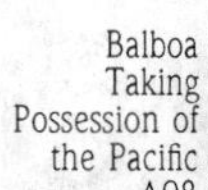

Balboa Taking Possession of the Pacific A98

Golden Altar of San José — A99

San Blas Indian Woman and Child — A101

Santo Tomas Hospital A100

Modern Highway A102

1942 Engr.; Flag on ½c Litho.

342 A95 ½c dl vio, bl & car .15 .15
343 A96 1c dk green .15 .15
344 A97 2c vermilion .16 .15
345 A98 5c dp bl & blk .20 .15
346 A99 10c car rose & org .35 .20
347 A100 15c lt bl & blk .60 .50
348 A101 50c org red & ol blk 1.40 1.00
349 A102 1b black 2.00 1.00
Nos. 342-349 (8) 5.01 3.30

See Nos. 357, 365, 376-377, 380, 395, 409.
For surcharges and overprints see Nos. 366-370, 373-375, 378-379, 381, 387-388, 396, C129-C130, RA23.

Catalogue values for unused stamps in this section, from this point to the end of the section, are for Never Hinged items.

Flag of Panama — A103

Arms of Panama — A104

Engraved; Flag on 2c Lithographed
1947, Apr. Unwmk. *Perf. 12½*

350 A103 2c car, bl & red .15 .15
351 A104 5c deep blue .15 .15

Second anniversary of the National Constitutional Assembly of 1945.

No. 241 Surcharged in Black

Habilitada
CORREOS
B/. 0.50

1947 *Perf. 12*

352 A53 50c on 24c yel brn 1.50 1.50
a. "Habilitada" 2.00 2.00

Nos. C6C, C75, C74 and C87 Surcharged in Black or Carmine

HABILITADA
CORREOS
B/. 0.0½

353 AP5 ½c on 8c gray blk .15 .15
a. "B/.0.0½ CORREOS" (transposed) 2.50 2.50
354 AP34 ½c on 8c dk ol brn & blk (C) .15 .15
355 AP34 1c on 7c rose car .15 .15
356 AP42 2c on 8c vio .16 .15
Nos. 352-356 (5) 2.11
Set value 1.38

Flag Type of 1942

1948 Engr. and Litho.

357 A95 ½c car, org, bl & dp car .15 .15

Monument to Firemen of Colon — A105

American-La France Fire Engine A106

20c, Firemen & hose cart. 25c, New Central Fire Station, Colon. 50c, Maximino Walker. 1b, J. J. A. Ducruet.

1948 Engr.

Center in Black

358 A105 5c dp car .35 .15
359 A106 10c orange .60 .20
360 A106 20c gray bl .90 .38
361 A106 25c chocolate .90 .50
362 A105 50c purple 1.00 .50
363 A105 1b dp grn 2.50 1.50
Nos. 358-363 (6) 6.25 3.23

50th anniversary of the founding of the Colon Fire Department.
For overprint see No. C125.

Cervantes — A107

1948 Unwmk. *Perf. 12½*

364 A107 2c car & blk .25 .15
Nos. 364,C105-C106 (3) .76 .55

400th anniv. of the birth of Miguel de Cervantes Saavedra, novelist, playwright and poet.

Oxcart Type of 1942 Redrawn
Inscribed: "ACARREO DE CANA"

1948 *Perf. 12*

365 A97 2c vermilion .60 .15

No. 365 Surcharged or Overprinted in Black

1949, May 23

366 A97 1c on 2c ver .16 .15
367 A97 2c vermilion .16 .15
a. Inverted overprint 3.00 3.00
Nos. 366-367,C108-C111 (6) 3.63 3.61

Incorporation of Chiriqui Province, cent.

Stamps and Types of 1942-48 Issues Overprinted in Black or Red

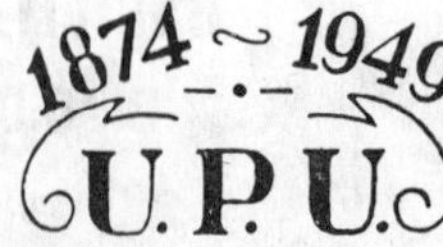

1949, Sept. Engr.

368 A96 1c dk green .15 .15
369 A97 2c ver (#365) .20 .15
370 A98 5c blue (R) .30 .18
Nos. 368-370,C114-C118 (8) 3.81 3.43

75th anniv. of the UPU.
Overprint on No. 368 is slightly different and smaller, 15½x12mm.

Francisco Javier de Luna — A108

Dr. Carlos J. Finlay — A109

1949, Dec. 7 *Perf. 12½*

371 A108 2c car & blk .22 .15

200th anniversary of the founding of the University of San Javier. See No. C119.

1950, Jan. 12 Unwmk. *Perf. 12*

372 A109 2c car & gray blk .35 .15

Issued to honor Dr. Carlos J. Finlay (1833-1915), Cuban physician and biologist who found that a mosquito transmitted yellow fever. See No. C120.

Nos. 343, 357 and 345, Overprinted or Surcharged in Carmine or Black

CENTENARIO
del Gral. José
de San Martín
17 de Agosto
de 1950

1950, Aug. 17

373 A96 1c dk green .15 .15
374 A95 2c on ½c car, org, bl & dp car (Bk) .16 .15
375 A98 5c dp bl & blk .30 .16
Nos. 373-375,C121-C125 (8) 4.21 3.51

Gen. José de San Martin, death cent.
The overprint is in four lines on No. 375.

Types of 1942

1950 Engr.

376 A97 2c ver & blk .15 .15
377 A98 5c blue .25 .15
Set value .15

No. 376 is inscribed "ACARREO DE CANA."

Nos. 376 and 377 Overprinted in Green or Carmine

Tercer Centenario del
Natalicio de San Juan
Bautista de La Salle.

1651-1951

1951, Sept. 26

378 A97 2c ver & blk (G) .15 .15
379 A98 5c blue (C) .22 .15

St. Jean-Baptiste de la Salle, 500th birth anniv.
The overprint exists (a) inverted on both stamps, (b) with top line omitted and second line repeated in its place. Value, each $12.50.

Altar Type of 1942

1952 Engr. *Perf. 12*

380 A99 10c pur & org .75 .25

No. 357 Surcharged "1952" and New Value in Black

1952

381 A95 1c on ½c multi .15 .15

Queen Isabella I and Arms — A110

1952, Oct. 20 Engr. *Perf. 12½*
Center in Black

382 A110 1c green .15 .15
383 A110 2c carmine .15 .15
384 A110 5c dk bl .20 .15
385 A110 10c purple .30 .30
Nos. 382-385,C131-C136 (10) 5.95 5.27

Queen Isabella I of Spain. 500th birth anniv.

No. 380 and Type of 1942 Surcharged "B/ .0.01 1953" in Black or Carmine

1953 *Perf. 12*

387 A99 1c on 10c pur & org .15 .15
388 A100 1c on 15c black (C) .15 .15
Set value .20 .15

A similar surcharge on No. 346 was privately applied.

A111 A112

2c, Baptism of the Flag. 5c, Manuel Amador Guerrero & Senora de Amador. 12c, Santos Jorge A. & Jeronimo de la Ossa. 20c, Revolutionary Junta. 50c, Old city hall. 1b, Natl. coinage.

1953, Nov. 3 Engr. *Perf. 12*

389 A111 2c purple .15 .15
390 A112 5c red orange .25 .15
391 A112 12c dp red vio .50 .15
392 A112 20c slate gray 1.00 .22
393 A111 50c org yel 1.50 .60
394 A112 1b blue 2.50 1.25
Nos. 389-394 (6) 5.90 2.52

Founding of the Republic of Panama, 50th anniv. See #C140-C145. For surcharge see #413.

Farm Girl Type of 1942

1954 Unwmk. *Perf. 12*

395 A96 1c dp car rose .15 .15

Surcharged with New Value

396 A96 3c on 1c dp car rose .15 .15
Set value .15 .15

Monument to Gen. Tomas Herrera — A113

1954 Litho. *Perf. 12½*

397 A113 3c purple .16 .15
Nos. 397,C148-C149 (3) 2.81 2.55

Centenary of the death of Gen. Tomas Herrera.

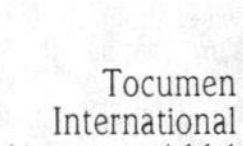

Tocumen International Airport — A114

1955

398 A114 ½c org brn .15 .15

For surcharges see Nos. 411-412.

Pres. José Antonio Remon Cantera, 1908-1955 — A115

1955, June 1

399 A115 3c lilac rose & blk .15 .15

See No. C153.

Victor de la Guardia y Ayala and Miguel Chiari A116

1955, Sept. 13

400 A116 5c violet .16 .15

Centenary of province of Coclé.

Ferdinand de Lesseps — A117

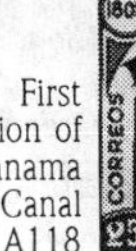

First Excavation of Panama Canal A118

Design: 50c, Theodore Roosevelt.

1955, Nov. 16

401 A117 3c rose brn, *rose* .30 .15
402 A118 25c vio bl, *lt bl* .75 .75
403 A117 50c vio, *lt vio* 1.50 1.00
Nos. 401-403,C155-C156 (5) 4.71 4.05

Ferdinand de Lesseps, 150th birth anniv., French promoter connected with building of Panama Canal. 75th anniv. of the 1st French excavations.

Imperfs exist, but were not sold at any post office.

Popes

A set of twelve stamps picturing various Popes exists. Value, approximately $50.

Arms of Panama City A119

Carlos A. Mendoza A120

Perf. 12½

1956, Aug. 17 Litho. Unwmk.

404 A119 3c green .15 .15

Sixth Inter-American Congress of Municipalities, Panama City, Aug. 14-19, 1956.

For souvenir sheet see C182a.

1956, Sept. 13 Wmk. 311

405 A120 10c rose red & dp grn .20 .15

Pres. Carlos A. Mendoza, birth cent.

National Archives A121

1956, Nov. 27

406 A121 15c shown .40 .20
407 A121 25c Pres. Belisario Porras .60 .50
Nos. 406-407,C183-C184 (4) 1.40 1.05

Centenary of the birth of Pres. Belisario Porras. For surcharge see No. 446.

Pan-American Highway, Panama A122

1957, Aug. 1

408 A122 3c gray green .15 .15
Nos. 408,C185-C187 (4) 3.05 3.05

7th Pan-American Highway Congress.

Hospital Type of 1942

1957 Unwmk. Engr. *Perf. 12*

409 A100 15c black .60 .45

Manuel Espinosa Batista — A123

Flags of 21 American Nations — A124

Perf. 12½

1957, Sept. 20 Litho. Wmk. 311

410 A123 5c grn & ultra .15 .15

Centenary of the birth of Manuel Espinosa B., independence leader.

No. 398 Surcharged "1957" and New Value in Violet or Black

1957 Unwmk.

411 A114 1c on ½c org brn (V) .15 .15
412 A114 3c on ½c org brn .15 .15
Set value .15 .15

No. 391 Surcharged "1958," New Value and Dots

1958 Engr. *Perf. 12*

413 A112 3c on 12c dp red vio .15 .15

Perf. 12½

1958, July 10 Litho. Unwmk.
Center yellow & black; flags in national colors

414 A124 1c lt gray .15 .15
415 A124 2c brt yel grn .15 .15
416 A124 3c red org .15 .15
417 A124 7c vio bl .22 .15
Nos. 414-417,C203-C206 (8) 3.48
Set value 2.60

Organization of American States, 10th anniv.

Brazilian Pavilion, Brussels Fair — A125

3c, Argentina. 5c, Venezuela. 10c, Great Britain.

1958, Sept. 8 Wmk. 311

418 A125 1c org yel & emer .15 .15
419 A125 3c lt bl & olive .15 .15
420 A125 5c lt brn & slate .15 .15
421 A125 10c aqua & redsh brn .20 .16
Nos. 418-421,C207-C209 (7) 2.95 2.86

World's Fair, Brussels, Apr. 17-Oct. 19.

Pope Pius XII as Young Man A126

UN Headquarters Building A127

Perf. 12½

1959, Jan. Wmk. 311 Litho.

422 A126 3c orange brown .15 .15
Nos. 422,C210-C212 (4) 1.60 1.35

Pope Pius XII, 1876-1958. See #C212a.

1959, Apr. 14 Wmk. 311

Design: 15c, Humanity looking into sun.

423 A127 3c maroon & olive .15 .15
424 A127 15c orange & emer .35 .22
Nos. 423-424,C213-C217 (7) 3.25 2.92

10th anniv. (in 1958) of the signing of the Universal Declaration of Human Rights.

For overprints see Nos. 425-426, C219-C221.

Nos. 423-424 Overprinted in Dark Blue

8A REUNION
C.E.P.A.L.
MAYO 1959

1959, May 16

425 A127 3c maroon & olive .15 .15
426 A127 15c orange & emer .35 .20
Nos. 425-426,C218-C221 (6) 3.06 2.80

Issued to commemorate the 8th Reunion of the Economic Commission for Latin America.

Eusebio A. Morales A128

National Institute A129

Perf. 12½

1959, July 27 Litho. Wmk. 311

427 A128 3c shown .15 .15
428 A128 13c Abel Bravo .25 .25
429 A129 21c shown .40 .25
Nos. 427-429,C222-C223 (5) 1.11
Set value .70

50th anniversary, National Institute.

Soccer — A130

Fencing — A131

1959, Oct. 26

430 A130 1c shown .15 .15
431 A130 3c Swimming .15 .15
432 A130 20c Hurdling .45 .40
Nos. 430-432,C224-C226 (6) 1.90
Set value 1.35

Issued to commemorate the 3rd Pan American Games, Chicago, Aug. 27-Sept. 7, 1959.

For overprint and surcharge see #C289, C349.

Perf. 12½

1960, Sept. 22 Litho. Wmk. 343

433 A131 3c shown .15 .15
434 A131 5c Soccer .16 .15
Nos. 433-434,C234-C237 (6) 2.16
Set value 1.30

17th Olympic Games, Rome, Aug. 25-Sept. 11.

For surcharges & overprints see #C249-C250, C254, C266-C270, C290, C298, C350, RA40.

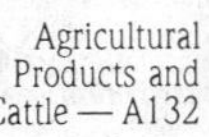

Agricultural Products and Cattle — A132

1961, Mar. 3 Wmk. 311 *Perf. 12½*

435 A132 3c blue green .15 .15

Issued to publicize the second agricultural and livestock census, Apr. 16, 1961.

Children's Hospital — A133

1961, May 2
436 A133 3c greenish blue .15 .15
Nos. 436,C284-C286 (4) .60 .60

25th anniv. of the Lions Club of Panama. See #C245-C247.

Flags of Panama and Costa Rica A134

1961, Oct. 2 Wmk. 343 *Perf. 12½*
437 A134 3c car & bl .15 .15

Meeting of Presidents Mario Echandi of Costa Rica and Roberto F. Chiari of Panama at Paso Canoa, Apr. 21, 1961. See No. C251.

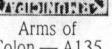

Arms of Colon — A135

Mercury and Cogwheel — A136

1962, Feb. 28 Litho. Wmk. 311
438 A135 3c car, yel & vio bl .15 .15

3rd Central American Municipal Assembly, Colon, May 13-17. See No. C255.

1962, Mar. 16 Wmk. 343
439 A136 3c red org .15 .15

First industrial and commercial census.

Social Security Hospital A137

1962, June 1 *Perf. 12½*
440 A137 3c vermilion & gray .15 .15

Opening of the Social Security Hospital.
For surcharge see No. 445.

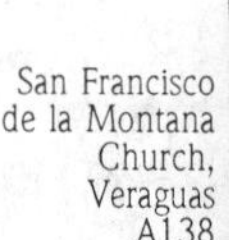
San Francisco de la Montana Church, Veraguas A138

Ruins of Old Panama Cathedral (1519-1671) — A139

Designs: 3c, David Cathedral. 5c, Natá Church. 10c, Don Bosco Church. 15c, Church of the Virgin of Carmen. 20c, Colon Cathedral. 25c, Greek Orthodox Temple. 50c, Cathedral of Panama. 1b, Protestant Church of Colon.

1962-64 Litho. Wmk. 343
Buildings in Black
441 A138 1c red & bl .15 .15
441A A139 2c red & yel .15 .15
441B A138 3c vio & yel .15 .15
441C A139 5c rose & lt grn .15 .15
441D A139 10c grn & yel .25 .20
441E A139 10c red & bl ('64) .25 .15
441F A139 15c ultra & lt grn .30 .16
441G A139 20c red & pink .40 .25
441H A138 25c grn & pink .50 .45
441I A139 50c ultra & pink 1.00 .42
441J A138 1b lilac & yel 2.00 1.50
Nos. 441-441J (11) 5.30 3.73

Freedom of religion in Panama.
Issued: #441E, 6/4/64; others, 7/20/62.
See #C256-C265; souvenir sheet #C264a.
For surcharges and overprints see Nos. 445A, 451, C288, C296-C297, C299.

Bridge of the Americas during Construction A140

1962, Oct. 12 *Perf. 12½*
442 A140 3c carmine & gray .15 .15

Opening of the Bridge of the Americas (Thatcher Ferry Bridge), Oct. 12, 1962. See No. C273. For surcharge see No. 445B.

Fire Brigade Exercises, Inauguration of Aqueduct, 1906 — A141

Portraits of Fire Brigade Officials: 3c, Lt. Col. Luis Carlos Endara P., Col. Raul Arango N. and Major Ernesto Arosemena A. 5c, Guillermo Patterson Jr., David F. de Castro, Pres. T. Gabriel Duque, Telmo Rugliancich and Tomas Leblanc.

1963 Wmk. 311 *Perf. 12½*
443 A141 1c emer & blk .15 .15
443A A141 3c vio bl & blk .15 .15
444 A141 5c mag & blk .15 .15
Nos. 443-444,C279-C281 (6) 1.45
Set value 1.05

75th anniversary (in 1962) of the Panamanian Fire Brigade.
For surcharge see No. 445C.

Nos. 440, 441A, 442, 443A and 407 Surcharged "VALE" and New Value in Black or Red

1963 Wmk. 343 *Perf. 12½*
445 A137 4c on 3c ver & gray .15 .15
445A A138 4c on 3c vio & yel .15 .15
445B A140 4c on 3c car & gray .15 .15
Wmk. 311
445C A141 4c on 3c vio bl & blk .15 .15
446 A121 10c on 25c dk car rose & bluish blk (R) .35 .15
Nos. 445-446 (5) .95
Set value .58

1964 Winter Olympics, Innsbruck — A141a

Perf. 14x13½, 13½x14 (#447A, 447C)
1963, Dec. 20 Litho.
447 A141a ½c Mountains
447A A141a 1c Speed skating
447B A141a 3c like No. 447
447C A141a 4c like No. 447A
447D A141a 5c Slalom skiing
447E A141a 15c like No. 447D
447F A141a 21c like No. 447D
447G A141a 31c like No. 447D
h. Souv. sheet of 2, #447F-447G, perf. 13½x14

#447D-447G are airmail. #447h exists imperf., with background colors switched.

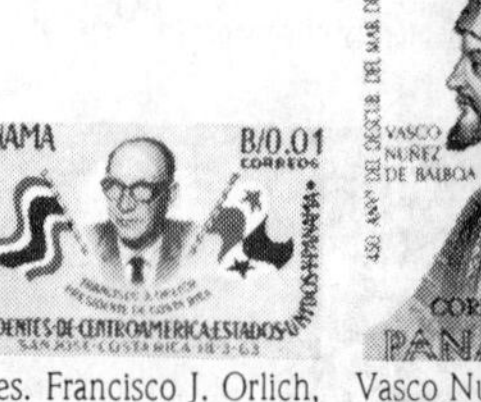
Pres. Francisco J. Orlich, Costa Rica — A142

Vasco Nuñez de Balboa — A143

Flags and Presidents: 2c, Luis A. Somoza, Nicaragua. 3c, Dr. Ramon Villeda M., Honduras. 4c, Roberto F. Chiari, Panama.

Perf. 12½x12
1963, Dec. 18 Litho. Unwmk.
Portrait in Slate Green
448 A142 1c lt grn, red & ultra .15 .15
448A A142 2c lt bl, red & ultra .15 .15
448B A142 3c pale pink, red & ultra .16 .15
448C A142 4c rose, red & ultra .20 .16
Nos. 448-448C,C292-C294 (7) 2.11 2.31

Meeting of Central American Presidents with Pres. John F. Kennedy, San José, Mar. 18-20, 1963.

1964, Jan. 22 Photo. *Perf. 13*
449 A143 4c green, *pale rose* .15 .15

450th anniv. of Balboa's discovery of the Pacific Ocean. See No. C295.

No. C231 Surcharged in Red: "Correos B/.0.10"

1964 Wmk. 311 Litho. *Perf. 12½*
450 AP74 10c on 21c lt bl .20 .15

Type of 1962 Overprinted in Red: "HABILITADA"

1964 Wmk. 343
451 A138 1b red, bl & blk 2.00 2.00

1964 Summer Olympics, Tokyo — A144

1964, Apr. *Perf. 13½x14*
452 A144 ½c shown
452A A144 1c Torch bearer
Perf. 14x13½
452B A144 5c Olympic stadium
452C A144 10c like No. 452B
452D A144 21c like No. 452B
452E A144 50c like No. 452B
f. Souv. sheet of 1, perf. 13½x14

Nos. 452B-452E are airmail. No. 452f exists imperf. with different colors.

Space Conquest — A145

½c, Projected Apollo spacecraft. 1c, Gemini, Agena spacecraft. 5c, Astronaut Walter M. Schirra. 10c, Astronaut L. Gordon Cooper. 21c, Schirra's Mercury capsule. 50c, Cooper's Mercury capsule.

1964, Apr. 21 *Perf. 14x14x13½*
453 A145 ½c bl grn & multi
453A A145 1c dk blue & multi
453B A145 5c yel bis & multi
453C A145 10c lilac rose & multi
453D A145 21c blue & multi
453E A145 50c violet & multi
f. Souvenir sheet of 1

Nos. 453B-453E are airmail. No. 453f exists imperf. with different colors.

Aquatic Sports A146

Perf. 14x13½, 13½x14
1964, Sept. 2
454 A146 ½c Water skiing
454A A146 1c Skin diving
454B A146 5c Fishing
454C A146 10c Sailing, vert.
454D A146 21c Hydroplane racing
454E A146 31c Water polo
f. Souvenir sheet of 1

Nos. 454B-454E are airmail. Nos. 454-454f exist imperf. with different colors.

Eleanor Roosevelt — A147

Perf. 12x12½
1964, Oct. 9 Litho. Unwmk.
455 A147 4c car & blk, *grnsh* .15 .15

Issued to honor Eleanor Roosevelt (1884-1962). See Nos. C330-C330a.

Canceled to Order
Canceled sets of new issues have been sold by the government. Postally used copies are worth more.

1964 Winter Olympics, Innsbruck — A147a

Olympic medals and winners: ½c, Women's slalom. 1c, Men's 500-meter speed skating. 2c, Four-man bobsled. 3c, Women's figure skating. 4c, Ski jumping. 5c, 15km cross country skiing. 6c, 50km cross country skiing. 7c, Women's 3000-meter speed skating. 10c, Men's figure skating. 21c, Two-man bobsled. 31c, Men's downhill skiing.

Litho. & Embossed
Perf. 13½x14
1964, Oct. 14 Unwmk.
456 A147a ½c bl grn & multi
456A A147a 1c dk bl & multi
456B A147a 2c brn vio & multi
456C A147a 3c lil rose & multi
456D A147a 4c brn lake & multi
456E A147a 5c brt vio & multi
456F A147a 6c grn bl & multi
456G A147a 7c dp vio & multi
456H A147a 10c emer grn & multi
456I A147a 21c ver & multi
456J A147a 31c ultra & multi
k. Souvenir sheet of 3, #456H-456J

Nos. 456E-456J are airmail. No. 456k exists imperf.
See Nos. 458-458J.

Satellites — A147b

Designs: ½c, Telstar 1. 1c, Transit 2A. 5c, OSO 1 Solar Observatory. 10c, Tiros 2 weather satellite. 21c, Weather station. 50c, Syncom 3.

1964, Dec. 21 *Perf. 14x14x13½*

457 A147b ½c ver & multi
457A A147b 1c violet & multi
457B A147b 5c lil rose & multi
457C A147b 10c blue & multi
457D A147b 21c bl grn & multi
457E A147b 50c green & multi
f. Souvenir sheet of 1

Nos. 457B-457E are airmail. No. 457f exists imperf. with different colors.
For overprints see Nos. 489-489b.

1964 Olympic Medals Type

Summer Olympic Medals and Winners: ½c, Parallel bars. 1c, Dragon-class sailing. 2c, Individual show jumping. 3c, Two-man kayak. 4c, Team road race cycling. 5c, Individual dressage. 6c, Women's 800-meter run. 7c, 3000-meter steeplechase. 10c, Men's floor exercises. 21c, Decathlon. 31c, Men's 100-meter freestyle swimming.

Litho. & Embossed

1964, Dec. 28 *Perf. 13½x14*

458 A147a ½c orange & multi
458A A147a 1c plum & multi
458B A147a 2c bl grn & multi
458C A147a 3c red brn & multi
458D A147a 4c lilac rose & multi
458E A147a 5c dull grn & multi
458F A147a 6c blue & multi
458G A147a 7c dk vio & multi
458H A147a 10c ver & multi
458I A147a 21c dl vio & multi
458J A147a 31c dk bl grn & multi
k. Souvenir sheet of 3, #458H-458J

#458E-458J are airmail. #458k exists imperf.

John F. Kennedy & Cape Kennedy — A147c

Designs: 1c, Launching of Titan II rocket, Gemini capsule. 2c, Apollo lunar module. 3c, Proposed Apollo command and service modules. 5c, Gemini capsule atop Titan II rocket. 6c, Soviet cosmonauts Komarov, Yegorov, Feoktistov. 11c, Ranger VII. 31c, Lunar surface.
Illustration reduced.

1965, Feb. 25 **Litho.** *Perf. 14*

459 A147c ½c vio bl & multi
459A A147c 1c blue & multi
459B A147c 2c plum & multi
459C A147c 3c ol grn & multi
459D A147c 5c lilac rose & multi
459E A147c 10c dull grn & multi
459F A147c 11c brt vio & multi
459G A147c 31c green & multi
h. Souvenir sheet of 1

Nos. 459D-459G are airmail. No. 459h exists imperf. with different color. For overprints see Nos. 491-491b.

Atomic Power for Peace — A147d

Designs: ½c, Nuclear powered submarine *Nautilus*. 1c, Nuclear powered ship *Savannah*. 4c, First nuclear reactor, Calderhall, England. 6c, Nuclear powered icebreaker *Lenin*. 10c, Nuclear powered observatory. 21c, Nuclear powered space vehicle.
Illustration reduced.

1965, May 12

460 A147d ½c blue & multi
460A A147d 1c green & multi
460B A147d 4c red & multi
460C A147d 6c dl bl grn & multi
460D A147d 10c blue grn & multi
460E A147d 21c dk violet & multi
f. Souvenir sheet of 2, #460D-460E

Nos. 460B-460E are airmail. Nos. 460-460fa exist imperf. with different colors.

John F. Kennedy Memorial — A147e

Kennedy and: ½c, PT109. 1c, Space capsule. 10c, UN emblem. 21c, Winston Churchill. 31c, Rocket launch at Cape Kennedy.

1965, Aug. 23 *Perf. 13½x13*

461 A147e ½c multicolored
461A A147e 1c multicolored
461B A147e 10c + 5c, multi
461C A147e 21c + 10c, multi
461D A147e 31c + 15c, multi
e. Souv. sheet of 2, #461A, 461D, perf. 12½x12

Nos. 461B-461D are airmail semipostal. Nos. 461-461e exist imperf. with different colors.
For overprints see Nos. C367A-C367B.

Keel-billed Toucan — A148

Song Birds: 2c, Scarlet macaw. 3c, Red-crowned woodpecker. 4c, Blue-gray tanager, horiz.

1965, Oct. 27 **Unwmk.** *Perf. 14*

462	A148	1c brt pink & multi	.15	.15
462A	A148	2c multicolored	.15	.15
462B	A148	3c brt vio & multi	.15	.15
462C	A148	4c org yel & multi	.15	.15
		Nos. 462-462C (4)	.60	
		Set value		.38

Snapper — A149

1965, Dec. 7 **Litho.**

463	A149	1c shown	.15	.15
463A	A149	2c Dorado	.15	.15
		Nos. 463-463A,C339-C342 (6)	1.70	
		Set value		1.00

Pope Paul VI, Visit to UN
A149a

Designs: ½c, Pope on Balcony of St. Peters, Vatican City. 1c, Pope Addressing UN General Assembly. 5c, Arms of Vatican City, Panama, UN emblem. 10c, Lyndon Johnson, Pope Paul VI, Francis Cardinal Spellman. 21c, Ecumenical Council, Vatican II. 31c, Earlybird satellite.

1966 Apr. 4 *Perf. 12x12½*

464 A149a ½c multicolored
464A A149a 1c multicolored
464B A149a 5c multicolored
464C A149a 10c multicolored
464D A149a 21c multicolored
464E A149a 31c multicolored
f. Souv. sheet of 2, #464B, 464E, perf. 13x13½

Nos. 464B-464E are airmail. No. 464f exists imperf. with different margin color.
For overprints see Nos. 490-490B.

Famous Men — A149b

Designs: ½c, William Shakespeare. 10c, Dante Alighieri. 31c, Richard Wagner.

1966, May 26 *Perf. 14*

465 A149b ½c multicolored
465A A149b 10c multicolored
465B A149b 31c multicolored
c. Souv. sheet of 2, #465A-465B, perf. 13½x14

Nos. 465A-465B are airmail. No. 465c exists imperf. with different margin color.

Works by Famous Artists — A149c

Paintings: ½c, Elizabeth Tucher by Durer. 10c, Madonna of the Rocky Grotto by Da Vinci. 31c, La Belle Jardiniere by Raphael.

1966, May 26

466 A149c ½c multicolored
466A A149c 10c multicolored
466B A149c 31c multicolored
c. Souv. sheet of 2, #466A-466B

Nos. 466A-466B are airmail. No. 466c exists imperf. with different margin color.

No. 441H Surcharged

1966, June 27 **Wmk. 343** *Perf. 12½*

467	A138	13c on 25c grn & pink	.40	.25

The "25c" has not been obliterated.

A149d A149e

1966, July 11 *Perf. 14*

468 A149d ½c shown
468A A149d .005b Uruguay, 1930, 1950
468B A149d 10c Italy, 1934, 1938
468C A149d 10c Brazil, 1958, 1962
468D A149d 21c Germany, 1954
468E A149d 21c Great Britain
f. Souv. sheet of 2, #468B, 468D
g. Souv. sheet of 2, #468, 468E, imperf.

World Cup Soccer Championships, Great Britain. Nos. 468B-468E are airmail. Imperfs. are different colors than perforated issues.
For overprints see Nos. 470-470g.

Perf. 12x12½, 12½x12

1966, Aug. 12

Italian Contributions to Space Research: ½c, Launch of Scout rocket, San Marco satellite. 1c, San Marco in orbit, horiz. 5c, Italian scientists, rocket. 10c, Arms of Panama, Italy, horiz. 21c, San Marco boosted into orbit, horiz.

469 A149e ½c multicolored
469A A149e 1c multicolored
469B A149e 5c multicolored
469C A149e 10c multicolored
469D A149e 21c multicolored
e. Souv. sheet of 2, #469C-469D, imperf.

Nos. 469B-469D are airmail.

Nos. 468-468g Ovptd.

Inglaterra vs Alemania
4 2
Wembley, 7-30-1966

1966, Sept. 28 *Perf. 14*

470 A149d ½c on #468
470A A149d .005b on #468A
470B A149d 10c on #468B
470C A149d 10c on #468C
470D A149d 21c on #468D
470E A149d 21c on #468E
f. on #468f
g. on #468g, imperf.

Nos. 470B-470E are airmail.

A149f

Religious Paintings
A149g

Paintings: ½c, Coronation of Mary. 1c, Holy Family with Angel. 2c, Adoration of the Magi. 3c, Madonna and Child. No. 471D, The Annunciation. No. 471E, The Nativity. No. 471h, Madonna and Child.

1966, Oct. 24 *Perf. 11*

Size of No. 471D: 32x34mm

471 A149f ½c Velazquez
471A A149f 1c Saraceni
471B A149g 2c Durer
471C A149f 3c Orazio
471D A149g 21c Rubens
471E A149f 21c Boticelli

Souvenir Sheet

Perf. 14

471F Sheet of 2
g. A149f 21c like No. 471E, black inscriptions
h. A149f 31c Mignard

Nos. 471D-471F are airmail. All exist imperf. with different colors.

Sir Winston Churchill, British Satellites — A149h

Churchill and: 10c, Blue Streak, NATO emblem. 31c, Europa 1, rocket engine.

1966, Nov. 25 *Perf. 12x12½*

No.	Type	Description
472	A149h	½c shown
472A	A149h	10c org & multi
472B	A149h	31c dk bl & multi
c.		Souv. sheet of 2, #472A-472B, perf. 13½x14

Nos. 472A-472B are airmail. No. 472c exists imperf. with different colors.
For overprints see Nos. 492-492B.

John F. Kennedy, 3rd Death Anniv. — A149i

1966, Nov. 25 *Perf. 14*

No.	Type	Description
473	A149i	½c shown
473A	A149i	10c Kennedy, UN bldg.
473B	A149i	31c Kennedy, satellites & map
c.		Souv. sheet of 2, #473A-473B

Nos. 473A-473B are airmail. No. 473c exists imperf. with different colors.

Jules Verne (1828-1905), French Space Explorations — A149j

Designs: ½c, Earth, A-1 satellite. 1c, Verne, submarine. 5c, Earth, FR-1 satellite. 10c, Verne, telescope. 21c, Verne, capsule heading toward Moon. 31c, D-1 satellite over Earth.

1966, Dec. 28 *Perf. 13½x14*

No.	Type	Description
474	A149j	½c bl & multi
474A	A149j	1c bl grn & multi
474B	A149j	5c ultra & multi
474C	A149j	10c lil, blk & red
474D	A149j	21c vio & multi
f.		Souv. sheet of 2, #474C, 474D, imperf.
474E	A149j	31c dl bl & multi
g.		Souvenir sheet of 1

Nos. 474B-474E are airmail. All imperfs. are in different colors.

Hen and Chicks A150

Domestic Animals: 3c, Rooster. 5c, Pig, horiz. 8c, Cow, horiz.

1967, Feb. 3 **Unwmk.** *Perf. 14*

No.	Type	Description	Unused	Used
475	A150	1c multi	.15	.15
475A	A150	3c multi	.15	.15
475B	A150	5c multi	.15	.15
475C	A150	8c multi	.25	.15
		Nos. 475-475C,C353-C356 (8)	3.00	
		Set value		1.55

Easter — A150a

Paintings: ½c, Christ at Calvary. 1c, The Crucifixion. 5c, Pieta, horiz. 10c, Body of Christ. 21c, The Arisen Christ. No. 476E, Christ Ascending into Heaven. No. 476F, Christ on the Cross. No. 476G, Madonna and Child.

Perf. 14x13½, 13½x14

1967, Mar. 13

No.	Type	Description
476	A150a	½c Giambattista Tiepolo
476A	A150a	1c Rubens
476B	A150a	5c Sarto
476C	A150a	10c Raphael Santi
476D	A150a	21c Multscher
476E	A150a	31c Grunewald

Souvenir Sheets

Perf. 12½x12x12½x13½

No.	Type	Description
476F	A150a	31c Van der Weyden

Imperf

No.	Type	Description
476G	A150a	31c Rubens

Nos. 476B-476G are airmail.

1968 Summer Olympics, Mexico City — A150b

Indian Ruins at: ½c, Teotihuacan. 1c, Tajin. 5c, Xochicalco. 10c, Monte Alban. 21c, Palenque. 31c, Chichen Itza.

1967, Apr. *Perf. 12x12½*

No.	Type	Description
477	A150b	½c plum & multi
477A	A150b	1c red lilac & multi
477B	A150b	5c blue & multi
477C	A150b	10c ver & multi
477D	A150b	21c green bl & multi
477E	A150b	31c green & multi

Nos. 477B-477E are airmail.

New World Anhinga A151

Birds: 1c, Quetzals. 3c, Turquoise-browed motmot. 4c, Double-collared aracari, horiz. 5c, Macaw. 13c, Belted kingfisher. 50c, Hummingbird.

1967, July 20 *Perf. 14*

No.	Type	Description	Unused	Used
478	A151	½c lt bl & multi	.15	.15
478A	A151	1c lt gray & multi	.15	.15
478B	A151	3c pink & multi	.15	.15
478C	A151	4c lt grn & multi	.15	.15
478D	A151	5c buff & multi	.20	.15
478E	A151	13c yel & multi	.50	.25
		Nos. 478-478E (6)	1.30	
		Set value		.75

Souvenir Sheet

Perf. 14½

No.	Type	Description
478F	A151	50c Sheet of 1

No. 478A exists imperf. with blue background.

Works of Famous Artists A151a

Paintings: No. 479, Maiden in the Doorway. No. 479A, Blueboy. No. 479B, The Promise of Louis XIII. No. 479C, St. George and the Dragon. No. 479D, The Blacksmith's Shop, horiz. No. 479E, St. Hieronymus. Nos. 479F-479K, Self-portraits.

Perf. 14x13½, 13½x14

1967, Aug. 23

No.	Type	Description
479	A151a	5c Rembrandt
479A	A151a	5c Gainsborough
479B	A151a	5c Ingres
479C	A151a	21c Raphael
479D	A151a	21c Velazquez
479E	A151a	21c Durer

Souvenir Sheets

Various Compound Perfs.

No.	Type	Description
479F	A151a	21c Gainsborough
479G	A151a	21c Rembrandt
479H	A151a	21c Ingres
479I	A151a	21c Raphael
479J	A151a	21c Velazquez
479K	A151a	21c Durer

Nos. 479C-479K are airmail.

Red Deer, by Franz Marc A152

Animal Paintings by Franz Marc: 3c, Tiger, vert. 5c, Monkeys. 8c, Blue Fox.

1967, Sept. 1 *Perf. 14*

No.	Type	Description	Unused	Used
480	A152	1c multi	.15	.15
480A	A152	3c multi	.15	.15
480B	A152	5c multi	.15	.15
480C	A152	8c multi	.25	.15
		Nos. 480-480C,C357-C360 (8)	2.15	
		Set value		1.25

Paintings by Goya A152a

Designs: 2c, The Water Carrier. 3c, Count Floridablanca. 4c, Senora Francisca Sebasa y Garcia. 5c, St. Bernard and St. Robert. 8c, Self-portrait. 10c, Dona Isabel Cobos de Porcel. 13c, Clothed Maja, horiz. 21c, Don Manuel Osoria de Zuniga as a child. 50c, Cardinal Luis of Bourbon and Villabriga.

Perf. 14x13½, 13½x14

1967, Oct. 17

No.	Type	Description
481	A152a	2c multicolored
481A	A152a	3c multicolored
481B	A152a	4c multicolored
481C	A152a	5c multicolored
481D	A152a	8c multicolored
481E	A152a	10c multicolored
481F	A152a	13c multi, horiz.
481G	A152a	21c multicolored

Souvenir Sheet

No.	Type	Description
481H	A152a	50c multicolored

Nos. 481C-481H are airmail.

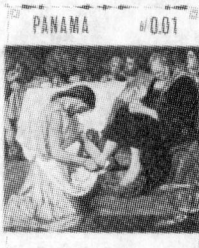

Life of Christ A152b

Paintings: No. 482, The Holy Family. No. 482A, Christ Washing Feet. 3c, Christ's Charge to Peter. 4c, Christ and the Money Changers in the Temple, horiz. No. 482D, Christ's Entry into Jerusalem, horiz. No. 482E, The Last Supper. No. 482l, Pastoral Adoration. No. 482m, The Holy Family. No. 482n, Christ with Mary and Martha. No. 482o, Flight from Egypt. No. 482p, St. Thomas. No. 482q, The Tempest. No. 482r, The Transfiguration. No. 482s, The Crucifixion. No. 482J, The Baptism of Christ, by Guido Reni. No. 482K, Christ at the Sea of Galilee, by Tintoretto, horiz.

1968, Jan. 10 *Perf. 14x13½x13½x14*

No.	Type	Description
482	A152b	1c Michaelangelo
482A	A152b	1c Brown
482B	A152b	3c Rubens
482C	A152b	4c El Greco
482D	A152b	21c Van Dyck
482E	A152b	21c de Juanes

Souvenir Sheets

Various Perfs.

No.	Type	Description
482F		Sheet of 2
l.	A152b	1c Schongauer
m.	A152b	21c Raphael
482G		Sheet of 2
n.	A152b	3c Tintoretto
o.	A152b	21c Caravaggio
482H		Sheet of 2
p.	A152b	21c Anonymous, 12th cent.
q.	A152b	31c multicolored
482I		Sheet of 2
r.	A152b	21c Raphael
s.	A152b	31c Montanez

Imperf

No.	Type	Description
482J	A152b	22c Sheet of 1
482K	A152b	24c Sheet of 1

Nos. 482C-482K are airmail.

Butterflies — A152c

1968, Feb. 23 *Perf. 14*

No.	Type	Description
483	A152c	½c Apodemia albinus
483A	A152c	1c Caligo ilioneus, vert.
483B	A152c	3c Meso semia tenera
483C	A152c	4c Pamphila epictetus
483D	A152c	5c Entheus peleus
483E	A152c	13c Tmetoglene drymo

Souvenir Sheet

Perf. 14½

No.	Type	Description
483F	A152c	50c Thymele chalco, vert.

Nos. 483D-483F are airmail. No. 483F exists imperf. with pink margin.

10th Winter Olympics, Grenoble — A152d

1968, May 7 *Perf. 14x13½, 13½x14*

No.	Type	Description
484	A152d	½c Emblem, vert.
484A	A152d	1c Ski jumper
484B	A152d	5c Skier
484C	A152d	10c Mountain climber
484D	A152d	21c Speed skater
484E	A152d	31c Two-man bobsled

Souvenir Sheets

Perf. 14

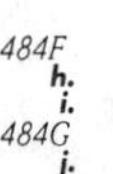

484F Sheet of 2
- **h.** A152d 10c Emblem, snowflake
- **i.** A152d 31c Figure skater

484G Sheet of 2
- **j.** A152d 31c Biathlon
- **k.** A152d 10c Skier on ski lift

Nos. 484B-484G are airmail.

Sailing Ships A152e

Paintings by: ½c, Gamiero, vert. 1c, Lebreton. 3c, Anonymous Japanese. 4c, Le Roi. 5c, Van de Velde. 13c, Duncan. 50c, Anonymous Portuguese, vert.

1968, May 7 *Perf. 14*

485 A152e ½c multicolored
485A A152e 1c multicolored
485B A152e 3c multicolored
485C A152e 4c multicolored
485D A152e 5c multicolored
485E A152e 13c multicolored

Souvenir Sheet

Perf. 14½

485F A152e 50c multicolored

Nos. 485D-485E are airmail. No. 485F exists imperf. with light blue margin.

Tropical Fish — A152f

1968, June 26 *Perf. 14*

486 A152f ½c Balistipus undulatus
486A A152f 1c Holacanthus ciliaris
486B A152f 3c Chaetodon ephippium
486C A152f 4c Epinephelus elongatus
486D A152f 5c Anisotremus verginicus
486E A152f 13c Balistoides conspicillum

Souvenir Sheet

Perf. 14½

486F A152f 50c Raja texana, vert.

Nos. 486D-486F are airmail. No. 486F exists imperf. with pink margin.

Olympic Medals and Winners, Grenoble — A152g

Olympic Medals and Winners: 1c, Men's giant slalom. 2c, Women's downhill. 3c, Women's figure skating. 4c, 5000-meter speed skating. 5c, 10,000-meter speed skating. 6c, Women's slalom. 8c, Women's 1000-meter speed skating. 13c, Women's 1500-meter speed skating. 30c, Two-man bobsled. 70c, Nordic combined.

Litho. & Embossed

1968, July 30 *Perf. 13½x14*

487 A152g 1c pink & multi
487A A152g 2c vio & multi
487B A152g 3c grn & multi
487C A152g 4c plum & multi
487D A152g 5c red brn & multi
487E A152g 6c brt vio & multi
487F A152g 8c Prus bl & multi
487G A152g 13c bl & multi
487H A152g 30c rose lil & multi

Souvenir Sheet

487I A152g 70c red & multi

Nos. 487G-487H are airmail.

Miniature Sheet

Music A152h

Paintings of Musicians, Instruments: 5c, Mandolin, by de la Hyre. 10c, Lute, by Caravaggio. 15c, Flute, by ter Brugghen. 20c, Chamber ensemble, by Tourmer. 25c, Violin, by Caravaggio. 30c, Piano, by Vermeer. 40c, Harp, by Memling.

1968, Sept. 11 **Litho.** *Perf. 13½x14*

488 Sheet of 6
- **a.** A152h 5c multicolored
- **b.** A152h 10c multicolored
- **c.** A152h 15c multicolored
- **d.** A152h 20c multicolored
- **e.** A152h 25c multicolored
- **f.** A152h 30c multicolored

Souvenir Sheet

Perf. 14

488A A152h 40c multicolored

Nos. 457, 457E Ovptd. in Black

OLIMPIADAS MEXICO
TRANSMITIDAS
VIA SATELITE
TELEVISION PANAMENA

1968, Oct. 17

489 A147b ½c on No. 457
489A A147b 50c on No. 457E
- **b.** Souv. sheet of 1, on No. 457f

Nos. 489-489A exist with gold overprint. Overprint differs on No. 489b.

Nos. 464, 464D & 464f Ovptd. in Black or Gold

VISITA S. S. PAULO VI
CONGRESO EUCARISTICO
LATINOAMERICANO
TRANSMITIDA «ATS-3»

1968, Oct. 18 *Perf. 12x12½*

490 A149a ½c on No. 464
490A A149a 21c on No. 464D

Souvenir Sheet

Perf. 13x13½

490B on No. 464f (G)

Nos. 490A-490B are airmail. No. 490B exists imperf. with different colored border. Overprint differs on No. 490B.

Nos. 459, 459G-459h Ovptd. in Black

INAUGURACION
COMUNICACIONES
POR SATELITE
PANAMA 5-OCT 1968

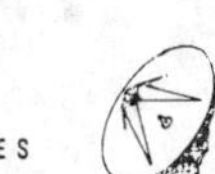

1968, Oct. 21 *Perf. 14*

491 A147c ½c on No. 459
491A A147c 31c on No. 459G
- **b.** on souv. sheet, No. 459h

Nos. 491A-491b are airmail. Nos. 491-491A exist overprinted in gold, and imperf., overprinted in gold. No. 491b exists imperf. with different colors and black or gold overprints.

Nos. 472-472A, 472c Overprinted in Black or Gold

PANAMA INAUGURA
COMUNICACIONES
VIA SATELITE
5-OCT.1968

1968, Oct. 22 *Perf. 12x12½*

492 A149h ½c on No. 472
492A A149h 10c on No. 472A

Souvenir Sheet

Perf. 13½x14

492B on No. 472c

Nos. 492A-492B are airmail. No. 492B exists imperf with different colors.

Hunting on Horseback — A152i

Paintings and Tapestries: 1c, Koller. 3c, Courbet. 5c, Tischbein (Ancien on stamp). 10c, Gobelin, vert. 13c, Oudry. 30c, Rubens.

1968, Oct. 29 *Perf. 14*

493 A152i 1c multicolored
493A A152i 3c multicolored
493B A152i 5c multicolored
493C A152i 10c multicolored
493D A152i 13c multicolored
493E A152i 30c multicolored

Nos. 493D-493E are airmail.

Miniature Sheet

Famous Race Horses — A152j

Horse Paintings: a, 5c, Lexington, by Edward Troye. b, 10c, American Eclipse, by Alvan Fisher. c, 15c, Plenipotentiary, by Abraham Cooper. d, 20c, Gimcrack, by George Stubbs. e, 25c, Flying Childers, by James Seymour. f, 30c, Eclipse, by Stubbs.

1968, Oct. 29 *Perf. 13½x14*

494 A152j Sheet of 6, #a.-f.

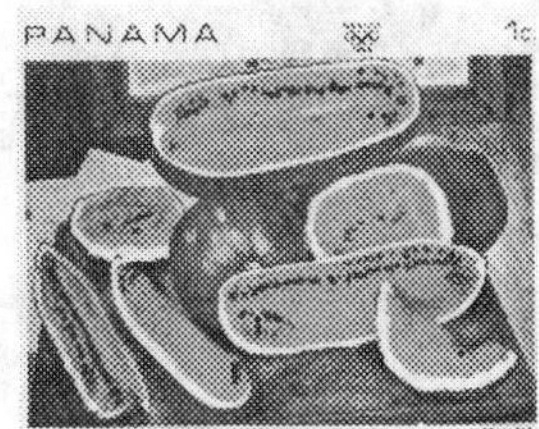

1968 Summer Olympics, Mexico City — A152k

Mexican art: 1c, Watermelons, by Diego Rivera. 2c, Women, by Jose Clemente Orozco. 3c, Flower Seller, by Miguel Covarrubias, vert. 4c, Nutall Codex, vert. 5c, Mayan statue, vert. 6c, Face sculpture, vert. 8c, Seated figure, vert. 13c. Ceramic angel, vert. 30c, Christ, by David Alfaro Siqueiros. 70c, Symbols of Summer Olympic events.

Perf. 13½x14, 14x13½

1968, Dec. 23

495 A152k 1c multicolored
495A A152k 2c multicolored
495B A152k 3c multicolored
495C A152k 4c multicolored
495D A152k 5c multicolored
495E A152k 6c multicolored
495F A152k 8c multicolored
495G A152k 13c multicolored
495H A152k 30c multicolored

Souvenir Sheet

Perf. 14

495I A152k 70c multicolored

Nos. 495G-495H are airmail.

First Visit of Pope Paul VI to Latin America A152l

Paintings: 1c-3c, 5c-6c, Madonna and Child. 4c, The Annunciation. 7c-8c, Adoration of the Magi. 10c, Holy Family. 50c, Madonna and Child, angel.

1969 *Perf. 14*

496 A152l 1c Raphael
496A A152l 2c Ferruzzi
496B A152l 3c Bellini
496C A152l 4c Portuguese School, 17th cent.
496D A152l 5c Van Dyck
496E A152l 6c Albani
496F A152l 7c Viennese master
496G A152l 8c Van Dyck
496H A152l 10c Portuguese School, 16th cent.

Souvenir Sheet

Perf. 14½

496I A152l 50c Del Sarto

Nos. 496E-496I are airmail.

Map of Panama, People and Houses A153

Design: 10c, Map of Americas and people, vert.

1969, Aug. **Photo.** **Wmk. 350**

500 A153	5c violet blue	.15	.15
501 A153	10c bright rose lilac	.30	.15
	Set value		.20

Issued to publicize the 1970 census.

Cogwheel A154

1969, Aug.

502 A154 13c yel & dk bl gray .35 .16

50th anniv. of Rotary International of Panama.

Cornucopia and Map of Panama — A155

Perf. 14½x15

1969, Oct. 10 **Litho.** **Unwmk.**

503 A155 10c lt bl & multi .25 .15

First anniversary of the October 11 Revolution.

Map of Panama and Ruins A156

Natá Church A157

Designs: 5c, Farmer, wife and mule. 13c, Hotel Continental. 20c, Church of the Virgin of Carmen. 21c, Gold altar, San José Church. 25c, Del Rey bridge. 30c, Dr. Justo Arosemena monument. 34c, Cathedral of Panama. 38c, Municipal Palace. 40c, French Plaza. 50c, Thatcher Ferry Bridge (Bridge of the Americas). 59c, National Theater.

Perf. 14½x15, 15x14½

1969-70		Litho.	Unwmk.	
504 A156	3c	org & blk	.15	.15
505 A156	5c	lt bl grn ('70)	.15	.15
506 A157	8c	dl brn ('70)	.20	.15
507 A156	13c	emer & blk	.30	.15
508 A157	20c	vio brn ('70)	.50	.22
509 A157	21c	yellow ('70)	.50	.40
510 A156	25c	lt bl grn ('70)	.60	.25
511 A157	30c	black ('70)	.75	.40
512 A156	34c	org brn ('70)	.80	.50
513 A156	38c	brt bl ('70)	.85	.40
514 A156	40c	org yel ('70)	1.00	.60
515 A156	50c	brt rose lil & blk	1.10	.70
516 A156	59c	brt rose lil ('70)	1.40	.90
		Nos. 504-516 (13)	8.30	4.97

For surcharges see Nos. 541, 543, 545-547, RA78-RA80.

Stadium and Discus Thrower A158

Flor del Espiritu Santo — A159

Perf. 13½

1970, Jan. 6		Litho.	Wmk. 365	
517 A158	1c	ultra & multi	.15	.15
518 A158	2c	ultra & multi	.15	.15
519 A158	3c	ultra & multi	.15	.15
520 A158	5c	ultra & multi	.20	.15
521 A158	10c	ultra & multi	.30	.15
522 A158	13c	ultra & multi	.40	.20
523 A159	13c	pink & multi	.40	.20
524 A158	25c	ultra & multi	.85	.50
525 A158	30c	ultra & multi	1.00	.75
		Nos. 517-525,C368-C369 (11)	4.90	3.45

11th Central American and Caribbean Games, Feb. 28-Mar. 14.

Office of Comptroller General, 1970 — A160

Designs: 5c, Alejandro Tapia and Martin Sosa, first Comptrollers, 1931-34, horiz. 8c, Comptroller's emblem. 13c, Office of Comptroller General, 1955-70, horiz.

1971, Feb. 25		Litho.	Wmk. 365	
526 A160	3c	yel & multi	.15	.15
527 A160	5c	brn, buff & gold	.15	.15
528 A160	8c	gold & multi	.16	.15
529 A160	13c	blk & multi	.25	.15
		Set value	.56	.32

Comptroller General's Office, 40th anniv.

Indian Alligator Design — A161

1971, Aug. 18 Wmk. 343 *Perf. 13½*

530 A161	8c	multicolored	.20	.20

SENAPI (Servicio Nacional de Artesania y Pequeñas Industrias), 5th anniv.

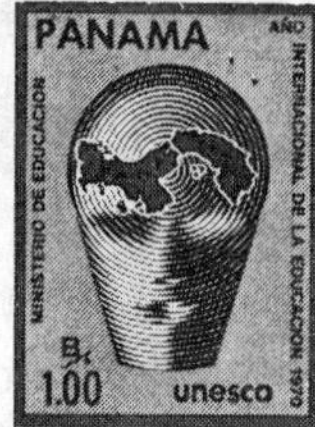

Education Year Emblem, Map of Panama — A162

1971, Aug. 19			Litho.	
531 A162	1b	multicolored	2.50	2.50

International Education Year, 1970.
For surcharge see No. 542.

Congress Emblem A163

1972, Aug. 25				
532 A163	25c	multicolored	.75	.60

9th Inter-American Conference of Saving and Loan Associations, Panama City, Jan. 23-29, 1971.

UPU Headquarters, Bern — A164

Design: 30c, UPU Monument, Bern, vert.

1971, Dec. 14			Wmk. 343	
533 A164	8c	multicolored	.20	.15
534 A164	30c	multicolored	.80	.60

Inauguration of Universal Postal Union Headquarters, Bern, Switzerland.
For surcharge see No. RA77.

Cow, Pig and Produce A165

1971, Dec. 15				
535 A165	3c	yel, brn & blk	.15	.15

3rd agricultural census.

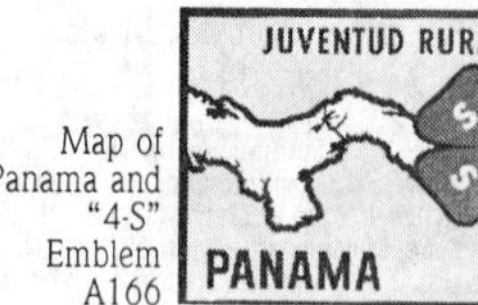

Map of Panama and "4-S" Emblem A166

1971, Dec. 16				
536 A166	2c	multicolored	.15	.15

Rural youth 4-S program.

UNICEF Emblem, Children A167

Perf. 13½

1972, Sept. 12		Litho.	Wmk. 365	
537 A167	1c	yel & multi	.15	.15
		Nos. 537,C390-C392 (4)	1.55	1.05

25th anniv. (in 1971) of UNICEF. See No. C392a.

Tropical Fruits A168

1972, Sept. 13				
538 A168	1c	shown	.15	.15
539 A168	2c	Isla de Noche	.15	.15
540 A168	3c	Carnival float, vert.	.15	.15
		Set value, #538-540, C393-C395	1.10	.65

Tourist publicity.
For surcharges see Nos. RA75-RA76.

VALE 10¢

CONSEJO DE SEGURIDAD
15 - 21 Marzo 1973

Nos. 516, 531 and 511 Surcharged in Red

Perf. 14½x15, 15x14½, 13½
Wmk. 343, Unwmkd.

1973, Mar. 16				
541 A156	8c	on 59c brt rose lil	.15	.15
542 A162	10c	on 1b multi	.20	.20
543 A157	13c	on 30c blk	.25	.25
		Nos. 541-543,C402 (4)	.90	.90

UN Security Council Meeting, Panama City, Mar. 15-21. Surcharges differ in size and are adjusted to fit shape of stamp.

José Daniel Crespo, Educator — A169

Perf. 13½

1973, June 20		Litho.	Wmk. 365	
544 A169	3c	lt bl & multi	.15	.15
		Nos. 544,C403-C413 (12)	5.31	3.57

For overprints and surcharges see Nos. C414-C416, C418-C421, RA81-RA82, RA84.

Nos. 511-512 and 509 Surcharged in Red **VALE 13¢**

Perf. 15x14½, 14½x15

1974, Nov. 11			Unwmk.	
545 A157	5c	on 30c blk	.15	.15
546 A156	10c	on 34c org brn	.20	.15
547 A157	13c	on 21c yel	.25	.15
		Set value, #545-547, C417-C421	1.25	.75

Surcharge vertical on No. 546.

Bolivar, Bridge of the Americas, Men with Flag — A170

Perf. 12½

1976, Mar. 30		Litho.	Unwmk.	
548 A170	6c	multicolored	.15	.15
		Nos. 548,C426-C428 (4)	2.15	1.23

150th anniversary of Congress of Panama.

Evibacus Princeps A171

Marine life: 3c, Ptitosarcus sinuosus, vert. 4c, Acanthaster planci. 7c, Starfish. 1b, Mithrax spinossimus.

Perf. 12½x13, 13x12½

1976, May 6		Litho.	Wmk. 377	
549 A171	2c	multi	.15	.15
550 A171	3c	multi	.15	.15
551 A171	4c	multi	.15	.15
552 A171	7c	multi	.20	.15
		Nos. 549-552,C429-C430 (6)	1.55	1.30

Souvenir Sheet
Imperf

553 A171	1b	multi	3.00	

Bolivar from Bolivar Monument A172

Bolivar and Argentine Flag — A173

Stamps of design A172 show details of Bolivar Monument, Panama City; design A173 shows head of Bolivar and flags of Latin American countries.

Perf. 13½

1976, June 22		Unwmk.	Litho.	
554 A172	20c	shown	.50	.50
555 A173	20c	shown	.50	.50
556 A173	20c	Bolivia	.50	.50
557 A173	20c	Brazil	.50	.50
558 A173	20c	Chile	.50	.50
559 A172	20c	Battle scene	.50	.50
560 A173	20c	Colombia	.50	.50
561 A173	20c	Costa Rica	.50	.50
562 A173	20c	Cuba	.50	.50
563 A173	20c	Ecuador	.50	.50
564 A173	20c	El Salvador	.50	.50
565 A173	20c	Guatemala	.50	.50
566 A173	20c	Guyana	.50	.50
567 A173	20c	Haiti	.50	.50
568 A172	20c	Assembly	.50	.50
569 A172	20c	Liberated people	.50	.50
570 A173	20c	Honduras	.50	.50
571 A173	20c	Jamaica	.50	.50
572 A173	20c	Mexico	.50	.50
573 A173	20c	Nicaragua	.50	.50
574 A173	20c	Panama	.50	.50
575 A173	20c	Paraguay	.50	.50
576 A173	20c	Peru	.50	.50
577 A173	20c	Dominican Rep.	.50	.50
578 A172	20c	Bolivar and flag bearer	.50	.50
579 A173	20c	Surinam	.50	.50
580 A173	20c	Trinidad-Tobago	.50	.50
581 A173	20c	Uruguay	.50	.50
582 A173	20c	Venezuela	.50	.50
583 A172	20c	Indian delegation	.50	.50
a.		Sheet of 30, #554-583	15.00	15.00

Souvenir Sheet

584		Sheet of 3	2.25	2.25
a.	A172 30c	Bolivar and flag bearer	.50	.50
b.	A172 30c	Monument, top	.50	.50
c.	A172 40c	Inscription tablet	.65	.65

Amphictyonic Congress of Panama, sesquicentennial. No. 584 comes perf. and imperf.

Nicanor Villalaz, Designer of Coat of Arms — A174

National Lottery Building, Panama City — A175

1976, Nov. 12 Litho. *Perf. 12½*

585 A174 5c dk blue .15 .15
586 A175 6c multicolored .15 .15
Set value .22 .15

Contadora Island
A176

1976, Dec. 29 *Perf. 12½*

587 A176 3c multicolored .15 .15

Pres. Carter and Gen. Omar Torrijos Signing Panama Canal Treaties — A177

Design: 23c, like No. 588. Design includes Alejandro Orfila, Secretary General of OAS.

1978, Jan. Litho. *Perf. 12*

Size: 90x40mm

588 A177 Strip of 3 2.00 2.00
a. 3c multicolored .15 .15
b. 40c multicolored .80 .50
c. 50c multicolored 1.00 *.75*

Perf. 14

Size: 36x26mm

589 A177 23c multicolored .45 .15

Signing of Panama Canal Treaties, Washington, DC, Sept. 7, 1977.

Pres. Carter and Gen. Torrijos Signing Treaties — A178

1978, Nov. 13 Litho. *Perf. 12*

590 A178 Strip of 3 2.00 2.00
a. 5c multi (30x40mm) .15 .15
b. 35c multi (30x40mm) .70 .35
c. 41c multi (45x40mm) .80 .40

Size: 36x26mm

591 A178 3c Treaty signing .15 .15

Signing of Panama Canal Treaties ratification documents, Panama City, Panama, June 6, 1978.

World Commerce Zone, Colon
A179

1978 Litho. *Perf. 12*

592 A179 6c multicolored .15 .15

Free Zone of Colon, 30th anniversary.

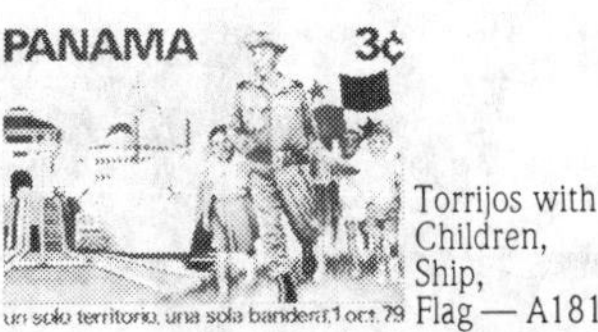

Melvin Jones, Lions Emblem
A180

1978, Dec. 5

593 A180 50c multicolored 1.00 .75

Birth centenary of Melvin Jones, founder of Lions International.

Torrijos with Children, Ship, Flag — A181

"75," Coat of Arms — A182

Rotary Emblem, "75" — A183

Gen. Torrijos and Pres. Carter, Flags, Ship — A184

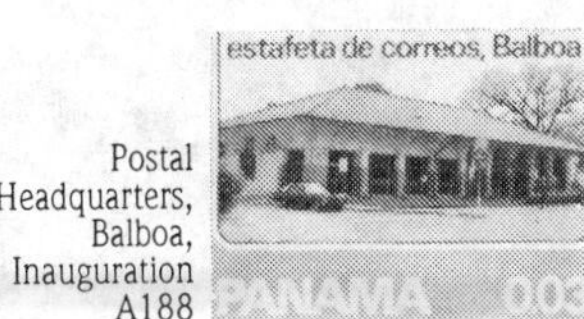

UPU Emblem, Globe — A185

Boy and Girl Inside Heart — A186

1979, Oct. 1 Litho. *Perf. 14*

594 A181 3c multicolored .15 .15
595 A182 6c multicolored .15 .15
596 A183 17c multicolored .35 .30
597 A184 23c multicolored .45 .20
598 A185 35c multicolored .70 .60
599 A186 50c multicolored 1.00 .50
Nos. 594-599 (6) 2.80 1.90

Return of Canal Zone to Panama, Oct. 1 (3c, 23c); Natl. Bank, 75th anniv.; Rotary Intl., 75th anniv.; 18th UPU Cong., Rio, Sept.-Oct., 1979; Intl. Year of the Child.

Colon Station, St. Charles Hotel, Engraving — A187

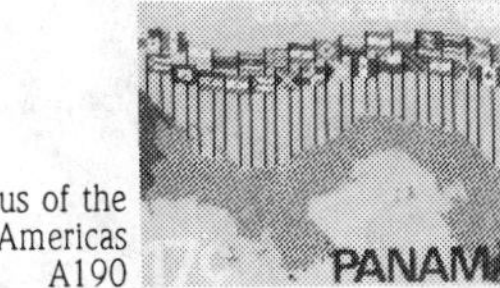

Postal Headquarters, Balboa, Inauguration
A188

Return of Canal Zone to Panama, Oct. 1, 1979 — A189

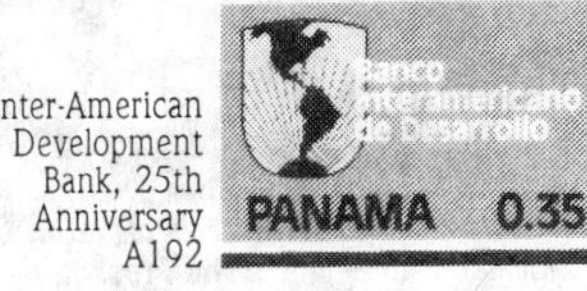

Census of the Americas
A190

Panamanian Tourist and Convention Center Opening
A191

Inter-American Development Bank, 25th Anniversary
A192

Canal Centenary
A193

Olympic Stadium, Moscow '80 Emblem
A194

1980, June 17 Litho. *Perf. 12*

600 A187 1c rose violet .15 .15
601 A188 3c multicolored .15 .15
602 A189 6c multicolored .15 .15
603 A190 17c multicolored .35 .25
604 A191 23c multicolored .45 .20
605 A192 35c multicolored .70 .30
606 A193 41c pale rose & blk .90 .45
607 A194 50c multicolored 1.00 .50
Nos. 600-607 (8) 3.85
Set value 1.80

Transpanamanian Railroad, 130th anniv. (1c); 22nd Summer Olympic Games, Moscow, July 19-Aug. 3 (50c).

La Salle Congregation, 75th Anniv. (1979) — A195

Louis Braille — A196

1981, May 15 Litho. *Perf. 12*

608 A195 17c multicolored .35 .16

1981, May 15

609 A196 23c multicolored .45 .20

Intl. Year of the Disabled.

Bull's Blood
A197

1981, June 26 Litho. *Perf. 12*

610 A197 3c shown .15 .15
611 A197 6c Lory, vert. .15 .15
612 A197 41c Hummingbird, vert. .90 .50
613 A197 50c Toucan 1.10 .42
Nos. 610-613 (4) 2.30
Set value 1.00

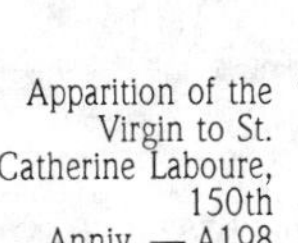

Apparition of the Virgin to St. Catherine Laboure, 150th Anniv. — A198

1981, June 26 Litho. *Perf. 12*

614 A198 35c multicolored .70 .35

Gen. Torrijos and Bayano Dam
A199

Perf. 10½

1982, Mar. Litho. Wmk. 311

615 A199 17c multicolored .35 .16

78th Anniv. of Independence Soldiers Institute — A200

1981, Nov. 30 Litho. *Perf. 10½*

616 A200 3c multicolored .15 .15

First Death Anniv. of Gen. Omar Torrijos Herrera
A201

1982, May 14 Litho. *Perf. 10½*

617 A201 5c Aerial view .15 .15
618 A201 6c Army camp .15 .15
619 A201 50c Felipillo Engineering Works 1.00 .40
Nos. 617-619,C433-C434 (5) 2.80
Set value 1.15

Ricardo J. Alfaro (1882-1977), Statesman — A202

1982, Aug. 18 Wmk. 382

620 A202 3c multicolored .15 .15

See Nos. C436-C437.

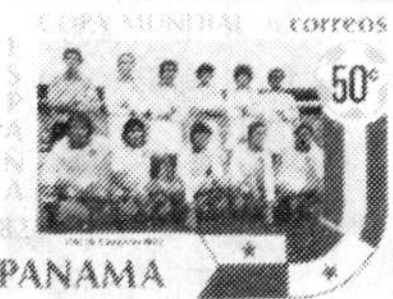

1982 World Cup — A203

1982, Dec. 27 Litho. *Perf. 10½*

621 A203 50c Italian team 1.00 .48

See Nos. C438-C440.

Expo Comer '83, Panama Intl. Commerce Exposition, Jan. 12-16 A204

1983 Litho. Wmk. 382 *Perf. 10½*
622 A204 17c multicolored .40 .30

Visit of Pope John Paul II — A205

Bank Emblem — A206

Various portraits of the Pope. 35c airmail.

Perf. 12x11

1983, Mar. 1 Litho. Wmk. 382
623 A205 6c multicolored .15 .15
624 A205 17c multicolored .35 .25
625 A205 35c multicolored .75 .25
Nos. 623-625 (3) 1.25 .65

1983, Mar. 18
626 A206 50c multicolored 1.00 .40

24th Council Meeting of Inter-American Development Bank, Mar. 21-23.

Simon Bolivar (1783-1830) — A207

1983, July 25 Litho. *Perf. 12*
627 A207 50c multicolored 1.00 .50

Souvenir Sheet

Imperf

628 A207 1b like 50c 2.00 .80

World Communications Year — A208

1983, Oct. 9 Litho. *Perf. 14*
629 A208 30c UPAE emblem .60 .22
630 A208 40c WCY emblem .80 .32
631 A208 50c UPU emblem 1.00 .40
632 A208 60c Dove in flight 1.25 .50
Nos. 629-632 (4) 3.65 1.44

Souvenir Sheet

Imperf

633 A208 1b multicolored 2.00 2.00

No. 633 contains designs of Nos. 629-632 without denominations.

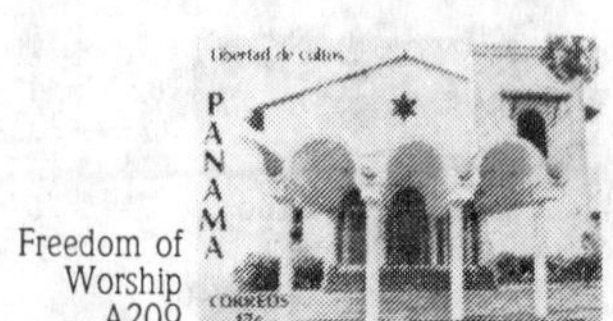

Freedom of Worship A209

1983, Oct. 21 Litho. *Perf. 11½*
634 A209 3c Panama Mosque .15 .15
635 A209 5c Bahai Temple .15 .15
636 A209 6c St. Francis Church .20 .15
637 A209 17c Kol Shearit Israel Synagogue .45 .25
Set value .80 .42

No. 637 incorrectly inscribed.

Ricardo Miro (1883-1940), Poet — A210

The Prophet, by Alfredo Sinclair — A211

Famous Men: 3c, Richard Newman (1883-1946), educator. 5c, Cristobal Rodriguez (1883-1943), politician. 6c, Alcibiades Arosemena (1883-1958), industrialist and financier. 35c, Cirilo Martinez (1883-1924), linguist.

1983, Nov. 8 Litho. *Perf. 14*
638 A210 1c multicolored .15 .15
639 A210 3c multicolored .15 .15
640 A210 5c multicolored .15 .15
641 A210 6c multicolored .15 .15
642 A210 35c multicolored .70 .35
Set value 1.00 .65

1983, Dec. 12 *Perf. 12*

#643, Village House, by Juan Manuel Cedeno. #644, Large Nude, by Manuel Chong Neto. 3c, On Another Occasion, by Spiros Vamvas. 6c, Punta Chame Landscape, by Guillermo Trujillo. 28c, Neon Light, by Alfredo Sinclair. 41c, Highland Girls, by Al Sprague. 1b, Bright Morning, by Ignacio Mallol Pibernat. Nos. 643-647, 650 horiz.

643 A211 1c multicolored .15 .15
644 A211 1c multicolored .15 .15
645 A211 3c multicolored .15 .15
646 A211 6c multicolored .15 .15
647 A211 28c multicolored .55 .22
648 A211 35c multicolored .70 .28
649 A211 41c multicolored .80 .35
650 A211 1b multicolored 2.00 .80
Nos. 643-650 (8) 4.65
Set value 1.80

Double Cup, Indian Period A212

Pottery: 40c, Raised dish, Tonosi period. 50c, Jug with face, Canazas period, vert. 60c, Bowl, Conte, vert.

1984, Jan. 16 Litho. *Perf. 12*
651 A212 30c multicolored .90 .20
652 A212 40c multicolored 1.00 .30
653 A212 50c multicolored 1.25 .40
654 A212 60c multicolored 1.50 .55
Nos. 651-654 (4) 4.65 1.45

Souvenir Sheet

Imperf

655 A212 1b like 30c 2.00 2.00

Pre-Olympics A213

1984, June Litho. *Perf. 14*
656 A213 19c Baseball .40 .35
657 A213 19c Basketball, vert. .40 .35
658 A213 19c Boxing .40 .35
659 A213 19c Swimming, vert. .40 .35
Nos. 656-659 (4) 1.60 1.40

Roberto Duran — A214

Paintings — A215

1984 Olympic Games — A214a

1984, June 14 Litho. *Perf. 14*
660 A214 26c multicolored .60 .25

1st Panamanian to hold 3 boxing championships.

1984 Litho. *Perf. 14*
660A A214a 6c Shooting .15 .15
660B A214a 30c Weight lifting .60 .20
660C A214a 37c Wrestling .75 .30
660D A214a 1b Long jump 2.00 1.50
Nos. 660A-660D (4) 3.50 2.15

Souvenir Sheet

660E A214a 1b Running 2.00 .80

Nos. 660B-660D are airmail. No. 660E contains one 45x45x64mm stamp.

1984, Sept. 17 Litho. *Perf. 14*

Paintings by Panamanian artists: 1c, Woman Thinking, by Manuel Chong Neto. 3c, The Child, by Alfredo Sinclair. 6c, A Day in the Life of Rumalda, by Brooke Alfaro. 30c, Highlands People, by Al Sprague. 37c, Intermission during the Dance, by Roberto Sprague. 44c, Punta Chame Forest, by Guillermo Trujillo. 50c, The Blue Plaza, by Juan Manuel Cedeno. 1b, Ira, by Spiros Vamvas.

661 A215 1c multi .15 .15
662 A215 3c multi, horiz. .15 .15
663 A215 6c multi, horiz. .15 .15
664 A215 30c multi .60 .20
665 A215 37c multi, horiz. .75 .25
666 A215 44c multi, horiz. .90 .35
667 A215 50c multi, horiz. 1.00 .40
668 A215 1b multi, horiz. 2.00 1.50
Nos. 661-668 (8) 5.70 3.15

Postal Sovereignty A216

1984, Oct. 1 Litho. *Perf. 12*
669 A216 19c Gen. Torrijos, canal .40 .25

Fauna A217

1984, Dec. 5 Engr. *Perf. 14*
670 A217 3c Manatee .15 .15
671 A217 30c Gato negro .60 .22
672 A217 44c Tigrillo congo .90 .38
673 A217 50c Puerco de monte 1.00 .40
Nos. 670-673 (4) 2.65 1.15

Souvenir Sheet

674 A217 1b Perezoso de tres dedos, vert. 2.00 2.00

Nos. 671-673 are airmail.

Coins A218

Perf. 11x12

1985, Jan. 17 Litho. Wmk. 353
675 A218 3c 1935 1c .15 .15
676 A218 3c 1904 10c .15 .15
677 A218 6c 1916 5c .15 .15
678 A218 30c 1904 50c .60 .22
679 A218 37c 1962 half-balboa .75 .35
680 A218 44c 1953 balboa .90 .45
Nos. 675-680 (6) 2.70
Set value 1.20

Nos. 678-680 are airmail.

Contadora Type of 1985

Souvenir Sheet

Perf. 13½x13

1985, Oct. 1 Litho. Unwmk.
680A AP108 1b Dove, flags, map 2.00 2.00

Cargo Ship in Lock — A219

1985, Oct. 16 *Perf. 14*
681 A219 19c multicolored .40 .25

Panama Canal, 70th anniv. (1984).

UN 40th Anniv. A220

1986, Jan. 17 Litho. *Perf. 14*
682 A220 23c multicolored .45 .35

Intl. Youth Year — A221

1986, Jan. 17
683 A221 30c multicolored .60 .35

Waiting Her Turn, by Al Sprague (b.1938) — A222

Oil paintings: 5c, Aerobics, by Guillermo Trujillo (b. 1927). 19c, Cardboard House, by Eduardo Augustine (b. 1954). 30c, Door to the Homeland, by Juan Manuel Cedeno (b. 1914). 36c, Supper for Three, by Brooke Alfaro (b. 1949). 42c, Tenderness, by Alfredo Sinclair (b. 1915). 50c, Woman and Character, by Manuel Chong Neto (b. 1927). 60c, Calla lillies, by Maigualida de Diaz (b. 1950).

1986, Jan. 21
684 A222 3c multicolored .15 .15
685 A222 5c multicolored .15 .15
686 A222 19c multicolored .38 .20
687 A222 30c multicolored .60 .35
688 A222 36c multicolored .70 .45
689 A222 42c multicolored .85 .52
690 A222 50c multicolored 1.00 .60
691 A222 60c multicolored 1.25 .72
Nos. 684-691 (8) 5.08 3.14

Miss Universe Pageant A223

1986, July 7 Litho. *Perf. 12*
692 A223 23c Atlapa Center .45 .28
693 A223 60c Emblem, vert. 1.25 .72

Halley's Comet A224

Designs: 30c, Old Panama Cathedral tower, vert.

1986, Oct. 30 Litho. *Perf. 13½*

694 A224 23c multicolored .45 .35
695 A224 30c multicolored .60 .35

Size: 75x86mm

Imperf

695A A224 1b multicolored 2.00

A225

A226

1986 World Cup Soccer Championships, Mexico: Illustrations from Soccer History, by Sandoval and Meron.

1986, Oct. 30

696 A225 23c Argentina, winner .45 .35
697 A225 30c Fed. Rep. of Germany, second .60 .35
698 A225 37c Argentina, Germany .75 .60
Nos. 696-698 (3) 1.80 1.30

Souvenir Sheet

698A A225 1b Argentina, diff. 2.00

1986, Nov. 21

699 A226 20c shown .40 .24
700 A226 23c Montage of events .45 .35

15th Central American and Caribbean Games, Dominican Republic.

Christmas — A227

1986, Dec. 18 Litho.

701 A227 23c shown .45 .30
702 A227 36c Green tree .70 .48
703 A227 42c Silver tree .85 .55
Nos. 701-703 (3) 2.00 1.33

Intl. Peace Year — A228

Tropical Carnival, Feb.-Mar. — A229

1986, Dec. 30 *Perf. 13½*

704 A228 8c multicolored .16 .15
705 A228 19c multicolored .38 .25

1987, Jan. 27 Litho. *Perf. 13½*

706 A229 20c Diablito Sucio mask .40 .30
707 A229 35c Sun .70 .52

Size: 74x84mm

Imperf

708 A229 1b like 35c 2.00 1.50
Nos. 706-708 (3) 3.10 2.32

1st Panamanian Eye Bank — A230

1987, Feb. 17 Litho. *Perf. 14*

709 A230 37c multicolored .75 .75

Panama Lions Club, 50th Anniv. (in 1985). Dated 1986.

Flowering Plants — A231

Birds — A232

1987, Mar. 5

710 A231 3c Brownea macrophylla .15 .15
711 A232 5c Thraupis episcopus .15 .15
712 A231 8c Solandra grandiflora .16 .15
713 A232 15c Tyrannus melancholicus .30 .22
714 A231 19c Barleria micans .38 .35
715 A232 23c Pelecanus occidentalis .45 .35
716 A231 30c Cordia dentata .60 .45
717 A232 36c Columba cayennensis .75 .55
Nos. 710-717 (8) 2.94 2.37

Dated 1986.

Monument and Octavio Mendez Pereira, Founder A233

1987, Mar. 26 Litho. *Perf. 14*

718 A233 19c multicolored .38 .28

University of Panama, 50th anniv. (in 1985). Stamp dated "1986."

UNFAO, 40th Anniv. (in 1985) A234

1987, Apr. 9 *Perf. 13½*

719 A234 10c blk, pale ol & yel org .20 .15
720 A234 45c blk, dk grn & yel grn .90 .70

Natl. Theater, 75th Anniv. A235

Baroque composers: 19c, Schutz (1585-1672). 37c, Bach. 60c, Handel. Nos. 721, 723-724 vert.

1987, Apr. 28 *Perf. 14*

721 A235 19c multicolored .38 .28
722 A235 30c shown .60 .45
723 A235 37c multicolored .75 .60
724 A235 60c multicolored 1.20 .90
Nos. 721-724 (4) 2.93 2.23

A236

A237

1987, May 13 Litho. *Perf. 14*

725 A236 23c multicolored .50 .45

Inter-American Development Bank, 25th anniv.

1987, Nov. 28 Litho. *Perf. 14*

726 A237 25c Fire wagon, 1887, and modern ladder truck .55 .42
727 A237 35c Fireman carrying victim .80 .60

Panama Fire Brigade, cent.

A238

A239

1987, Dec. 11

728 A238 15c Wrestling, horiz. .35 .26
729 A238 23c Tennis .50 .38
730 A238 30c Swimming, horiz. .65 .48
731 A238 41c Basketball .90 .70
732 A238 60c Cycling 1.30 1.00
Nos. 728-732 (5) 3.70 2.82

Souvenir Sheet

733 A238 1b Weight lifting 2.25 1.75

10th Pan American Games, Indianapolis.
For surcharges see Nos. 813, 817.

1987, Dec. 17

Christmas (Religious paintings): 22c, Adoration of the Magi, by Albrecht Nentz (d. 1479). 35c, Virgin Adored by Angels, by Matthias Grunewald (d. 1528). 37c, The Virgin and Child, by Konrad Witz (c. 1400-1445).

734 A239 22c multicolored .48 .35
735 A239 35c multicolored .80 .60
736 A239 37c multicolored .80 .60
Nos. 734-736 (3) 2.08 1.55

Intl. Year of Shelter for the Homeless A240

Designs: 45c, by A. Sinclair. 50c, Woman, boy, girl, shack, housing in perspective by A. Pulido.

1987, Dec. 29 *Perf. 14*

737 A240 45c multicolored 1.00 .75
738 A240 50c multicolored 1.10 .82

For surcharge see No. 814.

Reforestation Campaign — A241

Say No to Drugs — A242

1988, Jan. 14 Litho. *Perf. 14½x14*

739 A241 35c dull grn & yel grn .78 .60
740 A241 40c red & pink .90 .70
741 A241 45c brn & lemon 1.00 .75
Nos. 739-741 (3) 2.68 2.05

Dated 1987. For surcharge see No. 816.

1988, Jan. 14

742 A242 10c org lil rose .22 .16
743 A242 17c yel grn & lil rose .38 .28
744 A242 25c pink & sky blue .55 .42
Nos. 742-744 (3) 1.15 .86

Child Survival Campaign A243

1988, Feb. 29 Litho. *Perf. 14*

745 A243 20c Breast-feeding .45 .35
746 A243 31c Universal immunization .70 .60
747 A243 45c Growth and development, vert. 1.00 .90
Nos. 745-747 (3) 2.15 1.85

For surcharge see No. 816A.

Fish — A244

1988, Mar. 14

748 A244 7c Myripristis jacobus .16 .15
749 A244 35c Pomacanthus paru .80 .60
750 A244 60c Holocanthus tricolor 1.35 1.00
751 A244 1b Equetus punctatus 2.25 1.70
Nos. 748-751 (4) 4.56 3.45

The 7c actually shows the Holocanthus tricolor, the 60c the Myripristis jacobus.
For surcharge see No. 819.

Girl Guides, 75th Anniv. — A245

1988, Apr. 14

752 A245 35c multicolored .80 .60

Christmas A246

St. John Bosco (1815-1888) A247

Paintings: 17c, *Virgin and Gift-givers.* 45c, *Virgin of the Rosary and St. Dominic.*

1988, Dec. 29 Litho. *Perf. 12*

753 A246 17c multicolored .40 .30
754 A246 45c multicolored 1.00 .75

See No. C446.

1989, Jan. 31

755 A247 10c Portrait .25 .15
756 A247 20c Minor Basilica .50 .35

1988 Summer Olympics, Seoul A248

Athletes and medals.

1989, Mar. 17 Litho. *Perf. 12*

757 A248 17c Running .38 .30
758 A248 25c Wrestling .55 .42
759 A248 60c Weight lifting 1.30 1.00
Nos. 757-759 (3) 2.23 1.72

Souvenir Sheet

760 A248 1b Swimming, vert. 2.25 1.65

See No. C447.

A249 A250

1989, Apr. 12 Litho. *Perf. 12*

761 A249 40c red, blk & blue 1.00 .75
762 A249 1b Emergency and rescue services 2.40 1.80

Intl. Red Cross and Red Crescent organizations, 125th annivs.

1989, Oct. 12 Litho. *Perf. 12*

America Issue: Pre-Columbian artifacts.

767 A250 20c Monolith of Barriles .50 .38
768 A250 35c Vessel .88 .65

French Revolution, Bicent. A251

1989, Nov. 14 *Perf. 13½*

769 A251 25c multicolored .62 .48
Nos. 769,C450-C451 (3) 2.65 1.98

Christmas — A252

Designs: 17c, Holy family in Panamanian costume. 35c, Creche. 45c, Holy family, gift givers.

1989, Dec. 1

770 A252 17c multicolored .42 .32
771 A252 35c multicolored .88 .65
772 A252 45c multicolored 1.15 .85
Nos. 770-772 (3) 2.45 1.82

A253 A254

1990, Jan. 16

773 A253 23c brown .58 .45

Rogelio Sinan (b. 1902), writer.

1990, Mar. 14 Litho. *Perf. 13½*

774 A254 25c blue & black .60 .45
775 A254 35c Experiment .82 .60
776 A254 45c Beakers, test tubes, books 1.00 .75
Nos. 774-776 (3) 2.42 1.80

Dr. Guillermo Patterson, Jr., chemist.

Fruits A255

1990, May 15 *Perf. 13½*

777 A255 20c Byrsonima crassifolia .48 .35
778 A255 35c Bactris gasipaes .82 .60
779 A255 40c Anacardium occidentale .95 .68
Nos. 777-779 (3) 2.25 1.63

Tortoises A256

1990, July 17

780 A256 35c Pseudemys scripta .82 .60
781 A256 45c Lepidochelys olivacea 1.00 .75
782 A256 60c Geochelone carbonaria 1.40 1.00
Nos. 780-782 (3) 3.22 2.35

For surcharges see Nos. 815, 818.

Native American A257

1990, Oct. 12

783 A257 20c shown .65 .40
784 A257 35c Native, vert. 1.15 .85

Discovery of Isthmus of Panama, 490th Anniv. — A258

1991, Nov. 19 Litho. *Perf. 12*

785 A258 35c multicolored .90 .65

St. Ignatius of Loyola, 500th Birth Anniv. — A259

1991, Nov. 29

786 A259 20c multicolored .50 .32
a. Tete beche pair 1.00 .65

Society of Jesus, 450th anniv.

Christmas A260

1991, Dec. 2

787 A260 35c Luke 2:14 .90 .65
788 A260 35c Nativity scene .90 .65
a. Pair, #787-788 1.80 1.30

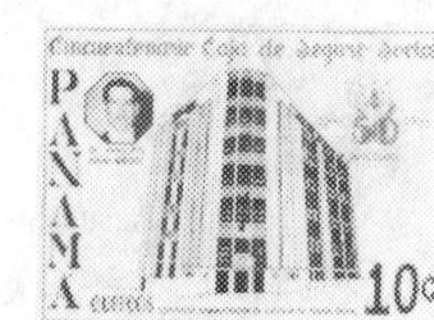

Social Security Administration, 50th Anniv. — A261

Design: No. 790, Dr. Arnulfo Arias Madrid (1901-1988), Constitution of Panama, 1941.

1991 Litho. *Perf. 12*

789 A261 10c multicolored .24 .15
790 A261 10c multicolored .24 .15

Women's citizenship rights, 50th anniv. (No. 790).

Epiphany — A262

1992, Feb. 5 Litho. *Perf. 12*

791 A262 10c multicolored .22 .15
a. Tete beche pair .50 .30

New Life Housing Project — A263

1992, Feb. 17

792 A263 5c multicolored .15 .15
a. Tete beche pair .22 .15

Border Treaty Between Panama and Costa Rica, 50th Anniv. — A264

Designs: a, 20c, Hands clasped. b, 40c, Map. c, 50c, Pres. Rafael A. Calderon, Costa Rica. and Pres. Arnulfo Arias Madrid, Panama.

1992, Feb. 20

793 A264 Strip of 3, #a.-c. 2.65 1.75

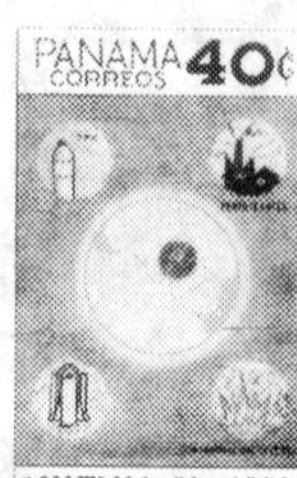

Causes of Hole in Ozone Layer — A265

1992, Feb. 24

794 A265 40c multicolored 1.00 .70
a. Tete beche pair 2.00 1.40

Expocomer '92, Intl. Commercial Exposition — A266

1992, Mar. 11

795 A266 10c multicolored .25 .18

A267 A268

Margot Fonteyn (1919-91), ballerina: a, 35c, Wearing dress. b, 45c, In costume.

1992, Mar. 12

796 A267 Pair, #a.-b. 1.90 1.40

1992, June 22 Litho. *Perf. 12*

797 A268 10c multicolored .25 .15
a. Tete beche pair .50 .30

Maria Olimpia de Obaldia (1891-1985), poet.

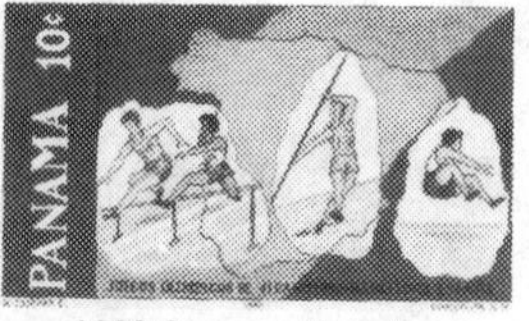

1992 Summer Olympics, Barcelona — A269

1992, June 24 Litho. *Perf. 12*

798 A269 10c multicolored .25 .18
a. Tete-beche pair .50 .36

Zion Baptist Church, Bocas del Toro, 1892 — A270

1992, Oct. 1 Litho. *Perf. 12*

799 A270 20c multicolored .50 .35
a. Tete beche pair 1.00 .70

Baptist Church in Panama, Cent.

Discovery of America, 500th Anniv. — A271

a, 20c, Columbus' fleet. b, 35c, Coming ashore.

1992, Oct. 12

800 A271 Pair, #a.-b. 1.40 .95

Endangered Wildlife — A272

Designs: a, 5c, Agouti paca. b, 10c, Harpia harpyja. c, 15c, Felis onca. d, 20c, Iguana iguana.

1992, Sept. 23

801 A272 Strip of 4, #a.-d. 1.25 .90

Expo '92, Seville — A273

Worker's Health Year — A274

1992, Dec. 21 Litho. *Perf. 12*

802 A273 10c multicolored .25 .18
 a. Tete beche pair .50 .30

1992, Dec. 21

803 A274 15c multicolored .40 .30
 a. Tete beche pair .80 .60

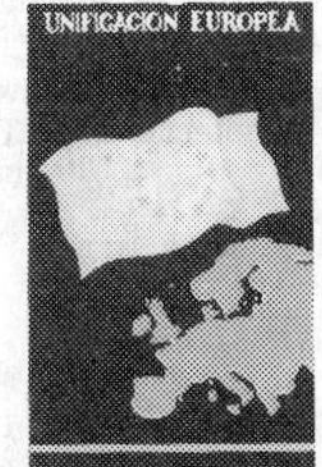

Unification of Europe — A275

1992, Dec. 21 Litho. *Perf. 12*

804 A275 10c multicolored .30 .15

Issued with se-tenant label.

Christmas — A276

a, 20c, Angel announcing birth of Christ. b, 35c, Mary and Joseph approaching city gate.

1992, Dec. 21

805 A276 Pair, #a.-b. 1.25 .95

Evangelism in America, 500th Anniv. (in 1992) — A277

1993, Apr. 13 Litho. *Perf. 12*

806 A277 10c multicolored .25 .15
 a. Tete beche pair .50 .30

Natl. Day for the Disabled A278

1993, May 10

807 A278 5c multicolored .20 .15
 a. Tete beche pair .40 .30

Dr. Jose de la Cruz Herrera (1876-1961), Humanitarian A279

1993, May 26

808 A279 5c multicolored .20 .15
 a. Tete beche pair .40 .30

1992 Intl. Conference on Nutrition, Rome — A280

1993, June 26 Litho. *Perf. 12*

809 A280 10c multicolored .25 .15
 a. Tete beche pair .50 .30

Columbus' Exploration of the Isthmus of Panama, 490th Anniv. — A281

1994, June 2 Litho. *Perf. 12*

810 A281 50c multicolored 1.25 .95
 a. Tete beche pair + 2 labels 2.50 2.00

Dated 1993.

Greek Community in Panama, 50th Anniv. A282

Designs: 20c, Greek influences in Panama, Panamanian flag, vert. No. 812a, Parthenon. No. 812b, Greek Orthodox Church.

1995, Feb. 16 Litho. *Perf. 12*

811 A282 20c multicolored .45 .32

Souvenir Sheet

812 A282 75c Sheet of 2, #a.-b. 3.25 2.50

Nos. 729, 731, 737, 741, 747, 750, 781-782 Surcharged

B/.0.20
1995

1995			*Perfs., Etc. as Before*		
813	A238	20c on 23c #729		.45	.35
814	A240	25c on 45c #737		.60	.42
815	A256	30c on 45c #781		.70	.52
816	A241	35c on 45c #741		.80	.60
816A	A243	35c on 45c No. 747		.85	.65
817	A238	40c on 41c #731		.95	.70
818	A256	50c on 60c #782		1.40	1.00
819	A244	1b on 60c No. 750		2.50	2.00
		Nos. 813-819 (8)		8.25	6.24

Issued: #813-815, 816A-818, 5/6; #816, 819, 4/3.

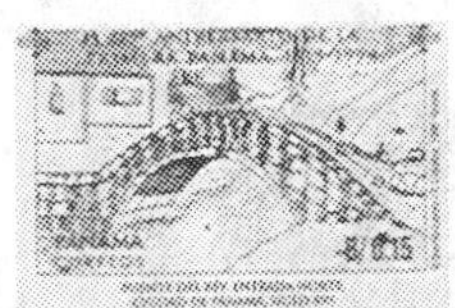

First Settlement of Panama, 475th Anniv. (in 1994) — A283

Designs: 15c, Horse and wagon crossing bridge. 20c, Arms of first Panama City, vert. 25c, Model of an original cathedral. 35c, Ruins of cathedral, vert.

1996, Oct. 11 Litho. *Perf. 14*

820 A283 15c beige, black & brown .40 .30
821 A283 20c multicolored .50 .40
822 A283 25c beige, black & brown .65 .45
823 A283 35c beige, black & brown .95 .70
 Nos. 820-823 (4) 2.50 1.85

Endangered Species A284

1996, Oct. 18 Litho. *Perf. 14*

824 A284 20c Tinamus major .50 .40

Mammals A285

Designs: a, Nasua narica. b, Tamandua mexicana. c, Cyclopes didactylus. d, Felis concolor.

1996, Oct. 18

825 A285 25c Block of 4, #a.-d. 2.50 1.90

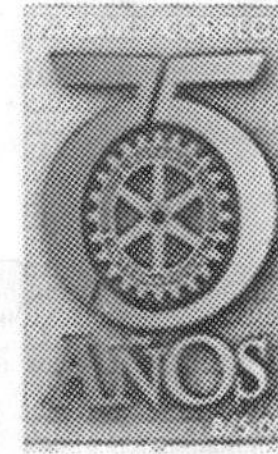

A286

A287

1996, Oct. 22 Litho. *Perf. 14*

826 A286 40c multicolored 1.00 .75

Kiwanis Clubs of Panama, 25th anniv. (in 1993.)

1996, Oct. 17

827 A287 5b multicolored 12.50 9.50

Rotary Clubs of Panama, 75th anniv. (in 1994).

A288

A289

1996, Oct. 21

828 A288 45c multicolored 1.15 .85

UN, 50th anniv. (in 1995).

1996, Oct. 21

Design: Ferdinand de Lesseps (1805-94), builder of Suez Canal.

829 A289 35c multicolored .95 .70

Andrés Bello Covenant, 25th Anniv. (in 1995) — A290

1996, Oct. 23

830 A290 35c multicolored .95 .70

Chinese Presence in Panama — A291

1996, June 10 *Perf. 14½*

831 A291 60c multicolored 1.50 1.10

Litho.

Imperf

Size: 80x68mm

Patterns depicting four seasons: 1.50b, Invierno, Primavera, Verano, Otono.

832 A291 1.50b multicolored 3.75 2.80

Radiology, Cent. (in 1995) A292

1996, Oct. 23 Litho. *Perf. 14*

833 A292 1b multicolored 2.50 1.90

University of Panama, 60th Anniv. A293

1996, Oct. 14

834 A293 40c multicolored 1.00 .75

Christmas — A295

1996, Oct. 24 Litho. *Perf. 14*

836 A295 35c multicolored .95 .70

Mail Train A296

1996, Dec. 10 Litho. *Perf. 14*

837 A296 30c multicolored .60 .45

America issue.

Christmas
A301

1997, Nov. 18 Litho. *Perf. 14x14½*
847 A301 35c multicolored .90 .70

AIR POST STAMPS

Special Delivery Stamp No. E3 Surcharged in Dark Blue

1929, Feb. 8 Unwmk. *Perf. 12½*
C1 SD1 25c on 10c org 1.00 .80
a. Inverted surcharge 22.50 22.50

Nos. E3-E4 Overprinted in Blue

CORREO AEREO

1929
C2 SD1 10c orange .50 .50
a. Inverted overprint 16.00 14.00
b. Double overprint 16.00 14.00

Some specialists claim the red overprint is a proof impression.

With Additional Surcharge of New Value
C3 SD1 15c on 10c org .50 .50
C4 SD1 25c on 20c dk brn 1.10 1.00
a. Double surcharge 14.00 14.00
Nos. C2-C4 (3) 2.10 2.00

No. E3 Surcharged in Blue

1930, Jan. 25
C5 SD1 5c on 10c org .50 .50

No. 219 Overprinted in Red

1930, Feb. 28 *Perf. 12*
C6 A39 1b dk vio & blk 16.00 12.50

Airplane over Map of Panama
AP5 AP6

1930-41 Engr. *Perf. 12*
C6A AP5 5c blue ('41) .15 .15
C6B AP5 7c rose car ('41) .22 .15
C6C AP5 8c gray blk ('41) .22 .15
C7 AP5 15c dp grn .30 .15
C8 AP5 20c rose .35 .15
C9 AP5 25c deep blue .65 .65
Nos. C6A-C9 (6) 1.89
Set value .92

See No. C112.
For surcharges and overprints see Nos. 353, C16-C16A, C53B, C69, C82-C83, C109, C122, C124.

1930, Aug. 4 *Perf. 12½*
C10 AP6 5c ultra .15 .15
C11 AP6 10c orange .35 .20
C12 AP6 30c dp vio 5.50 4.00
C13 AP6 50c dp red 1.50 .50
C14 AP6 1b black 5.50 4.00
Nos. C10-C14 (5) 13.00 8.85

For surcharge and overprints see Nos. C53A, C70-C71, C115.

Amphibian — AP7

1931, Nov. 24 Typo.
Without Gum
C15 AP7 5c deep blue .80 1.00
a. 5c gray blue .80 1.00
b. Horiz. pair, imperf. btwn. 50.00

For the start of regular airmail service between Panama City and the western provinces, but valid only on Nov. 28-29 on mail carried by hydroplane "3 Noviembre."

Many sheets have a papermaker's watermark "DOLPHIN BOND" in double-lined capitals.

No. C9 Surcharged in Red 19mm long

HABILITADA
20 c.

1932, Dec. 14 *Perf. 12*
C16 AP5 20c on 25c dp bl 5.00 .50

Surcharge 17mm long
C16A AP5 20c on 25c dp bl 150.00 2.50

Special Delivery Stamp No. E4 Overprinted in Red or Black

CORREO AEREO

1934 *Perf. 12½*
C17 SD1 20c dk brn 1.00 .50
C17A SD1 20c dk brn (Bk) 75.00 55.00

Surcharged In Black

CORREO AEREO
10
CENTESIMOS

1935, June
C18 SD1 10c on 20c dk brn .80 .50

Same Surcharge with Small "10"
C18A SD1 10c on 20c dk brn 40.00 5.00
b. Horiz. pair, imperf. vert. 100.00

Nos. 234 and 242 Surcharged in Blue

1936, Sept. 24
C19 A53 5c on ½c org 225.00 250.00
C20 A53 5c on 50c org 1.00 .80
a. Double surcharge 60.00 60.00

Centenary of the birth of President Pablo Arosemena.

It is claimed that No. C19 was not regularly issued. Counterfeits of No. C19 exist.

Urracá Monument — AP8

Human Genius Uniting the Oceans
AP9

20c, Panama City. 30c, Balboa Monument. 50c, Pedro Miguel Locks. 1b, Palace of Justice.

1936, Dec. 1 Engr. *Perf. 12*
C21 AP8 5c blue .55 .40
C22 AP9 10c yel org .70 .60
C23 AP9 20c red 1.65 1.50
C24 AP8 30c dk vio 3.00 2.50
C25 AP9 50c car rose 6.75 5.75
C26 AP9 1b black 8.00 6.00
Nos. C21-C26 (6) 20.65 16.75

4th Postal Congress of the Americas and Spain.

Nos. C21-C26 Overprinted in Red or Blue

1937, Mar. 29
C27 AP8 5c blue (R) .35 .35
a. Inverted overprint 35.00
C28 AP9 10c yel org (Bl) .55 .45
C29 AP9 20c red (Bl) 1.25 1.00
a. Double overprint 35.00
C30 AP8 30c dk vio (R) 3.25 3.25
C31 AP8 50c car rose (Bl) 13.00 13.00
a. Double overprint 120.00
C32 AP9 1b black (R) 16.00 13.00
Nos. C27-C32 (6) 34.40 31.05

Regular Stamps of 1921-26 Surcharged in Red

CORREO
AEREO
5¢

1937, June 30 *Perf. 12, 12½*
C33 A55 5c on 15c ultra .75 .75
C34 A55 5c on 20c brn .75 .75
C35 A47 10c on 10c vio 1.75 1.50

Regular Stamps of 1920-26 Surcharged in Red

CORREO AEREO
5¢

C36 A56 5c on 24c blk vio .75 .75
C37 A39 5c on 1b dk vio & blk .75 .50
C38 A56 10c on 50c blk 2.25 2.00
a. Inverted surcharge 20.00

No. 248 Overprinted in Red

CORREO
AEREO

C39 A54 5c dark blue .75 .75
a. Double overprint 18.00
Nos. C33-C39 (7) 7.75 7.00

Fire Dept. Badge
AP14

Florencio Arosemena
AP15

José Gabriel Duque — AP16

Perf. 14x14½
1937, Nov. 25 Photo. Wmk. 233
C40 AP14 5c blue .75 .60
C41 AP15 10c orange 1.00 1.00
C42 AP16 20c crimson 1.50 .75
Nos. C40-C42 (3) 3.25 2.35

50th anniversary of the Fire Department.

Basketball — AP17

Baseball
AP18

1938, Feb. 2 *Perf. 14x14½, 14½x14*
C43 AP17 1c shown .90 .22
C44 AP18 2c shown .90 .15
C45 AP18 7c Swimming 1.25 .25
C46 AP18 8c Boxing 1.25 .25
C47 AP17 15c Soccer 3.00 1.25
a. Souv. sheet of 5, #C43-C47 8.00 8.00
b. As "a," No. C43 omitted *2,500.*
Nos. C43-C47 (5) 7.30 2.12

4th Central American Caribbean Games.

US Constitution Type
Engr. & Litho.
1938, Dec. 7 Unwmk. *Perf. 12½*
Center in Black, Flags in Red and Ultramarine
C49 A83 7c gray .25 .18
C50 A83 8c brt ultra .35 .18
C51 A83 15c red brn .45 .45
C52 A83 50c orange 5.00 5.00
C53 A83 1b black 5.00 5.00
Nos. C49-C53 (5) 11.05 10.81

Nos. C12 and C7 Surcharged in Red

1938, June 5 *Perf. 12½, 12*
C53A AP6 7c on 30c dp vio .40 .40
c. Double surcharge 18.00
d. Inverted surcharge 27.50
C53B AP5 8c on 15c dp grn .40 .40
e. Inverted surcharge 22.50

Opening of the Normal School at Santiago, Veraguas Province, June 5, 1938. The 8c surcharge has no bars.

Belisario Porras — AP23

Designs: 2c, William Howard Taft. 5c, Pedro J. Sosa. 10c, Lucien Bonaparte Wise. 15c, Armando Reclus. 20c, Gen. George W. Goethals. 50c, Ferdinand de Lesseps. 1b, Theodore Roosevelt.

1939, Aug. 15 Engr.
C54 AP23 1c dl rose .35 .15
C55 AP23 2c dp bl grn .35 .15
C56 AP23 5c indigo .50 .15
C57 AP23 10c dk vio .60 .18
C58 AP23 15c ultra 1.40 .30
C59 AP23 20c rose pink 3.50 1.40
C60 AP23 50c dk brn 4.00 .70
C61 AP23 1b black 6.00 3.75
Nos. C54-C61 (8) 16.70 6.78

Opening of Panama Canal, 25th anniv.
For surcharges see Nos. C63, C65, G1, G3.

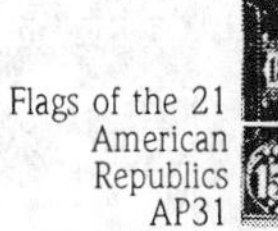

Flags of the 21 American Republics AP31

1940, Apr. 15 **Unwmk.**
C62 AP31 15c blue .42 .35

Pan American Union, 50th anniversary.
For surcharge see No. C66.

Stamps of 1939-40 Surcharged in Black:

a **5 5**

b **AEREO SIETE**

c **SIETE**

d **8— 8**

1940, Aug. 12
C63 AP23 (a) 5c on 15c lt ultra .22 .22
a. "7 AEREO 7" on 15c 40.00 40.00
C64 A84 (b) 7c on 15c ultra .40 .25
C65 AP23 (c) 7c on 20c rose pink .40 .25
C66 AP31 (d) 8c on 15c blue .40 .25
Nos. C63-C66 (4) 1.42 .97

Stamps of 1924-30 Overprinted in Black or Red:

e

CONSTITUCION
1941

f g

1941, Jan. 2 *Perf. 12½, 12*
C67 SD1 (e) 7c on 10c orange .80 .80
C68 A53 (f) 15c on 24c yel brn (R) 2.00 2.00
C69 AP5 (g) 20c rose 1.65 1.65
C70 AP6 (g) 50c deep red 5.00 3.25
C71 AP6 (g) 1b black (R) 11.00 8.00
Nos. C67-C71 (5) 20.45 15.70

New constitution of Panama which became effective Jan. 2, 1941.

Liberty — AP32

Black Overprint

1942, Feb. 19 **Engr.** *Perf. 12*
C72 AP32 20c chestnut brn 3.00 2.50

Costa Rica - Panama Type
Engr. & Litho.

1942, Apr. 25 **Unwmk.**
C73 A94 15c dp grn, dk bl & dp rose .55 .15

Swordfish AP34

J. D. Arosemena Normal School — AP35

Alejandro Meléndez G. — AP40

Designs: 8c, Gate of Glory, Portobelo. 15c, Taboga Island, Balboa Harbor. 50c, Firehouse. 1b, Gold animal figure.

1942, June 4 **Engr.** *Perf. 12*
C74 AP34 7c rose carmine .50 .16
C75 AP34 8c dk ol brn & blk .16 .15
C76 AP34 15c dark violet .25 .15
C77 AP35 20c red brown .35 .15
C78 AP34 50c olive green .65 .35
C79 AP34 1b blk & org yel 1.60 .80
Nos. C74-C79 (6) 3.51
Set value 1.50

See Nos. C96-C99, C113, C126. For surcharges and overprints see Nos. 354-355, C84-C86, C108, C110-C111, C114, C116, C118, C121, C123, C127-C128, C137.

1943, Dec. 16

Design: 5b, Ernesto T. Lefevre.

C80 AP40 3b dk olive gray 4.50 4.50
C81 AP40 5b dark blue 7.00 7.00

For overprint & surcharge see #C117, C128A.

Catalogue values for unused stamps in this section, from this point to the end of the section, are for Never Hinged items.

Nos. C6C and C7 Surcharged in Carmine

AEREO
B/. 0.10
1947

1947, Mar. 8 *Perf. 12*
C82 AP5 5c on 8c gray blk .15 .15
a. Double overprint 25.00
C83 AP5 10c on 15c dp grn .50 .40

Nos. C74 to C76 Surcharged in Black or Carmine

AEREO
B/. 0.10
1947

C84 AP34 5c on 7c rose car (Bk) .16 .16
a. Double surcharge 375.00
C85 AP34 5c on 8c dk ol brn & blk .16 .16
C86 AP34 10c on 15c dk vio .25 .22
a. Double surcharge 30.00 30.00
Nos. C82-C86 (5) 1.22 1.09

National Theater — AP42

1947, Apr. 7 **Engr.** **Unwmk.**
C87 AP42 8c violet .40 .25

Natl. Constitutional Assembly of 1945, 2nd anniv.
For surcharge see No. 356.

Manuel Amador Guerrero AP43

Manuel Espinosa B. — AP44

5c, José Agustín Arango. 10c, Federico Boyd. 15c, Ricardo Arias. 50c, Carlos Constantino Arosemena. 1b, Nicanor de Obarrio. 2b, Tomas Arias.

1948, Feb. 11 *Perf. 12½*
Center in Black
C88 AP43 3c blue .30 .18
C89 AP43 5c brown .30 .18
C90 AP43 10c orange .30 .18
C91 AP43 15c deep claret .30 .18
C92 AP44 20c deep carmine .55 .55
C93 AP44 50c dark gray 1.00 .80
C94 AP44 1b green 3.00 2.50
C95 AP44 2b yellow 6.50 6.00
Nos. C88-C95 (8) 12.25 10.57

Members of the Revolutionary Junta of 1903.

Types of 1942

1948, June 14 *Perf. 12*
C96 AP34 2c carmine .50 .15
C97 AP34 15c olive gray .25 .15
C98 AP35 20c green .25 .15
C99 AP34 50c rose carmine 4.00 3.00
Nos. C96-C99 (4) 5.00 3.45

Franklin D. Roosevelt and Juan D. Arosemena AP45

Four Freedoms AP46

Monument to F. D. Roosevelt AP47

Map showing Boyd-Roosevelt Trans-Isthmian Highway AP48

Franklin D. Roosevelt AP49

1948, Sept. 15 *Perf. 12½*
C100 AP45 5c dp car & blk .16 .15
C101 AP46 10c yellow org .30 .30
C102 AP47 20c dull green .35 .35
C103 AP48 50c dp ultra & blk .65 .60
C104 AP49 1b gray black 1.50 1.20
Nos. C100-C104 (5) 2.96 2.60

Franklin Delano Roosevelt (1882-1945).
For surcharges see Nos. RA28-RA29.

Monument to Cervantes AP50

Design: 10c, Don Quixote attacking windmill.

1948, Nov. 15
C105 AP50 5c dk blue & blk .16 .15
C106 AP50 10c purple & blk .35 .25

400th anniv. of the birth of Miguel de Cervantes Saavedra, novelist, playwright and poet.

No. C106 Overprinted in Carmine

"CENTENARIO DE JOSE GABRIEL DUQUE"

"18 de Enero de 1949"

1949, Jan.
C107 AP50 10c purple & blk .60 .38
a. Inverted overprint 50.00

José Gabriel Duque (1849-1918), newspaper publisher and philanthropist.

Nos. C96, C6A, C97 and C99 Overprinted in Black or Red

h

i

1949, May
C108 AP34(h) 2c carmine .16 .16
a. Double overprint 5.00
C109 AP5(i) 5c blue (R) .25 .25
C110 AP34(h) 15c olive gray (R) .65 .65
C111 AP34(h) 50c rose carmine 2.25 2.25
Nos. C108-C111 (4) 3.31 3.31

Centenary of the incorporation of Chiriqui Province.
No. C74 exists with this overprint.

Types of 1930-42

Design: 10c, Gate of Glory, Portobelo.

1949, Aug. 4 *Perf. 12*
C112 AP5 5c orange .16 .15
C113 AP34 10c dk blue & blk .20 .15
Set value .22

For surcharge see No. C137.

Stamps of 1943-49 Overprinted or Surcharged in Black, Green or Red

1949, Sept. 9
C114 AP34 2c carmine .15 .15
a. Inverted overprint 17.50
b. Double overprint 22.50
C115 AP5 5c orange (G) .38 .25
a. Inverted overprint 9.00
b. Double overprint 20.00
c. Double ovpt., one inverted 20.00
C116 AP34 10c dk bl & blk (R) .38 .30
C117 AP40 25c on 3b dk ol gray (R) .50 .50
C118 AP34 50c rose carmine 1.75 1.75
Nos. C114-C118 (5) 3.16 2.95

75th anniv. of the UPU.
No. C115 has small overprint, 15½x12mm, like No. 368. Overprint on Nos. C114, C116 and C118 as illustrated. Surcharge on No. C117 is arranged vertically, 29x18mm.

University of San Javier — AP51

1949, Dec. 7 **Engr.** *Perf. 12½*
C119 AP51 5c dk blue & blk .35 .15

See note after No. 371.

Mosquito — AP52

1950, Jan. 12 *Perf. 12*

C120 AP52 5c dp ultra & gray blk	1.40	.65

See note after No. 372.

Nos. C96, C112, C113 and C9 Overprinted in Black or Carmine (5 or 4 lines)

CENTENARIO del Gral. José de San Martín 17 de Agosto de 1950

1950, Aug. 17 **Unwmk.**

C121 AP34 2c carmine	.35	.25
C122 AP5 5c orange	.35	.35
C123 AP34 10c dk bl & blk (C)	.50	.40
C124 AP5 25c deep blue (C)	.80	.80

Same on No. 362, Overprinted "AEREO"

C125 A105 50c pur & blk (C)	1.60	1.25
Nos. C121-C125 (5)	3.60	3.05

Gen. José de San Martin, death cent.

Firehouse Type of 1942

1950, Oct. 30 **Engr.**

C126 AP34 50c deep blue	2.00	1.00

Nos. C113 and C81 Surcharged in Carmine or Orange

AEREO

B/. 0.02

X 1952 X

1952, Feb. 20

C127 AP34 2c on 10c	.16	.15
a. Pair, one without surch.	250.00	
C128 AP34 5c on 10c (O)	.20	.15
b. Pair, one without surch.	250.00	
C128A AP40 1b on 5b	20.00	20.00

The surcharge on No. C128A is arranged to fit stamp, with four bars covering value panel at bottom, instead of crosses.

Nos. 376 and 380 Surcharged "AEREO 1952" and New Value in Carmine or Black

1952, Aug. 1

C129 A97 5c on 2c ver & blk (C)	.15	.15
a. Inverted surcharge	22.50	
C130 A99 25c on 10c pur & org	1.00	1.00

Isabella Type of Regular Issue

Perf. 12½

1952, Oct. 20 **Unwmk.** **Engr.**

Center in Black

C131 A110 4c red orange	.15	.15
C132 A110 5c olive green	.15	.15
C133 A110 10c orange	.20	.25
C134 A110 25c gray blue	.65	.32
C135 A110 50c chocolate	1.00	.65
C136 A110 1b black	3.00	3.00
Nos. C131-C136 (6)	5.15	4.52

Queen Isabella I of Spain, 500th birth anniv.

No. C113 Surcharged "5 1953" in Carmine

1953, Apr. 22 *Perf. 12*

C137 AP34 5c on 10c dk bl & blk	.35	.15

Masthead of La Estrella — AP54

1953, July

C138 AP54 5c rose carmine	.16	.15
C139 AP54 10c blue	.22	.20

Panama's 1st newspaper, La Estrella de Panama, cent.
For surcharges see Nos. C146-C147.

Act of Independence — AP55

Senora de Remon and Pres. José A. Remon Cantera AP56

Designs: 7c, Pollera. 25c, National flower. 50c, Marcos A. Salazar, Esteban Huertas and Domingo Diaz A. 1b, Dancers.

1953, Nov.

C140 AP55 2c deep ultra	.15	.15
C141 AP56 5c deep green	.15	.15
C142 AP56 7c gray	.25	.15
C143 AP56 25c black	1.50	.65
C144 AP56 50c dark brown	1.00	.65
C145 AP56 1b red orange	2.50	1.00
Nos. C140-C145 (6)	5.55	2.75

Founding of republic, 50th anniversary.
For overprints see Nos. C227-C229.

Nos. C138-C139 Surcharged with New Value in Black or Red

1953-54

C146 AP54 1c on 5c rose car ('54)	.15	.15
C147 AP54 1c on 10c blue (R)	.15	.15
Set value	.15	.15

Gen. Herrera at Conference Table — AP57

Design: 1b, Gen. Herrera leading troops.

1954, Dec. 4 **Litho.** *Perf. 12½*

C148 AP57 6c deep green	.15	.15
C149 AP57 1b scarlet & blk	2.50	2.25

Death of Gen. Tomas Herrera, cent.
For surcharge see No. C198.

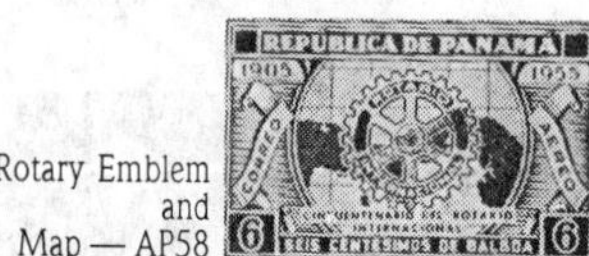

Rotary Emblem and Map — AP58

1955, Feb. 23

C150 AP58 6c rose violet	.15	.15
C151 AP58 21c red	.50	.35
C152 AP58 1b black	4.00	3.25
a. 1b violet black	4.50	4.50
Nos. C150-C152 (3)	4.65	3.75

Rotary International, 50th anniv.
For surcharge see No. C154.

Cantera Type

1955, June 1

C153 A115 6c rose vio & blk	.16	.15

Issued in tribute to Pres. José Antonio Remon Cantera, 1908-1955.
For surcharge see No. C188.

No. C151 Surcharged

B/.xxxxxxxx0.15

1955, Dec. 7

C154 AP58 15c on 21c red	.40	.35

Pedro J. Sosa — AP60

First Barge Going through Canal and de Lesseps AP61

Perf. 12½

1955, Nov. 22 **Unwmk.** **Litho.**

C155 AP60 5c grn, *lt grn*	.16	.15
C156 AP61 1b red lilac & blk	2.00	2.00

150th anniversary of the birth of Ferdinand de Lesseps. Imperforates exist.

Pres. Dwight D. Eisenhower AP62

Statue of Bolivar AP63

Bolivar Hall AP64

Portraits-Presidents: C158, Pedro Aramburu, Argentina. C159, Dr. Victor Paz Estenssoro, Bolivia. C160, Dr. Juscelino Kubitschek O., Brazil. C161, Gen. Carlos Ibanez del Campo, Chile. C162, Gen. Gustavo Rojas Pinilla, Colombia. C163, Jose Figueres, Costa Rica. C164, Gen. Fulgencio Batista y Zaldivar, Cuba. C165, Gen. Hector B. Trujillo Molina, Dominican Rep. C166, José Maria Velasco Ibarra, Ecuador. C167, Col. Carlos Castillo Armas, Guatemala. C168, Gen. Paul E. Magloire, Haiti. C169, Julio Lozano Diaz, Honduras. C170, Adolfo Ruiz Cortines, Mexico. C171, Gen. Anastasio Somoza, Nicaragua. C172, Ricardo Arias Espinosa, Panama. C173, Gen. Alfredo Stroessner, Paraguay. C174, Gen. Manuel Odria, Peru. C175, Col. Oscar Osorio, El Salvador. C176, Dr. Alberto F. Zubiria, Uruguay. C177, Gen. Marcos Perez Jimenez, Venezuela. 1b, Simon Bolivar.

1956, July 18

C157 AP62 6c rose car & vio bl	.40	.35
C158 AP62 6c brt grnsh bl & blk	.25	.20
C159 AP62 6c bister & blk	.25	.20
C160 AP62 6c emerald & blk	.25	.20
C161 AP62 6c lt grn & brn	.25	.20
C162 AP62 6c yellow & grn	.25	.20
C163 AP62 6c brt vio & grn	.25	.20
C164 AP62 6c dl pur & vio bl	.25	.20
C165 AP62 6c red lil & sl grn	.25	.20
C166 AP62 6c citron & vio bl	.25	.20
C167 AP62 6c ap grn & brn	.25	.20
C168 AP62 6c brn & vio bl	.25	.20
C169 AP62 6c brt car & grn	.25	.20
C170 AP62 6c red & brn	.35	.25
C171 AP62 6c lt bl & grn	.25	.20
C172 AP62 6c vio bl & grn	.25	.20
C173 AP62 6c orange & blk	.25	.20
C174 AP62 6c bluish gray & brn	.25	.20
C175 AP62 6c sal rose & blk	.25	.20
C176 AP62 6c dk grn & vio bl	.25	.20
C177 AP62 6c dk org brn & dk grn	.25	.20
C178 AP63 20c dk bluish gray	.55	.55
C179 AP64 50c green	1.00	1.00
C180 AP63 1b brown	2.00	1.25
Nos. C157-C180 (24)	9.05	7.20

Pan-American Conf., Panama City, July 21-22, 1956, and 130th anniv. of the 1st Pan-American Conf. Imperforates exist.

Ruins of First Town Council Building — AP65

Design: 50c, City Hall, Panama City.

1956, Aug. 17

C181 AP65 25c red	.50	.35
C182 AP65 50c black	1.00	.90
a. Souv. sheet of 3, #404, C181-C182, imperf.	2.25	2.25

6th Inter-American Congress of Municipalities, Panama City, Aug. 14-19, 1956.
No. C182a sold for 85c.
For overprint see No. C187a.

Monument AP66

St. Thomas Hospital AP67

1956, Nov. 27 **Wmk. 311**

C183 AP66 5c green	.15	.15
C184 AP67 15c dk carmine	.25	.20
Set value		.25

Centenary of the birth of Pres. Belisario Porras.

Highway Construction — AP68

20c, Road through jungle, Darien project. 1b, Map of Americas showing Pan-American Highway.

Perf. 12½

1957, Aug. 1 **Wmk. 311** **Litho.**

C185 AP68 10c black	.15	.15
C186 AP68 20c lt blue & blk	.50	.50
C187 AP68 1b green	2.25	2.25
a. AP65 Souvenir sheet of 3, unwmkd.	5.00	5.00
Nos. C185-C187 (3)	2.90	2.90

7th Pan-American Highway Congress.
No. C187a is No. C182a overprinted in black: "VII degree CONGRESSO INTERAMERICANO DE CARRETERAS 1957."

No. C153 Surcharged "1957" and New Value

1957, Aug. 13 **Unwmk.**

C188 AP59 10c on 6c rose vio & blk	.20	.16

Remon Polyclinic AP69

Customs House, Portobelo AP70

Buildings: #C191, Portobelo Castle. #C192, San Jeronimo Castle. #C193, Remon Hippodrome. #C194, Legislature. #C195, Interior & Treasury Department. #C196, El Panama Hotel. #C197, San Lorenzo Castle.

Perf. 12½

1957, Oct. Wmk. 311 Litho.

Design in Black

C189 AP69 10c lt blue .22 .15
C190 AP70 10c lilac .22 .15
C191 AP70 10c gray .22 .15
C192 AP70 10c lilac rose .22 .15
C193 AP70 10c ultra .22 .15
C194 AP70 10c brown ol .22 .15
C195 AP70 10c orange yel .22 .15
C196 AP70 10c yellow grn .22 .15
C197 AP70 1b red 2.25 1.60
Nos. C189-C197 (9) 4.01 2.80

No. C148 Surcharged with New Value and "1958" in Red

1958, Feb. 11 Unwmk.

C198 AP57 5c on 6c dp grn .20 .15

United Nations Emblem — AP71

Flags of Panama and UN — AP72

1958, Mar. 5 Litho. Wmk. 311

C199 AP71 10c brt green .15 .15
C200 AP71 21c lt ultra .35 .25
C201 AP71 50c orange 1.00 .85
C202 AP72 1b gray, ultra & car 2.00 1.60
a. Souv. sheet of 4, #C199-C202, imperf. 4.50 4.50
Nos. C199-C202 (4) 3.50 2.85

10th anniv. of the UN (in 1955).

The sheet also exists with the 10c and 50c omitted.

OAS Type of Regular Issue, 1958

Designs: 10c, 1b, Flags of 21 American Nations. 50c, Headquarters in Washington.

1958, July 10 Unwmk. *Perf. 12½*

Center yellow and black; flags in national colors

C203 A124 5c lt blue .15 .15
C204 A124 10c carmine rose .16 .15
C205 A124 50c gray .60 .60
C206 A124 1b black 1.90 1.60
Nos. C203-C206 (4) 2.81 2.50

Type of Regular Issue

Pavilions: 15c, Vatican City. 50c, United States. 1b, Belgium.

1958, Sept. 8 Wmk. 311 *Perf. 12½*

C207 A125 15c gray & lt vio .25 .20
C208 A125 50c dk gray & org brn .65 .65
C209 A125 1b brt vio & bluish grn 1.40 1.40
a. Souv. sheet of 7, #418-421, C207-C209 3.50 3.50
Nos. C207-C209 (3) 2.30 2.25

No. C209a sold for 2b.

Pope Type of Regular Issue

Portraits of Pius XII: 5c, As cardinal. 30c, Wearing papal tiara. 50c, Enthroned.

1959, Jan. 21 Litho. Wmk. 311

C210 A126 5c violet .15 .15
C211 A126 30c lilac rose .50 .40
C212 A126 50c blue gray .80 .65
a. Souv. sheet of 4, #422, C210-C212, imperf. 1.90 1.90
Nos. C210-C212 (3) 1.45 1.20

#C212a is watermarked sideways and sold for 1b. The sheet also exists with 30c omitted. #C212a with C.E.P.A.L. overprint is listed as #C221a.

Human Rights Issue Type

Designs: 5c, Humanity looking into sun. 10c, 20c, Torch and UN emblem. 50c, UN Flag. 1b, UN Headquarters building.

1959, Apr. 14 *Perf. 12½*

C213 A127 5c emerald & bl .15 .15
C214 A127 10c gray & org brn .15 .15
C215 A127 20c brown & gray .25 .20
C216 A127 50c green & ultra .70 .65
C217 A127 1b red & blue 1.50 1.40
Nos. C213-C217 (5) 2.75 2.55

Nos. C213-C215, C212a Overprinted and C216 Surcharged in Red or Dark Blue

8a REUNION
C.E.P.A.L.
MAYO 1959

1959, May 16

C218 A127 5c emer & bl (R) .15 .15
C219 A127 10c gray & org brn (Bl) .16 .15
C220 A127 20c brown & gray (R) .35 .25
C221 A127 1b on 50c grn & ultra (R) 1.90 1.90
a. Souvenir sheet of 4 4.00 4.00
Nos. C218-C221 (4) 2.56 2.45

8th Reunion of the Economic Commission for Latin America.

This overprint also exists on Nos. C216-C217. These have been disavowed by Panama's postmaster general.

No. C221a is No. C212a with two-line black overprint at top of sheet: "8a. REUNION DE LA C.E.P.A.L. MAYO 1959."

Type of Regular Issue, 1959

Portraits: 5c, Justo A. Facio, Rector. 10c, Ernesto de la Guardia, Jr., Pres. of Panama.

Perf. 12½

1959, July 27 Wmk. 311 Litho.

C222 A128 5c black .15 .15
C223 A128 10c black .16 .15
Set value .24 .15

Type of Regular Issue, 1959

1959, Oct. 26 Wmk. 311 *Perf. 12½*

C224 A130 5c Boxing .15 .15
C225 A130 10c Baseball .20 .15
C226 A130 50c Basketball .80 .65
Nos. C224-C226 (3) 1.15 .95

For surcharge see No. C349.

Nos. C143-C145 Overprinted in Vermilion, Red or Black

NACIONES UNIDAS
AÑO MUNDIAL.
REFUGIADOS.
1959–1960

Unwmk.

1960, Feb. 6 Engr. *Perf. 12*

C227 AP56 25c black (V) .75 .20
C228 AP56 50c dk brown (R) 1.00 .40
C229 AP56 1b red orange 1.75 1.25
Nos. C227-C229 (3) 3.50 1.85

World Refugee Year, July 1, 1959-June 30, 1960.

The revenues from the sale of Nos. C227-C229 went to the United Nations Refugee Fund.

Administration Building, National University AP74

Designs: 21c, Humanities building. 25c, Medical school. 30c, Dr. Octavio Mendez Pereria first rector of University.

Perf. 12½

1960, Mar. 23 Litho. Wmk. 311

C230 AP74 10c brt green .20 .15
C231 AP74 21c lt blue .40 .20
C232 AP74 25c ultra .50 .25
C233 AP74 30c black .60 .35
Nos. C230-C233 (4) 1.70 .95

National University, 25th anniv.

For surcharges see Nos. 450, C248, C253, C287, C291.

Olympic Games Type

5c, Basketball. 10c, Bicycling, horiz. 25c, Javelin thrower. 50c, Athlete with Olympic torch.

1960, Sept. 22 Wmk. 343 *Perf. 12½*

C234 A131 5c orange & red .15 .15
C235 A131 10c ocher & blk .20 .15
C236 A131 25c lt bl & dk bl .50 .35
C237 A131 50c brown & blk 1.00 .65
a. Souv. sheet of 2, #C236-C237 2.25 2.25
Nos. C234-C237 (4) 1.85 1.30

For surcharges see Nos. C249-C250, C254, C266-C270, C290, C350, RA40.

Citizens' Silhouettes AP75

Design: 10c, Heads and map of Central America.

1960 Litho. Wmk. 229

C238 AP75 5c black .15 .15
C239 AP75 10c brown .20 .15
Set value .20

6th census of population and the 2nd census of dwellings (No. C238), Dec. 11, 1960, and the All America Census, 1960 (No. C239).

Boeing 707 Jet Liner AP76

1960, Dec. 1 Wmk. 343 *Perf. 12½*

C240 AP76 5c lt grnsh blue .15 .15
C241 AP76 10c emerald .20 .15
C242 AP76 20c red brown .40 .25
Nos. C240-C242 (3) .75
Set value .45

1st jet service to Panama. For surcharge see No. RA41.

Souvenir Sheet

UN Emblem — AP77

Wmk. 311

1961, Mar. 7 Litho. *Imperf.*

C243 AP77 80c blk & car rose 1.60 1.60

15th anniv. (in 1960) of the UN.

Counterfeits without control number exist.

No. C243 Overprinted in Blue with Large Uprooted Oak Emblem and "Ano de los Refugiados"

1961, June 2

C244 AP77 80c blk & car rose 2.50 2.50

World Refugee Year, July 1, 1959-June 30, 1960.

Lions International Type

Designs: 5c, Helen Keller School for the Blind. 10c, Children's summer camp. 21c, Arms of Panama and Lions emblem.

1961, May 2 Wmk. 311 *Perf. 12½*

C245 A133 5c black .15 .15
C246 A133 10c emerald .20 .15
C247 A133 21c ultra, yel & red .40 .25
Nos. C245-C247 (3) .75
Set value .40

For overprints see Nos. C284-C286.

Nos. C230 and C236 Surcharged in Black or Red

HABILITADA
en
B/. 0.01

1961 Wmk. 311 (1c); Wmk. 343

C248 AP74 1c on 10c .15 .15
C249 A131 1b on 25c (Bk) 2.00 2.00
C250 A131 1b on 25c (R) 2.00 2.00
Nos. C248-C250 (3) 4.15 4.15

Pres. Roberto F. Chiari and Pres. Mario Echandi AP78

Perf. 12½

1961, Oct. 2 Wmk. 343 Litho.

C251 AP78 1b black & gold 2.00 1.25

Meeting of the Presidents of Panama and Costa Rica at Paso Canoa, Apr. 21, 1961.

Dag Hammarskjold — AP79

1961, Dec. 27 *Perf. 12½*

C252 AP79 10c black .20 .15

Dag Hammarskjold, UN Secretary General, 1953-61.

No. C230 Surcharged

Vale B/. 0.15

1962, Feb. 21 Wmk. 311

C253 AP74 15c on 10c brt grn .30 .20

No. C236 Surcharged

XX
VALE
B/. 1.00

Wmk. 343

C254 A131 1b on 25c 2.00 1.25

City Hall, Colon — AP80

1962, Feb. 28 Litho. Wmk. 311

C255 AP80 5c vio bl & blk .15 .15

Issued to publicize the third Central American Municipal Assembly, Colon, May 13-17.

Church Type of Regular Issue, 1962

Designs: 5c, Church of Christ the King. 7c, Church of San Miguel. 8c, Church of the Sanctuary. 10c, Saints Church. 15c, Church of St. Ann. 21c, Canal Zone Synagogue (Now used as USO Center). 25c, Panama Synagogue. 30c, Church of St. Francis. 50c, Protestant Church, Canal Zone. 1b, Catholic Church, Canal Zone.

Perf. 12½

1962-64 Wmk. 343 Litho.

Buildings in Black

C256 A138 5c purple & buff .15 .15
C257 A138 7c lil rose & brt pink .15 .15
C258 A139 8c purple & bl .16 .15
C259 A139 10c lilac & sal .20 .15
C259A A139 10c grn & dl red brn ('64) .20 .20
C260 A139 15c red & buff .30 .20
C261 A138 21c brown & blue .40 .40
C262 A138 25c blue & pink .50 .35
C263 A139 30c lil rose & bl .60 .42
C264 A138 50c lilac & lt grn 1.00 .65
a. Souv. sheet of 4, #441H-441J, C262, C264, imperf. 2.00 2.00
C265 A139 1b bl & sal 2.00 1.40
Nos. C256-C265 (11) 5.66 4.22

Freedom of religion in Panama. Issue dates: #C259A, June 4, 1964; others, July 20, 1962.

For overprints and surcharges see Nos. C288, C296-C297, C299.

Nos. C234 and C236 Overprinted and Surcharged "IX JUEGOS C.A. Y DEL CARIBE KINGSTON-1962" and Games Emblem in Black, Green, Orange or Red

1962 Wmk. 343 *Perf. 12½*

C266 A131 5c org & red .15 .15
C267 A131 10c on 25c (G) .20 .20
C268 A131 15c on 25c (O) .30 .30
C269 A131 20c on 25c (R) .40 .40
C270 A131 25c lt bl & dk bl .50 .50
Nos. C266-C270 (5) 1.55 1.55

Ninth Central American and Caribbean Games, Kingston, Jamaica, Aug. 11-25.

Nos. CB1-CB2 Surcharged

V
A
L
E

.20
¢

X X

1962, May 3 **Wmk. 311**
C271 SPAP1 10c on 5c + 5c 1.00 .75
C272 SPAP1 20c on 10c + 10c 1.50 1.50

Type of Regular Issue, 1962

Design: 10c, Canal bridge completed.

1962, Oct. 12 **Wmk. 343**
C273 A140 10c blue & blk .20 .15

John H. Glenn, "Friendship 7" Capsule — AP81

UPAE Emblem — AP82

Designs: 10c, "Friendship 7" capsule and globe, horiz. 31c, Capsule in space, horiz. 50c, Glenn with space helmet.

1962, Oct. 19 **Wmk. 311** *Perf. 12½*
C274 AP81 5c rose red .15 .15
C275 AP81 10c yellow .20 .16
C276 AP81 31c blue .80 .80
C277 AP81 50c emerald 1.00 1.00
a. Souv. sheet of 4, #C274-C277, imperf. 2.25 2.25
Nos. C274-C277 (4) 2.15 2.11

1st orbital flight of US astronaut Lt. Col. John H. Glenn, Jr., Feb. 20, 1962. No. C277a sold for 1b.
For surcharges see Nos. C290A-C290D, C367, CB4-CB7.

1963, Jan. 8 **Litho.** **Wmk. 343**
C278 AP82 10c multi .20 .15

50th anniversary of the founding of the Postal Union of the Americas and Spain, UPAE.

Type of Regular Issue

10c, Fire Engine "China", Plaza de Santa Ana. 15c, 14th Street team. 21c, Fire Brigade emblem.

1963, Jan. 22 **Wmk. 311** *Perf. 12½*
C279 A141 10c orange & blk .20 .15
C280 A141 15c lilac & blk .30 .20
C281 A141 21c gold, red & ultra .50 .50
Nos. C279-C281 (3) 1.00 .85

"FAO" and Wheat Emblem — AP83

1963, Mar. 21 **Litho.**
C282 AP83 10c green & red .20 .15
C283 AP83 15c ultra & red .25 .20

FAO "Freedom from Hunger" campaign.

No. C245 Overprinted in Yellow, Orange or Green: "XXII Convención / Leonística / Centroamericana / Panama, 18-21 / Abril 1963"

1963, Apr. 18 **Wmk. 311** *Perf. 12½*
C284 A133 5c black (Y) .15 .15
C285 A133 5c black (O) .15 .15
C286 A133 5c black (G) .15 .15
Set value .30 .30

22nd Central American Lions Congress, Panama, Apr. 18-21.

No. C230 Surcharged:

HABILITADO

Vale B/. 0.04

1963, June 11
C287 AP74 4c on 10c brt grn .15 .15

Nos. 445 and 432 Overprinted "AEREO" Vertically

1963 **Wmk. 343** *Perf. 12½*
C288 A139 10c green, yel & blk .20 .15

Wmk. 311

C289 A130 20c emerald & red brn .40 .22

No. C234 Overprinted: "LIBERTAD DE PRENSA 20-VIII-63"

1963, Aug. 20 **Wmk. 343**
C290 A131 5c orange & red .15 .15

Freedom of Press Day, Aug. 20, 1963.

"Visita Astronautas Glenn-Schirra Sheppard Cooper a Panamá"

Nos. C274, C277a Overprinted or Surcharged — a

HABILITADO

No. C274 Surcharged in Black — b

10¢

Perf. 12½

1963, Aug. 21 **Litho.** **Wmk. 311**
C290A AP81(a) 5c on #C274
C290B AP81(a) 10c on 5c #C274
C290C AP81(b) 10c on 5c #C274

Souvenir Sheet

Imperf.

C290D AP81(a) Sheet of 4, #C277a

Overprint on No. C290D has names in capital letters and covers all four stamps.

No. C232 Surcharged in Red: "VALE 10¢"

1963, Oct. 9 **Wmk. 311** *Perf. 12½*
C291 AP74 10c on 25c ultra .20 .15

Type of Regular Issue, 1963

Flags and Presidents: 5c, Julio A. Rivera, El Salvador. 10c, Miguel Ydigoras F., Guatemala. 21c, John F. Kennedy, US.

Perf. 12½x12

1963, Dec. 18 **Litho.** **Unwmk.**

Portrait in Slate Green

C292 A142 5c yel, red & ultra .15 .30
C293 A142 10c bl, red & ultra .30 .40
C294 A142 21c org yel, red & ultra 1.00 1.00
Nos. C292-C294 (3) 1.45 1.70

Balboa Type of Regular Issue, 1964

1964, Jan. 22 **Photo.** *Perf. 13*
C295 A143 10c dk vio, *pale pink* .20 .16

No. C261 Surcharged in Red: "VALE B/.0.50"

1964 **Wmk. 343** **Litho.** *Perf. 12½*
C296 A138 50c on 21c brn, bl & blk 1.00 .70

Type of 1962 Overprinted: "HABILITADA"

C297 A139 1b emer, yel & blk 2.00 2.00

Nos. 434 and 444 Surcharged: "Aéreo B/.0.10"

1964 **Wmk. 343** *Perf. 12½*
C298 A131 10c on 5c bl grn & emer .20 .15
C299 A139 10c on 5c rose, lt grn & blk .20 .15

St. Patrick's Cathedral, New York — AP84

Cathedrals: #C301, St. Stephen's, Vienna. #C302, St. Sofia's, Sofia. #C303, Notre Dame, Paris. #C304, Cologne. #C305, St. Paul's, London. #C306, Metropolitan, Athens. #C307, St. Elizabeth's, Kosice, Czechoslovakia (inscr. Kassa, Hungary). #C308, New Delhi. #C309, Milan. #C310, Guadalupe Basilica. #C311, New Church, Delft, Netherlands. #C312, Lima. #C313, St. John's Poland. #C314, Lisbon. #C315, St. Basil's, Moscow. #C316, Toledo. #C317, Stockholm. #C318, Basel. #C319, St. George's Patriarchal Church, Istanbul. 1b, Panama City. 2b, St. Peter's Basilica, Rome.

Unwmk.

1964, Feb. 17 **Engr.** *Perf. 12*

Center in Black

C300 AP84 21c olive .80 .80
C301 AP84 21c chocolate .80 .80
C302 AP84 21c aqua .80 .80
C303 AP84 21c red brown .80 .80
C304 AP84 21c magenta .80 .80
C305 AP84 21c red .80 .80
C306 AP84 21c orange red .80 .80
C307 AP84 21c blue .80 .80
C308 AP84 21c brown .80 .80
C309 AP84 21c green .80 .80
C310 AP84 21c violet bl .80 .80
C311 AP84 21c dk slate grn .80 .80
C312 AP84 21c violet .80 .80
C313 AP84 21c black .80 .80
C314 AP84 21c emerald .80 .80
C315 AP84 21c dp violet .80 .80
C316 AP84 21c olive grn .80 .80
C317 AP84 21c carmine rose .80 .80
C318 AP84 21c Prus green .80 .80
C319 AP84 21c dark brown .80 .80
C320 AP84 1b dark blue 4.00 4.00
C321 AP84 2b yellow green 7.75 7.75
a. Souv. sheet of 6 7.50 7.50
Nos. C300-C321 (22) 27.75 27.75

Vatican II, the 21st Ecumenical Council of the Roman Catholic Church.
No. C321a contains 6 imperf. stamps similar to Nos. C300, C303, C305, C315, C320 and C321. Size: 198x138mm. Sold for 3.85b.
Six stamps of this set (Nos. C300, C305, C309, C319, C321a) were overprinted "1964." The overprint is olive bister on the stamps, yellow on the souvenir sheet. The overprint is reported to exist also in yellow gold on the same six stamps and in olive bister on the souvenir sheet.

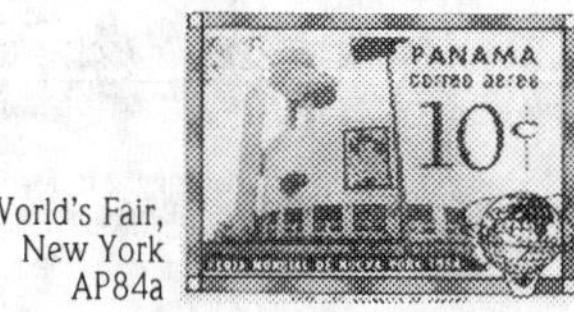

World's Fair, New York AP84a

5c, 10c, 15c, Various pavilions. 21c, Unisphere.

1964, Sept. 14 **Wmk. 311** *Perf. 12½*
C322 AP84a 5c yellow & blk
C323 AP84a 10c red & blk
C324 AP84a 15c green & blk
C325 AP84a 21c ultra & blk

Souvenir Sheet

Perf. 12

C326 AP84a 21c ultra & blk

No. C326 contains one 49x35mm stamp. Exists imperf.

AP84b

AP84c

Hammarskjold Memorial, UN Day: No. C327, C329a, Dag Hammarskjold. No. C328, C329b, UN emblem.

Perf. 13½x14

1964, Sept. 24 **Unwmk.**
C327 AP84b 21c black & blue
C328 AP84b 21c black & blue

Souvenir Sheet

Imperf

C329 Sheet of 2
a.-b. AP84b 21c blk & grn, any single

Nos. C327-C328 exist imperf. in black and green.

Roosevelt Type of Regular Issue

Perf. 12x12½

1964, Oct. 9 **Litho.** **Unwmk.**
C330 A147 20c grn & blk, *buff* .40 .30
a. Souv. sheet of 2, #455, C330, imperf. .55 .55

1964 *Perf. 13½x14*
C331 AP84c 21c shown
C332 AP84c 21c Papal coat of arms
a. Souv. sheet of 2, #C331-C332

Pope John XXIII (1881-1963). Nos. C331-C332 exist imperf in different colors.

Galileo, 400th Birth Anniv. — AP84d

21c, Galileo, studies of gravity.
Illustration reduced.

1965 *Perf. 14*
C333 AP84d 10c blue & multi
C334 AP84d 21c green & multi
a. Souv. sheet of 2, #C333-C334

Nos. C333-C334a exist imperf. with different colors.

Alfred Nobel (1833-1896), Founder of Nobel Prize — AP84e

Illustration reduced.

1965 **Litho. & Embossed**
C335 AP84e 10c Peace Medal, rev.
C336 AP84e 21c Peace Medal, obv.
a. Souv. sheet of 2, #C335-C336

Nos. C335-C336a exist imperf. with different colors.

Bird Type of Regular Issue, 1965

Song Birds: 5c, Common troupial, horiz. 10c, Crimson-backed tanager, horiz.

1965, Oct. 27 **Unwmk.** *Perf. 14*
C337 A148 5c dp orange & multi .15 .15
C338 A148 10c brt blue & multi .25 .15
Set value .18

Fish Type of Regular Issue

Designs: 8c, Shrimp. 12c, Hammerhead. 13c, Atlantic sailfish. 25c, Seahorse, vert.

1965, Dec. 7 **Litho.**
C339 A149 8c multi .20 .15
C340 A149 12c multi .30 .20
C341 A149 13c multi .30 .22
C342 A149 25c multi .60 .40
Nos. C339-C342 (4) 1.40 .97

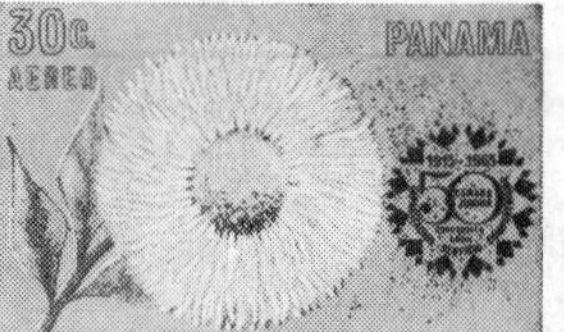

English Daisy and Emblem — AP85

Junior Chamber of Commerce Emblem and: #C344, Hibiscus. #C345, Orchid. #C346, Water lily. #C347, Gladiolus. #C348, Flor del Espiritu Santo.

1966, Mar. 16

C343	AP85	30c brt pink & multi	.75	.35
C344	AP85	30c salmon & multi	.75	.35
C345	AP85	30c pale yel & multi	.75	.35
C346	AP85	40c lt grn & multi	1.00	.35
C347	AP85	40c blue & multi	1.00	.35
C348	AP85	40c pink & multi	1.00	.35
		Nos. C343-C348 (6)	5.25	2.10

50th anniv. of the Junior Chamber of Commerce.

Nos. C224 and C236 Surcharged

1966, June 27 Wmk. 311 *Perf. 12½*

C349 A130 3c on 5c blk & red brn .15 .15

Wmk. 343

C350 A131 13c on 25c lt & dk bl .35 .25

The old denominations are not obliterated on Nos. C349-C350.

ITU Cent. AP85a

1966, Aug. 12 *Perf. 13½x14*

C351 AP85a 31c multicolored

Sovenir Sheet

Perf. 14

C352 AP85a 31c multicolored

No. C352 exists imperf. with blue green background.

Animal Type of Regular Issue, 1967

Domestic Animals: 10c, Pekingese dog. 13c, Zebu, horiz. 30c, Cat. 40c, Horse, horiz.

1967, Feb. 3 Unwmk. *Perf. 14*

C353	A150	10c multi	.25	.16
C354	A150	13c multi	.30	.20
C355	A150	30c multi	.75	.45
C356	A150	40c multi	1.00	.55
		Nos. C353-C356 (4)	2.30	1.36

Young Hare, by Durer AP86

10c, St. Jerome and the Lion, by Albrecht Durer. 20c, Lady with the Ermine, by Leonardo Da Vinci. 30c, The Hunt, by Delacroix, horiz.

1967, Sept. 1

C357	AP86	10c black, buff & car	.20	.15
C358	AP86	13c lt yellow & multi	.25	.16
C359	AP86	20c multicolored	.40	.22
C360	AP86	30c multicolored	.60	.40
		Nos. C357-C360 (4)	1.45	.93

Panama-Mexico Friendship — AP86a

Designs: 1b, Pres. Gustavo Diaz Ordaz of Mexico and Pres. Marco A. Robles of Panama, horiz.

1968, Jan. 20 *Perf. 14*

C361 AP86a 50c shown
C361A AP86a 1b multi
b. Souv. sheet of 2, #C361-C361A, imperf.

For overprints see Nos. C364-C364B.

Souvenir Sheet

Olympic Equestrian Events — AP86b

1968, Oct. 29 *Imperf.*

C362 Sheet of 2
a. AP86b 8c Dressage
b. AP86b 30c Show jumping

Intl. Human Rights Year — AP86c

1968, Dec. 18 *Perf. 14*

C363 AP86c 40c multicolored
a. Miniature sheet of 1

Nos. C361-C361b Ovptd. in Red or Black

"1a. EXPOSICION FILATELICA Y NUMISMA-TICA NAL. 29-8-68"

1969, Jan. 31

C364 AP86a 50c on #C361 (R)
C364A AP86a 1b on #C361A (B)

Souvenir Sheet

C364B on #C361a (R)

Intl. Philatelic and Numismatic Expo. Overprint larger on No. C364A, larger and in different arrangement on No. C364B.

Intl. Space Exploration — AP86d

1969, Mar. 14

C365 Sheet of 6
a. AP86d 5c France, Diadem I
b. AP86d 10c Italy, San Marco II
c. AP86d 15c Great Britain, UK 3
d. AP86d 20c US, Saturn V/Apollo 7
e. AP86d 25c US, Surveyor 7
f. AP86d 30c Europe/US, Esro 2

Satellite Transmission of Summer Olympics, Mexico, 1968 — AP86e

1969, Mar. 14 *Perf. 14½*

C366 AP86e 1b multi
a. Miniature sheet of 1

Decreto Nº 112 (de 6 de marzo de 1969)

B/. 0.05

Nos. CB4, 461B & 461C Surcharged

1969, Mar. 26 *Perf. 13½x13*

C367 AP81 5c on 5c+5c
C367A A147e 5c on 10c+5c
C367B A147e 10c on 21c+10c

Games Type of Regular Issue and

San Blas Indian Girl — AP87

Design: 13c, Bridge of the Americas.

1970, Jan. 6 Litho. *Perf. 13½*

C368	A158	13c multi	.40	.30
C369	AP87	30c multi	.90	.75
a.		"AEREO" omitted	*50.00*	*50.00*

See notes after No. 525.

Juan D. Arosemena and Arosemena Stadium AP88

Designs: 2c, 3c, 5c, like 1c. No. C374, Basketball. No. C375, New Panama Gymnasium. No. C376, Revolution Stadium. No. C377, Panamanian man and woman in Stadium. 30c, Stadium, eternal flame, arms of Mexico, Puerto Rico and Cuba.

1970, Oct. 7 Wmk. 365 *Perf. 13½*

C370	AP88	1c pink & multi	.15	.15
C371	AP88	2c pink & multi	.15	.15
C372	AP88	3c pink & multi	.15	.15
C373	AP88	5c pink & multi	.15	.15
C374	AP88	13c lt blue & multi	.30	.15
C375	AP88	13c lilac & multi	.30	.15
C376	AP88	13c yellow & multi	.30	.15
C377	AP88	13c pink & multi	.30	.15
C378	AP88	30c yellow & multi	.85	.50
a.		Souv. sheet of 1, imperf.	1.50	1.50
		Nos. C370-C378 (9)	2.65	
		Set value		1.45

11th Central American and Caribbean Games, Feb. 28-Mar. 14.

Astronaut on Moon — AP89

EXPO '70 Emblem and Pavilion — AP90

Design: No. C380, US astronauts Charles Conrad, Jr., Richard F. Gordon, Jr. and Alan L. Bean.

1971 Wmk. 343 *Perf. 13½*

C379 AP89 13c gold & multi .50 .35
C380 AP89 13c lt green & multi .50 .35

Man's first landing on the moon, Apollo 11, July 20, 1969 (No. C379) and Apollo 12 moon mission, Nov. 14-24, 1969.

Issued: No. C379, Aug. 20; No. C380, Aug. 23.

1971, Aug. 24 **Litho.**

C381 AP90 10c pink & multi .25 .25

EXPO '70 International Exposition, Osaka, Japan, Mar. 15-Sept. 13.

Flag of Panama AP91

Design: 13c, Map of Panama superimposed on Western Hemisphere, and tourist year emblem.

1971, Dec. 11 **Wmk. 343**

C382	AP91	5c multi	.15	.15
C383	AP91	13c multi	.25	.25
		Set value		.32

Proclamation of 1972 as Tourist Year of the Americas.

Mahatma Gandhi — AP92

1971, Dec. 17

C384 AP92 10c black & multi .60 .35

Centenary of the birth of Mohandas K. Gandhi (1869-1948), leader in India's fight for independence.

Central American Independence Issue

Flags of Central American States — AP92a

1971, Dec. 20

C385 AP92a 13c multi .35 .25

160th anniv. of Central America independence.

AP93 AP94

1971, Dec. 21

C386 AP93 8c Panama #4 .25 .25

2nd National Philatelic and Numismatic Exposition, 1970.

1972, Sept. 7 **Wmk. 365**

C387 AP94 40c Natá Church .80 .60

450th anniversary of the founding of Natá. For surcharges see Nos. C402, RA85.

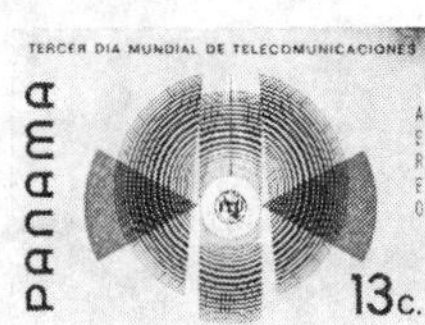

Telecommunications Emblem — AP95

1972, Sept. 8

C388 AP95 13c lt bl, dp bl & blk .40 .40

3rd World Telecommunications Day (in 1971).

Apollo 14 — AP96

1972, Sept. 11

C389 AP96 13c tan & multi .65 .50

Apollo 14 US moon mission, Jan. 1-Feb. 9, 1971.

Shoeshine Boy Counting Coins — AP97

1972, Sept. 12

C390 AP97 5c shown .15 .15
C391 AP97 8c Mother & Child .25 .25
C392 AP97 50c UNICEF emblem 1.00 .50
a. Souv. sheet of 1, imperf. 1.20 1.20
Nos. C390-C392 (3) 1.40 .90

25th anniv. (in 1971) of the UNICEF.

San Blas Cloth, Cuna Indians AP98

1972, Sept. 13

C393 AP98 5c shown .15 .15
C394 AP98 8c Beaded necklace, Guaymi Indians .25 .15
C395 AP98 25c View of Portobelo .60 .45
a. Souv. sheet of 2, #C393, C395, imperf. 1.00 1.00
Nos. C393-C395 (3) 1.00
Set value .60

Tourist publicity.
For surcharges see Nos. C417, RA83.

Baseball and Games' Emblem AP99

Designs (Games' Emblem and): 10c, Basketball, vert. 13c, Torch, vert. 25c, Boxing. 50c, Map and flag of Panama, Bolivar. 1b, Medals.

Perf. 12½

1973, Feb. 9 Litho. Unwmk.

C396 AP99 8c rose red & yel .20 .15
C397 AP99 10c black & ultra .25 .15
C398 AP99 13c blue & multi .35 .16
C399 AP99 25c blk, yel grn & red .60 .25
C400 AP99 50c green & multi 1.20 .60
C401 AP99 1b multicolored 2.25 1.00
Nos. C396-401 (6) 4.85 2.31

7th Bolivar Games, Panama City, Feb. 17-Mar. 3.

No. C387 Surcharged in Red Similar to No. 542

1973, Mar. 16 Wmk. 365 ***Perf. 13½***

C402 AP94 13c on 40c multi .30 .30

UN Security Council Meeting, Panama City, Mar. 15-21.

Portrait Type of Regular Issue 1973

Designs: 5c, Isabel Herrera Obaldia, educator. 8c, Nicolas Victoria Jaén, educator. 10c, Forest Scene, by Roberto Lewis. No. C406, Portrait of a Lady, by Manuel E. Amador. No. C407, Ricardo Miró, poet. 20c, Portrait, by Isaac Benitez. 21c, Manuel Amador Guerrero, statesman. 25c, Belisario Porras, statesman. 30c, Juan Demostenes Arosemena, statesman. 34c, Octavio Mendez Pereira, writer. 38c, Ricardo J. Alfaro, writer.

1973, June 20 Litho. ***Perf. 13½***

C403 A169 5c pink & multi .15 .15
C404 A169 8c pink & multi .16 .15
C405 A169 10c gray & multi .20 .15
C406 A169 13c pink & multi .35 .16
C407 A169 13c pink & multi .35 .16
C408 A169 20c blue & multi .50 .40
C409 A169 21c yellow & multi .50 .40
C410 A169 25c pink & multi .50 .40
C411 A169 30c gray & multi .65 .35
C412 A169 34c lt blue & multi .80 .60
C413 A169 38c lt blue & multi 1.00 .50
Nos. C403-C413 (11) 5.16 3.42

Famous Panamanians.
For overprints and surcharges see Nos. C414-C416, C418-C421.

Nos. C403, C410, and C412 Overprinted in Black or Red

1923
1973

Bodas de Oro
Escuela Profesional
Isabel Herrera Obaldia

1973, Sept. 14 Litho. ***Perf. 13½***

C414 A169 5c pink & multi .20 .20
C415 A169 25c pink & multi .60 .45
C416 A169 34c lt blue & multi (R) .90 .75
Nos. C414-C416 (3) 1.70 1.40

50th anniversary of the Isabel Herrera Obaldia Professional School.

Nos. C395, C408, C413, C412 and C409 Surcharged in Red

VALE 8¢

1974, Nov. 11 Litho. ***Perf. 13½***

C417 AP98 1c on 25c multi .15 .15
C418 A169 3c on 20c multi .15 .15
C419 A169 8c on 38c multi .16 .15
C420 A169 10c on 34c multi .20 .20
C421 A169 13c on 21c multi .25 .15
Set value .70 .50

Women's Hands, Panama Map, UN and IWY Emblems — AP100

Victoria Sugar Plant, Sugar Cane, Map of Veraguas Province — AP101

Perf. 12½

1975, May 6 Litho. Unwmk.

C422 AP100 17c blue & multi .50 .20
a. Souv. sheet, typo., imperf., no gum 1.00 1.00

International Women's Year 1975.

1975, Oct. 9 Litho. ***Perf. 12½***

Designs: 17c, Bayano electrification project and map of Panama, horiz. 33c, Tocumen International Airport and map, horiz.

C423 AP101 17c bl, buff & blk .35 .30
C424 AP101 27c ultra & yel grn .50 .35
C425 AP101 33c bl & multi .65 .45
Nos. C423-C425 (3) 1.50 1.10

Oct. 11, 1968, Revolution, 7th anniv.

Bolivar Statue and Flags — AP102

Bolivar Hall, Panama City AP103

Design: 41c, Bolivar with flag of Panama, ruins of Old Panama City.

1976, Mar.

C426 AP102 23c multi .50 .20
C427 AP103 35c multi .70 .28
C428 AP102 41c multi .80 .60
Nos. C426-C428 (3) 2.00 1.08

150th anniversary of Congress of Panama.
Issue dates: 23c, Mar. 15; others Mar. 30.

Marine Life Type of 1976

Marine life: 17c, Diodon hystrix, vert. 27c, Pocillopora damicornis.

Perf. 13x12½, 12½x13

1976, May 6 Litho. Wmk. 377

C429 A171 17c multi .35 .30
C430 A171 27c multi .55 .40

Cerro Colorado AP104

1976, Nov. 12 Litho. ***Perf. 12½***

C431 AP104 23c multi .45 .20

Cerro Colorado copper mines, Chiriqui Province.

Gen. Omar Torrijos Herrera (1929-1981) AP105

1982, Feb. Litho. ***Perf. 10½***

C432 AP105 23c multi .45 .20

Torrijos Type of 1982

Perf. 10½

1982, May 14 Litho. Wmk. 311

C433 A201 35c Security Council reunion, 1973 .70 .28
C434 A201 41c Torrijos Airport .80 .50

Souvenir Sheet

Imperf

C435 A201 23c like #C432 2.00 2.00

No. C435 sold for 1b.

Alfaro Type of 1982

Photos by Luiz Gutierrez Cruz.

1982, Aug. 18 Wmk. 382

C436 A202 17c multi .35 .15
C437 A202 23c multi .45 .18

World Cup Type of 1982

1982, Dec. 27 Litho. ***Perf. 10½***

C438 A203 23c Map .60 .18
C439 A203 35c Pele, vert. .80 .28
C440 A203 41c Cup, vert. 1.00 .40
Nos. C438-C440 (3) 2.40 .86

1b imperf. souvenir sheet exists in design of 23c; black control number. Size; 85x75mm.

Nicolas A. Solano (1882-1943), Tuberculosis Researcher — AP106

Wmk. 382 (Stars)

1983, Feb. 8 Litho. ***Perf. 10½***

C441 AP106 23c brown .45 .20

World Food Day — AP107

Contadora Group for Peace — AP108

1984, Oct. 16 Litho. ***Perf. 12***

C442 AP107 30c Hand grasping fork .60 .20

1985, Oct. 1 Litho. ***Perf. 14***

C443 AP108 10c multi .20 .15
C444 AP108 20c multi .40 .16
C445 AP108 30c multi .60 .22
Nos. C443-C445 (3) 1.20 .53

See No. 680A.

Christmas Type of 1988

1988, Dec. 29 Litho. ***Perf. 12***

C446 A246 35c *St. Joseph and the Infant* .80 .40

Olympics Type of 1989

1989, Mar. 17 Litho. ***Perf. 12***

C447 A248 35c Boxing .78 .40

Opening of the Panama Canal, 75th Anniv. AP109

1989, Sept. 29 Litho. ***Perf. 13½***

C448 AP109 35c *Ancon* in lock, 1914 .88 .65
C449 AP109 60c Ship in lock, 1989 1.50 1.15

Revolution Type of 1989

1989, Nov. 14 Litho.

C450 A251 35c Storming of the Bastille .88 .65
C451 A251 45c Anniv. emblem 1.15 .85

French revolution, bicent.

AIR POST SEMI-POSTAL STAMPS

Catalogue values for unused stamps in this section are for Never Hinged items.

"The World Against Malaria" — SPAP1

Perf. 12½

1961, Dec. 20 Wmk. 311 Litho.

CB1 SPAP1 5c + 5c car rose .50 .50
CB2 SPAP1 10c + 10c vio bl .50 .50
CB3 SPAP1 15c + 15c dk grn .50 .50
Nos. CB1-CB3 (3) 1.50 1.50

WHO drive to eradicate malaria.

For surcharges see Nos. C271-C272.

Nos. C274-C276 Surcharged in Red

1863 1963

+10c

Perf. 12½

1963, Mar. 4 Litho. Wmk. 311

CB4 AP81 5c +5c on #C274
CB5 AP81 10c +10c on #C275
CB6 AP81 15c +15c on #C276

Surcharge on No. CB4 differs to fit stamp. See No. CB7.

No. CB4 Surcharged in Black

"Centenario
Cruz Roja
Internacional"

XX

10¢

CB7 AP81 10c on 5c+5c
Intl. Red. Cross cent.

SPECIAL DELIVERY STAMPS

Nos. 211-212 Overprinted in Red **EXPRESO**

1926 Unwmk. *Perf. 12*

E1 A31 10c org & blk	7.50	3.25
a. "EXRPESO"	40.00	
E2 A32 20c brn & blk	10.00	3.25
a. "EXRPESO"	40.00	
b. Double overprint	35.00	35.00

Bicycle Messenger SD1

1929 Engr. *Perf. 12½*

E3 SD1 10c orange	1.25	1.00
E4 SD1 20c dk brn	4.75	2.50

For surcharges and overprints see Nos. C1-C5, C17-C18A, C67.

REGISTRATION STAMPS

Issued under Colombian Dominion

R1

1888 Unwmk. Engr. *Perf. 13½*

F1 R1 10c black, *gray* 8.00 5.25

Imperforate and part-perforate copies without gum and those on surface-colored paper are reprints.

R2

Magenta, Violet or Blue Black Handstamped Overprint

1898 *Perf. 12*

F2 R2 10c yellow 7.00 6.50

The handstamp on No. F2 was also used as a postmark.

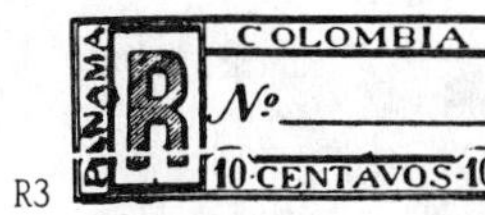

R3

1900 Litho. *Perf. 11*

F3 R3 10c blk, *lt bl* 4.00 3.50

1901

F4 R3 10c brown red 30.00 20.00

R4

Blue Black Surcharge

1902

F5 R4 20c on 10c brn red 20.00 16.00

Issues of the Republic Issued in the City of Panama

Registration Stamps of Colombia Handstamped

R9

Handstamped in Blue Black or Rose REPUBLICA DE PANAMA

1903-04 *Imperf.*

F6 R9 20c red brn, *bl*	45.00	42.50
F7 R9 20c blue, *blue* (R)	45.00	42.50

For surcharges and overprints see Nos. F8-F11, F16-F26.

Reprints exist of Nos. F6 and F7; see note after No. 64.

With Additional Surcharge in Rose 10.

F8 R9 10c on 20c red brn, *bl*	60.00	55.00
b. "10" in blue black	60.00	55.00
F9 R9 10c on 20c bl, *bl*	60.00	45.00

Handstamped in Rose

Panamá

.10

F10 R9 10c on 20c red brn, *bl*	60.00	55.00
F11 R9 10c on 20c blue, *blue*	45.00	42.50

Issued in Colon

Regular Issues Handstamped "R/COLON" in Circle (as on F2) Together with Other Overprints and Surcharges

Handstamped REPUBLICA DE PANAMA

1903-04 *Perf. 12*

F12 A4 10c yellow 3.00 2.50

Handstamped PANAMA

F13 A4 10c yellow 22.50

Overprinted in Red

PANAMA PANAMA

F14 A4 10c yellow 3.00 2.50

Overprinted in Black República de Panamá.

F15 A4 10c yellow 7.50 5.00

The handstamps on Nos. F12 to F15 are in magenta, violet or red; various combinations of these colors are to be found. They are struck in various positions, including double, inverted, one handstamp omitted, etc.

Colombia No. F13 Handstamped Like No. F12 in Violet

Imperf

F16 R9 20c red brn, *bl* 60.00 55.00

Overprinted Like No. F15 in Black

F17 R9 20c red brn, *bl* 6.00 5.75

No. F17 Surcharged in Manuscript

F18 R9 10c on 20c red brn, *bl* 60.00 55.00

No. F17 Surcharged in Purple 10

F19 R9 10c on 20c 82.50 80.00

No. F17 Surcharged in Violet 10

F20 R9 10c on 20c 82.50 80.00

The varieties of the overprint which are described after No. 138 are also to be found on the Registration and Acknowledgment of Receipt stamps. It is probable that Nos. F17 to F20 inclusive owe their existence more to speculation than to postal necessity.

Issued in Bocas del Toro

Colombia Nos. F17 and F13 Handstamped in Violet

R DE PANAMA

1903-04

F21 R9 20c blue, *blue*	125.00	120.00
F22 R9 20c red brn, *bl*	125.00	120.00

No. F21 Surcharged in Manuscript in Violet or Red

F23 R9 10c on 20c bl, *bl* 150.00 140.00

Colombia Nos. F13, F17 Handstamped in Violet Panama

Surcharged in Manuscript (a) "10" (b) "10cs" in Red

F25 R9 10 on 20c red brn, *bl*	70.00	65.00
F26 R9 10cs on 20c bl, *bl*	55.00	50.00
Nos. F21-F26 (5)	525.00	495.00

No. F25 without surcharge is bogus, according to leading experts.

General Issue

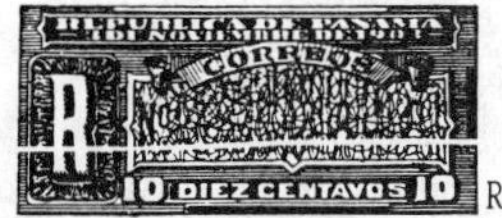

R5

1904 Engr. *Perf. 12*

F27 R5 10c green 1.00 .50

Nos. 190 and 213 Surcharged in Red

5 cts.

#F29-F30

#F29b

1916-17

F29 A11 5c on 8c pur & blk	3.00	2.25
a. "5" inverted	55.00	
b. Large, round "5"	50.00	
c. Inverted surcharge	12.50	11.00
d. Tête bêche surcharge		
F30 A33 5c on 8c vio & blk ('17)	3.50	.80
a. Inverted surcharge	10.00	8.25
b. Tête bêche surcharge		
c. Double surcharge		40.00

Stamps similar to No. F30, overprinted in green were unauthorized.

INSURED LETTER STAMPS

Stamps of 1939 Surcharged in Black

0 05 0 05
SEGURO
POSTAL

HABILITADO

1942 Unwmk. *Perf. 12½*

G1 AP23 5c on 1b blk	.50	.50
G2 A84 10c on 1b dk brn	.80	.80
G3 AP23 25c on 50c dk brn	2.00	2.00
Nos. G1-G3 (3)	3.30	3.30

ACKNOWLEDGMENT OF RECEIPT STAMPS

Issued under Colombian Dominion

Experts consider this handstamp- "A.R. / COLON / COLOMBIA"-to be a cancellation or a marking intended for a letter to receive special handling. It was applied at Colon to various stamps in 1897-1904 in different colored inks for philatelic sale. It exists on cover, usually with the bottom line removed by masking the handstamp.

Nos. 17-18 Handstamped in Rose

1902

H4 A4 5c blue	5.00	5.00
H5 A4 10c yellow	10.00	10.00

This handstamp was also used as a postmark.

Issues of the Republic Issued in the City of Panama

Colombia No. H3 Handstamped

AR2

Handstamped in Rose REPUBLICA DE PANAMA

1903-04 Unwmk. *Imperf.*

H9 AR2 10c blue, *blue* 10.00 8.00

Reprints exist of No. H9, see note after No. 64.

No. H9 Surcharged with New Value

H10 AR2 5c on 10c bl, *bl* 5.00 5.00

Colombia No. H3 Handstamped in Rose — **Panamá**

H11 AR2 10c blue, *blue* 17.50 14.00

Issued in Colon

Handstamped in Magenta or Violet — **REPUBLICA DE PANAMA**

Imperf

H17 AR2 10c blue, *blue* 15.00 15.00

Handstamped — **PANAMA**

H18 AR2 10c blue, *blue* 82.50 70.00

Overprinted in Black — *República de Panamá.*

H19 AR2 10c blue, *blue* 11.00 8.00

No. H19 Surcharged in Manuscript

H20 AR2 10c on 5c on 10c 100.00 82.50

Issued in Bocas del Toro

Colombia No. H3 Handstamped in Violet and Surcharged in Manuscript in Red Like Nos. F25-F26

1904

H21 AR2 5c on 10c blue, *blue*

No. H21, unused, without surcharge is bogus.

General Issue

AR3

1904 Engr. *Perf. 12*

H22 AR3 5c blue 1.00 .80

No. 199 Overprinted in Violet — **A. R.**

1916

H23 A20 2½c red orange 1.00 .80
- *a.* "R.A." for "A.R." 50.00
- *b.* Double overprint 8.00
- *c.* Inverted overprint 8.00

LATE FEE STAMPS

Issues of the Republic Issued in the City of Panama

LF3

Colombia No. I4 Handstamped in Rose or Blue Black — **REPUBLICA DE PANAMA**

1903-04 Unwmk. *Imperf.*

I1 LF3 5c pur, *rose* 12.50 9.00
I2 LF3 5c pur, *rose* (Bl Blk) 17.50 12.50

Reprints exist of #I1-I2; see note after #64.

General Issue

LF4

1904 Engr. *Perf. 12*

I3 LF4 2½c lake 1.00 .65

No. 199 Overprinted with Typewriter — **Retardo**

1910, Aug. 12

I4 A20 2½c red orange 120.00 100.00

Used only on Aug. 12-13.
Counterfeits abound.

Handstamped — **RETARDO**

1910

I5 A20 2½c red orange 60.00 50.00

Counterfeits abound.

No. 195 Surcharged in Green — ***RETARDO* UN CENTÉSIMO**

1917

I6 A17 1c on ½c orange .80 .80
- *a.* "UN CENTESIMO" inverted 50.00
- *b.* Double surcharge 10.00
- *c.* Inverted surcharge 6.50 6.50

Same Surcharge on No. 196

1921

I7 A17 1c on ½c rose 25.00 20.00

POSTAGE DUE STAMPS

San Lorenzo Castle Gate, Mouth of Chagres River — D1

Statue of Columbus — D2

Pedro J. Sosa — D4

D5

Design: 4c, Capitol, Panama City.

1915 Unwmk. Engr. *Perf. 12*

J1	D1	1c olive brown	3.00	.75
J2	D2	2c olive brown	4.50	.65
J3	D1	4c olive brown	6.00	1.25
J4	D4	10c olive brown	4.50	1.75
		Nos. J1-J4 (4)	18.00	4.40

Type D1 was intended to show a gate of San Lorenzo Castle, Chagres, and is so inscribed.

1930 *Perf. 12½*

J5	D5	1c emerald	.80	.60
J6	D5	2c dark red	.80	.60
J7	D5	4c dark blue	1.20	.80
J8	D5	10c violet	1.20	.80
		Nos. J5-J8 (4)	4.00	2.80

POSTAL TAX STAMPS

Pierre and Marie Curie — PT1

1939 Unwmk. Engr. *Perf. 12*

RA1	PT1	1c rose carmine	.50	.15
RA2	PT1	1c green	.50	.15
RA3	PT1	1c orange	.50	.15
RA4	PT1	1c blue	.50	.15
		Nos. RA1-RA4 (4)	2.00	.60

See Nos. RA6-RA18, RA24-RA27, RA30.

Stamp of 1924 Overprinted in Black

1940

RA5 A53 1c dark green 1.40 .75

Inscribed 1940

1941

RA6	PT1	1c rose carmine	.50	.15
RA7	PT1	1c green	.50	.15
RA8	PT1	1c orange	.50	.15
RA9	PT1	1c blue	.50	.15
		Nos. RA6-RA9 (4)	2.00	
		Set value		.40

Inscribed 1942

1942

RA10 PT1 1c violet .40 .15

Inscribed 1943

1943

RA11	PT1	1c rose carmine	.40	.15
RA12	PT1	1c green	.40	.15
RA13	PT1	1c orange	.40	.15
RA14	PT1	1c blue	.40	.15
		Nos. RA11-RA14 (4)	1.60	.60

Inscribed 1945

1945

RA15	PT1	1c rose carmine	.40	.16
RA16	PT1	1c green	.40	.16
RA17	PT1	1c orange	.40	.16
RA18	PT1	1c blue	.40	.16
		Nos. RA15-RA18 (4)	1.60	.64

Nos. 234 and 235 Surcharged in Black or Red — **CANCER B/. 0.01 1947**

1946 Unwmk. *Perf. 12*

RA19 A53 1c on ½c orange .60 .15
RA20 A53 1c on 1c dk grn (R) .60 .15

> Catalogue values for unused stamps in this section, from this point to the end of the section, are for Never Hinged items.

Same Surcharged in Black on Nos. 239 and 241

1947

RA21 A53 1c on 12c ol grn .40 .30
RA22 A53 1c on 24c yel brn .40 .30

Surcharged in Red on No. 342

RA23 A95 1c on ½c dl vio, bl & car .40 .15

Type of 1939
Inscribed 1947

1947

RA24	PT1	1c rose carmine	.40	.15
RA25	PT1	1c green	.40	.15
RA26	PT1	1c orange	.40	.15
RA27	PT1	1c blue	.40	.15
		Nos. RA24-RA27 (4)	1.60	
		Set value		.28

Nos. C100 and C101 Surcharged in Black

a

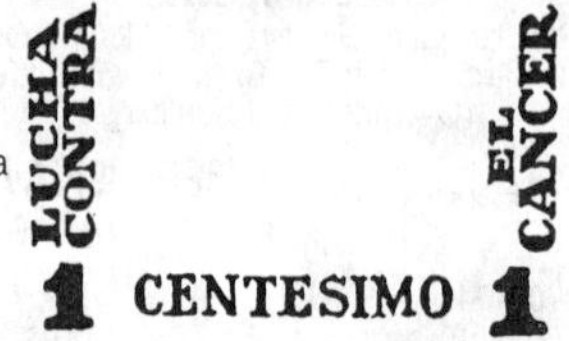

b

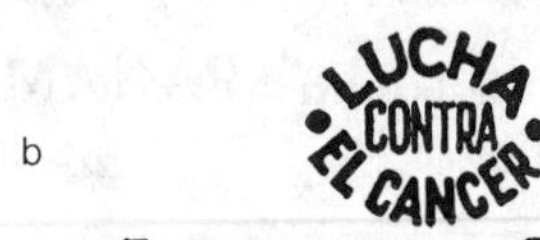

1949 Unwmk. *Perf. 12½*

RA28 AP45 (a) 1c on 5c .35 .15
- *a.* Inverted surcharge 10.00

RA29 AP46 (b) 1c on 10c yel org .35 .15
Set value .16

Type of 1939
Inscribed 1949

1949 *Perf. 12*

RA30 PT1 1c brown .50 .15

The tax from the sale of Nos. RA1-RA30 was used for the control of cancer.

Juan D. Arosemena Stadium — PT2

Torch Emblem — PT3

Discobolus — PT4

#RA33, Adan Gordon Olympic Swimming Pool.

1951 Unwmk. Engr. *Perf. 12½*

RA31	PT2	1c carmine & blk	.65	.16
RA32	PT3	1c dk bl & blk	.65	.16
RA33	PT2	1c grn & blk	.65	.16
		Nos. RA31-RA33 (3)	1.95	.48

1952

Design: No. RA34, Turners' emblem.

RA34 PT3 1c org & blk .65 .16
RA35 PT4 1c pur & blk .65 .16

The tax from the sale of Nos. RA31-RA35 was used to promote physical education.

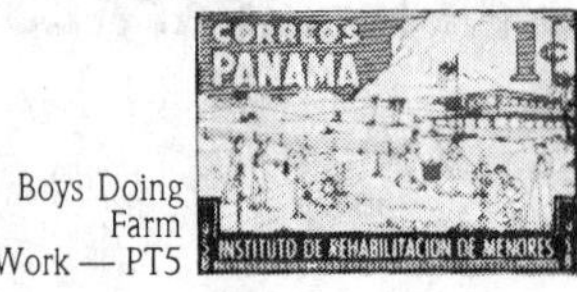

Boys Doing Farm Work — PT5

1958 Wmk. 311 Litho. *Perf. 12½*
Size: 35x24mm

RA36 PT5 1c rose red & gray .15 .15

Type of 1958
Inscribed 1959

1959 Size: 35x24mm

RA37 PT5 1c gray & emerald .15 .15
RA38 PT5 1c vio bl & gray .15 .15
Set value .16 .15

Type of 1958
Inscribed 1960

1960 Litho. Wmk. 334 *Perf. 13½*
Size: 32x23mm

RA39 PT5 1c carmine & gray .15 .15

Nos. C235 and C241 Surcharged in Black or Red — **XX 1¢ "Rehabilitación de Menores"**

1961 Wmk. 343 *Perf. 12½*

RA40 A131 1c on 10c ocher & blk .15 .15
RA41 AP76 1c on 10c emer (R) .15 .15
- *a.* Inverted surcharge

Set value .20 .15

Girl at Sewing Machine — PT6

Perf. 12½

1961, Nov. 24 Litho. Wmk. 343

RA42 PT6	1c brt vio		.15	.15
RA43 PT6	1c rose lilac		.15	.15
RA44 PT6	1c yellow		.15	.15
RA45 PT6	1c blue		.15	.15
RA46 PT6	1c emerald		.15	.15
	Set value		.35	.25

1961, Dec. 1

Design: Boy with hand saw.

RA47 PT6	1c red lilac	.15	.15
RA48 PT6	1c rose	.15	.15
RA49 PT6	1c orange	.15	.15
RA50 PT6	1c blue	.15	.15
RA51 PT6	1c gray	.15	.15
	Set value	.35	.25

Boy Scout — PT7 Map of Panama, Flags — PT8

Designs: Nos. RA57-RA61, Girl Scout.

1964, Feb. 7 Wmk. 343

RA52 PT7	1c olive	.15	.15
RA53 PT7	1c gray	.15	.15
RA54 PT7	1c lilac	.15	.15
RA55 PT7	1c carmine rose	.15	.15
RA56 PT7	1c blue	.15	.15
RA57 PT7	1c bluish green	.15	.15
RA58 PT7	1c violet	.15	.15
RA59 PT7	1c orange	.15	.15
RA60 PT7	1c yellow	.15	.15
RA61 PT7	1c brn org	.15	.15
	Set value	1.00	.50

The tax from Nos. RA36-RA61 was for youth rehabilitation.

1973, Jan. 22 Unwmk.

RA62 PT8	1c black	.15	.15

7th Bolivar Sports Games, Feb. 17-Mar. 3, 1973. The tax was for a new post office in Panama City.

Farm Cooperative — PT9

Designs: No. RA64, 5b silver coin. No. RA65, Victoriano Lorenzo. No. RA66, RA69, Cacique Urraca. No. RA67-RA68, RA70, Post Office.

1973-75

RA63 PT9	1c brt yel grn & ver	.15	.15
RA64 PT9	1c gray & red	.15	.15
RA65 PT9	1c ocher & red	.15	.15
RA66 PT9	1c org & red	.15	.15
RA67 PT9	1c bl & red	.15	.15
RA68 PT9	1c blue ('74)	.15	.15
RA69 PT9	1c orange ('74)	.15	.15
RA70 PT9	1c vermilion ('75)	.15	.15
	Set value	.80	.40

The tax was for a new post office in Panama City.

Stamps of 1969-1973 Surcharged in Violet Blue, Yellow, Black or Carmine

VALE 1¢
PRO EDIFICIO

1975

RA75 A168	1c on 1c (#538; VB)	.15	.15
RA76 A168	1c on 2c (#539; Y)	.15	.15
RA77 A164	1c on 30c (#534; B)	.15	.15
RA78 A157	1c on 30c (#511; B)	.15	.15
RA79 A156	1c on 40c (#514; B)	.15	.15
RA80 A156	1c on 50c (#515; B)	.15	.15
RA81 A169	1c on 20c (#C408; C)	.15	.15
RA82 A169	1c on 25c (#C410; B)	.15	.15
RA83 AP98	1c on 25c (#C395; B)	.15	.15
RA84 A169	1c on 30c (#C411; B)	.15	.15
RA85 AP94	1c on 40c (#C387; C)	.15	.15
	Set value	1.10	.85

The tax was for a new post office in Panama City. Surcharge vertical, reading down on No. RA75 and up on Nos. RA76, RA78 and RA83. Nos. RA75-RA85 were obligatory on all mail.

PT10 PT11

1980, Dec. 3 Litho. *Perf. 12*

RA86 PT10	2c Boys	.15	.15
RA87 PT10	2c Boy and chicks	.15	.15
RA88 PT10	2c Working in fields	.15	.15
RA89 PT10	2c Boys feeding piglet	.15	.15
a.	Souv. sheet of 4, #RA86-RA89	2.00	
	Set value	.20	.20

Tax was for Children's Village (Christmas 1980). Nos. RA86-RA89 se-tenant and were obligatory on all mail. #RA89a sold for 1b.

1981, Nov. 1 Litho. *Perf. 12*

RA90 PT11	2c Boy, pony	.15	.15
RA91 PT11	2c Nativity	.15	.15
RA92 PT11	2c Tree	.15	.15
RA93 PT11	2c Church	.15	.15
	Set value	.20	.20

Souvenir Sheet

RA94	Sheet of 4	*7.50*
a.-d.	PT11 2c, Children's drawings	

Tax was for Children's Village. Nos. RA90-RA93 se-tenant and were obligatory on all mail. No. RA94 sold for 5b.

PT12

1982, Nov. 1 Litho. *Perf. 13½x12½*

RA95 PT12	2c Carpentry	.15	.15
RA96 PT12	2c Beekeeping	.15	.15
RA97 PT12	2c Pig farming, vert.	.15	.15
RA98 PT12	2c Gardening, vert.	.15	.15
	Set value	.20	.20

Tax was for Children's Village (Christmas 1982). Nos. RA95-RA96 and RA97-RA98 se-tenant and were obligatory on all mail.

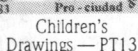

Children's Drawings — PT13 Boy — PT14

1983, Nov. 1 Litho. *Perf. 14½*

RA99 PT13	2c Annunciation	.15	.15
RA100 PT13	2c Bethlehem and Star	.15	.15
RA101 PT13	2c Church and Houses	.15	.15
RA102 PT13	2c Flight into Egypt	.15	.15
	Set value	.20	.20

Nos. RA100-RA102 are vert.

Souvenir sheets exist showing undenominated designs of Nos. RA99, RA101 and Nos. RA100, RA102 respectively. They sold for 2b each.

1984, Nov. 1 Litho. *Perf. 12x12½*

RA103 PT14	2c White-collared shirt	.15	.15
RA104 PT14	2c T-shirt	.15	.15
RA105 PT14	2c Checked shirt	.15	.15
RA106 PT14	2c Scout uniform	.15	.15
	Set value	.20	.20

Tax was for Children's Village. Obligatory on all mail. Issued se-tenant. An imperf. souvenir sheet sold for 2b, with designs similar to Nos. RA103-RA106, exists.

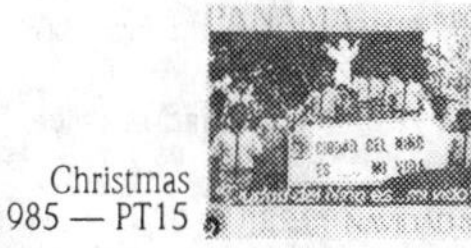

Christmas 1985 — PT15

Inscriptions: No. RA107, "Ciudad del Nino es . . . mi vida." No. RA108, "Feliz Navidad." No. RA109, "Feliz Ano Nuevo." No. RA110, "Gracias."

1985, Dec. 10 Litho. *Perf. 13½x13*

RA107 PT15	2c multi	.15	.15
RA108 PT15	2c multi	.15	.15
RA109 PT15	2c multi	.15	.15
RA110 PT15	2c multi	.15	.15
	Set value	.20	.20

Nos. RA107-RA110 obligatory on all mail: tax for Children's Village. A souvenir sheet, perf. and imperf., sold for 2b, with designs of Nos. RA107-RA110.

Children's Village, 20th Anniv. — PT16

Inscriptions and Embera, Cuna, Embera and Guaymies tribal folk figures: No. RA111, "1966-1986." No. RA112, "Ciudad del Nino es . . . mi vida." No. RA113, "20 anos de fundacion." No. RA114, "Gracias."

1986, Nov. 1 Litho. *Perf. 13½*

RA111 PT16	2c multi	.15	.15
RA112 PT16	2c multi	.15	.15
RA113 PT16	2c multi	.15	.15
RA114 PT16	2c multi	.15	.15
	Set value	.20	.20

Nos. RA111-RA114 obligatory on all mail through Nov., Dec. and Jan.; tax for Children's Village. Printed se-tenant. Sheets of 4 exist perf. and imperf. Sold for 2b.

PAPUA NEW GUINEA

'pa–pyə–wə 'nü 'gi–nē

LOCATION — Eastern half of island of New Guinea, north of Australia

GOVT. — Independent state in British Commonwealth.

AREA — 185,136 sq. mi.

POP. — 3,260,000 (est. 1984)

CAPITAL — Port Moresby

In 1884 a British Protectorate was proclaimed over this part of the island, called "British New Guinea." In 1905 the administration was transferred to Australia and in 1906 the name was changed to Territory of Papua.

In 1949 the administration of Papua and New Guinea was unified, as the 1952 issue indicates. In 1972 the name was changed to Papua New Guinea. In 1974 came self-government, followed by independence on September 16, 1975.

Issues of 1925-39 for the mandated Territory of New Guinea are listed under New Guinea.

12 Pence = 1 Shilling
20 Shillings = 1 Pound
100 Cents = 1 Dollar (1966)
100 Toea = 1 Kina (1975)

Catalogue values for unused stamps in this country are for Never Hinged items, beginning with Scott 122 in the regular postage section and Scott J1 in the postage due section.

Watermarks

Wmk. 13- Crown and Double-Lined A

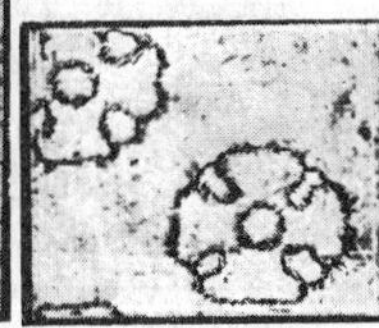

Wmk. 47- Multiple Rosette

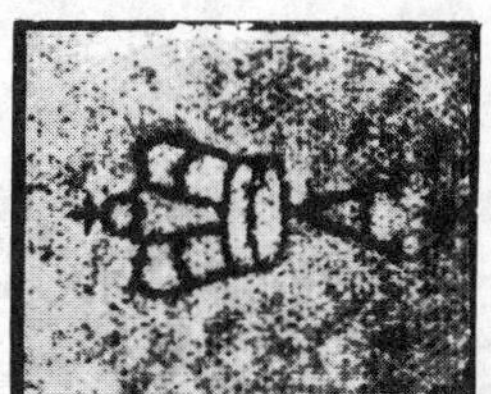

Wmk. 74- Crown and Single-Lined A Sideways

Wmk. 228- Small Crown and C of A Multiple

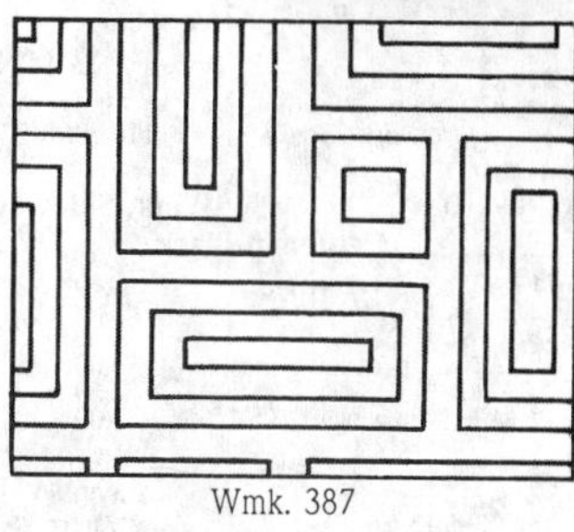

Wmk. 387

British New Guinea

Lakatoi — A1

Wmk. 47

1901, July 1 Engr. *Perf. 14*

Center in Black

1	A1	½p yellow green	4.00	3.75
2	A1	1p carmine	3.25	2.00
3	A1	2p violet	6.50	4.00
4	A1	2½p ultra	8.00	11.00
5	A1	4p black brown	30.00	35.00
6	A1	6p dark green	40.00	40.00
7	A1	1sh orange	52.50	70.00
8	A1	2sh6p brown ('05)	525.00	575.00
		Nos. 1-8 (8)	669.25	740.75

The paper varies in thickness and the watermark is found in two positions, with the greater width of the rosette either horizontal or vertical.

For overprints see Nos. 11-26.

Papua

Stamps of British New Guinea, Overprinted **Papua.**

1906, Nov. 8 Wmk. 47 *Perf. 14*

Center in Black

11	A1	½p yellow green	5.00	18.00
12	A1	1p carmine	8.50	14.00
13	A1	2p violet	4.50	4.00
14	A1	2½p ultra	4.00	14.00
15	A1	4p black brown	165.00	140.00
16	A1	6p dark green	25.00	37.50
17	A1	1sh orange	20.00	35.00
18	A1	2sh6p brown	125.00	150.00
		Nos. 11-18 (8)	357.00	412.50

Overprinted **Papua.**

1907 Center in Black

19	A1	½p yellow green	5.00	6.00
a.		Double overprint	1,750.	
20	A1	1p carmine	3.50	4.75
a.		Vertical overprint, up	1,750.	1,100.
21	A1	2p violet	4.25	3.00
22	A1	2½p ultra	7.00	17.50
a.		Double overprint		
23	A1	4p black brown	27.50	42.50
24	A1	6p dark green	25.00	32.50
a.		Double overprint	2,100.	3,750.
25	A1	1sh orange	30.00	40.00
a.		Double overprint		

26 A1 2sh6p brown 32.50 42.50
b. Vert. ovpt., down 3,250.
d. Double horiz. ovpt. 2,600.
Nos. 19-26 (8) 134.75 188.75

A2

Small "PAPUA"

Perf. 11, 12½

1907-08 Litho. Wmk. 13

Center in Black

28 A2 1p carmine ('08) 5.00 3.50
29 A2 2p violet ('08) 5.50 4.50
30 A2 2½p ultra ('08) 13.00 21.00
31 A2 4p black brown 4.00 6.50
32 A2 6p dk green ('08) 12.50 14.00
33 A2 1sh orange ('08) 16.00 17.50
Nos. 28-33 (6) 56.00 67.00

Perf. 12½

30a A2 2½p 45.00 65.00
31a A2 4p 8.50 8.75
33a A2 1sh 65.00 75.00
Nos. 30a-33a (3) 118.50 148.75

1909-10 Wmk. Sideways

Center in Black

34 A2 ½p yellow green 1.40 2.50
a. Perf. 11x12½ 2,000. 2,000.
b. Perf. 11 2.00 2.75
35 A2 1p carmine 6.00 8.25
a. Perf. 11 9.00 9.00
36 A2 2p violet ('10) 3.00 2.50
a. Perf. 11x12½ 900.00
b. Perf. 11 4.75 5.50
37 A2 2½p ultra ('10) 4.00 16.00
a. Perf. 12½ 7.00 25.00
38 A2 4p black brn ('10) 4.75 5.00
a. Perf. 11x12½ 6,750.
39 A2 6p dark green 14.00 14.00
a. Perf. 12½ 2,600. 3,500.
40 A2 1sh orange ('10) 12.00 22.50
a. Perf. 11 45.00 60.00
Nos. 34-40 (7) 45.15 70.75

One stamp in each sheet has a white line across the upper part of the picture which is termed the "rift in the clouds."

Large "PAPUA"

2sh6p:

Type I - The numerals are thin and irregular. The body of the "6" encloses a large spot of color. The dividing stroke is thick and uneven.

Type II - The numerals are thick and well formed. The "6" encloses a narrow oval of color. The dividing stroke is thin and sharp.

1910 Wmk. 13

Center in Black

41 A2 ½p yellow green 1.50 1.75
42 A2 1p carmine 5.00 3.50
43 A2 2p violet 4.25 4.00
44 A2 2½p blue violet 3.75 4.00
45 A2 4p black brown 5.00 8.25
46 A2 6p dark green 6.50 10.00
47 A2 1sh orange 8.25 12.50
48 A2 2sh6p brown, type II 55.00 70.00
a. Type I 55.00 70.00
Nos. 41-48 (8) 89.25 114.00

Wmk. Sideways

49 A2 2sh6p choc, type I 80.00 100.00

1911 Typo. Wmk. 74 Perf. 12½

50 A2 ½p yellow green .70 .70
51 A2 1p lt red 1.25 1.25
52 A2 2p lt violet 1.10 1.10
53 A2 2½p ultra 4.00 4.00
54 A2 4p olive green 4.50 5.50
55 A2 6p orange brown 4.25 4.25
56 A2 1sh yellow 8.00 11.00
57 A2 2sh6p rose 25.00 37.50
Nos. 50-57 (8) 48.80 65.30

For surcharges see Nos. 74-79.

1915, June Perf. 14

59 A2 1p light red 6.00 2.00

A3

1916-31

60 A3 ½p pale yel grn & myr grn ('19) .25 .25
61 A3 1p rose red & blk .90 .90
62 A3 1½p yel brn & gray bl ('25) .60 .60
63 A3 2p red vio & vio brn ('19) 2.50 1.00
64 A3 2p red brn & vio brn ('31) 3.25 2.25
a. 2p cop red & vio brn ('31) 35.00 7.50
65 A3 2½p ultra & dk grn ('19) 2.25 2.50
66 A3 3p emerald & blk 1.00 1.00
a. 3p dp bl grn & blk 2.00 2.00
67 A3 4p org & lt brn ('19) 3.75 3.75
68 A3 5p ol brn & sl ('31) 5.25 6.00
69 A3 6p vio & dl vio ('23) 2.25 2.50
70 A3 1sh ol grn & dk brn ('19) 3.00 3.25
71 A3 2sh6p rose & red brn ('19) 11.25 13.50
72 A3 5sh dp grn & blk 17.50 17.50
73 A3 10sh gray bl & grn ('25) 165.00 190.00
Nos. 60-73 (14) 218.75 245.00

Type A3 is a redrawing of type A2.

The lines of the picture have been strengthened, making it much darker, especially the sky and water.

For surcharges & overprints see #88-91, O1-O10.

Stamps of 1911 Surcharged **ONE PENNY**

1917 Perf. 12½

74 A2 1p on ½p yellow grn .45 1.00
75 A2 1p on 2p lt violet 10.50 10.00
76 A2 1p on 2½p ultra 1.10 4.50
77 A2 1p on 4p olive green 1.50 4.50
78 A2 1p on 6p orange brown 7.00 12.50
79 A2 1p on 2sh6p rose 1.25 4.50
Nos. 74-79 (6) 21.80 37.00

No. 62 Surcharged **TWO PENCE**

1931, Jan. 1 Perf. 14

88 A3 2p on 1½p yellow brn & gray blue 1.25 1.25

5d.

Nos. 70, 71 and 72 Surcharged in Black

FIVE PENCE

1931

89 A3 5p on 1sh #70 2.00 1.75
90 A3 9p on 2sh6p #71 3.50 8.00
91 A3 1sh3p on 5sh #72 5.00 12.50
Nos. 89-91 (3) 10.50 22.25

Type of 1916 Issue

1932 Wmk. 228 Perf. 11

92 A3 9p dp violet & gray 15.00 27.50
93 A3 1sh3p pale blue & gray blk 17.50 30.00

For overprints see Nos. O11-O12.

Motuan Girl — A5

Bird of Paradise and Boar's Tusk — A6

Mother and Child — A7

Papuan Motherhood — A8

Dubu (Ceremonial Platform) — A9

Fire Maker — A10

Designs: 1p, Steve, son of Oala. 1½p, Tree houses. 3p, Papuan dandy. 5p, Masked dancer. 9p, Shooting fish. 1sh3p, Lakatoi. 2sh, Delta art. 2sh6p, Pottery making. 5sh, Sgt.-Major Simoi. £1, Delta house.

Unwmk.

1932, Nov. 14 Engr. Perf. 11

94 A5 ½p orange & blk .20 .20
95 A5 1p yel green & blk .15 .15
96 A5 1½p red brn & blk .90 .90
97 A6 2p light red 2.00 .45
98 A5 3p blue & blk 2.50 2.25
99 A7 4p olive green 2.00 2.00
100 A5 5p grnsh sl & blk 2.25 2.25
101 A8 6p bister brown 4.00 3.75
102 A5 9p lilac & blk 7.50 9.00
103 A9 1sh bluish gray 3.00 3.00
104 A5 1sh3p brown & blk 12.50 14.50
105 A5 2sh bluish slate & blk 14.50 21.00
106 A5 2sh6p rose lilac & blk 21.00 32.50
107 A5 5sh olive & blk 45.00 45.00
108 A10 10sh gray lilac 82.50 82.50
109 A5 £1 lt gray & black 200.00 140.00
Nos. 94-109 (16) 400.00 359.45

For overprints see Nos. 114-117.

Hoisting Union Jack at Port Moresby — A21

H. M. S. "Nelson" at Port Moresby — A22

1934, Nov. 6

110 A21 1p dull green .90 .90
111 A22 2p red brown 1.10 1.10
112 A21 3p blue 2.75 2.75
113 A22 5p violet brown 6.25 6.25
Nos. 110-113 (4) 11.00 11.00
Set, never hinged 17.00

Declaration of British Protection, 50th anniv.

Silver Jubilee Issue

Stamps of 1932 Issue Overprinted in Black:

HIS MAJESTY'S JUBILEE.
1910 1935
a

HIS MAJESTY'S
JUBILEE.
1910 — 1935
b

1935, July 9

Glazed Paper

114 A5(a) 1p yellow grn & blk .25 .35
115 A6(b) 2p light red .65 .85
116 A5(a) 3p lt blue & blk 2.50 3.25
117 A5(a) 5p grnsh slate & blk 5.00 6.50
Nos. 114-117 (4) 8.40 10.95
Set, never hinged 14.00

25th anniv. of the reign of George V.

Coronation Issue

King George VI — A22a

Unwmk.

1937, May 14 Engr. Perf. 11

118 A22a 1p green .25 .20
119 A22a 2p salmon rose .25 .20
120 A22a 3p blue .25 .25
121 A22a 5p brown violet .35 .35
Nos. 118-121 (4) 1.10 1.00
Set, never hinged 2.00

Catalogue values for unused stamps in this section, from this point to the end of the section, are for Never Hinged items.

Papua and New Guinea

Tree-climbing Kangaroo — A23

Kiriwina Chief's House — A24

Copra Making A25

Designs: 1p, Buka head-dress. 2p, Youth. 2½p, Bird of paradise. 3p, Policeman. 3½p, Chimbu headdress. 7½p, Kiriwina yam house. 1sh, Trading canoe. 1sh6p, Rubber tapping. 2sh, Shields and spears. 2sh6p, Plumed shepherd. 10sh, Map. £1, Spearing fish.

Unwmk.

1952, Oct. 30 Engr. Perf. 14

122 A23 ½p blue green .20 .15
123 A23 1p chocolate .20 .15
124 A23 2p deep ultra .60 .15
125 A23 2½p orange 2.50 .50
126 A23 3p dark green .90 .15
127 A23 3½p dk carmine 1.10 .20
128 A24 6½p vio brown 1.75 .35
129 A24 7½p dp ultra 13.00 5.75
130 A25 9p chocolate 4.00 .80
131 A25 1sh yellow green 2.50 .45
132 A24 1sh6p dark green 7.25 1.10
133 A24 2sh deep blue 7.75 .90
134 A25 2sh6p dk red brown 8.75 1.50
135 A25 10sh gray black 72.50 15.00
136 A24 £1 chocolate 77.50 22.50
Nos. 122-136 (15) 200.50 49.65
Set, hinged 155.00

See Nos. 139-141. For surcharges and overprints see Nos. 137-138, 147, J1-J3, J5-J6.

Nos. 125 and 131 Surcharged with New Values and Bars

1957, Jan. 29 Perf. 14

137 A23 4p on 2½p orange .50 .30
138 A25 7p on 1sh yellow green 1.00 .80

Type of 1952 and

Klinki Plymill A26

Designs: 3½p, Chimbu headdress. 4p, 5p, Cacao. 8p, Klinki Plymill. 1sh7p, Cattle. 2sh5p, Cattle. 5sh, Coffee, vert.

1958-60 Engr. Perf. 14

139 A23 3½p black 8.50 4.50
140 A23 4p vermilion .60 .15
141 A23 5p green ('60) .60 .15
142 A26 7p gray green 3.75 .55
143 A26 8p dk ultra 2.75 1.25
144 A26 1sh7p red brown 40.00 20.00
145 A26 2sh5p vermilion 6.25 4.00
146 A26 5sh gray olive & brn red 8.00 2.00
Nos. 139-146 (8) 70.45 32.60

Issue dates: June 2, 1958, Nov. 10, 1960.

For surcharge see No. J4.

No. 122 Surcharged with New Value

1959, Dec. 1

147 A23 5p on ½p blue green .85 .30

Council Chamber and Frangipani Flowers A27

1961, Apr. 10 Photo. *Perf. 14½x14*

148 A27	5p	green & yellow	1.40	.70
149 A27	2sh3p	green & salmon	11.00	8.00

Reconstitution of the Legislative Council.

Woman's Head — A28

Red-plumed Bird of Paradise — A29

Port Moresby Harbor A30

Constable Ragas Amis Matia, Port Moresby A32

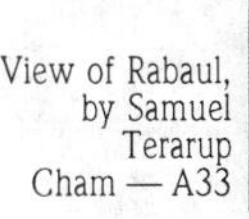

View of Rabaul, by Samuel Terarup Cham — A33

Woman Dancer A31

Elizabeth II A34

Designs: 3p, Man's head. 6p, Golden opossum. 2sh, Male dancer with drum. 2sh3p, Piaggio transport plane landing at Tapini.

Perf. 14 (A28, A31, A32), 11½ (A29, A33), 14x13½ (A30), 14½ (A34)

1961-63 Engr. Unwmk.

153 A28	1p	dk carmine	.15	.15
154 A28	3p	bluish black	.15	.15
		Photo.		
155 A29	5p	lt brn, red brn, blk & yel	.15	.15
156 A29	6p	gray, ocher & slate	.55	.55
		Engr.		
157 A30	8p	green	.25	.20
158 A31	1sh	gray green	3.50	.45
159 A31	2sh	rose lake	.85	.40
160 A30	2sh3p	dark blue	.70	.45
161 A32	3sh	green	.90	.70
		Photo.		
162 A33	10sh	multicolored	18.00	13.00
163 A34	£1	brt grn, blk & gold	12.00	7.50
		Nos. 153-163 (11)	37.20	23.70

The 5p and 6p are on granite paper.

Issued: 3sh, 9/5/62; 10sh, 2/13/63: 5p, 6p, 3/27/63; 8p, 2sh3p, 5/8/63; £1, 7/3/63; others, 7/26/61.

Malaria Eradication Emblem — A35

1962, Apr. 7 Litho. *Perf. 14*

164 A35	5p	lt blue & maroon	.30	.15
165 A35	1sh	lt brown & red	1.65	.95
166 A35	2sh	yellow green & blk	3.50	3.00
		Nos. 164-166 (3)	5.45	4.10

WHO drive to eradicate malaria.

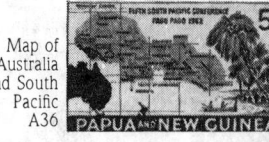

Map of Australia and South Pacific A36

1962, July 9 Engr. Unwmk.

167 A36	5p	dk red & lt green	.30	.15
168 A36	1sh6p	dk violet & yel	1.65	1.50
169 A36	2sh6p	green & lt blue	5.25	4.00
		Nos. 167-169 (3)	7.20	5.65

5th So. Pacific Conf., Pago Pago, July 1962.

High Jump — A37

Games Emblem — A38

1962, Oct. 24 Photo. *Perf. 11½*

Size: 26x21mm

Granite Paper

171 A37	5p	shown	.35	.15
172 A37	5p	Javelin	.35	.15
		Size: 32½x22½mm		
173 A37	2sh3p	runners	3.00	2.50
		Nos. 171-173 (3)	3.70	2.80

British Empire and Commonwealth Games, Perth, Australia, Nov. 22-Dec. 1.

Nos. 171 and 172 printed in alternating horizontal rows in sheet.

Red Cross Centenary Emblem — A38a

1963, May 1 *Perf. 13½*

174 A38a	5p	blue grn, gray & red	.70	.40

Centenary of the International Red Cross.

1963, Aug. 14 Engr. *Perf. 13½x14*

176 A38	5p	olive bister	.25	.15
177 A38	1sh	green	.95	.90

So. Pacific Games, Suva, Aug. 29-Sept. 7.

Top of Wooden Shield — A39

Casting Ballot — A40

Various Carved Heads.

Perf. 11½

1964, Feb. 5 Unwmk. Photo.

Granite Paper

178 A39	11p	multicolored	.25	.20
179 A39	2sh5p	multicolored	.85	.60
180 A39	2sh6p	multicolored	.70	.45
181 A39	5sh	multicolored	1.90	1.25
		Nos. 178-181 (4)	3.70	2.50

1964, Mar. 4 Unwmk. *Perf. 11½*

Granite Paper

182 A40	5p	dk brown & pale brn	.15	.15
183 A40	2sh3p	dk brown & lt blue	1.10	1.10

First Common Roll elections.

A41

A42

Designs: 5p, Patients at health center clinic. 8p, Dentist and school child patient. 1sh, Nurse holding infant. 1sh2p, Medical student using microscope.

1964, Aug. 5 Engr. *Perf. 14*

184 A41	5p	violet	.15	.15
185 A41	8p	green	.25	.25
186 A41	1sh	deep ultra	.35	.35
187 A41	1sh2p	rose brown	.45	.45
		Nos. 184-187 (4)	1.20	1.20

Territorial health services.

1964-65 Unwmk. Photo. *Perf. 11½*

Designs: 1p, Striped gardener bower birds. 3p, New Guinea regent bower birds. 5p, Blue birds of paradise. 6p, Lawes six-wired birds of paradise. 8p, Sickle-billed birds of paradise. 1sh, Emperor birds of paradise. 2sh, Brown sickle-billed bird of paradise. 2sh3p, Lesser bird of paradise. 3sh, Magnificent bird of paradise. 5sh, Twelve-wired bird of paradise. 10sh, Magnificent rifle birds.

Birds in Natural Colors

Size: 21x26mm

188 A42	1p	brt citron & dk brn	.15	.15
189 A42	3p	gray & dk brown	.20	.15
190 A42	5p	salmon pink & blk	.20	.15
191 A42	6p	pale grn & sepia	.25	.20
192 A42	8p	pale lilac & dk brn	.40	.25
		Size: 25x36mm		
193 A42	1sh	salmon & blk	.55	.40
194 A42	2sh	blue & dk brn	1.75	1.10
195 A42	2sh3p	lt green & dk brn	2.75	1.65
196 A42	3sh	yellow & dk brn	3.00	2.00
197 A42	5sh	lt ultra & dk brn	8.00	4.50
198 A42	10sh	gray & dk blue	7.00	5.50
		Nos. 188-198 (11)	24.25	16.05

Issued: 6p, 8p, 1sh, 10sh, 10/28/64; others, 1/20/65.

Carved Crocodile's Head — A43

Designs: Wood carvings from Sepik River Region used as ship's prows and as objects of religious veneration.

1965, Mar. 24 Photo. *Perf. 11½*

199 A43	4p	multicolored	.40	.20
200 A43	1sh2p	gray brown, bister & dk brown	1.50	1.50
201 A43	1sh6p	lilac, dk brn & buff	.65	.65
202 A43	4sh	blue, dk vio & mar	1.90	1.90
		Nos. 199-202 (4)	4.45	4.25

"Simpson and His Donkey" by Wallace Anderson — A43a

1965, Apr. 14 *Perf. 13½x13*

203 A43a	2sh3p	brt grn, sep & blk	1.00	1.00

ANZAC issue. See note after Australia No. 387.

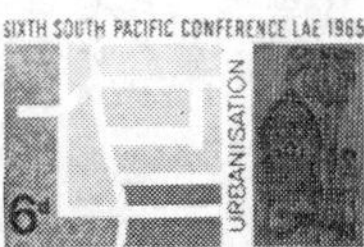

Urbanized Community and Stilt House — A44

Design: 1sh, Stilt house at left.

1965, July 7 Photo. *Perf. 11½*

204 A44	6p	multicolored	.15	.15
205 A44	1sh	multicolored	.25	.25

6th South Pacific Conf., Lae, July, 1965.

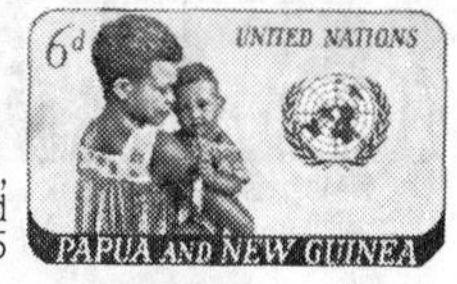

UN Emblem, Mother and Child — A45

UN Emblem and: 1sh, Globe and orbit, vert. 2sh, Four globes in orbit, vert.

1965, Oct. 13 Unwmk. *Perf. 11½*

206 A45	6p	brown, grnsh bl & dp bl	.15	.15
207 A45	1sh	dull pur, blue & org	.30	.30
208 A45	2sh	dp blue, pale grn & grn	.35	.35
		Nos. 206-208 (3)	.80	.80

20th anniversary of the United Nations.

New Guinea Birdwing — A46

Molala Harai and Paiva Streamer — A47

Discus — A48

Butterflies: 1c, Blue emperor, vert. 3c, White-banded map butterfly, vert. 4c, Mountain swallow-tail, vert. 5c, Port Moresby terinos, vert. 12c, Blue crow. 15c, Euchenor butterfly. 20c, White-spotted parthenos. 25c, Orange Jezebel. 50c, New Guinea emperor. $1, Blue-spotted leaf-wing. $2, Paradise birdwing.

Myths of Elema People: 7c, Marai, the fisherman. 30c, Meavea Kivovia and the Black Cockatoo. 60c, Toivita Tapaivita (symbolic face decorations).

1966 Photo. *Perf. 11½*

Granite Paper

209 A46	1c	salmon, blk & aqua	.15	.15
210 A47	2c	black & carmine	.15	.15
211 A46	3c	gray grn, brn & org	.15	.15
212 A46	4c	multicolored	.16	.15
213 A46	5c	multicolored	.20	.15
214 A47	7c	blue, blk & yel	.45	.40
215 A46	10c	multicolored	.40	.35
216 A46	12c	salmon & multi	1.00	1.00
217 A46	15c	pale vio, dk brn & buff	1.00	.80
218 A46	20c	yel bister, dk brn & yel orange	1.50	1.00
219 A46	25c	gray, blk & yel	3.00	2.00
220 A47	30c	blk, yel grn & car	1.50	.90
221 A46	50c	multicolored	4.50	3.25
222 A47	60c	blk, org & car	3.00	2.50
223 A46	$1	pale blue, dk brn & dp org	5.75	5.00
224 A46	$2	multicolored	10.00	9.00
		Nos. 209-224 (16)	32.91	26.95

In 1967 Courvoisier made new plates for the $1 and $2. Stamps from these plates show many minor differences and slight variations in shade.

Issued: 12c, 10/10: A47, 6/8; others, 2/14.

1966, Aug. 31 *Perf. 11½*

Granite Paper

225 A48	5c	shown	.15	.15
226 A48	10c	Soccer	.45	.45
227 A48	20c	Tennis	.60	.60
		Nos. 225-227 (3)	1.20	1.20

Second South Pacific Games, Noumea, New Caledonia, Dec. 8-18.

Papua New Guinea stamps can be mounted in the Scott Australian Dependencies album.

d'Albertis' Creeper — A49

Book and Pen ("Fine Arts") — A50

Flowers: 10c, Tecomanthe dendrophila. 20c, Rhododendron macgregoriae. 60c, Rhododendron konori.

1966, Dec. 7 Photo. *Perf. 11½*

228 A49 5c multicolored .15 .15
229 A49 10c multicolored .30 .30
230 A49 20c multicolored .50 .50
231 A49 60c multicolored 1.50 1.50
Nos. 228-231 (4) 2.45 2.45

1967, Feb. 8 Photo. *Perf. 12½x12*

Designs: 3c, "Surveying," transit, view finder and pencil. 4c, "Civil Engineering," buildings and compass. 5c, "Science," test tubes and chemical formula. 20c, "Justice," Justitia and scales.

232 A50 1c orange & multi .15 .15
233 A50 3c blue & multi .15 .15
234 A50 4c brown & multi .15 .15
235 A50 5c green & multi .15 .15
236 A50 20c pink & multi .45 .45
Set value .80 .80

Issued to publicize the development of the University of Papua and New Guinea and the Institute of Higher Technical Education.

Leaf Beetle — A51

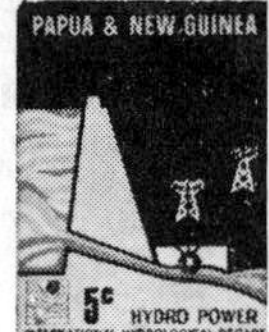

Hydroelectric Power — A52

Beetles: 10c, Eupholus schoenherri. 20c, Sphingnotus albertisi. 25c, Cyphogastra albertisi.

1967, Apr. 12 Unwmk. *Perf. 11½*

237 A51 5c blue & multi .15 .15
238 A51 10c lt green & multi .30 .30
239 A51 20c rose & multi .50 .50
240 A51 25c yellow & multi .65 .65
Nos. 237-240 (4) 1.60 1.60

1967, June 28 Photo. *Perf. 12x12½*

Designs: 10c, Pyrethrum (Chrysanthemum cinerariaefolium). 20c, Tea. 25c, like 5c.

241 A52 5c multicolored .15 .15
242 A52 10c multicolored .30 .30
243 A52 20c multicolored .50 .50
244 A52 25c multicolored .65 .65
Nos. 241-244 (4) 1.60 1.60

Completion of part of the Laloki River Hydroelectric Works near Port Moresby, and the Hydrological Decade (UNESCO), 1965-74.

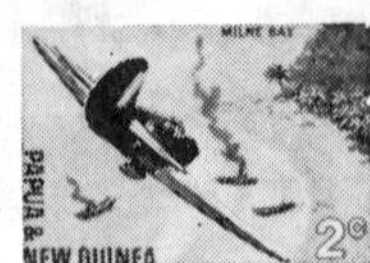

Battle of Milne Bay — A53

Designs: 5c, Soldiers on Kokoda Trail, vert. 20c, The coast watchers. 50c, Battle of the Coral Sea.

1967, Aug. 30 Unwmk. *Perf. 11½*

245 A53 2c multicolored .15 .15
246 A53 5c multicolored .15 .15
247 A53 20c multicolored .30 .30
248 A53 50c multicolored .75 .75
Nos. 245-248 (4) 1.35 1.35

25th anniv. of the battles in the Pacific, which stopped the Japanese from occupying Papua and New Guinea.

Pesquet's Parrot — A54

Chimbu District Headdress — A55

Parrots: 5c, Fairy lory. 20c, Dusk-orange lory. 25c, Edward's fig parrot.

1967, Nov. 29 Photo. *Perf. 12*

249 A54 5c multicolored .15 .15
250 A54 7c multicolored .30 .30
251 A54 20c multicolored .85 .85
252 A54 25c multicolored 1.10 1.10
Nos. 249-252 (4) 2.40 2.40

Perf. 12x12½, 12½x12

1968, Feb. 21 Photo. Unwmk.

Headdress from: 10c, Southern Highlands District, horiz. 20c, Western Highlands District, horiz. 60c, Chimbu District (different from 5c).

253 A55 5c multicolored .15 .15
254 A55 10c multicolored .20 .15
255 A55 20c multicolored .40 .30
256 A55 60c multicolored 1.25 .90
Nos. 253-256 (4) 2.00 1.50

Frogs — A56

1968, Apr. 24 Photo. *Perf. 11½*

257 A56 5c Tree .20 .20
258 A56 10c Tree, diff. .40 .40
259 A56 15c Swamp .60 .60
260 A56 20c Tree, diff. .80 .75
Nos. 257-260 (4) 2.00 1.95

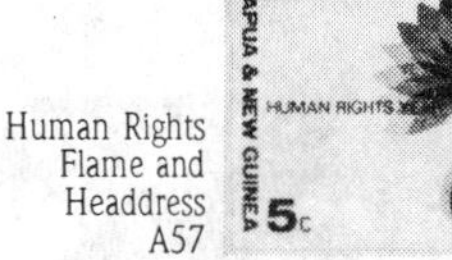

Human Rights Flame and Headdress A57

Symbolic Designs: 10c, Human Rights Flame surrounded by the world. 20c, 25c, "Universal Suffrage" in 2 abstract designs.

1968, June 26 Litho. *Perf. 14x13*

261 A57 5c black & multi .15 .15
262 A57 10c black & multi .25 .25
263 A57 20c black & multi .60 .40
264 A57 25c black & multi .65 .55
Nos. 261-264 (4) 1.65 1.35

Issued for Human Rights Year, 1968, and to publicize free elections.

Frilled Clam — A58

Sea Shells: 1c, Egg cowry. 3c, Crested stromb. 4c, Lithograph bone. 5c, Marble cone. 7c, Orange-spotted miter. 10c, Red volute. 12c, Checkerboard helmet shell. 15c, Scorpion shell. 25c, Chocolate-flamed Venus shell. 30c, Giant murex. 40c, Chambered nautilus. 60c, Triton's trumpet. $1, Emerald snails. $2, Glory of the sea, vert.

Perf. 12½x12, 12x12½

1968-69 Photo.

Granite Paper

265 A58 1c multicolored .15 .15
266 A58 3c multicolored .15 .15
267 A58 4c multicolored .15 .15
268 A58 5c multicolored .20 .15
269 A58 7c multicolored .30 .15
270 A58 10c multicolored .40 .25
271 A58 12c multicolored .60 .40
272 A58 15c multicolored .65 .45
273 A58 20c multicolored .75 .50
274 A58 25c multicolored 1.10 .75
275 A58 30c multicolored 1.40 1.00
276 A58 40c multicolored 2.25 1.40
277 A58 60c multicolored 2.75 1.75
278 A58 $1 multicolored 4.50 3.75
279 A58 $2 multicolored 11.00 7.75
Nos. 265-279 (15) 26.35 18.75

Issued: 5c, 20c, 25c, 30c, 60c, 8/28/68; 3c, 10c, 15c, 40c, $1, 10/30/68; others, 1/29/69.

Legend of Tito-Iko — A59

Fireball Class Sailboat, Port Moresby Harbor — A60

Myths of Elema People: No. 281, 5c inscribed "Iko." No. 282, 10c inscribed "Luvuapo." No. 283, 10c inscribed "Miro."

#280 & 282:
Perf. 12½x13½xRoul. 9xPerf. 13½
#281 & 283:
Roul. 9 x Perf. 13½x12½x13½

1969, Apr. 9 Litho. Unwmk.

280 A59 5c black, yellow & red .15 .15
281 A59 5c black, yellow & red .15 .15
a. Vert. pair, #280-281 .25 .25
282 A59 10c black, gray & red .30 .25
283 A59 10c black, gray & red .30 .25
a. Vert. pair, #282-283 .60 .60
Nos. 280-283 (4) .90 .80

Nos. 281a, 283a have continuous designs, rouletted between.

Perf. 14x14½, 14½x14

1969, June 25 Engr.

Designs: 10c, Games' swimming pool, Boroko, horiz. 20c, Main Games area, Konedobu, horiz.

284 A60 5c black .15 .15
285 A60 10c bright violet .35 .35
286 A60 20c green .65 .65
Nos. 284-286 (3) 1.15 1.15

3rd S. Pacific Games, Port Moresby, Aug. 13-23.

Dendrobium Ostrinoglossum A61

Potter A62

Orchids: 10c, Dendrobium lawesii. 20c, Dendrobium pseudofrigidum. 30c, Dendrobium conanthum.

1969, Aug. 27 Photo. *Perf. 11½*

Granite Paper

287 A61 5c multicolored .20 .20
288 A61 10c multicolored .50 .40
289 A61 20c multicolored .85 .85
290 A61 30c multicolored 1.50 1.40
Nos. 287-290 (4) 3.05 2.85

Issued to publicize the 6th World Orchid Conference, Sydney, Australia, Sept. 1969.

1969, Sept. 24 Photo. *Perf. 11½*

Granite Paper

291 A62 5c multicolored .30 .20

50th anniv. of the ILO.

Bird of Paradise A63

Seed Pod Rattle (Tareko) A64

Coil Stamps

1969-71 *Perf. 14½ Horiz.*

291A A63 2c red, dp blue & blk .15 .15
292 A63 5c orange & emerald .20 .15
Set value .30 .20

Issue dates: 5c, Sept. 24, 2c, Apr. 1, 1971.

1969, Oct. 29 Photo. *Perf. 12½*

Musical Instruments: 10c, Hand drum (garamut). 25c, Pan pipes (iviliko). 30c, Hourglass drum (kundu).

293 A64 5c multicolored .15 .15
294 A64 10c multicolored .25 .20
295 A64 25c multicolored .55 .45
296 A64 30c multicolored .70 .50
Nos. 293-296 (4) 1.65 1.30

Prehistoric Ambum Stone and Skull — A65

Designs: 10c, Masawa canoe of the Kula Circuit. 25c, Map of Papua and New Guinea made by Luis Valez de Torres, 1606. 30c, H.M.S. Basilisk, 1873.

1970, Feb. 11 Photo. *Perf. 12½*

297 A65 5c violet brown & multi .15 .15
298 A65 10c ocher & multi .25 .18
299 A65 25c orange brown & multi .55 .45
300 A65 30c olive green & multi .75 .55
Nos. 297-300 (4) 1.70 1.33

King of Saxony Bird of Paradise — A66

Birds of Paradise: 10c, King. 15c, Augusta Victoria. 25c, Multi-crested.

1970, May 13 Photo. *Perf. 11½*

301 A66 5c tan & multi .50 .20
302 A66 10c multicolored 1.00 .45
303 A66 15c lt blue & multi 2.00 1.40
304 A66 25c multicolored 3.50 2.00
Nos. 301-304 (4) 7.00 4.05

Canceled to Order

Starting in 1970 or earlier, the Philatelic Bureau at Port Moresby began to sell new issues canceled to order at face value.

Douglas DC-3 and Matupi Volcano — A67

Aircraft: No. 305, DC-6B and Mt. Wilhelm. No. 306, Lockheed Mark II Electra and Mt. Yule. No. 307, Boeing 727 and Mt. Giluwe. No. 308, Fokker F27 Friendship and Manam Island Volcano. 30c, Boeing 707 and Hombom's Bluff.

1970, July 8 Photo. *Perf. 14½x14*

305 A67 5c "TAA" on tail .15 .15
306 A67 5c Striped tail .15 .15
307 A67 5c "T" on tail .15 .15
308 A67 5c Red tail .15 .15
a. Block of 4, #305-308 .55 .55
309 A67 25c multicolored .90 .85
310 A67 30c multicolored 1.10 .90
Nos. 305-310 (6) 2.60 2.35

Development of air service during the last 25 years between Australia and New Guinea.

Nicolaus N. de Miklouho-Maclay, Explorer, and Mask — A68

Designs: 10c, Bronislaw Kaspar Malinowski, anthropologist, and hut. 15c, Count Tommaso Salvadori, ornithologist, and cassowary. 20c, Friedrich R. Schlechter, botanist, and orchid.

1970, Aug. 19 Photo. *Perf. 11½*

311 A68	5c brown, blk & lilac		.15	.15
312 A68	10c multicolored		.25	.20
313 A68	15c dull lilac & multi		.45	.35
314 A68	20c slate & multi		.80	.55
	Nos. 311-314 (4)		1.65	1.25

42nd Cong. of the Australian and New Zealand Assoc. for the Advancement of Science, Port Moresby, Aug. 17-21.

Wogeo Island Food Bowl — A69

Eastern Highlands Round House — A70

National Handicraft: 10c, Lime pot. 15c, Aibom sago storage pot. 30c, Manus Island bowl, horiz.

1970, Oct. 28 Photo. *Perf. 12½*

315 A69	5c multicolored	.15	.15
316 A69	10c multicolored	.25	.25
317 A69	15c multicolored	.40	.40
318 A69	30c multicolored	.80	.70
	Nos. 315-318 (4)	1.60	1.50

1971, Jan. 27 Photo. *Perf. 11½*

Local Architecture: 7c, Milne Bay house. 10c, Purari Delta house. 40c, Sepik or Men's Spirit House.

319 A70	5c dark olive & multi	.15	.15
320 A70	7c Prus blue & multi	.20	.20
321 A70	10c deep orange & multi	.30	.25
322 A70	40c brown & multi	.95	.80
	Nos. 319-322 (4)	1.60	1.40

Spotted Cuscus — A71

Basketball — A72

Animals: 10c, Brown and white striped possum. 15c, Feather-tailed possum. 25c, Spiny anteater, horiz. 30c, Good-fellow's tree-climbing kangaroo, horiz.

1971, Mar. 31 Photo. *Perf. 11½*

323 A71	5c blue green & multi	.25	.15
324 A71	10c multicolored	.65	.45
325 A71	15c multicolored	1.10	.75
326 A71	25c dull yellow & multi	1.65	.95
327 A71	30c olive & multi	2.25	1.25
	Nos. 323-327 (5)	5.90	3.55

1971, June 9 Litho. *Perf. 14*

328 A72	7c shown	.15	.15
329 A72	14c Yachting	.30	.25
330 A72	21c Boxing	.55	.40
331 A72	28c Field events	.60	.50
	Nos. 328-331 (4)	1.60	1.30

Fourth South Pacific Games, Papeete, French Polynesia, Sept. 8-19.

Bartering Fish for Coconuts and Taro — A73

Siaa Dancer — A74

Primary industries: 9c, Man stacking yams and taro. 14c, Market scene. 30c, Farm couple tending yams.

1971, Aug. 18 Photo. *Perf. 11½*

332 A73	7c multicolored	.20	.15
333 A73	9c multicolored	.35	.25
334 A73	14c multicolored	.50	.40
335 A73	30c multicolored	1.00	.90
	Nos. 332-335 (4)	2.05	1.70

1971, Oct. 27 Photo. *Perf. 11½*

Designs: 9c, Urasena masked dancer. 20c, Two Siassi masked dancers, horiz. 28c, Three Siaa dancers, horiz.

336 A74	7c orange & multi	.15	.15
337 A74	9c yel green & multi	.25	.25
338 A74	20c bister & multi	.65	.60
339 A74	28c multicolored	1.00	.90
	Nos. 336-339 (4)	2.05	1.90

Papua New Guinea and Australia Arms — A75

#341, Papua New Guinea & Australia flags.

1972, Jan. 26 *Perf. 12½x12*

340 A75	7c gray blue, org & blk	.40	.30
341 A75	7c gray blue, blk, red & yel	.40	.30
a.	Pair, #340-341	.80	.60

Constitutional development for the 1972 House of Assembly elections.

Papua New Guinea Map, South Pacific Commission Emblem — A76

#343, Man's head, So. Pacific Commission flag.

1972, Jan. 26

342 A76	15c brt green & multi	.70	.40
343 A76	15c brt green & multi	.70	.40
a.	Pair, #342-343	1.40	.80

South Pacific Commission, 25th anniv.

Pitted-shelled Turtle — A77

Designs: 14c, Angle-headed agamid. 21c, Green python. 30c, Water monitor.

1972, Mar. 15 Photo. *Perf. 11½*

344 A77	7c multicolored	.40	.20
345 A77	14c car rose & multi	1.25	.55
346 A77	21c yellow & multi	1.65	.80
347 A77	30c yel green & multi	2.00	1.25
	Nos. 344-347 (4)	5.30	2.80

Curtiss Seagull MF 6 and Ship A78

14c, De Havilland 37 & porters from gold fields. 20c, Junkers G 31 & heavy machinery. 25c, Junkers F 13 & Lutheran mission church.

1972, June 7

Granite Paper

348 A78	7c dp yellow & multi	.30	.25
349 A78	14c dp orange & multi	.85	.55
350 A78	20c olive & multi	1.40	.85
351 A78	25c multicolored	1.65	.90
	Nos. 348-351 (4)	4.20	2.55

50th anniv. of aviation in Papua New Guinea.

National Day Unity Emblem — A79

Designs: 10c, Unity emblem and kundu (drum). 30c, Unity emblem and conch.

1972, Aug. 16 *Perf. 12x12½*

352 A79	7c violet blue & multi	.15	.15
353 A79	10c orange & multi	.35	.20
354 A79	30c vermilion & multi	.75	.50
	Nos. 352-354 (3)	1.25	.85

National Day, Sept. 15, 1972.

Rev. Copland King — A80

Pioneering Missionaries: No. 356, Pastor Ruatoka. No. 357, Bishop Stanislaus Henry Verjus. No. 358, Rev. Dr. Johannes Flierl.

1972, Oct. 25 Photo. *Perf. 11½*

355 A80	7c dark blue & multi	.40	.30
356 A80	7c dark red & multi	.40	.30
357 A80	7c dark green & multi	.40	.30
358 A80	7c dark olive bister & multi	.40	.30
	Nos. 355-358 (4)	1.60	1.20

Christmas 1972.

Relay Station on Mt. Tomavatur — A81

1973, Jan. 24 Photo. *Perf. 12½*

359 A81	7c shown	.30	.15
360 A81	7c Mt. Kerigomna	.30	.15
361 A81	7c Sattelburg	.30	.15
362 A81	7c Wideru	.30	.15
a.	Block of 4, #359-362	1.25	.85
363 A81	9c Teleprinter	.50	.20
364 A81	30c Map of network	1.50	.85
	Nos. 359-364 (6)	3.20	1.65

Telecommunications development 1968-1972. No. 362a has a unifying frame.

Queen Carol's Bird of Paradise — A82

Birds of Paradise: 14c, Goldie's. 21c, Ribbon-tailed astrapia. 28c, Princess Stephanie's.

1973, Mar. 30 Photo. *Perf. 11½*

Size: 22½x38mm

365 A82	7c citron & multi	.70	.45
366 A82	14c dull green & multi	1.50	.85

Size: 17x48mm

367 A82	21c lemon & multi	2.00	1.25
368 A82	28c lt blue & multi	3.00	1.75
	Nos. 365-368 (4)	7.20	4.30

Wood Carver, Milne Bay — A83

Designs: 3c, Wig makers, Southern Highlands. 5c, Bagana Volcano, Bougainville. 6c, Pig Exchange, Western Highlands. 7c, Coastal village, Central District. 8c, Arawe mother, West New Britain. 9c, Fire dancers, East New Britain. 10c, Tifalmin hunter, West Sepik District. 14c, Crocodile hunters, Western District. 15c, Mt. Elimbari, Chimbu. 20c, Canoe racing, Manus District. 21c, Making sago, Gulf District. 25c, Council House, East Sepik. 28c, Menyamya bowmen, Morobe. 30c, Shark snaring, New Ireland. 40c, Fishing canoes, Madang. 60c, Women making tapa cloth, Northern District. $1, Asaro mudmen, Eastern Highlands. $2, Sing festival, Enga District.

1973-74 Photo. *Perf. 11½*

Granite Paper

369 A83	1c multicolored	.15	.15
370 A83	3c multi ('74)	.15	.15
371 A83	5c multicolored	.15	.15
372 A83	6c multi ('74)	.15	.15
373 A83	7c multicolored	.15	.15
374 A83	8c multi ('74)	.15	.15
375 A83	9c multicolored	.20	.15
376 A83	10c multi ('74)	.20	.15
377 A83	14c multicolored	.30	.15
378 A83	15c multicolored	.35	.20
379 A83	20c multi ('74)	.40	.30
380 A83	21c multicolored	.40	.30
381 A83	25c multicolored	.55	.35
382 A83	28c multicolored	.60	.40
383 A83	30c multicolored	.60	.40
385 A83	40c multicolored	.80	.60
386 A83	60c multi ('74)	1.25	.75
387 A83	$1 multi ('74)	4.50	2.75
388 A83	$2 multi ('74)	7.75	4.50
	Nos. 369-383,385-388 (19)	18.80	11.90

Issue dates: 1c, 7c, 9c, 15c, 25c, 40c, June 13. 5c, 14c, 21c, 28c, 30c, Aug.

Papua New Guinea No. 7 A84

1c, Ger. New Guinea #1-2. 6c, Ger. New Guinea #17. 7c, New Britain #43. 25c, New Guinea #1. 30c, Papua New Guinea #108.

Litho. (1c, 7c); Litho. & Engr. (others)

1973, Oct. 24 *Perf. 13½x14*

Size: 54x31mm

389 A84	1c gold, brn, grn & blk	.15	.15
390 A84	6c silver, blue & indigo	.20	.20
391 A84	7c gold, red, blk & buff	.25	.25

Perf. 14x14½

Size: 45x38mm

392 A84	9c gold, org, blk & brn	.30	.30
393 A84	25c gold & orange	.90	.90
394 A84	30c silver & dp lilac	1.00	1.00
	Nos. 389-394 (6)	2.80	2.80

75th anniv. of stamps in Papua New Guinea.

Masks — A85

1973, Dec. 5 Photo. *Perf. 12½*

Granite Paper

395 A85	7c multicolored	.35	.30
396 A85	10c violet blue & multi	.65	.55

Self-government.

Queen Elizabeth II — A86

1974, Feb. 22 Photo. *Perf. 14x14½*

397 A86	7c dp carmine & multi	.20	.20
398 A86	30c vio blue & multi	1.00	.90

Visit of Queen Elizabeth II and the Royal Family, Feb. 22-27.

Wreathed Hornbill A87

Size of No. 400, 32½x48mm.

Perf. 12, 11½ (10c)

1974, June 12 **Photo.**

Granite Paper

399	A87	7c shown	1.50	1.25
400	A87	10c Great cassowary	2.50	2.25
401	A87	30c Kapul eagle	6.00	5.50
		Nos. 399-401 (3)	10.00	9.00

Dendrobium Bracteosum — A88

Orchids: 10c, Dendrobium anosmum. 20c, Dendrobium smillieae. 30c, Dendrobium insigne.

1974, Nov. 20 **Photo.** ***Perf. 11½***

Granite Paper

402	A88	7c dark green & multi	.40	.20
403	A88	10c dark blue & multi	.60	.30
404	A88	20c bister & multi	1.25	.55
405	A88	30c green & multi	2.00	.80
		Nos. 402-405 (4)	4.25	1.85

Motu Lakatoi A89

Traditional Canoes: 10c, Tami two-master morobe. 25c, Aramia racing canoe. 30c, Buka Island canoe.

1975, Feb. 26 **Photo.** ***Perf. 11½***

Granite Paper

406	A89	7c multicolored	.20	.20
407	A89	10c orange & multi	.40	.30
408	A89	25c apple green & multi	1.10	.95
409	A89	30c citron & multi	1.40	1.10
		Nos. 406-409 (4)	3.10	2.55

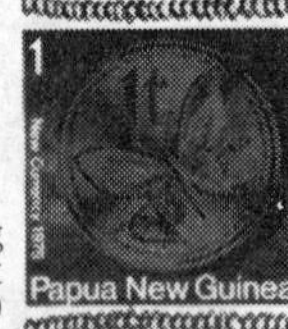

Paradise Birdwing Butterfly, 1t Coin — A90

Ornate Butterfly Cod on 2t and Plateless Turtle on 5t — A91

New coinage: 10t, Cuscus on 10t. 20t, Cassowary on 20t. 1k, River crocodiles on 1k coin with center hole; obverse and reverse of 1k.

Perf. 11, 11½ (A91)

1975, Apr. 21 **Photo.**

Granite Paper

410	A90	1t green & multi	.15	.15
411	A91	7t brown & multi	.30	.20
412	A90	10t violet blue & multi	.45	.25
413	A90	20t carmine & multi	.60	.50
414	A91	1k dull blue & multi	4.50	2.75
		Nos. 410-414 (5)	6.00	3.85

Ornithoptera Alexandrae — A92

Boxing and Games' Emblem — A93

Birdwing Butterflies: 10t, O. victoriae regis. 30t, O. allottei. 40t, O. chimaera.

1975, June 11 **Photo.** ***Perf. 11½***

Granite Paper

415	A92	7t multicolored	.30	.20
416	A92	10t multicolored	.45	.30
417	A92	30t multicolored	1.50	1.00
418	A92	40t multicolored	2.25	1.25
		Nos. 415-418 (4)	4.50	2.75

1975, Aug. 2 **Photo.** ***Perf. 11½***

Granite Paper

419	A93	7t shown	.20	.20
420	A93	20t Track and field	.55	.45
421	A93	25t Basketball	.70	.60
422	A93	30t Swimming	.95	.70
		Nos. 419-422 (4)	2.40	1.95

5th South Pacific Games, Guam, Aug. 1-10.

Map of South East Asia and Flag of PNG A94

Design: 30t, Map of South East Asia and Papua New Guinea coat of arms.

1975, Sept. 10 **Photo.** ***Perf. 11½***

Granite Paper

423	A94	7t red & multi	.20	.20
424	A94	30t blue & multi	.70	.70
	a.	Souvenir sheet of 2, #423-424	2.00	2.00

Papua New Guinea independence, Sept. 16, 1975.

M. V. Bulolo A95

Ships of the 1930's: 15t, M.V. Macdhui. 25t, M.V. Malaita. 60t, S.S. Montoro.

1976, Jan. 21 **Photo.** ***Perf. 11½***

Granite Paper

425	A95	7t multicolored	.25	.15
426	A95	15t multicolored	.40	.30
427	A95	25t multicolored	.70	.45
428	A95	60t multicolored	1.65	1.25
		Nos. 425-428 (4)	3.00	2.15

Rorovana Carvings — A96

Bougainville Art: 20t, Upe hats. 25t, Kapkaps (tortoise shell ornaments). 30t, Carved canoe paddles.

1976, Mar. 17 **Photo.** ***Perf. 11½***

Granite Paper

429	A96	7t multicolored	.20	.15
430	A96	20t blue & multi	.50	.45
431	A96	25t dp orange & multi	.65	.50
432	A96	30t multicolored	.75	.65
		Nos. 429-432 (4)	2.10	1.75

Houses — A97

1976, June 9 **Photo.** ***Perf. 11½***

Granite Paper

433	A97	7t Rabaul	.15	.15
434	A97	15t Aramia	.30	.20
435	A97	30t Telefomin	.55	.45
436	A97	40t Tapini	.80	.55
		Nos. 433-436 (4)	1.80	1.35

Boy Scouts and Scout Emblem — A98

De Havilland Sea Plane, Map of Pacific — A99

Designs: 15t, Sea Scouts on outrigger canoe, Scout emblem. 60t, Plane on water.

1976, Aug. 18 **Photo.** ***Perf. 11½***

Granite Paper

437	A98	7t multicolored	.20	.15
438	A99	10t lilac & multi	.25	.20
439	A98	15t multicolored	.50	.35
440	A99	60t multicolored	1.65	1.25
		Nos. 437-440 (4)	2.60	1.95

50th anniversaries: Papua New Guinea Boy Scouts; 1st flight from Australia.

Father Ross and Mt. Hagen — A100

1976, Oct. 28 **Photo.** ***Perf. 11½***

Granite Paper

441	A100	7t multicolored	.45	.30

Rev. Father William Ross (1896-1973), American missionary in New Guinea.

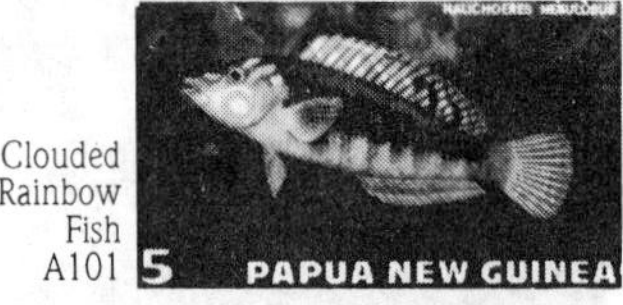

Clouded Rainbow Fish A101

Tropical Fish: 15t, Imperial angelfish. 30t, Freckled rock cod. 40t, Threadfin butterflyfish.

1976, Oct. 28

Granite Paper

442	A101	5t multicolored	.20	.15
443	A101	15t multicolored	.60	.40
444	A101	30t multicolored	1.25	.75
445	A101	40t multicolored	1.40	.95
		Nos. 442-445 (4)	3.45	2.25

Kundiawa Man — A102

Mekeo Headdress A103

Headdresses: 5t, Masked dancer, East Sepik Province. 10t, Dancer, Koiari area. 15t, Hanuabada woman. 20t, Young woman, Orokaiva. 25t, Haus Tambaran dancer, East Sepik Province. 30t, Asaro Valley man. 35t, Garaina man, Morobe. 40t, Waghi Valley man. 50t, Trobriand dancer, Milne Bay. 1k, Wasara.

Perf. 12 (15, 25, 30t), 11½ (others)

1977-78 **Photo.**

Sizes: 25x30mm (1, 5, 20t), 26x26mm (10, 15, 25, 30, 50t), 23x38mm (35, 40t)

446	A102	1t multicolored	.15	.15
447	A102	5t multicolored	.15	.15
448	A102	10t multicolored	.20	.20
449	A102	15t multicolored	.25	.25
450	A102	20t multicolored	.35	.35
451	A102	25t multicolored	.45	.45
452	A102	30t multicolored	.55	.55
453	A102	35t multicolored	.60	.60
454	A102	40t multicolored	.70	.70
455	A102	50t multicolored	.95	.95

Litho.

Perf. 14½x14

Size: 28x35½mm

456	A102	1k multicolored	1.90	1.90

Perf. 14½x15

Size: 33x23mm

457	A103	2k multicolored	3.50	3.50
		Nos. 446-457 (12)	9.75	9.75

Issued: #456-457, Jan. 12, 1977; #448, 450, 453, 455, June 7, 1978; others, Mar. 29, 1978.

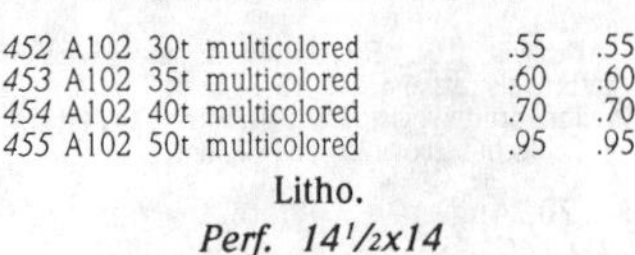

Elizabeth II and P.N.G. Arms A104

Designs: 7t, Queen and P.N.G. flag. 35t, Queen and map of P.N.G.

1977, Mar. 16 **Photo.** ***Perf. 15x14***

462	A104	7t multicolored	.20	.15
463	A104	15t multicolored	.45	.35
464	A104	35t multicolored	.95	.85
		Nos. 462-464 (3)	1.60	1.35

25th anniv. of the reign of Elizabeth II.

Whitebreasted Ground Dove — A105

Protected Birds: 7t, Victoria crowned pigeon. 15t, Pheasant pigeon. 30t, Orange-fronted fruit dove. 50t, Banded imperial pigeon.

1977, June 8 **Photo.** ***Perf. 11½***

Granite Paper

465	A105	5t multicolored	.15	.15
466	A105	7t multicolored	.25	.15
467	A105	15t multicolored	.50	.35
468	A105	30t multicolored	1.00	.65
469	A105	50t multicolored	1.75	1.10
		Nos. 465-469 (5)	3.65	2.40

Girl Guides and Gold Badge — A106

Designs (Girl Guides): 15t, Mapping and blue badge. 30t, Doing laundry in brook and red badge. 35t, Wearing grass skirts, cooking and green badge.

1977, Aug. 10 **Litho.** ***Perf. 14½***

470	A106	7t multicolored	.15	.15
471	A106	15t multicolored	.30	.25
472	A106	30t multicolored	.55	.45
473	A106	35t multicolored	.70	.60
		Nos. 470-473 (4)	1.70	1.45

Papua New Guinea Girl Guides, 50th anniv.

Legend of Kari Marupi — A107

Myths of Elema People: 20t, Savoripi Clan. 30t, Oa-Laea. 35t, Oa-Iriarapo.

1977, Oct. 19 **Litho.** ***Perf. 13½***

474	A107	7t black & multi	.15	.15
475	A107	20t black & multi	.45	.35
476	A107	30t black & multi	.60	.50
477	A107	35t black & multi	.80	.65
		Nos. 474-477 (4)	2.00	1.65

Blue-tailed Skink A108

Lizards: 15t, Green tree skink. 35t, Crocodile skink. 40t, New Guinea blue-tongued skink.

1978, Jan. 25 Photo. *Perf. 11½*
Granite Paper

478 A108	10t blue & multi	.28	.25
479 A108	15t lilac & multi	.40	.38
480 A108	35t olive & multi	.80	.75
481 A108	40t orange & multi	1.00	.85
	Nos. 478-481 (4)	2.48	2.23

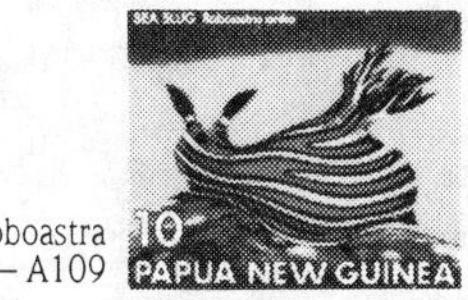

Roboastra Arika — A109

Sea Slugs: 15t, Chromodoris fidelis. 35t, Flabellina macassarana. 40t, Chromodoris trimarginata.

1978, Aug. 29 Photo. *Perf. 11½*

482 A109	10t multicolored	.25	.20
483 A109	15t multicolored	.35	.28
484 A109	35t multicolored	.85	.65
485 A109	40t multicolored	1.00	.85
	Nos. 482-485 (4)	2.45	1.98

Mandated New Guinea Constabulary A110

Constabulary and Badge: 10t, Royal Papua New Guinea. 20t, Armed British New Guinea. 25t, German New Guinea police. 30t, Royal Papua and New Guinea.

1978, Oct. 26 Photo. *Perf. 14½x14*

486 A110	10t multicolored	.20	.18
487 A110	15t multicolored	.30	.28
488 A110	20t multicolored	.40	.38
489 A110	25t multicolored	.50	.45
490 A110	30t multicolored	.60	.55
	Nos. 486-490 (5)	2.00	1.84

Ocarina, Chimbu Province — A111

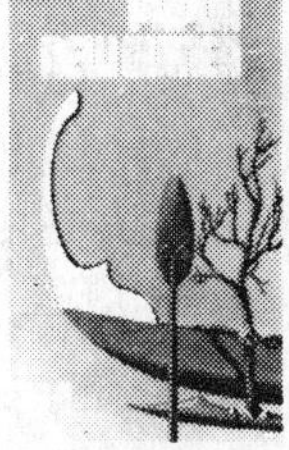
Prow and Paddle, East New Britain — A112

Musical Instruments: 20t, Musical bow, New Britain, horiz. 28t, Launut, New Ireland. 35t, Nose flute, New Hanover, horiz.

Perf. 14½x14, 14x14½
1979, Jan. 24 Litho.

491 A111	7t multicolored	.15	.15
492 A111	20t multicolored	.40	.38
493 A111	28t multicolored	.55	.50
494 A111	35t multicolored	.75	.65
	Nos. 491-494 (4)	1.85	1.68

1979, Mar. 28 Litho. *Perf. 14½*

Canoe Prows and Paddles: 21t, Sepik war canoe. 25t, Trobriand Islands. 40t, Milne Bay.

495 A112	14t multicolored	.25	.20
496 A112	21t multicolored	.30	.30
497 A112	25t multicolored	.40	.35
498 A112	40t multicolored	.65	.60
	Nos. 495-498 (4)	1.60	1.45

Belt of Shell Disks — A113

Traditional Currency: 15t, Tusk chest ornament. 25t, Shell armband. 35t, Shell necklace.

1979, June 6 Litho. *Perf. 12½x12*

499 A113	7t multicolored	.15	.15
500 A113	15t multicolored	.30	.30
501 A113	25t multicolored	.45	.40
502 A113	35t multicolored	.75	.65
	Nos. 499-502 (4)	1.65	1.50

Oenetus A114

Moths: 15t, Celerina vulgaris. 20t, Alcidis aurora, vert. 25t, Phyllodes conspicillator. 30t, Nyctalemon patroclus, vert.

1979, Aug. 29 Photo. *Perf. 11½*

503 A114	7t multicolored	.16	.16
504 A114	15t multicolored	.35	.35
505 A114	20t multicolored	.40	.40
506 A114	25t multicolored	.50	.50
507 A114	30t multicolored	.65	.65
	Nos. 503-507 (5)	2.06	2.06

Baby in String Bag Scale — A115

IYC (Emblem and): 7t, Mother nursing baby. 30t, Boy playing with dog and ball. 60t, Girl in classroom.

1979, Oct. 24 Litho. *Perf. 14x13½*

508 A115	7t multicolored	.15	.15
509 A115	15t multicolored	.25	.25
510 A115	30t multicolored	.45	.45
511 A115	60t multicolored	.80	.80
	Nos. 508-511 (4)	1.65	1.65

Mail Sorting, Mail Truck A116

UPU Membership: 25t, Wartime mail delivery. 35t, UPU monument, airport and city. 40t, Hand canceling, letter carrier.

1980, Jan. 23 Litho. *Perf. 13½x14*

512 A116	7t multicolored	.15	.15
513 A116	25t multicolored	.35	.35
514 A116	35t multicolored	.55	.55
515 A116	40t multicolored	.65	.65
	Nos. 512-515 (4)	1.70	1.70

Male Dancer, Betrothal Ceremony — A117

Third South Pacific Arts Festival, Port Moresby (Minj Betrothal Ceremony Mural): No. 516 has continuous design.

1980, Mar. 26 Photo. *Perf. 11½*
Granite Paper

516	Strip of 5	1.60	1.60
a.	A117 20t single stamp	.30	.30

National Census A118

1980, June 4 Litho. *Perf. 14*

517 A118	7t shown	.15	.15
518 A118	15t Population symbol	.20	.20
519 A118	40t P. N. G. map	.55	.55
520 A118	50t Faces	.75	.75
	Nos. 517-520 (4)	1.65	1.65

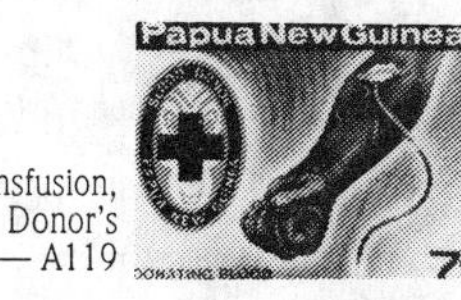

Blood Transfusion, Donor's Badge — A119

1980, Aug. 27 Litho. *Perf. 14½*

521 A119	7t shown	.15	.15
522 A119	15t Donating blood	.20	.20
523 A119	30t Map of donation centers	.45	.45
524 A119	60t Blood components and types	.80	.80
	Nos. 521-524 (4)	1.60	1.60

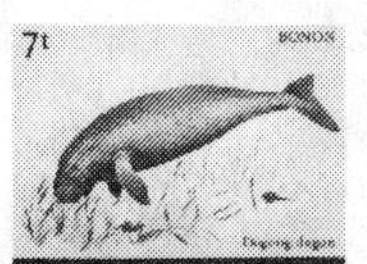

Dugong — A120

1980, Oct. 29 Photo. *Perf. 11½*

525 A120	7t shown	.15	.15
526 A120	30t Native spotted cat, vert.	.65	.65
527 A120	35t Tube-nosed bat, vert.	.75	.75
528 A120	45t Raffray's bandicoot	1.00	1.00
	Nos. 525-528 (4)	2.55	2.55

Beach Kingfisher A121

Mask A122

1981, Jan. 21 Photo. *Perf. 12*
Granite Paper

529 A121	3t shown	.15	.15
530 A121	7t Forest kingfisher	.15	.15
531 A121	20t Sacred kingfisher	.50	.50

Size: 26x45½mm

532 A121	25t White-tailed paradise kingfisher	.55	.55

Size: 26x36mm

533 A121	60t Blue-winged kookaburra	1.50	1.50
	Nos. 529-533 (5)	2.85	2.85

Coil Stamps
Perf. 14½ Horiz.
1981, Jan. 21 Photo.

534 A122	2t shown	.15	.15
535 A122	5t Hibiscus	.15	.15
	Set value	.20	.15

Defense Force Soldiers Firing Mortar A123

1981, Mar. 25 Photo. *Perf. 13½x14*

536 A123	7t shown	.15	.15
537 A123	15t DC-3 military plane	.25	.25
538 A123	40t Patrol boat Eitape	.65	.65
539 A123	50t Medics treating civilians	.80	.80
	Nos. 536-539 (4)	1.85	1.85

For surcharge see No. 615.

Missionary Aviation Fellowship Plane — A124

Planes of Missionary Organizations: 15t, Holy Ghost Society. 20t, Summer Institute of Linguistics. 30t, Lutheran Mission. 35t, Seventh Day Adventist.

1981, June 17 Litho. *Perf. 14*

540 A124	10t multicolored	.15	.15
541 A124	15t multicolored	.25	.25
542 A124	20t multicolored	.30	.30
543 A124	30t multicolored	.50	.50
544 A124	35t multicolored	.55	.55
	Nos. 540-544 (5)	1.75	1.75

Scoop Net Fishing A125

1981, Aug. 26

545 A125	10t shown	.15	.15
546 A125	15t Kite fishing	.25	.25
547 A125	30t Rod fishing	.45	.45
548 A125	60t Scissor net fishing	.95	.95
	Nos. 545-548 (4)	1.80	1.80

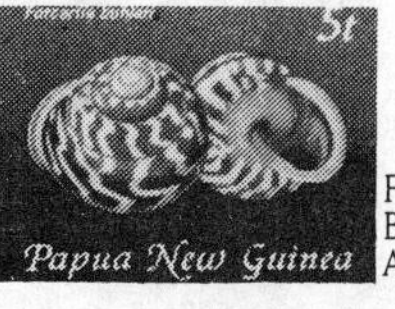

Forcartia Buhleri A126

1981, Oct. 28 Photo. *Perf. 12*
Granite Paper

549 A126	5t shown	.15	.15
550 A126	15t Naninia citrina	.30	.30
551 A126	20t Papuina adonis, papuina hermione	.35	.35
552 A126	30t Papustyla hindei, papustyla novaepommeraniae	.55	.55
553 A126	40t Rhynchotrochus strabo	.70	.70
	Nos. 549-553 (5)	2.05	2.05

75th Anniv. of Boy Scouts — A127

1982, Jan. 20 Photo. *Perf. 11½*
Granite Paper

554 A127	15t Lord Baden-Powell, flag raising	.30	.30
555 A127	25t Leader, campfire	.50	.50
556 A127	35t Scout, hut building	.65	.65
557 A127	50t Percy Chatterton, first aid	1.00	1.00
	Nos. 554-557 (4)	2.45	2.45

Wanigela Pottery A128

1982, Mar. 24 Litho. *Perf. 14*
Size: 29x29mm

558 A128	10t Boiken, East Sepik	.15	.15
559 A128	20t Gumalu, Madang	.30	.30

Perf. 14½
Size: 36x23mm

560 A128	40t shown	.60	.60
561 A128	50t Ramu Valley, Madang	.75	.75
	Nos. 558-561 (4)	1.80	1.80

Nutrition A129

1982, May 5 Litho. *Perf. 14½x14*
562 A129 10t Mother, child .20 .20
563 A129 15t Protein .30 .30
564 A129 30t Fruits, vegetables .55 .55
565 A129 40t Carbohydrates .75 .75
Nos. 562-565 (4) 1.80 1.80

Coral — A130

1982, July 21 Photo. *Perf. 11½*
Granite Paper
566 A130 1t Stylophora sp. .15 .15
567 A130 5t Acropora humilis .15 .15
568 A130 15t Distichopora sp. .30 .30
569 A130 1k Xenia sp. 2.00 2.00
Nos. 566-569 (4) 2.60 2.60

See Nos. 575-579, 588-591, 614.

Centenary of Catholic Church in Papua New Guinea — A131

1982, Sept. 15 Photo. *Perf. 11½*
570 Strip of 3 .80 .80
a. A131 10t any single .25 .25

12th Commonwealth Games, Brisbane, Australia, Sept. 30-Oct. 9 — A132

1982, Oct. 6 Litho. *Perf. 14½*
571 A132 10t Running .20 .20
572 A132 15t Boxing .30 .30
573 A132 45t Shooting .90 .90
574 A132 50t Lawn bowling 1.00 1.00
Nos. 571-574 (4) 2.40 2.40

Coral Type of 1982

1983, Jan. 12 Photo. *Perf. 11½*
Granite Paper
575 A130 3t Dendrophyllia .15 .15
576 A130 10t Dendronephthya .20 .20
577 A130 30t Dendrone-phthya, diff. .65 .65
578 A130 40t Antipathes .90 .70
579 A130 3k Distichopora 7.00 7.00
Nos. 575-579 (5) 8.90 8.70

Nos. 575-579 vert.

Commonwealth Day — A133

1983, Mar. 9 Litho. *Perf. 14*
580 A133 10t Flag, arms .15 .15
581 A133 15t Youth, recreation .25 .25
582 A133 20t Technical assistance .30 .30
583 A133 50t Export assistance .85 .85
Nos. 580-583 (4) 1.55 1.55

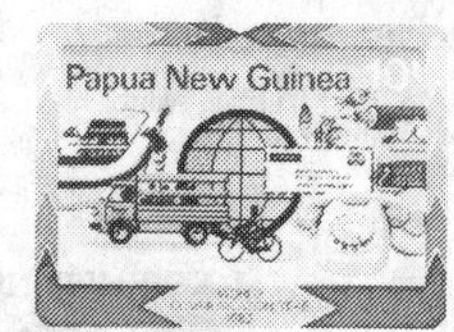

World Communications Year — A134

1983, Sept. 7 Litho. *Perf. 14*
584 A134 10t Mail transport .20 .20
585 A134 25t Writing & receiving letter .50 .50
586 A134 30t Telephone calls .60 .60
587 A134 60t Family reunion 1.20 1.20
Nos. 584-587 (4) 2.50 2.50

Coral Type of 1982

1983, Nov. 9 Photo. *Perf. 11½*
588 A130 20t Isis sp. .60 .60
589 A130 25t Acropora sp. 1.00 1.00
590 A130 35t Stylaster elegans 1.50 1.50
591 A130 45t Turbinarea sp. 1.90 1.90
Nos. 588-591 (4) 5.00 5.00

Nos. 588-591 vert.

Turtles — A135

1984, Feb. 8 Photo.
Granite Paper
592 A135 5t Chelonia depressa .15 .15
593 A135 10t Chelonia mydas .30 .30
594 A135 15t Eretkmochelys imbricata .50 .50
595 A135 20t Lepidochelys olivacea .60 .60
596 A135 25t Caretta caretta .80 .80
597 A135 40t Dermochelys coriacea 1.40 1.40
Nos. 592-597 (6) 3.75 3.75

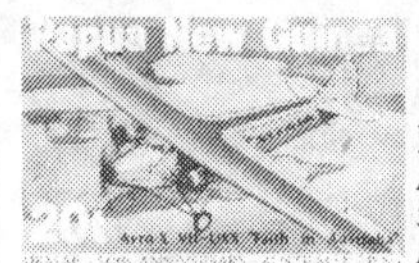

Papua-Australia Airmail Service, 50th Anniv. A136

Mail planes.

1984, May 9 Litho. *Perf. 14½x14*
598 A136 20t Avro X VH-UXX .45 .45
599 A136 25t DH86B VH-UYU Carmania .55 .55
600 A136 40t Westland Widgeon 1.00 1.00
601 A136 60t Consolidated Catalina NC777 1.40 1.40
Nos. 598-601 (4) 3.40 3.40

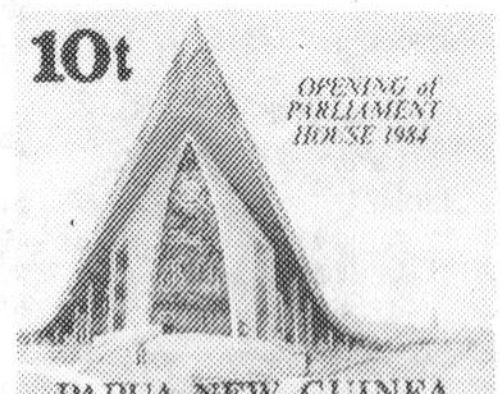

Parliament House Opening — A137

1984, Aug. 7 Litho. *Perf. 13½x14*
602 A137 10t multicolored .45 .45

Bird of Paradise — A138

1984, Aug. 7 Photo. *Perf. 11½*
Granite Paper
603 A138 5k multicolored 9.50 9.50

Ceremonial Shield — A139

1984, Sept. 21
604 A139 10t Central Province .25 .25
605 A139 20t West New Britain .60 .60
606 A139 30t Madang .90 .90
607 A139 50t East Sepik 1.65 1.65
Nos. 604-607 (4) 3.40 3.40

A140

British New Guinea Proclamation Centenary A141

1984, Nov. 6 Litho. *Perf. 14½x14*
608 Pair .55 .55
a. A140 10t Nelson, Port Moresby, 1884 .25 .25
b. A141 10t Port Moresby, 1984 .25 .25
609 Pair 2.50 2.50
a. A140 45t Rabaul, 1984 1.25 1.25
b. A141 45t Elizabeth, Rabaul, 1884 1.25 1.25

Chimbu Gorge — A142

1985, Feb. 6 Photo. *Perf. 11½*
610 A142 10t Fergusson Island, vert. .30 .30
611 A142 25t Sepik River, vert. .80 .80
612 A142 40t shown 1.25 1.25
613 A142 60t Dali Beach, Vanimo 2.00 2.00
Nos. 610-613 (4) 4.35 4.35

Coral Type of 1982

1985, May 29 Photo. *Perf. 11½*
614 A130 12t Dendronephthya sp. .50 .50

For surcharge see No. 686.

No. 536 Surcharged

1985, Apr. 1 Litho. *Perf. 13½x14*
615 A123 12t on 7t multi .75 .75
a. Inverted surcharge —

Ritual Structures — A143

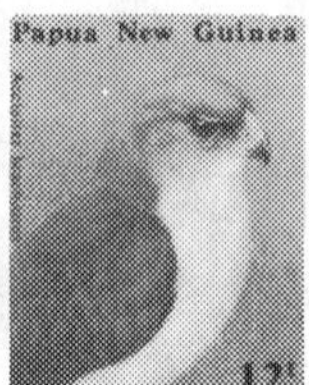

Indigenous Birds of Prey — A144

Designs: 15t, Dubu platform, Central Province. 20t, Tamuniai house, West New Britain. 30t, Yam tower, Trobriand Island. 60t, Huli grave, Tari.

1985, May 1 *Perf. 13x13½*
616 A143 15t multicolored .50 .50
617 A143 20t multicolored .70 .70
618 A143 30t multicolored 1.00 1.00
619 A143 60t multicolored 1.75 1.75
Nos. 616-619 (4) 3.95 3.95

1985, Aug. 26 *Perf. 14x14½*
620 A144 12t Accipiter brachyurus .50 .50
621 A144 12t In flight .50 .50
a. Pair, #620-621 1.00 1.00
622 A144 30t Megatriorchis doriae 1.25 1.25
623 A144 30t In flight 1.25 1.25
a. Pair, #622-623 2.50 2.50
624 A144 60t Henicopernis longicauda 2.50 2.50
625 A144 60t In flight 2.50 2.50
a. Pair, #624-625 5.00 5.00
Nos. 620-625 (6) 8.50 8.50

Flag and Gable of Parliament House, Port Moresby — A145

1985, Sept. 11 *Perf. 14½x15*
626 A145 12t multicolored .50 .50

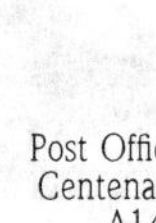
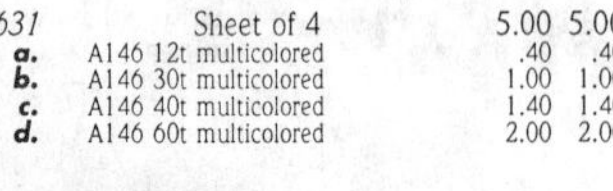

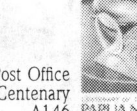

Post Office Centenary A146

Designs: 12t, No. 631a, 1901 Postal card, aerogramme, spectacles and inkwell. 30t, No. 631b, Queensland Type A15, No. 628. 40t, No. 631c, Plane and news clipping, 1885. 60t, No. 631d, 1892 German canceler, 1985 first day cancel.

1985, Oct. 9 *Perf. 14½x14*
627 A146 12t multicolored .35 .35
628 A146 30t multicolored .90 .90
629 A146 40t multicolored 1.25 1.25
630 A146 60t multicolored 1.90 1.90
Nos. 627-630 (4) 4.40 4.40

Souvenir Sheet
631 Sheet of 4 5.00 5.00
a. A146 12t multicolored .40 .40
b. A146 30t multicolored 1.00 1.00
c. A146 40t multicolored 1.40 1.40
d. A146 60t multicolored 2.00 2.00

Nombowai Cave Carved Funerary Totems — A147

1985, Nov. 13 *Perf. 11½*
632 A147 12t Bird Rulowlaw, headman .30 .30
633 A147 30t Barn owl Raus, headman .75 .75
634 A147 60t Melerawuk 1.50 1.50
635 A147 80t Cockerel, woman 2.00 2.00
Nos. 632-635 (4) 4.55 4.55

Conch Shells — A148

1986, Feb. 12 *Perf. 11½*
636 A148 15t Cypraea valentia .45 .45
637 A148 35t Oliva buelowi 1.10 1.10
638 A148 45t Oliva parkinsoni 1.40 1.40
639 A148 70t Cypraea aurantium 2.25 2.25
Nos. 636-639 (4) 5.20 5.20

Queen Elizabeth II 60th Birthday
Common Design Type

Designs: 15t, In ATS officer's uniform, 1945. 35t, Silver wedding anniv. portrait by Patrick Lichfield, Balmoral, 1972. 50t, Inspecting troops, Port Moresby, 1982. 60t, Banquet aboard Britannia, state tour, 1982. 70t, Visiting Crown Agents' offices, 1983.

Perf. 14½
1986, Apr. 21 Litho. Unwmk.
640 CD337 15t scar, blk & sil .30 .30
641 CD337 35t ultra & multi .70 .70
642 CD337 50t green & multi 1.00 1.00
643 CD337 60t violet & multi 1.10 1.10
644 CD337 70t rose vio & multi 1.40 1.40
Nos. 640-644 (5) 4.50 4.50

AMERIPEX '86
A149

Small birds.

1986, May 22 Photo. *Perf. 12½*
Granite Paper

645 A149 15t Pitta erythrogaster .65 .65
646 A149 35t Melanocharis striativentris 1.50 1.50
647 A149 45t Rhipidura rufifrons 1.90 1.90
648 A149 70t Poecilodryas placens, vert. 3.00 3.00
Nos. 645-648 (4) 7.05 7.05

Lutheran Church, Cent. — A150

1986, July 7 Litho. *Perf. 14x15*

649 A150 15t Monk, minister .55 .55
650 A150 70t Churches from 1886, 1986 2.50 2.50

Indigenous Orchids — A151

Folk Dancers — A152

1986, Aug. 4 Litho. *Perf. 14*

651 A151 15t Dendrobium vexillarius .65 .65
652 A151 35t Dendrobium lineale 1.50 1.50
653 A151 45t Dendrobium johnsoniae 1.90 1.90
654 A151 70t Dendrobium cuthbertsonii 3.00 3.00
Nos. 651-654 (4) 7.05 7.05

1986, Nov. 12 Litho. *Perf. 14*

655 A152 15t Maprik .65 .65
656 A152 35t Kiriwina 1.50 1.50
657 A152 45t Kundiawa 1.90 1.90
658 A152 70t Fasu 3.00 3.00
Nos. 655-658 (4) 7.05 7.05

Fish
A153

Unwmk.

1987, Apr. 15 Litho. *Perf. 15*

659 A153 17t White-cap anemonefish .50 .50
660 A153 30t Black anemonefish .85 .85
661 A153 35t Tomato clownfish 1.00 1.00
662 A153 70t Spine-cheek anemonefish 2.00 2.00
Nos. 659-662 (4) 4.35 4.35

For surcharges see Nos. 720, 823, 868.

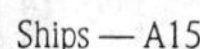
Ships — A154

1987-88 Photo. Unwmk. *Perf. 11½*
Granite Paper

663 A154 1t La Boudeuse, 1768 .15 .15
664 A154 5t Roebuck, 1700 .15 .15
665 A154 10t Swallow, 1767 .25 .25
666 A154 15t Fly, 1845 .35 .35
667 A154 17t like 15t .40 .40
668 A154 20t Rattlesnake, 1849 .45 .45
669 A154 30t Vitiaz, 1871 .75 .75
670 A154 35t San Pedrico, Zabre, 1606 .75 .75
671 A154 40t L'Astrolabe, 1827 .90 .90
672 A154 45t Neva, 1876 .90 .90
673 A154 60t Caravel of Jorge De Meneses, 1526 1.50 1.50
674 A154 70t Eendracht, 1616 1.50 1.50
675 A154 1k Blanche, 1872 2.75 2.75
676 A154 2k Merrie England, 1889 4.25 4.25
676A A154 3k Samoa, 1884 7.50 7.50
Nos. 663-676A (15) 22.55 22.55

Issued: 5, 35, 45, 70t, 2k, 6/15/87; 15, 20, 40, 60t, 2/17/88; 17t, 1k, 3/1/88; 1, 10, 30t, 3k, 11/16/88.

For surcharge see No. 824.

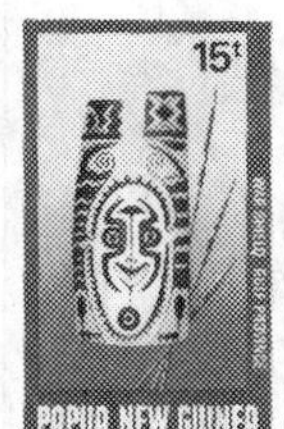

War Shields — A155

Perf. 11½x12

1987, Aug. 19 Photo. Unwmk.

677 A155 15t Elema shield, Gulf Province, c. 1880 .32 .32
678 A155 35t East Sepik Province .75 .75
679 A155 45t Simbai region, Madang Province .95 .95
680 A155 70t Telefomin region, West Sepik 1.45 1.45
Nos. 677-680 (4) 3.47 3.47

Starfish
A156

1987, Sept. 30 Litho. *Perf. 14*

682 A156 17t Protoreaster nodosus .40 .40
683 A156 35t Gomophia egeriae .90 .90
684 A156 45t Choriaster granulatus 1.10 1.10
685 A156 70t Neoferdina ocellata 1.75 1.75
Nos. 682-685 (4) 4.15 4.15

No. 614 Surcharged **15t**

1987, Sept. 23 Photo. *Perf. 11½*
Granite Paper

686 A130 15t on 12t multi .90 .90

Aircraft
A157

Designs: 15t, Cessna Stationair 6, Rabaraba Airstrip. 35t, Britten-Norman Islander over Hombrum Bluff. 45t, DHC Twin Otter over the Highlands. 70t, Fokker F28 over Madang.

Unwmk.

1987, Nov. 11 Litho. *Perf. 14*

687 A157 15t multicolored .45 .45
688 A157 35t multicolored 1.00 1.00
689 A157 45t multicolored 1.25 1.25
690 A157 70t multicolored 2.00 2.00
Nos. 687-690 (4) 4.70 4.70

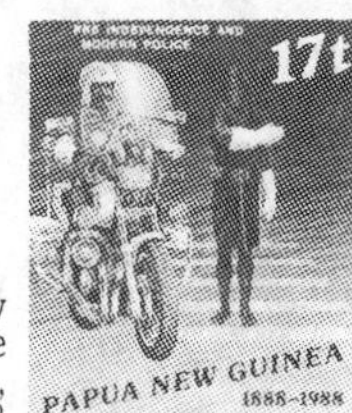

Royal Papua New Guinea Police Force, Cent. — A158

Historic and modern aspects of the force: 17t, Motorcycle constable and pre-independence officer wearing a lap-lap. 35t, Sir William McGregor, Armed Native Constabulary founder, 1890, and recruit. 45t, Badges. 70t, Albert Hahl, German official credited with founding the island's police movement in 1888, and badge, early officer.

Perf. 14x15

1988, June 15 Litho. Unwmk.

691 A158 17t multicolored .40 .40
692 A158 35t multicolored .75 .75
693 A158 45t multicolored 1.10 1.10
694 A158 70t multicolored 1.65 1.65
Nos. 691-694 (4) 3.90 3.90

Sydney Opera House and a Lakatoi (ship) — A159

Fireworks and Globes — A160

1988, July 30 Litho. *Perf. 13½*

695 A159 35t multicolored .80 .80
696 A160 Pair 1.60 1.60
a.-b. 35t any single .80 .80
c. Souvenir sheet of 2, #696a-696b 1.60 1.60

SYDPEX '88, Australia (No. 695); Australia bicentennial (No. 696).

World Wildlife Fund
A161

Metamorphosis of a Queen Alexandra's birdwing butterfly.

1988, Sept. 19 *Perf. 14½*

697 A161 5t Courtship *.30 .30*
698 A161 17t Ovipositioning and larvae, vert. *1.00 1.00*
699 A161 25t Emergence from pupa, vert. *1.50 1.50*
700 A161 35t Adult male on leaf *2.00 2.00*
Nos. 697-700 (4) *4.80 4.80*

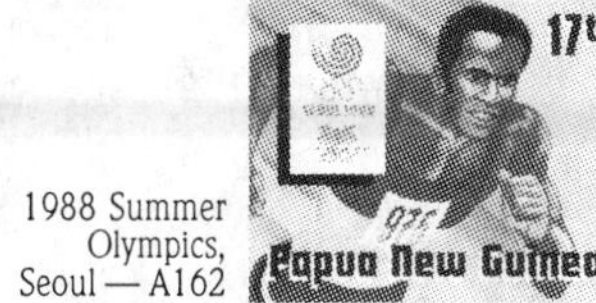

1988 Summer Olympics, Seoul — A162

1988, Sept. 19 Litho. *Perf. 13½*

701 A162 17t Running .40 .40
702 A162 45t Weight lifting 1.10 1.10

Rhododendrons
A163

Wmk. 387

1989, Jan. 25 Litho. *Perf. 14*

703 A163 3t *R. zoelleri* .15 .15
704 A163 20t *R. cruttwellii* .50 .50
705 A163 60t *R. superbum* 1.50 1.50
706 A163 70t *R. christianae* 1.75 1.75
Nos. 703-706 (4) 3.90 3.90

Intl. Letter Writing Week — A164

1989, Mar. 22 *Perf. 14½*

707 A164 20t Writing letter .40 .40
708 A164 35t Mailing letter .65 .65
709 A164 60t Stamping letter 1.10 1.10
710 A164 70t Reading letter 1.40 1.40
Nos. 707-710 (4) 3.55 3.55

Thatched Dwellings — A165

1989, May 17 Wmk. 387 *Perf. 15*

711 A165 20t Buka Is., 1880s .50 .50
712 A165 35t Koiari tree houses .90 .90
713 A165 60t Lauan, New Ireland, 1890s 1.50 1.50
714 A165 70t Basilaki, Milne Bay Province, 1930s 1.75 1.75
Nos. 711-714 (4) 4.65 4.65

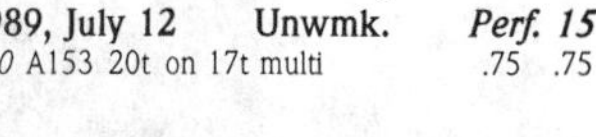

Small Birds — A166

1989, July 12 Unwmk. *Perf. 14½*

715 A166 20t *Oreocharis arfaki* female, shown .60 .60
716 A166 20t Male .60 .60
a. Pair, #715-716 1.25 1.25
717 A166 35t *Ifrita kowaldi* 1.10 1.10
718 A166 45t *Poecilodryas albonotata* 1.40 1.40
719 A166 70t *Sericornis nouhuysi* 2.25 2.25
Nos. 715-719 (5) 5.95 5.95

No. 659 Surcharged

1989, July 12 Unwmk. *Perf. 15*

720 A153 20t on 17t multi .75 .75

Traditional Dance — A167

Designs: 20t, Motumotu, Gulf Province. 35t, Baining, East New Britain Province. 60t, Vailala River, Gulf Province. 70t, Timbunke, East Sepik Province.

Perf. 14x14½

1989, Sept. 6 Litho. Wmk. 387

721 A167 20t multicolored .60 .60
722 A167 35t multicolored 1.00 1.00
723 A167 60t multicolored 1.75 1.75
724 A167 70t multicolored 2.00 2.00
Nos. 721-724 (4) 5.35 5.35

For surcharge see No. 860.

Christmas A168

Designs: 20t, Hibiscus, church and symbol from a gulf gope board, Kavaumai. 35t, Rhododendron, madonna and child, and mask, Murik Lakes region. 60t, D'Albertis creeper, candle, and shield from Oksapmin, West Sepik highlands. 70t, Pacific frangipani, peace dove and flute mask from Chungrebu, a Rao village in Ramu.

Perf. 14x14½

1989, Nov. 8 Litho. Unwmk.

725 A168 20t multicolored .55 .55
726 A168 35t multicolored .90 .90
727 A168 60t multicolored 1.75 1.75
728 A168 70t multicolored 2.00 2.00
Nos. 725-728 (4) 5.20 5.20

Waterfalls — A169

Unwmk.

1990, Feb. 1 Litho. *Perf. 14*

729 A169 20t Guni Falls .50 .50
730 A169 35t Rouna Falls .85 .85
731 A169 60t Ambua Falls 1.50 1.50
732 A169 70t Wawoi Falls 1.65 1.65
Nos. 729-732 (4) 4.50 4.50

For surcharges see Nos. 866, 870.

Natl. Census — A170

1990, May 2 *Perf. 14½x15*

733 A170 20t Three youths, form .50 .50
734 A170 70t Man, woman, child, form 1.65 1.65

For surcharge see No. 869.

Gogodala Dance Masks — A171

1990, July 11 Litho. *Perf. 13½*

735 A171 20t shown .50 .50
736 A171 35t multi, diff. .85 .85
737 A171 60t multi, diff. 1.50 1.50
738 A171 70t multi, diff. 1.65 1.65
Nos. 735-738 (4) 4.50 4.50

For surcharges see Nos. 867, 871.

Waitangi Treaty, 150th Anniv. — A172

Designs: 20t, Dwarf Cassowary, Great Spotted Kiwi. No. 740, Double Wattled Cassowary, Brown Kiwi. No. 741, Sepik mask and Maori carving.

1990, Aug. 24 Litho. *Perf. 14½*

739 A172 20t multicolored .50 .50
740 A172 35t multicolored .80 .80
741 A172 35t multicolored .80 .80
Nos. 739-741 (3) 2.10 2.10

No. 741 for World Stamp Exhibition, New Zealand 1990.

For surcharges see Nos. 862-863.

Birds — A173

1990, Sept. 26 Litho. *Perf. 14*

742 A173 20t Whimbrel .60 .60
743 A173 35t Sharp-tailed sandpiper .95 .95
744 A173 60t Ruddy turnstone 1.90 1.90
745 A173 70t Terek sandpiper 2.00 2.00
Nos. 742-745 (4) 5.45 5.45

Musical Instruments A174

1990, Oct. 31 Litho. *Perf. 13*

746 A174 20t Jew's harp .50 .50
747 A174 35t Musical bow .80 .80
748 A174 60t Wantoat drum 1.45 1.45
749 A174 70t Gogodala rattle 1.65 1.65
Nos. 746-749 (4) 4.40 4.40

For surcharge see No. 861.

Snail Shells A174a

Designs: 21t, Rhynchotrochus weigmani. 40t, Forcartia globula, Canefriula azonata. 50t, Planispira deaniana. 80t, Papuina chancel, Papuina xanthocheila.

1991, Mar. 6 Litho. *Perf. 14x14½*

750 A174a 21t multicolored .55 .55
751 A174a 40t multicolored 1.00 1.00
752 A174a 50t multicolored 1.25 1.25
753 A174a 80t multicolored 2.00 2.00
Nos. 750-753 (4) 4.80 4.80

For surcharge see No. 864.

A175

A176

1991-93 Litho. *Perf. 14½*

755 A175 1t Ptiloris magnificus .15 .15
756 A175 5t Loria loriae .15 .15
757 A175 10t Cnemophilus macgregorii .20 .20
758 A175 20t Parotia wahnesi .40 .40
759 A175 21t Manucodia chalybata .45 .45
760 A175 30t Paradisaea decora .60 .60
761 A175 40t Loboparadisea sericea .80 .80
762 A175 45t Cicinnurus regius .95 .95
763 A175 50t Paradigalla brevicauda 1.00 1.00
764 A175 60t Parotia carolae 1.30 1.30
765 A175 90t Paradisaea guilielmi 1.95 1.95
766 A175 1k Diphyllodes magnificus 2.00 2.00
767 A175 2k Lophorina superba 4.00 4.00
a. Strip of 4, #761, 763, 766-767 + label 8.00 8.00
768 A175 5k Phonygammus keraudrenii 10.00 10.00

Perf. 13

769 A176 10k Paradisaea minor 21.00 21.00
Nos. 755-769 (15) 44.95 44.95

No. 767a for Hong Kong '94 and sold for 4k.

Issued: 21t, 45t, 60t, 90t, 3/25/92; 5t, 40t, 50t, 1k, 2k, 9/2/92; 1t, 10t, 20t, 30t, 5k, 1993; 10k, 5/1/91; No. 767a, 2/18/94.

For surcharges see Nos. 863A, 865, 878A, 878C.

Large T — A176a

1993 Litho. *Perf. 14½*

770A A176a 21t like #758 .50 .50
770B A176a 45t like #762 1.00 1.00
770C A176a 60t like #764 1.40 1.40
770D A176a 90t like #765 2.25 2.25
Nos. 770A-770D (4) 5.15 5.15

Originally scheduled for release on Feb. 19, 1992, #770A-770D were withdrawn when the denomination was found to have an upper case "T." Corrected versions with a lower case "T" are #759, 762, 764-765. A quantity of the original stamps appeared in the market and to prevent speculation in these items, the Postal Administration of Papua New Guinea released the stamps with the upper case "T."

For surcharges see Nos. 863B, 865A, 878B, 878D.

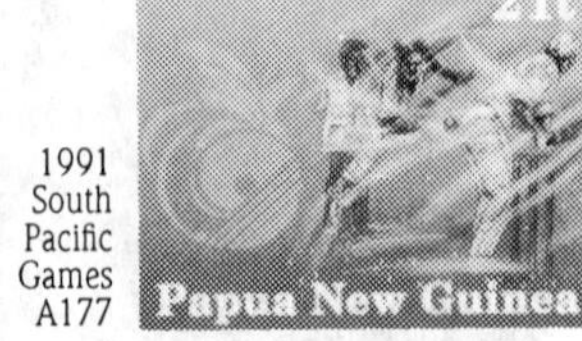

1991 South Pacific Games A177

1991, June 26 Litho. *Perf. 13*

771 A177 21t Cricket .50 .50
772 A177 40t Running .95 .95
773 A177 50t Baseball 1.20 1.20
774 A177 80t Rugby 1.90 1.90
Nos. 771-774 (4) 4.55 4.55

Anglican Church in Papua New Guinea, Cent. A178

Churches: 21t, Cathedral of St. Peter & St. Paul, Dogura. 40t, Kaieta Shrine, Anglican landing site. 80t, First thatched chapel, modawa tree.

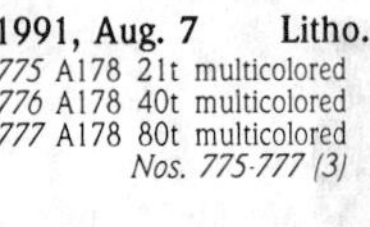

1991, Aug. 7 Litho. *Perf. 14½*

775 A178 21t multicolored .50 .50
776 A178 40t multicolored .95 .95
777 A178 80t multicolored 1.90 1.90
Nos. 775-777 (3) 3.35 3.35

Traditional Headdresses — A179

Designs: 21t, Rambutso, Manus Province. 40t, Marawaka, Eastern Highlands. 50t, Tufi, Oro Province. 80t, Sina Sina, Simbu Province.

1991, Oct. 16 Litho. *Perf. 13*

778 A179 21t multicolored .50 .50
779 A179 40t multicolored .95 .95
780 A179 50t multicolored 1.20 1.20
781 A179 80t multicolored 1.90 1.90
Nos. 778-781 (4) 4.55 4.55

Discovery of America, 500th Anniv. A180

1992, Apr. 15 Litho. *Perf. 14*

782 A180 21t Nina .45 .45
783 A180 45t Pinta .90 .90
784 A180 60t Santa Maria 1.30 1.30
785 A180 90t Columbus, ships 1.95 1.95
a. Souvenir sheet of 2, #784-785 2.75 2.75
Nos. 782-785 (4) 4.60 4.60

World Columbian Stamp Expo '92, Chicago. Issue date: No. 785a, June 3.

A181 A182

Papuan Gulf Artifacts: 21t, Canoe prow shield, Bamu. 45t, Skull rack, Kerewa. 60t, Ancestral figure, Era River. 90t, Gope (spirit) board, Urama.

1992, June 3 Litho. *Perf. 14*

786 A181 21t multicolored .50 .50
787 A181 45t multicolored 1.00 1.00
788 A181 60t multicolored 1.40 1.40
789 A181 90t multicolored 2.25 2.25
Nos. 786-789 (4) 5.15 5.15

1992, July 22 Litho. *Perf. 14*

Soldiers from: 21t, Papuan Infantry Battalion. 45t, Australian Militia. 60t, Japanese Nankai Force. 90t, US Army.

790 A182 21t multicolored .50 .50
791 A182 45t multicolored 1.00 1.00
792 A182 60t multicolored 1.40 1.40
793 A182 90t multicolored 2.25 2.25
Nos. 790-793 (4) 5.15 5.15

World War II, 50th anniv.

Flowering Trees — A183

1992, Oct. 28 Litho. *Perf. 14*

794 A183 21t Hibiscus tiliaceus .50 .50
795 A183 45t Castanospermum australe 1.00 1.00

796 A183 60t Cordia subcordata 1.40 1.40
797 A183 90t Acacia auriculiformis 2.00 2.00
Nos. 794-797 (4) 4.90 4.90

Mammals A184

1993, Apr. 7 Litho. *Perf. 14*

798 A184 21t Myoictis melas .50 .50
799 A184 45t Microperoryctes longicauda 1.10 1.10
800 A184 60t Mallomys rothschildi 1.50 1.50
801 A184 90t Pseudocheirus forbesi 2.25 2.25
Nos. 798-801 (4) 5.35 5.35

Small Birds — A185

1993, June 9 Litho. *Perf. 14*

802 A185 21t Clytomyias insignis .45 .45
803 A185 45t Pitta superba .95 .95
804 A185 60t Rhagologus leucostigma 1.25 1.25
805 A185 90t Toxorhamphus poliopterus 2.00 2.00
Nos. 802-805 (4) 4.65 4.65

Nos. 802-805 Redrawn with Taipei '93 emblem in Blue and Yellow

1993, Aug. 13 Litho. *Perf. 14*

806 A185 21t multicolored .50 .50
807 A185 45t multicolored 1.10 1.10
808 A185 60t multicolored 1.40 1.40
809 A185 90t multicolored 2.25 2.25
Nos. 806-809 (4) 5.25 5.25

Freshwater Fish A186

Designs: 21t, Iriatherina werneri. 45t, Tateurndina ocellicauda. 60t, Melanotaenia affinis. 90t, Pseudomugil connieae.

1993, Sept. 29 Litho. *Perf. 14x14½*

810 A186 21t multicolored .50 .50
811 A186 45t multicolored 1.00 1.00
812 A186 60t multicolored 1.40 1.40
813 A186 90t multicolored 2.00 2.00
Nos. 810-813 (4) 4.90 4.90

For surcharges see Nos. 876-878.

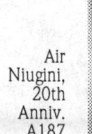

Air Niugini, 20th Anniv. A187

1993, Oct. 27 *Perf. 14*

814 A187 21t DC3 .50 .50
815 A187 45t F27 1.00 1.00
816 A187 60t Dash 7 1.40 1.40
817 A187 90t Airbus A310-300 2.00 2.00
Nos. 814-817 (4) 4.90 4.90

Souvenir Sheet

Paradisaea Rudolphi — A188

1993, Sept. 29 Litho. *Perf. 14*

818 A188 2k multicolored 5.25 5.25

Bangkok '93.

Huon Tree Kangaroo — A189

1994, Jan. 19 Litho. *Perf. 14½*

819 A189 21t Domesticated joey .45 .45
820 A189 45t Adult male 1.00 1.00
821 A189 60t Female, joey in pouch 1.40 1.40
822 A189 90t Adolescent 1.90 1.90
Nos. 819-822 (4) 4.75 4.75

No. 661 Surcharged

21t

No. 671 Surcharged

K1.20

1994, Mar. 23

Perfs. and Printing Methods as Before

823 A153 21t on 35t multi *3.00* .40
824 A154 1.20k on 40t multi *21.00* 2.50

Artifacts — A190

Designs: 1t, Hagen ceremonial axe, Western Highlands. 2t, Telefomin war shield, West Sepik. 20t, Head mask, Gulf of Papua. 21t, Kanganaman stool, East Sepik. 45t, Trobriand lime gourd, Milne Bay. 60t, Yuat River flute stopper, East Sepik. 90t, Tami island dish, Morobe. 1k, Kundu drum, Ramu River estuary. 5k, Gogodala dance mask, Western Province. 10k, Malanggan mask, New Ireland.

1994-95 Litho. *Perf. 14½*

825 A190 1t multicolored .15 .15
826 A190 2t multicolored .15 .15
828 A190 20t multicolored .35 .35
829 A190 21t multicolored .35 .35
833 A190 45t multicolored .80 .80
835 A190 60t multicolored 1.10 1.10
836 A190 90t multicolored 1.65 1.65
837 A190 1k multicolored 1.65 1.65
839 A190 5k multicolored 9.00 9.00
840 A190 10k multicolored 15.00 15.00
Nos. 825-840 (10) 30.20 30.20

Issued: 21, 45, 60, 90t, 3/23; 1, 2, 20t, 5k, 6/29/94; 1k, 10k, 4/12/95.
This is an expanding set. Numbers may change.

Classic Cars — A191

1994, May 11 Litho. *Perf. 14*

841 A191 21t Model T Ford .50 .50
842 A191 45t Chevrolet 490 1.00 1.00
843 A191 60t Baby Austin 1.40 1.40
844 A191 90t Willys Jeep 2.00 2.00
Nos. 841-844 (4) 4.90 4.90

PHILAKOREA '94 — A192

Tree kangaroos: 90t, Dendrolagus inustus. 1.20k, Dendrolagus dorianus.

1994, Aug. 10 Litho. *Perf. 14*

845 A192 Sheet of 2, #a.-b. 4.50 4.50

Moths A193

Designs: 21t, Daphnis hypothous pallescens. 45t, Tanaorhinus unipuncta. 60t, Neodiphthera sciron. 90t, Parotis maginata.

1994, Oct. 26 Litho. *Perf. 14*

846 A193 21t multicolored .45 .45
847 A193 45t multicolored 1.00 1.00
848 A193 60t multicolored 1.25 1.25
849 A193 90t multicolored 2.00 2.00
Nos. 846-849 (4) 4.70 4.70

Beatification of Peter To Rot — A194

1995, Jan. 11 Litho. *Perf. 14*

850 A194 21t Peter To Rot .45 .45
851 A194 1k on 90t Pope John Paul II 2.25 2.25
a. Pair, #850-851 + label 2.75 2.75

No. 851 was not issued without surcharge.

Tourism A195

#852, Cruising. #853, Handicrafts. #854, Jet. #855, Resorts. #856, Trekking adventure. #857, White-water rafting. #858, Boat, diver. #859, Divers, sunken plane.

1995, Jan. 11

852 A195 21t multicolored .45 .45
853 A195 21t multicolored .45 .45
a. Pair, #852-853 .90 .90
854 A195 50t on 45t multi 1.10 1.10
855 A195 50t on 45t multi 1.10 1.10
a. Pair, #854-855 2.25 2.25
856 A195 65t on 60t multi 1.40 1.40
857 A195 65t on 60t multi 1.40 1.40
a. Pair, #856-857 2.75 2.75
858 A195 1k on 90t multi 2.25 2.25
859 A195 1k on 90t multi 2.25 2.25
a. Pair, #858-859 4.50 4.50
Nos. 852-859 (8) 10.40 10.40

Nos. 854-859 were not issued without surcharge.

Nos. 662, 722, 730, 732, 734, 736, 738, 740-741, 747, 753, 762, 765, 770B, 770D Surcharged

5t

Thick "t" in Surcharge

21t

Thin "t" in Surcharge

1994-95 *Perfs., Etc. as Before*

860 A167 5t on 35t #722 .15 .15
861 A174 5t on 35t #747
862 A172 10t on 35t #740
863 A172 10t on 35t #741
863A A175 21t on 45t #762 .38 .38
863B A176a 21t on 45t #770B .38 .38
864 A174a 21t on 80t #753
865 A175 21t on 90t #765 .45 .45
865A A176a 21t on 90T #770D
866 A169 50t on 35t #730
867 A171 50t on 35t #736
868 A153 65t on 70t #662 1.40 1.40
869 A170 65t on 70t #734 1.40 1.40
870 A169 1k on 70t #732
871 A171 1k on 70t #738 2.00 2.00

Size, style and location of surcharge varies.
#863A-863B, 865-865A have thin type surcharge.
Issued: #862, 8/23/94; #864, 8/28/94; #861, 863, 864, 10/3/94; #860, 871, 10/6/94; #866-868, 869-870, 11/28/94; #863A-863B, 5/16/1995; #865, 3/27/95; #865A, 4/25/95.

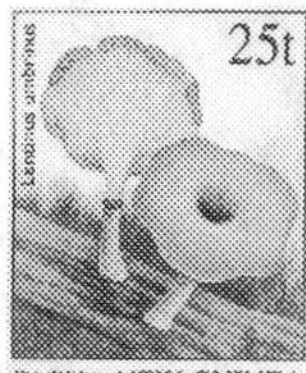

Mushrooms — A196

25t, Lentinus umbrinus. 50t, Amanita hemibapha. 65t, Boletellus emodensis. 1k, Ramaria zippellii.

1995, June 21 Litho. *Perf. 14*

872 A196 25t multicolored .40 .40
Complete booklet, 10 #872 4.00
873 A196 50t multicolored .85 .85
Complete booklet, 10 #873 8.50
874 A196 65t multicolored 1.10 1.10
875 A196 1k multicolored 1.75 1.75
Nos. 872-875 (4) 4.10 4.10

1996 Litho. *Perf. 12*

875A A196 25t like #872 2.50 2.50

No. 875A has a taller vignette, a smaller typeface for the description, denomination, and country name and does not have a date inscription like #872.

Nos. 811-813 Surcharged Thick "t"
Nos. 762, 765, 770B, 770D Surcharged Thin "t"

See illustrations above #860.

1995 Litho. *Perf. 14x14½*

876 A186 21t on 45t #811 .40 .40
877 A186 21t on 60t #812 .40 .40
878 A186 21t on 90t #813 .40 .40
878A A175 45t on 45t #762
878B A176a 45t on 45t #770B
878C A175 90t on 90t #765
878D A176a 90t on 90t #770D
Nos. 876-878 (3) 1.20 1.20

#878A, 878C dated 1993. #878B, 878D dated 1992. #878A, 878C exist dated 1992
Issued: #876-878, 6/20; #878A-878D, 8/4.

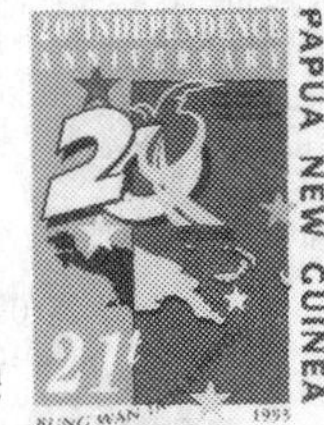

Independence, 20th Anniv. — A197

Designs: 50t, 1k, "20" emblem.

1995, Aug. 30 *Perf. 14*

879 A197 21t shown .40 .40
880 A197 50t blue & multi .90 .90
881 A197 1k green & multi 1.75 1.75
Nos. 879-881 (3) 3.05 3.05

Souvenir Sheet

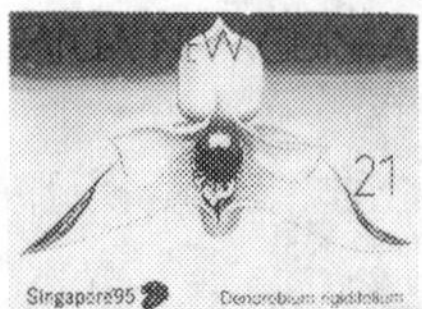

Singapore '95 — A198

Orchids: a, 21t, Dendrobium rigidifolium. b, 45t, Dendrobium convolutum. c, 60t, Dendrobium spectabile. d, 90t, Dendrobium tapiniense.

1995, Aug. 30 **Litho.** *Perf. 14*

882 A198 Sheet of 4, #a.-d. 4.50 4.50

No. 882 sold for 3k.

Souvenir Sheet

New Year 1995 (Year of the Boar) — A199

Illustration reduced.

1995, Sept. 14

883 A199 3k multicolored 4.50 4.50

Beijing '95.

Eruption of Rabaul Volcano, 1st Anniv. A200

1995, Sept. 19

884 A200 2k multicolored 3.00 3.00

Crabs — A201

1995, Oct. 25 **Litho.** *Perf. 14*

885 A201 21t Zosimus aeneus .40 .40
886 A201 50t Cardisoma carnifex 1.00 1.00
887 A201 65t Uca tetragonon 1.30 1.30
888 A201 1k Eriphia sebana 2.00 2.00
Nos. 885-888 (4) 4.70 4.70

Parrots — A202

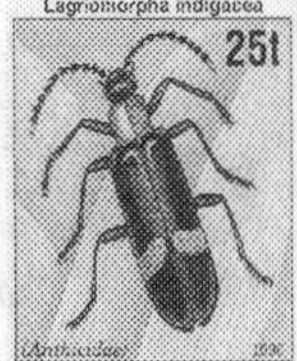

Beetles — A203

Designs: 25t, Psittrichas fulgidas. 50t, Trichoglossus haemotodus. 65t, Alisterus chloropterus. 1k, Aprosmictus erythropterus.

1996, Jan. 17 **Litho.** *Perf. 12*

889 A202 25t multicolored .40 .40
890 A202 50t multicolored .75 .75
891 A202 65t multicolored 1.00 1.00
892 A202 1k multicolored 1.50 1.50
Nos. 889-892 (4) 3.65 3.65

1996, Mar. 20 **Litho.** *Perf. 12*

Designs: 25t, Lagriomorpha indigacea. 50t, Eupholus geoffroyi. 65t, Promechus pulcher. 1k, Callistola pulchra.

893 A203 25t multicolored .65 .65
894 A203 50t multicolored 1.30 1.30
895 A203 65t multicolored 1.70 1.70
896 A203 1k multicolored 2.60 2.60

Souvenir Sheet

Zhongshan Memorial Hall, Guangzhou, China — A204

Illustration reduced.

1996, Apr. 22 **Litho.** *Perf. 14*

897 A204 70t multicolored 1.10 1.10

CHINA '96, 9th Asian Intl. Philatelic Exhibition.

1996 Summer Olympics, Atlanta A205

1996, July 24 **Litho.** *Perf. 12*

898 A205 25t Shooting .40 .40
899 A205 50t Track .75 .75
900 A205 65t Weight lifting 1.00 1.00
901 A205 1k Boxing 1.50 1.50
Nos. 898-901 (4) 3.65 3.65

Olymphilex '96.

Radio, Cent. A206

Designs: 25t, Air traffic control. 50t, Commercial broadcasting. 65t, Gerehu earth station. 1k, First transmission in Papua New Guinea.

1996, Sept. 11 **Litho.** *Perf. 12*

902 A206 25t multicolored .40 .40
903 A206 50t multicolored .75 .75
904 A206 65t multicolored 1.00 1.00
905 A206 1k multicolored 1.50 1.50
Nos. 902-905 (4) 3.65 3.65

Souvenir Sheet

Taipei '96, 10th Asian Intl. Philatelic Exhibition — A207

Designs: a, Dr. Sun Yat-sen (1866-1925). b, Dr. John Guise (1914-91). Illustration reduced.

1996, Oct. 16 **Litho.** *Perf. 14*

906 A207 65t Sheet of 2, #a.-b. 2.00 2.00

Flowers A208

Designs: 1t, Hibiscus rosa-sinensis. 5t, Bougainvillea spectabilis. 65t, Plumeria rubra. 1k, Mucuna novo-guineensis.

1996, Nov. 27 **Litho.** *Perf. 14*

907 A208 1t multicolored .15 .15
908 A208 5t multicolored .15 .15
909 A208 65t multicolored 1.00 1.00
910 A208 1k multicolored 1.50 1.50
Nos. 907-910 (4) 2.80 2.80

Souvenir Sheet

Oxen and Natl. Flag A209

1997, Feb. 3 **Litho.** *Perf. 14*

911 A209 1.50k multicolored 2.25 2.25

Hong Kong '97.

Boat Prows A210

1997, Mar. 19 **Litho.** *Perf. 14½x14*

912 A210 25t Gogodala .40 .40
913 A210 50t East New Britain .75 .75
914 A210 65t Trobriand Island 1.00 1.00
915 A210 1k Walomo 1.50 1.50
Nos. 912-915 (4) 3.65 3.65

Queen Elizabeth II and Prince Philip, 50th Wedding Anniv. — A211

Designs: No. 916, Princess Anne, polo players. No. 917, Queen up close. No. 918, Prince in riding attire. No. 919, Queen, another person riding horses. No. 920, Grandsons riding horses, Prince waving. No. 921, Queen waving, riding pony.

2k, Queen, Prince riding in open carriage.

1997, June 25 **Litho.** *Perf. 13½*

916 A211 25t multicolored .40 .40
917 A211 25t multicolored .40 .40
a. Pair, #916-917 .80 .80
918 A211 50t multicolored .75 .75
919 A211 50t multicolored .75 .75
a. Pair, #918-919 1.50 1.50
920 A211 1k multicolored 1.50 1.50
921 A211 1k multicolored 1.50 1.50
a. Pair, #920-921 3.00 3.00
Nos. 916-921 (6) 5.30 5.30

Souvenir Sheet

922 A211 2k multicolored 1.20 1.20

Souvenir Sheet

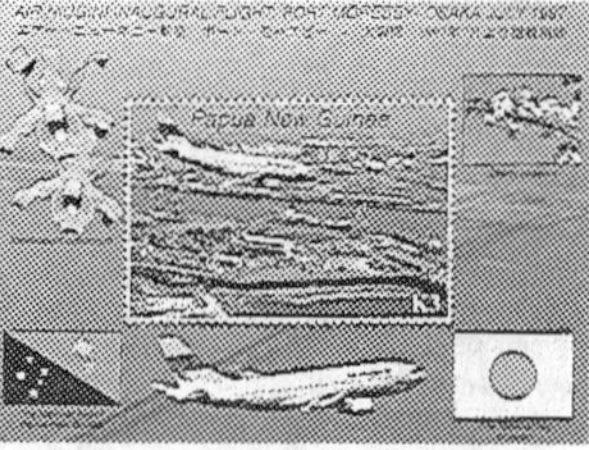

Air Niugini, First Flight, Port Moresby-Osaka — A212

Illustration reduced.

1997, July 19 **Litho.** *Perf. 12*

923 A212 3k multicolored 4.60 4.60

1997 Pacific Year of Coral Reef — A213

Designs: 25t, Pocillopora woodjonesi. 50t, Subergorgia mollis. 65t, Oxypora glabra. 1k, Turbinaria reinformis.

1997, Aug. 27 **Litho.** *Perf. 12*

924 A213 25t multicolored .40 .40
925 A213 50t multicolored .75 .75
926 A213 65t multicolored 1.00 1.00
927 A213 1k multicolored 1.50 1.50
Nos. 924-927 (4) 3.65 3.65

Flowers — A214

Designs: 10t, Thunbergia fragrans. 20t, Caesalpinia pulcherrima. 25t, Hoya. 30t, Heliconia. 50t, Amomum goliathensis.

1997, Nov. 26 **Litho.** *Perf. 12*

928 A214 10t multicolored .15 .15
929 A214 20t multicolored .30 .30
930 A214 25t multicolored .40 .40
931 A214 30t multicolored .45 .45
932 A214 50t multicolored .75 .75
Nos. 928-932 (5) 2.05 2.05

Birds A215

Designs: 25t, Tyto tenebricosa. 50t, Aepypodius afrakiamus. 65t, Accipiter poliocephalus. 1k, Zonerodius heliosylus.

1998 **Litho.** *Perf. 12*

933 A215 25t multicolored .40 .40
934 A215 50t multicolored .75 .75
935 A215 65t multicolored 1.00 1.00
936 A215 1k multicolored 1.50 1.50
Nos. 933-936 (4) 3.65 3.65

AIR POST STAMPS

AIR MAIL

Regular Issue of 1916 Overprinted

1929 Wmk. 74 *Perf. 14*

No.	Type	Description	Unused	Used
C1	A3	3p blue grn & dk gray	1.25	1.40
b.		Vert. pair, one without ovpt.	3,000.	
c.		Horiz. pair, one without ovpt.	3,000.	
d.		3p blue green & sepia black	50.00	62.50
e.		Overprint on back, vert.	2,500.	

No. C1 exists on white and on yellowish paper, No. C1d on yellowish paper only.

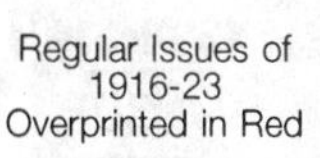
Regular Issues of 1916-23 Overprinted in Red

1930, Sept. 15 Wmk. 74

No.	Type	Description	Unused	Used
C2	A3	3p blue grn & blk	1.00	*2.50*
a.		Yellowish paper	1,000.	—
b.		Double overprint	1,400.	
C3	A3	6p violet & dull violet	3.50	*7.50*
a.		Yellowish paper	6.50	7.00
C4	A3	1sh ol green & ol brn	7.50	*10.00*
a.		Inverted overprint	3,500.	
b.		Yellowish paper	15.00	35.00
		Nos. C2-C4 (3)	12.00	*20.00*

Port Moresby — AP1

Unwmk.

1938, Sept. 6 Engr. *Perf. 11*

No.	Type	Description	Unused	Used
C5	AP1	2p carmine	1.25	1.40
C6	AP1	3p ultra	1.50	1.65
C7	AP1	5p dark green	2.00	2.25
C8	AP1	8p red brown	3.00	3.25
C9	AP1	1sh violet	12.50	7.50
		Nos. C5-C9 (5)	20.25	16.05
		Set, never hinged	45.00	

50th anniv. of Papua as a British possession.

Papuans Poling Rafts — AP2

1939-41

No.	Type	Description	Unused	Used
C10	AP2	2p carmine	2.50	2.00
C11	AP2	3p ultra	2.50	2.75
C12	AP2	5p dark green	4.00	3.25
C13	AP2	8p red brown	4.00	3.00
C14	AP2	1sh violet	6.00	3.50
C15	AP2	1sh6p lt olive ('41)	27.50	32.50
		Nos. C10-C15 (6)	46.50	47.00
		Set, never hinged	80.00	

POSTAGE DUE STAMPS

Catalogue values for unused stamps in this section are for Never Hinged items.

Nos. 128, 122, 129, 139 and 125 Surcharged in Black, Blue, Red or Orange

POSTAL CHARGES 6d.

1960 Unwmk. Engr. *Perf. 14*

No.	Type	Description	Unused	Used
J1	A24	1p on 6½p	8.00	6.00
J2	A23	3p on ½p (Bl)	12.00	8.00
a.		Double surcharge	525.00	
J3	A24	6p on 7½p (R)	20.00	12.00
a.		Double surcharge	525.00	
J4	A23	1sh3p on 3½p (O)	27.50	20.00
J5	A23	3sh on 2½p	35.00	32.50
		Nos. J1-J5 (5)	102.50	78.50

POSTAL CHARGES 6d.

No. 129 Surcharged with New Value in Red

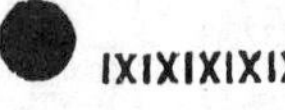

No.	Type	Description	Unused	Used
J6	A24	6p on 7½p	650.00	425.00
a.		Double surcharge	2,750.	1,750.

D1

Perf. 13½x14

1960, June 2 Litho. Wmk. 228

No.	Type	Description	Unused	Used
J7	D1	1p orange	.15	.15
J8	D1	3p ocher	.45	.20
J9	D1	6p light ultra	.75	.30
J10	D1	9p vermilion	1.25	.45
J11	D1	1sh emerald	1.75	.70
J12	D1	1sh3p bright violet	3.00	1.25
J13	D1	1sh6p light blue	3.50	2.75
J14	D1	3sh yellow	4.50	2.50
		Nos. J7-J14 (8)	15.35	8.30

OFFICIAL STAMPS

Nos. 60-63, 66-71, 92-93 Overprinted **O S**

1931 Wmk. 74 *Perf. 14½*

No.	Type	Description	Unused	Used
O1	A3	½p #60	.65	*2.25*
O2	A3	1p #61	.65	*2.75*
O3	A3	1½p #62	2.25	*6.50*
O4	A3	2p #63	2.75	*8.25*
O5	A3	3p #66	3.00	*10.00*
O6	A3	4p #67	3.00	*10.00*
O7	A3	5p #68	4.50	*14.00*
O8	A3	6p #69	5.00	*10.00*
O9	A3	1sh #70	6.50	*14.00*
O10	A3	2sh6p #71	27.50	*52.50*
		Nos. O1-O10 (10)	55.80	*130.25*

1932 Wmk. 228 *Perf. 11½*

No.	Type	Description	Unused	Used
O11	A3	9p #92	25.00	*50.00*
O12	A3	1sh3p #93	25.00	*52.50*

PARAGUAY

'par–ə–,gwī

LOCATION — South America, bounded by Bolivia, Brazil and Argentina
GOVT. — Republic
AREA — 157,042 sq. mi.
POP. — 3,477,000 (1983)
CAPITAL — Asuncion

10 Reales = 100 Centavos = 1 Peso
100 Centimos = 1 Guarani (1944)

Catalogue values for unused stamps in this country are for Never Hinged items, beginning with Scott 430 in the regular postage section, Scott B11 in the semi-postal section, and Scott C154 in the airpost section.

Watermarks

Wmk. 319 - Stars and R P Multiple

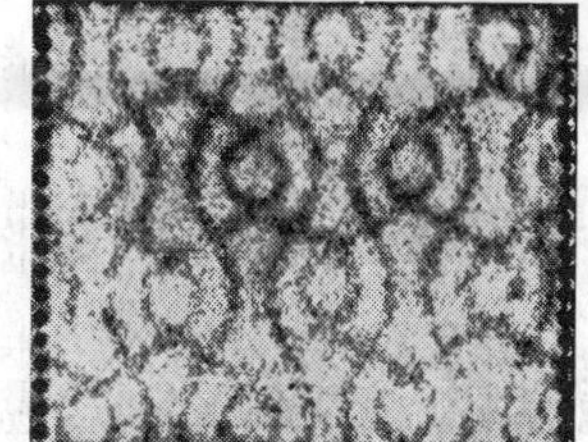
Wmk. 320 - Interlacing Lines

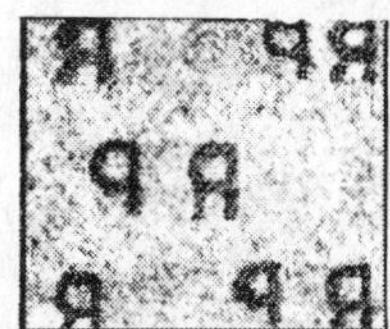
Wmk. 347 - RP Multiple

Vigilant Lion Supporting Liberty Cap
A1 A2

A3

Unwmk.

1870, Aug. 1 Litho. *Imperf.*

No.	Type	Description	Unused	Used
1	A1	1r rose	3.75	3.75
2	A2	2r blue	42.50	42.50
3	A3	3r black	100.00	100.00
		Nos. 1-3 (3)	146.25	146.25

Unofficial reprints of 2r in blue and other colors are on thicker paper than originals. They show a colored dot in upper part of "S" of "DOS" in upper right corner.

For surcharges see Nos. 4-9, 19.

Handstamp Surcharged

1878 Black Surcharge

No.	Type	Description	Unused	Used
4	A1	5c on 1r rose	40.00	40.00
5	A2	5c on 2r blue	175.00	160.00
5E	A3	5c on 3r black	300.00	250.00
		Nos. 4-5E (3)	515.00	450.00

Blue Surcharge

No.	Type	Description	Unused	Used
5F	A1	5c on 1r rose	40.00	40.00
5H	A2	5c on 2r blue	*600.00*	*600.00*
6	A3	5c on 3r black	175.00	175.00
		Nos. 5F-6 (3)	*815.00*	*815.00*

The surcharge may be found inverted, double, sideways and omitted.

The originals are surcharged in dull black or dull blue. The reprints are in intense black and bright blue. The reprint surcharges are overinked and show numerous breaks in the handstamp.

Handstamp Surcharged

Black Surcharge

No.	Type	Description	Unused	Used
7	A2	5c on 2r blue	300.00	225.00
8	A3	5c on 3r black	250.00	190.00

Blue Surcharge

No.	Type	Description	Unused	Used
9	A3	5c on 3r black	125.00	125.00
a.		Dbl. surch., large & small "5"	*675.00*	*675.00*
		Nos. 7-9 (3)	675.00	540.00

The surcharge on Nos. 7, 8 and 9 is usually placed sideways. It may be found double or inverted on Nos. 8 and 9.

Nos. 4 to 9 have been extensively counterfeited.

A4

A4a

1879 Litho. *Perf. 12½*

Thin Paper

No.	Type	Description	Unused	Used
10	A4	5r orange	.38	
11	A4	10r red brown	.45	
a.		Imperf.		
b.		Horiz. pair, imperf. vert.	11.25	

Nos. 10 and 11 were never placed in use.

For surcharges see Nos. 17-18.

1879-81 Thin Paper

No.	Type	Description	Unused	Used
12	A4a	5c orange brown	.90	.90
13	A4a	10c blue grn ('81)	1.25	1.25

Reprints of Nos. 10-13 are imperf., perf. 11½, 12, 12½ or 14. They have yellowish gum and the 10c is deep green.

A5

A6

A7

1881, Aug. Litho. *Perf. 11½-13½*

No.	Type	Description	Unused	Used
14	A5	1c blue	.45	.38
a.		Imperf., pair	1.75	1.75
15	A6	2c rose red	.45	.38
a.		2c dull orange red	.45	.38
b.		Imperf., pair	1.75	1.75
c.		Horiz. or vert. pair, imperf. btwn.	1.50	1.50
16	A7	4c brown	.45	.38
a.		Imperf., pair	1.75	1.75
b.		Horiz. or vert. pair, imperf. btwn.	1.50	1.50
		Nos. 14-16 (3)	1.35	1.14

No. 11 Surcharged

Handstamped in Black or Gray

1881, July *Perf. 12½*

No.	Type	Description	Unused	Used
17	A4	1c on 10c blue grn	4.50	4.50
18	A4	2c on 10c blue grn	4.50	4.50

No. 1 Surcharged

1884, May 8 Handstamped *Imperf.*

No.	Type	Description	Unused	Used
19	A1	1c on 1r rose	2.00	1.75

The surcharges on Nos. 17-19 exist double, inverted and in pairs with one omitted. Counterfeits exist.

Seal of the Treasury
A11 A12

1884, Aug. 3 Litho. *Perf. 11½, 12½*

No.	Type	Description	Unused	Used
20	A11	1c green	.25	.18
21	A11	2c rose red	.25	.18
22	A11	5c blue	.25	.18
		Nos. 20-22 (3)	.75	.54

Shades exist.

For overprints see Nos. O1, O8, O15.

Imperf., Pairs

No.	Type	Description	Unused	Used
20a	A11	1c green	1.00	
21a	A11	2c rose red	1.75	
22a	A11	5c blue	3.75	
		Nos. 20a-22a (3)	6.50	

Perf. 11½, 11½x12, 12½x11½

1887 Typo.

No.	Type	Description	Unused	Used
23	A12	1c green	.15	.15
24	A12	2c rose	.15	.15
25	A12	5c blue	.20	.15
26	A12	7c brown	.42	.30
27	A12	10c lilac	.30	.18
28	A12	15c orange	.30	.18
29	A12	20c pink	.30	.18
		Nos. 23-29 (7)	1.82	
		Set value		1.10

See #42-45. For surcharges & overprints see #46, 49-50, 71-72, 167-170A, O20-O41, O49.

Symbols of Liberty from Coat of Arms — A13

1889, Feb. Litho. *Perf. 11½*

30	A13 15c red violet	1.25	1.25
a.	Imperf., pair	5.00	5.00

For overprints see Nos. O16-O19.

Overprint Handstamped in Violet

1892, Oct. 12 *Perf. 12x12½*

31	A15 10c violet blue	4.50	2.00

Discovery of America by Columbus, 400th anniversary. Overprint reads: "1492 / 12 DE OCTUBRE / 1892." Sold only on day of issue.

Cirilo A. Rivarola — A15

Designs: 2c, Salvador Jovellanos. 4c, Juan B. Gil. 5c, Higinio Uriarte. 10c, Cándido Bareiro. 14c, Gen. Bernardino Caballero. 20c, Gen. Patricio Escobar. 30c, Juan G. González.

1892-96 Litho. *Perf. 12x12½*

32	A15 1c gray (centavos)	.15	.15
33	A15 1c gray (centavo) ('96)	.15	.15
34	A15 2c green	.15	.15
a.	Chalky paper ('96)	.15	.15
35	A15 4c carmine	.15	.15
a.	Chalky paper ('96)	.15	.15
36	A15 5c violet ('93)	.15	.15
a.	Chalky paper ('96)	.15	.15
37	A15 10c vio bl (punched) ('93)	.18	.15
	Unpunched ('96)	4.00	1.50
38	A15 10c dull blue ('96)	.15	.15
39	A15 14c yellow brown	.42	.38
40	A15 20c red ('93)	.65	.38
41	A15 30c light green	1.00	.65
	Nos. 32-41 (10)	3.15	
	Set value		1.90

The 10c violet blue (No. 37) was, until 1896, issued punched with a circular hole in order to prevent it being fraudulently overprinted as No. 31.

Nos. 33 and 38 are on chalky paper.

For surcharge see No. 70.

Seal Type of 1887

1892 Typo.

42	A12 40c slate blue	1.75	.90
43	A12 60c yellow	.75	.38
44	A12 80c light blue	.65	.38
45	A12 1p olive green	.65	.38
	Nos. 42-45 (4)	3.80	2.04

No. 46

CORREOS 5 CENTAVOS

Nos. 47-48

1895, Aug. 1 *Perf. 11½x12*

46	A12 5c on 7c brown, #26	.25	.15

Telegraph Stamps Surcharged

1896, Apr. Engr. *Perf. 11½*

Denomination in Black

47	5c on 2c brown & gray	.38	.25
a.	Inverted surcharge	10.00	10.00
48	5c on 4c yellow & gray	.38	.25
a.	Inverted surcharge	7.50	7.50

Nos. 28, 42 Surcharged

Provisorio
10
Centavos

1898-99 Typo.

49	A12 10c on 15c org ('99)	.45	.35
a.	Inverted surcharge	14.00	14.00
b.	Double surcharge	9.00	9.00
50	A12 10c on 40c slate bl	.20	.15

Surcharge on No. 49 has small "c."

Telegraph Stamps Surcharged

1900, May 14 Engr. *Perf. 11½*

50A	5c on 30c grn, gray & blk	1.25	.90
50B	10c on 50c dl vio, gray & blk	3.00	2.00

The basic telegraph stamps are like those used for Nos. 47-48, but the surcharges on Nos. 50A-50B consist of "5 5" and "10 10" above a blackout rectangle covering the engraved denominations.

A 40c red, bluish gray and black telegraph stamp (basic type of A24) was used provisionally in August, 1900, for postage. Value, postally used, $5.

Seal of the Treasury — A25

J. B. Egusquiza — A26

1900, Sept. Engr. *Perf. 11½, 12*

51	A25 2c gray	.15	.15
52	A25 3c orange brown	.15	.15
53	A25 5c dark green	.15	.15
54	A25 8c dark brown	.15	.15
55	A25 10c carmine rose	.15	.15
56	A25 24c deep blue	.30	.15
	Nos. 51-56 (6)	1.05	
	Set value		.60

See Nos. 57-67. For surcharges see Nos. 69, 74, 76, 156-157.

1901, Apr. Litho. *Perf. 11½*

Small Figures

57	A25 2c rose	.15	.15
58	A25 5c violet brown	.15	.15
59	A25 40c blue	.65	.22
	Nos. 57-59 (3)	.95	
	Set value		.40

1901-02

Larger Figures

60	A25 1c gray green ('02)	.15	.15
61	A25 2c gray	.15	.15
a.	Half used as 1c on cover		.38
62	A25 4c pale blue	.15	.15
63	A25 5c violet	.15	.15
64	A25 8c gray brown ('02)	.15	.15
65	A25 10c rose red ('02)	.18	.15
66	A25 28c orange ('02)	.30	.18
67	A25 40c blue	.30	.15
	Nos. 60-67 (8)	1.53	
	Set value		.84

Perf. 12x12½

1901, Sept. 24 Typo. Chalky Paper

68	A26 1p slate	.30	.20

For surcharge see No. 73.

No. 56 Surcharged

Habilitado
en
20
centavos

1902, Aug.

Red Surcharge

69	A25 20c on 24c dp blue	.25	.15
a.	Inverted surcharge	6.25	

Nos. 39, 43-44 Surcharged

Habilitado en un 1 cent.   Habilitado en cinco 5 cent.

1902, Dec. 22 *Perf. 12x12½*

70	A15 1c on 14c yellow brn	.18	.15
a.	No period after "cent"	.90	.75
b.	Comma after "cent"	.65	.50
c.	Accent over "Un"	.65	.50

1903 *Perf. 11½*

71	A12 5c on 60c yellow	.25	.15
72	A12 5c on 80c lt blue	.18	.15

Nos. 68, 64, 66 Surcharged

Habilitado en un 1 cent. — #73   Habilitado en 5 cent. — #74   Habilitado en cinco 5 cent. — #76

1902-03 *Perf. 12*

73	A26 1c on 1p slate ('03)	.15	.15
a.	No period after "cent"	1.65	1.50

Perf. 11½

74	A25 5c on 8c gray brown	.25	.15
a.	No period after "cent"	.90	.75
b.	Double surcharge	3.50	3.00
76	A25 5c on 28c orange	.25	.18
a.	No period after "cent"	.90	.75
b.	Comma after "cent"	.38	.30
	Nos. 73-76 (3)	.65	.48

The surcharge on Nos. 73 and 74 is found reading both upward and downward.

Sentinel Lion with Right Paw Ready to Strike for "Peace and Justice"
A32 A33

Perf. 11½

1903, Feb. 28 Litho. Unwmk.

77	A32 1c gray	.15	.15
78	A32 2c blue green	.18	.15
79	A32 5c blue	.25	.15
80	A32 10c orange brown	.30	.15
81	A32 20c carmine	.30	.15
82	A32 30c deep blue	.38	.15
83	A32 60c purple	1.00	.65
	Nos. 77-83 (7)	2.56	1.55

For surcharges and overprints see Nos. 139-140, 166, O50-O56.

1903, Sept.

84	A33 1c yellow green	.15	.15
85	A33 2c red orange	.15	.15
86	A33 5c dark blue	.15	.15
87	A33 10c purple	.20	.15
88	A33 20c dark green	.65	.30
89	A33 30c ultramarine	.75	.20
90	A33 60c ocher	.75	.50
	Nos. 84-90 (7)	2.80	
	Set value		1.38

Nos. 84-90 exist imperf. Value for pairs, $3 each for 1c-20c, $4 for 30c, $5 for 60c.

The three-line overprint "Gobierno provisorio Ago. 1904" is fraudulent.

Sentinel Lion at Rest
A35 A36

Perf. 11½, 12, 11½x12

1905-10 Engr.

Dated "1904"

91	A35 1c orange	.15	.15
92	A35 1c vermilion ('07)	.15	.15
93	A35 1c grnsh bl ('07)	.15	.15
94	A35 2c vermilion ('06)	.15	.15
95	A35 2c olive grn ('07)	30.00	
96	A35 2c car rose ('08)	.15	.15
97	A35 5c dark blue	.15	.15
98	A35 5c slate blue ('06)	.15	.15
99	A35 5c yellow ('06)	.15	.15
100	A35 10c bister ('06)	.15	.15
101	A35 10c emerald ('07)	.15	.15
102	A35 10c dp ultra ('08)	.15	.15
103	A35 20c violet ('06)	.30	.20
104	A35 20c bister ('07)	.30	.20
105	A35 20c apple grn ('07)	.25	.15
106	A35 30c turq bl ('06)	.30	.15
107	A35 30c blue gray ('07)	.30	.15
108	A35 30c dull lilac ('08)	.38	.18
109	A35 60c chocolate ('07)	.25	.15
110	A35 60c org brn ('07)	3.50	1.25
111	A35 60c salmon pink ('10)	3.50	1.25
	Nos. 91-94,96-111 (20)	10.73	
	Set value		4.35

All but Nos. 92 and 104 exist imperf. Value for pair, $3 each, except No. 95 at $17.50 and Nos. 109-111 at $7.50 each pair.

For surcharges and overprints see Nos. 129-130, 146-155, 174-190, 266.

1904, Aug. Litho. *Perf. 11½*

112	A36 10c blue	.25	.15
a.	Imperf., pair	3.00	

No. 112 Surcharged in Black

PAZ
12 Dic. 1904
30
centavos

1904, Dec.

113	A36 30c on 10c blue	.38	.25

Peace between a successful revolutionary party and the government previously in power.

Governmental Palace, Asunción — A37

Dated "1904"

1906-10 Engr. *Perf. 11½, 12*

Center in Black

114	A37 1p bright rose	1.25	.75
115	A37 1p brown org ('07)	.50	.25
116	A37 1p ol gray ('07)	.50	.25
117	A37 2p turquoise ('07)	.25	.18
118	A37 2p lake ('09)	.25	.20
119	A37 2p brn org ('10)	.30	.20
120	A37 5p red ('07)	.75	.50
121	A37 5p ol grn ('10)	.75	.50
122	A37 5p dull bl ('10)	.75	.50
123	A37 10p brown org ('07)	.70	.50
124	A37 10p dp blue ('10)	.70	.50
125	A37 10p choc ('10)	.75	.50
126	A37 20p olive grn ('07)	1.75	1.65
127	A37 20p violet ('10)	1.75	1.65
128	A37 20p yellow ('10)	1.75	1.65
	Nos. 114-128 (15)	12.70	9.78

Nos. 94 and 95 Surcharged

Habilitado
en
5
CENTAVOS

1907

129	A35 5c on 2c vermilion	.20	.15
a.	"5" omitted	1.00	1.00
b.	Inverted surcharge	3.50	3.50
c.	Double surcharge		
d.	Double surcharge, one inverted	1.00	1.00
e.	Double surcharge, both invtd.	6.00	6.00
130	A35 5c on 2c olive grn	.25	.15
a.	"5" omitted	1.00	1.00
b.	Inverted surcharge	1.00	1.00
c.	Double surcharge	2.00	2.00
d.	Bar omitted	2.00	2.00

Official Stamps of 1906-08 Surcharged

Habilitado
en
5
CENTAVOS

1908

131	O17 5c on 10c bister	.18	.15
a.	Double surcharge	3.00	3.00
132	O17 5c on 10c violet	.18	.15
a.	Inverted surcharge	2.25	2.25
133	O17 5c on 20c emerald	.18	.15
134	O17 5c on 20c violet	.18	.15
a.	Inverted surcharge	2.25	2.25
135	O17 5c on 30c slate bl	.65	.65
136	O17 5c on 30c turq bl	.65	.65
a.	Inverted surcharge		
b.	Double surcharge	6.00	6.00
137	O17 5c on 60c choc	.15	.15
a.	Double surcharge	6.00	6.00
138	O17 5c on 60c red brown	.20	.15
a.	Inverted surcharge	.38	.38
	Nos. 131-138 (8)	2.37	2.20

Same Surcharge on Official Stamps of 1903

139	A32 5c on 30c dp blue	1.25	1.10
140	A32 5c on 60c purple	.50	.30
a.	Double surcharge	2.50	2.50

Official Stamps of 1906-08 Overprinted **Habilitado**

141 O17 5c deep blue .20 .15
a. Inverted overprint 1.50 1.50
b. Bar omitted 4.50 4.50
c. Double overprint 2.00 2.00
142 O17 5c slate blue .25 .20
a. Inverted overprint 2.00 2.00
b. Double overprint 1.75 1.75
c. Bar omitted 4.50 4.50
143 O17 5c greenish blue .15 .15
a. Inverted overprint 1.25 1.25
b. Bar omitted 3.75 3.75
144 O18 1p brown org & blk .25 .22
a. Double overprint 1.00 1.00
b. Double overprint, one inverted 1.25 1.25
c. Triple overprint, two inverted 2.25 2.25
145 O18 1p brt rose & blk .42 .35
a. Bar omitted
Nos. 141-145 (5) 1.27 1.07

Regular Issues of 1906-08 Surcharged **Habilitado en 5 CENTAVOS**

1908
146 A35 5c on 1c grnsh bl .15 .15
a. Inverted surcharge 1.00 1.00
b. Double surcharge 1.50 1.50
c. "5" omitted 1.50 1.50
147 A35 5c on 2c car rose .15 .15
a. Inverted surcharge 1.75 1.75
b. "5" omitted 2.00 2.00
c. Double surcharge 3.50 3.50
d. Double surcharge, one invtd.
148 A35 5c on 60c org brn .15 .15
a. Inverted surcharge 2.50 2.50
b. "5" omitted 1.00 1.00
149 A35 5c on 60c sal pink .15 .15
a. Double surcharge .50 .50
b. Double surcharge, one invtd. 3.50 3.50
150 A35 5c on 60c choc .15 .15
a. Inverted surcharge 5.00 5.00
151 A35 20c on 1c grnsh bl .15 .15
a. Inverted surcharge 1.50 1.50
152 A35 20c on 2c ver 6.00 5.00
153 A35 20c on 2c car rose 3.50 3.00
a. Inverted surcharge 12.50
154 A35 20c on 30c dl lil .20 .18
a. Inverted surcharge 1.50 1.50
b. Double surcharge
155 A35 20c on 30c turq bl 1.50 1.50
Nos. 146-155 (10) 12.10 10.58

Same Surcharge on Regular Issue of 1901-02

156 A25 5c on 28c org 1.25 1.10
157 A25 5c on 40c dk bl .38 .30
a. Inverted surcharge 4.00 4.00

Same Surcharge on Official Stamps of 1908

158 O17 5c on 10c emer .18 .15
a. Double surcharge 7.00
159 O17 5c on 10c red lil .18 .15
a. Double surcharge 2.00 2.00
b. "5" omitted 1.50 1.50
160 O17 5c on 20c bis .38 .30
a. Double surcharge 1.25 1.25
161 O17 5c on 20c sal pink .38 .30
a. "5" omitted 1.75 1.75
162 O17 5c on 30c bl gray .15 .15
163 O17 5c on 30c yel .15 .15
a. "5" omitted 1.50 1.50
b. Inverted surcharge 1.25 1.25
164 O17 5c on 60c org brn .20 .15
a. Double surcharge 6.00 6.00
165 O17 5c on 60c dp ultra .15 .15
a. Inverted surcharge 2.50 2.50
b. "5" omitted 1.50
Nos. 158-165 (8) 1.77
Set value 1.20

Same Surcharge on No. O52

166 A32 20c on 5c blue 1.25 1.00
a. Inverted surcharge 3.00 3.75

Surcharged **Habilitado en 20 CENTAVOS**

1908

On Stamp of 1887

167 A12 20c on 2c car 2.50 2.00
a. Inverted surcharge 7.50

On Official Stamps of 1892

168 A12 5c on 15c org 2.50 1.75
169 A12 5c on 20c pink 40.00 32.50
170 A12 5c on 50c gray 17.50 12.50
170A A12 20c on 5c blue 1.50 1.25
b. Inverted surcharge 8.75 8.75
Nos. 167-170A (5) 64.00 50.00

Nos. 151, 152, 153, 155, 167, 170A, while duly authorized, all appear to have been sold to a single individual, and although they paid postage, it is doubtful whether they can be considered as ever having been placed on sale to the public.

Nos. O82-O84 Surcharged (Date in Red) **Habilitado 1908 UN CENTAVO**

1908-09
171 O18 1c on 1p brt rose & blk .20 .15
172 O18 1c on 1p lake & blk .18 .15
173 O18 1c on 1p brn org & blk ('09) .90 .65
Nos. 171-173 (3) 1.28 .95

Varieties of surcharge on Nos. 171-173 include: "CETTAVO"; date omitted, double or inverted; third line double or omitted.

Types of 1905-1910 Overprinted **1908**

1908, Mar. 5 *Perf. 11½*
174 A35 1c emerald .15 .15
175 A35 5c yellow .15 .15
176 A35 10c lilac brown .15 .15
177 A35 20c yellow orange .15 .15
178 A35 30c red .25 .20
179 A35 60c magenta .20 .18
180 A37 1p light blue .15 .15
Set value .90 .70

Overprinted *1909*

1909, Sept.
181 A35 1c blue gray .15 .15
182 A35 1c scarlet .15 .15
183 A35 5c dark green .15 .15
184 A35 5c deep orange .15 .15
185 A35 10c rose .15 .15
186 A35 10c bister brown .15 .15
187 A35 20c yellow .15 .15
188 A35 20c violet .15 .15
189 A35 30c orange brown .30 .20
190 A35 30c dull blue .30 .20
Set value 1.35 .95

Coat of Arms above Numeral of Value — A38

"The Republic" — A39

1910-21 **Litho.** *Perf. 11½*
191 A38 1c gray black .15 .15
192 A38 5c bright violet .15 .15
a. Pair, imperf. between 1.00 1.00
193 A38 5c blue grn ('19) .15 .15
194 A38 5c lt blue ('21) .15 .15
195 A38 10c yellow green .15 .15
196 A38 10c dp vio ('19) .15 .15
197 A38 10c red ('21) .15 .15
198 A38 20c red .15 .15
199 A38 50c car rose .30 .15
200 A38 75c deep blue .15 .15
a. Diag. half perforated ('11) .15 .15
Set value 1.05 .60

Nos. 191-200 exist imperforate.
No. 200a was authorized for use as 20c.
For surcharges see Nos. 208, 241, 261, 265.

1911 **Engr.**
201 A39 1c olive grn & blk .15 .15
202 A39 2c dk blue & blk .15 .15
203 A39 5c carmine & indigo .15 .15
204 A39 10c dp blue & brn .18 .15
205 A39 20c olive grn & ind .18 .15
206 A39 50c lilac & indigo .30 .15
207 A39 75c ol grn & red lil .30 .15
Nos. 201-207 (7) 1.41
Set value .72

Centenary of National Independence.
The 1c, 2c, 10c and 50c exist imperf. Value for pairs, $1.50 each.

No. 199 Surcharged **Habilitada en VEINTE**

1912
208 A38 20c on 50c car rose .15 .15
a. Inverted surcharge 1.25 1.25
b. Double surcharge 1.25 1.25
c. Bar omitted 1.75 1.75

National Coat of Arms — A40

1913 **Engr.** *Perf. 11½*
209 A40 1c gray .15 .15
210 A40 2c orange .15 .15
211 A40 5c lilac .15 .15
212 A40 10c green .15 .15
213 A40 20c dull red .15 .15
214 A40 40c rose .15 .15
215 A40 75c deep blue .15 .15
216 A40 80c yellow .15 .15
217 A40 1p light blue .15 .15
218 A40 1.25p pale blue .15 .15
219 A40 3p greenish blue .18 .15
Set value .85 .60

For surcharges see Nos. 225, 230-231, 237, 242, 253, 262-263, L3-L4.

Nos. J7-J10 Overprinted **HABILITADO 1918**

1918
220 D2 5c yellow brown .15 .15
221 D2 10c yellow brown .15 .15
222 D2 20c yellow brown .15 .15
223 D2 40c yellow brown .15 .15
Nos. 220-223 (4) .60 .60

Nos. J10 and 214 Surcharged **HABILITADO EN 0.05 1918**

224 D2 5c on 40c yellow brn .15 .15
225 A40 30c on 40c rose .15 .15
Set value .44 .38

Nos. 220-225 exist with surcharge inverted, double and double with one inverted.
The surcharge "Habilitado-1918-5 cents 5" on the 1c gray official stamps of 1914, is bogus.

No. J11 Overprinted **HABILITADO 1920**

1920
229 D2 1p yellow brown .15 .15
a. Inverted overprint .65 .65
e. "AABILITADO" .75 .75
f. "1929" for "1920" .75 .75
g. Overprint lines 8mm apart .20 .15

Nos. 216 and 219 Surcharged **HABILITADO en 0.50 1920**

230 A40 50c on 80c yellow .15 .15
231 A40 1.75p on 3p grnsh bl .75 .65

Same Surcharge on No. J12

232 D2 1p on 1.50p yel brn .22 .15
Nos. 229-232 (4) 1.27 1.10

Nos. 229-232 exist with various surcharge errors, including inverted, double, double inverted and double with one inverted. Those that were issued are listed.

Parliament Building — A41

1920 **Litho.** *Perf. 11½*
233 A41 50c red & black .22 .15
a. "CORRLOS" 1.50 1.50
234 A41 1p lt blue & blk .65 .30
235 A41 1.75p dk blue & blk .15 .15
236 A41 3p orange & blk 1.00 .15
Nos. 233-236 (4) 2.02 .75

50th anniv. of the Constitution.
All values exist imperforate and Nos. 233, 235 and 236 with center inverted. It is doubtful that any of these varieties were regularly issued.

No. 215 Surcharged **50**

1920
237 A40 50c on 75c deep blue .30 .15

Nos. 200, 215 Surcharged **50**

1921
241 A38 50c on 75c deep blue .15 .15
242 A40 50c on 75c deep blue .15 .15
Set value .15

A42

1922, Feb. 8 **Litho.** *Perf. 11½*
243 A42 50c car & dk blue .15 .15
a. Imperf. pair .50
b. Center inverted 10.00 10.00
244 A42 1p dk blue & brn .15 .15
a. Imperf. pair .50
b. Center inverted 12.50 12.50
Set value .20 .16

For overprints see Nos. L1-L2.

Rendezvous of Conspirators A43

1922-23
245 A43 1p deep blue .15 .15
246 A43 1p scar & dk bl ('23) .15 .15
247 A43 1p red vio & gray ('23) .15 .15
248 A43 1p org & gray ('23) .15 .15
249 A43 5p dark violet .38 .18
250 A43 5p dk bl & org brn ('23) .38 .18
251 A43 5p dl red & lt bl ('23) .38 .18
252 A43 5p emer & blk ('23) .38 .18
Nos. 245-252 (8) 2.12
Set value 1.00

National Independence.

No. 218 Surcharged "Habilitado en $1:-1924" in Red

1924
253 A40 1p on 1.25p pale blue .15 .15

This stamp was for use in Asunción. Nos. L3 to L5 were for use in the interior, as is indicated by the "C" in the surcharge.

Map of Paraguay — A44

1924 **Litho.** *Perf. 11½*
254 A44 1p dark blue .15 .15
255 A44 2p carmine rose .15 .15
256 A44 4p light blue .18 .15
a. Perf. 12 .38 .15
Set value .38 .20

#254-256 exist imperf. Value $3 each pair.
For surcharges and overprint see Nos. 267, C5, C15-C16, C54-C55, L7.

Gen. José E. Díaz — A45

Columbus — A46

1925-26 *Perf. 11½, 12*
257 A45 50c red .15 .15
258 A45 1p dark blue .15 .15
259 A45 1p emerald ('26) .15 .15
Set value .26 .18

#257-258 exist imperf. Value $1 each pair.
For overprints see Nos. L6, L8, L10.

1925 *Perf. 11½*
260 A46 1p blue .20 .15
a. Imperf., pair 2.00

For overprint see No. L9.

Nos. 194, 214-215, J12 Surcharged in Black or Red

Habilitado en 1 centavo

1926
261 A38 1c on 5c lt blue .15 .15
262 A40 7c on 40c rose .15 .15
263 A40 15c on 75c dp bl (R) .15 .15
264 D2 1.50p on 1.50p yel brn .15 .15
Set value .32 .24

Nos. 194, 179 and 256 Surcharged "Habilitado" and New Values

1927
265 A38 2c on 5c lt blue .15 .15
266 A35 50c on 60c magenta .15 .15
a. Inverted surcharge 2.00
267 A44 1.50p on 4p lt blue .15 .15

Official Stamp of 1914 Surcharged "Habilitado" and New Value

268 O19 50c on 75c dp bl .15 .15
Set value, #265-268 .28 .25

National Emblem A47

Pedro Juan Caballero A48

Map of Paraguay — A49

Fulgencio Yegros — A50

Ignacio Iturbe A51

Oratory of the Virgin, Asunción A52

Perf. 12, 11, 11½, 11x12

1927-38 **Typo.**
269 A47 1c lt red ('31) .15 .15
270 A47 2c org red ('30) .15 .15
271 A47 7c lilac .15 .15
272 A47 7c emerald ('29) .15 .15
273 A47 10c gray grn ('28) .15 .15
a. 10c light green ('31) .15 .15
274 A47 10c lil rose ('30) .15 .15
275 A47 10c light bl ('35) .15 .15
276 A47 20c dull bl ('28) .15 .15
277 A47 20c lil brn ('30) .15 .15
278 A47 20c lt vio ('31) .15 .15
279 A47 20c rose ('35) .15 .15
280 A47 50c ultramarine .15 .15
281 A47 50c dl red ('28) .15 .15
282 A47 50c orange ('30) .15 .15
283 A47 50c gray ('31) .15 .15
284 A47 50c brn vio ('34) .15 .15
285 A47 50c rose ('36) .15 .15
286 A47 70c ultra ('28) .15 .15
287 A48 1p emerald .15 .15
288 A48 1p org red ('30) .15 .15
289 A48 1p brn org ('34) .15 .15
290 A49 1.50p brown .15 .15
291 A49 1.50p lilac ('28) .15 .15
292 A49 1.50p rose red ('32) .15 .15
293 A50 2.50p bister .15 .15
294 A51 3p gray .20 .15
295 A51 3p rose red ('36) .15 .15
296 A51 3p brt vio ('36) .15 .15
297 A52 5p chocolate .20 .18
298 A52 5p violet ('36) .15 .15
299 A52 5p pale org ('38) .15 .15
300 A49 20p red ('29) 1.40 1.10
301 A49 20p emerald ('29) 1.40 1.10
302 A49 20p vio brn ('29) 1.40 1.10
Set value 6.25 5.00

No. 281 is also known perf. 10½x11½.
Papermaker's watermarks are sometimes found on No. 271 ("GLORIA BOND" in double-lined circle) and No. 280 ("Extra Vencedor Bond").
For surcharges and overprints see Nos. 312, C4, C6, C13-C14, C17-C18, C25-C32, C34-C35, L11-L30, O94-O96, O98.

Arms of Juan de Salazar de Espinosa A53

Columbus A54

1928, Aug. 15 *Perf. 12*
303 A53 10p violet brown 1.25 .90

Issued in commemoration of Juan de Salazar de Espinosa, founder of Asunción.
A papermaker's watermark ("INDIAN BOND EXTRA STRONG S.&C") is sometimes found on Nos 303, 305-307.

1928 **Litho.**
304 A54 10p ultra .50 .25
305 A54 10p vermilion .50 .25
306 A54 10p deep red .50 .25
Nos. 304-306 (3) 1.50 .75

For surcharge and overprint see Nos. C33, L37.

President Rutherford B. Hayes of US and Villa Occidental A55

1928, Nov. 20 *Perf. 12*
307 A55 10p gray brown 5.00 1.40
308 A55 10p red brown 5.00 1.40

50th anniv. of the Hayes' Chaco decision.

Portraits of Archbishop Bogarin — A56

1930, Aug. 15
309 A56 1.50p lake 1.00 .75
310 A56 1.50p turq blue 1.00 .75
311 A56 1.50p dull vio 1.00 .75
Nos. 309-311 (3) 3.00 2.25

Archbishop Juan Sinforiano Bogarin, first archbishop of Paraguay.
For overprints see Nos. 321-322.

No. 272 Surcharged

Habilitado en CINCO

1930
312 A47 5c on 7c emer .15 .15

A57

1930-39 **Typo.** *Perf. 11½, 12*
313 A57 10p brown .50 .20
314 A57 10p brn red, *bl* ('31) .50 .20
315 A57 10p dk bl, *pink* ('32) .50 .20
316 A57 10p gray brn ('36) .38 .18
317 A57 10p gray ('37) .38 .18
318 A57 10p blue ('39) .15 .15
Nos. 313-318 (6) 2.41 1.11

1st Paraguayan postage stamp, 60th anniv.
For overprint see No. L31.

Gunboat "Humaitá" — A58

1931 *Perf. 12*
319 A58 1.50p purple .38 .22
Nos. 319,C39-C53 (16) 6.15 5.86

Constitution, 60th anniv.
For overprint see No. L33.

View of San Bernardino — A59

1931, Aug.
320 A59 1p light green .25 .15

Founding of San Bernardino, 50th anniv.
For overprint see No. L32.

Nos. 309-310 Overprinted in Blue or Red

FELIZ AÑO NUEVO 1932

1931, Dec. 31
321 A56 1.50p lake (Bl) .75 .75
322 A56 1.50p turq blue (R) .75 .75

Map of the Gran Chaco — A60

1932-35 **Typo.** *Perf. 12*
323 A60 1.50p deep violet .15 .15
324 A60 1.50p rose ('35) .15 .15
Set value .18

For overprints see Nos. L34-L36, O97.

Nos. C74-C78 Surcharged

CORREOS 1 PESO FELIZ AÑO NUEVO 1933

1933 **Litho.**
325 AP18 50c on 4p ultra .25 .20
326 AP18 1p on 8p red .50 .38
327 AP18 1.50p on 12p bl grn .50 .38
328 AP18 2p on 16p dk vio .50 .38
329 AP18 5p on 20p org brn 1.25 1.00
Nos. 325-329 (5) 3.00 2.34

Flag of the Race Issue

Flag with Three Crosses: Caravels of Columbus — A61

1933, Oct. 10 **Litho.** *Perf. 11*
330 A61 10c multicolored .15 .15
331 A61 20c multicolored .15 .15
332 A61 50c multicolored .15 .15
333 A61 1p multicolored .15 .15
334 A61 1.50p multicolored .15 .15
335 A61 2p multicolored .25 .25
336 A61 5p multicolored .50 .50
337 A61 10p multicolored .50 .50
Set value 1.70 1.60

441st anniv. of the sailing of Christopher Columbus from the port of Palos, Aug. 3, 1492, on his first voyage to the New World.

Monstrance A62

Arms of Asunción A63

1937, Aug. **Unwmk.** *Perf. 11½*
338 A62 1p dk blue, yel & red .15 .15
339 A62 3p dk blue, yel & red .15 .15
340 A62 10p dk blue, yel & red .15 .15
Set value .22 .20

1st Natl. Eucharistic Congress, Asuncion.

1937, Aug.
341 A63 50c violet & buff .15 .15
342 A63 1p bis & lt grn .15 .15
343 A63 3p red & lt bl .15 .15
344 A63 10p car rose & buff .15 .15
345 A63 20p blue & drab .15 .15
Set value .40 .35

Founding of Asuncion, 400th anniv.

Oratory of the Virgin, Asunción — A64

Carlos Antonio Lopez — A65

José Eduvigis Diaz — A66

1938-39 **Typo.** *Perf. 11, 12*
346 A64 5p olive green .18 .15
347 A64 5p pale rose ('39) .25 .15
348 A64 11p violet brown .18 .15
Set value .28

Founding of Asuncion, 400th anniv.

1939 *Perf. 12*
349 A65 2p lt ultra & pale brn .18 .15
350 A66 2p lt ultra & brn .20 .15

Reburial of ashes of Pres. Carlos Antonio Lopez (1790-1862) and Gen. José Eduvigis Diaz in the National Pantheon, Asuncion.

Pres. Patricio Escobar and Ramon Zubizarreta
A67

Design: 5p, Pres. Bernardino Caballero and Senator José S. Decoud.

1939-40 Litho. *Perf. 11½*
Heads in Black

351	A67	50c dull org ('40)	.15	.15
352	A67	1p lt violet ('40)	.15	.15
353	A67	2p red brown ('40)	.18	.15
354	A67	5p lt ultra	.25	.15
		Nos. 351-354,C122-C123,O99-O104 (12)	9.03	8.85

Founding of the University of Asuncion, 50th anniv.

Varieties of this issue include inverted heads (50c, 1p, 2p); doubled heads; Caballero and Decoud heads in 50c frame: imperforates and part-perforates. Copies with inverted heads were not officially issued.

Coats of Arms — A69

Pres. Baldomir of Uruguay, Flags of Paraguay, Uruguay — A70

Designs: 2p, Pres. Benavides, Peru. 3p, US Eagle and Shield. 5p, Pres. Alessandri, Chile. 6p, Pres. Vargas, Brazil. 10p, Pres. Ortiz, Argentina.

1939 Engr.; Flags Litho. *Perf. 12*
Flags in National Colors

355	A69	50c violet blue	.15	.15
356	A70	1p olive	.15	.15
357	A70	2p blue green	.15	.15
358	A70	3p sepia	.25	.18
359	A70	5p orange	.20	.15
360	A70	6p dull violet	.50	.40
361	A70	10p bister brn	.38	.25
		Nos. 355-361,C113-C121 (16)	10.03	8.90

First Buenos Aires Peace Conference.
For overprint and surcharge see Nos. 387, B10.

Coats of Arms of New York and Asunción — A76

1939, Nov. 30

362	A76	5p scarlet	.15	.15
363	A76	10p deep blue	.25	.18
364	A76	11p dk blue grn	.35	.30
365	A76	22p olive blk	.45	.38
		Nos. 362-365,C124-C126 (7)	9.35	8.76

New York World's Fair.

Paraguayan Soldier — A77

Paraguayan Woman — A78

Cowboys — A79

Plowing — A80

View of Paraguay River — A81

Oxcart A82

Pasture A83

Pirareta Falls — A84

1940, Jan. 1 Photo. *Perf. 12½*

366	A77	50c deep orange	.15	.15
367	A78	1p brt red violet	.15	.15
368	A79	3p bright green	.15	.15
369	A80	5p chestnut	.16	.15
370	A81	10p magenta	.20	.15
371	A82	20p violet	.38	.32
372	A83	50p cobalt blue	.90	.45
373	A84	100p black	1.90	1.40
		Nos. 366-373 (8)	3.99	2.92

Second Buenos Aires Peace Conference.
For surcharge see No. 386.

Map of the Americas — A85

1940, May Engr. *Perf. 12*

374	A85	50c red orange	.15	.15
375	A85	1p green	.15	.15
376	A85	5p dark blue	.15	.15
377	A85	10p brown	.38	.38
		Nos. 374-377,C127-C130 (8)	4.21	3.41

Pan American Union, 50th anniversary.

Reproduction of Type A1 — A86

Sir Rowland Hill — A87

Designs: 6p, Type A2. 10p, Type A3.

1940, Aug. 15 Photo. *Perf. 13½*

378	A86	1p aqua & brt red vio	.50	.25
379	A87	5p dp yel grn & red brn	.65	.32
380	A86	6p org brn & ultra	1.50	.65
381	A86	10p ver & black	1.50	1.00
		Nos. 378-381 (4)	4.15	2.22

Postage stamp centenary.

Dr. José Francia
A90 A91

1940, Sept. 20 Engr. *Perf. 12*

382	A90	50c carmine rose	.15	.15
383	A91	50c plum	.15	.15
384	A90	1p bright green	.15	.15
385	A91	5p deep blue	.15	.15
		Set value	.48	.40

Centenary of the death of Dr. Jose Francia (1766-1840), dictator of Paraguay, 1814-1840.

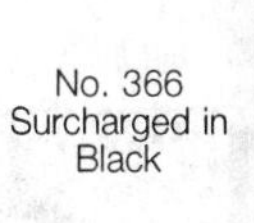

No. 366 Surcharged in Black

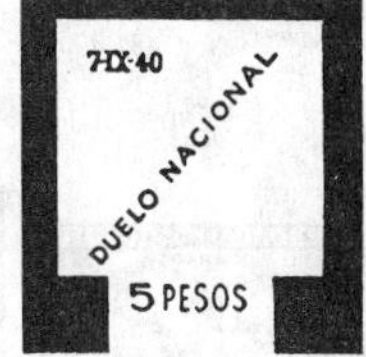

1940, Sept. 7 *Perf. 12½*

386	A77	5p on 50c dp org	.20	.20

In honor of Pres. Jose F. Estigarribia who died in a plane crash Sept. 7, 1940.

No. 360 Overprinted in Black **Visita al Paraguay Agosto de 1941**

1941, Aug. *Perf. 12*

387	A70	6p multi	.20	.20

Visit to Paraguay of Pres. Vargas of Brazil.

Nos. C113-C115 Overprinted "HABILITADO" and Bars in Blue or Red

1942, Jan. 17 *Perf. 12½*

388	A69	1p multi (Bl)	.15	.15
389	A69	3p multi (R)	.15	.15
390	A70	5p multi (R)	.18	.15
		Nos. 388-390 (3)	.48	
		Set value		.30

Coat of Arms — A92

1942-43 Litho. *Perf. 11, 12, 11x12*

391	A92	1p light green	.15	.15
392	A92	1p orange ('43)	.15	.15
393	A92	7p light blue	.15	.15
394	A92	7p yel brn ('43)	.15	.15
		Set value	.24	.20

The Indian Francisco — A93

Arms of Irala — A95

Domingo Martinez de Irala and His Vision — A94

1942, Aug. 15 Engr. *Perf. 12*

395	A93	2p green	.65	.30
396	A94	5p rose	.65	.30
397	A95	7p sapphire	.65	.25
		Nos. 395-397,C131-C133 (6)	7.95	5.85

400th anniversary of Asuncion.

Pres. Higinio Morinigo, Scenes of Industry & Agriculture
A96

Christopher Columbus
A97

1943, Aug. 15 Unwmk.

398	A96	7p blue	.15	.15

For surcharges see Nos. 404, 428.

1943, Aug. 15

399	A97	50c violet	.18	.15
400	A97	1p gray brn	.15	.15
401	A97	5p dark grn	.45	.15
402	A97	7p brt ultra	.25	.15
		Nos. 399-402 (4)	1.03	
		Set value		.46

Discovery of America, 450th anniv.
For surcharges see Nos. 405, 429.

No. 296 Surcharged in Black **Habilitado en un céntimo**

1944 *Perf. 12, 11, 11½, 11x12*

403	A51	1c on 3p brt vio	.15	.15

Nos. 398 and 402 Surcharged "1944 / 5 Centimos 5" in Red

1944 *Perf. 12*

404	A96	5c on 7p blue	.15	.15
405	A97	5c on 7p brt ultra	.15	.15
		Set value	.20	.15

Imperforates
Starting with No. 406, many Paraguayan stamps exist imperf.

Primitive Postal Service among Indians — A98

Ruins of Humaitá Church — A99

Locomotive of early Paraguayan Railroad — A100

Early Merchant Ship — A102

Marshal Francisco S. Lopez — A101

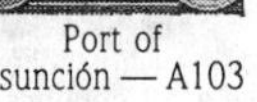

Port of Asunción — A103

Birthplace of Paraguay's Liberation — A104

Monument to Heroes of Itororó — A105

1944-45 Unwmk. Engr. *Perf. 12½*

406	A98	1c black	.15	.15
407	A99	2c copper brn ('45)	.15	.15
408	A100	5c light olive	.25	.15
409	A101	7c light blue ('45)	.15	.15
410	A102	10c green ('45)	.25	.20
411	A103	15c dark blue ('45)	.25	.20
412	A104	50c black brown	.45	.45
413	A105	1g dk rose car ('45)	.90	.50
		Nos. 406-413,C134-C146 (21)	10.41	9.38
		Nos. 406-413 (8)	2.55	1.95

See #435, 437, 439, 441, C158-C162.
For surcharges see #414, 427.

No. 409 Surcharged in Red

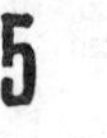

1945

414	A101	5c on 7c light blue	.15	.15

Handshake, Map and Flags of Paraguay and Panama — A106

Designs: 3c, Venezuela Flag. 5c, Colombia Flag. 2g, Peru Flag.

Engr.; Flags Litho. in Natl. Colors
1945, Aug. 15 Unwmk. *Perf. 12½*

415	A106	1c dark green	.15	.15
416	A106	3c lake	.15	.15
417	A106	5c blue blk	.15	.15
418	A106	2g brown	1.10	.75
		Nos. 415-418,C147-C153 (11)	5.31	4.95

Goodwill visits of Pres. Higinio Morinigo during 1943.

Nos. B6 to B9 Surcharged "1945" and New Value in Black

1945 Engr. *Perf. 12*

419	SP4	2c on 7p + 3p red brn	.15	.15
420	SP4	2c on 7p + 3p purple	.15	.15
421	SP4	2c on 7p + 3p car rose	.15	.15
422	SP4	2c on 7p + 3p saph	.15	.15
423	SP4	5c on 7p + 3p red brn	.15	.15
424	SP4	5c on 7p + 3p purple	.15	.15
425	SP4	5c on 7p + 3p car rose	.15	.15
426	SP4	5c on 7p + 3p saph	.15	.15
		Set value	.84	.60

Similar Surcharge in Red on Nos. 409, 398 and 402

Perf. 12½, 12

427	A101	5c on 7c lt blue	.15	.15
428	A96	5c on 7p blue	.15	.15
429	A97	5c on 7p brt ultra	.15	.15
		Nos. 427-429 (3)	.45	
		Set value		.30

Nos. 427-429 exist with black surcharge.

Catalogue values for unused stamps in this section, from this point to the end of the section, are for Never Hinged items.

Coat of Arms ("U.P.U." at bottom) — A110

1946 Litho. *Perf. 11, 12, 11x12*

430	A110	5c gray	.15	.15

See Nos. 459-463, 478-480, 498-506, 525-536, 646-658.
For overprints see Nos. 464-466.

Nos. B6 to B9 Surcharged "1946" and New Value in Black

1946 *Perf. 12*

431	SP4	5c on 7p + 3p red brn	.32	.25
432	SP4	5c on 7p + 3p purple	.32	.25
433	SP4	5c on 7p + 3p car rose	.32	.25
434	SP4	5c on 7p + 3p saph	.32	.25
		Nos. 431-434 (4)	1.28	1.00

Types of 1944-45 and

First Telegraph in South America — A111

Colonial Jesuit Altar — A113

Monument to Antequera A112

1946, Sept. 21 Engr. *Perf. 12½*

435	A102	1c rose car	.15	.15
436	A111	2c purple	.15	.15
437	A98	5c ultra	.15	.15
438	A112	10c org yel	.15	.15
439	A105	15c brn olive	.15	.15
440	A113	50c deep grn	.30	.20
441	A104	1g brt ultra	.65	.38
		Set value	1.35	.90

See Nos. C135-C138, C143.

Marshal Francisco Solano Lopez — A114

1947, May 15 *Perf. 12*

442	A114	1c purple	.15	.15
443	A114	2c org red	.15	.15
444	A114	5c green	.15	.15
445	A114	15c ultra	.15	.15
446	A114	50c dark grn	.25	.25
		Nos. 442-446,C163-C167 (10)	3.43	3.43

Juan Sinforiano Bogarin, Archbishop of Asunción — A115

Archbishopric Coat of Arms — A116

Projected Monument of the Sacred Heart of Jesus A117

Vision of Projected Monument A118

1948, Jan. 6 Engr. *Perf. 12½*

447	A115	2c dark blue	.15	.15
448	A116	5c deep car	.15	.15
449	A117	10c gray blk	.15	.15
450	A118	15c green	.20	.15
		Nos. 447-450,C168-C175 (12)	4.08	4.03

Archbishopric of Asunción, 50th anniv.

"Political Enlightenment" A119

1948, Sept. 11 Engr. & Litho.

451	A119	5c car red & bl	.15	.15
452	A119	15c red org, red & bl	.15	.15
		Nos. 451-452,C176-C177 (4)	2.80	2.55

Issued to honor the Barefeet, a political group.

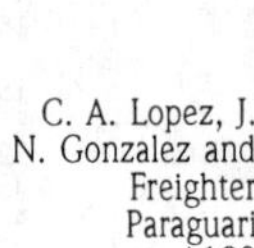

C. A. Lopez, J. N. Gonzalez and Freighter Paraguari A120

1949 Litho.

Centers in Carmine, Black, Ultramarine and Blue

453	A120	2c orange	.15	.15
454	A120	5c blue vio	.15	.15
455	A120	10c black	.15	.15
456	A120	15c violet	.15	.15
457	A120	50c blue grn	.15	.15
458	A120	1g dull vio brn	.20	.15
		Set value	.58	.40

Paraguay's merchant fleet centenary.

Type of 1946

1950 Unwmk. *Perf. 10½*

459	A110	5c red	.15	.15
460	A110	10c blue	.15	.15
461	A110	50c rose lilac	.15	.15
462	A110	1g pale violet	.15	.15

1951

Coarse Impression

463	A110	30c green	.15	.15
		Set value, #459-463	.28	.25

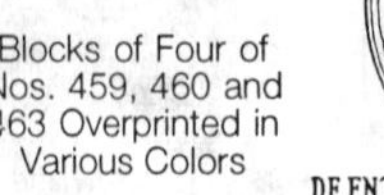

Blocks of Four of Nos. 459, 460 and 463 Overprinted in Various Colors

Illustration reduced one-half.

1951, Apr. 18

464	A110	5c red (Bk), block	.15	.15
465	A110	10c blue (R), block	.25	.18
466	A110	30c green (V), block	.38	.30

1st Economic Cong. of Paraguay, Apr. 18, 1951.

Columbus Lighthouse A121

1952, Feb. 11 *Perf. 10*

467	A121	2c org brn	.15	.15
468	A121	5c light ultra	.15	.15
469	A121	10c rose	.15	.15
470	A121	15c light blue	.15	.15
471	A121	20c lilac	.15	.15
472	A121	50c orange	.15	.15
473	A121	1g bluish grn	.18	.18
		Set value	.50	.50

Silvio Pettirossi, Aviator — A122

1954, Mar. Litho. *Perf. 10*

474	A122	5c blue	.15	.15
475	A122	20c rose pink	.15	.15
476	A122	50c vio brn	.15	.15
477	A122	60c lt vio	.15	.15
		Set value, #474-477, C201-C204	.64	.62

Arms Type of 1946

1954 *Perf. 11*

478	A110	10c vermilion	.15	.15

Perf. 10

478A	A110	10c ver, redrawn	.15	.15
479	A110	10g orange	.25	.20
480	A110	50g vio brn	1.25	1.00
		Set value	1.55	1.25

No. 478A measures 20½x24mm, has 5 frame lines at left and 6 at right. No. 478 measures 20x24½mm, has 6 frame lines at left and 5 at right.

Three National Heroes — A123

1954, Aug. 15 Litho. *Perf. 10*

481	A123	5c light vio	.15	.15
482	A123	20c light blue	.15	.15
483	A123	50c rose pink	.15	.15
484	A123	1g org brn	.15	.15
485	A123	2g blue grn	.15	.15
		Nos. 481-485,C216-C220 (10)	5.85	5.78

Marshal Francisco S. Lopez, Pres. Carlos A. Lopez and Gen. Bernardino Caballero.

Pres. Alfredo Stroessner and Pres. Juan D. Peron A124

Photo. & Litho.
1955, Apr. Wmk. 90 *Perf. 13x13½*

486	A124	5c multicolored	.15	.15
487	A124	10c multicolored	.15	.15
488	A124	50c multicolored	.15	.15
489	A124	1.30g multicolored	.15	.15
490	A124	2.20g multicolored	.15	.15
		Set value, #486-490, C221-C224	.75	.66

Visit of Pres. Juan D. Peron of Argentina.

Jesuit Ruins, Trinidad Belfry A125

Santa Maria Cornice — A126

Jesuit Ruins: 20c, Corridor at Trinidad. 2.50g, Tower of Santa Rosa. 5g, San Cosme gate. 15g, Church of Jesus. 25g, Niche at Trinidad.

Perf. 12½x12, 12x12½

1955, June 19 Engr. Unwmk.

491	A125	5c	org yel	.15	.15
492	A125	20c	olive bister	.15	.15
493	A126	50c	lt red brn	.15	.15
494	A126	2.50g	olive	.15	.15
495	A125	5g	yel brn	.15	.15
496	A125	15g	blue grn	.22	.15
497	A126	25g	deep grn	.45	.25
			Set value, #491-497, C225-C232	2.00	1.50

25th anniv. of the priesthood of Monsignor Rodriguez.

For surcharges see Nos. 545-551.

Arms Type of 1946

Perf. 10, 11 (No. 500)

1956-58 Litho. Unwmk.

498	A110	5c	brown ('57)	.15	.15
499	A110	30c	red brn ('57)	.15	.15
500	A110	45c	gray olive	.15	.15
500A	A110	90c	lt vio bl	.15	.15
501	A110	2g	ocher	.15	.15
502	A110	2.20g	lil rose	.15	.15
503	A110	3g	ol bis ('58)	.15	.15
503A	A110	4.20g	emer ('57)	.15	.15
504	A110	5g	ver ('57)	.15	.15
505	A110	10g	lt grn ('57)	.15	.15
506	A110	20g	blue ('57)	.30	.22
			Set value	.92	.75

No. 500A exists with four-line, carmine overprint: "DIA N. UNIDAS 24 Octubre 1945-1956". It was not regularly issued and no decree authorizing it is known.

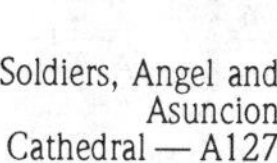

Soldiers, Angel and Asuncion Cathedral — A127

#513-519, Soldier & nurse in medallion & flags.

Perf. 13½

1957, June 12 Photo. Unwmk.

Granite Paper

Flags in Red and Blue

508	A127	5c	bl grn	.15	.15
509	A127	10c	carmine	.15	.15
510	A127	15c	ultra	.15	.15
511	A127	20c	dp claret	.15	.15
512	A127	25c	gray blk	.15	.15
513	A127	30c	lt blue	.15	.15
514	A127	40c	gray blk	.15	.15
515	A127	50c	dark car	.15	.15
516	A127	1g	bluish grn	.15	.15
517	A127	1.30g	ultra	.15	.15
518	A127	1.50g	dp claret	.15	.15
519	A127	2g	brt grn	.15	.15
			Set value	1.50	.55

Heroes of the Chaco war. See #C233-C245.

Statue of St. Ignatius (Guarani Carving) — A128

Blessed Roque Gonzales and St. Ignatius A129

1.50g, St. Ignatius and San Ignacio Monastery.

Wmk. 319

1958, Mar. 15 Litho. *Perf. 11*

520	A128	50c	dk red brn	.15	.15
521	A129	50c	lt bl grn	.15	.15
522	AP91	1.50g	brt vio	.15	.15
523	A128	3g	light bl	.15	.15
524	A129	6.25g	rose car	.15	.15
			Nos. 520-524 (5)	.75	
			Set value		.28

St. Ignatius of Loyola (1491-1556). See Nos. 704-707.

Arms Type of 1946

1958-64 Litho. *Perf. 10, 11*

525	A110	45c	gray olive	.15	.15
526	A110	50c	rose vio	.15	.15
527	A110	70c	lt brn ('59)	.15	.15
527A	A110	90c	vio blue	.15	.15
528	A110	1g	violet	.15	.15
529	A110	1.50g	lilac ('59)	.15	.15
529A	A110	2g	bister ('64)	.15	.15
530	A110	3g	ol bis ('59)	.15	.15
531	A110	4.50g	lt ultra ('59)	.15	.15
531A	A110	5g	rose red ('59)	.15	.15
531B	A110	10g	bl grn ('59)	.15	.15
532	A110	12.45g	yel green	.15	.15
533	A110	15g	dl orange	.15	.15
534	A110	30g	citron	.28	.20
535	A110	50g	brown red	.42	.30
536	A110	100g	gray vio	.85	.65
			Set value	2.40	1.90

Pres. Alfredo Stroessner — A130

Perf. 13½

1958, Aug. 15 Litho. Wmk. 320

Center in Slate

537	A130	10c	sal pink	.15	.15
538	A130	15c	violet	.15	.15
539	A130	25c	yel grn	.15	.15
540	A130	30c	light fawn	.15	.15
541	A130	50c	rose car	.15	.15
542	A130	75c	light ultra	.15	.15
543	A130	5g	lt bl grn	.15	.15
544	A130	10g	brown	.15	.15
			Nos. 537-544,C246-C251 (14)	4.40	
			Set value		3.65

Re-election of President General Alfredo Stroessner.

Nos. 491-497 Surcharged in Red

Perf. 12½x12, 12x12½

1959, May 14 Engr. Unwmk.

545	A125	1.50g	on 5c org yel	.15	.15
546	A125	1.50g	on 20c ol bis	.15	.15
547	A126	1.50g	on 50c lt red brn	.15	.15
548	A126	3g	on 2.50g ol	.15	.15
549	A125	6.25g	on 5g yel brn	.15	.15
550	A125	20g	on 15g bl grn	.25	.25
551	A126	30g	on 25g dp grn	.40	.40
			Nos. 545-551,C252-C259 (15)	5.53	4.43

The surcharge is made to fit the stamps. Counterfeits of surcharge exist.

Goalkeeper Catching Soccer Ball A131

WRY Emblem A132

1960, Mar. 18 Photo. *Perf. 12½*

556	A131	30c	brt red & bl grn	.15	.15
557	A131	50c	plum & dk bl	.15	.15
558	A131	75c	ol grn & org	.15	.15
559	A131	1.50g	dk vio & bl grn	.15	.15
			Nos. 556-559,C262-C264 (7)	1.35	
			Set value		.90

Olympic Games of 1960.

1960, Apr. 7 Litho. *Perf. 11*

560	A132	25c	sal & yel grn	.15	.15
561	A132	50c	lt yel grn & red org	.15	.15
562	A132	70c	lt brn & lil rose	.25	.20
563	A132	1.50g	lt bl & ultra	.25	.20
564	A132	3g	gray & bis brn	.50	.45
			Nos. 560-564,C265-C268 (9)	5.15	4.43

World Refugee Year, July 1, 1959-June 30, 1960 (1st issue).

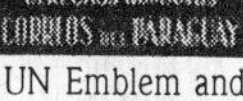

UN Emblem and Dove — A133

Flags of UN and Paraguay and UN Emblem — A134

UN Declaration of Human Rights: 3g, Hand holding scales. 6g, Hands breaking chains. 20g, Flame.

1960, Apr. 21 *Perf. 12½x13*

565	A133	1g	dk car & bl	.15	.15
566	A133	3g	blue & org	.15	.15
567	A133	6g	gray grn & sal	.15	.15
568	A133	20g	ver & yel	.15	.15
			Set value, #565-568, C269-C271	1.45	1.45

Miniature sheets exist, perf. and imperf., containing one each of Nos. 565-568, all printed in purple and orange.

Perf. 13x13½

1960, Oct. 24 Photo. Unwmk.

569	A134	30c	lt bl, red & bl	.15	.15
570	A134	75c	yel, red & bl	.15	.15
571	A134	90c	pale lil, red & bl	.15	.15
			Set value, #569-571, C272-C273	.25	.25

15th anniversary of the United Nations.

International Bridge, Arms of Brazil, Paraguay — A135

Truck Carrying Logs — A136

1961, Jan. 26 Litho. *Perf. 14*

572	A135	15c	green	.15	.15
573	A135	30c	dull blue	.15	.15
574	A135	50c	orange	.15	.15
575	A135	75c	vio blue	.15	.15
576	A135	1g	violet	.15	.15
			Set value, #572-575, C274-C277	1.05	.95

Inauguration of the International Bridge between Paraguay and Brazil.

Unwmk.

1961, Apr. 10 Photo. *Perf. 13*

90c, 2g, Logs on river barge. 1g, 5g, Radio tower.

577	A136	25c	yel grn & rose car	.15	.15
578	A136	90c	blue & yel	.15	.15
579	A136	1g	car rose & org	.15	.15
580	A136	2g	ol grn & sal	.15	.15
581	A136	5g	lilac & emer	.15	.15
			Set value, #577-581, C278-C281	1.65	1.40

Paraguay's progress, "Paraguay en Marcha."

P. J. Caballero, José G. R. Francia, F. Yegros, Revolutionary Leaders A137

1961, May 16 Litho. *Perf. 14½*

582	A137	30c	green	.15	.15
583	A137	50c	lil rose	.15	.15
584	A137	90c	violet	.15	.15
585	A137	1.50g	Prus bl	.15	.15
586	A137	3g	olive bis	.15	.15
587	A137	4g	ultra	.15	.15
588	A137	5g	brown	.15	.15
			Set value, #582-588, C282-C287	2.15	2.00

150th anniv. of Independence (1st issue).

"Chaco Peace" A138

Puma A139

1961, June 12 *Perf. 14x14½*

589	A138	25c	vermilion	.15	.15
590	A138	30c	green	.15	.15
591	A138	50c	red brn	.15	.15
592	A138	1g	bright vio	.15	.15
593	A138	2g	dk bl gray	.15	.15
			Set value, #589-593, C288-C290	1.40	1.30

Chaco Peace; 150th anniv. of Independence (2nd issue).

1961, Aug. 16 Unwmk. *Perf. 14*

594	A139	75c	dull vio	.15	.15
595	A139	1.50g	brown	.15	.15
596	A139	4.50g	green	.15	.15
597	A139	10g	Prus blue	.15	.15
			Nos. 594-597,C291-C293 (7)	3.15	3.00

150th anniv. of Independence (3rd issue).

University Seal — A140

Hotel Guarani — A141

1961, Sept. 18 *Perf. 14x14½*

598	A140	15c	ultra	.15	.15
599	A140	25c	dk red	.15	.15
600	A140	75c	bl grn	.15	.15
601	A140	1g	orange	.15	.15
			Set value, #598-601, C294-C296	.85	.85

Founding of the Catholic University in Asuncion; 150th anniv. of Independence (4th issue).

1961, Oct. 14 Litho. *Perf. 15*

602	A141	50c	slate bl	.15	.15
603	A141	1g	green	.15	.15
604	A141	4.50g	lilac	.15	.15
			Set value, #602-604, C297-C300	.90	.85

Opening of the Hotel Guarani; 150th anniv. of Independence (5th issue).

Tennis Racket and Balls in Flag Colors — A142

1961, Oct. 16 Litho. *Perf. 11*

605 A142 35c multi .15
606 A142 75c multi .15
607 A142 1.50g multi .15
608 A142 2.25g multi .15
609 A142 4g multi .15
Set value .28

28th South American Tennis Championships, Asuncion, Oct. 15-23 (1st issue). Some specialists question the status of this issue. See Nos. C301-C303.

Imperforates exist in changed colors as well as two imperf. souvenir sheets with stamps in changed colors.

Limited Distribution Issues Beginning with No. 610, sets with limited distribution are not valued.

Alan B. Shepard, First US Astronaut A143

18.15g, 36g, 50g, Shepard, Saturn, horiz.

1961, Dec. 22 Litho. *Perf. 11*

610 A143 10c blue & brown
611 A143 25c blue & car rose
612 A143 50c blue & yel org
613 A143 75c blue & green
614 A143 18.15g green & blue
615 A143 36g orange & blue
616 A143 50g car rose & blue
a. Souvenir sheet of 1

Nos. 614-616a are airmail.

Uprooted Oak Emblem — A145

1961, Dec. 30 Unwmk. *Perf. 11*

619 A145 10c ultra & lt bl .15
620 A145 25c maroon & org .15
621 A145 50c car rose & pink .15
622 A145 75c dk bl & yel grn .15
Set value .20

World Refugee Year, 1959-60 (2nd issue). Imperforates in changed colors and souvenir sheets exist. Some specialists question the status of this issue.

See Nos. C307-C309.

Europa A146

Design: 20g, 50g, Dove.

1961, Dec. 31

623 A146 50c multicolored
624 A146 75c multicolored
625 A146 1g multicolored
626 A146 1.50g multicolored
627 A146 4.50g multicolored
a. Souvenir sheet of 5, #623-627
628 A146 20g multicolored
629 A146 50g multicolored
a. Souvenir sheet of 1

Nos. 628-629 are airmail.

Tennis Player — A147

1962, Jan. 5 *Perf. 15x14½*

630 A147 35c Prussian bl .15 .15
631 A147 75c dark vio .15 .15
632 A147 1.50g red brn .15 .15
633 A147 2.25g emerald .15 .15
634 A147 4g carmine .15 .15
635 A147 12.45g red lil .20 .20
636 A147 20g bl grn .35 .35
637 A147 50g org brn .55 .55
Set value 1.35 1.35

28th South American Tennis Championships, 1961 (2nd issue) and the 150th anniv. of Independence (6th issue).

Nos. 634-637 are airmail.

Scout Bugler A148

Lord Baden-Powell A148a

1962, Feb. 6 *Perf. 11*

Olive Green Center

638 A148 10c dp magenta .15
639 A148 20c red orange .15
640 A148 25c dk brown .15
641 A148 30c emerald .15
642 A148 50c indigo .15
643 A148a 12.45g car rose & bl .25
644 A148a 36g car rose & emer .75
645 A148a 50g car rose & org yel 1.00
Set value 2.25

Issued to honor the Boy Scouts. Imperfs. in changed colors exist and imperf. souvenir sheets exist. Some specialists question the status of this issue.

Nos. 643-645 are airmail.

Arms Type of 1946

1962-68 Litho. Wmk. 347

646 A110 50c steel bl ('63) .15 .15
647 A110 70c dull lil ('63) .15 .15
648 A110 1.50g violet ('63) .15 .15
649 A110 3g dp bl ('68) .15 .15
650 A110 4.50g redsh brn ('67) .15 .15
651 A110 5g lilac ('64) .15 .15
652 A110 10g car rose ('63) .15 .15
653 A110 12.45g ultra .15 .15
654 A110 15.45g org ver .15 .15
655 A110 18.15g lilac .15 .15
656 A110 20g lt brn ('63) .15 .15
657 A110 50g dl red brn ('67) .35 .18
658 A110 100g bl gray ('63) .70 .42
Set value 1.85 1.25

Map and Laurel Branch A149

UN Emblem A150

Design: 20g, 50g, Hands holding globe.

Perf. 14x14½

1962, Apr. 14 Unwmk.

659 A149 50c ocher .15 .15
660 A149 75c vio blue .15 .15
661 A149 1g purple .15 .15
662 A149 1.50g brt grn .15 .15
663 A149 4.50g vermilion .15 .15
664 A149 20g lil rose .18 .18
665 A149 50g orange .38 .38
Set value .80 .80

Day of the Americas; 150th anniv. of Independence (7th issue).

Nos. 664-665 are airmail.

1962, Apr. 23 *Perf. 15*

Design: #670-673, UN Headquarters, NYC.

666 A150 50c bister brn .15 .15
667 A150 75c dp claret .15 .15
668 A150 1g Prussian bl .15 .15
669 A150 2g orange brn .15 .15
670 A150 12.45g dl vio .20 .20
671 A150 18.15g ol grn .30 .30
672 A150 23.40g brn red .45 .45
673 A150 30g carmine .50 .50
Set value 1.60 1.60

UN; Independence, 150th anniv. (8th issue).

Nos. 670-673 are airmail.

Malaria Eradication Emblem and Mosquito A151

Design: 75c, 1g, 1.50g, Microscope, anopheles mosquito and eggs. 3g, 4g, Malaria eradication emblem. 12.45g, 18.15g, 36g, Mosquito, UN emblem and microscope.

Perf. 14x13½

1962, May 23 Wmk. 346

674 A151 30c pink, ultra & blk .15
675 A151 50c bis, grn & blk .15
676 A151 75c rose red, blk & bis .15
677 A151 1g brt grn, blk & bis .15
678 A151 1.50g dl red brn, blk & bis .15
679 A151 3g bl, red & blk .15
680 A151 4g grn, red & blk .15
681 A151 12.45g ol bis, grn & blk .18
682 A151 18.15g rose lil, red & blk .38
683 A151 36g rose red, vio bl & blk 1.00
Set value 2.00

WHO drive to eradicate malaria. Imperforates exist in changed colors. Two souvenir sheets exist, one containing one copy of No. 683, the other an imperf. 36g in blue, red & black. Some specialists question the status of this issue.

Nos. 679-683 are airmail.

Stadium — A152

Soccer Players and Globe A152a

Perf. 13½x14

1962, July 28 Litho. Wmk. 346

684 A152 15c yel & dk brn .15
685 A152 25c brt grn & dk brn .15
686 A152 30c lt vio & dk brn .15
687 A152 40c dl org & dk brn .15
688 A152 50c brt yel grn & dk brn .15
689 A152a 12.45g brt rose, blk & vio .38
690 A152a 18.15g lt red brn, blk & vio .55
691 A152a 36g gray grn, blk & brn 1.10
Set value 2.25

World Soccer Championships, Chile, May 30-June 17. Some specialists question the status of this issue. Imperfs. exist. A souvenir sheet contains one No. 691.

Nos. 689-691 are airmail.

Freighter A153

Ship's Wheel — A153a

Designs: Various merchantmen. 44g, Like 12.45g with diagonal colorless band in background.

Perf. 14½x15

1962, July 31 Unwmk.

692 A153 30c bister brn .15 .15
693 A153 90c slate bl .15 .15
694 A153 1.50g brown red .15 .15
695 A153 2g green .15 .15
696 A153 4.20g vio blue .15 .15

Perf. 15x14½

697 A153a 12.45g dk red .15 .15
698 A153a 44g blue .38 .32
Set value .78 .70

Issued to honor the merchant marine.

Nos. 697-698 are airmail.

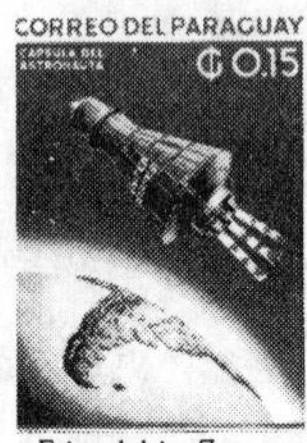

Friendship 7 over South America — A154

Lt. Col. John H. Glenn, Jr., Lt. Cmdr. Scott Carpenter — A154a

Perf. 13½x14

1962, Sept. 4 Litho. Wmk. 346

699 A154 15c dk bl & bis .15
700 A154 25c vio brn & bis .15
701 A154 30c dk sl grn & bis .15
702 A154 40c dk gray & bis .15
703 A154 50c dk vio & bis .15
704 A154a 12.45g car lake & gray .15
705 A154a 18.15g red lil & gray .20
706 A154a 36g dl cl & gray .40
Set value 1.00

US manned space flights. Imperfs. in changed colors and two souvenir sheets exist. Some specialists question the status of this issue.

Nos. 704-706 are airmail.

Discus Thrower — A155

Olympic flame and: 12.45g, Melbourne, 1956. 18.15g, Rome, 1960. 36g, Tokyo, 1964.

1962, Oct. 1 Litho.

707 A155 15c blk & yel .15
708 A155 25c blk & lt grn .15
709 A155 30c blk & pink .15
710 A155 40c blk & pale vio .15
711 A155 50c blk & lt bl .15
712 A155 12.45g brt grn, lt grn & choc .15
713 A155 18.15g ol brn, yel & choc .20
714 A155 36g rose red, pink & choc .40
Set value 1.00

Olympic Games from Amsterdam 1928 to Tokyo 1964. Each stamp is inscribed with date and place of various Olympic Games. Imperfs. in changed colors and two souvenir sheets exist. Some specialists question the status of this issue.

Nos. 712-714 are airmail.

Peace Dove and Cross A156

Dove Symbolizing Holy Ghost A156a

Perf. 14½

1962, Oct. 11 **Litho.** **Unwmk.**

715 A156	50c	olive	.15	.15
716 A156	70c	dark blue	.15	.15
717 A156	1.50g	bister	.15	.15
718 A156	2g	violet	.15	.15
719 A156	3g	brick red	.15	.15
720 A156a	5g	vio bl	.15	.15
721 A156a	10g	brt grn	.15	.15
722 A156a	12.45g	lake	.15	.15
723 A156a	18.15g	orange	.25	.20
724 A156a	23.40g	violet	.30	.22
725 A156a	36g	rose red	.50	.35
		Set value	1.60	1.25

Vatican II, the 21st Ecumenical Council of the Roman Catholic Church, which opened Oct. 11, 1962.

Nos. 720-725 are airmail.

Europa A157

1962, Dec. 17 *Perf. 11*

726 A157	4g	yel, red & brn	
727 A157	36g	multi, diff.	
a.		Souvenir sheet of 2, #726-727	

No. 727 is airmail.

Solar System A158

12.45g, 36g, 50g, Inner planets, Jupiter & rocket.

Perf. 14x13½

1962, Dec. 17 **Wmk. 346**

728 A158	10c	org & purple
729 A158	20c	org & brn vio
730 A158	25c	org & dark vio
731 A158	30c	org & ultra
732 A158	50c	org & dull green
733 A158	12.45g	org & brown
734 A158	36g	org & blue
735 A158	50g	org & green
a.		Souvenir sheet of 1

Nos. 733-735 are airmail.

The following stamps exist imperf. in different colors: Nos. 736-743a, 744-751a, 752-759a, 760-766a, 775-782a, 783-790a, 791-798a, 799-805a, 806-813a, 814-821a, 828-835a, 836-843, 841a, 850-857a, 858-865a, 871-878, 876a, 887-894a, 895-902, 900a, 903-910a, 911-918a, 919-926a, 927-934a, 943-950a, 951-958a, 959-966a, 978-985a, 986-993a, 994-1001a, 1002-1003, 1003d, 1004-1007a, 1051-1059, B12-B19.

Pierre de Coubertin (1836-1937), Founder of Modern Olympic Games — A159

Summer Olympic Games sites and: Nos. 12.45g, 18.15g, 36g, Torch bearer in stadium.

Perf. 14x13½

1963, Feb. 16 **Wmk. 346**

736 A159	15c	Athens, 1896
737 A159	25c	Paris, 1900
738 A159	30c	St. Louis, 1904
739 A159	40c	London, 1908
740 A159	50c	Stockholm, 1912
741 A159	12.45g	No games, 1916
742 A159	18.15g	Antwerp, 1920
743 A159	36g	Paris, 1924
a.		Souvenir sheet of 1

Nos. 741-743a are airmail.

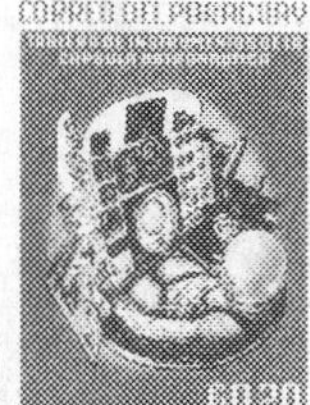

Walter M. Schirra, US Astronaut — A160

Design: 12.45g, 36g, 50g, Schirra.

1963, Mar. 16 *Perf. 13½x14*

744 A160	10c	brn org & blk
745 A160	20c	car & blk
746 A160	25c	lake & blk
747 A160	30c	ver & blk
748 A160	50c	mag & blk
749 A160	12.45g	bl blk & lake
750 A160	36g	dl gray vio & lake
751 A160	50g	dk grn bl & lake
a.		Souvenir sheet of 1

Nos. 749-751a are airmail.

Winter Olympics A161

Games sites and: 12.45g, 36g, 50g, Snowflake.

1963, May 16 *Perf. 14x13½*

752 A161	10g	Chamonix, 1924
753 A161	20c	St. Moritz, 1928
754 A161	25c	Lake Placid, 1932
755 A161	30c	Garmisch-Partenkirchen, 1936
756 A161	50c	St. Moritz, 1948
757 A161	12.45g	Oslo, 1952
758 A161	36g	Cortina d'Ampezzo, 1956
759 A161	50g	Squaw Valley, 1960
a.		Souvenir sheet of 1

Nos. 757-759a are airmail.

Freedom from Hunger A162

Perf. 13½x14, 14x13½

1963, May 31

760 A162	10c	yel grn & brn
761 A162	25c	lt bl & brn
762 A162	50c	lt grn bl & brn
763 A162	75c	lt lil & brn
764 A162	18.15g	yel org & brn
765 A162	36g	lt bl grn & brn
766 A162	50g	bis & brn
a.		Souvenir sheet of 1

#760-763 are vert. #764-766a are airmail.

Pres. Alfredo Stroessner — A163

1963, Aug. 6 **Wmk. 347** *Perf. 11*

767 A163	50c	ol gray & sep	.15	.15
768 A163	75c	buff & sepia	.15	.15
769 A163	1.50g	lt lil & sep	.15	.15
770 A163	3g	emer & sepia	.15	.15
771 A163	12.45g	pink & claret	.18	.15
772 A163	18.15g	pink & grn	.25	.22
773 A163	36g	pink & vio	.75	.50
		Set value	1.45	1.00

Third presidential term of Alfredo Stroessner. A 36g imperf. souvenir sheet exists.

Nos. 771-773 are airmail.

MUESTRA

Illustrations may show the word "MUESTRA." This means specimen and is not on the actual stamps. The editors would like to borrow copies so that replacement illustrations can be made.

Souvenir Sheet

Dag Hammarskjold, UN Secretary General — A164

1963, Aug. 21 **Unwmk.** *Imperf.*

774 A164 2g Sheet of 2

Project Mercury Flight of L. Gordon Cooper A165

12.45g, 18.15g, 50g, L. Gordon Cooper, vert.

Perf. 14x13½, 13½x14

1963, Aug. 23 **Litho.** **Wmk. 346**

775 A165	15c	brn & orange
776 A165	25c	brn & blue
777 A165	30c	brn & violet
778 A165	40c	brn & green
779 A165	50c	brn & red vio
780 A165	12.45g	brn & bl grn
781 A165	18.15g	brn & blue
782 A165	50g	brn & pink
a.		Souvenir sheet of 1

Nos. 780-782 are airmail.

1964 Winter Olympics, Innsbruck A166

Design: 12.45g, 18.15g, 50g, Innsbruck Games emblem, vert.

Perf. 14x13½, 13½x14

1963, Oct. 28 **Unwmk.**

783 A166	15c	choc & red
784 A166	25c	gray grn & red
785 A166	30c	plum & red
786 A166	40c	sl grn & red
787 A166	50c	dp bl & red
788 A166	12.45g	sep & red
789 A166	18.15g	grn bl & red
790 A166	50g	tan & red
a.		Souvenir sheet of 1

Nos. 788-790 are airmail.

1964 Summer Olympics, Tokyo — A167

12.45g, 18.15g, 50g, Tokyo games emblem.

1964, Jan. 8 *Perf. 13½x14*

791 A167	15c	blue & red
792 A167	25c	org & red
793 A167	30c	tan & red
794 A167	40c	vio brn & red
795 A167	50c	grn bl & red
796 A167	12.45g	vio & red
797 A167	18.15g	brn & red
798 A167	50g	grn bl & red
a.		Souvenir sheet of 1

Nos. 796-798 are airmail.

Intl. Red Cross, Cent. — A168

Designs: 10c, Helicopter. 25c, Space ambulance. 30c, Red Cross symbol, vert. 50c, Clara Barton, founder of American Red Cross, vert. 18.15g, Jean Henri Dunant, founder of Intl. Red Cross, vert. 36g, Red Cross space hospital, space ambulance. 50g, Plane, ship, ambulance, vert.

1964, Feb. 4 *Perf. 14x13½, 13½x14*

799 A168	10c	vio brn & red
800 A168	25c	bl grn & red
801 A168	30c	dk bl & red
802 A168	50c	ol blk & red
803 A168	18.15g	choc, red, & pink
804 A168	36g	grn bl & red
805 A168	50g	vio & red
a.		Souvenir sheet of 1

Nos. 803-805 are airmail.

Space Research A169

15c, 25c, 30c, Gemini spacecraft rendezvous with Agena rocket. 40c, 50c, Future Apollo and LunarModules. 12.45g, 18.15g, 50g, Telstar communications satellite, Olympic rings, vert.

1964, Mar. 11

806 A169	15c	vio & tan
807 A169	25c	grn & tan
808 A169	30c	bl & tan
809 A169	40c	brt bl & red
810 A169	50c	sl grn & red
811 A169	12.45g	dk bl & tan
812 A169	18.15g	dk grn bl & tan
813 A169	50g	dp vio & tan
a.		Souvenir sheet of 1

1964 Summer Olympic Games, Tokyo (#811-813a). Nos. 811-813a are airmail.

Rockets and Satellites A170

15c, 25c, Apollo command module mock-up. 30c, Tiros 7 weather satellite, vert. 40c, 50c, Ranger 6. 12.45g, 18.15g, 50g, Saturn I lift-off, vert.

1964, Apr. 25

814 A170	15c	brn & tan
815 A170	25c	vio & tan
816 A170	30c	Prus bl & lake
817 A170	40c	ver & tan
818 A170	50c	ultra & tan
819 A170	12.45g	grn bl & choc

820 A170 18.15g bl & choc
821 A170 50g lil rose & choc
a. Souvenir sheet of 1

Nos. 819-821a are airmail.

Popes Paul VI, John XXIII and St. Peter's, Rome — A171

Design: 12.45g, 18.15g, 36g, Asuncion Cathedral, Popes Paul VI and John XXIII.

1964, May 23 Wmk. 347

No.	Type	Denom.	Color	Unused	Used
822	A171	1.50g	claret & org	.15	.15
823	A171	3g	claret & dk grn	.15	.15
824	A171	4g	claret & bister	.15	.15
825	A171	12.45g	sl grn & lem	.18	.15
826	A171	18.15g	pur & lem	.25	.22
827	A171	36g	vio bl & lem	1.00	.80
			Set value	1.55	1.25

National holiday of St. Maria Auxiliadora (Our Lady of Perpetual Help).
Nos. 825-827 are airmail.

United Nations — A172

Designs: 15c, John F. Kennedy. 25c, 12.45g, Pope Paul VI and Patriarch Atenagoras. 30c, Eleanor Roosevelt, Chairman of UN Commission on Human Rights. 40c, Relay, Syncom and Telstar satellites. 50c, Echo 2 satellite. 18.15g, U Thant, UN Sec. Gen. 50g, Rocket, flags of Europe, vert.

Perf. 14x13½, 14 (15c, 25c, 12.45g)
1964, July 30 Unwmk.
Size: 35x35mm (#830, 834), 40x29mm (#831-832, 835)

828 A172 15c blk & brn
829 A172 25c blk, bl & red
830 A172 30c blk & ver
831 A172 40c dk bl & sep
832 A172 50c vio & car
833 A172 12.45g blk, grn & red
834 A172 18.15g blk & grn

Perf. 13½x14

835 A172 50g multicolored
a. Souvenir sheet of 1

Nos. 833-835a are airmail.

Space Achievements — A173

Designs: 10c, 30c, Ranger 7, Moon, vert. 15c, 12.45+6g, Wernher von Braun looking through telescope, vert. 20c, 20+10g, John F. Kennedy, rockets, vert. 40c, 18.15+9g, Rockets, von Braun.

1964, Sept. 12 ***Perf. 12½x12***

836 A173 10c bl & blk
837 A173 15c yel grn & brt pink
838 A173 20c yel org & bl
839 A173 30c mag & blk
840 A173 40c yel org, bl & blk
841 A173 12.45g +6g red & bl
a. Souvenir sheet of 2, #840-841
842 A173 18.15g +9g grn bl, brn & blk
843 A173 20g +10g red & bl

Nos. 841-843 are airmail.

Coats of Arms of Paraguay and France — A174

Designs: 3g, 12.45g, 36g, Presidents Stroessner and de Gaulle. 18.15g, Coats of Arms of Paraguay and France.

1964, Oct. 6 Wmk. 347

No.	Type	Denom.	Color	Unused	Used
844	A174	1.50g	brown	.15	.15
845	A174	3g	ultramarine	.15	.15
846	A174	4g	gray	.15	.15
847	A174	12.45g	lilac	.18	.15
848	A174	18.15g	bl grn	.25	.22
849	A174	36g	magenta	1.00	.80
			Set value	1.55	1.25

Visit of Pres. Charles de Gaulle of France.
Nos. 847-849 are airmail.

Boy Scout Jamborees — A175

Designs: 15c, 18.15g, Lord Robert Baden-Powell (1857-1941), Boy Scouts founder. 20c, 30c, 12.45g, Boy Scout emblem, map, vert.

1965, Jan. 15 Unwmk. ***Perf. 14***

850 A175 10c Argentina, 1961
851 A175 15c Peru, canceled
852 A175 20c Chile, 1959
853 A175 30c Brazil, 1954
854 A175 50c Uruguay, 1957
855 A175 12.45g Brazil, 1960
856 A175 18.15g Venezuela, 1964
857 A175 36g Brazil, 1963
a. Souvenir sheet of 1, perf. 12x12½

Nos. 855-857a are airmail.

A176 A177

Olympic and Paraguayan Medals: 25c, John F. Kennedy. 30c, Medal of Peace and Justice, reverse. 40c, Gens. Stroessner and DeGaulle, profiles. 50c, 18.15g, DeGaulle and Stroessner, in uniform. 12.45g, Medal of Peace and Justice, obverse.

Litho. & Embossed
1965, Mar. 30 ***Perf. 13½x13***

858 A176 15c multicolored
859 A176 25c multicolored
860 A176 30c multicolored

Perf. 12½x12

861 A176 40c multicolored
862 A176 50c multicolored
863 A176 12.45g multicolored
864 A176 18.15g multicolored
865 A176 50g multicolored
a. Souv. sheet of 1, perf. 13½x13

Nos. 863-865a are airmail. Medal on No. 865a is gold foil.

Overprint: "Centenario de la Epopeya Nacional 1.864-1.870"

Design: Map of Americas.

1965, Apr. 26 Wmk. 347 ***Perf. 11***

No.	Type	Denom.	Color	Unused	Used
866	A177	1.50g	dull grn	.15	.15
867	A177	3g	car red	.15	.15
868	A177	4g	dark blue	.15	.15
869	A177	12.45g	brn & blk	.15	.15
870	A177	36g	brt lil & blk	.50	.35
			Set value	.78	.60

Centenary of National Epic. Not issued without overprint.
Nos. 869-870 are airmail.

Scientists — A178

Unwmk.
1965, June 5 Litho. ***Perf. 14***

871 A178 10c Newton
872 A178 15c Copernicus
873 A178 20c Galileo
874 A178 30c like #871
875 A178 40c Einstein
876 A178 12.45g +6g like #873
a. Souvenir sheet of 2, #875-876
877 A178 18.15g +9g like #875
878 A178 20g +10g like #872

Nos. 876-878 are airmail.

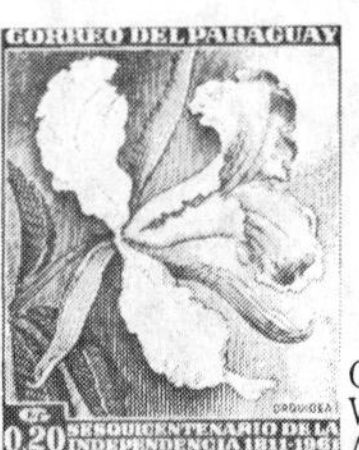

Cattleya Warscewiczii A179

Ceibo Tree — A179a

1965, June 28 Unwmk. ***Perf. 14½***

No.	Type	Denom.	Color	Unused	Used
879	A179	20c	purple	.15	.15
880	A179	30c	blue	.15	.15
881	A179	90c	bright mag	.15	.15
882	A179	1.50g	green	.15	.15
883	A179a	3g	brn red	.15	.15
884	A179a	4g	green	.15	.15
885	A179	4.50g	orange	.15	.15
886	A179a	66g	brn org	.75	.50
			Set value	1.10	.85

150th anniv. of Independence (1811-1961).
Nos. 883-884, 886 are airmail.

John F. Kennedy and Winston Churchill — A180

Designs: 15c, Kennedy, PT 109. 25c, Kennedy family. 30c, 12.45g, Churchill, Parliament building. 40c, Kennedy, Alliance for Progress emblem. 50c, 18.15g, Kennedy, rocket launch at Cape Canaveral. 50g, John Glenn, Kennedy, Lyndon Johnson examining Friendship 7.

1965, Sept. 4 ***Perf. 12x12½***

887 A180 15c bl & brn
888 A180 25c red & brn
889 A180 30c vio & blk
890 A180 40c org & sep
891 A180 50c bl grn & sep
892 A180 12.45g yel & blk
893 A180 18.15g car & blk
894 A180 50g grn & blk
a. Souvenir sheet of 1

Nos. 892-894a are airmail.

ITU, Cent. A181

Satellites: 10c, 40c, Ranger 7 transmitting to Earth. 15c, 20g+10g, Syncom, Olympic rings. 20c, 18.15g+9g, Early Bird. 30c, 12.45g+6g, Relay, Syncom, Telstar, and Echo 2.

1965, Sept. 30

895 A181 10c dull bl & sep
896 A181 15c lilac & sepia
897 A181 20c ol grn & sep
898 A181 30c blue & sepia
899 A181 40c grn & sep
900 A181 12.45g +6g ver & sep
a. Souvenir sheet of 2, #899-900
901 A181 18.15g +9g org & sep
902 A181 20g +10g vio & sep

Nos. 900-902 are airmail.

Pope Paul VI, Visit to UN A182

Designs: 10c, 50c, Pope Paul VI, U Thant, A. Fanfani. 15c, 12.45g, Pope Paul VI, Lyndon B. Johnson. 20c, 36g, Early Bird satellite, globe, papal arms. 30c, 18.15g, Pope Paul VI, Unisphere.

1966, Nov. 19

903 A182 10c multicolored
904 A182 15c multicolored
905 A182 20c multicolored
906 A182 30c multicolored
907 A182 50c multicolored
908 A182 12.45g multicolored
909 A182 18.15g multicolored
910 A182 36g multicolored
a. Souvenir sheet of 1

Nos. 908-910a are airmail.

Astronauts and Space Exploration — A183

Designs: 15c, 50g, Edward White walking in space, June 3, 1965. 25c, 18.15g, Gemini 7 & 8 docking, Dec. 16-18, 1965. 30c, Virgil I. Grissom and John W. Young, Mar. 23, 1965. 40c, 50c, Edward White and James McDivitt, June 3, 1965. 12.45g, Photographs of lunar surface.

1966, Feb. 19 ***Perf. 14***

911 A183 15c multicolored
912 A183 25c multicolored
913 A183 30c multicolored
914 A183 40c multicolored
915 A183 50c multicolored
916 A183 12.45g multicolored
917 A183 18.15g multicolored
918 A183 50g multicolored
a. Souvenir sheet of 1

Nos. 916-918a are airmail.

Events of 1965 — A184

10c, Meeting of Pope Paul VI & Cardinal Spellman, 10/4/65. 15c, Intl. Phil. Exposition, Vienna. 20c, OAS, 75th anniv. 30c, 36g, Intl. Quiet Sun Year, 1964-65. 50c, 18.15g, Saturn rockets at NY World's Fair. 12.45g, UN Intl. Cooperation Year.

1965, Mar. 9

No.	Type	Value	Description
919	A184	10c	multicolored
920	A184	15c	multicolored
921	A184	20c	multicolored
922	A184	30c	multicolored
923	A184	50c	multicolored
924	A184	12.45g	multicolored
925	A184	18.15g	multicolored
926	A184	36g	multicolored
a.			Souvenir sheet of 1

Nos. 924-926a are airmail.

1968 Summer Olympics, Mexico City — A185

Perf. 12½x12 (Nos. 927, 929, 931, 933), 13½x13

1966, Apr. 1

No.	Type	Value	Description
927	A185	10c	shown
928	A185	15c	God of Death
929	A185	20c	Aztec calendar stone
930	A185	30c	like No. 928
931	A185	50c	Zapotec deity
932	A185	12.45g	like No. 931
933	A185	18.15g	like No. 927
934	A185	36g	like No. 929
a.			Souvenir sheet of 1

Nos. 932-934a are airmail.

St. Ignatius Type of 1958 and

St. Ignatius and San Ignacio Monastery A185a

1966, Apr. 20 Wmk. 347 *Perf. 11*

No.	Type	Value	Description	Unused	Used
935	A129	15c	ultramarine	.15	.15
936	A129	25c	ultramarine	.15	.15
937	A129	75c	ultramarine	.15	.15
938	A129	90c	ultramarine	.15	.15
939	A185a	3g	brown	.15	.15
940	A185a	12.45g	sepia	.15	.15
941	A185a	18.15g	sepia	.15	.15
942	A185a	23.40g	sepia	.25	.20
			Set value	.75	.62

350th anniv. of the founding of San Ignacio Guazu Monastery.

Nos. 939-942 are airmail.

German Contributors in Space Research — A186

Designs: 10c, 36g, Paraguay #835, C97, Germany #C40. 15c, 50c, 18.15g, 3rd stage of Europa 1 rocket, vert. 20c, 12.45g, Hermann Oberth, jet propulsion engineer, vert. 30c, Reinhold K. Tiling, builder of 1st German rocket, 1931, vert.

Perf. 12x12½ (Nos. 943, 950), 12½x12 (Nos. 945, 947, 949), 13½x13

1966, May 16 Unwmk.

No.	Type	Value	Description
943	A186	10c	multicolored
944	A186	15c	multicolored
945	A186	20c	multicolored
946	A186	30c	multicolored
947	A186	50c	multicolored
948	A186	12.45g	multicolored
949	A186	18.15g	multicolored
950	A186	36g	multicolored
a.			Souvenir sheet of 1, perf. 12x13½x13x13½

Nos. 948-950a are airmail.

Writers — A187

1966, June 11 *Perf. 12x12½*

No.	Type	Value	Description
951	A187	10c	Dante
952	A187	15c	Moliere
953	A187	20c	Goethe
954	A187	30c	Shakespeare
955	A187	50c	like #952
956	A187	12.45g	like #953
957	A187	18.15g	like #954
958	A187	36g	like #951
a.			Souvenir sheet of 1, perf. 13½x14

Nos. 956-958a are airmail.

Italian Contributors in Space Research — A188

10c, 36g, Italian satellite, San Marco 1. 15c, 18.15g, Drafting machine, Leonardo Da Vinci. 20c, 12.45g, Map, Italo Balbo (1896-1940), aviator. 30c, 50c, Floating launch & control facility, satellite.

1966, July 11

No.	Type	Value	Description
959	A188	10c	multicolored
960	A188	15c	multicolored
961	A188	20c	multicolored
962	A188	30c	multicolored
963	A188	50c	multicolored
964	A188	12.45g	multicolored
965	A188	18.15g	multicolored
966	A188	36g	multicolored
a.			Souvenir sheet of 1, perf. 13x13½

Nos. 964-966a are airmail.

Rubén Dario — A189

"Paraguay de Fuego" by Dario — A189a

1966, July 16 Wmk. 347

No.	Type	Value	Description	Unused	Used
967	A189	50c	ultramarine	.15	.15
968	A189	70c	bister brn	.15	.15
969	A189	1.50g	rose car	.15	.15
970	A189	3g	violet	.15	.15
971	A189	4g	greenish bl	.15	.15
972	A189	5g	black	.15	.15
973	A189a	12.45g	blue	.15	.15
974	A189a	18.15g	red lil	.15	.15
975	A189a	23.40g	org brn	.25	.15
976	A189a	36g	brt grn	.38	.18
977	A189a	50g	rose car	.42	.20
			Nos. 967-977 (11)	2.25	
			Set value		1.50

50th death anniv. of Ruben Dario (pen name of Felix Rubén Garcia Sarmiento, 1867-1916), Nicaraguan poet, newspaper correspondent and diplomat.

Nos. 973-977 are airmail.

Space Missions — A190

1966, Aug. 25 Unwmk.

No.	Type	Value	Description
978	A190	10c	Gemini 8
979	A190	15c	Gemini 9
980	A190	20c	Surveyor 1 on moon
981	A190	30c	Gemini 10
982	A190	50c	like #981
983	A190	12.45g	like #980
984	A190	18.15g	like #979
985	A190	36g	like #978
a.			Souvenir sheet of 1, perf. 13x13½

Nos. 983-985a are airmail.

1968 Winter Olympics, Grenoble — A191

1966, Sept. 30 *Perf. 14*

No.	Type	Value	Description
986	A191	10c	Figure skating
987	A191	15c	Downhill skiing
988	A191	20c	Speed skating
989	A191	30c	2-man luge
990	A191	50c	like #989
991	A191	12.45g	like #988
992	A191	18.15g	like #987
993	A191	36g	like #986
a.			Souvenir sheet of 1

Nos. 987, 992, World Skiing Championships, Portillo, Chile, 1966. Nos. 991-993a are airmail.

Pres. John F. Kennedy, 3rd Death Anniv. — A192

Perf. 12x12½, 13½x14 (#997-998, 1001)

1966, Nov. 7

No.	Type	Value	Description
994	A192	10c	Echo 1 & 2
995	A192	15c	Telstar 1 & 2
996	A192	20c	Relay 1 & 2
997	A192	30c	Syncom 1, 2 & 3, Early Bird
998	A192	50c	like #997
999	A192	12.45g	like #996
1000	A192	18.15g	like #995
1001	A192	36g	like #994
a.			Souvenir sheet of 1, perf. 13x14x13½x14

Nos. 999-1001a are airmail.

Paintings — A193

Portraits of women by: No. 1002a, 10c, De Largilliere. b, 15c, Rubens. c, 20c, Titian. d, 30c, Hans Holbein. e, 50c, Sanchez Coello.

Paintings: No. 1003a, 12.45g, Mars and Venus with United by Love by Veronese. b, 18.15g, Allegory of Prudence, Peace and Abundance by Vouet. c, 36g, Madonna and Child by Andres Montegna.

1966, Dec. 10 *Perf. 14x13½*

No.	Type	Description
1002	A193	Strip of 5, #a.-e.
1003	A193	Strip of 3, #a.-c.
d.		Souvenir sheet of 1, #1003c

Nos. 1003a-1003d are airmail. No. 1003d has green pattern in border and is perf. 12½x12.

Holy Week Paintings A194

Life of Christ by: No. 1004a, 10c, Raphael. b, 15c, Rubens. c, 20c, Da Ponte. d, 30c, El Greco. e, 50c, Murillo, horiz.

12.45g, G. Reni. 18.15g, Tintoretto. 36g, Da Vinci, horiz.

Perf. 14x13½, 13½x14

1967, Feb. 28

No.	Type	Value	Description
1004	A194		Strip of 5, #a.-e.
1005	A194	12.45g	multicolored
1006	A194	18.15g	multicolored
1007	A194	36g	multicolored
a.			Souvenir sheet of 1

Nos. 1005-1007a are airmail. No. 1007a has salmon pattern in border and contains one 60x40mm, perf. 14 stamp.

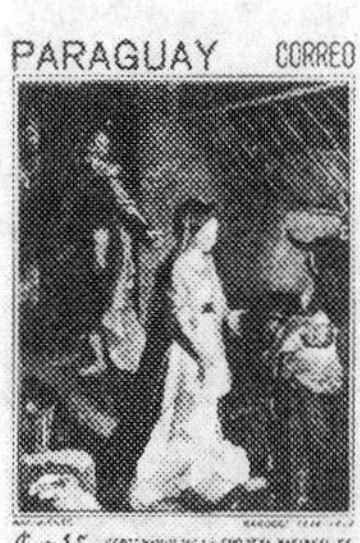

Birth of Christ by Barocci A195

16th Cent. Paintings: 12.45g, Madonna and Child by Caravaggio. 18.15g, Mary of the Holy Family (detail) by El Greco. 36g, Assumption of the Virgin by Vasco Fernandes.

1967, Mar. 10 *Perf. 14½*

No.	Type	Value	Description
1008	A195	10c	lt bl & multi
1009	A195	15c	lt grn & multi
1010	A195	20c	lt brn & multi
1011	A195	30c	lil & multi
1012	A195	50c	pink & multi
1013	A195	12.45g	lt bl grn & multi
1014	A195	18.15g	brt pink & multi
1015	A195	36g	lt vio & multi
a.			Souv. sheet of 1, sep & multi

Nos. 1013-1015a are airmail.

Exist imperf. with changed borders.

Globe and Lions Emblem — A196

Medical Laboratory "Health" — A196a

Designs: 1.50g, 3g, Melvin Jones. 4g, 5g, Lions' Headquarters, Chicago. 12.45g, 18.15g, Library "Education."

1967, May 9 Litho. Wmk. 347

1016	A196	50c	light vio	.15	.15
1017	A196	70c	blue	.15	.15
1018	A196	1.50g	ultra	.15	.15
1019	A196	3g	brown	.15	.15
1020	A196	4g	Prussian grn	.15	.15
1021	A196	5g	ol gray	.15	.15
1022	A196a	12.45g	dk brn	.15	.15
1023	A196a	18.15g	violet	.15	.15
1024	A196a	23.40g	rose cl	.15	.15
1025	A196a	36g	Prus blue	.30	.18
1026	A196a	50g	rose car	.35	.20
			Set value	1.20	.90

50th anniversary of Lions International.

Nos. 1022-1026 are airmail.

Vase of Flowers by Chardin A197

Still Life Paintings by: No. 1027b, 15c, Fontanesi, horiz. c, 20c, Cezanne. d, 30c, Van Gogh. e, 50c, Renoir.

Paintings: 12.45g, Cha-U-Kao at the Moulin Rouge by Toulouse-Lautrec. 18.15g, Gabrielle with Jean Renoir by Renoir. 36g, Patience Escalier, Shepherd of Provence by Van Gogh.

1967, May 16 *Perf. 12½x12*

1027	A197		Strip of 5, #a.-e.
1028	A197	12.45g	multicolored
1029	A197	18.15g	multicolored
1030	A197	36g	multicolored
a.			Souvenir sheet of 1, perf. 14x12x14x13½

Nos. 1028-1030a are airmail. No. 1030a has a green pattern in border.

Exist imperf. with changed borders.

Famous Paintings — A198

1967, July 16 *Perf. 12x12½*

1031 A198 10c Jan Steen

Perf. 14x13½, 13½x14

1032	A198	15c	Frans Hals, vert.
1033	A198	20c	Jordaens
1034	A198	25c	Rembrandt
1035	A198	30c	de Marees, vert.
1036	A198	50c	Quentin, vert.
1037	A198	12.45g	Nicolaes Maes, vert.
1038	A198	18.15g	Vigee-Lebrun, vert.
1039	A198	36g	Rubens, vert.

Souvenir Sheet

Perf. 12x12½

1040 A198 50g G. B. Tiepolo

Nos. 1037-1039 are airmail. An imperf. souvenir sheet of 3, #1037-1039 exists with dark green pattern in border.

John F. Kennedy, 50th Birth Anniv. A199

Kennedy and: 10c, Recovery of Alan Shepard's capsule, Lyndon Johnson, Mrs. Kennedy. 15c, John Glenn. 20c, Mr. and Mrs. M. Scott Carpenter. 25c, Rocket 2nd stage, Wernher Von Braun. 30c, Cape Canaveral, Walter Schirra. 50c, Syncom 2 satellite, horiz. 12.45g, Launch of Atlas rocket. 18.15g, Theorized lunar landing, horiz. 36g, Portrait of Kennedy by Torres. 50g, Apollo lift-off, horiz.

Perf. 14x13½, 13½x14

1967, Aug. 19

1041	A199	10c	multicolored
1042	A199	15c	multicolored
1043	A199	20c	multicolored
1044	A199	25c	multicolored
1045	A199	30c	multicolored
1046	A199	50c	multicolored
1047	A199	12.45g	multicolored
1048	A199	18.15g	multicolored
1049	A199	36g	multicolored

Souvenir Sheet

1050 A199 50g multicolored

Nos. 1047-1050 are airmail. An imperf. souvenir sheet of 3 containing #1047-1049 exists with violet border.

Sculptures A200

1967, Oct. 16 *Perf. 14x13½*

1051	A200	10c	Head of athlete
1052	A200	15c	Myron's Discobolus
1053	A200	20c	Apollo of Belvedere
1054	A200	25c	Artemis
1055	A200	30c	Venus De Milo
1056	A200	50c	Winged Victory of Samothrace
1057	A200	12.45g	Laocoon Group
1058	A200	18.15g	Moses
1059	A200	50g	Pieta

Nos. 1057-1059 are airmail.

Mexican Art — A201

Designs: 10c, Bowl, Veracruz. 15c, Knobbed vessel, Colima. 20c, Mixtec jaguar pitcher. 25c, Head, Veracruz. 30c, Statue of seated woman, Teotihuacan. 50c, Vessel depicting a woman, Aztec. 12.45g, Mixtec bowl, horiz. 18.15g, Three-legged vessel, Teotihuacan, horiz. 36g, Golden mask, Teotihuacan, horiz. 50g, The Culture of the Totonac by Diego Rivera, 1950, horiz.

1967, Nov. 29 *Perf. 14x13½*

1060	A201	10c	multicolored
1061	A201	15c	multicolored
1062	A201	20c	multicolored
1063	A201	25c	multicolored
1064	A201	30c	multicolored
1065	A201	50c	multicolored

Perf. 13½x14

1066	A201	12.45g	multicolored
1067	A201	18.15g	multicolored
1068	A201	36g	multicolored

Souvenir Sheet

Perf. 14

1069 A201 50g multicolored

1968 Summer Olympics, Mexico City (#1065-1069).

Nos. 1066-1069 are airmail. An imperf. souvenir sheet of 3 containing #1066-1068 exists with green pattern in border.

Paintings of the Madonna and Child A202

1968, Jan. 27 *Perf. 14x13½,13½x14*

1070	A202	10c	Bellini
1071	A202	15c	Raphael
1072	A202	20c	Correggio
1073	A202	25c	Luini
1074	A202	30c	Bronzino
1075	A202	50c	Van Dyck
1076	A202	12.45g	Vignon, horiz.
1077	A202	18.15g	de Ribera
1078	A202	36g	Botticelli

Nos. 1076-1078 are airmail and also exist as imperf. souvenir sheet of 3 with olive brown pattern in border.

Paintings of Winter Scenes — A203

1968 Winter Olympics Emblem A204

Perf. 13½x14, 14x13½

1968, Apr. 23

1079	A203	10c	Pissarro
1080	A203	15c	Utrillo, vert.
1081	A203	20c	Monet
1082	A203	25c	Breitner, vert.
1083	A203	30c	Sisley
1084	A203	50c	Brueghel, vert.
1085	A203	12.45g	Avercampe, vert.
1086	A203	18.15g	Brueghel, diff.
1087	A203	36g	P. Limbourg & brothers, vert.

Souvenir Sheet

1088 Sheet of 2
a. A204 50g multicolored

Nos. 1087-1088, 1088a are airmail. No. 1088 contains #1088a and #1087 with red pattern.

Paraguayan Stamps, Cent. (in 1970) — A205

Perf. 13½x14, 14x13½

1968, June 3 **Litho.**

1089	A205	10c	#1, 4
1090	A205	15c	#C21, 310, vert.
1091	A205	20c	#203, C140
1092	A205	25c	#C72, C61, vert.
1093	A205	30c	#638, 711
1094	A205	50c	#406, C38, vert.
1095	A205	12.45g	#B2, B7
1096	A205	18.15g	#C10, C11, vert.
1097	A205	36g	#828, C76, 616

Souvenir Sheet

Perf. 14

1098 Sheet of 2
a. A205 50g #929 & #379

Nos. 1095-1098a are airmail. No. 1098 contains No. 1098a and No. 1097 with light brown pattern in border.

Paintings A206

Designs: Nos. 1099-1106, paintings of children. Nos. 1107-1108, paintings of sailboats at sea.

1968, July 9 *Perf. 14x13½, 13½x14*

1099	A206	10c	Russell
1100	A206	15c	Velazquez
1101	A206	20c	Romney
1102	A206	25c	Lawrence
1103	A206	30c	Caravaggio
1104	A206	50c	Gentileschi
1105	A206	12.45g	Renoir
1106	A206	18.15g	Copley
1107	A206	36g	Sessions, horiz.

Souvenir Sheet

Perf. 14

1108 Sheet of 2
a. A206 50g Currier & Ives, horiz.

1968 Summer Olympics, Mexico City (Nos. 1107-1108).

Nos. 1106-1108a are airmail. No. 1108 contains No. 1108a and No. 1107 with a red pattern in border.

WHO Emblem

A207 A207a

1968, Aug. 12 Wmk. 347 *Perf. 11*

1109	A207	3g	bluish grn	.15	.15
1110	A207	4g	brt pink	.15	.15
1111	A207	5g	bister brn	.15	.15
1112	A207	10g	violet	.15	.15
1113	A207a	36g	blk brn	.30	.18
1114	A207a	50g	rose claret	.35	.22
1115	A207a	100g	brt bl	.75	.45
			Set value	1.55	1.00

WHO, 20th anniv.; cent. of the natl. epic.

39th Intl. Eucharistic Congress A208

Paintings of life of Christ by various artists (except No. 1125a).

Perf. 14x13½

1968, Sept. 25 Litho. Unwmk.

1116	A208	10c	Caravaggio
1117	A208	15c	El Greco
1118	A208	20c	Del Sarto
1119	A208	25c	Van der Weyden
1120	A208	30c	De Patinier
1121	A208	50c	Plockhorst
1122	A208	12.45g	Bronzino
1123	A208	18.15g	Raphael
1124	A208	36g	Correggio

Souvenir Sheet

Perf. 14

1125 Sheet of 2
a. A208 36g Pope Paul VI
b. A208 50g Tiepolo

Pope Paul VI's visit to South America (No. 1125). Nos. 1122-1125b are airmail.

Events of 1968 A209

Designs: 10c, Mexican 25p Olympic coin. 15c, Rentry of Echo 1 satellite. 20c, Visit of Pope Paul VI to Fatima, Portugal. 25c, Dr. Christian Barnard, 1st heart transplant. 30c, Martin Luther King, assasination. 50c, Pres. Alfredo Stroessner laying wreath at grave of Pres. Kennedy, vert. 12.45g, Pres. Stroessner, Pres. Lyndon B. Johnson. 18.15g, John F. Kennedy, Abraham Lincoln, Robert Kennedy. 50g, Summer Olympics, Mexico City, satellite transmissions, vert.

Perf. 13½x14, 14x13½

1968, Dec. 21

1126	A209	10c	multicolored
1127	A209	15c	multicolored
1128	A209	20c	multicolored
1129	A209	25c	multicolored
1130	A209	30c	multicolored
1131	A209	50c	multicolored
1132	A209	12.45g	multicolored
1133	A209	18.15g	multicolored
1134	A209	50g	multicolored

Nos. 1132-1134 are airmail. Set exists imperf. in sheets of 3 in changed colors.

1968 Summer Olympics, Mexico City — A210

Olympic Stadium A210a

Gold Medal Winners: 10c, Felipe Munoz, Mexico, 200-meter breast stroke. 15c, Daniel Rebillard, France, 4000-meter cycling. 20c, David Hemery, England, 400-meter hurdles. 25c, Bob Seagren, US, pole vault. 30c, Francisco Rodriguez, Venezuela, light flyweight boxing. 50c, Bjorn Ferm, Sweden, modern pentathlon. 12.45g, Klaus Dibiasi, Italy, platform diving. 50g, Ingrid Becker, West Germany, fencing, women's pentathlon.

1969, Feb. 13 *Perf. 14x13½*

1135	A210	10c	multicolored
1136	A210	15c	multicolored
1137	A210	20c	multicolored
1138	A210	25c	multicolored
1139	A210	30c	multicolored
1140	A210	50c	multicolored
1141	A210	12.45g	multicolored
1142	A210a	18.15g	multicolored
1143	A210	50g	multicolored

Nos. 1141-1143 are airmail. Set exists imperf. in sheets of 3 in changed colors.

Space Missions — A211

Designs: 10c, Apollo 7, John F. Kennedy. 15c, Apollo 8, Kennedy. 20c, Apollo 8, Kennedy, diff. 25c, Study of solar flares, ITU emblem. 30c, Canary Bird satellite. 50c, ESRO satellite. 12.45g, Wernher von Braun, rocket launch. 18.15g, Global satellite coverage, ITU emblem. 50g, Otto Lilienthal, Graf Zeppelin, Hermann Oberth, evolution of flight.

1969, Mar. 10 *Perf. 13½x14*

1144	A211	10c	multicolored
1145	A211	15c	multicolored
1146	A211	20c	multicolored
1147	A211	25c	multicolored
1148	A211	30c	multicolored
1149	A211	50c	multicolored
1150	A211	12.45g	multicolored
1151	A211	18.15g	multicolored
1152	A211	50g	multicolored

Nos. 1150-1152 are airmail. Set exists imperf. in sheets of 3 in changed colors.

"World United in Peace" — A212

1969, June 28 Wmk. 347 *Perf. 11*

1153	A212	50c	rose	.15	.15
1154	A212	70c	ultra	.15	.15
1155	A212	1.50g	light brn	.15	.15
1156	A212	3g	lil rose	.15	.15
1157	A212	4g	emerald	.15	.15
1158	A212	5g	violet	.15	.15
1159	A212	10g	brt lilac	.15	.15
			Set value	.45	.45

Peace Week.

Birds A213

Designs: 10c, Pteroglossus viridis. 15c, Phytotoma rutila. 20c, Porphyrula martinica. 25c, Oxyrunchus cristatus. 30c, Spizaetus ornatus. 50c, Phoenicopterus ruber. 75c, Amazona ochrocephala. 12.45g, Ara ararauna, Ara macao. 18.15g, Colibri coruscans.

Perf. 13½x14, 14x13½

1969, July 9 Unwmk.

1160	A213	10c	multicolored
1161	A213	15c	multicolored
1162	A213	20c	multicolored
1163	A213	25c	multicolored
1164	A213	30c	multicolored
1165	A213	50c	multicolored
1166	A213	75c	multicolored
1167	A213	12.45g	multicolored
1168	A213	18.15g	multicolored

Nos. 1167-1168 are airmail. Nos. 1161, 1164-1168 are vert.

Fauna A214

1969, July 9

1169	A214	10c	Porcupine
1170	A214	15c	Lemur, vert.
1171	A214	20c	3-toed sloth, vert.
1172	A214	25c	Puma
1173	A214	30c	Alligator
1174	A214	50c	Jaguar
1175	A214	75c	Anteater
1176	A214	12.45g	Tapir
1177	A214	18.15g	Capybara

Nos. 1176-1177 are airmail.

Olympic Soccer Champions, 1900-1968 A215

Designs: 10c, Great Britain, Paris, 1900. 15c, Canada, St. Louis, 1904. 20c, Great Britain, London, 1908 and Stockholm, 1912. 25c, Belgium, Antwerp, 1920. 30c, Uruguay, Paris, 1924 and Amsterdam, 1928. 50c, Italy, Berlin, 1936. 75c, Sweden, London, 1948; USSR, Melbourne, 1956. 12.45g, Yugoslavia, Rome, 1960. 18.15g, Hungary, Helsinki, 1952, Tokyo, 1964 and Mexico, 1968.

1969, Nov. 26 *Perf. 14*

1178	A215	10c	multicolored
1179	A215	15c	multicolored
1180	A215	20c	multicolored
1181	A215	25c	multicolored
1182	A215	30c	multicolored
1183	A215	50c	multicolored
1184	A215	75c	multicolored
1185	A215	12.45g	multicolored
1186	A215	18.15g	multicolored

Nos. 1185-1186 are airmail.

A216

World Cup or South American Soccer Champions: 10c, Paraguay, 1953. 15c, Uruguay, 1930. 20c, Italy, 1934. 25c, Italy, 1938. 30c, Uruguay, 1950. 50c, Germany, 1954, horiz. 75c, Brazil, 1958. 12.45g, Brazil, 1962. 18.15g, England, 1966. No. 1198, Trophy.

1969, Nov. 26 *Perf. 14*

1189	A216	10c	multicolored
1190	A216	15c	multicolored
1191	A216	20c	multicolored
1192	A216	25c	multicolored
1193	A216	30c	multicolored
1194	A216	50c	multicolored
1195	A216	75c	multicolored
1196	A216	12.45g	multicolored
1197	A216	18.15g	multicolored

Souvenir Sheet

Perf. 13½

1198 A216 23.40g multicolored

Nos. 1196-1198 are airmail. No. 1198 contains one 50x60mm stamp.

Paintings by Francisco de Goya (1746-1828) A217

Designs: 10c, Miguel de Lardibazal. 15c, Francisca Sabasa y Gracia. 20c, Don Manuel Osorio. 25c, Young Women with a Letter. 30c, The Water Carrier. 50c, Truth, Time and History. 75c, The Forge. 12.45g, The Spell. 18.15g, Duke of Wellington on Horseback. 23.40g, "La Maja Desnuda."

1969, Nov. 29 Litho. *Perf. 14x13½*

1200	A217	10c	multicolored
1201	A217	15c	multicolored
1202	A217	20c	multicolored
1203	A217	25c	multicolored
1204	A217	30c	multicolored
1205	A217	50c	multicolored
1206	A217	75c	multicolored
1207	A217	12.45g	multicolored
1208	A217	18.15g	multicolored

Souvenir Sheet

Perf. 14

1209 A217 23.40g multicolored

Nos. 1207-1209 are airmail.

Christmas A218

Various paintings of The Nativity or Madonna and Child.

1969, Nov. 29 *Perf. 14x13½*

1210	A218	10c	Master Bertram
1211	A218	15c	Procaccini
1212	A218	20c	Di Crediti
1213	A218	25c	De Flemalle
1214	A218	30c	Correggio
1215	A218	50c	Borgianni
1216	A218	75c	Botticelli
1217	A218	12.45g	El Greco

1218 A218 18.15g De Morales

Souvenir Sheet

Perf. ***13½***

1219 A218 23.40g Isenheimer Altar

Nos. 1217-1219 are airmail.

Souvenir Sheet

European Space Program — A219

1969, Nov. 29 Litho. ***Perf. 14***

1220 A219 23.40g ESRO 1B

Imperf

1221 A219 23.40g Ernst Stuhlinger

Francisco Solano — A220

1970, Mar. 1 Wmk. 347 ***Perf. 11***

1222 A220 1g bis brn .15 .15
1223 A220 2g violet .15 .15
1224 A220 3g brt pink .15 .15
1225 A220 4g rose claret .15 .15
1226 A220 5g blue .15 .15
1227 A220 10g bright grn .15 .15
1228 A220 15g lt Prus bl .15 .15
1229 A220 20g org brn .15 .15
1230 A220 30g gray grn .22 .15
1231 A220 40g gray brn .28 .20
Set value 1.00 .80

Marshal Francisco Solano Lopez (1827-1870), President of Paraguay. Nos. 1228-1231 are airmail.

1st Moon Landing, Apollo 11 — A221

Designs: 10c, Wernher von Braun, lift-off. 15c, Eagle and Columbia in lunar orbit. 20c, Deployment of lunar module. 25c, Landing on Moon. 30c, First steps on lunar surface. 50c, Gathering lunar soil. 75c, Lift-off from Moon. 12.45g, Rendevouz of Eagle and Columbia. 18.15g, Pres. Kennedy, von Braun, splashdown. No. 1241, Gold medal of Armstrong, Aldrin and Collins. No. 1242, Moon landing medal, Kennedy, von Braun. No. 1243, Apollo 12 astronauts Charles Conrad and Alan Bean on moon, and Dr. Kurt Debus.

1970, Mar. 11 Unwmk. ***Perf. 14***

1232 A221 10c multicolored
1233 A221 15c multicolored
1234 A221 20c multicolored
1235 A221 25c multicolored
1236 A221 30c multicolored
1237 A221 50c multicolored
1238 A221 75c multicolored
1239 A221 12.45g multicolored
1240 A221 18.15g multicolored

Souvenir Sheets

1241 A221 23.40g multicolored

Imperf

1242 A221 23.40g multicolored
1243 A221 23.40g multicolored

Nos. 1239-1243 are airmail. Nos. 1241-1242 contain one 50x60mm stamp, No. 1243 one 60x50mm stamp.

Easter A222

Designs: 10c, 15c, 20c, 25c, 30c, 50c, 75c, Stations of the Cross. 12.45g, Christ appears to soldiers, vert. 18.15g, Christ appears to disciples, vert. 23.40g, The sad Madonna, vert.

1970, Mar. 11

1244 A222 10c multicolored
1245 A222 15c multicolored
1246 A222 20c multicolored
1247 A222 25c multicolored
1248 A222 30c multicolored
1249 A222 50c multicolored
1250 A222 75c multicolored
1251 A222 12.45g multicolored
1252 A222 18.15g multicolored

Souvenir Sheet

Perf. ***13½***

1253 A222 23.40g multicolored

Nos. 1251-1253 are airmail. No. 1253 contains one 50x60mm stamp.

Paraguay No. 2 — A223

Designs (First Issue of Paraguay): 2g, 10g, #1. 3g, #3. 5g, #2. 15g, #3. 30g, #2. 36g, #1.

1970, Aug. 15 Litho. Wmk. 347

1254 A223 1g car rose .15 .15
1255 A223 2g ultra .15 .15
1256 A223 3g org brn .15 .15
1257 A223 5g violet .15 .15
1258 A223 10g lilac .15 .15
1259 A223 15g vio brn .22 .18
1260 A223 30g dp grn .45 .38
1261 A223 36g brt pink .50 .42
Set value 1.40 1.20

Centenary of stamps of Paraguay.

1972 Summer Olympics, Munich A224

No. 1262: a, 10c, Discus. b, 15c, Cycling. c, 20c, Men's hurdles. d, 25c, Fencing. e, 30c, Swimming, horiz.

50c, Shotput. 75c, Sailing. 12.45, Women's hurdles, horiz. 18.15g, Equestrian, horiz. No. 1267, Flags, Olympic coins. No. 1268, Frauenkirche Church, Munich. No. 1269, Olympic Village, Munich, horiz.

1970, Sept. 28 Unwmk. ***Perf. 14***

1262 A224 Strip of 5, #a.-e.
1263 A224 50c multicolored
1264 A224 75c multicolored
1265 A224 12.45g multicolored
1266 A224 18.15g multicolored

Souvenir Sheets

Perf. ***13½***

1267 A224 23.40g multicolored

Imperf

1268 A224 23.40g multicolored
1269 A224 23.40g multicolored

Nos. 1265-1269 are airmail. Nos. 1267-1269 each contain one 50x60mm stamp.

Paintings, Pinakothek, Munich, 1972 A225

Nudes by: No. 1270a, 10c, Cranach. b, 15c, Baldung. c, 20c, Tintoretto. d, 25c, Rubens. e, 30c, Boucher, horiz. 50c, Baldung, diff. 75c, Cranach, diff.

12.45g, Self-portrait, Durer. 18.15g, Alterpiece, Altdorfer. 23.40g, Madonna and Child.

1970, Sept. 28 ***Perf. 14***

1270 A225 Strip of 5, #a.-e.
1271 A225 50c multicolored
1272 A225 75c multicolored
1273 A225 12.45g multicolored
1274 A225 18.15g multicolored

Souvenir Sheet

Perf. ***13½***

1275 A225 23.40g multicolored

Nos. 1273-1275 are airmail. No. 1275 contains one 50x60mm stamp.

Apollo Space Program — A226

No. 1276: a, 10c, Ignition, Saturn 5. b, 15c, Apollo 1 mission emblem, vert. c, 20c, Apollo 7, Oct. 1968. d, 25c, Apollo 8, Dec. 1968. e, 30c, Apollo 9, Mar. 1969.

50c, Apollo 10, May 1969. 75c, Apollo 11, July 1969. 12.45g, Apollo 12, Nov. 1969. 18.15g, Apollo 13, Apr. 1970. No. 1281, Lunar landing sites. No. 1282, Wernher von Braun, rockets. No. 1283, James A. Lovell, John L. Swigert, Fred W. Haise.

1970, Oct. 19 ***Perf. 14***

1276 A226 Strip of 5, #a.-e.
1277 A226 50c multicolored
1278 A226 75c multicolored
1279 A226 12.45g multicolored
1280 A226 18.15g multicolored

Souvenir Sheets

Perf. ***13½***

1281 A226 23.40g multicolored

Imperf

1282 A226 23.40g multicolored
1283 A226 23.40g multicolored

Nos. 1279-1283 are airmail. Nos. 1281-1283 each contain one 60x50mm stamp.

1970, Oct. 19 ***Perf. 14***

Future Space Projects: No. 1284a, 10c, Space station, 2000. b, 15c, Lunar station, vert. c, 20c, Space transport. d, 25c, Lunar rover. e, 30c, Skylab.

50c, Space station, 1971. 75c, Lunar vehicle. 12.45g, Lunar vehicle, diff., vert. 18.15g, Vehicle rising above lunar surface. 23.40g, Moon stations, transport.

1284 A226 Strip of 5, #a.-e.
1285 A226 50c multicolored
1286 A226 75c multicolored
1287 A226 12.45g multicolored
1288 A226 18.15g multicolored

Souvenir Sheet

Perf. ***13½***

1289 A226 23.40g multicolored

Nos. 1287-1289 are airmail. No. 1289 contains one 50x60mm stamp. For overprints see Nos. 2288-2290, C653.

EXPO '70, Osaka, Japan A228

Paintings from National Museum, Tokyo: No. 1288a, 10c, Buddha. b, 15c, Fire, people. c, 20c, Demon, Ogata Korin. d, 25c, Japanese play, Hishikawa Moronobu. e, 30c, Birds.

50c, Woman, Utamaro. 75c, Samurai, Wantabe Kazan. 12.45c, Women Beneath Tree, Kano Hideroi. 18.15g, Courtesans, Torrii Kiyonaga. 50g, View of Mt. Fuji, Hokusai, horiz. No. 1296, Courtesan, Kaigetsudo Ando. No. 1297, Emblem of Expo '70. No. 1298, Emblem of 1972 Winter Olympics, Sapporo.

1970, Nov. 26 Litho. ***Perf. 14***

1290 A228 Strip of 5, #a.-e.
1291 A228 50c multicolored
1292 A228 75c multicolored
1293 A228 12.45g multicolored
1294 A228 18.15g multicolored
1295 A228 50g multicolored

Souvenir Sheets

Perf. ***13½***

1296 A228 20g multicolored
1297 A228 20g multicolored
1298 A228 20g multicolored

Nos. 1293-1298 are airmail. Nos. 1296-1298 each contain one 50x60mm stamp.

Flower Paintings A229

Artists: No. 1299a, 10c, Von Jawlensky. b, 15c, Purrmann. c, 20c, De Vlaminck. d, 25c, Monet. e, 30c, Renoir.

50c, Van Gogh. 75, Cezanne. 12.45g, Van Huysum. 18.15g, Ruysch. 50g, Walscappelle. 20g, Bosschaert.

1970, Nov. 26 ***Perf. 14***

1299 A229 Strip of 5, #a.-e.
1300 A229 50c multicolored
1301 A229 75c multicolored
1302 A229 12.45g multicolored
1303 A229 18.15g multicolored
1304 A229 50g multicolored

Souvenir Sheet

Perf. ***13½***

1305 A229 20g multicolored

Nos. 1302-1305 are airmail. No. 1305 contains one 50x60mm stamp.

Paintings from The Prado, Madrid — A230

Nudes by: No. 1306a, 10c, Titian. b, 15c, Velazquez. c, 20c, Van Dyck. d, 25c, Tintoretto. e, 30c, Rubens.

50c, Venus and Sleeping Adonis, Veronese. 75c, Adam and Eve, Titian. 12.45g, The Holy Family, Goya. 18.15g, Shepherd Boy, Murillo. 50g, The Holy Family, El Greco.

1970, Dec. 16 ***Perf. 14***

1306 A230 Strip of 5, #a.-e.
1307 A230 50c multicolored
1308 A230 75c multicolored

1309 A230 12.45g multicolored
1310 A230 18.15g multicolored
1311 A230 50g multicolored

#1309-1311 are airmail. #1307-1311 are vert.

1970, Dec. 16

Paintings by Albrecht Durer (1471-1528): No. 1312a, 10c, Adam and Eve. b, 15c, St. Jerome in the Wilderness. c, 20c, St. Eustachius and George. d, 25c, Piper and drummer. e, 30c, Lucretia's Suicide.

50c, Oswald Krel. 75c, Stag Beetle. 12.45g, Paul and Mark. 18.15g, Lot's Flight. 50g, Nativity.

1312 A230 Strip of 5, #a.-e.
1313 A230 50c multicolored
1314 A230 75c multicolored
1315 A230 12.45g multicolored
1316 A230 18.15g multicolored
1317 A230 50g multicolored

Nos. 1315-1317 are airmail. See No. 1273.

Christmas
A232

Paintings: No. 1318a, 10c, The Annunciation, Van der Weyden. b, 15c, The Madonna, Zeitblom. c, 20c, The Nativity, Von Soest. d, 25c, Adoration of the Magi, Mayno. e, 30c, Adoration of the Magi, Da Fabriano.

50c, Flight From Egypt, Masters of Martyrdom. 75c, Presentation of Christ, Memling. 12.45g, The Holy Family, Poussin, horiz. 18.15g, The Holy Family, Rubens. 20g, Adoration of the Magi, Giorgione, horiz. 50g, Madonna and Child, Batoni.

1971, Mar. 23

1318 A232 Strip of 5, #a.-e.
1319 A232 50c multicolored
1320 A232 75c multicolored
1321 A232 12.45g multicolored
1322 A232 18.15g multicolored
1323 A232 50g multicolored

Souvenir Sheet

Perf. 13½

1324 A232 20g multicolored

Nos. 1321-1324 are airmail. No. 1324 contains one 60x50mm stamp.

1972 Summer Olympics, Munich
A233

Olympic decathlon gold medalists: No. 1325a, 10c, Hugo Wieslander, Stockholm 1912. b, 15c, Helge Lovland, Antwerp 1920. c, 20c, Harald M. Osborn, Paris 1924. d, 25c, Paavo Yrjola, Amsterdam 1928. e, 30c, James Bausch, Los Angeles 1932.

50c, Glenn Morris, Berlin 1936. 75c, Bob Mathias, London 1948, Helsinki 1952. 12.45g, Milton Campbell, Melbourne 1956. 18.15g, Rafer Johnson, Rome 1960. 50g, Willi Holdorf, Tokyo 1964. No. 1331, Bill Toomey, Mexico City 1968.

No. 1332, Pole vaulter, Munich, 1972.

1971, Mar. 23 ***Perf. 14***

1325 A233 Strip of 5, #a.-e.
1326 A233 50c multicolored
1327 A233 75c multicolored
1328 A233 12.45g multicolored
1329 A233 18.15g multicolored
1330 A233 50g multicolored

Souvenir Sheets

Perf. 13½

1331 A233 20g multicolored
1332 A233 20g multicolored

Nos. 1328-1332 are airmail. Nos. 1331-1332 each contain one 50x60mm stamp.

Art
A234

Paintings by: No. 1333a, 10c, Van Dyck. b, 15c, Titian. c, 20c, Van Dyck, diff. d, 25c, Walter. e, 30c, Orsi.

50c, 17th cent. Japanese artist, horiz. 75c, David. 12.45g, Huguet. 18.15g, Perugino. 20g, Van Eyck. 50g, Witz.

1971, Mar. 26 ***Perf. 14***

1333 A234 Strip of 5, #a.-e.
1334 A234 50c multicolored
1335 A234 75c multicolored
1336 A234 12.45g multicolored
1337 A234 18.15g multicolored
1338 A234 50g multicolored

Souvenir Sheet

Perf. 13½

1339 A234 20g multicolored

Nos. 1336-1339 are airmail. No. 1339 contains one 50x60mm stamp.

Paintings from the Louvre, Paris

Portraits of women by: No. 1340a, 10c, De la Tour. b, 15c, Boucher. c, 20c, Delacroix. d, 25c, 16th cent. French artist. e, 30c, Ingres.

50c, Ingres, horiz. 75c, Watteau, horiz. 12.45g, 2nd cent. artist. 18.15g, Renoir. 20g, Mona Lisa, Da Vinci. 50g, Liberty Guiding the People, Delacroix.

1971, Mar. 26 ***Perf. 14***

1340 A234 Strip of 5, #a.-e.
1341 A234 50c multicolored
1342 A234 75c multicolored
1343 A234 12.45g multicolored
1344 A234 18.15g multicolored
1345 A234 50g multicolored

Souvenir Sheet

Perf. 13½

1346 A234 20g multicolored

Nos. 1343-1346 are airmail. No. 1346 contains one 50x60mm stamp.

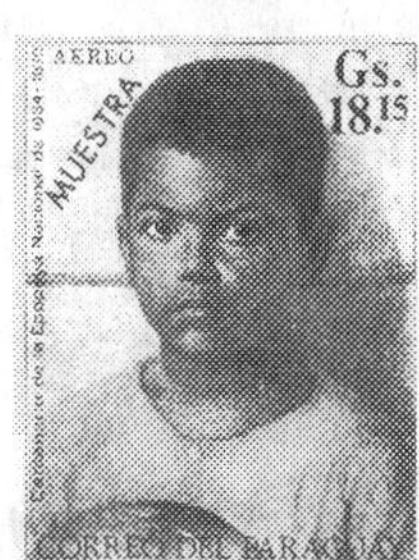

Paintings
A236

Artist: No. 1347a, 10c, Botticelli. b, 15c, Titian. c, 20c, Raphael. d, 25c, Pellegrini. e, 30c, Caracci.

50c, Titian, horiz. 75c, Ricci, horiz. 12.45g, Courtines. 18.15g, Rodas. 50g, Murillo.

1971, Mar. 29 ***Perf. 14***

1347 A236 Strip of 5, #a.-e.
1348 A236 50c multicolored
1349 A236 75c multicolored
1350 A236 12.45g multicolored
1351 A236 18.15g multicolored
1352 A236 50g multicolored

Nos. 1350-1352 are airmail.

Hunting Scenes — A237

Different Paintings by: No. 1353a, 10c, Gozzoli, vert. b, 15c, Velazquez, vert. c, 20c, Brun. d, 25c, Fontainebleau School, 1550, vert. e, 30c, Uccello, vert.

50c, P. De Vos. 75c, Vernet. 12.45g, 18.15g, 50g, Alken & Sutherland. No. 1359, Paul & Derveaux. No. 1360, Degas.

1971, Mar. 29

1353 A237 Strip of 5, #a.-e.
1354 A237 50c multicolored
1355 A237 75c multicolored
1356 A237 12.45g multicolored
1357 A237 18.15g multicolored
1358 A237 50g multicolored

Souvenir Sheets

Perf. 13½

1359 A237 20g multicolored
1360 A237 20g multicolored

Nos. 1356-1360 are airmail. Nos. 1359-1360 each contain one 60x50mm stamp.

Philatokyo '71
A238

Designs: Nos. 1361a-1361e, 10c, 15c, 20c, 25c, 30c, Different flowers, Gukei. 50c, Birds, Lu Chi. 75c, Flowers, Sakai Hoitsu. 12.45g, Man and Woman, Utamaro. 18.15g, Tea Ceremony, from Tea museum. 50g, Bathers, Utamaro. No. 1367, Woman, Kamakura Period. No. 1368, Japan #1, #821, #904, #1023.

1971, Apr. 7 ***Perf. 14***

1361 A238 Strip of 5, #a.-e.
1362 A238 50c multicolored
1363 A238 75c multicolored
1364 A238 12.45g multicolored
1365 A238 18.15g multicolored
1366 A238 50g multicolored

Souvenir Sheets

Perf. 13½

1367 A238 20g multicolored
1368 A238 20g multicolored

Nos. 1364-1368 are airmail. Nos. 1367-1368 each contain one 50x60mm stamp.

See Nos. 1375-1376.

1972 Winter Olympics, Sapporo
A239

Paintings of women by: No. 1369a, 10c, Harunobu. b, 15c, Hosoda. c, 20c, Harunobu, diff. d, 25c, Uemura Shoen. e, 30c, Ketao.

50c, Three Women, Torii. 75c, Old Man, Kakizahi. 12.45g, 2-man bobsled. 18.15g, Ice sculptures, horiz. 50g, Mt. Fuji, Hokusai, horiz. No. 1375, Skier, horiz. No. 1376, Sapporo Olympic emblems.

1971, Apr. ***Perf. 14***

1369 A239 Strip of 5, #a.-e.
1370 A239 50c multicolored
1371 A239 75c multicolored
1372 A239 12.45g multicolored
1373 A239 18.15g multicolored
1374 A239 50g multicolored

Souvenir Sheets

Perf. 14½

1375 A239 20g multicolored

Perf. 13½

1376 A239 20g multicolored

Nos. 1372-1376 are airmail. No. 1375 contains one 35x25mm stamp with PhilaTokyo 71 emblem. No. 1376 contains one 50x60mm stamp.

For Japanese painting stamps with white border and Winter Olympics emblem see #1409-1410.

UNESCO and Paraguay Emblems, Globe, Teacher and Pupil — A240

Wmk. 347

1971, May 18 **Litho.** ***Perf. 11***

1377	A240	3g	ultra	.15	.15
1378	A240	5g	lilac	.15	.15
1379	A240	10g	emerald	.15	.15
1380	A240	20g	claret	.15	.15
1381	A240	25g	brt pink	.18	.15
1382	A240	30g	brown	.20	.15
1383	A240	50g	gray olive	.35	.25
			Set value	1.00	.75

International Education Year.
Nos. 1380-1383 are airmail.

Paintings, Berlin-Dahlem Museum — A241

Artists: 10c, Caravaggio. No. 1385: a, 15c, b, 20c, Di Cosimo. 25c, Cranach. 30c, Veneziano. 50g, Holbein. 75c, Baldung. 12.45g, Cranach, diff. 18.15g, Durer. 50g, Schongauer.

1971, Dec. 24 **Unwmk.** ***Perf. 14***

1384 A241 10c multicolored
1385 A241 Pair, #a.-b.
1386 A241 25c multicolored
1387 A241 30c multicolored
1388 A241 50c multicolored
1389 A241 75c multicolored
1390 A241 12.45g multicolored
1391 A241 18.15g multicolored
1392 A241 50g multicolored

Nos. 1390-1392 are airmail. No. 1385 has continuous design.

Napoleon I, 150th Death Anniv.
A242

Paintings: No. 1393a, 10c, Desiree Clary, Gerin. b, 15c, Josephine de Beauharnais, Gros. c, 20c, Maria Luisa, Gerard. d, 25c, Juliette Recamier, Gerard. e, 30c, Maria Walewska, Gerard.

50c, Victoria Kraus, unknown artist, horiz. 75c, Napoleon on Horseback, Chabord. 12.45g, Trafalgar, A. Mayer, horiz. 18.15g, Napoleon Leading Army, Gautherot, horiz.

50g, Napoleon's tomb.

1971, Dec. 24

1393 A242 Strip of 5, #a.-e.
1394 A242 50c multicolored
1395 A242 75c multicolored
1396 A242 12.45g multicolored
1397 A242 18.15g multicolored
1398 A242 50g multicolored

Nos. 1396-1398 are airmail.

Locomotives — A243

Designs: No. 1399a, 10c, Trevithick, Great Britain, 1804. b, 15c, Blenkinsops, 1812. c, 20c, G. Stephenson #1, 1825. d, 25c, Marc Seguin, France, 1829. e, 30c, "Adler," Germany, 1835.
50c, Sampierdarena #1, Italy, 1854. 75c, Paraguay #1, 1861. 12.45g, "Munich," Germany, 1841. 18.15g, US, 1875. 20g, Japanese locomotives, 1872-1972. 50g, Mikado D-50, Japan, 1923.

1972, Jan. 6

1399 A243 Strip of 5, #a.-e.
1400 A243 50c multicolored
1401 A243 75c multicolored
1402 A243 12.45g multicolored
1403 A243 18.15g multicolored
1404 A243 50g multicolored

Souvenir Sheet

Perf. 13¹/₂

1405 A243 20g multicolored

Nos. 1402-1405 are airmail. No. 1405 contains one 60x50mm stamp.
See Nos. 1476-1480.

1972 Winter Olympics, Sapporo — A244

Designs: Nos. 1406a, 10c, Hockey player. b, 15c, Jean-Claude Killy. c, 20c, Gaby Seyfert. d, 25c, 4-Man bobsled. e, 30c, Luge.
50c, Ski jumping, horiz. 75c, Slalom skiing, horiz. 12.45g, Painting, Kuniyoshi. 18.15g, Winter Scene, Hiroshige, horiz. 50g, Ski lift, man in traditional dress.

1972, Jan. 6 ***Perf. 14***

1406 A244 Strip of 5, #a.-e.
1407 A244 50c multicolored
1408 A244 75c multicolored
1409 A244 12.45g multicolored
1410 A244 18.15g multicolored
1411 A244 50g multicolored

Souvenir Sheet

Perf. 13¹/₂

1412 A244 20g Skier
1413 A244 20g Flags

Nos. 1409-1413 are airmail. Nos. 1412-1413 each contain one 50x60mm stamp. For overprint see Nos. 2295-2297. For Winter Olympic stamps with gold border, see Nos. 1372-1373.

UNICEF, 25th Anniv. (in 1971) — A245

1972, Jan. 24

Granite Paper

1414	A245	1g	red brn	.15	.15
1415	A245	2g	ultra	.15	.15
1416	A245	3g	lil rose	.15	.15
1417	A245	4g	violet	.15	.15
1418	A245	5g	emerald	.15	.15
1419	A245	10g	claret	.15	.15
1420	A245	20g	brt bl	.15	.15
1421	A245	25g	lt ol	.18	.15
1422	A245	30g	dk brn	.20	.15
			Set value	.82	.65

Nos. 1420-1422 are airmail.

Race Cars — A246

No. 1423: a, 10c, Ferrari. b, 15c, B.R.M. c, 20c, Brabham. d, 25c, March. e, 30c, Honda.
50c, Matra-Simca MS 650. 75c, Porsche. 12.45g, Maserati-8 CTF, 1938. 18.15g, Bugatti 35B, 1929. 20g, Lotus 72 Ford. 50g, Mercedes, 1924.

1972, Mar. 20 **Unwmk.** ***Perf. 14***

1423 A246 Strip of 5, #a.-e.
1424 A246 50c multicolored
1425 A246 75c multicolored
1426 A246 12.45g multicolored
1427 A246 18.15g multicolored
1428 A246 50g multicolored

Souvenir Sheet

Perf. 13¹/₂

1429 A246 20g multicolored

Nos. 1426-1429 are airmail. No. 1429 contains one 60x50mm stamp.

Sailing Ships — A247

Paintings: No. 1430a, 10c, Holbein. b, 15c, Nagasaki print. c, 20c, Intrepid, Roux. d, 25c, Portuguese ship, unknown artist. e, 30c, Mount Vernon, US, 1798, Corne.
50c, Van Eertvelt, vert. 75c, Santa Maria, Van Eertvelt, vert. 12.45g, Royal Prince, 1679, Van Beecq. 18.15g, Van Bree. 50g, Book of Arms, 1497, vert.

1972, Mar. 29 ***Perf. 14***

1430 A247 Strip of 5, #a.-e.
1431 A247 50c multicolored
1432 A247 75c multicolored
1433 A247 12.45g multicolored
1434 A247 18.15g multicolored
1435 A247 50g multicolored

Nos. 1433-1435 are airmail.

Paintings in Vienna Museum A248

Nudes by: No. 1436a, 10c, Rubens. b, 15c, Bellini. c, 20c, Carracci. d, 25c, Cagnacci. e, 30c, Spranger.
50c, Mandolin Player, Strozzi. 75c, Woman in Red Hat, Cranach the elder. 12.45g, Adam and Eve, Coxcie. 18.15g, Legionary on Horseback, Poussin. 50g, Madonna and Child, Bronzino.

1972, May 22

1436 A248 Strip of 5, #a.-e.
1437 A248 50c multicolored
1438 A248 75c multicolored
1439 A248 12.45g multicolored
1440 A248 18.15g multicolored
1441 A248 50g multicolored

Nos. 1439-1441 are airmail.

Paintings in Asuncion Museum A249

No. 1442: a, 10c, Man in Straw Hat, Holden Jara. b, 15c, Portrait, Tintoretto. c, 20c, Indians, Holden Jara. d, 25c, Nude, Bouchard. e, 30c, Italian School.
50c, Reclining Nude, Berisso, horiz. 75c, Carracci, horiz. 12.45g, Reclining Nude, Schiaffino, horiz. 18.15g, Reclining Nude, Lostow, horiz. 50g, Madonna and Child, 17th cent. Italian School.

1972, May 22

1442 A249 Strip of 5, #a.-e.
1443 A249 50c multicolored
1444 A249 75c multicolored
1445 A249 12.45g multicolored
1446 A249 18.15g multicolored
1447 A249 50g multicolored

Nos. 1445-1447 are airmail.

Presidential Summit A250

No. 1448: a, 10c, Map of South America. b, 15c, Brazil natl. arms. c, 20c, Argentina natl. arms. d, 25c, Bolivia natl. arms. e, 30c, Paraguay natl. arms.
50c, Pres. Emilio Garrastazu, Brazil. 75c, Pres. Alejandro Lanusse, Argentina. 12.45g, Pres. Hugo Banzer Suarez, Bolivia. 18.15, Pres. Stroessner, Paraguay, horiz. 23.40g, Flags.

1972, Nov. 18

1448 A250 Strip of 5, #a.-e.
1449 A250 50c multicolored
1450 A250 75c multicolored
1451 A250 12.45g multicolored
1452 A250 18.15g multicolored

Souvenir Sheet

Perf. 13¹/₂

1453 A250 23.40g multicolored

Nos. 1451-1453 are airmail. No. 1453 contains one 50x60mm stamp. For overprint see No. 2144.

Pres. Stroessner's Visit to Japan A251

No. 1454: a, 10c, Departure of first Japanese mission to US & Europe, 1871. b, 15c, First railroad, Tokyo-Yokahama, 1872. c, 20c, Samurai. d, 25c, Geishas. e, 30c, Cranes, Hiroshige.
50c, Honda race car. 75c, Pres. Stroessner, Emperor Hirohito, Mt. Fuji, bullet train, horiz. 12.45g, Rocket. 18.15g, Stroessner, Hirohito, horiz. No. 1459, Mounted samurai, Masanobu, 1740. No. 1460, Hirohito's speech, state dinner, horiz. No. 1461, Delegations at Tokyo airport, horiz.

1972, Nov. 18 ***Perf. 14***

1454 A251 Strip of 5, #a.-e.
1455 A251 50c multicolored
1456 A251 75c multicolored
1457 A251 12.45g multicolored
1458 A251 18.15g multicolored

Souvenir Sheets

Perf. 13¹/₂

1459 A251 23.40g multicolored
1460 A251 23.40g multicolored

Imperf

1461 A251 23.40g multicolored

Nos. 1457-1461 are airmail. Nos. 1459-1460 each contain one 50x60mm stamp. No. 1461 contains one 85x42mm stamp with simulated perforations. For overprints see Nos. 2192-2194, 2267.

Wildlife — A252

Paintings: No. 1462a, 10c, Cranes, Botke. b, 15c, Tiger, Utamaro. c, 20c, Horses, Arenys. d, 25c, Pheasant, Dietzsch. e, 30c, Monkey, Brueghel, the Elder. All vert.
50c, Deer, Marc. 75c, Crab, Durer. 12.45g, Rooster, Jakuchu, vert. 18.15g, Swan, Asselyn.

1972, Nov. 18 ***Perf. 14***

1462 A252 Strip of 5, #a.-e.
1463 A252 50c multicolored
1464 A252 75c multicolored
1465 A252 12.45g multicolored
1466 A252 18.15g multicolored

Nos. 1465-1466 are airmail.

Acaray Dam A253

Designs: 2g, Francisco Solano Lopez monument. 3g, Friendship Bridge. 5g, Tebicuary River Bridge. 10g, Hotel Guarani. 20g, Bus and car on highway. 25g, Hospital of Institute for Social Service. 50g, "Presidente Stroessner" of state merchant marine. 100g, "Electra C" of Paraguayan airlines.

Perf. 13¹/₂x13

1972, Nov. 16 **Wmk. 347**

Granite Paper

1467	A253	1g	sepia	.15	.15
1468	A253	2g	brown	.15	.15
1469	A253	3g	brt ultra	.15	.15
1470	A253	5g	brt pink	.15	.15
1471	A253	10g	dl grn	.15	.15
1472	A253	20g	rose car	.15	.15
1473	A253	25g	gray	.18	.15
1474	A253	50g	violet	.35	.25
1475	A253	100g	brt lil	.70	.50
	Nos. 1467-1475 (9)			2.13	
			Set value		1.20

Tourism Year of the Americas.
Nos. 1472-1475 are airmail.

Locomotives Type

No. 1476: a, 10c, Stephenson's Rocket, 1829. b, 15c, First Swiss railroad, 1847. c, 20c, 1st Spanish locomotive, 1848. d, 2c, Norris, US, 1850. e, 30c, Ansaldo, Italy, 1859.
50c, Badenia, Germany, 1863. 75c, 1st Japanese locomotive, 1895. 12.45g, P.L.M., France, 1924. 18.15g, Stephenson's Northumbrian.

1972, Nov. 25 **Unwmk.** ***Perf. 14***

1476 A243 Strip of 5, #a.-e.
1477 A243 50c multicolored
1478 A243 75c multicolored
1479 A243 12.45g multicolored
1480 A243 18.15g multicolored

Nos. 1479-1480 are airmail.

South American Wildlife — A254

No. 1481: a, 10c, Tetradactyla. b, 15c, Nasua socialis. c, 20c, Priodontes giganteus. d, 25c, Blastocerus dichotomus. e, 30c, Felis pardalis.
50c, Aotes, vert. 75c, Rhea americana. 12.45g, Desmodus rotundus. 18.15g, Urocyon cinereoargenteus.

1972, Nov. 25

1481 A254 Strip of 5, #a.-e.
1482 A254 50c multicolored
1483 A254 75c multicolored
1484 A254 12.45g multicolored
1485 A254 18.15g multicolored

Nos. 1484-1485 are airmail.

1 G CORREO DEL PARAGUAY OAS Emblem — A255

Perf. 13x13½

1973 Litho. Wmk. 347

Granite Paper

1486 A255	1g multi		.15	.15
1487 A255	2g multi		.15	.15
1488 A255	3g multi		.15	.15
1489 A255	4g multi		.15	.15
1490 A255	5g multi		.15	.15
1491 A255	10g multi		.15	.15
1492 A255	20g multi		.15	.15
1493 A255	25g multi		.18	.15
1494 A255	50g multi		.35	.25
1495 A255	100g multi		.70	.50
		Set value	1.65	1.20

Org. of American States, 25th anniv.
Nos. 1492-1495 are airmail.

Paintings in Florence Museum A256

Artists: No. 1496: a, 10c, Cranach, the Elder. b, 15c, Caravaggio. c, 20c, Fiorentino. d, 25c, Di Credi. e, 30c, Liss. f, 50c, Da Vinci. g, 75c, Botticelli.
No. 1497: a, 5g, Titian, horiz. b, 10g, Del Piombo, horiz. c, 20g, De Michelino, horiz.

1973, Mar. 13 Unwmk. *Perf. 14*

1496 A256 Strip of 7, #a.-g.
1497 A256 Strip of 3, #a.-c.

No. 1497 is airmail.

Butterflies — A257

#1498: a, 10c, Catagramma patazza. b, 15c, Agrias narcissus. c, 20c, Papilio zagreus. d, 25c, Heliconius chestertoni. e, 30c, Metamorphadido. f, 50c, Catagramma astarte. g, 75c, Papilio brasiliensis.
No. 1499a, 5g, Agrias sardanapalus. b, 10g, Callithea saphhira. c, 20g, Jemadia hospita.

1973, Mar. 13

1498 A257 Strip of 7, #a.-g.
1499 A257 Strip of 3, #a.-c.

No. 1499 is airmail.

Cats A258

Faces of Cats: No. 1500: a, 10c, b, 15c. c, 20c, d, 25c, e, 30c. f, 50c. g, 75c.
No. 1501a, 5g, Cat under rose bush, by Desportes. b, 10g, Two cats, by Marc, horiz. c, 20g, Man with cat, by Rousseau.

1973, June 29

1500 A258 Strip of 7, #a.-g.
1501 A258 Strip of 3, #a.-c.

No. 1500 is airmail. For other cat designs, see type A287.

Flemish Paintings A259

Nudes by: No. 1502: a, 10c, Spranger. b, 15c, Jordaens. c, 20c, de Clerck. d, 25c, Spranger, diff. e, 30c, Goltzius. f, 50c, Rubens. g, 75c, Vase of flowers, J. Brueghel.
No. 1503a, 5g, Nude, de Clerck, horiz. b, 10g, Woman with mandolin, de Vos. c, 20g, Men, horses, Rubens, horiz.

1973, June 29 Litho. *Perf. 14*

1502 A259 Strip of 7, #a.-g.
1503 A259 Strip of 3, #a.-c.

No. 1503 is airmail.

Hand Holding Letter — A260

EXPOPAR 73, Paraguayan Industrial Exhib. — A261

Wmk. 347

1973, July 10 Litho. *Perf. 11*

1504 A260	2g lil rose & blk	.15	.15

No. 1504 was issued originally as a nonobligatory stamp to benefit mailmen, but its status was changed to regular postage.

1973, Aug. 11 *Perf. 13x13½*

Granite Paper

1505 A261	1g	org brn	.15	.15
1506 A261	2g	vermilion	.15	.15
1507 A261	3g	blue	.15	.15
1508 A261	4g	emerald	.15	.15
1509 A261	5g	lilac	.15	.15
1510 A261	20g	lilac rose	.15	.15
1511 A261	25g	rose claret	.18	.15
		Set value	.55	.45

Nos. 1510-1511 are airmail.

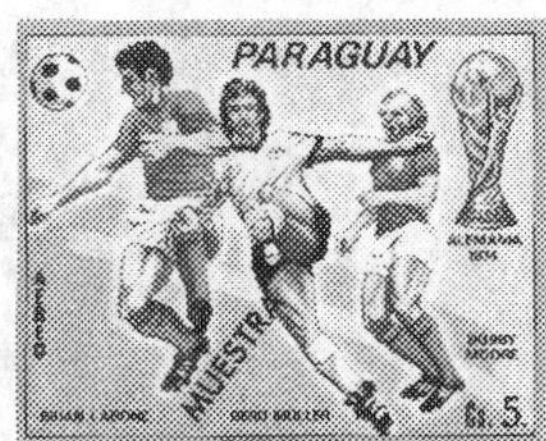

1974 World Cup Soccer Championships, Munich — A262

No. 1512: a, 10c, Uruguay vs. Paraguay. b, 15c, Crerand, England and Eusebio, Portugal. c, 20c, Bobby Charlton, England. d, 25c, Franz Beckenbauer, Germany. e, 30c, Erler, Germany and McNab, England. f, 50c, Pele, Brazil and Willi Schulz, Germany. g, 75c, Arsenio Erico, Paraguay.
5g, Brian Labone, Gerd Mueller, Bobby Moore. No. 1514a, 10g, Luigi Riva, Italy. No. 1514b, 20g, World Cup medals. No. 1515, World Cup trophy.

1973 Litho. Unwmk. *Perf. 14*

1512 A262 Strip of 7, #a.-g.
1513 A262 5g multicolored
1514 A262 Pair, #a.-b.

Souvenir Sheet

Perf. 13½

1515 A262 25g multicolored

Nos. 1513-1515 are airmail. Issue dates: Nos. 1512-1514, Oct. 8. No. 1515, June 29. For overprint see No. 2131.

Paintings A263

Details from paintings, artist: No. 1517a, 10c, Lion of St. Mark, Carpaccio. b, 15c, Venus and Mars, Pittoni. c, 20c, Rape of Europa, Veronese. d, 25c, Susannah and the Elders, Tintoretto. e, 30c, Euphrosyne, Amigoni. f, 50c, Allegory of Moderation, Veronese. g, 75c, Ariadne, Tintoretto.
5g, Pallas and Mars, Tintoretto. No. 1519a, 10g, Portrait of Woman in Fur Hat, G.D. Tiepolo. b, 20g, Dialectic of Industry, Veronese.

1973, Oct. 8 *Perf. 14*

1517 A263 Strip of 7, #a.-g.
1518 A263 5g multicolored
1519 A263 Pair, #a.-b.

Nos. 1518-1519 are airmail.

Birds A264

No. 1520: a, 10c, Tersina viridis. b, 15c, Pipile cumanensis. c, 20c, Pyrocephalus rubinus. d, 25c, Andigena laminirostris. e, 30c, Xipholena punicea. f, 50c, Tangara chilensis. g, 75, Polytmus guainumbi.
5g, Onychorhynchus mexicanus, vert. No. 1522a, 10g, Rhinocrypta lanceolata, vert. b, 20g, Trogon collaris, vert. 25g, Colibri florisuga mellivora, vert.

1973, Nov. 14

1520 A264 Strip of 7, #a.-g.
1521 A264 5g multicolored
1522 A264 Pair, #a.-b.

Souvenir Sheet

Perf. 13½

1523 A264 25g multicolored

Nos. 1521-1523 are airmail. No. 1523 contains one 50x60mm stamp.

Space Exploration — A265

No. 1524a, 10c, Apollo 11. b, 15c, Apollo 12. c, 20c, Apollo 13. d, 25c, Apollo 14. e, 30c, Apollo 15. f, 50c, Apollo 16. g, 75c, Apollo 17.
5g, Skylab. No. 1526a, 10g, Space shuttle. b, 20g, Apollo-Soyuz mission. No. 1527, Pioneer 11, Jupiter. No. 1528, Pioneer 10, Jupiter, vert.

1973, Nov. 14 *Perf. 14*

1524 A265 Strip of 7, #a.-g.
1525 A265 5g multicolored
1526 A265 Pair, #a.-b.

Souvenir Sheet

Perf. 14½

1527 A265 25g multicolored

Perf. 13½

1528 A265 25g multicolored

#1525-1528 are airmail. #1527 contains on 35x25mm stamp, #1528 one 50x60mm stamp.

Souvenir Sheet

Women of Avignon, Pablo Picasso — A266

Illustration reduced.

1973, Nov. 14 *Perf. 13½*

1529 A266 25g multicolored

Traditional Costumes A267

No. 1530: a, 25c, Indian girl. b, 50c, Bottle dance costume. c, 75c, Dancer balancing vase on head. d, 1g, Dancer with flowers. e, 1.50g, Weavers. f, 1.75g, Man, woman in dance costumes. g, 2.25g, Musicians in folk dress, horiz.

1973, Dec. 30 *Perf. 14*

1530 A267 Strip of 7, #a.-g.

Flowers A268

Designs: No. 1531a, 10c Passion flower. b, 20c, Dahlia. c, 25c, Bird of paradise. d, 30c, Freesia. e, 40c, Anthurium. f, 50c, Water lily. g, 75c, Orchid.

1973, Dec. 31
1531 A268 Strip of 7, #a.-g.

Roses
A269

Designs: No. 1532a, 10c, Hybrid perpetual. b, 15c, Tea scented. c, 20c, Japanese rose. d, 25c, Bouquet of roses and flowers. e, 30c, Rose of Provence. f, 50c, Hundred petals rose. g, 75c, Bouquet of roses, dragonfly.

1974, Feb. 2
1532 A269 Strip of 7, #a.-g.

Paintings in Gulbenkian Museum
A270

Designs and artists: No. 1533a, 10c, Cupid and Three Graces, Boucher. b, 15c, Bath of Venus, Burne-Jones. c, 20c, Mirror of Venus, Burne-Jones. d, 25c, Two Women, Natoire. e, 30c, Fighting Cockerels, de Vos. f, 50c, Portrait of a Young Girl, Bugiardini. g, 75c, Madonna and Child, J. Gossaert.

5g, Outing on Beach at Enoshima, Utamaro. No. 1534a, 10g, Woman with Harp, Lowrence. b, 20g, Centaurs Embracing, Rubens.

1974, Feb. 4
1533 A270 Strip of 7, #a.-g.
1534 A270 5g multicolored
1535 A270 Pair, #a.-b.

Nos. 1534-1535 are airmail.

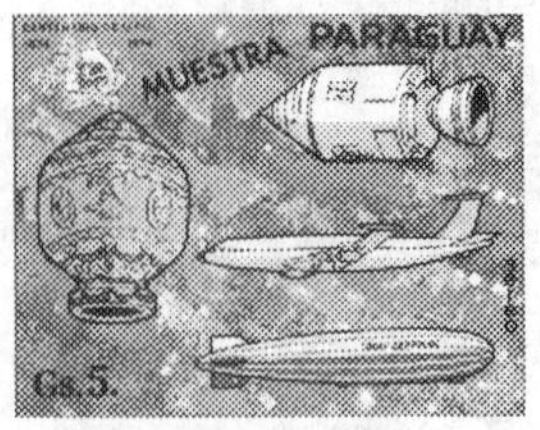

UPU Cent.
A271

Horse-drawn mail coaches: No. 1536a, 10c, London. b, 15c, France. c, 20c, England. d, 25c, Bavaria. e, 30c, Painting by C.C. Henderson. f, 50c, Austria, vert. g, 75c, Zurich, vert.

5g, Hot air balloon, Apollo spacecraft, airplane, Graf Zeppelin. No. 1538a, 10g, Steam locomotive. b, 20g, Ocean liner, sailing ship. No. 1539, Airship, balloon. No. 1540, Mail coach crossing river.

1974, Mar. 20 *Perf. 14*
1536 A271 Strip of 7, #a.-g.
1537 A271 5g multicolored
1538 A271 Pair, #a.-b.

Souvenir Sheets

Perf. 14½

1539 A271 15g multicolored

Perf. 13½

1540 A271 15g multicolored

Nos. 1537-1540 are airmail. No. 1539 contains one 50x35mm stamp, No. 1540 one 60x50mm stamp. Nos. 1539-1540 each include a 5g surtax for a monument to Francisco Solano Lopez. For overprint see No. 2127.

Paintings
A272

Details from works, artist: No. 1541a, 10c, Adam and Eve, Mabuse. b, 15c, Portrait, Piero di Cosimo. c, 20c, Bathsheba in her Bath, Cornelisz. d, 25c, Toilet of Venus, Boucher. e, 30c, The Bathers, Renoir. f, 50c, Lot and his Daughters, Dix. g, 75c, Bouquet of Flowers, van Kessel.

5g, King's Pet Horse, Seele. No. 1543a, 10g, Woman with Paintbrushes, Batoni. b, 20g, Three Musicians, Flemish master.

1974, Mar. 20
1541 A272 Strip of 7, #a.-g.
1542 A272 5g multicolored
1543 A272 Pair, #a.-b.

Nos. 1542-1543 are airmail.

Sailing Ships — A272a

Designs: No. 1544a, 5c, Ship, map. b, 10c, English ship. c, 15c, Dutch ship. d, 20c, Whaling ships. e, 25c, Spanish ship. f, 35c, USS Constitution. g, 40c, English frigate. h, 50c, "Fanny," 1832.

1974, Sept. 13 *Perf. 14½*
1544 A272a Strip of 8, #a.-h.

Strip price includes a 50c surtax.

Paintings in Borghese Gallery, Rome
A273

Details from works and artists: No. 1545a, 5c, Portrait, Romano. b, 10c, Boy Carrying Fruit, Caravaggio. c, 15c, A Sybil, Domenichino. d, 20c, Nude, Titian. e, 25c, The Danae, Correggio. f, 35c, Nude, Savoldo. g, 40c, Nude, da Vinci. h, 50c, Nude, Rubens. 15g, Christ Child, Piero di Cosimo.

1975, Jan. 15 *Perf. 14*
1545 A273 Strip of 8, #a.-h.

Souvenir Sheet

Perf. 14½

1546 A273 15g multicolored

No. 1546 is airmail and price includes a 5g surtax used for a monument to Francisco Solano Lopez.

Christmas
A274

Paintings, artists: No. 1547a, 5c, The Annunciation, della Robia. b, 10c, The Nativity, G. David. c, 15c, Madonna and Child, Memling. d, 20c, Adoration of the Shepherds, Giorgione. e, 25c, Adoration of the Magi, French school, 1400. f, Madonna and Child with Saints, 35c, Pulzone. g, 40c, Madonna and Child, van Orley. h, 50c, Flight From Egypt, Pacher. 15g, Adoration of the Magi, Raphael.

1975, Jan. 17 *Perf. 14*
1547 A274 Strip of 8, #a.-h.

Souvenir Sheet

Perf. 14½

1548 A274 15g multicolored

No. 1548 is airmail and price includes a 5g surtax for a monument to Francisco Solano Lopez.

"U.P.U.," Pantheon, Carrier Pigeon, Globe
A275

1975, Feb. Wmk. 347 *Perf. 13½x13*

1549	A275	1g	blk & lilac	.15	.15
1550	A275	2g	blk & rose red	.15	.15
1551	A275	3g	blk & ultra	.15	.15
1552	A275	5g	blk & blue	.15	.15
1553	A275	10g	blk & lil rose	.15	.15
1554	A275	20g	blk & brn	.15	.15
1555	A275	25g	blk & emer	.18	.15
			Set value	.58	.52

Centenary of Universal Postal Union.
Nos. 1554-1555 are airmail.

Paintings in National Gallery, London
A276

Details from paintings, artist: 5c, The Rokeby Venus, Velazquez, horiz. 10c, The Range of Love, Watteau. 15c, Venus (The School of Love), Correggio. 20c, Mrs. Sarah Siddons, Gainsborough. 25c, Cupid Complaining to Venus, L. Cranach the Elder. 35c, Portrait, Lotto. 40c, Nude, Rembrandt. 50c, Origin of the Milky Way, Tintoretto. 15g, Rider and Hounds, Pisanello.

1975, Apr. 25 Unwmk. *Perf. 14*
1556 A276 5c multicolored
1557 A276 10c multicolored
1558 A276 15c multicolored
1559 A276 20c multicolored
1560 A276 25c multicolored
1561 A276 35c multicolored
1562 A276 40c multicolored
1563 A276 50c multicolored

Souvenir Sheet

Perf. 13½

1564 A276 15g multicolored

No. 1564 is airmail, contains one 50x60mm stamp and price includes a 5g surtax for a monument to Francisco Solano Lopez.

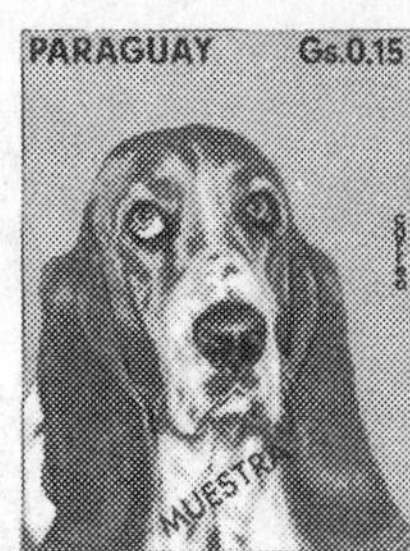

Dogs — A277

1975, June 7 *Perf. 14*
1565 A277 5c Boxer
1566 A277 10c Poodle
1567 A277 15c Basset hound
1568 A277 20c Collie
1569 A277 25c Chihuahua
1570 A277 35c German shepherd
1571 A277 40c Pekinese
1572 A277 50c Chow

Souvenir Sheet

Perf. 13½

1573 A277 15g Fox hound, horse

No. 1573 is airmail, contains one 39x57mm stamp and price includes a 5g surtax for a monument to Francisco Solano Lopez.

South American Fauna — A278

Designs: No. 1574a, 5c, Piranha (Pirana). b, 10c, Anaconda. c, 15c, Turtle (Tortuga). d, 20c, Iguana. e, 25c, Mono, vert. f, 35c, Mara. g, 40c, Marmota, vert. h, 50c, Peccary.

1975, Aug. 20 Litho. *Perf. 14*
1574 A278 Strip of 8, #a.-h.

Souvenir Sheet

Perf. 13½

1575 A278 15g Aguara guazu

No. 1575 is airmail, contains and one 60x50mm stamp and price includes a 5g surtax for a monument to Francisco Solano Lopez.

For overprints see Nos. 2197.

Michelangelo (1475-1564), Italian Sculptor and Painter
A279

No. 1583: Statues, a, 5c, David. b, 10c, Aurora.

Paintings, c, 15c, Original Sin. d, 20c, The Banishment. e, 25c, The Deluge. f, 35c, Eve. g, 40c, Mary with Jesus and John. h, 50c, Judgement Day.

4g, Adam Receiving Life from God, horiz. No. 1585a, 5g, Libyan Sybil. b, 10g, Delphic Sybil. No. 1586, God Creating the Heaven and the Earth, horiz. No. 1587, The Holy Family.

1975, Aug. 23 Litho. *Perf. 14*
1583 A279 Strip of 8, #a.-h.
1584 A279 4g multicolored
1585 A279 Pair, #a.-b.

Perf. 12

1586 A279 15g multicolored

Souvenir Sheet

Perf. 13½

1587 A279 15g multicolored

Nos. 1586-1587 sold for 20g with surtax for a monument to Francisco Solano Lopez. Nos. 1584-1587 are airmail.

Winter Olympics, Innsbruck, 1976 — A280

#1597a, 2g, Slalom skier. b, 3g, Cross country skier. c, 4g, Pair figure skating. d, 5g, Hockey.
#1598a, 10g, Speed skater. b, 15g, Downhill skier.

1975, Aug. 27 Litho. *Perf. 14*

1596 A280 1g Luge
1597 A280 Strip of 4, #a.-d.
1598 A280 Pair, #a.-b.
1599 A280 20g 4-Man bobsled

Souvenir Sheet

Perf. 13½

1600 A280 25g Ski jumper
1601 A280 25g Woman figure skater

Nos. 1596, 1598-1601 are horiz. Nos. 1598-1601 are airmail. Nos. 1600-1601 each contain one 60x50mm stamp.

Summer Olympics, Montreal, 1976 — A281

No. 1606: a, 1g, Weightlifting. b, 2g, Kayak. c, 3g, Hildegard Flack, 800 meter run. d, Lasse Viren, 5,000 meter run.
No. 1607: a, 5g, Dieter Kottysch, boxing. b, 10g, Lynne Evans, archery. c, 15g, Akinori Kakayama, balance rings. 20g, Heide Rosendahl, broad jump. No. 1609, Decathlon. No. 1610, Liselott Linsenhoff, dressage, horiz.

1975, Aug. 28 *Perf. 14*

1606 A281 Strip of 4, #a.-d.
1607 A281 Strip of 3, #a.-c.
1608 A281 20g multicolored

Souvenir Sheets

Perf. 14½

1609 A281 25g multicolored
1610 A281 25g multicolored

Nos. 1607b-1610 are airmail.

US, Bicent. — A282

Ships.

Unwmk.

1975, Oct. 20 Litho. *Perf. 14*

1616 A282 5c Sachem, vert.
1617 A282 10c Reprisal, Lexington
1618 A282 15c Wasp
1619 A282 20c Mosquito, Spy
1620 A282 25c Providence, vert.
1621 A282 35c Yankee Hero, Milford
1622 A282 40c Cabot, vert.
1623 A282 50c Hornet, vert.

Souvenir Sheet

1624 A282 15g Montgomery

No. 1624 is airmail and contains one 50x70mm stamp.

US, Bicent. — A283

Details from paintings, artists: No. 1625a, 5c, The Collector, Kahill. b, 10c, Morning Interlude, Brackman, vert. c, 15c, White Cloud, Catlin, vert. d, 20c, Man From Kentucky, Benton, vert. e, 25c, The Emigrants, Remington. f, 35c, Spirit of '76, Willard, vert. g, John Paul Jones capturing Serapis, unknown artist. h, 50c, Declaration of Independence, Trumbull. 15g, George Washington, Stuart and Thomas Jefferson, Peale.

1975, Nov. 20 *Perf. 14*

1625 A283 Strip of 8, #a.-h.

Souvenir Sheet

Perf. 13½

1625A A283 15g multicolored

No. 1625A is airmail, contains one 60x50mm stamp and price includes a 5g surtax for a monument to Francisco Solano Lopez.

Institute of Higher Education A284

Perf. 13½x13

1976, Mar. 16 Litho. Wmk. 347

1626 A284	5g vio, blk & red	.15	.15
1627 A284	10g ultra, blk & red	.15	.15
1628 A284	30g brn, blk & red	.22	.18
	Set value	.34	.28

Inauguration of Institute of Higher Education, Sept. 23, 1974.
No. 1628 is airmail.

Rotary Intl., 70th Anniv. — A285

1976, Mar. 16 *Perf. 13x13½*

1629 A285	3g blk, bl & citron	.15	.15
1630 A285	4g car, bl & citron	.15	.15
1631 A285	25g emer, bl & lemon	.18	.15
	Set value	.28	.22

No. 1631 is airmail.

IWY Emblem, Woman's Head — A286

1976, Mar. 16

1632 A286	1g ultra & brn	.15	.15
1633 A286	2g car & brn	.15	.15
1634 A286	20g grn & brn	.15	.15
	Set value	.24	.20

Intl Women's Year (1975).
No. 1634 is airmail.

Cats — A287

Various cats: No. 1635a, 5c. b, 10c. c, 15c. d, 20c. e, 25c. f, 35c. g, 40c. h, 50c. 15g.

1976, Apr. 2 Unwmk. *Perf. 14*

1635 A287 Strip of 8, #a.-h.

Souvenir Sheet

Perf. 13½

1636 A287 15g multicolored

No. 1636 is airmail, contains one 50x60mm stamp and price includes a 5g surtax for a monument to Francisco Solano Lopez.
See Nos. 2132-2133, 2201-2202, 2274-2275. For overprint see No. 2212.

Railroads, 150th Anniv. (in 1975) — A288

Locomotives: 1g, Planet, England, 1830. 2g, Koloss, Austria, 1844. 3g, Tarasque, France, 1846. 4g, Lawrence, Canada, 1853. 5g, Carlsruhe, Germany, 1854. 10g, Great Sagua, US, 1856. 15g, Berga, Spain. 20g, Encarnacion, Paraguay. 25g, English locomotive, 1825.

1976, Apr. 2 *Perf. 13x13½*

1637 A288 1g multicolored
1638 A288 2g multicolored
1639 A288 3g multicolored
1640 A288 4g multicolored
1641 A288 5g multicolored
1642 A288 10g multicolored
1643 A288 15g multicolored
1644 A288 20g multicolored

Souvenir Sheet

1645 A288 25g multicolored

Nos. 1642-1645 are airmail. No. 1645 contains one 40x27mm stamp.

Painting by Spanish Artists — A289

Paintings: 1g, The Naked Maja by Goya. 2g, Nude by J. de Torres. 3g, Nude holding oranges by de Torres, vert. 4g, Woman playing piano by Z. Velazquez, vert. 5g, Knight on white horse by Esquivel. 10g, The Shepherd, by Murillo. 15g, The Immaculate Conception by Antolinez, vert. 20g, Nude by Zuloaga. 25g, Prince Baltasar Carlos on Horseback by D. Velasquez.

1976, Apr. 2 *Perf. 13x13½,13½x13*

1646 A289 1g multicolored
1647 A289 2g multicolored
1648 A289 3g multicolored
1649 A289 4g multicolored
1650 A289 5g multicolored
1651 A289 10g multicolored
1652 A289 15g multicolored
1653 A289 20g multicolored

Souvenir Sheet

1654 A289 25g multicolored

Nos. 1651-1654 are airmail. No. 1654 contains one 58x82mm stamp.

Butterflies — A290

No. 1655: a, 5c, Prepona praeneste. b, 10c, Prepona proschion. c, 15c, Pereute leucodrosime. d, 20c, Agrias amydon. e, 25c, Morpho aegea gynandromorphe. f, 35c, Pseudatteria leopardina. g, 40c, Morpho helena. h, 50c, Morpho hecuba.

1976, May 12 Unwmk. *Perf. 14*

1655 A290 Strip of 8, #a.-h.

Farm Animals — A291

1976, June 15

1656 A291 1g Rooster, vert.
1657 A291 2g Hen, vert.
1658 A291 3g Turkey, vert.
1659 A291 4g Sow
1660 A291 5g Donkeys
1661 A291 10g Brahma cattle
1662 A291 15g Holstein cow
1663 A291 20g Horse

Nos. 1661-1663 are airmail.

US and US Post Office, Bicent. — A292

Designs: 1g, Pony Express rider. 2g, Stagecoach. 3g, Steam locomotive, vert. 4g, American steamship, Savannah. 5g, Curtiss Jenny biplane. 10g, Mail bus. 15g, Mail car, rocket train. 20g, First official missile mail, vert. No. 1672, First flight cover, official missile mail. No. 1673, US #C76 tied to cover by moon landing cancel.

1976, June 18

1664 A292 1g multicolored
1665 A292 2g multicolored
1666 A292 3g multicolored
1667 A292 4g multicolored
1668 A292 5g multicolored
1669 A292 10g multicolored
1670 A292 15g multicolored
1671 A292 20g multicolored

Souvenir Sheets

Perf. 14½

1672 A292 25g multicolored
1673 A292 25g multicolored

Nos. 1669-1673 are airmail and each contain one 50x40mm stamp.

Mythological Characters A293

Details from paintings, artists: No. 1674a, 1g, Jupiter, Ingres. b, 2g, Saturn, Rubens. c, 3g, Neptune, Tiepolo. d, 4g, Uranus and Aphrodite, Medina, horiz. e, 5g, Pluto and Prosperpine, Giordano, horiz. f, 10g, Venus, Ingres. g, 15g, Mercury, de la Hyre. 20g, Mars and Venus, Veronese.

25g, Viking Orbiter descending to Mars, horiz.

1976, July 18 *Perf. 14*
1674 A293 Strip of 7, #a.-g.
1675 A293 20g multicolored

Souvenir Sheet
Perf. 14½
1676 A293 25g multicolored

Nos. 1674f-1674g, 1675-1676 are airmail.

Sailing Ships A294

Paintings: No. 1677a, 1g, Venice frigate of the Spanish Armada, vert. b, 2g, Swedish war ship, Vasa, 1628, vert. c, 3g, Spanish galleon being attacked by pirates by Puget. d, 4g, Combat by Dawson. e, 5g, European boat in Japan, vert. f, 10g, Elizabeth Grange in Liverpool by Walters. g, 15g, Prussen, 1903, by Holst. 20g, Grand Duchess Elizabeth, 1902, by Bohrdt.

1976, July 15 *Perf. 14*
1677 A294 Strip of 7, #a.-g.
1678 A294 20g multicolored

Nos. 1677f-1678 are airmail.

German Sailing Ships — A295

Ship, artist: 1g, Bunte Kuh, 1402, Zeeden. 2g, Arms of Hamburg, 1667, Wichman, vert. 3g, Kaiser Leopold, 1667, Wichman, vert. 4g, Deutschland, 1848, Pollack, vert. 5g, Humboldt, 1851, Fedeler. 10g, Borussia, 1855, Seitz. 15g, Gorch Fock, 1958, Stroh, vert. 20g, Grand Duchess Elizabeth, 1902, Bohrdt. 25g, SS Pamir, Zeytline, vert.

Unwmk.
1976, Aug. 20 Litho. *Perf. 14*
1685 A295 1g multicolored
1686 A295 2g multicolored
1687 A295 3g multicolored
1688 A295 4g multicolored
1689 A295 5g multicolored
1690 A295 10g multicolored
1691 A295 15g multicolored
1692 A295 20g multicolored

Souvenir Sheet
Perf. 14½
1693 A295 25g multicolored

Intl. German Naval Exposition, Hamburg; NORDPOSTA '76 (No. 1693). Nos. 1690-1693 are airmail.

US Bicentennial A296

Western Paintings by: No. 1694a, 1g, E. C. Ward. b, 2g, William Robinson Leigh. c, 3g, A. J. Miller. d, 4g, Charles Russell. e, 5g, Frederic Remington. f, 10g, Remington, horiz. g, 15g, Carl Bodmer.

No. 1695, A. J. Miller. No. 1696, US #1, 2, 245, C76.

Unwmk.
1976, Sept. 9 Litho. *Perf. 14*
1694 A296 Strip of 7, #a.-g.
1695 A296 20g multicolored

Souvenir Sheet
Perf. 13x13½
1696 A296 25g multicolored

Nos. 1694f-1694g, 1695-1696 are airmail. No. 1696 contains one 65x55mm stamp.

1976 Summer Olympics, Montreal — A297

Gold Medal Winners: No. 1703a, 1g, Nadia Comaneci, Romania, gymnastics, vert. b, 2g, Kornelia Ender, East Germany, swimming. c, 3g, Luann Ryan, US, archery, vert. d, 4g, Jennifer Chandler, US, diving. e, 5g, Shirley Babashoff, US, swimming. f, 10g, Christine Stuckelberger, Switzerland, equestrian. g, 15g, Japan, volleyball, vert.

20g, Annegret Richter, W. Germany, running, vert. No. 1705, Bruce Jenner, US, decathlon. No. 1706, Alwin Schockemohle, equestrian. No. 1707, Medals list, vert.

Unwmk.
1976, Dec. 18 Litho. *Perf. 14*
1703 A297 Strip of 7, #a.-g.
1704 A297 20g multicolored

Souvenir Sheets
Perf. 14½
1705 A297 25g multicolored
1706 A297 25g multicolored
1707 A297 25g multicolored

Nos. 1703f-1703g, 1705-1707 are airmail. Nos. 1705-1706 each contain one 50x40mm stamp. No. 1707 contains one 50x70mm stamp.

Titian, 500th Birth Anniv. A298

Details from paintings: No. 1708a, 1g, Venus and Adonis. b, 2g, Diana and Callisto. c, 3g, Perseus and Andromeda. d, 4g, Venus of the Mirror. e, 5g, Venus Sleeping, horiz. f, 10g, Bacchanal, horiz. g, 15g, Venus, Cupid and the Lute Player. 20g, Venus and the Organist, horiz.

1976, Dec. 18 *Perf. 14*
1708 A298 Strip of 7, #a.-g.
1709 A298 20g multicolored

No. 1708f-1708g, 1709 are airmail.

Peter Paul Rubens, 400th Birth Anniv. A299

Paintings: No. 1710a, 1g, Adam and Eve. b, 2g, Tiger and Lion Hunt. c, 3g, Bathsheba Receiving David's Letter. d, 4g, Susanna in the Bath. e, 5g, Perseus and Andromeda. f, 10g, Andromeda Chained to the Rock. g, 15g, Shivering Venus. 20g, St. George Slaying the Dragon. 25g, Birth of the Milky Way, horiz.

1977, Feb. 18
1710 A299 Strip of 7, #a.-g.
1711 A299 20g multicolored

Souvenir Sheet
Perf. 14½
1712 A299 25g multicolored

Nos. 1710f-1710g, 1711-1712 are airmail.

US, Bicent. — A300

Space exploration: No. 1713a, 1g, John Glenn, Mercury 7. b, 2g, Pres. Kennedy, Apollo 11. c, 3g, Wernher von Braun, Apollo 17. d, 4g, Mercury, Venus, Mariner 10. e, 5g, Jupiter, Saturn, Jupiter 10/11. f, 10g, Viking, Mars. g, 15g, Viking A on Mars. 20g, Viking B on Mars. No. 1715, Future space projects on Mars, vert. No. 1716, Future land rover on Mars.

1977, Mar. 3 *Perf. 14*
1713 A300 Strip of 7, #a.-g.
1714 A300 20g multicolored

Souvenir Sheets
Perf. 13½
1715 A300 25g multicolored
1716 A300 25g multicolored

Nos. 1713f-1713g, 1714-1716 are airmail. No. 1715 contains one 50x60mm stamp, No. 1716 one 60x50mm stamp.

Olympic History A301

Designs: 1g, Spiridon Louis, marathon 1896, Athens, Pierre de Coubertin. 2g, Giuseppe Delfino, fencing 1960, Rome, Pope John XXIII. 3g, Jean Claude Killy, skiing 1968, Grenoble, Charles de Gaulle. 4g, Ricardo Delgado, boxing 1968, Mexico City, G. Diaz Ordaz. 5g, Hayata, gymnastics 1964, Tokyo, Emperor Hirohito. 10g, Klaus Wolfermann, javelin 1972, Munich, Avery Brundage. 15g, Michel Vaillancourt, equestrian 1976, Montreal, Queen Elizabeth II. 20g, Franz Klammer, skiing 1976, Innsbruck, Austrian national arms.

25g, Emblems of 1896 Athens games and 1976 Montreal games.

1977, June 7 *Perf. 14*
1717 A301 1g multicolored
1718 A301 2g multicolored
1719 A301 3g multicolored
1720 A301 4g multicolored
1721 A301 5g multicolored
1722 A301 10g multicolored
1723 A301 15g multicolored
1724 A301 20g multicolored

Souvenir Sheet
Perf. 13½
1725 A301 25g multicolored

Nos. 1722-1725 are airmail. No. 1725 contains one 49x60mm stamp.

LUPOSTA '77, Intl. Stamp Exibition, Berlin A302

Graf Zeppelin 1st South America flight and: 1g, German girls in traditional costumes. 2g, Bull fighter, Seville. 3g, Dancer, Rio de Janeiro. 4g, Gaucho breaking bronco, Uruguay. 5g, Like #1530b. 10g, Argentinian gaucho. 15g, Ceremonial indian costume, Bolivia. 20g, Indian on horse, US.

No. 1734, Zeppelin over sailing ship. No. 1735, Ferdinand Von Zeppelin, zeppelin over Berlin, horiz.

1977, June 9 *Perf. 14*
1726 A302 1g multicolored
1727 A302 2g multicolored
1728 A302 3g multicolored
1729 A302 4g multicolored
1730 A302 5g multicolored
1731 A302 10g multicolored
1732 A302 15g multicolored
1733 A302 20g multicolored

Souvenir Sheets
Perf. 13½
1734 A302 25g multicolored
1735 A302 25g multicolored

#1731-1735 are airmail. #1734 contains one 49x60mm stamp, #1735 one 60x49mm stamp.

FLOR DE MBURUCUYA
3 G CORREO DEL PARAGUAY
Mburucuya Flowers — A303

TEJEDORA DE NANDUTI
5 G CORREO DEL PARAGUAY
Weaver with Spider Web Lace — A304

Designs: 1g, Ostrich feather panel. 2g, Black palms. 20g, Rose tabebuia. 25g, Woman holding ceramic pot.

Perf. 13x13½

1977	**Litho.**	**Wmk. 347**	
1736 A304	1g multicolored	.15	.15
1737 A303	2g multicolored	.15	.15
1738 A303	3g multicolored	.15	.15
1739 A304	5g multicolored	.15	.15
1740 A303	20g multicolored	.25	.18
1741 A304	25g multicolored	.30	.20
	Set value	.75	.55

Issued: 2g, 3g, 20g, 4/25; 1g, 5g, 25g, 6/27.
Nos. 1740-1741 are airmail.

Aviation History — A305

Designs: No. 1742a, 1g, Orville and Wilbur Wright, Wright Flyer, 1903. b, 2g, Alberto Santos-Dumont, Canard, 1906. c, 3g, Louis Bleriot, Bleriot 11, 1909. d, 4g, Otto Lilienthal, Glider, 1891. e, 5g, Igor Sikorsky, Avion le Grande, 1913. f, 10g,

Juan de la Cierva, Autogiro. g, 15g, Silvio Pettirossi, Deperdussin acrobatic plane. No. 1743, Concorde jet. No. 1744, Lindbergh, Spirit of St. Louis, Statue of Liberty, Eiffel Tower. No. 1745, Design of flying machine by da Vinci.

1977, July 18 Unwmk. *Perf. 14*
1742 A305 Strip of 7, #a.-g.
1743 A305 20g multicolored

Souvenir Sheet

Perf. 14½

1744 A305 25g multicolored
1745 A305 25g multicolored

Nos. 1742f-1745 are airmail. No. 1745 contains one label.

Francisco Solano Lopez — A306

Perf. 13x13½

1977, July 24 Litho. Wmk. 347

1752 A306 10g brown	.15	.15
1753 A306 50g dk vio	.50	.38
1754 A306 100g green	1.00	.75

Marshal Francisco Solano Lopez (1827-1870), President of Paraguay.
Nos. 1753-1754 are airmail.

Paintings — A307

Paintings by: No. 1755a, 1g, Gabrielle Rainer Istvanffy. b, 2g, L. C. Hoffmeister. c, 3g, Frans Floris. d, 4g, Gerard de Lairesse. e, 5g, David Teniers I. f, 10g, Jacopo Zucchi. g, 15g, Pierre Paul Prudhon. 20g, Francois Boucher. 25g, Ingres. 5g-25g vert.

1977, July 25 *Perf. 14*
1755 A307 Strip of 7, #a.-g.
1756 A307 20g multicolored

Souvenir Sheet

Perf. 14½

1757 A307 25g multicolored

Nos. 1755f-1757 are airmail.

German Sailing Ships — A308

Designs: No. 1764a, 1g, De Beurs van Amsterdam. b, 2g, Katharina von Blankenese. c, 3g, Cuxhaven. d, 4g, Rhein. e, 5g, Churprinz and Marian. f, 10g, Bark of Bremen, vert. g, 15g, Elbe II, vert. 20g, Karacke. 25g, Admiral Karpeanger.

Unwmk.

1977, Aug. 27 Litho. *Perf. 14*
1764 A308 Strip of 7, #a.-g.
1765 A308 20g multicolored

Souvenir Sheet

Perf. 13½

1766 A308 25g multicolored

Nos. 1764f-1766 are airmail. No. 1766 contains one 40x30mm stamp.

Nobel Laureates for Literature — A309

Authors and scenes from books: No. 1773a, 1g, John Steinbeck, Grapes of Wrath, vert. b, 2g, Ernest Hemingway, Death in the Afternoon. c, 3g, Pearl S. Buck, The Good Earth, vert. d, 4g, George Bernard Shaw, Pygmalion, vert. e, 5g, Maurice Maeterlinck, Joan of Arc, vert. f, 10g, Rudyard Kipling, The Jungle Book. g, Henryk Sienkiewicz, Quo Vadis. 20g, C. Theodor Mommsen, History of Rome. 25g, Nobel prize medal.

1977, Sept. 5 *Perf. 14*
1773 A309 Strip of 7, #a.-g.
1774 A309 20g multicolored

Souvenir Sheet

Perf. 14½

1775 A309 25g multicolored

Nos. 1773f-1775 are airmail.

1978 World Cup Soccer Championships, Argentina — A310

Posters and World Cup Champions: No. 1782a, 1g, Uruguay, 1930. b, 2g, Italy, 1934. c, 3g, Italy, 1938. d, 4g, Uruguay, 1950. e, 5g, Germany, 1954. f, 10g, Soccer player by Fritz Genkinger. g, 15g, Soccer player, orange shirt by Genkinger.

No. 1783a, 1g, Brazil, 1958. b, 2g, Brazil, 1962. c, 3g, England, 1966. d, 4g, Brazil, 1970. e, 5g, Germany, 1974. f, 10g, Player #4 by Genkinger. g, 15g, Player #1 by Genkinger, horiz.

No. 1784, World Cup Trophy. No. 1785, German players, Argentina '78. No. 1786, The Loser, by Genkinger. No. 1787, The Defender, (player #11) by Genkinger.

1977, Oct. 28 Unwmk. *Perf. 14*
1782 A310 Strip of 7, #a.-g.
1783 A310 Strip of 7, #a.-g.
1784 A310 20g multicolored
1785 A310 20g multicolored

Souvenir Sheets

Perf. 14½

1786 A310 25g red & multi
1787 A310 25g black & multi

Nos. 1782f-1782g, 1783f-1783g, 1784-1787 are airmail.

Peter Paul Rubens, 400th Birth Anniv. A312

Details from paintings: No. 1788a, 1g, Rubens and Isabella Brant under Honeysuckle Bower. b, 2g, Judgment of Paris. c, 3g, Union of Earth and Water. d, 4g, Daughters of Kekrops Discovering Erichthonius. e, 5g, Holy Family with the Lamb. f, 10c, Adoration of the Magi. g, 15c, Philip II on Horseback.

20g, Education of Marie de Medici, horiz. 25g, Triumph of Eucharist Over False Gods.

1978, Jan. 19 Unwmk. *Perf. 14*
1788 A312 Strip of 7, #a.-g.
1789 A312 20g multicolored

Souvenir Sheet

Perf. 14½

1790 A312 25g multicolored

Nos. 1788f-1788g, 1789-1790 are airmail. No. 1790 contains one 50x70mm stamp and exists inscribed in gold or silver.

1978 World Chess Championships, Argentina — A313

Paintings of chess players: No. 1791a, 1g, De Cremone. b, 2g, L. van Leyden. c, 3g, H. Muehlich. d, 4g, Arabian artist. e, 5g, Benjamin Franklin playing chess, E. H. May. f, 10g, G. Cruikshank. g, 15g, 17th cent. tapestry. 20g, Napoleon playing chess on St. Helena. 25g, Illustration from chess book, Shah Name.

1978, Jan. 23 *Perf. 14*
1791 A313 Strip of 7, #a.-g.
1792 A313 20g multicolored

Souvenir Sheet

Perf. 14½

1793 A313 25g multicolored

Nos. 1791f-1791g, 1792-1793 are airmail. No. 1793 contains one 50x40mm stamp.

Jacob Jordaens, 300th Death Anniv. A314

Paintings: No. 1794a, 3g, Satyr and the Nymphs. b, 4g, Satyr with Peasant. c, 5g, Allegory of Fertility. d, 6g, Upbringing of Jupiter. e, 7g, Holy Family. f, 8g, Adoration of the Shepherds. g, 20g, Jordaens with his family. 10g, Meleagro with Atalanta, horiz. No. 1796, Feast for a King, horiz. No. 1797, Holy Family with Shepherds.

1978, Jan. 25 *Perf. 14*
1794 A314 Strip of 7, #a.-g.
1795 A314 10g multicolored
1796 A314 25g multicolored

Souvenir Sheet

Perf. 14½

1797 A314 25g multicolored

Nos. 1795-1797 are airmail. No. 1797 contains one 50x70mm stamp.

Albrecht Durer, 450th Death Anniv. A315

Monograms and details from paintings: No. 1804a, 3g, Temptation of the Idler. b, 4g, Adam and Eve. c, 5g, Satyr Family. d, 6g, Eve. e, 7g, Adam. f, 8g, Portrait of a Young Man. g, 20g, Squirrels and Acorn. 10g, Madonna and Child. No. 1806, Brotherhood of the Rosary (Lute-playing Angel). No. 1807, Soldier on Horseback with a Lance.

1978, Mar. 10 *Perf. 14*
1804 A315 Strip of 7, #a.-g.
1805 A315 10g multicolored
1806 A315 25g multicolored

Souvenir Sheet

Perf. 13½

1807 A315 25g blk, buff & sil

Nos. 1805-1807 are airmail. No. 1807 contains one 30x40mm stamp.

Francisco de Goya, 150th Death Anniv. A316

Paintings: No. 1814a, 3g, Allegory of the Town of Madrid. b, 4g, The Clothed Maja. c, 5g, The Parasol. d, 6g, Dona Isabel Cobos de Porcel. e, 7g, The Drinker. f, 8g, The 2nd of May 1908. g, 20g, General Jose Palafox on Horseback. 10g, Savages Murdering a Woman. 25g, The Naked Maja, horiz.

1978, May 11 *Perf. 14*
1814 A316 Strip of 7, #a.-g.
1815 A316 10g multicolored
1816 A316 25g multicolored

Nos. 1815-1816 are airmail.

Future Space Projects — A317

Various futuristic space vehicles and imaginary creatures: No. 1816a, 3g. b, 4g. c, 5g. d, 6g. e, 7g. f, 8g. g, 20g.

1978, May 16
1817 A317 Strip of 7, #a.-g.
1818 A317 10g multicolored
1819 A317 25g multi, diff.

Nos. 1818-1819 are airmail.

Racing Cars A318

No. 1820: a, 3g, Tyrell Formula I. b, 4g, Lotus Formula 1, 1978. c, 5g, McLaren Formula 1. d, 6g, Brabham Alfa Romeo Formula 1. e, 7g, Renault Turbo Formula 1. f, 8g, Wolf Formula 1. g, 20g, Porsche 935. 10g, Bugatti. 25g, Mercedes Benz W196, Stirling Moss, driver. No. 1823, Ferrari 312T.

1978, June 28 *Perf. 14*
1820 A318 Strip of 7, #a.-g.
1821 A318 10g multicolored
1822 A318 25g multicolored

Souvenir Sheet

Perf. 14½

1823 A318 25g multicolored

Nos. 1821-1823 are airmail. No. 1823 contains one 50x35mm stamp.

Paintings by Peter Paul Rubens A319

3g, Holy Family with a Basket. 4g, Amor Cutting a Bow. 5g, Adam 7 Eve in Paradise. 6g, Crown of Fruit, horiz. 7g, Kidnapping of Ganymede. 8g, The Hunting of Crocodile & Hippopotamus. 10g, The Reception of Marie de Medici at Marseilles. 20g, Two Satyrs. 25g, Felicity of the Regency.

1978, June 30 *Perf. 14*

1824 A319 3g multicolored
1825 A319 4g multicolored
1826 A319 5g multicolored
1827 A319 6g multicolored
1828 A319 7g multicolored
1829 A319 8g multicolored
1830 A319 10g multicolored
1831 A319 20g multicolored
1832 A319 25g multicolored

Nos. 1830, 1832 are airmail.

National College A320

Perf. 13½x13

1978 Litho. Wmk. 347

1833 A320	3g	claret	.15	.15
1834 A320	4g	violet blue	.15	.15
1835 A320	5g	lilac	.15	.15
1836 A320	20g	brown	.16	.15
1837 A320	25g	violet black	.20	.15
1838 A320	30g	bright green	.25	.18
		Set value	.75	.60

Centenary of National College in Asuncion.
Nos. 1836-1838 are airmail.

José Estigarribia, Bugler, Flag of Paraguay A321

1978 Litho. *Perf. 13x13½*

1839 A321	3g	multi	.15	.15
1840 A321	5g	multi	.15	.15
1841 A321	10g	multi	.15	.15
1842 A321	20g	multi	.16	.15
1843 A321	25g	multi	.20	.15
1844 A321	30g	multi	.25	.18
		Set value	.78	.60

Induction of Jose Felix Estigarribia (1888-1940), general and president of Paraguay, into Salon de Bronce (National Heroes' Hall of Fame).
Nos. 1842-1844 are airmail.

Queen Elizabeth II Coronation, 25th Anniv. A322

Flowers and: 3g, Barbados #234. 4g, Tristan da Cunha #13. 5g, Bahamas #157. 6g, Seychelles #172. 7g, Solomon Islands #88. 8g, Cayman Islands #150. 10g, New Hebrides #77. 20g, St. Lucia #156. 25g, St. Helena #139.

No. 1854, Solomon Islands #368a-368c, Gilbert Islands #312a-312c. No. 1855, Great Britain #313-316.

1978, July 25 Unwmk. *Perf. 14*

1845 A322 3g multicolored
1846 A322 4g multicolored
1847 A322 5g multicolored
1848 A322 6g multicolored
1849 A322 7g multicolored
1850 A322 8g multicolored
1851 A322 10g multicolored
1852 A322 20g multicolored
1853 A322 25g multicolored

Souvenir Sheets

Perf. 13½

1854 A322 25g multicolored
1855 A322 25g multicolored

Nos. 1851, 1853-1855 are airmail. Nos. 1854-1855 each contain one 60x40mm stamp.

Intl. Philatelic Exhibitions A323

Various paintings, ship, nudes, etc. for: No. 1856a, 3g, Nordposta '78. b, 4g, Riccione '78. c, 5g, Uruguay '79. d, 6g, ESSEN '78. e, 7g, ESPAMER '79. f, 8g, London '80. g, 20g, PRAGA '78. 10g, EUROPA '78. No. 1858, Eurphila '78.
No. 1859, Francisco de Pinedo, map of his flight.

1978, July 19 *Perf. 14*

1856 A323 Strip of 7, #a.-g.
1857 A323 10g multicolored
1858 A323 25g multicolored

Souvenir Sheet

Perf. 13½x13

1859 A323 25g multicolored

No. 1859 for Riccione '78 and Eurphila '78 and contains one 54x34mm stamp. Nos. 1857-1859 are airmail. Nos. 1856b-1858 are vert.

Intl. Year of the Child — A324

Grimm's Snow White and the Seven Dwarfs: No. 1866a, 3g, Queen pricking her finger. b, 4g, Queen and mirror. c, 5g, Man with dagger, Snow White. d, 6g, Snow White in forest. e, 7g, Snow White asleep, seven dwarfs. f, 8g, Snow White dancing with dwarfs. g, 20g, Snow White being offered apple. 10g, Snow White in repose. 25g, Snow White, Prince Charming on horseback.

1978, Oct. 26

1866 A324 Strip of 7, #a.-g.
1867 A324 10g multicolored
1868 A324 25g multicolored

Nos. 1867-1868 are airmail.
See Nos. 1893-1896, 1916-1919.

Mounted South American Soldiers A325

No. 1869a, 3g, Gen. Jose Felix Bogado (1771-1829). b, 4g, Colonel, First Volunteer Regiment, 1806. c, 5g, Colonel wearing dress uniform, 1860. d, 6g, Soldier, 1864-1870. e, 7g, Dragoon, 1865. f, 8g, Lancer. g, 20g, Soldier, 1865. 10g, Gen. Bernardo O'Higgins, 200th birth anniv. 25g, Jose de San Martin, 200th birth anniv.

1978, Oct. 31

1869 A325 Strip of 7, #a.-g.
1870 A325 10g multicolored
1871 A325 25g multicolored

Nos. 1870-1871 are airmail.

1978 World Cup Soccer Championships, Argentina — A326

Soccer Players: No. 1872a, 3g, Paraguay, vert. b, 4g, Austria, Sweden. c, 5g, Argentina, Poland. d, 6g, Italy, Brazil. e, 7g, Netherlands, Austria. f, 8g, Scotland, Peru. g, 20g, Germany, Italy. 10g, Argentina, Holland. 25g, Germany, Tunisia.
No. 1875, Stadium.

1979, Jan. 9 *Perf. 14*

1872 A326 Strip of 7, #a.-g.
1873 A326 10g multicolored
1874 A326 25g multicolored

Souvenir Sheet

Perf. 13½

1875 A326 25g multicolored

Nos. 1873-1875 are airmail. No. 1875 contains one 60x40mm stamp.
For overprint see No. C610.

Christmas A327

Paintings of the Nativity and Madonna and Child by: No. 1876a, 3g, Giorgione, horiz. b, 4g, Titian. c, 5g, Titian, diff. d, 6g, Raphael. e, 7g, Schongauer. f, 8g, Muratti. g, 20g, Van Oost. 10g, Memling. No. 1878, Rubens.
No. 1879, Madonna and Child Surrounded by a Garland and Boy Angels, Rubens.

1979, Jan. 10 Litho. *Perf. 14*

1876 A327 Strip of 7, #a.-g.
1877 A327 10g multicolored
1878 A327 25g multicolored

Souvenir Sheet

Photo. & Engr.

Perf. 12

1879 A327 25g multicolored

Nos. 1877-1879 are airmail.

First Powered Flight, 75th Anniv. (in 1978) — A328

Airplanes: No. 1880a, 3g, Eole, C. Ader, 1890. b, 4g, Flyer III, Wright Brothers. c, 5g, Voisin, Henri Farman, 1908. d, 6g, Curtiss, Eugene Ely, 1910. e, 7g, Etrich-Taube A11. f, 8g, Fokker EIII. g, 20g, Albatros C, 1915. 10g, Boeing 747 carrying space shuttle. No. 1882, Boeing 707. No. 1883, Zeppelin flight commemorative cancels.

1979, Apr. 24 Litho. *Perf. 14*

1880 A328 Strip of 7, #a.-g.
1881 A328 10g multicolored
1882 A328 25g multicolored

Souvenir Sheet

Perf. 14½

1883 A328 25g blue & black

Nos. 1881-1883 are airmail. Nos. 1880-1883 incorrectly commemorate 75th anniv. of ICAO. No. 1883 contains one 50x40mm stamp.

Albrecht Durer, 450th Death Anniv. (in 1978) A329

Paintings: No. 1884a, 3g, Virgin with the Dove. b, 4g, Virgin Praying. c, 5g, Mater Dolorosa. d, 6g, Virgin with a Carnation. e, 7g, Madonna and Sleeping Child. f, 8g, Virgin Before the Archway. g, 20g, Flight Into Egypt. No. 1885, Madonna of the Haller family. No. 1886, Virgin with a Pear.
No. 1887, Lamentation Over the Dead Christ for Albrecht Glimm. No. 1888, Space station, horiz., with Northern Hemisphere of Celestial Globe in margin.

1979, Apr. 28 *Perf. 14*

1884 A329 Strip of 7, #a.-g.
1885 A329 10g multicolored
1886 A329 25g multicolored

Souvenir Sheets

Perf. 13½

1887 A329 25g multicolored
1888 A329 25g multicolored

Intl. Year of the Child (#1885-1886).
Nos. 1885-1886, 1888 are airmail. No. 1887 contains one 30x40mm stamp, No. 1888 one 40x30mm stamp.

Sir Rowland Hill, Death Cent. — A330

Hill and: No. 1889a, 3g, Newfoundland #C1, vert. b, 4g, France #C14. c, 5g, Spain #B106. d, 6g, Similar to Ecuador #C2, vert. e, 7g, US #C3a. f, 8g, Gelber Hund inverted overprint, vert. g, 20g, Switzerland #C20a.
10g, Privately issued Zeppelin stamp. No. 1891, Paraguay #C82, #C96, vert. No. 1892, Italy #C49. No. 1892A, France #C3-C4.

1979, June 11 *Perf. 14*

1889 A330 Strip of 7, #a.-g.
1890 A330 10g multicolored
1891 A330 25g multicolored

Souvenir Sheet

Perf. 13½x13

1892 A330 25g multicolored

Perf. 14½

1892A A330 25g multicolored

Issue dates: No. 1892A, Aug. 28. Others, June 11. Nos. 1890-1892A are airmail.

Grimm's Fairy Tales Type of 1978

Cinderella: No. 1893a, 3g, Two stepsisters watch Cinderella cleaning. b, 4g, Cinderella, father, stepsisters. c, 5g, Cinderella with birds while working. d, 6g, Finding dress. e, 7g, Going to ball. f, 8g, Dancing with prince. g, 20g, Losing slipper leaving ball.

10g, Prince Charming trying slipper on Cinderella's foot. No. 1895, Couple riding to castle. No. 1896, Couple entering ballroom.

1979, June 24 *Perf. 14*

1893 A324 Strip of 7, #a.-g.
1894 A324 10g multicolored
1895 A324 25g multicolored

Souvenir Sheet

Perf. 13½

1896 A324 25g multicolored

Intl. Year of the Child.

Congress Emblem — A331

1979, Aug. Litho. *Perf. 13x13½*

1897 A331	10g red, blue & black	.15	.15
1898 A331	50g red, blue & black	.40	.30

22nd Latin-American Tourism Congress, Asuncion. No. 1898 is airmail.

1980 Winter Olympics, Lake Placid — A332

#1899: a, 3g, Monica Scheftschik, luge. b, 4g, E. Deufl, Austria, downhill skiing. c, 5g, G. Thoeni, Italy, slalom skiing. d, 6g, Canada Two-man bobsled. e, 7g, Germany vs. Finland, ice hockey. f, 8g, Hoenl, Russia, ski jump. g, 20g, Dianne De Leeuw, Netherlands, figure skating, vert.

10g, Hanni Wenzel, Liechtenstein, slalom skiing. No. 1901, Frommelt, Liechtenstein, slalom skiing, vert. No. 1902, Kulakova, Russia, cross country skier. No. 1903, Dorothy Hamill, US, figure skating, vert. No. 1904, Brigitte Totschning, skier.

1979 Unwmk. *Perf. 14*

1899 A332 Strip of 7, #a.-g.
1900 A332 10g multicolored
1901 A332 25g multicolored

Souvenir Sheets

Perf. 13½

1902 A332 25g multicolored
1903 A332 25g multicolored
1904 A332 25g multicolored

#1900-1904 are airmail. #1902-1903 each contain one 40x30mm stamp, #1904, one 25x36mm stamp.

Issued: #1899-1902, 8/22; #1903, 6/11; #1904, 4/24.

Sailing Ships A333

No. 1905: a, 3g, Caravel, vert. b, 4g, Warship. c, 5g, Warship, by Jan van Beeck. d, 6g, H.M.S. Britannia, vert. e, 7g, Salamis, vert. f, 8g, Ariel, vert. g, 20g, Warship, by Robert Salmon.

1979, Aug. 28 *Perf. 14*

1905 A333 Strip of 7, #a.-g.
1906 A333 10g Lisette
1907 A333 25g Holstein, vert.

Nos. 1906-1907 are airmail.

Intl. Year of the Child — A334

Various kittens: No. 1908a, 3g. b, 4g. c, 5g. d, 6g. e, 7g. f, 8g. g, 20g.

1979, Nov. 29 *Perf. 14*

1908 A334 Strip of 7, #a.-g.
1909 A334 10g multicolored
1910 A334 25g multicolored

Nos. 1909-1910 are airmail.

Grimm's Fairy Tales Type of 1978

Little Red Riding Hood: No. 1916a, 3g, Leaving with basket. b, 4g, Meets wolf. c, 5g, Picks flowers. d, 6g, Wolf puts on Granny's gown. e, 7g, Wolf in bed. f, 8g, Hunter arrives. g, 20g, Saved by the hunter.

10g, Hunter enters house. No. 1918, Hunter leaves. No. 1919, Overall scene.

1979, Dec. 4 *Perf. 14*

1916 A324 Strip of 7, #a.-g.
1917 A324 10g multicolored
1918 A324 25g multicolored

Souvenir Sheet

Perf. 14½

1919 A324 25g multicolored

Intl. Year of the Child. No. 1919 contains one 50x70mm stamp.

Greek Athletes A335

Paintings on Greek vases: No. 1926a, 3g, 3 runners. b, 4g, 2 runners. c, 5g, Throwing contest. d, 6g, Discus. e, 7g, Wrestlers. f, 8g, Wrestlers, diff. g, 20g, 2 runners, diff.

10g, Horse and rider, horiz. 25g, 4 warriors with shields, horiz.

1979, Dec. 20 *Perf. 14*

1926 A335 Strip of 7, #a.-g.
1927 A335 10g multicolored
1928 A335 25g multicolored

Nos. 1927-1928 are airmail.

Electric Trains — A336

No. 1929: a, 3g, First electric locomotive, Siemens, 1879, vert. b, 4g, Switzerland, 1897. c, 5g, Model E71 28, Germany. d, 6g, Mountain train, Switzerland. e, 7g, Electric locomotive used in Benelux countries. f, 8g, Locomotive "Rheinpfeil," Germany. g, 20g, Model BB-9004, France.

10g, 200-Km/hour train, Germany. 25g, Japanese bullet train.

1979, Dec. 24 Litho. *Perf. 14*

1929 A336 Strip of 7, #a.-g.
1930 A336 10g multicolored
1931 A336 25g multicolored

Nos. 1930-1931 are airmail.

Sir Rowland Hill, Death Cent. — A337

Hill and: No. 1938a, 3g, Spad S XIII, 1917-18. b, 4g, P-51 D Mustang, 1944-45. c, 5g, Mitsubishi A6M6c Zero-Sen, 1944. d, 6g, Depperdussin float plane, 1913. e, 7g, Savoia Marchetti SM 7911, 1936. f, 8g, Messerschmitt Me 262B, 1942-45. g, 20g, Nieuport 24bis, 1917-18.

10g, Zeppelin LZ 104-/159, 1917. No. 1940, Fokker Dr-1 Caza, 1917. No. 1941, Vickers Supermarine "Spitfire" Mk.IX, 1942-45.

1980, Apr. 8 *Perf. 14*

1938 A337 Strip of 7, #a.-g.
1939 A337 10g multicolored
1940 A337 25g multicolored

Souvenir Sheet

Perf. 13½

1941 A337 25g multicolored

Incorrectly commemorates 75th anniv. of ICAO. Nos. 1939-1941 are airmail. No. 1941 contains one 37x27mm stamp.

Sir Rowland Hill, Paraguayan Stamps A338

Hill and: No. 1948a, 3g, #1. b, 4g, #5. c, 5g, #6. d, 6g, #379. e, 7g, #381. f, 8g, #C384. g, 20g, #C389.

10g, #C83, horiz. No. 1950, #C92, horiz. No. 1951, #C54, horiz. No. 1952, #C1, horiz.

1980, Apr. 14 Litho. *Perf. 14*

1948 A338 Strip of 7, #a.-g.
1949 A338 10g multicolored
1950 A338 25g multicolored

Souvenir Sheets

Perf. 14½

1951 A338 25g multicolored
1952 A338 25g multicolored

#1949-1952 are airmail. #1951 contains one 50x40mm stamp. #1952 one 50x35mm stamp.

1980 Winter Olympics, Lake Placid A339

No. 1953: a, 3g, Thomas Wassberg, Sweden, cross country skiing. b, 4g, Scharer & Benz, Switzerland, 2-man bobsled. c, 5g, Annemarie Moser-Proll, Austria, women's downhill skiing. d, 6g, Hockey team, US. e, 7g, Leonhard Stock, Austria, men's downhill skiing. f, 8g, Anton (Toni) Innauer, Austria, ski jump. g, 20g, Christa Kinshofer, Germany, slalom skiing.

10g, Ingemar Stenmark, slalom, Sweden. No. 1955, Robin Cousins, figure skating, Great Britain. No. 1956, Eric Heiden, speed skating, US, horiz.

1980, June 4 *Perf. 14*

1953 A339 Strip of 7, #a.-g.
1954 A339 10g multi, horiz.
1955 A339 25g multi, horiz.

Souvenir Sheet

Perf. 13½

1956 A339 25g multicolored

Nos. 1954-1956 are airmail. No. 1956 contains one 60x49mm stamp.

Composers and Paintings of Young Ballerinas A340

Paintings of ballerinas by Cydney or Degas and: No. 1957a, 3g, Gioacchino Rossini. b, 4g, Johann Strauss, the younger. c, 5g, Debussy. d, 6g, Beethoven. e, 7g, Chopin. f, 8g, Richard Wagner. g, 20g, Johann Sebastian Bach, horiz. 10g, Robert Stoltz. 25g, Verdi.

1980, July 1 *Perf. 14*

1957 A340 Strip of 7, #a.-g.
1958 A340 10g multicolored
1959 A340 25g multicolored

Birth and death dates are incorrectly inscribed on 4g, 8g, 10g. No. 1957f is incorrectly inscribed "Adolph" Wagner. Nos. 1958-1959 are airmail. For overprints see Nos. 1998-1999.

Pilar City Bicentennial A341

Perf. 13½x13

1980, July 17 Litho. Wmk. 347

1966 A341 5g multi	.15	.15
1967 A341 25g multi	.20	.15
Set value	.25	.20

No. 1967 is airmail.

Christmas, Intl. Year of the Child — A342

No. 1968: a, 3g, Christmas tree. b, 4g, Santa filling stockings. c, 5g, Nativity scene. d, 6g, Adoration of the Magi. e, 7g, Three children, presents. f, 8g, Children, dove, fruit. g, 20g, Children playing with toys. 10g, Madonna and Child, horiz. No. 1970, Children blowing bubbles, horiz. No. 1971, Five children, horiz.

1980, Aug. 4 Unwmk. *Perf. 14*

1968 A342 Strip of 7, #a.-g.
1969 A342 10g multicolored
1970 A342 25g multicolored

Souvenir Sheet

1971 A342 25g multicolored

Nos. 1969-1970 are airmail.

Ships A343

Emblems and ships: No. 1972a, 3g, ESPAMER '80, Spanish Armada. b, 4g, NORWEX '80, Viking longboat. c, 5g, RICCIONE '80, Battle of Lepanto. d, 6g, ESSEN '80, Great Harry of Cruickshank. e, 7g, US Bicentennial, Mount Vernon. f, 8g, LONDON '80, H.M.S. Victory. g, 20g, ESSEN '80, Hamburg III, vert. 10g, ESSEN '80, Gorch Fock. 25g, PHILATOKYO '81, Nippon Maru, horiz.

1980, Sept. 15 *Perf. 14*

1972 A343 Strip of 7, #a.-g.
1973 A343 10g multicolored
1974 A343 25g multicolored

Nos. 1973-1974 are airmail. For overprint see No. 2278.

Souvenir Sheet

King Juan Carlos A344

1980, Sept. 19 *Perf. 14½*

1975 A344 25g multicolored

Paraguay Airlines Boeing 707 Service Inauguration — A345

Perf. 13½x13

1980, Sept. 17 Litho. Wmk. 347

1976 A345	20g multi	.16	.15
1977 A345	100g multi	.80	.65

No. 1977 is airmail.

A346

World Cup Soccer Championships, Spain — A346a

Various soccer players, winning country: No. 1978a, 3g, Uruguay 1930, 1950. b, 4g, Italy 1934, 1938. c, 5g, Germany 1954, 1974. d, 6g, Brazil 1958, 1962, 1970. e, 7g, England, 1966. f, 8g, Argentina, 1978. g, 20g, Espana '82 emblem.
10g, World Cup trophy, flags. 25g, Soccer player from Uruguay.

1980, Dec. 10 Unwmk. *Perf. 14*

1978 A346 Strip of 7, #a.-g.
1979 A346 10g multicolored
1980 A346 25g multicolored

Souvenir Sheet

Perf. 14½

1981 A346a 25g Sheet of 1 + 2 labels

Nos. 1979-1981 are airmail.

1980 World Chess Championships, Mexico — A347

Illustrations from The Book of Chess: No. 1982a, 3g, Two men, chess board. b, 4g, Circular chess board, players. c, 5g, Four-person chess match. d, 6g, King Alfonso X of Castile and Leon. e, 7g, Two players, chess board, horiz. f, 8g, Two veiled women, chess board, horiz. g, 20g, Two women in robes, chess board, horiz.
10g, Crusader knights, chess board, horiz. 25g, Three players, chess board, horiz.

1980, Dec. 15 Litho. *Perf. 14*

1982 A347 Strip of 7, #a.-g.
1983 A347 10g multicolored
1984 A347 25g multicolored

Nos. 1983-1984 are airmail.
See Nos. C506-C510. Compare with illustration AP199.

1980 Winter Olympics, Lake Placid A348

Olympic scenes, gold medalists: No. 1985a, 25c, Lighting Olympic flame. b, 50c, Hockey team, US. c, 1g, Eric Heiden, US, speed skating. d, 2g, Robin Cousins, Great Britain, figure skating. e, 3g, Thomas Wassberg, Sweden, cross country skiing. f, 4g, Annie Borckinck, Netherlands, speed skating. g, 5g, Gold, silver, and bronze medals.
No. 1986, Irene Epple, silver medal, slalom, Germany. 10g, Ingemar Stenmark, slalom, giant slalom, Sweden. 30g, Annemarie Moser-Proll, downhill, Austria. 25g, Baron Pierre de Coubertin.

1981, Feb. 4 Litho. *Perf. 14*

1985 A348 Strip of 7, #a.-g.
1986 A348 5g multicolored
1987 A348 10g multicolored
1988 A348 30g multicolored

Souvenir Sheet

Perf. 13½

1988A A348 25g multicolored

No. 1985 exists in strips of 4 and 3. Nos. 1986-1988A are airmail. No. 1988A contains one 30x40mm stamp.

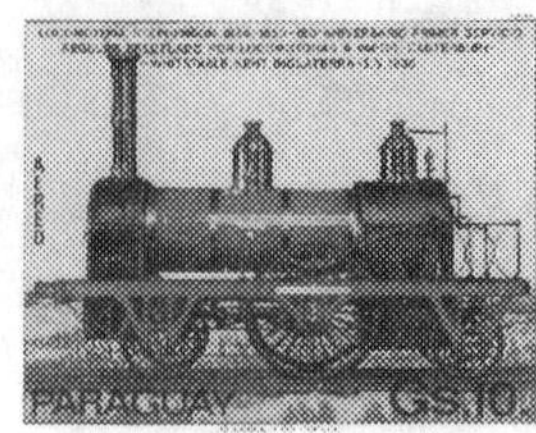

Locomotives — A349

No. 1989, 25c, Electric model 242, Germany. b, 50c, Electric, London-Midlands-Lancashire, England. c, 1g, Electric, Switzerland. d, 2g, Diesel-electric, Montreal-Vancouver, Canada. e, 3g, Electric, Austria. f, 4g, Electric inter-urban, Lyons-St. Etienne, France, vert. g, 5g, First steam locomotive in Paraguay.
No. 1991, Steam locomotive, Japan. 10g, Stephenson's steam engine, 1830 England. No. 1993, Crocodile locomotive, Switzerland. 30g, Stephenson's Rocket, 1829, England, vert.

1981, Feb. 9 Litho. *Perf. 14*

1989 A349 Strip of 7, #a.-g.
1990 A349 5g multicolored
1991 A349 10g multicolored
1992 A349 30g multicolored

Souvenir Sheet

Perf. 13½x13

1993 A349 25g multicolored

Electric railroads, cent. (#1989a-1989f), steam-powered railway service, 150th anniv. (#1989g, 1990-1991), Liverpool-Manchester Railway, 150th anniv. (#1992). Swiss Railways, 75th anniv. (#1993).
Nos. 1990-1993 are airmail. No. 1993 contains one 54x34mm stamp.

Intl. Year of the Child A350

Portraits of children with assorted flowers: No. 1994a, 10g. b, 25g. c, 50g. d, 100g. e, 200g. f, 300g. g, 400g.

1981, Apr. 13 Litho. *Perf. 14*

1994 A350 Strip of 7, #a.-g.
1995 A350 75g multicolored
1996 A350 500g multicolored
1997 A350 1000g multicolored

Nos. 1995-1997 are airmail.

Nos. 1957b and 1958 Overprinted in Red

1981, May 22

1998 A340 4g on #1957b
1999 A340 10g on #1958

No. 1999 is airmail.

The following stamps were issued in sheets of 8 with 1 label: Nos. 2001, 2013, 2037, 2044, 2047, 2055, 2140.
The following stamp was issued in sheets of 10 with 2 labels: No. 1994a.
The following stamps were issued in sheets of 6 with 3 labels: Nos. 2017, 2029, 2035, 2104, 2145.
The following stamps were issued in sheets of 3 with 6 labels: 2079, 2143.
The following stamps were issued in sheets of 5 with 4 labels: Nos. 2050-2051, 2057, 2059, 2061, 2067, 2069, 2077, 2082, 2089, 2092, 2107, 2117, 2120, 2121, 2123, 2125, 2129, 2135, 2138, 2142, 2146, 2148, 2151, 2160, 2163, 2165, 2169, 2172, 2176, 2179, 2182, 2190, 2196, 2202, 2204, 2214, 2222, 2224, 2232, 2244, 2246, 2248, 2261, 2263, 2265, 2271, 2273, 2275, 2277.
The following stamps were issued in sheets of 4 with 5 labels: Nos. 2307, 2310, 2313, 2316, 2324, 2329.

Royal Wedding of Prince Charles and Lady Diana Spencer — A351

Prince Charles, sailing ships: No. 2000a, 25c, Royal George. b, 50c, Great Britain. c, 1g, Taeping. d, 2g, Star of India. e, 3g, Torrens. f, 4g, Loch Etive. No. 2001, Medway.
No. 2002, Charles, flags, and Concorde. 10g, Flags, flowers, Diana, Charles. 25g, Charles, Diana, flowers, vert. 30g, Coats of arms, flags.

1981, June 27

2000 A351 Strip of 6, #a.-f.
2001 A351 5g multicolored
2002 A351 5g multicolored
2003 A351 10g multicolored
2004 A351 30g multicolored

Souvenir Sheet

Perf. 13½

2005 A351 25g multicolored

Nos. 2002-2005 are airmail. No. 2005 contains one 50x60mm stamp. For overprint see No. 2253.

Traditional Costumes and Itaipu Dam A352

Women in various traditional costumes: a, 10g. b, 25g. c, 50g. d, 100g. e, 200g. f, 300g. g, 400g, President Stroessner, Itaipu Dam.

1981, June 30 *Perf. 14*

2006 A352 Strip of 7, #a.-g.

For overprints see No. 2281.

UPU Membership Centenary — A353

1981, Aug. 18 Litho. *Perf. 13½x13*

2007 A353	5g rose lake & blk	.15	.15
2008 A353	10g lil & blk	.15	.15
2009 A353	20g grn & blk	.16	.15

2010 A353	25g lt red brn & blk		.20	.15
2011 A353	50g bl & blk		.40	.30
		Set value	.88	.68

Peter Paul Rubens, Paintings A354

Details from paintings: No. 2012: a, 25c, Madonna Surrounded by Saints. b, 50c, Judgment of Paris. c, 1g, Duke of Buckingham Conducted to the Temple of Virtus. d, 2g, Minerva Protecting Peace from Mars. e, 3g, Henry IV Receiving the Portrait of Marie de Medici. f, 4g, Triumph of Juliers. 5g, Madonna and Child Reigning Among Saints (Cherubs).

1981, July 9 Litho. *Perf. 14*

2012 A354 Strip of 6, #a.-f.
2013 A354 5g multicolored

Jean Auguste-Dominique Ingres (1780-1867), Painter — A355

Details from paintings: No. 2014: a, 25c, c, 1g, d, 2g, f, 4g, The Turkish Bath. b, 50c, The Water Pitcher. e, 3g, Oediphus and the Sphinx. g, 5g, The Bathing Beauty.

1981, Oct. 13

2014 A355 Strip of 7, #a.-g.

No. 2014f and 2014g exist in sheet of 8 (four each) plus label. For overprints see No. 2045.

Pablo Picasso, Birth Cent. — A356

Designs: No. 2015: a, 25c, Women Running on the Beach. b, 50c, Family on the Beach.
No. 2016: a, 1g, Still-life. b, 2g, Bullfighter. c, 3g, Children Drawing. d, 4g, Seated Woman. 5g, Paul as Clown.

1981, Oct. 19

2015 A356 Pair, #a.-b.
2016 A356 Strip of 4, #a.-d.
2017 A356 5g multicolored

Nos. 2015-2016 Ovptd. in Silver

1981, Oct. 22

2018 A356 on Nos. 2015a-2015b
2019 A356 on Nos. 2016a-2016d

Philatelia '81, Frankfurt.

Nos. 2015-2016 Ovptd. in Gold

1981, Oct. 25

2020 A356 on Nos. 2015a-2015b
2021 A356 on Nos. 2016a-2016d

Espamer '81 Philatelic Exhibition.

Royal Wedding of Prince Charles and Lady Diana A357

Designs: No. 2022a-2022c, 25c, 50c, 1g, Diana, Charles, flowers. d, 2g, Couple. e, 3g, Couple leaving church. f, 4g, Couple, Queen Elizabeth II waving from balcony. g, 5g, Diana. No. 2023, Wedding party, horiz. 10g, Riding in royal coach, horiz. 30g, Yeomen of the guard, horiz.

1981, Dec. 4 Litho. *Perf. 14*

2022 A357 Strip of 7, #a.-g.
2023 A357 5g multicolored
2024 A357 10g multicolored
2025 A357 30g multicolored

Souvenir Sheets

Perf. 14½

2026 A357 25g like #2022d
2027 A357 25g Wedding portrait

No. 2022g exists in sheets of 8 plus label. Nos. 2023-2027 are airmail. Nos. 2026-2027 contain one each 50x70mm stamp.

Christmas A358

Designs: No. 2028a, 25c, Jack-in-the-box. b, 50c, Jesus and angel. c, 1g, Santa, angels. d, 2g, Angels lighting candle. e, 3g, Christmas plant. f, 4g, Nativity scene. 5g, Children singing by Christmas tree.

1981, Dec. 17 *Perf. 14*

2028 A358 Strip of 6, #a.-f.

Size: 28x45mm

Perf. 13½

2029 A358 5g multicolored

Intl. Year of the Child (Nos. 2028-2029). For overprints see No. 2042.

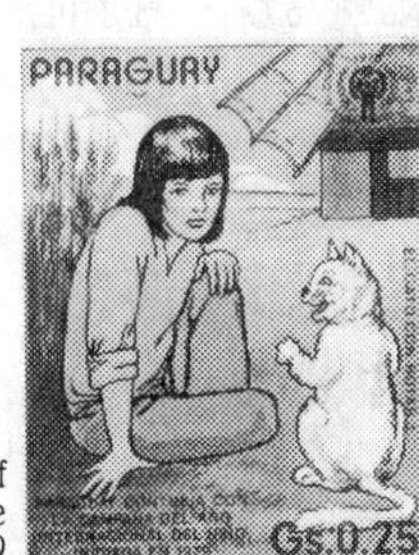

Intl. Year of the Child — A359

Story of Puss 'n Boots: No. 2030a, 25c, Boy, Puss. b, 50c, Puss, rabbits.
1g, Puss, king. 2g, Prince, princess, king. 3g, Giant ogre, Puss. 4g, Puss chasing mouse. 5g, Princess, prince, Puss.

1982, Apr. 16 Litho. *Perf. 14*

2030 A359 Pair, #a.-b.
2031 A359 1g multicolored
2032 A359 2g multicolored
2033 A359 3g multicolored
2034 A359 4g multicolored
2035 A359 5g multicolored

#2031-2034 printed se-tenant with label.

Scouting, 75th Anniv. and Lord Baden-Powell, 125th Birth Anniv. — A360

No. 2036: a, 25c, Tetradactyla, Scout hand salute. b, 50c, Nandu (rhea), Cub Scout and trefoil. c, 1g, Peccary, Wolf's head totem. d, 2g, Coatimundi, emblem on buckle. e, 3g, Mara, Scouting's Intl. Communications emblem. f, 4g, Deer, boy scout.
No. 2037, Aotes, Den mother, Cub Scout. No. 2038, Ocelot, scouts cooking. 10g, Collie, boy scout. 30g, Armadillo, two scouts planting tree. 25g, Lord Robert Baden-Powell, founder of Boy Scouts.

1982, Apr. 21

2036 A360 Strip of 6, #a.-f.
2037 A360 5g multicolored
2038 A360 5g multicolored
2039 A360 10g multicolored
2040 A360 30g multicolored

Souvenir Sheet

Perf. 14½

2041 A360 25g multicolored

Nos. 2038-2041 are airmail. For overprint see No. 2140.

No. 2028 Overprinted with ESSEN 82 Emblem

1982, Apr. 28 *Perf. 14*

2042 A358 on #2028a-2028f

Essen '82 Intl. Philatelic Exhibition.

Cats and Kittens — A361

Various cats or kittens: No. 2043a, 25c. b, 50c. c, 1g. d, 2g. e, 3g. f, 4g.

1982, June 7 *Perf. 14*

2043 A361 Strip of 6, #a.-f.
2044 A361 5g multi, vert.

For overprints see Nos. 2054-2055.

Nos. 2014a-2014e Ovptd. PHILEXFRANCE 82 Emblem ans "PARIS 11-21.6.82" in Blue

1982, June 11

2045 A355 Strip of 5, #a.-e.

Philexfrance '82 Intl. Philatelic Exhibition. Size of overprint varies.

World Cup Soccer Championships, Spain — A362

Designs: 2046a, 25c, Brazilian team. b, 50c, Chilean team. c, 1g, Honduran team. d, 2g, Peruvian team. e, 3g, Salvadoran team. f, 4g, Globe as soccer ball, flags of Latin American finalists. No. 2047, Ball of flags. No. 2048, Austrian team. No. 2049, Players from Brazil, Austria. No. 2050, Spanish team. No. 2051, Two players from Argentina, Brazil, vert. No. 2052, W. German team. No. 2053, Players from Argentina, Brazil. No. 2053A, World Cup trophy, world map on soccer balls. No. 2053B, Players from W. Germany, Mexico, vert.

1982 Litho. *Perf. 14*

2046 A362 Strip of 6, #a.-f.
2047 A362 5g multicolored
2048 A362 5g multicolored
2049 A362 5g multicolored
2050 A362 10g multicolored
2051 A362 10g multicolored
2052 A362 30g multicolored
2053 A362 30g multicolored

Souvenir Sheets

Perf. 14½

2053A A362 25g multicolored
2053B A362 25g multicolored

Issue dates: Nos. 2049, 2051, 2053, 2053A, Apr. 19. Others, June 13.
Nos. 2047 exists in sheets of 8 plus label. Nos. 2048-2053B are airmail.
For overprints see Nos. 2086, 2286, C593.

Nos. 2043-2044 Overprinted in Silver With PHILATECIA 82 and Intl. Year of the Child Emblems

1982, Sept. 12 *Perf. 14*

2054 A361 Strip of 5, #a.-e.
2055 A361 5g on #2044

Philatelia '82, Hanover, Germany and Intl. Year of the Child.

Raphael, 500th Birth Anniv. A363

Details from paintings: No. 2056a, 25c, Adam and Eve (The Fall). b, 50c, Creation of Eve. c, 1g, Portrait of a Young Woman (La Fornarina). d, 2g The Three Graces. e, 3g, f, 4g, Cupid and the Three Graces. 5g. Leda and the Swan.

1982, Sept. 27

2056 A363 Strip of 6, #a.-f.
2057 A363 5g multicolored

Nos. 2056e-2056f have continuous design.

Christmas A364

Entire works or details from paintings by Raphael: No. 2058a, 25c, The Belvedere Madonna. b, 50c, The Ansidei Madonna. c, 1g, La Belle Jardiniere. d, 2g, The Aldobrandini (Garvagh) Madonna. e, 3g, Madonna of the Goldfinch. f, 4g, The Alba Madonna. No. 2059, Madonna of the

Grand Duke. No. 2060, Madonna of the Linen Window. 10g, The Alba Madonna, diff. 25g, The Holy Family with St. Elizabeth and the Infant St. John and Two Angels. 30g, The Canigiani Holy Family.

1982 *Perf. 14, 13x13½ (#2061)*
2058 A364 Strip of 6, #a.-f.
2059 A364 5g multicolored
2060 A364 5g multicolored
2061 A364 10g multicolored
2062 A364 30g multicolored

Souvenir Sheet
Perf. 14½
2063 A364 25g multicolored

Issued: #2058-2059, 9/30; others, 12/17.
Nos. 2058a-2058f and 2059 exist perf. 13. Nos. 2060-2063 are airmail and have silver lettering. For overprint see No. 2087.

Life of Christ, by Albrecht Durer A365

Details from paintings: No. 2064a, 25c, The Flight into Egypt. b, 50c, Christ Among the Doctors. c, 1g, Christ Carrying the Cross. d, 2g, Nailing of Christ to the Cross. e, 3g, Christ on the Cross. f, 4g, Lamentation Over the Dead Christ. 5g, The Circumcision of Christ.

1982, Dec. 14 *Perf. 14*
2064 A365 Strip of 6, #a.-f.
Perf. 13x13½
2065 A365 5g multicolored

For overprint see No. 2094.

South American Locomotives — A366

Locomotives from: No. 2066a, 25c, Argentina. b, 50c, Uruguay. c, 1g, Ecuador. d, 2g, Bolivia. e, 3g, Peru. f, 4g, Brazil. 5g, Paraguay.

1983, Jan. 17 Litho. *Perf. 14*
2066 A366 Strip of 6, #a.-f.
2067 A366 5g multicolored

For overprint see No. 2093.

Race Cars A367

No. 2068: a, 25c, ATS-Ford D 06. b, 50c, Ferrari 126 C 2. c, 1g, Brabham-BMW BT 50. d, 2g, Renault RE 30 B. e, 3g, Porsche 956. f, 4g, Talbot-Ligier-Matra JS 19. 5g, Mercedes Benz C-111.

1983, Jan. 19 *Perf. 14*
2068 A367 Strip of 6, #a.-f.
Perf. 13½x13
2069 A367 5g multicolored

For overprint see No. 2118.

Itaipua Dam, Pres. Stroessner — A368

1983, Jan. 22	**Litho.**	**Wmk. 347**	
2070 A368	3g multi	.15	.15
2071 A368	5g multi	.15	.15
2072 A368	10g multi	.15	.15
2073 A368	20g multi	.16	.15
2074 A368	25g multi	.20	.15
2075 A368	50g multi	.40	.30
	Set value	.92	.70

25th anniv. of Stroessner City.
Nos. 2073-2075 airmail.

1984 Winter Olympics, Sarajevo — A369

Ice skaters: No. 2076a, 25c, Marika Kilius, Hans-Jurgens Baumler, Germany, 1964. b, 50c, Tai Babilonia, Randy Gardner, US, 1976. c, 1g, Anett Poetzsch, E. Germany, 1980, vert. d, 2g, Tina Riegel, Andreas Nischwitz, Germany, 1980, vert. e, Dagmar Lurz, Germany, 1980, vert. f, 4g, Trixi Schuba, Austria, 1972, vert. 5g, Peggy Fleming, US, 1968, vert.

Perf. 13½x13, 13x13½
1983, Feb. 23 **Unwmk.**
2076 A369 Strip of 6, #a.-f.
2077 A369 5g multicolored

For overprints see Nos. 2177, 2266.

Pope John Paul II A370

#2078: a, 25c, Virgin of Caacupe. b, 50c, Cathedral of Caacupe. c, 1g, Cathedral of Asuncion. d, 2g, Pope holding crucifix. e, 3g, Our Lady of the Assumption. f, 4g, Pope giving blessing. 5g, Pope with hands clasped. 25g, Madonna & child.

1983, June 11 Litho. *Perf. 14*
2078 A370 Strip of 6, #a.-f.
2079 A370 5g multicolored

Souvenir Sheet
Perf. 14½
2080 A370 25g multicolored

No. 2080 is airmail. For overprint see No. 2143.

Antique Automobiles — A371

No. 2081: a, 25c, Bordino Steamcoach, 1854. b, 50c, Panhard & Levassor, 1892. c, 1g, Benz Velo, 1894. d, 2g, Peugeot-Daimler, 1894. e, 3g, 1st car with patented Lutzmann system, 1898. f, 4g, Benz Victory, 1891-92. No. 2082, Ceirano 5CV. No. 2083, Mercedes Simplex PS 32 Turismo, 1902. 10g, Stae Electric, 1909. 25g, Benz Velocipede, 1885. 30g, Rolls Royce Silver Ghost, 1913.

1983, July 18 *Perf. 14*
2081 A371 Strip of 6, #a.-f.
2082 A371 5g multicolored
2083 A371 5g multicolored
2084 A371 10g multicolored
2085 A371 30g multicolored

Souvenir Sheet
Perf. 14½
2085A A371 25g Sheet of 1 + label

Nos. 2083-2085A are airmail.

No. 2046 Ovptd. in Red, No. 2058 Ovptd. in Black with "52o CONGRESO F.I.P." and Brasiliana 83 Emblem

1983, July 27 *Perf. 14*
2086 A362 Strip of 6, #a.-f.
2087 A364 Strip of 6, #a.-f.

Brasiliana '83, Rio de Janiero and 52nd FIP Congress. No. 2087 exists perf. 13.

Aircraft Carriers — A372

Carriers and airplanes: No. 2088a, 25c, 25 de Mayo, A-4Q Sky Hawk, Argentina. b, 50c, Minas Gerais, Brazil. c, 1g, Akagi, A6M3 Zero, Japan. d, 2g, Guiseppe Miraglia, Italy. e, 3g, Enterprise, S-3A Viking, US. f, 4g, Dedalo, AV-8A Matador, Spain. 5g, Schwabenland, Dornier DO-18, Germany. No aircraft on Nos. 2088b, 2088d.
25g, US astronauts Donn Eisele, Walter Schirra & Walt Cunningham, Earth & Apollo 7.

1983, Aug. 29 *Perf. 14*
2088 A372 Strip of 6, #a.-f.
2089 A372 5g multicolored

Souvenir Sheet
Perf. 13½
2090 A372 25g multicolored

No. 2090 is airmail and contains one 55x45mm stamp.

Birds A373

#2091: a, 25c, Pulsatrix perspicillata. b, 50c, Ortalis ruficauda. c, 1g, Chloroceryle amazona. d, 2g, Trogon violaceus. e, 3g, Pezites militaris. f, 4g, Bucco capensis. 5g, Cyanerpes cyaneus.

1983, Oct. 22 *Perf. 14*
2091 A373 Strip of 6, #a.-f.
Perf. 13
2092 A373 5g multicolored

No. 2066 Ovptd. for PHILATELICA 83 in Silver

1983, Oct. 28
2093 A366 Strip of 6, #a.-f.

Philatelia '83, Dusseldorf, Germany.

No. 2064 Overprinted in Silver for EXFIVIA - 83

1983, Nov. 5
2094 A365 Strip of 6, #a.-f.

Exfivia '83 Philatelic Exhibition, La Paz, Bolivia.

Re-election of President Stroessner — A374

10g, Passion flower, vert. 25g, Miltonia phalaenopsis, vert. 50g, Natl. arms, Chaco soldier. 75g, Acaray hydroelectric dam. 100g, Itaipu hydroelectric dam. 200g, Pres. Alfredo Stroessner, vert.

1983, Nov. 24 *Perf. 14*
2095 A374 10g multicolored
2096 A374 25g multicolored
2097 A374 50g multicolored
2098 A374 75g multicolored
Perf. 13
2099 A374 100g multicolored
2100 A374 200g multicolored

#2099-2100 are airmail. #2096 exists perf 13. For overprint see #C577.

Montgolfier Brothers' 1st Flight, Bicent. — A375

No. 2101: a, 25c, Santos-Dumont's Biplane, 1906. b, 50c, Airship. No. 2102a, 1g, Paulhan's biplane over Juvisy. b, 2g, Zeppelin LZ-3, 1907. No. 2103a, 3g, Biplane of Henri Farman. b, 4g, Graf Zeppelin over Friedrichshafen. 5g, Lebaudy's dirigible. 25g, Detail of painting, Great Week of Aviation at Betheny, 1910.

1984, Jan. 7 *Perf. 13*
2101 A375 Pair, #a.-b.
2102 A375 Pair, #a.-b.
2103 A375 Pair, #a.-b.
Perf. 14
2104 A375 5g multicolored

Souvenir Sheet
Perf. 13½
2105 A375 25g multicolored

No. 2105 is airmail and contains one 75x55mm stamp. For overprint see No. 2145.

Dogs A376

#2106: a, 25c, German Shepherd. b, 50c, Great Dane, vert. c, 1g, Poodle, vert. d, 2g, Saint Bernard. e, 3g, Greyhound. f, 4g, Dachshund. 5g, Boxer.

1984, Jan. 11 Litho. *Perf. 14*
2106 A376 Strip of 6, #a.-f.
2107 A376 5g multicolored

Animals, Anniversaries — A377

1984, Jan. 24 *Perf. 13*
2108 A377 10g Puma
2109 A377 25g Alligator
2110 A377 50g Jaguar
2111 A377 75g Peccary
2112 A377 100g Simon Bolivar, vert.
2113 A377 200g Girl scout, vert.

Simon Bolivar, birth bicent. and Girl Scouts of Paraguay, 76th anniv.
Nos. 2112-2113 are airmail.

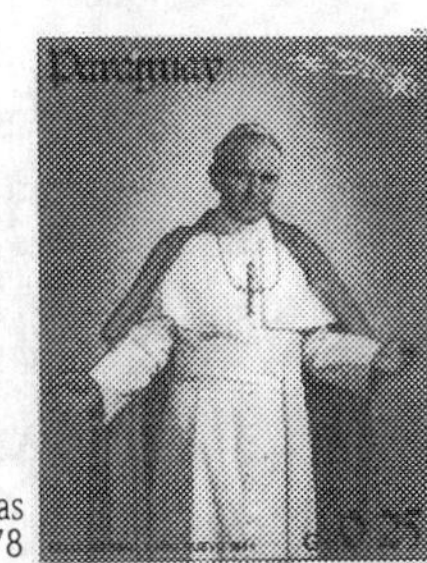
Christmas A378

Designs: No. 2114a, 25c, Pope John Paul II. b, 50c, Christmas tree. c, 1g, Children. d, 2g, Nativity Scene. e, 3g, Three Kings. f, 4g, Madonna and Child. No. 2115, Madonna and Child by Raphael.

1984, Mar. 23 *Perf. 13x13½*
2114 A378 Strip of 6, #a.-f.
2115 A378 5g multicolored

Troubadour Knights A379

Illustrations of medieval miniatures: No. 2116a, 25c, Ulrich von Liechtenstein. b, 50c, Ulrich von Gutenberg. c, 1g, Der Putter. d, 2g, Walther von Metz. e, 3g, Hartman von Aue. f, 4g, Lutok von Seuen. 5g, Werner von Teufen.

1984, Mar. 27 *Perf. 14*
2116 A379 Strip of 6, #a.-f.
Perf. 13
2117 A379 5g multicolored

For overprint see No. 2121.

No. 2068 Ovptd. in Silver with ESSEN 84 Emblem

1984, May 10
2118 A367 Strip of 6, #a.-f.

Essen '84 Intl. Philatelic Exhibition.

Endangered Animals — A380

Designs: No. 2119a, 25c, Priodontes giganteus. b, 50c, Catagonus wagneri. c, 1g, Felis pardalis. d, 2g, Chrysocyon brachyurus. e, 3g, Burmeisteria retusa. f, 4g, Myrmecophaga tridactyla. 5g, Caiman crocodilus.

1984, June 16 *Perf. 14*
2119 A380 Strip of 6, #a.-f.
Perf. 13
2120 A380 5g multicolored

For overprint see No. 2129.

No. 2117 Ovptd. in Silver with Emblems, etc., for U.P.U. 19th World Congress, Hamburg

1984, June 19 *Perf. 13*
2121 A379 5g on #2117

UPU Congress, Hamburg '84 — A381

Sailing ships: No. 2122a, 25c, Admiral of Hamburg. b, 50c, Neptune. c, 1g, Archimedes. d, 2g, Passat. e, 3g, Finkenwerder cutter off Heligoland. f, 4g, Four-masted ship. 5g, Deutschland.

1984, June 19 *Perf. 13*
2122 A381 Strip of 6, #a.-f.
2123 A381 5g multicolored

For overprints see Nos. 2146, 2279-2280.

British Locomotives — A382

No. 2124: a, 25c, Pegasus 097, 1868. b, 50c, Pegasus 097, diff. c, 1g, Cornwall, 1847. d, 2g, Cornwall, 1847, diff. e, 3g, Patrick Stirling #1, 1870. f, 4g, Patrick Stirling #1, 1870, diff. 5g, Stepney Brighton Terrier, 1872.

1984, June 20 *Perf. 14*
2124 A382 Strip of 6, #a.-f.
Perf. 13
2125 A382 5g multicolored

No. C486 Overprinted in Blue on Silver with UN emblem and "40o Aniversario de la / Fundacion de las / Naciones Unidas 26.6.1944"

1984, Aug. 1 **Litho.** *Perf. 14½*
2126 AP161 25g on No. C486

No. 1536 Ovptd. in Orange (#a.-d.) or Silver (#e.-g.) with AUSIPEX 84 Emblem and:

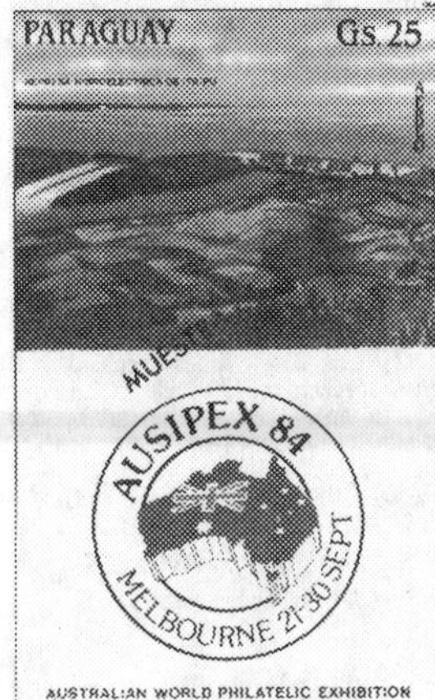

A383

1984, Aug. 21 *Perf. 14*
2127 A271 Strip of 7, #a.-g.

Souvenir Sheet
Perf. 14½
2128 A383 25g multicolored

Ausipex '84 Intl. Philatelic Exhibition, Melbourne, Australia. No. 2128 is airmail.

Nos. 2120 and C551 Ovptd. in Black and Red

PHILA KOREA 1984
COREA SEDE DE FUTUROS JUEGOS OLIMPICOS DE VERANO
1988

1984 *Perf. 13*
2129 A380 5g on #2120
Perf. 14
2130 AP178 30g on #C551

Issued: #2129, Sept. 20; #2130, Aug. 30.
No. 2130 is airmail.

No. 1512 Ovptd. "VER STUTTGART CAMPEON NACIONAL DE FUTBOL DE ALEMANIA 1984" and Emblem

1984, Sept. 5 *Perf. 14*
2131 A263 Strip of 7, #a.-g.

VFB Stuttgart, 1984 German Soccer Champions.

Cat Type of 1976

Various cats: No. 2132: a, 25c. b, 50c. c, 1g. d, 2g. e, 3g. f, 4g.

1984, Sept. 10 *Perf. 13x13½*
2132 A287 Strip of 6, #a.-f.
2133 A287 5g multicolored

1984 Summer Olympics, Los Angeles — A384

Gold medalists: No. 2134a, 25c Michael Gross, W. Germany, swimming. b, 50c, Peter Vidmar, US, gymnastics. c, 1g, Fredy Schmidtke, W. Germany, cycling. d, 2g, Philippe Boisse, France, fencing. e, 3g, Ulrike Meyfarth, W. Germany, women's high jump. f, 4g, Games emblem. 5g, Mary Lou Retton, US, women's all-around gymnastics, vert. 30g, Rolf Milser, W. Germany, weight lifting, vert.

1985, Jan. 16 **Litho.** *Perf. 13*
2134 A384 Strip of 6, #a.-f.
2135 A384 5g multicolored

Souvenir Sheet
Perf. 13½
2136 A384 30g multicolored

No. 2136 is airmail and contains one 50x60mm stamp. For overprints see Nos. 2174, 2199, 2200. Compare with type A399.

Mushrooms A385

#2137: a, 25c, Boletus luteus. b, 50c, Agaricus campester. c, 1g, Pholiota spectabilis. d, 2g, Tricholoma terreum. e, 3g, Laccaria laccata. f, 4g, Amanita phalloides. 5g, Scleroderna verrucosum.

1985, Jan. 19 *Perf. 14*
2137 A385 Strip of 6, #a.-f.
2138 A385 5g multicolored

See Nos. 2166-2167.

World Wildlife Fund — A386

Endangered or extinct species: No. 2139a, 25c, Capybara. b, 50c, Mono titi, vert. c, 1g, Rana cornuda adornada. d, 2g, Priodontes giganteus, digging. e, 3g, Priodontes giganteus, by water. f, 4g, Myrmecophaga tridactyla. g, 5g, Myrmecophaga tridactyla, with young.

1985, Mar. 13 *Perf. 14*
2139 A386 Strip of 7, #a.-g.

See No. 2252.

No. 2037 Ovptd. in Red with ISRAPHIL Emblem

1985, Apr. 10
2140 A360 5g on No. 2037

Israel '85 Intl. Philatelic Exhibition.

John James Audubon, Birth Bicent. A387

Birds: No. 2141a, 25c, Piranga flava. b, 50c, Polyborus plancus. c, 1g, Chiroxiphia caudata. d, 2g, Xolmis irupero. e, 3g, Phloeoceastes leucopogon. f, 4g, Thraupis bonariensis. 5g, Parula pitiayumi, horiz.

1985, Apr. 18 *Perf. 13*
2141 A387 Strip of 6, #a.-f.
2142 A387 5g multicolored

No. 2079 Ovptd. in Silver with Italia '85 Emblem

1985, May 20 *Perf. 14*
2143 A370 5g on #2079

Italia '85 Intl. Philatelic Exhibition.

No. 1448e Ovptd. in Red on Silver

12 de Junio 1935 · 1985
Cincuentenario de la
PAZ del CHACO

1985, June 12
2144 A250 30c on #1448e

No. 2104 Ovptd. in Silver and Blue with LUPO 85 Congress Emblem

1985, July 5
2145 A375 5g on No. 2104

LUPO '85, Lucerne, Switzerland.

No. 2123 Ovptd. in Silver and Blue with MOPHILA 85 Emblem and "HAMBURGO 11-12. 9. 85"

1985, July 5 *Perf. 13*
2146 A381 5g on #2123

Mophila '85 Intl. Philatelic Exhibition, Hamburg.

Intl. Youth Year A388

Scenes from Tom Sawyer and Huckleberry Finn: No. 2147a, 25c, Mississippi riverboat. b, 50c, Finn.

c, 1g, Finn and friends by campfire. d, 2g, Finn and Joe, sinking riverboat. e, 3g, Finn, friends, riverboat. f, 4g, Cemetery. 5g, Finn, Sawyer. 25g, Raft, riverboat.

1985, Aug. 5 *Perf. 13½x13*
2147 A388 Strip of 6, #a.-f.
2148 A388 5g multicolored

Souvenir Sheet
Perf. 14½
2149 A388 25g multicolored

No. 2149 is airmail. For overprint see No. C612.

German Railroads, 150th Anniv. — A389

Locomotives: No. 2150a, 25c, T3, 1883. b, 50c, T18, 1912. c, 1g, T16, 1914. d, 2g, #01 118, Historic Trains Society, Frankfurt. e, 3g, #05 001 Express, Nuremberg Transit Museum. f, 4g, #10 002 Express, 1957. 5g, Der Adler, 1835. 25g, Painting of 1st German Train, Dec. 7, 1835.

1985, Aug. 8 *Perf. 14*
2150 A389 Strip of 6, #a.-f.
Perf. 13
2151 A389 5g multicolored

Souvenir Sheet
Perf. 13½
2152 A389 25g multicolored

No. 2152 is airmail and contains one 75x53mm stamp. For overprint see No. 2165.

Development Projects — A390

Pres. Stroessner and: 10g, Soldier, map, vert. 25g, Model of Yaci Reta Hydroelectric Project. 50g, Itaipu Dam. 75g, Merchantman Lago Ipoa. 100g, 1975 Coin, vert. 200g, Asuncion Intl. Airport.

1985, Sept. 17 Litho. *Perf. 13*
2153 A390 10g multicolored
2154 A390 25g multicolored
2155 A390 50g multicolored
2156 A390 75g multicolored
2157 A390 100g multicolored
2158 A390 200g multicolored

Chaco Peace Agreement, 50th Anniv. (#2153, 2157). Nos. 2157-2158 are airmail. For overprints see Nos. 2254-2259.

Nudes by Peter Paul Rubens A391

Details from paintings: No. 2159a, 25c, b, 50c, Venus in the Forge of Vulcan. c, 1g, Cimon and Iphigenia, horiz. d, 2g, The Horrors of War. e, 3g, Apotheosis of Henry IV and the Proclamation of the Regency. f, 4g, The Reception of Marie de Medici at Marseilles. 5g, Union of Earth and Water. 25g, Nature Attended by the Three Graces.

1985, Oct. 18 *Perf. 14*
2159 A391 Strip of 6, #a.-f.
Perf. 13x13½
2160 A391 5g multicolored

Souvenir Sheet
Perf. 14
2161 A391 25g multicolored

No. 2161 is airmail.

1986, Jan. 16 *Perf. 14*

Nudes by Titian: details from paintings. No. 2162a, 25c, Venus, an Organist, Cupid and a Little Dog. b, 50c, c, 1g, Diana and Actaeon. d, 2g, Danae. e, 3g, Nymph and a Shepherd. f, 4g, Venus of Urbino. 5g, Cupid Blindfolded by Venus, vert. 25g, Diana and Callisto, vert.

2162 A391 Strip of 6, #a.-f.
Perf. 13
2163 A391 5g multicolored

Souvenir Sheet
Perf. 13½
2164 A391 25g multicolored

No. 2164 is airmail and contains one 50x60mm stamp.

Nos. 2150 Ovptd. in Red **ESSEN 86**

1986, Feb. 25 *Perf. 14*
2165 A389 Strip of 6, #a.-f.

Essen '86 Intl. Philatelic Exhibition.

Mushrooms Type of 1985

Designs: No. 2166a, 25g, Lepiota procera. b, 50c, Tricholoma albo-brunneum. c, 1g, Clavaria. d, 2g, Volvaria. e, 3g, Licoperdon perlatum. f, 4g, Dictyophora duplicata. 5g, Polyporus rubrum.

1986, Mar. 17 *Perf. 14*
2166 A385 Strip of 6, #a.-f.
Perf. 13
2167 A385 5g multicolored

Automobile, Cent. — A393

No. 2168: a, 25c, Wolseley, 1904. b, 50c, Peugeot, 1892. c, 1g, Panhard, 1895. d, 2g, Cadillac, 1903. e, 3g, Fiat, 1902. f, 4g, Stanley Steamer, 1898. 5g, Carl Benz Velocipede , 1885. 25g, Carl Benz (1844-1929), automotive engineer.

1986, Apr. 28 Litho. *Perf. 13½x13*
2168 A393 Strip of 6, #a.-f.
2169 A393 5g multicolored

Souvenir Sheet
Perf. 13½
2170 A393 25g multicolored

No. 2170 is airmail and contains one 30x40mm stamp.

World Cup Soccer Championships, Mexico City — A394

Various match scenes, Paraguay vs.: No. 2171a, 25c, b, 50c, US, 1930. c, 1g, d, 2g, Belgium, 1930. e, 3g, Bolivia, 1985. f, 4g, Brazil, 1985. 5g, Natl. Team, 1986. 25g, Player, vert.

1986, Mar. 12 *Perf. 13½x13*
2171 A394 Strip of 6, #a.-f.
2172 A394 5g multicolored

Souvenir Sheet
Perf. 14½
2173 A394 25g multicolored

No. 2173 is airmail. For overprints see Nos. 2283, 2287.

No. 2135 Ovptd. in Silver "JUEGOS / PANAMERICANOS / INDIANAPOLIS / 1987"

1986, June 9 *Perf. 13*
2174 A384 5g on No. 2135

1987 Pan American Games, Indianapolis.

Maybach Automobiles — A395

Designs: No. 2175a, 25c, W-6, 1930-36. b, 50c, SW-38 convertible. c, 1g, SW-38 hardtop, 1938. d, 2g, W-6/DSG, 1933. e, 3g, Zeppelin DS-8, 1931. f, 4g, Zeppelin DS-8, 1936. 5g, Zeppelin DS-8 aerodynamic cabriolet, 1936.

1986, June 19 *Perf. 13½x13*
2175 A395 Strip of 6, #a.-f.
2176 A395 5g multicolored

No. 2077 Overprinted in Bright Blue with Olympic Rings and "CALGARY 1988"

1986, July 9 *Perf. 13*
2177 A369 5g on #2077

1988 Winter Olympics, Calgary.

Statue of Liberty, Cent. — A396

Passenger liners: No. 2178a, 25c, City of Paris, England, 1867. b, 50c, Mauretania, England. c, 1g, Normandie, France, 1932. d, 2g, Queen Mary, England, 1938. e, 3g, Kaiser Wilhelm the Great II, Germany, 1897. f, 4g, United States, US, 1952. 5g, Bremen, Germany, 1928. 25g, Sailing ship Gorch Fock, Germany, 1976, vert.

1986, July 25 *Perf. 13*
2178 A396 Strip of 6, #a.-f.
2179 A396 5g multicolored

Souvenir Sheet
Perf. 14½
2180 A396 25g multicolored

No. 2180 is airmail and contains one 50x70mm stamp.

Dog Type of 1984

#2181: a, 25c, German shepherd. b, 50c, Icelandic shepherd. c, 1g, Collie. d, 2g, Boxer. e, 3g, Scottish terrier. f, 4g, Welsh springer spaniel. 5g, Painting of Labrador retriever by Ellen Krebs, vert.

1986, Aug. 28 *Perf. 13x13½*
2181 A376 Strip of 6, #a.-f.
Perf. 13½x13
2182 A376 5g multicolored

Paraguay Official Stamps, Cent. — A397

Designs: Nos. 2183-2185, No. O1. Nos. 2186-2188, No. O4.

1986, Aug. 28 Litho. *Perf. 13x13½*

2183 A397	5g multi		.15	.15
2184 A397	15g multi		.15	.15
2185 A397	40g multi		.15	.15
2186 A397	65g multi		.18	.15
2187 A397	100g multi		.25	.18
2188 A397	150g multi		.38	.28
		Set value	1.00	.75

Nos. 2186-2188 are airmail.

Tennis Players A398

Designs: No. 2189a, Victor Pecci, Paraguay. b, 50c, Jimmy Connors, US. c, 1g, Gabriela Sabatini, Argentina. d, 2g, Boris Becker, W. Germany. e, 3g, Claudia Kohde, E. Germany. f, 4g, Sweden, 1985 Davis Cup team champions, horiz. 5g, Steffi Graf, W. Germany. 25g, 1986 Wimbledon champions Martina Navratilova and Boris Becker, horiz.

Perf. 13x13½, 13½x13
1986, Sept. 17 **Unwmk.**
2189 A398 Strip of 6, #a.-f.
2190 A398 5g multicolored

Souvenir Sheet
Perf. 13½
2191 A398 25g multicolored

No. 2191 is airmail and contains one 75x55mm stamp. For overprints see No. 2229.

Nos. 1454-1456 Ovptd. in Red or Silver (#2192c, 2192d): "Homenage a la visita de Sus Altezas Imperiales los Principees Hitachi --28.9-3.10.86"

1986, Sept. 28 *Perf. 14*
2192 A251 Strip of 5, #a.-e.
2193 A251 50c on #1455
2194 A251 75c on #1456

1988 Summer Olympics, Seoul — A399

Athletes, 1984 Olympic medalists: No. 2195a, 25c, Runner. b, 50c, Boxer. c, 1g, Joaquim Cruz, Brazil, 800-meter run. d, 2g, Mary Lou Retton, US, individual all-around gymnastics. e, 3g, Carlos Lopes, Portugal, marathon. f, 4g, Fredy Schmidtke, W. Germany, 1000-meter cycling, horiz. 5g, Joe Fargis, US, equestrian, horiz.

1986, Oct. 29 *Perf. 13x13½,13½x13*
2195 A399 Strip of 6, #a.-f.
2196 A399 5g multicolored

For overprints see Nos. 2227-2228, 2230.

Nos. 1574c-1574g Ovptd. in Silver, Ship Type of 1983 Ovptd. in Red

1987, Mar. 20 Litho. *Perf. 14*
2197 A278 Strip of 5, #a.-e.
2198 AP176 10g multicolored

500th Anniv. of the discovery of America and the 12th Spanish-American Stamp & Coin Show, Madrid.

Olympics Type of 1985 Overprinted in Silver with Olympic Rings and 500th Anniv. of the Discovery of America Emblems and "BARCELONA 92 / Sede de las Olimpiadas en el ano del 500o Aniversario del Descubrimiento de America"

Designs like Nos. 2134a-2134f.

1987, Apr. 24 *Perf. 14*
2199 A384 Strip of 6, #a.-f.

1992 Summer Olympics, Barcelona and discovery of America. 500th anniv. in 1992.

No. 2135 Overprinted in Silver "ROMA / OLYMPHILEX" / Olympic Rings / "SEOUL / CALGARY / 1988"

1987, Apr. 30 *Perf. 13*
2200 A384 5g on No. 2135

Olymphilex '87 Intl. Philatelic Exhibition, Rome.

Cat Type of 1976

Various cats and kittens: No. 2201: a, 1g. b, 2g. c, 3g. d, 5g. 60g, Black cat.

1987, May 22 *Perf. 13x13½*
2201 A287 Strip of 4, #a.-d.
2202 A287 60g multicolored

No. 2202 also exists perf. 14. For overprint see No. 2212.

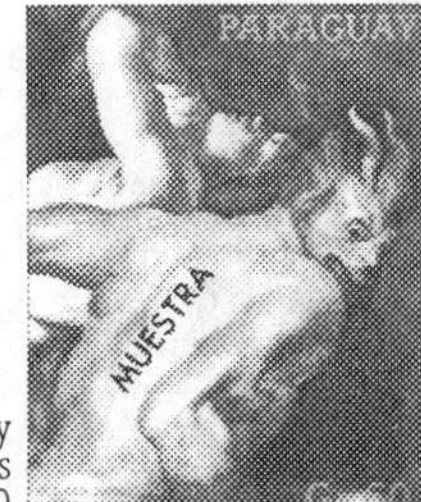
Paintings by Rubens A400

No. 2203: a, 1g, The Four Corners of the World, horiz. b, 2g, Jupiter and Calisto. c, 3g, Susanna and the Elders. d, 5g, Marriage of Henry IV and Marie de Medici in Lyon.

60g, The Last Judgment. 100g, The Holy Family with St. Elizabeth and John the Baptist. No. 2205A, War and Peace.

1987 Litho. *Perf. 13x13½, 13½x13*
2203 A400 Strip of 4, #a.-d.
2204 A400 60g multicolored

Souvenir Sheets

2205 A400 100g multicolored
2205A A400 100g multicolored

Christmas 1986 (#2205).
Issued: No. 2204, May 25; No. 2205, May 26.
Nos. 2205-2205A are airmail and contain one 54x68mm stamp.

Places and Events A401

Designs: 10g, ACEPAR Industrial Plant. 25g, Franciscan monk, native, vert. 50g, Yaguaron Church altar, vert. 75g, Founding of Asuncion, 450th anniv. 100g, Paraguay Airlines passenger jet. 200g, Pres. Stoessner, vert.

1987, June 2 Litho. *Perf. 13*
2206 A401 10g multicolored
2207 A401 25g multicolored
2208 A401 50g multicolored
2209 A401 75g multicolored
2210 A401 100g multicolored
2211 A401 200g multicolored

Nos. 2210-2211 are airmail. For overprints see Nos. 2225-2226, C685, C722.

No. 2201 Ovptd. in Blue CAPEX 87

1987, June 12 *Perf. 13x13½*
2212 A287 Strip of 4, #a.-d.

Discovery of America, 500th Anniv. (in 1992) — A402

Discovery of America anniv. emblem and ships: No. 2213a, 1g, Spanish galleon, 17th cent. b, 2g, Victoria, 1st to circumnavigate the globe, 1519-22. c, 3g, San Hermenegildo. 5g, San Martin, c.1582. 60g, Santa Maria, c.1492, vert.

1987, Sept. 9 *Perf. 14*
2213 A402 Strip of 4, #a.-d.

Perf. 13x13½

2214 A402 60g multicolored

Colorado Party, Cent. A403

Bernardino Caballero (founder), President Stroessner and: 5g, 10g, 25g, Three-lane highway. 150g, 170g, 200g, Power lines.

Perf. 13½x13

1987, Sept. 11 Wmk. 347

2215	A403	5g multi	.15	.15
2216	A403	10g multi	.15	.15
2217	A403	25g multi	.15	.15
2218	A403	150g multi	.35	.26
2219	A403	170g multi	.38	.28
2220	A403	200g multi	.45	.35
		Set value	1.30	1.00

Nos. 2218-2220 are airmail.

Berlin, 750th Anniv. A404

Berlin Stamps and Coins: No. 2221: a, 1g, #9NB145. b, 2g, #9NB154. c, 3g, #9N57, vert. d, 5g, #9N170, vert. 60g, 1987 Commemorative coin, vert.

Perf. 13½x13, 13½x13

1987, Sept. 12 Unwmk.
2221 A404 Strip of 4, #a.-d.
2222 A404 60g multicolored

For overprints see Nos. 2239, 2294.

Race Cars A405

No. 2223: a, 1g, Audi Sport Quattro. b, 2g, Lancia Delta S 4. c, 3g, Fiat 131. d, 5g, Porsche 911 4x4. 60g, Lancia Rally.

1987, Sept. 27 *Perf. 13*
2223 A405 Strip of 4, #a.-d.

Perf. 14

2224 A405 60g multicolored

Nos. 2209-2210 Ovptd. in Bright Blue

EXFIVIA 87
Bolivia
4 al 13.12.87

1987, Sept. 30 *Perf. 13*
2225 A401 75g on #2209
2226 A401 100g on #2210

EXFIVIA '87 Intl. Philatelic Exhibition, LaPaz, Bolivia. No. 2226 is airmail.

Nos. 2195d-2195f, 2196 Overprinted in Black or Silver

1987, Oct. 1 *Perf. 13½x13*
2227 A399 Strip of 3, #a.-c.
2228 A399 5g on No. 2196 (S)

Olymphilex '87 Intl. Phil. Exhib., Seoul.

No. 2189 Ovptd. with Emblem and "PHILATELIA '87," etc.

Perf. 13x13½, 13½x13

1987, Oct. 15
2229 A398 Strip of 6, #a.-f.

PHILATELIA '87 Intl. Phil. Exhib., Cologne. Size and configuration of overprint varies.

Nos. 2195a-2195b Ovptd. in Bright Blue for EXFILNA '87 and BARCELONA 92

1987, Oct. 24 *Perf. 13x13½*
2230 A399 Pair, #a.-b.

Exfilna '87 Intl. Philatelic Exhibition.

Ship Paintings A406

No. 2231: a, 1g, San Juan Nepomuceno. b, 2g, San Eugenio. c, 3g, San Telmo. d, 5g, San Carlos. 60g, Spanish galleon, 16th cent. 100g, One of Columbus' ships.

1987 Litho. *Perf. 14*
2231 A406 Strip of 4, #a.-d.

Perf. 13x13½

2232 A406 60g multicolored

Souvenir Sheet

Perf. 13½

2233 A406 100g multicolored

Discovery of America, 500th anniv. in 1992 (#2233). Issue dates: Nos. 2231-2232, Dec. 10. No. 2233, Dec. 12.
No. 2233 is airmail and contains one 54x75mm stamp.

1988 Winter Olympics, Calgary — A407

#2237: a, 5g, Joel Gaspoz. b, 60g, Peter Mueller.

1987, Dec. 31 *Perf. 14*
2234 A407 1g Maria Walliser
2235 A407 2g Erika Hess
2236 A407 3g Pirmin Zurbriggen

Miniature Sheet

Perf. 13½x13

2237 A407 Sheet of 4 each #2237a, 2237b+label

Souvenir Sheet

Perf. 14½

2238 A407 100g Walliser, Zurbriggen

No. 2238 is airmail. For overprints see Nos. 2240-2242.

No. 2221 Ovptd. in Silver "AEROPEX 88 / ADELAIDE"

1988, Jan. 29 *Perf. 13*
2239 A404 Strip of 4, #a.-d.

Aeropex '88, Adelaide, Australia.

Nos. 2234-2236 Ovptd. in Gold with Olympic Rings and "OLYMPEX / CALGARY 1988"

1988, Feb. 13 *Perf. 14*
2240 A407 1g on #2234
2241 A407 2g on #2235
2242 A407 3g on #2236

Olympex '88, Calgary. Size and configuration of overprint varies.

1988 Summer Olympics, Seoul — A408

Equestrians: No. 2243a, 1g, Josef Neckermann, W. Germany, on Venetia. b, 2g, Henri Chammartin, Switzerland. c, 3g, Christine Stueckelberger, Switzerland, on Granat. d, 5g, Liselott Linsenhoff, W. Germany, on Piaff. 60g, Hans-Guenter Winkler, W. Germany.

1988, Mar. 7 *Perf. 13*
2243 A408 Strip of 4, #a.-d.

Perf. 13½x13

2244 A408 60g multicolored

For overprint see No. 2291.

Berlin, 750th Anniv. A409

Paintings: No. 2245a, 1g, Virgin and Child, by Jan Gossaert. b, 2g, Virgin and Child, by Rubens. c, 3g, Virgin and Child, by Hans Memling. d, 5g, Madonna, by Albrecht Durer. 60g, Adoration of the Shepherds, by Martin Schongauer.

1988, Apr. 8 *Perf. 13*
2245 A409 Strip of 4, #a.-d.
2246 A409 60g multicolored

Christmas 1987. See Nos. C727-C731.

Visit of Pope John Paul II A410

Religious art: No. 2247a, 1g, Pope John Paul II, hands clasped. b, 2g, Statue of the Virgin. c, 3g, Czestochowa Madonna. d, 5g, Our Lady of Caacupe. Nos. 2247a-2247d are vert.

1988, Apr. 11 *Perf. 13*
2247 A410 Strip of 4, #a.-d.
2248 A410 60g multicolored

Visit of Pope John Paul II — A411

Rosette window and crucifix.

1988, May 5 **Litho.** *Perf. 13x13½*

2249 A411	10g blue & blk		.15	.15
2250 A411	20g blue & blk		.15	.15
2251 A411	50g blue & blk		.22	.16
	Set value		.36	.28

World Wildlife Fund Type of 1985

Endangered Animals: No. 2252a, 1g, like #2139g. b, 2g, like #2139f. c, 3g, like #2139d. d, 5g, like #2139e.

1988, June 14 **Unwmk.** *Perf. 14*
2252 A386 Strip of 4, #a.-d.

Nos. 2252a-2252d have denomination and border in blue.

Nos. 2000a-2000d Ovptd. in Gold with Emblem and "Bicentenario de / AUSTRALIA / 1788-1988"

1988, June 17
2253 A351 Strip of 4, #a.-d.

Australia, bicent.

Types of 1985 Overprinted in 2 or 4 Lines in Gold "NUEVO PERIODO PRESIDENCIAL CONSTITUCIONAL 1988-1993"

1988, Aug. 12 *Perf. 14*
2254 A390 10g like #2153
2255 A390 25g like #2154
2256 A390 50g like #2155
2257 A390 75g like #2156
2258 A390 100g like #2157
2259 A390 200g like #2158

Pres. Stroessner's new term in office. Nos. 2258-2259 are airmail.

Olympic Tennis, Seoul A412

Designs: No. 2260a, 1g, Steffi Graf, W. Germany. b, 2g, Olympic gold medal, horiz. c, 3g, Boris Becker, W. Germany. d, 5g, Emilio Sanchez, Spain. 60g, Steffi Graf, diff.

1988, Aug. 16 *Perf. 13*
2260 A412 Strip of 4, #a.-d.
2261 A412 60g multicolored

1992 Summer Olympics, Barcelona — A413

Olympic medalists from Spain: No. 2262a, 1g, Ricardo Zamora, soccer, Antwerp, 1920, vert. b, 2g, Equestrian team, Amsterdam, 1928. c, 3g, Angel Leon, shooting, Helsinki, 1952. d, 5g, Kayak team, Montreal, 1976. 60g, Francisco Fernandez Ochoa, slalom, Sapporo, 1972, vert. 100g, Olympic Stadium, Barcelona, vert.

1989, Jan. 5 *Perf. 14*
2262 A413 Strip of 4, #a.-d.

Perf. 13
2263 A413 60g multicolored

Souvenir Sheet

Perf. 13½
2264 A413 100g multicolored

Discovery of America 500th anniv. (in 1992). No. 2264 is airmail and contains one 50x60mm stamp. For overprint see No. 2293.

Columbus Space Station A414

1989, Jan. 7 **Litho.** *Perf. 13x13½*
2265 A414 60g multicolored

Discovery of America 500th anniv. (in 1992).

No. 2076 Overprinted in Silver, Red and Blue with Olympic Rings, "1992" and Emblem

Perf. 13½x13, 13x13½

1989, Jan. 10
2266 A369 Strip of 6, #a.-f.

1992 Winter Olympics, Albertville. Location and configuration of overprint varies.

No. 1454 Ovptd. in Silver "HOMENAJE AL EMPERADOR HIROITO DE JAPON 29.IV,1901-6.1.1989"

1989, Feb. 8 *Perf. 14*
2267 A251 Strip of 5, #a.-e.

Death of Emperor Hirohito of Japan.

Formula 1 Drivers, Race Cars — A415

No. 2268: a, 1g, Stirling Moss, Mercedes W196. b, 2g, Emerson Fittipaldi, Lotus. c, 3g, Nelson Piquet, Lotus. d, 5g, Niki Lauda, Ferrari 312 B. 60g, Juan Manuel Fangio, Maserati 250F.

1989, Mar. 6 *Perf. 13*
2268 A415 Strip of 4, #a.-d.
2269 A415 60g multicolored

Paintings by Titian A416

No. 2270: a, 1g, Bacchus and Ariadne (Bacchus). b, 2g, Bacchus and Ariadne (tutelary spirit). c, 3g, Death of Actaeon. d, 5g, Portrait of a Young Woman with a Fur Cape. 60g, Concert in a Field. 100g, Holy Family with Donor.

1989, Apr. 17 *Perf. 13x13½*
2270 A416 Strip of 4, #a.-d.
2271 A416 60g multicolored

Souvenir Sheet

Perf. 13½
2271A A416 100g multicolored

No. 2271A is airmail and contains one 60x49mm stamp. Issue date: May 27.

1994 Winter Olympics, Lillehammer — A417

Athletes: No. 2272a, 1g, Torbjorn Lokken, 1987 Nordic combined world champion. b, 2g, Atle Skardal, skier, Norway. c, 3g, Geir Karlstad, Norway, world 10,000-meter speed skating champion, 1987. d, 5g, Franck Piccard, France, 1988 Olympic medalist, skiing. 60g, Roger Ruud, ski jumper, Norway.

1989, May 23 *Perf. 13½x13*
2272 A417 Strip of 4, #a.-d.
2273 A417 60g multicolored

Cat Type of 1976

Various cats: #2274a, 1g. b, 2g. c, 3g. d, 5g.

1989, May 25 *Perf. 13*
2274 A287 Strip of 4, #a.-d.
2275 A287 60g Siamese

Federal Republic of Germany, 40th Anniv. — A418

Famous men and automobiles: No. 2276a, 1g, Konrad Adenauer, chancellor, 1949-1963, Mercedes. b, 2g, Ludwig Erhard, chancellor, 1963-1966, Volkswagen Beetle. c, 3g, Felix Wankel, engine designer, 1963 NSU Spider. d, 5g, Franz Josef Strauss, President of Bavarian Cabinet, BMW 502. 60g, Pres. Richard von Weizsacker and Dr. Josef Neckermann.

1989, May 27 *Perf. 13½x13*
2276 A418 Strip of 4, #a.-d.
2277 A418 60g multicolored

For overprints see No. 2369.

Ship Type of 1980 Overprinted with Discovery of America, 500th Anniv. Emblem in Red on Silver

1989, May 29 *Perf. 14½*

Miniature Sheet

2278 A343 Sheet of 7+label, like #1972

Discovery of America 500th anniv. (in 1992).

No. 2122a Overprinted with Hamburg Emblem and Nos. 2122b-2122f, 2123 Ovptd. with Diff. Emblem in Red on Silver

1989, May 30 **Litho.** *Perf. 13½x13*
2279 A381 Strip of 6, #a.-f.
2280 A381 5g on #2123

City of Hamburg, 800th anniv.

Nos. 2006a-2006b Ovptd. "BRASILIANA / 89"

1989, July 5 *Perf. 14*
2281 A352 Pair, #a.-b.

No. 2171 Overprinted in Metallic Red and Silver with FIFA and Italia 90 Emblems and "PARAGUAY PARTICIPO EN 13 CAMPEONATOS MUNDIALES"

1989, Sept. 14 **Litho.** *Perf. 13½x13*
2283 A394 Strip of 6, #a.-f.

Size and configuration of overprint varies.

Nos. C738, C753 Overprinted in metallic red with Italia '90 emblem and "SUDAMERICA-GRUPO 2 / PARAGUAY-COLOMBIA / PARAGUAY-ECUADOR / COLOMBIA-PARAGUAY / ECUADOR-PARAGUAY" and in metallic red on silver with FIFA emblem

1989, Sept. 14 **Litho.** *Perf. 13*
2284 AP228 25g on #C738
2285 AP232 25g on #C753

Nos. 2046, 2172 Overprinted in Metallic Red and Silver "PARAGUAY CLASIFICADO EN 1930, 1950, 1958 Y 1986" and Emblems or "ITALIA '90"

1989, Sept. 15 **Litho.** *Perf. 14*
2286 A362 Strip of 6, #a.-f.

Perf. 13½x13
2287 A394 5g multicolored

1990 World Cup Soccer Championships, Italy. Location and size of overprint varies.

Nos. 1284-1286 Ovptd. in Gold "...BIEN ESTUVIMOS EN LA LUNA AHORA NECESITAMOS LOS MEDIOS PARA LLEGAR A LOS PLANETAS" Wernher von Braun's Signature and UN and Space Emblems

1989, Sept. 16 *Perf. 14*
2288 A226 Strip of 5, #a.-e.
2289 A226 50c multicolored
2290 A226 75c multicolored

Location, size and configuration of overprint varies.

Nos. 2243, C764 Overprinted in Silver or Gold with Emblem and "ATENAS 100 ANOS DE LOS JUEGOS OLIMPICOS 1896-1996"

1989, Sept. 18 *Perf. 13*
2291 A408 Strip of 4, #a.-d.
2292 AP233 25g on #C764 (G)

1992 Summer Olympics Barcelona, Spain. Size and location of overprint varies.

Nos. 2262a-2262d Ovptd. in Silver with Heads of Steffi Graf or Boris Becker and: "WIMBLEDON 1988 / SEUL 1988 / WIMBLEDON 1989 / EL TENIS NUEVAMENTE EN / LAS OLIMPIADAS 1988-1992" or Similar

1989, Sept. 19 *Perf. 14*
2293 A413 Strip of 4, #a.-d.

Addition of tennis as an Olympic sport in 1992. Size and configuration of overprint varies.

No. 2221 Ovptd. in Gold and Blue "PRIMER AEROPUERTO PARA / /COHETES, BERLIN 1930 OBERTH, / NEBEL, RITTER, VON BRAUN" space emblem and "PROF. DR. HERMANN / OBERTH 95o ANIV. / NACIMIENTO 25.6.1989"

Perf. 13½x13, 13x13½

1989, Sept. 20
2294 A404 Strip of 4, #a.-d.

Dr. Hermann Oberth, rocket scientist, 95th birth anniv. Overprint size, etc, varies.

Nos. 1406-1408 Ovptd. in Metallic Red and Silver with Emblems and "OLIMPIADAS / DE INVIERNO / ALBERTVILLE 1992" in 2 or 3 Lines

1989, Sept. 21 *Perf. 14*
2295 A244 Strip of 5, #a.-e.
2296 A244 50c multicolored
2297 A244 75c multicolored

1992 Winter Olympics, Albertville. Size and configuration of overprint varies.

Nos. 2251, C724 Overprinted **PARAFIL 89**

Perf. 13½, 13½x13

1989, Oct. 9 Litho. Wmk. 347
2298 A411 50g on #2251
2299 AP226 120g on #C724

Parafil '89, Paraguay-Argentina philatelic exhibition.

Birds Facing Extinction A419

Perf. 13½x13

1989, Dec. 19 Litho. Wmk. 347
2300 A419 50g Ara chloroptera .15 .15
2301 A419 100g Mergus octosetaceus .16 .15
2302 A419 300g Rhea americana .50 .40
2303 A419 500g Ramphastos toco .80 .65
2304 A419 1000g Crax fasciolota 1.65 1.35
2305 A419 2000g Ara ararauna 3.25 2.60
Nos. 2300-2305 (6) 6.51 5.30

Nos. 2302-2305 airmail. Nos. 2300 & 2305 vert. Frames and typestyles vary greatly. Watermark on 50g, 100g, 300g is 8mm high.

1992 Summer Olympics, Barcelona A420

Athletes: No. 2306a, 1g, A. Fichtel and S. Bau, W. Germany, foils, 1988. b, 2g, Spanish basketball team, 1984. c, 3g, Jackie Joyner-Kersee, heptathalon and long jump, 1988, horiz. d, 5g, L. Beerbaum, W. Germany, show jumping, team, 1988. 60g, W. Brinkmann, W. Germany, show jumping, team, 1988. 100g, Emilio Sanchez, tennis.

Unwmk.

1989, Dec. 26 Litho. *Perf. 14*
2306 A420 Strip of 4, #a.-d.

Perf. 13

2307 A420 60g multicolored

Souvenir Sheet

Perf. 13½

2308 A420 100g multicolored

No. 2308 is airmail and contains one 47x57mm stamp.

World Cup Soccer Championships, Italy — A421

1986 World Cup soccer players in various positions: No. 2309a, 1g, England vs. Paraguay. b, 2g, Spain vs. Denmark. c, 3g, France vs. Italy. d, 5g, Germany vs. Morocco. 60g, Mexico vs. Paraguay. 100g, Germany vs. Argentina.

1989, Dec. 29 *Perf. 14*
2309 A421 Strip of 4, #a.-d.

Perf. 13½

2310 A421 60g multicolored

Souvenir Sheet

Perf. 14½

2311 A421 100g multicolored

No. 2311 is airmail and contains one 40x50mm stamp.

For overprints see Nos. 2355-2356.

1992 Summer Olympics, Barcelona — A422

Barcelona '92, proposed Athens '96 emblems and: No. 2312a, 1g, Greece #128. b, 2g, Greece #126, vert. c, 3g, Greece #127, vert. d, 5g, Greece #123, vert. 60g, Paraguay #736. 100g, Horse and rider, vert.

1990, Jan. 4 *Perf. 13½x13, 13x13½*
2312 A422 Strip of 4, #a.-d.
2313 A422 60g multicolored

Souvenir Sheet

Perf. 13½

2314 A422 100g multicolored

No. 2314 is airmail and contains one 50x60mm stamp and exists with either white or yellow border. Stamps inscribed 1989.

For overprints see No. 2357.

Swiss Confederation, 700th Anniv. — A423

#2315: a, 3g, Monument to William Tell. b, 5g, Manship Globe, UN Headquarters, Geneva. 60g, 15th cent. messenger, Bern. #2317, 1st Swiss steam locomotive, horiz. #2318, Jean Henri Dunant, founder of the Red Cross, horiz.

1990, Jan. 25 *Perf. 14*
2315 A423 Pair, #a.-b.

Perf. 13

2316 A423 60g multicolored

Souvenir Sheets

Perf. 14½

2317 A423 100g multicolored
2318 A423 100g multicolored

Nos. 2317-2318 are airmail. For overprints see Nos. 2352-2354.

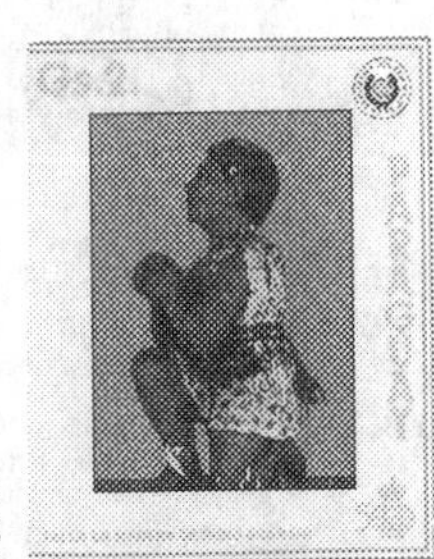

Wood Carving A424

Discovery of America, 500th anniv. emblem &: #2319: a, 1g, 1st cathechism in Guarani. b, 2g, shown. #2319 has continuous design.

1990, Jan. 26 *Perf. 14*
2319 A424 Pair, #a.-b. + label

Organization of American States, Cent. — A425

Perf. 13½x13

1990, Feb. 9 Litho. Wmk. 347
2320 A425 50g multicolored .15 .15
2321 A425 100g multicolored .30 .25
2322 A425 200g Map of Paraguay .60 .48
Nos. 2320-2322 (3) 1.05 .88

1992 Winter Olympics, Albertville — A426

Calgary 1988 skiers: No. 2323a, 1g, Alberto Tomba, Italy, slalom and giant slalom. b, 2g, Vreni Schneider, Switzerland, women's slalom and giant slalom, vert. c, 3g, Luc Alphand, France, skier, vert. d, 5g, Matti Nykaenen, Finland, ski-jumping.

60g, Marina Kiehl, W. Germany, women's downhill. 100g, Frank Piccard, France, super giant slalom.

1990, Mar. 7 Unwmk. *Perf. 14*
2323 A426 Strip of 4, #a.-d.

Perf. 13

2324 A426 60g multicolored

Souvenir Sheet

Perf. 14½

2325 A426 100g multicolored

No. 2325 is airmail, contains one 40x50mm stamp and exists with either white or yellow border.

Pre-Columbian Art, Customs — A427

UPAE Emblem and: 150g, Pre-Columbian basket. 500g, Aboriginal ceremony.

1990, Mar. 8 Wmk. 347 *Perf. 13*
2326 A427 150g multicolored .45 .38
2327 A427 500g multicolored 1.50 1.20

No. 2327 is airmail.

For overprints see Nos. 2345-2346.

First Postage Stamp, 150th Anniv. — A428

Penny Black, Mail Transportation 500th anniv. emblem and: No. 2328a, 1g, Penny Black on cover. b, 2g, Mauritius #1-2 on cover. c, 3g, Baden #4b on cover. d, 5g, Roman States #4 on cover. 60g, Paraguay #C38 and four #C54 on cover.

1990, Mar. 12 Unwmk. *Perf. 14*
2328 A428 Strip of 4, #a.-d.

Perf. 13½x13

2329 A428 60g multicolored

Postal Union of the Americas and Spain (UPAE) — A429

1990, July 2 *Perf. 13x13½*
2330 A429 200g Map, flags .35 .30
2331 A429 250g Paraguay #1 .40 .35
2332 A429 350g FDC of #2326-2327, horiz. .60 .45
Nos. 2330-2332 (3) 1.35 1.10

National University, Cent. (in 1989) — A430

1990, Sept. 8
2333 A430 300g Future site .90 .70
2334 A430 400g Present site 1.20 .95
2335 A430 600g Old site 1.80 1.45
Nos. 2333-2335 (3) 3.90 3.10

Franciscan Churches A431

Perf. 13½x13

1990, Sept. 25 Litho. Wmk. 347
2336 A431 50g Guarambare .15 .15
2337 A431 100g Yaguaron .30 .25
2338 A431 200g Ita .60 .48
Nos. 2336-2338 (3) 1.05 .88

For overprints see Nos. 2366-2368.

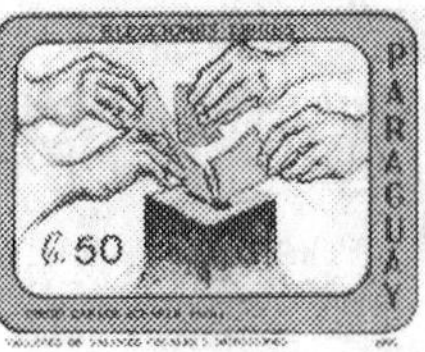

Democracy in Paraguay A432

Designs: 100g, State and Catholic Church, vert. 200g, Human rights, vert. 300g, Freedom of the Press, vert. 500g, Return of the exiles. 3000g, People and democracy.

Perf. 13½x13, 13x13½

1990, Oct. 5 Litho. Wmk. 347
2339 A432 50g multicolored .15 .15
2340 A432 100g multicolored .20 .18
2341 A432 200g multicolored .40 .36
2342 A432 300g multicolored .60 .55
2343 A432 500g multicolored 1.00 .90
2344 A432 3000g multicolored 6.00 5.50
Nos. 2339-2344 (6) 8.35 7.64

Nos. 2343-2344 are airmail.

Nos. 2326-2327 Overprinted in Magenta

Visita de Sus
Majestades Los
Reyes de España
22-24 Octubre 1990

1990 Litho. Wmk. 347 *Perf. 13*

2345 A427	150g multicolored		.45	.38
2346 A427	500g multicolored		1.50	1.20

No. 2346 is airmail.

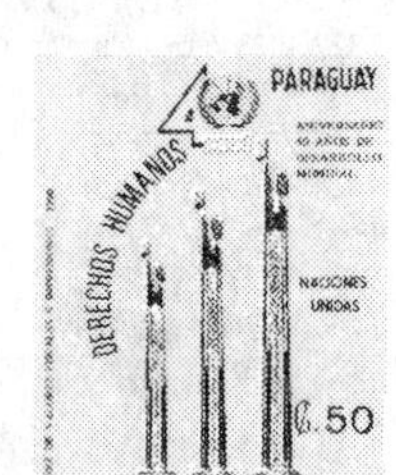

UN Development Program, 40th Anniv. A433

Designs: 50m, Human Rights, sculpture by Hugo Pistilli. 100m, United Nations, sculpture by Hermann Guggiari. 150m, Miguel de Cervantes Literature Award, won by Augusto Roa Bastos.

1990, Oct. 26

2347 A433	50g lilac & multi	.15	.15
2348 A433	100g gray & multi	.30	.25
2349 A433	150g green & multi	.45	.38
	Nos. 2347-2349 (3)	.90	.78

America A434

50g, Paraguay River banks. 250g, Chaco land.

Perf. 13½x13

1990, Oct. 31 Wmk. 347

2350 A434	50g multicolored	.15	.15
2351 A434	250g multicolored	.50	.42

No. 2351 is airmail.

Nos. 2315-2316, 2318 Ovptd. in Metallic Red and Silver

700 Aniv.
Confederación
Helvética
1291-1991

Unwmk.

1991, Apr. 2 Litho. *Perf. 14*

2352 A423 Pair, #a.-b.

Perf. 13

2353 A423 60g on #2316

Souvenir Sheet

Perf. 14½

2354 A423 100g on #2318

Swiss Confederation, 700th anniv. and Red Cross, 125th anniv. No. 2354 is airmail. No. 2352 exists perf. 13. Location of overprint varies.

Nos. 2309-2310 Ovptd. in Silver

Adjudicación
Campeonato Mundial
de Fútbol
USA 94

1991, Apr. 4 *Perf. 14*

2355 A421 Strip of 4, #a.-d.

Perf. 13x13½

2356 A421 60g on #2310

1994 World Cup Soccer Championships. Location of overprint varies.

Nos. 2312, C822, C766 Ovptd. in Silver

Participación de
Alemania Unificada
en las Olimpíadas
Barcelona 92

200 Aniv. 1791-1991

1991, Apr. 4 *Perf. 13*

2357 A422 Strip of 4, #a.-d.
2358 AP246 25g on #C822

Perf. 13x13½

2359 AP233 30g on #C766

Participation of reunified Germany in 1992 Summer Olympics. Nos. 2358-2359 are airmail. Location of overprint varies.

Professors — A435

Designs: 50g, Julio Manuel Morales, gynecologist. 100g, Carlos Gatti, clinician. 200g, Gustavo Gonzalez, geologist. 300g, Juan Max Boettner, physician and musician. 350g, Juan Boggino, pathologist. 500g, Andres Barbero, physician, founder of Paraguayan Red Cross.

Perf. 13x13½

1991, Apr. 5 Wmk. 347

2360 A435	50g multicolored	.15	.15
2361 A435	100g multicolored	.20	.18
2362 A435	200g multicolored	.40	.36
2363 A435	300g multicolored	.60	.55
2364 A435	350g multicolored	.70	.60
2365 A435	500g multicolored	1.00	.90
	Nos. 2360-2365 (6)	3.05	2.74

Nos. 2364-2365 are airmail.

Nos. 2336-2338 Ovptd. in Black and Red

1991 Wmk. 347 *Perf. 13½x13*

2366 A431	50g on #2336	.15	.15
2367 A431	100g on #2337	.20	.18
2368 A431	200g on #2338	.40	.36
	Nos. 2366-2368 (3)	.75	.69

Espamer '91 Philatelic Exhibition.

Nos. 2276a-2276b Ovptd. in Silver

Unificación de Alemania
para la Paz del Mundo

200 Aniv 1791-1991

Nos. 2276c-2276d Ovptd. in Silver

Unificación de Alemania
para la Paz del Mundo

1991 Unwmk. *Perf. 13*

2369 A418 Strip of 4, #a.-d.

Writers and Muscians A436

Designs: 50g, Ruy Diaz de Guzman, historian. 100g, Maria Talavera, war correspondent, vert. 150g, Augusto Roa Bastos, writer, vert. 200g, Jose Asuncion Flores, composer, vert. 250g, Felix Perez Cardozo, harpist. 300g, Juan Carlos Moreno Gonzalez, composer.

Perf. 13½x13,13x13½

1991, Aug. 27 Litho. Wmk. 347

2373 A436	50g multicolored	.15	.15
2374 A436	100g multicolored	.25	.22
2375 A436	150g multicolored	.38	.35
2376 A436	200g multicolored	.48	.45
2377 A436	250g multicolored	.60	.55
2378 A436	300g multicolored	.75	.65
	Nos. 2373-2378 (6)	2.61	2.37

Nos. 2376-2378 are airmail.

America — A437

100g, War of Tavare. 300g, Arrival of Spanish explorer Domingo Martinez de Irala in Paraguay.

Perf. 13x13½

1991, Oct. 9 Litho. Wmk. 347

2379 A437	100g multicolored	.25	.22
2380 A437	300g multicolored	.75	.65

No. 2380 is airmail.

Paintings — A438

Designs: 50g, Compass of Life, by Alfredo Moraes. 100g, The Lighted Alley, by Michael Burt. 150g, Earring, by Lucy Yegros. 200g, Migrant Workers, by Hugo Bogado Barrios. 250g, Passengers Without a Ship, by Bernardo Ismachoviez. 300g, Native Guarani, by Lotte Schulz.

Perf. 13x13½

1991, Nov. 12 Litho. Wmk. 347

2381 A438	50g multicolored	.15	.15
2382 A438	100g multicolored	.25	.22
2383 A438	150g multicolored	.38	.35
2384 A438	200g multicolored	.48	.45
2385 A438	250g multicolored	.60	.55
2386 A438	300g multicolored	.75	.65
	Nos. 2381-2386 (6)	2.61	2.37

Nos. 2384-2386 are airmail.

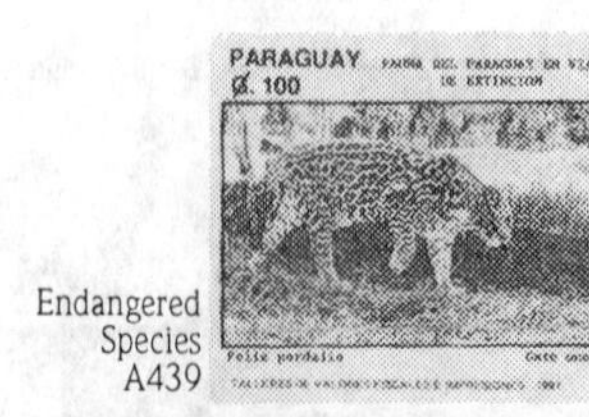

Endangered Species A439

Perf. 13x13½, 13½x13

1992, Jan. 28 Litho. Wmk. 347

2387 A439	50g Catagonus wagneris, vert.	.15	.15
2388 A439	100g Felis pardalis	.25	.22
2389 A439	150g Tapirus terrestri	.38	.35
2390 A439	200g Chrysocyon brachyurus	.48	.45
	Nos. 2387-2390 (4)	1.26	1.17

Tile Designs of Christianized Indians — A440

Perf. 13x13½

1992, Mar. 2 Litho. Wmk. 347

2391 A440	50g Geometric	.15	.15
2392 A440	100g Church	.18	.15
2393 A440	150g Missionary ship	.28	.25
2394 A440	200g Plant	.38	.35
	Nos. 2391-2394 (4)	.99	.90

Discovery of America, 500th anniv.

Leprosy Society of Paraguay, 60th Anniv. — A441

Designs: 50g, Society emblem, Malcolm L. Norment, founder. 250g, Gerhard Henrik Armauer Hansen (1841-1912), discoverer of leprosy bacillus.

Perf. 13x13½

1992, Apr. 28 Litho. Wmk. 347

2395 A441	50g multicolored	.15	.15
2396 A441	250g multicolored	.60	.55

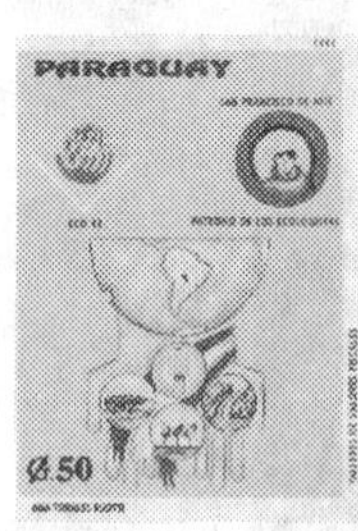

Earth Summit, Rio de Janeiro — A442

Earth Summit emblem, St. Francis of Assisi, and: 50g, Hands holding symbols of clean environment. 100g, Butterfly, industrial pollution. 250g, Globe, calls for environmental protection.

1992, June 9

2397 A442	50g multicolored	.15	.15
2398 A442	100g multicolored	.25	.22
2399 A442	250g multicolored	.60	.55
	Nos. 2397-2399 (3)	1.00	.92

For overprints see Nos. 2422-2424.

Natl. Census A443

Perf. 13½x13, 13x13½

1992. July 30

2400 A443	50g Economic activity	.15	.15
2401 A443	200g Houses, vert.	.48	.45
2402 A443	250g Population, vert.	.60	.55
2403 A443	300g Education	.75	.65
	Nos. 2400-2403 (4)	1.98	1.80

1992 Summer Olympics, Barcelona A444

Perf. 13x13½, 13½x13

1992, Sept. 1

2404	A444	50g Soccer, vert.	.15	.15
2405	A444	100g Tennis, vert.	.25	.22
2406	A444	150g Running, vert.	.38	.35
2407	A444	200g Swimming	.48	.42
2408	A444	250g Judo, vert.	.60	.55
2409	A444	350g Fencing	.85	.75
		Nos. 2404-2409 (6)	2.71	2.44

Evangelism in Paraguay, 500th Anniv. — A445

Designs: 50g, Friar Luis Bolanos. 100g, Friar Juan de San Bernardo. 150g, San Roque Gonzalez de Santa Cruz. 200g, Father Amancio Gonzalez. 250g, Monsignor Juan Sinforiano Bogarin, vert.

Rough Perf. 13½x13, 13x13½

1992, Oct. 9 **Unwmk.**

2410	A445	50g multicolored	.15	.15
2411	A445	100g multicolored	.25	.22
2412	A445	150g multicolored	.38	.35
2413	A445	200g multicolored	.48	.45
2414	A445	250g multicolored	.60	.55
		Nos. 2410-2414 (5)	1.86	1.72

For overprints see Nos. 2419-2421.

America A446

Designs: 150g, Columbus, fleet arriving in New World. 350g, Columbus, vert.

Rough Perf. 13½x13, 13x13½

1992, Oct. 12

2415	A446	150g multicolored	.38	.35
2416	A446	350g multicolored	.85	.75

No. 2416 is airmail.

Ovptd. "PARAFIL 92" in Blue

1992, Nov. 9

2417	A446	150g multicolored	.38	.35
2418	A446	350g multicolored	.85	.75

No. 2418 is airmail.

Navidad 92

Nos. 2410-2412 Ovptd. in Green

1992, Nov. 6 *Rough Perf. 13½x13*

2419	A445	50g multicolored	.15	.15
2420	A445	100g multicolored	.25	.22
2421	A445	150g multicolored	.38	.35
		Nos. 2419-2421 (3)	.78	.72

Nos. 2397-2399 Ovptd. in Blue

NACIONES UNIDAS

1992-30 AÑOS CENTRO INFORMACION ONU EN PARAGUAY

Perf. 13x13½

1992, Oct. 24 **Wmk. 347**

2422	A442	50g multicolored	.15	.15
2423	A442	100g multicolored	.25	.22
2424	A442	250g multicolored	.60	.55
		Nos. 2422-2424 (3)	1.00	.92

Inter-American Institute for Cooperation in Agriculture, 50th Anniv. — A447

Designs: 50g, Field workers. 100g, Test tubes, cattle in pasture. 200g, Hands holding flower. 250g, Cows, corn, city.

Perf. 13x13½

1992, Nov. 27 **Unwmk.**

2425	A447	50g multicolored	.15	.15
2426	A447	100g multicolored	.25	.22
2427	A447	200g multicolored	.50	.45
2428	A447	250g multicolored	.60	.55
		Nos. 2425-2428 (4)	1.50	1.37

For overprints see Nos. 2461-2462.

Notary College of Paraguay, Cent. A448

Designs: 50g, Yolanda Bado de Artecona. 100g, Jose Ramon Silva. 150g, Abelardo Brugada Valpy. 200g, Tomas Varela. 250g, Jose Livio Lezcano. 300g, Francisco I. Fernandez.

1992, Nov. 29 *Rough Perf. 13½x13*

2429	A448	50g multicolored	.15	.15
2430	A448	100g multicolored	.25	.22
2431	A448	150g multicolored	.38	.35
2432	A448	200g multicolored	.50	.45
2433	A448	250g multicolored	.60	.55
2434	A448	300g multicolored	.70	.65
		Nos. 2429-2434 (6)	2.58	2.37

Opening of Lopez Palace, Cent. — A449

Paintings of palace by: 50g, Michael Burt. 100g, Esperanza Gill. 200g, Emili Aparici. 250g, Hugo Bogado Barrios, vert.

1993, Mar. 9 *Perf. 13½x13, 13x13½*

2435	A449	50g multicolored	.15	.15
2436	A449	100g multicolored	.25	.22
2437	A449	200g multicolored	.50	.45
2438	A449	250g multicolored	.60	.55
		Nos. 2435-2438 (4)	1.50	1.37

For overprints see Nos. 2453-2456.

Treaty of Asuncion, 1st Anniv. — A450

Rough Perf. 13x13½

1993, Mar. 10 **Wmk. 347**

2439	A450	50g Flags, map	.15	.15
2440	A450	350g Flags, globe	.85	.75

Santa Isabel Leprosy Assoc., 50th Anniv. — A451

Various flowers.

Perf. 13x13½

1993, May 24 **Unwmk.**

2441	A451	50g multicolored	.15	.15
2442	A451	200g multicolored	.50	.45
2443	A451	250g multicolored	.60	.55
2444	A451	350g multicolored	.85	.75
		Nos. 2441-2444 (4)	2.10	1.90

Goethe College, Cent. — A452

Designs: 50g, Goethe, by Johann Heinrich Lips, inscription. 100g, Goethe (close-up), by Johann Heinrich Wilhelm Tischbein.

1993, June 18

2445	A452	50g multicolored	.15	.15
2446	A452	200g multicolored	.50	.45

For overprints see Nos. 2451-2452.

World Friendship Crusade, 35th Anniv. — A453

Designs: 50g, Stylized globe. 100g, Map, Dr. Ramon Artemio Bracho. 200g, Children. 250g, Two people embracing.

1993, July 1

2447	A453	50g multicolored	.15	.15
2448	A453	100g multicolored	.25	.22
2449	A453	200g multicolored	.50	.45
2450	A453	250g multicolored	.60	.55
		Nos. 2447-2450 (4)	1.50	1.37

For overprint see No. 2486.

Nos. 2445-2446 Ovptd. "BRASILIANA 93"

1993, July 12

2451	A452	50g multicolored	.15	.15
2452	A452	200g multicolored	.50	.45

Nos. 2435-2438 Ovptd.

TRANSMISION DEL MANDO PRESIDENCIAL GRAL. ANDRES RODRIGUEZ ING. JUAN C. WASMOSY 15 DE AGOSTO 1993

Perf. 13½x13, 13x13½

1993, Aug. 13

2453	A449	50g multicolored	.15	.15
2454	A449	100g multicolored	.25	.22
2455	A449	200g multicolored	.50	.45
2456	A449	250g multicolored	.60	.55
		Nos. 2453-2456 (4)	1.50	1.37

Size of overprint varies.

Church of the Incarnation, Cent. — A454

Design: 50g, Side view of church, vert.

Unwmk.

1993, Oct. 8 **Litho.** *Perf. 13*

2457	A454	50g multicolored	.15	.15
2458	A454	350g multicolored	.40	.35

Endangered Animals A455

America: 50g, Myrmecophaga tridactyla. 250g, Speothos venaticus.

1993, Oct. 27

2459	A455	50g multicolored	.15	.15
2460	A455	250g multicolored	.30	.25

No. 2459 is airmail.

Nos. 2426-2427 Ovptd.

'30 ANOS DEL PROGRAMA MUNDIANDE ALIMENTOS'

1993, Nov. 16 *Perf. 13x13½*

2461	A447	100g multicolored	.15	.15
2462	A447	200g multicolored	.22	.18

Christmas A456

1993, Nov. 24

2463	A456	50g shown	.15	.15
2464	A456	250g Stars, wise men	.30	.25

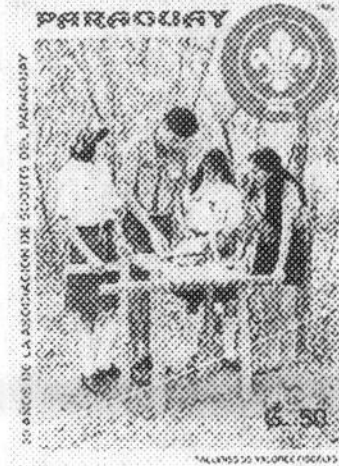

Scouting in Paraguay, 80th Anniv. — A457

50g, Girl scouts watching scout instuctor. 100g, Boy scouts learning crafts. 200g, Lord Robert Baden-Powell. 250g, Girl scout with flag.

1993, Dec. 30

2465	A457	50g multicolored	.15	.15
2466	A457	100g multicolored	.15	.15
2467	A457	200g multicolored	.22	.18
2468	A457	250g multicolored	.30	.25
		Nos. 2465-2468 (4)	.82	.73

First Lawyers to Graduate from Natl. University of Ascuncion, Cent. A458

1994, Apr. 8 *Perf. 13*

2469 A458	50g	Cecilio Baez	.15	.15
2470 A458	100g	Benigno Riquelme, vert.	.15	.15
2471 A458	250g	Emeterio Gonzalez	.30	.25
2472 A458	500g	J. Gaspar Villamayor	.52	.48
		Nos. 2469-2472 (4)	1.12	1.03

Phoenix Sports Corporation, 50th Anniv. — A459

Designs: 50g, Basketball player, vert. 200g, Soccer players, vert. 250g, Pedro Andrias Garcia Arias, founder, tennis player.

1994, May 20 **Litho.** *Perf. 13*

2473 A459	50g	multicolored	.15	.15
2474 A459	200g	multicolored	.22	.18
2475 A459	250g	multicolored	.30	.25
		Nos. 2473-2475 (3)	.67	.58

1994 World Cup Soccer Championships, US — A460

Various soccer plays.

1994, June 2

2476 A460	250g	multicolored	.30	.25
2477 A460	500g	multicolored	.52	.48
2478 A460	1000g	multicolored	1.00	.85
		Nos. 2476-2478 (3)	1.82	1.58

For overprints see Nos. 2483-2485.

Intl. Olympic Committee, Cent. — A461

Unwmk.

1994, June 23 **Litho.** *Perf. 13*

2479 A461	350g	Runner	.40	.35
2480 A461	400g	Lighting Olympic flame	.45	.38

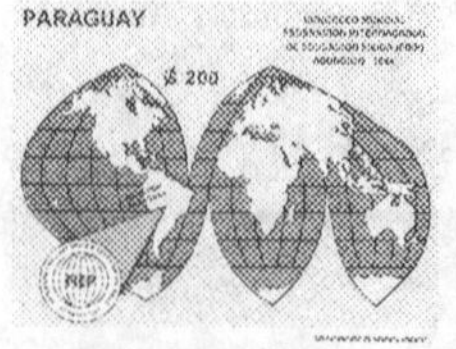

World Congress on Physical Education, Asuncion A462

Designs: 1000g, Stylized family running to break finish line, vert.

Perf. 13½x13, 13x13½

1994, July 19 **Litho.**

2481 A462	200g	multicolored	.38	.32
2482 A462	1000g	multicolored	1.75	1.50

Nos. 2476-2478 Ovptd.

BRASIL
Campeón Mundial de Fútbol
Estados Unidos '94

1994, Aug. 2 *Perf. 13*

2483 A460	250g	multicolored	.45	.38
2484 A460	500g	multicolored	.90	.75
2485 A460	1000g	multicolored	1.75	1.50
		Nos. 2483-2485 (3)	3.10	2.63

No. 2448 Ovptd.

25 Años, Conquista de la Luna por el hombre 1969 - 1994

1994, Aug. 3 *Perf. 13x13½*

2486 A453	100g	multicolored	.20	.15

Agustin Pio Barrios Mangore (1885-1944), Musician — A463

1994, Aug. 5 *Perf. 13x13½*

2487 A463	250g	In tuxedo	.45	.38
2488 A463	500g	In traditional costume	.90	.75

Paraguayan Police, 151st Anniv. — A464

50g, 1913 Guardsman on horseback. 250g, Pedro Nolasco Fernandez, 1st capital police chief; Carlos Bernadino Cacabelos, 1st commissioner.

1994, Aug. 26 *Perf. 13x13½*

2489 A464	50g	multicolored	.15	.15
2490 A464	250g	multicolored	.45	.38

For overprint see Nos. 2569-2570.

Parafil '94 A465

Birds: 100g, Ciconia maquari. 150g, Paroaria capitata. 400g, Chloroceryle americana, vert. 500g, Jabiru mycteria, vert.

1994, Sept. 9 *Perf. 13*

2491 A465	100g	multicolored	.18	.15
2492 A465	150g	multicolored	.28	.22
2493 A465	400g	multicolored	.75	.60
2494 A465	500g	multicolored	.90	.75
		Nos. 2491-2494 (4)	2.11	1.72

Solar Eclipse — A466

Designs: 50g, Eclipse, Copernicus. 200g, Sundial, Johannes Keplar.

Unwmk.

1994, Sept. 23 **Litho.** *Perf. 13*

2495 A466	50g	multicolored	.15	.15
2496 A466	200g	multicolored	.40	.32

America Issue A467

1994, Oct. 11 *Perf. 13½*

2497 A467	100g	Derelict locomotive	.20	.16
2498 A467	1000g	Motorcycle	2.00	1.65

Intl. Year of the Family — A468

1994, Oct. 25 *Perf. 13x13½*

2499 A468	50g	Mother, child	.15	.15
2500 A468	250g	Family faces	.50	.40

Christmas A469

Ceramic figures: 150g, Nativity. 700g, Joseph, infant Jesus, Mary, vert.

1994, Nov. 4 *Perf. 13½*

2501 A469	150g	multicolored	.30	.25
2502 A469	700g	multicolored	1.40	1.10

Paraguayan Red Cross, 75th Anniv. — A470

Designs: 150g, Boy Scouts, Jean-Henri Dunant. 700g, Soldiers, paramedics, Dr. Andres Barbero.

1994, Nov. 25 *Perf. 13½x13*

2503 A470	150g	multicolored	.30	.25
2504 A470	700g	multicolored	1.40	1.10

A 500g showing "75" inside a red cross, with ambulance and emblem with black cross in center was part of thgis set. When it was discovered that the emblem contained a black instead of a red cross it was withdrawn. The editors are garthering information on this stamp.

San Jose College, 90th Anniv. — A471

Pope John Paul II and: 200g, Eternal flame. 250g, College entrance.

1994, Dec. 4

2505 A471	200g	multicolored	.40	.32
2506 A471	250g	multicolored	.50	.40

Louis Pasteur (1822-95) A472

1995, Mar. 24 **Litho.** *Perf. 13½*

2507 A472	1000g	multicolored	1.50	1.00

Fight Against AIDS — A473

1995, May 4

2508 A473	500g	Faces	.75	.50
2509 A473	1000g	shown	1.50	1.00

FAO, 50th Anniv. A474

1995, June 23

2510 A474	950g	Bread, pitcher	1.40	1.00
2511 A474	2000g	Watermelon	3.00	2.00

Fifth Neotropical Ornithological Congress — A475

1995, July 6

2512 A475	100g	Parula pitiayumi	.15	.15
2513 A475	200g	Chirroxiphia caudata	.30	.20
2514 A475	600g	Icterus icterus	.90	.65
2515 A475	1000g	Carduelis magellanica	1.50	1.00
		Nos. 2512-2515 (4)	2.85	2.00

Fifth Intl. Symposium on Municipalities, Ecology & Tourism — A476

Designs: 1150g, Rio Monday rapids. 1300g, Areguá Railroad Station.

1995, Aug. 4 Litho. *Perf. 13½*

2516 A476 1150g multicolored 1.25 .85
2517 A476 1300g multicolored 1.30 .90

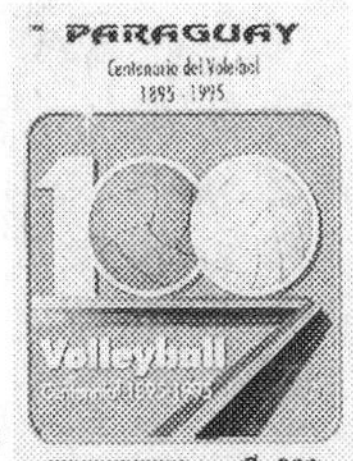

Volleyball, Cent. — A477

1995, Sept. 28

2518 A477 300g shown .30 .20
2519 A477 600g Ball, net .60 .40
2520 A477 1000g Hands, ball, net 1.00 .70
Nos. 2518-2520 (3) 1.90 1.30

America Issue A478

Preserve the environment: 950g, Macizo Monument, Achay. 2000g, Tinfunique Reserve, Chaco, vert.

1995, Oct. 12

2521 A478 950g multicolored 1.00 .65
2522 A478 2000g multicolored 2.00 1.40

UN, 50th Anniv. — A479

Designs: 200g, Flags above olive branch. 3000g, UN emblem, stick figures.

1995, Oct. 20

2523 A479 200g multicolored .20 .15
2524 A479 3000g multicolored 3.00 2.00

Christmas — A480

1995, Nov. 7

2525 A480 200g shown .20 .15
2526 A480 1000g Nativity 1.00 .70

Jose Marti (1853-95) A481

Designs: 200g, Hedychium coronarium, Marti, vert. 1000g, Hedychium coronarium, map & flag of Cuba, Marti.

1995, Dec. 19 Litho. *Perf. 13½*

2527 A481 200g multicolored .25 .15
2528 A481 1000g multicolored 1.10 .75

Lion's Clubs of South America & the Caribbean, 25th Anniv. A482

1996, Jan. 11

2529 A482 200g Railway station .25 .15
2530 A482 1000g Viola House 1.10 .75

Orchids A483

Designs: 100g, Cattleya nobilior. 200g, Oncidium varicosum. 1000g, Oncidium jonesianum, vert. 1150g, Sophronitis cernua.

Perf. 13½x13, 13x13½

1996, Apr. 22 Litho.

2531 A483 100g multicolored .15 .15
2532 A483 200g multicolored .20 .15
2533 A483 1000g multicolored 1.00 .60
2534 A483 1150g multicolored 1.10 .65
Nos. 2531-2534 (4) 2.45 1.55

1996 Summer Olympic Games, Atlanta A484

1996, June 6 *Perf. 13½x13*

2535 A484 500g Diving .50 .30
2536 A484 1000g Running 1.00 .60

Founding of Society of Salesian Fathers in Paraguay, Cent. A485

Pope John Paul II, St. John Bosco (1815-88), and: 200g, Men, boys from Salesian Order, natl. flag. 300g, Madonna and Child, vert. 1000g, Map of Paraguay, man following light.

Perf. 13½x13, 13x13½

1996, July 22

2537 A485 200g multicolored .20 .15
2538 A485 300g multicolored .30 .20
2539 A485 1000g multicolored 1.00 .60
Nos. 2537-2539 (3) 1.50 .95

UNICEF, 50th Anniv. A486

Children's paintings: 1000g, Outdoor scene, by S. Báez, 1300g, Four groups of children, by C. Pérez.

1996, Sept. 27 *Perf. 13½x13*

2540 A486 1000g multicolored 1.00 .60
2541 A486 1300g multicolored 1.25 .85

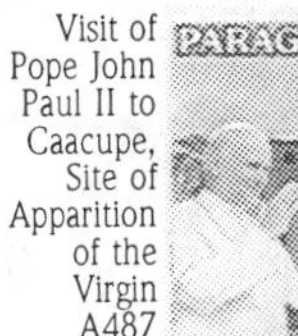

Visit of Pope John Paul II to Caacupe, Site of Apparition of the Virgin A487

Design: 200g, Pope John Paul II, church, Virgin of Caacupe, vert.

1996, Oct. 4 *Perf. 13x13½, 13½x13*

2542 A487 200g multicolored .20 .15
2543 A487 1300g multicolored 1.25 .85

Traditional Costumes — A488

America issue: 500g, Woman in costume. 1000g, Woman, man, in costumes.

1996, Oct. 11 *Perf. 13x13½*

2544 A488 500g multicolored .50 .30
2545 A488 1000g multicolored 1.00 .60

UN Year for Eradication of Poverty — A489

Perf. 13½x13, 13x13½

1996, Oct. 17

2546 A489 1000g Food products 1.00 .60
2547 A489 1150g Boy, fruit, vert. 1.10 .75

Christmas — A490

Madonna and Child, by: 200g, Koki Ruíz. 1000g, Hernán Miranda.

1996, Nov. 7 *Perf. 13x13½*

2548 A490 200g multicolored .20 .15
2549 A490 1000g multicolored 1.00 .60

Butterflies A491

Designs: 200g, Eryphanis automedon. 500g, Dryadula phaetusa. 1000g, Vanessa myrinna. 1150g, Heliconius ethilla.

1997, Mar. 5 Litho. *Perf. 13x13½*

2550 A491 200g multicolored .20 .15
2551 A491 500g multicolored .50 .30
2552 A491 1000g multicolored .95 .55
2553 A491 1150g multicolored 1.10 .65
Nos. 2550-2553 (4) 2.75 1.65

Official Buildings A492

200g, 1st Legistlature. 1000g, Postal Headquarters.

1997, May 5 *Perf. 13½x13*

2554 A492 200g multicolored .20 .15
2555 A492 1000g multicolored 1.10 .65

1997, Year of Jesus Christ — A493

1997, June 10 *Perf. 13x13½*

2556 A493 1000g Crucifix, Pope John Paul II .95 60

11th Summit of the Rio Group Chiefs of State, Asunción A494

1997, Aug. 23 *Perf. 13½x13*

2557 A494 1000g multicolored .95 .60

Environmental and Climate Change — A495

Flowers: 300g, Opunita elata. 500g, Bromelia balansae, 1000g, Monvillea kroenlaini.

Perf. 13½x13, 13x13½

1997, Aug. 25

2558 A495 300g multi .30 .20
2559 A495 500g multi, vert. .50 .30
2560 A495 1000g multi 1.00 .60
Nos. 2558-2560 (3) 1.80 1.10

1st Philatelic Exposition of MERCOSUR Countries, Chile and Bolivia — A496

Fauna: 200g, Felis tigrina. 1000g, Alouatta caraya, vert. 1150g, Agouti paca.

Perf. 13½x13, 13x13½

1997, Aug. 29

2561 A496	200g multicolored	.20	.15
2562 A496	1000g multicolored	.95	.60
2563 A496	1150g multicolored	1.10	.65
	Nos. 2561-2563 (3)	2.25	1.40

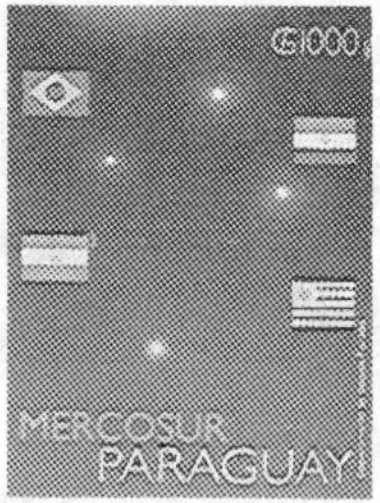

MERCOSUR (Common Market of Latin America) A497

1997, Sept. 26 *Perf. 13x13½*

2564 A497 1000g multicolored .95 .60

See Argentina #1975, Brazil #2646, Urugray #1681.

America Issue A498

Life of a postman: 1000g, Postman, letters going around the world, vert. 1150g, Window with six panes showing weather conditions, different roads, postman.

Perf. 13x13½, 13½x13

1997, Oct. 10

2565 A498	1000g multicolored	1.00	.60
2566 A498	1150g multicolored	1.10	.65

Natl. Council on Sports, 50th Anniv. — A499

200g, Neri Kennedy throwing javelin. 1000g, Ramón Milciades Giménez Gaona throwing discus.

1997, Oct. 16 *Perf. 13x13½*

2567 A499	200g multicolored	.25	.15
2568 A499	1000g multicolored	1.25	.75

Nos. 2489-2490 Ovptd. in Red

MEVIFIL '97

1997, Nov. 14

2569 A464	50g multicolored	.50	.30
2570 A464	250g multicolored	2.50	1.50

Christmas — A500

Paintings of Madonna and Child: 200g, By Olga Blinder. 1000g, By Hermán Miranda.

1997, Nov. 17

2571 A500	200g multicolored	.20	.15
2572 A500	1000g multicolored	1.10	.65

UN Fund for Children of the World with AIDS — A501

Children's paintings: 500g, Boy. 1000g, Girl.

1997, Dec. 5

2573 A501	500g multicolored	.50	.30
2574 A501	1000g multicolored	1.00	.60

Rotary Club of Asunción, 70th Anniv. — A502

1997, Dec. 11

2575 A502 1150g multicolored 1.10 .65

SEMI-POSTAL STAMPS

Red Cross Nurse — SP1

Unwmk.

1930, July 22 **Typo.** *Perf. 12*

B1 SP1	1.50p + 50c gray violet	1.00	.65
B2 SP1	1.50p + 50c deep rose	1.00	.65
B3 SP1	1.50p + 50c dark blue	1.00	.65
	Nos. B1-B3 (3)	3.00	1.95

The surtax was for the benefit of the Red Cross Society of Paraguay.

College of Agriculture — SP2

1930

B4 SP2 1.50p + 50c blue, *pink* .25 .25

Surtax for the Agricultural Institute.

The sheet of No. B4 has a papermaker's watermark: "Vencedor Bond."

A 1.50p+50c red on yellow was prepared but not regularly issued. Value, 20 cents.

Red Cross Headquarters — SP3

Our Lady of Asunción — SP4

1932

B5 SP3 50c + 50c rose .25 .20

1941 **Engr.**

B6 SP4	7p + 3p red brown	.30	.25
B7 SP4	7p + 3p purple	.30	.25
B8 SP4	7p + 3p carmine rose	.30	.25
B9 SP4	7p + 3p sapphire	.30	.25
	Nos. B6-B9 (4)	1.20	1.00

For surcharges see Nos. 419-426, 431-434.

No. 361 Surcharged in Black

1944

B10 A70 10c on 10p multicolored .35 .25

The surtax was for the victims of the San Juan earthquake in Argentina.

Catalogue values for unused stamps in this section, from this point to the end of the section, are for Never Hinged items.

No. C169 Surcharged in Carmine "AYUDA AL ECUADOR 5 + 5"

1949 **Unwmk.** *Perf. 12½*

B11 A117 5c + 5c on 30c dk blue .15 .15

Surtax for the victims of the Ecuador earthquake.

38th Intl. Eucharistic Congress, Bombay — SP5

Various coins and coat of arms.

Perf. 12x12½

1964, Dec. 11 **Litho. & Engr.**

B12 SP5	20g +10g multicolored	
B13 SP5	30g +15g multicolored	
B14 SP5	50g +25g multicolored	
B15 SP5	100g +50g multicolored	
a.	Souvenir sheet of 4, #B12-B15	

Buildings and Ancient Vatican Coins SP6

1964, Dec. 12

B16 SP6	20g +10g multicolored	
B17 SP6	30g +15g multicolored	
B18 SP6	50g +25g multicolored	
B19 SP6	100g +50g multicolored	
a.	Souvenir sheet of 4, #B16-B19	

AIR POST STAMPS

Official Stamps of 1913 Surcharged

Correo Aéreo Habilitado en $ 2:85

1929, Jan. 1 **Unwmk.** *Perf. 11½*

C1 O19	2.85p on 5c lilac	.75	.65
C2 O19	5.65p on 10c grn	.50	.38
C3 O19	11.30p on 50c rose	.75	.50
	Nos. C1-C3 (3)	2.00	1.53

Counterfeits of surcharge exist.

Regular Issues of 1924-27 Surcharged as in 1929

1929, Feb. 26 *Perf. 12*

C4 A51	3.40p on 3p gray	1.75	1.10
a.	Surch. "Correo / en $3.40 / Habilitado / Aereo"	8.75	
b.	Double surcharge	8.75	
c.	"Aéro" instead of "Aéreo"		
C5 A44	6.80p on 4p lt bl	1.75	1.10
a.	Surch. "Correo / Aereo / en $6.80 / Habilitado"	8.75	
C6 A52	17p on 5p choc	1.75	1.10
a.	Surch. "Correo / Habilitado / Habilitado / en 17p"	4.50	
b.	Double surcharge	8.75	
	Nos. C4-C6 (3)	5.25	3.30

Wings AP1

Pigeon with Letter AP2

Airplanes AP3

1929-31 **Typo.** *Perf. 12*

C7 AP1	2.85p gray green	.50	.45
a.	Imperf., pair	37.50	
C8 AP1	2.85p turq grn ('31)	.25	.20
C9 AP2	5.65p brown	.75	.38
C10 AP2	5.65p scar ('31)	.38	.25
C11 AP3	11.30p chocolate	.50	.38
a.	Imperf., pair	37.50	
C12 AP3	11.30p dp blue ('31)	.25	.25
	Nos. C7-C12 (6)	2.63	1.91

Sheets of these stamps sometimes show portions of a papermaker's watermark "Indian Bond C. Extra Strong."

Excellent counterfeits are plentiful.

Regular Issues of 1924-28 Surcharged in Black or Red

Correo Aéreo Habilitado en $ 3.40

1929 *Perf. 11½, 12*

C13 A47	95c on 7c lilac	.20	.15
C14 A47	1.90p on 20c dull bl	.20	.15
C15 A44	3.40p on 4p lt bl (R)	.25	.20
a.	Double surcharge	2.00	
C16 A44	4.75p on 4p lt bl (R)	.45	.38
a.	Double surcharge	2.00	
C17 A51	6.80p on 3p gray	.50	.50
a.	Double surcharge	3.00	
C18 A52	17p on 5p choc	1.50	1.50
a.	Horiz. pair, imperf. between	25.00	
	Nos. C13-C18 (6)	3.10	2.88

Six stamps in the sheet of No. C17 have the "$" and numerals thinner and narrower than the normal type.

Airplane and Arms — AP4

Cathedral of Asunción — AP5

Airplane and Globe — AP6

1930 *Perf. 12*

C19 AP4 95c dp red, *pink* .25 .25
C20 AP4 95c dk bl, *blue* .25 .25
C21 AP5 1.90p lt red, *pink* .25 .25
C22 AP5 1.90p violet, *blue* .25 .25
C23 AP6 6.80p blk, *lt bl* .25 .25
C24 AP6 6.80p green, *pink* .25 .30
Nos. C19-C24 (6) 1.50 1.55

Sheets of Nos. C19-C24 have a papermaker's watermark: "Extra Vencedor Bond."
Counterfeits exist.

Stamps and Types of 1927-28 Overprinted in Red **CORREO AEREO**

1930

C25 A47 10c olive green .15 .15
a. Double overprint 3.00
C26 A47 20c dull blue .15 .15
a. "CORREO CORREO" instead of "CORREO AEREO" 2.50
b. "AEREO AEREO" instead of "CORREO AEREO" 2.50
C27 A48 1p emerald .50 .50
C28 A51 3p gray .50 .50
Nos. C25-C26 (2) .30 .30

Nos. 273, 282, 286, 288, 300, 302, 305 Surcharged in Red or Black

CORREO AEREO CINCO #C29-C30, C32

CORREO AEREO VEINTE CENTAVOS #C31

CORREO AEREO SEIS #C33

CORREO AEREO DIEZ #C34-C35

1930

Red or Black Surcharge

C29 A47 5c on 10c gray grn (R) .15 .15
a. "AEREO" omitted 15.00
C30 A47 5c on 70c ultra (R) .15 .15
a. Vert. pair, imperf. between 20.00
C31 A48 20c on 1p org red .18 .18
a. "CORREO" double 3.00 3.00
b. "AEREO" double 3.00 3.00
C32 A47 40c on 50c org (R) .15 .15
a. "AEREO" omitted 4.50 4.50
b. "CORREO" double 3.00 3.00
c. "AEREO" double 3.00 3.00
C33 A54 6p on 10p red .75 .65
C34 A49 10p on 20p red 3.00 2.75
C35 A49 10p on 20p vio brn 3.00 2.75
Nos. C29-C35 (7) 7.38 6.78

Declaration of Independence AP11

1930, May 14 **Typo.**

C36 AP11 2.85p dark blue .25 .25
C37 AP11 3.40p dark green .25 .20
C38 AP11 4.75p deep lake .25 .20
Nos. C36-C38 (3) .75 .65

Natl. Independence Day, May 14, 1811.

Gunboat Type

Gunboat "Paraguay."

1931-39 *Perf. 11½, 12*

C39 A58 1p claret .15 .15
C40 A58 1p dk blue ('36) .15 .15
C41 A58 2p orange .15 .15
C42 A58 2p dk brn ('36) .15 .15
C43 A58 3p turq green .24 .24
C44 A58 3p lt ultra ('36) .25 .25
C45 A58 3p brt rose ('39) .20 .20
C46 A58 6p dk green .28 .28
C47 A58 6p violet ('36) .35 .32
C48 A58 6p dull bl ('39) .25 .25
C49 A58 10p vermilion .70 .60
C50 A58 10p bluish grn ('35) 1.00 1.00
C51 A58 10p yel brn ('36) .75 .75
C52 A58 10p dk blue ('36) .50 .50
C53 A58 10p lt pink ('39) .65 .65
Nos. C39-C53 (15) 5.77 5.64

1st constitution of Paraguay as a Republic and the arrival of the "Paraguay" and "Humaita."
Counterfeits of #C39-C53 are plentiful.

Regular Issue of 1924 Surcharged

3 3 Correo Aéreo

"Graf Zeppelin"

1931, Aug. 22

C54 A44 3p on 4p lt bl 6.00 5.00

Overprinted **Correo Aéreo**

"Graf Zeppelin"

C55 A44 4p lt blue 4.50 3.75

On Nos. C54-C55 the Zeppelin is hand-stamped. The rest of the surcharge or overprint is typographed.

War Memorial — AP13

Orange Tree and Yerba Mate — AP14

Yerba Mate — AP15

Palms — AP16

Eagle — AP17

1931-36 **Litho.**

C56 AP13 5c lt blue .15 .15
a. Horiz. pair, imperf. btwn. 6.25
C57 AP13 5c dp grn ('33) .15 .15
C58 AP13 5c lt red ('33) .15 .15
C59 AP13 5c violet ('35) .15 .15
C60 AP14 10c dp violet .15 .15
C61 AP14 10c brn lake ('33) .15 .15
C62 AP14 10c yel brn ('33) .15 .15
C63 AP14 10c ultra ('35) .15 .15
a. Imperf., pair 5.50
C64 AP15 20c red .15 .15
C65 AP15 20c dl blue ('33) .15 .15
C66 AP15 20c emer ('33) .15 .15
C67 AP15 20c yel brn ('35) .15 .15
a. Imperf., pair 3.75
C68 AP16 40c dp green .15 .15
C69 AP16 40c slate bl ('35) .15 .15
C70 AP16 40c red ('36) .15 .15
C71 AP17 80c dull blue .15 .15
C72 AP17 80c dl grn ('33) .15 .15
C73 AP17 80c scar ('33) .15 .15
Set value 1.60 1.25

Airship "Graf Zeppelin" — AP18

1932, Apr. **Litho.**

C74 AP18 4p ultra .85 .85
a. Imperf., pair 5.00
C75 AP18 8p red 1.40 1.00
C76 AP18 12p blue grn 1.10 .85
C77 AP18 16p dk violet 2.25 1.50
C78 AP18 20p orange brn 2.25 2.00
Nos. C74-C78 (5) 7.85 6.20

For surcharges see Nos. 325-329.

"Graf Zeppelin" over Brazilian Terrain — AP19

"Graf Zeppelin" over Atlantic AP20

1933, May 5

C79 AP19 4.50p dp blue 1.25 1.00
C80 AP19 9p dp rose 2.50 2.00
a. Horiz. pair, imperf. between 150.00
C81 AP19 13.50p blue grn 2.50 2.00
C82 AP20 22.50p bis brn 6.25 5.00
C83 AP20 45p dull vio 8.75 8.75
Nos. C79-C83 (5) 21.25 18.75

Excellent counterfeits are plentiful.
For overprints see Nos. C88-C97.

Posts and Telegraph Building, Asunción AP21

1934-37 *Perf. 11½*

C84 AP21 33.75p ultra 1.50 1.25
C85 AP21 33.75p car ('35) 1.50 1.25
a. 33.75p rose ('37) 1.25 1.25
C86 AP21 33.75p emerald ('36) 2.00 1.50
C87 AP21 33.75p bis brn ('36) .50 .50
Nos. C84-C87 (4) 5.50 4.50

For surcharge see No. C107.

Nos. C79-C83 Overprinted in Black **1 9 3 4**

1934, May 26

C88 AP19 4.50p deep bl 1.50 1.25
C89 AP19 9p dp rose 1.75 1.50
C90 AP19 13.50p blue grn 5.00 4.50
C91 AP20 22.50p bis brn 4.00 3.50
C92 AP20 45p dull vio 7.00 6.00
Nos. C88-C92 (5) 19.25 16.75

Types of 1933 Issue Overprinted in Black **1935**

1935

C93 AP19 4.50p rose red 2.00 1.10
C94 AP19 9p lt green 2.50 1.50
C95 AP19 13.50p brown 7.50 4.50
C96 AP20 22.50p violet 6.25 4.50
C97 AP20 45p blue 17.50 11.00
Nos. C93-C97 (5) 35.75 22.60

Tobacco Plant AP22

1935-39 **Typo.**

C98 AP22 17p lt brown 2.00 2.00
C99 AP22 17p carmine 3.75 3.75
C100 AP22 17p dark blue 2.50 2.50
C101 AP22 17p pale yel grn ('39) 1.50 1.50
Nos. C98-C101 (4) 9.75 9.75

Excellent counterfeits are plentiful.

Church of Incarnation AP23

1935-38

C102 AP23 102p carmine 3.00 2.25
C103 AP23 102p blue 3.00 2.25
C103A AP23 102p indigo ('36) 1.90 1.90
C104 AP23 102p yellow brn 2.00 2.00
a. Imperf., pair 15.00
C105 AP23 102p violet ('37) .95 .95
C106 AP23 102p brn org ('38) .85 .85
Nos. C102-C106 (6) 11.70 10.20

Excellent counterfeits are plentiful.
For surcharges see Nos. C108-C109.

Types of 1934-35 Surcharged in Red **Habilitado en $ 24.—**

1937, Aug. 1

C107 AP21 24p on 33.75p sl bl .50 .38
C108 AP23 65p on 102p ol bis 1.25 .90
C109 AP23 84p on 102p bl grn 1.25 .75
Nos. C107-C109 (3) 3.00 2.03

Plane over Asunción AP24

1939, Aug. 3 **Typo.** *Perf. 10½, 11½*

C110 AP24 3.40p yel green .50 .50
C111 AP24 3.40p orange brn .30 .25
C112 AP24 3.40p indigo .30 .25
Nos. C110-C112 (3) 1.10 1.00

Buenos Aires Peace Conference Type and

Map of Paraguay with New Chaco Boundary — AP28

Designs: 1p, Flags of Paraguay and Bolivia. 5p, Pres. Ortiz of Argentina, flags of Paraguay, Argentina. 10p, Pres. Vargas, Brazil. 30p, Pres. Alessandri, Chile. 50p, US Eagle and Shield. 100p, Pres. Benavides, Peru. 200p, Pres. Baldomir, Uruguay.

Engr.; Flags Litho.

1939, Nov. *Perf. 12½*

Flags in National Colors

C113 A69 1p red brown .15 .15
C114 A69 3p dark blue .15 .15
C115 A70 5p olive blk .15 .15
C116 A70 10p violet .15 .15
C117 A70 30p orange .18 .15
C118 A70 50p black brn .22 .15
C119 A70 100p brt green .35 .32
C120 A70 200p green 1.90 1.25
C121 AP28 500p black 5.00 5.00
Nos. C113-C121 (9) 8.25 7.47

For overprints see Nos. 388-390.

University of Asuncion Type

Pres. Bernardino Caballero and Senator José S. Decoud.

1939, Sept. **Litho.** *Perf. 12*

C122 A67 28p rose & blk 3.25 3.25
C123 A67 90p yel grn & blk 4.00 4.00

Map with Asunción to New York Air Route — AP35

1939, Nov. 30 — **Engr.**

C124	AP35	30p brown	1.90	1.50
C125	AP35	80p orange	2.25	2.25
C126	AP35	90p purple	4.00	4.00
		Nos. C124-C126 (3)	8.15	7.75

New York World's Fair.

Pan American Union Type

1940, May — *Perf. 12*

C127	A85	20p rose car	.18	.15
C128	A85	70p violet bl	.45	.18
C129	A85	100p Prus grn	.50	.50
C130	A85	500p dk violet	2.25	1.75
		Nos. C127-C130 (4)	3.38	2.58

Asuncion 400th Anniv. Type

1942, Aug. 15

C131	A93	20p deep plum	.50	.40
C132	A94	70p fawn	1.50	1.10
C133	A95	500p olive gray	4.00	3.50
		Nos. C131-C133 (3)	6.00	5.00

> Imperforates
> Starting with No. C134, many Paraguayan air mail stamps exist imperforate.

Port of Asunción AP40

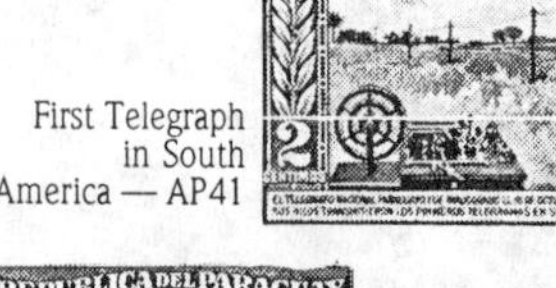

First Telegraph in South America — AP41

Early Merchant Ship — AP42

Birthplace of Paraguay's Liberation AP43

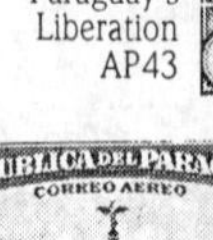

Monument to Antequera AP44

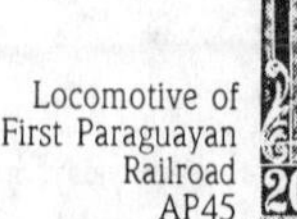

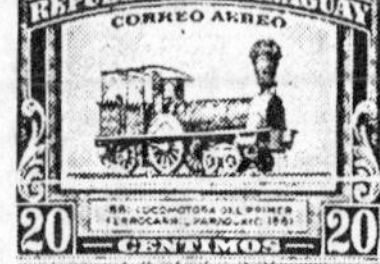

Locomotive of First Paraguayan Railroad AP45

Monument to Heroes of Itororó — AP46

Primitive Postal Service among Indians — AP48

Government House — AP47

Colonial Jesuit Altar — AP49

Ruins of Humaitá Church — AP50

Oratory of the Virgin — AP51

Marshal Francisco S. Lopez — AP52

1944-45 — **Unwmk.** — *Perf. 12½*

C134	AP40	1c blue	.15	.15
C135	AP41	2c green	.15	.15
C136	AP42	3c brown vio	.15	.15
C137	AP43	5c brt bl grn	.15	.15
C138	AP44	10c dk violet	.15	.15
C139	AP45	20c dk brown	.18	.15
C140	AP46	30c lt blue	.15	.15
C141	AP47	40c olive	.18	.18
C142	AP48	70c brown red	.30	.25
C143	AP49	1g orange yel	.70	.50
C144	AP50	2g copper brn	.85	.70
C145	AP51	5g black brn	1.75	1.75
C146	AP52	10g indigo	3.00	3.00
		Nos. C134-C146 (13)	7.86	7.43

See Nos. C158-C162. For surcharges see Nos. C154-C157.

Flags Type

Flags: 20c, Ecuador. 40c, Bolivia. 70c, Mexico. 1g, Chile. 2g, Brazil. 5g, Argentina. 10g, US.

Engr.; Flags Litho. in Natl. Colors

1945, Aug. 15

C147	A106	20c orange	.15	.15
C148	A106	40c olive	.15	.15
C149	A106	70c lake	.16	.15
C150	A106	1g slate bl	.30	.30
C151	A106	2g blue vio	.40	.40
C152	A106	5g green	.60	.60
C153	A106	10g brown	2.00	2.00
		Nos. C147-C153 (7)	3.76	3.75

Sizes: Nos. C147-C151, 30x26mm; 5g, 32x28mm; 10g, 33x30mm.

> Catalogue values for unused stamps in this section, from this point to the end of the section, are for Never Hinged items.

Nos. C139-C142 Surcharged "1946" and New Value in Black

1946 — **Engr.** — *Perf. 12½*

C154	AP45	5c on 20c dk brn	.40	.40
C155	AP46	5c on 30c lt blue	.40	.40
C156	AP47	5c on 40c olive	.40	.40
C157	AP48	5c on 70c brn red	.40	.40
		Nos. C154-C157 (4)	1.60	1.60

Types of 1944-45

1946, Sept. 21 — **Engr.**

C158	AP50	10c dp car	.15	.15
C159	AP40	20c emerald	.15	.15
C160	AP47	1g brown org	.30	.30
C161	AP52	5g purple	.90	.90
C162	AP51	10g rose car	2.50	2.50
		Nos. C158-C162 (5)	4.00	4.00

Marshal Francisco Solano Lopez Type

1947, May. 15 — *Perf. 12*

C163	A114	32c car lake	.15	.15
C164	A114	64c orange brn	.18	.18
C165	A114	1g Prus green	.25	.25
C166	A114	5g Prus grn & brn vio	.75	.75
C167	A114	10g dk car rose & dk yel grn	1.25	1.25
		Nos. C163-C167 (5)	2.58	2.58

Archbishopric of Asunción Types

1948, Jan. 6 — **Unwmk.** — *Perf. 12½*

Size: 25½x31mm

C168	A116	20c gray blk	.15	.15
C169	A117	30c dark blue	.15	.15
C170	A118	40c lilac	.15	.15
C171	A115	70c orange red	.15	.15
C172	A112	1g brown red	.18	.18
C173	A118	2g red	.50	.50

Size: 25½x34mm

C174	A115	5g brt car & dk bl	.90	.90
C175	A116	10g dk grn & brn	1.25	1.25
		Nos. C168-C175 (8)	3.43	3.43

For surcharges see Nos. B11, C178.

Type of Regular Issue of 1948 Inscribed "AEREO"

1948, Sept. 11 — **Engr. & Litho.**

C176	A119	69c dk grn, red & bl	.50	.50
C177	A119	5g dk bl, red & bl	2.00	1.75

The Barefeet, a political group.

No. C171 Surcharged in Black

DUELO NACIONAL
5 CENTIMOS 5

1949, June 29

C178	A115	5c on 70c org red	.15	.15

Archbishop Juan Sinforiano Bogarin (1863-1949).

Symbols of UPU AP65

Franklin D. Roosevelt AP66

1950, Sept. 4 — **Engr.** — *Perf. 13½x13*

C179	AP65	20c green & violet	.15	.15
C180	AP65	30c rose vio & brn	.15	.15
C181	AP65	50c gray & green	.15	.15
C182	AP65	1g blue & brown	.15	.15
C183	AP65	5g rose & black	.38	.38
		Nos. C179-C183 (5)	.98	.98

UPU, 75th anniv. (in 1949).

Engr.; Flags Litho.

1950, Oct. 2 — *Perf. 12½*

Flags in Carmine & Violet Blue.

C184	AP66	20c red	.15	.15
C185	AP66	30c black	.15	.15
C186	AP66	50c claret	.15	.15
C187	AP66	1g dk gray grn	.15	.15
C188	AP66	5g deep blue	.38	.38
		Set value	.78	.78

Franklin D. Roosevelt (1882-1945).

Urn Containing Remains of Columbus AP67

1952, Feb. 11 — **Litho.** — *Perf. 10*

C189	AP67	10c ultra	.15	.15
C190	AP67	20c green	.15	.15
C191	AP67	30c lilac	.15	.15
C192	AP67	40c rose	.15	.15
C193	AP67	50c bister brn	.15	.15
C194	AP67	1g blue	.15	.15
C195	AP67	2g orange	.15	.15
C196	AP67	5g red brown	.30	.30
		Set value	.78	.78

Queen Isabella I — AP68

1952, Oct. 12

C197	AP68	1g vio blue	.15	.15
C198	AP68	2g chocolate	.15	.15
C199	AP68	5g dull green	.25	.25
C200	AP68	10g lilac rose	.55	.55
		Nos. C197-C200 (4)	1.10	1.10

500th birth anniv. of Queen Isabella I of Spain (in 1951).

Pettirossi Type

1954, Mar.

C201	A122	40c brown	.15	.15
C202	A122	55c green	.15	.15
C203	A122	80c ultra	.15	.15
C204	A122	1.30g gray blue	.22	.22
		Set value	.38	.38

Church of San Roque — AP70

1954, June 20 — **Engr.** — *Perf. 12x13*

C205	AP70	20c carmine	.15	.15
C206	AP70	30c brown vio	.15	.15
C207	AP70	50c ultra	.15	.15
C208	AP70	1g red brn & bl grn	.15	.15
C209	AP70	1g red brn & lil rose	.15	.15
C210	AP70	1g red brn & blk	.15	.15
C211	AP70	1g red brn & org	.15	.15
a.		Min. sheet of 4, #C208-C211, perf. 12x12½	.30	.30
C212	AP70	5g dk red brn & vio	.15	.15
C213	AP70	5g dk red brn & ol grn	.15	.15
C214	AP70	5g dk red brn & org yel	.15	.15
C215	AP70	5g dk red brn & yel org	.15	.15
a.		Min. sheet of 4, #C212-C215, perf. 12x12½	.65	.65
		Set value	.95	.95

Centenary (in 1953) of the establishment of the Church of San Roque, Asuncion.

Nos. C211a and C215a issued without gum.

Heroes Type

Unwmk.

1954, Aug. 15 — **Litho.** — *Perf. 10*

C216	A123	5g violet	.15	.15
C217	A123	10g olive green	.25	.25
C218	A123	20g gray brown	.45	.38
C219	A123	50g vermilion	1.00	1.00
C220	A123	100g blue	3.25	3.25
		Nos. C216-C220 (5)	5.10	5.03

Peron Visit Type

Photo. & Litho.

1955, Apr. — **Wmk. 90** — *Perf. 13x13½*

Frames & Flags in Blue & Carmine

C221	A124	60c ol grn & cream	.15	.15
C222	A124	2g bl grn & cream	.15	.15
C223	A124	3g brn org & cream	.15	.15
C224	A124	4.10g brt rose pink & cr	.18	.15
		Set value	.42	.38

Monsignor Rodriguez Type

Jesuit Ruins: 3g, Corridor at Trinidad. 6g, Tower of Santa Rosa. 10g, San Cosme gate. 20g, Church of Jesus. 30g, Niche at Trinidad. 50g, Sacristy at Trinidad.

Perf. 12½x12, 12x12½

1955, June 19 — **Engr.** — **Unwmk.**

C225	A125	2g aqua	.15	.15
C226	A125	3g olive grn	.15	.15
C227	A126	4g lt blue grn	.15	.15
C228	A126	6g brown	.15	.15
C229	A125	10g rose	.15	.15
C230	A125	20g brown ol	.15	.15

C231 A126 30g dk green .30 .25
C232 A126 50g dp aqua .35 .30
Set value 1.00 .90

For surcharges see Nos. C252-C259.

Soldier and Flags — AP75

"Republic" and Soldier — AP76

1957, June 12 Photo. *Perf. 13½*

Granite Paper

Flags in Red and Blue

C233 AP75 10c ultra .15 .15
C234 AP75 15c dp claret .15 .15
C235 AP75 20c red .15 .15
C236 AP75 25c light blue .15 .15
C237 AP75 50c bluish grn .15 .15
C238 AP75 1g rose car .15 .15
C239 AP76 1.30g dp claret .15 .15
C240 AP76 1.50p light blue .15 .15
C241 AP76 2g emerald .15 .15
C242 AP76 4.10g red .15 .15
C243 AP76 5g gray black .15 .15
C244 AP76 10g bluish grn .15 .15
C245 AP76 25g ultra .25 .20
Set value .90 .80

Heroes of the Chaco war.

Stroessner Type of Regular Issue

1958, Aug. 16 Litho. Wmk. 320

Center in Slate

C246 A130 12g rose lilac .25 .25
C247 A130 18g orange .30 .30
C248 A130 23g orange brn .50 .50
C249 A130 36g emerald .50 .50
C250 A130 50g citron .65 .65
C251 A130 65g gray 1.00 1.00
Nos. C246-C251 (6) 3.20 3.20

Re-election of Pres. General Alfredo Stroessner.

Nos. C225-C232 Surcharged like #545-551 in Red

Perf. 12½x12, 12x12½

1959, May 26 Engr. Unwmk.

C252 A125 4g on 2g aqua .15 .15
C253 A125 12.45g on 3g ol grn .18 .15
C254 A126 18.15g on 6g brown .25 .22
C255 A125 23.40g on 10g rose .35 .28
C256 A125 34.80g on 20g brn ol .50 .38
C257 A126 36g on 4g lt bl grn .55 .40
C258 A126 43.95g on 30g dk grn .65 .45
C259 A126 100g on 50g deep aqua 1.50 1.00
Nos. C252-C259 (8) 4.13 3.03

The surcharge is made to fit the stamps. Counterfeits of surcharge exist.

UN Emblem — AP77

Unwmk.

1959, Aug. 27 Typo. *Perf. 11*

C260 AP77 5g ocher & ultra .50 .40

Visit of Dag Hammarskjold, Secretary General of the UN, Aug. 27-29.

Map and UN Emblem AP78

Uprooted Oak Emblem AP79

1959, Oct. 24 Litho. *Perf. 10*

C261 AP78 12.45g blue & salmon .20 .15

United Nations Day, Oct. 24, 1959.

Olympic Games Type of Regular Issue

Design: Basketball.

1960, Mar. 18 Photo. *Perf. 12½*

C262 A131 12.45g red & dk bl .15 .15
C263 A131 18.15g lilac & gray ol .20 .20
C264 A131 36g bl grn & rose car .40 .40
Nos. C262-C264 (3) .75 .75

The Paraguayan Philatelic Agency reported as spurious the imperf. souvenir sheet reproducing one of No. C264.

1960, Apr. 7 Litho. *Perf. 11*

C265 AP79 4g green & pink .45 .38
C266 AP79 12.45g bl & yel grn .90 .65
C267 AP79 18.15g car & ocher 1.25 .75
C268 AP79 23.40g red org & bl 1.25 1.50
Nos. C265-C268 (4) 3.85 3.28

World Refugee Year, July 1, 1959-June 30, 1960 (1st issue).

Human Rights Type of Regular Issue, 1960

Designs: 40g, UN Emblem. 60g, Hands holding scales. 100g, Flame.

1960, Apr. 21 *Perf. 12½x13*

C269 A133 40g dk ultra & red .25 .25
C270 A133 60g grnsh bl & org .30 .30
C271 A133 100g dk ultra & red .65 .65
Nos. C269-C271 (3) 1.20 1.20

An imperf. miniature sheet exists, containing one each of Nos. C269-C271, all printed in green and vermilion.

UN Type of Regular Issue

Perf. 13x13½

1960, Oct. 24 Photo. Unwmk.

C272 A134 3g orange, red & bl .15 .15
C273 A134 4g pale grn, red & bl .15 .15
Set value .15 .15

International Bridge, Paraguay-Brazil AP80

1961, Jan. 26 Litho. *Perf. 14*

C274 AP80 3g carmine .15 .15
C275 AP80 12.45g brown lake .18 .15
C276 AP80 18.15g Prus grn .20 .18
C277 AP80 36g dk blue .38 .35
a. Souv. sheet of 4, #C274-C277, imperf. .75 .75
Nos. C274-C277 (4) .91 .83

Inauguration of the International Bridge between Paraguay and Brazil.

"Paraguay en Marcha" Type of 1961

12.45g, Truck carrying logs. 18.15g, Logs on river barge. 22g, Radio tower. 36g, Jet plane.

1961, Apr. 10 Photo. *Perf. 13*

C278 A136 12.45g yel & vio bl .25 .20
C279 A136 18.15g pur & ocher .30 .25
C280 A136 22g ultra & ocher .38 .30
C281 A136 36g brt grn & yel .40 .38
Nos. C278-C281 (4) 1.33 1.13

Declaration of Independence AP81

1961, May 16 Litho. *Perf. 14½*

C282 AP81 12.45g dl red brn .15 .15
C283 AP81 18.15g dk blue .20 .18
C284 AP81 23.40g green .25 .22
C285 AP81 30g lilac .30 .28
C286 AP81 36g rose .40 .38
C287 AP81 44g olive .50 .45
Nos. C282-C287 (6) 1.80 1.66

150th anniv. of Independence (1st issue).

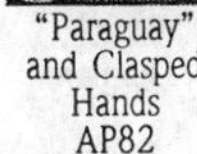

"Paraguay" and Clasped Hands AP82

South American Tapir AP83

1961, June 12 *Perf. 14x14½*

C288 AP82 3g vio blue .15 .15
C289 AP82 4g rose claret .15 .15
C290 AP82 100g gray green .90 .80
Nos. C288-C290 (3) 1.20 1.10

Chaco Peace; 150th anniv. of Independence (2nd issue).

1961, Aug. 16 Unwmk. *Perf. 14*

C291 AP83 12.45g claret .65 .50
C292 AP83 18.15g ultra .65 .65
C293 AP83 34.80g red brown 1.25 1.25
Nos. C291-C293 (3) 2.55 2.40

150th anniv. of Independence (3rd issue).

Catholic University Type of 1961

1961, Sept. 18 *Perf. 14x14½*

C294 A140 3g bister brn .15 .15
C295 A140 12.45g lilac rose .20 .20
C296 A140 36g blue .40 .40
Nos. C294-C296 (3) .75 .75

Hotel Guarani Type of 1961

Design: Hotel Guarani, different view.

1961, Oct. 14 Litho. *Perf. 15*

C297 A141 3g dull red brn .15 .15
C298 A141 4g ultra .15 .15
C299 A141 18.15g orange .25 .22
C300 A141 36g rose car .40 .38
Set value .75 .70

Tennis Type

1961, Oct. 16 Unwmk. *Perf. 11*

C301 A142 12.45g multi .25
C302 A142 20g multi .45
C303 A142 50g multi 1.00
Nos. C301-C303 (3) 1.70

Some specialists question the status of this issue.

Two imperf. souvenir sheets exist containing four 12.45g stamps each in a different color with simulated perforations and black marginal inscription.

WRY Type

Design: Oak emblem rooted in ground, wavy-lined frame.

1961, Dec. 30

C307 A145 18.15g brn & red .20
C308 A145 36g car & emer .45
C309 A145 50g emer & org .65
Nos. C307-C309 (3) 1.30

Imperforates in changed colors and souvenir sheets exist. Some specialists question the status of this issue.

Pres. Alfredo Stroessner and Prince Philip — AP84

1962, Mar. 9 Litho.

Portraits in Ultramarine

C310 AP84 12.45g grn & buff .15 .15
C311 AP84 18.15g red & pink .18 .18
C312 AP84 36g brn & yel .32 .32
Nos. C310-C312 (3) .65 .65

Visit of Prince Philip, Duke of Edinburgh. perf. and imperf. souvenir sheets exist.

Illustrations AP85-AP89, AP92-AP94, AP96-AP97, AP99-AP105, AP107-AP110, AP113-AP115, AP117, AP123, AP127a, AP132-AP133, AP136, AP138, AP140, AP142, AP144-AP145, AP149-AP150, AP152-AP153, AP156, AP158-AP159, AP165, AP167, AP171, AP180, AP183-AP184, AP187, AP196, AP202, AP205, AP208, AP211, AP221-AP222, AP224-AP225, AP229, AP234-AP235, AP237 and AP240 are reduced.

Souvenir Sheet

Abraham Lincoln (1809-1865), 16th President of US — AP85

1963, Aug. 21 Litho. *Imperf.*

C313 AP85 36g gray & vio brn

Limited Distribution Issues
Beginning with No. C313, stamps with limited distribution are not valued.

Souvenir Sheet

1960 Summer Olympics, Rome — AP86

1963, Aug. 21 Litho. & Engr.

C314 AP86 50g lt bl, vio brn & sep

MUESTRA

Illustrations may show the word "MUESTRA." This means specimen and is not on the actual stamps.

Souvenir Sheet

Cattleya Cigas — AP87

1963, Aug. 21 **Litho.**
C315 AP87 66g multicolored

Souvenir Sheet

Pres. Alfredo Stroessner — AP88

1964, Nov. 3
C316 AP88 36g multicolored

Souvenir Sheet

Saturn V Rocket, Pres. John F. Kennedy — AP89

1968, Jan. 27 *Perf. 14*
C317 AP89 50g multicolored

Pres. Kennedy, 4th death anniv. (in 1967).

Torch, Book, Houses — AP90

1969, June 28 **Wmk. 347** *Perf. 11*

C318 AP90 36g blue		.50
C319 AP90 50g bister brn		.65
C320 AP90 100g rose car		1.25
Nos. C318-C320 (3)		2.40

National drive for teachers' homes.

Souvenir Sheets

US Space Program — AP91

John F. Kennedy, Wernher von Braun, moon and: No. C321, Apollo 11 en route to moon. No. C322, Saturn V lift-off. No. C323, Apollo 9. No. C324, Apollo 10.

1969, July 9 *Perf. 14*
C321 AP91 23.40g multicolored
C322 AP91 23.40g multicolored

Imperf

C323 AP91 23.40g multicolored
C324 AP91 23.40g multicolored

Nos. C323-C324 each contain one 56x46mm stamp.

Souvenir Sheets

Events and Anniversaries — AP92

#C325, Apollo 14. #C326, Dwight D. Eisenhower, 1st death anniv. #C327, Napoleon Bonaparte, birth bicent. #C328, Brazil, winners of Jules Rimet World Cup Soccer Trophy.

1970, Dec. 16 *Perf. 13½*
C325 AP92 20g multicolored
C326 AP92 20g multicolored
C327 AP92 20g multicolored
C328 AP92 20g multicolored

Souvenir Sheets

Paraguayan Postage Stamps, Cent. — AP93

No. C329, Marshal Francisco Solano Lopez, Pres. Alfredo Stroessner, Paraguay #1. No. C330, #3, 1014, 1242. No. C331, #1243, C8, C74.

1971
C329 AP93 20g multicolored
C330 AP93 20g multicolored
C331 AP93 20g multicolored

Issued: #C329, 3/23; #C330-C331, 3/29.

Souvenir Sheets

Emblems of Apollo Space Missions — AP94

Designs: No. C332, Apollo 7, 8, 9, & 10. No. C333, Apollo 11, 12, 13, & 14.

1971, Mar. 26
C332 AP94 20g multicolored
C333 AP94 20g multicolored

Souvenir Sheet

Charles de Gaulle — AP95

1971, Dec. 24 *Perf. 14*
C334 AP95 20g multicolored

Souvenir Sheet

Taras Shevchenko (1814-1861), Ukrainian Poet — AP96

1971, Dec. 24 *Perf. 13½*
C335 AP96 20g multicolored

Souvenir Sheets

Johannes Kepler (1571-1630), German Astronomer — AP97

Kepler and: No. C336, Apollo lunar module over moon. No. C337, Astronaut walking in space.

1971, Dec. 24
C336 AP97 20g multicolored
C337 AP97 20g multicolored

Souvenir Sheet

10 years of US Space Program — AP98

1972, Jan. 61 *Perf. 13½*
C338 AP98 20g multicolored

Souvenir Sheet

Apollo 16 Moon Mission — AP99

1972, Mar. 29 **Litho.** *Perf. 13½*
C339 AP99 20g multicolored

Souvenir Sheets

History of the Olympics — AP100

Designs: No. C340, Pierre de Coubertin (1863-1937), founder of modern Olympics. No. C341, Skier, Garmisch-Partenkirchen, 1936. No. C342, Olympic flame, Sapporo, 1972. No. C343, French, Olympic flags. No. C344, Javelin thrower, Paris, 1924. No. C345, Equestrian event.

1972, Mar. 29 *Perf. 14½*
C340 AP100 20g multicolored
C341 AP100 20g multicolored
C342 AP100 20g multicolored
C343 AP100 20g multicolored
C344 AP100 20g multicolored
C345 AP100 20g multicolored

Souvenir Sheet

Medal Totals, 1972 Winter Olympics, Sapporo — AP101

1972, Nov. 18 *Perf. 13½*
C346 AP101 23.40g multicolored

Souvenir Sheets

French Contributions to Aviation and Space Exploration — AP102

Georges Pompidou, Charles de Gaulle and: No. C347, Concorde. No. C348, Satellite D2A, Mirage G 8 jets.

1972, Nov. 25
C347 AP102 23.40g multicolored
C348 AP102 23.40g multicolored

Souvenir Sheets

Summer Olympic Gold Medals, 1896-1972 — AP103

1972, Nov. 25
C349 AP103 23.40g 9 medals, 1896-1932, vert.
C350 AP103 23.40g 8 medals, 1936-1972

Souvenir Sheet

Adoration of the Shepherds by Murillo — AP104

1972, Nov. 25
C351 AP104 23.40g multicolored

Christmas.

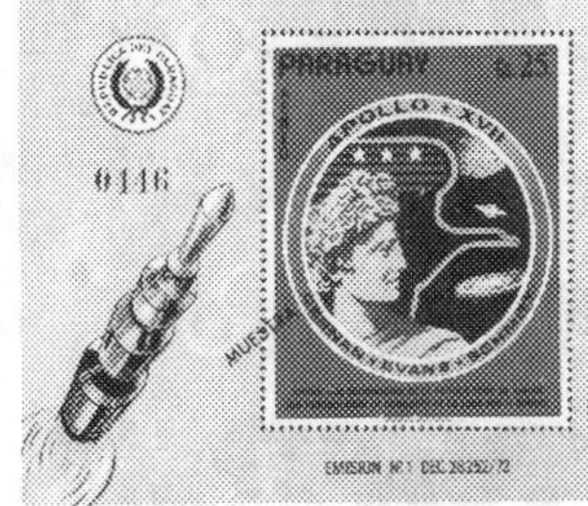

Apollo 17 Moon Mission — AP105

1973, Mar. 13
C352 AP105 25g multicolored

Souvenir Sheet

192 Olympic Winners — AP106

1973, Mar. 15 *Perf. 13½*
C353 AP106 20g multicolored

Souvenir Sheets

The Holy Family by Peter Paul Rubens — AP107

Design: No. C355, In the Forest at Pierrefonds by Alfred de Dreux.

1973, Mar. 15
C354 AP107 25g multicolored
C355 AP107 25g multicolored

Souvenir Sheet

German Championship Soccer Team F.C. Bayern, Bavaria #2 — AP108

1973, June 29 *Imperf.*
C356 AP108 25g multicolored

IBRA '73 Intl. Philatelic Exhibition, Munich,

Souvenir Sheet

Copernicus, 500th Birth Anniv. and Space Exploration — AP109

#C357, Lunar surface, Apollo 11. #C358, Copernicus, position of Earth at soltices and equinoxes, vert. #C359, Skylab space laboratory.

1973, June 29 *Perf. 13½*
C357 AP109 25g multicolored
C358 AP109 25g multicolored
C359 AP109 25g multicolored

Souvenir Sheets

Exploration of Mars — AP110

1973, Oct. 8
C360 AP110 25g Mariner 9
C361 AP110 25g Viking probe, horiz.

Pres. Stroessner's Visit to Europe and Morocco — AP111

Designs: No. C362a, 5g, Arms of Paraguay, Spain, Canary Islands. b, 10g, Gen. Franco, Stroessner, vert. c, 25g, Arms of Paraguay, Germany. d, 50g, Stroessner, Giovanni Leone, Italy, vert. No. C363, Itaipu Dam between Paraguay and Brazil.

1973, Dec. 30 *Perf. 14*
C362 AP111 Strip of 4, #a.-d.
C363 AP111 150g multicolored

Souvenir Sheet

Imperf

C364 AP111 100g Country flags

No. C364 contains one 60x50mm stamp.

1974 World Cup Soccer Championships, Munich — AP112

Abstract paintings of soccer players: No. C366a, 10g, Player seated on globe. b, 20g, Player as viewed from under foot. No. C367, Player kicking ball. No. C368, Goalie catching ball, horiz.

1974, Jan. 31 *Perf. 14*
C365 AP112 5g shown
C366 AP112 Pair, #a.-b.

Souvenir Sheets

Perf. 13½

C367 AP112 25g multicolored
C368 AP112 25g multicolored

Nos. C367-C368 each contain one 50x60mm stamp.

Souvenir Sheets

Tourism Year — AP113

Design: No. C370, Painting, Birth of Christ by Louis le Nain (1593-1648), horiz.

1974, Feb. 4 *Perf. 13½*
C369 AP113 25g multicolored
C370 AP113 25g multicolored

Christmas (No. C370).

Souvenir Sheets

Events and Anniversaries — AP114

1974, Mar. 20
C371 AP114 25g Rocket lift-off
C372 AP114 25g Solar system, horiz.
C373 AP114 25g Skylab 2 astronauts, horiz.

Souvenir Sheet

C374 AP114 25g Olympic Flame

UPU centennial (#C371-C372). 1976 Olympic Games (#C374).

President Stroessner Type of 1973

Designs: 100g, Stroessner, Georges Pompidou. 200g, Stroessner and Pope Paul VI.

1974, Apr. 25 *Perf. 14*

C375 AP111 100g multicolored

Souvenir Sheet

Perf. 13½

C376 AP111 200g multicolored

No. C376 contains one 60x50mm stamp.

Souvenir Sheet

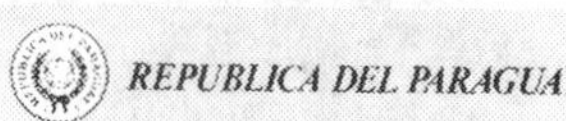

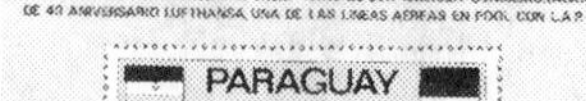

Lufthansa Airlines Intercontinental Routes, 40th Anniv. — AP115

1974, July 13 *Perf. 13½*

C377 AP115 15g multicolored

No. C377 face value was 15g plus 5g extra for a monument to Francisco Solano Lopez.

Reserve #C378 (AP115) for Hermann Oberth, 80th birth anniv. souv. sheet.

1974 World Cup Soccer Championships, West Germany — AP116

1974, July 13 *Perf. 14*

C379 AP116 4g Goalie

C380 AP116 5g Soccer ball

C381 AP116 10g shown

Souvenir Sheet

Perf. 13½

C382 AP116 15g Soccer ball, diff.

No. C382 contains one 53x46mm stamp. No. C382 face value was 15g plus 5g extra for a monument for Francisco Solano Lopez.

Souvenir Sheet

First Balloon Flight over English Channel — AP117

1974, Sept. 13 *Imperf.*

C383 AP117 15g multicolored

No. C383 face value was 15g plus 5g extra for a monument for Francisco Solano Lopez.

Anniversaries and Events — AP118

Designs: 4g, US #C76 on covers that went to Moon. No. C385a, 5g, Pres. Pinochet of Chile. No. C385b, 10g, Pres. Stroessner's visit to South Africa. No. C386, Mariner 10 over Mercury, horiz. No. C387, Paraguay permanent member of UPU. No. C388, UPU cent., Rousseau's "Zeppelins."

1974, Dec. 2 *Perf. 14*

C384 AP118 4g multicolored

C385 AP118 Pair #a.-b.

Souvenir Sheets

Perf. 13½

C386 AP118 15g multicolored

C387 AP118 15g multicolored

Perf. 14½

C388 AP118 15g multicolored

Nos. C386-C387 contain one 60x50mm stamp, No. C388 one 50x35mm stamp. Face value was 15g plus 5g extra for a monument to Francisco Solano Lopez. Compare No. C386 with No. C392.

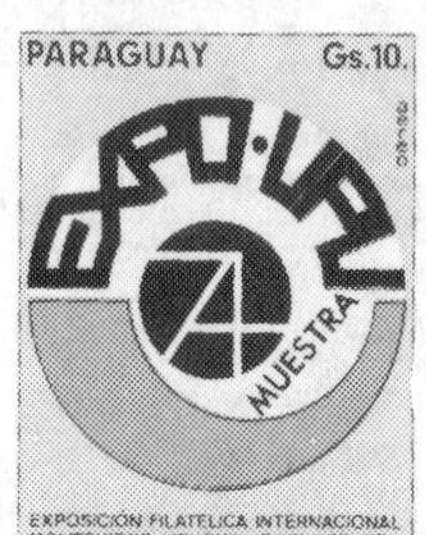

Anniversaries and Events AP119

Designs: 4g, UPU, cent. 5g, 17th Congress, UPU, Lausanne. 10g, Intl. Philatelic Exposition, Montevideo, Uruguay. No. C392, Mariner 10 orbiting Mercury, horiz. No. C393, Figure skater, horiz. No. C394, Innsbruck Olympic emblem.

1974, Dec. 7 *Perf. 14*

C389 AP119 4g multicolored

C390 AP119 5g multicolored

C391 AP119 10g multicolored

Souvenir Sheets

Perf. 13½

C392 AP119 15g bl & multi

C393 AP119 15g multicolored

C394 AP119 15g multicolored

UPU centennial (#C389). Nos. C392-C394 each contain one 60x50mm stamp and face value was 15g plus 5g extra for a monument to Francisco Solano Lopez.

German World Cup Soccer Champions — AP120

1974, Dec. 20 *Perf. 14*

C395 AP120 4g Holding World Cup trophy, vert.

C396 AP120 5g Team on field

C397 AP120 10g Argentina '78 emblem, vert.

Souvenir Sheet

Perf. 13½

C398 AP120 15g Players holding trophy, vert.

No. C398 contains one 50x60mm stamp and face value was 15g plus 5g extra for a monument to Francisco Solano Lopez.

Souvenir Sheet

Apollo-Soyuz — AP121

1974, Dec. 20 *Perf. 13½*

C400 AP121 15g multicolored

Expo '75 AP122

1975, Feb. 24 *Perf. 14*

C401 AP122 4g Ryukyumurasaki, vert.

C402 AP122 5g Hibiscus

C403 AP122 10g Ancient sailing ship

Souvenir Sheet

Perf. 14½

C404 AP122 15g Expo emblem, vert.

No. C404 face value was 15g plus 5g extra for a monument to Francisco Solano Lopez.

Souvenir Sheets

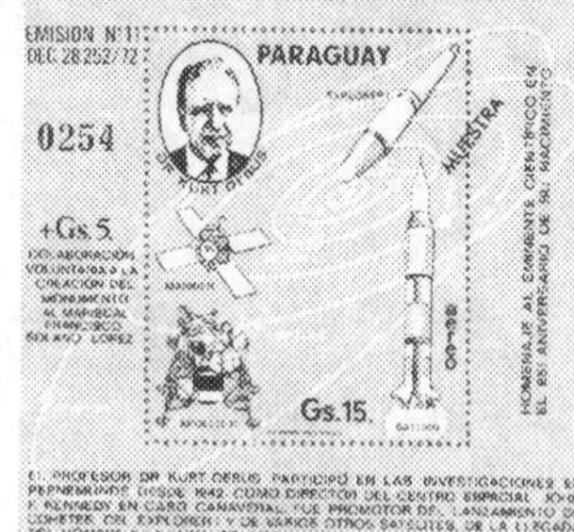

Anniversaries and Events — AP123

Designs: No. C405, Dr. Kurt Debus, space scientist, 65th birth anniv. No. C406, 1976 Summer Olympics, Montreal, horiz.

1975, Feb. 24 *Perf. 13½*

C405 AP123 15g multicolored

C406 AP123 15g multicolored

Nos. C405-C406 face value was 15g plus 5g extra for a monument to Francisco Solano Lopez.

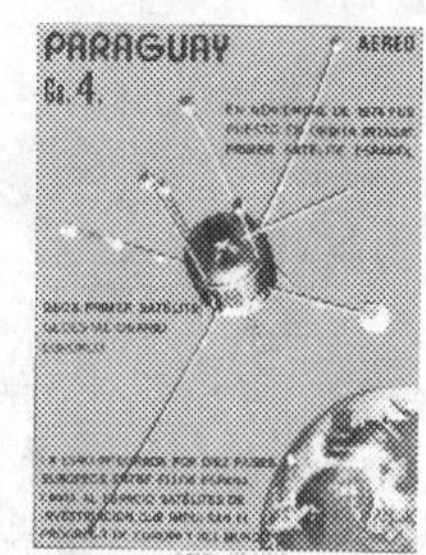

GEOS Satellite AP124

Designs: No. C408a, 5g, ESPANA 75. b, 10g, Mother and Child, Murillo.

1975, Aug. 21 *Perf. 14*

C407 AP124 4g shown

C408 AP124 Pair, #1.-b.

Souvenir Sheet

Perf. 13½

C409 AP124 15g Spain #1139, 1838, C167, charity stamp

C410 AP124 15g Zeppelin, plane, satellites

Perf. 14½

C411 AP124 15g Jupiter

Nos. C409-C411 face value was 15g plus 5g extra for a monument to Francisco Solano Lopez.
Size of stamps: No. C409, 45x55mm; C410, 55x45mm; C411, 32x22mm.

Souvenir Sheets

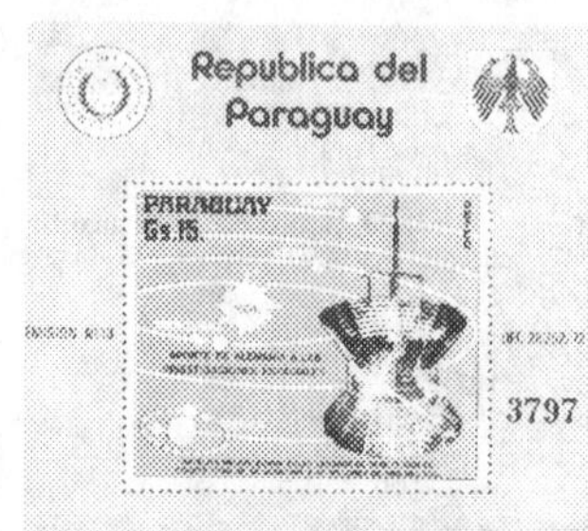

Anniversaries and Events — AP125

Designs: No. C413, UN emblem, Intl. Women's Year, vert. No. C414, Helios space satellite.

1975, Aug. 26 *Perf. 13½*

C413 AP125 15g multicolored

C414 AP125 15g multicolored

Nos. C413-C414 face value was 15g plus 5g extra for a monument to Francisco Solano Lopez.

Souvenir Sheets

Anniversaries and Events — AP126

No. C418, Zeppelin, boats. No. C419, Soccer, Intelsat IV, vert. No. C420, Viking Mars landing.

1975, Oct. 13 *Perf. 13½*

C418 AP126 15g multicolored

C419 AP126 15g multicolored

C420 AP126 15g multicolored

Nos. C418-C420 face value was 15g plus 5g extra for a monument to Francisco Solano Lopez.

United States, Bicent. — AP127

#C421: a, 4g, Lunar rover. b, 5g, Ford Elite, 1975. c, 10g, Ford, 1896. No. C422, Airplanes and spacecraft. No. C423, Arms of Paraguay & US.

1975, Nov. 28 Litho. *Perf. 14*
C421 AP127 Strip of 3, #a.-c.

Souvenir Sheets
Perf. 13½

C422 AP127 15g multicolored
C423 AP127 15g multicolored

Nos. C422-C423 each contain one 60x50mm stamp and face value was 15g plus 20g with 5g surtax for a monument to Francisco Solano Lopez.

Souvenir Sheet

0726

+Gs.5

La Musique by Francois Boucher — AP127a

1975, Nov. 28 *Perf. 13½*
C424 AP127a 15g multicolored

No. C424 face value was 15g plus 5g extra for a monument to Francisco Solano Lopez.

Anniversaries and Events — AP128

Designs: 4g, Flight of Concorde jet. 5g, JU 52/3M, Lufthansa Airlines, 50th anniv. 10g, EXFILMO '75 and ESPAMER '75. No. C428, Concorde, diff. No. C429, Dr. Albert Schweitzer, missionary and Konrad Adenauer, German statesman. No. C430, Ferdinand Porsche, auto designer, birth cent., vert.

1975, Dec. 20 *Perf. 14*
C425 AP128 4g multicolored
C426 AP128 5g multicolored
C427 AP128 10g multicolored

Souvenir Sheets
Perf. 13½

C428 AP128 15g multicolored
C429 AP128 15g multicolored
C430 AP128 15g multicolored

Nos. C428-C430 face value was 15g plus 5g extra for a monument to Francisco Solano Lopez. No. C428 contains one 54x34mm stamp, No. C429 one 60x50mm stamp, No. C430 one 30x40mm stamp.

Anniversaries and Events — AP129

Details: 4g, The Transfiguration by Raphael, vert. 5g, Nativity by Del Mayno. 10g, Nativity by Vignon. No. C434, Detail from Adoration of the Shepherds by Ghirlandaio. No. C435, Austria, 1000th anniv., Leopold I, natl. arms, vert. No. C436, Sepp Herberger and Helmut Schon, coaches for German soccer team.

1976, Feb. 2 Litho. *Perf. 14*
C431 AP129 4g multicolored
C432 AP129 5g multicolored
C433 AP129 10g multicolored

Souvenir Sheets
Perf. 13½

C434 AP129 15g multicolored
C435 AP129 15g multicolored

Perf. 13½x13

C436 AP129 15g multicolored

Nos. C434-C436 face value was 15g plus 5g extra for a monument to Francisco Solano Lopez. No. C434 contains one 40x30mm stamp, No. C435 one 30x40mm stamp, No. C436 one 54x34mm stamp.

Souvenir Sheet

Apollo-Soyuz — AP130

1976, Apr. 2 *Perf. 13½x13*
C437 AP130 25g multicolored

Souvenir Sheet

Lufthansa, 50th Anniv. — AP131

1976, Apr. 7 *Perf. 13½x13*
C438 AP131 25g multicolored

Souvenir Sheet

Interphil '76 — AP132

1976, May 12 *Perf. 13½*
C439 AP132 15g multicolored

No. C439 face value was 15g plus 5g extra for a monument to Francisco Solano Lopez.

Souvenir Sheets

Anniversaries and Events — AP133

Designs: No. C440, Alexander Graham Bell, telephone cent. No. C441, Gold, silver, and bronze medals, 1976 Winter Olympics, Innsbruck. No. C442, Gold medalist Rosi Mittermaier, downhill and slalom, vert. No. C443, Viking probe on Mars. No. C444, UN Postal Administration, 25th anniv. and UPU, cent., vert. No. C445, Prof. Hermann Oberth, Wernher von Braun. No. C446, Madonna and Child by Durer, vert.

1976 *Perf. 13½*
C440 AP133 25g multicolored
C441 AP133 25g multicolored
C442 AP133 25g multicolored

Perf. 14½

C443 AP133 25g multicolored
C444 AP133 25g multicolored
C445 AP133 25g multicolored
C446 AP133 25g multicolored

No. C442 contains one 35x54mm stamp, No. C443 one 46x36mm stamp, No. C444 one 25x35mm stamp.

Issue dates: Nos. C440-C441, June 15. No. C443, July 8. Nos. C442, C444, July 15. No. C445, Aug. 20. No. C446, Sept. 9.

Souvenir Sheet

UN Offices in Geneva #22, UN #42 — AP136

1976, Dec. 18 *Perf. 13½*
C447 AP136 25g multicolored

UN Postal Administration, 25th anniv. and telephone, cent.

Reserved #C448 AP137 for Ludwig Beethoven souvenir sheet.

Souvenir Sheet

Alfred Nobel, 80th Death Anniv. and First Nobel Prize, 75th Anniv. — AP138

1977, June 7 *Perf. 13½*
C449 AP138 25g multicolored

Souvenir Sheet

Coronation of Queen Elizabeth II, 25th Anniv. — AP139

1977, July 25 *Perf. 14½*
C450 AP139 25g multicolored

Souvenir Sheet

Uruguay '77 Intl. Philatelic Exhibition — AP140

1977, Aug. 27 Litho. *Perf. 13½*
C451 AP140 25g multicolored

Souvenir Sheets

Exploration of Mars — AP141

1977, Sept. 5 *Perf. 13½*
C452 AP141 25g Martian craters

1977, Oct. 28 Litho. *Perf. 13½*
C454 AP141 25g Projected Martian lander

Souvenir Sheet

Sepp Herberger, German Soccer Team Coach — AP142

1978, Jan. 23 Litho. *Perf. 13½*
C455 AP142 25g multicolored

Souvenir Sheet

Austria #B331, Canada #681, US #716, Russia #B66 — AP143

1978, Mar. 10 Litho. *Perf. 14½*
C456 AP143 25g multicolored

Inner perforations are simulated.

Souvenir Sheet

Alfred Nobel — AP144

1978, Mar. 15 Litho. *Perf. 13½*
C457 AP144 25g multicolored

Souvenir Sheets

Anniversaries and Events — AP145

Designs: No. C458, Queen Elizabeth II wearing St. Edward's Crown, holding orb and scepter. No. C459, Queen Elizabeth II presenting World Cup Trophy to English team captain. No. C460, Flags of nations participating in 1978 World Cup Soccer Championships. No. C461, Soccer action. No. C462, Argentina, 1978 World Cup Champions.

1978 *Perf. 14½, 13½ (#C461)*
C458 AP145 25g multicolored
C459 AP145 25g multicolored
C460 AP145 25g multicolored
C461 AP145 25g multicolored
C462 AP145 25g multicolored

Coronation of Queen Elizabeth II, 25th Anniv. (#C458-C459). 1978 World Cup Soccer Championships, Argentina (#C460-C462).

No. C460 contains one 70x50mm stamp, No. C461 one 39x57mm stamp.

Issued: No. C458, May 11. Nos. C459-C460, May 16. No. C461, June 30. No. C462, Oct. 26.

Souvenir Sheet

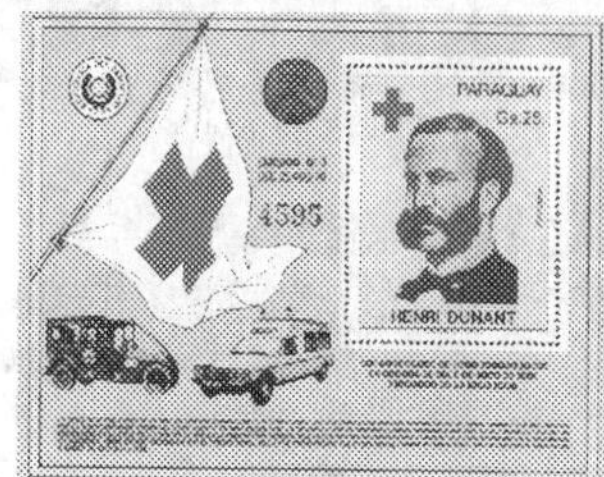

Jean-Henri Dunant, 150th Birth Anniv. — AP146

1978, June 28 *Perf. 14½*
C463 AP146 25g multicolored

Souvenir Sheet

Capt. James Cook, 250th Birth Anniv. — AP147

1978, July 19 *Perf. 13½*
C464 AP147 25g multicolored

Discovery of Hawaii, Death of Capt. Cook, bicentennial; Hawaii Statehood, 20th anniv.

Souvenir Sheet

Adoration of the Magi by Albrecht Durer — AP149

1978, Oct. 31 *Perf. 13½*
C468 AP149 25g multicolored

Souvenir Sheet

Prof. Hermann Oberth, 85th Birth Anniv. — AP150

1979, Aug. 28 *Perf. 14½*
C469 AP150 25g multicolored

Souvenir Sheet

World Cup Soccer Championships — AP151

1979, Nov. 29
C470 AP151 25g multicolored

Souvenir Sheet

Helicopters — AP152

1979, Nov. 29 Litho. *Perf. 13½*
C471 AP152 25g multicolored

Souvenir Sheet

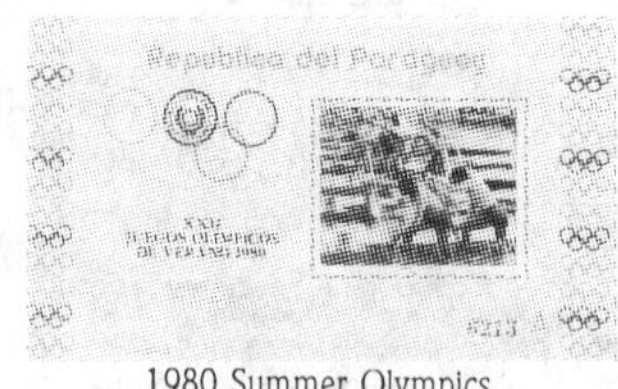

1980 Summer Olympics, Moscow — AP153

1979, Dec. 20 *Perf. 14½*
C472 AP153 25g Two-man canoe

Souvenir Sheet

1982 World Cup Soccer Championships, Spain — AP154

1979, Dec. 24 Litho. *Perf. 13x13½*
C473 AP154 25g Sheet of 1 + label

Souvenir Sheet

Maybach DS-8 "Zeppelin" — AP155

1980, Apr. 8 *Perf. 14½*
C474 AP155 25g multicolored

Wilhelm Maybach, 50th death anniv. Karl Maybach, 100th birth anniv.

Souvenir Sheet

Rotary Intl., 75th Anniv. — AP156

1980, July 1 Litho. *Perf. 14½*
C475 AP156 25g multicolored

Apollo 11 Type of 1970
Souvenir Sheet

Design: 1st steps on lunar surface.

1980, July 30 *Perf. 13½*
Size: 36x26mm
C476 A221 25g multicolored

Souvenir Sheet

Virgin Surrounded by Animals by Albrecht Durer
AP158

Photo. & Engr.
1980, Sept. 24 *Perf. 12*
C477 AP158 25g multicolored

Souvenir Sheet

1980 Olympic Games — AP159

1980, Dec. 15 Litho. *Perf. 14*
C478 AP159 25g multi

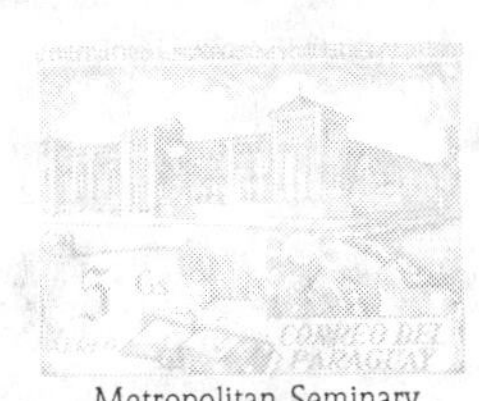

Metropolitan Seminary Centenary — AP160

1981, Mar. 26 Litho. Wmk. 347

C479 AP160	5g ultra	.15	.15
C480 AP160	10g red brn	.15	.15
C481 AP160	25g green	.20	.15
C482 AP160	50g gray	.40	.30
	Set value	.72	.55

Anniversaries and Events AP161

Designs: 5g, George Washington, 250th birth anniv. (in 1982). 10g, Queen Mother Elizabeth, 80th birthday (in 1980). 30g, Phila Tokyo '81.

No. C486, Emperor Hirohito, 80th birthday. No. C487, Washington Crossing the Delaware.

1981, July 10 Unwmk. *Perf. 14*

C483 AP161 5g multicolored
C484 AP161 10g multicolored
C485 AP161 30g multicolored

Souvenir Sheets

Perf. 14½

C486 AP161 25g multicolored
C487 AP161 25g multicolored

No. C484 issued in sheets of 8 plus label. For overprints see Nos. 2126, C590-C591, C611.

First Space Shuttle Mission — AP162

Pres. Ronald Reagan and: 5g, Columbia in Earth orbit. 10g, Astronauts John Young and Robert Crippen. 30g, Columbia landing.

George Washington and: No. C491, Columbia re-entering atmosphere. No. C492, Columbia inverted above Earth.

1981, Oct. 9 *Perf. 14*

C488 AP162 5g multicolored
C489 AP162 10g multicolored
C490 AP162 30g multicolored

Souvenir Sheets

Perf. 13½

C491 AP162 25g multicolored
C492 AP162 25g multicolored

Nos. C491-C492 each contain one 60x50mm stamp. Inauguration of Pres. Reagan, George Washington, 250th birth anniv. (in 1982) (#C491-C492).

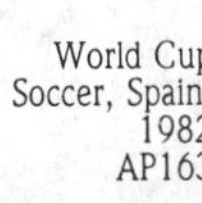

World Cup Soccer, Spain, 1982 AP163

1981, Oct. 15 *Perf. 14*

Color of Shirts

C493 AP163 5g yellow, green
C494 AP163 10g blue, white
C495 AP163 30g white & black, orange

Souvenir Sheet

Perf. 14½

C496 AP163 25g Goalie

No. C494 exists in sheets of 5 plus 4 labels.

Christmas AP164

Paintings: 5g, Virgin with the Child by Stefan Lochner. 10g, Our Lady of Caacupe. 25g, Altar of the Virgin by Albrecht Durer. 30g, Virgin and Child by Matthias Grunewald.

1981, Dec. 21 *Perf. 14*

C497 AP164 5g multicolored
C498 AP164 10g multicolored
C499 AP164 30g multicolored

Souvenir Sheet

Perf. 13½

C500 AP164 25g multicolored

No. C500 contains one 54x75mm stamp.

Souvenir Sheet

Graf Zeppelin's First Flight to South America, 50th Anniv. — AP165

1981, Dec. 28 *Perf. 14½*

C501 AP165 25g multicolored

Mother Maria Mazzarello (1837-1881), Co-Founder of Daughters of Mary — AP166

Perf. 13x13½

1981, Dec. 30 Litho. Wmk. 347

C502 AP166	20g blk & grn	.16	.15
C503 AP166	25g blk & red brn	.20	.15
C504 AP166	50g blk & gray vio	.40	.30

Souvenir Sheet

The Magus (Dr. Faust) by Rembrandt — AP167

Litho. & Typo.

1982, Apr. 23 Unwmk. *Perf. 14½*

C505 AP167 25g blk, buff & gold

Johann Wolfgang von Goethe, 150th death anniv.

The following stamps were issued 4 each in sheets of 8 with 1 label: Nos. C590-C591, C669-C670, C677-C678, C682-C683, C690-C691, C699-C700, C718-C719, C747-C748.

The following stamps were issued in sheets of 4 with 5 labels: Nos. C765-C766, C774, C779-C780, C785, C803, C813, C818, C823.

The following stamps were issued in sheets of 3 with 6 labels: Nos. C739, C754.

The following stamps were issued in sheets of 5 with 4 labels: Nos. C507, C512, C515, C519, C524, C529, C535, C539, C542, C548, C550, C559, C569, C572, C579, C582, C585, C588, C596, C598, C615, C622, C626, C634, C642, C647, C650, C656, C705, C711, C731, C791, C798, C808.

The following stamp was issued in sheets of 7 with 2 labels: No. C660.

World Chess Championships Type of 1980

Illustrations from The Book of Chess: 5g, The Game of the Virgins. 10g, Two gothic ladies. 30g, Chess game at apothecary shop.

No. C509, Christians and Jews preparing to play in garden. No. C510, Indian prince introducing chess to Persia.

1982, June 10 Litho. *Perf. 14*

C506 A347 5g multicolored
C507 A347 10g multicolored
C508 A347 30g multicolored

Souvenir Sheets

Perf. 13½

C509 A347 25g multicolored

Perf. 14½

C510 A347 25g multicolored

No. C509 contains one 50x60mm stamp, No. C510 one 50x70mm stamp. For overprint see No. C665.

Italy, Winners of 1982 World Cup Soccer Championships — AP168

Players: 5g, Klaus Fischer, Germany. 10g, Altobelli holding World Cup Trophy. 25g, Forster, Altobelli, horiz. 30g, Fischer, Gordillo.

1982, Oct. 20 *Perf. 14*

C511 AP168 5g multicolored
C512 AP168 10g multicolored
C513 AP168 30g multicolored

Souvenir Sheet

C513A AP168 25g multicolored

Christmas — AP169

Paintings by Peter Paul Rubens: 5g, The Massacre of the Innocents. 10g, The Nativity, vert. 25g, The Madonna Adored by Four Penitents and Saints. 30g, The Flight to Egypt.

1982, Oct. 23

C514 AP169 5g multicolored
C515 AP169 10g multicolored
C516 AP169 30g multicolored

Souvenir Sheet

Perf. 14½

C517 AP169 25g multicolored

No. C517 contains one 50x70mm stamp.

The Sampling Officials of the Draper's Guild by Rembrandt — AP170

Details from Rembrandt Paintings: 10g, Self portrait, vert. 25g, Night Watch, vert. 30g, Self portrait, diff., vert.

1983, Jan. 21 *Perf. 14, 13 (10g)*

C518 AP170 5g multicolored
C519 AP170 10g multicolored
C520 AP170 30g multicolored

Souvenir Sheet

Perf. 13½

C521 AP170 25g multicolored

No. C521 contains one 50x60mm stamp.

Souvenir Sheet

1982 World Cup Soccer Championships, Spain — AP171

1983, Jan. 21 *Perf. 13½*

C522 AP171 25g Fuji blimp

German Rocket Scientists — AP172

Designs: 5g, Dr. Walter R. Dornberger, V2 rocket ascending. 10g, Nebel, Ritter, Oberth, Riedel, and

Von Braun examining rocket mock-up. 30g, Dr. A. F. Staats, Cyrus B research rocket.
No. C526, Dr. Eugen Sanger, rocket design. No. C527, Fritz Von Opel, Opel-Sander rocket plane. No. C528, Friedrich Schmiedl, first rocket used for mail delivery.

1983 *Perf. 14*
C523 AP172 5g multicolored
C524 AP172 10g multicolored
C525 AP172 30g multicolored

Souvenir Sheets
Perf. 14½
C526 AP172 25g multicolored
C527 AP172 25g multicolored
C528 AP172 25g multicolored

Issue dates: No. C528, Apr. 13; others, Jan. 24.

First Manned Flight, 200th Anniv. AP173

Balloons: 5g, Montgolfier brothers, 1783. 10g, Baron von Lutgendorf's, 1786. 30g, Adorne's, 1784.
No. C532, Montgolfier brothers, diff. No. C533, Profiles of Montgolfier Brothers. No. C534, Bicentennial emblem, nova.

1983 *Perf. 14, 13 (10g)*
C529 AP173 5g multicolored
C530 AP173 10g multicolored
C531 AP173 30g multicolored

Souvenir Sheets
Perf. 13½
C532 AP173 25g multicolored
C533 AP173 25g multicolored
C534 AP173 25g multicolored

Nos. C532-C533 each contain one 50x60mm stamp, No. C534 one 30x40mm stamp.
Issued: #C529-C533, 2/25; #C534, 10/19.

1984 Summer Olympics, Los Angeles AP174

1932 Gold medalists: 5g, Wilson Charles, US, 100-meter dash. 10g, Ellen Preis, Austria, fencing. 25g, Rudolf Ismayr, Germany, weight lifting. 30g, John Anderson, US, discus.

1983, June 13 *Perf. 14*
C535 AP174 5g multicolored
C536 AP174 10g multicolored
C537 AP174 30g multicolored

Souvenir Sheet
Perf. 14½
C538 AP174 25g Sheet of 1 + label

No. C535 incorrectly credits Charles with gold medal.

Flowers AP175

1983, Aug. 31 *Perf. 14*
C539 AP175 5g Episcia reptans
C540 AP175 10g Lilium
C541 AP175 30g Heliconia

Intl. Maritime Organization, 25th Anniv. AP176

5g, Brigantine Undine. 10g, Training ship Sofia, 1881, horiz. 30g, Training ship Stein, 1879.
No. C545, Santa Maria. No. C546, Santa Maria and Telstar communications satellite.

Perf. 14, 13½x13 (10g)
1983, Oct. 24 **Litho.**
C542 AP176 5g multicolored
C543 AP176 10g multicolored
C544 AP176 30g multicolored

Souvenir Sheets
Perf. 14½
C545 AP176 25g multicolored
Perf. 13½
C546 AP176 25g multicolored

No. C546 contains one 90x57mm stamp. Discovery of America, 490th Anniv. (in 1982) (#C545-C546). For overprint see No. 2198.

Space Achievements — AP177

Designs: 5g, Space shuttle Challenger. 10g, Pioneer 10, vert. 30g, Herschel's telescope, Cerro Tololo Obervatory, Chile, vert.

1984, Jan. 9 *Perf. 14*
C547 AP177 5g multicolored
C548 AP177 10g multicolored
C549 AP177 30g multicolored

Summer Olympics, Los Angeles AP178

5g, 400-meter hurdles. 10g, Small bore rifle, horiz. 25g, Equestrian, Christine Stuckleberger. 30g, 100-meter dash.

1984, Jan. *Perf. 14*
C550 AP178 5g multicolored
C551 AP178 10g multicolored
C552 AP178 30g multicolored

Souvenir Sheet
Perf. 14½
C553 AP178 25g multicolored

For overprint see No. 2130.

1984 Winter Olympics, Sarajevo AP179

Perf. 14, 13x13½ (10g)
1984, Mar. 24
C554 AP179 5g Steve Podborski, downhill
C555 AP179 10g Olympic Flag
C556 AP179 30g Gaetan Boucher, speed skating

No. C555 printed se-tenant with label.

Souvenir Sheets

Cupid and Psyche by Peter Paul Rubens — AP180

Design: No. C558, Satyr and Maenad (copy of Rubens' Bacchanal) by Jean-Antoine Watteau (1684-1721).

1984, Mar. 26 *Perf. 13½*
C557 AP180 25g multicolored
C558 AP180 25g multicolored

No. C558 contains one 78x57mm stamp.

1982, 1986 World Cup Soccer Championships, Spain, Mexico City — AP181

Soccer players: 5g, Tardelli, Breitner. 10g, Zamora, Stielke. 30g, Walter Schachner, player on ground.
No. C562, Player from Paraguay. No. C563, World Cup Trophy, Spanish, Mexican characters, horiz.

1984, Mar. 29 *Perf. 14, 13 (10g)*
C559 AP181 5g multicolored
C560 AP181 10g multicolored
C561 AP181 30g multicolored

Souvenir Sheets
Perf. 14½
C562 AP181 25g multicolored
C563 AP181 25g multicolored

Souvenir Sheet

ESPANA '84 — AP182

1984, Mar. 31
C564 AP182 25g multicolored

No. C564 has one stamp and a label.

Souvenir Sheets

ESPANA '84 — AP183

No. C565, Holy Family of the Lamb by Raphael. No. C566, Adoration of the Magi by Rubens.

1984, Apr. 16 *Perf. 13½*
C565 AP183 25g multicolored
C566 AP183 25g multicolored

Souvenir Sheet

19th UPU Congress — AP184

1984, June 9
C567 AP184 25g multicolored

Intl. Chess Federation, 60th Anniv. AP185

Perf. 14, 13x13½ (10g)

1984, June 18

C568 AP185 5g shown
C569 AP185 10g Woman holding chess piece
C570 AP185 30g Bishop, knight

First Europe to South America Airmail Flight by Lufthansa, 50th Anniv. — AP186

Designs: 5g, Lockheed Superconstellation. 10g, Dornier Wal. 30g, Boeing 707.

Perf. 14, 13½x13 (10g)

1984, June 22

C571 AP186 5g multicolored
C572 AP186 10g multicolored
C573 AP186 30g multicolored

For overprint see No. C592.

Souvenir Sheets

First Moon Landing, 15th Anniv. — AP187

1984, June 23 *Perf. 14½*

C574 AP187 25g Apollo 11 lunar module
C575 AP187 25g Prof. Hermann Oberth

Hermann Oberth, 90th Birthday (#C575).

Souvenir Sheet

The Holy Family with John the Baptist — AP188

1984, Aug. 3 Photo. & Engr. *Perf. 14*

C576 AP188 20g multicolored

Raphael, 500th birth anniv. (in 1983).

No. 2099 Overprinted in Red: ANIVERSARIO GOBIERNO CONSTRUCTIVO Y DE LA PAZ DEL PRESIDENTE CONSTITUCIONAL GRAL. DE EJERCITO ALFREDO STROESSNER 15 / 8 / 1964

1984, Aug. 15 *Perf. 13*

C577 A374 100g on No. 2099

1984 Winter Olympics, Sarajevo — AP189

Gold medalists: 5g, Max Julen, giant slalom, Switzerland. 10g, Hans Stanggassinger, Franz Wembacher, luge, West Germany. 30g, Peter Angerer, biathlon, Germany.

Perf. 14, 13½x13 (10g)

1984, Sept. 12

C578 AP189 5g multicolored
C579 AP189 10g multicolored
C580 AP189 30g multicolored

For overprint see No. C596.

Motorcycles, Cent. — AP190

1984, Nov. 9 *Perf. 14, 13½x13 (10g)*

C581 AP190 5g Reitwagen, Daimler-Maybach, 1885
C582 AP190 10g BMW, 1980
C583 AP190 30g Opel, 1930

Christmas AP191

1985, Jan. 18 *Perf. 13*

C584 AP191 5g shown
C585 AP191 10g Girl playing guitar
C586 AP191 30g Girl, candle, basket

1986 World Cup Soccer Championships, Mexico — AP192

Various soccer players.

Perf. 13x13½, 13½x13

1985, Jan. 21

Color of Shirt

C587 AP192 5g red & white
C588 AP192 10g white & black, horiz.
C589 AP192 30g blue

No. C484 Ovptd. in Silver

1985, Feb. 6 *Perf. 14*

C590 AP161 10g INTERPEX / 1985
C591 AP161 10g STAMPEX / 1985

No. C572 Ovptd. in Vermilion

STUTTGART 85

1985, Feb. 16 *Perf. 13½x13*

C592 AP186 10g on No. C572

No. 2053A Ovptd. "FINAL / ALEMANIA 1 : 3 ITALIA"

1985, Mar. 7 *Perf. 14½*

C593 A362 25g multicolored

Souvenir Sheets

Rotary Intl., 80th Anniv. — AP193

Designs: No. C594, Paul Harris, founder of Rotary Intl. No. C595, Rotary Intl. Headquarters, Evanston, IL, horiz.

1985, Mar. 11

C594 AP193 25g multicolored
C595 AP193 25g multicolored

No. C579 Ovptd. "OLYMPHILEX 85" in Black and Olympic Rings in Silver

1985, Mar. 18 *Perf. 13½x13*

C596 AP189 10g on No. C579

Music Year AP194

Designs: 5g, Agustin Barrios (1885-1944), musician, vert. 10g, Johann Sebastian Bach, composer, score. 30g, Folk musicians.

Perf. 14, 13½x13 (10g)

1985, Apr. 16

C597 AP194 5g multicolored
C598 AP194 10g multicolored
C599 AP194 30g multicolored

1st Paraguayan Locomotive, 1861 — AP195

1985, Apr. 20 *Perf. 14*

C600 AP195 5g shown
C601 AP195 10g Transrapid 06, Germany
C602 AP195 30g TGV, France

Souvenir Sheet

Visit of Pope John Paul II to South America — AP196

1985, Apr. 22 Litho. *Perf. 13½*

C603 AP196 25g silver & multi

No. C603 also exists with gold inscriptions.

Inter-American Development Bank, 25th Anniv. — AP197

1985, Apr. 25 Litho. Wmk. 347

C604	AP197	3g	dl red brn, org & yel	.15	.15
C605	AP197	5g	vio, org & yel	.15	.15
C606	AP197	10g	rose vio, org & yel	.15	.15
C607	AP197	50g	sep, org & yel	.15	.15
C608	AP197	65g	bl, org & yel	.15	.15
C609	AP197	95g	pale bl grn, org & yel	.15	.15
			Set value	.42	.35

No. 1875 Ovptd. in Black in Margin "V EXPOSICION MUNDIAL / ARGENTINA 85" and

1985, May 24 Unwmk. *Perf. 13½*

C610 A326 25g on No. 1875

No. C485 Ovptd. in Dark Blue with Emblem and: "Expo '85/TSUKUBA"

1985, July 5 *Perf. 14*

C611 AP161 30g on No. C485

No. 2149 Ovptd. in Dark Blue in Margin with UN emblem and "26.6.1985 - 40-ANIVERSARIO DE LA / FUNDACION DE LAS NACIONES UNIDAS"

1985, Aug. 5 *Perf. 14½*

C612 A388 25g on No. 2149

Jean-Henri Dunant, Founder of Red Cross, 75th Death Anniv. — AP198

Dunant and: 5g, Enclosed ambulance. 10g, Nobel Peace Prize, Red Cross emblem. 30g, Open ambulance with passengers.

1985, Aug. 6 *Perf. 13*
C614 AP198 5g multicolored
C615 AP198 10g multicolored
C616 AP198 30g multicolored

World Chess Congress, Austria — AP199

5g, The Turk, copper engraving, Book of Chess by Racknitz, 1789. 10g, King seated, playing chess, Book of Chess, 14th cent. 25g, Margrave Otto von Brandenburg playing chess with his wife, Great Manuscript of Heidelberg Songs, 13th cent. 30g, Three men playing chess, Book of Chess, 14th cent.

1985, Aug. 9 **Litho.** *Perf. 13*
C617 AP199 5g multicolored
C618 AP199 10g multicolored
C619 AP199 30g multicolored

Souvenir Sheet
Perf. 13½
C620 AP199 25g multicolored

No. C620 contains one 60x50mm stamp.

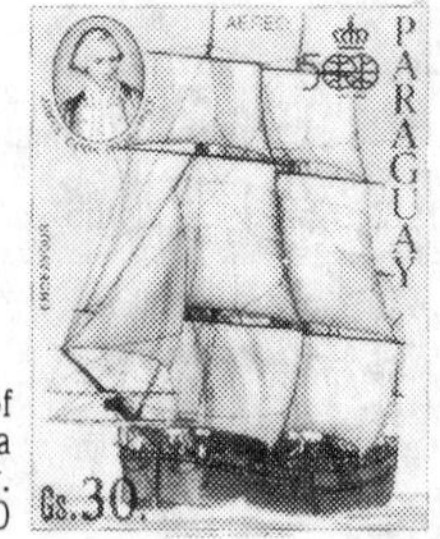

Discovery of America 500th Anniv. AP200

Explorers, ships: 5g, Marco Polo and ship. 10g, Vicente Yanez Pinzon, Nina, horiz. 25g, Christopher Columbus, Santa Maria. 30g, James Cook, Endeavor.

Perf. 14, 13½x13 (10g)
1985, Oct. 19 **Litho.**
C621 AP200 5g multicolored
C622 AP200 10g multicolored
C623 AP200 30g multicolored

Souvenir Sheet
Perf. 14½
C624 AP200 25g multicolored

Year of Cook's death is incorrect on No. C623. For overprint see No. C756.

ITALIA '85 — AP201

Nudes (details): 5g, La Fortuna, by Guido Reni, vert. 10g, The Triumph of Galatea, by Raphael. 25g, The Birth of Venus, by Botticelli, vert. 30g, Sleeping Venus, by Il Giorgione.

1985, Dec. 3 *Perf. 14*
C625 AP201 5g multicolored
C626 AP201 10g multicolored
C627 AP201 30g multicolored

Souvenir Sheet
Perf. 13½
C628 AP201 25g multicolored

No. C628 contains one 49x60mm stamp.

Souvenir Sheet

Maimonides, Philosopher, 850th Birth Anniv. — AP202

1985, Dec. 31 *Perf. 13½*
C629 AP202 25g multicolored

UN, 40th Anniv. — AP203

1986, Feb. 27 **Wmk. 392**

C630 AP203	5g bl & sepia	.15	.15
C631 AP203	10g bl & gray	.15	.15
C632 AP203	50g bl & grysh brn	.15	.15
	Set value	.24	.22

For overprint see No. C726.

AMERIPEX '86 — AP204

Discovery of America 500th anniv. emblem and: 5g, Spain #424. 10g, US #233. 25g, Spain #426, horiz. 30g, Spain #421.

Perf. 14, 13½x13 (10g)
1986, Mar. 19 **Unwmk.**
C633 AP204 5g multicolored
C634 AP204 10g multicolored
C635 AP204 30g multicolored

Souvenir Sheet
Perf. 13½
C636 AP204 25g multicolored

No. C636 contains one 60x40mm stamp. For overprint see No. C755.

Souvenir Sheet

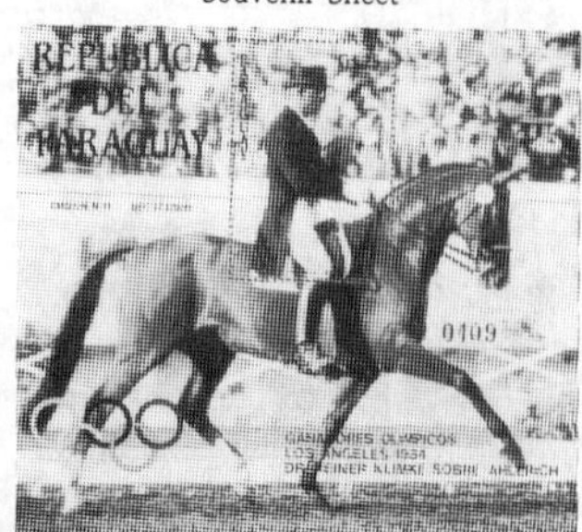

1984 Olympic Gold Medalist, Dr. Reiner Klimke on Ahlerich — AP205

1986, Mar. 20 *Perf. 14½*
C637 AP205 25g multicolored

Tennis Players AP206

Designs: 5g, Martina Navratilova, US. 10g, Boris Becker, W. Germany. 30g, Victor Pecci, Paraguay.

1986, Mar. 26 *Perf. 14, 13 (10g)*
C638 AP206 5g multicolored
C639 AP206 10g multicolored
C640 AP206 30g multicolored

Nos. C638-C640 exist with red inscriptions, perf. 13. For overprints see Nos. C672-C673.

Halley's Comet — AP207

5g, Bayeux Tapestry, c. 1066, showing comet. 10g, Edmond Halley, comet. 25g, Comet, Giotto probe. 30g, Rocket lifting off, Giotto probe, vert.

Perf. 14, 13½x13 (10g)
1986, Apr. 30
C641 AP207 5g multicolored
C642 AP207 10g multicolored
C643 AP207 30g multicolored

Souvenir Sheet
Perf. 14½
C644 AP207 25g multicolored

Souvenir Sheet

Madonna by Albrecht Durer — AP208

1986, June 4 **Typo.** *Rough Perf. 11*
Self-Adhesive
C645 AP208 25g black & red

No. C645 was printed on cedar.

Locomotives — AP209

1986, June 23 **Litho.** *Perf. 13*
C646 AP209 5g #3038
C647 AP209 10g Canadian Pacific A1E, 1887
C648 AP209 30g 1D1 #483, 1925

1986 World Cup Soccer Championships — AP210

Paraguay vs.: 5g, Colombia. 10g, Chile. 30g, Chile, diff.
25g, Paraguay Natl. team.

Perf. 13, 13½x13 (10g)
1986, June 24
C649 AP210 5g multicolored
C650 AP210 10g multicolored
C651 AP210 30g multicolored

Souvenir Sheet
Perf. 14½
C652 AP210 25g multicolored

No. C652 contains one 81x75mm stamp. For overprints see Nos. C693-C695.

No. 1289 Ovptd. in Silver on Dark Blue with Mercury Capsule and "MERCURY / 5-V-1961 / 25 Anos Primer / Astronauta / Americano / Alan B. Shepard / 1986"

1986, July 11 *Perf. 13½*
C653 A226 23.40g on No. 1289

Souvenir Sheet

Trajectory Diagram of Halley's Comet, Giotto Probe — AP211

1986, July 28
C654 AP211 25g multicolored

German Railroads, 150th Anniv. — AP212

Design: 25g, Christening of the First German Train, 1835, by E. Shilling and B. Goldschmidt.

1986, Sept. 1 *Perf. 13½x13*
C655 AP212 5g VT 10 501DB, 1954
C656 AP212 10g 1st Electric, 1879
C657 AP212 30g Hydraulic diesel, class 218

Souvenir Sheet
Perf. 13½
C658 AP212 25g multicolored

No. C658 contains one 54x75mm stamp.

Intl. Peace Year AP213

Details from The Consequences of War by Rubens: 5g, Two women. 10g, Woman nursing child. 30g, Two men.

1986, Oct. 27 *Perf. 13*
C659 AP213 5g multicolored
C660 AP213 10g multicolored
C661 AP213 30g multicolored

Japanese Emigrants in Paraguay, 50th Anniv. AP214

1986, Nov. 6 *Perf. 13½x13, 13x13½*
C662 AP214 5g La Colemna Vineyard .15 .15
C663 AP214 10g Cherry, lapacho flowers .15 .15
C664 AP214 20g Integration monument, vert. .15 .15
Set value .15 .15

No. C507 Ovptd. in Silver "XXVII-DUBAI / Olimpiada de / Ajedrez - 1986"

1986, Dec. 30 **Unwmk.** *Perf. 14*
C665 A347 10g on No. C507

1986 World Cup Soccer Championships, Mexico — AP214a

Match scenes.

1987, Feb. 19 *Perf. 14*
C666 AP214a 5g England vs. Paraguay
C667 AP214a 10g Larios catching ball
C668 AP214a 20g Trejo, Ferreira

Perf. 13½x13
C669 AP214a 25g Torales, Flores, Romero
C670 AP214a 30g Mendonza

Souvenir Sheet
Perf. 14½
C671 AP214a 100g Romero

Nos. C669-C670 are horiz. No. C671 contains one 40x50mm stamp.

Nos. C639-C640 Ovptd. in Silver including Olympic Rings and "NUEVAMENTE EL / TENIS EN LAS / OLYMPIADAS 1988 / SEOUL COREA"

1987, Apr. 15 *Perf. 13*
C672 AP206 10g on No. C639
C673 AP206 30g on No. C640

Automobiles — AP215

1987, May 29 **Litho.** *Perf. 13½*
C674 AP215 5g Mercedes 300 SEL 6.3
C675 AP215 10g Jaguar Mk II 3.8
C676 AP215 20g BMW 635 CSI
C677 AP215 25g Alfa Romeo GTA
C678 AP215 30g BMW 1800 Tisa

1988 Winter Olympics, Calgary — AP216

Gold medalists or Olympic competitors: 5g, Michela Figini, Switzerland, downhill, 1984, vert. 10g, Hanni Wenzel, Liechtenstein, slalom and giant slalom, 1980. 20g, 4-Man bobsled, Switzerland, 1956, 1972. 25g, Markus Wasmeier, downhill. 30g, Ingemar Stenmark, Sweden, slalom and giant slalom, 1980. 100g, Pirmin Zurbriggen, Switzerland, vert. (downhill, 1988).

1987, Sept. 10 *Perf. 14*
C679 AP216 5g multicolored
C680 AP216 10g multicolored
C681 AP216 20g multicolored

Perf. 13½x13
C682 AP216 25g multicolored
C683 AP216 30g multicolored

Souvenir Sheet
Perf. 13½
C684 AP216 100g multicolored

No. C684 contains one 45x57mm stamp.

Nos. 2211 and C467 Ovptd. in Red on Silver "11.IX.1887 - 1987 / Centenario de la fundacion de / la A.N.R. (Partido Colarado) / Bernardino Caballero Fundador / General de Ejercito / D. Alfredo Stroessner Continuador"

1987, Sept. 11 *Perf. 13, 14*
C685 A401 200g on No. 2211
C686 AP148 1000g on No. C467

1988 Summer Olympics, Seoul — AP217

Medalists and competitors: 5g, Sabine Everts, West Germany, javelin. 10g, Carl Lewis, US, 100 and 200-meter run, 1984. 20g, Darrell Pace, US, archery, 1976, 1984. 25g, Juergen Hingsen, West Germany, decathalon, 1984. 30g, Claudia Losch, West Germany, shot put, 1984. 100g, Fredy Schmidtke, West Germany, cycling, 1984.

1987, Sept. 22 *Perf. 14*
C687 AP217 5g multi
C688 AP217 10g multi, vert.
C689 AP217 20g multi

Perf. 13½x13
C690 AP217 25g multi, vert.
C691 AP217 30g multi, vert.

Souvenir Sheet
Perf. 14½
C692 AP217 100g multi, vert.

Nos. C650-C652 Ovptd. in Violet or Blue (#C694) with Soccer Ball and "ZURICH 10.VI.87 / Lanzamiento ITALIA '90 / Italia 3 - Argentina 1"

Perf. 13½x13, 13

1987, Oct. 19 **Litho.**
C693 AP210 10g on No. C650
C694 AP210 30g on No. C651

Souvenir Sheet
Perf. 14½
C695 AP210 25g on No. C652

Paintings by Rubens AP218

Details from: 5g, The Virtuous Hero Crowned. 10g, The Brazen Serpent, 1635. 20g, Judith with the Head of Holofernes, 1617. 25g, Assembly of the Gods of Olympus. 30g, Venus, Cupid, Bacchus and Ceres.

1987, Dec. 14 *Perf. 13*
C696 AP218 5g multicolored
C697 AP218 10g multicolored
C698 AP218 20g multicolored

Perf. 13x13½
C699 AP218 25g multicolored
C700 AP218 30g multicolored

Christmas AP219

Details from paintings: 5g, Virgin and Child with St. Joseph and St. John the Baptist, anonymous. 10g, Madonna and Child under the Veil with St. Joseph and St. John, by Marco da Siena. 20g, Sacred Conversation with the Donors, by Titian. 25g, The Brotherhood of the Rosary, by Durer. 30g, Madonna with Standing Child, by Rubens. 100g, Madonna and Child, engraving by Albrecht Durer.

1987 **Litho.** *Perf. 14*
C701 AP219 5g multicolored
C702 AP219 10g multicolored
C703 AP219 20g multicolored
C704 AP219 25g multicolored

Perf. 13x13½
C705 AP219 30g multicolored

Souvenir Sheet
Perf. 14½
C706 AP219 100g multi

Issued: #C701-C705, 12/16; #C706, 12/17.

Austrian Railways, Sesquicentennial — AP220

Locomotives: 5g, Steam #3669, 1899. 10g, Steam #GZ 44074. 20g, Steam, diff. 25g, Diesel-electric. 30g, Austria No. 1067. 100g, Steam, vert.

1988, Jan. 2 *Perf. 14*
C707 AP220 5g multicolored
C708 AP220 10g multicolored
C709 AP220 20g multicolored
C710 AP220 25g multicolored

Perf. 13½x13
C711 AP220 30g multicolored

Souvenir Sheet
Perf. 13½
C712 AP220 100g multicolored

No. C712 contains one 50x60mm stamp.

Souvenir Sheet

Christmas — AP221

1988, Jan. 4 *Perf. 13½*
C713 AP221 100g Madonna, by Rubens

Souvenir Sheet

1988 Summer Olympics, Seoul — AP222

1988, Jan. 18 *Perf. 14½*
C714 AP222 100g gold & multi

Exists with silver lettering and frame.

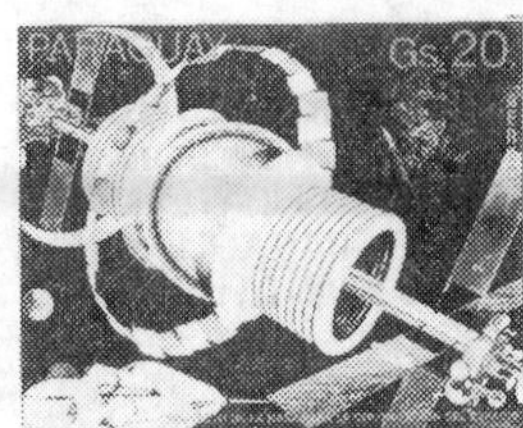

Colonization of Space — AP223

Designs: 5g, NASA-ESA space station. 10g, Eurospace module Columbus docked at space station. 20g, NASA space sation. 25g, Ring section of space station, vert. 30g, Space station living quarters in central core, vert.

1988, Mar. 9 **Litho.** *Perf. 13½x13*
C715 AP223 5g multicolored
C716 AP223 10g multicolored
C717 AP223 20g multicolored

Perf. 13x13½
C718 AP223 25g multicolored
C719 AP223 30g multicolored

Souvenir Sheet

Berlin, 750th Anniv. — AP224

1988, Mar. 10 Litho. *Perf. 14½*
C720 AP224 100g multicolored

LUPOSTA '87.

Souvenir Sheet

Apollo 15 Launch, 1971 — AP225

1988, Apr. 12
C721 AP225 100g multicolored

No. 2210 Ovptd. in Metallic Red with

1988, Apr. 28 *Perf. 13*
C722 A401 100g on No. 2210

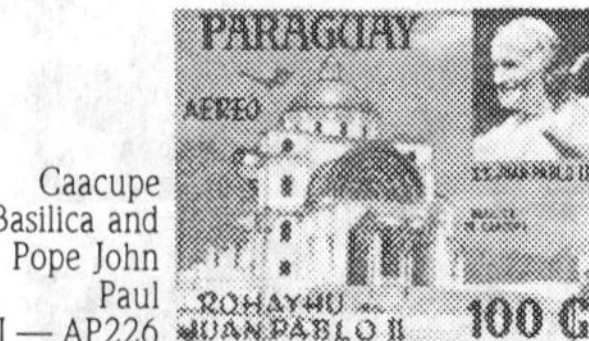

Caacupe Basilica and Pope John Paul II — AP226

Perf. 13½x13
1988, May 5 Litho. Wmk. 347
C723 AP226 100g multi .45 .35
C724 AP226 120g multi .55 .42
C725 AP226 150g multi .68 .52
Nos. C723-C725 (3) 1.68 1.29

Visit of Pope John Paul II.

No. C631 Overprinted

*** 75° ANIVERSARIO**
DE FUNDACION
CENTRO FILATELICO
DEL PARAGUAY
15 JUNIO-1913 - 1988

Perf. 13x13½
1988, June 15 Wmk. 392
C726 AP203 10g blue & gray .15 .15

Paraguay Philatelic Center, 75th Anniv.

Berlin, 750th Anniv. Paintings Type of 1988

Paintings: 5g, Venus and Cupid, 1742, by Francois Boucher. 10g, Perseus Liberates Andromeda, 1662, by Rubens. 20g, Venus and the Organist by Titian. 25g, Leda and the Swan by Correggio. 30g, St. Cecilia by Rubens.

1988, June 15 Unwmk. *Perf. 13*
C727 A409 5g multi, horiz.
C728 A409 10g multi, horiz.
C729 A409 20g multi, horiz.
C730 A409 25g multi, horiz.

Perf. 13x13½
C731 A409 30g multicolored

Founding of "New Germany" and 1st Cultivation of Herbal Tea, Cent. AP227

Perf. 13x13½, 13½x13
1988, June 18 Litho. Wmk. 347
C732 AP227 90g Cauldron, vert. .42 .32
C733 AP227 105g Farm workers carrying crop .48 .35
C734 AP227 120g like 105g .55 .42
Nos. C732-C734 (3) 1.45 1.09

1990 World Cup Soccer Championships, Italy — AP228

5g, Machine slogan cancel from Montevideo, May 21, 1930. 10g, Italy #324, vert. 20g, France #349. 25g, Brazil #696, vert. 30g, Paraguayan commemorative cancel for ITALIA 1990.

1988, Aug. 1 Unwmk. *Perf. 13*
C735 AP228 5g multicolored
C736 AP228 10g multicolored
C737 AP228 20g multicolored
C738 AP228 25g multicolored

Perf. 13½x13
C739 AP228 30g multicolored

For overprint see No. 2284.

Souvenir Sheet

Count Ferdinand von Zeppelin, Airship Designer, Birth Sesquicentennial — AP229

1988, Aug. 3 *Perf. 14½*
C740 AP229 100g multicolored

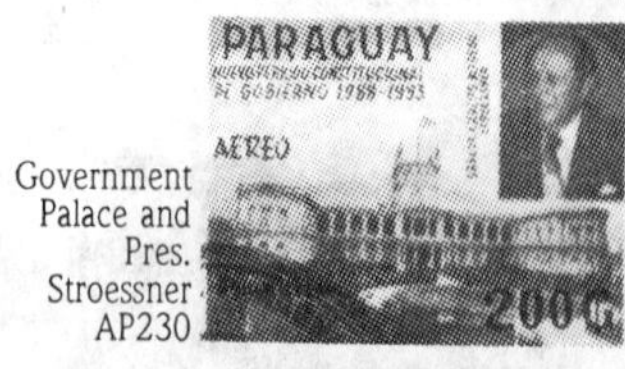

Government Palace and Pres. Stroessner AP230

Perf. 13½
1988, Aug. 5 Litho. Wmk. 347
C741 AP230 200g multi .40 .30
C742 AP230 500g multi 1.00 1.00
C743 AP230 1000g multi 2.00 2.00
Nos. C741-C743 (3) 3.40 3.30

Pres. Stroessner's new term in office, 1988-1993. Size of letters in watermark on 200g, 1000g: 5mm. On 500g, 10mm.

1988 Winter Olympics, Calgary — AP231

Gold medalists: 5g, Hubert Strolz, Austria, Alpine combined. 10g, Alberto Tomba, Italy, giant slalom and slalom. 20g, Franck Piccard, France, super giant slalom. 25g, Thomas Muller, Hans-Peter Pohl and Hubert Schwarz, Federal Republic of Germany, Nordic combined team, vert. 30g, Vreni Schneider, Switzerland, giant slalom and slalom, vert. 100g, Marina Kiehl, Federal Republic of Germany, downhill, vert.

Perf. 13½x13
1988, Sept. 2 Unwmk.
C744 AP231 5g multicolored
C745 AP231 10g multicolored
C746 AP231 20g multicolored

Perf. 13x13½
C747 AP231 25g multicolored
C748 AP231 30g multicolored

Souvenir Sheet
Perf. 14½
C749 AP231 100g multicolored

1990 World Cup Soccer Championships, Italy — AP232

Designs: 5g, Mexico #C350. 10g, Germany #1146. 20g, Argentina #1147, vert. 25g, Spain #2211. 30g, Italy #1742.

1988, Oct. 4 *Perf. 13*
C750 AP232 5g multicolored
C751 AP232 10g multicolored
C752 AP232 20g multicolored
C753 AP232 25g multicolored

Perf. 14
C754 AP232 30g multicolored

For overprint see No. 2285.

No. C635 Ovptd. in Metallic Red:

1988, Nov. 25 *Perf. 14*
C755 AP204 30g on No. C635

No. C623 Ovptd. in Gold

1988, Nov. 25 *Perf. 14*
C756 AP200 30g on No. C623

1988 Summer Olympics, Seoul — AP233

Gold medalists: No. C757, Nicole Uphoff, individual dressage. No. C758, Anja Fichtel, Sabine Bau, Zita Funkenhauser, Anette Kluge and Christine Weber, team foil. No. C759, Silvia Sperber, smallbore standard rifle. No. C760, Mathias Baumann, Claus Erhorn, Thies Kaspareit and Ralph Ehrenbrink, equestrian team 3-day event. No. C761, Anja Fichtel, individual foil, vert. No. C762, Franke Sloothaak, Ludger Beerbaum, Wolfgang Brinkmann and Dirk Hafemeister, equestrian team jumping. No. C763, Arnd Schmitt, individual epee, vert. No. C764, Jose Luis Doreste, Finn class yachting. No. C765, Steffi Graf, tennis. No. C766, Michael Gross, 200-meter butterfly, vert. No. C767, West Germany, coxed eights. No. C768, Nicole Uphoff, Monica Theodorescu, Ann Kathrin Linsenhoff and Reiner Klimke, team dressage.

1989 *Perf. 13*
C757 AP233 5g multicolored
C758 AP233 5g multicolored
C759 AP233 10g multicolored
C760 AP233 10g multicolored
C761 AP233 20g multicolored
C762 AP233 20g multicolored
C763 AP233 25g multicolored
C764 AP233 25g multicolored

Perf. 13½x13
C765 AP233 30g multicolored
C766 AP233 30g multicolored

Souvenir Sheets
Perf. 14½
C767 AP233 100g multicolored
C768 AP233 100g multicolored

Nos. C767-C768 each contain one 80x50mm stamp.

Issue dates: Nos. C757, C759, C761, C763, C765, and C767, Mar. 3. Others, Mar. 20.

For overprints see Nos. 2292, 2359.

Souvenir Sheet

Intl. Red Cross, 125th Anniv. (in 1988) — AP234

1989, Apr. 17 Litho. *Perf. 13½*
C769 AP234 100g #803 in changed colors

No. C769 has perforated label picturing Nobel medal.

Olympics Type of 1989

1988 Winter Olympic medalists or competitors: 5g, Pirmin Zurbriggen, Peter Mueller, Switzerland, and Franck Piccard, France, Alpine skiing. 10g, Sigrid Wolf, Austria, super giant slalom, vert. 20g, Czechoslovakia vs. West Germany, hockey, vert. 25g, Piccard, skiing, vert. 30g, Piccard, wearing medal, vert.

1989, Apr. 17 *Perf. 13½x13*
C770 AP233 5g multicolored

Perf. 13x13½
C771 AP233 10g multicolored
C772 AP233 20g multicolored
C773 AP233 25g multicolored
C774 AP233 30g multicolored

Souvenir Sheet

1990 World Cup Soccer Championships, Italy — AP235

1989, Apr. 21 *Perf. 14½*
C775 AP235 100g Sheet of 1 + label

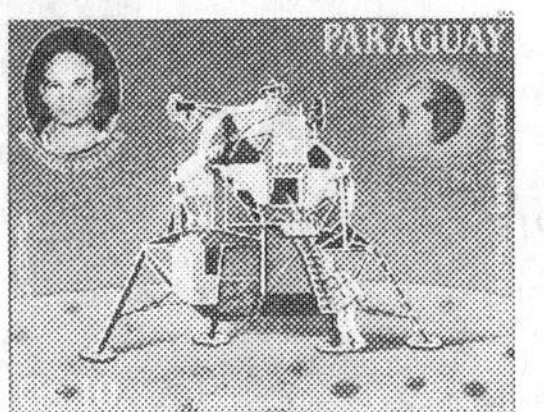

1st Moon Landing, 20th Anniv. — AP236

Designs: 5g, Wernher von Braun, Apollo 11 launch, vert. 10g, Michael Collins, lunar module on moon. 20g, Neil Armstrong, astronaut on lunar module ladder, vert. 25g, Buzz Aldrin, solar wind experiment, vert. 30g, Kurt Debus, splashdown of Columbia command module, vert.

1989, May 24 *Perf. 13*
C776 AP236 5g multicolored
C777 AP236 10g multicolored
C778 AP236 20g multicolored
C779 AP236 25g multicolored
C780 AP236 30g multicolored

Luis Alberto del Parana and the Paraguayans — AP237

1989, May 25 *Perf. 14½*
C780A AP237 100g multicolored

A clear plastic phonograph record is affixed to the souvenir sheet.

Hamburg, 800th Anniv. — AP238

Hamburg anniv. emblem, SAIL '89 emblem, and: 5g, Galleon and Icarus, woodcut by Pieter Brueghel. 10g, Windjammer, vert. 20g, Bark in full sail. 25g, Old Hamburg by A.E. Schliecker, vert. 30g, Commemorative coin issued by Federal Republic of Germany. 100g, Hamburg, 13th cent. illuminated manuscript, vert.

Perf. 13½x13, 13x13½

1989, May 26
C781 AP238 5g multicolored
C782 AP238 10g multicolored
C783 AP238 20g multicolored
C784 AP238 25g multicolored
C785 AP238 30g multicolored

Souvenir Sheet

Perf. 14½
C786 AP238 100g multicolored

No. C786 contains one 40x50mm stamp.

French Revolution, Bicent. — AP239

Details from paintings: 5g, Esther Adorns Herself for her Presentation to King Ahasuerus, by Theodore Chasseriau, vert. 10g, Olympia, by Manet, vert. 20g, The Drunker Erigone with a Panther, by Louis A. Reisener. 25g, Anniv. emblem and natl. coats of arms. 30g, Liberty Leading the People, by Delacroix, vert. 100g, The Education of Maria de Medici, by Rubens, vert.

Perf. 13x13½, 13½x13

1989, May 27
C787 AP239 5g multicolored
C788 AP239 10g multicolored
C789 AP239 20g multicolored
C790 AP239 25g multicolored
C791 AP239 30g multicolored

Souvenir Sheet

Perf. 14½
C792 AP239 100g multicolored

Souvenir Sheet

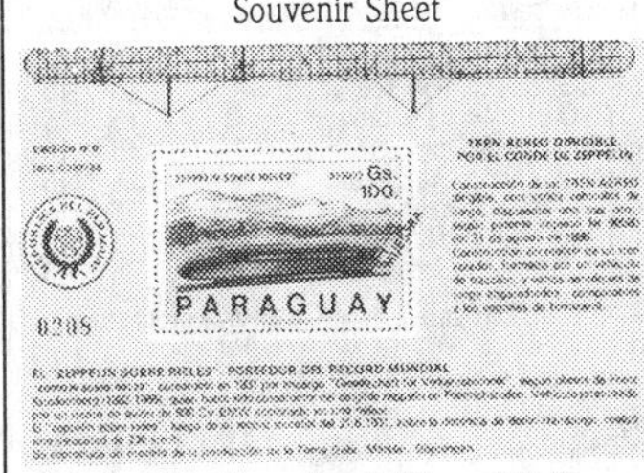

Railway Zeppelin, 1931 — AP240

1989, May 27 **Litho.** *Perf. 13½*
C793 AP240 100g multicolored

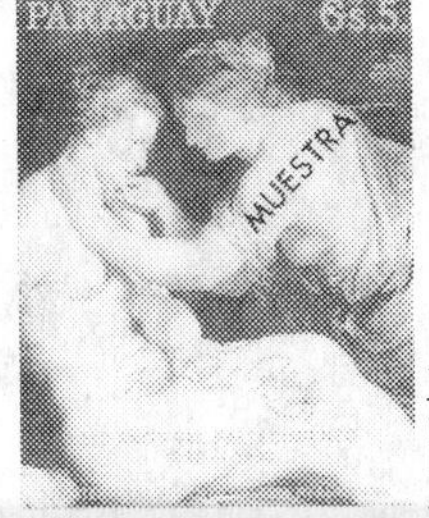

Jupiter and Calisto by Rubens AP241

Details from paintings by Rubens: 10g, Boreas Abducting Oreithyia (1619-20). 20g, Fortuna (1625). 25g, Mars with Venus and Cupid (1625). 30g, Virgin with Child (1620).

1989, Dec. 27 **Litho.** *Perf. 14*
C794 AP241 5g multicolored
C795 AP241 10g multicolored
C796 AP241 20g multicolored
C797 AP241 25g multicolored

Perf. 13
C798 AP241 30g multicolored

Death of Rubens, 350th anniversary.

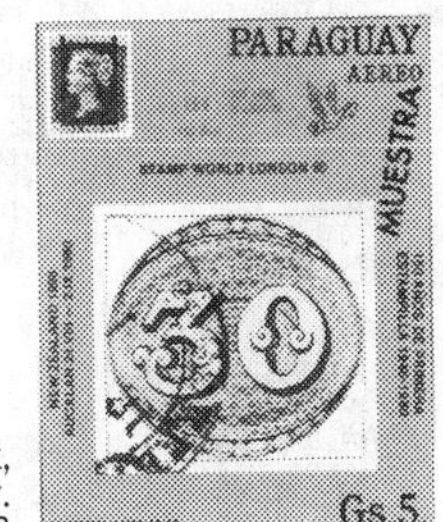

Penny Black, 150th Anniv. AP242

Penny Black, 500 years of postal services emblem, Stamp World '90 emblem and: 5g, Brazil #1. 10g, British Guiana #2. 20g, Chile #1. 25g, Uruguay #1. 30g, Paraguay #1.

1989, Dec. 30 *Perf. 14*
C799 AP242 5g multicolored
C800 AP242 10g multicolored
C801 AP242 20g multicolored
C802 AP242 25g multicolored

Perf. 13
C803 AP242 30g multicolored

Animals AP243

Designs: 5g, Martucha. 10g, Mara. 20g, Lobo de crin. 25g, Rana cornuda tintorera, horiz. 30g, Jaguar, horiz. Inscribed 1989.

1990, Jan. 8 *Perf. 13x13½, 13½x13*
C804 AP243 5g multicolored
C805 AP243 10g multicolored
C806 AP243 20g multicolored
C807 AP243 25g multicolored
C808 AP243 30g multicolored

Columbus' Fleet AP244

Discovery of America 500th anniversary emblem and: 10g, Olympic rings, stylized basketball player, horiz. 20g, Medieval nave, Expo '92 emblem. 25g, Four-masted barkentine, Expo '92 emblem, horiz. 30g, Similar to Spain Scott 2571, Expo '92 emblem.

1990, Jan. 27 *Perf. 14*
C809 AP244 5g multicolored
C810 AP244 10g multicolored
C811 AP244 20g multicolored
C812 AP244 25g multicolored

Perf. 13½x13
C813 AP244 30g multicolored

Postal Transportation, 500th Anniv. — AP245

500th Anniv. Emblem and: 5g, 10g, 20g, 25g, Penny Black and various post coaches, 10g, vert. 30g, Post coach.

1990, Mar. 9 *Perf. 13½x13, 13x13½*
C814 AP245 5g multicolored
C815 AP245 10g multicolored
C816 AP245 20g multicolored
C817 AP245 25g multicolored
C818 AP245 30g multicolored

Fort and City of Arco by Durer — AP246

Paintings by Albrecht Durer, postal transportation 500th anniversary emblem and: 10g, Trent Castle. 20g, North Innsbruck. 25g, Fort yard of Innsbruck, vert. 30g, Virgin of the Animals. No. C824, Madonna and Child, vert. No. C825, Postrider, vert.

1990, Mar. 14 *Perf. 14*
C819 AP246 5g multicolored
C820 AP246 10g multicolored
C821 AP246 20g multicolored
C822 AP246 25g multicolored

Perf. 13
C823 AP246 30g multicolored

Souvenir Sheets

Perf. 14½
C824 AP246 100g multicolored
C825 AP246 100g multicolored

Nos. C824-C825 each contain one 40x50mm stamp.

For overprint see No. 2358.

AP247

1988? **Photo.** **Wmk. 347** *Perf. 11*

C826 AP247 40g red lilac	1.00	.85
C827 AP247 60g bright green	1.50	1.25

POSTAGE DUE STAMPS

D1

D2

1904 **Unwmk.** **Litho.** *Perf. 11½*

J1 D1 2c green	.20	.18
J2 D1 4c green	.20	.18
J3 D1 10c green	.20	.18
J4 D1 20c green	.20	.18
Nos. J1-J4 (4)	.80	.72

1913 **Engr.**

J5 D2 1c yellow brown	.15	.15
J6 D2 2c yellow brown	.15	.15
J7 D2 5c yellow brown	.15	.15
J8 D2 10c yellow brown	.15	.15
J9 D2 20c yellow brown	.15	.15
J10 D2 40c yellow brown	.15	.15
J11 D2 1p yellow brown	.15	.15
J12 D2 1.50p yellow brown	.15	.15
Set value	.55	.40

For overprints and surcharges see Nos. 220-224, 229, 232, 264, L5.

INTERIOR OFFICE ISSUES

The "C" signifies "Campana" (rural). These stamps were sold by Postal Agents in country districts, who received a commission on their sales. These stamps were available for postage in the interior but not in Asunción or abroad.

Nos. 243-244 Overprinted in Red

1922

L1	A42	50c car & dk bl	.15	.15
L2	A42	1p dk bl & brn	.15	.15
		Set value	.22	.15

The overprint on Nos. L1-L2 exists double or inverted. Counterfeits exist.

Nos. 215, 218, J12 Surcharged

C
Habilitado
en
$ 1:—
1924

1924

L3	A40	50c on 75c deep bl	.15	.15
L4	A40	1p on 1.25p pale bl	.15	.15
L5	D2	1p on 1.50p yel brn	.15	.15
		Set value	.24	.15

Nos. L3-L4 exist imperf.

Nos. 254, 257-260 Overprinted in Black or Red **C**

1924-26

L6	A45	50c red ('25)	.15	.15
L7	A44	1p dk blue (R)	.15	.15
L8	A45	1p dk bl (R) ('25)	.15	.15
L9	A46	1p blue (R) ('25)	.15	.15
L10	A45	1p emerald ('26)	.15	.15
		Set value	.26	.25

Nos. L6, L8-L9 exist imperf. Value $2.50 each pair.

Same Overprint on Stamps and Type of 1927-36 in Red or Black

1927-39

L11	A47	50c ultra (R)	.15	.15
L12	A47	50c dl red ('28)	.15	.15
L13	A47	50c orange ('29)	.15	.15
L14	A47	50c lt bl ('30)	.15	.15
L15	A47	50c gray (R) ('31)	.15	.15
L16	A47	50c bluish grn (R) ('33)	.15	.15
L17	A47	50c vio (R) ('34)	.15	.15
L18	A48	1p emerald	.15	.15
L19	A48	1p org red ('29)	.15	.15
L20	A48	1p lil brn ('31)	.15	.15
L21	A48	1p dk bl (R) ('33)	.15	.15
L22	A48	1p brt vio (R) ('35)	.15	.15
L23	A49	1.50p brown	.15	.15
a.		Double overprint	1.50	
L24	A49	1.50p lilac ('28)	.15	.15
L25	A49	1.50p dull bl (R)	.15	.15
L26	A50	2.50p bister ('28)	.15	.15
L27	A50	2.50p vio (R) ('36)	.15	.15
L28	A51	3p gray (R)	.15	.15
L29	A51	3p rose red ('39)	.15	.15
L30	A52	5p vio (R) ('36)	.15	.15
L31	A57	10p gray brn (R) ('36)	.30	.25
		Set value	1.40	1.00

Types of 1931-35 and No. 305 Overprinted in Black or Red **C**

1931-36

L32	A59	1p light red	.15	.15
L33	A58	1.50p dp bl (R)	.15	.15
L34	A60	1.50p bis brn ('32)	.15	.15
L35	A60	1.50p grn (R) ('34)	.15	.15
L36	A60	1.50p bl (R) ('36)	.15	.15
L37	A54	10p vermilion	1.25	1.25
		Set value	1.50	1.40

OFFICIAL STAMPS

O1

O2

O3

O4

O5

O6

O7

Unwmk.

1886, Aug. 20 **Litho.** ***Imperf.***

O1	O1	1c orange	3.00	3.00
O2	O2	2c violet	3.00	3.00
O3	O3	5c red	3.00	3.00
O4	O4	7c green	3.00	3.00
O5	O5	10c brown	3.00	3.00
O6	O6	15c slate blue	3.00	3.00
a.		Wavy lines on face of stamp		
b.		"OFICIAL" omitted	1.25	
O7	O7	20c claret	3.00	3.00
		Nos. O1-O7 (7)	21.00	21.00

Nos. O1 to O7 have the date and various control marks and letters printed on the back of each stamp in blue and black.

The overprints exist inverted on all values.

Nos. O1 to O7 have been reprinted from new stones made from slightly retouched dies.

Types of 1886 With Overprint

1886 ***Perf. 11½***

O8	O1	1c dark green	.50	.50
O9	O2	2c scarlet	.50	.50
O10	O3	5c dull blue	.50	.50
O11	O4	7c orange	.50	.50
O12	O5	10c lake	.50	.50
O13	O6	15c brown	.50	.50
O14	O7	20c blue	.50	.50
		Nos. O8-O14 (7)	3.50	3.50

The overprint exists inverted on all values. Value, each $1.50.

No. 20 Overprinted **OFICIAL**

1886, Sept. 1

O15	A11	1c dark green	1.50	1.50

Types of 1889 Regular Issue Surcharged

Handstamped Surcharge in Black

1889 ***Imperf.***

O16	A13	3c on 15c violet	1.50	1.00
O17	A13	5c on 15c red brn	1.50	1.00
		Perf. 11½		
O18	A13	1c on 15c maroon	1.50	1.00
O19	A13	2c on 15c maroon	1.50	1.00
		Nos. O16-O19 (4)	6.00	4.00

Counterfeits of Nos. O16-O19 abound.

Regular Issue of 1887 Handstamp Overprinted in Violet **OFICIAL**

Perf. 11½-12½ & Compounds

1890 **Typo.**

O20	A12	1c green	.15	.15
O21	A12	2c rose red	.15	.15
O22	A12	5c blue	.15	.15
O23	A12	7c brown	3.75	2.50
O24	A12	10c lilac	.15	.15
O25	A12	15c orange	.45	.25
O26	A12	20c pink	.38	.30
		Nos. O20-O26 (7)	5.18	3.65

Nos. O20-O26 exist with double overprint and all but the 20c with inverted overprint.

Nos. O20-O22, O24-O26 exist with blue overprint. The status is questioned. Value, set $15.

Stamps and Type of 1887 Regular Issue Overprinted in Black **OFICIAL**

1892

O33	A12	1c green	.15	.15
O34	A12	2c rose red	.15	.15
O35	A12	5c blue	.15	.15
O36	A12	7c brown	1.75	1.00
O37	A12	10c lilac	.65	.22
O38	A12	15c orange	.18	.15
O39	A12	20c pink	.22	.15
O40	A12	50c gray	.15	.15
		Nos. O33-O40 (8)	3.40	
		Set value		1.70

No. 26 Overprinted

1893

O41	A12	7c brown	10.00	5.00

Counterfeits of No. O41 exist.

O16

1901, Feb. **Engr.** ***Perf. 11½, 12½***

O42	O16	1c dull blue	.20	.20
O43	O16	2c rose red	.15	.15
O44	O16	4c dark brown	.15	.15
O45	O16	5c dark green	.15	.15
O46	O16	8c orange brn	.15	.15
O47	O16	10c car rose	.15	.15
O48	O16	20c deep blue	.15	.15
		Set value	.75	.68

A 12c deep green, type O16, was prepared but not issued.

No. 45 Overprinted **Oficial**

1902 ***Perf. 12x12½***

O49	A12	1p olive grn	.15	.15
a.		Inverted overprint	10.00	

Counterfeits of No. O49a exist.

Regular Issue of 1903 Overprinted

1903 ***Perf. 11½***

O50	A32	1c gray	.15	.15
O51	A32	2c blue green	.15	.15
O52	A32	5c blue	.15	.15
O53	A32	10c orange brn	.15	.15
O54	A32	20c carmine	.15	.15
O55	A32	30c deep blue	.15	.15
O56	A32	60c purple	.15	.15
		Set value	.60	.40

O17

O18

1905-08 **Engr.** ***Perf. 11½, 12***

O57	O17	1c gray grn	.15	.15
O58	O17	1c ol grn ('05)	.20	.15
O59	O17	1c brn org ('06)	.45	.15
O60	O17	1c ver ('08)	.25	.15
O61	O17	2c brown org	.15	.15
O62	O17	2c gray grn ('05)	.15	.15
O63	O17	2c red ('06)	.75	.25
O64	O17	2c gray ('08)	.38	.20
O65	O17	5c deep bl ('06)	.20	.15
O66	O17	5c gray bl ('08)	1.50	1.00
O67	O17	5c grnsh bl ('08)	.75	.65
O68	O17	10c violet ('06)	.15	.15
O69	O17	20c violet ('08)	.65	.38
		Nos. O57-O69 (13)	5.73	
		Set value		3.20

1908

O70	O17	10c bister	3.50
O71	O17	10c emerald	3.50
O72	O17	10c red lilac	4.50
O73	O17	20c bister	3.00
O74	O17	20c salmon pink	3.50
O75	O17	20c green	3.50
O76	O17	30c turquoise bl	3.35
O77	O17	30c blue gray	3.50
O78	O17	30c yellow	1.50
O79	O17	60c chocolate	3.50
O80	O17	60c orange brn	4.00
O81	O17	60c deep ultra	3.00
O82	O18	1p brt rose & blk	22.50
O83	O18	1p lake & blk	22.50
O84	O18	1p brn org & blk	22.50
		Nos. O70-O84 (15)	107.85

Nos. O70-O84 were not issued, but were surcharged or overprinted for use as regular postage stamps. See Nos. 131-138, 141-145, 158-165, 171-173.

O19

1913 ***Perf. 11½***

O85	O19	1c gray	.15	.15
O86	O19	2c orange	.15	.15
O87	O19	5c lilac	.15	.15
O88	O19	10c green	.15	.15
O89	O19	20c dull red	.15	.15
O90	O19	50c rose	.15	.15
O91	O19	75c deep blue	.15	.15
O92	O19	1p dull blue	.15	.15
O93	O19	2p yellow	.15	.15
		Set value	.50	.50

For surcharges see Nos. 268, C1-C3.

Type of Regular Issue of 1927-38 Overprinted in Red **OFICIAL**

1935

O94	A47	10c light ultra	.15	.15
O95	A47	50c violet	.15	.15
O96	A48	1p orange	.15	.15
O97	A60	1.50p green	.15	.15
O98	A50	2.50p violet	.15	.15
		Set value	.30	.25

Overprint is diagonal on 1.50p.

University of Asunción Type

1940 **Litho.** ***Perf. 12***

O99	A67	50c red brn & blk	.15	.15
O100	A67	1p rose pink & blk	.15	.15
O101	A67	2p lt bl grn & blk	.15	.15
O102	A67	5p ultra & blk	.15	.15
O103	A67	10p lt vio & blk	.15	.15
O104	A67	50p dp org & blk	.30	.25
		Set value	.55	.45

PENRHYN ISLAND

pen-'rin 'ī-lənd

(Tongareva)

AREA — 3 sq. mi.
POP. — 395 (1926)

Stamps of Cook Islands were used in Penrhyn from 1932 until 1973.

12 Pence = 1 Shilling

Catalogue values for unused stamps in this country are for Never Hinged items, beginning with Scott 35 in the regular postage section, Scott B1 in the semi-postal section and Scott O1 in the officials section.

Watermarks

Wmk. 61- N Z and Star Close Together

Wmk. 63- Double-lined N Z and Star

On watermark 61 the margins of the sheets are watermarked "NEW ZEALAND POSTAGE" and parts of the double-lined letters of these words are frequently found on the stamps. It occasionally happens that a stamp shows no watermark whatever.

Stamps of New Zealand Surcharged in Carmine, Vermilion, Brown or Blue:

PENRHYN ISLAND.
½ PENI.
½ pence

PENRHYN ISLAND.
TAI PENI.
1 pence

PENRHYN ISLAND.
2½ PENI.
2½ pence

1902 Wmk. 63 *Perf. 14*
1 A18 ½p green (C) 1.25 *2.50*
a. No period after "ISLAND" 90.00 100.00
2 A35 1p carmine (Br) 3.25 *5.00*
a. Perf. 11 *1,000.* *1,000.*
b. Perf. 11x14 *1,000.* *1,000.*

Wmk. 61 *Perf. 14*
5 A18 ½p green (V) 1.00 *2.50*
a. No period after "ISLAND" 60.00 65.00
6 A35 1p carmine (Bl) 1.00 *2.75*
a. No period after "ISLAND" 40.00 40.00
b. Perf. 11x14 *9,000.* *8,500.*

Unwmk. *Perf. 11*
8 A22 2½p blue (C) 2.50 *5.00*
a. "½" and "PENI" 2mm apart 10.50 *16.00*
9 A22 2½p blue (V) 2.50 *5.00*
a. "½" and "PENI" 2mm apart 10.50 *16.00*
Nos. 1-9 (6) 11.50 *22.75*

Stamps with compound perfs. also exist perf. 11 or 14 on one or more sides.

PENRHYN ISLAND.

PENRHYN ISLAND.

Toru Pene.
d

Ono Pene.
e

PENRHYN ISLAND.

Tahi Silingi.
f

1903 Wmk. 61
10 A23(d) 3p yellow brn (Bl) 9.00 *19.00*
11 A26(e) 6p rose (Bl) 15.00 *32.50*
12 A29(f) 1sh orange red (Bl) 45.00 *55.00*
a. 1sh bright red (Bl) 45.00 *55.00*
b. 1sh brown red (Bl) 45.00 *55.00*
Nos. 10-12 (3) 69.00 *106.50*

1914-15 *Perf. 14, 14x14½*
13 A41(a) ½p yellow grn (C) 1.25 3.00
a. No period after "ISLAND" 32.50 *50.00*
b. No period after "PENI" 75.00 *90.00*
14 A41(a) ½p yel grn (V) ('15) .90 4.75
a. No period after "ISLAND" 13.00 22.50
b. No period after "PENI" 37.50 *50.00*
15 A41(e) 6p carmine rose (Bl) 27.50 37.50
16 A41(f) 1sh vermilion (Bl) 40.00 *62.50*
Nos. 13-16 (4) 69.65 *107.75*

New Zealand Stamps of 1915-19 Overprinted in Red or Dark Blue

PENRHYN ISLAND.

Perf. 14x13½, 14x14½
1917-20 Typo.
17 A43 ½p yel grn (R) ('20) .75 1.65
18 A47 1½p gray black (R) 5.75 4.00
19 A47 1½p brn org (R) ('19) .55 *4.00*
20 A43 3p choc (Bl) ('19) 3.00 4.50

Engr.
21 A44 2½p dull bl (R) ('20) 1.75 2.75
22 A45 3p vio brn (Bl) ('18) 8.25 *16.00*
23 A45 6p car rose (Bl) ('18) 4.50 *11.00*
24 A45 1sh vermilion (Bl) 10.50 *22.50*
Nos. 17-24 (8) 35.05 *66.40*

Landing of Capt. Cook A10

Avarua Waterfront A11

Capt. James Cook — A12

Coconut Palm — A13

Arorangi Village, Rarotonga — A14

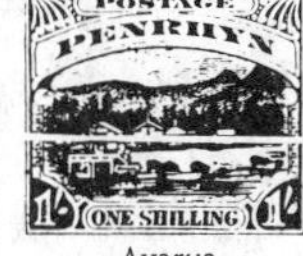
Avarua Harbor — A15

1920 Unwmk. *Perf. 14*
25 A10 ½p emerald & blk 1.00 *5.00*
a. Center inverted 625.00
26 A11 1p red & black 1.25 *5.00*
a. Center inverted 850.00
27 A12 1½p violet & blk 5.00 *10.00*
28 A13 3p red org & blk 3.75 *7.50*
29 A14 6p dk brn & red brn 4.50 *17.50*
30 A15 1sh dull bl & blk 10.00 *20.00*
Nos. 25-30 (6) 25.50 *65.00*

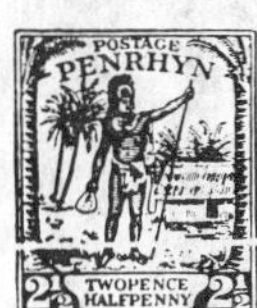
Rarotongan Chief (Te Po) — A16

1927 Engr. Wmk. 61
31 A16 2½p blue & red brn 2.00 *4.00*

Types of 1920 Issue

1928-29
33 A10 ½p yellow grn & blk 4.00 *4.00*
34 A11 1p carmine rose & blk 4.50 *5.25*

PENRHYN

Northern Cook Islands

POP. — 2,030 (1976).

The Northern Cook Islands include six besides Penrhyn that are inhabited: Nassau, Palmerston (Avarua), Manihiki (Humphrey), Rakahanga (Reirson), Pukapuka (Danger) and Suwarrow (Anchorage).

100 Cents = 1 Dollar

Catalogue values for unused stamps in this section are for Never Hinged items.

Cook Islands Nos. 200-201, 203, 205-208, 211-212, 215-217 Overprinted

PENRHYN
NORTHERN

1973 Photo. Unwmk. *Perf. 14x13½*
35 A34 1c gold & multi .15 .15
36 A34 2c gold & multi .15 .15
37 A34 3c gold & multi .15 .15
38 A34 4c gold & multi .15 .15
a. Overprinted on #204
39 A34 5c gold & multi .15 .15
40 A34 6c gold & multi .20 .20
41 A34 8c gold & multi .25 .25
42 A34 15c gold & multi .45 .45
43 A34 20c gold & multi .55 .55
44 A34 50c gold & multi 1.75 1.75
45 A35 $1 gold & multi 1.90 1.90
46 A35 $2 gold & multi 4.25 4.25
Nos. 35-46 (12) 10.10 10.10

Nos. 45-46 are overprinted "Penrhyn" only. Overprint exists with broken "E" or "O."

Issue dates: #35-45, Oct. 24; #46, Nov. 14.

Cook Islands Nos. 369-371 Overprinted in Silver: "PENRHYN / NORTHERN"

1973, Nov. 14 Photo. *Perf. 14*
47 A60 25c Princess Anne .80 .80
48 A60 30c Mark Phillips 1.10 1.10
49 A60 50c Princess and Mark Phillips 1.25 1.25
Nos. 47-49 (3) 3.15 3.15

Wedding of Princess Anne and Capt. Mark Phillips.

Fluorescence

Starting with No. 50, stamps carry a "fluorescent security underprinting" in a multiple pattern combining a sailing ship, "Penrhyn Northern Cook Islands" and stars.

Ostracion A17

Aerial View of Penrhyn Atoll — A18

Designs: ½c-$1, Various fish of Penrhyn. $5, Map showing Penrhyn's location.

1974-75 Photo. *Perf. 13½x14*
50 A17 ½c multicolored .15 .15
51 A17 1c multicolored .15 .15
52 A17 2c multicolored .15 .15
53 A17 3c multicolored .15 .15
54 A17 4c multicolored .15 .15
55 A17 5c multicolored .15 .15
56 A17 8c multicolored .20 .20
57 A17 10c multicolored .20 .20
58 A17 20c multicolored .45 .45
59 A17 25c multicolored .50 .50
60 A17 60c multicolored 1.25 1.25
61 A17 $1 multicolored 2.00 2.00
62 A18 $2 multicolored 4.00 4.00
63 A18 $5 multicolored 9.50 9.50
Nos. 50-63 (14) 19.00 19.00

Issue dates: $2, Feb. 12, 1975; $5, Mar. 12, 1975; others Aug. 15, 1974.

For surcharges and overprints see Nos. 72, 352-353, O1-O12.

Map of Penrhyn and Nos. 1-2 — A19

UPU, cent.: 50c, UPU emblem, map of Penrhyn and Nos. 27-28.

1974, Sept. 27 *Perf. 13*
64 A19 25c violet & multi .40 .40
65 A19 50c slate grn & multi .80 .80

Penrhyn Island stamps can be mounted in the Scott New Zealand Dependencies album.

Adoration of the Kings, by Memling — A20

Christmas: 10c, Adoration of the Shepherds, by Hugo van der Goes. 25c, Adoration of the Kings, by Rubens. 30c, Holy Family, by Orazio Borgianni.

1974, Oct. 30
66 A20 5c multicolored .15 .15
67 A20 10c multicolored .20 .20
68 A20 25c multicolored .50 .50
69 A20 30c multicolored .60 .60
Nos. 66-69 (4) 1.45 1.45

Churchill Giving "V" Sign — A21

1974, Nov. 30 Photo.
70 A21 30c shown .60 .60
71 A21 50c Portrait .90 .90

Winston Churchill (1874-1965).

No. 63 Overprinted  KIA ORANA ASTRONAUTS

1975, July 24 *Perf. 13½x13*
72 A18 $5 multicolored 4.00 4.00

Safe splashdown of Apollo space capsule.

Madonna, by Dirk Bouts A22

Pietà, by Michelangelo A23

Madonna Paintings: 15c, by Leonardo da Vinci. 35c, by Raphael.

1975, Nov. 21 Photo. *Perf. 14½x13*
73 A22 7c gold & multi .20 .20
74 A22 15c gold & multi .45 .45
75 A22 35c gold & multi 1.00 1.00
Nos. 73-75 (3) 1.65 1.65

Christmas 1975.

1976, Mar. 19 Photo. *Perf. 14x13*
76 A23 15c gold & dark brown .25 .25
77 A23 20c gold & deep purple .35 .35
78 A23 35c gold & dark green .55 .55
a. Souvenir sheet of 3, #76-78 1.50 1.50
Nos. 76-78 (3) 1.15 1.15

Easter and for the 500th birth anniv. of Michelangelo Buonarroti (1475-1564), Italian sculptor, painter and architect.

The Spirit of '76, by Archibald M. Willard — A24

No. 79, Washington Crossing the Delaware, by Emmanuel Leutze.

1976, May 20 Photo. Perf. 13½

79 A24 Strip of 3 1.10 1.10
a. 30c Boatsman .35 .35
b. 30c Washington .35 .35
c. 30c Men in boat .35 .35
80 A24 Strip of 3 2.00 2.00
a. 50c Drummer boy .55 .55
b. 50c Old drummer .55 .55
c. 50c Fifer .55 .55
d. Souvenir sheet, #79-80 4.00 4.00

American Bicentennial. Nos. 79-80 printed in sheets of 15, 5 strips of 3 and 3-part corner labels.

For overprint see No. O13.

Running A25

Montreal Olympic Games Emblem and: 30c, Long jump. 75c, Javelin.

1976, July 9 Photo. Perf. 13½

81 A25 25c multicolored .25 .25
82 A25 30c multicolored .30 .30
83 A25 75c multicolored .95 .95
a. Souvenir sheet of 3, #81-83, perf. 14½x13½ 2.00 2.00
Nos. 81-83 (3) 1.50 1.50

21st Olympic Games, Montreal, Canada, July 17-Aug. 1. Nos. 81-83 printed in sheets of 6 (2x3).

Flight into Egypt, by Dürer — A26

Etchings by Albrecht Dürer: 15c, Adoration of the Shepherds. 35c, Adoration of the Kings.

1976, Oct. 20 Photo. Perf. 13x13½

84 A26 7c silver & dk brown .15 .15
85 A26 15c silver & slate grn .25 .25
86 A26 35c silver & purple .60 .60
Nos. 84-86 (3) 1.00 1.00

Christmas. Nos. 84-86 printed in sheets of 8 (2x4) with decorative border.

Elizabeth II and Westminster Abbey — A27

$1, Elizabeth II & Prince Philip. $2, Elizabeth II.

1977, Mar. 24 Photo. Perf. 13½x13

87 A27 50c silver & multi .15 .15
88 A27 $1 silver & multi .40 .40
89 A27 $2 silver & multi .80 .80
a. Souvenir sheet of 3, #87-89 1.65 1.65
Nos. 87-89 (3) 1.35 1.35

25th anniversary of reign of Queen Elizabeth II. Nos. 87-89 issued in sheets of 4.

For overprints see Nos. O14-O15.

Annunciation A28

Designs: 15c, Announcement to Shepherds. 35c, Nativity. Designs from "The Bible in Images," by Julius Schnorr von Carolsfeld (1794-1872).

1977, Sept. 23 Photo. Perf. 13½

90 A28 7c multicolored .25 .25
91 A28 15c multicolored .50 .50
92 A28 35c multicolored 1.25 1.25
Nos. 90-92 (3) 2.00 2.00

Christmas. Issued in sheets of 6.

Red Sickle-bill (I'wii) — A29

Chief's Feather Cloak — A30

Designs: No. 95, Crimson creeper (apapane). No. 96, Feathered head of Hawaiian god. No. 97, Hawaiian gallinule (alae). No. 98, Chief's regalia: feather cape, staff (kahili) and helmet. No. 99, Yellow-tufted bee-eater (o'o). No. 100, Scarlet feathered image (head). Birds are extinct; their feathers were used for artifacts shown.

1978, Jan. 19 Photo. Perf. 12½x13

93 A29 20c silver & multi .40 .40
94 A30 20c silver & multi .40 .40
95 A29 30c silver & multi .60 .60
96 A30 30c silver & multi .60 .60
97 A29 35c silver & multi .65 .65
98 A30 35c silver & multi .65 .65
99 A29 75c silver & multi 1.40 1.40
a. Souv. sheet of 4, #93, 95, 97, 99 3.75 3.75
100 A30 75c silver & multi 1.40 1.40
a. Souv. sheet of 4, #94, 96, 98, 100 3.75 3.75
Nos. 93-100 (8) 6.10 6.10

Bicentenary of Capt. Cook's arrival in Hawaii. Stamps of same denomination printed se-tenant in sheets of 8 (4x2).

A31 A32

Rubens' Paintings: 10c, St. Veronica by Rubens. 15c, Crucifixion. 35c, Descent from the Cross.

1978, Mar. 10 Photo. Perf. 13½x13
Size: 25x36mm

101 A31 10c multicolored .20 .20
102 A31 15c multicolored .30 .30
103 A31 35c multicolored .70 .70
a. Souvenir sheet of 3 1.25 1.25
Nos. 101-103 (3) 1.20 1.20

Easter and 400th birth anniv. of Peter Paul Rubens (1577-1640). Nos. 101-103 issued in sheets of 6. No. 103a contains one each of Nos. 101-103 (27x36mm).

Miniature Sheet

1978, May 24 Photo. Perf. 13

104 Sheet of 6 2.50 2.50
a. A32 90c Arms of United Kingdom .40 .30
b. A32 90c shown .40 .30
c. A32 90c Arms of New Zealand .40 .30
d. Souvenir sheet of 3, #104a-104c 3.00 2.50

25th anniv. of coronation of Elizabeth II.

No. 104 contains 2 horizontal se-tenant strips of Nos. 104a-104c, separated by horizontal gutter showing coronation.

A33 A34

Paintings by Dürer: 30c, Virgin and Child. 35c, Virgin and Child with St. Anne.

1978, Nov. 29 Photo. Perf. 14x13½

105 A33 30c multicolored .60 .60
106 A33 35c multicolored .75 .75
a. Souvenir sheet of 2, #105-106 1.40 1.40

Christmas and 450th death anniv. of Albrecht Dürer (1471-1528), German painter. Nos. 105-106 issued in sheets of 6.

1979, Sept. 26 Photo. Perf. 14

Designs: No. 107, Penrhyn #64-65. No. 108, Rowland Hill, Penny Black. No. 109, Penrhyn #104b. No. 110, Hill portrait.

107 A34 75c multicolored .60 .60
108 A34 75c multicolored .60 .60
109 A34 90c multicolored .75 .75
110 A34 90c multicolored .75 .75
a. Souvenir sheet of 4, #107-110 3.25 3.25
Nos. 107-110 (4) 2.70 2.70

Sir Rowland Hill (1795-1879), originator of penny postage. Nos. 107-108 and 109-110 issued se-tenant in sheets of 8.

Max and Moritz, IYC Emblem — A35

IYC: Scenes from Max and Moritz, by Wilhelm Busch (1832-1908).

1979, Nov. 20 Photo. Perf. 13x12½

111 Sheet of 4 .75
a. A35 12c shown .15
b. A35 12c Looking down chimney .15
c. A35 12c With stolen chickens .15
d. A35 12c Woman and dog, empty pan .15
112 Sheet of 4 .90
a. A35 15c Sawing bridge .20
b. A35 15c Man falling into water .20
c. A35 15c Broken bridge .20
d. A35 15c Running away .20
113 Sheet of 4 1.25
a. A35 20c Baker .30
b. A35 20c Sneaking into bakery .30
c. A35 20c Falling into dough .30
d. A35 20c Baked into breads .30
Nos. 111-113 (3) 2.90

A36 A37

Easter (15th Century Prayerbook Illustrations): 12c, Jesus Carrying the Cross. 20c, Crucifixion, by William Vreland. 35c, Descent from the Cross.

1980, Mar. 28 Photo. Perf. 13x13½

114 A36 12c multicolored .20 .20
115 A36 20c multicolored .35 .35
116 A36 35c multicolored .60 .60
a. Souvenir sheet of 3, #114-116 1.10 1.10
Nos. 114-116 (3) 1.15 1.15

See Nos. B4-B6.

1980, Sept. 17 Photo. Perf. 13

117 A37 $1 multicolored 1.65 1.65

Souvenir Sheet

118 A37 $2.50 multicolored 3.00 3.00

Queen Mother Elizabeth, 80th birthday.

A38 A39

Designs: Nos. 119-120, Platform diving. Nos. 121-122, Archery. Nos. 123-124, Soccer. Nos. 125-126, Running. Stamps of same denomination se-tenant in continuous design.

1980, Nov. 14 Photo. Perf. 13½

119 A38 10c Falk Hoffman, DDR .15 .15
120 A38 10c Martina Jaschke .15 .15
121 A38 20c Tomi Polkolainen .20 .20
122 A38 20c Kete Losaberidse .20 .20
123 A38 30c Czechoslovakia, gold .30 .30
124 A38 30c DDR, silver .30 .30
125 A38 50c Barbel Wockel .50 .50
126 A38 50c Pietro Mennea .50 .50
a. Souvenir sheet of 8, #119-126 2.50 2.50
Nos. 119-126 (8) 2.30 2.30

22nd Summer Olympic Games, Moscow, July 19-Aug. 3.

1980, Dec. 5 Photo. Perf. 13

Christmas (15th Century Virgin and Child Paintings by): 20c, Virgin and Child, by Luis Dalmau. 35c, Serra brothers. 50c, Master of the Porciuncula.

127 A39 20c multicolored .25 .25
128 A39 35c multicolored .35 .35
129 A39 50c multicolored .45 .45
a. Souvenir sheet of 3, #127-129 1.75 1.75
Nos. 127-129 (3) 1.05 1.05

See Nos. B7-B9.

Amatasi — A40

A41

Cutty Sark, 1869 A42

1981 Photo. Perf. 14

130 A40 1c shown .15 .15
131 A40 1c Ndrua .15 .15
132 A40 1c Waka .15 .15
133 A40 1c Tongiaki .15 .15
134 A40 3c Va'a teu'ua .15 .15
135 A40 3c Victoria, 1500 .15 .15
136 A40 3c Golden Hinde, 1560 .15 .15
137 A40 3c Boudeuse, 1760 .15 .15
138 A40 4c Bounty, 1787 .15 .15
139 A40 4c Astrolabe, 1811 .15 .15
140 A40 4c Star of India, 1861 .15 .15
141 A40 4c Great Rep., 1853 .15 .15
142 A40 6c Balcutha, 1886 .15 .15
143 A40 6c Coonatto, 1863 .15 .15
144 A40 6c Antiope, 1866 .15 .15
145 A40 6c Teaping, 1863 .15 .15
146 A40 10c Preussen, 1902 .20 .20
147 A40 10c Pamir, 1921 .20 .20
148 A40 10c Cap Hornier, 1910 .20 .20
149 A40 10c Patriarch, 1869 .20 .20

Perf. 13½x14½

150 A41 15c shown .30 .30
151 A41 15c Ndrua .30 .30
152 A41 15c Waka .30 .30
153 A41 15c Tongiaki .30 .30
154 A41 20c Va'a Teu'ua .40 .40
155 A41 20c Victoria, 1500 .40 .40
156 A41 20c Golden Hind, 1560 .40 .40
157 A41 20c Boudeuse, 1760 .40 .40
158 A41 30c Bounty, 1787 .60 .60
159 A41 30c Astrolabe, 1811 .60 .60
160 A41 30c Star of India, 1861 .60 .60
161 A41 30c Great Rep., 1853 .60 .60
162 A41 50c Balcutha, 1886 1.00 1.00
163 A41 50c Coonatto, 1863 1.00 1.00
164 A41 50c Antiope, 1866 1.00 1.00
165 A41 50c Teaping, 1863 1.00 1.00
166 A41 $1 Preussen, 1902 2.00 2.00
167 A41 $1 Pamir, 1921 2.00 2.00
168 A41 $1 Cap Hornier, 1910 2.00 2.00
169 A41 $1 Patriarch, 1869 2.00 2.00

Perf. 13½

170 A42 $2 shown 4.00 4.00
171 A42 $4 Mermerus, 1872 8.00 8.00
172 A42 $6 Resolution, Discovery, 1776 12.00 12.00
Nos. 130-172 (43) 44.40 44.40

Stamps of same denomination se-tenant.

Issue dates: 1c-10c, Feb. 16. 15c-50c, Mar. 16. $1, May 15. $2, $4, June 26. $6, Sept. 21.

For surcharges and overprints see Nos. 232-243, 251, 254, 395, O35, O37, O39.

Christ with Crown of Thorns, by Titan — A44

Easter: 30c, Jesus at the Grove, by Paolo Veronese. 50c, Pieta, by Van Dyck.

1981, Apr. 5 *Perf. 14*

173 A44	30c multicolored		.50	.50
174 A44	40c multicolored		.65	.65
175 A44	50c multicolored		.80	.80
a.	Souv. sheet of 3, #173-175, perf. 13½		2.25	2.25
	Nos. 173-175 (3)		1.95	1.95

See Nos. B10-B12.

A45 A46

Designs: Portraits of Prince Charles.

1981, July 10 **Photo.** *Perf. 14*

176 A45	40c multicolored	.20	.20
177 A45	50c multicolored	.25	.25
178 A45	60c multicolored	.30	.30
179 A45	70c multicolored	.40	.40
180 A45	80c multicolored	.45	.45
a.	Souv. sheet of 5, #176-180+label	2.00	2.00
	Nos. 176-180 (5)	1.60	1.60

Royal wedding. Nos. 176-180 each issued in sheets of 5 plus label showing couple.

For overprints and surcharges see Nos. 195-199, 244-245, 248, 299-300, B13-B18.

1981, Dec. 7 **Photo.** *Perf. 13*

#181: a, Red shirt. b, Striped shirt. c, Blue shirt.
#182: a, Blue shirt. b, Red shirt. c, Striped shirt.
#183: a, Orange shirt. b, Purple shirt. c, Black shirt.

181	Strip of 3	.50	.50
a.-c.	A46 15c, any single	.15	.15
182	Strip of 3	1.25	1.25
a.-c.	A46 35c, any single	.40	.40
183	Strip of 3	1.75	1.75
a.-c.	A46 50c, any single	.55	.55
	Nos. 181-183 (3)	3.50	3.50

1982 World Cup Soccer. See No. B19.

Christmas — A47

21st Birthday of Princess Diana — A48

Dürer Engravings: 30c, Virgin on a Crescent, 1508. 40c, Virgin at the Fence, 1503. 50c, Holy Virgin and Child, 1505.

1981, Dec. 15 **Photo.** *Perf. 13x13½*

184 A47	30c multicolored	.45	.45
185 A47	40c multicolored	.60	.60
186 A47	50c multicolored	.75	.75
a.	Souvenir sheet of 3	2.00	2.00
	Nos. 184-186 (3)	1.80	1.80

Souvenir Sheets

Perf. 14x13½

187 A47	70c + 5c like #184	1.50	1.50
188 A47	70c + 5c like #185	1.50	1.50
189 A47	70c + 5c like #186	1.50	1.50

No. 186a contains Nos. 184-186 each with 2c surcharge. Nos. 187-189 each contain one 25x40mm stamp. Surtaxes were for childrens' charities.

1982, July 1 **Photo.** *Perf. 14*

Designs: Portraits of Diana.

190 A48	30c multicolored	.30	.30
191 A48	50c multicolored	.50	.50
192 A48	70c multicolored	.75	.75
193 A48	80c multicolored	.90	.90
194 A48	$1.40 multicolored	1.50	1.50
a.	Souv. sheet of 5, #190-194 + label	4.00	4.00
	Nos. 190-194 (5)	3.95	3.95

For new inscriptions, overprints and surcharges, see Nos. 200-204, 246-247, 249-250, 301-302.

Nos. 176-180a Overprinted: "BIRTH OF PRINCE WILLIAM OF WALES 21 JUNE 1982"

1982, July 30

195 A45	40c multicolored	.65	.65
196 A45	50c multicolored	.80	.80
197 A45	60c multicolored	1.00	1.00
198 A45	70c multicolored	1.10	1.10
199 A45	80c multicolored	1.25	1.25
a.	Souv. sheet of 5, #195-199 + label	7.00	7.00
	Nos. 195-199 (5)	4.80	4.80

Nos. 190-194a Inscribed in Silver: 21 JUNE 1982 BIRTH OF/PRINCE WILLIAM OF WALES or COMMEMORATING THE BIRTH OF/PRINCE WILLIAM OF WALES

1982 **Photo.** *Perf. 14*

200 A48	30c 21 June 1982	.30	.30
200A A48	30c Commem...	.30	.30
201 A48	50c 21 June 1982	.50	.50
201A A48	50c Commem...	.50	.50
202 A48	70c 21 June 1982	.75	.75
202A A48	70c Commem...	.75	.75
203 A48	80c 21 June 1982	.85	.85
203A A48	80c Commem...	.85	.85
204 A48	$1.40 21 June 1982	1.50	1.50
204A A48	$1.40 Commem...	1.50	1.50
b.	Souv. sheet of 5, #200, 201, 202, 203, 204 + label	4.00	4.00
	Nos. 200-204A (10)	7.80	7.80

Miniature sheets of each denomination were issued containing 2 "21 JUNE 1982...," 3 "COMMEMORATING...," and a label.

For surcharges see Nos. 247, 250, 253.

A49 A50

Christmas: Virgin and Child Paintings.

1982, Dec. 10 **Photo.** *Perf. 14*

205 A49	35c Joos Van Cleve (1485-1540)	.50	.50
206 A49	48c Filippino Lippi (1457-1504)	.65	.65
207 A49	60c Cima Da Conegliano (1459-1517)	.80	.80
a.	Souvenir sheet of 3	2.25	2.25
	Nos. 205-207 (3)	1.95	1.95

Souvenir Sheets

208 A49	70c + 5c like 35c	.90	.90
209 A49	70c + 5c like 48c	.90	.90
210 A49	70c + 5c like 60c	.90	.90

No. 207a contains Nos. 205-207 each with 2c surcharge. Nos. 208-210 each contain one stamp, perf. 13½. Surtaxes were for childrens' charities.

1983, Mar. 14 *Perf. 13½x13*

211 A50	60c Red coral	.80	.80
212 A50	60c Aerial view	.80	.80
213 A50	60c Eleanor Roosevelt, grass skirt	.80	.80
214 A50	60c Map	.80	.80
	Nos. 211-214 (4)	3.20	3.20

Commonwealth day. Nos. 211-214 se-tenant.

For surcharges see Nos. O27-O30.

Scouting Year A51

Emblem and various tropical flowers.

1983, Apr. 5 *Perf. 13½x14½*

215 A51	36c multicolored	.60	.60
216 A51	48c multicolored	.80	.80
217 A51	60c multicolored	1.00	1.00
	Nos. 215-217 (3)	2.40	2.40

Souvenir Sheet

218 A51	$2 multicolored	3.25	3.25

Nos. 215-218 Overprinted: "XV / WORLD JAMBOREE / CANADA / 1983"

1983, July 8 **Photo.** *Perf. 13½x14½*

219 A51	36c multicolored	.60	.60
220 A51	48c multicolored	1.00	1.00
221 A51	60c multicolored	1.00	1.00
	Nos. 219-221 (3)	2.60	2.60

Souvenir Sheet

222 A51	$2 multicolored	3.25	3.25

15th World Boy Scout Jamboree.

Save the Whales Campaign A52

Various whale hunting scenes.

1983, July 29 **Photo.** *Perf. 13*

223 A52	8c multicolored	.15	.15
224 A52	15c multicolored	.25	.25
225 A52	35c multicolored	.60	.60
226 A52	60c multicolored	1.00	1.00
227 A52	$1 multicolored	1.75	1.75
	Nos. 223-227 (5)	3.75	3.75

World Communications Year — A53

Designs: Cable laying Vessels.

1983, Sept. **Photo.** *Perf. 13*

228 A53	36c multicolored	.60	.60
229 A53	48c multicolored	.80	.80
230 A53	60c multicolored	1.00	1.00
	Nos. 228-230 (3)	2.40	2.40

Souvenir Sheet

231	Sheet of 3	2.50	2.50
a.	A53 36c + 3c like No. 228	.65	.65
b.	A53 48c + 3c like No. 229	.85	.85
c.	A53 60c + 3c like No. 230	.95	.95

Surtax was for local charities.

Nos. 146-149, 154-161, 170, 172, 178-180, 192-194, 202-204 Surcharged

Perf. 14, 13½x14½, 13½

1983 **Photo.**

232	A40	18c on 10c #146	.35	.35
233	A40	18c on 10c #147	.35	.35
234	A40	18c on 10c #148	.35	.35
235	A40	18c on 10c #149	.35	.35
236	A41	36c on 20c #154	.70	.70
237	A41	36c on 20c #155	.70	.70
238	A41	36c on 20c #156	.70	.70
239	A41	36c on 20c #157	.70	.70
240	A41	36c on 30c #158	.70	.70
241	A41	36c on 30c #159	.70	.70
242	A41	36c on 30c #160	.70	.70
243	A41	36c on 30c #161	.70	.70
244	A45	48c on 60c multi	.90	.90
245	A45	72c on 70c multi	1.50	1.50
246	A48	72c on 70c #192	1.50	1.50
247	A48	72c on 70c #202	1.50	1.50
247A	A48	72c on 70c #202A	1.50	1.50
248	A45	96c on 80c multi	1.75	1.75
249	A48	96c on 80c #193	1.75	1.75
250	A48	96c on 80c #203	1.75	1.75
250A	A48	96c on 80c #203A	1.75	1.75
251	A42	$1.20 on $2 multi	2.25	2.25
252	A48	$1.20 on $1.40 #194	2.25	2.25
253	A48	$1.20 on $1.40 #204	2.25	2.25
253A	A48	$1.20 on $1.40 #204A	2.25	2.25
254	A42	$5.60 on $6 multi	10.50	10.50
		Nos. 232-254 (26)	40.40	40.40

Issued: #232-243, 245, 251, Sept. 26; #244, 246, 249, 252, 254, Oct. 28; others Dec. 1.

First Manned Balloon Flight, 200th Anniv. — A54

Designs: 36c, Airship, Sir George Cayley (1773-1857). 48c, Man-powered airship, Dupuy de Lome (1818-1885). 60c, Brazilian Aviation Pioneer, Alberto Santos Dumont (1873-1932). 96c, Practical Airship, Paul Lebaudy (1858-1937). $1.32, L-Z 127 Graf Zeppelin.

1983, Oct. 31 **Litho.** *Perf. 13*

255 A54	36c multicolored	.60	.60
256 A54	48c multicolored	.80	.80
257 A54	60c multicolored	.95	.95
258 A54	96c multicolored	1.50	1.50
259 A54	$1.32 multicolored	2.25	2.25
a.	Souvenir sheet of 5, #255-259	6.00	6.00
	Nos. 255-259 (5)	6.10	6.10

Nos. 255-259 se-tenant with labels. Sheets of 5 for each value exist.

Nos. 255-259 are misspelled "ISLANS." For correcting overprints see Nos. 287-291.

Christmas — A55

Raphael Paintings: 36c, Madonna in the Meadow. 42c, Tempi Madonna. 48c, Small Cowper Madonna. 60c, Madonna Della Tenda.

1983, Nov. 30 **Photo.** *Perf. 13x13½*

260 A55	36c multicolored	.55	.55
261 A55	42c multicolored	.65	.65
262 A55	48c multicolored	.75	.75
263 A55	60c multicolored	.95	.95
a.	Souvenir sheet of 4	3.00	3.00
	Nos. 260-263 (4)	2.90	2.90

Souvenir Sheets

Perf. 13½

264 A55	75c + 5c like #260	1.25	1.25
265 A55	75c + 5c like #261	1.25	1.25
266 A55	75c + 5c like #262	1.25	1.25
267 A55	75c + 5c like #263	1.25	1.25

No. 263a contains Nos. 260-263 each with 3c surcharge. Nos. 264-267 each contain one 29x41mm stamp. Issued Dec. 28. Surtaxes were for children's charities.

Waka Canoe — A56

1984 **Photo.** *Perf. 14½*

268 A56	2c shown	.15	.15
269 A56	4c Amatasi fishing boat	.15	.15
270 A56	5c Ndrua canoe	.15	.15
271 A56	8c Tongiaki canoe	.15	.15
272 A56	10c Victoria, 1500	.15	.15
273 A56	18c Golden Hind, 1560	.25	.25
274 A56	20c Boudeuse, 1760	.30	.30
275 A56	30c Bounty, 1787	.40	.40
276 A56	36c Astrolabe, 1811	.50	.50
277 A56	48c Great Republic, 1853	.65	.65
278 A56	50c Star of India, 1861	.70	.70
279 A56	60c Coonatto, 1863	.80	.80
280 A56	72c Antiope, 1866	1.00	1.00
281 A56	80c Balcutha, 1886	1.10	1.10
282 A56	96c Cap Hornier, 1910	1.40	1.40
283 A56	$1.20 Pamir, 1921	1.60	1.60

Perf. 13

Size: 42x34mm

284 A56	$3 Mermerus, 1872	3.00	3.00
285 A56	$5 Cutty Sark, 1869	4.75	4.75
286 A56	$9.60 Resolution, Discovery	9.00	9.00
	Nos. 268-286 (19)	26.20	26.20

Issue dates: Nos. 268-277, Feb. 8. Nos. 278-283, Mar. 23. Nos. 284-286 June 15.

For overprints and surcharges see Nos. O16-O26, O31-O34, O36, O38, O40.

Nos. 255-259a Ovptd. with Silver Bar and "NORTHERN COOK ISLANDS" in Black

1984 Litho. *Perf. 13*

287 A54 36c multicolored .90 .90
288 A54 48c multicolored 1.20 1.20
289 A54 60c multicolored 1.50 1.50
290 A54 96c multicolored 2.40 2.40
291 A54 $1.32 multicolored 3.25 3.25
a. Souvenir sheet of 5, #287-291 9.25 9.25
Nos. 287-291 (5) 9.25 9.25

1984 Los Angeles Summer Olympic Games A57

1984, July 20 Photo. *Perf. 13½x13*

292 A57 35c Olympic flag .38 .38
293 A57 60c Torch, flags .60 .60
294 A57 $1.80 Classic runners, Memorial Coliseum 1.90 1.90
Nos. 292-294 (3) 2.88 2.88

Souvenir Sheet

295 Sheet of 3 + label 2.75 2.75
a. A57 35c + 5c like #292 .30 .30
b. A57 50c + 5c like #293 .55 .55
c. A57 $1.80 + 5c like #294 1.90 1.90

Surtax for amateur sports.

AUSIPEX '84 — A57a

1984, Sept. 20

296 A57a 60c Nos. 136, 108, 180, 104b .60 .60
297 A57a $1.20 Map of South Pacific 1.25 1.25

Souvenir Sheet

298 Sheet of 2 2.00 2.00
a. A57a 96c like #296 1.00 1.00
b. A57a 96c like #297 1.00 1.00

For surcharge see No. 345.

Nos. 176-177, 190-191 Ovptd. "Birth of/Prince Henry/15 Sept. 1984" and Surcharged in Black or Gold

1984, Oct. 18 *Perf. 14*

299 A45 $2 on 40c 2.25 2.25
300 A45 $2 on 50c 2.25 2.25
301 A48 $2 on 30c 2.25 2.25
302 A48 $2 on 50c 2.25 2.25
Nos. 299-302 (4) 9.00 9.00

Nos. 209-302 printed in sheets of 5 plus one label each picturing a portrait of the royal couple or an heraldic griffin.

Christmas 1984 — A58

Paintings: 36c, Virgin and Child, by Giovanni Bellini. 48c, Virgin and Child, by Lorenzo di Credi. 60c, Virgin and Child, by Palma, the Older. 96c, Virgin and Child, by Raphael.

1984, Nov. 15 Photo. *Perf. 13x13½*

303 A58 36c multicolored .32 .32
304 A58 48c multicolored .45 .45
305 A58 60c multicolored .55 .55
306 A58 96c multicolored .90 .90
a. Souvenir sheet of 4 3.00 3.00
Nos. 303-306 (4) 2.22 2.22

Souvenir Sheets

307 A58 96c + 10c like #303 1.20 1.20
308 A58 96c + 10c like #304 1.20 1.20
309 A58 96c + 10c like #305 1.20 1.20
310 A58 96c + 10c like #306 1.20 1.20

No. 306a contains Nos. 303-306, each with 5c surcharge. Nos. 307-310 issued Dec. 10. Surtax for children's charities.

Audubon Bicentenary A59

1985, Apr. 9 Photo. *Perf. 13*

311 A59 20c Harlequin duck .18 .18
312 A59 55c Sage grouse .50 .50
313 A59 65c Solitary sandpiper .60 .60
314 A59 75c Red-backed sandpiper .70 .70
Nos. 311-314 (4) 1.98 1.98

Souvenir Sheets

Perf. 13½x13

315 A59 95c Like #311 .85 .85
316 A59 95c Like #312 .85 .85
317 A59 95c Like #313 .85 .85
318 A59 95c Like #314 .85 .85

For surcharges see Nos. 391-394.

Queen Mother, 85th Birthday — A60

1985, June 24 Photo. *Perf. 13x13½*

319 A60 75c Photograph, 1921 .75 .75
320 A60 95c New mother, 1926 .90 .90
321 A60 $1.20 Coronation day, 1937 1.10 1.10
322 A60 $2.80 70th birthday 2.75 2.75
a. Souvenir sheet of 4, #319-322 6.00 6.00
Nos. 319-322 (4) 5.50 5.50

Souvenir Sheet

323 A60 $5 Portrait, c. 1980 4.75 4.75

No. 322a issued on 8/4/86, for 86th birthday.

Intl. Youth Year — A61

Grimm Brothers' fairy tales.

1985, Sept. 10 *Perf. 13x13½*

324 A61 75c House in the Wood .90 .90
325 A61 95c Snow White and Rose Red 1.15 1.15
326 A61 $1.15 Goose Girl 1.40 1.40
Nos. 324-326 (3) 3.45 3.45

Christmas 1985 A62

Paintings (details) by Murillo: 75c, No. 330a, The Annunciation. $1.15, No. 330b, Adoration of the Shepherds. $1.80, No. 330c, The Holy Family.

1985, Nov. 25 Photo. *Perf. 14*

327 A62 75c multicolored .90 .90
328 A62 $1.15 multicolored 1.40 1.40
329 A62 $1.80 multicolored 2.25 2.25
Nos. 327-329 (3) 4.55 4.55

Souvenir Sheets

Perf. 13½

330 Sheet of 3 3.50 3.50
a.-c. A62 95c any single 1.15 1.15
331 A62 $1.20 like #327 1.25 1.25
332 A62 $1.45 like #328 1.50 1.50
333 A62 $2.75 like #329 2.75 2.75

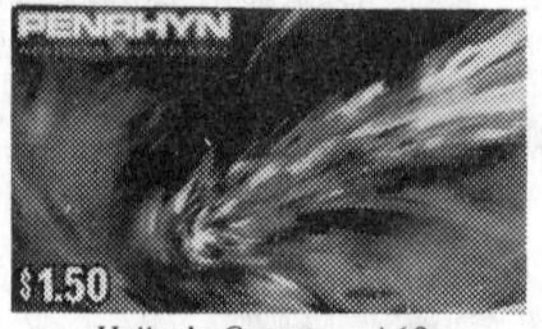

Halley's Comet — A63

Fire and Ice, by Camille Rendal. Nos. 334-335 se-tenant in continuous design.

1986, Feb. 4 *Perf. 13½x13*

334 A63 $1.50 Comet head 1.75 1.75
335 A63 $1.50 Comet tail 1.75 1.75

Size: 109x43mm

Imperf

336 A63 $3 multicolored 3.50 3.50
Nos. 334-336 (3) 7.00 7.00

Elizabeth II, 60th Birthday A64

1986, Apr. 21 *Perf. 14*

337 A64 95c Age 3 1.15 1.15
338 A64 $1.45 Wearing crown 1.75 1.75

Size: 60x34mm

Perf. 13½x13

339 A64 $2.50 Both portraits 3.00 3.00
Nos. 337-339 (3) 5.90 5.90

A65

A66

Statue of Liberty, Cent.: 95c, Statue, scaffolding. $1.75 Removing copper facade. $3, Restored statue on Liberty Island.

1986, June 27 Photo. *Perf. 13½*

340 A65 95c gold, pale grn & sep 1.00 1.00
341 A65 $1.75 gold, pale grn & sep 1.90 1.90
342 A65 $3 gold, pale grn & sep 3.25 3.25
Nos. 340-342 (3) 6.15 6.15

1986, July 23 *Perf. 13x13½*

343 A66 $2.50 Portraits 2.75 2.75
344 A66 $3.50 Profiles 4.00 4.00

Wedding of Prince Andrew and Sarah Ferguson. Nos. 343-344 each printed in sheets of 4 plus 2 center decorative labels.

No. 298 Surcharged with Gold Circle, Bar, New Value in Black and Exhibition Emblem in Gold and Black

1986, Aug. 4

345 Sheet of 2 4.50 4.50
a. A57a $2 on 96c #298a 2.25 2.25
b. A57a $2 on 96c #298b 2.25 2.25

STAMPEX '86, Adelaide, Aug. 4-10.

Christmas — A67

Engravings by Rembrandt: 65c, No. 349a, Adoration of the Shepherds. $1.75, No. 349b, Virgin and Child. $2.50, No. 349c, The Holy Family.

1986, Nov. 20 Litho. *Perf. 13x13½*

346 A67 65c gold, hn brn & buff .70 .70
347 A67 $1.75 gold, hn brn & buff 1.85 1.85
348 A67 $2.50 gold, hn brn & buff 2.65 2.65
Nos. 346-348 (3) 5.20 5.20

Souvenir Sheet

Perf. 13½x13

349 Sheet of 3 4.80 4.80
a.-c. A67 $1.50 any single 1.60 1.60

Corrected inscription is black on silver.
For surcharges see Nos. B20-B23.

Souvenir Sheets

Statue of Liberty, Cent. A68

Photographs: No. 350a, Workmen, crown. No. 350b, Ellis Is., aerial view. No. 350c, Immigration building, Ellis Is. No. 350d, Buildings, opposite side of Ellis Is. No. 350e, Workmen inside torch structure. No. 351a, Liberty's head and torch. No. 351b, Torch. No. 351c, Workmen on scaffold. No. 351d, Statue, full figure. No. 351e, Workmen beside statue. Nos. 351a-351e vert.

1987, Apr. 15 Litho. *Perf. 14*

350 Sheet of 5 + label 3.50 3.50
a.-e. A68 65c any single .70 .70
351 Sheet of 5 + label 3.50 3.50
a.-e. A68 65c any single .70 .70

Nos. 62-63 Ovptd. "Fortieth Royal Wedding / Anniversary 1947-87" in Lilac Rose

1987, Nov. 20 Photo. *Perf. 13½x14*

352 A18 $2 multicolored 2.00 2.00
353 A18 $5 multicolored 5.25 5.25

Christmas — A69

Paintings (details) by Raphael: 95c, No. 357a, The Garvagh Madonna, the National Gallery, London. $1.60, No. 357b, The Alba Madonna, the National Gallery of Art, Washington. $2.25, No. 357c, $4.80, The Madonna of the Fish, Prado Museum, Madrid.

1987, Dec. 11 Photo. *Perf. 13½*

354 A69 95c multicolored 1.25 1.25
355 A69 $1.60 multicolored 2.05 2.05
356 A69 $2.25 multicolored 2.90 2.90
Nos. 354-356 (3) 6.20 6.20

Souvenir Sheets

357 Sheet of 3 + label 4.35 4.35
a.-c. A69 $1.15 any single 1.45 1.45
358 A69 $4.80 multicolored 6.25 6.25

No. 358 contains one 31x39mm stamp.

1988 Summer Olympics, Seoul — A70

Events and: 55c, $1.25, Seoul Games emblem. 95c, Obverse of a $50 silver coin issued in 1987 to commemorate the participation of Cook Islands atheletes in the Olympics for the 1st time. $1.50, Coin reverse.

Perf. 13½x13, 13x13½

1988, July 29 **Photo.**

359 A70 55c Running .70 .70
360 A70 95c High jump, vert. 1.25 1.25
361 A70 $1.25 Shot put 1.50 1.50
362 A70 $1.50 Tennis, vert. 1.75 1.75
Nos. 359-362 (4) 5.20 5.20

Souvenir Sheet

363 Sheet of 2 5.00 5.00
a. A70 $2.50 like 95c 2.25 2.25
b. A70 $2.50 like $1.50 2.25 2.25

Nos. 359-363 Ovptd. for Olympic Gold Medalists

a. "CARL LEWIS / UNITED STATES / 100 METERS"
b. "LOUISE RITTER / UNITED STATES / HIGH JUMP"
c. "ULF TIMMERMANN / EAST GERMANY / SHOT-PUT"
d. "STEFFI GRAF / WEST GERMANY / WOMEN'S TENNIS"
e. "JACKIE / JOYNER-KERSEE / United States / Heptathlon"
f. "STEFFI GRAF / West Germany / Women's Tennis / MILOSLAV MECIR / Czechoslovakia / Men's Tennis"

Perf. 13½x13, 13x13½

1988, Oct. 14 **Photo.**

364 A70(a) 55c on No. 359 .75 .75
365 A70(b) 95c on No. 360 1.30 1.30
366 A70(c) $1.25 on No. 361 1.70 1.70
367 A70(d) $1.50 on No. 362 2.00 2.00
Nos. 364-367 (4) 5.75 5.75

Souvenir Sheet

368 Sheet of 2 6.75 6.75
a. A70(e) $2.50 on No. 363a 3.35 3.35
b. A70(f) $2.50 on No. 363b 3.35 3.35

Christmas — A71

Virgin and Child paintings by Titian.

1988, Nov. 9 *Perf. 13x13½*

369 A71 70c multicolored .80 .80
370 A71 85c multi, diff. .95 .95
371 A71 95c multi, diff. 1.00 1.00
372 A71 $1.25 multi, diff. 1.40 1.40
Nos. 369-372 (4) 4.15 4.15

Souvenir Sheet

Perf. 13

373 A71 $6.40 multi, diff. 7.00 7.00

No. 373 contains one diamond-shaped stamp, size: 55x55mm.

1st Moon Landing, 20th Anniv. A72

Apollo 11 mission emblem, US flag and: 55c, First step on the Moon. 75c, Astronaut carrying equipment. 95c, Conducting experiment. $1.25, Crew members Armstrong, Collins and Aldrin. $1.75, Armstrong and Aldrin aboard lunar module.

1989, July 24 **Photo.** *Perf. 14*

374 A72 55c multicolored .65 .65
375 A72 75c multicolored .90 .90
376 A72 95c multicolored 1.15 1.15
377 A72 $1.25 multicolored 1.50 1.50
378 A72 $1.75 multicolored 2.10 2.10
Nos. 374-378 (5) 6.30 6.30

Christmas — A73

Details from *The Nativity,* by Albrecht Durer, 1498, center panel of the Paumgartner altarpiece: 55c, Madonna. 70c, Christ child, cherubs. 85c, Joseph. $1.25, Attendants. $6.40, Entire painting.

1989, Nov. 17 **Photo.** *Perf. 13x13½*

379 A73 55c multicolored .65 .65
380 A73 70c multicolored .82 .82
381 A73 85c multicolored 1.00 1.00
382 A73 $1.25 multicolored 1.45 1.45
Nos. 379-382 (4) 3.92 3.92

Souvenir Sheet

383 A73 $6.40 multicolored 6.75 6.75

No. 383 contains one 31x50mm stamp.

Queen Mother, 90th Birthday — A74

1990, July 24 **Photo.** *Perf. 13½*

384 A74 $2.25 multicolored 2.75 2.75

Souvenir Sheet

385 A74 $7.50 multicolored 8.75 8.75

Christmas — A75

Paintings: 55c, Adoration of the Magi by Veronese. 70c, Virgin and Child by Quentin Metsys. 85c, Virgin and Child Jesus by Van Der Goes. $1.50, Adoration of the Kings by Jan Gossaert. $6.40, Virgin and Child with Saints Francis, John the Baptist, Zenobius and Lucy by Domenico Veneziano.

1990, Nov. 26 **Litho.** *Perf. 14*

386 A75 55c multicolored .68 .68
387 A75 70c multicolored .85 .85
388 A75 85c multicolored 1.00 1.00
389 A75 $1.50 multicolored 1.85 1.85
Nos. 386-389 (4) 4.38 4.38

Souvenir Sheet

390 A75 $6.40 multicolored 7.00 7.00

Nos. 311-314 Surcharged in Red or Black **$1.50**

1990, Dec. 5 **Photo.** *Perf. 13*

391 A59 $1.50 on 20c (R) 1.85 1.85
392 A59 $1.50 on 55c 1.85 1.85
393 A59 $1.50 on 65c 1.85 1.85
394 A59 $1.50 on 75c (R) 1.85 1.85
Nos. 391-394 (4) 7.40 7.40

Birdpex '90, 20th Intl. Ornithological Cong., New Zealand. Surcharge appears in various locations.

No. 172 Overprinted "COMMEMORATING 65th BIRTHDAY OF H.M. QUEEN ELIZABETH II"

1991, Apr. 22 **Photo.** *Perf. 13½*

395 A42 $6 multicolored 7.00 7.00

Christmas A76

Paintings: 55c, Virgin and Child with Saints, by Gerard David. 85c, The Nativity, by Tintoretto. $1.15, Mystic Nativity, by Botticelli. $1.85, Adoration of the Shepherds, by Murillo. $6.40, Madonna of the Chair, by Raphael.

1991, Nov. 11 **Litho.** *Perf. 14*

396 A76 55c multicolored .65 .65
397 A76 85c multicolored 1.00 1.00
398 A76 $1.15 multicolored 1.35 1.35
399 A76 $1.85 multicolored 2.15 2.15
Nos. 396-399 (4) 5.15 5.15

Souvenir Sheet

400 A76 $6.40 multicolored 7.40 7.40

1992 Summer Olympics, Barcelona — A77

1992, July 27 **Litho.** *Perf. 14*

401 A77 75c Runners .90 .90
402 A77 95c Boxing 1.20 1.20
403 A77 $1.15 Swimming 1.45 1.45
404 A77 $1.50 Wrestling 1.90 1.90
Nos. 401-404 (4) 5.45 5.45

6th Festival of Pacific Arts, Rarotonga — A78

Festival poster and: $1.15, Marquesan canoe. $1.75, Statue of Tangaroa. $1.95, Manihiki canoe.

1992, Oct. 16 **Litho.** *Perf. 14x15*

405 A78 $1.15 multicolored 1.20 1.20
406 A78 $1.75 multicolored 1.80 1.80
407 A78 $1.95 multicolored 2.00 2.00
Nos. 405-407 (3) 5.00 5.00

Overprinted "ROYAL VISIT"

1992, Oct. 16

408 A78 $1.15 on #405 1.20 1.20
409 A78 $1.75 on #406 1.80 1.80
410 A78 $1.95 on #407 2.00 2.00
Nos. 408-410 (3) 5.00 5.00

Christmas A79

Paintings by Ambrogio Borgognone: 55c, $6.40, Virgin with Child and Saints. 85c, Virgin on Throne. $1.05, Virgin on Carpet. $1.85, Virgin of the Milk.

1992, Nov. 18 **Litho.** *Perf. 13½*

411 A79 55c multicolored .58 .58
412 A79 85c multicolored .90 .90
413 A79 $1.05 multicolored 1.10 1.10
414 A79 $1.85 multicolored 1.90 1.90
Nos. 411-414 (4) 4.48 4.48

Souvenir Sheet

415 A79 $6.40 multicolored 6.50 6.50

No. 415 contains one 38x48mm stamp.

Discovery of America, 500th Anniv. — A80

Designs: $1.15, Vicente Yanez Pinzon, Nina. $1.35, Martin Alonso Pinzon, Pinta. $1.75, Columbus, Santa Maria.

1992, Dec. 4 *Perf. 15x14*

416 A80 $1.15 multicolored 1.20 1.20
417 A80 $1.35 multicolored 1.40 1.40
418 A80 $1.75 multicolored 1.85 1.85
Nos. 416-418 (3) 4.45 4.45

Coronation of Queen Elizabeth II, 40th Anniv. — A81

1993, June 4 **Litho.** *Perf. 14x14½*

419 A81 $6 multicolored 6.75 6.75

Marine Life — A82

Marine Life — A82a

1993-97 **Litho.** *Perf. 14*

420 A82 5c Helmet shell .15 .15
421 A82 10c Daisy coral .15 .15
422 A82 15c Hydroid coral .18 .18
423 A82 20c Feather star .22 .22
424 A82 25c Sea star .28 .28
425 A82 30c Nudibranch .35 .35
426 A82 50c Smooth sea star .58 .58
427 A82 70c Black pearl oyster .80 .80
428 A82 80c Pyjama nudibranch .90 .90
429 A82 85c Prickly sea cucumber .95 .95
430 A82 90c Organ pipe coral 1.00 1.00
431 A82 $1 Aeolid nudibranch 1.10 1.10
432 A82 $2 Textile cone shell 2.25 2.25
433 A82a $3 pink & multi 3.25 3.25
434 A82a $5 lilac & multi 5.50 5.50

Perf. 14x13½

435 A82a $8 blue & multi 11.00 11.00
Nos. 420-435 (16) 28.66 28.66

Issued: 80c, 85c, 90c, $1, $2, 12/3/93; $3, $5, 11/21/94; $8, 11/17/97; others, 10/18/93.

This is an expanding set. Numbers will change if necessary.

Christmas — A83

Details from Virgin on Throne with Child, by Cosimo Tura: 55c, Madonna and Child. 85c, Musicians. $1.05, Musicians, diff. $1.95, Woman. $4.50, Entire painting.

1993, Nov. 2 Litho. *Perf. 14*
436 A83 55c multicolored .60 .60
437 A83 85c multicolored .95 .95
438 A83 $1.05 multicolored 1.10 1.10
439 A83 $1.95 multicolored 2.25 2.25

Size: 32x47mm
Perf. 13½
440 A83 $4.50 multicolored 5.00 5.00
Nos. 436-440 (5) 9.90 9.90

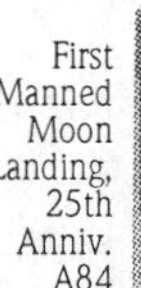

First Manned Moon Landing, 25th Anniv. A84

1994, July 20 Litho. *Perf. 14*
441 A84 $3.25 multicolored 3.50 3.50

Christmas — A85

Details or entire paintings: No. 442a, Virgin and Child with Saints Paul & Jerome, by Vivarini. b, The Virgin and Child with St. John, by B. Luini. c, The Virgin and Child with Saints Jerome & Dominic, by F. Lippi. d, Adoration of Shepherds, by Murillo.

No. 443a, Adoration of the Kings, by Reni. b, Madonna & Child with the Infant Baptist, by Raphael. c, Adoration of the Kings, by Reni, diff. d, Virgin and Child, by Bergognone.

1994, Nov. 30 Litho. *Perf. 14*
442 A85 90c Block of 4, #a.-d. 4.50 4.50
443 A85 $1 Block of 4, #a.-d. 5.00 5.00

End of World War II, 50th Anniv. — A86

Designs: a, Battleships on fire, Pearl Harbor, Dec. 7, 1941. b, B-29 bomber Enola Gay, A-bomb cloud, Aug. 1945.

1995, Sept. 4 Litho. *Perf. 13*
444 A86 $3.75 Pair, #a.-b. 10.00 10.00

Queen Mother, 95th Birthday A87

1995, Sept. 14 Litho. *Perf. 13½*
445 A87 $4.50 multicolored 6.00 6.00

No. 445 was issued in sheets of 4.

UN, 50th Anniv. — A88

1995, Oct. 20 Litho. *Perf. 13½*
446 A88 $4 multicolored 5.25 5.25

No. 446 was issued in sheets of 4.

1995, Year of the Sea Turtle — A89

No. 447: a, Loggerhead. b, Hawksbill.
No. 448: a, Olive ridley. b, Green.

1995, Dec. 7 Litho. *Perf. 13½*
447 A89 $1.15 Pair, #a.-b. 3.00 3.00
448 A89 $1.65 Pair, #a.-b. 4.50 4.50

Queen Elizabeth II, 70th Birthday A90

1996, June 20 Litho. *Perf. 14*
449 A90 $4.25 multicolored 6.00 6.00

No. 449 was issued in sheets of 4.

1996 Summer Olympic Games, Atlanta A91

1996, July 12 Litho. *Perf. 14*
450 A91 $5 multicolored 6.90 6.90

Queen Elizabeth II and Prince Philip, 50th Wedding Anniv. A92

1997, Nov. 20 Litho. *Perf. 14*
451 A92 $3 multicolored 4.25 4.25

Souvenir Sheet
452 A92 $4 multicolored 5.50 5.50

No. 452 is a continuous design.

SEMI-POSTAL STAMPS

Catalogue values for unused stamps in this section are for Never Hinged items.

Easter Type of 1978
Souvenir Sheets

Rubens Paintings: No. B1, like #101. No. B2, like #102. No. B3, like #103.

1978, Apr. 17 Photo. *Perf. 13½x13*
B1 A31 60c + 5c multi .75 .75
B2 A31 60c + 5c multi .75 .75
B3 A31 60c + 5c multi .75 .75

Surtax was for school children.

Easter Type of 1980
Souvenir Sheets

1980, Mar. 28 Photo. *Perf. 13x13½*
B4 A36 70c + 5c like #114 .75 .75
B5 A36 70c + 5c like #115 .75 .75
B6 A36 70c + 5c like #116 .75 .75

Surtax was for local charities.

Christmas Type of 1980
Souvenir Sheets

1980, Dec. 5 Photo. *Perf. 13*
B7 A39 70c + 5c like #127 1.00 1.00
B8 A39 70c + 5c like #128 1.00 1.00
B9 A39 70c + 5c like #129 1.00 1.00

Surtax was for local charities.

Easter Type of 1981
Souvenir Sheets

1981, Apr. 5 Photo. *Perf. 13½*
B10 A44 70c + 5c like #173 .90 .90
B11 A44 70c + 5c like #174 .90 .90
B12 A44 70c + 5c like #175 .90 .90

Surtax was for local charities.

Nos. 176-180a Surcharged

1981, Nov. 30 Photo. *Perf. 14*
B13 A45 40c + 5c like #176 .35 .35
B14 A45 50c + 5c like #177 .40 .40
B15 A45 60c + 5c like #178 .50 .50
B16 A45 70c + 5c like #179 .60 .60
B17 A45 80c + 5c like #180 .65 .65
Nos. B13-B17 (5) 2.50 2.50

Souvenir Sheet
B18 Sheet of 5 4.75 4.75
a. A45 40c + 10c like #176 .65 .65
b. A45 50c + 10c like #177 .75 .75
c. A45 60c + 10c like #178 .90 .90
d. A45 70c + 10c like #179 1.10 1.10
e. A45 80c + 10c like #180 1.25 1.25

Intl. Year of the Disabled. Surtax was for the disabled.

Soccer Type of 1981

1981, Dec. 7 *Perf. 13*
B19 A46 Sheet of 9 5.50 5.50

No. B19 contains Nos. 181-183. Surtax was for local sports.

Nos. 346-349 Surcharged ".SOUTH PACIFIC PAPAL VISIT . 21 TO 24 NOVEMBER 1986" in Metallic Blue

1986, Nov. 24 Litho. *Perf. 13x13½*
B20 A67 65c + 10c multi .80 .80
B21 A67 $1.75 + 10c multi 2.00 2.00
B22 A67 $2.50 + 10c multi 2.75 2.75
Nos. B20-B22 (3) 5.55 5.55

Souvenir Sheet
Perf. 13½x13
B23 Sheet of 3 5.25 5.25
a.-c. A67 $1.50 + 10c on #349a-349c 1.75 1.75

No. B23 inscribed "COMMEMORATING FIRST PAPAL VISIT TO SOUTH PACIFIC / VISIT OF POPE JOHN PAUL II . NOVEMBER 1986."

OFFICIAL STAMPS

Catalogue values for unused stamps in this section are for Never Hinged items.

Nos. 51-60, 80, 88-89 Overprinted or Surcharged in Black, Silver or Gold **O.H.M.S**

Perf. 13½x14, 13½, 13½x13
1978, Nov. 14 Photo.
O1 A17 1c multi .15 .15
O2 A17 2c multi .15 .15
O3 A17 3c multi .15 .15
O4 A17 4c multi .15 .15
O5 A17 5c multi .15 .15
O6 A17 8c multi .15 .15
O7 A17 10c multi .18 .18
O8 A17 15c on 60c multi .25 .25
O9 A17 18c on 60c multi .35 .35
O10 A17 20c multi .38 .38
O11 A17 25c multi (S) .40 .40
O12 A17 30c on 60c multi .60 .60
O13 A24 Strip of 3, multi 2.75 2.75
a. 50c, No. 80a (G) .80 .80
b. 50c, No. 80b (G) .80 .80
c. 50c, No. 80c (G) .80 .80
O14 A27 $1 multi (S) 2.00 2.00
O15 A27 $2 multi (G) 4.00 4.00
Nos. O1-O15 (15) 11.81 11.81

Overprint on No. O14 diagonal.

Nos. 268-276, 278, 277, 211-214, 280, 282, 281, 283, 170, 284, 171, 285, 172, 286 Surcharged with Bar and New Value or Ovptd. "O.H.M.S." in Silver or Metallic Red

1985-87 Photo. *Perfs. as before*
O16 A56 2c multi .15 .15
O17 A56 4c multi .15 .15
O18 A56 5c multi .15 .15
O19 A56 8c multi .15 .15
O20 A56 10c multi .15 .15
O21 A56 18c multi .20 .20
O22 A56 20c multi .22 .22
O23 A56 30c multi .35 .35
O24 A56 40c on 36c .45 .45
O25 A56 50c multi .55 .55
O26 A56 55c on 48c .62 .62
O27 A50 65c on 60c #211 .72 .72
O28 A50 65c on 60c #212 .72 .72
O29 A50 65c on 60c #213 .72 .72
O30 A50 65c on 60c #214 .72 .72
O31 A56 75c on 72c .85 .85
O32 A56 75c on 96c .85 .85
O33 A56 80c multi .90 .90
O34 A56 $1.20 multi 1.35 1.35
O35 A42 $2 multi (R) 2.25 2.25
O36 A56 $3 multi 3.35 3.35
O37 A42 $4 multi (R) 4.50 4.50
O38 A56 $5 multi 6.00 6.00
O39 A42 $6 multi (R) 7.25 7.25
O40 A56 $9.60 multi 11.75 11.75
Nos. O16-O40 (25) 45.07 45.07

Issue dates: Nos. O16-O30, Aug. 15; Nos. O31-O37, Apr. 29, 1986; Nos. O38-O40, Nov. 2, 1987.

15-Cent Minimum Value
The minimum catalogue value is 15 cents. Separating se-tenant pieces into individual stamps does not increase the value of the stamps since demand for the separated stamps may be small.

PERU

pə-'rü

LOCATION — West coast of South America
GOVT. — Republic
AREA — 496,093 sq. mi.
POP. — 18,300,000 (est. 1982)
CAPITAL — Lima

8 Reales = 1 Peso (1857)
100 Centimos = 8 Dineros =
4 Pesetas = 1 Peso (1858)
100 Centavos = 1 Sol (1874)
100 Centimos = 1 Inti (1985)
100 Centimos = 1 Sol (1991)

Catalogue values for unused stamps in this country are for Never Hinged items, beginning with Scott 426 in the regular postage section, Scott B1 in the semi-postal section, Scott C78 in the airpost section, Scott CB1 in the airpost semi-postal section, and Scott RA31 in the postal tax section.

Watermark

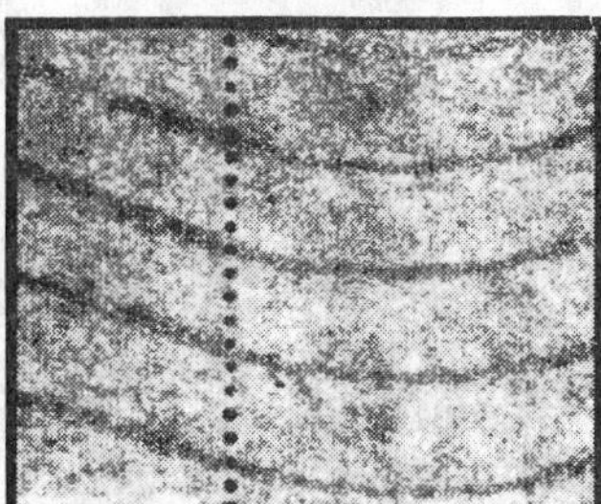

Wmk. 346- Parallel Curved Lines

Sail and Steamship — A1

Design: 2r, Ship sails eastward.

1857, Dec. 1 Unwmk. Engr. *Imperf.*

1	A1 1r blue, *blue*	1,250.	1,450.
2	A1 2r brn red, *blue*	1,350.	1,600.

The Pacific Steam Navigation Co. gave a quantity of these stamps to the Peruvian government so that a trial of prepayment of postage by stamps might be made.

Stamps of 1 and 2 reales, printed in various colors on white paper, laid and wove, were prepared for the Pacific Steam Navigation Co. but never put in use. Value $50 each on wove paper, $400 each on laid paper.

Coat of Arms
A2 A3

A4

Wavy Lines in Spandrels

1858, Mar. 1 Litho.

3	A2 1d deep blue	200.	28.
4	A3 1p rose red	850.	130.
5	A4 ½peso rose red	*3,750.*	*3,000.*
6	A4 ½peso buff	*1,600.*	300.
a.	½peso orange yellow	*1,600.*	300.

A5 A6

Large Letters

1858, Dec.

Double-lined Frame

7	A5 1d slate blue	250.00	27.50
8	A6 1p red	250.00	37.50

A7 A8

1860-61

Zigzag Lines in Spandrels

9	A7 1d blue	100.00	6.50
a.	1d Prussian blue	100.00	12.00
b.	Cornucopia on white ground	225.00	47.50
c.	Zigzag lines broken at angles	125.00	14.00
10	A8 1p rose	250.00	25.00
a.	1p brick red	250.00	25.00
b.	Cornucopia on white ground	250.00	30.00

Retouched, 10 lines instead of 9 in left label

11	A8 1p rose	130.00	25.00
a.	Pelure paper	200.00	25.00
	Nos. 9-11 (3)	480.00	56.50

A9 A10

1862-63 Embossed

12	A9 1d red	13.00	2.75
a.	Arms embossed sideways	425.00	90.00
b.	Thick paper	27.50	8.00
c.	Diag. half used on cover		140.00
13	A10 1p brown ('63)	72.50	22.50
a.	Diag. half used on cover		1,000.

Counterfeits of Nos. 13 and 15 exist.

A11

1868-72

14	A11 1d green	11.00	2.25
a.	Arms embossed inverted	*1,200.*	*700.00*
b.	Diag. half used on cover		350.00
15	A10 1p orange ('72)	90.00	32.50
a.	Diag. half used on cover		—

Nos. 12-15, 19 and 20 were printed in horizontal strips. Stamps may be found printed on two strips of paper where the strips were joined by overlapping.

Llamas — A12

A13

A14

1866-67 Engr. *Perf. 12*

16	A12 5c green	6.00	.65
17	A13 10c vermilion	6.00	1.40
18	A14 20c brown	20.00	4.00
a.	Diagonal half used on cover		375.00
	Nos. 16-18 (3)	32.00	6.05

See Nos. 109, 111, 113.

Locomotive and Arms — A15

Llama — A16

1871, Apr. Embossed *Imperf.*

19	A15 5c scarlet	75.00	25.00
a.	5c pale red	75.00	25.00

20th anniv. of the first railway in South America, linking Lima and Callao.

The so-called varieties "ALLAO" and "CALLA" are due to over-inking.

1873, Mar. *Rouletted Horiz.*

20	A16 2c dk ultra	30.00	*250.00*

Counterfeits are plentiful.

Sun God of the Incas — A17

Coat of Arms
A18 A19

A20 A21

A22 A23

Embossed with Grill

1874-84 Engr. *Perf. 12*

21	A17 1c orange ('79)	.50	.40
22	A18 2c dk violet	.65	.50
23	A19 5c blue ('77)	.85	.25
24	A19 5c ultra ('79)	8.50	2.00
25	A20 10c green ('76)	.25	.22
a.	Imperf., pair	25.00	
26	A20 10c slate ('84)	2.00	.25
a.	Diag. half used as 5c on cover		—
27	A21 20c brown red	2.00	.65
28	A22 50c green	9.00	2.50
29	A23 1s rose	1.50	1.50
	Nos. 21-29 (9)	25.25	8.27

No. 25a lacks the grill.

No. 26 with overprint "DE OFICIO" is said to have been used to frank mail of Gen. A. A. Caceres during the civil war against Gen. Miguel Iglesias, provisional president. Experts question its status.

1880

30	A17 1c green	2.00
31	A18 2c rose	2.00

Nos. 30 and 31 were prepared for use but not issued without overprint.

See Nos. 104-108, 110, 112, 114-115.

For overprints see Nos. 32-103, 116-128, J32-J33, O2-O22, N11-N23, 1N1-1N9, 3N11-3N20, 5N1, 6N1-6N2, 7N1-7N2, 8N7, 8N10-8N11, 9N1-9N3, 10N3-10N8, 10N10-10N11, 11N1-11N5, 12N1-12N3, 13N1, 14N1-14N16, 15N5-15N8, 15N13-15N18, 16N1-16N22.

Stamps of 1874-80 Overprinted in Red, Blue or Black

Reduced illustration

1880, Jan. 5

32	A17 1c green (R)	.50	.40
a.	Inverted overprint	10.00	10.00
b.	Double overprint	13.50	13.50
33	A18 2c rose (Bl)	1.00	.65
a.	Inverted overprint	10.00	10.00
b.	Double overprint	14.00	12.00
34	A18 2c rose (Bk)	45.00	35.00
a.	Inverted overprint		
b.	Double overprint		
35	A19 5c ultra (R)	2.00	1.00
a.	Inverted overprint	10.00	10.00
b.	Double overprint	14.00	14.00
36	A22 50c green (R)	27.50	17.50
a.	Inverted overprint	45.00	45.00
b.	Double overprint	55.00	55.00
37	A23 1s rose (Bl)	70.00	45.00
a.	Inverted overprint	110.00	110.00
b.	Double overprint	110.00	110.00
	Nos. 32-37 (6)	146.00	99.55

Stamps of 1874-80 Overprinted in Red or Blue

Reduced illustration

1881, Jan. 28

38	A17 1c green (R)	.75	.60
a.	Inverted overprint	8.25	8.25
b.	Double overprint	14.00	14.00
39	A18 2c rose (Bl)	14.00	9.00
a.	Inverted overprint	17.50	15.00
b.	Double overprint	25.00	20.00
40	A19 5c ultra (R)	1.50	.75
a.	Inverted overprint	14.00	14.00
b.	Double overprint	20.00	20.00
41	A22 50c green (R)	450.00	250.00
a.	Inverted overprint	600.00	
42	A23 1s rose (Bl)	82.50	55.00
a.	Inverted overprint	150.00	

Reprints of Nos. 38 to 42 were made in 1884. In the overprint the word "PLATA" is 3mm high instead of 2½mm. The cross bars of the letters "A" of that word are set higher than on the original stamps. The 5c is printed in blue instead of ultramarine.

For stamps of 1874-80 overprinted with Chilean arms or small UPU "horseshoe," see Nos. N11-N23.

Stamps of 1874-79 Handstamped in Black or Blue

1883

65	A17 1c orange (Bk)	.85	.65
66	A17 1c orange (Bl)	45.00	
68	A19 5c ultra (Bk)	7.50	5.00
69	A20 10c green (Bk)	.75	.65
70	A20 10c green (Bl)	5.00	4.00
71	A22 50c green (Bk)	7.00	3.50
73	A23 1s rose (Bk)	10.00	6.00
	Nos. 65-73 (7)	76.10	

This overprint is found in 11 types.

The 1c green, 2c dark violet and 20c brown red, overprinted with triangle, are fancy varieties made for sale to collectors and never placed in regular use.

Overprinted Triangle and "Union Postal Universal Peru" in Oval

1883

77	A22 50c grn (R & Bk)	120.00	60.00
78	A23 1s rose (Bl & Bk)	140.00	90.00

The 1c green, 2c rose and 5c ultramarine, over printed with triangle and "U. P. U. Peru" oval, were never placed in regular use.

Overprinted Triangle and "Union Postal Universal Lima" in Oval

1883

79	A17 1c grn (R & Bl)	50.00	37.50
80	A17 1c grn (R & Bk)	4.00	4.00
a.	Oval overprint inverted		
b.	Double overprint of oval		
81	A18 2c rose (Bl & Bk)	4.00	4.00
82	A19 5c ultra (R & Bk)	6.50	6.00
83	A19 5c ultra (R & Bl)	6.50	6.00
84	A22 50c grn (R & Bk)	140.00	90.00
85	A23 1s rose (Bl & Bk)	150.00	125.00
	Nos. 79-85 (7)	361.00	272.50

Some authorities question the status of No. 79.

Nos. 80, 81, 84, and 85 were reprinted in 1884. They have the second type of oval overprint with "PLATA" 3mm high.

Overprinted Triangle and

86	A17	1c grn (Bk & Bk)	1.00	.80
a.		Horseshoe inverted	10.00	
87	A17	1c grn (Bl & Bk)	5.00	3.50
88	A18	2c ver (Bk & Bk)	1.00	.75
89	A19	5c bl (Bk & Bk)	1.25	1.00
90	A19	5c bl (Bl & Bk)	7.00	6.50
91	A19	5c bl (R & Bk)	*1,500.*	*1,100.*

Overprinted Horseshoe Alone

1883, Oct. 23

95	A17	1c green	1.25	1.25
96	A18	2c vermilion	1.20	*4.00*
a.		Double overprint		
97	A19	5c blue	2.00	2.00
98	A19	5c ultra	20.00	15.00
99	A22	50c rose	57.50	57.50
100	A23	1s ultra	30.00	22.50
		Nos. 95-100 (6)	111.95	102.25

The 2c violet overprinted with the above design in red and triangle in black also the 1c green overprinted with the same combination plus the horseshoe in black, are fancy varieties made for sale to collectors.

No. 23 Overprinted in Black

1884, Apr. 28

103	A19	5c blue	.65	.40
a.		Double overprint	5.00	5.00

Stamps of 1c and 2c with the above overprint, also with the above and "U. P. U. LIMA" oval in blue or "CORREOS LIMA" in a double-lined circle in red, were made to sell to collectors and were never placed in use.

Without Overprint or Grill

1886-95

104	A17	1c dull violet	.50	.16
105	A17	1c vermilion ('95)	.40	.22
106	A18	2c green	.75	.16
107	A18	2c dp ultra ('95)	.35	.22
108	A19	5c orange	.60	.30
109	A12	5c claret ('95)	1.25	.50
110	A20	10c slate	.40	.15
111	A13	10c orange ('95)	.60	.35
112	A21	20c blue	5.00	.65
113	A14	20c dp ultra ('95)	6.00	1.40
114	A22	50c red	1.50	.65
115	A23	1s brown	1.25	.50
		Nos. 104-115 (12)	18.60	5.26

Overprinted Horseshoe in Black and Triangle in Rose Red

1889

116	A17	1c green	.75	.50
a.		Horseshoe inverted	7.50	

Nos. 30 and 25 Overprinted "Union Postal Universal Lima" in Oval in Red

1889, Sept. 1

117	A17	1c green	1.50	1.25
117A	A20	10c green	1.50	1.50

The overprint on Nos. 117 and 117A is of the second type with "PLATA" 3mm high.

Stamps of 1874-80 Overprinted in Black

Pres. Remigio Morales Bermúdez

1894, Oct. 23

118	A17	1c orange	.60	.42
a.		Inverted overprint	7.00	7.00
b.		Double overprint	7.00	7.00
119	A17	1c green	.40	.35
a.		Inverted overprint	3.50	3.50
b.		Dbl. inverted ovpt.	5.00	5.00
120	A18	2c violet	.40	.35
a.		Diagonal half used as 1c		
b.		Inverted overprint	7.00	7.00
c.		Double overprint	7.00	
121	A18	2c rose	.40	.35
a.		Double overprint	7.00	7.00
b.		Inverted overprint	7.00	7.00
122	A19	5c blue	2.50	1.75
122A	A19	5c ultra	4.25	2.00
b.		Inverted overprint	10.00	10.00
123	A20	10c green	.40	.35
a.		Inverted overprint	7.00	7.00
124	A22	50c green	1.40	1.20
a.		Inverted overprint	10.00	10.00
		Nos. 118-124 (8)	10.35	6.77

Same, with Additional Overprint of Horseshoe

125	A18	2c vermilion	.35	.25
a.		Head inverted	2.50	2.50
b.		Head double	5.00	5.00
126	A19	5c blue	1.00	.50
a.		Head inverted	7.00	7.00
127	A22	50c rose	42.50	30.00
a.		Head double	55.00	45.00
b.		Head inverted		
128	A23	1s ultra	100.00	90.00
a.		Both overprints inverted	125.00	110.00
b.		Head double	125.00	110.00
		Nos. 125-128 (4)	143.85	120.75

A23a

1895 Vermilion Surcharge ***Perf. 11½***

129	A23a	5c on 5c grn	10.00	7.50
130	A23a	10c on 10c ver	8.00	6.00
131	A23a	20c on 20c brn	8.50	6.50
132	A23a	50c on 50c ultra	10.00	7.50
133	A23a	1s on 1s red brn	10.00	8.00
		Nos. 129-133 (5)	46.50	35.50

Nos 129-133 were used only in Tumbes. The basic stamps were prepared by revolutionaries in northern Peru.

"Liberty"
A23b A23c

1895, Sept. 8 **Engr.**

134	A23b	1c gray violet	1.25	.80
135	A23b	2c green	1.25	.65
136	A23b	5c yellow	1.25	.65
137	A23b	10c ultra	1.25	.65
138	A23c	20c orange	1.25	1.00
139	A23c	50c dark blue	7.25	4.50
140	A23c	1s car lake	37.50	25.00
		Nos. 134-140 (7)	51.00	33.25

Success of the revolution against the government of General Caceres and of the election of President Pierola.

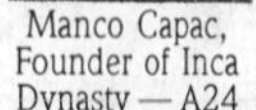
Manco Capac, Founder of Inca Dynasty — A24

Francisco Pizarro Conqueror of the Inca Empire — A25

General José de La Mar — A26

1896-1900

141	A24	1c ultra	.50	.15
a.		1c blue (error)	40.00	35.00
142	A24	1c yel grn ('98)	.50	.15
143	A24	2c blue	.50	.15
144	A24	2c scar ('99)	.50	.15
145	A25	5c indigo	.75	.16
146	A25	5c green ('97)	.75	.15
147	A25	5c grnsh bl ('99)	.50	.15
148	A25	10c yellow	1.00	.22
149	A25	10c gray blk ('00)	1.00	.15
150	A25	20c orange	2.00	.22
151	A26	50c car rose	5.00	.80
152	A26	1s orange red	7.50	1.00
153	A26	2s claret	2.25	.80
		Nos. 141-153 (13)	22.75	4.25

The 5c in black is a chemical changeling.

For surcharges and overprints see Nos. 187-188, E1, O23-O26.

Paucartambo Bridge — A27

Post and Telegraph Building, Lima — A28

Pres. Nicolás de Piérola — A29

1897, Dec. 31

154	A27	1c dp ultra	.65	.35
155	A28	2c brown	.65	.22
156	A29	5c bright rose	1.00	.25
		Nos. 154-156 (3)	2.30	.82

Opening of new P.O. in Lima.

A30 A31

1897, Nov. 8

157	A30	1c bister	.50	.45
a.		Inverted overprint	2.50	2.50
b.		Double overprint	10.00	10.00

1899

158	A31	5s orange red	1.65	1.65
159	A31	10s blue green	500.00	350.00

For surcharge see No. J36.

Pres. Eduardo de Romaña — A32

Admiral Miguel L. Grau — A33

1900 **Frame Litho., Center Engr.**

160	A32	22c yel grn & blk	8.00	.85

1901, Jan.

2c, Col. Francisco Bolognes. 5c, Pres. Romaña.

161	A33	1c green & blk	1.00	.22
162	A33	2c red & black	1.00	.22
163	A33	5c dull vio & blk	1.00	.22
		Nos. 161-163 (3)	3.00	.66

Advent of 20th century.

A34

Municipal Hygiene Institute Lima — A35

1902 **Engr.**

164	A34	22c green	.35	.20

1905

165	A35	12c dp blue & blk	1.00	.22

For surcharges see Nos. 166-167, 186, 189.

Same Surcharged in Red or Violet

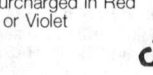

1907

166	A35	1c on 12c (R)	.25	.20
a.		Inverted surcharge	8.00	8.00
b.		Double surcharge	8.00	8.00
167	A35	2c on 12c (V)	.50	.35
a.		Double surcharge	8.00	8.00
b.		Inverted surcharge	8.00	8.00

Monument of Bolognesi — A36

Admiral Grau — A37

Llama — A38

Statue of Bolivar — A39

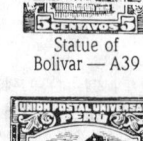

City Hall, Lima, formerly an Exhibition Building — A40

School of Medicine, Lima — A41

Post and Telegraph Building, Lima — A42

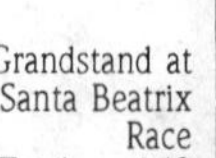

Grandstand at Santa Beatrix Race Track — A43

Columbus Monument — A44

1907

168	A36	1c yel grn & blk	.35	.15
169	A37	2c red & violet	.35	.15
170	A38	4c olive green	5.50	.75
171	A39	5c blue & blk	.60	.15
172	A40	10c red brn & blk	1.00	.22
173	A41	20c dk grn & blk	22.50	.50
174	A42	50c black	22.50	1.00
175	A43	1s purple & grn	125.00	2.50
176	A44	2s dp bl & blk	125.00	100.00
		Nos. 168-176 (9)	302.80	105.42

For surcharges and overprint see #190-195, E2.

Manco Capac A45

Columbus A46

Pizarro — A47

San Martin — A48

Bolívar — A49

La Mar — A50

Ramón Castilla — A51

Grau — A52

Bolognesi — A53

1909

177	A45	1c gray	.20	.15
178	A46	2c green	.20	.15
179	A47	4c vermilion	.30	.15
180	A48	5c violet	.20	.15
181	A49	10c deep blue	.50	.15
182	A50	12c pale blue	1.00	.15
183	A51	20c brown red	1.10	.22
184	A52	50c yellow	5.00	.35
185	A53	1s brn red & blk	10.00	.35
		Nos. 177-185 (9)	18.50	
		Set value		1.45

See types A54, A78-A80, A81-A89.
For surcharges and overprint see Nos. 196-200, 208, E3.

No. 165 Surcharged in Red

1913, Jan.

186	A35	8c on 12c dp bl & blk	.65	.22

Stamps of 1899-1908 Surcharged in Magenta

UN CENTAVO 1915
a

UN CENTAVO 1915
b

2 CENTAVOS 1915
c

1915

On Nos. 142, 149

187	A24(a)	1c on 1c	16.50	12.00
a.		Inverted surcharge	22.50	18.00
188	A25(a)	1c on 10c	.80	.75

On No. 165

189	A35(c)	2c on 12c	.22	.20
a.		Inverted surcharge		

On Nos. 168-170, 172-174

190	A36(a)	1c on 1c	.65	.65
191	A37(a)	1c on 2c	1.00	1.00
192	A38(b)	1c on 4c	1.65	1.65
a.		Inverted surcharge	6.00	6.00
193	A40(b)	1c on 10c	.35	.30
a.		Inverted surcharge	2.50	2.50
193C	A40(c)	2c on 10c	100.00	80.00
194	A41(c)	2c on 20c	14.00	12.00
195	A42(c)	2c on 50c	2.00	2.00
		Nos. 187-195 (10)	137.17	110.55

Nos. 182-184, 179, 185 Surcharged in Red, Green or Violet

d

VALE 2 CENTAVOS 1916
e

VALE 10 CENTAVOS 1916
f

1916

196	A50(d)	1c on 12c (R)	.16	.15
a.		Double surcharge	2.00	2.00
b.		Green surcharge	4.50	4.50
197	A51(d)	1c on 20c (G)	.16	.15
198	A52(d)	1c on 50c (G)	.16	.15
a.		Inverted surcharge	2.00	2.00
199	A47(e)	2c on 4c (V)	.16	.15
200	A53(f)	10c on 1s (G)	.50	.25
a.		"VALF"	3.50	3.50
		Nos. 196-200 (5)	1.14	.85

Official Stamps of 1909-14 Overprinted or Surcharged in Green or Red:

FRANQUEO 1916
g

FRANQUEO VALE 2 Cts 1916
h

1916

201	O1	1c red (G)	.15	.15
202	O1	2c on 50c ol grn (R)	.16	.16
203	O1	10c bis brn (G)	.20	.15

Postage Due Stamps of 1909 Surcharged in Violet-Black

204	D7	2c on 1c brown	.40	.40
205	D7	2c on 5c brown	.15	.15
206	D7	2c on 10c brown	.15	.15
207	D7	2c on 50c brown	.15	.15
		Nos. 201-207 (7)	1.36	1.31

Many copies of Nos. 187 to 207 have a number of pin holes. It is stated that these holes were made at the time the surcharges were printed.

The varieties which we list of the 1915 and 1916 issues were sold to the public at post offices. Many other varieties which were previously listed are now known to have been delivered to one speculator or to have been privately printed by him from the surcharging plates which he had acquired.

No. 179 Surcharged in Black

1917

208	A47	1c on 4c ver	.22	.16
a.		Double surcharge	4.00	4.00
b.		Inverted surcharge	4.00	4.00

San Martín A54

Columbus at Salamanca A62

Funeral of Atahualpa — A63

Battle of Arica, "Arica, the Last Cartridge" — A64

Designs: 2c, Bolivar. 4c, José Gálvez. 5c, Manuel Pardo. 8c, Grau. 10c, Bolognesi. 12c, Castilla. 20c, General Cáceres.

1918 **Engr.**

Centers in Black

209	A54	1c orange	.15	.15
210	A54	2c green	.20	.15
211	A54	4c lake	.30	.15
212	A54	5c dp ultra	.25	.15
213	A54	8c red brn	.75	.25
214	A54	10c grnsh bl	.35	.15
215	A54	12c dl vio	1.00	.16
216	A54	20c ol grn	1.25	.16
217	A62	50c vio brn	5.00	.35
218	A63	1s greenish bl	12.00	.50
219	A64	2s deep ultra	21.00	.65
		Nos. 209-219 (11)	42.25	
		Set value		2.40

For surcharges see Nos. 232-233, 255-256.

Augusto B. Leguía — A65

1919, Dec. **Litho.**

220	A65	5c bl & blk	.16	.16
a.		Imperf.	.35	.35
b.		Center inverted	11.00	11.00
221	A65	5c brn & blk	.15	.16
a.		Imperf.	.35	.35
b.		Center inverted	11.00	11.00

Constitution of 1919.

San Martín — A66

Thomas Cochrane — A70

Oath of Independence — A69

Designs: 2c, Field Marshal Arenales. 4c, Field Marshal Las Heras. 10c, Martin Jean Guisse. 12c, Vidal. 20c, Leguia. 50c, San Martin monument. 1s, San Martin and Leguia.

1921, July 28 **Engr.; 7c Litho.**

222	A66	1c ol brn & red brn	.28	.16
a.		Center inverted	350.00	325.00
223	A66	2c green	.28	.20
224	A66	4c car rose	.80	.60
225	A69	5c ol brn	.40	.15
226	A70	7c violet	.65	.28
227	A66	10c ultra	.80	.40
228	A66	12c blk & slate	2.50	.60
229	A66	20c car & gray blk	2.50	.80
230	A66	50c vio brn & dl vio	7.25	2.50
231	A69	1s car rose & yel grn	12.00	3.75
		Nos. 222-231 (10)	27.46	9.44

Centenary of Independence.

Nos. 213, 212 Surcharged in Black or Red Brown

CINCO Centavos 1923

CUATRO Centavos 1924

1923-24

232	A54	5c on 8c No. 213	.50	.25
233	A54	4c on 5c (RB) ('24)	.35	.16
a.		Inverted surcharge	5.00	5.00
b.		Double surcharge, one inverted	6.00	6.00

Simón Bolívar
A78 A79 A80

Perf. 14, 14x14½, 14½, 13½

1924 **Engr.; Photo. (4c, 5c)**

234	A78	2c olive grn	.28	.15
235	A79	4c yellow grn	.52	.15
236	A79	5c black	1.00	.15
237	A80	10c carmine	.60	.15
238	A78	20c ultra	1.25	.15
239	A78	50c dull violet	3.75	.80
240	A78	1s yellow brn	10.00	2.50
241	A78	2s dull blue	20.00	10.00
		Nos. 234-241 (8)	37.40	14.05

Centenary of the Battle of Ayacucho which ended Spanish power in South America.
No. 237 exists imperf.

José Tejada Rivadeneyra A81

Mariano Melgar A82

Iturregui A83

Leguía A84

José de La Mar — A85

Monument of José Olaya — A86

Statue of María Bellido — A87

De Saco — A88

José Leguía — A89

1924-29 Engr. *Perf. 12*
Size: 18½x23mm

242 A81 2c olive gray .20 .15
243 A82 4c dk grn .20 .15
244 A83 8c black 2.00 2.00
245 A84 10c org red .20 .15
245A A85 15c dp bl ('28) .60 .16
246 A86 20c blue .80 .15
247 A86 20c yel ('29) 1.50 .16
248 A87 50c violet 5.00 .32
249 A88 1s bis brn 9.00 .80
250 A89 2s ultra 22.50 5.00
Nos. 242-250 (10) 42.00 9.04

See Nos. 258, 260, 276-282.
For surcharges and overprint see Nos. 251-253, 257-260, 262, 268-271, C1.

No. 246 Surcharged in Red:

DOS Centavos 1925 a — **DOS Centavos 1925** b

1925
251 A86(a) 2c on 20c blue *350.00*
252 A86(b) 2c on 20c blue .80 .50
a. Inverted surcharge 35.00 35.00
b. Double surch., one inverted 50.00 50.00

No. 245 Overprinted **Plebiscito**

1925
253 A84 10c org red 1.00 1.00
a. Inverted overprint 17.50 17.50

This stamp was for exclusive use on letters from the plebiscite provinces of Tacna and Arica, and posted on the Peruvian transport "Ucayali" anchored in the port of Africa.

No. 213 Surcharged

Habilitada 2 Cts. 1929 a — **Habilitada 2 centavos 1929** b

1929
255 A54(a) 2c on 8c .75 .75
256 A54(b) 2c on 8c .75 .75

No. 247 Surcharged **Habilitada 15 cts. 1929**

257 A86 15c on 20c yellow .75 .75
a. Inverted surcharge 7.50 7.50
Nos. 255-257 (3) 2.25 2.25

Stamps of 1924 Issue
Coil Stamps

1929 *Perf. 14 Horizontally*
258 A81 2c olive gray 40.00 20.00
260 A84 10c orange red 45.00 17.50

Postal Tax Stamp of 1928 Overprinted **Habilitada Franqueo**

1930 *Perf. 12*
261 PT6 2c dark violet .35 .35
a. Inverted overprint 2.50 2.50

No. 247 Surcharged **Habilitada 2 Cts. 1930**

262 A86 2c on 20c yellow .22 .22

Air Post Stamp of 1928 Surcharged **Habilitada Franqueo 2 Cts. 1930**

263 AP1 2c on 50c dk grn .20 .15
a. "Habitada" 1.00 1.00

Coat of Arms — A91

Lima Cathedral — A92

10c, Children's Hospital. 50c, Madonna & Child.

Perf. 12x11½, 11½x12
1930, July 5 Litho.
264 A91 2c green .70 .70
265 A92 5c scarlet 1.65 1.25
266 A92 10c dark blue 1.10 1.00
267 A91 50c bister brown 18.00 12.00
Nos. 264-267 (4) 21.45 14.95

6th Pan American Congress for Child Welfare. By error the stamps are inscribed "Seventh Congress."

Type of 1924 Overprinted in Black, Green or Blue

1930, Dec. 22 Photo. *Perf. 15x14*
Size: 18¼x22mm
268 A84 10c orange red (Bk) .20 .15
a. Inverted overprint 10.00 10.00
b. Without overprint 6.50 6.50
c. Double surcharge 5.00 5.00

Same with Additional Surcharge of Numerals in Each Corner

269 A84 2c on 10c org red (G) .15 .15
a. Inverted surcharge 12.00
270 A84 4c on 10c org red (G) .20 .20
a. Double surcharge 8.25 8.25

Engr.
Perf. 12
Size: 19x23½mm
271 A84 15c on 10c org red (Bl) .30 .15
a. Inverted surcharge 10.00 10.00
b. Double surcharge 10.00 10.00
Nos. 268-271 (4) .85
Set value, #268-271 .44

Bolívar — A95

1930, Dec. 16 Litho.
272 A95 2c buff .35 .35
273 A95 4c red .65 .50
274 A95 10c blue green .35 .25
275 A95 15c slate gray .65 .65
Nos. 272-275 (4) 2.00 1.75

Death cent. of General Simón Bolívar.
For surcharges see Nos. RA14-RA16.

Types of 1924-29 Issues
Size: 18x22mm

1931 Photo. *Perf. 15x14*
276 A81 2c olive green .25 .15
277 A82 4c dark green .25 .15
279 A85 15c deep blue .75 .15
280 A86 20c yellow 1.25 .20
281 A87 50c violet 1.25 .25
282 A88 1s olive brown 2.00 .35
Nos. 276-282 (6) 5.75
Set value 1.00

Pizarro — A96

Old Stone Bridge, Lima — A97

1931, July 28 Litho. *Perf. 11*
283 A96 2c slate blue 1.65 1.40
284 A96 4c deep brown 1.65 1.40
285 A96 15c dark green 1.65 1.40
286 A97 10c rose red 1.65 1.40
287 A97 10c mag & lt grn 1.65 1.40
288 A97 15c yel & bl gray 1.65 1.40
289 A97 15c dk slate & red 1.65 1.40
Nos. 283-289 (7) 11.55 9.80

1st Peruvian Phil. Exhib., Lima, July, 1931.

Manco Capac — A99

Sugar Cane Field — A102

Oil Refinery A100

Guano Deposits A104

Picking Cotton — A103

Mining — A105

Llamas — A106

Arms of Piura — A107

1931-32 *Perf. 11, 11x11½*
292 A99 2c olive black .25 .15
293 A100 4c dark green .50 .16
295 A102 10c red orange 1.00 .15
a. Vertical pair, imperf. between 30.00
296 A103 15c turq blue 1.50 .16
297 A104 20c yellow 5.00 .25
298 A105 50c gray lilac 6.00 .25
299 A106 1s brown olive 13.00 1.00
Nos. 292-299 (7) 27.25 2.12

1932, July 28 *Perf. 11½x12*
300 A107 10c dark blue 6.00 6.00
301 A107 15c deep violet 6.00 6.00
Nos. 300-301,C3 (3) 32.00 31.00

400th anniv. of the founding of the city of Piura. On sale one day. Counterfeits exist.

Parakas A108

Chimu A109

Inca — A110

Perf. 11½, 12, 11½x12
1932, Oct. 15
302 A108 10c dk vio .20 .15
303 A109 15c brn red .40 .15
304 A110 50c dk brn .90 .16
Nos. 302-304 (3) 1.50
Set value .30

4th cent. of the Spanish conquest of Peru.

Arequipa and El Misti — A111

President Luis M. Sánchez Cerro — A112

Monument to Simón Bolívar at Lima A115

Statue of Liberty A116

1932-34 Photo. *Perf. 13½*
305 A111 2c black .16 .15
306 A111 2c blue blk .16 .15
307 A111 2c grn ('34) .16 .15
308 A111 4c dk brn .16 .15
309 A111 4c org ('34) .16 .15
310 A112 10c vermilion 13.00 10.00
311 A115 15c ultra .35 .15
312 A115 15c mag ('34) .35 .15
313 A115 20c red brn .75 .15
314 A115 20c vio ('34) .75 .15
315 A115 50c dk grn ('33) .75 .15
316 A115 1s dp org 6.00 .22
317 A115 1s org brn 7.50 .35
Nos. 305-317 (13) 30.25 12.07

For overprint see No. RA24.

1934
318 A116 10c rose .50 .15

Pizarro — A117

The Inca — A119

Coronation of Huascar — A118

1934-35 *Perf. 13*
319 A117 10c crimson .25 .15
320 A117 15c ultra .75 .15
321 A118 20c deep bl ('35) 1.25 .15
322 A118 50c dp red brn 1.00 .15
323 A119 1s dark vio 3.00 .35
Nos. 319-323 (5) 6.25
Set value .65

For surcharges and overprint see Nos. 354-355, J54, O32.

Pizarro and the Thirteen A120

Belle of Lima — A122

Francisco Pizarro — A123

4c, Lima Cathedral. 1s, Veiled woman of Lima.

1935, Jan. 18 *Perf. 13½*

No.	Type	Description	Unused	Used
324	A120	2c brown	.35	.20
325	A120	4c violet	.50	.38
326	A122	10c rose red	.50	.20
327	A123	15c ultra	.80	.60
328	A120	20c slate gray	1.40	.75
329	A122	50c olive grn	2.00	1.50
330	A122	1s Prus bl	4.50	3.00
331	A123	2s org brn	10.50	8.00
		Nos. 324-331,C6-C12 (15)	66.10	46.08

Founding of Lima, 4th cent.

View of Ica — A125

Lake Huacachina, Health Resort A126

Grapes — A127 Cotton Boll — A128

Zuniga y Velazco and Philip IV — A129

Supreme God of the Nazcas — A130

Engr.; Photo. (10c)

1935, Jan. 17 *Perf. 12½*

No.	Type	Description	Unused	Used
332	A125	4c gray blue	.80	.80
333	A126	5c dark car	.28	.80
334	A127	10c magenta	3.25	1.65
335	A126	20c green	1.25	1.25
336	A128	35c dark car	6.50	4.00
337	A129	50c org & brn	4.50	4.00
338	A130	1s pur & red	13.00	10.00
		Nos. 332-338 (7)	29.58	22.50

Founding of the City of Ica, 300th anniv.

Pizarro and the Thirteen — A131

1935-36 **Photo.** *Perf. 13½*

No.	Type	Description	Unused	Used
339	A131	2c dp claret	.25	.15
340	A131	4c bl grn ('36)	.25	.15
		Set value		.15

For surcharge and overprints see Nos. 353, J53, RA25-RA26.

"San Cristóbal," First Peruvian Warship — A132

Grand Marshal José de La Mar — A138

Naval College at Punta — A133

Independence Square, Callao A134

Aerial View of Callao A135

Plan of Walls of Callao in 1746 A137

Packetboat "Sacramento" A139

Viceroy José Antonio Manso de Velasco — A140

Fort Maipú — A141

Plan of Fort Real Felipe — A142

Design: 15c, Docks and Custom House.

1936, Aug. 27 **Photo.** *Perf. 12½*

No.	Type	Description	Unused	Used
341	A132	2c black	.52	.40
342	A133	4c bl grn	.52	.25
343	A134	5c yel brn	.52	.25
344	A135	10c bl gray	.52	.25
345	A135	15c green	.52	.25
346	A137	20c dk brn	.52	.25
347	A138	50c purple	1.10	.50
348	A139	1s olive grn	9.50	2.00

Engr.

No.	Type	Description	Unused	Used
349	A140	2s violet	13.00	6.00
350	A141	5s carmine	18.00	14.00
351	A142	10s red org & brn	45.00	35.00
		Nos. 341-351,C13 (12)	92.22	60.55

Province of Callao founding, cent.

Nos. 340, 321 and 323 Surcharged in Black

Habilitado

S. 0.10 Cts.

1936 *Perf. 13½, 13*

No.	Type	Description	Unused	Used
353	A131	2c on 4c bl grn	.15	.15
a.		"0.20" for "0.02"	3.50	3.50
354	A118	10c on 20c dp bl	.25	.15
a.		Double surcharge	3.50	
b.		Inverted surcharge	3.50	
355	A119	10c on 1s dk vio	.35	.35
		Nos. 353-355 (3)	.75	
		Set value		.54

Many varieties of the surcharge are found on these stamps: no period after "S," no period after "Cts," period after "2," "S" omitted, various broken letters, etc.

The surcharge on No. 355 is horizontal.

Peruvian Cormorants (Guano Deposits) — A143

Oil Well at Talara — A144

Avenue of the Republic, Lima — A146

San Marcos University at Lima — A148

Post Office, Lima — A149

Viceroy Manuel de Amat y Junyent — A150

Designs: 10c, "El Chasqui" (Inca Courier). 20c, Municipal Palace and Museum of Natural History. 5s, Joseph A. de Pando y Riva. 10s, Dr. José Dávila Condemarín.

1936-37 **Photo.** *Perf. 12½*

No.	Type	Description	Unused	Used
356	A143	2c lt brn	.60	.15
357	A143	2c grn ('37)	.75	.15
358	A144	4c blk brn	.60	.22
359	A144	4c int blk ('37)	.35	.15
360	A143	10c crimson	.35	.15
361	A143	10c ver ('37)	.20	.15
362	A146	15c ultra	.65	.15
363	A146	15c brt bl ('37)	.35	.15
364	A146	20c black	.65	.16
365	A146	20c blk brn ('37)	.25	.15
366	A148	50c org yel	2.50	.50
367	A148	50c dk gray vio ('37)	.75	.16
368	A149	1s brn vio	5.00	.65
369	A149	1s ultra ('37)	1.50	.20

Engr.

No.	Type	Description	Unused	Used
370	A150	2s ultra	11.00	2.50
371	A150	2s dk vio ('37)	3.50	.50
372	A150	5s slate bl	11.00	3.50
373	A150	10s dk vio & brn	60.00	22.50
		Nos. 356-373 (18)	100.00	32.09

No. 370 Surcharged in Black

Habilit.

Un Sol

1937

No.	Type	Description	Unused	Used
374	A150	1s on 2s ultra	2.50	2.50

Children's Holiday Center, Ancón — A153

Chavin Pottery — A154

Highway Map of Peru — A155

Archaeological Museum, Lima — A156

Industrial Bank of Peru — A157

Worker's Houses, Lima — A158

Toribio de Luzuriaga A159

Historic Fig Tree A160

Idol from Temple of Chavin — A161

Mt. Huascarán — A162

Imprint: "Waterlow & Sons Limited, Londres"

1938, July 1 **Photo.** *Perf. 12½, 13*

No.	Type	Description	Unused	Used
375	A153	2c emerald	.15	.15
376	A154	4c org brn	.15	.15
377	A155	10c scarlet	.20	.15
378	A156	15c ultra	.24	.15
379	A157	20c magenta	.15	.15
380	A158	50c greenish blue	.40	.15
381	A159	1s dp claret	1.00	.15
382	A160	2s green	3.00	.15

Engr.

No.	Type	Description	Unused	Used
383	A161	5s dl vio & brn	7.00	.40
384	A162	10s blk & ultra	12.00	.52
		Nos. 375-384 (10)	24.29	
		Set value		1.50

See Nos. 410-418, 426-433, 438-441.

For surcharges see Nos. 388, 406, 419, 445-446A, 456, 758.

Palace Square
A163

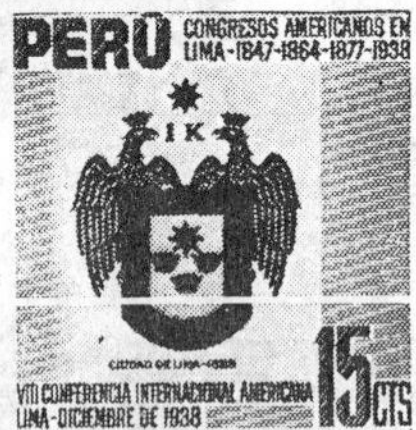

Lima Coat of Arms — A164

Government Palace — A165

1938, Dec. 9 Photo. *Perf. 12½*

385	A163	10c slate green	.50	.30

Engraved and Lithographed

386	A164	15c blk, gold, red & bl	.80	.40

Photo.

387	A165	1s olive	2.00	1.00
		Nos. 385-387,C62-C64 (6)	6.80	4.20

8th Pan-American Conf., Lima, Dec. 1938.

No. 377 Surcharged in Black

Habilitada 5 cts.

1940 *Perf. 13*

388	A155	5c on 10c scarlet	.15	.15
a.		Inverted surcharge		

National Radio Station — A166

Overprint: "FRANQUEO POSTAL"

1941 Litho. *Perf. 12*

389	A166	50c dull yel	2.00	.15
390	A166	1s violet	2.00	.20
391	A166	2s dl gray grn	4.00	.60
392	A166	5s fawn	22.50	6.75
393	A166	10s rose vio	35.00	5.25
		Nos. 389-393 (5)	65.50	12.95

Gonzalo Pizarro and Orellana
A167

Francisco de Orellana
A168

Francisco Pizarro — A169

Map of South America with Amazon as Spaniards Knew It in 1542 — A170

Gonzalo Pizarro
A171

Discovery of the Amazon River
A172

1943, Feb. *Perf. 12½*

394	A167	2c crimson	.15	.15
395	A168	4c slate	.16	.15
396	A169	10c yel brn	.20	.15
397	A170	15c vio blue	.50	.16
398	A171	20c yel olive	.16	.16
399	A172	25c dull org	1.65	.40
400	A168	30c dp magenta	.40	.20
401	A170	50c blue grn	.40	.32
402	A167	70c violet	2.25	.80
403	A171	80c lt bl	2.25	.80
404	A172	1s cocoa brn	4.00	.60
405	A169	5s intense blk	8.00	4.00
		Nos. 394-405 (12)	20.12	7.89

400th anniv. of the discovery of the Amazon River by Francisco de Orellana in 1542.

No. 377 Surcharged in Black

1943 *Perf. 13*

406	A155	10c on 10c scar	.15	.15

Samuel Finley Breese Morse — A173

1944 *Perf. 12½*

407	A173	15c light blue	.16	.15
408	A173	30c olive gray	.50	.16

Centenary of invention of the telegraph.

Types of 1938
Imprint: "Columbian Bank Note Co."

1945-47 Litho. *Perf. 12½*

410	A153	2c green	.15	.15
411	A154	4c org brn ('46)	.15	.15
412	A156	15c ultra	.15	.15
413	A157	20c magenta	1.65	.15
414	A158	50c grnsh bl	.15	.15
415	A159	1s vio brn	.25	.15
416	A160	2s dl grn	.65	.15
417	A161	5s dl vio & brn	4.00	.50
418	A162	10s blk & ultra ('47)	5.00	.75
		Nos. 410-418 (9)	12.15	
		Set value		1.60

No. 415 Surcharged in Black

Habilitada S|o. 0.20

1946

419	A159	20c on 1s vio brn	.30	.15
a.		Surcharge reading down	8.25	8.25

A174

A175

A176

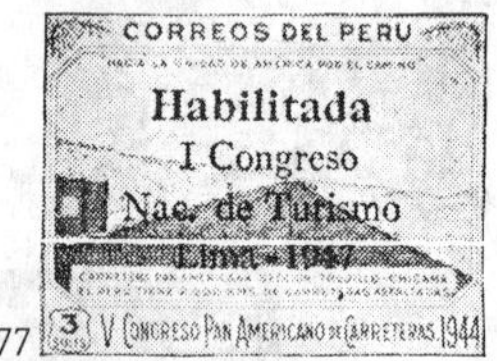

A177

A178

Overprinted in Black

Perf. 12½

1947, Apr. 15 Litho. Unwmk.

420	A174	15c blk & car	.25	.15
421	A175	1s olive brn	.38	.30
422	A176	1.35s yel grn	.38	.35
423	A177	3s Prus blue	.80	.75
424	A178	5s dull grn	1.90	1.50
		Nos. 420-424 (5)	3.71	3.05

1st National Tourism Congress, Lima. The basic stamps were prepared, but not issued, for the 5th Pan American Highway Congress of 1944.

Catalogue values for unused stamps in this section, from this point to the end of the section, are for Never Hinged items.

Types of 1938
Imprint: "Waterlow & Sons Limited, Londres."

Perf. 13x13½, 13½x13

1949-51 Photo.

426	A154	4c chocolate	.15	.15
427	A156	15c aquamarine	.15	.15
428	A157	20c blue vio	.15	.15
429	A158	50c red brn	.25	.15
430	A159	1s blk brn	.50	.15
431	A160	2s ultra	1.00	.15

Engr.

Perf. 12½

432	A161	5s ultra & red brn ('50)	.90	.38
433	A162	10s dk bl grn & blk ('51)	3.00	.75
		Nos. 426-433 (8)	6.10	
		Set value		1.50

Monument to Admiral Miguel L. Grau — A179

1949, June 6 *Perf. 12½*

434	A179	10c ultra & bl grn	.15	.15

Types of 1938
Imprint: "Inst. de Grav. Paris."

1951 *Perf. 12½x12, 12x12½*

438	A156	15c peacock grn	.15	.15
439	A157	20c violet	.15	.15
440	A158	50c org brn	.20	.15
441	A159	1s dark brn	.30	.15
		Nos. 438-441 (4)	.80	
		Set value		.22

Nos. 375 and 438 Surcharged in Black

HABILITADA S|. 0.01

1951-52 *Perf. 12½, 12½x12*

445	A153	1c on 2c	.15	.15
446	A156	10c on 15c	.15	.15
446A	A156	10c on 15c ('52)	.15	.15
		Set value	.30	.15

On No. 446A "Sl. 0.10" is in smaller type measuring 11½mm. See No. 456.

Nos. 445-446A exist with surcharge double.

Water Promenade — A180

Post Boy — A181

Designs: 4c, 50c, 1s, 2s, Various buildings, Lima. 20c, Post Office Street, Lima. 5s, Lake Llangamuco, Ancachs. 10s, Ruins of Machu-Picchu.

Overprint: "V Congreso Panamericano de Carreteras 1951"

1951, Oct. 13 Unwmk. *Perf. 12*

Black Overprint

447	A180	2c dk grn	.15	.15
448	A180	4c brt red	.15	.15
449	A181	15c gray	.15	.15
450	A181	20c ol brn	.20	.15
451	A180	50c dp plum	.25	.15
452	A180	1s blue	.30	.15
453	A180	2s deep blue	.45	.20
454	A180	5s brn lake	1.25	1.25
455	A181	10s chocolate	2.25	1.25
		Nos. 447-455 (9)	5.15	
		Set value		3.10

5th Pan-American Congress of Highways, 1951.

No. 438 Surcharged in Black

HABILITADA S|o. 0.05

1952 Unwmk. *Perf. 12½x12*

456	A156	5c on 15c pck grn	.15	.15

Tourist Hotel, Tacna — A182

Vicuña — A183

Contour Farming, Cuzco
A184

Gen. Marcos Perez Jimenez
A185

Designs: 5c, Fishing boat and principal fish. 10c, Matarani. 15c, Locomotive No. 80 and coaches. 25c, Engineering school. 30c, Ministry of Public Health and Social Assistance. 1s, Paramonga fortress. 2s, Monument to Native Farmer.

Imprint: "Thomas De La Rue & Co. Ltd."

Perf. 13, 12 (A184)

1952-53 Litho. Unwmk.

457	A182	2c	red lil ('53)	.15	.15
458	A182	5c	green	.15	.15
459	A182	10c	yel grn ('53)	.15	.15
460	A182	15c	gray ('53)	.15	.15
461	A183	20c	red brn ('53)	.38	.15
462	A182	25c	rose red	.15	.15
463	A182	30c	indigo ('53)	.15	.15
464	A184	50c	green ('53)	.45	.15
465	A184	1s	brown	.30	.15
466	A184	2s	Prus grn ('53)	.35	.15
			Set value	2.00	.62

See Nos. 468-478, 483-488, 497-501, C184-C185, C209.

For surcharges see Nos. C434, C437, C440-C441, C454, C494.

1956, July 25 Engr. *Perf. 13½x13*

467	A185	25c	brown	.15	.15

Visit of Gen. Marcos Perez Jimenez, Pres. of Venezuela, June 1955.

Types of 1952-53

Imprint: "Thomas De La Rue & Co. Ltd."

Designs as before.

1957-59 Litho. *Perf. 13, 12*

468	A182	15c	brown ('59)	.40	.15
469	A182	25c	green ('59)	.40	.15
470	A182	30c	rose red	.20	.15
471	A184	50c	dull pur	.30	.15
472	A184	1s	lt vio bl	.40	.15
473	A184	2s	gray ('58)	.50	.15
			Nos. 468-473 (6)	2.20	
			Set value		.40

Types of 1952-53

Imprint: "Joh. Enschedé en Zonen-Holland"

Designs as before.

Perf. 12½x13½, 13½x12½, 13x14

1960 Litho. Unwmk.

474	A183	20c	lt red brn	.18	.15
475	A182	30c	lilac rose	.15	.15
476	A184	50c	rose vio	.15	.15
477	A184	1s	lt vio bl	.20	.15
478	A184	2s	gray	.42	.15
			Nos. 474-478 (5)	1.10	
			Set value		.30

#475 measures 33x22mm, #470 32x22½mm.

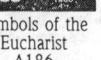

Symbols of the Eucharist
A186

Trumpeting Angels
A187

1960, Aug. 10 Photo. *Perf. 11½*

479	A186	50c	Cross and "JHS"	.15	.15
480	A186	1s	shown	.25	.25

Nos. 479-480 were intended for voluntary use to help finance the 6th National Eucharistic Congress at Piura, Aug. 25-28, 1960. Authorized for payment of postage on day of issue only, Aug. 10, but through misunderstanding within the Peruvian postal service they were accepted for payment of postage by some post offices until late in December. Reauthorized for postal use, they were again sold and used, starting in July, 1962. See Nos. RA37-RA38.

1961, Dec. 20 Litho. *Perf. 10½*

481	A187	20c	bright blue	.28	.15

Christmas. Valid for postage for one day, Dec. 20. Used thereafter as a voluntary seal to benefit a fund for postal employees.

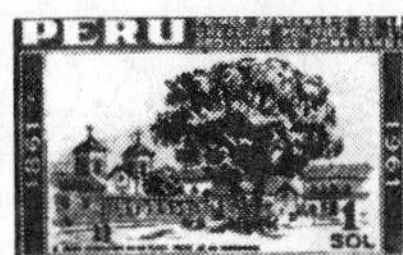

Centenary Cedar, Main Square, Pomabamba
A188

Unwmk.

1962, Sept. 7 Engr. *Perf. 13*

482	A188	1s	red & green	.40	.15

Cent. (in 1961) of Pomabamba province.

Types of 1952-53

Designs: 20c, Vicuña. 30c, Port of Matarani. 40c, Gunboat. 50c, Contour farming. 60c, Tourist hotel, Tacna. 1s, Paramonga, Inca fortress.

Imprint: "Thomas De La Rue & Co. Ltd."

Perf. 13x13½, 13½x13, 12 (A184)

1962, Nov. 19 Litho. Wmk. 346

483	A183	20c	rose claret	.15	.15
484	A182	30c	dark blue	.15	.15
485	AP49	40c	orange	.15	.15
486	A184	50c	lt bluish grn	.15	.15
487	A182	60c	grnsh blk	.16	.15
488	A184	1s	rose	.22	.15
			Nos. 483-488 (6)	.98	
			Set value		.38

Wheat Emblem and Symbol of Agriculture, Industry — A189

1963, July 23 Unwmk. *Perf. 12½*

489	A189	1s	red org & ocher	.15	.15

FAO "Freedom from Hunger" campaign. See No. C190.

Alliance for Progress Emblem
A190

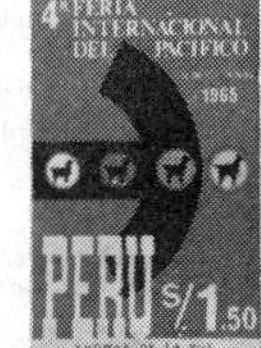

Pacific Fair Emblem
A191

1964, June 22 Litho. *Perf. 12x12½*

490	A190	40c	multi	.15	.15
			Nos. 490,C192-C193 (3)	.55	.52

Alliance for Progress. See note after US No. 1234.

1965, Oct. 30 Litho. *Perf. 12x12½*

491	A191	1.50s	multi	.15	.15
492	A191	2.50s	multi	.20	.15
493	A191	3.50s	multi	.25	.20
			Nos. 491-493 (3)	.60	
			Set value		.40

4th Intl. Pacific Fair, Lima, Oct. 30-Nov. 14.

Santa Claus and Letter — A192

1965, Nov. 2 *Perf. 11*

494	A192	20c	red & blk	.15	.15
495	A192	50c	grn & blk	.16	.15
496	A192	1s	bl & blk	.35	.15
			Nos. 494-496 (3)	.66	
			Set value		.25

Christmas. Valid for postage for one day, Nov. 2. Used Nov. 3, 1965-Jan. 31, 1966, as voluntary seals for the benefit of a fund for postal employees. See #522-524. For surcharges see #641-643.

Types of 1952-62

20c, Vicuña. 30c, Port of Matarani. 40c, Gunboat. 50c, Contour farming. 1s, Paramonga, Inca fortress.

Imprint: "I.N.A."

Perf. 12, 13½x14 (A184)

1966, Aug. 8 Litho. Unwmk.

497	A183	20c	brn red	.15	.15
498	A182	30c	dk bl	.15	.15
499	AP49	40c	orange	.15	.15
500	A184	50c	gray grn	.15	.15
501	A184	1s	rose	.15	.15
			Set value	.50	.25

Postal Tax Stamps Nos. RA40, RA43 Surcharged

XHabilitadoX

XX
Habilitado

S.0.10 a

S/. 0.10 b

Perf. 14x14½, 12½x12

1966, May 9 Litho.

501A	PT11	(a)	10c on 2c lt brn	.15	.15
501B	PT14	(b)	10c on 3c lt car	.15	.15

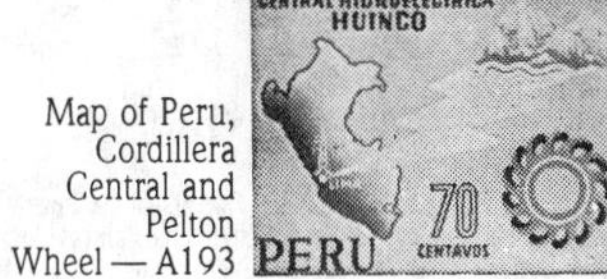

Map of Peru, Cordillera Central and Pelton Wheel — A193

1966, Nov. 24 Photo. *Perf. 13½x14*

502	A193	70c	bl, blk & vio bl	.15	.15

Opening of the Huinco Hydroelectric Center. See No. C205.

Inca Wind Vane and Sun — A194

Perf. 13½x14

1967, Apr. 18 Photo. Unwmk.

503	A194	90c	dp lil rose, blk & gold	.15	.15

6-year building program. See No. C212.

Pacific Fair Emblem
A195

Indian and Wheat
A197

Gold Alligator, Mochica Culture
A196

1967, Oct. 9 Photo. *Perf. 12*

504	A195	1s	gold, dk grn & blk	.15	.15

5th Intl. Pacific Fair, Lima, Oct. 27-Nov. 12. See No. C216.

1968, Aug. 16 Photo. *Perf. 12*

Designs (gold sculptures of the pre-Inca Yunca tribes): 2.60s, Bird, vert. 3.60s, Lizard. 4.60s, Bird, vert. 5.60s, Jaguar.

Sculptures in Gold Yellow and Brown

505	A196	1.90s	dp magenta	.25	.15
506	A196	2.60s	black	.35	.20
507	A196	3.60s	dp magenta	.40	.30
508	A196	4.60s	black	.50	.35
509	A196	5.60s	dp magenta	.50	.35
			Nos. 505-509 (5)	2.00	1.35

See Nos. B1-B5. For surcharge see No. 685.

1969, Mar. 3 Litho. *Perf. 11*

Designs: 3s, 4s, Farmer digging in field.

Black Surcharge

510	A197	2.50s	on 90c brn & yel	.15	.15
511	A197	3s	on 90c lil & brn	.16	.15
512	A197	4s	on 90c rose & grn	.22	.16
			Nos. 510-512,C232-C233 (5)	1.13	.82

Agrarian Reform Law.
#510-512 were not issued without surcharge.

Flag, Worker Holding Oil Rig and Map — A198

1969, Apr. 9 Litho. *Perf. 12*

513	A198	2.50s	multi	.15	.15
514	A198	3s	gray & multi	.16	.15
515	A198	4s	lil & multi	.20	.16
516	A198	5.50s	lt bl & multi	.25	.20
			Nos. 513-516 (4)	.76	.66

Nationalization of the Brea Parinas oilfields, Oct. 9, 1968.

Kon Tiki Raft. Globe and Jet — A199

1969, June 17 Litho. *Perf. 11*

517	A199	2.50s	dp bl & multi	.15	.15
			Nos. 517,C238-C241 (5)	.83	
			Set value		.55

1st Peruvian Airlines (APSA) flight to Europe.

Capt. José A. Quiñones Gonzales (1914-41), Military Aviator — A200

1969, July 23 Litho. *Perf. 11*

518	A200	20s	red & multi	1.20	.60

See No. C243.

Freed Andean Farmer
A201

1969, Aug. 28 Litho. *Perf. 11*

519	A201	2.50s	dk bl, lt bl & red	.15	.15
			Set value, #519, C246-C247	.35	.25

Enactment of the Agrarian Reform Law of June 24, 1969.

Adm. Miguel Grau — A202

1969, Oct. 8 Litho. *Perf. 11*

520 A202 50s dk bl & multi 3.00 2.25

Issued for Navy Day.

Flags and "6" — A203

1969, Nov. 14

521 A203 2.50s gray & multi .20 .20
Nos. 521,C251-C252 (3) .65
Set value .40

6th Intl. Pacific Trade Fair, Lima, Nov. 14-30.

Santa Claus Type of 1965

Design: Santa Claus and letter inscribed "FELIZ NAVIDAD Y PROSPERO AÑO NUEVO."

1969, Dec. 1 Litho. *Perf. 11*

522 A192 20c red & blk .15 .15
523 A192 20c org & blk .15 .15
524 A192 20c brn & blk .15 .15
Set value .15 .15

Christmas. Valid for postage for one day, Dec. 1, 1969. Used after that date as postal tax stamps.

Gen. Francisco Bolognesi and Soldier — A204

Puma-shaped Jug, Vicus Culture — A205

1969, Dec. 9

525 A204 1.20s lt ultra, blk & gold .15 .15

Army Day, Dec. 9. See No. C253.

1970, Feb. 23 Litho. *Perf. 11*

526 A205 2.50s buff, blk & brn .20 .20
Nos. 526,C281-C284 (5) 1.26 1.26

Ministry of Transport and Communications A206

1970, Apr. 1 Litho. *Perf. 11*

527 A206 40c org & gray .15 .15
528 A206 40c gray & lt gray .15 .15
529 A206 40c brick red & gray .15 .15
530 A206 40c brt pink & gray .15 .15
531 A206 40c org brn & gray .15 .15
Set value .25 .25

Ministry of Transport and Communications, 1st anniv.

Anchovy A207

Fish: No. 533, Pacific hake.

1970, Apr. 30 Litho. *Perf. 11*

532 A207 2.50s vio bl & multi .20 .20
533 A207 2.50s vio bl & multi .20 .20
a. Strip of 5, #532-533, C285-C287 1.10 1.10

Composite Head; Soldier and Farmer — A208

1970, June 24 Litho. *Perf. 11*

534 A208 2.50s gold & multi .16 .15
Nos. 534,C290-C291 (3) .71
Set value .30

"United people and army building a new Peru."

Cadets, Chorrillos College, and Arms A209

Coat of Arms and: No. 536, Cadets of La Punta Naval College. No. 537, Cadets of Las Palmas Air Force College.

1970, July 27 Litho. *Perf. 11*

535 A209 2.50s blk & multi .42 .16
536 A209 2.50s blk & multi .42 .16
537 A209 2.50s blk & multi .42 .16
a. Strip of 3, #535-537 1.30 .75

Peru's military colleges.

Courtyard, Puruchuco Fortress, Lima — A210

1970, Aug. 6

538 A210 2.50s multi .15 .15
Nos. 538,C294-C297 (5) 1.28 1.28

Issued for tourist publicity.

Nativity, Cuzco School A211

Christmas paintings: 1.50s, Adoration of the Kings, Cuzco School. 1.80s, Adoration of the Shepherds, Peruvian School.

1970, Dec. 23 Litho. *Perf. 11*

539 A211 1.20s multi .15 .15
540 A211 1.50s multi .15 .15
541 A211 1.80s multi .15 .15
Set value .22 .15

St. Rosa of Lima — A212

1971, Apr. 12 Litho. *Perf. 11*

542 A212 2.50s multi .15 .15

300th anniv. of the canonization of St. Rosa of Lima (1586-1617), first saint born in the Americas.

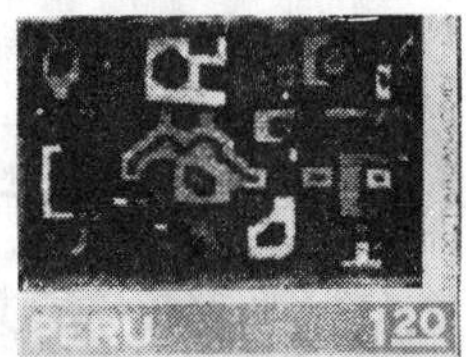

Tiahuanacoide Cloth — A213

Design: 2.50s, Chancay cloth.

1971, Apr. 19

543 A213 1.20s bl & multi .15 .15
544 A213 2.50s yel & multi .20 .15
Nos. 543-544,C306-C308 (5) 1.37
Set value .42

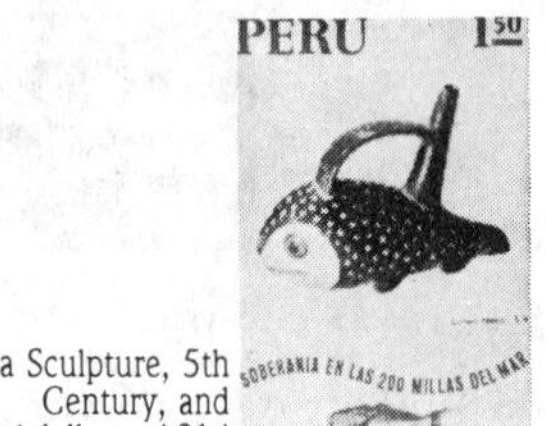

Nazca Sculpture, 5th Century, and Seriolella — A214

1971, June 7 Litho. *Perf. 11*

545 A214 1.50s multi .15 .15
Nos. 545,C309-C312 (5) 2.03
Set value .62

Publicity for 200-mile zone of sovereignty of the high seas.

Mateo Garcia Pumacahua A215

#547, Mariano Melgar. #548, Micaela Bastidas. #549, Jose Faustino Sanchez Carrion. #550, Francisco Antonia de Zela. #551, Jose Baquijano y Carrillo. #552, Martin Jorge Guise.

1971

546 A215 1.20s ver & blk .15 .15
547 A215 1.20s gray & multi .15 .15
548 A215 1.50s dk bl & multi .15 .15
549 A215 2s dk bl & multi .15 .15
550 A215 2.50s ultra & multi .20 .15
551 A215 2.50s gray & multi .20 .15
552 A215 2.50s dk bl & multi .20 .15
Nos. 546-552,C313-C325 (20) 4.04
Set value 2.50

150th anniv. of independence, and to honor the heroes of the struggle for independence.

Issue dates: Nos. 546, 550, May 10; Nos. 547, 551, July 5; Nos. 548-549, 552, July 27.

Gongora Portentosa — A216

Designs: Various Peruvian orchids.

1971, Sept. 27 *Perf. 13½x13*

553 A216 1.50s pink & multi .20 .15
554 A216 2s pink & multi .25 .15
555 A216 2.50s pink & multi .30 .15
556 A216 3s pink & multi .35 .15
557 A216 3.50s pink & multi .40 .15
Nos. 553-557 (5) 1.50
Set value .32

"Progress of Liberation," by Teodoro Nuñez Ureta — A217

3.50s, Detail from painting by Nuñez Ureta.

1971, Nov. 4 *Perf. 13x13½*

558 A217 1.20s multi .15 .15
559 A217 3.50s multi .20 .20
Nos. 558-559,C331 (3) 3.35

2nd Ministerial meeting of the "Group of 77."

Plaza de Armas, Lima, 1843 — A218

Design: 3.50s, Plaza de Armas, Lima, 1971.

1971, Nov. 6

560 A218 3s pale grn & blk .35 .15
561 A218 3.50s lt brick red & blk .40 .20

3rd Annual Intl. Stamp Exhibition, EXFILIMA '71, Lima, Nov. 6-14.

Army Coat of Arms — A219

1971, Dec. 9 Litho. *Perf. 13½x13*

562 A219 8.50s multi .75 .20

Sesquicentennial of Peruvian Army.

Flight into Egypt A220

Old Stone Sculptures of Huamanga: 2.50s, Three Kings. 3s, Nativity.

1971, Dec. 18 *Perf. 13x13½*

563 A220 1.80s multi .18 .15
564 A220 2.50s multi .25 .15
565 A220 3s gray & multi .35 .20
Nos. 563-565 (3) .78 .50

Christmas. See Nos. 597-599.

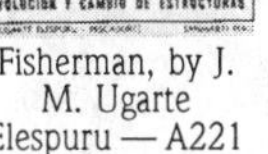
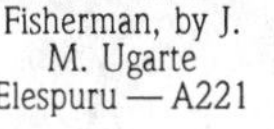

Fisherman, by J. M. Ugarte Elespuru — A221

Gold Statuette, Chimu, c. 1500 — A222

Paintings by Peruvian Workers: 4s, Threshing Grain in Cajamarca, by Camilo Blas. 6s, Huanca Highlanders, by José Sabogal.

1971, Dec. 30 *Perf. 13½x13*

566 A221 3.50s blk & multi .35 .15
567 A221 4s blk & multi .42 .15
568 A221 6s blk & multi .60 .15
Nos. 566-568 (3) 1.37 .45

To publicize the revolution and change of order.

1972, Jan. 31 Litho. *Perf. 13½x13*

Ancient Jewelry: 4s, Gold drummer, Chimu. 4.50s, Quartz figurine, Lambayeque culture, 5th century. 5.40s, Gold necklace and pendant, Mochiqua, 4th century. 6s, Gold insect, Lambayeque culture, 14th century.

569 A222 3.90s red, blk & ocher .40 .15
570 A222 4s red, blk & ocher .40 .15
571 A222 4.50s brt bl, blk & ocher .50 .15
572 A222 5.40s red, blk & ocher .60 .15
573 A222 6s red, blk & ocher .60 .15
Nos. 569-573 (5) 2.50
Set value .55

Popeye Catalufa A223

Fish: 1.50s, Guadara. 2.50s, Jack mackerel.

1972, Mar. 20 *Perf. 13x13½*

574 A223 1.20s lt bl & multi .25 .15
575 A223 1.50s lt bl & multi .25 .15
576 A223 2.50s lt bl & multi .25 .15
Nos. 574-576,C333-C334 (5) 1.55 .75

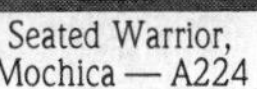

Seated Warrior, Mochica — A224

"Bringing in the Harvest" (July) — A225

Painted pottery jugs of Mochica culture, 5th century: 1.50s, Helmeted head. 2s, Kneeling deer. 2.50s, Helmeted head. 3s, Kneeling warrior.

1972, May 8 *Perf. 13½x13*

Emerald Background

577 A224 1.20s multi .20 .15
578 A224 1.50s multi .25 .15
579 A224 2s multi .30 .15
580 A224 2.50s multi .35 .15
581 A224 3s multi .40 .15
Nos. 577-581 (5) 1.50 .75

1972-73 Litho. *Perf. 13½x13*

Monthly woodcuts from Calendario Incaico.

Black Vignette & Inscriptions

582 A225 2.50s red brn *(July)* .35 .15
583 A225 3s grn *(Aug.)* .60 .15
584 A225 2.50s rose *(Sept.)* .35 .15
585 A225 3s lt bl *(Oct.)* .50 .15
586 A225 2.50s org *(Nov.)* .50 .15
587 A225 3s lil *(Dec.)* .50 .15
588 A225 2.50s brn *(Jan.)* ('73) .35 .15
589 A225 3s pale grn *(Feb.)* ('73) .50 .15
590 A225 2.50s bl *(Mar.)* ('73) .35 .15
591 A225 3s org *(Apr.)* ('73) .50 .15
592 A225 2.50s lil rose *(May)* ('73) .35 .15

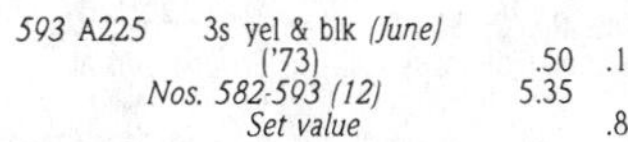

593 A225 3s yel & blk *(June)* ('73) .50 .15
Nos. 582-593 (12) 5.35
Set value .85

400th anniv. of publication of the Calendario Incaico by Felipe Guaman Poma de Ayala.

Family Tilling Field — A226

Oil Derricks — A228

Sovereignty of the Sea (Inca Frieze) A227

Perf. 13½x13, 13x13½

1972, Oct. 31 Litho.

594 A226 2s multi .25 .20
595 A227 2.50s multi .25 .20
596 A228 3s gray & multi .25 .20
Nos. 594-596 (3) .75 .60

4th anniversaries of land reforms and the nationalization of the oil industry and 15th anniv. of the claim to a 200-mile zone of sovereignty of the sea.

Christmas Type of 1971

Sculptures from Huamanga, 17-18th cent.: 1.50s, Holy Family, wood, vert. 2s, Holy Family with lambs, stone. 2.50s, Holy Family in stable, stone, vert.

1972, Nov. 30

597 A220 1.50s buff & multi .15 .15
598 A220 2s buff & multi .15 .15
599 A220 2.50s buff & multi .16 .15
Nos. 597-599 (3) .46
Set value .30

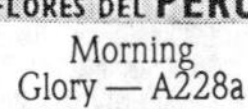

Morning Glory — A228a

Mayor on Horseback, by Fierro — A229

1972, Dec. 29 Litho. *Perf. 13*

600 A228a 1.50s shown .15 .15
601 A228a 2.50s Amaryllis .25 .15
602 A228a 3s Liabum excelsum .30 .15
603 A228a 3.50s Bletia (orchid) .45 .15
604 A228a 5s Cantua buxifolia .35 .15
Nos. 600-604 (5) 1.50 .75

1973, Aug. 13 Litho. *Perf. 13*

Paintings by Francisco Pancho Fierro (1803-1879): 2s, Man and Woman, 1830. 2.50s, Padre Abregu Riding Mule. 3.50s, Dancing Couple. 4.50s, Bullfighter Estevan Arredondo on Horseback.

605 A229 1.50s salmon & multi .15 .15
606 A229 2s salmon & multi .20 .15
607 A229 2.50s salmon & multi .25 .15
608 A229 3.50s salmon & multi .35 .20
609 A229 4.50s salmon & multi .55 .20
Nos. 605-609 (5) 1.50 .85

Presentation in the Temple A230

Christmas Paintings of the Cuzqueña School: 2s, Holy Family, vert. 2.50s, Adoration of the Kings.

1973, Nov. 30 Litho. *Perf. 13x13½*

610 A230 1.50s multi .15 .15
611 A230 2s multi .15 .15
612 A230 2.50s multi .15 .15
Set value .32 .16

Peru No. 20 — A231

1974, Mar. 1 Litho. *Perf. 13*

613 A231 6s gray & dk bl .50 .25

Peruvian Philatelic Assoc., 25th anniv.

Non-ferrous Smelting Plant, La Oroya A232

Colombia Bridge, San Martin A233

Designs: 8s, 10s, Different views, Santiago Antunez Dam, Tayacaja.

1974 Litho. *Perf. 13x13½*

614 A232 1.50s blue .15 .15
615 A233 2s multi .15 .15
616 A232 3s rose claret .20 .15
617 A232 4.50s green .25 .15
618 A233 8s multi .35 .16
619 A233 10s multi .45 .20
Nos. 614-619 (6) 1.55
Set value .65

"Peru Determines its Destiny."
Issued: 2s, 8s, 10s, 7/1; 1.50s, 3s, 4.50s, 12/6.

Battle of Junin, by Felix Yañez A234

2s, 3s, Battle of Ayacucho, by Felix Yañez.

1974 Litho. *Perf. 13x13½*

620 A234 1.50s multi .15 .15
621 A234 2s multi .20 .15
622 A234 2.50s multi .25 .15
623 A234 3s multi .30 .15
Nos. 620-623 (4) .90
Set value .40

Sesquicentennial of the Battles of Junin and Ayacucho.

Issue dates: 1.50s, 2.50s, Aug. 6. 2s, 3s, Oct. 9.

See Nos. C400-C404.

Indian Madonna — A235

1974, Dec. 20 Litho. *Perf. 13½x13*

624 A235 1.50s multi .15 .15

Christmas. See No. C417.

Maria Parado de Bellido A236

International Women's Year Emblem — A237

IWY Emblem, Peruvian Colors and: 2s, Micaela Bastidas. 2.50s, Juana Alarco de Dammert.

Perf. 13x13½, 13½x13

1975, Sept. 8 Litho.

625 A236 1.50s bl grn, red & blk .15 .15
626 A237 2s blk & red .15 .15
627 A236 2.50s pink, blk & red .20 .15
628 A237 3s red, blk & ultra .25 .15
Nos. 625-628 (4) .75
Set value .20

International Women's Year.

St. Juan Macias — A238

1975, Nov. 14 *Perf. 13½x13*

629 A238 5s blk & multi .25 .20

Canonization of Juan Macias in 1975.

Louis Braille A239

1976, Mar. 2 Litho. *Perf. 13x13½*

630 A239 4.50s gray, red & blk .20 .20

Sesquicentennial of the invention of Braille system of writing for the blind by Louis Braille (1809-1852).

Peruvian Flag — A240

1976, Aug. 29 Litho. *Perf. 13x13½*

631 A240 5s gray, blk & red .20 .20

Revolutionary Government, phase II, 1st anniv.

St. Francis, by El Greco — A241

Indian Mother — A242

1976, Dec. 9 Litho. *Perf. 13½x13*

632	A241	5s gold, buff & brn	.25	.20

St. Francis of Assisi, 750th death anniv.

1976, Dec. 23

633	A242	4s multi	.25	.15

Christmas.

Chasqui Messenger — A243

"X" over Flags — A244

1977 Litho. *Perf. 13½x13*

634	A243	6s grnsh bl & blk	.25	.20
635	A243	8s red & blk	.25	.20
636	A243	10s ultra & blk	.50	.35
637	A243	12s lt grn & blk	.50	.35
		Nos. 634-637,C465-C467 (7)	4.35	2.60

For surcharge see No. C502.

1977, Nov. 25 Litho. *Perf. 13½x13*

638	A244	10s multi	.20	.20

10th Intl. Pacific Fair, Lima, Nov. 16-27.

Republican Guard Badge — A245

Indian Nativity — A246

1977, Dec. 1

639	A245	12s multi	.25	.25

58th anniversary of Republican Guard.

1977, Dec. 23

640	A246	8s multi	.15	.15

Christmas. See No. C484.

Nos. 495, 494, 496 Surcharged with New Value and Bar in Red, Dark Blue or Black: "FRANQUEO / 10.00 / RD-0161-77"

1977, Dec. *Perf. 11*

641	A192	10s on 50c (R)	.25	.15
642	A192	20s on 20c (DB)	.50	.30
643	A192	30s on 1s (B)	.65	.40
		Nos. 641-643 (3)	1.40	.85

Inca Head — A247

1978 Litho. *Perf. 13½x13*

644	A247	6s bright green	.15	.15
645	A247	10s red	.15	.15
646	A247	16s red brown	.20	.20
		Nos. 644-646,C486-C489 (7)	3.37	2.75

For surcharges see Nos. C498-C499, C501.

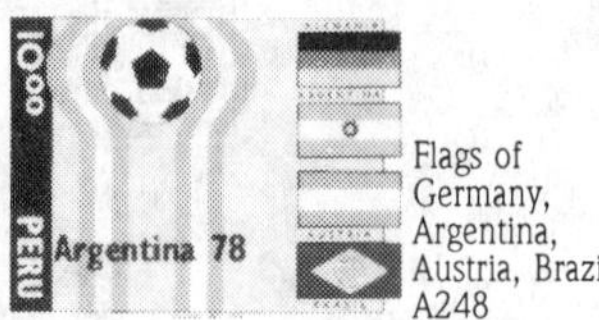

Flags of Germany, Argentina, Austria, Brazil A248

Argentina '78 Emblem and Flags of Participants: No. 648, 652, Hungary, Iran, Italy, Mexico. No. 649, 653, Scotland, Spain, France, Netherlands. No. 650, 654, Peru, Poland, Sweden and Tunisia. No. 651, like No. 647.

1978 Litho. *Perf. 13x13½*

647	A248	10s blue & multi	.30	.20
648	A248	10s blue & multi	.30	.20
649	A248	10s blue & multi	.30	.20
650	A248	10s blue & multi	.30	.20
a.		Block of 4, #647-650	1.25	1.00
651	A248	16s blue & multi	.30	.20
652	A248	16s blue & multi	.30	.20
653	A248	16s blue & multi	.30	.20
654	A248	16s blue & multi	.30	.20
a.		Block of 4, #651-654	1.25	1.00
		Nos. 647-654 (8)	2.40	1.60

11th World Soccer Cup Championship, Argentina, June 1-25.

Issued: #647-650, June 28; #651-654, Dec. 4.

Thomas Faucett, Planes of 1928, 1978 A249

1978, Oct. 19 Litho. *Perf. 13*

655	A249	40s multicolored	.40	.25

Faucett Aviation, 50th anniversary.

Nazca Bowl, Huaco A250

1978-79 Litho. *Perf. 13x13½*

656	A250	16s violet bl ('79)	.15	.15
657	A250	20s green ('79)	.18	.15
658	A250	25s lt green ('79)	.22	.22
659	A250	35s rose red ('79)	.38	.18
660	A250	45s dk brown	.45	.25
661	A250	50s black	.55	.28
662	A250	55s car rose ('79)	.55	.28
663	A250	70s lilac rose ('79)	.65	.55
664	A250	75s blue	.75	.45
665	A250	80s salmon ('79)	.75	.45
667	A250	200s brt vio ('79)	1.90	1.40
		Nos. 656-667 (11)	6.53	4.36

For surcharges see Nos. 715, 731.

Peruvian Nativity — A252

Ministry of Education, Lima — A253

1978, Dec. 28 Litho. *Perf. 13½x13*

672	A252	16s multicolored	.15	.15

1979, Jan. 4

673	A253	16s multicolored	.15	.15

National Education Program.

Nos. RA40, B1-B5 and 509 Surcharged in Various Colors. No. RA40 Surcharged also:

Habilitado
Dif.-Porte
S/. 2.00
a

SOBRE
TASA
OFICIAL
S/. 3.00
b

Habilitado
R.D. N° 0118
S/. 35.00
c

1978, July-Aug.

674	PT11(a)	2s on 2c (O)	.15	.15
675	PT11(b)	3s on 2c (Bk)	.15	.15
676	PT11(a)	4s on 2c (G)	.15	.15
677	PT11(a)	5s on 2c (V)	.15	.15
678	PT11(b)	6s on 2c (DBl)	.15	.15
679	SP1	20s on 1.90s + 90c (G)	.75	.75
680	SP1	30s on 2.60s + 1.30s (Bl)	.75	.75
681	PT11(c)	35s on 2c (C)	.30	.30
682	PT11(c)	50s on 2c (LtBl)	2.00	2.00
683	SP1	55s on 3.60s + 1.80s (VBl)	1.00	1.00
684	SP1	65s on 4.60s + 2.30s (Go)	1.00	1.00
685	A196	80s on 5.60s (VBl)	.75	.75
686	SP1	85s on 20s + 10s (Bk)	1.50	1.50
		Nos. 674-686 (13)	8.80	8.80

Surcharge on Nos. 679-680, 683-684, 686 includes heavy bar over old denomination.

Battle of Iquique A254

Heroes' Crypt — A255

Col. Francisco Bolognesi — A256

War of the Pacific: No. 688, Col. Jose J. Inclan. No. 689, Corvette Union running Arica blockade. No. 690, Battle of Angamos, Aguirre, Miguel Grau (1838-1879), Perre. No. 690A, Lt. Col. Pedro Ruiz Gallo. 85s, Marshal Andres A. Caceres. No. 692, Naval Battle of Angamos. No. 697, Col. Bolognesi's Reply, by Angeles de la Cruz. No. 698, Col. Alfonso Ugarte on horseback.

Perf. 13½x13, 13x13½

1979-80 Litho.

687	A254	14s multicolored	.15	.15
688	A256	25s multicolored	.35	.20
689	A254	25s multicolored	.16	.20
690	A254	25s multicolored	.22	.20
690A	A256	25s multicolored ('80)	.16	.20
691	A256	85s multicolored	.55	.50
692	A254	100s multicolored	.65	.30
693	A256	100s multicolored	.65	.30
694	A256	115s multicolored	1.20	.75
695	A255	200s multicolored	4.00	3.00
696	A256	200s multicolored	1.20	1.00
697	A254	200s multicolored	1.20	1.00
698	A254	200s multicolored	1.20	1.00
		Nos. 687-698 (13)	11.69	8.80

For surcharges see Nos. 713, 732.

Peruvian Red Cross, Cent. — A257

1979, May 4 *Perf. 13x13½*

699	A257	16s multicolored	.15	.15

Billiard Balls — A258

Arms of Cuzco — A259

1979, June 4 *Perf. 13½x13*

700	A258	34s multicolored	.25	.25

For surcharge see No. 714.

1979, June 24

701	A259	50s multicolored	.35	.20

Inca Sun Festival, Cuzco.

Peru Colors, Tacna Monument — A260

Telecom 79 — A261

1979, Aug. 28 Litho. *Perf. 13½x13*

702	A260	16s multicolored	.15	.15

Return of Tacna Province to Peru, 50th anniv. For surcharge see No. 712.

1979, Sept. 20

703	A261	15s multicolored	.15	.15

3rd World Telecommunications Exhibition, Geneva, Sept. 20-26.

Caduceus — A262

Gold Jewelry — A264

World Map, "11," Fair Emblem A263

1979, Nov. 13

704	A262	25s multicolored	.20	.20

Stomatology Academy of Peru, 50th anniv.; 4th Intl. Congress.

1979, Nov. 24

705	A263	55s multicolored	.38	.25

11th Pacific Intl. Trade Fair, Lima, Nov. 14-25.

1979, Dec. 19 *Perf. 13½x13*

706	A264	85s multicolored	.55	.40

Larco Herrera Archaeological Museum.

Christmas A265

1979, Dec. 27 Litho. *Perf. 13x13½*

707	A265	25s multicolored	.20	.20

Queen Sofia and King Juan Carlos I, Visit to Peru — A266

1979 Litho. *Perf. 13x13½*

708	A266	75s multicolored	.55	.25

No. RA40 Surcharged in Black, Green or Blue

1979, Oct. 8

709	PT11	7s on 2c brown	.15	.15
710	PT11	9s on 2c brown (G)	.15	.15
711	PT11	15s on 2c brown (B)	.20	.15
		Set value	.42	.35

Nos. 702, 687, 700, 663 Surcharged
Perf. 13½x13, 13x13½

1980, Apr. 14 Litho.

712	A260	20s on 16s multi	.25	.20
713	A254	25s on 14s multi	.30	.25
714	A258	65s on 34s multi	.50	.40
715	A250	80s on 70s lilac rose	.75	.30
		Nos. 712-715,C501-C502 (6)	2.50	1.70

Liberty Holding Arms of Peru — A267 Chimu Cult Cup — A268

Civic duties: 15s, Respect the Constitution. 20s, Honor country. 25s, Vote. 30s, Military service. 35s, Pay taxes. 45s, Contribute to national progress. 50s, Respect rights.

1980 Litho.

716	A267	15s greenish blue	.15	.15
717	A267	20s salmon pink	.15	.15
718	A267	25s ultra	.16	.16
719	A267	30s lilac rose	.20	.20
720	A267	35s black	.22	.16
721	A267	45s light blue green	.30	.22
722	A267	50s brown	.50	.22
		Nos. 716-722 (7)	1.68	1.26

1980, July 9 Litho.

723	A268	35s multicolored	.22	.16

Map of Peru and Liberty — A269

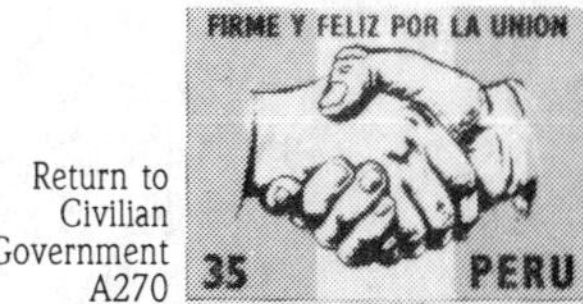

Return to Civilian Government A270

Perf. 13½x13, 13x13½

1980, Sept. 9 Litho.

724	A269	25s multicolored	.16	.16
725	A270	35s multicolored	.22	.22

For surcharge see No. 730.

Machu Picchu A271

1980, Nov. 10 Litho. *Perf. 13x13½*

726	A271	25s multicolored	.16	.16

World Tourism Conf., Manila, Sept. 27.

Tupac Amaru Rebellion Bicent. — A272 150th Death Anniv. of Simon Bolivar (in 1980) — A274

Christmas A273

1980, Dec. 22 Litho. *Perf. 13½x13*

727	A272	25s multicolored	.20	.20

1980, Dec. 31 Litho. *Perf. 13*

728	A273	15s multicolored	.15	.15

1981, Jan. 28 Litho. *Perf. 13½x13*

729	A274	40s multicolored	.30	.22

Nos. 725, 667, 694 Surcharged

1981 Litho. *Perf. 13x13½*

730	A270	25s on 35s multi	.20	.20
731	A250	85s on 200s brt violet	.65	.50
732	A256	100s on 115s multi	.75	.60
		Nos. 730-732 (3)	1.60	1.30

Return to Constitutional Government, July 28, 1980 — A275

1981, Mar. 26 Litho. *Perf. 13½x13*

733	A275	25s multicolored	.25	.15

For surcharges see Nos. 736-737, 737C.

Tupac Amaru and Micaela Bastidas, Bronze Sculptures, by Miguel Baca-Rossi A276

1981, May 18 Litho. *Perf. 13x13½*

734	A276	60s multicolored	.45	.35

Rebellion of Tupac Amaru and Micaela Bastidas, bicentenary.

Nos. 733, RA41 and Voluntary Postal Tax Stamps of 1965 Surcharged in Black, Dull Brown or Lake

Cross, Unleavened Bread, Wheat — A276a Chalice, Host — A276b

Perf. 13½x13, Rouletted 11 (#735, 737B), 11½ (#737A)

1981 Litho., Photo. (#737A-737B)

735	PT17	40s on 10c #RA41	.15	.15
736	A275	40s on 25s #733	.15	.15
737	A275	130s on 25s #733 (DB)	.30	.20
737A	A276a	140s on 50c brn, yel & red	.32	.20
737B	A276b	140s on 1s multi	.32	.20
737C	A275	140s on 25s #733 (L)	.32	.20
		Nos. 735-737C (6)	1.56	1.10

Issued: #735, Apr. 12. #736, 737, 737C, Apr. 6. #737A, Apr. 15. #737B, Apr. 28.

Carved Stone Head, Pallasca Tribe — A277

#739, 742, 749 Pottery vase, Inca, vert. #740, Head, diff., vert. #743, 749A-749B, Huaco idol (fish), Nazca. 100s, Pallasca, vert. 140s, Puma.

Perf. 13½x13, 13x13½

1981-82 Litho.

738	A277	30s dp rose lilac	.25	.25
739	A277	40s orange ('82)	.30	.18
740	A277	40s ultra	.30	.18
742	A277	80s brown ('82)	.75	.50
743	A277	80s red ('82)	.75	.38
745	A277	100s lilac rose	.75	.50
748	A277	140s lt blue grn	1.00	.70
749	A277	180s green ('82)	1.75	1.25
749A	A277	240s grnsh blue ('82)	1.00	.70
749B	A277	280s violet ('82)	1.40	1.00
		Nos. 738-749B (10)	8.25	5.64

For surcharges see Nos. 789, 798-799, 1026.

A278 A279

1981, May 31 *Perf. 13½x13*

750	A278	130s multicolored	.60	.60

Postal and Philatelic Museum, 50th anniv.

1981, Oct. 7 Litho. *Perf. 13½x13*

751	A279	30s purple & gray	.22	.22

1979 Constitution Assembly President Victor Raul Haya de la Torre.

Inca Messenger, by Guaman Poma (1526-1613) A280 Intl. Year of the Disabled A280a

1981 Litho. *Perf. 12*

752	A280	30s lilac & blk	.22	.15
753	A280	40s vermilion & blk	.18	.38
754	A280	130s brt yel grn & blk	.50	.38
755	A280	140s brt blue & blk	.50	.50
756	A280	200s yellow brn & blk	.75	.75
		Nos. 752-756 (5)	2.15	2.16

Christmas. Issue dates: 30s, 40s, 200s, Dec. 21; others, Dec. 31.

1981 Litho. *Perf. 13½x13*

756A	A280a	100s multicolored	.60	.38

Nos. 377, C130, C143, J56, O33, RA36, RA39, RA40, RA42, RA43 Surcharged in Brown, Black, Orange, Red, Green or Blue

1982

757	PT11	10s on 2c (#RA40, Br)	.25	.25
758	A155	10s on 10c (#377)	.15	.15
758A	AP60	40s on 1.25s (#C143)	.15	.15
758B	PT15	70s on 5c (#RA36, R)	.20	.20
759	D7	80s on 10c (#J56)	.18	.18
760	O1	80s on 10c (#O33)	.18	.18
761	PT14	80s on 3c (#RA43, O)	.18	.18
762	PT17	100s on 10c (#RA42, R)	.25	.25
763	AP57	100s on 2.20s (#C130, R)	.25	.25
764	PT14	150s on 3c (#RA39, G)	.35	.35
765	PT14	180s on 3c (#RA43, R)	.40	.40
766	PT14	200s on 3c (#RA43, Bl)	.50	.50
767	AP60	240s on 1.25s (#C143, R)	.60	.60
768	PT15	280s on 5c (#RA36)	.70	.70
		Nos. 757-768 (14)	4.34	4.34

Nos. 758A, 763, 767 airmail. Nos. 759 and 760 surcharged "Habilitado / Franq. Postal / 80 Soles".

Jorge Basadre (1903-1908), Historian — A281

Julio C. Tello (1882-1947), Archaeologist A282

Perf. 13½x13, 13x13½

1982, Oct. 13 Litho.

769	A281	100s pale green & blk	.25	.15
770	A282	200s lt green & dk bl	.50	.30

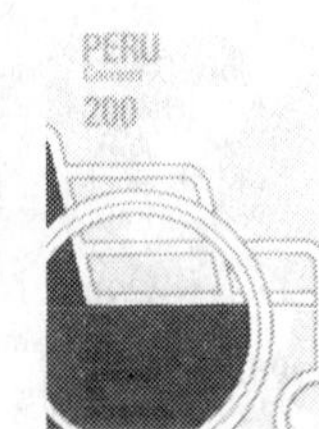

9th Women's World Volleyball Championship, Sept. 12-26 — A283 Rights of the Disabled — A284

1982, Oct. 18 *Perf. 12*

771	A283	80s black & red	.20	.20

For surcharge see No. 791.

1982, Oct. 22

772	A284	200s blue & red	.35	.25

Brena Campaign Centenary A285

1982, Oct. 26 *Perf. 13x13½*

773	A285	70s Andres Caceres medallion	.15	.15

For surcharge see No. 790.

1982 World Cup — A286
16th Intl. Congress of Latin Notaries, Lima, June — A287

1982, Nov. 2 *Perf. 12*
774 A286 80s multicolored .15 .15
For surcharge see No. 800.

1982, Nov. 6
775 A287 500s Emblem .90 .60

Handicrafts Year — A288

1982, Nov. 24 *Perf. 13x13½*
776 A288 200s Clay bull figurine .35 .25

Christmas — A289
Pedro Vilcapaza — A290

1982 *Perf. 13½x13*
777 A289 280s Holy Family .50 .50
For surcharge see No. 797.

1982, Dec. 2 *Perf. 13½x13*
778 A290 240s black & lt brn .45 .30
Death centenary of Indian leader against Spanish during Andes Rebellion.
For surcharges see Nos. 792.

Jose Davila Condemarin (1799-1882), Minister of Posts (1849-76) A291

1982, Dec. 10 *Perf. 13x13½*
779 A291 150s blue & blk .25 .25

10th Anniv. of Intl. Potato Study Center, Lima — A292

1982, Dec. 27 *Perf. 13x13½*
780 A292 240s multicolored .45 .30
For surcharge see No. 793.

450th Anniv. of City of San Miguel de Piura — A293

1982, Dec. 31 *Perf. 13x13½*
781 A293 280s Arms .50 .50
For surcharge see No. 795.

TB Bacillus Centenary A294

1983, Jan. 18 *Perf. 12*
782 A294 240s Microscope, slide .45 .45
For surcharge see No. 794.

St. Teresa of Jesus of Avila (1515-1582), by Jose Espinoza de los Monteros, 1682 — A295

1983, Mar. 1
783 A295 100s multicolored .18 .15

10th Anniv. of State Security Service A296

1983, Mar. 8
784 A296 100s blue & orange .18 .15

Horseman's Ornamental Silver Shoe, 19th Cent. — A297

1983, Mar. 18
785 A297 250s multicolored .45 .30

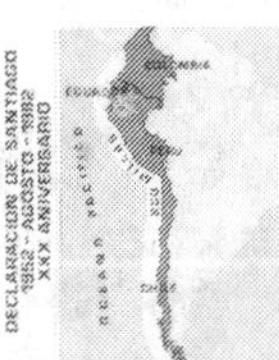

30th Anniv. of Santiago Declaration A298
75th Anniv. of Lima and Callao State Lotteries A300

25th Anniv. of Lima-Bogota Airmail Service A299

1983, Mar. 25
786 A298 280s Map .50 .50
For surcharge see No. 796.

1983, Apr. 8
787 A299 150s Jet .28 .18

1983, Apr. 26
788 A300 100s multicolored .18 .18

Nos. 739, 773, 771, 778, 780, 782, 781, 786, 777, 749, 774 Surcharged in Black or Green

1983 **Litho.**
789 A277 100s on 40s orange .22 .15
790 A285 100s on 70s multi .22 .15
791 A283 100s on 80s blk & red .22 .15
792 A290 100s on 240s multi .22 .15
793 A292 100s on 240s multi .22 .22
794 A294 100s on 240s ol grn .22 .22
795 A293 150s on 280s multi (G) .30 .30
796 A298 150s on 280s multi .30 .30
797 A289 200s on 280s multi .45 .35
798 A277 300s on 180s green .70 .45
799 A277 400s on 180s green .90 .90
800 A286 500s on 80s multi 1.10 1.10
Nos. 789-800 (12) 5.07 4.44

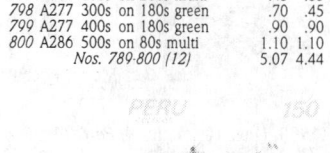

Military Ships — A301

1983, May 2 *Perf. 12*
801 A301 150s Cruiser Almirante Grau, 1907 .25 .18
802 A301 350s Submarine Ferre, 1913 .65 .40

Simon Bolivar Birth Bicentenary — A302
Christmas — A303

1983, Dec. 13 **Litho.** *Perf. 14*
803 A302 100s black & lt bl .18 .15

1983, Dec. 16
804 A303 100s Virgin and Child .18 .15

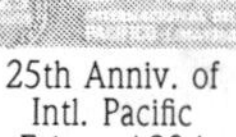

25th Anniv. of Intl. Pacific Fair — A304
Col. Leoncio Prado (1853-83) — A306

World Communications Year (in 1983) — A305

1983
805 A304 350s multicolored .65 .40

1984, Jan. 27 **Litho.** *Perf. 14*
806 A305 700s multicolored 1.25 .90

1984, Feb. 3 **Litho.** *Perf. 14*
807 A306 150s ol & ol brn .15 .15

Postal Building A307

Pottery — A308
Arms of City of Callao — A310

Shipbuilding and Repair A309

Peruvian Flora — A311
Peruvian Fauna — A312

1984 **Litho.** *Perf. 14*
808 A307 50s Ministry of Posts, Lima .15 .15
809 A308 100s Water jar .15 .15
810 A308 150s Llama .15 .15
811 A308 200s Painted vase .15 .15
812 A309 250s shown .18 .15
813 A309 300s Mixed cargo ship .25 .15
814 A310 350s shown .28 .15
815 A310 400s Arms of Cajamarca .28 .15
816 A310 500s Arms of Ayacucho .40 .18
817 A311 700s Canna edulis ker .52 .28
818 A312 1000s Lagothrix flavicauda .75 .38
Nos. 808-818 (11) 3.26
Set value 1.60

Issue dates: 50s, Aug. 29; 100s-200s, May 9; 250s-300s, Feb. 22; 350s, Apr. 23; 400s, June 21; 500s, June 22; 700s, Sept. 12; 1000s, July 3.
See Nos. 844-853, 880-885.

A313
A315

Designs: 50s, Hipolito Unanue (1758-1833). 200s, Ricardo Palma (1833-1919), Writer.

1984 **Litho.** *Perf. 14*
819 A313 50s dull green .15 .15
820 A313 200s purple .15 .15

Issue dates: 50s, Nov. 14; 200s, Mar. 20.
See No. 828.

1984, Mar. 30
821 A315 500s Shooting .35 .22
822 A315 750s Hurdles .50 .35
1984 Summer Olympics.

Independence Declaration Act — A316

1984, July 18 **Litho.** *Perf. 14*
823 A316 350s Signing document .20 .15

Admiral Grau — A317

Naval Battle A318

1984, Oct. 8 Litho. *Perf. 12½*

824 Block of 4 1.15 .75
a. A317 600s Knight of the Seas, by Pablo Muniz .28 .18
b. A318 600s Battle of Angamos .28 .18
c. A317 600s Congressional seat .28 .18
d. A318 600s Battle of Iquique .28 .18

Admiral Miguel Grau, 150th birth anniv.

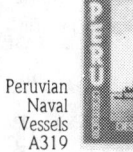

Peruvian Naval Vessels A319

1984, Dec. Litho. *Perf. 14*

825 A319 250s Destroyer Almirante Guise, 1934 .15 .15
826 A319 400s Gunboat America, 1905 .18 .15

Christmas A320

1984, Dec. 11 Litho. *Perf. 13x13½*

827 A320 1000s multi .45 .30

Famous Peruvians Type of 1984

1984, Dec. 14 Litho. *Perf. 14*

828 A313 100s brown lake .22 .15

Victor Andres Belaunde (1883-1967), Pres. of UN General Assembly, 1959-60.

450th Anniv., Founding of Cuzco — A322

1984, Dec. 20 Litho. *Perf. 13½x13*

829 A322 1000s Street scene .42 .28

15th Pacific Intl. Fair, Lima — A323

1984, Dec. 28 Litho. *Perf. 13x13½*

830 A323 1000s Llama .42 .28

450th Anniv., Lima — A324

Visit of Pope John Paul II — A325

1985, Jan. 17 Litho. *Perf. 13½x13*

831 A324 1500s The Foundation of Lima, by Francisco Gamarra .50 .35

1985, Jan. 31 Litho. *Perf. 13½x13*

832 A325 2000s Portrait .52 .35

Microwave Tower — A326

Jose Carlos Mariategui (1894-1924), Author — A327

1985, Feb. 28 Litho. *Perf. 13½x13*

833 A326 1100s multi .50 .15

ENTEL Peru, Natl. Telecommunications Org., 15th anniv.

1985-86 Photo. *Perf. 13½x13*

Designs: 500s, Francisco Garcia Calderon (1832-1905), president. No. 838, Oscar Miro Quesada (1884-1981), jurist. No. 839, Cesar Vallejo (1892-1938), author. No. 840, Jose Santos Chocano (1875-1934), poet.

836 A327 500s lt olive grn .15 .15
837 A327 800s dull red .18 .15
838 A327 800s dk olive grn .18 .18
839 A327 800s Prus blue ('86) .15 .15
840 A327 800s dk red brn ('86) .15 .15
Set value .60 .45

See Nos. 901-905.

American Air Forces Cooperation System, 25th Anniv. — A328

1985, Apr. 16

842 A328 400s Member flags, emblem .15 .15

Jose A. Quinones Gonzales (1914-1941), Air Force Captain A329

1985, Apr. 22 *Perf. 13x13½*

843 A329 1000s Portrait, bomber .22 .15

Types of 1984

Design: 200s, Entrance arch and arcade, Central PO admin. building, vert. No. 845, Spotted Robles Moqo bisque vase, Pacheco, Ica. No. 846, Huaura bisque cat. No. 847, Robles Moqo bisque llama head. No. 848, Huancavelica city arms. No. 849, Huanuco city arms. No. 850, Puno city arms. No. 851, Llama wool industry. No. 852, Hymenocallis amancaes. No. 853, Penguins, Antarctic landscape.

1985-86 Litho. *Perf. 13½x13*

844 A307 200s slate blue .15 .15
845 A308 500s bister brn .22 .15
846 A308 500s dull yellow brn .22 .15
847 A308 500s black brn .22 .15
848 A310 700s brt org yel .32 .15
849 A310 700s brt bl ('86) .32 .15
850 A310 900s brown ('86) .40 .15
851 A309 1100s multicolored .50 .15
852 A311 1100s multicolored .50 .15
853 A312 1500s multicolored .70 .15
Nos. 844-853 (10) 3.55
Set value .65

Natl. Aerospace Institute Emblem, Globe — A330

1985, May 24 *Perf. 13x13½*

858 A330 900s ultra .20 .15

14th Inter-American Air Defense Day.

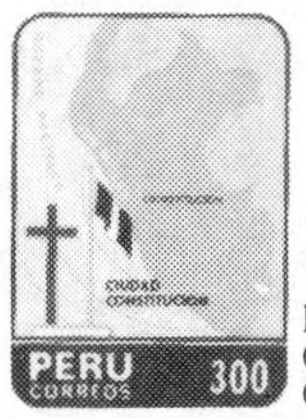

Founding of Constitution City — A333

1985, July Litho. *Perf. 13½x13*

859 A333 300s Map, flag, crucifix .15 .15

Natl. Radio Society, 55th Anniv. — A334

1985, July 24 *Perf. 13x13½*

860 A334 1300s bl & brt org .16 .15

San Francisco Convent Church — A335

Doctrina Christiana Frontispiece, 1585, Lima — A336

1985, Oct. 12 *Perf. 13½x13*

861 A335 1300s multicolored .16 .15

1985, Oct. 23

862 A336 300s pale buff & blk .15 .15

1st printed book in South America, 400th anniv.

Intl. Civil Aviation Org., 40th Anniv. A337

1985, Oct. 31 *Perf. 13x13½*

863 A337 1100s 1920 Curtis Jenny .18 .15

Christmas — A338

Postman, Child — A338a

1985, Dec. 30 Litho. *Perf. 13½x13*

864 A338 2.50i Virgin and child, 17th cent. .40 .15

1985, Dec. 30 Litho. *Perf. 13½x13*

864A A338a 2.50i multi .28 .22

Christmas charity for children's and postal workers' funds.

Founding of Trujillo, 450th Anniv. — A339

1986, Mar. 5 Litho. *Perf. 13½x13*

865 A339 3i City arms .40 .25

Restoration of Chan Chan Ruins, Trujillo Province A340

1986, Apr. 5 Litho. *Perf. 13x13½*

866 A340 50c Bas-relief .15 .15

Saint Rose of Lima, Birth Quadricent. A341

16th Intl. Pacific Fair A342

1986, Apr. 30 Litho. *Perf. 13½x13*

867 A341 7i multicolored .90 .60

1986, May 20

868 A342 1i Natl. products symbols .38 .15

Intl. Youth Year — A343

1986, May 23 *Perf. 13x13½*

869 A343 3.50i multicolored .42 .28

A344

A346

A345

1986, June 27 Litho. ***Perf. 13½x13***
870 A344 50c brown .18 .15

Pedro Vilcapaza (1740-81), independence hero.

1986, Aug. 8 Litho. ***Perf. 13x13½***
871 A345 3.50i multi .65 .30

UN, 40th anniv.

1986, Aug. 11 ***Perf. 13½x13***
872 A346 50c grysh brown .24 .15

Fernando and Justo Albujar Fayaque, Manuel Guarniz Lopez, natl. heroes.

Peruvian Navy — A347

1986, Aug. 19 ***Perf. 13x13½***
873 A347 1.50i R-1, 1926 .18 .15
874 A347 2.50i Abtao, 1954 .30 .22

Flora Type of 1984

1986 Litho. ***Perf. 13½x13***
880 A311 80c Tropaeolum majus .15 .15
881 A311 80c Datura candida .15 .15
884 A312 2i Canis nudus .30 .22
885 A312 2i Penelope albipennis .35 .28
Nos. 880-885 (4) .95 .80

Canchis Province Folk Costumes — A348

1986, Aug. 26 Litho. ***Perf. 13½x13***
890 A348 3i multicolored .35 .25

Tourism Day — A349

1986, Aug. 29 ***Perf. 13x13½***
891 A349 4i Sacsayhuaman .48 .35

1986, Oct. 12 Litho. ***Perf. 13x13½***
891A A349 4i Intihuatana, Cuzco .50 .38

Interamerican Development Bank, 25th Anniv. A350

1986, Sept. 4
892 A350 1i multicolored .25 .15

Beatification of Sr. Ana de Los Angeles A351

1986, Sept. 15
893 A351 6i Sr. Ana, Pope John Paul II .72 .55

Jorge Chavez (1887-1910), Aviator, and Bleriot XI 1M — A352

VAN '86 — A353

1986, Sept. 23 ***Perf. 13½x13***
894 A352 5i multicolored .85 .45

Chavez's flight over the Alps, 75th anniv.

1986, Sept. 26
895 A353 50c light blue .15 .15

Ministry of Health vaccination campaign, Sept. 27-28, Oct. 25-26, Nov. 22-23.

Natl. Journalism Day — A354

1986, Oct. 1
896 A354 1.50i multi .18 .15

Peruvian Navy — A355

1986, Oct. 7 Litho. ***Perf. 13x13½***
897 A355 1i Brigantine Gamarra, 1848 .15 .15
898 A355 1i Monitor Manco Capac, 1880 .15 .15
Set value .24

Institute of Higher Military Studies, 35th Anniv. — A356

1986, Oct. 31 Litho. ***Perf. 13x13½***
899 A356 1i multicolored .18 .15

Boy, Girl — A357

1986, Nov. 3 ***Perf. 13½x13***
900 A357 2.50i red, brn & blk .38 .30

Christmas charity for children and postal workers' funds.

Famous Peruvians Type of 1985

1986-87
901 A327 50c Carrion .15 .15
902 A327 50c Barrenechea .15 .15
904 A327 80c Jose de la Riva Aguero .15 .15
905 A327 80c Barrenechea .15 .15
Set value .28 .22

Issued: #904, 10/22/87; #905, 11/9/87.
This is an expanding set. Numbers will change if necessary.

Christmas — A358

SENATI, 25th Anniv. — A359

1986, Dec. 3
908 A358 5i St. Joseph and Child .75 .58

1986, Dec. 19 ***Perf. 13½x13***
909 A359 4i multicolored .70 .45

Shipibo Tribal Costumes — A360

World Food Day — A361

1987, Apr. 24 Litho. ***Perf. 13½x13***
910 A360 3i multicolored .45 .35

1987, May 26
911 A361 50c multicolored .18 .15

Preservation of the Nasca Lines — A362

Design: Nasca Lines and Dr. Maria Reiche (b. 1903), archaeologist.

1987, June 13 Litho. ***Perf. 13x13½***
912 A362 8i multicolored 1.20 .90

A363

A365

A364

1987, July 15 Litho. ***Perf. 13½x13***
913 A363 50c violet .18 .15

Mariano Santos (1850-1900), "The Hero of Tarapaca," 1879, Chilean war. Dated 1986.

1987, July 19 ***Perf. 13x13½***
914 A364 3i multicolored .45 .35

Natl. Horse Club, 50th anniv. Dated 1986.

1987, Aug 13 ***Perf. 13½x13***
915 A365 2i multicolored .30 .22

Gen. Felipe Santiago Salaverry (1806-1836), revolution leader. Dated 1986.

Colca's Canyon — A366

AMIFIL '87 — A367

1987, Sept. 8 Litho. ***Perf. 13½x13***
916 A366 6i multicolored .52 .38

10th Natl. Philatelic Exposition, Arequipa. Dated 1986.

1987, Sept. 10
917 A367 1i Nos. 1-2 .20 .15

Dated 1986.

Jose Maria Arguedas (b. 1911), Anthropologist, Author — A368

1987, Sept. 19
918 A368 50c brown .15 .15

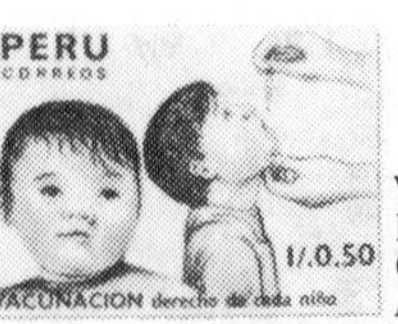

Arequipa Chamber of Commerce & Industry A369

1987, Sept. 23 ***Perf. 13x13½***
919 A369 2i multicolored .22 .16

Vaccinate Every Child Campaign A370

1987, Sept. 30 Litho. ***Perf. 13x13½***
920 A370 50c orange brown .15 .15

Argentina, Winner of the 1986 World Cup Soccer Championships — A371

1987, Nov. 18
921 A371 4i multicolored .32 .22

Restoration of Chan Chan Ruins, Trujillo Province A372

Chimu culture (11th-15th cent.) bas-relief.

1987, Nov. 27
922 A372 50c multicolored .15 .15

See No. 936.

Halley's Comet A373

1987, Dec. 7
923 A373 4i Comet, Giotto satellite .32 .22

Jorge Chavez Dartnell (1887-1910), Aviator — A374

Founding of Lima, 450th Anniv. (in 1985) — A375

1987, Dec. 15 *Perf. 13½x13*
924 A374 2i yel bis, claret brn & gold .30 .15

1987, Dec. 18 Litho. *Perf. 13½x13*
925 A375 2.50i Osambela Palace .30 .15

Dated 1985.

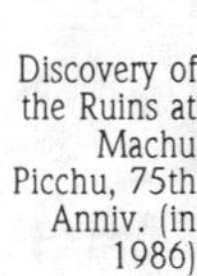

Discovery of the Ruins at Machu Picchu, 75th Anniv. (in 1986) A376

1987, Dec. *Perf. 13x13½*
926 A376 9i multicolored .65 .48

Dated 1986.

St. Francis's Church, Cajamarca A377

1988, Jan. 23 Litho. *Perf. 13x13½*
927 A377 2i multicolored .30 .15

Cultural Heritage. Dated 1986.

Participation of Peruvian Athletes in the Olympics, 50th Anniv. — A378

Design: Athletes on parade, poster publicizing the 1936 Berlin Games.

1988, Mar. 1 Litho. *Perf. 13½x13*
928 A378 1.50i multicolored .40 .15

Dated 1986.

Ministry of Education, 150th Anniv. A379

1988, Mar. 10 *Perf. 13x13½*
929 A379 1i multicolored .18 .15

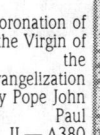

Coronation of the Virgin of the Evangelization by Pope John Paul II — A380

1988, Mar. 14 Litho. *Perf. 13x13½*
930 A380 10i multicolored .48 .24

Dated 1986.

Rotary Intl. Involvement in Anti-Polio Campaign A381

1988, Mar. 16
931 A381 2i org, gold & dark blue .15 .15

Postman, Cathedral — A382

St. John Bosco (1815-1888), Educator — A384

Meeting of 8 Latin-American Presidents, Acapulco, 1st Anniv. — A383

1988, Apr. 29 Litho. *Perf. 13½x13*
932 A382 9i brt blue .28 .15

Christmas charity for children and postal workers' funds.

1988, May 4 *Perf. 13x13½*
933 A383 9i multicolored .28 .15

1988, June 1 *Perf. 13½x13*
934 A384 5i multicolored .15 .15

1st Peruvian Scientific Expedition to the Antarctic A385

1988, June 2 *Perf. 13x13½*
935 A385 7i Ship Humboldt, globe .16 .15

Restoration of Chan-Chan Ruins, Trujillo Province A386

1988, June 7
936 A386 4i Bas-relief .15 .15

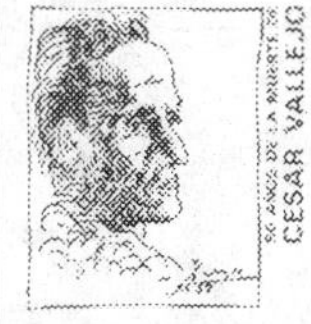

Cesar Vallejo (1892-1938), Poet — A387

Journalists' Fund — A388

1988, June 15 *Perf. 13½x13*
937 A387 25i buff, blk & brn .58 .30

1988, July 12 Litho. *Perf. 13½x13*
938 A388 4i buff & deep ultra .18 .15

Type A44 — A389

1988, Sept. 1 Litho. *Perf. 13½x13*
939 A389 20i blk, lt pink & ultra .16 .15

EXFILIMA '88, discovery of America 500th anniv.

17th Intl. Pacific Fair — A390

1988, Sept. 6 *Perf. 13x13½*
940 A390 4i multicolored .15 .15

Painting by Jose Sabogal (1888-1956) A391

1988, Sept. 7
941 A391 12i multicolored .18 .15

Peru Kennel Club Emblem, Dogs — A392

1988, Sept. 9 *Perf. 13½x13*
942 A392 20i multicolored .16 .15

CANINE '88 Intl. Dog Show, Lima.

Alfonso de Silva (1902-1934), Composer, and Score to Esplendido de Flores A393

1988, Sept. 27 Litho. *Perf. 13x13½*
943 A393 20i multicolored .16 .15

2nd State Visit of Pope John Paul II — A394

1988 Summer Olympics, Seoul — A395

1988, Oct. 10 *Perf. 13½x13*
944 A394 50i multicolored .40 .20

1988, Nov. 10 Litho. *Perf. 13½x13*
945 A395 25i Women's volleyball .38 .15

Women's Volleyball Championships (1982) — A396

Chavin Culture Ceramic Vase — A397

1988, Nov. 16 *Perf. 12*

Surcharged in Red

946 A396 95i on 300s multi .78 .40

No. 946 not issued without overprint.

Christmas charity for children's and postal workers' funds.

1988 Litho. *Perf. 12*

Surcharged in Henna or Black

947 A397 40i on 100s red brn .16 .15
948 A397 80i on 10s blk .32 .16
Set value .24

Nos. 947-948 not issued without surcharge. Issue dates: 40i, Dec. 15. 80i, Dec. 22.

Rain Forest Border Highway — A398

Codex of the Indian Kings, 1681 — A399

1989, Jan. 27 Litho. *Perf. 12*
Surcharged in Black
949 A398 70i on 80s multi .20 .15

Not issued without surcharge.

1989, Feb. 10
Surcharged in Olive Brown
950 A399 230i on 300s multi .50 .25

Not issued without surcharge.

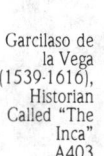

Credit Bank of Peru, Cent. — A400

1989, Apr. 9 Litho. *Perf. 13x13½*
951 A400 500i Huari Culture weaving .75 .35

Postal Services A401

1989, Apr. 20 *Perf. 13*
952 A401 50i SESPO, vert. .15 .15
953 A401 100i CAN .18 .15
Set value .26 .15

El·Comercio, 150th Anniv. — A402

1989, May 15
954 A402 600i multi .60 .30

Garcilaso de la Vega (1539-1616), Historian Called "The Inca" A403

1989, July 11 Litho. *Perf. 12½*
955 A403 300i multi .32 .16

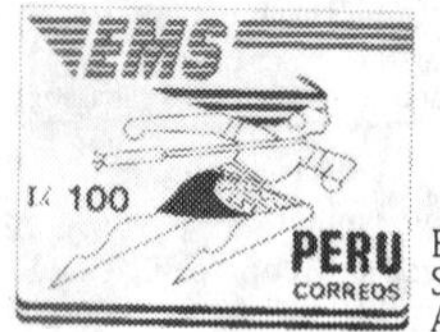

Express Mail Service A404

1989, July 12
956 A404 100i dark red, org & dark blue .20 .15

Federation Emblem and Roca A405

1989, Aug. 29 Litho. *Perf. 13*
957 A405 100i multi .21 .15

Luis Loli Roca (1925-1988), founder of the Federation of Peruvian Newspaper Publishers.

Restoration of Chan Chan Ruins, Trujillo Province A406

Chimu culture (11th-15th cent.) bas-relief.

1989, Sept. 17 *Perf. 12½*
958 A406 400i multi .44 .22

Geographical Society of Lima, Cent. — A407

1989, Sept. 18 *Perf. 13*
959 A407 600i Early map of So. America .65 .32

Founders of Independence Soc. — A408

1989, Sept. 28 Litho. *Perf. 12½*
960 A408 300i multicolored .30 .15

3rd Meeting of the Presidential Consultation and Planning Board — A409

1989, Oct. 12 *Perf. 13*
961 A409 1300i Huacachina Lake 1.40 .70

For surcharge see No. 1017.

Children Mailing Letters — A410

1989, Nov. 29 Litho. *Perf. 12½*
962 A410 1200i multicolored .32

Christmas charity for children's and postal workers' funds.

Cacti A411

1989, Dec. 21 Litho. *Perf. 13*
963 A411 500i *Loxanthocereus acanthurus* .20
964 A411 500i *Corryocactus huincoensis* .20
965 A411 500i *Haageocereus clavispinus* .20
966 A411 500i *Trichocereus peruvianus* .20
967 A411 500i *Matucana cereoides* .20
Nos. 963-967 (5) 1.00

Nos. 965-967 vert. For surcharges see Nos. 1028-1031

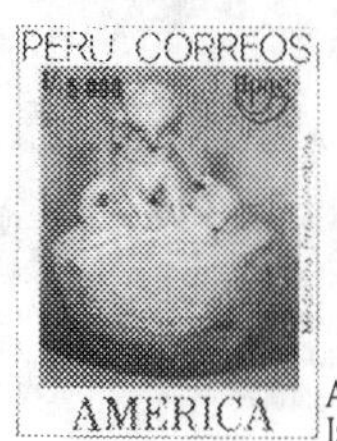

America Issue — A412

UPAE emblem and pre-Columbian medicine jars.

1989, Dec. 28 *Perf. 12½*
968 A412 5000i shown 2.00
969 A412 5000i multi, diff. 2.00

Belen Church, Cajamarca A413

1990, Feb. 1 Litho. *Perf. 12½*
970 A413 600i multicolored .20

Historic patrimony of Cajamarca and culture of the Americas.

Huascaran Natl. Park — A414

1990, Feb. 4 *Perf. 13*
971 A414 900i Llanganuco Lagoons .15
972 A414 900i Mountain climber, Andes, vert. .15
973 A414 1000i Alpamayo mountain .16
974 A414 1000i *Puya raimondi*, vert. .16
975 A414 1100i Condor and Quenual .17
976 A414 1100i El Huascaran .17
Nos. 971-976 (6) .96

Pope and Icon of the Virgin — A415

1990, Feb. 6 *Perf. 12½*
977 A415 1250i multicolored .52

Visit of Pope John Paul II. For surcharge see No. 1039.

Butterflies A416

1990, Feb. 11 *Perf. 13*
978 A416 1000i *Amydon* .15
979 A416 1000i *Agrias beata*, female .15
980 A416 1000i *Sardanapalus*, male .15
981 A416 1000i *Sardanapalus*, female .15
982 A416 1000i *Agrias beata*, male .15
Nos. 978-982 (5) .75

For surcharges see Nos. 1033-1037.

A417

A418

Victor Raul Haya de La Torre and Seat of Government.

1990, Feb. 24 *Perf. 12½*
983 A417 2100i multicolored .55

Return to constitutional government, 10th anniv.

1990, May 24 Litho. *Perf. 12½*
984 A418 300i multicolored .28

Peruvian Philatelic Assoc., 50th anniv. Dated 1989. For surcharge see No. 1038.

Prenfil '88 A419

1990, May 29
985 A419 300i multicolored .20

World Exposition of Stamp & Literature Printers, Buenos Aires. Dated 1989. For surcharge see No. 1032.

French Revolution, Bicentennial A420

#986, Liberty. #987, Storming the Bastille. #988, Lafayette celebrating the Republic. #989, Rousseau & symbols of the Revolution.

1990, June 5
986 A420 2000i multicolored .50
987 A420 2000i multicolored .50
988 A420 2000i multicolored .50
989 A420 2000i shown .50
a. Strip of 4, #986-989 + label 2.00

Dated 1989.

Arequipa, 450th Anniv. A421

1990, Aug. 15 Litho. *Perf. 13*
990 A421 50,000i multi .50

Lighthouse A422

Design: 230,000i, Hospital ship Morona.

1990, Sept. 19 *Perf. 12½*
Surcharged in Black
991 A422 110,000i on 200i blue .85
992 A422 230,000i on 400i blue 1.75

Not issued without surcharge.

A423 A424

1990-91 Litho. *Perf. 13*

993 A423 110,000i Torch bearer .55
994 A423 280,000i Shooting 1.40
995 A423 290,000i Running, horiz. 1.45
996 A423 300,000i Soccer 1.50
997 A423 560,000i Swimming, horiz. 2.30
998 A423 580,000i Equestrian 2.40
999 A423 600,000i Sailing 2.50
1000 A423 620,000i Tennis 2.55
Nos. 993-1000 (8) 14.65

4th South American Games, Lima. Issue dates: #993-996, Oct. 19. #997-1000, Feb. 5, 1991.

1990, Nov. 22 Litho. *Die Cut*
Self-Adhesive

1001 A424 250,000i No. 1 1.50
1002 A424 350,000i No. 2 2.25

Pacific Steam Navigation Co., 150th anniv.

Postal Workers' Christmas Fund A425

1990, Dec. 7 Litho. *Perf. 12½*

1003 A425 310,000i multi 1.70

Maria Jesus Castaneda de Pardo, First Woman President of Peruvian Red Cross — A426

1991, May 15 Litho. *Perf. 12½*

1004 A426 .15im on 2500i red & blk .60

Dated 1990. Not issued without surcharge.

2nd Peruvian Scientific Expedition to Antarctica — A427

.40im, Penguins, man. .45im, Peruvian research station, skua. .50im, Whale, map, research station.

1991, June 20

1005 A427 .40im on 50,000i 1.60
1006 A427 .45im on 80,000i 1.80
1007 A427 .50im on 100,000i 2.00
Nos. 1005-1007 (3) 5.40

Not issued without surcharge.

A428 A429

St. Anthony Natl. Univ., Cuzco, 300th Anniv.: 10c, Siphoonandra ellipitica. 20c, Don Manuel de Mollinedo y Angulo, founder. 1s, University coat of arms.

1991, Sept. 26 Litho. *Perf. 13½x13*

1008 A428 10c multicolored .24
1009 A428 20c multicolored .48
1010 A428 1s multicolored 2.40
Nos. 1008-1010 (3) 3.12

1991, Dec. 3 Litho. *Perf. 13½x13*

Paintings: No. 1011, Madonna and child. No. 1012, Madonna with lambs and angels.

1011 A429 70c multicolored 1.50
1012 A429 70c multicolored 1.50

Postal Workers' Christmas fund.

America Issue A430

1991, Dec. 23 *Perf. 13*

1013 A430 .50im Mangrove swamp 1.10
1014 A430 .50im Gera waterfall, vert. 1.10

Dated 1990.

Sir Rowland Hill and Penny Black A431

1992, Jan. 15 Litho. *Perf. 13*

1015 A431 .40im gray, blk & bl .85

Penny Black, 150th anniv. (in 1990).

A432 A433

1992, Jan. 28

1016 A432 .30im multicolored .65

Our Lady of Guadalupe College, 150th anniv. (in 1990)

1992, Jan. 30 *Perf. 13½x13*

1017 A433 10c multicolored .16

Entre Nous Society, 80th anniv.

Peru-Bolivia Port Access Agreement — A434

1992, Feb. 25 Litho. *Perf. 12½*

1018 A434 20c multicolored .32

Restoration of Chan-Chan Ruins — A435

1992, Mar. 17

1019 A435 .15im multicolored .35

Dated 1990.

Antonio Raimondi, Naturalist and Publisher, Death Cent. — A436

1992, Mar. 31

1020 A436 .30im multicolored .75

Dated 1990.

Newspaper "Diario de Lima", Bicent. (in 1990) — A437

1992, May 22 Litho. *Perf. 13*

1021 A437 .35im pale yel & black .65

Dated 1990.

Mariano Melgar (1790-1815), Poet A438

1992, Aug. 5 Litho. *Perf. 12½x13*

1022 A438 60c multicolored .85

8 Reales, 1568, First Peruvian Coinage A439

1992, Aug. 7 *Perf. 13x12½*

1023 A439 70c multicolored 1.00

Catholic Univeristy of Peru, 75th Anniv. — A440

1992, Aug. 18 *Perf. 12½*

1024 A440 90c black & tan 1.30

Pan-American Health Organization, 90th Anniv. — A441

1992, Dec. 2 Litho. *Die Cut*
Self-Adhesive

1025 A441 3s multicolored 3.75

Nos. 749, 961 Surcharged

S/. 0.50

Perf. 13½x13, 13
1992, Nov. 18 Litho.

1026 A277 50c on 180s #749 .65
1027 A409 1s on 1300i #961 1.25

Nos. 963, 965-967, 977-982, & 984-985 Surcharged

S/. 0.40

1992, Dec. 24 Litho. *Perfs. as Before*

1028 A411 40c on 500i #963
1029 A411 40c on 500i #965
1030 A411 40c on 500i #966
1031 A411 40c on 500i #967
1032 A419 50c on 300i #985
1033 A416 50c on 1000i #978
1034 A416 50c on 1000i #979
1035 A416 50c on 1000i #980
1036 A416 50c on 1000i #981
1037 A416 50c on 1000i #982
1038 A418 1s on 300i #984
1039 A415 1s on 1250i #977

Virgin with a Spindle, by Urbina — A442

1993, Feb. 10 Litho. *Die Cut*
Self-Adhesive

1040 A442 80c multicolored .95

Sican Culture A443

Various artifacts.

1993, Feb. 10
Self-Adhesive

1041 A443 2s multicolored 2.35
1042 A443 5s multi, vert. 6.00

Evangelization in Peru, 500th Anniv. — A444

1993, Feb. 12
Self-Adhesive

1043 A444 1s multicolored 1.20

Fruit Sellers, by Angel Chavez — A445

Dancers, by Monica Rojas — A446

1993, Feb. 12
Self-Adhesive

1044 A445 1.50s multicolored 1.80
1045 A446 1.50s multicolored 1.80

Statue of Madonna and Child — A447

1993, Feb. 24 Litho. *Die Cut*
Self-Adhesive

1046 A447 70c multicolored 1.15

Salesian Brothers in Peru, cent. (in 1991).

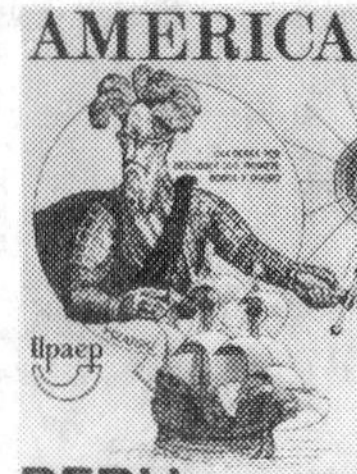

America Issue — A448

UPAEP: No. 1047a, 90c, Francisco Pizarro, sailing ship. b, 1s, Sailing ship, map of northwest coast of South America.

1993, Mar. 19 *Perf. 12½*

1047 A448 Pair, #a.-b. 2.45

Sipan Gold Head — A449

1993, Apr. 1

1048 A449 50c multicolored .68

Beatification of Josemaria Escriva, 1st Anniv. — A450

1993, July 7 Litho. *Die Cut*
Self-Adhesive

1049 A450 30c multicolored .52

Peru-Japan Treaty of Peace and Trade, 120th Anniv. — A451

Designs: 1.50s, Flowers. 1.70s, Peruvian, Japanese children, mountains.

1993, Aug. 21 Litho. *Perf. 11*

1050 A451 1.50s multicolored 2.00
1051 A451 1.70s multicolored 2.25

Sea Lions — A452

1993, Sept. 20 Litho. *Perf. 11*

1052 A452 90c shown 1.00
1053 A452 1s Parrot, vert. 1.10

Amifil '93 (#1052). Brasiliana '93 (#1053).

Based on available currency exchange rates, the face value of Nos. 1056-1057 is about $2.53. It appears that Peruvian stamps are appearing in the market at significantly higher prices. We have left some of Peru's new issues unvalued until we have more information on the relationship between face value and current retail prices.

A453

A454

1993, Nov. 9 Litho. *Die Cut*
Self-Adhesive

1054 A453 50c olive brown

Honorio Delgado, Physician and Author, Birth Cent. (in 1992).

1993, Nov. 12
Self-Adhesive

1055 A454 80c orange brown

Rosalia De LaValle De Morales Macedo, Social Reformer, Birth Cent.

A455

Intl. Pacific Fair, Lima — A456

Sculptures depicting Peruvian ethnic groups.

1993, Nov. 22
Self-Adhesive

1056 A455 2s Quechua
1057 A455 3.50s Orejon

1993, Nov. 25 Litho. *Perf. 11*

1058 A456 1.50s multicolored

Christmas A457

Cultural Artifacts A458

Design: 1s, Madonna of Loreto.

1993, Nov. 30 *Perf. 11*

1059 A457 1s multicolored

1993, Nov. 30 *Die Cut*

2.50s, Sican artifacts. 4s, Sican mask. 10s, Chancay ceramic statue, vert. 20s, Chancay textile.

Self-Adhesive

1060 A458 2.50s multicolored
1061 A458 4s multicolored
1062 A458 10s multicolored
1063 A458 20s multicolored

See Nos. 1079-1082.

Prevention of AIDS — A459

1993, Dec. 1 Litho. *Perf. 11*

1064 A459 1.50s multicolored

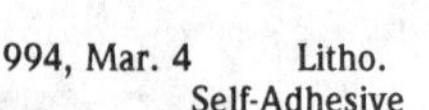

A460

A461

1994, Mar. 4 Litho. *Die Cut*
Self-Adhesive

1065 A460 1s multicolored 1.65

Natl. Council on Science and Technology (Concytec), 25th Anniv. Dated 1993.

1994

20c, 40c, 50c, Bridge of Huaman Poma de Ayala.

Self-Adhesive

1066 A461 20c blue .35
1067 A461 40c orange .65
1068 A461 50c purple .85
Nos. 1066-1068 (3) 1.85

Litho.
Perf. 12x11

1073 A461 30c brown .50
1074 A461 40c black .70
1075 A461 50c vermilion .85
Nos. 1073-1075 (3) 2.05

Issued: Nos. 1066-1068, 3/11/94; Nos. 1073-1075, 5/13/94.
This is an expanding set. Numbers may change.

Cultural Artifacts Type of 1993

No. 1079, Engraved silver container, vert. No. 1080, Engraved medallion. No. 1081, Carved bull, Pucara. No. 1082, Plate with fish designs.

1994, Mar. 25
Self-Adhesive

1079 A458 1.50s multicolored 2.50
1080 A458 1.50s multicolored 2.50
1081 A458 3s multicolored 4.75
1082 A458 3s multicolored 4.75
Nos. 1079-1082 (4) 14.50

Sipan Artifacts — A464

1994, May 19 Litho. *Perf. 11*

1083 A464 3s Peanut-shaped beads 4.75
1084 A464 5s Mask, vert. 8.00

El Brujo Archaelogical Site, Trujillo A465

1994, Nov. 3 Litho. *Perf. 14*

1085 A465 70c multicolored .65

Christmas A466

Ceramic figures: 1.80s, Christ child. 2s, Nativity scene. Dated 1994.

1995, Mar. 17 Litho. *Perf. 13x13½*

1086 A466 1.80s multicolored 1.65
1087 A466 2s multicolored 1.75

1994 World Cup Soccer Championships, US — A467

1995, Mar. 20 *Perf. 13½x13*

1088 A467 60c shown .50
1089 A467 4.80s Mascot, flags 4.25

Dated 1994.

Ministry of Transportation, 25th Anniv. A468

1995, Mar. 22 *Perf. 13x13½*

1090 A468 20c multicolored .15

Dated 1994.

Cultural Artifacts — A469

Mochican art: 40c, Pitcher with figures beneath blanket. 80c, Jeweled medallion. 90c, Figure holding severed head.

1995, Mar. 27 *Perf. 14*

1091 A469 40c multicolored .35
1092 A469 80c multicolored .70
1093 A469 90c multicolored .80
Nos. 1091-1093 (3) 1.85

Dated 1994.

Juan Parra del Riego, Birth Cent. — A470

No. 1095, Jose Carlos Mariategui, birth cent.

1995, Mar. 28 *Perf. 14*
1094 A470 90c multicolored .80

Perf. 13½x13
1095 A470 90c multicolored .80

Dated 1994.

Las Carmelitas Monastery, 350th Anniv. A471

1995, Mar. 31 **Litho.** *Perf. 13*
1096 A471 70c multicolored 1.10

Dated 1994.

Peru's Volunteer Fireman's Assoc. A472

Fire trucks: 50c, Early steam ladder. 90c, Modern aerial ladder.

1995, Apr. 12 *Perf. 14*
1097 A472 50c multicolored .85
1098 A472 90c multicolored 1.50

Dated 1994.

Musical Instruments — A473

1995, Apr. 10 **Litho.** *Perf. 13½x13*
1099 A473 20c Cello .35
1100 A473 40c Drum .70

Union Club, Fountain, Plaza of Arms — A474

Design: 1s, Santo Domingo Convent, Lima.

1995, Apr. 19 **Litho.** *Perf. 14*
1101 A474 90c multicolored 1.50
1102 A474 1s multicolored 1.75

Cultural history of Lima.

Ethnic Groups — A475

1995, Apr. 26 *Perf. 13½x13*
1103 A475 1s Bora girl 1.75
1104 A475 1.80s Aguaruna man 3.00
sa

World Food Program, 30th Anniv. A476

1995, May 3 *Perf. 13x13½*
1105 A476 1.80s multicolored 3.00

Solanum Ambosinum A477

Reed Boat, Lake Titicaca A478

Design: 2s, Mochica ceramic representation of papa flower.

1995, May 8 *Perf. 13½x13*
1106 A477 1.80s multicolored 3.00
1107 A477 2s multicolored 3.50

1995, May 12
1108 A478 2s multicolored 3.50

Fauna — A479

Perf. 13½x13, 13x13½
1995, May 18
1109 A479 1s American owl, vert. 1.75
1110 A479 1.80s Jaguar 3.00

Andes Development Corporation, 25th Anniv. — A480

1995, Aug. 29 **Litho.** *Perf. 14*
1111 A480 5s multicolored 8.00

World Tourism Day — A481

1995, Sept. 27 *Perf. 13x13½*
1112 A481 5.40s multicolored 8.50

Dated 1994.

World Post Day — A482

1995, Oct. 9 *Perf. 14*
1113 A482 1.80s Antique mail box 2.75

Dated 1994.

America Issue A483

Perf. 13½x14, 14x13½ (#1115)
1995, Oct. 12
1114 A483 1.50s Landing of Columbus 2.50
1115 A483 1.70s Guanaco, vert. 2.75
1116 A483 1.80s Early mail cart 2.75
1117 A483 2s Postal trucks 3.25
Nos. 1114-1117 (4) 11.25

No. 1116-1117 are dated 1994.

UN, 50th Anniv. A484

Design: 90c, Peruvian delegates, 1945.

1995, Oct. 28 *Perf. 14*
1118 A484 90c multicolored 1.50

Entrys, Lima Cathedrals — A485

Designs: 30c, St. Apolonia. 70c, St. Louis, side entry to St. Francis.

1995, Oct. 20
1119 A485 30c multicolored .55
1120 A485 70c multicolored 1.25

Dated 1994.

Artifacts from Art Museums — A486

Carvings and sculptures: No. 1121, St. James on horseback, 19th cent. No. 1122, Church. 40c, Woman on pedestal. 50c, Archangel.

1995, Oct. 31 *Perf. 14½x14*
1121 A486 20c multicolored .35
1122 A486 20c multicolored .35
1123 A486 40c multicolored .65
1124 A486 50c multicolored .80
Nos. 1121-1124 (4) 2.15

Dated 1994.

Scouting — A487

Designs: a, 80c, Lady Olave Baden-Powell. b, 1s, Lord Robert Baden-Powell.

1995, Nov. 9 **Litho.** *Perf. 13½x13*
1125 A487 Pair, #a.-b. 2.75

Dated 1994.

A488 A489

Folk Dances: 1,80s, Festejo. 2s, Marinera limeña, horiz.

1995, Nov. 16 *Perf. 14*
1126 A488 1.80s multicolored 2.75
1127 A488 2s multicolored 3.00

Dated 1994.

1995, Nov. 23

Biodiversity: 50c, Manu Natl. Park. 90c, Anolis punctatus, horiz.

1128 A489 50c multicolored .85
1129 A489 90c multicolored 1.50

Dated 1994.

A490 A491

Electricity for Development: 20c, Toma de Huinco. 40c, Antacoto Lake.

1995, Nov. 27
1130 A490 20c multicolored .30
1131 A490 40c multicolored .60

Dated 1994.

1995, Dec. 4

Peruvian Saints: 90c, St. Toribio de Mogrovejo. 1s, St. Francisco Solano.

1132 A491 90c multicolored 1.40
1133 A491 1s multicolored 1.50

Dated 1994.

FAO, 50th Anniv. A492

1996, Apr. 24 **Litho.** *Perf. 14*
1134 A492 60c multicolored .90

Christmas 1995 A493

Local crafts: 30c, Nativity scene with folding panels, vert. 70c, Carved statues of three Magi.

1996, May 2
1135 A493 30c multicolored .45
1136 A493 70c multicolored 1.00

America Issue — A494

Designs: 30c, Rock formations of Lachay. 70c, Coastal black crocodile.

1996, May 9

1137 A494 30c multicolored .45
1138 A494 70c multicolored 1.00

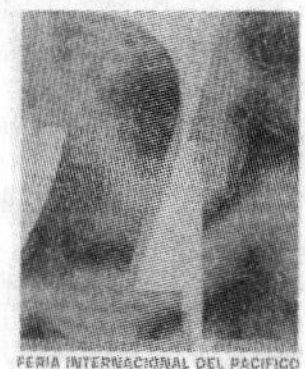

Intl. Pacific Fair — A495

1996, May 16

1139 A495 60c multicolored .90

1992 Summer Olympic Games, Barcelona A496

a, Shooting. b, Tennis. c, Swimming. d, Weight lifting.

1996, June 10 **Litho.** ***Perf. 12½***

1140 A496 60c Block of 4, #a.-d. 2.90

Dated 1992.

Expo '92, Seville — A497

1996, June 17

1141 A497 1.50s multicolored 2.20

Dated 1992.

Cesar Vallejo (1892-1938), Writer — A498

1996, June 25

1142 A498 50c black & gray .75

Dated 1992.

Lima, City of Culture — A499

1996, July 1

1143 A499 30c brown & tan .45

Dated 1992.

Kon-Tiki Expedition, 50th Anniv. — A500

1997, Apr. 28 **Litho.** ***Perf. 12½***

1144 A500 3.30s multicolored 2.50

UNICEF, 50th Anniv. (in 1996) A501

Mochica Pottery A502

1997, Aug. 7 **Litho.** ***Perf. 13½x14***

Granite Paper

1145 A501 1.80s multicolored 2.40

1997, Aug. 18 **Litho.** ***Perf. 14½***

Designs: 20c, Owl. 30c, Ornamental container. 50c, Goose jar. 1s, Two monkies on jar. 1.30s, Duck pitcher. 1.50s, Cat pitcher.

1146 A502 20c green .25
1147 A502 30c lilac .40
1148 A502 50c black .65
1149 A502 1s red brown 1.25
1150 A502 1.30s red 1.75
1151 A502 1.50s brown 2.00
Nos. 1146-1151 (6) 6.30

1996 Summer Olympics, Atlanta — A503

a, Shooting. b, Gymnastics. c, Boxing. d, Soccer.

1997, Aug. 25 ***Perf. 14x13½***

Granite paper

1152 A503 2.70s Strip of 4, #a.-d. 8.25

College of Biology, 25th Anniv. — A504

1997, Aug. 26

Granite Paper

1153 A504 5s multicolored 3.75

Scouting, 90th Anniv. — A505

1997, Aug. 29

Granite Paper

1154 A505 6.80s multicolored 5.25

8th Intl. Conference Against Corruption, Lima A506

1997, Sept. 7 ***Perf. 13½x14***

Granite Paper

1155 A506 2.70s multicolored 2.00

Montreal Protocol on Substances that Deplete Ozone Layer, 10th Anniv. — A507

1997, Sept. 16 ***Perf. 14x13½***

Granite Paper

1156 A507 6.80s multicolored 5.25

Lord of Sipan Artifacts A508

Designs: 2.70s, Animal figure with large hands, feet. 3.30s, Medallion with warrior figure, vert. 10s, Tomb of Lord of Sipan, vert.

1997 **Litho.** ***Perf. 13½x14***

Granite Paper

1157 A508 2.70s multicolored 3.50
1158 A508 3.30s multicolored 4.30

Souvenir Sheet

1159 A508 10s multicolored 13.00

Peruvian Indians — A509

1997 **Litho.** ***Perf. 14x13½***

Granite Paper

1160 A509 2.70s Man 3.50
1161 A509 2.70s Woman 3.50

America Issue. Nos. 1160-1161 are dated 1996.

Heinrich von Stephan (1831-97) — A510

1997

Granite Paper

1162 A510 10s multicolored 13.00

America Issue — A511

1997

Granite Paper

1163 A511 2.70s Early post carrier 3.50
1164 A511 2.70s Modern letter carrier 3.50

13th Bolivar Games — A512

a, Tennis. b, Soccer. c, Basketball. d, Shot put.

1997 **Litho.** ***Perf. 14x13½***

Granite Paper

1165 A512 2.70s Block of 4, #a.-d. 14.00

Marshal Ramon Castilla (1797-1867) A513

1997

Granite Paper

1166 A513 1.80s multicolored 2.50

Treaty of Tlatelolco Banning Nuclear Weapons in Latin America, 30th Anniv. — A514

1997

Granite Paper

1167 A514 20s multicolored 26.00

Manu Natl. Park — A515

Birds: a, Kingfisher. b, Woodpecker. c, Crossbill. d, Eagle. e, Jabiru. f, Owl.

1997

Granite Paper

Sheet of 6

1168 A515 3.30s #a.-f. + label 25.00

8th Peruvian Antarctic Scientific Expedition A516

1997

Granite Paper

1169 A516 6s multicolored 7.75

Christmas — A517

1997

Granite Paper

1170 A517 2.70s multicolored 3.50

Hipolito Unanue Agreement, 25th Anniv. — A518

1997, Dec. 18 Litho. ***Perf. 14x13½***

Granite Paper

1171 A518 1s multicolored 1.30

Souvenir Sheet

Peruvian Gold Libra, Cent. — A519

1997, Dec. 18

Granite Paper

1172 A519 10s multicolored 13.00

Dept. of Post and Telegraph, Cent. — A520

1997, Dec. 31

Granite Paper

1173 A520 1s multicolored 1.30

SEMI-POSTAL STAMPS

> Catalogue values for unused stamps in this section are for Never Hinged items.

Gold Funerary Mask SP1

Designs: 2.60s+1.30s, Ceremonial knife, vert. 3.60s+1.80s, Ceremonial vessel. 4.60s+2.30s, Goblet with precious stones, vert. 20s+10s, Earplug.

Perf. 12x12½, 12½x12

1966, Aug. 16 Photo. Unwmk.

B1	SP1	1.90s + 90c multi	.40	.40
B2	SP1	2.60s + 1.30s multi	.50	.50
B3	SP1	3.60s + 1.80s multi	.75	.75
B4	SP1	4.60s + 2.30s multi	1.00	1.00
B5	SP1	20s + 10s multi	4.00	4.00
		Nos. B1-B5 (5)	6.65	6.65

The designs show gold objects of the 12th-13th centuries Chimu culture. The surtax was for tourist publicity.

For surcharges see Nos. 679-680, 683-684, 686.

AIR POST STAMPS

No. 248 Overprinted in Black **Servicio Aéreo**

1927, Dec. 10 Unwmk. ***Perf. 12***

C1 A87 50c violet 37.50 20.00

Two types of overprint. Counterfeits exist.

President Augusto Bernardino Leguía — AP1

1928, Jan. 12 Engr.

C2 AP1 50c dark green .65 .35

For surcharge see No. 263.

Coat of Arms of Piura Type

1932, July 28 Litho.

C3 A107 50c scarlet 20.00 19.00

Counterfeits exist.

Airplane in Flight — AP3

1934, Feb. Engr. ***Perf. 12½***

C4	AP3	2s blue	4.00	.35
C5	AP3	5s brown	8.00	.75

Funeral of Atahualpa AP4

Palace of Torre-Tagle — AP7

Designs: 35c, Mt. San Cristobal. 50c, Avenue of Barefoot Friars. 10s, Pizarro and the Thirteen.

1935, Jan. 18 Photo. ***Perf. 13½***

C6	AP4	5c emerald	.25	.15
C7	AP4	35c brown	.35	.30
C8	AP4	50c orange yel	.70	.60
C9	AP4	1s plum	1.25	.90
C10	AP7	2s red orange	2.00	1.75
C11	AP4	5s dp claret	8.50	5.25
C12	AP4	10s dk blue	32.50	22.50
		Nos. C6-C12 (7)	45.55	31.45

4th centenary of founding of Lima.

Nos. C6-C12 overprinted "Radio Nacional" are revenue stamps.

"La Callao," First Locomotive in South America AP9

1936, Aug. 27 ***Perf. 12½***

C13 AP9 35c gray black 2.50 1.40

Founding of the Province of Callao, cent.

Nos. C4-C5 Surcharged "Habilitado" and New Value, like Nos. 353-355

1936, Nov. 4

C14	AP3	5c on 2s blue	.35	.15
C15	AP3	25c on 5s brown	.65	.35
a.		Double surcharge	13.50	13.50
b.		No period btwn. "O" & "25 Cts"	1.40	1.40
c.		Inverted surcharge	16.50	
		Set value		.42

There are many broken letters in this setting.

La Mar Park, Lima — AP10

Jorge Chávez AP14

Aerial View of Peruvian Coast — AP16

View of the "Sierra" — AP17

St. Rosa of Lima — AP22

Designs: 15c, Mail Steamer "Inca" on Lake Titicaca. 20c, Native Queña (flute) Player and Llama. 30c, Ram at Model Farm, Puno. 50c, Mines of Peru. 1s, Train in Mountains. 1.50s, Jorge Chavez Aviation School. 2s, Transport Plane. 5s, Aerial View of Virgin Forests.

1936-37 Photo. ***Perf. 12½***

C16	AP10	5c brt green	.15	.15
C17	AP10	5c emerald ('37)	.20	.15
C18	AP10	15c lt ultra	.40	.15
C19	AP10	15c blue ('37)	.25	.15
C20	AP10	20c gray blk	1.10	.15
C21	AP10	20c pale ol grn ('37)	.70	.22
C22	AP14	25c magenta ('37)	.32	.15
C23	AP10	30c henna brn	3.50	.80
C24	AP10	30c dk ol brn ('37)	1.00	.15
C25	AP14	35c brown	2.00	1.75
C26	AP10	50c yellow	.32	.25
C27	AP10	50c brn vio ('37)	.50	.15
C28	AP16	70c Prus grn	4.25	3.75
C29	AP16	70c pck grn ('37)	.70	.55
C30	AP17	80c brn blk	5.00	3.75
C31	AP17	80c ol blk ('37)	1.00	.38
C32	AP10	1s ultra	3.50	.30
C33	AP10	1s red brn ('37)	1.75	.20
C34	AP14	1.50s red brn	5.50	4.25
C35	AP14	1.50s org yel ('37)	3.50	.32
		Engr.		
C36	AP10	2s deep blue	10.00	5.50
C37	AP10	2s yel grn ('37)	6.75	.55
C38	AP16	5s green	12.50	2.75
C39	AP22	10s car & brn	100.00	80.00
		Nos. C16-C39 (24)	164.89	106.52

Nos. C23, C25, C28, C30, C36 Surcharged in Black or Red **Habilit. Un Sol**

1936, June 26

C40	AP10	15c on 30c hn brn	.52	.30
C41	AP14	15c on 35c brown	.52	.18
C42	AP16	15c on 70c Prus grn	3.25	2.75
C43	AP17	25c on 80c brn blk (R)	3.25	2.75
C44	AP10	1s on 2s dp bl	5.25	3.75
		Nos. C40-C44 (5)	12.79	9.73

Surcharge on No. C43 is vertical, reading down.

First Flight in Peru, 1911 AP23

Jorge Chávez AP24

Airport of Limatambo at Lima — AP25

Map of Aviation Lines from Peru — AP26

Designs: 10c, Juan Bielovucic (1889-?) flying over Lima race course, Jan. 14, 1911. 15c, Jorge Chavez-Dartnell (1887-1910), French-born Peruvian aviator who flew from Brixen to Domodossola in the Alps and died of plane-crash injuries.

1937, Sept. 15 Engr. *Perf. 12*

C45	AP23	10c violet	.35	.15
C46	AP24	15c dk green	.50	.15
C47	AP25	25c gray brn	.35	.15
C48	AP26	1s black	1.65	1.20
		Nos. C45-C48 (4)	2.85	1.65

Inter-American Technical Conference of Aviation, Sept. 1937.

Government Restaurant at Callao — AP27

Monument on the Plains of Junin — AP28

Rear Admiral Manuel Villar — AP29

View of Tarma — AP30

Dam, Ica River — AP31

View of Iquitos — AP32

Highway and Railroad Passing — AP33

Mountain Road — AP34

Plaza San Martín, Lima — AP35

National Radio of Peru — AP36

Stele from Chavin Temple — AP37

Ministry of Public Works, Lima — AP38

Crypt of the Heroes, Lima — AP39

Imprint: "Waterlow & Sons Limited, Londres."

1938, July 1 Photo. *Perf. 12½, 13*

C49	AP27	5c violet brn	.15	.15
C50	AP28	15c dk brown	.15	.15
C51	AP29	20c dp magenta	.32	.15
C52	AP30	25c dp green	.15	.15
C53	AP31	30c orange	.15	.15
C54	AP32	50c green	.25	.16
C55	AP33	70c slate bl	.40	.15
C56	AP34	80c olive	.70	.15
C57	AP35	1s slate grn	5.50	2.50
C58	AP36	1.50s purple	1.25	.15

Engr.

C59	AP37	2s ind & org brn	2.00	.50
C60	AP38	5s brown	10.00	1.00
C61	AP39	10s ol grn & ind	40.00	24.00
		Nos. C49-C61 (13)	61.02	29.36

See Nos. C73-C75, C89-C93, C103.

For surcharges see Nos. C65, C76-C77, C82-C88, C108C.

Torre-Tagle Palace — AP40

National Congress Building AP41

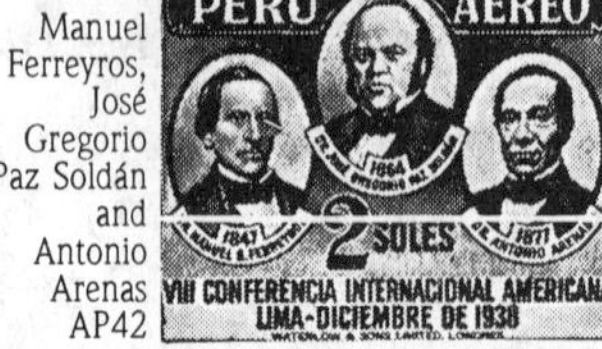

Manuel Ferreyros, José Gregorio Paz Soldán and Antonio Arenas AP42

1938, Dec. 9 Photo. *Perf. 12½*

C62	AP40	25c brt ultra	.65	.45
C63	AP41	1.50s brown vio	1.75	1.50
C64	AP42	2s black	1.10	.55
		Nos. C62-C64 (3)	3.50	2.50

8th Pan-American Conference at Lima.

No. C52 Surcharged in Black

Habilit.
0.15

1942 *Perf. 13*

C65	AP30	15c on 25c dp grn	1.00	.15

Types of 1938

Imprint: "Columbian Bank Note Co."

1945-46 Unwmk. Litho. *Perf. 12½*

C73	AP27	5c violet brn	.15	.15
C74	AP31	30c orange	.20	.15
C75	AP36	1.50s purple ('46)	.32	.25
		Nos. C73-C75 (3)	.67	
		Set value		.35

Nos. C73 and C54 Overprinted in Black

1947, Sept. 25 *Perf. 12½, 13*

C76	AP27	5c violet brn	.15	.15
C77	AP32	50c green	.15	.15
		Set value	.15	.15

1st Peru Intl. Airways flight from Lima to New York City, Sept. 27-28, 1947.

Catalogue values for unused stamps in this section, from this point to the end of the section, are for Never Hinged items.

Peru-Great Britain Air Route — AP43

Basketball Players — AP44

Designs: 5s, Discus thrower. 10s, Rifleman.

1948, July 29 Photo. *Perf. 12½*

C78	AP43	1s blue	2.25	1.50

Carmine Overprint, "AEREO"

C79	AP44	2s red brown	3.00	2.00
C80	AP44	5s yellow grn	5.00	3.25
C81	AP44	10s yellow	6.25	4.00
a.		Souv. sheet, #C78-C81, perf 13	17.50	17.50
		Nos. C78-C81 (4)	16.50	10.75

Peru's participation in the 1948 Olympic Games held at Wembley, England, during July and August. Postally valid for four days, July 29-Aug. 1, 1948. Proceeds went to the Olympic Committee.

A surtax of 2 soles on No. C81a was for the Children's Hospital.

Remainders of Nos. C78-C81 and C81a were overprinted "Melbourne 1956" and placed on sale Nov. 19, 1956, at all post offices as "voluntary stamps" with no postal validity. Clerks were permitted to postmark them to please collectors, and proceeds were to help pay the cost of sending Peruvian athletes to Australia. On April 14, 1957, postal authorities declared these stamps valid for one day, April 15, 1957. The overprint was applied to 10,000 sets and 21,000 souvenir sheets. Value, set, $10; sheet, $10.

No. C55 Surcharged in Red

Habilitada.
S/. 0.10

1948, Dec. *Perf. 13*

C82	AP33	10c on 70c slate bl	.15	.15
C83	AP33	20c on 70c slate bl	.15	.15
C84	AP33	55c on 70c slate bl	.16	.15
		Nos. C82-C84 (3)	.46	
		Set value		.15

Nos. C52, C55 and C56 Surcharged in Black

Habilitada
S/. 0.10

1949, Mar. 25

C85	AP30	5c on 25c dp grn	.15	.15
C86	AP30	10c on 25c dp grn	.15	.15
C87	AP33	15c on 70c slate bl	.15	.15
C88	AP34	30c on 80c olive	.65	.15
		Set value	.90	.30

The surcharge reads up, on No. C87.

Types of 1938

Imprint: "Waterlow & Sons Limited, Londres."

Perf. 13x13½, 13½x13

1949-50 Photo.

C89	AP27	5c olive bis	.15	.15
C90	AP31	30c red	.15	.15
C91	AP33	70c blue	.25	.15
C92	AP34	80c cerise	.40	.15
C93	AP36	1.50s vio brn ('50)	.50	.20
		Nos. C89-C93 (5)	1.45	
		Set value		.50

Air View, Reserva Park, Lima — AP45

Flags of the Americas and Spain — AP46

Designs: 30c, National flag. 55c, Huancayo Hotel. 95c, Blanca-Ancash Cordillera. 1.50s, Arequipa Hotel. 2s, Coal chute and dock, Chimbote. 5s, Town hall, Miraflores. 10s, Hall of National Congress, Lima.

Overprinted "U. P. U. 1874-1949" in Red or Black

1951, Apr. 2 Engr. *Perf. 12*

C94	AP45	5c blue grn	.15	.15
C95	AP45	30c black & car	.15	.15
a.		Inverted overprint		
C96	AP45	55c yel grn (Bk)	.15	.15
C97	AP45	95c dk green	.15	.15
C98	AP45	1.50s dp car (Bk)	.20	.15
C99	AP45	2s deep blue	.25	.16
C100	AP45	5s rose car (Bk)	3.00	2.50
C101	AP45	10s purple	4.00	3.50
C102	AP46	20s dk brn & ultra	6.75	5.50
		Nos. C94-C102 (9)	14.80	12.41

UPU, 75th anniv. (in 1949).

Nos. C94-C102 exist without overprint, but were not regularly issued. Value, set, $200.

Type of 1938

Imprint: "Inst. de Grav. Paris."

1951, May Engr. *Perf. 12½x12*

C103	AP27	5c olive bister	.15	.15

Type of 1938 Surcharged in Black

HABILITADA
S|o. 0.25

1951

C108	AP31	25c on 30c rose red	.15	.15

Thomas de San Martin y Contreras and Jerónimo de Aliaga y Ramirez AP47

San Marcos University AP48

Designs: 50c, Church and convent of Santo Domingo. 1.20s, P. de Peralta Barnuevo, T. de San Martin y Contreras and J. Baquijano y Carrillo de Cordova. 2s, T. Rodriguez de Mendoza, J. Hipolito Unanue y Pavon and J. Cayetano Heredia y Garcia. 5s, Arms of the University, 1571 and 1735.

Perf. 11½x12½

1951, Dec. 10 Litho.

C109	AP47	30c gray	.15	.15
C110	AP48	40c ultra	.15	.15
C111	AP48	50c car rose	.15	.15
C112	AP47	1.20s emerald	.15	.15

C113 AP47 2s slate .25 .15
C114 AP47 5s multicolored 1.10 .15
Nos. C109-C114 (6) 1.95
Set value .55

400th anniv. of the founding of San Marcos University.

River Gunboat Marañon AP49

Peruvian Cormorants AP50

National Airport, Lima — AP51

Tobacco Plant AP52

Manco Capac Monument AP54

Garcilaso de la Vega — AP53

Designs: 1.50s, Housing Unit No. 3. 2.20s, Inca Solar Observatory.

Imprint: "Thomas De La Rue & Co. Ltd."

1953-60 Unwmk. *Perf. 13, 12*
C115 AP49 40c yellow grn .15 .15
a. 40c blue green ('57) .15 .15
C116 AP50 75c dk brown .75 .15
C116A AP50 80c pale brn red ('60) .40 .15
C117 AP51 1.25s blue .20 .15
C118 AP49 1.50s cerise .20 .15
C119 AP51 2.20s dk blue .80 .25
C120 AP52 3s brown .90 .22
C121 AP53 5s bister .75 .15
C122 AP54 10s dull vio brn 1.75 .35
Nos. C115-C122 (9) 5.90
Set value 1.35

See #C158-C162, C182-C183, C186-C189, C210-C211.
For surcharges see #C420-C422, C429-C433, C435-C436, C438, C442-C443, C445-C450, C455, C471-C474, C476, C478-C479, C495.

Queen Isabella I — AP55

Fleet of Columbus AP56

Perf. 12½x11½, 11½x12½
1953, June 18 Engr. Unwmk.
C123 AP55 40c dp carmine .15 .15
C124 AP56 1.25s emerald .20 .16
C125 AP55 2.15s dp plum .42 .30
C126 AP56 2.20s black .65 .30
Nos. C123-C126 (4) 1.42 .91

500th birth anniv. (in 1951) of Queen Isabella I of Spain.
For surcharge see No. C475.

Arms of Lima and Bordeaux AP57

Designs: 50c, Eiffel Tower and Cathedral of Lima. 1.25s, Admiral Dupetit-Thouars and frigate "La Victorieuse." 2.20s, Presidents Coty and Prado and exposition hall.

1957, Sept. 16 *Perf. 13*
C127 AP57 40c claret, grn & ultra .15 .15
C128 AP57 50c grn, blk & hn brn .15 .15
C129 AP57 1.25s bl, ind & dk grn .16 .15
C130 AP57 2.20s bluish blk, bl & red brn .35 .35
Set value .65 .60

French Exposition, Lima, Sept. 15-Oct. 1.
For surcharges see Nos. 763, C503-C505.

Pre-Stamp Postal Markings — AP58

10c, 1r Stamp of 1857. 15c, 2r Stamp of 1857. 25c, 1d Stamp of 1860. 30c, 1p Stamp of 1858. 40c, ½p Stamp of 1858. 1.25s, José Davila Condemarin. 2.20s, Ramon Castilla. 5s, Pres. Manuel Prado. 10s, Shield of Lima containing stamps.

Perf. 12½x13
1957, Dec. 1 Engr. Unwmk.
C131 AP58 5c silver & blk .15 .15
C132 AP58 10c lil rose & bl .15 .15
C133 AP58 15c grn & red brn .15 .15
C134 AP58 25c org yel & bl .15 .15
C135 AP58 30c vio brn & org brn .15 .15
C136 AP58 40c black & bis .15 .15
C137 AP58 1.25s dk bl & dk brn .30 .25
C138 AP58 2.20s red & sl bl .50 .50
C139 AP58 5s lil rose & mar 1.25 1.00
C140 AP58 10s ol grn & lil 2.00 1.75
Set value 4.30 3.70

Centenary of Peruvian postage stamps. No. C140 issued to publicize the Peruvian Centenary Phil. Exhib. (PEREX).

Carlos Paz Soldan — AP59

Port of Callao and Pres. Manuel Prado — AP60

Design: 1s, Ramon Castilla.

Perf. 14x13½, 13½x14
1958, Apr. 7 Litho. Wmk. 116
C141 AP59 40c brn & pale rose .15 .15
C142 AP59 1s grn & lt grn .15 .15
C143 AP60 1.25s dull pur & ind .20 .15
Nos. C141-C143 (3) .50
Set value .26

Centenary of the telegraph connection between Lima and Callao and the centenary of the political province of Callao.
For surcharge see No. 767.

Flags of France and Peru — AP61

Cathedral of Lima and Lady — AP62

1.50s, Horseback rider & mall in Lima. 2.50s, Map of Peru showing national products.

Perf. 12½x13, 13x12½
1958, May 20 Engr. Unwmk.
C144 AP61 50c dl vio, bl & car .15 .15
C145 AP62 65c multi .15 .15
C146 AP62 1.50s bl, brn vio & ol .20 .15
C147 AP61 2.50s sl grn, grnsh bl & claret .25 .16
Set value .62 .40

Peruvian Exhib. in Paris, May 20-July 10.

Bro. Martin de Porres Velasquez AP63

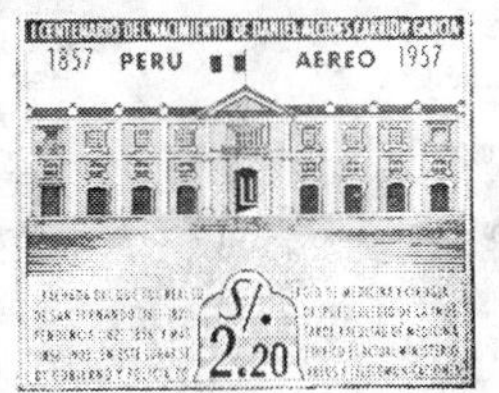

First Royal School of Medicine (Now Ministry of Government and Police) — AP64

Designs: 1.20s, Daniel Alcides Carrion Garcia. 1.50s, Jose Hipolito Unanue Pavon.

Perf. 13x13½, 13½x13
1958, July 24 Litho. Unwmk.
C148 AP63 60c multi .15 .15
C149 AP63 1.20s multi .15 .15
C150 AP63 1.50s multi .15 .15
C151 AP64 2.20s black .20 .16
Nos. C148-C151 (4) .65
Set value .38

Daniel A. Carrion (1857-85), medical martyr.

Gen. Ignacio Alvarez Thomas AP65

1958, Nov. 13 *Perf. 13x12½*
C152 AP65 1.10s brn lake, bis & ver .16 .15
C153 AP65 1.20s blk, bis & ver .20 .16

General Thomas (1787-1857), fighter for South American independence.

"Justice" and Emblem — AP66

1958, Nov. 13
Star in Blue and Olive Bister
C154 AP66 80c emerald .15 .15
C155 AP66 1.10s red orange .15 .15
C156 AP66 1.20s ultra .15 .15
C157 AP66 1.50s lilac rose .16 .15
Set value .46 .36

Lima Bar Assoc., 150th anniv.

Types of 1953-57

Designs: 80c, Peruvian cormorants. 3.80s, Inca Solar Observatory.

Imprint: "Joh. Enschedé en Zonen-Holland"

Perf. 12½x14, 14x13, 13x14
1959, Dec. 9 Unwmk.
C158 AP50 80c brown red .15 .15
C159 AP52 3s lt green .60 .22
C160 AP51 3.80s orange 1.00 .25
C161 AP53 5s brown .60 .25
C162 AP54 10s orange ver 1.20 .40
Nos. C158-C162 (5) 3.55 1.27

WRY Emblem, Dove, Rainbow and Farmer — AP67

Peruvian Cormorant Over Ocean — AP68

1960, Apr. 7 Litho. *Perf. 14x13*
C163 AP67 80c multi .25 .25
C164 AP67 4.30s multi .55 .55
a. Souv. sheet of 2, #C163-C164, imperf. 5.50 5.50

World Refugee Year, July 1, 1959-June 30, 1960.
No. C164a sold for 15s.

1960, May 30 *Perf. 14x13½*
C165 AP68 1s multi .35 .15

Intl. Pacific Fair, Lima, 1959.

Lima Coin of 1659 — AP69

1961, Jan. 19 Unwmk. *Perf. 13x14*
C166 AP69 1s org brn & gray .15 .15
C167 AP69 2s Prus bl & gray .20 .16
Set value .24

1st National Numismatic Exposition, Lima, 1959; 300th anniv. of the first dated coin (1659) minted at Lima.

The Earth — AP70

1961, Mar. 8 Litho. *Perf. 13½x14*
C168 AP70 1s multicolored .15 .15

International Geophysical Year.

Frigate Amazonas
AP71

1961, Mar. 8 Engr. *Perf. 13½*

C169 AP71 50c brown & grn .15 .15
C170 AP71 80c dl vio & red org .15 .15
C171 AP71 1s green & sepia .20 .20
Set value .36 .36

Centenary (in 1958) of the trip around the world by the Peruvian frigate Amazonas.

Machu Picchu Sheet

A souvenir sheet was issued Sept. 11, 1961, to commemorate the 50th anniversary of the discovery of the ruins of Machu Picchu, ancient Inca city in the Andes, by Hiram Bingham. It contains two bi-colored imperf. airmail stamps, 5s and 10s, lithographed in a single design picturing the mountaintop ruins. The sheet was valid for one day and was sold in a restricted manner. Value $7.50.

Olympic Torch, Laurel and Globe — AP72

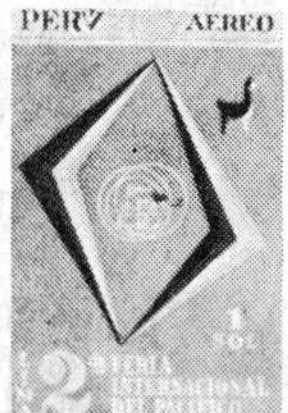

Fair Emblem and Llama — AP73

1961, Dec. 13 Unwmk. *Perf. 13*

C172 AP72 5s gray & ultra .40 .35
C173 AP72 10s gray & car .80 .60
a. Souv. sheet of 2, #C172-C173, imperf. 2.25 2.25

17th Olympic Games, Rome, 8/25-9/11/60.

1962, Jan. Litho. *Perf. 10½x11*

C174 AP73 1s multi .16 .15

2nd International Pacific Fair, Lima, 1961.

Map Showing Disputed Border, Peru-Ecuador
AP74

1962, May 25 *Perf. 10½*

Gray Background

C175 AP74 1.30s blk, red & car rose .16 .16
C176 AP74 1.50s blk, red & emer .20 .20
C177 AP74 2.50s blk, red & dk bl .25 .25
Nos. C175-C177 (3) .61 .61

Settlement of the border dispute with Ecuador by the Protocol of Rio de Janeiro, 20th anniv.

Cahuide and Cuauhtémoc
AP75

Designs: 2s, Tupac Amaru (Jose G. Condorcanqui) and Miguel Hidalgo. 3s, Pres. Manuel Prado and Pres. Adolfo Lopez Mateos of Mexico.

1962, May 25 Engr. *Perf. 13*

C178 AP75 1s dk car rose, red & brt grn .15 .15
C179 AP75 2s grn, red & brt grn .20 .15
C180 AP75 3s brn, red & brt grn .25 .16
Nos. C178-C180 (3) .60 .46

Exhibition of Peruvian art treasures in Mexico.

Agriculture, Industry and Archaeology
AP76

1962, Sept. 7 Litho. *Perf. 14x13½*

C181 AP76 1s black & gray .15 .15

Cent. (in 1961) of Pallasca Ancash province.

Types of 1953-60

Designs: 1.30s, Guanayes. 1.50s, Housing Unit No. 3. 1.80s, Locomotive No. 80 (like No. 460). 2s, Monument to Native Farmer. 3s, Tobacco plant. 4.30s, Inca Solar Observatory. 5s, Garcilaso de la Vega. 10s, Inca Monument.

Imprint: "Thomas De La Rue & Co. Ltd."

1962-63 Wmk. 346 Litho. *Perf. 13*

C182 AP50 1.30s pale yellow .20 .15
C183 AP49 1.50s claret .22 .15
C184 A182 1.80s dark blue .25 .15

Perf. 12

C185 A184 2s emerald ('63) .25 .15
C186 AP52 3s lilac rose .35 .16
C187 AP51 4.30s orange .65 .25
C188 AP53 5s citron .65 .35

Perf. 13½x14

C189 AP54 10s vio bl ('63) 1.20 .50
Nos. C182-C189 (8) 3.77 1.86

Freedom from Hunger Type

1963, July 23 Unwmk. *Perf. 12½*

C190 A189 4.30s lt grn & ocher .50 .50

Jorge Chávez and Wing — AP77

Fair Poster — AP78

1964, Feb. 20 Engr. *Perf. 13*

C191 AP77 5s org brn, dk brn & bl .65 .35

1st crossing of the Alps by air (Sept. 23, 1910) by the Peruvian aviator Jorge Chávez, 50th anniv.

Alliance for Progress Type

Design: 1.30s, Same, horizontal.

Perf. 12½x12, 12x12½

1964, June 22 Litho.

C192 A190 1.30s multi .15 .15
C193 A190 3s multi .25 .22

1965, Jan. 15 Unwmk. *Perf. 14½*

C194 AP78 1s multi .15 .15

3rd International Pacific Fair, Lima 1963.

Basket, Globe, Pennant
AP79

St. Martin de Porres
AP80

1965, Apr. 19 *Perf. 12x12½*

C195 AP79 1.30s violet & red .25 .25
C196 AP79 4.30s bis brn & red .55 .55

4th Women's Intl. Basketball Championship.
For surcharge see No. C493.

1965, Oct. 29 Litho. *Perf. 11*

Designs: 1.80s, St. Martin's miracle: dog, cat and mouse feeding from same dish. 4.30s, St. Martin with cherubim in Heaven.

C197 AP80 1.30s gray & multi .15 .15
C198 AP80 1.80s gray & multi .20 .15
C199 AP80 4.30s gray & multi .50 .50
Nos. C197-C199 (3) .85
Set value .68

Canonization of St. Martin de Porres Velasquez (1579-1639), on May 6, 1962.
For surcharges see Nos. C439, C496.

Victory Monument, Lima, and Battle Scene — AP81

Designs: 3.60s, Monument and Callao Fortress. 4.60s, Monument and José Galvez.

1966, May 2 Photo. *Perf. 14x13½*

C200 AP81 1.90s multicolored .25 .25
C201 AP81 3.60s brn, yel & bis .40 .40
C202 AP81 4.60s multicolored .60 .60
Nos. C200-C202 (3) 1.25 1.25

Centenary of Peru's naval victory over the Spanish Armada at Callao, May, 1866.

Civil Guard Emblem
AP82

1.90s, Various activities of Civil Guard.

1966, Aug. 30 Photo. *Perf. 13½x14*

C203 AP82 90c multicolored .15 .15
C204 AP82 1.90s dp lil rose, gold & blk .16 .15
Set value .24 .22

Centenary of the Civil Guard.

Hydroelectric Center Type of Regular Issue

1966, Nov. 24 Photo. *Perf. 13½x14*

C205 A193 1.90s lil, blk & vio bl .16 .15

Sun Symbol, Ancient Carving — AP83

Designs: 3.60s, Map of Peru and spiral, horiz. 4.60s, Globe with map of Peru.

Perf. 14x13½, 13½x14

1967, Feb. 16 Litho.

C206 AP83 2.60s red org & blk .22 .16
C207 AP83 3.60s dp blue & blk .35 .22
C208 AP83 4.60s tan & multi .40 .30
Nos. C206-C208 (3) .97 .68

Photography exhibition "Peru Before the World" which opened simultaneously in Lima, Madrid, Santiago de Chile and Washington, Sept. 27, 1966.
For surcharges see Nos. C444, C470, C492.

Types of 1953-60

2.60s, Monument to Native Farmer. 3.60s, Tobacco plant. 4.60s, Inca Solar Observatory.

Imprint: "I.N.A."

1967, Jan. *Perf. 13½x14, 14x13½*

C209 A184 2.60s brt green .22 .16
C210 AP52 3.60s lilac rose .35 .20
C211 AP51 4.60s orange .40 .25
Nos. C209-C211 (3) .97 .61

Wind Vane and Sun Type of Regular Issue

1967, Apr. 18 Photo. *Perf. 13½x14*

C212 A194 1.90s yel brn, blk & gold .16 .16

St. Rosa of Lima by Angelino Medoro — AP84

Lions Emblem — AP85

St. Rosa Painted by: 2.60s, Carlo Maratta. 3.60s, Cuzquena School, 17th century.

1967, Aug. 30 Photo. *Perf. 13½*

C213 AP84 1.90s blk, gold & multi .25 .15
C214 AP84 2.60s blk, gold & multi .42 .16
C215 AP84 3.60s blk, gold & multi .60 .22
Nos. C213-C215 (3) 1.27 .53

350th death anniv. of St. Rosa of Lima.
For surcharge see No. C477.

Fair Type of Regular Issue

1967, Oct. 27 Photo. *Perf. 12*

C216 A195 1s gold, brt red lil & blk .15 .15

1967, Dec. 29 Litho. *Perf. 14x13½*

C217 AP85 1.60s brt bl & vio bl, *grysh* .20 .20

50th anniversary of Lions International.

Decorated Jug, Nazca Culture — AP86

Antarqui, Inca Messenger — AP87

Painted pottery jugs of pre-Inca Nazca culture: 2.60s, Falcon. 3.60s, Round jug decorated with grain-eating bird. 4.60s, Two-headed snake. 5.60s, Marine bird.

1968, June 4 Photo. *Perf. 12*

C218 AP86 1.90s multi .15 .15
C219 AP86 2.60s multi .16 .15
C220 AP86 3.60s black & multi .22 .20
C221 AP86 4.60s brown & multi .30 .25
C222 AP86 5.60s gray & multi .38 .35
Nos. C218-C222 (5) 1.21 1.10

For surcharges see #C451-C453, C497, C500.

1968, Sept. 2 Litho. *Perf. 12*

Design: 5.60s, Alpaca and jet liner.

C223 AP87 3.60s multi .30 .30
C224 AP87 5.60s red, blk & brn .45 .45

12th anniv. of Peruvian Airlines (APSA).
For surcharges see Nos. C480-C482.

Human Rights Flame — AP88

1968, Sept. 5 Photo. *Perf. 14x13½*

C225 AP88 6.50s brn, red & grn .22 .20

International Human Rights Year.

Discobolus and Mexico Olympics Emblem
AP89

1968, Oct. 19 Photo. *Perf. 13½*

C226 AP89 2.30s yel, brn & dk bl .15 .15
C227 AP89 3.50s yel grn, sl bl & red .18 .18
C228 AP89 5s brt pink, blk & ultra .25 .16
C229 AP89 6.50s lt bl, mag & brn .38 .30
C230 AP89 8s lil, ultra & car .40 .25
C231 AP89 9s org, vio & grn .42 .30
Nos. C226-C231 (6) 1.78 1.34

19th Olympic Games, Mexico City, Oct. 12-27.

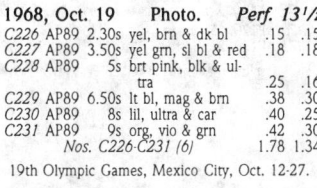

Hand, Corn and Field — AP90

1969, Mar. 3 Litho. *Perf. 11*

C232 AP90 5.50s on 1.90s grn & yel .25 .16
C233 AP90 6.50s on 1.90s bl, grn & yel .35 .20

Agrarian Reform Law. Not issued without surcharge.

Peruvian Silver 8-reales Coin, 1568 — AP91

1969, Mar. 17 Litho. *Perf. 12*

C234 AP91 5s yellow, gray & blk .20 .15
C235 AP91 5s bl grn, gray & blk .20 .15

400th anniv. of the first Peruvian coinage.

Ramon Castilla Monument — AP92

Design: 10s, Pres. Ramon Castilla.

1969, May 30 Photo. *Perf. 13½*

Size: 27x40mm

C236 AP92 5s emerald & indigo .35 .15

Perf. 12

Size: 21x37mm

C237 AP92 10s plum & brn .65 .30

Ramon Castilla (1797-1867), president of Peru (1845-1851 and 1855-1862), on the occasion of the unveiling of the monument in Lima.

Airline Type of Regular Issue

1969, June 17 Litho. *Perf. 11*

C238 A199 3s org & multi .15 .15
C239 A199 4s multi .15 .15
C240 A199 5.50s ver & multi .18 .15
C241 A199 6.50s vio & multi .20 .16
Nos. C238-C241 (4) .68
Set value .48

First Peruvian Airlines (APSA) flight to Europe.

Radar Antenna, Satellite and Earth — AP93

1969, July 14 Litho. *Perf. 11*

C242 AP93 20s multi 1.25 .55
a. Souv. sheet 1.50 1.50

Opening of the Lurin satellite earth station near Lima.

No. C242a contains one imperf. stamp with simulated perforations similar to No. C242.

Gonzales Type of Regular Issue

1969, July 23 Litho. *Perf. 11*

C243 A200 20s red & multi 1.20 .55

WHO Emblem AP94

1969, Aug. 14 Photo. *Perf. 12*

C244 AP94 5s gray, red brn, gold & blk .16 .15
C245 AP94 6.50s dl org, gray bl, gold & blk .20 .16

WHO, 20th anniv.

Agrarian Reform Type of Regular Issue

1969, Aug. 28 Litho. *Perf. 11*

C246 A201 3s lil & blk .15 .15
C247 A201 4s brn & buff .15 .15
Set value .24 .20

Garcilaso de la Vega — AP95

Designs: 2.40s, De la Vega's coat of arms. 3.50s, Title page of "Commemtarios Reales que tratan del origen de los Yncas," Lisbon, 1609.

1969, Sept. 18 Litho. *Perf. 12x12½*

C248 AP95 2.40s emer, sil & blk .15 .15
C249 AP95 3.50s ultra, buff & blk .15 .15
C250 AP95 5s sil, yel, blk & brn .20 .15
a. Souv. sheet of 3, #C248-C250, imperf. .90 .90
Nos. C248-C250 (3) .50
Set value .38

Garcilaso de la Vega, called "Inca" (1539-1616), historian of Peru.

Fair Type of Regular Issue, 1969

1969, Nov. 14 Litho. *Perf. 11*

C251 A203 3s bis & multi .20 .15
C252 A203 4s multi .25 .15
Set value .18

Bolognesi Type of Regular Issue

1969, Dec. 9 Litho. *Perf. 11*

C253 A204 50s lt brn, blk & gold 3.00 1.40

Arms of Amazonas — AP96

1970, Jan. 6 Litho. *Perf. 11*

C254 AP96 10s multi .50 .50

ILO Emblem AP97

1970, Jan. 16

C278 AP97 3s dk vio bl & lt ultra .25 .25

ILO, 50th anniv.

Motherhood and UNICEF Emblem AP98

1970, Jan. 16 Photo. *Perf. 13½x14*

C279 AP98 5s yel, gray & blk .22 .15
C280 AP98 6.50s brt pink, gray & blk .35 .20

Vicus Culture Type of Regular Issue

Ceramics of Vicus Culture, 6th-8th Centuries: 3s, Squatting warrior. 4s, Jug. 5.50s, Twin jugs. 6.50s, Woman and jug.

1970, Feb. 23 Litho. *Perf. 11*

C281 A205 3s buff, blk & brn .16 .16
C282 A205 4s buff, blk & brn .20 .20
C283 A205 5.50s buff, blk & brn .30 .30
C284 A205 6.50s buff, blk & brn .40 .40
Nos. C281-C284 (4) 1.06 1.06

Fish Type of Regular Issue

1970, Apr. 30 Litho. *Perf. 11*

C285 A207 3s Swordfish .20 .20
C286 A207 3s Yellowfin tuna .20 .20
C287 A207 5.50s Wolf fish .30 .30
Nos. C285-C287 (3) .70 .70

Telephone — AP99

UN Headquarters, NY — AP100

1970, June 12 Litho. *Perf. 11*

C288 AP99 5s multi .25 .15
C289 AP99 10s multi .55 .22

Nationalization of the Peruvian telephone system, Mar. 25, 1970.

Soldier-Farmer Type of Regular Issue

1970, June 24 Litho. *Perf. 11*

C290 A208 3s gold & multi .20 .15
C291 A208 5.50s gold & multi .35 .15
Set value .20

1970 June 26

C292 AP100 3s vio bl & lt bl .15 .15

25th anniversary of United Nations.

Rotary Club Emblem AP101

1970, July 18

C293 AP101 10s blk, red & gold .70 .50

Rotary Club of Lima, 50th anniversary.

Tourist Type of Regular Issue

3s, Ruins of Sun Fortress, Trujillo. 4s, Sacsayhuaman Arch, Cuzco. 5.50s, Arch & Lake Titicaca, Puno. 10s, Machu Picchu, Cuzco.

1970, Aug. 6 Litho. *Perf. 11*

C294 A210 3s multi .15 .15
C295 A210 4s multi, vert. .20 .20
C296 A210 5.50s multi, vert. .28 .28
C297 A210 10s multi, vert. .50 .50
a. Souvenir sheet of 5 1.65 1.65
Nos. C294-C297 (4) 1.13 1.13

No. C297a contains 5 imperf. stamps similar to Nos. 538, C294-C297 with simulated perforations.

Procession, Lord of Miracles — AP102

4s, Cockfight, by T. Nuñez Ureta. 5.50s, Altar of Church of the Nazarene, vert. 6.50s, Procession, by J. Vinatea Reinoso. 8s, Procession, by José Sabogal, vert.

1970, Nov. 30 Litho. *Perf. 11*

C298 AP102 3s blk & multi .15 .15
C299 AP102 4s blk & multi .20 .15
C300 AP102 5.50s blk & multi .25 .15
C301 AP102 6.50s blk & multi .35 .16
C302 AP102 8s blk & multi .40 .20
Nos. C298-C302 (5) 1.35
Set value .66

October Festival in Lima.

"Tight Embrace" (from ancient monolith) AP103

1971, Feb. 8 Litho. *Perf. 11*

C303 AP103 4s ol gray, yel & red .22 .15
C304 AP103 5.50s dk bl, pink & red .30 .15
C305 AP103 6.50s sl, buff & red .35 .16
Nos. C303-C305 (3) .87 .46

Issued to express Peru's gratitude to the world for aid after the Ancash earthquake, May 31, 1970.

Textile Type of Regular Issue

Designs: 3s, Chancay tapestry, vert. 4s, Chancay lace. 5.50s, Paracas cloth, vert.

1971, Apr. 19 Litho. *Perf. 11*

C306 A213 3s multi .25 .15
C307 A213 4s grn & multi .35 .15
C308 A213 5.50s multi .42 .15
Nos. C306-C308 (3) 1.02
Set value .30

Fish Type of Regular Issue

Fish Sculptures and Fish: 3.50s, Chimu Inca culture, 14th century and Chilean sardine. 4s, Mochica culture, 5th century, and engraulis ringens. 5.50s, Chimu culture, 13th century, and merluccios peruanos. 8.50s, Nazca culture, 3rd century, and brevoortis maculatachilcae.

1971, June 7 Litho. *Perf. 11*

C309 A214 3.50s multi .30 .15
C310 A214 4s multi .38 .15
C311 A214 5.50s multi .50 .15
C312 A214 8.50s multi .70 .20
Nos. C309-C312 (4) 1.88
Set value .52

Independence Type of 1971

Paintings: No. C313, Toribio Rodriguez de Mendoza. No. C314, José de la Riva Aguero. No. C315, Francisco Vidal. 3.50s, José de San Martin. No. C317, Juan P. Viscardo y Guzman. No. C318, Hipolito Unanue. 4.50s, Liberation Monument, Paracas. No. C320, José G. Condorcanqui-Tupac Amaru. No. C321, Francisco J. de Luna Pizarro. 6s, March of the Numancia Battalion, horiz. 7.50s, Peace Tower, monument for Alvarez de Arenales, horiz. 9s, Liberators' Monument, Lima, horiz. 10s, Independence Proclamation in Lima, horiz.

1971 Litho. *Perf. 11*

C313 A215 3s brt mag & blk .15 .15
C314 A215 3s gray & multi .15 .15
C315 A215 3s dk bl & multi .15 .15
C316 A215 3.50s dk bl & multi .15 .15
C317 A215 4s emer & blk .16 .15
C318 A215 4s gray & multi .16 .15
C319 A215 4.50s dk bl & multi .18 .15
C320 A215 5.50s brn & blk .22 .15
C321 A215 5.50s gray & multi .22 .15
C322 A215 6s dk bl & multi .22 .15
C323 A215 7.50s dk bl & multi .30 .18
C324 A215 9s dk bl & multi .38 .20
C325 A215 10s dk bl & multi .40 .20
Nos. C313-C325 (13) 2.84
Set value 1.60

150th anniversary of independence, and to honor the heroes of the struggle for independence. Sizes: 6s, 10s, 45x35mm, 7.50s, 9s, 41x39mm. Others 31x49mm.

Issue dates: Nos. C313, C317, C320, May 10; Nos. C314, C318, C321, July 5; others July 27.

Ricardo Palma — AP104

Weight Lifter — AP105

1971, Aug. 27 *Perf. 13*

C326 AP104 7.50s ol bis & blk .75 .18

Sesquicentennial of National Library. Ricardo Palma (1884-1912) was a writer and director of the library.

1971, Sept. 15

C327 AP105 7.50s brt bl & blk .50 .18

25th World Weight Lifting Championships, Lima.

Flag, Family, Soldier's Head — AP106

1971, Oct. 4

C328 AP106 7.50s blk, lt bl & red .50 .18
a. Souv. sheet of 1, imperf. 1.00 1.00

3rd anniv. of the revolution of the armed forces.

"Sacramento" AP107

1971, Oct. 8

C329 AP107 7.50s lt bl & dk bl .38 .18

Sesquicentennial of Peruvian Navy.

Peruvian Order of the Sun — AP108

1971, Oct. 8

C330 AP108 7.50s multi .40 .40

Sequicentennial of the Peruvian Order of the Sun.

Liberation Type of Regular Issue

Design: 50s, Detail from painting "Progress of Liberation," by Teodoro Nuñez Ureta.

1971, Nov. 4 Litho. *Perf. 13x13½*

C331 A217 50s multi 3.00 1.50

2nd Ministerial meeting of the "Group of 77."

Fair Emblem — AP109

1971, Nov. 12 *Perf. 13*

C332 AP109 4.50s multi .30 .15

7th Pacific International Trade Fair.

Fish Type of Regular Issue

3s, Pontinus furcirhinus dubius. 5.50s, Hogfish.

1972, Mar. 20 Litho. *Perf. 13x13½*

C333 A223 3s lt bl & multi .30 .15
C334 A223 5.50s lt bl & multi .50 .15
Set value .22

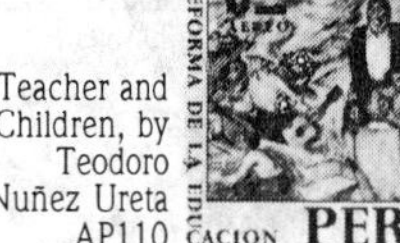

Teacher and Children, by Teodoro Nuñez Ureta AP110

1972, Apr. 10 Litho. *Perf. 13x13½*

C335 AP110 6.50s multi .50 .16

Enactment of Education Reform Law.

White-tailed Trogon — AP111

1972, June 19 Litho. *Perf. 13½x13*

C336 AP111 2s shown .15 .15
C337 AP111 2.50s Amazonian umbrel-la bird .18 .15
C338 AP111 3s Peruvian cock-of-the-rock .22 .15
C339 AP111 6.50s Cuvier's toucan .45 .15
C340 AP111 8.50s Blue-crowned motmot .65 .22
Nos. C336-C340 (5) 1.65
Set value .55

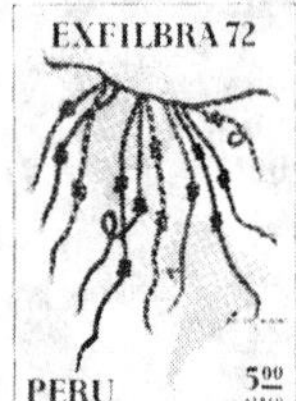

Quipu and Map of Americas — AP112

Inca Runner, Olympic Rings — AP113

1972, Aug. 21

C341 AP112 5s blk & multi .30 .15

4th Interamerican Philatelic Exhibition, EXFILBRA, Rio de Janeiro, Aug. 26-Sept. 2.

1972, Aug. 28

C342 AP113 8s buff & multi .55 .35

20th Olympic Games, Munich, Aug. 26-Sept. 11.

Woman of Catacaos, Piura — AP114

Funerary Tower, Sillustani, Puno — AP115

Regional Costumes: 2s, Tupe (Yauyos) woman of Lima. 4s, Indian with bow and arrow, from Conibo, Loreto. 4.50s, Man with calabash, Cajamarca. 5s, Moche woman, Trujillo. 6.50s, Man and woman of Ocongate, Cuzco. 8s, Chucupana woman, Ayacucho. 8.50s, Cotuncha woman, Junin. 10s, Woman of Puno dancing "Pandilla."

1972-73

C343 AP114 2s blk & multi .15 .15
C344 AP114 3.50s blk & multi .30 .30
C345 AP114 4s blk & multi .35 .35
C346 AP114 4.50s blk & multi .40 .40
C346A AP114 5s blk & multi .40 .40
C347 AP114 6.50s blk & multi .50 .50
C347A AP114 8s blk & multi .60 .60
C347B AP114 8.50s blk & multi .65 .65
C348 AP114 10s blk & multi .75 .75
Nos. C343-C348 (9) 4.10 4.10

Issued: 3.50s, 4s, 6.50s, 9/29/72; 2s, 4.50s, 10s, 4/30/73; 5s, 8s, 8.50s, 10/15/73.

Perf. 13½x13, 13x13½

1972, Oct. 16 Litho.

Archaeological Monuments: 1.50s, Stone of the 12 angles, Cuzco. 3.50s, Ruins of Chavin, Ancash, horiz. 5s, Wall and gate, Chavin, Ancash, horiz. 8s, Ruins of Machu Picchu, horiz.

C349 AP115 1.50s multi .15 .15
C350 AP115 3.50s multi .22 .22
C351 AP115 4s multi .25 .15
C352 AP115 5s multi .35 .15
C353 AP115 8s multi .65 .35
Nos. C349-C353 (5) 1.62 1.02

AP116

AP117

Designs: Inca ponchos, various textile designs.

1973, Jan. 29 Litho. *Perf. 13½x13*

C354 AP116 2s multi .15 .15
C355 AP116 3.50s multi .20 .15
C356 AP116 4s multi .20 .15
C357 AP116 5s multi .25 .20
C358 AP116 8s multi .50 .25
Nos. C354-C358 (5) 1.30 .90

1973, Mar. 19 Litho. *Perf. 13½x13*

Antique Jewelry: 1.50s, Goblets and Ring, Mochica, 10th cent. 2.50s, Golden hands and arms, Lambayeque, 12th cent. 4s, Gold male statuette, Mochica, 8th ceny. 5s, Two gold brooches, Nazca, 8th cent. 8s, Flayed puma, Mochica, 8th cent.

C359 AP117 1.50s multi .15 .15
C360 AP117 2.50s multi .15 .15
C361 AP117 4s multi .20 .20
C362 AP117 5s multi .25 .25
C363 AP117 8s multi .50 .20
Nos. C359-C363 (5) 1.25 .95

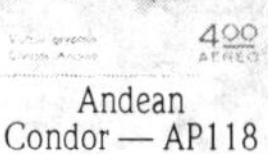

Andean Condor — AP118

Indian Guide, by José Sabogal — AP119

Protected Animals: 5s, Vicuña. 8s, Spectacled bear.

1973, Apr. 16 Litho. *Perf. 13½x13*

C364 AP118 4s blk & multi .20 .15
C365 AP118 5s blk & multi .25 .20
C366 AP118 8s blk & multi .42 .20
Nos. C364-C366 (3) .87 .55

See Nos. C372-C376, C411-C412.

1973, May 7 Litho. *Perf. 13½x13*

Peruvian Paintings: 8.50s, Portrait of a Lady, by Daniel Hernandez. 20s, Man Holding Figurine, by Francisco Laso.

C367 AP119 1.50s multi .15 .15
C368 AP119 8.50s multi .38 .30
C369 AP119 20s multi .90 .50
Nos. C367-C369 (3) 1.43 .95

Basket and World Map AP120

1973, May 26 *Perf. 13x13½*

C370 AP120 5s green .25 .15
C371 AP120 20s lil rose 1.10 .50

1st International Basketball Festival.

Darwin's Rhea — AP121 Orchid — AP122

1973, Sept. 3 Litho. *Perf. 13½x13*

C372 AP121 2.50s shown .20 .20
C373 AP121 3.50s Giant otter .25 .25
C374 AP121 6s Greater flamingo .40 .40
C375 AP121 8.50s Bush dog, horiz. .55 .55
C376 AP121 10s Chinchilla, horiz. .60 .60
Nos. C372-C376 (5) 2.00 2.00

Protected animals.

1973, Sept. 27

Designs: Various orchids.

C377 AP122 1.50s blk & multi .15 .15
C378 AP122 2.50s blk & multi .25 .15
C379 AP122 3s blk & multi .30 .20
C380 AP122 3.50s blk & multi .35 .20
C381 AP122 8s blk & multi .75 .20
Nos. C377-C381 (5) 1.80 .90

Pacific Fair Emblem — AP123

1973, Nov. 14 Litho. *Perf. 13½x13*

C382 AP123 8s blk, red & gray .50 .30

8th International Pacific Fair, Lima.

Cargo Ship ILO — AP124

Designs: 2.50s, Boats of Pescaperu fishing organization. 8s, Jet and seagull.

1973, Dec. 14 Litho. *Perf. 13*

C383 AP124 1.50s multi .15 .15
C384 AP124 2.50s multi .30 .30
C385 AP124 8s multi .60 .16
Nos. C383-C385 (3) 1.05 .61

Issued to promote government enterprises.

Lima Monument AP125

1973, Nov. 27 *Perf. 13*

C386 AP125 8.50s red & multi .50 .16

50th anniversary of Air Force Academy. Monument honors Jorge Chavez, Peruvian aviator.

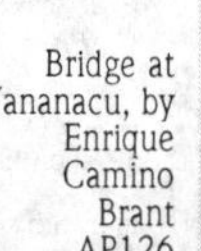

Bridge at Yananacu, by Enrique Camino Brant AP126

Paintings: 10c, Peruvian Birds, by Teodoro Nuñez Ureta, vert. 50s, Boats of Totora, by Jorge Vinatea Reinoso.

Perf. 13x13½, 13½x13

1973, Dec. 28

C387 AP126 8s multi .40 .20
C388 AP126 10s multi .50 .25
C389 AP126 50s multi 2.25 1.25
Nos. C387-C389 (3) 3.15 1.70

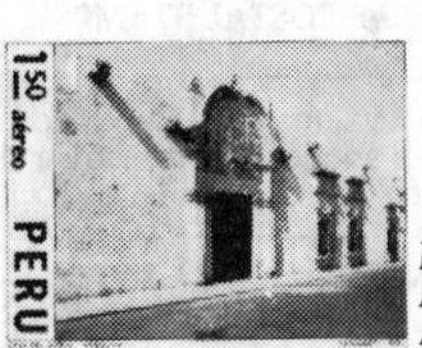

Moral House, Arequipa AP127

2.50s, El Misti Mountain, Arequipa. 5s, Puya Raymondi (cacti), vert. 6s, Huascaran Mountain. 8s, Lake Querococha. Views on 5s, 6s, 8s are views in White Cordilleras Range, Ancash Province.

1974, Feb. 11

C390 AP127 1.50s multi .15 .15
C391 AP127 2.50s multi .20 .15
C392 AP127 5s multi .30 .15
C393 AP127 6s multi .40 .15
C394 AP127 8s multi .65 .16
Nos. C390-C394 (5) 1.70
Set value .60

San Jeronimo's, Cuzco — AP128

Churches of Peru: 3.50s, Cajamarca Cathedral. 5s, San Pedro's, Zepita-Puno, horiz. 6s, Cuzco Cathedral. 8.50s, Santo Domingo, Cuzco.

1974, May 6

C395 AP128 1.50s multi .15 .15
C396 AP128 3.50s multi .20 .15
C397 AP128 5s multi .30 .15
C398 AP128 6s multi .35 .15
C399 AP128 8.50s multi .50 .16
Nos. C395-C399 (5) 1.50
Set value .60

Surrender at Ayacucho, by Daniel Hernandez AP129

Designs: 6s, Battle of Junin, by Felix Yañex. 7.50s, Battle of Ayachucho, by Felix Yañez.

1974 Litho. *Perf. 13x13½*

C400 AP129 3.50s multi .20 .15
C401 AP129 6s multi .35 .15
C402 AP129 7.50s multi .40 .15
C403 AP129 8.50s multi .50 .18
C404 AP129 10s multi .65 .20
Nos. C400-C404 (5) 2.10
Set value .70

Sesquicentennial of the Battles of Junin and Ayacucho and of the surrender at Ayacucho.

Issued: 7.50s, Aug. 6; 6s, Oct. 9; others, Dec. 9.

Chavin Stone, Ancash AP130

Machu Picchu, Cuzco AP131

#C407, C409, Different bas-reliefs from Chavin Stone. #C408, Baths of Tampumacchay, Cuzco. #C410, Ruins of Kencco, Cuzco.

Perf. 13½x13, 13x13½

1974, Mar. 25

C405 AP130 3s multi .20 .15
C406 AP131 3s multi .20 .15
C407 AP130 5s multi .30 .15
C408 AP131 5s multi .30 .15
C409 AP130 10s multi .60 .20
C410 AP131 10s multi .60 .20
Nos. C405-C410 (6) 2.20 1.00

Cacajao Rubicundus AP132

1974, Oct. 21 *Perf. 13½x13*

C411 AP132 8s multi .40 .25
C412 AP132 20s multi 1.00 .40

Protected animals.

Inca Gold Mask AP133

1974, Nov. 8 *Perf. 13x13½*

C413 AP133 8s yel & multi .40 .16

8th World Mining Congress, Lima.

Chalan, Horseman's Cloak — AP134

1974, Nov. 11 Litho. *Perf. 13½x13*

C414 AP134 5s multi .25 .15
C415 AP134 8.50s multi .50 .25

Pedro Paulet and Aerial Torpedo AP135

1974, Nov. 28 Litho. *Perf. 13x13½*

C416 AP135 8s bl & vio .40 .30

UPU, cent. Pedro Paulet, inventor of the mail-carrying aerial torpedo.

Christmas Type of 1974

Design: 6.50s, Indian Nativity scene.

1974, Dec. 20 *Perf. 13½x13*

C417 A235 6.50s multi .25 .25

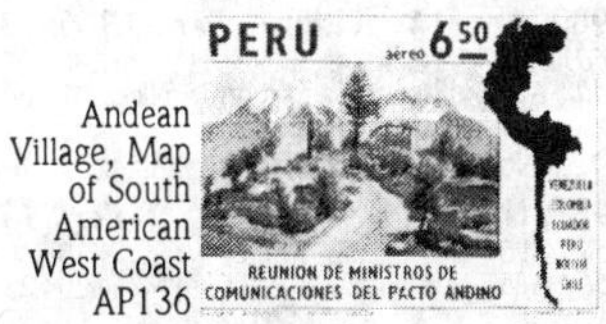

Andean Village, Map of South American West Coast AP136

1974, Dec. 30

C418 AP136 6.50s multi .35 .25

Meeting of Communications Ministers of Andean Pact countries.

Map of Peru, Modern Buildings, UN Emblem — AP137

1975, Mar. 12 Litho. *Perf. 13x13*

C419 AP137 6s blk, gray & red .20 .20

2nd United Nations Industrial Development Organization Conference, Lima.

Nos. C187, C211 and C160 Surcharged with New Value and Heavy Bar in Dark Blue

Wmk. 346

1975, April Litho. *Perf. 12*

C420 AP51 2s on 4.30s org .20 .15

Perf. 13½x14, 13x14

Unwmk.

C421 AP51 2.50s on 4.60s org .25 .15
C422 AP51 5s on 3.80s org .25 .20
Nos. C420-C422 (3) .70 .50

World Map and Peruvian Colors AP138

1975, Aug. 25 Litho. *Perf. 13x13½*

C423 AP138 6.50s lt bl, vio bl & red .25 .20

Conference of Foreign Ministers of Nonaligned Countries.

Map of Peru and Flight Route AP139

1975, Oct. 23 Litho. *Perf. 13x13½*

C424 AP139 8s red, pink & blk .35 .16

AeroPeru's first flights: Lima-Rio de Janeiro, Lima-Los Angeles.

Fair Poster — AP140

Col. Francisco Bolognesi — AP141

1975, Nov. 21 Litho. *Perf. 13½x13*

C425 AP140 6s blk, bis & red .50 .25

9th International Pacific Fair, Lima, 1975.

1975, Dec. 23 Litho. *Perf. 13½x13*

C426 AP141 20s multi .80 .50

160th birth anniv. of Col. Francisco Bolognesi.

Indian Mother and Child — AP142

Inca Messenger, UPAE Emblem — AP143

1976, Feb. 23 Litho. *Perf. 13½x13*

C427 AP142 6s gray & multi .35 .25

Christmas 1975.

1976, Mar. 19 Litho. *Perf. 13½x13*

C428 AP143 5s red, blk & tan .40 .25

11th Congress of the Postal Union of the Americas and Spain, UPAE.

Nos. C187, C211, C160, C209, C210 Surcharged in Dark Blue or Violet Blue (No Bar)

1976 **As Before**

C429 AP51 2s on 4.30s org .15 .15
C430 AP51 3.50s on 4.60s org .16 .15
C431 AP51 4.50s on 3.80s org .20 .20
C432 AP51 5s on 4.30s org .25 .20
C433 AP51 6s on 4.60s org .35 .25
C434 A184 10s on 2.60s brt grn .50 .20
C435 AP52 50s on 3.60s lil rose (VB) 2.00 1.75
Nos. C429-C435 (7) 3.61 2.90

Stamps of 1962-67 Surcharged with New Value and Heavy Bar in Black, Red, Green, Dark Blue or Orange

1976-77 **As Before**

C436 AP52 1.50s on 3.60s (Bk) #C210 .15 .15
C437 A184 2s on 2.60s (R) #C209 ('77) .20 .15
C438 AP52 2s on 3.60s (G) #C210 .20 .15
C439 AP80 2s on 4.30s (Bk) #C199 .20 .15
C440 A184 3s on 2.60s (Bk) #C209 ('77) .20 .15
C441 A184 4s on 2.60s (DBl) #C209 .25 .15
C442 AP52 4s on 3.60s (DBl) #C210 ('77) .25 .15
C443 AP51 5s on 4.30s (R) #C187 .30 .15
C444 AP83 6s on 4.60s (Bk) #C208 ('77) .35 .20
C445 AP51 6s on 4.60s (DBl) #C211 ('77) .35 .20
C446 AP51 7s on 4.30s (Bk) #C187 ('77) .25 .20
C447 AP52 7.50s on 3.60s (DBl) #C210 .45 .25
C448 AP52 8s on 3.60s (O) #C210 .50 .16
C449 AP51 10s on 4.30s (Bk) #C187 ('77) .30 .20
C450 AP51 10s on 4.60s (DBl) #C211 .60 .20
C451 AP86 24s on 3.60s (Bk) #C220 ('77) 1.75 .60
C452 AP86 28s on 4.60s (Bk) #C221 ('77) 1.00 .60
C453 AP86 32s on 5.60s (Bk) #C222 ('77) 1.00 .60
C454 A184 50s on 2.60s (O) #C209 ('77) 2.50 1.00
C455 AP52 50s on 3.60s (G) #C210 2.00 1.25
Nos. C436-C455 (20) 12.80 6.66

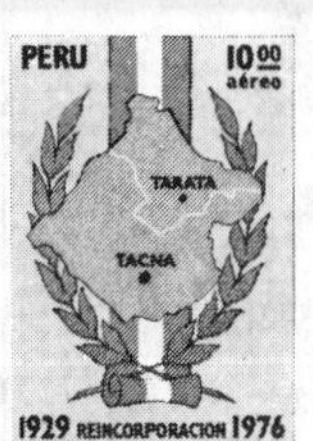

AP144

AP145

Map of Tacna and Tarata Provinces.

1976, Aug. 28 Litho. *Perf. 13½x13*

C456 AP144 10s multi .35 .25

Re-incorporation of Tacna Province into Peru, 47th anniversary.

1976, Sept. 15 Litho. *Perf. 13½x13*

Investigative Police badge.

C457 AP145 20s multi .65 .35

Investigative Police of Peru, 54th anniv.

AP146

AP147

"Declaration of Bogota."

1976, Sept. 22

C458 AP146 10s multi .35 .25

Declaration of Bogota for cooperation and world peace, 10th anniversary.

1976, Nov. 2 Litho. *Perf. 13½x13*

Pal Losonczi and map of Hungary.

C459 AP147 7s ultra & blk .35 .20

Visit of Pres. Pal Losonczi of Hungary, Oct. 1976.

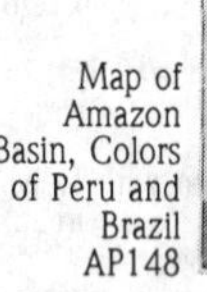

Map of Amazon Basin, Colors of Peru and Brazil AP148

1976, Dec. 16 Litho. *Perf. 13*

C460 AP148 10s bl & multi .35 .25

Visit of Gen. Ernesto Geisel, president of Brazil, Nov. 5, 1976.

Liberation Monument, Lima AP149

1977, Mar. 9 Litho. *Perf. 13x13½*

C461 AP149 20s red buff & blk .50 .50

Army Day.

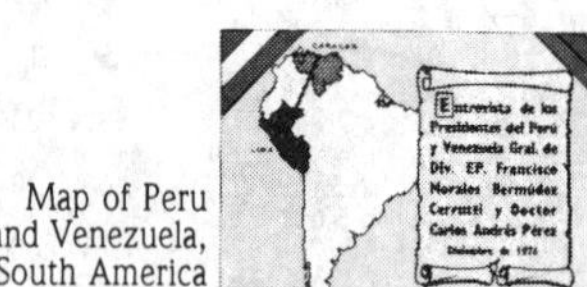

Map of Peru and Venezuela, South America AP150

1977, Mar. 14

C462 AP150 12s buff & multi .50 .30

Meeting of Pres. Francisco Morales Bermudez Cerrutti of Peru and Pres. Carlos Andres Perez of Venezuela, Dec. 1976.

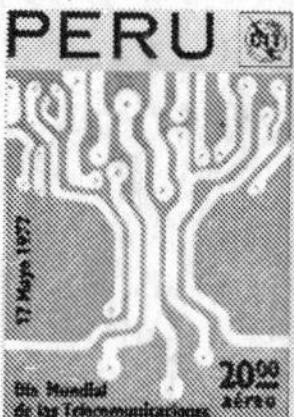

Electronic Tree — AP151

Map of Peru, Refinery, Tanker — AP152

1977, May 30 Litho. *Perf. 13½x13*

C463 AP151 20s gray, red & blk .65 .35

World Telecommunications Day.

1977, July 13 Litho. *Perf. 13½x13*

C464 AP152 14s multi .42 .30

Development of Bayovar oil complex.

Messenger Type of 1977

1977 Litho. *Perf. 13½x13*

C465 A243 24s mag & blk .65 .40
C466 A243 28s bl & blk 1.40 .50
C467 A243 32s rose brn & blk .80 .60
Nos. C465-C467 (3) 2.85 1.50

Arms of Arequipa — AP153

Gen. Jorge Rafael Videla — AP154

1977, Sept. 3 Litho. *Perf. 13½x13*

C468 AP153 10s multi .20 .15

Gold of Peru Exhibition, Arequipa 1977.

1977, Oct. 8 Litho. *Perf. 13½x13*

C469 AP154 36s multi .65 .25

Visit of Jorge Rafael Videla, president of Argentina.

Stamps of 1953-67 Surcharged with New Value and Heavy Bar in Black, Dark Blue or Green

1977 As Before

C470 AP83 2s on 3.60s #C207 .15 .15
C471 AP51 2s on 4.60s (DB) #C211 .15 .15
C472 AP51 4s on 4.60s (DB) #C211 .15 .15
C473 AP51 5s on 4.30s #C187 .35 .15
C474 AP52 5s on 3.60s #C210 .20 .15
C475 AP55 10s on 2.15s #C125 .40 .20
C476 AP52 10s on 3.60s (DB) #C210 .65 .20
C477 AP84 10s on 3.60s #C215 .50 .20
C478 AP52 20s on 3.60s (DB) #C210 .50 .25
C479 AP51 100s on 3.80s (G) #C160 2.00 1.75
Nos. C470-C479 (10) 5.05 3.35

Nos. C223-C224 Surcharged with New Value, Heavy Bars and: "FRANQUEO"

1977 Litho. *Perf. 12*

C480 AP87 6s on 3.60s multi .40 .30
C481 AP87 8s on 3.60s multi .50 .35
C482 AP87 10s on 5.60s multi .50 .40
Nos. C480-C482 (3) 1.40 1.05

Adm. Miguel Grau — AP155

1977, Dec. 15 Litho. *Perf. 13½x13*

C483 AP155 28s multi .38 .25

Navy Day. Miguel Grau (1838-1879), Peruvian naval commander.

Christmas Type of 1977

1977, Dec. 23

C484 A246 20s Indian Nativity .50 .20

Andrés Bello, Flag and Map of Participants AP156

1978, Jan. 12 Litho. *Perf. 13*

C485 AP156 30s multi .40 .30

8th Meeting of Education Ministers honoring Andrés Bello, Lima.

Inca Type of 1978

1978 Litho. *Perf. 13½x13*

C486 A247 24s dp rose lil .32 .30
C487 A247 30s salmon .40 .30
C488 A247 65s brt bl .90 .65
C489 A247 95s dk bl 1.25 1.00
Nos. C486-C489 (4) 2.87 2.25

Antenna, ITU Emblem AP157

1978, July 3 Litho. *Perf. 13x13½*

C490 AP157 50s gray & multi .65 .65

10th World Telecommunications Day.

San Martin, Flag Colors of Peru and Argentina — AP158

1978, Sept. 4 Litho. *Perf. 13½x13*

C491 AP158 30s multi .40 .40

Gen. José de San Martin (1778-1850), soldier and statesman, protector of Peru.

Stamps of 1965-67 Surcharged "Habilitado / R.D. No. O118" and New Value in Red, Green, Violet Blue or Black

1978 Litho.

C492 AP83 34s on 4.60s multi (R) #C208 .30 .25
C493 AP79 40s on 4.30s multi (G) #C196 .35 .30
C494 A184 70s on 2.60s brt grn (VB) #C209 .60 .50
C495 AP52 110s on 3.60s lil rose (Bk) #C210 .90 .75
C496 AP80 265s on 4.30s gray & multi (Bk) #C199 2.25 2.00
Nos. C492-C496 (5) 4.40 3.80

Stamps and Type of 1968-78 Surcharged in Violet Blue, Black or Red

1978 Litho.

C497 AP86 25s on 4.60s (VB) #C221 .25 .25
C498 A247 45s on 28s dk grn (Bk) .40 .22
C499 A247 75s on 28s dk grn (R) .65 .40
C500 AP86 105s on 5.60s (R) #C222 1.25 1.00
Nos. C497-C500 (4) 2.55 1.87

Nos. C498-C499 not issued without surcharge.

Nos. C486, C467 Surcharged

1980, Apr. 14 Litho. *Perf. 13½x13*

C501 A247 35s on 24s dp rose lil .30 .25
C502 A243 45s on 32s rose brn & blk .40 .30

No. C130 Surcharged in Black

1981, Nov. Engr. *Perf. 13*

C503 AP57 30s on 2.20s multi .30 .30
C504 AP57 40s on 2.20s multi .30 .25

No. C130 Surcharged and Overprinted in Green: "12 Feria / Internacional / del / Pacifico 1981"

1981, Nov. 30

C505 AP57 140s on 2.20s multi 1.10 .75

12th Intl. Pacific Fair.

AIR POST SEMI-POSTAL STAMPS

Catalogue values for unused stamps in this section are for Never Hinged items.

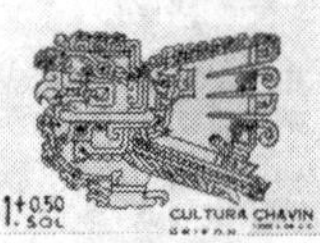

Chavin Griffin — SPAP1

1.50s+1s, Bird. 3s+2.50s, Cat. 4.30s+3s, Mythological figure, vert. 6s+ 4s, Chavin god, vert.

Perf. 12½x12, 12x12½

1963, Apr. 18 Litho. Wmk. 346

Design in Gray and Brown

CB1 SPAP1 1s + 50c sal pink .20 .20
CB2 SPAP1 1.50s + 1s blue .20 .20
CB3 SPAP1 3s + 2.50s lt grn .50 .50
CB4 SPAP1 4.30s + 3s green .80 .80
CB5 SPAP1 6s + 4s citron 1.00 1.00
Nos. CB1-CB5 (5) 2.70 2.70

The designs are from ceramics found by archaeological excavations of the 14th century Chavin culture. The surtax was for the excavations fund.

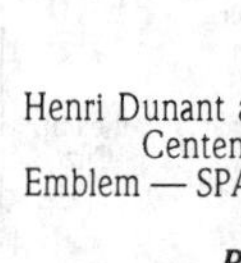

Henri Dunant and Centenary Emblem — SPAP2

Perf. 12½x12

1964, Jan. 29 Unwmk.

CB6 SPAP2 1.30s + 70c multi .16 .16
CB7 SPAP2 4.30s + 1.70s multi .42 .42

Centenary of International Red Cross.

SPECIAL DELIVERY STAMPS

No. 149 Overprinted in Black

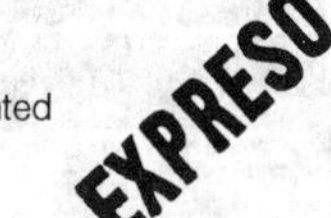

1908 Unwmk. *Perf. 12*

E1 A25 10c gray black 20.00 15.00

No. 172 Overprinted in Violet

EXPRESO

1909

E2 A40 10c red brn & blk 25.00 14.00

No. 1819 Handstamped in Violet

EXPRESO

1910

E3 A49 10c deep blue 14.00 12.00

Two handstamps were used to make No. E2. Impressions from them measure 22½x6½mm and 24x6½mm.

Counterfeits exist of Nos. E1-3.

POSTAGE DUE STAMPS

Coat of Arms — D1

Steamship and Llama
D2 D3

D4 D5

1874-86 Unwmk. Engr. *Perf. 12*
With Grill

J1 D1 1c bister ('79) .25 .15
J2 D2 5c vermilion .30 .16
J3 D3 10c orange .35 .25
J4 D4 20c blue .60 .35
J5 D5 50c brown 9.00 3.50
Nos. J1-J5 (5) 10.50 4.41

A 2c green exists, but was not regularly issued.
For overprints and surcharges see Nos. 157, J6-J31, J37-J38, 8N14-8N15, 14N18.

1886
Without Grill

J1a D1 1c bister .15
J2a D2 5c vermilion .15
J3a D3 10c orange .20
J4a D4 20c blue .35
J5a D5 50c brown 3.50
Nos. J1a-J5a (5) 4.35

Nos. J1-J5 Overprinted in Blue or Red

1881
"PLATA" 2½mm High

J6 D1 1c bis (Bl) 3.50 2.50
J7 D2 5c ver (Bl) 6.50 6.00
a. Double overprint
b. Inverted overprint 17.00 17.00
J8 D3 10c org (Bl) 6.50 6.50
a. Inverted overprint 17.00 17.00
J9 D4 20c bl (R) 25.00 20.00
J10 D5 50c brn (Bl) 55.00 50.00
Nos. J6-J10 (5) 96.50 85.00

In the reprints of this overprint "PLATA" is 3mm high instead of 2½mm. Besides being struck in the regular colors it was also applied to the 1, 5, 10 and 50c in red and the 20c in blue.

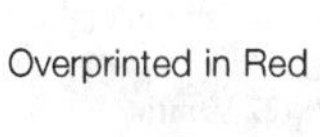

Overprinted in Red

1881

J11 D1 1c bister 5.00 5.00
J12 D2 5c vermilion 6.50 6.00
J13 D3 10c orange 8.00 6.50
J14 D4 20c blue 25.00 20.00
J15 D5 50c brown 80.00 65.00
Nos. J11-J15 (5) 124.50 102.50

Originals of Nos. J11 to J15 are overprinted in brick-red, oily ink; reprints in thicker, bright red ink. The 5c exists with reprinted overprint in blue.

Overprinted "Union Postal Universal Lima Plata", in Oval in first named color and Triangle in second named color

1883

J16 D1 1c bis (Bl & Bk) 5.00 3.50
J17 D1 1c bis (Bk & Bl) 7.50 7.00
J18 D2 5c ver (Bl & Bk) 7.50 7.00
J19 D3 10c org (Bl & Bk) 7.50 6.00
J20 D4 20c bl (R & Bk) *450.00 450.00*
J21 D5 50c brn (Bl & Bk) 55.00 42.50

Reprints of Nos. J16 to J21 have the oval overprint with "PLATA" 3mm. high. The 1c also exists with the oval overprint in red.

Overprinted in Black

1884

J22 D1 1c bister .50 .50
J23 D2 5c vermilion .50 .50
J24 D3 10c orange .50 .50
J25 D4 20c blue 1.00 .50
J26 D5 50c brown 3.00 .90
Nos. J22-J26 (5) 5.50 2.90

The triangular overprint is found in 11 types.

Overprinted "Lima Correos" in Circle in Red and Triangle in Black

1884

J27 D1 1c bister 12.50 11.00

Reprints of No. J27 have the overprint in bright red. At the time they were made the overprint was also printed on the 5, 10, 20 and 50c Postage Due stamps.

Postage Due stamps overprinted with Sun and "CORREOS LIMA" (as shown above No. 103), alone or in combination with the "U. P. U. LIMA" oval or "LIMA CORREOS" in double-lined circle, are fancy varieties made to sell to collectors and never placed in use.

Overprinted

1896-97

J28 D1 1c bister .35 .30
a. Double overprint
J29 D2 5c vermilion .45 .25
a. Double overprint
b. Inverted overprint
J30 D3 10c orange .55 .35
a. Inverted overprint
J31 D4 20c blue .65 .50
a. Double overprint
J32 A22 50c red ('97) .75 .50
J33 A23 1s brn ('97) 1.00 .65
a. Double overprint
b. Inverted overprint
Nos. J28-J33 (6) 3.75 2.55

Liberty — D6

1899 Engr.

J34 D6 5s yel grn 1.00 *5.00*
J35 D6 10s dl vio 900.00 900.00

For surcharge see No. J39.

DÉFICIT

UN CENTAVO

DEFICIT CINCO CENTAVOS

1902

On No. 159

J36 A31 5c on 10s bl grn 1.00 .80
a. Double surcharge 12.00 12.00

On No. J4

J37 D4 1c on 20c blue .50 .40
a. "DEFICIT" omitted 6.50 2.00
b. "DEFICIT" double 6.50 2.00
c. "UN CENTAVO" double 6.00 2.00
d. "UN CENTAVO" omitted 8.25 6.00

Surcharged Vertically

J38 D4 5c on 20c blue 1.50 1.00

On No. J35

J39 D6 1c on 10s dull vio .60 .50
Nos. J36-J39 (4) 3.60 2.70

D7

1909 Engr. *Perf. 12*

J40 D7 1c red brown .50 .15
J41 D7 5c red brown .50 .15
J42 D7 10c red brown .60 .16
J43 D7 50c red brown .90 .20
Nos. J40-J43 (4) 2.50 .66

1921
Size: 18¼x22mm

J44 D7 1c violet brown .25 .16
J45 D7 2c violet brown .25 .20
J46 D7 5c violet brown .35 .20
J47 D7 10c violet brown .50 .25
J48 D7 50c violet brown 1.65 .75
J49 D7 1s violet brown 7.50 3.00
J50 D7 2s violet brown 12.00 3.50
Nos. J44-J50 (7) 22.50 8.06

Nos. J49 and J50 have the circle at the center replaced by a shield containing "S/.", in addition to the numeral.

In 1929 during a shortage of regular postage stamps, some of the Postage Due stamps of 1921 were used instead.

See Nos. J50A-J52, J55-J56. For surcharges see Nos. 204-207, 757.

Type of 1909-22
Size: 18¾x23mm

J50A D7 2c violet brown .75 .16
J50B D7 10c violet brown .75 .16

Type of 1909-22 Issues

1932 Photo. *Perf. 14½x14*

J51 D7 2c violet brown .75 .25
J52 D7 10c violet brown .75 .25

Regular Stamps of 1934-35 Overprinted in Black **"Deficit"**

1935 *Perf. 13*

J53 A131 2c deep claret .75 .50
J54 A117 10c crimson .75 .50

Type of 1909-32
Size: 19x23mm
Imprint: "Waterlow & Sons, Limited, Londres."

1936 Engr. *Perf. 12½*

J55 D7 2c light brown .15 .15
J56 D7 10c gray green .50 .50

OFFICIAL STAMPS

Regular Issue of 1886 Overprinted in Red

a

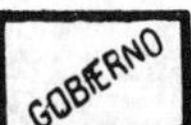

1890, Feb. 2

O2 A17 1c dl vio 1.40 1.40
a. Double overprint 8.25 8.25
O3 A18 2c green 1.40 1.40
a. Double overprint
b. Inverted overprint 8.25 8.25
O4 A19 5c orange 2.00 1.65
a. Inverted overprint 8.25 8.25
b. Double overprint 8.25 8.25
O5 A20 10c slate 1.00 .65
a. Double overprint 8.25 8.25
b. Inverted overprint 8.25 8.25
O6 A21 20c blue 3.00 2.00
a. Double overprint 8.25 8.25
b. Inverted overprint 8.25 8.25
O7 A22 50c red 4.00 2.00
a. Inverted overprint 12.00
b. Double overprint
O8 A23 1s brown 5.00 4.50
a. Double overprint 17.00 17.00
b. Inverted overprint 17.00 17.00
Nos. O2-O8 (7) 17.80 13.60

Nos. 118-124 (Bermudez Ovpt.) Overprinted Type "a" in Red

1894, Oct.

O9 A17 1c green 1.40 1.40
a. "Gobierno" and head invtd. 6.50 5.50
b. Dbl. ovpt. of "Gobierno"
O10 A17 1c orange 22.50 20.00
O11 A18 2c rose 1.40 1.40
a. Overprinted head inverted 10.00 10.00
b. Both overprints inverted
O12 A18 2c violet 1.40 1.40
a. "Gobierno" double
O13 A19 5c ultra 22.50 20.00
a. Both overprints inverted
O14 A19 5c blue 10.00 9.00
O15 A20 10c green 3.50 3.50
O16 A22 50c green 5.00 5.00
Nos. O9-O16 (8) 67.70 61.70

Nos. 125-126 ("Horseshoe" Ovpt.) Overprinted Type "a" in Red

O17 A18 2c vermilion 2.00 2.00
O18 A19 5c blue 2.00 2.00

Nos. 105, 107, 109, 113 Overprinted Type "a" in Red

1895, May

O19 A17 1c vermilion 8.25 8.25
O20 A18 2c dp ultra 8.25 8.25
O21 A12 5c claret 6.50 6.50
O22 A14 20c dp ultra 6.50 6.50
Nos. O19-O22 (4) 29.50 29.50

Nos. O2-O22 have been extensively counterfeited.

Nos. 141, 148, 149, 151 Overprinted in Black

1896-1901

O23 A24 1c ultra .15 .15
O24 A25 10c yellow 1.00 .50
a. Double overprint
O25 A25 10c gray blk ('01) .15 .15
O26 A26 50c brt rose .40 .25
Nos. O23-O26 (4) 1.70 1.05

O1

1909-14 Engr. *Perf. 12*
Size: 18½x22mm

O27 O1 1c red .20 .15
a. 1c brown red .20 .15
O28 O1 1c orange ('14) .50 .35
O29 O1 10c bis brn ('14) .20 .15
a. 10c violet brown .20 .15
O30 O1 50c ol grn ('14) .65 .35
a. 50c blue green 1.00 .35

Size: 18¾x23½mm

O30B O1 10c vio brn .50 .16
Nos. O27-O30B (5) 2.05
Set value 1.00

See Nos. O31, O33-O34. For overprints and surcharge see Nos. 201-203, 760.

1933 Photo. *Perf. 15x14*

O31 O1 10c violet brown .50 .15

No. 319 Overprinted in Black **"Servicio Oficial"**

1935 Unwmk. *Perf. 13*

O32 A117 10c crimson .20 .20

Type of 1909-33
Imprint: "Waterlow & Sons, Limited, Londres."

1936 Engr. *Perf. 12½*
Size: 19x23mm

O33 O1 10c light brown .15 .15
O34 O1 50c gray green .35 .35

PARCEL POST STAMPS

PP1

PP2

PP3

1897 Typeset Unwmk. *Perf. 12*

Q1 PP1 1c dull lilac 2.25 1.90
Q2 PP2 2c bister 2.50 2.25
 a. 2c olive 2.50 2.25
 b. 2c yellow 2.50 2.25
 c. Laid paper 65.00 65.00
Q3 PP2 5c dk bl 10.00 6.50
 a. Tête bêche pair *375.00*
Q4 PP3 10c vio brn 14.00 10.00
Q5 PP3 20c rose red 17.00 14.00
Q6 PP3 50c bl grn 45.00 37.50
 Nos. Q1-Q6 (6) 90.75 72.15

Surcharged in Black

UN CENTAVO

1903-04

Q7 PP3 1c on 20c rose red 12.00 10.00
Q8 PP3 1c on 50c bl grn 12.00 10.00
Q9 PP3 5c on 10c vio brn 80.00 65.00
 a. Inverted surcharge 120.00 110.00
 b. Double surcharge
 Nos. Q7-Q9 (3) 104.00 85.00

POSTAL TAX STAMPS

Plebiscite Issues

These stamps were not used in Tacna and Arica (which were under Chilean occupation) but were used in Peru to pay a supplementary tax on letters, etc.

It was intended that the money derived from the sale of these stamps should be used to help defray the expenses of the plebiscite.

Morro Arica — PT1

Adm. Grau and Col. Bolognesi Reviewing Troops PT2

Bolognesi Monument — PT3

1925-26 Unwmk. Litho. *Perf. 12*

RA1 PT1 5c dp bl 1.50 .35
RA2 PT1 5c rose red .80 .22
RA3 PT1 5c yel grn .70 .22
RA4 PT2 10c brown 3.00 .80
RA5 PT3 50c bl grn 19.00 9.00
 Nos. RA1-RA5 (5) 25.00 10.59

PT4

1926

RA6 PT4 2c orange .30 .15

PT5

1927-28

RA7 PT5 2c dp org .60 .15
RA8 PT5 2c red brn .60 .15
RA9 PT5 2c dk bl .60 .15
RA10 PT5 2c gray vio .40 .15
RA11 PT5 2c bl grn ('28) .40 .15
RA12 PT5 20c red 2.50 1.00
 Nos. RA7-RA12 (6) 5.10 1.75

PT6

1928 **Engr.**

RA13 PT6 2c dk vio .20 .15

The use of the Plebiscite stamps was discontinued July 26, 1929, after the settlement of the Tacna-Arica controversy with Chile.

For overprint see No. 261.

Unemployment Fund Issues

These stamps were required in addition to the ordinary postage, on every letter or piece of postal matter. The money obtained by their sale was to assist the unemployed.

Nos. 273-275 Surcharged

Habilitada Pro Desocupados 2 Cts.

1931

RA14 A95 2c on 4c red .65 .50
 a. Inverted surcharge 3.50 3.50
RA15 A95 2c on 10c bl grn .50 .50
 a. Inverted surcharge 3.50 3.50
RA16 A95 2c on 15c sl gray .50 .50
 a. Inverted surcharge 3.50 3.50
 Nos. RA14-RA16 (3) 1.65 1.50

"Labor" PT7

Blacksmith PT8

Two types of Nos. RA17-RA18:
I - Imprint 15mm.
II - Imprint 13¾mm.

Perf. 12x11½, 11½x12

1931-32 **Litho.**

RA17 PT7 2c emer (I) .15 .15
 a. Type II .15
RA18 PT7 2c rose car (I) ('32) .15 .15
 a. Type II .15
 Set value .20 .15

1932-34

RA19 PT8 2c dp gray .15 .15
RA20 PT8 2c pur ('34) .15 .15
 Set value .20 .15

Monument of 2nd of May — PT9

Perf. 13, 13½, 13x13½

1933-35 **Photo.**

RA21 PT9 2c bl vio .20 .15
RA22 PT9 2c org ('34) .20 .15
RA23 PT9 2c brn vio ('35) .20 .15
 Nos. RA21-RA23 (3) .60
 Set value .18

For overprint see No. RA27.

No. 307 Overprinted in Black

a **Pro-Desocupados**

1934 *Perf. 13½*

RA24 A111 2c green .15 .15
 a. Inverted overprint 2.00 2.00

No. 339 Overprinted in Black

Pro Desocupados

1935

RA25 A131 2c deep claret .15 .15

No. 339 Overprinted Type "a" in Black

1936 Unwmk. *Perf. 13½*

RA26 A131 2c deep claret .15 .15

No. RA23 Overprinted in Black

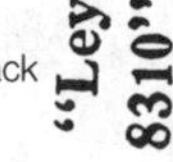

1936 *Perf. 13x13½*

RA27 PT9 2c brn vio .15 .15
 a. Double overprint 1.40
 b. Overprint reading down 1.40
 c. Overprint double, reading down 1.40

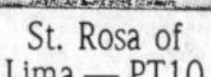
St. Rosa of Lima — PT10

"Protection" by John Q. A. Ward — PT11

1937 Engr. *Perf. 12*

RA28 PT10 2c car rose .15 .15

Nos. RA27 and RA28 represented a tax to help erect a church.

Imprint: "American Bank Note Company"

1938 **Litho.**

RA29 PT11 2c brown .20 .15

The tax was to help the unemployed.

See Nos. RA30, RA34, RA40. For surcharges see Nos. 501A, 674-678, 681-682, 709-711, 757.

Type of 1938 Redrawn
Imprint: "Columbian Bank Note Company."

1943 *Perf. 12½*

RA30 PT11 2c dl claret brn .20 .15

See note above #RA14. See #RA34, RA40.

Catalogue values for unused stamps in this section, from this point to the end of the section, are for Never Hinged items.

PT12

PT13

1949 *Perf. 12½, 12*

Black Surcharge

RA31 PT12 3c on 4c vio bl .55 .15
RA32 PT13 3c on 10c blue .55 .15
 Set value .16

The tax was for an education fund.

Symbolical of Education PT14

Emblem of Congress PT15

1950 Typo. *Perf. 14*

Size: 16½x21mm

RA33 PT14 3c dp car .15 .15

See Nos. RA35, RA39, RA43.

For surcharges see Nos. 501B, 761, 764-766, RA45-RA48, RA58.

Type of 1938
Imprint: "Thomas De La Rue & Co. Ltd."

1951 **Litho.**

RA34 PT11 2c lt redsh brn .15 .15

Type of 1950
Imprint: "Thomas De La Rue & Company, Limited."

1952 Unwmk. *Perf. 14, 13*

Size: 16½x21½mm

RA35 PT14 3c brn car .20 .15

1954 *Rouletted 13*

RA36 PT15 5c bl & red .22 .15

The tax was to help finance the National Marian Eucharistic Congress.

For surcharges see Nos. 758B, 768.

Piura Arms and Congress Emblem — PT16

1960 Litho. *Perf. 10½*

RA37 PT16 10c ultra, red, grn & yel .18 .15
 a. Green ribbon inverted
RA38 PT16 10c ultra & red .25 .15
 Set value .15

Nos. RA37-RA38 were used to help finance the 6th National Eucharistic Congress, Piura, Aug. 25-28. Obligatory on all domestic mail until Dec. 31, 1960. Both stamps exist imperf.

Type of 1950
Imprint: "Bundesdruckerei Berlin"

1961 *Perf. 14*

Size: 17½x22½mm

RA39 PT14 3c dp car .15 .15

Type of 1938
Imprint: "Harrison and Sons Ltd"

1962, Apr. Litho. *Perf. 14x14½*

RA40 PT11 2c lt brn .15 .15

Symbol of Eucharist — PT17

1962, May 8 *Rouletted 11*

RA41 PT17 10c bl & org .15 .15

Issued to raise funds for the Seventh National Eucharistic Congress, Huancayo, 1964. Obligatory on all domestic mail.

See No. RA42. For surcharges and overprint see Nos. 735, 762, RA44.

1962

Imprint: "Iberia"

RA42 PT17 10c bl & org .15 .15

Type of 1950

1965, Apr. Litho. *Perf. 12½x12*

Imprint: "Thomas de La Rue"

Size: 18x22mm

RA43 PT14 3c light carmine .20 .15

Type of 1962 Overprinted in Red with three "X," Bars and: "Periodista / Peruano / LEY / 16078"

1966, July 2 Litho. *Pin Perf.*

Imprint: "Iberia"

RA44 PT17 10c vio & org .15 .15

No. RA43 Surcharged in Green or Black

HABILITADO
"Fondo del
Periodista
Peruano"
Ley 16078
S/o. 0.10
b

Habilitado
«Fondo del
Periodista
Peruano»
Ley 16078
S/. 0.10
c

HABILITADO
"Fondo del
Periodista
Peruano"
Ley 16078
S/o. 0.10
d

1966-67 *Perf. 12x12½*

RA45 PT14 (b) 10c on 3c (G)	.80	.15
RA46 PT14 (c) 10c on 3c (Bk)	.80	.15
RA47 PT14 (c) 10c on 3c (G)	.20	.15
RA48 PT14 (d) 10c on 3c (G)	.25	.15
Nos. RA45-RA48 (4)	2.05	
Set value		.46

The surtax of Nos. RA44-RA48 was for the Peruvian Journalists' Fund.

Pen Made of Newspaper PT18

Temple at Chan-Chan PT19

1967, Dec. Litho. *Perf. 11*

RA49 PT18 10c dk red & blk .15 .15

The surtax was for the Peruvian Journalists' fund.

For surcharges see Nos. RA56-RA57.

1967, Dec. 27

Designs: No. RA51, Side view of temple. Nos. RA52-RA55, Various stone bas-reliefs from Chan-Chan.

RA50 PT19 20c bl & grn	.15	.15
RA51 PT19 20c multi	.15	.15
RA52 PT19 20c brt bl & blk	.15	.15
RA53 PT19 20c emer & blk	.15	.15
RA54 PT19 20c sep & blk	.15	.15
RA55 PT19 20c lil rose & blk	.15	.15
Set value	.42	.30

The surtax was for the excavations at Chan-Chan, northern coast of Peru. (Mochica-Chimu pre-Inca period).

Type of 1967 Surcharged in Red: "VEINTE / CENTAVOS / R.S. 16-8-68"

Designs: No. RA56, Handshake. No. RA57, Globe and pen.

1968, Oct. Litho. *Perf. 11*

RA56 PT18 20c on 50c multi	.50	.50
RA57 PT18 20c on 1s multi	.50	.50

Nos. RA56-RA57 without surcharge were not obligatory tax stamps.

No. C199 surcharged "PRO NAVIDAD/ Veinte Centavos/R.S. 5-11-68" was not a compulsory postal tax stamp.

#RA43 Surchd. Similar to Type "c"

1968, Oct. *Perf. 12½x12*

RA58 PT14 20c on 3c lt car .15 .15

Surcharge lacks quotation marks and 4th line reads: Ley 17050.

OCCUPATION STAMPS

Issued under Chilean Occupation

Stamps formerly listed as Nos. N1-N10 are regular issues of Chile canceled in Peru.

Stamps of Peru, 1874-80, Overprinted in Red, Blue or Black

1881-82 *Perf. 12*

N11 A17 1c org (Bl)	.50	1.00
a. Inverted overprint		
N12 A18 2c dk vio (Bk)	.50	4.00
a. Inverted overprint	16.50	
b. Double overprint	22.50	
N13 A18 2c rose (Bk)	1.65	*18.00*
a. Inverted overprint		
N14 A19 5c bl (R)	55.00	62.50
a. Inverted overprint		
N15 A19 5c ultra (R)	90.00	100.00
N16 A20 10c grn (R)	.50	*1.65*
a. Inverted overprint	6.50	6.50
b. Double overprint	12.00	12.00
N17 A21 20c brn red (Bl)	80.00	120.00
Nos. N11-N17 (7)	228.15	307.15

Reprints of No. N17 have the overprint in bright blue; on the originals it is in dull ultramarine. Nos. N11 and N12 exist with reprinted overprint in red or yellow. There are numerous counterfeits with the overprint in both correct and fancy colors.

Same, with Additional Overprint in Black

1882

N19 A17 1c grn (R)	.50	.80
a. Arms inverted	8.25	10.00
b. Arms double	5.50	6.50
c. Horseshoe inverted	12.00	13.50
N20 A19 5c bl (R)	.80	.80
a. Arms inverted	13.50	15.00
b. Arms double	13.50	15.00
N21 A22 50c rose (Bk)	1.65	2.00
a. Arms inverted	10.00	
N22 A22 50c rose (Bl)	1.65	2.75
N23 A23 1s ultra (R)	3.25	4.50
a. Arms inverted	13.50	
b. Horseshoe inverted	16.50	
c. Arms and horseshoe inverted	20.00	
d. Arms double	13.50	
Nos. N19-N23 (5)	7.85	10.85

PROVISIONAL ISSUES

Stamps Issued in Various Cities of Peru during the Chilean Occupation of Lima and Callao

During the Chilean-Peruvian War which took place in 1879 to 1882, the Chilean forces occupied the two largest cities in Peru, Lima & Callao. As these cities were the source of supply of postage stamps, Peruvians in other sections of the country were left without stamps and were forced to the expedient of making provisional issues from whatever material was at hand. Many of these were former canceling devices made over for this purpose. Counterfeits exist of many of the overprinted stamps.

ANCACHS

(See Note under "Provisional Issues")

Regular Issue of Peru, Overprinted in Manuscript in Black

Alerta

1884 Unwmk. *Perf. 12*

1N1 A19 5c blue 57.50 55.00

Regular Issues of Peru, Overprinted in Black

Overprinted **FRANCA**

1N2 A19 5c blue 18.00 16.50

Overprinted

1N3 A19 5c blue	90.00	82.50
1N4 A20 10c green	55.00	40.00
1N5 A20 10c slate	55.00	35.00

Same, with Additional Overprint "FRANCA"

1N6 A20 10c green 82.50 42.50

Overprinted

1N7 A19 5c blue	30.00	25.00
1N8 A20 10c green	30.00	25.00

Same, with Additional Overprint "FRANCA"

1N9 A20 10c green

A1

Revenue Stamp of Peru, 1878-79, Overprinted in Black "CORREO Y FISCAL" and "FRANCA"

1N10 A1 10c yellow 37.50 37.50

APURIMAC

(See Note under "Provisional Issues")

Provisional Issue of Arequipa Overprinted in Black

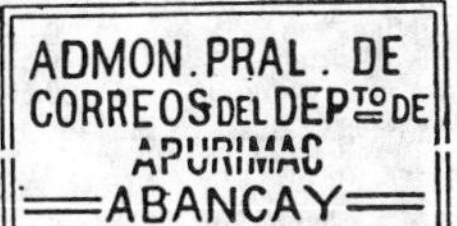

Overprint Covers Two Stamps

1885 Unwmk. *Imperf.*

2N1 A6 10c gray 100.00 90.00

Some experts question the status of No. 2N1.

AREQUIPA

(See Note under "Provisional Issues")

Coat of Arms

A1 A2

Overprint ("PROVISIONAL 1881-1882") in Black

1881, Jan. Unwmk. *Imperf.*

3N1 A1 10c blue	2.50	3.50
a. 10c ultramarine	2.50	4.00
b. Double overprint	12.00	13.50
c. Overprinted on back of stamp	8.25	10.00
3N2 A2 25c rose	2.50	6.00
a. "2" in upper left corner invtd.	8.25	
b. "Cevtavos"	8.25	10.00
c. Double overprint	12.00	13.50

The overprint also exists on 5s yellow.

The overprints "1883" in large figures or "Habilitado 1883" are fraudulent.

For overprints see Nos. 3N3, 4N1, 8N1, 10N1, 15N1-15N3.

With Additional Overprint Handstamped in Red

1881, Feb.

3N3 A1 10c blue	3.50	3.50
a. 10c ultramarine	13.50	8.25

A4

1883 **Litho.**

3N7 A4 10c dull rose	3.50	5.00
a. 10c vermilion	3.50	5.00

Overprinted in Blue like No. 3N3

3N9 A4 10c vermilion	5.00	4.00
a. 10c dull rose	5.00	4.00

See No. 3N10. For overprints see Nos. 8N2, 8N9, 10N2, 15N4.

Reprints of No. 3N9 are in different colors from the originals, orange, bright red, etc. They are printed in sheets of 20 instead of 25.

Redrawn

3N10 A4 10c brick red (Bl) 165.00

The redrawn stamp has small triangles without arabesques in the lower spandrels. The palm branch at left of the shield and other parts of the design have been redrawn.

Same Overprint in Black, Violet or Magenta On Regular Issues of Peru

1884 Embossed with Grill *Perf. 12*

3N11 A17 1c org (Bk, V or M)	6.50	6.50
3N12 A18 2c dk vio (Bk)	6.50	6.50
3N13 A19 5c bl (Bk, V or M)	2.00	1.35
a. 5c ultramarine (Bk or M)	8.25	6.50
3N15 A20 10c sl (Bk)	3.50	2.50
3N16 A21 20c brn red (Bk, V or M)	25.00	25.00
3N18 A22 50c grn (Bk or V)	25.00	25.00
3N20 A23 1s rose (Bk or V)	35.00	35.00
Nos. 3N11-3N20 (7)	103.50	101.85

A5

A6

Rear Admiral M. L. Grau A7

Col. Francisco Bolognesi A8

Same Overprint as on Previous Issues

1885 *Imperf.*

3N22 A5 5c olive (Bk)	5.25	5.25
3N23 A6 10c gray (Bk)	5.25	4.75
3N25 A7 5c blue (Bk)	5.25	4.75
3N26 A8 10c olive (Bk)	5.25	3.25
Nos. 3N22-3N26 (4)	21.00	18.00

For overprints see Nos. 2N1, 8N5-8N6, 8N12-8N13, 10N9, 10N12, 15N10-15N12.

These stamps have been reprinted without overprint; they exist however with forged overprint.

Originals are on thicker paper with distinct mesh, reprints on paper without mesh.

Without Overprint

3N22a A5	5c olive		5.25	5.25
3N23a A6	10c gray		4.00	3.25
3N25a A7	5c blue		4.00	3.25
3N26a A8	10c olive		4.00	3.25
	Nos. 3N22a-3N26a (4)		17.25	15.00

AYACUCHO

(See Note under "Provisional Issues")

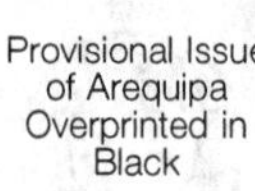
Provisional Issue of Arequipa Overprinted in Black

1881 Unwmk. *Imperf.*

4N1 A1 10c blue		82.50	70.00
a. 10c ultramarine		82.50	70.00

CHACHAPOYAS

(See Note under "Provisional Issues")

Regular Issue of Peru Overprinted in Black

1884 Unwmk. *Perf. 12*

5N1 A19 5c ultra 100.00 90.00

CHALA

(See Note under "Provisional Issues")

Regular Issues of Peru Overprinted in Black

1884 Unwmk. *Perf. 12*

6N1 A19 5c blue	8.25	6.50
6N2 A20 10c slate	10.00	8.25

CHICLAYO

(See Note under "Provisional Issues")

Regular Issue of Peru Overprinted in Black

1884 Unwmk. *Perf. 12*

7N1 A19 5c blue 16.50 10.00

Same, Overprinted **FRANCA**

7N2 A19 5c blue 35.00 22.50

CUZCO

(See Note under "Provisional Issues")

Provisional Issues of Arequipa Overprinted in Black

1881-85 Unwmk. *Imperf.*

8N1 A1 10c blue	70.00	60.00
8N2 A4 10c red	70.00	60.00

Overprinted "CUZCO" in an oval of dots

8N5 A5 5c olive	110.00	100.00
8N6 A6 10c gray	80.00	75.00

Regular Issue of Peru Overprinted in Black "CUZCO" in a Circle

Perf. 12

8N7 A19 5c blue 50.00 50.00

Provisional Issues of Arequipa Overprinted in Black CUZCO

1883 *Imperf.*

8N9 A4 10c red 10.00 10.00

Same Overprint in Black on Regular Issues of Peru

1884 *Perf. 12*

8N10 A19 5c blue	16.50	10.00
8N11 A20 10c slate	16.50	10.00

Same Overprint in Black on Provisional Issues of Arequipa

Imperf

8N12 A5 5c olive	27.50	27.50
8N13 A6 10c gray	8.00	8.00

Postage Due Stamps of Peru Surcharged in Black

Perf. 12

8N14 D1 10c on 1c bis	110.00	100.00
8N15 D3 10c on 10c org	110.00	100.00

HUACHO

(See Note under "Provisional Issues")

Regular Issues of Peru Overprinted in Black

1884 Unwmk. *Perf. 12*

9N1 A19 5c blue	8.00	8.00
9N2 A20 10c green	6.00	6.00
9N3 A20 10c slate	16.50	16.50
Nos. 9N1-9N3 (3)	30.50	30.50

MOQUEGUA

(See Note under "Provisional Issues")

Provisional Issues of Arequipa Overprinted in Violet

Overprint 27mm wide (illustration reduced).

1881-83 Unwmk. *Imperf.*

10N1 A1 10c blue	42.50	40.00
10N2 A4 10c red ('83)	42.50	40.00

Same Overprint on Regular Issues of Peru in Violet

1884 *Perf. 12*

10N3 A17 1c orange	42.50	40.00
10N4 A19 5c blue	37.50	30.00

Red Overprint

10N5 A19 5c blue 30.00 20.00

Same Overprint in Violet on Provisional Issues of Peru of 1880

Perf. 12

10N6 A17 1c grn (R)	8.25	6.50
10N7 A18 2c rose (Bl)	10.00	10.00
10N8 A19 5c bl (R)	20.00	20.00

Same Overprint in Violet on Provisional Issue of Arequipa

1885 *Imperf.*

10N9 A6 10c gray 57.50 50.00

Regular Issues of Peru Overprinted in Violet MOQUEA.

Perf. 12

10N10 A19 5c blue	110.00	65.00
10N11 A20 10c slate	45.00	25.00

Same Overprint in Violet on Provisional Issue of Arequipa

Imperf

10N12 A6 10c gray 70.00 65.00

PAITA

(See Note under "Provisional Issues")

Regular Issues of Peru Overprinted

Black Overprint

1884 Unwmk. *Perf. 12*

11N1 A19 5c blue	22.50	22.50
a. 5c ultramarine		
11N2 A20 10c green	15.00	15.00
11N3 A20 10c slate	22.50	22.50

Red Overprint

11N4 A19 5c blue 22.50 22.50

Overprint lacks ornaments on Nos. 11N4-11N5.

Violet Overprint. Letters 5 1/2mm High

11N5 A19 5c ultra	22.50	22.50
a. 5c blue		

PASCO

(See Note under "Provisional Issues")

Regular Issues of Peru Overprinted in Magenta or Black

1884 Unwmk. *Perf. 12*

12N1 A19 5c blue (M)	16.50	12.00
a. 5c ultramarine (M)	22.50	22.50
12N2 A20 10c green (Bk)	35.00	30.00
12N3 A20 10c slate (Bk)	65.00	57.50
Nos. 12N1-12N3 (3)	116.50	99.50

PISCO

(See Note under "Provisional Issues")

Regular Issue of Peru Overprinted in Black

1884 Unwmk. *Perf. 12*

13N1 A19 5c blue 190.00 165.00

PIURA

(See Note under "Provisional Issues")

Regular Issues of Peru Overprinted in Black PIURA

1884 Unwmk. *Perf. 12*

14N1 A19 5c blue	20.00	10.00
a. 5c ultramarine	25.00	13.50
14N2 A21 20c brn red	82.50	82.50
14N3 A22 50c green	200.00	200.00

Same Overprint in Black on Provisional Issues of Peru of 1881

14N4 A17 1c grn (R)	22.50	22.50
14N5 A18 2c rose (Bl)	40.00	40.00
14N6 A19 5c ultra (R)	50.00	50.00

Regular Issues of Peru Overprinted in Violet, Black or Blue PIURA

14N7 A19 5c bl (V)	16.50	10.00
a. 5c ultramarine (V)	16.50	10.00
b. 5c ultramarine (Bk)	16.50	10.00
14N8 A21 20c brn red (Bk)	82.50	82.50
14N9 A21 20c brn red (Bl)	82.50	82.50

Same Overprint in Black on Provisional Issues of Peru of 1881

14N10 A17 1c grn (R)	20.00	20.00
14N11 A19 5c bl (R)	22.50	22.50
a. 5c ultramarine (R)	40.00	40.00

Regular Issues of Peru Overprinted in Black

14N13 A19 5c blue	4.00	3.50
14N14 A21 20c brn red	82.50	82.50

Regular Issues of Peru Overprinted in Black

14N15 A19 5c ultra	70.00	65.00
14N16 A21 20c brn red	135.00	120.00

Same Overprint on Postage Due Stamp of Peru

14N18 D3 10c orange 80.00 67.50

PUNO

(See Note under "Provisional Issues")

Provisional Issue of Arequipa Overprinted in Violet or Blue

Diameter of outer circle 20 1/2mm, PUNO 11 1/2mm wide, M 3 1/2mm wide.

Other types of this overprint are fraudulent.

1882-83 Unwmk. *Imperf.*

15N1 A1 10c blue (V)	16.50	16.50
a. 10c ultramarine (V)	20.00	20.00
15N3 A2 25c red (V)	25.00	20.00
15N4 A4 10c dl rose (Bl)	25.00	25.00
a. 10c vermilion (Bl)	25.00	25.00

The overprint also exists on 5s yellow of Arequipa.

Same Overprint in Magenta on Regular Issues of Peru

1884 *Perf. 12*

15N5 A17 1c orange	12.00	12.00
15N6 A18 2c violet	35.00	35.00
15N7 A19 5c blue	8.25	8.25

Violet Overprint

15N8 A19 5c blue	8.25	8.25
a. 5c ultramarine	12.00	12.00

Same Overprint in Black on Provisional Issues of Arequipa

1885 *Imperf.*

15N10 A5 5c olive	16.50	13.50
15N11 A6 10c gray	5.50	5.50
15N12 A8 10c olive	10.00	10.00

Regular Issues of Peru Overprinted in Magenta PUNO 1 ABR M

1884 *Perf. 12*

15N13 A17 1c orange	10.00	8.25
15N14 A18 2c violet	13.50	12.00
15N15 A19 5c blue	5.50	5.50
a. 5c ultramarine	11.00	11.00
15N16 A20 10c green		
15N17 A21 20c brn red	82.50	82.50
15N18 A22 50c green		

YCA

(See Note under "Provisional Issues")

Regular Issues of Peru Overprinted in Violet

1884	Unwmk.	*Perf. 12*	
16N1 A17	1c orange	40.00	40.00
16N3 A19	5c blue	12.00	6.75
	Black Overprint		
16N5 A19	5c blue	10.00	5.25
	Magenta Overprint		
16N6 A19	5c blue	10.00	5.25
16N7 A20	10c slate	30.00	30.00

Regular Issues of Peru Overprinted in Black

16N12 A19	5c blue	150.00	135.00
16N13 A21	20c brown	190.00	165.00

Regular Issues of Peru Overprinted in Carmine

16N14 A19	5c blue	150.00	135.00
16N15 A20	10c slate	190.00	165.00

Same, with Additional Overprint

16N21 A19	5c blue	165.00	150.00
16N22 A21	20c brn red	250.00	225.00

Various other stamps exist with the overprints "YCA" and "YCA VAPOR" but they are not known to have been issued. Some of them were made to fill a dealer's order and others are reprints or merely cancellations.

PHILIPPINES

ˌfi–lə–ˈpēnz

LOCATION — Group of about 7,100 islands and islets in the Malay Archipelago, north of Borneo, in the North Pacific Ocean

GOVT. — Republic

AREA — 115,830 sq. mi.

POP. — 53,350,000 (est. 1984)

CAPITAL — Quezon City

The islands were ceded to the United States by Spain in 1898. On November 15, 1935, they were given their independence, subject to a transition period which ended July 4, 1946. On that date the Commonwealth became the Republic of the Philippines.

20 Cuartos = 1 Real
100 Centavos de Peso = 1 Peso (1864)
100 Centimos de Escudo = 1 Escudo (1871)
100 Centimos de Peseta = 1 Peseta (1872)
1000 Milesimas de Peso = 100 Centimos or Centavos = 1 Peso (1878)
100 Cents = 1 Dollar (1899)
100 Centavos = 1 Peso (1906)
100 Centavos (Sentimos) = 1 Peso (Piso) (1946)

Catalogue values for unused stamps in this country are for Never Hinged items, beginning with Scott 500 in the regular postage section, Scott B1 in the semi-postal section, Scott C64 in the air post section, Scott E11 in the special delivery section, Scott J23 in the postage due section, and Scott O50 in the officials section.

Watermarks

Wmk. 104- Loops

Wmk. 257- Curved Wavy Lines

Wmk. 190PI- Single-lined PIPS

Wmk. 191PI- Double-lined PIPS

Watermark 191 has double-lined USPS.

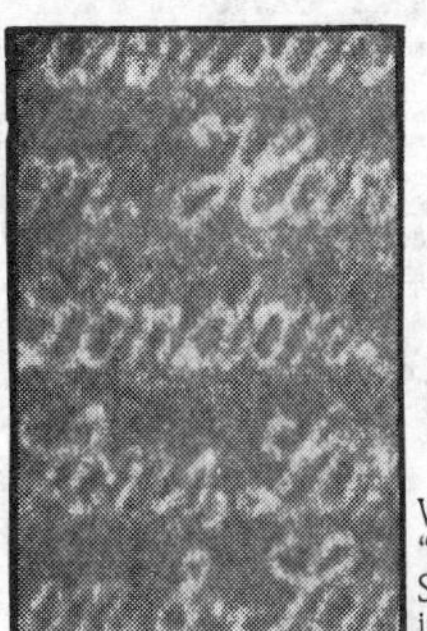

Wmk. 233- "Harrison & Sons, London." in Script

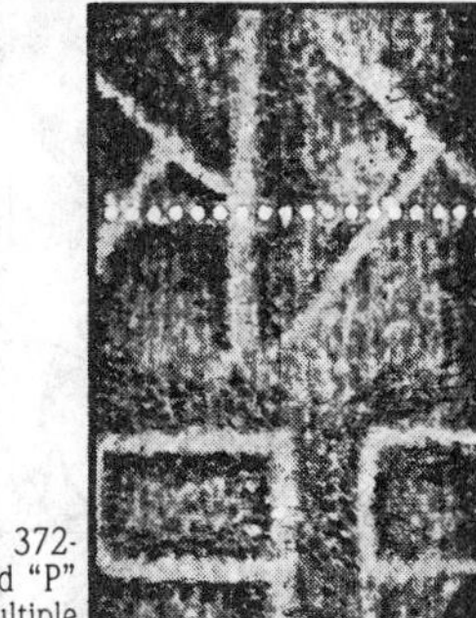

Wmk. 372- "K" and "P" Multiple

Wmk. 385

Wmk. 389

Wmk. 391- Natl. Crest, Rising Sun and Eagle

Issued under Spanish Dominion

The stamps of Philippine Islands punched with a round hole were used on telegraph receipts or had been withdrawn from use and punched to indicate that they were no longer available for postage. In this condition they sell for only a trifle, as compared to postally used copies.

Queen Isabella II
A1 A2

1854	Unwmk.	Engr.	*Imperf.*
1 A1	5c orange	1,250.	225.
a.	5c brown orange	1,500.	275.
2 A1	10c carmine	375.	165.
a.	10c pale rose	600.	250.
4 A2	1r blue	425.	190.
a.	1r slate blue	575.	200.
b.	1r ultramarine	575.	200.
c.	"CORROS," (pos. 26)	*2,600.*	*1,000.*
5 A2	2r green	600.	125.
a.	2r yellow green	700.	300.

Forty varieties of each value.
For overprints see Nos. 25-25A.

A3

1855			Litho.
6 A3	5c pale vermilion	1,200.	300.

Four varieties.

Redrawn

7 A3	5c vermilion	*7,000.*	*800.*

In the redrawn stamp the inner circle is smaller and is not broken by the labels at top and bottom. Only one variety.

The 10c black was not issued.

Cuba A1

A 1r green on blue and 2r carmine on blue can only be distinguished from Cuba Nos. 2-3 by the cancellations. Value, $85 and $125 respectively with identifiable Philippines cancellation.

For overprints see Nos. 26-27.

Queen Isabella II — A5

1859, Jan. 1	Litho.	Unwmk.	
10 A5	5c vermilion	10.00	5.00
a.	5c scarlet	14.00	7.00
b.	5c orange	21.00	10.00
11 A5	10c rose	10.00	11.00

Four varieties of each value.
For overprint see No. 28.

Dot after CORREOS
A6 A7

1861-62			
12 A6	5c vermilion	25.00	8.50
13 A7	5c dull red ('62)	90.00	37.50

For overprint see No. 29.

Colon after CORREOS — A8

A8a

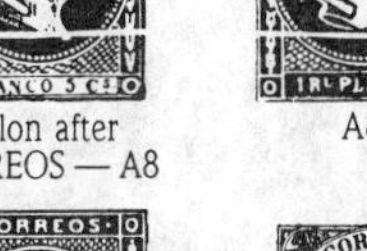

A9 A10

1863			
14 A8	5c vermilion	8.50	6.50
15 A8	10c carmine	25.00	40.00
16 A8	1r violet	475.00	300.00
17 A8	2r blue	375.00	250.00
18 A8a	1r gray grn	190.00	90.00

20 A9 1r emerald 100.00 35.00
a. 1r green 110.00 37.50
Nos. 14-20 (6) 1,173. 721.50

No. 18 has "CORREOS" 10 1/2mm long, the point of the bust is rounded and is about 1mm from the circle which contains 94 pearls.

No. 20 has "CORREOS" 11mm long, and the bust ends in a sharp point which nearly touches the circle of 96 pearls.

For overprints see Nos. 30-34.

1864 **Typo.**

21 A10 3 1/8c blk, *buff* 2.50 1.25
22 A10 6 2/8c grn, *rose* 2.50 .75
23 A10 12 4/8c blue, *sal* 4.75 .75
24 A10 25c red, *buff* 6.50 2.50
Nos. 21-24 (4) 16.25 5.25

For overprints see Nos. 35-38.

Cuba Nos. 2-3 and Preceding Issues Handstamped

HABILITADO POR LA NACION

1868-74

25 A2 1r sl bl ('74) *1,900. 800.00*
b. "CORROS," (pos. 26) *2,750.*
25A A2 2r grn ('74) *3,500. 775.00*
26 A1 1r grn, *bl* ('73) 140.00 60.00
27 A1 2r car, *bl* ('73) 250.00 110.00
28 A5 10c rose ('74) 50.00 35.00
29 A7 5c dull red ('73) 60.00 30.00
30 A8 5c ver ('72) 65.00 25.00
31 A8 1r vio ('72) 400.00 325.00
32 A8 2r bl ('72) 400.00 225.00
33 A8a 1r gray grn ('71) 125.00 35.00
34 A9 1r emer ('71) 35.00 15.00
35 A10 3 1/8c blk, *buff* 7.50 3.50
36 A10 6 2/8c grn, *rose* 7.50 3.50
37 A10 12 4/8c bl, *salmon* 25.00 12.00
38 A10 25c ver, *buff* 22.50 8.00

Illustration for #26-27 (Cuba A1) follows #7.

Imperforates

Imperforates of designs A11-A14 probably are from proof or trial sheets.

"Spain"
A11

King Amadeo
A12

1871 **Typo.** ***Perf. 14***

39 A11 5c blue 40.00 4.50
40 A11 10c deep green 5.50 3.75
41 A11 20c brown 47.50 25.00
42 A11 40c rose 60.00 13.00
Nos. 39-42 (4) 153.00 46.25

1872

43 A12 12c rose 9.00 3.25
44 A12 16c blue 90.00 24.00
a. 16c ultramarine 100.00 50.00
45 A12 25c gray lilac 7.00 3.25
a. 25c lilac 11.00 6.50
46 A12 62c violet 21.00 6.00
47 A12 1p25c yellow brn 40.00 19.00
Nos. 43-47 (5) 167.00 55.50

The 12c is known in dark blue and the 62c in rose. They were not regularly issued.

"Peace"
A13

King Alfonso XII
A14

1874

48 A13 12c gray lilac 10.00 3.00
49 A13 25c ultra 3.50 1.40
50 A13 62c rose 30.00 3.00
51 A13 1p25c brown 150.00 47.50
Nos. 48-51 (4) 193.50 54.90

1875-77

52 A14 2c rose 1.50 .45
53 A14 2c dk blue ('77) 135.00 62.50
54 A14 6c orange ('77) 7.00 *10.00*
55 A14 10c blue ('77) 2.50 .50
56 A14 12c lilac ('76 2.50 .50
57 A14 20c vio brn ('76 9.00 7.00
58 A14 25c dp green ('76 7.00 .50
Nos. 52-58 (7) 164.50 81.45

Nos. 52, 63 Handstamp Surcharged in Black or Blue

HABILITADO 12 Cs PTA

1877-79

59 A14 12c on 2c rose (Bk) 60.00 21.00
60 A16 12c on 25m blk (Bk) ('79) 60.00 21.00
61 A16 12c on 25m blk (Bl) ('79) 200.00 165.00
Nos. 59-61 (3) 320.00 207.00

Surcharge exists inverted and double.

A16

1878-79 **Typo.**

62 A16 0.0625 (62 1/2m) gray 40.00 12.00
63 A16 25m black 2.00 .30
64 A16 25m green ('79) 42.50 20.00
65 A16 50m dull lilac 21.00 8.00
66 A16 100m car ('79) 70.00 30.00
67 A16 100m yel grn ('79) 6.50 2.00
68 A16 125m blue 3.50 .35
69 A16 200m rose ('79) 22.50 4.50
70 A16 200m vio rose ('79) 200.00 110.00
71 A16 250m bister ('79) 8.00 2.00
Nos. 62-71 (10) 416.00 189.15

Imperforates of type A16 probably are from proof or trial sheets.

For surcharges see Nos. 60-61, 72-75.

Stamps of 1878-79 Surcharged:

UNIVERSAL DE CONVENIO CORREOS HABILITADO 2 cént de peso
a

UNIVERSAL DE CONVENIO CORREOS HABILITADO 2 cént de peso
b

1879

72 A16 (a) 2c on 25m grn 32.50 7.00
a. Double surcharge
b. Inverted surcharge 225.00 150.00
73 A16 (a) 8c on 100m car 27.50 5.50
a. "COREROS" 82.50 50.00
74 A16 (b) 2c on 25m grn 125.00 35.00
75 A16 (b) 8c on 100m car 125.00 35.00
Nos. 72-75 (4) 310.00 82.50

A19

Original state: The medallion is surrounded by a heavy line of color of nearly even thickness, touching the line below "Filipinas"; the opening in the hair above the temple is narrow and pointed.

1st retouch: The line around the medallion is thin, except at the upper right, and does not touch the horizontal line above it; the opening in the hair is slightly wider and rounded; the lock of hair above the forehead is shaped like a broad "V" and ends in a point; there is a faint white line below it, which is not found on the original. The shape of the hair and the width of the white line vary.

2nd retouch: The lock of hair is less pointed; the white line is much broader.

1880-88 **Typo.**

76 A19 2c carmine .60 *2.00*
77 A19 2 1/2c brown 5.75 1.25
78 A19 2 4/8c ultra ('82) .80 1.50
79 A19 2 4/8c ultra, 1st retouch ('83) .60 1.25
80 A19 2 4/8c ultra, 2nd retouch ('86) 7.50 3.00
81 A19 5c gray ('82) .60 .50
a. 5c gray blue 1.00 1.50
82 A19 6 2/8c dp green ('82) 4.75 8.00
83 A19 8c yellow brn 25.00 4.50
84 A19 10c green ('88) 250.00 175.00
85 A19 10c brn lil ('82) 2.50 1.25
a. 10c brown violet 10.00 5.00
86 A19 12 4/8c brt rose ('82) 1.25 1.25
87 A19 20c bis brn ('82) 2.50 1.25
88 A19 25c dk brown ('82) 3.25 1.25
Nos. 76-83,85-88 (12) 55.10 27.00

See #137-139. For surcharges see #89-108, 110-111.

Surcharges exist double or inverted on many of Nos. 89-136.

Stamps and Type of 1880-86 Handstamp Surcharged in Black, Green or Red:

c

d

e

f

1881-88

Design A19

Black Surcharge

89 (c) 2c on 2 1/2c brn 3.00 1.75
91 (f) 10c on 2 4/8c ultra (#80) ('87) 4.50 1.40
92 (d) 20c on 8c brn ('83) 6.75 2.25
93 (d) 1r on 2c car ('83) 50.00 —
94 (d) 2r on 2 4/8c ultra (#78; '83) 4.50 1.50

Most used copies of No. 93 are hole puched. Postally used copies are rare.

Green Surcharge

95 (e) 8c on 2c car ('83) 5.00 1.65
95A (d+e) 8c on 1r on 2c car ('83) 80.00 —
96 (d) 10c on 2c car ('83) 3.75 1.65
97 (d) 1r on 2c car ('83) 95.00 30.00
98 (d) 1r on 5c gray bl ('83) 4.50 2.25
99 (d) 1r on 8c brn ('83) 6.75 2.25

Red Surcharge

100 (f) 1c on 2 4/8c ultra (#79; '87) .75 .60
101 (f) 1c on 2 4/8c ultra (#80; '87) 2.50 1.25
102 (d) 16c on 2 4/8c ultra (#78; '83) 6.75 2.25
103 (d) 1r on 2c car ('83) 4.50 2.25
104 (d) 1r on 5c bl gray ('83) 12.50 3.75

Handstamp Surcharged in Magenta

g

h

1887

105 A19 (g) 8c on 2 4/8c (#79) .75 .45
106 A19 (g) 8c on 2 4/8c (#80) 3.00 2.00

1888

107 A19 (h) 2 4/8c on 1c gray grn 1.25 .75
108 A19 (h) 2 4/8c on 5c bl gray 1.50 .70
109 N1 (h) 2 4/8c on 1/8c grn 1.50 1.00
110 A19 (h) 2 4/8c on 50m bis 1.40 .65
111 A19 (h) 2 4/8c on 10c grn 1.25 .50
Nos. 107-111 (5) 6.90 3.60

No. 109 is surcharged on a newspaper stamp of 1886-89 and has the inscriptions shown on cut N1.

On Revenue Stamps

R1

R2

R3

Handstamp Surcharged in Black, Yellow, Green, Red, Blue or Magenta:

HABILITADO PARA CORREOS 2 4/8 CMS.
j

HABILITADO CORREOS 6 2/8 CENS.
k

m

HABILITADO
PARA
CORREOS

1881-88

Black Surcharge

112 R1 (c) 2c on 10c bis 35.00 9.00
113 R1 (j) 2 4/8c on 10c bis 2.25 .75
114 R1 (j) 2 4/8c on 2r bl 150.00 67.50
115 R1 (j) 8c on 10c bis *250.00 125.00*
116 R1 (j) 8c on 2r bl 5.75 1.50
118 R1 (d) 1r on 12 4/8c gray bl ('83) 5.50 2.75
119 R1 (d) 1r on 10c bis ('82) 8.50 3.00

Yellow Surcharge

120 R2 (e) 2c on 200m grn ('82) 4.50 2.00
121 R1 (d) 16c on 2r bl ('83) 3.75 1.90

Green Surcharge

122 R1 (d) 1r on 10c bis ('83) 8.00 2.75

Red Surcharge

123 R1(d+e) 2r on 8c on 2r blue 30.00 15.00
a. On 8c on 2r blue (d+d)
124 R1(d) 1r on 12 4/8c gray bl ('83) 11.00 5.50
125 R1(k) 6 2/8c on 12 4/8c gray bl ('85) 4.50 2.00
126 R3(d) 1r on 10p bis ('83) 70.00 19.00
127 R1(m) 1r green 225.00 140.00
127A R1(m) 2r blue 425.00 82.50
128 R2(d) 1r on 1p grn ('83) 25.00 12.00
129 R2(d) 1r on 200m grn ('83) 60.00 35.00
129A R1(d) 2r on 2r blue *200.00 150.00*

The surcharge on No. 129A is pale red.

Blue Surcharge

129B R1(m) 10c bister ('81) *250.00* —

Magenta Surcharge

130 R2(h) 2 4/8c on 200m grn ('88) 3.00 1.25
131 R2(h) 2 4/8c on 20c brn ('88) 9.00 4.50

On Telegraph Stamps

T1

T2

Surcharged in Red, or Black

1883-88

132 T1 (d) 2r on 250m ultra (R) 6.00 3.00
133 T1 (d) 20c on 250m ultra *200.00* —
134 T1 (d) 2r on 250m ultra 7.50 3.75
135 T1 (d) 1r on 20c on 250m ultra (R & Bk) 6.75 3.75

Magenta Surcharge

136 T2 (h) 2 4/8c on 1c bis ('88) .70 .50

Most, if not all, copies of No. 133 are hole-punched.

Type of 1880-86 Redrawn

1887-89

137 A19 50m bister .50 .25
138 A19 1c gray green ('88) .50 .20
a. yellow green ('89) .55 .25
139 A19 6c yellow brn ('88) 8.00 *15.00*
Nos. 137-139 (3) 9.00 15.45

King Alfonso XIII — A36

1890-97 **Typo.**

No.	Type	Description	Unused	Used
140	A36	1c violet ('92)	.50	.20
141	A36	1c rose ('95)	4.25	2.25
142	A36	1c blue grn ('96)	1.75	.55
143	A36	1c claret ('97)	10.00	15.00
144	A36	2c claret	.15	.15
145	A36	2c violet ('92)	.20	.15
146	A36	2c dk brown ('94)	.20	.20
147	A36	2c ultra ('96)	.30	.30
148	A36	2c gray brn ('96)	.20	.20
149	A36	2 4/8c dull blue	.35	.15
150	A36	2 4/8c ol gray ('92)	.20	.15
151	A36	5c dark blue	.30	.15
152	A36	5c dk ol gray	.60	.20
152A	A36	5c violet black		
153	A36	5c green ('92)	.50	.45
155	A36	5c violet brn ('96)	7.00	3.00
156	A36	5c blue grn ('96)	4.50	1.75
157	A36	6c brown vio ('92)	.20	.15
158	A36	6c red orange ('94)	.75	.65
159	A36	6c car rose ('96)	4.50	3.00
160	A36	8c yellow grn	.15	.15
161	A36	8c ultra ('92)	.50	.20
162	A36	8c red brown ('94)	.60	.20
163	A36	10c blue grn	1.25	.15
164	A36	10c pale claret ('91)	.80	.30
165	A36	10c claret ('92)	.45	.15
166	A36	10c yellow brn ('96)	.60	.15
167	A36	12 4/8c yellow grn	.20	.15
168	A36	12 4/8c orange ('92)	.60	.15
169	A36	15c red brown ('92)	.60	.20
170	A36	15c rose ('94)	1.50	.65
171	A36	15c blue grn ('96)	1.65	1.65
172	A36	20c rose	52.50	27.50
173	A36	20c salmon ('91)	8.00	2.50
174	A36	20c gray brn ('92)	1.50	.25
175	A36	20c dk violet ('94)	12.50	6.00
176	A36	20c orange ('96)	3.50	1.75
177	A36	25c brown	7.00	1.40
178	A36	25c dull blue ('91)	1.65	.20
179	A36	40c dk violet ('97)	17.50	15.00
180	A36	80c claret ('97)	25.00	40.00

The 5c lilac is a perforated proof. Many of Nos. 140-180 exist imperf.

The existence of No. 152A has been questioned.

Stamps of Previous Issues Handstamp Surcharged in Blue, Red, Black or Violet

1897

Blue Surcharge

No.	Type	Description	Unused	Used
181	A36	5c on 5c green	1.65	.90
182	A36	15c on 15c red brn	2.25	.90
183	A36	20c on 20c gray brn	5.50	5.50

Red Surcharge

No.	Type	Description	Unused	Used
185	A36	5c on 5c green	1.90	1.10

Black Surcharge

No.	Type	Description	Unused	Used
187	A36	5c on 5c green	17.50	17.50
188	A36	15c on 15c rose	2.50	1.65
189	A36	20c on 20c dk vio	14.00	8.50
190	A36	20c on 25c brown	10.00	10.00

Violet Surcharge

No.	Type	Description	Unused	Used
191	A36	15c on 15c rose	8.75	6.25
		Nos. 181-191 (9)	64.05	52.30

Inverted, double and other variations of this surcharge exist.

The 5c on 5c blue gray was released during US Administration. The surcharge is a mixture of red and black inks.

Impressions in violet black are believed to be reprints. The following varieties are known: 5c on 5c blue green, 15c on 15c rose, 15c on 15c red brown, 20c on 20c gray brown, 20c on 20c dark violet, 20c on 25c brown. These surcharges are to be found double, inverted, etc.

King Alfonso XIII — A39

1898 **Typo.**

No.	Type	Description	Unused	Used
192	A39	1m orange brown	.15	.15
193	A39	2m orange brown	.15	.15
194	A39	3m orange brown	.15	.15
195	A39	4m orange brown	5.75	5.75
196	A39	5m orange brown	.15	.15
197	A39	1c black violet	.15	.15
198	A39	2c dk bl grn	.15	.15
199	A39	3c dk brown	.15	.15
200	A39	4c orange	11.00	30.00
201	A39	5c car rose	.15	.15
202	A39	6c dk blue	.70	.40
203	A39	8c gray brown	.35	.15
204	A39	10c vermilion	1.25	.75
205	A39	15c dull ol grn	1.25	.60
206	A39	20c maroon	1.25	.90
207	A39	40c violet	.70	.60
208	A39	60c black	3.00	2.25
209	A39	80c red brown	3.75	2.25
210	A39	1p yellow green	9.00	9.00
211	A39	2p slate blue	12.50	11.50
		Nos. 192-211 (20)	51.70	65.35

Nos. 192-211 exist imperf. Value $1,000.

The Spanish surrendered in May 1898. Some Filipinos continued to fight until 1901. During this period provisional stamps were created in several areas. Some of these stamps may have been totally philatelic. See the Scott Specialized Catalogue of U. S. Stamps for stamps issued by Gen. Aguinaldo's Filipino Revolutionary Government.

Issued under US Administration

Regular Issues of the United States Overprinted in Black

On US No. 260

1899-1900 **Unwmk.** ***Perf. 12***

No.	Type	Description	Unused	Used
212	A96	50c orange	400.00	250.00

On US Nos. 279, 279d, 267, 268, 281, 282C, 283, 284, 275 and 275a

Wmk. 191

No.	Type	Description	Unused	Used
213	A87	1c yellow grn	3.00	.60
a.		Inverted overprint	13,500.	
214	A88	2c org red, III	1.25	.60
a.		2c car, type III	1.90	.90
b.		Booklet pane of 6 ('00)	300.00	*150.00*
215	A89	3c purple	5.75	1.25
216	A91	5c blue	5.50	.90
a.		Inverted overprint		*3,750.*
217	A94	10c brown, I	17.50	4.00
217A	A94	10c org brn, II	200.00	32.50
218	A95	15c olive grn	32.50	8.00
219	A96	50c orange	140.00	37.50
a.		50c red orange	*275.00*	
		Nos. 213-219 (8)	405.50	85.35

On US Nos. 280b, 282 and 272

1901

No.	Type	Description	Unused	Used
220	A90	4c orange brn	22.50	4.50
221	A92	6c lake	27.50	7.00
222	A93	8c violet brn	27.50	7.50

On US Nos. 276, 276A, 277a and 278

Red Overprint

No.	Type	Description	Unused	Used
223	A97	$1 blk, type I	425.00	240.00
223A	A97	$1 blk, type II	2,250.	675.00
224	A98	$2 dk blue	475.00	250.00
225	A99	$5 dk green	850.00	650.00

On US Nos. 300-313 and shades

1903-04

No.	Type	Description	Unused	Used
226	A115	1c blue green	4.00	.30
227	A116	2c carmine	7.50	1.10
228	A117	3c brt violet	67.50	12.50
229	A118	4c brown ('04)	75.00	22.50
a.		4c orange brown	75.00	20.00
230	A119	5c blue	11.00	1.00
231	A120	6c brnsh lake ('04)	80.00	22.50
232	A121	8c vio blk ('04)	40.00	12.50
233	A122	10c pale red brn ('04)	20.00	2.25
a.		10c red brown	25.00	3.00
b.		Pair, one without ovpt.		*1,500.*
234	A123	13c purple blk	32.50	17.50
a.		13c brown violet	32.50	17.50
235	A124	15c olive grn	60.00	15.00
236	A125	50c orange	130.00	35.00
		Nos. 226-236 (11)	527.50	142.15

Red Overprint

No.	Type	Description	Unused	Used
237	A126	$1 black	450.00	250.00
238	A127	$2 dk blue ('04)	750.00	750.00
239	A128	$5 dk green ('04)	1,000.	900.00

On US Nos. 319, 319c in Black

1904

No.	Type	Description	Unused	Used
240	A129	2c carmine	5.50	2.25
a.		Booklet pane of 6	*1,100.*	
b.		2c scarlet	6.25	2.75

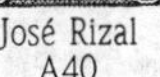

José Rizal A40

Arms of Manila A41

4c, McKinley. 6c, Magellan. 8c, Miguel Lopez de Legaspi. 10c, Gen. Henry W. Lawton. 12c, Lincoln. 16c, Adm. William T. Sampson. 20c, Washington. 26c, Francisco Carriedo. 30c, Franklin.

Each Inscribed "Philippine Islands / United States of America"

1906, Sept. 8 **Engr.** **Wmk. 191PI**

No.	Type	Description	Unused	Used
241	A40	2c dp green	.25	.15
a.		2c yellow green ('10)	.40	.15
b.		Booklet pane of 6	425.00	
242	A40	4c carmine	.30	.15
a.		4c carmine lake ('10)	.60	.15
b.		Booklet pane of 6	600.00	
243	A40	6c violet	1.25	.20
244	A40	8c brown	2.50	.65
245	A40	10c blue	1.75	.20
246	A40	12c brown lake	5.00	2.00
247	A40	16c violet blk	3.75	.20
248	A40	20c orange brn	4.00	.30
249	A40	26c violet brn	6.00	2.25
250	A40	30c olive grn	4.75	1.50
251	A41	1p orange	27.50	7.00
252	A41	2p black	35.00	1.25
253	A41	4p dk blue	100.00	15.00
254	A41	10p dk green	225.00	70.00
		Nos. 241-254 (14)	417.05	100.85

See Nos. 255-304, 326-353. For surcharges see Nos. 368-369, 450. For overprints see Nos. C1-C28, C36-C46, C54-C57, O5-O14.

Change of Colors

1909-13 ***Perf. 12***

No.	Type	Description	Unused	Used
255	A40	12c red orange	8.50	2.50
256	A40	16c olive green	3.50	.75
257	A40	20c yellow	7.50	1.25
258	A40	26c blue green	1.75	.75
259	A40	30c ultra	10.00	3.25
260	A41	1p pale violet	30.00	5.00
260A	A41	2p vio brn ('13)	85.00	2.75
		Nos. 255-260A (7)	146.25	16.25

1911 **Wmk. 190PI** ***Perf. 12***

No.	Type	Description	Unused	Used
261	A40	2c green	.65	.15
a.		Booklet pane of 6	475.00	
262	A40	4c car lake	2.50	.15
a.		4c carmine	—	—
b.		Booklet pane of 6	525.00	
263	A40	6c dp violet	2.00	.15
264	A40	8c brown	8.50	.45
265	A40	10c blue	3.25	.15
266	A40	12c orange	2.50	.45
267	A40	16c olive grn	2.50	.15
268	A40	20c yellow	2.00	.15
a.		20c orange	2.00	.15
269	A40	26c blue green	3.00	.20
270	A40	30c ultra	3.50	.45
271	A41	1p pale violet	22.50	.55
272	A41	2p violet brn	27.50	.75
273	A41	4p dp blue	625.00	80.00
274	A41	10p dp green	225.00	25.00
		Nos. 261-274 (14)	930.40	108.75

1914

No.	Type	Description	Unused	Used
275	A40	30c gray	10.00	.40

1914-23 ***Perf. 10***

No.	Type	Description	Unused	Used
276	A40	2c green	1.75	.15
a.		Booklet pane of 6	400.00	
277	A40	4c carmine	1.75	.15
a.		Booklet pane of 6	400.00	
278	A40	6c lt violet	37.50	9.00
a.		6c deep violet	42.50	6.00
279	A40	8c brown	40.00	10.00
280	A40	10c dk blue	25.00	.20
281	A40	16c olive grn	75.00	4.50
282	A40	20c orange	22.50	.85
283	A40	30c gray	55.00	2.75
284	A41	1p pale vio	110.00	3.00
		Nos. 276-284 (9)	368.50	30.60

1918-26 ***Perf. 11***

No.	Type	Description	Unused	Used
285	A40	2c green	20.00	4.25
a.		Booklet pane of 6	*650.00*	
286	A40	4c carmine	25.00	2.50
a.		Booklet pane of 6	*1,250.*	
287	A40	6c dp violet	35.00	1.75
287A	A40	8c lt brown	200.00	25.00
288	A40	10c dk blue	52.50	1.50
289	A40	16c olive grn	90.00	6.75
289A	A40	20c orange	60.00	7.50
289C	A40	30c gray	55.00	12.50
289D	A41	1p pale violet	70.00	14.00
		Nos. 285-289D (9)	607.50	75.75

1917-25 **Unwmk.** ***Perf. 11***

No.	Type	Description	Unused	Used
290	A40	2c yellow grn	.15	.15
a.		2c dark green	.15	.15
b.		Vert. pair, imperf. horiz.	1,500.	
c.		Horiz. pair, imperf. btwn.	*1,500.*	—
d.		Vert. pair, imperf. btwn.	*1,750.*	
e.		Booklet pane of 6	*27.50*	
291	A40	4c carmine	.15	.15
a.		4c light rose	.15	.15
b.		Booklet pane of 6	17.50	—
292	A40	6c deep violet	.30	.15
a.		6c lilac	.35	.15
b.		6c red violet	.35	.15
c.		Booklet pane of 6	*550.00*	—
293	A40	8c yellow brown	.20	.15
a.		8c orange brown	.20	.15
294	A40	10c deep blue	.20	.15
295	A40	12c red orange	.30	.15
296	A40	16c lt ol grn	55.00	.25
a.		16c olive bister	55.00	.40
297	A40	20c orange yel	.30	.15
298	A40	26c green	.45	.45
a.		26c blue green	.55	.25
299	A40	30c gray	.55	.15
300	A41	1p pale violet	27.50	1.00
a.		1p red lilac	27.50	1.00
b.		1p pale rose lilac	27.50	1.10
301	A41	2p violet brn	25.00	.75
302	A41	4p blue	22.50	.45
a.		4p dark blue	22.50	.45
		Nos. 290-302 (13)	132.60	4.10

1923-26

Design: 16c, Adm. George Dewey.

No.	Type	Description	Unused	Used
303	A40	16c olive bister	.90	.15
a.		16c olive green	1.30	.20
304	A41	10p deep green ('26)	45.00	5.00

Legislative Palace — A42

1926, Dec. 20 **Unwmk.** ***Perf. 12***

No.	Type	Description	Unused	Used
319	A42	2c green & blk	.40	.25
a.		Horiz. pair, imperf. btwn.	*275.00*	
b.		Vert. pair, imperf. btwn.	*500.00*	
320	A42	4c carmine & blk	.40	.35
a.		Horiz. pair, imperf. btwn.	*275.00*	
b.		Vert. pair, imperf. btwn.	*500.00*	
321	A42	16c ol grn & blk	.75	.65
a.		Horiz. pair, imperf. btwn.	*350.00*	
b.		Vert. pair, imperf. btwn.	*550.00*	
c.		Double impression of center	*575.00*	
322	A42	18c lt brown & blk	.85	.50
a.		Double impression of center	*575.00*	
b.		Vert. pair, imperf. btwn.	*550.00*	
323	A42	20c orange & blk	1.20	.80
a.		20c orange & brown	*500.00*	—
b.		Imperf., pair	*450.00*	*450.00*
c.		As "a," imperf., pair	*850.00*	
d.		Vert. pair, imperf. btwn.	*550.00*	
324	A42	24c gray & blk	.85	.55
a.		Vert. pair, imperf. btwn.	*550.00*	
325	A42	1p rose lil & blk	45.00	30.00
a.		Vert. pair, imperf. btwn.	*625.00*	
		Nos. 319-325 (7)	49.45	33.10

Opening of the Legislative Palace.

For overprints see Nos. O1-O4.

Coil Stamp

Rizal Type of 1906

1928 ***Perf. 11 Vertically***

No.	Type	Description	Unused	Used
326	A40	2c green	7.50	15.00

Types of 1906-23

1925-31 **Unwmk.** ***Imperf.***

No.	Type	Description	Unused	Used
340	A40	2c yellow grn ('31)	.15	.15
a.		2c green ('25)	.25	.15
341	A40	4c car rose ('31)	.15	.15
a.		4c carmine ('25)	.40	.20
342	A40	6c violet ('31)	1.00	1.00
a.		6c deep violet('25)	8.00	4.00
343	A40	8c brown ('31)	.90	.90
a.		8c yellow brown ('25)	6.00	3.00
344	A40	10c blue ('31)	1.00	1.00
a.		10c deep blue ('25)	10.00	5.00
345	A40	12c dp orange ('31)	1.50	1.50
a.		12c red orange('25)	10.00	5.00
346	A40	16c ol grn *(Dewey)* ('31)	1.10	1.10
a.		16c bister green ('25)	8.50	4.00
347	A40	20c orange yel ('31)	1.10	1.10
a.		20c yellow ('25)	8.50	4.00
348	A40	26c green ('31)	1.10	1.10
a.		26c blue green ('25)	10.00	5.00
349	A40	30c lt gray ('31)	1.25	1.25
a.		30c gray ('25)	10.00	5.00
350	A41	1p lt violet ('31)	4.00	4.00
a.		1p violet ('25)	70.00	30.00
351	A41	2p brown vio ('31)	10.00	10.00
a.		2p violet brown ('25)	150.00	50.00
352	A41	4p blue ('31)	30.00	30.00
a.		4p deep blue ('25)	700.00	300.00
353	A41	10p green ('31)	90.00	90.00
a.		10p deep green ('25)	1,000.	500.00
		Nos. 340-353 (14)	143.25	143.25
		Nos. 340a-353a (14)	1,991.	915.35

Mount Mayon, Luzon — A43

Post Office, Manila — A44

Pier No. 7, Manila Bay A45

(See footnote) A46

Rice Planting — A47

Rice Terraces — A48

Baguio Zigzag — A49

1932, May 3 *Perf. 11*

354 A43	2c	yellow green	.40	.20
355 A44	4c	rose carmine	.35	.25
356 A45	12c	orange	.50	.50
357 A46	18c	red orange	17.50	9.00
358 A47	20c	yellow	.65	.55
359 A48	24c	deep violet	1.00	.65
360 A49	32c	olive brown	1.00	.70
		Nos. 354-360 (7)	21.40	11.85

The 18c vignette was intended to show Pagsanjan Falls in Laguna, central Luzon, and is so labeled. Through error the stamp pictures Vernal Falls in Yosemite National Park, California.

For overprints see #C29-C35, C47-C51, C63.

Nos. 302, 302a Surcharged in Orange or Red

1932

368 A41	1p on 4p blue (O)	2.00	.45
a.	1p on 4p dark blue (O)	2.75	1.30
369 A41	2p on 4p dk bl (R)	3.50	.75
a.	2p on 4p blue (R)	3.50	.75

Tennis Player — A51

Basketball Players — A52

Baseball Players — A50

1934, Apr. 14 **Typo.** *Perf. 11½*

380 A50	2c	yellow brn	*1.50*	*.80*
381 A51	6c	ultra	.25	.20
a.		Vert. pair, imperf. btwn.	*1,250.*	

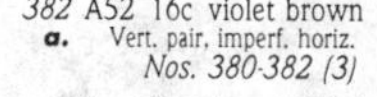

382 A52	16c	violet brown	.50	.50
a.		Vert. pair, imperf. horiz.	*1,250.*	
		Nos. 380-382 (3)	*2.25*	*1.50*

Tenth Far Eastern Championship Games.

José Rizal — A53

Woman and Carabao — A54

La Filipina — A55

Pearl Fishing — A56

Fort Santiago — A57

Salt Spring — A58

Magellan's Landing, 1521 A59

"Juan de la Cruz" A60

Rice Terraces — A61

"Blood Compact," 1565 — A62

Barasoain Church, Malolos — A63

Battle of Manila Bay, 1898 — A64

Montalban Gorge — A65

George Washington — A66

1935, Feb. 15 **Engr.** *Perf. 11*

383 A53	2c	rose	.15	.15
384 A54	4c	yellow grn	.20	.15
385 A55	6c	dk brown	.15	.15
386 A56	8c	violet	.15	.15
387 A57	10c	rose car	.15	.15
388 A58	12c	black	.15	.15
389 A59	16c	dk blue	.15	.15
390 A60	20c	lt ol grn	.20	.15
391 A61	26c	indigo	.25	.25
392 A62	30c	orange red	.25	.25
393 A63	1p	red org & blk	1.65	1.25
394 A64	2p	bister brn & blk	4.00	1.25
395 A65	4p	blue & blk	4.00	2.75
396 A66	5p	green & blk	8.00	2.00
		Nos. 383-396 (14)	19.45	8.95

For overprints see Nos. 411-424, 433-446, 463-466, 468, 472-474, 478-484, 485-494, C52-C53, O15-O36, O38, O40-O43, N2-N3, NO6. For surcharges see Nos. 449, N4-N9, N28, NO2-NO5.

Commonwealth Issues

The Temples of Human Progress A67

1935, Nov. 15

397 A67	2c	carmine rose	.15	.15
398 A67	6c	dp violet	.20	.15
399 A67	16c	blue	.20	.15
400 A67	36c	yellow grn	.35	.30
401 A67	50c	brown	.55	.55
		Nos. 397-401 (5)	1.45	1.30

Inauguration of the Philippine Commonwealth, Nov. 15, 1935.

Jose Rizal — A68

President Manuel L. Quezon — A69

1936, June 19 *Perf. 12*

402 A68	2c	yellow brown	.15	.15
403 A68	6c	slate blue	.15	.15
a.		Horiz. pair, imperf. vert.	*1,350.*	
404 A68	36c	red brown	.50	.45
		Nos. 402-404 (3)	.80	
		Set value		.60

75th anniv. of the birth of José Rizal.

1936, Nov. 15 *Perf. 11*

408 A69	2c	orange brown	.15	.15
409 A69	6c	yellow green	.15	.15
410 A69	12c	ultra	.15	.15
		Set value	.30	.25

1st anniversary of the Commonwealth.

For overprints see Nos. 467, 475.

Stamps of 1935 Overprinted in Black

COMMON-
WEALTH
a

COMMONWEALTH
b

1936-37 *Perf. 11*

411 A53 (a)	2c	rose	.15	.15
a.		Booklet pane of 6	2.50	*.65*
412 A54 (b)	4c	yel grn ('37)	.50	
413 A55 (a)	6c	dark brown	.20	.15
414 A56 (b)	8c	violet ('37)	.25	.20
415 A57 (b)	10c	rose carmine	.20	.15
a.		"Commonwealt"		—
416 A58 (b)	12c	black ('37)	.20	.15
417 A59 (b)	16c	dk blue	.20	.15
418 A60 (a)	20c	lt ol grn ('37)	.65	.40
419 A61 (b)	26c	indigo ('37)	.45	.35
420 A62 (b)	30c	orange red	.35	.15
421 A63 (b)	1p	red org & blk	.65	.20
422 A64 (b)	2p	bis brn & blk ('37)	5.00	2.75
423 A65 (b)	4p	bl & blk ('37)	17.50	3.00
424 A66 (b)	5p	grn & blk ('37)	1.75	1.25
		Nos. 411-424 (14)	28.05	
		Nos. 411,413-424 (13)		9.05

Map of Philippines A70

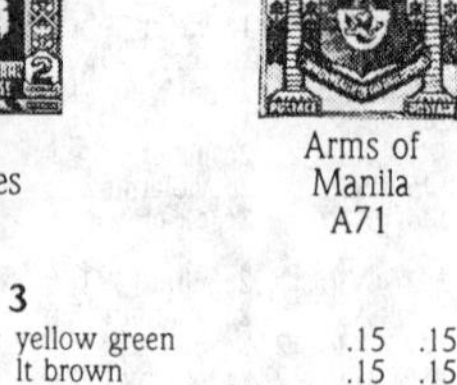
Arms of Manila A71

1937, Feb. 3

425 A70	2c	yellow green	.15	.15
426 A70	6c	lt brown	.15	.15
427 A70	12c	sapphire	.15	.15
428 A70	20c	dp orange	.25	.15
429 A70	36c	dp violet	.55	.40
430 A70	50c	carmine	.65	.35
		Nos. 425-430 (6)	1.90	
		Set value		1.00

33rd Eucharistic Congress.

1937, Aug. 27 *Perf. 11*

431 A71	10p	gray	4.25	2.00
432 A71	20p	henna brown	2.25	1.40

For overprints see Nos. 495-496. For surcharges see Nos. 451, C58.

Stamps of 1935 Overprinted in Black

COMMON-
WEALTH
a

COMMONWEALTH
b

1938-40 *Perf. 11*

433 A53 (a)	2c	rose ('39)	.15	.15
a.		Booklet pane of 6	3.50	*.65*
b.		"WEALTH COMMON-"	*4,000.*	—
c.		Hyphen omitted	—	—
434 A54 (b)	4c	yel grn ('40)	1.25	—
435 A55 (a)	6c	dk brn ('39)	.15	.15
a.		6c golden brown	.15	.15
436 A56 (b)	8c	violet ('39)	.15	.15
a.		"Commonwealt"	65.00	
437 A57 (b)	10c	rose car ('39)	.15	.15
a.		"Commonwealt"		—
438 A58 (b)	12c	black ('40)	.15	.15
439 A59 (b)	16c	dk blue	.15	.15
440 A60 (a)	20c	lt ol grn ('39)	.15	.15
441 A61 (b)	26c	indigo ('40)	.20	.20
442 A62 (b)	30c	org red ('39)	1.40	.70
443 A63 (b)	1p	red org & blk	.40	.20
444 A64 (b)	2p	bis brn & blk	2.75	.75
445 A65 (b)	4p	bl & blk ('40)	100.00	75.00
446 A66 (b)	5p	grn & blk ('40)	4.50	2.75
		Nos. 433-446 (14)	111.55	
		Nos. 433,435-446 (13)		80.65

Overprint "b" measures 18½x1¾mm. No. 433b occurs in booklet pane, No. 433a, position 5; all copies are straight-edged, left and bottom.

Stamps of 1917-37 Surcharged in Red, Violet or Black

FIRST
FOREIGN
a

TRADE
WEEK
2
CENTAVOS
MAY 21-27,1939

FIRST FOREIGN
TRADE WEEK
MAY 21-27, 1939
6CENTAVOS6
b

50CENTAVOS50
FIRST FOREIGN
TRADE WEEK
MAY 21-27,1939
c

1939, July 5

449 A54	2c on 4c yel grn (R)	.15	.15
450 A40	6c on 26c bl grn (V)	.15	.15
a.	6c on 26c green	.65	.30
451 A71	50c on 20p hn brn (Bk)	1.00	1.00
	Nos. 449-451 (3)	1.30	1.30

Foreign Trade Week.

Triumphal Arch — A72

Malacañan Palace — A73

1939, Nov. 15 *Perf. 11*

452	A72	2c yellow green	.15	.15
453	A72	6c carmine	.15	.15
454	A72	12c bright blue	.20	.15
		Set value	.35	.20

For overprints see Nos. 469, 476.

1939, Nov. 15

455	A73	2c green	.15	.15
456	A73	6c orange	.15	.15
457	A73	12c carmine	.20	.15
		Set value	.35	.20

Nos. 452-457 commemorate the 4th anniv. of the Commonwealth.
For overprint see No. 470.

Pres. Quezon Taking Oath of Office — A74

1940, Feb. 8

458	A74	2c dk orange	.15	.15
459	A74	6c dk green	.15	.15
460	A74	12c purple	.25	.15
		Nos. 458-460 (3)	.55	
		Set value		.25

4th anniversary of Commonwealth.
For overprints see Nos. 471, 477.

José Rizal — A75

Rotary Press Printing

1941, Apr. 14 *Perf. 11x10½*

Size: 19x22½mm

461	A75	2c apple green	.15	.15

Flat Plate Printing

1941-43 Size: 18¾x22mm *Perf. 11*

462	A75	2c apple green ('43)	.15	.15
a.		2c pale apple green	.20	.15
b.		Bklt. pane of 6, #462 ('43)	1.25	*1.25*
c.		Bklt. pane of 6, #462A	2.50	*2.75*

No. 462 was issued only in booklet panes and all copies have straight edges.
Further printings were made in 1942 and 1943 in different shades from the first supply of stamps sent to the islands.
For type A75 overprinted see Nos. 464, O37, O39, N1, NO1.

Philippine Stamps of 1935-41, Handstamped in Violet **VICTORY**

1944 *Perf. 11, 11x10½*

463	A53	2c rose (#411)	*260.00*	*95.00*
a.		Booklet pane of 6	*2,000.*	
463B	A53	2c rose (#433)	*1,200.*	*1,200.*
464	A75	2c ap grn (#461)	2.50	2.25
465	A54	4c yel grn (#384)	*25.00*	*25.00*
466	A55	6c dk brn (#385)	*1,500.*	*1,350.*
467	A69	6c yel grn (#409)	*110.00*	*85.00*
468	A55	6c dk brn (#413)	*650.00*	*600.00*
469	A72	6c car (#453)	*135.00*	*110.00*
470	A73	6c org (#456)	*600.00*	*550.00*
471	A74	6c dk grn (#459)	*160.00*	*150.00*
472	A56	8c vio (#436)	15.00	20.00
473	A57	10c rose car (#415)	*110.00*	*75.00*
474	A57	10c rose car (#437)	*135.00*	*110.00*
475	A69	12c ultra (#410)	*400.00*	*175.00*
476	A72	12c brt bl (#454)	*3,500.*	*2,000.*
477	A74	12c pur (#460)	*190.00*	*135.00*
478	A59	16c dk bl (#389)	*700.00*	
479	A59	16c dk bl (#417)	*450.00*	*325.00*
480	A59	16c dk bl (#439)	*160.00*	*100.00*
481	A60	20c lt ol grn (#440)	27.50	27.50
482	A62	30c org red (#420)	*225.00*	*160.00*
483	A62	30c org red (#442)	*325.00*	*250.00*
484	A63	1p red org & blk (#443)	*5,500.*	*4,000.*

Types of 1935-37 Overprinted

VICTORY COMMON-WEALTH — a

VICTORY COMMONWEALTH — b

1945 *Perf. 11*

485	A53 (a)	2c rose	.15	.15
486	A54 (b)	4c yellow grn	.15	.15
487	A55 (a)	6c golden brn	.15	.15
488	A56 (b)	8c violet	.15	.15
489	A57 (b)	10c rose car	.15	.15
490	A58 (b)	12c black	.20	.15
491	A59 (b)	16c dk blue	.25	.15
492	A60 (a)	20c lt olive grn	.30	.15
493	A62 (b)	30c orange red	.40	.35
494	A63 (b)	1p red org & blk	1.10	.25

Nos. 431-432 Overprinted in Black **VICTORY**

495	A71	10p gray	40.00	13.50
496	A71	20p henna brown	35.00	15.00
		Nos. 485-496 (12)	78.00	30.30

José Rizal — A76

Rotary Press Printing

1946, May 28 *Perf. 11x10½*

497	A76	2c sepia	.15	.15

For overprints see Nos. 503, O44.

Catalogue values for unused stamps in this section, from this point to the end of the section, are for Never Hinged items.

Republic

Philippine Girl Holding Flag of the Republic — A77

1946, July 4 Unwmk. Engr. *Perf. 11*

500	A77	2c carmine	.20	.20
501	A77	6c green	.35	.20
502	A77	12c blue	.50	.35
		Nos. 500-502 (3)	1.05	.75

Independence of the Philippines, July 4, 1946.

No. 497 Overprinted in Brown

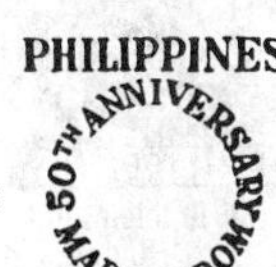

1946, Dec. 30 *Perf. 11x10½*

503	A76	2c sepia	.20	.15

50th anniv. of the execution of José Rizal.

Rizal Monument A78

Bonifacio Monument A79

Jones Bridge — A80

Santa Lucia Gate — A81

Mayon Volcano — A82

Avenue of Palms — A83

1947 Engr. *Perf. 12*

504	A78	4c black brown	.15	.15
505	A79	10c red orange	.16	.15
506	A80	12c deep blue	.22	.15
507	A81	16c slate gray	1.35	.80
508	A82	20c red brown	.40	.15
509	A83	50c dull green	1.00	.65
510	A83	1p violet	2.00	.50
		Nos. 504-510 (7)	5.28	
		Set value		2.20

For surcharges see Nos. 613-614, 809. For overprints see Nos. 609, O50-O52, O54-O55.

Manuel L. Quezon — A84

1947, May 1 **Typo.**

511	A84	1c green	.15	.15

See No. 515.

Pres. Manuel A. Roxas Taking Oath of Office — A85

1947, July 4 Unwmk. *Perf. 12½*

512	A85	4c carmine rose	.20	.15
513	A85	6c dk green	.45	.45
514	A85	16c purple	1.00	.65
		Nos. 512-514 (3)	1.65	1.25

First anniversary of republic.

Quezon Type
Souvenir Sheet

1947, Nov. 28 *Imperf.*

515		Sheet of 4	.50	.50
a.		A84 1c bright green	.15	.15

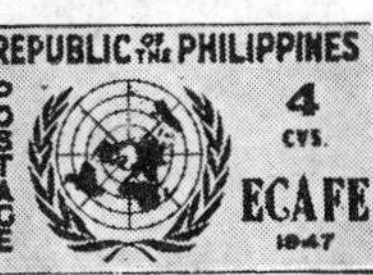

United Nations Emblem A87

1947, Nov. 24 *Perf. 12½*

516	A87	4c dk car & pink	1.40	1.20
a.		Imperf.	2.00	2.00
517	A87	6c pur & pale vio	2.00	2.00
a.		Imperf.	2.00	2.00
518	A87	12c dp bl & pale bl	2.25	2.25
a.		Imperf.	2.00	2.00
		Nos. 516-518 (3)	5.65	5.45

Conference of the Economic Commission in Asia and the Far East, held at Baguio.

Gen. Douglas MacArthur — A88

1948, Feb. 3 Engr. *Perf. 12*

519	A88	4c purple	.45	.20
520	A88	6c rose car	.90	.60
521	A88	16c brt ultra	1.40	.60
		Nos. 519-521 (3)	2.75	1.40

Threshing Rice — A89

1948, Feb. 23 Typo. *Perf. 12½*

522	A89	2c grn & pale yel grn	.75	.50
523	A89	6c brown & cream	.90	.65
524	A89	18c dp bl & pale bl	2.50	2.00
		Nos. 522-524 (3)	4.15	3.15

Conf. of the FAO held at Baguio. No. 524 exists imperf. See No. C67.

Manuel A. Roxas A90

José Rizal A91

1948, July 15 **Engr.** ***Perf. 12***

525 A90 2c black	.20	.15
526 A90 4c black	.25	.20

Issued in tribute to President Manuel A. Roxas who died April 15, 1948.

1948, June 19 **Unwmk.**

527 A91 2c bright green	.15	.15
a. Booklet pane of 6	1.25	

For surcharges see Nos. 550, O56. For overprint see No. O53.

Scout Saluting — A92

Sampaguita, National Flower — A93

1948, Oct. 31 **Typo.** ***Imperf.***

528 A92 2c chocolate & green	.35	.15
a. Perf. 11½	1.00	.50
529 A92 4c chocolate & pink	.40	.25
a. Perf. 11½	1.20	.70

25th anniversary of the foundation of the Boy Scouts of the Philippines.
No. 528 exists part perforate.

1948, Dec. 8 ***Perf. 12½***

530 A93 3c blk, pale bl & grn	.32	.25

UPU Monument, Bern — A94

1949, Oct. 9 **Unwmk.** **Engr.** ***Perf. 12***

531 A94 4c green	.15	.15
532 A94 6c dull violet	.15	.15
533 A94 18c blue gray	.60	.20
Nos. 531-533 (3)	.90	
Set value		.34

Souvenir Sheet

Imperf

534 Sheet of 3	.55	.45
a. A94 4c green	.15	.15
b. A94 6c dull violet	.16	.15
c. A94 18c blue	.20	.20

75th anniv. of the UPU.
In 1960 an unofficial, 3-line overprint ("President D. D. Eisenhower /Visit to the Philippines/June 14-16, 1960") was privately applied to No. 534.
For surcharge & overprint see Nos. 806, 901.

Gen. Gregorio del Pilar at Tirad Pass — A95

1949, Dec. 2 ***Perf. 12***

535 A95 2c red brown	.15	.15
536 A95 4c green	.25	.22

50th anniversary of the death of Gen. Gregorio P. del Pilar and fifty-two of his men at Tirad Pass.

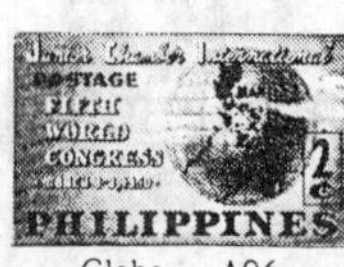
Globe — A96

Red Lauan Tree — A97

1950, Mar. 1

537 A96 2c purple	.15	.15
538 A96 6c dk green	.22	.15
539 A96 18c dp blue	.50	.15
Nos. 537-539,C68-C69 (5)	1.90	
Set value		.58

5th World Cong. of the Junior Chamber of Commerce, Manila, Mar. 1-8, 1950.
For surcharge see No. 825.

1950, Apr. 14

540 A97 2c green	.15	.15
541 A97 4c purple	.35	.20
Set value		.26

50th anniversary of the Bureau of Forestry.

F. D. Roosevelt with his Stamps — A98

Lions Club Emblem — A99

1950, May 22

542 A98 4c dark brown	.22	.18
543 A98 6c carmine rose	.38	.35
544 A98 18c blue	.90	.70
Nos. 542-544 (3)	1.50	1.23

Honoring Franklin D. Roosevelt and for the 25th anniv. of the Philatelic Association of the Philippines. See No. C70.

1950, June 4 **Engr.**

545 A99 2c orange	.42	.42
546 A99 4c violet	.55	.55
Nos. 545-546,C71-C72 (4)	2.27	2.02

Convention of the Lions Club, Manila, June 1950.

Pres. Elpidio Quirino Taking Oath — A100

1950, July 4 **Unwmk.** ***Perf. 12***

547 A100 2c car rose	.15	.15
548 A100 4c magenta	.15	.15
549 A100 6c blue green	.20	.15
Set value	.38	.35

4th anniversary of the Republic of the Philippines.

No. 527 Surcharged in Black

1950, Sept. 20

550 A91 1c on 2c bright green	.15	.15

Dove over Globe — A101

1950, Oct. 23

551 A101 5c green	.25	.20
552 A101 6c rose carmine	.25	.20
553 A101 18c ultra	.55	.42
Nos. 551-553 (3)	1.05	.82

Baguio Conference of 1950.
For surcharge see No. 828.

Headman of Barangay Inspecting Harvest A102

1951, Mar. 31 **Litho.** ***Perf. 12½***

554 A102 5c dull green	.16	.15
555 A102 6c red brown	.25	.25
556 A102 18c violet blue	.65	.65
Nos. 554-556 (3)	1.06	1.05

The government's Peace Fund campaign.

Imperf., Pairs

554a A102 5c dull green	.16	.16
555a A102 6c red brown	.25	.25
556a A102 18c violet blue	.65	.65
Nos. 554a-556a (3)	1.06	1.06

Arms of Manila A103

Arms of Cebu A104

Arms of Zamboanga A105

Arms of Iloilo A106

1951 **Engr.** ***Perf. 12***

Various Frames

557 A103 5c purple	.40	.35
558 A103 6c gray	.25	.22
559 A103 18c bright ultra	.40	.35

Various Frames

560 A104 5c crimson rose	.40	.35
561 A104 6c bister brown	.25	.22
562 A104 18c violet	.40	.35

Various Frames

563 A105 5c blue green	.45	.38
564 A105 6c red brown	.30	.22
565 A105 18c light blue	.45	.38

Various Frames

566 A106 5c bright green	.55	.42
567 A106 6c violet	.38	.25
568 A106 18c deep blue	.55	.42
Nos. 557-568 (12)	4.78	3.91

Issue dates: A103, Feb. 3. A104, Apr. 27. A105, June 19. A106, Aug. 26.
For surcharges see Nos. 634-636.

UN Emblem and Girl Holding Flag — A107

Liberty Holding Declaration of Human Rights — A108

1951, Oct. 24 **Unwmk.** ***Perf. 11½***

569 A107 5c red	.55	.25
570 A107 6c blue green	.45	.25
571 A107 18c violet blue	1.10	.70
Nos. 569-571 (3)	2.10	1.20

United Nations Day, Oct. 24, 1951.

1951, Dec. 10 ***Perf. 12***

572 A108 5c green	.40	.22
573 A108 6c red orange	.55	.40
574 A108 18c ultra	1.00	.60
Nos. 572-574 (3)	1.95	1.22

Universal Declaration of Human Rights.

Students and Department Seal — A109

1952, Jan. 31

575 A109 5c orange red	.40	.32

50th anniversary (in 1951) of the Philippine Educational System.

Milkfish and Map — A111

1952, Oct. 27 ***Perf. 12½***

578 A111 5c orange brown	.90	.55
579 A111 6c deep blue	.55	.45

4th Indo-Pacific Fisheries Council Meeting, Quezon City, Oct. 23-Nov. 7, 1952.

Maria Clara — A112

1952, Nov. 16

580 A112 5c deep blue	.40	.15
581 A112 6c brown	.40	.15
Nos. 580-581,C73 (3)	1.65	1.00

1st Pan-Asian Philatelic Exhibition, PANAPEX, Manila, Nov. 16-22.

Wright Park, Baguio City — A113

Francisco Baltazar, Poet — A114

1952, Dec. 15 ***Perf. 12***

582 A113 5c red orange	.60	.60
583 A113 6c dp blue green	.90	.75

3rd Lions District Convention, Baguio City.

1953, Mar. 27

584 A114 5c citron	.35	.30

National Language Week.

"Gateway to the East" — A115

Presidents Quirino and Sukarno — A116

1953, Apr. 30

585 A115 5c turq green	.25	.15
586 A115 6c vermilion	.32	.15
Set value		.20

Philippines International Fair.

1953, Oct. 5 **Engr. & Litho.**

587 A116 5c multicolored	.15	.15
588 A116 6c multicolored	.20	.20
Set value		.28

2nd anniversary of the visit of Indonesia's President Sukarno.

Marcelo H. del Pilar — A117

1c, Manuel L. Quezon. 2c, José Abad Santos (diff. frame). 3c, Apolinario Mabini (diff. frame). 10c, Father José Burgos. 20c, Lapu-Lapu. 25c, Gen. Antonio Luna. 50c, Cayetano Arellano. 60c, Andres Bonifacio. 2p, Graciano L. Jaena.

Perf. 12, 12½, 13, 14x13½

1952-60 **Engr.**

589 A117	1c red brn ('53)	.15	.15
590 A117	2c gray ('60)	.15	.15
591 A117	3c brick red ('59)	.15	.15
592 A117	5c crim rose	.15	.15
595 A117	10c ultra ('55)	.15	.15
597 A117	20c car lake ('55)	.25	.15
598 A117	25c yel grn ('58)	.35	.16
599 A117	50c org ver ('59)	.65	.22
600 A117	60c car rose ('58)	.80	.35
601 A117	2p violet	2.50	.80
	Nos. 589-601 (10)	5.30	
	Set value		1.80

For overprints & surcharges see #608, 626, 641-642, 647, 830, 871, 875-877, O57-O61.

Doctor Examining Boy — A118

1953, Dec. 16

603 A118	5c lilac rose	.25	.22
604 A118	6c ultra	.32	.30

50th anniversary of the founding of the Philippine Medical Association.

First Philippine Stamps, Magellan's Landing and Manila Scene A119

1954, Apr. 25 *Perf. 13*

Stamp of 1854 in Orange

605 A119	5c purple	.50	.32
606 A119	18c deep blue	1.00	.85
607 A119	30c green	2.25	2.00
	Nos. 605-607,C74-C76 (6)	9.90	8.37

Centenary of Philippine postage stamps. For surcharge see No. 829.

Nos. 592 and 509 Overprinted or Surcharged in Black

1954, Apr. 23 *Perf. 12*

608 A117	5c crimson rose	1.00	.85
609 A83	18c on 50c dull grn	1.75	1.25

1st National Boy Scout Jamboree, Quezon City, April 23-30, 1954.

The surcharge on No. 609 is reduced to fit the size of the stamp.

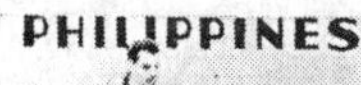

Discus Thrower and Games Emblem A120

1954, May 31 *Perf. 13*

610 A120	5c shown	.70	.50
611 A120	18c Swimmer	1.10	.85
612 A120	30c Boxer	1.75	1.50
	Nos. 610-612 (3)	3.55	2.85

2nd Asian Games, Manila, May 1-9.

Nos. 505 and 508 Surcharged in Blue

5 MANILA CONFERENCE OF 5 1954

1954, Sept. 6 *Perf. 12*

613 A79	5c on 10c red org	.15	.15
614 A82	18c on 20c red brn	.55	.52

Issued to publicize the Manila Conference, 1954.

The surcharge is arranged to obliterate the original denomination.

Allegory of Independence A121

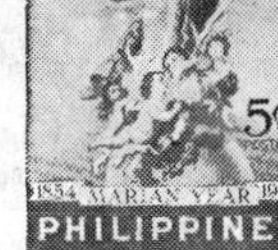

"Immaculate Conception," by Murillo A122

1954, Nov. 30 *Perf. 13*

615 A121	5c dark carmine	.22	.16
616 A121	18c deep blue	.65	.40

56th anniversary of the declaration of the first Philippine Independence.

For surcharge see No. 826.

1954, Dec. 30 *Perf. 12*

617 A122	5c blue	.38	.25

Issued to mark the end of the Marian Year.

Mayon Volcano, Moro Vinta and Rotary Emblem A123

1955, Feb. 23 **Engr.** *Perf. 13*

618 A123	5c dull blue	.20	.15
619 A123	18c dk car rose	.65	.50
	Nos. 618-619,C77 (3)	2.10	1.50

Rotary Intl., 50th anniv. For surcharge see #827.

Allegory of Labor — A124

Pres. Ramon Magsaysay — A125

1955, May 26 *Perf. 13x12½*

620 A124	5c brown	.35	.25

Issued in connection with the Labor-Management Congress, Manila, May 26-28, 1955.

1955, July 4 *Perf. 12½*

621 A125	5c blue	.16	.15
622 A125	20c red	.50	.50
623 A125	30c green	.80	.80
	Nos. 621-623 (3)	1.46	1.45

9th anniversary of the Republic.

Village Well A126

1956, Mar. 16 *Perf. 12½x13½*

624 A126	5c violet	.25	.25
625 A126	20c dull green	.60	.55

Issued to publicize the drive for improved health conditions in rural areas.

No. 592 Overprinted

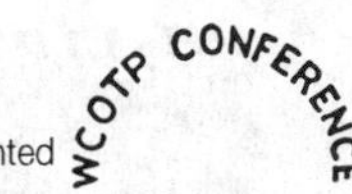

1956, Aug. 1 **Unwmk.** *Perf. 12*

626 A117	5c crimson rose	.32	.30

5th Annual Conf. of the World Confederation of Organizations of the Teaching Profession, Manila, Aug. 1-8, 1956.

Nurse and Disaster Victims — A127

Engraved; Cross Lithographed in Red

1956, Aug. 30

627 A127	5c violet	.42	.40
628 A127	20c gray brown	.55	.45

50 years of Red Cross Service in the Philippines.

Monument to US Landing, Leyte — A128

1956, Oct. 20 **Litho.** *Perf. 12½*

629 A128	5c carmine rose	.15	.15
a.	Imperf. ('57)	.42	.42

Landing of US forces under Gen. Douglas MacArthur on Leyte, Oct. 20, 1944.

Issue date: No. 629a, Feb. 16.

Santo Tomas University A129

1956, Nov. 13 **Photo.** *Perf. 11½*

630 A129	5c brown car & choc	.32	.22
631 A129	60c lilac & red brn	1.25	1.10

Issued in honor of the University of Santo Tomas.

Statue of Christ by Rizal — A130

1956, Nov. 28 **Engr.** *Perf. 12*

632 A130	5c gray olive	.25	.20
633 A130	20c rose carmine	.55	.52

2nd Natl. Eucharistic Cong., Manila, Nov. 28-Dec. 2, and for the centenary of the Feast of the Sacred Heart.

Nos. 561, 564 and 567 Surcharged with New Value in Blue or Black

1956 **Unwmk.** *Perf. 12*

634 A104	5c on 6c bis brn (Bl)	.15	.15
635 A105	5c on 6c red brn (Bl)	.15	.15
636 A106	5c on 6c vio (Bk)	.15	.15
	Set value	.36	.36

Girl Scout, Emblem and Tents — A131

1957, Jan. 19 **Litho.** *Perf. 12½*

637 A131	5c dark blue	.32	.32
a.	Imperf.	.42	.42

Centenary of the Scout movement and for the Girl Scout World Jamboree, Quezon City, Jan. 19-Feb. 2, 1957.

Copies of Nos. 637 and 637a (No. 48 in sheet) exist with heavy black rectangular handstamps obliterating erroneous date at left, denomination and cloverleaf emblem.

Pres. Ramon Magsaysay (1907-57) — A132

1957, Aug. 31 **Engr.** *Perf. 12*

638 A132	5c black	.15	.15

"Spoliarium" by Juan Luna — A133

1957, Oct. 23 *Perf. 14x14½*

639 A133	5c rose carmine	.15	.15

Centenary of the birth of Juan Luna, painter.

Sergio Osmena and First National Assembly — A134

1957, Oct. 16 *Perf. 12½x13½*

640 A134	5c blue green	.15	.15

1st Philippine Assembly and honoring Sergio Osmeña, Speaker of the Assembly.

Nos. 595 and 597 Surcharged in Carmine or Black

1957, Dec. 30 *Perf. 14x13½*

641 A117	5c on 10c ultra (C)	.15	.15
642 A117	10c on 20c car lake	.22	.22

Inauguration of Carlos P. Garcia as president and Diosdado Macapagal as vice-president, Dec. 30.

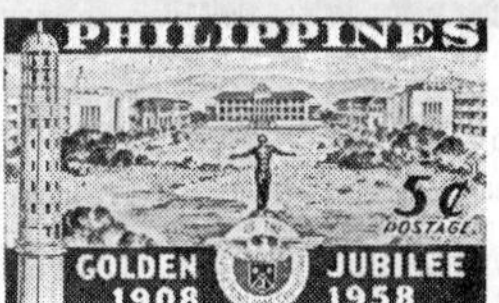

University of the Philippines — A135

1958 **Engr.** *Perf. 13½x13*

643 A135	5c dk carmine rose	.30	.15

50th anniversary of the founding of the University of the Philippines.

Pres. Carlos P. Garcia — A136

1958 **Photo.** ***Perf. 11½***
Granite Paper

644 A136 5c multicolored .15 .15
645 A136 20c multicolored .40 .30
Set value .38

12th anniversary of Philippine Republic.

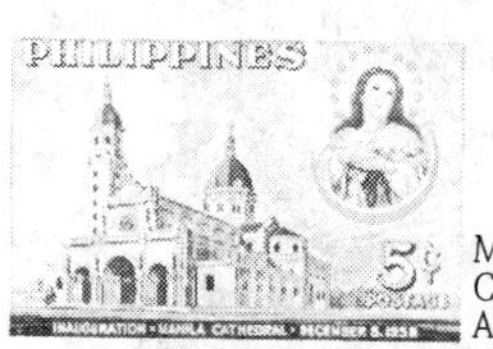

Manila Cathedral A137

Perf. 13x13½, 12
1958, Dec. 8 **Engr.**
646 A137 5c multicolored .20 .15

Issued to commemorate the inauguration of the rebuilt Manila Cathedral, Dec. 8, 1958.

No. 592 Surcharged **OneCentavo**

1959 ***Perf. 12***
647 A117 1c on 5c crim rose .15 .15

Nos. B4-B5 Surcharged with New Values and Bars

1959, Feb. 3 ***Perf. 13***
648 SP4 1c on 2c + 2c red .15 .15
649 SP5 6c on 4c + 4c vio .15 .15
Set value .15 .15

14th anniversary of the liberation of Manila from the Japanese forces.

Philippine Flag — A138

1959, Feb. 8 **Unwmk.** ***Perf. 13***
650 A138 6c dp ultra, yel & dp car .15 .15
651 A138 20c dp car, yel & dp ultra .15 .15
Set value .22 .22

Seal of Bulacan Province — A139 Seal of Bacolod City — A140

1959 **Engr.** ***Perf. 13***
652 A139 6c lt yellow grn .15 .15
653 A139 20c rose red .22 .15
Set value .22

60th anniversary of the Malolos constitution. For surcharge see No. 848.

1959

Design: 6c, 25c, Seal of Capiz Province and portrait of Pres. Roxas.

654 A139 6c lt brown .15 .15
655 A139 25c purple .22 .20
Set value .28 .26

Pres. Manuel A. Roxas, 11th death anniv.

1959
656 A140 6c blue green .15 .15
657 A140 10c rose lilac .15 .15
Set value .16

Nos. 658-803 were reserved for the rest of a projected series showing seals and coats of arms of provinces and cities.

Camp John Hay Amphitheater, Baguio — A141

Perf. 13½ (6c, 25c), 12 (6c)
1959, Sept. 1
804 A141 6c bright green .15 .15
805 A141 25c rose red .25 .20

50th anniversary of the city of Baguio.

No. 533 Surcharged in Red

6¢

1959, Oct. 24 ***Perf. 12***
806 A94 6c on 18c blue .15 .15

Issued for United Nations Day, Oct. 24.

Maria Cristina Falls — A142

1959, Nov. 18 **Photo.** ***Perf. 13½, 12***
807 A142 6c vio & dp yel grn .15 .15
808 A142 30c green & brown .35 .25
Set value .32

No. 504 Surcharged with New Value and Bars

1959 **Engr.** ***Perf. 12***
809 A78 1c on 4c blk brn .15 .15

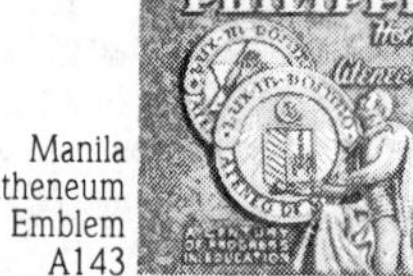

Manila Atheneum Emblem A143

1959, Dec. 10 ***Perf. 13½, 12***
810 A143 6c ultra .15 .15
811 A143 30c rose red .35 .25
Set value .42 .32

Centenary of the Manila Atheneum (Ateneo de Manila), a school, and to mark a century of progress in education.

Manuel Quezon A144 José Rizal A145

1959-60 **Engr.** ***Perf. 13***
812 A144 1c olive gray ('60) .15 .15
Perf. 14x12
813 A145 6c gray blue .15 .15
Set value .16 .15

A146

Perf. 12½x13½
1960 **Unwmk.** **Photo.**
814 A146 6c brown & gold .15 .15

25th anniversary of the Philippine Constitution. See No. C82.

Site of Manila Pact A147

1960 **Engr.** ***Perf. 12½***
815 A147 6c emerald .15 .15
816 A147 25c orange .30 .22
Set value .36 .28

5th anniversary (in 1959) of the Congress of the Philippines establishing the South-East Asia Treaty Organization (SEATO).
For overprints see Nos. 841-842.

Sunset at Manila Bay and Uprooted Oak Emblem A148

1960, Apr. 7 **Photo.** ***Perf. 13½***
817 A148 6c multicolored .15 .15
818 A148 25c multicolored .30 .22
Set value .36 .28

World Refugee Year, July 1, 1959-June 30, 1960.

A149

1960, July 29 ***Perf. 13½***
819 A149 5c lt grn, red & gold .15 .15
820 A149 6c bl, red & gold .15 .15
Set value .22 .16

Philippine Tuberculosis Society, 50th anniv.

Basketball A150

1960, Nov. 30 ***Perf. 13x13½***
821 A150 6c shown .15 .15
822 A150 10c Runner .15 .15
Set value .16

17th Olympic Games, Rome, Aug. 25-Sept. 11. See Nos. C85-C86.

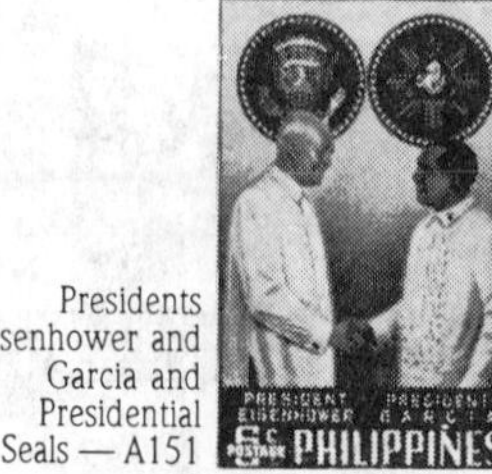

Presidents Eisenhower and Garcia and Presidential Seals — A151

1960, Dec. 30 ***Perf. 13½***
823 A151 6c multi .15 .15
824 A151 20c ultra, red & yel .40 .20

Visit of Pres. Dwight D. Eisenhower to the Philippines, June 14, 1960.

Nos. 539, 616, 619, 553, 606 and 598 Surcharged with New Values and Bars in Red or Black

1960-61 **Engr.** ***Perf. 12, 13, 12½***
825 A96 1c on 18c dp bl (R) .15 .15
826 A121 5c on 18c dp bl (R) .15 .15
827 A123 5c on 18c dp car rose .20 .15
828 A101 10c on 18c ultra (R) .15 .15
829 A119 10c on 18c dp bl & org (R) .20 .15
830 A117 20c on 25c yel grn ('61) .20 .15
Nos. 825-830 (6) 1.05
Set value .65

On No. 830, no bars are overprinted, the surcharge "20 20" serving to cancel the old denomination.

Mercury and Globe — A152

1961, Jan. 23 **Photo.** ***Perf. 13½***
831 A152 6c red brn, bl, blk & gold .15 .15

Issued to commemorate the Manila Postal Conference, Jan. 10-23. See also No. C87.

Nos. B10, B11 and B11a Surcharged "2nd National Boy Scout Jamboree Pasonanca Park" and New Value in Black or Red

1961, May 2 **Engr.** ***Perf. 13***
Yellow Paper
832 SP8 10c on 6c + 4c car .15 .15
833 SP8 30c on 25c + 5c bl (R) .32 .32
a. Tete beche, *wht* (10c on 6c + 4c & 30c on 25c + 5c) (Bk) .50 .50

Issued to publicize the Second National Boy Scout Jamboree, Pasonanca Park, Zamboanga City.

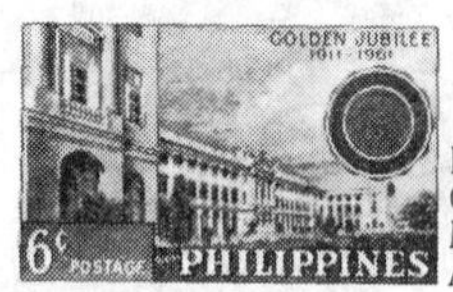

De la Salle College, Manila A153

1961, June 16 **Photo.** ***Perf. 11½***
834 A153 6c multi .15 .15
835 A153 10c multi .15 .15
Set value .22 .16

De la Salle College, Manila, founding, 50th anniv.

José Rizal as Student A154

6c, Rizal & birthplace at Calamba, Laguna. 10c, Rizal & parents. 20c, Rizal with Juan Luna & F. R. Hidalgo in Madrid. 30c, Rizal's execution.

1961 **Unwmk.** ***Perf. 13½***
836 A154 5c multi .15 .15
837 A154 6c multi .15 .15
838 A154 10c grn & red brn .15 .15
839 A154 20c brn red & grnsh bl .22 .20
840 A154 30c vio, lil & org brn .32 .25
Set value .84 .72

Centenary of the birth of José Rizal.

Nos. 815-816 Overprinted

I
K
A
15 **KAARAWAN**
Republika ng Pilipinas
Hulyo 4, 1961

1961, July 4 Engr. *Perf. 12½*
841 A147 6c emerald .20 .20
842 A147 25c orange .32 .32

15th anniversary of the Republic.

Colombo Plan Emblem and Globe Showing Member Countries — A155

1961, Oct. 8 Photo. *Perf. 13x11½*
843 A155 5c multi .15 .15
844 A155 6c multi .15 .15
Set value .15 .15

7th anniversary of the admission of the Philippines to the Colombo Plan.

Government Clerk A156

1961, Dec. 9 Unwmk. *Perf. 12½*
845 A156 6c vio, bl & red .15 .15
846 A156 10c gray bl & red .30 .15
Set value .22

Honoring Philippine government employees.

No. C83 Surcharged

6¢

PAAF
GOLDEN JUBILEE
1911 1961

1961, Nov. 30 Engr. *Perf. 14x14½*
847 AP11 6c on 10c car .15 .15

Philippine Amateur Athletic Fed., 50th anniv.

No. 655 Surcharged with New Value and: "MACAPAGAL-PELAEZ INAUGURATION DEC. 30, 1961"

1961, Dec. 30 *Perf. 12½*
848 A139 6c on 25c pur .15 .15

Inauguration of President Diosdado Macapagal and Vice-President Emanuel Pelaez.

No. B8 Surcharged

6 s

1962, Jan. 23 Photo. *Perf. 13½x13*
849 SP7 6c on 5c grn & red .15 .15

Vanda Orchids A157

Apolinario Mabini A158

Orchids: 6c, White mariposa. 10c, Sander's dendrobe. 20c, Sanggumay.

1962, Mar. 9 Photo. *Perf. 13½x14*
Dark Blue Background
850 A157 5c rose, grn & yel .15 .15
851 A157 6c grn & yel .15 .15
852 A157 10c grn, car & brn .15 .15
853 A157 20c lil, brn & grn .25 .25
a. Block of 4, #850-853 .65 .65
b. As "a," imperf. .90 .90

Perf. 13½; 14 (1s); 13x12 (#857, 10s)
1962-69 Engr. Unwmk.

Portraits: 1s, Manuel L. Quezon. 5s, Marcelo H. del Pilar. 6s, José Rizal. No. 857A Rizal (wearing shirt). 10s, Father José Burgos. 20s, Lapu-Lapu. 30s, Rajah Soliman. 50s, Cayetano Arellano. 70s, Sergio Osmena. 1p (No. 863), Emilio Jacinto. 1p (No. 864), José M. Panganiban.

854 A158 1s org brn ('63) .15 .15
855 A158 3s rose red .15 .15
856 A158 5s car rose ('63) .15 .15
857 A158 6s dk red brn .15 .15
857A A158 6s pck bl ('64) .15 .15
858 A158 10s brt pur ('63) .15 .15
859 A158 20s Prus bl ('63) .15 .15
860 A158 30s vermilion .24 .15
861 A158 50s vio ('63) .40 .15
862 A158 70s brt bl ('63) .50 .22
863 A158 1p grn ('63) 1.00 .20
864 A158 1p dp org ('69) .60 .25
Set value 3.20 1.10

For surcharges see #873-874, 969, 1054, 1209.
For overprints see #946, 1119, O63-O69.

Pres. Macapagal Taking Oath of Office A159

1962 Photo. *Perf. 13½*
Vignette Multicolored
865 A159 6s blue .15 .15
866 A159 10s green .15 .15
867 A159 30s violet .30 .15
Set value .46 .22

Issued to commemorate the swearing in of President Diosdado Macapagal, Dec. 30, 1961.

Volcano in Lake Taal and Malaria Eradication Emblem A160

1962, Oct. 24 Unwmk. *Perf. 11½*
Granite Paper
868 A160 6s multi .15 .15
869 A160 10s multi .15 .15
870 A160 70s multi .70 .50
Set value .86 .64

Issued on UN Day for the WHO drive to eradicate malaria.

No. 598 Surcharged in Red

1762 1962
BICENTENNIAL
Diego Silang
Revolt
20

1962, Nov. 15 Engr. *Perf. 12*
871 A117 20s on 25c yel grn .20 .15

Issued to commemorate the bicentennial of the Diego Silang revolt in Ilocos Province.

No. B6 Overprinted with Sideways Chevron Obliterating Surtax

1962, Dec. 23 *Perf. 12*
872 SP6 5c on 5c + 1c dp bl .15 .15

Nos. 855, 857 Surcharged with New Value and Old Value Obliterated

1963 *Perf. 13½*
873 A158 1s on 3s rose red .15 .15

Perf. 13x12
874 A158 5s on 6s dk red brn .15 .15
Set value .15 .15

No. 601 Surcharged

1963, June 12 *Perf. 12*
875 A117 6s on 2p vio .15 .15
876 A117 20s on 2p vio .22 .22
877 A117 70s on 2p vio .65 .55

Diego Silang Bicentennial Art and Philatelic Exhibition, ARPHEX, Manila, May 28-June 30.

Pres. Manuel Roxas A161

1963-73 Engr. *Perf. 13½*
878 A161 6s brt bl & blk, *bluish* .15 .15
879 A161 30s brn & blk .35 .15

Pres. Ramon Magsaysay
880 A161 6s lil & blk .15 .15
881 A161 30s yel grn & blk .30 .15

Pres. Elpidio Quirino
882 A161 6s grn & blk ('65) .15 .15
883 A161 30s rose lil & blk ('65) .30 .15

Gen. (Pres.) Emilio Aguinaldo
883A A161 6s dp cl & blk ('66) .15 .15
883B A161 30s bl & blk ('66) .30 .15

Pres. José P. Laurel
883C A161 6s lt red brn & blk ('66) .15 .15
883D A161 30s bl & blk ('66) .30 .15

Pres. Manuel L. Quezon
883E A161 10s bl gray & blk ('67) .15 .15
883F A161 30s lt vio & blk ('67) .30 .15

Pres. Sergio Osmeña
883G A161 10s rose lil & blk ('70) .15 .15
883H A161 40s grn & blk ('70) .30 .15

Pres. Carlos P. Garcia
883I A161 10s multi ('73) .15 .15
883J A161 30s multi ('73) .30 .15
Set value, #878-883J 3.00 1.00

Nos. 878-883J honor former presidents.
For surcharges see Nos. 984-985, 1120, 1146, 1160-1161.

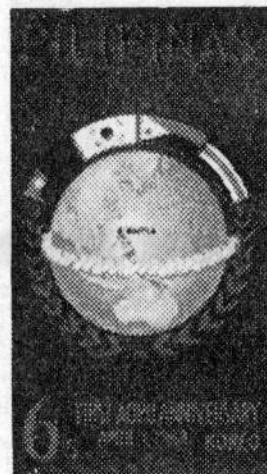

Globe, Flags of Thailand, Korea, China, Philippines A162

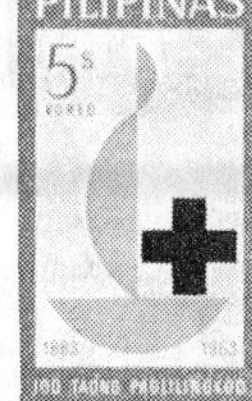

Red Cross Centenary Emblem A163

1963, Aug. 26 Photo. *Perf. 13½x13*
884 A162 6s dk grn & multi .15 .15
885 A162 20s dk grn & multi .18 .15
Set value .26 .16

1st anniv. of the Asian-Oceanic Postal Union.
For surcharge see No. 1078.

1963, Sept. 1 *Perf. 11½*
886 A163 5s lt vio, gray & red .15 .15
887 A163 6s ultra, gray & red .15 .15
888 A163 20s grn, gray & red .20 .15
Set value .34 .22

Centenary of the International Red Cross.

Bamboo Dance A164

Folk Dances: 6s, Dance with oil lamps. 10s, Duck dance. 20s, Princess Gandingan's rock dance.

1963, Sept. 15 Unwmk. *Perf. 14*
889 A164 5s multi .15 .15
890 A164 6s multi .15 .15
891 A164 10s multi .15 .15
892 A164 20s multi .22 .22
a. Block of 4, #889-892 .50 .50

For surcharges and overprints see #1043-1046.

Pres. Macapagal and Filipino Family — A165

1963, Sept. 28 *Perf. 14*
893 A165 5s bl & multi .15 .15
894 A165 6s yel & multi .15 .15
895 A165 20s lil & multi .15 .15
Set value .30 .22

Issued to publicize Pres. Macapagal's 5-year Socioeconomic Program.
For surcharge see No. 1181.

Presidents Lopez Mateos and Macapagal A166

1963, Sept. 28 Photo. *Perf. 13½*
896 A166 6s multi .15 .15
897 A166 30s multi .20 .15
Set value .28 .20

Issued to commemorate the visit of Pres. Adolfo Lopez Mateos of Mexico to the Philippines.
For surcharge see No. 1166.

Andres Bonifacio — A167

1963, Nov. 30 Unwmk. *Perf. 12*
898 A167 5s gold, brn, gray & red .15 .15
899 A167 6s sil, brn, gray & red .15 .15
900 A167 25s brnz, brn, gray & red .24 .22
Set value .38 .32

Issued to commemorate the centenary of the birth of Andres Bonifacio, national hero and poet.
For surcharges see Nos. 1147, 1162.

No. 534 Overprinted: "UN ADOPTION/DECLARATION OF HUMAN RIGHTS/15TH ANNIVERSARY DEC. 10, 1963"

1963, Dec. 10 Engr. *Imperf.*
Souvenir Sheet
901 A94 Sheet of 3 .55 .55

15th anniv. of the Universal Declaration of Human Rights.

Woman holding Sheaf of Rice — A168

1963, Dec. 20 Photo. *Perf. 13½x13*

902 A168 6s brn & multi .15 .15

FAO "Freedom from Hunger" campaign. See Nos. C88-C89.

Bamboo Organ — A169 Apolinario Mabini — A170

1964, May 4 *Perf. 13½*

903 A169 5s multi .15 .15
904 A169 6s multi .15 .15
905 A169 20s multi .20 .15
Set value .34 .22

The bamboo organ in the Church of Las Pinas, Rizal, was built by Father Diego Cera, 1816-1822. For surcharge see No. 1055.

Perf. 14½

1964, July 23 Photo. Wmk. 233

906 A170 6s pur & gold .15 .15
907 A170 10s red brn & gold .15 .15
908 A170 30s brt grn & gold .22 .15
Set value .38 .26

Apolinario Mabini (1864-1903), national hero and a leader of the 1898 revolution. For surcharge see No. 1056.

Flags Surrounding SEATO Emblem A171 Pres. Macapagal Signing Code A172

Unwmk.

1964, Sept. 8 Photo. *Perf. 13*

Flags and Emblem Multicolored

909 A171 6s dk bl & yel .15 .15
910 A171 10s dp grn & yel .15 .15
911 A171 25s dk brn & yel .20 .15
Set value .38 .26

10th anniversary of the South-East Asia Treaty Organization (SEATO). For surcharge see No. 1121.

1964, Dec. 21 Wmk. 233 *Perf. 14½*

912 A172 3s multi .15 .15
913 A172 6s multi .15 .15
Set value .15 .15

Signing of the Agricultural Land Reform Code. See No. C90. For surcharges see Nos. 970, 1234.

Basketball — A173

Sport: 10s, Women's relay race. 20s, Hurdling. 30s, Soccer.

1964, Dec. 28 *Perf. 14½x14*

915 A173 6s lt bl, dk brn & gold .15 .15
916 A173 10s gold, pink & dk brn .15 .15
b. Gold omitted
917 A173 20s gold, dk brn & yel .22 .15
918 A173 30s emer, dk brn & gold .30 .22
Nos. 915-918 (4) .82 .67
Set value .50

18th Olympic Games, Tokyo, Oct. 10-25. For overprints see Nos. 962-965. For surcharge see No. 1079.

Imperf., Pairs

915a A173 6s .15 .15
916a A173 10s .15 .15
917a A173 20s .32 .32
918a A173 30s .40 .40
Nos. 915a-918a (4) 1.02 1.02

Presidents Lubke and Macapagal and Coats of Arms A174

1965, Apr. 19 Unwmk. *Perf. 13½*

919 A174 6s ol grn & multi .15 .15
920 A174 10s multi .15 .15
921 A174 25s dp bl & multi .18 .15
Set value .35 .25

Issued to commemorate the visit of Pres. Heinrich Lubke of Germany, Nov. 18-23, 1964. For surcharge see No. 1167.

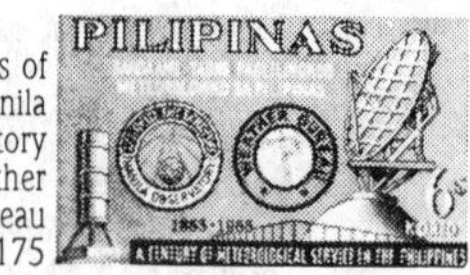

Emblems of Manila Observatory and Weather Bureau A175

1965, May 22 Photo. *Perf. 13½*

922 A175 6s lt ultra & multi .15 .15
923 A175 20s lt vio & multi .15 .15
924 A175 50s bl grn & multi .40 .25
Set value .60 .38

Issued to commemorate the centenary of the Meteorological Service in the Philippines. For surcharge see No. 1069.

Pres. John F. Kennedy (1917-63) — A176

Perf. 14½x14

1965, May 29 Wmk. 233

Center Multicolored

925 A176 6s gray .15 .15
926 A176 10s brt vio .15 .15
927 A176 30s ultra .35 .20
Nos. 925-927 (3) .65
Set value .32

Nos. 925-927 exist with ultramarine of tie omitted.

The 6s and 30s exist imperf. Value, each $30. For surcharges see Nos. 1148, 1210.

King and Queen of Thailand, Pres. and Mrs. Macapagal — A177

Perf. 12½x13

1965, June 12 Unwmk.

928 A177 2s brt bl & multi .15 .15
929 A177 6s bis & multi .15 .15
930 A177 30s red & multi .22 .15
Set value .34 .22

Visit of King Bhumibol Adulyadej and Queen Sirikit of Thailand, July 1963. For surcharge see No. 1122.

Princess Beatrix and Evangelina Macapagal A178

Perf. 13x12½

1965, July 4 Photo. Unwmk.

931 A178 2s bl & multi .15 .15
932 A178 6s blk & multi .15 .15
933 A178 10s multi .15 .15
Set value .22 .16

Issued to commemorate the visit of Princess Beatrix of the Netherlands, Nov. 21-23, 1962. For surcharge see No. 1188.

Cross and Rosary Held Before Map of Philippines — A179

Design: 6s, Map of Philippines, cross and Legaspi-Urdaneta monument.

1965, Oct. 4 Unwmk. *Perf. 13*

934 A179 3s multi .15 .15
935 A179 6s multi .15 .15
Set value .16 .15

400th anniv. of the Christianization of the Philippines. See Nos. C91-C92 and souvenir sheet No. C92a. For overprint see No. C108.

Presidents Sukarno and Macapagal and Prime Minister Tunku Abdul Rahman A180

1965, Nov. 25 *Perf. 13*

936 A180 6s multi .15 .15
937 A180 10s multi .15 .15
938 A180 25s multi .20 .15
Set value .34 .24

Signing of the Manila Accord (Mapilindo) by Malaya, Philippines and Indonesia. For surcharge see No. 1182.

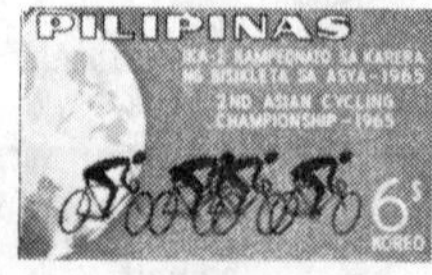

Bicyclists and Globe A181

1965, Dec. 5 *Perf. 13½*

939 A181 6s multi .15 .15
940 A181 10s multi .15 .15
941 A181 25s multi .20 .15
Set value .35 .24

Second Asian Cycling Championship, Philippines, Nov. 28-Dec. 5.

Nos. B21-B22 Surcharged

10s

MARCOS-LOPEZ
INAUGURATION
DEC. 30, 1965

1965, Dec. 30 Engr. *Perf. 13*

942 SP12 10s on 6s + 4s .15 .15
943 SP12 30s on 30s + 5s .24 .24

Inauguration of President Ferdinand Marcos and Vice-President Fernando Lopez.

Antonio Regidor — A182

1966, Jan. 21 *Perf. 12x11*

944 A182 6s blue .15 .15
945 A182 30s brown .22 .20
Set value .28 .25

Dr. Antonio Regidor, Secretary of the High Court of Manila and President of Public Instruction. For surcharges see Nos. 1110-1111.

No. 857A Overprinted in Red: "HELP ME STOP / SMUGGLING / Pres. MARCOS"

1966, May 1 Engr. *Perf. 13½*

946 A158 6s peacock blue .15 .15

Anti-smuggling drive.

Exists with overprint inverted, double, double inverted and double with one inverted. For surcharge see No. 1209.

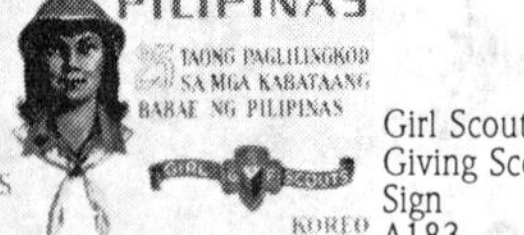

Girl Scout Giving Scout Sign A183

1966, May 26 Litho. *Perf. 13x12½*

947 A183 3s ultra & multi .15 .15
948 A183 6s emer & multi .15 .15
949 A183 20s brn & multi .20 .15
Set value .32 .22

Philippine Girl Scouts, 25th anniversary. For surcharge see No. 1019.

Pres. Marcos Taking Oath of Office — A184

1966, June 12 *Perf. 12½*

950 A184 6s bl & multi .15 .15
951 A184 20s emer & multi .15 .15
952 A184 30s yel & multi .22 .20
Set value .38 .32

Issued to commemorate the inauguration of President Ferdinand E. Marcos, Dec. 30, 1965. For overprints see Nos. 960-961. For surcharge see No. 1050.

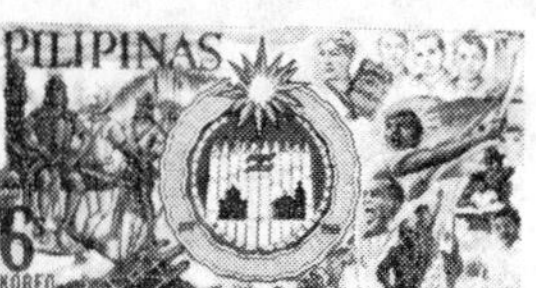

Seal of Manila and Historical Scenes — A185

1966, June 24

953 A185	6s multi	.15	.15
954 A185	30s multi	.20	.15
	Set value	.26	.22

Adoption of the new seal of Manila.
For surcharges see Nos. 1070, 1118, 1235.

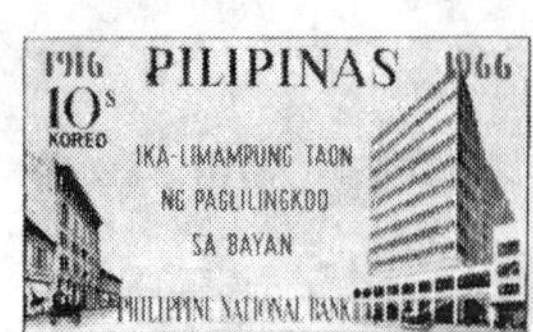

Old and New Philippine National Bank Buildings — A186

Designs: 6s, Entrance to old bank building and 1p silver coin.

1966, July 22 Photo. *Perf. 14x13½*

955 A186 6s gold, ultra, sil & blk	.15	.15
956 A186 10s multi	.15	.15
Set value	.22	.15

50th anniv. of the Philippine Natl. Bank. See #C93. For surcharges see #1071, 1100, 1236.

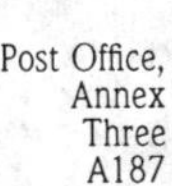

Post Office, Annex Three A187

1966, Oct. 1 Wmk. 233 *Perf. 14½*

957 A187 6s lt vio, yel & grn	.15	.15
958 A187 10s rose cl, yel & grn	.15	.15
959 A187 20s ultra, yel & grn	.20	.15
Set value	.35	.22

60th anniversary of Postal Savings Bank.
For surcharges see Nos. 1104, 1112, 1189.

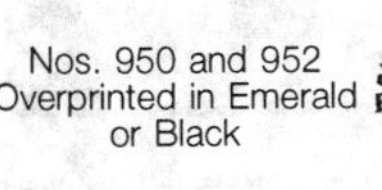
Nos. 950 and 952 Overprinted in Emerald or Black

Perf. 12½
1966, Oct. 24 Litho. Unwmk.

960 A184 6s multi (E)	.15	.15
961 A184 30s multi	.25	.22
Set value	.32	.28

Manila Summit Conference, Oct. 23-27.

Nos. 915a-918a Overprinted

50th ANNIVERSARY LIONS INTERNATIONAL 1967

Wmk. 233
1967, Jan. 14 Photo. *Imperf.*

962 A173 6s lt bl, dk brn & gold	.15	.15
963 A173 10s gold, dk brn & pink	.15	.15
964 A173 20s gold, dk brn & yel	.20	.15
965 A173 30s emer, dk brn & gold	.30	.30
Set value	.68	.55

Lions Intl., 50th anniv. The Lions emblem is in the lower left corner on the 6s, in the upper left corner on the 10s and in the upper right corner on the 30s.

"Succor" by Fernando Amorsolo — A188

Unwmk.
1967, May 15 Litho. *Perf. 14*

966 A188 5s sepia & multi	.15	.15
967 A188 20s blue & multi	.20	.15
968 A188 2p green & multi	1.75	1.00

25th anniversary of the Battle of Bataan.

Nos. 857A and 913 Surcharged

1967, Aug. Engr. *Perf. 13½*

969 A158 4s on 6s pck bl	.15	.15

Perf. 14½
Photo. Wmk. 233

970 A172 5s on 6s multi	.15	.15
Set value	.16	.15

Issue dates: 4s, Aug. 10; 5s, Aug. 7.

Gen. Douglas MacArthur and Paratroopers Landing on Corregidor — A189

Unwmk.
1967, Aug. 31 Litho. *Perf. 14*

971 A189 6s multi	.15	.15
972 A189 5p multi	3.25	3.25

25th anniversary, Battle of Corregidor.

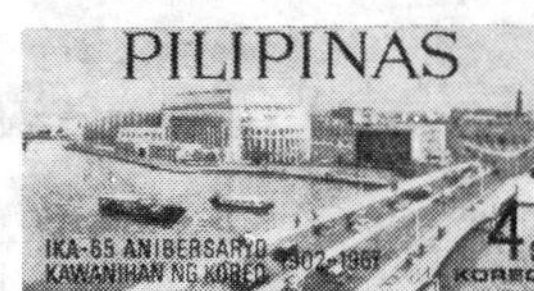

Bureau of Posts, Manila, Jones Bridge over Pasig River — A190

1967, Sept. 15 Litho. *Perf. 14x13½*

973 A190 4s multi & blk	.15	.15
974 A190 20s multi & red	.15	.15
975 A190 50s multi & vio	.32	.25
Nos. 973-975 (3)	.62	
Set value		.44

65th anniversary of the Bureau of Posts.
For overprint see No. 1015.

Philippine Nativity Scene — A191

1967, Dec. 1 Photo. *Perf. 13½*

976 A191 10s multi	.15	.15
977 A191 40s multi	.30	.22

Christmas 1967.

Chinese Garden, Rizal Park, Presidents Marcos and Chiang Kai-shek — A192

Presidents' heads & scenes in Chinese Garden, Rizal Park, Manila: 10s, Gate. 20s, Landing pier.

1967-68 Photo. *Perf. 13½*

978 A192 5s multi	.15	.15
979 A192 10s multi ('68)	.15	.15
980 A192 20s multi	.15	.15
Set value	.25	.20

Sino-Philippine Friendship Year 1966-67.

Makati Center Post Office, Mrs. Marcos and Rotary Emblem — A193

1968, Jan. 9 Litho. *Perf. 14*

981 A193 10s bl & multi	.15	.15
982 A193 20s grn & multi	.15	.15
983 A193 40s multi	.30	.30
Nos. 981-983 (3)	.60	.60

1st anniv. of the Makati Center Post Office.

Nos. 882, 883C and B27 Surcharged with New Value and Two Bars

10s

1968

984 A161 5s on 6s grn & blk	.15	.15
985 A161 5s on 6s lt red brn & blk	.15	.15
986 SP14 10s on 6s + 5s ultra & red	.15	.15
Set value	.20	.15

For similar surcharge see No. 1586.

Felipe G. Calderon, Barasoain Church and Malolos Constitution — A194

1968, Apr. 4 Litho. *Perf. 14*

987 A194 10s lt ultra & multi	.15	.15
988 A194 40s grn & multi	.35	.25
989 A194 75s multi	.65	.60
Nos. 987-989 (3)	1.15	1.00

Calderon (1868-1909), lawyer and author of the Malolos Constitution.

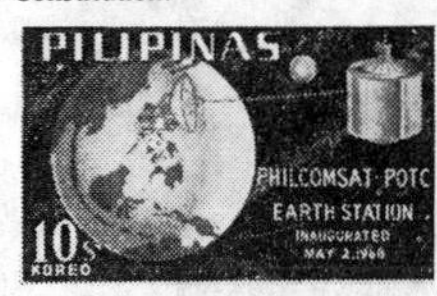

Earth and Transmission from Philippine Station to Satellite A195

1968, Oct. 21 Photo. *Perf. 13½*

990 A195 10s blk & multi	.15	.15
991 A195 40s multi	.45	.35
992 A195 75s multi	.75	.60
Nos. 990-992 (3)	1.35	1.10

Issued to commemorate the inauguration of the Philcomsat Station in Tany, Luzon, May 2, 1968.

Tobacco Industry and Tobacco Board's Emblem — A196

1968, Nov. 15 Photo. *Perf. 13½*

993 A196 10s blk & multi	.15	.15
994 A196 40s bl & multi	.35	.30
995 A196 70s crim & multi	.60	.50
Nos. 993-995 (3)	1.10	.95

Philippine tobacco industry.

Kudyapi A197

Philippine Musical Instruments: 20s, Ludag (drum). 30s, Kulintangan. 50s, Subing (bamboo flute).

1968, Nov. 22 Photo. *Perf. 13½*

996 A197 10s multi	.15	.15
997 A197 20s multi	.15	.15
998 A197 30s multi	.28	.25
999 A197 50s multi	.45	.40
Nos. 996-999 (4)	1.03	
Set value		.82

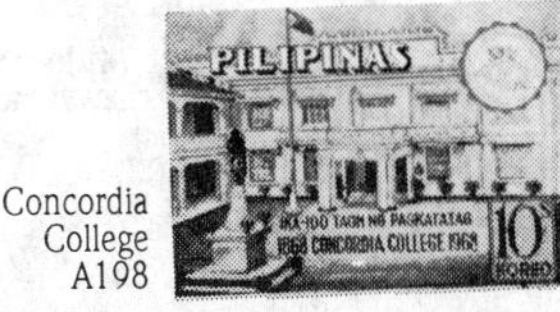

Concordia College A198

1968, Dec. 8 *Perf. 13x13½*

1000 A198 10s multi	.15	.15
1001 A198 20s multi	.15	.15
1002 A198 70s multi	.40	.32
Set value	.60	.50

Centenary of the Colegio de la Concordia, Manila, a Catholic women's school. Issued Dec. 8 (Sunday), but entered the mail Dec. 9.

Singing Children — A199

1968, Dec. 16 *Perf. 13½*

1003 A199 10s multi	.15	.15
1004 A199 40s multi	.40	.35
1005 A199 75s multi	.75	.60
Nos. 1003-1005 (3)	1.30	1.10

Christmas 1968.

Animals A200

1969, Jan. 8 Photo. *Perf. 13½*

1006 A200 2s Tarsier	.15	.15
1007 A200 10s Tamarau	.15	.15
1008 A200 20s Carabao	.15	.15
1009 A200 75s Mouse deer	.50	.40
Set value	.72	.58

Opening of the hunting season.

Emilio Aguinaldo and Historical Building, Cavite — A201

1969, Jan. 23 Litho. *Perf. 14*

1010 A201 10s yel & multi	.15	.15
1011 A201 40s bl & multi	.45	.28
1012 A201 70s multi	.75	.60
Nos. 1010-1012 (3)	1.35	1.03

Emilio Aguinaldo (1869-1964), commander of Filipino forces in rebellion against Spain.

Guard Turret, San Andres Bastion, Manila, and Rotary Emblem — A202

1969, Jan. 29 Photo. *Perf. 12½*
1013 A202 10s ultra & multi .15 .15
Nos. 1013,C96-C97 (3) .92 .75

50th anniv. of the Manila Rotary Club.

Senator Claro M. Recto (1890-1960), Lawyer and Supreme Court Judge — A203

1969, Feb. 10 Engr. *Perf. 13*
1014 A203 10s bright rose lilac .15 .15

No. 973 Overprinted

PHILATELIC WEEK
NOV. 24-30, 1968

1969, Feb. 14 Litho. *Perf. 14x13½*
1015 A190 4s multi & blk .15 .15

Philatelic Week, Nov. 24-30, 1968.

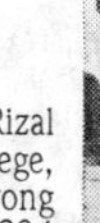

José Rizal College, Mandaluyong A204

1969, Feb. 19 Photo. *Perf. 13*
1016 A204 10s multicolored .15 .15
1017 A204 40s multicolored .35 .25
1018 A204 50s multicolored .45 .38
Nos. 1016-1018 (3) .95 .78

Founding of Rizal College, 50th anniv.

No. 948 Surcharged in Red with New Value, 2 Bars and: "4th NATIONAL BOY / SCOUT JAMBOREE / PALAYAN CITY-MAY, 1969"

1969, May 12 Litho. *Perf. 13x12½*
1019 A183 5s on 6s multi .15 .15

A205 A206

Map of Philippines, Red Crescent, Cross, Lion and Sun emblems.

1969, May 26 Photo. *Perf. 12½*
1020 A205 10s gray, ultra & red .15 .15
1021 A205 40s lt ultra, dk bl & red .40 .25
1022 A205 75s bister, brn & red .60 .55
Nos. 1020-1022 (3) 1.15 .95

League of Red Cross Societies, 50th anniv.

1969, June 13 Photo. *Perf. 14*

Pres. and Mrs. Marcos harvesting miracle rice.

1023 A206 10s multicolored .15 .15
1024 A206 40s multicolored .40 .30
1025 A206 75s multicolored .60 .55
Nos. 1023-1025 (3) 1.15 1.00

Introduction of IR8 (miracle) rice, produced by the International Rice Research Institute.

Holy Child of Leyte and Map of Leyte A207

1969, June 30 *Perf. 13½*
1026 A207 5s emerald & multi .15 .15
1027 A207 10s crimson & multi .15 .15
Set value .16 .15

80th anniv. of the return of the image of the Holy Child of Leyte to Tacloban. See No. C98.

Philippine Development Bank — A208

1969, Sept. 12 Photo. *Perf. 13½*
1028 A208 10s dk bl, blk & grn .15 .15
1029 A208 40s rose car, blk & grn .50 .25
1030 A208 75s brown, blk & grn .75 .55
Nos. 1028-1030 (3) 1.40 .95

Inauguration of the new building of the Philippine Development Bank in Makati, Rizal.

Common Birdwing A209

Butterflies: 20s, Tailed jay. 30s, Red Helen. 40s, Birdwing.

1969, Sept. 15 Photo. *Perf. 13½*
1031 A209 10s multicolored .15 .15
1032 A209 20s multicolored .15 .15
1033 A209 30s multicolored .20 .15
1034 A209 40s multicolored .30 .18
Set value .68 .42

World's Children and UNICEF Emblem A210

1969, Oct. 6
1035 A210 10s blue & multi .15 .15
1036 A210 20s multicolored .15 .15
1037 A210 30s multicolored .15 .15
Set value .32 .26

15th anniversary of Universal Children's Day.

Monument and Leyte Landing — A211

1969, Oct. 20 *Perf. 13½x14*
1038 A211 5s lt grn & multi .15 .15
1039 A211 10s yellow & multi .15 .15
1040 A211 40s pink & multi .30 .18
Set value .48 .30

25th anniv. of the landing of the US forces under Gen. Douglas MacArthur on Leyte, Oct. 20, 1944.

Philippine Cultural Center, Manila A212

1969, Nov. 4 Photo. *Perf. 13½*
1041 A212 10s ultra .15 .15
1042 A212 30s brt rose lilac .20 .15
Set value .28 .22

Cultural Center of the Philippines, containing theaters, a museum and libraries.

Nos. 889-892 Surcharged or Overprinted: "1969 PHILATELIC WEEK"

1969, Nov. 24 Photo. *Perf. 14*
1043 A164 5s multicolored .15 .15
1044 A164 5s on 6s multi .15 .15
1045 A164 10s multicolored .15 .15
1046 A164 10s on 20s multi .15 .15
Set value .34 .30

Philatelic Week, Nov. 23-29.

Melchora Aquino — A213

1969, Nov. 30 *Perf. 12½*
1047 A213 10s multicolored .15 .15
1048 A213 20s multicolored .15 .15
1049 A213 30s dk bl & multi .25 .15
Nos. 1047-1049 (3) .55
Set value .30

Melchora Aquino (Tandang Sora; 1812-1919), the Grand Old Woman of the Revolution.

No. 950 Surcharged with New Value, 2 Bars and: "PASINAYA, IKA -2 PANUNUNGKULAN / PANGULONG FERDINAND E. MARCOS / DISYEMBRE 30, 1969"

1969, Dec. 30 Litho. *Perf. 12½*
1050 A184 5s on 6s multi .20 .15

Inauguration of Pres. Marcos and Vice Pres. Fernando Lopez for a 2nd term, Dec. 30.

Pouring Ladle and Iligan Steel Mills — A214

1970, Jan. 20 Photo. *Perf. 13½*
1051 A214 10s ver & multi .15 .15
1052 A214 20s multicolored .15 .15
1053 A214 30s ultra & multi .25 .18
Nos. 1051-1053 (3) .55
Set value .36

Iligan Integrated Steel Mills, Northern Mindanao, the first Philippine steel mills.

Nos. 857A, 904 and 906 Surcharged with New Value and Two Bars

1970, Apr. 30 As Before
1054 A158 4s on 6s peacock bl .15 .15
1055 A169 5s on 6s multi .15 .15
1056 A170 5s on 6s pur & gold .15 .15
Set value .15 .15

New UPU Headquarters and Monument, Bern — A215

Perf. 13½

1970, May 20 Unwmk. Photo.
1057 A215 10s bl, dk bl & yel .15 .15
1058 A215 30s lt grn, dk bl & yel .32 .18
Set value .24

Opening of the new UPU Headquarters in Bern.

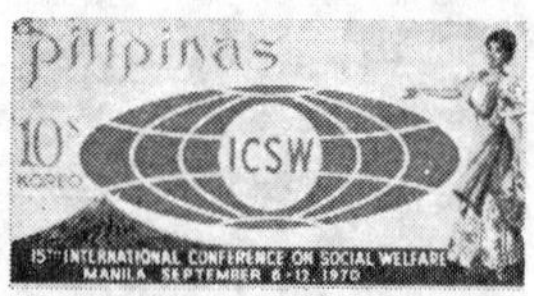

Emblem, Mayon Volcano and Filipina — A216

1970, Sept. 6 Photo. *Perf. 13½x14*
1059 A216 10s brt blue & multi .15 .15
1060 A216 20s multicolored .18 .15
1061 A216 30s multicolored .30 .15
Nos. 1059-1061 (3) .63
Set value .36

Issued to publicize the 15th International Conference on Social Welfare, Manila, Sept. 6-12.

Crab, by Alexander Calder, and Map of Philippines A217

1970, Oct. 5 *Perf. 13x13½*
1062 A217 10s emerald & multi .15 .15
1063 A217 40s multicolored .35 .20
1064 A217 50s ultra & multi .50 .30
Nos. 1062-1064 (3) 1.00 .65

Campaign against cancer.

Scaled Tridacna — A218

Sea Shells: 10s, Royal spiny oyster. 20s, Venus comb. 40s, Glory of the sea.

1970, Oct. 19 Photo. *Perf. 13½*
1065 A218 5s black & multi .15 .15
1066 A218 10s dk grn & multi .15 .15
1067 A218 20s multicolored .15 .15
1068 A218 40s dk blue & multi .32 .20
Set value .60 .38

Nos. 922, 953 and 955 Surcharged

4S
FOUR

Photogravure; Lithographed

1970, Oct. 26 *Perf. 13½, 12½*
1069 A175 4s on 6s multi .15 .15
1070 A185 4s on 6s multi .15 .15
1071 A186 4s on 6s multi .15 .15
Set value .15 .15

One line surcharge on No. 1071.

Map of Philippines and FAPA Emblem — A219

1970, Nov. 16 Photo. *Perf. 13½*
1072 A219 10s dp orange & multi .15 .15
1073 A219 50s lt violet & multi .40 .20
Set value .26

Opening of the 4th General Assembly of the Federation of Asian Pharmaceutical Assoc. (FAPA) & the 3rd Asian Cong. of Pharmaceutical Sciences.

Hundred Islands of Pangasinan, Peddler's Cart — A220

Designs: 20s, Tree house in Pasonanca Park, Zamboanga City. 30s, Sugar industry, Negros Island, Mt. Kanlaon, Woman and Carabao statue, symbolizing agriculture. 2p, Miagao Church, Iloilo, and horse-drawn calesa.

1970, Nov. 12 *Perf. 12½x13½*

1074 A220 10s multicolored .15 .15
1075 A220 20s multicolored .15 .15
1076 A220 30s multicolored .18 .16
1077 A220 2p multicolored 1.10 .65
Nos. 1074-1077 (4) 1.58 1.11

Tourist publicity. See Nos. 1086-1097.

No. 884 Surcharged: "UPU-AOPU / Regional Seminar / Nov. 23-Dec. 5, 1970 / TEN 10s"

1970, Nov. 22 Photo. *Perf. 13½x13*

1078 A162 10s on 6s multi .15 .15

Universal Postal Union and Asian-Oceanic Postal Union Regional Seminar, Nov. 23-Dec. 5.

No. 915 Surcharged Vertically: "1970 PHILATELIC WEEK"

Perf. 14½x14

1970, Nov. 22 Wmk. 233

1079 A173 10s on 6s multi .15 .15

Philatelic Week, Nov. 22-28.

Pope Paul VI, Map of Far East and Australia — A221

Perf. 13½x14

1970, Nov. 27 Photo. Unwmk.

1080 A221 10s ultra & multi .15 .15
1081 A221 30s multicolored .18 .15
Nos. 1080-1081,C99 (3) .61
Set value .35

Visit of Pope Paul VI, Nov. 27-29, 1970.

Mariano Ponce — A222

1970, Dec. 30 Engr. *Perf. 14½*

1082 A222 10s rose carmine .15 .15

Mariano Ponce (1863-1918), editor and legislator. See Nos. 1136-1137. For surcharges see Nos. 1190, 1231. For overprint see No. O70.

PATA Emblem A223

1971, Jan. 21 Photo. *Perf. 14½*

1083 A223 5s brt green & multi .15 .15
1084 A223 10s blue & multi .15 .15
1085 A223 70s brown & multi .30 .22
Set value .46 .35

Pacific Travel Association (PATA), 20th annual conference, Manila, Jan. 21-29.

Tourist Type of 1970

Designs: 10s, Filipina and Ang Nayong (7 village replicas around man-made lagoon). 20s, Woman and fisherman, Estancia. 30s, Pagsanjan Falls. 5p, Watch Tower, Punta Cruz, Boho.

Perf. 12½x13½

1971, Feb. 15 Photo.

1086 A220 10s multicolored .15 .15
1087 A220 20s multicolored .15 .15
1088 A220 30s multicolored .15 .15
1089 A220 5p multicolored 1.25 1.25
Nos. 1086-1089 (4) 1.70 1.70

1971, Apr. 19

Designs: 10s, Cultured pearl farm, Davao. 20s, Coral divers, Davao, Mindanao. 40s, Moslem Mosque, Zamboanga. 1p, Rice terraces, Banaue.

1090 A220 10s multicolored .15 .15
1091 A220 20s multicolored .15 .15
1092 A220 40s multicolored .15 .15
1093 A220 1p multicolored .35 .30
Set value .68 .55

1971, May 3

10s, Spanish cannon, Zamboanga. 30s, Magellan's cross, Cebu City. 50s, Big Jar monument in Calamba, Laguna. 70s, Mayon Volcano, Legaspi.

1094 A220 10s multicolored .15 .15
1095 A220 30s multicolored .15 .15
1096 A220 50s multicolored .15 .15
1097 A220 70s multicolored .32 .20
Set value .65 .48

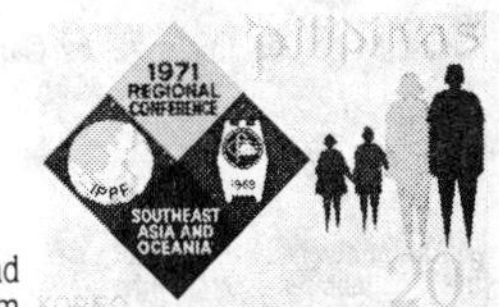

Family and Emblem A224

1971, Mar. 21 Photo. *Perf. 13½*

1098 A224 20s lt grn & multi .15 .15
1099 A224 40s pink & multi .15 .15
Set value .22 .18

Regional Conf. of the Intl. Planned Parenthood Federation for SE Asia & Oceania, Baguio City, Mar. 21-27.

No. 955 Surcharged **FIVE 5s**

1971, June 10 Photo. *Perf. 14x13½*

1100 A186 5s on 6s multi .15 .15

Allegory of Law A225

1971, June 15 Photo. *Perf. 13*

1101 A225 15s orange & multi .15 .15

60th anniversary of the University of the Philippines Law College. See No. C100.

Manila Anniversary Emblem — A226

1971, June 24

1102 A226 10s multicolored .15 .15

Founding of Manila, 400th anniv. See #C101.

Santo Tomas University, Arms of Schools of Medicine and Pharmacology — A227

1971, July 8 Photo. *Perf. 13½*

1103 A227 5s yellow & multi .15 .15

Centenary of the founding of the Schools of Medicine and Surgery, and Pharmacology at the University of Santo Tomas, Manila. See No. C102.

No. 957 Surcharged

1971, July 11 Wmk. 233 *Perf. 14½*

1104 A187 5s on 6s multi .15 .15

World Congress of University Presidents, Manila.

Our Lady of Guia Appearing to Filipinos and Spanish Soldiers — A228

1971, July 8 Photo. *Perf. 13½*

1105 A228 10s multi .15 .15
1106 A228 75s multi .32 .30
Set value .38

4th centenary of appearance of the statue of Our Lady of Guia, Ermita, Manila.

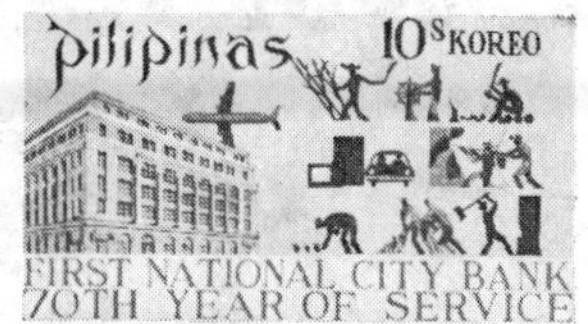

Bank Building, Plane, Car and Workers — A229

1971, Sept. 14 *Perf. 12½*

1107 A229 10s blue & multi .15 .15
1108 A229 30s lt grn & multi .18 .15
1109 A229 1p multicolored .40 .32
Nos. 1107-1109 (3) .73
Set value .52

1st Natl. City Bank in the Philippines, 70th anniv.

No. 944 Surcharged **FOUR**

Perf. 12x11

1971, Nov. 24 Engr. Unwmk.

1110 A182 4s on 6s blue .15 .15
1111 A182 5s on 6s blue .15 .15
Set value .15 .15

No. 957 Surcharged

Perf. 14½

1971, Nov. 24 Wmk. 233 Photo.

1112 A187 5s on 6s multi .15 .15

Philatelic Week, 1971.

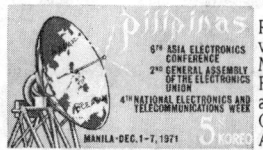

Radar with Map of Far East and Oceania A230

1972, Feb. 29 Photo. *Perf. 14x14½*

1113 A230 5s org yel & multi .15 .15
1114 A230 40s red org & multi .32 .20
Set value .40 .25

Electronics Conferences, Manila, Dec. 1-7, 1971.

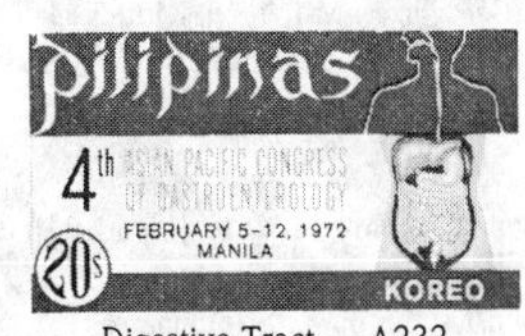

Fathers Gomez, Burgos and Zamora — A231

1972, Apr. 3 *Perf. 13x12½*

1115 A231 5s gold & multi .15 .15
1116 A231 60s gold & multi .25 .25
Set value .30 .30

Centenary of the deaths of Fathers Mariano Gomez, José Burgos and Jacinto Zamora, martyrs for Philippine independence from Spain.

Digestive Tract — A232

1972, Apr. 11 Photo. *Perf. 12½x13*

1117 A232 20s ultra & multi .15 .15

4th Asian Pacific Congress of Gastroenterology, Manila, Feb. 5-12. See No. C103.

No. 953 Surcharged

1972, Apr. 20 *Perf. 12½*

1118 A185 5s on 6s multi .15 .15

No. O69 with Two Bars over "G." and "O."

1972, May 16 Engr. *Perf. 13½*

1119 A158 50s violet .25 .15

Nos. 883A, 909 and 929 Surcharged with New Value and 2 Bars

1972, May 29

1120 A161	10s on 6s dp cl & blk	.15	.15
1121 A171	10s on 6s multi	.15	.15
1122 A177	10s on 6s multi	.15	.15
	Set value	.20	.15

Independence Monument, Manila — A233

1972, May 31 Photo. *Perf. 13x12½*

1123 A233	5s brt blue & multi	.15	.15
1124 A233	50s red & multi	.50	.15
1125 A233	60s emerald & multi	.65	.20
	Nos. 1123-1125 (3)	1.30	
	Set value		.38

Visit ASEAN countries (Association of South East Asian Nations).

"K," Skull and Crossbones — A234

Development of Philippine Flag: No. 1126, 3 "K's" in a row ("K" stands for Katipunan). No. 1127, 3 "K's" as triangle. No. 1128, One "K." No. 1130, 3 "K's," sun over mountain on white triangle. No. 1131, Sun over 3 "K's." No. 1132, Tagalog "K" in sun. No. 1133, Sun with human face. No. 1134, Tricolor flag, forerunner of present flag. No. 1135, Present flag. Nos. 1126, 1128, 1130-1131, 1133, 1135 inscribed in Tagalog.

1972, June 12 Photo. *Perf. 13*

1126 A234	30s ultra & red	.18	.15
1127 A234	30s ultra & red	.18	.15
1128 A234	30s ultra & red	.18	.15
1129 A234	30s ultra & blk	.18	.15
1130 A234	30s ultra & red	.18	.15
1131 A234	30s ultra & red	.18	.15
1132 A234	30s ultra & red	.18	.15
1133 A234	30s ultra & red	.18	.15
1134 A234	30s ultra, red & blk	.18	.15
1135 A234	30s ultra, yel & red	.18	.15
a.	Block of 10	1.90	1.50

Portrait Type of 1970

40s, Gen. Miguel Malvar. 1p, Julian Felipe.

1972 Engr. *Perf. 14*

1136 A222	40s rose red	.20	.15
1137 A222	1p deep blue	.55	.20
	Set value		.25

Honoring Gen. Miguel Malvar (1865-1911), revolutionary leader, and Julian Felipe (1861-1944), composer of Philippine national anthem.

Issue dates: 40s, July 10; 1p, June 26.

Parrotfish A235

1972, Aug. 14 Photo. *Perf. 13*

1138 A235	5s shown	.15	.15
1139 A235	10s Sunburst butterflyfish	.15	.15
1140 A235	20s Moorish idol	.15	.15
	Set value, #1138-1140, C104	.70	.40

Tropical fish.

Development Bank of the Philippines A236

1972, Sept. 12

1141 A236	10s gray blue & multi	.15	.15
1142 A236	20s lilac & multi	.15	.15
1143 A236	60s tan & multi	.32	.20
	Set value	.50	.32

Development Bank of the Philippines, 25th anniv.

Pope Paul VI A237

1972, Sept. 26 Unwmk. *Perf. 14*

1144 A237	10s lt green & multi	.15	.15
1145 A237	50s lt violet & multi	.25	.20
	Set value	.30	.25

First anniversary (in 1971) of the visit of Pope Paul VI to the Philippines, and for his 75th birthday. See No. C105.

Nos. 880, 899 and 925 Surcharged with New Value and 2 Bars

1972, Sept. 29 As Before

1146 A161	10s on 6s lil & blk	.15	.15
1147 A167	10s on 6s multi	.15	.15
1148 A176	10s on 6s multi	.15	.15
	Set value	.24	.15

Charon's Bark, by Resurrección Hidalgo — A238

Paintings: 10s, Rice Workers' Meal, by F. Amorsolo. 30s, "Spain and the Philippines," by Juan Luna, vert. 70s, Song of Maria Clara, by F. Amorsolo.

Perf. 14x13

1972, Oct. 16 Unwmk. Photo.

Size: 38x40mm

1149 A238	5s silver & multi	.15	.15
1150 A238	10s silver & multi	.15	.15

Size: 24x56mm

1151 A238	30s silver & multi	.15	.15

Size: 38x40mm

1152 A238	70s silver & multi	.32	.32
	Set value	.58	.58

25th anniversary of the organization of the Stamp and Philatelic Division.

PHILIPPINE NURSES ASSOCIATION 1922 · 50th ANNIVERSARY · 1972

Lamp, Nurse, Emblem — A239

1972, Oct. 22 *Perf. 12½x13½*

1153 A239	5s violet & multi	.15	.15
1154 A239	10s blue & multi	.15	.15
1155 A239	70s orange & multi	.25	.22
	Set value	.36	.32

Philippine Nursing Association, 50th anniv.

Heart, Map of Philippines A240

1972, Oct. 24 *Perf. 13*

1156 A240	5s purple, emer & red	.15	.15
1157 A240	10s blue, emer & red	.15	.15
1158 A240	30s emerald, bl & red	.15	.15
	Set value	.26	.22

"Your heart is your health," World Health Month.

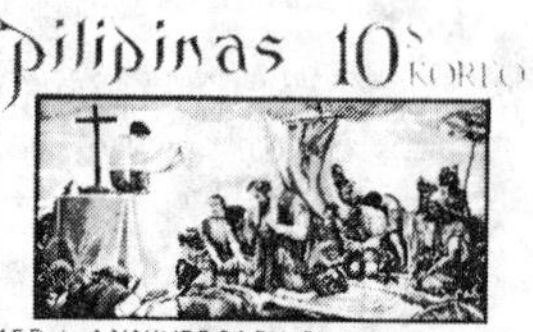

First Mass on Limasawa, by Carlos V. Francisco — A241

1972, Oct. 31 *Perf. 14*

1159 A241	10s brown & multi	.15	.15

450th anniversary of the first mass in the Philippines, celebrated by Father Valderama on Limasawa, Mar. 31, 1521. See No. C106.

Nos. 878, 882, 899 Surcharged: "ASIA PACIFIC SCOUT CONFERENCE NOV. 1972"

1972, Nov. 13 As Before

1160 A161	10s on 6s bl & blk	.15	.15
1161 A161	10s on 6s grn & blk	.15	.15
1162 A167	10s on 6s multi	.15	.15
	Set value	.30	.20

Asia Pacific Scout Conference, Nov. 1972.

Torch, Olympic Emblems — A242

Perf. 12½x13½

1972, Nov. 15 Photo.

1163 A242	5s blue & multi	.15	.15
1164 A242	10s multicolored	.15	.15
1165 A242	70s orange & multi	.32	.25
	Set value	.44	.36

20th Olympic Games, Munich, Aug. 26-Sept. 11. For surcharges see Nos. 1297, 1759-1760.

Nos. 896 and 919 Surcharged with New Value, Two Bars and: "1972 PHILATELIC WEEK"

1972, Nov. 23 Photo. *Perf. 13½*

1166 A166	10s on 6s multi	.15	.15
1167 A174	10s on 6s multi	.15	.15
	Set value	.15	.15

Philatelic Week 1972.

Manunggul Burial Jar, 890-710 B.C. — A243

#1169, Ngipet Duldug Cave ritual earthenware vessel, 155 B.C. #1170, Metal age chalice, 200-600 A.D. #1171, Earthenware vessel, 15th cent.

1972, Nov. 29

1168 A243	10s green & multi	.15	.15
1169 A243	10s lilac & multi	.15	.15
1170 A243	10s blue & multi	.15	.15
1171 A243	10s yellow & multi	.15	.15
	Set value	.32	.20

College of Pharmacy and Univ. of the Philippines Emblems — A244

1972, Dec. 11 *Perf. 12½x13½*

1172 A244	5s lt vio & multi	.15	.15
1173 A244	10s yel grn & multi	.15	.15
1174 A244	30s ultra & multi	.20	.15
	Set value	.35	.22

60th anniversary of the College of Pharmacy of the University of the Philippines.

Christmas Lantern Makers, by Jorgé Pineda A245

1972, Dec. 14 Photo. *Perf. 12½*

1175 A245	10s dk bl & multi	.15	.15
1176 A245	30s brown & multi	.15	.15
1177 A245	50s green & multi	.25	.22
	Set value	.46	.36

Christmas 1972.

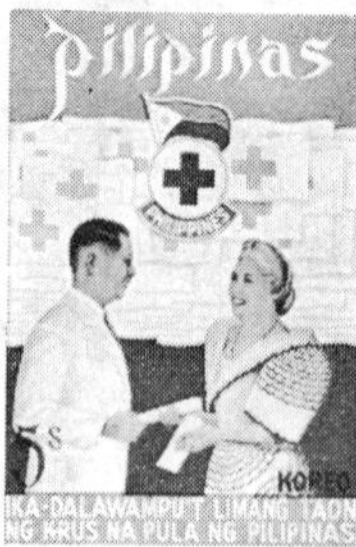

Red Cross Flags, Pres. Roxas and Mrs. Aurora Quezon — A246

1972, Dec. 21

1178 A246	5s ultra & multi	.15	.15
1179 A246	20s multicolored	.15	.15
1180 A246	30s brown & multi	.15	.15
	Set value	.30	.25

25th anniv. of the Philippine Red Cross.

Nos. 894 and 936 Surcharged with New Value and 2 Bars

1973, Jan. 22 Photo. *Perf. 14, 13*

1181 A165	10s on 6s multi	.15	.15
1182 A180	10s on 6s multi	.15	.15
	Set value	.16	.15

San Luis University, Luzon — A247

1973, Mar. 1 Photo. *Perf. 13½x14*

1183 A247 5s multicolored .15 .15
1184 A247 10s yellow & multi .15 .15
1185 A247 75s multicolored .30 .25
Set value .40 .35

60th anniversary of San Luis University, Baguio City, Luzon.
For surcharge see No. 1305.

Jesus Villamor and Fighter Planes — A248

1973, Apr. 9 Photo. *Perf. 13½x14*

1186 A248 10s multicolored .15 .15
1187 A248 2p multicolored .70 .70

Col. Jesus Villamor (1914-1971), World War II aviator who fought for liberation of the Philippines.
For surcharge see No. 1230.

Nos. 932, 957, O70 Surcharged with New Values and 2 Bars

1973, Apr. 23 As Before

1188 A178 5s on 6s multi .15 .15
1189 A187 5s on 6s multi .15 .15
1190 A222 15s on 10s rose car .15 .15
Set value .24 .15

Two additional bars through "G.O." on No. 1190.

ITI Emblem, Performance and Actor Vic Silayan — A249

1973, May 15 Photo. *Perf. 13x12½*

1191 A249 5s blue & multi .15 .15
1192 A249 10s yel grn & multi .15 .15
1193 A249 50s orange & multi .20 .15
1194 A249 70s rose & multi .30 .18
Set value .62 .40

1st Third World Theater Festival, sponsored by the UNESCO affiliated International Theater Institute, Manila, Nov. 19-30, 1971.
For surcharge see No. 1229.

Josefa Llanes Escoda — A250

#1196, Gabriela Silang. No. 1197, Rafael Palma. 30s, Jose Rizal. 60s, Marcela Agoncillo. 90s, Teodoro R. Yangco. 1.10p, Dr. Pio Venezuela. 1.20p, Gregoria de Jesus. #1204, Pedro A. Paterno. #1205, Teodora Alonso. 1.80p, Edilberto Evangelista. 5p, Fernando M. Guerrero.

1973-78 Engr. *Perf. 14½*

1195 A250 15s sepia .15 .15

Litho. *Perf. 12½*

1196 A250 15s violet ('74) .15 .15
1197 A273 15s emerald ('74) .15 .15
1198 A250 30s vio bl ('78) .15 .15
1199 A250 60s dl red brn .22 .22
1200 A273 90s brt bl ('74) .30 .15
1202 A273 1.10p brt bl ('74) .38 .18
1203 A250 1.20p dl red ('78) .25 .15
1204 A250 1.50p lil rose .50 .42
1205 A273 1.50p brown ('74) .50 .20
1206 A250 1.80p green .60 .55
1208 A250 5p blue 1.65 1.65
Nos. 1195-1208 (12) 5.00 4.12

1973-74 *Imperf.*

1196a A250 15s violet ('74) .15 .15
1197a A273 15s emerald ('74) .15 .15
1199a A250 60s dull red brown .30 .30
1200a A273 90s bright blue ('74) .45 .40
1202a A273 1.10p bright blue ('74) .52 .52
1204a A250 1.50p lilac rose .60 .52
1205a A273 1.50p brown ('74) .70 .70
1206a A250 1.80p green .70 .70
1208a A250 5p blue 2.00 2.00
Nos. 1196a-1208a (9) 5.57 5.44

Honoring: Escoda (1898-194?), leader of Girl Scouts and Federation of Women's Clubs. Silang (1731-63), "the Ilocana Joan of Arc". Palma (1874-1939), journalist, statesman, educator. Rizal (1861-96), natl. hero. Agoncillo (1859-1946), designer of 1st Philippine flag, 1898. Yangco (1861-1939), patriot and philanthropist. Valenzuela (1869-1956), physician and newspaperman.
Gregoria de Jesus, independence leader. Paterno (1857-1911), lawyer, writer, patriot. Alonso (1827-1911), mother of Rizal. Evangelista (1862-97), army engineer, patriot. Guerrero (1873-1929), journalist, political leader.
For overprint see No. 1277. For surcharges see Nos. 1311, 1470, 1518.

No. 946 surcharged with New Value

1973, June 4 Engr. *Perf. 13½*

1209 A158 5s on 6s peacock bl .15 .15

Anti-smuggling campaign.

No. 925 Surcharged

1973, June 4 Wmk. 233

1210 A176 5s on 6s multi .15 .15

10th anniv. of death of John F. Kennedy.

Pres. Marcos, Farm Family, Unfurling of Philippine Flag — A251

Perf. 12½x13½

1973, Sept. 24 Photo. Unwmk.

1211 A251 15s ultra & multi .15 .15
1212 A251 45s red & multi .15 .15
1213 A251 90s multi .32 .32
Nos. 1211-1213 (3) .62 .62

75th anniversary of Philippine independence and 1st anniversary of proclamation of martial law.

Imelda Romualdez Marcos, First Lady of the Philippines A252

1973, Oct. 31 Photo. *Perf. 13*

1214 A252 15s dl bl & multi .15 .15
1215 A252 50s multicolored .18 .18
1216 A252 60s lil & multi .22 .22
Set value .46 .46

Presidential Palace, Manila, Pres. and Mrs. Marcos — A253

1973, Nov. 15 Litho. *Perf. 14*

1217 A253 15s rose & multi .15 .15
1218 A253 50s ultra & multi .15 .15
Set value .22 .22

See No. C107.

INTERPOL Emblem — A254

1973, Dec. 18 Photo. *Perf. 13*

1219 A254 15s ultra & multi .15 .15
1220 A254 65s lt grn & multi .30 .15
Set value .22

Intl. Criminal Police Organization, 50th anniv.

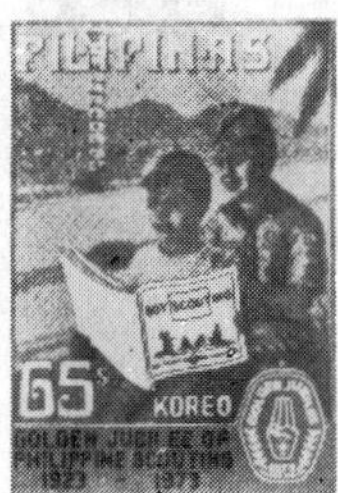

Cub and Boy Scouts — A255

15s, Various Scout activities; inscribed in Tagalog.

1973, Dec. 28 Litho. *Perf. 12½*

1221 A255 15s bister & emer .15 .15
a. Imperf. ('74) .15 .15
1222 A255 65s bister & brt bl .28 .22
a. Imperf. ('74) .40 .40
Set value .36 .28

50th anniv. of Philippine Boy Scouts.
Nos. 1221a-1222a issued Feb. 4, although first day covers are dated Dec. 28, 1973.

Manila, Bank Emblem and Farmers — A256

Designs: 60s, Old bank building. 1.50p, Modern bank building.

1974, Jan. 3 Photo. *Perf. 12½x13½*

1223 A256 15s silver & multi .15 .15
1224 A256 60s silver & multi .20 .15
1225 A256 1.50p silver & multi .50 .30
Nos. 1223-1225 (3) .85
Set value .48

Central Bank of the Philippines, 25th anniv.

UPU Emblem, Maria Clara Costume — A257

Filipino Costumes: 60s, Balintawak and UPU emblem. 80s, Malong costume and UPU emblem.

1974, Jan. 15 *Perf. 12½*

1226 A257 15s multicolored .15 .15
1227 A257 60s multicolored .20 .15
1228 A257 80s multicolored .30 .18
Nos. 1226-1228 (3) .65
Set value .36

Centenary of Universal Postal Union.

No. 1192 Surcharged in Red with New Value, 2 Bars and: "1973 / PHILATELIC WEEK"

1974, Feb. 4 Photo. *Perf. 13x12½*

1229 A249 15s on 10s multi .15 .15

Philatelic Week, 1973. First day covers exist dated Nov. 26, 1973.

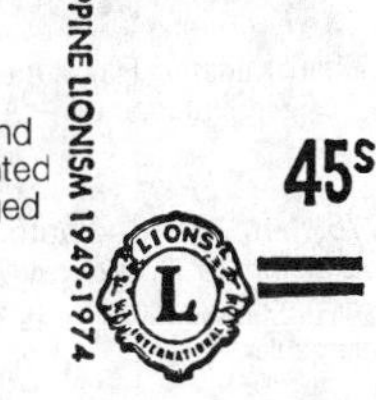

Nos. 1186 and 1136 Overprinted and Surcharged

1974, Mar. 25 Photo. *Perf. 13½x14*

1230 A248 15s on 10s multi .15 .15

Engr. *Perf. 14*

1231 A222 45s on 40s rose red .15 .15
Set value .22 .18

25th anniversary of Lions International of the Philippines. The overprint on No. 1230 arranged to fit shape of stamp.

Pediatrics Congress Emblem and Map of Participating Countries A258

1974, Apr. 30 Litho. *Perf. 12½*

1232 A258 30s brt bl & red .15 .15
a. Imperf. .15 .15
1233 A258 1p dl grn & red .32 .20
a. Imperf. .42 .32
Set value .28

Asian Congress of Pediatrics, Manila, Apr. 30-May 4.

Nos. 912, 954-955 Surcharged with New Value and Two Bars

1974, Aug. 1 As Before

1234 A172 5s on 3s multi .15 .15
1235 A185 5s on 6s multi .15 .15
1236 A186 5s on 6s multi .15 .15
Set value .15 .15

WPY Emblem A259

1974, Aug. 15 Litho. *Perf. 12½*

1237 A259 5s org & bl blk .15 .15
a. Imperf. .15 .15
1238 A259 2p lt grn & dk bl .60 .32
a. Imperf. .65 .50
Set value .65 .36

World Population Year, 1974.

Red Feather Community Chest Emblem A260

Perf. 12½

1974, Sept. 5 Litho. Wmk. 372

1239 A260 15s brt bl & red .15 .15
1240 A260 40s emer & red .15 .15
1241 A260 45s red brn & red .20 .15
Set value .42 .25

Philippine Community Chest, 25th anniv.

Imperf.

1239a A260 15s .15 .15
1240a A260 40s .20 .20
1241a A260 45s .20 .20

Sultan Kudarat, Flag, Order and Map of Philippines — A261

Perf. 13½x14

1975, Jan. 13 Photo. Unwmk.

1242 A261 15s multicolored .15 .15

Sultan Mohammad Dipatuan Kudarat, 16th-17th century ruler.

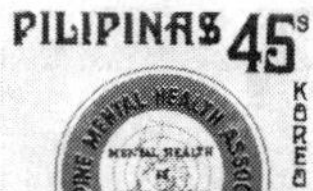

Mental Health Association Emblem — A262

Perf. 12½

1975, Jan. 20 Wmk. 372 Litho.

1243 A262 45s emer & org .15 .15
a. Imperf. .20 .20
1244 A262 1p emer & pur .25 .20
a. Imperf. .32 .32

Philippine Mental Health Assoc., 25th anniv.

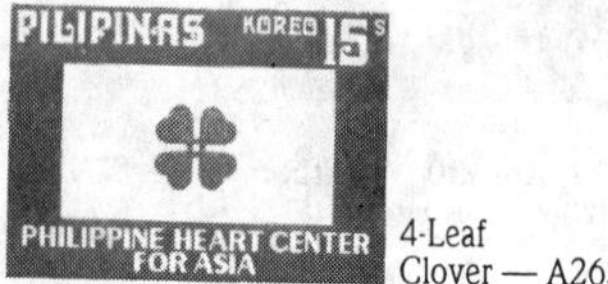

4-Leaf Clover — A263

1975, Feb. 14

1245 A263 15s vio bl & red .15 .15
a. Imperf. .15 .15
1246 A263 50s emer & red .15 .15
a. Imperf. .18 .18
Set value .20 .16

Philippine Heart Center for Asia, inauguration.

Military Academy, Cadet and Emblem — A264

Perf. 13½x14

1975, Feb. 17 Unwmk.

1247 A264 15s grn & multi .15 .15
1248 A264 45s plum & multi .24 .15
Set value .22

Philippine Military Academy, 70th anniv.

Helping the Disabled — A265

Perf. 12½, Imperf.

1975, Mar. 17 Wmk. 372

1249 A265 Block of 10 1.65 1.25
a.-j. 45s grn, any single .15 .15

25th anniversary (in 1974) of Philippine Orthopedic Association.
For surcharge see No. 1635.

Nos. B43, B50-B51 Surcharged with New Value and Two Bars

1975, Apr. 15 Unwmk.

1250 SP18 5s on 15s + 5s .15 .15
1251 SP16 60s on 70s + 5s .22 .20
1252 SP18 1p on 1.10p + 5s .25 .22
Set value .52 .46

"Grow and Preserve Forests"
A266 A267

1975, May 19 Litho. *Perf. 14½*

1253 A266 45s blk, brn & grn .15 .15
1254 A267 45s blk, brn & grn .15 .15
a. Pair, #1253-1254 .25 .25

Forest conservation.

Jade Vine — A268

1975, June 9 Photo. *Perf. 14½*

1255 A268 15s multicolored .15 .15

Imelda R. Marcos, IWY Emblem — A269

Civil Service Emblem — A270

Perf. 12½

1975, July 2 Litho. Wmk. 372

1256 A269 15s bl & blk .15 .15
a. Imperf. .15 .15
1257 A269 80s pink, bl & grn .32 .25
a. Imperf. .32 .32
Set value .40 .32

International Women's Year 1975.
For surcharges see Nos. 1500, 1505.

1975, Sept. 19 Litho. *Perf. 12½*

1258 A270 15s multicolored .15 .15
a. Imperf. .15 .15
1259 A270 50s multicolored .20 .15
a. Imperf. .20 .20
Set value .28 .18

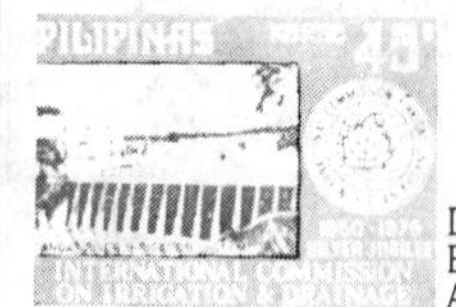

Dam and Emblem A271

1975, Sept. 30

1260 A271 40s org & vio bl .15 .15
a. Imperf. .15 .15
1261 A271 1.50p brt rose & vio bl .42 .32
a. Imperf. .52 .52

For surcharges see Nos. 1517, 1520.

Manila Harbor, 1875 A272

1975, Nov. 4 Unwmk. *Perf. 13x13½*

1262 A272 1.50p red & multi .42 .25

Hong Kong and Shanghai Banking Corporation, centenary of Philippines service.

Norberto Romualdez (1875-1941), Scholar and Legislator — A273

Jose Rizal Monument, Luneta Park — A273a

Noted Filipinos: No. 1264, Rafael Palma (1874-1939), journalist, statesman, educator. No. 1265, Rajah Kalantiaw, chief of Panay, author of ethical-penal code (1443). 65s, Emilio Jacinto (1875-1899), patriot. No. 1269, Gen. Gregorio del Pilar (1875-1899), military hero. No. 1270, Lope K. Santos (1879-1963), grammarian, writer. 1.60p, Felipe Agoncillo (1859-1941), lawyer, cabinet member.

Perf. 12½

1975-81 Wmk. 372 Litho.

1264 A273 30s brn ('77) .15 .15
1265 A273 30s dp rose ('78) .15 .15
1266 A273a 40s yel & blk ('81) .15 .15
1267 A273 60s violet .15 .15
a. Imperf. .22 .22
1268 A273 65s lilac rose .15 .15
a. Imperf. .24 .24
1269 A273 90s lilac rose .20 .15
a. Imperf. .32 .32
1270 A273 90s grn ('78) .15 .15
1272 A273 1.60p blk ('76) .50 .15
Nos. 1264-1272 (8) 1.60
Set value .60

See Nos. 1195-1208. For overprints see Nos. 1278. For surcharges see Nos. 1310, 1367, 1440, 1469, 1514, 1562, 1574, 1758-1760.

A274

1975, Nov. 22 Litho. *Perf. 12½*

1275 A274 60s multicolored .15 .15
1276 A274 1.50p multicolored .40 .32

1st landing of the Pan American World Airways China Clipper in the Philippines, 40th anniv.

Nos. 1199 and 1205 Overprinted

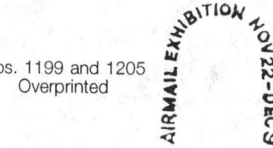

AIRMAIL EXHIBITION NOV22-DEC9

1975, Nov. 22 Unwmk.

1277 A250 60s dl red brn .15 .15
1278 A273 1.50p brown .32 .32

Airmail Exhibition, Nov. 22-Dec. 9.

APO Emblem — A275

1975, Nov. 24 Wmk. 372

1279 A275 5s ultra & multi .15 .15
a. Imperf. .15 .15
1280 A275 1p bl & multi .35 .25
a. Imperf. .40 .40
Set value .42 .30

Amateur Philatelists' Org., 25th anniv.
For surcharge see No. 1338.

San Agustin Church — A276

Philippine Churches: 30s, Morong Church, horiz. 45s, Basilica of Taal, horiz. 60s, San Sebastian Church.

1975, Dec. 23 Litho. *Perf. 12½*

1281 A276 20s bluish grn .15 .15
1282 A276 30s yel org & blk .15 .15
1283 A276 45s rose, brn & blk .15 .15
1284 A276 60s yel, bis & blk .20 .15
Set value .52 .40

Holy Year 1975.

Imperf.

1281a A276 20s .15 .15
1282a A276 30s .15 .15
1283a A276 45s .20 .20
1284a A276 60s .32 .32

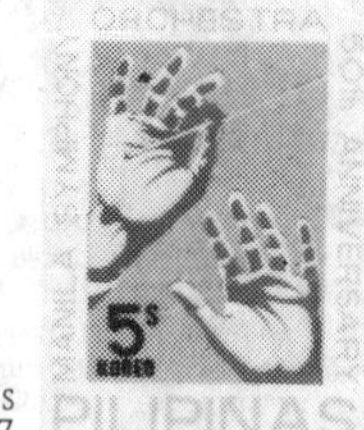

Conductor's Hands — A277

1976, Jan. 27

1285 A277 5s org & multi .15 .15
1286 A277 50s multicolored .20 .15
Set value .25 .20

Manila Symphony Orchestra, 50th anniversary.

PAL Planes of 1946 and 1976 A278

1976, Feb. 14

1287 A278 60s bl & multi .15 .15
1288 A278 1.50p red & multi .42 .32

Philippine Airlines, 30th anniversary.

National University — A279

1976, Mar. 30

1289 A279 45s bl, vio bl & yel .15 .15
1290 A279 60s lt bl, vio bl & pink .20 .15
Set value .22

National University, 75th anniversary.

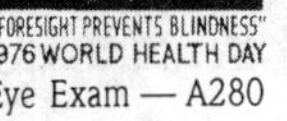

Eye Exam — A280 Book and Emblem — A281

1976, Apr. 7 Litho. *Perf. 12½*
1291 A280 15s multicolored .15 .15

World Health Day: "Foresight prevents blindness."

1976, May 24 Unwmk.
1292 A281 1.50p grn & multi .45 .40

National Archives, 75th anniversary.

Santo Tomas University, Emblems A282

1976, June 7 Wmk. 372
1293 A282 15s yel & multi .15 .15
1294 A282 50s multicolored .15 .15
Set value .22 .16

Colleges of Education and Science, Santo Tomas University, 50th anniversary.

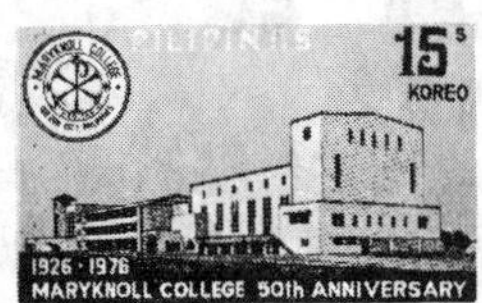

Maryknoll College A283

Perf. 12½
1976, July 26 Litho. Wmk. 372
1295 A283 15s lt bl & multi .15 .15
1296 A283 1.50p bis & multi .42 .32
Set value .36

Maryknoll College, Quezon City, 50th anniv.

No. 1164 Surcharged in Dark Violet

15s ==
Montreal 1976
21st OLYMPICS
CANADA

Perf. 12½x13½
1976, July 30 Photo.
1297 A242 15s on 10s multi .15 .15

21st Olympic Games, Montreal, Canada, July 17-Aug. 1.

Police College, Manila — A284

1976, Aug. 8 Litho. *Perf. 12½*
1298 A284 15s multicolored .15 .15
a. Imperf. .15 .15
1299 A284 60s multicolored .20 .15
a. Imperf. .32 .32
Set value .28 .20

Philippine Constabulary, 75th anniversary.

Surveyors — A285

1976, Sept. 2 Wmk. 372
1300 A285 80s multicolored .22 .20

Bureau of Lands, 75th anniversary.

Monetary Fund and World Bank Emblems — A286 Virgin of Antipollo — A287

1976, Oct. 4 Litho. *Perf. 12½*
1301 A286 60s multicolored .15 .15
1302 A286 1.50p multicolored .42 .32

Joint Annual Meeting of the Board of Governors of the International Monetary Fund and the World Bank, Manila, Oct. 4-8.
For surcharge see No. 1575.

1976, Nov. 26 *Perf. 12½*
1303 A287 30s multicolored .15 .15
1304 A287 90s multicolored .20 .15
Set value .28 .22

Virgin of Antipolo, Our Lady of Peace and Good Voyage, 350th anniv. of arrival of statue in the Philippines and 50th anniv. of the canonical coronation.

No. 1184 Surcharged with New Value and 2 Bars and Overprinted: "1976 PHILATELIC WEEK"

Perf. 13½x14
1976, Nov. 26 Photo. Unwmk.
1305 A247 30s on 10s multi .15 .15

Philatelic Week 1976.

People Going to Church A288

Perf. 12½
1976, Dec. 1 Litho. Wmk. 372
1306 A288 15s bl & multi .15 .15
1307 A288 30s bl & multi .15 .15
Set value .16 .15

Christmas 1976.

Symbolic Diamond and Book A289 Galicano Apacible A290

1976, Dec. 13
1308 A289 30s grn & multi .15 .15
1309 A289 75s grn & multi .22 .15
Set value .22

Philippine Educational System, 75th anniversary.

No. 1202 and 1208 Surcharged with New Value and 2 Bars

1977, Jan. 17 Unwmk.
1310 A273 1.20p on 1.10p bl .32 .20
1311 A250 3p on 5p bl .65 .60

1977 Litho. Wmk. 372 *Perf. 12½*

Design: 30s, José Rizal.

1313 A290 30s multicolored .15 .15
1318 A290 2.30p multicolored .52 .35
Set value .40

Dr. José Rizal (1861-1896) physician, poet and national hero (30s). Dr. Galicano Apacible (1864-1949), physician, statesman (2.30p).
Issue dates: 30s, Feb. 16; 2.30p, Jan. 24.

Emblem, Flags, Map of AOPU A291

1977, Apr. 1 Wmk. 372
1322 A291 50s multicolored .15 .15
1323 A291 1.50p multicolored .32 .25
Set value .32

Asian-Oceanic Postal Union (AOPU), 15th anniv.

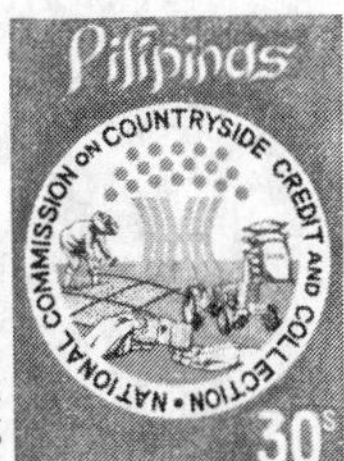

Cogwheels and Worker — A292

1977, Apr. 21 *Perf. 12½*
1324 A292 90s blk & multi .25 .22
1325 A292 2.30p blk & multi .50 .42

Asian Development Bank, 10th anniversary.

Farmer at Work and Receiving Money — A293

1977, May 14 Litho. Wmk. 372
1326 A293 30s org red & multi .15 .15

National Commission on Countryside Credit and Collection, campaign to strengthen the rural credit system.

Solicitor General's Emblem A294

1977, June 30 Litho. *Perf. 12½*
1327 A294 1.65p multicolored .32 .20

Office of the Solicitor General, 75th anniversary.
For surcharges see Nos. 1483, 1519.

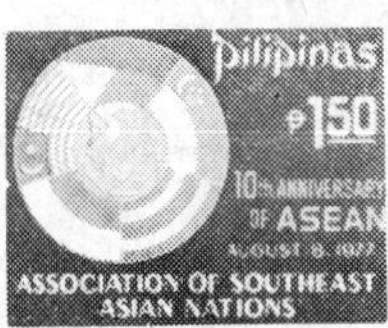

Conference Emblem A295

1977, July 29 Litho. *Perf. 12½*
1328 A295 2.20p bl & multi .45 .25

8th World Conference of the World Peace through Law Center, Manila, Aug. 21-26.
For surcharge see No. 1576.

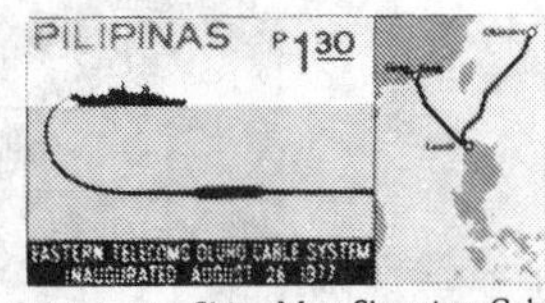

ASEAN Emblem A296

1977, Aug. 8
1329 A296 1.50p grn & multi .35 .20

Association of South East Asian Nations (ASEAN), 10th anniversary.
For surcharge see No. 1559.

Cable-laying Ship, Map Showing Cable Route — A297

1977, Aug. 26 Litho. *Perf. 12½*
1330 A297 1.30p multicolored .30 .20

Inauguration of underwater telephone cable linking Okinawa, Luzon and Hong Kong.

President Marcos A298

1977, Sept. 11 Wmk. 372
1331 A298 30s multicolored .15 .15
1332 A298 2.30p multicolored .55 .35
Set value .40

Ferdinand E. Marcos, president of the Philippines, 60th birthday.

People Raising Flag — A299

1977, Sept. 21 Litho. *Perf. 12½*
1333 A299 30s multicolored .15 .15
1334 A299 2.30p multicolored .55 .35
Set value .40

5th anniversary of "New Society."

Bishop Gregorio Aglipay — A300

1977, Oct. 1 **Litho.** ***Perf. 12½***
1335 A300 30s multicolored .15 .15
1336 A300 90s multicolored .22 .15
Set value .28 .16

Philippine Independent Aglipayan Church, 75th anniversary.

Fairchild FC-2 over World Map A301

1977, Oct. 28 **Wmk. 372**
1337 A301 2.30p multicolored .52 .32

First scheduled Pan American airmail service, Key West to Havana, 50th anniversary.

No. 1280 Surcharged with New Value, 2 Bars and Overprinted in Red: "1977 / PHILATELIC / WEEK"

1977, Nov. 22 **Litho.** ***Perf. 12½***
1338 A275 90s on 1p multi .20 .15

Philatelic Week.

Children Celebrating and Star from Lantern — A302

1977, Dec. 1 **Unwmk.**
1339 A302 30s multicolored .15 .15
1340 A302 45s multicolored .15 .15
Set value .22 .15

Christmas 1977.

Scouts and Map showing Jamboree Locations A303

1977, Dec. 27
1341 A303 30s multicolored .15 .15

National Boy Scout Jamboree, Tumauini, Isabela; Capitol Hills, Cebu City; Mariano Marcos, Davao, Dec. 27, 1977-Jan. 5, 1978.

Far Eastern University Arms — A304

1978, Jan. 26 **Litho.** **Wmk. 372**
1342 A304 30s gold & multi .15 .15

Far Eastern University, 50th anniversary.

Sipa A305

Designs: Various positions of Sipa ball-game.

1978, Feb. 28 ***Perf. 12½***
1343 A305 5s bl & multi .15 .15
1344 A305 10s bl & multi .15 .15
1345 A305 40s bl & multi .15 .15
1346 A305 75s bl & multi .24 .15
a. Block, #1343-1346 .45 .35

No. 1346a has continuous design.

Arms of Meycauayan A306

1978, Apr. 21 **Litho.** ***Perf. 12½***
1347 A306 1.05p multicolored .22 .15

Meycauayan, founded 1578-1579.
For surcharge see No. 1560.

Moro Vinta and UPU Emblem — A307

2.50p, No. 1350b, Horse-drawn mail cart. No. 1350a, like 5p. No. 1350c, Steam locomotive. No. 1350d, Three-master.

1978, June 9 **Litho.** ***Perf. 13½***
1348 A307 2.50p multicolored .60 .40
1349 A307 5p multicolored 1.10 .80

Souvenir Sheet

Perf. 12½x13

1350 Sheet of 4 10.00
a.-d. A307 7.50p, any single 2.00 2.00

CAPEX International Philatelic Exhibition, Toronto, Ont., June 9-18. No. 1350 contains 36½x25mm stamps.

No. 1350 exists imperf. in changed colors.

Andres Bonifacio Monument, by Guillermo Tolentino — A308

Perf. 12½

1978, July 10 **Litho.** **Wmk. 372**
1351 A308 30s multicolored .15 .15

PILIPINAS 30s
KARPOV KORCHNOI
WORLD CHESS CHAMPIONSHIP BAGUIO CITY, PHILIPPINES · JULY 17 1978

Rook, Knight and Globe A309

1978, July 17
1352 A309 30s vio bl & red .15 .15
1353 A309 2p vio bl & red .42 .30
Set value .48 .35

World Chess Championship, Anatoly Karpov and Viktor Korchnoi, Baguio City, 1978.

Miners A310

1978, Aug. 12 **Litho.** ***Perf. 12½***
1354 A310 2.30p multicolored .45 .25

75th anniversary of Benguet gold mining industry.

Manuel Quezon and Quezon Memorial — A311

1978, Aug. 19
1355 A311 30s multicolored .15 .15
1356 A311 1p multicolored .22 .15
Set value .30 .15

Manuel Quezon (1878-1944), first president of Commonwealth of the Philippines.

Law Association Emblem, Philippine Flag — A312

1978, Aug. 27 **Litho.** ***Perf. 12½***
1357 A312 2.30p multicolored .45 .32

58th International Law Conference, Manila, Aug. 27-Sept. 2.

Pres. Sergio Osmeña (1878-1961) A313

1978, Sept. 8
1358 A313 30s multicolored .15 .15
1359 A313 1p multicolored .22 .15
Set value .30 .15

For surcharge see No. 1501.

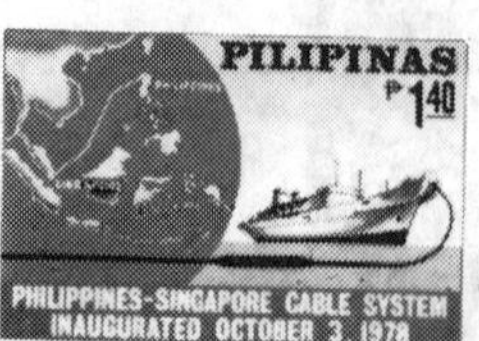

Map Showing Cable Route, Cablelaying Ship — A314

1978, Sept. 30
1360 A314 1.40p multicolored .30 .18

ASEAN Submarine Cable Network, Philippines-Singapore cable system, inauguration.

Basketball, Games' Emblem A315

1978, Oct. 1
1361 A315 30s multicolored .15 .15
1362 A315 2.30p multicolored .45 .32
Set value .36

8th Men's World Basketball Championship, Manila, Oct. 1-15.

San Lazaro Hospital and Dr. Catalino Gavino A316

1978, Oct. 13 **Litho.** ***Perf. 12½***
1363 A316 50s multicolored .15 .15
1364 A316 90s multicolored .20 .15
Set value .16

San Lazaro Hospital, 400th anniversary.
For surcharge see No. 1512.

Pilipinas 30s
SMALLPOX TARGET ZERO
GLOBAL ERADICATION OF SMALLPOX

Nurse Vaccinating Child — A317

1978, Oct. 24
1365 A317 30s multicolored .15 .15
1366 A317 1.50p multicolored .35 .20
Set value .42 .25

Eradication of smallpox.

No. 1268 Surcharged

1978 PHILATELIC WEEK
60s

1978, Nov. 23
1367 A273 60s on 65s lil rose .15 .15

Philatelic Week.

PHILIPPINE LONG DISTANCE TELEPHONE COMPANY
50th ANNIVERSARY
Pilipinas 30s ₱2.00
ACROSS THE COUNTRY AROUND THE WORLD

"The Telephone Across Country and World"
A318 A319

Perf. 12½

1978, Nov. 28 **Litho.** **Wmk. 372**
1368 A318 30s multicolored .15 .15
1369 A319 2p multicolored .42 .30
a. Pair, #1368-1369 .50 .40

Philippine Long Distance Telephone Company, 50th anniversary.

Traveling Family A320 DECADE OF THE FILIPINO CHILD

1978, Nov. 28

1370 A320	30s multicolored	.15	.15
1371 A320	1.35p multicolored	.32	.15
	Set value	.38	.16

Decade of Philippine children.
For surcharges see Nos. 1504, 1561.

Church and Arms of Agoo — A321

1978, Dec. 7 Litho. *Perf. 12½*

1372 A321	30s multicolored	.15	.15
1373 A321	45s multicolored	.15	.15
	Set value	.20	.15

400th anniversary of the founding of Agoo.

Church and Arms of Balayan A322

1978, Dec. 8

1374 A322	30s multicolored	.15	.15
1375 A322	90s multicolored	.22	.15
	Set value	.28	.15

400th anniv. of the founding of Balayan.

Dr. Honoria Acosta Sison (1888-1970), 1st Philippine Woman Physician — A323

1978, Dec. 15

1376 A323	30s multicolored	.15	.15

Family, Houses, UN Emblem A324

1978, Dec. Litho. *Perf. 12½*

1377 A324	30s multicolored	.15	.15
1378 A324	3p multicolored	.65	.40
	Set value		.45

30th anniversary of Universal Declaration of Human Rights.

Chaetodon Trifasciatus — A325

Fish: 1.20p, Balistoides niger. 2.20p, Rhinecanthus aculeatus. 2.30p, Chelmon rostratus. No. 1383, Chaetodon mertensi. No. 1384, Euxiphipops xanthometapon.

1978, Dec. 29 *Perf. 14*

1379 A325	30s multi	.15	.15
1380 A325	1.20p multi	.25	.15
1381 A325	2.20p multi	.42	.22
1382 A325	2.30p multi	.45	.25
1383 A325	5p multi	1.00	.55
1384 A325	5p multi	1.00	.55
	Nos. 1379-1384 (6)	3.27	1.87

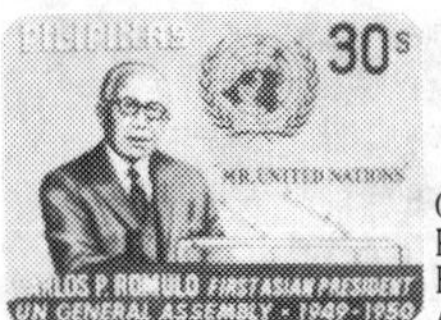

Carlos P. Romulo, UN Emblem A326

1979, Jan. 14 Litho. *Perf. 12½*

1385 A326	30s multi	.15	.15
1386 A326	2p multi	.50	.25
	Set value		.30

Carlos P. Romulo (1899-1985), pres. of UN General Assembly and Security Council.

Rotary Emblem and "60" A327

Rosa Sevilla de Alvero A328

1979, Jan. 26 **Wmk. 372**

1387 A327	30s multi	.15	.15
1388 A327	2.30p multi	.55	.22
	Set value		.26

Rotary Club of Manila, 60th anniversary.

1979, Mar. 4 Litho. *Perf. 12½*

1389 A328	30 rose	.15	.15

Rosa Sevilla de Alvero, educator and writer, birth centenary.
For surcharges see Nos. 1479-1482.

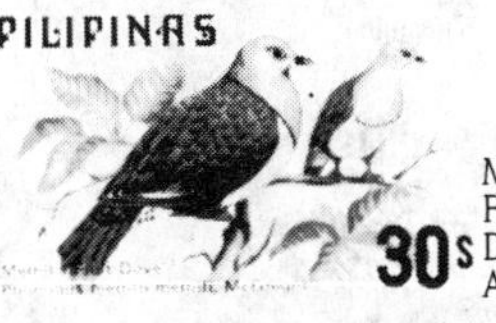

Oil Well and Map of Palawan A329

Perf. 12½

1979, Mar. 21 Litho. **Wmk. 372**

1390 A329	30s multi	.15	.15
1391 A329	45s multi	.15	.15
	Set value	.20	.15

First Philippine oil production, Nido Oil Reef Complex, Palawan.

Merrill's Fruit Doves A330

Birds: 1.20p, Brown tit babbler. 2.20p, Mindoro imperial pigeons. 2.30p, Steere's pittas. No. 1396, Koch's and red-breasted pittas. No. 1397, Philippine eared nightjar.

Perf. 14x13½

1979, Apr. 16 **Unwmk.**

1392 A330	30s multi	.15	.15
1393 A330	1.20p multi	.25	.15
1394 A330	2.20p multi	.42	.22
1395 A330	2.30p multi	.45	.25
1396 A330	5p multi	1.00	.55
1397 A330	5p multi	1.00	.55
	Nos. 1392-1397 (6)	3.27	1.87

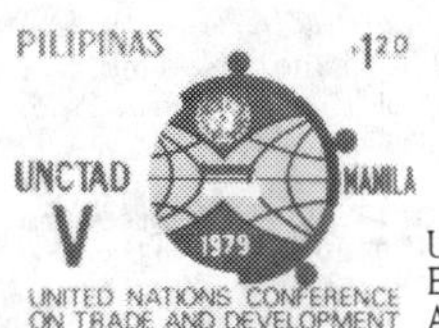

Association Emblem and Reader A331

Perf. 12½

1979, Apr. 3 Litho. **Wmk. 372**

1398 A331	30s multi	.15	.15
1399 A331	75s multi	.15	.15
1400 A331	1p multi	.22	.15
	Set value	.44	.20

Association of Special Libraries of the Philippines, 25th anniversary.

UNCTAD Emblem A332

Perf. 12½

1979, May 3 Litho. **Wmk. 372**

1401 A332	1.20p multi	.22	.15
1402 A332	2.30p multi	.50	.20

5th Session of United Nations Conference on Trade and Development, Manila, May 3-June 1.

Civet Cat A333

Philippine Animals: 1.20p, Macaque. 2.20p, Wild boar. 2.30p, Dwarf leopard. No. 1407, Asiatic dwarf otter. No. 1408, Anteater.

1979, May 14 *Perf. 14*

1403 A333	30s multi	.15	.15
1404 A333	1.20p multi	.25	.15
1405 A333	2.20p multi	.42	.22
1406 A333	2.30p multi	.45	.25
1407 A333	5p multi	1.00	.55
1408 A333	5p multi	1.00	.55
	Nos. 1403-1408 (6)	3.27	1.87

Dish Antenna — A334

1979, May 17 *Perf. 12½*

1409 A334	90s shown	.18	.15
1410 A334	1.30p World map	.24	.15
	Set value		.16

11th World Telecommunications Day, May 17.

Mussaenda Donna Evangelina — A335

Philippine Mussaendas: 1.20p, Dona Esperanza. 2.20p, Dona Hilaria. 2.30p, Dona Aurora. No. 1415, Gining Imelda. No. 1416, Dona Trining.

1979, June 11 Litho. *Perf. 14*

1411 A335	30s multi	.15	.15
1412 A335	1.20p multi	.15	.15
1413 A335	2.20p multi	.42	.22
1414 A335	2.30p multi	.45	.25
1415 A335	5p multi	1.00	.55
1416 A335	5p multi	1.00	.55
	Nos. 1411-1416 (6)	3.17	1.87

Manila Cathedral, Coat of Arms — A336

1979, June 25 *Perf. 12½*

1417 A336	30s multi	.15	.15
1418 A336	75s multi	.15	.15
1419 A336	90s multi	.20	.15
	Set value	.42	.22

Archdiocese of Manila, 400th anniversary.

Patrol Boat, Naval Arms — A337

1979, June 26

1420 A337	30s multi	.15	.15
1421 A337	45s multi	.15	.15
	Set value	.16	.15

Philippine Navy Day.

Man Breaking Chains, Broken Syringe — A338

1979, July 23 Litho. *Perf. 12½*

1422 A338	30s multi	.15	.15
1423 A338	90s multi	.20	.15
1424 A338	1.05p multi	.24	.15
	Set value	.50	.26

Fight drug abuse.
For surcharge see No. 1513.

Afghan Hound A339

Designs: 90s, Striped tabbies. 1.20p, Dobermann pinscher. 2.20p, Siamese cats. 2.30p, German shepherd. 5p, Chinchilla cats.

1979, Aug. 6 *Perf. 14*

1425 A339	30s multi	.15	.15
1426 A339	90s multi	.20	.15
1427 A339	1.20p multi	.24	.15
1428 A339	2.20p multi	.45	.15
1429 A339	2.30p multi	.50	.42
1430 A339	5p multi	1.00	.50
	Nos. 1425-1430 (6)	2.54	1.52

Children Playing IYC Emblem A340

Designs: Children playing and IYC emblem, diff.

1979, Aug. 31 Litho. *Perf. 12½*

1431 A340	15s multi	.15	.15
1432 A340	20s multi	.15	.15
1433 A340	25s multi	.15	.15
1434 A340	1.20p multi	.20	.15
	Set value	.40	.25

International Year of the Child.

Hands Holding Emblem — A341

1979, Sept. 27 Litho. *Perf. 12½*

1435	A341	30s multi	.15	.15
1436	A341	1.35p multi	.25	.15
		Set value	.32	.15

Methodism in the Philippines, 80th anniversary.

Emblem and Coins A342

Perf. 12½

1979, Nov. 15 Litho. Wmk. 372

1437	A342	30s multi	.15	.15

Philippine Numismatic and Antiquarian Society, 50th anniversary.

Concorde over Manila and Paris A343

Design: 2.20p, Concorde over Manila.

1979, Nov. 22

1438	A343	1.05p multi	.20	.15
1439	A343	2.20p multi	.45	.32

Air France service to Manila, 25th anniversary.

No. 1272 Surcharged in Red

1979, Nov. 23

1440	A273	90s on 1.60 blk	.20	.15

Philatelic Week. Surcharge similar to No. 1367.

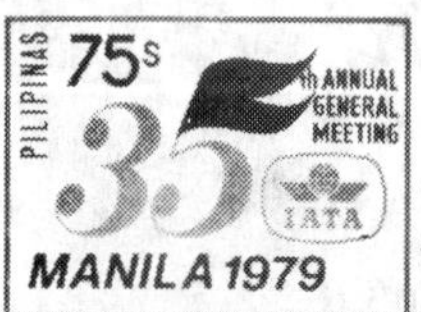
Transport Association Emblem A344

1979, Nov. 27

1441	A344	75s multi	.18	.15
1442	A344	2.30p multi	.48	.35

International Air Transport Association, 35th annual general meeting, Manila.

Local Government Year A345

Mother and Children, Ornament A346

1979, Dec. 14 Litho. *Perf. 12½*

1443	A345	30s multi	.15	.15
1444	A345	45s multi	.15	.15
		Set value	.20	.15

1979, Dec. 17

1445	A346	30s shown	.15	.15
1446	A346	90s Stars	.24	.15
		Set value	.32	.20

Christmas. For surcharge see No. 1515.

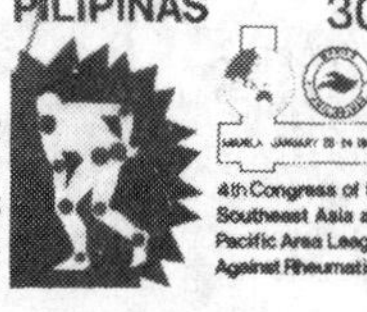
Rheumatic Pain Spots and Congress Emblem A347

Perf. 12½

1980, Jan. 20 Litho. Wmk. 372

1447	A347	30s multi	.15	.15
1448	A347	90s multi	.32	.15
		Set value		.20

Southeast Asia and Pacific Area League Against Rheumatism, 4th Congress, Manila, Jan. 19-24.

Gen. Douglas MacArthur — A348

30s, MacArthur's birthplace (Little Rock, AR) & burial place (Norfolk, VA). 2.30p, MacArthur's cap, Sunglasses & pipe. 5p, MacArthur & troops wading ashore at Leyte, Oct. 20, 1944.

1980, Jan. 26 Wmk. 372 *Perf. 12½*

1449	A348	30s multi	.15	.15
1450	A348	75s multi	.22	.15
1451	A348	2.30p multi	.70	.50
		Nos. 1449-1451 (3)	1.07	
		Set value		.66

Souvenir Sheet

Imperf

1452	A348	5p multi	1.90	1.00

Gen. Douglas MacArthur (1880-1964).
For overprint see No. 2198.

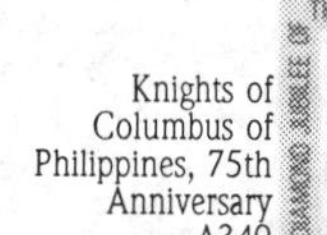
Knights of Columbus of Philippines, 75th Anniversary A349

1980, Feb. 14

1453	A349	30s multi	.15	.15
1454	A349	1.35p multi	.48	.28
		Set value		.32

Philippine Military Academy, 75th Anniversary A350

Perf. 12½

1980, Feb. 17 Litho. Wmk. 372

1455	A350	30s multi	.15	.15
1456	A350	1.20p multi	.42	.20
		Set value		.25

Philippines Women's University, 75th Anniversary — A351

1980, Feb. 21

1457	A351	30s multi	.15	.15
1458	A351	1.05p multi	.38	.18
		Set value		.22

Disaster Relief A352

Rotary International, 75th Anniversary (Paintings by Carlos Botong Francisco): Nos. 1459 and 1460 each in continuous design.

1980, Feb. 23 *Perf. 12½*

1459		Strip of 5	.60	.28
a.	A352	30s single stamp	.15	.15
1460		Strip of 5	4.00	1.90
a.	A352	2.30p single stamp	.80	.38

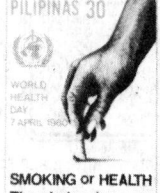

A353

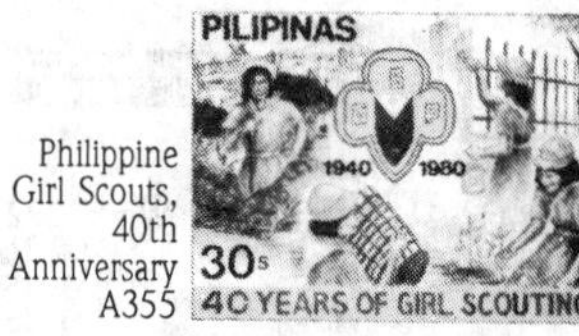
A354

Perf. 12½

1980, Mar. 28 Litho. Wmk. 372

1461	A353	30s multi	.15	.15
1462	A353	1.30p multi	.45	.20
		Set value		.25

6th centenary of Islam in Philippines.

1980, Apr. 14

Hand crushing cigarette, WHO emblem.

1463	A354	30s multi	.15	.15
1464	A354	75s multi	.24	.15
		Set value		.18

World Health Day (Apr. 17); anti-smoking campaign.

Philippine Girl Scouts, 40th Anniversary A355

Perf. 12½

1980, May 26 Litho. Wmk. 372

1465	A355	30s multi	.15	.15
1466	A355	2p multi	.38	.18
		Set value		.22

Jeepney (Public Jeep) — A356

1980, June 24 Litho. *Perf. 12½*

1467	A356	30s Jeepney, diff.	.15	.15
1468	A356	1.20p shown	.40	.20
		Set value		.25

For surcharge see No. 1503.

Nos. 1272, 1206 Surcharged in Red

Wmk. 372 (1.35p)

1980, Aug. 1 Litho. *Perf. 12½*

1469	A273	1.35p on 1.60p blk	.52	.26
1470	A250	1.50p on 1.80p grn	.60	.30

Independence, 82nd Anniversary.

Association Emblem — A357

1980, Aug. 1 Wmk. 372

1471	A357	30s multi	.15	.15
1472	A357	2.30p multi	.80	.75

International Association of Universities, 7th General Conference, Manila, Aug. 25-30.

Congress Emblem, Map of Philippines A358

Perf. 12½

1980, Aug. 18 Litho. Wmk. 372

1473	A358	30s lt grn & blk	.15	.15
1474	A358	75s lt bl & blk	.28	.16
1475	A358	2.30p sal & blk	.90	.48
		Nos. 1473-1475 (3)	1.33	.79

Intl. Federation of Library Associations and Institutions, 46th Congress, Manila, Aug. 18-23.

Kabataang Barangay (New Society), 5th Anniversary — A359

1980, Sept. 19 Litho. *Perf. 12½*

1476	A359	30s multi	.15	.15
1477	A359	40s multi	.15	.15
1478	A359	1p multi	.38	.20
		Nos. 1476-1478 (3)	.68	
		Set value		.32

Nos. 1389, 1422, 1443, 1445, 1327 Surcharged in Blue, Black or Red

Perf. 12½

1980, Sept. 26 Litho. Wmk. 372

1479	A328	40s on 30s rose (Bl)	.16	.15
1480	A338	40s on 30s multi	.16	.15
1481	A345	40s on 30s multi	.16	.15
1482	A346	40s on 30s multi (R)	.16	.15
1483	A294	2p on 1.65p multi (R)	.80	.40
		Nos. 1479-1483 (5)	1.44	
		Set value		.68

Catamaran, Conference Emblem A360

1980, Sept. 27

1484	A360	30s multi	.15	.15
1485	A360	2.30p multi	.85	.52
		Set value		.58

World Tourism Conf., Manila, Sept. 27.

Stamp Day — A361

UN, 35th Anniv. — A362

1980, Oct. 9

1486	A361	40s multi	.16	.15
1487	A361	1p multi	.40	.20
1488	A361	2p multi	.80	.40
		Set value		.66

1980, Oct. 20

Designs: 40s, UN Headquarters and Emblem, Flag of Philippines. 3.20p, UN and Philippine flags, UN headquarters.

1489 A362 40s multi .16 .15
1490 A362 3.20p multi 1.25 .85

Murex Alabaster A363

1980, Nov. 2

1491 A363 40s *shown* .16 .15
1492 A363 60s *Bursa bubo* .22 .15
1493 A363 1.20p *Homalocantha zamboi* .42 .20
1494 A363 2p *Xenophora pallidula* .80 .38
Nos. 1491-1494 (4) 1.60 .88

INTERPOL Emblem on Globe — A364

1980, Nov. 5 Litho. Wmk. 372

1495 A364 40s multi .16 .15
1496 A364 1p multi .40 .18
1497 A364 3.20p multi 1.25 .85
Nos. 1495-1497 (3) 1.81 1.18

49th General Assembly Session of INTERPOL (Intl. Police Organization), Manila, Nov. 13-21.

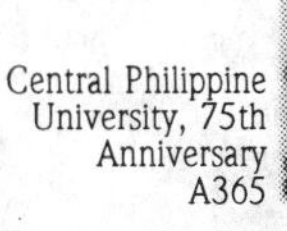

Central Philippine University, 75th Anniversary A365

1980, Nov. 17 Unwmk.

1498 A365 40s multi .15 .15
1499 A365 3.20p multi 1.25 .80

No. 1257 Surcharged

Perf. 12½

1980, Nov. 21 Litho. Wmk. 372

1500 A269 1.20p on 80s multi .42 .20

Philatelic Week. Surcharge similar to No. 1367.

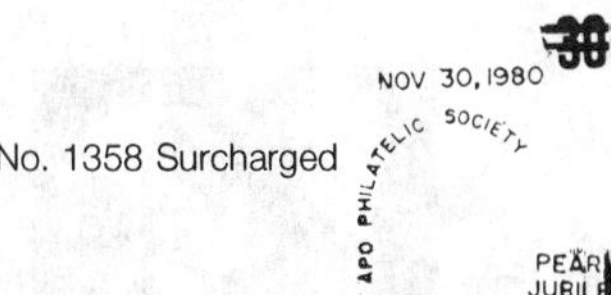

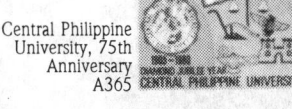

No. 1358 Surcharged

1980, Nov. 30

1501 A313 40s on 30s multi .16 .15

APO Philatelic Society, 30th anniversary.

Christmas Tree, Present and Candy Cane — A366

Perf. 12½

1980, Dec. 15 Litho. Unwmk.

1502 A366 40s multi .16 .15

Christmas 1980.

No. 1467 Surcharged

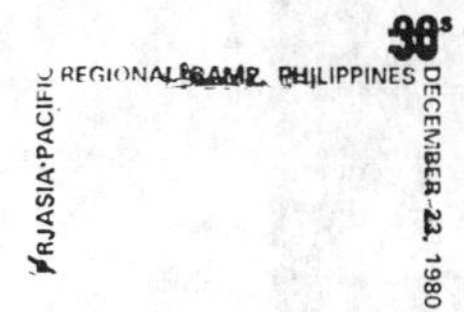

1981, Jan. 2

1503 A356 40c on 30s multi .16 .15

Nos. 1370, 1257 Surcharged in Red or Black

1981

1504 A320 10s on 30s (R) multi .15 .15
1505 A269 85s on 80s multi .32 .16
Set value .36 .20

Issue dates: 10s, Jan. 12; 85s, Jan. 2.

Heinrich Von Stephan, UPU Emblem — A367

1981, Jan. 30

1506 A367 3.20p multi 1.25 .60

Heinrich von Stephan (1831-1897), founder of UPU, birth sesquicentennial.

Pope John Paul II Greeting Crowd — A368

Designs: 90s, Pope, signature, vert. 1.20p, Pope, cardinals, vert. 3p, Pope giving blessing, Vatican arms, Manila Cathedral. 7.50p, Pope, light on map of Philippines, vert.

Perf. 13½x14

1981, Feb. 17 Unwmk.

1507 A368 90s multi .35 .16
1508 A368 1.20p multi .45 .22
1509 A368 2.30p multi .90 .42
1510 A368 3p multi 1.10 .55
Nos. 1507-1510 (4) 2.80 1.35

Souvenir Sheet

1511 A368 7.50p multi 3.00 1.40

Visit of Pope John Paul, Feb. 17-22.

Nos. 1364, 1423, 1268, 1446, 1261, 1206, 1327 Surcharged

1981 Litho. *Perf. 12½*

1512 A316 40s on 90s multi .16 .15
1513 A338 40s on 90s multi .16 .15
1514 A273 40s on 65s lil rose .16 .15
1515 A346 40s on 90s multi .16 .15
1517 A271 1p on 1.50p brt rose & vio bl .42 .18
1518 A250 1.20p on 1.80p grn .45 .22
1519 A294 1.20p on 1.65p multi .45 .22
1520 A271 2p on 1.50p brt rose & vio bl .85 .35
Nos. 1512-1520 (8) 2.81
Set value 1.25

A369

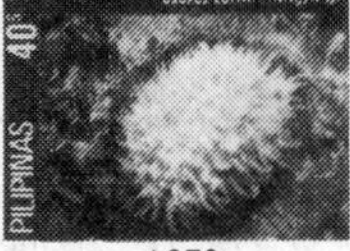

A370

1981, Apr. 20 Wmk. 372

1521 A369 2p multi .80 .38
1522 A369 3.20p multi 1.25 .65

68th Spring Meeting of the Inter-Parliamentary Union, Manila, Apr. 20-25.

Unless otherwise stated, all issues on granite paper.

Perf. 12½

1981, May 22 Litho. Wmk. 372

1523 A370 40s Bubble coral .16 .15
1524 A370 40s Branching coral .16 .15
1525 A370 40s Brain coral .16 .15
1526 A370 40s Table coral .16 .15
a. Block of 4, #1523-1526 .65 .40
Set value .28

Philippine Motor Assoc., 50th Anniv. — A371

Vintage cars.

1981, May 25

1527 A371 40s Presidents car .16 .15
1528 A371 40s 1930 .16 .15
1529 A371 40s 1937 .16 .15
1530 A371 40s shown .16 .15
a. Block of 4, #1527-1530 .65 .40
Set value .28

Re-inauguration of Pres. Ferdinand E. Marcos — A372

1981, June 30

1531 A372 40s multi .16 .15

Souvenir Sheet

Imperf

1532 A372 5p multi 1.90 .90

No. 1531 exists imperf.
For overprint see No. 1753.

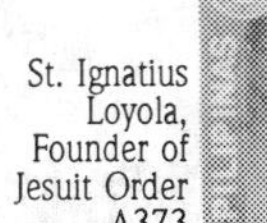

St. Ignatius Loyola, Founder of Jesuit Order A373

400th Anniv. of Jesuits in Philippines: No. 1534, Jose Rizal, Ateneo University. No. 1535, Father Federico Faura, Manila Observatory. No. 1536, Father Saturnino Urios, map of Philippines.

1981, July 31

1533 A373 40s multi .16 .15
1534 A373 40s multi .16 .15
1535 A373 40s multi .16 .15
1536 A373 40s multi .16 .15
Nos. 1533-1536 (4) .64
Set value .28

Souvenir Sheet

Imperf

1537 A373 2p multi .90 .35

No. 1537 contains vignettes of Nos. 1533-1536.
For surcharge see No. 1737.

A374

A375

Design: 40s, Isabelo de los Reyes (1867-1938), labor union founder. 1p, Gen. Gregorio del Pilar (1875-1899). No. 1540, Magsaysay. No. 1541, Francisco Dagohoy. No. 1543, Ambrosia R. Bautista, signer of Declaration of Independence, 1898, No. 1544, Juan Sumulong (1875-1942), statesman. 2.30p, Nicanor Abelardo (1893-1934), composer. 3.20p, Gen. Vicente Lim (1888-1945), first Philippine graduate of West Point.

Perf. 12½

1981-82 Litho. Wmk. 372

1538 A374 40s grnsh bl ('82) .16 .15
1539 A374 1p blk & red brn .42 .18
1540 A374 1.20p blk & lt red brn .45 .22
1541 A374 1.20p brown ('82) .45 .22
1543 A374 2p blk & red brn .85 .35
1544 A374 2p rose lil ('82) .85 .35
1545 A374 2.30p lt red brn ('82) .90 .38
1546 A374 3.20p gray bl ('82) 1.25 .65
Nos. 1538-1546 (8) 5.33 2.50

See Nos. 1672-1680, 1682-1683, 1685. For surcharges see Nos. 1668-1669.

1981, Sept. 2

1551 A375 40s multi .16 .15

Chief Justice Fred Ruiz Castro, 67th birth anniv.

A376

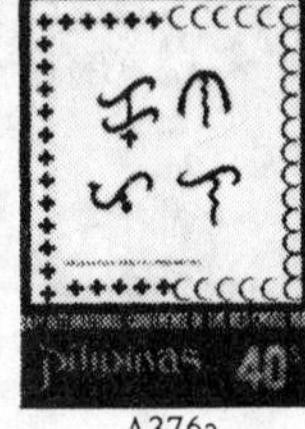

A376a

Perf. 12½

1981, Oct. 24 Litho. Wmk. 372

1552 A376 40s multi .16 .15
1553 A376 3.20p multi 1.25 .65

Intl. Year of the Disabled.

1981, Nov. 7

1554 A376a 40s multi .15 .15
1555 A376a 2p multi .80 .35
1556 A376a 3.20p multi 1.20 .60
Nos. 1554-1556 (3) 2.15 1.10

24th Intl. Red Cross Conf., Manila, Nov. 7-14.

Intramuros Gate, Manila — A377

1981, Nov. 13

1557 A377 40s black .16 .15

Manila Park Zoo Concert Series, Nov. 20-30 A378

1981, Nov. 20

1558 A378 40s multi .16 .15

No. 1329 Overprinted "1981 Philatelic Week" and Surcharged

Perf. 12½

1981, Nov. 23 Litho. Wmk. 372

1559 A296 1.20p on 1.50p multi .45 .22

Nos. 1205, 1347, 1371 Surcharged

1981, Nov. 25 Litho. *Perf. 12½*

1560 A306 40s on 1.05p multi .16 .15
1561 A320 40s on 1.35p multi .16 .15
1562 A273 1.20p on 1.50p brn .45 .22
Nos. 1560-1562 (3) .77
Set value .35

11th Southeast Asian Games, Manila, Dec. 6-15 — A379

1981, Dec. 3

1563 A379 40s Running .16 .15
1564 A379 1p Bicycling .45 .18
1565 A379 2p Pres. Marcos, Intl. Olympic Pres. Samaranch .90 .35
1566 A379 2.30p Soccer .90 .42
1567 A379 2.80p Shooting 1.10 .50
1568 A379 3.20p Bowling 1.25 .65
Nos. 1563-1568 (6) 4.76 2.25

Manila Intl. Film Festival, Jan. 18-29 A380

Perf. 12½

1982, Jan. 18 Litho. Wmk. 372

1569 A380 40s Film Center .16 .15
1570 A380 2p Golden trophy, vert. .90 .35
1571 A380 3.20p Trophy, diff., vert. 1.25 .65
Nos. 1569-1571 (3) 2.31 1.15

Manila Metropolitan Waterworks and Sewerage System Centenary A381

1982, Jan. 22

1572 A381 40s blue .16 .15
1573 A381 1.20p brown .45 .22
Set value .28

Nos. 1268, 1302, 1328 Surcharged

1982, Jan. 28

1574 A273 1p on 65s lil rose .45 .20
1575 A286 1p on 1.50p multi .45 .20
1576 A295 3.20p on 2.20p multi 1.25 .65
Nos. 1574-1576 (3) 2.15 1.05

Scouting Year — A382

1982, Feb. 22

1577 A382 40s Portrait .16 .15
1578 A382 2p Scout giving salute .90 .35
Set value .42

25th Anniv. of Children's Museum and Library Foundation A383

1982, Feb. 25

1579 A383 40s Mural .16 .15
1580 A383 1.20p Children playing .45 .22
Set value .28

77th Anniv. of Philippine Military Academy — A384

Perf. 12½

1982, Mar. 25 Litho. Wmk. 372

1581 A384 40s multi .16 .15
1582 A384 1p multi .45 .20
Set value .26

40th Bataan Day — A385

1982, Apr. 9

1583 A385 40s Soldier .16 .15
1584 A385 2p "Reunion for Peace" .90 .35
Set value .42

Souvenir Sheet

Imperf

1585 A385 3.20p Cannon, flag 1.25 .70

No. 1585 contains one 38x28mm stamp. No. 1585 comes on two different papers, the second being thicker with cream gum.

For surcharge see No. 2114.

10s

No. B27 Surcharged

1982 Photo. *Perf. 13½*

1586 SP14 10s on 6 + 5s multi .15 .15

A386

A387

1982, Apr. 28 Litho. *Perf. 12½*

1587 A386 1p rose pink .45 .20

Aurora Aragon Quezon (1888-1949), former First Lady. See No. 1684.

1982, May 1

1588 A387 40s Man holding award .16 .15
1589 A387 1.20p Award .45 .22
Set value .28

7th Towers Awards.

UN Conf. on Human Environment, 10th Anniv. A388

1982, June 5

1590 A388 40s Turtle .16 .15
1591 A388 3.20p Philippine eagle 1.25 .65

75th Anniv. of Univ. of Philippines College of Medicine A389

1982, June 10

1592 A389 40s multi .16 .15
1593 A389 3.20p multi 1.25 .65

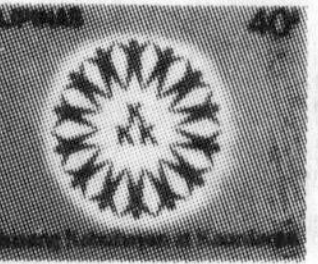

Natl. Livelihood Movement A390

1982, June 12

1594 A390 40s multi .16 .15

See #1681-1681A. For overprint see #1634.

Adamson Univ., 50th Anniv. — A391

1982, June 21

1595 A391 40s bl & multi .16 .15
1596 A391 1.20p lt vio & multi .45 .22
Set value .28

Social Security, 25th Anniv. — A392

Pres. Marcos, 65th Birthday — A393

1982, Sept. 1 *Perf. 13½x13*

1597 A392 40s multi .16 .15
1598 A392 1.20p multi .45 .22
Set value .28

1982, Sept. 11 *Perf. 13½x13*

1599 A393 40s sil & multi .16 .15
1600 A393 3.20p sil & multi 1.25 .65
a. Souv. sheet of 2, #1599-1600, imperf. 1.40 .70

For surcharge see No. 1666.

15th Anniv. of Assoc. of Southeast Asian Nations (ASEAN) — A394

1982, Sept. 22 Litho. *Perf. 12½*

1601 A394 40s Flags .16 .15

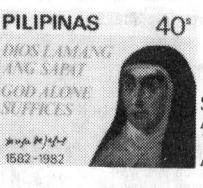

St. Teresa of Avila (1515-1582) A395

1982, Oct. 15 *Perf. 13x13½*

1602 A395 40s Text .16 .15
1603 A395 1.20p Map .45 .22
1604 A395 2p like #1603 .90 .35
Nos. 1602-1604 (3) 1.51 .72

10th Anniv. of Tenant Farmers' Emancipation Decree — A396

Perf. 13x13½

1982, Oct. 21 Litho. Wmk. 372

1605 A396 40s Pres. Marcos signing law .16 .15

See No. 1654.

350th Anniv. of St. Isabel College A397

1982, Oct. 22

1606 A397 40s multi .16 .15
1607 A397 1p multi .45 .20
Set value .26

Reading Campaign A398

1982, Nov. 4

1608 A398 40s yel & multi .16 .15
1609 A398 2.30p grn & multi .90 .38

For surcharge see No. 1713.

42nd Skal Club World Congress, Manila, Nov. 7-12 A399

1982, Nov. 7

1610 A399 40s Heads .16 .15
1611 A399 2p Chief .90 .35
Set value .42

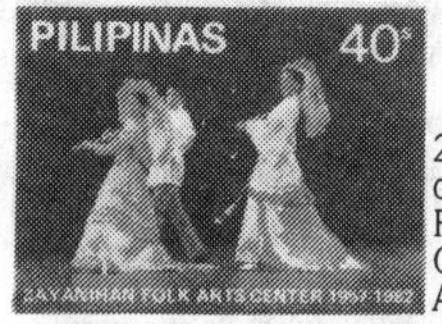

25th Anniv. of Bayanihan Folk Arts Center A400

Designs: Various folk dances.

1982, Nov. 10 Litho. *Perf. 13x13½*

1612 A400 40s multi .16 .15
1613 A400 2.80p multi 1.10 .50

TB Bacillus Centenary A401

1982, Dec. 7 Wmk. 372

1614 A401 40s multi .16 .15
1615 A401 2.80p multi 1.10 .50

Christmas 1982 A402

1982, Dec. 10

1616 A402 40s multi .16 .15
1617 A402 1p multi .45 .20
Set value .26

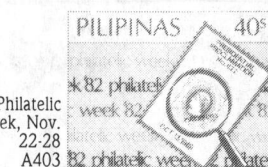

Philatelic Week, Nov. 22-28 A403

Perf. 13x13½

1982, Nov. 28 Litho. Wmk. 372

1618 A403 40s yel & multi .16 .15
1619 A403 1p sil & multi .45 .20
Set value .26

For surcharge see No. 1667.

Visit of Pres. Marcos to the US, Sept. A404

1982, Dec. 18

1620 A404 40s multi .16 .15
1621 A404 3.20p multi 1.25 .60
a. Souv. sheet of 2, #1620-1621 1.50 .70

UN World Assembly on Aging, July 26-Aug. 6 A405

Senate Pres. Eulogio Rodriguez, Sr. (1883-1964) A406

1982, Dec. 24

1622 A405 1.20p Woman .45 .22
1623 A405 2p Man .90 .35

1983, Jan. 21

1624 A406 40s grn & multi .16 .15
1625 A406 1.20p org & multi .45 .22
Set value .28

1983 Manila Intl. Film Festival, Jan. 24-Feb. 4 — A407

1983, Jan. 24

1626 A407 40s blk & multi .16 .15
1627 A407 3.20p pink & multi 1.25 .60

Beatification of Lorenzo Ruiz (1981) A408

Perf. 13x13½

1983, Feb. 18 Litho. Wmk. 372

1628 A408 40s multi .16 .15
1629 A408 1.20p multi .45 .22

400th Anniv. of Local Printing Press A409

1983, Mar. 14

1630 A409 40s blk & grn .16 .15

Safety at Sea — A410

1983, Mar. 17 ***Perf. 13½x13***

1631 A410 40s multi .16 .15

25th anniv. of Inter-Governmental Maritime Consultation Org. Convention.

Intl. Org. of Supreme Audit Institutions, 11th Congress, Manila, Apr. 19-27 A411

Perf. 13x13½

1983, Apr. 8 Litho. Wmk. 372

1632 A411 40s Symbols .16 .15
1633 A411 2.80p Emblem 1.10 .50
a. Souv. sheet of 2, 1632-1633, imperf. 1.40 .65

No. 1633a comes on two papers: cream gum, normal watermark; white gum, watermark made up of smaller letters.

Type of 1982 Overprinted in Red: "7th BSP NATIONAL JAMBOREE 1983"

1983, Apr. 13 ***Perf. 12½***

1634 A390 40s multi .16 .15

Boy Scouts of Philippines jamboree.

No. 1249 Surcharged

1983, Apr. 15

1635 Block of 10 1.65 .70
a.-j. A265 40s on 45s, any single .16 .15

A412 A413

Perf. 13½x13

1983, May 9 Litho. Wmk. 372

1636 A412 40s multi .16 .15

75th anniv. of Dental Assoc.

Perf. 13½x13

1983, June 17 Litho. Wmk. 372

1637 A413 40s Statue .16 .15
1638 A413 1.20p Statue, diff., diamond .45 .22
Set value .28

75th anniv. of University of the Philippines.

Visit of Japanese Prime Minister Yasuhiro Nakasone, May 6-8 — A414

Perf. 13x13½

1983, June 20 Litho. Wmk. 372

1639 A414 40s multi .16 .15

25th Anniv. of Natl. Science and Technology Authority A415

1983, July 11

1640 A415 40s Animals, produce .16 .15
1641 A415 40s Heart, food, pill .16 .15
1642 A415 40s Factories, windmill, car .16 .15
1643 A415 40s Chemicals, house, book .16 .15
a. Block of 4, #1640-1643 .65 .35

Science Week.

World Communications Year — A416

Perf. 12½

1983, Oct. 24 Litho. Wmk. 372

1644 A416 3.20p multi 1.25 .60

Philippine Postal System Bicentennial A417

1983, Oct. 31

1645 A417 40s multi .16 .15

Christmas — A418

Star of the East and Festival Scene in continuous design.

1983, Nov. 15 Litho. ***Perf. 12½***

1646 Strip of 5 .80 .35
a.-e. A418 40s single stamp .16 .15
f. Souvenir sheet .80

Xavier University, 50th Anniv. A419

1983, Dec. 1 Litho. ***Perf. 14***

1647 A419 40s multi .16 .15
1648 A419 60s multi .24 .15
Set value .16

A420 A421

1983, Dec. 8 Litho. ***Perf. 12½***

1649 A420 40s brt ultra & multi .16 .15
1650 A420 60s gold & multi .24 .15
Set value .16

Ministry of Labor and Employment, golden jubilee.

1983, Dec. 7

1651 A421 40s multi .16 .15
1652 A421 60s multi .24 .15
Set value .16

50th anniv. of Women's Suffrage Movement.

Philatelic Week A422

Stamp Collecting: a, Cutting. b, Sorting. c, Soaking. d, Affixing hinges. e, Mounting stamp.

1983, Dec. 20

1653 Strip of 5 *2.50* .40
a.-e. A422 50s any single .25 .15

Emancipation Type of 1982

1983 Litho. ***Perf. 13***

Size: 32x22mm

1654 A396 40s multi .15 .15

Philippine Cockatoo — A423

Princess Tarhata Kiram — A424

1984, Jan. 9 Unwmk. ***Perf. 14***

1655 A423 40s shown .15 .15
1656 A423 2.30p Guaiabero .24 .15
1657 A423 2.80p Crimson-spotted racket-tailed parrots .28 .15
1658 A423 3.20p Large-billed parrot .32 .15
1659 A423 3.60p Tanygnathus sumatranus .35 .15
1660 A423 5p Hanging parakeets .50 .20
Nos. 1655-1660 (6) 1.84
Set value .72

1984, Jan. 16 Wmk. 372 ***Perf. 13***

1661 A424 3p grn & red .30 .15

Order of Virgin Mary, 300th Anniv. A425

Dona Concha Felix de Calderon A426

1984, Jan. 23 ***Perf. 13½x13***

1662 A425 40s blk & multi .15 .15
1663 A425 60s red & multi .15 .15
Set value .15 .15

1984, Feb. 9 ***Perf. 13***

1664 A426 60s blk & bl grn .15 .15
1665 A426 3.60p red & bl grn .35 .15
Set value .40 .18

Nos. 1546, 1599, 1618 Surcharged

1984, Feb. 20

1666 A393 60s on 40s (R) .15 .15
1667 A403 60s on 40s .15 .15
1668 A374 3.60p on 3.20p (R) .35 .15
Set value .46 .24

No. 1685 Surcharged

1985, Oct. 21 Litho. *Perf. 12½*

1669 A374 3.60p on 4.20p rose lil .28 .15

Portrait Type of 1981

Designs: No. 1672, Gen. Artemio Ricarte. No. 1673, Teodoro M. Kalaw. No. 1674, Pres. Carlos P. Garcia. No. 1675, Senator Quintin Paredes. No. 1676, Dr. Deogracias V. Villadolid (1896-1976), 1st director, Bureau of Fisheries. No. 1677, Santiago Fonacier (1885-1940), archbishop. No. 1678, 2p, Vicente Orestes Romualdez (1885-1970), lawyer. 3p, Francisco Dagohoy.

Types of 3p:
Type I - Medium size "PILIPINAS," large, heavy denomination.
Type II - Large "PILIPINAS," medium denomination.

Perf. 13, 12½ (2p), 12½x13 (3p)

1984-85 Litho.

1672 A374 60s blk & lt brn .15 .15
1673 A374 60s blk & pur .15 .15
1674 A374 60s black .15 .15
1675 A374 60s dull blue .15 .15
1676 A374 60s brn blk ('85) .15 .15
1677 A374 60s dk red ('85) .15 .15
1678 A374 60s cobalt blue ('85) .15 .15
1679 A374 2p brt rose ('85) .16 .15
1680 A374 3p pale brn, type I .25 .15
1680A A374 3p pale brn, type II .25 .15
Set value, Nos. 1672-1680A (10) 1.25 .70

Issued: #1672, 3/22; #1673, 3/31; #1674, 6/14; #1675, 9/12; #1676, 3/22; #1677, 5/21; #1678, 2p, 7/3; 3p, 9/7.

Types of 1982

1984

1681 A390 60s green & multi .15 .15
1681A A390 60s red & multi .15 .15
1682 A374 1.80p #1546 .18 .15
1683 A374 2.40p #1545 .25 .15
1684 A386 3.60p Quezon .35 .15
1685 A374 4.20p #1544 .40 .18
Nos. 1681-1685 (6) 1.48
Set value .60

Issued: 4.20p, 3/26; #1581A, 1984; others 5/5.

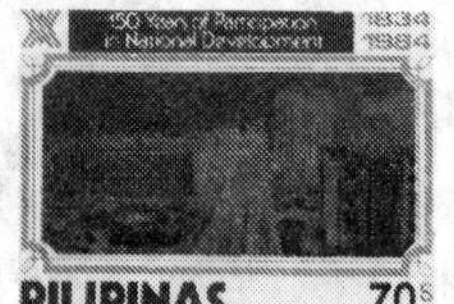

Ayala Corp. Sesquicentenary — A427

Night Views of Manila.

1984, Apr. 25 Litho. *Perf. 13x13½*

1686 A427 70s multi .15 .15
1687 A427 3.60p multi .35 .15
Set value .42 .18

ESPANA '84 — A428

Designs: 2.50p, No. 1690d, Our Lady of the Most Holy Rosary with St. Dominic, by C. Francisco. 5p, No. 1690a, Spoliarium, by Juan Luna. No. 1690b, Blessed Virgin of Manila as Patroness of Voyages, Galleon showing map of Panama-Manila. No. 1690c. Illustrations from The Monkey and the Turtle, by Rizal (first children's book published in Philippines, 1885.)

1984, Apr. 27 *Perf. 14*

1688 A428 2.50p multi .28 .15
1689 A428 5p multi .55 .25
a. Pair, #1688-1689 .85 .40

Souvenir Sheet

Perf. 14½x15, Imperf.

1690 Sheet of 4 3.50 1.55
a.-d. A428 7.50p, any single .85 .38

Maria Pax Mendoza Guazon — A429

1984, May 26 *Perf. 13*

1691 A429 60s brt blue & red .15 .15
1692 A429 65s brt blue, red & blk .15 .15
Set value .15 .15

Butterflies A430

1984, Aug. 2 Litho. *Perf. 14*

1693 A430 60s Adolias amlana .15 .15
1694 A430 2.40p Papilio daedalus .20 .15
1695 A430 3p Prothoe frankii semperi .25 .15
1696 A430 3.60p Troides magellanus .28 .15
1697 A430 4.20p Yoma sabina vasuki .35 .18
1698 A430 5p Chilasa idaeoides .40 .20
Nos. 1693-1698 (6) 1.63
Set value .78

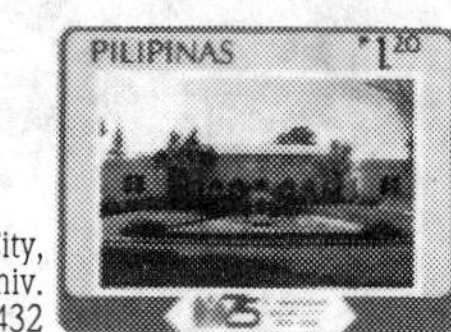

Baguio City, 75th Anniv. A432

1984, Aug. 24 Litho. *Perf. 12½*

1706 A432 1.20p The Mansion .15 .15

Light Rail Transit A433

1984, Sept. 10 *Perf. 13x13½*

1707 A433 1.20p multi .15 .15

A similar unlisted issue shows a streecar facing left on the 1.20p.

No. 1, Australia No. 59 and Koalas A434

1984, Sept. 21 *Perf. 14½x15*

1708 A434 3p multi .25 .15
1709 A434 3.60p multi .28 .15

Souvenir Sheet

1710 Sheet of 3 5.00 2.50
a. A434 20p multi 1.65 .80

AUSIPEX '84. No. 1710 exists imperf.

No. 1609 Surcharged with 2 Black Bars and Ovptd. "14-17 NOV. 84 / R.I. ASIA REGIONAL CONFERENCE"

1984, Nov. 11 Litho. *Perf. 13x13½*

1713 A398 1.20p on 2.30p multi .15 .15

Philatelic Week — A435

1984, Nov. 22 *Perf. 13½x13*

1714 A435 1.20p Gold medal .15 .15
1715 A435 3p Winning stamp exhibit .25 .15
a. Pair, #1714-1715 .40 .20

AUSIPEX '84 and Mario Que, 1st Philippine exhibitor to win FIP Gold Award.

Ships A436

1984, Nov. Litho. *Perf. 13½x13*

1718 A436 60s Caracao canoes .15 .15
1719 A436 1.20p Chinese junk .15 .15
1720 A436 6p Spanish galleon .50 .25
1721 A436 7.20p Casco .60 .30
1722 A436 8.40p Steamboat .70 .35
1723 A436 20p Cruise liner 1.65 .80
Nos. 1718-1723 (6) 3.75 2.00

Ateneo de Manila University, 125th Anniv. A438

1984, Dec. 7 Litho. *Perf. 13x13½*

1730 A438 60s ultra & gold .15 .15
1731 A438 1.20p dk ultra & sil .15 .15
Set value .16 .15

Christmas A439

Jaycees, Youth Development A440

1984, Dec. 8 *Perf. 13½x13*

1732 A439 60s Madonna and Child .15 .15
1733 A439 1.20p Holy family .15 .15
a. Pair, #1732-1733 .16 .15

1984, Dec. 19

Abstract painting by Raoul G. Isidro.

1734 Strip of 10 2.50 .85
a.-e. A440 60s, any single .15 .15
f.-j. A440 3p, any single .25 .15

Natl. Jaycees Awards, 25th anniv.

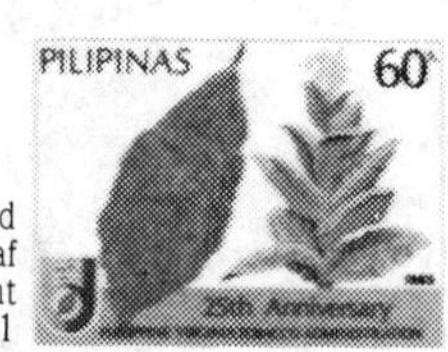

Dried Tobacco Leaf and Plant A441

1985, Jan. 14 *Perf. 13x13½*

1735 A441 60s multicolored .15 .15
1736 A441 3p multicolored .25 .15
Set value .30 .16

Philippine-Virginia Tobacco Admin., 25th anniv.

No. 1537 Surcharged

1985, Jan. Litho. *Imperf.*

1737 A373 3p on 2p multi .35 .15

Comes with missing period ("p300").

Natl. Research Council Emblem A442

1985, Feb. 3 Litho. *Perf. 13x13½*

1738 A442 60s bl, dk bl & blk .15 .15
1739 A442 1.20p org, dk bl & blk .18 .15
Set value .25 .15

Pacific Science Assoc., 5th intl. congress, Manila, Feb. 3-7.

Medicinal Plants A443

1985, Mar. 15 *Perf. 12½*

1740 A443 60s Carmona retusa .15 .15
1741 A443 1.20p Orthosiphon aristatus .15 .15
1742 A443 2.40p Vitex negundo .20 .15
1743 A443 3p Aloe barbadensis .25 .15
1744 A443 3.60p Quisqualis indica .28 .15
1745 A443 4.20p Blumea balsamifera .35 .18
Nos. 1740-1745 (6) 1.38
Set value .62

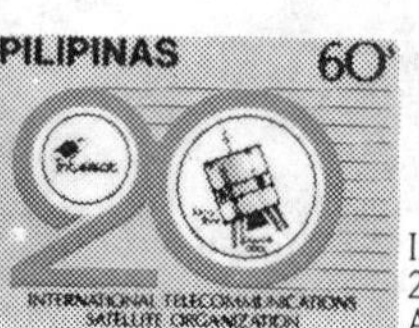

INTELSAT, 20th Anniv. A444

1985, Apr. 6 *Perf. 13x13½*

1746 A444 60s multicolored .15 .15
1747 A444 3p multicolored .25 .15
Set value .30 .16

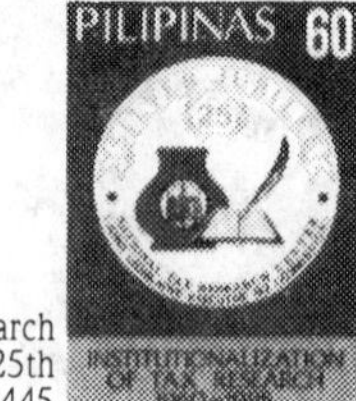

Tax Research Institute, 25th Anniv. — A445

1985, Apr. 22 *Perf. 13½x13*

1748 A445 60s multicolored .15 .15

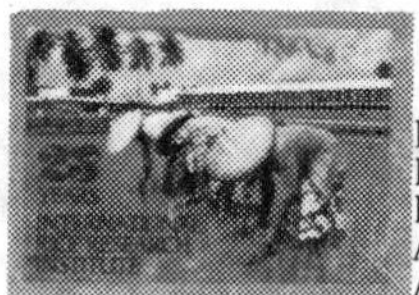

Intl. Rice Research Institute, 25th Anniv. A446

1985, May 27 *Perf. 13x13½*

1749 A446 60s Planting .15 .15
1750 A446 3p Paddies .15 .15
Set value .16 .15

1st Spain-Philippines Peace Treaty, 420th Anniv. — A447

Designs: 1.20p, Blessed Infant of Cebu, statue, shrine and basilica. 3.60p, King Tupas of Cebu and Miguel Lopez de Legaspi signing treaty, 1565.

1985, June 4 *Perf. 12½*

1751 A447 1.20p multi .15 .15
1752 A447 3.60p multi .28 .15
a. Pair, #1751-1752 + label .45 .45
Set value .18

No. 1532 Ovptd. "10th Anniversary Philippines and People's Republic of China Diplomatic Relations 1975-1985"

1985, June 8 *Imperf.*

1753 A372 5p multi .40 .20

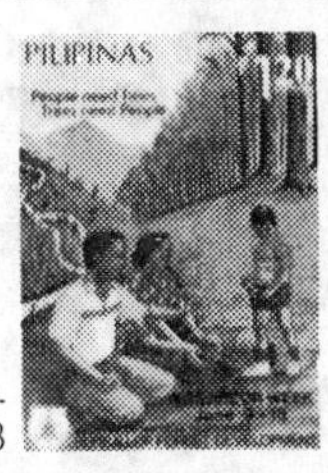

Arbor Week, June 9-15 — A448

1985, June 9 *Perf. 13½x13*
1754 A448 1.20p multi .15 .15

Battle of Bessang Pass, 40th Anniv. A449

1985, June 14 *Perf. 13x13½*
1755 A449 1.20p multi .15 .15

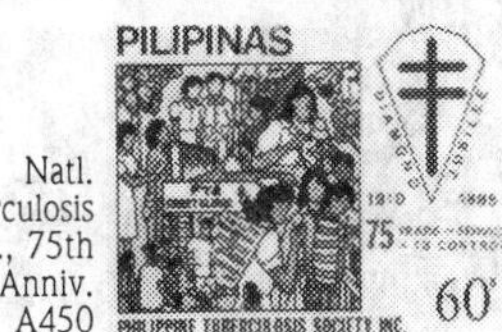

Natl. Tuberculosis Soc., 75th Anniv. A450

1985, July 29
1756 A450 60s Immunization, research .15 .15
1757 A450 1.20p Charity seal .15 .15
a. Pair, #1756-1757 .18 .16

No. 1297 Surcharged with Bars, New Value and Scout Emblem in Gold, Ovptd. "GSP" and "45th Anniversary Girl Scout Charter" in Black

Perf. 12½x13½

1985, Aug. 19 **Photo.**
1758 A242 2.40p on 15s on 10s .20 .15
1759 A242 4.20p on 15s on 10s .35 .18
1760 A242 7.20p on 15s on 10s .60 .30
Nos. 1758-1760 (3) 1.15 .63

Virgin Mary Birth Bimillennium A451

Statues and paintings.

1985, Sept. 8 **Litho.** *Perf. 13½x13*
1761 A451 1.20p Fatima .15 .15
1762 A451 2.40p Beaterio .20 .15
1763 A451 3p Penafrancia .25 .15
1764 A451 3.60p Guadalupe .30 .15
Nos. 1761-1764 (4) .90
Set value .40

Intl. Youth Year — A452

Prize-winning children's drawings.

1985, Sept. 23 *Perf. 13x13½*
1765 A452 2.40p Agriculture .20 .15
1766 A452 3.60p Education .30 .15
Set value .24

Girl and Rice Terraces A453

1985, Sept. 26
1767 A453 2.40p multi .20 .15

World Tourism Organization, 6th general assembly, Sofia, Bulgaria, Sept. 17-26.

Export Year — A454 UN, 40th Anniv. — A455

1985, Oct. 8 *Perf. 13½x13*
1768 A454 1.20p multi .15 .15

1985, Oct. 24
1769 A455 3.60p multi .30 .15

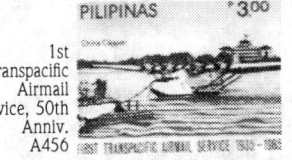

1st Transpacific Airmail Service, 50th Anniv. A456

1985, Nov. 22 *Perf. 13x13½*
1770 A456 3p China Clipper on water .25 .15
1771 A456 3.60p China Clipper, map .30 .15

Natl. Bible Week A457

1985, Dec. 3 *Perf. 12½*
1774 A457 60s multicolored .15 .15
1775 A457 3p multicolored .25 .15
Set value .30 .16

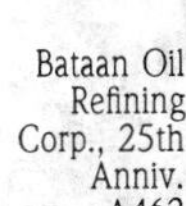

Christmas 1985 A458

1985, Dec. 8 *Perf. 13x13½*
1776 A458 60s Panuluyan .15 .15
1777 A458 3p Pagdalaw .25 .15
Set value .30 .16

Scales of Justice A459

1986, Jan. 12
1778 A459 60s lilac rose & blk .15 .15
1779 A459 3p brt grn, lil rose & blk .25 .15

University of the Philippines, College of Law, 75th anniv.

See No. 1838.

Flores de Heidelberg, by Jose Rizal — A460

Design: 60s, Noli Me Tangere.

1986 **Litho.** **Wmk.** *Perf. 13*
1780 A460 60s violet .15 .15
1781 A460 1.20p bluish grn .15 .15
1782 A460 3.60p redsh brn .28 .15
Set value .42 .24

Issue dates: 60s, 1.20p, Feb. 21. 3.60p, July 10.

For surcharges see Nos. 1834, 1913.

Philippine Airlines, 45th Anniv. — A461

Aircraft: No. 1783a, Douglas DC3, 1946. b, Douglas DC4 Skymaster, 1946. c, Douglas DC6, 1948. d, Vickers Viscount 784, 1957.

No. 1784a, Fokker Friendship F27 Mark 100, 1960. b, Douglas DC8 Series 50, 1962. c, Bac One Eleven Series 500, 1964. d, McDonnell Douglas DC10 Series 30, 1974.

No. 1785a, Beech Model 18, 1941. b, Boeing 747, 1980.

1986, Mar. 15 **Wmk.**
1783 Block of 4 .25 .20
a.-d. A461 60s, any single .15 .15
1784 Block of 4 .80 .40
a.-d. A461 2.40p, any single .20 .15
1785 Pair .60 .28
a.-b. A461 3.60p, any single .30 .15
Nos. 1783-1785 (3) 1.65 .88

See No. 1842.

Bataan Oil Refining Corp., 25th Anniv. A462

Perf. 13½x13, 13x13½

1986, Apr. 12 **Wmk.**
1786 A462 60s Refinery, vert. .15 .15
1787 A462 3p shown .25 .15
Set value .30 .16

EXPO '86, Vancouver A463

1986, May 2 **Wmk.** *Perf. 13x13½*
1788 A463 60s multicolored .15 .15
1789 A463 3p multicolored .25 .15
Set value .30 .16

Asian Productivity Organization, 25th Anniv. — A464

1986 **Wmk.**
1790 A464 60s multicolored .15 .15
1791 A464 3p multicolored .25 .15
Set value .30 .16

Wmk. *Perf. 13*
Size: 30x22mm
1792 A464 3p pale brown .25 .15

Issued: #1790-1791, May 15; #1792, July 10.

AMERIPEX '86 — A465 Election of Corazon Aquino, 7th Pres. — A466

1986, May 22 **Wmk.** *Perf. 13½x13*
1793 A465 60s No. 241 .15 .15
1794 A465 3p No. 390 .25 .15
Set value .30 .16

See No. 1835.

1986, May 25 **Wmk.**

Portrait of Aquino and: 60s, Salvador Laurel, vice-president, and hands in symbolic gestures of peace and freedom. 1.20p, Symbols of communication and transportation. 2.40p, Parade. 3p, Military. 7.20p, Vice-president, parade, horiz.

1795 A466 60s multi .15 .15
1796 A466 1.20p multi .15 .15
1797 A466 2.40p multi .16 .15
1798 A466 3p multi .20 .15
Set value .48 .28

Souvenir Sheet

Imperf

1799 A466 7.20p multi .45 .22

For surcharge see No. 1939.

De La Salle University, 75th Anniv. A467

60s, Statue of St. John the Baptist de la Salle, Paco buildings, 1911, & university, 1986. 2.40p, St. Miguel Febres Cordero, buildings, 1911. 3p, St. Benilde, buildings, 1986. 7.20p, Founding fathers.

1986, June 16 **Wmk.** *Perf. 13x13½*
1800 A467 60s grn, blk & pink .15 .15
1801 A467 2.40p grn, blk & bl .20 .15
1802 A467 3p grn, blk & yel .25 .15
Set value .50 .26

Souvenir Sheet

Imperf

1803 A467 7.20p grn & blk .55 .28

For surcharge see No. 1940.

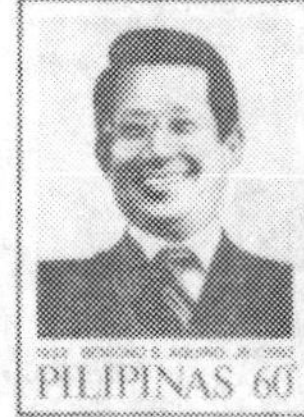

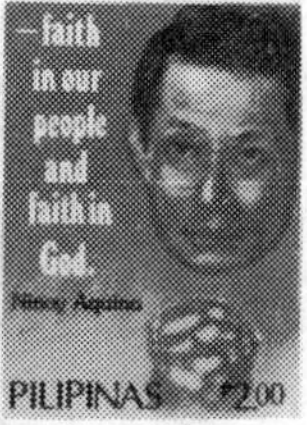

Memorial to Benigno S. Aquino, Jr. (1932-83)

A468 A469

Perf. 13½x13, 13x13½

1986, Aug. 21 **Wmk.**
1804 A468 60s dl bluish grn .15 .15
1805 A469 2p shown .16 .15
1806 A469 3.60p The Filipino is worth dying for, horiz. .30 .15
Set value .52 .26

Souvenir Sheet

Imperf

1807 A469 10p Hindi ka nag-iisa, horiz. .80 .40

See No. 1836. For surcharge see No. 1914.

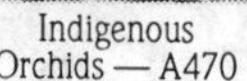

Indigenous Orchids — A470

Quiapo District, 400th Anniv. — A471

1986, Aug. 28 Wmk. *Perf. 13½x13*

1808 A470 60s Vanda sanderiana *.50* .15
1809 A470 1.20p Epigeneium lyonii *.85* .15
1810 A470 2.40p Paphiopedilum philippinense *1.65* .15
1811 A470 3p Amesiella philippinensis *2.00* .15
Nos. 1808-1811 (4) *5.00*
Set value .35

For surcharge see No. 1941.

Perf. 13½x13, 13x13½

1986, Aug. 29 Wmk.

60s, Our Lord Jesus the Nazarene, statue, Quiapo church. 3.60p, Quiapo church, 1930, horiz.

1812 A471 60s pink, blk & lake .15 .15
1813 A471 3.60p pale grn, blk & dk ultra .30 .15
Set value .36 .18

For surcharge see No. 1915.

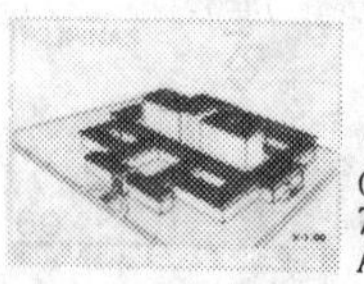

General Hospital, 75th Anniv. — A472

1986, Sept. 1 Wmk. *Perf. 13½x13*

1814 A472 60s bl & multi .15 .15
1815 A472 3p grn & multi .25 .15
Set value .30 .16

See No. 1841. For surcharge see No. 1888.

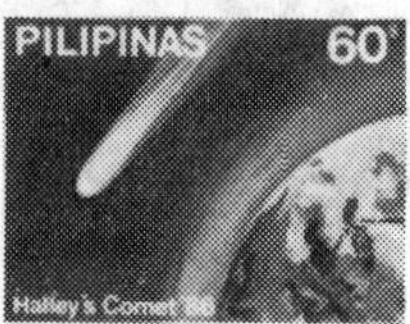

Halley's Comet A473

1986, Sept. 25 Wmk. *Perf. 13x13½*

1816 A473 60s Comet, Earth .15 .15
1817 A473 2.40p Comet, Earth, Moon .20 .15
Set value .26 .15

For surcharge see No. 1942.

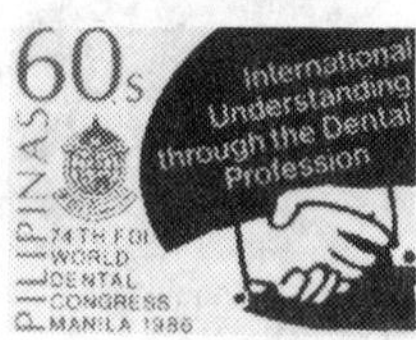

74th FDI World Dental Congress, Manila A474

Perf. 13x13½

1986, Nov. 10 Litho. Wmk.

1818 A474 60s Handshake .15 .15
1819 A474 3p Jeepney bus *5.00* .20
Set value .25

See Nos. 1837, 1840.

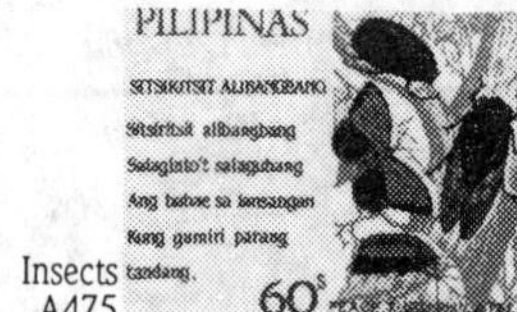

Insects A475

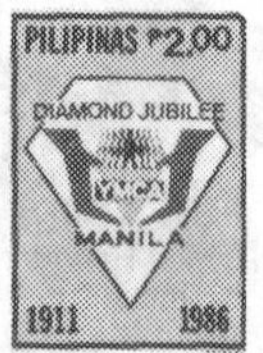

Intl. Peace Year — A476

Manila YMCA, 75th Anniv. — A477

Perf. 13x13½, 13½x13

1986, Nov. 21 Wmk.

1820 A475 60s Butterfly, beetles *.65* .15
1821 A476 1p blue & blk *1.10* .15
1822 A475 3p Dragonflies *3.25* .20
Nos. 1820-1822 (3) *5.00*
Set value .30

Philately Week.

1986, Nov. 28 Wmk. *Perf. 13x13½*

1823 A477 2p blue *1.50* .15
1824 A477 3.60p red *2.50* .20

See No. 1839. For surcharge see No. 1916.

Philippine Normal College, 85th Anniv. A478

Various arrangements of college crest and buildings, 1901-1986.

1986, Dec. 12 Wmk.

1825 A478 60s multi *2.75* .15
1826 A478 3.60p buff, ultra & gldn brn .42 .20
Set value .25

For surcharge see No. 1917.

Christmas A479

Perf. 13½x13, 13x13½

1986, Dec. 15 Wmk.

1827 A479 60s Holy family *.25* .15
1828 A479 60s Mother and child, doves *.25* .15
1829 A479 60s Child touching mother's face *.25* .15
1830 A479 1p Adoration of the shepherds *.45* .15
1831 A479 1p Mother, child signaling peace *.45* .15
1832 A479 1p Holy family, lamb *.45* .15
1833 A479 1p Mother, child blessing food *.45* .15
Nos. 1827-1833 (7) *2.55* 1.05
Set value .35

Nos. 1827-1829, vert.

No. 1780 Surcharged

1987, Jan. 6 Litho. Wmk. *Perf. 13*

1834 A460 1p on 60s vio .15 .15

Types of 1986

Designs: 75s, No. 390, AMERIPEX '86. 1p, Benigno S. Aquino, Jr. 3.25p, Handshake, 74th World Dental Congress. 3.50p, Scales of Justice. 4p, Manila YMCA emblem. 4.75p, Jeepney bus. 5p, General Hospital. 5.50p, Boeing 747, 1980.

4p
Type I - "4" is taller than "0's."
Type II - "4" is same height as "0's."

1987 Wmk. Litho. *Perf. 13*

Size: 22x31mm, 31x22mm

1835 A465 75s brt yel grn .15 .15
1836 A468 1p blue .15 .15
1837 A474 3.25p dull grn .40 .20
1838 A459 3.50p dark car .42 .20
1839 A477 4p blue, type I .45 .22
1839A A477 4p blue, type II *5.00* *.50*
1840 A474 4.75p dl yel grn .55 .28
1841 A472 5p olive bister .65 .32
1842 A461 5.50p dk bl gray .65 .32
Nos. 1835-1842 (9) *8.42* 2.34

All No. 1839A dated "1-1-87."
Issued: No. 1839A, 12/16/87; others, 1/16/87.

Manila Hotel, 75th Anniv. A480

1987, Jan. 30 Wmk. *Perf. 13x13½*

1843 A480 1p Hotel, c. 1912 .15 .15
1844 A480 4p Hotel, 1987 .45 .22
1845 A480 4.75p Lobby .55 .28
1846 A480 5.50p Foyer .65 .32
Nos. 1843-1846 (4) 1.80 .97

Intl. Eucharistic Congress, Manila, 50th Anniv. A481

Perf. 13½x13, 13x13½

1987, Feb. 7 Wmk.

1847 A481 75s Emblem, vert. .15 .15
1848 A481 1p shown .15 .15
Set value .20 .15

Pres. Aquino Taking Oath A482

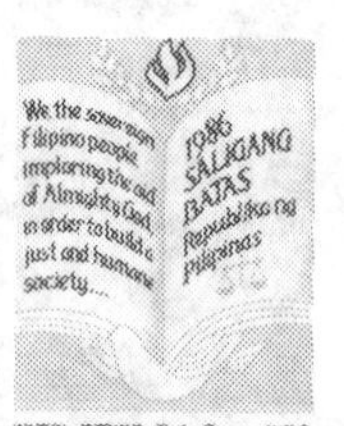

Text — A483

Perf. 13½x13, 13x13½

1987, Mar. 4 Wmk. 391

1849 A482 1p multi .15 .15
1850 A483 5.50p blue & deep bister .70 .35
Set value .40

Ratification of the new constitution.
See No. 1905. For surcharge see No. 2005.

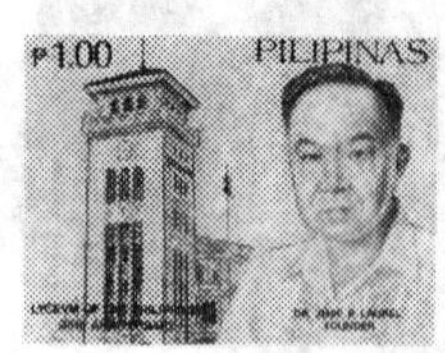

Lyceum College and Founder, Jose P. Laurel A484

Perf. 13x13½

1987, May 7 Litho. Wmk.

1851 A484 1p multi .15 .15
1852 A484 2p multi .16 .15
Set value .24 .15

Lyceum of the Philippines, 35th anniv.

Government Service Insurance System — A485

1987, June 1 *Perf. 13½x13*

1853 A485 1p Salary and policy loans .15 .15
1854 A485 1.25p Disability, medicare .16 .15
1855 A485 2p Retirement benefits .25 .15
1856 A485 3.50p Life insurance .42 .20
Nos. 1853-1856 (4) .98
Set value .45

Davao City, 50th Anniv. A486

Perf. 13x13½

1987, Mar. 16 Litho. Wmk.

1857 A486 1p Falconer, woman planting, city seal .15 .15

Salvation Army in the Philippines, 50th Anniv. — A487

Natl. League of Women Voters, 50th Anniv. — A488

Perf. 13½x13

1987, June 5 Photo. Wmk.

1858 A487 1p multi .15 .15

1987, July 15 Wmk.

1859 A488 1p pink & blue .15 .15

A489

A490

#1851, Gen. Vicente Lukban (1860-1916). #1862, Wenceslao Q. Vinzons (1910-1942). #1863, Brig.-gen. Mateo M. Capinpin (1887-1958). #1864, Jesus Balmori (1882-1948).

Perf. 13x13½, 12½ (#1862)

1987 Litho. Wmk.

1861 A489 1p olive grn .15 .15
1862 A489 1p dull greenish blue .15 .15
1863 A489 1p dull red brn .15 .15
1864 A489 1p rose red & rose claret .15 .15
Set value .36 .22

Issue dates: No. 1861, July 31. No. 1862, Sept. 9. No. 1863, Oct. 15. No. 1864, Dec. 17.
This is an expanding set. Numbers will change if necessary.

Perf. 13½x13

1987, July 22 Litho. Wmk.

Nuns (1862-1987), children, Crucifix, Sacred Heart.

1881 A490 1p multi .15 .15

Daughters of Charity of St. Vincent de Paul in the Philippines, 125th anniv.

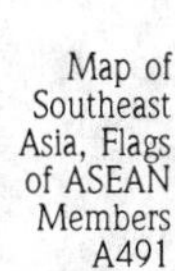

Map of Southeast Asia, Flags of ASEAN Members A491

1987, Aug. 7 Wmk. *Perf. 13x13½*

1882 A491 1p multi .15 .15

ASEAN, 20th anniv.

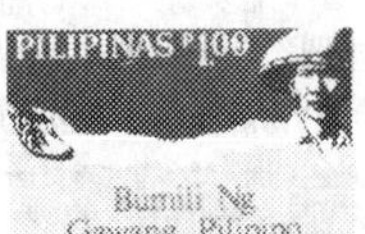

Exports Campaign A492

1987, Aug. 11 Wmk. *Perf. 13*

1883	A492	1p shown	.15	.15
1884	A492	2p Worker, gearwheel	.16	.15
		Set value	.24	.15

See No. 1904.

Canonization of Lorenzo Ruiz by Pope John Paul II, Oct. 18 — A493

First Filipino saint: 1p, Ruiz, stained glass window showing Crucifixion. 5.50p, Ruiz at prayer, execution in 1637.

Perf. 13½x13

1987, Oct. 10 Litho. Wmk. 389

1885	A493	1p multi	.15	.15
1886	A493	5.50p multi	.48	.25

Size: 57x57mm

Imperf

1887	A493	8p like 5.50p	.70	.35
		Set value		.65

No. 1887 has denomination at LL.

No. 1841 Surcharged **P4.75**

1987, Oct. 12 Wmk. *Perf. 13*

1888 A472 4.75p on 5p olive bis .40 .20

Order of the Good Shepherd Sisters in Philippines, 65th Anniv. A494

Perf. 13x13½

1987, Oct. 27 Wmk. 389

1889 A494 1p multi .15 .15

Natl. Boy Scout Movement, 50th Anniv. A495

Founders: J. Vargas, M. Camus, J.E.H. Stevenot, A.N. Luz, V. Lim, C. Romulo and G.A. Daza.

Perf. 13x13½

1987, Oct. 28 Litho. Wmk. 389

1890 A495 1p multi .15 .15

Philippine Philatelic Club, 50th Anniv. A496

1987, Nov. 7 *Perf. 13x13½*

1891 A496 1p multi .15 .15

Order of the Dominicans in the Philippines, 400th Anniv. A497

Designs: 1p, First missionaries shipwrecked, church and image of the Virgin, vert. 4.75p, J.A. Jeronimo Guerrero, Br., Diego de St. Maria and Letran Dominican College. 5.50p, Pope with Dominican representatives.

Perf. 13½x13, 13x13½

1987, Nov. 11

1892	A497	1p multi	.15	.15
1893	A497	4.75p multi	.40	.20
1894	A497	5.50p multi	.48	.25
		Nos. 1892-1894 (3)	1.03	
		Set value		.50

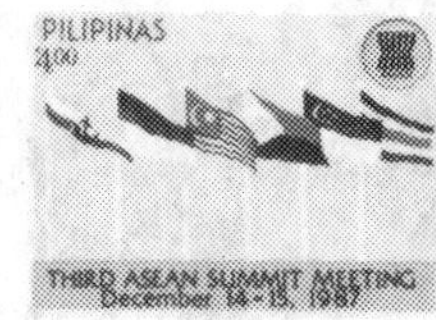

3rd ASEAN Summit Meeting, Dec. 14-15 A498

Perf. 13x13½

1987, Dec. 5 Wmk. 389

1895 A498 4p multi .32 .16

Christmas 1987 — A499

1987, Dec. 8 *Perf. 13½x13*

1896	A499	1p Postal service	.15	.15
1897	A499	1p 5-Pointed stars	.15	.15
1898	A499	4p Procession, church	.32	.16
1899	A499	4.75p Gift exchange	.38	.18
1900	A499	5.50p Bamboo cannons	.42	.20
1901	A499	8p Pig, holiday foods	.60	.32
1902	A499	9.50p Traditional foods	.75	.38
1903	A499	11p Serving meal	.85	.42
		Nos. 1896-1903 (8)	3.62	1.96

Exports Type of 1987

Design: Worker, gearwheel.

Wmk. 391

1987, Dec. 16 Litho. *Perf. 13*

1904 A492 4.75p lt blue & blk .38 .20

Constitution Ratification Type of 1987

1987, Dec. 16 Wmk. 391 *Perf. 13*

Size: 22x31½mm

1905 A483 5.50p brt yel grn & fawn .42 .20

Grand Masonic Lodge of the Philippines, 75th Anniv. A500

Perf. 13x13½

1987, Dec. 19 Wmk. 389

1906 A500 1p multi .15 .15

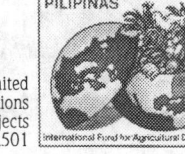

United Nations Projects A501

Designs: a, Intl. Fund for Agricultural Development (IFAD). b, Transport and Communications Decade for Asia and the Pacific. c, Intl. Year of Shelter for the Homeless (IYSH). d, World Health Day, 1987.

Perf. 13x13½

1987, Dec. 22 Litho. Wmk. 389

1907		Strip of 4 + label	*3.50*	.20
a.-d.	A501	1p, any single	.25	.15

Label pictures UN emblem.

7th Opening of Congress A502

Designs: 1p, Official seals of the Senate and Quezon City House of Representatives, gavel, vert. 5.50p, Congress in session.

Perf. 13½x13, 13x13½

1988, Jan. 25 Wmk. 389

1908	A502	1p multi	.15	.15
1909	A502	5.50p multi	.58	.30
		Set value		.36

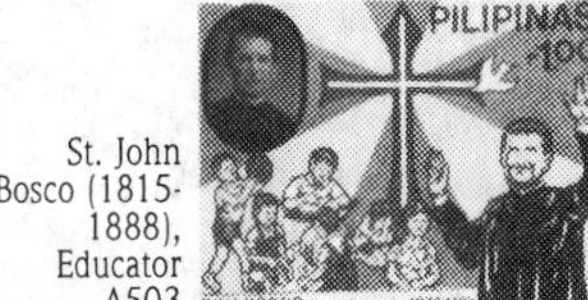

St. John Bosco (1815-1888), Educator A503

1988, Jan. 31 *Perf. 13x13½*

1910	A503	1p multi	.15	.15
1911	A503	5.50p multi	.58	.30
		Set value		.36

Buy Philippine Goods — A504

Perf. 13½x13

1988, Feb. 1 Litho. Wmk. 389

1912 A504 1p buff, ultra, blk & scar .15 .15

Nos. 1782, 1806, 1813, 1824, 1826 Surcharged

Wmk. (#1913, 1916) 389 (#1914, 1917), 391 (#1915)

Perf. 13 (#1782), 13x13½

1988, Feb. 14

1913	A460	3p on 3.60p redsh brn	.32	.16
1914	A469	3p on 3.60p multi	.32	.16
1915	A471	3p on 3.60p pale grn, blk & dark ultra	.32	.16
1916	A477	3p on 3.60p red	.32	.16
1917	A478	3p on 3.60p buff, ultra & golden brn	.32	.16
		Nos. 1913-1917 (5)	1.60	.80

Use Zip Codes — A505

1988, Feb. 25 Wmk. *Perf. 13*

1918	A505	60s multi	.22	.15
1919	A505	1p multi	.32	.15
		Set value		.15

Insects That Prey on Other Insects — A506

1988, Mar. 11 Wmk. 390 *Perf. 13*

1920	A506	1p Vesbius purpureus	*.35*	.15
1921	A506	5.50p Campsomeris aurulenta	*1.65*	.30
		Set value		.36

Solar Eclipse 1988 A507

Perf. 13x13½

1988, Mar. 18 Unwmk.

1922	A507	1p multi	*.35*	.15
1923	A507	5.50p multi	*1.65*	.30
		Set value		.36

Toribio M. Teodoro (1887-1965), Shoe Manufacturer A508

1988, Apr. 27 Litho. Wmk. *Perf. 13*

1924	A508	1p buff, dark olive bister & brt rose	.15	.15
1925	A508	1.20p pale blue grn, blk & scar	.15	.15
		Set value	.26	.15

A509 A510

College of the Holy Spirit, 75th anniv.: 1p, Emblem and motto "Truth in Love." 4p, Arnold Janssen, founder, and Sr. Edelwina, director 1920-1947.

Perf. 13½x13

1988, May 22 Unwmk.

1926	A509	1p blk, maroon & gold	.15	.15
1927	A509	4p blk, olive grn & maroon	.48	.24
		Set value		.30

Perf. 13½x13

1988, June 4 Litho. Unwmk.

1928 A510 4p dark ultra, brt blue & blk .42 .20

Intl. Conference of Newly Restored Democracies.

A511

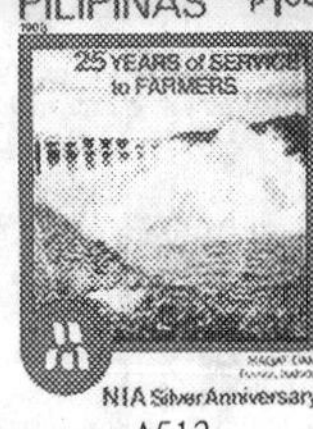

A512

Juan Luna and Felix Hidalgo.

1988, June 15 Wmk. *Perf. 13*

1929 A511	1p multi		.15	.15
1930 A511	5.50p multi		.45	.22
	Set value			.26

First Natl. Juan Luna and Felix Resurreccion Hidalgo Commemorative Exhibition, June 15-Aug. 15. Artists Luna and Hidalgo won medals at the 1884 Madrid Fine Arts Exhibition.

Perf. 13¹/₂x13

1988, June 22 Litho. Wmk. 372

1931 A512	1p multi	.15	.15
1932 A512	5.50p multi	.55	.28
	Set value		.32

Natl. Irrigation Administration, 25th anniv.

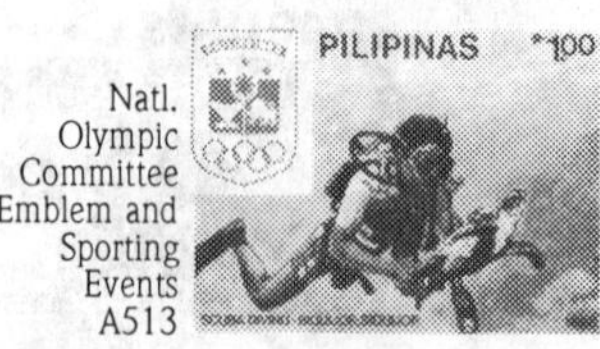

Natl. Olympic Committee Emblem and Sporting Events A513

Designs: 1p, Scuba diving, Siquijor Is. 1.20p, Big game fishing, Aparri, Cagayan Province. 4p, Yachting, Manila Central. 5.50p, Climbing Mt. Apo. 8p, Golf, Cebu, Cebu Is. 11p, Cycling through Marawi, Mindanao Is.

1988, July 11 *Perf. 13x13¹/₂*

1933 A513	1p multi	.15	.15
1934 A513	1.20p multi	*.20*	.15
1935 A513	4p multi	*.60*	.20
1936 A513	5.50p multi	*.90*	.30
1937 A513	8p multi	*1.25*	.40
1938 A513	11p multi	*1.75*	.55
	Nos. 1933-1938 (6)	*4.85*	1.75

4p, 8p, 1p and 5.50p also exist in strips of 4 plus center label picturing torch and inscribed "Philippine Olympic Week, May 1-7, 1988."

Nos. 1797, 1801, 1810 and 1817 Surcharged with 2 Bars and New Value in Black or Gold

1988, Aug. 1 As Before

1939 A466	1.90p on 2.40p #1797	.20	.15
1940 A467	1.90p on 2.40p #1801	.20	.15
1941 A470	1.90p on 2.40p #1810	.20	.15
1942 A473	1.90p on 2.40p #1817 (G)	.20	.15
	Nos. 1939-1942 (4)	.80	
	Set value		.40

Land Bank of the Philippines, 25th Anniv. A514

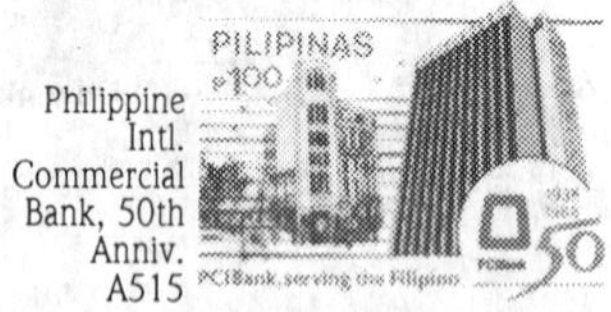

Philippine Intl. Commercial Bank, 50th Anniv. A515

Perf. 13x13¹/₂

1988, Aug. 8 Litho. Wmk. 372

1943 A514	1p shown	.15	.15
1944 A515	1p shown	.15	.15
1945 A514	5.50p like No. 1943	.55	.28
1946 A515	5.50p like No. 1944	.55	.28
	Nos. 1943-1946 (4)	1.40	
	Set value		.65

Nos. 1943-1944 and 1945-1946 exist in se-tenant pairs from center rows of the sheet.

Profile of Francisco Balagtas Baltasar (b. 1788), Tagalog Language Poet, Author — A516

1988, Aug. 8 Litho. Wmk. *Perf. 13*

1947 A516	1p Facing right	.15	.15
1948 A516	1p Facing left	.15	.15
a.	Pair, #1947-1948	.20	.15

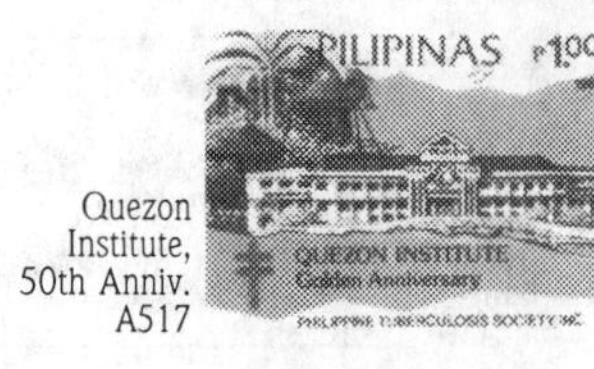

Quezon Institute, 50th Anniv. A517

Perf. 13x13¹/₂

1988, Aug. 18 Litho. Wmk. 372

1949 A517	1p multi	.15	.15
1950 A517	5.50p multi	.55	.28
	Set value		.32

Philippine Tuberculosis Soc.

Mushrooms A518

1988 Summer Olympics, Seoul A519

1988, Sept. 13 Wmk. 391 *Perf. 13*

1951 A518	60s Brown	.15	.15
1952 A518	1p Rat's ear fungus	.15	.15
1953 A518	2p Abalone	.20	.15
1954 A518	4p Straw	.40	.20
	Set value	.75	.40

1988, Sept. 19 *Perf. 13¹/₂x13*

1955 A519	1p Women's archery	.15	.15
1956 A519	1.20p Women's tennis	.15	.15
1957 A519	4p Boxing	.40	.20
1958 A519	5.50p Women's running	.55	.28
1959 A519	8p Swimming	.80	.40
1960 A519	11p Cycling	1.10	.55
	Nos. 1955-1960 (6)	3.15	1.73

Souvenir Sheet

Imperf

1961	Sheet of 4	2.25	1.15
a.	A519 5.50p Weight lifting	.55	.28
b.	A519 5.50p Basketball, horiz.	.55	.28
c.	A519 5.50p Judo	.55	.28
d.	A519 5.50p Shooting, horiz.	.55	.28

Department of Justice, Cent. A520

1988, Sept. 26 *Perf. 13x13¹/₂*

1962 A520	1p multi	.15	.15

Intl. Red Cross and Red Crescent Organizations, 125th Annivs. — A521

Christian Children's Fund, 50th Anniv. — A522

1988, Sept. 30 *Perf. 13¹/₂x13*

1963 A521	1p multi	.15	.15
1964 A521	5.50p multi	.55	.28
	Set value		.32

1988, Oct. 6

1965 A522	1p multi	.15	.15

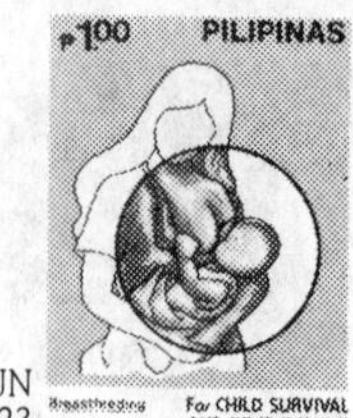

UN Campaigns — A523

Designs: a, Breast-feeding. b, Growth monitoring. c, Immunization. d, Oral rehydration. e, Oral rehydration therapy. f, Youth on crutches.

Perf. 13¹/₂x13

1988, Oct. 24 Litho. Wmk. 392

1966	Strip of 5	*2.00*	.25
a.-e.	A523 1p any single	.20	.15

Child Survival Campaign (Nos. 1966a-1966d); Decade for Disabled Persons (No. 1966e).

Bacolod City Charter, 50th Anniv. A524

1988, Oct. 19 Litho. *Perf. 13x13¹/₂*

1967 A524	1p multi	.15	.15

UST Graduate School, 50th Anniv. — A525

Dona Aurora Aragon Quezon (b. 1888) — A526

Perf. 13¹/₂x13

1988, Dec. 20 Litho. Unwmk.

1968 A525	1p multi	.15	.15

1988, Nov. 7 Wmk. 391 *Perf. 13*

1969 A526	1p multi	.15	.15
1970 A526	5.50p multi	.58	.30
	Set value		.35

Malate Church, 400th Anniv. A527

a, Church, 1776. b, Statue & anniv. emblem. c, Church, 1880. d, Church, 1988. Continuous design.

1988, Dec. 16

1971	Block of 4	.45	.20
a.-d.	A527 1p any single	.15	.15

UN Declaration of Human Rights, 40th Anniv. A528

1988, Dec. 9 Wmk. *Perf. 13¹/₂x13*

1972 A528	1p shown	.15	.15
1973 A528	1p Commission on human rights	.15	.15
	Set value	.24	.15

Nos. 1972-1973 exist in se-tenant pair, value 50c.

Long Distance Telephone Company — A529

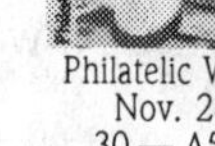

Philatelic Week, Nov. 24-30 — A530

1988, Nov. 28 Wmk.

1974 A529	1p Communications tower	.15	.15

1988, Nov. 24 Wmk. 391 *Perf. 13*

Emblem and: a, Post Office, "1938." b, Stamp counter. c, Framed stamp exhibits, four people. d, Exhibits, 8 people. Has a continuous design.

1975	Block of 4	.45	.20
a.-d.	A530 1p any single	.15	.15

Christmas A531

Designs: 75s, Handshake, peave dove, vert. 1p, Children making ornaments. 2p, Boy carrying decoration. 3.50p, Tree, vert. 4.75p, Candle, vert. 5.50p, Man, star, heart.

1988, Dec. 2 Wmk. 391

1976 A531	75s multi	.15	.15
1977 A531	1p multi	.15	.15
1978 A531	2p multi	.20	.15
1979 A531	3.50p multi	.35	.18
1980 A531	4.75p multi	.50	.25
1981 A531	5.50p multi	.58	.30
	Nos. 1976-1981 (6)	1.93	
	Set value		.90

Gen. Santos City, 50th Anniv. A532

Perf. 13x13¹/₂

1989, Feb. 27 Litho. Wmk.

1982 A532	1p multi	.15	.15

Guerrilla Fighters — A533

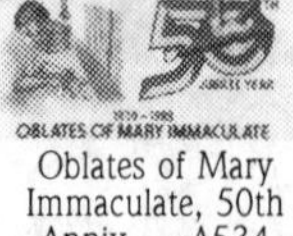

Oblates of Mary Immaculate, 50th Anniv. — A534

Emblem and: No. 1983, Miguel Z. Ver (1918-42). No. 1984, Eleuterio L. Adevoso (1922-75). Printed in continuous design.

1989, Feb. 18 Wmk. 391

1983 A533	1p multi	.15	.15
1984 A533	1p multi	.15	.15
a.	Pair, #1983-1984	.24	.20

1989, Feb. 17 Wmk. *Perf. 13¹/₂x13*

1985 A534	1p multicolored	.15	.15

Fiesta Islands '89 — A535

Perf. 13 (Nos. 1991, 1994, 1997), 13½x14

1989-90 Litho. Wmk. 391

1986	A535	60s	Turumba	.15	.15
1987	A535	75s	Pahiyas	.15	.15
1988	A535	1p	Pagoda Sa Wawa	.15	.15
1989	A535	1p	Masskara	.15	.15
1990	A535	3.50p	Independence Day	.35	.18
1990A	A535	4p	like #1995	.42	.42
1991	A535	4.75p	Sinulog	.52	.25
1992	A535	4.75p	Cagayan de Oro	.52	.25
1993	A535	4.75p	Grand Canao	.50	.25
1994	A535	5.50p	Lenten festival	.60	.30
1995	A535	5.50p	Penafrancia	.60	.30
1996	A535	5.50p	Fireworks	.60	.30
1997	A535	6.25p	Iloilo Paraw regatta	.68	.35
			Nos. 1986-1997 (13)	5.39	
			Set value		2.35

Issued: #1991, 1994, 6.25p, 3/1/89; 60s, 75s, 3.50p, 6/28/89; #1988, 1992, 1995, 9/1/89; #1989, 1993, 1996, 12/1/89; 4p, 8/6/90.

Great Filipinos — A536

Men and women: a, Don Tomas B. Mapua (1888-), educator. b, Camilo O. Osias (1889-), educator. c, Dr. Olivia D. Salamanca (1889-), physician. d, Dr. Francisco S. Santiago (1889-), composer. e, Leandro H. Fernandez (1889-), educator.

Perf. 14x13½

1989, May 18 Litho. Unwmk.

1998	Strip of 5	.60	.30
a.-e.	A536 1p any single	.15	.15

See Nos. 2022, 2089, 2151, 2240, 2307, 2360, 2414, 2486.

26th World Congress of the Intl. Federation of Landscape Architects A537

Designs: a, Adventure Pool. b, Paco Park. c, Beautification of Malacanang area streets. d, Erosion control at an upland farm.

1989, May 31 Wmk. 391

1999	Block of 4	.45	.20
a.-d.	A537 1p any single	.15	.15

Printed in continuous design.

French Revolution, Bicent. A538

1989, July 1 Perf. 14

2000	A538	1p	multi	.15	.15
2001	A538	5.50p	multi	.52	.25
			Set value		.30

Supreme Court — A539

1989, June 11

2002	A539	1p	multi	.18	.15

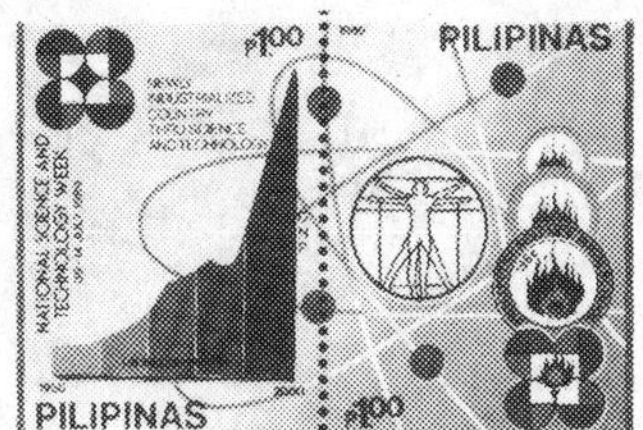

Natl. Science and Technology Week
A540 A541

1989, July 14

2003	A540	1p	GNP chart	.15	.15
2004	A541	1p	Science High School emblem	.15	.15
a.			Pair, #2003-2004	.24	.20

No. 1905 Surcharged

Wmk. 391

1989, Aug. 21 Litho. Perf. 13

2005	A483	4.75p on 5.50p		.50	.25

Philippine Environment Month
A542 A543

Wmk. 391

1989, June 5 Litho. Perf. 14

2006	A542	1p	Palawan peacock pheasant	.15	.15
2007	A543	1p	Palawan bear cat	.15	.15
a.			Pair, #2006-2007	.24	.20

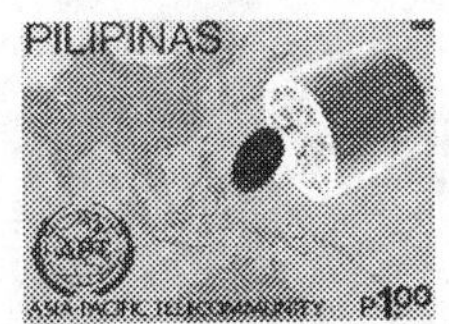

Asia-Pacific Telecommunity, 10th Anniv. — A544

Wmk. 372

1989, Oct. 30 Litho. Perf. 14

2008	A544	1p	multicolored	.18	.15

Dept. of Natl. Defense, 50th Anniv. — A545

1989, Oct. 23

2009	A545	1p	multicolored	.18	.15

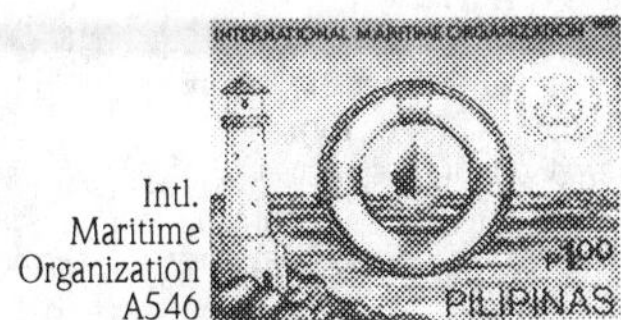

Intl. Maritime Organization A546

1989, Nov. 13 Unwmk. Perf. 14

2010	A546	1p	multicolored	.16	.15

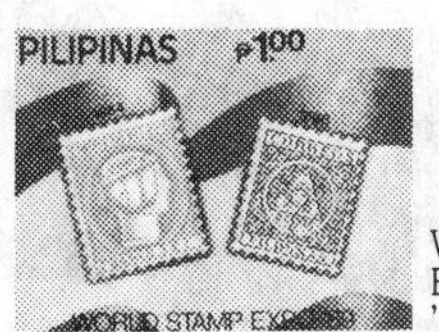

World Stamp Expo '89 — A546a

Unwmk.

1989, Nov. 17 Litho. Perf. 14

2010A	A546a	1p	#1, Y1	
2010B	A546a	4p	#219, 398	
2010C	A546a	5.50p	#N1, 500	
			Nos. 2010A-2010C (3)	5.00

Nos. 2010A-2010C withdrawn from sale week of release.

Teaching Philately in the Classroom, Close-up of Youth Collectors A547

1989, Nov. 20 Perf. 14x13½

2011	A547	1p	shown	.15	.15
2012	A547	1p	Class, diff.	.15	.15
			Set value	.28	.15

Christmas — A548

1989 Perf. 13½x14

2013	A548	60s	Annunciation	.15	.15
2014	A548	75s	Visitation	.15	.15
2015	A548	1p	Journey to Bethlehem	.15	.15
2016	A548	2p	Search for the inn	.22	.15
2017	A548	4p	Appearance of the star	.42	.22
2018	A548	4.75p	Birth of Jesus Christ	.52	.25
			Set value	1.40	.70

11th World Cardiology Congress A549

1990, Feb. 12 Photo. Wmk. Perf. 14

2019	A549	5.50p	black, dark red & deep blue	.60	.30

Beer Production, Cent. A550

1990, Apr. 16 Wmk.

2020	A550	1p	multicolored	.15	.15
2021	A550	5.50p	multicolored	.60	.30
			Set value		.35

Great Filipinos Type of 1989

Designs: a, Claro M. Recto (1890-1960), politician. b, Manuel H. Bernabe. c, Guillermo E. Tolentino. d, Elpidio R. Quirino (1890-1956), politician. e, Bienvenido Ma. Gonzalez.

Perf. 14x13½

1990, June 1 Litho. Unwmk.

2022	Strip of 5	.60	.30
a.-e.	A536 1p any single	.15	.15

1990 Census — A551

Wmk. 391

1990, Apr. 30 Photo. Perf. 14

Color of Buildings

2023	A551	1p	light blue	.15	.15
2024	A551	1p	beige	.15	.15
a.			Pair, #2023-2024	.24	.15

No. 2024a printed in continuous design.

Legion of Mary, 50th Anniv. — A552

Wmk. 391

1990, July 21 Photo. Perf. 14

2025	A552	1p	multicolored	.15	.15

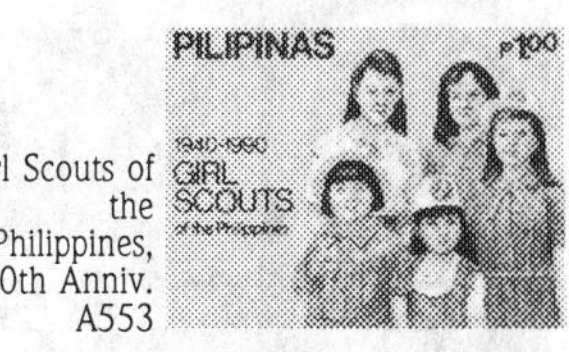

Girl Scouts of the Philippines, 50th Anniv. A553

1990, May 21

2026	A553	1p	yellow & multi	.15	.15
2027	A553	1.20p	lt lilac & multi	.15	.15
			Set value		.15

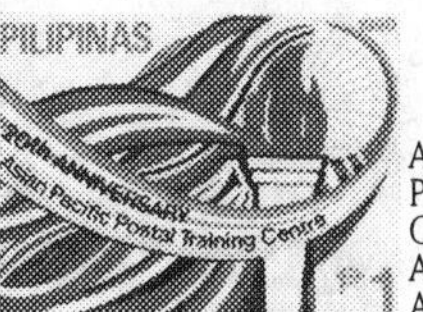

Asian Pacific Postal Training Center, 20th Anniv. A554

Wmk. 391

1990, Sept. 10 Photo. Perf. 14

2028	A554	1p	red & multi	.15	.15
2029	A554	4p	blue & multi	.45	.34
			Set value		.40

Natl. Catechetical Year — A555

1990, Sept. 28

2030	A555	1p	blk & multi	.15	.15
2031	A555	3.50p	grn & multi	.40	.20
			Set value		.26

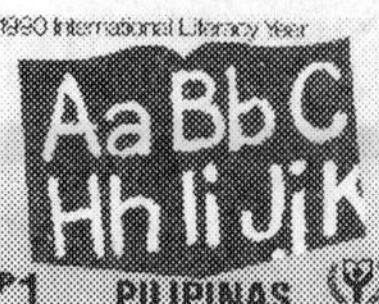

Intl. Literacy Year — A556

Wmk. 391

1990, Oct. 24 Photo. Perf. 14

2032	A556	1p	blk, org & grn	.15	.15
2033	A556	5.50p	blk, yel & grn	.60	.30
			Set value		.36

UN Development Program, 40th Anniv. A557

1990, Oct. 24

No.	Type	Denom.	Description	Unused	Used
2034	A557	1p	yel & multi	.15	.15
2035	A557	5.50p	orange & multi	.60	.30
			Set value		.36

Flowers — A558

1990 Photo. Wmk. 391 *Perf. 14*

No.	Type	Denom.	Description	Unused	Used
2036	A558	1p	Waling waling	.15	.15
2037	A558	4p	Sampaguita	.48	.24
			Set value		.30

29th Orient and Southeast Asian Lions forum. Issued: 1p, Oct. 3; 4p, Oct. 18.

Christmas
A559 A560

Drawings of the Christmas star: a, Yellow star, pink beading. b, Yellow star, white beading. c, Green, blue, yellow and orange star. d, Red star, white outlines.

1990, Dec. 3

No.	Type	Denom.	Description	Unused	Used
2038			Strip of 4	.48	.24
a.-d.	A559	1p	any single	.15	.15
2039	A560	5.50p	multicolored	.60	.30

Blind Safety Day — A561

Wmk. 391

1990, Dec. 7 Photo. *Perf. 14*

No.	Type	Denom.	Description	Unused	Used
2040	A561	1p	bl, blk & yel	.18	.15

Publication of Rizal's "Philippines After 100 Years," Cent. A562

1990, Dec.17

No.	Type	Denom.	Description	Unused	Used
2041	A562	1p	multicolored	.18	.15

Philatelic Week A563

Paintings: 1p, Family by F. Amorsolo. 4.75p, The Builders by V. Edades. 5.50p, Laughter by A. Magsaysay-Ho.

1990, Nov. 16

No.	Type	Denom.	Description	Unused	Used
2042	A563	1p	multicolored	.18	.15
2043	A563	4.75p	multi, vert.	.85	.42
2044	A563	5.50p	multi, vert.	1.00	.50
			Nos. 2042-2044 (3)	2.03	1.07

A564

A565

1991, Jan. 30 Wmk. 391

No.	Type	Denom.	Description	Unused	Used
2045	A564	1p	multicolored	.18	.15

2nd Plenary Council of the Philippines.

Wmk. 391

1991, Mar. 15 Litho. *Perf. 14*

No.	Type	Denom.	Description	Unused	Used
2046	A565	1p	multicolored	.15	.15
2047	A565	5.50p	multicolored	.50	.25

Philippine Airlines, 50th anniv. No. 2047 is airmail.

Flowers — A566

Flowers: 1p, 2p, Plumeria. 4p, 6p, Ixora. 4.75p, 7p, Bougainvillea. 5.50p, 8p, Hibiscus.

1991 Photo. *Perf. 14x13½*

No.	Type	Denom.	Description	Unused	Used
2048	A566	60s	Gardenia	.15	.15
2049	A566	75s	Allamanda	.15	.15
2050	A566	1p	yellow	.15	.15
2051	A566	1p	red	.15	.15
2052	A566	1p	salmon	.15	.15
2053	A566	1p	white	.15	.15
a.			Block of 4, #2050-2053	.35	.18
2053B	A566	1p	like #2049	.15	.15
2054	A566	1.20p	Nerium	.15	.15
2055	A566	1.50p	like #2048	.15	.15
2056	A566	2p	yellow	.20	.15
2057	A566	2p	red	.20	.15
2058	A566	2p	rose & yellow	.20	.15
2059	A566	2p	white	.20	.15
a.			Block of 4, #2055-2059	.80	.40
2060	A566	3p	like #2054	.30	.15
2061	A566	3.25p	Cananga	.28	.15
2062	A566	4p	dull rose	.35	.18
2063	A566	4p	pale yellow	.35	.18
2064	A566	4p	orange yel	.35	.18
2065	A566	4p	scarlet	.35	.18
a.			Block of 4, #2062-2065	1.40	.75
2066	A566	4.75p	vermilion	.40	.20
2067	A566	4.75p	brt rose lil	.40	.20
2068	A566	4.75p	white	.40	.20
2069	A566	4.75p	lilac rose	.40	.20
a.			Block of 4, #2066-2069	1.60	.80
2070	A566	5p	Canna	.42	.22
2071	A566	5p	like #2061	.50	.25
2072	A566	5.50p	red	.48	.24
2073	A566	5.50p	yellow	.48	.24
2074	A566	5.50p	white	.48	.24
2075	A566	5.50p	pink	.48	.24
a.			Block of 4, #2072-2075	2.00	1.00
2076	A566	6p	dull rose	.60	.30
2077	A566	6p	pale yellow	.60	.30
2078	A566	6p	orange yellow	.60	.30
2079	A566	6p	scarlet	.60	.30
a.			Block of 4, #2076-2079	2.40	1.20
2080	A566	7p	vermilion	.70	.35
2081	A566	7p	brt rose lilac	.70	.35
2082	A566	7p	white	.70	.35
2083	A566	7p	deep lil rose	.70	.35
a.			Block of 4, #2080-2083	2.80	1.40
2084	A566	8p	red	.80	.40
2085	A566	8p	yellow	.80	.40
2086	A566	8p	white	.80	.40
2087	A566	8p	deep pink	.80	.40
a.			Block of 4, #2084-2087	3.20	1.60
2088	A566	10p	like #2070	1.00	.50
			Nos. 2048-2088 (42)	17.97	9.90

Issue dates: 60s, 75s, No. 2053a, 5.50p, Mar. 30; 1.20p, 4p, 4.75p, May 17 (FDC, on sale June 7), No. 2053B, Jan. 23, 1993.

Inscribed "1991" except for No. 2053B, which is inscribed "1992.".

Nos. 2048, 2059a, 2060, 2070, 2079a, 2083a, 2087a, 2088 exist with "1992."

Great Filipinos Type of 1989

Designs: a, Jorge B. Vargas (1890-1980). b, Ricardo M. Paras (1891-1984). c, Jose P. Laurel (1891-1959), politician. d, Vincente Fabella (1891-1959). e, Maximo M. Kalaw (1891-1954).

Perf. 14x13½

1991, June 3 Litho. Wmk. 372

No.	Type	Denom.	Description	Unused	Used
2089	A536	1p	Strip of 5, #a.-e.	.45	.22

12th Asia-Pacific Boy Scout Jamboree A567

Perf. 14x13½

1991, Apr. 22 Wmk. 391

No.	Type	Denom.	Description	Unused	Used
2090	A567	1p	Square knot	.15	.15
2091	A567	4p	Sheepshank knot	.35	.18
2092	A567	4.75p	Figure 8 knot	.40	.20
a.			Souv. sheet of 3, #2090-2092, imperf.	1.75	.90
			Nos. 2090-2092 (3)	.90	.53

No. 2092a sold for 16.50p and has simulated perfs.

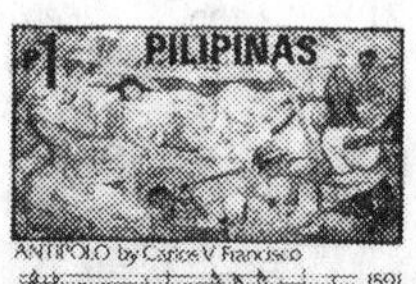

Antipolo by Carlos V. Francisco A568

1991, June 23 Litho. Wmk. *Perf. 14*
Granite Paper

No.	Type	Denom.	Description	Unused	Used
2093	A568	1p	multicolored	.18	.15

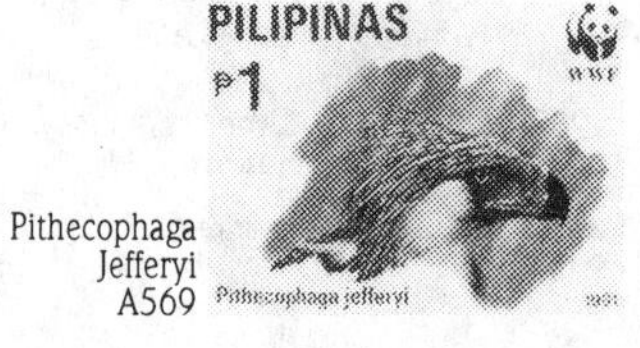

Pithecophaga Jefferyi A569

1991, July 31 Photo. Wmk. 391

No.	Type	Denom.	Description	Unused	Used
2094	A569	1p	Head	.15	.15
2095	A569	4.75p	Perched on limb	.50	.25
2096	A569	5.50p	In flight	.58	.28
2097	A569	8p	Feeding young	.85	.42
			Nos. 2094-2097 (4)	2.08	1.10

World Wildlife Fund.

Philippine Bar Association, Cent. — A570

Wmk. 391

1991, Aug. 20 Photo. *Perf. 14*

No.	Type	Denom.	Description	Unused	Used
2098	A570	1p	multicolored	.18	.15

A571

1991, Aug. 29

No.	Type	Denom.	Description	Unused	Used
2099	A571	1p	multicolored	.18	.15

Size: 82x88mm

Imperf

No.	Type	Denom.	Description	Unused	Used
2100	A571	16p	like #2099	1.70	.85

Induction of Filipinos into USAFFE (US Armed Forces in the Far East), 50th Anniv. For overprint see No. 2193.

A572 A573

Independence Movement, cent.: a, Basil at graveside. b, Simon carrying lantern. c, Father Florentino, treasure chest. d, Sister Juli with rosary.

1991, Sept. 18

No.	Type	Denom.	Description	Unused	Used
2101	A572	1p	Block of 4, #a.-d.	.45	.22

Wmk. 391

1991, Oct. 15 Photo. *Perf. 14*

No.	Type	Denom.	Description	Unused	Used
2102	A573	1p	multicolored	.18	.15

Size: 60x60mm

Imperf

No.	Type	Denom.	Description	Unused	Used
2103	A573	16p	multicolored	1.70	.85

St. John of the Cross, 400th death anniv.

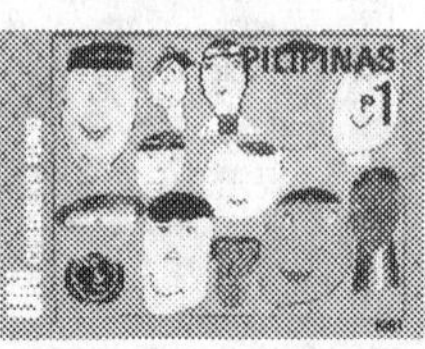

United Nations Agencies A574

Designs: 1p, UNICEF, children. 4p, High Commissioner for Refugees, hands supporting boat people. 5.50p, Postal Administration, 40th anniv., UN #29, #C3.

1991, Oct. 24 *Perf. 14*

No.	Type	Denom.	Description	Unused	Used
2104	A574	1p	multicolored	.15	.15
2105	A574	4p	multicolored	.42	.20
2106	A574	5.50p	multicolored	.60	.30
			Nos. 2104-2106 (3)	1.17	.65

Philatelic Week A575

Paintings: 2p, Bayanihan by Carlos Francisco. 7p, Sari-sari Vendor by Mauro Malang Santos. 8p, Give Us This Day by Vincente Manansala.

1991, Nov. 20

No.	Type	Denom.	Description	Unused	Used
2107	A575	2p	multicolored	.22	.15
2108	A575	7p	multicolored	.75	.38
2109	A575	8p	multicolored	.85	.42
			Nos. 2107-2109 (3)	1.82	.95

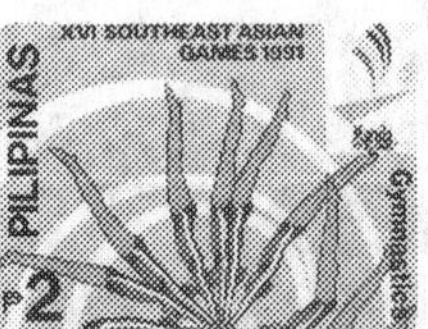

16th Southeast Asian Games, Manila A576

#2110, Gymnastics, games emblem at UR. #2111, Gymnastics, games emblem at LR. #2112, Martial arts, games emblem at LL, vert. #2113, Martial arts, games emblem at LR, vert.

Wmk. 391

1991, Nov. 22 Photo. *Perf. 14*

No.	Type	Denom.	Description	Unused	Used
2110	A576	2p	multicolored	.18	.15
2111	A576	2p	multicolored	.18	.15
a.			Pair, #2110-2111	.36	.18
2112	A576	6p	multicolored	.50	.25
2113	A576	6p	multicolored	.50	.25
a.			Pair, #2112-2113	1.00	.50
b.			Souv. sheet of 2, #2112-2113, imperf.	1.40	.70
c.			Souv. sheet of 4, #2110-2113	1.05	.52
			Nos. 2110-2113 (4)	1.36	.80

No. 2113b has simulated perforations.

No. 1585 Surcharged in Red
Souvenir Sheet

1991, Nov. 27 Wmk. 372 *Imperf.*

No.	Type	Denom.	Description	Unused	Used
2114	A385	4p	on 3.20p	.70	.35

First Philippine Philatelic Convention.

Children's Christmas Paintings — A577

1991, Dec. 4 Wmk. 391 *Perf. 14*

2115 A577 2p shown .18 .15
2116 A577 6p Wrapped gift .50 .25
2117 A577 7p Santa, tree .60 .30
2118 A577 8p Tree, star .70 .35
Nos. 2115-2118 (4) 1.98 1.05

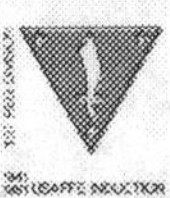

Insignias of Military Groups Inducted into USAFFE — A578

White background: No. 2119a, 1st Regular Div. b, 2nd Regular Div. c, 11th Div. d, 21st Div. e, 31st Div. f, 41st Div. g, 51st Div. h, 61st Div. i, 71st Div. j, 81st Div. k, 91st Div. l, 101st Div. m, Bataan Force. n, Philippine Div. o, Philippine Army Air Corps. p, Offshore Patrol.

Nos. 2120a-2120p, like #2119a-2119p with yellow background.

Perf. 14x13½

1991, Dec. 8 Photo. Wmk. 391

2119 A578 2p Block of 16, #a.-p. 5.75 2.85
2120 A578 2p Block of 16, #a.-p. 5.75 2.85
q. Block of 32, #2119-2120 *30.00*

Induction of Filipinos into USAFFE, 50th anniv.

Nos. 2119-2120 were printed in sheets of 200 containing 5 #2120q plus five blocks of 8.

Basketball, Cent. — A579

Designs: 2p, PBA Games, vert. 6p, Map, player dribbling. 7p, Early players. 8p, Men shooting basketball, vert. 16p, Tip-off.

Wmk. 391

1991, Dec. 19 Litho. *Perf. 14*

2121 A579 2p multicolored .18 .15
2122 A579 6p multicolored .50 .25
2123 A579 7p multicolored .60 .30
2124 A579 8p multicolored .70 .35
a. Souv. sheet of 4, #2121-2124 2.00 1.05
Nos. 2121-2124 (4) 1.98 1.05

Souvenir Sheet

Imperf

2125 A579 16p multicolored 1.45 .72

No. 2125 has simulated perforations.

New Year 1992, Year of the Monkey A580

Wmk. 391

1991, Dec. 27 Litho. *Perf. 14*

2126 A580 2p violet & multi .18 .15
2127 A580 6p green & multi .52 .25
Set value .34

See Nos. 2459a, 2460a.

Services and Products A581

Wmk. 391

1992, Jan. 15 Litho. *Perf. 14*

2128 A581 2p Mailing center .18 .15
2129 A581 6p Housing project .50 .25
2130 A581 7p Livestock .60 .30
2131 A581 8p Handicraft .70 .35
Nos. 2128-2131 (4) 1.98 1.05

Medicinal Plants — A582

Wmk. 391

1992, Feb. 7 Litho. *Perf. 14*

2132 A582 2p Curcuma longa .18 .15
2133 A582 6p Centella asiatica .52 .25
2134 A582 7p Cassia alata .60 .30
2135 A582 8p Ervatamia pandacaqui .70 .35
Nos. 2132-2135 (4) 2.00 1.05

Love A583

"I Love You" in English on Nos. 2137a-2140a, in Filipino on Nos. 2137b-2140b with designs: No. 2137, Letters, map. No. 2138, Heart, doves. No. 2139, Bouquet of flowers. No. 2140, Map, Cupid with bow and arrow.

Wmk. 391

1992, Feb. 10 Photo. *Perf. 14*

2137 A583 2p Pair, #a.-b. .35 .18
2138 A583 6p Pair, #a.-b. 1.05 .52
2139 A583 7p Pair, #a.-b. 1.20 .60
2140 A583 8p Pair, #a.-b. 1.40 .70
Nos. 2137-2140 (4) 4.00 2.00

A584 A585

Wmk. 391

1992, Apr. 12 Litho. *Perf. 14*

2141 A584 2p blue & multi .18 .15
2142 A584 8p red vio & multi .70 .35

Our Lady of Sorrows of Porta Vaga, 400th anniv.

1992, Mar. 27

Expo '92, Seville: 2p, Man and woman celebrating. 8p, Philippine discovery scenes. 16p, Pavilion, horiz.

2143 A585 2p multicolored .18 .15
2144 A585 8p multicolored .70 .35

Souvenir Sheet

Imperf

2145 A585 16p multicolored 1.40 .70

Department of Agriculture, 75th Anniv. A586

a, Man planting seed. b, Fish trap. c, Pigs.

1992, May 4

2146 A586 2p Strip of 3, #a.-c. .52 .25

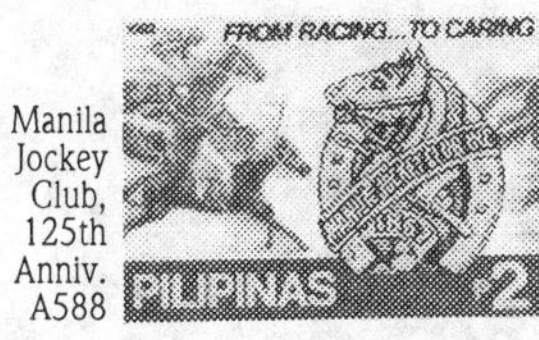

Manila Jockey Club, 125th Anniv. A588

Wmk. 391

1992, May 14 Litho. *Perf. 14*

2149 A588 2p multicolored .20 .15

Souvenir Sheet

Imperf

2150 A588 8p multicolored .70 .35

No. 2150 has simulated perfs.

Great Filipinos Type of 1989

Designs: a, Pres. Manuel A. Roxas (1892-1948). b, Justice Natividad Almeda-Lopez (1892-1977). c, Justice Roman A. Ozaeta (b. 1892). d, Engracia Cruz-Reyes (1892-1975). e, Fernando Amorsolo (1892-1972).

Perf. 14x13½

1992, June 1 Wmk. 391

2151 A536 2p Strip of 5, #a.-e. .90 .45

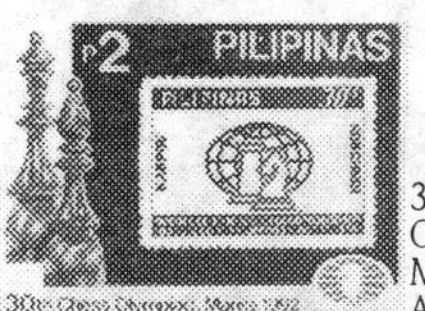

30th Chess Olympiad, Manila A589

Designs: No. 2154a, like #2152. b, like #2153.

1992, June 7 *Perf. 14*

2152 A589 2p No. 1352 .18 .15
2153 A589 6p No. B21 .52 .25

Souvenir Sheet

Imperf

2154 A589 8p Sheet of 2, #a.-b. 1.40 .70

No. 2154 has simulated perfs.

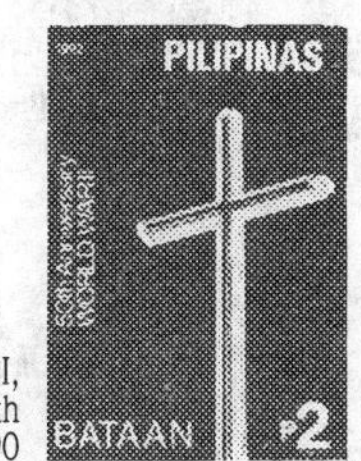

World War II, 50th Anniv. — A590

Designs: 2p, Bataan, cross. 6p, Insignia of defenders of Bataan and Corregidor. 8p, Corregidor, Monument. No. 2158, Cross, map of Bataan. No. 2159, Monument, map of Corregidor.

Wmk. 391

1992, June 12 Photo. *Perf. 14*

2155 A590 2p multicolored .18 .15
2156 A590 6p multicolored .52 .25
2157 A590 8p multicolored .70 .35

Size: 63x76mm, 76x63mm

Imperf

2158 A590 16p multicolored 1.90 .95
2159 A590 16p multicolored 1.90 .95
Nos. 2155-2159 (5) 5.20 2.65

Nos. 2158-2159 have simulated perforations.

President Corazon C. Aquino and President-Elect Fidel V. Ramos — A591

1992, June 30 *Perf. 14*

2160 A591 2p multicolored .22 .15

Anniversary of Democracy.

Jose Rizal's Exile to Dapitan, Cent. A592

1992, June 17

2161 A592 2p Dapitan shrine .18 .15
2162 A592 2p Portrait, vert. .18 .15
Set value .18

ASEAN, 25th Anniv. A593

Contemporary paintings: Nos. 2163, 2165, Spirit of ASEAN. Nos. 2164, 2166, ASEAN Sea.

Wmk. 391

1992, July 18 Litho. *Perf. 14*

2163 A593 2p multicolored .20 .15
2164 A593 2p multicolored .20 .15
2165 A593 6p multicolored .60 .30
2166 A593 6p multicolored .60 .30
Nos. 2163-2166 (4) 1.60 .90

Founding of Katipunan, Cent. A594

Details or entire paintings of revolutionaries, by Carlos "Botong" Francisco: No. 2167a, Preparing for battle, vert. No. 2167b, Attack leader (detail), vert. No. 2168a, Attack. No. 2168b, Signing papers.

Wmk. 391

1992, July 27 Photo. *Perf. 14*

2167 A594 2p Pair, #a.-b. .36 .18
2168 A594 2p Pair, #a.-b. .36 .18

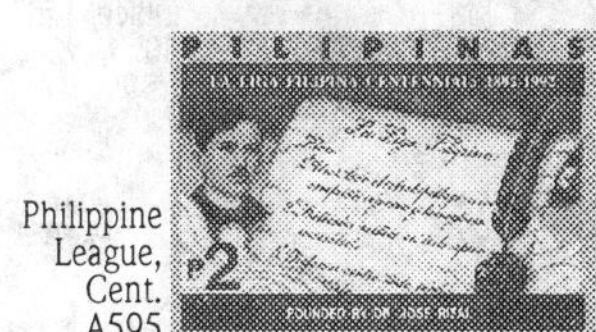

Philippine League, Cent. A595

Wmk. 391

1992, July 31 Photo. *Perf. 14*

2169 A595 2p multicolored .20 .15

1992 Summer Olympics, Barcelona A596

Wmk. 391

1992, Aug. 4 Litho. *Perf. 14*

2170 A596 2p Swimming .20 .15
2171 A596 7p Boxing .70 .35
2172 A596 8p Hurdling .80 .40
Nos. 2170-2172 (3) 1.70 .90

Souvenir Sheet

Imperf

2172A A596 Sheet of 3, #2171-2172, 2172b 1.75 .85
b. 1p like #2170 .15 .15

No. 2172A has simulated perforations.

Religious of the Assumption in Philippines, Cent. A597

Cathedral of San Sebastian, Cent. — A597a

Wmk. 391

1992, Aug. 15 Photo. *Perf. 14*

2173 A597 2p multicolored .18 .15
2174 A597a 2p multicolored .18 .15
Set value .18

Founding of Nilad Masonic Lodge, Cent. — A598

Various Masonic symbols and: 6p, A. Luna. 8p, M.H. Del Pilar.

Wmk. 391

1992, Aug. 15 Photo. *Perf. 14*

2175 A598 2p green & black .18 .15
2176 A598 6p yellow, black & brown .52 .28
2177 A598 8p blue, black & violet .70 .35
Nos. 2175-2177 (3) 1.40 .78

Pres. Fidel V. Ramos Taking Oath of Office, June 30, 1992 A599

1992, July 30

2178 A599 2p Ceremony, people .18 .15
2179 A599 8p Ceremony, flag .70 .35

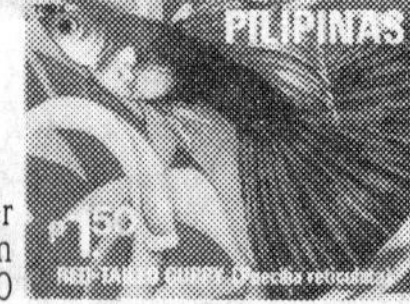

Freshwater Aquarium Fish — A600

Designs: No. 2180a, Red-tailed guppy, b, Tiger lacetail guppy. c, Flamingo guppy. d, Neon tuxedo guppy. e, King cobra guppy.

No. 2181a, Black moor. b, Bubble eye. c, Pearl scale goldfish. d, Red cap. e, Lionhead goldfish.

No. 2182, Golden arowana.

No. 2183a, Delta topsail variatus. b, Orange spotted hi-fin platy. c, Red lyretail swordtail. d, Bleeding heart hi-fin platy.

No. 2184a, 6p, Green discus. b, 6p, Brown discus. c, 7p, Red discus. d, 7p, Blue discus.

1992, Sept. 9 *Perf. 14*

2180 A600 1.50p Strip of 5, #a.-e. .65 .32
2181 A600 2p Strip of 5, #a.-e. .90 .45

Imperf

Size: 65x45mm

2182 A600 8p multicolored .70 .35

Souvenir Sheets

Perf. 14

2183 A600 4p Sheet of 4, #a.-d. 1.40 .70
2184 A600 Sheet of 4, #a.-d. 2.25 1.15

See Nos. 2253-2257.

Birthday Greetings — A601

1992, Sept 28 *Perf. 14*

2185 A601 2p Couple dancing .18 .15
2186 A601 6p like #2185 .52 .25
2187 A601 7p Cake, balloons .60 .30
2188 A601 8p like #2187 .70 .35
Nos. 2185-2188 (4) 2.00 1.05

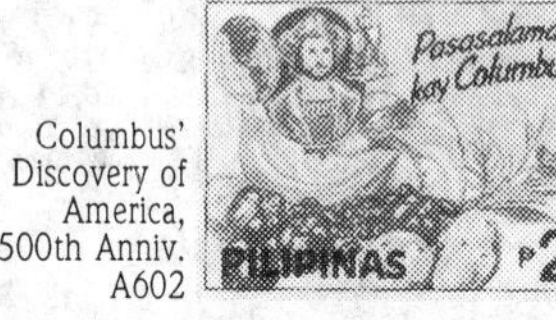

Columbus' Discovery of America, 500th Anniv. A602

Various fruits and vegetables.

1992, Oct. 14

2189 A602 2p multicolored .18 .15
2190 A602 6p multi, diff. .52 .25
2191 A602 8p multi, diff. .70 .35
Nos. 2189-2191 (3) 1.40 .75

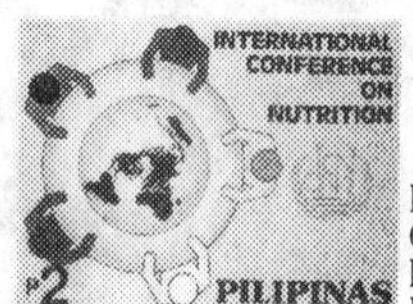

Intl. Conference on Nutrition, Rome — A603

1992, Oct. 27

2192 A603 2p multicolored .18 .15

No. 2100 Ovptd. in Blue "Second / National Philatelic Convention / Cebu, Philippines, Oct. 22-24, 1992"

Wmk. 391

1992, Oct. 15 Photo. *Imperf.*

2193 A571 16p multicolored 1.40 1.40

Christmas — A604

Various pictures of mother and child.

Wmk. 391

1992, Nov. 5 Litho. *Perf. 14*

2194 A604 2p multicolored .18 .15
2195 A604 6p multicolored .52 .25
2196 A604 7p multicolored .60 .30
2197 A604 8p multicolored .70 .35
Nos. 2194-2197 (4) 2.00 1.05

No. 1452 Ovptd. "INAUGURATION OF THE PHILIPPINE POSTAL MUSEUM / AND PHILATELIC LIBRARY, NOVEMBER 10, 1992" in Red

Wmk. 372

1992, Nov. 10 Litho. *Imperf.*

Souvenir Sheet

2198 A348 5p multicolored .60 .30

A605 A606

Wmk. 391

1992, Nov. 15 Litho. *Perf. 14*

2199 A605 2p People, boat .18 .15
2200 A605 8p People, boat, diff. .70 .35

Fight Against Drug Abuse.

1992, Nov. 24

Paintings: 2p, Family, by Cesar Legaspi. 6p, Pounding Rice, by Nena Saguil. 7p, Fish Vendors, by Romeo V. Tabuena.

2201 A606 2p multicolored .18 .15
2202 A606 6p multicolored .52 .26
2203 A606 7p multicolored .60 .30
Nos. 2201-2203 (3) 1.30 .71

Philatelic Week.

Birds A607

Designs: No. 2204a, Black shama. b, Philippine cockatoo. c, Sulu hornbill. d, Mindoro imperial pigeon. e, Blue-headed fantail.

No. 2205a, Philippine trogon, vert. b, Rufous hornbill, vert. c, White-bellied woodpecker, vert. d, Spotted wood kingfisher, vert.

No. 2206a, Brahminy kite. b, Philippine falconet. c, Pacific reef egret. d, Philippine mallard.

Wmk. 391

1992, Nov. 25 Litho. *Perf. 14*

2204 A607 2p Strip of 5, #a.-e. 1.05 .52

Souvenir Sheets

2205 A607 2p Sheet of 4, #a.-d. .90 .45
2206 A607 2p Sheet of 4, #a.-d. .90 .45

No. 2204 printed in sheets of 10 with designs in each row shifted one space to the right from the preceding row. Two rows in each sheet are tete-beche.

The 1st printing of this set was rejected. The unissued stamps do not have the frame around the birds. The denominations on the sheet stamps and the 2nd souvenir sheet are larger. On the 1st souvenir sheet they are smaller.

For overprint see No. 2405.

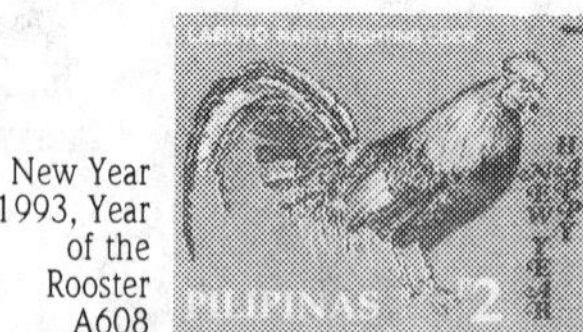

New Year 1993, Year of the Rooster A608

1992

2207 A608 2p Native fighting cock .18 .15
2208 A608 6p Legendary Maranao bird .52 .25
a. Souvenir sheet of 2, #2207-2208 + 2 labels .90 .45
b. As "a," ovptd. in sheet margin .90 .45
Set value .34

Nos. 2208a and 2208b exist imperf. Overprint on No. 2208b reads: "PHILIPPINE STAMP EXHIBIT / TAIPEI, DECEMBER 1-3, 1992" in English and Chinese.

Issue dates: Nos. 2207-2208, 2208a, Nov. 27. No. 2208b, Dec. 1.

See Nos. 2459b, 2460b.

Guerrilla Units of World War II — A609

Units: a, Bulacan Military Area, Anderson's Command, Luzon Guerrilla Army Forces. b, Marking's Fil-American Guerrillas, Hunters ROTC Guerrillas, President Quezon's Own Guerrillas. c, 61st Division, 71st Division, Cebu Area Command. d, 48th Chinese Guerrilla Squadron, 101st Division, Vinzons Guerrillas.

1992, Dec. 7

2209 A609 2p Block of 4, #a.-d. .70 .35

Tree — A610 Fish — A610c

Flower

A610a A610b

Flag

A610d A610e

Animal

A610f A610g

Bird

A610h A610i

Leaf

A610j A610k

Costume

A610l A610m

Fruit

A610n A610o

House — A610p

Natl. Symbols: #2219n, like #2213. #2215a, 2217a, 2219b, Natl. hero, Dr. Jose P. Rizal. #2215b, 2217b, 2219c, House. #2215c, 2217c, 2219d, Costume. #2215d, 2217d, 2219e, Natl. dance. #2215e, 2217e, 2219f, Natl. sport. #2215f, 2219g, Philippine eagle. #2217f, Maya bird. #2215g, 2217g, 2219a, Flag, "Pilipinas" at top. #2215h, 2217h, 2219i, Animal. #2215i, 2217i, 2219j, Flower. #2215j, 2217j, 2219k, Tree. #2215k, 2217k, 2219 l, Fruit. #2215 l, 2217 l, 2219m, Leaf. #2215m, 2217m, 2219n, Fish. #2215n, 2217n, 2219h, Flag, "Pilipinas" at bottom.

#2231: a, Flag. b, House. c, Costume. d, Tree. e, Flower (pink). f, Fruit. g, Leaf. h, Fish. i, Animal. j, Bird.

#2232: a, 2p, Aguinaldo. b, 3p, Rizal. c, 2p, Barasoain. d, 3p, Mabini.

Natl. flag and 1872 Cavite Mutiny: #2233; a, 2p, Cavite Arsenal. b, 3p, La Fuerza de San Felipe-Cavite. c, 2p, Commemorative marker. d, 3p, Cristanto de Los Reyes y Mendoza.

Nat'l Flag, 1896 Philippine Revolution: #2234: a, Cry of Pugadlawin. b, Battle of Pinaglabanan. c, Cry of Nueva Ecija. d, Battle of Binakayan.

(Some positions from blocks of 14 or souvenir sheets may be identical or similar: #2215i (red "Pilipinas")and #2463A (blue "Pilipinas"), #2217n ("1993" level with top of "Pilipinas")and #2216A ("1993" level with bottom of "Pilipinas"), #2334e and #2211 (color of flower).

No. 2235: a, Edilberto Evangelista. b, Vicente Alvarez. c, Francisco Del Castillo. d, Pantaleon Villegas.

Perf. 14x13½

1993-97 Litho. Wmk. 391

Unwmk.

(#2212A, 2214, 2215, 2216A, 2218A, 2219, 2220, 2222)

2210	A610	60s	multicolored	.15	.15
2211	A610b	1p	Red "Pilipinas"	.15	.15
2212	A610a	1p	multicolored	.15	.15
2212A	A610b	1p	Blue "Pilipinas"	.15	.15
2213	A610c	1.50p	Red "Pilipinas"	.15	.15
2214	A610c	1.50p	Blue "Pilipinas"	.20	.15
2215		2p	Block of 14, #a.-n.	4.25	2.00
2216	A610d	2p	multicolored	.18	.15
2216A	A610e	2p	multicolored	.15	.15
2217		2p	Block of 14, #a.-l., #2216, 2216A	3.00	1.50
2218	A610f	3p	multicolored	.32	.16
2218A	A610g	3p	multicolored	.45	.20
2219		4p	Block of 14, #a.-n.	8.50	4.25
2220	A610g	4p	like #2218A	.60	.30
a.			Block of 14, #2219a-2219h, 2220, 2219j-2219n	8.50	4.25
2221	A610h	5p	multicolored	.55	.28
2222	A610i	5p	multicolored	.75	.35
2223	A610j	6p	multicolored	.52	.25
2223A	A610k	6p	Blue "Pilipinas"	.80	.40
2223B	A610k	6p	Red "Pilipinas"	.80	.40
2224	A610l	7p	multicolored	.60	.30
2224A	A610m	7p	Blue "Pilipinas"	.85	.40
2224B	A610m	7p	Red "Pilipinas"	.85	.40
2225	A610n	8p	multicolored	.70	.35
2226	A610o	8p	Red "Pilipinas"	1.25	.65
2227	A610o	8p	Blue "Pilipinas"	.95	.50
2228	A610p	10p	Red "Pilipinas"	1.10	.55
2229	A610p	10p	Blue "Pilipinas"	1.20	.60
			Nos. 2210-2229 (27)	29.32	15.04

Souvenir Sheets

2231	A610	1p	Sheet of 10, #a.-j.	1.50	.75

Perf. 13½

Unwmk.

2232	A610		Sheet of 4, #a.-d.	.75	.38
2233	A610		Sheet of 4, #a.-d.	.75	.40
2234	A610	4p	Sheet of 4, #a.-d.	2.00	1.00
2235	A610	4p	Sheet of 4, #a.-d.	2.00	2.00

Nos. 2216, 2216A issued in sheets of 200 and with No. 2217.

No. 2215 has blue compressed security printing at top, smaller vignettes, "Pilipinas" in orange red, and is dated "1995." No. 2216 has "Pilipinas" in orange brown at UL. No. 2216A has "Pilipinas" in red at bottom of stamp and is dated "1993."

Nos. 2212A, 2214, 2215, 2218A, 2219, 2220, 2222, 2223A, 2224A, 2227, 2229 have blue compressed security printing at top, smaller vignettes, "Philipinas" in red (#2215) or dark blue.

No. 2219 is dated "1995;" No. 2220a, "1996."

Nos. 2218, 2221, 2228 exist dated "1994;" Nos. 2211, 2213, 2218, 2221, 2223B, 2224B, 2226, 2228, "1995." Nos. 2218A, 2222, 2223A, 2227, 2229, "1997."

No. 2220 was released because postal forgeries of No. 2219j were discovered.

Issued: #2212, 2216, 2223, 2224, 2225, 4/29/93; #2210, 2213, 2218, 2221, 2228, 2231, 6/12/93; #2217, 10/28/93; #2216A, 2/10/94: #2211, 53/94; #2232, 6/12/94; #2224B, 7/6/94; #2226, 10/4/94; #2223B, 12/1/94; #2233, 6/12/95; #2215, 11/2/95; #2219, 1/8/96; #2212A, 2214, 2218A, 2220, 2222, 2/12/96; #2224A, 2227, 2229, 4/19/96; #2234, 6/12/96; #2223A, 11/21/96; #2235, 6/12/97.

See Nos. 2463-2469.

Butterflies A611

Designs: No. 2237a, Euploea mulciber. b, Cheritra orpheus. c, Delias henningia. d, Mycalesis ita. e, Delias diaphana.

No. 2238a, Papilio rumanzobia. b, Papilio palinurus. c, Trogonoptera trojana. d, Graphium agamemnon.

No. 2239, Papilio lowi, Valeria boebera, Delias themis.

1993 Litho. Wmk. 391 *Perf. 14*

2237	A611	2p	Strip of 5, #a.-e.	.95	.48

Souvenir Sheets

2238	A611	2p	Sheet of 4, #a.-d.	.75	.75
e.			Ovptd. in sheet margin	.75	.75
2239	A611	10p	multicolored	.95	.95
a.			Ovptd. in sheet margin	.95	.95
b.			Ovptd. in blue in sheet margin	.95	.95

Issue dates: Nos. 2237-2239, May 28. Nos. 2238e, 2239a, May 29. No. 2239b, July 1.

Nos. 2238a-2238d are vert. No. 2239 contains one 116x28mm stamp.

Overprint on Nos. 2238e, 2239a reads "INDOPEX '93 / INDONESIA PHILATELIC EXHIBITION 1993" and "6th ASIAN INTERNATIONAL PHILATELIC EXHIBITION / 29th MAY-4th JUNE 1993 SURABAYA-INDONESIA."

Overprint on No. 2239b reads "Towards the Year 2000 / 46th PAF Anniversary 1 July 1993" and includes Philippine Air Force emblem and jet.

Great Filipinos Type of 1989

Designs: a, Nicanor Abelardo, composer. b, Pilar Hidalgo-Lim, mathematician, educator. c, Manuel Viola Gallego, lawyer, educator. d, Maria Ylagan Orosa (1893-1943), pharmacist, health advocate. e, Eulogio B. Rodriguez, historian.

1993, June 10 *Perf. 13½*

2240	A536	2p	Strip of 5, #a.-e.	.95	.48

17th South East Asia Games, Singapore A612

No. 2241: a, Weight lifting, archery, fencing, shooting. b, Boxing, judo. c, Track, cycling, gymnastics, golf.

No. 2242: a, Table tennis, soccer, volleyball, badminton. b, Billiards, bowling. c, Swimming, water polo, yachting, diving.

No. 2243, Basketball, vert.

1993, June 18 *Perf. 13*

2241	A612	2p	Strip of 3, #a.-c.	.58	.30
2242	A612	6p	Strip of 3, #a.-c.	1.75	.90

Souvenir Sheet

2243	A612	10p	multicolored	.95	.95

#2241a, 2241c, 2242a, 2242c are 80x30mm. No. 2243 contains one 30x40mm stamp. No. 2242a exists inscribed "June 13-20, 1993."

Orchids — A613

No. 2244: a, Spathoglottis chrysantha. b, Arachnis longicaulis. c, Phalaenopsis mariae. d, Coelogyne marmorata. e, Dendrobium sanderae.

No. 2245: a, Dendrobium serratilabium. b, Phalaenopsis equestris. c, Vanda merrillii. d, Vanda luzonica. e, Grammatophyllum martae.

No. 2246, Aerides quinquevulnera. No. 2247, Vanda lamellata.

1993, Aug. 14 Unwmk. *Perf. 14*

2244	A613	2p	Block of 5, #a.-e.	.95	.48
2245	A613	3p	Block of 5, #a.-e.	1.40	.70

Souvenir Sheets

2246	A613	8p	multicolored	.75	.75
a.			With additional inscription	2.50	2.50

Imperf

2247	A613	8p	multicolored	.75	.75
a.			With additional inscription	2.50	2.50

No. 2246 contains one 27x78mm stamp.

Nos. 2246a, 2247a inscribed in sheet margin with Taipei '93 emblem in blue and yellow. Additional black inscription in English and Chinese reads: "ASIAN INTERNATIONAL INVITATION STAMP EXHIBITION / TAIPEI '93."

Greetings A614

"Thinking of You" in English on Nos. 2248a-2251a, in Filipino on Nos. 2248b-2251b with designs: 2p, Flowers, dog at window. 6p, Dog looking at alarm clock. 7p, Dog looking at calendar. 8p, Dog with slippers.

Wmk. 391

1993, Aug. 20 Litho. *Perf. 14*

2248	A614	2p	Pair, #a.-b.	.85	.42
2249	A614	6p	Pair, #a.-b.	2.50	1.25
2250	A614	7p	Pair, #a.-b.	3.00	1.50
2251	A614	8p	Pair, #a.-b.	3.50	1.75
			Nos. 2248-2251 (4)	9.85	4.92

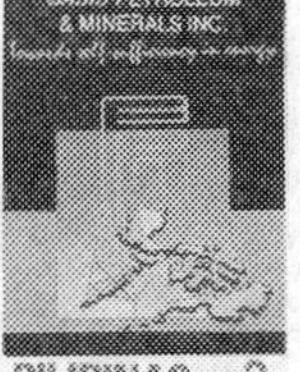

A615 A616

1993, Aug. 24

2252	A615	2p	multicolored	.25	.15

Natl. Coconut Week.

Fish Type of 1992

No. 2253: a, Paradise fish. b, Pearl gourami. c, Red-tailed black shark. d, Tiger barb. e, Cardinal tetra.

No. 2254: a, Albino ryukin goldfish. b, Black oranda goldfish. c, Lionhead goldfish. d, Celestial-eye goldfish. e, Pompon goldfish.

No. 2255: a, Pearl-scale angelfish. b, Zebra angelfish. c, Marble angelfish. d, Black angelfish.

No. 2256: a, Neon betta. b, Libby betta. c, Split-tailed betta. d, Butterfly betta.

No. 2257, Albino oscar.

1993 Unwmk. *Perf. 14*

2253	A600	2p	Strip of 5, #a.-e.	1.10	.55
2254	A600	2p	Strip of 5, #a.-e.	1.10	.55

Souvenir Sheets

Perf. 14

2255	A600	2p	Sheet of 4, #a.-d.	.65	.65
2256	A600	3p	Sheet of 4, #a.-d.	1.25	1.25
e.			Ovptd. in margin	1.25	1.25

Imperf

Stamp Size: 70x45mm

2257	A600	6p	multicolored	.65	.65
a.			Ovptd. in margin	.65	.65

Nos. 2256e, 2257a overprinted in black "QUEEN SIRIKIT NATIONAL CONVENTION CENTER / 1-10 OCTOBER 1993," "BANGKOK WORLD PHILATELIC EXHIBITION 1993" with Bangkok '93 show emblem in purple in margin.

Nos. 2255a-2255d are vert.

Issued: #2256e, 2257a, 9/20; others, 9/9.

Wmk. 391

1993, Sept. 20 Photo. *Perf. 14*

2258	A616	2p	multicolored	.22	.15

Basic Petroleum and Minerals, Inc., 25th anniv.

16th World Law Conference, Manila A617

6p, Globe on scales, gavel, flag, vert. 7p, Justice holding scales, courthouse. 8p, Fisherman, vert.

Unwmk.

1993, Sept. 30 Litho. *Perf. 14*

2259	A617	2p	multicolored	.20	.15
2260	A617	6p	multicolored	.60	.30
2261	A617	7p	multicolored	.70	.35
2262	A617	8p	multicolored	.80	.40
			Nos. 2259-2262 (4)	2.30	1.20

Our Lady of the Rosary of la Naval, 400th Anniv. A618

1993, Oct. 18 Wmk. 391

2263	A618	2p	multicolored	.20	.15

Intl. Year of Indigenous People — A619

People wearing traditional costumes.

1993, Oct. 24 Unwmk.

2264	A619	2p	multicolored	.20	.15
2265	A619	6p	multicolored	.60	.30
2266	A619	7p	multicolored	.70	.35
2267	A619	8p	multicolored	.80	.40
			Nos. 2264-2267 (4)	2.30	1.20

Environmental Protection — A620

Paintings: 2p, Trees. 6p, Marine life. 7p, Bird, trees. 8p, Man and nature.

1993, Nov. 22

2268	A620	2p	multicolored	.20	.15
2269	A620	6p	multicolored	.60	.30
2270	A620	7p	multicolored	.70	.35
2271	A620	8p	multicolored	.80	.40
			Nos. 2268-2271 (4)	2.30	1.20

Philately Week.

A621

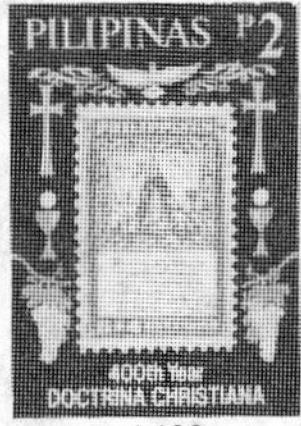

A622

Designs: a, Lunar buggy. b, Floating power tiller.

Unwmk.

1993, Nov. 30 Litho. *Perf. 14*

2272 A621 2p Pair, #a.-b. .40 .20

Filipino Inventors Society, Inc., 50th Anniv.

1993, Nov. 30

2273 A622 2p multicolored .20 .15

Printing of Doctrina Christiana in Spanish and Tagalog, 400th anniv.

A623

A624

Christmas: 2p, Nativity scene. 6p, Church, people. 7p, Water buffalo carrying fruits, vegetables, sea food. 8p, Christmas lantern, carolers.

1993, Dec. 1

2274 A623 2p multicolored .20 .15
2275 A623 6p multicolored .60 .30
2276 A623 7p multicolored .70 .35
2277 A623 8p multicolored .80 .40
Nos. 2274-2277 (4) 2.30 1.20

1993, Dec. 10

Maps, Philippine guerrilla units of World War II: a, US Army Forces in the Philippines Northern Luzon. b, Bohol Area Command. c, Leyete Area Command. d, Palawan Special Battalion, Sulu Area Command.

2278 A624 2p Block or strip of 4, #a.-d. .80 .40

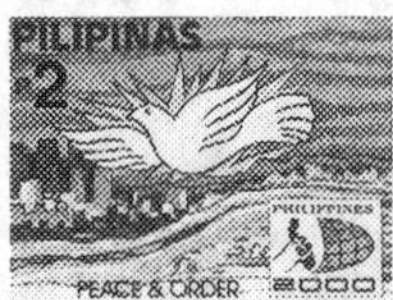

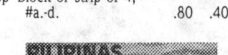

Philippines 2000 — A625

Designs: 2p, Peace and Order. 6p, Transportation, communications. 7p, Infrastructure, industry. No. 2282, People empowerment. No. 2283, Transportation, communications, buildings, people.

Unwmk.

1993, Dec. 14 Litho. *Perf. 14*

2279 A625 2p multicolored .20 .15
2280 A625 6p multicolored .60 .30
2281 A625 7p multicolored .70 .35
2282 A625 8p multicolored .80 .40

Imperf

Size: 110x85mm

2283 A625 8p multicolored .80 .40
Nos. 2279-2282 (4) 2.30 1.20

New Year 1994 (Year of the Dog) A626

Unwmk.

1993, Dec. 15 Litho. *Perf. 14*

2284 A626 2p Manigong bagong taon .20 .15
2285 A626 6p Happy new year .60 .30
a. Souvenir sheet of 2, #2284-2285 + 2 labels .80 .40

No. 2285a exists imperf.
See Nos. 2459c, 2460c.

First ASEAN Scout Jamboree, Mt. Makiling — A627

Designs: 2p, Flags of ASEAN countries, Boy Scout emblem. 6p, Flags, Boy Scout, emblem.

1993, Dec. 28

2286 A627 2p multicolored .20 .15
2287 A627 6p multicolored .60 .30
a. Souvenir sheet of 2, #2286-2287 .80 .40

Rotary Club of Manila, 75th Anniv. A628

Unwmk.

1994, Jan. 19 Litho. *Perf. 14*

2288 A628 2p multicolored .15 .15

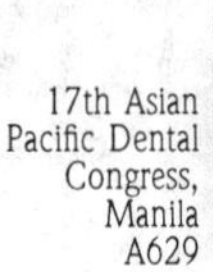
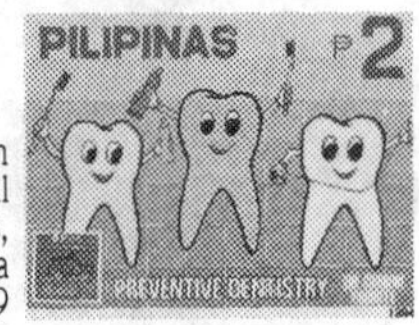

17th Asian Pacific Dental Congress, Manila A629

2p, Healthy teeth. 6p, Globe, flags, teeth.

1994, Feb. 3

2289 A629 2p multicolored .15 .15
2290 A629 6p multicolored .45 .22
Set value .28

Corals A630

#2291: a, Acropora micropthalma. b, Seriatopora hystrix. c, Acropora latistella. d, Millepora tenella. e, Millepora tenella, up close. f, Pachyseris valenciennesi. g, Pavona decussata. h, Galaxea fascicularis. i, Acropora formosa. j, Acropora humilis.

#2292: a, Isis. b, Plexaura. c, Dendronepthya. d, Heteroxenia.

#2293: a, Xenia puertogalerae. b, Plexaura, diff. c, Dendrophyllia gracilis. d, Plerogyra sinuosa.

1994, Feb. 15 Litho. *Perf. 14*

2291 A630 2p Block of 10, #a.-j. 3.00 1.50

Souvenir Sheets

2292 A630 2p Sheet of 4, #a.-d. .60 .30
2293 A630 3p Sheet of 4, #a.-d. .90 .45
e. With added inscription .90 .45

No. 2293e is inscribed in sheet margin "NAPHILCON '94 / 1ST NATIONAL / PHILATELIC CONGRESS / 21 FEBRUARY - 5 MARCH 1994 / PHILATELY 2000."

Issued: No. 2293e, 2/21.

Hong Kong '94 — A631

2p, Nos. 2126, 2207. 6p, Nos. 2284, 2285.

1994, Feb. 18

2294 A631 2p multicolored .15 .15
a. Souv. sheet of 2, #2294-2295, green .30 .15
2295 A631 6p multicolored .45 .22
a. Souv. sheet of 2, #2294-2295, blue .90 .45

A632

A633

1994, Feb. 20

2296 A632 2p multicolored .15 .15

Philippine Military Academy Class of 1944, 50th Anniv.

1994, Mar. 1

2297 A633 2p multicolored .15 .15

Federation of Filipino-Chinese Chambers of Commerce and Industry, 40th Anniv.

A634

A635

"Congratulations" in English on Nos. 2298a-2301a, in Tagalog on Nos. 2293b-2301b with designs: No. 2298, Books, diploma, mortarboard. No. 2299, Baby carried by stork. No. 2300, Valentine bouquet with portraits in heart. No. 2301, Bouquet.

1994, Apr. 15

2298 A634 2p Pair, #a.-b. .30 .15
2299 A634 2p Pair, #a.-b. .30 .15
2300 A634 2p Pair, #a.-b. .30 .15
2301 A634 2p Pair, #a.-b. .30 .15
Nos. 2298-2301 (4) 1.20 .60

1994, May 5 Litho. *Perf. 14*

1994 Miss Universe Pageant, Manila: Nos. 2302a (2p), 2304a, Gloria Diaz, 1969 winner. No. 2302b (6p), Crown, Philippine jeepney. Nos. 2303a (2p), 2304b, Margie Moran, 1973 winner. No. 2303b (7p), Pageant participant, Kalesa horse-drawn cart.

2302 A635 Pair, #a.-b. .60 .30
2303 A635 Pair, #a.-b. .70 .35

Souvenir Sheet

2304 A635 8p Sheet of 2, #a.-b. 1.20 .60

Great Filipinos Type of 1989

Designs: a, Antonio J. Molina, musician. b, Jose Yulo, politician. c, Josefa Jara-Martinez, social worker. d, Nicanor Reyes, Sr., accountant. e, Sabino B. Padilla, lawyer.

1994, June 10

2307 A536 2p Strip of 5, #a.-e. .75 .38

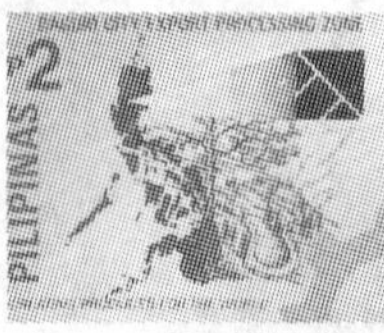

Philippine Export Processing Zones A637

No. 2308: a, Baguio City. b, Bataan. c, Mactan. d, Cavite.

No. 2309a, 7p, Map of Philippines, export products. b, 8p, Export products flowing around world map.

Unwmk.

1994, July 4 Litho. *Perf. 14*

2308 A637 2p Block of 4, #a.-d. .60 .30
2309 A637 Pair, #a.-b. 1.10 .55

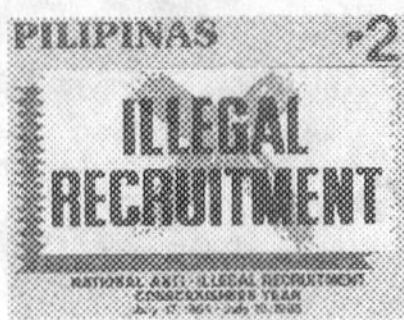

Fight Illegal Recruitment Year — A638

1994, July 15

2310 A638 2p multicolored .15 .15

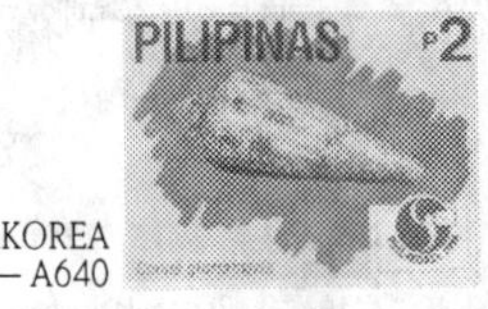

Wildlife A639

Designs: a, Palawan bearcat. b, Philippine tarsier. c, Scaly anteater. d, Palawan porcupine.
12p, Visayan spotted deer.

1994, Aug. 12 Litho. *Perf. 14*

2311 A639 6p Block of 4, #a.-d. 1.90 .95

Souvenir Sheet

2312 A639 12p multicolored .95 .95
a. Ovptd. in margin .95 .95

No. 2312a overprinted in white, black and red in sheet margin with "SINGPEX '94 / 31 August-3 September 1994" and show emblem.

PHILAKOREA '94 — A640

Shells: a, Conus gloriamaris. b, Conus striatus. c, Conus geographus. d, Conus textile.

No. 2314a, Conus marmoreus. No. 2314b, Conus geographus, diff. No. 2315a, Conus striatus, diff. No. 2315b, Conus marmoreus, diff.

1994, Aug. 16

2313 A640 2p Block of 4, #a.-d. .62 .30

Souvenir Sheets

2314 A640 6p Sheet of 2, #a.-b. .95 .48
2315 A640 6p Sheet of 2, #a.-b. .95 .48

Landings at Leyte Gulf, 50th Anniv. A641

Designs: a, Pres. Sergio Osmena, Sr. b, Gen. MacArthur wading ashore. c, Dove of Peace. d, Carlos P. Romulo.

1994, Sept. 15

2316 A641 2p Block of 4, #a.-d. .62 .30

See Nos. 2391a-2391d.

1994 International Year of the Family

Intl. Anniversaries & Events A642

Unwmk.

1994, Oct. 24 Litho. *Perf. 14*

2317 A642 2p Family .16 .15
2318 A642 6p Labor workers .48 .25
2319 A642 7p Feather, clouds .55 .28
Nos. 2317-2319 (3) 1.19 .68

Intl. Year of the Family (#2317). ILO, 75th anniv. (#2318). ICAO, 50th anniv. (#2319).

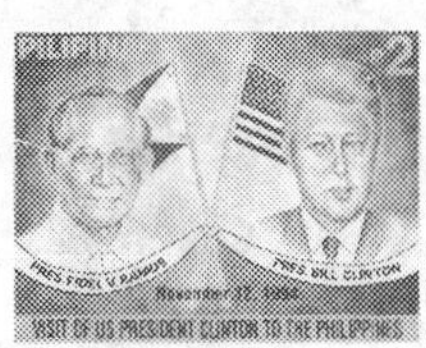

Visit of US Pres. Bill Clinton A643

1994, Nov. 12

2320 A643 2p green & multi .16 .15
2321 A643 8p blue & multi .65 .32

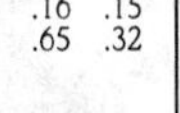

East Asean Business Convention, Davao — A644

1994, Nov. 15

2322 A644 2p violet & multi .16 .15
2323 A644 6p brown & multi .48 .25

Nos. 2322-2323 not issued without overprint "Nov. 15-20, 1994" and obliterator covering original date at lower left.

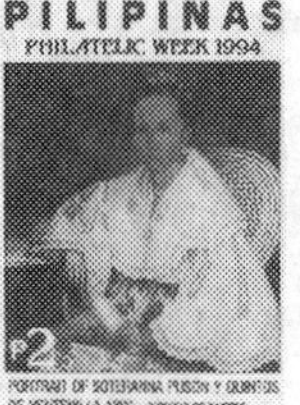

Philatelic Week — A645

Christmas — A646

Portraits by Philippine artists: 2p, Soteranna Puson Y Quintos de Ventenilla, by Dionisio de Castro. 6p, Quintina Castor de Sadie, by Simon Flores y de la Rosa. 7p, Artist's mother, by Felix Eduardo Resurreccion Hidalgo y Padilla. 8p, Una Bulaquena, by Juan Luna y Novicio.

12p, Cirilo and Severina Quiason Family, by Simon Flores y de la Rosa.

1994, Nov. 21

2324 A645 2p multicolored .16 .15
2325 A645 6p multicolored .48 .25
2326 A645 7p multicolored .55 .28
2327 A645 8p multicolored .65 .32
Nos. 2323-2327 (5) 2.32 1.25

Souvenir Sheet

2328 A645 12p multicolored .95 .48

No. 2328 contains one 29x80mm stamp.

1994, Nov. 25

2329 A646 2p Wreath .16 .15
2330 A646 6p Angels .48 .25
2331 A646 7p Bells .55 .28
2332 A646 8p Basket .65 .32
Nos. 2329-2332 (4) 1.84 1.00

ASEANPEX '94 A647

Designs: No. 2333a, Blue-naped parrot. b, Bleeding heart pigeon. c, Palawan peacock pheasant. d, Koch's pitta.

No. 2334, Philippine eagle, vert.

1994

2333 A647 2p Block of 4, #a.-d. .65 .32

Souvenir Sheet

2334 A647 12p multicolored .95 .48

A648

Philippine Guerrilla Units in World War II — A649

No. 2335: a, Troops entering prison. b, Prisoners escaping.

Bombed building and: No. 2336a, Emblem of East Central Luzon Guerrilla Area. b, Map, Mindoro Provincial Batallion, Marinduque Guerrilla Force. c, Map, Zambales Military District, Masbate Guerrilla Regiment. d, Map, Samar Area Command.

1994 Litho. Unwmk. *Perf. 14*

2335 A648 2p Pair, #a.-b. .32 .16
2336 A649 2p Block of 4, #a.-d. .65 .32

No. 2335 is a continuous design.
See Nos. 2392a-2392b.

New Year 1995 (Year of the Boar) — A650

1994

2337 A650 2p shown .16 .15
2338 A650 6p Boy, girl pigs .48 .25
a. Souvenir sheet of 2, #2337-2338 + 2 labels .65 .32

No. 2338 exists imperf.
See Nos. 2459d, 2460d.

Kalayaan, Cent. (in 1998) — A651

a, Flag, 1898. b, Philippine flag. c, Cent. emblem.

1994

2339 A651 2p Strip of 3, #a.-c. .48 .25

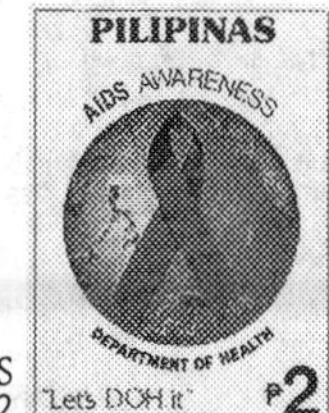

AIDS Awareness — A652

1994

2340 A652 2p multicolored .16 .15

Visit of Pope John Paul II A653

Pope John Paul II and: #2342, Papal arms, globe showing Philippines. 6p, Emblem, map of Asia. #2344, Children.

#2341, a, Archdiocese of Manila. b, Diocese of Cebu. c, Diocese of Caceres. d, Diocese of Nueva Segovia.

#2345, Pres. Fidel V. Ramos, Pope John Paul II.

1995, Jan. 2

2341 A653 2p Block of 4, #a.-d. .65 .32
2342 A653 2p multicolored .16 .15
2343 A653 6p multicolored .48 .25
2344 A653 8p multicolored .65 .32
Nos. 2341-2344 (4) 1.94 1.04

Souvenir Sheet

2345 A653 8p multicolored .65 .32
a. Overprinted in margin .65 .32

Federation of Asian Bishops' Conferences (#2343). 10th World Youth Day (#2344).

Overprint in margin of No. 2345a reads "CHRISTYPEX '95 / JANUARY 4-16, 1995 / University of Santo Tomas, Manila / PHILIPPINE PHILATELIC FEDERATION."

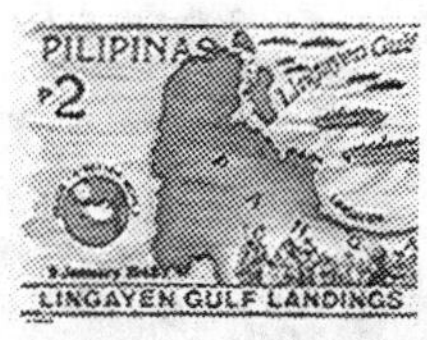

Lingayen Gulf Landings, 50th Anniv. A654

a, Map of Lingayen Gulf, ships, troops. b, Map, emblems of 6th, 37th, 40th, 43rd Divisions.

1995, Jan. 9

2346 A654 2p Pair, #a.-b. .32 .16

No. 2346 is a continuous design.
See Nos. 2391e-2391f.

Liberation of Manila, 50th Anniv. — A655

Statue honoring victims and: 2p, 8p, Various destroyed buildings. Illustration reduced.

1995, Feb. 3

2347 A655 2p magenta & multi .16 .15
2348 A655 8p blue & multi .65 .32

See Nos. 2392m, 2392r.

Jose W. Diokno (1922-87), Politician — A656

1995, Feb. 26

2349 A656 2p multicolored .16 .15

Intl. School, Manila, 75th Anniv. A657

Unwmk.

1995, Mar. 4 Litho. *Perf. 14*

2350 A657 2p shown .15 .15
2351 A657 8p Globe, cut out figures .65 .32

Wildlife A658

No. 2352: a, Mousedeeer. b, Tamaraw. c, Visayan warty pig. d, Palm civet.

No. 2353, vert: a, Flying lemur. b, Philippine deer.

1995, Mar. 20

2352 A658 2p Block of 4, #a.-d. .65 .30

Souvenir Sheet

2353 A658 8p Sheet of 2, #a.-b. 1.25 .65

Battles of World War II, 50th Anniv. A659

Unit emblems and and maps showing: No. 2354, Battle of Nichols Airbase and Ft. Mckinley. No. 2355: a, Nasugbu landings. b, Tagaytay landings.

1995, Apr. 9

2354 A659 2p multicolored .15 .15
2355 A659 2p Pair, #a.-b. .35 .15

See Nos. 2391g-2391h, 2392c.

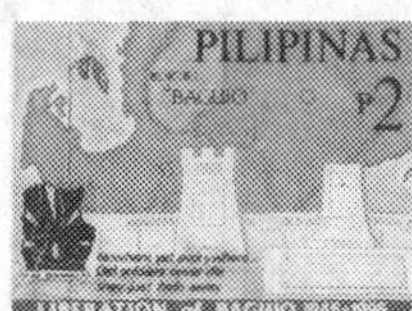

Liberation of Baguio, 50th Anniv. A660

1995, Apr. 27

2356 A660 2p multicolored .25 .15

See No. 2392d.

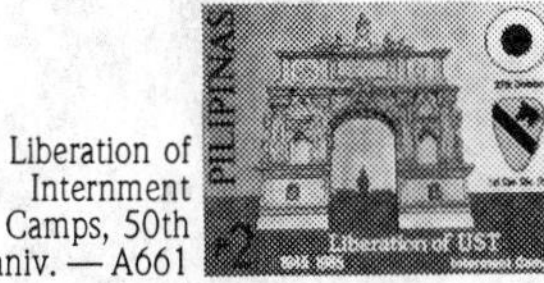

Liberation of Internment Camps, 50th Anniv. — A661

1995, May 28

2357 A661 2p UST .25 .15
2358 A661 2p Cabanatuan .25 .15
2359 A661 2p Los Banos .25 .15
Nos. 2357-2359 (3) .75 .45

See Nos. 2392e-2392g.

Great Filipinos Type of 1989

Persons born in 1895: a, Victorio C. Edades. b, Jovita Fuentes. c, Candido M. Africa. d, Asuncion Arriola-Perez. e, Eduardo A. Quisumbing.

Perf. 14x13½

1995, June 1 Litho. Unwmk.

2360 A536 2p Strip of 5, #a.-e. 1.25 .60

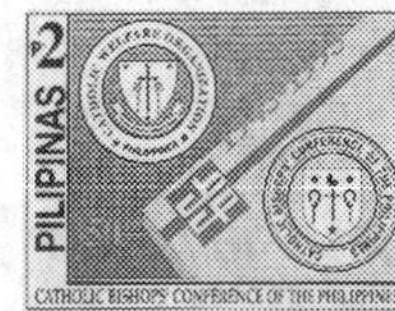

Catholic Bishops' Conference of the Philippines, 50th Anniv. A662

1995, July 22 *Perf. 14*

2361 A662 2p multicolored .25 .15

A663 A664

1995, Aug. 2

2362 A663 2p multicolored .25 .15

Jaime N. Ferrer (1916-87).

1995, Aug. 4

Jars: No. 2363a, Manunggul. b, Non-anthropomorphic. c, Anthropomorphic. d, Leta-leta yawning jarlet.

12p, Double spouted and legged vessel, presentation tray.

2363 A664 2p Block of 4, #a.-d. 1.00 .50

Souvenir Sheet

2364 A664 12p multicolored 1.50 .75

Archaeological finds. No. 2364 contains one 80x30mm stamp. Jakarta '95 (#2364).

ASEAN Environment Year 1995 — A665

Designs: Nos. 2365a, 2366a, Left hand holding turtle, wildlife scene. Nos. 2365b, 2366b, Right hand below fish, bird, wildlife scene.

1995, Aug. 10

2365 A665 2p Pair, #a.-b. .50 .25

Souvenir Sheet

2366 A665 6p Sheet of 2, #a.-b. 1.50 .75

Nos. 2365-2366 are each continuous designs.

Souvenir Sheet

Philippine Eagle, New Natl. Bird — A666

Illustration reduced.

1995, Aug. 11

2367 A666 16p multicolored 4.00 2.00

Mercury Drug Co., 50th Anniv. A667

1995, Aug. 15

2368 A667 2p multicolored .25 .15

Parish of St. Louis Bishop, 400th Anniv. A668

1995, Aug. 18

2369 A668 2p multicolored .25 .15

Asian-Pacific Postal Training Center, 25th Anniv. A669

Unwmk.

1995, Sept. 1 Litho. *Perf. 14*

2370 A669 6p multicolored .90 .45

UN, 50th Anniv. — A670

Filipinos serving in UN: No. 2371a, #2372, Carlos P. Romulo. b, Rafael M. Salas. c, Salvador P. Lopez. d, Jose D. Ingles.

1995, Sept. 25

2371 A670 2p Block of 4, #a.-d. 1.25 .65

2371E A670 2p Cesar C. Bengzon

f. Block of 4, #2371b-2371d, 2371E 50.00

Souvenir Sheet

2372 A670 16p multicolored 2.50 1.25

No. 2371E was issued with the wrong portrait and was withdrawn after two days.

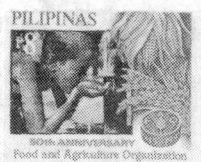

FAO, 50th Anniv. — A671

1995, Sept. 25

2373 A671 8p multicolored 1.25 .65

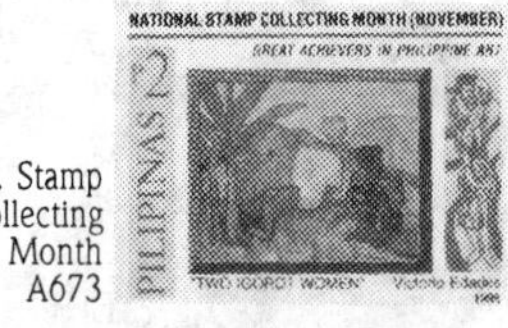

A671a A672

Unwmk.

1995, Oct. 5 Litho. *Perf. 14*

2373A A671a 2p multicolored .15 .15

Manila Overseas Press Club, 50th anniv.

1995, Oct. 24

2374 A672 2p Total Eclipse of the Sun .30 .15

Natl. Stamp Collecting Month A673

Paintings: 2p, Two Igorot Women, by Victorio Edades. 6p, Serenade, by Carlos "Botong" Francisco. 7p, Tuba Drinkers, by Vincente Manansala. 8p, Genesis, by Hernando Ocampo.

12p, The Builders, by Edades.

1995, Nov. 6

2375 A673 2p multicolored .30 .15

2376 A673 6p multicolored .90 .45

2377 A673 7p multicolored 1.00 .50

2378 A673 8p multicolored 1.25 .65

Nos. 2375-2378 (4) 3.45 1.75

Souvenir Sheet

2379 A673 12p multicolored 1.75 .90

No. 2379 contains one 76x26mm stamp.

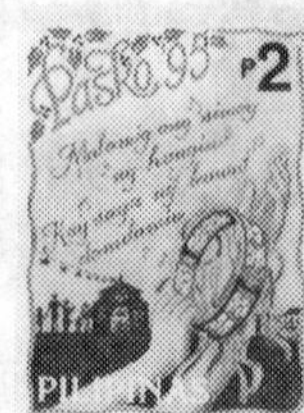

Christmas — A674

Musical instruments, Christmas carols.

1995, Nov. 22

2380 A674 2p Tambourine .30 .15

2381 A674 6p Maracas .90 .45

2382 A674 7p Guitar 1.00 .50

2383 A674 8p Drum 1.25 .65

Nos. 2380-2383 (4) 3.45 1.75

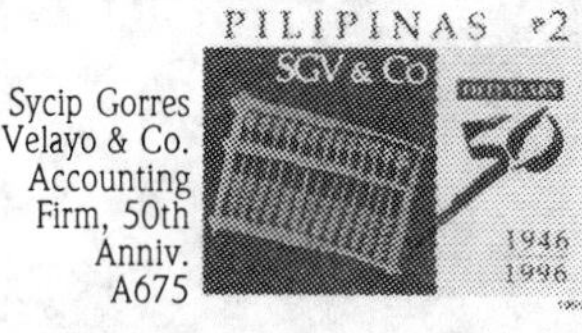

Sycip Gorres Velayo & Co. Accounting Firm, 50th Anniv. A675

1995, Nov. 27

2384 A675 2p Abacus .30 .15

Souvenir Sheet

Pres. Fidel V. Ramos Proclaiming November as Natl. Stamp Collecting Month — A676

1995, Nov. 29

2385 A676 8p multicolored 1.25 .65

New Year 1996 (Year of the Rat) — A677

1995, Dec. 1

2386 A677 2p shown .30 .15

2387 A677 6p Outline of rat .90 .45

a. Souv. sheet, #2386-2387+2 labels 1.25 .65

No. 2387a exists imperf.

See Nos. 2459e, 2460e.

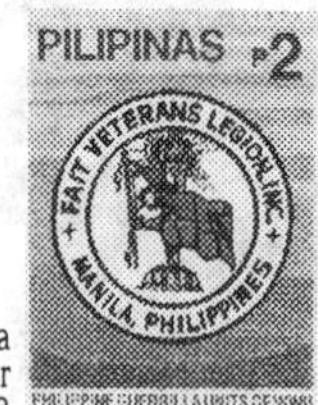

Philippine Guerrilla Units of World War II — A678

Designs: a, Emblem, FIL-American Irregular Troops (FAIT). b, Emblem, BICOL Brigade. c, Map, FIL-American Guerrilla Forces (Cavite), Hukbalahap Unit (Pampanga). d, Map, South Tarlac, Northwest Pampanga Military Districts.

1995, Dec. 8 Litho. *Perf. 14*

2388 A678 2p Block of 4, #a.-d. 1.25 .60

Significant Events of World War II, 50th Anniv. A679

Designs: a, Map, liberation of Panay and Romblon, 61st Division. b, Map, Liberation of Cebu, Americal Division. c, Battle of Ipo Dam, 43rd Division, FIL-American Guerrillas. d, Map, Battle of Bessang Pass, 37th Division. e, Sculpture, surrender of Gen. Yamashita.

1995, Dec. 15

2389 A679 2p Strip of 5, #a.-e. 1.50 .75

See Nos. 2392h-2392 l.

Revolutionary Heroes — A680

a, Jose P. Rizal (1861-96) b, Andres Bonifacio, (1863-97). c, Apolinario Mabini (1864-1903).

1995, Dec. 27

2390 A680 2p Set of 3, #a.-c. .90 .45

Miniature Sheets

World War II Types of 1994-95 and

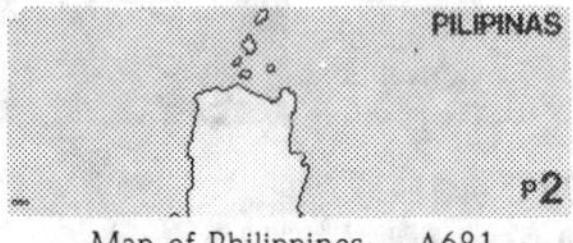

Map of Philippines — A681

Color of Pilipinas and denomination: Nos. 2391a-2391d, like #2316, red. Nos. 2391e-2391f, like #2346, red. Nos. 2391g-2391h, like #2355, red. Nos. 2391i-2391l, map of Philippines with blue background showing sites of Allied landings.

No. 2392: a-b, like #2335, white. c, like #2354, red. d, like #2356, white. e, like #2358, white. f, like #2357, white. g, like #2359, white. h.-l., like #2389a-2389e, purple. m, like #2347, red. n.-q., map of Philippines with green background showing location of prison camps. r, like #2348, red.

1995, Dec. 27 Litho. *Perf. 14*

2391 A681 2p Sheet of 12, #a.-l. 4.25 4.25

2392 A681 2p Sheet of 18, #a.-r. 6.25 6.25

23rd Intl. Congress of Internal Medicine — A682

1996, Jan. 10 Litho. *Perf. 14*

2393 A682 2p multicolored .30 .15

Sun Life Assurance Company of Canada in the Philippines, Cent. — A683

1996, Jan. 26

2394 A683 2p shown .30 .15

2395 A683 8p Sun over horizon 1.25 .60

Valentine's Day — A684

"I Love You" on Nos. 2396a-2399a, "Happy Valentine" on Nos. 2396b-2399b and: No. 2396, Pair of love birds. No. 2397, Cupid with bow and arrow. No. 2398, Box of chocolates. No. 2399, Bouquet of roses, butterfly.

1996, Feb. 9

2396 A684 2p Pair, #a.-b. .60 .30

2397 A684 6p Pair, #a.-b. 1.80 .90

2398 A684 7p Pair, #a.-b. 2.25 1.15

2399 A684 8p Pair, #a.-b. 2.50 1.25

Nos. 2396-2399 (4) 7.15 3.60

St. Thomas University Hospital, 50th Anniv. A685

1996, Mar. 5

2400 A685 2p multicolored .30 .15

Gregorio Araneta University Foundation, 50th Anniv. — A686

1996, Mar. 5

2401 A686 2p multicolored .30 .15

Fish — A687

No. 2402: a, Emperor fish. b, Mandarinfish. c, Regal angelfish. d, Clown triggerfish. e, Raccoon butterflyfish. g, Powder brown tang. h, Two-banded anemonefish. i, Moorish idol. j, Blue tang. k, Majestic angelfish.

No. 2403: a, like #2402d. b, like #2402k. c, like #2402c. d, like #2402h.

1996, Mar. 12

2402 A687 4p Strip of 5, #a.-e. 3.00 1.50
2402F A687 4p Strip of 5, #g.-k. 3.00 1.50

Miniature Sheet

2403 A687 4p Sheet of 4, #a.-d. 2.50 1.25
e. #2403 with new inscriptions 2.50 1.25

Souvenir Sheet

2404 A687 12p Lionfish 1.80 .90
a. #2404 with new inscriptions 1.80 .90

Nos. 2402, 2402F have blue compressed security printing at left, black denomination, white background, margin. Nos. 2403-2404 have blue background, violet denomination, continuous design.

ASEANPEX '96 (No. 2403-2404).

Nos. 2403e, 2404a inscribed in sheet margins with various INDONESIA '96 exhibition emblems.

Issued: Nos. 2403e, 2404a, 3/21/96.

See Nos. 2410-2413.

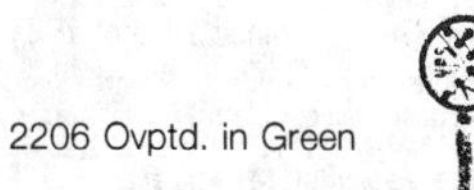

No. 2206 Ovptd. in Green

1996 Litho. Wmk. 391 *Perf. 14*

2405 A607 2p Sheet of 4, #a.-d. 1.80 .90

Ovpt. in sheet margin reads: "THE YOUNG PHILATELISTS' SOCIETY 10TH ANNIVERSARY".

Souvenir Sheet

Basketball — A688

Illustration reduced.

1996, Apr. 14

2406 A688 10p multicolored .50 .25

PALARONG/PAMBANSA '96.

Francisco B. Ortigas, Sr. — A689

1996, Apr. 30 Unwmk.

2407 A689 4p multicolored .20 .15

Discovery of Radioactivity, Cent. — A690

1996, Apr. 30

2408 A690 4p multicolored .20 .15

Congregation of Dominican Sisters of St. Catherine of Siena, 300th Anniv. A691

1996, Apr. 30

2409 A691 4p multicolored .20 .15

Fish Type of 1996

No. 2410: a, Long-horned cowfish. b, Queen angelfish. c, Long-nosed butterflyfish. d, Yellow tang. e, Blue-faced angelfish.

No. 2411: a, Saddleback butterflyfish. b, Sailfin tang. c, Harlequin tuskfish. d, Clown wrasse. e, Spotted boxfish.

No. 2412: a, like #2410e. b, like #2410c. c, like #2410b. d, like #2411c.

No. 2413, vert: a, Purple firefish. b, Pacific seahorse. c, Red-faced batfish. d, Long-nosed hawksfish.

1996

2410 A687 4p Strip of 5, #a.-e. 2.25 1.10
2411 A687 4p Strip of 5, #a.-e. 2.25 1.10
2412 A687 4p Sheet of 4, #a.-d. 1.75 .90
e. With added inscription 1.75 .90
2413 A687 4p Sheet of 4, #a.-d. 1.75 .90
e. With added inscription 1.75 .90

Nos. 2412-2413 have white background. Nos. 2410-2411 have blue background.

ASEANPEX '96 (#2412-2413). Added inscription in sheet margin of #2412e, 2413e includes CHINA '96 emblem and "CHINA '96 - 9th Asian International Exhibition" in red.

Issued: Nos. 2410-2413, 5/10/96. Nos. 2412e, 2413e, 5/16/96.

Great Filipinos Type of 1989

Designs: a, Carlos P. Garcia (1896-1971), politician. b, Casimiro del Rosario (1896-1962), physicist. c, Geronima T. Pecson (1896-1989), politician. d, Cesar C. Bengson (1896-1992), lawyer. e, Jose Corazon de Jesus (1896-1932), writer.

Perf. 13½

1996, June 1 Litho. Unwmk.

2414 A536 4p Strip of 5, #a.-e. 1.75 .90

ABS CBN (Broadcasting Network), 50th Anniv. A692

1996, June 13 *Perf. 14*

2415 A692 4p shown .50 .25
2416 A692 8p Rooster, world map .85 .40

Manila, Convention City — A693

1996, June 24

2417 A693 4p multicolored .50 .25

Jose Cojuangco, Sr. (1896-1976), Businessman, Public Official — A694

1996, July 3

2418 A694 4p multicolored .50 .25

Philippine-American Friendship Day — A695

Symbols of Philippines, US: 4p, Hats. 8p, National birds. 16p, Flags, vert.

1996, July 4

2419 A695 4p multicolored .50 .25
2420 A695 8p multicolored 1.00 .50

Souvenir Sheet

2421 A695 16p multicolored 1.00 .50

Modern Olympic Games, Cent. A696

4p, No. 2426a, Boxing. 6p, No. 2426b, Athletics. 7p, No. 2426c, Swimming. 8p, No. 2426d, Equestrian.

Unwmk.

1996, July 19 Litho. *Perf. 14*

2422 A696 4p multicolored .50 .25
2423 A696 6p multicolored .75 .40
2424 A696 7p multicolored .90 .45
2425 A696 8p multicolored 1.00 .50
Nos. 2422-2425 (4) 3.15 1.60

Miniature Sheet

2426 A696 4p Sheet of 4, #a.-d. 2.00 1.00

Nos. 2422-2425 have colored background, blue security code at right, denominations at LR. Nos. 2426a-2426d have colored circles on white background, blue security code at top, and denominations at UR, UL, LR, LL, respectively.

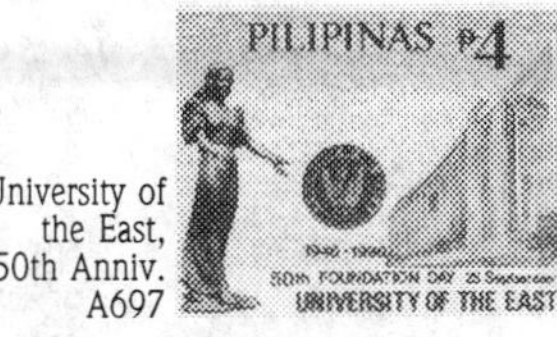

University of the East, 50th Anniv. A697

1996, Aug. 15

2427 A697 4p multicolored .50 .25

Orchids A698

No. 2428a, Dendrobium anosmum. b, Phalaenopsis. equestris-alba. c, Aerides lawrenceae. d, Vanda javierii.

No. 2429a, Renanthera philippinensis. b, Dendrobium schuetzei. c, Dendrobium taurinum. d, Vanda lamellata.

No. 2430a, Coelogyne pandurata. b, Vanda merrilii. c, Cymbidium aliciae. d, Dendrobium topaziacum.

1996, Sept. 26

2428 A698 4p Block or strip of 4, #a.-d. 2.00 1.00
2429 A698 4p Block or strip of 4, #a.-d. 2.00 1.00

Miniature Sheet

2430 A698 4p Sheet of 4, #a.-d. 2.00 1.00

Nos. 2428-2429 were printed in sheets of 4 each.

ASEANPEX '96 (#2430). Complete sheets of Nos. 2428-2429 have ASEANPEX emblem in selvage.

6th Asian Pacific Intl. Trade Fair — A699

1996, Sept. 30

2431 A699 4p multicolored .50 .25

UNICEF, 50th Anniv. — A700 TAIPEX '96 — A701

Children in montage of scenes studying, working, playing: No. 2432a, Blue & multi. b, Purple & multi. c, Green & multi. d, Red & multi.

16p, Four children, horiz.

1996, Oct. 9

2432 A700 4p Block of 4, #a.-d. 2.00 1.00

Souvenir Sheet

2433 A700 16p multicolored 2.00 1.00

1996, Oct. 21 Litho. *Perf. 14*

Orchids: No. 2434: a, Fran's Fantasy "Alea." b, Malvarosa Green Goddess "Nani." c, Ports of Paradise "Emerald Isle." d, Mem. Conrada Perez "Nani."

No. 2435: a, Pokai tangerine "Lea." b, Mem. Roselyn Reisman "Diana." c, C. Moscombe x Toshi Aoki. d, Mem. Benigno Aquino "Flying Aces."

12p, Pamela Hetherington "Coronation," Living Gold "Erin Treasure," Eleanor Spicer "White Bouquet."

2434 A701 4p Block of 4, #a.-d. 2.25 1.10
2435 A701 4p Block of 4, #a.-d. 2.25 1.10

Souvenir Sheet

2436 A701 12p multicolored 1.75 .85

Nos. 2434-2435 were issued in sheets of 16 stamps. No. 2436 contains one 80x30mm stamp.

1996 Asia-Pacific Economic Cooperation A702

Winning entries of stamp design competition: 4p, Sun behind mountains, airplane, skyscrapers, tower, ship, satellite dish, vert. 7p, Skyscrapers. 8p, Flags of nations beside path, globe, skyscrapers, sun, vert.

1996, Oct. 30

2437 A702 4p multicolored .55 .25
2438 A702 6p shown .80 .40
2439 A702 7p multicolored .90 .45
2440 A702 8p multicolored 1.00 .50
Nos. 2437-2440 (4) 3.25 1.60

Christmas A703

Designs: 4p, Philippine Nativity scene, vert. 6p, Midnight Mass. 7p, Carolers. 8p, Carolers with Carabao, vert.

1996, Nov. 5

2441 A703 4p multicolored .55 .25
2442 A703 6p multicolored .80 .40
2443 A703 7p multicolored .90 .45
2444 A703 8p multicolored 1.00 .50
Nos. 2441-2444 (4) 3.25 1.60

Eugenio P. Perez (1896-1957), Politician — A704

1996, Nov. 11 Litho. *Perf. 14*

2445 A704 4p multicolored .55 .25

New Year 1997 (Year of the Ox) — A705

1996, Dec. 1

2446 A705 4p Carabao .55 .25
2447 A705 6p Tamaraw .80 .40
a. Souv. sheet, #2446-2447 + 2 labels 1.35 .65

No. 2447a exists imperf.
See Nos. 2459f, 2460f.

ASEANPEX '96, Intl. Philatelic Exhibition, Manila — A706

Independence, Cent. (in 1998) — A707

Jose P. Rizal (1861-96): No. 2448: a, At 14 years. b, At 18. c, At 25. d, At 31.

No. 2449: a, "Noli Me Tangere." b, Gomburza to whom Rizal dedicated "El Filbusterismo." c, Oyang Dapitana, by Rizal. d, Ricardo Camicero, by Rizal.

No. 2450, horiz: a, Rizal's house, Calamba. b, University of St. Tomas, Manila, 1611. c, Orient Hotel, Manila. d, Dapitan during Rizal's time.

No. 2451, horiz: a, Central University, Madrid. b, British Museum, London. c, Botanical Garden, Madrid. d, Heidelberg, Germany.

No. 2452, Rizal at 14, horiz. No. 2453, Rizal at 18, horiz. No. 2454, Rizal at 25, horiz. No. 2455, Rizal at 31, horiz.

1996

2448 A706 4p Block of 4, #a.-d. 2.20 1.10
2449 A706 4p Block of 4, #a.-d. 2.20 1.10
2450 A706 4p Block of 4, #a.-d. 2.20 1.10
2451 A706 4p Block of 4, #a.-d. 2.20 1.10

Souvenir Sheets

2452 A706 12p multicolored 1.60 .80
2453 A706 12p multicolored 1.60 .80
2454 A706 12p multicolored 1.60 .80
2455 A706 12p multicolored 1.60 .80

Issued: Nos. 2448, 2452, 12/14/96; Nos. 2449, 2453, 12/15/96; Nos. 2450, 2454, 12/16/96; Nos. 2451, 2455, 12/17/96. Nos. 2448-2451 were issued in sheets of 16 stamps.

1996, Dec. 20

Revolutionary heroes: a, Fr. Mariano C. Gomez (1799-1872). b, Fr. Jose A. Burgos (1837-72). c, Fr. Jacinto Zamora (1835-72).

2456 A707 4p Strip of 3, #a.-c. 1.65 .85

Jose Rizal — A709

1996, Dec. 30 Litho. *Perf. 14*

2458 A709 4p multicolored .55 .25

New Year Types of 1991-96

Unwmk.

1997, Feb. 12 Litho. *Perf. 14*

2459 Sheet of 6 3.30 1.65
a. A580 4p like #2126 .55 .25
b. A608 4p like #2208 .55 .25
c. A626 4p like #2284 .55 .25
d. A650 4p like #2337 .55 .25
e. A677 4p like #2386 .55 .25
f. A705 4p like #2446 .55 .25
2460 Sheet of 6 4.80 2.40
a. A580 6p like #2127 .80 .40
b. A608 6p like #2207 .80 .40
c. A626 6p like #2285 .80 .40
d. A650 6p like #2338 .80 .40
e. A677 6p like #2387 .80 .40
f. A705 6p like #2447 .80 .40

Hong Kong '97.

Nos. 2459a-2459b, 2460a-2460b have white margins, color differences. Nos. 2459c-2459d, 2459f, 2460c-2460d, 2460f have color differences. Nos. 2459e, 2460e, do not have blue security printing, and have color differences.

Nos. 2459a-2459f, 2460a-2460f are all dated "1997."

Holy Rosary Seminary, Bicent. A710

1997, Feb. 18

2461 A710 4p multicolored .55 .25

Philippine Army, Cent. — A711

1997, Feb. 18

2462 A711 4p multicolored .55 .25

Natl. Symbols Type of 1993-96

Gem — A711a

1997 Litho. Unwmk. *Perf. 14x13½*

2463 A610b 1p like #2212A .15 .15
2463A A610b 2p like #2212A .25 .15
2464 A711a 4p multicolored .30 .15
2465 A610i 5p like #2222 .35 .20
2466 A610k 6p like #2223A .40 .20
2467 A610m 7p like #2224A .50 .25
2468 A610o 8p like #2227 .55 .30
2469 A610p 10p like #2229 .70 .35
Nos. 2463-2469 (8) 3.20 1.75

Nos. 2463, #2465-2469 do not have blue compressed security printing at top and are dated "1997."

Nos. 2463A, 2464 have blue compressed security printing at top and are dated "1997."

Issued: 5p, 2/26; 1p, 10p, 2/27; 8p, 3/6; 7p, 3/7; 6p, 3/10; 2p, 4/15; 4p, 6/10.

Dept. of Finance, Cent. — A712

1997, Apr. 8 *Perf. 14*

2471 A712 4p multicolored .55 .25

Philippine Red Cross, 50th Anniv. A713

1997, Apr. 8

2472 A713 4p multicolored .55 .25

Philamlife Insurance Co., 50th Anniv. A714

1997, Apr. 8

2473 A714 4p multicolored .55 .25

J. Walter Thompson Advertising, 50th Anniv. in Philippines A715

1997, Apr. 18

2474 A715 4p multicolored .55 .25

Souvenir Sheet

Philippine-American Friendship Day, Republic Day, 50th Anniv. — A716

Illustration reduced.

1997, May 29

2475 A716 16p multicolored 2.50 1.25

PACIFIC 97.

Wild Animals A717

World Wildlife Fund: No. 2476, Visayan spotted deer. No. 2477, Visayan spotted deer (doe & fawn). No. 2478, Visayan warty pig. No. 2479, Visayan warty pig (adult, young).

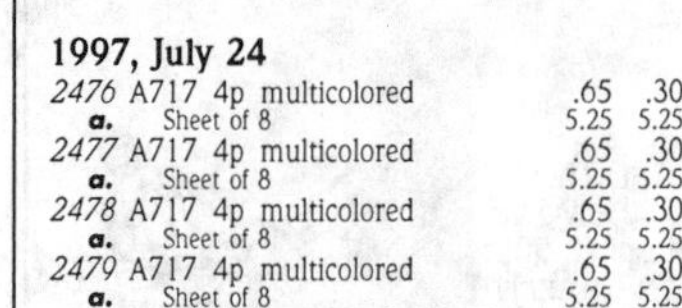

1997, July 24

2476 A717 4p multicolored .65 .30
a. Sheet of 8 5.25 5.25
2477 A717 4p multicolored .65 .30
a. Sheet of 8 5.25 5.25
2478 A717 4p multicolored .65 .30
a. Sheet of 8 5.25 5.25
2479 A717 4p multicolored .65 .30
a. Sheet of 8 5.25 5.25
b. Block or strip of 4, #2476-2479 2.60 2.60

No. 2479b was issued in sheets of 16 stamps.

ASEAN, 30th Anniv. A718

Founding signatories: No. 2480, Adam Malik, Indonesia, Tun Abdul Razak, Malaysia, Narcisco Ramos, Philippines, S. Rajaratnam, Singapore, Thanat Khoman, Thailand. No. 2481, Natl. flags of founding signatories. No. 2482, Flags of current ASEAN countries. No. 2483, Flags of ASEAN countries surrounding globe.

1997, Aug. 7 *Perf. 14*

2480 A718 4p multicolored .50 .25
2481 A718 4p multicolored .50 .25
a. Pair, #2480-2481 1.00 .50
2482 A718 6p multicolored .75 .40
2483 A718 6p multicolored .75 .40
a. Pair, #2482-2483 1.50 .80
Nos. 2480-2483 (4) 2.50 1.30

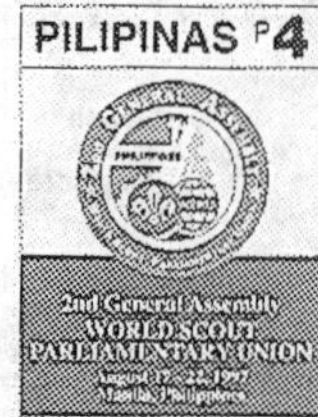

World Scout Parliamentary Union, 2nd General Assembly — A719

1997, Aug. 17

2484 A719 4p multicolored .50 .25

Manuel L. Quezon University, 50th Anniv. A720

1997, Aug. 19

2485 A720 4p multicolored .50 .25

Great Filipinos Type of 1989

Famous people: a, Justice Roberto Regala (1897-1979). b, Doroteo Espiritu, dental surgeon, inventor (b. 1897). c, Elisa R. Ochoa (1897-1978), nurse, tennis champion. d, Mariano Marcos (1897-1945), lawyer, educator. e, Jose F. Romero (1897-1978), editor.

Perf. 14x13½

1997, June 1 Litho. Unwmk.

2486 A536 4p Strip of 5, #a.-e. 1.75 .90

Battle of Candon, 1898 A721

4p, Don Federico Isabelo Abaya, revolutionary leader against Spanish. 6p, Soldier on horseback.

1997, Sept. 24 *Perf. 14*

2487 A721 4p multi, vert. .55 .25
2488 A721 6p multi .80 .40

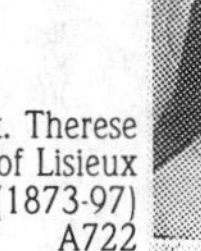
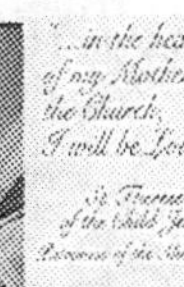
St. Therese of Lisieux (1873-97) A722

1997, Oct. 16
2489 A722 6p multicolored .80 .40

Stamp and Philatelic Division, 50th Anniv. A723

Abstract art: 4p, Homage to the Heroes of Bessang Pass, by Hernando Ruiz Ocampo. 6p, Jardin III, by Fernando Zobel. 7p, Abstraction, by Nena Saguil, vert. 8p, House of Life, by Jose Joya, vert. 16p, Dimension of Fear, by Jose Joya.

1997, Oct. 16
2490 A723 4p multicolored .55 .25
2491 A723 6p multicolored .80 .40
2492 A723 7p multicolored .95 .50
2493 A723 8p multicolored 1.10 .55
Nos. 2490-2493 (4) 3.40 1.70

Souvenir Sheet
2494 A723 16p multicolored 2.20 1.10

No. 2494 contains one 80x30mm stamp.

Heinrich von Stephan (1831-97) A724

1997, Oct. 24 Litho. *Perf. 14*
2495 A724 4p multicolored .50 .25

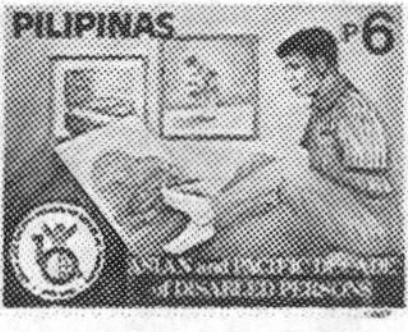
Asian and Pacific Decade of Disabled Persons A725

1997, Oct. 24 Litho. *Perf. 14*
2496 A725 6p multicolored .75 .40

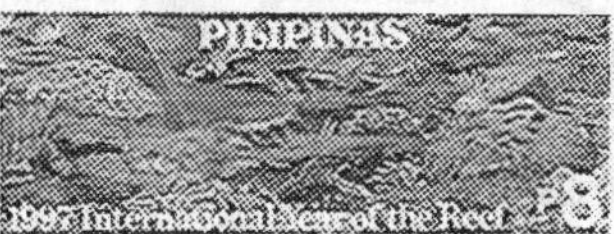
Intl. Year of the Reef — A726

Illustration reduced.

1997, Oct. 24 Litho. *Perf. 14*
2497 A726 8p multicolored 1.00 .50

Souvenir Sheet
2498 A726 16p multicolored 2.00 1.00

No. 2498 is a continuous design.

Christmas — A727 Independence, Cent. — A728

Various stained glass windows.

1997, Nov. 7
2499 A727 4p multicolored .50 .25
2500 A727 6p multicolored .80 .40
2501 A727 7p multicolored .90 .45
2502 A727 8p multicolored 1.00 .50
Nos. 2499-2502 (4) 3.20 1.60

1997, Nov. 30

Various monuments to Andres Bonifacio (1863-97), revolutionary, founder of the Katipunan: a, red & multi. b, yellow & multi. c, blue & multi.

2503 A728 4p Strip of 3, #a.-c. 1.75 .85

New Year 1998 (Year of the Tiger) A729

1997, Dec. 1
2504 A729 4p shown .50 .25
2505 A729 6p Tigers, diff. .80 .40
a. Souvenir sheet, #2504-2505 + 2 labels 1.30 .65

No. 2505a exists imperf.

Philippine Eagle — A730

1997, Dec. 5
2506 A730 20p Looking right 2.50 1.25
2507 A730 30p Looking forward 3.75 1.80
2508 A730 50p On cliff 6.25 3.25
Nos. 2506-2508 (3) 12.50 6.30

Game Cocks A731

No. 2509: a, Hatch grey. b, Spangled roundhead. c, Racey mug. d, Silver grey.
No. 2510, vert: a, Grey. b, Kelso. c, Bruner roundhead. d, Democrat.
No. 2511, Cock fight, vert. No. 2512, Cocks facing each other ready to fight.

1997, Dec. 18
2509 A731 4p Block of 4, #a.-d. 2.00 1.00
2510 A731 4p Block of 4, #a.-d. 2.00 1.00

Souvenir Sheets
2511 A731 12p multicolored 1.50 .75
2512 A731 16p multicolored 2.00 1.00

No. 2512 contains one 80x30mm stamp.

Art Association of the Philippines, 50th Anniv. A732

Stylized designs: No. 2513, Colors of flag, sunburst. No. 2514, Association's initials, clenched fist holding artist's implements.

Unwmk.
1998, Feb. 14 Litho. *Perf. 14*
2513 A732 4p multicolored .40 .20
2514 A732 4p multicolored .40 .20
a. Pair, #2513-2514 .80 .40

Club Filipino Social Organization, Cent. — A733 Blessed Marie Eugenie (1817-98) — A734

1998, Feb. 25
2515 A733 4p multicolored .45 .25

1998, Feb. 25
2516 A734 4p multicolored .45 .25

Fulbright Educational Exchange Program in the Philippines, 50th Anniv. A735

1998, Feb. 25
2517 A735 4p multicolored .45 .25

SEMI-POSTAL STAMPS

Catalogue values for unused stamps in this section are for Never Hinged items.

Republic

Epifanio de los Santos, Trinidad H. Pardo and Teodoro M. Kalaw SP1

Doctrina Christiana, Cover Page — SP2 "Noli Me Tangere," Cover Page — SP3

Unwmk.
1949, Apr. 1 Engr. *Perf. 12*
B1 SP1 4c + 2c sepia .80 .60
B2 SP2 6c + 4c violet 2.50 1.65
B3 SP3 18c + 7c blue 3.00 2.75
Nos. B1-B3 (3) 6.30 5.00

The surtax was for restoration of war-damaged public libraries.

War Widow and Children — SP4 Disabled Veteran — SP5

1950, Nov. 30
B4 SP4 2c + 2c red .15 .15
B5 SP5 4c + 4c violet .28 .28
Set value .35 .36

The surtax was for war widows and children and disabled veterans of World War II.
For surcharges see Nos. 648-649.

Mrs. Manuel L. Quezon SP6

1952, Aug. 19 *Perf. 12*
B6 SP6 5c + 1c dp bl .15 .15
B7 SP6 6c + 2c car rose .28 .28

The surtax was used to encourage planting and care of fruit trees among Philippine children. For surcharge see No. 872.

Quezon Institute SP7

1958, Aug. 19 Photo. *Perf. 13½, 12*
Cross in Red
B8 SP7 5c + 5c grn .15 .15
B9 SP7 10c + 5c dp vio .32 .32

These stamps were obligatory on all mail from Aug. 19-Sept. 30.
For surcharges see Nos. 849, B12-B13, B16.

The surtax on all semi-postals from Nos. B8-B9 onward was for the Philippine Tuberculosis Society unless otherwise stated.

Scout Cooking — SP8

1959 Engr. *Perf. 13*
Yellow Paper
B10 SP8 6c + 4c shown .15 .15
B11 SP8 25c + 5c Archery .42 .42
a. Nos. B10-B11 tête bêche, *white* .85 .85
Nos. B10-B11,CB1-CB3 (5) 2.42 2.42

Issued to publicize the 10th Boy Scout World Jamboree, Makiling National Park, July 17-26. The surtax was to finance the Jamboree.
For souvenir sheet see No. CB3a. For surcharges see Nos. 832-833, C111.

Nos. B8-B9 Surcharged in Red

HELP
FIGHT
TB
3+5

1959 Photo. *Perf. 13½, 12*
B12 SP7 3c + 5c on 5c + 5c .15 .15
a. "3 + 5" and bars omitted
B13 SP7 6c + 5c on 10c + 5c .15 .15
Set value .24 .20

Bohol Sanatorium — SP9

1959, Aug. 19 Engr. *Perf. 12*

Cross in Red

Stamp	Unused	Used
B14 SP9 6c + 5c yel grn	.15	.15
B15 SP9 25c + 5c vio bl	.35	.28

No. B8 Surcharged "Help Prevent TB" and New Value

1960, Aug. 19 Photo. *Perf. 13½, 12*

Stamp	Unused	Used
B16 SP7 6c + 5c on 5c + 5c	.18	.15

Roxas Memorial T.B. Pavilion SP10

Perf. 11½

1961, Aug. 19 Unwmk. Photo.

Stamp	Unused	Used
B17 SP10 6c + 5c brn & red	.18	.15

Emiliano J. Valdes T.B. Pavilion SP11

1962, Aug. 19

Cross in Red

Stamp	Unused	Used
B18 SP11 6s + 5s dk vio	.15	.15
B19 SP11 30s + 5s ultra	.35	.25
B20 SP11 70s + 5s brt bl	.80	.65
Nos. B18-B20 (3)	1.30	1.05

José Rizal Playing Chess SP12

Design: 30s+5s, Rizal fencing.

1962, Dec. 30 Engr. *Perf. 13*

Stamp	Unused	Used
B21 SP12 6s + 4s grn & rose lil	.20	.20
B22 SP12 30s + 5s brt bl & claret	.42	.42

Surtax for Rizal Foundation.
For surcharges see Nos. 942-943.

Map of Philippines and Cross — SP13

1963, Aug. 19 Unwmk. *Perf. 13*

Stamp	Unused	Used
B23 SP13 6s + 5s vio & red	.15	.15
B24 SP13 10s + 5s grn & red	.15	.15
B25 SP13 50s + 5s brn & red	.52	.35
Nos. B23-B25 (3)	.82	
Set value		.50

Negros Oriental T.B. Pavilion SP14

1964, Aug. 19 Photo. *Perf. 13½*

Cross in Red

Stamp	Unused	Used
B26 SP14 5s + 5s brt pur	.15	.15
B27 SP14 6s + 5s ultra	.15	.15
B28 SP14 30s + 5s brown	.35	.25
B29 SP14 70s + 5s green	.65	.60
Nos. B26-B29 (4)	1.30	
Set value		.90

For surcharges see Nos. 986, 1586.

No. B27 Surcharged in Red with New Value and Two Bars

1965, Aug. 19

Cross in Red

Stamp	Unused	Used
B30 SP14 1s + 5s on 6s + 5s	.15	.15
B31 SP14 3s + 5s on 6s + 5s	.18	.15
Set value	.30	.15

Stork-billed Kingfisher — SP15

Birds: 5s+5s, Rufous hornbill. 10s+5s, Monkey-eating eagle. 30s+5s, Great-billed parrot.

1967, Aug. 19 Photo. *Perf. 13½*

Stamp	Unused	Used
B32 SP15 1s + 5s multi	.15	.15
B33 SP15 5s + 5s multi	.15	.15
B34 SP15 10s + 5s multi	.15	.15
B35 SP15 30s + 5s multi	.35	.35
Set value	.58	.58

1969, Aug. 15 Litho. *Perf. 13½*

Birds: 1s+5s, Three-toed woodpecker. 5s+5s, Philippine trogon. 10s+5s, Mt. Apo lorikeet. 40s+5s, Scarlet minivet.

Stamp	Unused	Used
B36 SP15 1s + 5s multi	.15	.15
B37 SP15 5s + 5s multi	.15	.15
B38 SP15 10s + 5s multi	.18	.15
B39 SP15 40s + 5s multi	.35	.25
Set value	.70	.55

Julia V. de Ortigas and Tuberculosis Society Building — SP16

1970, Aug. 3 Photo. *Perf. 13½*

Stamp	Unused	Used
B40 SP16 1s + 5s multi	.15	.15
B41 SP16 5s + 5s multi	.15	.15
B42 SP16 30s + 5s multi	.45	.45
B43 SP16 70s + 5s multi	.55	.55
Nos. B40-B43 (4)	1.30	1.30

Mrs. Julia V. de Ortigas was president of the Philippine Tuberculosis Society, 1932-1969.
For surcharge see No. 1251.

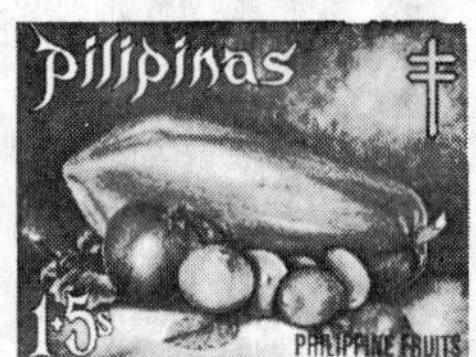
Mabolo, Santol, Chico, Papaya SP17

Philippine Fruits: 10s+5s, Balimbing, atis, mangosteen, macupa, bananas. 40s+5s, Susong-kalabao, avocado, duhat, watermelon, guava, mango. 1p+5s, Lanzones, oranges, sirhuelas, pineapple.

1972, Aug. 1 Litho. *Perf. 13*

Stamp	Unused	Used
B44 SP17 1s + 5s multi	.15	.15
B45 SP17 10s + 5s multi	.15	.15
B46 SP17 40s + 5s multi	.25	.25
B47 SP17 1p + 5s multi	.50	.50
Set value	.86	.86

Nos. B45-B46 Surcharged with New Value and 2 Bars

1973, June 15

Stamp	Unused	Used
B48 SP17 15s + 5s on 10s + 5s	.15	.15
B49 SP17 60s + 5s on 40s + 5s	.32	.32

Dr. Basilio J. Valdes and Veterans Memorial Hospital — SP18

1974, July 8 Litho. *Perf. 12½*

Cross in Red

Stamp	Unused	Used
B50 SP18 15s + 5s blue grn	.15	.15
a. Imperf.	.15	.15
B51 SP18 1.10p + 5s vio blue	.20	.15
a. Imperf.	.25	.25
Set value	.25	.22
Set value, imperf.	.30	.30

Dr. Valdes (1892-1970) was president of Philippine Tuberculosis Society.

For surcharges see Nos. 1250, 1252.

AIR POST STAMPS

Madrid-Manila Flight Issue

Regular Issue of 1917-26 Overprinted in Red or Violet

1926, May 13 Unwmk. *Perf. 11*

Stamp	Unused	Used
C1 A40 2c green (R)	7.50	3.50
C2 A40 4c carmine	10.00	4.25
a. Inverted overprint	*2,000.*	—
C3 A40 6c lilac (R)	47.50	14.00
C4 A40 8c orange brn	47.50	14.00
C5 A40 10c dp blue (R)	47.50	14.00
C6 A40 12c red orange	47.50	25.00
C7 A40 16c lt ol grn *(Sampson)*	*1,650.*	*1,550.*
C8 A40 16c ol bis *(Sampson)* (R)	*3,250.*	*2,600.*
C9 A40 16c ol grn *(Dewey)*	55.00	25.00
C10 A40 20c orange yel	55.00	25.00
C11 A40 26c blue green	55.00	27.50
C12 A40 30c gray	55.00	27.50
C13 A41 2p vio brn (R)	475.00	260.00
C14 A41 4p dk blue (R)	675.00	450.00
C15 A41 10p dp green	1,050.	625.00

Same Overprint on No. 269

Perf. 12

Wmk. 190PI

Stamp	Unused	Used
C16 A40 26c blue green	*2,400.*	

Same Overprint on No. 284

Perf. 10

Stamp	Unused	Used
C17 A41 1p pale violet	175.00	100.00

Flight of Spanish aviators Gallarza and Loriga from Madrid to Manila.

London-Orient Flight Issue

Regular Issue of 1917-25 Overprinted in Red

1928, Nov. 9 Unwmk. *Perf. 11*

Stamp	Unused	Used
C18 A40 2c green	.40	.25
C19 A40 4c carmine	.50	.40
C20 A40 6c violet	1.75	1.40
C21 A40 8c orange brn	1.90	1.60
C22 A40 10c dp blue	1.90	1.60
C23 A40 12c red orange	2.75	2.25
C24 A40 16c ol grn *(Dewey)*	2.00	1.50
C25 A40 20c orange yel	2.75	2.25
C26 A40 26c blue green	8.00	5.50
C27 A40 30c gray	8.00	5.50

Same Overprint on No. 271

Perf. 12

Wmk. 190PI

Stamp	Unused	Used
C28 A41 1p pale violet	45.00	25.00
Nos. C18-C28 (11)	74.95	47.25

Commemorating an airplane flight from London to Manila.

Nos. 354-360 Overprinted

1932, Sept. 27 Unwmk. *Perf. 11*

Stamp	Unused	Used
C29 A43 2c yellow green	.40	.30
C30 A44 4c rose carmine	.40	.30
C31 A45 12c orange	.60	.50
C32 A46 18c red orange	3.50	3.25
C33 A47 20c yellow	1.75	1.50
C34 A48 24c deep violet	1.75	1.50
C35 A49 32c olive brown	1.75	1.50
Nos. C29-C35 (7)	10.15	8.85

Visit of Capt. Wolfgang von Gronan on his round-the-world flight.

Regular Issue of 1917-25 Overprinted

1933, Apr. 11

Stamp	Unused	Used
C36 A40 2c green	.40	.35
C37 A40 4c carmine	.45	.35
C38 A40 6c deep violet	.80	.75
C39 A40 8c orange brn	2.50	1.50
C40 A40 10c dk blue	2.25	1.00
C41 A40 12c orange	2.00	1.00
C42 A40 16c ol grn *(Dewey)*	2.00	1.00
C43 A40 20c yellow	2.00	1.00
C44 A40 26c green	2.25	1.50
a. 26c blue green	3.00	1.80
C45 A40 30c gray	3.00	1.75
Nos. C36-C45 (10)	17.65	10.20

Commemorating the flight from Madrid to Manila of aviator Fernando Rein y Loring.

No. 290a Overprinted

1933, May 26 Unwmk. *Perf. 11*

Stamp	Unused	Used
C46 A40 2c green	.50	.40

Regular Issue of 1932 Overprinted

Stamp	Unused	Used
C47 A44 4c rose carmine	.20	.15
C48 A45 12c orange	.30	.15
C49 A47 20c yellow	.30	.20
C50 A48 24c deep violet	.40	.25
C51 A49 32c olive brown	.50	.35
Nos. C46-C51 (6)	2.20	1.50

Nos. 387, 392 Overprinted in Gold

1935, Dec. 2

Stamp	Unused	Used
C52 A57 10c rose carmine	.30	.20
C53 A62 30c orange red	.50	.35

China Clipper flight from Manila to San Francisco, December 2-5, 1935.

Regular Issue of 1917-25 Surcharged in Various Colors

MANILA-MADRID
ARNACAL
FLIGHT-1936
2CENTAVOS2

1936, Sept. 6 *Perf. 11*

Stamp	Unused	Used
C54 A40 2c on 4c car (Bl)	.15	.15
C55 A40 6c on 12c red org (V)	.15	.15
C56 A40 16c on 26c bl grn (Bk)	.25	.20
a. 16c on 26c green	1.25	.70
Set value	.40	.35

Manila-Madrid flight by aviators Antonio Arnaiz and Juan Calvo.

Regular Issue of 1917-37 Surcharged in Black or Red

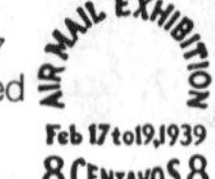

1939, Feb. 17

Stamp	Unused	Used
C57 A40 8c on 26c bl grn (Bk)	.75	.40
a. 8c on 26c green (Bk)	1.60	.55
C58 A71 1p on 10p gray (R)	3.00	2.25

1st Air Mail Exhibition, held Feb. 17-19, 1939.

Moro Vinta and Clipper — AP1

1941, June 30
C59 AP1 8c carmine 1.00 .60
C60 AP1 20c ultra 1.20 .45
C61 AP1 60c blue green 1.75 1.00
C62 AP1 1p sepia .70 .50
Nos. C59-C62 (4) 4.65 2.55

For overprint see No. NO7. For surcharges see Nos. N10-N11, N35-N36.

No. C47 Handstamped in Violet **VICTORY**

1944, Dec. 3 Unwmk. Perf. 11
C63 A44 4c rose carmine 1,600. 1,600.

Catalogue values for unused stamps in this section, from this point to the end of the section, are for Never Hinged items.

Republic

Manuel L. Quezon and Franklin D. Roosevelt AP2

Unwmk.
1947, Aug. 19 Engr. Perf. 12
C64 AP2 6c dark green .52 .52
C65 AP2 40c red orange 1.00 1.00
C66 AP2 80c deep blue 2.75 2.75
Nos. C64-C66 (3) 4.27 4.27

FAO Type
1948, Feb. 23 Typo. Perf. 12½
C67 A89 40c dk car & pink 12.50 6.50

Junior Chamber Type
1950, Mar. 1 Engr. Perf. 12
C68 A96 30c deep orange .38 .15
C69 A96 50c carmine rose .65 .15

F. D. Roosevelt Type
Souvenir Sheet
1950, May 22 Imperf.
C70 A98 80c deep green 1.25 1.25

Lions Club Type
1950, June 2 Perf. 12
C71 A99 30c emerald .60 .45
C72 A99 50c ultra .70 .60
a. Souvenir sheet of 2, #C71-C72 1.40 1.40

Maria Clara Type
1952, Nov. 16 Perf. 12½
C73 A112 30c rose carmine .85 .70

Postage Stamp Cent. Type
1954, Apr. 25 Perf. 13
1854 Stamp in Orange
C74 A119 10c dark brown 1.00 .85
C75 A119 20c dark green 1.65 1.35
C76 A119 50c carmine 3.50 3.00
Nos. C74-C76 (3) 6.15 5.20

Rotary Intl. Type
1955, Feb. 23
C77 A123 50c blue green 1.25 .85

Lt. José Gozar AP10

20c, 50c, Lt. Gozar. 30c, 70c, Lt. Basa.

1955 Engr. Perf. 13
C78 AP10 20c deep violet .45 .15
C79 AP10 30c red .52 .15
C80 AP10 50c bluish green .70 .20
C81 AP10 70c blue 1.10 .88
Nos. C78-C81 (4) 2.77 1.38

Issued in honor of Lt. José Gozar and Lt. Cesar Fernando Basa, Filipino aviators in World War II.

Constitution Type of Regular Issue
1960, Feb. 8 Photo. Perf. 12½x13½
C82 A146 30c brt bl & silver .32 .25

Air Force Plane of 1935 and Saber Jet AP11

1960, May 2 Engr. Perf. 14x14½
C83 AP11 10c carmine .18 .15
C84 AP11 20c ultra .35 .25

25th anniversary of Philippine Air Force.
For surcharge see No. 847.

Olympic Type of Regular Issue
30c, Sharpshooter. 70c, Woman swimmer.

1960, Nov. 30 Photo. Perf. 13x13½
C85 A150 30c orange & brn .42 .35
C86 A150 70c grnsh bl & vio brn .85 .70

Postal Conference Type
1961, Feb. 23 Perf. 13½x13
C87 A152 30c multicolored .28 .22

Freedom from Hunger Type
1963, Dec. 20 Photo.
C88 A168 30s lt grn & multi .28 .20
C89 A168 50s multicolored .45 .35

Land Reform Type
1964, Dec. 21 Wmk. 233 Perf. 14½
C90 A172 30s multicolored .25 .20

Mass Baptism by Father Andres de Urdaneta, Cebu — AP12

70s, World map showing route of the Cross from Spain to Mexico to Cebu, and two galleons.

Unwmk.
1965, Oct. 4 Photo. Perf. 13
C91 AP12 30s multicolored .25 .15
C92 AP12 70s multicolored .55 .32
a. Souvenir sheet of 4 1.40 1.40

400th anniv. of the Christianization of the Philippines. No. C92a contains four imperf. stamps similar to Nos. 934-935 and C91-C92 with simulated perforation.
For surcharge see No. C108.

Souvenir Sheet

Family and Progress Symbols — AP13

1966, July 22 Photo. Imperf.
C93 AP13 70s multicolored .65 .65

50th anniv. of the Philippine Natl. Bank. No. C93 contains one stamp with simulated perforation superimposed on a facsimile of a 50p banknote of 1916.

Eruption of Taal Volcano and Refugees AP14

1967, Oct. 1 Photo. Perf. 13½x13
C94 AP14 70s multicolored .52 .45

Eruption of Taal Volcano, Sept. 28, 1965.

Eruption of Taal Volcano — AP15

1968, Oct. 1 Litho. Perf. 13½
C95 AP15 70s multicolored .52 .52

Eruption of Taal Volcano, Sept. 28, 1965.

Rotary Type of 1969
1969, Jan. 29 Photo. Perf. 12½
C96 A202 40s green & multi .25 .18
C97 A202 75s red & multi .52 .42

Holy Child Type of Regular Issue
1969, June 30 Photo. Perf. 13½
C98 A207 40s ultra & multi .28 .20

Pope Type of Regular Issue
1970, Nov. 27 Photo. Perf. 13½x14
C99 A221 40s violet & multi .28 .20

Law College Type of Regular Issue
1971, June 15 Perf. 13
C100 A225 1p green & multi .45 .42

Manila Type of Regular Issue
1971, June 24
C101 A226 1p multi & blue .65 .45

Santo Tomas Type of Regular Issue
1971, July 8 Photo. Perf. 13½
C102 A227 2p lt blue & multi .90 .80

Congress Type of Regular Issue
1972, Apr. 11 Photo. Perf. 13½x13
C103 A232 40s green & multi .25 .20

Tropical Fish Type of Regular Issue
1972, Aug. 14 Photo. Perf. 13
C104 A235 50s Dusky angelfish .42 .20

Pope Paul VI Type of Regular Issue
1972, Sept. 26 Photo. Perf. 14
C105 A237 60s lt blue & multi .32 .32

First Mass Type of Regular Issue
1972, Oct. 31 Photo. Perf. 14
C106 A241 60s multicolored .28 .25

Presidential Palace Type of Regular Issue
1973, Nov. 15 Litho. Perf. 14
C107 A253 60s multicolored .20 .20

No. C92a Surcharged and Overprinted with US Bicentennial Emblems and: "U.S.A. BICENTENNIAL / 1776-1976" in Black

Unwmk.
1976, Sept. 23 Photo. Imperf.
C108 Sheet of 4 .45 .45
a. A179 5s on 3s multi .15 .15
b. A179 5s on 6s multi .15 .15
c. AP12 15s on 30s multi .15 .15
d. AP12 50s on 70s multi .25 .25

American Bicentennial. Nos. C108a-C108d are overprinted with Bicentennial emblem and 2 bars over old denomination. Inscription and 2 Bicentennial emblems overprinted in margin. Overprint and surcharges exist in red.

Souvenir Sheet

Netherlands No. 1 and Philippines No. 1 and Windmill AP16

1977, May 26 Litho. Perf. 14½
C109 Sheet of 3 6.50 6.50
a. AP16 7.50p multicolored 1.90 1.90

AMPHILEX '77, International Stamp Exhibition, Amsterdam, May 26-June 5.
Exists imperf. Value $12.50.

Souvenir Sheet

Philippines and Spain Nos. 1, Bull and Matador AP17

1977, Oct. 7 Litho. Perf. 12½x13
C110 Sheet of 3 8.00 8.00
a. AP17 7.50p multicolored 2.00 2.00

ESPAMER '77 (Exposicion Filatelica de America y Europa), Barcelona, Spain, Oct. 7-13.
Exists imperf. Value $12.50.

Nos. B10 and CB3a Surcharged

50s
JULY 4-14, 1979
QUEZON CITY

1979, July 5 Engr. Perf. 13
C111 SP8 90s on 6c + 4c car, yel .18 .18

Souvenir Sheet
White Paper
C112 Sheet of 5 .70 .70
a. SP8 50s on 6c + 4c carmine .15
b. SP8 50s on 25c + 5c blue .15
c. SP8 50s on 30c + 10c green .15
d. SP8 50s on 70c + 20c red brown .15
e. SP8 50s on 80c + 20c violet .15

First Scout Philatelic Exhibition, Quezon City, July 4-14, commemorating 25th anniversary of First National Jamboree.
Surcharge on No. C111 includes "AIRMAIL." Violet marginal inscriptions on No. C112 overprinted with heavy bars; new commemorative inscriptions and Scout emblem added.

AIR POST SEMI-POSTAL STAMPS

Catalogue values for unused stamps in this section are for Never Hinged items.

Type of Semi-Postal Issue, 1959

Designs: 30c+10c, Bicycling. 70c+20c, Scout with plane model. 80c+20c, Pres. Carlos P. Garcia and scout shaking hands.

Unwmk.
1959, July 17 Engr. Perf. 13
CB1 SP8 30c + 10c green .30 .30
CB2 SP8 70c + 20c red brown .65 .65
CB3 SP8 80c + 20c violet .90 .90
a. Souvenir sheet of 5 2.75 2.75
Nos. CB1-CB3 (3) 1.85 1.85

10th Boy Scout World Jamboree, Makiling Natl. Park, July 17-26. Surtax was for the Jamboree.
No. CB3a measures 171x89mm. and contains one each of Nos. CB1-CB3 and types of Nos. B10-B11 on white paper. Sold for 4p.
For surcharge see No. C112.

SPECIAL DELIVERY STAMPS

United States No. E5 Overprinted in Red **PHILIPPINES**

1901, Oct. 15 Wmk. 191 Perf. 12
E1 SD3 10c dark blue 110.00 100.00

Special Delivery Messenger SD2

1906 Engr. Wmk. 191PI
E2 SD2 20c ultra 30.00 7.50
b. 20c pale ultra 30.00 7.50

See Nos. E3-E6. For overprints see Nos. E7-E10, EO1.

Special Printing

Overprinted in Red as No. E1 on United States No. E6

1907

E2A SD4 10c ultra *2,250.*

Type of 1906

1911 **Wmk. 190PI**

E3 SD2 20c dp ultra 20.00 1.75

1916 ***Perf. 10***

E4 SD2 20c dp ultra 175.00 50.00

1919 **Unwmk.** ***Perf. 11***

E5 SD2 20c ultra .60 .20
a. 20c pale blue .75 .20
b. 20c dull violet .60 .20

1925-31 ***Imperf.***

E6 SD2 20c dull vio ('31) 20.00 *17.50*

Type of 1919 Overprinted in Black — COMMONWEALTH

1939 ***Perf. 11***

E7 SD2 20c blue violet .25 .20

Nos. E5b and E7, Handstamped in Violet — VICTORY

1944 ***Perf. 11***

E8 SD2 20c dull vio (#E5b) *700.00 500.00*
E9 SD2 20c blue vio (#E7) *190.00 150.00*

Type SD2 Overprinted "VICTORY" As No. 486

1945

E10 SD2 20c blue violet .70 .55
a. "IC" close together 3.25 2.75

Catalogue values for unused stamps in this section, from this point to the end of the section, are for Never Hinged items.

Republic

Manila Post Office and Messenger SD3

Unwmk.

1947, Dec. 22 **Engr.** ***Perf. 12***

E11 SD3 20c rose lilac .55 .40

Post Office Building, Manila, and Hands with Letter — SD4

1962, Jan. 23 ***Perf. 13½x13***

E12 SD4 20c lilac rose .25 .20

SPECIAL DELIVERY OFFICIAL STAMP

Type of 1906 Issue Overprinted — O.B.

1931 **Unwmk.** ***Perf. 11***

EO1 SD2 20c dull violet .65 .40
a. No period after "B" 20.00 15.00
b. Double overprint —

POSTAGE DUE STAMPS

Postage Due Stamps of the United States Nos. J38 to J44 Overprinted in Black — PHILIPPINES

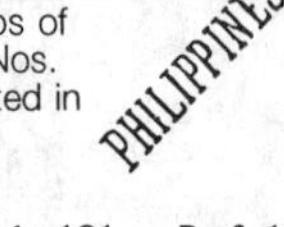

1899, Aug. 16 **Wmk. 191** ***Perf. 12***

J1 D2 1c deep claret 5.75 1.25
J2 D2 2c deep claret 6.00 1.10
J3 D2 5c deep claret 15.00 2.25
J4 D2 10c deep claret 19.00 4.75
J5 D2 50c deep claret 200.00 90.00

1901, Aug. 31

J6 D2 3c deep claret 17.50 6.00
J7 D2 30c deep claret 225.00 95.00
Nos. J1-J7 (7) 488.25 200.35

No. J1 was used to pay regular postage September 5-19, 1902.

Post Office Clerk — D3

Unwmk.

1928, Aug. 21 **Engr.** ***Perf. 11***

J8 D3 4c brown red .15 .15
J9 D3 6c brown red .15 .15
J10 D3 8c brown red .15 .15
J11 D3 10c brown red .15 .15
J12 D3 12c brown red .15 .15
J13 D3 16c brown red .15 .15
J14 D3 20c brown red .15 .15
Set value .90 .90

For overprints see Nos. O16-O22, NJ1. For surcharge see No. J15.

No. J8 Surcharged in Blue — 3 CVOS. 3

1937

J15 D3 3c on 4c brown red .20 .15

Nos. J8 to J14 Handstamped in Violet — VICTORY

1944

J16 D3 4c brown red *125.00* —
J17 D3 6c brown red *80.00* —
J18 D3 8c brown red *85.00* —
J19 D3 10c brown red *80.00* —
J20 D3 12c brown red *80.00* —
J21 D3 16c brown red *85.00* —
J22 D3 20c brown red *85.00* —
Nos. J16-J22 (7) *620.00*

Catalogue values for unused stamps in this section, from this point to the end of the section, are for Never Hinged items.

Republic

D4

Unwmk.

1947, Oct. 20 **Engr.** ***Perf. 12***

J23 D4 3c rose carmine .15 .15
J24 D4 4c brt violet blue .30 .25
J25 D4 6c olive green .38 .38
J26 D4 10c orange .50 .50
Nos. J23-J26 (4) 1.33 1.28

OFFICIAL STAMPS

Official Handstamped Overprints

"Officers purchasing stamps for government business may, if they so desire, overprint them with the letters 'O.B.' either in writing with black ink or by rubber stamps but in such a manner as not to obliterate the stamp that postmasters will be unable to determine whether the stamps have been previously used." C. M. Cotterman, Director of Posts, Dec. 26, 1905. Beginning with Jan. 1, 1906, all branches of the Insular Government used postage stamps to prepay postage instead of franking them as before. Some officials used manuscript, some utilized typewriters, some made press-printed overprints, but by far the larger number used rubber stamps. The majority of these read "O.B." but other forms were: "OFFICIAL BUSINESS" or "OFFICIAL MAIL" in two lines, with variations on many of these. These "O.B." overprints are known on US 1899-1901 stamps; on 1903-06 stamps in red and blue; on 1906 stamps in red, blue, black, yellow and green. "O.B." overprints were also made on the centavo and peso stamps of the Philippines, per order of May 25, 1907. Beginning in 1926 the stamps were overprinted and issued by the Post Office, but some government offices continued to handstamp "O.B."

Regular Issue of 1926 Overprinted in Red — OFFICIAL

1926, Dec. 20 **Unwmk.** ***Perf. 12***

O1 A42 2c green & blk 2.25 1.00
O2 A42 4c carmine & blk 2.25 1.20
a. Vert. pair, imperf. btwn. *750.00*
O3 A42 18c lt brn & blk 7.00 4.00
O4 A42 20c orange & blk 6.75 1.75
Nos. O1-O4 (4) 18.25 7.95

Opening of the Legislative Palace.

Regular Issue of 1917-26 Overprinted — O.B.

1931 ***Perf. 11***

O5 A40 2c green .15 .15
a. No period after "B" 15.00 5.00
b. No period after "O" —
O6 A40 4c carmine .15 .15
a. No period after "B" 15.00 5.00
O7 A40 6c dp violet .20 .15
O8 A40 8c yellow brn .20 .15
O9 A40 10c deep blue .30 .15
O10 A40 12c red orange .25 .15
a. No period after "B" 32.50
O11 A40 16c lt ol grn *(Dewey)* .25 .15
a. 16c olive bister 1.25 .20
O12 A40 20c orange yel .25 .15
a. No period after "B" 22.50 15.00
O13 A40 26c green .40 .30
a. 26c blue green 1.00 .65
O14 A40 30c gray .30 .25
Nos. O5-O14 (10) 2.45
Set value 1.25

Same Overprint on Nos. 383-392

1935

O15 A53 2c rose .15 .15
a. No period after "B" 15.00 5.00
O16 A54 4c yellow green .15 .15
a. No period after "B" 15.00 8.50
O17 A55 6c dk brown .15 .15
a. No period after "B" 20.00 17.50
O18 A56 8c violet .15 .15
O19 A57 10c rose carmine .20 .15
O20 A58 12c black .20 .15
O21 A59 16c dark blue .20 .15
O22 A60 20c lt olive grn .20 .15
O23 A61 26c indigo .25 .20
O24 A62 30c orange red .30 .25
Set value 1.60 1.00

Same Overprint on Nos. 411, 418

1937-38 ***Perf. 11***

O25 A53 2c rose .15 .15
a. No period after "B" 4.25 2.25
O26 A60 20c lt ol grn ('38) .65 .50
Set value .70 .55

Nos. 383-392 Overprinted in Black:

O. B. / COMMON-WEALTH — a

O. B. / COMMONWEALTH — b

1938-40 ***Perf. 11***

O27 A53(a) 2c rose .15 .15
a. Hyphen omitted 20.00 20.00
b. No period after "B" 25.00 25.00
O28 A54(b) 4c yellow grn .15 .15
O29 A55(a) 6c dk brown .15 .15
O30 A56(b) 8c violet .15 .15
O31 A57(b) 10c rose car .15 .15
a. No period after "O" 30.00 30.00
O32 A58(b) 12c black .15 .15
O33 A59(b) 16c dark blue .20 .15
O34 A60(a) 20c lt ol grn ('40) .25 .25
O35 A61(b) 26c indigo .30 .30
O36 A62(b) 30c orange red .25 .25
Set value 1.60 1.25

No. 461 Overprinted in Black — c — O. B.

Perf. 11x10½

1941, Apr. 14 **Unwmk.**

O37 A75 2c apple green .15 .15

Official Stamps Handstamped in Violet — VICTORY

1944 ***Perf. 11, 11x10½***

O38 A53 2c (#O27) *200.* *110.*
O39 A75 2c (#O37) *6.50* *3.*
O40 A54 4c (#O16) *37.50* *25.*
O40A A55 6c (#O29) *4,250.* —
O41 A57 10c (#O31) *135.*
O42 A60 20c (#O22) *6,000.*
O43 A60 20c (#O26) *1,550.*

No. 497 Overprinted Type "c" in Black

Perf. 11x10½

1946, June 19 **Unwmk.**

O44 A76 2c sepia .15 .15

Catalogue values for unused stamps in this section, from this point to the end of the section, are for Never Hinged items.

Republic

Nos. 504, 505 and 507 Overprinted in Black — d — O. B.

1948 **Unwmk.** ***Perf. 12***

O50 A78 4c black brown .15 .15
a. Inverted overprint 25.00
b. Double overprint 25.00
O51 A79 10c red orange .20 .15
O52 A81 16c slate gray 1.40 .52
Nos. O50-O52 (3) 1.75
Set value .62

The overprint on No. O51 comes in two sizes: 13mm, applied in Manila, and 12½mm, applied in New York.

Nos. 527, 508 and 509 Overprinted in Black — e — O. B.

Overprint Measures 14mm

O53 A91 2c bright green .38 .15

1949

O54 A82 20c red brown .52 .15

Overprint Measures 12mm

O55 A83 50c dull green .90 .52

No. 550 Overprinted Type "e" in Black
Overprint Measures 14mm

1950

O56 A91 1c on 2c brt green .15 .15

Nos. 589, 592, 595 and 597 Overprinted in Black — f — O. B.

Overprint Measures 15mm

1952-55

O57 A117 1c red brown ('53) .15 .15
O58 A117 5c crim rose .15 .15
O59 A117 10c ultra ('55) .18 .15
O60 A117 20c car lake ('55) .42 .15
Set value .75 .20

No. 647 Overprinted — g — O B

1959 **Engr.** ***Perf. 12***

O61 A117 1c on 5c crim rose .15 .15

No. 813 Overprinted Type "f"
Overprint measures 16½mm

1959

O62 A145 6c gray blue .15 .15

Nos. 856-861 Overprinted

G. O. — h

G. O. — j

G. O. — k

G.O. — l

1962-64 ***Perf. 13½***

O63 A158(j) 5s car rose ('63) .15 .15

Perf. 13x12

O64 A158(h) 6s dk red brn .15 .15

Perf. 13½

O65 A158(k) 6s pck blue ('64) .15 .15
O66 A158(j) 10s brt purple ('63) .15 .15
O67 A158(j) 20s Prus blue ('63) .15 .15
O68 A158(j) 30s vermilion .28 .15
O69 A158(k) 50s violet ('63) .42 .15
Set value 1.05 .45

"G.O." stands for "Gawaing Opisyal," Tagalog for "Official Business."
On 6s overprint "k" is 10mm wide.
For overprint see No. 1119.

No. 1082 Overprinted Type "l"

1970, Dec. 30 **Engr.** ***Perf. 14***

O70 A222 10s rose carmine .15 .15

NEWSPAPER STAMPS

N1

N2

1886-89 Unwmk. Typo. *Perf. 14*

P1 N1 1/8c yellow green .25 3.00
P2 N1 1m rose ('89) .25 20.00
P3 N1 2m blue ('89) .25 20.00
P4 N1 5m dk brown ('89) .25 20.00
Nos. P1-P4 (4) 1.00 63.00

1890-96

P5 N2 1/8c dark violet .15 .15
P6 N2 1/8c green ('92) .80 2.00
P7 N2 1/8c orange brn ('94) .20 .20
P8 N2 1/8c dull blue ('96) .75 .55
P9 N2 1m dark violet .15 .15
P10 N2 1m green ('92) 2.00 5.00
P11 N2 1m olive gray ('94) .20 .20
P12 N2 1m ultra ('96) .20 .15
P13 N2 2m dark violet .15 .15
P14 N2 2m green ('92) 2.25 12.00
P15 N2 2m olive gray ('94) .20 .20
P16 N2 2m brown ('96) .20 .15
P17 N2 5m dark violet .15 .15
P18 N2 5m green ('92) 125.00 30.00
P19 N2 5m olive gray ('94) .20 .20
P20 N2 5m dp blue grn ('96) 2.25 1.25

Imperfs. exist of Nos. P8, P9, P11, P12, P16, P17 and P20.

OCCUPATION STAMPS

Issued under Japanese Occupation

Nos. 461, 438 and 439 Overprinted with Bars in Black

1942-43 Unwmk. *Perf. 11x10 1/2, 11*

N1 A75 2c apple green .15 .15
a. Pair, one without overprint —
N2 A58 12c black ('43) .15 .15
N3 A59 16c dark blue 5.00 3.75
Nos. N1-N3 (3) 5.30 4.05

Nos. 435, 442, 443 and 423 Surcharged in Black

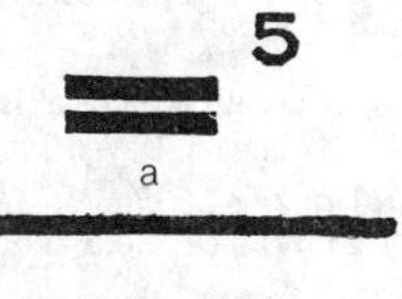

a

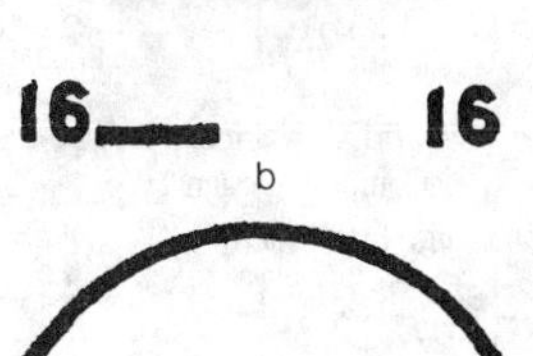

b

c

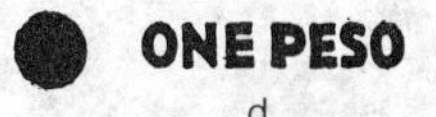

d

Perf. 11

N4 A55 5c on 6c gldn brn .15 .15
a. Top bar shorter, thinner .20 .20
b. 5(c) on 6c dk brn .20 .20
c. As "b," top bar shorter and thinner .20 .20
N5 A62 16c on 30c ('43) .25 .25
N6 A63 50c on 1p ('43) .60 .60
a. Double surcharge 300.00
N7 A65 1p on 4p ('43) 110.00 120.00

On Nos. N4 and N4b, the top bar measures 1 1/2x22 1/2mm. On Nos. N4a and N4c, the top bar measures 1x21mm and the "5" is smaller and thinner.

No. 384 Surcharged in Black

CONGRATULATIONS
FALL OF
BATAAN AND
CORREGIDOR
1942
2

1942, May 18

N8 A54 2c on 4c yel grn 6.00 6.00

Japan's capture of Bataan and Corregidor. The American-Filipino forces finally surrendered May 7, 1942.

No. 384 Surcharged in Black

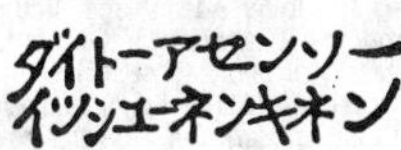

12-8-1942 5

1942, Dec. 8

N9 A54 5c on 4c yel grn .50 .50

1st anniversary of the "Greater East Asia War."

Nos. C59 and C62 Surcharged in Black

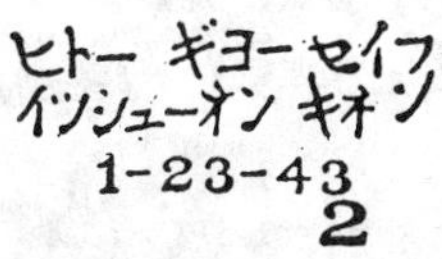

1943, Jan. 23

N10 AP1 2c on 8c carmine .25 .25
N11 AP1 5c on 1p sepia .50 .50

1st anniversary of the Philippine Executive Commission.

Nipa Hut
OS1

Rice Planting
OS2

Mt. Mayon and
Mt. Fuji — OS3

Moro
Vinta — OS4

Engr., Typo. (2c, 6c, 25c)

1943-44 Wmk. 257 *Perf. 13*

N12 OS1 1c deep orange .15 .15
N13 OS2 2c bright green .15 .15
N14 OS1 4c slate green .15 .15
N15 OS3 5c orange brown .15 .15
N16 OS2 6c red .15 .15
N17 OS3 10c blue green .15 .15
N18 OS4 12c steel blue 1.00 1.00
N19 OS4 16c dark brown .15 .15
N20 OS1 20c rose violet 1.25 1.25
N21 OS3 21c violet .15 .15
N22 OS2 25c pale brown .15 .15
N23 OS3 1p deep carmine .75 .75
N24 OS4 2p dull violet 5.00 5.00
N25 OS4 5p dark olive 8.50 8.50
Nos. N12-N25 (14) 17.85 17.85

For surcharges see Nos. NB5-NB7.

Map of Manila Bay Showing Bataan and Corregidor OS5

1943, May 7 Photo. Unwmk.

N26 OS5 2c carmine red .15 .15
N27 OS5 5c bright green .25 .25
Set value .35 .35

1st anniversary of the fall of Bataan and Corregidor.

No. 440 Surcharged in Black

Limbagan
1593 - 1943
12 12

1943, June 20 Engr. *Perf. 11*

N28 A60 12c on 20c lt ol grn .20 .20
a. Double surcharge —

350th anniversary of the printing press in the Philippines. "Limbagan" is Tagalog for "printing press."

Rizal Monument, Filipina and Philippine Flag — OS6

1943, Oct. 14 Photo. *Perf. 12*

N29 OS6 5c light blue .15 .15
a. Imperf. .15 .15
N30 OS6 12c orange .15 .15
a. Imperf. .15 .15
N31 OS6 17c rose pink .20 .20
a. Imperf. .20 .20
Set value .35 .35
Set value, imperf. .35 .35

"Independence of the Philippines." Japan granted "independence" Oct. 14, 1943, when the puppet republic was founded.

The imperforate stamps were issued without gum. See No. NB4.

José Rizal
OS7

Rev. José Burgos
OS8

Design: 17c, Apolinario Mabini.

1944, Feb. 17 Litho. *Perf. 12*

N32 OS7 5c blue .20 .20
a. Imperf. .15 .15
N33 OS8 12c carmine .15 .15
a. Imperf. .15 .15
N34 OS7 17c deep orange .15 .15
a. Imperf. .15 .15
Set value .35 .35
Set value, imperf. .35 .35

See No. NB8.

Nos. C60 and C61 Surcharged in Black

REPUBLIKA
NG PILIPINAS
5-7-44
5

1944, May 7 *Perf. 11*

N35 AP1 5c on 20c ultra .50 .35
N36 AP1 12c on 60c blue grn 1.25 .85

2nd anniv. of the fall of Bataan and Corregidor.

José P. Laurel — OS10

1945, Jan. 12 Litho. *Imperf.*

Without Gum

N37 OS10 5c dull violet brn .15 .15
N38 OS10 7c blue green .15 .15
N39 OS10 20c chalky blue .15 .15
Set value .25 .20

Issued belatedly on Jan. 12, 1945, to commemorate the first anniversary of the puppet Philippine Republic, Oct. 14, 1944. "S" stands for "sentimos."

OCCUPATION SEMI-POSTAL STAMPS

Woman, Farming and Cannery — OSP1

Unwmk.

1942, Nov. 12 Litho. *Perf. 12*

NB1 OSP1 2c + 1c pale violet .15 .15
NB2 OSP1 5c + 1c brt green .25 .15
NB3 OSP1 16c + 2c orange 25.00 25.00

Issued to promote the campaign to produce and conserve food. The surtax aided the Red Cross.

"Independence of the Philippines" Type
Souvenir Sheet

1943, Oct. 14 *Imperf.*

Without Gum

NB4 Sheet of 3 45.00 6.00

No. NB4 contains one each of Nos. N29a-N31a. Lower inscription from Rizal's "Last Farewell." Size: 127x177mm. Sold for 2.50p.

Nos. N18, N20 and N21 Surcharged in Black

BAHA
1943
+21

1943, Dec. 8 Wmk. 257 *Perf. 13*

NB5 OS4 12c + 21c steel blue .15 .15
NB6 OS1 20c + 36c rose violet .15 .15
NB7 OS3 21c + 40c violet .15 .15
Set value .30 .30

The surtax was for the benefit of victims of a Luzon flood. "Baha" is Tagalog for "flood."

Type of 1944
Souvenir Sheet

1944, Feb. 9 Unwmk. Litho. *Imperf.*

Without Gum

NB8 Sheet of 3 5.00 3.00

No. NB8 contains one each of Nos. N32a-N34a.

Sheet sold for 1p, surtax going to a fund for the care of heroes' monuments.

OCCUPATION POSTAGE DUE STAMP

No. J15 Overprinted with Bar in Blue

1942, Oct. 14 Unwmk. *Perf. 11*

NJ1 D3 3c on 4c brown red 35.00 20.00

On copies of No. J15, two lines were drawn in India ink with a ruling pen across "United States of America" by employees of the Short Paid Section of the Manila Post Office to make a provisional 3c postage due stamp which was used from Sept. 1, 1942, (when the letter rate was raised from 2c to 5c) until Oct. 14 when No. NJ1 went on sale.

OCCUPATION OFFICIAL STAMPS

Nos. 461, 413, 435, 435a and 442 Overprinted or Surcharged in Black with Bars and

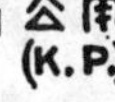

1943-44 Unwmk. *Perf. 11x10½, 11*

NO1 A75 2c apple green .15 .15
a. Double overprint 500.00
NO2 A55 5(c) on 6c dk brn (#413) ('44) 35.00 35.00
NO3 A55 5(c) on 6c gldn brn (#435a) .15 .15
a. Narrower spacing between bars .15 .15
b. 5(c) on 6c dark brown (#435) .15 .15
c. As "b," narrower spacing between bars .15 .15
d. Double overprint —
NO4 A62 16c on 30c org red .30 .30
a. Wider spacing between bars .30 .30

On Nos. NO3 and NO3b, the bar deleting "United States of America" is 9¾mm to 10mm above the bar deleting "Common-." On Nos. NO3a and NO3c, the spacing is 8mm to 8½mm.

On No. NO4 the center bar is 19mm long, 3½mm below the top bar and 6mm above the Japanese characters. On No. NO4a, the center bar is 20½mm long, 9mm below the top bar and 1mm above the Japanese characters.

"K. P." stands for Kagamitang Pampamahalaan, "Official Business" in Tagalog.

Nos. 435 and 435a Surcharged in Black

1944 *Perf. 11*

NO5 A55 5c on 6c golden brown .15 .15
a. 5c on 6c dark brown .15 .15

Nos. O34 and C62 Overprinted in Black

Pilipinas
REPUBLIKA

a

K.P.

b

(K. P.)

NO6 A60(a) 20c light olive green .25 .25
NO7 AP1(b) 1p sepia .65 .65
Nos. NO5-NO7 (3) 1.05 1.05

PITCAIRN ISLANDS

'pit-,karn 'ī-lənds

LOCATION — South Pacific Ocean, nearly equidistant from Australia and South America
GOVT. — British colony under the British High Commissioner in New Zealand
AREA — 1.75 sq. mi.
POP. — 57 (1984)

The district of Pitcairn also includes the uninhabited islands of Ducie, Henderson and Oeno.

Postal affairs are administered by Fiji.

12 Pence = 1 Shilling
100 Cents = 1 Dollar (1967)

Catalogue values for all unused stamps in this country are for Never Hinged items.

Cluster of Oranges — A1

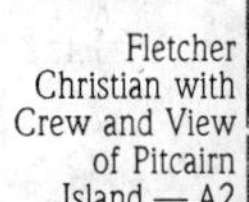
Fletcher Christian with Crew and View of Pitcairn Island — A2

John Adams and His House — A3

William Bligh and H. M. Armed Vessel "Bounty" — A4

Map of Pitcairn and Pacific Ocean — A5

Bounty Bible — A6

H.M. Armed Vessel "Bounty" A7

Pitcairn School, 1949 — A8

Fletcher Christian and View of Pitcairn Island — A9

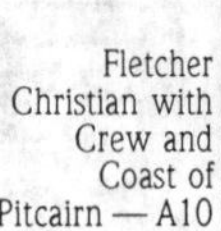
Fletcher Christian with Crew and Coast of Pitcairn — A10

Perf. 12½, 11½x11

1940-51 Engr. Wmk. 4

1 A1 ½p blue grn & org .50 .25
2 A2 1p red lil & rose vio .75 .40
3 A3 1½p rose car & blk .75 .65
4 A4 2p dk brn & brt grn 1.75 1.00
5 A5 3p dk blue & yel grn 1.50 1.25
5A A6 4p dk blue grn & blk 14.00 6.50
6 A7 6p sl grn & dp brn 5.00 2.00
6A A8 8p lil rose & grn 14.00 6.50
7 A9 1sh slate & vio 4.00 2.25
8 A10 2sh6p dk brn & brt grn 8.00 5.00
Nos. 1-8 (10) 50.25 25.80

Nos. 1-5, 6 and 7-8 exist in a booklet of eight panes of one.

Issued: 4p, 8p, 9/1/51; others, 10/15/40.

Common Design Types pictured following the introduction.

Peace Issue

Common Design Type

1946, Dec. 2 *Perf. 13½x14*

9 CD303 2p brown .35 .35
10 CD303 3p deep blue .65 .65

Silver Wedding Issue

Common Design Types

1949, Aug. 1 Photo. *Perf. 14x14½*

11 CD304 1½p scarlet 1.50 .75

Engraved; Name Typographed

Perf. 11½x11

12 CD305 10sh purple 70.00 *55.00*

UPU Issue

Common Design Types

Engr.; Name Typo. on 3p & 6p

1949, Oct. 10 *Perf. 13½, 11x11½*

13 CD306 2½p red brown 5.00 2.50
14 CD307 3p indigo 5.00 2.50
15 CD308 6p green 10.00 5.00
16 CD309 1sh rose violet 17.50 10.00
Nos. 13-16 (4) 37.50 20.00

Coronation Issue

Common Design Type

1953, June 2 *Perf. 13½x13*

19 CD312 4p dk green & blk 2.50 1.00

Ti Plant — A11

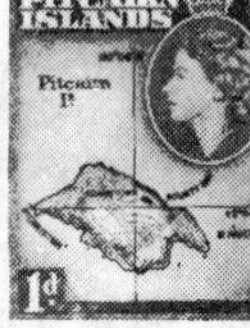

Map — A12

Designs: 2p, John Adams and Bounty Bible. 2½p, Handicraft (Carving). 3p, Bounty Bay. 4p, School (actually Schoolteacher's House). 6p, Fiji-Pitcairn connection (Map). 8p, Inland scene. 1sh, Handicraft (Ship model). 2sh, Wheelbarrow. 2sh6p, Whaleboat.

Perf. 13x12½, 12½x13

1957, July 2 Engr. Wmk. 4

20 A11 ½p lilac & green .35 .15
21 A12 1p olive grn & blk .50 .20
22 A12 2p blue & brown .60 .26
23 A11 2½p orange & brn .85 .30
24 A11 3p ultra & emer .95 .40
25 A11 4p ultra & rose red *(Pitcairn School)* 3.50 1.25
26 A11 6p indigo & buff 2.00 .70
27 A11 8p magenta & grn 2.50 .80
28 A11 1sh brown & blk 2.75 1.00
29 A12 2sh dp orange & grn 21.00 7.25
30 A11 2sh6p magenta & ultra 14.00 6.00
Nos. 20-30 (11) 49.00 18.31

See Nos. 31, 38.

Type of 1957 Corrected

1958, Nov. 5 *Perf. 13x12½*

31 A11 4p ultra & rose red *(Schoolteacher's House)* .75 .50

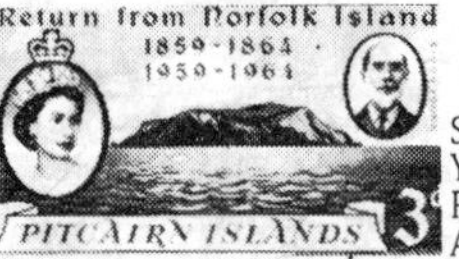

Simon Young and Pitcairn A13

Designs: 6p, Maps of Norfolk and Pitcairn Islands. 1sh, Schooner Mary Ann.

Perf. 14½x13½

1961, Nov. 15 Photo. Wmk. 314

32 A13 3p yellow & black .70 .50
33 A13 6p blue & red brown 1.25 .90
34 A13 1sh brt green & dp org 3.00 2.25
Nos. 32-34 (3) 4.95 3.65

Pitcairn Islanders return from Norfolk Island.

Freedom from Hunger Issue

Common Design Type

1963, June 4 *Perf. 14x14½*

35 CD314 2sh6p ultra 17.50 6.50

Red Cross Centenary Issue

Common Design Type

1963, Dec. 9 Litho. *Perf. 13*

36 CD315 2p black & red .50 .30
37 CD315 2sh6p ultra & red 12.00 10.00

Type of 1957

Perf. 13x12½

1963, Dec. 4 Engr. Wmk. 314

38 A11 ½p lilac & green 1.00 1.00

Pitcairn Longboat A14

Queen Elizabeth II — A15

Designs: 1p, H.M. Armed Vessel Bounty. 2p, Oarsmen rowing longboat. 3p, Great frigate bird. 4p, Fairy tern 6p, Pitcairn reed warbler. 8p, Red-footed booby. 10p, Red-tailed tropic birds. 1sh, Henderson Island flightless rail. 1sh6p, Henderson Island lory. 2sh6p, Murphy's petrel. 4sh, Henderson Island fruit pigeon.

1964-65 Photo. *Perf. 14x14½*

39 A14 ½p multicolored .15 .15
40 A14 1p vio bl, blk & tan .15 .15
41 A14 2p multicolored .15 .15
42 A14 3p ocher & multi .20 .15
43 A14 4p multicolored .30 .20
44 A14 6p multicolored .50 .30
45 A14 8p multicolored .50 .35
a. Gray (beak) omitted 100.00
46 A14 10p blue, blk & org .70 .45
47 A14 1sh multicolored .80 .60
48 A14 1sh6p multicolored 1.00 .80
49 A14 2sh6p multicolored 3.00 2.00
50 A14 4sh brown & multi 4.00 3.50
51 A15 8sh multicolored 11.00 9.00
Nos. 39-51 (13) 22.45 17.80

Issued: ½p-4sh, 8/5/64; 8sh, 4/5/65.

For surcharges see Nos. 72-84.

ITU Issue

Common Design Type

1965, May 17 Litho. *Perf. 11x11½*

52 CD317 1p red lilac & org brn .40 .20
53 CD317 2sh6p grnsh blue & ultra 15.00 11.00

Intl. Cooperation Year Issue

Common Design Type

1965, Oct. 25 *Perf. 14½*

54 CD318 1p bl grn & claret .35 .20
55 CD318 1sh6p lt vio & grn 14.00 11.00

Churchill Memorial Issue

Common Design Type

1966, Jan. 24 Photo. *Perf. 14*

Design in Black, Gold and Carmine Rose

56 CD319 2p brt blue 1.00 .50
57 CD319 3p green 1.50 1.00
58 CD319 6p brown 4.00 3.00
59 CD319 1sh violet 12.50 10.00
Nos. 56-59 (4) 19.00 14.50

World Cup Soccer Issue

Common Design Type

1966, Aug. 1 Litho. *Perf. 14*

60 CD321 4p multi 1.00 .75
61 CD321 2sh6p multi 6.50 5.00

WHO Headquarters Issue

Common Design Type

1966, Sept. 20 Litho. *Perf. 14*

62 CD322 8p multi 2.00 1.50
63 CD322 1sh6p multi 11.00 6.50

UNESCO Anniversary Issue

Common Design Type

1966, Dec. 1 Litho. *Perf. 14*

64 CD323 ½p "Education" .20 .15
65 CD323 10p "Science" 2.00 1.50
66 CD323 2sh "Culture" 12.00 8.00
Nos. 64-66 (3) 14.20 9.65

Mangarevan Canoe, c. 1325, and Pitcairn Island — A16

Designs: 1p, Pedro Fernandez de Quiros and galleon, 1606. 8p, "San Pedro," 17th century Spanish brigantine, 1606. 1sh, Capt. Philip Carteret and H.M.S. Swallow. 1sh6p, "Hercules," 1819.

Perf. 14½

1967, Mar. 1 Photo. Wmk. 314

No.	Type	Denom.	Description	Unused	Used
67	A16	½p	multicolored	.15	.15
68	A16	1p	multicolored	.15	.15
69	A16	8p	multicolored	.30	.25
70	A16	1sh	multicolored	.50	.40
71	A16	1sh6p	multicolored	.75	.70
			Nos. 67-71 (5)	1.85	1.65

Bicentenary of the discovery of Pitcairn Islands by Capt. Philip Carteret.

Nos. 39-51 Surcharged in Gold

20c

1967, July 10 *Perf. 14x14½*

No.	Type	Denom.	Description	Unused	Used
72	A14	½c on ½p		.15	.15
a.			Brown omitted	400.00	
73	A14	1c on 1p		.15	.15
74	A14	2c on 2p		.15	.15
75	A14	2½c on 3p		.20	.15
76	A14	3c on 4p		.30	.25
77	A14	5c on 6p		.50	.50
78	A14	10c on 8p		.80	.75
a.			"10c" omitted	240.00	
79	A14	15c on 10p		1.25	1.00
80	A14	20c on 1sh		1.75	1.50
81	A14	25c on 1sh6p		2.00	2.00
82	A14	30c on 2sh6p		2.50	2.00
83	A14	40c on 4sh		4.00	4.00
84	A15	45c on 8sh		6.00	6.00
			Nos. 72-84 (13)	19.75	18.60

Size of gold rectangle and anchor varies. The anchor symbol is designed after the anchor of H.M.S. Bounty.

Admiral Bligh and Bounty's Launch A17

Designs: 8c, Bligh and his followers adrift in a boat. 20c, Bligh's tomb, St. Mary's Cemetery, Lambeth, London.

Unwmk.

1967, Dec. 7 Litho. *Perf. 13*

No.	Type	Denom.	Description	Unused	Used
85	A17	1c	ultra, lt blue & blk	.15	.15
86	A17	8c	brt rose, yel & blk	.25	.25
87	A17	20c	brown, yel & blk	.60	.50
			Nos. 85-87 (3)	1.00	.90

150th anniv. of the death of Admiral William Bligh (1754-1817), capt. of the Bounty.

Human Rights Flame A18

Perf. 13½x13

1968, Mar. 4 Litho. Wmk. 314

No.	Type	Denom.	Description	Unused	Used
88	A18	1c	rose & multi	.15	.15
89	A18	2c	ocher & multi	.15	.15
90	A18	25c	multicolored	.50	.40
			Nos. 88-90 (3)	.80	.70

International Human Rights Year.

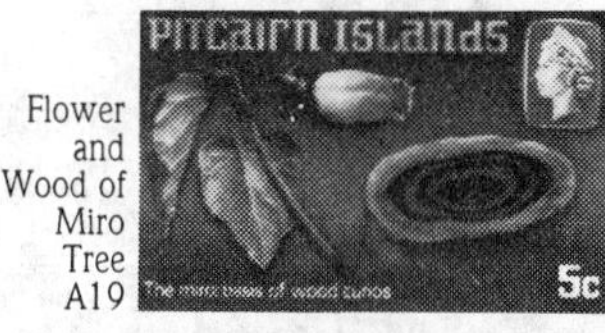

Flower and Wood of Miro Tree A19

Pitcairn Handicraft: 10c, Carved flying fish. 15c, Two "hand" vases, vert. 20c, Old and new woven baskets, vert.

Perf. 14½x14, 14x14½

1968, Aug. 19 Photo. Wmk. 314

No.	Type	Denom.	Description	Unused	Used
91	A19	5c	chocolate & multi	.15	.15
92	A19	10c	dp green & multi	.20	.15
93	A19	15c	brt violet & multi	.30	.25
94	A19	20c	black & multi	.40	.30
			Nos. 91-94 (4)	1.05	.85

See Nos. 194-197.

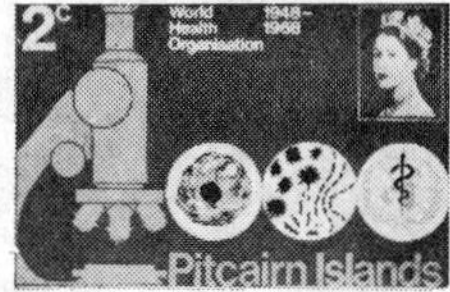

Microscope, Cell, Germs and WHO Emblem A20

20c, Hypodermic and jars containing pills.

1968, Nov. 25 Litho. *Perf. 14*

No.	Type	Denom.	Description	Unused	Used
95	A20	2c	vio blue, grnsh bl & blk	.15	.15
96	A20	20c	black, magenta & org	.60	.50

20th anniv. of WHO.

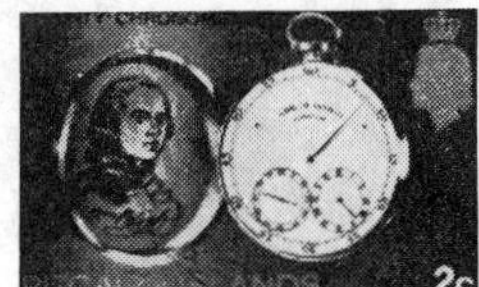

Capt. Bligh and his Larcum-Kendall Chronometer — A21

Designs: 1c, Pitcairn Island. 3c, Bounty's anchor, vert. 4c, Plan of the Bounty, drawn 1787. 5c, Breadfruit and method of transporting young plants. 6c, Bounty Bay. 8c, Pitcairn longboat. 10c, Ship Landing Point and palms. 15c, Fletcher Christian's Cave. 20c, Thursday October Christian's house. 25c, "Flying Fox" cable system (for hauling cargo), vert. 30c, Radio Station at Taro Ground. 40c, Bounty Bible.

Perf. 13x12½, 12½x13

1969, Sept. 17 Litho. Wmk. 314

No.	Type	Denom.	Description	Unused	Used
97	A21	1c	brn, yel & gold	.15	.15
98	A21	2c	brn, blk & gold	.15	.15
99	A21	3c	red, blk & gold	.20	.15
100	A21	4c	buff, brn & gold	.25	.15
101	A21	5c	gold & multi	.30	.20
102	A21	6c	gold & multi	.40	.30
103	A21	8c	gold & multi	.60	.40
104	A21	10c	gold & multi	1.25	.75
105	A21	15c	gold & multi	1.40	1.00
a.			Gold (Queen's head) omitted	500.00	
106	A21	20c	gold & multi	1.75	1.40
107	A21	25c	gold & multi	3.25	2.25
108	A21	30c	gold & multi	4.00	3.25
109	A21	40c	red lil, blk & gold	5.50	3.50
			Nos. 97-109 (13)	19.20	13.65

For overprint see No. 118.

Lantana — A22

Pitcairn Flowers: 2c, Indian shot (canna indica). 5c, Pulau (hibiscus tiliaceus). 25c, Wild gladioli.

1970, Mar. 23 Litho. *Perf. 14*

No.	Type	Denom.	Description	Unused	Used
110	A22	1c	black & multi	.15	.15
111	A22	2c	black & multi	.20	.15
112	A22	5c	black & multi	.45	.20
113	A22	25c	black & multi	3.50	1.75
			Nos. 110-113 (4)	4.30	2.25

Rudderfish (Dream Fish) A23

Fish: 5c, Groupers (Auntie and Ann). 15c, Wrasse (Elwyn's trousers). 20c, Wrasse (Whistling daughter).

Perf. 14½x14

1970, Oct. 12 Photo. Wmk. 314

No.	Type	Denom.	Description	Unused	Used
114	A23	5c	black & multi	1.10	.40
115	A23	10c	grnsh bl & blk	2.25	.70
116	A23	15c	multicolored	3.25	1.00
117	A23	20c	multicolored	4.50	1.25
			Nos. 114-117 (4)	11.10	3.35

No. 104 Overprinted in Silver: "ROYAL VISIT 1971"

1971, Feb. 22 Litho. *Perf. 13x12½*

No.	Type	Denom.	Description	Unused	Used
118	A21	10c	gold & multi	2.50	1.50

Polynesian Artifacts — A24

Polynesian Art on Pitcairn: 5c, Rock carvings, vert. 15c, Making of stone fishhook. 20c, Seated deity, vert.

1971, May 3 Litho. *Perf. 13½*

Queen's Head in Gold

No.	Type	Denom.	Description	Unused	Used
119	A24	5c	dk brown & bis	.75	.75
120	A24	10c	ol green & blk	1.50	1.50
121	A24	15c	black & lt vio	2.75	2.25
122	A24	20c	black & rose red	3.50	2.50
			Nos. 119-122 (4)	8.50	7.00

Health Care A25

Designs: 4c, South Pacific Commission flag and Southern Cross, vert. 18c, Education (elementary school). 20c, Economy (country store).

1972, Apr. 4 Litho. *Perf. 14x14½*

No.	Type	Denom.	Description	Unused	Used
123	A25	4c	vio blue, yel & ultra	.80	.50
124	A25	8c	brown & multi	1.25	1.00
125	A25	18c	yellow grn & multi	2.00	1.50
126	A25	20c	orange & multi	2.25	1.75
			Nos. 123-126 (4)	6.30	4.75

So. Pacific Commission, 25th anniv.

Silver Wedding Issue, 1972

Common Design Type

Design: Queen Elizabeth II, Prince Philip, skuas and longboat.

1972, Nov. 20 Photo. Wmk. 314

No.	Type	Denom.	Description	Unused	Used
127	CD324	4c	slate grn & multi	.25	.15
128	CD324	20c	ultra & multi	.85	.60

Pitcairn Coat of Arms A26

1973, Jan. 2 Litho. *Perf. 14½x14*

No.	Type	Denom.	Description	Unused	Used
129	A26	50c	multicolored	3.50	3.50

Rose Apple — A27

1973, June 25 *Perf. 14*

No.	Type	Denom.	Description	Unused	Used
130	A27	4c	shown	.90	.40
131	A27	8c	Mountain apple	1.50	.75
132	A27	15c	Lata (myrtle)	2.25	1.40
133	A27	20c	Cassia	2.50	1.75
134	A27	35c	Guava	5.00	3.50
			Nos. 130-134 (5)	12.15	7.80

Princess Anne's Wedding Issue

Common Design Type

1973, Nov. 14 Litho. *Perf. 14*

No.	Type	Denom.	Description	Unused	Used
135	CD325	10c	lilac & multi	.20	.15
136	CD325	25c	gray green & multi	.40	.35

Miter and Horn Shells A28

1974, Apr. 15

No.	Type	Denom.	Description	Unused	Used
137	A28	4c	shown	.50	.40
138	A28	10c	Dove shells	1.25	1.00
139	A28	18c	Limpets and false limpet	2.00	1.75
140	A28	50c	Lucine shells	5.50	5.00
a.			Souvenir sheet of 4, #137-140	11.00	6.00
			Nos. 137-140 (4)	9.25	8.15

Pitcairn Post Office, UPU Emblem A29

UPU, cent.: 20c, Stampless cover, "Posted at Pitcairn Island No Stamps Available." 35c, Longboat leaving Bounty Bay for ship offshore.

1974, July 22 Wmk. 314 *Perf. 14½*

No.	Type	Denom.	Description	Unused	Used
141	A29	4c	multicolored	.15	.15
142	A29	20c	multicolored	.60	.50
143	A29	35c	multicolored	1.25	1.00
			Nos. 141-143 (3)	2.00	1.65

Churchill: "Lift up your hearts . . ." — A30

Design: 35c, Churchill and "Give us the tools and we will finish the job."

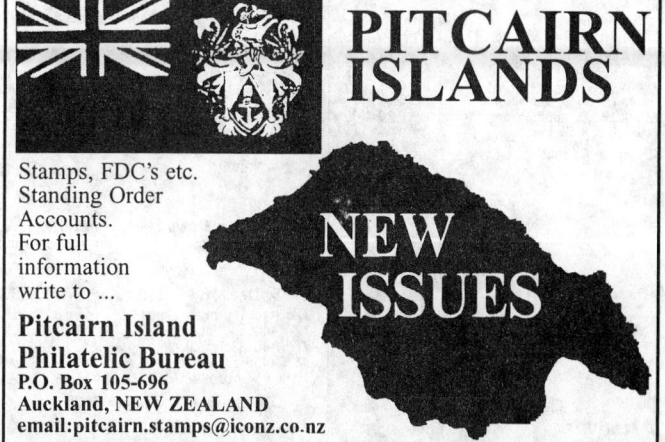

1974, Nov. 30 Litho. Wmk. 373

144 A30 20c black & citron .50 .40
145 A30 35c black & yellow .75 .60

Sir Winston Churchill (1874-1965).

Queen Elizabeth II — A31

1975, Apr. 21 Wmk. 314 *Perf. 14½*

146 A31 $1 multicolored 9.50 9.50

Mailboats A32

1975, July 22 Litho. *Perf. 14½*

147 A32 4c Seringapatam, 1830 .25 .20
148 A32 10c Pitcairn, 1890 .65 .60
149 A32 18c Athenic, 1901 1.25 1.00
150 A32 50c Gothic, 1948 3.25 2.75
a. Souvenir sheet of 4, #147-150, perf. 14 12.50 10.00
Nos. 147-150 (4) 5.40 4.55

Pitcairn Wasp A33

Insects: 6c, Grasshopper. 10c, Pitcairn moths. 15c, Dragonfly. 20c, Banana moth.

Perf. 14½

1975, Nov. 9 Litho. Wmk. 314

151 A33 4c blue grn & multi .40 .20
152 A33 6c carmine & multi .65 .35
153 A33 10c purple & multi 1.00 .60
154 A33 15c black & multi 1.50 .85
155 A33 20c multicolored 1.75 1.00
Nos. 151-155 (5) 5.30 3.00

Fletcher Christian — A34

H.M.S. Bounty — A35

American Bicentennial: 30c, George Washington. 50c, Mayflower.

1976, July 4 Wmk. 373 *Perf. 13½*

156 A34 5c multicolored .20 .15
157 A35 10c multicolored .40 .35
158 A34 30c multicolored 1.00 .90
a. Pair, #156, 158 1.40 1.40
159 A35 50c multicolored 1.25 1.00
a. Pair, #157, 159 1.65 1.65
Nos. 156-159 (4) 2.85 2.40

Prince Philip's Arrival, 1971 Visit — A36

20c, Chair of homage. 50c, The enthronement.

1977, Feb. 6 *Perf. 13*

160 A36 8c silver & multi .15 .15
161 A36 20c silver & multi .25 .20
162 A36 50c silver & multi .60 .55
Nos. 160-162 (3) 1.00 .90

25th anniv. of the reign of Elizabeth II.

Building Longboat A37

Designs: 1c, Man ringing Island Bell, vert. 5c, Landing cargo. 6c, Sorting supplies. 9c, Cleaning wahoo (fish), vert. 10c, Farming. 15c, Sugar mill. 20c, Women grating coconuts and bananas. 35c, Island church. 50c, Gathering miro logs, Henderson Island. 70c, Burning obsolete stamps, vert. $1, Prince Philip and "Britannia." $2, Elizabeth II, vert.

1977-81 Litho. *Perf. 14½*

163 A37 1c multicolored .15 .15
164 A37 2c multicolored .15 .15
165 A37 5c multicolored .15 .15
166 A37 6c multicolored .15 .15
167 A37 9c multicolored .15 .15
168 A37 10c multicolored .15 .15
168A A37 15c multicolored .20 .20
169 A37 20c multicolored .25 .25
170 A37 35c multicolored .45 .45
171 A37 50c multicolored .60 .60
171A A37 70c multicolored .85 .85
172 A37 $1 multicolored 1.25 1.25
173 A37 $2 multicolored 2.50 2.50
Nos. 163-173 (13) 7.00 7.00

Issued: #168A, 171A, 10/1/81; others, 9/12/77.

Building "Bounty" Model A38

Bounty Day: 20c, Bounty model afloat. 35c, Burning Bounty.

1978, Jan. 9 *Perf. 14½*

174 A38 6c yellow & multi .20 .15
175 A38 20c yellow & multi .85 .65
176 A38 35c yellow & multi 1.25 1.00
a. Souvenir sheet of 3, #174-176 8.00 7.00
Nos. 174-176 (3) 2.30 1.80

Souvenir Sheet

Elizabeth II in Coronation Regalia — A39

Wmk. 373

1978, Sept. Litho. *Perf. 12*

177 A39 $1.20 silver & multi 2.00 2.00

25th anniv. of coronation of Elizabeth II.

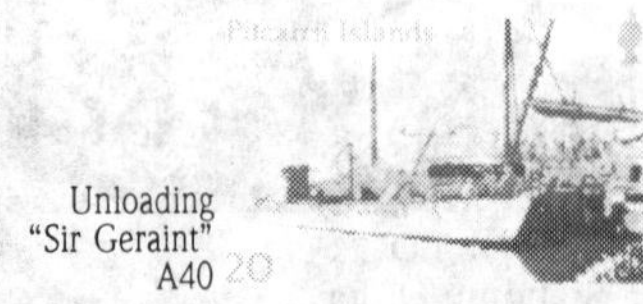

Unloading "Sir Geraint" A40

Designs: 15c, Harbor before development. 30c, Work on the jetty. 35c, Harbor after development.

Perf. 13½

1978, Dec. 18 Litho. Wmk. 373

178 A40 15c multicolored .20 .20
179 A40 20c multicolored .35 .35
180 A40 30c multicolored .60 .60
181 A40 35c multicolored .65 .65
Nos. 178-181 (4) 1.80 1.80

Development of new harbor on Pitcairn.

John Adams A41

Design: 70c, John Adams' grave.

1979, Mar. 5 Litho. *Perf. 14½*

182 A41 35c multicolored .30 .30
183 A41 70c multicolored .60 .60

John Adams (1760-1829), founder of Pitcairn Colony, 150th death anniversary.

Pitcairn Island Seen from "Amphitrite" — A42

Engravings (c. 1850): 9c, Bounty Bay and Pitcairn Village, 20c, Lookout Ridge. 70c, Church and schoolhouse.

1979, Sept. 12 Litho. *Perf. 14*

184 A42 6c multicolored .15 .15
185 A42 9c multicolored .15 .15
186 A42 20c multicolored .20 .20
187 A42 70c multicolored .50 .50
Nos. 184-187 (4) 1.00 1.00

Taking Presents to the Square, IYC Emblem — A43

IYC Emblem and Children's Drawings: 9c, Decorating trees with presents. 20c, Distributing presents. 35c, Carrying the presents home.

Perf. 13½

1979, Nov. 28 Litho. Wmk. 373

188 A43 6c multicolored .15 .15
189 A43 9c multicolored .15 .15
190 A43 20c multicolored .30 .30
191 A43 35c multicolored .50 .50
a. Souvenir sheet of 4, #188-191 2.00 2.00
Nos. 188-191 (4) 1.10 1.10

Christmas and IYC.

Souvenir Sheet

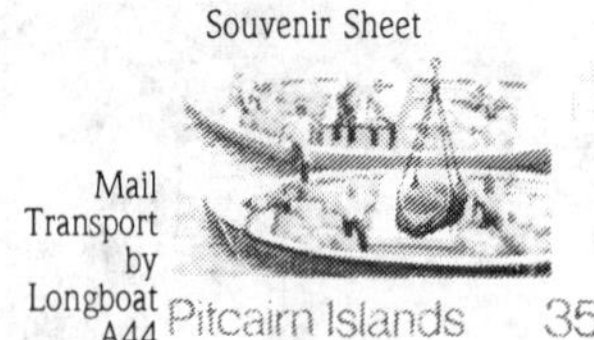

Mail Transport by Longboat A44

Perf. 14½

1980, May 6 Litho. Wmk. 373

192 Sheet of 4 1.25 1.25
a. A44 35c shown .25 .25
b. A44 35c Mail crane lift .25 .25
c. A44 35c Tractor transport .25 .25
d. A44 35c Arrival at post office .25 .25

London 80 Intl. Phil. Exhib., May 6-14.

Queen Mother Elizabeth Birthday Issue

Common Design Type

Wmk. 373

1980, Aug. 4 Litho. *Perf. 14*

193 CD330 50c multicolored .50 .50

Handicraft Type of 1968

Perf. 14½x14, 14x14½

1980, Sept. 29 Litho. Wmk. 373

194 A19 9c Turtles .15 .15
195 A19 20c Wheelbarrow .20 .20
196 A19 35c Gannet, vert. .35 .35
197 A19 40c Bonnet and fan, vert. .40 .40
Nos. 194-197 (4) 1.10 1.10

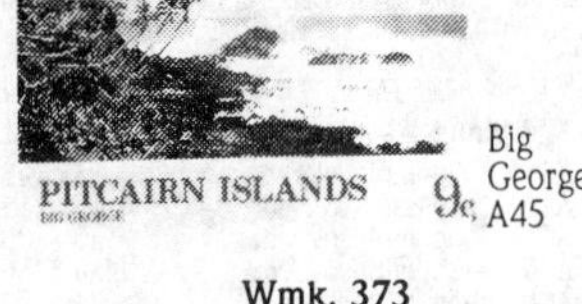

Big George A45

Wmk. 373

1981, Jan. 22 Litho. *Perf. 14*

198 A45 6c View of Adamstown .15 .15
199 A45 9c shown .15 .15
200 A45 20c Christian's Cave, Gannet's Ridge .20 .20
201 A45 35c Pawala Valley Ridge .30 .30
202 A45 70c Tatrimoa .60 .60
Nos. 198-202 (5) 1.40 1.40

Citizens Departing for Norfolk Island A46

1981, May 3 Photo. *Perf. 13x14½*

203 A46 9c shown .15 .15
204 A46 35c Norfolk Isld. from Morayshire .35 .35
205 A46 70c Morayshire .70 .70
Nos. 203-205 (3) 1.20 1.20

Migration to Norfolk Is., 125th anniv.

Royal Wedding Issue

Common Design Type

Wmk. 373

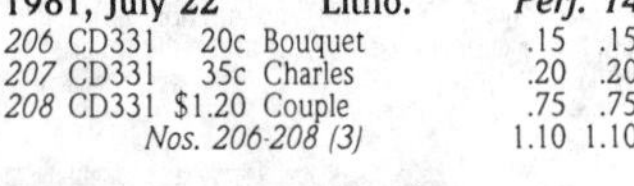

1981, July 22 Litho. *Perf. 14*

206 CD331 20c Bouquet .15 .15
207 CD331 35c Charles .20 .20
208 CD331 $1.20 Couple .75 .75
Nos. 206-208 (3) 1.10 1.10

Lemon A47

1982, Feb. 23 Litho. *Perf. 14½*

209 A47 9c shown .15 .15
210 A47 20c Pomegranate .20 .20
211 A47 35c Avocado .30 .30
212 A47 70c Pawpaw .60 .60
Nos. 209-212 (4) 1.25 1.25

Princess Diana Issue

Common Design Type

1982, July 1 Litho. *Perf. 14½x14*

213 CD333 6c Arms .15 .15
214 CD333 9c Diana .15 .15
215 CD333 70c Wedding .55 .55
216 CD333 $1.20 Portrait .90 .90
Nos. 213-216 (4) 1.75 1.75

Christmas — A48

Designs: Various paintings of angels by Raphael. 50c, $1 vert.

1982, Oct. 19 Litho. *Perf. 14*

217 A48 15c multicolored .15 .15
218 A48 20c multicolored .20 .20
219 A48 50c multicolored .45 .45
220 A48 $1 multicolored 1.00 1.00
Nos. 217-220 (4) 1.80 1.80

A48a

1983, Mar. 14
221 A48a 6c Radio operator .15 .15
222 A48a 9c Postal clerk .15 .15
223 A48a 70c Fisherman .60 .60
224 A48a $1.20 Artist 1.00 1.00
Nos. 221-224 (4) 1.90 1.90

Commonwealth Day.

175th Anniv. of Capt. Folger's Discovery of the Settlers A49

Wmk. 373

1983, June 14 Litho. *Perf. 14*
225 A49 6c Topaz off Pitcairn Isld. .15 .15
226 A49 20c Topaz, islanders .30 .30
227 A49 70c John Adams welcoming Folger 1.10 1.10
228 A49 $1.20 Presentation of Chronometer 1.75 1.75
Nos. 225-228 (4) 3.30 3.30

Local Trees A50

1983, Oct. 6 Litho. *Perf. 13½*
229 Pair .90 .90
a. A50 35c Hattie .45 .45
b. A50 35c Branch, wood painting .45 .45
230 Pair 1.50 1.50
a. A50 70c Pandanus .75 .75
b. A50 70c Branch, basket weaving .75 .75

See Nos. 289-290.

Pseudojuloides Atavai — A51

Perf. 14½

1984, Jan. 11 Litho. Wmk. 373
231 A51 1c shown .15 .15
232 A51 4c Halichoeres melasmapomus .15 .15
233 A51 6c Scarus longipinnis .15 .15
234 A51 9c Variola louti .15 .15
235 A51 10c Centropyge hotumatua .15 .15
236 A51 15c Stegastes emeryi .25 .25
237 A51 20c Chaetodon smithi .30 .30
238 A51 35c Xanthichthys mento .50 .50
239 A51 50c Chrysiptera galba .70 .70
240 A51 70c Genicanthus spinus 1.00 1.00
241 A51 $1 Myripristis tiki 1.25 1.25
242 A51 $1.20 Anthias ventralis 1.25 1.25
243 A51 $2 Pseudocaranx dentex 2.75 2.75
Nos. 231-243 (13) 8.75 8.75

See Nos. 295-296.

Constellations — A52

1984, May 14 Wmk. 373
244 A52 15c Crux Australis .15 .15
245 A52 20c Piscis Australis .25 .25
246 A52 70c Canis Minor .90 .90
247 A52 $1 Virgo 1.25 1.25
Nos. 244-247 (4) 2.55 2.55

Souvenir Sheet

AUSIPEX '84 — A53

Longboats.

1984, Sept. 21 Litho. Wmk. 373
248 Sheet of 2 3.00 3.00
a. A53 50c multicolored .60 .60
b. A53 $2 multicolored 2.40 2.40

HMS Portland off Bounty Bay, by J. Linton Palmer, 1853 — A54

Paintings by J. Linton Palmer, 1853, and William Smyth, 1825: 9c, Christian's Look Out at Pitcairn Island. 35c, The Golden Age. $2, View of Village, by Smyth.

Wmk. 373

1985, Jan. 16 Litho. *Perf. 14*
249 A54 6c multicolored .15 .15
250 A54 9c multicolored .15 .15
251 A54 35c multicolored .50 .50

Size: 48x32mm
252 A54 $2 multicolored 2.00 2.00
Nos. 249-252 (4) 2.80 2.80

Copies of No. 252 with "1835" date were not issued. Value, $45.
See Nos. 291-294.

Queen Mother 85th Birthday
Common Design Type
Perf. 14½x14

1985, June 7 Litho. Wmk. 384
253 CD336 6c In Dundee, 1964 .15 .15
254 CD336 35c At 80th birthday celebration .30 .30
255 CD336 70c Queen Mother .55 .55
256 CD336 $1.20 Holding Prince Henry 1.00 1.00
Nos. 253-256 (4) 2.00 2.00

Souvenir Sheet
257 CD336 $2 In coach at the Races, Ascot 2.00 2.00

Act 6 — A55

Essi Gina A56

1985, Aug. 28 *Perf. 14½x14*
258 A55 50c shown .90 .90
259 A55 50c Columbus Louisiana .90 .90

Perf. 14
260 A56 50c shown .90 .90
261 A56 50c Stolt Spirit .90 .90
Nos. 258-261 (4) 3.60 3.60

See Nos. 281-284.

Christmas — A57

Madonna & child paintings: 6c, by Raphael. 9c, by Krause. 35c, by Andreas Mayer. $2, by an unknown Austrian master.

1985, Nov. 26 *Perf. 14*
262 A57 6c multicolored .15 .15
263 A57 9c multicolored .15 .15
264 A57 35c multicolored .45 .45
265 A57 $2 multicolored 2.50 2.50
Nos. 262-265 (4) 3.25 3.25

Turtles A58

Designs: 9c, 20c, Chelonia mydas. 70c, $1.20, Eretmochelys imbricata.

Perf. 14½

1986, Feb. 12 Litho. Wmk. 384
266 A58 9c multicolored .15 .15
267 A58 20c multi, diff. .40 .40
268 A58 70c multicolored 1.50 1.50
269 A58 $1.20 multi, diff. 2.75 2.75
Nos. 266-269 (4) 4.80 4.80

Queen Elizabeth II 60th Birthday
Common Design Type

Designs: 6c, In Royal Lodge garden, Windsor, 1946. 9c, Wedding of Princess Anne and Capt. Mark Philips, 1973. 20c, Wearing mantle and robes of Order of St. Paul's Cathedral, 1961. $1.20, Concert, Royal Festival Hall, London, 1971. $2, Visting Crown Agents' offices, 1983.

1986, Apr. 21 Litho. *Perf. 14½*
270 CD337 6c multi .15 .15
271 CD337 9c multi .15 .15
272 CD337 20c multi .20 .20
273 CD337 $1.20 multi 1.00 1.00
274 CD337 $2 multi 1.75 1.75
Nos. 270-274 (5) 3.25 3.25

Royal Wedding Issue, 1986
Common Design Type

Designs: 20c, Informal portrait. $1.20, Andrew aboard royal navy vessel.

Wmk. 384

1986, July 23 Litho. *Perf. 14*
275 CD338 20c multi .30 .30
276 CD338 $1.20 multi 2.00 2.00

7th Day Adventist Church, Cent. — A59

Designs: 6c, First church, 1886, and John I. Tay, missionary. 20c, Second church, 1907, and mission ship Pitcairn, 1890. 35c, Third church, 1945, baptism and Down Isaac. $2, Church, 1954, and sailing ship.

1986, Oct. 18
277 A59 6c multicolored .15 .15
278 A59 20c multicolored .45 .45
279 A59 35c multicolored .75 .75
280 A59 $2 multicolored 4.25 4.25
Nos. 277-280 (4) 5.60 5.60

Ship Type of 1985

1987, Jan. 20 *Perf. 14x14½*
281 A55 50c Brussel 1.25 1.25
282 A55 50c Samoan Reefer 1.25 1.25

Perf. 14
283 A56 50c Australian Exporter 1.25 1.25
284 A56 50c Taupo 1.25 1.25
Nos. 281-284 (4) 5.00 5.00

Island Houses A60

1987, May 21 Wmk. 373 *Perf. 14*
285 A60 70c lt greenish blue, bluish grn & blk .70 .70
286 A60 70c cream, yel bister & blk .70 .70
287 A60 70c lt blue, brt blue & blk .70 .70
288 A60 70c lt lil, brt vio & blk .70 .70
Nos. 285-288 (4) 2.80 2.80

Tree Type of 1983

1987, Aug. 10 Wmk. 384 *Perf. 14½*
289 Pair 1.25 1.25
a. A50 40c Leaves, blossoms .50 .50
b. A50 40c Monkey puzzle tree .50 .50
290 Pair 5.00 5.00
a. A50 $1.80 Leaves, blossoms, nuts 2.00 2.00
b. A50 $1.80 Duduinut tree 2.00 2.00

Art Type of 1985

Paintings by Lt. Conway Shipley, 1848: 20c, House and Tomb of John Adams. 40c, Bounty Bay, with H.M.S. Calypso. 90c, School House and Chapel. $1.80, Pitcairn Island with H.M.S. Calypso.

1987, Dec. 7 Litho. *Perf. 14*
291 A54 20c multi .25 .25
292 A54 40c multi .50 .50
293 A54 90c multi 1.25 1.25

Size: 48x32mm
294 A54 $1.80 multi 2.50 2.50
Nos. 291-294 (4) 4.50 4.50

Fish Type of 1984
Perf. 14½

1988, Jan. 14 Litho. Wmk. 384
295 A51 90c Variola louti 2.25 2.25
296 A51 $3 Gymnothorax eurostus 6.75 6.75

Souvenir Sheet

Australia Bicentennial — A61

1988, May 9 Wmk. 384 *Perf. 14*
297 A61 $3 HMS *Bounty* replica under sail 4.00 4.00

Visiting Ships A62

Perf. 13½

1988, Aug. 14 Litho. Wmk. 373
298 A62 5c HMS *Swallow,* 1767 .15 .15
299 A62 10c HMS *Pandora,* 1791 .15 .15
300 A62 15c HMS *Briton* and HMS *Tagus,* 1814 .15 .15
301 A62 20c HMS *Blossom,* 1825 .20 .20
a. Wmk. 384 .75 .75
b. Booklet pane of 4, #301a .80
302 A62 30c S.V. *Lucy Anne,* 1831 .30 .30
303 A62 35c S.V. *Charles Doggett,* 1831 .35 .35
304 A62 40c HMS *Fly,* 1838 .40 .40
305 A62 60c LMS *Camden,* 1840 .60 .60
306 A62 90c HMS *Virago,* 1853 .85 .85
a. Wmk. 384 .85 .85
b. Booklet pane of 4, #306a 3.50
307 A62 $1.20 S.S. *Rakaia,* 1867 1.15 1.15
308 A62 $1.80 HMS *Sappho,* 1882 1.75 1.75
309 A62 $5 HMS *Champion,* 1893 4.50 4.50
Nos. 298-309 (12) 10.55 10.55

20c, 90c exist dated "1990."
Issued: #301a-301b, 306a-306b, May 3, 1990.

Constitution, 150th Anniv. — A63

Text and: 20c, Raising the Union Jack. 40c, Signing of the constitution aboard the H.M.S. "Fly," 1838. $1.05, Suffrage. $1.80, Equal education.

1988, Nov. 30 Wmk. 373 *Perf. 14*

315 A63 20c multicolored .20 .20
316 A63 40c multicolored .45 .45
317 A63 $1.05 multicolored 1.25 1.25
318 A63 $1.80 multicolored 2.00 2.00
Nos. 315-318 (4) 3.90 3.90

Christmas A64

Designs: a, Angel, animals in stable. b, Holy Family. c, Two Magi. d, Magus and shepherd boy.

1988, Nov. 30 Wmk. 384 *Perf. 14*

319 Strip of 4 4.00 4.00
a.-d. A64 90c any single 1.00 1.00

Miniature Sheets

Pitcairn Isls., Bicent. A65

No. 320 (*Bounty* sets sail for the South Seas, Dec. 23, 1787): a, Fitting out the *Bounty* at Deptford. b, *Bounty* leaving Spithead. c, *Bounty* trying to round Cape Horn. d, Anchored in Adventure Bay, Tasmania. e, Ship's mates collecting breadfruit. f, Breadfruit in great cabin.

No. 321 (the mutiny, Apr. 28, 1789): a, *Bounty* leaving Matavai Bay. b, Mutineers waking Capt. Bligh. c, Confrontation between Fletcher Christian and Bligh. d, Bligh and crew members set adrift in an open boat. e, Castaways. f, Throwing breadfruit overboard.

No. 322: a, like No. 321e. b, Isle of Man #393. c, Norfolk Is. #453.

1989 Litho. Wmk. 373

320 Sheet of 6 4.50 4.50
a.-f. A65 20c any single .50 .50
321 Sheet of 6 12.00 12.00
a.-f. A65 90c any single 1.50 1.50

Souvenir Sheet

Wmk. 384

322 Sheet of 3 + label 5.00 5.00
a.-c. A65 90c any single 1.25 1.25

See #331, Isle of Man #389-394 and Norfolk Is. #452-456.

Issued: #320, Feb. 22; #321-322, Apr. 28.

Difference between #. 321e and 322a is inscription at bottom of #322a: "C. Abbott 1989 BOT."

Aircraft — A66

Perf. 14½

1989, July 25 Litho. Wmk. 384

323 A66 20c RNZAF Orion .25 .25
324 A66 80c Beechcraft Queen Air 1.25 1.25
325 A66 $1.05 Navy helicopter, USS *Breton* 1.75 1.75
326 A66 $1.30 RNZAF Hercules 2.25 2.25
Nos. 323-326 (4) 5.50 5.50

Second mail drop on Pitcairn, Mar. 21, 1985 (20c); photo mission from Tahiti, Jan. 14, 1983 (80c); diesel fuel delivery by the navy, Feb. 12, 1969 ($1.05); and parachute delivery of a bulldozer, May 31, 1983 ($1.30).

The Islands A67

Wmk. 373

1989, Oct. 23 Litho. *Perf. 14*

327 A67 15c Ducie Is. .20 .20
328 A67 90c Henderson Is. 1.00 1.00
329 A67 $1.05 Oeno Is. 1.25 1.25
330 A67 $1.30 Pitcairn Is. 1.75 1.75
Nos. 327-330 (4) 4.20 4.20

Bicentennial Type of 1989

Miniature Sheet

Designs: a, Mutineers aboard *Bounty* anticipating landing on Pitcairn. b, Landing. c, Exploration of the island. d, Carrying goods ashore. e, Burning the *Bounty*. f, Settlement.

1990, Jan. 15 Wmk. 384 *Perf. 14*

331 Sheet of 6 + 3 labels 6.00 6.00
a.-f. A65 40c any single .75 .75

Stamp World London '90 — A68

Links with the UK: 80c, Peter Heywood and Ennerdale, Cumbria. 90c, John Adams and The Tower of St. Augustine, Hackney. $1.05, William Bligh and The Citadel Gateway, Plymouth. $1.30, Fletcher Christian and birthplace, Cockermouth.

1990, May 3 Wmk. 373 *Perf. 14*

332 A68 80c multicolored .95 .95
333 A68 90c multicolored 1.05 1.05
334 A68 $1.05 multicolored 1.25 1.25
335 A68 $1.30 multicolored 1.55 1.55
Nos. 332-335 (4) 4.80 4.80

Queen Mother 90th Birthday

Common Design Types

1990, Aug. 4 Wmk. 384 *Perf. 14x15*

336 CD343 40c Portrait, 1937 .50 .50

Perf. 14½

337 CD344 $3 King, Queen in carriage 4.00 4.00

First Pitcairn Island Postage Stamps, 50th Anniv — A69

Historical items and Pitcairn Islands stamps.

Perf. 13½x14

1990, Oct. 15 Wmk. 373

338 A69 20c Chronometer, #2 .25 .25
339 A69 80c Bounty's Bible, #31 1.00 1.00
340 A69 90c Bounty's Bell, #108 1.25 1.25
341 A69 $1.05 Bounty, #172 1.50 1.50
342 A69 $1.30 Penny Black, #300 2.00 2.00
Nos. 338-342 (5) 6.00 6.00

Birds — A70

1990, Dec. 5 Wmk. 373 *Perf. 14*

343 A70 20c Redbreast .25 .25
344 A70 90c Wood pigeon 1.25 1.25
345 A70 $1.30 Sparrow 1.75 1.75
346 A70 $1.80 Flightless chicken 2.50 2.50
Nos. 343-346 (4) 5.75 5.75

Birdpex '90, 20th Intl. Ornithological Congress, New Zealand.

Miniature Sheet

Pitcairn Islands, Bicent. A71

Bicentennial celebrations: a, Re-enacting the landing. b, Commemorative plaque. c, Memorial church service. d, Cricket match. e, Bounty model burning. f, Fireworks.

Perf. 14½

1991, Mar. 24 Litho. Wmk. 384

347 A71 80c Sheet of 6, #a.-f. 10.00 10.00

Elizabeth & Philip, Birthdays

Common Design Types

Perf. 14½

1991, July 12 Litho. Wmk. 384

348 CD346 20c multicolored .25 .25
349 CD345 $1.30 multicolored 2.25 2.25
a. Pair, #348-349 + label 2.50 2.50

Cruise Ships A72

1991, June 17

350 A72 15c Europa .25 .25
351 A72 80c Royal Viking Star 1.25 1.25
352 A72 $1.30 World Discoverer 2.10 2.10
353 A72 $1.80 Sagafjord 3.00 3.00
Nos. 350-353 (4) 6.60 6.60

Island Vehicles A73

1991, Sept. 25 Wmk. 373 *Perf. 14*

354 A73 20c Bulldozer .25 .25
355 A73 80c Motorcycle 1.00 1.00
356 A73 $1.30 Tractor 1.75 1.75
357 A73 $1.80 All-terrain vehicle 2.50 2.50
Nos. 354-357 (4) 5.50 5.50

Christmas — A74

1991, Nov. 18 *Perf. 14x14½*

358 A74 20c The Annunciation .25 .25
359 A74 80c Shepherds 1.00 1.00
360 A74 $1.30 Nativity scene 1.75 1.75
361 A74 $1.80 Three wise men 2.50 2.50
Nos. 358-361 (4) 5.50 5.50

Queen Elizabeth II's Accession to the Throne, 40th Anniv.

Common Design Type

Wmk. 384

1992, Feb. 6 Litho. *Perf. 14*

362 CD349 20c multicolored .25 .25
363 CD349 60c multicolored .75 .75
364 CD349 90c multicolored 1.00 1.00
365 CD349 $1 multicolored 1.25 1.25

Wmk. 373

366 CD349 $1.80 multicolored 2.50 2.50
Nos. 362-366 (5) 5.75 5.75

Sharks A75

Designs: 20c, Carcharhinus galapagensis. $1, Eugomphodus taurus. $1.50, Carcharhinus melanopterus. $1.80, Carcharhinus amblyrhynchos.

Perf. 15x14½

1992, June 30 Litho. Wmk. 373

367 A75 20c multicolored .25 .25
368 A75 $1 multicolored 1.25 1.25
369 A75 $1.50 multicolored 1.75 1.75
370 A75 $1.80 multicolored 2.50 2.50
Nos. 367-370 (4) 5.75 5.75

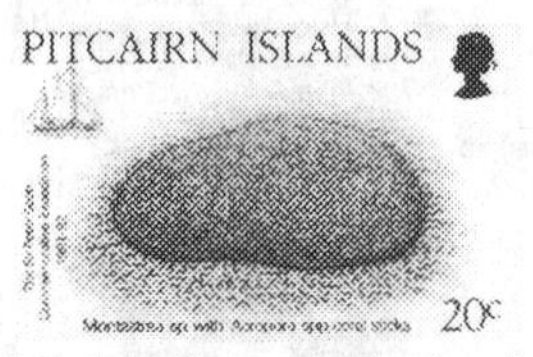

Sir Peter Scott Commemorative Expedition to Pitcairn Islands, 1991-92 — A76

Designs: 20c, Montastrea, acropora coral sticks. $1, Henderson sandalwood. $1.50, Murphy's petrel. $1.80, Henderson hawkmoth.

Perf. 14x15

1992, Sept. 11 Litho. Wmk. 373

371 A76 20c multicolored .25 .25
372 A76 $1 multicolored 1.25 1.25
373 A76 $1.50 multicolored 1.75 1.75
374 A76 $1.80 multicolored 2.50 2.50
Nos. 371-374 (4) 5.75 5.75

Captain William Bligh, 175th Anniv. of Death A77

20c, Bligh's birthplace, St. Tudy, Cornwall, HMS Resolution. $1, On deck of HMAV Bounty, breadfruit plant. $1.50, Voyage in open boat, Bligh's answers at court martial. $1.80, Portrait by Rachel H. Combe, Battle of Camperdown, 1797.

Perf. 14½

1992, Dec. 7 Litho. Wmk. 373

375 A77 20c multicolored .25 .25
376 A77 $1 multicolored 1.25 1.25
377 A77 $1.50 multicolored 1.75 1.75
378 A77 $1.80 multicolored 2.00 2.00
Nos. 375-378 (4) 5.25 5.25

Royal Naval Vessels A78

Wmk. 384

1993, Mar. 10 Litho. *Perf. 14*

379 A78 15c HMS Chichester .20 .20
380 A78 20c HMS Jaguar .30 .30
381 A78 $1.80 HMS Andrew 2.75 2.75
382 A78 $3 HMS Warrior 4.50 4.50
Nos. 379-382 (4) 7.75 7.75

Coronation of Queen Elizabeth II, 40th Anniv. A79

Wmk. 373

1993, June 17 Litho. *Perf. 13*

383 A79 $5 multicolored 7.00 7.00

Scenic Views A80

10c, Pawala Valley Ridge. 90c, St. Pauls. $1.20, Matt's Rocks from Water Valley. $1.50, Ridge Rope to St. Paul's Pool. $1.80, Ship Landing Point.

Wmk. 373

1993, Sept. 8 Litho. *Perf. 14*

384 A80 10c multicolored .15 .15
385 A80 90c multicolored .95 .95
386 A80 $1.20 multicolored 1.25 1.25
387 A80 $1.50 multicolored 1.65 1.65
388 A80 $1.80 multicolored 1.90 1.90
Nos. 384-388 (5) 5.90 5.90

Lizards A81

Designs: 20c, Indopacific tree gecko. No. 390, Stump-toed gecko. No. 391, Mourning gecko. $1, Moth skink No. 393, Snake-eyed skink. No. 394, White-bellied skink.

Perf. 13x13½

1993, Dec. 14 Litho. Wmk. 373

389 A81 20c multicolored .25 .25
390 A81 45c multicolored .50 .50
391 A81 45c multicolored .50 .50
a. Pair, #390-391 1.00 1.00
392 A81 $1 multicolored 1.10 1.10
393 A81 $1.50 multicolored 1.75 1.75
394 A81 $1.50 multicolored 1.75 1.75
a. Pair, #393-394 3.50 3.50
Nos. 389-394 (6) 5.85 5.85

Nos. 390-391, 393-394 Ovptd. with Hong Kong '94 Emblem

Perf. 13x13½

1994, Feb. 18 Litho. Wmk. 373

395 A81 45c on #390 .75 .75
396 A81 45c on #391 .75 .75
a. Pair, #395-396 1.50 1.50
397 A81 $1.50 on #393 2.75 2.75
398 A81 $1.50 on #394 2.75 2.75
a. Pair, #397-398 5.50 5.50
Nos. 395-398 (4) 7.00 7.00

Early Pitcairners — A82

Designs: 5c, Friday October Christian. 20c, Moses Young. $1.80, James Russell McCoy. $3, Rosalind Amelia Young.

1994, Mar. 7 *Perf. 14*

399 A82 5c multicolored .15 .15
400 A82 20c multicolored .25 .25
401 A82 $1.80 multicolored 2.00 2.00
402 A82 $3 multicolored 3.25 3.25
Nos. 399-402 (4) 5.65 5.65

Shipwrecks A83

20c, Wildwave, Oeno Island, 1858. 90c, Cornwallis, Pitcairn Island, 1875. $1.80, Acadia, Ducie Island, 1881. $3, Oregon, Oeno Island, 1883.

Wmk. 373

1994, June 22 Litho. *Perf. 14*

403 A83 20c multicolored .25 .25
404 A83 90c multicolored 1.00 1.00
405 A83 $1.80 multicolored 2.00 2.00
406 A83 $3 multicolored 3.50 3.50
Nos. 403-406 (4) 6.75 6.75

Corals A84

Designs: 20c, Fire coral, vert. 90c, Cauliflower coral, arc-eye hawkfish. $1, Snubnose chub, lobe coral, vert.
$3, Coral garden, butterflyfish, vert.

Wmk. 373

1994, Sept. 15 Litho. *Perf. 14*

407 A84 20c multicolored .25 .25
408 A84 90c multicolored 1.10 1.10
409 A84 $1 multicolored 1.25 1.25
Nos. 407-409 (3) 2.60 2.60

Souvenir Sheet

410 A84 $3 multicolored 3.75 3.75

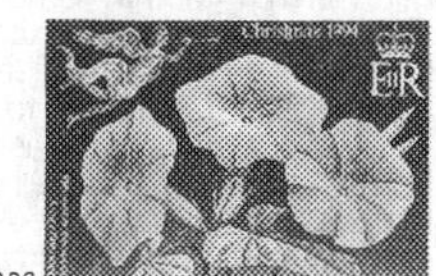

Christmas A85

Flowers: 20c, Morning glory. 90c, Hibiscus, vert. $1, Frangipani. $3, Ginsey, vert.

Wmk. 373

1994, Nov. 24 Litho. *Perf. 14*

411 A85 20c multicolored .25 .25
412 A85 90c multicolored 1.10 1.10
413 A85 $1 multicolored 1.25 1.25
414 A85 $3 multicolored 3.75 3.75
Nos. 411-414 (4) 6.35 6.35

Birds A86

Designs: 5c, Fairy tern. 10c, Red-tailed tropicbird chick, vert. 15c, Henderson rail. 20c, Red-footed booby, vert. 45c, Blue-gray noddy. 50c, Henderson reed warbler. 90c, Common noddy. $1, Masked booby, chick, vert. $1.80, Henderson fruit dove. $2, Murphy's petrel. $3, Christmas shearwater. $5, Red-tailed tropicbird juvenile.

1995, Mar. 8 *Perf. 13½*

415 A86 5c multicolored .15 .15
416 A86 10c multicolored .15 .15
417 A86 15c multicolored .18 .18
418 A86 20c multicolored .25 .25
419 A86 45c multicolored .55 .55
420 A86 50c multicolored .62 .62
421 A86 90c multicolored 1.10 1.10
422 A86 $1 multicolored 1.25 1.25
423 A86 $1.80 multicolored 2.25 2.25
424 A86 $2 multicolored 2.50 2.50
425 A86 $3 multicolored 3.75 3.75
426 A86 $5 multicolored 6.25 6.25
Nos. 415-426 (12) 19.00 19.00

Oeno Island Vacation — A87

Designs: 20c, Boating. 90c, Volleyball on the beach. $1.80, Picnic. $3, Sing-a-long.

1995, June 26 *Perf. 14x15*

427 A87 20c multicolored .25 .25
428 A87 90c multicolored 1.25 1.25
429 A87 $1.80 multicolored 2.50 2.50
430 A87 $3 multicolored 4.00 4.00
Nos. 427-430 (4) 8.00 8.00

Souvenir Sheet

Queen Mother, 95th Birthday — A88

1995, Aug. 4 *Perf. 14½*

431 A88 $5 multicolored 6.75 6.75

Radio, Cent. — A89

Designs: 20c, Guglielmo Marconi, radio equipment, 1901. $1, Man, Pitcairn radio, 1938. $1.50, Woman, satellite earth station equipment, 1994. $3, Satellite in orbit, 1992.

1995, Sept. 5 *Perf. 13*

432 A89 20c multicolored .25 .25
433 A89 $1 multicolored 1.25 1.25
434 A89 $1.50 multicolored 2.00 2.00
435 A89 $3 multicolored 4.00 4.00
Nos. 432-435 (4) 7.50 7.50

UN, 50th Anniv.

Common Design Type

Designs: 20c, Lord Mayor's Show. $1, RFA Brambleleaf. $1.50, UN ambulance. $3, Royal Air Force Tristar.

Wmk. 373

1995, Oct. 24 Litho. *Perf. 14*

436 CD353 20c multicolored .25 .25
437 CD353 $1 multicolored 1.25 1.25
438 CD353 $1.50 multicolored 2.00 2.00
439 CD353 $3 multicolored 4.00 4.00
Nos. 436-439 (4) 7.50 7.50

Supply Ship Day A90

1996, Jan. 30 *Perf. 14x14½*

440 A90 20c Early morning .30 .30
441 A90 40c Meeting ship .55 .55
442 A90 90c Unloading supplies 1.20 1.20
443 A90 $1 Landing work 1.30 1.30
444 A90 $1.50 Supply sorting 2.00 2.00
445 A90 $1.80 Last load 2.40 2.40
Nos. 440-445 (6) 7.75 7.75

Queen Elizabeth II, 70th Birthday

Common Design Type

Various portraits of Queen, scenes from Pitcairn Islands: 20c, Bounty Bay. 90c, Jetty, Landing Point, Bounty Bay. $1.80, Matt's Rocks. $3, St. Paul's.

1996, Apr. 21 *Perf. 13½x14*

446 CD354 20c multicolored .30 .30
447 CD354 90c multicolored 1.25 1.25
448 CD354 $1.80 multicolored 2.50 2.50
449 CD354 $3 multicolored 4.25 4.25
Nos. 446-449 (4) 8.30 8.30

CHINA '96, 9th Asian Intl. Philatelic Exhibition — A91

No. 450, Chinese junk. No. 451, HMAV Bounty. No. 452: a, Chinese rat. b, Polynesian rat.

1996, May 17 *Perf. 14*

450 A91 $1.80 multicolored 2.50 2.50
451 A91 $1.80 multicolored 2.50 2.50

Souvenir Sheet

452 A91 90c Sheet of 2, #a.-b. 2.50 2.50

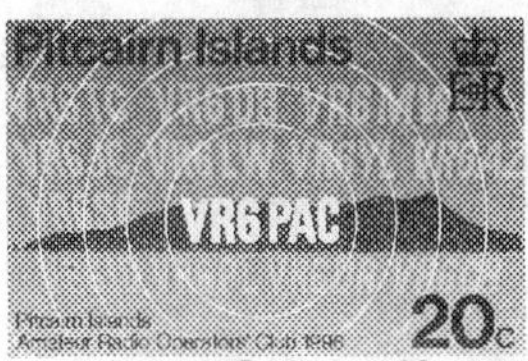

Amateur Radio — A92

Designs: 20c, Call signs of members in Amateur Radio Operator's Club, 1996. No. 454, VR6 1M calling for medical assistance. No. 455, Operator receiving transmission, physician standing by. $2.50, Andrew Young, Pitcairn's first operator, 1938.

1996, Sept. 4 Wmk. 384 *Perf. 14*

453 A92 20c multicolored .30 .30
454 A92 $1.50 multicolored 2.10 2.10
455 A92 $1.50 multicolored 2.10 2.10
a. Pair, #454-455 4.25 4.25
456 A92 $2.50 multicolored 3.50 3.50
Nos. 453-456 (4) 8.00 8.00

Birds A93

World Wildlife Fund: 5c, Henderson Island reed-warbler, vert. 10c, Stephen's lorikeet, vert. 20c, Henderson Island rail, vert. 90c, Henderson Island fruit-dove, vert. No. 461, Masked booby. No. 462, Common fairy-tern.

1996, Nov. 20 Wmk. 373

457 A93 5c multicolored .15 .15
458 A93 10c multicolored .15 .15
459 A93 20c multicolored .30 .30
460 A93 90c multicolored 1.30 1.30
461 A93 $2 multicolored 2.80 2.80
462 A93 $2 multicolored 2.80 2.80
Nos. 457-462 (6) 7.50 7.50

Souvenir Sheet

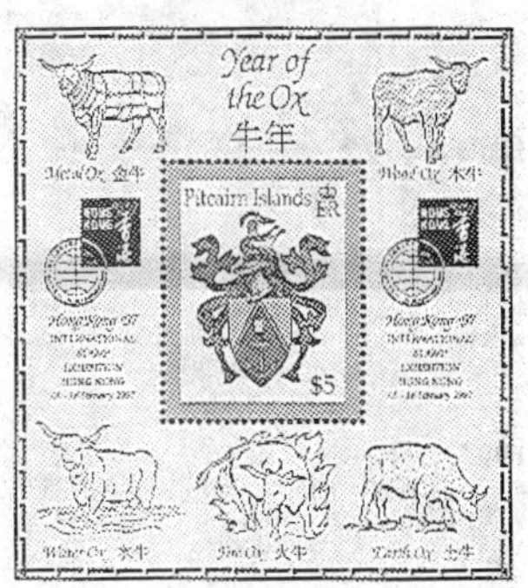

Coat of Arms — A94

Illustration reduced.

1997, Feb. 12 *Perf. 14½x14*

463 A94 $5 multicolored 7.00 7.00

Hong Kong '97.

South Pacific Commission, 50th Anniv. — A95

Designs: a, MV David Baker. b, MV McLachlan.

Perf. 13½x14

1997, May 26	Litho.	Wmk. 373	
464 A95 $2.50 Sheet of 2, #a.-b.		7.00	7.00

Health Care A96

Designs: 20c, New Health Center. $1, Resident nurse treating patient. $1.70, Dental officer treating patient. $3, Patient being taken aboard ship.

Wmk. 373

1997, Sept. 12	Litho.	*Perf. 14*	
465 A96	20c multicolored	.25	.25
466 A96	$1 multicolored	1.25	1.25
467 A96	$1.70 multicolored	2.10	2.10
468 A96	$3 multicolored	3.75	3.75
	Nos. 465-468 (4)	7.35	7.35

Queen Elizabeth II and Prince Philip, 50th Wedding Anniv. — A97

Designs: No. 469, Prince driving team of horses. No. 470, Queen wearing wide-brimmed hat. No. 471, Prince in formal riding attire. No. 472, Queen, horse. No. 473, Queen and Prince standing behind flowers. No. 474, Prince Charles riding horse.

Wmk. 373

1997, Nov. 20	Litho.	*Perf. 13*	
469 A97	20c multicolored	.25	.25
470 A97	20c multicolored	.25	.25
a.	Pair, #469-470	.50	.50
471 A97	$1 multicolored	1.25	1.25
472 A97	$1 multicolored	1.25	1.25
a.	Pair, #471-472	2.50	2.50
473 A97	$1.70 multicolored	2.10	2.10
474 A97	$1.70 multicolored	2.10	2.10
a.	Pair, #473-474	4.20	4.20
	Nos. 469-474 (6)	7.20	7.20

Christmas A98

Flower, picture: 20c, Gardenia taitensis, view of Island at night. 80c, Bauhinia variegata, ringing public bell. $1.20, Metrosideros collina, children's baskets hanging on line. $3, Hibiscus tiliaceus, Pitcairn Church, Square at Adamstown.

Perf. 13½

1997, Dec. 1	Litho.	Wmk. 373	
475 A98	20c multicolored	.25	.25
476 A98	80c multicolored	.95	.95
477 A98	$1.20 multicolored	1.40	1.40
478 A98	$3 multicolored	3.50	3.50
	Nos. 475-478 (4)	6.10	6.10

Views of Christian's Cave — A99

5c, Dorcas Apple, looking across Adamstown. 20c, Rocks near Betty's Edge looking past Tatinanny. 35c, Cave mouth. $5, Cave from road near where Fletcher Christian built home.

Perf. 13½

1998, Feb. 9	Litho.	Wmk. 384	
479 A99	5c multi, vert.	.15	.15
480 A99	20c multi	.25	.25
481 A99	35c multi, vert.	.40	.40
482 A99	$5 multi, vert.	5.75	5.75
	Nos. 479-482 (4)	6.55	6.55

POLAND

'pō-lənd

LOCATION — Europe between Russia and Germany
GOVT. — Republic
AREA — 120,628 sq. mi.
POP. — 36,399,000 (est. 1983)
CAPITAL — Warsaw

100 Kopecks = 1 Ruble
100 Fenigi = 1 Marka (1918)
100 Halerzy = 1 Korona (1918)
100 Groszy = 1 Zloty (1924)

Catalogue values for unused stamps in this country are for Never Hinged items, beginning with Scott 534 in the regular postage section, Scott B63 in the semi-postal section, Scott C28 in the airpost section, Scott CB1 in the airpost semi-postal section, and Scott J146 in the postage due section.

Watermarks

Wmk. 145- Wavy Lines

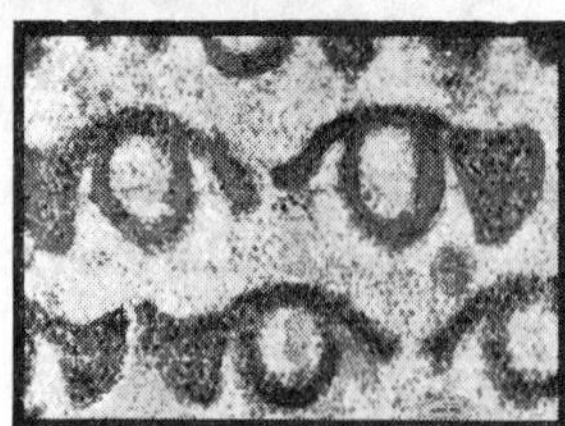

Wmk. 234- Multiple Post Horns

Wmk. 326- Multiple Post Horns

Issued under Russian Dominion

Coat of Arms — A1

Perf. 11½ to 12½

1860	Typo.	Unwmk.	
1 A1	10k blue & rose	800.	200.
a.	10k blue & carmine	950.	275.
b.	10k dark blue & rose	950.	275.
c.	Added blue frame for inner oval	1,400.	475.
d.	Imperf.		

Used for letters within the Polish territory and to Russia. Postage on all foreign letters was paid in cash.

These stamps were superseded by those of Russia in 1865.

Counterfeits exist.

Issues of the Republic

Local issues were made in various Polish cities during the German occupation. In the early months of the Republic many issues were made by overprinting the German occupation stamps with the words "Poczta Polska" and an eagle or bars often with the name of the city. These issues were not authorized by the Government but were made by the local authorities and restricted to local use. In 1914 two stamps were issued for the Polish Legion and in 1918 the Polish Expeditionary Force used surcharged Russian stamps. The regularity of these issues is questioned.

Warsaw Issues

Statue of Sigismund III — A2

Coat of Arms of Warsaw — A3

Polish Eagle — A4

Sobieski Monument — A5

Stamps of the Warsaw Local Post Surcharged

1918, Nov. 17	Wmk. 145	*Perf. 11½*	
11 A2	5f on 2gr brn & buff	1.25	.80
a.	Inverted surcharge	37.50	32.50
12 A3	10f on 6gr grn & buff	1.25	.75
a.	Inverted surcharge	4.50	4.00
13 A4	25f on 10gr rose & buff	2.75	1.65
a.	Inverted surcharge	9.00	8.00
14 A5	50f on 20gr bl & buff	7.75	4.75
a.	Inverted surcharge	130.00	100.00
	Nos. 11-14 (4)	13.00	7.95

Counterfeits exist.

Occupation Stamps Nos. N6-N16 Overprinted or Surcharged:

Poczta Polska (a)

5 Poczta Polska (b)

1918-19	Wmk. 125	*Perf. 14, 14½*	
15 A16	3pf brown ('19)	19.00	12.00
16 A22	5pf on 2½pf gray	.30	.30
17 A16	5pf on 3pf brown	3.50	2.25
18 A16	5pf green	.65	.50
19 A16	10pf carmine	.15	.15
20 A22	15pf dark violet	.15	.15
21 A16	20pf blue	.20	.20
a.	20pf ultramarine	*350.00*	*350.00*
23 A22	25pf on 7½pf org	.30	.15
24 A16	30pf org & blk, *buff*	.15	.15
25 A16	40pf lake & black	.45	.45
26 A16	60pf magenta	.65	.65
	Nos. 15-26 (11)	25.50	16.95

There are two settings of this overprint. The first printing, issued Dec. 5, 1918, has space of 3½mm between the middle two bars. The second printing, issued Jan. 15, 1919, has space of 4mm. No. 15 comes only in the second setting; all others in both. The German overprint on No. 21a is very glossy.

Varieties of this overprint and surcharge are numerous: double; inverted; misspellings (Pocata, Poczto, Pelska); letters omitted, inverted or wrong font; 3 bars instead of 4, etc.

Counterfeits exist.

Lublin Issue

Austrian Military Semi-Postal Stamps of 1918 Overprinted

1918, Dec. 5	Unwmk.	*Perf. 12½x13*	
27 MSP7	10h gray green	7.25	7.25
a.	Inverted overprint	19.00	19.00
28 MSP8	20h magenta	7.25	7.25
a.	Inverted overprint	19.00	19.00
29 MSP7	45h blue	7.25	7.25
a.	Inverted overprint	19.00	19.00
	Nos. 27-29 (3)	21.75	21.75

Austrian Military Stamps of 1917 Surcharged

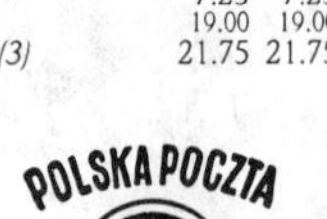

1918-19		*Perf. 12½*	
30 M3	3hal on 3h ol gray	21.00	19.00
a.	Inverted surcharge	225.00	225.00
b.	Perf. 11½	30.00	21.00
c.	Perf. 11½x12½	40.00	40.00
31 M3	3hal on 15h brt rose	2.75	2.00
a.	Inverted surcharge	20.00	20.00

Surcharged in Black

32 M3	10hal on 30h sl grn	3.00	1.75
a.	Inverted surcharge	20.00	20.00
b.	Brown surcharge (error)	60.00	50.00
34 M3	25hal on 40h ol bis	4.50	2.75
a.	Inverted surcharge	30.00	30.00
b.	Perf. 11½	15.00	9.00
35 M3	45hal on 60h rose	3.25	2.25
a.	Inverted surcharge	20.00	20.00
36 M3	45hal on 80h dl blue	5.50	4.25
a.	Inverted surcharge	30.00	30.00
37 M3	50hal on 60h rose	3.25	2.50
a.	Inverted surcharge	20.00	20.00

Similar surcharge with bars instead of stars over original value

38 M3	45hal on 80h dl blue	6.00	4.75
a.	Inverted surcharge	20.00	20.00

Overprinted

39 M3	50h deep green	26.00	17.00
a.	Inverted overprint	80.00	80.00
40 M3	90h dark violet	4.00	2.75
a.	Inverted overprint	20.00	20.00
	Nos. 30-40 (10)	79.25	59.00

Cracow Issues

Austrian Stamps of 1916-18 Overprinted

POCZTA
POLSKA

1919, Jan. 17		Typo.	
41 A37	3h brt violet	190.00	190.00
42 A37	5h lt green	190.00	190.00
43 A37	6h deep orange	19.00	19.00
a.	Inverted overprint	*6,000.*	
44 A37	10h magenta	190.00	190.00
45 A37	12h lt blue	19.00	19.00

46 A39 40h olive green 13.00 13.00
a. Inverted overprint 100.00 100.00
b. Double overprint 400.00
47 A39 50h blue green 7.00 7.00
a. Inverted overprint *8,000.*
48 A39 60h deep blue 4.50 4.50
a. Inverted overprint 100.00 75.00
49 A39 80h orange brown 4.50 5.00
a. Inverted overprint. 100.00 100.00
b. Double overprint *125.00 125.00*
50 A39 90h red violet 625.00 725.00
51 A39 1k carmine, *yel* 7.50 6.25

Engr.

52 A40 2k blue 4.50 4.75
53 A40 3k carmine rose 50.00 55.00
54 A40 4k yellow green 72.50 72.50
55 A40 10k deep violet *3,250. 3,750.*

The 3k is on granite paper.

The overprint on Nos. 52-55 is litho. and slightly larger than illustration with different ornament between lines of type.

Same Overprint on Nos. 168-171

1919 **Typo.**

56 A42 15h dull red 7.25 6.25
57 A42 20h dark green 85.00 125.00
58 A42 25h blue 1,250. 725.00
59 A42 30h dull violet 165.00 190.00

Austria No. 157 Surcharged

POLSKA
POCZTA
25

1919, Jan. 24

60 A39 25h on 80h org brn 2.75 2.75
a. Inverted surcharge 60.00 60.00

Excellent counterfeits of Nos. 27 to 60 exist.

Polish Eagle — A9

1919, Feb. 25 **Litho.** ***Imperf.***

Without gum

Yellowish Paper

61 A9 2h gray .30 .35
62 A9 3h dull violet .30 .35
63 A9 5h green .15 .15
64 A9 6h orange 13.00 19.00
65 A9 10h lake .15 .15
66 A9 15h brown .15 .15
67 A9 20h olive green .30 .35

Bluish Paper

68 A9 25h carmine .15 .15
69 A9 50h indigo .15 .15
70 A9 70h deep blue .30 .35
71 A9 1k ol gray & car .55 .95
Nos. 61-71 (11) 15.50 22.10

Nos. 61-71 exist with privately applied perforations.

Counterfeits exist.

For surcharges see Nos. J35-J39.

Posen (Poznan) Issue

Germany Nos. 84-85, 87, 96, 98 Overprinted in Black

5 5 10 10
Poczta Poczta
Polska Polska

Perf. 14, 14½

1919, Aug. 5 **Wmk. 125**

72 A22 5pf on 2pf gray 18.00 15.00
73 A22 5pf on 7½pf org 1.90 1.25
a. Inverted surcharge 100.00
74 A16 5pf on 20pf bl vio 1.50 1.10
75 A16 10pf on 25pf org & blk, *yel* 3.75 3.00
76 A16 10pf on 40pf lake & blk 2.00 1.25
Nos. 72-76 (5) 27.15 21.60

Counterfeits exist.

Germany Nos. 96 and 98 Surcharged in Red or Green

5 **10**

1919, Sept. 15

77 A22 5pf on 2pf (R) 200.00 150.00
a. Inverted surcharge *4,250.*
78 A22 10pf on 7½pf (G) 175.00 110.00

Nos. 77-78 are a provisional issue for use in Gniezno. Counterfeit surcharges abound.

Eagle and Fasces, Symbolical of United Poland
A10 A11

"Agriculture" A12 "Peace" A13

Polish Cavalryman — A14

For Northern Poland

Denominations as "F" or "M"

1919, Jan. 27 ***Imperf.***

Wove or Ribbed Paper

81 A10 3f bister brn .15 .15
82 A10 5f green .15 .15
83 A10 10f red violet .15 .15
84 A10 15f deep rose .15 .15
85 A11 20f deep blue .15 .15
86 A11 25f olive green .15 .15
87 A11 50f blue green .15 .15
88 A12 1m violet 1.90 1.65
89 A12 1.50m deep green 3.75 2.25
90 A12 2m dark brown 3.00 2.25
91 A13 2.50m orange brn 13.00 10.00
92 A14 5m red violet 17.00 10.00
Nos. 81-92 (12) 39.70 27.20

Perf. 10, 11, 11½, 10x11½, 11½x10

1919-20

93 A10 3f bister brn .15 .15
94 A10 5f green .15 .15
95 A10 10f red violet .15 .15
96 A10 10f brown ('20) .15 .15
97 A10 15f deep rose .15 .15
98 A10 15f vermilion ('20) .15 .15
99 A11 20f deep blue .15 .15
100 A11 25f olive green .15 .15
101 A11 40f brt violet ('20) .15 .15
102 A11 50f blue green .15 .15
103 A12 1m violet .45 .20
105 A12 1.50m deep green .90 .40
106 A12 2m dark brown .90 .40
107 A13 2.50m orange brn 1.40 1.10
108 A14 5m red violet 2.25 1.10
Nos. 93-108 (15) 7.40
Set value 3.90

Several denominations among Nos. 81-132 are found with double impression or in pairs imperf. between.

See Nos. 109-132, 140-152C, 170-175. For surcharges and overprints see Nos. 153, 199-200, B1-B14, 2K1-2K10.

For Southern Poland

Denominations as "H" or "K"

1919, Jan. 27 ***Imperf.***

109 A10 3h red brown .15 .15
110 A10 5h emerald .15 .15
111 A10 10h orange .15 .15
112 A10 15h vermilion .15 .15
113 A11 20h gray brown .15 .15
114 A11 25h light blue .15 .15
115 A11 50h orange brn .15 .15
116 A12 1k dark green .15 .15
117 A12 1.50k red brown 4.75 4.00
118 A12 2k dark blue 2.25 2.25
119 A13 2.50k dark violet 11.00 6.50
120 A14 5k slate blue 13.00 8.25
Nos. 109-120 (12) 32.20 22.20

Perf. 10, 11½, 10x11½, 11½x10

121 A10 3h red brown .15 .15
122 A10 5h emerald .15 .15
123 A10 10h orange .15 .15
124 A10 15h vermilion .15 .15
125 A11 20h gray brown .15 .15
126 A11 25h light blue .15 .15
127 A11 50h orange brn .15 .15
128 A12 1k dark green .50 .40
129 A12 1.50k red brown 1.25 .55
130 A12 2k dark blue 1.25 .55
131 A13 2.50k dark violet 1.40 .70
132 A14 5k slate blue 2.25 1.25
Nos. 121-132 (12) 7.70
Set value 3.75

National Assembly Issue

A20

Ignacy Jan Paderewski — A21

Adalbert Trampczynski — A22

Eagle Watching Ship — A24

Designs: 25f, Gen. Josef Pilsudski. 1m, Griffin.

1919-20 ***Perf. 11½***

Wove or Ribbed Paper

133 A20 10f red violet .15 .15
134 A21 15f brown red .40 .25
a. Imperf., pair 25.00
135 A22 20f dp brown (21x25mm) .30 .25
136 A22 20f dp brown (17x20mm) ('20) .60 .80
137 A21 25f olive green .15 .15
138 A24 50f Prus blue .25 .15
139 A24 1m purple .30 .25
Nos. 133-139 (7) 2.15 2.00

First National Assembly of Poland.

General Issue

1919 ***Perf. 9 to 14½ and Compound***

Thin Laid Paper

140 A11 25f olive green .15 .15
141 A11 50f blue green .15 .15
142 A12 1m dark gray .35 .15
143 A12 2m bister brn 1.10 .15
144 A13 3m red brown .50 .15
a. Pair, imperf. vert. 5.00 5.75
145 A14 5m red violet .20 .15
146 A14 6m deep rose .20 .15
a. Pair, imperf. vert. 6.50 6.50
147 A14 10m brown red .35 .25
a. Horizontal pair, imperf. 6.50 6.50
148 A14 20m gray green .65 .50
Nos. 140-148 (9) 3.65 1.80

Type of 1919 Redrawn

Perf. 9 to 14½ and Compound

1920-22

Thin Laid or Wove Paper

149 A10 1m red .15 .15
150 A10 2m gray green .15 .15
151 A10 3m light blue .15 .15
152 A10 4m rose red .15 .15
152A A10 5m dark violet .15 .15
b. Horiz. pair, imperf. vert. 5.25 5.25
152C A10 8m gray brown ('22) .35 .25
Set value .85 .60

The word "POCZTA" is in smaller letters and the numerals have been enlarged.

The color of No. 152A varies from dark violet to red brown.

No. 101 Surcharged

3 Mk.

Perf. 10, 11½, 10x11½, 11½x10

1921, Jan. 25

Thick Wove Paper

153 A11 3m on 40f brt vio .15 .15
a. Double surcharge 20.00 20.00
b. Inverted surcharge 20.00 20.00

Sower and Rainbow of Hope — A27

Perf. 9 to 14½ and Compound

1921 **Litho.**

Thin Laid or Wove Paper

Size: 28x22mm

154 A27 10m slate blue .15 .15
155 A27 15m light brown .40 .15
155A A27 20m red .15 .15
Nos. 154-155A (3) .70
Set value .35

Signing of peace treaty with Russia.

See No. 191. For surcharges see Nos. 196-198.

Sun (Peace) Breaking into Darkness (Despair) — A28

"Peace" and "Agriculture" A29

"Peace" A30

Perf. 11, 11½, 12, 12½, 13 and Compound

1921, May 2

156 A28 2m green 1.40 .60
157 A28 3m blue 1.40 .60
158 A28 4m red .90 .60
a. 4m carmine rose (error) 200.00
159 A29 6m carmine rose 1.40 .65
160 A29 10m slate blue 1.00 .80
161 A30 25m dk violet 2.50 1.90
162 A30 50m slate bl & buff 1.50 1.10
Nos. 156-162 (7) 10.10 6.25

Issued to commemorate the Constitution.

Polish Eagle — A31

Perf. 9 to 14½ and Compound

1921-23

163 A31 25m violet & buff .15 .15
164 A31 50m carmine & buff .15 .15
a. Vert. pair, imperf. horiz.
165 A31 100m blk brn & org .15 .15
166 A31 200m black & rose ('23) .35 .15
167 A31 300m olive grn ('23) .35 .15
168 A31 400m brown ('23) .35 .15
169 A31 500m brn vio ('23) .35 .15
169A A31 1000m orange ('23) .35 .15
169B A31 2000m dull blue ('23) .35 .15
Nos. 163-169B (9) 2.55 1.35

For surcharge see No. 195.

Type of 1919 and

Miner — A32

Perf. 9 to 14½ and Compound

1922-23

170 A10 5f blue .15 .15
171 A10 10f lt violet .15 .15
172 A11 20f pale red .15 .15
173 A11 40f violet brn .15 .15
174 A11 50f orange .15 .15
175 A11 75f blue green .15 .15
176 A32 1m black .15 .15
177 A32 1.25m dark green .15 .20
178 A32 2m deep rose .15 .20
179 A32 3m emerald .15 .20
180 A32 4m deep ultra .15 .20
181 A32 5m yellow brn .15 .20
182 A32 6m red orange .15 .20
183 A32 10m lilac brn .15 .20
184 A32 20m deep violet .15 .25
185 A32 50m olive green .20 .30
187 A32 80m vermilion ('23) .40 .85
188 A32 100m violet ('23) .40 .85
189 A32 200m orange ('23) 1.50 2.50
190 A32 300m pale blue ('23) 4.50 4.00
Nos. 170-190 (20) 9.25 11.20

This issue was to commemorate the union of Upper Silesia with Poland.

There were 2 printings of Nos. 176 to 190, the 1st being from flat plates, the 2nd from rotary press on thin paper, perf. 12½.

Nos. 173 and 175 are printed from new plates showing larger value numerals and a single "f."

Sower Type Redrawn
Size: 25x21mm

1922 **Thick or Thin Wove Paper**

191 A27 20m carmine .35 .20

In this stamp the design has been strengthened and made more distinct, especially the ground and the numerals in the upper corners.

Nicolaus Copernicus — A33

Father Stanislaus Konarski — A34

1923 *Perf. 10 to 12½*

192 A33 1000m indigo .80 .32
193 A34 3000m brown .45 .32
a. "Konapski" 15.00 15.00
194 A33 5000m rose .80 .32
Nos. 192-194 (3) 2.05 .96

Nicolaus Copernicus (1473-1543), astronomer (Nos. 192, 194); Stanislaus Konarski (1700-1773), educator, and the creation by the Polish Parliament of the Commission of Public Instruction (No. 193).

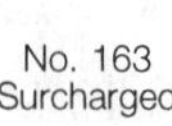

No. 163 Surcharged

1923 *Perf. 9 to 14½ and Compound*

195 A31 10000m on 25m .30 .15
a. Double surcharge 5.00
b. Inverted surcharge 7.50

Stamps of 1921 Surcharged MK MK 25,000

196 A27 25000m on 20m red .60 .15
a. Double surcharge 5.00 5.00
b. Inverted surcharge 10.00
197 A27 50000m on 10m grnsh bl .30 .15
a. Double surcharge 5.00 5.00
b. Inverted surcharge 7.50 7.50

No. 191 Surcharged MK MK 25,000

198 A27 25000m on 20m carmine .50 .15
a. Double surcharge 5.00 5.00
b. Inverted surcharge 7.50

No. 150 Surcharged with New Value

1924

199 A10 20000m on 2m gray grn .70 .15
a. Inverted surcharge 7.50 7.50
b. Double surcharge 5.00 5.00

Type of 1919 Issue Surcharged with New Value

200 A10 100000m on 5m red brn .30 .15
a. Double surcharge 5.00 5.00
b. Inverted surcharge 7.50 7.50
Set value, #195-200 .60

Arms of Poland — A35

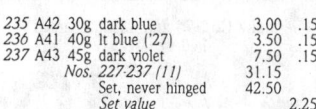

Perf. 10 to 14½ and Compound

1924 **Litho.**

Thin Paper

205 A35 10,000m lilac brn .30 .25
206 A35 20,000m olive grn .30 .15
207 A35 30,000m scarlet 1.10 .35
208 A35 50,000m apple grn 2.25 .35
209 A35 100,000m brown org .60 .30
210 A35 200,000m lt blue .30 .15
211 A35 300,000m red vio .60 .35
212 A35 500,000m brown .60 .65
213 A35 1,000,000m pale rose .60 *2.75*
214 A35 2,000,000m dk green 1.10
Nos. 205-214 (10) 7.75
Set, never hinged 13.00

Arms of Poland A36

President Stanislaus Wojciechowski A37

Perf. 10 to 13½ and Compound

1924

215 A36 1g orange brown .35 .15
216 A36 2g dark brown .35 .15
217 A36 3g orange .40 .15
218 A36 5g olive green .90 .15
219 A36 10g blue green 1.10 .15
220 A36 15g red 1.10 .15
221 A36 20g blue 2.25 .15
222 A36 25g red brown 3.00 .35
a. 25g indigo *3,000.* *4,250.*
223 A36 30g deep violet 21.00 .25
a. 30g gray blue *250.00*
224 A36 40g indigo 4.00 .35
225 A36 50g magenta 3.75 .30

Perf. 11½, 12

226 A37 1z scarlet 22.50 1.25
Nos. 215-226 (12) 60.70
Set, never hinged 100.00
Set value 3.00

For overprints see Nos. 1K1-1K11.

Holy Gate of Wilno (Vilnius) A38

Poznan Town Hall A39

Sigismund Monument, Warsaw — A40

Wawel Castle at Cracow — A41

Sobieski Statue at Lwow — A42

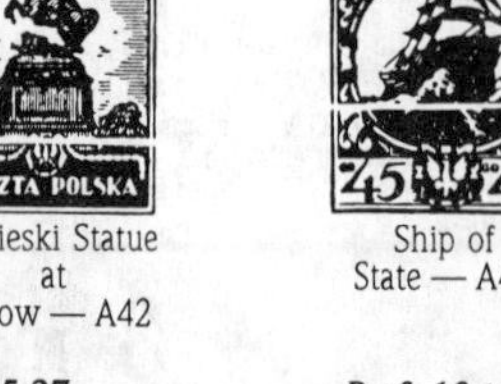

Ship of State — A43

1925-27 *Perf. 10 to 13*

227 A38 1g bister brown .40 .15
228 A42 2g brown olive .45 .25
229 A40 3g blue 1.75 .15
230 A39 5g yellow green 1.75 .15
231 A40 10g violet 1.75 .15
232 A41 15g rose red 1.65 .15
233 A43 20g dull red 1.90 .15
234 A38 24g gray blue 7.50 1.10
235 A42 30g dark blue 3.00 .15
236 A41 40g lt blue ('27) 3.50 .15
237 A43 45g dark violet 7.50 .15
Nos. 227-237 (11) 31.15
Set, never hinged 42.50
Set value 2.25

For overprints see Nos. 1K11A-1K17.

1926-27 **Redrawn**

238 A40 3g blue 2.75 .45
239 A39 5g yellow green 3.25 .20
240 A40 10g violet 4.75 .20
241 A41 15g rose red 4.75 .20
Nos. 238-241 (4) 15.50 1.05
Set, never hinged 22.50

On Nos. 229-232 the lines representing clouds touch the numerals. On the redrawn stamps the numerals have white outlines, separating them from the cloud lines.

Marshal Pilsudski A44

Frederic Chopin A45

1927 **Typo.** *Perf. 12½, 11½*

242 A44 20g red brown 3.25 .50
243 A45 40g deep ultra 16.00 1.75
Set, never hinged 27.50

See No. 250. For overprint see No. 1K18.

President Ignacy Moscicki — A46

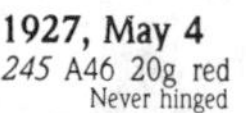

1927, May 4 *Perf. 11½*

245 A46 20g red 5.50 .45
Never hinged 7.00

Dr. Karol Kaczkowski A47

Juliusz Slowacki A48

1927, May 27 *Perf. 11½, 12½*

246 A47 10g gray green 2.75 2.25
247 A47 25g carmine 6.50 3.00
248 A47 40g dark blue 8.75 3.00
Nos. 246-248 (3) 18.00 8.25
Set, never hinged 40.00

4th Intl. Congress of Military Medicine and Pharmacy, Warsaw, May 30-June 4.

1927, June 28 *Perf. 12½*

249 A48 20g rose 6.00 .50
Never hinged 8.00

Transfer from Paris to Cracow of the remains of Julius Slowacki, poet.

Pilsudski Type of 1927
Design Redrawn

1928 *Perf. 11½, 12x11½, 12½x13*

250 A44 25g yellow brown 2.75 .25
Never hinged 6.00

Souvenir Sheet

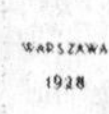

A49

1928, May 3 **Engr.** *Perf. 12½*

251 A49 Sheet of 2 250.00 325.00
Never hinged 375.00
a. 50g black brown 110.00 140.00
b. 1z black brown 110.00 140.00

1st Natl. Phil. Exhib., Warsaw, May 3-13.

Sold to each purchaser of a 1.50z ticket to the Warsaw Philatelic Exhibition.

Counterfeits exist.

Marshal Pilsudski A49a

Pres. Moscicki A50

Perf. 10½ to 14 and Compound

1928-31

Wove Paper

253 A49a 50g bluish slate 4.00 .20
254 A49a 50g blue grn ('31) 12.50 .20
Set, never hinged 22.50

See No. 315.

Perf. 12x12½, 11½ to 13½ and Compound

1928

Laid Paper

255 A50 1z black, *cream* 11.00 .20
Never hinged 17.00
a. Horizontally laid paper ('30) 70.00 2.50
Never hinged 90.00

See Nos. 305, 316. For surcharges and overprints see Nos. J92-J94, 1K19, 1K24.

General Josef Bem A51

Henryk Sienkiewicz A52

1928, May **Typo.** *Perf. 12½*

Wove Paper

256 A51 25g rose red 4.00 .25
Never hinged 5.25

Return from Syria to Poland of the ashes of General Josef Bem.

1928, Oct.

257 A52 15g ultra 2.00 .20
Never hinged 3.25

For overprint see No. 1K23.

Eagle Arms — A53

"Swiatowid," Ancient Slav God — A54

1928-29 *Perf. 12x12½*

258 A53 5g dark violet .35 .15
259 A53 10g green 1.00 .15
260 A53 25g red brown .55 .15
Nos. 258-260 (3) 1.90
Set, never hinged 3.75
Set value .25

See design A58. For overprints see Nos. 1K20-1K22.

1928, Dec. 15 *Perf. 12½x12*

261 A54 25g brown 2.50 .20
Never hinged 3.25

Poznan Agricultural Exhibition.

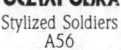

King John III Sobieski
A55

Stylized Soldiers
A56

1930, July *Perf. 12x12½*
262 A55 75g claret 5.75 .25
Never hinged 7.50

1930, Nov. 1 *Perf. 12½*
263 A56 5g violet brown .35 .15
264 A56 15g dark blue 2.25 .35
265 A56 25g red brown 1.25 .15
266 A56 30g dull red 6.25 3.75
Nos. 263-266 (4) 10.10 4.40
Set, never hinged 20.00

Centenary of insurrection of 1830.

Kosciuszko, Washington, Pulaski
A57

1932, May 3 *Perf. 11½*
Laid Paper
267 A57 30g brown 2.75 .30
Never hinged 3.50

200th birth anniv. of George Washington.

A58

A59

Perf. 12x12½
1932-33 Typo. Wmk. 234
268 A58 5g dull vio ('33) .35 .15
269 A58 10g green .35 .15
270 A58 15g red brown ('33) .35 .15
271 A58 20g gray .75 .15
272 A58 25g buff .95 .15
273 A58 30g deep rose 3.25 .15
274 A58 60g blue 19.00 .35
Nos. 268-274 (7) 25.00
Set, never hinged 32.50
Set value .60

For overprints and surcharge see Nos. 280-281, 284, 292, 1K25-1K27.

1933, Jan. 2 Engr. *Perf. 11½*
275 A59 60g Torun City Hall 37.50 .75
Never hinged 80.00

700th anniversary of the founding of the City of Torun by the Grand Master of the Knights of the Teutonic Order.
See No. B28.

Altar Panel of St. Mary's Church, Cracow
A60

Perf. 11½-12½ & Compound
1933, July 10 Unwmk.
Laid Paper
277 A60 80g red brown 15.00 1.50
Set, never hinged 21.00

400th death anniv. of Veit Stoss, sculptor and woodcarver.
For surcharge see No. 285.

John III Sobieski and Allies before Vienna, painted by Jan Matejko
A61

1933, Sept. 12 Laid Paper
278 A61 1.20z indigo 37.50 6.00
Never hinged 60.00

250th anniv. of the deliverance of Vienna by the Polish and allied forces under command of John III Sobieski, King of Poland, when besieged by the Turks in 1683.
For surcharge see No. 286.

Cross of Independence
A62

Josef Pilsudski
A63

Perf. 12½
1933, Nov. 11 Typo. Wmk. 234
279 A62 30g scarlet 7.50 .40
Never hinged 8.75

15th anniversary of independence.

Type of 1932 Overprinted in Red or Black

Wyst. Filat.
1934
Katowice

1934, May 5 *Perf. 12*
280 A58 20g gray (R) 30.00 24.00
281 A58 30g deep rose 30.00 24.00
Set, never hinged 100.00

Katowice Philatelic Exhibition. Counterfeits exist.

Perf. 11½ to 12½ and Compound
1934, Aug. 6 Engr. Unwmk.
282 A63 25g gray blue 1.25 .25
283 A63 30g black brown 3.00 .40
Set, never hinged 5.25

Polish Legion, 20th anniversary.
For overprint see No. 293.

Nos. 274, 277-278 Surcharged in Black or Red

1934 Wmk. 234 *Perf. 12x12½*
284 A58 55g on 60g blue 6.00 .50
Perf. 11½-12½ & Compound
Unwmk.
285 A60 25g on 80g red brn 6.50 .65
286 A61 1z on 1.20z ind (R) 16.00 2.50
a. Figure "1" in surcharge 5mm high instead of 4½mm 18.00 2.50
Never hinged 21.00
Nos. 284-286 (3) 28.50 3.65
Set, never hinged 37.50

Surcharge of No. 286 includes bars.

Pilsudski Mourning Issue

Marshal Pilsudski — A64

1935 *Perf. 11 to 13 and Compound*
287 A64 5g black .90 .15
288 A64 15g black .90 .25
289 A64 25g black 1.75 .20
290 A64 45g black 4.25 1.40
291 A64 1z black 8.50 4.25
Nos. 287-291 (5) 16.30 6.25
Set, never hinged 24.00

Nos. 287-288 are typo., Nos. 290-291 litho. No. 289 exists both typo. and litho.

See No. B35b.

Nos. 270, 282 Overprinted in Blue or Red

Kopiec
Marszalka
Pilsudskiego

1935 Wmk. 234 *Perf. 12x12½*
292 A58 15g red brown 1.00 .45
Perf. 11½, 11½x12½
Unwmk.
293 A63 25g gray blue (R) 3.25 1.50
Set, never hinged 5.75

Issued in connection with the proposed memorial to Marshal Pilsudski, the stamps were sold at Cracow exclusively.

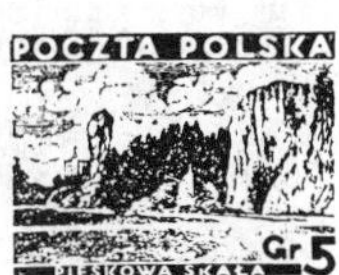

"The Dog Cliff"
A65

President Ignacy Moscicki
A75

Designs: 10g, "Eye of the Sea." 15g, M. S. "Pilsudski." 20g, View of Pieniny. 25g, Belvedere Palace. 30g, Castle in Mira. 45g, Castle at Podhorce. 50g, Cloth Hall, Cracow. 55g, Raczynski Library, Poznan. 1z, Cathedral, Wilno.

1935-36 Typo. *Perf. 12½x13*
294 A65 5g violet blue .60 .15
295 A65 10g yellow green .60 .15
296 A65 15g Prus green 1.90 .15
297 A65 20g violet black .95 .15
Engr.
298 A65 25g myrtle green .80 .15
299 A65 30g rose red 2.00 .30
300 A65 45g plum ('36) 1.00 .30
301 A65 50g black ('36) 1.00 .30
302 A65 55g blue ('36) 9.50 .60
303 A65 1z brown ('36) 3.75 1.65
304 A75 3z black brown 2.25 2.50
Nos. 294-304 (11) 24.35 6.40
Set, never hinged 32.50

See Nos. 308-311. For overprints see Nos. 306-307, 1K28-1K32.

Type of 1928 Inscribed "1926. 3. VI. 1936" on Bottom Margin

1936, June 3
305 A50 1z ultra 7.50 6.00
Never hinged 9.50

Presidency of Ignacy Moscicki, 10th anniv.

Nos. 299, 302 Overprinted in Blue or Red

GORDON-BENNETT 30.VIII.
1936

1936, Aug. 15
306 A65 30g rose red 12.00 6.00
307 A65 55g blue (R) 12.00 6.00
Set, never hinged 30.00

Gordon-Bennett Intl. Balloon Race. Counterfeits exist.

Scenic Type of 1935-36

Designs: 5g, Church at Czestochowa. 10g, Maritime Terminal, Gdynia. 15g, University, Lwow. 20g, Municipal Building, Katowice.

1937 Engr. *Perf. 12½*
308 A65 5g violet blue .15 .15
309 A65 10g green .55 .15
310 A65 15g red brown .40 .15
311 A65 20g orange brown .55 .15
Nos. 308-311 (4) 1.65
Set, never hinged 3.00
Set value .30

For overprints see Nos. 1K31-1K32.

Marshal Smigly-Rydz
A80

President Moscicki
A81

1937 *Perf. 12½x13*
312 A80 25g slate green .25 .15
313 A80 55g blue .60 .15
Set, never hinged 1.50
Set value .25

For surcharges see Nos. N30, N32.

Types of 1928-37
Souvenir Sheets

1937
314 Sheet of 4 25.00 25.00
a. A80 25g, dark brown 2.75 2.75
315 Sheet of 4 25.00 25.00
a. A49a 50g, deep blue 2.75 2.75
316 Sheet of 4 25.00 25.00
a. A50 1z, gray black 2.75 2.75
Set, never hinged 110.00

Visit of King Carol of Romania to Poland, June 26-July 1.
See No. B35c.

1938, Feb. 1 *Perf. 12½*
317 A81 15g slate green .15 .15
318 A81 30g rose violet .60 .15
Set, never hinged 1.10
Set value .25

71st birthday of President Moscicki.
For surcharge see No. N31.

Kosciuszko, Paine and Washington and View of New York City — A82

1938, Mar. 17 *Perf. 12x12½*
319 A82 1z gray blue 1.25 1.75
Never hinged 2.00

150th anniv. of the US Constitution.

Boleslaus I and Emperor Otto III at Gnesen — A83

Marshal Pilsudski — A95

Designs: 10g, King Casimir III. 15g, King Ladislas II Jagello and Queen Hedwig. 20g, King Casimir IV. 25g, Treaty of Lublin. 30g, King Stephen Bathory commending Wielock, the peasant. 45g, Stanislas Zolkiewski and Jan Chodkiewicz. 50g, John III Sobieski entering Vienna. 55g, Union of nobles, commoners and peasants. 75g, Dabrowski, Kosciuszko and Poniatowski. 1z, Polish soldiers. 2z, Romuald Traugutt.

1938, Nov. 11 Engr. *Perf. 12½*
320 A83 5g red orange .15 .15
321 A83 10g green .15 .15
322 A83 15g fawn .30 .15
323 A83 20g peacock blue .40 .15
324 A83 25g dull violet .15 .15
325 A83 30g rose red .65 .15
326 A83 45g black .40 .15
327 A83 50g brt red vio 2.75 .15
328 A83 55g ultra .85 .15
329 A83 75g dull green 2.00 1.50
330 A83 1z orange 1.65 1.40
331 A83 2z carmine rose 11.00 8.00
332 A95 3z gray black 9.00 14.00
Nos. 320-332 (13) 29.45 26.25
Set, never hinged 39.00

20th anniv. of Poland's independence. See No. 339. For surcharges see Nos. N33-N47.

Souvenir Sheet

Marshal Pilsudski, Gabriel Narutowicz, President Moscicki, Marshal Smigly-Rydz
A96

1938, Nov. 11 *Perf. 12½*

333 A96 Sheet of 4 16.00 18.00
Never hinged 21.00
a. 25g dull violet (Pilsudski) 1.65 1.75
b. 25g dull violet (Narutowicz) 1.65 1.75
c. 25g dull violet (Moscicki) 1.65 1.75
d. 25g dull violet (Smigly-Rydz) 1.65 1.75

20th anniv. of Poland's independence.

Poland Welcoming Teschen People — A97

Skier — A98

1938, Nov. 11

334 A97 25g dull violet 1.50 .45
Never hinged 2.00

Restoration of the Teschen territory ceded by Czechoslovakia.

1939, Feb. 6

335 A98 15g orange brown 1.25 1.10
336 A98 25g dull violet 1.65 .50
337 A98 30g rose red 2.50 1.10
338 A98 55g brt ultra 7.75 4.00
Nos. 335-338 (4) 13.15 6.70
Set, never hinged 21.00

Intl. Ski Meet, Zakopane, Feb. 11-19.

Type of 1938

Design: 15g, King Ladislas II Jagello and Queen Hedwig.

Re-engraved

1939, Mar. 2 *Perf. 12½*

339 A83 15g redsh brown .25 .20
Never hinged .55

No. 322 with crossed swords and helmet at lower left. No. 339, swords and helmet have been removed.

Marshal Pilsudski Reviewing Troops — A99

1939, Aug. 1 **Engr.**

340 A99 25g dull rose violet .60 .50
Never hinged .80

Polish Legion, 25th anniv. See No. B35a.

Polish Peoples Republic

Romuald Traugutt A100

Tadeusz Kosciuszko A101

Design: 1z, Jan Henryk Dabrowski.

Perf. 11½

1944, Sept. 7 **Litho.** **Unwmk.**

Without Gum

341 A100 25g crimson rose 37.50 40.00
342 A101 50g deep green 45.00 52.50
343 A101 1z deep ultra 40.00 52.50
Nos. 341-343 (3) 122.50 145.00

Counterfeits exist.
For surcharges see Nos. 362-363.

Polish Eagle — A103

Grunwald Monument, Cracow — A104

1944, Sept. 13 **Photo.** *Perf. 12½*

344 A103 25g deep red .60 .35
a. 25g dull red, typo. .85
Never hinged 1.10
345 A104 50g dk slate green .45 .15
Set, never hinged 1.65

No. 344a was not put on sale without surcharge. See Nos. 346, 349a. For surcharges see Nos. 345A-356, 364, B54, C19-C20.

No. 344 Surcharged in Black

— 1 zł —

31.XII.1943

K. R. N.

31.XII.1944

a

— 2 zł —

P. K. W. N.

31.XII.1944

b

— 3 zł —

31.XII.1944

R. T. R. P.

c

1944-45

345A A103 1z on 25g 1.90 2.00
345B A103 2z on 25g ('45) 1.90 2.00
345C A103 3z on 25g ('45) 1.90 2.00
Nos. 345A-345C (3) 5.70 6.00
Set, never hinged 7.00

Issued to honor Polish government agencies. K. R. N. - Krajowa Rada Narodowa (Polish National Council), P. K. W. N. - Polski Komitet Wyzwolenia Narodu (Polish National Liberation Committee) and R. T. R. P. - Rzad Tymczasowy Rzeczypospolitej Polskiej (Temporary Administration of the Polish Republic).

Counterfeits exist.

No. 344a Surcharged in Brown

1'50
ZL

1945, Sept. 1

346 A103 1.50z on 25g dull red .45 .20
Never hinged .70
a. 1.50z on 25g deep red, #344 350.00 250.00

Counterfeits of No. 346a exist.

— 3 zł —

No. 344 Surcharged in Blue

Kielce

15. I. 1945

1945, Feb. 12

347 A103 3z on 25g 4.25 6.25
348 A103 3z on 25g *(Radom, 16. I. 1945)* 3.00 3.50
349 A103 3z on 25g *(Warszawa, 17. I. 1945)* 6.25 7.00
a. 3z on 25g dull red, #344a 110.00 125.00
350 A103 3z on 25g *(Czestochowa, 17. I. 1945)* 3.00 3.50
351 A103 3z on 25g *(Krakow, 19. I. 1945)* 3.00 3.50
352 A103 3z on 25g *(Lodz, 19. I. 1945)* 3.00 3.50
353 A103 3z on 25g *(Gniezno, 22. I. 1945)* 3.00 3.50
354 A103 3z on 25g *(Bydgoszcz, 23. I. 1945)* 3.00 3.50
355 A103 3z on 25g *(Kalisz, 24. I. 1945)* 3.00 3.50
356 A103 3z on 25g *(Zakopane, 29. I. 1945)* 3.00 3.50
Nos. 347-356 (10) 34.50 41.25
Set, never hinged 42.50

Dates overprinted are those of liberation for each city.

Counterfeits exist.

Grunwald Monument, Cracow — A105

Kosciuszko Statue, Cracow — A106

Cloth Hall, Cracow A107

Copernicus Memorial A108

Wawel Castle — A109

1945, Apr. 10 **Photo.** *Perf. 10½, 11*

357 A105 50g dk violet brn .15 .15
a. 50g dark brown .45 .35
Never hinged 1.00
358 A106 1z henna brown .30 .24
359 A107 2z sapphire .45 .35
360 A108 3z dp red violet 1.25 .48
361 A109 5z blue green 2.75 3.25
Nos. 357-361 (5) 4.90 4.47
Set, never hinged 6.25

Liberation of Cracow Jan. 19, 1945.

Nos. 357-361 exist imperforate.

No. 357a is a coarser printing from a new plate showing designer's name (J. Wilczyk) in lower left margin. No. 357 does not show his name.

Nos. 341-342 Surcharged in Black or Red:

5 zł ■

22.I.1863.

d

5 zł.

24. III. 1794

e

1945 *Perf. 11½*

362 A100(d) 5z on 25g 27.50 32.50
363 A101(e) 5z on 50g (R) 6.00 9.00
Never hinged 7.00

No. 362 was issued without gum.

No. 345 Surcharged in Brown

1 ZŁ

1945, Sept. 10 *Perf. 12½*

364 A104 1z on 50g dk sl grn .38 .18
Never hinged .60

Lodz Skyline — A110

Kosciuszko Monument, Lodz — A111

Flag Bearer Carrying Wounded Comrade — A112

1945 **Litho.** *Perf. 11, 9 (3z)*

365 A110 1z deep ultra .55 .15
366 A111 3z dull red violet .60 .45
367 A112 5z deep carmine 2.00 1.90
Nos. 365-367 (3) 3.15 2.50
Set, never hinged 4.00

Nos. 365 and 367 commemorate the liberation of Lodz and Warsaw.

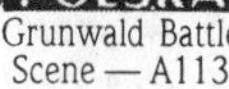

Grunwald Battle Scene — A113

Eagle Breaking Fetters and Manifesto of Freedom — A114

1945, July 16

368 A113 5z deep blue 8.00 9.00
Never hinged 10.00

Battle of Grunwald (Tannenberg), July 15, 1410.

1945, July 22

369 A114 3z rose carmine 12.00 15.00
Never hinged 15.00

1st anniv. of the liberation of Poland.

Crane Tower, Gdansk A115

Stock Tower, Gdansk A116

Ancient High Gate, Gdansk — A117

1945, Sept. 15 Photo. Unwmk.

No.	Type	Description	Unused	Used
370	A115	1z olive	.15	.15
371	A116	2z sapphire	.15	.15
372	A117	3c dark violet	.60	.26
		Nos. 370-372 (3)	.90	.56
		Set, never hinged	1.50	

Recovery of Poland's access to the sea at Gdansk (Danzig).
Exist imperf. Value, set $25.

Civilian and Soldiers in Rebellion — A118

1945, Nov. 29

No.	Type	Description	Unused	Used
373	A118	10z black	7.75	9.00
		Never hinged	9.00	

115th anniv. of the "November Uprising" against the Russians, Nov. 29, 1830.

Warsaw Castle, 1939 and 1945 A119

Views of Warsaw, 1939 and 1945: 3z, Cathedral of St. John. 3.50z, City Hall. 6z, Post Office. 8z, Army General Staff Headquarters. 10z, Holy Cross Church.

1945-46 Unwmk. *Imperf.*

No.	Type	Description	Unused	Used
374	A119	1.50z crimson	.20	.15
375	A119	3z dark blue	.38	.15
376	A119	3.50z lt blue grn	.95	.42
377	A119	6z gray black ('46)	.38	.22
378	A119	8z brown ('46)	1.90	.42
379	A119	10z dark violet ('46)	.80	.22
		Nos. 374-379 (6)	4.61	1.58
		Set, never hinged	6.00	

Nos. 374-379 Overprinted in Black

WARSZAWA
WOLNA
17 Styczeń
1945—1946

1946, Jan. 17

No.	Type	Description	Unused	Used
383	A119	1.50z crimson	1.25	2.00
384	A119	3z dark blue	1.25	2.00
385	A119	3.50z lt blue grn	1.25	2.00
386	A119	6z gray black	1.25	2.00
387	A119	8z brown	1.25	2.00
388	A119	10z dark violet	1.25	2.00
		Nos. 383-388 (6)	7.50	12.00
		Set, never hinged	9.50	

Liberation of Warsaw, Jan. 17, 1945, 1st anniv.
Counterfeits exist.

Polish Revolutionist A125

Infantry Advancing A126

1946, Jan. 22 *Perf. 11*

No.	Type	Description	Unused	Used
389	A125	6z slate blue	6.00	8.00
		Never hinged	7.50	

Revolt of Jan. 22, 1863.

1946, May 9

No.	Type	Description	Unused	Used
390	A126	3z brown	.30	.15
		Never hinged	.50	

Polish freedom, first anniversary.

Premier Edward Osubka-Morawski Pres. Boleslaw Bierut and Marshal Michael Rola-Zymierski — A127

Perf. 11x10½

1946, July 22 Unwmk.

No.	Type	Description	Unused	Used
391	A127	3z purple	3.00	4.00
		Never hinged	4.00	

For surcharge see No. B53.

Bedzin Castle — A128

Duke Henry IV of Silesia, from Tomb at Wroclaw — A129

Lanckrona Castle — A130

1946, Sept. 1 Photo. *Imperf.*

No.	Type	Description	Unused	Used
392	A128	5z olive gray	.15	.15
393	A128	5z brown	.15	.15
		Perf. 10½		
394	A129	6z gray black	.30	.15
		Imperf		
395	A130	10z deep blue	.65	.20
		Nos. 392-395 (4)	1.25	
		Set, never hinged	2.00	
		Set value		.50

Perforated copies of Nos. 392, 393 and 395 have been privately made.
For surcharge see No. 404.

Jan Matejko, Jacek Malczewski, Josef Chelmonski A131

Adam Chmielowski (Brother Albert) — A132

Designs: 3z, Chopin. 5z, Wojciech Boguslawski, Helena Modjeska and Stefan Jaracz. 6z, Alexander Swietockowski, Stephen Zeromski and Boleslaw Prus. 10z, Marie Sklodowska Curie. 15z, Stanislaw Wyspianski, Juliusz Slowacki and Jan Kasprowicz. 20z, Adam Mickiewicz.

1947 *Perf. 11*

No.	Type	Description	Unused	Used
396	A131	1z blue	.20	.15
397	A132	2z brown	.40	.16
398	A132	3z Prus green	.50	.16
399	A131	5z olive green	.65	.16
400	A131	6z gray green	1.25	.65
401	A132	10z gray brown	1.00	.16
402	A131	15z sepia	1.50	.50
403	A132	20z gray black	1.50	.70
		Nos. 396-403 (8)	7.00	2.64
		Set, never hinged	9.00	

Set exists imperf, value $12.

No. 394 Surcharged in Red

1947, Feb. 25 *Perf. 10½*

No.	Type	Description	Unused	Used
404	A129	5z on 6z gray blk	.40	.15
		Never hinged	.70	

Types of 1947

1947 Photo. *Perf. 11, Imperf.*

No.	Type	Description	Unused	Used
405	A131	1z slate gray	.20	.15
406	A132	2z orange	.20	.15
407	A132	3z olive green	1.40	.35
408	A131	5z olive brown	.30	.15
409	A131	6z carmine rose	.52	.20
410	A132	10z blue	.90	.18
411	A131	15z chestnut brn	.70	.32
412	A132	20z dark violet	.52	.50
a.		Souvenir sheet of 8, #405-412	150.00	200.00
		Never hinged	175.00	
		Nos. 405-412 (8)	4.74	2.00
		Set, never hinged	6.00	

No. 412a sold for 500z.

Laborer A139

Farmer A140

Fisherman A141

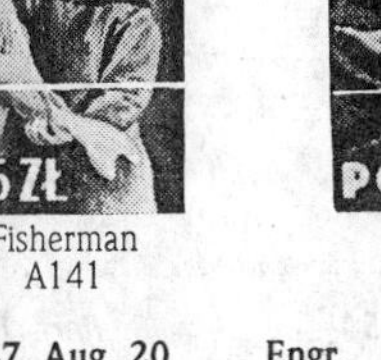

Miner A142

1947, Aug. 20 Engr. *Perf. 13*

No.	Type	Description	Unused	Used
413	A139	5z rose brown	.70	.15
414	A140	10z brt blue green	.16	.15
415	A141	15z dark blue	.75	.15
416	A142	20z brown black	.50	.15
		Nos. 413-416 (4)	2.11	
		Set, never hinged	3.00	
		Set value		.50

Allegory of the Revolution A143

Insurgents A144

1948, Mar. 15 Photo. *Perf. 11*

No.	Type	Description	Unused	Used
417	A143	15z brown	.25	.15
		Never hinged	.50	

Revolution of 1848. See Nos. 430-432.

1948, Apr. 19

No.	Type	Description	Unused	Used
418	A144	15z gray black	1.25	1.40
		Never hinged	1.75	

5th anniv. of the ghetto uprising, Warsaw, Apr. 19, 1943.

Decorated Bicycle Wheel — A145

1948, May 1

No.	Type	Description	Unused	Used
419	A145	15z brt rose & blue	2.25	1.10
		Never hinged	3.00	

1st Intl. Bicycle Peace Race, Warsaw-Prague-Warsaw.

Launching Ship — A146

Loading Freighter — A147

35z, Racing yacht "Gen. Mariusz Zaruski."

1948, June 22

No.	Type	Description	Unused	Used
420	A146	6z violet	1.10	1.50
421	A147	15z brown car	1.25	1.50
422	A147	35z slate gray	2.25	2.50
		Nos. 420-422 (3)	4.60	5.50
		Set, never hinged	6.00	

Polish Merchant Marine.

Cyclists — A148

A149

1948, June 22

No.	Type	Description	Unused	Used
423	A148	3z gray	1.75	1.40
424	A148	6z brown	1.75	2.50
425	A148	15z green	1.75	3.25
		Nos. 423-425 (3)	5.25	7.15
		Set, never hinged	6.00	

Poland Bicycle Race, 7th Circuit, June 22-July 4.

1948, July 15

No.	Type	Description	Unused	Used
426	A149	6z blue	.32	.28
427	A149	15z red	.75	.30
428	A149	18z rose brown	.65	.15
429	A149	35z dark brown	.65	.30
		Nos. 426-429 (4)	2.37	1.03
		Set, never hinged	3.75	

Exhibition to commemorate the recovery of Polish territories, Wroclaw, 1948.

Gen. Henryk Dembinski and Gen. Josef Bem — A150

Symbolical of United Youth — A151

Designs: 35z, S. Worcell, P. Sciegienny and E. Dembowski. 60z, Friedrich Engels and Karl Marx.

1948, July 15

No.	Type	Description	Unused	Used
430	A150	30z dark brown	.50	.38
431	A150	35z olive green	2.25	.38
432	A150	60z bright rose	.70	.55
		Nos. 430-432 (3)	3.45	1.31
		Set, never hinged	5.00	

Revolution of 1848, cent. See No. 417.

1948, Aug. 8

No.	Type	Description	Unused	Used
433	A151	15z blue	.42	.25
		Never hinged	.75	

Intl. Congress of Democratic Youth, Warsaw, Aug.

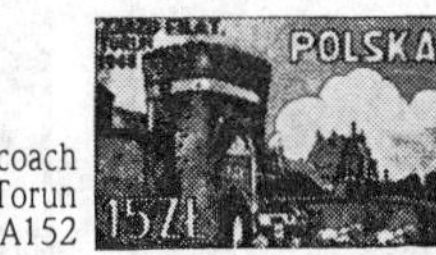

Stagecoach Leaving Torun Gate — A152

1948, Sept. 4

No.	Type	Description	Unused	Used
434	A152	15z brown	.48	.30
		Never hinged	.75	

Philatelic Exhibition, Torun, Sept.

Clock Dial and Locomotive — A153

Pres. Boleslaw Bierut — A154

1948, Oct. 6 *Perf. 11½*
435 A153 18z blue 4.00 4.00
Never hinged 5.00

European Railroad Schedule Conference, Cracow.

1948-49 Unwmk. *Perf. 11, 11½*
436 A154 2z orange ('49) .15 .15
437 A154 3z blue grn ('49) .15 .15
438 A154 5z brown .15 .15
439 A154 6z slate .40 .15
440 A154 10z violet ('49) .15 .15
441 A154 15z dp carmine .15 .15
442 A154 18z gray green .45 .25
443 A154 30z blue .75 .15
444 A154 35z violet brown 2.00 .35
Nos. 436-444 (9) 4.35
Set, never hinged 8.00
Set value 1.20

Workers Carrying Flag — A155

Designs: 15z, Marx, Engels, Lenin and Stalin. 25z, Ludwig Warynski.

Inscribed: "Kongres Jednosci Klasy Robotniczej 8. XII. 1948."

1948, Dec. 8 *Perf. 11*
445 A155 5z crimson .50 .22
446 A155 15z dull violet .50 .65
447 A155 25z brown 1.25 .55
Nos. 445-447 (3) 2.25 1.42
Set, never hinged 3.50

Redrawn
Dated: "XII. 1948"

Designs as before.

1948, Dec. 15 *Perf. 11½*
448 A155 5z brown carmine 1.75 1.25
449 A155 15z bright blue 1.75 1.25
450 A155 25z dark green 2.50 2.50
Nos. 448-450 (3) 6.00 5.00
Set, never hinged 7.50

Congress of the Union of the Working Class, Warsaw, Dec. 1948.

"Socialism" A156

Designs: 5z, "Labor." 15z, "Peace."

Perf. 11½
1949, May 31 Unwmk. Photo.
451 A156 3z carmine rose 1.00 1.00
452 A156 5z deep blue 1.00 1.00
453 A156 15z deep green 1.40 1.40
Nos. 451-453 (3) 3.40 3.40
Set, never hinged 4.00

8th Trade Union Congress, June 5, 1949.

Warsaw Scene — A157

Pres. Boleslaw Bierut — A158

Radio Station — A159

Perf. 13x12½, 12½x13
1949, July 22 Litho.
454 A157 10z gray black 2.00 1.25
455 A158 15z lilac rose 1.25 1.40
456 A159 35z gray blue 1.25 1.25
Nos. 454-456 (3) 4.50 3.90
Set, never hinged 6.00

5th anniv. of "People's Poland."

A160 A161

UPU, 75th Anniv.: 6z, Stagecoach and world map. 30z, Ship and map. 80z, Plane and map.

1949, Oct. 10 Engr. *Perf. 13x12½*
457 A160 6z gray purple .70 1.40
458 A160 30z blue 1.75 1.40
459 A160 80z dull green 3.75 3.00
Nos. 457-459 (3) 6.20 5.80
Set, never hinged 7.25

1949 *Perf. 13½x13*

Symbolical of United Poland.

460 A161 5z brown red .85 .15
461 A161 10z rose red .22 .15
462 A161 15z green .22 .15
463 A161 35z dark brown .70 .40
Nos. 460-463 (4) 1.99
Set, never hinged 2.75
Set value .70

Congress of the People's Movement for Unity.

Adam Mickiewicz A162

Frederic Chopin A163

Design: 35z, Juliusz Slowacki.

1949, Dec. 5 *Perf. 12½*
464 A162 10z brown violet 2.00 1.40
465 A163 15z brown rose 2.75 2.25
466 A162 35z deep blue 2.00 1.40
Nos. 464-466 (3) 6.75 5.05
Set, never hinged 8.75

Mail Delivery A164

Adam Mickiewicz and Pushkin A165

1950, Jan. 21
467 A164 15z red violet 2.25 1.50
Never hinged 3.00

3rd Congress of PTT Trade Unions, Jan. 21-23, 1950.

1949, Dec. 15
468 A165 15z lilac 2.25 2.00
Never hinged 3.00

Polish-Soviet friendship.

Pres. Boleslaw Bierut A166

Julian Marchlewski A167

1950, Feb. 25 Engr. *Perf. 12x12½*
469 A166 15z red .28 .15
Never hinged .90

See Nos. 478-484, 490-496. For surcharge see No. 522.

1950, Mar. 23 Photo. *Perf. 11x10½*
470 A167 15z gray black .55 .30
Never hinged 1.00

25th death anniv. of Julian Marchlewski, author and political leader.

Reconstruction, Warsaw — A168

Perf. 11, 12 and Compounds of 13
1950, Apr. 15
471 A168 5z dark brown .15 .15
Never hinged .25

See No. 497.

Worker Holding Hammer, Flag and Olive Branch — A169

Workers of Three Races with Flag — A170

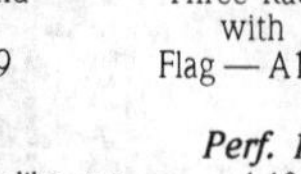

1950, Apr. 26 *Perf. 11½*
472 A169 10z deep lilac rose 1.10 .20
473 A170 15z brown olive 1.10 .15
Set, never hinged 3.25

60th anniversary of Labor Day.

Freedom Monument, Poznan A171

Dove on Globe A172

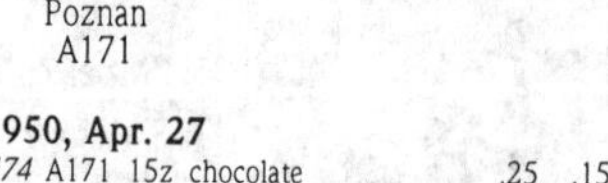

1950, Apr. 27
474 A171 15z chocolate .25 .15
Never hinged .40

Poznan Fair, Apr. 29-May 14, 1950.

1950, May 15 Unwmk.
475 A172 10z dark green .65 .15
476 A172 15z dark brown .32 .15
Set, never hinged 1.50
Set value .25

Day of Intl. Action for World Peace.

Polish Workers A173

Hibner, Kniewski and Rutkowski A174

1950, July 20 *Perf. 12½x13*
477 A173 15z violet blue .15 .15
Never hinged .30

Poland's 6-year plan. See Nos. 507A-510, 539.

Bierut Type of 1950, No Frame
1950 Engr. *Perf. 12x12½*
478 A166 5z dull green .15 .15
479 A166 10z dull red .15 .15
480 A166 15z deep blue .65 .15
481 A166 20z violet brown .18 .15
482 A166 25z yellow brown .30 .15
482A A166 30z rose brown .35 .15
483 A166 40z brown .25 .15
484 A166 50z olive 1.10 .24
Nos. 478-484 (8) 3.13
Set, never hinged 6.00
Set value .75

1950, Aug. 18 Photo. *Perf. 11*
485 A174 15z gray black 1.65 .70
Never hinged 2.25

25th anniv. of the execution of three Polish revolutionists, Wladyslaw Hibner, Wladyslaw Kniewski and Henryk Rutkowski.

Worker and Dove — A175

Dove by Picasso — A176

1950, Aug. 31 Engr. *Perf. 12½*
486 A175 15z gray green .28 .15
Never hinged .50

Polish Peace Congress, Warsaw, 1950.

"GROSZY"

To provide denominations needed as a result of the currency revaluation of Oct. 28, 1950, each post office was authorized to surcharge stamps of its current stock with the word "Groszy." Many types and sizes of this surcharge exist. The surcharge was applied to most of Poland's 1946-1950 issues. All stamps of that period could receive the surcharge upon request of anyone. Counterfeits exist.

1950, Nov. 13
487 A176 40g blue 1.25 .30
488 A176 45g brown red .38 .15
Set, never hinged 2.50

2nd World Peace Congress.

Josef Bem and Battle Scene — A177

1950, Dec. 10
489 A177 45g blue 2.00 1.00
Never hinged 3.00

Death centenary of Gen. Josef Bem.

Type of 1950 with Frame Omitted
Perf. 12x12½
1950, Dec. 16 Engr. Unwmk.
490 A166 5g brown violet .15 .15
491 A166 10g bluish green .15 .15
492 A166 15g dp yellow grn .15 .15
493 A166 25g dark red .15 .15
493A A166 30g red .22 .15
494 A166 40g vermilion .15 .15
495 A166 45g deep blue .95 .18
496 A166 75g brown .60 .15
Set value 2.20 .76
Set, never hinged 4.00

Reconstruction Type of 1950
Perf. 11, 11x11½, 13x11
1950 Photo.
497 A168 15g green .15 .15
Never hinged .25

Woman and Doves — A178

1951, Mar. 2 Engr. *Perf. 12½*
498 A178 45g dark red .28 .15
Never hinged .50

Congress of Women, Mar. 3-4, 1951.

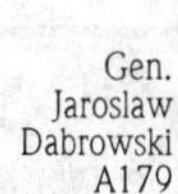

Gen. Jaroslaw Dabrowski A179

1951, Mar. 24 *Perf. 12x12½*
499 A179 45g dark green .20 .15
Never hinged .35

80th anniv. of the Insurrection of Paris and the death of Gen. Jaroslaw Dabrowski.

Dove Type of 1950 Surcharged

1951, Apr. 20 *Perf. 12½*
500 A176 45g on 15z brn red .40 .15
Never hinged .60

Worker and Flag — A180

Steel Mill, Nowa Huta — A181

1951, Apr. 25 Photo. *Perf. 14x11*
501 A180 45g scarlet .35 .15
Never hinged .55

Labor Day, May 1.

1951 Engr. *Perf. 12½*
502 A181 40g dark blue .15 .15
503 A181 45g black .15 .15
504 A181 60g brown .20 .15
505 A181 90g dark carmine .38 .15
Nos. 502-505 (4) .88
Set, never hinged 2.50
Set value .28

Pioneer Saluting A182

Boy and Girl Pioneers A183

1951, Apr. 1 Photo.
506 A182 30g olive brown .80 .50
507 A183 45g brt grnsh blue 6.75 .70
Set, never hinged 9.00

Issued to publicize Children's Day, June 1, 1951.

Workers Type of 1950

1951 Unwmk. Engr. *Perf. 12½x13*
507A A173 45g violet blue .15 .15
508 A173 75g black brown .15 .15
509 A173 1.15z dark green .40 .20
510 A173 1.20z dark red .25 .20
Nos. 507A-510 (4) .95
Set, never hinged 2.50
Set value .55

Issued to publicize Poland's 6-year plan.

Stanislaw Staszyk — A184

Congress Emblem — A186

Z. F. von Wroblewski and Karol S. Olszewski A185

Portraits: 40g, Marie Sklodowska Curie. 60g, Marceli Nencki. 1.15z, Nicolaus Copernicus.

Perf. 12½, 14x11

1951, Apr. 25 Photo.
511 A184 25g carmine rose 1.90 1.40
512 A184 40g ultra .25 .20
513 A185 45g purple 7.00 1.40
514 A184 60g green .55 .20
515 A184 1.15z claret 1.90 .70
516 A186 1.20z gray 1.40 .55
Nos. 511-516 (6) 13.00 4.45
Set, never hinged 16.00

1st Congress of Polish Science.

Feliks E. Dzerzhinski — A187

1951, July 5 Engr. *Perf. 12x12½*
517 A187 45g chestnut brown .20 .15
Never hinged .30

25th death anniv. of Feliks E. Dzerzhinski, Polish revolutionary, organizer of Russian secret police.

Pres. Boleslaw Bierut — A188

1951, July 22 *Perf. 12½*
518 A188 45g dark carmine .55 .15
519 A188 60g deep green 13.00 6.75
520 A188 90g deep blue 1.10 .40
Nos. 518-520 (3) 14.65 7.30
Set, never hinged 18.00

7th anniv. of the formation of the Polish People's Republic.

Flag and Sports Emblem A189

Youths Encircling Globe A190

Perf. 12½, 14x11

1951, Sept. 8 Photo.
521 A189 45g green 1.00 .50
Never hinged 1.65

National Sports Festival, 1951.

Type of 1950 with Frame Omitted Surcharged with New Value in Black

1951, Sept. 1 Engr. *Perf. 12½x11½*
522 A166 45g on 35z org red .20 .15
Never hinged .30

1951, Aug. 5 Photo. *Perf. 12½x11*
523 A190 40g deep ultra .60 .20
Never hinged .95

3rd World Youth Festival, Berlin, Aug. 5-19.

Joseph V. Stalin — A191

Frederic Chopin and Stanislaw Moniuszko — A192

1951, Oct. 30 Engr. *Perf. 12½*
524 A191 45g lake .20 .15
525 A191 90g gray black .40 .15
Set, never hinged 1.25

Month of Polish-Soviet friendship, Nov. 1951.

1951, Nov. 15 Unwmk.
526 A192 45g gray .20 .15
527 A192 90g brownish red .90 .24
Set, never hinged 1.75
Set value .30

Festival of Polish Music, 1951.

Apartment House Construction A193

Coal Mining A194

Design: #529-530, Electrical installation.

1951-52

Inscribed: "Plan 6," etc.

528 A193 30g dull green .15 .15
529 A193 30g gray black ('52) .15 .15
530 A193 45g red ('52) .22 .15
531 A194 90g chocolate .38 .15
532 A193 1.15z violet brn ('52) .42 .15
533 A194 1.20z deep blue ('52) .42 .18
Nos. 528-533,B68-B69A (9) 2.99
Set, never hinged 4.00
Set value 1.38

Poland's 6-year plan.

Catalogue values for unused stamps in this section, from this point to the end of the section, are for Never Hinged items.

Pawel Finder — A195

Flag, Workman, Mother and Child — A196

Portrait: 1.15z, Malgorzata Fornalska.

1952, Jan. 18
534 A195 90g chocolate .25 .15
535 A195 1.15z red orange .30 .20
Nos. 534-535,B63 (3) .73
Set value .40

Polish Workers Party, 10th anniv. See No. B63.

1952, Mar. 8 *Perf. 12½x12*
536 A196 1.20z deep carmine .42 .15

Intl. Women's Day. See No. B64.

Gen. Karol Swierczewski-Walter A197

Pres. Boleslaw Bierut A198

1952, Mar. 28 *Perf. 12½*
537 A197 90g blue gray .38 .20

Gen. Karol Swierczewski-Walter (1896-1947). See No. B65.

1952, Apr. 18
538 A198 90g dull green .70 .45
Nos. 538,B66-B67 (3) 1.74 .83

60th birth anniv. of Pres. Boleslaw Bierut.

Souvenir Sheet

A199

1951, Nov. 15
539 A199 Sheet of 4 20.00 11.50
a. 45g red brown (A173) 1.40 1.00
b. 75g red brown (A173) 1.40 1.00
c. 1.15z red brown (A173) 1.40 1.00
d. 1.20z red brown (A173) 1.40 1.00

Polish Philatelic Association Congress, Warsaw, 1951. Sold for 5 zloty.

Workers with Flag A200

J. I. Kraszewski A201

1952, May 1 Unwmk. *Perf. 12½*
540 A200 75g deep green .45 .15

Labor Day, May 1, 1952. See No. B70.

1952, May

1z, Hugo Kollontaj. 1.15z, Maria Konopnicka.

Various Frames

541 A201 25g brown violet .35 .15
542 A201 1z yellow green .38 .15
543 A201 1.15z red brown .75 .35
Nos. 541-543,B71-B72 (5) 2.25

Nikolai Gogol A202

Gymnast A203

1952, June 5
544 A202 25g deep green .75 .38

100th death anniv. of Nikolai V. Gogol, writer.

1952, June 21 Photo. *Perf. 13*
545 A203 1.15z Runners 1.40 .90
546 A203 1.20z shown .60 .52
Nos. 545-546,B75-B76 (4) 7.50 3.17

Racing Cyclists — A204

Shipyard Worker and Collier — A205

1952, Apr. 25 *Perf. 13½*
547 A204 40g blue 1.25 .42

5th Intl. Peace Bicycle Race, Warsaw-Berlin-Prague.

1952, June 28 Engr. *Perf. 12½*
548 A205 90g violet brown .95 .32
Nos. 548,B77-B78 (3) 4.40 1.14

Shipbuilders' Day, 1952.

Concrete Works, Wierzbica — A206

Bugler — A207

1952, June 17

549 A206 3z gray .95 .38
550 A206 10z brown red 1.50 .25

1952, July 17 *Perf. 12½x12*

551 A207 90g brown .45 .15

Youth Festival, 1952. See Nos. B79-B80.

Celebrating New Constitution A208

Power Plant, Jaworzno A209

1952, July 22 **Photo.** *Perf. 12½*

552 A208 3z vio & dk brn .42 .24

Proclamation of a new constitution. See No. B81.

1952, Aug. 7 **Engr.**

553 A209 1z black .65 .25
554 A209 1.50z deep green .65 .15
Nos. 553-554,B82 (3) 1.95 .55

Grywald — A210

Parachute Descent — A211

1952, Aug. 18

555 A210 60g dark green .50 .40
556 A210 1z red ("Niedzica") .80 .15
a. 1z red ("Niedziga") 3.50 .75
Nos. 555-556,B85 (3) 2.30 .80

1952, Aug. 23

557 A211 90g deep blue .70 .45
Nos. 557,B86-B87 (3) 3.50 1.65

Aviation Day, Aug. 23.

Avicenna A212

Shipbuilding A213

Portrait: 90g, Victor Hugo.

1952, Sept. 1

558 A212 75g red brown .35 .15
559 A212 90g sepia .25 .15
Set value .20

Anniversaries of the births of Avicenna (1000th) and Victor Hugo (150th).

1952, Sept. 10

560 A213 5g deep green .15 .15
561 A213 15g red brown .15 .15
Set value .25 .15

Reconstruction of Gdansk shipyards.

Assault on the Winter Palace, 1917 A214

1952, Nov. 7 *Perf. 12x12½*

562 A214 60g dark brown .55 .32

Russian Revolution, 35th anniv. See #B92. #562, B92 exist imperf. Value $30.

Auto Assembly Plant, Zeran — A215

Dove — A216

1952, Dec. 12 *Perf. 12½*

563 A215 1.15z brown .48 .15

See No. B99.

1952, Dec. 12 **Photo.**

564 A216 30g green .55 .20
565 A216 60g ultra 1.25 .52

Congress of Nations for Peace, Vienna, Dec. 12-19, 1952.

Soldier with Flag — A217

Karl Marx — A218

1953, Feb. 2 **Unwmk.** *Perf. 11*

Flag in Carmine

566 A217 60g olive gray 4.50 .85
567 A217 80g blue gray 1.00 .40

10th anniv. of the Battle of Stalingrad.

1953, Mar. 14 *Perf. 12½*

568 A218 60g dull blue 20.00 8.25
569 A218 80g dark brown 1.00 .32

70th death anniv. of Karl Marx.

Cyclists and Arms of Warsaw — A219

Flag and Globe — A220

Arms: No. 571, Berlin. No. 572, Prague.

1953, Apr. 30

570 A219 80g dark brown 1.10 .35
571 A219 80g dark green 1.10 .35
572 A219 80g red 13.00 8.75
Nos. 570-572 (3) 15.20 9.45

6th Intl. Peace Bicycle Race, Warsaw-Berlin-Prague.

1953, Apr. 28

573 A220 60g vermilion 4.25 3.25
574 A220 80g carmine .70 .35

Labor Day, May 1, 1953.

Boxer — A221

Design: 95g, Boxing match.

1953, May 17

575 A221 40g red brown 1.00 .45
576 A221 80g orange 10.00 5.75
577 A221 95g violet brown 1.50 1.65
Nos. 575-577 (3) 12.50 7.85

European Championship Boxing Matches, Warsaw, May 17-24, 1953.

Copernicus Watching Heavens, by Jan Matejko A222

Nicolaus Copernicus — A223

Perf. 12x12½, 12½x12

1953, May 22 **Engr.**

578 A222 20g brown 1.50 .55
579 A223 80g deep blue 12.00 8.75

480th birth anniv. of Nicolaus Copernicus, astronomer.

Fishing Boat A224

Old Part of Warsaw A225

Design: 1.35z, Freighter "Czech."

1953, July 15 *Perf. 12½*

580 A224 80g dark green 1.10 .45
581 A224 1.35z deep blue 2.00 1.50

Issued for Merchant Marine Day.

1953, July 15 **Photo.**

582 A225 20g red brown .40 .35
583 A225 2.35z blue 3.50 3.00

36th anniv. of the proclamation of "People's Poland."

Students of Two Races — A226

Schoolgirl and Dove — A227

Design: 1.35z, Congress badge (similar to AP7).

1953, Aug. 24

584 A226 40g dark brown .42 .20
585 A227 1.35z green 1.00 .15
586 A227 1.50z blue 2.50 2.00
Nos. 584-586,C32-C33 (5) 6.42 3.85

3rd World Congress of Students, Warsaw, 1953.

Nurse Feeding Baby — A228

Design: 1.75z, Nurse instructing mother.

1953, Nov. 21

587 A228 80g rose carmine 8.25 5.00
588 A228 1.75z deep green .45 .15

Poland's Social Health Service.

Mieczyslaw Kalinowski A229

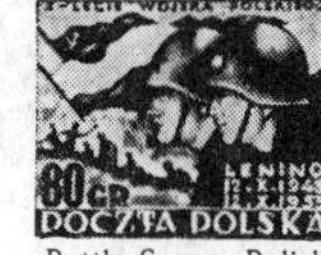

Battle Scene, Polish and Soviet Flags A230

Portrait: 1.75z, Roman Pazinski.

1953, Oct. 10

589 A229 45g brown 3.50 2.25
590 A230 80g brown lake .55 .15
591 A229 1.75z olive gray .55 .20
Nos. 589-591 (3) 4.60 2.60

10th anniv. of Poland's People's Army.

Jan Kochanowski A231

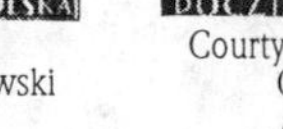

Courtyard, Wawel Castle A232

Portrait: 1.35z, Mikolaj Rej.

1953, Nov. 10 **Engr.**

592 A231 20g red brown .20 .15
593 A232 80g deep plum .40 .15
594 A231 1.35z gray black 1.75 1.00
Nos. 592-594 (3) 2.35 1.30

Issued for the "Renaissance Year."
For surcharges see Nos. 733-736.

Palace of Culture, Warsaw A233

Designs: 1.75z, Constitution Square. 2z, Old Section, Warsaw.

1953, Nov. 30 *Perf. 12x12½*

595 A233 80g vermilion 9.00 1.25
596 A233 1.75z deep blue .65 .40
597 A233 2z violet brown 5.50 2.50
Nos. 595-597 (3) 15.15 4.15

Issued for the reconstruction of Warsaw.

Ice Dancer — A236

Skier — A237

Design: 2.85z, Ice hockey player.

1953, Dec. 31 **Litho.** *Perf. 12½*

602 A236 80g blue 1.25 .30
603 A237 95g blue green 1.75 .50
604 A236 2.85z dark red 4.75 2.00
Nos. 602-604 (3) 7.75 2.80

Canceled to Order

The government stamp agency began late in 1951 to sell canceled sets of new issues. Until 1990, at least, values in the second ("used") column are for these canceled-to-order stamps. Postally used copies are worth more.

Children at Play — A238

Designs: 80g, Girls on the way to school. 1.50z, Two students in class.

1953, Dec. 31 **Photo.**

605 A238 10g violet .20 .15
606 A238 80g red brown .85 .30
607 A238 1.50z dark green 5.75 2.00
Nos. 605-607 (3) 6.80 2.45

Krynica Spa A239

Dunajec Canyon, Pieniny Mountains A240

Designs: 80g, Morskie Oko, Tatra Mts. 2z, Windmill and framework, Ciechocinek.

1953, Dec. 16

608 A239 20g blue & rose brn .18 .15
609 A240 80g bl grn & dk vio 1.90 1.10
610 A240 1.75z ol bis & dk grn .75 .15
611 A239 2z brick red & blk 1.10 .18
Nos. 608-611 (4) 3.93 1.58

Electric Passenger Train A241

Spinning Mill, Worker A242

Design: 80g, Electric locomotive and cars.

1954, Jan. 26 **Engr.**

612 A241 60g deep blue 6.00 4.00
613 A241 80g red brown .52 .18

1954, Mar. 24 **Photo.**

Designs: 40g, Woman letter carrier. 80g, Woman tractor driver.

614 A242 20g deep green 1.50 .45
615 A242 40g deep blue .60 .15
616 A242 80g dark brown .40 .15
Nos. 614-616 (3) 2.50 .75

Flags and May Flowers A243

"Peace" Uniting Three Capitals A244

1954, Apr. 28

617 A243 40g chocolate .65 .30
618 A243 60g deep blue .65 .15
619 A243 80g carmine rose .65 .25
Nos. 617-619 (3) 1.95 .70

Labor Day, May 1, 1954.

1954, Apr. 29 ***Perf. 12½x12***

Design: No. 621, Dove, olive branch and wheel.

620 A244 80g red brown .50 .15
621 A244 80g deep blue .52 .15
Set value .24

7th Intl. Bicycle Tour, May 2-17, 1954.

A245

Glider and Framed Clouds — A246

1954, Apr. 30 **Engr.** ***Perf. 11½***

622 A245 25g gray .95 .20
623 A245 80g brown carmine .30 .15
Set value .26

3rd Trade Union Congress, Warsaw 1954.

1954, May 31 **Photo.** ***Perf. 12½***

60g, Glider & flags. 1.35z, Glider & large cloud.

624 A246 45g dark green .55 .15
625 A246 60g purple 2.00 .80
626 A246 60g brown 1.10 .15
627 A246 1.35z blue 1.40 .28
Nos. 624-627 (4) 5.05 1.38

Intl. Glider Championships, Leszno.

Fencing — A247

Handstand on Horizontal Bars — A248

Design: 1z, Relay racers.

1954, July 17

628 A247 25g violet brown 1.40 .30
629 A248 60g Prus blue 1.40 .15
630 A247 1z violet blue 2.75 .45
Nos. 628-630 (3) 5.55 .90

Javelin Throwers — A249

Studzianki Battle Scene — A250

1954, July 17 ***Perf. 12***

631 A249 60g rose brn & dk red brn 1.25 .22
632 A249 1.55z gray & black 1.10 .35

Nos. 628-632 were issued to publicize the second Summer Spartacist Games, 1954.

1954, Aug. 24 ***Perf. 12½***

Design: 1z, Soldier and flag bearer.

633 A250 60g dark green 1.40 .40
634 A250 1z violet blue 6.00 1.25

10th anniversary, Battle of Studzianki.

Railway Signal — A251

Farmer Picking Fruit — A252

Design: 60g, Modern train.

1954, Sept. 9

635 A251 40g dull blue 2.25 .85
636 A251 60g black 2.25 .38

Issued to publicize Railwaymen's Day.

1954, Sept. 15

637 A252 40g violet 1.40 .60
638 A252 60g black .60 .16

Month of Polish-Soviet friendship.

View of Elblag — A253

Chopin and Piano — A254

Cities: 45g, Gdansk. 60g, Torun. 1.40z, Malbork. 1.55z, Olsztyn.

1954, Oct. 16 **Engr.** ***Perf. 12x12½***

639 A253 20g dk car, *bl* 5.50 .70
640 A253 45g brown, *yel* .50 .15
641 A253 60g dk green, *cit* .60 .15
642 A253 1.40z dk blue, *pink* 1.40 .15
643 A253 1.55z dk vio brn, *cr* 2.00 .15
Nos. 639-643 (5) 10.00
Set value 1.05

Pomerania's return to Poland, 500th anniv. For overprint see No. 866.

1954, Nov. 8 **Photo.** ***Perf. 12½***

644 A254 45g dark brown .50 .15
645 A254 60g dark green .95 .15
646 A254 1z dark blue 2.25 .55
Nos. 644-646 (3) 3.70 .85

5th Intl. Competition of Chopin's Music.

Coal Mine — A255

Designs: 20g, Soldier, flag and map. 25g, Steel mill. 40g, Relaxing worker in deck chair. 45g, Building construction. 60g, Tractor in field. 1.15z, Lublin Castle. 1.40z, Books and publications. 1.55z, Loading ship. 2.10z, Attacking tank.

Photo.; Center Engr.

1954-55 ***Perf. 12½x12***

647 A255 10g red brn & choc 1.25 .15
648 A255 20g rose & grnsh blk .65 .30
649 A255 25g bister & blk 1.50 .18
650 A255 40g yel org & choc .48 .18
651 A255 45g claret & vio brn .95 .18
652 A255 60g emerald & red brn .95 .22
653 A255 1.15z brt bl grn & sep .95 .50
654 A255 1.40z orange & choc 9.25 2.25
655 A255 1.55z blue & indigo 1.75 .65
656 A255 2.10z ultra & indigo 3.00 1.40
Nos. 647-656 (10) 20.73 6.01

10th anniversary of "People's Poland." Issued: 25g, 60g, 1955; others, Dec. 23, 1954.

1954, Oct. 30 **Photo.; Center Litho.**

656A A255 25g bister & blk 2.50 1.50
656B A255 60g emer & red brn 1.25 1.00

Insurgents Attacking Russians — A256

60g, Gen. Tadeusz Kosciuszko and insurgents. 1.40z, Kosciuszko leading attack in Cracow.

1954, Nov. 30 **Engr.** ***Perf. 12½***

657 A256 40g grnsh black .40 .15
658 A256 60g violet brown .60 .16
659 A256 1.40z dark gray 1.65 .70
Nos. 657-659 (3) 2.65 1.01

160th anniv. of the Insurrection of 1794.

Bison — A257

60g, European elk. 1.90z, Chamois. 3z, Beaver.

Engr.; Background Photo.

1954, Dec. 22

660 A257 45g yel grn & blk brn .40 .20
661 A257 60g emerald & dk brn .40 .20
662 A257 1.90z blue & blk brn .60 .20
663 A257 3z bl grn & dk brn 1.75 .50
Nos. 660-663 (4) 3.15 1.10

Exist imperf. Value, set $4.50.

Liberators Entering Warsaw — A258

Frederic Chopin — A259

60g, Allegory of freedom (Warsaw Mermaid).

1955, Jan. 17 **Photo.**

664 A258 40g red brown .85 .32
665 A258 60g dull blue 2.25 .65

Liberation of Warsaw, 10th anniversary.

1955, Feb. 22 **Engr.**

666 A259 40g dark brown .35 .15
667 A259 60g indigo .65 .20
Set value .26

5th Intl. Competition of Chopin's Music, Feb. 22-Mar. 21.

Brothers in Arms Monument A260

Sigismund III A261

Warsaw monuments: 5g, Mermaid. 10g, Feliks E. Dzerzhinski. 40g, Nicolaus Copernicus. 45g, Marie Sklodowska Curie. 60g, Adam Mickiewicz. 1.55z, Jan Kilinski.

1955, May 3 **Unwmk.** ***Perf. 12½***

668 A260 5g dk grn, *grnsh* .15 .15
669 A260 10g vio brn, *yel* .15 .15
670 A261 15g blk brn, *bluish* .15 .15
671 A260 20g dk bl, *pink* .15 .15
672 A260 40g vio, *vio* .60 .15
673 A261 45g vio brn, *cr* .80 .25
674 A260 60g dk bl, *gray* .60 .15
675 A261 1.55z sl bl, *grysh* 1.65 .30
Nos. 668-675 (8) 4.25
Set value .95

See Nos. 737-739.

Palace of Culture and Flags of Poland and USSR — A262

Design: 60g, Monument.

Perf. 12½x12, 11

1955, Apr. 21 **Photo.**

676 A262 40g rose red .20 .15
677 A262 40g lt brown .60 .30
678 A262 60g Prus blue .25 .15
679 A262 60g dk olive brn .25 .15
Nos. 676-679 (4) 1.30
Set value .50

Polish-USSR treaty of friendship, 10th anniv.

Arms and Bicycle Wheels A263

Poznan Town Hall and Fair Emblem A264

Design: 60g, Three doves above road.

1955, Apr. 25 *Perf. 12*

No.	Type	Value	Color	Unused	Used
680	A263	40g	chocolate	.40	.15
681	A263	60g	ultra	.25	.15
			Set value		.20

8th Intl. Peace Bicycle Race, Prague-Berlin-Warsaw.

1955, June 10 Photo. *Perf. 12½*

No.	Type	Value	Color	Unused	Used
682	A264	40g	brt ultra	.30	.15
683	A264	60g	dull red	.15	.15
			Set value		.20

24th Intl. Fair at Poznan, July 3-24, 1955.

"Laikonik" Carnival Costume — A265

A265a

1955, June 16 Typo. *Perf. 12*

Multicolored Centers

No.	Type	Value	Color	Unused	Used
684	A265	20g	emerald & henna	.30	.22
685	A265a	40g	brt org & lil	.42	.15
686	A265	60g	blue & carmine	1.25	.30
			Nos. 684-686 (3)	1.97	.67

Cracow Celebration Days.

Pansies — A266

40g, 60g, (#690), Dove & Tower of Palace of Science & Culture. 45g, Pansies. 60g, (#691), 1z, "Peace" (POKOJ) & Warsaw Mermaid.

1955, July 13 Litho. *Perf. 12*

No.	Type	Value	Color	Unused	Used
687	A266	25g	vio brn, org & car	.20	.15
688	A266	40g	gray bl & gray blk	.20	.15
689	A266	45g	brn lake, yel & car	.35	.15
690	A266	60g	sepia & orange	.30	.15
691	A266	60g	ultra & lt blue	.30	.15
692	A266	1z	purple & lt blue	.90	.50
			Nos. 687-692 (6)	2.25	
			Set value		1.00

5th World Festival of Youth, Warsaw, July 31-Aug. 14, 1955.
Exist imperf. Value, set $3.

Motorcyclists A267

Stalin Palace of Culture and Science, Warsaw A268

1955, July 20 Photo. *Perf. 12½*

No.	Type	Value	Color	Unused	Used
693	A267	40g	chocolate	.30	.20
694	A267	60g	dark green	.24	.15
			Set value		.25

13th Intl. Motorcycle Race in the Tatra Mountains, Aug. 7-9, 1955.

1955, July 21

No.	Type	Value	Color	Unused	Used
695	A268	60g	ultra	.20	.15
696	A268	60g	gray	.20	.15
697	A268	75g	blue green	.45	.15
698	A268	75g	brown	.45	.15
			Nos. 695-698 (4)	1.30	
			Set value		.45

Polish National Day, July 22, 1955. Sheets contain alternating copies of the 60g values or the 75g values respectively.

Athletes A269

Stadium A270

Designs: 40g, Hammer throwing. 1z, Basketball. 1.35z, Sculling. 1.55z, Swimming.

1955, July 27 Unwmk. *Perf. 12½*

No.	Type	Value	Color	Unused	Used
699	A269	20g	chocolate	.15	.15
700	A269	40g	plum	.15	.15
701	A270	60g	dull blue	.30	.15
702	A269	1z	orange ver	.55	.15
703	A269	1.35z	dull violet	.70	.15
704	A269	1.55z	peacock green	1.25	.50
			Nos. 699-704 (6)	3.10	
			Set value		.95

2nd International Youth Games, 1955. Exist imperf. Value, set $4.

Town Hall, Szczecin (Stettin) — A271

Rebels with Flag — A272

Designs: 40g, Cathedral, Wroclaw (Breslau) 60g, Town Hall, Zielona Gora (Grunberg). 95g, Town Hall, Opole (Oppeln).

1955, Sept. 22 Engr. *Perf. 11½*

No.	Type	Value	Color	Unused	Used
705	A271	25g	dull green	.20	.15
706	A271	40g	red brown	.25	.15
707	A271	60g	violet blue	.60	.15
708	A271	95g	dark gray	.90	.28
			Nos. 705-708 (4)	1.95	
			Set value		.60

10th anniv. of the acquisition of Western Polish Territories.

1955, Sept. 30 Photo. *Perf. 12x12½*

No.	Type	Value	Color	Unused	Used
709	A272	40g	dark brown	.25	.20
710	A272	60g	dk carmine rose	.25	.15

Revolution of 1905, 50th anniversary.

Adam Mickiewicz A273

Mickiewicz Monument, Paris — A274

Designs: 60g, Death mask. 95g, Statue, Warsaw.

1955, Oct. 10 *Perf. 12x12½, 12½*

No.	Type	Value	Color	Unused	Used
711	A273	20g	dark brown	.15	.15
712	A274	40g	brn org & dk brn	.18	.15
713	A274	60g	green & brown	.25	.15
714	A274	95g	brn red & blk	1.50	.50
			Nos. 711-714 (4)	2.08	
			Set value		.75

Death centenary of Adam Mickiewicz, poet, and to publicize the celebration of Mickiewicz year.

Teacher and Child — A275

Rook and Hands — A276

Design: 60g, Flame and open book.

Perf. 12½x13

1955, Oct. 21 Unwmk.

No.	Type	Value	Color	Unused	Used
715	A275	40g	brown	1.50	.25
716	A275	60g	ultra	2.50	.85

50th anniv. of the Polish Teachers' Trade Union.

1956, Feb. 9 *Perf. 12½*

Design: 60g, Chess knight and hands.

No.	Type	Value	Color	Unused	Used
717	A276	40g	dark red	1.90	.85
718	A276	60g	blue	1.50	.15

First World Chess Championship of the Deaf and Dumb, Feb. 9-23.

Captain and S. S. Kilinski A277

Designs: 10g, Sailor and barges. 20g, Dock worker and S. S. Pokoj. 45g, Shipyard and worker. 60g, Fisherman, S. S. Chopin and trawlers.

1956, Mar. 16 Engr. *Perf. 12x12½*

No.	Type	Value	Color	Unused	Used
719	A277	5g	green	.15	.15
720	A277	10g	carmine lake	.15	.15
721	A277	20g	deep ultra	.15	.15
722	A277	45g	rose brown	.70	.25
723	A277	60g	violet blue	.55	.15
			Nos. 719-723 (5)	1.70	
			Set value		.50

Snowflake and Ice Skates — A278

Cyclist — A279

Designs: 40g, Snowflake and Ice Hockey sticks. 60g, Snowflake and Skis.

1956, Mar. 7 Photo. *Perf. 12½*

No.	Type	Value	Color	Unused	Used
724	A278	20g	brt ultra & blk	4.00	1.50
725	A278	40g	brt grn & vio bl	.55	.15
726	A278	60g	lilac & lake	.55	.15
			Nos. 724-726 (3)	5.10	1.80

XI World Students Winter Sport Championship, Mar. 7-13.

1956, Apr. 25

No.	Type	Value	Color	Unused	Used
727	A279	40g	dark blue	1.25	.40
728	A279	60g	dark green	.20	.15

9th Intl. Peace Bicycle Race, Warsaw-Berlin-Prague, May 1-15.

Zakopane Mountains and Shelter — A280

40g, Map, compass & knapsack. 60g, Map of Poland & canoe. 1.15z, Skis & mountains.

1956, May 25

No.	Type	Value	Color	Unused	Used
729	A280	30g	dark green	.30	.15
730	A280	40g	lt red brown	.30	.15
731	A280	60g	blue	1.10	.50
732	A280	1.15z	dull purple	.55	.15
			Nos. 729-732 (4)	2.25	
			Set value		.75

Polish Tourist industry.

No. 593 Surcharged with New Values

1956, July 6 Engr. *Perf. 12½*

No.	Type	Value	Color	Unused	Used
733	A232	10g	on 80g dp plum	.35	.20
734	A232	40g	on 80g dp plum	.30	.20
735	A232	60g	on 80g dp plum	.55	.20
736	A232	1.35z	on 80g dp plum	1.25	.70
			Nos. 733-736 (4)	2.45	1.30

The size and type of surcharge and obliteration of old value differ for each denomination.

Type of 1955

Warsaw Monuments: 30g, Ghetto Monument. 40g, John III Sobieski. 1.55z, Prince Joseph Poniatowski.

1956, July 10

No.	Type	Value	Color	Unused	Used
737	A260	30g	black	.25	.15
738	A260	40g	red brn, *grnsh*	.50	.25
739	A260	1.55z	vio brn, *pnksh*	.70	.25
			Nos. 737-739 (3)	1.45	.65

No. 737 measures 22½x28mm, instead of 21x27mm.

Polish and Russian Dancers A281

Design: 60g, Open book and cogwheels.

1956, Sept. 14 Litho. *Perf. 12*

No.	Type	Value	Color	Unused	Used
740	A281	40g	brn red & brn	.35	.20
741	A281	60g	bister & red	.15	.15

Polish-Soviet Friendship month.

Ludwiga Warzynska and Children A282

Bee on Clover and Beehive A283

1956, Sept. 17 Photo. *Perf. 12½*

No.	Type	Value	Color	Unused	Used
742	A282	40g	dull red brown	.70	.20
743	A282	60g	blue	.32	.15
			Set value		.26

Issued in honor of a heroic school teacher who saved three children from a burning house.

1956, Oct. 30 Litho. Unwmk.

Design: 60g, Father Jan Dzierzon.

No.	Type	Value	Color	Unused	Used
744	A283	40g	org yel & brn	.95	.35
745	A283	60g	yellow & brn	.30	.15

50th death anniv. of Father Jan Dzierzon, the inventor of the modernized beehive.

"Lady with the Ermine" by Leonardo da Vinci — A284

40g, Niobe. 60g, Madonna by Veit Stoss.

1956 Engr. *Perf. 11½x11*

No.	Type	Value	Color	Unused	Used
746	A284	40g	dark green	2.50	.75
747	A284	60g	dark violet	.80	.25
748	A284	1.55z	chocolate	1.65	.25
			Nos. 746-748 (3)	4.95	1.25

Intl. Museum Week (UNESCO), Oct. 8-14.

Fencer A285

Designs: 20g, Boxer. 25g, Sculling. 40g, Steeplechase racer. 60g, Javelin thrower. No. 755, Woman gymnast. No. 756, Woman broad jumper.

1956 Engr. *Perf. 11½*

No.	Type	Value	Color	Unused	Used
750	A285	10g	slate & chnt	.15	.15
751	A285	20g	lt brn & dl vio	.25	.15
a.			Center inverted		

752 A285 25g lt blue & blk .40 .15
753 A285 40g brt bl grn & redsh brn .30 .15
754 A285 60g rose car & ol brn .40 .15
755 A285 1.55z lt vio & sepia 1.50 1.00
756 A285 1.55z orange & chnt 1.00 .25
Nos. 750-756 (7) 4.00
Set value 1.70

16th Olympic Games, Melbourne, 11/22-12/8.

15th Century Mailman — A286

Lithographed and Engraved

1956, Nov. 30 Unwmk. *Perf. 12½*

757 A286 60g lt blue & blk 1.65 .80

Reopening of the Postal Museum in Wroclaw.

Skier and Snowflake A287 — Ski Jumper and Snowflake A288

Design: 1z, Skier in right corner.

1957, Jan. 18 Photo. *Perf. 12½*

758 A287 40g blue .25 .15
759 A288 60g dark green .25 .15
760 A287 1z purple .50 .30
Nos. 758-760 (3) 1.00
Set value .45

50 years of skiing in Poland.

Globe and Tree — A289

UN Emblem — A290

UN Building, NY — A291

1957, Feb. 26 Photo. *Perf. 12*

761 A289 5g mag & brt grnsh bl .35 .20
762 A290 15g blue & gray .40 .20
763 A291 40g brt bl grn & gray .75 .45
Nos. 761-763 (3) 1.50 .85

Issued in honor of the United Nations.
Exist imperf. Value, set $4.25.
An imperf. souvenir sheet exists, containing a 1.50z stamp in a redrawn design similar to A291. The stamp is blue and bright bluish green Value, $25 unused, $14 canceled.

Skier — A292

Sword, Foil and Saber on World Map — A293

1957, Mar. 22 *Perf. 12½*

764 A292 60g blue .60 .22
765 A292 60g brown .80 .28

12th anniv. of the death of the skiers Bronislaw Czech and Hanna Marusarzowna.

1957, Apr. 20 Unwmk. *Perf. 12½*

Designs: No. 767, Fencer facing right. No. 768, Fencer facing left.

766 A293 40g deep plum .55 .32
767 A293 60g carmine .38 .15
768 A293 60g ultra .38 .15
a. Pair, #767-768 1.25 .50
Set value .45

World Youth Fencing Championships, Warsaw.
No. 768a has continuous design.

Dr. Sebastian Petrycy A294

Bicycle Wheel and Carnation A295

Doctors' Portraits: 20g Wojciech Oczko. 40g, Jedrzej Sniadecki. 60g, Tytus Chalubinski. 1z, Wladyslaw Bieganski. 1.35z, Jozef Dietl. 2.50z, Benedykt Dybowski. 3z, Henryk Jordan.

Portraits Engr., Inscriptions Typo.

1957 *Perf. 11½*

769 A294 10g sepia & ultra .15 .15
770 A294 20g emerald & claret .15 .15
771 A294 40g gray & org red .15 .15
772 A294 60g blue & pale brn .35 .16
773 A294 1z orange & dk blue .15 .15
774 A294 1.35z gray brn & grn .20 .15
775 A294 2.50z dull vio & lil rose .42 .15
776 A294 3z violet & ol brn .50 .15
Set value 1.75 .55

1957, May 4 Photo. *Perf. 12½*

777 A295 60g shown .55 .20
778 A295 1.50z Cyclist .20 .15

10th Intl. Peace Bicycle Race, Warsaw-Berlin-Prague.

Poznan Fair Emblem A296

Turk's Cap A297

1957, June 8 Litho. Unwmk.

779 A296 60g ultramarine .22 .15
780 A296 2.50z lt blue green .30 .15
Set value .20

Issued to publicize the 26th Fair at Poznan.

1957, Aug. 12 Photo. *Perf. 12*

Flowers: No. 782, Carline Thistle. No. 783, Sea Holly. No. 784, Edelweiss. No. 785, Lady's-slipper.

781 A297 60g bl grn & claret .24 .15
782 A297 60g gray, grn & yel .24 .15
783 A297 60g lt blue & grn .24 .15
784 A297 60g gray & yel grn .24 .15
785 A297 60g lt grn, mar & yel 1.00 .28
Nos. 781-785 (5) 1.96
Set value .60

Fire Fighter A298

Town Hall, Leipzig and Congress Emblem A299

60g, Child & flames. 2.50z, Grain & flames.

1957, Sept. 11 *Perf. 12*

786 A298 40g black & red .15 .15
787 A298 60g dk grn & org red .15 .15
788 A298 2.50z violet & red .50 .20
Set value .60 .30

Intl. Fire Brigade Conf., Warsaw.

1957, Sept. 25 Photo. *Perf. 12½*

789 A299 60g violet .15 .15

4th Intl. Trade Union Cong., Leipzig, Oct. 4-15.

"Girl Writing Letter" by Fragonard — A300

Karol Libelt — A301

1957, Oct. 9 *Perf. 12*

790 A300 2.50z dark blue green .50 .15

Issued for Stamp Day, Oct. 9.

1957, Nov. 15 Photo. *Perf. 12½*

791 A301 60g carmine lake .15 .15

Centenary of the Poznan Scientific Society and to honor Karol Libelt, politician and philosopher.

Broken Chain and Flag — A302

Jan A. Komensky (Comenius) — A303

Design: 2.50z, Lenin Statue, Poronin.

1957, Nov. 7

792 A302 60g brt blue & red .15 .15
793 A302 2.50z black & red brn .25 .15
Set value .20

40th anniv. of the Russian Revolution.

1957, Dec. 11 *Perf. 12*

794 A303 2.50z brt carmine .25 .15

300th anniv. of the publication of "Didactica Opera Omnia."

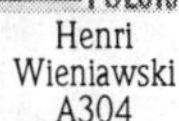

Henri Wieniawski A304

Andrzej Strug A305

1957, Dec. 2 *Perf. 12½*

795 A304 2.50z blue .25 .15

3rd Wieniawski Violin Competition in Poznan.

1957, Dec. 16 Unwmk. *Perf. 12½*

796 A305 2.50z brown .20 .15

20th death anniv. of Andrzej Strug, novelist.

Joseph Conrad and "Torrens" A306

1957, Dec. 30 Engr. *Perf. 12x12½*

797 A306 60g brown, *grnsh* .15 .15
798 A306 2.50z dk blue, *pink* .45 .18
Set value .25

Birth cent. of Joseph Conrad, Polish-born English writer.

Postilion and Stylized Plane — A307

Town Hall at Biecz — A308

Designs: 40g, Tomb of Prosper Prowano, globe with plane and satellite. 60g, St. Mary's Church, Cracow, mail coach and plane. 95g, Mail coach and postal bus. 2.10z, Medieval postman and train. 3.40z, Medieval galleon and modern ships.

1958 Litho. *Perf. 12½*

799 A307 40g lt blue & vio brn .15 .15
800 A307 60g pale vio & blk .15 .15
801 A307 95g lemon & violet .15 .15
802 A307 2.10z gray & ultra .45 .35
803 A307 2.50z brt blue & blk .35 .15
804 A307 3.40z aqua & maroon .35 .15
Set value 1.30 .65

400th anniversary of the Polish posts. Imperfs. exist of all but No. 803.

1958, Mar. 29 Engr. *Perf. 12½*

Town Halls: 40g, Wroclaw. 60g, Tarnow, horiz. 2.10z, Danzig. 2.50z, Zamosc.

805 A308 20g green .15 .15
806 A308 40g brown .15 .15
807 A308 60g dark blue .15 .15
808 A308 2.10z rose lake .30 .15
809 A308 2.50z violet .45 .15
Set value .95 .35

Giant Pike Perch — A309

Fishes: 60g, Salmon, vert. 2.10z, Pike, vert. 2.50z, Trout, vert. 6.40z, Grayling.

1958, Apr. 22 Photo. *Perf. 12*

810 A309 40g bl, blk, grn & yel .15 .15
811 A309 60g yel grn, dk grn & bl .15 .15
812 A309 2.10z dk bl, grn & yel .40 .15
813 A309 2.50z pur, blk & yel grn 1.50 .30
814 A309 6.40z bl grn, brn & red .90 .35
Nos. 810-814 (5) 3.10
Set value .90

Casimir Palace, Warsaw University — A310

Stylized Glider and Cloud — A311

1958, May 14 Unwmk. *Perf. 12½*

815 A310 2.50z violet blue .20 .15

140th anniv. of the University of Warsaw.

1958, June 14 Litho.

Design: 2.50z, Design reversed.

816 A311 60g gray blue & blk .15 .15
817 A311 2.50z gray & blk .35 .15
Set value .20

7th Intl. Glider Competitions.

The Scott Catalogue value is a retail value; that is, what you could expect to pay for the stamp in a grade of Very Fine. The value listed reflects recent actual dealer selling prices.

Fair Emblem A312

Armed Postman and Mail Box A313

1958, June 9

818 A312 2.50z black & rose .20 .15

27th Fair at Poznan.

1958, Sept. 1 Engr. *Perf. 11*

819 A313 60g dark blue .15 .15

19th anniv. of the defense of the Polish post office at Danzig (Gdansk). Inscribed: "You were the first."

Letter, Quill and Postmark A314

Polar Bear A315

1958, Oct. 9 Litho.

820 A314 60g blk, bl grn & ver .50 .25

Issued for Stamp Day. Exists imperf.

1958, Sept. 30 Photo. *Perf. 12½x12*

Design: 2.50z, Rocket and Sputnik.

821 A315 60g black .18 .15
822 A315 2.50z dark blue .55 .15
Set value .20

Intl. Geophysical Year.

Partisan's Cross — A316

Designs: 60g, Virtuti Militari Cross. 2.50z, Grunwald Cross.

1958, Oct. 10 *Perf. 11*

823 A316 40g black, grn & ocher .15 .15
824 A316 60g black, blue & yel .15 .15
825 A316 2.50z multicolored .60 .20
Nos. 823-825 (3) .90
Set value .34

Polish People's Army, 15th anniv.

17th Century Ship — A317

UNESCO Building, Paris — A318

Design: 2.50z, Polish immigrants.

1958, Oct. 29 *Perf. 11*

826 A317 60g dk slate grn .15 .15
827 A317 2.50z dk carmine rose .25 .15
Set value .18

350th anniversary of the arrival of the first Polish immigrants in America.

1958, Nov. 3 Unwmk.

828 A318 2.50z yellow grn & blk .45 .15

UNESCO Headquarters in Paris, opening, Nov. 3.

Stagecoach — A319

Perf. 12½

1958, Oct. 26 Engr. Wmk. 326

829 A319 2.50z slate, *buff* 1.00 .50
a. Souvenir sheet of 6 9.00 9.00

Philatelic exhibition in honor of the 400th anniv. of the Polish post, Warsaw, Oct. 25-Nov. 10.

Souvenir Sheet

1958, Dec. 12 Unwmk. *Imperf.*

Printed on Silk

830 A319 50z dark blue 14.00 10.00

400th anniversary of the Polish posts.

Stanislaw Wyspianski A320

Kneeling Figure A321

Portrait: 2.50z, Stanislaw Moniuszko.

1958, Nov. 25 Engr. *Perf. 12½*

831 A320 60g dark violet .15 .15
832 A320 2.50z dk slate grn .35 .15
Set value .20

Stanislaw Wyspianski, painter and poet, and Stanislaw Moniuszko, composer.

1958, Dec. 10 Litho.

833 A321 2.50z lt brn & red brn .35 .15

Signing of the Universal Declaration of Human Rights, 10th anniv.

Red Flag — A322

Sailing — A323

1958, Dec. 16 Photo.

834 A322 60g plum & red .15 .15

40th anniv. of the Communist Party of Poland.

1959, Jan. 3

Sports: 60g, Girl archer. 95g, Soccer. 2z, Horsemanship.

835 A323 40g lt bl & vio bl .20 .15
836 A323 60g salmon & brn vio .20 .15
837 A323 95g green & brn vio .30 .20
838 A323 2z dp bl & lt grn .30 .20
Nos. 835-838 (4) 1.00 .70

Hand at Wheel — A324

Wheat, Hammer and Flag — A325

1959, Mar. 10 Wmk. 326 *Perf. 12½*

839 A324 40gr shown .15 .15
840 A325 60gr shown .15 .15
841 A324 1.55z Factory .42 .15
Set value .60 .30

3rd Workers Congress.

Amanita Phalloides — A326

Designs: Various mushrooms.

1959, May 8 Photo. *Perf. 11½*

842 A326 20g yellow, grn & brn 1.40 .55
843 A326 30g multicolored .20 .15
844 A326 40g multicolored .60 .15
845 A326 60g yel grn, brn & ocher .60 .15
846 A326 1z multicolored .38 .15
847 A326 2.50z blue, grn & brn .80 .15
848 A326 3.40z multicolored 1.10 .38
849 A326 5.60z dl yel, brn & grn 3.00 1.50
Nos. 842-849 (8) 8.08 3.18

"Storks," by Jozef Chelmonski A327

Paintings by Polish Artists: 60g, Mother and Child, Stanislaw Wyspianski, vert. 1z, Mme. de Romanet, Henryk Rodakowski, vert. 1.50z, Old Man and Death, Jacek Malczewski, vert. 6.40z, River Scene, Aleksander Gierymski.

1959 Engr. *Perf. 12, 12½x12*

850 A327 40g gray green .20 .15
851 A327 60g dull purple .25 .15
852 A327 1z intense black .30 .15
853 A327 1.50z brown .50 .30
854 A327 6.40z blue 2.25 .70
Nos. 850-854 (5) 3.50 1.45

Nos. 850 and 854 measure 36x28mm; Nos. 851 and 853, 28x36mm; No. 852, 28x37mm.

Miner and Globe — A328

Map of Poland and Symbol of Agriculture — A329

1959, July 1 Litho.

855 A328 2.50z multicolored .45 .15

3rd Miners' Conf., Katowice, July 1959.

Perf. 12x12½

1959, July 21 Wmk. 326

Map of Poland and: 60g, Symbol of industry. 1.50z, Symbol of art and science.

856 A329 40g black, bl & grn .15 .15
857 A329 60g black & ver .15 .15
858 A329 1.50z black & blue .15 .15
Set value .40 .20

15 years of the Peoples' Republic of Poland.

Lazarus Ludwig Zamenhof A330

Map of Austria and Flower A331

Design: 1.50z, Star, globe and flag.

1959, July 24 *Perf. 12½*

859 A330 60g blk & grn, *ol* .15 .15
860 A330 1.50z ultra, grn & red, *gray* .42 .15
Set value .20

Centenary of the birth of Lazarus Ludwig Zamenhof, author of Esperanto, and in conjunction with the Esperanto Congress in Warsaw.

1959, July 27 Litho.

861 A331 60g sep, red & grn, *yel* .15 .15
862 A331 2.50z bl, red, & grn, *gray* .45 .20
Set value .26

7th World Youth Festival, Vienna, July 26-Aug. 14.

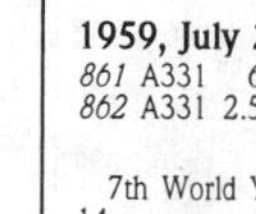

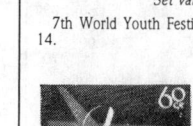

Symbolic Plane — A332

1959, Aug. 24 Wmk. 326 *Perf. 12½*

863 A332 60g vio bl, grnsh bl & blk .15 .15

30th anniv. of LOT, the Polish airline.

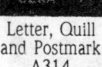

Sejm (Parliament) Building A333

1959, Aug. 27 Photo. *Perf. 12x12½*

864 A333 60g lt grn, blk & red .15 .15
865 A333 2.50z vio gray, blk & red .40 .15

48th Interparliamentary Conf., Warsaw.

No. 640 Overprinted in Blue: "BALPEX I - GDANSK 1959"

1959, Aug. 30 Engr. Unwmk.

866 A253 45g brown, *yel* .65 .50

Intl. Phil. Exhib. of Baltic States at Gdansk.

Stylized Dove and Globe — A334

Red Cross Nurse — A335

Perf. 12½

1959, Sept. 1 Photo. Wmk. 326

867 A334 60g blue & gray .15 .15

World Peace Movement, 10th anniv.

1959, Sept. 21 Litho. *Perf. 12½*

Designs: 60g, Nurse. 2.50z, Henri Dunant.

Size: 21x26mm

868 A335 40g red, lt grn & blk .15 .15
869 A335 60g bis brn, brn & red .15 .15

Perf. 11

Size: 23x23mm

870 A335 2.50z red, pink & blk .65 .35
Nos. 868-870 (3) .95
Set value .50

Polish Red Cross, 40th anniv.; Red Cross, cent.

Polish-Chinese Friendship Society Emblem — A336

Flower Made of Stamps — A337

Wmk. 326

1959, Sept. 28 Litho. *Perf. 11*

871 A336 60g multicolored .45 .16
872 A336 2.50z multicolored .30 .15

Polish-Chinese friendship.

1959, Oct. 9 *Perf. 12½*

873 A337 60g lt grnsh bl, grn & red .15 .15
874 A337 2.50z red, grn & vio .35 .16
Set value .25

Issued for Stamp Day, 1959.

Sputnik 3 — A338

60g, Rocket. 2.50z, Earth, moon, Sputnik 2.

1959, Nov. 7 Photo. Wmk. 326

875 A338 40g Prus blue & gray .22 .15
876 A338 60g maroon & black .32 .20
877 A338 2.50z green & dk blue .90 .48
Nos. 875-877 (3) 1.44 .83

42nd anniv. of the Russian Revolution and the landing of the Soviet moon rocket.
Exist imperf. Value, set $3.

Child Doing Homework A339

Charles Darwin A340

Design: 60g, Three children leaving school.

Lithographed and Engraved

1959, Nov. 14 ***Perf. 11½***

878 A339 40g green & dk brn .15 .15
879 A339 60g blue & red .15 .15
Set value .16

"1,000 Schools" campaign for the 1,000th anniversary of Poland.

1959, Dec. 10 Engr. *Perf. 11*

Scientists: 10g, Dmitri I. Mendeleev. 60g, Albert Einstein. 1.50z, Louis Pasteur. 1.55z, Isaac Newton. 2.50z, Nicolaus Copernicus.

880 A340 20g dark blue .15 .15
881 A340 40g olive gray .15 .15
882 A340 60g claret .15 .15
883 A340 1.50g dk violet brn .15 .15
884 A340 1.55z dark green .45 .15
885 A340 2.50z violet 1.00 .48
Nos. 880-885 (6) 2.05
Set value .80

Man from Rzeszow — A341

Woman from Rzeszow — A342

Regional Costumes: 40g, Cracow. 60g, Kurpiow. 1z, Silesia. 2z, Lowicz. 2.50z, Mountain people. 3.10z, Kujawy. 3.40z, Lublin. 5.60z, Szamotuli. 6.50z, Lubuski.

Engraved and Photogravure

1959-60 Wmk. 326 *Perf. 12, Imperf.*

886 A341 20g slate grn & blk .15 .15
887 A342 20g slate grn & blk .15 .15
888 A341 40g lt bl & rose car ('60) .15 .15
889 A342 40g rose car & bl ('60) .15 .15
890 A341 60g black & pink .15 .15
891 A342 60g black & pink .15 .15
892 A341 1z grnsh red & dk red .15 .15
893 A342 1z grnsh bl & dk red .15 .15
894 A341 2z yellow & ultra ('60) .20 .15
895 A342 2z yellow & ultra ('60) .20 .15
896 A341 2.50z green & rose lil .30 .20
897 A342 2.50z green & rose lil .30 .20
898 A341 3.10z yel grn & sl grn ('60) .40 .25
899 A342 3.10z yel grn & sl grn ('60) .40 .25
900 A341 3.40z gray grn & brn ('60) .50 .30
901 A342 3.40z gray grn & brn ('60) .50 .30
902 A341 5.60z yel grn & gray bl 1.25 .50
903 A342 5.60z yel grn & gray bl 1.25 .50
904 A341 6.50z vio & gray grn ('60) 1.25 .50
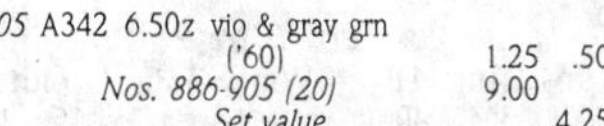
905 A342 6.50z vio & gray grn ('60) 1.25 .50
Nos. 886-905 (20) 9.00
Set value 4.25

The male and female costume stamps of each denomination were printed se-tenant in sheets of 56.

Piano — A343

Frederic Chopin — A344

Design: 1.50z, Musical note and manuscript.

1960, Feb. 22 Litho. *Perf. 12*

906 A343 60g brt violet & blk .40 .32
907 A343 1.50z black, gray & red .60 .22

Perf. 12½x12

Engr.

908 A344 2.50z black 2.50 .90
Nos. 906-908 (3) 3.50 1.44

150th anniversary of the birth of Frederic Chopin and to publicize the Chopin music competition.

Stamp of 1860 — A345

Designs: 60g, Ski meet stamp of 1939. 1.35z, Design from 1860 issue. 1.55z, 1945 liberation stamp. 2.50z, 1957 stamp day stamp.

Litho. (40g, 1.35z); Litho. and Photo.

Perf. 11½x11

1960, Mar. 21 Wmk. 326

909 A345 40g multicolored .16 .15
910 A345 60g violet, ultra & blk .32 .16
911 A345 1.35z gray, red & bl .75 .40
912 A345 1.55z green, car & blk .75 .25
913 A345 2.50z ap grn, dk grn & blk 1.00 .45
Nos. 909-913 (5) 2.98 1.41

Centenary of Polish stamps. Nos. 909-913 were also issued in sheets of 4. Value, $275.
For overprint see No. 934.

Discus Thrower, Amsterdam 1928 A346

Polish Olympic Victories: No. 915, Runner. No. 916, Bicyclist. No. 917, Steeplechase. No. 918, Trumpeters. No. 919, Boxers. No. 920, Olympic flame. No. 921 Woman jumper.

Lithographed and Embossed

Perf. 12x12½

1960, June 15 Unwmk.

914 A346 60g blue & blk .20 .15
915 A346 60g car rose & blk .20 .15
916 A346 60g violet & blk .20 .15
917 A346 60g blue grn & blk .20 .15
a. Block of 4, #914-917 .80 .40
918 A346 2.50z ultra & blk .60 .25
919 A346 2.50z chestnut & blk .60 .25
920 A346 2.50z red & blk .60 .25
921 A346 2.50z emerald & blk .60 .25
a. Block of 4, #918-921 2.50 1.00
Nos. 914-921 (8) 3.20
Set value 1.50

17th Olympic Games, Rome, Aug. 25-Sept. 11.
Nos. 917a and 921a have continuous design forming the stadium oval.
Nos. 914-921 exist imperf. Value, set $5.

Tomb of King Wladyslaw II Jagiello — A347

Battle of Grunwald by Jan Matejko — A348

Design: 90g, Detail from Grunwald monument.

Perf. 11x11½

1960 Wmk. 326 Engr.

922 A347 60g violet brown .35 .15
923 A347 90g olive gray .70 .32

Size: 78x37mm

924 A348 2.50z dark gray 2.00 1.10
Nos. 922-924 (3) 3.05 1.57

550th anniversary, Battle of Grunwald.

The Annunciation A349

Carvings by Veit Stoss, St. Mary's Church, Cracow: 30g, Nativity. 40g, Adoration of the Kings. 60g, The Resurrection. 2.50z, The Ascension. 5.60z, Descent of the Holy Ghost. 10z, The Assumption of the Virgin, vert.

1960 Wmk. 326 Engr. *Perf. 12*

925 A349 20g Prus blue .25 .15
926 A349 30g lt red brown .15 .15
927 A349 40g violet .28 .15
928 A349 60g dull green .28 .15
929 A349 2.50z rose lake .90 .22
930 A349 5.60z dark brown 5.75 2.75
Nos. 925-930 (6) 7.61 3.57

Miniature Sheet

Imperf

931 A349 10z black 6.00 5.50

No. 931 contains one vertical stamp which measures 72x95mm.

A350

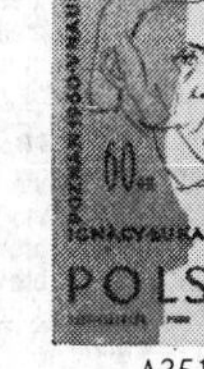

A351

1960, Sept. 26 *Perf. 12½*

932 A350 2.50z black .35 .15

Birth cent. of Ignacy Jan Paderewski, statesman and musician.

Engr. & Photo.

1960, Sept. 14 *Perf. 11*

Lukasiewicz and kerosene lamp.

933 A351 60g citron & black .15 .15

5th Pharmaceutical Congress; Ignacy Lukasiewicz, chemist-pharmacist.

No. 909 Overprinted: "DZIEN ZNACZKA 1960"

1960 Litho. *Perf. 11½x11*

934 A345 40g multicolored 1.25 .60

Issued for Stamp Day, 1960.

Great Bustard A352

Birds: 20g, Raven. 30g, Great cormorant. 40g, Black stork. 50g, Eagle owl. 60g, White-tailed sea eagle. 75g, Golden eagle. 90g, Short-toed eagle. 2.50z, Rock thrush. 4z, European kingfisher. 5.60z, Wall creeper. 6.50z, European roller.

1960 Unwmk. Photo. *Perf. 11½*

Birds in Natural Colors

935 A352 10g gray & blk .15 .15
936 A352 20g gray & blk .15 .15
937 A352 30g gray & blk .15 .15
938 A352 40g gray & blk .22 .15
939 A352 50g pale grn & blk .28 .15
940 A352 60g pale grn & blk .40 .15
941 A352 75g pale grn & blk .40 .15
942 A352 90g pale grn & blk .55 .16
943 A352 2.50z pale ol gray & blk 4.00 1.65
944 A352 4z pale ol gray & blk 2.50 .60
945 A352 5.60z pale ol gray & blk 4.25 .65
946 A352 6.50z pale ol gray & blk 6.50 2.00
Nos. 935-946 (12) 19.55 6.11

Gniezno A353

Front Page of "Merkuriusz" A354

Historic Towns: 10g, Cracow. 20g, Warsaw. 40g, Poznan. 50g, Plock. 60g, Kalisz. No. 952A, Tczew. 80g, Frombork. 90g, Torun. 95g, Puck (ships). 1z, Slupsk. 1.15z, Gdansk (Danzig). 1.35z, Wroclaw. 1.50z, Szczecin. 1.55z, Opole. 2z, Kolobrzeg. 2.10z, Legnica. 2.50z, Katowice. 3.10z, Lodz. 5.60z, Walbrzych.

1960-61 Engr. *Perf. 11½, 13x12½*

947 A353 5g red brown .15 .15
948 A353 10g green .15 .15
949 A353 20g dark brown .15 .15
950 A353 40g vermilion .15 .15
951 A353 50g violet .15 .15
952 A353 60g rose claret .15 .15
952A A353 60g lt ultra ('61) .30 .15
953 A353 80g blue .20 .15
954 A353 90g brown ('61) .30 .15
955 A353 95g olive gray .20 .15

Engraved and Lithographed

956 A353 1z orange & gray .20 .15
957 A353 1.15z slate grn & sal .20 .15
958 A353 1.35z lil rose & lt grn .20 .15
959 A353 1.50z sep & pale grn .20 .15
960 A353 1.55z car lake & buff .20 .15
961 A353 2z dk blue & pink .30 .15
962 A353 2.10z sepia & yel .25 .15
963 A353 2.50z dl vio & pale grn .40 .15
964 A353 3.10z ver & gray .45 .15
965 A353 5.60z sl grn & lt grn 1.10 .20
Nos. 947-965 (20) 5.40
Set value 2.00

Lithographed and Embossed

1961 Wmk. 326 *Perf. 12*

Newspapers: 60g, "Proletaryat," first issue, Sept. 15, 1883. 2.50z, "Rzeczpospolita," first issue, July 23, 1944.

966 A354 40g black, ultra & emer .50 .20
967 A354 60g black, org brn & yel .50 .20
968 A354 2.50z black, violet & bl 3.00 2.50
Nos. 966-968 (3) 4.00 2.90

300th anniv. of the Polish newspaper Merkuriusz.

Ice Hockey A355 — Part of Cogwheel A356

60g, Ski jump. 1z, Soldiers on skis. 1.50z, Slalom.

1961, Feb. 1 Litho. Wmk. 326

969 A355 40g lt violet, blk & yel .40 .15
970 A355 60g lt ultra, blk & car 1.10 .50
971 A355 1z lt blue, ol & red 5.25 2.00
972 A355 1.50z grnsh bl, blk & yel .90 .32
Nos. 969-972 (4) 7.65 2.97

1st Winter Spartacist Games of Friendly Armies.

1961, Feb. 11 ***Perf. 12½***

973 A356 60g red & black .15 .15

Fourth Congress of Polish Engineers.

Maj. Yuri A. Gagarin A357

Design: 60g, Globe and path of rocket.

1961, Apr. 27 Photo. ***Perf. 12***

974 A357 40g dark red & black .75 .32
975 A357 60g ultra, black & car .45 .20

1st man in space, Yuri A. Gagarin, Apr. 12, 1961.

Emblem of Poznan Fair A358

1961, May 25 Litho. ***Perf. 12½x12***

977 A358 40g brt bl, blk & red org .15 .15
978 A358 1.50z red org, blk & brt bl .18 .15
a. Souvenir sheet of 2 2.00 1.90
Set value .26 .16

30th Intl. Fair at Poznan.

No. 978a contains two of No. 978 with simulated perforation and blue marginal inscriptions. Sold for 4.50z. Issued July 29, 1961.

Tadeusz Kosciuszko A359

Famous Poles: No. 979, Mieszko I. No. 980, Casimir Wielki. No. 981, Casimir Jagiello. No. 982, Nicolaus Copernicus. No. 983, Andrzej Frycz-Modrzewski.

Photogravure and Engraved

1961, June 15 ***Perf. 11x11½***

Black Inscriptions and Designs

979 A359 60g chalky blue .15 .15
980 A359 60g deep rose .15 .15
981 A359 60g slate .15 .15
982 A359 60g dull violet .65 .20
983 A359 60g lt brown .15 .15
984 A359 60g olive gray .15 .15
Set value 1.18 .54

See Nos. 1059-1064, 1152-1155.

Trawler — A360

Designs: Various Polish Cargo Ships.

Unwmk.

1961, June 24 Litho. ***Perf. 11***

985 A360 60g multicolored .35 .15
986 A360 1.55z multicolored .45 .15
987 A360 2.50z multicolored .75 .30
988 A360 3.40z multicolored .90 .50
989 A360 4z multicolored 1.50 .90
990 A360 5.60z multicolored 3.50 1.65
Nos. 985-990 (6) 7.45 3.65

Polish ship industry. Sizes (width): 60g, 2.50z, 54mm; 1.55z, 3.40z, 4z, 80mm; 5.60z, 108mm.

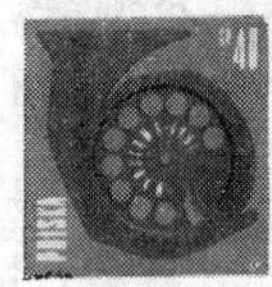

Post Horn and Telephone Dial — A361

Post horn and: 60g, Radar screen. 2.50z, Conference emblem, globe.

1961, June 26

991 A361 40g sl, gray & red org .15 .15
992 A361 60g gray, yel & vio .15 .15
993 A361 2.50z ol bis, brt bl & vio bl .35 .25
a. Souvenir sheet of 3, #991-993 2.75 1.50
Nos. 991-993 (3) .65
Set value .40

Conference of Communications Ministers of Communist Countries, Warsaw.

No. 993a sold for 5z.

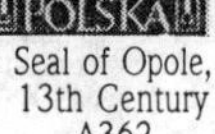

Seal of Opole, 13th Century A362 — Cement Works, Opole A363

Designs: No. 996, Tombstone of Henry IV and seal, Wroclaw. No. 997, Apartment houses, Wroclaw. No. 998, Seal of Conrad II and Silesian eagle. No. 999, Steel works, Gorzow. No. 1000, Seal of Prince Barnim I. No. 1001, Seaport, Szczecin. No. 1002, Seal of Princess Elizabeth. No. 1003, Factory, Szczecinek. No. 1004, Seal of Unislaw. No. 1005, Shipyard, Gdansk. No. 1005A, Tower, Frombork Cathedral. No. 1005B, Chemical Laboratory, Kortowo.

1961-62 Wmk. 326 Engr. ***Perf. 11***

Western Territories

994 A362 40g brown, *grysh* .15 .15
995 A363 40g brown, *grysh* .15 .15
996 A362 60g violet, *pink* .15 .15
997 A363 60g violet, *pink* .15 .15
998 A362 95g green, *bluish* .15 .15
999 A363 95g green, *bluish* .15 .15
1000 A362 2.50z ol grn, *grnsh* .32 .15
1001 A363 2.50z ol grn, *grnsh* .32 .15

Northern Territories

1002 A362 60g vio bl, *bluish* .15 .15
1003 A363 60g vio bl, *bluish* .15 .15
1004 A362 1.55z brown, *buff* .15 .15
1005 A363 1.55z brown, *buff* .15 .15
1005A A362 2.50z slate bl, *grysh* .32 .15
1005B A363 2.50z slate bl, *grysh* .32 .15
Set value 2.40 1.30

Sheets of 56 with alternating rows of horizontal and vertical stamps. The horizontal stamps also alternate with a label with commemorative inscription. Each sheet contains 28 se-tenant pairs of types A362-A363 with label.

Issued: #994-997, 1000-1001, 7/21; 85g, 2/23/62; #1002-1005B, 1308-1313, 7/21/62.

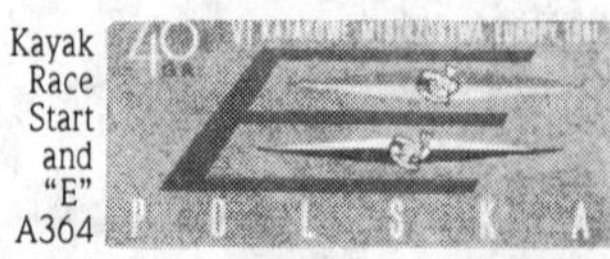

Kayak Race Start and "E" A364

Designs: 60g, Four-man canoes and "E." 2.50z, Paddle, Polish flag and "E," vert.

Perf. 12½

1961, Aug. 18 Wmk. 326 Litho.

1006 A364 40g bl grn, yel & red .15 .15
1007 A364 60g multicolored .15 .15
1008 A364 2.50z multicolored .90 .38
Nos. 1006-1008 (3) 1.20
Set value .50

6th European Canoe Championships, Poznan, Aug. 18-20. Exist imperf. Value, set $2.

Maj. Gherman Titov, Star, Globe, Orbit A365

Dove and Earth A366

Perf. 12x12½

1961, Aug. 24 Photo. Unwmk.

1009 A365 40g pink, blk & red .30 .15
1010 A366 60g blue & black .30 .15
Set value .20

Manned space flight of Vostok 2, Aug. 6-7, in which Russian Maj. Gherman Titov orbited the earth 17 times.

Insurgents' Monument, St. Ann's Mountain — A367

Design: 1.55z, Cross of Silesian Insurgents.

Wmk. 326

1961, Sept. 15 Litho. ***Perf. 12***

1011 A367 60g gray & emerald .15 .15
1012 A367 1.55z gray & blue .20 .15
Set value .20

40th anniv. of the third Silesian uprising.

"PKO," Initials of Polish Savings Bank — A368

Initials and: #1014, Bee and clover. #1015, Ant. #1016, Squirrel. 2.50z, Savings bankbook.

1961, Oct. 2 Wmk. 326 ***Perf. 12***

1013 A368 40g ver, blk & org .15 .15
1014 A368 60g blue, blk & brt pink .15 .15
1015 A368 60g bis brn, blk & ocher .15 .15
1016 A368 60g brt grn, blk & dl red .15 .15
1017 A368 2.50z car rose, gray & blk 1.75 1.40
Nos. 1013-1017 (5) 2.35
Set value 1.70

Issued to publicize Savings Month.

Mail Cart, by Jan Chelminski A369

1961, Oct. 9 Engr. ***Perf. 12x12½***

1018 A369 60g deep green .25 .15
1019 A369 60g violet brown .25 .15
Set value .18

Polish Postal Museum, 40th anniv; Stamp Day.

Congress Emblem A370

1961, Nov. 20 Wmk. 326 ***Perf. 12***

1020 A370 60g black .15 .15

Issued to publicize the Fifth World Congress of Trade Unions, Moscow, Dec. 4-16.

Seal of Kopasyni Family, 1284 A371 — Child and Syringe A372

60g, Seal of Bytom, 14th century. 2.50z, Emblem of International Miners Congress, 1958.

1961, Dec. 4 Litho. ***Perf. 11x11½***

1021 A371 40g multicolored .15 .15
1022 A371 60g bl, gray bl & vio bl .15 .15
1023 A371 2.50z yel grn, grn & blk .45 .24
Nos. 1021-1023 (3) .75
Set value .38

1,000 years of the Polish mining industry.

Perf. 12½x12, 12x12½

1961, Dec. 11

Designs: 60g, Children of three races, horiz. 2.50z, Mother, child and milk bottle.

1024 A372 40g lt blue & blk .15 .15
1025 A372 60g orange & blk .15 .15
1026 A372 2.50z brt bl grn & blk .50 .24
Nos. 1024-1026 (3) .80
Set value .38

15th anniversary of UNICEF.

Emblem A373

Design: 60g, Map with oil pipe line from Siberia to Central Europe.

1961, Dec. 12 Wmk. 326 ***Perf. 12***

1027 A373 40g dk red, yel & vio bl .15 .15
1028 A373 60g vio bl, bl & red .15 .15
Set value .18

15th session of the Council of Mutual Economic Assistance of the Communist States.

Ground Beetle — A374

Black Apollo Butterfly A375

Insects: 30g, Violet runner. 40g, Alpine longicorn beetle. 50g, Great oak capricorn beetle. 60g, Gold runner. 80g, Stag-horned beetle. 1.35z, Death's-head moth. 1.50z, Tiger-striped swallowtail butterfly. 1.55z, Apollo butterfly. 2.50z, Red ant. 5.60z, Bumble bee.

Perf. 12½x12

1961, Dec. 30 Photo. Unwmk.

Insects in Natural Colors

1029 A374 20g bister brown .15 .15
1030 A374 30g pale gray grn .15 .15
1031 A374 40g pale yellow grn .15 .15
1032 A374 50g blue green .15 .15
1033 A374 60g dull rose lilac .15 .15
1034 A374 80g pale green .24 .15

Perf. 11½

1035 A375 1.15z ultra .32 .15
1036 A375 1.35z sapphire .32 .15
1037 A375 1.50z bluish green .55 .15
1038 A375 1.55z brt purple .48 .15
1039 A375 2.50z brt green 1.90 .45
1040 A375 5.60z orange brown 9.00 3.50
Nos. 1029-1040 (12) 13.56 5.45

Worker with Gun — A376

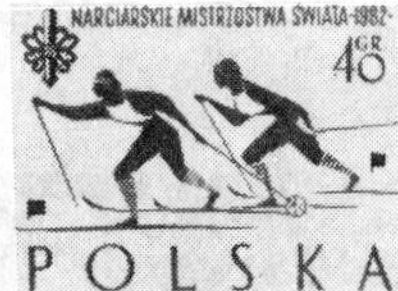

Women Skiers — A377

#1042, Worker with trowel and gun. #1043, Worker with hammer. #1044, Worker at helm. #1045, Worker with dove and banner.

Perf. 12½x12

1962, Jan. 5 Litho. Unwmk.

1041 A376 60g red, blk & green .15 .15
1042 A376 60g red, blk & slate .15 .15
1043 A376 60g blk & vio bl, *red* .15 .15
1044 A376 60g blk & bis, *red* .15 .15
1045 A376 60g blk & gray, *red* .15 .15
Set value .52 .46

Polish Workers' Party, 20th anniversary.

Lithographed and Embossed

1962, Feb. 14 *Perf. 12*

Designs: 60g, Long distance skier. 1.50z, Ski jump, vert. 10z, FIS emblem, vert.

1046 A377 40g gray, red & gray bl .15 .15
a. 40g sepia, red & dull blue .45 .15
1047 A377 60g gray, red & gray bl .15 .15
a. 60g sepia, red & dull blue .55 .30
1048 A377 1.50z gray, red & gray bl .30 .20
a. 1.50z gray, lilac & red 1.65 .80
Nos. 1046-1048 (3) .60
Set value .35

Souvenir Sheet

Imperf

1049 A377 10z gray, red & gray bl 3.00 2.50

World Ski Championships at Zakopane (FIS).

No. 1049 contains one stamp with simulated perforation. The sheet sold for 15z.

Each of Nos. 1046-1048 exists in a souvenir sheet of four. Value, set of 3, $57.50.

Broken Flower and Prison Cloth (Auschwitz) — A378

Majdanek Concentration Camp — A379

Design: 1.50z, Proposed memorial, Treblinka concentration camp.

Perf. 11½

1962, Apr. 3 Wmk. 326 Engr.

1050 A378 40g slate blue .15 .15
1051 A379 60g dark gray .24 .15
1052 A378 1.50z dark violet .52 .22
Nos. 1050-1052 (3) .91
Set value .38

Issued during International Resistance Movement Month to commemorate the millions who died in concentration camps, 1940-45.

Bicyclist A380

Designs: 2.50z, Cyclists in race. 3.40z, Wheel and arms of Berlin, Prague and Warsaw.

Unwmk.

1962, Apr. 27 Litho. *Perf. 12*

1053 A380 60g blue & blk .15 .15
1054 A380 2.50z yellow & blk .35 .15
1055 A380 3.40z lilac & blk .52 .20
Nos. 1053-1055 (3) 1.02
Set value .40

15th Intl. Peace Bicycle Race, Warsaw-Berlin-Prague.

Size of #1053, 1055: 36x22mm, #1054: 74x22mm.

Lenin in Bialy Dunajec A381

Karol Swierczewski-Walter A382

Designs: 60g, Lenin. 2.50z, Lenin and Cracow fortifications.

Engraved and Photogravure

Perf. 11x11½

1962, May 25 Wmk. 326

1056 A381 40g pale grn & Prus grn .50 .15
1057 A381 60g pink & dp claret .15 .15
1058 A381 2.50z yellow & dk brn .32 .15
Nos. 1056-1058 (3) .97
Set value .36

50th anniv. of Lenin's arrival in Poland.

Famous Poles Type of 1961

Famous Poles: No. 1059, Adam Mickiewicz. No. 1060, Juliusz Slowacki. No. 1061, Frederic Chopin. No. 1062, Romuald Traugutt. No. 1063, Jaroslaw Dabrowski. No. 1064, Maria Konopnicka.

1962, June 20 Engr. & Photo.

Black Inscriptions and Designs

1059 A359 60g dull green .20 .15
1060 A359 60g brown orange .15 .15

Perf. 12x12½

Litho.

1061 A359 60g dull blue .15 .15
1062 A359 60g brown olive .15 .15
1063 A359 60g rose lilac .15 .15
1064 A359 60g blue green .15 .15
Set value .80 .52

Perf. 11x11½

1962, July 14 Engr. Unwmk.

1065 A382 60g black .15 .15

15th death anniv. of General Karol Swierczewski-Walter, organizer of the new Polish army.

Crocus A383

The Poisoned Well by Jacek Malczewski A384

Flowers: No. 1067, Orchid. No. 1068, Monkshood. No. 1069, Gas plant. No. 1070, Water lily. No. 1071, Gentian. No. 1072, Daphne mezereum. No. 1073, Cowbell. No. 1074, Anemone. No. 1075, Globeflower. No. 1076, Snowdrop. No. 1077, Adonis vernalis.

Unwmk.

1962, Aug. 8 Photo. *Perf. 12*

Flowers in Natural Colors

1066 A383 60g dull yel & red .20 .15
1067 A383 60g redsh brn & vio 1.00 .42
1068 A383 60g pink & lilac .15 .15
1069 A383 90g olive & green .20 .15
1070 A383 90g yel grn & red .20 .15
1071 A383 90g lt ol grn & red .20 .15
1072 A383 1.50z gray bl & bl .32 .15
1073 A383 1.50z yel grn & dk grn .60 .18
1074 A383 1.50z Prus grn & dk bl .32 .15
1075 A383 2.50z gray grn & dk bl .80 .48
1076 A383 2.50z dk bl grn & dk bl .80 .48
1077 A383 2.50z gray bl & grn 1.25 .55
Nos. 1066-1077 (12) 6.04 3.16

1962, Aug. 15 Engr. Wmk. 326

1078 A384 60g black, *buff* .30 .15

Issued in sheets of 40 with alternating label for FIP Day (Federation Internationale de Philatelie), Sept. 1. Also issued in miniature sheet of 4. Value, $40.

Pole Vault — A385

Designs: 60g, Relay race. 90g, Javelin. 1z, Hurdles. 1.50z, High jump. 1.55z, Discus. 2.50z, 100m. dash. 3.40z, Hammer throw.

Unwmk.

1962, Sept. 12 Litho. *Perf. 11*

1079 A385 40g multicolored .15 .15
1080 A385 60g multicolored .15 .15
1081 A385 90g multicolored .15 .15
1082 A385 1z multicolored .15 .15
1083 A385 1.50z multicolored .15 .15
1084 A385 1.55z multicolored .20 .15
1085 A385 2.50z multicolored .35 .15
1086 A385 3.40z multicolored .90 .25
Nos. 1079-1086 (8) 2.20
Set value .80

7th European Athletic Championships, Belgrade, Sept. 12-16.

Exist imperf. Value, set $4.

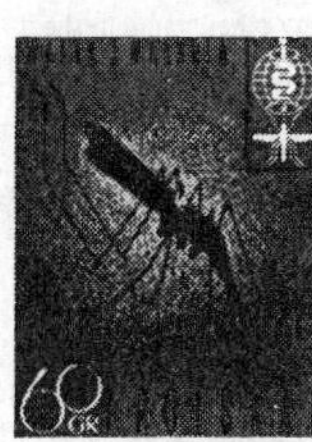
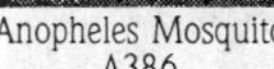

Anopheles Mosquito A386

Pavel R. Popovich and Andrian G. Nikolayev A387

Designs: 1.50z, Malaria blood cells. 2.50z, Cinchona flowers. 3z, Anopheles mosquito.

1962, Oct. 1 Wmk. 326 *Perf. 13x12*

1087 A386 60g ol blk, dk brn & bl grn .15 .15
1088 A386 1.50z red, gray & brt vio .16 .15
1089 A386 2.50z multicolored .38 .16
Nos. 1087-1089 (3) .69
Set value .28

Miniature Sheet

Imperf

1090 A386 3z multicolored 1.00 .60

WHO drive to eradicate malaria.

1962, Oct. 6 *Perf. 12½x12*

Design: 2.50z, Two stars in orbit around earth. 10z, Two stars in orbit.

1091 A387 60g violet, blk & cit .15 .15
1092 A387 2.50z Prus bl, blk & red .24 .15
Set value .22

Souvenir Sheet

Perf. 12x11

1093 A387 10z sl bl, blk & red 2.25 1.50

1st Russian group space flight, Vostoks III and IV, Aug. 11-15, 1962.

Woman Mailing Letter Warsaw — A388

1962, Oct. 9 Engr. *Perf. 12½x12*

1094 A388 60g black .15 .15
1095 A388 2.50z red brown .48 .15
Set value .25

Stamp Day. The design is from the painting "A Moment of Decision," by Anthony Kamienski.

Mazovian Princes' Mansion, — A389

1962, Oct. 13 Litho.

1096 A389 60g red & black .15 .15

25th anniversary of the founding of the Polish Democratic Party.

Cruiser "Aurora" — A390

Photo. & Engr.

1962, Nov. 3 *Perf. 11*

1097 A390 60g red & dk blue .15 .15

45th anniv. of the Russian October revolution.

Janusz Korczak by K. Dunikowski A391

King on Horseback A392

Illustrations from King Matthew books: 90g, King giving fruit to Island girl. 1z, King handcuffed and soldier with sword. 2.50z, King with dead bird. 5.60z, King ice skating in moonlight.

Perf. 13x12

1962, Nov. 12 Unwmk. Litho.

1098 A391 40g brown, bis & sep .15 .15
1099 A392 60g multicolored .15 .15
1100 A392 90g multicolored .30 .15
1101 A392 1z multicolored .30 .15
1102 A392 2.50z brn, yel & brt grn .55 .32
1103 A392 5.60z brn, dk bl & grn 2.00 .85
Nos. 1098-1103 (6) 3.45
Set value 1.50

20th anniversary of the death of Dr. Janusz Korczak (Henryk Goldszmit), physician, pedagogue and writer, in the Treblinka concentration camp, Aug. 5, 1942.

View of Old Warsaw — A393

1962, Nov. 26 Wmk. 326 *Perf. 11*

1104 A393 3.40z multicolored .42 .22
a. Sheet of 4 5.00 5.00

5th Trade Union Congress, Warsaw, Nov. 26-Dec. 1.

Orphan Mary and the Dwarf — A394

Various Scenes from "Orphan Mary and the Dwarfs" by Maria Konopnicka.

Perf. 13x12

1962, Dec. 31 Unwmk. Litho.

1105 A394 40g multicolored .30 .15
1106 A394 60g multicolored 2.00 1.00
1107 A394 1.50z multicolored .50 .15
1108 A394 1.55z multicolored .50 .15
1109 A394 2.50z multicolored .60 .35
1110 A394 3.40z multicolored 2.00 1.25
Nos. 1105-1110 (6) 5.90 3.05

120th anniversary of the birth of Maria Konopnicka, poet and fairy tale writer.

Romuald Traugutt A395

Perf. 11½x11

1963, Jan. 31 Wmk. 326

1111 A395 60g aqua, blk & pale pink .15 .15

Centenary of the 1863 insurrection and to honor its leader, Romuald Traugutt.

Tractor and Wheat — A396

Designs: 60g, Man reaping and millet. 2.50z, Combine and rice.

Perf. 12x12½

1963, Feb. 25 Litho. Wmk. 326

1112 A396 40g gray, bl, blk & ocher .15 .15
1113 A396 60g brn red, blk, brn & grn .52 .22
1114 A396 2.50z yel, buff, blk & grn .42 .15
Nos. 1112-1114 (3) 1.09
Set value .42

FAO "Freedom from Hunger" campaign.

Cocker Spaniel — A397

Dogs: 30g, Polish sheep dog. 40g, Boxer. 50g, Airedale terrier, vert. 60g, French bulldog, vert. 1z, Poodle, vert. 2.50z, Hunting dog. 3.40z, Sheep dog, vert. 6.50z, Great Dane.

1963, Mar. 25 Unwmk. *Perf. 12½*

1115 A397 20g lil, blk & org brn .15 .15
1116 A397 30g rose car & blk .15 .15
1117 A397 40g lil, blk & yel grn .20 .15
1118 A397 50g multicolored .30 .15
1119 A397 60g lt blue & blk .38 .15
1120 A397 1z yellow grn & blk .70 .55
1121 A397 2.50z orange, blk & brn 1.25 .52
1122 A397 3.40z red orange & blk 2.75 1.10
1123 A397 6.50z brt yellow & blk 4.75 3.00
Nos. 1115-1123 (9) 10.63 5.92

Egyptian Ship — A398

Fighter and Ruins of Warsaw Ghetto — A399

Ancient Ships: 10g, Phoenician merchant ship. 20g, Greek trireme. 30g, 3rd century merchantman. 40g, Scandinavian "Gokstad." 60g, Frisian "Kogge." 1z, 14th century "Holk." 1.15z, 15th century "Caraca."

Photo. (Background) & Engr.

1963, Apr. 5 *Perf. 11½*

1124 A398 5g brown, *tan* .15 .15
1125 A398 10g green, *gray grn* .15 .15
1126 A398 20g ultra, *gray* .15 .15
1127 A398 30g black, *gray ol* .15 .15
1128 A398 40g lt bl, *bluish* .15 .15
1129 A398 60g claret, *gray* .15 .15
1130 A398 1z black, *bl* .15 .15
1131 A398 1.15z grn, *pale rose* .35 .15
Set value .85 .50

See Nos. 1206-1213, 1299-1306.

Perf. 11½x11

1963, Apr. 19 Wmk. 326

1132 A399 2.50z gray brn & gray .32 .15

Warsaw Ghetto Uprising, 20th anniv.

Centenary Emblem — A400

Perf. 12½x12

1963, May 8 Litho. Unwmk.

1133 A400 2.50z blue, yel & red .40 .15

Intl. Red Cross, cent. Every other stamp in sheet inverted.

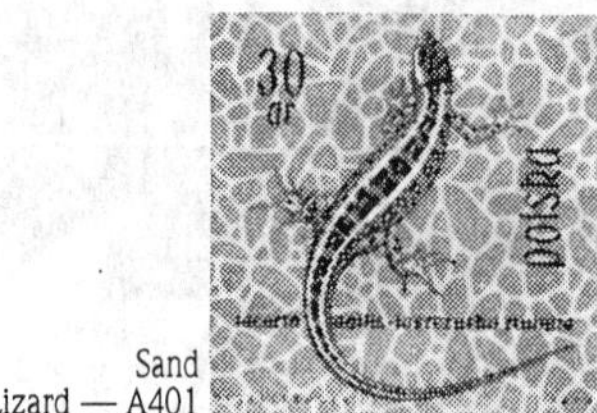

Sand Lizard — A401

40g, Smooth snake. 50g, European pond turtle. 60g, Grass snake. 90g, Slow worm. 1.15z, European tree frog. 1.35z, Alpine newt. 1.50z, Crested newt. 1.55z, Green toad. 2.50z, Firebellied toad. 3z, Fire salamander. 3.40z, Natterjack.

Perf. 11½

1963, June 1 Unwmk. Photo.

Reptiles and Amphibians in Natural Colors

1134 A401 30g grnsh gray & blk .15 .15
1135 A401 40g gray ol & blk .15 .15
1136 A401 50g bis brn & blk .16 .15
1137 A401 60g tan & blk .16 .15
1138 A401 90g gray grn & blk .16 .15
1139 A401 1.15z gray & blk .16 .15
1140 A401 1.35z gray bl & dk bl .35 .16
1141 A401 1.50z bluish grn & blk .42 .25
1142 A401 1.55z bluish gray & blk .35 .16
1143 A401 2.50z gray vio & blk .35 .16
1144 A401 3z gray grn & blk .75 .32
1145 A401 3.40z gray & blk 2.25 1.50
Nos. 1134-1145 (12) 5.41
Set value 3.00

Foil, Saber, Sword and Helmet A402

Designs: 40g, Fencers and knights in armor. 60g, Fencers and dragoons. 1.15z, Contemporary and 18th cent. fencers. 1.55z, Fencers and old houses, Gdansk. 6.50z, Arms of Gdansk, vert.

Perf. 12x12½, 12½x12

1963, June 29 Litho. Unwmk.

1146 A402 20g brown & orange .15 .15
1147 A402 40g dk blue & blue .15 .15
1148 A402 60g red & dp orange .15 .15
1149 A402 1.15z green & emerald .15 .15
1150 A402 1.55z violet & lilac .35 .15
1151 A402 6.50z yel brn, mar & yel 1.25 .45
Nos. 1146-1151 (6) 2.20
Set value .88

28th World Fencing Championships, Gdansk, July 15-28. A souvenir sheet exists containing one each of Nos. 1147-1150. Value, $40.

Famous Poles Type of 1961

No. 1152, Ludwik Warynski. No. 1153, Ludwik Krzywicki. No. 1154, Marie Sklodowska Curie. No. 1155, Karol Swierczewski-Walter.

Perf. 12x12½

1963, July 20 Wmk. 326

Black Inscriptions and Designs

1152 A359 60g red brown .15 .15
1153 A359 60g gray brown .15 .15
1154 A359 60g blue .30 .15
1155 A359 60g green .15 .15
Set value .50 .38

Valeri Bykovski — A403

Designs: 60g, Valentina Tereshkova. 6.50z, Rockets "Falcon" and "Mew" and globe.

Unwmk.

1963, Aug. 26 Litho. *Perf. 11*

1156 A403 40g ultra, emer & blk .15 .15
1157 A403 60g green, ultra & blk .15 .15
1158 A403 6.50z multicolored 1.25 .40
Nos. 1156-1158 (3) 1.55
Set value .55

Space flights of Valeri Bykovski June 14-19, and Valentina Tereshkova, first woman cosmonaut, June 16-19, 1963.

For overprints see Nos. 1175-1177.

Basketball A404

Designs: Various positions of ball, hands and players. 10z, Town Hall, People's Hall and Arms of Wroclaw.

1963, Sept. 16 Unwmk. *Perf. 11½*

1159 A404 40g multicolored .15 .15
1160 A404 50g fawn, grn & blk .15 .15
1161 A404 60g red, lt grn & blk .15 .15
1162 A404 90g multicolored .15 .15
1163 A404 2.50z multicolored .25 .15
1164 A404 5.60z multicolored 1.25 .28
Set value 1.75 .65

Souvenir Sheet

Imperf

1165 A404 10z multicolored 2.50 1.25

13th European Men's Basketball Championship, Wroclaw, Oct. 4-13. No. 1165 contains one stamp; inscription on margin also commemorates the simultaneous European Sports Stamp Exhibition. Sheet sold for 15z.

Eagle and Ground-to-Air Missile A405

Eagle and: 40g, Destroyer. 60g, Jet fighter plane. 1.15z, Radar. 1.35z, Tank. 1.55z, Self-propelled rocket launcher. 2.50z, Amphibious troop carrier. 3z, Swords and medieval and modern soldiers.

1963, Oct. 1 *Perf. 12x12½*

1166 A405 20g multicolored .15 .15
1167 A405 40g violet, grn & red .15 .15
1168 A405 60g multicolored .15 .15
1169 A405 1.15z multicolored .16 .15
1170 A405 1.35z multicolored .16 .15
1171 A405 1.55z multicolored .16 .15
1172 A405 2.50z multicolored .25 .15
1173 A405 3z multicolored .55 .18
Set value 1.50 .60

Polish People's Army, 20th anniversary.

"Love Letter" by Wladyslaw Czachórski — A406

Perf. 11½

1963, Oct. 9 Unwmk. Engr.

1174 A406 60g dark red brown .20 .15

Issued for Stamp Day.

Nos. 1156-1158 Overprinted: "23-28 X. 1963" and name of astronaut

1963 Litho. *Perf. 11*

1175 A403 40g ultra, emer & blk .25 .15
1176 A403 60g green, ultra & blk .30 .15
1177 A403 6.50z multicolored 1.50 .80
Nos. 1175-1177 (3) 2.05 1.10

Visit of Valentina Tereshkova and Valeri Bykovski to Poland, Oct. 23-28. The overprints are: 40g, W. F. Bykowski / w Polsce; 60g, W. W. Tierieszkowa / w Polsce; 6.50z, W. F. BYKOWSKI I W. W. TIERIESZKOWA W POLSCE.

Konstantin E. Tsiolkovsky's Rocket and Rocket Speed Formula — A407

American and Russian Spacecrafts: 40g, Sputnik 1. 50g, Explorer 1. 60g, Lunik 2. 1z, Lunik 3. 1.50z, Vostok 1. 1.55z, Friendship 7. 2.50z, Vostoks 3 & 4. 5.60z, Mariner 2. 6.50z, Mars 1.

Perf. 12½x12

1963, Nov. 11 Litho. Unwmk.

Black Inscriptions

1178 A407 30g dull bl grn & gray .15 .15
1179 A407 40g lt ol grn & gray .15 .15
1180 A407 50g violet bl & gray .15 .15
1181 A407 60g brown org & gray .15 .15
1182 A407 1z brt green & gray .15 .15
1183 A407 1.50z orange red & gray .15 .15
1184 A407 1.55z blue & gray .15 .15
1185 A407 2.50z lilac & gray .15 .15
1186 A407 5.60z brt yel grn & gray .50 .25
1187 A407 6.50z grnsh blue & gray .90 .30
Set value 2.00 1.00

Conquest of space. A souvenir sheet contains 2 each of Nos. 1186-1187. Value $40.

Arab Stallion "Comet" — A408

Horses from Mazury Region — A409

Horses: 30g, Tarpans (wild horses). 40g, Horse from Sokolka. 50g, Arab mares and foals, horiz. 90g, Steeplechasers, horiz. 1.55z, Arab stallion "Witez II." 2.50z, Head of Arab horse, facing right. 4z, Mixed breeds, horiz. 6.50z, Head of Arab horse, facing left.

Perf. 11½x11 (A408); 12½x12, 12

1963, Dec. 30 Photo.

1188 A408 20g black, yel & car .15 .15
1189 A408 30g multicolored .16 .15
1190 A408 40g multicolored .16 .15

Sizes: 75x26mm (50g, 90g, 4z); 28x38mm (60g, 1.55z, 2.50z, 6.50z)

1191 A409 50g multicolored .20 .15
1192 A409 60g yel, dp rose & blk .20 .15
1193 A409 90g multicolored .28 .15
1194 A409 1.55z multicolored .48 .18
1195 A409 2.50z multicolored .60 .18
1196 A409 4z multicolored 1.40 .48
1197 A409 6.50z yel, dl bl & blk 2.50 1.50
Nos. 1188-1197 (10) 6.13 3.24

Issued to publicize Polish horse breeding.

Ice Hockey A410

Sports: 30g, Slalom. 40g, Skiing. 60g, Speed skating. 1z, Ski jump. 2.50z, Tobogganing. 5.60z, Cross-country skiing. 6.50z, Figure skating pair.

1964, Jan. 25 Litho. *Perf. 12x12½*

1198 A410 20g multicolored .15 .15
1199 A410 30g multicolored .15 .15
1200 A410 40g multicolored .15 .15
1201 A410 60g multicolored .15 .15
1202 A410 1z multicolored .28 .15
1203 A410 2.50z multicolored .48 .18
1204 A410 5.60z multicolored .75 .35
1205 A410 6.50z multicolored 1.25 .70
Nos. 1198-1205 (8) 3.36
Set value 1.50

9th Winter Olympic Games, Innsbruck, Jan. 29-Feb. 9. A souvenir sheet contains 2 each of Nos. 1203, 1205. Value $35.

Ship Type of 1963

Sailing Ships: 1.35z, Caravel of Columbus, vert. 1.50z, Galleon. 1.55z, Polish warship, 1627, vert. 2z, Dutch merchant ship, vert. 2.10z, Line ship. 2.50z, Frigate. 3z, 19th century merchantman. 3.40z, "Dar Pomorza," 20th century school ship, vert.

1964, Mar. 19 Engr. *Perf. 12½*

1206 A398 1.35z ultra .15 .15
1207 A398 1.50z claret .15 .15
1208 A398 1.55z black .15 .15
1209 A398 2z violet .15 .15
1210 A398 2.10z green .15 .15
1211 A398 2.50z carmine rose .25 .15
1212 A398 3z olive green .40 .15
1213 A398 3.40z brown .55 .15
Nos. 1206-1213 (8) 1.95
Set value .75

European Cat — A411

40g, 60g, 1.55z, 2.50z, 6.50z, Various European cats. 50g, Siamese cat. 90g, 1.35z, 3.40z, Various Persian cats. 60g, 90g, 1.35z, 1.55z horiz.

1964, Apr. 30 Litho. *Perf. 12½*

Cats in Natural Colors; Black Inscriptions

1216 A411 30g yellow .15 .15
1217 A411 40g orange .15 .15
1218 A411 50g yellow .15 .15
1219 A411 60g brt green .38 .15
1220 A411 90g lt brown .15 .15
1221 A411 1.35z emerald .15 .15
1222 A411 1.55z violet blue .55 .20
1223 A411 2.50z lilac 1.50 .60
1224 A411 3.40z rose 1.90 1.00
1225 A411 6.50z violet 3.50 1.65
Nos. 1216-1225 (10) 8.58 4.35

King Casimir III, the Great — A412

Designs: No. 1227, Hugo Kollataj. No. 1228, Jan Dlugosz. No. 1229, Nicolaus Copernicus. 2.50z, King Wladyslaw II Jagiello and Queen Jadwiga.

1964, May 5 Engr. *Perf. 11x11½*

Size: 22x35mm

1226 A412 40g dull claret .15 .15
1227 A412 40g green .15 .15
1228 A412 60g violet .15 .15
1229 A412 60g dark blue .15 .15

Size: 35½x37mm

1230 A412 2.50z gray brown .35 .15
Set value .78 .35

Jagiellonian University, Cracow, 600th anniv.

Lapwing A413

Waterfowl: 40g, White-spotted bluethroat. 50g, Black-tailed godwit. 60g, Osprey. 90g, Gray heron. 1.35z, Little gull. 1.55z, Shoveler. 5.60z, Arctic loon. 6.50z, Great crested grebe.

Perf. 11½

1964, June 5 Unwmk. Photo.

Birds in Natural Colors; Black Inscriptions

Size: 34x34mm

1231 A413 30g chalky blue .15 .15
1232 A413 40g bister .15 .15
1233 A413 50g brt yellow grn .15 .15

Perf. 11½x11

Size: 34x48mm

1234 A413 60g blue .15 .15
1235 A413 90g lemon .15 .15
1236 A413 1.35z green .30 .15

Perf. 11½

Size: 34x34mm

1237 A413 1.55z olive .30 .16
1238 A413 5.60z blue green .90 .40
1239 A413 6.50z brt green 1.50 .60
Nos. 1231-1239 (9) 3.75
Set value 1.45

Hands Holding Red Flag — A414

Designs: No. 1241, Red and white ribbon around hammer. No. 1242, Hammer and rye. No. 1243, Brick wall under construction and red flag.

1964, June 15 Litho. *Perf. 11*

1240 A414 60g ol bis, red, blk & pink .15 .15
1241 A414 60g red, gray & black .15 .15
1242 A414 60g magenta, blk & yel .15 .15
1243 A414 60g gray, red, sal & blk .15 .15
Set value .36 .32

4th congress of the Polish United Workers Party.

Symbols of Peasant-Worker Alliance — A415

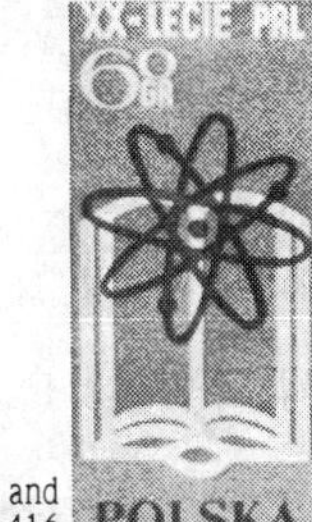

Atom Symbol and Book — A416

Shipyard, Gdansk — A417

Designs: No. 1245, Stylized oak. No. 1247, Factory and cogwheel. No. 1248, Tractor and grain. No. 1249, Pen, brush, mask and ornament. No. 1251, Lenin Metal Works, Nowa Huta. No. 1252, Cement factory, Chelm. No. 1253, Power Station, Turoszow. No. 1254, Oil refinery, Plock. No. 1255, Sulphur mine, Tarnobrzeg.

1964 Litho. *Perf. 12x12½*

1244 A415 60g red, org & blk .15 .15
1245 A415 60g grn, red, ocher, bl & blk .15 .15

Photo.

Perf. 11

1246 A416 60g gray & dp vio bl .15 .15
1247 A416 60g brt blue & blk .15 .15
1248 A416 60g emerald & blk .15 .15
1249 A416 60g orange & red .15 .15

Photogravure and Engraved

1250 A417 60g dl bl grn & ultra .15 .15
1251 A417 60g brt pink & pur .15 .15
1252 A417 60g gray & gray brn .15 .15
1253 A417 60g grn & slate grn .15 .15
1254 A417 60g salmon & claret .15 .15
1255 A417 60g citron & sepia .15 .15
Set value .95 .70

20th anniversary of the Polish People's Republic.

Warsaw Fighters, 1944 — A418

1964, Aug. 1 Litho. *Perf. 12½x12*

1256 A418 60g multicolored .15 .15

20th anniv. of the Warsaw insurrection against German occupation.

Running — A419

Women's High Jump — A420

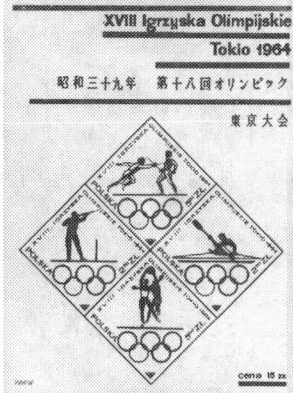

XVIII Igrzyska Olimpijskie
Tokio 1964
昭和三十九年 第十八回オリンピック
東京大会

Olympic Sports — A421

Sport: 40g, Rowing (single). 60g, Weight lifting. 90g, Relay race (square). 1z, Boxing (square). 2.50z, Soccer (square). 6.50z, Diving.

Unwmk.

1964, Aug. 17 Litho. *Perf. 11*

1257 A419 20g multicolored .15 .15
1258 A419 40g grnsh bl, bl & yel .15 .15
1259 A419 60g vio bl, red & rose lil .15 .15
1260 A419 90g dk brown, red & yel .18 .15
1261 A419 1z dk violet, lil & gray .18 .15
1262 A419 2.50z multicolored .38 .20
1263 A420 5.60z multicolored .95 .48
1264 A420 6.50z multicolored 1.50 .80
Nos. 1257-1264 (8) 3.64
Set value 1.80

Souvenir Sheet

Imperf

1265 A421 Sheet of 4 3.50 1.65
a. 2.50z Sharpshooting .45 .22
b. 2.50z Canoeing .45 .22
c. 5z Fencing .45 .22
d. 5z Basketball .45 .22

18th Olympic Games, Tokyo, Oct. 10-25. Size of stamps in No. 1265: 24x24mm. A souvenir sheet containing 2 each of Nos. 1263-1264 with black marginal inscription exists. Value $45.

Warsaw Mermaid and Stars A422

Stefan Zeromski by Monika Zeromska A423

1964, Sept. 7 *Perf. 12½x12*

1266 A422 2.50z violet & black .40 .15

15th Astronautical Congress, Warsaw, Sept. 7-12.

1964, Sept. 21 Photo. *Perf. 12½*

1267 A423 60g olive gray .20 .15

Stefan Zeromski (1864-1925), writer.

Gun and Hand Holding Hammer — A424

Globe and Red Flag — A425

1964, Sept. 21 Litho. *Perf. 11*

1268 A424 60g brt grn, blk & red .15 .15

3rd Miners' Militia Cong., Warsaw, Sept. 24-26.

1964, Sept. 28 Photo. *Perf. 12½*

1269 A425 60g black & red orange .15 .15

First Socialist International, centenary.

Stagecoach by Jozef Brodowski — A426

1964, Oct. 9 Engr. *Perf. 11½*

1270 A426 60g green .15 .15
1271 A426 60g lt brown .15 .15
Set value .16

Issued for Stamp Day.

Eleanor Roosevelt (1884-1962) — A427

1964, Oct. 10 *Perf. 12½*

1272 A427 2.50z black .20 .15

Proposed Monument for Defenders of Westerplatte, 1939 — A428

Polish Soldiers Crossing Oder River, 1945 A429

Designs: No. 1274, Virtuti Military Cross. No. 1275, Nike, proposed monument for the martyrs of Bydgoszcz (woman with sword and torch). No. 1277, Battle of Studzianki, 1944.

Perf. 12x11, 11x12

1964, Nov. 16 Engr. Unwmk.

1273 A428 40g blue violet .15 .15
1274 A428 40g slate .15 .15
1275 A428 60g dark blue .15 .15
1276 A429 60g dark blue grn .15 .15
1277 A429 60g grnsh black .15 .15
Set value .45 .25

Struggle and martyrdom of the Polish people, 1939-45. The vertical stamps are printed in sheets of 56 stamps (8x7) with 7 labels in each outside vertical row. The horizontal stamps are printed in sheets of 50 stamps (5x10) with 10 labels in each outside vertical row. See Nos. 1366-1368.

Souvenir Sheet

Col. Vladimir M. Komarov, Boris B. Yegorov and Dr. Konstantin Feoktistov — A430

1964, Nov. 21 Litho. *Perf. 11½x11*

1278 A430 Sheet of 3 1.25 .70
a. 60g red & black (Komarov) .35 .15
b. 60g brt grn & blk (Feoktistov) .35 .15
c. 60g ultra & blk (Yegorov) .35 .15

Russian three-manned space flight in space ship Voskhod, Oct. 12-13, 1964. Size of stamps: 27x36mm.

Cyclamen A431

Garden Flowers: 30g, Freesia. 40g, Monique rose. 50g, Peony. 60g, Royal lily. 90g, Oriental poppy. 1.35z, Tulip. 1.50z, Narcissus. 1.55z, Begonia. 2.50z, Carnation. 3.40z, Iris. 5.60z, Camellia.

1964, Nov. 30 Photo. *Perf. 11*

Size: 35½x35½mm

Flowers in Natural Colors

1279 A431 20g violet .15 .15
1280 A431 30g deep lilac .15 .15
1281 A431 40g blue .15 .15
1282 A431 50g violet blue .15 .15
1283 A431 60g lilac .15 .15
1284 A431 90g deep green .15 .15

Size: 26x37½mm

1285 A431 1.35z dark blue .15 .15
1286 A431 1.50z deep carmine .42 .26
1287 A431 1.55z green .15 .15
1288 A431 2.50z ultra .38 .15
1289 A431 3.40z redsh brown .75 .26
1290 A431 5.60z olive gray 1.40 .65
Nos. 1279-1290 (12) 4.15
Set value 1.75

Future Interplanetary Spacecraft — A432

Designs: 30g, Launching of Russian rocket. 40g, Dog Laika and launching tower. 60g, Lunik 3 photographing far side of the Moon. 1.55z, Satellite exploring the ionosphere. 2.50z, Satellite "Elektron 2" exploring radiation belt. 5.60z, "Mars 1" between Mars and Earth.

Perf. 12½x12

1964, Dec. 30 Litho. Unwmk.

1291 A432 20g multicolored .15 .15
1292 A432 30g multicolored .15 .15
1293 A432 40g ol grn, blk & bl .15 .15
1294 A432 60g dk bl, blk & dk red .15 .15
1295 A432 1.55z gray & multi .25 .15
1296 A432 2.50z multicolored .52 .15
1297 A432 5.60z multicolored .90 .40
Nos. 1291-1297,B108 (8) 3.77
Set value 1.45

Issued to publicize space research.

Warsaw Mermaid, Ruins and New Buildings A433

1965, Jan. 15 Engr. *Perf. 11x11½*

1298 A433 60g slate green .15 .15

Liberation of Warsaw, 20th anniversary.

Ship Type of 1963

Designs as before.

1965, Jan. 25 Engr. *Perf. 12½*

1299 A398 5g dark brown .15 .15
1300 A398 10g slate green .15 .15
1301 A398 20g slate blue .15 .15
1302 A398 30g gray olive .15 .15
1303 A398 40g dark blue .15 .15
1304 A398 60g claret .15 .15
1305 A398 1z red brown .15 .15
1306 A398 1.15z dk red brown .15 .15
Set value .65 .50

Edaphosaurus — A434

Dinosaurs: 30g, Cryptocleidus, vert. 40g, Brontosaurus. 60g, Mesosaurus, vert. 90g, Stegosaurus. 1.15z, Brachiosaurus, vert. 1.35z, Styracosaurus. 3.40z, Corythosaurus, vert. 5.60z, Rhamphorhynchus, vert. 6.50z, Tyrannosaurus.

1965, Mar. 5 Litho. *Perf. 12½*

1307 A434 20g multicolored .15 .15
1308 A434 30g multicolored .15 .15
1309 A434 40g multicolored .15 .15
1310 A434 60g multicolored .15 .15
1311 A434 90g multicolored .32 .15
1312 A434 1.15z multicolored .16 .15
1313 A434 1.35z multicolored .18 .15
1314 A434 3.40z multicolored .48 .16
1315 A434 5.60z multicolored 1.10 .35
1316 A434 6.50z multicolored 1.65 .90
Nos. 1307-1316 (10) 4.49
Set value 2.00

See Nos. 1395-1403.

Symbolic Wax Seal — A435

Russian and Polish Flags, Oil Refinery-Chemical Plant, Plock — A436

1965, Apr. 21 *Perf. 12½x12, 12½*

1317 A435 60g multicolored .15 .15
1318 A436 60g multicolored .15 .15
Set value .20 .16

20th anniversary of the signing of the Polish-Soviet treaty of friendship, mutual assistance and postwar cooperation.

Polish Eagle and Town Coats of Arms — A437

1965, May 8 Engr. *Perf. 11½*

1319 A437 60g carmine rose .15 .15

20th anniversary of regaining the Western and Northern Territories.

Dove — A438

1965, May 8 Litho. *Perf. 12x12½*

1320 A438 60g red & black .15 .15

Victory over Fascism, 20th anniversary.

ITU Emblem — A439

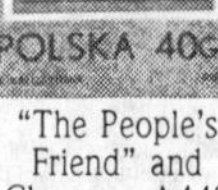

"The People's Friend" and Clover — A440

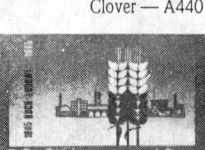

Factory and Rye — A441

Perf. 12½x12

1965, May 17 Litho. Unwmk.

1321 A439 2.50z brt bl, lil, yel & blk .45 .15

ITU, cent.

1965, June 5 *Perf. 11*

1322 A440 40g multicolored .15 .15
1323 A441 60g multicolored .15 .15
Set value .20 .15

"Popular Movement" in Poland, 70th anniv.

Finn Class Yachts A442

Yachts: 30g, Dragon class. 40g, 5.5-m. class. 50g, Group of Finn class. 60g, V-class. 1.35z, Group of Cadet class. 4z, Group of Star class. 5.60z, Two Flying Dutchmen. 6.50z, Two Amethyst class. 15z, Finn class race. (30g, 40g, 60g, 5.60z vertical.)

1965, June 14 Litho. *Perf. 12½*

1324 A442 30g multicolored .15 .15
1325 A442 40g multicolored .15 .15
1326 A442 50g multicolored .15 .15
1327 A442 60g multicolored .15 .15
1328 A442 1.35z multicolored .16 .15
1329 A442 4z multicolored .55 .22
1330 A442 5.60z multicolored 1.00 .42
1331 A442 6.50z multicolored 1.65 .70
Nos. 1324-1331 (8) 3.96
Set value 1.75

Miniature Sheet

Perf. 11

1332 A442 15z multicolored 2.00 1.25

World Championships of Finn Class Yachts, Gdynia, July 22-29. No. 1332 contains one stamp 48x22mm.

Marx and Lenin — A443

Photogravure and Engraved

1965, June 14 *Perf. 11½x11*

1333 A443 60g black, *ver* .15 .15

6th Conference of Ministers of Post of Communist Countries, Peking, June 21-July 15.

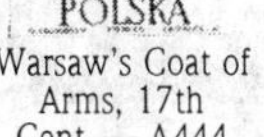

Warsaw's Coat of Arms, 17th Cent. — A444

Old Town Hall, 18th Cent. — A445

Designs: 10g, Artifacts, 13th century. 20g, Tombstone of last Duke of Mazovia. 60g, Barbican, Gothic-Renaissance castle. 1.50z, Arsenal, 19th century. 1.55z, National Theater. 2.50z, Staszic Palace. 3.40z, Woman with sword from Heroes' Memorial and Warsaw Mermaid seal.

Perf. 11x11½, 11½x11, 12x12½, 12½x12

1965, July 21 **Engr.** **Unwmk.**

1334 A444 5g carmine rose .15 .15
1335 A444 10g green .15 .15
1336 A445 20g violet blue .15 .15
1337 A445 40g brown .15 .15
1338 A445 60g orange .15 .15
1339 A445 1.50z black .15 .15
1340 A445 1.55z gray blue .15 .15
1341 A445 2.50z lilac .25 .15

Perf. 11½

Photogravure and Engraved

1342 A444 3.40z citron & blk .90 .60
Set value 1.60 1.05

700th anniversary of Warsaw.

No. 1342 is perforated all around, with lower right quarter perforated to form a 21x26mm stamp within a stamp. It was issued in sheets of 25 (5x5).

For surcharges see Nos. 1919-1926.

IQSY Emblem A446

Designs: 2.50z, Radar screen, Torun. 3.40z, Solar system.

1965, Aug. 9 **Litho.**

1343 A446 60g vio, ver, brt grn & blk .15 .15
a. 60g ultra, org, yel, bl & blk .15 .15
1344 A446 2.50z red, yel, pur & blk .25 .15
a. 2.50z red brn, yel, gray & blk .25 .15
1345 A446 3.40z orange & multi .32 .15
a. 3.40z ol gray & multi .32 .15
Nos. 1343-1345 (3) .72
Nos. 1343a-1345a (3) .72
Set value .26
Set value, #1343a-1345a .26

International Quiet Sun Year, 1964-65.

Odontoglossum Grande — A447

Weight Lifting — A448

Orchids: 30g, Cypripedium hibridum. 40g, Lycaste skinneri. 50g, Cattleya. 60g, Vanda sanderiana. 1.35z, Cypripedium hibridum. 4z, Sobralia. 5.60z, Disa grandiflora. 6.50z, Cattleya labiata.

1965, Sept. 6 **Photo.** *Perf. 12½x12*

1346 A447 20g multicolored .15 .15
1347 A447 30g multicolored .15 .15
1348 A447 40g multicolored .15 .15
1349 A447 50g multicolored .15 .15
1350 A447 60g multicolored .15 .15
1351 A447 1.35z multicolored .25 .15
1352 A447 4z multicolored .60 .30
1353 A447 5.60z multicolored 1.25 .40
1354 A447 6.50z multicolored 2.00 .75
Nos. 1346-1354 (9) 4.85
Set value 1.95

1965, Oct. 8 **Photo.** **Unwmk.**

Sport: 40g, Boxing. 50g, Relay race, men. 60g, Fencing. 90g, Women's 80-meter hurdles. 3.40z, Relay race, women. 6.50z, Hop, step and jump. 7.10z, Volleyball, women.

1355 A448 30g gold & multi .15 .15
1356 A448 40g gold & multi .15 .15
1357 A448 50g silver & multi .15 .15
1358 A448 60g gold & multi .15 .15
1359 A448 90g silver & multi .15 .15
1360 A448 3.40z gold & multi .50 .15
1361 A448 6.50z gold & multi .85 .42
1362 A448 7.10z bronze & multi 1.00 .60
Nos. 1355-1362 (8) 3.10
Set value 1.50

Victories won by the Polish team in 1964 Olympic Games. Each denomination printed in sheets of eight stamps and two center labels showing medals.

Mail Coach, by Piotr Michalowski A449

Design: 2.50z, Departure of Coach, by Piotr Michalowski.

1965, Oct. 9 **Engr.** *Perf. 11x11½*

1363 A449 60g brown .15 .15
1364 A449 2.50z slate green .22 .15
Set value .15

Issued for Stamp Day, 1965. Sheets of 50 with labels se-tenant inscribed "Dzien Znaczka 1965 R."

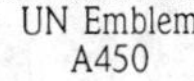

UN Emblem A450

Memorial, Plaszow A451

1965, Oct. 24 **Litho.** *Perf. 12½x12*

1365 A450 2.50z ultra .35 .15

20th anniversary of United Nations.

Perf. 12x11, 11x12

1965, Nov. 29 **Engr.**

Designs: No. 1367, Kielce Memorial. No. 1368, Chelm Memorial, horiz.

1366 A451 60g grnsh gray .15 .15
1367 A451 60g chocolate .15 .15
1368 A451 60g black .15 .15
Nos. 1366-1368 (3) .45
Set value .20

Note after #1277 applies also to #1366-1368.

Wolf — A452

1965, Nov. 30 **Photo.** *Perf. 11½*

1369 A452 20g shown .15 .15
1370 A452 30g Lynx .15 .15
1371 A452 40g Red fox .15 .15
1372 A452 50g Badger .15 .15
1373 A452 60g Brown bear .15 .15
1374 A452 1.50z Wild Boar .50 .15
1375 A452 2.50z Red deer .50 .15
1376 A452 5.60z European bison 1.10 .45
1377 A452 7.10z Moose 1.40 .90
Nos. 1369-1377 (9) 4.25
Set value 2.00

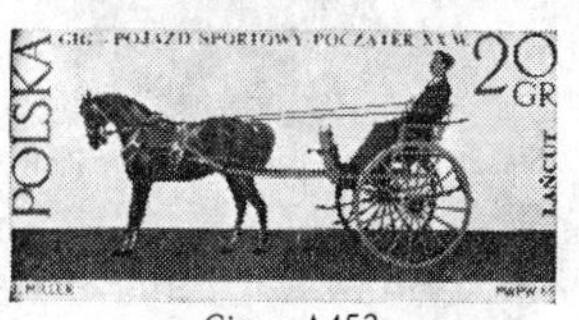

Gig — A453

Horse-drawn carriages, Lancut Museum: 40g, Coupé. 50g, Lady's basket. 60g, Vis-a-vis. 90g, Cab. 1.15z, Berlinka. 2.50z, Hunting break. 6.50z, Caleche à la Daumont. 7.10z, English break.

1965, Dec. 30 **Litho.** *Perf. 11*

Size: 50x23mm

1378 A453 20g multicolored .15 .15
1379 A453 40g lilac & multi .15 .15
1380 A453 50g orange & multi .15 .15
1381 A453 60g fawn & multi .15 .15
1382 A453 90g yellow & multi .15 .15

Size: 76x23mm

1383 A453 1.15z multicolored .15 .15
1384 A453 2.50z olive & multi .42 .20
1385 A453 6.50z multicolored 1.10 .45

Size: 103x23mm

1386 A453 7.10z blue & multi 2.00 .90
Nos. 1378-1386 (9) 4.42
Set value 1.90

Cargo Ship (No. 1389) — A454

Designs: No. 1387, Supervising Technical Organization (NOT) emblem, symbols of industry. No. 1388, Pit head and miners' badge, vert. No. 1390, Chemical plant, Plock. No. 1391, Combine. No. 1392, Railroad train. No. 1393, Building crane, vert. No. 1394, Pavilion and emblem of 35th International Poznan Fair.

1966 **Litho.** *Perf. 11*

1387 A454 60g multicolored .15 .15
1388 A454 60g multicolored .15 .15
1389 A454 60g multicolored .15 .15
1390 A454 60g multicolored .15 .15
1391 A454 60g multicolored .15 .15
1392 A454 60g multicolored .15 .15
1393 A454 60g multicolored .15 .15
1394 A454 60g multicolored .15 .15
Set value .75 .65

20th anniversary of the nationalization of Polish industry. No. 1394 also commemorates the 35th International Poznan Fair. Nos. 1387-1388 issued in connection with the 5th Congress of Polish Technicians, Katowice. Printed in sheets of 20 stamps and 20 labels with commemorative inscription within cogwheel on each label.

Issued: #1387-1388, Feb. 10; others, May 21.

Dinosaur Type of 1965

Prehistoric Vertebrates: 20g, Dinichthys. 30g, Eusthenopteron. 40g, Ichthyostega. 50g, Mastodonsaurus. 60g, Cynognathus. 2.50z, Archaeopteryx, vert. 3.40z, Brontotherium. 6.50z, Machairodus. 7.10z, Mammoth.

1966, Mar. 5 **Litho.** *Perf. 12½*

1395 A434 20g multicolored .15 .15
1396 A434 30g multicolored .15 .15
1397 A434 40g multicolored .15 .15
1398 A434 50g multicolored .15 .15
1399 A434 60g multicolored .28 .15
1400 A434 2.50z multicolored .35 .15
1401 A434 3.40z multicolored .55 .20
1402 A434 6.50z multicolored 1.25 .45
1403 A434 7.10z multicolored 2.00 .90
Nos. 1395-1403 (9) 5.03
Set value 1.95

Henryk Sienkiewicz A455

Photogravure and Engraved

1966, Mar. 30 *Perf. 11½*

1404 A455 60g black, *dl yel* .20 .15

Henryk Sienkiewicz (1846-1916), author and winner of 1905 Nobel Prize.

Soccer Game A456

Peace Dove and War Memorial A457

Designs: Various phases of soccer. Each stamp inscribed with the place and the result of final game in various preceding soccer championships.

1966, May 6 *Perf. 13x12*

1405 A456 20g multicolored .15 .15
1406 A456 40g multicolored .15 .15
1407 A456 60g multicolored .15 .15
1408 A456 90g multicolored .18 .15
1409 A456 1.50z multicolored .35 .18
1410 A456 3.40z multicolored .60 .24
1411 A456 6.50z multicolored 1.25 .60
1412 A456 7.10z multicolored 1.65 .95
Nos. 1405-1412 (8) 4.48 2.57

World Cup Soccer Championship, Wembley, England, July 11-30. Each denomination printed in sheets of 10 (5x2).

See No. B109.

Typo. & Engr.

1966, May 9 *Perf. 11½*

1413 A457 60g silver & multi .15 .15

21st anniversary of victory over Fascism.

Women's Relay Race — A458

Designs: 20g, Start of men's short distance race, vert. 60g, Javelin, vert. 90g, Women's 80-meter hurdles. 1.35z, Discus, vert. 3.40z, Finish of men's medium distance race. 6.50z, Hammer throw, vert 7.10z, High jump.

Perf. 11½x11, 11x11½

1966, June 18 **Litho.**

1414 A458 20g multicolored .15 .15
1415 A458 40g multicolored .15 .15
1416 A458 60g multicolored .15 .15
1417 A458 90g multicolored .15 .15
1418 A458 1.35z multicolored .16 .15
1419 A458 3.40z multicolored .48 .15
1420 A458 6.50z multicolored .65 .32
1421 A458 7.10z multicolored .85 .50
Nos. 1414-1421 (8) 2.74
Set value 1.30

Souvenir Sheet

Design: 5z, Long distance race.

Imperf

1422 A458 5z multicolored 1.75 .90

European Athletic Championships, Budapest, August, 1966. No. 1422 contains one 57x27mm stamp.

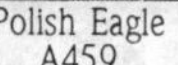

Polish Eagle
A459

Flowers and Farm Produce
A460

Designs: Nos. 1424, 1426, Flag of Poland. No. 1425, Polish Eagle.

Photogravure and Embossed
Perf. 12½x12

1966, July 21 Unwmk.
1423 A459 60g gold, red & blk .15 .15
1424 A459 60g gold, red & blk .15 .15
1425 A459 2.50z gold, red & blk .25 .15
1426 A459 2.50z gold, red & blk .25 .15
Set value .68 .40

1000th anniversary of Poland. Nos. 1423-1424 and 1425-1426 printed in 2 sheets of 10 (5x2); top row in each sheet in eagle design, bottom row in flag design.

1966, Aug. 15 Photo. *Perf. 11*

Designs: 60g, Woman holding loaf of bread. 3.40z, Farm girls holding harvest wreath.

Size: 22x50mm
1427 A460 40g gold & multi .22 .15
1428 A460 60g gold & multi .22 .15

Size: 48x50mm
1429 A460 3.40z violet bl & multi .55 .35
Nos. 1427-1429 (3) .99
Set value .50

Issued to publicize the harvest festival.

Chrysanthemum — A461

Flowers: 20g, Poinsettia. 30g, Centaury. 40g, Rose. 60g, Zinnias. 90g, Nasturtium. 5.60z, Dahlia. 6.50z, Sunflower. 7.10z, Magnolia.

1966, Sept. 1 *Perf. 11½*
Flowers in Natural Colors
1430 A461 10g gold & black .15 .15
1431 A461 20g gold & black .15 .15
1432 A461 30g gold & black .15 .15
1433 A461 40g gold & black .15 .15
1434 A461 60g gold & black .15 .15
1435 A461 90g gold & black .60 .25
1436 A461 5.60z gold & black .75 .25
1437 A461 6.50z gold & black 1.10 .52
1438 A461 7.10z gold & black .85 .65
Nos. 1430-1438 (9) 4.05
Set value 1.90

Map Showing Tourist Attractions — A462

Designs: 20g, Lighthouse, Hel. 40g, Amethyst yacht on Masurian Lake. No. 1442, Poniatowski Bridge, Warsaw, and sailboat. No. 1443, Mining Academy, Kielce. 1.15z, Dunajec Gorge. 1.35z, Old oaks, Rogalin. 1.55z, Planetarium, Katowice. 2z, M.S. Batory and globe.

Perf. 12½x12, 11½x12

1966, Sept. 15 Engr.
1439 A462 10g carmine rose .15 .15
1440 A462 20g olive gray .15 .15
1441 A462 40g grysh blue .15 .15
1442 A462 60g redsh brown .15 .15
1443 A462 60g black .15 .15
1444 A462 1.15z green .15 .15
1445 A462 1.35z vermilion .15 .15
1446 A462 1.55z violet .15 .15
1447 A462 2z dark gray .15 .15
Set value 1.10 .60

Stableman with Percherons, by Piotr Michalowski — A463

2.50z, "Horses and Dogs" by Michalowski.

1966, Sept. 8 *Perf. 11x11½*
1448 A463 60g gray brown .15 .15
1449 A463 2.50z green .18 .15
Set value .18

Issued for Stamp Day, 1966.

Capital of Romanesque Column from Tyniec and Polish Flag — A464

Engraved and Photogravure
1966, Oct. 7 *Perf. 11½*
1450 A464 60g dark brown & rose .15 .15

Polish Cultural Congress.

Soldier — A465

1966, Oct. 20 Litho. *Perf. 11x11½*
1451 A465 60g blk, ol grn, & dl red .15 .15

Participation of the Polish Jaroslaw Dabrowski Brigade in the Spanish Civil War.

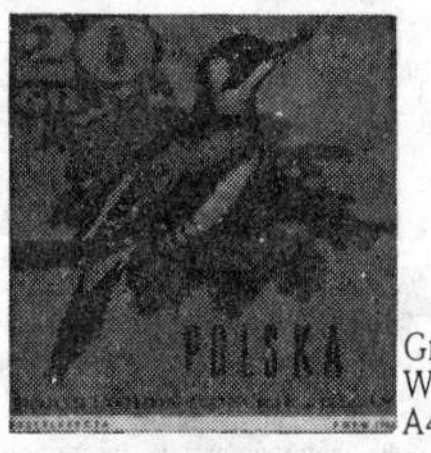

Green Woodpecker A466

Forest Birds: 10g, The eight birds of the set combined. 30g, Eurasian jay. 40g, European golden oriole. 60g, Hoopoe. 2.50z, European redstart. 4z, Siskin (finch). 6.50z, Chaffinch. 7.10z, Great tit.

1966, Nov. 17 Photo. *Perf. 11½*
Birds in Natural Colors; Black Inscription
1452 A466 10g lt green .15 .15
1453 A466 20g dull violet bl .15 .15
1454 A466 30g dull green .15 .15
1455 A466 40g gray .15 .15
1456 A466 60g gray green .15 .15
1457 A466 2.50z lt olive grn .40 .16
1458 A466 4z dull violet 1.40 .38
1459 A466 6.50z green 1.10 .45
1460 A466 7.10z gray blue 2.00 .75
Nos. 1452-1460 (9) 5.65 2.49

Ceramic Ram, c. 4000 B.C. — A467

Designs: No. 1462, Bronze weapons and ornaments, c. 3500 B.C., horiz. No. 1463, Biskupin, settlement plan, 2500 B.C.

1966, Dec. 10 Engr. *Perf. 11x11½*
1461 A467 60g dull violet blue .15 .15
1462 A467 60g brown .15 .15
1463 A467 60g green .15 .15
Set value .30 .24

Polish Eagle, Hammer and Grain — A468

Designs: 60g, Eagle and map of Poland.

1966, Dec. 20 Litho. *Perf. 11*
1464 A468 40g brn, red & bluish lil .15 .15
1465 A468 60g brn, red & ol grn .15 .15
Set value .16 .15

Millenium of Poland.

Gemini, American Spacecraft — A469

Spacecraft: 20g, Vostok (USSR). 60g, Ariel 2 (Great Britain). 1.35z, Proton 1 (USSR). 1.50z, FR 1 (France). 3.40z, Alouette (Canada). 6.50z, San Marco 1 (Italy). 7.10z, Luna 9 (USSR).

1966, Dec. 20 *Perf. 11½x11*
1466 A469 20g tan & multi .15 .15
1467 A469 40g brown & multi .15 .15
1468 A469 60g gray & multi .15 .15
1469 A469 1.35z multicolored .20 .15
1470 A469 1.50z multicolored .20 .15
1471 A469 3.40z multicolored .50 .16
1472 A469 6.50z multicolored 1.10 .22
1473 A469 7.10z multicolored 1.40 .48
Nos. 1466-1473 (8) 3.85
Set value 1.15

Dressage — A470

Horses: 20g, Horse race. 40g, Jump. 60g, Steeplechase. 90g, Trotting. 5.90z, Polo. 6.60z, Stallion "Ofir." 7z, Stallion "Skowronek."

1967, Feb. 25 Photo. *Perf. 12½*
1474 A470 10g ultra & multi .15 .15
1475 A470 20g orange & multi .15 .15
1476 A470 40g ver & multi .15 .15
1477 A470 60g multicolored .15 .15
1478 A470 90g green & multi .25 .15
1479 A470 5.90z multicolored .95 .20
1480 A470 6.60z multicolored 1.25 .45
1481 A470 7z violet & multi 2.25 1.00
Nos. 1474-1481 (8) 5.30
Set value 2.00

Janov Podlaski stud farm, 150th anniv.

Memorial at Auschwitz (Oswiecim) A471

Emblem of Memorials Administration — A472

Memorials at: No. 1484, Oswiecim-Monowice. No. 1485, Westerplatte (Walcz). No. 1486, Lodz-Radugoszcz. No. 1487, Stutthof. No. 1488, Lambinowice-Jencom. No. 1489, Zagan.

1967 Engr. *Perf. 11½x11, 11x11½*
1482 A471 40g brown olive .15 .15
1483 A472 40g dull violet .15 .15
1484 A472 40g black .15 .15
1485 A472 40g green .15 .15
1486 A472 40g black .15 .15
1487 A471 40g ultra .15 .15
1488 A471 40g brown .15 .15
1489 A472 40g deep plum .15 .15
Set value .64 .50

Issued to commemorate the martyrdom and fight of the Polish people, 1939-45.

Issue dates: Nos. 1482-1484, Apr. 10. Nos. 1485-1487, Oct. 9. Nos. 1488-1489, Dec. 28.

See Nos. 1620-1624.

Striped Butterflyfish A473

Tropical fish: 10g, Imperial angelfish. 40g, Barred butterflyfish. 60g, Spotted triggerfish. 90g, Undulate triggerfish. 1.50z, Striped triggerfish. 4.50z, Black-eye butterflyfish. 6.60z, Blue angelfish. 7z, Saddleback butterflyfish.

1967, Apr. 1 Litho. *Perf. 11x11½*
1492 A473 5g multicolored .15 .15
1493 A473 10g multicolored .15 .15
1494 A473 40g multicolored .15 .15
1495 A473 60g multicolored .15 .15
1496 A473 90g multicolored .15 .15
1497 A473 1.50z multicolored .20 .15
1498 A473 4.50z multicolored .70 .30
1499 A473 6.60z multicolored .85 .45
1500 A473 7z multicolored 1.50 .75
Nos. 1492-1500 (9) 4.00
Set value 1.90

Bicyclists — A474

1967, May 5 Litho. *Perf. 11*
1501 A474 60g multicolored .15 .15

20th Warsaw-Berlin-Prague Bicycle Race.

Men's 100-meter Race A475

Sports and Olympic Rings: 40g, Steeplechase. 60g, Women's relay race. 90g, Weight lifter. 1.35z, Hurdler. 3.40z, Gymnast on vaulting horse. 6.60z, High jump. 7z, Boxing.

1967, May 24 Litho. *Perf. 11*
1502 A475 20g multicolored .15 .15
1503 A475 40g multicolored .15 .15
1504 A475 60g multicolored .15 .15
1505 A475 90g multicolored .15 .15
1506 A475 1.35z multicolored .15 .15
1507 A475 3.40z multicolored .38 .15
1508 A475 6.60z multicolored .75 .24
1509 A475 7z multicolored .90 .52
Nos. 1502-1509 (8) 2.78
Set value 1.20

19th Olympic Games, Mexico City, 1968. Nos. 1502-1509 printed in sheets of 8, (2x4) with label showing emblem of Polish Olympic Committee between each two horizontal stamps. See No. B110.

Badge of Socialist Working Brigade A476

1967, June 2

No.	Type	Description	Unused	Used
1510	A476	60g multicolored	.15	.15

6th Congress of Polish Trade Unions. Printed in sheets of 20 stamps and 20 labels and in miniature sheets of 4 stamps and 4 labels.

Mountain Arnica — A477

Medicinal Plants: 60g, Columbine. 3.40z, Gentian. 4.50z, Ground pine. 5z, Iris sibirica. 10z, Azalea pontica.

1967, June 14 ***Perf. 11½x11***

Flowers in Natural Colors

No.	Type	Description	Unused	Used
1511	A477	40g black & brn org	.15	.15
1512	A477	60g black & lt blue	.15	.15
1513	A477	3.40z black & dp org	.35	.15
1514	A477	4.50z black & lt vio	.38	.15
1515	A477	5z black & maroon	.40	.15
1516	A477	10z black & bister	1.00	.42
		Nos. 1511-1516 (6)	2.43	
		Set value		.92

Monument for Silesian Insurgents A478

1967, July 21 **Litho.** ***Perf. 11½***

No.	Type	Description	Unused	Used
1517	A478	60g multicolored	.15	.15

Unveiling of the monument for the Silesian Insurgents of 1919-21 at Katowice, July, 1967.

Marie Curie — A479

Designs: No. 1519, Curie statue, Warsaw. No. 1520, Nobel Prize diploma.

1967, Aug. 1 **Engr.** ***Perf. 11½x11***

No.	Type	Description	Unused	Used
1518	A479	60g dk carmine rose	.18	.15
1519	A479	60g violet	.15	.15
1520	A479	60g sepia	.18	.15
		Nos. 1518-1520 (3)	.51	
		Set value		.24

Marie Sklodowska Curie (1867-1934), discoverer of radium and polonium.

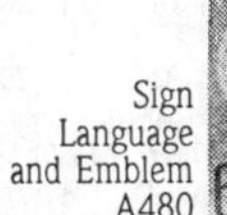

Sign Language and Emblem A480

1967, Aug. 1 **Litho.** ***Perf. 11x11½***

No.	Type	Description	Unused	Used
1521	A480	60g brt blue & blk	.15	.15

5th Congress of the World Federation of the Deaf, Warsaw, Aug. 10-17.

Flowers of the Meadows A481

Flowers: 40g, Poppy. 60g, Morning glory. 90g, Pansy. 1.15z, Common pansy. 2.50z, Corn cockle. 3.40z, Wild aster. 4.50z, Common pimpernel. 7.90z, Chicory.

1967, Sept. 5 **Photo.** ***Perf. 11½***

No.	Type	Description	Unused	Used
1522	A481	20g multicolored	.15	.15
1523	A481	40g multicolored	.15	.15
1524	A481	60g multicolored	.15	.15
1525	A481	90g multicolored	.15	.15
1526	A481	1.15z multicolored	.15	.15
1527	A481	2.50z multicolored	.32	.18
1528	A481	3.40z multicolored	.50	.18
1529	A481	4.50z multicolored	1.00	.52
1530	A481	7.90z multicolored	1.25	.52
		Nos. 1522-1530 (9)	3.82	
		Set value		1.75

Wilanow Palace, by Wincenty Kasprzycki A482

Engraved and Photogravure

1967, Oct. 9 ***Perf. 11½***

No.	Type	Description	Unused	Used
1531	A482	60g olive blk & lt bl	.15	.15

Issued for Stamp Day, 1967.

Cruiser Aurora — A483

Designs: No. 1533, Lenin and library. No. 1534, Luna 10, earth and moon.

1967, Oct. 9 **Litho.** ***Perf. 11***

No.	Type	Description	Unused	Used
1532	A483	60g gray, red & blk	.15	.15
1533	A483	60g gray, dull red & blk	.15	.15
1534	A483	60g gray, red & blk	.15	.15
		Nos. 1532-1534 (3)	.45	
		Set value		.26

Russian Revolution, 50th anniv.

Tadeusz Kosciusko — A485

Engraved and Photogravure

1967, Oct. 14 ***Perf. 12x11***

No.	Type	Description	Unused	Used
1540	A485	60g choc & ocher	.15	.15
1541	A485	2.50z sl grn & rose car	.15	.15
		Set value	.22	.22

Tadeusz Kosciusko (1746-1817), Polish patriot and general in the American Revolution.

Vanessa Butterfly A486

Designs: Various Butterflies.

1967, Oct. 14 **Litho.** ***Perf. 11½***

Butterflies in Natural Colors

No.	Type	Description	Unused	Used
1542	A486	10g green	.15	.15
1543	A486	20g lt violet bl	.15	.15
1544	A486	40g yellow green	.15	.15
1545	A486	60g gray	.15	.15
1546	A486	2z lemon	.25	.15
1547	A486	2.50z Prus green	.30	.15
1548	A486	3.40z blue	.50	.15
1549	A486	4.50z rose lilac	1.65	.45
1550	A486	7.90z bister	2.75	1.00
		Nos. 1542-1550 (9)	6.05	
		Set value		2.10

Polish Woman, by Antoine Watteau A487

Paintings from Polish Museums: 20g, Lady with the Ermine, by Leonardo da Vinci. 60g, Dog Fighting Heron, by Abraham Hondius. 2z, Guitarist after the Hunt, by J. Baptiste Greuze. 2.50z, Tax Collectors, by Marinus van Reymerswaele. 3.40z, Portrait of Daria Flodorowna, by Fiodor St. Rokotov. 4.50z, Still Life with Lobster, by Jean de Heem, horiz. 6.60z, Landscape (from the Good Samaritan), by Rembrandt, horiz.

Perf. 11½x11, 11x11½

1967, Nov. 15 **Photo.**

No.	Type	Description	Unused	Used
1551	A487	20g gold & multi	.15	.15
1552	A487	40g gold & multi	.15	.15
1553	A487	60g gold & multi	.15	.15
1554	A487	2z gold & multi	.20	.15
1555	A487	2.50z gold & multi	.28	.15
1556	A487	3.40z gold & multi	.40	.15
1557	A487	4.50z gold & multi	.95	.42
1558	A487	6.60z gold & multi	1.10	.70
		Nos. 1551-1558 (8)	3.38	
		Set value		1.75

Printed in sheets of 5 + label.

Ossolinski Medal, Book and Flags — A488

1967, Dec. 12 **Litho.** ***Perf. 11***

No.	Type	Description	Unused	Used
1559	A488	60g lt bl, red & lt brn	.15	.15

150th anniversary of the founding of the Ossolineum, a center for scientific and cultural activities, by Count Josef Maximilian Ossolinski.

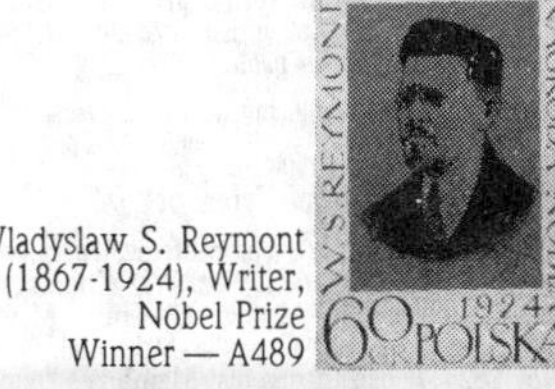

Wladyslaw S. Reymont (1867-1924), Writer, Nobel Prize Winner — A489

1967, Dec. 12

No.	Type	Description	Unused	Used
1560	A489	60g dk brn, ocher & red	.15	.15

Ice Hockey A490

Designs: 60g, Skiing. 90g, Slalom. 1.35z, Speed skating. 1.55z, Long-distance skiing. 2z, Sledding. 7z, Biathlon. 7.90z, Ski jump.

1968, Jan. 10

No.	Type	Description	Unused	Used
1561	A490	40g multicolored	.15	.15
1562	A490	60g multicolored	.15	.15
1563	A490	90g multicolored	.15	.15
1564	A490	1.35z multicolored	.15	.15
1565	A490	1.55z multicolored	.15	.15
1566	A490	2z multicolored	.20	.15
1567	A490	7z multicolored	.52	.35
1568	A490	7.90z multicolored	.85	.52
		Nos. 1561-1568 (8)	2.32	
		Set value		1.30

10th Winter Olympic Games, Grenoble, France, Feb. 6-18, 1968.

Puss in Boots — A491

Fairy Tales: 40g, The Fox and the Raven. 60g, Mr. Twardowski (man flying on a cock). 2z, The Fisherman and the Fish. 2.50z, Little Red Riding Hood. 3.40z, Cinderella. 5.50z, Thumbelina. 7z, Snow White.

1968, Mar. 15 **Litho.** ***Perf. 12½***

No.	Type	Description	Unused	Used
1569	A491	20g multicolored	.15	.15
1570	A491	40g lt violet & multi	.15	.15
1571	A491	60g multicolored	.15	.15
1572	A491	2z olive & multi	.28	.15
1573	A491	2.50z ver & multi	.35	.15
1574	A491	3.40z multicolored	.65	.16
1575	A491	5.50z multicolored	.90	.42
1576	A491	7z multicolored	1.50	.70
		Nos. 1569-1576 (8)	4.13	
		Set value		1.70

Bird-of-Paradise Flower A492

Exotic Flowers: 10g, Clianthus dampieri. 20g, Passiflora quadrangularis. 40g, Coryphanta vivipara. 60g, Odontonia. 90g, Protea cynaroides.

1968, May 15 **Litho.** ***Perf. 11½***

No.	Type	Description	Unused	Used
1577	A492	10g sepia & multi	.15	.15
1578	A492	20g multicolored	.15	.15
1579	A492	30g brown & multi	.15	.15
1580	A492	40g ultra & multi	.15	.15
1581	A492	60g multicolored	.15	.15
1582	A492	90g multicolored	.20	.15
		Nos. 1577-1582,B111-B112 (8)	3.40	
		Set value		1.65

"Peace" by Henryk Tomaszewski A493

2.50z, Poster for Gounod's Faust, by Jan Lenica.

1968, May 29 **Litho.** ***Perf. 11½x11***

No.	Type	Description	Unused	Used
1583	A493	60g gray & multi	.15	.15
1584	A493	2.50z gray & multi	.18	.15
		Set value		.18

2nd Intl. Poster Biennial Exhibition, Warsaw.

Zephyr Glider
A494

Polish Gliders: 90g, Storks. 1.50z, Swallow. 3.40z, Flies. 4z, Seal. 5.50z, Pirate.

1968, May 29 *Perf. 12½*

1585 A494 60g multicolored .15 .15
1586 A494 90g multicolored .15 .15
1587 A494 1.50z multicolored .15 .15
1588 A494 3.40z multicolored .55 .15
1589 A494 4z multicolored .80 .30
1590 A494 5.50z multicolored .95 .40
Nos. 1585-1590 (6) 2.75
Set value 1.00

11th Intl. Glider Championships, Leszno.

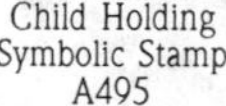
Child Holding Symbolic Stamp
A495

Sosnowiec Memorial
A496

No. 1592, Balloon over Poznan Town Hall.

1968, July 2 Litho. *Perf. 11½x11*

1591 A495 60g multicolored .15 .15
1592 A495 60g multicolored .15 .15
Set value .24 .15

75 years of Polish philately; "Tematica 1968" stamp exhibition in Poznan. Printed in sheets of 12 (4x3) se-tenant, arranged checkerwise.

Photogravure and Engraved

1968, July 20 *Perf. 11x11½*

1593 A496 60g brt rose lilac & blk .15 .15

The monument by Helena and Roman Husarski and Witold Ceckiewicz was unveiled Sept. 16, 1967, to honor the revolutionary deeds of Silesian workers and miners.

Relay Race and Sculptured Head — A497

Sports and Sculptures: 40g, Boxing. 60g, Basketball. 90g, Long jump. 2.50z, Women's javelin. 3.40z, Athlete on parallel bars. 4z, Bicycling. 7.90z, Fencing.

1968, Sept. 2 Litho. *Perf. 11x11½*
Size: 35x26mm

1594 A497 30g sepia & multi .15 .15
1595 A497 40g brn org, brn & blk .15 .15
1596 A497 60g gray & multi .15 .15
1597 A497 90g violet & multi .15 .15
1598 A497 2.50z multicolored .25 .15
1599 A497 3.40z brt grn, blk & lt ultra .38 .15
1600 A497 4z multicolored .40 .22
1601 A497 7.90z multicolored .80 .42
Nos. 1594-1601,B113 (9) 4.33
Set value 2.25

19th Olympic Games, Mexico City, Oct. 12-27.

Jewish Woman with Lemons, by Aleksander Gierymski
A498

Polish Paintings: 40g, Knight on Bay Horse, by Piotr Michalowski. 60g, Fisherman, by Leon Wyczolkowski. 1.35z, Eliza Parenska, by Stanislaw Wyspianski. 1.50z, "Manifest," by Wojciech Weiss. 4.50z, Stancyk (Jester), by Jan Matejko, horiz. 5z, Children's Band, by Tadeusz Makowski, horiz. 7z, Feast II, by Zygmunt Waliszewski, horiz.

Perf. 11½x11, 11x11½

1968, Oct. 10 Litho.

1602 A498 40g gray & multi .15 .15
1603 A498 60g gray & multi .15 .15
1604 A498 1.15z gray & multi .15 .15
1605 A498 1.35z gray & multi .18 .15
1606 A498 1.50z gray & multi .35 .18
1607 A498 4.50z gray & multi .48 .25
1608 A498 5z gray & multi .80 .32
1609 A498 7z gray & multi .90 .55
Nos. 1602-1609 (8) 3.16
Set value 1.60

Issued in sheets of 4 stamps and 2 labels inscribed with painter's name.

"September, 1939" by M. Bylina — A499

Paintings: No. 1611, Partisans, by L. Maciag. No. 1612, Tank in Battle, by M. Bylina. No. 1613, Monte Cassino, by A. Boratynski. No. 1614, Tanks Approaching Warsaw, by S. Garwatowski. No. 1615, Battle on the Neisse, by M. Bylina. No. 1616, On the Oder, by K. Mackiewicz. No. 1617, "In Berlin," by M. Bylina. No. 1618, Warship "Blyskawica" by M. Mokwa. No. 1619, "Pursuit" (fighter planes), by T. Kulisiewicz.

Litho., Typo. & Engr.

1968, Oct. 12 *Perf. 11½*

1610 A499 40g pale yel, ol & vio .15 .15
1611 A499 40g lil, red lil & ind .15 .15
1612 A499 40g gray, dk bl & ol .15 .15
1613 A499 40g pale sal, org brn & blk .15 .15
1614 A499 40g pale grn, dk grn & plum .15 .15
1615 A499 60g gray, vio bl & blk .15 .15
1616 A499 60g pale grn, ol grn & vio brn .15 .15
1617 A499 60g pink, car & grnsh blk .15 .15
1618 A499 60g pink, brn & grn .15 .15
1619 A499 60g lt bl, grnsh bl & blk .15 .15
Set value 1.00 .65

Polish People's Army, 25th anniversary.

Memorial Types of 1967

Designs: No. 1620, Tomb of the Unknown Soldier, Warsaw. No. 1621, Nazi War Crimes Memorial, Zamosc. No. 1622, Guerrilla Memorial, Plichno. No. 1623, Guerrilla Memorial, Kartuzy. No. 1624, Polish Insurgents' Memorial, Poznan.

Perf. 11½x11, 11x11½

1968, Nov. 15 Engr.

1620 A471 40g slate .15 .15
1621 A472 40g dull red .15 .15
1622 A472 40g dark blue .15 .15
1623 A471 40g sepia .15 .15
1624 A472 40g sepia .15 .15
Set value .35 .25

Issued to commemorate the martyrdom and fight of the Polish people, 1939-45.

Strikers, S. Lentz
A500

No. 1626, "Manifesto," by Wojciech Weiss. No. 1627, Party members, by F. Kowarski, horiz.

Perf. 11½x11, 11x11½

1968, Nov. 11 Litho.

1625 A500 60g dark red & multi .15 .15
1626 A500 60g dark red & multi .15 .15
1627 A500 60g dark red & multi .15 .15
Set value .30 .18

5th Congress of the Polish United Workers' Party.

Departure for the Hunt, by Wojciech Kossak — A501

Hunt Paintings: 40g, Hunting with Falcon, by Juliusz Kossak. 60g, Wolves' Raid, by A. Wierusz-Kowalski. 1.50z, Bear Hunt, by Julian Falat. 2.50z, Fox Hunt, by T. Sutherland. 3.40z, Boar Hunt, by Frans Snyders. 4.50z, Hunters' Rest, by W. G. Pierow. 8.50z, Lion Hunt in Morocco, by Delacroix.

1968, Nov. 20 *Perf. 11*

1628 A501 20g multicolored .15 .15
1629 A501 40g multicolored .15 .15
1630 A501 60g multicolored .15 .15
1631 A501 1.50z multicolored .20 .15
1632 A501 2.50z multicolored .18 .15
1633 A501 3.40z multicolored .40 .15
1634 A501 4.50z multicolored .80 .40
1635 A501 8.50z multicolored 1.40 .80
Nos. 1628-1635 (8) 3.43
Set value 1.60

Afghan Greyhound
A502

Dogs: 20g, Maltese. 40g, Rough-haired fox terrier, vert. 1.50z, Schnauzer. 2.50z, English setter. 3.40z, Pekinese. 4.50z, German shepherd. 8.50z, Pointer.

1969, Feb. 2 *Perf. 11x11½, 11½x11*
Dogs in Natural Colors

1636 A502 20g gray & brt grn .15 .15
1637 A502 40g gray & orange .28 .15
1638 A502 60g gray & lilac .28 .15
1639 A502 1.50z gray & black .28 .15
1640 A502 2.50z gray & brt pink .45 .22
1641 A502 3.40z gray & dk grn .75 .30
1642 A502 4.50z gray & ver 1.40 .55
1643 A502 8.50z gray & violet 2.75 1.25
Nos. 1636-1643 (8) 6.34 2.92

General Assembly of the Intl. Kennel Federation, Warsaw, May 1969.

Eagle-on-Shield House Sign — A503

1969, Feb. 23 Litho. *Perf. 11½x11*

1644 A503 60g gray, red & blk .15 .15

9th Congress of Democratic Movement.

Sheaf of Wheat
A504

1969, Mar. 29 Litho. *Perf. 11½x11*

1645 A504 60g multicolored .15 .15

5th Congress of the United Peasant Party, Warsaw, March 29-31.

Runner — A505

Olympic Rings and: 20g, Woman gymnast. 40g, Weight lifting. 60g, Women's javelin.

1969, Apr. 25 Litho. *Perf. 11½x11*

1646 A505 10g orange & multi .15 .15
1647 A505 20g ultra & multi .15 .15
1648 A505 40g yellow & multi .15 .15
1649 A505 60g red & multi .15 .15
Nos. 1646-1649,B114-B117 (8) 2.90
Set value 1.25

50th anniv. of the Polish Olympic Committee, and the 75th anniv. of the Intl. Olympic Committee.

Sailboat and Lighthouse, Kolobrzeg Harbor — A506

40g, Tourist map of Swietokrzyski National Park. 60g, Ruins of 16th cent. castle, Niedzica, vert. 1.50z, Castle of the Dukes of Pomerania & ship, Szczecin. 2.50z, View of Torun & Vistula. 3.40z, View of Klodzko, vert. 4z, View of Sulejow. 4.50z, Market Place, Kazimierz Dolny, vert.

1969, May 20 Litho. *Perf. 11*

1650 A506 40g multicolored .15 .15
1651 A506 60g multicolored .15 .15
1652 A506 1.35z multicolored .15 .15
1653 A506 1.50z multicolored .15 .15
1654 A506 2.50z multicolored .16 .15
1655 A506 3.40z multicolored .25 .15
1656 A506 4z multicolored .35 .18
1657 A506 4.50z multicolored .60 .24
Nos. 1650-1657 (8) 1.96
Set value .95

Issued for tourist publicity. Printed in sheets of 15 stamps and 15 labels. Domestic plants on labels of 40g, 60g and 1.35z, coats of arms on others.

See Nos. 1731-1735.

World Map and Sailboat Opty
A507

1969, June 21 Litho. *Perf. 11x11½*

1658 A507 60g multicolored .15 .15

Leonid Teliga's one-man voyage around the world, Casablanca, Jan. 21, 1967, to Las Palmas, Apr. 16, 1969.

Nicolaus Copernicus, Woodcut by Tobias Stimer — A508

Designs: 60g, Copernicus, by Jeremias Falck, 15th century globe and map of constellations. 2.50z, Copernicus, painting by Jan Matejko and map of heliocentric system.

Photo., Engr. & Litho.

1969, June 26 *Perf. 11½*

1659	A508	40g	dl yel, sep & dp car	.15	.15
1660	A508	60g	grnsh gray, blk & dp car	.15	.15
1661	A508	2.50z	lt vio brn, ol & dp car	.42	.16
			Nos. 1659-1661 (3)	.72	
			Set value		.30

Copernicus (1473-1543), astronomer.

"Memory" Pathfinders' Cross and Protectors' Badge — A509

Frontier Guard and Embossed Arms of Poland — A510

Coal Miner — A511

Designs: No. 1663, "Defense," military eagle and Pathfinders' cross. No. 1664, "Labor," map of Poland and Pathfinders' cross.

Photo., Engr. & Litho.

1969, July 19 *Perf. 11x11½*

1662	A509	60g	ultra, blk & red	.15	.15
1663	A509	60g	green, blk & red	.15	.15
1664	A509	60g	carmine, blk & grn	.15	.15
			Set value	.30	.24

5th National Alert of Polish Pathfinders' Union.

1969, July 21 **Litho. & Embossed**

Designs: No. 1666, Oil refinery-chemical plant, Plock. No. 1667, Combine harvester. No. 1668, Rebuilt Grand Theater, Warsaw. No. 1669, Marie Sklodowska-Curie Monument and University, Lublin. No. 1671, Chemical industry (sulphur) worker. No. 1672, Steelworker. No. 1673, Ship builder and ship.

1665	A510	60g	red & multi	.15	.15
1666	A510	60g	red & multi	.15	.15
1667	A510	60g	red & multi	.15	.15
1668	A510	60g	red & multi	.15	.15
1669	A510	60g	red & multi	.15	.15
a.			Strip of 5, #1665-1669	.40	.40

Perf. 11½x11

Litho.

1670	A511	60g	gray & multi	.15	.15
1671	A511	60g	gray & multi	.15	.15
1672	A511	60g	gray & multi	.15	.15
1673	A511	60g	gray & multi	.15	.15
a.			Strip of 4, #1670-1673	.32	.32
			Set value (9)	.72	.45

25th anniv. of the Polish People's Republic.

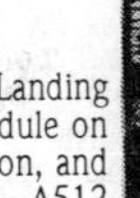

Landing Module on Moon, and Earth — A512

1969, Aug. 21 **Litho.** *Perf. 12x12½*

1674	A512	2.50z	multicolored	.80	.42

Man's first landing on the moon, July 20, 1969. US astronauts Neil A. Armstrong and Col. Edwin E. Aldrin, Jr., with Lieut. Col. Michael Collins piloting Apollo 11. Issued in sheets of 8 stamps and 2 tabs with decorative border. One tab shows Apollo 11 with lunar landing module, the other shows module's take-off from moon. Value, sheet. $20.

Motherhood, by Stanislaw Wyspianski — A513

Polish Paintings: 40g, "Hamlet," by Jacek Malczewski. 60g, Indian Summer (sleeping woman), by Jozef Chelmonski. 2z, Two Girls, by Olga Boznanska, vert. 2.50z, "The Sun of May" (Breakfast on the Terrace), by Jozef Mehoffer, vert. 3.40z, Woman Combing her Hair, by Wladyslaw Slewinski. 5.50z, Still Life, by Jozef Pankiewicz. 7z, The Abduction of the King's Daughter, by Witold Wojtkiewicz.

Perf. 11x11½, 11½x11

1969, Sept. 4 **Photo.**

1675	A513	20g	gold & multi	.15	.15
1676	A513	40g	gold & multi	.15	.15
1677	A513	60g	gold & multi	.15	.15
1678	A513	2z	gold & multi	.20	.15
1679	A513	2.50z	gold & multi	.20	.15
1680	A513	3.40z	gold & multi	.32	.15
1681	A513	5.50z	gold & multi	.80	.32
1682	A513	7z	gold & multi	1.25	.52
			Nos. 1675-1682 (8)	3.22	
			Set value		1.35

Issued in sheets of 4 stamps and 2 labels inscribed with painter's name.

Nike — A514

1969, Sept. 19 **Litho.** *Perf. 11½x11*

1683	A514	60g	gray, red & bister	.15	.15

4th Congress of the Union of Fighters for Freedom and Democracy.

Details from Memorial, Majdanek Concentration Camp — A515

1969, Sept. 20 *Perf. 11*

1684	A515	40g	brt lil, gray & blk	.15	.15

Unveiling of a monument to the victims of the Majdanek concentration camp. The monument was designed by the sculptor Wiktor Tolkin.

Costumes from Krczonow, Lublin — A516

Regional Costumes: 60g, Lowicz, Lodz. 1.15z, Rozbark, Katowice. 1.35z, Lower Silesia, Wroclaw. 1.50z, Opoczno, Lodz. 4.50z, Sacz, Cracow. 5z, Highlanders, Cracow. 7z, Kurpiow, Warsaw.

1969, Sept. 30 **Litho.** *Perf. 11½x11*

1685	A516	40g	multicolored	.15	.15
1686	A516	60g	multicolored	.15	.15
1687	A516	1.15z	multicolored	.15	.15
1688	A516	1.35z	multicolored	.15	.15
1689	A516	1.50z	multicolored	.16	.15
1690	A516	4.50z	multicolored	.52	.24
1691	A516	5z	multicolored	.80	.42
1692	A516	7z	multicolored	.65	.30
			Nos. 1685-1692 (8)	2.73	
			Set value		1.30

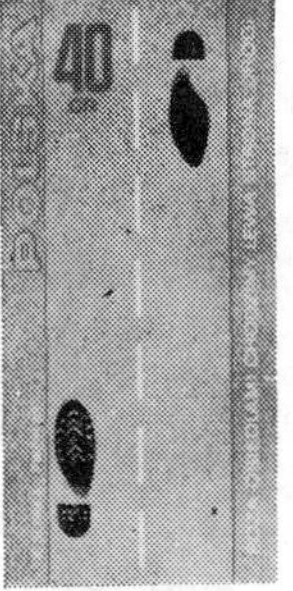
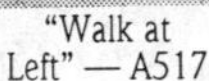

"Walk at Left" — A517

ILO Emblem and Welder's Mask — A518

Traffic safety: 60g, "Drive Carefully" (horses on road). 2.50z, "Lower your Lights" (automobile on road).

1969, Oct. 4 *Perf. 11*

1693	A517	40g	multicolored	.15	.15
1694	A517	60g	multicolored	.15	.15
1695	A517	2.50z	multicolored	.18	.15
			Set value	.30	.16

1969, Oct. 20 *Perf. 11x11½*

1696	A518	2.50z	violet bl & ol	.15	.15

ILO, 50th anniversary.

Bell Foundry A519

Miniatures from Behem's Code, completed 1505: 60g, Painter's studio. 1.35z, Wood carvers. 1.55z, Shoemaker. 2.50z, Cooper. 3.40z, Bakery. 4.50z, Tailor. 7z, Bowyer's shop.

1969, Nov. 12 **Litho.** *Perf. 12½*

1697	A519	40g	gray & multi	.15	.15
1698	A519	60g	gray & multi	.15	.15
1699	A519	1.35z	gray & multi	.15	.15
1700	A519	1.55z	gray & multi	.15	.15
1701	A519	2.50z	gray & multi	.20	.15
1702	A519	3.40z	gray & multi	.28	.15
1703	A519	4.50z	gray & multi	.40	.22
1704	A519	7z	gray & multi	.85	.40
			Set value	2.05	1.10

Angel — A520

Folk Art (Sculptures): 40g, Sorrowful Christ (head). 60g, Sorrowful Christ (seated figure). 2z, Crying woman. 2.50z, Adam and Eve. 3.40z, Woman with birds.

1969, Dec. 19 **Litho.** *Perf. 12½*

Size: 21x36mm

1705	A520	20g	lt blue & multi	.15	.15
1706	A520	40g	lilac & multi	.15	.15
1707	A520	60g	multicolored	.15	.15
1708	A520	2z	multicolored	.18	.15
1709	A520	2.50z	multicolored	.20	.15
1710	A520	3.40z	multicolored	.28	.18
			Nos. 1705-1710,B118-B119 (8)	2.33	
			Set value		1.10

Leopold Staff (1878-1957) A521

Polish Writers: 60g, Wladyslaw Broniewski (1897-1962). 1.35z, Leon Kruczkowski (1900-1962). 1.50z, Julian Tuwim (1894-1953). 1.55z, Konstanty Ildefons Galczynski (1905-1953). 2.50z, Maria Dabrowska (1889-1965). 3.40z, Zofia Nalkowska (1885-1954).

Litho., Typo. & Engr.

1969, Dec. 30 *Perf. 11x11½*

1711	A521	40g	ol grn & blk, *grnsh*	.15	.15
1712	A521	60g	dp car & blk, *pink*	.15	.15
1713	A521	1.35z	vio bl & blk, *grysh*	.15	.15
1714	A521	1.50z	pur & blk, *pink*	.15	.15
1715	A521	1.55z	dp grn & blk, *grnsh*	.15	.15
1716	A521	2.50z	ultra & blk, *gray*	.20	.15
1717	A521	3.40z	red brn & blk, *pink*	.28	.15
			Set value	1.00	.50

Statue of Nike and Polish Colors A522

1970, Jan. 17 **Photo.** *Perf. 11½*

1718	A522	60g	sil, gold, red & blk	.15	.15

Warsaw liberation, 25th anniversary.

Medieval Print Shop and Modern Color Proofs — A523

1970, Jan. 20 **Litho.** *Perf. 11½x11*

1719	A523	60g	multicolored	.15	.15

Centenary of Polish printers' trade union.

Ringnecked Pheasant A524

Game Birds: 40g, Mallard drake. 1.15z, Woodcock. 1.35z, Ruffs (males). 1.50z, Wood pigeon. 3.40z, Black grouse. 7z, Gray partridges (cock and hen). 8.50z, Capercaillie cock giving mating call.

1970, Feb. 28 Litho. *Perf. 11½*

1720 A524 40g multicolored .15 .15
1721 A524 60g multicolored 1.25 .15
1722 A524 1.15z multicolored .15 .15
1723 A524 1.35z multicolored .15 .15
1724 A524 1.50z multicolored .35 .15
1725 A524 3.40z multicolored .35 .15
1726 A524 7z multicolored 1.65 .65
1727 A524 8.50z multicolored 1.90 .85
Nos. 1720-1727 (8) 5.95
Set value 2.10

Lenin in his Kremlin Study, Oct. 1918, and Polish Lenin Steel Mill — A525

Designs: 60g, Lenin addressing 3rd International Congress in Leningrad, 1920, and Luna 13. 2.50z, Lenin with delegates to 10th Russian Communist Party Congress, Moscow, 1921, dove and globe.

Engr. & Typo.

1970, Apr. 22 *Perf. 11*

1728 A525 40g grnsh blk & dl red .15 .15
1729 A525 60g sep & dp lil rose .15 .15
a. Souvenir sheet of 4 1.25 .48
1730 A525 2.50z bluish blk & ver .18 .15
Nos. 1728-1730 (3) .48
Set value .18

Lenin (1870-1924), Russian communist leader.
No. 1729a commemorates the Cracow Intl. Phil. Exhib.

Tourist Type of 1969

#1731, Townhall, Wroclaw, vert. #1732, Cathedral, Piast Castle tower and church towers, Opole. #1733, Castle, Legnica. #1734, Castle Tower, Bolkow. #1735, Town Hall, Brzeg.

1970, May 9 Litho. *Perf. 11*

1731 A506 60g Wroclaw .15 .15
1732 A506 60g Opole .15 .15
1733 A506 60g Legnica .15 .15
1734 A506 60g Bolkow .15 .15
1735 A506 60g Brzeg .15 .15
Nos. 1731-1735 (5) .75
Set value .40

Issued for tourist publicity. Printed in sheets of 15 stamps and 15 labels, showing coats of arms.

Polish and Russian Soldiers before Brandenburg Gate — A526

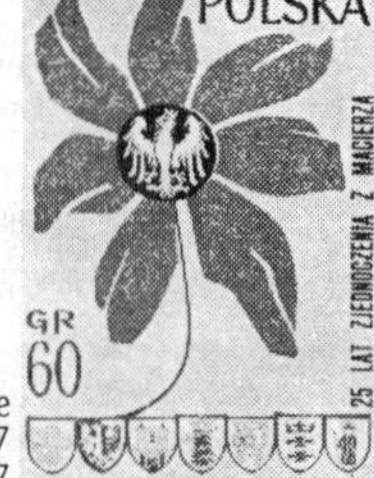

Flower, Eagle and Arms of 7 Cities — A527

Lithographed and Engraved

1970, May 9 *Perf. 11*

1736 A526 60g tan & multi .15 .15

Perf. 11½

1737 A527 60g silver, red & sl grn .15 .15
Set value .18 .16

25th anniv. of victory over Germany and of Polish administration of the Oder-Neisse border area.

Peasant Movement Flag — A528

1970, May 15 Litho. *Perf. 11½*

1738 A528 60g olive & multi .15 .15

Polish peasant movement, 75th anniv.

A529

A530

1970, May 20

1739 A529 2.50z blue & vio bl .15 .15

Inauguration of new UPU headquarters, Bern.

1970, May 30 *Perf. 11½x11*

1740 A530 60g multicolored .25 .15

European Soccer Cup Finals. Printed in sheets of 15 stamps and 15 se-tenant labels inscribed with the scores of the games.

Lamp of Learning — A531

1970, June 3 *Perf. 11½*

1741 A531 60g black, bis & red .15 .15

Plock Scientific Society, 150th anniversary.

Cross-country Race — A532

Designs: No. 1743, Runners from ancient Greek vase. No. 1744, Archer, drawing by W. Skoczylas.

1970, June 16 Photo. *Perf. 11x11½*

1742 A532 60g yellow & multi .15 .15
1743 A532 60g black & multi .15 .15
1744 A532 60g dark blue & multi .15 .15
Nos. 1742-1744 (3) .45
Set value .20

10th session of the Intl. Olympic Academy. See No. B120.

Copernicus, by Bacciarelli and View of Bologna — A533

Designs: 60g, Copernicus, by W. Lesseur and view of Padua. 2.50z, Copernicus, by Zinck Nora and view of Ferrara.

Photo., Engr. & Typo.

1970, June 26 *Perf. 11½*

1745 A533 40g orange & multi .15 .15
1746 A533 60g olive & multi .15 .15
1747 A533 2.50z multicolored .38 .15
Set value .54 .28

Aleksander Orlowski (1777-1832), Self-portrait A534

Miniatures: 40g, Jan Matejko (1838-1893), self-portrait. 60g, King Stefan Batory (1533-1586), anonymous painter. 2z, Maria Leszczynska (1703-1768), anonymous French painter. 2.50z, Maria Walewska (1789-1817), by Jacquotot Marie-Victoire. 3.40z, Tadeusz Kosciuszko (1746-1817), by Jan Rustem. 5.50z, Samuel Bogumil Linde (1771-1847), by G. Landolfi. 7z, Michal Oginski (1728-1800), by Windisch Nanette.

Litho. & Photo.

1970, Aug. 27 *Perf. 11½*

1748 A534 20g gold & multi .15 .15
1749 A534 40g gold & multi .15 .15
1750 A534 60g gold & multi .15 .15
1751 A534 2z gold & multi .15 .15
1752 A534 2.50z gold & multi .25 .15
1753 A534 3.40z gold & multi .38 .24
1754 A534 5.50z gold & multi .65 .35
1755 A534 7z gold & multi 1.10 .52
Nos. 1748-1755 (8) 2.98
Set value 1.60

Nos. 1748-1755 printed in sheets of 4 stamps and 2 labels. The miniatures show famous Poles and are from collections in the National Museums in Warsaw and Cracow.

Poster for Chopin Competition — A535

Photogravure and Engraved

1970, Sept. 8 *Perf. 11x11½*

1756 A535 2.50z black & vio .25 .15

8th Intl. Chopin Piano Competition, Warsaw, Oct. 7-25.

UN Emblem A536

1970, Sept. 8 Photo. *Perf. 11½*

1757 A536 2.50z multicolored .25 .15

United Nations, 25th anniversary.

Poles — A537

Design: 60g, Family, home and Polish flag.

1970, Sept. 15 Litho. *Perf. 11½x11*

1758 A537 40g gray & multi .15 .15
1759 A537 60g multicolored .18 .15
Set value .20

National Census, Dec. 8, 1970.

Grunwald Cross and Warship Piorun (Thunderbolt) — A538

Grunwald Cross and Warship: 60g, Orzel (Eagle). 2.50z, Garland.

1970, Sept. 25 Engr. *Perf. 11½x11*

1760 A538 40g sepia .15 .15
1761 A538 60g black .15 .15
1762 A538 2.50z deep brown .45 .15
Nos. 1760-1762 (3) .75
Set value .28

Polish Navy during World War II.

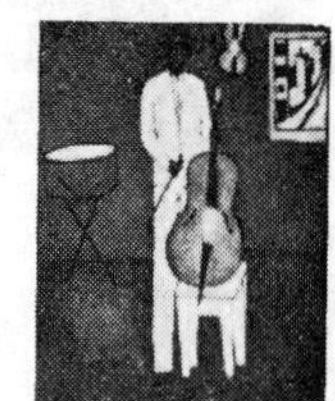

Cellist, by Jerzy Nowosielski — A539

Paintings: 40g, View of Lodz, by Benon Liberski. 60g, Studio Concert, by Waclaw Taranczewski. 1.50z, Still Life, by Zbigniew Pronaszko. 2z, Woman Hanging up Laundry, by Andrzej Wroblewski. 3.40z, "Expressions," by Maria Jarema, horiz. 4z, Canal in the Forest, by Piotr Potworowski, horiz. 8.50z, "The Sun," by Wladyslaw Strzeminski, horiz.

1970, Oct. 9 Photo. *Perf. 11½*

1763 A539 20g multicolored .15 .15
1764 A539 40g multicolored .15 .15
1765 A539 60g multicolored .15 .15
1766 A539 1.50z multicolored .16 .15
1767 A539 2z multicolored .18 .15
1768 A539 3.40z multicolored .28 .15
1769 A539 4z multicolored .48 .22
1770 A539 8.50z multicolored 1.00 .48
Nos. 1763-1770 (8) 2.55
Set value 1.15

Issued for Stamp Day.

Luna 16 Landing on Moon — A540 Stag — A541

1970, Nov. 20 Litho. *Perf. 11½x11*

1771 A540 2.50z multicolored .38 .15

Luna 16 Russian unmanned, automatic moon mission, Sept. 12-24. Issued in sheets of 8 stamps and 2 tabs. One tab shows rocket launching; the other, parachute landing of capsule. Value, sheet $16.

1970, Dec. 23 Photo. *Perf. 11½x12*

16th Cent. Tapestries in Wawel Castle: 1.15z, Stork. 1.35z, Leopard fighting dragon. 2z, Man's head. 2.50z, Child holding bird. 4z, God, Adam & Eve. 4.50z, Panel with monogram of King Sigismund Augustus. 5.50z, Poland's coat of arms.

1772 A541 60g multicolored .15 .15
1773 A541 1.15z purple & multi .15 .15
1774 A541 1.35z multicolored .15 .15
1775 A541 2z sepia & multi .20 .15
1776 A541 2.50z dk blue & multi .25 .15

1777 A541 4z green & multi .60 .22
1778 A541 4.50z multicolored .75 .32
Nos. 1772-1778 (7) 2.25
Set value .95

Souvenir Sheet

Imperf

1779 A541 5.50z black & multi 1.00 .50

No. 1779 contains one 48x57mm stamp. See No. B121.

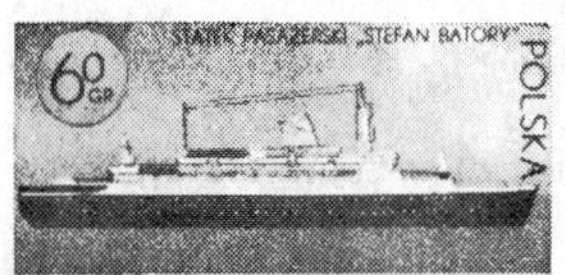

Transatlantic Liner Stefan Batory — A542

Polish Ships: 40g, School sailing ship Dar Pomorza. 1.15z, Ice breaker Perkun. 1.35z, Rescue ship R-1. 1.50z, Freighter Ziemia Szczecinska. 2.50z, Tanker Beskidy. 5z, Express freighter Hel. 8.50z, Ferry Gryf.

1971, Jan. 30 Photo. *Perf. 11*

1780 A542 40g ver & multi .15 .15
1781 A542 60g multicolored .15 .15
1782 A542 1.15z blue & multi .15 .15
1783 A542 1.35z yellow & multi .15 .15
1784 A542 1.50z multicolored .18 .15
1785 A542 2.50z violet & multi .24 .15
1786 A542 5z multicolored .52 .24
1787 A542 8.50z blue & multi .85 .42
Set value 2.10 1.10

Checiny Castle A543

Polish Castles: 40g, Wisnicz. 60g, Bedzin. 2z, Ogrodzieniec. 2.50z, Niedzica. 3.40z, Kwidzyn. 4z, Pieskowa Skala. 8.50z, Lidzbark Warminski.

1971, Mar. 5 Litho. *Perf. 11*

1788 A543 20g multicolored .15 .15
1789 A543 40g multicolored .15 .15
1790 A543 60g multicolored .15 .15
1791 A543 2z multicolored .16 .15
1792 A543 2.50z multicolored .18 .15
1793 A543 3.40z multicolored .28 .15
1794 A543 4z multicolored .35 .18
1795 A543 8.50z multicolored .75 .42
Nos. 1788-1795 (8) 2.17
Set value 1.00

Fighting in Pouilly Castle, Jaroslaw Dabrowski and Walery Wroblewski — A544

1971, Mar. 3 *Perf. 12½x12½*

1796 A544 60g vio bl, brn & red .15 .15

Centenary of the Paris Commune.

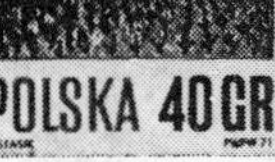

Seedlings — A545

Bishop Marianos — A546

1971, Mar. 30 Photo. *Perf. 11½x11*

Sizes: 26x34mm (40g, 1.50z); 26x47mm (60g)

1797 A545 40g shown .15 .15
1798 A545 60g Forest .15 .15
1799 A545 1.50z Clearing .25 .15
Set value .45 .25

Proper forest management.

1971, Apr. 20

Frescoes from Faras Cathedral, Nubia, 8th-12th centuries: 60g, St. Anne. 1.15z, 1.50z, 7z, Archangel Michael (diff. frescoes). 1.35z, Hermit Anamon of Tuna el Gabel. 4.50z, Cross with symbols of four Evangelists. 5z, Christ protecting Nubian dignitary.

1800 A546 40g gold & multi .15 .15
1801 A546 60g gold & multi .15 .15
1802 A546 1.15z gold & multi .15 .15
1803 A546 1.35z gold & multi .15 .15
1804 A546 1.50z gold & multi .15 .15
1805 A546 4.50z gold & multi .50 .20
1806 A546 5z gold & multi .52 .22
1807 A546 7z gold & multi .65 .32
Nos. 1800-1807 (8) 2.42
Set value 1.10

Polish archaeological excavations in Nubia.

Silesian Insurrectionists — A547

1971, May 3 Photo. *Perf. 11*

1808 A547 60g dk red brn & gold .15 .15
a. Souv. sheet of 3+3 labels 1.65 .60

50th anniversary of the 3rd Silesian uprising. Printed in sheets of 15 stamps and 15 labels showing Silesian Insurrectionists monument in Katowice.

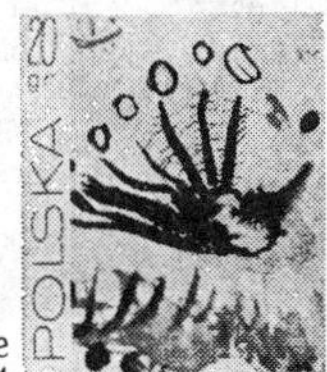

Peacock on the Lawn, by Dorota, 4 years old — A548

Children's Drawings and UNICEF Emblem: 40g, Our Army, horiz. 60g, Spring. 2z, Cat with Ball, horiz. 2.50z, Flowers in Vase. 3.40z, Friendship, horiz. 5.50z, Clown. 7z, The Unknown Planet, horiz.

Perf. 11½x11, 11x11½

1971, May 20

1809 A548 20g multicolored .15 .15
1810 A548 40g multicolored .15 .15
1811 A548 60g multicolored .15 .15
1812 A548 2z multicolored .18 .15
1813 A548 2.50z multicolored .18 .15
1814 A548 3.40z multicolored .32 .15
1815 A548 5.50z multicolored .50 .22
1816 A548 7z multicolored .80 .35
Nos. 1809-1816 (8) 2.43
Set value 1.00

25th anniversary of UNICEF.

Fair Emblem — A549

1971, June 1 Photo. *Perf. 11½x11*

1817 A549 60g ultra, blk & dk car .15 .15

40th International Poznan Fair, June 13-22.

Collegium Maius, Cracow — A550

40g, Copernicus House, Torun, vert. 2.50z, Olsztyn Castle. 4z, Frombork Cathedral, vert.

1971, June Litho. *Perf. 11*

1818 A550 40g multicolored .15 .15
1819 A550 60g blk, red brn & sep .15 .15
1820 A550 2.50z multicolored .25 .15
1821 A550 4z multicolored .45 .18
Nos. 1818-1821 (4) 1.00
Set value .42

Nicolaus Copernicus (1473-1543), astronomer. Printed in sheets of 15 with labels showing portrait of Copernicus, page from "Euclid's Geometry," astrolabe or drawing of heliocentric system, respectively.

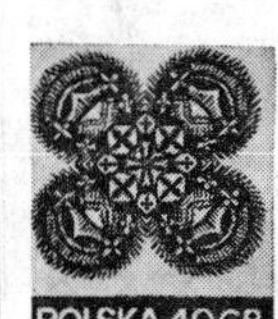

Paper Cut-out — A551

Worker, by Xawery Dunikowski — A552

Designs: Various paper cut-outs (folk art).

Photo., Engr. & Typo.

1971, July 12 *Perf. 12x11½*

1822 A551 20g blk & brt grn, *bluish* .15 .15
1823 A551 40g sl grn & dk ol, *lt gray* .15 .15
1824 A551 60g brn & bl, *gray* .15 .15
1825 A551 1.15z plum & brn, *buff* .15 .15
1826 A551 1.35z dk grn & ver, *yel grn* .15 .15
Set value .38 .34

1971, July 21 Photo. *Perf. 11½x12*

Sculptures: No. 1828, Founder, by Xawery Dunikowski. No. 1829, Miners, by Magdalena Wiecek. No. 1830, Woman harvester, by Stanislaw Horno-Poplawski.

1827 A552 40g silver & multi .15 .15
1828 A552 40g silver & multi .15 .15
1829 A552 60g silver & multi .15 .15
1830 A552 60g silver & multi .15 .15
a. Souv. sheet of 4, #1827-1830 2.50 .85
Set value .40 .28

Punched Tape and Cogwheel A553

1971, Sept. 2 Litho. *Perf. 11x11½*

1831 A553 60g purple & red .15 .15

6th Congress of Polish Technicians, held at Poznan, February, 1971.

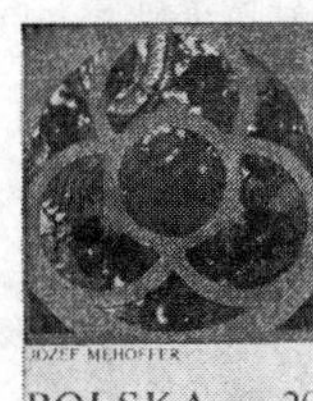

Angel, by Jozef Mehoffer, 1901 A554

Water Lilies, by Wyspianski A555

Stained Glass Windows: 60g, Detail from "The Elements" by Stanislaw Wyspianski. 1.35z, Apollo, by Wyspianski, 1904. 1.55z, Two Kings, 14th century. 3.40z, Flight into Egypt, 14th century. 5.50z, St. Jacob the Elder, 14th century.

1971, Sept. 15 Photo. *Perf. 11½x11*

1832 A554 20g gold & multi .15 .15
1833 A555 40g gold & multi .15 .15
1834 A555 60g gold & multi .15 .15
1835 A555 1.35z gold & multi .16 .15
1836 A554 1.55z gold & multi .20 .15
1837 A554 3.40z gold & multi .30 .15
1838 A554 5.50z gold & multi .45 .22
Nos. 1832-1838,B122 (8) 2.51 1.67

Mrs. Fedorowicz, by Witold Pruszkowski (1846-1896) A556

Paintings of Women: 50g, Woman with Book, by Tytus Czyzewski (1885-1945). 60g, Girl with Chrysanthemums, by Olga Boznanska (1865-1940). 2.50z, Girl in Red Dress, by Jozef Pankiewicz (1866-1940), horiz. 3.40z, Nude, by Leon Chwistek (1884-1944), horiz. 4.50z, Strange Garden (woman), by Jozef Mehoffer (1869-1946). 5z, Artist's Wife with White Hat, by Zbigniew Pronaszko (1885-1958).

Perf. 11½x11, 11x11½

1971, Oct. 9 Litho.

1839 A556 40g gray & multi .15 .15
1840 A556 50g gray & multi .15 .15
1841 A556 60g gray & multi .15 .15
1842 A556 2.50z gray & multi .20 .15
1843 A556 3.40z gray & multi .28 .15
1844 A556 4.50z gray & multi .42 .22
1845 A556 5z gray & multi .55 .32
Nos. 1839-1845,B123 (8) 2.60
Set value 1.25

Stamp Day, 1971. Printed in sheets of 4 stamps and 2 labels inscribed "Women in Polish Paintings."

Royal Castle, Warsaw A557

1971, Oct. 14 Photo. *Perf. 11x11½*

1846 A557 60g gold, blk & brt red .15 .15

P-11C Dive Bombers A558

Planes and Polish Air Force Emblem: 1.50z, PZL 23-A Karas fighters. 3.40z, PZL Los bomber.

1971, Oct. 14

1847 A558 90g multicolored .15 .15
1848 A558 1.50z blue, red & blk .18 .15
1849 A558 3.40z multicolored .38 .15
Nos. 1847-1849 (3) .71
Set value .28

Martyrs of the Polish Air Force, 1939.

Lunar Rover and Astronauts A559

Design: No. 1851, Lunokhod 1 on moon, vert.

Perf. 11x11½, 11½x11

1971, Nov. 17

1850 A559 2.50z multicolored .50 .15
1851 A559 2.50z multicolored .50 .15
Set value .24

Apollo 15 US moon exploration mission, July 26-Aug. 7 (No. 1850); Luna 17 unmanned automated USSR moon mission, Nov. 10-17 (No. 1851). Printed in sheets of 6 stamps and 2 labels, with marginal inscriptions.

Worker at Helm — A560

Shipbuilding A561

No. 1853, Worker. No. 1855, Apartment houses under construction. No. 1856, "Bison" combine harvester. No. 1857, Polish Fiat 125. No. 1858, Mining tower. No. 1859, Chemical plant.

1971, Dec. 8 *Perf. 11½x11*

1852	A560	60g	gray, ultra & red	.15	.15
1853	A560	60g	red & gray	.15	.15
a.			Pair, #1852-1853 + label	.20	.16

Perf. 11x11½

1854	A561	60g	red, gold & blk	.15	.15
1855	A561	60g	red, gold & blk	.15	.15
1856	A561	60g	red, gold & blk	.15	.15
1857	A561	60g	red, gold & blk	.15	.15
1858	A561	60g	red, gold & blk	.15	.15
1859	A561	60g	red, gold & blk	.15	.15
a.			Souv. sheet of 6, #1854-1859	.90	.50
b.			Block of 6, #1854-1859	.60	.50
			Set value	.80	.64

6th Congress of the Polish United Worker's Party. No. 1859b has outline of map of Poland extending over the block.

Cherry Blossoms — A562

Blossoms: 20g, Niedzwiecki's apple. 40g, Pear. 60g, Peach. 1.15z, Japanese magnolia. 1.35z, Red hawthorne. 2.50z, Apple. 3.40z, Red chestnut. 5z, Acacia robinia. 8.50z, Cherry.

1971, Dec. 28 Litho. *Perf. 12½*

Blossoms in Natural Colors

1860	A562	10g	dull blue & blk	.15	.15
1861	A562	20g	grnsh blue & blk	.15	.15
1862	A562	40g	lt violet & blk	.15	.15
1863	A562	60g	green & blk	.15	.15
1864	A562	1.15z	Prus bl & blk	.15	.15
1865	A562	1.35z	ocher & blk	.15	.15
1866	A562	2.50z	green & blk	.20	.15
1867	A562	3.40z	ocher & blk	.40	.20
1868	A562	5z	tan & blk	.55	.25
1869	A562	8.50z	bister & blk	1.10	.52
			Nos. 1860-1869 (10)	3.15	
			Set value		1.45

Fighting Worker, by J. Jarnuszkiewicz — A563

Photogravure and Engraved

1972, Jan. 5 *Perf. 11½*

1870	A563	60g	red & black	.15	.15

Polish Workers' Party, 30th anniversary.

Luge and Sapporo '72 Emblem — A564

Sapporo '72 Emblem and: 60g, Women's slalom, vert. 1.65z, Biathlon, vert. 2.50z, Ski jump.

1972, Jan. 12 Photo. *Perf. 11*

1871	A564	40g	silver & multi	.15	.15
1872	A564	60g	silver & multi	.15	.15
1873	A564	1.65z	silver & multi	.22	.15
1874	A564	2.50z	silver & multi	.45	.22
			Set value	.85	.48

11th Winter Olympic Games, Sapporo, Japan, Feb. 3-13. See No. B124.

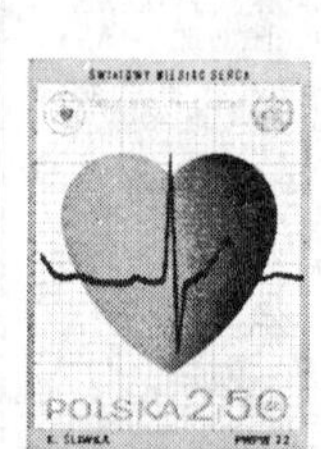

Heart and Electro-cardiogram A565

Bicyclists Racing A566

1972, Mar. 28 Photo. *Perf. 11½x11*

1875	A565	2.50z	blue, red & blk	.20	.15

"Your heart is your health," World Health Day.

1972, May 2 *Perf. 11*

1876	A566	60g	silver & multi	.15	.15

25th Warsaw-Berlin-Prague Bicycle Race.

Berlin Monument — A567

Olympic Runner — A568

1972, May 9 Engr. *Perf. 11½x11*

1877	A567	60g	grnsh black	.15	.15

Unveiling of monument for Polish soldiers and German anti-Fascists in Berlin, May 14.

1972, May 20 *Perf. 11½x11*

Olympic Rings and "Motion" Symbol and: 30g, Archery. 40g, Boxing. 60g, Fencing. 2.50z, Wrestling. 3.40z, Weight lifting. 5z, Bicycling. 8.50z, Sharpshooting.

1878	A568	20g	multicolored	.15	.15
1879	A568	30g	multicolored	.15	.15
1880	A568	40g	multicolored	.15	.15
1881	A568	60g	gray & multi	.15	.15
1882	A568	2.50z	multicolored	.22	.15
1883	A568	3.40z	multicolored	.40	.18
1884	A568	5z	blue & multi	.52	.24
1885	A568	8.50z	multicolored	.90	.50
			Nos. 1878-1885 (8)	2.64	
			Set value		1.20

20th Olympic Games, Munich, Aug. 26-Sept. 10. See No. B125.

Vistula and Cracow — A569

1972, May 28 Photo. *Perf. 11½x11*

1886	A569	60g	red, grn & ocher	.15	.15

50th anniversary of Polish Immigrants Society in Germany (Rodlo).

Knight of King Mieszko I — A570

1972, June 12

1887	A570	60g	gold, red brn, yel & blk	.15	.15

Millennium of the Battle of Cedynia (Cidyny).

Zoo Animals — A571

1972, Aug. 20 Litho. *Perf. 12½*

1888	A571	20g	Cheetah	.15	.15
1889	A571	40g	Giraffe, vert	.15	.15
1890	A571	60g	Toco toucan	.15	.15
1891	A571	1.35z	Chimpanzee	.22	.15
1892	A571	1.65z	Gibbon	.25	.15
1893	A571	3.40z	Crocodile	.35	.18
1894	A571	4z	Kangaroo	1.25	.45
1895	A571	4.50z	Tiger, vert	2.25	1.00
1896	A571	7z	Zebra	2.75	1.25
			Nos. 1888-1896 (9)	7.52	3.63

Ludwik Warynski — A572

1972, Sept. 1 Photo. *Perf. 11*

1897	A572	60g	multicolored	.15	.15

90th anniversary of Proletariat Party, founded by Ludwik Warynski. Printed in sheets of 25 stamps each se-tenant with label showing masthead of party newspaper "Proletariat."

Feliks Dzerzhinski A573

1972, Sept. 11 Litho. *Perf. 11x11½*

1898	A573	60g	red & black	.15	.15

Feliks Dzerzhinski (1877-1926), Russian politician of Polish descent.

Congress Emblem — A574

1972, Sept. 15 Photo. *Perf. 11½x11*

1899	A574	60g	multicolored	.15	.15

25th Congress of the International Cooperative Union, Warsaw, Sept. 1972.

"In the Barracks," by Moniuszko A575

Scenes from Operas or Ballets by Moniuszko: 20g, The Countess. 40g, The Frightful Castle. 60g, Halka. 1.15z, A New Don Quixote. 1.35z, Verbum Nobile. 1.55z, Ideal. 2.50z, Paria.

Photogravure and Engraved

1972, Sept. 15 *Perf. 11½*

1900	A575	10g	gold & violet	.15	.15
1901	A575	20g	gold & dk brn	.15	.15
1902	A575	40g	gold & slate grn	.15	.15
1903	A575	60g	gold & indigo	.15	.15
1904	A575	1.15z	gold & dk blue	.15	.15
1905	A575	1.35z	gold & dk blue	.15	.15
1906	A575	1.55z	gold & grnsh blk	.15	.15
1907	A575	2.50z	gold & dk brown	.32	.18
			Set value	.90	.60

Stanislaw Moniuszko (1819-1872), composer.

"Amazon," by Piotr Michalowski A576

Paintings: 40g, Ostafi Daszkiewicz, by Jan Matejko. 60g, "Summer Rain" (dancing woman), by Wojciech Gerson. 2z, Woman from Naples, by Aleksander Kotsis. 2.50z, Girl Taking Bath, by Pantaleon Szyndler. 3.40z, Count of Thun (child), by Artur Grottger. 4z, Rhapsodist (old man), by Stanislaw Wyspianski. 60g and 2.50z inscribed "DZIEN ZNACZKA 1972."

1972, Sept. 28 Photo. *Perf. 10½x11*

1908	A576	30g	gold & multi	.15	.15
1909	A576	40g	gold & multi	.15	.15
1910	A576	60g	gold & multi	.15	.15
1911	A576	2z	gold & multi	.18	.15
1912	A576	2.50z	gold & multi	.18	.15
1913	A576	3.40z	gold & multi	.35	.15
1914	A576	4z	gold & multi	.75	.40
			Nos. 1908-1914,B126 (8)	3.41	
			Set value		1.60

Stamp Day.

Copernicus, by Jacob van Meurs, 1654, Heliocentric System A577

Portraits of Copernicus: 60g, 16th century etching and Prussian coin, 1530. 2.50z, by Jeremiah Falck, 1645, and coat of arms of King of Prussia, 1520. 3.40z, Copernicus with lily of the valley, and page from Theophilactus Simocatta's "Letters on Customs."

1972, Sept. 28 Litho. *Perf. 11x11½*

1915 A577 40g brt blue & blk .15 .15
1916 A577 60g ocher & blk .15 .15
1917 A577 2.50z red & blk .25 .15
1918 A577 3.40z yellow grn & blk .55 .26
Nos. 1915-1918 (4) 1.10
Set value .50

See No. B127.

Nos. 1337-1338 Surcharged in Red or Black

50 GR X (a) — 1 50 ZŁ (b)

1972 Engr. *Perf. 11½x11*

1919 A445(a) 50g on 40g (R) .15 .15
1920 A445(a) 90g on 40g (R) .15 .15
1921 A445(a) 1z on 40g (R) .15 .15
1922 A445(b) 1.50z on 60g .15 .15
1923 A445(a) 2.70z on 40g (R) .18 .15
1924 A445(b) 4z on 60g .32 .15
1925 A445(b) 4.50z on 60g .35 .15
1926 A445(b) 4.90z on 60g .42 .15
Nos. 1919-1926 (8) 1.87
Set value .65

Issued: Nos. 1919-1920, Nov. 17; others, Oct. 2.

The Little Soldier, by E. Piwowarski A578

1972, Oct. 16 Litho. *Perf. 11½*

1927 A578 60g rose & black .15 .15

Children's health center (Centrum Zdrowia Dzieck), to be built as memorial to children killed during Nazi regime.

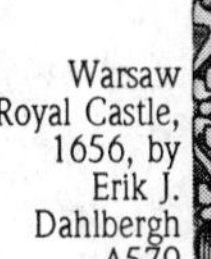

Warsaw Royal Castle, 1656, by Erik J. Dahlbergh A579

1972, Oct. 16 Photo. *Perf. 11x11½*

1928 A579 60g violet, bl & blk .15 .15

Rebuilding of Warsaw Castle, destroyed during World War II.

Ribbons with Symbols of Trade Union Activities — A580

Mountain Lodge, Chocholowska Valley — A581

1972, Nov. 13 *Perf. 11½x11*

1929 A580 60g multicolored .15 .15

7th and 13th Polish Trade Union congresses, Nov. 13-15.

1972, Nov. 13 *Perf. 11*

Mountain Lodges in Tatra National Park: 60g, Hala Ornak, West Tatra, horiz. 1.55z, Hala Gasienicowa. 1.65z, Pieciu Stawow Valley, horiz. 2.50z, Morskie Oko, Rybiego Potoku Valley

1930 A581 40g multicolored .15 .15
1931 A581 60g multicolored .15 .15
1932 A581 1.55z multicolored .15 .15
1933 A581 1.65z multicolored .15 .15
1934 A581 2.50z multicolored .28 .15
Set value .72 .40

Japanese Azalea — A582

Flowering Shrubs: 50g, Alpine rose. 60g, Pomeranian honeysuckle. 1.65z, Chinese quince. 2.50z, Viburnum. 3.40z, Rhododendron. 4z, Mock orange. 8.50z, Lilac.

1972, Dec. 15 Litho. *Perf. 12½*

1935 A582 40g gray & multi .15 .15
1936 A582 50g blue & multi .15 .15
1937 A582 60g multicolored .15 .15
1938 A582 1.65z ultra & multi .18 .15
1939 A582 2.50z ocher & multi .28 .15
1940 A582 3.40z multicolored .35 .20
1941 A582 4z multicolored .65 .22
1942 A582 8.50z multicolored 1.25 .52
Nos. 1935-1942 (8) 3.16
Set value 1.30

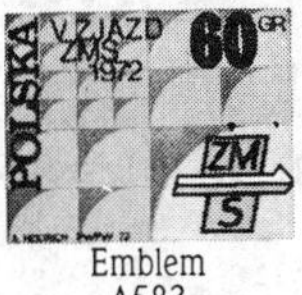

Emblem A583

Copernicus A584

1972, Dec. 15 Photo. *Perf. 11½*

1943 A583 60g red & multi .15 .15

5th Congress of Socialist Youth Union.

Coil Stamps

1972, Dec. 28 Photo. *Perf. 14*

1944 A584 1z deep claret .15 .15
1945 A584 1.50z yellow brown .18 .15
Set value .16

Nicolaus Copernicus (1473-1543), astronomer. Black control number on back of every 5th stamp.

Piast Knight, 10th Century A585

Polish Cavalry: 40g, Knight, 13th century. 60g, Knight of Ladislas Jagello, 15th century, horiz. 1.35z, Hussar, 17th century. 4z, National Guard Uhlan, 18th century. 4.50z, Congress Kingdom Period, 1831. 5z, Light cavalry, 1939, horiz. 7z, Light cavalry, People's Army, 1945.

1972, Dec. 28 *Perf. 11*

1946 A585 20g violet & multi .15 .15
1947 A585 40g multicolored .15 .15
1948 A585 60g orange & multi .15 .15
1949 A585 1.35z orange & multi .15 .15
1950 A585 4z orange & multi .38 .15
1951 A585 4.50z orange & multi .48 .22
1952 A585 5z brown & multi .80 .32
1953 A585 7z multicolored 1.10 .50
Nos. 1946-1953 (8) 3.36
Set value 1.40

Man and Woman, Sculpture by Wiera Muchina — A586

Design: 60g, Globe with Red Star.

1972, Dec. 30

1954 A586 40g gray & multi .15 .15
1955 A586 60g blk, red & vio bl .15 .15
Set value .16 .15

50th anniversary of the Soviet Union.

Nicolaus Copernicus, by M. Bacciarelli — A587

Portraits of Copernicus: 1.50z, painted in Torun, 16th century. 2.70z, by Zinck Nor. 4z, from Strasbourg clock. 4.90z, Copernicus in his Observatory, by Jan Matejko, horiz.

Perf. 11½x11, 11x11½

1973, Feb. 18 Photo.

1956 A587 1z brown & multi .15 .15
1957 A587 1.50z multicolored .15 .15
1958 A587 2.70z multicolored .20 .15
1959 A587 4z multicolored .35 .20
1960 A587 4.90z multicolored .50 .28
Nos. 1956-1960 (5) 1.35
Set value .75

Piast Coronation Sword, 12th Century — A588

Lenin Monument, Nowa Huta — A589

Polish Art: No. 1962, Kruzlowa Madonna, c. 1410. No. 1963, Hussar's armor, 17th century. No. 1964, Wawel head, wood, 16th century. No. 1965, Cock, sign of Rifle Fraternity, 16th century. 2.70z, Cover of Queen Anna Jagiellonka's prayer book (eagle), 1582. 4.90z, Skarbimierz Madonna, wood, c. 1340. 8.50z, The Nobleman Tenczynski, portrait by unknown artist, 17th century.

1973, Mar. 28 Photo. *Perf. 11½x11*

1961 A588 50g violet & multi .15 .15
1962 A588 1z lt blue & multi .15 .15
1963 A588 1z ultra & multi .15 .15
1964 A588 1.50z blue & multi .15 .15
1965 A588 1.50z green & multi .15 .15
1966 A588 2.70z multicolored .20 .15
1967 A588 4.90z multicolored .38 .15
1968 A588 8.50z black & multi 1.10 .42
Set value 2.10 1.00

1973, Apr. 28 Litho. *Perf. 11x11½*

1969 A589 1z multicolored .15 .15

Unveiling of Lenin Monument at Nowa Huta.

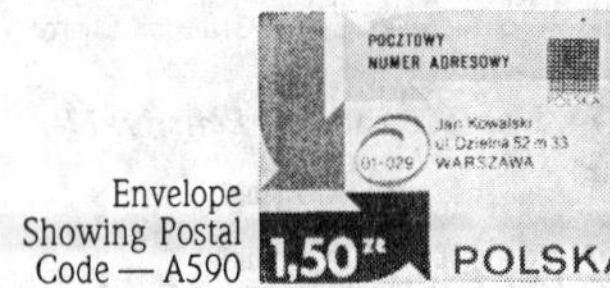

Envelope Showing Postal Code — A590

1973, May 5 *Perf. 11x11½*

1970 A590 1.50z multicolored .15 .15

Introduction of postal code system in Poland.

Wolf — A591

1973, May 21 Photo. *Perf. 11*

1971 A591 50g shown .15 .15
1972 A591 1z Mouflon .15 .15
1973 A591 1.50z Moose .15 .15
1974 A591 2.70z Capercaillie .32 .15
1975 A591 3z Deer .40 .15
1976 A591 4.50z Lynx .55 .20
1977 A591 4.90z European hart 1.50 .42
1978 A591 5z Wild boar 1.65 .70
Nos. 1971-1978 (8) 4.87
Set value 1.65

Intl. Hunting Committee Congress and 50th anniv. of Polish Hunting Assoc.

US Satellite "Copernicus" over Earth — A592

No. 1980, USSR satellite Salyut over earth.

1973, June 20

1979 A592 4.90z multicolored .45 .25
1980 A592 4.90z multicolored .45 .25

American and Russian astronomical observatories in space. No. 1979 and No. 1980 issued in sheets of 6 stamps and 2 labels.

Flame Rising from Book — A593

1973, June 26 Litho.

1981 A593 1.50z blue & multi .15 .15

2nd Polish Science Cong., Warsaw, June 26-29.

Arms of Poznan on 14th Century Seal A594

Marceli Nowotko A595

Polska '73 Emblem and: 1.50z, Tombstone of Nicolas Tomicki, 1524. 2.70z, Kalisz paten, 12th century. 4z, Lion knocker from bronze gate, Gniezno, 12th century, horiz.

Perf. 11½x11, 11x11½

1973, June 30

1982 A594 1z pink & multi .15 .15
1983 A594 1.50z orange & multi .15 .15
1984 A594 2.70z buff & multi .22 .15
1985 A594 4z yellow & multi .40 .15
Nos. 1982-1985 (4) .92
Set value .38

POLSKA '73 Intl. Phil. Exhib., Poznan, Aug. 19-Sept. 2. See No. B128.

1973, Aug. 8 Litho. *Perf. 11½x11*

1986 A595 1.50z red & black .15 .15

Marceli Nowotko (1893-1942), labor leader, member of Central Committee of Communist Party of Poland.

Emblem and Orchard — A596

Human Environment Emblem and: 90g, Grazing cows. 1z, Stork's nest. 1.50z, Pond with fish and water lilies. 2.70z, Flowers on meadow. 4.90z, Underwater fauna and flora. 5z, Forest scene. 6.50z, Still life.

1973, Aug. 30 Photo. *Perf. 11*

1987	A596	50g	black & multi	.15	.15
1988	A596	90g	black & multi	.15	.15
1989	A596	1z	black & multi	.15	.15
1990	A596	1.50z	black & multi	.15	.15
1991	A596	2.70z	black & multi	.18	.15
1992	A596	4.90z	black & multi	.60	.20
1993	A596	5z	black & multi	.90	.25
1994	A596	6.50z	black & multi	1.50	.40
			Nos. 1987-1994 (8)	3.78	
			Set value		1.20

Protection of the environment.

Motorcyclist — A597

1973, Sept. 2 *Perf. 11½*

1995	A597	1.50z	silver & multi	.15	.15

Finals in individual world championship motorcycle race on cinder track, Chorzów, Sept. 2.

Tank A598

1973, Oct. 12 Litho. *Perf. 12½*

1996	A598	1z	shown	.15	.15
1997	A598	1z	Fighter plane	.15	.15
1998	A598	1.50z	Missile	.16	.15
1999	A598	1.50z	Warship	.16	.15
			Set value	.48	.28

Polish People's Army, 30th anniversary.

Grzegorz Piramowicz — A599

Design: 1.50z, J. Sniadecki, Hugo Kollataj and Julian Ursyn Niemcewicz.

Photogravure and Engraved

1973, Oct. 13 *Perf. 11½x11*

2000	A599	1z	buff & dk brn	.15	.15
2001	A599	1.50z	gray & sl grn	.15	.15
			Set value	.25	.16

National Education Commission, bicentenary.

Henryk Arctowski, and Penguins A600

Polish Scientists: No. 2003, Pawel Edmund Strzelecki and Kangaroo. No. 2004, Benedykt Tadeusz Dybowski and Lake Baikal. No. 2005, Stefan Rogozinski, sailing ship "Lucja-Malgorzata." 2z, Bronislaw Malinowski, Trobriand Island drummers. 2.70z, Stefan Drzewiecki and submarine. 3z, Edward Adolf Strasburger and plants. 8z, Ignacy Domeyko, geological strata.

1973, Nov. 30 Photo. *Perf. 10½x11*

2002	A600	1z	gold & multi	.15	.15
2003	A600	1z	gold & multi	.15	.15
2004	A600	1.50z	gold & multi	.15	.15
2005	A600	1.50z	gold & multi	.15	.15
2006	A600	2z	gold & multi	.15	.15
2007	A600	2.70z	gold & multi	.20	.15
2008	A600	3z	gold & multi	.28	.15
2009	A600	8z	gold & multi	.95	.42
			Set value	1.95	.90

Polish Flag — A601

1973, Dec. 15 Photo. *Perf. 11½x11*

2010	A601	1.50z	dp ultra, red & gold	.15	.15

Polish United Workers' Party, 25th anniv.

Jelcz-Berliet Bus — A602

Designs: Polish automotives.

1973, Dec. 28 Photo. *Perf. 11x11½*

2011	A602	50g	shown	.15	.15
2012	A602	90g	Jelcz 316	.15	.15
2013	A602	1z	Polski Fiat 126p	.15	.15
2014	A602	1.50z	Polski Fiat 125p	.15	.15
2015	A602	4z	Nysa M-521 bus	.38	.18
2016	A602	4.50z	Star 660 truck	.48	.22
			Set value	1.20	.65

Iris — A603

Flowers: 1z, Dandelion. 1.50z, Rose. 3z, Thistle. 4z, Cornflowers. 4.50z, Clover. (Paintings by Stanislaw Wyspianski.)

1974, Jan. 22 Engr. *Perf. 12x11½*

2017	A603	50g	lilac	.15	.15
2018	A603	1z	green	.15	.15
2019	A603	1.50z	red orange	.15	.15
2020	A603	3z	deep violet	.28	.15
2021	A603	4z	violet blue	.42	.15
2022	A603	4.50z	emerald	.50	.18
			Set value	1.42	.58

Cottage, Kurpie A604

Designs: 1.50z, Church, Sekowa. 4z, Town Hall, Sulmierzyce. 4.50z, Church, Lachowice. 4.90z, Windmill, Sobienie-Jeziory. 5z, Orthodox Church, Ulucz.

1974, Mar. 5 Photo. *Perf. 11x11½*

2023	A604	1z	multicolored	.15	.15
2024	A604	1.50z	yellow & multi	.15	.15
2025	A604	4z	pink & multi	.28	.15
2026	A604	4.50z	lt blue & multi	.30	.15
2027	A604	4.90z	multicolored	.35	.15
2028	A604	5z	pink & multi	.45	.18
			Nos. 2023-2028 (6)	1.68	
			Set value		.74

Mail Coach and UPU Emblem — A605

Embroidery from Cracow — A606

1974, Mar. 30 *Perf. 11½x12*

2029	A605	1.50z	multicolored	.15	.15

Centenary of Universal Postal Union.

1974, May 7 Photo. *Perf. 11½x11*

Embroideries from: 1.50z, Lowicz. 4z, Slask.

2030	A606	50g	multicolored	.15	.15
2031	A606	1.50z	multicolored	.15	.15
2032	A606	4z	multicolored	.38	.18
a.			Souvenir sheet of 3, #2030-2032, imperf.	1.75	1.25
b.			As "a," perf. 11½x11	6.00	4.50
			Set value	.56	.30

SOCPHILEX IV International Philatelic Exhibition, Katowice, May 18-June 2.

No. 2032a sold for 17z.

No. 2032b sold for 17z plus 15z for 4 envelopes.

Association Emblem A607

Soldier and Dove A608

1974, May 8 Litho. *Perf. 12x11½*

2033	A607	1.50z	gray & red	.15	.15

5th Congress of the Assoc. of Combatants for Liberty & Democracy, Warsaw, May 8-9.

1974, May 9 *Perf. 11½x11*

2034	A608	1.50z	org, lt bl & blk	.15	.15

29th anniversary of victory over Fascism.

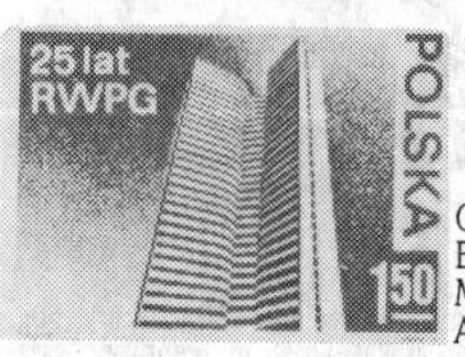

Comecon Building, Moscow A609

1974, May 15 *Perf. 11x11½*

2035	A609	1.50z	gray bl, bis & red	.15	.15

25th anniv. of the Council of Mutual Economic Assistance.

Soccer Ball and Games' Emblem A610

Design: No. 2037, Soccer players, Olympic rings and 1972 medal.

1974, June 15 Photo. *Perf. 11x11½*

2036	A610	4.90z	olive & multi	.50	.20
a.			Souvenir sheet of 4 + 2 labels	4.50	2.00
2037	A610	4.90z	olive & multi	.50	.20
a.			Souv. sheet, 2 each #2036-2037	14.00	7.50

World Cup Soccer Championship, Munich, June 13-July 7.

No. 2036a issued to commemorate Poland's silver medal in 1974 Championship.

Sailing Ship, 16th Century A611

Chess, by Jan Kochanowski A612

Polish Sailing Ships: 1.50z, "Dal," 1934. 2.70z, "Opty," sailed around the world, 1969. 4z, "Dar Pomorza," winner "Operation Sail," 1972. 4.90z, "Polonez," sailed around the world, 1973.

1974, June 29 Litho. *Perf. 11½x11*

2038	A611	1z	multicolored	.15	.15
2039	A611	1.50z	multicolored	.15	.15
2040	A611	2.70z	multicolored	.20	.15
2041	A611	4z	green & multi	.42	.22
2042	A611	4.90z	dp blue & multi	.60	.28
			Nos. 2038-2042 (5)	1.52	
			Set value		.74

1974, July 15 Litho. *Perf. 11½x11*

Design: 1.50z, "Education," etching by Daniel Chodowiecki.

2043	A612	1z	multicolored	.15	.15
2044	A612	1.50z	multicolored	.22	.15
			Set value		.20

10th International Chess Festival, Lublin.

Man and Map of Poland — A613

Polish Eagle — A614

1974, July 21 Photo. *Perf. 11½x11*

2045	A613	1.50z	black, gold & red	.15	.15
2046	A614	1.50z	silver & multi	.15	.15
2047	A614	1.50z	red & multi	.15	.15
			Set value	.36	.24

People's Republic of Poland, 30th anniv.

Lazienkowska Bridge Road — A615

1974, July 21 *Perf. 11x11½*

2048	A615	1.50z	multicolored	.15	.15

Opening of Lazienkowska Bridge over Vistula south of Warsaw.

Strawberries and Congress Emblem — A616

1974, Sept. 10 Photo. *Perf. 11½*

2049	A616	50g	shown	.15	.15
2050	A616	90g	Black currants	.15	.15
2051	A616	1z	Apples	.15	.15
2052	A616	1.50z	Cucumbers	.15	.15
2053	A616	2.70z	Tomatoes	.17	.15
2054	A616	4.50z	Peas	.38	.18

2055 A616 4.90z Pansies .60 .22
2056 A616 5z Nasturtiums 1.25 .40
Nos. 2049-2056 (8) 3.00
Set value 1.10

19th Intl. Horticultural Congress, Warsaw, Sept.

Civic Militia and Security Service Badge — A617

Polish Child, by Lukasz Orlowski — A618

1974, Oct. 3 Photo. ***Perf. 11½x11***
2057 A617 1.50g multicolored .15 .15

30th anniv. of the Civic Militia and the Security Service.

1974, Oct. 9

Polish paintings of Children: 90g, Girl with Pigeon, Anonymous artist, 19th century. 1z, Girl, by Stanislaw Wyspianski. 1.50z, The Orphan from Poronin, by Wladyslaw Slewinski. 3z, Peasant Boy, by Kazimierz Sichulski. 4.50z, Florentine Page, by Aleksander Gierymski. 4.90z, The Artist's Son Tadeusz, by Piotr Michalowski. 6.50z, Boy with Doe, by Aleksander Kotsis.

2058 A618 50g multicolored .15 .15
2059 A618 90g multicolored .15 .15
2060 A618 1z multicolored .15 .15
2061 A618 1.50z multicolored .15 .15
2062 A618 3z multicolored .25 .15
2063 A618 4.50z multicolored .38 .15
2064 A618 4.90z multicolored .45 .22
2065 A618 6.50z multicolored .60 .28
Nos. 2058-2065 (8) 2.28
Set value .96

Children's Day. The 1z and 1.50z are inscribed "Dzien Znaczka (Stamp Day) 1974."

Cracow Manger — A619

King Sigismund Vasa — A620

Masterpieces of Polish art: 1.50z, Flight into Egypt, 1465. 4z, King Jan Olbracht.

1974, Dec. 2 Litho. ***Perf. 11½x11***
2066 A619 1z multicolored .15 .15
2067 A620 1.50z multicolored .16 .15
2068 A620 2z multicolored .22 .15
2069 A619 4z multicolored .60 .20
Nos. 2066-2069 (4) 1.13
Set value .44

Angler — A621

Designs: 1.50z, Hunter with bow and arrow. 4z, Boy snaring geese. 4.50z, Beekeeper. Designs from 16th century woodcuts.

1974-77 Engr. ***Perf. 11½x11***
2070 A621 1z black .15 .15
2071 A621 1.50z indigo .15 .15
2071A A621 4z slate green .22 .15
2071B A621 4.50z dark brown .25 .15
Set value .66 .38

Issued: 1z-1.50z, 12/30; 4z-4.50z, 12/12/77.

Pablo Neruda, by Osvaldo Guayasamin — A622

1974, Dec. 31 Litho. ***Perf. 11½x11***
2072 A622 1.50z multicolored .15 .15

Pablo Neruda (1904-1973), Chilean poet.

Nike Monument and Opera House, Warsaw — A623

1975, Jan. 17 Photo. ***Perf. 11***
2073 A623 1.50z multicolored .15 .15

30th anniversary of the liberation of Warsaw.

Hobby Falcon A624

"Auschwitz" A625

1975, Jan. 23 ***Perf. 11½x12***
2074 A624 1z Lesser kestrel, male .15 .15
2075 A624 1z same, female .15 .15
a. Pair, #2074-2075 .25 .20
2076 A624 1.50z Red-footed falcon, male .18 .15
2077 A624 1.50z same, female .18 .15
a. Pair, #2076-2077 .36 .25
2078 A624 2z shown .35 .15
2079 A624 3z Kestrel .52 .22
2080 A624 4z Merlin 1.65 .45
2081 A624 8z Peregrine 2.25 .90
Nos. 2074-2081 (8) 5.43
Set value 2.00

Falcons.

Photogravure and Engraved

1975, Jan. 27 ***Perf. 11½x11***
2082 A625 1.50z red & black .25 .15

30th anniversary of the liberation of Auschwitz (Oswiecim) concentration camp.

Women's Hurdle Race A626

Designs: 1.50z, Pole vault. 4z, Hop, step and jump. 4.90z, Sprinting.

1975, Mar. 8 Litho. ***Perf. 11x11½***
2083 A626 1z multicolored .15 .15
2084 A626 1.50z olive & multi .15 .15
2085 A626 4z multicolored .35 .15
2086 A626 4.90z green & multi .42 .22
Nos. 2083-2086 (4) 1.07
Set value .48

6th European Indoor Athletic Championships, Katowice, Mar. 1975.

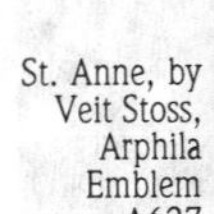

St. Anne, by Veit Stoss, Arphila Emblem A627

1975, Apr. 15 Photo. ***Perf. 11x11½***
2087 A627 1.50z multicolored .15 .15

ARPHILA 75, International Philatelic Exhibition, Paris, June 6-10.

Amateur Radio Union Emblem, Globe A628

1975, Apr. 15 Litho. ***Perf. 11½***
2088 A628 1.50z multicolored .15 .15

International Amateur Radio Union Conference, Warsaw, Apr. 1975.

Mountain Guides' Badge and Sudetic Mountains — A629

Designs: No. 2089, Pine, badge and Tatra Mountains, vert. No. 2090, Gentian and Tatra Mountains, vert. No. 2092, Yew branch with berries, and Sudetic Mountains. No. 2093, River, Beskids Mountains and badge, vert. No. 2094, Arnica and Beskids Mountains, vert.

1975, Apr. 30 Photo. ***Perf. 11***
2089 A629 1z multicolored .15 .15
2090 A629 1z multicolored .15 .15
a. Pair, #2089-2090 .20 .15
2091 A629 1.50z multicolored .15 .15
2092 A629 1.50z multicolored .15 .15
a. Pair, #2091-2092 .30 .20
2093 A629 4z multicolored .40 .18
2094 A629 4z multicolored .40 .18
a. Pair, #2093-2094 .80 .40
Set value 1.10 .60

Centenary of Polish Mountain Guides Organizations. Pairs have continuous design.

Hands Holding Tulips and Rifle — A630

Warsaw Treaty Members' Flags — A631

1975, May 9 ***Perf. 11½x11***
2095 A630 1.50z blue & multi .15 .15

End of WWII, 30th anniv.; victory over Fascism.

1975, May 14
2096 A631 1.50z blue & multi .15 .15

20th anniversary of the signing of the Warsaw Treaty (Bulgaria, Czechoslovakia, German Democratic Rep., Hungary, Poland, Romania, USSR).

Cock and Hen, Congress Emblem — A632

1975, June 23 Photo. ***Perf. 12x11½***
2097 A632 50g shown .15 .15
2098 A632 1z Geese .15 .15
2099 A632 1.50z Cattle .16 .15
2100 A632 2z Cow .28 .15
2101 A632 3z Arabian stallion .42 .15
2102 A632 4z Wielkopolska horses .50 .15
2103 A632 4.50z Pigs .85 .35
2104 A632 5z Sheep 1.75 .52
Nos. 2097-2104 (8) 4.26
Set value 1.35

20th Congress of the European Zootechnical Federation, Warsaw.

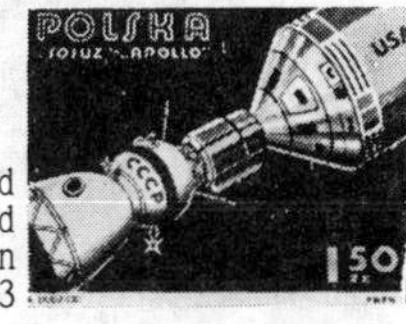

Apollo and Soyuz Linked in Space — A633

1975, July 15 ***Perf. 11x11½***
2105 A633 1.50z shown .20 .15
2106 A633 4.90z Apollo .50 .22
2107 A633 4.90z Soyuz .50 .22
a. Souv. sheet, 2 each #2106-2107 + 2 labels 7.50 4.00
b. Pair, #2106-2107 1.00 .50
Nos. 2105-2107 (3) 1.20 .59

Apollo Soyuz space test project (Russo-American cooperation), launching July 15; link-up, July 17.

Health Fund Emblem — A634

1975, July 12 ***Perf. 11½x11***
2108 A634 1.50z silver, blk & bl .15 .15

National Fund for Health Protection.

"E" and Polish Flag — A635

1975, July 30 Litho. ***Perf. 11x11½***
2109 A635 4z lt blue, red & blk .32 .15

European Security and Cooperation Conference, Helsinki, July 30-Aug. 1.

UN Emblem and Sunburst A636

1975, July 25
2110 A636 4z blue & multi .32 .15

30th anniversary of the United Nations.

Bolek and Lolek A637

Cartoon Characters and Children's Health Center Emblem: 1z, Jacek and Agatka. 1.50z, Reksio, the dog. 4z, Telesfor, the dragon.

1975, Aug. 30 Photo. *Perf. 11x11½*

2111 A637	50g violet bl & multi	.15	.15
2112 A637	1z multicolored	.15	.15
2113 A637	1.50z multicolored	.15	.15
2114 A637	4z multicolored	.45	.18
	Set value	.70	.40

Children's television programs.

Circular Bar Graph and Institute's Emblem — A638

IWY Emblem, White, Yellow and Brown Women — A639

1975, Sept. 1 Litho. *Perf. 11½x11*

2115 A638 1.50z multicolored .15 .15

International Institute of Statistics, 40th session, Warsaw, Sept. 1975.

1975, Sept. 8 Photo.

2116 A639 1.50z multicolored .15 .15

International Women's Year.

First Poles Arriving on "Mary and Margaret" 1608 A640

George Washington — A641

Designs: 1.50z, Polish glass blower and glass works, Jamestown, 1608. 2.70z, Helena Modrzejewska (1840-1909), Polish actress, came to US in 1877. 4z, Casimir Pulaski (1747-1779), and 6.40z, Tadeusz Kosciusko (1748-1817), heroes of American War of Independence.

1975, Sept. 24 Litho. *Perf. 11x11½*

2117 A640	1z black & multi	.15	.15
2118 A640	1.50z black & multi	.15	.15
2119 A640	2.70z black & multi	.20	.15
2120 A640	4z black & multi	.32	.15
2121 A640	6.40z black & multi	.48	.22
	Nos. 2117-2121 (5)	1.30	
	Set value		.58

Souvenir Sheet

Perf. 12

2122	Sheet of 3+3 labels	1.75	1.50
a.	A641 4.90z shown	.55	.30
b.	A641 4.90z Kosciusko	.55	.30
c.	A641 4.90z Pulaski	.55	.30

American Revolution, bicentenary.

Albatross Biplane, 1918-1925 A642

Design: 4.90z, IL 62 jet, 1975.

1975, Sept. 25 *Perf. 11x11½*

2123 A642	2.40z buff & multi	.15	.15
2124 A642	4.90z gray & multi	.42	.20
	Set value		.26

50th anniversary of Polish air post stamps.

Frederic Chopin A643

Dunikowski, Self-portrait A644

1975, Oct. 7 Photo.

2125 A643 1.50z gold, lt vio & blk .20 .15

9th International Chopin Piano Competition, Warsaw, Oct. 7-28.

Printed in sheets of 50 stamps with alternating labels with commemorative inscription.

1975, Oct. 9 *Perf. 11½x11*

Sculptures: 1z, "Breath." 1.50z "Maternity."

2126 A644	50g silver & multi	.15	.15
2127 A644	1z silver & multi	.15	.15
2128 A644	1.50z silver & multi	.15	.15
	Set value	.26	.20

Stamp Day; Xawery Dunikowski (1875-1964), sculptor. See No. B131.

Town Hall, Zamosc A645

Lodz, by Wladyslaw Strzeminski A646

Design: 1z, Arcades, Kazimierz Dolny, horiz.

Coil Stamps

1975, Nov. 11 Photo. *Perf. 14*

2129 A645	1z olive green	.15	.15
2130 A645	1.50z rose brown	.15	.15
	Set value	.20	.15

European Architectural Heritage Year. Black control number on back of every fifth stamp of Nos. 2129-2130.

1975, Nov. 22 Litho. *Perf. 12½*

2131 A646	4.50z multicolored	.45	.18
a.	Souvenir sheet	.90	.50

Lodz 75, 12th Polish Philatelic Exhibition, for 25th anniv. of Polish Philatelists Union.

Piast Family Eagle A647

1.50z, Seal of Prince Boleslaw of Legnica. 4z, Coin of Prince Jerzy Wilhelm (1660-1675).

1975, Nov. 29 Engr. *Perf. 11x11½*

2132 A647	1z green	.15	.15
2133 A647	1.50z brown	.15	.15
2134 A647	4z dull violet	.28	.15
	Set value	.46	.26

Piast dynasty's influence on the development of Silesia.

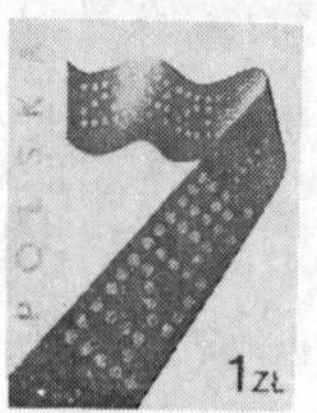

"7" Inscribed "ZJAZD" and "PZPR" — A648

"VII ZJAZD PZPR" — A649

1975, Dec. 8 Photo. *Perf. 11½x11*

2135 A648	1z lt blue & multi	.15	.15
2136 A649	1.50z silver, red & ultra	.15	.15
	Set value	.25	.15

7th Congress of Polish United Workers' Party.

Ski Jump — A650

Designs (Winter Olympic Games Emblem and): 1z, Ice hockey. 1.50z, Slalom. 2z, Speed skating. 4z, Luge. 6.40z, Biathlon.

1976, Jan. 10 *Perf. 11x11½*

2137 A650	50g silver & multi	.15	.15
2138 A650	1z silver & multi	.15	.15
2139 A650	1.50z silver & multi	.15	.15
2140 A650	2z silver & multi	.18	.15
2141 A650	4z silver & multi	.38	.15
2142 A650	6.40z silver & multi	.65	.25
	Set value	1.45	.64

12th Winter Olympic Games, Innsbruck, Austria, Feb. 4-15.

Engine by Richard Trevithick, 1803 — A651

Locomotives by: 1z, M. Murray and J. Blenkinsop, 1810. No. 2145, George Stephenson's Rocket, 1829. No. 2146, Polish electric locomotive, 1969. 2.70z, Stephenson, 1837. 3z, Joseph Harrison, 1840. 4.50z, Thomas Rogers, 1855. 4.90z, Chrzanow (Polish), 1922.

1976, Feb. 13 Photo. *Perf. 11½x12*

2143 A651	50g multicolored	.15	.15
2144 A651	1z multicolored	.15	.15
2145 A651	1.50z multicolored	.15	.15
2146 A651	1.50z multicolored	.15	.15
2147 A651	2.70z multicolored	.22	.15
2148 A651	3z multicolored	.22	.15
2149 A651	4.50z multicolored	.85	.48
2150 A651	4.90z multicolored	.90	.55
	Nos. 2143-2150 (8)	2.79	
	Set value		1.50

History of the locomotive.

Telephone, Radar and Satellites, ITU Emblem — A652

1976, Mar. 10 *Perf. 11*

2151 A652 1.50z multicolored .15 .15

Centenary of first telephone call by Alexander Graham Bell, Mar. 10, 1876.

Atom Symbol and Flags of Communist Countries A653

1976, Mar. 10 Litho. *Perf. 11½*

2152 A653 1.50z multicolored .15 .15

Joint Institute of Nuclear Research, Dubna, USSR, 20th anniversary.

Ice Hockey — A654

Design: 1.50z, like 1z, reversed.

1976, Apr. 8 Photo. *Perf. 11½x11*

2153 A654	1z multicolored	.15	.15
2154 A654	1.50z multicolored	.15	.15
	Set value	.22	.15

Ice Hockey World Championship 1976, Katowice.

Soldier and Map of Sinai A655

1976, Apr. 30 Photo. *Perf. 11x11½*

2155 A655 1.50z multicolored .15 .15

Polish specialist troops serving with UN Forces in Sinai Peninsula.

No. 2155 printed se-tenant with label with commemorative inscription.

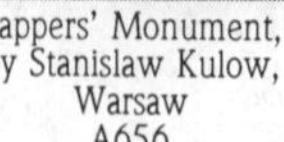

Sappers' Monument, by Stanislaw Kulow, Warsaw A656

Interphil 76, Philadelphia A657

Design: No. 2157, First Polish Army Monument, by Bronislaw Koniuszy, Warsaw.

1976, May 8 *Perf. 11½*

2156 A656	1z gold & multi	.15	.15
2157 A656	1z silver & multi	.15	.15
	Set value	.15	.15

Memorials unveiled on 30th anniv. of WWII victory.

1976, May 20 Litho. *Perf. 11½x11*

2158 A657 8.40z gray & multi .70 .32

Interphil 76, Intl. Phil. Exhib., Philadelphia, May 29-June 6.

Wielkopolski Park and Owl — A658

National Parks: 1z, Wolinski Park and eagle. 1.50z, Slowinski Park and sea gull. 4.50z, Bieszczadzki Park and lynx. 5z, Ojcowski Park and bat. 6z, Kampinoski Park and elk.

1976, May 22 Photo. *Perf. 12x11½*

2159 A658 90g multicolored .15 .15
2160 A658 1z multicolored .15 .15
2161 A658 1.50z multicolored .15 .15
2162 A658 4.50z multicolored .35 .15
2163 A658 5z multicolored .38 .18
2164 A658 6z multicolored .48 .22
Set value 1.45 .75

UN Headquarters, Dove-shaped Globe A659

1976, June 29 Litho. *Perf. 11x11½*

2165 A659 8.40z multicolored .70 .32

UN postage stamps, 25th anniversary.

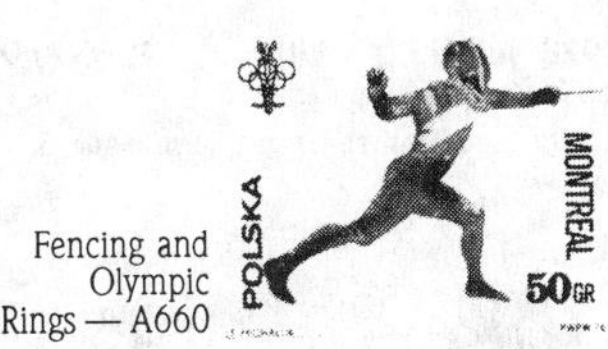

Fencing and Olympic Rings — A660

1976, June 30 Photo.

2166 A660 50g shown .15 .15
2167 A660 1z Bicycling .15 .15
2168 A660 1.50z Soccer .15 .15
2169 A660 4.20z Boxing .35 .15
2170 A660 6.90z Weight lifting .55 .28
2171 A660 8.40z Running .65 .35
Nos. 2166-2171 (6) 2.00
Set value .95

21st Olympic Games, Montreal, Canada, July 17-Aug. 1. See No. B132.

Polish Theater, Poznan — A662

1976, July 12 Litho. *Perf. 11x11½*

2173 A662 1.50z gray ol & org .15 .15

Polish Theater in Poznan, centenary.

Czekanowski, Lake Baikal — A663

1976, Sept. 3 Photo. *Perf. 11x11½*

2174 A663 1.50z silver & multi .15 .15

Aleksander Czekanowski (1833-1876), geologist, death centenary.

Siren A664

Designs: 1z, Sphinx, vert. 2z, Lion. 4.20z, Bull. 4.50z, Goat. Designs from Corinthian vases, 7th century B.C.

Perf. 11x11½, 11½x11

1976, Oct. 30 Photo.

2175 A664 1z gold & multi .15 .15
2176 A664 1.50z gold & multi .15 .15
2177 A664 2z gold & multi .15 .15
2178 A664 4.20z gold & multi .28 .16
2179 A664 4.50z gold & multi .30 .18
Nos. 2175-2179,B133 (6) 2.13
Set value 1.05

Stamp Day.

Warszawa M20 — A665

Automobiles: 1.50z, Warszawa 223. 2z, Syrena 104. 4.90z, Polski Fiat 125.

1976, Nov. 6 Photo. *Perf. 11*

2180 A665 1z multicolored .15 .15
2181 A665 1.50z multicolored .15 .15
2182 A665 2z multicolored .15 .15
2183 A665 4.90z multicolored .35 .16
a. Souvenir sheet of 4, #2180-2183 + 2 labels 1.25 .55
Set value .65 .36

Zeran Automobile Factory, Warsaw, 25th anniv.

Pouring Ladle — A666

Virgin and Child, Epitaph, 1425 — A667

1976, Nov. 26 Litho. *Perf. 11*

2184 A666 1.50z multicolored .15 .15

First steel production at Katowice Foundry.

1976, Dec. 15

6z, The Beautiful Madonna, sculpture, c. 1410.

2185 A667 1z multicolored .15 .15
2186 A667 6z multicolored .40 .20
Set value .26

Polish Trade Union Emblem — A668

1976, Dec. 29

2187 A668 1.50z multicolored .15 .15

8th Polish Trade Union Congress.

Tanker Zawrat Unloading, Gdansk — A669

Polish Ports: No. 2189, Ferry "Gryf" and cars at pier, Gdansk. No. 2190, Loading containers, Gdynia. No. 2191, "Stefan Batory" and "People of the Sea" monument, Gdynia. 2z, Barge and cargoship "Ziemia Szczecinska", Szczecin. 4.20z, Coal loading installations, Swinoujscie. 6.90z, Liner, hydrofoil and lighthouse, Kolobrzeg. 8.40z, Map of Polish Coast with ports, ships and emblem of Union of Polish Ports.

1976, Dec. 29 Photo. *Perf. 11*

2188 A669 1z multicolored .15 .15
2189 A669 1z multicolored .15 .15
2190 A669 1.50z multicolored .15 .15
2191 A669 1.50z multicolored .15 .15
2192 A669 2z multicolored .15 .15
2193 A669 4.20z multicolored .30 .15
2194 A669 6.90z multicolored .55 .24
2195 A669 8.40z multicolored .60 .28
Nos. 2188-2195 (8) 2.20
Set value 1.00

Nurse Helping Old Woman — A670

Civilian Defense Medal — A671

1977, Jan. 24 Litho. *Perf. 11½x11*

2196 A670 1.50z multicolored .15 .15

Polish Red Cross.

1977, Feb. 26 Litho. *Perf. 11*

2197 A671 1.50z multicolored .15 .15

Civilian Defense.

Ball on the Road — A672

1977, Mar. 12 Photo.

2198 A672 1.50z olive & multi .15 .15

Social Action Committee (founded 1966), "Stop, Child on the Road!"

Forest Fruits — A673

1977, Mar. 17 *Perf. 11½x11*

2199 A673 50g Dewberry .15 .15
2200 A673 90g Cranberry .15 .15
2201 A673 1z Wild strawberry .15 .15
2202 A673 1.50z Bilberry .15 .15
2203 A673 2z Raspberry .16 .15
2204 A673 4.50z Blueberry .38 .15
2205 A673 6z Dog rose .48 .20
2206 A673 6.90z Hazelnut .60 .24
Nos. 2199-2206 (8) 2.22
Set value .88

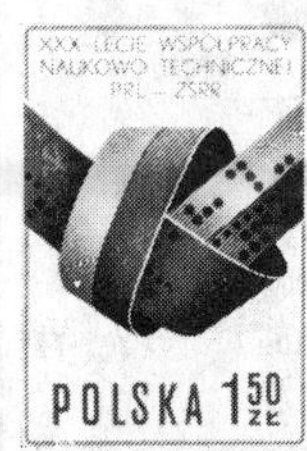

Flags of USSR and Poland as Computer Tape — A674

Emblem and Graph — A675

1977, Apr. 4 Litho. *Perf. 11½x11*

2207 A674 1.50z red & multi .15 .15

Scientific and technical cooperation between Poland and USSR, 30th anniversary.

1977, Apr. 22

2208 A675 1.50z red & multi .15 .15

7th Congress of Polish Engineers.

Venus, by Rubens A676

Paintings by Flemish painter Peter Paul Rubens (1577-1640): 1.50z, Bathsheba. 5z, Helene Fourment. 6z, Self-portrait.

1977, Apr. 30 *Perf. 11½*

Frame in Gray Brown

2209 A676 1z multicolored .16 .15
2210 A676 1.50z multicolored .24 .15
2211 A676 5z multicolored .75 .20
2212 A676 6z multicolored .80 .25
Nos. 2209-2212 (4) 1.95
Set value .60

See No. B134.

Peace Dove A677

1977, May 6 *Perf. 11x11½*

2213 A677 1.50z black, ultra & yel .15 .15

Congress of World Council of Peace, Warsaw, May 6-11.

Bicyclist A678

1977, May 6 Photo.

2214 A678 1.50z gray & multi .15 .15

30th International Peace Bicycling Race, Warsaw-Berlin-Prague.

Wolf A679

Violinist, by Jacob Toorenvliet A680

Wildlife Fund Emblem and: No. 2216, Great bustard. No. 2217, Kestrel. 6z, Otter.

1977, May 12 Photo. *Perf. 11½x11*

2215 A679 1z silver & multi .15 .15
2216 A679 1.50z silver & multi .15 .15
2217 A679 1.50z silver & multi .15 .15
2218 A679 6z silver & multi .50 .20
Nos. 2215-2218 (4) .95
Set value .42

Wildlife protection.

1977, May 16

2219 A680 6z gold & multi .42 .25

AMPHILEX '77 Intl. Phil. Exhib., Amsterdam, May 26-June 5. No. 2219 issued in sheets of 6.

Midsummer Bonfire A681

Folk Customs: 1z, Easter cock. 1.50z, Dousing the women on Easter Monday. 3z, Harvest festival. 6z, Christmas procession with crèche. 8.40z, Wedding dance. 1z, 1.50z, 3z, 6z vertical.

Perf. 11x11½, 11½x11

1977, June 13 **Photo.**

2220 A681 90g multicolored .15 .15
2221 A681 1z multicolored .15 .15
2222 A681 1.50z multicolored .15 .15
2223 A681 3z multicolored .22 .15
2224 A681 6z multicolored .45 .18
2225 A681 8.40z multicolored .65 .24
Nos. 2220-2225 (6) 1.77
Set value .65

Henryk Wieniawski and Musical Symbol — A682

1977, June 30 **Litho.** ***Perf. 11½x11***

2226 A682 1.50z gold, blk & red .15 .15

Wieniawski Music Festivals, Poznan: 5th Intl. Lute Competition, June 30-July 10, and 7th Intl. Violin Competition, Nov. 13-27.

Parnassius Apollo — A683

Butterflies: No. 2228, Nymphalis polychloros. No. 2229, Papilio machaon. No. 2230, Nymphalis antiopa. 5z, Fabriciana adippe. 6.90z, Argynnis paphia.

1977, Aug. 22 **Photo.** ***Perf. 11***

2227 A683 1z multicolored .15 .15
2228 A683 1z multicolored .15 .15
2229 A683 1.50z multicolored .15 .15
2230 A683 1.50z multicolored .15 .15
2231 A683 5z multicolored .52 .15
2232 A683 6.90z multicolored .90 .40
Set value 1.75 .75

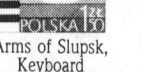

Arms of Slupsk, Keyboard A684

Feliks Dzerzhinski A685

1977, Sept. 3 ***Perf. 11½***

2233 A684 1.50z multicolored .15 .15

Slupsk Piano Festival.

1977, Sept. 10 **Litho.** ***Perf. 11½x11***

2234 A685 1.50z olive bis & sepia .15 .15

Feliks E. Dzerzhinski (1877-1926), organizer and head of Russian Secret Police (Cheka).

Earth and Sputnik — A686

1977, Oct. 1 **Litho.** ***Perf. 11x11½***

2235 A686 1.50z ultra & car .15 .15
a. Souvenir sheet of 3+3 labels .90 .60

60th anniv. of the Russian Revolution and 20th anniv. of Sputnik space flight. Printed in sheets of 15 stamps and 15 carmine labels showing Winter Palace, Leningrad.

Boleslaw Chrobry's Denarius, 11th Century — A687

Silver Coins: 1z, King Kazimierz Wielki's Cracow groszy, 14th century. 1.50z, Legniza-Brzeg-Wolow thaler, 17th century. 4.20z, King Augustus III guilder, Gdansk, 18th century. 4.50z, 5z (ship), 1936. 6z, 100z, Poland's millenium, 1966.

1977, Oct. 9 **Photo.** ***Perf. 11½x11***

2236 A687 50g silver & multi .15 .15
2237 A687 1z silver & multi .15 .15
2238 A687 1.50z silver & multi .15 .15
2239 A687 4.20z silver & multi .32 .15
2240 A687 4.50z silver & multi .40 .20
2241 A687 6z silver & multi .65 .25
Set value 1.55 .75

Stamp Day.

Monastery, Przasnysz A688

Architectural landmarks: No. 2242, Wolin Gate, vert. No. 2243, Church, Debno, vert. No. 2245, Cathedral, Plock. 6z, Castle, Kornik. 6.90z, Palace and Garden, Wilanow.

Perf. 11½x11, 11x11½

1977, Nov. 21 **Photo.**

2242 A688 1z multicolored .15 .15
2243 A688 1z multicolored .15 .15
2244 A688 1.50z multicolored .15 .15
2245 A688 1.50z multicolored .15 .15
2246 A688 6z multicolored .42 .15
2247 A688 6.90z multicolored .55 .22
Nos. 2242-2247 (6) 1.57
Set value .65

Vostok (USSR) and Mercury (USA) A689

1977, Dec. 28 **Photo.** ***Perf. 11x11½***

2248 A689 6.90z ultra & multi .48 .28
a. Souvenir sheet of 6 4.50 3.50

20 years of space conquest. No. 2248a contains 6 No. 2248 (2 tete-beche pairs) and 2 labels, one showing Sputnik 1 and "4.X.1957," the other Explorer 1 and "31.1.1958."

DN Class Iceboats — A690

Design: No. 2250, One iceboat.

1978, Feb. 6 **Litho.** ***Perf. 11***

2249 A690 1.50z lt ultra & blk .15 .15
2250 A690 1.50z lt ultra & blk .15 .15
a. Pair, #2249-2250 + label .30 .20

6th World Iceboating Championships, Feb. 6-11.

Electric Locomotive, Katowice Station, 1957 — A691

Locomotives in Poland: No. 2252, Narrow-gauge engine and Gothic Tower, Znin. No. 2253, Pm36 and Cegielski factory, Poznan, 1936. No. 2254, Electric train and Otwock Station, 1936. No. 2255, Marki Train and Warsaw Stalow Station, 1907. 4.50z, Ty51 coal train and Gdynia Station, 1933. 5z, Tr21 and Chrzanow factory, 1920. 6z, "Cockerill" and Vienna Station, 1848.

1978, Feb. 28 **Photo.** ***Perf. 12x11½***

2251 A691 50g multicolored .15 .15
2252 A691 1z multicolored .15 .15
2253 A691 1z multicolored .15 .15
2254 A691 1.50z multicolored .15 .15
2255 A691 1.50z multicolored .15 .15
2256 A691 4.50z multicolored .38 .15
2257 A691 5z multicolored .40 .15
2258 A691 6z multicolored .48 .22
Nos. 2251-2258 (8) 2.01
Set value .75

Pierwsze Wzloty, 1896, and Czeslaw Tanski A692

Polish Sport Planes: 1z, Zwyciezcy-Challenge, 1932, F. Zwirko and S. Wigura, vert. 1.50z, RWD-5 bis over South Atlantic, 1933, and S. Skarzynski, vert. 4.20z, MI-2 helicopter over mountains, Pezetel emblem, vert. 6.90z, PZL-104 Wilga 35, Pezetel emblem. 8.40z, Motoszybowiec SZD-45 Ogar.

Perf. 11x11½, 11½x11

1978, Apr. 15

2259 A692 50g multicolored .15 .15
2260 A692 1z multicolored .15 .15
2261 A692 1.50z multicolored .16 .15
2262 A692 4.20z multicolored .42 .15
2263 A692 6.90z multicolored .65 .22
2264 A692 8.40z multicolored .80 .24
Nos. 2259-2264 (6) 2.33
Set value .75

Soccer — A693 Poster — A694

Design: 6.90z, Soccer ball, horiz.

Perf. 11½x11, 11x11½

1978, May 12 **Litho.**

2265 A693 1.50z multicolored .15 .15
2266 A693 6.90z multicolored .50 .25
Set value .32

11th World Cup Soccer Championships, Argentina, June 1-25.

1978, June 1 ***Perf. 12x11½***

2267 A694 1.50z multicolored .15 .15

7th International Poster Biennale, Warsaw.

Fair Emblem — A695

1978, June 10 ***Perf. 11***

2268 A695 1.50z multicolored .15 .15

50th International Poznan Fair.

Polonez Passenger Car — A696

1978, June 10 **Photo.** ***Perf. 11***

2269 A696 1.50z multicolored .15 .15

Maj. Miroslaw Hermaszewski A697

6.90z, Hermaszewski, globe & trajectory.

Perf. 11½x11, 11x11½

1978, June 27 **Photo.**

2270 A697 1.50z multi .15 .15
a. Without date .28 .28
2271 A697 6.90z multi, horiz. .50 .24
a. Without date 1.00 1.00
Set value .30

1st Polish cosmonaut on Russian space mission. Nos. 2270a, 2271a printed in sheets of 6 stamps and 2 labels.

Stamps and sheets showing Zenon Jankowski were prepared but not issued.

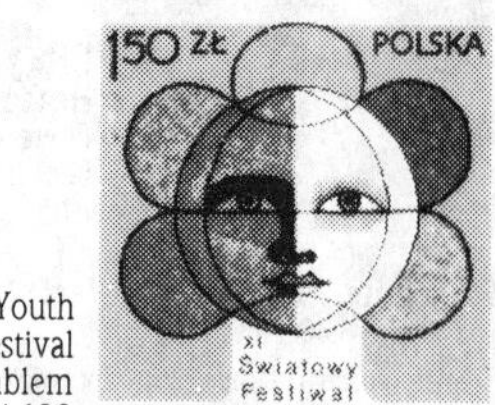

Youth Festival Emblem A698

1978, July 12 **Litho.** ***Perf. 11½***

2272 A698 1.50z multicolored .15 .15

11th Youth Festival, Havana, July 28-Aug. 5.

Souvenir Sheet

Flowers — A699

Illustration reduced.

1978, July 20 ***Perf. 11½x11***

2273 A699 1.50z gold & multi .30 .15

30th anniv. of Polish Youth Movement.

Anopheles Mosquito and Blood Cells — A700

Design: 6z, Tsetse fly and blood cells.

1978, Aug. 19 **Litho.** ***Perf. 11½x11***

2274 A700 1.50z multicolored .15 .15
2275 A700 6z multicolored .45 .20
Set value .28

4th International Parasitological Congress.

Norway Maple, Environment Emblem — A701

Jan Zizka, Battle of Grunwald, by Jan Matejko — A702

Human Environment Emblem and: 1z, English oak. 1.50z, White poplar. 4.20z, Scotch pine. 4.50z, White willow. 6z, Birch.

1978, Sept. 6 Photo. *Perf. 14*

2276 A701	50g gold & multi		.15	.15
2277 A701	1z gold & multi		.15	.15
2278 A701	1.50z gold & multi		.15	.15
2279 A701	4.20z gold & multi		.35	.15
2280 A701	4.50z gold & multi		.38	.15
2281 A701	6z gold & multi		.50	.18
	Nos. 2276-2281 (6)		1.68	
	Set value			.55

Protection of the environment.

Souvenir Sheet

1978, Sept. 8 *Perf. 11½x11*

2282 A702 6z gold & multi .90 .35

PRAGA '78 Intl. Phil. Exhib., Prague, Sept. 8-17.

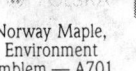

Letter, Telephone and Satellite — A703

1978, Sept. 20 Litho. *Perf. 11*

2283 A703 1.50z multicolored .15 .15

20th anniversary of the Organization of Ministers of Posts and Telecommunications of Warsaw Pact countries.

Peace, by Andre le Brun — A704

1978-79 Litho. *Perf. 11½ (1z), 12½*

2284 A704	1z violet	.15	.15
2285 A704	1.50z steel blue ('79)	.18	.15
2286 A704	2z brown ('79)	.15	.15
2287 A704	2.50z ultra ('79)	.20	.15
	Nos. 2284-2287 (4)	.68	
	Set value		.36

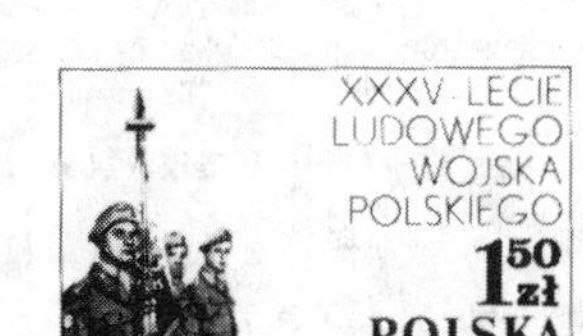

Polish Unit, UN Middle East Emergency Force — A706

Designs: No. 2289, Color Guard, Kosziusko Division (4 soldiers). No. 2290, Color Guard, field training (3 soldiers).

1978, Oct. 6 Photo. *Perf. 12x11½*

2289 A706	1.50z multicolored	.15	.15
2290 A706	1.50z multicolored	.15	.15
2291 A706	1.50z multicolored	.15	.15
	Set value	.40	.24

35th anniversary of People's Army.

Young Man, by Raphael A707

1978, Oct. 9 *Perf. 11*

2292 A707 6z multicolored .42 .15

Stamp Day.

Dr. Korczak and Children — A708

1978, Oct. 11 Litho. *Perf. 11½x11*

2293 A708 1.50z multicolored .15 .15

Dr. Janusz Korczak, physician, educator, writer, birth centenary.

Wojciech Boguslawski (1757-1829) A709

Polish dramatists: 1z, Aleksander Fredro (1793-1878). 1.50z, Juliusz Slowacki (1809-1849). 2z, Adam Mickiewicz (1798-1855). 4.50z, Stanislaw Wyspianski (1869-1907). 6z, Gabriela Zapolska (1857-1921).

1978, Nov. 11 Litho. *Perf. 11½*

2294 A709	50g multicolored	.15	.15
2295 A709	1z multicolored	.15	.15
2296 A709	1.50z multicolored	.15	.15
2297 A709	2z multicolored	.16	.15
2298 A709	4.50z multicolored	.35	.15
2299 A709	6z multicolored	.48	.18
	Set value	1.20	.50

Polish Combatants Monument, and Eiffel Tower, Paris A710

1978, Nov. 2 Photo. *Perf. 11x11½*

2300 A710 1.50z brown, red & bl .15 .15

Przewalski Mare and Colt A711

Animals: 1z, Polar bears. 1.50z, Indian elephants. 2z, Jaguars. 4.20z, Gray seals. 4.50z, Hartebeests. 6z, Mandrills.

1978, Nov. 10

2301 A711	50g multicolored	.15	.15
2302 A711	1z multicolored	.15	.15
2303 A711	1.50z multicolored	.15	.15
2304 A711	2z multicolored	.16	.15
2305 A711	4.20z multicolored	.28	.15
2306 A711	4.50z multicolored	.35	.15
2307 A711	6z multicolored	.48	.15
	Set value	1.50	.55

Warsaw Zoological Gardens, 50th anniv.

Adolf Warski (1868-1937) A712

Party Emblem A713

Portraits: No. 2309, Julian Lenski (1889-1937). No. 2310, Aleksander Zawadzki (1899-1964). No. 2311, Stanislaw Dubois (1901-1942).

Perf. 11½x11, 11x11½

1978, Dec. 15 Photo.

2308 A712	1.50z red & brown	.15	.15
2309 A712	1.50z red & black	.15	.15
2310 A712	1.50z red & dk vio	.15	.15
2311 A712	1.50z red & dk blue	.15	.15
2312 A713	1.50z black, red & gold	.15	.15
	Set value	.50	.30

Polish United Workers' Party, 30th anniv.

LOT Planes, 1929 and 1979 A714

1979, Jan. 2 Photo. *Perf. 11x11½*

2313 A714 6.90z gold & multi .45 .18

LOT, Polish airline, 50th anniversary.

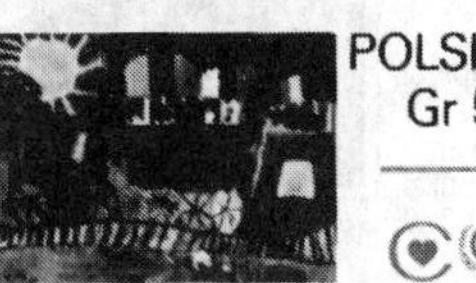

Train and IYC Emblem — A715

Children's Paintings: 1z, Children with toys. 1.50z, Children in meadow. 6z, Family.

1979, Jan. 13 *Perf. 11*

2314 A715	50g multicolored	.15	.15
2315 A715	1z multicolored	.15	.15
2316 A715	1.50z multicolored	.15	.15
2317 A715	6z multicolored	.50	.15
	Set value	.75	.30

International Year of the Child.

Artist's Wife, by Karol Mondral — A716

Modern Polish Graphic Arts: 50g, "Lightning," by Edmund Bartlomiejcyk, horiz. 1.50z, Musicians, by Tadeusz Kulisiewicz. 4.50z, Portrait of a Brave Man, by Wladyslaw Skoczylas.

Perf. 11½x12, 12x11½

1979, Mar. 5 Engr.

2318 A716	50g brt violet	.15	.15
2319 A716	1z slate green	.15	.15
2320 A716	1.50z blue gray	.15	.15
2321 A716	4.50z violet blue	.35	.15
	Set value	.60	.28

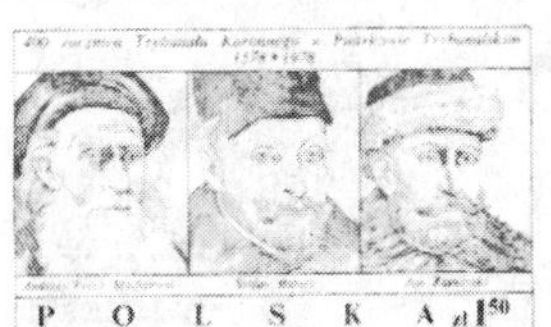

Andrzej Frycz-Modrzewski, Stefan Batory, Jan Zamoyski — A717

Photogravure and Engraved

1979, Mar. 12 *Perf. 12x11½*

2322 A717 1.50z cream & sepia .15 .15

Royal Tribunal in Piotrkow Trybunalski, 400th anniversary.

Pole Vault and Olympic Emblem — A718

Olympic Emblem and: 1.50z, High jump. 6z, Cross-country skiing. 8.40z, Equestrian.

1979, Mar. 26 Photo. *Perf. 12x11½*

2323 A718	1z multicolored	.15	.15
2324 A718	1.50z multicolored	.15	.15
2325 A718	6z multicolored	.42	.15
2326 A718	8.40z multicolored	.65	.20
	Nos. 2323-2326 (4)	1.37	
	Set value		.46

1980 Olympic Games.

Flounder — A720

Fish and Environmental Protection Emblem: 90g, Perch. 1z, Grayling. 1.50z, Salmon. 2z, Trout. 4.50z, Pike. 5z, Carp. 6z, Catfish and frog.

1979, Apr. 26 Photo. *Perf. 11½x11*

2327 A720	50g multicolored	.15	.15
2328 A720	90g multicolored	.15	.15
2329 A720	1z multicolored	.15	.15
2330 A720	1.50z multicolored	.15	.15
2331 A720	2z multicolored	.15	.15
2332 A720	4.50z multicolored	.40	.15
2333 A720	5z multicolored	.50	.15
2334 A720	6z multicolored	.60	.20
	Nos. 2327-2334 (8)	2.25	
	Set value		.75

Polish angling, centenary, and protection of the environment.

A721

1979, Apr. 30 Litho. *Perf. 11x11½*

2335 A721 1.50z multicolored .15 .15

Council for Mutual Economic Aid of Socialist Countries, 30th anniversary.

Faces and Emblem — A722

1979, May 7 *Perf. 11*

2336 A722 1.50z red & black .15 .15

6th Congress of Association of Fighters for Liberty and Democracy, Warsaw, May 7-8.

St. George's Church, Sofia
A722a

1979, May 15 Photo. *Perf. 11x11½*
2337 A722a 1.50z multicolored .15 .15

Philaserdica '79 Phil. Exhib., Sofia, Bulgaria, May 18-27.

Pope John Paul II, Cracow Cathedral
A723

Designs: 8.40z, Pope John Paul II, Auschwitz-Birkenau Memorial. 50z, Pope John Paul II.

1979, June 2 Photo. *Perf. 11x11½*
2338 A723 1.50z multicolored .18 .15
2339 A723 8.40z multicolored .80 .32
Set value .40

Souvenir Sheet
Perf. 11½x11
2340 A723 50z multicolored 6.00 3.50

Visit of Pope John Paul II to Poland, June 2-11. No. 2340 contains one 26x35mm stamp.
A variety of #2340 with silver margin exists.

Paddle Steamer Prince Ksawery and Old Warsaw — A724

Designs: 1.50z, Steamer Gen. Swierczewski and Gdansk, 1914. 4.50z, Tug Aurochs and Plock, 1960. 6z, Motor ship Mermaid and modern Warsaw, 1959.

1979, June 15 Litho. *Perf. 11*
2341 A724 1z multicolored .15 .15
2342 A724 1.50z multicolored .15 .15
2343 A724 4.50z multicolored .32 .15
2344 A724 6z multicolored .48 .18
Nos. 2341-2344 (4) 1.10
Set value .42

Vistula River navigation, 150th anniversary.

Kosciuszko Monument, Philadelphia — A725

1979, July 1 Photo. *Perf. 11½*
2345 A725 8.40z multicolored .60 .25

Gen. Tadeusz Kosziuszko (1746-1807), Polish soldier and statesman who served in American Revolution.

Mining Machinery
A726

Eagle and People
A727

Design: 1.50z, Salt crystals.

1979, July 14 Photo. *Perf. 14*
2346 A726 1z lt brown & blk .15 .15
2347 A726 1.50z blue grn & blk .15 .15
Set value .25 .15

Wieliczka ancient rock-salt mines.

1979, July 21 *Perf. 11½x11*

No. 2349, Man with raised hand and flag.

2348 A727 1.50z red, blue & gray .15 .15
2349 A727 1.50z silver, red & blk .15 .15
Set value .25 .16

35 years of Polish People's Republic.

Souvenir Sheet
1979, Sept. 2 Photo. *Perf. 11½x11*
2350 A727 Sheet of 2, #2348-2349 + label .50 .45

13th National Philatelic Exhibition.

Poland No. 1, Rowland Hill (1795-1879), Originator of Penny Postage
A728

1979, Aug. 16 Litho. *Perf. 11½x11*
2351 A728 6z multicolored .40 .18

Souvenir Sheet

The Rape of Europa, by Bernardo Strozzi
A729

1979, Aug. 20 Photo. *Perf. 11x11½*
2352 A729 10z multicolored .75 .50

Europhil '79, Intl. Phil. Exhib.

Wojciech Jastrzebowski
A730

1979, Aug. 27 *Perf. 11½x11*
2353 A730 1.50z multicolored .15 .15

Economic Congress.

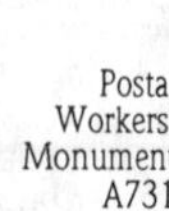

Postal Workers' Monument
A731

1979, Sept. 1 *Perf. 11x11½*
2354 A731 1.50z multicolored .15 .15

40th anniversary of Polish postal workers' resistance to Nazi invaders. See No. B137.

ITU Emblem, Radio Antenna
A732

1979, Sept. 24 *Perf. 11x11½*
2355 A732 1.50z multicolored .15 .15

Intl. Radio Consultative Committee (CCIR) of the ITU, 50th anniv.

Violin
A733

1979, Sept. 25 Litho.
2356 A733 1.50z dk blue, org, grn .15 .15

Henryk Wieniawski Young Violinists' Competition, Lublin.

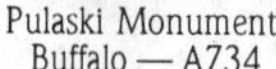
Pulaski Monument, Buffalo — A734

Gen. Franciszek Jozwiak — A735

1979, Oct. 1 Photo. *Perf. 11½x12*
2357 A734 8.40z multicolored .48 .22

Gen. Casimir Pulaski (1748-1779), Polish nobleman who served in American Revolutionary War.

1979, Oct. 3 *Perf. 11½x11*
2358 A735 1.50z gray blue, dk blue & gold .15 .15

35th anniv. of Civil and Military Security Service, founded by Gen. Franciszek Jozwiak (1895-1966).

Drive-in Post Office — A736

Designs: 1.50z, Parcel sorting. 4.50z, Loading mail train. 6z, Mobile post office.

1979, Oct. 9 *Perf. 11½*
2359 A736 1z multicolored .15 .15
2360 A736 1.50z multicolored .15 .15
2361 A736 4.50z multicolored .38 .15
2362 A736 6z multicolored .52 .18
Set value 1.00 .44

Stamp Day.

Holy Family — A737

Design: 6.90z, Nativity, horiz.

Perf. 11½x11, 11x11½
1979, Dec. 4 Photo.
2363 A737 2z multicolored .15 .15
2364 A737 6.90z multicolored .45 .20
Set value .28

A738

A739

Space Achievements: 1z, Soyuz 30 and Salyut 6. 1.50z, Kopernik 500 and Copernicus satellite. 2z, Lunik 2 and Ranger 7. 4.50z, Yuri Gagarin and Vostok. 6.90z, Neil Armstrong and Apollo 11.

1979, Dec. 28 Photo. *Perf. 11½x11*
2365 A738 1z multi .15 .15
2366 A738 1.50z multi .15 .15
2367 A738 2z multi .15 .15
2368 A738 4.50z multi .35 .15
2369 A738 6.90z multi .48 .18
a. Souvenir sheet of 5 1.65 1.00
Nos. 2365-2369 (5) 1.28
Set value .50

No. 2369a contains Nos. 2365-2369, tete beche plus label.

1980, Jan. 31 Photo. *Perf. 11½x12*

Designs: Horse Paintings.

2370 A739 1z Stagecoach .15 .15
2371 A739 2z Horse, trainer .15 .15
2372 A739 2.50z Trotters .15 .15
2373 A739 3z Fox hunt .24 .15
2374 A739 4z Sled .28 .15
2375 A739 6z Hay cart .50 .16
2376 A739 6.50z Pairs .52 .16
2377 A739 6.90z Hurdles .52 .18
Nos. 2370-2377 (8) 2.51
Set value .88

Sierakov horse stud farm, 150th anniv.

Party Slogan on Map of Poland — A740
Worker, by Janusz Stanny — A741

1980, Feb. 11 Photo. *Perf. 11½x11*
2378 A740 2.50z multi .20 .15
2379 A741 2.50z multi .20 .15
Set value .18

Polish United Workers' Party, 8th Congress.

Equestrian, Olympic Rings — A742

1980, Mar. 31 *Perf. 12x11½*
2380 A742 2z shown .16 .15
2381 A742 2.50z Archery .20 .15
2382 A742 6.50z Biathlon .52 .20
2383 A742 8.40z Volleyball .65 .25
Nos. 2381-2383 (3) 1.37
Set value .62

13th Winter Olympic Games, Lake Placid, NY, Feb. 12-24 (6.50z); 22nd Summer Olympic Games, Moscow, July 19-Aug. 3. See No. B138.

Map and Old Town Hall, 1591, Zamosc
A743

1980, Apr. 3 Litho. Perf. 11½
2384 A743 2.50z multi .20 .15

Zamosc, 400th anniversary.

Arms of Poland and Russia
A744

1980, Apr. 21 Litho. Perf. 11½
2385 A744 2.50z multi .20 .15

Treaty of Friendship, Cooperation and Mutual Assistance between Poland and USSR, 35th anniversary.

Lenin, 110th Birth Anniversary
A745

1980, Apr. 22 Photo. Perf. 11
2386 A745 2.50z multi .25 .15

Workers Marching — A746

Dove Over Liberation Date — A747

1980, May 1 Perf. 11½x11
2387 A746 2.50z multi .20 .15

Revolution of 1905, 75th anniversary.

1980, May 9 Perf. 11½x12
2388 A747 2.50z multi .20 .15

Victory over fascism, 35th anniversary.

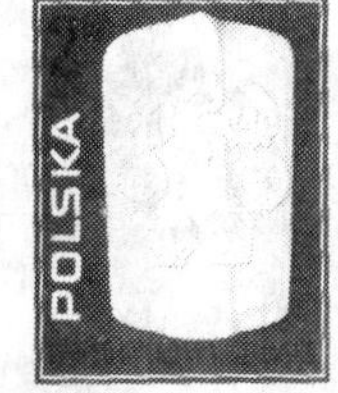

Arms of Treaty-signing Countries — A748

1980, May 14 Litho. Perf. 11½x11
2389 A748 2z red & blk .20 .15

Signing of Warsaw Pact (Bulgaria, Czechoslovakia, German Democratic Rep., Hungary, Poland, Romania, USSR), 25th anniversary.

Caverns, (1961 Expedition) Map of Cuba — A749

1980, May 22 Photo. Perf. 14
2390 A749 2z shown .18 .15
2391 A749 2z Seals, Antarctica, 1959 .18 .15
2392 A749 2.50z Ethnology, Mongolia, 1963 .22 .15
2393 A749 2.50z Archaeology, Syria, 1959 .22 .15
2394 A749 6.50z Mountain climbing, Nepal, 1978 .52 .18
2395 A749 8.40z Paleontology, Mongolia, 1963 .65 .22
Nos. 2390-2395 (6) 1.97
Set value .72

Malachowski Lyceum, Arms of Polish Order of Labor — A750

Xerocomus Parasiticus — A751

1980, June 7 Photo. Perf. 11x12
2396 A750 2z blk & dl grn .15 .15

Malachowski Lyceum (oldest school in Plock), 800th anniversary.

1980, June 30 Perf. 11½x11
2397 A751 2z shown .18 .15
2398 A751 2z Clathrus ruber .18 .15
2399 A751 2.50z Phallus hadriani .22 .15
2400 A751 2.50z Strobilomyces floccopus .22 .15
2401 A751 8z Sparassis crispa .60 .22
2402 A751 10.50z Langermannia gigantea .80 .28
Nos. 2397-2402 (6) 2.20
Set value .82

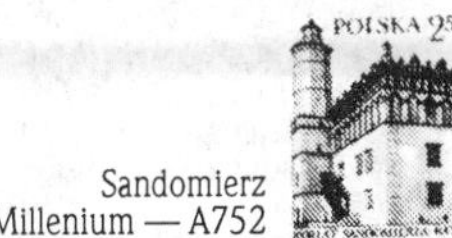

Sandomierz Millenium — A752

1980, July 12 Photo. Perf. 11x11½
2403 A752 2.50z dk brown .22 .15

"Lwow," T. Ziolkowski — A753

Ships and Teachers: 2.50z, Antoni Garnuszewski, A. Garnuszewski. 6z, Zenit, A. Ledochowski. 6.50z, Jan Turlejski, K. Porebski. 6.90z, Horyzon, G. Kanski. 8.40z, Dar Pomorza, K. Maciejewicz.

1980, July 21 Litho. Perf. 11
2404 A753 2z multi .20 .15
2405 A753 2.50z multi .24 .15
2406 A753 6z multi .50 .20
2407 A753 6.50z multi .58 .22
2408 A753 6.90z multi .58 .24
2409 A753 8.40z multi .70 .30
Nos. 2404-2409 (6) 2.80 1.26

Marize Maritime High School.

A754 A755

Designs: Medicinal plants.

1980, Aug. 15 Litho. Perf. 11½x11
2410 A754 2z Atropa belladonna .18 .15
2411 A754 2.50z Datura innoxia .22 .15
2412 A754 3.40z Valeriana .25 .15
2413 A754 5z Mentha piperita .45 .18
2414 A754 6.50z Calendula .55 .25
2415 A754 8z Salvia officinalis .60 .28
Nos. 2410-2415 (6) 2.25
Set value 1.00

1980, Aug. 20 Perf. 11
2416 A755 2.50z multi .25 .15

Jan Kochanowski (1530-1584), poet.

United Nations, 35th Anniversary — A756

1980, Sept. 19 Photo. Perf. 11x11½
2417 A756 8.40z multi .75 .32

Chopin Piano Competition
A757

1980, Oct. 2 Litho. Perf. 11½
2418 A757 6.90z blk & tan .60 .32

Mail Pick-up — A758

1980, Oct. 9 Photo. Perf. 12x11½
2419 A758 2z shown .18 .15
2420 A758 2.50z Letter sorting .22 .15
2421 A758 6z Loading mail plane .55 .22
2422 A758 6.50z Mail boxes .55 .24
a. Souvenir sheet of 4, #2419-2422 4.25 3.00
Nos. 2419-2422 (4) 1.50
Set value .64

Stamp Day.

Girl Embracing Dove, UN Emblem
A759

1980, Nov. 21 Litho. Perf. 11x11½
2423 A759 8.40z multicolored .75 .35

UN Declaration on the Preparation of Societies for Life in Peace.

Battle of Olzynska Grochowska, by W. Kossak — A760

1980, Nov. 29 Photo. Perf. 11
2424 A760 2.50z multicolored .25 .15

Battle of Olzynska Grochowska, 1830.

Horse-drawn Fire Engine — A761

Designs: Horse-drawn vehicles.

1980, Dec. 16
2425 A761 2z shown .18 .15
2426 A761 2.50z Passenger coach .22 .15
2427 A761 3z Beer wagon .24 .15
2428 A761 5z Sled .45 .18
2429 A761 6z Bus .50 .25
2430 A761 6.50z Two-seater .55 .25
Nos. 2425-2430 (6) 2.14 1.13

Honor to the Silesian Rebels, by Jan Borowczak
A762

Pablo Picasso
A763

1981, Jan. 22 Engr. Perf. 11½
2431 A762 2.50z gray grn .18 .15

Silesian uprising, 60th anniversary.

1981, Mar. 10 Photo. Perf. 11½x11
2432 A763 8.40z multi .55 .32
a. Miniature sheet of 2 + 2 labels 2.50 1.25

Pablo Picasso (1881-1973), artist, birth centenary. No. 2432 se-tenant with label showing A Crying Woman. Sold for 20.80z.

Balloon Flown by Pilatre de Rozier, 1783 — A764

Gordon Bennett Cup (Balloons): No. 2434, J. Blanchard, J. Jeffries, 1875. 2.50z, F. Godard, 1850. 3z, F. Hynek, Z. Burzynski, 1933. 6z, Z. Burzynski, N. Wysocki, 1935. 6.50z, B. Abruzzo, M. Anderson, P. Newman, 1978. 10.50z, Winners' names, 1933-1935, 1938.

1981, Mar. 25 Photo. *Perf. 11½x12*

2433 A764 2z multi .18 .15
2434 A764 2z multi .18 .15
2435 A764 2.50z multi .24 .15
2436 A764 3z multi .25 .15
2437 A764 6z multi .55 .24
2438 A764 6.50z multi .60 .25
Nos. 2433-2438 (6) 2.00
Set value .85

Souvenir Sheet

Imperf

2439 A764 10.50z multi .95 .70

Iphegenia, by Franz Anton Maulbertsch (1724-1796), WIPA '81 Emblem A765

1981, May 11 Litho. *Perf. 11½*

2440 A765 10.50z multi 1.00 .48

WIPA '81 Intl. Phil. Exhib., Vienna, May 22-31.

Wroclaw, 1493 A766

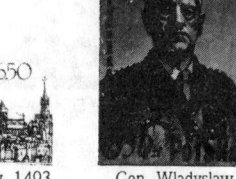

Gen. Wladyslaw Sikorski (1881-1943) A767

1981, May 15 Photo. *Perf. 14*

2441 A766 6.50z brown .50 .22

See #2456-2459. For surcharges see #2526, 2939.

1981, May 20 *Perf. 11½x11*

2442 A767 6.50z multi .42 .22

Kwan Vase, 18th Cent. — A768

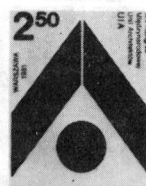

Intl. Architects Union, 14th Congress, Warsaw — A769

1981, June 15

2443 A768 1z shown .15 .15
2444 A768 2z Cup, saucer, 1820 .22 .15
2445 A768 2.50z Jug, 1820 .25 .15
2446 A768 5z Portrait plate, 1880 .52 .15
2447 A768 6.50z Vase, 1900 .65 .20
2448 A768 8.40z Basket, 1840 .75 .24
Nos. 2443-2448 (6) 2.54
Set value .80

1981, July 15 Litho.

2449 A769 2.50z multi .18 .15

Moose, Rifle and Pouch — A770

A770a

1981, July 30

2450 A770 2z shown .15 .15
2451 A770 2z Boar .15 .15
2452 A770 2.50z Fox .25 .15
2453 A770 2.50z Elk .25 .15
2454 A770 6.50z Greylag goose, horiz. .65 .20
2455 A770 6.50z Fen duck .65 .20
Nos. 2450-2455 (6) 2.10
Set value .72

City Type of 1981

Perf. 11x11½, 11½x13

1981, July 28 Photo.

2456 A766 4z Gdansk, 1652, vert. .30 .15
2457 A766 5z Krakow, 1493, vert. .40 .18
2458 A766 6z Legnica, 1744 .50 .22
2459 A766 8z Warsaw, 1618 .65 .28
Nos. 2456-2459 (4) 1.85 .83

1982, Nov. 2 Photo. *Perf. 11½*

2461 A770a 12z Vistula River .22 .15
2463 A770a 17z Kasimierz Dolny .32 .15
2466 A770a 25z Gdansk .45 .22
Nos. 2461-2466 (3) .99
Set value .44

Wild Bison — A771

1981, Aug. 27 *Perf. 11½x11*

2471 Strip of 5 3.25 1.25
a.-e. A771 6.50z, any single .60 .22

60th Anniv. of Polish Tennis Federation A772

1981, Sept. 17 Photo. *Perf. 11x11½*

2472 A772 6.50z multi .60 .25

Model Airplane — A773

1981, Sept. 24 *Perf. 14*

2473 A773 1z shown .15 .15
2474 A773 2z Boats .22 .15
2475 A773 2.50z Racing cars .25 .15
2476 A773 4.20z Gliders .45 .15
2477 A773 6.50z Radio-controlled racing cars .65 .18
2478 A773 8z Yachts .70 .22
Nos. 2473-2478 (6) 2.42
Set value .75

Intl. Year of the Disabled — A774

Stamp Day — A775

1981, Sept. 25 Litho. *Perf. 11½x11*

2479 A774 8.40z multi .75 .28

1981, Oct. 9 Photo. *Perf. 14*

2480 A775 2.50z Pistol, 18th cent., horiz. .25 .15
2481 A775 8.40z Sword, 18th cent. .75 .24
Set value .32

A776

A777

1981, Oct. 10 *Perf. 11½x12*

2482 A776 2.50z multi .25 .15

Henryk Wieniawski (1835-1880), violinist and composer.

1981, Oct. 15 Litho.

Working Movement Leaders: 50g, Bronislaw Wesolowski (1870-1919). 2z, Malgorzata Fornalska (1902-1944). 2.50z, Maria Koszutska (1876-1939). 6.50z, Marcin Kasprzak (1860-1905).

2483 A777 50g grn & blk .15 .15
2484 A777 2z bl & blk .16 .15
2485 A777 2.50z brn & blk .18 .15
2486 A777 6.50z lil rose & blk .45 .18
Nos. 2483-2486 (4) .94
Set value .38

World Food Day — A778

1981, Oct. 16 *Perf. 11½x11*

2487 A778 6.90z multi .65 .25

Old Theater, Cracow, 200th Anniv. — A779

Theater Emblem and: 2z, Helena Modrzejewska (1840-1909), actress. 2.50z, Stanislaw Kozmian (1836-1922), theater director, 1865-1885, founder of Cracow School. 6.50z, Konrad Swinarski (1929-1975), stage manager.

Photo. & Engr.

1981, Oct. 17 *Perf. 12x11½*

2488 A779 2z multi .24 .15
2489 A779 2.50z multi .30 .15
2490 A779 6.50z multi .58 .20
2491 A779 8z multi .75 .24
Nos. 2488-2491 (4) 1.87 .74

Souvenir Sheet

Vistula River Project — A780

1981, Dec. 20 Litho. *Perf. 11½x12*

2492 A780 10.50z multi 1.25 .75

Flowering Succulent Plants — A781

1981, Dec. 22 Photo. *Perf. 13*

2493 A781 90g Epiphyllopsis gaertneri .15 .15
2494 A781 1z Cereus tonduzii .15 .15
2495 A781 2z Cylindropuntia leptocaulis .18 .15
2496 A781 2.50z Cylindroppuntia fulgida .25 .15
2497 A781 2.50z Caralluma lugardi .25 .15
2498 A781 6.50z Nopalea cochenillifera .50 .20
2499 A781 6.50z Lithopsps helmutii .50 .20
2500 A781 10.50z Cylindropuntia spinosior 1.00 .35
Nos. 2493-2500 (8) 2.98
Set value 1.10

Polish Workers' Party, 40th Anniv. — A782

Stoneware Plate, 1890 — A783

1982, Jan. 5 Photo. *Perf. 11½x11*

2501 A782 2.50z multi .25 .15

1982, Jan. 20

Porcelain or Stoneware: 2z, Plate, mug, 1790. 2.50z, Soup tureen, gravy dish, 1830. 6z, Salt and pepper dish, 1844, 8z, Stoneware jug, 1840. 10.50z, Stoneware figurine, 1740.

2502 A783 1z multi .15 .15
2503 A783 2z multi .18 .15
2504 A783 2.50z multi .24 .15
2505 A783 6z multi .60 .25
2506 A783 8z multi .80 .32
2507 A783 10.50z multi 1.00 .42
Nos. 2502-2507 (6) 2.97
Set value 1.20

Ignacy Lukasiewicz (1822-1882), Oil Lamp Inventor — A784

Designs: Various oil lamps.

1982, Mar. 22 Photo. *Perf. 11½x11*

2508 A784 1z multi .15 .15
2509 A784 2z multi .15 .15
2510 A784 2.50z multi .24 .15
2511 A784 3.50z multi .32 .15
2512 A784 9z multi .85 .35
2513 A784 10z multi .90 .40
Nos. 2508-2513 (6) 2.61
Set value 1.12

Karol Szymanowski (1882-1937), Composer — A785

1982, Apr. 8

2514	A785	2.50z dk brn & gold	.25	.15

Victory in Challenge Trophy Flights A786

1982, May 5 Photo. *Perf. 11x11½*

2515	A786	27z RWD-6 monoplane	1.25	.65
2516	A786	31z RWD-9	1.75	.85
a.		Souv. sheet of 2, #2515-2516	3.25	2.25

Henryk Sienkiewicz (1846-1916), Writer — A787

1982 World Cup — A788

Polish Nobel Prize Winners: 15z, Wladyslaw Reymont (1867-1925), writer, 1924. 25z, Marie Curie (1867-1934), physicist 1903, 1911. 31z, Czeslaw Milosz (b. 1911), poet, 1980.

1982, May 10 Litho. *Perf. 11½x11*

2517	A787	3z black & dk grn	.15	.15
2518	A787	15z black & brown	.65	.24
2519	A787	25z black	1.10	.40
2520	A787	31z black & gray	1.25	.52
		Nos. 2517-2520 (4)	3.15	1.31

Perf. 11½x11, 11x11½

1982, May 28 Photo.

2521	A788	25z Ball	1.25	.60
2522	A788	27z Bull, ball, horiz.	1.50	.65

Souvenir Sheet

Maria Kaziera Sobieska — A789

1982, June 11 Photo. *Perf. 11½x11*

2523	A789	65z multi	3.25	2.25

PHILEXFRANCE '82 Intl. Stamp Exhibition, Paris, June 11-21.

Assoc. Presidents Stanislaw Sierakowski and Boleslaw Domanski A790

1982, July 20 Litho.

2524	A790	4.50z multi	.45	.15

Assoc. of Poles in Germany, 60th anniv.

2nd UN Conference on Peaceful Uses of Outer Space, Vienna, Aug. 9-21 — A791

1982, Aug. 9 Photo.

2525	A791	31z Globe	1.25	.65

No. 2441 Surcharged

1982, Aug. 20

2526	A766	10z on 6.50z brn	.40	.22

Black Madonna of Jasna Gora, 600th Anniv. — A792

2.50z, Father Augustin Kordecki (1603-1673). 25z, Siege of Jasna Gora by Swedes, 1655, horiz.

1982, Aug. 26 *Perf. 11*

2527	A792	2.50z multi	.15	.15
2528	A792	25z multi	.80	.28
2529	A792	65z multi	2.50	1.10
		Nos. 2527-2529 (3)	3.45	1.53

A souvenir sheet of 2 No. 2529 exists.

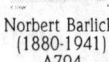

Workers' Movement A793

1982, Sept. 3 *Perf. 11½x11*

2530	A793	6z multicolored	.35	.15

Norbert Barlicki (1880-1941) A794

Carved Head, Wawel Castle A795

Workers' Activists: 6z, Pawel Finder (1904-1944). 15z, Marian Buczek (1896-1939). 20z, Cezaryna Wojnarowska (1861-1911). 29z, Ignacy Daszynski (1866-1936).

1982, Sept. 10 *Perf. 12x11½*

2531	A794	5z multi	.28	.15
2532	A794	6z multi	.30	.15
2533	A794	15z multi	.75	.28
2534	A794	20z multi	.95	.32
2535	A794	29z multi	1.10	.40
		Nos. 2531-2535 (5)	3.38	1.30

1982, Sept. 25

2536	A795	60z Woman's head	2.25	1.00
2537	A795	100z Man's head	3.25	1.75

TB Bacillus Centenary A796

St. Maximilian Kolbe (1894-1941) A797

1982, Sept. 22 *Perf. 11½x11*

2538	A796	10z Koch	.40	.15
2539	A796	25z Oko Bujwid (1857-1942), bacteriologist	1.00	.40

1982, Oct.

2540	A797	27z multi	1.00	.45

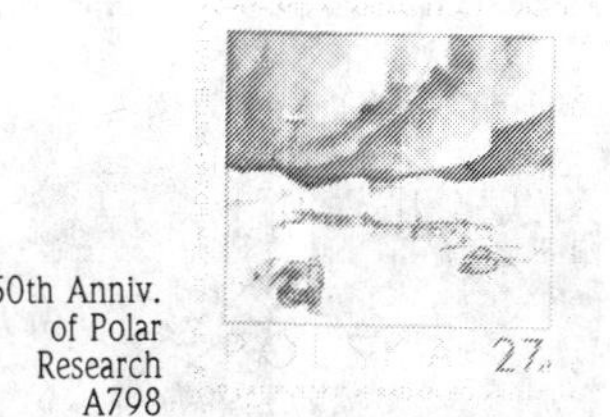

50th Anniv. of Polar Research A798

1982, Oct. 25 Litho. *Perf. 11½*

2541	A798	27z multi	1.00	.45

Stanislaw Zaremba (1863-1942), Mathematician — A799

Mathematicians: 6z, Waclaw Sierpinski (1882-1969). 12z, Zygmunt Janiszewski (1888-1920). 15z, Stefan Banach (1892-1945).

1982, Nov. 23 Photo. *Perf. 11x11½*

2542	A799	5z multicolored	.18	.15
2543	A799	6z multicolored	.25	.15
2544	A799	12z multicolored	.50	.28
2545	A799	15z multicolored	.60	.25
		Nos. 2542-2545 (4)	1.53	.83

First Anniv. of Military Rule — A800

1982, Dec. 13 *Perf. 12x11½*

2546	A800	2.50z Medal obverse and reverse	.15	.15

Cracow Monuments Restoration A801

1982, Dec. 20 Litho. *Perf. 11½x11*

2547	A801	15z Deanery portal	.50	.25
2548	A801	25z Law College portal	.80	.40

Souvenir Sheet

Lithographed and Engraved

Imperf

2549	A801	65z City map	1.25	1.00

No. 2549 contains one stamp 22x27mm.

See Nos. 2593-2594, 2656-2657, 2717-2718, 2809, 2847.

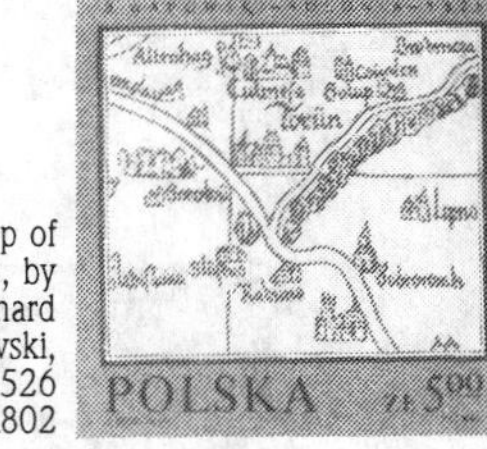

Map of Poland, by Bernard Wapowski, 1526 A802

Maps: 6z, Warsaw, Polish Kingdom Quartermaster, 1839. 8z, Poland, Romer's Atlas, 1908. 25z, Krakow, by A. Buchowiecki, 1703, astrolabe, 17th cent.

1982, Dec. 28 Litho. *Perf. 11½*

2550	A802	5z multicolored	.15	.15
2551	A802	6z multicolored	.20	.15
2552	A802	8z multicolored	.30	.15
2553	A802	25z multicolored	.85	.40
		Nos. 2550-2553 (4)	1.50	
		Set value		.70

120th Anniv. of 1863 Uprising — A803

1983, Jan. 22 Photo. *Perf. 12x11½*

2554	A803	6z The Battle, by Arthur Grottger (1837-67)	.25	.15

Warsaw Theater Sesquicentennial — A804

1983, Feb. 24 Photo. *Perf. 11*

2555	A804	6z multicolored	.25	.15

10th Anniv. of UN Conference on Human Environment, Stockholm — A805

1983, Mar. 24 Litho. *Perf. 11½*

2556	A805	5z Wild flowers	.18	.15
2557	A805	6z Swan, carp, eel	.22	.15
2558	A805	17z Hoopoe	.55	.32
2559	A805	30z Fish	1.00	.50
2560	A805	31z Deer, fawn, buffalo	1.00	.50
2561	A805	38z Fruit	1.10	.60
		Nos. 2556-2561 (6)	4.05	2.22

Karol Kurpinski (1785-1857), Composer — A806

Famous People: 6z, Maria Jasnorzewska Pawlikowska (1891-1945), poet. 17z, Stanislaw Szober (1879-1938), linguist. 25z, Tadeusz Banachiewicz (1882-1954), astronomer. 27z, Jaroslaw Iwaszkiewicz (1894-1980), writer. 31z, Wladyslaw

Tatarkiewicz (1886-1980), philosopher, art historian.

1983, Mar. 25 Photo. *Perf. 11½x11*

2562 A806 5z tan & brn .20 .15
2563 A806 6z pink & vio .25 .15
2564 A806 17z dk grn & lt grn .55 .28
2565 A806 25z bister & brn .85 .42
2566 A806 27z lt bl & dk bl .95 .45
2567 A806 31z violet & pur 1.10 .55
Nos. 2562-2567 (6) 3.90 2.00

Polish Medalists in 22nd Olympic Games, 1980 A807

1983, Apr. 5 *Perf. 11x11½*

2568 A807 5z Steeplechase .15 .15
2569 A807 6z Equestrian .20 .15
2570 A807 15z Soccer, 1982 World Cup .50 .25
2571 A807 27z + 5z Pole vault 1.00 .50
Nos. 2568-2571 (4) 1.85 1.05

Warsaw Ghetto Uprising, 40th Anniv. — A808

Customs Cooperation Council, 30th Anniv. — A809

1983, Apr. 19 Photo. *Perf. 11½x11*

2572 A808 6z Heroes' Monument, by Natan Rappaport .25 .15

Se-tenant with label showing anniversary medal.

1983, Apr. 28

2573 A809 5z multicolored .15 .15

Second Visit of Pope John Paul II — A810

Portraits of Pope. 31z vert.

1983, June 16 Photo. *Perf. 11*

2574 A810 31z multicolored 1.10 .50
2575 A810 65z multicolored 2.25 1.10
a. Souvenir sheet 2.50 1.75

Army of King John III Sobieski — A811

1983, July 5 *Perf. 11½x11*

2576 A811 5z Dragoons .15 .15
2577 A811 5z Knight in armor .15 .15
2578 A811 6z Non-commissioned infantry officers .20 .15
2579 A811 15z Light cavalryman .50 .25
2580 A811 27z Hussars .90 .45
Nos. 2576-2580 (5) 1.90
Set value .95

750th Anniv. of Torun Municipality — A812

1983, Aug. 25 Photo. *Perf. 11*

2581 A812 6z multicolored .25 .15
a. Souvenir sheet of 4 3.00 2.75

No. 2581a had limited distribution.

60th Anniv. of Polish Boxing Union — A813

1983, Nov. 4 Litho. *Perf. 11½x11*

2582 A813 6z multicolored .25 .15

Enigma Decoding Machine, 50th Anniv. — A813a

Girl Near House — A813b

1983, Aug. 16 Litho. *Perf. 11½x11*

2582A A813a 5z multicolored .15 .15

1983 Photo. *Perf. 11½x12*

2582B A813b 6z multicolored .25 .15

Public courtesy campaign.

Portrait of King John III Sobieski A814

King's Portraits by: #2584, Unknown court painter. #2585, Sobieski on Horseback, by Francesco Trevisani (1656-1746). 25z, Jerzy Eleuter Szymonowicz-Siemiginowski (1660-1711). 65z+10z, Sobieski at Vienna, by Jan Matejko (1838-1893).

1983, Sept. 12 *Perf. 11*

2583 A814 5z multicolored .18 .15
2584 A814 6z multicolored .24 .15
2585 A814 6z multicolored .24 .15
2586 A814 25z multicolored .95 .40
Nos. 2583-2586 (4) 1.61
Set value .68

Souvenir Sheet

Imperf

2587 A814 65z + 10z multi 2.50 2.00

Victory over the Turks in Vienna, 300th anniv.

Polish Peoples' Army, 40th Anniv. — A815

Designs: No. 2588, General Zygmunt Berling (1896-1980). No. 2589, Wanda Wasilewska (1905-1964). No. 2591, Troop formation.

1983, Oct. 12 Photo. *Perf. 11*

2588 A815 5z multicolored .15 .15
2589 A815 5z multicolored .15 .15
2590 A815 6z multicolored .20 .15
2591 A815 6z multi, horiz. .20 .15
Nos. 2588-2591 (4) .70
Set value .36

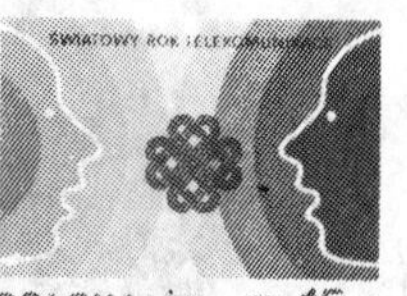

World Communications Year — A816

1983, Oct. 18 Photo. *Perf. 11*

2592 A816 15z multicolored .50 .25

Cracow Restoration Type of 1982

1983, Nov. 25 Litho. *Perf. 11*

2593 A801 5z Cloth Hall, horiz. .18 .15
2594 A801 6z Town Hall Tower .28 .15
Set value .22

Traditional Hats — A818

Natl. People's Council, 40th Anniv. — A819

1983, Dec. 16 Photo. *Perf. 11½x11*

2595 A818 5z Biskupianski .16 .15
2596 A818 5z Rozbarski .16 .15
2597 A818 6z Warminsko-Mazurski .18 .15
2598 A818 6z Cieszynski .18 .15
2599 A818 25z Kurpiowski .75 .38
2600 A818 38z Lubuski 1.10 .55
Nos. 2595-2600 (6) 2.53
Set value 1.25

1983, Dec. 31

2601 A819 6z Hand holding sword (poster) .25 .15

People's Army, 40th Anniv. A820

Musical Instruments A821

1984, Jan. 1 Litho. *Perf. 11½x11*

2602 A820 5z Gen. Bem Brigade badge .20 .15

1984, Feb. 10 Photo.

2603 A821 5z Dulcimer .16 .15
2604 A821 6z Drum, tambourine .18 .15
2605 A821 10z Accordion .35 .15
2606 A821 15z Double bass .40 .20
2607 A821 17z Bagpipes .60 .24
2608 A821 29z Figurines by Tadeusz Żak 1.10 .38
Nos. 2603-2608 (6) 2.79
Set value 1.10

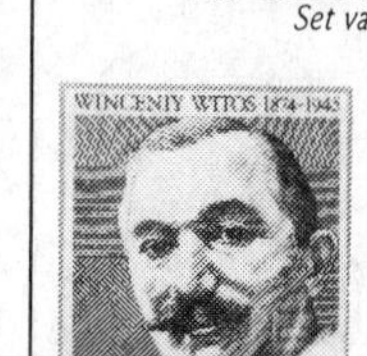

Wincenty Witos (1874-1945), Prime Minister — A822

1984, Mar. 2 Litho. *Perf. 11½x11*

2609 A822 6z green & sepia .20 .15

Local Flowers (Clematis Varieties) A823

1984, Mar. 26 Photo. *Perf. 11x11½*

2610 A823 5z Lanuginosa .18 .15
2611 A823 6z Tangutica .24 .15
2612 A823 10z Texensis .30 .15
2613 A823 17z Alpina .65 .24
2614 A823 25z Vitalba .90 .35
2615 A823 27z Montana 1.00 .38
Nos. 2610-2615 (6) 3.27
Set value 1.25

The Ecstasy of St. Francis, by El Greco A824

1984, Apr. 21 *Perf. 11*

2616 A824 27z multicolored 1.00 .32

1984 Olympics A825

1984, Apr. 25 Litho. *Perf. 11x11½*

2617 A825 5z Handball .17 .15
2618 A825 6z Fencing .22 .15
2619 A825 15z Bicycling .55 .20
2620 A825 16z Running .60 .22
2621 A825 17z Running, diff. .65 .24
a. Souv. sheet of 2, #2620-2621 1.50 1.25
2622 A825 31z Skiing 1.00 .45
Nos. 2617-2622 (6) 3.19 1.41

No. 2621a sold for 43z.

Battle of Monte Cassino, 40th Anniv. — A826

1984, May 18 Photo. *Perf. 11½x11*

2623 A826 15z Memorial Cross .50 .20

View of Warsaw from the Praga Bank, by Bernardo Belotto Canaletto — A827

Paintings of Vistula River views: 6z, Trumpet Festivity, by Aleksander Gierymski. 25z, The Vistula near the Bielany District, by Jozef Rapacki. 27z, Steamship Harbor in the Powisle District, by Franciszek Kostrzewski.

1984, June 20 Photo. *Perf. 11*

2624 A827 5z multicolored .16 .15
2625 A827 6z multicolored .20 .15
2626 A827 25z multicolored .80 .35
2627 A827 27z multicolored .80 .40
Nos. 2624-2627 (4) 1.96
Set value .92

Warrior's Head, Wawel Castle — A828

Sculptures: 3.50z, Eastern ruler. No. 2628A, Woman wearing wreath. 10z, Man wearing hat.

1984-85 Photo. *Perf. 11½x12*

2628 A828 3.50z brown .15 .15
2628A A828 5z dark claret .15 .15
2628B A828 10z brt ultra .30 .15
Set value .50 .30

Coil Stamp

Perf. 13½x14

2629 A828 5z dark blue green .20 .15

Issue dates: 3.50z, Jan. 24, 1985. No. 2628A, 10z, July 8, 1985. No. 2629, July 10, 1984.
No. 2629 has black control number on back of every fifth stamp.
See Nos. 2738-2744.

Order of Grunwald Cross — A829

Designs: 6z, Order of Revival of Poland. 10z, Order of the Banner of Labor, First Class. 16z, Order of Builders of People's Poland.

1984, July 21 Photo. *Perf. 11½*

2630 A829 5z multicolored .15 .15
2631 A829 6z multicolored .20 .15
2632 A829 10z multicolored .32 .15
2633 A829 16z multicolored .52 .24
a. Sheet of 4, #2630-2633, perf. 11½x12 3.25 3.00
Nos. 2630-2633 (4) 1.19
Set value .56

40th anniversary of July Manifesto (Origin of Polish People's Republic).

Warsaw Uprising, 40th Anniv. A830

1984, Aug. 1

2634 A830 4z multicolored .15 .15
2635 A830 5z multicolored .15 .15
2636 A830 6z multicolored .18 .15
2637 A830 25z multicolored .75 .35
Nos. 2634-2637 (4) 1.23
Set value .56

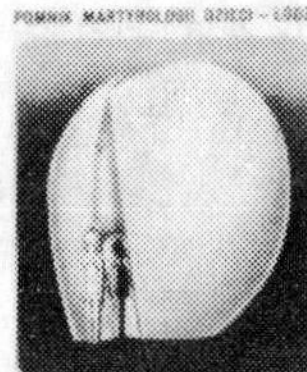

Broken Heart Monument, Lodz — A831

1984, Aug. 31

2638 A831 16z multicolored .50 .25

Defense of Oksywie Holm, Col. S. Dabek — A832

1984, Sept. 1

2639 A832 5z shown .18 .15
2640 A832 6z Bzura River battle, Gen. T. Kutrzeba .22 .15
Set value .20

Invasion of Poland, 45th anniversary.
See Nos. 2692-2693, 2757, 2824-2826, 2864-2866, 2922-2925.

Polish Militia, 40th Anniv. A833

1984, Sept. 29 Photo. *Perf. 11½*

2641 A833 5z shown .18 .15
2642 A833 6z Militiaman at Control Center .22 .15
Set value .20

Polish Aviation A834

1984, Nov. 6 Photo. *Perf. 11x11½*

2643 A834 5z Balloon ascent, 1784 .15 .15
2644 A834 5z Powered flight, 1911 .15 .15
2645 A834 6z Balloon Polonez, 1983 .20 .15
2646 A834 10z Modern gliders .30 .16
2647 A834 16z Wilga, 1983 .50 .30
2648 A834 27z Farman, 1914 .90 .48
2649 A834 31z Los and PZL P-7 .95 .48
Nos. 2643-2649 (7) 3.15 1.87

Protected Animals A835

1984, Dec. 4 Photo. *Perf. 11x11½*

2650 A835 4z Mustela nivalis .15 .15
2651 A835 5z Martes foina .18 .15
2652 A835 5z Mustela erminea .18 .15

Perf. 11½x11

2653 A835 10z Castor fiber, vert. .32 .15
2654 A835 10z Lutra lutra, vert. .32 .15
2655 A835 65z Marmota marmota, vert. 1.90 .70
Nos. 2650-2655 (6) 3.05
Set value 1.20

Cracow Restoration Type of 1982

Perf. 11½x11, 11x11½

1984, Dec. 10 Litho.

2656 A801 5z Royal Cathedral, Wawel .15 .15
2657 A801 15z Royal Castle, Wawel, horiz. .32 .15
Set value .22

Religious Buildings — A837

Perf. 11½x12, 12x11½

1984, Dec. 28 Photo.

2658 A837 5z Protestant Church, Warsaw .15 .15
2659 A837 10z Saint Andrew Church, Cracow .28 .15
2660 A837 15z Greek Orthodox Church, Rychwald .45 .16
2661 A837 20z Orthodox Church, Warsaw .55 .20
2662 A837 25z Tykocin Synagogue, horiz. .70 .25
2663 A837 31z Tartar Mosque, Kruszyniany, horiz. .80 .30
Nos. 2658-2663 (6) 2.93 1.21

Classic and Contemporary Fire Engines — A838

Designs: 4z, Horse-drawn fire pump, 19th cent. 10z, Polski Fiat, c. 1930. 12z, Jelcz 315, 1970s. 15z, Horse-drawn hand pump, 1899. 20z, Jelcz engine, Magirus power ladder, 1970s. 30z, Hand pump, 18th cent.

1985, Feb. 25 Photo. *Perf. 11x11½*

2664 A838 4z multicolored .16 .15
2665 A838 10z multicolored .28 .15
2666 A838 12z multicolored .32 .15
2667 A838 15z multicolored .40 .18
2668 A838 20z multicolored .55 .22
2669 A838 30z multicolored .85 .35
Nos. 2664-2669 (6) 2.56
Set value 1.00

Battle of Raclawice, April, 1794, by Jan Styka, 1894 — A839

1985, Apr. 4 *Perf. 11*

2670 A839 27z multicolored .75 .30

Kosciuszko Insurrection cent.

A840 A841

1985, Apr. 11 Litho. *Perf. 11½*

2671 A840 10z sal rose & dk vio bl .25 .15

Wincenty Rzymowski (1883-1950),Democratic Party founder.

1985, Apr. 25 Photo. *Perf. 11½x11*

2672 A841 15z Blue jeans, badge .35 .15

Intl. Youth Year.

Prince Boleslaw Krzywousty (1085-1138) A842

Regional maps and: 10z, Wladyslaw Gomulka (1905-82), sec.-gen. of the Polish Workers Party, prime minister 1945-49. 20z, Piotr Zaremba (b. 1910), president of Gdansk Province 1945-50.

1985, May 8 Litho. *Perf. 11½*

2673 A842 5z multicolored .15 .15
2674 A842 10z multicolored .25 .15
2675 A842 20z multicolored .55 .20
Nos. 2673-2675 (3) .95
Set value .38

Restoration of the Western & Northern Territories to Polish control, 40th anniv.

Victory Berlin 1945, by Jozef Mlynarski (b. 1925) — A843

Painting: Polish and Soviet soldiers at Brandenburg Gate, May 9, 1945.

1985, May 9 Photo. *Perf. 12x11½*

2676 A843 5z multicolored .15 .15

Liberation from German occupation, 40th anniv.

Warsaw Treaty Org., 30th Anniv. — A844

1985, May 14 Litho. *Perf. 11½x11*

2677 A844 5z Emblem, member flags .15 .15

World Wildlife Fund A845

Endangered Wildlife: Canis lupus.

1985, May 25 Photo. *Perf. 11x11½*

2678 A845 5z Wolves, winter landscape .15 .15
2679 A845 10z Female, cubs .25 .15
2680 A845 10z Wolf .25 .15
2681 A845 20z Wolves, summer landscape .55 .20
Nos. 2678-2681 (4) 1.20
Set value .48

A846 A847

Folk instruments.

1985, June 25 *Perf. 11½x11*

2682 A846 5z Wooden rattle .15 .15
2683 A846 10z Jingle .30 .15
2684 A846 12z Clay whistles .32 .15
2685 A846 20z Wooden fiddles .60 .22
2686 A846 25z Tuned bells .70 .24
2687 A846 31z Shepherd's flutes, ram's horn, ocarina .90 .35
Nos. 2662-2687 (6) 2.97 1.26

Photogravure and Engraved
1985, June 29

Design: O.R.P. Iskra and emblem.

2688 A847 5z bluish blk & yel .15 .15

Polish Navy, 40th anniv.

Tomasz Nocznicki (1862-1944) A848

Polish Labor Movement founders: 20z, Maciej Rataj (1884-1940).

1985, July 26 Engr. *Perf. 11x11½*

2689 A848 10z grnsh black .28 .15
2690 A848 20z brown black .52 .24

Natl. labor movement, 90th anniv.

Polish Field Hockey Assn., 50th Anniv. A849

1985, Aug. 22 Litho. *Perf. 11½x11*

2691 A849 5z multicolored .25 .15

World War II Battles Type of 1984

Designs: 5z, Defense of Wizny, Capt. Wladyslaw Raginis. 10z, Attack on Mlawa, Col. Wilhelm Andrzej Liszka-Lawicz.

1985, Sept. 1 Photo. *Perf. 12x11½*

2692 A832 5z multicolored .15 .15
2693 A832 10z multicolored .35 .15
Set value .20

Pafawag Railway Rolling Stock Co. — A850

1985, Sept. 18 Litho. *Perf. 11½*

2694 A850 5z Box car .15 .15
2695 A850 10z 201 E locomotive .28 .15
2696 A850 17z Two-axle coal car .48 .24
2697 A850 20z Passenger car .60 .28
Nos. 2694-2697 (4) 1.51 .82

Wild Ducks A851

1985, Oct. 21 Photo. *Perf. 11x11½*

2698 A851 5z Anas crecca .15 .15
2699 A851 5z Anas querquedula .15 .15
2700 A851 10z Aythya fuligula .28 .15
2701 A851 15z Bucephala clangula .40 .18
2702 A851 25z Somateria mollissima .65 .30
2703 A851 29z Netta rufina .80 .35
Nos. 2698-2703 (6) 2.43
Set value 1.05

UN, 40th Anniv. A852

1985, Oct. 24 Litho. *Perf. 11½x11*

2704 A852 27z multicolored .75 .30

Polish Ballet, 200th Anniv. — A853

1985, Dec. 4

2705 A853 5z Prima ballerina .18 .15
2706 A853 15z Male dancer .42 .18
Set value .24

Paintings by Stanislaw Ignacy Witkiewicz (1885-1939) — A854

5z, Marysia and Burek in Ceylon. No. 2708, Woman with a Fox. No. 2709, Self-portrait, 1931. 20z, Compositions, 1917. 25z, Portrait of Nena Stachurska, 1929. Nos. 2707, 2709-2711 vert.

Perf. 11½x11, 11x11½
1985, Dec. 6 Photo.

2707 A854 5z multicolored .15 .15
2708 A854 10z multicolored .28 .15
2709 A854 10z multicolored .28 .15
2710 A854 20z multicolored .55 .24
2711 A854 25z multicolored .70 .30
Nos. 2707-2711 (5) 1.96
Set value .84

Souvenir Sheet

Johann Sebastian Bach — A855

1985, Dec. 30 *Perf. 11½x11*

2712 A855 65z multicolored 1.75 1.00
a. With inscription 8.00 8.00

No. 2712a inscribed "300 Rocznica Urodzin Jana Sebastiana Bacha." Distribution was limited.

Profile, Emblem, Sigismond III Column, Royal Castle Tower — A856

Intl. Peace Year — A858

Halley's Comet A857

1986, Jan. 16 *Perf. 11½x11*

2713 A856 10z lt ultra, brt ultra & ultra .25 .15

Congress of Intellectuals for World Peace, Warsaw.

1986, Feb. 7 Photo. *Perf. 11½*

Designs: No. 2714, Michal Kamienski (1879-1973), astronomer, orbit diagram. No. 2715, Comet, Vega, Giotto, Planet-A, ICE-3 space probes.

2714 A857 25z multicolored .60 .30
2715 A857 25z multicolored .60 .30

1986, Mar. 20 Photo. *Perf. 11½x11*

2716 A858 25z turq bl, yel & ultra .60 .38

Cracow Restoration Type of 1982

Designs: 5z, Collegium Maius, Jagiellonian Museum. 10z, Town Hall, Kazimierz.

1986, Mar. 20 Litho. *Perf. 11½*

2717 A801 5z multicolored .15 .15
2718 A801 10z multicolored .25 .15

Wildlife A859

1986, Apr. 15 Photo. *Perf. 11½x11*

2719 A859 5z Perdix perdix .15 .15
2720 A859 5z Oryctolagus cuniculus .15 .15
2721 A859 10z Dama dama .20 .15
2722 A859 10z Phasianus colchicus .20 .15
2723 A859 20z Lepus europaeus .42 .20
2724 A859 40z Ovis ammon .80 .35
Nos. 2719-2724 (6) 1.92
Set value .86

Nos. 2719-2720, 2723-2724 vert.

Stanislaw Kulczynski (1895-1975), Scientist, Party Leader — A860

Photogravure and Engraved
1986, May 3 *Perf. 11½x11*

2725 A860 10z buff & choc .22 .15

Warsaw Fire Brigade, 150th Anniv. — A861

Painting detail: The Fire Brigade on the Cracow Outskirts on Their Way to a Fire, 1871, by Josef Brodowski (1828-1900).

1986, May 16 *Perf. 11*

2726 A861 10z dl brn & dk brn .22 .15

Paderewski — A862

1986, May 22 *Perf. 11½x11*

2727 A862 65z multicolored 1.50 .70

AMERIPEX'86.

1986 World Cup Soccer Championships, Mexico — A863

1986, May 26 *Perf. 11½*

2728 A863 25z multicolored .50 .22

Ferryboats — A864

1986, June 18 Photo. *Perf. 11*

2729 A864 10z Wilanow .20 .15
2730 A864 10z Wawel .20 .15
a. Souv. sheet of 2, #2729-2730 1.65 1.65
2731 A864 15z Pomerania .30 .15
2732 A864 25z Rogalin .55 .25
a. Souv. sheet of 2, #2731-2732 3.25 3.25
Nos. 2729-2732 (4) 1.25 .70

Nos. 2729-2732 printed se-tenant with labels picturing historic sites from the names of cities serviced. No. 2730a sold for 30z; No. 2732a for 55z. Surtax for the Natl. Assoc. of Philatelists.

Antarctic Agreement, 25th Anniv. A865

Map of Antarctica and: 5z, A. B. Dobrowolski, Kopernik research ship. 40z, H. Arctowski, Professor Siedlecki research ship.

1986, June 23 Litho. *Perf. 11½x11*

2733 A865 5z ver, pale grn & blk .15 .15
2734 A865 40z org, pale vio & dk vio 1.10 .40
Set value .45

Polish United Workers' Party, 10th Congress
A866

1986, July 29 Photo. *Perf. 11x11½*
2735 A866 10z red & dk gray bl .25 .15

Wawel Heads Type of 1984-85

Designs: 15z, Woman wearing a wreath (like No. 2628A). No. 2739, Thinker. No. 2740, Eastern ruler. 40z, Youth wearing beret. 60z, Warrior. 200z, Man's head.

Perf. 11½x12, 14 (15z, No. 2740, 60z)
Engr., Photo. (15z, No. 2740, 60z)
1986-89

2738 A828 15z rose brown .18 .15
2739 A828 20z green .38 .18
2740 A828 20z peacock blue .20 .15
2742 A828 40z gray .75 .35
2743 A828 60z dark green .25 .15
2744 A828 200z dark gray 3.75 1.75
Nos. 2738-2744 (6) 5.51 2.73

Issue dates: 15z, Sept. 22, 1988. Nos. 2739, 2742, July 30, 1986. No. 2740, Mar. 31, 1989. 60z, Dec. 15, 1989. No. 2744, Nov. 11, 1986.

No. 2740 and 60z are coil stamps, have black control number on back of every 5th stamp.

For surcharge see No. 2954.

This is an expanding set. Numbers will change if necessary.

Jasna Gora Monastery Collection — A867

Designs: No. 2746, The Paulinite Church on Skalka in Cracow, oil painting detail, circa 1627. No. 2747, Jesse's Tree, oil on wood, 17th cent. No. 2748, Gilded chalice, 18th cent. No. 2749, Virgin Mary embroidery, 15th cent.

1986, Aug. 15 Photo. *Perf. 11½x11*
2746 A867 5z multicolored .15 .15
2747 A867 5z multicolored .15 .15
2748 A867 20z multicolored .40 .20
2749 A867 40z multicolored .80 .40
Nos. 2746-2749 (4) 1.50
Set value .72

Victories of Polish Athletes at 1985 World Championships — A868

Designs: No. 2750, Precision Flying, Kissimmee, Florida, won by Waclaw Nycz. No. 2751, Wind Sailing, Tallinn, USSR, won by Malgorzata Palasz-Piasecka. No. 2752, Glider Acrobatics, Vienna, won by Jerzy Makula. No. 2753, Greco-Roman Wrestling (82kg), Kolboten, Norway, won by Bogdan Daras. No. 2754, Road Cycling, Giavera del Montello, Italy, won by Lech Piasecki. No. 2755, Women's Modern Pentathlon, Montreal, won by Barbara Kotowska.

1986, Aug. 21 *Perf. 11½*
2750 A868 5z multicolored .15 .15
2751 A868 10z multicolored .24 .15
2752 A868 10z multicolored .24 .15
2753 A868 15z multicolored .35 .15
2754 A868 20z multicolored .55 .20
2755 A868 30z multicolored .70 .28
Nos. 2750-2755 (6) 2.23
Set value .88

STOCKHOLMIA '86 — A869

1986, Aug. 28 *Perf. 11x11½*
2756 A869 65z multicolored 1.50 .75
a. Souvenir sheet 1.50 .75

World War II Battles Type of 1984

Design: Battle of Jordanow, Col. Stanislaw Maczek, motorized cavalry 10th brigade commander-in-chief.

1986, Sept. 1 *Perf. 12x11½*
2757 A832 10z multicolored .25 .15

Albert Schweitzer A870

World Post Day A871

Photogravure and Engraved
1986, Sept. 26 *Perf. 12x11½*
2758 A870 5z pale bl vio, sep & buff .15 .15

1986, Oct. 9 Litho. *Perf. 11x11½*
2759 A871 40z orange, ultra & sep .75 .35
a. Souvenir sheet of 2 10.00 10.00

No. 2759a sold for 120z.

Folk and Fairy Tale Legends A872

Designs: No. 2760, Basilisk. No. 2761, Duke Popiel, vert. No. 2762, Golden Duck. No. 2763, Boruta, the Devil, vert. No. 2764, Janosik the Thief, vert. No. 2765, Lajkonik, conqueror of the Tartars, 13th cent., vert.

1986, Oct. 28 Photo. *Perf. 11½x11*
2760 A872 5z multicolored .15 .15
2761 A872 5z multicolored .15 .15
2762 A872 10z multicolored .20 .15
2763 A872 10z multicolored .20 .15
2764 A872 20z multicolored .35 .18
2765 A872 50z multicolored .95 .42
Nos. 2760-2765 (6) 2.00
Set value .88

Prof. Tadeusz Kotarbinski (1886-1981) — A873

1986, Nov. 19 Litho. *Perf. 11½*
2766 A873 10z sepia, buff & brn blk .28 .15

17th-20th Cent. Architecture A874

Designs: No. 2767, Church, Baczal Dolny. No. 2768, Windmill, Zygmuntow. 10z, Oravian cottage, Zubrzyca Gorna. 15z, Kashubian Arcade cottage, Wazydze. 25z, Barn, Grzawa. 30z, Water mill, Molkowice Stare.

Perf. 11x11½, 11½x11
1986, Nov. 26 Photo.
2767 A874 5z multicolored .15 .15
2768 A874 5z multi, vert. .15 .15
2769 A874 10z multicolored .20 .15
2770 A874 15z multicolored .28 .15
2771 A874 25z multicolored .50 .22
2772 A874 30z multicolored .55 .28
Nos. 2767-2772 (6) 1.83
Set value .80

Royalty A875

Photogravure and Engraved
1986, Dec. 4 *Perf. 11*
2773 A875 10z Mieszko I .20 .15
2774 A875 25z Dobrava .50 .25

See Nos. 2838-2839, 2884-2885, 2932-2933, 3033-3034, 3068-3069, 3141-3144, 3191-3192, 3222-3225, 3309-3312, 3366-3369. For surcharges see Nos. 3016-3017.

New Year 1987 — A876

1986, Dec. 12 Photo. *Perf. 11x11½*
2775 A876 25z multicolored .50 .30

Warsaw Cyclists Soc., Cent. A877

Designs: No. 2776, First trip to Bielany, uniformed escort, 1887. No. 2777, Jan Stanislaw Skrodzki (1867-1957), 1895 record-holder. No. 2778, Dynasy Society building, 1892-1937. No. 2779, Mieczyslaw Baranski, champion, 1896. No. 2780, Karolina Kociecka (b. 1875), female competitor. No. 2781, Henryk Weiss (d. 1912), Dynasy champion, 1904-1908.

Perf. 13x12½, 12½x13
1986, Dec. 19 Litho.
2776 A877 5z multicolored .15 .15
2777 A877 5z multicolored .15 .15
2778 A877 10z multicolored .20 .15
2779 A877 10z multicolored .20 .15
2780 A877 30z multicolored .55 .28
2781 A877 50z multicolored .95 .45
Nos. 2776-2781 (6) 2.20
Set value 1.00

Nos. 2777-2781 vert.

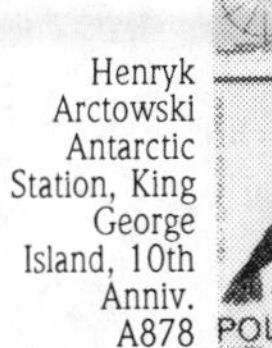

Henryk Arctowski Antarctic Station, King George Island, 10th Anniv. A878

Wildlife and ships: No. 2782, Euphausia superba, training freighter Antoni Garnuszewski. No. 2783, Notothenia rossi, Dissostichus mawsoni, Zulawy transoceanic ship. No. 2784, Fulmarus glacialoides, yacht Pogoria. No. 2785, Pigoscelis adeliae, yacht Gedania. 30z, Arctocephalus, research boat Dziunia. 40z, Hydrurga leptonyx, ship Kapitan Ledochowski.

1987, Feb. 13 Litho. *Perf. 11½*
2782 A878 5z multicolored .15 .15
2783 A878 5z multicolored .15 .15
2784 A878 10z multicolored .20 .15
2785 A878 10z multicolored .20 .15
2786 A878 30z multicolored .60 .28
2787 A878 40z multicolored .85 .38
Nos. 2782-2787 (6) 2.15
Set value .98

Paintings by Leon Wyczolkowski (1852-1936) — A879

1987, Mar. 20 Photo. *Perf. 11*
2788 A879 5z Cineraria Flowers, 1924 .15 .15
2789 A879 10z Portrait of a Woman, 1883 .20 .15
2790 A879 10z Wood Church, 1910 .20 .15
2791 A879 25z Harvesting Beetroot, 1910 .50 .25
2792 A879 30z Wading Fishermen, 1891 .60 .30
2793 A879 40z Self-portrait, 1912 .80 .40
Nos. 2788-2793 (6) 2.45
Set value 1.20

Nos. 2789 and 2791 vert.

The Ravage, 1866, by Artur Grottger (1837-1867) — A880

1987, Mar. 26 Photo. *Perf. 11*
2794 A880 15z dk brown & buff .25 .15

Gen. Karol Swierczewski-Walter (1897-1947) — A881

1987, Mar. 27 Engr. *Perf. 11½x12*
2795 A881 15z olive green .25 .15

Pawel Edmund Strzelecki (1797-1873), Explorer — A882

1987, Apr. 23 Photo. *Perf. 11½x11*
2796 A882 65z olive black 1.10 .65

Colonization of Australia, bicentennial.

2nd PRON Congress A883

1987, May 8 Litho. *Perf. 11½*
2797 A882 10z pale gray, brn, red & brt ultra .20 .15

Patriotic Movement of the National Renaissance Congress.

Motor Vehicles A884

1987, May 19 Photo. *Perf. 12x11½*

2798	A884	10z	1936 Saurer-Zawrat	.20	.15
2799	A884	10z	1928 CWS T-1	.20	.15
2800	A884	15z	1928 Ursus-A	.30	.15
2801	A884	15z	1936 Lux-Sport	.30	.15
2802	A884	25z	1939 Podkowa 100	.50	.25
2803	A884	45z	1935 Sokol 600 RT	.90	.45
			Nos. 2798-2803 (6)	2.40	1.30

Royal Castle, Warsaw — A885

1987, June 5

2804	A885	50z	multicolored	.90	.50

A souvenir sheet of 1 exists.

A886

State Visit of Pope John Paul II — A887

1987, June 8 *Perf. 11*

2805	A886	15z	shown	.30	.15
2806	A886	45z	Portrait, diff.	.90	.45
a.			Pair, #2805-2806	1.20	.60

Souvenir Sheet

Perf. 12x11½

2807	A887	50z	shown	1.00	1.00

No. 2806a has continuous design.

Cracow Restoration Type of 1982

1987, July 6 Litho. *Perf. 11½*

2809	A801	10z	Barbican Gate, Wawel, horiz.	.20	.15

Esperanto Language, Cent. A890

1987, July 25 Litho. *Perf. 11½*

2811	A890	45z	Ludwig L. Zamenhof	.80	.38

A891

A892

Poznan and Town Hall, by Stanislaw Wyspianski.

1987, Aug. 3

2812	A891	15z	black & pale salmon	.25	.15

POZNAN '87, Aug. 8-16.

1987, Aug. 20 Photo. *Perf. 11½x11*

2813	A892	10z	Queen	.16	.15
2814	A892	10z	Worker	.16	.15
2815	A892	15z	Drone	.28	.15
2816	A892	15z	Box hive, orchard	.28	.15
2817	A892	40z	Bee collecting pollen	.75	.40
2818	A892	50z	Beekeeper collecting honey	.90	.50
			Nos. 2813-2818 (6)	2.53	1.50

31st World Apiculture Congress, Warsaw.

Success of Polish Athletes at World Championship Events — A894

1987, Sept. 24 Litho. *Perf. 14*

2820	A894	10z	Acrobatics, France	.16	.15
2821	A894	15z	Kayak, Canada	.24	.15
2822	A894	20z	Marksmanship, E. Germany	.32	.16
2823	A894	25z	Wrestling, Hungary	.40	.20
			Nos. 2820-2823 (4)	1.12	
			Set value		.56

World War II Battles Type of 1984

Designs: No. 2824, Battle of Mokra, Julian Filipowicz. No. 2825, Battle scene near Oleszycami, Brig.-Gen. Josef Rudolf Kustron. 15z, Air battles over Warsaw, pilot Stefan Pawlikowski.

1987, Sept. 1 Photo. *Perf. 12x11½*

2824	A832	10z	multicolored	.20	.15
2825	A832	10z	multicolored	.20	.15
2826	A832	15z	multicolored	.30	.15
			Nos. 2824-2826 (3)	.70	
			Set value		.35

Jan Hevelius (1611-1687), Astronomer, and Constellations — A895

1987, Sept. 15 Litho. *Perf. 11½*

2827	A895	15z	Hevelius, sextant, vert.	.24	.15
2828	A895	40z	shown	.65	.35

Souvenir Sheet

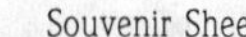

1st Artificial Satellite, Sputnik, 30th Anniv. — A896

1987, Oct. 2 Photo. *Perf. 11½x11*

2829	A896	40z	Stacionar 4 satellite	1.00	1.00

World Post Day — A897

Design: Ignacy Franciszek Przebendowski (1730-1791), postmaster general, and post office building, 19th cent., Krakowskie Przedmiescie, Warsaw.

1987, Oct. 9 Litho.

2830	A897	15z	lt olive grn & rose claret	.25	.15

Col. Stanislaw Wieckowski — A898

Photo. & Engr.

1987, Oct. 16 *Perf. 12x11½*

2831	A898	15z	deep blue & blk	.25	.15

Col. Wieckowski (1884-1942), physician and social reformer executed by the Nazis at Auschwitz.

HAFNIA '87 — A899

Fairy tales by Hans Christian Andersen (1805-1875): No. 2832, The Little Mermaid. No. 2833, The Nightingale. No. 2834, The Wild Swan. No. 2835, The Match Girl. 30z, The Snow Queen. 40z, The Brave Toy Soldier.

1987, Oct. 16 Photo. *Perf. 11x11½*

2832	A899	10z	multicolored	.20	.15
2833	A899	10z	multicolored	.20	.15
2834	A899	20z	multicolored	.40	.20
2835	A899	20z	multicolored	.40	.20
2836	A899	30z	multicolored	.60	.30
2837	A899	40z	multicolored	.80	.40
			Nos. 2832-2837 (6)	2.60	1.40

Royalty Type of 1986

1987, Dec. 4 Photo. & Engr. *Perf. 11*

2838	A875	10z	Boleslaw I Chrobry	.18	.15
2839	A875	15z	Mieszko II	.28	.15

No. 2838 exists with label.

New Year 1988 — A900

1987, Dec. 14 Photo. *Perf. 11x11½*

2840	A900	15z	multicolored	.25	.15

Dragonflies A901

Perf. 11x11½, 11½x11

1988, Feb. 23 Photo.

2841	A901	10z	Anax imperator	.18	.15
2842	A901	15z	Libellula quadrimaculata, vert.	.26	.15
2843	A901	15z	Calopteryx splendens	.26	.15
2844	A901	20z	Cordulegaster annulatus, vert.	.35	.18
2845	A901	30z	Sympetrum pedemontanum	.52	.26
2846	A901	50z	Aeschna viridis, vert.	.90	.45
			Nos. 2841-2846 (6)	2.47	1.34

Cracow Restoration Type of 1982

1988, Mar. 8 Litho. *Perf. 11½x11*

2847	A801	15z	Florianska Gate, 1300	.25	.15

Intl. Year of Graphic Design A903

1988, Apr. 28 Photo. *Perf. 11x11½*

2848	A903	40z	multicolored	.50	.25

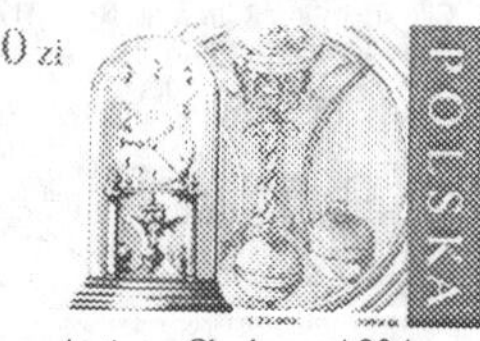
Antique Clocks — A904

Clocks in the Museum of Artistic and Precision Handicrafts, Warsaw, and clockworks: No. 2849, Frisian wall clock, 17th cent., vert. No. 2850, Anniversary clock and rotary pendulum, 20th cent. No. 2851, Carriage clock, 18th cent., vert. No. 2852, Louis XV rococo bracket clock, 18th cent., vert. 20z, Pocket watch, 19th cent. 40z, Gdansk six-sided clock signed by Benjamin Zoll, 17th cent.

Perf. 11½x12, 12x11½

1988, May 19 Photo.

2849	A904	10z	lt green & multi	.16	.15
2850	A904	10z	purple & multi	.16	.15
2851	A904	15z	dull org & multi	.25	.15
2852	A904	15z	brown & multi	.25	.15
2853	A904	20z	multicolored	.32	.16
2854	A904	40z	multicolored	.65	.32
			Nos. 2849-2854 (6)	1.79	
			Set value		.88

1988 Summer Olympics, Seoul — A905

1988, June 27 Photo. *Perf. 11x11½*

2855	A905	15z	Triple jump	.26	.15
2856	A905	20z	Wrestling	.35	.18
2857	A905	20z	Two-man kayak	.35	.18
2858	A905	25z	Judo	.45	.22
2859	A905	40z	Shooting	.70	.35
2860	A905	55z	Swimming	.95	.48
			Nos. 2855-2860 (6)	3.06	1.56

See No. B148.

Natl. Industry A906

1988, Aug. 23 Photo. *Perf. 11x11½*
Size: 35x27mm

2861 A906 45z Los "Elk" aircraft .75 .38

State Aircraft Works, 60th anniv.
See Nos. 2867, 2871, 2881-2883.

16th European Regional FAO Conference, Cracow — A907

Designs: 15z, Computers and agricultural growth. 40z, Balance between industry and nature.

1988, Aug. 22 *Perf. 11½x11*

2862 A907 15z multicolored .22 .15
2863 A907 40z multicolored .60 .30

World War II Battles Type of 1984

Battle scenes and commanders: 15z, Modlin, Brig.-Gen. Wiktor Thommee. No. 2865, Warsaw, Brig.-Gen. Walerian Czuma. No. 2866, Tomaszow Lubelski, Brig.-Gen. Antoni Szylling.

1988, Sept. 1 Photo. *Perf. 12x11½*

2864 A832 15z multicolored .24 .15
2865 A832 20z multicolored .32 .16
2866 A832 20z multicolored .32 .16
Nos. 2864-2866 (3) .88 .47

Natl. Industries Type of 1988

Design: Stalowa Wola Ironworks, 50th anniv.

1988, Sept. 5 *Perf. 11x11½*
Size: 35x27mm

2867 A906 15z multicolored .25 .15

World Post Day — A909

Design: Postmaster Tomasz Arciszewski (1877-1955), Post and Telegraph Administration emblem used from 1919 to 1927.

1988, Oct. 9 Litho. *Perf. 11½x11*

2868 A909 20z multicolored .25 .15

Also printed in sheet of 12 plus 12 labels.

World War II Combat Medals — A910

1988, Oct. 12 Photo.

2869 A910 20z Battle of Lenino Cross .32 .16
2870 A910 20z shown .32 .16

See Nos. 2930-2931.

Natl. Industries Type of 1988

Design: Air Force Medical Institute, 60th anniv.

1988, Oct. 12 *Perf. 11x11½*
Size: 38x27mm

2871 A906 20z multicolored .25 .15

Stanislaw Malachowski, Kazimierz Nestor Sapieha — A912

1988, Oct. 16 *Perf. 11*

2872 A912 20z multicolored .25 .15

Four Years' Sejm (Parliament) (1788-1792), bicent.

National Leaders — A913

1988, Nov. 11 *Perf. 12x11½*

2873 A913 15z Wincenty Witos .22 .15
2874 A913 15z Ignacy Daszynski .22 .15
2875 A913 20z Wojciech Korfanty .25 .15
2876 A913 20z Stanislaw Wojciechowski .25 .15
2877 A913 20z Julian Marchlewski .25 .15
2878 A913 200z Ignacy Paderewski 2.75 1.00
2879 A913 200z Jozef Pilsudski 2.75 1.00
2880 A913 200z Gabriel Narutowicz 2.75 1.00
a. Souvenir sheet of 3, #2878-2880 12.50 12.50
Nos. 2873-2880 (8) 9.44 3.75

Natl. independence, 70th anniv.

Natl. Industry Types of 1988

Designs: 15z, Wharf, Gdynia. 20z, Industrialist Hipolit Cegielski, 1883 steam locomotive. 40z, Poznan fair grounds, Upper Silesia Tower.

1988 Photo. *Perf. 11x11½*
Size: 39x27mm

2881 A906 15z multicolored .30 .15
2882 A906 20z multicolored .40 .20

Size: 35x27mm

2883 A906 40z multicolored .80 .40
Nos. 2881-2883 (3) 1.50 .75

70th anniv. of Polish independence. Gdynia Port, 65th anniv (15z); Metal Works in Poznan, 142nd anniv. (20z); and Poznan Intl. Fair 60th anniv. (40z).

Issued: 15z, 12/12; 20z, 11/28; 40z, 12/21.

Royalty Type of 1986

1988, Dec. 4 Photo. & Engr. *Perf. 11*

2884 A875 10z Rycheza .20 .15
2885 A875 15z Kazimierz I Odnowiciel .30 .15

New Year 1989 A914

1988, Dec. 9 Photo. *Perf. 11x11½*

2886 A914 20z multicolored .30 .20

Unification of Polish Workers' Unions, 40th Anniv. — A915

1988, Dec. 15 *Perf. 11½x12*

2887 A915 20z black & ver .30 .20

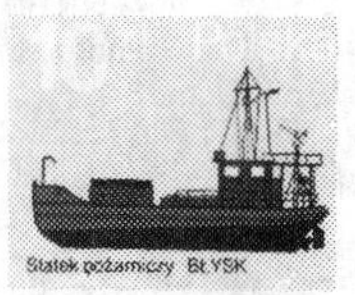

Fire Boats — A916

1988, Dec. 29 Litho. *Perf. 14*

2888 A916 10z Blysk .16 .15
2889 A916 15z Zar .25 .15
2890 A916 15z Plomien .25 .15
2891 A916 20z Strazak 4 .32 .16
2892 A916 20z Strazak 11 .32 .16
2893 A916 45z Strazak 25 .75 .38
Nos. 2888-2893 (6) 2.05 1.15

Horses — A917

1989, Mar. 6 Photo. *Perf. 11*

2894 A917 15z Lippizaner .26 .15
2895 A917 15z Arden, vert. .26 .15
2896 A917 20z English .35 .18
2897 A917 20z Arabian, vert. .35 .18
2898 A917 30z Wielkopolski .52 .26
2899 A917 70z Polish, vert. 1.25 .60
Nos. 2894-2899 (6) 2.99 1.52

Dogs — A918 Battle of Monte Cassino, 45th Anniv. — A919

1989, May 3 Photo. *Perf. 11½x11*

2900 A918 15z Wire-haired dachshund .15 .15
2901 A918 15z Cocker spaniel .15 .15
2902 A918 20z Czech fousek pointer .16 .15
2903 A918 20z Welsh terrier .16 .15
2904 A918 25z English setter .20 .15
2905 A918 45z Pointer .38 .20
Nos. 2900-2905 (6) 1.20
Set value .58

1989, May 18 *Perf. 11½x12*

Design: 165z, Battle of Falaise, General Stanislaw Maczek, horiz. 210z, Battle of Arnhem, Gen. Stanislaw Sosabowski, vert.

2906 A919 80z Gen. W. Anders .45 .22
2907 A919 165z multicolored .85 .42
2907A A919 210z multicolored 1.20 .60
Nos. 2906-2907 (2) 1.30 .64

1st Armored Division at the Battle of Falaise, 45th anniv. Battle of Arnhem, 45th anniv.
See No. 2968.

A 50z stamp for Gen. Grzegorz Korczynski was prepared but not released.

Woman Wearing a Phrygian Cap — A920

1989, July 3 Litho. *Perf. 11½x11*

2908 A920 100z blk, dark red & dark ultra .70 .30
a. Souv. sheet of 2+2 labels 2.00 2.00

French revolution bicent., PHILEXFRANCE '89. No. 2908 printed se-tenant with inscribed label picturing exhibition emblem. No. 2908a sold for 270z. Surcharge benefited the Polish Philatelic Union.

Polonia House, Pultusk — A921

1989, July 16 Photo. *Perf. 11½*

2909 A921 100z multicolored .70 .30

First Moon Landing, 20th Anniv. A922

1989, July 21 *Perf. 11x11½*

2910 A922 100z multicolored .70 .30
a. Souvenir sheet of 1 .70 .30

No. 2910a exists imperf.

Polish People's Republic, 45th Anniv. — A923

Winners of the Order of the Builders of People's Poland: No. 2911, Ksawery Dunikowski (1875-1964), artist. No. 2912, Stanislaw Mazur (1897-1964), agriculturist. No. 2913, Natalia Gasiorowska (1881-1964), historian. No. 2914, Wincenty Pstrowski (1904-1948), coal miner.

1989, July 21 *Perf. 11½x11*

2911 A923 35z multicolored .25 .15
2912 A923 35z multicolored .25 .15
2913 A923 35z multicolored .25 .15
2914 A923 35z multicolored .25 .15
Nos. 2911-2914 (4) 1.00
Set value .44

Security Service and Militia, 45th Anniv. A924

1989, July 21 *Perf. 11x11½*

2915 A924 35z dull brn & slate blue .35 .15

World Fire Fighting Congress, July 25-30, Warsaw — A925

1989, July 25 *Perf. 11½x11*

2916 A925 80z multicolored .55 .28

Daisy — A926

Designs: 60z, Juniper. 150z, Daisy. 500z, Wild rose. 1000z, Blue corn flower.

1989 Photo. *Perf. 11x12*

2917 A926 40z slate green .15 .15
2918 A926 60z violet blue .15 .15
2919 A926 150z rose lake .18 .15
2920 A926 500z bright violet .55 .28
2921 A926 1000z bright blue 1.10 .55
Nos. 2917-2921 (5) 2.13
Set value 1.00

Issue dates: 40z, 60z, Aug. 25. 150z, Dec. 4; 500z, 1000z, Dec. 19.
See Nos. 2978-2979, 3026. For surcharge see No. 2970.

World War II Battles Type of 1984

Battle scenes and commanders: No. 2922, Westerplatte, Capt. Franciszek Dabrowski. No. 2923, Hel, Artillery Capt. B. Przybyszewski. No. 2924, Kock, Brig.-Gen. Franciszek Kleeberg. No. 2925, Lwow, Brig.-Gen. Wladyslaw Langner.

1989, Sept. 1 *Perf. 12x11½*

2922 A832 25z multicolored .16 .15
2923 A832 25z multicolored .16 .15
2924 A832 35z multicolored .24 .15
2925 A832 35z multicolored .24 .15
Nos. 2922-2925 (4) .80
Set value .34

Nazi invasion of Poland, 50th anniv.

Caricature Museum — A927

1989, Sept. 15 Photo. *Perf. 11½x11*

2926 A927 40z multicolored .20 .15

Teaching Surgery at Polish Universities, Bicent., and Surgeon's Soc. Cent. — A928

Surgeons: 40z, Rafal Jozef Czerwiakowski (1743-1813), 1st professor of surgery and founder of the 1st surgical department, Jagellonian University, Cracow. 60z, Ludwik Rydygier (1850-1920), founder of the Polish Surgeons Society.

1989, Sept. 18 *Perf. 11½x12*

2927 A928 40z black & brt ultra .20 .15
2928 A928 60z black & brt green .30 .15

World Post Day — A929

Design: Emil Kalinski (1890-1973), minister of the Post and Telegraph from 1933-1939.

1989, Oct. 9 *Perf. 12x11½*

2929 A929 60z multicolored .30 .15

Printed se-tenant with label picturing postal emblem of the second republic.

WWII Decorations Type of 1988

Medals: No. 2930, Participation in the Struggle for Control of the Nation. No. 2931, Defense of Warsaw, 1939-45.

1989, Oct. 12 Photo. *Perf. 11½x11*

2930 A910 60z multicolored .24 .15
2931 A910 60z multicolored .24 .15

Royalty Type of 1986

Photo. & Engr.

1989, Oct. 18 *Perf. 11*

2932 A875 20z Boleslaw II Szczodry .15 .15
2933 A875 30z Wladyslaw I Herman .15 .15

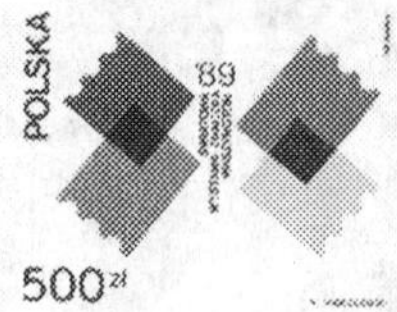

World Stamp Expo '89, Washington, DC, Nov. 17-Dec.3 A930

1989, Nov. 14 Photo. *Perf. 11x11½*

2934 A930 500z multicolored 1.65 .80

Exists imperf.

Polish Red Cross Soc., 70th Anniv. — A931

1989, Nov. 17 *Perf. 11½x11*

2935 A931 200z blk, brt yel grn & scar .75 .30

Treaty of Versailles, 70th Anniv. A932

Design: State arms and representatives of Poland who signed the treaty, including Ignacy Jan Paderewski (1860-1941), pianist, composer, statesman, and Roman Dmowski (1864-1939), statesman.

1989, Nov. 21 *Perf. 11x11½*

2936 A932 350z multicolored 1.25 .50

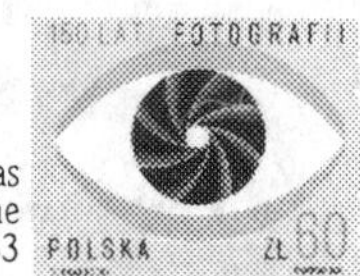

Camera Shutter as the Iris of the Eye — A933

Designs: 40z, Photographer in silhouette, Maksymilian Strasz (1804-1870), pioneer of photography in Poland.

Perf. 11½x12, 12x11½

1989, Nov. 27

2937 A933 40z multicolored .15 .15
2938 A933 60z shown .20 .15
Set value .15

Photography, 150th anniv.

No. 2456 Surcharged

1989, Nov. 30 Photo. *Perf. 11x11½*

2939 A766 500z on 4z dark violet 1.25 .50

Flowers, Still-life Paintings in the National Museum, Warsaw A934

1989, Dec. 18 *Perf. 13*

2940 A934 25z Jan Ciaglinski .15 .15
2941 A934 30z Wojciech Weiss .15 .15
2942 A934 35z Antoni Kolasinski .15 .15
2943 A934 50z Stefan Nacht-Samborski .15 .15
2944 A934 60z Jozef Pankiewicz .15 .15
2945 A934 85z Henryka Beyer .22 .15
2946 A934 110z Wladyslaw Slewinski .30 .18
2947 A934 190z Czeslaw Wdowiszewski .50 .32
Nos. 2940-2947 (8) 1.77
Set value 1.00

Religious Art — A935

1989, Dec. 21 *Perf. 11½x11*

2948 A935 50z Jesus, shroud .25 .20
2949 A935 60z Two saints .25 .20
2950 A935 90z Three saints .25 .20

Perf. 11x11½

2951 A935 150z Jesus, Mary, Joseph .45 .22
2952 A935 200z Madonna and Child Enthroned .60 .30
2953 A935 350z Holy Family with angels 1.25 .52
Nos. 2948-2953 (6) 3.05 1.64

Nos. 2951-2953 vert.

Republic of Poland

No. 2738 Surcharged

1990, Jan. 31 Photo. *Perf. 11½x12*

2954 A828 350z on 15z rose brn .25 .15

Opera Singers — A936

Portraits: 100z, Krystyna Jamroz (1923-1986). 150z, Wanda Werminska (1900-1988). 350z, Ada Sari (1882-1968). 500z, Jan Kiepura (1902-1966).

1990, Feb. 9 *Perf. 12x11½*

2955 A936 100z multicolored .15 .15
2956 A936 150z multicolored .15 .15
2957 A936 350z multicolored .20 .15
2958 A936 500z multicolored .28 .15
Nos. 2955-2958 (4) .78
Set value .30

Yachting A937

1990, Mar. 29 *Perf. 11x11½*

2959 A937 100z shown .15 .15
2960 A937 200z Rugby .15 .15
2961 A937 400z High jump .20 .15
2962 A937 500z Figure skating .25 .15
2963 A937 500z Diving .25 .15
2964 A937 1000z Rhythmic gymnastics .50 .26
Nos. 2959-2964 (6) 1.50
Set value .75

Roman Kozlowski (1889-1977), Paleontologist A938

1990, Apr. 17 Photo. *Perf. 11x11½*

2965 A938 500z red & olive bister .30 .15

Pope John Paul II, 70th Birthday A939

1990, May 18 *Perf. 11*

2966 A939 1000z multicolored .55 .25

Souvenir Sheet

First Polish Postage Stamp, 130th Anniv. — A940

Design includes No. 1 separated by simulated perforations from 1000z commemorative version at right.

1990, May 25 *Perf. 11½*

2967 A940 1000z multicolored .55 .25

Battle Type of 1989

Design: Battle of Narvik, 1940, General Z. Bohusz-Szyszko.

1990, May 28 *Perf. 11½x12*

2968 A919 1500z multicolored .60 .25

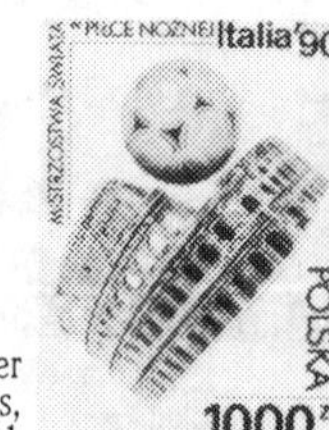

World Cup Soccer Championships, Italy — A941

1990, June 8 *Perf. 11½x11*

2969 A941 1000z multicolored .60 .30

No. 2918 Surcharged in Vermilion

700 zł

1990, June 18 Photo. *Perf. 11x12*

2970 A926 700z on 60z vio bl .40 .20

Memorial to Victims of June 1956 Uprising, Poznan — A942

1990, June 28 Photo. *Perf. 12x11½*

2971 A942 1500z multicolored .70 .30

Social Insurance Institution, 70th Anniv. — A943

1990, July 5 *Perf. 11x11½*

2972 A943 1500z multicolored .75 .35

Shells — A944

#2973, Mussel. #2974, Fresh water snail.

1990, July 16 *Perf. 14*

2973 A944 B (500z) dk pur .15 .15
2974 A944 A (700z) olive grn .35 .15
Set value .25

Katyn Forest Massacre, 50th Anniv. — A945

1990, July 20

2975 A945 1500z gray, red & blk .75 .35

Polish Meteorological Service — A946

1990, July 27 *Perf. 11x11½*

2976 A946 500z shown .25 .15
2977 A946 700z Thermometer .40 .15
Set value .25

Flower Type of 1989

Designs: 2000z, Nuphar. 5000z, German iris.

1990, Aug. 13 *Die Cut*

Self Adhesive

2978 A926 2000z olive grn 1.00 .55
2979 A926 5000z violet 2.50 .95

World Kayaking Championships, Poznan — A947

Design: 1000z, One-man kayak.

1990, Aug. 22 Photo. *Perf. 11x11½*

2980 A947 700z multicolored .40 .20
2981 A947 1000z multicolored .60 .30
a. Souv. sheet of 1 + label 4.50 4.50

A948

A949

1990, Aug. 31 *Perf. 11½x11*

2982 A948 1500z blk, red & gray .75 .35

Solidarity, 10th anniv.

1990, Sept. 24 Photo. *Perf. 11½x11*

Flowers.

2983 A949 200z Polemonium coeruleum .15 .15
2984 A949 700z Nymphoides peltata .35 .16
2985 A949 700z Dracocephalum ruyschiana .35 .16
2986 A949 1000z Helleborus purpurascens .55 .25
2987 A949 1500z Daphne cneorum .80 .30
2988 A949 1700z Dianthus superbus .90 .40
Nos. 2983-2988 (6) 3.10 1.42

Cmielow Porcelain Works, Bicentennial A950

Designs: 700z, Platter, 1870-1887. 800z, Plate, 1887-1890, vert. No. 2991, Figurine, 1941-1944, vert. No. 2992, Cup, saucer, c. 1887. 1500z, Candy box, 1930-1990. 2000z, Vase, 1979, vert.

1990, Oct. 31 Photo. *Perf. 11*

2989 A950 700z multicolored .40 .15
2990 A950 800z multicolored .42 .15
2991 A950 1000z multicolored .55 .20
2992 A950 1000z multicolored .55 .20
2993 A950 1500z multicolored .85 .30
2994 A950 2000z multicolored 1.10 .40
Nos. 2989-2994 (6) 3.87 1.40

Owls — A951

1990, Nov. 6 Litho. *Perf. 14*

2995 A951 200z Athene noctua .15 .15
2996 A951 500z shown .30 .15
2997 A951 500z Strix aluco, winter .30 .15
2998 A951 1000z Asio flammeus .60 .25
2999 A951 1500z Asio otus .90 .40
3000 A951 2000z Tyto alba 1.25 .50
Nos. 2995-3000 (6) 3.50 1.60

Pres. Lech Walesa, 1983 Nobel Peace Prize Winner A952

1990, Dec. 12 Litho. *Perf. 11x11½*

3001 A952 1700z multicolored 1.00 .45

A953

A954

1990, Dec. 21 Photo. *Perf. 11½x11*

3002 A953 1500z multicolored .75 .35

Polish participation in Battle of Britain, 50th anniv.

1990, Dec. 28 Litho. *Perf. 11½*

Architecture: 700z, Collegiate Church, 12th cent., Leczyca. 800z, Castle, 14th cent., Reszel. 1500z, Town Hall, 16th cent., Chelmno. 1700z, Church of the Nuns of the Visitation, 18th cent., Warsaw.

3003 A954 700z multicolored .35 .15
3004 A954 800z multicolored .40 .18
3005 A954 1500z multicolored .80 .32
3006 A954 1700z multicolored .90 .35
Nos. 3003-3006 (4) 2.45 1.00

No. 3006 printed with se-tenant label for World Philatelic Exhibition, Poland '93.

Art Treasures of the Natl. Gallery, Warsaw A955

Paintings: 500z, King Sigismund Augustus. 700z, The Adoration of the Magi, Pultusk Codex. 1000z, St. Matthew, Pultusk Codex. 1500z, Christ Removing the Moneychangers by Mikolaj Haberschrack. 1700z, The Annunciation. 2000z, The Three Marys by Haberschrack.

1991, Jan. 11 Photo. *Perf. 11*

3007 A955 500z multicolored .15 .15
3008 A955 700z multicolored .30 .15
3009 A955 1000z multicolored .35 .15
3010 A955 1500z multicolored .50 .18
3011 A955 1700z multicolored .55 .22
3012 A955 2000z multicolored .65 .28
Nos. 3007-3012 (6) 2.50 1.13

Pinecones — A956

1991, Feb. 22 *Perf. 12x11½*

3013 A956 700z Abies alba .20 .15
3014 A956 1500z Pinus strobus .40 .20

See Nos. 3163-3164, 3231-3232.

Radziwill Palace A957

1991, Mar. 3 Photo. *Perf. 11x12*

3015 A957 1500z multicolored .40 .20

Admission to CEPT.

Royalty Type of 1986 Surcharged in Red

1000 zł

Designs: 1000z, Boleslaw III Krzywousty. 1500z, Wladyslaw II Wygnaniec.

Photo. & Engr.

1991, Mar. 25 *Perf. 11*

3016 A875 1000z on 40z, grn & blk .30 .15
3017 A875 1500z on 50z, red vio & gray blk .50 .25

Not issued without surcharge.

Brother Albert (Adam Chmielowski, 1845-1916) — A958

1991, Mar. 29 Photo. *Perf. 12x11½*

3018 A958 2000z multicolored .50 .25

Battle of Legnica, 750th Anniv. A959

Photo. & Engr.

1991, Apr. 9 *Perf. 14½x14*

3019 A959 1500z multicolored .45 .25

See Germany No. 1635.

Polish Icons — A960

Designs: 500z, 1000z, 1500z, Various paintings of Madonna and Child. 700z, 2000z, 2200z, Various paintings of Jesus.

1991, Apr. 22 Photo. *Perf. 11*

3020 A960 500z multicolored .16 .15
3021 A960 700z multicolored .24 .15
3022 A960 1000z multicolored .35 .15
3023 A960 1500z multicolored .52 .22
3024 A960 2000z multicolored .70 .30
3025 A960 2200z multicolored .75 .32
Nos. 3020-3025 (6) 2.72 1.29

Flower Type of 1989

Design: 700z, Lily of the Valley.

1991, Apr. 26 Litho. *Perf. 14*

3026 A926 700z dk blue green .25 .15

Royalty Type of 1986

Designs: 1000z, Boleslaw IV Kedzierzawy. 1500z, Mieszko III Stary.

Photo. & Engr.

1991, Apr. 30 *Perf. 11x11½*

3033 A875 1000z brn red & black .35 .15
3034 A875 1500z brt bl & bluish blk .60 .20

A961

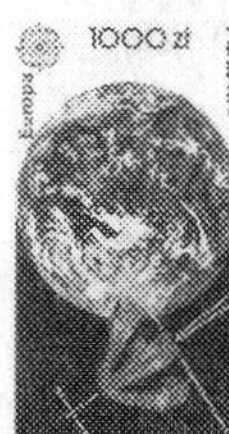
A962

Designs: 2000z, Title page of act. 2500z, Debate in the Sejm. 3000z, Adoption of Constitution, May 3, 1791, by Jan Matejko (1838-1893).

1991, May 2 Litho. *Perf. 11½*

3035 A961 2000z brown & ver .50 .20
3036 A961 2500z brown & ver .70 .40

Souvenir Sheet

3037 A961 3000z multicolored 1.25 .75

May 3, 1791 Polish constitution, bicent.

1991, May 6 Litho. *Perf. 11½x11*

3038 A962 1000z multicolored .40 .15

Europa.

European Conference for Protection of Cultural Heritage, Cracow — A963

1991, May 27 Litho. *Perf. 11½*

3039 A963 2000z blue & lake .75 .30

Sinking of the Bismarck, 50th Anniv. — A964

1991, May 27

3040 A964 2000z multicolored .75 .30

A965

A966

Designs: 1000z, Pope John Paul II. 2000z, Pope wearing white.

1991, June 1 Litho. *Perf. 11½x11*

3041 A965 1000z multicolored .30 .15
3042 A965 2000z multicolored .70 .30

1991, June 21 Litho. *Perf. 11½*

3043 A966 2000z multicolored .60 .25

Antarctic Treaty, 30th anniv.

Polish Paper Industry, 500th Anniv. A967

1991, July 8

3044 A967 2500z lake & gray .75 .30

Victims of Stalin — A968

1991, July 29 Litho. *Perf. 11½x12*

3045 A968 2500z black & red .75 .30

Souvenir Sheet

Pope John Paul II — A969

1991, Aug. 15 Photo. *Perf. 11½x11*

3046 A969 3500z multicolored 1.00 .50

Basketball, Cent. A970

1991, Aug. 19 Litho. *Perf. 11x11½*

3047 A970 2500z multicolored .75 .30

Leon Wyczolkowski (1852-1936), painter — A971

1991, Sept. 7 Photo. *Perf. 11½x12*

3048 A971 3000z olive brown .80 .40
a. Sheet of 4 4.50 4.50

16th Polish Philatelic Exhibition, Bydgoszcz '91.

Kazimierz Twardowski (1866-1938) — A972

1991, Oct. 10 *Perf. 11x11½*

3049 A972 2500z sepia & blk .60 .30

Butterflies — A973

1991, Nov. 16 Litho. *Perf. 12½*

3050 A973 1000z Papilio machaon .20 .15
3051 A973 1000z Mormonia sponsa .20 .15
3052 A973 1500z Vanessa cardui .30 .15
3053 A973 1500z Iphiclides podalirius .30 .15
3054 A973 2500z Panaxia dominula .50 .30
3055 A973 2500z Nymphalis io .50 .30
a. Block of 6, #3050-3055 2.00 1.10

Souvenir Sheet

3056 A973 15,000z Aporia crataegi 5.00 5.00

No. 3056 has a holographic image on the stamp and comes se-tenant with a Phila Nippon '91 label. The image may be affected by soaking in water. Varieties such as missing hologram, double and shifted images, and imperfs exist.

On Jan. 15, 1994, the Polish postal administration demonetized No. 3056.

Nativity Scene, by Francesco Solimena A974

1991, Nov. 25 Photo. *Perf. 11*

3057 A974 1000z multicolored .30 .15

Polish Armed Forces at Tobruk, 50th Anniv. — A975

1991, Dec. 10 Photo. *Perf. 11½*

3058 A975 2000z Gen. Stanislaw Kopanski .60 .30

A976

A977

World War II Commanders: 2000z, Brig. Gen. Michal Tokarzewski-Karaszewicz (1893-1964). 2500z, Gen. Kazimierz Sosukowski (1885-1969). 3000z, Gen. Stefan Rowecki (1895-1944). 5000z, Gen. Tadeusz Komorowski (1895-1966). 6500z, Brig. Gen. Leopold Okulicki (1898-1946).

1991, Dec. 20 Litho.

3059 A976 2000z vermilion & blk .60 .20
3060 A976 2500z violet bl & lake .75 .30
3061 A976 3000z magenta & dk bl .95 .40
3062 A976 5000z olive & brn 1.50 .60
3063 A976 6500z brn org & brn 2.00 1.00
Nos. 3059-3063 (5) 5.80 2.50

1991, Dec. 30 Photo. *Perf. 12x11½*

Boy Scouts in Poland, 80th anniv.: 1500z, Lord Robert Baden-Powell, founder of Boy Scouts. 2000z, Andrzej Malkowski (1889-1919), founder of Boy Scouts in Poland. 2500z, Scout standing guard, 1920. 3500z, Soldier scout, 1944.

3064 A977 1500z multicolored .45 .20
3065 A977 2000z multicolored .55 .25
3066 A977 2500z multicolored .70 .35
3067 A977 3500z multicolored 1.00 .55
Nos. 3064-3067 (4) 2.70 1.35

Royalty Type of 1986

Designs: 1500z, Kazimierz II Sprawiedliwy. 2000z, Leszek Bialy.

1992, Jan. 15 Photo. & Engr. *Perf. 11*

3068 A875 1500z olive green & brn .22 .15
3069 A875 2000z gray blue & blk .30 .15

Paintings A978

Paintings (self-portraits except for 2200z) by: 700z, Sebastien Bourdon. 1000z, Sir Joshua Reynolds. 1500z, Sir Gottfried Kneller. 2000z, Murillo. 2200z, Rubens. 3000z, Diego de Silva y Velazquez.

1992, Jan. 16 Photo.

3070 A978 700z multicolored .15 .15
3071 A978 1000z multicolored .15 .15
3072 A978 1500z multicolored .22 .15
3073 A978 2000z multicolored .30 .15
3074 A978 2200z multicolored .32 .16
3075 A978 3000z multicolored .45 .25
Nos. 3070-3075 (6) 1.59
Set value .80

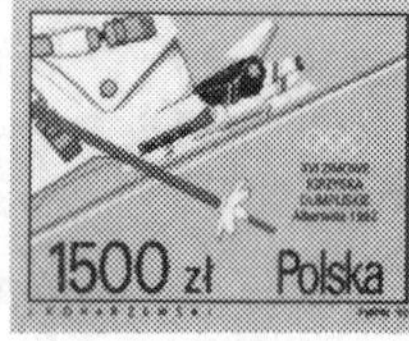
1992 Winter Olympics, Albertville A979

1992, Feb. 8 Litho. *Perf. 11x11½*

3076 A979 1500z Skiing .22 .15
3077 A979 2500z Hockey .35 .20

See Nos. 3095-3098.

Tadeusz Manteuffel (1902-1970), Historian — A980

1992, Mar. 5 Photo. *Perf. 11½x11*

3078 A980 2500z brown .95 .40

Famous Poles — A981

Designs: 1500z, Nicolaus Copernicus, astronomer. 2000z, Frederic Chopin, composer. 2500z, Henryk Sienkiewicz, novelist. 3500z, Marie Sklodowska Curie, scientist. 5000z, Casimir Funk, biochemist.

1992, Mar. 5 Litho. *Perf. 11x11½*

3079 A981 1500z multicolored .60 .25
3080 A981 2000z multicolored .75 .30
3081 A981 2500z multicolored .95 .40
3082 A981 3500z multicolored 1.30 .55
Nos. 3079-3082 (4) 3.60 1.50

Souvenir Sheet

3083 A981 5000z multicolored 1.50 .60

Expo '92, Seville (#3083).

Discovery of America, 500th Anniv. — A982

1992, May 5

3084 A982 1500z Columbus, chart .50 .25
3085 A982 3000z Chart, Santa Maria 1.00 .50
a. Pair, #3084-3085 1.50 .75

Europa.

Waterfalls — A983

1992, June 1 Litho. *Perf. 11½*

3086 A983 2000z Pstrag (trout) .35 .15
3087 A983 2500z Zimorodek (kingfisher) .45 .18
3088 A983 3000z Jelec (whiting) .52 .22
3089 A983 3500z Pluszcz .60 .25
Nos. 3086-3089 (4) 1.92 .80

Order of Virtuti Militari, Bicent. A984

Designs: 1500z, Prince Jozef Poniatowski (1763-1813). 3000z, Marshal Jozef Pilsudski (1867-1935). No. 3092, Black Madonna of Czestochowa.

1992, June 18 *Perf. 11*

3090 A984 1500z multi .25 .15
3091 A984 3000z multi .52 .25

Souvenir Sheet

Imperf

3092 A984 20,000z multi 3.50

No. 3092 contains one 39x60mm stamp.

Children's Drawings of Love — A985

Designs: 1500z, Heart between woman and man. 3000z, Butterfly, animals with sun and rain.

1992, June 26 Litho. *Perf. 11½x11*

3093 A985 1500z multicolored .25 .15
3094 A985 3000z multicolored .52 .25
a. Pair, #3093-3094 .80 .35

Olympics Type of 1992

1992, July 25 Litho. *Perf. 11x11½*

3095 A979 1500z Fencing .30 .15
3096 A979 2000z Boxing .40 .20
3097 A979 2500z Sprinting .45 .22
3098 A979 3000z Cycling .75 .38
Nos. 3095-3098 (4) 1.90 .95

1992 Summer Olympics, Barcelona.

Souvenir Sheet

OLYMPHILEX '92, Barcelona — A986

1992, July 29

3099 A986 20,000z Runners 5.00 2.50

Exists imperf.

Janusz Korczak (1879-1942), Physician, Concentration Camp Victim — A987

1992, Aug. 5 Photo. *Perf. 11x11½*

3100 A987 1500z multicolored .35 .15

Polish Emigrants Assoc. World Meeting — A988

1992, Aug. 19 *Perf. 12x11½*

3101 A988 3000z multicolored .70 .35

World War II Combatants World Meeting — A989

1992, Aug. 14 *Perf. 11½x11*

3102 A989 3000z multicolored .75 .38

Stefan Cardinal Wyszynski (1901-1981) — A990

3000z, Pope John Paul II embracing person.

1992, Aug. 15 Litho.

3103 A990 1500z multicolored .40 .20
3104 A990 3000z multicolored .85 .40
a. Block of 2, #3103-3104 + 2 labels 1.25

6th World Youth Cong., Czestochowa (#3104).

Adampol, Polish Village in Turkey, 150th Anniv. A991

1992, Sept. 15 Photo. *Perf. 11x11½*

3105 A991 3500z multicolored .85 .42

World Post Day — A992

1992, Oct. 9 *Perf. 11½x11*

3106 A992 3500z multicolored .85 .42

Bruno Schulz (1892-1942), Author — A993

1992, Oct. 26 Litho. *Perf. 11x11½*

3107 A993 3000z multicolored .70 .35

Polish Sculptures, Natl. Museum, Warsaw A994

Designs: 2000z, Seated Girl, by Henryk Wicinski. 2500z, Portrait of Tytus Czyzewski, by Zbigniew Pronaszko. 3000z, Polish Nike, by Edward Wittig. 3500z, The Nude, by August Zamoyski.

1992, Oct. 29 *Perf. 11½*

3108 A994 2000z multicolored .55 .28
3109 A994 2500z multicolored .70 .35
3110 A994 3000z multicolored .80 .40
3111 A994 3500z multicolored .95 .48
a. Souvenir sheet of 4, #3108-3111 3.00 1.50
Nos. 3108-3111 (4) 3.00 1.51

Polska '93 (#3111a).

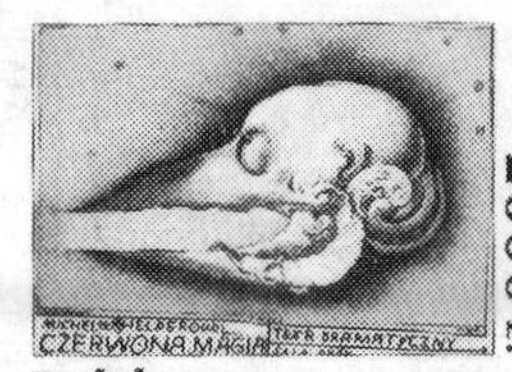

Posters — A995

Designs: 1500z, 10th Theatrical Summer in Zamosc, by Jan Mlodozeniec, vert. 2000z, Red Magic, by Franciszek Starowieyski. 2500z, Circus, by Waldemar Swierzy, vert. 3500z, Mannequins, by Henryk Tomaszewski.

1992, Oct. 30 *Perf. 13½*

3112 A995 1500z multicolored .35 .18
3113 A995 2000z multicolored .45 .22
3114 A995 2500z multicolored .60 .30
3115 A995 3500z multicolored .80 .40
Nos. 3112-3115 (4) 2.20 1.10

Illustrations by Edward Lutczyn A996

Designs: 1500z, Girl using snake as jump rope. 2000z, Boy on rocking horse with rockers reversed. 2500z, Boy using bird as arrow. 3500z, Girl with ladder, wind-up giraffe with keys on back.

1992, Nov. 16 Photo. *Perf. 11*

3116 A996 1500z multicolored .28 .15
3117 A996 2000z multicolored .38 .20
3118 A996 2500z multicolored .48 .24
3119 A996 3500z multicolored .65 .32
Nos. 3116-3119 (4) 1.79 .91

Polska '93.

Home Army A997

1992, Nov. 20 Litho. *Perf. 13½*

3120 A997 1500z shown .28 .15
3121 A997 3500z Soldiers, diff. .65 .32
a. Pair, #3120-3121 .95 .48

Souvenir Sheet

3122 A997 20,000z +500z "WP AK," vert. 4.00 2.00

Christmas A998

1992, Nov. 25 Photo. *Perf. 11½*

3123 A998 1000z multicolored .25 .15

A999 A1000

1992, Dec. 5 Photo. *Perf. 11½x11*

3124 A999 1500z Wheat stalks .40 .20
3125 A999 3500z Food products 1.00 .50

Intl. Conference on Nutrition, Rome.

1992, Dec. 10 Litho.

3126 A1000 3000z multicolored .70 .35

Postal Agreement with the Sovereign Military Order of Malta, Aug. 1, 1991.

Natl. Arms — A1001

1992, Dec. 14 Photo. *Perf. 12x11½*

3127 A1001 2000z 1295 .55 .28
3128 A1001 2500z 15th cent. .70 .35
3129 A1001 3000z 18th cent. .85 .40
3130 A1001 3500z 1919 1.00 .45
3131 A1001 5000z 1990 1.40 .65
Nos. 3127-3131 (5) 4.50 2.13

Polish Philatelic Society, Cent. A1002

1993, Jan. 6 Photo. *Perf. 11½*
3132 A1002 1500z multicolored .50 .25

A1003 A1004

1993, Feb. 5 *Perf. 11½x11*
3133 A1003 3000z multicolored 1.00 .50

1993 Winter University Games, Zakopane.

1993, Feb. 14

Design: I Love You.

3134 A1004 1500z shown .50 .25
3135 A1004 3000z Heart on envelope 1.00 .50

Amber — A1005

Various pieces of amber.

1993, Jan. 29 Litho. *Perf. 13½*
3136 A1005 1500z multicolored .40 .20
3137 A1005 2000z multicolored .55 .28
3138 A1005 2500z multicolored .68 .35
3139 A1005 3000z multicolored .82 .40
Nos. 3136-3139 (4) 2.45 1.23

Souvenir Sheet

3140 A1005 20,000z Necklace, map, horiz. 5.00 2.50

Polska '93 (#3140).

Royalty Type of 1986

Designs: 1500z, Wladyslaw Laskonogi. 2000z, Henryk I Brodaty (1201-38). 2500z, Konrad I Mazowiecki. 3000z, Boleslaw V Wstydliwy.

Photo. & Engr.

1993, Mar. 25 *Perf. 11*
3141 A875 1500z yellow grn & brn .40 .20
3142 A875 2000z red vio & indigo .55 .28
3143 A875 2500z gray & black .68 .35
3144 A875 3000z yellow brn & brn .82 .40
Nos. 3141-3144 (4) 2.45 1.23

#3144 printed with se-tenant label for Polska '93.

Battle of the Arsenal, 50th Anniv. — A1006

1993, Mar. 26 Photo. *Perf. 11½*
3145 A1006 1500z multicolored .40 .20

Intl. Medieval Knights' Tournament, Golub-Dobrzyn — A1007

Various knights on horseback.

1993, Mar. 29 *Perf. 11x11½*
3146 A1007 1500z multicolored .40 .20
3147 A1007 2000z multicolored .55 .28
3148 A1007 2500z multicolored .68 .35
3149 A1007 3500z multicolored .92 .45
Nos. 3146-3149 (4) 2.55 1.28

City of Szczecin, 750th Anniv. A1008

1993, Apr. 3 Litho. *Perf. 11½x11*
3150 A1008 1500z multicolored .42 .20

Warsaw Ghetto Uprising, 50th Anniv. — A1009

1993, Apr. 19 Litho. *Perf. 14*
3151 A1009 4000z gray, black & yel 1.15 .60

See Israel No. 1163.

Europa — A1010

Contemporary art by: No. 3152, A. Szapocznikow and J. Lebenstein. No. 3153, S. Gierowski and B. Linke.

1993, Apr. 30 Photo. *Perf. 11x11½*
3152 A1010 1500z multicolored .42 .20
3153 A1010 4000z multicolored 1.15 .60
a. Pair, #3152-3153 1.60 .80

Polish Parliament (Sejm), 500th Anniv. — A1011

1993, May 2 Photo. *Perf. 11*
3154 A1011 2000z multicolored .56 .28

Death of Francesco Nullo, 130th Anniv. A1012

1993, May 5 Litho. *Perf. 11x11½*
3155 A1012 2500z multicolored .70 .35

Souvenir Sheet

Legend of the White Eagle — A1013

1993, May 7 Engr. *Perf. 13½*
3156 A1013 50,000z dark brown 9.00 5.00

Polska '93.

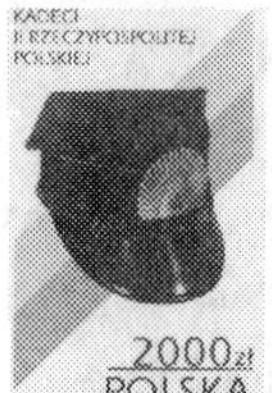

Cadets of Second Polish Republic — A1014

1993, May 21 Litho. *Perf. 11x11½*
3157 A1014 2000z multicolored .56 .28

Nicolaus Copernicus (1473-1543) A1015

1993, May 24
3158 A1015 2000z multicolored .56 .28

Kornel Makuszymski, 40th Death Anniv. — A1016

Illustrations: 1500z, Lion, monkey. 2000z, Goat walking. 3000z, Monkey. 5000z, Goat riding bird.

1993, June 1
3159 A1016 1500z multicolored .42 .20
3160 A1016 2000z multicolored .56 .28
3161 A1016 3000z multicolored .85 .42
3162 A1016 5000z multicolored 1.40 .70
Nos. 3159-3162 (4) 3.23 1.60

Pine Cone Type of 1991

1993, June 30 Photo. *Perf. 12x11½*
3163 A956 10,000z Pinus cembra 2.10 1.00
3164 A956 20,000z Pinus sylvestris 4.25 2.00

Birds — A1017

1993, July 15 Litho. *Perf. 11½*
3165 A1017 1500z Passer montanus .25 .15
3166 A1017 2000z Motacilla alba .32 .16
3167 A1017 3000z Dendrocopos syriacus .50 .25
3168 A1017 4000z Carduelis carduelis .65 .32
3169 A1017 5000z Sturnus vulgaris .80 .40
3170 A1017 6000z Pyrrhula pyrrhula .95 .48
Nos. 3165-3170 (6) 3.47 1.76

Polish Natl. Anthem, Bicent. A1018

1993, July 20 Photo. *Perf. 11x11½*
3171 A1018 1500z multicolored .25 .15

See No. 3206.

Madonna and Child A1019

Syncopate Perf Type A

Designs: 1500z, Stone carving from Basilica, Lesna Podlaska. 2000z, Statue, Swieta Lipska.

Type A: On the two longer sides, the oval hole equal in width to 3 holes is the 4th hole from a short side, followed by normal round perfs on the balance of the long side. The larger number of normal holes varies from stamp to stamp.

Perf. 11x11½ Syncopated Type A (2 Sides)

1993, Aug. 15
3172 A1019 1500z multicolored .20 .15
3173 A1019 2000z multicolored .25 .15
Set value .22

World Post Day — A1020

Photo. & Engr.

1993, Oct. 9 *Perf. 11½x11*
3174 A1020 2500z multicolored .32 .16

Polish Parachute Brigade A1021

Perf. 11x11½, Syncopated Type A (2 Sides)

1993, Sept. 25 Photo.
3175 A1021 1500z multicolored .25 .15

Death of St. Hedwig (Jadwiga), 750th Anniv. — A1022

1993, Oct. 14 Litho. *Perf. 14*
3176 A1022 2500z multicolored .35 .18

See Germany No. 1816.

35th Intl. Jazz Jamboree A1023

Perf. 11½ Syncopated Type A (2 Sides)

1993, Sept. 27 **Litho.**
3177 A1023 2000z multicolored .25 .15

Souvenir Sheet

Election of Pope John Paul II, 15th Anniv. — A1024

1993, Oct. 16
3178 A1024 20,000z multicolored 3.00 2.00

A1025

Christmas — A1026

1993, Nov. 11
3179 A1025 4000z Eagle, crown .50 .25

Souvenir Sheet

3180 A1025 20,000z Dove 2.75 1.40

Independence, 75th anniv. No. 3180 has a continuous design.

1993, Nov. 25
3181 A1026 1500z multicolored .25 .15

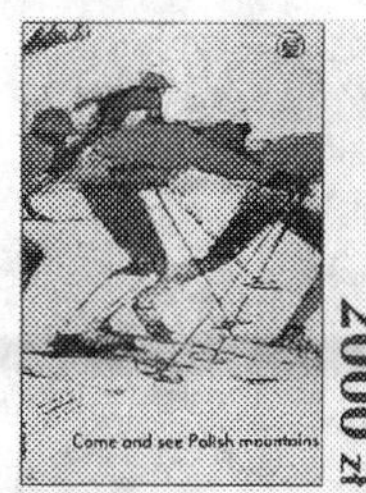
Posters A1027

Designs: 2000z, "Come and see Polish mountains." 5000z, Alban Berg Wozzeck.

1993, Dec. 10
3182 A1027 2000z multicolored .30 .15
3183 A1027 5000z multicolored .65 .32

See Nos. 3203-3204, 3259-3260.

"I Love You" — A1028

A1029

Perf. 11½x11 Syncopated Type A (2 Sides)

1994, Jan. 14 **Litho.**
3184 A1028 1500z multicolored .25 .15

1994, Feb. 12 Photo. *Perf. 11½x11*
3185 A1029 2500z Cross-country skiing .30 .15
3186 A1029 5000z Ski jumping .60 .30

Souvenir Sheet

3187 A1029 10,000z Downhill skiing 1.50 1.50

1994 Winter Olympics, Lillehammer. Intl. Olympic Committee, cent. (#2187).

Kosciuszko Insurrection, Bicent. — A1030

Perf. 11½x11 Syncopated Type A (2 Sides)

1994, Mar. 24 **Photo.**
3188 A1030 2000z multicolored .30 .15

Zamosc Academy, 400th Anniv. — A1031

1994, Mar. 15
3189 A1031 5000z brn, blk & gray .65 .30

Gen. Jozef Bem (1794-1850) A1032

Perf. 11½ Syncopated Type A (2 Sides)

1994, Mar. 14
3190 A1032 5000z multicolored .65 .30

Royalty Type of 1986 with Denomination at Bottom

Photo. & Engr.

1994, Apr. 15 *Perf. 11*
3191 A875 2500z Leszek Czarny .30 .15
3192 A875 5000z Przemysl II .60 .30

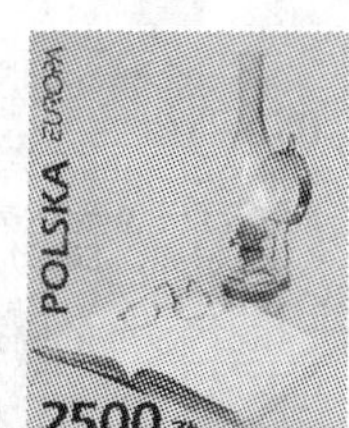
Inventions A1033

Europa: 2500z, Petroleum lamp, invented by I. Lukasiewicz (1822-82). 6000z, Astronomical sighting device, with profile of Copernicus (1473-1543).

Perf. 11½x11 Syncopated Type A (2 Sides)

1994, Apr. 30 **Litho.**
3193 A1033 2500z multicolored .30 .15
3194 A1033 6000z multicolored .70 .35

St. Mary's Sanctuary — A1034

Design: 4000z, Our Lady of Kalwaria Zebrzydowska.

Perf. 11½x11 Syncopated Type A (2 Sides)

1994, May 16 **Litho.**
3195 A1034 4000z multicolored .55 .25

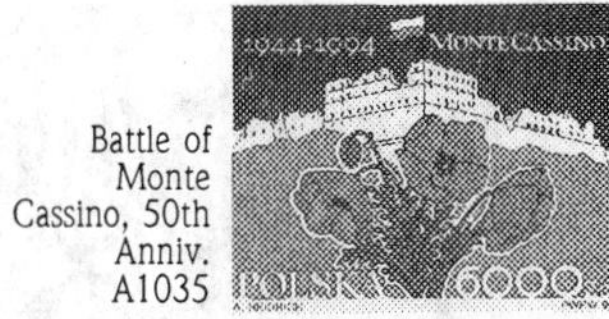
Battle of Monte Cassino, 50th Anniv. A1035

Perf. 11x11½ Syncopated Type A (2 Sides)

1994, May 18
3196 A1035 6000z multicolored .80 .40

Traditional Dances — A1036

Perf. 11½ Syncopated Type A (2 Sides)

1994, May 25
3197 A1036 3000z Mazurka .35 .20
3198 A1036 4000z Goralski .50 .25
3199 A1036 9000z Krakowiak 1.25 .60
Nos. 3197-3199 (3) 2.10 1.05

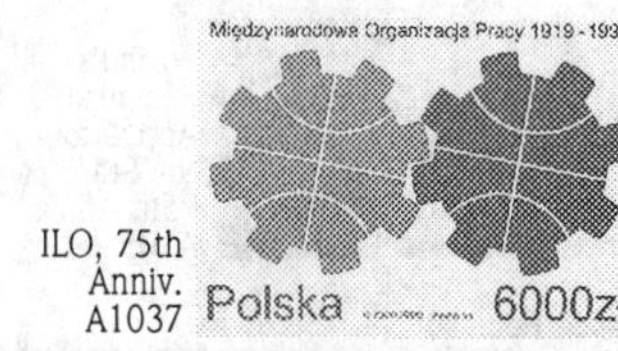
ILO, 75th Anniv. A1037

Perf. 11½x11 Syncopated Type A (2 Sides)

1994, June 7 **Litho.**
3200 A1037 6000z multicolored .75 .35

Polish Electricians Assoc., 75th Anniv. A1038

Perf. 11x11½ Syncopated Type A (2 Sides)

1994, June 10
3201 A1038 4000z multicolored .55 .30

1994 World Soccer Cup Championships, US — A1039

Perf. 11½x11 Syncopated Type A (2 Sides)

1994, June 17
3202 A1039 6000z multicolored .75 .38

Poster Art Type of 1993

4000z, Mr. Fabre, by Wiktor Gorka. 6000z, VIII OISTAT Congress, by Hubert Hilscher, horiz.

11x11½, 11½x11 Syncopated Type A (2 Sides)

1994, July 4 **Litho.**
3203 A1027 4000z multicolored .60 .30
3204 A1027 6000z multicolored .90 .45

Florian Znaniecki (1882-1958), Sociologist — A1040

11½ Syncopated Type A (2 Sides)

1994, July 15 **Litho.**
3205 A1040 9000z multicolored 1.10 .55

Polish Natl. Anthem Type of 1993

Design: 2500z, Battle of Raclawice, 1794.

1994, July 20 Photo. *Perf. 11x11½*
3206 A1018 2500z multicolored .35 .18

A1042

A1043

11½x11 Syncopated Type A (2 Sides)

1994, Aug. 1 **Litho.**
3207 A1042 2500z Natl. arms .35 .18

Warsaw Uprising, 50th anniv.

1994, Aug. 16
3208 A1043 4000z PHILAKOREA '94 .50 .25

Stamp Day.

Basilica of St. Brigida, Gdansk — A1044

1994, Aug. 28
3209 A1044 4000z multicolored .50 .25

Modern Olympic Games, Cent. — A1045

Perf. 11x11½ Syncopated Type A (2 Sides)

1994, Sept. 5
3210 A1045 4000z multicolored .70 .35

Krzysztof Komeda (1931-69), Jazz Muscian A1046

Perf. 11½ Syncopated Type A (2 Sides)

1994, Sept. 22 **Litho.**
3211 A1046 6000z multicolored .70 .35

Aquarium Fish — A1047

Designs: No. 3212a, Ancistrus dolichopterus. b, Pterophyllum scalare. c, Xiphophorus helleri, paracheirodon innesi. d, Poecilia reticulata.

Perf. 11½x11 Syncopated Type A (2 Sides)

1994, Sept. 28 **Litho.**
3212 Strip of 4 2.00 1.00
a.-d. A1047 4000z any single .50 .25

World Post Day — A1048

1994, Oct. 9
3213 A1048 4000z Postal Arms, 1858 .50 .25

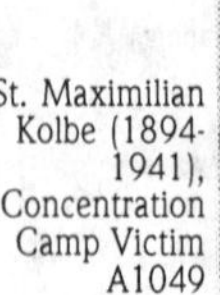

St. Maximilian Kolbe (1894-1941), Concentration Camp Victim A1049

1994, Oct. 24 **Photo.** ***Perf. 11x11½***
3214 A1049 2500z multicolored .35 .15

Pigeons A1050

Designs: a, Mewka polska. b, Krymka biatostacka. c, Srebrniak polski. d, Sokot gdanski. 10,000z, Polski golab pocztowy.

Perf. 11x11½ Syncopated Type A (2 Sides)

1994, Oct. 28 **Litho.**
3215 Block of 4 2.25 1.10
a.-b. A1050 4000z any single .45 .20
c.-d. A1050 6000z any single .65 .30

Souvenir Sheet

3216 A1050 10,000z multicolored 1.25 .60

Christmas A1051

11x11½ Syncopated Type A (2 Sides)

1994, Nov. 25 **Litho.**
3217 A1051 2500z multicolored .35 .15

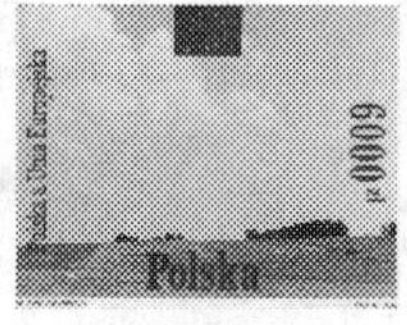

European Union A1052

1994, Dec. 15
3218 A1052 6000z multicolored .75 .35

Love Stamp — A1053

Perf. 11½x11 Syncopated Type A (2 Sides)

1995, Jan. 31 **Litho.**
3219 A1053 35g dk bl & rose car .40 .20

Hydro-Meteorological Service, 75th Anniv. — A1054

Perf. 11x11½ Syncopated Type A (2 Sides)

1995, Jan. 31
3220 A1054 60g multicolored .50 .25

Poland's Renewed Access to the Sea, 75th Anniv. A1055

1995, Feb. 10
3221 A1055 45g multicolored .48 .25

Polish Royalty Type of 1986 with Denomination at Bottom

Photo. & Engr.

1995, Feb. 28 ***Perf. 11***
3222 A875 35g Waclaw II .40 .20
3223 A875 45g Wladyslaw I Lotiek .45 .25
3224 A875 60g Kazimierz III, the Great .65 .30
3225 A875 80g Ludwik Wegierski .80 .40
Nos. 3222-3225 (4) 2.30 1.15

St. John of God (1495-1550), Initiator of Order — A1056

Perf. 12x11½ Syncopated Type A (2 Sides)

1995, Mar. 8 **Litho.**
3226 A1056 60g multicolored .70 .35

Easter Eggs A1057

Each stamp showing various designs on 3 eggs.

Perf. 11½ Syncopated Type A (2 Sides)

1995, Mar. 16

Background Color

3227 A1057 35g dull red .35 .20
3228 A1057 35g violet .35 .20
3229 A1057 45g bright blue .45 .25
3230 A1057 45g blue green .45 .25
Nos. 3227-3230 (4) 1.60 .90

Pinecone Type of 1991

1995, Mar. 27 **Photo.** ***Perf. 11½***
3231 A956 45g Larix decidua .45 .25
3232 A956 80g Pinus mugo .80 .40

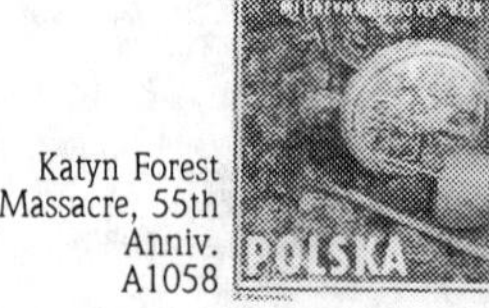

Katyn Forest Massacre, 55th Anniv. A1058

Perf. 11½ Syncopated Type A (2 Sides)

1995, Apr. 13 **Litho.**
3233 A1058 80g multicolored .85 .45

Europa A1060

Perf. 11x11½ Syncopated Type A (2 Sides)

1995, Apr. 28 **Litho.**
3234 A1060 35g shown .35 .18
3235 A1060 80g Flowers in helmet .85 .42

Ruturn of Western Polish Territories, 50th Anniv. A1061

Perf. 11½ Syncopated Type A (2 Sides)

1995, May 6 **Litho.**
3236 A1061 45g multicolored .50 .25

Pope John Paul II, 75th Birthday — A1062

Perf. 11½ Syncopated Type A (2 Sides)

1995, May 18 **Litho.**
3237 A1062 80g multicolored .85 .45

Groteska Theatre of Fairy Tales, 50th Anniv. A1063

Designs: No. 3238, Two performing. No. 3239, Stage scene. No. 3240, Puppet leaning on barrel, vert. No. 3241, Character holding flower, vert.

1995, May 25
3238 A1063 35g multicolored .35 .20
3239 A1063 35g multicolored .35 .20
a. Pair, #3238-3239 .70 .35
3240 A1063 45g multicolored .50 .25
3241 A1063 45g multicolored .50 .25
a. Pair, #3240-3241 1.00 .50
Nos. 3238-3241 (4) 1.70 .90

Polish Railways, 150th Anniv. A1064

Designs: 35g, Warsaw-Vienna steam train, 1945. 60g, Combustion fuel powered train, 1927. 80g, Electric train, 1936. 1z, Euro City Sobieski, Warsaw-Vienna, 1992.

1995, June 9
3242 A1064 35g multicolored .35 .20
3243 A1064 60g multicolored .65 .30
a. Pair, #3242-3243 1.00 .50
3244 A1064 80g multicolored .85 .45
3245 A1064 1z multicolored 1.10 .55
a. Pair, #3244-3245 2.00 1.00
Nos. 3242-3245 (4) 2.95 1.50

UN, 50th Anniv. A1065

Perf. 11½ Syncopated Type A (2 Sides)

1995, June 26 **Litho.**
3246 A1065 80g multicolored .90 .45

Handlowy Bank, Warsaw, 125th Anniv. A1066

1995, June 30
3247 A1066 45g multicolored .50 .25

Polish Peasants' Movement, Cent. A1067

Perf. 11½ Syncopated Type A (2 Sides)

1995, July 13 **Litho.**
3248 A1067 45g multicolored .50 .25

Polish Natl. Anthem, Bicent. A1068

1995, July 20 **Photo.** ***Perf. 11x11½***
3249 A1068 35g multicolored .40 .20

Deciduous Trees — A1069

1995, July 31 *Perf. 12x11½*

3250 A1069	(B) Quercus petraea		.40	.20
3551 A1069	(A) Sorbus aucuparia		.50	.25

On day of issue No. 3250 was valued at 35g and No. 3551 was valued at 45g.

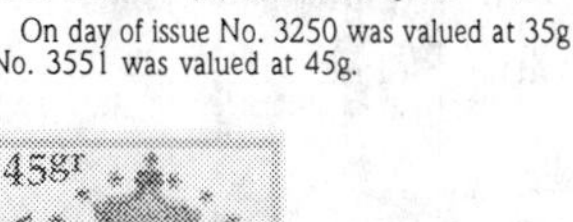

St. Mary of Consolation, Holy Trinity and All Saints Basilica, Lezajsk — A1070

Perf. 11½ Syncopated Type A (2 Sides)

1995, Aug. 2 **Litho.**

3252 A1070 45g multicolored .45 .20

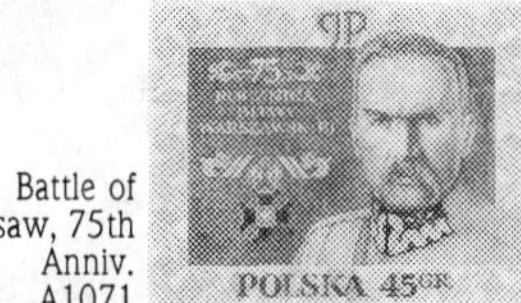
Battle of Warsaw, 75th Anniv. A1071

Design: 45g, Jósef Pilsudski (1867-1935).

1995, Aug. 14

3253 A1071 45g multicolored .45 .20

Horse-Equipage Driving World Championships, Poznan — A1072

Designs: 60g, Horses pulling carriage, men in formal attire. 80g, Marathon race through water, around pylons.

Perf. 11½ Syncopated Type A (2 Sides)

1995, Aug. 23 **Litho.**

3254 A1072	60g multicolored	.65	.30
3255 A1072	80g multicolored	.85	.45
a.	Pair, #3254-3255	1.50	.75

18th All Polish Philatelic Exhibition, Warsaw — A1073

Designs: 35g, Warsaw Technical University, School of Architecture. 1z, Warsaw Castle Place, Old Town, horiz.

Perf. 11½ Syncopated Type A (2 Sides)

1995, Aug. 30 **Litho.**

3256 A1073 35g multicolored .35 .20

Souvenir Sheet

3257 A1073 1z multicolored 1.10 .55

11th World Congress of Space Flight Participants, Warsaw — A1074

Perf. 11½ Syncopated Type A (2 Sides)

1995, Sept. 10 **Litho.**

3258 A1074 80g multicolored .80 .40

Poster Art Type of 1993

35g, The Crazy Locomotive, by Jan Sawka. 45g, The Wedding, by Eugeniusz Get Stankiewicz.

Perf. 11½ Syncopated Type A (2 Sides)

1995, Sept. 27 **Litho.**

3259 A1027	35g multicolored	.35	.20
3260 A1027	45g multicolored	.50	.25

13th Intl. Chopin Piano Festival A1076

Perf. 11½ Syncopated Type A (2 Sides)

1995, Oct. 1 **Litho.**

3261 A1076 80g Polonaise score .80 .40

A1077

A1078

World Post Day 45g, Postman in uniform, Polish Kingdom. 80g, Feather, wax seal of Stanislaw II Poniatowski.

1995, Oct. 9

3262 A1077	45g multicolored	.45	.20
3263 A1077	80g multicolored	.80	.40

1995, Oct. 26

3264 A1078 45g multicolored .45 .20

Acrobatic Sports World Championships, Wroclaw.

Janusz Groszkowski (1898-1984), Physicist — A1079

Perf. 11½ Syncopated Type A (2 Sides)

1995, Nov. 10 **Litho.**

3265 A1079 45g multicolored .50 .25

Christmas — A1080

1995, Nov. 27

3266 A1080	35g Nativity	.35	.20
3267 A1080	45g Magi, tree	.50	.25
a.	Pair, Nos. 3266-3267	.85	.45

No. 3267a is a continuous design.

Songbird Chicks A1081

Designs: a, 35g, Parus caeruleus. b, 45g, Aegithalos caudatus. c, 60g, Lanius excubitor. d, 80g, Coccothraustes.

1995, Dec. 15

3268 A1081 Block of 4, #a.-d. 2.25 1.10

See No. 3377.

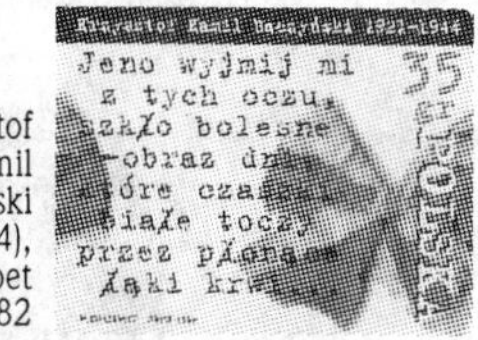
Krzysztof Kamil Baczynski (1921-44), Poet A1082

Perf. 11½ Syncopated Type A (2 Sides)

1996, Jan. 22 **Litho.**

3269 A1082 35g multicolored .35 .20

Love — A1083

1996, Jan. 31

3270 A1083 40g Cherries .40 .20

Architecture A1084

40g, Romanesque style church, Inowlodz, 11-12th cent. 55g, Gothic syle, St. Virgin Mary's Church, Cracow, 14th cent. 70g, Renaissance period, St. Sigismundus Chapel of Cracow, Wawel Castle, 1519-33. 1z, Order of Holy Sacrament Nuns Baroque Church, Warsaw, 1688-92.

Perf. 11½ Syncopated Type A (2 Sides)

1996, Feb. 27 **Litho.**

3271 A1084	40g multicolored	.35	.20
3272 A1084	55g multicolored	.50	.25
3273 A1084	70g multicolored	.65	.30
3274 A1084	1z multicolored	.90	.45
	Nos. 3271-3274 (4)	2.40	1.20

Polish Sailing Ships A1085

Designs: a, 40g, Topmast schooner, "Oceania," 1985. b, 55c, Staysail schooner, "Zawisza Czarny," 1961. c, 70g, Schooner, "General Zaruski," 1939. d, 75g, Brig, "Fryderyk Chopin," 1992.

1996, Mar. 11

3275 A1085 Strip of 4, #a.-d. 2.20 1.10

Warsaw, Capital of Poland, 400th Anniv. A1086

1996, Mar. 18

3276 A1086 55g multicolored .55 .25

Signs of the Zodiac — A1087

1996 **Photo.** *Perf. 12x11½*

3277 A1087	5g Aquarius	.15	.15
3278 A1087	10g Pisces	.15	.15
3279 A1087	20g Taurus	.20	.15
3280 A1087	25g Gemini	.25	.15
3281 A1087	30g Cancer	.30	.15
3282 A1087	40g Virgo	.40	.20
3283 A1087	50g Leo	.50	.25
3284 A1087	55g Libra	.55	.25
3285 A1087	70g Aries	.65	.30
3286 A1087	1z Scorpio	.95	.50
3287 A1087	2z Sagittarius	1.90	.95
3288 A1087	5z Capricorn	4.75	2.40
	Nos. 3277-3288 (12)	10.75	5.60

Issued: 70g, 3/21; 20g, 4/21; 25g, 5/10; 30g, 5/20; 40g, 50g, 5/31; 55g, 6/10; 1z, 6/20; 2z, 6/28; 5z, 7/10; 5g, 7/19; 10g, 7/31.

Famous Women — A1088

Europa: 40g, Hanka Ordonówa (1902-50), singer. 1z, Pola Negri (1896-1987), actress.

Perf. 11½ Syncopated Type A (2 Sides)

1996, Apr. 30 **Litho.**

3289 A1088	40g multicolored	.35	.20
3290 A1088	1z multicolored	.90	.45

3rd Silesian Uprising, 75th Anniv. A1089

Perf. 11 ½ Syncopated Type A (2 Sides)

1996, May 2 **Litho.**

3291 A1089 55g multicolored .50 .25

UNICEF, 50th Anniv. — A1090

Illustrations from tales of Jan Brzechwa: No. 3292, Cat and mouse. No. 3293. Man at table, waiters. No. 3294, People with "onion heads." No. 3295, Chef, duck, vegetables at table. No. 3296,

Man talking to bird with human head. No. 3297, Fox standing in front of bears.

1996, May 31

3292 A1090 40g multicolored .35 .20
3293 A1090 40g multicolored .35 .20
3294 A1090 55g multicolored .50 .25
3295 A1090 55g multicolored .50 .25
3296 A1090 70g multicolored .65 .30
3297 A1090 70g multicolored .65 .30
Nos. 3292-3297 (6) 3.00 1.50

Drawings by Stanislaw Noakowski (1867-1928) A1091

Designs: 40g, Renaissance building. 55g, Renaissance bedroom. 70g, Gothic village church. 1z, Stanislaw August Library, 18th cent.

1996, June 28

3298 A1091 40g multicolored .35 .20
3299 A1091 55g multicolored .50 .25
3300 A1091 70g multicolored .65 .30
3301 A1091 1z multicolored .90 .45
Nos. 3298-3301 (4) 2.40 1.20

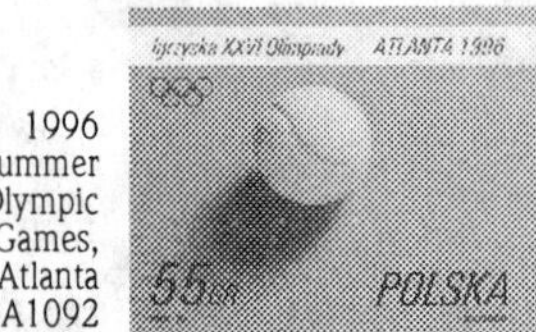

1996 Summer Olympic Games, Atlanta A1092

Designs: 40g, Discus as medallion, vert. 55g, Tennis ball. 70g, Polish flag, Olympic rings. 1z, Tire & wheel of mountain bicycle, vert.

1996, July 5

3302 A1092 40g multicolored .35 .20
3303 A1092 55g multicolored .50 .25
3304 A1092 70g multicolored .65 .30
3305 A1092 1z multicolored .90 .45
Nos. 3302-3305 (4) 2.40 1.20

OLYMPHILEX '96, Atlanta — A1093

1996, July 5

3306 A1093 1z multicolored .90 .45

National Anthem, Bicent. A1094

1996, July 20 Photo. *Perf. 11x11½*

3307 A1094 40g multicolored .35 .20

Madonna and Child, St. Mary's Ascension Church, Przeczyce — A1095

Perf. 11½x11 Syncopated Type A (2 Sides)

1996, Aug. 2 **Litho.**

3308 A1095 40g multicolored .40 .20

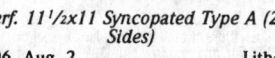

Royalty Type of 1986

Designs: 40g, Jadwiga. 55g, Wladyslaw II Jagiello. 70g, Wladyslaw II Warnenczyk. 1z, Kazimierz Jagiellonczyk.

1996, Aug. 29 Engr. *Perf. 11*

3309 A875 40g olive brown & brown .40 .20
3310 A875 55g red violet & violet .55 .25
3311 A875 70g gray & black .65 .30
3312 A875 1z yellow green & green .95 .50
Nos. 3309-3312 (4) 2.55 1.25

Mountain Scenes, Tatra Natl. Park A1096

Perf. 11½ Syncopated Type A (2 Sides)

1996, Sept. 5 **Litho.**

3313 A1096 40g Giewont .35 .20
3314 A1096 40g Krzesanica .35 .20
3315 A1096 55g Swinica .50 .25
3316 A1096 55g Koscielec .50 .25
3317 A1096 70g Rysy .65 .30
3318 A1096 70g Miguszowieckie Szczyty .65 .30
Nos. 3313-3318 (6) 3.00 1.50

Zbigniew Seifert (1946-79), Jazz Musician — A1097

Perf. 11½ Syncopated Type A (2 Sides)

1996, Sept. 25 **Litho.**

3319 A1097 70g multicolored .65 .30

Post and Telecommunications Museum, Wroclaw, 75th Anniv. — A1098

Paintings: 40g, Horse Exchange and Post Station, by M. Watorski. 1z+20g, Stagecoach in Jagniatkowo, by Prof. Täger.

1996, Oct. 9 Photo. *Perf. 12x11½*

3320 A1098 40g multicolored .35 .20

Souvenir Sheet

Perf. 11x11½

3321 A1098 1z +20g multi 1.15 .60

Nos. 3321 contains one 43x31mm stamp.

Christmas — A1099

Perf. 11½ Syncopated Type A (2 Sides)

1996, Nov. 27 **Litho.**

3322 A1099 40g Santa in sleigh .40 .20
3323 A1099 55g Carolers .50 .25

Bison Bonasus — A1100

1996, Dec. 4

3324 A1100 55g shown .50 .25
3325 A1100 55g Facing .50 .25
3326 A1100 55g Two animals .50 .25
3327 A1100 55g Adult male .50 .25
a. Strip of 4, #3324-3327 2.00 1.00

Wislaws Szymborska, 1996 Nobel Laureate in Literature — A1101

1996, Dec. 10

3328 A1101 1z multicolored .95 .50

Queen of Hearts A1102

Perf. 11x11½ Syncopated Type A

1997, Jan. 14 **Litho.**

3329 A1102 B King of Hearts .40 .20
3330 A1102 A Queen of Hearts .50 .25
a. Pair, #3329-3330 .90 .45
Complete booklet, 4 #3330a 3.60

Nos. 3329-3330 sold for 40g and 55g, respectively, on day of issue.

Easter Traditions A1103

50g, Man, woman in traditional costumes holding palms. 60g, Decorating eggs. 80g, Blessing the Easter meal. 1.10z, Man pouring water on woman.

Perf. 11x11½ Syncopated Type A

1997, Mar. 14 **Litho.**

3331 A1103 50g multicolored .40 .20
3332 A1103 60g multicolored .50 .25
3333 A1103 80g multicolored .65 .30
3334 A1103 1.10z multicolored .90 .45
Nos. 3331-3334 (4) 2.45 1.20

St. Adalbert (955?-97)
A1104 A1105

Design: 50g, St. Adalbert among heathen, horiz.

1997 Engr. *Perf. 11x11½x 11½x11*

3335 A1104 50g brown .50 .25
3336 A1104 60g slate .60 .30
3337 A1105 1.10z purple 1.00 .50
Nos. 3335-3337 (3) 2.10 1.05

See Czech Republic No. 3012, Germany No. 1964, Hungary No. 3569, Vatican City No. 1040.

Issued: Nos. 3335-3336, 4/19; No. 3337, 4/23.

Stories and Legends — A1106

Europa: 50g, shown. 1.10z, Mermaid.

Perf. 11½ Syncopated Type A

1997, May 5

3338 A1106 50g multicolored .50 .25
3339 A1106 1.10z multicolored 1.00 .50

46th Eucharistic Congress A1107

1997, May 6

3340 A1107 50g multicolored .50 .25

Souvenir Sheet

Pope John Paul II — A1108

Perf. 11x11½ Syncopated Type A

1997, May 28

3341 A1108 1.10z multicolored 1.00 1.00

POLSKA 50 GR

City of Gdansk, 1000th Anniv. — A1109

Design: 1.10z, View of city, horiz.

Perf. 11½x11, 11x11½

1997, Apr. 18 **Engr.**

3342 A1109 50g multicolored .50 .25

Souvenir Sheet

3343 A1109 1.10z multicolored block 1.10 .55

Polish Country Estates — A1110

1997 Photo. *Perf. 11½x12*

3344 A1110 50g Lopusznej .15 .15
3345 A1110 60g Zyrzyna .15 .15
3346 A1110 1.10z Ozarowie .15 .15
3347 A1110 1.70z Tulowicach .20 .15
3348 A1110 2.20z Kuznocinie .25 .15
3349 A1110 10z Koszutach 1.00 .50
Nos. 3344-3349 (6) 1.90 1.25

Issued: 50g, 60g, 4/26/97; 1.10z, 1.70z, 2.20z, 10z, 5/23/97.

PACIFIC 97 — A1111

Design: San Francisco-Oakland Bay Bridge.

Perf. 11½ Syncopated Type A

1997, May 20 **Litho.**

3350 A1111 1.30z multicolored	1.00	.50

Bats — A1113

50g, Plecotus auritus. 60g, Nyctalus noctula. 80g, Myotis myotis. 1.30z, Vespertilio murinus.

1997, May 30

3352 A1113 50g multicolored	.45	.20
3353 A1113 60g multicolored	.55	.25
3354 A1113 80g multicolored	.70	.35
3355 A1113 1.30z multicolored	1.15	.60
Nos. 3352-3355 (4)	2.85	1.40

Jagiellon University School of Theology, 600th Anniv. A1114

Painting by Jan Matejko.

1997, June 6 ***Perf. 11***

3356 A1114 80g multicolored	.70	.35

Polish Settlement in Argentina, Cent. — A1115

Perf. 11½ Syncopated Type A

1997, June 6

3357 A1115 1.40z multicolored	1.25	.60

Paintings, by Juliusz Kossak (1824-99) — A1116

Designs: 50g, Man on horse, woman, child. 60g, Men on galloping horses, carriage. 80g, Feeding horses in stable. 1.10z, Man with horses.

1997, July 4 **Photo.** ***Perf. 11***

3358 A1116 50g multicolored	.45	.20
3359 A1116 60g multicolored	.50	.25
3360 A1116 80g multicolored	.70	.35
3361 A1116 1.10z multicolored	.95	.50
Nos. 3358-3361 (4)	2.60	1.30

Polish Natl. Anthem, Bicent. A1117

Designs: 50g, People in city waving hats at Gen. Jan Henryk Dabrowski.
1.10z, Words to Natl. Anthem, Dabrowski.

1997, July 18 ***Perf. 11x11½***

3362 A1117 50g multicolored	.45	.20

Souvenir Sheet

3363 A1117 1.10z multicolored	.95	.50

Pawel Edmund Strzelecki (1797-1873), Geographer — A1118

Perf. 11½ Syncopated Type A

1997, July 20 **Litho.**

3364 A1118 1.50z multicolored	1.30	.65

Virgin of Consolation, Church of the Virgin of Consolation and St. Michael Archangel, Gorka Duchowna — A1119

Perf. 11½x11 Syncopated Type A

1997, Aug. 28

3365 A1119 50g multicolored	.45	.20

Royalty Type of 1986

Kings: 50g, Jan I Olbracht (1459-1501). 60g, Aleksander (1461-1506). 80g, Sigismundus I Stary (1467-48). 1.10z, Sigismundus II Augustus (1520-72).

1997, Sept. 22 **Engr.** ***Perf. 11***

3366 A875 50g brn & dk brn	.40	.20
3367 A875 60g blue & dp brn	.50	.25
3368 A875 80g grn & dk slate	.65	.35
3369 A875 1.10z mag & dk mag	.90	.45
Nos. 3366-3369 (4)	2.45	1.25

Mieczyslaw Kosz (1944-73), Jazz Musician A1120

World Post Day A1121

Perf. 11½ Syncopated Type A (2 Sides)

1997, Oct. 3 **Litho.**

3370 A1120 80g multicolored	.65	.35

1997, Oct. 9

3371 A1121 50g multicolored	.45	.20

Moscow '97 Intl. Philatelic Exhibition A1122

Type B: On the two longer sides, the oval hole equal in width to three holes is located in the center, with an equal number of normal round holes to either side.

Perf. 11½ Syncopated Type B (2 Sides)

1997, Oct. 13

3372 A1122 80g multicolored	.70	.35

Theater Poster Art — A1123

#3373, "Sam Pierze Radion," black cat becoming white cat, by T. Gronowski, 1926. #3374, "Szewcy" (Bootmakers), by R. Cieslewicz, 1971. #3375, "Goya," by W. Sadowski, 1983. #3376, "Maz i zona," by A. Pagowski, 1977.

Perf. 11x11½, 11½x11 Syncopated Type A (2 Sides)

1997 **Litho.**

3373 A1123 50g multi	.55	.30
3374 A1123 50g multi, vert.	.55	.30
3375 A1123 60g multi, vert.	.65	.35
3376 A1123 60g multi, vert.	.65	.35
Nos. 3373-3376 (4)	2.40	1.30

Chick Type of 1995

Designs: a, Tadorna tadorna. b, Mergus merganser. c, Gallinago gallinago. d, Gallinula chloropus.

1997 ***Perf. 11½ Syncopated Type A***

3377 A1081 50g Block of 4, #a.-d.	1.60	.80

Christmas A1124

50g, Nativity. 60g, Food, candles. 80g, Outdoor winter scene, star, church. 1.10z, Carolers.

Perf. 11½x11, 11x11½ Syncopated Type A (2 Sides)

1997

3378 A1124 50g multi, vert.	.55	.25
3379 A1124 60g multi	.65	.35
3380 A1124 80g multi	.90	.45
3381 A1124 1.10z multi, vert.	1.20	.60
Nos. 3378-3381 (4)	3.30	1.65

SEMI-POSTAL STAMPS

Regular Issue of 1919 Surcharged in Violet

I POLSKA WYSTAWA MAREK 5F + F5 — a

I POLSKA WYSTAWA MAREK 5 + 5 — b

1919, May 3 **Unwmk.** ***Imperf.***

B1 A10(a) 5f + 5f grn	.16	.20
B2 A10(a) 10f + 5f red vio	2.00	1.40
B3 A10(a) 15f + 5f dp red	.38	.20
B4 A11(b) 25f + 5f ol grn	.38	.20
B5 A11(b) 50f + 5f bl grn	.60	.32

Perf. 11½

B6 A10(a) 5f + 5f grn	.25	.16
B7 A10(a) 10f + 5f red vio	.50	.16
B8 A10(a) 15f + 5f dp red	.25	.16
B9 A11(b) 25f + 5f ol grn	.30	.16
B10 A11(b) 50f + 5f bl grn	1.00	.42
Nos. B1-B10 (10)	5.82	3.38

First Polish Philatelic Exhibition. The surtax benefited the Polish White Cross Society.

Regular Issue of 1920 Surcharged in Carmine  30MK

1921, Mar. 5 *Perf. 9*

Thin Laid Paper

B11 A14 5m + 30m red vio 5.00 7.00
B12 A14 6m + 30m dp rose 5.00 7.00
B13 A14 10m + 30m lt red 12.00 12.00
B14 A14 20m + 30m gray grn 37.50 35.00
Nos. B11-B14 (4) 59.50 61.00

Counterfeits, differently perforated, exist of Nos. B11-B14.

SP1

Light of Knowledge — SP2

1925, Jan. 1 **Typo.** *Perf. 12½*

B15 SP1 1g orange brn 12.00 14.00
B16 SP1 2g dk brown 12.00 14.00
B17 SP1 3g orange 12.00 14.00
B18 SP1 5g olive grn 12.00 14.00
B19 SP1 10g blue grn 12.00 14.00
B20 SP1 15g red 12.00 14.00
B21 SP1 20g blue 12.00 14.00
B22 SP1 25g red brown 12.00 14.00
B23 SP1 30g dp violet 12.00 14.00
B24 SP1 40g indigo 35.00 14.00
B25 SP1 50g magenta 12.00 14.00
Nos. B15-B25 (11) 155.00 154.00
Set, never hinged 200.00

"Na Skarb" means "National Funds." These stamps were sold at a premium of 50 groszy each, for charity.

1927, May 3 *Perf. 11½*

B26 SP2 10g + 5g choc & grn 7.00 4.50
B27 SP2 20g + 5g dk bl & buff 7.00 4.50
Set, never hinged 24.00

"NA OSWIATE" means "For Public Instruction." The surtax aided an Association of Educational Societies.

Torun Type of 1933

1933, May 21 **Engr.**

B28 A59 60g (+40g) red brn, *buff* 16.00 12.00
Never hinged 21.00

Philatelic Exhibition at Torun, May 21-28, 1933, and sold at a premium of 40g to aid the exhibition funds.

Souvenir Sheet

Stagecoach and Wayside Inn — SP3

1938, May 3 **Engr.** *Perf. 12, Imperf.*

B29 SP3 Sheet of 4 72.50 65.00
Never hinged 90.00
a. 45g green 7.50 7.50
b. 55g blue 7.50 7.50

5th Phil. Exhib., Warsaw, May 3-8. The sheet contains two 45g and two 55g stamps. Sold for 3z.

Souvenir Sheet

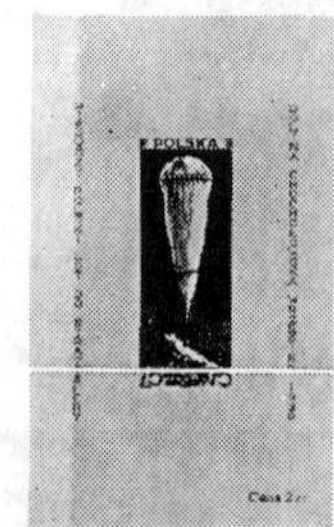
Stratosphere Balloon over Mountains — SP4

1938, Sept. 15 *Perf. 12½*

B31 SP4 75g dp vio, sheet 55.00 60.00
Never hinged 75.00

Issued in advance of a proposed Polish stratosphere flight. Sold for 2z.

Winterhelp Issue

SP5

1938-39

B32 SP5 5g + 5g red org .55 .95
B33 SP5 25g + 10g dk vio ('39) .90 1.40
B34 SP5 55g + 15g brt ultra ('39) 1.75 2.25
Nos. B32-B34 (3) 3.20 4.60
Set, never hinged 5.00

For surcharges see Nos. N48-N50.

Souvenir Sheet

SP6

1939, Aug. 1

B35 SP6 Sheet of 3, dark blue gray 27.50 20.00
Never hinged 32.50
a. 25g Marshal Pilsudski Reviewing Troops 4.75 3.50
b. 25g Marshal Pilsudski 4.75 3.50
c. 25g Marshal Smigly-Rydz 4.75 3.50

25th anniv. of the founding of the Polish Legion. The sheets sold for 1.75z, the surtax going to the National Defense fund.
See types A64, A80, A99.

Polish People's Republic

Polish Warship SP7

Sailing Vessel — SP8

Polish Naval Ensign and Merchant Flag — SP9

Crane and Crane Tower, Gdansk SP10

1945, Apr. 24 **Typo.** *Perf. 11*

B36 SP7 50g + 2z red 2.50 4.25
B37 SP8 1z + 3z dp bl 2.50 4.25
B38 SP9 2z + 4z dk car 2.50 4.25
B39 SP10 3z + 5z ol grn 2.50 4.25
Nos. B36-B39 (4) 10.00 17.00
Set, never hinged 13.00

Polish Maritime League, 25th anniv.

City Hall, Poznan SP11

1945, June 16 **Photo.**

B40 SP11 1z + 5z green 15.00 20.00
Never hinged 20.00

Postal Workers' Convention, Poznan, June 16, 1945. Exists imperf.

Last Stand at Westerplatte — SP12

1945, Sept. 1

B41 SP12 1z + 9z steel blue 12.00 20.00
Never hinged 15.00

Polish army's last stand at Westerplatte, Sept. 1, 1939. Exists imperf.

"United Industry" — SP13

1945, Nov. 18 **Unwmk.** *Perf. 11*

B42 SP13 1.50z + 8.50z sl blk 5.00 7.50
Never hinged 7.00

Trade Unions Congress, Warsaw, Nov. 18.

Polish Volunteers in Spain — SP14

1946, Mar. 10

B43 SP14 3z + 5z red 3.00 4.25
Never hinged 4.00

Participation of the Jaroslaw Dabrowski Brigade in the Spanish Civil War.

14th Century Piast Eagle and Soldiers — SP15

"Death" Spreading Poison Gas over Majdanek Prison Camp — SP16

1946, May 2

B44 SP15 3z + 7z brn .60 .50
Never hinged 1.00

Silesian uprisings of 1919-21, 1939-45.

1946, Apr. 29

B45 SP16 3z + 5z Prus grn 2.00 3.00
Never hinged 3.00

Issued to recall Majdanek, a concentration camp of World War II near Lublin.

Bydgoszcz (Bromberg) Canal — SP17

Map of Polish Coast and Baltic Sea — SP18

1946, Apr. 19 **Unwmk.** *Perf. 11*

B46 SP17 3z + 2z ol blk 2.25 6.00
Never hinged 3.75

600th anniv. of Bydgoszcz (Bromberg).

1946, July 21

B47 SP18 3z + 7z dp bl 1.25 2.00
Never hinged 2.00

Maritime Holiday of 1946. The surtax was for the Polish Maritime League.

Salute to P.T.T. Casualty and Views of Gdansk — SP19

1946, Sept. 14

B48 SP19 3z + 12z slate 1.40 2.00
Never hinged 2.00

Polish postal employees killed in the German attack on Danzig (Gdansk), Sept. 1939.

School Children — SP20

Designs: 6z+24z, Courtyard of Jagiellon University, Cracow. 11z+19z, Gregor Piramowicz (1735-1801), founder of Education Commission.

1946, Oct. 10 **Unwmk.** *Perf. 11½*

B49 SP20 3z + 22z dk red 22.50 35.00
B49A SP20 6z + 24z dk bl 22.50 35.00
B49B SP20 11z + 19z dk grn 22.50 35.00
c. Souv. sheet of 3, #B49-B49B 315.00 375.00
Never hinged 400.00
Nos. B49-B49B (3) 67.50 105.00
Never hinged 77.50

Polish educational work. Surtax was for International Bureau of Education.
No. B49Bc sold for 100z.

Stanislaw Stojalowski, Jakob Bojko, Jan Stapinski and Wincenty Witos — SP21

1946, Dec. 1

B50 SP21 5z + 10z bl grn 1.00 1.40
B51 SP21 5z + 10z dull blue 1.00 1.40
B52 SP21 5z + 10z dk olive 1.00 1.40
Nos. B50-B52 (3) 3.00 4.20
Never hinged 4.00

50th anniv. of the Peasant Movement. The surtax was for education and cultural improvement among the Polish peasantry.

No. 391 Surcharged in Red

1947, Feb. 4 *Perf. 11x10½*

B53 A127 3z + 7z purple 5.50 8.00
Never hinged 6.75

Opening of the Polish Parliament, Jan. 19, 1947.

No. 344 Surcharged in Blue

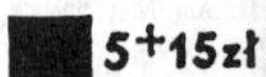

1947, Feb. 21 *Perf. 12½*
B54 A103 5z + 15z on 25g 1.25 3.50
Never hinged 2.50

Ski Championship Meet, Zakopane. Counterfeits exist.

Emil Zegadlowicz SP22

1947, Mar. 1 **Photo.** *Perf. 11*
B55 SP22 5z + 15z dl gray grn 1.25 1.50
Never hinged 1.50

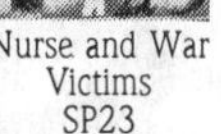

Nurse and War Victims SP23

Adam Chmielowski SP24

1947, June 1 *Perf. 10½*
B56 SP23 5z + 5z ol blk & red 2.50 3.50
Never hinged 3.25

The surtax was for the Red Cross.

1947, Dec. 21 *Perf. 11*
B57 SP24 2z + 18z dk vio 1.25 2.25
Never hinged 1.65

Zamkowy Square and Proposed Highway — SP25

1948, Nov. 1
B58 SP25 15z + 5z green .30 .25
Never hinged .50

The surtax was to aid in the reconstruction of Warsaw.

Infant and TB Crosses — SP26

Various Portraits of Children

1948, Dec. 16 *Perf. 11½*
B59 SP26 3z + 2z dl grn 2.00 2.50
B60 SP26 5z + 5z brn 2.00 2.50
B61 SP26 6z + 4z vio 1.65 2.50
B62 SP26 15z + 10z car lake 1.65 2.50
Nos. B59-B62 (4) 7.30 10.00
Set, never hinged 9.00

Alternate vertical rows of stamps was ten different labels. The surtax was for anti-tuberculosis work among children.

Catalogue values for unused stamps in this section, from this point to the end of the section, are for Never Hinged items.

Workers Party Type of 1952
Perf. 12½

1952, Jan. 18 **Engr.** **Unwmk.**
B63 A195 45g + 15g Marceli Nowotko .18 .15

Women's Day Type of 1952

1952, Mar. 8 *Perf. 12½x12*
B64 A196 45g + 15g chocolate .32 .15

Swierczewski-Walter Type of 1952

1952, Mar. 28 *Perf. 12½*
B65 A197 45g + 15g chocolate .38 .15

Bierut Type of 1952

1952, Apr. 18
B66 A198 45g + 15g red .52 .20
B67 A198 1.20z + 15g ultra .52 .18

Type of Regular Issue of 1951-52 Inscribed "Plan 6," etc.

Design: 45g+15g, Electrical installation.

1952
B68 A193 30g + 15g brn red .35 .18
B69 A193 45g + 15g chocolate .60 .30
B69A A194 1.20z + 15g red org .30 .22
Nos. B68-B69A (3) 1.25 .70

Labor Day Type of Regular Issue of 1952

1952, May 1
B70 A200 45g + 15g car rose .28 .15

Similar to Regular Issue of 1952

#B71, Maria Konopnicka. #B72, Hugo Kollataj.

1952, May
Different Frames
B71 A201 30g + 15g blue green .52 .15
B72 A201 45g + 15g brown .25 .15
Set value .24

Issued: No. B71, May 10. No. B72, May 20.

Leonardo da Vinci — SP28

1952, June 1
B73 SP28 30g + 15g ultra .85 .50

500th birth anniv. of Leonardo da Vinci.

Pres. Bierut and Children — SP29

1952, June 1 **Photo.** *Perf. 13½x14*
B74 SP29 45g + 15g blue 2.50 .60

Intl. Children's Day, June 1.

Sports Type

1952, June 21 *Perf. 13*

Design: 45g+15g, Soccer players and trophy.

B75 A203 30g + 15g blue 3.75 1.40
B76 A203 45g + 15g purple 1.75 .35

Yachts SP31

"Dar Pomorza" SP32

1952, June 28 **Engr.** *Perf. 12½*
B77 SP31 30g + 15g dp bl grn 2.75 .60
B78 SP32 45g + 15g dp ultra .70 .22

Shipbuilders' Day, 1952.

Workers on Holiday — SP33

Students SP34

Perf. 12½x12, 12x12½

1952, July 17
B79 SP33 30g + 15g dp grn .32 .20
B80 SP34 45g + 15g red .70 .15

Issued to publicize the Youth Festival, 1952.

Constitution Type of Regular Issue

1952, July 22 **Photo.** *Perf. 11*
B81 A208 45g + 15g lt bl grn & dk brn 1.10 .24

Power Plant Type of Regular Issue

1952, Aug. 7 **Engr.** *Perf. 12½*
B82 A209 45g + 15g red .65 .15

Ludwik Warynski SP36

Church of Frydman SP37

1952, July 31
B83 SP36 30g + 15g dk red .42 .15
B84 SP36 45g + 15g blk brn .40 .20

70th birth anniv. of Ludwik Warynski, political organizer.

1952, Aug. 18
B85 SP37 45g + 15g vio brn 1.00 .25

Aviator Watching Glider SP38

Henryk Sienkiewicz SP39

Design: 45g+15g, Pilot entering plane.

1952, Aug. 23
B86 SP38 30g + 15g grn .55 .30
B87 SP38 45g + 15g brn red 2.25 .90

Aviation Day, Aug. 23.

1952, Oct. 25
B88 SP39 45g + 15g vio brn .35 .22

Henryk Sienkiewicz (1846-1916), author of "Quo Vadis" and other novels, Nobel prizewinner (literature, 1905).

Revolution Type of Regular Issue

1952, Nov. 7 *Perf. 12x12½*
B92 A214 45g + 15g red brn .70 .15

Exists imperforate. See #562.

Lenin — SP42

Miner — SP43

1952, Nov. 7 *Perf. 12½*
B93 SP42 30g + 15g vio brn .28 .15
B94 SP42 45g + 15g brn .70 .32
a. "LENIN" omitted 20.00

Month of Polish-Soviet friendship, Nov. 1952.

1952, Dec. 4
B95 SP43 45g + 15g blk brn .18 .15
B96 SP43 1.20z + 15g brn .52 .20

Miners' Day, Dec. 4.

Henryk Wieniawski and Violin — SP44

Truck Factory, Lublin — SP45

1952, Dec. 5 **Photo.**
B97 SP44 30g + 15g dk grn .55 .32
B98 SP44 45g + 15g purple 2.75 .60

Henryk Wieniawski; 2nd Intl. Violin Competition.

Type of Regular Issue of 1952

1952, Dec. 12 **Engr.**
B99 A215 45g + 15g dp grn .28 .20

1953, Feb. 20
B100 SP45 30g + 15g dp bl .20 .16
B101 SP45 60g + 20g vio brn .40 .15
Set value .25

Souvenir Sheet

Town Hall in Poznan — SP46

1955, July 7 **Photo. & Litho.** *Imperf.*
B102 SP46 2z pck grn & ol grn 3.50 2.00
B103 SP46 3z car rose & ol blk 19.00 10.50

6th Polish Philatelic Exhibition in Poznan. Sheets sold for 3z and 4.50z respectively.

Souvenir Sheet

"Peace" (POKOJ) and Warsaw Mermaid — SP47

Design: 1z, Pansies (A266) and inscription on map of Europe, Africa and Asia.

1955, Aug. 3
B104 SP47 1z bis, rose vio & yel 4.25 1.50
B105 SP47 2z ol gray, ultra & lt bl 20.00 7.50

Intl. Phil. Exhib., Warsaw, Aug. 1-14, 1955. Sheets sold for 2z and 3z respectively.

Souvenir Sheet

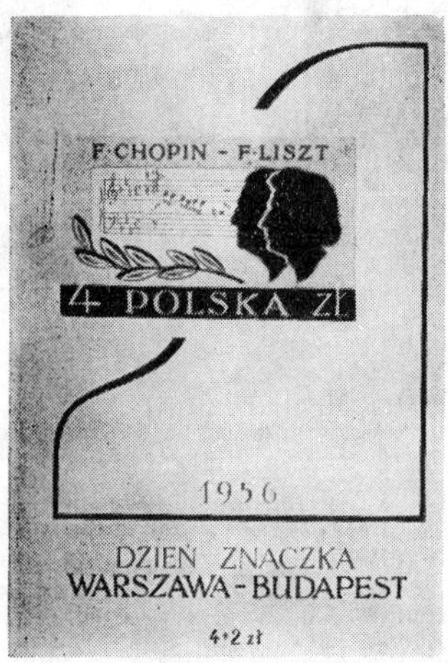

Chopin and Liszt — SP48

1956, Oct. 25 Photo. *Imperf.*
B106 SP48 4z dk blue grn 30.00 16.00

Day of the Stamp; Polish-Hungarian friendship. The sheet sold for 6z.

Souvenir Sheet

Stamp of 1860 SP49

Wmk. 326

1960, Sept. 4 Litho. *Perf. 11*
B107 SP49 Sheet of 4 40.00 35.00
a. 10z + 10z blue, red & black 9.00 9.00

Intl. Phil. Exhib. "POLSKA 60" Warsaw, 9/3-11. Sold only with 5z ticket to exhibition.

Type of Space Issue, 1964

Design: Yuri A. Gagarin in space capsule.

Perf. 12½x12
1964, Dec. 30 Unwmk.
B108 A432 6.50z + 2z Prus grn & multi 1.50 .65

> ***Set Values***
> *A 15-cent minimum now applies to individual stamps and sets. Where the 15-cent minimum per stamp would increase the value of a set beyond retail, there is a "Set Value" notation giving the retail value of the set.*

Miniature Sheet

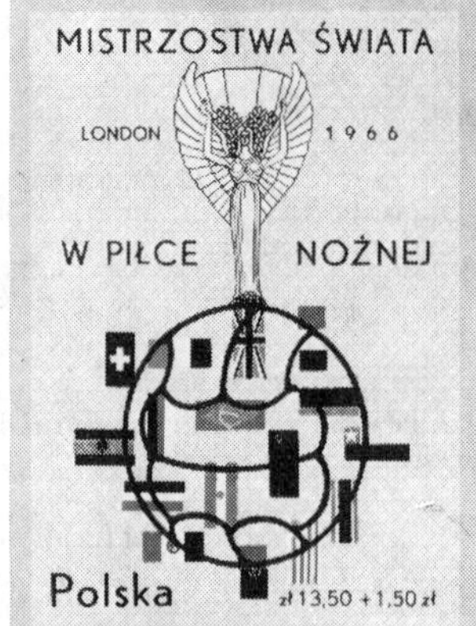

Jules Rimet Cup and Flags of Participating Countries — SP50

1966, May 9 Litho. *Imperf.*
B109 SP50 13.50z + 1.50z multi 2.50 1.50

World Cup Soccer Championship, Wembley, England, July 11-30.

Souvenir Sheet

J. Kusocinski, Olympic Winner 10,000-Meter Race, 1932 — SP51

1967, May 24 Litho. *Imperf.*
B110 SP51 10z + 5z multi 1.50 1.00

19th Olympic Games, Mexico City, 1968. Simulated perforations.

Flower Type of Regular Issue

Flowers: 4z+2z, Abutilon. 8z+4z, Rosa polyantha hybr.

1968, May 15 Litho. *Perf. 11½*
B111 A492 4z + 2z vio & multi .80 .35
B112 A492 8z + 4z lt vio & multi 1.65 .80

Olympic Type of Regular Issue, 1968

Design: 10z+5z, Runner with Olympic torch and Chin cultic carved stone disc showing Mayan ball player and game's scoreboard.

1968, Sept. 2 Litho. *Perf. 11½*
Size: 56x45mm
B113 A497 10z + 5z multi 1.90 1.10

19th Olympic Games, Mexico City, Oct. 12-27. The surtax was for the Polish Olympic Committee.

Olympic Type of Regular Issue, 1969

Olympic Rings and: 2.50z+50g, Women's discus. 3.40z+1z, Running. 4z+1.50z, Boxing. 7z+2z, Fencing.

1969, Apr. 25 Litho. *Perf. 11½x11*
B114 A505 2.50z + 50g multi .30 .15
B115 A505 3.40z + 1z multi .40 .18
B116 A505 4z + 1.50z multi .60 .25
B117 A505 7z + 2z multi 1.00 .50
Nos. B114-B117 (4) 2.30 1.08

Folk Art Type of Regular Issue

5.50z+1.50z, Choir. 7z+1.50z, Organ grinder.

1969, Dec. 19 Litho. *Perf. 11½x11*
Size: 24x36mm
B118 A520 5.50z + 1.50z multi .52 .24
B119 A520 7z + 1.50z multi .70 .30

Sports Type of Regular Issue
Souvenir Sheet

Design: "Horse of Glory," by Z. Kaminski.

1970, June 16 Photo. *Imperf.*
B120 A532 10z + 5z multi 1.75 1.00

The surtax was for the Polish Olympic Committee. No. B120 contains one imperf. stamp with simulated perforations.

Tapestry Type of Regular Issue
Souvenir Sheet

Design: 7z+3z, Satyrs holding monogram of King Sigismund Augustus.

1970, Dec. 23 Photo. *Imperf.*
B121 A541 7z + 3z multi 1.75 1.00

Type of Regular Issue

Design: 8.50z+4z, Virgin Mary, 15th century stained glass window.

1971, Sept. 15 *Perf. 11½x11*
B122 A555 8.50z + 4z multi .95 .55

Painting Type of Regular Issue

7z+1z, Nude, by Wojciech Weiss (1875-1950).

1971, Oct. 9 Litho.
B123 A556 7z + 1z multi .70 .35

Winter Olympic Type of Regular Issue
Souvenir Sheet

Design: Slalom and Sapporo '72 emblem, vert.

1972, Jan. 12 Photo. *Imperf.*
B124 A564 10z + 5z multi 2.00 1.25

No. B124 contains one stamp with simulated perforations, 27x52mm.

Summer Olympic Type of Regular Issue
Souvenir Sheet

Design: 10z+5z, Archery (like 30g).

1972, May 20 Photo. *Perf. 11½x11*
B125 A568 10z + 5z multi 1.75 1.00

Painting Type of Regular Issue, 1972

Design: 8.50z+4z, Portrait of a Young Lady, by Jacek Malczewski, horiz.

1972, Sept. 28 Photo. *Perf. 11x10½*
B126 A576 8.50z + 4z multi 1.50 .65

Souvenir Sheet

Copernicus — SP52

Engraved and Photogravure
1972, Sept. 28 *Perf. 11½*
B127 SP52 10z + 5z vio bl, gray & car 1.50 .85

Nicolaus Copernicus (1473-1543), astronomer. No. B127 shows the Ptolemaic and Copernican concepts of solar system from L'Harmonica Microcosmica, by Cellarius, 1660.

Souvenir Sheet

Poznan, 1740, by F. B. Werner — SP53

1973, Aug. 19 *Imperf.*
B128 SP53 10z + 5z ol & dk brn 2.00 .90
a. 10z + 5z pale lilac & dk brn 6.00 4.00

POLSKA 73 Intl. Phil. Exhib., Poznan, Aug. 19-Sept. 2. No. B128 contains one stamp with simulated perforations.

No. B128a was sold only in combination with an entrance ticket.

Copernicus, by Marcello Baciarelli — SP54

1973, Sept. 27 Photo. *Perf. 11x11½*
B129 SP54 4z + 2z multi .50 .28

Stamp Day. The surtax was for the reconstruction of the Royal Castle in Warsaw.

Souvenir Sheet

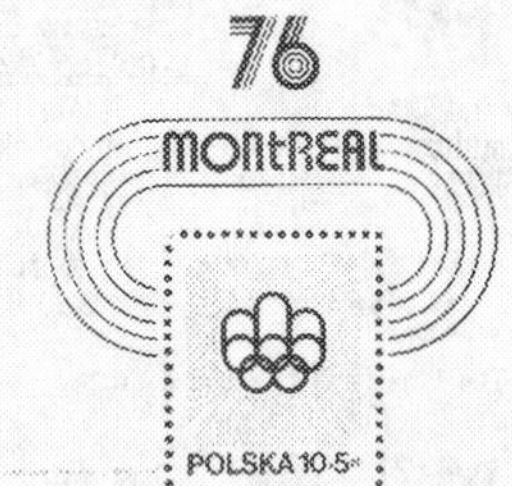

Montreal Olympic Games Emblem — SP55

Photo. & Engr.
1975, Mar. 8 *Perf. 12*
B130 SP55 10z + 5z sil & grn 1.50 1.00

21st Olympic Games, Montreal, July 17-Aug. 8, 1976.

Outer edge of souvenir sheet is perforated.

Dunikowski Type of 1975

Design: 8z+4z, Mother and Child, from Silesian Insurrectionist Monument, by Dunikowski.

1975, Oct. 9 Photo. *Perf. 11½x11*
B131 A644 8z + 4z multi 1.00 .45

Souvenir Sheet

Volleyball — SP56

Engraved and Photogravure
1976, June 30 *Perf. 11½*
B132 SP56 10z + 5z blk & car 1.40 .70

21st Olympic Games, Montreal, Canada, July 17-Aug. 1. No. B132 contains one perf. 11½ stamp and is perf. 11½ all around.

Corinthian Art Type 1976

Design: 8z+4z, Winged Sphinx, vert.

1976, Oct. 30 Photo. *Perf. 11½x11*
B133 A664 8z + 4z multi 1.10 .50

Souvenir Sheet

Stoning of St. Stephen, by Rubens — SP57

1977, Apr. 30 Engr. *Perf. 12x11½*
B134 SP57 8z + 4z sepia 1.10 .65

Peter Paul Rubens (1577-1640), Flemish painter.
Outer edge of souvenir sheet is perforated.

Souvenir Sheet

Kazimierz Gzowski — SP58

1978, June 6 Photo. *Perf. 11½x11*
B135 SP58 8.40z + 4z multi 1.10 .55

CAPEX, '78 Canadian Intl. Phil. Exhib., Toronto, June 9-18.
K. S. Gzowski (1813-1898), Polish engineer and lawyer living in Canada, built International Bridge over Niagara River.

Souvenir Sheet

Olympic Rings — SP59

1979, May 19 Engr. *Imperf.*
B136 SP59 10z + 5z black 1.00 .75

1980 Olympic Games.

Monument Type of 1979
Souvenir Sheet

1979, Sept. 1 Photo. *Imperf.*
B137 A731 10z + 5z multi 1.25 .75

Surtax was for monument.

Summer Olympic Type of 1980
Souvenir Sheet

1980, Mar. 31 Photo. *Perf. 11x11½*
B138 A742 10.50z + 5z Kayak 1.00 .75

No. B138 contains one stamp 42x30mm.

Souvenir Sheet

Intercosmos Cooperative Space Program — SP60

1980, Apr. 12 *Perf. 11½x11*
B139 SP60 6.90z + 3z multi .85 .75

SP61

SP62

1970 Uprising Memorial: 2.50z + 1z, Triple Crucifix, Gdansk (27x46mm). 6.50z + 1z, Monument, Gdynia.

1981, Dec. 16 Photo. *Perf. 11½x12*
B140 SP61 2.50 + 1z blk & red .70 .32
B141 SP61 6.50 + 1z blk & lil 1.00 .70

1984, May 15 Photo. *Perf. 11½x12*

Portrait of a German Princess, by Lucas Cranach

B142 SP62 27z + 10z multi 1.50 .80

1984 UPU Congress, Hamburg. No. B142 issued se-tenant with multicolored label showing UPU emblem and text.

Souvenir Sheet

Madonna with Child, St. John and the Angel, by Sandro Botticelli (1445-1510), Natl. Museum, Warsaw
SP63

1985, Sept. 25 Photo. *Perf. 11*
B143 SP63 65z + 15z multi 2.25 1.25
a. Inscribed: 35 LAT POLSKIEGO . . . 4.50 4.50

ITALIA '85. Surtax for Polish Association of Philatelists.
No. B143a was for the 35th anniv. of the Polish Philatelic Union. Distribution was limited.

Joachim Lelewel (1786-1861), Historian — SP64

1986, Dec. 22 Photo. *Perf. 11½x12*
B144 SP64 10z + 5z multi .30 .18

Surtax for the Natl. Committee for School Aid.

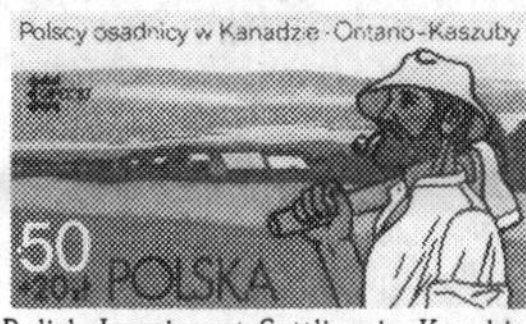

Polish Immigrant Settling in Kasubia, Ontario — SP65

1987, June 13 Photo. *Perf. 12x11½*
B145 SP65 50z + 20z multi 1.40 .70

CAPEX '87, Toronto, Canada. Surtaxed for the Polish Philatelists' Union.

Souvenir Sheet

OLYMPHILEX '87, Rome — SP66

1987, Aug. 28 Litho. *Perf. 14*
B146 SP66 45z + 10z like #2617 1.10 1.10

FINLANDIA '88 — SP67

1988, June 1 Photo. *Perf. 12x11½*
B147 SP67 45z +20z Salmon, reindeer 1.25 .65

Souvenir Sheet

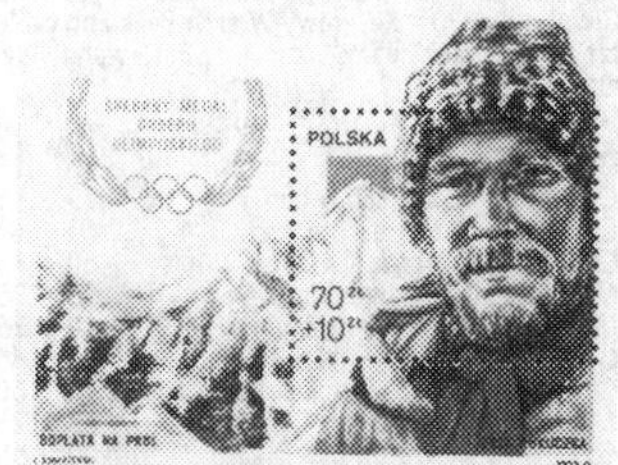

Jerzy Kukuczka, Mountain Climber Awarded Medal by the Intl. Olympic Committee for Climbing the Himalayas — SP68

1988, Aug. 17 Photo. *Perf. 11x11½*
B148 SP68 70z +10z multi 1.50 .80

Surtax for the Polish Olympic Fund.

Aid for Victims of 1997 Oder River Flood — SP69

1997, Aug. 18 Photo. *Perf. 11½x12*
B149 SP69 60g +30g multi .80 .40

AIR POST STAMPS

Biplane — AP1

Perf. 12½

1925, Sept. 10 Typo. Unwmk.

C1	AP1	1g lt blue	.65	2.25
C2	AP1	2g orange	.65	2.25
C3	AP1	3g yellow brn	.65	2.25
C4	AP1	5g dk brown	.65	.85
C5	AP1	10g dk green	1.65	.75
C6	AP1	15g red violet	2.50	.85
C7	AP1	20g olive grn	10.50	4.25
C8	AP1	30g dull rose	6.75	1.50
C9	AP1	45g dk violet	8.50	4.25
		Nos. C1-C9 (9)	32.50	19.20
		Set, never hinged	45.00	

Counterfeits exist.
For overprint see No. C11.

Capt. Franciszek Zwirko and Stanislaus Wigura
AP2

Perf. 11½ to 12½ and Compound

1933, Apr. 15 Engr. Wmk. 234
C10 AP2 30g gray green 14.00 1.00
Never hinged 20.00

Winning of the circuit of Europe flight by two Polish aviators in 1932. The stamp was available for both air mail and ordinary postage.
For overprint see No. C12.

Nos. C7 and C10 Overprinted in Red

Challenge 1934

1934, Aug. 28 Unwmk. *Perf. 12½*
C11 AP1 20g olive green 12.50 6.75

Wmk. 234
Perf. 11½

C12 AP2 30g gray green 7.00 2.25
Set, never hinged 26.00

Polish People's Republic

Douglas Plane over Ruins of Warsaw — AP3

Unwmk.

1946, Mar. 5 Photo. *Perf. 11*

C13	AP3	5z grnsh blk	.40	.15
a.		Without control number	4.00	.40
		Never hinged	6.00	
C14	AP3	10z dk violet	.40	.15
C15	AP3	15z blue	1.25	.25
C16	AP3	20z rose brn	.80	.15
C17	AP3	25z dk bl grn	1.65	.38
C18	AP3	30z red	2.50	.55
		Nos. C13-C18 (6)	7.00	1.63
		Set, never hinged	10.00	

The 10z, 20z and 30z were issued only with control number in lower right stamp margin. The 15z and 25z exist only without number. The 5z comes both ways.
Nos. C13-C18 exist imperforate.

Nos. 345, 344 and 344a Surcharged in Red or Black

a

Zł 40 Zł
LOTNICZA

b

LOTNICZA
Zł 50 Zł

1947, Sept. 10 *Perf. 12½*

C19	A104(a)	40z on 50g (R)	1.65	.90
C20	A103(b)	50z on 25g dl red	1.90	1.75
a.		50z on 25g deep red	2.75	2.50
		Never hinged, #C20a	3.50	
		Set, never hinged	5.50	

Counterfeits exist.

Centaur — AP4

1948 *Perf. 11*

C21	AP4	15z dk violet	1.50	.25
C22	AP4	25z deep blue	.80	.18
C23	AP4	30z brown	.65	.45
C24	AP4	50z dk green	1.25	.45

C25	AP4	75z gray black	1.50	.55
C26	AP4	100z red orange	1.50	.45
		Nos. C21-C26 (6)	7.20	2.33
		Set, never hinged	9.50	

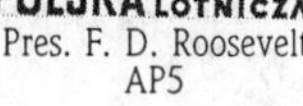

Pres. F. D. Roosevelt
AP5

Airplane Mechanic and Propeller
AP5a

100z, Casimir Pulaski. 120z, Tadeusz Kosciusko.

1948, Dec. 30 Photo. *Perf. 11½*

Granite Paper

C26A	AP5	80z blue blk	13.00	*22.50*
C26B	AP5	100z purple	14.00	*19.00*
C26C	AP5	120z deep blue	14.00	*19.00*
d.		Souvenir sheet of 3	140.00	*190.00*
		Never hinged	200.00	
		Nos. C26A-C26C (3)	41.00	*60.50*
		Set, never hinged	50.00	

No. C26Cd contains stamps similar to Nos. C26A-C26C with colors changed: 80z ultramarine, 100z carmine rose, 120z dark green. Sold for 500z.

1950, Feb. 6 Engr. *Perf. 12½*

C27	AP5a	500z rose lake	3.25	3.50
		Never hinged	5.00	

Catalogue values for unused stamps in this section, from this point to the end of the section, are for Never Hinged items.

Seaport
AP6

Designs: 90g, Mechanized farm. 1.40z, Warsaw. 5z, Steel mill.

1952, Apr. 10 *Perf. 12x12½*

C28	AP6	55g intense blue	.15	.15
C29	AP6	90g dull green	.30	.15
C30	AP6	1.40z violet brn	.45	.18
C31	AP6	5z gray black	1.65	.60
		Nos. C28-C31 (4)	2.55	1.08

Nos. C28-C31 exist imperf. Value $15.

Congress Badge — AP7

1953, Aug. 24 Photo. *Imperf.*

C32	AP7	55g brown lilac	1.00	.40
C33	AP7	75g brown org	1.50	1.10

3rd World Congress of Students, Warsaw 1953.

Souvenir Sheet

AP8

1954, May 23 Engr. *Perf. 12x12½*

C34	AP8	5z gray green	30.00	20.00

3rd congress of the Polish Phil. Assoc., Warsaw, 1954. Sold for 7.50 zlotys. A similar sheet, imperf. and in dark blue, was issued but had no postal validity.

Paczkow Castle, Luban
AP9

Plane over "Peace" Steelworks
AP10

80g, Kazimierz Dolny. 1.15z, Wawel castle, Cracow. 1.50z, City Hall, Wroclaw. 1.55z, Lazierski Square, Warsaw. 1.95z, Cracow gate, Lublin.

1954, July 9 *Perf. 12½*

C35	AP9	60g dk gray grn	.15	.15
C36	AP9	80g red	.15	.15
C37	AP9	1.15z black	1.00	.40
C38	AP9	1.50z rose lake	.40	.20
C39	AP9	1.55z dp gray bl	.40	.15
C40	AP9	1.95z chocolate	.80	.35
		Nos. C35-C40 (6)	2.90	1.40

Wmk. 326 ('58 Values); Unwmkd.

1957-58 Engr. & Photo. *Perf. 12½*

Plane over: 1.50z, Castle Square, Warsaw. 3.40z, Old Market, Cracow. 3.90z, King Boleslaw Chrobry Wall, Szczecin. 4z, Karkonosze mountains. 5z, Gdansk. 10z, Ruins of Liwa Castle. 15z, Old City, Lublin. 20z, Kasprowy Wierch Peak and cable car. 30z, Porabka dam. 50z, M. S. Batory and Gdynia harbor.

C41	AP10	90g black & pink	.15	.15
C42	AP10	1.50z brn & salmon	.15	.15
C43	AP10	3.40z sep & buff	.35	.15
C44	AP10	3.90z dk brn & cit	.60	.45
C45	AP10	4z ind & lt grn	.30	.15
C46	AP10	5z maroon & gray	.55	.15
C47	AP10	10z sepia & grn	1.10	.25
C48	AP10	15z vio bl & pale bl	1.40	.45
C49	AP10	20z vio blk & lem	2.75	.60
C50	AP10	30z ol gray & bis	3.75	1.25
C51	AP10	50z dk bl & gray	6.00	1.65
		Nos. C41-C51 (11)	17.10	5.40

Issue dates: 5z, 10z, 20z, 30z, 50z, Dec. 15, 1958. Others, Dec. 6, 1957.

1959, May 23 Litho. Wmk. 326

C52	AP10	10z sepia	1.75	1.50
a.		With 5z label	2.00	2.00

65th anniv. of the Polish Philatelic Society. Sheet of 6 stamps and 2 each of 3 different labels. Each label carries an added charge of 5z for a fund to build a Society clubhouse in Warsaw.

Jantar Glider — AP11

Contemporary aviation: 10z, Mi6 transport helicopter. 20z, PZL-106 Kruk, crop spraying plane. 50z, Plane over Warsaw Castle.

1976-78 Unwmk. Engr. *Perf. 11½*

C53	AP11	5z dk blue grn	.40	.25
C54	AP11	10z dk brown	.80	.50
C55	AP11	20z grnsh black	1.50	.75
C56	AP11	50z claret	3.00	1.90
		Nos. C53-C56 (4)	5.70	3.40

Issued: 5z, 10z, 3/27/76; 20z, 2/15/77; 50z, 2/2/78.

AIR POST SEMI-POSTAL STAMP

Catalogue values for unused stamps in this section are for Never Hinged items.

Polish People's Republic

Wing of Jet Plane and Letter — SPAP1

Perf. 11½

1957, Mar. 28 Unwmk. Photo.

CB1	SPAP1	4z + 2z blue	3.00	3.50
a.		Souv. sheet of 1, ultra, imperf.	10.00	4.50

7th Polish National Philatelic Exhibition, Warsaw. Sheet of 12 with 4 diagonally arranged gray labels.

POSTAGE DUE STAMPS

Cracow Issues

Postage Due Stamps of Austria, 1916, Overprinted in Black or Red

POCZTA
◇
POLSKA

1919, Jan. 10 Unwmk. *Perf. 12½*

J1	D4	5h rose red	7.00	6.00
J2	D4	10h rose red	*1,750.*	*1,750.*
J3	D4	15h rose red	3.75	3.00
a.		Inverted overprint	150.00	
J4	D4	20h rose red	275.00	275.00
J5	D4	25h rose red	17.50	15.00
J6	D4	30h rose red	*800.00*	*750.00*
J7	D4	40h rose red	*700.00*	*600.00*
J8	D5	1k ultra (R)	*2,400.*	*2,400.*
J9	D5	5k ultra (R)	*2,400.*	*2,400.*
J10	D5	10k ultra (R)	*10,000.*	*9,000.*
a.		Black overprint	*14,000.*	—

Overprint on Nos. J1-J7, J10a is type. Overprint on Nos. J8-J10 is slightly larger than illustration, has a different ornament between lines of type and is litho.

D6

Type of Austria, 1916-18, Surcharged in Black

1919, Jan. 10

J11	D6	15h on 36h vio	300.00	200.00
J12	D6	50h on 42h choc	30.00	30.00
a.		Double surcharge	—	*8,000.*

Counterfeits exist of Nos. J1-J12.

Regular Issues

Numerals of Value
D7 D8

1919 Typo. *Perf. 11½*

For Northern Poland

J13	D7	2f red orange	.38	.32
J14	D7	4f red orange	.16	.18
J15	D7	5f red orange	.15	.15
J16	D7	10f red orange	.15	.15
J17	D7	20f red orange	.15	.15
J18	D7	30f red orange	.15	.15
J19	D7	50f red orange	.15	.15
J20	D7	100f red orange	.75	.45
J21	D7	500f red orange	1.75	1.25

For Southern Poland

J22	D7	2h dark blue	.15	.15
J23	D7	4h dark blue	.15	.15
J24	D7	5h dark blue	.15	.15
J25	D7	10h dark blue	.15	.15
J26	D7	20h dark blue	.15	.15
J27	D7	30h dark blue	.15	.15
J28	D7	50h dark blue	.15	.15
J29	D7	100h dark blue	.32	.22
J30	D7	500h dark blue	1.40	1.10
		Nos. J13-J30 (18)	6.56	
		Set value		4.50

Counterfeits exist.

1920 *Perf. 9, 10, 11½*

Thin Laid Paper

J31	D7	20f dark blue	.70	.48
J32	D7	100f dark blue	.35	.24
J33	D7	200f dark blue	.60	.48
J34	D7	500f dark blue	.35	.24
		Nos. J31-J34 (4)	2.00	1.44

Regular Issue of 1919 Surcharged

6 Mk.

dopłata

1921, Jan. 25 *Imperf.*

Wove Paper

J35	A9	6m on 15h brown	.45	.42
J36	A9	6m on 25h car	.45	.42
J37	A9	20m on 10h lake	1.25	1.10
J38	A9	20m on 50h indigo	1.40	1.40
J39	A9	35m on 70h dp bl	12.00	12.00
		Nos. J35-J39 (5)	15.55	15.34

Counterfeits exist.

Perf. 9 to 14½ and Compound

1921-22 Typo.

Thin Laid or Wove Paper

Size: 17x22mm

J40	D8	1m indigo	.32	.15
J41	D8	2m indigo	.32	.15
J42	D8	4m indigo	.32	.15
J43	D8	6m indigo	.32	.15
J44	D8	8m indigo	.32	.15
J45	D8	20m indigo	.32	.15
J46	D8	50m indigo	.32	.15
J47	D8	100m indigo	.60	.18
		Nos. J40-J47 (8)	2.84	
		Set value		1.00

Nos. J44-J45, J41 Surcharged

Perf. 9 to 14½ and Compound

1923, Nov.

J48	D8	10,000(m) on 8m indigo	.35	.15
J49	D8	20,000(m) on 20m indigo	.35	.15
J50	D8	50,000(m) on 2m indigo	2.25	.70
		Nos. J48-J50 (3)	2.95	1.00

Type of 1921-22 Issue

1923 Typo. *Perf. 12½*

Size: 19x24mm

J51	D8	50m indigo	.15	.15
J52	D8	100m indigo	.15	.15
J53	D8	200m indigo	.15	.15
J54	D8	500m indigo	.15	.15
J55	D8	1000m indigo	.15	.15
J56	D8	2000m indigo	.15	.15
J57	D8	10,000m indigo	.15	.15
J58	D8	20,000m indigo	.15	.15
J59	D8	30,000m indigo	.15	.15
J60	D8	50,000m indigo	.38	.15
J61	D8	100,000m indigo	.38	.15
J62	D8	200,000m indigo	.45	.15
J63	D8	300,000m indigo	.45	.32
J64	D8	500,000m indigo	.65	.18
J65	D8	1,000,000m indigo	1.50	.60
J66	D8	2,000,000m indigo	2.75	.60
J67	D8	3,000,000m indigo	3.00	.85
		Nos. J51-J67 (17)	10.91	
		Set value		3.80

D9

D10

Perf. 10 to 13½ and Compound

1924

Size: 20x25½mm

J68	D9	1g brown	.28	.22
J69	D9	2g brown	.28	.22
J70	D9	4g brown	.28	.22
J71	D9	6g brown	.55	.22
J72	D9	10g brown	3.25	.22
J73	D9	15g brown	2.50	.40
J74	D9	20g brown	6.00	.40
J75	D9	25g brown	5.00	.40
J76	D9	30g brown	1.10	.40
J77	D9	40g brown	1.10	.40
J78	D9	50g brown	1.10	.40
J79	D9	1z brown	1.00	.55
J80	D9	2z brown	1.00	.55
J81	D9	3z brown	1.90	2.25
J82	D9	5z brown	1.90	.85
		Nos. J68-J82 (15)	27.24	7.70

Nos. J68-J69 and J72-J75 exist measuring 19½x24½mm.

For surcharges see Nos. J84-J91.

1930, July *Perf. 12½*

J83 D10 5g olive brown .70 .20
Never hinged 1.00

Postage Due Stamps of 1924 Surcharged

50 groszy

Perf. 10 to 13½ and Compound

1934-38

J84 D9 10g on 2z brown ('38) .40 .28
J85 D9 15g on 2z brown .40 .28
J86 D9 20g on 1z brown .40 .28
J87 D9 20g on 5z brown 2.00 .55
J88 D9 25g on 40g brown 1.25 .55
J89 D9 30g on 40g brown .85 .55
J90 D9 50g on 40g brown .85 .70
J91 D9 50g on 3z brown ('35) 1.75 1.00
Nos. J84-J91 (8) 7.90 4.19
Set, never hinged 15.00

No. 255a Surcharged in Red or Indigo

DOPŁATA 25 GR

1934-36 **Laid Paper**

J92 A50 10g on 1z (R) ('36) .80 .15
a. Vertically laid paper (No. 255) 25.00 18.00
J93 A50 20g on 1z (R) ('36) 2.50 .80
J94 A50 25g on 1z (I) .80 .30
a. Vertically laid paper (No. 255) 30.00 18.00
Nos. J92-J94 (3) 4.10 1.25
Set, never hinged 5.00

D11

1938-39 **Typo.** *Perf. 12½x12*

J95 D11 5g dark blue green .15 .15
J96 D11 10g dark blue green .15 .15
J97 D11 15g dark blue green .15 .15
J98 D11 20g dark blue green .60 .20
J99 D11 25g dark blue green .15 .16
J100 D11 30g dark blue green .42 .20
J101 D11 50g dark blue green .80 1.25
J102 D11 1z dark blue green 2.50 1.65
Nos. J95-J102 (8) 4.92 3.91
Set, never hinged 12.00

For surcharges see Nos. N51-N55.

Polish People's Republic

Post Horn with Thunderbolts
D12

Polish Eagle
D13

Perf. 11x10½

1945, May 20 **Litho.** **Unwmk.**

Size: 25½x19mm

J103 D12 1z orange brown .15 .15
J104 D12 2z orange brown .20 .15
J105 D12 3z orange brown .25 .20
J106 D12 5z orange brown .35 .30
Nos. J103-J106 (4) .95 .80
Set, never hinged 2.00

Type of 1945

Perf. 11, 11½ (P) or Imperf. (I)

1946-49 **Photo.**

Size: 29x21½mm

J106A D12 1z org brn (P) ('49) .20 .15
J107 D12 2z org brn (P,I) .20 .15
J108 D12 3z org brn (P,I) .20 .15
J109 D12 5z org brn (I) .20 .15
J110 D12 6z org brn (I) .20 .15
J111 D12 10z org brn (I) .25 .20
J112 D12 15z org brn (P,I) .35 .30
J113 D12 25z org brn (P,I) .50 .45
J114 D12 100z brn (P) ('49) 1.00 .50
J115 D12 150z brn (P) ('49) 1.75 .50
Nos. J106A-J115 (10) 4.85 2.70
Set, never hinged 6.00

1950 **Engr.** *Perf. 12x12½*

J116 D13 5z red brown .15 .15
J117 D13 10z red brown .15 .15
J118 D13 15z red brown .15 .15
J119 D13 20z red brown .28 .15
J120 D13 25z red brown .32 .18
J121 D13 50z red brown .48 .35
J122 D13 100z red brown 1.00 .70
Nos. J116-J122 (7) 2.53
Set, never hinged 3.50
Set value 1.55

1951-52

J123 D13 5g red brown .15 .15
J124 D13 10g red brown .15 .15
J125 D13 15g red brown .15 .15
J126 D13 20g red brown .15 .15
J127 D13 25g red brown .16 .15
J128 D13 30g red brown .22 .15
J129 D13 50g red brown .25 .20
J130 D13 60g red brown .30 .20
J131 D13 90g red brown .38 .25
J132 D13 1z red brown .60 .45
J133 D13 2z red brown .95 .75
J134 D13 5z brown violet 2.00 1.75
Nos. J123-J134 (12) 5.46 4.50
Set, never hinged 7.00

1953, Apr. **Photo.** **Without imprint**

J135 D13 5g red brown .15 .15
J136 D13 10g red brown .15 .15
J137 D13 15g red brown .15 .15
J138 D13 20g red brown .15 .15
J139 D13 25g red brown .16 .15
J140 D13 30g red brown .25 .15
J141 D13 50g red brown .42 .25
J142 D13 60g red brown .50 .30
J143 D13 90g red brown .60 .50
J144 D13 1z red brown .80 .50
J145 D13 2z red brown 1.50 1.25
Nos. J135-J145 (11) 4.83 3.70
Set, never hinged 6.25

Catalogue values for unused stamps in this section, from this point to the end of the section, are for Never Hinged items.

1980, Sept. 2 **Litho.** *Perf. 12½*

J146 D13 1z lt red brown .15 .15
J147 D13 2z gray olive .18 .15
J148 D13 3z dull violet .28 .15
J149 D13 5z brown .45 .20
Nos. J146-J149 (4) 1.06
Set value .45

OFFICIAL STAMPS

O1

Perf. 10, 11½, 10x11½, 11½x10

1920, Feb. 1 **Litho.** **Unwmk.**

O1 O1 3f vermilion .15 .15
O2 O1 5f vermilion .15 .18
O3 O1 10f vermilion .15 .18
O4 O1 15f vermilion .15 .18
O5 O1 25f vermilion .15 .18
O6 O1 50f vermilion .15 .18
O7 O1 100f vermilion .28 .25
O8 O1 150f vermilion .28 .38
O9 O1 200f vermilion .52 .38
O10 O1 300f vermilion .28 .38
O11 O1 600f vermilion .52 .38
Nos. O1-O11 (11) 2.78 2.82

Numerals Larger
Stars inclined outward

1920, Nov. 20 *Perf. 11½*

Thin Laid Paper

O12 O1 5f red .15 .15
O13 O1 10f red .50 .45
O14 O1 15f red .35 .35
O15 O1 25f red 1.10 1.10
O16 O1 50f red .65 .65
Nos. O12-O16 (5) 2.75 2.70

Polish Eagle
O3 O4

Perf. 12x12½

1933, Aug. 1 **Typo.** **Wmk. 234**

O17 O3 (30g) vio (Zwyczajna) .95 .15
O18 O3 (80g) red (Polecona) 2.25 .30
Set, never hinged 4.00

1935, Apr. 1

O19 O4 (25g) bl vio (Zwyczajna) .15 .15
O20 O4 (55g) car (Polecona) .30 .15
Set, never hinged .75

Stamps inscribed "Zwyczajna" or "Zwykla" were for ordinary official mail. Those with "Polecona" were for registered official mail.

Polish People's Republic

Polish Eagle — O5

Perf. 11, 14

1945, July 1 **Photo.** **Unwmk.**

O21 O5 (5z) bl vio (Zwykla) .35 .15
a. Imperf. 1.00 1.00
O22 O5 (10z) red (Polecona) .65 .18
a. Imperf. 1.65 1.25
Set, never hinged, #O21, O22 2.00
Set, never hinged, #O21a, O22a 4.00
Set value .25

Control number at bottom right: M-01705 on No. O21; M-01706 on No. O22.

Type of 1945 Redrawn

1946, July 31

O23 O5 (5z) dl bl vio (Zwykla) .30 .15
O24 O5 (10z) dl rose red (Polecona) .50 .22
Set, never hinged 1.50

The redrawn stamps appear blurred and the eagle contains fewer lines of shading.

Control number at bottom right: M-01709 on Nos. O23-O26.

Redrawn Type of 1946

1946, July 31 *Imperf.*

O25 O5 (60g) dl bl vio (Zwykla) .40 .15
O26 O5 (1.55z) dl rose red (Polecona) .40 .20
Set, never hinged 1.25

Type of 1945, 2nd Redrawing
No Control Number at Lower Right

Perf. 11, 11½, 11x12½

1950-53 **Unwmk.**

O27 O5 (60g) blue (Zwykla) .22 .15
O28 O5 (1.55z) red (Polecona) ('53) .38 .20
Set, never hinged .80

Redrawn Type of 1952

1954 *Perf. 13x11, 11½, 14*

O29 O5 (60g) slate gray (Zwykla) 1.10 .50
Never hinged 1.50

O6

Perf. 11x11½, 12x12½

1954, Aug. 15 **Engr.**

O30 O6 (60g) dark blue (Zwykla) .25 .15
O31 O6 (1.55z) red (Polecona) .45 .24
Set, never hinged 1.00

Polish People's Republic, 10th anniversary.

NEWSPAPER STAMPS

Austrian Newspaper Stamps of 1916 Overprinted

POCZTA ◇ POLSKA

1919, Jan. 10 **Unwmk.** *Imperf.*

P1 N9 2h brown 9.00 9.00
P2 N9 4h green 3.00 2.50
P3 N9 6h dark blue 3.00 2.50
P4 N9 10h orange 35.00 35.00
P5 N9 30h claret 5.00 4.50
Nos. P1-P5 (5) 55.00 53.50

Poland German Occupation stamps can be mounted in the Scott Germany album part 2.

OCCUPATION STAMPS

Issued under German Occupation

German Stamps of 1905 Overprinted

Perf. 14, 14½

1915, May 12 **Wmk. 125**

N1 A16 3pf brown 1.00 .45
N2 A16 5pf green 1.25 .55
N3 A16 10pf carmine 1.25 .55
N4 A16 20pf ultra 1.90 .80
N5 A16 40pf lake & blk 10.50 4.25
Nos. N1-N5 (5) 15.90 6.60

German Stamps of 1905-17 Overprinted

Gen.-Gouv. Warschau

1916-17

N6 A22 2½pf gray .22 .35
N7 A16 3pf brown .90 .45
N8 A16 5pf green .90 1.00
N9 A22 7½pf orange .70 .15
N10 A16 10pf carmine .90 .35
N11 A22 15pf yel brn 4.25 2.25
N12 A22 15pf dk vio ('17) .55 .35
N13 A16 20pf ultra 1.40 .65
N14 A16 30pf org & blk, *buff* 6.25 3.75
N15 A16 40pf lake & blk 2.25 .15
N16 A16 60pf magenta 3.00 1.50
Nos. N6-N16 (11) 21.32 10.95

For overprints and surcharges see Nos. 15-26.

6 Groschen 6

German Stamps of 1934 Surcharged in Black

Deutsche Post OSTEN

1939, Dec. 1 **Wmk. 237** *Perf. 14*

N17 A64 6g on 3pf bister .26 .32
N18 A64 8g on 4pf dl bl .26 .35
N19 A64 12g on 6pf dk grn .26 .32
N20 A64 16g on 8pf vermilion .70 1.00
N21 A64 20g on 10pf choc .26 .32
N22 A64 24g on 12pf dp car .26 .32
N23 A64 30g on 15pf maroon .80 .90
N24 A64 40g on 20pf brt bl .70 .42
N25 A64 50g on 25pf ultra .70 .75
N26 A64 60g on 30pf ol grn .70 .42
N27 A64 80g on 40pf red vio .80 .90
N28 A64 1z on 50pf dk grn & blk 2.00 1.40
N29 A64 2z on 100(pf) org & blk 3.75 3.00
Nos. N17-N29 (13) 11.45 10.42
Set, never hinged 16.00

Stamps of Poland 1937, Surcharged in Black or Brown

1940 **Unwmk.** *Perf. 12½, 12½x13*

N30 A80 24g on 25g sl grn 1.10 1.75
N31 A81 40g on 30g rose vio .40 .65
N32 A80 50g on 55g blue .35 .52

Similar Surcharge on Stamps of 1938-39

N33 A83 2g on 5g red org .22 .35
N34 A83 4(g) on 5g red org .22 .35
N35 A83 6(g) on 10g grn .22 .35
N36 A83 8(g) on 10g grn (Br) .28 .45
N37 A83 10(g) on 10g grn .22 .35
N38 A83 12(g) on 15g redsh brn (#339) .22 .35
N39 A83 16(g) on 15g redsh brn (#339) .28 .45
N40 A83 24g on 25g dl vio .22 .35
N41 A83 30(g) on 30g rose red .28 .45
N42 A83 50(g) on 50g brt red vio .35 .55
N43 A83 60(g) on 55g ultra 7.50 9.25
N44 A83 80(g) on 75g dl grn 7.50 9.25
N45 A83 1z on 1z org 7.50 9.25
N46 A83 2z on 2z car rose 5.00 5.50
N47 A95 3z on 3z gray blk 5.00 5.50

Similar Surcharge on Nos. B32-B34

N48 SP5 30g on 5g+5g .35 .55
N49 SP5 40g on 25g+10g .35 .55

N50 SP5 1z on 55g+15g 7.25 6.50

Similar Surcharge on Nos. J98-J102

Perf. 12½x12

N51 D11 50(g) on 20g .65 1.10
N52 D11 50(g) on 25g 13.00 13.00
N53 D11 50(g) on 30g 40.00 35.00
N54 D11 50(g) on 50g .65 .90
N55 D11 50(g) on 1z 1.10 .90
Nos. N30-N55 (26) 100.21 104.17
Set, never hinged 140.00

The surcharge on Nos. N30 to N55 is arranged to fit the shape of the stamp and obliterate the original denomination. On some values, "General Gouvernement" appears at the bottom. Counterfeits exist.

St. Florian's Gate, Cracow — OS1

Palace, Warsaw — OS13

Designs: 8g, Watch Tower, Cracow. 10g, Cracow Gate, Lublin. 12g, Courtyard and statue of Copernicus. 20g, Dominican Church, Cracow. 24g, Wawel Castle, Cracow. 30g, Church, Lublin. 40g, Arcade, Cloth Hall, Cracow. 48g, City Hall, Sandomierz. 50g, Court House, Cracow. 60g, Courtyard, Cracow. 80g, St. Mary's Church, Cracow.

1940-41 Unwmk. Photo. *Perf. 14*

N56 OS1 6g brown .28 .55
N57 OS1 8g brn org .28 .55
N58 OS1 8g bl blk ('41) .28 .38
N59 OS1 10g emerald .15 .24
N60 OS1 12g dk grn 3.00 .30
N61 OS1 12g dp vio ('41) .28 .16
N62 OS1 20g dk ol brn .15 .15
N63 OS1 24g hn brn .15 .15
N64 OS1 30g purple .15 .16
N65 OS1 30g vio brn ('41) .15 .32
N66 OS1 40g slate blk .15 .16
N67 OS1 48g chnt brn ('41) .60 .80
N68 OS1 50g brt bl .15 .16
N69 OS1 60g slate grn .15 .24
N70 OS1 80g dull pur .25 .30
N71 OS13 1z rose lake 2.00 1.10
N72 OS13 1z Prus grn ('41) .55 .55
Nos. N56-N72 (17) 8.72 6.27
Set, never hinged 11.00

For surcharges see Nos. NB1-NB4.

Cracow Castle and City, 15th Century OS14

1941, Apr. 20 Engr. *Perf. 14½*

N73 OS14 10z red & ol blk 2.00 2.00
Never hinged 2.50

Printed in sheets of 8.

Rondel and Florian's Gate, Cracow OS15

Design: 4z, Tyniec Monastery, Vistula River.

1941 *Perf. 13½x14*

N74 OS15 2z dk ultra .35 .45
N75 OS15 4z slate grn .48 .60
Set, never hinged 1.25

Adolf Hitler — OS17

1941-43 Unwmk. Photo. *Perf. 14*

N76 OS17 2g gray blk .15 .16
N77 OS17 6g golden brn .15 .16
N78 OS17 8g slate blue .15 .16
N79 OS17 10g green .15 .15
N80 OS17 12g purple .15 .15
N81 OS17 16g org red .50 .48
N82 OS17 20g blk brn .15 .16
N83 OS17 24g henna .15 .15
N84 OS17 30g rose vio .45 .16
N85 OS17 32g dk bl grn .50 .38
N86 OS17 40g brt blue .15 .16
N87 OS17 48g chestnut .55 .42
N88 OS17 50g vio bl ('43) .15 .16
N89 OS17 60g dk olive ('43) .15 .16
N90 OS17 80g dk vio ('43) .15 .16
Nos. N76-N90 (15) 3.65 3.17
Set, never hinged 4.50

A 20g black brown exists with head of Hans Frank substituted for that of Hitler. It was printed and used by Resistance movements.

Nos. N76-N80, N82-N90 exist imperf.

1942-44 Engr. *Perf. 12½*

N91 OS17 50g vio bl .40 .48
N92 OS17 60g dk ol .40 .48
N93 OS17 80g dk red vio .40 .48
N94 OS17 1z slate grn .40 .48
a. Perf. 14 ('44) .52 .60
N95 OS17 1.20z dk brn .45 .55
a. Perf. 14 ('44) .60 .80
N96 OS17 1.60z bl vio .50 .60
a. Perf. 14 ('44) .75 1.10
Nos. N91-N96 (6) 2.55 3.07
Set, never hinged 3.50
Set, #N94a, N95a, N96a, never hinged 3.00

Exist imperf.

Rondel and Florian's Gate, Cracow OS18

Designs: 4z, Tyniec Monastery, Vistula River. 6z, View of Lwow. 10z, Cracow Castle and City, 15th Century.

1943-44 *Perf. 13½x14*

N100 OS18 2z slate grn .15 .15
N101 OS18 4z dk gray vio .28 .35
N102 OS18 6z sepia ('44) .48 .50
N103 OS18 10z org brn & gray blk .52 .60
Nos. N100-N103 (4) 1.43 1.60
Set, never hinged 1.90

OCCUPATION SEMI-POSTAL STAMPS

Issued under German Occupation

Types of 1940 Occupation Postage Stamps Surcharged in Red

Unwmk.

1940, Aug. 17 Photo. *Perf. 14*

NB1 OS1 12g + 8g olive gray 3.00 3.50
NB2 OS1 24g + 16g olive gray 3.00 3.50
NB3 OS1 50g + 50g olive gray 3.50 4.00
NB4 OS1 80g + 80g olive gray 3.50 4.00
Nos. NB1-NB4 (4) 13.00 15.00
Set, never hinged 15.00

German Peasant Girl in Poland — OSP1

Designs: 24g+26g, Woman wearing scarf. 30g+20g, Similar to type OSP4.

1940, Oct. 26 Engr. *Perf. 14½*

Thick Paper

NB5 OSP1 12g + 38g dk sl grn 2.25 2.75
NB6 OSP1 24g + 26g cop red 2.25 2.75
NB7 OSP1 30g + 20g dk pur 2.75 3.75
Nos. NB5-NB7 (3) 7.25 9.25
Set, never hinged 8.50

1st anniversary of the General Government.

German Peasant — OSP4

1940, Dec. 1 *Perf. 12*

NB8 OSP4 12g + 8g dk grn 1.00 .90
NB9 OSP4 24g + 16g rose red 1.65 1.65
NB10 OSP4 30g + 30g vio brn 2.00 2.00
NB11 OSP4 50g + 50g ultra 2.75 2.50
Nos. NB8-NB11 (4) 7.40 7.05
Set, never hinged 9.25

The surtax was for war relief.

Adolf Hitler — OSP5

Unwmk.

1942, Apr. 20 Engr. *Perf. 11*

Thick Cream Paper

NB12 OSP5 30g + 1z brn car .30 .35
NB13 OSP5 50g + 1z dk ultra .30 .35
NB14 OSP5 1.20z + 1z brown .30 .35
Nos. NB12-NB14 (3) .90 1.05
Set, never hinged 1.40

To commemorate Hitler's 53rd birthday. Printed in sheets of 25.

Ancient Lublin — OSP6

Designs: 24g+6g, 1z+1z, Modern Lublin.

1942, Aug. 15 Photo. *Perf. 12½*

NB15 OSP6 12g + 8g rose vio .15 .15
NB16 OSP6 24g + 6g henna .15 .15
NB17 OSP6 50g + 50g dp bl .18 .25
NB18 OSP6 1z + 1z dp grn .40 .55
Nos. NB15-NB18 (4) 1.10
Set, never hinged 1.40
Set value .78

600th anniversary of Lublin.

Veit Stoss — OSP8

Adolf Hitler — OSP13

Designs: 24g+26g, Hans Durer. 30g+30g, Johann Schuch. 50g+50g, Joseph Elsner. 1z+1z, Nicolaus Copernicus.

1942, Nov. 20 Engr. *Perf. 13½x14*

NB19 OSP8 12g + 18g dl pur .15 .20
NB20 OSP8 24g + 26g dl henna .15 .20
NB21 OSP8 30g + 30g dl rose vio .15 .20
NB22 OSP8 50g + 50g dl bl vio .20 .25
NB23 OSP8 1z + 1z dl myr grn .40 .45
Nos. NB19-NB23 (5) 1.05 1.30
Set, never hinged 1.40

For overprint see No. NB27.

1943, Apr. 20

NB24 OSP13 12g + 1z purple .15 .22
NB25 OSP13 24g + 1z rose car .15 .22
NB26 OSP13 84g + 1z myrtle grn .38 .42
Nos. NB24-NB26 (3) .68 .86
Set, never hinged 1.20

To commemorate Hitler's 54th birthday.

Type of 1942 Overprinted in Black

24. MAI 1543
24. MAI 1943

1943, May 24

NB27 OSP8 1z + 1z rose lake .80 1.10
Never hinged 1.10

Nicolaus Copernicus (1473-1543), astronomer.

Printed in sheets of 10, with marginal inscription.

Cracow Gate, Lublin — OSP14

Adolf Hitler — OSP19

Designs: 24g+76g, Cloth Hall, Cracow. 30g+70g, New Government Building, Radom. 50g+1z, Bruhl Palace, Warsaw. 1z+2z, Town Hall, Lwow.

The center of the designs is embossed with the emblem of the National Socialist Party.

1943 Photogravure, Embossed

NB28 OSP14 12g + 38g dk grn .15 .15
NB29 OSP14 24g + 76g red .15 .15
NB30 OSP14 30g + 70g rose vio .15 .15
NB31 OSP14 50g + 1z brt bl .15 .15
NB32 OSP14 1z + 2z bl blk .20 .35
Nos. NB28-NB32 (5) .95
Set value .65
Set, never hinged .90

3rd anniversary of the National Socialist Party in Poland.

1944, Apr. 20 Photo. *Perf. 14x13½*

NB33 OSP19 12g + 1z green .15 .18
NB34 OSP19 24g + 1z brn red .15 .18
NB35 OSP19 84g + 1z dk vio .15 .18
Nos. NB33-NB35 (3) .54
Set, never hinged .55
Set value .35

To commemorate Hitler's 55th birthday. Printed in sheets of 25.

Conrad Celtis — OSP20

Designs: 24g+26g, Andreas Schluter. 30g+30g, Hans Boner. 50g+50g, Augustus II. 1z+1z, Georg Gottlieb Pusch.

1944, July 15 Engr. *Perf. 13½x14*

NB36 OSP20 12g + 18g dk grn .15 .15
NB37 OSP20 24g + 26g dk red .15 .15
NB38 OSP20 30g + 30g rose vio .15 .15
NB39 OSP20 50g + 50g ultra .15 .32
NB40 OSP20 1z + 1z dl red brn .15 .32
Set value .54 .88
Set, never hinged .85

Cracow Castle OSP25

1944, Oct. 26 *Perf. 14½*

NB41 OSP25 10z + 10z red & blk 7.50 12.00
Never hinged 11.00
a. Imperf. 9.00
Never hinged 12.00
b. 10z + 10z car & greenish blk 12.50 18.00

5th anniv. of the General Government, Oct. 26, 1944. Printed in sheets of 8.

OCCUPATION RURAL DELIVERY STAMPS

Issued under German Occupation

OSD1

Perf. 13½

1940, Dec. 1 Photo. Unwmk.

NL1	OSD1	10g	red orange	.45	*.65*
NL2	OSD1	20g	red orange	.45	*1.00*
NL3	OSD1	30g	red orange	.45	*1.00*
NL4	OSD1	50g	red orange	1.10	*2.00*
			Nos. NL1-NL4 (4)	2.45	*4.65*
			Set, never hinged	4.00	

OCCUPATION OFFICIAL STAMPS

Issued under German Occupation

Eagle and Swastika OOS1

Perf. 12, 13½x14

1940, Apr. Photo. Unwmk.

Size: 31x23mm

NO1	OOS1	6g	lt brown	.95	1.50
NO2	OOS1	8g	gray	.95	1.50
NO3	OOS1	10g	green	.95	1.50
NO4	OOS1	12g	dk green	1.10	1.90
NO5	OOS1	20g	dk brown	1.10	3.25
NO6	OOS1	24g	henna brn	17.50	.50
NO7	OOS1	30g	rose lake	1.50	2.75
NO8	OOS1	40g	dl violet	1.50	4.50
NO9	OOS1	48g	dl olive	6.25	4.75
NO10	OOS1	50g	royal bl	1.25	2.75
NO11	OOS1	60g	dk ol grn	.95	1.90
NO12	OOS1	80g	rose vio	.95	1.90

Size: 35x26mm

NO13	OOS1	1z	gray blk & brn vio	3.00	4.75
NO14	OOS1	3z	gray blk & chnt	3.00	4.50
NO15	OOS1	5z	gray blk & org brn	4.25	6.25
			Nos. NO1-NO15 (15)	45.20	44.20
			Set, never hinged	65.00	

1940 *Perf. 12*

Size: 21¼x16¼mm

NO16	OOS1	6g	brown	.65	1.10
NO17	OOS1	8g	slate	1.10	1.75
NO18	OOS1	10g	dp grn	1.75	2.00
NO19	OOS1	12g	slate grn	1.75	2.00
NO20	OOS1	20g	blk brn	.90	1.10
NO21	OOS1	24g	cop brn	.65	1.10
NO22	OOS1	30g	rose lake	1.10	1.75
NO23	OOS1	40g	dl pur	1.75	2.00
NO24	OOS1	50g	royal blue	1.75	2.00
			Nos. NO16-NO24 (9)	11.40	14.80
			Set, never hinged	16.00	

Nazi Emblem and Cracow Castle — OOS2

1943 Photo. *Perf. 14*

NO25	OOS2	6g	brown	.15	.15
NO26	OOS2	8g	slate blue	.15	.15
NO27	OOS2	10g	green	.15	.15
NO28	OOS2	12g	dk vio	.35	.24
NO29	OOS2	16g	red org	.15	.15
NO30	OOS2	20g	dk brn	.18	.15
NO31	OOS2	24g	dk red	.35	.15
NO32	OOS2	30g	rose vio	.18	.15
NO33	OOS2	40g	blue	.18	.15
NO34	OOS2	60g	olive grn	.18	.15
NO35	OOS2	80g	dull claret	.28	.15
NO36	OOS2	100g	slate blk	.35	.60
			Nos. NO25-NO36 (12)	2.65	2.34
			Set, never hinged	3.50	

POLISH OFFICES ABROAD

OFFICES IN DANZIG

Poland Nos. 215-225 Overprinted **PORT GDAŃSK**

1925, Jan. 5 Unwmk. *Perf. 11½x12*

1K1	A36	1g	orange brn	.45	1.10
1K2	A36	2g	dk brown	.60	3.25
1K3	A36	3g	orange	.60	1.10
1K4	A36	5g	olive grn	15.00	7.50
1K5	A36	10g	blue grn	5.00	2.25
1K6	A36	15g	red	30.00	5.75
1K7	A36	20g	blue	1.75	1.10
1K8	A36	25g	red brown	1.75	1.10
1K9	A36	30g	dp violet	2.00	1.10
1K10	A36	40g	indigo	2.00	1.10
1K11	A36	50g	magenta	5.50	1.65
			Nos. 1K1-1K11 (11)	64.65	27.00

Same Ovpt. on Poland Nos. 230-231

1926 *Perf. 11½, 12*

1K11A	A39	5g	yellow grn	52.50	37.50
1K12	A40	10g	violet	12.50	15.00

Counterfeit overprints are known on Nos. 1K1-1K32.

No. 232 Overprinted **PORT GDAŃSK**

1926-27

1K13	A41	15g	rose red	45.00	40.00

Same Overprint on Redrawn Stamps of 1926-27

Perf. 13

1K14	A39	5g	yellow grn	2.00	1.75
1K15	A40	10g	violet	2.00	1.75
1K16	A41	15g	rose red	4.00	3.75
1K17	A43	20g	dull red	3.25	2.25
			Nos. 1K14-1K17 (4)	11.25	9.50

Same Ovpt. on Poland Nos. 250, 255a

1928-30 *Perf. 12½*

1K18	A44	25g	yellow brn	4.75	1.50

Laid Paper

Perf. 11½x12, 12½x11½

1K19	A50	1z	blk, *cr* ('30)	30.00	30.00
			Set, never hinged	47.50	

Poland Nos. 258-260 Overprinted **PORT GDAŃSK**

1929-30 *Perf. 12x12½*

1K20	A53	5g	dk violet	1.65	1.40
1K21	A53	10g	green ('30)	1.65	1.40
1K22	A53	25g	red brown	2.75	1.40
			Nos. 1K20-1K22 (3)	6.05	4.20
			Set, never hinged	8.00	

Same Overprint on Poland No. 257

1931, Jan. 5 *Perf. 12½*

1K23	A52	15g	ultra	3.50	4.00
			Never hinged	5.00	

Poland No. 255 Overprinted in Dark Blue **PORT GDAŃSK**

1933, July 1 *Perf. 11½*

Laid Paper

1K24	A50	1z	black, *cream*	82.50	100.00
			Never hinged	110.00	

Poland Nos. 268-270 Overprinted in Black **PORT GDAŃSK**

1934-36 Wmk. 234 *Perf. 12x12½*

1K25	A58	5g	dl violet	3.25	3.75
1K26	A58	10g	green ('36)	35.00	*72.50*
1K27	A58	15g	red brown	3.25	3.75
			Nos. 1K25-1K27 (3)	41.50	*80.00*
			Set, never hinged	60.00	

Poland Nos. 294, 296, 298 Overprinted in Black in one or two lines **PORT GDANSK**

1935-36 Unwmk. *Perf. 12½x13*

1K28	A65	5g	violet blue	3.50	3.00
1K29	A65	15g	Prus green	3.50	4.75
1K30	A65	25g	myrtle green	3.50	2.00
			Nos. 1K28-1K30 (3)	10.50	9.75
			Set, never hinged	14.00	

Same Overprint in Black on Poland Nos. 308, 310

1937, June 5

1K31	A65	5g	violet blue	1.10	1.75
1K32	A65	15g	red brown	1.10	1.75
			Set, never hinged	3.25	

Polish Merchants Selling Wheat in Danzig, 16th Century — A2

1938, Nov. 11 Engr. *Perf. 12½*

1K33	A2	5g	red orange	.65	.95
1K34	A2	15g	red brown	.65	.95
1K35	A2	25g	dull violet	.65	1.65
1K36	A2	55g	brt ultra	1.65	3.00
			Nos. 1K33-1K36 (4)	3.60	6.55
			Set, never hinged	5.25	

OFFICES IN THE TURKISH EMPIRE

Stamps of Poland 1919, Overprinted in Carmine

LEVANT

1919, May Unwmk. *Perf. 11½*

Wove Paper

2K1	A10	3f	bister brn	27.50	24.00
2K2	A10	5f	green	27.50	24.00
2K3	A10	10f	red vio	27.50	24.00
2K4	A10	15f	red	27.50	24.00
2K5	A11	20f	dp blue	27.50	24.00
2K6	A11	25f	olive grn	27.50	24.00
2K7	A11	50f	blue grn	27.50	24.00

Overprinted **L E V A N T**

2K8	A12	1m	violet	27.50	24.00
2K9	A12	1.50m	dp green	27.50	24.00
2K10	A12	2m	dk brown	27.50	24.00
2K11	A13	2.50m	orange brn	27.50	24.00
2K12	A14	5m	red violet	27.50	24.00
			Nos. 2K1-2K12 (12)	330.00	288.00

Counterfeit cancellations are plentiful.

Counterfeits exist of Nos. 2K1-2K12.

Reissues are lighter, shiny red. Value, set $17.50.

Polish stamps with "P.P.C." overprint (Poste Polonaise Constantinople) were used on consular mail for a time.

Seven stamps with these overprints were not issued. Value, set $20.

EXILE GOVERNMENT IN GREAT BRITAIN

These stamps were issued by the Polish government in exile for letters posted from Polish merchant ships and warships.

United States Embassy Ruins, Warsaw — A1

Polish Ministry of Finance Ruins, Warsaw — A2

Destruction of Mickiewicz Monument, Cracow — A3

Polish Submarine "Orzel" — A8

Ruins of Warsaw A4

Polish Machine Gunners A5

Armored Tank — A6

Polish Planes in Great Britain A7

Perf. 12½, 11½x12

1941, Dec. 15 Engr. Unwmk.

3K1	A1	5g	rose violet	.35	.52
3K2	A2	10g	dk bl grn	.75	.70
3K3	A3	25g	black	1.25	1.25
3K4	A4	55g	dark blue	1.50	1.50
3K5	A5	75g	olive grn	3.75	3.75
3K6	A6	80g	dk car rose	3.75	3.75
3K7	A7	1z	slate blue	3.75	3.75
3K8	A8	1.50z	copper brn	3.75	4.25
			Nos. 3K1-3K8 (8)	18.85	19.47
			Set, never hinged	25.00	

These stamps were used for correspondence carried on Polish ships and, on certain days, in Polish Military camps in Great Britain.

For surcharges see Nos. 3K17-3K20.

Polish Air Force in Battle of the Atlantic — A9

Polish Army in France, 1939-40 — A11

Polish Merchant Navy A10

Polish Army in Narvik, Norway, 1940 — A12

The Homeland Fights On — A15

Polish Army in Libya, 1941-42
A13

General Sikorsky and Polish Soldiers in the Middle East, 1943
A14

The Secret Press in Poland
A16

1943, Nov. 1

3K9	A9	5g rose lake	.32	.65
3K10	A10	10g dk bl grn	.65	1.00
3K11	A11	25g dk vio	.65	1.00
3K12	A12	55g sapphire	1.00	1.65
3K13	A13	75g brn car	1.65	2.25
3K14	A14	80g rose car	2.25	2.75
3K15	A15	1z olive blk	2.25	2.75
3K16	A16	1.50z black	3.00	3.25
		Nos. 3K9-3K16 (8)	11.77	15.30
		Set, never hinged	15.00	

Nos. 3K5 to 3K8 Surcharged in Blue

MONTE CASSINO
18. V. 1944

Gr55

Perf. 12½, 11½x12

1944, June 27 **Unwmk.**

3K17	A5	45g on 75g	6.00	6.00
3K18	A6	55g on 80g	6.00	6.00
3K19	A7	80g on 1z	6.00	6.00
3K20	A8	1.20z on 1.50z	6.00	6.00
		Nos. 3K17-3K20 (4)	24.00	24.00
		Set, never hinged	32.50	

Capture of Monte Cassino by the Poles, May 18, 1944.

EXILE GOVERNMENT IN GREAT BRITAIN SEMI-POSTAL STAMP

Heroic Defenders of Warsaw — SP1

Perf. 11½

1945, Feb. 3 **Unwmk.** **Engr.**

3KB1	SP1	1z + 2z slate green	3.75	7.50
		Never hinged	6.00	

Warsaw uprising, Aug. 1-Oct. 3, 1944.

PONTA DELGADA

ˌpän-tə del-ˈgä-də

LOCATION — Administrative district of the Azores comprising the islands of Sao Miguel and Santa Maria
GOVT. — A district of Portugal
AREA — 342 sq. mi.
POP. — 124,000 (approx.)
CAPITAL — Ponta Delgada

1000 Reis = 1 Milreis

King Carlos
A1 A2

Perf. 11½, 12½, 13½

1892-93 **Typo.** **Unwmk.**

1	A1	5r yellow	2.75	1.25
a.		Diagonal half used as 2½r on piece		17.50
b.		Perf. 11½	6.00	1.75
2	A1	10r reddish vio	2.75	1.50
3	A1	15r chocolate	3.25	2.00
4	A1	20r lavender	3.25	2.00
a.		Perf. 13½	6.00	2.00
5	A1	25r deep green	7.50	1.00
6	A1	50r ultra	7.50	2.25
7	A1	75r carmine	6.75	4.50
8	A1	80r yellow grn	11.00	6.50
9	A1	100r brn, *yel*	11.00	5.00
10	A1	150r car, *rose*	62.50	30.00
11	A1	200r dk bl, *bl*	62.50	42.50
12	A1	300r dk bl, *salmon*	62.50	42.50
		Nos. 1-12 (12)	243.25	141.00

The reprints are on paper slightly thinner than that of the originals, and unsurfaced. They have white gum and clean-cut perf. 13½ or 11½. Lowest valued, Nos. 1-9, $4 each, Nos. 10-12, $20 each.

1897-1905 *Perf. 11½*

Name and Value in Black except Nos. 25 and 34

13	A2	2½r gray	.55	.30
14	A2	5r orange	.55	.30
15	A2	10r lt green	.55	.30
16	A2	15r brown	7.75	6.00
17	A2	15r gray grn ('99)	2.00	1.00
18	A2	20r dull violet	2.00	1.00
19	A2	25r sea green	2.50	1.00
20	A2	25r rose red ('99)	2.00	.35
21	A2	50r blue	2.50	1.10
22	A2	50r ultra ('05)	16.00	10.00
23	A2	65r slate blue ('98)	1.25	.40
24	A2	75r rose	6.25	1.10
25	A2	75r brn & car, *yel* ('05)	12.50	6.00
26	A2	80r violet	1.75	1.10
27	A2	100r dk bl, *bl*	3.75	1.10
28	A2	115r org brn, *rose* ('98)	3.00	1.10
29	A2	130r gray brn, *buff* ('98)	2.00	1.10
30	A2	150r lt brn, *buff*	2.00	1.25
31	A2	180r sl, *pnksh* ('98)	2.00	1.25
32	A2	200r red vio, *pnksh*	6.75	5.00
33	A2	300r blue, *rose*	6.75	5.00
a.		Perf. 12½	40.00	27.50
34	A2	500r blk & red, *bl*	14.00	9.00
a.		Perf. 12½	20.00	12.00
		Nos. 13-34 (22)	98.40	54.75

Imperfs are proofs.

The stamps of Ponta Delgada were superseded by those of the Azores, which in 1931 were replaced by those of Portugal.

PORTUGAL

ˈpōr–chi–gəl

LOCATION — Southern Europe, on the western coast of the Iberian Peninsula
GOVT. — Republic
AREA — 35,516 sq. mi.
POP. — 9,930,000 (est. 1983)
CAPITAL — Lisbon

Figures for area and population include the Azores and Madeira, which are integral parts of the republic. The republic was established in 1910. See Azores, Funchal, Madeira.

1000 Reis = 1 Milreis
10 Reis = 1 Centimo
100 Centavos = 1 Escudo (1912)

Catalogue values for unused stamps in this country are for Never Hinged items, beginning with Scott 662 in the regular postage section, Scott C11 in the airpost section, Scott J65 in the postage due section, and Scott O2 in the officials section.

Queen Maria II
A1 A2

A3 A4

Typo. & Embossed

1853 **Unwmk.** *Imperf.*

1	A1	5r reddish brown	2,900.	675.00
2	A2	25r blue	900.00	12.00
3	A3	50r dp yellow grn	3,250.	675.00
a.		50r blue green	6,250.	1,050.
4	A4	100r lilac	27,500.	1,300.

The stamps of the 1853 issue were reprinted in 1864, 1885, 1905 and 1953. Many stamps of subsequent issues were reprinted in 1885 and 1905. The reprints of 1864 are on thin white paper with white gum. The originals have brownish gum which often stains the paper. The reprints of 1885 are on a stout, very white paper. They are usually ungummed, but occasionally have a white gum with yellowish spots. The reprints of 1905 are on creamy white paper of ordinary quality with shiny white gum.

When perforated the reprints of 1885 have a rather rough perforation 13½ with small holes; those of 1905 have a clean-cut perforation 13½ with large holes making sharp pointed teeth.

The colors of the reprints usually differ from those of the originals, but actual comparison is necessary.

The reprints are often from new dies which differ slightly from those used for the originals.

5 reis: There is a defect in the neck which makes the Adam's apple appear very large in the first reprint. The later ones can be distinguished by the paper and the shades and by the absence of the pendant curl.

25 reis: The burelage of the ground work in the original is sharp and clear, while in the 1864 reprints it is blurred in several places; the upper and lower right hand corners are very thick and blurred. The central oval is less than ½mm from the frame at the sides in the originals and fully ¾mm in the 1885 and 1905 reprints.

50 reis: In the reprints of 1864 and 1885 there is a small break in the upper right hand diagonal line of the frame, and the initials of the engraver (F. B. F.), which in the originals are plainly discernible in the lower part of the bust, do not show. The reprints of 1905 have not the break in the frame and the initials are distinct.

100 reis: The small vertical lines at top and bottom at each side of the frame are heavier in the reprints of 1864 than in the originals. The reprints of 1885 and 1905 can be distinguished only by the paper, gum and shades.

Reprints of 1953 have thick paper, no gum and dates "1853/1953" on back.

Values of lowest-cost reprints (1885) of Nos. 1-3, $50 each; of No. 4, $100.

King Pedro V
A5 A6

A7 A8

1855 **With Straight Hair**

TWENTY-FIVE REIS:
Type I - Pearls mostly touch each other and oval outer line.
Type II - Pearls are separate from each other and oval outer line.

5	A5	5r red brown	8,500.	650.00
6	A6	25r blue, type II	950.00	17.50
a.		25r blue, type I	1,100.	20.00
7	A7	50r green	500.00	50.00
8	A8	100r lilac	650.00	75.00

Several types of No. 5 exist, differing in number of pearls encircling head (74 to 89) and other details.

All values were reprinted in 1885 and 1905. Value for lowest-cost, $15 each.
See note after No. 4.

1856 **With Curled Hair**

TWENTY-FIVE REIS:
Type I - The network is fine (single lines).
Type II - The network is coarse (double lines).

9	A5	5r brown (shades)	400.00	47.50
10	A6	25r blue, type II	375.00	10.00
a.		25r blue, type I	8,500.	40.00

1858

11	A6	25r rose, type II	275.00	3.25

The 5r dark brown, formerly listed and sold at about $1, is now believed by the best authorities to be a reprint made before 1866. It is printed on thin yellowish white paper with yellowish white gum and is known only unused. The same remarks will apply to a 25r blue which is common unused but not known used. It is printed from a die which was not used for the issued stamps but the differences are slight and can only be told by expert comparison.

Nos. 9 and 10, also 10a in rose, were reprinted in 1885 and Nos. 9, 10, 10a and 11 in 1905. Value of lowest-cost reprints, $15 each.
See note after No. 4.

King Luiz
A9 A10

A11 A12

A13

1862-64

FIVE REIS:
Type I - The distance between "5" and "reis" is 3mm.
Type II - The distance between "5" and "reis" is 2mm.

12	A9	5r brown, type I	125.00	10.00
a.		5r brown, type II	165.00	20.00
13	A10	10r orange	140.00	35.00
14	A11	25r rose	100.00	3.25
15	A12	50r yellow green	725.00	55.00
16	A13	100r lilac ('64)	775.00	65.00
		Nos. 12-16 (5)	1,865.	168.25

All values were reprinted in 1885 and all except the 25r in 1905. Value of lowest-cost reprints, $10 each.
See note after No. 4.

King Luiz
A14 A15

1866-67 *Imperf.*

17	A14	5r black	110.00	6.50
18	A14	10r yellow	200.00	100.00
19	A14	20r bister	175.00	42.50
20	A14	25r rose ('67)	200.00	5.25
21	A14	50r green	250.00	47.50
22	A14	80r orange	250.00	47.50
23	A14	100r dk lilac ('67)	275.00	67.50
24	A14	120r blue	300.00	50.00
		Nos. 17-24 (8)	1,760.	366.75

Some values with unofficial percé en croix (diamond) perforation were used in Madeira.

All values were reprinted in 1885 and 1905. Value $10 each.
See note after No. 4.

Typographed & Embossed

1867-70 *Perf. 12½*

No.	Type	Description	Unused	Used
25	A14	5r black	125.00	32.50
26	A14	10r yellow	250.00	77.50
27	A14	20r bister ('69)	300.00	77.50
28	A14	25r rose	65.00	4.50
29	A14	50r green ('68)	250.00	77.50
30	A14	80r orange ('69)	350.00	77.50
31	A14	100r lilac ('69)	250.00	77.50
32	A14	120r blue	300.00	47.50
33	A14	240r pale violet ('70)	1,000.	300.00
		Nos. 25-33 (9)	2,890.	772.00

Nos. 25-33 frequently were separated with scissors. Slightly blunted perfs on one or two sides are to be expected for stamps of this issue.

Two types each of 5r and 100r differ in the position of the "5" at upper right and the "100" at lower right in relation to the end of the label.

Nos. 25-33 were reprinted in 1885 and 1905. Some of the 1885 reprints were perforated 12½ as well as 13½. Value of the lowest-cost reprints, $10 each.

See note after No. 4.

1870-84 *Perf. 12½, 13½*

No.	Type	Description	Unused	Used
34	A15	5r black	55.00	4.00
a.		Imperf.	450.00	
b.		Perf. 11		500.00
c.		Perf. 14	200.00	77.50
35	A15	10r yellow ('71)	77.50	19.00
a.		Imperf.	450.00	
b.		Perf. 11		500.00
c.		Perf. 14	400.00	175.00
36	A15	10r blue grn ('79)	375.00	150.00
37	A15	10r yellow grn ('80)	125.00	18.00
38	A15	15r lilac brn ('75)	100.00	19.00
39	A15	20r bister	77.50	16.00
a.		Imperf.	450.00	
b.		Perf. 11		500.00
40	A15	20r rose ('84)	300.00	30.00
41	A15	25r rose	30.00	2.25
a.		Imperf.	450.00	
b.		Perf. 11		500.00
c.		Perf. 14	400.00	14.00
42	A15	50r pale green	140.00	14.00
b.		Perf. 11		500.00
43	A15	50r blue ('79)	325.00	35.00
44	A15	80r orange	125.00	12.00
a.		Perf. 14	1,000.	475.00
b.		Perf. 11		500.00
45	A15	100r pale lilac ('71)	60.00	6.00
a.		Perf. 14	1,250.	475.00
46	A15	120r bl, perf. 12½ ('71)	275.00	40.00
a.		Perf. 13½		—
47	A15	150r pale bl ('76)	350.00	75.00
b.		Perf. 13½	750.00	200.00
48	A15	150r yellow ('80)	140.00	9.00
49	A15	240r pale violet ('73)	1,500.	800.00
b.		Perf. 11		—
50	A15	300r dull violet ('76)	125.00	19.00
51	A15	1000r black ('84)	225.00	45.00

Two types each of 15r, 20r and 80r differ in the distance between the figures of value.

Imperfs probably are proofs.

For overprints and surcharges see Nos. 86-87, 94-96.

All values of the issues of 1870-84 were reprinted in 1885 and 1905. Value of the lowest-cost reprints, $10 each.

See note after No. 4.

King Luiz
A16 A17

A18

A19

1880-81 **Typo.** *Perf. 12½, 13½*

No.	Type	Description	Unused	Used
52	A16	5r black	27.50	2.75
53	A17	25r bluish gray	325.00	19.00
54	A18	25r gray	30.00	2.50
55	A18	25r brown vio ('81)	30.00	2.50
56	A19	50r blue ('81)	325.00	9.50
		Nos. 52-56 (5)	737.50	36.25

All values were reprinted in 1885 and 1905. Value of the lowest-cost reprints, $5 each.

See note after No. 4.

A20

A21

King Luiz
A22 A23

A24

A24a

1882-87 *Perf. 11½, 12½, 13½*

No.	Type	Description	Unused	Used
57	A20	2r black ('84)	22.50	10.00
58	A21	5r black ('83)	14.00	.90
59	A22	10r green ('84)	37.50	2.75
60	A23	25r brown	27.50	1.65
61	A24	50r blue	45.00	2.00
62	A24a	500r black ('84)	500.00	200.00
63	A24a	500r vio, perf. 12½ ('87)	275.00	35.00
a.		Perf. 13½	575.00	250.00
		Nos. 57-63 (7)	921.50	252.30

For overprints see Nos. 79-82, 85, 88-89, 93.

The stamps of the 1882-87 issues were reprinted in 1885, 1893 and 1905. Value of the lowest-cost reprints, $5 each.

See note after No. 4.

A25

A26

1887 *Perf. 11½*

No.	Type	Description	Unused	Used
64	A25	20r rose	45.00	12.00
65	A26	25r violet	30.00	2.00
66	A26	25r lilac rose	30.00	2.00
		Nos. 64-66 (3)	105.00	16.00

For overprints see Nos. 83-84, 90-92.

Nos. 64-66 were reprinted in 1905. Value $5 each. See note after No. 4.

King Carlos — A27

1892-93 *Perf. 11½, 12½, 13½*

No.	Type	Description	Unused	Used
67	A27	5r orange	12.00	1.25
68	A27	10r redsh violet	30.00	1.40
69	A27	15r chocolate	30.00	2.75
70	A27	20r lavender	35.00	6.50
71	A27	25r dk green	27.50	1.25
72	A27	50r blue	35.00	3.75
73	A27	75r carmine ('93)	67.50	5.25
a.		Perf. 11½	325.00	8.50
74	A27	80r yellow grn	90.00	35.00
75	A27	100r brn, *buff* ('93)	65.00	4.25
a.		Perf. 11½	375.00	10.50
76	A27	150r car, *rose* ('93)	165.00	35.00
77	A27	200r dk bl, *bl* ('93)	165.00	30.00
78	A27	300r dk bl, *sal* ('93)	175.00	45.00
		Nos. 67-78 (12)	897.00	171.40

Nos. 76-78 were reprinted in 1900 (perf. 11½), and all values in 1905 (perf. 13½). Values of the lowest-cost reprints of Nos. 67-75, $6 each; of Nos. 76-78, $12 each.

See note after No. 4.

Stamps and Types of Previous Issues Overprinted in Black or Red:

PROVISORIO
a

PROVISORIO
b

c

1892

No.	Type	Description	Unused	Used
79	A21 (a)	5r gray blk	17.00	6.50
a.		Double overprint	650.00	275.00
80	A22 (b)	10r green	17.00	6.50
a.		Inverted overprint	—	—
b.		Double overprint	650.00	275.00

1892-93

No.	Type	Description	Unused	Used
81	A21 (c)	5r gray blk (R)	17.00	5.00
82	A22 (c)	10r green (R)	17.00	6.50
a.		Inverted overprint	150.00	92.50
83	A25 (c)	20r rose	40.00	14.00
a.		Inverted overprint	225.00	200.00
84	A26 (c)	25r rose lilac	14.00	4.00
a.		Perf. 12½	500.00	47.50
85	A24 (c)	50r blue (R) ('93)	77.50	42.50
		Nos. 81-85 (5)	165.50	72.00

1893

No.	Type	Description	Unused	Used
86	A15 (c)	15r bister brn (R)	17.00	9.00
87	A15 (c)	80r yellow	110.00	60.00

Nos. 86-87 are found in two types each. See note below No. 51.

Some of Nos. 79-87 were reprinted in 1900 and all values in 1905. Value of lowest-cost reprint, $10.

See note after No. 4.

Stamps and Types of Previous Issues Overprinted or Surcharged in Black or Red:

d e

1893 *Perf. 11½, 12½*

No.	Type	Description	Unused	Used
88	A21 (d)	5r gray blk (R)	27.50	15.00
89	A22 (d)	10r green (R)	25.00	16.00
a.		"1938"	225.00	160.00
b.		"1863"	225.00	160.00
c.		"1838"	225.00	160.00
d.		Perf. 12½	1,500.	650.00
90	A25 (d)	20r rose	45.00	24.00
a.		Inverted overprint	110.00	65.00
b.		"1938"	250.00	165.00
91	A26 (e)	20r on 25r lil rose	55.00	32.50
92	A26 (d)	25r lilac rose	110.00	65.00
a.		Inverted overprint	250.00	150.00
93	A24 (d)	50r blue (R)	110.00	72.50

Perf. 12½

No.	Type	Description	Unused	Used
94	A15 (e)	50r on 80r yel	125.00	72.50
95	A15 (e)	75r on 80r yel	77.50	47.50
96	A15 (d)	80r yellow	110.00	60.00
		Nos. 88-96 (9)	685.00	405.00

Nos. 94-96 are found in two types each. See note below No. 51.

Some of Nos. 88-96 were reprinted in 1900 and all values in 1905. Value of lowest-cost reprint, $10 each.

See note after No. 4.

Prince Henry on his Ship — A46

Prince Henry Directing Fleet Maneuvers — A47

Symbolic of Prince Henry's Studies — A48

1894 **Litho.** *Perf. 14*

No.	Type	Description	Unused	Used
97	A46	5r orange	3.25	.70
98	A46	10r magenta	3.25	.70
99	A46	15r red brown	8.50	1.75
100	A46	20r dull violet	8.50	2.25
101	A47	25r gray green	8.50	.80
102	A47	50r blue	21.00	3.75
103	A47	75r car rose	40.00	6.50
104	A47	80r yellow grn	40.00	8.00
105	A47	100r lt brn, *pale buff*	32.50	7.75

Engr.

No.	Type	Description	Unused	Used
106	A48	150r lt car, *pale rose*	80.00	16.00
107	A48	300r dk bl, *sal buff*	100.00	18.00
108	A48	500r dp vio, *pale lil*	225.00	42.50
109	A48	1000r gray blk, *grysh*	400.00	55.00
		Nos. 97-109 (13)	970.50	163.70

5th centenary of the birth of Prince Henry the Navigator.

King Carlos — A49

1895-1905 Typo. *Perf. 11½*

Value in Black or Red (#122, 500r)

110	A49	2½r gray	.25	.15
111	A49	5r orange	.25	.20
112	A49	10r lt green	.45	.15
113	A49	15r brown	77.50	1.75
114	A49	15r gray grn ('99)	37.50	1.75
115	A49	20r gray violet	.60	.30
116	A49	25r sea green	55.00	.20
117	A49	25r car rose ('99)	.30	.15
118	A49	50r blue	70.00	.35
119	A49	50r ultra ('05)	.50	.20
120	A49	65r slate bl ('98)	.50	.20
121	A49	75r rose	100.00	3.00
122	A49	75r brn, *yel* ('05)	1.25	.65
123	A49	80r violet	1.90	.85
124	A49	100r dk bl, *bl*	.80	.30
125	A49	115r org brn, *pink* ('98)	4.25	2.00
126	A49	130r gray brn, *straw* ('98)	3.00	1.10
127	A49	150r lt brn, *straw*	125.00	15.00
128	A49	180r sl, *pnksh* ('98)	13.00	6.00
129	A49	200r red lil, *pnksh*	5.50	.90
130	A49	300r blue, *rose*	3.50	1.40
131	A49	500r blk, *bl* ('96)	9.00	3.75
a.		Perf. 12½	110.00	17.00
		Nos. 110-131 (22)	510.05	40.35

Several values of the above type exist without figures of value, also with figures inverted or otherwise misplaced but they were not regularly issued.

St. Anthony and his Vision — A50

St. Anthony Ascends to Heaven — A52

St. Anthony Preaching to Fishes — A51

St. Anthony, from Portrait — A53

Perf. 11½, 12½ and Compound

1895 Typo.

132	A50	2½r black	4.75	1.00

Litho.

133	A51	5r brown org	4.75	1.00
134	A51	10r red lilac	14.00	5.50
135	A51	15r chocolate	15.00	5.50
136	A51	20r gray violet	16.00	6.75
137	A51	25r green & vio	13.00	1.25
138	A52	50r blue & brn	32.50	16.00
139	A52	75r rose & brn	52.50	26.00
140	A52	80r lt grn & brn	65.00	40.00
141	A52	100r choc & blk	57.50	22.50
142	A53	150r carmine & bis	175.00	70.00
143	A53	200r blue & bis	165.00	70.00
144	A53	300r slate & bis	225.00	85.00
145	A53	500r vio brn & grn	400.00	200.00
146	A53	1000r violet & grn	650.00	225.00
		Nos. 132-146 (15)	1,890.	775.50

7th centenary of the birth of Saint Anthony of Padua. Stamps have eulogy in Latin printed on the back.

Common Design Types pictured following the introduction.

Vasco da Gama Issue

Common Design Types

1898 Engr. *Perf. 12½ to 16*

147	CD20	2½r blue green	1.25	.35
148	CD21	5r red	1.25	.35
149	CD22	10r red violet	7.75	1.40
150	CD23	25r yellow green	4.50	.35
151	CD24	50r dark blue	9.25	2.50
152	CD25	75r violet brown	37.50	8.25
153	CD26	100r bister brown	27.50	7.50
154	CD27	150r bister	60.00	20.00
		Nos. 147-154 (8)	149.00	40.70

For overprints and surcharges see Nos. 185-192, 199-206.

King Manuel II
A62 A63

1910 Typo. *Perf. 14½x15*

156	A62	2½r violet	.25	.15
157	A62	5r black	.25	.15
158	A62	10r gray green	.40	.15
159	A62	15r lilac brown	3.00	1.00
160	A62	20r carmine	1.00	.55
161	A62	25r violet brn	.65	.20
162	A62	50r dark blue	1.65	.50
163	A62	75r bister brn	10.00	3.50
164	A62	80r slate	2.75	1.65
165	A62	100r brn, *lt grn*	10.50	2.00
166	A62	200r dk grn, *sal*	6.00	3.00
167	A62	300r blk, *azure*	7.25	3.50
168	A63	500r ol grn & vio brn	14.00	8.00
169	A63	1000r dk bl & blk	32.50	17.50
		Nos. 156-169 (14)	90.20	41.85

For overprint see No. RA1.

Preceding Issue Overprinted in Carmine or Green

1910

170	A62	2½r violet	.40	.15
171	A62	5r black	.40	.15
172	A62	10r gray green	3.00	.75
173	A62	15r lilac brn	1.10	.60
174	A62	20r carmine (G)	4.50	1.65
175	A62	25r violet brn	.95	.20
176	A62	50r dk blue	6.50	1.75
177	A62	75r bister brn	9.50	3.00
178	A62	80r slate	3.50	1.75
179	A62	100r brn, *lt grn*	2.00	.55
180	A62	200r dk grn, *sal*	2.50	1.10
181	A62	300r blk, *azure*	4.00	2.00
182	A63	500r ol grn & vio brn	10.00	5.50
183	A63	1000r dk bl & blk	25.00	14.00
		Nos. 170-183 (14)	73.35	33.15

The numerous inverted and double overprints on this issue were unofficially and fraudulently made. The 50r with blue overprint is a fraud.

Vasco da Gama Issue Overprinted or Surcharged:

REPUBLICA
a

REPUBLICA REPUBLICA

REIS 15 REIS
b

1$000
c

1911 *Perf. 12½ to 16*

185	CD20(a)	2½r blue green	.50	.30
a.		Inverted overprint	12.50	8.00
186	CD21(b)	15r on 5r red	.80	.40
a.		Inverted surcharge	10.00	6.00
187	CD23(a)	25r yellow grn	.60	.50
188	CD24(a)	50r dark blue	3.00	1.10
a.		Inverted overprint		
189	CD25(a)	75r violet brn	40.00	20.00
190	CD27(b)	80r on 150r bis	5.75	3.25
191	CD26(a)	100r bister brn	5.75	1.75
a.		Inverted overprint	25.00	22.50
192	CD22(c)	1000r on 10r red vio	57.50	25.00
		Nos. 185-192 (8)	113.90	52.30

Postage Due Stamps of 1898 Overprinted or Surcharged for Regular Postage:

REPUBLICA

REPUBLICA
d

Rs 300 Rs
e

1911 *Perf. 12*

193	D1(d)	5r black	1.50	1.50
a.		Double ovpt., one inverted	16.00	16.00
194	D1(d)	10r magenta	1.65	1.65
195	D1(d)	20r orange	4.00	2.75
196	D1(d)	200r brn, *buff*	70.00	50.00
197	D1(e)	300r on 50r slate	50.00	35.00
198	D1(e)	500r on 100r car, *pink*	22.50	15.00
a.		Inverted surcharge	60.00	60.00
		Nos. 193-198 (6)	149.65	105.90

Vasco da Gama Issue of Madeira Overprinted or Surcharged Types "a," "b" and "c"

1911 *Perf. 12½ to 16*

199	CD20(a)	2½r blue grn	8.00	6.00
a.		Double overprint		
200	CD21(b)	15r on 5r red	2.00	2.00
a.		Inverted surcharge	12.50	12.50
201	CD23(a)	25r yellow grn	3.75	3.50
202	CD24(a)	50r dk blue	7.00	6.50
a.		Inverted overprint		
203	CD25(a)	75r violet brn	7.00	5.00
a.		Inverted overprint		
204	CD27(b)	80r on 150r bis	8.00	7.50
a.		Inverted surcharge		
205	CD26(a)	100r bister brn	25.00	7.00
a.		Inverted overprint	75.00	75.00
206	CD22(c)	1000r on 10r red vio	25.00	17.00
		Nos. 199-206 (8)	85.75	54.50

Ceres — A64

With Imprint

1912-31 Typo. *Perf. 15x14, 12x11½*

207	A64	¼c dark olive	.35	.25
208	A64	½c black	.35	.25
209	A64	1c deep green	.60	.15
210	A64	1c choc ('18)	.15	.15
211	A64	1½c chocolate	5.00	2.25
212	A64	1½c dp green ('18)	.15	.15
213	A64	2c carmine	5.00	2.25
214	A64	2c orange ('18)	.15	.15
215	A64	2c yellow ('24)	.50	.25
216	A64	2c choc ('26)	1.25	*1.25*
217	A64	2½c violet	.15	.15
218	A64	3c car rose ('17)	.15	.15
219	A64	3c ultra ('21)	.45	.25
220	A64	3½c lt green ('18)	.15	.15
221	A64	4c lt green ('19)	.15	.15
222	A64	4c orange ('26)	1.25	1.25
223	A64	5c deep blue	5.00	.50
224	A64	5c yellow brn ('18)	.90	.35
225	A64	5c olive brn ('23)	.25	.25
226	A64	5c black brn ('31)	.15	.15
227	A64	6c pale rose ('20)	.15	.15
228	A64	6c brown ('24)	.50	.25
229	A64	6c red brn ('30)	.15	.15
230	A64	7½c yellow brn	11.00	2.25
231	A64	7½c dp blue ('18)	.15	.15
232	A64	8c slate	.20	.15
233	A64	8c blue grn ('22)	.40	.25
234	A64	8c orange ('24)	.40	.25
235	A64	10c orange brn	.40	.25
236	A64	10c red ('31)	.40	.25
237	A64	12c bl gray ('20)	1.10	.60
238	A64	12c dp green ('21)	.40	.35
239	A64	13½c chlky bl ('20)	1.25	.40
240	A64	14c dk bl, *yel* ('20)	1.25	.85
241	A64	14c brt violet ('21)	.50	.40
242	A64	15c plum	1.65	.75
243	A64	15c black ('23)	.35	.25
244	A64	16c brt ultra ('24)	.80	.60
245	A64	20c vio brn, *grn*	12.00	1.40
246	A64	20c brn, *buff* ('20)	14.00	3.25
247	A64	20c dk brown ('21)	.45	.25
248	A64	20c dp green ('23)	.15	.15
249	A64	20c gray ('24)	.15	.15
250	A64	24c grnsh bl ('21)	.40	.25
251	A64	25c salmon pink ('23)	.40	.25
252	A64	25c lt gray ('26)	.40	.25
253	A64	25c blue grn ('30)	.80	.25
254	A64	30c brn, *pink*	95.00	8.50
255	A64	30c lt brn, *yel* ('17)	8.00	1.50
256	A64	30c gray brn ('21)	.45	.25
257	A64	30c dk brown ('24)	4.50	1.50
258	A64	32c dp green ('24)	.50	.35
259	A64	36c red ('21)	1.65	.40
260	A64	40c dk bl ('23)	.80	.50
261	A64	40c choc ('24)	.40	.40
262	A64	40c green ('26)	.20	.15
263	A64	48c rose ('24)	5.00	3.00
264	A64	50c org, *sal*	11.00	1.00
265	A64	50c yellow ('21)	1.50	.60
266	A64	50c bister ('30)	2.00	1.25
267	A64	50c red brn ('30)	2.00	.80
268	A64	60c blue ('21)	1.25	.55
269	A64	64c pale ultra ('24)	6.00	4.00
270	A64	75c dull rose ('23)	11.00	5.00
271	A64	75c car rose ('30)	2.00	.80
272	A64	80c brn rose ('21)	1.25	.95
273	A64	80c violet ('24)	.90	.40
274	A64	80c dk green ('30)	2.00	.80
275	A64	90c chalky bl ('21)	1.50	.60
276	A64	96c dp rose ('26)	25.00	22.50
277	A64	1e dp grn, *bl*	6.00	1.00
278	A64	1e violet ('21)	3.50	1.75
a.		Perf. 15x14	125.00	70.00
279	A64	1e dk blue ('23)	4.50	2.00
280	A64	1e gray vio ('24)	1.40	.80
281	A64	1e brn lake ('30)	6.00	.80
282	A64	1.10e yel brn ('21)	3.50	1.50
283	A64	1.20e yel grn ('21)	2.00	1.25
284	A64	1.20e buff ('24)	45.00	30.00
285	A64	1.20e pur brn ('31)	4.00	.80
286	A64	1.25e dk bl ('31)	4.00	.80
287	A64	1.50e blk vio ('23)	12.00	3.00
288	A64	1.50e lilac ('24)	12.00	4.50
289	A64	1.60e dp bl ('24)	17.00	4.50
290	A64	2e sl grn ('21)	50.00	5.00
291	A64	2e red vio ('31)	20.00	6.00
292	A64	2.40e ap grn ('26)	150.00	100.00
293	A64	3e pink ('26)	150.00	90.00
294	A64	3.20e gray grn ('24)	30.00	11.00
295	A64	4.50e org ('31)	60.00	32.50
296	A64	5e emer ('24)	32.50	8.00
297	A64	10e pink ('24)	125.00	45.00
298	A64	20e pale turq ('24)	250.00	150.00
		Nos. 207-298 (92)	1,244.	580.95

See design A85. For surcharges & overprints see #453-495, RA2.

Presidents of Portugal and Brazil and Aviators Cabral and Coutinho — A65

1923 Litho. *Perf. 14*

299	A65	1c brown	.15	*.30*
300	A65	2c orange	.15	*.30*
301	A65	3c ultra	.15	*.30*
302	A65	4c yellow grn	.15	*.30*
303	A65	5c bister brn	.15	*.30*
304	A65	10c brown org	.15	*.30*
305	A65	15c black	.15	*.30*
306	A65	20c blue grn	.15	*.30*
307	A65	25c rose	.15	*.30*
308	A65	30c olive brn	.80	*.80*
309	A65	40c chocolate	.40	*.35*
310	A65	50c yellow	.40	*.40*
311	A65	75c violet	.50	*.80*
312	A65	1e dp blue	.80	*1.00*
313	A65	1.50e olive grn	1.25	*2.50*
314	A65	2e myrtle grn	.70	*2.00*
		Nos. 299-314 (16)	6.20	*10.55*

Flight of Sacadura Cabral and Gago Coutinho from Portugal to Brazil.

Camoens at Ceuta — A66

Camoens Saving the Lusiads — A67

Luis de Camoens — A68

First Edition of the Lusiads — A69

Monument to Camoens — A72

Camoens Dying — A70

Tomb of Camoens A71

Engr.; Values Typo. in Black

1924, Nov. 11 *Perf. 14, 14½*

No.	Type	Value	Color	Unused	Used
315	A66	2c	lt blue	.15	.15
316	A66	3c	orange	.15	.15
317	A66	4c	dk gray	.15	.15
318	A66	5c	yellow grn	.15	.15
319	A66	6c	lake	.15	.15
320	A67	8c	orange brn	.15	.15
321	A67	10c	gray vio	.15	.15
322	A67	15c	olive grn	.15	.15
323	A67	16c	violet brn	.15	.15
324	A67	20c	dp orange	.15	.15
325	A68	25c	lilac	.15	.15
326	A68	30c	dk brown	.15	.15
327	A68	32c	dk green	.80	.80
328	A68	40c	ultra	.15	.15
329	A68	48c	red brown	1.65	1.25
330	A69	50c	red orange	2.00	1.00
331	A69	64c	green	2.00	1.25
332	A69	75c	dk violet	2.00	1.25
333	A69	80c	bister	1.50	1.00
334	A69	96c	lake	1.50	1.00
335	A70	1e	slate	1.25	.80
336	A70	1.20e	lt brown	6.00	3.00
337	A70	1.50e	red	2.00	1.00
338	A70	1.60e	dk blue	2.00	1.00
339	A70	2e	apple grn	6.00	3.00
340	A71	2.40e	green, *grn*	5.00	2.50
341	A71	3e	dk bl, *bl*	2.00	.80
a.			Value double	60.00	
b.			Value omitted		
342	A71	3.20e	blk, *green*	2.00	.80
343	A71	4.50e	blk, *orange*	5.00	3.25
344	A71	10e	dk brn, *pnksh*	8.00	5.00
345	A72	20e	dk vio, *lil*	12.00	5.00
			Nos. 315-345 (31)	64.65	35.65

Birth of Luis de Camoens, poet, 400th anniv.

For overprints see Nos. 1S6-1S71.

Castello-Branco's House at Sao Miguel de Seide — A73

Castello-Branco's Study — A74

Camillo Castello-Branco A75

Teresa de Albuquerque A76

Mariana and Joao de Cruz — A77

Simao de Botelho — A78

1925, Mar. 26 *Perf. 12½*

No.	Type	Value	Color	Unused	Used
346	A73	2c	orange	.15	.15
347	A73	3c	green	.15	.15
348	A73	4c	ultra	.15	.15
349	A73	5c	scarlet	.15	.15
350	A73	6c	brown vio	.15	.15
a.			"6" and "C" omitted		
351	A73	8c	black brn	.15	.15
352	A74	10c	pale blue	.15	.15
353	A75	15c	olive grn	.15	.15
354	A74	16c	red orange	.50	.40
355	A74	20c	dk violet	.50	.40
356	A75	25c	car rose	.50	.40
357	A74	30c	bister brn	.50	.40
358	A74	32c	green	1.40	.85
359	A75	40c	green & blk	.80	.45
360	A74	48c	red brn	3.00	1.75
361	A76	50c	blue green	1.00	.50
362	A76	64c	orange brn	3.50	2.00
363	A76	75c	gray blk	1.40	.80
364	A75	80c	brown	1.40	.80
365	A76	96c	car rose	2.00	.90
366	A76	1e	gray vio	1.40	.60
367	A76	1.20e	yellow grn	2.25	1.50
368	A77	1.50e	dk bl, *bl*	30.00	11.00
369	A75	1.60e	indigo	6.50	3.00
370	A77	2e	dk grn, *grn*	7.50	3.00
371	A77	2.40e	red, *org*	65.00	24.00
372	A77	3e	lake, *bl*	80.00	35.00
373	A77	3.20e	*green*	40.00	24.00
374	A75	4.50e	red & blk	15.00	2.75
375	A77	10e	brn, *yel*	15.00	2.75
376	A78	20e	*orange*	16.00	2.75
			Nos. 346-376 (31)	296.35	121.20

Centenary of the birth of Camillo Castello-Branco, novelist.

First Independence Issue

Alfonso the Conqueror, First King of Portugal — A79

Batalha Monastery and King John I — A80

Battle of Aljubarrota — A81

Filipa de Vilhena Arming her Sons — A82

King John IV (The Duke of Braganza) A83

Independence Monument, Lisbon A84

1926, Aug. 13 *Perf. 14, 14½*

Center in Black

No.	Type	Value	Color	Unused	Used
377	A79	2c	orange	.25	*.25*
378	A80	3c	ultra	.25	*.25*
379	A79	4c	yellow grn	.25	*.25*
380	A80	5c	black brn	.25	*.25*
381	A79	6c	ocher	.25	*.25*
382	A80	15c	dk green	.60	*.25*
383	A79	16c	dp blue	.80	*.60*
384	A81	20c	dull violet	.80	*.60*
385	A82	25c	scarlet	.80	*.60*
386	A81	32c	dp green	1.10	*.85*
387	A82	40c	yellow brn	.60	.40
388	A80	46c	carmine	4.00	*2.50*
389	A82	50c	olive bis	4.00	*2.50*
390	A83	64c	blue green	5.50	*3.00*
391	A82	75c	red brown	5.50	*3.00*
392	A84	96c	dull red	8.00	*4.50*
393	A83	1e	black vio	8.00	*5.25*
394	A81	1.60e	myrtle grn	11.00	*7.00*
395	A84	3e	plum	30.00	*22.50*
396	A84	4.50e	olive grn	40.00	*25.00*
397	A81	10e	carmine	65.00	*40.00*
			Nos. 377-397 (21)	186.95	*119.80*

The use of these stamps instead of the regular issue was obligatory on Aug. 13th and 14th, Nov. 30th and Dec. 1st, 1926.

Surcharged with Bars and

2 C.

1926

Center in Black

No.	Type	Surcharge		Unused	Used
397A	A80	2c	on 5c blk brn	1.50	*1.10*
397B	A80	2c	on 46c car	1.50	*1.10*
397C	A83	2c	on 64c bl grn	1.50	*1.00*
397D	A82	3c	on 75c red brn	1.50	*1.00*
397E	A84	3c	on 96c dull red	2.50	*1.40*
397F	A83	3c	on 1e blk vio	2.00	*1.25*
397G	A81	4c	on 1.60e myr grn	12.50	*8.00*
397H	A84	4c	on 3e plum	5.00	*3.00*
397J	A84	6c	on 4.50e ol grn	5.00	*3.00*
397K	A81	6c	on 10e carmine	5.00	*3.00*
			Nos. 397A-397K (10)	38.00	*23.85*

There are two styles of the ornaments in these surcharges.

Ceres — A85

Without Imprint

1926, Dec. 2 **Typo.** *Perf. 13½x14*

No.	Type	Value	Color	Unused	Used
398	A85	2c	chocolate	.15	.15
399	A85	3c	brt blue	.15	.15
400	A85	4c	dp orange	.15	.15
401	A85	5c	dp brown	.15	.15
402	A85	6c	orange brn	.15	.15
403	A85	10c	orange red	.15	.15
404	A85	15c	black	.15	.15
405	A85	16c	ultra	.15	.15
406	A85	25c	gray	.15	.15
407	A85	32c	dp green	.15	.25
408	A85	40c	blue green	.15	.15
409	A85	48c	rose	1.50	1.25
410	A85	50c	ocher	2.00	1.00
411	A85	64c	deep blue	2.00	1.00
412	A85	80c	violet	4.50	.40
413	A85	96c	car rose	2.50	1.25
414	A85	1e	red brown	11.00	.80
415	A85	1.20e	yellow brn	11.00	.80
416	A85	1.60e	dark blue	3.00	.15
417	A85	2e	green	18.00	.60
418	A85	3.20e	olive grn	8.00	1.00
419	A85	4.50e	yellow	8.00	1.00
420	A85	5e	brown olive	100.00	2.00
421	A85	10e	red	10.00	1.25
			Nos. 398-421 (24)	183.15	14.25

See design A64.

Second Independence Issue

Gonçalo Mendes da Maia — A86

Dr. Joao das Regras — A88

Guimaraes Castle — A87

Battle of Montijo — A89

Brites de Almeida — A90

Joao Pinto Ribeiro — A91

1927, Nov. 29 **Engr.** *Perf. 14*

Center in Black

No.	Type	Value	Color	Unused	Used
422	A86	2c	brown	.15	.15
423	A87	3c	ultra	.15	.15
424	A86	4c	orange	.15	.15
425	A88	5c	olive brn	.15	.15
426	A89	6c	orange brn	.15	.15

427	A87	15c black brn	.80	.60
428	A88	16c deep blue	1.25	*.80*
429	A86	25c gray	1.25	*.80*
430	A89	32c blue grn	2.40	*1.65*
431	A90	40c yellow grn	.80	*.55*
432	A86	48c brown red	13.00	*7.50*
433	A87	80c dk violet	15.00	*10.00*
434	A90	96c dull red	15.00	*10.00*
435	A88	1.60e myrtle grn	18.00	*12.00*
436	A91	4.50e bister	25.00	*17.00*
		Nos. 422-436 (15)	93.25	*61.65*

The use of these stamps instead of the regular issue was compulsory on Nov. 29-30, Dec. 1-2, 1927. The money derived from their sale was used for the purchase of a palace for a war museum, the organization of an international exposition in Lisbon, in 1940, and for fêtes to be held in that year in commemoration of the 8th cent. of the founding of Portugal and the 3rd cent. of its restoration.

Third Independence Issue

Gualdim Paes — A93

The Siege of Santarem — A94

Battle of Rolica — A95

Battle of Atoleiros — A96

Joana de Gouveia — A97

Matias de Albuquerque — A98

1928, Nov. 28

Center in Black

437	A93	2c lt blue	.60	.40
438	A94	3c lt green	.60	.40
439	A95	4c lake	.60	.40
440	A96	5c olive grn	.60	.40
441	A97	6c orange brn	.60	.40
442	A94	15c slate	.80	*.55*
443	A95	16c dk violet	.80	*.55*
444	A93	25c ultra	.80	*.55*
445	A97	32c dk green	3.50	*2.50*
446	A96	40c olive brn	.80	*.70*
447	A95	50c red orange	10.00	*5.00*
448	A94	80c lt gray	10.00	*6.00*
449	A97	96c carmine	20.00	*11.00*
450	A96	1e claret	32.50	*21.00*
451	A93	1.60e dk blue	14.00	*9.00*
452	A98	4.50e yellow	16.00	*9.00*
		Nos. 437-452 (16)	112.20	*67.85*

Obligatory Nov. 27-30. See note after No. 436.

Type and Stamps of 1912-28 Surcharged in Black

1928-29 *Perf. 12x11½, 15x14*

453	A64	4c on 8c orange	.15	.15
454	A64	4c on 30c dk brn	.15	.15
455	A64	10c on ¼c dk ol	.15	.15
a.		Inverted surcharge	5.00	
456	A64	10c on ½c blk (R)	.40	.40
a.		Perf. 15x14	.80	.45
457	A64	10c on 1c choc	.15	.15
a.		Perf. 15x14	*60.00*	*45.00*
458	A64	10c on 4c grn	.15	.15
a.		Perf. 15x14	*70.00*	*55.00*
459	A64	10c on 4c orange	.15	.15
460	A64	10c on 5c ol brn	.15	.15
461	A64	15c on 16c blue	.15	.20
462	A64	15c on 16c ultra	.90	.75
463	A64	15c on 20c brown	25.00	25.00
464	A64	15c on 20c gray	.15	.20
465	A64	15c on 24c grnsh bl	2.00	1.40
466	A64	15c on 25c gray	.15	.15
467	A64	15c on 25c sal pink	.15	.15
468	A64	16c on 32c dp grn	.75	.75
469	A64	40c on 2c orange	.15	.15
470	A64	40c on 2c yellow	4.00	3.00
471	A64	40c on 2c choc	.15	.15
472	A64	40c on 3c ultra	.15	.15
473	A64	40c on 50c yellow	.15	.15
474	A64	40c on 60c dull bl	.65	.60
a.		Perf. 15x14	8.00	6.50
475	A64	40c on 64c pale ultra	.80	.80
476	A64	40c on 75c dl rose	.80	.80
477	A64	40c on 80c violet	.50	.45
478	A64	40c on 90c chlky bl	3.50	2.50
a.		Perf. 15x14	9.00	7.50
479	A64	40c on 1e gray vio	.65	.65
480	A64	40c on 1.10e yel brn	.70	.70
481	A64	80c on 6c pale rose	.70	.70
482	A64	80c on 6c choc	.70	.65
483	A64	80c on 48c rose	.90	.85
484	A64	80c on 1.50e lilac	1.65	.85
485	A64	96c on 1.20e yel grn	3.00	2.00
486	A64	96c on 1.20e buff	3.00	2.50
487	A64	1.60e on 2e slate grn	27.50	21.00
488	A64	1.60e on 3.20e gray grn	8.00	6.00
489	A64	1.60e on 20e pale turq	11.00	7.50
		Nos. 453-489 (37)	99.35	82.20

Stamps of 1912-26 Overprinted in Black or Red **Revalidado**

1929 *Perf. 12x11½*

490	A64	10c orange brn	.15	.15
a.		Perf. 15x14	175.00	175.00
491	A64	15c black (R)	.15	.15
492	A64	40c lt green	.40	.40
493	A64	40c chocolate	.40	.40
494	A64	96c dp rose	4.00	3.50
495	A64	1.60e brt blue	17.00	13.00
a.		Double overprint		
		Nos. 490-495 (6)	22.10	17.60

Liberty A100

"Portugal" Holding Volume of "Lusiads" A101

1929, May *Perf. 12x11½*

496	A100	1.60e on 5c red brn	11.00	9.00

1931-38 **Typo.** *Perf. 14*

497	A101	4c bister brn	.15	.15
498	A101	5c olive gray	.15	.15
499	A101	6c lt gray	.15	.15
500	A101	10c dk violet	.15	.15
501	A101	15c gray blk	.15	.15
502	A101	16c brt blue	1.00	.40
503	A101	25c deep green	3.00	.15
504	A101	25c brt bl ('33)	3.00	.25
505	A101	30c dk grn ('33)	1.40	.25
506	A101	40c orange red	5.00	.15
507	A101	48c fawn	.95	.50
508	A101	50c lt brown	.15	.15
509	A101	75c car rose	4.00	1.25
510	A101	80c emerald	.15	.15
511	A101	95c car rose ('33)	13.00	5.00
512	A101	1e claret	25.00	.15
513	A101	1.20e olive grn	2.00	.80
514	A101	1.25e dk blue	1.50	.15
515	A101	1.60e dk blue ('33)	25.00	3.25
516	A101	1.75e dk blue ('38)	.15	.15
517	A101	2e dull violet	.60	.15
518	A101	4.50e orange	1.25	.15
519	A101	5e yellow grn	1.25	.15
		Nos. 497-519 (23)	89.15	13.95

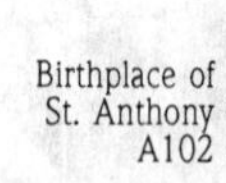

Birthplace of St. Anthony A102

Font where St. Anthony was Baptized A103

Lisbon Cathedral A104

St. Anthony with Infant Jesus A105

Santa Cruz Cathedral A106

St. Anthony's Tomb at Padua A107

1931, June **Typo.** *Perf. 12*

528	A102	15c plum	.80	.40

Litho.

529	A103	25c gray & pale grn	.85	.40
530	A104	40c gray brn & buff	.80	.40
531	A105	75c dl rose & pale rose	30.00	11.00
532	A106	1.25e gray & pale bl	70.00	22.50
533	A107	4.50e gray vio & lil	32.50	2.50
		Nos. 528-533 (6)	134.95	37.20

7th centenary of the death of St. Anthony of Padua and Lisbon.

For surcharges see Nos. 543-548.

Nuno Alvares Pereira (1360-1431), Portuguese Warrior and Statesman — A108

1931, Nov. 1 **Typo.** *Perf. 12x11½*

534	A108	15c black	1.40	1.00
535	A108	25c gray grn & blk	1.40	1.00
536	A108	40c orange	3.50	.60
a.		Value omitted	120.00	120.00
537	A108	75c car rose	26.00	17.00
538	A108	1.25e dk bl & pale bl	35.00	15.00
539	A108	4.50e choc & lt grn	150.00	40.00
a.		Value omitted	300.00	300.00
		Nos. 534-539 (6)	217.30	74.60

For surcharges see Nos. 549-554.

Nos. 528-533 Surcharged **40 C.**

1933 *Perf. 12*

543	A104	15c on 40c	.80	.45
544	A102	40c on 15c	4.00	1.75
545	A103	40c on 25c	.80	.45
546	A105	40c on 75c	8.00	3.25
547	A106	40c on 1.25e	8.00	3.25
548	A107	40c on 4.50e	8.00	3.25
		Nos. 543-548 (6)	29.60	12.40

Nos. 534-539 Surcharged **15 C.**

1933 *Perf. 12x11½*

549	A108	15c on 40c	1.40	.80
550	A108	40c on 15c	2.25	.80
551	A108	40c on 25c	2.25	.80
552	A108	40c on 75c	8.00	4.00
553	A108	40c on 1.25e	8.00	4.00
554	A108	40c on 4.50e	8.00	4.00
		Nos. 549-554 (6)	29.90	14.40

President Carmona A109

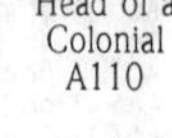
Head of a Colonial A110

1934, May 28 **Typo.** *Perf. 11½*

556	A109	40c brt violet	13.00	.30

1934, July *Perf. 11½x12*

558	A110	25c dk brown	4.00	.80
559	A110	40c scarlet	22.50	.40
560	A110	1.60e dk blue	40.00	11.00
		Nos. 558-560 (3)	66.50	12.20

Colonial Exposition.

Roman Temple, Evora A111

Prince Henry the Navigator A112

"All for the Nation" A113

Coimbra Cathedral A114

1935-41 *Perf. 11½x12*

561	A111	4c black	.15	.15
562	A111	5c blue	.15	.15
563	A111	6c choc ('36)	.15	.15

Perf. 11½, 12x11½ (1.75e)

564	A112	10c turq grn	.60	.15
565	A112	15c red brown	.15	.15
a.		Booklet pane of 4		
566	A113	25c dp blue	4.75	.15
a.		Booklet pane of 4		
567	A113	40c brown	1.00	.15
a.		Booklet pane of 4		
568	A113	1e rose red	7.50	.40
568A	A114	1.75e blue	60.00	1.00
568B	A113	10e gray blk ('41)	17.00	2.00
569	A113	20e turq grn ('41)	24.00	1.50
		Nos. 561-569 (11)	115.45	5.95

For overprint see No. O1.

Queen Maria — A115

Rod and Bowl of Aesculapius — A116

Typographed, Head Embossed

1935, June 1 *Perf. 11½*

570	A115	40c scarlet	1.25	.15

First Portuguese Philatelic Exhibition.

1937, July 24 **Typo.** *Perf. 11½x12*

571	A116	25c blue	8.00	.80

Centenary of the establishment of the School of Medicine in Lisbon and Oporto.

Gil Vicente A117

Grapes A118

1937

572 A117	40c dark brown		14.00	.15
573 A117	1e rose red		2.00	.15
	Set value			.20

400th anniversary of the death of Gil Vicente (1465-1536), Portuguese playwright. Design shows him in cowherd role in his play, "Auto do Vaqueiro."

1938 *Perf. 11½*

575 A118	15c brt purple	.80	.60
576 A118	25c brown	1.75	1.40
577 A118	40c dp red lilac	6.00	.40
578 A118	1.75e dp blue	20.00	20.00
	Nos. 575-578 (4)	28.55	22.40

International Vineyard and Wine Congress.

Emblem of Portuguese Legion — A119

1940, Jan. 27 Unwmk. *Perf. 11½*

579 A119	5c dull yellow	.25	.30
580 A119	10c violet	.25	.30
581 A119	15c brt blue	.30	.30
582 A119	25c brown	10.00	.80
583 A119	40c dk green	20.00	.40
584 A119	80c yellow grn	1.25	.50
585 A119	1e brt red	24.00	2.25
586 A119	1.75e dark blue	4.00	2.00
a.	Souvenir sheet of 8, #579-586	90.00	275.00
	Nos. 579-586 (8)	60.05	6.85

Issued in honor of the Portuguese Legion.
No. 586a sold for 5.50e, the proceeds going to various charities.

Portuguese World Exhibition A120

King John IV — A121

Discoveries Monument, Belém — A122

King Alfonso I — A123

1940 Engr. *Perf. 12x11½, 11½x12*

587 A120	10c brown violet	.20	.15
588 A121	15c dk grnsh bl	.20	.15
589 A122	25c dk slate grn	.70	.40
590 A121	35c yellow green	.60	.50
591 A123	40c olive bister	1.40	.15
592 A120	80c dk violet	3.00	.40
593 A122	1e dark red	6.00	1.25
594 A123	1.75e ultra	4.00	1.65
a.	Souv. sheet of 8, #587-594 ('41)	25.00	60.00
	Nos. 587-594 (8)	16.10	4.65

Portuguese Intl. Exhibition, Lisbon (10c, 80c); restoration of the monarchy, 300th anniv (15c, 35c); Portuguese independence, 800th anniv (40c, 1.75e).
No. 594a sold for 10e.

Sir Rowland Hill — A124

1940, Aug. 12 Typo. *Perf. 11½x12*

595 A124	15c dk violet brn	.20	.15
596 A124	25c dp orange brn	.20	.15
597 A124	35c green	.20	.15
598 A124	40c brown violet	.35	.15
599 A124	50c turq green	10.50	3.00
600 A124	80c lt blue	1.25	1.25
601 A124	1e crimson	12.00	2.50
602 A124	1.75e dk blue	3.25	3.00
a.	Souv. sheet of 8, #595-602 ('41)	22.50	65.00
	Nos. 595-602 (8)	27.95	10.35

Postage stamp centenary.
No. 602a sold for 10e.

Fisherwoman of Nazare A126

Native of Coimbra A127

Native of Saloio — A128

Fisherwoman of Lisbon — A129

Native of Olhao — A130

Native of Aveiro — A131

Native of Madeira A132

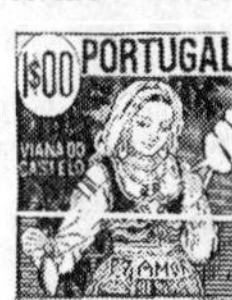
Native of Viana do Castelo A133

Rancher of Ribatejo A134

Peasant of Alentejo A135

1941, Apr. 4 Typo. *Perf. 11½*

605 A126	4c sage green	.20	.15
606 A127	5c orange brn	.20	.15
607 A128	10c red violet	1.65	1.10
608 A129	15c lt yel grn	.20	.30
609 A130	25c rose violet	1.00	.40
610 A131	40c yellow grn	.20	.15
611 A132	80c lt blue	1.65	1.40
612 A133	1e rose red	4.00	1.00

613 A134	1.75e dull blue	5.25	3.50
614 A135	2e red orange	21.00	17.00
a.	Sheet of 10, #605-614	40.00	120.00
	Nos. 605-614 (10)	35.35	25.15

No. 614a sold for 10e.

Ancient Sailing Vessel — A136

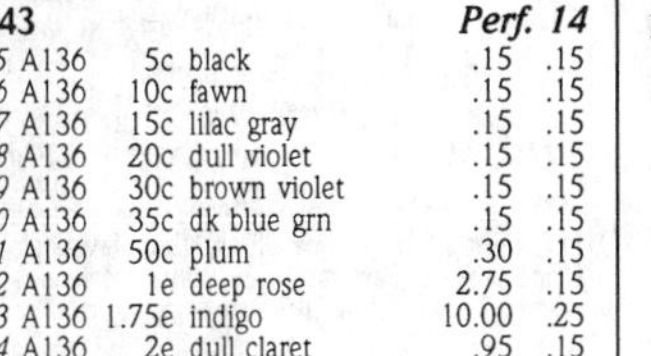

1943 *Perf. 14*

615 A136	5c black	.15	.15
616 A136	10c fawn	.15	.15
617 A136	15c lilac gray	.15	.15
618 A136	20c dull violet	.15	.15
619 A136	30c brown violet	.15	.15
620 A136	35c dk blue grn	.15	.15
621 A136	50c plum	.30	.15
622 A136	1e deep rose	2.75	.15
623 A136	1.75e indigo	10.00	.25
624 A136	2e dull claret	.95	.15
625 A136	2.50e crim rose	1.40	.15
626 A136	3.50e grnsh blue	5.25	.35
627 A136	5e dp orange	.75	.15
628 A136	10e blue gray	1.65	.15
629 A136	15e blue green	14.00	.75
630 A136	20e olive gray	45.00	.20
631 A136	50e salmon	145.00	.55
	Nos. 615-631 (17)	227.95	
	Set value		3.00

See Nos. 702-710.

Farmer A137

Postrider A138

1943, Oct. *Perf. 11½*

632 A137	10c dull blue	.70	.20
633 A137	50c red	1.10	.20

Congress of Agricultural Science.

1944, May Unwmk.

634 A138	10c dk violet brn	.40	.15
635 A138	50c purple	.40	.15
636 A138	1e cerise	2.50	.52
637 A138	1.75e brt blue	2.50	1.25
a.	Sheet of 4, #634-637	18.00	30.00
	Nos. 634-637 (4)	5.80	2.07

3rd Philatelic Exhibition, Lisbon.
No. 637a sold for 7.50e.

Portrait of Avellar Brotero — A139

Statue of Brotero — A140

1944, Nov. 23 Typo. *Perf. 11½x12*

638 A139	10c chocolate	.15	.15
639 A140	50c dull green	.80	.15
640 A140	1e carmine	3.25	.50
641 A139	1.75e dark blue	2.50	1.10
a.	Sheet of 4,#638-641 ('45)	22.50	30.00
	Nos. 638-641 (4)	6.70	1.90

Avellar Brotero, botanist, 200th birth anniv.
No. 641a sold for 7.50e.

Gil Eannes — A141

Designs: 30c, Joao Goncalves Zarco. 35c, Bartolomeu Dias. 50c, Vasco da Gama. 1e, Pedro Alvares Cabral. 1.75e, Fernando Magellan. 2e, Goncalo Velho. 3.50e, Diogo Cao.

1945, July 29 Engr. *Perf. 13½*

642 A141	10c violet brn	.15	.15
643 A141	30c yellow brn	.15	.15
644 A141	35c blue green	.30	.30
645 A141	50c dk olive grn	.60	.30
646 A141	1e vermilion	1.65	.75
647 A141	1.75e slate blue	2.50	1.40
648 A141	2e black	2.75	1.40
649 A141	3.50e carmine rose	5.00	3.25
a.	Sheet of 8, #642-649	15.00	25.00
	Nos. 642-649 (8)	13.10	7.70

Portuguese navigators of 15th and 16th centuries.
No. 649a sold for 15e.

Pres. Antonio Oscar de Fragoso Carmona A149

Astrolabe A150

Perf. 11½

1945, Nov. 12 Photo. Unwmk.

650 A149	10c bright violet	.15	.15
651 A149	30c copper brown	.15	.15
652 A149	35c dark green	.15	.15
653 A149	50c dark olive	.45	.30
654 A149	1e dark red	5.00	1.25
655 A149	1.75e dark blue	4.00	2.75
656 A149	2e deep claret	22.50	3.50
657 A149	3.50e slate black	14.00	5.00
a.	Sheet of 8, #650-657	67.50	85.00
	Nos. 650-657 (8)	46.40	13.25

No. 657a sold for 15e.

1945, Dec. 27 Litho.

658 A150	10c light brown	.15	.15
659 A150	50c gray green	.20	.15
660 A150	1e brown red	1.75	.80
661 A150	1.75e dull chalky blue	1.75	1.75
a.	Sheet of 4, #658-661 ('46)	15.00	22.50
	Nos. 658-661 (4)	3.85	2.85

Centenary of the Portuguese Naval School.
No. 661a, issued Apr. 29, sold for 7.50e.

Catalogue values for unused stamps in this section, from this point to the end of the section, are for Never Hinged items.

Silves Castle A151

Almourol Castle A152

Castles: 30c, Leiria. 35c, Feira. 50c, Guimaraes. 1.75e, Lisbon. 2e, Braganca. 3.50e, Ourem.

1946, June 1 Engr.

662 A151	10c brown vio	.15	.15
663 A151	30c brown red	.15	.15
664 A151	35c olive grn	.15	.15
665 A151	50c gray blk	.35	.30
666 A152	1e brt carmine	10.00	.50
667 A152	1.75e dk blue	8.00	1.00
a.	Sheet of 4	75.00	80.00
668 A152	2e dk gray grn	21.00	1.25
669 A152	3.50e orange brn	13.00	1.40
	Nos. 662-669 (8)	52.80	4.90

No. 667a printed on buff granite paper, size 135x102mm, sold for 12.50e.

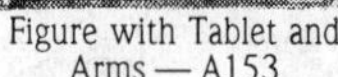

Figure with Tablet and Arms — A153

Madonna and Child — A154

1946, Nov. 19 *Perf. 12x11½*

670 A153 50c dark blue .60 .15
a. Sheet of 4 70.00 70.00

Establishment of the Bank of Portugal, cent.
No. 670a measures 155x143½mm and sold for 7.50e.

1946, Dec. 8 Unwmk. *Perf. 13½*

671 A154 30c gray black .40 .25
672 A154 50c deep green .40 .25
673 A154 1e rose car 2.25 .80
674 A154 1.75e brt blue 4.00 1.00
a. Sheet of 4, #671-674 ('47) 35.00 42.50
Nos. 671-674 (4) 7.05 2.30

300th anniv. of the proclamation making the Virgin Mary patroness of Portugal.
No. 674a sold for 7.50e.

Shepherdess, Caramullo A155

Surrender of the Moors, 1147 A163

30c, Timbrel player, Malpique. 35c, Flute player, Monsanto. 50c, Woman of Avintes. 1e, Field laborer, Maia. 1.75e, Woman of Algarve. 2e, Bastonet player, Miranda. 3.50e, Woman of the Azores.

1947, Mar. 1 Photo. *Perf. 11½*

675 A155 10c rose violet .15 .15
676 A155 30c dark red .15 .15
677 A155 35c dk olive grn .15 .15
678 A155 50c dark brown .30 .15
679 A155 1e red 5.00 .25
680 A155 1.75e slate blue 5.75 1.75
681 A155 2e peacock bl 27.50 1.25
682 A155 3.50e slate blk 13.00 2.00
a. Sheet of 8, #675-682 160.00 190.00
Nos. 675-682 (8) 52.00 5.85

No. 682a sold for 15e.

1947, Oct. 13 Engr. *Perf. 12½*

683 A163 5c blue green .15 .15
684 A163 20c dk carmine .15 .15
685 A163 50c violet .25 .15
686 A163 1.75e dark blue 2.75 2.75
687 A163 2.50e chocolate 4.00 5.00
688 A163 3.50e slate black 6.75 8.00
Nos. 683-688 (6) 14.05 16.20

Conquest of Lisbon from the Moors, 800th anniv.

St. John de Britto
A164 A165

1948, May 28 *Perf. 11½x12*

689 A164 30c green .15 .15
690 A165 50c dark brown .15 .15
691 A164 1e rose carmine 4.50 .60
692 A165 1.75e blue 5.50 .70
Nos. 689-692 (4) 10.30 1.60

Birth of St. John de Britto, 300th anniv.

Architecture and Engineering — A166

King John I — A167

1948, May 28 *Perf. 13x12½*

693 A166 50c violet brn .15 .15

Exposition of public Works and Natl. Congress of Engineering and Architecture, 1948.

Perf. 11½

1949, May 6 Unwmk. Photo.

Designs: 30c, Philippa of Lancaster. 35c, Prince Ferdinand. 50c, Prince Henry the Navigator. 1e, Nuno Alvarez Pereira. 1.75e, John das Regras. 2e, Fernao Lopes. 3.50e, Affonso Domingues.

694 A167 10c brn vio & cr .15 .15
695 A167 30c dk bl grn & cr .15 .15
696 A167 35c dk ol grn & cr .15 .15
697 A167 50c dp blue & cr .55 .15
698 A167 1e dk red & cr .55 .15
699 A167 1.75e dk gray & cr 10.00 4.25
700 A167 2e dk gray bl & cr 5.50 .60
701 A167 3.50e dk brn & gray 16.00 11.00
a. Sheet of 8, #694-701 35.00 27.50
Nos. 694-701 (8) 33.05 16.60

No. 701a sold for 15e.

Ship Type of 1942

1948-49 Typo. *Perf. 14*

702 A136 80c dp green 2.75 .15
703 A136 1e dp claret ('48) 1.65 .15
704 A136 1.20e dp carmine 2.75 .15
705 A136 1.50e olive 18.00 .15
706 A136 1.80e yellow org 18.00 .90
707 A136 2e deep blue 3.50 .20
708 A136 4e orange 22.50 .60
709 A136 6e yellow grn 40.00 .65
710 A136 7.50e grnsh gray 18.00 .90
Nos. 702-710 (9) 127.15 3.85

Angel, Coimbra Museum A168

Symbols of the UPU A169

1949, Dec. 20 Engr. *Perf. 13x14*

711 A168 1e red brown 4.50 .15
712 A168 5e olive brown .60 .15

16th Intl. Congress of History and Art.

1949, Dec. 29

713 A169 1e brown violet .15 .15
714 A169 2e deep blue .25 .15
715 A169 2.50e deep green 1.40 .32
716 A169 4e brown red 4.25 2.00
Nos. 713-716 (4) 6.05 2.62

75th anniv. of the UPU.

Madonna of Fatima A170

St. John of God Helping Ill Man A171

1950, May 13 *Perf. 11½x12*

717 A170 50c dark green .35 .15
718 A170 1e dark brown 1.75 .15
719 A170 2e blue 3.50 .95
720 A170 5e lilac 50.00 11.00
Nos. 717-720 (4) 55.60 12.25

Holy Year, 1950, and to honor "Our Lady of the Rosary" at Fatima.

1950, Oct. 30 Engr. Unwmk.

721 A171 20c gray violet .15 .15
722 A171 50c cerise .25 .15
723 A171 1e olive grn .80 .15
724 A171 1.50e deep orange 6.50 1.25
725 A171 2e blue 5.75 .35
726 A171 4e chocolate 22.50 2.25
Nos. 721-726 (6) 35.95 4.30

400th anniv. of the death of St. John of God.

Guerra Junqueiro — A172

Fisherman and Catch — A173

1951, Mar. 2 Litho. *Perf. 13½*

727 A172 50c dark brown 1.50 .30
728 A172 1e dk slate gray .38 .20

Birth centenary of Guerra Junqueiro, poet.

1951, Mar. 9

729 A173 50c gray grn, *buff* 1.50 .30
730 A173 1e rose lake, *buff* .45 .15

3rd National Congress of Fisheries.

Dove — A174

Pope Pius XII — A175

1951, Oct. 11

731 A174 20c dk brn & buff .25 .15
732 A174 90c dk ol grn & cr 4.50 .55
733 A175 1e dp cl & pink 4.00 .15
734 A175 2.30e dk bl grn & bl 5.00 .50
Nos. 731-734 (4) 13.75
Set value 1.15

End of the Holy Year.

15th Century Colonists, Terceira — A176

1951, Oct. 24 *Perf. 13x13½*

735 A176 50c dk bl, *salmon* 1.00 .25
736 A176 1e dk brn, *cream* .45 .25

500th anniversary (in 1950) of the colonizing of the island of Terceira.

Student, Soldiers and Workers — A177

1951, Nov. 22 *Perf. 13½x13*

737 A177 1e violet brown 1.10 .15
738 A177 2.30e dark blue .90 .28
Set value .35

25th anniversary of the national revolution.

16th Century Coach — A178

Designs: Various coaches.

Perf. 13x13½

1952, Jan. 8 Engr. Unwmk.

739 A178 10c purple .15 .15
740 A178 20c olive gray .15 .15
741 A178 50c steel blue .35 .15
742 A178 90c green 1.10 1.25
743 A178 1e red orange .55 .15
744 A178 1.40e rose pink 3.00 3.50
745 A178 1.50e rose brown 3.50 2.00
746 A178 2.30e deep ultra 1.10 1.25
Nos. 739-746 (8) 9.90 8.60

National Museum of Coaches.

Symbolical of NATO — A179

1952, Apr. 4 Litho. *Perf. 12½*

747 A179 1e green & blk 7.25 .32
748 A179 3.50e gray & vio bl 115.00 15.00
Set, hinged 55.00

North Atlantic Treaty signing, 3rd anniv.

Hockey Players on Roller Skates — A180

1952, June 28 *Perf. 13x13½*

749 A180 1e dk blue & gray 1.75 .15
750 A180 3.50e dk red brown 2.75 1.75

Issued to publicize the 8th World Championship Hockey-on-Skates matches.

Francisco Gomes Teixeira — A181

St. Francis and Two Boys — A182

1952, Nov. 25 *Perf. 14x14½*

751 A181 1e cerise .50 .15
752 A181 2.30e deep blue 2.50 1.75

Centenary of the birth of Francisco Gomes Teixeira (1851-1932), mathematician.

1952, Dec. 23 *Perf. 13½*

753 A182 1e dark green .40 .15
754 A182 2e dp claret 1.10 .25
755 A182 3.50e chalky blue 15.00 5.00
756 A182 5e dark purple 27.50 1.10
Nos. 753-756 (4) 44.00 6.50

400th anniv. of the death of St. Francis Xavier.

Marshal Carmona Bridge A183

Designs: 1.40e, "28th of May" Stadium. 2e, University City, Coimbra. 3.50e, Salazar Dam.

1952, Dec. 10 Unwmk. *Perf. 12½*

Buff Paper

757 A183 1e red brown .35 .20
758 A183 1.40e dull purple 5.00 3.00
759 A183 2e dark green 3.75 1.00
760 A183 3.50e dark blue 6.00 2.50
Nos. 757-760 (4) 15.10 6.70

Centenary of the foundation of the Ministry of Public Works.

Equestrian Seal of King Diniz — A184

1953-56 **Litho.**

761 A184 5c green, *citron* .15 .15
762 A184 10c ind, *salmon* .15 .15
763 A184 20c org red, *cit* .15 .15
763A A184 30c rose lil, *cr* ('56) .15 .15
764 A184 50c gray .15 .15
765 A184 90c dk grn, *cit* 5.25 .20
766 A184 1e vio brn, *rose* .20 .15
767 A184 1.40e rose red 5.25 .35
768 A184 1.50e red, *cream* .20 .15
769 A184 2e gray .20 .15
770 A184 2.30e blue 8.50 .25
771 A184 2.50e gray blk, *sal* .30 .15
772 A184 5e rose vio, *cr* .30 .15
773 A184 10e blue, *citron* .90 .15
774 A184 20e bis brn, *cit* 2.00 .15
775 A184 50e rose violet 2.50 .15
Nos. 761-775 (16) 26.35
Set value 1.50

St. Martin of Braga A185

Guilherme Gomes Fernandes A186

Perf. 13x13½

1953, Feb. 26 **Unwmk.**

776 A185 1e gray blk & gray .50 .15
777 A185 3.50e dk brn & yel 4.50 3.50

14th centenary of the arrival of St. Martin of Dume on the Iberian peninsula.

1953, Mar. 28 *Perf. 13*

778 A186 1e red violet .45 .15
779 A186 2.30e deep blue 3.75 3.00

Birth of Guilherme Gomes Fernandes, General Inspector of the Firemen of Porto.

Emblems of Automobile Club A187

1953, Apr. 15 *Perf. 12½*

780 A187 1e dk grn & yel grn .45 .15
781 A187 3.50e dk brn & buff 4.75 2.75

Portuguese Automobile Club, 50th anniv.

Princess St. Joanna — A188

Queen Maria II — A189

Perf. 14½x14

1953, May 14 **Litho.** **Unwmk.**

782 A188 1e blk & gray grn 1.00 .15
783 A188 3.50e dk blue & blue 5.00 3.75

Birth of Princess St. Joanna, 500th anniv.

1953, Oct. 3 **Photo.** *Perf. 13½*

Background of Lower Panel in Gold

784 A189 50c red brown .15 .15
785 A189 1e claret brn .15 .15
786 A189 1.40e dk violet .95 .45
787 A189 2.30e dp blue 2.25 1.25
788 A189 3.50e violet blue 2.25 1.25
789 A189 4.50e dk blue grn 1.90 .55
790 A189 5e dk ol grn 3.50 .45
791 A189 20e red violet 32.50 6.25
Nos. 784-791 (8) 43.65 10.50

Centenary of Portugal's first postage stamp.

Allegory — A190

1954, Sept. 22 *Perf. 13*

792 A190 1e bl & dk grnsh bl .60 .15
793 A190 1.50e buff & dk brn 1.25 .30

150th anniversary of the founding of the State Secretariat for Financial Affairs.

Open Textbook — A191

Cadet and College Arms — A192

1954, Oct. 15 **Litho.**

794 A191 50c blue .15 .15
795 A191 1e red .15 .15
796 A191 2e dk green 11.00 .25
797 A191 2.50e orange brn 9.50 .48
Nos. 794-797 (4) 20.80
Set value .82

National literacy campaign.

1954, Nov. 17

798 A192 1e choc & lt grn .75 .15
799 A192 3.50e dk bl & gray grn 2.00 1.25

150th anniversary of the Military College.

Manuel da Nobrega and Crucifix — A193

King Alfonso I — A194

1954, Dec. 17 **Engr.** *Perf. 14x13*

800 A193 1e brown .30 .15
801 A193 2.30e deep blue 19.00 15.00
802 A193 3.50e gray green 5.50 2.00
803 A193 5e green 17.00 3.00
Nos. 800-803 (4) 41.80 20.15

Founding of Sao Paulo, Brazil, 400th anniv.

1955, Mar. 17 *Perf. 13½x13*

Kings: 20c, Sancho I. 50c, Alfonso II. 90c, Sancho II. 1e, Alfonso III. 1.40e, Diniz. 1.50e, Alfonso IV. 2e, Pedro I. 2.30e, Ferdinand I.

804 A194 10c rose violet .15 .15
805 A194 20c dk olive grn .15 .15
806 A194 50c dk blue grn .15 .15
807 A194 90c green 1.10 .65
808 A194 1e red brown .50 .15
809 A194 1.40e carmine rose 3.00 1.75
810 A194 1.50e olive brn 1.25 .55
811 A194 2e deep orange 3.75 1.65
812 A194 2.30e violet blue 3.75 1.40
Nos. 804-812 (9) 13.80 6.60

Telegraph Pole — A195

A. J. Ferreira da Silva — A196

1955, Sept. 16 **Litho.** *Perf. 13½*

813 A195 1e ocher & hn brn .40 .15
814 A195 2.30e gray grn & Prus bl 6.50 1.50
815 A195 3.50e lemon & dp grn 6.50 .80
Nos. 813-815 (3) 13.40 2.45

Centenary of the telegraph system in Portugal.

1956, May 8 **Photo.** **Unwmk.**

816 A196 1e blue & dk blue .50 .15
817 A196 2.30e grn & dk grn 3.00 1.75

Centenary of the birth of Prof. Antonio Joaquim Ferreira da Silva, chemist.

Steam Locomotive, 1856 A197

Madonna, 15th Century A198

Design: 1.50e, 2e, Electric train, 1956.

1956, Oct. 28 **Litho.** *Perf. 13*

818 A197 1e lt & dk ol grn .40 .15
819 A197 1.50e Prus bl & lt grnsh bl 1.50 .15
820 A197 2e dk org brn & bis 12.00 .45
821 A197 2.50e choc & brn 14.00 .60
Nos. 818-821 (4) 27.90 1.35

Centenary of the Portuguese railways.

1956, Dec. 8 **Photo.**

822 A198 1e dp grn & lt ol grn .22 .15
823 A198 1.50e dk red brn & ol bis .42 .25
Set value .32

Mothers' Day, Dec. 8.

J. B. Almeida Garrett A199

1957, Mar. 7 **Engr.** *Perf. 13½x14*

824 A199 1e sepia .35 .15
825 A199 2.30e lt purple 12.50 4.00
826 A199 3.50e dull green 2.50 .65
827 A199 5e rose carmine 20.00 5.50
Nos. 824-827 (4) 35.35 10.30

Issued in honor of Joao Baptista da Silva Leitao de Almeida Garrett, poet.

Cesario Verde A200

Exhibition Emblems A201

1957, Dec. 12 **Litho.** *Perf. 13½*

828 A200 1e citron & brown .50 .15
829 A200 3.30e gray grn, yel grn & dk ol 1.50 .60

Jose Joaquim de Cesario Verde (1855-86), poet.

1958, Apr. 7

830 A201 1e multicolored .20 .15
831 A201 3.30e multicolored .75 .55
Set value .60

Universal & Intl. Exposition at Brussels.

Queen St. Isabel — A202

Institute for Tropical Medicine — A203

Design: 2e, 5e, St. Teotonio.

Perf. 14½x14

1958, July 10 **Photo.** **Unwmk.**

832 A202 1e rose brn & buff .15 .15
833 A202 2e dk green & buff .30 .15
834 A202 2.50e purple & buff 1.00 .20
835 A202 5e brown & buff 2.00 .25
Nos. 832-835 (4) 3.45
Set value .65

1958, Sept. 4 **Litho.** *Perf. 13*

836 A203 1e dk grn & lt gray .75 .15
837 A203 2.50e bl & pale bl 2.00 .35
Set value .40

6th Intl. Cong. for Tropical Medicine and Malaria, Lisbon, Sept. 1958, and opening of the new Tropical Medicine Institute.

Cargo Ship and Loading Crane — A204

1958, Nov. 27 **Unwmk.** *Perf. 13*

838 A204 1e brn & dk brn 1.50 .15
839 A204 4.50e vio bl & dk bl 1.25 .55
Set value .60

2nd Natl. Cong. of the Merchant Marine, Porto.

Queen Leonor — A205

1958, Dec. 17

840 A205 1e multi .20 .15
841 A205 1.50e bis, blk, bl & dk bis brn 1.90 .15
a. Dark bister brown omitted
842 A205 2.30e multi 1.50 .20
843 A205 4.10e multi 1.50 .30
Nos. 840-843 (4) 5.10
Set value .60

500th anniv. of the birth of Queen Leonor.

Arms of Aveiro — A206

Symbols of Hope and Peace — A207

1959, Aug. 30 **Litho.** *Perf. 13*

844 A206 1e ol bis, brn, gold & sil .40 .15
845 A206 5e grnsh gray, gold & sil 2.75 .35

Millennium of Aveiro.

1960, Mar. 2 *Perf. 12½*

846 A207 1e lt violet & blk .40 .15
847 A207 3.50e gray & dk grn 1.75 1.75

10th anniversary (in 1959) of NATO.

Open Door to "Peace" and WRY Emblem A208

Glider A209

1960, Apr. 7 **Unwmk.** *Perf. 13*

848 A208 20c multi .15 .15
849 A208 1e multi .32 .15
850 A208 1.80e yel grn, org & blk .35 .42
Nos. 848-850 (3) .82
Set value .58

World Refugee Year, 7/1/59-6/30/60.

1960, May 2

Designs: 1.50e, Plane. 2e, Plane and parachutes. 2.50e, Model plane.

851 A209 1e yellow, gray & blue .15 .15
852 A209 1.50e multicolored .52 .22
853 A209 2e bl grn, yel & blk .75 .35
854 A209 2.50e grnsh bl, ocher & red 1.40 .45
Nos. 851-854 (4) 2.82 1.17

Aero Club of Portugal, 50th anniv. (in 1959).

Father Cruz — A210

University of Evora Seal — A211

1960, July 18 Unwmk. *Perf. 13*

855 A210 1e deep brown .15 .15
856 A210 4.30e Prus blue & blk 2.75 2.50

Father Cruz, "father of the poor."

1960, July 18 Litho.

857 A211 50c violet blue .15 .15
858 A211 1e red brn & yel .20 .15
859 A211 1.40e rose cl & rose 1.65 .50
Nos. 857-859 (3) 2.00
Set value .62

Founding of the University of Evora, 400th anniv.

Arms of Prince Henry — A212

Arms of Lisbon and Symbolic Ship — A213

Designs: 2.50e, Caravel. 3.50e, Prince Henry. 5e, Prince Henry's motto. 8e, Prince Henry's sloop. 10e, Old chart of Sagres region of Portugal.

1960, Aug. 4 Photo. *Perf. 12x12½*

860 A212 1e gold & multi .15 .15
861 A212 2.50e gold & multi 1.10 .32
862 A212 3.50e gold & multi 1.25 1.10
863 A212 5e gold & multi 2.25 .42
864 A212 8e gold & multi .50 .42
865 A212 10e gold & multi 3.75 1.65
Nos. 860-865 (6) 9.00 4.06

500th anniversary of the death of Prince Henry the Navigator.

Europa Issue, 1960
Common Design Type

1960, Sept. 16 Litho. *Perf. 13*
Size: 31x21mm

866 CD3 1e ultra & gray blue .16 .15
867 CD3 3.50e brn red & rose red 1.65 1.65

1960, Nov. 17 *Perf. 13*

868 A213 1e gray ol, blk & vio bl .28 .15
869 A213 3.30e bl, blk & ultra 2.50 2.50

5th Natl. Philatelic Exhibition, Lisbon, part of the Prince Henry the Navigator festivities. (The ship in the design is in honor of Prince Henry).

Flag and Laurel — A214

1960, Dec. 20 Litho. *Perf. 13*

870 A214 1e multicolored .22 .20

50th anniversary of the Republic.

King Pedro V — A215

1961, Aug. 3 Engr. *Perf. 13*

871 A215 1e gray brn & dk grn .22 .15
872 A215 6.50e dk blue & blk .95 .45

Centenary of the founding of the Faculty of Letters, Lisbon University.

Setubal Sea Gate and Ships — A216

1961, Aug. 24 Litho. *Perf. 12x11½*

873 A216 1e gold & multi .20 .15
874 A216 4.30e gold & multi 4.25 3.00

Centenary of the city of Setubal.

Clasped Hands and CEPT Emblem — A217

Tomar Castle and River Nabao — A218

Europa Issue, 1961

1961, Sept. 18 *Perf. 13½x13*

875 A217 1e blue & lt blue .15 .15
876 A217 1.50e green & brt green .60 .60
877 A217 3.50e brown, pink & red .90 .90
Nos. 875-877 (3) 1.65 1.65

1962, Jan. 26 *Perf. 11½x12*

878 A218 1e gold & multi .15 .15
879 A218 3.50e gold & multi .95 .90

800th anniversary of the city of Tomar.

National Guardsman A219

Archangel Gabriel A220

1962, Feb. 20 Unwmk. *Perf. 13½*

880 A219 1e multi .15 .15
881 A219 2e multi 1.10 .30
882 A219 2.50e multi .90 .25
Nos. 880-882 (3) 2.15
Set value .60

50th anniv. of the Republican National Guard.

1962, Mar. 24 Litho. *Perf. 13*

883 A220 1e ol, pink & red brn .50 .15
884 A220 3.50e ol, pink & dk grn .30 .30
Set value .36

Issued for St. Gabriel's Day. St. Gabriel is patron of telecommunications.

Tents and Scout Emblem — A221

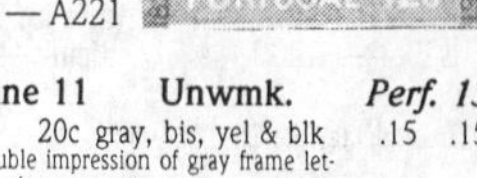

1962, June 11 Unwmk. *Perf. 13*

885 A221 20c gray, bis, yel & blk .15 .15
a. Double impression of gray frame lettering
886 A221 50c multi .15 .15
887 A221 1e multi .32 .15
888 A221 2.50e multi 1.50 .25
889 A221 3.50e multi .35 .30
890 A221 6.50e multi .35 .30
Nos. 885-890 (6) 2.82
Set value 1.08

50th anniv. of the Portuguese Boy Scouts and the 18th Boy Scout World Conf., Sept. 19-24, 1961.

Children Reading — A222

Designs: 1e, Vaccination. 2.80e, Children playing ball. 3.50e, Guarding sleeping infant.

1962, Sept. 10 Litho. *Perf. 13½*

891 A222 50c bluish grn, yel & blk .15 .15
892 A222 1e pale bl, yel & blk .42 .15
893 A222 2.80e dp org yel & blk .85 .50
894 A222 3.50e dl rose, yel & blk 1.25 .85
Nos. 891-894 (4) 2.67
Set value 1.45

10th Intl. Cong. of Pediatrics, Lisbon, Sept. 9-15.

19-Cell Honeycomb A223

1962, Sept. 17

895 A223 1e bl, dk bl & gold .15 .15
896 A223 1.50e lt & dk grn & gold .52 .40
897 A223 3.50e dp rose, mar & gold .50 .65
Nos. 895-897 (3) 1.17 1.20

Europa. The 19 cells represent the 19 original members of the Conference of European Postal and Telecommunications Administrations, C.E.P.T.

St. Zenon, the Courier A224

European Soccer Cup and Emblem A225

1962, Dec. 1 Unwmk. *Perf. 13½*

898 A224 1e multi .15 .15
899 A224 2e multi .52 .50
900 A224 2.80e multi 1.00 1.00
Nos. 898-900 (3) 1.67 1.65

Issued for Stamp Day.

1963, Feb. 5 *Perf. 13½*

901 A225 1e multi .38 .15
902 A225 4.30e multi .75 .75

Victories of the Benfica Club of Lisbon in the 1961 and 1962 European Soccer Championships.

Wheat Emblem — A226

1963, Mar. 21 Litho.

903 A226 1e multi .15 .15
904 A226 3.30e multi .60 .70
905 A226 3.50e multi .70 .50
Nos. 903-905 (3) 1.45 1.35

FAO "Freedom from Hunger" campaign.

Stagecoach A227

1963, May 7 *Perf. 12x11½*

906 A227 1e gray, lt & dk bl .15 .15
907 A227 1.50e bis, dk brn & lil rose .80 .25
908 A227 5e org brn, dk brn & rose lil .18 .22
Nos. 906-908 (3) 1.13 .62

1st Intl. Postal Conference, Paris, 1863.

St. Vincent de Paul by Monsaraz — A228

1963, July 10 Photo. *Perf. 13½x14*
Gold Inscription

909 A228 20c lt blue & ultra .15 .15
a. Gold inscription omitted 55.00
910 A228 1e gray & slate .16 .15
911 A228 2.80e green & slate .80 .80
a. Gold inscription omitted 65.00
912 A228 5e dp rose car & sl .80 .38
Nos. 909-912 (4) 1.91
Set value 1.30

Tercentenary of the death of St. Vincent de Paul.

Emblem of Order and Knight A229

1963, Aug. 13 Litho. *Perf. 11½*

913 A229 1e multi .15 .15
914 A229 1.50e multi .18 .15
915 A229 2.50e multi 1.25 .32
Nos. 913-915 (3) 1.58
Set value .46

800th anniv. of the Military Order of Avis.

Europa Issue, 1963

Stylized Bird — A230

1963, Sept. 16 *Perf. 13½*

916 A230 1e lt bl, gray & blk .16 .15
917 A230 1.50e grn, gray & blk 1.10 .48
918 A230 3.50e red, gray & blk 1.40 1.10
Nos. 916-918 (3) 2.66 1.73

Jet Plane — A231

Apothecary Jar — A232

1963, Dec. 1 Unwmk. *Perf. 13½*

919 A231 1e dk bl & lt bl .15 .15
920 A231 2.50e dk grn & yel grn .65 .28
921 A231 3.50e org brn & org .85 .55
Nos. 919-921 (3) 1.65 .98

Transportes Aéreos Portugueses, TAP, 10th anniv.

1964, Apr. 9 Litho.

922 A232 50c brn ol, dk brn & blk .15 .15
923 A232 1e rose brn, dp cl & blk .15 .15
924 A232 4.30e dk gray, sl & blk 3.25 3.25
Nos. 922-924 (3) 3.55 3.55

4th centenary of the publication (in Goa, Apr. 10, 1563) of "Coloquios Dos Simples e Drogas" (Herbs and Drugs in India) by Garcia D'Orta.

Emblem of National Overseas Bank — A233

Mt. Sameiro Church — A234

1964, May 19 Unwmk. Perf. 13 1/2
925 A233 1e bister, yel & dk bl .15 .15
926 A233 2.50e ocher, yel & grn 1.00 .38
927 A233 3.50e bister, yel & brn .70 .50
Nos. 925-927 (3) 1.85 1.03

Centenary of National Overseas Bank.

1964, June 5 Litho.
928 A234 1e red brn, bis & dl brn .15 .15
929 A234 2e brn, bis & dl brn .52 .30
930 A234 5e dk vio bl, bis & gray .75 .48
Nos. 928-930 (3) 1.42 .93

Centenary of the Shrine of Our Lady of Mt. Sameiro, Braga.

Europa Issue, 1964
Common Design Type

1964, Sept. 14 Unwmk. Perf. 13 1/2
Size: 19x32mm.
931 CD7 1e bl, lt bl & dk bl .20 .15
932 CD7 3.50e rose brn, buff & dk brn .90 .55
933 CD7 4.30e grn, yel grn & dk grn 1.40 2.00
Nos. 931-933 (3) 2.50 2.70

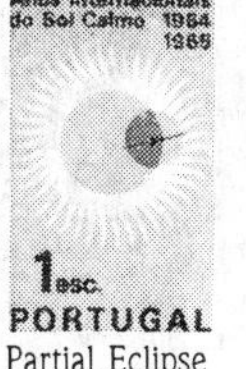

Partial Eclipse of Sun — A235

Olympic Rings, Emblems of Portugal and Japan — A236

1964
934 A235 1e multicolored .18 .15
935 A235 8e multicolored .70 .45
Set value .50

International Quiet Sun Year, 1964-65.

1964, Dec. 1 Unwmk. Perf. 13 1/2
Black Inscriptions; Olympic Rings in Pale Yellow
936 A236 20c tan, red & vio bl .15 .15
937 A236 1e ultra, red & vio bl .15 .15
938 A236 1.50e yel grn, red & vio bl .90 .45
939 A236 6.50e rose lil, red & vio bl 1.00 1.00
Nos. 936-939 (4) 2.20 1.75

18th Olympic Games, Tokyo, Oct. 10-25.

Eduardo Coelho — A237

Traffic Signs and Signals — A238

1964, Dec. 28 Litho. Perf. 13 1/2
940 A237 1e multicolored .15 .15
941 A237 5e multicolored .85 .65

Centenary of the founding of Portugal's first newspaper, "Diario de Noticias," and to honor the founder, Eduardo Coelho, journalist.

1965, Feb. 15 Litho.
942 A238 1e yellow, red & emer .15 .15
943 A238 3.30e multicolored 1.75 2.00
944 A238 3.50e red, yellow & emer .85 .45
Nos. 942-944 (3) 2.75 2.60

1st National Traffic Cong., Lisbon, Feb. 15-19.

Ferdinand I, Duke of Braganza — A239

Coimbra Gate, Angel with Censer and Sword — A240

1965, Mar. 16 Unwmk. Perf. 13 1/2
945 A239 1e rose brown & blk .15 .15
946 A239 10e Prus green & blk .90 .65

500th anniv. of the city of Braganza (in 1964).

1965, Apr. 27 Perf. 11 1/2x12
947 A240 1e blue & multi .15 .15
948 A240 2.50e multi .90 .40
949 A240 5e multi 1.00 .65
Nos. 947-949 (3) 2.05 1.20

9th centenary (in 1964) of the capture of the city of Coimbra from the Moors.

ITU Emblem — A241

1965, May 17 Perf. 13 1/2
950 A241 1e bis brn, ol grn & ol .15 .15
951 A241 3.50e ol, rose cl & dp cl .80 .40
952 A241 6.50e yel grn, dl bl & sl bl .45 .35
Nos. 950-952 (3) 1.40 .90

International Telecommunication Union, cent.

Calouste Gulbenkian A242

1965, July 20 Litho. Perf. 13 1/2
953 A242 1e multicolored .35 .15
954 A242 8e multicolored .35 .30
Set value .36

Gulbenkian (1869-1955), oil industry pioneer and sponsor of the Gulbenkian Foundation.

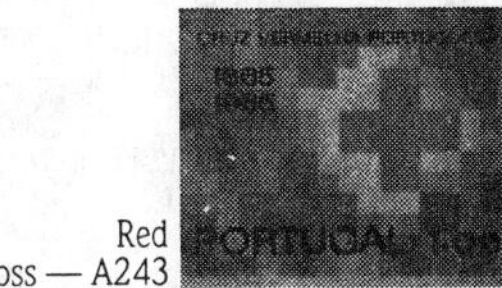
Red Cross — A243

1965, Aug. 17 Unwmk. Perf. 13 1/2
955 A243 1e green, red & blk .15 .15
956 A243 4e olive, red & blk .75 .60
957 A243 4.30e lt rose brn, red & blk 4.50 4.50
Nos. 955-957 (3) 5.40 5.25

Centenary of the Portuguese Red Cross.

Europa Issue, 1965
Common Design Type

1965, Sept. 27 Litho. Perf. 13
Size: 31x24mm
958 CD8 1e saph, grnsh bl & dk bl .15 .15
959 CD8 3.50e rose brn, sal & brn 1.10 1.10
960 CD8 4.30e grn, yel grn & dk grn 3.25 2.25
Nos. 958-960 (3) 4.50 3.50

Military Plane — A244

1965, Oct. 20 Perf. 13 1/2
961 A244 1e ol grn, red & dk grn .15 .15
962 A244 2e sepia, red & dk grn .65 .30
963 A244 5e chlky bl, red & dk grn 1.10 .60
Nos. 961-963 (3) 1.90 1.05

Portuguese Air Force founding, 50th anniv.

Woman — A245

Chrismon with Alpha and Omega — A246

Designs: Characters from Gil Vicente Plays.

1965, Dec. 1 Litho. Perf. 13 1/2
964 A245 20c ol, pale yel & blk .15 .15
965 A245 1e brn, pale yel & blk .15 .15
966 A245 2.50e dk red, buff & blk 1.25 .22
967 A245 6.50e blue, gray & blk .25 .22
Nos. 964-967 (4) 1.80
Set value .58

Gil Vicente (1465?-1536?).

1966, Mar. 28 Litho. Perf. 13 1/2
968 A246 1e ol bis, gold & blk .18 .15
969 A246 3.30e gray, gold & blk 1.75 1.50
970 A246 5e rose cl, gold & blk 1.00 .45
Nos. 968-970 (3) 2.93 2.10

Congress of the International Committee for the Defense of Christian Civilization, Lisbon.

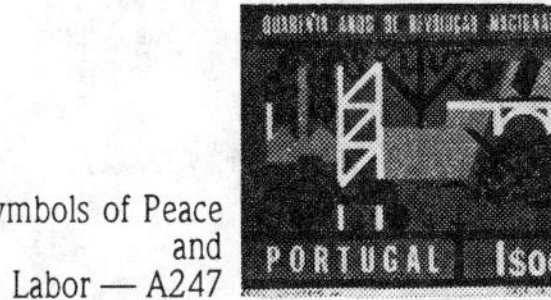

Symbols of Peace and Labor — A247

1966, May 28 Litho. Perf. 13 1/2
971 A247 1e dk bl, sl bl & lt sl bl .15 .15
972 A247 3.50e ol, ol brn, & lt ol .75 .42
973 A247 4e dk brn, brn car & dl rose .60 .35
Nos. 971-973 (3) 1.50 .92

40th anniversary of National Revolution.

Knight Giraldo on Horseback A248

1966, June 8
974 A248 1e multicolored .30 .15
975 A248 8e multicolored .35 .35
Set value .42

Conquest of Evora from the Moors, 800th anniv.

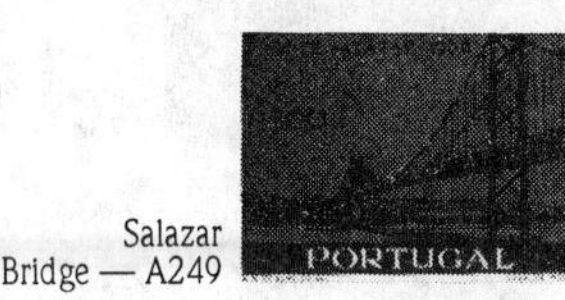

Salazar Bridge — A249

Designs: 2.80e, 4.30e, View of bridge, vert.

1966, Aug. 6 Litho. Perf. 13 1/2
976 A249 1e gold & red .15 .15
977 A249 2.50e gold & ultra .90 .35
978 A249 2.80e silver & dp ultra 1.00 .90
979 A249 4.30e silver & dk grn 1.00 .90
Nos. 976-979 (4) 3.05 2.30

Issued to commemorate the opening of the Salazar Bridge over the Tejo River, Lisbon.

Europa Issue, 1966
Common Design Type

1966, Sept. 26 Litho. Perf. 11 1/2x12
Size: 26x32mm
980 CD9 1e blue & blk .15 .15
981 CD9 3.50e red brn & blk 1.65 1.65
982 CD9 4.30e yel grn & blk 1.65 1.65
Nos. 980-982 (3) 3.45 3.45

Pestana A250

Bocage A251

Portraits: 20c, Camara Pestana (1863-1899), bacteriologist. 50c, Egas Moniz (1874-1955), neurologist. 1e, Antonio Pereira Coutinho (1851-1939), botanist. 1.50e, José Corrêa da Serra (1750-1823), botanist. 2e, Ricardo Jórge (1858-1938), hygienist and anthropologist. 2.50e, J. Liete de Vasconcelos (1858-1941), ethnologist. 2.80e, Maximiano Lemos (1860-1923), medical historian. 4.30e, José Antonio Serrano, anatomist.

1966, Dec. 1 Litho. Perf. 13 1/2
Portrait and Inscription in Dark Brown and Bister
983 A250 20c gray green .15 .15
984 A250 50c orange .15 .15
985 A250 1e lemon .15 .15
986 A250 1.50e bister brn .15 .15
987 A250 2e brown org .85 .15
988 A250 2.50e pale green 1.10 .15
989 A250 2.80e salmon 1.25 1.25
990 A250 4.30e Prus blue 1.65 1.40
Nos. 983-990 (8) 5.45
Set value 3.10

Issued to honor Portuguese scientists.

1966, Dec. 28 Litho. Perf. 11 1/2x12
991 A251 1e bis, grnsh gray & blk .15 .15
992 A251 2e brn org, grnsh gray & blk .35 .20
993 A251 6e gray, grnsh gray & blk .60 .48

200th anniversary of the birth of Manuel Maria Barbosa du Bocage (1765-1805), poet.

Europa Issue, 1967
Common Design Type

1967, May 2 Litho. Perf. 13
Size: 21 1/2x31mm
994 CD10 1e lt bl, Prus bl & blk .15 .15
995 CD10 3.50e sal, brn red & blk 1.10 1.10
996 CD10 4.30e yel grn, ol grn & blk 1.65 1.65
Nos. 994-996 (3) 2.90 2.90

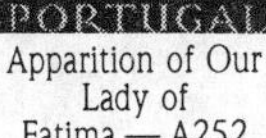

Apparition of Our Lady of Fatima — A252

Statues of Roman Senators — A253

Designs: 2.80e, Church and Golden Rose. 3.50e, Statue of the Pilgrim Virgin, with lilies and doves. 4e, Doves holding crown over Chapel of the Apparition.

1967, May 13 Perf. 11 1/2x12
997 A252 1e multicolored .15 .15
998 A252 2.80e multicolored .48 .80
999 A252 3.50e multicolored .20 .20
1000 A252 4e multicolored .26 .25
Nos. 997-1000 (4) 1.09 1.40

50th anniversary of the apparition of the Virgin Mary to 3 shepherd children at Fatima.

1967, June 1 Litho. Perf. 13
1001 A253 1e gold & rose claret .15 .15
1002 A253 2.50e gold & dull blue .90 .42
1003 A253 4.30e gold & gray green .52 .52
Nos. 1001-1003 (3) 1.57 1.09

Introduction of a new civil law code.

Shipyard, Margueira, Lisbon — A254

Design: 2.80e, 4.30e, Ship's hull and map showing location of harbor.

1967, June 23

1004 A254 1e aqua & multi .15 .15
1005 A254 2.80e multicolored .40 .45
1006 A254 3.50e multicolored .40 .24
1007 A254 4.30e multicolored .50 .48
Nos. 1004-1007 (4) 1.45 1.32

Issued to commemorate the inauguration of the Lisnave Shipyard at Margueira, Lisbon.

Symbols of Healing A255

Flags of EFTA Nations A256

1967, Oct. 8 Litho. *Perf. 13½*

1008 A255 1e multicolored .15 .15
1009 A255 2e multicolored .52 .20
1010 A255 5e multicolored .85 .60
Nos. 1008-1010 (3) 1.52 .95

Issued to publicize the 6th European Congress of Rheumatology, Lisbon, Oct. 8-13.

1967, Oct. 24 Litho. *Perf. 13½*

1011 A256 1e bister & multi .15 .15
1012 A256 3.50e buff & multi .50 .50
1013 A256 4.30e gray & multi 1.50 1.50
Nos. 1011-1013 (3) 2.15 2.15

Issued to publicize the European Free Trade Association. See note after Norway No. 501.

Tables of the Law — A257

1967, Dec. 27 Litho. *Perf. 13½*

1014 A257 1e olive .15 .15
1015 A257 2e red brown .45 .20
1016 A257 5e green .75 .55
Nos. 1014-1016 (3) 1.35 .90

Centenary of abolition of death penalty.

Bento de Goes — A258

1968, Feb. 14 Engr. *Perf. 12x11½*

1017 A258 1e olive, indigo & dk brn .40 .15
1018 A258 8e org brn, dl pur & ol grn .65 .48

360th anniversary (in 1967) of the death of Bento de Goes (1562-1607), Jesuit explorer of the route to China.

Europa Issue, 1968
Common Design Type

1968, Apr. 29 Litho. *Perf. 13*
Size: 31x21mm

1019 CD11 1e multicolored .15 .15
1020 CD11 3.50e multicolored 1.25 1.25
1021 CD11 4.30e multicolored 2.75 2.75
Nos. 1019-1021 (3) 4.15 4.15

Mother's and Child's Hands — A259

1968, May 26 Litho. *Perf. 13½*

1022 A259 1e lt gray, blk & red .15 .15
1023 A259 2e salmon, blk & red .60 .25
1024 A259 5e lt bl, blk & red .85 .65
Nos. 1022-1024 (3) 1.60 1.05

Mothers' Organization for Natl. Education. 30th anniv.

"Victory over Disease" and WHO Emblem A260

1968, July 10 Litho. *Perf. 12½*

1025 A260 1e multicolored .15 .15
1026 A260 3.50e multicolored .40 .28
1027 A260 4.30e tan & multi 3.00 3.00
Nos. 1025-1027 (3) 3.55 3.43

20th anniv. of WHO.

Madeira Grapes and Wine — A261

Joao Fernandes Vieira — A262

Designs: 1e, Fireworks on New Year's Eve. 1.50e, Mountains and valley. 3.50e, Woman doing Madeira embroidery. 4.30e, Joao Gonçalves Zarco. 20e, Muschia aurea (flower.)

Perf. 12x11½, 11½x12

1968, Aug. 17 Litho.

1028 A261 50c multi .15 .15
1029 A261 1e multi .15 .15
1030 A261 1.50e multi .15 .15
1031 A262 2.80e multi 1.00 1.00
1032 A262 3.50e multi .70 .35
1033 A262 4.30e multi 3.00 3.00
1034 A262 20e multi 1.65 .50
Nos. 1028-1034 (7) 6.80 5.30

Issued to publicize Madeira and the Lubrapex 1968 stamp exhibition.

Design descriptions in Portuguese, French and English printed on back of stamps.

Pedro Alvares Cabral A263

Cabral's Fleet A264

Design: 3.50e, Cabral's coat of arms, vert.

Perf. 12x12½, 12½x12

1969, Jan. 30 Engr.

1035 A263 1e vio bl, bl & gray bl .15 .15
1036 A263 3.50e deep claret 1.50 1.00

Litho.

1037 A264 6.50e green & multi 1.10 1.10
Nos. 1035-1037 (3) 2.75 2.25

5th cent. of the birth of Pedro Alvarez Cabral (1468-1520), navigator, discoverer of Brazil. Nos. 1035-1037 have description of the designs printed on the back in Portuguese, French and English.

Europa Issue, 1969
Common Design Type

1969, Apr. 28 Litho. *Perf. 13*
Size: 31x22½mm

1038 CD12 1e dp blue & multi .35 .15
1039 CD12 3.50e multicolored 3.50 1.00
1040 CD12 4.30e green & multi 5.50 1.50
Nos. 1038-1040 (3) 9.35 2.65

King José I and Arms of National Press — A265

1969, May 14 Litho. *Perf. 11½x12*

1041 A265 1e multicolored .15 .15
1042 A265 2e multicolored .55 .20
1043 A265 8e multicolored .42 .42
Nos. 1041-1043 (3) 1.12 .77

Bicentenary of the National Press.

ILO Emblem — A266

1969, May 28 *Perf. 13*

1044 A266 1e bluish grn, blk & sil .15 .15
1045 A266 3.50e red, blk & sil .60 .30
1046 A266 4.30e brt bl, blk & sil 1.00 .85
Nos. 1044-1046 (3) 1.75 1.30

50th anniversary of the ILO.

Juan Cabrillo Rodriguez — A267

Vianna da Motta, by Columbano Bordalo Pinheiro — A268

1969, July 16 Litho. *Perf. 11½x12*

1047 A267 1e multi .15 .15
1048 A267 2.50e multi .75 .25
1049 A267 6.50e multi .55 .55
Nos. 1047-1049 (3) 1.45 .95

Bicent. of San Diego, Calif., & honoring Juan Cabrillo Rodriguez, explorer of California coast.

Backs inscribed. See note below No. 1034.

1969, Sept. 24 Litho. *Perf. 12*

1050 A268 1e multicolored .40 .15
1051 A268 9e gray & multi .42 .55

Centenary of the birth of Vianna da Motta (1868-1948), pianist and composer.

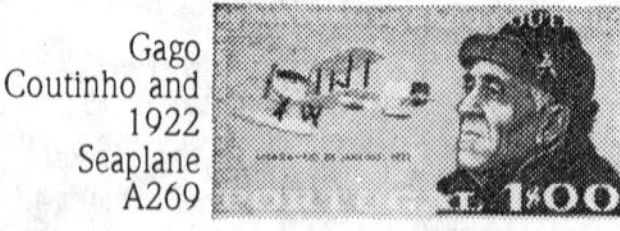
Gago Coutinho and 1922 Seaplane A269

Design: 2.80e, 4.30e, Adm. Coutinho and Coutinho sextant.

1969, Oct. 22

1052 A269 1e grnsh gray, dk & lt brn .15 .15
1053 A269 2.80e yel bis, dk & lt brn .65 .65
1054 A269 3.30e gray bl, dk & lt brn 1.00 1.00
1055 A269 4.30e lt rose brn, dk & lt brn 1.40 1.25
Nos. 1052-1055 (4) 3.20 3.05

Admiral Carlos Viegas Gago Coutinho (1869-1959), explorer and aviation pioneer.

Vasco da Gama — A270

Designs: 2.80e, Da Gama's coat of arms. 3.50e, Map showing route to India and compass rose, horiz. 4e, Da Gama's fleet, horiz.

Perf. 12x11½, 11½x12

1969, Dec. 30 Litho.

1056 A270 1e multi .15 .15
1057 A270 2.80e multi 1.65 1.65
1058 A270 3.50e multi 1.25 .70
1059 A270 4e multi 1.00 .42
Nos. 1056-1059 (4) 4.05 2.92

Vasco da Gama (1469-1525), navigator who found sea route to India.

Design descriptions in Portuguese, French and English printed on back of stamps.

Europa Issue, 1970
Common Design Type

1970, May 4 Litho. *Perf. 13½*
Size: 31x22mm

1060 CD13 1e multicolored .60 .60
1061 CD13 3.50e multicolored 3.75 3.75
1062 CD13 4.30e multicolored 5.75 5.25
Nos. 1060-1062 (3) 10.10 9.60

Distillation Plant — A271

Design: 2.80e, 6e, Catalytic cracking tower.

1970, June 5 Litho. *Perf. 13*

1063 A271 1e dk bl & dl bl .15 .15
1064 A271 2.80e sl grn & pale grn .75 .75
1065 A271 3.30e dk ol grn & ol .60 .55
1066 A271 6e dk brn & dl ocher .50 .35
Nos. 1063-1066 (4) 2.00 1.80

Opening of the Oporto Oil Refinery.

Marshal Carmona and Oak Leaves A272

Designs: 2.50e, Carmona, Portuguese coat of arms and laurel. 7e, Carmona and ferns.

Perf. 12x12½

1970, July 1 Litho. & Engr.

1067 A272 1e ol grn & blk .15 .15
1068 A272 2.50e red, ultra & blk .60 .30
1069 A272 7e slate bl & blk .55 .55
Nos. 1067-1069 (3) 1.30 1.00

Centenary of the birth of Marshal Antonio Oscar de Fragoso Carmona (1869-1951), President of Portugal, 1926-1951.

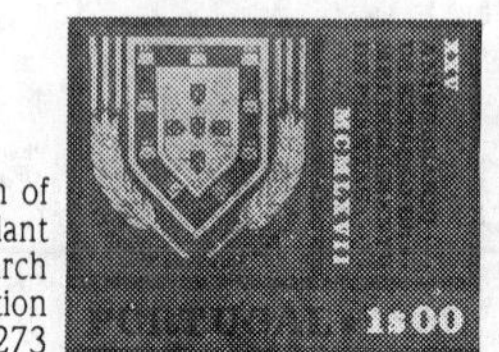
Emblem of Plant Research Station A273

1970, July 29 Litho.

1070 A273 1e multi .15 .15
1071 A273 2.50e multi .60 .22
1072 A273 5e multi .85 .45
Nos. 1070-1072 (3) 1.60 .82

25th anniv. of the Plant Research Station at Elvas.

Compass Rose and EXPO Emblem — A274

Designs: 5e, Monogram of Christ (IHS) and EXPO emblem. 6.50e, "Portugal and Japan" as written in old manuscripts, and EXPO emblem.

1970, Sept. 16 Litho. *Perf. 13*

1073 A274 1e gold & multi .15 .15
1074 A274 5e silver & multi .65 .22
1075 A274 6.50e multicolored 1.25 1.25
Nos. 1073-1075,C11 (4) 2.40 1.82

EXPO '70 International Exhibition, Osaka, Japan, Mar. 15-Sept. 13.

Castle (from Arms of Santarem) A275

#1077, Star & wheel, from Covilha coat of arms. 2.80e, Ram & Covilha coat of arms. 4e, Knights on horseback & Santarem coat of arms.

1970, Oct. 7 Litho. *Perf. 12x11½*

1076 A275 1e multicolored .15 .15
1077 A275 1e ultra & multi .15 .15
1078 A275 2.80e red & multi 1.10 1.10
1079 A275 4e gray & multi .45 .35
Nos. 1076-1079 (4) 1.85 1.75

City of Santarem, cent. (#1076, 1079); City of Covilha, cent. (#1077-1078).

Paddlesteamer Great Eastern Laying Cable — A276

Designs: 2.80e, 4e, Cross section of cable.

1970, Nov. 21 Litho. *Perf. 14*

1080 A276 1e multi .15 .15
1081 A276 2.50e multi .90 .35
1082 A276 2.80e multi 1.25 1.25
1083 A276 4e multi .90 .65
Nos. 1080-1083 (4) 3.20 2.40

Centenary of the Portugal-Great Britain submarine telegraph cable.

Grapes and Woman Filling Baskets A277

Designs: 1e, Worker carrying basket of grapes, and jug. 3.50e, Glass of wine, and barge with barrels on River Douro. 7e, Wine bottle and barrels.

1970, Dec. 20 Litho. *Perf. 12x11½*

1084 A277 50c multi .15 .15
1085 A277 1e multi .15 .15
1086 A277 3.50e multi .50 .15
1087 A277 7e multi .50 .45
Nos. 1084-1087 (4) 1.30
Set value .68

Publicity for port wine export.

Mountain Windmill, Bussaco Hills — A278

Francisco Franco (1885-1955) — A279

Windmills: 50c, Beira Litoral Province. 1e, Estremadura Province. 2e, St. Miguel, Azores. 3.30e, Porto Santo, Madeira. 5e, Pico, Azores.

1971, Feb. 24 Litho. *Perf. 13*

1088 A278 20c multicolored .15 .15
1089 A278 50c lt blue & multi .15 .15
1090 A278 1e gray & multi .15 .15
1091 A278 2e multicolored .38 .15
1092 A278 3.30e ocher & multi 1.00 1.10
1093 A278 5e multicolored .85 .30
Nos. 1088-1093 (6) 2.68
Set value 1.60

Backs inscribed. See note below No. 1034.

Europa Issue, 1971

Common Design Type

1971, May 3 Photo. *Perf. 14*

Size: 32x22mm

1094 CD14 1e dk bl, lt grn & blk .50 .50
1095 CD14 3.50e red brn, yel & blk 3.25 3.25
1096 CD14 7.50e olive, yel & blk 5.00 5.00
Nos. 1094-1096 (3) 8.75 8.75

Perf. 11½x12½; 13½ (2.50e, 4e)

1971, July 7 Engr.

Portuguese Sculptors: 1e, Antonio Teixeira Lopes (1866-1942). 1.50e, Antonio Augusto da Costa Mota (1862-1930). 2.50e, Rui Roque Gameiro (1906-1935). 3.50e, José Simoes de Almedia (nephew; 1880-1950). 4e, Francisco dos Santos (1878-1930).

1097 A279 20c black .15 .15
a. Perf. 13½ 1.10 .22
1098 A279 1e claret .15 .15
1099 A279 1.50e sepia .20 .15
1100 A279 2.50e dark blue .45 .15
1101 A279 3.50e carmine rose .48 .18
1102 A279 4e gray green .95 .80
Nos. 1097-1102 (6) 2.38
Set value 1.35

Pres. Antonio Salazar — A280

1971, July 27 Engr. *Perf. 13½*

1103 A280 1e multicolored .15 .15
a. Perf. 12½x12 35.00 1.10
1104 A280 5e multicolored .52 .20
1105 A280 10e multicolored .85 .40
a. Perf. 12½x12 15.00 .65
Nos. 1103-1105 (3) 1.52 .75

Wolframite Crystals A281

Minerals: 2.50e, Arsenopyrite (gold). 3.50e, Beryllium. 6.50e, Chalcopyrite (copper).

1971, Sept. 24 Litho. *Perf. 12*

1106 A281 1e multicolored .15 .15
1107 A281 2.50e carmine & multi .75 .28
1108 A281 3.50e green & multi .30 .15
1109 A281 6.50e blue & multi .45 .30
Nos. 1106-1109 (4) 1.65 .88

Spanish-Portuguese-American Economic Geology Congress.

Town Gate, Castelo Branco — A282

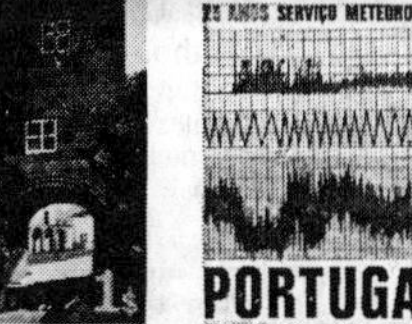

Weather Recording Station and Barograph Charts — A283

Designs: 3e, Memorial column. 12.50e, Arms of Castelo Branco, horiz.

1971, Oct. 7 *Perf. 14*

1110 A282 1e multi .15 .15
1111 A282 3e multi .75 .32
1112 A282 12.50e multi .60 .30
Nos. 1110-1112 (3) 1.50 .77

Bicentenary of Castelo Branco as a town.

1971, Oct. 29 *Perf. 13½*

Designs: 4e, Stratospheric weather balloon and weather map of southwest Europe and North Africa. 6.50e, Satellite and aerial map of Atlantic Ocean off Portugal.

1113 A283 1e buff & multi .15 .15
1114 A283 4e multicolored 1.10 .52
1115 A283 6.50e blk, dl red brn & org .48 .30
Nos. 1113-1115 (3) 1.73 .97

25 years of Portuguese meteorological service.

Missionaries and Ship — A284

1971, Nov. 24

1116 A284 1e gray, ultra & blk .15 .15
1117 A284 3.30e dp bis, lil & blk .75 .75
1118 A284 4.80e olive, grn & blk .75 .75
Nos. 1116-1118 (3) 1.65 1.65

400th anniv. of the martyrdom of a group of Portuguese missionaries on the way to Brazil.

"Man" A285

Nature Conservation: 3.30e, "Earth" (animal, vegetable, mineral). 3.50e, "Air" (birds). 4.50e, "Water" (fish).

1971, Dec. 22 Litho. *Perf. 12*

1119 A285 1e brown & multi .15 .15
1120 A285 3.30e lt bl, yel & grn .28 .20
1121 A285 3.50e lt bl, rose & vio .30 .15
1122 A285 4.50e lt bl, grn & ultra 1.10 .75
Nos. 1119-1122 (4) 1.83 1.25

City Hall, Sintra — A286

Designs: 5c, Aqueduct, Lisbon. 50c, University, Coimbra. 1e, Torre dos Clerigos, Porto. 1.50e, Belem Tower, Lisbon. 2.50e, Castle, Vila da Feira. 3e, Misericordia House, Viana do Castelo. 3.50e, Window, Tomar Convent. 8e, Ducal Palace, Guimaraes. 10e, Cape Girao, Madeira. 20e, Episcopal Garden, Castelo Branco. 100e, Lakes of Seven Cities, Azores.

1972-73 Litho. *Perf. 12½*

Size: 22x17½mm

1123 A286 5c gray, grn & blk .35 .28
1124 A286 50c gray bl, blk & org .18 .15
1125 A286 1e green, blk & brn .15 .15
1126 A286 1.50e blue, bis & blk .15 .15
1127 A286 2.50e brn, dk brn & gray .35 .15
1128 A286 3e yellow, blk & brn .50 .15
1129 A286 3.50e dp org, sl & brn .35 .15
1130 A286 8e blk, ol & grn 3.50 .28

Perf. 13½

Size: 31x22mm

1131 A286 10e gray & multi 1.10 .25
1132 A286 20e green & multi 7.00 .35
1133 A286 50e gray bl, ocher & blk 2.00 .35
1134 A286 100e green & multi 4.75 1.10
Nos. 1123-1134 (12) 20.38
Set value 3.00

"CTT" and year date printed in minute gray multiple rows on back of stamps.

Issue dates: 1e, 1.50e, 50e, 100e, Mar. 1; 50c, 3e, 10e, 20e, Dec. 6, 1972; 5c, 2.50e, 3.50e, 8e, Sept. 5, 1973.

See Nos. 1207-1214.

Tagging

Starting in 1975, phosphor (bar or L-shape) was applied to the face of most definitives and commemoratives.

Stamps issued both with and without tagging include Nos. 1124-1125, 1128, 1130-1131, 1209, 1213-1214, 1250, 1253, 1257, 1260, 1263.

Window, Pinhel Church — A287

Heart and Pendulum — A288

1e, Arms of Pinhel, horiz. 7.50e, Stone lantern.

1972, Mar. 29 *Perf. 13½*

1135 A287 1e blue & multi .15 .15
a. Perf. 11½x12½ 16.00 .45
1136 A287 2.50e multicolored .60 .20
1137 A287 7.50e blue & multi .50 .40
Nos. 1135-1137 (3) 1.25 .75

Bicentenary of Pinhel as a town.

1972, Apr. 24

Designs: 4e, Heart and spiral pattern. 9e, Heart and continuing coil pattern.

1138 A288 1e violet & red .15 .15
1139 A288 4e green & red 1.25 .80
1140 A288 9e brown & red .52 .48
Nos. 1138-1140 (3) 1.92 1.43

"Your heart is your health," World Health Day.

Europa Issue 1972

Common Design Type

1972, May 1 *Perf. 13½*

Size: 21x31mm

1141 CD15 1e gray & multi .30 .30
1142 CD15 3.50e salmon & multi 3.25 3.25
1143 CD15 6e green & multi 4.50 4.50
Nos. 1141-1143 (3) 8.05 8.05

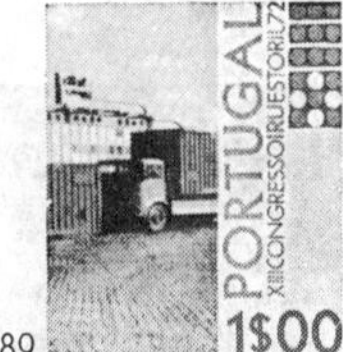

Trucks — A289

1972, May 17 Litho. *Perf. 13½*

1144 A289 1e shown .15 .15
1145 A289 4.50e Taxi .75 .45
1146 A289 8e Autobus .60 .40
Nos. 1144-1146 (3) 1.50 1.00

13th Congress of International Union of Road Transport (I.R.U.), Estoril, May 15-18.

Soccer, Olympic Rings — A290

1972, July 26 Litho. *Perf. 14*

1147 A290 50c shown .15 .15
1148 A290 1e Running .15 .15
1149 A290 1.50e Equestrian .15 .15
1150 A290 3.50e Swimming, women's .38 .18
1151 A290 4.50e Yachting .52 .50
1152 A290 5e Gymnastics, women's .90 .38
Nos. 1147-1152 (6) 2.25
Set value 1.25

20th Olympic Games, Munich, Aug. 26-Sept. 11.

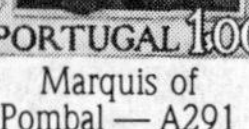

Marquis of Pombal — A291

Tomé de Sousa — A292

1972, Aug. 28 *Perf. 13½*

1153 A291 1e shown .15 .15
1154 A291 2.50e Scientific apparatus .75 .28
1155 A291 8e Seal of Univ. of Coimbra .60 .45
Nos. 1153-1155 (3) 1.50 .88

Bicentenary of the Pombaline reforms of University of Coimbra.

1972, Oct. 5 **Litho.** *Perf. 13½*

Designs: 2.50e, José Bonifacio. 3.50e, Dom Pedro IV. 6e, Allegory of Portuguese-Brazilian Community.

1156 A292 1e gray & multi .15 .15
1157 A292 2.50e green & multi .32 .15
1158 A292 3.50e multicolored .32 .18
1159 A292 6e blue & multi .60 .30
Nos. 1156-1159 (4) 1.39 .78

150th anniv. of Brazilian independence.

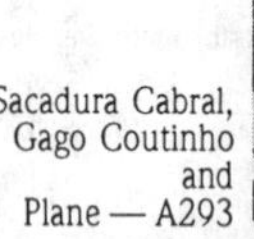

Sacadura Cabral, Gago Coutinho and Plane — A293

2.50e, 3.80e, Map of flight from Lisbon to Rio.

1972, Nov. 15 *Perf. 11½x12½*

1160 A293 1e blue & multi .15 .15
a. Perf. 13½ 10.50 1.25
1161 A293 2.50e multi .52 .15
1162 A293 2.80e multi .60 .60
1163 A293 3.80e multi .70 .70
a. Perf. 13½ *25.00 16.00*
Nos. 1160-1163 (4) 1.97 1.60

50th anniv. of the Lisbon to Rio flight by Commander Arturo de Sacadura Cabral and Adm. Carlos Viegas Gago Coutinho, Mar. 30-June 5, 1922.

Luiz Camoens A294

Designs: 3e, Hand saving manuscript from sea. 10e, Symbolic of man's questioning and discovering the unknown.

1972, Dec. 27 **Litho.** *Perf. 13*

1164 A294 1e org brn, buff & blk .15 .15
1165 A294 3e dull bl, lt grn & blk .65 .24
1166 A294 10e red brn, buff & yel .90 .42
Nos. 1164-1166 (3) 1.70 .81

4th centenary of the publication of The Lusiads by Luiz Camoens (1524-1580).

Graphs and Sequence Count — A295

1973, Apr. 11 **Litho.** *Perf. 14½*

1167 A295 1e shown .15 .15
1168 A295 4e Odometer .65 .28
1169 A295 9e Graphs .48 .25
Nos. 1167-1169 (3) 1.28 .68

Productivity Conference '72, Jan. 17-22, 1972.

Europa Issue 1973

Common Design Type

1973, Apr. 30 *Perf. 13*

Size: 31x29mm

1170 CD16 1e multicolored .30 .15
1171 CD16 4e brn red & multi 3.25 1.90
1172 CD16 6e green & multi 5.75 2.50
Nos. 1170-1172 (3) 9.30 4.55

Gen. Medici, Arms of Brazil and Portugal A296

2.80e, 4.80e, Gen. Medici and world map.

Lithographed and Engraved

1973, May 16 *Perf. 12x11½*

1173 A296 1e dk grn, blk & sep .15 .15
1174 A296 2.80e olive & multi .40 .35
1175 A296 3.50e dk bl, blk & buff .40 .30
1176 A296 4.80e multicolored .32 .25
Nos. 1173-1176 (4) 1.27 1.05

Visit of Gen. Emilio Garrastazu Medici, President of Brazil, to Portugal.

Child and Birds — A297

Designs: 4e, Child and flowers. 7.50e, Child.

1973, May 28 **Litho.** *Perf. 13*

1177 A297 1e ultra & multi .15 .15
1178 A297 4e multicolored .60 .20
1179 A297 7.50e bister & multi .75 .45
Nos. 1177-1179 (3) 1.50 .80

To pay renewed attention to children.

Transportation, Weather Map — A298

Designs: 3.80e, Communications: telegraph, telephone, radio, satellite. 6e, Postal service: mailbox, truck, mail distribution diagram.

1973, June 25

1180 A298 1e multi .15 .15
1181 A298 3.80e multi .22 .18
1182 A298 6e multi .52 .40
Nos. 1180-1182 (3) .89
Set value .62

Ministry of Communications, 25th anniv.

Pupil and Writing Exercise — A299

Designs: 4.50e, Illustrations from 18th century primer. 5.30e, School and children, by 9-year-old Marie de Luz, horiz. 8e, Symbolic chart of teacher-pupil link, horiz.

1973, Oct. 24 **Litho.** *Perf. 13*

1183 A299 1e blue & multi .15 .15
1184 A299 4.50e brown & multi .55 .20
1185 A299 5.30e lt blue & multi .48 .35
1186 A299 8e green & multi .90 .55
Nos. 1183-1186 (4) 2.08 1.25

Primary state school education, bicent.

Oporto Streetcar, 1910 A300

Designs: 1e, Horse-drawn streetcar, 1872. 3.50e, Double-decker Leyland bus, 1972.

1973, Nov. 7

Size: 31½x34mm

1187 A300 1e brown, yel & blk .15 .15
1188 A300 3.50e choc & multi 1.00 .60

Size: 37½x27mm

Perf. 12½

1189 A300 7.50e buff & multi .90 .55
Nos. 1187-1189 (3) 2.05 1.30

Cent. of public transportation in Oporto.

Servicemen's League Emblem A301

Death of Nuño Gonzalves A302

Designs: 2.50e, Sailor, soldier and aviator. 11e, Military medals.

1973, Nov. 28 **Litho.** *Perf. 13*

1190 A301 1e multi .15 .15
1191 A301 2.50e multi .95 .45
1192 A301 11e dk blue & multi .65 .52
Nos. 1190-1192 (3) 1.75 1.12

50th anniv. of the Servicemen's League.

1973, Dec. 19

1193 A302 1e slate blue & org .15 .15
1194 A302 10e violet brn & org .55 .42

600th anniv. of the heroism of Nuno Gonzalves, alcaide of Faria Castle.

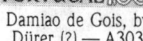

Damiao de Gois, by Dürer (?) — A303

"The Exile," by Soares dos Reis — A304

Designs: 4.50e, Title page of Cronica de Principe D. Joao. 7.50e, Lute and score of Dodecachordon.

1974, Apr. 5 **Litho.** *Perf. 12*

1195 A303 1e multi .15 .15
1196 A303 4.50e multi .80 .30
1197 A303 7.50e multi .90 .35
Nos. 1195-1197 (3) 1.85 .80

400th anniversary of the death of Damiao de Gois (1502-1574), humanist, writer, composer.

Europa Issue 1974

1974, Apr. 29 **Litho.** *Perf. 13*

1198 A304 1e multicolored .50 .50
1199 A304 4e dk red & multi 7.75 3.00
1200 A304 6e dk green & multi 9.00 6.00
Nos. 1198-1200 (3) 17.25 9.50

Pattern of Light Emission A305

Designs: 4.50e, Spiral wave radiation pattern. 5.30e, Satellite and earth.

1974, June 26 **Litho.** *Perf. 14*

1201 A305 1.50e gray olive .15 .15
1202 A305 4.50e dark blue 1.00 .45
1203 A305 5.30e brt rose lilac .32 .30
Nos. 1201-1203 (3) 1.47 .90

Establishment of satellite communications network via Intelsat among Portugal, Angola and Mozambique.

Diffusion of Hertzian Waves A306

Designs (Symbolic): 3.30e, Messages through space. 10e, Navigation help.

1974, Sept. 4 **Litho.** *Perf. 12*

1204 A306 1.50e multi .15 .15
1205 A306 3.30e multi .50 .45
1206 A306 10e multi 1.10 .60
Nos. 1204-1206 (3) 1.75 1.20

Guglielmo Marconi (1874-1937), Italian electrical engineer and inventor.

Buildings Type of 1972-73

Designs: 10c, Ponte do Lima (Roman bridge). 30c, Alcobaça Monastery, interior. 2e, City Hall, Bragança. 4e, New Gate, Braga. 4.50e, Dolmen of Carrazeda. 5e, Roman Temple, Evora. 6e, Leca do Balio Monastery. 7.50e, Almourol Castle.

1974, Sept. 18 **Litho.** *Perf. 12½*

Size: 22x17½mm

1207 A286 10c multi .15 .15
1208 A286 30c multi .15 .15
1209 A286 2e multi .15 .15
1210 A286 4e multi .35 .15
1211 A286 4.50e multi .60 .15
1212 A286 5e multi 6.25 .15
1213 A286 6e multi 1.75 .18
1214 A286 7.50e multi .90 .15
Nos. 1207-1214 (8) 10.30
Set value .75

"CTT" and year date printed in minute gray multiple rows on back of stamps.

Postilion, Truck and Letter A307

Designs: 2e, Hand holding letter. 3.30e, Packet and steamship. 4.50e, Pigeon and letters. 5.30e, Hand holding sealed letter. 20e, Old and new locomotives.

1974, Oct. 9 **Litho.** *Perf. 13*

1220 A307 1.50e brown & multi .15 .15
1221 A307 2e multicolored .45 .15
1222 A307 3.30e olive & multi .15 .15
1223 A307 4.50e multicolored .45 .42
1224 A307 5.30e multicolored .35 .30
1225 A307 20e multicolored 1.25 1.00
a. Souvenir sheet of 6 5.00 5.00
Nos. 1220-1225 (6) 2.80 2.17

Centenary of UPU. No. 1225a contains one each of Nos. 1220-1225, arranged to show a continuous design with a globe in center. Sold for 50e.

Luisa Todi, Singer (1753-1833) A308

Marcos Portugal, Composer (1762-1838) A309

Portuguese Musicians: 2e, Joao Domingos Bomtempo (1775-1842). 2.50e, Carlos Seixas (1704-1742). 3e, Duarte Lobo (1565-1646). 5.30e, Joao de Sousa Carvalho (1745-1798).

1974, Oct. 30 **Litho.** *Perf. 12*

1226 A308 1.50e brt pink .15 .15
1227 A308 2e vermilion .60 .22
1228 A308 2.50e brown .50 .15
1229 A308 3e bluish black .35 .22

1230	A308	5.30e slate green	.38	.35
1231	A309	11e rose lake	.38	.35
		Nos. 1226-1231 (6)	2.36	1.44

Coat of Arms of Beja — A310

2,000th Anniv. of Beja: 3.50e, Men of Beja in costumes from Roman times to date. 7e, Moorish Arches and view across plains.

1974, Nov. 13

1232	A310	1.50e multi	.15	.15
1233	A310	3.50e multi	.60	.50
1234	A310	7e multi	1.00	.50
		Nos. 1232-1234 (3)	1.75	1.15

Annunciation A311

Rainbow and Dove A312

Christmas: 4.50e, Adoration of the Shepherds. 10e, Flight into Egypt. Designs show Portuguese costumes from Nazare township.

1974, Dec. 4 — Litho. — *Perf. 13*

1235	A311	1.50e red & multi	.15	.15
1236	A311	4.50e multicolored	1.25	.30
1237	A311	10e blue & multi	.85	.42
		Nos. 1235-1237 (3)	2.25	.87

1974, Dec. 18 — *Perf. 12*

1238	A312	1.50e multi	.15	.15
1239	A312	3.50e multi	1.50	.42
1240	A312	5e multi	1.00	.25
		Nos. 1238-1240 (3)	2.65	.82

Armed Forces Movement of Apr. 25, 1974.

Egas Moniz — A313

Soldier as Farmer, Farmer as Soldier — A314

Designs: 3.30e, Lobotomy probe and Nobel Prize medal, 1949. 10e, Cerebral angiograph, 1927.

1974, Dec. 27 — Engr. — *Perf. 11½x12*

1241	A313	1.50e yellow & multi	.15	.15
1242	A313	3.30e brown & ocher	.22	.35
1243	A313	10e gray & ultra	1.00	.35
		Nos. 1241-1243 (3)	1.37	.85

Egas Moniz (1874-1955), brain surgeon, birth centenary.

1975, Mar. 21 — Litho. — *Perf. 12*

1244	A314	1.50e green & multi	.15	.15
1245	A314	3e gray & multi	.85	.20
1246	A314	4.50e multicolored	1.10	.40
		Nos. 1244-1246 (3)	2.10	.75

Cultural progress and citizens' guidance campaign.

Hands and Dove — A315

Designs: 4.50e, Brown hands reaching for dove. 10e, Dove with olive branch and arms of Portugal.

1975, Apr. 23 — Litho. — *Perf. 13½*

1247	A315	1.50e red & multi	.15	.15
1248	A315	4.50e brown & multi	1.10	.40
1249	A315	10e green & multi	1.25	.52
		Nos. 1247-1249 (3)	2.50	1.07

Movement of April 25th, first anniversary. Slogans in Portuguese, French and English printed on back of stamps.

God's Hand Reaching Down — A316

Designs: 4.50e, Jesus' hand holding up cross. 10e, Dove (Holy Spirit) descending.

1975, May 13 — Litho. — *Perf. 13½*

1250	A316	1.50e multicolored	.15	.15
1251	A316	4.50e plum & multi	1.40	.48
1252	A316	10e blue & multi	1.40	.60
		Nos. 1250-1252 (3)	2.95	1.23

Holy Year 1975.

Horseman of the Apocalypse, 12th Century — A317

Europa: 10e, The Poet Fernando Pessoa, by Almada Negreiros (1893-1970).

1975, May 26

1253	A317	1.50e multi	.75	.30
1254	A317	10e multi	13.00	10.00

Assembly Building A318

1975, June 2 — Litho. — *Perf. 13½*

1255	A318	2e red, blk & yel	.15	.15
1256	A318	20e emer, blk & yel	1.75	1.00

Opening of Constituent Assembly.

Hikers — A319

Designs: 4.50e, Campsite on lake. 5.30e, Mobile homes on the road.

1975, Aug. 4 — Litho. — *Perf. 13½*

1257	A319	2e multicolored	.50	.15
1258	A319	4.50e multicolored	.90	.35
1259	A319	5.30e multicolored	.35	.45
		Nos. 1257-1259 (3)	1.75	.95

36th Rally of the International Federation of Camping and Caravanning, Santo Andre Lake.

People and Sapling — A320

Designs (UN Emblem and): 4.50e, People and dove. 20e, People and grain.

1975, Sept. 17 — Litho. — *Perf. 13½*

1260	A320	2e green & multi	.20	.15
1261	A320	4.50e vio & multi	.90	.20
1262	A320	20e multicolored	2.00	.55
		Nos. 1260-1262 (3)	3.10	.90

United Nations, 30th anniversary.

Icarus and Rocket — A321

Designs: 4.50e, Apollo and Soyuz in space. 5.30e, Robert H. Goddard, Robert Esnault-Pelterie, Hermann Oberth and Konstantin Tsiolkovski. 10e, Sputnik, man in space, moon landing module.

1975, Sept. 26 — Litho. — *Perf. 13½*

Size: 30½x26½mm

1263	A321	2e green & multi	.20	.15
1264	A321	4.50e brown & multi	.90	.30
1265	A321	5.30e lilac & multi	.30	.30

Size: 65x28mm

1266	A321	10e blue & multi	2.00	.52
		Nos. 1263-1266 (4)	3.40	1.27

26th Congress of International Astronautical Federation, Lisbon, Sept. 1975.

Land Survey A322

Designs: 8e, Ocean survey. 10e, People of many races and globe.

1975, Nov. 19 — Litho. — *Perf. 12x12½*

1267	A322	2e ocher & multi	.20	.15
1268	A322	8e blue & multi	.60	.52
1269	A322	10e dk vio & multi	1.40	.55
		Nos. 1267-1269 (3)	2.20	1.22

Centenary of Lisbon Geographical Society.

Arch and Trees — A323

Designs: 8e, Plan, pencil and ruler. 10e, Hand, old building and brick tower.

1975, Nov. 28 — *Perf. 13½*

1270	A323	2e dk bl & gray	.18	.15
1271	A323	8e dk car & gray	1.50	1.40
1272	A323	10e ocher & multi	1.65	1.50
		Nos. 1270-1272 (3)	3.33	3.05

European Architectural Heritage Year 1975.

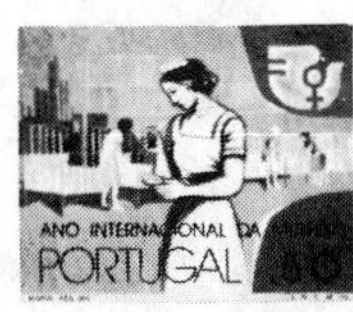

Nurse and Hospital Ward — A324

Designs (IWY Emblem and): 2e, Farm workers. 3.50e, Secretary. 8e, Factory worker.

1975, Dec. 30 — Litho. — *Perf. 13½*

1273	A324	50c multicolored	.15	.15
1274	A324	2e multicolored	.55	.15
1275	A324	3.50e multicolored	.55	.28
1276	A324	8e multicolored	.60	.55
a.		Souvenir sheet of 4	2.50	2.50
		Nos. 1273-1276 (4)	1.85	1.13

International Women's Year 1975. No. 1276a contains 4 stamps similar to Nos. 1273-1276 in slightly changed colors. Sold for 25e.

Pen Nib as Plowshare A325

1976, Feb. 6 — Litho. — *Perf. 12*

1277	A325	3e dk bl & red org	.22	.15
1278	A325	20e org, ultra & red	2.00	.95

Portuguese Society of Writers, 50th anniversary.

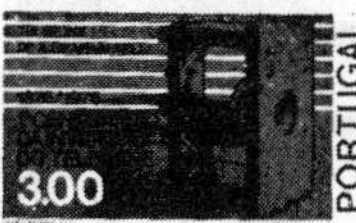

Telephones, 1876, 1976 — A326

10.50e, Alexander Graham Bell & telephone.

1976, Mar. 10 — Litho. — *Perf. 12x12½*

1279	A326	3e yel grn, grn & blk	.60	.15
1280	A326	10.50e rose, red & blk	1.65	.52

Centenary of first telephone call by Alexander Graham Bell, March 10, 1876.

Industry and Shipping — A327

Design: 1e, Garment, food and wine industries.

1976, Apr. 7 — Litho. — *Perf. 12½*

1281	A327	50c red brown	.20	.15
1282	A327	1e slate	.30	.15
		Set value		.24

Support of national production.

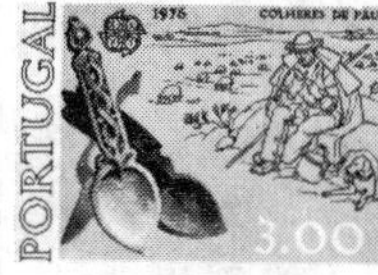

Carved Spoons, Olive Wood — A328

Europa: 20e, Gold filigree pendant, silver box and CEPT emblem.

1976, May 3 — Litho. — *Perf. 12x12½*

1283	A328	3e olive & multi	.75	.15
1284	A328	20e tan & multi	15.00	5.25

Stamp Collectors A329

Designs: 7.50e, Stamp exhibition and hand canceler. 10e, Printing and designing stamps.

1976, May 29 — Litho. — *Perf. 14½*

1285	A329	3e multicolored	.15	.15
1286	A329	7.50e multicolored	.42	.30
1287	A329	10e multicolored	1.10	.30
		Nos. 1285-1287 (3)	1.67	.75

Interphil 76, International Philatelic Exhibition, Philadelphia, Pa., May 29-June 6.

King Ferdinand I — A330

Designs: 5e, Plowshare, farmers chasing off hunters. 10e, Harvest.

1976, July 2 — Litho. — *Perf. 12*

1288	A330	3e lt bl & multi	.15	.15
1289	A330	5e yel grn & multi	.90	.60
1290	A330	10e multicolored	.95	.90
a.		Souv. sheet of 3, #1288-1290	3.00	3.00
		Nos. 1288-1290 (3)	2.00	1.65

Agricultural reform law (compulsory cultivation of uncultivated lands), 600th anniversary. No. 1290a sold for 30e.

Torch Bearer A331

7e, Women's relay race. 10.50e, Olympic flame.

1976, July 16 *Perf. 13½*

1291	A331	3e red & multi	.15	.15
1292	A331	7e red & multi	.85	.60
1293	A331	10.50e red & multi	1.10	.52
		Nos. 1291-1293 (3)	2.10	1.27

21st Olympic Games, Montreal, Canada, July 17-Aug. 1.

Farm A332

1976, Sept. 15 **Litho.** *Perf. 12*

1294	A332	3e shown	.48	.15
1295	A332	3e Ship	.48	.15
1296	A332	3e City	.48	.15
1297	A332	3e Factory	.80	.15
b.		Souv. sheet of 4, #1294-1297	8.00	8.00
		Nos. 1294-1297 (4)	2.24	.60

Fight against illiteracy. #1297b sold for 25e.

Perf. 13½

1294a	A332	3e	*30.00*	*15.00*
1295a	A332	3e	1.50	1.10
1296a	A332	3e	*35.00*	*18.00*
1297a	A332	3e	.60	.45
		Nos. 1294a-1297a (4)	67.10	34.55

Azure-winged Magpie — A333

Designs: 5e, Lynx. 7e, Portuguese laurel cherry. 10.50e, Little wild carnations.

1976, Sept. 30 **Litho.** *Perf. 12*

1298	A333	3e multi	.24	.15
1299	A333	5e multi	.70	.15
1300	A333	7e multi	.70	.52
1301	A333	10.50e multi	.90	.70
		Nos. 1298-1301 (4)	2.54	1.52

Portucale 77, 2nd International Thematic Exhibition, Oporto, Oct. 29-Nov. 6, 1977.

Exhibition Hall — A334

Design: 20e, Symbolic stamp and emblem.

1976, Oct. 9 **Litho.** *Perf. 13½*

1302	A334	3e bl & multi	.18	.15
1303	A334	20e ocher & multi	1.75	1.10
a.		Souv. sheet of 2, #1302-1303	3.00	3.00

6th Luso-Brazilian Phil. Exhib., LUBRAPEX 76, Oporto, Oct. 9. #1303a sold for 30e.

Bank Emblem and Family A335

7e, Grain. 15e, Cog wheels.

1976, Oct. 29 *Perf. 12*

1304	A335	3e org & multi	.15	.15
1305	A335	7e grn & multi	.95	.45
1306	A335	15e bl & multi	1.10	.55
		Nos. 1304-1306 (3)	2.20	1.15

Trust Fund Bank centenary.

Sheep Grazing on Marsh A336

Designs: 3e, Drainage ditches. 5e, Fish in water. 10e, Ducks flying over marsh.

1976, Nov. 24 **Litho.** *Perf. 14*

1307	A336	1e multicolored	.18	.15
1308	A336	3e multicolored	.45	.18
1309	A336	5e multicolored	.95	.30
1310	A336	10e multicolored	1.25	.45
		Nos. 1307-1310 (4)	2.83	1.08

Protection of wetlands.

"Liberty" — A337

1976, Nov. 30 **Litho.** *Perf. 13½*

1311	A337	3e gray, grn & ver	.45	.15

Constitution of 1976.

Mother Examining Child's Eyes — A338

Designs: 5e, Welder with goggles. 10.50e, Blind woman reading Braille.

1976, Dec. 13

1312	A338	3e multicolored	.15	.15
1313	A338	5e multicolored	.65	.15
1314	A338	10.50e multicolored	.95	.65
		Nos. 1312-1314 (3)	1.75	.95

World Health Day and campaign against blindness.

Hydroelectric Energy A339

Abstract Designs: 4e, Fossil fuels. 5e, Geothermal energy. 10e, Wind power. 15e, Solar energy.

1976, Dec. 30

1315	A339	1e multicolored	.16	.15
1316	A339	4e multicolored	.30	.15
1317	A339	5e multicolored	.32	.15
1318	A339	10e multicolored	.60	.40
1319	A339	15e multicolored	1.10	.70
		Nos. 1315-1319 (5)	2.48	1.55

Sources of energy.

Map of Council of Europe Members A340

1977, Jan. 28 **Litho.** *Perf. 12*

1320	A340	8.50e multicolored	.50	.50
1321	A340	10e multicolored	.50	.50

Portugal's joining Council of Europe.

Alcoholic and Bottle — A341

Designs (Bottle and): 5e, Symbolic figure of broken life. 15e, Bars blotting out the sun.

1977, Feb. 4 *Perf. 13*

1322	A341	3e multicolored	.15	.15
1323	A341	5e ocher & multi	.38	.20
1324	A341	15e org & multi	.90	.70
		Nos. 1322-1324 (3)	1.43	1.05

Anti-alcoholism Day and 10th anniversary of Portuguese Anti-alcoholism Society.

Trees Tapped for Resin — A342

Designs: 4e, Trees stripped for cork. 7e, Trees and logs. 15e, Trees at seashore as windbreakers.

1977, Mar. 21 **Litho.** *Perf. 13½*

1325	A342	1e multicolored	.15	.15
1326	A342	4e multicolored	.24	.15
1327	A342	7e multicolored	.90	.35
1328	A342	15e multicolored	1.00	.65
		Nos. 1325-1328 (4)	2.29	1.30

Forests, a natural resource.

"Suffering" A343

6e, Man exercising. 10e, Group exercising. All designs include emblems of WHO & Portuguese Institute for Rheumatology.

1977, Apr. 13 **Litho.** *Perf. 12x12½*

1329	A343	4e blk, brn & ocher	.15	.15
1330	A343	6e blk, bl & vio	.60	.52
1331	A343	10e blk, pur & red	.52	.24
		Nos. 1329-1331 (3)	1.27	.91

International Rheumatism Year.

Southern Plains Landscape A344

Europa: 8.50e, Northern mountain valley.

1977, May 2

1332	A344	4e multi	.38	.25
1333	A344	8.50e multi	1.65	1.10
a.		Min. sheet, 2 each #1332-1333	15.00	15.00

Pope John XXI Enthroned A345

Petrus Hispanus, the Physician A346

1977, May 20 **Litho.** *Perf. 13½*

1334	A345	4e multicolored	.25	.15
1335	A346	15e multicolored	.60	.60

Pope John XXI (Petrus Hispanus), only Pope of Portuguese descent, 7th death centenary.

Compass Rose, Camoens Quotation A347

1977, June 8 *Perf. 12*

1336	A347	4e multi	.18	.15
1337	A347	8.50e multi	.55	.52

Camoens Day and to honor Portuguese overseas communities.

Student, Computer and Book — A348

Designs (Book and): No. 1339, Folk dancers, flutist and boat. No. 1340, Tractor drivers. No. 1341, Atom and people.

1977, July 20 **Litho.** *Perf. 12x12½*

1338	A348	4e multicolored	.22	.18
1339	A348	4e multicolored	.22	.18
1340	A348	4e multicolored	.22	.18
1341	A348	4e multicolored	.22	.18
a.		Souv. sheet of 4, #1338-1341	3.50	3.50
		Nos. 1338-1341 (4)	.88	.72

Continual education. #1341a sold for 20e.

Pyrites, Copper, Chemical Industry A349

Designs: 5e, Marble, statue, public buildings. 10e, Iron ore, girders, crane. 20e, Uranium ore, atomic diagram.

1977, Oct. 4 **Litho.** *Perf. 12x11½*

1342	A349	4e multicolored	.15	.15
1343	A349	5e multicolored	.42	.16
1344	A349	10e multicolored	.45	.22
1345	A349	20e multicolored	1.25	.55
		Nos. 1342-1345 (4)	2.27	1.08

Natural resources from the subsoil.

Alexandre Herculano A350

1977, Oct. 19 **Engr.** *Perf. 12x11½*

1346	A350	4e multicolored	.15	.15
1347	A350	15e multicolored	.55	.50

Alexandre Herculano de Carvalho Araujo (1810-1877), historian, novelist, death centenary.

Maria Pia Bridge A351

Design: 4e, Arrival of first train, ceramic panel by Jorge Colaco, St. Bento railroad station.

1977, Nov. 4 **Litho.** *Perf. 12x11½*

1348	A351	4e multicolored	.16	.15
1349	A351	10e multicolored	.80	.80

Centenary of extension of railroad across Douro River.

Poveiro Bark — A352

Coastal Fishing Boats: 3e, Do Mar bark. 4e, Nazaré bark. 7e, Algarve skiff. 10e, Xavega bark. 15e, Bateira de Buarcos.

1977, Nov. 19 *Perf. 12*

1350	A352	2e multicolored	.32	.15
1351	A352	3e multicolored	.16	.15
1352	A352	4e multicolored	.16	.16
1353	A352	7e multicolored	.24	.16
1354	A352	10e multicolored	.40	.40
1355	A352	15e multicolored	.90	.65
a.		Souv. sheet of 6, #1350-1355	3.00	3.00
		Nos. 1350-1355 (6)	2.18	1.67

PORTUCALE 77, 2nd International Topical Exhibition. Oporto, Nov. 19-20. No. 1355a sold for 60e.

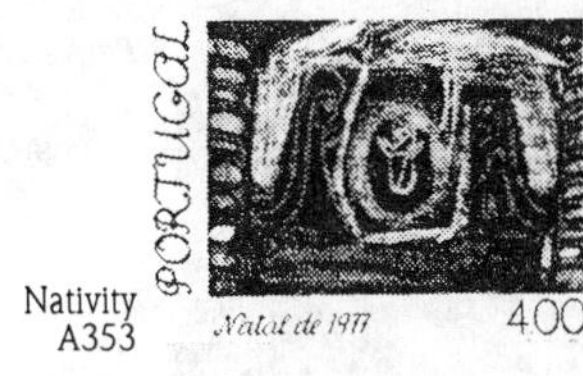

Nativity
A353

Children's Drawings: 7e, Nativity. 10e, Holy Family, vert. 20e, Star and Christ Child, vert.

Perf. 12x11½, 11½x12

1977, Dec. 12 Litho.

1356 A353 4e multicolored .15 .15
1357 A353 7e multicolored .45 .32
1358 A353 10e multicolored .45 .35
1359 A353 20e multicolored 1.65 .75
Nos. 1356-1359 (4) 2.70 1.57

Christmas 1977.

Old Desk and Computer — A354

Designs: Work tools, old and new.

1978-83 Litho. *Perf. 12½*

Size: 22x17mm

1360 A354 50c Medical .15 .15
1361 A354 1e Household .15 .15
1362 A354 2e Communications .15 .15
1363 A354 3e Garment making .15 .15
1364 A354 4e Office .15 .15
1365 A354 5e Fishing craft .15 .15
1366 A354 5.50e Weaving .15 .15
1367 A354 6e Plows .16 .15
1368 A354 6.50e Aviation .15 .15
1369 A354 7e Printing .20 .15
1370 A354 8e Carpentry .18 .15
1371 A354 8.50e Potter's wheel .20 .15
1372 A354 9e Photography .20 .15
1373 A354 10e Saws .20 .15
1373A A354 12.50e Compasses ('83) .18 .15
1373B A354 16e Mail processing ('83) .18 .15

Perf. 13½

Size: 31x22mm

1374 A354 20e Construction .55 .35
1375 A354 30e Steel industry .65 .32
a. Incomplete arch .65 .32
1376 A354 40e Transportation .75 .70
1377 A354 50e Chemistry 1.10 .55
1378 A354 100e Shipbuilding 2.00 .90
1379 A354 250e Telescopes 4.75 2.75
Nos. 1360-1379 (22) 12.50
Set value 7.00

Red Mediterranean Soil — A355

Designs: 5e, Stone formation. 10e, Alluvial soil. 20e, Black soil.

1978, Mar. 6 Litho. *Perf. 12*

1380 A355 4e multicolored .16 .15
1381 A355 5e multicolored .20 .15
1382 A355 10e multicolored .32 .32
1383 A355 20e multicolored 1.25 .55
Nos. 1380-1383 (4) 1.93 1.17

Soil, a natural resource.

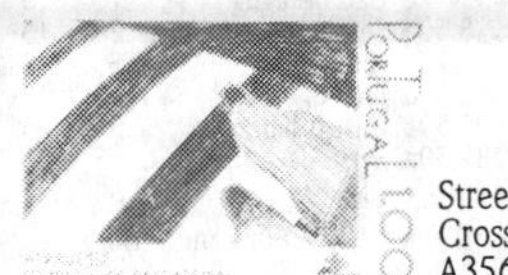

Street Crossing A356

Designs: 2e, Motorcyclist. 2.50e, Children in back seat of car. 5e, Hands holding steering wheel. 9e, Driving on country road. 12.50e, "Avoid drinking and driving."

1978, Apr. 19 Litho. *Perf. 12*

1384 A356 1e multi .15 .15
1385 A356 2e multi .15 .15
1386 A356 2.50e multi .22 .15
1387 A356 5e multi .38 .15
1388 A356 9e multi .55 .30
1389 A356 12.50e multi .65 .60
Nos. 1384-1389 (6) 2.10
Set value 1.20

Road safety campaign.

Roman Tower, Belmonte A357

Europa: 40e, Belém Monastery of Hieronymite monks (inside).

1978, May 2

1390 A357 10e multicolored .40 .40
1391 A357 40e multicolored 1.65 1.65
a. Souv. sheet, 2 each #1390-1391 8.00 8.00

No. 1391a sold for 120e.

Trajan's Bridge — A358

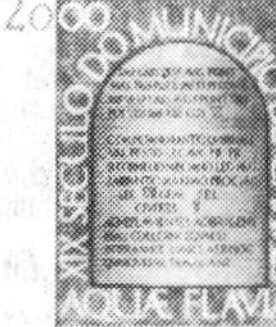

Roman Tablet from Bridge — A359

1978, June 14 Litho. *Perf. 13½*

1392 A358 5e multicolored .16 .15
1393 A359 20e multicolored .95 .95

1900th anniv. of Chaves (Aquae Flaviae).

Running A360

1978, July 24 Litho. *Perf. 12*

1394 A360 5e shown .15 .15
1395 A360 10e Bicycling .30 .18
1396 A360 12.50e Watersport .45 .45
1397 A360 15e Soccer .45 .30
Nos. 1394-1397 (4) 1.35 1.08

Sport for all the people.

Pedro Nunes A361

Design: 20e, "Nonio" navigational instrument and diagram from "Tratado da Rumaçao do Globo."

1978, Aug. 9 Litho. *Perf. 12x11½*

1398 A361 5e multicolored .15 .15
1399 A361 20e multicolored .75 .50

Nunes (1502-78), navigator and cosmographer.

Trawler, Frozen Fish Processing, Can of Sardines A362

Fishing Industry: 9e, Deep-sea trawler, loading and unloading at dock. 12.50e, Trawler with radar and instruction in use of radar. 15e, Trawler with echo-sounding equipment, microscope and test tubes.

1978, Sept. 16 Litho. *Perf. 12x11½*

1400 A362 5e multi .15 .15
1401 A362 9e multi .18 .15
1402 A362 12.50e multi .45 .40
1403 A362 15e multi .55 .30
Nos. 1400-1403 (4) 1.33 1.00

Natural resources.

Postrider A363

Designs: No. 1405, Carrier pigeon. No. 1406, Envelopes. No. 1407, Pen.

1978, Oct. 30 Litho. *Perf. 12*

1404 A363 5e yel & multi .24 .18
1405 A363 5e bl gray & multi .24 .18
1406 A363 5e grn & multi .24 .18
1407 A363 5e red & multi .24 .18
Nos. 1404-1407 (4) .96 .72

Introduction of Postal Code.

Human Figure, Flame Emblem A364

Design: 40e, Human figure pointing the way and flame emblem.

1978, Dec. 7 Litho. *Perf. 12*

1408 A364 14e multicolored .25 .25
1409 A364 40e multicolored 1.10 1.10
a. Souv. sheet, 2 each #1408-1409 3.75 3.75

Universal Declaration of Human Rights, 30th anniv. and 25th anniv. of European Declaration.

Sebastiao Magalhaes Lima A365

1978, Dec. 7

1410 A365 5e multicolored .20 .15

Sebastiao Magalhaes Lima (1850-1928), lawyer, journalist, statesman.

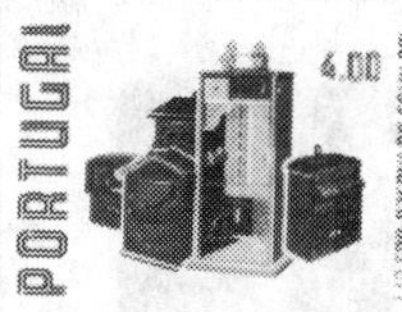

Mail Boxes and Scale — A366

Designs: 5e, Telegraph and condenser lens. 10e, Portugal Nos. 2-3 and postal card printing press, 1879. 14e, Book and bookcases, 1879, 1979.

1978, Dec. 20

1411 A366 4e multicolored .16 .15
1412 A366 5e multicolored .20 .15
1413 A366 10e multicolored .32 .16
1414 A366 14e multicolored .75 .65
a. Souv. sheet of 4, #1411-1414 1.65 1.65
Nos. 1411-1414 (4) 1.43 1.11

Centenary of Postal Museum and Postal Library; 125th anniversary of Portuguese stamps (10e). No. 1414a sold for 40e.

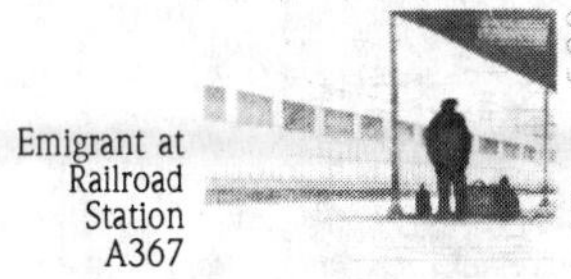

Emigrant at Railroad Station A367

Designs: 14e, Farewell at airport. 17e, Emigrant greeting child at railroad station.

1979, Feb. 21 Litho. *Perf. 12*

1415 A367 5e multicolored .15 .15
1416 A367 14e multicolored .30 .30
1417 A367 17e multicolored .75 .65
Nos. 1415-1417 (3) 1.20 1.10

Portuguese emigration.

Automobile Traffic — A368

Combat noise pollution: 5e, Pneumatic drill. 14e, Man with bull horn.

1979, Mar. 14 *Perf. 13½*

1418 A368 4e multicolored .15 .15
1419 A368 5e multicolored .15 .15
1420 A368 14e multicolored .35 .35
Nos. 1418-1420 (3) .65 .65

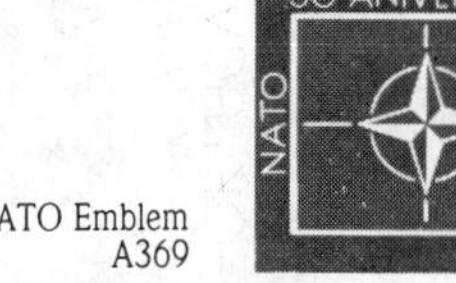

NATO Emblem A369

1979, Apr. 4 Litho. *Perf. 12*

1421 A369 5e multicolored .15 .15
1422 A369 50e multicolored 1.40 1.25
a. Souv. sheet, 2 each #1421-1422 3.25 3.25

NATO, 30th anniv.

Mail Delivery, 16th Century A370

Europa: 40e, Mail delivery, 19th century.

1979, Apr. 30 Litho. *Perf. 12*

1423 A370 14e multicolored .32 .32
1424 A370 40e multicolored .80 .80
a. Souv. sheet, 2 each #1423-1424 5.25 5.25

Mother, Infant, Dove — A371

Designs (IYC Emblem and): 5.50e, Children playing ball. 10e, Child in nursery school. 14e, Black and white boys.

1979, June 1 Litho. *Perf. 12x12½*

1425 A371 5.50e multi .15 .15
1426 A371 6.50e multi .18 .15
1427 A371 10e multi .25 .18
1428 A371 14e multi .45 .35
a. Souv. sheet of 4, #1425-1428 1.50 1.50
Nos. 1425-1428 (4) 1.03
Set value .72

Intl. Year of the Child. No. 1428a sold for 40e.

Salute to the Flag — A372

1979, June 8

1429 A372 6.50e multicolored .22 .18
a. Souvenir sheet of 9 2.00 2.00

Portuguese Day.

Pregnant Woman A373

Designs: 17e, Boy sitting in a cage. 20e, Face, and hands using hammer.

1979, June 6 Litho. *Perf. 12x12½*

1430 A373 6.50e multi .20 .20
1431 A373 17e multi .48 .48
1432 A373 20e multi .52 .52
Nos. 1430-1432 (3) 1.20 1.20

Help for the mentally retarded.

Children Reading Book, UNESCO Emblem A374

17e, Teaching deaf child, and UNESCO emblem.

1979, June 25

1433 A374 6.50e multi .20 .15
1434 A374 17e multi .48 .48

Intl. Bureau of Education, 50th anniv.

Water Cart, Brasiliana '79 Emblem A375

Brasiliana '79 Philatelic Exhibition: 5.50e, Wine sledge. 6.50e, Wine cart. 16e, Covered cart. 19e, Mogadouro cart. 20e, Sand cart.

1979, Sept. 15 Litho. *Perf. 12*

1435 A375 2.50e multi .15 .15
1436 A375 5.50e multi .15 .15
1437 A375 6.50e multi .18 .18
1438 A375 16e multi .35 .35
1439 A375 19e multi .40 .35
1440 A375 20e multi .45 .30
Nos. 1435-1440 (6) 1.68 1.48

Antonio Jose de Almeida (1866-1929) — A376

Republican Leaders: 6.50e, Afonso Costa (1871-1937). 10e, Teofilo Braga (1843-1924). 16e, Bernardino Machado (1851-1944). 19.50e, Joao Chagas (1863-1925). 20e, Elias Garcia (1830-1891).

1979, Oct. 4 *Perf. 12½x12*

1441 A376 5.50e multi .15 .15
1442 A376 6.50e multi .15 .15
1443 A376 10e multi .20 .15
1444 A376 16e multi .30 .30
1445 A376 19.50e multi .35 .60
1446 A376 20e multi .35 .30
Nos. 1441-1446 (6) 1.50 1.65

See Nos. 1454-1459.

Red Cross and Family — A377

20e, Doctor examining elderly man.

1979, Oct. 26 *Perf. 12x12½*

1447 A377 6.50e multi .15 .15
1448 A377 20e multi .55 .55

National Health Service Campaign.

Holy Family, 17th Century Mosaic — A378

Mosaics, Lisbon Tile Museum: 6.50e, Nativity, 16th century. 16e, Flight into Egypt, 18th century.

1979, Dec. 5 Litho. *Perf. 12x12½*

1449 A378 5.50e multi .15 .15
1450 A378 6.50e multi .18 .18
1451 A378 16e multi .45 .45
Nos. 1449-1451 (3) .78 .78

Christmas 1979.

Rotary International, 75th Anniversary A379

1980, Feb. 22 *Perf. 12x11½*

1452 A379 16e shown .42 .42
1453 A379 50e Emblem, torch 1.10 1.10

Portrait Type of 1979

Leaders of the Republican Movement: 3.50e, Alvaro de Castro (1878-1928). 5.50e, Antonio Sergio (1883-1969). 6.50e, Norton de Matos (1867-1955). 11e, Jaime Cortesao (1884-1960). 16e, Teixeira Gomes (1860-1941). 20e, Jose Domingues dos Santos (1885-1958). Nos. 1454-1459 horizontal.

1980, Mar. 19

1454 A376 3.50e multi .15 .15
1455 A376 5.50e multi .18 .15
1456 A376 6.50e multi .18 .15
1457 A376 11e multi .35 .35
1458 A376 16e multi .48 .38
1459 A376 20e multi .48 .32
Nos. 1454-1459 (6) 1.82 1.50

Europa Issue

Serpa Pinto (1864-1900), Explorer of Africa — A380

1980, Apr. 14

1460 A380 16e shown .20 .20
1461 A380 60e Vasco da Gama .85 .85
a. Souv. sheet, 2 each #1460-1461 3.00 3.00

Barn Owl — A381

1980, May 6 Litho. *Perf. 12x11½*

1462 A381 6.50e shown .25 .18
1463 A381 16e Red fox .52 .52
1464 A381 19.50e Timber wolf .60 .50
1465 A381 20e Golden eagle .60 .52
a. Souv. sheet of 4, #1462-1465 2.25 2.25
Nos. 1462-1465 (4) 1.97 1.72

European Campaign for the Protection of Species and their Habitat (Lisbon Zoo animals); London 1980 International Stamp Exhibition, May 6-14.

Luiz Camoens (1524-80) — A382

Lithographed & Engraved

1980, June 9 *Perf. 11½x12*

1466 A382 6.50e multi .15 .15
1467 A382 20e multi .50 .50

Nos. 1466-1467 each se-tenant with label.

Mendes Pinto and Chinese Men A383

1980, June 30 Litho. *Perf. 12x11½*

1468 A383 6.50e shown .20 .18
1469 A383 10e Battle at sea .28 .28

A Peregrinacao (The Peregrination,) by Fernao Mendes Pinto (1509-1583), written in 1580, published in 1614.

St. Vincent and Old Lisbon — A384

Designs: 8e, Lantern Tower, Evora Cathedral. 11e, Jesus with top hat, Miranda do Douro Cathedral, and mountain. 16e, Our Lady of the Milk, Braga Cathedral, and Canicada Dam. 19.50e, Pulpit, Santa Cruz Monastery, Coimbra, and Aveiro River. 20e, Algarve chimney, and Rocha Beach.

1980, Sept. 17 Litho. *Perf. 12x12½*

1470 A384 6.50e multi .16 .15
1471 A384 8e multi .20 .16
1472 A384 11e multi .25 .20
1473 A384 16e multi .35 .35
1474 A384 19.50e multi .42 .42
1475 A384 20e multi .42 .32
Nos. 1470-1475 (6) 1.80 1.60

World Tourism Conf., Manila, Sept. 27.

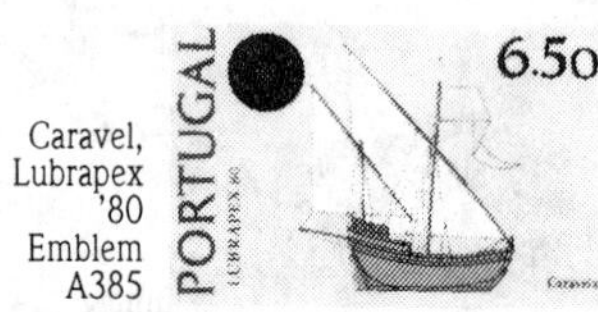

Caravel, Lubrapex '80 Emblem A385

1980, Oct. 18 Litho. *Perf. 12x11½*

1476 A385 6.50e shown .18 .15
1477 A385 8e Three-master Nau .22 .16
1478 A385 16e Galleon .42 .42
1479 A385 19.50e Paddle steamer .48 .32
a. Souv. sheet of 4, #1476-1479 3.00 3.00
Nos. 1476-1479 (4) 1.30 1.05

Lubrapex '80 Stamp Exhib., Lisbon, Oct. 18-26.

Car Emitting Gas Fumes A386

1980, Oct. 31

1480 A386 6.50e Light bulbs .20 .15
1481 A386 16e shown .40 .40

Energy conservation.

Student, School and Sextant A387

1980, Dec. 19 Litho. *Perf. 12x11½*

1482 A387 6.50e Founder, book, emblem .16 .15
1483 A387 19.50e shown .42 .40

Lisbon Academy of Science bicentennial.

Man with Diseased Heart and Lungs, Hand Holding Cigarette A388

1980, Dec. 19 *Perf. 13½*

1484 A388 6.50e shown .18 .15
1485 A388 19.50e Healthy man rejecting cigarette .48 .48

Anti-smoking campaign.

Census Form and Houses A389

1981, Jan. 28 Litho. *Perf. 13½*

1486 A389 6.50e Form, head .20 .15
1487 A389 16e shown .40 .40

Fragata on Tejo River — A390

1981, Feb. 23 Litho. *Perf. 12x12½*

1488 A390 8e shown .20 .15
1489 A390 8.50e Rabelo, Douro River .20 .15
1490 A390 10e Moliceiro, Aveiro River .20 .15
1491 A390 16e Barco, Lima River .32 .28
1492 A390 19.50e Carocho, Minho River .35 .32
1493 A390 20e Varino, Tejo River .35 .24
Nos. 1488-1493 (6) 1.62 1.29

Rajola Tile, Valencia, 15th Century — A391

Designs: No. 1495, Moresque tile, Coimbra 16th cent. No. 1496, Arms of Duke of Braganza, 1510. No. 1497, Pisanos design, 1595.

1981 Litho. *Perf. 11½x12*

1494 A391 8.50e multi .22 .15
a. Miniature sheet of 6 1.90 1.90
1495 A391 8.50e multi .22 .15
a. Miniature sheet of 6 1.90 1.90
1496 A391 8.50e multi .22 .15
a. Miniature sheet of 6 1.90 1.90
1497 A391 8.50e multi .22 .15
a. Miniature sheet of 6 1.90 1.90
b. Souv. sheet of 4, #1494-1497 1.50 1.50
Nos. 1494-1497 (4) .88 .60

Issued: #1494, Mar. 16; #1495, June 13; #1496, Aug. 28; #1497, Dec. 16. See Nos. 1528-1531, 1563-1566, 1593-1596, 1617-1620.

Perdigueiro A392

1981, Mar. 16 *Perf. 12*

1498 A392 7e Cao de agua .16 .15
1499 A392 8.50e Serra de aires .24 .15
1500 A392 15e shown .35 .18
1501 A392 22e Podengo .50 .35
1502 A392 25.50e Castro laboreiro .55 .35
1503 A392 33.50e Serra da estrela .75 .35
Nos. 1498-1503 (6) 2.55 1.53

Portuguese Kennel Club, 50th anniversary.

Workers and Rainbow A393

1981, Apr. 30 Litho. *Perf. 12x12½*

1504 A393 8.50e shown .22 .22

1505 A393 25.50e Rainbow, demonstration .50 .50

International Workers' Day.

Europa Issue

Dancer in National Costume — A394

1981, May 11 *Perf. 13½*

1506 A394 22e shown .28 .28

1507 A394 48e Painted boat, horiz. .75 .75

a. Souv. sheet, 2 each #1506-1507 2.50 2.50

St. Anthony Writing A395

St. Anthony of Lisbon, 750th Anniversary of Death: 70e, Blessing people.

1981, June 13 *Perf. 12x11½*

1508 A395 8.50e multi .20 .20

1509 A395 70e multi 1.40 1.40

500th Anniv. of King Joao II — A396

1981, Aug. 28 *Perf. 12x11½*

1510 A396 8.50e shown .30 .30

1511 A396 27e Joao II leading army .95 .95

125th Anniv. of Portuguese Railroads A397

Designs: Locomotives.

1981, Oct. 28 Litho. *Perf. 12x11½*

1512 A397 8.50e Dom Luis, 1862 .22 .15

1513 A397 19e Pacific 500, 1925 .38 .35

1514 A397 27e ALCO 1500, 1948 .55 .45

1515 A397 33.50e BB 2600 ALSTHOM, '74 .75 .38

Nos. 1512-1515 (4) 1.90 1.33

Pearier Pump Fire Engine, 1856 — A398

1981, Nov. 18 Litho. *Perf. 12x12½*

1516 A398 7e shown .16 .15

1517 A398 8.50e Ford, 1927 .22 .15

1518 A398 27e Renault, 1914 .55 .40

1519 A398 33.50e Snorkel, Ford 1978 .70 .50

Nos. 1516-1519 (4) 1.63 1.20

A399 A400

Christmas: Clay creches.

1981, Dec. 16 *Perf. 12½x12*

1520 A399 7e multi .20 .15

1521 A399 8.50e multi .22 .15

1522 A399 27e multi .70 .48

Nos. 1520-1522 (3) 1.12

Set value .65

1982, Jan. 20 Litho. *Perf. 12½x12*

1523 A400 8.50e With animals .22 .15

1524 A400 27e Building church .60 .45

800th birth anniv. of St. Francis of Assisi.

Centenary of Figueira da Foz — A401

1982, Feb. 24 Litho. *Perf. 13½*

1525 A401 10e St. Catherine Fort .22 .15

1526 A401 19e Tagus Bridge, ships .40 .30

Set value .38

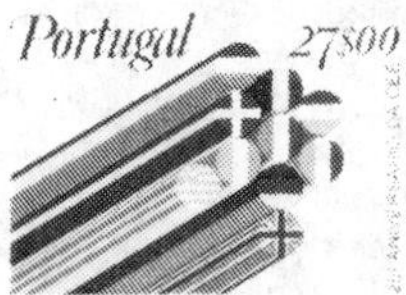

25th Anniv. of European Economic Community A402

1982, Feb. 24 *Perf. 12x11½*

1527 A402 27e multi .65 .42

a. Souvenir sheet of 4 2.75 2.75

Tile Type of 1981

Designs: No. 1528, Italo-Flemish pattern, 17th cent. No. 1529, Oriental fabric pattern altar frontal, 17th cent. No. 1530, Greek cross, 1630-1640. No. 1531, Blue and white design, Mother of God Convent, Lisbon, 1670.

1982 Litho. *Perf. 12x11½*

1528 A391 10e multi .22 .15

a. Miniature sheet of 6 1.65 1.65

1529 A391 10e multi .20 .15

a. Miniature sheet of 6 1.65 1.65

1530 A391 10e multi .18 .15

a. Miniature sheet of 6 1.65 1.65

1531 A391 10e red & blue .18 .15

a. Miniature sheet of 6 1.65 1.65

b. Souv. sheet of 4, #1528-1531 1.40 1.40

Nos. 1528-1531 (4) .78 .60

Issued: No. 1528, Mar. 24; No. 1529, June 11; No. 1530, Sept. 22; No. 1531, Dec. 15.

A403 A404

Major Sporting Events of 1982: 27e, Lisbon Sail. 33.50e, 25th Roller-hockey Championships, Lisbon and Barcelos, May 1-16. 50e, Intl. 470 Class World Championships, Cascais Bay. 75e, Espana '82 World Cup Soccer.

1982, Mar. 24 *Perf. 12x12½*

1532 A403 27e multi .60 .35

1533 A403 33.50e multi .70 .45

1534 A403 50e multi 1.10 .65

1535 A403 75e multi 1.65 1.00

Nos. 1532-1535 (4) 4.05 2.45

1982, Apr. 14 Litho. *Perf. 11½x12*

1536 A404 10e Phone, 1882 .20 .15

1537 A404 27e 1887 .55 .42

Telephone centenary.

Europa 1982 — A405

Embassy of King Manuel to Pope Leo X, 1514.

1982, May 3 *Perf. 12x11½*

1538 A405 33.50e multi .65 .42

a. Miniature sheet of 4 3.00 3.00

Visit of Pope John Paul II — A406

Designs: Pope John Paul and cathedrals.

1982, May 13 *Perf. 14*

1539 A406 10e Fatima .32 .20

1540 A406 27e Sameiro .85 .52

1541 A406 33.50e Lisbon 1.00 .65

a. Min. sheet, 2 each #1539-1541 4.75 4.75

Nos. 1539-1541 (3) 2.17 1.37

Tejo Estuary Nature Reserve Birds — A407

1982, June 11 *Perf. 11½x12*

1542 A407 10e Dunlin .22 .15

1543 A407 19e Red-crested pochard .45 .28

1544 A407 27e Greater flamingo .65 .40

1545 A407 33.50e Black-winged stilt .85 .48

Nos. 1542-1545 (4) 2.17 1.31

PHILEXFRANCE '82 Stamp Exhibition, Paris, June 11-21.

TB Bacillus Centenary A408

1982, July 27 *Perf. 12x11½*

1546 A408 27e Koch .55 .32

1547 A408 33.50e Virus, lungs .70 .25

Don't Drink and Drive! — A409

1982, Sept. 22 *Perf. 12*

1548 A409 10e multicolored .22 .15

Boeing 747 A410

Lubrapex '82 Stamp Exhibition (Historic Flights): 10e, South Atlantic crossing, 1922. 19e, South Atlantic night crossing, 1927. 33.50e, Lisbon-Rio de Janeiro discount fare flights, 1960-1967. 50e, Portugal-Brazil service, 10th anniv.

1982, Oct. 15 *Perf. 12x11½*

1549 A410 10e Fairey III D MK2 .22 .15

1550 A410 19e Dornier DO .40 .22

1551 A410 33.50e DC-7C .65 .40

1552 A410 50e shown 1.00 .60

a. Souv. sheet of 4, #1549-1552 2.75 2.75

Nos. 1549-1552 (4) 2.27 1.37

Marques de Pombal, Statesman, 200th Anniv. of Death — A411

1982, Nov. 24 Litho. *Perf. 12x11½*

1553 A411 10e multicolored .22 .15

75th Anniv. of Port Authority of Lisbon — A412

1983, Jan. 5 *Perf. 12½*

1554 A412 10e Ships .22 .15

French Alliance Centenary A413

1983, Jan. 5 *Perf. 12x11½*

1555 A413 27e multicolored .55 .35

Export Effort A414

1983, Jan. 28

1556 A414 10e multicolored .20 .15

World Communications Year — A415

1982, Feb. 23 Litho. *Perf. 11½x12*

1557 A415 10e blue & multi .20 .15

1558 A415 33.50e lt brown & multi .65 .40

Naval Uniforms and Ships — A416

1983, Feb. 23 *Perf. 13½*

1559 A416 12.50e Midshipman, 1782, Vasco da Gama .24 .15

1560 A416 25e Sailor, 1845, Estefania .45 .30

1561 A416 30e Sergeant, 1900, Adamastor .60 .35

1562 A416 37.50e Midshipman, 1892, Comandante Joao Belo .75 .45

a. Bklt. pane of 4, #1559-1562 3.00

Nos. 1559-1562 (4) 2.04 1.25

See Nos. 1589-1592.

Tile Type of 1981

No. 1563, Hunting scene, 1680. No. 1564, Birds, 18th cent. No. 1565, Flowers and Birds, 18th cent. No. 1566, Figurative tile, 18th cent.

1983 ***Perf. 12x11½***

1563 A391 12.50e multi .25 .15
a. Miniature sheet of 6 1.75 1.75
1564 A391 12.50e multi .28 .18
a. Miniature sheet of 6 1.75 1.75
1565 A391 12.50e multi .22 .15
a. Miniature sheet of 6 1.75 1.75
1566 A391 12.50e multi .22 .15
a. Miniature sheet of 6 1.75 1.75
b. Souv. sheet of 4, #1563-1566 1.25 1.25
Nos. 1563-1566 (4) .97 .63

Issued: No. 1563, Mar. 16; No. 1563, June 16; No. 1563, Oct. 19; No. 1563, Nov. 23.

17th European Arts and Sciences Exhibition, Lisbon — A417

Portuguese Discoveries and Renaissance Europe: 11e, Helmet, 16th cent. 12.50e, Astrolabe. 25e, Ships, Flemish tapestry. 30e, Column capital, 12th cent. 37.50e, Hour glass. 40e, Chinese panel painting.

1983, Apr. 6

1567 A417 11e multi .25 .16
1568 A417 12.50e multi .28 .18
1569 A417 25e multi .55 .32
1570 A417 30e multi .65 .40
1571 A417 37.50e multi .85 .50
1572 A417 40e multi .90 .52
a. Souv. sheet of 6, #1567-1572 3.75 3.75
Nos. 1567-1572 (6) 3.48 2.08

Europa Issue

Antonio Egas Moniz (1874-1955), Cerebral Angiography and Pre-frontal Leucotomy Pioneer A418

1983, May 5 Litho. ***Perf. 12½***

1573 A418 37.50e multi .60 .60
a. Souvenir sheet of 4 2.50 2.50

European Conference of Ministers of Transport — A419

1983, May 16

1574 A419 30e multi .85 .38

Endangered Sea Mammals A420

1983, July 29 Litho. ***Perf. 12x11½***

1575 A420 12.50e Sea wolf .18 .15
1576 A420 30e Dolphin .45 .28
1577 A420 37.50e Killer whale .55 .35
1578 A420 80e Humpback whale 1.25 .75
a. Souv. sheet of 4, #1575-1578 3.25 3.25
Nos. 1575-1578 (4) 2.43 1.53

BRASILIANA '83 Intl. Stamp Exhibition, Rio de Janeiro, July 29-Aug. 7.

600th Anniv. of Revolution of 1383 — A421

1983, Sept. 14 ***Perf. 13½***

1579 A421 12.50e Death of Joao Fernandes Andeiro .25 .15
1580 A421 30e Rebellion .60 .32

First Manned Balloon Flight A422

Designs: 16e, Bartolomeu Lourenco de Gusmao, Passarola flying machine. 51e, Montgolfier Balloon, first flight.

1983, Nov. 9 Litho. ***Perf. 12x11½***

1581 A422 16e multicolored .28 .18
1582 A422 51e multicolored .85 .52

Christmas 1983 — A423

Stained Glass Windows, Monastery at Batalha: 12.50e, Adoration of the Magi. 30e, Flight to Egypt.

1983, Nov. 23 ***Perf. 12½***

1583 A423 12.50e multi .22 .15
1584 A423 30e multi .52 .32

Lisbon Zoo Centenary A424

1984, Jan. 18 Litho. ***Perf. 12x11½***

1585 A424 16e Siberian tigers .50 .30
1586 A424 16e White rhinoceros .50 .30
1587 A424 16e Damalisco Albifronte .50 .30
1588 A424 16e Cheetahs .50 .30
a. Strip of 4, #1585-1588 2.00 1.25

Military Type of 1983

Air Force Dress Uniforms and Planes: 16e, 1954; Hawker Hurricane II, 1943. 35e, 1960; Republic F-84G Thunderjet. 40e, Paratrooper, 1966; 2502 Nord Noratlas, 1960. 51e, 1966; Corsair II, 1982.

1984, Feb. 5 Litho. ***Perf. 13½***

1589 A416 16e multi .25 .15
1590 A416 35e multi .55 .35
1591 A416 40e multi .65 .40
1592 A416 51e multi .80 .48
a. Bklt. pane of 4, #1589-1592 2.90
Nos. 1589-1592 (4) 2.25 1.38

Tile Type of 1981

Design: No. 1593, Royal arms, 19th cent. No. 1594, Pombal Palace wall tile, 19th cent. No. 1595, Facade covering, 19th cent. No. 1596, Grasshoppers, by Rafael Bordaro Pinhiero, 19th cent.

1984, Mar. 8 Litho. ***Perf. 12x11½***

1593 A391 16e multi .25 .15
a. Miniature sheet of 6 1.65 1.65
1594 A391 16e multi .25 .15
a. Miniature sheet of 6 1.65 1.65
1595 A391 16e multi .25 .15
a. Miniature sheet of 6 1.65 1.65
1596 A391 16e multi .24 .15
a. Miniature sheet of 6 1.65 1.65
b. Souv. sheet of 4, #1593-1596 1.25 1.25
Nos. 1593-1596 (4) .99 .60

Issued: No. 1593, Mar. 8; No. 1594, July 18; No. 1595, Aug. 3; No. 1596, Oct. 17 .

25th Intl. Fair, May 9-13 A425

Events: 40e, World Food Day. 51e, 15th Rehabilitation Intl. World Congress, Lisbon, June 4-8, vert.

1984, Apr. 3

1597 A425 35e multicolored .75 .35
1598 A425 40e multicolored .90 .40
1599 A425 51e multicolored 1.10 .48
Nos. 1597-1599 (3) 2.75 1.23

April 25th Revolution, 10th Anniv. — A426

1984, Apr. 25 ***Perf. 13½***

1600 A426 16e multicolored .40 .18

Europa (1959-84) A427

1984, May 2 ***Perf. 12x11½***

1601 A427 51e multicolored .80 .48
a. Souvenir sheet of 4 4.00 4.00

LUBRAPEX '84 and Natl. Early Art Museum Centenary A428

Paintings: 16e, Nun, 15th cent. 40e, St. John, by Master of the Retable of Santiago, 16th cent. 51e, View of Lisbon, 17th cent. 66e, Cabeca de Jovem, by Domingos Sesqueira, 19th cent.

1984, May 9 Litho. ***Perf. 12x11½***

1602 A428 16e multicolored .30 .18
1603 A428 40e multicolored .70 .40
1604 A428 51e multicolored .95 .52
1605 A428 66e multicolored 1.10 .60
a. Souv. sheet of 4, #1602-1605 3.75 2.75
Nos. 1602-1605 (4) 3.05 1.70

1984 Summer Olympics A429

1984, June 5

1606 A429 35e Fencing .52 .32
1607 A429 40e Gymnastics .60 .38
1608 A429 51e Running .75 .45
1609 A429 80e Pole vault 1.25 .75
Nos. 1606-1609 (4) 3.12 1.90

Souvenir Sheet

1610 A429 100e Hurdles 2.25 1.50

Historical Events A430

Designs: 16e, Gil Eanes, explorer who reached west coast of Africa, 1434. 51e, King Peter I of Brazil and IV of Portugal.

1984, Sept. 24 ***Perf. 12x11½***

1611 A430 16e multicolored .32 .18
1612 A430 51e multicolored .85 .45

See Brazil No. 1954.

Infantry Grenadier, 1740 — A431

1985, Jan. 23 Litho. ***Perf. 13½***

1613 A431 20e shown .30 .15
1614 A431 46e 5th Cavalry Regiment Officer, 1810 .70 .35
1615 A431 60e Artillery Corporal, 1892 .90 .45
1616 A431 100e Engineering Soldier, 1985 1.50 .75
a. Bklt. pane of 4, #1613-1616 3.50
Nos. 1613-1616 (4) 3.40 1.70

Tile Type of 1981

Designs: No. 1617, Tile from entrance hall of Lisbon's Faculdade de Letras, by Jorge Barradas, 20th cent.; No. 1618, Explorer and sailing ship, detail from tile panel by Maria Keil, Avenida Infante Santo, Lisbon; No. 1619, Profile and key, detail from a 20th century tile mural by Querubim Lapa; No. 1620, Geometric designs and flowers, by Manuel Cargaleiro.

1985 Litho. ***Perf. 12x11½***

1617 A391 20e multicolored .30 .15
a. Miniature sheet of 6 1.80 1.80
1618 A391 20e multicolored .25 .15
a. Miniature sheet of 6 1.50 1.50
1619 A391 20e multicolored .28 .15
a. Miniature sheet of 6 1.75 1.75
1620 A391 20e multicolored .25 .15
a. Miniature sheet of 6 1.50 1.50
b. Souv. sheet of 4, #1617-1620 1.00 1.00
Nos. 1617-1620 (4) 1.08 .60

Issued: No. 1617, Feb. 13; No. 1617, June 11; No. 1617, Aug. 20; No. 1617, Nov. 15.

Kiosks — A432

1985, Mar. 19 Litho. ***Perf. 11½x12***

1621 A432 20e Green kiosk .50 .15
1622 A432 20e Red kiosk .50 .15
1623 A432 20e Gray kiosk .50 .15
1624 A432 20e Blue kiosk .50 .15
a. Strip of 4, #1621-1624 2.00

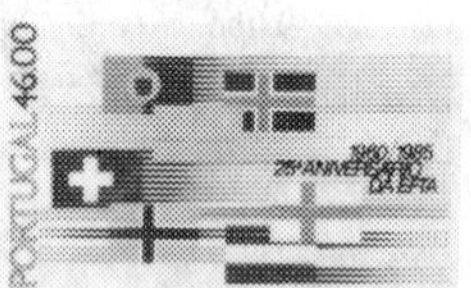

25th Anniv., European Free Trade Association — A433

1985, Apr. 10 Litho. ***Perf. 12x11½***

1625 A433 46e Flags of members .80 .30

Intl. Youth Year — A434

1985, Apr. 10 Litho.

1626 A434 60e Heads of boy and girl 1.10 .40

Europa 1985-Music — A435

1985, May 6 Litho. *Perf. 11½x12*

1627 A435 60e Woman playing tambourine .80 .40
a. Souvenir sheet of 4 3.50 3.50

Historic Anniversaries — A436

20e, King John I at the Battle of Aljubarrota, 1385. 46e, Queen Leonor (1458-1525) founding the Caldas da Rainha Hospital. 60e, Cartographer Pedro Reinel, earliest Portuguese map, c. 1483.

1985, July 5 Litho. *Perf. 12x11½*

1628 A436 20e multicolored .28 .15
1629 A436 46e multicolored .60 .30
1630 A436 60e multicolored .80 .40
Nos. 1628-1630 (3) 1.68 .85

See Nos. 1678-1680.

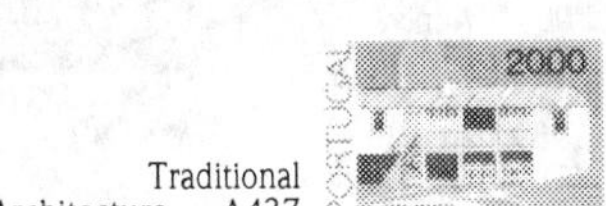

Traditional Architecture — A437

1985-89 Litho. *Perf. 12*

1631 A437 50c Saloia, Estremadura .15 .15
1632 A437 1e Beira interior .15 .15
1633 A437 1.50e Ribatejo .15 .15
1634 A437 2.50e Transmontanas .15 .15
1635 A437 10e Minho and Douro Litoral .15 .15
1636 A437 20e Farm house, Minho .28 .15
1637 A437 22.50e Alentejo .32 .16
1638 A437 25e African Sitio, Algarve .35 .18
1639 A437 27e Beira Interior .45 .22
1640 A437 29e Hill country .45 .22
1641 A437 30e Algarve .50 .25
1642 A437 40e Beira Interior .62 .30
1643 A437 50e Private home, Beira Litoral .70 .35
1644 A437 55e Tras-os-Montes .90 .45
1645 A437 60e Beira Litoral .95 .48
1646 A437 70e Estremadura Sul and Alentejo 1.10 .55
1647 A437 80e Estremadura 1.10 .55
1648 A437 90e Minho 1.25 .62
1649 A437 100e Adobe Monte, Alentejo 1.30 .65
1650 A437 500e Algarve 7.40 3.70
Nos. 1631-1650 (20) 18.42 9.58

Issue dates: 20e, 25e, 50e, 100e, Aug. 20, 1985. 2.50e, 22.50e, 80e, 90e, Mar. 10, 1986. 10e, 40e, 60e, 70e, Mar. 6, 1987. 1.50e, 27e, 30e, 55e, Mar. 15, 1988. 50c, 1e, 29e, 500e, Mar. 8, 1989.

Aquilino Ribeiro (1885-1963), Author — A438

46e, Fernando Pessoa (1888-1935), poet.

1985, Oct. 2 Litho. *Perf. 12*

1651 A438 20e multicolored .25 .15
1652 A438 46e multicolored .60 .30

Natl. Parks and Reserves A439

1985, Oct. 25

1653 A439 20e Berlenga Island .25 .15
1654 A439 40e Estrela Mountain Chain .58 .28
1655 A439 46e Boquilobo Marsh .70 .35
1656 A439 80e Formosa Lagoon 1.10 .55
Nos. 1653-1656 (4) 2.63 1.33

Souvenir Sheet

1657 A439 100e St. Jacinto Dunes 1.25 1.25

ITALIA '85.

Christmas 1985 — A440

Illuminated codices from The Prayer Times Book, Book of King Manuel, 1517-1538.

1985, Nov. 15 *Perf. 11½x12*

1658 A440 20e The Nativity .25 .15
1659 A440 46e Adoration of the Magi .60 .30

Postrider — A441

1985, Dec. 13 Litho. *Perf. 13½*

1660 A441 A(22.50e) lt yel grn & dp yel grn .32 .16

See No. 1938 for another stamp with postrider inscribed "Serie A."

Flags of EEC Member Nations A442

Design: 57.50e, Map of EEC, flags.

1986, Jan. 7 Litho. *Perf. 12*

1661 A442 20e multi .25 .15
1662 A442 57.50e multi .75 .38
a. Souv. sheet, 2 each #1661-1662 2.25 2.25

Admission of Portugal and Spain to the European Economic Community, Jan. 1. See Spain Nos. 2463-2466.

No. 1662a contains 2 alternating pairs of Nos. 1661-1662.

Castles A443

1986, Feb. 18 Litho. *Perf. 12*

1663 A443 22.50e Beja .32 .16
a. Booklet pane of 4 1.30
1664 A443 22.50e Feira .32 .16
a. Booklet pane of 4 1.30

1986, Apr. 10

1665 A443 22.50e Guimaraes .32 .16
a. Booklet pane of 4 1.30
1666 A443 22.50e Braganca .32 .16
a. Booklet pane of 4 1.30

1986, Sept. 18

1667 A443 22.50e Montemor-o-Velho .32 .16
a. Booklet pane of 4 1.30
1668 A443 22.50e Belmonte .32 .16
a. Booklet pane of 4 1.30
Nos. 1663-1668 (6) 1.92 .96

See Nos. 1688-1695, 1723-1726.

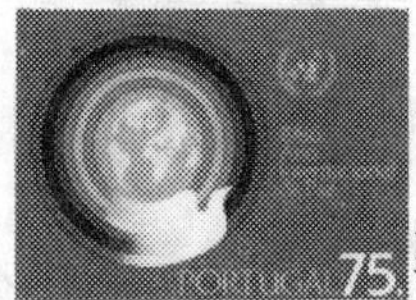

Intl. Peace Year — A445

1986, Feb. 18 Litho. *Perf. 12*

1669 A445 75e multicolored 1.00 .50

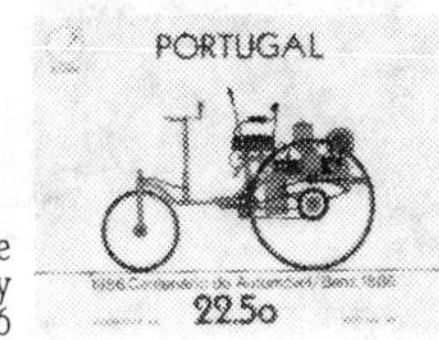

Automobile Centenary A446

1986, Apr. 10 Litho. *Perf. 12*

1670 A446 22.50e 1886 Benz .32 .16
1671 A446 22.50e 1886 Daimler .32 .16
a. Pair, #1670-1671 .65 .40

Europa 1986 — A447

1986, May 5 Litho.

1672 A447 68.50e Shad 1.05 .52
a. Souvenir sheet of 4 4.25 4.25

Horse Breeds A448

1986, May 22 Litho. *Perf. 12*

1673 A448 22.50e Alter .32 .16
1674 A448 47.50e Lusitano .68 .35
1675 A448 52.50e Garrano .75 .38
1676 A448 68.50e Sorraia 1.00 .50
Nos. 1673-1676 (4) 2.75 1.39

Souvenir Sheet

Halley's Comet A449

1986, June 24

1677 A449 100e multi 4.00 4.00

Anniversaries Type of 1985

Designs: 22.50e, Diogo Cao, explorer, heraldic pillar erected at Cape Lobo, 1484, 1st expedition. No. 1679, Manuel Passos, Corinthian column. No. 1680, Joao Baptista Ribeiro, painter, Oporto Academy director, c. 1836, and musicians.

1986, Aug. 28 Litho.

1678 A436 22.50e multi .32 .16
1679 A436 52.50e multi .75 .38
1680 A436 52.50e multi .75 .38
Nos. 1678-1680 (3) 1.82 .92

Diogo Cao's voyages, 500th anniv. Academies of Fine Art, 150th anniv.

Stamp Day — A450

Natl. Guard, 75th Anniv. — A451

Order of Engineers, 50th Anniv. — A452

No. 1681, Postal card, 100th anniv.

1986, Oct. 24 Litho.

1681 A450 22.50e multi .32 .16
1682 A451 47.50e multi .68 .35
1683 A452 52.50e multi .75 .38
Nos. 1681-1683 (3) 1.75 .89

Watermills A453

1986, Nov. 7

1684 A453 22.50e Duoro .32 .15
1685 A453 47.50e Coimbra .68 .35
1686 A453 52.50e Gerez .75 .38
1687 A453 90e Braga 1.25 .62
a. Souvenir sheet of 4, #1684-1687 3.00 3.00
Nos. 1684-1687 (4) 3.00 1.50

LUBRAPEX '86. #1687a issued Nov. 21.

Castle Type of 1986

1987-88 Litho.

1688 A443 25e Silves .35 .18
a. Booklet pane of 4 1.40
1689 A443 25e Evora Monte .35 .18
a. Booklet pane of 4 1.40
1690 A443 25e Leiria .38 .20
a. Booklet pane of 4 1.55
1691 A443 25e Trancoso .38 .20
a. Booklet pane of 4 1.55
1692 A443 25e St. George .38 .20
a. Booklet pane of 4 1.55
1693 A443 25e Marvao .38 .20
a. Booklet pane of 4 1.55
1694 A443 27e Fernando's Walls of Oporto .45 .22
a. Booklet pane of 4 1.80
1695 A443 27e Almourol .45 .22
a. Booklet pane of 4 1.80
Nos. 1688-1695 (8) 3.12 1.60

Issued: Nos. 1688-1689, Jan. 16; Nos. 1690-1691, Apr. 10; Nos. 1692-1693, Sept. 15; Nos. 1694-1695, Jan. 19, 1988.

Natl. Tourism Organization, 75th Anniv. A454

1987, Feb. 10 Litho. *Perf. 12*

1696 A454 25e Beach houses, Tocha .40 .20
1697 A454 57e Boats, Espinho .90 .45
1698 A454 98e Chafariz Fountain, Arraioles 1.50 .75
Nos. 1696-1698 (3) 2.80 1.40

European Nature Conservation Year — A455

1987, Mar. 20 *Perf. 12x12½*

1699 A455 25e shown .40 .20

1700 A455 57e Hands, flower, map .90 .45

1701 A455 74.50e Hands, star, rainbow 1.15 .58

Nos. 1699-1701 (3) 2.45 1.23

Europa 1987 — A456

Modern architecture: Bank Borges and Irmao Agency, 1986, Vila do Conde.

1987, May 5 **Litho.** *Perf. 12*

1702 A456 74.50e multi 1.25 .62

a. Souvenir sheet of 4 5.00 5.00

A457 A458

Lighthouses

1987, June 12 *Perf. 11½x12*

1703 A457 25e Aveiro .40 .20

1704 A457 25e Berlenga .40 .20

1705 A457 25e Cape Mondego .40 .20

1706 A457 25e Cape St. Vincente .40 .20

a. Strip of 4, #1703-1706 1.60 .80

1987, Aug. 27 **Litho.** *Perf. 12*

1707 A458 74.50e multi 1.10 .55

Amadeo de Souza-Cardoso (1887-1919), painter.

Portguese Royal Library, Rio de Janeiro, 150th anniv. A459

1987, Aug. 27 *Perf. 12x11½*

1708 A459 125e multicolored 2.00 1.00

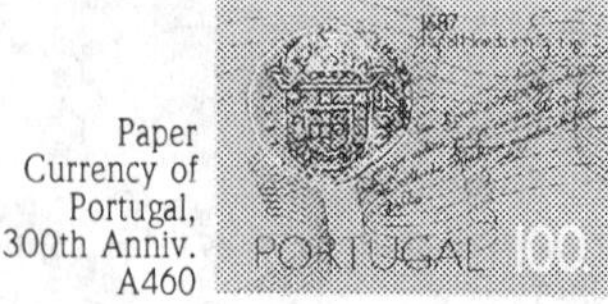

Paper Currency of Portugal, 300th Anniv. A460

1987, Aug. 27 *Perf. 12x11½*

1709 A460 100e multicolored 1.50 .75

Voyages of Bartolomeu Dias (d. 1499), 500th Anniv. A461

1987, Aug. 27 *Perf. 12x11½*

1710 A461 25e Departing from Lisbon, 1487 .38 .20

1711 A461 25e Discovering the African Coast, 1488 .38 .20

a. Pair, #1710-1711 .80 .50

No. 1711a has continuous design.

See Nos. 1721-1722.

Souvenir Sheet

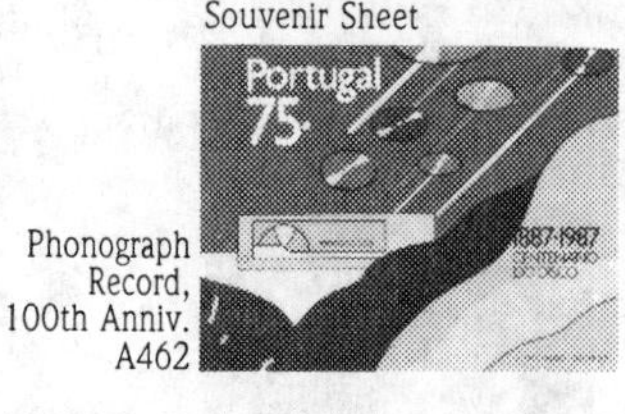

Phonograph Record, 100th Anniv. A462

1987, Oct. 9 **Litho.** *Perf. 12*

1712 Sheet of 2 3.00 3.00

a. A462 75e Compact-disc player 1.10 1.10

b. A462 125e Gramophone 1.90 1.90

Christmas A463

Various children's drawings, Intl. Year of the Child emblem.

1987, Nov. 6

1713 A463 25e Angels, magi, tree .38 .20

1714 A463 57e Friendship circle .88 .45

1715 A463 74.50e Santa riding dove 1.10 .58

a. Souv. sheet of 3, #1713-1715 2.40 2.40

Nos. 1713-1715 (3) 2.36 1.23

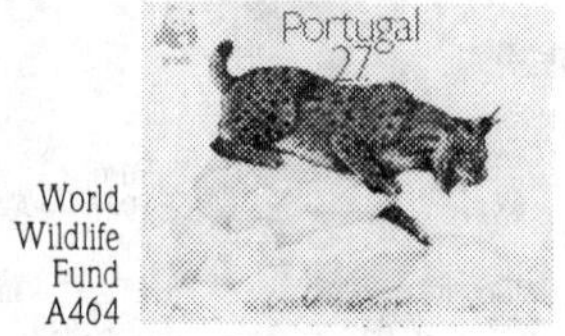

World Wildlife Fund A464

Lynx, *Lynx pardina.*

1988, Feb. 3 **Litho.** *Perf. 12*

1716 A464 27e Stalking .45 .22

1717 A464 27e Carrying prey .45 .22

1718 A464 27e Two adults .45 .22

1719 A464 27e Adult, young .45 .22

a. Strip of 4, Nos. 1716-1719 1.80 1.80

Printed in a continuous design.

Journey of Pero da Covilha to the East, 500th Anniv. A465

1988, Feb. 3

1720 A465 105e multi 1.65 .82

Bartolomeu Dias Type of 1987

Discovery of the link between the Atlantic and Indian Oceans by Dias, 500th Anniv.: No. 1721, Tidal wave, ship. No. 1722, Henricus Martelus Germanus's map (1489), picturing the African coast and linking the two oceans.

1988, Feb. 3

1721 A461 27e multi .45 .22

1722 A461 27e multi .45 .22

a. Bklt. pane of 4, Nos. 1710-1711, 1721-1722 1.70

b. Pair, #1721-1722 1.00 .60

No. 1722b has continuous design.

Castle Type of 1986

1988, Mar. 15 **Litho.** *Perf. 12*

1723 A443 27e Vila Nova de Cerveira .45 .22

a. Bklt. pane of 4 1.80

1724 A443 27e Palmela .45 .22

a. Bklt. pane of 4 1.80

1988, July 1

1725 A443 27e Chaves .45 .22

a. Bklt. pane of 4 1.80

1726 A443 27e Penedono .45 .22

a. Bklt. pane of 4 1.80

Nos. 1723-1726 (4) 1.80 .88

Europa 1988 — A466

Transportation: Mail coach, Lisbon-Oporto route, 1855-1864.

1988, Apr. 21 **Litho.** *Perf. 12*

1735 A466 80e multi 1.35 .68

a. Souv. sheet of 4 5.40 5.40

Jean Monnet (1888-1979), Economist A467

1988, May 9 **Litho.**

1736 A467 60e multi .98 .50

Souvenir Sheet

National Heritage (Patrimony) — A468

Design: 150e, Belvedere of Cordovil House and Fountain of Porta de Moura reflected in the Garcia de Resende balcony window, Evora, 16th cent.

1988, May 13 *Perf. 13½x12½*

1737 A468 150e multi 2.50 2.50

No. 1737 has inscribed margin picturing LUBRAPEX '88 and UNESCO emblems.

20th Cent. Paintings by Portuguese Artists — A469

Designs: 27e, *Viola,* c. 1916, by Amadeo de Souza-Cardoso (1887-1918). 60e, *Jugglers and Tumblers Do Not Fall,* 1949, by Jose de Almada Negreiros (1893-1970). 80e, *Still-life with Guitar,* c. 1940, by Eduardo Viana (1881-1967).

1988, Aug. 23 **Litho.** *Perf. 11½x12*

1738 A469 27e multi .42 .20

1739 A469 60e multi .90 .45

1740 A469 80e multi 1.20 .60

a. Min. sheet of 3, #1738-1740 2.55 2.55

Nos. 1738-1740 (3) 2.52 1.25

See Nos. 1748-1750, 1754-1765.

1988 Summer Olympics, Seoul — A470

1988, Sept. 16 **Litho.** *Perf. 12x11½*

1741 A470 27e Archery .40 .20

1742 A470 55e Weight lifting .82 .40

1743 A470 60e Judo .90 .45

1744 A470 80e Tennis 1.20 .60

Nos. 1741-1744 (4) 3.32 1.65

Souvenir Sheet

1745 A470 200e Yachting 3.00 3.00

Remains of the Roman Civilization in Portugal A471

Mozaics: 27e, "Winter Image," detail of *Mosaic of the Four Seasons,* limestone and glass, 3rd cent., House of the Waterworks, Coimbra. 80e, *Fish in Marine Water,* limestone, 3rd-4th cent., cover of a tank wall, public baths, Faro.

1988, Oct. 18 **Litho.** *Perf. 12*

1746 A471 27e multi .40 .20

1747 A471 80e multi 1.15 .58

20th Cent. Art Type of 1988

Paintings by Portuguese artists: 27e, *Burial,* 1938, by Mario Eloy. 60e, *Lisbon Roofs,* c. 1936, by Carlos Botelho. 80e, *Avejao Lirico,* 1939, by Antonio Pedro.

1988, Nov. 18 **Litho.** *Perf. 11½x12*

1748 A469 27e multi .42 .20

1749 A469 60e multi .92 .45

1750 A469 80e multi 1.25 .62

a. Souv. sheet of 3, #1748-1750 2.60 2.60

b. Souv. sheet of 6, #1738-1740, 1748-1750 5.25 5.25

Nos. 1748-1750 (3) 2.59 1.27

Braga Cathedral, 900th Anniv. A472

1989, Jan. 20 *Perf. 12*

1751 A472 30e multi .45 .22

INDIA '89 — A473

Designs: 55e, Caravel, Sao Jorge da Mina Fort, 1482. 60e, Navigator using astrolabe, 16th cent.

1989, Jan. 20

1752 A473 55e multi .85 .42

1753 A473 60e multi .92 .45

20th Cent. Art Type of 1988

Paintings by Portuguese artists: 29e, *Antithesis of Calm,* 1940, by Antonio Dacosta. 60c, *Lunch of the Unskilled Mason,* c. 1926, by Julio Pomar. 87e, *Simums,* 1949, by Vespeira.

1989, Feb. 15 **Litho.** *Perf. 11½x12*

1754 A469 29e multi .40 .20

1755 A469 60e multi .82 .40

1756 A469 87e multi 1.20 .60

a. Souv. sheet of 3, #1754-1756 2.50 2.50

Nos. 1754-1756 (3) 2.42 1.20

1989, July 7

Paintings by Portuguese artists: 29e, *046-72,* 1972, by Fernando Lanhas. 60e, *Les Spirales,* 1954, by Nadir Afonso. 87e, *Sim,* 1987, by Carlos Calvet.

1757 A469 29e multi .35 .18

1758 A469 60e multi .75 .38

1759 A469 87e multi 1.10 .55

a. Souv. sheet of 3, #1757-1759 2.20 2.20

b. Souv. sheet of 6, #1754-1759 4.75 4.75

Nos. 1757-1759 (3) 2.20 1.11

1990, Feb. 14

Paintings by Portuguese artists: 32e, *Aluenda-Tordesillas* by Joaquim Rodrigo. 60e, *Pintura* by Noronha da Costa. 95e, *Pintura* by Vasco Costa (1917-1985).

1760 A469 32e multicolored .42 .22

1761 A469 60e multicolored .78 .40

1762 A469 95e multicolored 1.25 .65

a. Souv. sheet of 3, #1760-1762 2.50 2.50

Nos. 1760-1762 (3) 2.45 1.27

1990, Sept. 21

Paintings by Portuguese artists: 32e, Costa Pinheiro. 60e, Paula Rego. 95e, Jose De Guimaraes.

1763 A469 32e multicolored .42 .22
1764 A469 60e multicolored .80 .40
1765 A469 95e multicolored 1.30 .65
a. Min. sheet of 3, #1763-1765 2.50 2.50
b. Min. sheet of 6, #1760-1765 5.00 5.00
Nos. 1763-1765 (3) 2.52 1.27

Special Occasions — A474

1989, Feb. 15 Litho. *Perf. 12*

1772 A474 29e multi .40 .20
a. Bklt. pane of 8 3.25
1773 A474 60e With love .80 .40
a. Bklt. pane of 8 6.40

European Parliament Elections — A475

1989, Mar. 8 Litho. *Perf. 11½x12*

1774 A475 60e multi .90 .45

Europa 1989 — A476

Children's toys.

1989, Apr. 26 Litho. *Perf. 12*

1775 A476 80e Top 1.20 .60

Souvenir Sheet

1776 Sheet of 4, 2 each #1775, 1776a 4.80 4.80
a. A476 80e Tops 1.20 1.20

Surface Transportation, Lisbon — A477

29e, Carris Co. elevated railway, Bica Street. 65e, Carris electric tram. 87e, Carmo Elevator, Santa Justa Street. 100e, Carris doubledecker bus. 250e, Transtejo Co. riverboat *Cacilheiro*, horiz.

1989, May 22 Litho.

1777 A477 29e multi .45 .22
1778 A477 65e multi .98 .50
1779 A477 87e multi 1.30 .65
1780 A477 100e multi 1.50 .75
Nos. 1777-1780 (4) 4.23 2.12

Souvenir Sheet

1781 A477 250e multi 3.75 3.75

Windmills A478

1989, June 14 Litho.

1782 A478 29e Ansiao .45 .22
1783 A478 65e Santiago do Cacem .98 .50
1784 A478 87e Afife 1.30 .65
1785 A478 100e Caldas da Rainha 1.50 .75
a. Bklt. pane of 4, #1782-1785 4.25
Nos. 1782-1785 (4) 4.23 2.12

Souvenir Sheet

French Revolution, 200th Anniv. — A479

1989, July 7 Litho. *Perf. 11½x12*

1786 A479 250e Drummer 3.00 3.00

No. 1786 has multicolored inscribed margin picturing the PHILEXFRANCE '89 emblem and the storming of the Bastille.

Natl. Palaces A480

1989, Oct. 18 Litho. *Perf. 12*

1787 A480 29e Ajuda, Lisbon, and King Luiz I .35 .18
1788 A480 60e Queluz .75 .38

Death cent. of King Luiz.

Exhibition Emblem and Wildflowers — A481

1989, Nov. 17 Litho.

1789 A481 29e *Armeria pseudarmeria* .38 .20
1790 A481 60e *Santolina impressa* .75 .38
1791 A481 87e *Linaria lamarckii* 1.10 .55
1792 A481 100e *Limonium multiforum* 1.25 .62
a. Bklt. pane of 4, #1789-1792 3.50
Nos. 1789-1792 (4) 3.48 1.75

World Stamp Expo '89, Washington, DC.

Portuguese Faience, 17th Cent. A482

1990, Jan. 24 Litho. *Perf. 12x11½*

1793 A482 33e shown .45 .22
1794 A482 33e Nobleman (plate) .45 .22
1795 A482 35e Urn .48 .24
1796 A482 60e Fish (pitcher) .80 .40
1797 A482 60e Crown, shield (plate) .80 .40
1798 A482 60e Lidded bowl .80 .40
Nos. 1793-1798 (6) 3.78 1.88

Souvenir Sheet

Perf. 12

1799 A482 250e Plate 3.35 3.35

No. 1799 contains one 52x45mm stamp. See Nos. 1829-1835, 1890-1896.

Score, Alfred Keil and Henrique Lopes de Mondonca A483

1990, Mar. 6 *Perf. 12x11½*

1804 A483 32e multicolored .42 .22

A Portuguesa, the Natl. Anthem, cent. (32e).

University Education in Portugal, 700th Anniv. — A484

1990, Mar. 6 *Perf. 11½x12*

1805 A484 70e multicolored .95 .48

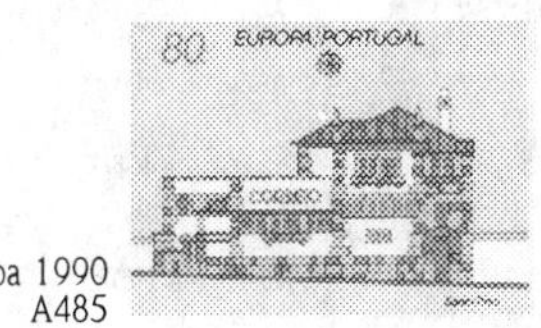

Europa 1990 A485

1990, Apr. 11 *Perf. 12x11½*

1806 A485 80e Santo Tirso P.O. 1.10 .55

Souvenir Sheet

1807 Sheet of 4, 2 each #1806, 1807a 4.40 4.40
a. A485 80e Mala Posta P.O. 1.10 1.10

Souvenir Sheet

Gentleman Using Postage Stamp, 1840 — A486

1990, May 3

1808 A486 250e multicolored 3.35 3.35

Stamp World London '90 and 150th anniv. of the Penny Black.

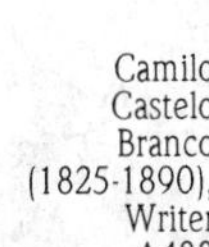

Greetings Issue — A487

"FELICITACOES" and street scenes.

1990, June 5 Litho. *Perf. 12*

1809 A487 60e Stairway .80 .40
1810 A487 60e Automobile .80 .40
1811 A487 60e Man in street .80 .40
1812 A487 60e shown .80 .40
Nos. 1809-1812 (4) 3.20 1.60

Perf. 13 Vert.

1809a A487 60e .80 .40
1810a A487 60e .80 .40
1811a A487 60e .80 .40
1812a A487 60e .80 .40
b. Bklt. pane of 4, #1809a-1812a 3.25

Camilo Castelo Branco (1825-1890), Writer A488

Designs: 70e, Friar Bartolomeu dos Martires (1514-1590), theologian.

1990, July 11 Litho. *Perf. 12x11½*

1813 A488 65e multicolored .90 .45
1814 A488 70e multicolored .95 .48

Ships — A489

1990, Sept. 21 Litho. *Perf. 12*

1815 A489 32e Barca .42 .22
1816 A489 60e Caravela Pescareza .80 .40
1817 A489 70e Barinel .95 .48
1818 A489 95e Caravela 1.30 .65
Nos. 1815-1818 (4) 3.47 1.75

Perf. 13½ Vert.

1815a A489 32e .42 .22
1816a A489 60e .80 .40
1817a A489 70e .95 .48
1818a A489 95e 1.30 .65
b. Bklt. pane of 4, #1815a-1818a 3.45

National Palaces — A490

1990, Oct. 11 *Perf. 12*

1819 A490 32e Pena .45 .22
1820 A490 60e Vila .82 .40
1821 A490 70e Mafra .95 .48
1822 A490 120e Guimaraes 1.65 .82
Nos. 1819-1822 (4) 3.87 1.92

Francisco Sa Carneiro (1934-1980), Politician A491

1990, Nov. 7

1823 A491 32e ol brn & blk .45 .22

Rossio Railway Station, Cent. — A492

Various locomotives.

1990, Nov. 7

1824 A492 32e Steam, 1887 .45 .22
1825 A492 60e Steam, 1891 .82 .40
1826 A492 70e Steam, 1916 .95 .48
1827 A492 95e Electric, 1956 1.30 .65
Nos. 1824-1827 (4) 3.52 1.75

Souvenir Sheet

1828 A492 200e Railway station 3.00 3.00

Ceramics Type of 1990

1991, Feb. 7 Litho. *Perf. 12*

1829 A482 35e Lavabo .50 .25
1830 A482 35e Tureen and plate .50 .25
1831 A482 35e Flower vase .50 .25
1832 A482 60e Finger bowl .85 .45
1833 A482 60e Coffee pot .85 .45
1834 A482 60e Mug .85 .45
Nos. 1829-1834 (6) 4.05 2.10

Souvenir Sheet

1835 A482 250e Plate 4.00 4.00

No. 1835 contains one 52x44mm stamp.

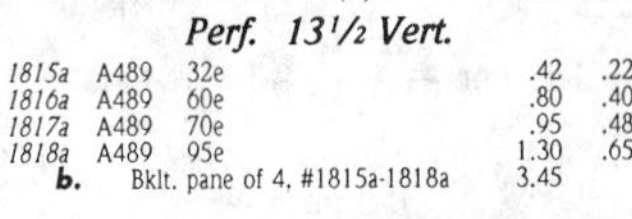

European Tourism Year — A494

1991, Mar. 6 Litho. *Perf. 12*
1836 A494 60e Flamingos .95 .48
1837 A494 110e Chameleon 1.70 .85

Souvenir Sheet
1838 A494 250e Deer 4.00 4.00

Portuguese Navigators — A495

1990-94 Litho. *Perf. 12x11½*
Design A495
1839 2e Joao Goncalves Zarco .15 .15
1840 3e Pedro Lopes de Sousa .15 .15
1841 4e Duarte Pacheco Pereira .15 .15
1842 5e Tristao Vaz Teixeira .15 .15
1843 6e Pedro Alvares Cabral .15 .15
1844 10e Joao de Castro .15 .15
1845 32e Bartolomeu Perestrelo .42 .22
1846 35e Gil Eanes .50 .25
1847 38e Vasco da Gama .58 .28
1848 42e Joao de Lisboa .58 .30
1849 45e Joaoa Rodriques Cabrillo .65 .35
1850 60e Nuno Tristao .85 .45
1851 65e Joao da Nova 1.00 .50
1852 70e Ferdinand Magellan 1.00 .50
1853 75e Pedro Fernandes de Queiros 1.10 .55
1854 80e Diogo Gomes 1.15 .60
1855 100e Diogo de Silves 1.35 .68
1856 200e Estevao Gomes 2.75 1.40
1857 250e Diogo Cao 3.60 1.80
1858 350e Bartolomeu Dias 5.30 2.65
Nos. 1839-1858 (20) 21.73 11.43

Issued: 2e, 5e, 32e, 100e, Mar. 6, 1990; 6e, 38e, 65e, 350e, Mar. 6, 1991; 35e, 60e, 80e, 250e, Mar. 6, 1992; 4e, 42e, 70e, 200e, Apr. 6, 1993; 3e, 10e, 45e, 75e, Apr. 29, 1994.

Europa A496

1991, Apr. 11 Litho. *Perf. 12*
1859 A496 80e Eutelsat II 1.10 .60

Souvenir Sheet
1860 Sheet, 2 each #1859, 1860a 4.50 4.50
a. A496 80e Olympus I 1.10 1.10

Souvenir Sheet

Princess Isabel & Philip le Bon — A497

1991, May 27 Litho. *Perf. 12½*
1861 A497 300e multicolored 4.00 4.00

Europalia '91. See Belgium No. 1402.

Discovery Ships — A498

1991, May 27 Litho. *Perf. 12*
1862 A498 35e Caravel .50 .25
1863 A498 75e Nau 1.10 .55
1864 A498 80e Nau, stern 1.15 .60
1865 A498 110e Galleon 1.70 .85
Nos. 1862-1865 (4) 4.45 2.25

Perf. 13½ Vert.
1862a A498 35e .50 .25
1863a A498 75e 1.10 .55
1864a A498 80e 1.15 .60
1865a A498 110e 1.70 .85
b. Bklt. pane of 4, #1862a-1865a 4.50

Portuguese Crown Jewels — A499

Designs: 35e, Running knot, diamonds & emeralds, 18th cent. 60e, Royal scepter, 19th cent. 70e, Sash of the Grand Cross, ruby & diamonds, 18th cent. 80e, Court saber, gold & diamonds in hilt, 19th cent. 140e, Royal crown, 19th cent.

1991, July 8 Litho. *Perf. 12*
1866 A499 35e multicolored .50 .25
1867 A499 60e multicolored .88 .44
1868 A499 80e multicolored 1.15 .62
1869 A499 140e multicolored 2.00 1.00
Nos. 1866-1869 (4) 4.53 2.31

Perf. 13½ Vert.
1870 A499 70e multicolored 1.00 .50
a. Booklet pane of 5 5.00

See Nos. 1898-1902.

Antero de Quental (1842-1891), Poet — A500

First Missionaries to Congo, 500th Anniv. A501

1991, Aug. 2 *Perf. 12*
1871 A500 35e multicolored .50 .25
1872 A501 110e multicolored 1.70 .85

Architectural Heritage A502

Designs: 35e, School of Architecture, Oporto University, by Siza Vieira. 60e, Torre do Tombo, by Ateliers Associates of Arsenio Cordeiro. 80e, Railway Bridge over Douro River, by Edgar Cardoso. 110e, Setubal-Braga highway bridge.

1991, Sept. 4 Litho. *Perf. 12*
1873 A502 35e multicolored .50 .25
1874 A502 60e multicolored .88 .44
1875 A502 80e multicolored 1.15 .62
1876 A502 110e multicolored 1.70 .85
Nos. 1873-1876 (4) 4.23 2.16

1992 Summer Olympics, Barcelona A503

1991, Oct. 9 Litho. *Perf. 12*
1877 A503 35e Equestrian .55 .28
1878 A503 60e Fencing .90 .45
1879 A503 80e Shooting 1.15 .60
1880 A503 110e Sailing 1.70 .85
Nos. 1877-1880 (4) 4.30 2.18

History of Portuguese Communications — A504

Designs: 35e, King Manuel I appointing first Postmaster, 1520. 60e, Mailbox, telegraph, 1881. 80e, Automobile, telephone, 1911. 110e, Airplane, mail truck, 1991.

1991, Oct. 9
1881 A504 35e multicolored .55 .28
1882 A504 60e multicolored .90 .45
1883 A504 80e multicolored 1.15 .60
Nos. 1881-1883 (3) 2.60 1.33

Souvenir Sheet
1884 A504 110e multicolored 1.75 1.75

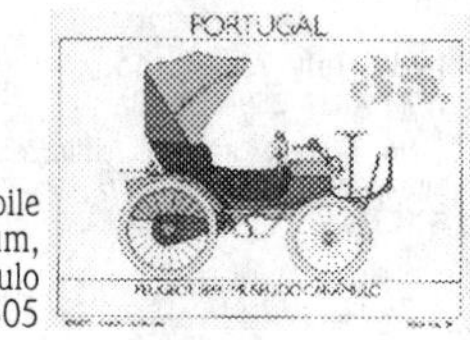

Automobile Museum, Caramulo A505

Designs: No. 1889a, Mercedes 380K, 1934. b, Hispano-Suiza, 1924.

1991, Nov. 15
1885 A505 35e Peugeot, 1899 .55 .28
1886 A505 60e Rolls Royce, 1911 .90 .45
1887 A505 80e Bugatti 35B, 1930 1.15 .60
1888 A505 110e Ferrari 195 Inter, 1950 1.70 .85
Nos. 1885-1888 (4) 4.30 2.18

Souvenir Sheet
1889 Sheet, 2 each #1889a-1889b 4.25 4.25
a.-b. A505 70e any single 1.00 1.00

Phila Nippon '91 (#1889). See #1903-1906A.

Ceramics Type of 1990

1992, Jan. 24 Litho. *Perf. 12*
1890 A482 40e Tureen with lid .60 .30
1891 A482 40e Plate .60 .30
1892 A482 40e Pitcher with lid .60 .30
1893 A482 65e Violin .95 .48
1894 A482 65e Bottle in form of woman .95 .48
1895 A482 65e Man seated on barrel .95 .48
Nos. 1890-1895 (6) 4.65 2.34

Souvenir Sheet
1896 A482 260e Political caricature 3.85 3.85

No. 1896 contains one 51x44mm stamp.

Portuguese Presidency of the European Community Council of Ministers A506

1992, Jan. 24
1897 A506 65e multicolored .95 .48

Crown Jewels Type of 1991

Designs: 38e, Coral flowers, 19th cent. 65e, Clock of gold, enamel, ivory and diamonds, 20th cent. 70e, Tobacco box encrusted with diamonds and emeralds, 1755. 85e, Royal scepter, 1828. 125e, Eighteen star necklace with diamonds, 1863.

1992, Feb. 7 Litho. *Perf. 11½x12*
1898 A499 38e multicolored .58 .28
1899 A499 70e multicolored 1.05 .58
1900 A499 85e multicolored 1.30 .65
1901 A499 125e multicolored 1.90 .95

Perf. 13½ Vert.
1902 A499 65e multicolored 1.00 .50
a. Booklet pane of 5 5.00
Nos. 1898-1902 (5) 5.83 2.96

Automobile Museum Type of 1991

Designs: 38e, Citroen Torpedo, 1922. 65e, Rochet Schneider, 1914. 85e, Austin Seven, 1933. 120e, Mercedes Benz 770, 1938. No. 1906b, Renault, 1911. c, Ford Model T, 1927.

1992, Mar. 6 Litho. *Perf. 12*
1903 A505 38e multicolored .58 .28
1904 A505 65e multicolored 1.00 .50
1905 A505 85e multicolored 1.30 .65
1906 A505 120e multicolored 1.80 .90
Nos. 1903-1906 (4) 4.68 2.33

Souvenir Sheet
1906A Sheet of 2 each, #b.-c. 4.25 4.25
b.-c. A505 70e any single 1.00 1.00

Automobile Museum, Oeiras.

Portuguese Arrival in Japan, 450th Anniv. A508

Granada '92: 120e, Three men with gifts, Japanese.

1992, Apr. 24 Litho. *Perf. 12*
1907 A508 38e shown .58 .30
1908 A508 120e multicolored 1.80 .90

Portuguese Pavilion, Expo '92, Seville — A509

1992, Apr. 24 Litho. *Perf. 11½x12*
1909 A509 65e multicolored 1.10 .55

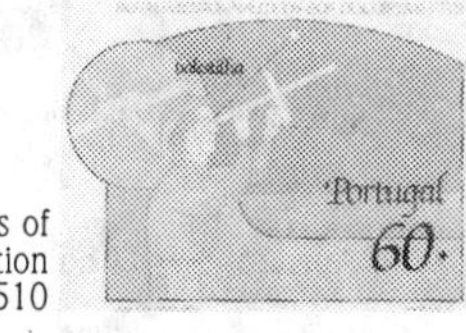

Instruments of Navigation A510

1992, May 9 Litho. *Perf. 12x11½*
1910 A510 60e Cross staff .95 .48
1911 A510 70e Quadrant 1.10 .55
1912 A510 100e Astrolabe 1.60 .80
1913 A510 120e Compass 1.90 .95
a. Souv. sheet of 4, #1910-1913 5.75 5.75
Nos. 1910-1913 (4) 5.55 2.78

Lubrapex '92 (#1913a).

Royal Hospital of All Saints, 500th Anniv. A511

1992, May 11
1914 A511 38e multicolored .60 .30

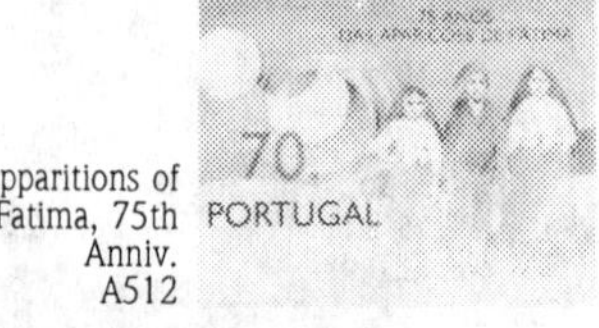

Apparitions of Fatima, 75th Anniv. A512

1992, May 11
1915 A512 70e multicolored 1.10 .55

Port of Leixoes, Cent. — A513

1992, May 11
1916 A513 120e multicolored 1.90 .95

A514

Voyages of Columbus — A515

Designs: 85e, King John II with Columbus. No. 1918, Columbus in sight of land. No. 1919, Landing of Columbus. No. 1920, Columbus soliciting aid from Queen Isabella. No. 1921, Columbus welcomed at Barcelona. No. 1922, Columbus presenting natives. No. 1923, Columbus.

Nos. 1918-1923 are similar in design to US Nos. 230-231, 234-235, 237, 245.

1992, May 22 Litho. *Perf. 12x11½*

1917 A514 85e gold & multi 1.40 .70

Souvenir Sheets

Perf. 12

1918 A515 260e blue 4.10 4.10
1919 A515 260e brown violet 4.10 4.10
1920 A515 260e brown 4.10 4.10
1921 A515 260e violet black 4.10 4.10
1922 A515 260e black 4.10 4.10
1923 A515 260e black 4.10 4.10

Europa.

See US Nos. 2624-2629, Italy Nos. 1883-1888, and Spain Nos. 2677-2682.

UN Conference on Environmental Development — A516

70e, Bird flying over polluted water system. 120e, Clean water system, butterfly, bird, flowers.

1992, June 12 Litho. *Perf. 12x11½*

1924 A516 70e multicolored 1.15 .58
1925 A516 120e multicolored 2.00 1.00
a. Pair, #1924-1925 3.15 1.58

1992 Summer Olympics, Barcelona — A517

1992, July 29 Litho. *Perf. 11½x12*

1926 A517 38e Women's running .65 .32
1927 A517 70e Soccer 1.15 .58
1928 A517 85e Hurdles 1.40 .70
1929 A517 120e Roller hockey 2.00 1.00
Nos. 1926-1929 (4) 5.20 2.60

Souvenir Sheet

Perf. 12

1930 A517 250e Basketball 4.10 4.10

Olymphilex '92 (#1930).

Campo Pequeno Bull Ring, Lisbon, Cent. — A518

Various scenes of picadors.

1992, Aug. 18 *Perf. 12x11½*

1931 A518 38e multicolored .65 .32
1932 A518 65e multicolored 1.10 .55
1933 A518 70e multicolored 1.15 .58
1934 A518 155e multicolored 2.55 1.30
Nos. 1931-1934 (4) 5.45 2.75

Souvenir Sheet

Perf. 13½x12½

1935 A518 250e Bull ring, vert. 4.10 4.10

No. 1935 contains one 35x50mm stamp.

Single European Market A519

1992, Nov. 4 Litho. *Perf. 12x11½*

1936 A519 65e multicolored .95 .48

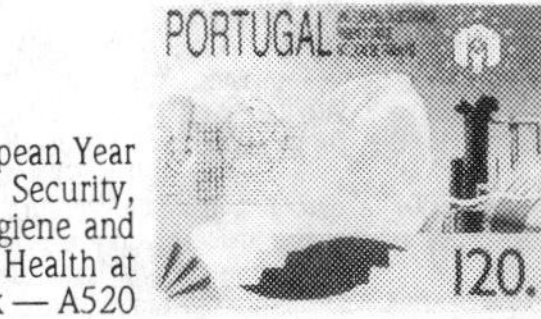

European Year for Security, Hygiene and Health at Work — A520

1992, Nov. 4 *Perf. 12x11½*

1937 A520 120e multicolored 1.80 .90

Postrider A521

1993, Mar. 9 Litho. *Perf. 12x12½*

1938 A521 (A) henna brown, gray & black .65 .30

No. 1938 sold for 42e on date of issue.

Almada Negreiros (1893-1970), Artist — A522

1993, Mar. 9 Litho. *Perf. 11½x12*

1939 A522 40e Portrait .58 .30
1940 A522 65e Ships .95 .48

Instruments of Navigation A523

1993, Apr. 6 *Perf. 12x11½*

1941 A523 42e Hourglass .60 .30
1942 A523 70e Nocturlabe 1.00 .50
1943 A523 90e Kamal 1.30 .65
1944 A523 130e Backstaff 1.90 .95
Nos. 1941-1944 (4) 4.80 2.40

Contemporary Paintings by Jose Escada (1934-1980) A524

Europa: No. 1945, Cathedral, 1979. No. 1946a, Abstract shapes, 1966.

1993, May 5 Litho. *Perf. 12x11½*

1945 A524 90e multicolored 1.25 .62

Souvenir Sheet

1946 Sheet, 2 each #1945, 1946a 5.00 5.00
a. A524 90e multicolored 1.25 1.25

Assoc. of Volunteer Firemen of Lisbon, 125th Anniv. A525

1993, June 21 Litho. *Perf. 12x11½*

1947 A525 70e multicolored .90 .45

Sao Carlos Natl. Theatre, Bicent. A526

1993, June 21

1948 A526 42e Rossini .52 .25
1949 A526 70e Verdi .90 .45
1950 A526 90e Wagner 1.15 .55
1951 A526 130e Mozart 1.65 .80
Nos. 1948-1951 (4) 4.22 2.05

Souvenir Sheet

1952 A526 300e Theatre 3.75 3.75

Union of Portuguese Speaking Capitals — A527

1993, July 30 Litho. *Perf. 11½x12*

1953 A527 130e multicolored 1.65 .80
a. Miniature sheet of 4 + 2 labels 6.75 3.25

Brasiliana '93 (#1953a).

Sculpture — A528

Designs: 42e, Annunciation Angel, 12th cent. 70e, St. Mark, 16th cent., horiz. No. 1956, Virgin and Child, 17th cent. 90e, Archangel St. Michael, 18th cent. 130e, Conde de Ferreira, 19th cent. 170e, Modern sculpture, 20th cent.

No. 1960a, Head of Agrippina, the Elder, 1st cent. No. 1960b, Virgin of the Annunciation, 16th cent. No. 1960c, The Widow, 19th cent. No. 1960d, Love Ode, 20th cent.

Perf. 11½x12, 12x11½

1993, Aug. 18

1954 A528 42e multicolored .55 .28
1955 A528 70e multicolored .90 .45
1956 A528 75e multicolored .95 .48
1957 A528 90e multicolored 1.10 .58
1958 A528 130e multicolored 1.65 .80
1959 A528 170e multicolored 2.25 1.10
Nos. 1954-1959 (6) 7.40 3.69

Souvenir Sheet

1960 Sheet of 4 4.00 4.00
a.-d. A528 75e any single .95 .95

See Nos. 2001-2007, 2067-2073.

Railway World Congress A529

90e, Cars on railway overpass, train. 130e, Traffic jam, train. 300e, Train, track skirting tree.

1993, Sept. 6 *Perf. 12x11½*

1961 A529 90e multicolored 1.10 .55
1962 A529 130e multicolored 1.65 .80

Souvenir Sheet

1963 A529 300e multicolored 3.75 3.75

Portuguese Arrival in Japan, 450th Anniv. A530

Designs: 42e, Japanese using musket. 130e, Catholic priests. 350e, Exchanging items of trade.

1993, Sept. 22 Litho. *Perf. 12*

1964 A530 42e multicolored .55 .28
1965 A530 130e multicolored 1.65 .85
1966 A530 350e multicolored 4.50 2.25
Nos. 1964-1966 (3) 6.70 3.38

See Macao Nos. 704-706.

Trawlers A531

1993, Oct. 1 Litho. *Perf. 12x11½*

1967 A531 42e Twin-mast .55 .28
1968 A531 70e Single-mast .90 .45
1969 A531 90e SS Germano 3 1.10 .55
1970 A531 130e Steam-powered 1.75 .85
Nos. 1967-1970 (4) 4.30 2.13

Perf. 11½

1967a A531 42e .55 .28
1968a A531 70e .90 .45
1969a A531 90e 1.10 .55
1970a A531 130e 1.75 .85
b. Booklet pane of 4, #1967a-1970a 4.30

A532

A533

Mailboxes: 42e, Rural mail bag, 1880. 70e, Railroad wall-mounted mailbox, 19th cent. 90e, Free-standing mailbox, 19th cent. 130e, Modern mailbox, 1992. 300e, Mailbox from horse-drawn postal vehicle, 19th cent.

1993, Oct. 9 Litho. *Perf. 12*

1971 A532 42e multicolored .48 .25
1972 A532 70e multicolored .80 .40
1973 A532 90e multicolored 1.00 .50
1974 A532 130e multicolored 1.50 .75
Nos. 1971-1974 (4) 3.78 1.90

Souvenir Sheet

1975 A532 300e multicolored 3.50 3.50

No. 1975 has continuous design.

1993, Oct. 9

Endangered birds of prey.

1976 A533 42e Imperial eagle .48 .25
1977 A533 70e Royal eagle owl .80 .40
1978 A533 130e Peregrine falcon 1.50 .75
1979 A533 350e Hen harrier 4.00 2.00
Nos. 1976-1979 (4) 6.78 3.40

Brazil-Portugal Treaty of Consultation and Friendship, 40th Anniv. A534

1993, Nov. 3

1980 A534 130e multicolored 1.50 .75

See Brazil No. 2430.

Souvenir Sheet

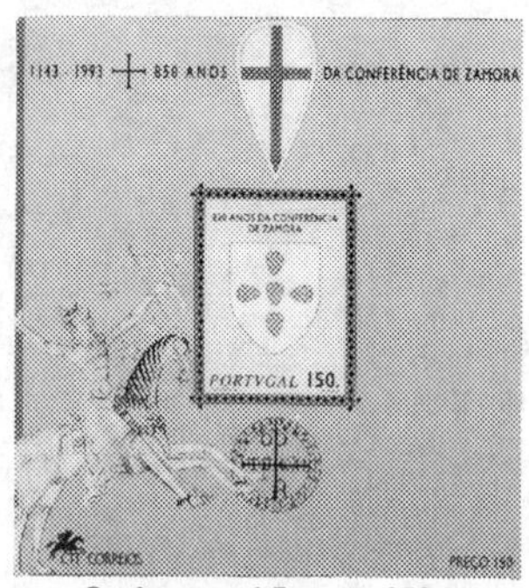

Conference of Zamora, 850th Anniv. — A535

1993, Dec. 9

1981 A535 150e multicolored 1.65 1.65

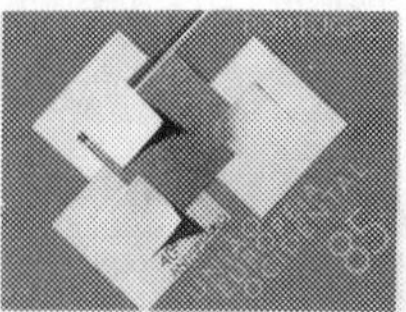

West European Union, 40th Anniv. A536

1994, Jan. 27 Litho. *Perf. 12*

1982 A536 85e multicolored 1.10 .55

Intl. Olympic Committee, Cent. A537

Design: No. 1984, Olympic torch, rings.

1994, Jan. 27

1983 A537 100e multicolored 1.25 .65
1984 A537 100e multicolored 1.25 .65

Issued in sheets of 8, 4 each + label.

Oliveira Martins (1845-94), Historian A538

100e, Florbela Espanca (1894-1930), poet.

1994, Feb. 21

1985 A538 45e multicolored .60 .30
1986 A538 100e multicolored 1.25 .65

Prince Henry the Navigator (1394-1460) — A539

Illustration reduced.

1994, Mar. 4

1987 A539 140e multicolored 1.75 .85

See Brazil No. 2463, Cape Verde No. 664, Macao No. 719.

Transfer of Power, 20th Anniv. A540

1994, Apr. 22 Litho. *Perf. 12x11½*

1988 A540 75e multicolored .90 .45

Europa A541

1994, May 5 Litho. *Perf. 12x11½*

1989 A541 100e People of Ormuz 1.25 .65

Souvenir Sheet

1990 Sheet of 4, 2 each #1989, 1990a 5.00 5.00
a. A541 100e Ears of corn 1.25 1.25

Intl. Year of the Family A542

1994, May 15 Litho. *Perf. 12x11½*

1991 A542 45e black, red & brown .55 .28
1992 A542 140e black, red & green 1.75 .85

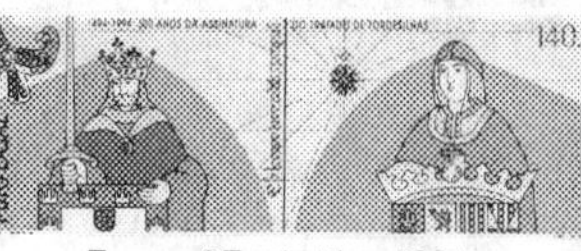

Treaty of Tordesillas, 500th Anniv. — A543

Illustration reduced.

1994, June 7 Litho. *Perf. 12x11½*

1993 A543 140e multicolored 1.75 .90

1994 World Cup Soccer Championships, US — A544

1994, June 7

1994 A544 100e shown 1.25 .60
1995 A544 140e Ball, 4 shoes 1.90 .95

Lisbon '94, European Capital of Culture A545

Birds and: 45e, Music. 75e, Photography. 100e, Theater and ballet. 145e, Art.

1994, July 1

1996 A545 45e multicolored .55 .28
1997 A545 75e multicolored .95 .48
1998 A545 100e multicolored 1.25 .60
1999 A545 140e multicolored 1.90 .95
a. Souvenir sheet of 4, #1996-1999 4.75 4.75
Nos. 1996-1999 (4) 4.65 2.31

Year of Road Safety — A545a

1994, Aug. 16 Litho. *Perf. 11½x12*

2000 A545a 45e black, red & green .58 .30

Sculpture Type of 1993

Designs: 45e, Pedra Formosa, Castreja culture. No. 2002, Carved pilaster, 7th cent., vert. 80e, Capital carved with figures, 12th cent. 100e, Laying Christ in the Tomb, 16th cent. 140e, Reliquary chapel, 17th cent. 180e, Bas relief, 20th cent.

No. 2007: a, Sarcophagus of Queen Urraca, 13th cent. b, Sarcophagus of Dom Afonso. c, Tomb of Dom Joao de Noronha and Dona Isabel de Sousa, 16th cent. d, Mausoleum of Adm. Machado Santos, 20th cent.

Perf. 12x11½, 11½x12

1994, Aug. 16

2001 A528 45e multicolored .58 .30
2002 A528 75e multicolored .95 .48
2003 A528 80e multicolored 1.00 .50
2004 A528 100e multicolored 1.25 .60
2005 A528 140e multicolored 1.75 .85
2006 A528 180e multicolored 2.25 1.10
Nos. 2001-2006 (6) 7.78 3.83

Souvenir Sheet

Perf. 12x11½

2007 Sheet of 4 4.00 4.00
a.-d. A528 75e any single .95 .95

Falconry A546

Designs: 45e, Falconer, hooded bird, dog. 75e, Falcon flying after prey. 100e, Falcon, prey on ground. 140e, Three falcons on perches. 250e, Hooded falcon.

1994, Sept. 16 Litho. *Perf. 12*

2008 A546 45e multicolored .58 .30
2009 A546 75e multicolored .95 .48
2010 A546 100e multicolored 1.25 .62
2011 A546 140e multicolored 1.75 .85
Nos. 2008-2011 (4) 4.53 2.25

Souvenir Sheet

2012 A546 250e multicolored 3.25 3.25

Trawlers A547

1994, Sept. 16 *Perf. 12x11½*

2013 A547 45e Maria Arminda .58 .30
2014 A547 75e Bom Pastor .95 .48
2015 A547 100e With triplex haulers 1.25 .62
2016 A547 140e Sueste 1.75 .85
Nos. 2013-2016 (4) 4.53 2.25

Perf. 11½ Vert.

2013a A547 45e .58 .30
2014a A547 75e .95 .48
2015a A547 100e 1.25 .62
2016a A547 140e 1.75 .85
b. Booklet pane of 4, #2013a-2016a 4.55

Modern Railway Transport — A548

Designs: 45e, Sintra Railway, electric multiple car unit. 75e, 5600 series locomotives. 140e, Lisbon subway cars. Illustration reduced.

1994, Oct. 10 Litho. *Perf. 12*

2017 A548 45e multicolored .55 .28
2018 A548 75e multicolored .90 .45
2019 A548 140e multicolored 1.75 .90
Nos. 2017-2019 (3) 3.20 1.63

Vehicles of Postal Transportation A549

45e, Horse-drawn mail coach, 19th cent. 75e, Railway postal ambulance, 1910. 100e, Mercedes station wagon, No. 222, 1950. 140e, Volkswagen van, 1952. 250e, DAF 2500 truck, 1983.

1994, Oct. 10

2020 A549 45e multicolored .55 .28
2021 A549 75e multicolored .90 .45
2022 A549 100e multicolored 1.25 .65
2023 A549 140e multicolored 1.75 .90
Nos. 2020-2023 (4) 4.45 2.28

Souvenir Sheet

2024 A549 250e multicolored 3.25 3.25

First Savings Bank in Portugal, 150th Anniv. A550

1994, Oct. 31

2025 A550 45e Pelican medallion .55 .28
2026 A550 100e Modern coins 1.25 .65

World Wide Savings Day (#2026).

American Society of Travel Agents, 64th Congress, Lisbon A551

1994, Nov. 7

2027 A551 140e multicolored 1.75 .90

Historical Inns — A552

Designs: 45e, S. Filipe Fort, Setubal. 75e, Obidos Castle. 100e, Dos Loios Convent, Evora. 140e, St. Marinha Guimaraes Monastery.

1994, Nov. 7

2028 A552 45e multicolored .55 .28
2029 A552 75e multicolored .90 .45
2030 A552 100e multicolored 1.25 .60
2031 A552 140e multicolored 1.75 .90
Nos. 2028-2031 (4) 4.45 2.23

Evangelization and Meeting of Cultures — A553

Designs: 45e, Carving of missionary, Mozambique, 19th cent., vert. 75e, Sculpture, young Jesus ministering to the people, India, 17th cent., vert. 100e, Chalice, Macao, 17th cent., vert. 140e, Carving of native, Angola, 19th cent.

1994, Nov. 17 Litho. *Perf. 12*

2032 A553 45e multicolored .55 .28
2033 A553 75e multicolored .95 .45
2034 A553 100e multicolored 1.25 .60
2035 A553 140e multicolored 1.75 .90
Nos. 2032-2035 (4) 4.50 2.23

Arrival of Portuguese in Senegal, 550th Anniv. A554

1994, Nov. 17

2036 A554 140e multicolored 1.75 .90

See Senegal No. 1083.

Souvenir Sheet

Battle of Montijo, 350th Anniv. — A555

Illustration reduced.

1994, Dec. 1

2037 A555 150e multicolored 1.90 1.90

Souvenir Sheet

Christmas A556

1994, Dec. 8

2038 A556 150e Magi 1.90 .95

Nature Conservation in Europe A557

Designs: 42e, Otis tarda. 90e, Pandion haliaetus. 130e, Lacerta schreiberi.

1995, Feb. 22 Litho. *Perf. 12*

2039 A557 42e multicolored .58 .30
2040 A557 90e multicolored 1.25 .62
2041 A557 130e multicolored 1.75 .85
a. Souvenir sheet of 3, #2039-2041 3.75 3.75
Nos. 2039-2041 (3) 3.58 1.77

St. Joao de Deus (1495-1550), Founder of Order of Hospitalers — A558

1995, Mar. 8 Litho. *Perf. 12*

2042 A558 45e multicolored .60 .30

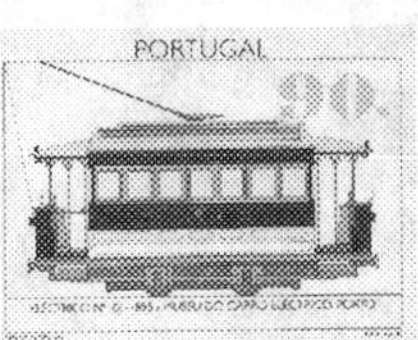

Trams & Automobiles in Portugal, Cent. — A559

Designs: 90e, 1895 Electric tram, 1895. 130e, 1895 Panhard & Levassor automobile.

1995, Mar. 8

2043 A559 90e multicolored 1.25 .60
2044 A559 130e multicolored 1.90 .95

19th Century Professions — A560

Designs: 1e, Baker woman. 20e, Spinning wheel and spoon vendor. 45e, Junk dealer. 50e, Fruit vendor. 75e, Whitewasher.

1995, Apr. 20 Litho. *Perf. 12*

2045 A560 1e multicolored .15 .15
2046 A560 20e multicolored .28 .15
2047 A560 45e multicolored .60 .30
Complete booklet, 10 #2047 6.00
2048 A560 50e multicolored .70 .35
2049 A560 75e multicolored 1.00 .50
Complete booklet, 10 #2049 10.00
Nos. 2045-2049 (5) 2.73 1.45

See Nos. 2088-2092, 2147-2151.

Peace & Freedom — A561

Europa: No. 2050, People awaiting ships for America, Aristides de Sousa Mendes signing entrance visas, 1940. No. 2051, Transportion of refugees from Gibraltar to Madeira, 1940.
Illustration reduced.

1995, May 5 Litho. *Perf. 12*

2050 A561 95e multicolored 1.25 .65
2051 A561 95e multicolored 1.25 .65

UN, 50th Anniv. A562

Design: 135e, like #2052, clouds in background.

1995, May 5

2052 A562 75e multicolored 1.00 .50
2053 A562 135e multicolored 1.75 .90
a. Souvenir sheet, 2 each #2052-2053 5.50 5.50

A563

St. Anthony of Padua (1195-1231) — A564

1995, June 13 Litho. *Perf. 12*

2054 A563 45e shown .60 .30
2055 A564 75e shown 1.00 .50
2056 A563 135e Statue holding Christ 1.90 .95
Nos. 2054-2056 (3) 3.50 1.75

Souvenir Sheet

2057 A563 250e Statue holding 3.50 3.50

See Italy Nos. 2040-2041, Brazil No. 2539..

Firemen in Portugal, 600th Anniv. A565

Designs: No. 2058, Carpenters with axes, women with pitchers, 1395. No. 2059, Dutch firemen, water pumper, 1701. 75e, Fireman of Lisbon, water wagon, 1780, firemen, 1782. 80e, Firemen pulling pumper, carrying water kegs, 1834. 95e, Fire chief directing firemen on Merryweather steam pumper, 1867. 135e, Firemen, hydrant, early fire truck, 1908.

1995, July 4 Litho. *Perf. 12*

2058 A565 45e multicolored .60 .30
2059 A565 45e multicolored .60 .30
a. Miniature sheet of 4 2.50 1.25
2060 A565 75e multicolored 1.00 .50
a. Miniature sheet of 4 4.00 2.00
2061 A565 80e multicolored 1.10 .55
2062 A565 95e multicolored 1.25 .65
2063 A565 135e multicolored 1.90 .90
Nos. 2058-2063 (6) 6.45 3.20

Dom Manuel I, 500th Anniv. of Acclamation — A566

1995, Aug. 4 Litho. *Perf. 12*

2064 A566 45e buff, brown & red .60 .30
a. Miniature sheet of 4 2.50 2.50

New Electric Railway Tram — A567

Illustration reduced.

1995, Sept. 1

2066 A567 80e multicolored 1.10 .55
a. Booklet pane of 4 4.50
Complete booklet, No. 2066a 4.50

Sculpture Type of 1993

Designs: 45e, Warrior, Castreja culture. 75e, Two-headed fountain. 80e, Statue, "The Truth," by Texeira Lopes. 95e, Monument to the war dead. 135e, Statue of Fernão Lopes, by Martins Correia. 190e, Monument to Fernando Pessoa, by Lagoa Henriques.

Equestrian statues: No. 2073: a, Medieval cavalryman. b, D. José I. c, D. João IV. d, Vímara Peres.

1995, Sept. 27 Litho. *Perf. 11½x12*

2067 A528 45e multicolored .60 .30
2068 A528 75e multicolored 1.00 .50
2069 A528 80e multicolored 1.10 .55
2070 A528 95e multicolored 1.25 .65
2071 A528 135e multicolored 1.80 .90
2072 A528 190e multicolored 2.50 1.25
Nos. 2067-2072 (6) 8.25 4.15

Souvenir Sheet

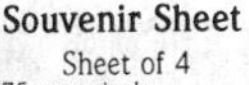

2073 Sheet of 4 4.00 4.00
a.-d. A528 75e any single 1.00 1.00

Portuguese Expansion Period Art — A568

45e, Statue of the Guardian Angel of Portugal. 75e, Reliquary of Queen D. Leonor. 80e, Statue of Dom Manuel. 95e, Painting, St. Anthony, by Nuno Goncalves. 135e, Painting, Adoration of the Magi, by Vasco Fernandez. 190e, Painting, Christ on the Way to Mount Calvary, by Jorge Afonso.

200e, Altarpiece for Convent of St. Vincent, by Nuno Goncalves.

1995, Oct. 9 Litho. *Perf. 12*

2074 A568 45e multicolored .60 .30
2075 A568 75e multicolored 1.00 .50
2076 A568 80e multicolored 1.00 .50
2077 A568 95e multicolored 1.25 .60
2078 A568 135e multicolored 1.75 .90
2079 A568 190e multicolored 2.50 1.25
Nos. 2074-2079 (6) 8.10 4.05

Souvenir Sheet

2080 A568 200e multicolored 2.75 2.75

No. 2080 contains one 76x27mm stamp.

José Maria Eca de Queiroz (1845-1900), Writer A569

1995, Oct. 27 Litho. *Perf. 12*

2081 A569 135e multicolored 1.75 .90

Christmas — A570

1995, Nov. 14

2082 A570 80e Annunciation angel 1.00 .50
a. "PORTUGAL" omitted 1.00 .50
b. Miniature sheet, 4 #2082 4.00 4.00
c. Miniature sheet, 4 #2082a 4.00 4.00

TAP Air Portugal, 50th Anniv. A571

1995, Nov. 14

2083 A571 135e Airbus A340/300 1.75 .90

Oceanographic Voyages of King Charles I of Portugal and Prince Albert I of Monaco, Cent. — A572

Designs: 95e, Ship, King Charles I holding sextant, microscope, sea life. 135e, Fish in sea, net, Prince Albert I holding binoculars, ship.
Illustration reduced.

1996, Feb. 1

2084 A572 95e multicolored 1.25 .60
2085 A572 135e multicolored 1.75 .90

See Monaco Nos. 1992-1993.

Natl. Library, Bicent. A573

1996, Feb. 29
2086 A573 80e multicolored 1.00 .50

Use of Portuguese as Official Language, 700th Anniv. A574

1996, Feb. 29
2087 A574 200e multicolored 2.50 1.25

Type of 1995

Designs: 3e, Exchange broker. 47e, Woman selling chestnuts. 78e, Cloth - seller. 100e, Black woman selling mussels. 250e, Water seller.

1996, Mar. 20 Litho. *Perf. 11½x12*
2088 A560 3e multicolored .15 .15
2089 A560 47e multicolored .60 .30
a. Booklet pane, 10 #2089 6.00
Complete booklet, #2089a 6.00
2090 A560 78e multicolored 1.00 .50
a. Booklet pane, 10 #2090 10.00
Complete booklet, #2090a 10.00
2091 A560 100e multicolored 1.25 .65
2092 A560 250e multicolored 3.20 1.60
Nos. 2088-2092 (5) 6.20 3.20

Joao de Deus (1830-96), Founder of New Method to Teach Reading A576

1996, Apr. 12 *Perf. 12*
2093 A576 78e multicolored 1.00 .50

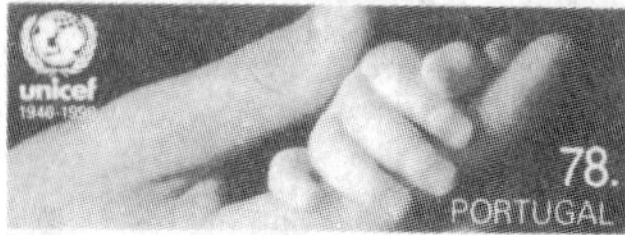
UNICEF, 50th Anniv. — A577

Illustration reduced.

1996, Apr. 12
2094 A577 78e shown 1.00 .50
2095 A577 140e Children 1.75 .90
a. Booklet pane, 2 each #2094-2095 5.50
Complete booklet, #2095a 5.50

Joao de Barros (1496-1570), Writer A578

1996, Apr. 12
2096 A578 140e multicolored 1.75 .90

Helena Vieira da Silva (1908-92), Painter — A579

1996, May 3
2097 A579 98e multicolored 1.25 .60
a. Souvenir sheet of 3 3.75 1.90

Europa.

Euro '96, European Soccer Championships, Great Britain — A580

1996, June 7 Litho. *Perf. 12*
2098 A580 78e Soccer players 1.00 .50
2099 A580 140e Soccer players, diff. 1.80 .90
a. Souvenir sheet, #2098-2099 2.80 2.80

Joao Vaz Corte-Real, Explorer, 500th Death Anniv. — A581

Illustration reduced.

1996, June 7
2100 A581 140e multicolored 1.80 .90

Souvenir Sheet
2101 A581 315e like #2100 4.00 4.00

No. 2101 contains one 40x31 stamp with a continuous design.

1996 Summer Olympics, Atlanta A582

1996, June 24
2102 A582 47e Wrestling .60 .30
2103 A582 78e Equestrian 1.00 .50
2104 A582 98e Boxing 1.30 .65
2105 A582 140e Running 1.80 .90
Nos. 2102-2105 (4) 4.70 2.35

Souvenir Sheet
2106 A582 300e Early track event 4.00 4.00

Olymphilex '96 (#2106).

Augusto Hilário (1864-96), Singer A583

1996, July 1 Litho. *Perf. 12x11½*
2107 A583 80e multicolored 1.00 .50

Alphonsine Condification of Statutes, 550th Anniv. — A584

1996, Aug. 7
2108 A584 350e multicolored 4.50 2.25

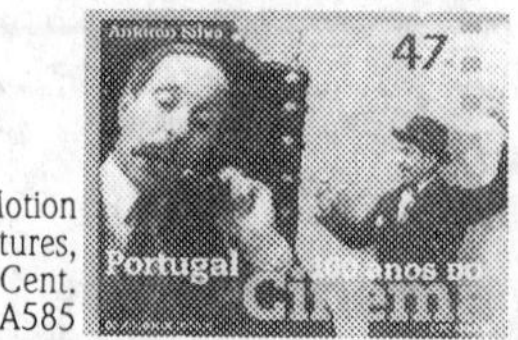
Motion Pictures, Cent. A585

Directors, stars of motion pictures: 47e, António Silva. 78e, Vasco Santana. 80e, Laura Alves. 98e, Aurélio Pais dos Reis. 100e, Leitao de Barros. 140e, António Lopes Ribeiro.

1996, Aug. 7
2109 A585 47e multicolored .60 .30
2110 A585 78e multicolored 1.00 .50
2111 A585 80e multicolored 1.00 .50
a. Souvenir sheet, #2109-2111 2.60 2.60
2112 A585 98e multicolored 1.30 .65
2113 A585 100e multicolored 1.30 .65
2114 A585 140e multicolored 1.80 .90
a. Souvenir sheet, #2112-2114 4.50 4.50
b. Souvenir sheet, #2109-2114 7.00 7.00
Nos. 2109-2114 (6) 7.00 3.50

Azeredo Perdigao (1896-1993), Lawyer, Chairman of Calouste Gulbenkian Foundation A586

1996, Sept. 19 Litho. *Perf. 12*
2115 A586 47e multicolored .60 .30

Arms of the Districts of Portugal A587

1996, Sept. 27
2116 A587 47e Aveiro .60 .30
2117 A587 78e Beja 1.00 .50
2118 A587 80e Braga 1.00 .50
a. Souvenir sheet, #2116-2118 2.60 2.60
2119 A587 98e Branganca 1.30 .65
2120 A587 100e Castelo Branco 1.30 .65
2121 A587 140e Coimbra 1.80 .90
a. Souvenir sheet, #2119-2121 4.50 4.50
Nos. 2116-2121 (6) 7.00 3.50

County of Portucale, 900th Anniv. A588

1996, Oct. 9
2122 A588 47e multicolored .60 .30

Home Mail Delivery, 175th Anniv. — A589

Designs: 47e, Mail carrier, 1821. 78e, Postman, 1854. 98e, Rural mail distrubutor, 1893. 100e, Postman, 1939. 140e, Postman, 1992.

1996, Oct. 9
2123 A589 47e multicolored .60 .30
2124 A589 78e multicolored 1.00 .50
2125 A589 98e multicolored 1.30 .65
2126 A589 100e multicolored 1.30 .65
2127 A589 140e multicolored 1.80 .90
Nos. 2123-2127 (5) 6.00 3.00

Traditional Food A590

47e, Minho-style pork. 78e, Trout, Boticas. 80e, Tripe, Oporto. 98e, Baked codfish, potatoes. 100e, Eel chowder, Aveiro. 140e, Lobster, Peniche.

1996, Oct. 9
2128 A590 47e multicolored .60 .30
2129 A590 78e multicolored 1.00 .50
2130 A590 80e multicolored 1.00 .50
2131 A590 98e multicolored 1.30 .65
2132 A590 100e multicolored 1.30 .65
2133 A590 140e multicolored 1.80 .90
Nos. 2128-2133 (6) 7.00 3.50

See Nos. 2170-2175.

Bank of Portugal, 150th Anniv. A591

1996, Nov. 12 Litho. *Perf. 12*
2134 A591 78e multicolored 1.00 .50

Rights of the People of East Timor A592

1996, Nov. 12
2135 A592 140e black & red 1.75 .90

Discovery of Maritime Route to India, 500th Anniv. — A593

Voyage of Vasco da Gama: 47e, Visit of D. Manuel I to shipyards. 78e, Departure from Lisbon, July 8, 1497. 98e, Trip over Atlantic Ocean. 140e, Passing Cape of Good Hope.
315e, Dream of Manuel.

1996, Nov. 12 *Perf. 13½*
2136 A593 47e multicolored .60 .30
2137 A593 78e multicolored 1.00 .50
2138 A593 98e multicolored 1.25 .60
2139 A593 140e multicolored 1.75 .85
Nos. 2136-2139 (4) 4.60 2.25

Souvenir Sheet
2140 A593 315e multicolored 4.00 4.00

See Nos. 2191-2195.

Souvenir Sheet

1996 Organization for Security and Cooperation in Europe Summit, Lisbon — A594

Illustration reduced.

1996, Dec. 2 *Perf. 12*
2141 A594 200e multicolored 2.50 2.50

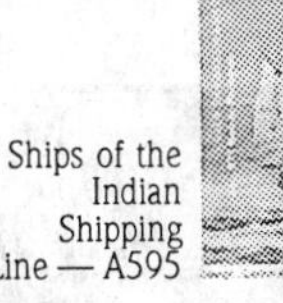

Ships of the Indian Shipping Line — A595

Designs: 49e, Portuguese galleon, 16th cent. 0e, "Principe da Beira," 1780. 100e, Bow of Frig-te "D. Fernando II e Gloria," 1843. 140e, Stern of D. Fernando II e Gloria."

997, Feb. 12 Litho. *Perf. 12*

142 A595 49e multicolored .60 .30
143 A595 80e multicolored .95 .45
144 A595 100e multicolored 1.15 .60
145 A595 140e multicolored 1.65 .80
Nos. 2142-2145 (4) 4.35 2.15

Project Life — A596

997, Feb. 20

2146 A596 80e multicolored .95 .45
a. Booklet pane of 5 4.75
Complete booklet, #2146a 4.75

19th Cent. Professions Type of 1995

Designs: 2e, Laundry woman. 5e, Broom seller. 0e, Olive oil seller. 49e, Woman with cape. 80e, Errand boy.

997, Mar. 12 Litho. *Perf. 11½x12*

2147 A560 2e multicolored .15 .15
2148 A560 5e multicolored .15 .15
2149 A560 30e multicolored .35 .20
2150 A560 49e multicolored .60 .30
a. Booklet pane of 10 6.00
Complete booklet, #2150a 6.00
2151 A560 80e multicolored .95 .50
a. Booklet pane of 10 9.50
Complete booklet, #2151a 9.50
Nos. 2147-2151 (5) 2.20 1.30

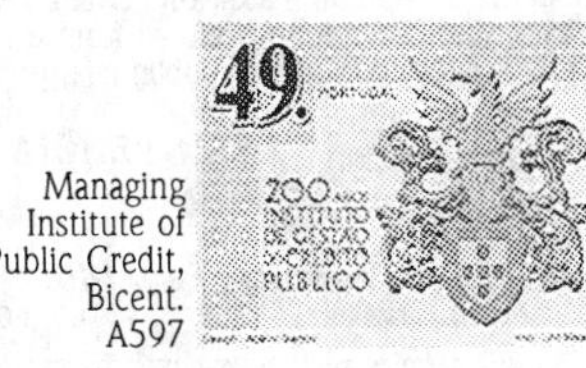

Managing Institute of Public Credit, Bicent. A597

1997, Mar. 12 Litho. *Perf. 12*

2152 A597 49e multicolored .60 .30

World Wildlife Fund — A598

Galemys pyreanicus: No. 2153, Looking upward. No. 2154, Paws around nose. No. 2155, Eating earthworm. No. 2156, Heading downward.

1997, Mar. 12 *Perf. 12*

2153 A598 49e multicolored .60 .30
2154 A598 49e multicolored .60 .30
2155 A598 49e multicolored .60 .30
2156 A598 49e multicolored .60 .30
a. Strip of 4, #2153-2156 2.40 1.20

Stories and Legends — A599

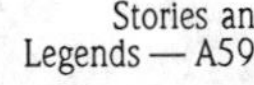

Europa: Moorish girl watching over treasures.

1997, May 5 Litho. *Perf. 12*

2157 A599 100e multicolored 1.05 .55
a. Souvenir sheet of 3 3.25 3.25

Sports A600

#2162: a, BMX bike riding. b, Hang gliding.

1997, May 29 *Perf. 12*

2158 A600 49e Surfing .50 .25
2159 A600 80e Skate boarding .85 .40
2160 A600 100e Roller blading 1.10 .55
2161 A600 140e Parasailing 1.50 .75
Nos. 2158-2161 (4) 3.95 1.95

Souvenir Sheet

2162 Sheet of 2 3.25 3.25
a.-b. A600 150e any single 1.60 1.60

Capture of Lisbon and Santarém from the Moors, 850th Anniv. — A601

Designs: No. 2163, Soldier on horse, front of fortress of Lisbon. No. 2164, Soldiers climbing ladders into Santareém at night.

1997, June 9 *Perf. 12*

2163 A601 80e multicolored .85 .40
2164 A601 80e multicolored .85 .40
a. Pair, #2163-2164 1.70 .80
b. Souvenir sheet, 2 #2164a 3.40 3.40

Fr. Luís Fróis (1532-97), Missionary, Historian — A602

Fr. José de Anchieta (1534-97), Missionary in Brazil — A603

80e, Fróis on mission in Orient. #2166, Fróis holding hands across chest. #2167, Fróis, church.

1997, June 9

2165 A602 80e multi, horiz. .85 .45
2166 A602 140e multi 1.50 .75
2167 A602 140e multi 1.50 .75
Nos. 2165-2167 (3) 3.85 1.95

1997, June 9

Design: No. 2169, Fr. António Vieira (1608-97), missionary in Brazil, diplomat.

2168 A603 140e multicolored 1.50 .75
2169 A603 350e multicolored 3.75 1.90

Traditional Food Type of 1996

10e, Roasted kid, Beira Baixa. 49e, Fried shad. 80e, Lamb stew. 100e, Fish chowder. 140e, Swordfish fillets with corn. 200e, Stewed octopus, Azores.

1997, July 5 Litho. *Perf. 12*

2170 A590 10e multicolored .15 .15
2171 A590 49e multicolored .60 .30
2172 A590 80e multicolored 1.00 .50
2173 A590 100e multicolored 1.25 .65
2174 A590 140e multicolored 1.70 .85
2175 A590 200e multicolored 2.50 1.25
Nos. 2170-2175 (6) 7.20 3.70

Souvenir Sheet

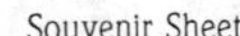

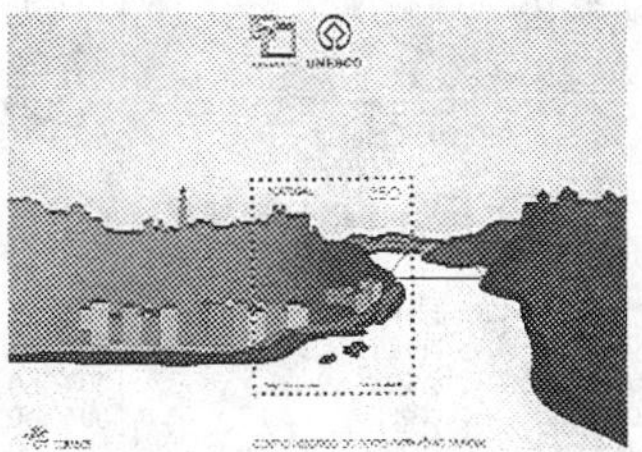

City of Oporto, UNESCO World Heritage Site — A605

Illustration reduced.

1997, July 5 Litho. *Perf. 12*

2176 A605 350e multicolored 3.75 3.75

A606

A607

1997, July 19 Litho. *Perf. 12*

2177 A606 100e multicolored 1.25 .65

Brotherhood of the Yeoman of Beja, 700th anniv.

1997, Aug. 29 Litho. *Perf. 12*

2178 A607 50e multicolored .55 .30

Natl. Laboratory of Civil Engineering, 50th anniv.

Treaty of Alcanices, 700th Anniv. A608

1997, Sept. 12

2179 A608 80e multicolored .90 .45

Arms of the Districts of Portugal A609

1997, Sept. 17

2180 A609 10e Evora .15 .15
2181 A609 49e Faro .55 .30
2182 A609 80e Guarda .90 .45
2183 A609 100e Leiria 1.10 .55
2184 A609 140e Lisboa 1.60 .80
a. Souvenir sheet, #2180, #2182, #2184 2.65 1.35
2185 A609 200e Portalegre 2.25 1.15
a. Souvenir sheet, #2181, 2183, #2185 4.00 4.00
Nos. 2180-2185 (6) 6.55 3.40

Incorporation of Postal Service in State Administration, Bicent. — A610

1997, Oct. 9

2186 A610 80e multicolored .90 .45

Portuguese Cartography — A611

Designs: 49e, Map from atlas of Lopo Homen-Reineis, 1519. 80e, Map from atlas of Joao Freire, 1546. 100e, Chart by Diogo Ribeiro, 1529. 140e, Anonymous map, 1630.

1997, Oct. 9

2187 A611 49e multicolored .55 .30
2188 A611 80e multicolored .90 .45
2189 A611 100e multicolored 1.15 .60
2190 A611 140e multicolored 1.60 .80
a. Souvenir sheet, #2187-2190 4.25 4.25
Nos. 2187-2190 (4) 4.20 2.15

Discovery of Maritime Route to India Type of 1996

Voyage of Vasco da Gama: 49e, St. Gabriel's cross, Quelimane. 80e, Stop at island off Mozambique. 100e, Arrival in Mombasa. 140e, Reception for king of Melinde.
315e, Trading with natives, Natal.

1997, Nov. 5 *Perf. 13½*

2191 A593 49e multicolored .55 .30
2192 A593 80e multicolored .90 .45
2193 A593 100e multicolored 1.15 .60
2194 A593 140e multicolored 1.60 .80
Nos. 2191-2194 (4) 4.20 2.15

Souvenir Sheet

2195 A593 315e multicolored 3.50 3.50

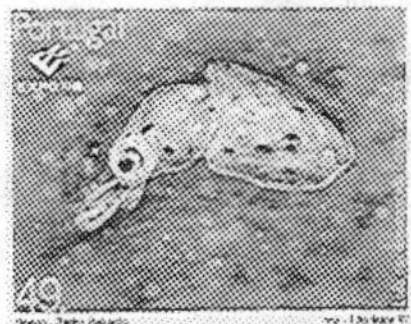

Expo '98 — A612

Plankton: 49e, Loligo vulgaris. 80e, Scyllarus arctus. 100e, Pontellina plumata. 140e, Solea senegalensis.
No. 2200: a, Calcidiscus leptoporus. b, Tabellaria.

1997, Nov. 5 *Perf. 12*

2196 A612 49e multicolored .55 .30
2197 A612 80e multicolored .90 .45
2198 A612 100e multicolored 1.10 .55
2199 A612 140e multicolored 1.60 .80
Nos. 2196-2199 (4) 4.15 2.10

Souvenir Sheet

Perf. 12½

2200 Sheet of 2 2.25 2.25
a.-b. A612 100e any single 1.10 1.10

Souvenir Sheet

Sintra, UNESCO World Heritage Site — A613

1997, Dec. 5 *Perf. 12*

2201 A613 350e multicolored 4.00 4.00

AIR POST STAMPS

Symbol of Aviation AP1

Perf. 12x11½

1936-41 Unwmk. Typo.

C1 AP1 1.50e dark blue .70 .70
C2 AP1 1.75e red orange 1.10 .70
C3 AP1 2.50e rose red 1.40 .70
C4 AP1 3e brt blue ('41) 8.00 10.00
C5 AP1 4e dp yel grn ('41) 13.00 15.00
C6 AP1 5e carmine lake 2.00 .70
C7 AP1 10e brown lake 2.75 .60
C8 AP1 15e orange ('41) 8.50 9.00
C9 AP1 20e black brn 8.50 2.50
C10 AP1 50e brn vio ('41) 100.00 60.00
Nos. C1-C10 (10) 145.95 99.90
Never hinged 300.00

Nos. C1-C10 exist imperf.

> Catalogue values for unused stamps in this section, from this point to the end of the section, are for Never Hinged items.

EXPO Type of Regular Issue

1970, Sept. 16 Litho. *Perf. 13*

C11 A274 3.50e silver & multi .35 .20

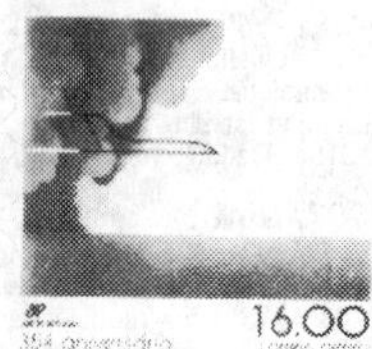

TAP-Airline of Portugal 35th Anniversary AP2

Design: 19e, Jet flying past sun.

1979, Sept. 21 Litho. *Perf. 12x11½*

C12 AP2 16e multicolored .35 .35
C13 AP2 19e multicolored .45 .45

POSTAGE DUE STAMPS

Vasco da Gama Issue

The Zamorin of Calicut Receiving Vasco da Gama — D1

Unwmk.

1898, May 1 Typo. *Perf. 12*

Denomination in Black

J1 D1 5r black 3.00 1.50
a. Value and "Continente" omitted 10.00 5.00
J2 D1 10r lilac & blk 4.00 1.75
J3 D1 20r orange & blk 6.50 2.25
J4 D1 50r slate & blk 52.50 9.00
J5 D1 100r car & blk, *pink* 87.50 32.50
J6 D1 200r brn & blk, *buff* 92.50 42.50
Nos. J1-J6 (6) 246.00 89.50

For overprints and surcharges see Nos. 193-198.

D2

D3

1904 *Perf. 11½x12*

J7 D2 5r brown .45 .50
J8 D2 10r orange 3.00 .70
a. Imperf. —
J9 D2 20r lilac 8.75 2.75
J10 D2 30r gray green 5.75 2.25
J11 D2 40r gray violet 7.00 2.25
J12 D2 50r carmine 52.50 3.75
a. Imperf.
J13 D2 100r dull blue 8.75 4.50
a. Imperf.
Nos. J7-J13 (7) 86.20 16.70

Preceding Issue Overprinted in Carmine or Green

1910

J14 D2 5r brown .50 .25
J15 D2 10r orange .50 .25
J16 D2 20r lilac 1.50 .70
J17 D2 30r gray green 1.40 .25
J18 D2 40r gray violet 1.40 .25
J19 D2 50r carmine (G) 6.00 3.25
J20 D2 100r dull blue 6.50 3.75
Nos. J14-J20 (7) 17.80 8.70

See note after No. 183.

1915, Mar. 18 Typo.

J21 D3 ½c brown .60 .60
J22 D3 1c orange .60 .60
J23 D3 2c claret .60 .60
J24 D3 3c green .60 .60
J25 D3 4c gray violet .60 .60
J26 D3 5c carmine .60 .60
J27 D3 10c dark blue .60 .60
Nos. J21-J27 (7) 4.20 4.20

1921-27

J28 D3 ½c gray green ('22) .15 .15
J29 D3 4c gray green ('27) .15 .15
J30 D3 8c gray green ('23) .15 .15
J31 D3 10c gray green ('22) .40 .40
J32 D3 12c gray green .40 .40
J33 D3 16c gray green ('23) .40 .40
J34 D3 20c gray green .40 .40
J35 D3 24c gray green .40 .40
J36 D3 32c gray green ('23) .40 .40
J37 D3 36c gray green .70 .65
J38 D3 40c gray green ('23) .70 .65
J39 D3 48c gray green ('23) .50 .50
J40 D3 50c gray green .50 .50
J41 D3 60c gray green .50 .50
J42 D3 72c gray green .50 .50
J43 D3 80c gray green ('23) 3.25 3.00
J44 D3 1.20e gray green 1.65 1.50
Nos. J28-J44 (17) 11.15 10.65

D4

D5

1932-33

J45 D4 5c buff .40 .40
J46 D4 10c lt blue .40 .40
J47 D4 20c pink .80 .60
J48 D4 30c blue green 1.00 .80
J49 D4 40c lt green 1.00 .80
J50 D4 50c gray 1.25 .80
J51 D4 60c rose 2.50 2.00
J52 D4 80c violet brn 5.00 4.00
J53 D4 1.20e gray ol ('33) 7.00 6.00
Nos. J45-J53 (9) 19.35 15.80

1940, Feb. 1 Unwmk. *Perf. 12½*

J54 D5 5c bister, perf. 14 .15 .50
J55 D5 10c rose lilac .15 .50
J56 D5 20c dk car rose .15 .50
J57 D5 30c purple .15 .50
J58 D5 40c cerise .15 .50
J59 D5 50c brt blue .15 .50
J60 D5 60c yellow grn .15 .50
J61 D5 80c scarlet .60 .55
J62 D5 1e brown 1.25 .55
J63 D5 2e dk rose vio 1.70 .55
J64 D5 5e org yel, perf. 14 5.00 5.00
a. Perf. 12½
Nos. J54-J64 (11) 9.60 10.15

Nos. J54-J64 were first issued perf. 14. In 1955 all but the 5c were reissued in perf. 12½.

> Catalogue values for unused stamps in this section, from this point to the end of the section, are for Never Hinged items.

D6

1967-84 Litho. *Perf. 11½*

J65 D6 10c dp org, red brn & yel .15 .15
J66 D6 20c bis, dk brn & yel .15 .15
J67 D6 30c org, red brn & yel .15 .15
J68 D6 40c ol bis, dk brn & yel .15 .15
J69 D6 50c ultra, dk bl & lt bl .15 .15
J70 D6 60c grnsh bl, dk grn & lt bl .15 .15
J71 D6 80c bl, dk bl & lt bl .15 .15
J72 D6 1e vio bl, dk bl & lt bl .15 .15
J73 D6 2e grn, dk grn & lt grn .15 .15
J74 D6 3e lt grn, grn & yel ('75) .15 .15
J75 D6 4e bl grn, dk grn & yel ('75) .15 .15
J76 D6 5e cl, dp cl & pink .15 .15
J77 D6 9e vio, dk vio & pink ('75) .28 .28
J78 D6 10e lil, pur & pale vio ('75) .28 .28
J79 D6 20e red, brn & pale vio ('75) .52 .52
J80 D6 40e dp red lil, rose vio & blu-ish lil ('84) 1.05 1.05
J81 D6 50e lil, brn & pale gray ('84) 1.35 1.35
Set value 4.25 4.25

D7

1992-93 Litho. *Perf. 12x11½*

J82 D7 1e multicolored .15 .15
J83 D7 2e multicolored .15 .15
J84 D7 5e multicolored .15 .15
J85 D7 10e multicolored .15 .15
J86 D7 20e multicolored .25 .25
J87 D7 50e multicolored .65 .65
J88 D7 100e multicolored 1.25 1.25
J89 D7 200e multicolored 2.50 2.50
Nos. J82-J89 (8) 5.25 5.25

Issued: 1e, 2e, 5e, 200e, 10/7/92; 10e, 20e, 50e, 100e, 3/9/93.

Type D7 Inscribed "CTT CORREIOS"

1995

J90 D7 3e multicolored .15 .15
J91 D7 4e multicolored .15 .15
J92 D7 9e multicolored .15 .15
J93 D7 40e multicolored .55 .55

1995-96

J94 D7 5e multicolored .15 .15
J95 D7 10e multicolored .15 .15
J96 D7 20e multicolored .25 .25
J97 D7 50e multicolored .60 .60
J98 D7 100e multicolored 1.20 1.20
Nos. J90-J98 (9) 3.35 3.35

Issued: 3e, 4e, 9e, 40e, 4/20/95; 50e, 5/22/95; 5e, 10e, 20e, 100e, 5/24/96.

This is an expanding set. Numbers will change when complete.

OFFICIAL STAMPS

No. 567 Overprinted in Black **OFICIAL**

1938 Unwmk. *Perf. 11½*

O1 A113 40c brown .18 .15

> Catalogue values for unused stamps in this section, from this point to the end of the section, are for Never Hinged items.

O1

1952, Sept. Litho. *Perf. 12½*

O2 O1 black & cream .15 .15

1975, June

O3 O1 black & yellow .55 .40

NEWSPAPER STAMPS

N1

Perf. 11½, 12½, 13½

1876 Typo. Unwmk.

P1 N1 2½r bister 14.00 .90
a. 2½r olive green 14.00 .90

Various shades.

PARCEL POST STAMPS

Mercury and Commerce PP1

1920-22 Unwmk. Typo. *Perf. 1*

Q1 PP1 1c lilac brown .15 .15
Q2 PP1 2c orange .15 .15
Q3 PP1 5c lt brown .15 .15
Q4 PP1 10c red brown .15 .15
Q5 PP1 20c gray blue .25 .15
Q6 PP1 40c carmine rose .25 .22
Q7 PP1 50c black .35 .30
Q8 PP1 60c dk blue ('21) .35 .30
Q9 PP1 70c gray brn ('21) 1.25 1.25
Q10 PP1 80c ultra ('21) 1.65 1.65
Q11 PP1 90c lt vio ('21) 1.50 1.50
Q12 PP1 1e lt green 1.50 .60
Q13 PP1 2e pale lilac ('22) 4.25 2.00
Q14 PP1 3e olive ('22) 5.00 2.00
Q15 PP1 4e ultra ('22) 14.00 5.00
Q16 PP1 5e gray ('22) 15.00 3.00
Q17 PP1 10e chocolate ('22) 32.50 5.50
Nos. Q1-Q17 (17) 78.45 24.07

Parcel Post Package PP2

1936 *Perf. 11½*

Q18 PP2 50c olive brown .15 .16
Q19 PP2 1e bister brown .15 .16
Q20 PP2 1.50e purple .15 .16
Q21 PP2 2e carmine lake 1.10 .16
Q22 PP2 2.50e olive green 1.10 .16
Q23 PP2 4.50e brown lake 1.40 .16
Q24 PP2 5e violet 3.50 .24
Q25 PP2 10e orange 4.25 .70
Nos. Q18-Q25 (8) 11.80 1.90

POSTAL TAX STAMPS

These stamps represent a special fee for the delivery of postal matter on certain days in each year. The money derived from their sale is applied to works of public charity.

Regular Issues Overprinted in Carmine **ASSISTENCIA**

1911, Oct. 4 Unwmk. *Perf. 14½x15*

RA1 A62 10r gray green 7.00 2.00

The 20r carmine of this type was for use on telegrams.

1912, Oct. 4 *Perf. 15x14½*

RA2 A64 1c deep green 5.00 1.65

The 2c carmine of this type was for use on telegrams.

"Lisbon" — PT1 "Charity" — PT2

1913, June 8 Litho. *Perf. 12x11½*

RA3 PT1 1c dark green .80 .80

The 2c dark brown of this type was for use on telegrams.

1915, Oct. 4 Typo.

RA4 PT2 1c carmine .40 .30

The 2c plum of this type was for use on telegrams.

See No. RA6.

No. RA4 Surcharged **15 ctvs.**

1924, Oct. 4
RA5 PT2 15c on 1c dull red 1.25 .70

The 30c on 2c claret of this type was for use on telegrams.

Charity Type of 1915 Issue

1925, Oct. 4 *Perf. 12½*
RA6 PT2 15c carmine .25 .20

The 30c brown violet of this type was for use on telegrams.

Comrades of the Great War Issue

Muse of History with Tablet — PT3

1925, Apr. 8 Litho. *Perf. 11*
RA7 PT3 10c brown .45 .40
RA8 PT3 10c green .45 .40
RA9 PT3 10c rose .45 .40
RA10 PT3 10c ultra .45 .40
Nos. RA7-RA10 (4) 1.80 1.60

The use of these stamps, in addition to the regular postage, was obligatory on certain days of the year. If the tax represented by these stamps was not prepaid, it was collected by means of Postal Tax Due Stamp No. RAJ1.

Pombal Issue

Common Design Types

Engraved; Value and "Continente" Typographed in Black

1925, May 8 *Perf. 12½*
RA11 CD28 15c ultra .15 .15
RA12 CD29 15c ultra .35 .45
RA13 CD30 15c ultra .35 .45
Nos. RA11-RA13 (3) .85 1.05

Olympic Games Issue

Hurdler — PT7

1928 Litho. *Perf. 12*
RA14 PT7 15c dull red & blk 4.00 *6.00*

The use of this stamp, in addition to the regular postage, was obligatory on May 22-24, 1928. 10% of the money thus obtained was retained by the Postal Administration; the balance was given to a Committee in charge of Portuguese participation in the Olympic games at Amsterdam.

POSTAL TAX DUE STAMPS

PTD1

PTD2

Comrades of the Great War Issue

1925 Unwmk. Typo. *Perf. 11x11½*
RAJ1 PTD1 20c brown orange .90 1.00

See Note after No. RA10.

Pombal Issue

Common Design Types

1925 *Perf. 12½*
RAJ2 CD28 30c ultra 1.00 1.10
RAJ3 CD29 30c ultra 1.00 1.10
RAJ4 CD30 30c ultra 1.00 1.10

When the compulsory tax was not paid by the use of stamps Nos. RA11 to RA13, double the amount was collected by means of Nos. RAJ2 to RAJ4.

Olympic Games Issue

1928 Litho. *Perf. 11½*
RAJ5 PTD2 30c lt red & blk 1.65 *1.75*

FRANCHISE STAMPS

These stamps are supplied by the Government to various charitable, scientific and military organizations for franking their correspondence. This franking privilege was withdrawn in 1938.

FOR THE RED CROSS SOCIETY

F1

Perf. 11½

1889-1915 Unwmk. Typo.
1S1 F1 rose & blk ('15) 1.25 .45
a. Vermilion & black ('08) 5.00 1.10
b. Red & black, perf. 12½ 67.50 5.00

No. 1S1 Overprinted in Green

COMISSÃO PORTUGUESA DOS PRISIONEIROS DE GUERRA

1917
1S3 F1 rose & black 60.00 50.00
a. Inverted overprint 150.00 150.00

"Charity" Extending Hope to Invalid — F1a

1926 Litho. *Perf. 14*

Inscribed "LISBOA"

1S4 F1a black & red 6.00 6.00

Inscribed "DELEGACOES"

1S5 F1a black & red 6.00 6.00

No. 1S4 was for use in Lisbon. No. 1S5 was for the Red Cross chapters outside Lisbon.
For overprints see Nos. 1S72-1S73.

Camoens Issue of 1924 Overprinted in Black or Red

CRUZ VERMELHA
Porte franco
1927

1927
1S6 A68 40c ultra .90 *.90*
1S7 A68 48c red brown .90 *.90*
1S8 A69 64c green .90 *.90*
1S9 A69 75c dk violet .90 *.90*
1S10 A71 4.50e blk, *org* (R) .90 *.90*
1S11 A71 10e dk brn, *pnksh* .90 *.90*
Nos. 1S6-1S11 (6) 5.40 *5.40*

Camoens Issue of 1924 Overprinted in Red

1928
1S12 A67 15c olive grn .90 *1.00*
1S13 A67 16c violet brn .90 *1.00*
1S14 A68 25c lilac .90 *1.00*
1S15 A68 40c ultra .90 *1.00*
1S16 A70 1.20e lt brown .90 *1.00*
1S17 A70 2e apple green .90 *1.00*
Nos. 1S12-1S17 (6) 5.40 *6.00*

Camoens Issue of 1924 Overprinted in Red

1929
1S18 A68 30c dk brown .90 *.90*
1S19 A68 40c ultra .90 *.90*
1S20 A69 80c bister .90 *.90*
1S21 A70 1.50e red .90 *.90*
1S22 A70 1.60e dark blue .90 *.90*
1S23 A71 2.40e green, *grn* .90 *.90*
Nos. 1S18-1S23 (6) 5.40 *5.40*

Same Overprint Dated "1930"

1930
1S24 A68 40c ultra .90 *.90*
1S25 A69 50c red orange .90 *.90*
1S26 A69 96c lake .90 *.90*
1S27 A70 1.60e dk blue .90 *.90*
1S28 A71 3e dk blue, *bl* .90 *.90*
1S29 A72 20e dk violet, *lil* .90 *.90*
Nos. 1S24-1S29 (6) 5.40 *5.40*

Camoens Issue of 1924 Overprinted in Red

1931
1S30 A68 25c lilac 1.00 *1.00*
1S31 A68 32c dk green 1.00 *1.00*
1S32 A68 40c ultra 1.00 *1.00*
1S33 A69 96c lake 1.00 *1.00*
1S34 A70 1.60e dark blue 1.00 *1.00*
1S35 A71 3.20e black, *green* 1.00 *1.00*
Nos. 1S30-1S35 (6) 6.00 *6.00*

Same Overprint Dated "1932"

1931
1S36 A67 20c dp orange 1.25 *1.25*
1S37 A68 40c ultra 1.25 *1.25*
1S38 A68 48c red brown 1.25 *1.25*
1S39 A69 64c green 1.25 *1.25*
1S40 A70 1.60e dark blue 1.25 *1.25*
1S41 A71 10e dk brown, *pnksh* 1.25 *1.25*
Nos. 1S36-1S41 (6) 7.50 *7.50*

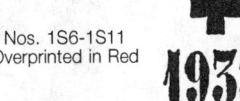

Nos. 1S6-1S11 Overprinted in Red

1932
1S42 A68 40c ultra 1.25 *1.40*
1S43 A68 48c red brown 1.25 *1.40*
1S44 A69 64c green 1.25 *1.40*
1S45 A69 75c dk violet 1.25 *1.40*
1S46 A71 4.50e blk, *orange* 1.25 *1.40*
1S47 A71 10e dk brn, *pnksh* 1.25 *1.40*
Nos. 1S42-1S47 (6) 7.50 *8.40*

Dated "1934"

1933
1S48 A68 40c ultra 1.75 *1.75*
1S49 A68 48c red brown 1.75 *1.75*
1S50 A69 64c green 1.75 *1.75*
1S51 A69 75c dark violet 1.75 *1.75*
1S52 A71 4.50e blk, *orange* 1.75 *1.75*
1S53 A71 10e dk brown, *pnksh* 1.75 *1.75*
Nos. 1S48-1S53 (6) 10.50 *10.50*

Dated "1935"

1935
1S54 A68 40c ultra 2.25 *2.25*
1S55 A68 48c red brown 2.25 *2.25*
1S56 A69 64c green 2.25 *2.25*
1S57 A69 75c dk violet 2.25 *2.25*
1S58 A71 4.50e black, *orange* 2.25 *2.25*
1S59 A71 10e dk brn, *pnksh* 2.25 *2.25*
Nos. 1S54-1S59 (6) 13.50 *13.50*

Camoens Issue of 1924 Overprinted in Black or Red

Cruz
Vermelha
Porte
Franco
1936

1935
1S60 A68 25c lilac .90 *.90*
1S61 A68 40c ultra (R) .90 *.90*
1S62 A69 50c red orange .90 *.90*
1S63 A70 1e slate .90 *.90*
1S64 A70 2e apple green .90 *.90*
1S65 A72 20e dk violet, *lilac* .90 *.90*
Nos. 1S60-1S65 (6) 5.40 *5.40*

Camoens Issue of 1924 Overprinted in Red

1936
1S66 A68 30c dk brown .90 *.90*
1S67 A68 32c dk green .90 *.90*
1S68 A69 80c bister .90 *.90*
1S69 A70 1.20e lt brown .90 *.90*
1S70 A71 3e dk blue, *bl* .90 *.90*
1S71 A71 4.50e black, *yel* .90 *.90*
Nos. 1S66-1S71 (6) 5.40 *5.40*

No. 1S4 Overprinted "1935"

1936 Unwmk. *Perf. 14*
1S72 F1a black & red 7.00 7.00

Same Stamp with Additional Overprint "Delegacoes"

1S73 F1a black & red 7.00 7.00

After the government withdrew the franking privilege in 1938, the Portuguese Red Cross Society distributed charity labels which lacked postal validity.

FOR CIVILIAN RIFLE CLUBS

Rifle Club Emblem — F2

Perf. 11½x12

1899-1910 Typo. Unwmk.
2S1 F2 bl grn & car ('99) 10.00 10.00
2S2 F2 brn & yel grn ('00) 10.00 10.00
2S3 F2 car & buff ('01) 1.50 1.50
2S4 F2 bl & org ('02) 1.50 1.50
2S5 F2 grn & org ('03) 1.50 1.50
2S6 F2 lt brn & car ('04) 1.50 1.50
2S7 F2 mar & ultra ('05) 1.50 1.50
2S8 F2 ultra & buff ('06) 1.50 1.50
2S9 F2 choc & yel ('07) 1.50 1.50
2S10 F2 car & ultra ('08) 1.50 1.50
2S11 F2 bl & yel grn ('09) 1.50 1.50
2S12 F2 bl grn & brn, *pink* ('10) 1.50 1.50
Nos. 2S1-2S12 (12) 35.00 35.00

FOR THE GEOGRAPHICAL SOCIETY OF LISBON

Coat of Arms
F3 F4

1903-34 Unwmk. Litho. *Perf. 11½*
3S1 F3 blk, rose, bl & red 14.00 3.25
3S2 F3 bl, yel, red & grn ('09) 16.00 4.00
3S3 F4 blk, org, bl & red ('11) 2.00 .75
3S4 F4 blk & brn org ('22) 3.50 2.75
3S5 F4 blk & bl ('24) 8.50 4.50
3S6 F4 blk & rose ('26) 3.25 2.25
3S7 F4 blk & grn ('27) 3.25 2.25
3S8 F4 bl, yel & red ('29) 2.75 1.50
3S9 F4 bl, red & vio ('30) 2.75 1.50
3S10 F4 dp bl, lil & red ('31) 2.75 1.50
3S11 F4 bis brn & red ('32) 2.75 1.50
3S12 F4 lt grn & red ('33) 2.75 1.50
3S13 F4 blue & red ('34) 2.75 1.50
Nos. 3S1-3S13 (13) 67.00 28.75

No. 3S12 with three-line overprint, "C.I.C.I. Portugal 1933," was not valid for postage and was sold only to collectors.

No. 3S2 was reprinted in 1933. Green vertical lines behind "Porte Franco" omitted. Value $7.50.

F5

1934 Litho. *Perf. 11½*
3S15 F5 blue & red 1.50 1.25

1935-38 *Perf. 11*

3S16 F5 blue 6.00 6.00
3S17 F5 dk bl & red ('36) 2.50 2.00
3S18 F5 lil & red ('37) 2.50 1.00
3S19 F5 blk, grn & car ('38) 2.50 1.00
Nos. 3S16-3S19 (4) 13.50 10.00

The inscription in the inner circle is omitted on No. 3S16.

FOR THE NATIONAL AID SOCIETY FOR CONSUMPTIVES

F10

Perf. 11½x12

1904, July **Typo.** **Unwmk.**

4S1 F10 brown & green 4.00 4.00
4S2 F10 carmine & yellow 4.00 4.00

AZORES

Starting in 1980, stamps inscribed Azores and Madeira were valid and sold in Portugal.

Azores No. 2 — A33

Design: 19.50e, Azores No. 6.

1980, Jan. 2 **Litho.** *Perf. 12*

314 A33 6.50e multi .15 .15
315 A33 19.50e multi .50 .20
a. Souvenir sheet of 2, #314-315 .90 .90
Set value .25

No. 315a exists overprinted for Capex 87.

Map of Azores A34

1980, Sept. 17 **Litho.** *Perf. 12x11½*

316 A34 50c shown .15 .15
317 A34 1e Cathedral .15 .15
318 A34 5e Windmill .15 .15
319 A34 6.50e Local women .15 .15
320 A34 8e Coastline .20 .15
321 A34 30e Ponta Delgada .60 .32
Set value 1.15 .65

World Tourism Conf., Manila, Sept. 27.

Europa Issue 1981

St. Peter's Cavalcade, St. Miguel Island — A35

1981, May 11 **Litho.** *Perf. 12*

322 A35 22e multicolored .52 .25
a. Souvenir sheet of 2 1.10 1.10

Bulls Attacking Spanish Soldiers A36

Battle of Salga Valley, 400th Anniv.: 33.50e, Friar Don Pedro leading citizens.

1981, July 24 **Litho.** *Perf. 12x11½*

323 A36 8.50e multi .18 .15
324 A36 33.50e multi .80 .45

Tolpis Azorica — A37

Designs: Local flora.

1981, Sept. 21 **Litho.** *Perf. 12½x12*

325 A37 7e shown .16 .15
326 A37 8.50e Ranunculus azoricus .20 .15
327 A37 20e Platanthera micranta .38 .15
328 A37 50e Laurus azorica 1.00 .32
a. Booklet pane of 4, #325-328 1.90
Nos. 325-328 (4) 1.74
Set value .64

1982, Jan. 29

329 A37 4e Myosotis azorica .15 .15
330 A37 10e Lactuca watsoniana .24 .16
331 A37 27e Vicia dennesiana .60 .22
332 A37 33.50e Azorina vidalii .75 .25
a. Booklet pane of 4 1.90
Nos. 329-332 (4) 1.74 .78

See Nos. 338-341.

Europa Type of Portugal

Design: Heroes of Mindelo embarkation, 1832.

1982, May 3 **Litho.** *Perf. 12x11½*

333 A405 33.50e multi .65 .32
a. Souvenir sheet of 3 2.00 2.00

Chapel of the Holy Ghost — A39

Designs: Various Chapels of the Holy Ghost.

1982, Nov. 24 **Litho.** *Perf. 12½x12*

334 A39 27e multi .75 .25
335 A39 33.50e multi .95 .40

Europa 1983 — A40

1983, May 5 **Litho.** *Perf. 12½*

336 A40 37.50e Geothermal energy .70 .35
a. Souvenir sheet of 3 2.50 2.50

Flag of the Autonomous Region — A41

1983, May 23 **Litho.** *Perf. 12x11½*

337 A41 12.50e multi .30 .15

Flower Type of 1981

1983, June 16 *Perf. 12½x12*

338 A37 12.50e St. John's wort .25 .15
339 A37 30e Prickless bramble .60 .30
340 A37 37.50e Romania bush .75 .38
341 A37 100e Common juniper 1.90 1.00
a. Booklet pane of 4, #338-341 3.50
Nos. 338-341 (4) 3.50 1.83

Woman Wearing Terceira Cloaks — A42

1984, Mar. 8 **Litho.** *Perf. 13½*

342 A42 16e Jesters costumes, 18th cent. .30 .15
343 A42 51e shown .90 .45

Europa Type of Portugal

1984, May 2 *Perf. 12x11½*

344 A427 51e multicolored .90 .40
a. Souvenir sheet of 3 2.75 2.75

Megabombus Ruderatus A44

1984, Sept. 3 **Litho.** *Perf. 12x11½*

345 A44 16e shown .24 .15
346 A44 35e Pieris brassicae azorensis .52 .26
347 A44 40e Chrysomela banksi .60 .30
348 A44 51e Phlogophora interrupta .75 .38
Nos. 345-348 (4) 2.11 1.09

Perf. 12 Vert.

345a A44 16e .24 .15
346a A44 35e .52 .26
347a A44 40e .60 .30
348a A44 51e .75 .38
b. Bklt. pane of 4, #345a-348a 2.50

1985, Feb. 13 *Perf. 12x11½*

349 A44 20e Polyspilla polyspilla .30 .15
350 A44 40e Sphaerophoria nigra .65 .32
351 A44 46e Colias croceus .75 .38
352 A44 60e Hipparchia azorina 1.00 .50
Nos. 349-352 (4) 2.70 1.35

Perf. 12 Vert.

349a A44 20e .30 .15
350a A44 40e .65 .32
351a A44 46e .75 .38
352a A44 60e 1.00 .50
b. Bklt. pane of 4, #349a-352a 3.00

Europa Type of Portugal

1985, May 6 **Litho.** *Perf. 11½x12*

353 A435 60e Man playing folia drum 1.00 .40
a. Souvenir sheet of 3 3.00 3.00

Native Boats — A46

1985, June 19 **Litho.** *Perf. 12x12½*

354 A46 40e Jeque .60 .25
355 A46 60e Bote .90 .38

Europa Type of Portugal

1986, May **Litho.**

356 A447 68.50e Pyrrhula murina 1.05 .52
a. Souvenir sheet of 3 3.25 3.25

Regional Architecture — A48

19th Century fountains: 22.50e, Alto das Covas, Angra do Heroismo. 52.50e, Faja de Baixo, San Miguel. 68.50e, Gates of St. Peter, Terceira. 100e, Agua d'Alto, San Miguel.

1986, Sept. 18 **Litho.** *Perf. 12*

357 A48 22.50e multi .35 .18
358 A48 52.50e multi .80 .40
359 A48 68.50e multi 1.05 .52
360 A48 100e multi 1.50 .75
a. Booklet pane of 4, #357-360 3.75
Nos. 357-360 (4) 3.70 1.85

Traditional Modes of Transportation A49

1986, Nov. 7 **Litho.**

361 A49 25e Isle of Santa Maria ox cart .35 .18
362 A49 75e Ram cart 1.05 .52

Europa Type of Portugal

Modern architecutre: Regional Assembly, Horta, designed by Manuel Correia Fernandes and Luis Miranda.

1987, May 5 **Litho.** *Perf. 12*

363 A456 74.50e multicolored 1.20 .60
a. Souvenir sheet of 4 5.00 5.00

Windows and Balconies A51

1987, July 1 *Perf. 12*

364 A51 51e Santa Cruz, Graciosa .80 .40
365 A51 74.50e Ribiera Grande, San Miguel 1.15 .58

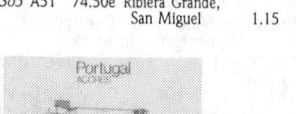

Aviation History A52

Seaplanes.

1987, Oct. 9 *Perf. 12x11½*

366 A52 25e NC-4 Curtiss Flyer, 1919 .38 .20
367 A52 57e Dornier DO-X, 1932 .88 .45
368 A52 74.50e Savoia-Marchetti S 55-X, 1933 1.15 .58
369 A52 125e Lockheed Sirius, 1933 1.90 .95
Nos. 366-369 (4) 4.31 2.18

Perf. 12 Vert.

366a A52 25e .38 .20
367a A52 57e .88 .45
368a A52 74.50e 1.15 .58
369a A52 125e 1.90 .95
b. Bklt. pane of 4, #366a-369a 4.25

Europa Type of Portugal

1988, Apr. 21 **Litho.** *Perf. 12*

370 A466 80e multicolored 1.35 .68
a. Souvenir sheet of 4 5.40 5.40

Birds — A54

1988, Oct. 18 **Litho.**

371 A54 27e Columba palambus azorica .40 .20
372 A54 60e Scolopax rusticola .88 .45
373 A54 80e Sterna dougallii 1.15 .58
374 A54 100e Buteo buteo 1.45 .72
a. Booklet pane of 4, #371-374 3.90
Nos. 371-374 (4) 3.88 1.95

Portugal Regional Issues of Azores can be mounted in the annual Scott Portugal supplement.

Coats of Arms — A55

1988, Nov. 18 **Litho.**
375 A55 55e Dominion of Azores .85 .42
376 A55 80e Bettencourt family 1.20 .60

Wildlife Conservation A56

Various kinglets, *Regulus regulus.*

1989, Jan. 20 **Litho.**
377 A56 30e Adult on branch .45 .22
378 A56 30e Two adults .45 .22
379 A56 30e Adult, nest .45 .22
380 A56 30e Bird in flight .45 .22
a. Strip of 4, Nos. 377-380 1.80 .88

See Nos. 385-388.

Europa Type of Portugal

Children's toys.

1989, Apr. 26 **Litho.**
381 A476 80e Tin boat 1.20 .60

Souvenir Sheet

Sheet, 2 each #381, 382a 4.80 4.80
a. A476 80e Tin boat, diff. 1.20 1.20

Settlement of the Azores, 550th Anniv. — A58

1989, Sept. 20 **Litho.**
383 A58 29e Friar Goncalho Velho .38 .20
384 A58 87e Settlers farming 1.10 .55

Bird Type of 1989 With World Wildlife Fund Emblem

Various *Pyrrhula murina.*

1990, Feb. 14 **Litho.** ***Perf. 12***
385 A56 32e Adult on branch .45 .22
386 A56 32e Two adults .45 .22
387 A56 32e Brooding .45 .22
388 A56 32e Bird in flight .45 .22
a. Strip of 4, #385-388 1.80 .88

No. 388a has continuous design.

Europa Type of Portugal

1990, Apr. 11 **Litho.** ***Perf. 12x11½***
389 A486 80e Vasco da Gama P.O. 1.10 .55

Souvenir Sheet

390 Sheet of 4, 2 each #389, 390a 4.40 4.40
a. A486 80e Maia P.O. 1.10 1.10

Professions A61

1990, July 11 **Litho.** ***Perf. 12***
391 A61 5e Cart maker .15 .15
392 A61 32e Potter .44 .44
393 A61 60e Metal worker .80 .80
394 A61 100e Cooper 1.35 1.35
Nos. 391-394 (4) 2.74 2.74

Perf. 13½ Vert.
391a A61 5e .15 .15
392a A61 32e .44 .44
393a A61 60e .80 .80
394a A61 100e 1.35 1.35
b. Bklt. pane of 4, #391a-394a 2.85

See Nos. 397-400, 406-409.

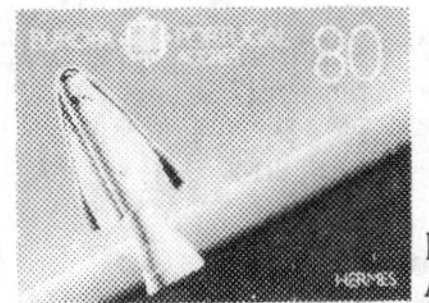

Europa A62

1991, Apr. 11 **Litho.** ***Perf. 12***
395 A62 80e Hermes space shuttle 1.15 .60

Souvenir Sheet

396 Sheet, 2 each #395, 396a 4.60 2.40
a. A62 80e Sanger 1.15 .60

Professions Type of 1990

1991, Aug. 2 **Litho.** ***Perf. 12x11½***
397 A61 35e Tile makers .50 .25
398 A61 65e Mosaic artists .95 .48
399 A61 70e Quarrymen 1.00 .50
400 A61 110e Stonemasons 1.60 .80
Nos. 397-400 (4) 4.05 2.03

Perf. 13½ Vert.
397a A61 35e .50 .25
398a A61 65e .95 .48
399a A61 70e 1.00 .50
400a A61 110e 1.60 .80
b. Bklt. pane of 4, #397a-400a 4.05

Transportation in the Azores — A63

Ships and Planes: 35e, Schooner Helena, 1918. 60e, Beechcraft CS, 1947. 80e, Yacht, Cruzeiro do Canal, 1987. 110e, British Aerospace ATP, 1991.

1991, Nov. 15 **Litho.** ***Perf. 12x11½***
401 A63 35e multicolored .52 .25
402 A63 60e multicolored .90 .45
403 A63 80e multicolored 1.20 .60
404 A63 110e multicolored 1.65 .80
Nos. 401-404 (4) 4.27 2.10

See Nos. 410-413.

Europa Type of Portugal

Europa: 85e, Columbus aboard Santa Maria.

1992, May 22 **Litho.** ***Perf. 12x11½***
405 A514 85e gold & multi 1.40 .70

Professions Type of 1990

1992, June 12 **Litho.** ***Perf. 12x11½***
406 A61 10e Guitar maker .16 .15
407 A61 38e Carpenter .65 .32
408 A61 85e Basket maker 1.40 .70
409 A61 120e Boat builders 2.00 1.00
Nos. 406-409 (4) 4.21 2.17

Perf. 13½ Vert.
406a A61 10e .16 .15
407a A61 38e .65 .32
408a A61 85e 1.40 .70
409a A61 120e 2.00 1.00
b. Bklt. pane of 4, #406a-409a 4.25

Transportation Type of 1991

Ships.

1992, Oct. 7 **Litho.** ***Perf. 12x11½***
410 A63 38e Insulano .58 .28
411 A63 65e Carvalho Araujo 1.00 .50
412 A63 85e Funchal 1.25 .65
413 A63 120e Terceirense 1.80 .90
Nos. 410-413 (4) 4.63 2.33

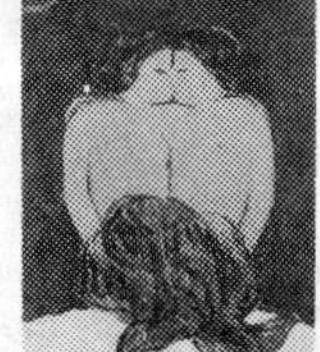

Contemporary Paintings by Antonio Dacosta (1914-90) — A64

Europa: No. 414, Two Mermaids at the Entrance to a Cave, 1980. No. 415a, Acoriana, 1986.

1993, May 5 **Litho.** ***Perf. 12x11½***
414 A64 90e multicolored 1.25 .62

Souvenir Sheet

415 Sheet, 2 each #414, 415a 5.00 2.50
a. A64 90e multicolored 1.25 .62

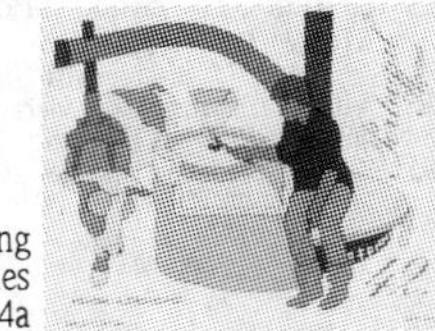

Grinding Stones A64a

Designs: 42e, Animal-powered mill. 130e, Woman using hand-driven mill.

1993, May 5 **Litho.** ***Perf. 12x11***
416 A64a 42e multicolored .50 .25
417 A64a 130e multicolored 1.50 .75

Architecture — A65

Church of Praia da Vitoria: 42e, Main entry. 70e, South entry.

Church of Ponta Delgada: 90e, Main entry. 130e, South entry.

1993, Nov. 3 **Litho.** ***Perf. 12***
418 A65 42e multicolored .48 .25
419 A65 70e multicolored .80 .40
420 A65 90e multicolored 1.00 .50
421 A65 130e multicolored 1.50 .75
Nos. 418-421 (4) 3.78 1.90

Tile Used in Religious Architecture A66

Designs: 40e, Blue and white pattern, Caloura church, Sao Miguel. 70e, Blue, white and yellow pattern, Caloura church, Sao Miguel. 100e, Drawing of Adoration of the Wise Men, by Bartolomeu Antunes, Esperanca monastery, Ponta Delgada. 150e, Drawing, frontal altar, Nossa Senhora dos Anjos chapel.

1994, Mar. 28 **Litho.** ***Perf. 12***
422 A66 40e multicolored .52 .25
423 A66 70e multicolored .90 .45
424 A66 100e multicolored 1.25 .65
425 A66 150e multicolored 2.00 .50
Nos. 422-425 (4) 4.67 1.85

Perf. 11½ Vert.
422a A66 40e .52 .25
423a A66 70e .90 .45
424a A66 100e 1.25 .65
425a A66 150e 2.00 .50
b. Booklet pane of 4, #422a-425a 4.75

Europa Type of Portugal

Wildlife, country: No. 426, Monkey, Brazil. No. 427a, Armadillo, Africa.

1994, May 5 **Litho.** ***Perf. 12***
426 A541 100e multicolored 1.25 .60

Souvenir Sheet

427 Sheet, 2 each #426, 427a 5.00 5.00
a. A541 100e multicolored 1.25 .60

Architecture Type of 1993

Designs: 45e, Church of Santa Barbara, Manueline Entry, Cedros. 140e, Railed window, Ribeira Grande.

1994, Sept. 16 **Litho.** ***Perf. 12***
428 A65 45e multicolored .58 .30
429 A65 140e multicolored 1.75 .85

Advocates of Local Autonomy A67

Designs: 42e, Aristides Moreira da Motta (1855-1942). 130e, Gil Mont'Alverne de Sequeira (1859-1931).

1995, Mar. 2 **Litho.** ***Perf. 12***
430 A67 42e multicolored .60 .30
431 A67 130e multicolored 1.90 .95

19th Century Architecture — A68

Designs: 45e, Santana Palace, Ponta Delgada. 80e, Our Lady of Victories Chapel, Furnas Lake. 95e, Hospital of the Santa Casa da Misericórdia, Ponta Delgada. 135e, Residence of Ernesto do Canto, Myrthes Park, Furnas Lake

1995, Sept. 1 **Litho.** ***Perf. 12***
432 A68 45e multicolored .60 .30
433 A68 80e multicolored 1.00 .50
434 A68 95e multicolored 1.25 .60
435 A68 135e multicolored 1.75 .90
Nos. 432-435 (4) 4.60 2.30

Perf. 11½ Vert.
432a A68 45e .60 .60
433a A68 80e 1.00 1.00
434a A68 95e 1.25 .60
435a A68 135e 1.75 .90
b. Booklet pane, Nos. 432a-435a 4.75
Complete booklet, No. 435b 4.75

Natália Correia (1923-93), Writer — A69

1996, May 3 **Litho.** ***Perf. 12***
436 A69 98e multicolored 1.25 .60
a. Souvenir sheet of 3 3.75 1.90

Europa.

Lighthouses — A70

Designs: 47e, Contendas, Terceira Island. 78e, Molhe, Port of Ponte Delgada, San Miguel Island. 98e, Arnel, San Miguel. 140e, Santa Clara, San Miguel. 200e, Ponta da Barca, Graciosa Island.

Illustration reduced.

1996, May 3
437 A70 47e multicolored .60 .30
438 A70 78e multicolored .90 .45
439 A70 98e multicolored 1.25 .60
440 A70 140e multicolored 1.75 .90
Nos. 437-440 (4) 4.50 2.25

Souvenir Sheet

441 A69 200e multicolored 2.50 1.25

Carved Work from Church Altar Pieces — A71

49e, Leaves, berries, bird, St. Peter Church, Ponta Delgada, Sao Miguel. 80e, Cherub, Church of the Convent of St. Peter de Alcântara, Sao Roque, Pico. 100e, Cherub, All Saints Church, former Jesuits' College, Ponta Delgada. 140e, Figure holding scroll above head, St. Joseph Church, Ponta Delgada.

1997, Apr. 16 **Litho.** ***Perf. 12***
442 A71 49e multicolored .55 .30
443 A71 80e multicolored .90 .45
444 A71 100e multicolored 1.15 .60
445 A71 140e multicolored 1.60 .80
Nos. 442-445 (4) 4.20 2.15

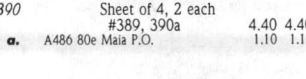

Perf. 11½ Vert.

442a A71 49e .55 .30
443a A71 80e .90 .45
444a A71 100e 1.15 .60
445a A71 140e 1.60 .80
b. Booklet pane, Nos. 442a-445a 4.20
Complete booklet, #445b 4.20

Stories and Legends Type of Portugal

Europa: Man on ship from "Legend of the Island of Seven Cities," horiz.

1997, May 5 Litho. *Perf. 12*
446 A599 100e multicolored 1.10 .55
a. Souvenir sheet of 3 3.30 1.70

MADEIRA

Type of Azores, 1980

6.50e, Madeira No. 2. 19.50e, Madeira No. 5.

1980, Jan. 2 Litho. *Perf. 12*
66 A33 6.50e multi .15 .15
67 A33 19.50e multi .50 .20
a. Souvenir sheet of 2, #66-67 .90 .90
Set value .25

No. 67a exists overprinted for Capex 87.

Grapes and Wine — A7

1980, Sept. 17 Litho. *Perf. 12x11½*
68 A7 50c Bullock cart .15 .15
69 A7 1e shown .15 .15
70 A7 5e Produce map of Madeira .15 .15
71 A7 6.50e Basket and lace .16 .15
72 A7 8e Orchid .20 .15
73 A7 30e Madeira boat .55 .35
Set value 1.10 .70

World Tourism Conf., Manila, Sept. 27.

Europa Issue 1981

O Bailinho Folk Dance — A8

1981, May 11 Litho. *Perf. 12*
74 A8 22e multi .42 .22
a. Souvenir sheet of 2 1.50 1.10

Explorer Ship — A9

1981, July 1 Litho. *Perf. 12x11½*
75 A9 8.50e shown .15 .15
76 A9 33.50e Map .60 .20
Set value .26

Discovery of Madeira anniv.

A10 A12

Designs: Local flora.

1981, Oct. 6 Litho. *Perf. 12½x12*
77 A10 7e Dactylorhiza foliosa .15 .15
78 A10 8.50e Echium candicans .18 .15
79 A10 20e Geranium maderense .40 .15
80 A10 50e Isoplexis sceptrum .95 .35
a. Booklet pane of 4, #77-80 1.90
Nos. 77-80 (4) 1.68 .80

See Nos. 82-85, 90-93.

Europa Type of Portugal

1982, May 3 Litho. *Perf. 12x11½*
81 A405 33.50e Sugar mills, 15th cent. .60 .30
a. Souvenir sheet of 3 2.00 2.00

1982, Aug. 31 Litho. *Perf. 12½x12*
82 A10 9e Goodyera macrophylla .15 .15
83 A10 10e Armeria maderensis .18 .15
84 A10 27e Viola paradoxa .35 .20
85 A10 33.50e Scilla maderensis .90 .45
a. Booklet pane of 4, #82-85 1.65
Nos. 82-85 (4) 1.58
Set value .80

1982, Dec. 15 Litho. *Perf. 13½*
86 A12 27e Brinco dancing dolls .65 .40
87 A12 33.50e Dancers .85 .50

Europa 1983 — A13

1983, May 5 Litho. *Perf. 12½*
88 A13 37.50e Levadas irrigation system .70 .32
a. Souvenir sheet of 3 2.25 2.25

Flag of the Autonomous Region — A14

1983, July 1 Litho. *Perf. 12x11½*
89 A14 12.50e multi .30 .30

Flower Type of 1981

1983, Oct. 19 Litho. *Perf. 12½x12*
90 A10 12.50e Matthiola maderensis .30 .30
91 A10 30e Erica maderensis .65 .30
92 A10 37.50e Cirsium latifolium .75 .30
93 A10 100e Clethra arborea 2.00 1.00
a. Booklet pane of 4, #90-93 3.75
Nos. 90-93 (4) 3.70 1.90

Europa Type of Portugal

1984, May 2 Litho. *Perf. 12x11½*
94 A427 51e multi .80 .40
a. Souvenir sheet of 3 3.00 3.00

Madeira Rally (Auto Race), 25th Anniv. — A16

Various cars.

1984, Aug. 3 Litho. *Perf. 11½x12*
95 A16 16e multicolored .40 .20
96 A16 51e multicolored 1.00 .50

Traditional Means of Transportation A17

1984, Nov. 22 *Perf. 12*
97 A17 16e Mountain sledge .25 .15
98 A17 35e Hammock .52 .25
99 A17 40e Winebag carriers' procession .60 .30
100 A17 51e Carreira Boat .75 .38
a. Booklet pane of 4, Nos. 97-100 2.15
Nos. 97-100 (4) 2.12 1.08

See Nos. 104-107.

Europa Type of Portugal

1985, May 6 Litho. *Perf. 11½x12*
101 A435 60e Man playing guitar 1.00 .40
a. Souvenir sheet of 3 4.00 4.00

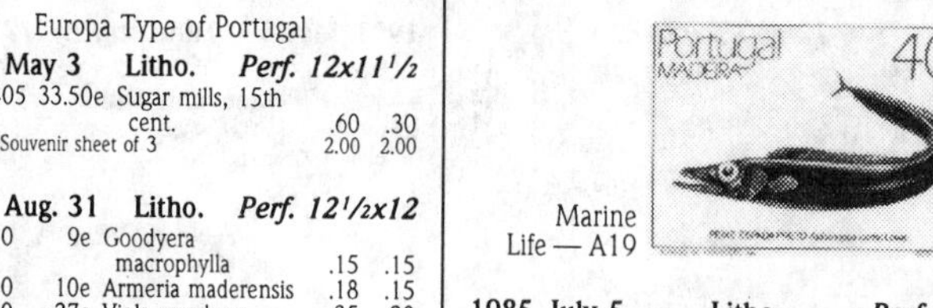

Marine Life — A19

1985, July 5 Litho. *Perf. 12*
102 A19 40e Aphanopus carbo .52 .28
103 A19 60e Lampris guttatus .80 .40

See Nos. 108-109.

Transportation type of 1984

1985, Sept. 11 Litho. *Perf. 12x11½*
104 A17 20e Ox-drawn sledge .35 .16
105 A17 40e Mountrain train .65 .32
106 A17 46e Fish vendors .75 .38
107 A17 60e Coastal steamer 1.00 .50
a. Booklet pane of 4, Nos. 104-107 2.20
Nos. 104-107 (4) 2.75 1.36

Marine Life Type of 1985

1986, Jan. 7 Litho.
108 A19 20e Thunnus obesus .25 .15
109 A19 75e Beryx decadactylus 1.00 .50

Europa Type of Portugal

1986, May 5 Litho.
110 A447 68.50e Great Shearwater 1.05 .52
a. Souvenir sheet of 3 3.25 3.25

Forts in Funchal and Machico A21

1986, July 1 Litho. *Perf. 12*
111 A21 22.50e Sao Lourenco, 1583 .32 .16
112 A21 52.50e Sao Joao do Pico, 1611 .75 .38
113 A21 68.50e Sao Tiago, 1614 1.00 .50
114 A21 100e Sao do Amparo, 1706 1.45 .75
a. Booklet pane of 4, #111-114 3.75
Nos. 111-114 (4) 3.52 1.79

A22 A24

Indigenous birds.

1987, Mar. 6 Litho.
115 A22 25e Regulus ignicapillus madeirensis .40 .20
116 A22 57e Columba trocaz .90 .45
117 A22 74.50e Tyto alba schmitzi 1.15 .58
118 A22 125e Pterodroma madeira 1.95 1.00
a. Booklet pane of 4, #115-118 4.50
Nos. 115-118 (4) 4.40 2.23

See Nos. 123-126.

Europa Type of Portugal

Modern Architecture: Social Services Center, Funchal, designed by Raul Chorao Ramalho.

1987, May 5 Litho. *Perf. 12*
119 A456 74.50e multicolored 1.20 .60
a. Souvenir sheet of 4 5.00 5.00

1987, July 1 *Perf. 12x12½*

Natl. monuments.

120 A24 51e Funchal Castle, 15th cent. .80 .40
121 A24 74.50e Old Town Hall, Santa Cruz, 16th cent. 1.15 .58

Europa Type of Portugal

Transportation Modern mail boat PS 13 TL.

1988, Apr. 21 Litho. *Perf. 12*
122 A466 80e multicolored 1.35 .68
a. Souvenir sheet of 4 5.40 5.40

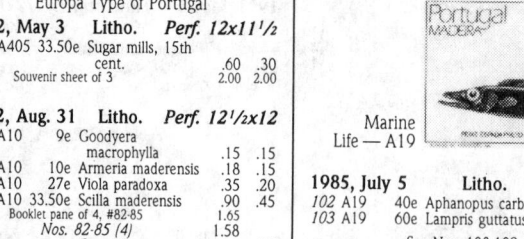

Bird Type of 1987

1988, June 15 Litho.
123 A22 27e Erithacus rubecula .45 .22
124 A22 60e Petronia .98 .50
125 A22 80e Fringilla coelebs 1.30 .65
126 A22 100e Accipiter nisus 1.65 .82
a. Booklet pane of 4, #123-126 4.40
Nos. 123-126 (4) 4.38 2.19

Portraits of Christopher Columbus and Purported Residences on Madeira A27

1988, July 1 Litho.
127 A27 55e Funchal, 1480-1481, vert. .88 .45
128 A27 80e Porto Santo 1.30 .65

Europa Type of Portugal

Children's toys.

1989, Apr. 26 Litho.
129 A476 80e Kite 1.20 .60

Souvenir Sheet

130 Sheet, 2 each #129, 130a 4.80 4.80
a. A476 80e Kite, diff. 1.20 1.20

Monuments — A29

Churches: 29e, Church of the Colegio (St. John the Evangelist Church). 87e, Santa Clara Church and convent.

1989, July 28 Litho.
131 A29 29e multi .35 .18
132 A29 87e multi 1.05 .52

Fish — A30

1989, Sept. 20 Litho.
133 A30 29e *Argyropelecus aculeatus* .38 .20
134 A30 60e *Pseudolepidaplois scrofa* .78 .40
135 A30 87e *Coris julis* 1.10 .55
136 A30 100e *Scorpaena maderensis* 1.30 .65
a. Booklet pane of 4, #133-136 3.60
Nos. 133-136 (4) 3.56 1.80

Europa Type of Portugal

1990, Apr. 11 Litho. *Perf. 12x11½*
137 A486 80e Zarco P.O. 1.10 .55

Souvenir Sheet

138 Sheet, 2 each #137, 138a 4.40 4.40
a. A486 80e Porto da Cruz P.O. 1.10 1.10

Subtropical Fruits and Plants — A32

1990, June 5 Litho. *Perf. 12*
139 A32 5e Banana .15 .15
140 A32 32e Avocado .42 .20
141 A32 60e Sugar apple .80 .40
142 A32 100e Passion fruit 1.35 .68
Nos. 139-142 (4) 2.72 1.43

Perf. 13½ Vert.

139a A32 5e .15 .15
140a A32 32e .42 .42
141a A32 60e .80 .80
142a A32 100e 1.35 1.35
b. Bklt. pane of 4, #139a-142a 2.65

See Nos. 153-160.

Boats of Madeira A33

1990, Aug. 24 *Perf. 12*

143 A33 32e Tuna .42 .20
144 A33 60e Desert islands .80 .40
145 A33 70e Maneiro .95 .48
146 A33 95e Chavelha 1.25 .64
Nos. 143-146 (4) 3.42 1.72

See Nos. 162-165.

Columba Trocaz Heineken — A34

1991, Jan. 23 **Litho.** *Perf. 12*

147 A34 35e shown .50 .25
148 A34 35e On branch .50 .25
149 A34 35e In flight .50 .25
150 A34 35e On nest .50 .35
a. Strip of 4, #147-150 2.00 1.00

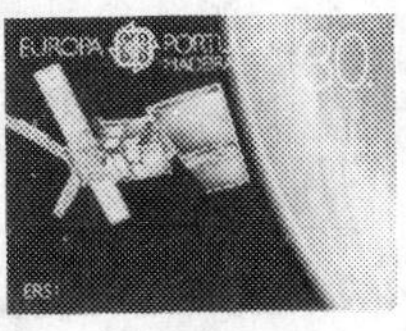

Europa A35

1991, Apr. 11 **Litho.** *Perf. 12*

151 A35 80e ERS-1 1.15 .60

Souvenir Sheet

152 Sheet, 2 each #151, 152a 4.60 2.40
a. A35 80e SPOT 1.15 .60

Subtropical Fruits Type of 1990

1991, June 7 **Litho.** *Perf. 12*

153 A32 35e Mango .50 .25
154 A32 65e Surinam cherry .90 .45
155 A32 70e Brazilian guava .95 .48
156 A32 110e Papaya 1.50 .75
Nos. 153-156 (4) 3.85 1.93

Perf. 13½ Vert.

153a A32 35e .50 .25
154a A32 65e .90 .45
155a A32 70e .95 .48
156a A32 110e 1.50 .75
b. Bklt. pane of 4, #153a-156a 3.85

1992, Feb. 21 **Litho.** *Perf. 11½x12*

157 A32 10e Prickly pear .15 .15
158 A32 38e Tree tomato .42 .22
159 A32 85e Ceriman 1.30 .65
160 A32 125e Guava 1.90 .95
Nos. 157-160 (4) 3.77 1.97

Perf. 13½ Vert.

157a A32 10e .15 .15
158a A32 38e .42 .22
159a A32 85e 1.30 .65
160a A32 125e 1.90 .95
b. Bklt. pane of 4, #157a-160a 3.80

Europa Type of Portugal

Europa: 85e, Columbus at Funchal.

1992, May 22 **Litho.** *Perf. 12x11½*

161 A514 85e gold & multi 1.40 .70

Ships Type of 1990

1992, Sept. 18 **Litho.** *Perf. 12x11½*

162 A33 38e Gaviao .65 .32
163 A33 65e Independencia 1.10 .55
164 A33 85e Madeirense 1.40 .70
165 A33 120e Funchalense 2.00 1.00
Nos. 162-165 (4) 5.15 2.57

Contemporary Paintings by Lourdes Castro — A36

Europa: No. 166, Shadow Projection of Christa Maar, 1968. No. 167a, Shadow Projection of a Dahlia, c. 1970.

1993, May 5 **Litho.** *Perf. 11½x12*

166 A36 90e multicolored 1.25 .62

Souvenir Sheet

167 Sheet, 2 each #166, 167a 5.00 2.50
a. A36 90e multicolored 1.25 .62

Nature Preservation — A37

Monachus monachus: No. 168, Adult on rock. No. 169, Swimming. No. 170, Mother nursing pup. No. 171, Two on rocks.

1993, June 30 **Litho.** *Perf. 12x11½*

168 A37 42e multicolored .52 .25
169 A37 42e multicolored .52 .25
170 A37 42e multicolored .52 .25
171 A37 42e multicolored .52 .25
a. Strip of 4, #168-171 2.25 1.00

Architecture — A38

Designs: 42e, Window from Sao Francisco Convent, Funchal. 130e, Window of Mercy (Old Hospital), Funchal.

1993, July 30 *Perf. 11½x12*

172 A38 42e multicolored .52 .25
173 A38 130e multicolored 1.65 .80

Europa Type of Portugal

Discoveries: No. 174, Native with bow and arrows. No. 175a, Palm tree.

1994, May 5 **Litho.** *Perf. 12*

174 A541 100e multicolored 1.25 .60

Souvenir Sheet

175 Sheet, 2 each, #174-175a 5.00 5.00
a. A541 100e multicolored 1.25 .60

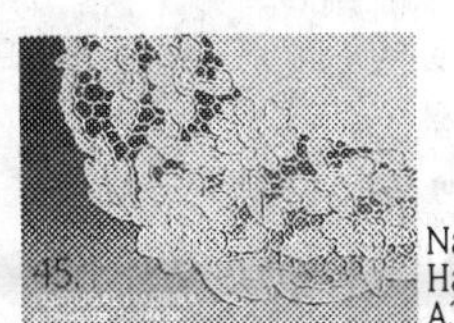

Native Handicrafts A39

1994, May 5 *Perf. 12x11½*

176 A39 45e Embroidery .55 .28
177 A39 75e Tapestry .90 .45
178 A39 100e Shoes 1.25 .60
179 A39 140e Wicker work 1.65 .85
Nos. 176-179 (4) 4.35 2.18

Perf. 11½ Vert.

176a A39 45e .55 .28
177a A39 75e .90 .45
178a A39 100e 1.25 .60
179a A39 140e 1.65 .85
b. Booklet pane of 4, #176a-179a 4.50

Portugal Regional Issues of Madeira can be mounted in the annual Scott Portugal supplement.

Arms of Madeira Districts — A40

1994, July 1 **Litho.** *Perf. 11½x12*

180 A40 45e Funchal .55 .28
181 A40 140e Porto Santo 1.90 .95

Traditional Arts & Crafts — A41

Designs: 45e, Chicken puppets made of flour paste. 80e, Inlaid wood furniture piece. 95e, Wicker bird cage. 135e, Knitted wool bonnet.

1995, June 30 **Litho.** *Perf. 11½x12*

182 A41 45e multicolored .60 .30
183 A41 80e multicolored 1.10 .55
184 A41 95e multicolored 1.25 .65
185 A41 135e multicolored 1.90 .95
Nos. 182-185 (4) 4.85 2.45

Perf. 11½ Vert.

182a A41 45e .60 .30
183a A41 80e 1.10 .55
184a A41 95e 1.25 .65
185a A41 135e 1.90 .95
b. Booklet pane, #182a-185a 4.85
Complete booklet, #185b 4.85

Famous Woman Type of Azores, 1996

Europa: Guiomar Vilhena (1705-89), entrepeneur.

1996, May 3 **Litho.** *Perf. 12*

186 A69 98e multicolored 1.25 .60
a. Souvenir sheet of 3 3.75 1.90

Paintings from Flemish Group, Museum of Sacred Paintings of Funchal (Madeira) A42

Designs: 47e, The Adoration of the Magi, vert. 78e, St. Mary Magdalene, vert. 98e, Annunciation. 140e, St. Peter, St. Paul and St. Andrew.

Perf. 11½x12, 12x11½

1996, July 1 **Litho.**

187 A42 47e multicolored .60 .30
188 A42 78e multicolored 1.00 .50
189 A42 98e multicolored 1.30 .65
190 A42 140e multicolored 1.80 .90
Nos. 187-190 (4) 4.70 2.35

Perf. 11½ on 2 Sides

187a A42 47e .60 .30
188a A42 78e 1.00 .50
189a A42 98e 1.30 .65
190a A42 140e 1.80 .90
b. Booklet pane, #187a-190a 4.70
Complete booklet, #190b 4.70

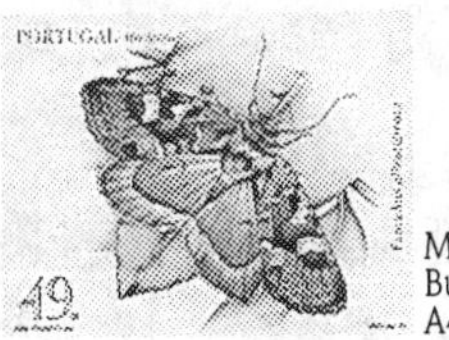

Moths & Butterflies A43

Designs: 49e, Eumichtis albostigmata. 80e, Menophra maderae. 100e, Vanessa indica vulcania. 140e, Pieris brassicae wollastoni.

1997, Feb. 12 **Litho.** *Perf. 12*

191 A43 49e multicolored .60 .30
192 A43 80e multicolored .95 .45
193 A43 100e multicolored 1.15 .60
194 A43 140e multicolored 1.65 .80
Nos. 191-194 (4) 4.35 2.15

Perf. 11½ Vert.

191a A43 49e multicolored .60 .30
192a A43 80e multicolored .95 .45
193a A43 100e multicolored 1.15 .60
194a A43 140e multicolored 1.65 .80
b. Booklet pane, #191a-194a 4.35
Complete booklet, #194b 4.35

Stories and Legends Type of Portugal

Europa: Man holding woman from "Legend of Machico," horiz.

1997, May 5 **Litho.** *Perf. 12*

195 A599 100e multicolored 1.10 .55
a. Souvenir sheet of 3 3.30 1.70

PORTUGUESE AFRICA

'pōr–chə–,gēz 'a–fri–kə

For use in any of the Portuguese possessions in Africa.

1000 Reis = 1 Milreis
100 Centavos = 1 Escudo

Common Design Types pictured following the introduction.

Vasco da Gama Issue
Common Design Types
Inscribed "Africa - Correios"
Perf. 13½ to 15½

1898, Apr. 1 **Engr.** **Unwmk.**

1 CD20 2½r blue green .90 .90
2 CD21 5r red .90 .90
3 CD22 10r red violet .90 .90
4 CD23 25r yellow green .90 .90
5 CD24 50r dark blue 1.10 1.10
6 CD25 75r violet brown 6.25 6.25
7 CD26 100r bister brown 5.00 4.50
8 CD27 150r bister 7.50 6.25
Nos. 1-8 (8) 23.45 21.70

Vasco da Gama's voyage to India.

POSTAGE DUE STAMPS

D1

1945 **Unwmk.** **Typo.** *Perf. 11½x12*
Denomination in Black

J1 D1 10c claret .70 .70
J2 D1 20c purple .70 .70
J3 D1 30c deep blue .70 .70
J4 D1 40c chocolate .70 .70
J5 D1 50c red violet .75 1.25
J6 D1 1e orange brown 1.50 3.75
J7 D1 2e yellow green 3.25 5.00
J8 D1 3e bright carmine 8.00 8.50
J9 D1 5e orange yellow 13.00 14.00
Nos. J1-J9 (9) 29.30 35.30

WAR TAX STAMPS

Liberty WT1

Perf. 12x11½, 15x14

1919 **Typo.** **Unwmk.**
Overprinted in Black, Orange or Carmine

MR1 WT1 1c green (Bk) .75 .75
MR2 WT1 4c green (O) 1.00
MR3 WT1 5c green (C) .75 .75
Nos. MR1-MR3 (3) 2.50

Some authorities consider No. MR2 a revenue stamp.

PORTUGUESE CONGO

'pōr–chi–gēz 'käŋ–(,)gō

LOCATION — The northernmost district of the Portuguese Angola Colony on the southwest coast of Africa
CAPITAL — Cabinda

Stamps of Angola replaced those of Portuguese Congo.

1000 Reis = 1 Milreis
100 Centavos = 1 Escudo (1913)

King Carlos
A1 A2

Perf. 11½, 12½, 13½

1894, Aug. 5 Typo. Unwmk.

1 A1 5r yellow .85 .75
a. Perf. 13½ 15.00 12.50
2 A1 10r redsh violet 1.65 .80
a. Perf. 13½ 17.50 14.00
3 A1 15r chocolate 2.75 2.00
4 A1 20r lavender 2.50 1.75
5 A1 25r green 1.50 .80
6 A1 50r light blue 2.75 2.00
7 A1 75r rose 4.50 3.75
a. Perf. 12½ 18.00 15.00
8 A1 80r yellow green 7.00 6.00
a. Perf. 12½ 17.50 12.50
9 A1 100r brown, *yel* 5.25 3.25
a. Perf. 13½ 30.00 15.00
10 A1 150r carmine, *rose* 10.00 9.00
11 A1 200r dk blue, *bl* 10.00 9.00
12 A1 300r dk blue, *salmon* 12.50 11.00
Nos. 1-12 (12) 61.25 50.10

For surcharges and overprints see Nos. 36-47, 127-131.

1898-1903 *Perf. 11½*
Name & Value in Black except 500r

13 A2 2½r gray .35 .25
14 A2 5r orange .35 .25
15 A2 10r lt green .55 .35
16 A2 15r brown 1.50 1.10
17 A2 15r gray grn ('03) .90 .55
18 A2 20r gray violet .90 .60
19 A2 25r sea green 1.40 .90
20 A2 25r car rose ('03) .90 .45
21 A2 50r deep blue 1.65 1.25
22 A2 50r brown ('03) 2.75 1.75
23 A2 65r dull blue ('03) 7.50 6.50
24 A2 75r rose 3.00 2.25
25 A2 75r red lilac ('03) 2.75 2.25
26 A2 80r violet 3.00 2.50
27 A2 100r dk bl, *bl* 2.25 1.75
28 A2 115r org brn, *pink* ('03) 6.00 5.00
29 A2 130r brn, *straw* ('03) 12.00 11.00
30 A2 150r brown, *buff* 3.00 2.50
31 A2 200r red lilac, *pnksh* 4.25 3.00
32 A2 300r dk blue, *rose* 4.25 3.25
33 A2 400r dl bl, *straw* ('03) 11.00 9.50
34 A2 500r blk & red, *bl* ('01) 15.00 9.00
35 A2 700r vio, *yelsh* ('01) 25.00 17.50
Nos. 13-35 (23) 110.25 83.45

For overprints and surcharges see Nos. 49-53, 60-74, 117-126, 136-138.

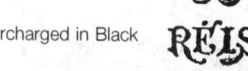

Surcharged in Black

1902 *Perf. 11½, 12½, 13½*
On Issue of 1894

36 A1 65r on 15r choc 3.50 3.00
a. Perf. 11½ 15.00 7.50
37 A1 65r on 20r lav 4.00 3.00
38 A1 65r on 25r green 4.00 3.00
a. Perf. 11½ 15.00 9.00
39 A1 65r on 300r bl, *sal* 4.50 4.50
40 A1 115r on 10r red vio 4.00 3.00
41 A1 115r on 50r lt bl 3.75 2.50
42 A1 130r on 5r yellow 4.00 2.75
a. Inverted surcharge 27.50 27.50
43 A1 130r on 75r rose 3.50 3.00
a. Perf. 12½ 7.00 6.00
44 A1 130r on 100r brn, *yel* 5.00 3.75
a. Inverted surcharge 40.00 35.00
b. Perf. 11½ 18.00 12.50
45 A1 400r on 80r yel grn 1.75 1.25
46 A1 400r on 150r car, *rose* 2.25 1.50
47 A1 400r on 200r bl, *bl* 2.25 1.50

On Newspaper Stamp of 1894

48 N1 115r on 2½r brn 3.75 2.50
a. Inverted surcharge 25.00 25.00
Nos. 36-48 (13) 46.25 35.25

Nos. 16, 19, 21 and 24 Overprinted in Black PROVISORIO

1902 *Perf. 11½*

49 A2 15r brown 2.00 1.25
50 A2 25r sea green 2.00 1.40
51 A2 50r blue 2.00 1.40
52 A2 75r rose 4.00 2.75
Nos. 49-52 (4) 10.00 6.80

No. 23 Surcharged 50 RÉIS

1905

53 A2 50r on 65r dull blue 3.50 2.25

Angola Stamps of 1898-1903 (Port. Congo type A2) Overprinted or Surcharged:

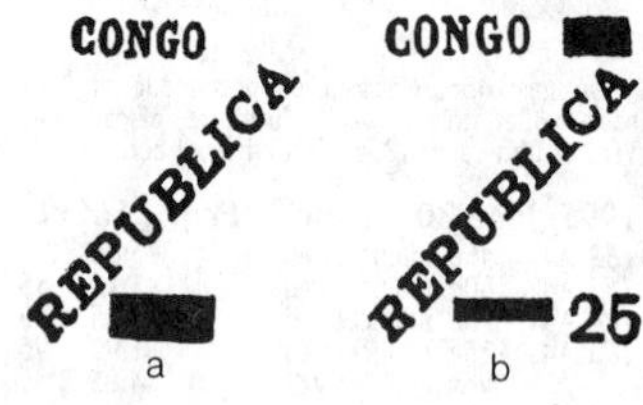

1911

54 (a) 2½r gray 1.00 .90
55 (a) 5r orange 1.40 1.25
56 (a) 10r lt green 1.40 1.25
a. "REPUBLICA" inverted 17.50 17.50
57 (a) 15r gray green 1.40 1.25
a. "REPUBLICA" inverted 17.50 17.50
58 (b) 25r on 200r red vio, *pnksh* 2.25 2.00
a. "REPUBLICA" inverted 17.50 17.50
b. "CONGO" double 17.50 17.50

Thin Bar and "CONGO" as Type "b"

59 (a) 2½r gray 1.10 .90
Nos. 54-59 (6) 8.55 7.55

Issue of 1898-1903 Overprinted in Carmine or Green — c REPUBLICA

1911

60 A2 2½r gray .15 .15
61 A2 5r orange .25 .20
62 A2 10r lt green .25 .20
63 A2 15r gray grn .25 .25
64 A2 20r gray vio .40 .25
65 A2 25r car rose (G) .50 .25
66 A2 50r brown .60 .30
67 A2 75r red lilac 1.00 .50
68 A2 100r dk bl, *bl* .80 .55
69 A2 115r org brn, *pink* 1.90 1.25
70 A2 130r brown, *straw* 1.90 1.25
71 A2 200r red vio, *pnksh* 2.75 1.75
72 A2 400r dull bl, *straw* 2.75 2.25
73 A2 500r blk & red, *bl* 3.75 2.00
74 A2 700r violet, *yelsh* 3.75 2.00
Nos. 60-74 (15) 21.00 13.15

Numerous inverts and doubles exist. These are printer's waste or made to order.

Vasco da Gama Issue of Various Portuguese Colonies Surcharged REPUBLICA CONGO ¼ C.

1913

On Stamps of Macao

75 CD20 ¼c on ½a bl grn 1.40 1.40
76 CD21 ½c on 1a red 1.40 1.40
77 CD22 1c on 2a red vio 1.40 1.40
78 CD23 2½c on 4a yel grn 1.40 1.40
79 CD24 5c on 8a dk blue 1.40 1.40
80 CD25 7½c on 12a vio brn 2.75 2.75
81 CD26 10c on 16a bis brn 2.00 2.00
82 CD27 15c on 24a bister 2.00 2.00
Nos. 75-82 (8) 13.75 13.75

On Stamps of Portuguese Africa

83 CD20 ¼c on 2½r bl grn .90 .90
84 CD21 ½c on 5r red .90 .90
85 CD22 1c on 10r red vio .90 .90
86 CD23 2½c on 25r yel grn .90 .90
87 CD24 5c on 50r dk bl 1.25 1.25
88 CD25 7½c on 75r vio brn 2.25 2.25
89 CD26 10c on 100r bis brn 1.40 1.40
a. Inverted surcharge 22.50 22.50
90 CD27 15c on 150r bister 1.75 1.50
Nos. 83-90 (8) 10.25 10.00

On Stamps of Timor

91 CD20 ¼c on ½a bl grn 1.40 1.40
92 CD21 ½c on 1a red 1.40 1.40
93 CD22 1c on 2a red vio 1.40 1.40
94 CD23 2½c on 4a yel grn 1.40 1.40
95 CD24 5c on 8a dk blue 1.40 1.40
a. Double surcharge 22.50 22.50
96 CD25 7½c on 12a vio brn 2.75 2.75
97 CD26 10c on 16a bis brn 2.50 2.50
98 CD27 15c on 24a bister 2.50 2.50
Nos. 91-98 (8) 14.75 14.75
Nos. 75-98 (24) 38.75 38.50

Ceres — A3

1914 Typo. *Perf. 15x14*
Name and Value in Black

99 A3 ¼c olive brn .30 .45
a. Inscriptions inverted
100 A3 ½c black .55 .90
101 A3 1c blue grn 2.75 3.75
102 A3 1½c lilac brn 1.10 1.25
103 A3 2c carmine 1.10 1.25
104 A3 2½c lt violet .35 .80
105 A3 5c dp blue .65 1.25
106 A3 7½c yellow brn .90 1.25
107 A3 8c slate 1.50 3.00
108 A3 10c orange brn 1.50 3.00
109 A3 15c plum 1.75 3.00
110 A3 20c yellow grn 2.00 3.00
111 A3 30c brown, *grn* 2.50 4.50
112 A3 40c brown, *pink* 4.00 6.00
113 A3 50c orange, *salmon* 4.00 6.00
114 A3 1e green, *blue* 5.00 8.00
Nos. 99-114 (16) 29.95 47.40

Issue of 1898-1903 Overprinted Locally in Green or Red

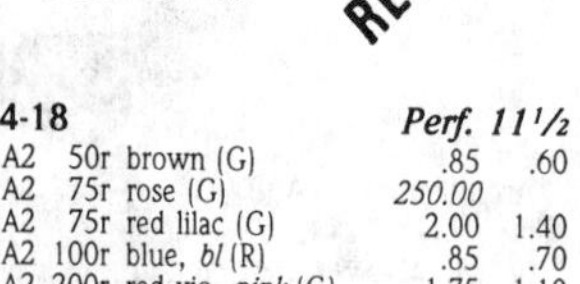

1914-18 *Perf. 11½*

117 A2 50r brown (G) .85 .60
118 A2 75r rose (G) 250.00
119 A2 75r red lilac (G) 2.00 1.40
120 A2 100r blue, *bl* (R) .85 .70
121 A2 200r red vio, *pink* (G) 1.75 1.10
122 A2 400r dl bl, *straw* (R) ('18) 72.50 50.00
123 A2 500r blk & red, *bl* (R) 57.50 37.50

Same on Nos. 51-52

124 A2 50r blue (R) .85 .65
125 A2 75r rose (G) 1.40 1.00

Same on No. 53

126 A2 50r on 65r dl bl (R) 1.10 1.00
Nos. 117,119-126 (9) 138.80 93.95

No. 118 was not regularly issued.

Provisional Issue of 1902 Overprinted Type "c" in Red

1915 *Perf. 11½, 12½, 13½*

127 A1 115r on 10r red vio .25 .20
a. Perf. 13½ 15.00 12.50
128 A1 115r on 50r lt bl .25 .20
a. Perf. 11½ 1.75 .60
129 A1 130r on 5r yellow .30 .25
130 A1 130r on 75r rose 1.40 .60
131 A1 130r on 100r brn, *buff* .40 .35
135 N1 115r on 2½r brn .40 .35

Nos. 49, 51 Overprinted Type "c"

136 A2 15r brown .60 .50
137 A2 50r blue .40 .35

No. 53 Overprinted Type "c"

138 A2 50r on 65r dull blue .50 .35
Nos. 127-138 (9) 4.50 3.15

NEWSPAPER STAMP

N1

Perf. 12½, 13½

1894, Aug. 5 Typo. Unwmk.

P1 N1 2½r brown .90 .55

For surcharge and overprint see Nos. 48, 135.

PORTUGUESE GUINEA

'pōr–chi–gēz 'gi–nē

LOCATION — On the west coast of Africa between Senegal and Guinea
GOVT. — Portuguese Overseas Territory
AREA — 13,944 sq. mi.
POP. — 560,000 (est. 1970)
CAPITAL — Bissau

The territory, including the Bissagos Islands, became an independent republic on Sept. 10, 1974. See Guinea-Bissau in Vol. 3.

1000 Reis = 1 Milreis
100 Centavos = 1 Escudo (1913)

Catalogue values for unused stamps in this country are for Never Hinged items, beginning with Scott 273 in the regular postage section, Scott J40 in the postage due section, and Scott RA17 in the postal tax section.

Stamps of Cape Verde, 1877-85 Overprinted in Black GUINÉ

1881 Unwmk. *Perf. 12½*
Without Gum (Nos. 1-7)

1 A1 5r black *1,000. 800.*
1A A1 10r yellow *1,250. 800.*
2 A1 20r bister *475. 250.*
3 A1 25r rose *1,250. 750.*
4 A1 40r blue *1,250. 800.*
a. Cliché of Mozambique in Cape Verde plate *15,000. 11,000.*
4B A1 50r green *1,300. 725.*
5 A1 100r lilac 275. 150.
6 A1 200r orange *550. 375.*
7 A1 300r brown *550. 400.*

Overprinted in Red or Black GUINÉ

1881-85 *Perf. 12½, 13½*

8 A1 5r black (R) 3.75 2.50
9 A1 10r yellow 150.00 110.00
10 A1 10r green ('85) 5.75 5.50
11 A1 20r bister 2.75 1.75
12 A1 20r rose ('85) 6.25 5.00
a. Double overprint
13 A1 25r carmine 2.25 1.25
a. Perf. 13½ 67.50 37.50
14 A1 25r violet ('85) 2.75 1.75
a. Double overprint
15 A1 40r blue 165.00 77.50
a. Cliché of Mozambique in Cape Verde plate *1,250. 800.00*
16 A1 40r yellow ('85) 1.75 1.25
a. Cliché of Mozambique in Cape Verde plate 37.50 25.00
b. Imperf.
c. As "a," imperf.
d. Double overprint
17 A1 50r green 165.00 77.50
18 A1 50r blue ('85) 4.75 2.50
a. Imperf.
b. Double overprint
19 A1 100r lilac 7.50 4.00
a. Inverted overprint
20 A1 200r orange 11.00 6.50
21 A1 300r yellow brn 13.00 10.00
a. 300r lake brown 16.00 12.50

Varieties of this overprint may be found without accent on "E" of "GUINE," or with grave instead of acute accent.

Stamps of the 1879-85 issues were reprinted on a smooth white chalky paper, ungummed, and on thin white paper with shiny white gum and clean-cut perforation 13½.

King Luiz — A3

1886 Typo. *Perf. 12½, 13½*

22 A3 5r gray black 5.50 3.75
a. Imperf.
23 A3 10r green 6.75 3.25
a. Perf. 13½ 7.75 4.75
b. Imperf.

24	A3	20r carmine	9.50	4.75
25	A3	25r red lilac	9.50	4.25
a.		Imperf.		
26	A3	40r chocolate	7.75	5.00
a.		Perf. 12½	75.00	45.00
27	A3	50r blue	16.00	4.25
a.		Imperf.		
28	A3	80r gray	14.00	11.00
a.		Perf. 12½	75.00	47.50
29	A3	100r brown	14.00	12.00
a.		Perf. 12½	35.00	20.00
30	A3	200r gray lilac	35.00	20.00
31	A3	300r orange	45.00	30.00
a.		Perf. 13½	200.00	165.00
		Nos. 22-31 (10)	163.00	98.25

For surcharges and overprints see Nos. 67-76, 80-183.

Reprinted in 1905 on thin white paper with shiny white gum and clean-cut perforation 13½.

King Carlos

A4 A5

1893-94 *Perf. 11½*

32	A4	5r yellow	1.65	.90
a.		Perf. 12½	2.00	1.25
33	A4	10r red violet	1.65	1.10
34	A4	15r chocolate	2.25	1.25
35	A4	20r lavender	2.25	1.25
36	A4	25r blue green	2.25	1.25
37	A4	50r lt blue	4.00	2.25
a.		Perf. 12½	15.00	8.50
38	A4	75r rose	10.50	7.50
39	A4	80r lt green	10.50	7.50
40	A4	100r brn, *buff*	11.00	7.50
41	A4	150r car, *rose*	10.50	8.00
42	A4	200r dk bl, *bl*	11.00	10.00
43	A4	300r dk bl, *sal*	16.00	10.00
		Nos. 32-43 (12)	83.55	58.50

Almost all of Nos. 32-43 were issued without gum.

For surcharges and overprints see #77-88, 184-188, 203-205.

1898-1903 *Perf. 11½*

Name & Value in Black except 500r

44	A5	2½r gray	.35	.30
45	A5	5r orange	.35	.30
46	A5	10r lt green	.35	.30
47	A5	15r brown	3.00	2.00
48	A5	15r gray grn ('03)	1.65	1.10
49	A5	20r gray violet	1.25	1.00
50	A5	25r sea green	1.65	.80
51	A5	25r carmine ('03)	.90	.50
52	A5	50r dark blue	2.50	1.25
53	A5	50r brown ('03)	3.00	2.00
54	A5	65r dl blue ('03)	8.50	8.00
55	A5	75r rose	15.00	7.25
56	A5	75r lilac ('03)	3.50	2.00
57	A5	80r brt violet	2.75	1.75
58	A5	100r dk bl, *bl*	2.50	1.75
a.		Perf. 12½	47.50	20.00
59	A5	115r org brn, *pink* ('03)	7.75	5.50
60	A5	130r brn, *straw* ('03)	9.00	6.75
61	A5	150r lt brn, *buff*	10.00	3.00
62	A5	200r red lilac, *pnksh*	9.00	3.00
63	A5	300r blue, *rose*	7.50	3.75
64	A5	400r dl bl, *straw* ('03)	12.00	9.00
65	A5	500r blk & red, *bl* ('01)	11.00	7.00
66	A5	700r vio, *yelsh* ('01)	15.00	9.00
		Nos. 44-66 (23)	128.50	77.30

Stamps issued in 1903 were without gum.

For overprints and surcharges see Nos. 90-115, 190-194, 197.

Issue of 1886 Surcharged in Black or Red

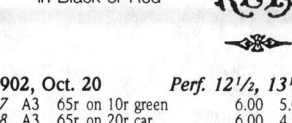

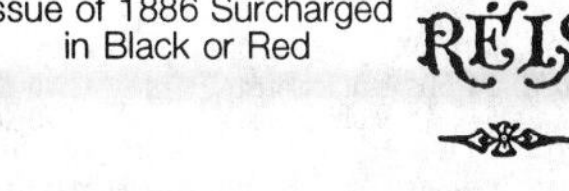

1902, Oct. 20 *Perf. 12½, 13½*

67	A3	65r on 10r green	6.00	5.00
68	A3	65r on 20r car	6.00	4.50
69	A3	65r on 25r red lilac	6.00	4.50
70	A3	115r on 40r choc	5.25	4.00
a.		Perf. 13½	12.00	8.75
71	A3	115r on 50r blue	5.25	4.00
72	A3	115r on 300r orange	6.50	5.25
73	A3	130r on 80r gray	6.50	4.50
74	A3	130r on 100r brown	7.00	5.25
a.		Perf. 13½	18.00	12.50
75	A3	400r on 200r gray lil	12.00	8.00
76	A3	400r on 5r gray blk (R)	30.00	21.00
		Nos. 67-76 (10)	90.50	66.00

Reprints of No. 76 are in black and have clean-cut perforation 13½.

Same Surcharge on Issue of 1893-94

Perf. 11½, 12½, 13½

77	A4	65r on 10r red vio	5.25	3.25
78	A4	65r on 15r choc	5.25	3.25
79	A4	65r on 20r lav	5.25	3.25
80	A4	65r on 50r lt bl	2.75	2.00
81	A4	115r on 5r yel	5.00	2.75
a.		Inverted surcharge	40.00	40.00
b.		Perf. 12½	50.00	35.00
82	A4	115r on 25r bl grn	5.50	3.00
83	A4	130r on 150r car, *rose*	5.50	3.00
84	A4	130r on 200r dk bl, *bl*	6.00	4.00
85	A4	130r on 300r dk bl, *sal*	6.00	4.00
86	A4	400r on 75r rose	4.00	2.75
87	A4	400r on 80r lt grn	2.75	1.50
88	A4	400r on 100r brn, *buff*	3.50	1.50

Same Surcharge on No. P1

89	N1	115r on 2½r brn	4.00	3.00
		Nos. 77-89 (13)	60.75	37.25

Issue of 1898 Overprinted in Black PROVISORIO

1902, Oct. 20 *Perf. 11½*

90	A5	15r brown	2.25	1.10
91	A5	25r sea green	2.25	1.50
92	A5	50r dark blue	2.75	1.50
93	A5	75r rose	5.25	3.50
		Nos. 90-93 (4)	12.50	7.60

No. 54 Surcharged in Black 50 RÉIS

1905

94	A5	50r on 65r dull blue	4.00	2.25

Issue of 1898-1903 Overprinted in Carmine or Green

1911 *Perf. 11½*

95	A5	2½r gray	.35	.30
a.		Inverted overprint	17.50	17.50
96	A5	5r orange	.35	.30
97	A5	10r lt green	.65	.45
98	A5	15r gray green	.65	.45
99	A5	20r gray violet	.65	.45
100	A5	25r carmine (G)	.65	.45
a.		Double overprint	14.00	14.00
101	A5	50r brown	.40	.35
102	A5	75c lilac	.40	.35
103	A5	100r dk bl, *bl*	1.40	.70
104	A5	115r org brn, *pink*	1.40	.90
105	A5	130r brn, *straw*	1.40	.90
106	A5	200r red lil, *pink*	6.00	3.00
107	A5	400r dl bl, *straw*	2.25	1.35
108	A5	500r blk & red, *bl*	2.50	1.35
109	A5	700r vio, *yelsh*	3.75	2.00
		Nos. 95-109 (15)	22.80	13.30

Issued without gum: #101-102, 104-105, 107.

Issue of 1898-1903 Overprinted in Red

1913 *Perf. 11½*

Without Gum (Nos. 110-115)

110	A5	15r gray grn	9.00	6.00
111	A5	75r lilac	9.00	6.00
a.		Inverted overprint		
112	A5	100r bl, *bl*	5.50	4.00
a.		Inverted overprint		
113	A5	200r red lil, *pnksh*	27.50	22.50
a.		Inverted overprint		

Same Overprint on Nos. 90, 93 in Red

114	A5	15r brown	9.00	6.50
a.		"REPUBLICA" double		
b.		"REPUBLICA" inverted	27.50	27.50
115	A5	75r rose	9.00	6.50
a.		"REPUBLICA" inverted		
		Nos. 110-115 (6)	69.00	51.50

Vasco da Gama Issue of Various Portuguese Colonies Surcharged REPUBLICA GUINE ¼ C.

1913

On Stamps of Macao

116	CD20	¼c on ½a bl grn	1.50	1.50
117	CD21	½c on 1a red	1.50	1.50
118	CD22	1c on 2a red vio	1.50	1.50
119	CD23	2½c on 4a yel grn	1.50	1.50
120	CD24	5c on 8a dk bl	1.50	1.50
121	CD25	7½c on 12a vio brn	3.00	3.00
122	CD26	10c on 16a bis brn	1.50	1.50
a.		Inverted surcharge	27.50	27.50
123	CD27	15c on 24a bis	2.50	2.50
		Nos. 116-123 (8)	14.50	14.50

On Stamps of Portuguese Africa

124	CD20	¼c on 2½c bl grn	1.25	1.25
125	CD21	½c on 5r red	1.25	1.25
126	CD22	1c on 10r red vio	1.25	1.25
127	CD23	2½c on 25r yel grn	1.25	1.25
128	CD24	5c on 50r dk bl	1.25	1.25
129	CD25	7½c on 75r vio brn	2.75	2.75
130	CD26	10c on 100r bis brn	1.25	1.25
131	CD27	15c on 150r bis	3.50	3.50
		Nos. 124-131 (8)	13.75	13.75

On Stamps of Timor

132	CD20	¼c on ½a bl grn	1.50	1.50
133	CD21	½c on 1a red	1.50	1.50
134	CD22	1c on 2a red vio	1.50	1.50
135	CD23	2½c on 4a yel grn	1.50	1.50
136	CD24	5c on 8a dk blue	1.50	1.50
137	CD25	7½c on 12a vio brn	2.75	2.75
138	CD26	10c on 16a bis brn	1.50	1.50
139	CD27	15c on 24a bister	2.75	2.75
		Nos. 132-139 (8)	14.50	14.50
		Nos. 116-139 (24)	42.75	42.75

Ceres — A6

1914-26 *Perf. 15x14, 12x11½*

Name and Value in Black

140	A6	¼c olive brown	.20	.15
141	A6	½c black	.20	.15
142	A6	1c blue green	1.25	1.25
143	A6	1c yel grn ('22)	.15	.15
144	A6	1½c lilac brn	.20	.15
145	A6	2c carmine	.20	.15
146	A6	2c gray ('25)	.20	1.50
147	A6	2½c lt violet	.15	.15
148	A6	3c orange ('22)	.20	1.50
149	A6	4c deep red ('22)	.20	1.50
150	A6	4½c gray ('22)	.20	1.50
151	A6	5c deep blue	.60	.50
152	A6	5c brt blue ('22)	.20	.15
153	A6	6c lilac ('22)	.20	1.50
154	A6	7c ultra ('22)	.30	1.50
155	A6	7½c yellow brn	.20	.15
156	A6	8c slate	.20	.15
157	A6	10c orange brn	.15	.15
158	A6	12c blue grn ('22)	.60	.45
159	A6	15c plum	7.50	6.50
160	A6	15c brn rose ('22)	.45	.30
161	A6	20c yellow grn	.20	.15
162	A6	24c ultra ('25)	1.75	1.50
163	A6	25c brown ('25)	2.25	2.00
164	A6	30c brown, *grn*	6.25	5.50
165	A6	30c gray grn ('22)	.80	.25
166	A6	40c brown, *pink*	3.25	3.00
167	A6	40c turq bl ('22)	.80	.35
168	A6	50c orange, *salmon*	3.25	3.00
169	A6	50c violet ('25)	1.75	.85
170	A6	60c dk blue ('22)	1.75	.85
171	A6	60c dp rose ('26)	2.25	1.65
172	A6	80c brt rose ('22)	1.50	.90
173	A6	1e green, *blue*	3.50	3.25
174	A6	1e pale rose ('22)	2.50	1.40
175	A6	1e indigo ('26)	3.25	2.50
176	A6	2e dk violet ('22)	2.75	1.40
177	A6	5e buff ('25)	12.00	9.50
178	A6	10e pink ('25)	25.00	16.00
179	A6	20e pale turq ('25)	55.00	30.00
		Nos. 140-179 (40)	143.35	103.55

For surcharges see Nos. 195-196, 211-213.

Provisional Issue of 1902 Overprinted in Carmine

1915 *Perf. 11½, 12½, 13½*

180	A3	115r on 40r choc	1.00	.60
a.		Perf. 13½	12.00	7.75
181	A3	115r on 50r blue	1.25	.70
182	A3	130r on 80r gray	4.00	1.75
a.		Perf. 12½	25.00	20.00
183	A3	130r on 100r brn	3.25	1.75
a.		Perf. 13½	13.00	10.00
184	A4	115r on 5r yellow	.75	.60
a.		Perf. 11½	4.50	4.00
185	A4	115r on 25r bl grn	.70	.60
186	A4	130r on 150r car, *rose*	1.10	.75
187	A4	130r on 200r bl, *bl*	.75	.65
188	A4	130r on 300r dk bl, *sal*	1.00	.75
189	N1	115r on 2½r brn	1.10	.80
a.		Perf. 13½	25.00	25.00
b.		Inverted overprint	20.00	20.00

On Nos. 90, 92, 94

Perf. 11½

190	A5	15r brown	.75	.65
191	A5	50r dark blue	.75	.65
192	A5	50r on 65r dl bl	.75	.65
		Nos. 180-192 (13)	17.15	10.90

Nos. 64, 66 Overprinted REPUBLICA

1919 **Without Gum** *Perf. 11½*

193	A5	400r dl bl, *straw*	22.50	19.00
194	A5	700r vio, *yelsh*	10.00	5.75

Nos. 140, 141 and 59 Surcharged:

$04 centavos
a

$12 CENTAVOS
b

1920, Sept. *Perf. 15x14, 11½*

Without Gum

195	A6(a)	4c on ¼c	3.00	2.50
196	A6(a)	6c on ½c	3.50	2.50
197	A5(b)	12c on 115r	5.00	4.00
		Nos. 195-197 (3)	11.50	9.00

Nos. 86-88 Surcharged República 40 C.

1925 *Perf. 11½*

203	A4	40c on 400r on 75r	.85	.70
204	A4	40c on 400r on 80r	.65	.50
205	A4	40c on 400r on 100r	.65	.50
		Nos. 203-205 (3)	2.15	1.70

Nos. 171-172, 176 Surcharged 70 C.

1931 *Perf. 12x11½*

211	A6	50c on 60c dp rose	2.75	1.50
212	A6	70c on 80c pink	2.75	1.75
213	A6	1.40e on 2e dk vio	5.25	3.50
		Nos. 211-213 (3)	10.75	6.75

Ceres — A7

1933 **Wmk. 232** *Perf. 12 x 11½*

214	A7	1c bister	.15	.15
215	A7	5c olive brn	.15	.15
216	A7	10c violet	.16	.15
217	A7	15c black	.20	.15
218	A7	20c gray	.20	.15
219	A7	30c dk green	.22	.15
220	A7	40c red orange	.42	.20
221	A7	45c lt blue	1.00	.75
222	A7	50c lt brown	1.00	.50
223	A7	60c olive grn	1.25	.50
224	A7	70c orange brn	1.25	.60
225	A7	80c emerald	1.40	.75
226	A7	85c deep rose	2.75	1.25
227	A7	1e red brown	1.25	.80
228	A7	1.40e dk blue	6.00	2.00
229	A7	2e red violet	4.00	1.75
230	A7	5e apple green	9.00	5.25
231	A7	10e olive bister	16.00	8.75
232	A7	20e orange	50.00	22.50
		Nos. 214-232 (19)	96.40	46.50

Common Design Types pictured following the introduction.

Common Design Types

Engr.; Name & Value Typo. in Black

1938 **Unwmk.** *Perf. 13½x13*

233	CD34	1c gray grn	.15	.15
234	CD34	5c orange brn	.15	.15
235	CD34	10c dk carmine	.15	.15
236	CD34	15c dk vio brn	.15	.15
237	CD34	20c slate	.35	.20
238	CD35	30c rose violet	.55	.25
239	CD35	35c brt green	.60	.30

240 CD35 40c brown .70 .30
241 CD35 50c brt red vio .70 .30
242 CD36 60c gray black .75 .30
243 CD36 70c brown vio .75 .30
244 CD36 80c orange 1.40 .65
245 CD36 1e red 1.40 .45
246 CD37 1.75e blue 1.90 .90
247 CD37 2e brown car 4.50 1.25
248 CD37 5e olive grn 5.00 2.00
249 CD38 10e blue vio 6.75 2.50
250 CD38 20e red brown 20.00 4.00
Nos. 233-250 (18) 45.95 14.30

Fort of Cacheu — A8

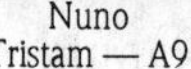

Nuno Tristam — A9

Ulysses S. Grant — A10

Designs: 3.50e, Teixeira Pinto. 5e, Honorio Barreto. 20e, Bissau Church.

Unwmk.

1946, Jan. 12 Litho. *Perf. 11*
251 A8 30c gray & lt gray .60 .50
252 A9 50c black & pink .60 .30
253 A9 50c gray grn & lt grn .60 .30
254 A10 1.75e blue & lt blue 2.50 1.25
255 A10 3.50e red & pink 3.50 2.00
256 A10 5e lt brn & buff 7.75 4.25
257 A8 20e vio & lt vio 11.00 5.50
a. Sheet of 7, #251-257 ('47) 60.00 60.00
Nos. 251-257 (7) 26.55 14.10

Discovery of Guinea, 500th anniversary.
No. 257a sold for 40 escudos.

Guinea Village — A11

UPU Symbols — A12

Designs: 10c, Crowned crane. 20c, 3.50e, Tribesman. 35c, 5e, Woman in ceremonial dress. 50c, Musician. 70c, Man. 80c, 20e, Girl. 1e, 2e, Drummer. 1.75e, Antelope.

1948, Apr. Photo. *Perf. 11½*
258 A11 5c chocolate .15 .15
259 A11 10c lt violet .60 .60
260 A11 20c dull rose .40 .25
261 A11 35c green .35 .25
262 A11 50c dp orange .35 .15
263 A11 70c dp gray bl .40 .25
264 A11 80c dk ol grn .85 .30
265 A11 1e rose red .85 .40
266 A11 1.75e ultra 3.50 2.00
267 A11 2e blue 7.50 1.00
268 A11 3.50e orange brn 2.50 .80
269 A11 5e slate 3.00 1.25
270 A11 20e violet 8.00 3.00
a. Sheet of 13, #258-270 + 2 labels 60.00 60.00
Nos. 258-270 (13) 28.45 10.40

No. 270a sold for 40 escudos.

Lady of Fatima Issue
Common Design Type

1948, Oct. Litho. *Perf. 14½*
271 CD40 50c deep green 3.00 2.25

1949, Oct. *Perf. 14*
272 A12 2e dp org & cream 2.75 2.25

Universal Postal Union, 75th anniversary.

Catalogue values for unused stamps in this section, from this point to the end of the section, are for Never Hinged items.

Holy Year Issue
Common Design Types

1950, May *Perf. 13x13½*
273 CD41 1e brown lake 1.25 1.00
274 CD42 3e blue green 1.90 1.40

Holy Year Extension Issue
Common Design Type

1951, Oct. *Perf. 14*
275 CD43 1e choc & pale brn .90 .60

Medical Congress Issue
Common Design Type

Design: Physical examination.

1952 *Perf. 13½*
276 CD44 50c purple & choc .40 .30

Exhibition Entrance A13

Stamp of Portugal and Arms of Colonies A14

1953, Jan. Litho. *Perf. 13*
277 A13 10c brn lake & ol .15 .15
278 A13 50c dk blue & bister .48 .22
279 A13 3e blk, dk brn & sal 1.50 .90
Nos. 277-279 (3) 2.13 1.27

Exhibition of Sacred Missionary Art held at Lisbon in 1951.

1953 Photo. Unwmk.
280 A14 50c multicolored .60 .50

Centenary of Portugal's first postage stamps.

Analeptes Trifasciata — A15

1953 *Perf. 11½*
Various Beetles in Natural Colors
281 A15 5c yellow .15 .15
282 A15 10c blue .15 .15
283 A15 30c org vermilion .15 .15
284 A15 50c yellow grn .15 .15
285 A15 70c gray brn .40 .25
286 A15 1e orange .40 .25
287 A15 2e pale ol grn 1.00 .25
288 A15 3e lilac rose 1.50 .70
289 A15 5e lt blue grn 2.50 .80
290 A15 10e lilac 4.00 1.00
Nos. 281-290 (10) 10.40 3.85

Sao Paulo Issue
Common Design Type

1954 Litho. *Perf. 13½*
291 CD46 1e lil rose, bl gray & blk .30 .15

Belem Tower, Lisbon, and Colonial Arms — A16

1955, Apr. 14
292 A16 1e blue & multi .25 .15
293 A16 2.50e gray & multi .55 .20

Visit of Pres. Francisco H. C. Lopes.

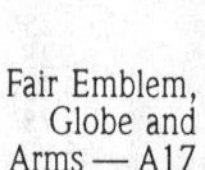

Fair Emblem, Globe and Arms — A17

1958 Unwmk. *Perf. 12x11½*
294 A17 2.50e multicolored .60 .50

World's Fair at Brussels.

Tropical Medicine Congress Issue
Common Design Type

Design: Maytenus senegalensis.

1958 *Perf. 13½*
295 CD47 5e multicolored 1.90 1.00

Honorio Barreto A18

Nautical Astrolabe A19

1959, Apr. 29 Litho. *Perf. 13½*
296 A18 2.50e multicolored .25 .20

Centenary of the death of Honorio Barreto, governor of Portuguese Guinea.

1960, June 25 *Perf. 13½*
297 A19 2.50e multicolored .25 .20

500th anniversary of the death of Prince Henry the Navigator.

Traveling Medical Unit — A20

1960 Unwmk. *Perf. 14½*
298 A20 1.50e multicolored .25 .20

10th anniv. of the Commission for Technical Cooperation in Africa South of the Sahara (C.C.T.A.).

Sports Issue
Common Design Type

1962, Jan. 18 Litho. *Perf. 13½*
299 CD48 50c Automobile race .15 .15
300 CD48 1e Tennis .60 .22
301 CD48 1.50e Shot put .22 .15
302 CD48 2.50e Wrestling .55 .15
303 CD48 3.50e Trapshooting .60 .18
304 CD48 15e Volleyball 1.65 .80
Nos. 299-304 (6) 3.77 1.65

Anti-Malaria Issue
Common Design Type

Design: Anopheles gambiae.

1962 Unwmk. *Perf. 13½*
305 CD49 2.50e multicolored .60 .30

African Spitting Cobra — A21

Snakes: 35c, African rock python. 70c, Boomslang. 80c, West African mamba. 1.50e, Smythe's water snake. 2e, Common night adder, horiz. 2.50e, Green swamp snake. 3.50e, Brown house snake. 4e, Spotted wolf snake. 5e, Common puff adder. 15e, Striped beauty snake. 20e, African egg eating snake, horiz.

1963, Jan. 17 Litho. *Perf. 13½*
306 A21 20c multicolored .15 .15
307 A21 35c multicolored .15 .15
308 A21 70c multicolored .35 .25
309 A21 80c multicolored .35 .25
310 A21 1.50e multicolored .55 .25
311 A21 2e multicolored .40 .15
312 A21 2.50e multicolored 1.25 .25
313 A21 3.50e multicolored .60 .20
314 A21 4e multicolored .60 .25
315 A21 5e multicolored .60 .25
316 A21 15e multicolored 1.00 .50
317 A21 20e multicolored 1.65 .60
Nos. 306-317 (12) 7.65 3.25

For overprints see Guinea-Bissau Nos. 696-703.

Airline Anniversary Issue
Common Design Type

1963 Litho. *Perf. 14½*
318 CD50 2.50e lt brown & multi .60 .30

National Overseas Bank Issue
Common Design Type

Design: 2.50e, Joao de Andrade Córvo.

1964, May 16 *Perf. 13½*
319 CD51 2.50e multicolored .60 .35

ITU Issue
Common Design Type

1965, May 17 Unwmk. *Perf. 14½*
320 CD52 2.50e lt blue & multi 1.75 .70

Soldier, 1548 — A22

Sacred Heart of Jesus Monument and Chapel of the Apparition — A23

40c, Rifleman, 1578. 60c, Rifleman, 1640. 1e, Grenadier, 1721. 2.50e, Fusiliers captain, 1740. 4.50e, Infantryman, 1740. 7.50e, Sergeant major, 1762. 10e, Engineers' officer, 1806.

1966, Jan. 8 Litho. *Perf. 13½*
321 A22 25c multicolored .20 .15
322 A22 40c multicolored .20 .15
323 A22 60c multicolored .30 .15
324 A22 1e multicolored .40 .20
325 A22 2.50e multicolored 1.10 .35
326 A22 4.50e multicolored 1.90 1.00
327 A22 7.50e multicolored 1.90 1.25
328 A22 10e multicolored 2.50 1.50
Nos. 321-328 (8) 8.50 4.75

National Revolution Issue
Common Design Type

Design: 2.50e, Berta Craveiro Lopes School and Central Pavilion of Bissau Hospital.

1966, May 28 Litho. *Perf. 11½*
329 CD53 2.50e multicolored .50 .30

Navy Club Issue
Common Design Type

Designs: 50c, Capt. Oliveira Muzanty and cruiser Republica. 1e, Capt. Afonso de Cerqueira and torpedo boat Guadiana.

1967, Jan. 31 Litho. *Perf. 13*
330 CD54 50c multicolored .40 .22
331 CD54 1e multicolored .90 .60

1967, May 13 *Perf. 12½x13*
332 A23 50c multicolored .20 .15

50th anniv. of the appearance of the Virgin Mary to three shepherd children at Fatima.

Pres. Rodrigues Thomas — A24

Cabral's Coat of Arms — A25

1968, Feb. 2 Litho. *Perf. 13½*

333 A24 1e multicolored .20 .15

Issued to commemorate the 1968 visit of Pres. Americo de Deus Rodrigues Thomaz.

1968, Apr. 22 Litho. *Perf. 14*

334 A25 2.50e multicolored .50 .20

Pedro Alvares Cabral, navigator who took possession of Brazil for Portugal, 500th birth anniv.

Admiral Coutinho Issue
Common Design Type

Design: 1e, Adm. Coutinho and astrolabe.

1969, Feb. 17 Litho. *Perf. 14*

335 CD55 1e multicolored .30 .20

Da Gama Coat of Arms — A26

Arms of King Manuel I — A27

Vasco da Gama Issue

1969, Aug. 29 Litho. *Perf. 14*

336 A26 2.50e multicolored .30 .15

Vasco da Gama (1469-1524), navigator.

Administration Reform Issue
Common Design Type

1969, Sept. 25 Litho. *Perf. 14*

337 CD56 50c multicolored .20 .15

King Manuel I Issue

1969, Dec. 1 Litho. *Perf. 14*

338 A27 2e multicolored .30 .20

Pres. Ulysses S. Grant and View of Bolama — A28

1970, Oct. 25 Litho. *Perf. 13½*

339 A28 2.50e multicolored .40 .20

Centenary of Pres. Grant's arbitration in 1868 of Portuguese-English dispute concerning Bolama.

Marshal Carmona Issue
Common Design Type

Design: 1.50e, Antonio Oscar Carmona in general's uniform.

1970, Nov. 15 Litho. *Perf. 14*

340 CD57 1.50e multicolored .30 .20

Luiz Camoens — A29

1972, May 25 Litho. *Perf. 13*

341 A29 50c brn org & multi .20 .15

4th centenary of publication of The Lusiads by Luiz Camoens (1524-1580).

Olympic Games Issue
Common Design Type

Design: 2.50e, Weight lifting, hammer throw and Olympic emblem.

1972, June 20 *Perf. 14x13½*

342 CD59 2.50e multicolored .40 .20

Lisbon-Rio de Janeiro Flight Issue
Common Design Type

Design: 1e, "Lusitania" taking off from Lisbon.

1972, Sept. 20 Litho. *Perf. 13½*

343 CD60 1e multicolored .20 .15

WMO Centenary Issue
Common Design Type

1973, Dec. 15 Litho. *Perf. 13*

344 CD61 2e lt brown & multi .40 .30

sa

AIR POST STAMPS

Common Design Type
Perf. 13½x13

1938, Sept. 19 Engr. Unwmk.
Name and Value in Black

C1	CD39	10c scarlet	.38	.30
C2	CD39	20c purple	.45	.30
C3	CD39	50c orange	.45	.30
C4	CD39	1e ultra	.55	.38
C5	CD39	2e lilac brown	4.75	3.25
C6	CD39	3e dark green	1.25	.85
C7	CD39	5e red brown	3.50	.95
C8	CD39	9e rose carmine	3.50	2.00
C9	CD39	10e magenta	8.50	2.75
		Nos. C1-C9 (9)	23.33	11.08

No. C7 exists with overprint "Exposicao Internacional de Nova York, 1939-1940" and Trylon and Perisphere.

POSTAGE DUE STAMPS

D1

D2

1904 Unwmk. Typo. *Perf. 12*
Without Gum

J1	D1	5r yellow green	.55	.40
J2	D1	10r slate	.55	.40
J3	D1	20r yellow brown	.60	.48
J4	D1	30r red orange	1.75	1.50
J5	D1	50r gray brown	1.75	1.50
J6	D1	60r red brown	3.75	2.50
J7	D1	100r lilac	3.75	2.50
J8	D1	130r dull blue	3.00	1.90
J9	D1	200r carmine	6.00	4.75
J10	D1	500r violet	10.00	5.50
		Nos. J1-J10 (10)	31.70	21.43

Same Overprinted in Carmine or Green

REPUBLICA

1911
Without Gum

J11	D1	5r yellow green	.22	.18
J12	D1	10r slate	.22	.18
J13	D1	20r yellow brown	.32	.28
J14	D1	30r red orange	.32	.28
J15	D1	50r gray brown	.32	.28
J16	D1	60r red brown	.90	.75
J17	D1	100r lilac	1.75	1.25
J18	D1	130r dull blue	1.75	.90
J19	D1	200r carmine (G)	1.75	1.40
J20	D1	500r violet	1.00	.90
		Nos. J11-J20 (10)	8.55	6.40

Nos. J2-J10 Overprinted **REPUBLICA**

1919
Without Gum

J21	D1	10r slate	7.50	7.50
J22	D1	20r yellow brown	8.25	8.25
J23	D1	30r red orange	6.00	5.25
J24	D1	50r gray brown	2.25	1.90
J25	D1	60r red brown	300.00	200.00
J26	D1	100r lilac	2.00	1.75
J27	D1	130r dull blue	20.00	17.50
J28	D1	200r carmine	2.50	2.25
J29	D1	500r violet	21.00	18.00
		Nos. J21-J24,J26-J29 (8)	69.50	62.40

No. J25 was not regularly issued but exists on genuine covers.

1921

J30	D2	½c yellow green	.15	.15
J31	D2	1c slate	.15	.15
J32	D2	2c orange brown	.15	.15
J33	D2	3c orange	.15	.15
J34	D2	5c gray brown	.15	.15
J35	D2	6c light brown	.15	.15
J36	D2	10c red violet	.25	.25
J37	D2	13c dull blue	.25	.25
J38	D2	20c carmine	.30	.30
J39	D2	50c gray	.30	.30
		Nos. J30-J39 (10)	2.00	
		Set value		1.70

Catalogue values for unused stamps in this section, from this point to the end of the section, are for Never Hinged items.

Common Design Type
Photogravure and Typographed
1952 Unwmk. *Perf. 14*
Numeral in Red, Frame Multicolored

J40	CD45	10c olive green	.15	.15
J41	CD45	30c purple	.15	.15
J42	CD45	50c dark green	.15	.15
J43	CD45	1e violet blue	.30	.30
J44	CD45	2e olive black	.45	.45
J45	CD45	5e brown red	.90	.90
		Set value	1.85	1.85

WAR TAX STAMPS

WT1

Perf. 11½x12

1919, May 20 Typo. Unwmk.

MR1	WT1	10r brn, buff & blk	40.00	25.00
MR2	WT1	40r brn, buff & blk	35.00	20.00
MR3	WT1	50r brn, buff & blk	37.50	22.50
		Nos. MR1-MR3 (3)	112.50	67.50

The 40r is not overprinted "REPUBLICA."
Some authorities consider Nos. MR2-MR3 to be revenue stamps.

NEWSPAPER STAMP

N1

Perf. 12½, 13½

1893 Typo. Unwmk.

P1 N1 2½r brown 1.10 .70

For surcharge and overprint see Nos. 89, 189.

POSTAL TAX STAMPS

Pombal Issue
Common Design Types

1925 Unwmk. Engr. *Perf. 12½*

RA1	CD28	15c red & black	.65	.60
RA2	CD29	15c red & black	.65	.60
RA3	CD30	15c red & black	.65	.60
		Nos. RA1-RA3 (3)	1.95	1.80

Coat of Arms PT7

1934, Apr. 1 Typo. *Perf. 11½*
Without Gum

RA4 PT7 50c red brn & grn 7.25 4.00

Coat of Arms
PT8 PT9

1938-40
Without Gum

RA5	PT8	50c ol bis & citron	7.00	4.25
RA6	PT8	50c lt grn & ol brn ('40)	7.00	4.25

1942 *Perf. 11*
Without Gum

RA7 PT9 50c black & yellow 2.00 1.10

1959, July Unwmk.
Without Gum

RA8 PT9 30c dark ocher & blk .20 .20

See Nos. RA24-RA26.

Lusignian Cross
PT10 PT11

1967 Typo. *Perf. 11x11½*
Without Gum

RA9	PT10	50c pink, red & blk	1.25	1.25
RA10	PT10	1e grn, red & blk	1.25	1.25
RA11	PT10	5e gray, red & blk	2.00	2.00
RA12	PT10	10e lt bl, red & blk	4.00	4.00
		Nos. RA9-RA12 (4)	8.50	8.50

The tax was for national defense.
A 50e was used for revenue only.

1967, Aug. Typo. *Perf. 11*
Without Gum

RA13	PT11	50c pink, blk & red	.95	.95
RA14	PT11	1e pale grn, blk & red	.95	.95
RA15	PT11	5e gray, blk & red	1.65	1.65
RA16	PT11	10e lt bl, blk & red	2.50	2.50
		Nos. RA13-RA16 (4)	6.05	6.05

The tax was for national defense.

Catalogue values for unused stamps in this section, from this point to the end of the section, are for Never Hinged items.

Carved Figurine — PT12

Art from Bissau Museum: 1e, Tree of Life, with 2 birds, horiz. #RA19, Man wearing horned headgear ("Vaca Bruto"). #RA20, as #RA19, inscribed "Tocador de Bombolon." 2.50e, The Magistrate. 5e, Man bearing burden on head. 10e, Stylized pelican.

1968 Litho. *Perf. 13½*

RA17	PT12	50c gray & multi	.15	.15
a.		Yellow paper	.75	
RA18	PT12	1e multi	.15	.15
RA19	PT12	2e *(Vaca Bruto)*	.16	.15
RA20	PT12	2e *(Tocador de Bombolon)*	*10.00*	
RA21	PT12	2.50e multi	.28	.20
RA22	PT12	5e multi	.42	.35
RA23	PT12	10e multi	.90	.70
		Nos. RA17-RA19,RA21-RA23 (6)	2.06	1.70

Obligatory on all inland mail Mar. 15-Apr. 15 and Dec. 15-Jan. 15, and all year on parcels.

A souvenir sheet embracing Nos. RA17-RA19 and RA21-RA23 exists. The stamps have simulated perforations. Value $3.50.

For surcharges see Nos. RA27-RA28.

Arms Type of 1942

1968 Typo. *Perf. 11*

Without Gum

RA24	PT9	2.50e lt blue & blk	.40	.40
RA25	PT9	5e green & blk	.75	.75
RA26	PT9	10e dp blue & blk	1.50	1.50
		Nos. RA24-RA26 (3)	2.65	2.65

No. RA20 Surcharged

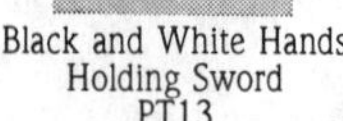

1968 Litho. *Perf. 13½*

RA27	PT12	50c on 2e multi	.45	.45
RA28	PT12	1e on 2e multi	.45	.45

Black and White Hands Holding Sword
PT13

Mother and Children
PT14

1968 Litho. *Perf. 13½*

RA29	PT13	50c pink & multi	.15	.15
RA30	PT13	1e multicolored	.15	.15
RA31	PT13	2e yellow & multi	.30	.30
RA32	PT13	2.50e buff & multi	.45	.45
RA33	PT13	3e multicolored	.50	.50
RA34	PT13	4e gray & multi	.55	.55
RA35	PT13	5e multicolored	.75	.75
RA36	PT13	10e multicolored	1.75	1.75
		Nos. RA29-RA36 (8)	4.60	4.60

The surtax was for national defense. Other denominations exist: 8e, 9e, 15e.

1971, June Litho. *Perf. 13½*

RA37	PT14	50c multicolored	.15	.15
RA38	PT14	1e multicolored	.15	.15
RA39	PT14	2e multicolored	.20	.20
RA40	PT14	3e multicolored	.30	.30
RA41	PT14	4e multicolored	.35	.35
RA42	PT14	5e multicolored	.60	.60
RA43	PT14	10e multicolored	1.10	1.10
		Nos. RA37-RA43 (7)	2.85	2.85

A 20e exists.

POSTAL TAX DUE STAMPS

Pombal Issue

Common Design Types

1925 Unwmk. *Perf. 12½*

RAJ1	CD28	30c red & black	.60	.50
RAJ2	CD29	30c red & black	.60	.50
RAJ3	CD30	30c red & black	.60	.50
		Nos. RAJ1-RAJ3 (3)	1.80	1.50

PORTUGUESE INDIA

'pōr–chi–gēz 'in–dē–ə

LOCATION — West coast of the Indian peninsula
GOVT. — Portuguese colony
AREA — 1,537 sq. mi.
POP. — 649,000 (1958)
CAPITAL — Panjim (Nova-Goa)

The colony was seized by India on Dec. 18, 1961, and annexed by that republic.

1000 Reis = 1 Milreis
12 Reis = 1 Tanga (1881-82)
(Real = singular of Reis)
16 Tangas = 1 Rupia
100 Centavos = 1 Escudo (1959)

Catalogue values for unused stamps in this country are for Never Hinged items, beginning with Scott 490 in the regular postage section, Scott J43 in the postage due section, and Scott RA6 in the postal tax section.

Expect Nos. 1-55, 70-112 to have rough perforations. Stamps frequently were cut apart because of the irregular and missing perforations. Scissor separations that do not remove perfs do not negatively affect value.

Numeral of Value
A1 A2

A1: Large figures of value.
"REIS" in Roman capitals. "S" and "R" of "SERVICO" smaller and "E" larger than the other letters. 33 lines in background. Side ornaments of four dashes.

A2: Large figures of value.
"REIS" in block capitals. "S," "E" and "R" same size as other letters of "SERVICO." 44 lines in background. Side ornaments of five dots.

Handstamped from a Single Die
Perf. 13 to 18 & Compound

1871, Oct. 1 Unwmk.

Thin Transparent Brittle Paper

1	A1	10r black	700.	350.
2	A1	20r dk carmine	1,500.	300.
3	A1	40r Prus blue	525.	350.
4	A1	100r yellow grn	625.	425.
5	A1	200r ocher yel	800.	475.

1872

Thick Soft Wove Paper

5A	A1	10r black	*1,700.*	350.
6	A1	20r dk carmine	*1,800.*	300.
7	A1	20r orange ver	*1,800.*	300.
8	A1	200r ocher yel	*1,700.*	600.
9	A1	300r dp red violet		*2,250.*

The 600r and 900r of type A1 are bogus.

See Nos. 24-28. For surcharges see Nos. 70-71, 73, 83, 94, 99, 104, 108.

Perf. 12½ to 14½ & Compound

1872

10	A2	10r black	250.00	100.00
11	A2	20r vermilion	250.00	90.00
a.		"20" omitted		*1,100.*
12	A2	40r blue	70.00	70.00
a.		Tête bêche pair	*6,000.*	
13	A2	100r deep green	75.00	65.00
14	A2	200r yellow	300.00	275.00
15	A2	300r red violet	300.00	225.00
a.		Imperf.		
16	A2	600r red violet	175.00	125.00
a.		"600" double	*675.00*	
17	A2	900r red violet	190.00	200.00
		Nos. 10-17 (8)	1,610.	1,150.

An unused 100r blue green exists with watermark of lozenges and gray burelage on back. Experts believe it to be a proof.

White Laid Paper

18	A2	10r black	35.00	22.50
a.		Tête bêche pair		*7,000.*
19	A2	20r vermilion	40.00	20.00
20	A2	40r blue	50.00	32.50
a.		"40" double	*400.00*	
b.		Tête bêche pair	*1,800.*	*1,800.*
21	A2	100r green	60.00	40.00
a.		"100" double	*400.00*	
22	A2	200r yellow	200.00	185.00
		Nos. 18-22 (5)	385.00	300.00

See No. 23. For surcharges see Nos. 72, 82, 95-96, 100-101, 105-106, 109-110.

1873

Re-issues

Thin Bluish Toned Paper

23	A2	20r vermilion	200.00	175.00
24	A1	10r black	12.00	7.25
a.		"1" inverted	150.00	125.00
b.		"10" double	450.00	
25	A1	20r vermilion	8.00	6.00
a.		"20" double	450.00	
b.		"20" inverted		
26	A1	300r dp violet	75.00	70.00
a.		"300" double	500.00	
27	A1	600r dp violet	85.00	80.00
a.		"600" double	550.00	
b.		"600" inverted	700.00	
28	A1	900r dp violet	85.00	80.00
a.		"900" double	550.00	
b.		"900" triple	1,100.	
		Nos. 23-28 (6)	465.00	418.25

Nos. 23 to 26 are re-issues of Nos. 11, 5A, 7, and 9. The paper is thinner and harder than that of the 1871-72 stamps and slightly transparent. It was originally bluish white but is frequently stained yellow by the gum.

A3 A4

A3: Same as A1 with small figures.
A4: Same as A2 with small figures.

1874

Thin Bluish Toned Paper

29	A3	10r black	37.50	30.00
30	A3	20r vermilion	625.00	300.00
a.		"20" double		700.00

For surcharge see No. 84.

1875

31	A4	10r black	40.00	25.00
32	A4	15r rose	11.00	10.00
a.		"15" inverted	500.00	
b.		"15" double		
33	A4	20r vermilion	57.50	30.00
a.		"0" missing	750.00	
b.		"20" sideways	750.00	
c.		"20" double		
		Nos. 31-33 (3)	108.50	65.00

For surcharges see Nos. 74, 78, 85.

A5 A6

A5: Re-cutting of A1.
Small figures. "REIS" in Roman capitals. Letters larger. "V" of "SERVICO" barred. 33 lines in background. Side ornaments of five dots.

A6: First re-cutting of A2.
Small figures. "REIS" in block capitals. Letters recut. "V" of "SERVICO" barred. 41 lines above and 43 below "REIS." Side ornaments of five dots.

Perf. 12½ to 13½ & Compound

1876

34	A5	10r black	20.00	14.00
35	A5	20r vermilion	15.00	12.00
a.		"20" double		
36	A6	10r black	5.50	4.00
a.		Double impression		
b.		"10" double	500.00	
37	A6	15r rose	375.00	340.00
a.		"15" omitted	*1,100.*	
38	A6	20r vermilion	18.00	15.00
39	A6	40r blue	105.00	95.00
40	A6	100r green	165.00	140.00
a.		Imperf.		
41	A6	200r yellow	900.00	700.00
42	A6	300r violet	600.00	500.00
a.		"300" omitted		
43	A6	600r violet	900.00	750.00
44	A6	900r violet	1,100.	850.00

For surcharges see Nos. 75-76, 78C-80, 86-87, 91-92, 98, 102, 107, 111.

A7

A8

A9

A7: Same as A5 with addition of a star above and a bar below the value.

A8: Second re-cutting of A2. Same as A6 but 41 lines both above and below "REIS." Star above and bar below value.

A9: Third re-cutting of A2. 41 lines above and 38 below "REIS." Star above and bar below value. White line around central oval.

1877

45	A7	10r black	32.50	27.50
46	A8	10r black	40.00	30.00
47	A9	10r black	30.00	27.50
a.		"10" omitted		
48	A9	15r rose	35.00	30.00
49	A9	20r vermilion	8.00	7.00
50	A9	40r blue	17.50	15.00
a.		"40" omitted		
51	A9	100r green	70.00	65.00
a.		"100" omitted		
52	A9	200r yellow	77.50	72.50
53	A9	300r violet	100.00	75.00
54	A9	600r violet	100.00	80.00
55	A9	900r violet	100.00	80.00
		Nos. 45-55 (11)	610.50	509.50

No. 47, 20r, 40r and 200r exist imperf.

For surcharges see Nos. 77, 81, 88-90, 93, 112.

Portuguese Crown — A10

Perf. 12½, 13½

1877, July 15 Typo.

56	A10	5r black	4.00	3.25
57	A10	10r yellow	10.00	8.00
a.		Imperf.		
58	A10	20r bister	10.50	6.75
59	A10	25r rose	11.00	9.00
60	A10	40r blue	15.00	12.50
a.		Perf. 12½	175.00	135.00
61	A10	50r yellow grn	35.00	22.50
62	A10	100r lilac	17.00	13.00
63	A10	200r orange	22.50	19.00
64	A10	300r yel brn	32.50	27.50
		Nos. 56-64 (9)	157.50	121.50

1880-81

65	A10	10r green	9.00	7.25
66	A10	25r slate	42.50	32.50
a.		Perf. 12½	92.50	72.50
67	A10	25r violet	30.00	21.00
68	A10	40r yellow	37.50	30.00
69	A10	50r dk blue	21.00	17.00
		Nos. 65-69 (5)	140.00	107.75

For surcharges see Nos. 113-161.

The stamps of the 1877-81 issues were reprinted in 1885, on stout very white paper, ungummed and with rough perforation 13½. They were again reprinted in 1905 on thin white paper with shiny white gum and clean-cut perforation 13½ with large holes. Value of the lowest-cost reprint, $1 each.

Stamps of 1871-77 Surcharged with New Values

Black Surcharge

1881

70	A1	1½r on 20r (#2)		*600.00*
71	A1	1½r on 20r (#7)		*500.00*
72	A2	1½r on 20r (#11)		*400.00*
73	A1	1½r on 20r (#25)	225.00	200.00
74	A4	1½r on 20r (#33)	135.00	125.00
a.		Inverted surcharge		
75	A5	1½r on 20r (#35)	110.00	80.00
76	A6	1½r on 20r (#38)	125.00	110.00
77	A9	1½r on 20r (#49)	200.00	140.00
78	A4	5r on 15r (#32)	2.50	2.50
a.		Double surcharge		
b.		Inverted surcharge		

78C A6 5r on 15r (#37) 175.00 165.00
79 A5 5r on 20r (#35) 2.75 2.75
a. Double surcharge
b. Inverted surcharge
80 A6 5r on 20r (#38) 2.75 2.00
a. Double surcharge
b. Inverted surcharge
81 A9 5r on 20r (#49) 5.00 4.50
a. Double surcharge
b. Invtd. surcharge

Red Surcharge

82 A2 5r on 10r (#18) *425.00 325.00*
83 A1 5r on 10r (#24) *475.00 275.00*
84 A3 5r on 10r (#29) *1,600.*
85 A4 5r on 10r (#31) *110.00 110.00*
86 A5 5r on 10r (#34) 5.50 5.50
a. Double surcharge
87 A6 5r on 10r (#36) 8.75 7.00
a. Inverted surcharge
88 A7 5r on 10r (#45) 80.00 45.00
a. Inverted surcharge
89 A8 5r on 10r (#46) 175.00 75.00
90 A9 5r on 10r (#47) 35.00 30.00
a. Inverted surcharge
b. Double surcharge

Similar Surcharge, Handstamped
Black Surcharge

1883

91 A5 1½r on 10r (#34) *750.00*
92 A6 1½r on 10r (#36) *750.00*
93 A9 1½r on 10r (#47) *750.00 550.00*
94 A1 4½r on 40r (#3) *700.00*
95 A2 4½r on 40r (#12) 32.50 32.50
96 A2 4½r on 40r (#20) 32.50 32.50
98 A6 4½r on 40r (#39) 32.50 32.50
99 A1 4½r on 100r (#4) *700.00*
100 A2 4½r on 100r (#13) 40.00 37.50
101 A2 4½r on 100r (#21) 40.00 37.50
102 A6 4½r on 100r (#40) 35.00 37.50
104 A1 6r on 100r (#4) *1,100.*
105 A2 6r on 100r (#13) *250.00*
106 A2 6r on 100r (#21) *250.00 200.00*
107 A6 6r on 100r (#40) *325.00 250.00*
108 A1 6r on 200r (#5) *750.00 550.00*
109 A2 6r on 200r (#14) *200.00*
110 A2 6r on 200r (#22) *200.00 200.00*
111 A6 6r on 200r (#41) *400.00*
112 A9 6r on 200r (#52) *500.00 500.00*

Stamps of 1877-81 Surcharged in Black — 1½

1881-82

113 A10 1½r on 5r blk 1.25 1.00
a. With additional surcharge "4½" in blue 75.00 60.00
114 A10 1½r on 10r grn 1.25 1.00
a. With additional surch. "6" 100.00 80.00
115 A10 1½r on 20r bis 10.50 8.00
a. Inverted surcharge
b. Double surcharge
c. Pair, one without surcharge
116 A10 1½r on 25r slate 35.00 30.00
117 A10 1½r on 100r lil 55.00 42.50
118 A10 4½r on 10r grn 165.00 150.00
119 A10 4½r on 20r bis 3.50 2.50
a. Inverted surcharge
120 A10 4½r on 25r vio 10.50 10.00
121 A10 4½r on 100r lil 105.00 95.00
122 A10 6r on 10r yel 42.50 40.00
123 A10 6r on 10r grn 9.25 7.25
124 A10 6r on 20r bis 15.00 14.00
125 A10 6r on 25r slate 30.00 25.00
126 A10 6r on 25r vio 2.00 1.65
127 A10 6r on 40r blue 75.00 62.50
128 A10 6r on 40r yel 37.50 30.00
129 A10 6r on 50r grn 42.50 35.00
130 A10 6r on 50r blue 60.00 50.00
Nos. 113-130 (18) 700.75 605.40

Surcharged in Black — 1 T

131 A10 1t on 10r grn 200.00 110.00
a. With additional surch. "6"
132 A10 1t on 20r bis 42.50 37.50
133 A10 1t on 25r slate 32.50 27.50
134 A10 1t on 25r vio 12.00 8.25
135 A10 1t on 40r blue 17.00 16.00
136 A10 1t on 50r grn 50.00 42.50
137 A10 1t on 50r blue 22.50 17.00
138 A10 1t on 100r lil 21.00 12.00
139 A10 1t on 200r org 42.50 37.50
140 A10 2t on 25r slate 32.50 30.00
a. Small "T" 50.00 35.00
141 A10 2t on 25r vio 12.50 10.50
142 A10 2t on 40r blue 37.50 30.00
143 A10 2t on 40r yel 47.50 37.50
144 A10 2t on 50r grn 14.00 12.00
a. Inverted surcharge
145 A10 2t on 50r blue 80.00 67.50
146 A10 2t on 100r lil 10.50 8.50
147 A10 2t on 200r org 35.00 30.00
148 A10 2t on 300r brn 30.00 27.50
149 A10 4t on 10r grn 12.50 10.50
a. Inverted surcharge
150 A10 4t on 50r grn 12.00 9.25
a. With additional surch. "2" 150.00 95.00
151 A10 4t on 200r org 35.00 30.00
152 A10 8t on 20r bis 30.00 21.00
153 A10 8t on 25r rose 165.00 150.00
154 A10 8t on 40r blue 42.50 35.00
155 A10 8t on 100r lil 35.00 30.00
156 A10 8t on 200r org 30.00 27.50
157 A10 8t on 300r brn 42.50 35.00
Nos. 131-157 (27) 1,144. 910.00

1882

Blue Surcharge

158 A10 4½r on 5r black 11.00 9.50

Similar Surcharge, Handstamped

1883

159 A10 1½r on 5r black 22.50 10.00
160 A10 1½r on 10r grn 22.50 7.00
161 A10 4½r on 100r lil *190.00 165.00*

The "2" in "½" is 3mm high, instead of 2mm as on Nos. 113, 114 and 121.

The handstamp is known double on #159-161.

A12

1882-83 **Typo.**

With or Without Accent on "E" of "REIS"

162 A12 1½r black .50 .40
a. "½" for "1½"
163 A12 4½r olive bister .50 .40
164 A12 6r green .60 .40
165 A12 1t rose .60 .40
166 A12 2t blue .60 .40
167 A12 4t lilac 2.75 2.50
168 A12 8t orange 2.75 2.50
Nos. 162-168 (7) 8.30 7.00

There were three printings of the 1882-83 issue. The first had "REIS" in thick letters with acute accent on the "E." The second had "REIS" in thin letters with accent on the "E." The third had the "E" without accent. In the first printing the "E" sometimes had a grave or circumflex accent.

The third printing may be divided into two sets, with or without a small circle in the cross of the crown.

Stamps doubly printed or with value omitted, double, inverted or misplaced are printer's waste.

Nos. 162-168 were reprinted on thin white paper, with shiny white gum and clean-cut perforation 13½. Value of lowest-cost reprint, $1 each.

"REIS" no serifs — A13

"REIS" with serifs — A14

1883 **Litho.** ***Imperf.***

169 A13 1½r black 1.25 1.00
a. Tête bêche pair
b. "1½" double 375.00 300.00
170 A13 4½r olive grn 12.50 11.00
a. "4½" omitted 325.00 250.00
171 A13 6r green 12.50 11.00
a. Tête bêche pair 1,100.
b. "6" omitted 350.00 275.00
172 A14 1½r black 65.00 25.00
a. "1½" omitted 325.00 300.00
173 A14 6r green 57.50 45.00
a. "6" omitted 375.00 325.00
Nos. 169-173 (5) 148.75 93.00

Nos. 169-171 exist with unofficial perf. 12.

King Luiz — A15

King Carlos — A16

Perf. 12½, 13½

1886, Apr. 29 **Embossed**

174 A15 1½r black 1.65 1.25
a. Perf. 13½ 105.00 62.50
175 A15 4½r bister 1.65 1.40
a. Perf. 13½ 27.50 12.50
176 A15 6r dp green 2.25 1.65
a. Perf. 13½ 30.00 14.00
177 A15 1t brt rose 3.75 2.75
178 A15 2t deep blue 6.00 4.00
179 A15 4t gray vio 7.00 4.00
180 A15 8t orange 7.00 4.25
Nos. 174-180 (7) 29.30 19.30

For surcharges and overprints see Nos. 224-230, 277-278, 282, 317-323, 354, 397.

Nos. 178-179 were reprinted. Originals have yellow gum. Reprints have white gum and clean-cut perforation 13½. Value, $4 each.

Perf. 11½, 12½, 13½

1895-96 **Typo.**

181 A16 1½r black .90 .40
182 A16 4½r pale orange .90 .40
a. Perf. 13½ 7.25 1.50
183 A16 6r green .90 .40
a. Perf. 12½ 2.75 1.00
184 A16 9r gray lilac 3.75 2.75
185 A16 1t lt blue 1.25 .50
a. Perf. 12½ 5.00 2.25
186 A16 2t rose .90 .50
a. Perf. 12½ 3.75 2.00
187 A16 4t dk blue 1.50 .75
a. Perf. 12½ 4.75 3.00
188 A16 8t brt violet 3.00 2.50
Nos. 181-188 (8) 13.10 8.20

For surcharges and overprints see Nos. 231-238,275-276, 279-281, 324-331, 352.

No. 184 was reprinted. Reprints have white gum, and clean-cut perforation 13½. Value $10.

Vasco da Gama Issue

Common Design Types

1898, May 1 **Engr.** ***Perf. 14 to 15***

189 CD20 1½r blue green .90 .80
190 CD21 4½r red .90 .80
191 CD22 6r red violet .90 .70
192 CD23 9r yellow green .90 .90
193 CD24 1t dk blue 1.50 1.50
194 CD25 2t violet brn 2.00 1.75
195 CD26 4t bister brn 2.00 1.75
196 CD27 8t bister 4.00 3.50
Nos. 189-196 (8) 13.10 11.70

For overprints and surcharges see Nos. 290-297, 384-389.

King Carlos — A17

1898-1903 **Typo.** ***Perf. 11½***

Name and Value in Black except No. 219

197 A17 1r gray ('02) .30 .15
198 A17 1½r orange .30 .25
199 A17 1½r slate ('02) .40 .25
200 A17 2r orange ('02) .30 .25
201 A17 2½r yel brn ('02) .40 .25
202 A17 3r dp blue ('02) .40 .25
203 A17 4½r lt green .65 .50
204 A17 6r brown .65 .50
205 A17 6r gray grn ('02) .40 .25
206 A17 9r dull vio .75 .50
a. 9r gray lilac 1.65 1.65
208 A17 1t sea green .75 .45
209 A17 1t car rose ('02) .55 .25
210 A17 2t blue 1.25 .50
a. Perf. 13½ 27.50 7.00
211 A17 2t brown ('02) 3.00 1.90
212 A17 2½t dull bl ('02) 8.25 6.00
213 A17 4t blue, *blue* 3.00 2.00
214 A17 5t brn, *straw* ('02) 3.00 1.90
215 A17 8t red lil, *pnksh* 3.00 1.25
216 A17 8t red vio, *pink* ('02) 4.50 2.75
217 A17 12t blue, *pink* 3.00 2.00
218 A17 12t grn, *pink* ('02) 4.50 3.00
219 A17 1rp blk & red, *bl* 8.50 6.00
220 A17 1rp dl bl, *straw* ('02) 10.00 6.50
221 A17 2rp vio, *yelsh* 11.00 7.50
222 A17 2rp gray blk, *straw* ('03) 15.00 11.00
Nos. 197-222 (25) 83.85 56.15

Several stamps of this issue exist without value or with value inverted but they are not known to have been issued in this condition. The 1r and 6r in carmine rose are believed to be color trials.

For surcharges and overprints see Nos. 223, 239-259, 260C-274, 283-289, 300-316, 334-350, 376-383, 390-396, 398-399.

No. 210 Surcharged in Black — 1½ Reis

1900

223 A17 1½r on 2t blue 2.75 .80
a. Inverted surcharge
b. Perf. 13½ 32.50 20.00

Stamps of 1885-96 Surcharged in Black or Red — 1 REAL

On Stamps of 1886

1902 ***Perf. 12½, 13½***

224 A15 1r on 2t blue .85 .45
225 A15 2r on 4½r bis .30 .25
a. Inverted surcharge *20.00 20.00*
b. Double surcharge
226 A15 2½r on 6r green .30 .25
227 A15 3r on 1t rose .30 .25
228 A15 2½t on 1½r blk (R) 1.65 1.25
229 A15 2½t on 4t gray vio 2.25 1.25
230 A15 5t on 8t orange 1.25 .60
a. Perf. 12½ 25.00 15.00

On Stamps of 1895-96

Perf. 11½, 12½, 13½

231 A16 1r on 6r green .45 .25
232 A16 2r on 8t brt vio .30 .25
233 A16 2½r on 9r gray vio .30 .30
234 A16 3r on 4½r yel 1.65 .90
a. Inverted surcharge 21.00 21.00
235 A16 3r on 1t lt bl 1.25 .80
236 A16 2½t on 1½r blk (R) 2.00 .75
237 A16 5t on 2t rose 2.00 .75
a. Perf. 12½ 32.50 20.00
238 A16 5t on 4t dk bl 2.00 .75
a. Perf. 12½ 32.50 20.00
Nos. 224-238 (15) 16.85 9.05

Nos. 224, 229, 231, 233, 234, 235 and 238 were reprinted in 1905. They have whiter gum than the originals and very clean-cut perf. 13½. Value $2.50 each.

Nos. 204, 208, 210 Overprinted — PROVISORIO

1902 ***Perf. 11½***

239 A17 6r brown 1.65 1.25
a. Inverted overprint
240 A17 1t sea green 2.00 1.25
241 A17 2t blue 1.50 1.25
a. Perf. 13½ 135.00 90.00
Nos. 239-241 (3) 5.15 3.75

No. 212 Surcharged in Black — 2 TANGAS

1905

243 A17 2t on 2½t dull blue 1.75 1.50

Stamps of 1898-1903 Overprinted in Lisbon in Carmine or Green

1911

244 A17 1r gray .15 .15
a. Inverted overprint 10.00 10.00
245 A17 1½r slate .15 .15
a. Double overprint 10.00 10.00
246 A17 2r orange .25 .20
a. Double overprint
b. Inverted overprint 10.00 10.00
247 A17 2½r yellow brn .25 .15
248 A17 3r deep blue .25 .15
249 A17 4½r light green .30 .20
250 A17 6r gray green .20 .15
251 A17 9r gray lilac .30 .20
252 A17 1t car rose (G) .30 .20
253 A17 2t brown .30 .20
254 A17 4t blue, *blue* 1.25 .95
255 A17 5t brn, *straw* 1.25 .95
256 A17 8t vio, *pink* 3.75 2.25
257 A17 12t grn, *pink* 4.00 2.25
258 A17 1rp dl bl, *straw* 5.25 4.25
259 A17 2rp gray blk, *straw* 8.00 6.75
Nos. 244-259 (16) 25.95 19.15

A18

Values are for pairs, both halves.

1911 **Perforated Diagonally**

260 A18 1r on 2r orange .75 .65
a. Without diagonal perf. 4.00 3.50
b. Cut diagonally instead of perf. 3.25 3.00

Stamps of Preceding Issues Perforated Vertically through the Middle and Each Half Surcharged with New Value:

3 REIS

3 REIS a — 6 REIS — 6 REIS b

Values are for pairs, both halves of the stamp.

1912-13

On Issue of 1898-1903

260C A17(a) 1r on 2r org .25 .20
261 A17(a) 1r on 1t car .25 .20
262 A17(a) 1r on 5t brn, *straw* 95.00 65.00
263 A17(b) 1r on 5t brn, *straw* 7.00 5.50
264 A17(a) 1 1/2r on 2 1/2r yel brn .70 .60
264C A17(a) 1 1/2r on 4 1/2r lt grn 11.00 7.00
265 A17(a) 1 1/2r on 9r gray lil .50 .40
266 A17(a) 1 1/2r on 4t bl, *bl* .50 .40
267 A17(a) 2r on 2 1/2r yel brn .65 .40
268 A17(a) 2r on 4t bl, *bl* .90 .65
269 A17(a) 3r on 2 1/2r yel brn .65 .40
270 A17(a) 3r on 2t brown .65 .45
271 A17(a) 6r on 4 1/2r lt grn .65 .55
272 A17(a) 6r on 9r gray lil .65 .50
273 A17(a) 6r on 9r dull vio 4.00 3.25
274 A17(b) 6r on 8t red vio, *pink* 1.50 .90

On Nos. 237-238, 230, 226, 233

275 A16(b) 1r on 5t on 2t 18.00 15.00
276 A16(b) 1r on 5t on 4t 9.00 8.50
277 A15(b) 1r on 5t on 8t 4.50 3.00
278 A15(a) 2r on 2 1/2r on 6r 3.75 3.00
279 A16(a) 2r on 2 1/2r on 9r 22.50 21.00
280 A16(b) 3r on 5t on 2t 7.00 5.75
281 A16(b) 3r on 5t on 4t 7.00 5.75
282 A15(b) 3r on 5t on 8t 2.25 1.50

On Issue of 1911

283 A17(a) 1r on 1r gray .25 .25
283B A17(a) 1r on 2r org .25 .25
284 A17(a) 1r on 1t car .30 .25
285 A17(a) 1r on 5t brn, *straw* .30 .25
285A A17(b) 1r on 5t brn, *straw*
285B A17(a) 1 1/2r on 4 1/2r lt grn .60 .45
286 A17(a) 3r on 2t brown 10.50 7.75
289 A17(a) 6r on 9r gray lil .50 .40

There are several settings of these surcharges and many minor varieties of the letters and figures, notably a small "6." Nos. 260-289 were issued mostly without gum.

More than half of Nos. 260C-289 exist with inverted or double surcharge, or with bisecting perforation omitted. The legitimacy of these varieties is questioned. Price of inverted surcharges, $3-$15; double surcharges, $1-$4; perf. omitted, $1.50-$15.

Similar surcharges made without official authorization on stamps of type A17 are: 2r on 2 1/2r, 3r on 2 1/2r, 3r on 5t, and 6r on 4 1/2r.

Common Design Types pictured following the introduction.

Vasco da Gama Issue Overprinted REPUBLICA

1913

290 CD20 1 1/2r blue green .30 .25
291 CD21 4 1/2r red .30 .25
a. Double overprint
292 CD22 6r red violet .40 .35
a. Double overprint
293 CD23 9r yellow grn .40 .35
294 CD24 1t dark blue .90 .50
295 CD25 2t violet brown 2.00 1.10
296 CD26 4t orange brn 1.10 .90
297 CD27 8t bister 2.00 1.25
Nos. 290-297 (8) 7.40 4.95

Issues of 1898-1913 Overprinted Locally in Red

1913-15

On Issues of 1898-1903

300 A17 2r orange 4.50 4.00
301 A17 2 1/2r yellow brn .85 .75
302 A17 3r dp blue 8.00 7.00
303 A17 4 1/2r lt green 1.75 1.50
304 A17 6r gray grn 20.00 16.00
305 A17 9r gray lilac 1.75 1.25
306 A17 1t sea green 20.00 16.00
307 A17 2t blue 26.00 14.00
309 A17 4t blue, *blue* 19.00 12.50
310 A17 5t brn, *straw* 25.00 16.00
311 A17 8t red vio, *pink* 27.50 22.50
312 A17 12t grn, *pink* 3.50 2.50
313 A17 1rp blk & red, *bl* 30.00 22.50
314 A17 1rp dl bl, *straw* 20.00 12.50
315 A17 2rp gray blk, *straw* 22.50 14.00
316 A17 2rp vio, *yelsh* 17.50 10.00
Nos. 300-316 (16) 247.85 173.00

Inverted or double overprints exist on 2 1/2r, 4 1/2r, 9r, 1rp and 2rp.

Nos. 300-316 were issued without gum except 4 1/2r and 9r.

Nos. 302, 304, 306, 307, 310, 311 and 313 were not regularly issued. Nor were the 1 1/2r, 2t brown and 12t blue on pink with preceding overprint.

Same Overprint in Red or Green On Provisional Issue of 1902

317 A15 1r on 2t blue 14.00 10.00
a. "REPUBLICA" inverted
318 A15 2r on 4 1/2r bis 14.00 10.00
a. "REPUBLICA" inverted
319 A15 2 1/2r on 6r grn .70 .60
a. "REPUBLICA" inverted 17.00 17.00
320 A15 3r on 1t rose (R) 10.00 8.00
321 A15 2 1/2t on 4t gray vio 40.00 19.00
323 A15 5t on 8t org (G) 10.00 7.50
a. Red overprint 10.00 7.50
324 A16 1r on 6r grn 10.00 7.50
325 A16 2r on 8t vio 10.00 7.50
a. Inverted surcharge
327 A16 3r on 4 1/2r yel 30.00 25.00
328 A16 3r on 1t lt bl 30.00 25.00
329 A16 5t on 2t rose (G) 3.25 2.75
330 A16 5t on 4t bl (G) 3.25 2.75
331 A16 5t on 4t bl (R) 3.75 3.75
a. "REPUBLICA" inverted
b. "REPUBLICA" double
Nos. 317-331 (13) 178.95 129.35

The 2 1/2r on 1 1/2r of types A15 and A16, the 3r on 1t (A15) and 2 1/2r on 9r (A16) were clandestinely printed.

Some authorities question the status of No. 317-318, 320-321, 324, 327-328.

Same Overprint on Nos. 240-241

1913-15

334 A17 1t sea green 7.00 5.00
335 A17 2t blue 6.50 6.00

This overprint was applied to No. 239 without official authorization.

On Issue of 1912-13 Perforated through the Middle

Values are for pairs, both halves of the stamp.

336 A17(a) 1r on 2r org 6.00 5.50
340 A17(a) 1 1/2r on 4 1/2r lt grn 6.00 5.50
341 A17(a) 1 1/2r on 9r gray lil 6.00
342 A17(a) 1 1/2r on 4t bl, *bl* 7.50
343 A17(a) 2r on 2 1/2r yel brn 5.50
344 A17(a) 2r on 4t bl, *bl* 7.50 6.50
345 A17(a) 3r on 2 1/2r yel brn 6.00
346 A17(a) 3r on 2t brn 5.00 4.75
347 A17(a) 6r on 4 1/2r lt grn 1.00 .80
348 A17(a) 6r on 9r gray lil 1.50 1.50
350 A17(b) 6r on 8t red vio, *pink* 1.50 1.50
352 A16(b) 1r on 5t on 4t bl 37.50
354 A15(a) 2r on 2 1/2r on 6r grn 9.00
Nos. 334-354 (15) 113.50

The 1r on 5t (A15), 1r on 1t (A17), 1 1/2r on 2 1/2r (A17), 3r on 5t on 8t (A15), and 6r on 9r (A17) were clandestinely printed.

Nos. 336, 347 exist with inverted surcharge.

Some authorities question the status of Nos. 341-345, 352 and 354.

Ceres — A21

1913-21 Typo. ***Perf. 12x11 1/2, 15x14***

Name and Value in Black

357 A21 1r olive brn .30 .25
358 A21 1 1/2r yellow grn .30 .25
a. Imperf.
359 A21 2r black .35 .30
360 A21 2 1/2r olive grn .35 .40
361 A21 3r lilac .35 .20
362 A21 4 1/2r orange brn .35 .20
363 A21 5r blue green .65 .45
364 A21 6r lilac brown .35 .20
365 A21 9r ultra .55 .25
366 A21 10r carmine .85 .50
367 A21 1t lt violet .40 .25
368 A21 2t deep blue .85 .30
369 A21 3t yellow brown 1.75 .90
370 A21 4t slate 2.00 1.10
371 A21 8t plum 4.00 3.50
372 A21 12t brown, *green* 3.50 3.00
373 A21 1rp brown, *pink* 21.00 16.00
374 A21 2rp org, *salmon* 14.00 11.00
375 A21 3rp green, *blue* 20.00 15.00
Nos. 357-375 (19) 71.90 54.05

The 1, 2, 2 1/2, 3, 4 1/2r, 1, 2, and 4t exist with the black inscriptions inverted and the 2 1/2r with them double, one inverted, but it is not known that any of these were regularly issued.

See Nos. 401-410. For surcharges see Nos. 400, 420, 423.

Nos. 249, 251-253, 256-259 Surcharged in Black — 1 1/2 REIS

1914

376 A17 1 1/2r on 4 1/2r grn .30 .25
377 A17 1 1/2r on 9r gray lil .40 .30
378 A17 1 1/2r on 12t grn, *pink* .50 .45
379 A17 3r on 1t car rose .40 .35
380 A17 3r on 2t brn 3.00 2.50
381 A17 3r on 8t red vio, *pink* 2.25 2.00
382 A17 3r on 1rp dl bl, *straw* .95 .55
383 A17 3r on 2rp gray blk, *straw* 1.00 .80

There are 3 varieties of the "2" in "1 1/2."

Nos. 376-377 exist with inverted surcharge.

Vasco da Gama Issue Surcharged in Black — REPUBLICA 1 1/2 REIS

384 CD21 1 1/2r on 4 1/2r red .35 .28
385 CD23 1 1/2r on 9r yel grn .45 .30
386 CD24 3r on 1t dk bl .35 .28
387 CD25 3r on 2t vio brn .55 .45
388 CD26 3r on 4t org brn .28 .22
389 CD27 3r on 8t bister 1.20 1.10
Nos. 376-389 (14) 11.98 9.83

Double, inverted and other surcharge varieties exist on Nos. 384-386, 389.

Stamps of 1898-1903 Surcharged in Red

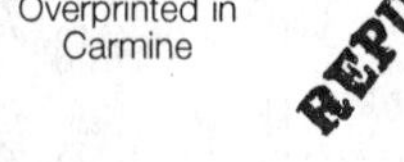

1 1/2 REIS

1915

390 A17 1 1/2r on 4 1/2r grn 27.50 20.00
a. "REPUBLICA" omitted 42.50 42.50
b. "REPUBLICA" inverted
391 A17 1 1/2r on 9r gray lil 10.00 7.50
a. "REPUBLICA" omitted
392 A17 1 1/2r on 12t grn, *pink* 1.25 1.00
396 A17 3r on 2rp gray blk, *straw* 12.50 4.00
Nos. 390-396 (4) 51.25 32.50

Nos. 390, 390a, 390b, 391, and 391a were not regularly issued. The 3r on 2 1/2r (A17) was surcharged without official authorization.

Preceding Issues Overprinted in Carmine — REPUBLICA

1915

On No. 230

397 A15 5t on 8t org 1.50 1.40

On Nos. 241, 243

398 A17 2t blue 1.25 1.25
399 A17 2t on 2 1/2t dl bl 1.50 1.25
Nos. 397-399 (3) 4.25 3.90

No. 359 Surcharged in Carmine — 1 1/2 REAL

1922

400 A21 1 1/2r on 2r black .50 .42

Ceres Type of 1913-21

1922-25 Typo. ***Perf. 12x11 1/2***

Name and Value in Black

401 A21 4r blue 1.25 1.10
402 A21 1 1/2t gray green 1.25 .85
403 A21 2 1/2t turq blue 1.40 1.10
404 A21 3t4r yellow brn 5.00 4.00
405 A21 4t gray ('25) 2.00 1.10
406 A21 8t dull rose 7.00 5.00
407 A21 1rp gray brn 16.50 15.00
408 A21 2rp yellow 22.50 16.00
409 A21 3rp bluish grn 30.00 24.00
410 A21 5rp carmine rose 35.00 27.50
Nos. 401-410 (10) 121.90 95.65

Vasco da Gama and Flagship — A22

1925, Jan. 30 **Litho.**

Without Gum

411 A22 6r brown 4.50 3.00
412 A22 1t red violet 6.25 4.50

400th anniv. of the death of Vasco da Gama (1469?-1524), Portuguese navigator.

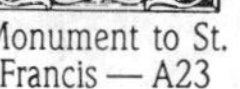

Monument to St. Francis — A23

Image of St. Francis — A25

Autograph of St. Francis A24

Image of St. Francis — A26

Tomb of St. Francis — A28

Church of Bom Jesus at Goa — A27

1931, Dec. 3 ***Perf. 14***

414 A23 1r gray green .50 .45
415 A24 2r brown .50 .45
416 A25 6r red violet 1.50 .50
417 A26 1 1/2t yellow brn 5.25 3.25
418 A27 2t deep blue 6.25 3.75
419 A28 2 1/2t light red 10.50 3.75
Nos. 414-419 (6) 24.50 12.15

Exposition of St. Francis Xavier at Goa, in December, 1931.

Nos. 371 and 404 Surcharged

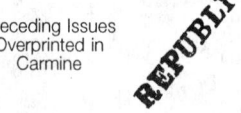

2 1/2 T.

1931-32 ***Perf. 15x14, 12x11 1/2***

420 A21 1 1/2r on 8t plum ('32) 1.40 1.00
423 A21 2 1/2t on 3t4r yel brn 25.00 20.00

"Portugal" and Vasco da Gama's Flagship "San Gabriel" — A29

Perf. 11 1/2x12

1933 Typo. Wmk. 232

424 A29 1r bister .15 .15
425 A29 2r olive brn .15 .15
426 A29 4r violet .15 .15
427 A29 6r dk green .15 .15
428 A29 8r black .20 .15
429 A29 1t gray .25 .15

430 A29 1½t dp rose .30 .15
431 A29 2t brown .35 .20
432 A29 2½t dk blue 2.00 .40
433 A29 3t brt blue 2.25 .40
434 A29 5t red orange 2.25 .40
435 A29 1rp olive grn 9.00 3.00
436 A29 2rp maroon 15.00 6.75
437 A29 3rp orange 22.50 8.00
438 A29 5rp apple grn 40.00 30.00
Nos. 424-438 (15) 94.70 50.20

For surcharges see Nos. 454-463, 472-474, J34-J36.

Common Design Types
Perf. 13½x13

1938, Sept. 1 Engr. Unwmk.
Name and Value in Black

439 CD34 1r gray grn .15 .15
440 CD34 2r orange brn .15 .15
441 CD34 3r dk vio brn .15 .15
442 CD34 6r brt green .15 .15
443 CD35 10r dk carmine .35 .22
444 CD35 1t brt red vio .65 .22
445 CD35 1½t red .80 .22
446 CD37 2t orange .80 .22
447 CD37 2½t blue .80 .22
448 CD37 3t slate 1.25 .28
449 CD36 5t rose vio 1.65 .45
450 CD36 1rp brown car 4.00 .80
451 CD36 2rp olive grn 6.25 2.50
452 CD38 3rp blue vio 10.00 6.00
453 CD38 5rp red brown 20.00 3.25
Nos. 439-453 (15) 47.15 14.98

For surcharges see Nos. 492-495, 504-505.

Stamps of 1933 Surcharged in Black

1 tanga

1941, June Wmk. 232 *Perf. 11½x12*

454 A29 1t on 1½t dp rose 2.00 1.40
455 A29 1t on 1rp olive grn 2.00 1.40
456 A29 1t on 2rp maroon 2.00 1.40
457 A29 1t on 5rp apple grn 2.00 1.40
Nos. 454-457 (4) 8.00 5.60

Nos. 430-431 Surcharged

3 RÉIS

1943

458 A29 3r on 1½t dp rose 1.50 .75
459 A29 1t on 2t brown 2.50 2.00

Nos. 434, 428, 437 and 432 Surcharged in Dark Blue or Carmine

1 REAL — a

6 Rëis — b

1945-46 Wmk. 232 *Perf. 11½x12*

460 A29(a) 1r on 5t red org (DB) .65 .45
461 A29(b) 2r on 8r blk (C) .50 .40
462 A29(b) 3r on 3rp org (DB) ('46) 1.40 1.25
463 A29(b) 6r on 2½t dk bl (C) 1.50 1.50
Nos. 460-463 (4) 4.05 3.60

St. Francis Xavier A30

Luis de Camoens A31

Garcia de Orta — A32

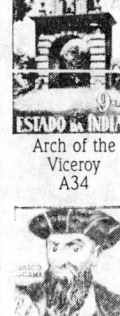

St. John de Britto — A33

Arch of the Viceroy A34

Affonso de Albuquerque A35

Vasco da Gama — A36

Francisco de Almeida — A37

Perf. 11½

1946, May 28 Litho. Unwmk.

464 A30 1r black & gray blk .45 .25
465 A31 2r rose brn & pale rose brn .45 .25
466 A32 6r ocher & dl yel .45 .25
467 A33 7r vio & pale vio 2.00 2.00
468 A34 9r sepia & buff 2.00 .50
469 A35 1t dk sl grn & sl grn 2.00 .50
470 A36 3½t ultra & pale ultra 2.25 1.10
471 A37 1rp choc & bis brn 5.00 1.40
a. Miniature sheet of 8, #464-471 19.00 19.00
Nos. 464-471 (8) 14.60 6.25

No. 471a sold for 1½ rupias.
See #476. For surcharges see #595, J43-J46.

No. 428, 431 and 433 Surcharged in Carmine or Black

1 Real

1946 Wmk. 232 *Perf. 11½x12*

472 A29 (c) 1r on 8r blk (C) .60 .50
473 A29 (b) 3r on 2t brn .60 .55
474 A29 (b) 6r on 3t brt bl 2.00 1.75
Nos. 472-474 (3) 3.20 2.80

Type of 1946 and

Joao de Castro — A38

José Vaz — A39

Luis de Ataide — A40

Duarte Pacheco Pereira — A41

1948 Unwmk. Litho. *Perf. 11½*

475 A38 3r brt ultra & lt bl .90 .50
476 A30 1t dk grn & yel grn 1.25 .60
477 A39 1½t dk pur & dl vio 2.00 1.10
478 A40 2½t brt ver 2.25 1.65
479 A41 7½t dk brn & org brn 4.00 2.25
a. Miniature sheet of 5 19.00 19.00
Nos. 475-479 (5) 10.40 6.10

No. 476 measures 21x31mm.

No. 479a measures 106x146mm. and contains one each of Nos. 475-479. Marginal inscriptions in gray. The sheet sold for 1 rupia.

For surcharge see No. 591.

Lady of Fatima Issue
Common Design Type

1948 *Perf. 14½*

480 CD40 1t dk blue green 2.25 2.00

Our Lady of Fatima — A42

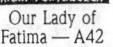

UPU Symbols — A42a

1949 Litho. *Perf. 14*

481 A42 1r blue .60 .50
482 A42 3r orange yel .60 .50
483 A42 9r dk car rose 1.10 .70
484 A42 2t green 2.75 1.75
485 A42 9t orange red 3.00 1.25
486 A42 2rp dk vio brn 5.75 2.75
487 A42 5rp olive grn 12.00 4.50
488 A42 8rp violet blue 27.50 12.00
Nos. 481-488 (8) 53.30 23.95

Our Lady of the Rosary at Fatima, Portugal.

1949, Oct.

489 A42a 2½t scarlet & pink 2.25 1.50

UPU, 75th anniversary.

Catalogue values for unused stamps in this section, from this point to the end of the section, are for Never Hinged items.

Holy Year Issue
Common Design Types

1950, May *Perf. 13x13½*

490 CD41 1r olive bister .60 .55
491 CD42 2t dk gray green 1.00 .55

See Nos. 496-503.

No. 443 Surcharged in Black

1 Real

1950 *Perf. 13½x13*

492 CD35 1r on 10r dk car .25 .25
493 CD35 2r on 10r dk car .25 .25

Similar Surcharge on No. 447 in Black or Red

494 CD37 1r on 2½t blue .25 .25
495 CD37 3r on 2½t blue (R) .25 .25
Nos. 492-495 (4) 1.00 1.00

Letters with serifs, small (lower case) "r" in "real" and "réis."

Holy Year Issue
Common Design Types

1951 Litho. *Perf. 13½*

496 CD41 1r dp car rose .22 .22
497 CD41 2r emerald .30 .25
498 CD42 3r red brown .30 .25
499 CD41 6r gray .35 .35
500 CD42 9r brt pink .75 .65
501 CD41 1t blue violet .50 .45
502 CD42 2t yellow .85 .55
503 CD41 4t violet brown .85 .55
Nos. 496-503 (8) 4.12 3.27

No. 447 with Surcharge Similar to Nos. 492-493 in Red

1951 *Perf. 13½x13*

504 CD37 6r on 2½t blue .30 .30
505 CD37 1t on 2½t blue .25 .25

Letters with serifs, small (lower case) "r" in "réis."

Holy Year Extension Issue
Common Design Type

1951 Litho. *Perf. 14*

506 CD43 1rp bl vio & pale vio 1.50 1.00

José Vaz — A43

Ruins of Sancoale Church — A44

Design: 12t, Altar.

1951 Litho. *Perf. 14½*
Dated: "1651-1951"

507 A43 1r Prus bl & pale bl .15 .15
508 A44 2r ver & red brn .15 .15
509 A43 3r gray blk & gray .40 .25
510 A44 1t vio bl & ind .16 .15
511 A43 2t dp cl & cl .25 .15
512 A44 3t ol grn & blk .40 .20
513 A43 9t indigo & ultra .50 .40
514 A44 10t lilac & vio .85 .50
515 A44 12t blk brn & brn 1.25 .75
Nos. 507-515 (9) 4.11 2.70

300th anniversary of the birth of José Vaz.

Medical Congress Issue
Common Design Type

Design: Medical School, Goa.

1952 Unwmk. *Perf. 13½*

516 CD44 4½t blk & lt blue 3.00 1.65

St. Francis Xavier Issue

Statue of Saint Francis Xavier — A44a

A45

QUARTO CENTENÁRIO DA MORTE DE S.FRANCISCO XAVIER

ÍNDIA PORTUGUESA

St. Francis Xavier and his Tomb, Goa — A46

Designs: 2t, Miraculous Arm of St. Francis. 4t, 5t, Tomb of St. Francis.

1952, Oct. 25 Litho. *Perf. 14*

517 A44a 6r aqua & multi .25 .20
518 A44a 2t cream & multi 2.00 .55
519 A44a 5t pink & silver 3.50 1.25
Nos. 517-519 (3) 5.75 2.00

Souvenir Sheets
Perf. 13

520 A45 9t brn & dk brn 8.50 8.50
521 A46 Sheet of 2 8.50 8.50
a. 4t orange buff & black 2.50 2.50
b. 8t slate & black 2.50 2.50

400th anniv. of the death of St. Francis Xavier.

Numeral A47

St. Francis Xavier A48

1952, Dec. 4 Litho. *Perf. 13½*

522 A47 3t black 3.00 3.00
523 A48 5t dk violet & blk 3.00 3.00
a. Strip of 2 + label 7.00 7.00

Issued to publicize Portuguese India's first stamp exhibition, Goa, 1952.

No. 523a consists of a tête bêche pair of Nos. 522-523 separated by a label publicizing the exhibition.

Statue of Virgin Mary — A49

Stamp of Portugal and Arms of Colonies — A49a

1953, Jan.

524 A49 6r dk & lt blue .15 .15
525 A49 1t brown & buff .75 .50
526 A49 3t dk pur & pale ol 2.50 1.25
Nos. 524-526 (3) 3.40 1.90

Exhibition of Sacred Missionary Art held at Lisbon in 1951.

For surcharge see No. 594.

Stamp Centenary Issue

1953 Typo.

527 A49a 1t multicolored .60 .50

Centenary of Portugal's first postage stamps.

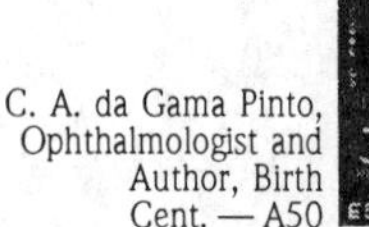
C. A. da Gama Pinto, Ophthalmologist and Author, Birth Cent. — A50

1954, Apr. 10 Litho. *Perf. 11½*

528 A50 3r gray & ol grn .25 .20
529 A50 2t black & gray blk .15 .15

Sao Paulo Issue
Common Design Type

1954, Oct. 2 Unwmk. *Perf. 13½*

530 CD46 2t dk Prus bl, bl & blk .25 .25

For surcharge see No. 593.

Affonso de Albuquerque School — A51

Msgr. Sebastiao Rodolfo Dalgado — A52

1955, Feb. 26

531 A51 9t multicolored .85 .60

Centenary (in 1954) of the founding of the Affonso de Albuquerque National School.

1955, Nov. 15 Unwmk. *Perf. 13½*

532 A52 1r multicolored .20 .20
533 A52 1t multicolored .50 .25

Birth cent. of Msgr. Sebastiao Rodolfo Dalgado.

Francisco de Almeida — A53

Manuel Antonio de Susa — A54

Map of Bassein by Pedro Barreto de Resendo, 1635 — A55

Portraits: 9r, Affonso de Albuquerque. 1t, Vasco da Gama. 1½t, Filipe Nery Xavier. 3t, Nuno da Cunha. 4t, Agostino Vicente Lourenco. 8t, Jose Vaz. 9t, Manuel Godinho de Heredia. 10t, Joao de Castro. 2rp, Antonio Caetano Pacheco. 3rp, Constantino de Braganca.

Maps of ancient forts, drawn in 1635: 2½t, Mombaim (Bombay). 3½t, Damao (Daman). 5t, Diu. 12t, Cochin. 1rp, Goa.

Inscribed: "450 Aniversario da Fundacao do Estado da India 1505-1955."

Perf. 11½x12 (A53), 14½ (A54), 12½ (A55)

1956, Mar. 24 Unwmk.

534 A53 3r multicolored .15 .15
535 A54 6r multicolored .15 .15
536 A53 9r multicolored .32 .30
537 A53 1t multicolored .32 .30
538 A54 1½t multicolored .15 .15
539 A55 2t multicolored 1.90 1.40
540 A55 2½t multicolored 1.25 .90
541 A53 3t multicolored .32 .15
542 A55 3½t multicolored 1.40 .90
543 A54 4t multicolored .15 .15
544 A55 5t multicolored .60 .40
545 A54 8t multicolored .50 .38
546 A54 9t multicolored .50 .38
547 A53 10t multicolored .48 .35
548 A55 12t multicolored 1.10 .80
549 A55 1rp multicolored 2.00 1.40
550 A54 2rp multicolored 1.90 1.10
551 A53 3rp multicolored 2.50 1.50
Nos. 534-551 (18) 15.69 10.86

Portuguese settlements in India, 450th anniv.

For surcharges see Nos. 575-577, 579-581, 592.

Map of Damao and Nagar Aveli — A56

Arms of Vasco da Gama — A57

1957 Litho. *Perf. 11½*

Map and Inscriptions in Black, Red, Ocher and Blue

552 A56 3r gray & buff .15 .15
553 A56 6r bl grn & pale lem .15 .15
554 A56 3t pink & lt gray .15 .15
555 A56 6t blue .35 .35
556 A56 11t ol bis & lt vio gray .75 .55
557 A56 2rp lt vio & pale gray 1.75 1.10
558 A56 3rp citron & pink 2.00 1.50
559 A56 5rp magenta & pink 2.25 1.75
Nos. 552-559 (8) 7.55 5.70

For surcharges see Nos. 571, 578, 584-585, 588-590.

1958, Apr. 3 Unwmk. *Perf. 13x13½*

Arms of: 6r, Lopo Soares de Albergaria. 9r, Francisco de Almeida. 1t, Garcia de Noronha. 4t, Alfonso de Albuquerque. 5t, Joao de Castro. 11t, Luis de Ataide. 1r, Nuno da Cunha.

Arms in Original Colors
Inscriptions in Black and Red

560 A57 2r buff & ocher .15 .15
561 A57 6r gray & ocher .15 .15
562 A57 9r pale blue & emer .15 .15
563 A57 1t pale citron & brn .20 .15
564 A57 4t pale bl grn & lil .25 .15
565 A57 5t buff & blue .30 .30
566 A57 11t pink & lt brn .50 .40
567 A57 1rp pale grn & maroon .80 .60
Nos. 560-567 (8) 2.50 2.05

For surcharges see Nos. 570, 572-574, 582-583, 586-587.

Exhibition Emblem and View — A58

1958, Dec. 15 Litho. *Perf. 14½*

568 A58 1rp multicolored .50 .50

World's Fair, Brussels, Apr. 17-Oct. 19.

For surcharge see No. 597.

Tropical Medicine Congress Issue
Common Design Type

Design: Holarrhena antidysenterica.

1958, Dec. 15 *Perf. 13½*

569 CD47 5t gray, brn, grn & red 1.00 .70

For surcharge see No. 596.

Stamps of 1955-58 Surcharged with New Values and Bars

1959, Jan. 1 Litho. Unwmk.

570 A57 5c on 2r (#560) .15 .15
571 A56 10c on 3r (#552) .15 .15
572 A57 15c on 6r (#561) .15 .15
573 A57 20c on 9r (#562) .15 .15
574 A57 30c on 1t (#563) .15 .15
575 A55 40c on 2t (#539) .15 .15
576 A55 40c on 2½t (#540) .40 .32
577 A55 40c on 3½t (#542) .15 .15
578 A56 50c on 3t (#554) .15 .15
579 A53 80c on 3t (#541) .15 .15
580 A53 80c on 10t (#547) .85 .75
581 A53 80c on 3rp (#551) 1.00 .85
582 A57 1e on 4t (#564) .15 .15
583 A57 1.50e on 5t (#565) .15 .15
584 A56 2e on 6t (#555) .38 .32
585 A56 2.50e on 11t (#556) .45 .25
586 A57 4e on 11t (#566) .60 .50
587 A57 4.50e on 1rp (#567) .65 .50
588 A56 5e on 2rp (#557) .65 .50
589 A56 10e on 3rp (#558) 2.00 1.50
590 A56 30e on 5rp (#559) 4.50 2.00
Nos. 570-590 (21) 13.13 9.14

Types of 1946-1958 Surcharged with New Values, Old Values Obliterated

1959 Litho. Unwmk.

591 A39 40c on 1½t dl pur .38 .15
592 A54 40c on 1½t multi .38 .15
593 CD46 40c on 2t bl & gray 1.00 .75
594 A49 80c on 3t blk & pale cit .38 .15
595 A36 80c on 3½t dk bl .55 .15
596 CD47 80c on 5t gray, brn, grn & red .55 .40
597 A58 80c on 1rp multi 1.25 .65
Nos. 591-597 (7) 4.49 2.40

Coin, Manuel I — A59

Arms of Prince Henry — A60

Various Coins from the Reign of Manuel I (1495-1521) to the Republic.

Perf. 13½x13

1959, Dec. 1 Litho. Unwmk.

Inscriptions in Black and Red

598 A59 5c lt bl & gold .15 .15
599 A59 10c pale brn & gold .15 .15
600 A59 15c pale grn & gray .15 .15
601 A59 30c salmon & gray .15 .15
602 A59 40c pale yel & gray .15 .15
603 A59 50c lilac & gray .15 .15
604 A59 60c pale yel grn & gray .15 .15
605 A59 80c lt bl & gray .15 .15
606 A59 1e ocher & gray .15 .15
607 A59 1.50e blue & gray .15 .15
608 A59 2e pale bl & gold .22 .15
609 A59 2.50e pale gray & gold .30 .15
610 A59 3e citron & gray .32 .18
611 A59 4e pink & gray .45 .20
612 A59 4.40e pale bis & vio brn .55 .30
613 A59 5e pale dl vio & gray .70 .40
614 A59 10e brt yel & gray 1.00 .70
615 A59 20e beige & gray 2.25 1.65
616 A59 30e brt yel grn & lt cop brn 2.50 2.50
617 A59 50e lt gray & gray 4.00 4.00
Nos. 598-617 (20) 13.79 11.73

1960, June 25 *Perf. 13½*

618 A60 3e multicolored .50 .50

500th anniversary of the death of Prince Henry the Navigator.

Portugal continued to print special-issue stamps for its lost colony after its annexation by India Dec. 18, 1961. Stamps of India were first used on Dec. 29. Stamps of Portuguese India remained valid until Jan. 5, 1962.

AIR POST STAMPS

Common Design Type

Perf. 13½x13

1938, Sept. 1 Engr. Unwmk.

Name and Value in Black

C1 CD39 1t scarlet .50 .25
C2 CD39 2½t purple .60 .25
C3 CD39 3½t orange .60 .25
C4 CD39 4½t ultra 1.50 .42
C5 CD39 7t lilac brown 1.65 .50
C6 CD39 7½t dark green 2.25 .75
C7 CD39 9t red brown 4.00 1.10
C8 CD39 11t magenta 4.50 1.10
Nos. C1-C8 (8) 15.60 4.62

No. C4 exists with overprint "Exposicao Internacional de Nova York, 1939-1940" and Trylon and Perisphere.

POSTAGE DUE STAMPS

D1

1904 Unwmk. Typo. *Perf. 11½*

Name and Value in Black

J1 D1 2r gray green .45 .30
J2 D1 3r yellow grn .45 .30
J3 D1 4r orange .45 .40
J4 D1 5r slate .45 .45
J5 D1 6r gray .45 .45
J6 D1 9r yellow brn .55 .55
J7 D1 1t red orange 1.10 .75
J8 D1 2t gray brown 2.25 1.50
J9 D1 5t dull blue 3.00 2.75
J10 D1 10t carmine 4.00 3.25
J11 D1 1rp dull vio 12.00 6.75
Nos. J1-J11 (11) 25.15 17.45

Nos. J1-J11 Overprinted in Carmine or Green

1911

J12 D1 2r gray grn .15 .15
J13 D1 3r yellow grn .15 .15
J14 D1 4r orange .15 .15
J15 D1 5r slate .15 .15
J16 D1 6r gray .20 .20
J17 D1 9r yellow brn .35 .30
J18 D1 1t red org .35 .30
J19 D1 2t gray brn .60 .50
J20 D1 5t dull blue 1.50 1.25
J21 D1 10t carmine (G) 2.50 1.75
J22 D1 1rp dull violet 4.50 3.00
Nos. J12-J22 (11) 10.60 7.90

Nos. J1-J11 Overprinted

REPÚBLICA

1914

J23 D1 2r gray grn .25 .25
J24 D1 3r yellow grn .25 .25
J25 D1 4r orange .25 .25

J26 D1	5r slate	.25	.25
J27 D1	6r gray	.50	.40
J28 D1	9r yellow brn	.50	.50
J29 D1	1t red org	.75	.50
J30 D1	2t gray brn	3.25	1.50
J31 D1	5t dull blue	3.25	2.00
J32 D1	10t carmine	7.00	2.50
J33 D1	1rp dull violet	14.00	4.25
	Nos. J23-J33 (11)	30.25	12.65

Nos. 432, 433 and 434 Surcharged In Red or Black

3 RÉIS Porteado

1943 Wmk. 232 *Perf. 11½x12*

J34 A29	3r on 2½t dk bl (R)	.60	.40
J35 A29	6r on 3t brt bl (R)	.80	.80
J36 A29	1t on 5t red org (Bk)	1.75	1.50
	Nos. J34-J36 (3)	3.15	2.70

D2

1945 Typo. Unwmk.

Country Name and Denomination in Black

J37 D2	2r brt carmine	.90	.90
J38 D2	3r blue	.90	.90
J39 D2	4r orange yel	.90	.90
J40 D2	6r yellow grn	.90	.90
J41 D2	1t bister brn	.90	.90
J42 D2	2t chocolate	.90	.90
	Nos. J37-J42 (6)	5.40	5.40

Catalogue values for unused stamps in this section, from this point to the end of the section, are for Never Hinged items.

Nos. 467 and 471 Surcharged in Carmine or Black

Porteado 2 Réis

1951, Jan. 1 *Perf. 11½*

J43 A33	2r on 7r vio & pale vio (C)	.55	.55
J44 A33	3r on 7r vio & pale vio (C)	.55	.55
J45 A37	1t on 1rp choc & bis brn	.55	.55
J46 A37	2t on 1rp choc & bis brn	.55	.55
	Nos. J43-J46 (4)	2.20	2.20

Common Design Type

Photogravure and Typographed

1952 *Perf. 14*

Numeral in Red; Frame Multicolored

J47 CD45	2r olive	.15	.15
J48 CD45	3r black	.15	.15
J49 CD45	6r dark blue	.15	.15
J50 CD45	1t dk carmine	.30	.20
J51 CD45	2t orange	.50	.50
J52 CD45	10t violet blue	2.00	2.00
	Nos. J47-J52 (6)	3.25	3.15

Nos. J47-J49 and J51-J52 Surcharged with New Value and Bars

1959, Jan.

Numeral in Red; Frame Multicolored

J53 CD45	5c on 2r olive	.15	.15
J54 CD45	10c on 3r black	.15	.15
J55 CD45	15c on 6r dk blue	.25	.20
J56 CD45	60c on 2t orange	.90	.90
J57 CD45	60c on 10t vio blue	1.75	1.75
	Nos. J53-J57 (5)	3.20	3.15

WAR TAX STAMPS

WT1

Overprinted in Black or Carmine

Perf. 15x14

1919, Apr. 15 Typo. Unwmk.

Denomination in Black

MR1 WT1	0:00:05,48rp grn	1.40	1.10
MR2 WT1	0:01:09,94rp grn	4.00	2.75
MR3 WT1	0:02:03,43rp grn (C)	4.00	2.75
	Nos. MR1-MR3 (3)	9.40	6.60

Some authorities consider No. MR2 a revenue stamp.

POSTAL TAX STAMPS

Pombal Issue

Common Design Types

1925 Unwmk. *Perf. 12½*

RA1 CD28	6r rose & black	.45	.45
RA2 CD29	6r rose & black	.45	.45
RA3 CD30	6r rose & black	.45	.45
	Nos. RA1-RA3 (3)	1.35	1.35

Mother and Child — PT1

1948 Litho. *Perf. 11*

RA4 PT1	6r yellow green	2.75	2.50
RA5 PT1	1t carmine	2.75	2.50

See Nos. RA7-RA7A, RA9, RA12. For surcharge and overprint see Nos. RA6, RA8.

Catalogue values for unused stamps in this section, from this point to the end of the section, are for Never Hinged items.

Type of 1948 Surcharged with New Value and Bar in Black

1951

RA6 PT1	1t on 6r carmine	3.00	2.00

Type of 1948

1952-53

RA7 PT1	1t gray	2.50	1.65
RA7A PT1	1t red orange ('53)	2.75	1.90

No. RA5 Overprinted in Black

«Revalidado» P. A. P.

1953

RA8 PT1	1t carmine	7.25	6.00

Type of 1948

1954 **Typo.**

RA9 PT1	6r pale bister	4.00	3.75

Mother and Child
PT2 PT3

Surcharged in Black

1956 Typo. *Perf. 11*

RA10 PT2	1t on 4t lt blue	11.00	10.00

Litho. *Perf. 13*

RA11 PT3	1t blk, pale grn & red	1.25	.90

See No. RA14. For surcharges see Nos. RA13, RA15-RA16.

Type of 1948 Redrawn

1956 *Perf. 11*

Without Gum

RA12 PT1	1t bluish green	3.25	3.00

Denomination in white oval at left.

No. RA11 Surcharged with New Value and Bars in Red

1957 *Perf. 13½*

RA13 PT3	6r on 1t	.90	.75

Type of 1956

1958 Unwmk. *Perf. 13*

RA14 PT3	1t dk bl, sal & grn	.90	.60

No. RA14 Surcharged with New Values and Four Bars

1959, Jan. Litho. *Perf. 13*

RA15 PT3	20c on 1t	.55	.55
RA16 PT3	40c on 1t	.55	.55

Arms and People Seeking Help — PT4

1960 *Perf. 13½*

RA17 PT4	20c brown & red	.25	.25

POSTAL TAX DUE STAMPS

Pombal Issue

Common Design Types

1925 Unwmk. *Perf. 12½*

RAJ1 CD28	1t rose & black	.60	.60
RAJ2 CD29	1t rose & black	.60	.60
RAJ3 CD30	1t rose & black	.60	.60
	Nos. RAJ1-RAJ3 (3)	1.80	1.80

See note after Portugal No. RAJ4.

PUERTO RICO

ˌpwer-tə-ˈrē-(ˌ)kō

(Porto Rico)

LOCATION — A large island in the West Indies, east of Hispaniola
GOVT. — Former Spanish Colony
AREA — 3,435 sq. mi.
POP. — 953,243 (1899)
CAPITAL — San Juan

The island was ceded to the United States by the Treaty of 1898.

100 Centimes = 1 Peseta
1000 Milesimas = 100 Centavos = 1 Peso (1881)
100 Cents = 1 Dollar (1898)

Values for unused stamps are for examples with original gum as defined in the catalogue introduction. Very fine examples of Nos. 1-170, MR1-MR13 will have perforations clear of the design but will be noticeably poorly centered. Extremely fine examples will be well centered; these are scarce and command substantial premiums.

Issued under Spanish Dominion

Puerto Rican stamps of 1855-73, a part of the Spanish colonial period, were also used in Cuba. They are listed as Cuba Nos. 1-4, 9-14, 18-21, 31-34, 39-41, 47-49, 51-53, 55-57.

Stamps of Cuba Overprinted in Black:

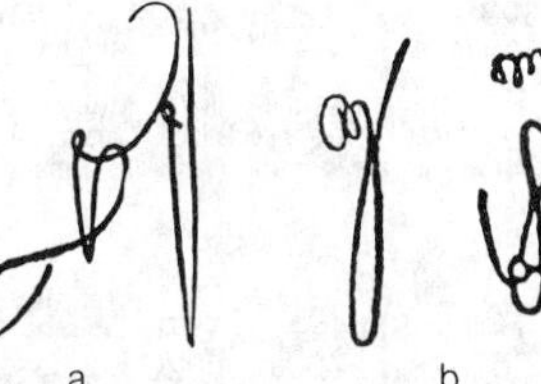
a b

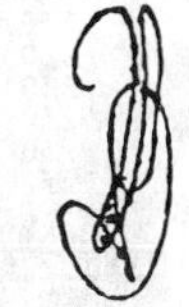

c d

1873 Unwmk. *Perf. 14*

1 A10 (a)	25c gray	30.00	1.50
2 A10 (a)	50c brown	80.00	4.50
3 A10 (a)	1p red brown	190.00	15.00
	Nos. 1-3 (3)	300.00	21.00

1874

4 A11 (b)	25c ultra	25.00	2.00
a.	Double overprint	150.00	
b.	Inverted overprint	150.00	

1875

5 A12 (b)	25c ultra	18.00	2.00
a.	Inverted overprint	55.00	35.00
6 A12 (b)	50c green	25.00	2.25
a.	Inverted overprint	*125.00*	*65.00*
7 A12 (b)	1p brown	100.00	11.00
	Nos. 5-7 (3)	143.00	15.25

1876

8 A13 (c)	25c pale violet	3.25	1.50
9 A13 (c)	50c ultra	7.50	2.50
10 A13 (c)	1p black	32.50	9.00
11 A13 (d)	25c blue gray	25.00	1.00
12 A13 (d)	1p black	55.00	8.00
	Nos. 8-12 (5)	123.25	22.00

Varieties of overprint on Nos. 8-11 include: inverted, double, partly omitted and sideways.

Counterfeit overprints exist.

King Alfonso XII
A5 A6

1877 **Typo.**

13 A5	5c yellow brown	5.25	2.00
a.	5c carmine (error)	200.00	—
14 A5	10c carmine	16.00	4.75
a.	10c brown (error)	200.00	—
15 A5	15c deep green	24.00	9.50
16 A5	25c ultra	10.00	1.50
17 A5	50c bister	16.00	4.00
	Nos. 13-17 (5)	71.25	21.75

Dated "1878"

1878

18 A5	5c ol bister	12.00	12.00
19 A5	10c red brown	190.00	67.50
20 A5	25c deep green	1.50	.90
21 A5	50c ultra	5.50	2.00
22 A5	1p bister	10.00	4.50
	Nos. 18-22 (5)	219.00	86.90

Dated "1879"

1879

23 A5	5c lake	10.00	4.50
24 A5	10c dark brown	10.00	4.50
25 A5	15c dk olive grn	10.00	4.50
26 A5	25c blue	3.50	1.50
27 A5	50c dark green	10.00	4.50
28 A5	1p gray	47.50	20.00
	Nos. 23-28 (6)	91.00	39.50

Imperforates of type A5 are from proof or trial sheets.

1880

29 A6	¼c deep green	21.00	16.00
30 A6	½c brt rose	5.50	2.00
31 A6	1c brown lilac	9.50	8.00
32 A6	2c gray lilac	5.50	3.75
33 A6	3c buff	5.50	3.75
34 A6	4c black	5.50	3.75
35 A6	5c gray green	2.75	1.50
36 A6	10c rose	3.25	1.75
37 A6	15c yellow brn	5.50	2.75
38 A6	25c gray blue	2.75	1.25
39 A6	40c gray	11.00	1.40
40 A6	50c dark brown	22.50	12.50
41 A6	1p olive bister	77.50	16.00
	Nos. 29-41 (13)	177.75	74.40

Dated "1881"

1881

42 A6	½m lake	.25	.25
43 A6	1m violet	.25	.15
44 A6	2m pale rose	.40	.25
45 A6	4m brt yellowish green	.70	.20
46 A6	6m brown lilac	.70	.40
47 A6	8m ultra	1.75	1.00
48 A6	1c gray green	2.75	1.00
49 A6	2c lake	3.50	2.75

50	A6	3c dark brown	7.50	4.50
51	A6	5c grayish ultra	2.50	.30
52	A6	8c brown	2.50	1.25
53	A6	10c slate	22.50	7.00
54	A6	20c olive bister	27.50	12.50
		Nos. 42-54 (13)	72.80	31.55

Alfonso XII — A7

Alfonso XIII — A8

1882-86

55	A7	½m rose	.25	.15
a.		½m salmon rose	.50	.30
56	A7	½m lake ('84)	.50	.40
57	A7	1m pale lake	.80	1.00
58	A7	1m brt rose ('84)	.25	.15
59	A7	2m violet	.25	.15
60	A7	4m brown lilac	.25	.15
61	A7	6m brown	.40	.15
62	A7	8m yellow green	.40	.15
63	A7	1c gray green	.25	.15
64	A7	2c rose	1.00	.15
65	A7	3c yellow	3.50	2.00
a.		Cliché of 8c in plate of 3c	110.00	
66	A7	3c yellow brn ('84)	3.50	.75
a.		Cliché of 8c in plate of 3c	22.50	
67	A7	5c gray blue	13.00	1.10
68	A7	5c gray bl, 1st retouch ('84)	13.00	2.50
69	A7	5c gray bl, 2nd retouch ('86)	100.00	5.00
70	A7	8c gray brown	3.25	.15
71	A7	10c dark green	3.25	.25
72	A7	20c gray lilac	4.75	.25
a.		20c olive brown (error)	*100.00*	
73	A7	40c blue	35.00	13.00
74	A7	80c olive bister	50.00	18.00
		Nos. 55-74 (20)	233.60	45.60

For differences between the original and the retouched stamps see note on the 1883-86 issue of Cuba.

1890-97

75	A8	½m black	.25	.15
76	A8	½m olive gray ('92)	.15	.15
77	A8	½m red brn ('94)	.15	.15
78	A8	½m dull vio ('96)	.20	.15
79	A8	1m emerald	.25	.15
80	A8	1m dk violet ('92)	.15	.15
81	A8	1m ultra ('94)	.15	.15
82	A8	1m dp brown ('96)	.20	.15
83	A8	2m lilac rose	.20	.15
84	A8	2m violet brn ('92)	.15	.15
85	A8	2m red orange ('94)	.15	.15
86	A8	2m yellow grn ('96)	.20	.15
87	A8	4m dk olive grn	10.00	5.00
88	A8	4m ultra ('92)	.15	.15
89	A8	4m yellow brn ('94)	.15	.15
90	A8	4m blue grn ('96)	.90	.30
91	A8	6m dk brown	32.50	13.00
92	A8	6m pale rose ('92)	.15	.15
93	A8	8m olive bister	25.00	19.00
94	A8	8m yellow grn ('92)	.15	.15
95	A8	1c yellow brown	.25	.15
96	A8	1c blue grn ('91)	.50	.15
97	A8	1c violet brn ('94)	5.25	.40
98	A8	1c claret ('96)	.60	.15
99	A8	2c brownish violet	.90	.75
100	A8	2c red brown ('92)	.85	.15
101	A8	2c lilac ('94)	2.00	.40
102	A8	2c orange brn ('96)	.60	.15
103	A8	3c slate blue	6.50	.90
104	A8	3c orange ('92)	.80	.15
105	A8	3c ol gray ('94)	5.25	.40
106	A8	3c blue ('96)	19.00	.30
107	A8	3c claret brn ('97)	.25	.15
108	A8	4c slate bl ('94)	1.25	.40
109	A8	4c gray brn ('96)	.65	.15
110	A8	5c brown violet	11.00	.40
111	A8	5c yellow grn ('94)	5.00	1.00
112	A8	5c blue green ('92)	.80	.15
113	A8	5c blue ('96)	.25	.15
114	A8	6c orange ('94)	.40	.15
115	A8	6c violet ('96)	.30	.15
116	A8	8c ultra	14.00	1.50
117	A8	8c gray brown ('92)	.15	.15
118	A8	8c dull vio ('94)	11.00	4.25
119	A8	8c car rose ('96)	2.50	1.25
120	A8	10c rose	4.00	1.00
a.		10c salmon rose	10.00	2.25
121	A8	10c lilac rose ('92)	1.25	.30
122	A8	20c red orange	4.50	4.00
123	A8	20c lilac ('92)	2.00	.50
124	A8	20c car rose ('94)	1.40	.40
125	A8	20c olive gray ('96)	6.00	1.25
126	A8	40c orange	100.00	42.50
127	A8	40c slate blue ('92)	5.00	3.50
128	A8	40c claret ('94)	6.50	11.00
129	A8	40c salmon ('96)	6.00	1.40
130	A8	80c yellow green	400.00	150.00
131	A8	80c orange ('92)	12.50	10.00
132	A8	80c black ('97)	24.00	20.00

Imperforates of type A8 were not issued and are variously considered to be proofs or printer's waste.

For overprints see Nos. 154A-170, MR1-MR13.

Landing of Columbus on Puerto Rico
A9

Alfonso XIII
A10

1893 Litho. *Perf. 12*

133	A9	3c dark green	165.00	50.00

400th anniversary, landing of Columbus on Puerto Rico. Counterfeits exist.

1898 Typo.

135	A10	1m orange brown	.15	.15
136	A10	2m orange brown	.15	.15
137	A10	3m orange brown	.15	.15
138	A10	4m orange brown	1.25	.50
139	A10	5m orange brown	.15	.15
140	A10	1c black violet	.15	.15
a.		Tête bêche pair	*900.00*	
141	A10	2c dk blue green	.15	.15
142	A10	3c dk brown	.15	.15
143	A10	4c orange	1.25	1.00
144	A10	5c brt rose	.15	.15
145	A10	6c dark blue	.50	.15
146	A10	8c gray brown	.15	.15
147	A10	10c vermilion	.15	.15
148	A10	15c dull olive grn	.15	.15
149	A10	20c maroon	1.50	.45
150	A10	40c violet	1.10	1.25
151	A10	60c black	1.10	1.25
152	A10	80c red brown	4.00	4.50
153	A10	1p yellow green	9.00	9.00
154	A10	2p slate blue	21.00	12.50
		Nos. 135-154 (20)	42.35	32.25

Nos. 135-154 exist imperf. Value, set $900.

Stamps of 1890-97 Handstamped in Rose or Purple

Habilitado
PARA
1898 y 99.

1898

154A	A8	½m dull violet	14.00	8.00
155	A8	1m deep brown	1.25	1.25
156	A8	2m yellow green	.35	.35
157	A8	4m blue green	.35	.35
158	A8	1c claret	3.50	3.50
159	A8	2c orange brown	.50	.70
160	A8	3c blue	30.00	13.00
161	A8	3c claret brn	2.50	2.50
162	A8	4c gray brn	.60	.60
163	A8	4c slate blue	17.50	12.00
164	A8	5c yellow grn	8.00	6.25
165	A8	5c blue	.60	.60
166	A8	6c violet	.60	.40
167	A8	8c car rose (P)	1.00	.75
a.		Rose overprint	16.00	16.00
168	A8	20c olive gray	1.00	1.00
169	A8	40c salmon	2.50	2.50
170	A8	80c black	30.00	20.00
		Nos. 154A-170 (17)	114.25	73.75

As usual with handstamps there are many inverted, double and similar varieties. Counterfeits of Nos. 154A-170 abound.

Issued under US Administration

A11

A12

Ponce Issue

1898 Unwmk. *Imperf.*

200	A11	5c vio, *yelsh*	*7,000.*	

The only way No. 200 is known used is handstamped on envelopes. Both unused stamps and used envelopes have a violet control mark. Counterfeits exist of Nos. 200-201.

Coamo Issue

1898 Unwmk. *Imperf.*

201	A12	5c black	650.00	1,050.

There are ten varieties in the setting (See the Scott United States Specialized Catalogue). The stamps bear the control mark "F. Santiago" in violet.

United States Nos. 279, 267, 281, 272 and 282C Overprinted in Black at 36 degree angle

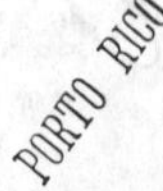

1899 Wmk. 191 *Perf. 12*

210	A87	1c yellow green	5.00	1.40
a.		Ovpt. at 25 degree angle	7.50	2.25
211	A88	2c car, type III	4.25	1.25
a.		Ovpt. at 25 degree angle	5.50	2.25
212	A91	5c blue	9.00	2.50
213	A93	8c violet brown	27.50	17.50
a.		Ovpt. at 25 degree angle	32.50	18.50
c.		"PORTO RIC"	125.00	110.00
214	A94	10c brown, type I	17.50	6.00
		Nos. 210-214 (5)	63.25	28.65

Misspellings of the overprint, actually broken letters (PORTO RICU, PORTU RICO, FORTO RICO), are found on 1c, 2c, 8c and 10c.

United States Nos. 279 and 267 Overprinted Diagonally in Black

1900

215	A87	1c yellow green	6.00	1.40
216	A88	2c carmine	4.75	1.25
a.		2c orange red	5.25	1.25
b.		Inverted overprint		*8,250.*

Stamps of Puerto Rico were replaced by those of the United States.

POSTAGE DUE STAMPS

United States Nos. J38, J39 and J42 Overprinted in Black at 36 degree angle

1899 Wmk. 191 *Perf. 12*

J1	D2	1c deep claret	22.50	5.50
a.		Overprint at 25 degree angle	22.50	7.50
J2	D2	2c deep claret	11.00	6.00
a.		Overprint at 25 degree angle	15.00	7.00
J3	D2	10c deep claret	160.00	60.00
a.		Overprint at 25 degree angle	180.00	85.00
		Nos. J1-J3 (3)	193.50	71.50

WAR TAX STAMPS

Stamps of 1890-94 Overprinted or Surcharged by Handstamp

IMPUESTO
DE GUERRA

1898 Unwmk. *Perf. 14*

Purple Overprint or Surcharge

MR1	A8	1c yellow brn	5.50	*4.00*
MR2	A8	2c on 2m orange	2.50	2.00
MR3	A8	2c on 5c blue grn	3.25	2.50
MR4	A8	2c dark violet	.65	.65
MR5	A8	2c lilac	.60	.60
MR6	A8	2c red brown	.30	.20
MR7	A8	5c blue green	1.25	1.25
MR8	A8	5c on 5c bl grn	6.00	4.00

Rose Surcharge

MR9	A8	2c on 2m orange	1.25	1.25
MR10	A8	5c on 1m dk vio	.20	.20
MR11	A8	5c on 1m dl bl	.55	.55

Magenta Surcharge

MR12	A8	5c on 1m dk vio	.30	.20
MR13	A8	5c on 1m dl bl	2.00	2.00
		Nos. MR1-MR13 (13)	24.35	19.40

Nos. MR2-MR13 were issued as War Tax Stamps (2c on letters or sealed mail; 5c on telegrams) but, during the early days of the American occupation, they were accepted for ordinary postage.

Double, inverted and similar varieties of overprints are numerous in this issue.

Counterfeit overprints exist.

QATAR

'kät–ər

LOCATION — A peninsula in eastern Arabia

GOVT. — Independent state

AREA — 4,575 sq. mi.

POP. — 260,000 (est. 1982)

CAPITAL — Doha

Qatar was a British protected sheikdom until Sept. 1, 1971, when it declared its independence. Stamps of Muscat were used until 1957.

100 Naye Paise = 1 Rupee

100 Dirhams = 1 Riyal (1967)

Catalogue values for all unused stamps in this country are for Never Hinged items.

Great Britain Nos. 317-325, 328, 332-333 and 309-311 Surcharged "QATAR" and New Value in Black

Perf. 14½x14

1957, Apr. 1 Photo. Wmk. 308

1	A129	1np on 5p lt brn	.15	.1
2	A126	3np on ½p red org	.15	.1
3	A126	6np on 1p ultra	.15	.1
4	A126	9np on 1½p grn	.15	.1
5	A126	12np on 2p red brn	.15	.1
6	A127	15np on 2½p scarlet	.25	.1
7	A127	20np on 3p dk pur	.25	.1
8	A128	25np on 4p ultra	.40	.3
9	A129	40np on 6p lil rose	.40	.3
10	A130	50np on 9p dp ol grn	.70	.4
11	A132	75np on 1sh3p dk grn	1.75	.7
12	A131	1ru on 1sh6p dk bl	2.50	.7

Engr. *Perf. 11x1*

13	A133	2ru on 2sh6p dk brn	4.00	1.5
14	A133	5ru on 5sh crimson	10.00	5.0
15	A133	10ru on 10sh brt ultra	20.00	10.0
		Nos. 1-15 (15)	41.00	20.0

Both typeset and stereotyped overprints were used on Nos. 13-15. The typeset have bars close together and thick, bold letters. The stereotyped have bars wider apart and thinner letters.

Great Britain Nos. 334-336 Surcharged "QATAR," New Value and Square of Dots in Black

Perf. 14½x14

1957, Aug. 1 Photo. Wmk. 308

16	A138	15np on 2½p scarlet	.45	.3
17	A138	25np on 4p ultra	.90	.7
18	A138	75np on 1sh3p dk grn	1.40	1.2
		Nos. 16-18 (3)	2.75	2.3

50th anniv. of the Boy Scout movement and the World Scout Jubilee Jamboree, Aug. 1-12.

Great Britain Nos. 353-358, 362 Surcharged "QATAR" and New Value

1960 Wmk. 322 *Perf. 14½x14*

19	A126	3np on ½p red org	.90	2.0
20	A126	6np on 1p ultra	1.50	3.0
21	A126	9np on 1½p grn	1.25	1.2
22	A126	12np on 2p red brn	6.00	10.0
23	A127	15np on 2½p scar	.40	.3
24	A127	20np on 3p dk pur	.40	.3
25	A129	40np on 6p lil rose	1.00	.6
		Nos. 19-25 (7)	11.45	17.5

Sheik Ahmad bin Ali al Thani — A1

Peregrine Falcon — A2

Oil Derrick — A3

Designs: 75np, Dhow. 5r, 10r, Mosque.

Perf. 14½

1961, Sept. 2 Unwmk. Photo

26	A1	5np rose carmine	.15	.1
27	A1	15np brown black	.15	.1
28	A1	20np claret	.15	.1
29	A1	30np deep green	.22	.1
30	A2	40np red	.35	.1
31	A2	50np sepia	.45	.3
32	A2	75np ultra	.70	.4

Engr. *Perf. 13*

33 A3 1ru rose red .80 .45
34 A3 2ru blue 1.65 1.10
35 A3 5ru green 4.00 2.75
36 A3 10ru black 8.50 5.00
Nos. 26-36 (11) 17.12 10.85

Nos. 31-32, 34-36 Overprinted or Surcharged

1964, Oct. 25 Photo. *Perf. 14½*

37 A2 50np sepia .65 .90
38 A2 75np ultra .90 1.40

Engr. *Perf. 13*

39 A3 1ru on 10r black 1.75 1.40
40 A3 2ru blue 4.25 2.75
41 A3 5ru green 10.00 6.25
Nos. 37-41 (5) 17.55 12.70

18th Olympic Games, Tokyo, Oct. 10-25.
For surcharges see Nos. 110-110D.

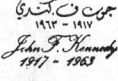

Nos. 31-32, 34-36 with Typographed Overprint or Surcharge

1964, Nov. 22 Photo. *Perf. 14½*

42 A2 50np sepia .70 .50
43 A2 75np ultra .90 .75

Engr. *Perf. 13*

44 A3 1ru on 10ru blk 1.75 1.50
45 A3 2ru blue 4.25 4.00
46 A3 5ru green 10.00 8.25
Nos. 42-46 (5) 17.60 15.00

Pres. John F. Kennedy (1917-63).
For surcharges see Nos. 111-111D.

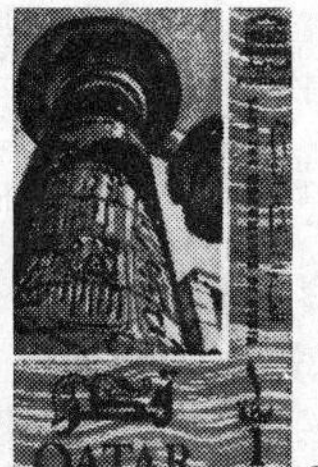

Column — A4

Designs: 2np, 1.50r, Isis Temple and Colonnade, Philae. 3np, 1r, Trajan's kiosk, Philae.

Perf. 14½x14

1965, Jan. 17 Photo. Unwmk.

47 A4 1np multicolored .75 .15
48 A4 2np multicolored .75 .15
49 A4 3np multicolored .75 .15
50 A4 1ru multicolored 1.10 .40
51 A4 1.50ru multicolored 2.25 .60
52 A4 2ru multicolored .75 .50
Nos. 47-52 (6) 6.35
Set value 1.65

UNESCO world campaign to save historic monuments in Nubia.

Qatar Scout Emblem, Tents and Sheik Ahmad — A5

Scouts Saluting and Sheik Ahmad — A6

Designs: 1np, 4np, Qatar scout emblem.

Perf. 14 (A5), 14½x14 (A6)

1965, May 22 Photo. Unwmk.

53 A5 1np ol grn & dk red brn .20 .15
54 A5 2np sal & dk vio bl .20 .15
55 A5 3np dk vio bl & grn .20 .15
56 A5 4np bl & dk red brn .20 .15
57 A5 5np dk vio bl & grnsh bl .20 .15
58 A6 30np multi .65 .45
59 A6 40np multi .80 .60
60 A6 1ru multi 2.00 1.25
Nos. 53-60 (8) 4.45
Set value 2.50

Issued to honor the Qatar Boy Scouts. Perf. and imperf. souvenir sheets contain one each of Nos. 58-60 with red brown marginal inscription. Size: 108x76mm.
For surcharges see Nos. 113-113G.

Eiffel Tower, Telstar, ITU Emblem and "Qatar" in Morse Code — A7

Designs: 2np, 1ru, Tokyo Olympic Games emblem and Syncom III. 3np, 40np, Radar tracking station and Relay satellite. 4np, 50np, Post Office Tower, London, and Echo II, Syncom III, Telstar and Relay satellites around globe.

Perf. 13½x14

1965, Oct. 16 Photo. Unwmk.

61 A7 1np dk bl & red brn .25 .15
62 A7 2np bl & dk red brn .25 .15
63 A7 3np dp yel grn & brt pur .25 .15
64 A7 4np org brn & brt bl .25 .15
65 A7 5np dl vio & dk ol bis .25 .15
66 A7 40np dk car rose & blk .65 .40
67 A7 50np sl grn & bis .85 .50
68 A7 1ru emer & car 1.65 1.00
a. Souvenir sheet of 2, #67-68 5.00 3.50
Nos. 61-68 (8) 4.40
Set value 2.15

Cent. of the ITU. #68a also exists imperf.
For overprints and surcharges see Nos. 91-98, 114-114G, 117-117G.

Triggerfish — A8

Various Fish, including: 2np, 50np, Clown grunt. 2np, 10ru, Saddleback butterflyfish. 4np, 5ru, Butterflyfish. 15np, 3ru, Paradisefish. 20np, 1ru, Rio Grande perch. 75np, Triggerfish.

1965, Oct. 18 *Perf. 14x14½*

69 A8 1np multi & black .15 .15
70 A8 2np multi & black .15 .15
71 A8 3np multi & black .15 .15
72 A8 4np multi & black .15 .15
73 A8 5np multi & black .20 .15
74 A8 15np multi & black .50 .15
75 A8 20np multi & black .55 .15
76 A8 30np multi & black .65 .22
77 A8 40np multi & black .90 .25
78 A8 50np multi & gold 1.25 .35
79 A8 75np multi & gold 2.00 .50
80 A8 1ru multi & gold 2.25 .65
81 A8 2ru multi & gold 5.25 1.25
82 A8 3ru multi & gold 7.75 1.90
83 A8 4ru multi & gold 10.00 2.50
84 A8 5ru multi & gold 14.00 3.50
85 A8 10ru multi & gold 30.00 6.50
Nos. 69-85 (17) 75.90 18.67

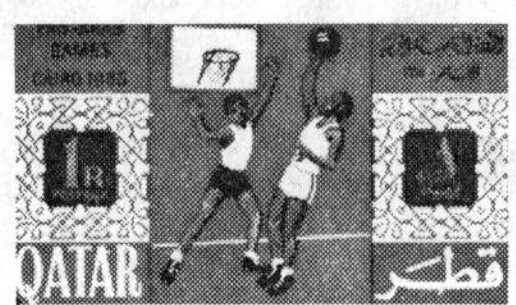

Basketball — A9

Sports: No. 87, Horse jumping. No. 88, Running. No. 89, Soccer. No. 90, Weight lifting.

1966, Jan. 10 Photo. *Perf. 11½*

Granite Paper

86 A9 1ru gray, blk & dk red 1.00 .60
87 A9 1ru brn & ol grn 1.00 .60
88 A9 1ru dull rose & blue 1.00 .60
89 A9 1ru grn & blk 1.00 .60
90 A9 1ru bl & brn 1.00 .60
Nos. 86-90 (5) 5.00 3.00

4th Pan Arab Games, Cairo, Sept. 2-11. Nos. 86-90 are printed in one sheet of 25 in horizontal rows of five.

Nos. 61-68 Overprinted in Black

1966, Feb. 9 Photo. *Perf. 13½x14*

91 A7 1np dk bl & red brn .18 .15
92 A7 2np bl & dk red brn .18 .15
93 A7 3np dp yel grn & brt pur .18 .15
94 A7 4np org brn & brt bl .18 .15
95 A7 5np dl vio & dk ol bis .18 .15
96 A7 40np dk car rose & blk .65 .25
97 A7 50np slate grn & bis .75 .30
98 A7 1ru emer & car 1.50 .60
Nos. 91-98 (8) 3.80
Set value 1.40

Issued to commemorate the rendezvous in space of Gemini 6 and 7, Dec. 15, 1965.
Exist overprinted in blue.
For surcharges see Nos. 117-117G.

Sheik Ahmad A9a

Designs: 3np, 5np, 40np, 80np, 2ru, 10ru, Reverse of coin with Arabic inscription.

Litho. & Embossed Gold or Silver Foil

1966, Feb. 24 *Imperf.*

99 A9a 1np ol & lil (S)
99A A9a 3np blk & org (S)
99B A9a 4np pur & red
99C A9a 5np brt grn & red brn

Diameter: 55mm

99D A9a 10np brn & brt vio (S)
99E A9a 40np org red & bl (S)
99F A9a 70np Prus bl & bl vio
99G A9a 80np car & grn

Diameter: 65mm

99H A9a 1ru red vio & blk (S)
99J A9a 2ru bl grn & cl (S)
99K A9a 5ru red lil & ver
99L A9a 10ru bl vio & brn car

John F. Kennedy, UN Headquarters, NY, and ICY Emblem — A10

Designs (ICY emblem and): #100, UN emblem. #100B, Dag Hammarskjold and UN General Assembly. #100C, Jawaharlal Nehru and dove.

1966, Mar. 8 *Perf. 11½*

Granite Paper

100 A10 40np brt bl, vio bl & red brn 1.50 1.00
100A A10 40np brt grn, vio & brn 1.50 1.00
100B A10 40np red brn, brt bl & blk 1.50 1.00
100C A10 40np dk vio & brt grn 1.50 1.00
d. Block of 4, #100-100C 6.00 4.00

UN Intl. Cooperation Year, 1965. Printed in sheets of 16 + 9 lables in shape of a cross.
An imperf. souvenir sheet of 4 contains one each of Nos. 100-100C.

Nos. 100-100C Overprinted in Black

U.N. 20th ANNIVERSARY

Telstar, Rocket — A10a

Designs: No. 101, John F. Kennedy, "In Memoriam / John F. Kennedy / 1917-1963." No. 101A, Olive branches, Churchill quote and "In Memoriam / 1874-1965." No. 101B, like #101 portrait facing left, no overprint. No. 101C, Eternal flame, Arabic inscription.

1966, Mar. 8

Granite Paper

101 A10a 5np bl grn, car & blk
101A A10a 5np bl grn, rose & blk
101B A10a 5np bl grn & blk
101C A10a 5np bl grn, rose & blk
101D A10a 5np bl brn, car & blk
101E A10 40np on No. 100
101F A10 40np on No. 100A
101G A10 40np on No. 100B
101H A10 40np on No. 100C

Nos. 101-101H were made from the sheets of Nos. 100-100C. The 4 outer labels and the center label were surcharged to create Nos. 101-101D. The other 4 labels were overprinted but have no denomination. Exists with red overprints. The imperf. souvenir sheet exists with overprint in margin:"IN VICTORY, / MAGNAMIMITY. / IN PEACE / GOODWILL / WINSTON CHURCHILL." The margin overprint overlaps onto No. 101A on upper left quarter of stamp.
exist imperf.
For surcharges see Nos. 118-118C.

John F. Kennedy (1917-1963) — A10b

Kennedy and: #102c, 10np, #102f, 70np, NYC. #102d, 30np, #102g, 80np, Rocket lifting off at Cape Kennedy. #102e, 60np, #102h, 1ru, Statue of Liberty. No. 102B, Statue of Liberty.

1966, July 18 *Perf. 13½*

102 A10b Strip of 3, #c.-e.
102A A10b Strip of 3, #f.-h.

Souvenir Sheet

Imperf

102B A10b 50np multicolored

Nos. 102-102A exist imperf. For surcharges see Nos. 119-119B.

1968 Summer Olympics, Mexico City A10c

Designs: #103c, 1np, #103f, 70np, #103B, Equestrian. #103d, 4np, #103g, 80np, Running. #103e, 5np, #103h, 90np, Javelin.

1966, July 20 *Perf. 13½*

103 A10c Strip of 3, #c.-e.
103A A10c Strip of 3, #f.-h.

Souvenir Sheet

Imperf

103B A10c 50np multicolored

Nos. 103-103A exist imperf. For surcharges see Nos. 120-120B.

A10d

American Astronauts — A10e

Astronaut and space vehicle: No. 104c, 5np, James A. Lovell. d, 10np, Thomas P. Stafford. e, 15np, Alan B. Shepard.

No. 104f, 20np, John H. Glenn. g, 30np, M. Scott Carpenter. h, 40np, Walter M. Schirra. i, 50np, Virgil I. Grissom. j, 60np, L. Gordon Cooper, Jr.

No. 104B, Stafford, Schirra, Frank Borman, Lovell and diagram of space rendezvous.

1966, Aug. 20 *Perf. 12*

104 A10d Strip of 3, #c.-e.
104A A10e Strip of 5, #f.-j.

Souvenir Sheet

Imperf

Size: 115x75mm

104B A10e 50np multicolored

The name of James A. Lovell is spelled "Lovel" on No. 104c. Nos. 104-104A exist imperf. For surcharges see Nos. 121-121B.

1966 World Cup Soccer Championships, London
A10h A10i

Designs: 1np-4np, Jules Rimet Cup. 60np, #107H, Hands holding Cup, soccer ball. 70np, #107J, Cup, soccer ball. 80np, #107K, Soccer players, ball. 90np, #107L, Wembley Stadium.

1966, Nov. 27 **Photo.** *Perf. 13½*

107 A10h 1np blue
107A A10h 2np blue
107B A10h 3np blue
107C A10h 4np blue
m. Block of 4, #107-107C
107D A10i 60np multicolored
107E A10i 70np multicolored
107F A10i 80np multicolored
107G A10i 90np multicolored
n. Block of 4, #107D-107G

Souvenir Sheets

Imperf

107H A10i 25np multicolored
107J A10i 25np multicolored
107K A10i 25np multicolored
107L A10i 25np multicolored

Nos. 107-107C are airmail. Issued in sheets of 36 containing 5 #107m and 4 #107n. Nos. 107-107G exist imperf.

Nos. 37-41 Surcharged with New Currency in Gray or Red

1966 **Photo.** *Perf. 14½*

110 A2 50d on 50np #37 (G)
110A A2 75d on 75np #38

Engr.

Perf. 13

110B A3 1r on 1ru on 10ru #39
110C A3 2r on 2ru #40
110D A3 5r on 5ru #41

Nos. 42-46 Surcharged with New Currency in Gray or Red

1966 **Photo.** *Perf. 14½*

111 A2 50d on 50np #42 (G)
111A A2 75d on 75np #43

Engr.

Perf. 13

111B A3 1r on 1ru on 10ru #44
111C A3 2r on 2ru #45
111D A3 5r on 5ru #46

Nos. 53-60 Surcharged with New Currency

Perf. 14 (A5), 14½x14 (A6)

1966 **Photo.**

113 A5 1d on 1np #53
113A A5 2d on 2np #54
113B A5 3d on 3np #55
113C A5 4d on 4np #56
113D A5 5d on 5np #57
113E A6 30d on 30np #58
113F A6 40d on 40np #59
113G A6 1r on 1ru #60

Exist imperf. Perf and imperf souvenir sheets contain one each of #113E-113G surcharged with new currency.

Nos. 61-68 Surcharged with New Currency in Black or Red

1966 *Perf. 13½x14*

114 A7 1d on 1np #61
114A A7 2d on 2np #62
114B A7 3d on 3np #63
114C A7 4d on 4np #64
114D A7 5d on 5np #65
114E A7 40d on 40np #66
114F A7 50d on 50np #67
114G A7 1r on 1ru #68

Exist imperf.

Nos. 91-95 Surcharged with New Currency

1966 **Photo.** *Perf. 13½x14*

117 A7 1d on 1np #91
117A A7 2d on 2np #92
117B A7 3d on 3np #93
117C A7 4d on 4np #94
117D A7 5d on 5np #95

Numbers have been reserved for additional values in this set.

Nos. 101E-101H with Red Overprint Surcharged with New Currency

1966 **Photo.** *Perf. 11½*

Granite Paper

118 A10a 40d on 40np #101E
118A A10a 40d on 40np #101F
118B A10a 40d on 40np #101G
118C A10a 40d on 40np #101H
d. Block of 4, #118-118C

Exist imperf. Imperf. souvenir sheets mentioned after Nos. 100C, 101H exist surcharged with new currency.

Nos. 102-102B Surcharged with New Currency

1966 *Perf. 13½*

119 Strip of 3
c. A10b 10d on 10np #102c
d. A10b 30d on 30np #102d
e. A10b 60d on 60np #102e
119A Strip of 3
f. A10b 70d on 70np #102f
g. A10b 80d on 80np #102g
h. A10b 1r on 1ru #102h

Souvenir Sheet

Imperf

119B A10b 50d on 50np #102B

Nos. 119-119A exist imperf.

Nos. 103-103B Surcharged with New Currency

1966 *Perf. 13½*

120 Strip of 3
c. A10c 1d on 1np #103c
d. A10c 4d on 4np #103d
e. A10c 5d on 5np #103e
120A Strip of 3
f. A10c 70d on 70np #103f
g. A10c 80d on 80np #103g
h. A10c 90d on 90np #103h

Souvenir Sheet

Imperf

120B A10c 50d on 50np #103

Nos. 120-120 exist imperf.

Nos. 104-104B Surcharged with New Currency

1966 *Perf. 12*

121 Strip of 3
c. A10d 5d on 5np #104c
d. A10d 10d on 10np #104d
e. A10d 15d on 15np #104e
121A Strip of 5
f. A10e 20d on 20np #104f
g. A10e 30d on 30np #104g
h. A10e 40d on 40np #104h
i. A10e 50d on 50np #104i
j. A10e 60d on 60np #104j

Souvenir Sheet

Imperf

121B A10e 50d on 50np #104B

Nos. 121-121A printed se-tenant with five labels showing Arabic inscription.

Arab Postal Union Emblem
A11

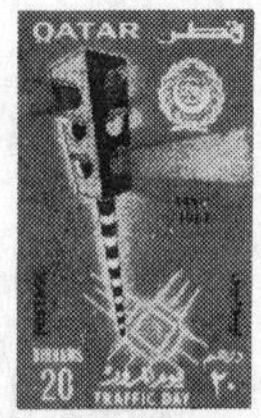

Traffic Light and Intersection
A12

Apollo Project
A11a

1967, Apr. 15 **Photo.** *Perf. 11x11½*

122 A11 70d magenta & sepia 1.40 .30
122A A11 80d dull blue & sepia 1.90 .35

Qatar's joining the Arab Postal Union.

1967, May 1 *Perf. 12½*

Designs: 5d, 70d, Two astronauts on Moon. 10d, 80d, Command and lunar modules in lunar orbit. 20d, 1r, Lunar module on Moon. 30d, 1.20r, Lunar module ascending from Moon. 40d, 2r, Saturn 5 rocket.

123 A11a 5d multicolored
123A A11a 10d multicolored
123B A11a 20d multicolored
123C A11a 30d multicolored
123D A11a 40d multicolored
123E A11a 70d multicolored
123F A11a 80d multicolored
123G A11a 1r multicolored
123H A11a 1.20r multicolored
123J A11a 2r multicolored

#123J exists in an imperf. souvenir sheet of one.

1967, May 24 **Litho.** *Perf. 13½*

124 A12 20d vio & multi .30 .15
124A A12 30d multi .50 .15
124B A12 50d multi .80 .20
124C A12 1r ultra & multi 1.65 .40
Nos. 124-124C (4) 3.25 .90

Issued for Traffic Day.

Boy Scouts and Sheik Ahmad — A13

Designs: 1d, First Boy Scout camp, Brownsea Island, 1907, and tents, Idaho, US, 1967. 2d, Lord Baden-Powell. 5d, Boy Scout canoeing. 15d, Swimming. 75d, Mountain climbing. 2r, Boy Scout saluting flag and emblem of 12th World Jamboree. 1d and 2d lack head of Sheik Ahmad.

1967, Sept. 15 **Litho.** *Perf. 11½x11*

125 A13 1d multicolored .35 .15
125A A13 2d buff & multi .35 .15

Litho. and Engr.

125B A13 3d rose & multi .35 .15
125C A13 5d lilac & multi .35 .15
125D A13 15d multicolored .55 .25
125E A13 75d green & multi 1.10 .80
125F A13 2r sepia & multi 5.00 3.25
Nos. 125-125F (7) 8.05 4.90

Nos. 125-125A for 60th anniv. of the Boy Scouts, Nos. 125B-125F for 12th Boy Scout World Jamboree, Farragut State Park, Idaho, Aug. 1-9.

Viking Ship (from Bayeux Tapestry)
A14

Famous Ships: 2d, Santa Maria (Columbus). 3d, San Gabriel (Vasco da Gama). 75d, Victoria (Ferdinand Magellan). 1r, Golden Hind (Sir Francis Drake). 2r, Gipsy Moth IV (Sir Francis Chichester).

1967, Nov. 27 **Litho.** *Perf. 13½*

126 A14 1d org & multi .25 .15
126A A14 2d lt bl, tan & blk .25 .15
126B A14 3d lt bl & multi .25 .15
126C A14 75d fawn & multi .80 .60
126D A14 1r gray, yel grn & red 1.50 1.25
126E A14 2r multi 3.50 2.50
Nos. 126-126E (6) 6.55 4.80

Professional Letter Writer — A15

Designs: 2d, Carrier pigeon and man releasing pigeon, vert. 3d, Postrider. 60d, Mail transport by rowboat, vert. 1.25r, Mailman riding camel, jet plane and modern buildings. 2r, Qatar No. 1, hand holding pen, paper, envelopes and inkwell.

1968, Feb. 14

127 A15 1d multicolored .25 .15
127A A15 2d multicolored .25 .15
127B A15 3d multicolored .25 .15
127C A15 60d multicolored 1.25 .70
127D A15 1.25r multicolored 2.50 1.40
127E A15 2r multicolored 4.25 2.25
Nos. 127-127E (6) 8.75 4.80

Ten years of Qatar postal service.

Human Rights Flame and Barbed Wire
A16

2d, Arab refugee family leaving concentration camp. 3d, Scales of Justice. 60d, Hands opening gates to the sun. 1.25r, Family and sun, vert. 2r, Stylized family groups.

1968, Apr. 10

128 A16 1d gray & multi .20 .15
129 A16 2d multicolored .20 .15
130 A16 3d brt grn, org & blk .20 .15
131 A16 60d org, brn & blk 1.00 .70
132 A16 1.25r brt grn, blk & yel 1.75 1.40
133 A16 2r multicolored 3.00 2.25
Nos. 128-133 (6) 6.35 4.80

International Human Rights Year.

Nurse Attending Premature Baby
A17

Designs (WHO Emblem and): 2d, Operating room. 3d, Dentist. 60d, X-ray examination. 1.25r, Medical laboratory. 2r, State Hospital.

1968, June 20

134 A17 1d multi .20 .15
135 A17 2d multi .20 .15
136 A17 3d multi .20 .15
137 A17 60d multi 1.00 .70
138 A17 1.25r multi 2.00 1.40
139 A17 2r multi 3.50 2.25
Nos. 134-139 (6) 7.10 4.80

20th anniv. of the World Health Organization.

Olympic Rings and Gymnast A18

Designs (Olympic Rings and): 1d, Discobolus and view of Mexico City. 2d, Runner and flaming torch. 60d, Weight lifting and torch. 1.25r, Olympic flame as a mosaic, vert. 2r, Mythological bird.

1968, Aug. 24

140 A18 1d multicolored .16 .15
141 A18 2d red yel & dk grn .16 .15
142 A18 3d dk brn gray grn & ocher .16 .15
143 A18 60d org brn pink & bl grn .70 .52
144 A18 1.25r multicolored 1.40 1.00
145 A18 2r yellow & multi 2.50 1.65
Nos. 140-145 (6) 5.08 3.62

Issued to publicize the 19th Olympic Games, Mexico City, Oct. 12-27.

Sheik Ahmad bin Ali al Thani
A19 A21

Dhow A20

Designs: 40d, Desalination plant. 60d, Loading platform and oil tanker. 70d, Qatar Mosque. 1r, Clock Tower, Market Place, Doha. 1.25r, Doha Fort. 1.50r, Falcon.

1968 Litho. *Perf. 13½*

146 A19 5d blue & green .15 .15
147 A19 10d brt bl & red brn .18 .15
148 A19 20d blk & vermilion .25 .15
149 A19 25d brt mag & brt grn .35 .15

Lithographed and Engraved

Perf. 13

150 A20 35d grn & brt pink .55 .30
151 A20 40d pur, lt bl & org .55 .35
152 A20 60d lt bl, brn & lil .80 .50
153 A20 70d blk, lt bl & brt grn 1.00 .60
154 A20 1r vio bl, yel & brt grn 1.40 .90
155 A20 1.25r ind, brt bl & ocher 1.90 1.10
156 A20 1.50r lt bl, dk grn & rose lil 2.00 1.25

Perf. 11½

157 A21 2r brn, ocher & bl gray 2.25 1.75
158 A21 5r grn, lt grn & pur 6.50 4.50
159 A21 10r ultra, lt bl & sep 19.00 9.00
Nos. 146-159 (14) 36.88 20.85

UN Headquarters, NY, and Flags — A22

1d, Flags. 4d, World map and dove. 60d, Classroom. 1.50r, Farmers, wheat and tractor. 2r, Sec. Gen. U Thant and General Assembly Hall.

1968, Oct. 24 Litho. *Perf. 13½x13*

160 A22 1d multi .15 .15
161 A22 4d multi .15 .15
162 A22 5d multi .15 .15
163 A22 60d multi 1.10 .55
164 A22 1.50r multi 2.50 1.25
165 A22 2r multi 3.00 1.75
Nos. 160-165 (6) 7.05 4.00

United Nations Day, Oct. 24, 1968.

Fishing Vessel Ross Rayyan A23

Progress in Qatar: 4d, Elementary School and children playing. 5d, Doha Intl. Airport. 60d, Cement factory and road building. 1.50r, Power station. 2r, Housing development.

1969, Jan. 13

166 A23 1d brt bl & multi .15 .15
167 A23 4d green & multi .15 .15
168 A23 5d dl org & multi .18 .15
169 A23 60d lt brn & multi 1.10 .50
170 A23 1.50r brt lil & multi 2.50 1.25
171 A23 2r buff & multi 3.00 1.50
Nos. 166-171 (6) 7.08 3.70

Armored Cars A24

Designs: 2d, Traffic police. 3d, Military helicopter. 60d, Military band. 1.25r, Field gun. 2r, Mounted police.

1969, May 6 Litho. *Perf. 13½*

172 A24 1d multicolored .15 .15
173 A24 2d lt blue & multi .20 .15
174 A24 3d gray & multi .25 .15
175 A24 60d multicolored 1.00 .35
176 A24 1.25r multi 3.00 1.00
177 A24 2r blue & multi 4.50 1.50
Nos. 172-177 (6) 9.10 3.30

Issued to honor the public security forces.

Oil Tanker A25

2d, Research laboratory. 3d, Off-shore oil rig, helicopter. 60d, Oil rig, storage tanks. 1.50r, Oil refinery. 2r, Oil tankers, 1890-1968.

1969, July 4

178 A25 1d gray & multi .15 .15
179 A25 2d olive & multi .15 .15
180 A25 3d ultra & multi .20 .15
181 A25 60d lilac & multi 1.65 .80
182 A25 1.50r red brn & multi 4.00 2.00
183 A25 2r brown & multi 5.25 2.50
Nos. 178-183 (6) 11.40 5.75

Qatar oil industry.

Boy Scouts Building Boats A26

Designs: 2d, Scouts at work and 10 symbolic candles. 3d, Parade. 60d, Gate to camp interior. 1.25r, Main camp gate. 2r, Hoisting Qatar flag, and Sheik Ahmad.

1969, Sept. 18 Litho. *Perf. 13½x13*

184 A26 1d multicolored .15 .15
185 A26 2d multicolored .15 .15
186 A26 3d multicolored .15 .15
187 A26 60d multicolored 1.40 .70
a. Souvenir sheet of 4, #184-187 5.50 3.25
188 A26 1.25r multicolored 3.00 1.40
189 A26 2r multicolored 4.50 2.25
Nos. 184-189 (6) 9.35 4.80

10th Qatar Boy Scout Jamboree. No. 187a sold for 1r.

Neil A. Armstrong — A27

Designs: 2d, Col. Edwin E. Aldrin, Jr. 3d, Lt. Col. Michael Collins. 60d, Astronaut walking on moon. 1.25r, Blast-off from moon. 2r, Capsule and raft in Pacific, horiz.

1969, Dec. 6 *Perf. 13x13½, 13½x13*

190 A27 1d blue & multi .15 .15
191 A27 2d multicolored .15 .15
192 A27 3d grn & multi .30 .15
193 A27 60d multicolored 1.10 .55
194 A27 1.25r pur & multi 2.50 1.25
195 A27 2r multicolored 3.25 1.75
Nos. 190-195 (6) 7.45 4.00

See note after US No. C76.

UPU Emblem, Boeing Jet Loading in Qatar A28

2d, Transatlantic ocean liner. 3d, Mail truck and mail bags. 60d, Qatar Post Office. 1.25r, UPU Headquarters, Bern. 2r, UPU emblem.

1970, Jan. 31 Litho. *Perf. 13½x13*

196 A28 1d multi .15 .15
197 A28 2d multi .15 .15
198 A28 3d multi .25 .15
199 A28 60d multi 1.00 .60
200 A28 1.25r multi 2.00 1.25
201 A28 2r brt yel grn, blk & lt brn 3.25 2.25
Nos. 196-201 (6) 6.80 4.55

Qatar's admission to the UPU.

Map of Arab League Countries, Flag and Emblem A28a

1970, Mar. *Perf. 13x13½*

202 A28a 35d yellow & multi .60 .42
203 A28a 60d blue & multi .85 .55
204 A28a 1.25r multi 1.90 1.25
205 A28a 1.50r vio & multi 2.50 1.75
Nos. 202-205 (4) 5.85 3.97

25th anniversary of the Arab League.

VC10 Touching down for Landing A29

Designs: 2d, Hawk, and VC10 in flight. 3d, VC10 and airport. 60d, Map showing route Doha to London. 1.25r, VC10 over Gulftown. 2r, Tail of VC10 with emblem of Gulf Aviation.

1970, Apr. 5 *Perf. 13½x13*

206 A29 1d multi .15 .15
207 A29 2d multi .15 .15
208 A29 3d multi .15 .15
209 A29 60d multi 1.00 .70
210 A29 1.25r multi 1.90 1.40
211 A29 2r multi 3.50 2.00
Nos. 206-211 (6) 6.85 4.55

Issued to publicize the first flight to London from Doha by Gulf Aviation Company.

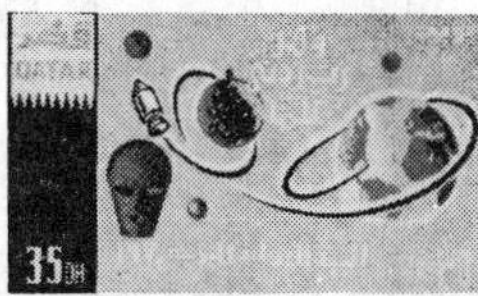

Education Year Emblem, Spaceship Trajectory, Koran Quotation — A30

1970, May 24 *Perf. 13x12½*

212 A30 35d blue & multi .90 .35
213 A30 60d blue & multi 1.90 .75

Intl. Education Year. Translation of Koran quotation: "And say, O God, give me more knowledge."

Flowers — A31

1970, July 2 *Perf. 13x13½*

214 A31 1d Freesia .25 .15
215 A31 2d Azalea .25 .15
216 A31 3d Ixia .30 .20
217 A31 60d Amaryllis 1.10 .70
218 A31 1.25r Cineraria 2.25 1.50
219 A31 2r Rose 3.75 2.00
Nos. 214-219 (6) 7.90 4.70

For surcharges see Nos. 287-289.

EXPO Emblem and Fisherman on Shikoku Beach — A32

1d, Toyahama fishermen honoring ocean gods, horiz. 2d, Map of Japan, horiz. 60d, Mt. Fuji. 1.50r, Camphorwood torii, horiz. 2r, Tower of Motherhood, EXPO Tower and Mt. Fuji.

Perf. 13½x13, 13x13½

1970, Sept. 29

220 A32 1d multi .15 .15
221 A32 2d multi .15 .15
222 A32 3d multi .16 .15
223 A32 60d multi .70 .50
a. Souvenir sheet of 4 5.00 4.00
224 A32 1.50r multi 2.00 1.50
225 A32 2r multi 2.50 2.00
Nos. 220-225 (6) 5.66 4.45

EXPO '70 Intl. Exhib., Osaka, Japan, Mar. 15-Sept. 13. No. 223a contains 4 imperf. stamps similar to Nos. 220-223 with simulated perforations. Sold for 1r.

Globe and UN Emblem — A33

UN, 25th anniv.: 2d, Cannon used as flower vase. 3d, Birthday cake and dove. 35d, Emblems of UN agencies forming wall. 1.50r, Trumpet and emblems of UN agencies. 2r, Two men, black and white, embracing, and globe.

1970, Dec. 7 Litho. *Perf. 14x13½*

226 A33 1d blue & multi .15 .15
227 A33 2d multicolored .15 .15
228 A33 3d brt pur & multi .15 .15
229 A33 35d green & multi .35 .20

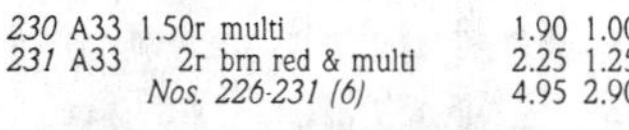

No.	Type	Description	Unused	Used
230	A33	1.50r multi	1.90	1.00
231	A33	2r brn red & multi	2.25	1.25
		Nos. 226-231 (6)	4.95	2.90

Al Jahiz and Old World Map A34

Designs: 2d, Sultan Saladin and palace. 3d, Al Farabi, sailboat and musical instruments. 35d, Iben al Haithum and palace. 1.50r, Al Motanabbi and camels. 2r, Avicenna and old world map.

1971, Feb. 20 *Perf. 13½x14*

No.	Type	Description	Unused	Used
232	A34	1d brt pink & multi	.15	.15
233	A34	2d pale bl & multi	.15	.15
234	A34	3d dl yel & multi	.16	.15
235	A34	35d lt bl & multi	.50	.32
236	A34	1.50r yel grn & multi	2.00	1.40
237	A34	2r pale grn & multi	3.00	2.00
		Nos. 232-237 (6)	5.96	4.17

Famous men of Islam.

Cormorant A35

Designs: 2d, Lizard and prickly pear. 3d, Flamingos and palms. 60d, Oryx and yucca. 1.25r, Gazelle and desert dandelion. 2r, Camel, palm and bronzed chenopod.

1971, Apr. 14 **Litho.** *Perf. 11x12*

No.	Type	Description	Unused	Used
238	A35	1d multi	.18	.15
239	A35	2d multi	.18	.15
240	A35	3d multi	.18	.15
241	A35	60d multi	.90	.60
242	A35	1.25r multi	1.75	1.10
243	A35	2r multi	3.00	1.75
		Nos. 238-243 (6)	6.19	3.90

Goonhilly Satellite Tracking Station A36

Designs: 2d, Cable ship, and section of submarine cable. 3d, 35d, London Post Office Tower, and television control room. 4d, Various telephones. 5d, 75d, Video telephone. 3r, Telex machine and tape.

1971, May 17 *Perf. 13½x13*

No.	Type	Description	Unused	Used
244	A36	1d vio bl & multi	.15	.15
245	A36	2d multicolored	.15	.15
246	A36	3d rose red & multi	.15	.15
247	A36	4d magenta & multi	.20	.15
248	A36	5d rose red & multi	.20	.15
249	A36	35d multicolored	.65	.16
250	A36	75d magenta & multi	1.40	.35
251	A36	3r ocher & multi	5.75	1.50
		Nos. 244-251 (8)	8.65	
		Set value		2.25

3rd World Telecommunications Day.

State of Qatar

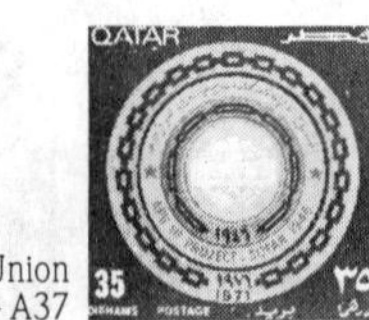

Arab Postal Union Emblem — A37

1971, Sept. 4 *Perf. 13*

No.	Type	Description	Unused	Used
252	A37	35d red & multi	.75	.20
253	A37	55d blue & multi	.90	.32
254	A37	75d brown & multi	1.50	.45
255	A37	1.25r violet & multi	2.50	.75
		Nos. 252-255 (4)	5.65	1.72

25th anniv. of the Conf. of Sofar, Lebanon, establishing the Arab Postal Union.

Boy Reading — A38

1971, Aug. 10 *Perf. 13x13½*

No.	Type	Description	Unused	Used
256	A38	35d brown & multi	.70	.25
257	A38	55d ultra & multi	1.00	.40
258	A38	75d green & multi	1.25	.50
		Nos. 256-258 (3)	2.95	1.15

International Literacy Day, Sept. 8.

Men Splitting Racism A39

Designs: 2d, 3r, People fighting racism. 3d, Soldier helping war victim. 4d, Men of 4 races rebuilding, vert. 5d, Children on swing, vert. 35d, Wave of racism engulfing people. 75d, like 1d.

Perf. 13½x13, 13x13½

1971, Oct. 12 **Litho.**

No.	Type	Description	Unused	Used
259	A39	1d multi	.15	.15
260	A39	2d multi	.15	.15
261	A39	3d multi	.15	.15
262	A39	4d multi	.15	.15
263	A39	5d multi	.15	.15
264	A39	35d multi	.25	.20
265	A39	75d multi	.60	.50
266	A39	3r multi	2.75	2.50
		Set value	3.50	3.50

Intl. Year Against Racial Discrimination.

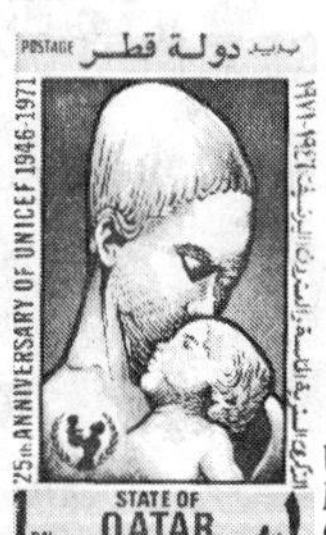

UNICEF Emblem, Mother and Child — A40

UNICEF, 25th anniv.: 2d, Child's head, horiz. 3d, 75d, Child with book. 4d, Nurse and child, horiz. 5d, Mother and child, horiz. 35d, Woman and daffodil. 3r, like 1d.

1971, Dec. 6 *Perf. 14x13½, 13½x14*

No.	Type	Description	Unused	Used
267	A40	1d blue & multi	.15	.15
268	A40	2d lil rose & multi	.15	.15
269	A40	3d blue & multi	.15	.15
270	A40	4d yellow & multi	.15	.15
271	A40	5d blue & multi	.15	.15
272	A40	35d lil rose & multi	.35	.25
273	A40	75d yellow & multi	.50	.40
274	A40	3r multicolored	2.50	1.65
		Set value	3.50	2.75

Sheik Ahmad, Flags of Arab League and Qatar A41

"International Cooperation" A42

75d, Sheik Ahmad, flags of United Nations and Qatar. 1.25r, Sheik Ahmad bin Ali al Thani.

Perf. 13½x13, 13x13½

1972, Jan. 17

No.	Type	Description	Unused	Used
275	A41	35d black & multi	.50	.20
276	A41	75d black & multi	.90	.45
277	A42	1.25r lt brn & blk	1.25	.65
278	A42	3r multicolored	3.75	1.75
a.		Souvenir sheet	6.00	3.50
		Nos. 275-278 (4)	6.40	3.05

Independence 1971. No. 278a contains one stamp with simulated perforations.

European Roller — A43

Birds: 2d, European kingfisher. 3d, Rock thrush. 4d, Caspian tern. 5d, Hoopoe. 35d, European bee-eater. 75d, European golden oriole. 3r, Peregrine falcon.

1972, Mar. 1 **Litho.** *Perf. 12x11*

No.	Type	Description	Unused	Used
279	A43	1d sepia & multi	.15	.15
280	A43	2d emerald & multi	.15	.15
281	A43	3d bister & multi	.15	.15
282	A43	4d lt blue & multi	.15	.15
283	A43	5d yellow & multi	.15	.15
284	A43	35d vio bl & multi	.45	.20
285	A43	75d pink & multi	1.10	.50
286	A43	3r blue & multi	4.50	2.00
		Nos. 279-286 (8)	6.80	
		Set value		2.90

Nos. 217-219 Surcharged

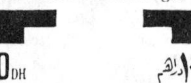

1972, Mar. 7 *Perf. 13x13½*

No.	Type	Description	Unused	Used
287	A31	10d on 60d multi	.20	.15
288	A31	1r on 1.25r multi	2.25	.90
289	A31	5r on 2r multi	10.00	4.00
		Nos. 287-289 (3)	12.45	5.05

Sheik Khalifa bin Hamad al Thani
A44 A44a

1972 *Perf. 14*

Size: 23x27mm

No.	Type	Description	Unused	Used
290	A44	5d pur & ultra	.15	.15
291	A44	10d brn & rose red	.20	.15
291A	A44a	10d lt brown & lt red		
291B	A44a	25d violet & emerald		
292	A44	35d org & dl grn	.50	.24
293	A44	55d brt grn & lil	.75	.38
294	A44	75d vio & lil rose	.85	.50

Size: 26½x32mm

No.	Type	Description	Unused	Used
295	A44	1r bister & blk	1.50	.75
296	A44	1.25r olive & blk	1.75	.80
297	A44	5r blue & blk	8.00	3.50
298	A44	10r red & blk	15.00	7.00
		Nos. 290-298 (9)	28.70	13.47

Issued: Type A44, Mar. 7.

Book Year Emblem A45

1972, Apr. 23 *Perf. 13½x13*

No.	Type	Description	Unused	Used
299	A45	35d lt ultra & blk	.40	.30
300	A45	55d lt brown & blk	.65	.50
301	A45	75d green & blk	.90	.70
302	A45	1.25r violet & blk	1.25	1.00
		Nos. 299-302 (4)	3.20	2.50

International Book Year 1972.

Olympic Rings, Soccer A46

2d, 3r, Running. 3d, Bicycling. 4d, Gymnastics. 5d, Basketball. 35d, Discus. 75d, Like 1d.

1972, June 12 *Perf. 13½x13*

No.	Type	Description	Unused	Used
303	A46	1d green & multi	.15	.15
304	A46	2d yel grn & multi	.15	.15
305	A46	3d blue & multi	.15	.15
306	A46	4d lilac & multi	.15	.15
307	A46	5d blue & multi	.15	.15
308	A46	35d gray & multi	.40	.16
a.		Souvenir sheet of 6	3.25	1.50
309	A46	75d green & multi	.80	.35
310	A46	3r multicolored	3.25	1.40
		Set value	3.60	2.10

20th Olympic Games, Munich, Aug. 26-Sept. 10. No. 308a contains stamps with simulated perforations similar to Nos. 303-308.

Installation of Underwater Pipe Line — A47

1972, Aug. 8 **Litho.** *Perf. 13x13½*

No.	Type	Description	Unused	Used
311	A47	1d Drilling for oil, vert.	.15	.15
312	A47	4d shown	.15	.15
313	A47	5d Drilling platform	.20	.15
314	A47	35d Ship searching for oil	.55	.30
315	A47	75d like 1d, vert.	1.25	.68
316	A47	3r like 5d	5.00	2.50
		Nos. 311-316 (6)	7.30	3.93

Oil from the sea.

Government Palace — A48

Designs: 35d, Clasped hands, Qatar flag. 75d, Clasped hands, UN flag. 1.25r, Sheik Khalifa bin Hamad al-Thani, vert.

Perf. 13½x13, 13x13½

1972, Sept. 3

No.	Type	Description	Unused	Used
317	A48	10d yel & multi	.15	.15
318	A48	35d blk & multi	.60	.25
319	A48	75d blk & multi	1.25	.50
320	A48	1.25r gold & multi	2.00	.75
a.		Souvenir sheet of 1	4.00	3.00
		Nos. 317-320 (4)	4.00	1.65

Independence Day, 1st anniv. of independence.

No. 320a contains one stamp with simulated perforations similar to No. 320.

Qatar Flag, Council Emblem and Flag — A49

1972, Dec. 4 **Litho.** *Perf. 14x13½*

No.	Type	Description	Unused	Used
321	A49	25d blue & multi	1.10	.45
322	A49	30d vio bl & multi	1.40	.60

Civil Aviation Council of Arab States, 10th session.

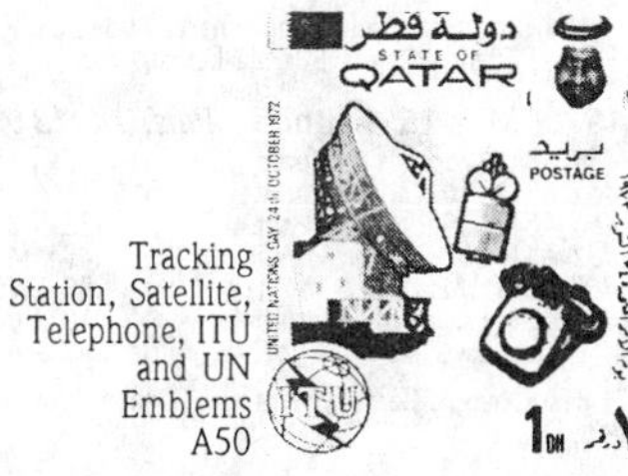
Tracking Station, Satellite, Telephone, ITU and UN Emblems
A50

Designs (Agency and UN Emblems): 2d, Surveyor, artist; UNESCO. 3d, Tractor, helicopter, fish, grain and fruit; FAO. 4d, Reading children, teacher; UNICEF. 5d, Weather satellite and map; WMO. 25d, Workers and crane; ILO. 55d, Health clinic; WHO. 1r, Mail plane and post office; UPU.

1972, Oct. 24 *Perf. 13½x14*

323	A50	1d multicolored	.15	.15
324	A50	2d multicolored	.15	.15
325	A50	3d multicolored	.15	.15
326	A50	4d multicolored	.15	.15
327	A50	5d multicolored	.15	.15
328	A50	25d multicolored	.38	.20
329	A50	55d multicolored	.85	.45
330	A50	1r multicolored	1.40	.75
		Nos. 323-330 (8)	3.38	
		Set value		1.75

United Nations Day, Oct. 24, 1972. Each stamp dedicated to a different UN agency.

Road Building
A51

1973, Feb. 22 **Litho.** *Perf. 13x13½*

331	A51	2d shown	.15	.15
332	A51	3d Housing development	.15	.15
333	A51	4d Operating room	.15	.15
334	A51	5d Telephone operators	.15	.15
335	A51	15d School, classroom	.15	.15
336	A51	20d Television studio	.25	.15
337	A51	35d Sheik Khalifa	.35	.28
338	A51	55d New Gulf Hotel	.60	.40
339	A51	1r Fertilizer plant	.90	.80
340	A51	1.35r Flour mill	1.65	1.10
		Nos. 331-340 (10)	4.50	
		Set value		3.00

1st anniv. of the accession of Sheik Khalifa bin Hamad al Thani as Emir of Qatar.

Aerial Pest Control — A52

WHO, 25th anniv.: 3d, Medicines. 4d, Poliomyelitis prevention. 5d, Malaria control. 55d, Mental health. 1r, Pollution control.

1973, May 14 **Litho.** *Perf. 14*

341	A52	2d blue & multi	.15	.15
342	A52	3d blue & multi	.15	.15
343	A52	4d blue & multi	.15	.15
344	A52	5d blue & multi	.15	.15
345	A52	55d blue & multi	1.50	.65
346	A52	1r blue & multi	2.25	1.50
		Nos. 341-346 (6)	4.35	
		Set value		2.45

Weather Ship
A53

Designs (WMO Emblem and): 3d, Launching of radiosonde balloon. 4d, Plane and meteorological data checking. 5d, Cup anemometers and meteorological station. 10d, Weather plane in flight. 1r, Nimbus I weather satellite. 1.55r, Launching of rocket carrying weather satellite.

1973, July **Litho.** *Perf. 14x13*

347	A53	2d multicolored	.15	.15
348	A53	3d multicolored	.15	.15
349	A53	4d multicolored	.15	.15
350	A53	5d multicolored	.15	.15
351	A53	10d multicolored	.15	.15
352	A53	1r multicolored	1.50	.65
353	A53	1.55r multicolored	2.25	1.00
		Nos. 347-353 (7)	4.50	
		Set value		2.00

Cent. of intl. meteorological cooperation.

Sheik Khalifa — A54

Clock Tower, Doha — A55

1973-74 **Litho.** *Perf. 14*

Size: 18x27mm

354	A54	5d green & multi	.15	.15
355	A54	10d lt bl & multi	.15	.15
356	A54	20d ver & multi	.20	.15
357	A54	25d orange & multi	.35	.15
358	A54	35d purple & multi	.50	.30
359	A54	55d dk gray & multi	.80	.40

Engr.

Perf. 13½

360	A55	75d lil, bl & yel grn	1.10	.60

Photo.

Perf. 13

Size: 27x32mm

360A	A54	1r multicolored	1.65	.85
360B	A54	5r multicolored	8.00	4.50
360C	A54	10r multicolored	16.00	11.00
		Nos. 354-360C (10)	28.90	18.25

Issue dates: 20d, 75d, July 3, 1973; 1r-10r, July 1974; others, Jan. 27, 1973.

Flag of Qatar, Handclasp, Sheik Khalifa — A56

Designs (Flag, Sheik and): 35d, Harvest. 55d, Government Building. 1.35r, Market and Clock Tower, Doha. 1.55r, Illuminated fountain.

1973, Oct. 4 **Litho.** *Perf. 13*

361	A56	15d red & multi	.15	.15
362	A56	35d buff & multi	.30	.16
363	A56	55d multi	.60	.30
364	A56	1.35r vio & multi	1.50	.80
365	A56	1.55r multi	2.00	1.00
		Nos. 361-365 (5)	4.55	2.41

2nd anniversary of independence.

Planting Tree, Qatar and UN Flags, UNESCO Emblem — A57

Designs (Qatar and UN Flags and): 4d, UN Headquarters and flags. 5d, Pipe laying, cement mixer, helicopter and ILO emblem. 35d, Nurse, patient and UNICEF emblem. 1.35r, Telecommunications and ITU emblem. 3r, Cattle, wheat disease analysis and FAO emblem.

1973, Oct. 24

366	A57	2d multi	.15	.15
367	A57	4d multi	.15	.15
368	A57	5d multi	.25	.15
369	A57	35d multi	.50	.20
370	A57	1.35r multi	2.00	.90
371	A57	3r multi	5.00	2.50
		Nos. 366-371 (6)	8.05	
		Set value		2.30

United Nations Day.

Prison Gates Opening — A58

4d, Marchers with flags. 5d, Scales of Justice. 35d, Teacher and pupils. 1.35r, UN General Assembly. 3r, Human Rights flame, vert.

1973, Dec. **Litho.** *Perf. 13x13½*

372	A58	2d yellow & multi	.15	.15
373	A58	4d pale lil & multi	.15	.15
374	A58	5d rose & multi	.15	.15
375	A58	35d ocher & multi	.40	.25
376	A58	1.35r lt bl & multi	1.75	1.00
377	A58	3r citron & multi	3.00	2.00
		Nos. 372-377 (6)	5.60	3.70

25th anniversary of the Universal Declaration of Human Rights.

Highway Overpass — A59

1974, Feb. 22 *Perf. 14x13½*

378	A59	2s shown	.15	.15
379	A59	3d Symbol of learning	.15	.15
380	A59	5d Oil field	.15	.15
381	A59	35d Gulf Hotel, Doha	.35	.20
382	A59	1.55r Radar station	1.90	1.00
383	A59	2.25r Sheik Khalifa	2.50	1.50
		Nos. 378-383 (6)	5.20	3.15

Accession of Sheik Khalifa as Emir, 2nd, anniv.

Mail Truck, Camel Caravan and UPU Emblem
A60

UPU cent.: 3d, Old and new trains, Arab Postal Union emblem. 10d, Old and new ships and Qatar coat of arms. 35d, Old and new planes. 75d, Mail sorting by hand and computer, and Arab Postal Union emblem. 1.25r, Old and new post offices, and Qatar coat of arms.

1974, May 22 **Litho.** *Perf. 13½*

384	A60	2d brt yel & multi	.15	.15
385	A60	3d lt bl & multi	.15	.15
386	A60	10d dp org & multi	.15	.15
387	A60	35d slate & multi	.45	.30
388	A60	75d yellow & multi	.90	.60
389	A60	1.25r lt bl & multi	1.65	1.00
		Nos. 384-389 (6)	3.45	
		Set value		2.10

Doha Hospital
A61

1974, July 13 **Litho.** *Perf. 13½*

390	A61	5d shown	.15	.15
391	A61	10d WPY emblem and people	.15	.15
392	A61	15d WPY emblem	.15	.15
393	A61	35d World map	.30	.20
394	A61	1.75r Clock and infants	1.50	1.00
395	A61	2.25r Family	1.90	1.25
		Nos. 390-395 (6)	4.15	2.90

World Population Year 1974.

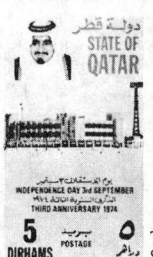

Television Station — A62

1974, Sept. 2 *Perf. 13½x13*

399	A62	5d shown	.15	.15
400	A62	10d Palace of Doha	.15	.15
401	A62	15d Teachers' College	.15	.15
402	A62	75d Clock Tower and Mosque	.75	.50
403	A62	1.55r Traffic circle, Doha	1.25	.75
404	A62	2.25r Sheik Khalifa	1.90	1.25
		Nos. 399-404 (6)	4.35	2.95

3rd anniversary of independence.

Operating Room and WHO Emblem — A63

United Nations Day: 10d, Satellite earth station and ITU emblem. 20d, Tractor, UN and FAO emblems. 25d, School children, UN and UNESCO emblems. 1.75r, Open air court, UN Headquarters, emblems. 2r, UPU and UN emblems.

1974, Oct. 24 **Litho.** *Perf. 13x13½*

405	A63	5d multi	.15	.15
406	A63	10d multi	.15	.15
407	A63	20d multi	.15	.15
408	A63	25d multi	.25	.15
409	A63	1.75r multi	1.40	1.00
410	A63	2r multi	1.75	1.25
		Nos. 405-410 (6)	3.85	2.85

VC-10, Gulf Aviation Airliner
A64

Arab League and Qatar Flags, Civil Aviation Emblem
A65

Design: 25d, Doha Airport.

1974, Dec. 1 **Litho.** *Perf. 13½*

411	A64	20d multi	.25	.20
412	A64	25d yel & dk bl	.32	.25
413	A65	30d multi	.40	.30
414	A65	50d multi	.65	.50
		Nos. 411-414 (4)	1.62	1.25

Arab Civil Aviation Day.

Caspian Terns, Hoopoes and Shara'o Island
A66

Dhow by Moonlight — A67

5d, Clock Tower, Doha, vert. 15d, Zubara Fort. 35d, Gulf Hotel & sailboats. 75d, Arabian oryx. 1.25r, Khor Al-Udein. 1.75r, Ruins, Wakrah.

1974, Dec. 21 Litho. *Perf. 13½*

No.	Type	Description	Unused	Used
415	A66	5d multi	.15	.15
416	A66	10d multi	.15	.15
417	A66	15d multi	.15	.15
418	A66	35d multi	.25	.18
419	A67	55d multi	.45	.35
420	A66	75d multi	.65	.50
421	A67	1.25r multi	1.20	.90
422	A66	1.75r multi	1.75	1.25
		Nos. 415-422 (8)	4.75	3.63

Traffic Circle, Doha A68

Sheik Khalifa — A69

Designs: 35d, Pipe line from offshore platform. 55d, Laying underwater pipe line. 1r, Refinery.

1975, Feb. 22 Litho. *Perf. 13½*

No.	Type	Description	Unused	Used
423	A68	10d multi	.15	.15
424	A68	35d multi	.55	.40
425	A68	55d multi	.80	.60
426	A68	1r multi	1.75	1.20
427	A69	1.35r sil & multi	2.00	1.50
428	A69	1.55r gold & multi	2.50	1.75
		Nos. 423-428 (6)	7.75	5.60

3rd anniversary of the accession of Sheik Khalifa.

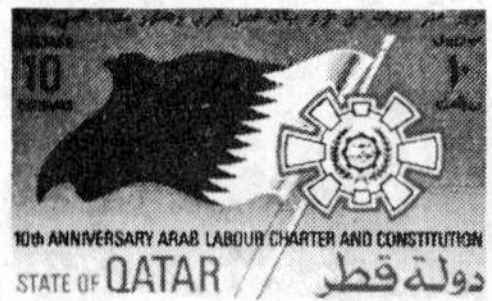

Qatar Flag and Arab Labor Charter Emblem A70

1975, May 28 Litho. *Perf. 13*

No.	Type	Description	Unused	Used
429	A70	10d bl, red brn & blk	.20	.15
430	A70	35d multicolored	.65	.35
431	A70	1r green & multi	1.75	1.00
		Nos. 429-431 (3)	2.60	1.50

Arab Labor Charter and Constitution, 10th anniversary.

Flintlock Pistol with Ornamental Grip — A71

Designs: 3d, Ornamental mosaic. 35d, View of museum. 75d, Arch and museum, vert. 1.25r, Flint arrowheads and tool. 3r, Gold necklace, vert.

1975, June 23 *Perf. 13*

No.	Type	Description	Unused	Used
432	A71	2d multi	.15	.15
433	A71	3d ver blk & gold	.16	.15
434	A71	35d bis & multi	.40	.25
435	A71	75d ver & multi	.90	.55
436	A71	1.25r vio & multi	1.50	.90
437	A71	3r fawn & multi	3.50	2.00
		Nos. 432-437 (6)	6.61	4.00

Opening of Qatar National Museum.

Traffic Signs, Policeman, Doha — A72

Designs: 15d, 55d, Cars, arrows, traffic lights, Doha Clock Tower. 35d, like 5d.

1975, June 24

No.	Type	Description	Unused	Used
438	A72	5d lt green & multi	.15	.15
439	A72	15d lt blue & multi	.50	.18
440	A72	35d lemon & multi	1.25	.45
441	A72	55d lt violet & multi	1.90	.75
		Nos. 438-441 (4)	3.80	1.53

Traffic Week.

Constitution, Arabic Text — A73

5d, Government buildings, horiz. 15d, Museum & Clock Tower, horiz. 55d, 1.25r, Sheik Khalifa & Qatar flag. 75d, Constitution, English text.

1975, Sept. 2

No.	Type	Description	Unused	Used
442	A73	5d multi	.15	.15
443	A73	15d multi	.40	.25
444	A73	35d multi	.45	.30
445	A73	55d multi	.70	.45
446	A73	75d multi	.95	.60
447	A73	1.25r multi	1.50	1.00
		Nos. 442-447 (6)	4.15	2.75

4th anniversary of independence.

Satellite over Globe, ITU Emblem A74

UN, 30th anniv.: 15d, UN Headquarters, NY and UN emblem. 35d, UPU emblem over Eastern Arabia, UN emblem. 1r, Nurses and infant, WHO emblem. 1.25r, Road building equipment, ILO emblem. 2r, Students, UNESCO emblem.

1975, Oct. 25 Litho. *Perf. 13x13½*

No.	Type	Description	Unused	Used
448	A74	5d multi	.20	.15
449	A74	15d multi	.30	.15
450	A74	35d multi	.40	.18
451	A74	1r multi	1.10	.50
452	A74	1.25r multi	1.25	.60
453	A74	2r multi	2.25	1.00
		Nos. 448-453 (6)	5.50	2.58

Fertilizer Plant A75

Designs: 10d, Flour mill, vert. 35d, Natural gas plant. 75d, Oil refinery. 1.25r, Cement works. 1.55r, Steel mill.

1975, Dec. 6

No.	Type	Description	Unused	Used
454	A75	5d salmon & multi	.20	.15
455	A75	10d yellow & multi	.25	.15
456	A75	35d multi	.55	.25
457	A75	75d multi	1.10	.60
458	A75	1.25r mag & multi	2.00	1.00
459	A75	1.55r multi	3.00	1.40
		Nos. 454-459 (6)	7.10	3.55

Modern Building, Doha A76

10d, 35d, 1.55r, Various modern buildings. 55d, 75d, Sheik Khalifa & Qatar flag, diff.

1976, Feb. 22 Litho. *Perf. 13*

No.	Type	Description	Unused	Used
460	A76	5d multi	.15	.15
461	A76	10d multi	.15	.15
462	A76	35d multi	.35	.20
463	A76	55d multi	.55	.30
464	A76	75d multi	.80	.45
465	A76	1.55r multi	1.50	.90
		Nos. 460-465 (6)	3.50	2.15

4th anniversary of accession of Sheik Khalifa.

Satellite Earth Station — A77

Designs: 55d, 1r, Satellite. 75d, Like 35d.

1976, Mar. 1

No.	Type	Description	Unused	Used
466	A77	35d multicolored	.65	.22
467	A77	55d dp bis & multi	.80	.30
468	A77	75d vermilion & multi	1.25	.45
469	A77	1r violet & multi	1.75	.60
		Nos. 466-469 (4)	4.45	1.57

Inauguration of satellite earth station in Qatar.

Telephones, 1876 and 1976 — A78

Arabian Soccer League Emblem — A79

1976, Mar. 10

No.	Type	Description	Unused	Used
470	A78	1r rose & multi	1.25	.75
471	A78	1.35r lt bl & multi	1.75	1.00

Centenary of first telephone call by Alexander Graham Bell, Mar. 10, 1876.

1976, Mar. 25 Litho. *Perf. 13½x13*

Designs: 10d, 1.25r, Stadium, Doha. 35d, Like 5d. 55d, Players. 75d, One player.

No.	Type	Description	Unused	Used
472	A79	5d lil & multi	.15	.15
473	A79	10d pink & multi	.15	.15
474	A79	35d bl grn & multi	.30	.25
475	A79	55d multi	.48	.40
476	A79	75d multi	.72	.60
477	A79	1.25r multi	1.25	1.00
		Nos. 472-477 (6)	3.05	2.55

4th Arabian Gulf Soccer Cup Tournament, Doha, Mar. 22-Apr.

Dhow A80

Designs: Various dhows.

1976, Apr. 19 *Perf. 13½x14*

No.	Type	Description	Unused	Used
478	A80	10d blue & multi	.15	.15
479	A80	35d blue & multi	.50	.20
480	A80	80d blue & multi	1.00	.45
481	A80	1.25r blue & multi	1.65	.75
482	A80	1.50r blue & multi	2.00	.90
483	A80	2r blue & multi	3.25	1.40
		Nos. 478-483 (6)	8.55	3.85

Soccer — A81

10d, Yachting. 35d, Steeplechase. 80d, Boxing. 1.25r, Weight lifting. 1.50r, Basketball.

1976, May 15 Litho. *Perf. 14x13½*

No.	Type	Description	Unused	Used
484	A81	5d multicolored	.15	.15
485	A81	10d blue & multi	.15	.15
486	A81	35d orange & multi	.22	.20
487	A81	80d bister & multi	.45	.40
488	A81	1.25r lilac & multi	.85	.75
489	A81	1.50r rose & multi	1.10	1.00
		Nos. 484-489 (6)	2.92	2.65

21st Olympic Games, Montreal, Canada, July 17-Aug. 1.

Village and Emblems — A82

35d, Emblems. 80d, Village. 1.25r, Sheik Khalifa.

1976, May 31 *Perf. 13½x14*

No.	Type	Description	Unused	Used
490	A82	10d orange & multi	.15	.15
491	A82	35d yellow & multi	.45	.20
492	A82	80d citron & multi	.90	.45
493	A82	1.25r dp blue & multi	1.50	.75
		Nos. 490-493 (4)	3.00	1.55

Habitat, UN Conf. on Human Settlements, Vancouver, Canada, May 31-June 11.

Snowy Plover A83

Birds: 10d, Great cormorant. 35d, Osprey. 80d, Flamingo. 1.25r, Rock thrush. 2r, Saker falcon. 35d, 80d, 1.25r, 2r, vertical.

Perf. 13½x14, 14x13½

1976, July 19 Litho.

No.	Type	Description	Unused	Used
494	A83	5d multi	.45	.15
495	A83	10d multi	1.00	.15
496	A83	35d multi	2.75	.28
497	A83	80d multi	5.25	.65
498	A83	1.25r multi	9.00	1.10
499	A83	2r multi	10.00	1.60
		Nos. 494-499 (6)	28.45	3.93

Sheik Khalifa and Qatar Flag — A84

Government Building — A85

Designs: 10d, like 5d. 80d, Government building. 1.25r, Offshore oil platform. 1.50r, UN emblem and Qatar coat of arms.

Perf. 14x13½, 13½x14

1976, Sept. 2

No.	Type	Description	Unused	Used
500	A84	5d gold & multi	.15	.15
501	A84	10d silver & multi	.15	.15
502	A85	40d multicolored	.45	.25
503	A85	80d multicolored	.80	.50
504	A85	1.25r multicolored	1.25	.75
505	A85	1.50r multicolored	1.65	.90
		Nos. 500-505 (6)	4.45	2.70

5th anniversary of independence.

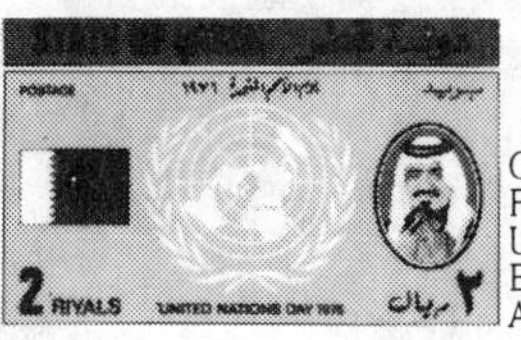

Qatar Flag and UN Emblem A86

1976, Oct. 24 Litho. *Perf. 13½x14*

506 A86 2r multi		2.00	1.00
507 A86 3r multi		2.75	1.50

United Nations Day 1976.

A87 Sheik Khalifa — A88 Sheik Khalifa

1977, Feb. 22 Litho. *Perf. 14x13½*

508 A87	20d silver & multi	.25	.15
509 A87	1.80r gold & multi	2.50	1.40

5th anniversary of the accession of Sheik Khalifa.

1977, Mar. 1 Litho. *Perf. 14x14½*

Size: 22x27mm

510 A88	5d multicolored	.15	.15
511 A88	10d aqua & multi	.15	.15
512 A88	35d orange & multi	.45	.15
513 A88	80d multicolored	1.00	.32

Perf. 13½

Size: 25x30mm

514 A88	1r vio bl & multi	1.65	.45
515 A88	5r yellow & multi	6.00	2.25
516 A88	10r multicolored	15.00	4.50
	Nos. 510-516 (7)	24.40	7.97

Letter, APU Emblem, Flag — A89

1977, Apr. 12 *Perf. 14x13½*

517 A89	35d blue & multi	.50	.25
518 A89	1.35r blue & multi	1.75	1.00

Arab Postal Union, 25th anniversary.

Waves and Sheik Khalifa A90

1977, May 17 Litho. *Perf. 13½x14*

519 A90	35d multi	.35	.25
520 A90	1.80r multi	2.00	1.50

World Telecommunications Day.

Sheik Khalifa — A90a

Perf. 13½x13

1977, June 29 Litho. Wmk. 368

520A A90a	5d multi	.15	.15
520B A90a	10d multi	.15	.15
520C A90a	35d multi	.20	.20
520D A90a	80d multi	.45	.45
e.	Bklt. pane, 4 5d, 3 10d, 2 35d, 80d	8.50	6.00
	Set value	.75	.75

Issued in booklets only.

Parliament, Clock Tower, Minaret — A91

Designs: No. 522, Main business district, Doha. No. 523, Highway crossings, Doha.

1977, Sept. 1 Litho. *Perf. 13x13½*

521 A91	80d multicolored	1.00	.65
522 A91	80d multicolored	1.00	.65
523 A91	80d multicolored	1.00	.65
	Nos. 521-523 (3)	3.00	1.95

6th anniversary of independence.

UN Emblem, Flag — A92

1977, Oct. 24 Litho. *Perf. 13½x14*

524 A92	20d green & multi	.25	.15
525 A92	1r blue & multi	1.25	.75

United Nations Day.

Surgery A93

20d, Steel mill. 1r, Classroom. 5r, Sheik Khalifa.

1978, Feb. 22 Litho. *Perf. 13½x14*

526 A93	20d multicolored	.15	.15
527 A93	80d multicolored	.50	.40
528 A93	1r multicolored	.60	.50
529 A93	5r multicolored	3.00	2.50
	Nos. 526-529 (4)	4.25	3.55

6th anniversary of the accession of Sheik Khalifa.

Oil Refinery — A94

Designs: 80d, Office buildings, Doha. 1.35r, Traffic Circle, Doha. 1.80r, Sheik Khalifa and flag.

1978, Aug. 31 Litho. *Perf. 13½x14*

530 A94	35d multi	.30	.20
531 A94	80d multi	.75	.50
532 A94	1.35r multi	1.25	.75
533 A94	1.80r multi	1.75	1.00
	Nos. 530-533 (4)	4.05	2.45

7th anniversary of independence.

Man Learning to Read A95

1978, Sept. 8 Litho. *Perf. 13½x14*

534 A95	35d multicolored	.40	.20
535 A95	80d multicolored	1.40	.65

International Literacy Day.

Flag and UN Emblem A96

1978, Oct. 14 *Perf. 13x13½*

536 A96	35d multi	.40	.20
537 A96	80d multi	1.40	.65

United Nations Day.

Human Rights Emblem — A97 — IYC Emblem — A98

Designs: 80d, like 35d. 1.25r, 1.80r, Scales and Human Rights emblem.

1978, Dec. 10 Litho. *Perf. 14x13½*

538 A97	35d multi	.30	.22
539 A97	80d multi	.70	.60
540 A97	1.25r multi	.90	.80
541 A97	1.80r multi	1.50	1.25
	Nos. 538-541 (4)	3.40	2.87

30th anniversary of Universal Declaration of Human Rights.

Wmk. JEZ Multiple (368)

1979, Jan. 1 Litho. *Perf. 13½x13*

542 A98	35d multi	.40	.25
543 A98	1.80r multi	1.50	1.25

International Year of the Child.

Sheik Khalifa

A99 — A100

1979, Jan. 15 Unwmk. *Perf. 14*

544 A99	5d multi	.15	.15
545 A99	10d multi	.15	.15
546 A99	20d multi	.20	.15
547 A99	25d multi	.25	.15
548 A99	35d multi	.35	.16
549 A99	60d multi	.90	.30
550 A99	80d multi	1.00	.40

Size: 27x32mm

551 A99	1r multi	1.25	.50
552 A99	1.25r multi	1.40	.60
553 A99	1.35r multi	1.90	.75
554 A99	1.80r multi	2.00	.90
555 A99	5r multi	6.00	2.50
556 A99	10r multi	12.00	5.00
	Nos. 544-556 (13)	27.55	11.71

1979, Feb. 22 Wmk. 368

557 A100	35d multi	.30	.20
558 A100	80d multi	.65	.50
559 A100	1r multi	.80	.60
560 A100	1.25r multi	1.00	.75
	Nos. 557-560 (4)	2.75	2.05

7th anniv. of accession of Sheik Khalifa.

Cables and People — A101

1979, May 17 Litho. *Perf. 14x13½*

561 A101	2r multi	1.25	1.10
562 A101	2.80r multi	1.65	1.40

World Telecommunications Day.

Children Holding Globe, UNESCO Emblem A102

Perf. 13x13½

1979, July 15 Litho. Unwmk.

563 A102	35d multicolored	.30	.20
564 A102	80d multicolored	1.40	.60

International Bureau of Education, Geneva, 50th anniversary.

Rolling Mill — A103 — UN Day — A104

Perf. 13½

1979, Sept. 2 Litho. Wmk. 368

565 A103	5d shown	.15	.15
566 A103	10d Doha, aerial view	.15	.15
567 A103	1.25r Qatar flag	.85	.75
568 A103	2r Sheik Khalifa	1.40	1.00
	Nos. 565-568 (4)	2.55	2.05

Independence, 8th anniversary.

1979, Oct. 24 Litho. *Perf. 13½x13*

569 A104	1.25r multi	1.00	.75
570 A104	2r multi	1.75	1.25

Conference Emblem — A105

1979, Nov. 24 *Perf. 13x13½*

571 A105	35d multi	.55	.25
572 A105	1.80r multi	2.25	1.25

Hegira (Pilgrimage Year); 3rd World Conference on Prophets.

Sheik Khalifa, 8th Anniversary of Accession — A106

1980, Feb. 22 Litho. *Perf. 13x13½*

573 A106	20d multi	.15	.15
574 A106	60d multi	.45	.35
575 A106	1.25r multi	.85	.65
576 A106	2r multi	1.75	1.25
	Nos. 573-576 (4)	3.20	2.40

Map of Arab Countries — A107

1980, Mar. 1 Litho. *Perf. 13½x14*

577	A107	2.35r multi	1.75	.95
578	A107	2.80r multi	2.25	1.15

6th Congress of Arab Town Organization, Doha, Mar. 1-4.

Oil Refinery A108

1980, Sept. 2 Litho. *Perf. 14½*

579	A108	10d shown	.20	.15
580	A108	35d View of Doha	.50	.25
581	A108	2r Oil rig	2.25	1.10
582	A108	2.35r Hospital	2.75	1.65
		Nos. 579-582 (4)	5.70	3.15

9th anniversary of independence.

Men Holding OPEC Emblem — A109 United Nations Day 1980 — A110

1980, Sept. 15 *Perf. 14x13½*

583	A109	1.35r multi	.90	.60
584	A109	2r multi	1.40	.90

OPEC, 20th anniversary.

1980, Oct. 24

585	A110	1.35r multi	1.10	.60
586	A110	1.80r multi	1.50	.80

Hegira (Pilgrimage Year) — A111

1980, Nov. 8 Litho. *Perf. 14½*

587	A111	10d multi	.15	.15
588	A111	35d multi	.24	.24
589	A111	1.25r multi	.80	.80
590	A111	2.80r multi	1.90	1.90
		Nos. 587-590 (4)	3.09	3.09

International Year of the Disabled — A112

1981, Jan. 5 Photo. *Perf. 11½*
Granite Paper

591	A112	2r multi	1.40	1.00
592	A112	3r multi	2.00	1.50

Education Day — A113

Sheik Khalifa, 9th Anniversary of Accession — A114

Perf. 14x13½
1981, Feb. 22 Litho. Wmk. 368

593	A113	2r multi	1.65	.80
594	A113	3r multi	2.50	1.25

1981, Feb. 22

595	A114	10d multi	.15	.15
596	A114	35d multi	.20	.15
597	A114	80d multi	.50	.35
598	A114	5r multi	4.25	2.25
		Nos. 595-598 (4)	5.10	2.90

A115

A116

1981, May 17 Litho. *Perf. 13½x13*

599	A115	2r multi	1.50	.95
600	A115	2.80r multi	1.90	1.25

13th World Telecommunications Day.

1981, June 11 Litho. *Perf. 14x13½*

Championship emblem.

601	A116	1.25r multi	1.65	.55
602	A116	2.80r multi	3.75	1.25

30th Intl. Military Soccer Championship, Doha.

10th Anniv. of Independence — A117

Perf. 13½x14
1981, Sept. 2 Litho. Wmk. 368

603	A117	5d multicolored	.15	.15
604	A117	60d multicolored	.50	.32
605	A117	80d multicolored	.65	.40
606	A117	5r multicolored	3.75	2.75
		Nos. 603-606 (4)	5.05	3.62

World Food Day A118

1981, Oct. 16 Litho. *Perf. 13*

607	A118	2r multi	2.00	.80
608	A118	2.80r multi	2.75	1.15

Red Crescent Society — A119

1982, Jan. 16 Litho. *Perf. 14x13½*

609	A119	20d multi	.30	.15
610	A119	2.80r multi	4.00	2.00

10th Anniv. of Sheik Khalifa's Accession — A120

Perf. 13½x14
1982, Feb. 22 Litho. Wmk. 368

611	A120	10d multi	.15	.15
612	A120	20d multi	.25	.15
613	A120	1.25r multi	1.50	.65
614	A120	2.80r multi	3.00	1.40
		Nos. 611-614 (4)	4.90	2.35

Sheik Khalifa A121

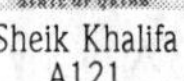

Oil Refinery A122

Designs: 5r, 10r, 15r, Hoda Clock Tower.

1982, Mar. 1 Photo. *Perf. 11½x12*
Granite Paper

615	A121	5d multi	.15	.15
616	A121	10d multi	.15	.15
617	A121	15d multi	.15	.15
618	A121	20d multi	.15	.15
619	A121	25d multi	.15	.15
620	A121	35d multi	.20	.15
621	A121	60d multi	.35	.25
622	A121	80d multi	.45	.35
623	A122	1r multi	.60	.45
624	A122	1.25r multi	.75	.55
625	A122	2r multi	1.20	.90
626	A122	5r multi	3.00	2.25
627	A122	10r multi	6.00	4.50
628	A122	15r multi	8.50	6.50
		Nos. 615-628 (14)	21.80	16.65

Hamad General Hospital A123

1982, Mar. Litho. *Perf. 13x13½*

629	A123	10d multi	.15	.15
630	A123	2.35r multi	2.75	1.40

6th Anniv. of United Arab Shipping Co. A124

1982, Mar. 6 Litho. *Perf. 13x13½*

631	A124	20d multi	.25	.15
632	A124	2.35r multi	3.00	1.40

A125 A126

1982, Apr. 12 Litho. *Perf. 13½x13*

633	A125	35d yellow & multi	.25	.20
634	A125	2.80r blue & multi	2.00	1.40

30th anniv. of Arab Postal Union.

1982, Sept. 2 Litho. *Perf. 13½x13*

635	A126	10d multi	.25	.15
636	A126	80d multi	.70	.40
637	A126	1.25r multi	1.25	.65
638	A126	2.80r multi	2.50	1.40
		Nos. 635-638 (4)	4.70	2.60

11th anniv. of Independence.

World Communications Year — A127

1983, Jan. 10 Litho. *Perf. 13½x13*

639	A127	35d multi	.45	.15
640	A127	2.80r multi	3.00	1.15

Gulf Postal Org., 2nd Conference, Doha, Apr. — A128

1983, Apr. 9 Litho. *Perf. 13½x14*

641	A128	1r multi	.75	.40
642	A128	1.35r multi	1.00	.55

A129 A130

1983, Sept. 2 Litho. *Perf. 14*

643	A129	10d multi	.15	.15
644	A129	35d multi	.30	.15
645	A129	80d multi	.70	.32
646	A129	2.80r multi	2.75	1.15
		Nos. 643-646 (4)	3.90	1.77

12th anniv. of Independence.

1983, Nov. 7 Litho. *Perf. 13½x14*

647	A130	35d multi	.30	.15
648	A130	2.80r multi	2.25	1.10

GCC Supreme Council, 4th regular session.

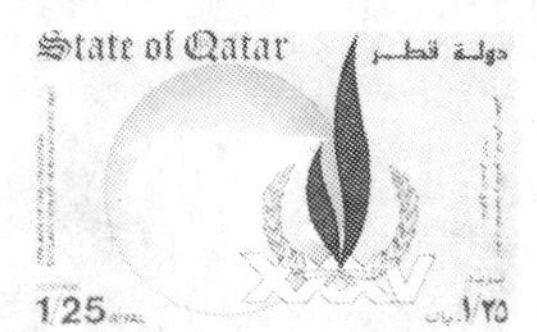

35th Anniv. of UN Declaration of Human Rights — A131

1983, Dec. 10 Litho. *Perf. 13½x14*

649 A131 1.25r Globe, emblem 1.75 .68
650 A131 2.80r Scale 3.00 1.50

A132

A133

1984, Mar. 1 Litho. *Perf. 13x13½*

651 A132 15d multi .15 .15
652 A132 40d multi .28 .25
653 A132 50d multi .35 .32

Perf. 14½x13½

654 A133 1r multi .65 .60
655 A133 1.50r multi 1.00 .90
656 A133 2.50r multi 1.65 1.50
657 A133 3r multi 1.90 1.75
658 A133 5r multi 3.25 3.00
659 A133 10r multi 6.50 6.00
Nos. 651-659 (9) 15.73 14.47

See Nos. 707-709, 792-801.

13th Anniv. of Independence A134

1984, Sept. 2 Photo. *Perf. 12*

660 A134 15d multi .15 .15
661 A134 1r multi .90 .55
662 A134 2.50r multi 2.00 1.35
663 A134 3.50r multi 3.00 1.90
Nos. 660-663 (4) 6.05 3.95

Literacy Day, 1984 — A135

40th Anniv., ICAO — A136

1984, Sept. 8 Litho. *Perf. 14x13½*

664 A135 1r lilac & multi 1.00 .55
665 A135 1r orange & multi 1.00 .55

1984, Dec. 7 Litho. *Perf. 13½x13*

666 A136 20d multi .25 .15
667 A136 3.50r multi 3.75 1.90

League of Arab States, 40th Anniv. A137

1985, Mar. 22 Photo. *Perf. 11½*

668 A137 50d multi .50 .25
669 A137 4r multi 3.50 2.00

Intl. Youth Year — A138

Traffic Crossing — A139

Perf. 11½x12

1985, Mar. 4 Granite Paper

670 A138 50d multi 1.00 .25
671 A138 1r multi 2.00 .50

1985, Mar. 9 *Perf. 14x13½*

672 A139 1r lt bl & multi 1.25 .50
673 A139 1r pink & multi 1.25 .50

Gulf Cooperation Council Traffic Safety Week, Mar. 16-22.

Natl. Independence, 14th Anniv. — A140

Perf. 11½x12

1985, Sept. 2 Granite Paper

674 A140 40d Doha .35 .20
675 A140 50d Earth satellite station .40 .25
676 A140 1.50r Oil refinery 1.25 .75
677 A140 4r Storage facility 3.25 2.00
Nos. 674-677 (4) 5.25 3.20

Org. of Petroleum Exporting Countries, 25th Anniv. — A141

1985, Sept. 14 *Perf. 13½x14*

678 A141 1r brt yel grn & multi 1.00 .50
679 A141 1r salmon rose & multi 1.00 .50

UN, 40th Anniv. A142

1985, Oct. 24 Litho. *Perf. 13½x14*

680 A142 1r multi .85 .50
681 A142 3r multi 2.50 1.50

Population and Housing Census — A143

1986, Mar. 1 Photo. *Perf. 11½x12*

682 A143 1r multi .80 .55
683 A143 3r multi 2.25 1.65

United Arab Shipping Co., 10th Anniv. — A144

1986, May 30 Litho. *Perf. 13½x14*

684 A144 1.50r Qatari ibn al Fuja'a 1.25 .85
685 A144 4r Al Wajba 3.25 2.25

Natl. Independence, 15th Anniv. — A145

Perf. 13x13½

1986, Sept. 2 Litho. Unwmk.

686 A145 40d multi .35 .25
687 A145 50d multi .45 .30
688 A145 1r multi .90 .60
689 A145 4r multi 3.25 2.25
Nos. 686-689 (4) 4.95 3.40

Sheik Khalifa — A146

1987, Jan. 1 Photo. *Perf. 11½x12*

Granite Paper

690 A146 15r multi 9.00 8.50
691 A146 20r multi 12.00 11.00
692 A146 30r multi 19.00 17.00
Nos. 690-692 (3) 40.00 36.50

15th Anniv. of Sheik Khalifa's Accession A147

1987, Feb. 22 *Perf. 12x11½*

Granite Paper

693 A147 50d multi .35 .30
694 A147 1r multi .65 .58
695 A147 1.50r multi 1.00 .85
696 A147 4r multi 2.75 2.25
Nos. 693-696 (4) 4.75 3.98

Arab Postal Union, 35th Anniv. — A148

Perf. 14x13½

1987, Apr. 12 Litho. Unwmk.

697 A148 1r multi .58 .58
698 A148 1.50r multi .85 .85

Natl. Independence, 16th Anniv. — A149

1987, Sept. 2 Litho. *Perf. 13x13½*

699 A149 25d Housing complex .20 .15
700 A149 75d Water tower, city .55 .45
701 A149 2r Modern office building 1.40 1.15
702 A149 4r Oil refinery 3.00 2.25
Nos. 699-702 (4) 5.15 4.00

A150

A151

Perf. 13½x13

1987, Sept. 8 Litho. Unwmk.

703 A150 1.50r multi 1.25 .85
704 A150 4r multi 3.00 2.25

Intl. Literacy Day.

Perf. 14x13½

1987, Apr. 24 Litho. Wmk. 368

705 A151 1r multicolored 1.00 .60
706 A151 4r multicolored 3.75 2.25

Gulf Environment Day.

Sheik Type of 1984

1988, Jan. 1 *Perf. 13x13½*

Size of 25d, 75d: 22x27mm

707 A133 25d multicolored .20 .15
708 A133 75d multicolored .60 .45

Perf. 14½x13

709 A133 2r multicolored 1.50 1.15

This is an expanding set. Numbers will change if necessary.

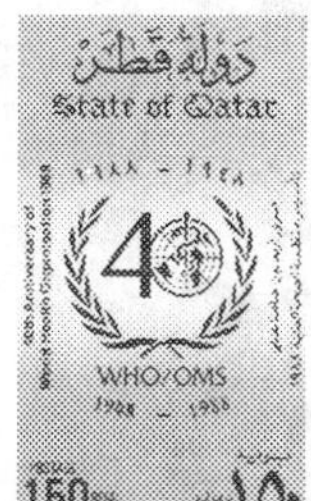

WHO, 40th Anniv. — A152

1988, Apr. 7 *Perf. 14x13½*

714 A152 1.50r multicolored 1.25 .90
715 A152 2r multicolored 1.65 1.15

Independence, 17th Anniv. — A153

Perf. 11½x12

1988, Sept. 2 Litho. Unwmk.

Granite Paper

716 A153 50d multicolored .40 .30
717 A153 75d multicolored .60 .45
718 A153 1.50r multicolored 1.15 .88
719 A153 2r multicolored 1.50 1.15
Nos. 716-719 (4) 3.65 2.78

Opening of the Doha General P.O. — A154

1988, Sept. 3 *Perf. 13x13½*

720 A154 1.50r multicolored 1.15 .88
721 A154 4r multicolored 3.00 2.25

Arab Housing Day — A155

Perf. 11½x12

1988, Oct. 3 Granite Paper

722 A155 1.50r multicolored 1.15 .88
723 A155 4r multicolored 3.00 2.25

A156 A157

Perf. 14x13½

1988, Dec. 10 Wmk. 368

724 A156 1.50r multicolored 1.15 .88
725 A156 2r multicolored 1.50 1.15

Declaration of Human Rights, 40th anniv.

Perf. 12x11½

1989, May 17 Unwmk.

Granite Paper

726 A157 2r multicolored 1.50 1.15
727 A157 4r multicolored 3.00 2.25

World Telecommunications Day.

Qatar Red Crescent Soc., 10th Anniv. — A158

Perf. 13½x14

1989, Aug. 8 Wmk. 368

728 A158 4r multicolored 3.00 2.30

Natl. Independence, 18th Anniv. — A159

Perf. 13x13½

1989, Sept. 2 Unwmk.

729 A159 75d multicolored .60 .45
730 A159 1r multicolored .80 .60
731 A159 1.50r multicolored 1.15 .88
732 A159 2r multicolored 1.50 1.15
Nos. 729-732 (4) 4.05 3.08

Gulf Air, 40th Anniv. A160

1990, Mar. 24 Litho. *Perf. 13x13½*

733 A160 50d multicolored .30 .20
734 A160 75d multicolored .45 .30
735 A160 4r multicolored 2.40 1.60
Nos. 733-735 (3) 3.15 2.10

Independence, 19th Anniv. A161

Designs: 75d, Map, sunburst. 1.50r, 2r, Swordsman, musicians.

1990, Sept. 2 *Perf. 14x13½*

736 A161 50d multicolored .30 .20
737 A161 75d multicolored .45 .30
738 A161 1.50r multicolored .90 .60
739 A161 2r multicolored 1.20 .80
Nos. 736-739 (4) 2.85 1.90

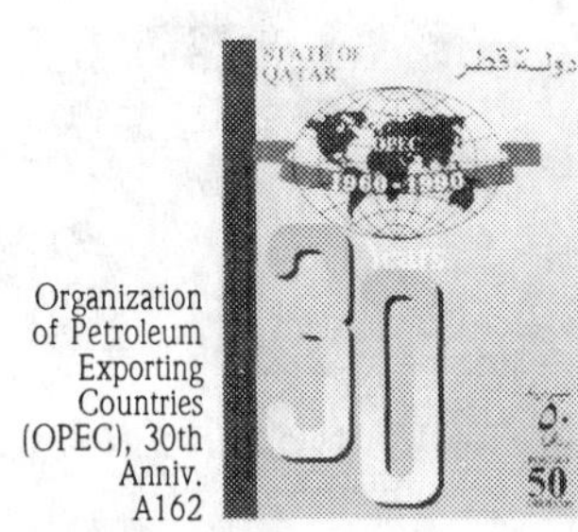

Organization of Petroleum Exporting Countries (OPEC), 30th Anniv. A162

1990, Sept. 14

740 A162 50d shown .30 .20
741 A162 1.50r Flags .90 .60

GCC Supreme Council, 11th Regular Session — A163

Designs: 1r, Leaders of member nations. 1.50r, Flag, council emblem. 2r, State seal, emblem.

Perf. 14x13½

1990, Dec. 22 Litho. Wmk. 368

742 A163 50d multicolored .30 .20
743 A163 1r multicolored .55 .40
744 A163 1.50r multicolored .85 .60
745 A163 2r multicolored .55 .40
Nos. 742-745 (4) 2.25 1.60

Plants — A164

Perf. 12½x13½

1991, June 20 Litho. Wmk. 368

747 A164 10d Glossonema edule .15 .15
750 A164 25d Lycium shawii .22 .15
752 A164 50d Acacia tortilis .45 .30
754 A164 75d Acacia ehrenbergiana .68 .45
756 A164 1r Capparis spinosa .90 .60
759 A164 4r Cymhopogon parkeri 3.60 2.40
Nos. 747-759 (6) 6.00 4.05

This is an expanding set. Numbers may change.

Independence, 20th Anniv. — A165

1991, Aug. 15 Litho. *Perf. 14x14½*

Granite Paper

762 A165 25d shown .20 .15
763 A165 75d red vio & multi .60 .28

Perf. 14½x14

764 A165 1r Doha skyline, horiz. .85 .38
765 A165 1.50r Palace, horiz. 1.25 .58
Nos. 762-765 (4) 2.90 1.39

Fish A166

Various species of fish.

1991, Dec. 1 *Perf. 14x13½*

767 A166 10d multicolored .15 .15
768 A166 15d multicolored .15 .15
770 A166 25d multicolored .15 .15
772 A166 50d multicolored .28 .20
773 A166 75d multicolored .42 .28
774 A166 1r multicolored .58 .38
775 A166 1.50r multicolored .90 .58
776 A166 2r multicolored 1.15 .78
Nos. 767-776 (8) 3.78 2.67

This is an expanding set. Numbers may change.

Sheik Khalifa, 20th Anniv. of Accession
A167 A168

Perf. 14x13½

1992, Feb. 22 Litho. Wmk. 368

781 A167 25d multicolored .15 .15
782 A167 50d multicolored .30 .18
783 A168 75d multicolored .45 .28
784 A168 1.50r multicolored .90 .58
Nos. 781-784 (4) 1.80 1.19

World Health Day A169

1992, Apr. 7 *Perf. 14x13½, 13½x14*

785 A169 50d Heart with face, vert. .30 .18
786 A169 1.50r shown .90 .58

Children's Paintings A170

1992, June 15 Unwmk. *Perf. 11½*

787 A170 25d Girls dancing .15 .15
788 A170 50d Children playing .30 .18
789 A170 75d Ships .45 .28
790 A170 1.50r Fishing from boats .90 .58
a. Souvenir sheet of 4, #787-790
Nos. 787-790 (4) 1.80 1.19

Type of 1984 with Smaller Arabic Inscription and

A171 A172

Designs: 25d, 1.50r, Offshore oil field. 50d, 2r, 5r, Map. 75d, 3r, Storage tanks, horiz. 1r, 4r, 10r, Oil refinery, horiz.

1992 Litho. *Perf. 13x13½*

791 A171 10d multicolored *.15 .15*
792 A132 25d multicolored *.18 .15*
793 A132 50d multicolored *.38 .25*

Perf. 13½x13

794 A132 75d multicolored *.55 .35*
795 A132 1r multicolored *.75 .50*

Size: 25x32mm

Perf. 14½x13, 13x14½

796 A132 1.50r multicolored *1.10 .72*
797 A132 2r multicolored *1.50 1.00*
798 A132 3r multicolored *2.25 1.50*
799 A132 4r multicolored *3.00 2.00*
800 A132 5r multicolored *3.75 2.50*
801 A132 10r multicolored *7.50 5.00*
802 A172 15r multicolored *11.00 7.50*
803 A172 20r multicolored *15.00 10.00*
804 A172 30r multicolored *22.50 15.00*
Nos. 791-804 (14) *69.61 46.62*

Issue dates: 10d, 25d, 50d, 1.50r, 2r, 5r, 15r, 30r, Feb. 15. Others, May 14.

1992 Summer Olympics, Barcelona A174

1992, July 25 Litho. *Perf. 15*

805 A174 50d Running .30 .20
806 A174 1.50r Soccer .90 .58

11th Persian Gulf Soccer Cup A175

1992, Nov. 27 Litho. *Perf. 14½*

807 A175 50d shown .30 .20
808 A175 1r Ball, net, vert. .60 .20

A176

Independence, 21st Anniv. — A177

Sheik Khalifa and: No. 810, "21" in English and Arabic. No. 811, Tree, dhow in harbor. No. 812, Natural gas well, pen, dhow.

Unwmk.

1992, Sept. 2 Litho. *Perf. 12*

Granite Paper

809 A176 50d shown .30 .20
810 A176 50d multicolored .30 .20
811 A177 1r multicolored .60 .40
812 A177 1r multicolored .60 .40
a. Strip of 8, 2 each #809-812 5.50 4.00
Nos. 809-812 (4) 1.80 1.20

Intl. Conference on Nutrition, Rome — A178

1992, Dec. 12 *Perf. 14½*

813 A178 50d Globe, emblems, vert. .30 .20
814 A178 1r Cornucopia .60 .40

Qatar Broadcasting, Silver Jubilee A179

Designs: 25d, Man at microphone, satellite dish. 50d, Rocket lift-off, satellite. 75d, Communications building. 1r, Technicians working on books.

1993, June 25 Photo. *Perf. 12x11½*

Granite Paper

819 A179 25d multicolored .15 .15
820 A179 50d multicolored .30 .20
821 A179 75d multicolored .45 .30
822 A179 1r multicolored .60 .40
a. Souvenir sheet of 4, #819-822
Nos. 819-822 (4) 1.50 1.05

Ruins A180

Mosque with: a, Minaret (at left, shown). b, Minaret with side projections (at right). c, Minaret with catwalk, inside wall. d, Minaret at right, outside wall.

1993, May 10 Litho. *Perf. 12*

Granite Paper

823 A180 1r Strip of 4, #a.-d. 2.50 1.65

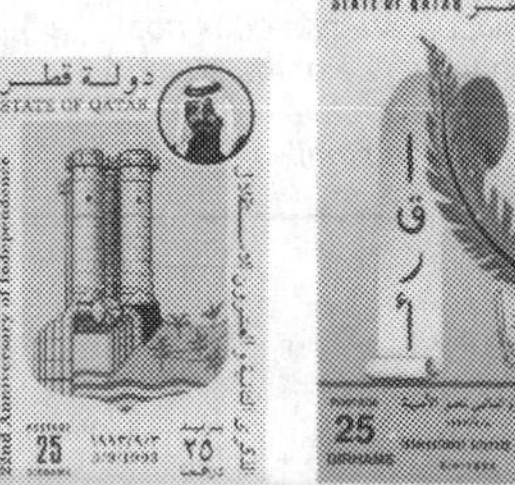

Independence, 22nd Anniv. — A181

Intl. Literacy Day — A182

Designs: 25c, Oil pumping station. 50d, Flag, clock tower. 75d, Coat of arms, "22." 1.50r, Flag, fortress tower.

1993, Sept. 2 Litho. *Perf. 11½*

Granite Paper

824 A181 25d multicolored .15 .15
825 A181 50d multicolored .30 .20
826 A181 75d multicolored .45 .30
827 A181 1.50r multicolored .90 .60
Nos. 824-827 (4) 1.80 1.25

Perf. 14x13½

1993, Sept. 2 Litho. Wmk. 368

Designs: 25d, Quill, paper. 50d, Papers with English letters, pen. 75d, Papers with Arabic letters, pen. 1.50r, Scroll, Arabic letters, pen.

828 A182 25d multicolored .15 .15
829 A182 50d multicolored .30 .20
830 A182 75d multicolored .45 .30
831 A182 1.50r multicolored .90 .60
Nos. 828-831 (4) 1.80 1.25

Children's Games A183

Designs: 25d, Girls with thread and spinners. 50d, Boys with stick and disk, vert. 75r, Children guiding wheels with sticks, vert. 1.50r, Girls with jump rope.

1993, Dec. 5 Litho. *Perf. 11½*

Granite Paper

832 A183 25d multicolored .15 .15
833 A183 50d multicolored .30 .20
834 A183 75d multicolored .45 .30
a. Souvenir sheet, 2 each #833, #834
835 A183 1.50r multicolored .90 .60
a. Souvenir sheet, 2 each #832, #835
Nos. 832-835 (4) 1.80 1.25

Falcons — A184 A185

1993, Dec. 22

Granite Paper

836 A184 25d Lanner .15 .15
837 A184 50d Saker .35 .20
838 A184 75d Barbary .55 .30
839 A184 1.50r Peregrine 1.10 .60
a. Souvenir sheet, #836-839
Nos. 836-839 (4) 2.15 1.25

1994, May 6 Litho. *Perf. 14*

Society for Handicapped Welfare and Rehabilition: 75d, Hands above and below handicapped symbol.

840 A185 25d shown .15 .15
841 A185 75d multi .45 .30

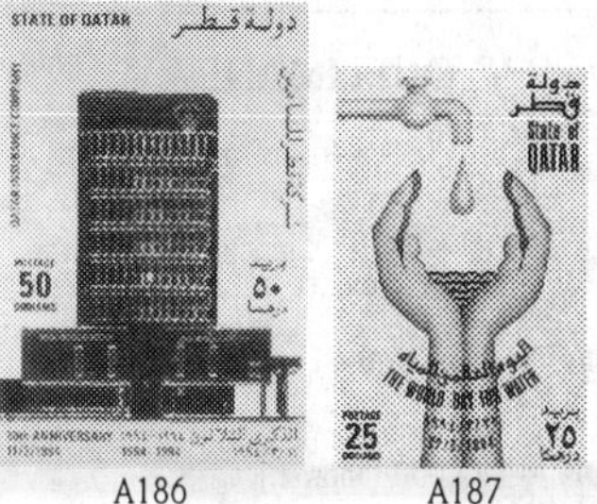

A186 A187

Perf. 14½

1994, Mar. 11 Litho. Unwmk.

Qatar Insurance Co., 30th Anniv.: 50d, Building. 1.50r, Co. arms, global tourist attractions.

842 A186 50d gold & multi .30 .20
843 A186 1.50r gold & multi .90 .60

1994, Mar. 22 Litho. *Perf. 11½*

World Day for Water: 1r, UN emblem, hands catching water drop, tower, grain.

844 A187 25d shown .15 .15
845 A187 1r multicolored .55 .35

A188 A189

1994, Mar. 22 Litho. *Perf. 11½*

846 A188 75d shown .42 .28
847 A188 2r Scales, gavel 1.10 .75

Intl. Law Conference.

Perf. 12x11½

1994, July 16 Litho. Unwmk.

848 A189 25d shown .15 .15
849 A189 1r Family, UN emblem .60 .40

Intl. Year of the Family.

Independence, 23rd Anniv. A190

25d, 2r, Text. 75d, Island. 1r, Oil drilling plant.

1994, Sept. 2 Photo. *Perf. 12*

Granite Paper

850 A190 25d green & multi .15 .15
851 A190 75d multicolored .45 .30
852 A190 1r multicolored .60 .40
853 A190 2r pink & multi 1.25 .80
Nos. 850-853 (4) 2.45 1.65

ILO, 75th Anniv. — A191

1994, May 28 *Perf. 14*

854 A191 25d salmon & multi .15 .15
855 A191 2r green & multi, diff. 1.10 .75

ICAO, 50th Anniv. A192

1994, Dec. 7 *Perf. 13½x14*

856 A192 25d shown .15 .15
857 A192 75d Emblem, airplane .42 .28

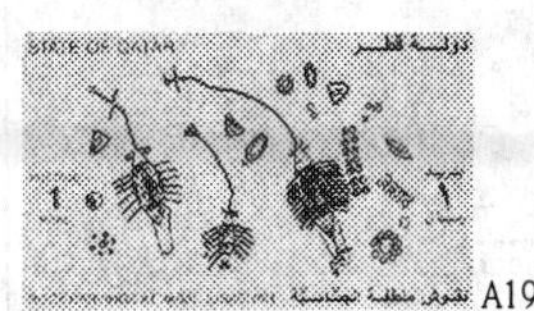

A193

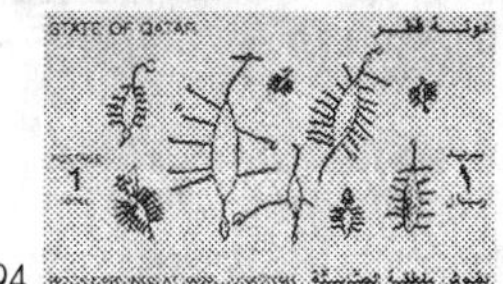

A194

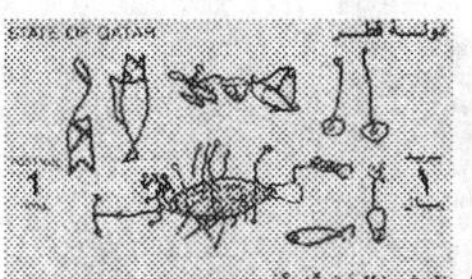

A195

A196

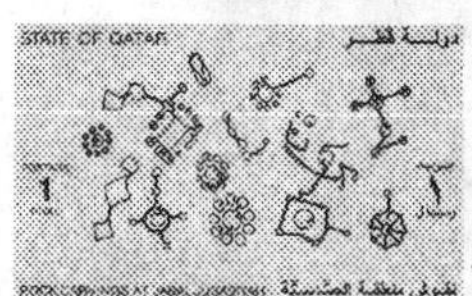

Rock Carvings at Jabal Jusasiyah A197

1995, Mar. 18 Litho. *Perf. 14½x15*

858 A193 1r multicolored .55 .35
859 A194 1r multicolored .55 .35
860 A195 1r multicolored .55 .35
861 A196 1r multicolored .55 .35
862 A197 1r multicolored .55 .35
863 A197 1r multi, diff. .55 .35
a. Vert. strip of 6, #858-863 3.25 2.25

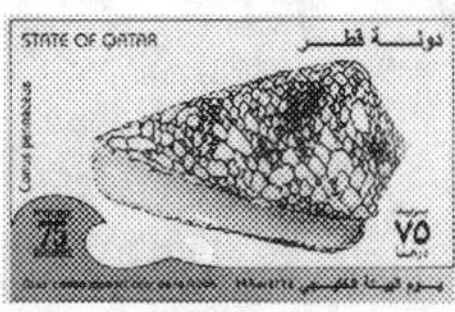

Gulf Environment Day — A198

Shells: No. 864a, Conus pennaceus. b, Cerithidea cingulata. c, Hexaplex kuesterianus. d, Epitonium scalare.

No. 865a, Murex scolopax. b, Thais mutabilis. c, Fusinus arabicus. d, Lambis truncata sebae.

1995, Apr. 24

864 A198 75d Strip of 4, #a.-d. 1.65 1.10
865 A198 1r Strip of 4, #a.-d. 2.25 1.50

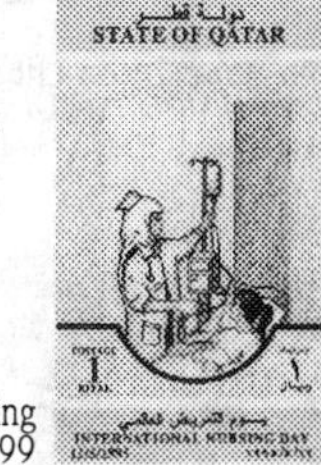

Intl. Nursing Day — A199

Designs: 1r, Nurse adjusting IV for patient. 1.50r, Injecting shot into arm of infant.

1995, May 12

866 A199 1r multicolored .55 .38
867 A199 1.50r multicolored .85 .55

Independence, 24th Anniv. — A200

Designs: a, 1.50r, Shipping dock, city. b, 1r, Children in classroom. c, 1.50r, Aerial view of city. d, 1r, Palm trees.

1995, Sept. 2 Litho. *Perf. 13½x14*

868 A200 Block of 4, #a.-d. 2.75 1.40

UN, 50th Anniv. — A201

1995, Oct. 24 *Perf. 13 1/2*

869 A201 1.50r multicolored .85 .55

Gazelles A202

Designs: No. 870a, 75c, Gazella dorcas pelzelni. b, 50d, Dorcatragus megalotis. c, 25d, Gazella dama. d, 1.50r, Gazella spekei. e, 2r, Gazella soemmeringi. f, 1r, Gazella dorcas.

3r, Gazella spekei, gazella dorcas pelzelni, gazella soemmeringi.

1996, Jan. **Litho.** *Perf. 11 1/2*

870 A202 Strip of 6, #a.-f. 5.00 3.00

Size: 121x81mm

Imperf

871 A202 3r multicolored *30.00 25.00*

Fight Against Drug Abuse — A203

1996, June 26 **Litho.** *Perf. 14x13*

872 A203 50d shown .30 .20

873 A203 1r "NO," needles, hand .60 .40

1996 Summer Olympic Games, Atlanta — A204

Designs: a, 10d, Olympic emblem, map of Qatar. b, 15d, Shooting. c, 25d, Bowling. d, 50d, Table tennis. e, 1r, Athletics. f, 1.50r, Yachting.

1996, July 19 **Litho.** *Perf. 14x13 1/2*

874 A204 Strip of 6, #a.-f. 2.00 1.30

Independence, 25th Anniv. — A204a

1996, Sept. 2 **Litho. & Typo.** *Perf. 12*

Granite Paper

875 A204a 1.50r silver & multi .85 .55

876 A204a 2r gold & multi 1.10 .75

Forts A204b

Designs: 25d, Al-Wajbah, vert. 75d, Al-Zubarah. 1r, Al-Kout. 3r, Umm Salal Mohammed.

1997, Jan. 15 **Litho.** *Perf. 14 1/2*

877 A204b 25d multicolored .15 .15

878 A204b 75d multicolored .45 .30

879 A204b 1r multicolored .60 .35

880 A204b 3r multicolored 1.80 1.20

Nos. 877-880 (4) 3.00 2.00

Sheik Khalifa
A205 A206

1996, Nov. 16 **Photo.** *Perf. 11 1/2x12*

Granite Paper

881 A205 25d pink & multi .15 .15

882 A205 50d green & multi .30 .20

883 A205 75d bl green & multi .45 .30

884 A205 1r gray & multi .60 .40

Perf. 11 1/2

885 A206 1.50r green bl & multi .90 .60

886 A206 2r green & multi 1.20 .80

887 A206 4r vermilion & multi 2.40 1.60

888 A206 5r purple & multi 3.00 2.00

889 A206 10r brown & multi 6.00 4.00

890 A206 20r blue & multi 12.00 8.00

891 A206 30r orange & multi 18.00 12.00

Nos. 881-891 (11) 45.00 30.05

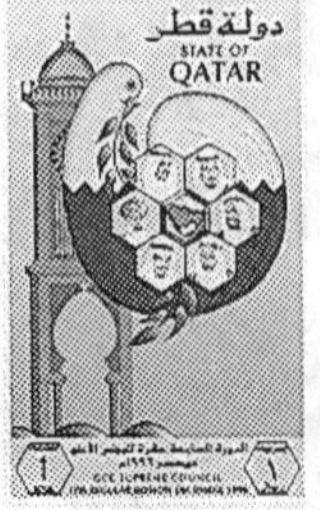

A207 A208

UNICEF, 50th Anniv.: No. 893, Children, open book emblem.

1996, Dec. 11 **Litho.** *Perf. 14 1/2*

892 A207 75d blue & multi .45 .30

893 A207 75d violet & multi .45 .30

1996, Dec. 7

17th Session of GCC Supreme Council: 1.50r, Emblem, dove with olive branch, Sheik Khalifa.

894 A208 1r multicolored .60 .40

895 A208 1.50r multicolored .90 .60

Opening of Port of Ras Laffan — A209

Illustration reduced.

1997, Feb. 24 **Litho.** *Perf. 13 1/2*

896 A209 3r multicolored 1.65 .85

Arabian Horses A210

1997, Mar. 19 **Photo.** *Perf. 12x11 1/2*

897 A210 25d Red horse with tan mane .15 .15

898 A210 75d Black horse .45 .30

899 A210 1r White horse .55 .30

900 A210 1.50r Red brown horse .85 .45

Nos. 897-900 (4) 2.00 1.20

Size: 115x75mm

Imperf

901 A210 3r Mares, foals *25.00*

Independence, 26th Anniv. — A211

1997 **Photo.** *Perf. 11 1/2x12*

Granite Paper

902 A211 1r shown .55 .30

903 A211 1.50r Oil refinery .85 .60

Doha '97, Doha-Mena Economic Conference — A212

1997 **Litho.** *Perf. 11*

904 A212 2r multicolored 1.10 .75

QUELIMANE

ˌkel-ə-ˈmän-ə

LOCATION — A district of the Mozambique Province in Portuguese East Africa

GOVT. — Part of the Portuguese East Africa Colony

AREA — 39,800 sq. mi.

POP. — 877,000 (approx.)

CAPITAL — Quelimane

This district was formerly a part of Zambezia. Quelimane stamps were replaced by those of Mozambique.

100 Centavos = 1 Escudo

Vasco da Gama Issue of Various Portuguese Colonies Surcharged as

REPUBLICA
QUELIMANE
1/4 C.

1913 **Unwmk.** *Perf. 12 1/2 to 16*

On Stamps of Macao

1 CD20 1/4c on 1/2a bl grn 2.50 3.50
2 CD21 1/2c on 1a red 2.00 3.00
3 CD22 1c on 2a red vio 2.00 3.00
4 CD23 2 1/2c on 4a yel grn 2.00 3.00
5 CD24 5c on 8a dk bl 2.00 3.00
6 CD25 7 1/2c on 12a vio brn 2.50 4.50
7 CD26 10c on 16a bis brn 2.00 3.00
a. Inverted surcharge 22.50
8 CD27 15c on 24a bister 2.00 3.00
Nos. 1-8 (8) 17.00 26.00

On Stamps of Portuguese Africa

9 CD20 1/4c on 2 1/2r bl grn 2.00 3.00
10 CD21 1/2c on 5r red 2.00 3.00
11 CD22 1c on 10r red vio 2.00 3.00
12 CD23 2 1/2c on 25r yel grn 2.00 3.00
13 CD24 5c on 50r dk bl 2.00 3.25
14 CD25 7 1/2c on 75r vio brn 2.50 4.50
15 CD26 10c on 100r bister 2.00 3.00
16 CD27 15c on 150r bister 2.00 3.00
Nos. 9-16 (8) 16.50 25.75

On Stamps of Timor

17 CD20 1/4c on 1/2a bl grn 2.00 3.00
18 CD21 1/2c on 1a red 2.00 3.00
19 CD22 1c on 2a red vio 2.00 3.00
20 CD23 2 1/2c on 4a yel grn 2.00 3.00
21 CD24 5c on 8a dk bl 2.00 3.00
22 CD25 7 1/2c on 12a vio brn 2.50 4.50
23 CD26 10c on 16a bis brn 2.00 3.00
24 CD27 15c on 24a bister 2.00 3.00
Nos. 17-24 (8) 16.50 25.50
Nos. 1-24 (24) 50.00 77.25

Ceres — A1

1914 **Typo.** *Perf. 15x14*

Name and Value in Black

25 A1 1/4c olive brown .80 *3.00*
26 A1 1/2c black 1.25 *3.00*
27 A1 1c blue green 1.10 *3.00*
a. Imperf.
28 A1 1 1/2c lilac brown 1.65 *3.00*
29 A1 2c carmine 1.75 *3.00*
30 A1 2 1/2c light violet .50 *1.50*
31 A1 5c deep blue 1.25 *3.00*
32 A1 7 1/2c yellow brown 1.25 *3.00*
33 A1 8c slate 1.35 *3.00*
34 A1 10c orange brown 1.25 *3.00*
35 A1 15c plum 3.00 *5.00*
36 A1 20c yellow green 1.50 *2.50*
37 A1 30c brown, *green* 4.00 *8.50*
38 A1 40c brown, *pink* 4.00 *8.50*
39 A1 50c orange, *salmon* 4.00 *9.50*
40 A1 1e green, *blue* 5.00 *11.00*
Nos. 25-40 (16) 33.65 *73.50*

15-Cent Minimum Value

The minimum catalogue value is 15 cents. Separating se-tenant pieces into individual stamps does not increase the value of the stamps since demand for the separated stamps may be small.

RAS AL KHAIMA

ˌräs al 'kī–mə

LOCATION — Oman Peninsula, Arabia, on Persian Gulf
GOVT. — Sheikdom under British protection

Ras al Khaima was the 7th Persian Gulf sheikdom to join the United Arab Emirates, doing so in Feb. 1972.

See United Arab Emirates.

100 Naye Paise = 1 Rupee

Catalogue values for all unused stamps in this country are for Never Hinged items.

Sheik Saqr bin Mohammed al Qasimi — A1

Seven Palm Trees — A2

Dhow — A3

Perf. 14½x14

1964, Dec. 21 Photo. Unwmk.

1	A1	5np brown & black	.25	.15
2	A1	15np deep blue & blk	.50	.25
3	A2	30np ocher & black	1.00	.50
4	A2	40np blue & black	1.25	.60
5	A2	75np brn red & blk	2.50	1.25
6	A3	1r lt grn & sepia	3.50	1.75
7	A3	2r brt vio & sepia	5.00	2.50
8	A3	5r blue gray & sepia	16.00	8.00
		Nos. 1-8 (8)	30.00	15.00

RHODESIA

rō–'dē–zh(ē–)ə

(British South Africa)

LOCATION — Southeastern Africa
GOVT. — Administered by the British South Africa Company
AREA — 440,653 sq. mi.
POP. — 1,738,000 (estimated 1921)
CAPITAL — Salisbury

In 1923 the area was divided and the portion south of the Zambezi River became the British Crown Colony of Southern Rhodesia. In the following year the remaining territory was formed into the Protectorate of Northern Rhodesia. The Federation of Rhodesia and Nyasaland (comprising Southern Rhodesia, Northern Rhodesia and Nyasaland) was established Sept. 3, 1953.

12 Pence = 1 Shilling
20 Shillings = 1 Pound

A1

A2

Coat of Arms — A3

Thin Paper

Engr. (A1, A3); Engr., Typo. (A2)

1890-94 Unwmk. *Perf. 14, 14½*

1	A2	½p	blue & ver ('91)	2.25	1.00
2	A1	1p	black	8.50	1.00
3	A2	2p	gray grn & ver ('91)	8.00	1.25
4	A2	3p	gray & grn ('91)	7.50	1.25
5	A2	4p	red brn & blk ('91)	8.00	1.50
6	A1	6p	ultra	47.50	18.00
7	A1	6p	deep blue	21.00	3.75
8	A2	8p	rose & bl ('91)	8.50	2.75
9	A1	1sh	gray brown	25.00	10.00
10	A1	2sh	vermilion	35.00	22.50
11	A1	2sh6p	dull lilac	22.50	25.00
			Revenue cancellation		.60
12	A2	3sh	brn & grn ('94)	90.00	65.00
			Revenue cancellation		2.00
13	A2	4sh	gray & ver ('93)	42.50	25.00
			Revenue cancellation		.80
14	A1	5sh	yellow	35.00	42.50
			Revenue cancellation		1.00
15	A1	10sh	deep green	65.00	65.00
			Revenue cancellation		1.00
16	A3	£1	dark blue	*165.00*	*125.00*
			Revenue cancellation		3.00
17	A3	£2	rose	*350.00*	*140.00*
			Revenue cancellation		4.00
18	A3	£5	yellow grn	*1,750.*	*500.00*
			Revenue cancellation		6.00
19	A3	£10	orange brn	*2,250.*	*900.00*
			Revenue cancellation		10.00
			Nos. 1-16 (16)	591.25	*410.50*

The paper of the 1891 issue has the trademark and initials of the makers in a monogram watermarked in each sheet. Some of the lower values were also printed on a slightly thicker paper without watermark.

Copies of #16-19 with cancellations removed are frequently offered as unused specimens.

See #24-25, 58.

For surcharges see #20-23, 40-42. For overprints see British Central Africa #1-20.

Nos. 6 and 9 Surcharged in Black

½d.

1891, Mar.

20	A1	½p on 6p ultra	65.00	*100.00*
21	A1	2p on 6p ultra	70.00	*125.00*
22	A1	4p on 6p ultra	75.00	*175.00*
23	A1	8p on 1sh brown	110.00	*250.00*
		Nos. 20-23 (4)	320.00	*650.00*

Beware of forged surcharges.

Thick Soft Paper

1895 *Perf. 12½*

24	A2	2p green & red	20.00	4.00
25	A2	4p ocher & black	22.50	*8.00*
a.		Imperf., pair	1,750.	

A4

1896 Engraved, Typo. *Perf. 14*

26	A4	½p	slate & violet	.65	.40
27	A4	1p	scarlet & emer	1.00	1.00
28	A4	2p	brown & rose lil	1.75	.75
29	A4	3p	red brown & ultra	.90	.40
30	A4	4p	blue & red lil	.90	.30
a.			4p ultra & red lilac	3.00	2.25
b.			Horiz. pair, imperf. btwn.		
31	A4	6p	vio & pale rose	1.75	.45
a.			6p violet & pink	60.00	10.00
32	A4	8p	dp grn & vio, *buff*	3.50	.85
a.			Imperf. pair	3,000.	
b.			Horiz. pair, imperf. btwn.		
33	A4	1sh	brt grn & ultra	15.00	2.50
34	A4	2sh	dk bl & grn, *buff*	17.50	5.00
35	A4	2sh6p	brn & vio, *yel*	45.00	37.50
36	A4	3sh	grn & red vio, *bl*	45.00	25.00
a.			Imperf. pair	3,500.	
37	A4	4sh	red & bl, *grn*	35.00	3.00
38	A4	5sh	org red & grn	30.00	12.00
39	A4	10sh	sl & car, *rose*	100.00	60.00
			Nos. 26-39 (14)	297.95	149.15

The plates for this issue were made from two dies. Stamps of die I have a small dot at the right of the tail of the supporter at the right of the shield, and the body of the lion is not fully shaded. Stamps of die II have not the dot and the lion is heavily shaded.

See type A7.

Nos. 4, 13-14 Surcharged in Black

One Penny — THREE PENCE.

1896, Apr. *Perf. 14*

40	A2	1p on 3p	350.00	350.00
a.		"P" of "Penny" inverted	*10,000.*	
41	A2	1p on 4sh	375.00	275.00
a.		"P" of "Penny" inverted	*10,000.*	
b.		Single bar in surch.	2,000.	2,500.
c.		"y" of "Penny" inverted	*10,000.*	
42	A1	3p on 5s yellow	210.00	*250.00*
a.		"T" of "THREE" inverted	*10,000.*	
b.		"R" of "THREE" inverted	*10,000.*	
		Nos. 40-42 (3)	935.00	875.00

Cape of Good Hope Stamps Overprinted in Black

BRITISH SOUTH AFRICA COMPANY.

1896, May 22 Wmk. 16

43	A6	½p	slate	6.25	10.00
44	A15	1p	carmine	8.00	10.50
45	A6	2p	bister brown	8.50	6.00
46	A6	4p	deep blue	10.00	10.00
a.			"COMPANY" omitted	*10,000.*	
47	A3	6p	violet	40.00	47.50
48	A6	1sh	yellow buff	80.00	85.00

Wmk. 2

49	A6	3p	claret	37.50	45.00
			Nos. 43-49 (7)	190.25	214.00

Forgeries are plentiful.

Remainders

Rhodesian authorities made available remainders in large quantities of all stamps in 1897, 1898-1908, 1905, 1909 and 1910 issues, CTO. Some varieties exist only as remainders. See notes following Nos. 100 and 118.

A7

Type A7 differs from type A4 in having the ends of the scroll which is below the shield curved between the hind legs of the supporters instead of passing behind one leg of each. There are other minor differences.

Perf. 13½ to 16

1897 Unwmk. Engr.

50	A7	½p	slate & violet	2.50	1.25
51	A7	1p	ver & gray grn	2.75	1.25
52	A7	2p	brown & lil rose	2.00	.50
53	A7	3p	red brn & gray bl	2.00	.50
a.			Vert. pair, imperf. btwn.	*1,500.*	
54	A7	4p	ultra & red lilac	2.75	.35
a.			Horiz. pair, imperf. btwn.	*5,000.*	*5,000.*
55	A7	6p	violet & salmon	2.75	1.00
56	A7	8p	dk grn & vio, *buff*	11.50	1.25
57	A7	£1	black & red, *grn*	425.00	200.00
			Revenue cancellation		10.00
			Nos. 50-56 (7)	26.25	6.10

Thick Paper

Perf. 15

58	A3	£2	bright red	*1,300.*	425.00
			Revenue cancellation		*10.00*

See note on remainders following No. 49.

A8

A9

A10

1898-1908 *Perf. 13½ to 16*

59	A8	½p	yellow green	1.00	.15
a.			Imperf. pair	900.00	
b.			Horiz. pair, imperf. vert.	900.00	
60	A8	1p	rose	1.10	.15
a.			1p red	.75	.15
b.			Horiz. or vert. pair, imperf. btwn.	*500.00*	
d.			Imperf. pair	*500.00*	*500.00*
61	A8	2p	brown	1.00	.15
62	A8	2½p	cobalt bl ('03)	3.00	.40
a.			Horiz. pair, imperf. between	*750.00*	*750.00*
63	A8	3p	claret ('08)	3.00	.40
a.			Vert. pair, imperf. between	*900.00*	
64	A8	4p	olive green	3.00	.15
a.			Vert. pair, imperf. between	*700.00*	
65	A8	6p	lilac	5.50	1.50
a.			Vert. pair, imperf. between		
66	A9	1sh	olive bister	6.50	1.00
a.			Imperf., pair	*3,500.*	
b.			Horiz. or vert. pair, imperf. btwn.	*3,500.*	
67	A9	2sh6p	bluish gray ('06)	27.50	.65
a.			Vert. pair, imperf. between	*1,300.*	*750.00*
68	A9	3sh	purple ('08)	7.00	1.00
69	A9	5sh	orange ('01)	18.00	8.00
70	A9	7sh6p	black ('01)	35.00	14.00
71	A9	10sh	bluish grn ('08)	12.00	2.00
72	A10	£1	gray vio ('01)	140.00	50.00
			Revenue cancellation		1.00
73	A10	£2	red brown ('08)	55.00	10.00
74	A10	£5	dk blue ('01)	*2,250.*	
			Revenue cancellation		6.00
75	A10	£10	blue lil ('01)	*2,750.*	
			Revenue cancellation		5.50
			Nos. 59-73 (15)	318.60	89.55

For overprints and surcharges see #82-100.
See note on remainders following #49.

Victoria Falls — A11

1905, July 13 *Perf. 13½ to 15*

No.	Type	Description	Unused	Used
76	A11	1p rose red	2.25	3.25
77	A11	2½p ultra	6.50	3.25
78	A11	5p magenta	15.00	35.00
79	A11	1sh blue green	16.00	20.00
a.		Imperf., pair	*12,500.*	
b.		Horiz. pair, imperf. vert.	*12,000.*	
c.		Horiz. pair, imperf. btwn.	*15,000.*	
d.		Vert. pair, imperf. btn.	*15,000.*	
80	A11	2sh6p black	85.00	*125.00*
81	A11	5sh violet	72.50	40.00
		Nos. 76-81 (6)	197.25	*226.50*

Opening of the Victoria Falls bridge across the Zambezi River.

See note on remainders following No. 49.

Stamps of 1898-1908 Overprinted or Surcharged:

RHODESIA.

RHODESIA.
5d

1909 *Perf. 14, 15*

No.	Type	Description	Unused	Used
82	A8	½p yellow green	.15	.15
83	A8	1p red	.15	.15
a.		Horiz. pair, imperf., vert.	*450.00*	
84	A8	2p brown	.90	.90
85	A8	2½p cobalt blue	.30	.15
86	A8	3p claret	.60	.20
b.		Double overprint		
87	A8	4p olive green	2.25	.45
88	A8	5p on 6p lilac	3.00	1.65
89	A8	6p lilac	4.25	.60
90	A9	7½p on 2sh6p	.75	.60
91	A9	10p on 3sh pur	1.25	1.25
92	A9	1sh olive bis	4.00	.35
93	A9	2sh on 5sh org	5.00	1.65
94	A9	2sh6p bluish gray	14.00	3.50
95	A9	3sh purple	13.00	6.00
96	A9	5sh orange	21.00	5.50
97	A9	7sh6p black	60.00	22.50
98	A9	10sh bluish grn	25.00	6.00
99	A10	£1 gray violet	95.00	60.00
a.		Pair, one without overprint	*15,000.*	
b.		Violet overprint	250.00	180.00
100	A10	£2 red brown	*2,400.*	325.00
		Nos. 82-99 (18)	250.60	111.60

See note on remainders following No. 49. The remainders included inverted overprints of the 3p ($35), 4p ($15) and 2s6p ($27.50).

Nos. 82-87, 89, 92, 94, 96 and 98 exist without period after "Rhodesia."

Queen Mary and King George V
A12 A13

1910 Engr. *Perf. 14, 15x14, 14x15*

No.	Type	Description	Unused	Used
101	A12	½p green	6.00	1.00
a.		½p olive green	14.00	1.25
b.		Perf. 15	225.00	13.00
c.		Imperf., pair	*6,000.*	*6,750.*
d.		Perf. 13½	250.00	37.50
102	A12	1p rose carmine	9.00	.50
a.		Vertical pair, imperf. btwn.	*18,500.*	
b.		Perf. 15	200.00	7.00
c.		Perf. 13½	*1,500.*	55.00
103	A12	2p gray & blk	27.50	6.00
a.		Horiz. pair, imperf. btwn.		
b.		Perf. 15	650.00	27.50
104	A12	2½p ultramarine	10.50	6.00
a.		2½p light blue	12.50	6.00
b.		Perf. 15	75.00	37.50
c.		Perf. 13½	30.00	37.50
105	A12	3p ol yel & vio	20.00	8.50
a.		Perf. 15	1,600.	55.00
106	A12	4p orange & blk	22.50	10.00
a.		4p orange & violet blk	52.50	35.00
b.		Perf. 15x14	550.00	
c.		Perf. 15	35.00	67.50
107	A12	5p ol grn & brn	20.00	27.50
a.		5p olive yel & brn (error)	400.00	115.00
b.		Perf. 15	450.00	115.00
108	A12	6p claret & brn	20.00	10.00
a.		Perf. 15	1,000.	55.00
109	A12	8p brn vio & gray blk	90.00	55.00
a.		Perf. 13½	50.00	150.00
110	A12	10p plum & rose red	25.00	42.50
111	A12	1sh turq grn & black	27.50	10.00
a.		Horiz. pair, imperf. btwn.		
b.		Perf. 15	550.00	35.00
112	A12	2sh gray bl & black	50.00	40.00
a.		Perf. 15	900.00	325.00
113	A12	2sh6p car rose & blk	325.00	275.00
114	A12	3sh vio & bl grn	120.00	120.00
115	A12	5sh yel grn & brn red	250.00	225.00
116	A12	7sh6p brt bl & car	500.00	450.00
117	A12	10sh red org & bl grn	300.00	200.00
a.		10sh red org & myr grn	500.00	250.00
118	A12	£1 bluish sl & car	900.00	350.00
a.		£1 black & red	1,000.	300.00
c.		Perf. 15	*15,000.*	4,750.
		Nos. 101-118 (18)	2,723.	1,837.

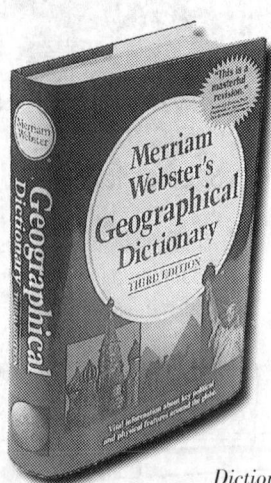

See note on remainders following No. 49. The £1 in plum and red is from the remainders.

1913-19 *Perf. 14*

No.	Type	Description	Unused	Used
119	A13	½p green	3.00	.55
a.		Horiz. pair, imperf. vert.	*525.00*	*525.00*
b.		Perf. 15	4.00	2.50
c.		Perf. 14x15	*2,000.*	200.00
d.		Perf. 15x14	*2,000.*	225.00
120	A13	1p brown rose	2.75	.15
a.		1p bright rose	4.00	.50
b.		Horiz. pair, imperf. btwn.	525.00	525.00
c.		Perf. 15	2.25	2.50
121	A13	1½p bister	2.50	.50
a.		Perf. 15	20.00	3.25
b.		Perf. 15x14		
c.		Vert. pair, imperf. btwn.	*525.00*	*525.00*
d.		Horiz. pair, imperf. btwn.	*525.00*	*525.00*
122	A13	2p vio blk & blk	3.00	1.10
a.		2p gray & blk	4.00	3.00
b.		Perf. 15	3.00	3.00
c.		Horiz. pair, imperf. btwn.	*3,250.*	*3,500.*
123	A13	2½p ultra	3.50	*12.00*
a.		Perf. 15	14.00	20.00
124	A13	3p orange yel & blk	3.50	1.25
a.		3p yellow & blk	5.00	3.00
b.		Perf. 15	6.00	5.25
125	A13	4p orange red & blk	7.00	3.25
a.		Perf. 15	30.00	13.00
126	A13	5p yel grn & blk	3.75	6.00
127	A13	6p lilac & blk	4.00	1.50
a.		Perf. 15	4.00	4.00
128	A13	8p gray grn & violet	10.00	25.00
a.		Perf. 15	30.00	30.00
129	A13	10p car rose & bl, perf. 15	6.50	*16.00*
a.		Perf. 14	8.50	*18.00*
130	A13	1sh turq bl & blk	5.00	2.50
a.		Perf. 15	6.50	1.75
131	A13	1sh lt grn & blk ('19)	45.00	15.00
132	A13	2sh brn & blk, perf. 14	11.00	8.00
a.		Perf. 15	11.00	20.00
133	A13	2sh6p ol gray & vio bl	20.00	8.50
a.		2sh6p gray & blue	20.00	22.50
b.		Perf. 15	20.00	20.00
134	A13	3sh brt blue & red brown	25.00	13.00
a.		Perf. 15	140.00	100.00
135	A13	5sh green & blue	55.00	45.00
a.		Perf. 15	75.00	75.00
136	A13	7sh6p black & vio, perf. 15	82.50	110.00
a.		Perf. 14	165.00	165.00
137	A13	10sh yel grn & car	140.00	140.00
a.		Perf. 15	140.00	225.00
138	A13	£1 violet & blk	450.00	*550.00*
a.		£1 magenta & black	450.00	*550.00*
b.		Perf. 15	650.00	650.00
		Nos. 119-138 (20)	883.00	*959.30*

Three dies were used for the stamps of this issue: 1) Outline at top of cap absent or very faint and broken. Left ear not shaded or outlined and appears white; 2) Outline at top of cap faint and broken. Ear shaded all over, with no outline; 3) Outline at top of cap continuous. Ear shaded all over, with continuous outline.

No. 120 Surcharged in Dark Violet:

Half Penny — No. 139

Half- Penny. — No. 140

1917

No.	Type	Description	Unused	Used
139	A13	½p on 1p	2.50	1.00
a.		Inverted surcharge	*1,500.*	*1,600.*
140	A13	½p on 1p	2.00	.65

Nos. 141-190 are accorded to Rhodesia and Nyasaland.

RHODESIA AND NYASALAND

rō-ˈdē-zh(ē-)ə ən(d) nī-ˈa-sə-ˌland

LOCATION — Southern Africa
GOVT. — Federal State in British Commonwealth
AREA — 486,973 sq. mi.
POP. — 8,510,000 (est. 1961)
CAPITAL — Salisbury, Southern Rhodesia

The Federation of Southern Rhodesia, Northern Rhodesia and Nyasaland was created in 1953, dissolved at end of 1963.

12 Pence = 1 Shilling
20 Shillings = 1 Pound

Catalogue values for all unused stamps in this country are for Never Hinged items.

A14

A15

Queen Elizabeth II
A16

Perf. 13½ (A14), 13½x13 (A15), 14x13 (A16)

1954-56 Engr. Unwmk.

No.	Type	Description	Unused	Used
141	A14	½p vermilion	.15	.15
a.		Booklet pane of 6	1.25	
b.		Perf. 12½x13½	.60	.40
142	A14	1p ultra	.15	.15
a.		Booklet pane of 6	1.25	
b.		Perf. 12½x13½	.80	.50
143	A14	2p emerald	.15	.15
a.		Booklet pane of 6	1.65	
143B	A14	2½p ocher ('56)	2.00	.15
144	A14	3p carmine	.15	.15
145	A14	4p red brown	.45	.15
146	A14	4½p blue green	.20	.15
147	A14	6p red lilac	1.40	.15
148	A14	9p purple	.60	.35
149	A14	1sh gray	1.25	.15
150	A15	1sh3p ultra & ver	2.25	.15
151	A15	2sh brn & dp bl	6.25	.70
152	A15	2sh6p carmine & blk	5.25	.55
153	A15	5sh olive & pur	12.00	1.40
154	A16	10sh red orange & aqua	15.00	7.00
155	A16	£1 brn car & ol	22.50	12.50
		Nos. 141-155 (16)	69.75	24.00

Issue dates: 2½p, Feb. 15, others, July 1.

Victoria Falls
A17 A18

1955, June 15 *Perf. 13½*

No.	Type	Description	Unused	Used
156	A17	3p Plane	.30	.15
157	A18	1sh David Livingstone	.85	.55

Centenary of discovery of Victoria Falls.

Tea Picking
A19

Rhodes' Grave, Matopos
A20

Designs: 1p, V. H. F. Mast. 2p, Copper mining. 2½p, Kingsley Fairbridge Memorial. 4p, Boat on Lake Bangweulu. 6p, Victoria Falls. 9p, Railroad trains. 1sh, Tobacco. 1sh3p, Ship on Lake Nyasa. 2sh, Chirundu Bridge, Zambezi River. 2sh6p, Salisbury Airport. 5sh, Cecil Rhodes statue, Salisbury. 10sh, Mlanje mountain. £1, Coat of arms.

Perf. 13½x14, 14x13½

1959-63 Engr. Unwmk.

Size: 18½x22½mm, 22½x18½mm

No.	Type	Description	Unused	Used
158	A19	½p emerald & blk	.50	.15
a.		Perf. 12½x13½	2.75	.65

159 A19 1p blk & rose red .15 .15
a. Perf. 12½x13½ 2.75 .65
b. Rose red (center) omitted 400.00
160 A19 2p ocher & violet .90 .15
161 A19 2½p slate & lil, perf. 14½ .35 .30
162 A20 3p blue & black .15 .15
a. Booklet pane of 4 ('63) 1.50
b. Black omitted

Perf. 14½

Size: 24x27mm, 27x24mm

163 A19 4p olive & mag 1.10 .15
164 A19 6p green & ultra .50 .15
164A A20 9p pur & ocher ('62) 6.25 2.75
165 A20 1sh ultra & yel grn .70 .20
166 A20 1sh3p sep & brt grn, perf. 14 2.75 .20
167 A20 2sh lake & grn 3.00 1.00
168 A20 2sh6p ocher & blue 3.75 1.00

Perf. 11½

Size: 32x27mm

169 A20 5sh yel grn & choc 5.25 1.65
170 A20 10sh brt rose & ol 22.50 9.50
171 A20 £1 violet & blk 37.50 19.00
Nos. 158-171 (15) 85.35 36.50

Nos. 158a and 159a are coils.
Issue dates: 9p, May 15, others, Aug. 12.

Kariba Gorge, 1955 — A21

Designs: 6p, Power lines. 1sh, View of dam. 1sh3p, View of dam and lake. 2sh6p, Power station. 5sh, Dam and Queen Mother Elizabeth.

1960, May 17 Photo. *Perf. 14½x14*

172 A21 3p orange & sl grn .40 .15
a. Orange omitted —
173 A21 6p yel brn & brn .55 .35
174 A21 1sh dull bl & emer 1.10 1.10
175 A21 1sh3p grnsh bl & ocher 1.75 1.75
176 A21 2sh6p org ver & blk 4.00 4.00
177 A21 5sh grnsh bl & lilac 7.75 7.75
Nos. 172-177 (6) 15.55 15.10

Miner with Drill — A22

Design: 1sh3p, Mining surface installations.

1961, May 8 Unwmk.

178 A22 6p chnt brn & ol grn .40 .35
179 A22 1sh3p lt blue & blk .70 .65

7th Commonwealth Mining and Metallurgical Cong., Apr. 10-May 20.

DH Hercules Biplane A23

Designs: 1sh3p, Flying boat over Zambezi River. 2sh6p, DH Comet, Salisbury Airport.

1962, Feb. 6

180 A23 6p ver & ol grn .45 .45
181 A23 1sh3p bl, blk, grn & yel 1.00 1.00
182 A23 2sh6p dk pur & car rose 6.50 6.50
Nos. 180-182 (3) 7.95 7.95

30th anniv. of the inauguration of the Rhodesia-London airmail service.

RHODESIA & NYASALAND Tobacco Plant — A24

Designs: 6p, Tobacco field. 1sh3p, Auction floor. 2sh6p, Cured tobacco.

1963, Feb. 18 Photo. *Perf. 14x14½*

184 A24 3p gray brown & grn .15 .15
185 A24 6p blue, grn & brn .15 .15
186 A24 1sh3p slate & red brn .35 .35
187 A24 2sh6p brown & org yel 1.50 1.50
Nos. 184-187 (4) 2.15 2.15

3rd World Tobacco Scientific Cong., Salisbury, Feb. 18-26 and the 1st Intl. Tobacco Trade Cong., Salisbury, March 6-16.

Red Cross — A25

1963, Aug. 6 *Perf. 14½x14*

188 A25 3p red .80 .20

Centenary of the International Red Cross.

"Round Table" Emblem A26

1963, Sept. 11 Unwmk.

189 A26 6p multicolored .45 .45
190 A26 1sh3p multicolored .70 .70

World Council of Young Men's Service Clubs at University College of Rhodesia and Nyasaland, Sept. 8-15.

POSTAGE DUE STAMPS

D1

Perf. 12½

1961, Apr. 19 Unwmk. Typo.

J1 D1 1p vermilion 1.50 3.00
a. Horiz. pair, imperf. btwn. 475.00
J2 D1 2p dark blue 2.00 2.50
J3 D1 4p emerald 2.50 7.00
J4 D1 6p dark purple 3.75 7.00
a. Horiz. pair, imperf. btwn. —
Nos. J1-J4 (4) 9.75 19.50

Nos. 142-143 exist with provisional "Poastage Due" handstamp.

RHODESIA

rō-ˈdē-zh(ē-)ə

Self-Governing State (formerly Southern Rhodesia)

LOCATION — Southeastern Africa, bordered by Zambia, Mozambique, South Africa and Botswana
GOVT. — Self-governing member of British Commonwealth
AREA — 150,333 sq. mi.
POP. — 4,670,000 (est. 1968)
CAPITAL — Salisbury

In Oct. 1964, Southern Rhodesia assumed the name Rhodesia. On Nov. 11, 1965, the white minority government declared Rhodesia independent. Rhodesia became Zimbabwe on Apr. 18, 1980. For earlier issues, see Southern Rhodesia and Rhodesia and Nyasaland.

12 Pence = 1 Shilling
20 Shillings = 1 Pound
100 Cents = 1 Dollar (1967)

Catalogue values for all unused stamps in this country are for Never Hinged items.

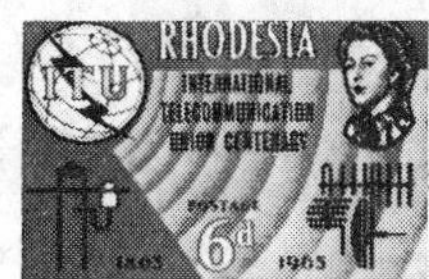

ITU Emblem, Old and New Communication Equipment — A27

Unwmk.

1965, May 17 Photo. *Perf. 14*

200 A27 6p apple grn & brt vio .80 .35
201 A27 1sh3p brt vio & dk vio 1.25 1.00
202 A27 2sh6p org brn & dk vio 4.25 4.25
Nos. 200-202 (3) 6.30 5.60

Cent. of the ITU.

Bangala Dam — A28

Designs: 4p, Irrigation canal through sugar plantation. 2sh6p, Worker cutting sugar cane.

1965, July 19 Photo. *Perf. 14*

203 A28 3p dull bl, grn & ocher .25 .15
204 A28 4p blue, grn & brn .70 .70
205 A28 2sh6p multicolored 4.00 3.25
Nos. 203-205 (3) 4.95 4.10

Issued to publicize Conservation Week of the Natural Resources Board.

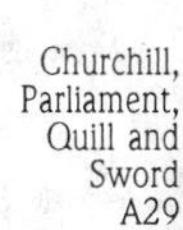

Churchill, Parliament, Quill and Sword A29

1965, Aug. 16

206 A29 1sh3p ultra & black .70 .40

Sir Winston Spencer Churchill (1874-1965), statesman and WWII leader.
For surcharge see No. 222.

Issues of Smith Government

Arms of Rhodesia A30

1965, Dec. 8 Photo. *Perf. 11*

207 A30 2sh6p violet & multi .25 .20
a. Imperf., pair 825.00

Declaration of independence by the government of Prime Minister Ian Smith.

Southern Rhodesia Nos. 95-108 Overprinted

INDEPENDENCE
11th November 1965

Perf. 14½

1966, Jan. 17 Unwmk. Photo.

Size: 23x19mm

208 A30 ½p lt bl, yel & grn .15 .15
209 A30 1p ocher & purple .15 .15
210 A30 2p violet & org yel .15 .15
211 A30 3p lt blue & choc .15 .15
212 A30 4p sl green & org .15 .15

Perf. 13½x13

Size: 27x23mm

213 A30 6p dull grn, red & yel .15 .15
a. Pair, one without overprint
214 A30 9p ol grn, yel & brn .25 .20
a. Double overprint 125.00
b. Inverted overprint
215 A30 1sh ocher & brt grn .30 .25
a. Double overprint 150.00
216 A30 1sh3p grn, vio & dk red .35 .30
217 A30 2sh dull bl & yel 1.00 .90
218 A30 2sh6p ultra & red .65 .55
a. Red omitted

Perf. 14½x14

Size: 32x27mm

Overprint 26mm Wide

219 A30 5sh bl, grn, ocher & lt brn 13.00 9.25
220 A30 10sh ocher, blk, red & bl 3.25 3.00
221 A30 £1 rose, sep, ocher & grn 6.00 5.50
Nos. 208-221 (14) 25.70 20.85

No. 206 Surcharged in Red

INDEPENDENCE
11th November
1965
= 5/-

Perf. 14

222 A29 5sh on 1sh3p 21.00 45.00

Ansellia Orchid — A31

Designs: 1p, Cape Buffalo. 2p, Oranges. 3p, Kudu. 4p, Emeralds. 6p, Flame lily. 9p, Tobacco. 1sh, Corn. 1sh3p, Lake Kyle. 2sh, Aloe. 2sh6p, Tigerfish. 5sh, Cattle. 10sh, Gray-breasted helmet guinea fowl. £1, Arms of Rhodesia.

Printed by Harrison & Sons, London.

1966, Feb. 9 Photo. *Perf. 14½*

Size: 23x19mm

223 A31 1p ocher & pur .15 .15
224 A31 2p slate grn & org .15 .15
225 A31 3p lt blue & choc .15 .15
b. Queen's head omitted
c. Booklet pane of 4 .85
226 A31 4p gray & brt grn .50 .15

Perf. 13½x13

Size: 27x23mm

227 A31 6p dull grn, red & yel .15 .15
228 A31 9p purple & ocher .15 .15
229 A31 1sh lt blue, yel & grn .15 .15
230 A31 1sh3p dull blue & yel .25 .15
231 A31 1sh6p ol grn, yel & brn 1.65 .35
232 A31 2sh lt ol grn, vio & dk red 1.10 1.10
233 A31 2sh6p brt grnsh bl, ultra & ver .50 .25

Perf. 14½x14

Size: 32x27mm

234 A31 5sh bl, grn, ocher & lt brn .55 .55
235 A31 10sh dl yel, blk, red & bl 3.25 3.25
236 A31 £1 sal pink, sep, ocher & grn 12.00 12.00
Nos. 223-236 (14) 20.70 18.70

See Nos. 245-248A.

Printed by Mardon Printers, Salisbury

1966-68 Litho. *Perf. 14½*

223a A31 1p ocher & purple .15 .15
224a A31 2p sl grn & org ('68) .15 .15
225a A31 3p lt bl & choc ('68) .20 .20
226a A31 4p sepia & brt grn .30 .30
227a A31 6p gray grn, red & yel .45 .45
228a A31 9p pur & ocher ('68) .60 .60
230a A31 1sh3p dl bl & yel .80 .80
232a A31 2sh lt ol grn, vio & dk red 3.25 3.25

Perf. 14

234a A31 5sh brt bl, grn, ocher & brn 8.25 8.25
235a A31 10sh ocher, blk, red & bl 27.50 27.50
236a A31 £1 sal pink, sep, ocher & grn 40.00 40.00
Nos. 223a-236a (11) 81.65 81.65

Zeederberg Coach A32

Designs: 9p, Sir Rowland Hill. 1sh6p, Penny Black. 2sh6p, Rhodesia No. 18, £5.

Perf. 14½

1966, May 2 Litho. Unwmk.

237 A32 3p blue, org & blk .20 .15
238 A32 9p beige & brown .25 .25
239 A32 1sh6p blue & black .65 .50

240 A32 2sh6p rose, yel grn & blk 1.10 1.10
a. Souvenir sheet of 4, #237-240 16.00 25.00
Nos. 237-240 (4) 2.20 2.00

28th Cong. of the Southern Africa Phil. Fed. and the RHOPEX Exhib., Bulawayo, May 2-7.

No. 240a was printed in sheets of 12 and comes with perforations extending through the margins in four different versions. Many have holes in the top margin made when the sheet was cut into individual panes. Sizes of panes vary.

De Havilland Dragon Rapide — A33

Planes: 1sh3p, Douglas DC-3. 2sh6p, Vickers Viscount. 5sh, Jet.

1966, June 1

241 A33 6p multicolored .80 .60
242 A33 1sh3p multicolored 1.40 .70
243 A33 2sh6p multicolored 3.50 2.75
244 A33 5sh blue & black 6.00 4.25
Nos. 241-244 (4) 11.70 8.30

20th anniv. of Central African Airways.

Dual Currency Issue

Type of 1966 with Denominations in Cents and Pence-Shillings

1967-68 Litho. Perf. 14½

245 A31 3p/2½c lt blue & choc .60 .20
246 A31 1sh/10c multi .75 .45
247 A31 1sh6p/15c multi 4.00 .90
248 A31 2sh/20c multi 7.75 9.00
248A A31 2sh6p/25c multi 40.00 52.50
Nos. 245-248A (5) 53.10 63.05

These locally printed stamps were issued to acquaint Rhodesians with the decimal currency to be introduced in 1969-1970.

Issued: 3p, Mar. 15, 1967. 1sh, Nov. 1, 1967. 1sh6p, 2sh, Mar. 11, 1968. 2sh6p, Dec. 9, 1968.

Leander Starr Jameson, by Frank Moss Bennett A34

1967, May 17

249 A34 1sh6p emerald & multi .40 .40

Dr. Leander Starr Jameson (1853-1917), pioneer with Cecil Rhodes and Prime Minister of Cape Colony. See No. 262.

Soapstone Sculpture, by Joram Mariga A35

9p, Head of Burgher of Calais, by Auguste Rodin. 1sh3p, "Totem," by Roberto Crippa. 2sh6p, St. John the Baptist, by Michele Tosini.

1967, July 12 Litho. Perf. 14

250 A35 3p brn, blk & ol grn .15 .15
251 A35 9p brt bl, blk & ol grn .15 .15
252 A35 1sh3p multicolored .20 .20
253 A35 2sh6p multicolored .50 .45
Nos. 250-253 (4) 1.00 .95

10th anniv. of the Rhodes Natl. Gallery, Salisbury.

White Rhinoceros A36

Designs: No. 255, Parrot's beak gladioli, vert. No. 256, Baobab tree. No. 257, Elephants.

1967, Sept. 6 Unwmk. Perf. 14½

254 A36 4p olive & black .25 .25
255 A36 4p dp orange & blk .25 .25
256 A36 4p brown & blk .25 .25
257 A36 4p gray & blk .25 .25
Nos. 254-257 (4) 1.00 1.00

Issued to publicize nature conservation.

Wooden Hand Plow, c. 1820 A37

Designs: 9p, Ox-drawn plow, c. 1860. 1sh6p, Steam tractor and plows, c. 1905. 2sh6p, Tractor and moldboard plow, 1968.

1968, Apr. 26 Litho. Perf. 14½

258 A37 3p multicolored .15 .15
259 A37 9p multicolored .15 .15
260 A37 1sh6p multicolored .30 .30
261 A37 2sh6p multicolored .80 .80
Nos. 258-261 (4) 1.40 1.40

15th world plowing contest, Kent Estate, Norton.

Portrait Type of 1967

Design: 1sh6p, Alfred Beit (portrait at left).

1968, July 15 Unwmk. Perf. 14½

262 A34 1sh6p orange, blk & red .45 .45

Alfred Beit (1853-1906), philanthropist and friend of Cecil Rhodes.

Allan Wilson, Matopos Hills — A38

Matabeleland, 75th Anniversary: 3p, Flag raising, Bulawayo, 1893. 9p, Bulawayo arms, view of Bulawayo.

1968, Nov. 4 Litho. Perf. 14½

263 A38 3p multicolored .15 .15
264 A38 9p multicolored .25 .25
265 A38 1sh6p multicolored .45 .45
Nos. 263-265 (3) .85 .85

William Henry Milton (1854-1930), Adminstrator A39

1969, Jan. 15

266 A39 1sh6p multicolored .50 .50

See Nos. 298-303.

Locomotive, 1890's A40

Beira-Salisbury Railroad, 70th Anniversary: 9p, Steam locomotive, 1901. 1sh6p, Garratt articulated locomotive, 1950, 2sh6p, Diesel, 1955.

1969, May 22

267 A40 3p multicolored .50 .20
268 A40 9p multicolored 1.50 .85
269 A40 1sh6p multicolored 6.00 4.50
270 A40 2sh6p multicolored 9.50 7.75
Nos. 267-270 (4) 17.50 13.30

Low Level Bridge — A41

Bridges: 9p, Mpudzi River. 1sh6p, Umniati River. 2sh6p, Birchenough over Sabi River.

1969, Sept. 18

271 A41 3p multicolored .25 .20
272 A41 9p multicolored .90 .50
273 A41 1sh6p multicolored 3.25 2.25
274 A41 2sh6p multicolored 4.25 2.75
Nos. 272-274 (3) 8.40 5.50

Blast Furnace — A42

Devil's Cataract, Victoria Falls — A43

Designs: 1c, Wheat harvest. 2½c, Ruins, Zimbabwe. 3c, Trailer truck. 3½c, 4c, Cecil Rhodes statue. 5c, Mining. 6c, Hydrofoil, "Seaflight." 7½c, like 8c. 10c, Yachting, Lake McIlwaine. 12½c, Hippopotamus. 14c, 15c, Kariba Dam. 20c, Irrigation canal. 25c, Bateleur eagles. 50c, Radar antenna and Viscount plane. $1, "Air Rescue." $2, Rhodesian flag.

1970-73 Litho. Perf. 14½

Size: 22x18mm

275 A42 1c multicolored .15 .15
a. Booklet pane of 4 .25
b. Min. sheet of 4, Rhophil 2.50
276 A42 2c multicolored .15 .15
277 A42 2½c multicolored .15 .15
a. Booklet pane of 4 .20
b. Min. sheet of 4, Rhophil 2.50
278 A42 3c multi ('73) 1.40 .20
a. Booklet pane of 4 7.25
279 A42 3½c multicolored .15 .15
a. Booklet pane of 4 .70
b. Min. sheet of 4, Rhophil 2.50
280 A42 4c multi ('73) 1.65 .25
a. Booklet pane of 4 8.00
281 A42 5c multicolored .15 .15

Size: 27x23mm

282 A43 6c multi ('73) 4.00 1.00
283 A43 7½c multi ('73) 8.00 3.25
284 A43 8c multicolored 1.25 .80
285 A43 10c multicolored .50 .25
286 A43 12½c multicolored 1.00 .25
287 A43 14c multi ('73) 16.00 2.75
288 A43 15c multi 2.50 .40
289 A43 20c multicolored 1.65 .45

Size: 30x25mm

290 A43 25c multicolored 3.25 1.00
291 A43 50c multicolored 2.25 4.00
292 A43 $1 multicolored 3.25 8.50
293 A43 $2 multicolored 11.00 25.00
Nos. 275-293 (19) 58.45 48.85

Booklet panes and miniature sheets were made by altering the plates used to print the stamps, eliminating every third horizontal and vertical row of stamps. The perforations extend through the margins in four different versions. In 1972 sheets of 4 overprinted in the margins were issued for Rhophil '72 Philatelic Exhibition.

Issue dates: Feb. 17, 1970, Jan. 1, 1973.

Despatch Rider, c. 1890 — A44

Posts and Telecommunications Corporation, Inauguration: 3½c, Loading mail, Salisbury Airport. 15c, Telegraph line construction, c.1890. 25c, Telephone and telecommunications equipment.

1970, July 1

294 A44 2½c multicolored .25 .25
295 A44 3½c multicolored .55 .55
296 A44 15c multicolored 1.75 1.75
297 A44 25c multicolored 3.00 3.00
Nos. 294-297 (4) 5.55 5.55

Famous Rhodesians Type of 1969

Portraits: 13c Dr. Robert Moffat (1795-1883), missionary. No. 299, Dr. David Livingstone (1813-73), explorer. No. 300, George Pauling (1854-1919), engineer No. 301, Thomas Baines (1820-75), self-portrait. No. 302, Mother Patrick (1863-1900), Dominican nurse and teacher. No. 303, Frederick Courteney Selous (1851-1917), explorer, big game hunter.

1970-75 Litho. Perf. 14½

298 A39 13c multi ('72) 1.50 1.50
299 A39 14c multi ('73) 1.00 1.00
300 A39 14c multi ('74) 1.50 1.50
301 A39 14c multi ('75) 1.25 1.25
302 A39 15c multi .75 .75
303 A39 15c multi ('71) .70 .70
Nos. 298-303 (6) 6.70 6.70

Issued: Feb. 14, 1972, Apr. 2, 1973, May 15, 1974, Feb. 12, 1975, Nov. 16, 1970, Mar. 1, 1971.

African Hoopoe — A45

Porphyritic Granite — A46

Birds: 2½c, Half-collared kingfisher, horiz. 5c, Golden-breasted bunting. 7½c, Carmine bee-eater. 8c, Red-eyed bulbul. 25c, Wattled plover, horiz.

1971, June 1

304 A45 2c multicolored 1.00 .45
305 A45 2½c multicolored 1.25 .50
306 A45 5c multicolored 2.75 1.10
307 A45 7½c multicolored 3.50 1.75
308 A45 8c multicolored 3.50 1.75
309 A45 25c multicolored 10.00 4.25
Nos. 304-309 (6) 22.00 9.80

1971, Aug. 30

Granite '71, Geological Symposium, Aug. 30-Sept. 19: 7½c, Muscovite mica, seen through microscope. 15c, Granite, seen through microscope. 25c, Geological map of Rhodesia.

310 A46 2½c multicolored .45 .35
311 A46 7½c multicolored 1.75 1.25
312 A46 15c multicolored 2.75 2.00
313 A46 25c multicolored 4.00 3.25
Nos. 310-313 (4) 8.95 6.85

"Be Airwise" A47

Prevent Pollution: 3½c, Antelope (Be Countrywise). 7c, Fish (Be Waterwise). 13c, City (Be Citywise).

1972, July 17

314 A47 2½c multicolored .15 .15
315 A47 3½c multicolored .20 .20
316 A47 7c multicolored .40 .40
317 A47 13c multicolored .60 .60
Nos. 314-317 (4) 1.35 1.35

The Three Kings — A48

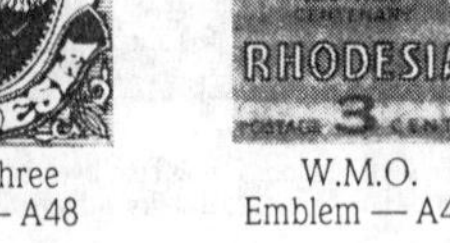

W.M.O. Emblem — A49

1972, Oct. 18

318 A48 2c multicolored .15 .15
319 A48 5c multicolored .15 .15
320 A48 13c multicolored .55 .55
Nos. 318-320 (3) .85 .85

Christmas.

1973, July 2

321 A49 3c multicolored .15 .15
322 A49 14c multicolored .70 .70
323 A49 25c multicolored 1.40 1.40
Nos. 321-323 (3) 2.25 2.25

Intl. Meteorological Cooperation, cent.

Arms of Rhodesia A50

1973, Oct. 10

No.	Type	Description	Unused	Used
324	A50	2½c multicolored	.15	.15
325	A50	4c multicolored	.20	.20
326	A50	7½c multicolored	.50	.50
327	A50	14c multicolored	.90	.90
		Nos. 324-327 (4)	1.75	1.75

Responsible Government, 50th Anniversary.

Kudu A51 — Thunbergia A52

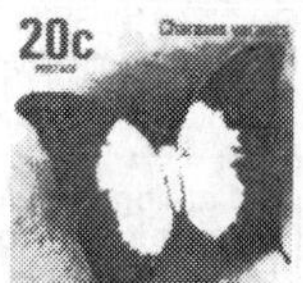

Pearl Charaxes — A53

1974-76 Litho. *Perf. 14½*

No.	Type	Description	Unused	Used
328	A51	1c shown	.15	.15
329	A51	2½c Eland	.50	.15
330	A51	3c Roan antelope	.15	.15
331	A51	4c Reedbuck	.15	.15
332	A51	5c Bushbuck	.20	.15
333	A52	6c shown	.30	.15
334	A52	7½c Flame lily	3.25	1.75
335	A52	8c like 7½c ('76)	.25	.15
336	A52	10c Devil thorn	.25	.15
337	A52	12c Hibiscus ('76)	.40	.20
338	A52	12½c Pink sabi star	3.25	1.75
339	A52	14c Wild pimpernel	4.75	2.50
340	A52	15c like 12½c ('76)	.50	.25
341	A52	16c like 14c ('76)	.50	.25
342	A53	20c shown	.50	.25
343	A53	24c Yellow pansy ('76)	.95	.50
344	A53	25c like 24c	4.75	2.50
345	A53	50c Queen purple tip	1.25	.65
346	A53	$1 Striped swordtail	2.50	1.25
347	A53	$2 Guinea fowl butterfly	4.75	2.50
		Nos. 328-347 (20)	29.30	15.55

Issue dates: Aug. 14, 1974, July 1, 1976.
For surcharges see Nos. 364-366.

Mail Collection and UPU Emblem A54

1974, Nov. 20 *Perf. 14½*

No.	Type	Description	Unused	Used
348	A54	3c shown	.30	.30
349	A54	4c Mail sorting	.40	.40
350	A54	7½c Mail delivery	.75	.75
351	A54	14c Parcel post	1.25	1.25
		Nos. 348-351 (4)	2.70	2.70

Universal Postal Union Centenary.

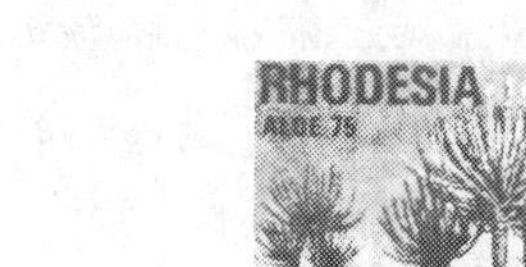

Euphorbia Confinalis — A55

1975, July 16

No.	Type	Description	Unused	Used
352	A55	2½c shown	.15	.15
353	A55	3c Aloe excelsa	.20	.20
354	A55	4c Hoodia lugardii	.35	.25
355	A55	7½c Aloe ortholopha	.65	.50
356	A55	14c Aloe musapana	1.50	1.25
357	A55	25c Aloe saponaria	2.00	1.90
		Nos. 352-357 (6)	4.85	4.25

Intl. Succulent Cong., Salisbury, July 1975.

Head Injury and Safety Helmet — A56

Occupational Safety: 4c, Bandaged hand and safety glove. 7½c, Injured eye and safety eyeglass. 14c, Blind man and protective shield.

1975, Oct. 15

No.	Type	Description	Unused	Used
358	A56	2½c multicolored	.15	.15
359	A56	4c multicolored	.30	.30
360	A56	7½c multicolored	.40	.40
361	A56	14c multicolored	.75	.75
		Nos. 358-361 (4)	1.60	1.60

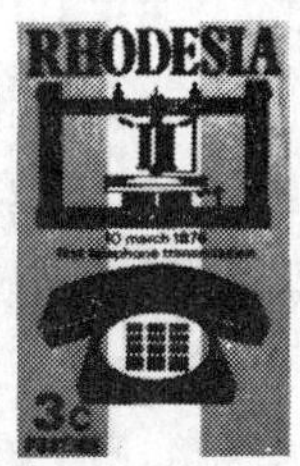

Telephones, 1876 and 1976 — A57 — Alexander Graham Bell — A58

1976, Mar. 10

No.	Type	Description	Unused	Used
362	A57	3c light blue & blk	.15	.15
363	A58	14c buff & black	.25	.25

Centenary of first telephone call, by Alexander Graham Bell, Mar. 10, 1876.

Nos. 334, 339 and 344 Surcharged with New Value and Two Bars

1976, July 1

No.	Type	Description	Unused	Used
364	A52	8c on 7½c multi	.15	.15
365	A52	16c on 14c multi	.20	.20
366	A53	24c on 25c multi	.60	.60
		Nos. 364-366 (3)	.95	.95

Wildlife Protection A59

1976, July 21

No.	Type	Description	Unused	Used
367	A59	4c Roan Antelope	.20	.20
368	A59	6c Brown hyena	.30	.30
369	A59	8c Wild dog	.40	.40
370	A59	16c Cheetah	.80	.80
		Nos. 367-370 (4)	1.70	1.70

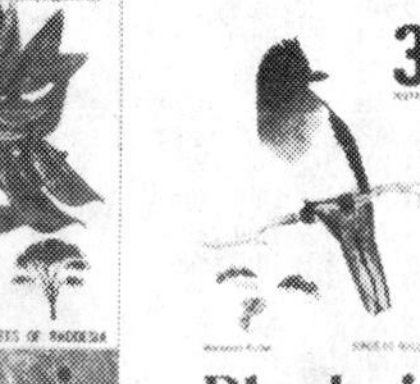

Brachystegia Spiciformis — A60 — Black-eyed Bulbul — A61

1976, Nov. 17

No.	Type	Description	Unused	Used
371	A60	4c shown	.15	.15
372	A60	6c Red mahogany	.15	.15
373	A60	8c Pterocarpus angolensis	.25	.25
374	A60	16c Rhodesian teak	.50	.50
		Nos. 371-374 (4)	1.05	1.05

Flowering trees.

1977, Mar. 16

Birds: 4c, Yellow-mantled whydah. 6c, Orange-throated longclaw. 8c, Long-tailed shrike. 16c, Lesser blue-eared starling. 24c, Red-billed wood hoopoe.

No.	Type	Description	Unused	Used
375	A61	3c multicolored	.15	.15
376	A61	4c multicolored	.20	.20
377	A61	6c multicolored	.30	.30
378	A61	8c multicolored	.45	.45
379	A61	16c multicolored	.90	.90
380	A61	24c multicolored	1.10	1.10
		Nos. 375-380 (6)	3.10	3.10

Lake Kyle, by Joan Evans — A62

Landscape Paintings: 4c, Chimanimani Mountains, by Evans. 6c, Rocks near Bonsor Reef, by Alice Balfour. 8c, Dwala (rock) near Devil's Pass, by Balfour. 16c, Zimbabwe, by Balfour. 24c, Victoria Falls, by Thomas Baines.

1977, July 20 Litho. *Perf. 14½*

No.	Type	Description	Unused	Used
381	A62	3c multicolored	.15	.15
382	A62	4c multicolored	.15	.15
383	A62	6c multicolored	.15	.15
384	A62	8c multicolored	.25	.25
385	A62	16c multicolored	.45	.45
386	A62	24c multicolored	.70	.70
		Nos. 381-386 (6)	1.85	1.85

Virgin and Child A63 — Fair Spire and Fairgrounds A64

1977, Nov. 16

No.	Type	Description	Unused	Used
387	A63	3c multicolored	.15	.15
388	A63	6c multicolored	.15	.15
389	A63	8c multicolored	.20	.20
390	A63	16c multicolored	.40	.40
		Nos. 387-390 (4)	.90	.90

Christmas.

1978, Mar. 15

19th Rhodesian Trade Fair, Bulawayo: 8c, Fair spire.

No.	Type	Description	Unused	Used
391	A64	4c multicolored	.15	.15
392	A64	8c multicolored	.25	.25

Morganite A65 — Black Rhinoceros A66

Odzani Falls — A67

1978, Aug. 16 Litho. *Perf. 14½*

No.	Type	Description	Unused	Used
393	A65	1c shown	.15	.15
394	A65	3c Amethyst	.15	.15
395	A65	4c Garnet	.15	.15
396	A65	5c Citrine	.15	.15
397	A65	7c Blue topaz	.15	.15
398	A66	9c shown	.15	.15
399	A66	11c Lion	.15	.15
400	A66	13c Warthog	.15	.15
401	A66	15c Giraffe	.15	.15
402	A66	17c Zebra	.15	.15
403	A67	21c shown	.15	.15
404	A67	25c Goba Falls	.20	.20
405	A67	30c Inyangombe Falls	.25	.25
406	A67	$1 Bridal Veil Falls	.95	.95
407	A67	$2 Victoria Falls	1.90	1.25
		Nos. 393-407 (15)	4.95	
		Set value		3.65

Wright's Flyer A A68

1978, Oct. 18

No.	Type	Description	Unused	Used
408	A68	4c shown	.15	.15
409	A68	5c Bleriot XI	.15	.15
410	A68	7c Vickers Vimy	.15	.15
411	A68	9c A.W. 15 Atalanta	.15	.15
412	A68	17c Vickers Viking 1B	.30	.30
413	A68	25c Boeing 720	.45	.45
		Set value	1.00	1.00

75th anniversary of powered flight.

POSTAGE DUE STAMPS

Type of Rhodesia and Nyasaland, 1961, Inscribed "RHODESIA"

Hyphen Hole Perf. 5

1965, June 17 Typo. Unwmk.

No.	Type	Description	Unused	Used
J5	D1	1p vermilion	.90	*2.00*
a.		Rouletted 9½	3.00	*12.00*

Rouletted 9½

No.	Type	Description	Unused	Used
J6	D1	2p dark blue	.45	.90
J7	D1	4p emerald	.70	*1.50*
J8	D1	6p purple	1.50	*3.00*
		Nos. J5-J8 (4)	3.55	*7.40*

Soapstone Zimbabwe Bird — D2

1966, Dec. 15 Litho. *Perf. 14½*

No.	Type	Description	Unused	Used
J9	D2	1p crimson	.65	*1.65*
J10	D2	2p violet blue	.85	*2.00*
J11	D2	4p emerald	1.50	*3.50*
J12	D2	6p lilac	1.65	*4.00*
J13	D2	1sh dull red brown	2.25	*5.00*
J14	D2	2sh black	3.50	*8.00*
		Nos. J9-J14 (6)	10.40	*24.15*

1970-73 Litho. *Perf. 14½*

Size: 26x22½mm

No.	Type	Description	Unused	Used
J15	D2	1c bright green	.45	*.85*
J16	D2	2c ultramarine	.90	*1.65*
J17	D2	5c red violet	1.40	*2.50*
J18	D2	6c lemon	4.50	*8.00*
J19	D2	10c rose red	3.25	*6.00*
		Nos. J15-J19 (5)	10.50	*19.00*

Issued: 6c, 5/7/73; others, 2/1/70.

RIO DE ORO

ˌrē-ō dē ˈōr-(ˌ)ō

LOCATION — On the northwest coast of Africa, bordering on the Atlantic Ocean
GOVT. — Spanish Colony
AREA — 71,600 sq. mi.
POP. — 24,000
CAPITAL — Villa Cisneros

Rio de Oro became part of Spanish Sahara.

100 Centimos = 1 Peseta

King Alfonso XIII
A1 A2

Control Numbers on Back in Blue

1905 Unwmk. Typo. *Perf. 14*

No.	Type	Description	Unused	Used
1	A1	1c blue green	3.00	1.75
2	A1	2c claret	3.00	1.75
3	A1	3c bronze green	3.00	1.75
4	A1	4c dark brown	3.00	1.75
5	A1	5c orange red	3.00	1.75
6	A1	10c dk gray brown	3.00	1.75
7	A1	15c red brown	3.00	1.75
8	A1	25c dark blue	60.00	21.00
9	A1	50c dark green	30.00	8.75
10	A1	75c dark violet	30.00	12.00
11	A1	1p orange brown	18.00	5.25
12	A1	2p buff	62.50	30.00
13	A1	3p dull violet	40.00	12.00
14	A1	4p blue green	40.00	12.00
15	A1	5p dull blue	55.00	22.50
16	A1	10p pale red	125.00	77.50
		Nos. 1-16 (16)	481.50	213.25

For surcharges see Nos. 17, 34-36, 60-66.

No. 8 Handstamp Surcharged in Rose

a

1907

17 A1 15c on 25c dk blue 190.00 55.00

The surcharge exists inverted, double and in violet, normally positioned.

Control Numbers on Back in Blue

1907 **Typo.**

18 A2 1c claret 2.25 1.75
19 A2 2c black 2.25 1.75
20 A2 3c dark brown 2.25 1.75
21 A2 4c red 2.25 1.75
22 A2 5c black brown 2.25 1.75
23 A2 10c chocolate 2.25 1.75
24 A2 15c dark blue 2.25 1.75
25 A2 25c deep green 5.50 2.75
26 A2 50c black violet 5.50 2.75
27 A2 75c orange brown 5.50 2.75
28 A2 1p orange 10.00 2.75
29 A2 2p dull violet 3.50 1.75
30 A2 3p blue green 3.50 1.75
a. Cliché of 4p in plate of 3p 200.00 140.00
31 A2 4p dark blue 5.50 2.75
32 A2 5p red 5.50 2.75
33 A2 10p deep green 6.50 6.00
Nos. 18-33 (16) 66.75 38.25

For surcharges see Nos. 38-43, 67-70.

Nos. 9-10 Handstamp Surcharged in Red — **1907 10 Cens**

1907

34 A1 10c on 50c dk green 60.00 14.00
a. "10" omitted 125.00 70.00
35 A1 10c on 75c dk violet 45.00 14.00

No. 12 Handstamp Surcharged in Violet — **1908 2 Cens**

1908

36 A1 2c on 2p buff 40.00 14.00

No. 36 is found with "1908" measuring 11mm and 12mm.

Same Surcharge in Red on No. 26

38 A2 10c on 50c blk vio 22.50 4.75

A 5c on 10c (No. 23) was not officially issued.

Nos. 25, 27-28 Handstamp Surcharged Type "a" in Red, Violet or Green

1908

39 A2 15c on 25c dp grn (R) 22.50 5.25
40 A2 15c on 75c org brn (V) 32.50 7.00
a. Green surcharge 37.50 14.00
41 A2 15c on 1p org (V) 30.00 7.00
42 A2 15c on 1p org (R) 30.00 10.50
43 A2 15c on 1p org (G) 30.00 10.50
Nos. 39-43 (5) 145.00 40.25

As this surcharge is handstamped, it exists in several varieties: double, inverted, in pairs with one surcharge omitted, etc.

A3

1908 ***Imperf.***

44 A3 5c on 50c green (C) 80.00 32.50
45 A3 5c on 50c green (V) 115.00 55.00

The surcharge, which is handstamped, exists in many variations.

Nos. 44-45 are found with and without control numbers on back.

King Alfonso XIII — A4

Control Numbers on Back in Blue

1909 **Typo.** ***Perf. 14½***

46 A4 1c red .50 .30
47 A4 2c orange .50 .30
48 A4 5c dark green .50 .30
49 A4 10c orange red .50 .30
50 A4 15c blue green .50 .30
51 A4 20c dark violet 1.50 .50
52 A4 25c deep blue 1.50 .50
53 A4 30c claret 1.50 .50
54 A4 40c chocolate 1.50 .50
55 A4 50c red violet 2.50 .50
56 A4 1p dark brown 3.50 2.00
57 A4 4p carmine rose 4.00 3.00
58 A4 10p claret 8.50 5.00
Nos. 46-58 (13) 27.00 14.00

Stamps of 1905 Handstamped in Black — **1910 10 Céntimos**

1910

60 A1 10c on 5p dull bl 12.00 8.75
a. Red surcharge 47.50 27.50
62 A1 10c on 10p pale red 12.00 8.75
a. Violet surcharge 72.50 37.50
b. Green surcharge 72.50 37.50
65 A1 15c on 3p dull vio 12.00 8.75
a. Imperf. 72.50
66 A1 15c on 4p blue grn 12.00 8.75
a. 10c on 4p bl grn 700.00 200.00
Nos. 60-66 (4) 48.00 35.00

See note after No. 43.

Nos. 31 and 33 Surcharged in Red or Violet — **2 Cents**

1911-13

67 A2 2c on 4p dk blue (R) 8.50 3.50
68 A2 5c on 10p dp grn (V) 22.50 3.50

Nos. 29-30 Surcharged in Black — **10 Céntimos**

69 A2 10c on 2p dull vio 10.50 3.50
69A A2 10c on 3p bl grn ('13) 125.00 15.00

Nos. 30, 32 Handstamped Type "a"

69B A2 15c on 3p bl grn ('13) 110.00 8.50
70 A2 15c on 5p red 8.50 3.75
Nos. 67-70 (6) 285.00 37.75

King Alfonso XIII
A5 A6

Control Numbers on Back in Blue

1912 **Typo.** ***Perf. 13½***

71 A5 1c carmine rose .25 .15
72 A5 2c lilac .25 .15
73 A5 5c deep green .25 .15
74 A5 10c red .25 .15
75 A5 15c brown orange .25 .15
76 A5 20c brown .25 .15
77 A5 25c dull blue .25 .15
78 A5 30c dark violet .25 .15
79 A5 40c blue green .25 .15
80 A5 50c lake .25 .15
81 A5 1p red 2.00 .45
82 A5 4p claret 4.50 2.00
83 A5 10p dark brown 6.00 3.00
Nos. 71-83 (13) 15.00 6.95

For overprints see Nos. 97-109.

Control Numbers on Back in Blue

1914 ***Perf. 13***

84 A6 1c olive black .25 .15
85 A6 2c maroon .25 .15
86 A6 5c deep green .25 .15
87 A6 10c orange red .25 .15
88 A6 15c orange red .25 .15
89 A6 20c deep claret .25 .15
90 A6 25c dark blue .25 .15
91 A6 30c blue green .25 .15
92 A6 40c brown orange .25 .15
93 A6 50c dark brown .25 .15
94 A6 1p dull lilac 1.90 1.40
95 A6 4p carmine rose 4.75 1.40
96 A6 10p dull violet 6.00 4.25
Nos. 84-96 (13) 15.15 8.55

Nos. 71-83 Overprinted in Black — **1917**

1917 ***Perf. 13½***

97 A5 1c carmine rose 7.25 .65
98 A5 2c lilac 7.25 .65
99 A5 5c deep green 2.25 .65
100 A5 10c red 2.25 .65
101 A5 15c orange brn 2.25 .65
102 A5 20c brown 2.25 .65
103 A5 25c dull blue 2.25 .65
104 A5 30c dark violet 2.25 .65
105 A5 40c blue green 2.25 .65
106 A5 50c lake 2.25 .65
107 A5 1p red 11.00 3.00
108 A5 4p claret 14.00 4.50
109 A5 10p dark brown 25.00 6.75
Nos. 97-109 (13) 82.50 20.75

Nos. 97-109 exist with overprint inverted or double (value 50 percent over normal) and in dark blue (value twice normal).

King Alfonso XIII — A7

Control Numbers on Back in Blue

1919 **Typo.** ***Perf. 13***

114 A7 1c brown .60 .35
115 A7 2c claret .60 .35
116 A7 5c light green .60 .35
117 A7 10c carmine .60 .35
118 A7 15c orange .60 .35
119 A7 20c orange .60 .35
120 A7 25c blue .60 .35
121 A7 30c green .60 .35
122 A7 40c vermilion .60 .35
123 A7 50c brown .60 .35
124 A7 1p lilac 4.50 2.50
125 A7 4p rose 7.75 4.50
126 A7 10p violet 12.00 7.50
Nos. 114-126 (13) 30.25 18.00

A8 A9

Control Numbers on Back in Blue

1920 ***Perf. 13***

127 A8 1c gray lilac .60 .40
128 A8 2c rose .60 .40
129 A8 5c light red .60 .40
130 A8 10c lilac .60 .40
131 A8 15c light brown .60 .40
132 A8 20c greenish blue .60 .40
133 A8 25c yellow .60 .40
134 A8 30c dull blue 4.00 3.25
135 A8 40c orange 2.00 1.40
136 A8 50c dull rose 2.00 1.40
137 A8 1p gray green 2.00 1.40
138 A8 4p lilac rose 4.00 2.75
139 A8 10p brown 10.00 7.00
Nos. 127-139 (13) 28.20 20.00

Control Numbers on Back in Blue

1922

140 A9 1c yellow .60 .35
141 A9 2c red brown .60 .35
142 A9 5c blue green .60 .35
143 A9 10c pale red .60 .35
144 A9 15c myrtle green .60 .35
145 A9 20c turq blue .60 .35
146 A9 25c deep blue .60 .35
147 A9 30c deep rose 1.25 .90
148 A9 40c violet 1.25 .90
149 A9 50c orange 1.25 .90
150 A9 1p lilac 3.50 1.40
151 A9 4p claret 7.00 3.00
152 A9 10p dark brown 10.00 7.00
Nos. 140-152 (13) 28.45 16.55

For subsequent issues see Spanish Sahara.

RIO MUNI

ˌrē-ō 'mü-nē

LOCATION — West Africa, bordering on Cameroun and Gabon Republics
GOVT. — Province of Spain
AREA — 9,500 sq. mi.
POP. — 183,377 (1960)
CAPITAL — Bata

Rio Muni and the island of Fernando Po are the two provinces that constitute Spanish Guinea. Separate stamp issues for the two provinces were decreed in 1960.

Spanish Guinea Nos. 1-84 were used only in the territory now called Rio Muni.

Rio Muni united with Fernando Po on Oct. 12, 1968, to form the Republic of Equatorial Guinea.

100 Centimos = 1 Peseta

Catalogue values for all unused stamps in this country are for Never Hinged items.

Boy Reading and Missionary
A1

Quina Plant
A2

1960 **Unwmk.** **Photo.** ***Perf. 13x12½***

1 A1 25c dull vio bl .15 .15
2 A1 50c olive brown .15 .15
3 A1 75c dull grysh pur .15 .15
4 A1 1p orange ver .15 .15
5 A1 1.50p brt blue grn .15 .15
6 A1 2p red lilac .15 .15
7 A1 3p sapphire .30 .15
8 A1 5p red brown .85 .15
9 A1 10p lt olive grn 1.50 .25
Set value 3.10 .75

1960 ***Perf. 13x12½***

10 A2 35c shown .15 .15
11 A2 80c Croton plant .15 .15
Set value .20 .15

See Nos. B1-B2.

Map of Rio Muni — A3

Designs: 50c, 1p, Gen. Franco. 70c, Government Palace.

1961, Oct. 1 ***Perf. 12½x13***

12 A3 25c gray violet .15 .15
13 A3 50c olive brown .15 .15
14 A3 70c brt green .15 .15
15 A3 1p red orange .15 .15
Set value .32 .20

25th anniversary of the nomination of Gen. Francisco Franco as Chief of State.

Rio Muni Headdress — A4

Design: 50c, Rio Muni idol.

1962, July 10 *Perf. 13x12½*

16 A4 25c violet .15 .15
17 A4 50c green .15 .15
18 A4 1p orange brown .15 .15
Set value .28 .15

Issued for child welfare.

Cape Buffalo — A5

Design: 35c, Gorilla, vert.

Perf. 13x12½, 12½x13

1962, Nov. 23 Photo. Unwmk.

19 A5 15c dark olive grn .15 .15
20 A5 35c magenta .15 .15
21 A5 1p brown orange .20 .15
Set value .32 .15

Issued for Stamp Day.

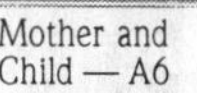

Mother and Child — A6

Father Joaquin Juanola — A7

1963, Jan. 29 *Perf. 13x12½*

22 A6 50c green .15 .15
23 A6 1p brown orange .15 .15
Set value .20 .15

Issued to help the victims of the Seville flood.

1963, July 6 *Perf. 13x12½*

Design: 50c, Blessing hand, cross and palms.

24 A7 25c dull violet .15 .15
25 A7 50c brown olive .15 .15
26 A7 1p orange red .15 .15
Set value .25 .15

Issued for child welfare.

Praying Child and Arms — A8

Branch of Copal Tree — A9

1963, July 12

27 A8 50c dull green .15 .15
28 A8 1p redsh brown .15 .15
Set value .20 .15

Issued for Barcelona flood relief.

Perf. 13x12½, 12½x13

1964, Mar. 6 Photo.

Design: 50c, Flowering quina, horiz.

29 A9 25c brt violet .15 .15
30 A9 50c blue green .15 .15
31 A9 1p dk carmine rose .15 .15
Set value .25 .15

Issued for Stamp Day 1963.

Tree Pangolin A10

Design: 50c, Chameleon.

1964, June 1 *Perf. 13x12½*

32 A10 25c violet blk .15 .15
33 A10 50c olive gray .15 .15
34 A10 1p fawn .15 .15
Set value .26 .15

Issued for child welfare.

Dwarf Crocodile A11

Designs: 15c, 70c, 3p, Dwarf crocodile. 25c, 1p, 5p, Leopard. 50c, 1.50p, 10p, Black rhinoceros.

1964, July 1

35 A11 15c lt brown .15 .15
36 A11 25c violet .15 .15
37 A11 50c olive .15 .15
38 A11 70c green .15 .15
39 A11 1p brown car .38 .15
40 A11 1.50p blue green .38 .15
41 A11 3p dark blue .60 .15
42 A11 5p brown 1.50 .60
43 A11 10p green 4.25 1.25
Nos. 35-43 (9) 7.71
Set value 2.15

Greshoff's Tree Frog — A12

Stamp Day: 1p, Helmet guinea fowl, vert.

Perf. 13x12½, 12½x13

1964, Nov. 23 Photo. Unwmk.

44 A12 50c green .15 .15
45 A12 1p deep claret .15 .15
46 A12 1.50p blue green .15 .15
Set value .26 .15

Issued for Stamp Day, 1964.

Woman's Head — A13

Woman Chemist — A14

1964 Photo. *Perf. 13x12½*

47 A13 50c shown .15 .15
48 A14 1p shown .15 .15
49 A14 1.50p Logger .15 .15
Set value .26 .15

Issued to commemorate 25 years of peace.

Goliath Beetle A15

Beetle: 1p, Acridoxena hewaniana.

1965, June 1 Photo. *Perf. 12½x13*

50 A15 50c Prus green .15 .15
51 A15 1p sepia .15 .15
52 A15 1.50p black .15 .15
Set value .26 .15

Issued for child welfare.

Ring-necked Pheasant — A16

Leopard and Arms of Rio Muni A17

Perf. 13x12½, 12½x13

1965, Nov. 23 Photo.

53 A16 50c grnsh gray .15 .15
54 A17 1p sepia .30 .15
55 A16 2.50p lilac 1.40 .55
Nos. 53-55 (3) 1.85 .85
Set value .65

Issued for Stamp Day, 1965.

Elephant and Parrot A18

Design: 1.50p, Lion and boy.

Perf. 12½x13

1966, June 1 Photo. Unwmk.

56 A18 50c olive .15 .15
57 A18 1p dk purple .15 .15
58 A18 1.50p brt Prus blue .15 .15
Set value .26 .15

Issued for child welfare.

Water Chevrotain — A19

Designs: 40c, 4p, Tree pangolin, vert.

1966, Nov. 23 Photo. *Perf. 13*

59 A19 10c brown & yel brn .15 .15
60 A19 40c brown & yellow .15 .15
61 A19 1.50p blue & rose lilac .15 .15
62 A19 4p dk bl & emerald .25 .15
Set value .40 .30

Issued for Stamp Day, 1966.

A20

Potto — A21

Designs: 40c, 4p, Vine creeper.

1967, June 1 Photo. *Perf. 13*

63 A20 10c green & yellow .15 .15
64 A20 40c blk, rose car & grn .15 .15
65 A20 1.50p blue & orange .15 .15
66 A20 4p black & green .25 .15
Set value .40 .30

Issued for child welfare.

1967, Nov. 23 Photo. *Perf. 13*

Designs: 1p, River hog, horiz. 3.50p, African golden cat, horiz.

67 A21 1p black & red brn .15 .15
68 A21 1.50p brown & grn .15 .15
69 A21 3.50p org brn & grn .30 .20
Set value .42 .32

Issued for Stamp Day 1967.

Zodiac Issue

Cancer — A22

1.50p, Taurus. 2.50p, Gemini.

1968, Apr. 25 Photo. *Perf. 13*

70 A22 1p brt mag, *lt yel* .15 .15
71 A22 1.50p brown, *pink* .15 .15
72 A22 2.50p dk vio, *yel* .25 .15
Set value .36 .26

Issued for child welfare.

SEMI-POSTAL STAMPS

Type of Regular Issue, 1960

Designs: 10c+5c, Croton plant. 15c+5c, Flower and leaves of croton.

1960 Unwmk. Photo. *Perf. 13x12½*

B1 A2 10c + 5c maroon .15 .15
B2 A2 15c + 5c bister brn .15 .15
Set value .15 .15

The surtax was for child welfare.

Bishop Juan de Ribera — SP1

Design: 20c+5c, The clown Pablo de Valladolid by Velazquez. 30c+10c, Juan de Ribera statue.

1961 *Perf. 13x12½*

B3 SP1 10c + 5c rose brn .15 .15
B4 SP1 20c + 5c dk slate grn .15 .15
B5 SP1 30c + 10c olive brn .15 .15
B6 SP1 50c + 20c brown .15 .15
Set value .32 .24

Issued for Stamp Day, 1960.

Mandrill SP2

Design: 25c+10c, Elephant, vert.

Perf. 12½x13, 13x12½

1961, June 21 Unwmk.

B7 SP2 10c + 5c rose brn .15 .15
B8 SP2 25c + 10c gray vio .15 .15
B9 SP2 80c + 20c dk grn .15 .15
Set value .26 .18

The surtax was for child welfare.

Statuette — SP3

Design: 25c+10c, 1p+10c, Male figure.

1961, Nov. 23 *Perf. 13x12½*

B10 SP3 10c + 5c rose brn .15 .15
B11 SP3 25c + 10c dark pur .15 .15
B12 SP3 30c + 10c olive blk .15 .15
B13 SP3 1p + 10c red org .15 .15
Set value .32 .24

Issued for Stamp Day 1961.

ROMANIA

rō-'mā-nē-ə

(Rumania, Roumania)

LOCATION — Southeastern Europe, bordering on the Black Sea
GOVT. — Republic
AREA — 91,699 sq. mi.

POP. — 22,600,000 (est. 1984)
CAPITAL — Bucharest

Romania was formed in 1861 from the union of the principalities of Moldavia and Walachia in 1859. It became a kingdom in 1881. Following World War I, the original territory was considerably enlarged by the addition of Bessarabia, Bukovina, Transylvania, Crisana, Maramures and Banat. The republic was established in 1948.

40 Parale = 1 Piaster
100 Bani = 1 Leu (plural "Lei") (1868)

Catalogue values for unused stamps in this country are for Never Hinged items, beginning with Scott 475 in the regular postage section, Scott B82 in the semi-postal section, Scott C24 in the airpost section, Scott CB1 in the airpost semi-postal section, Scott J82 in the postage due section, Scott O1 in the official section, Scott RA16 in the postal tax section, and Scott RAJ1 in the postal tax postage due section.

Watermarks

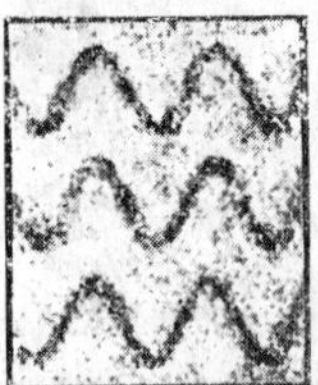
Wmk. 95- Wavy Lines

Wmk. 163- Coat of Arms

No. 163 is not a true watermark, having been impressed after the paper was manufactured.

Wmk. 164- PR

Wmk. 165- PR Interlaced

Wmk. 167- Coat of Arms Covering 25 Stamps

Reduced illustration.

Wmk. 200- PR

Wmk. 225 - Crown over PTT, Multiple

Wmk. 230- Crowns and Monograms

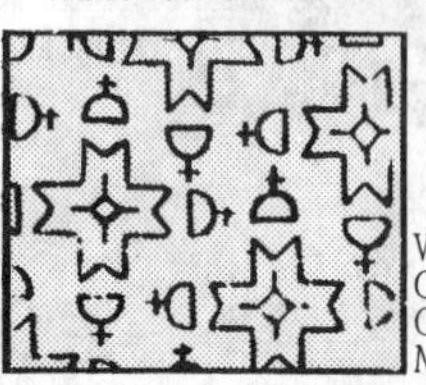
Wmk. 276- Cross and Crown Multiple

Wmk. 289- RPR Multiple

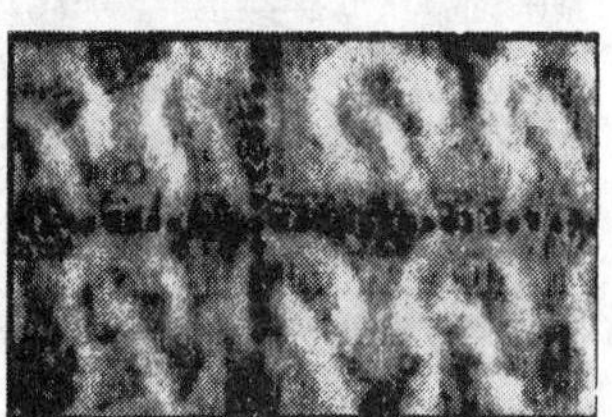
Wmk. 358- RPR Multiple in Endless Rows

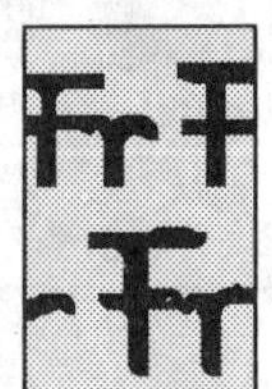
Wmk. 398- Fr Multiple

Values for unused stamps are for examples with original gum as defined in the catalogue introduction except for Nos. 1-4 which are valued without gum.

Moldavia

Coat of Arms
A1 A2

Handstamped

1858, July Unwmk. *Imperf.*

Laid Paper

1	A1	27pa blk, *rose*	*19,000*	*5,000.*
a.		Tête bêche pair		
2	A1	54pa blue, *grn*	*4,200.*	*2,000.*
3	A1	108pa blue, *rose*	*14,000.*	*4,500.*

Wove Paper

4	A1	81pa blue, *bl*	*21,000.*	*21,000.*

Cut to shape or octagonally, Nos. 1-4 sell for one-fourth to one-third of these prices.

1858

Bluish Wove Paper

5	A2	5pa black	*11,500.*	*4,250.*
a.		Tête bêche pair		
6	A2	40pa blue	150.	100.
a.		Tête bêche pair	*650.*	*1,750.*
7	A2	80pa red	*6,750.*	*300.*
a.		Tête bêche pair		

1859

White Wove Paper

8	A2	5pa black	*8,000.*	*4,250.*
a.		Tête bêche pair		
b.		Frame broken at bottom	75.	
c.		As "b," tête bêche pair	300.	
9	A2	40pa blue	90.	65.
b.		Tête bêche pair	375.	*1,000.*
10	A2	80pa red	250.	140.
b.		Tête bêche pair	*975.*	*3,000.*

No. 8b has a break in the frame at bottom below "A." It was never placed in use.

Moldavia-Walachia

Coat of Arms — A3

Printed by Hand from Single Dies

1862

White Laid Paper

11	A3	3pa orange	200.00	*2,250.*
a.		3pa yellow	200.00	*2,250.*
12	A3	6pa carmine	175.00	200.00
13	A3	6pa red	175.00	200.00
14	A3	30pa blue	45.00	75.00
		Nos. 11-14 (4)	595.00	

White Wove Paper

15	A3	3pa orange yel	50.00	*150.00*
a.		3pa lemon	100.00	*150.00*
16	A3	6pa carmine	40.00	*100.00*
17	A3	6pa vermilion	25.00	*65.00*
18	A3	30pa blue	50.00	25.00
		Nos. 15-18 (4)	165.00	

Tête bêche pairs

11b	A3	3pa orange		
12a	A3	6pa carmine		
14a	A3	30pa blue	150.00	
15b	A3	3pa orange yellow	120.00	*1,000.*
16a	A3	6pa carmine	110.00	
17a	A3	6pa vermilion	82.50	
18a	A3	30pa blue	110.00	

Nos. 11-18 were printed with a hand press, one at a time, from single dies. The impressions were very irregularly placed and occasionally overlapped. Sheets of 32 (4x8). The 3rd and 4th rows were printed inverted, making the second and third rows tête bêche. All values come in distinct shades, frequently even on the same sheet. The paper of this and the following issues through No. 52 often shows a bluish, grayish or yellowish tint.

1864 Typographed from Plates

White Wove Paper

19	A3	3pa yellow	27.50	*1,250.*
a.		Tête bêche pair	200.00	
b.		Pair, one sideways	70.00	
20	A3	6pa deep rose	3.50	
a.		Tête bêche pair	27.50	
b.		Pair, one sideways	9.00	
21	A3	30pa deep blue	4.50	*60.00*
a.		Tête bêche pair	30.00	
b.		Pair, one sideways	10.00	
c.		Bluish wove paper	*125.00*	
		Nos. 19-21 (3)	35.50	

Stamps of 1862 issue range from very clear to blurred impressions but rarely have broken or deformed characteristics. The 1864 issue, though rarely blurred, usually have various imperfections in the letters and numbers. These include breaks, malformations, occasional dots at left of the crown or above the "R" of "PAR," a doton the middle stroke of the "F," and many other bulges, breaks and spots of color.

The 1864 issue were printed in sheets of 40 (5x8). The first and second rows were inverted. Clichés in the third row were placed sideways, 4 with head to right and 4 with head to left, making one tête bêche pair. The fourth and fifth rows were normally placed.

No. 20 was never placed in use.

All values exist in shades, light to dark.

Counterfeit cancellations exist on #11-21.

Three stamps in this design- 2pa, 5pa, 20pa- were printed on white wove paper in 1864, but never placed in use. Value, set $7.50.

Romania

Prince Alexandru Ioan Cuza — A4

TWENTY PARALES:

Type I - The central oval does not touch the inner frame. The "I" of "DECI" extends above and below the other letters.

Type II - The central oval touches the frame at the bottom. The "I" of the "DECI" is the same height as the other letters.

1865, Jan. Unwmk. Litho. *Imperf.*

22	A4	2pa orange	30.00	*110.00*
a.		2pa yellow	40.00	*150.00*
b.		2pa ocher	90.00	*175.00*
23	A4	5pa blue	10.00	*140.00*
24	A4	20pa red, type I	3.75	7.00
a.		Bluish paper	150.00	
25	A4	20pa red, type II	3.75	7.00
a.		Bluish paper	150.00	
		Nos. 22-25 (4)	47.50	

The 20pa types are found se-tenant.

White Laid Paper

26	A4	2pa orange	25.00	*80.00*
a.		2pa ocher	65.00	
27	A4	5pa blue	40.00	*225.00*

Prince Carol — A5

Type I — A6

Type II — A7

TWENTY PARALES:

Type I - A6. The Greek border at the upper right goes from right to left.

Type II - A7. The Greek border at the upper right goes from left to right.

1866-67

Thin Wove Paper

29	A5	2pa blk, *yellow*	4.00	*45.00*
a.		Thick paper	40.00	*200.00*
30	A5	5pa blk, *dk bl*	25.00	*250.00*
a.		5pa black, *indigo*	70.00	—
b.		Thick paper	40.00	*275.00*
31	A6	20pa blk, *rose*, (I)	5.00	6.00
a.		Dot in Greek border, thin paper	350.00	125.00
b.		Thick paper	95.00	45.00
c.		Dot in Greek border, thick paper	125.00	72.50
32	A7	20pa blk, *rose*, (II)	6.00	9.00
a.		Thick paper	87.50	42.50
		Nos. 29-32 (4)	40.00	

The 20pa types are found se-tenant.

Faked cancellations are known on Nos. 22-27, 29-32.

The white dot of Nos. 31a and 31c occurs in extreme upper right border.

Thick paper was used in 1866, thin in 1867.

Prince Carol
A8 A9

1868-70

33	A8	2b orange	14.00	11.00
a.		2b yellow	27.50	25.00
34	A8	3b violet ('70)	20.00	15.00
35	A8	4b dk blue	40.00	22.50
36	A8	18b scarlet	150.00	7.00
a.		18b rose	150.00	7.00
		Nos. 33-36 (4)	224.00	55.50

1869

37	A9	5b orange yel	45.00	15.00
a.		5b deep orange	47.50	*50.00*

38 A9 10b blue 22.50 10.00
a. 10b ultramarine 55.00 15.00
b. 10b indigo 60.00 22.50
40 A9 15b vermilion 45.00 12.00
41 A9 25b orange & blue 25.00 10.00
42 A9 50b blue & red 150.00 15.00
a. 50b indigo & red 165.00 15.00
Nos. 37-42 (5) 287.50 62.00

No. 40 on vertically laid paper was not issued. Value $1,250.

Prince Carol
A10 A11

1871-72 ***Imperf.***

43 A10 5b rose 30.00 8.00
a. 5b vermilion 35.00 10.00
44 A10 10b orange yel 45.00 15.00
a. Vertically laid paper 500.00 500.00
45 A10 10b blue 125.00 25.00
46 A10 15b red 100.00 60.00
47 A10 25b olive brown 30.00 20.00
Nos. 43-47 (5) 330.00 128.00

1872

48 A10 10b ultra 18.00 25.00
a. Vertically laid paper 75.00 110.00
b. 10b greenish blue 110.00 110.00
49 A10 50b blue & red 150.00 165.00

No. 48 is a provisional issue printed from a new plate in which the head is placed further right.

Faked cancellations are found on No. 49.

1872 ***Perf. 12½***

Wove Paper

50 A10 5b rose 32.50 15.00
a. 5b vermilion 900.00 400.00
51 A10 10b blue 45.00 16.00
a. 10b ultramarine 47.50 25.00
52 A10 25b dark brown 16.00 15.00
Nos. 50-52 (3) 93.50 46.00

No. 43a with faked perforation is frequently offered as No. 50a.

Paris Print, Fine Impression

1872 **Typo.** ***Perf. 14x13½***

Tinted Paper

53 A11 1½b brnz grn, *bluish* 3.25 .50
54 A11 3b green, *bluish* 9.50 .75
55 A11 5b bis, *pale buff* 6.00 .90
56 A11 10b blue 6.00 1.10
57 A11 15b red brn, *pale buff* 60.00 3.50
58 A11 25b org, *pale buff* 65.00 4.00
59 A11 50b rose, *pale rose* 75.00 8.75
Nos. 53-59 (7) 224.75 19.50

Nos. 53-59 exist imperf.

Bucharest Print, Rough Impression

Perf. 11, 11½, 13½, and Compound

1876-79

60 A11 1½b brnz grn, *bluish* 4.00 .25
61 A11 5b bis, *yelsh* 12.00 .30
b. Printed on both sides 75.00
62 A11 10b bl, *yelsh* ('77) 14.00 .35
a. 10b pale bl, *yelsh* 12.00 .35
b. 10b dark blue, *yelsh* 20.00 .50
d. Cliché of 5b in plate of 10b ('79) 185.00 80.00
63 A11 10b ultra, *yelsh* ('77) 20.00 .50
64 A11 15b red brn, *yelsh* 40.00 .60
a. Printed on both sides 100.00
65 A11 30b org red, *yelsh* ('78) 110.00 6.00
a. Printed on both sides 210.00
Nos. 60-65 (6) 200.00 8.00

#60-65 are valued in the grade of fine.

#62d has been reprinted in dark blue. The originals are in dull blue. Value of reprint, $35.

Perf. 11, 11½, 13½ and Compound

1879

66 A11 1½b blk, *yelsh* 1.75 .15
b. Imperf. 12.00
67 A11 3b ol grn, *bluish* 5.75 .45
a. Diagonal half used as 1½b on cover
68 A11 5b green, *bluish* 2.00 .15
69 A11 10b rose, *yelsh* 6.75 .15
b. Cliché of 5b in plate of 10b 100.00 475.00
70 A11 15b rose red, *yelsh* 30.00 2.50
71 A11 25b blue, *yelsh* 24.00 2.25
72 A11 50b bister, *yelsh* 47.50 2.25
Nos. 66-72 (7) 117.75 7.90

#66-72 are valued in the grade of fine.

There are two varieties of the numerals on the 15b and 50b.

No. 69b has been reprinted in dark rose. Originals are in pale rose. Value of reprint, $40.

King Carol I
A12 A13

1880

White Paper

73 A12 15b brown 7.00 .25
74 A12 25b blue 12.50 .35

#73-74 are valued in the grade of fine. No. 74 exists imperf.

Perf. 13½, 11½ & Compound

1885-89

75 A13 1½b black 1.75 .35
a. Printed on both sides
76 A13 3b violet 5.00 .45
a. Half used as 1½b on cover
77 A13 5b green 50.00 4.00
78 A13 15b red brown 9.50 .70
79 A13 25b blue 9.50 .70
Nos. 75-79 (5) 75.75 6.20

Tinted Paper

80 A13 1½b blk, *bluish* 3.00 .55
81 A13 3b vio, *bluish* 4.25 .75
82 A13 3b ol grn, *bluish* 4.25 .35
83 A13 5b bl grn, *bluish* 3.50 .55
84 A13 10b rose, *pale buff* 6.00 .55
85 A13 15b red brn, *pale buff* 15.00 .55
86 A13 25b bl, *pale buff* 15.00 .95
87 A13 50b bis, *pale buff* 50.00 3.75
Nos. 80-87 (8) 101.00 8.00

1889 **Wmk. 163**

Thin Pale Yellowish Paper

88 A13 1½b black 27.50 2.00
89 A13 3b violet 21.00 2.00
90 A13 5b green 21.00 2.00
91 A13 10b rose 21.00 2.00
92 A13 15b red brown 57.50 4.50
93 A13 25b dark blue 45.00 3.75
Nos. 88-93 (6) 193.00 16.25

King Carol I
A14 A15

1890 ***Perf. 13½, 11½ & Compound***

94 A14 1½b maroon 4.25 .80
95 A14 3b violet 22.50 1.00
96 A14 5b emerald 9.50 1.00
97 A14 10b red 11.00 1.75
a. 10b rose 15.00 2.75
98 A14 15b dk brown 17.50 1.40
99 A14 25b gray blue 13.00 1.40
100 A14 50b orange 65.00 12.50
Nos. 94-100 (7) 142.75 19.85

1891 **Unwmk.**

101 A14 1½b lilac rose 1.10 .15
b. Printed on both sides 65.00
102 A14 3b lilac .85 .20
a. 3b violet 3.00 .30
b. Printed on both sides
c. Impressions of 5b on back 100.00 75.00
103 A14 5b emerald 1.65 .20
104 A14 10b pale red 7.00 .30
a. Printed on both sides 140.00 110.00
105 A14 15b gray brown 8.25 .25
106 A14 25b gray blue 5.50 .30
107 A14 50b orange 50.00 3.00
Nos. 101-107 (7) 74.35 4.40

Nos. 101-107 exist imperf.

1891

108 A15 1½b claret 1.40 1.25
109 A15 3b lilac 1.40 1.25
110 A15 5b emerald 1.90 1.75
111 A15 10b red 1.90 1.75
112 A15 15b gray brown 1.90 1.75
Nos. 108-112 (5) 8.50 7.75

25th year of the reign of King Carol I.

1894 **Wmk. 164**

113 A14 3b lilac 5.50 2.50
114 A14 5b pale green 5.50 2.50
115 A14 25b gray blue 8.00 4.00
116 A14 50b orange 16.00 8.00
Nos. 113-116 (4) 35.00 17.00

King Carol I
A17 A18

A19 A20

A21 A23

1893-98 **Wmk. 164 & 200**

117 A17 1b pale brown 1.00 .15
118 A17 1½b black .70 .15
119 A18 3b chocolate 1.00 .15
120 A19 5b blue 1.40 .15
a. Cliché of the 25b in the plate of 5b 47.50 60.00
121 A19 5b yel grn ('98) 4.00 .35
a. 5b emerald 4.00 .35
122 A20 10b emerald 2.00 .15
123 A20 10b rose ('98) 4.00 .30
124 A21 15b rose 2.00 .15
125 A21 15b black ('98) 4.00 .30
126 A19 25b violet 3.00 .15
127 A19 25b indigo ('98) 7.00 .45
128 A19 40b gray grn 17.50 .50
129 A19 50b orange 8.50 .25
130 A23 1 l bis & rose 17.50 .35
131 A23 2 l orange & brn 21.00 .55
Nos. 117-131 (15) 94.60 4.10

This watermark may be found in four versions (Wmks. 164, 200 and variations). The paper also varies in thickness.

A 3b orange of type A18; 10b brown, type A20; 15b rose, type A21, and 25b bright green with similar but different border, all watermarked "P R," were prepared but never issued. Value, each $10.

See Nos. 132-157, 224-229. For overprints see Romanian Post Offices in the Turkish Empire Nos. 10-11.

King Carol I — A24

Perf. 11½, 13½ and Compound

1900-03 **Unwmk.**

Thin Paper, Tinted Rose on Back

132 A17 1b pale brown .75 .25
133 A24 1b brown ('01) .75 .25
134 A24 1b black ('03) .75 .25
135 A18 3b red brown 1.00 .15
136 A19 5b emerald 1.50 .15
137 A20 10b rose 1.25 .15
138 A21 15b black 1.50 .15
139 A21 15b lil gray ('01) 1.50 .20
140 A21 15b dk vio ('03) 1.50 .25
141 A19 25b blue 2.50 .25
142 A19 40b gray grn 5.25 .35
143 A19 50b orange 10.50 .35
144 A23 1 l bis & rose ('01) 21.00 .60
145 A23 1 l grn & blk ('03) 15.00 .80
146 A23 2 l org & brn ('01) 15.00 .80
147 A23 2 l red brn & blk ('03) 13.00 .90
Nos. 132-147 (16) 92.75 5.85

#132 inscribed BANI; #133-134 BAN.

1900, July **Wmk. 167**

148 A17 1b pale brown 7.25 1.90
149 A18 3b red brown 5.75 1.90
150 A19 5b emerald 5.75 1.90
151 A20 10b rose 5.75 1.90
152 A21 15b black 8.75 2.75
153 A19 25b blue 10.00 3.25
154 A19 40b gray grn 17.50 3.75
155 A19 50b orange 17.50 3.75
156 A23 1 l bis & rose 20.00 4.75
157 A23 2 l orange & brn 26.00 5.75
Nos. 148-157 (10) 124.25 31.60

Mail Coach Leaving PO — A25

King Carol I and Façade of New Post Office — A26

1903 **Unwmk.** ***Perf. 14x13½***

Thin Paper, Tinted Rose on Face

158 A25 1b gray brown *1.50* .65
159 A25 3b brown violet *2.50* .80
160 A25 5b pale green *5.00* 1.40
161 A25 10b rose *4.00* 1.40
162 A25 15b black *4.00* 1.65
163 A25 25b blue *12.00* 6.00
164 A25 40b dull green *15.00* 6.75
165 A25 50b orange *27.50* 16.00
Nos. 158-165 (8) *71.50* 34.65

Counterfeits are plentiful. See note after No. 172. See No. 428.

1903 **Engr.** ***Perf. 13½x14***

Thick Toned Paper

166 A26 15b black 1.40 .95
167 A26 25b blue 3.25 1.75
168 A26 40b gray grn 4.50 2.25
169 A26 50b orange 4.50 2.25
170 A26 1 l dk brown 4.50 2.25
171 A26 2 l dull red 37.50 17.50
a. 2 l orange (error) 57.50 40.00
172 A26 5 l dull violet 45.00 26.00
Nos. 166-172 (7) 100.65 52.95

Opening of the new PO in Bucharest (Nos. 158-172).

Counterfeits exist.

Prince Carol Taking Oath of Allegiance, 1866 — A27

Prince in Royal Carriage — A28

Prince Carol at Calafat in 1877 — A29

Prince Carol Shaking Hands with His Captive, Osman Pasha — A30

Carol I as Prince in 1866 and King in 1906 — A31

Romanian Army Crossing Danube — A32

Romanian Troops Return to Bucharest in 1878 — A33

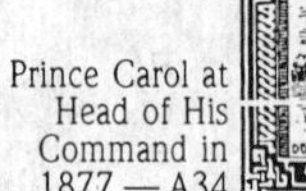

Prince Carol at Head of His Command in 1877 — A34

King Carol I at the Cathedral in 1896 — A35

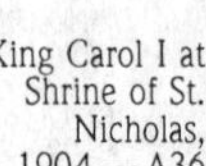

King Carol I at Shrine of St. Nicholas, 1904 — A36

1906 **Engr.** ***Perf. 12***

176	A27	1b bister & blk	.20	.15
177	A28	3b red brn & blk	.40	.15
178	A29	5b dp grn & blk	.50	.15
179	A30	10b carmine & blk	.30	.15
180	A31	15b dull vio & blk	.30	.15
181	A32	25b ultra & blk	2.50	1.40
a.		25b olive green & black	2.50	1.40
182	A33	40b dk brn & blk	.65	.35
183	A34	50b bis brn & blk	.75	.35
184	A35	1 l vermilion & blk	.75	.45
185	A36	2 l orange & blk	.90	.60
		Nos. 176-185 (10)	7.25	3.90

40 years' rule of Carol I as Prince & King.

No. 181a was never placed in use. Cancellations were by favor.

King Carol I — A37

1906

186	A37	1b bister & blk	.40	.15
187	A37	3b red brn & blk	1.00	.25
188	A37	5b dp grn & blk	.60	.20
189	A37	10b carmine & blk	.60	.20
190	A37	15b dl vio & blk	.60	.20
191	A37	25b ultra & blk	5.50	2.50
192	A37	40b dk brn & blk	1.50	.40
193	A37	50b bis brn & blk	1.50	.40
194	A37	1 l red & blk	1.50	.40
195	A37	2 l orange & blk	1.50	.40
		Nos. 186-195 (10)	14.70	5.10

25th anniversary of the Kingdom.

Plowman and Angel — A38

Exposition Building — A39

Exposition Buildings
A40 A41

King Carol I — A42

Queen Elizabeth (Carmen Sylva) — A43

1906 **Typo.** ***Perf. 11½, 13½***

196	A38	5b yel grn & blk	1.50	.40
197	A38	10b carmine & blk	1.50	.40
198	A39	15b violet & blk	2.50	.70
199	A39	25b blue & blk	2.50	.70
200	A40	30b red & blk brn	3.00	.60
201	A40	40b green & blk brn	3.50	.75
202	A41	50b orange & blk	3.00	.95
203	A41	75b lt brn & dk brn	3.00	.95
204	A42	1.50 l red lil & blk brn	32.50	13.00
a.		Center inverted		
205	A42	2.50 l yellow & brn	12.50	8.00
a.		Center inverted		
206	A43	3 l brn org & brn	8.25	8.00
		Nos. 196-206 (11)	73.75	34.45

General Exposition. They were sold at post offices July 29-31, 1906, and were valid only for those three days. Those sold at the exposition are overprinted "S E" in black. Remainders were sold privately, both unused and canceled to order, by the Exposition promoters.

King Carol I
A44 A45 A46

Perf. 11½, 13½ & Compound

1908-18 **Engr.**

207	A44	5b pale yel grn	1.50	.20
208	A44	10b carmine	.50	.15
209	A45	15b purple	8.25	1.90
210	A44	25b deep blue	.95	.15
211	A44	40b brt green	.60	.15
212	A44	40b dk brn ('18)	3.75	1.90
213	A44	50b orange	.45	.15
214	A44	50b lt red ('18)	1.50	.60
215	A44	1 l brown	1.25	.30
216	A44	2 l red	7.50	1.90
		Nos. 207-216 (10)	26.25	7.40

Perf. 13½x14, 11½, 13½ & Compound

1909-18 **Typo.**

217	A46	1b black	.45	.15
218	A46	3b red brown	.90	.15
219	A46	5b yellow grn	.45	.15
220	A46	10b rose	.90	.15
221	A46	15b dull violet	13.00	8.75
222	A46	15b olive green	.90	.15
223	A46	15b red brn ('18)	.80	.50
		Nos. 217-223 (7)	17.40	10.00

Nos. 217-219, 222 exist imperf.

No. 219 in black is a chemical changeling.

For surcharge and overprints see Nos. 240-242, 245-247, J50-J51, RA1-RA2, RA11-RA12, Romanian Post Offices in the Turkish Empire 7-9.

Types of 1893-99

1911-19 **White Paper** **Unwmk.**

224	A17	1½b straw	1.25	.35
225	A19	25b deep blue ('18)	.40	.15
226	A19	40b gray brn ('19)	.75	.20
227	A19	50b dull red ('19)	.75	.20
228	A23	1 l gray grn ('18)	1.25	.15
229	A23	2 l orange ('18)	1.40	.20
		Nos. 224-229 (6)	5.80	1.25

For overprints see Romanian Post Offices in the Turkish Empire Nos. 10-11.

Romania Holding Flag — A47

Romanian Crown and Old Fort on Danube — A48

Troops Crossing Danube — A49

View of Turtucaia — A50

Mircea the Great and Carol I — A51

View of Silistra — A52

Perf. 11½x13½, 13½x11½

1913, Dec. 25

230	A47	1b black	.40	.15
231	A48	3b ol gray & choc	1.00	.40
232	A49	5b yel grn & blk brn	.80	.15
233	A50	10b org & gray	.40	.15
234	A51	15b bister & vio	1.00	.40
235	A52	25b blue & choc	1.40	.55
236	A49	40b bis & red vio	2.00	.90
237	A48	50b yellow & bl	2.50	1.90
238	A48	1 l bl & ol bis	7.00	4.75
239	A48	2 l org red & rose	9.00	5.50
		Nos. 230-239 (10)	25.50	14.85

Romania's annexation of Silistra.

No. 217 Handstamped in Red

25
BANI

Perf. 13½x14, 11½, 13½ & Compound

1918, May 1

240	A46	25b on 1b black	.20	.15

This handstamp is found inverted.

No. 219 and 220 Overprinted in Black

1918

241	A46	5b yellow green	.30	.20
a.		Inverted overprint	9.00	5.00
b.		Double overprint	9.00	
242	A46	10b rose	.30	.20
a.		Inverted overprint	9.00	5.00
b.		Double overprint	9.00	

Nos. 217, 219 and 220 Overprinted in Red or Black

1919, Nov. 8

245	A46	1b black (R)	.15	.15
a.		Inverted overprint	6.00	
b.		Double overprint	9.00	2.00
246	A46	5b yel grn (Bk)	.15	.15
a.		Double overprint	9.00	2.75
b.		Inverted overprint	6.00	1.75
247	A46	10b rose (Bk)	.15	.15
a.		Inverted overprint	6.00	1.75
b.		Double overprint	9.00	2.50
		Nos. 245-247 (3)	.45	
		Set value		.40

Recovery of Transylvania and the return of the King to Bucharest.

King Ferdinand
A53 A54

1920-22 **Typo.**

248	A53	1b black	.20	.15
249	A53	5b yellow grn	.15	.15
250	A53	10b rose	.15	.15
251	A53	15b red brown	.65	.25
252	A53	25b deep blue	1.25	.35
253	A53	25b brown	.65	.25
254	A53	40b gray brown	1.10	.30
255	A53	50b salmon	.30	.15
256	A53	1 l gray grn	1.10	.20
257	A53	1 l rose	.65	.25
258	A53	2 l orange	1.10	.25
259	A53	2 l dp blue	1.10	.25
260	A53	2 l rose ('22)	2.50	1.65
		Nos. 248-260 (13)	10.90	4.35

Nos. 248-260 are printed on two papers: coarse, grayish paper with bits of colored fiber, and thinner white paper of better quality.

Nos. 248-251, 253 exist imperf.

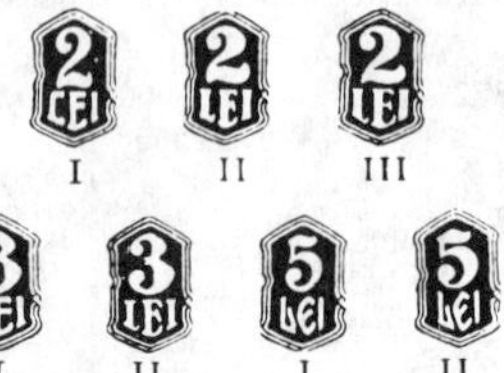

TWO LEI:

Type I - The "2" is thin, with tail 2½mm wide. Top of "2" forms a hook.

Type II - The "2" is thick, with tail 3mm wide. Top of "2" forms a ball.

Type III - The "2" is similar to type II. The "E" of "LEI" is larger and about 2mm wide.

THREE LEI:

Type I - Top of "3" begins in a point. Top and middle bars of "E" of "LEI" are without serifs.

Type II - Top of "3" begins in a ball. Top and middle bars of "E" of "LEI" have serifs.

FIVE LEI:

Type I - The "5" is 2½mm wide. The end of the final stroke of the "L" of "LEI" almost touches the vertical stroke.

Type II - The "5" is 3mm wide and the lines are broader than in type I. The end of the final stroke of the "L" of "LEI" is separated from the vertical by a narrow space.

Perf. 13½x14, 11½, 13½ & Compound

1920-26

261	A54	3b black	.15	.15
262	A54	5b black	.15	.15
263	A54	10b yel grn ('25)	.15	.15
a.		10b olive green ('25)	.35	
264	A54	25b bister brn	.15	.15
265	A54	25b salmon	.15	.15
266	A54	30b violet	.20	.15
267	A54	50b orange	.15	.15
268	A54	60b gray grn	.90	.40
269	A54	1 l violet	.20	.15
270	A54	2 l rose (I)	1.10	.25
a.		2 l claret (I)	*25.00*	
271	A54	2 l lt green (II)	.60	.15
a.		2 l light green (I)	.85	.15
b.		2 l light green (III)	.70	.15
272	A54	3 l blue (I)	2.25	.30
273	A54	3 l buff (II)	2.25	.25
a.		3 l buff (I)	*10.00*	.55
274	A54	3 l salmon (II)	.20	.15
a.		3 l salmon (I)	1.40	.90
275	A54	3 l car rose (II)	.55	.15
276	A54	5 l emer (I)	1.90	.25
277	A54	5 l lt brn (II)	.40	.15
a.		5 l light brown (I)	1.40	.50
278	A54	6 l blue	2.25	.75
279	A54	6 l carmine	5.25	1.25
280	A54	6 l ol grn ('26)	2.25	.40
281	A54	7½ l pale bl	1.90	.25
282	A54	10 l deep blue	1.90	.25
		Nos. 261-282 (22)	25.00	
		Set value		4.25

#273 and 273a, 274 and 274a, exist se-tenant.

The 50b exists in three types.

For surcharge see No. Q7.

Alba Iulia Cathedral A55

King Ferdinand A56

Coat of Arms — A57

Queen Marie as Nurse — A58

Michael the Brave and King Ferdinand A59

King Ferdinand A60

Queen Marie — A61

Perf. 13½x14, 13½, 11½ & Compound

1922, Oct. 15 Photo. Wmk. 95

283 A55	5b black		.30	.25
a.	Engraver's name omitted		*12.00*	1.40
284 A56	25b chocolate		.75	.35
285 A57	50b dp green		.75	.50
286 A58	1 l olive grn		.90	.70
287 A59	2 l carmine		.90	.70
288 A60	3 l blue		1.75	1.10
289 A61	6 l violet		6.50	6.00
	Nos. 283-289 (7)		11.85	9.60

Coronation of King Ferdinand I and Queen Marie on Oct. 15, 1922, at Alba Iulia. All values exist imperforate.

King Ferdinand
A62 A63

1926, July 1 Unwmk. *Perf. 11*

291 A62	10b yellow grn	.15	.15
292 A62	25b orange	.15	.15
293 A62	50b orange brn	.15	.15
294 A63	1 l dk violet	.15	.15
295 A63	2 l dk green	.15	.15
296 A63	3 l brown car	.15	.15
297 A63	5 l black brn	.15	.15
298 A63	6 l dk olive	.15	.15
a.	6 l bright blue (error)	70.00	70.00
300 A63	9 l slate	.15	.15
301 A63	10 l brt blue	.15	.15
b.	10 l brown carmine (error)	70.00	70.00
	Nos. 291-301 (10)	1.50	1.50

60th birthday of King Ferdinand.

Exist imperf. Imperf. examples with watermark 95 are proofs.

King Carol I and King Ferdinand A69

King Ferdinand A70

A71

1927, Aug. 1 *Perf. 13½*

308 A69	25b brown vio	.20	.20
309 A70	30b gray blk	.20	.20
310 A71	50b dk green	.20	.20
311 A69	1 l bluish slate	.20	.20
312 A70	2 l dp green	.25	.25
313 A70	3 l violet	.35	.35
314 A71	4 l dk brown	.40	.40
315 A71	4.50 l henna brn	1.50	1.25
316 A70	5 l red brown	.40	.40
317 A71	6 l carmine	1.00	.85
318 A69	7.50 l grnsh bl	.60	.60
319 A69	10 l brt blue	1.00	.85
	Nos. 308-319 (12)	6.30	5.75

50th anniversary of Romania's independence from Turkish suzerainty.

Some values exist imperf. All exist imperf. and with value numerals omitted.

King Michael
A72 A73

Perf. 13½x14 (25b, 50b); 13½

1928-29 Typo. Unwmk.

Size: 19x25mm

320 A72	25b black	.15	.15
321 A72	30b fawn ('29)	.25	.15
322 A72	50b olive grn	.15	.15

Photo.

Size: 18½x24½mm

323 A73	1 l violet	.25	.15
324 A73	2 l dp green	.35	.15
325 A73	3 l brt rose	.40	.15
326 A73	5 l red brown	.70	.15
327 A73	7.50 l ultra	3.00	.45
328 A73	10 l blue	2.50	.20
	Nos. 320-328 (9)	7.75	
	Set value		1.40

See Nos. 343-345, 353-357. For overprints see Nos. 359-368A.

Parliament House, Bessarabia A74

Designs: 1 l, 2 l, Parliament House, Bessarabia. 3 l, 5 l, 20 l, Hotin Fortress. 7.50 l, 10 l, Fortress Cetatea Alba.

1928, Apr. 29 Wmk. 95 *Perf. 13½*

329 A74	1 l deep green	.50	.35
330 A74	2 l deep brown	.50	.35
331 A74	3 l black brown	.50	.35
332 A74	5 l carmine lake	.65	.40
333 A74	7.50 l ultra	.65	.40
334 A74	10 l Prus blue	1.50	1.10
335 A74	20 l black vio	2.00	1.40
	Nos. 329-335 (7)	6.30	4.35

Reunion of Bessarabia with Romania, 10th anniv.

King Carol I and King Michael A77

View of Constanta Harbor A78

Trajan's Monument at Adam Clisi — A79

Cernavoda Bridge A80

1928, Oct. 25

336 A77	1 l blue green	.45	.30
337 A78	2 l red brown	.45	.30
338 A77	3 l gray black	.60	.30
339 A79	5 l dull lilac	.75	.40
340 A79	7.50 l ultra	1.00	.40
341 A80	10 l blue	1.50	1.00
342 A80	20 l carmine rose	2.25	1.25
	Nos. 336-342 (7)	7.00	3.95

Union of Dobruja with Romania, 50th anniv.

Michael Types of 1928-29

Perf. 13½x14

1928, Sept. 1 Typo. Wmk. 95

343 A72	25b black	.50	.15

Photo.

344 A73	7.50 l ultra	1.50	.75
345 A73	10 l blue	3.00	.50
	Nos. 343-345 (3)	5.00	1.40

Ferdinand I; Stephen the Great; Michael the Brave; Corvin and Constantine Brancoveanu A81

Union with Transylvania A82

Avram Jancu A83

Prince Michael the Brave — A84

Castle Bran — A85

King Ferdinand I — A86

1929, May 10 Photo. Wmk. 95

347 A81	1 l dark violet	1.10	.60
348 A82	2 l olive green	1.10	.60
349 A83	3 l violet brown	1.50	.75
350 A84	4 l cerise	1.50	.90
351 A85	5 l orange	1.75	.90
352 A86	10 l brt blue	2.00	1.50
	Nos. 347-352 (6)	8.95	5.25

Union of Transylvania and Romania.

Michael Type of 1928

1930 Unwmk. *Perf. 14½x14*

Size: 18x23mm

353 A73	1 l deep violet	.45	.15
354 A73	2 l deep green	.70	.15
355 A73	3 l carmine rose	1.40	.15
356 A73	7.50 l ultra	2.75	.50
357 A73	10 l deep blue	9.50	3.50
	Nos. 353-357 (5)	14.80	4.45

Stamps of 1928-30 Overprinted **8 IUNIE 1930**

On Nos. 320-322, 326, 328

Perf. 13½x14, 13½

1930, June 8 Typo.

359 A72	25b black	.20	.15
360 A72	30b fawn	.25	.15
361 A72	50b olive green	.25	.15

Photo.

Size: 18½x24½mm

362 A73	5 l red brown	.50	.15
362A A73	10 l brt blue	2.50	.55

On Nos. 353-357

Perf. 14½x14

Size: 18x23mm

363 A73	1 l deep violet	.30	.55
364 A73	2 l deep green	.25	.15
365 A73	3 l carmine rose	.50	.15
366 A73	7.50 l ultra	1.50	.35
367 A73	10 l deep blue	1.25	.20

On Nos. 343-344

Perf. 13½x14, 13½

Typo. Wmk. 95

368 A72	25b black	.50	.15

Photo.

Size: 18½x24½mm

368A A73	7.50 l ultra	2.00	.50
	Nos. 359-368A (12)	10.00	
	Set value		2.65

Accession to the throne by King Carol II. This overprint exists on Nos. 323, 345.

King Carol II
A87 A88 A89

Perf. 13½, 14, 14x13½

1930 Wmk. 225

369 A87	25b black	.15	.15
370 A87	50b chocolate	.25	.20
371 A87	1 l dk violet	.15	.15
372 A87	2 l gray green	.20	.15
373 A88	3 l carmine rose	.35	.15
374 A88	4 l orange red	.35	.15
375 A88	6 l carmine brn	.45	.15
376 A88	7.50 l ultra	.50	.15
377 A89	10 l deep blue	1.25	.15
378 A89	16 l peacock grn	3.00	.15
379 A89	20 l orange	3.75	.25
	Nos. 369-379 (11)	10.40	
	Set value		.95

Exist imperf. See Nos. 405-414.

A90

A91

1930, Dec. 24 Unwmk. *Perf. 13½*

380 A90	1 l dull violet	.50	.20
381 A91	2 l green	.80	.20
382 A91	4 l vermilion	1.00	.20
383 A91	6 l brown carmine	2.25	.20
	Nos. 380-383 (4)	4.55	.80

First census in Romania.

King Carol II — A92

King Carol I — A93

King Ferdinand — A96

King Carol II — A94

King Carol II, King Ferdinand and King Carol I — A95

1931, May 10 Photo. Wmk. 225

No.	Type	Value	Color	Unused	Used
384	A92	1 l	gray violet	3.00	1.75
385	A93	2 l	green	3.50	1.75
386	A94	6 l	red brown	5.00	2.75
387	A95	10 l	blue	8.00	5.00
388	A96	20 l	orange	9.00	6.75
			Nos. 384-388 (5)	28.50	18.00

50th anniversary of Romanian Kingdom.

Using Bayonet — A97

Romanian Infantryman 1870 — A98

Romanian Infantry 1830 — A99

King Carol I — A100

Infantry Advance A101

King Ferdinand A102

King Carol II — A103

1931, May 10

No.	Type	Value	Color	Unused	Used
389	A97	25b	gray black	.85	.50
390	A98	50b	dk red brn	1.40	.65
391	A99	1 l	gray violet	1.75	.80
392	A100	2 l	deep green	3.00	1.00
393	A101	3 l	carmine rose	5.50	3.00
394	A102	7.50 l	ultra	7.50	6.50
395	A103	16 l	blue green	10.00	3.00
			Nos. 389-395 (7)	30.00	15.45

Centenary of the Romanian Army.

Naval Cadet Ship "Mircea" — A104

King Carol II — A108

10 l, Ironclad. 16 l, Light cruiser. 20 l, Destroyer.

1931, May 10

No.	Type	Value	Color	Unused	Used
396	A104	6 l	red brown	3.25	2.00
397	A104	10 l	blue	4.50	2.25
398	A104	16 l	blue green	17.00	2.75
399	A104	20 l	orange	7.50	4.75
			Nos. 396-399 (4)	32.25	11.75

50th anniversary of the Romanian Navy.

1931 Unwmk. Engr. *Perf.* 12

No.	Type	Value	Color	Unused	Used
400	A108	30 l	ol bis & dk bl	.35	.15
401	A108	50 l	red & dk bl	1.25	.35
402	A108	100 l	dk grn & dk bl	1.50	.50
			Nos. 400-402 (3)	3.10	1.00

Exist imperf.

Carol II, Ferdinand, Carol I — A109

***Perf.* 13½**

1931, Nov. 1 Photo. Wmk. 230

No.	Type	Value	Color	Unused	Used
403	A109	16 l	Prus green	7.50	.40

Exists imperf.

Carol II Types of 1930-31

***Perf.* 13½, 14, 14½ and Compound**

1932 Wmk. 230

No.	Type	Value	Color	Unused	Used
405	A87	25b	black	.35	.15
406	A87	50b	dark brown	.50	.15
407	A87	1 l	dark violet	.85	.15
408	A87	2 l	gray green	.85	.15
409	A88	3 l	carmine rose	1.50	.15
410	A88	4 l	orange red	2.50	.15
411	A88	6 l	carmine brn	4.50	.15
412	A88	7.50 l	ultra	6.50	.45
413	A89	10 l	deep blue	75.00	.45
414	A89	20 l	orange	75.00	5.00
			Nos. 405-414 (10)	167.55	6.95

Alexander the Good A110

King Carol II A111

1932, May *Perf.* 13½

No.	Type	Value	Color	Unused	Used
415	A110	6 l	carmine brown	8.50	5.75

500th death anniv. of Alexander the Good, Prince of Moldavia, 1400-1432.

1932, June

No.	Type	Value	Color	Unused	Used
416	A111	10 l	brt blue	9.00	.40

Exists imperf.

Cantacuzino and Gregory Ghika, Founders of Coltea and Pantelimon Hospitals A112

Session of the Congress A113

Aesculapius and Hygeia A114

1932, Sept. *Perf.* 13½

No.	Type	Value	Color	Unused	Used
417	A112	1 l	carmine rose	5.00	3.50
418	A113	6 l	deep orange	12.50	5.50
419	A114	10 l	brt blue	20.00	10.00
			Nos. 417-419 (3)	37.50	19.00

9th Intl. History of Medicine Congress, Bucharest.

Bull's Head and Post Horn A116

Lion Rampant and Bridge A117

Dolphins A118

Eagle and Castles A119

Coat of Arms — A120

Eagle and Post Horn — A121

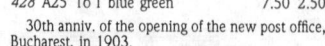

Bull's Head and Post Horn — A122

1932, Nov. 20 Typo. *Imperf.*

No.	Type	Value	Color	Unused	Used
421	A116	25b	black	.90	.25
422	A117	1 l	violet	1.40	.40
423	A118	2 l	green	1.90	.45
424	A119	3 l	car rose	2.00	.60
425	A120	6 l	red brown	2.75	.75
426	A121	7.50 l	lt blue	2.75	.75
427	A122	10 l	dk blue	3.50	1.10
			Nos. 421-427 (7)	15.20	4.30

75th anniv. of the first Moldavian stamps.

Mail Coach Type of 1903

1932, Nov. 20 *Perf.* 13½

No.	Type	Value	Color	Unused	Used
428	A25	16 l	blue green	7.50	2.50

30th anniv. of the opening of the new post office, Bucharest, in 1903.

Arms of City of Turnu-Severin, Ruins of Tower of Emperor Severus A123

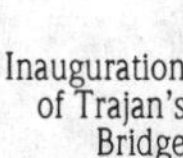

Inauguration of Trajan's Bridge A124

Prince Carol Landing at Turnu-Severin A125

Bridge over the Danube A126

1933, June 2 Photo. *Perf.* 14½x14

No.	Type	Value	Color	Unused	Used
429	A123	25b	gray green	.22	.15
430	A124	50b	dull blue	.45	.20
431	A125	1 l	black brn	.45	.24
432	A126	2 l	olive blk	1.10	.35
			Nos. 429-432 (4)	2.22	.94

Centenary of the incorporation in Walachia of the old Roman City of Turnu-Severin.
Exist imperf.

Queen Elizabeth and King Carol I — A127

Profiles of Kings Carol I, Ferdinand and Carol II — A128

Castle Peles, Sinaia A129

1933, Aug.

No.	Type	Value	Color	Unused	Used
433	A127	1 l	dark violet	2.00	1.25
434	A128	3 l	olive brown	2.00	1.25
435	A129	6 l	vermilion	3.25	1.65
			Nos. 433-435 (3)	7.25	4.15

50th anniversary of the erection of Castle Peles, the royal summer residence at Sinaia.
Exist imperf.

A130

A131

King Carol II — A132

1934, Aug. *Perf.* 13½

No.	Type	Value	Color	Unused	Used
436	A130	50b	brown	.55	.20
437	A131	2 l	gray green	1.00	.25
438	A131	4 l	red	1.50	.32
439	A132	6 l	deep claret	4.50	.20
			Nos. 436-439 (4)	7.55	.97

See Nos. 446-460 for stamps inscribed "Posta."
Nos. 436, 439 exist imperf.

Child and Grapes — A133

Woman and Fruit — A134

1934, Sept. 14

440	A133	1 l dull green	1.40	1.10
441	A134	2 l violet brown	1.40	1.10

Natl. Fruit Week, Sept. 14-21. Exist imperf.

Crisan, Horia and Closca A135

1935, Feb. 28

442	A135	1 l shown	.35	.25
443	A135	2 l Crisan	.50	.40
444	A135	6 l Closca	1.00	.50
445	A135	10 l Horia	2.00	1.00
		Nos. 442-445 (4)	3.85	2.15

150th anniversary of the death of three Romanian martyrs. Exist imperf.

A139

A140

A141

A142

King Carol II — A143

Perf. 13½

1935-40 Photo. Wmk. 230

446	A139	25b	black brn	.15	.15
447	A142	50b	brown	.15	.15
448	A140	1 l	purple	.15	.15
449	A141	2 l	green	.15	.15
449A	A141	2 l	dk bl grn ('40)	.25	.25
450	A142	3 l	deep rose	.15	.15
450A	A142	3 l	grnsh bl ('40)	.30	.30
451	A141	4 l	vermilion	.40	.15
452	A140	5 l	rose car ('40)	.40	.40
453	A143	6 l	maroon	.35	.15
454	A140	7.50 l	ultra	.60	.20
454A	A142	8 l	magenta ('40)	.60	.60
455	A141	9 l	brt ultra ('40)	.90	.90
456	A142	10 l	brt blue	.30	.20
456A	A143	12 l	sl bl ('40)	.50	.50
457	A139	15 l	dk brn ('40)	.50	.50
458	A143	16 l	Prus blue	.60	.15
459	A143	20 l	orange	.40	.20
460	A143	24 l	dk car ('40)	.85	.85
			Nos. 446-460 (19)	7.70	
			Set value		5.40

Exist imperf.

Nos. 454, 456 Overprinted in Red

CEHOSLOVACIA YUGOSLAVIA 1920-1936

1936, Dec. 5

461	A140	7.50 l ultra	2.25	1.75
462	A142	10 l brt blue	2.25	1.75

16th anniversary of the Little Entente. Overprints in silver or gold are fraudulent.

Birthplace of Ion Creanga A144

Ion Creanga A145

1937, May 15

463	A144	2 l green	.50	.35
464	A145	3 l carmine rose	.50	.35
465	A144	4 l dp violet	.75	.50
466	A145	6 l red brown	.75	.65
		Nos. 463-466 (4)	2.50	1.85

Creanga (1837-89), writer. Exist imperf.

Cathedral at Curtea de Arges — A146

1937, July 1

467	A146	7.50 l ultra	1.25	.40
468	A146	10 l blue	2.25	.35

The Little Entente (Romania, Czechoslovakia, Yugoslavia). Exist imperf.

Souvenir Sheet

A146a

Surcharged in Black with New Values

1937, Oct. 25 Unwmk. ***Perf. 13½***

469 A146a	Sheet of 4	3.00	3.00
a.	2 l on 20 l orange	.30	.30
b.	6 l on 10 l bright blue	.30	.30
c.	10 l on 6 l maroon	.30	.30
d.	20 l on 2 l green	.30	.30

Promotion of the Crown Prince Michael to the rank of Lieutenant on his 17th birthday.

Arms of Romania, Greece, Turkey and Yugoslavia — A147

Perf. 13x13½

1938, Feb. 10 Wmk. 230

470	A147	7.50 l ultra	.75	.50
471	A147	10 l blue	1.25	.50

The Balkan Entente.

A148

King Carol II

A149 A150

1938, May 10 ***Perf. 13½***

472	A148	3 l dk carmine	.35	.15
473	A149	6 l violet brn	.35	.15
474	A150	10 l blue	.50	.20
		Nos. 472-474 (3)	1.20	.50

New Constitution of Feb. 27, 1938.

Catalogue values for unused stamps in this section, from this point to the end of the section, are for Never Hinged items.

Prince Carol at Calatorie, 1866 A151

Examining Plans for a Monastery A153

Prince Carol and Carmen Sylva (Queen Elizabeth) A155

Sigmaringen and Peles Castles A154

Prince Carol, Age 6 — A156

Equestrian Statue — A159

Battle of Plevna A160

On Horseback A161

Cathedral of Curtea de Arges — A164

King Carol I and Queen Elizabeth A163

Designs: 50b, At Calafat. 4 l, In 1866. 5 l, In 1877. 12 l, in 1914.

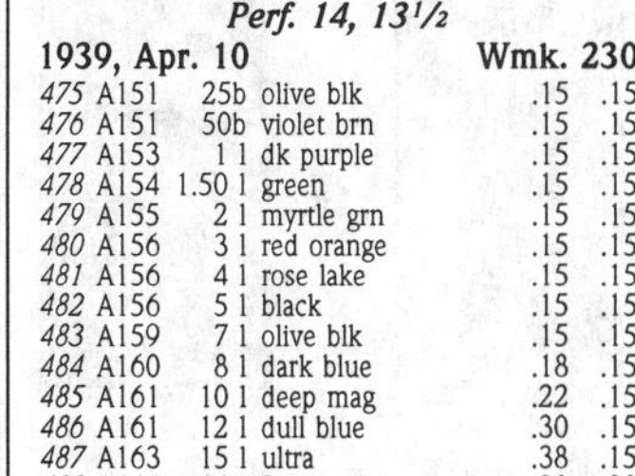

Perf. 14, 13½

1939, Apr. 10 Wmk. 230

475	A151	25b	olive blk	.15	.15
476	A151	50b	violet brn	.15	.15
477	A153	1 l	dk purple	.15	.15
478	A154	1.50 l	green	.15	.15
479	A155	2 l	myrtle grn	.15	.15
480	A156	3 l	red orange	.15	.15
481	A156	4 l	rose lake	.15	.15
482	A156	5 l	black	.15	.15
483	A159	7 l	olive blk	.15	.15
484	A160	8 l	dark blue	.18	.15
485	A161	10 l	deep mag	.22	.15
486	A161	12 l	dull blue	.30	.15
487	A163	15 l	ultra	.38	.15
488	A164	16 l	Prus green	.90	.38
			Set value (14)	2.80	1.30

Centenary of the birth of King Carol I.

Souvenir Sheets

1939 ***Perf. 14x13½***

488A	Sheet of 3, #475-476, 478	1.50	1.50
d.	Imperf. ('40)	3.50	3.50

Perf. 14x15½

488B	Sheet of 4, #480-482, 486	1.50	1.50
e.	Imperf. ('40)	3.50	3.50
488C	Sheet of 4, #479, 483-485	1.50	1.50
f.	Imperf. ('40)	3.50	3.50

No. 488A sold for 20 l, Nos. 488B-488C for 50 l, the surtax for national defense.

Nos. 488A-488C and 488Ad-488Cf were overprinted "PRO-PATRIA 1940" to aid the armament fund. Value, set of 6, $100.

Nos. 488A-488C exist with overprint of "ROMA BERLIN 1940" and bars, but these are not recognized as having been officially issued.

Romanian Pavilion A165

Romanian Pavilion A166

1939, May 8 ***Perf. 14x13½, 13½***

489	A165	6 l brown carmine	.30	.30
490	A166	12 l brt blue	.30	.30

New York World's Fair.

Mihail Eminescu

A167 A168

1939, May 22 ***Perf. 13½***

491	A167	5 l olive gray	.35	.35
492	A168	7 l brown carmine	.35	.35

Mihail Eminescu, poet, 50th death anniv.

Three Types of Locomotives A169

Modern Train A170

Wood-burning Locomotive A171

Streamlined Locomotive A172

Railroad Terminal A173

1939, June 10 Typo. *Perf. 14*

493	A169	1 l red violet	.40	.30
494	A170	4 l deep rose	.55	.30
495	A171	5 l gray lilac	.60	.30
496	A171	7 l claret	.70	.35
497	A172	12 l blue	1.00	1.00
498	A173	15 l green	2.00	1.25
		Nos. 493-498 (6)	5.25	3.50

Romanian Railways, 70th anniversary.

Arms of Romania, Greece, Turkey and Yugoslavia — A174

Perf. 13½

1940, May 27 Photo. Wmk. 230

504	A174	12 l lt ultra	.35	.35
505	A174	16 l dull blue	.35	.35

The Balkan Entente.

King Michael — A175

1940-42 Wmk. 230 *Perf. 14*

506	A175	25b Prus green	.15	.15
506A	A175	50b dk grn ('42)	.15	.15
507	A175	1 l purple	.15	.15
508	A175	2 l red orange	.15	.15
508A	A175	4 l slate ('42)	.15	.15
509	A175	5 l rose pink	.15	.15
509A	A175	7 l dp blue ('42)	.15	.15
510	A175	10 l dp magenta	.24	.15
511	A175	12 l dull blue	.15	.15
511A	A175	13 l dk vio ('42)	.15	.15
512	A175	16 l Prus blue	.24	.15
513	A175	20 l brown	1.25	.15
514	A175	30 l yellow grn	.15	.15
515	A175	50 l olive brn	.20	.15
516	A175	100 l rose brown	.28	.15
		Set value (15)	2.85	.80

See Nos. 535A-553.

Prince Duca — A176

1941, Oct. 6 *Perf. 13½*

517	A176	6 l lt brown	.15	.15
518	A176	12 l dk violet	.20	.20
519	A176	24 l brt blue	.25	.25
		Nos. 517-519 (3)	.60	.60

Crossing of the Dniester River by Romanian forces invading Russia.

Nos. 517-519 each exist in an imperf., ungummed souvenir sheet of 4. These were prepared by the civil government of Trans-Dniestria to be sold for 300 lei apiece to aid the Red Cross, but were not recognized by the national government at Bucharest. The sheets reached philatelic channels in 1946.

See Nos. 554-557.

Hotin Chapel, Bessarabia — A177 Sucevita Monastery, Bucovina — A179

Inscribed "Basarabia" or "Bucovina" at bottom

Designs: 50b, 9.50 l, Hotin Fortress, Bessarabia. 1.50 l, Soroca Fortress, Bessarabia. 2 l, 5.50 l, Tighina Fortress, Bessarabia. 3 l, Dragomirna Monastery, Bucovina. 6.50 l, Cetatea Alba Fortress, Bessarabia. 10 l, 130 l, Putna Monastery, Bucovina. 13 l, Milisauti Monastery, Bucovina. 26 l, St. Nicholas Monastery, Suceava, Bucovina. 39 l, Rughi Monastery, Bessarabia.

1941, Dec. 1 *Perf. 13½*

520	A177	25b rose car	.15	.15
521	A179	50b red brn	.15	.15
522	A179	1 l dp vio	.15	.15
523	A179	1.50 l green	.15	.15
524	A179	2 l brn org	.15	.15
525	A177	3 l dk ol grn	.15	.15
526	A177	5 l olive blk	.15	.15
527	A179	5.50 l brown	.15	.15
528	A179	6.50 l magenta	.28	.22
529	A179	9.50 l gray blk	.28	.22
530	A179	10 l dk vio brn	.18	.15
531	A177	13 l slate blue	.24	.15
532	A179	17 l brn car	.28	.15
533	A179	26 l gray grn	.35	.24
534	A179	39 l bl grn	.52	.38
535	A179	130 l yel org	2.00	1.50
		Nos. 520-535 (16)	5.33	
		Set value		3.25

See Nos. B179-B187.

Type of 1940-42

1943-45 Wmk. 276 *Perf. 14*

535A	A175	25b Prus grn ('44)	.15	.15
536	A175	50b dk grn ('44)	.15	.15
537	A175	1 l dk vio ('43)	.15	.15
538	A175	2 l red org ('43)	.15	.15
539	A175	3 l red brn ('44)	.15	.15
540	A175	3.50 l brn ('43)	.15	.15
541	A175	4 l slate	.15	.15
542	A175	4.50 l dk brn ('43)	.15	.15
543	A175	5 l rose car	.15	.15
544	A175	6.50 l dl vio	.15	.15
545	A175	7 l dp bl	.15	.15
546	A175	10 l dp mag	.15	.15
547	A175	11 l brt ultra	.15	.15
548	A175	12 l dark blue	.15	.15
549	A175	15 l royal blue	.15	.15
550	A175	16 l dp blue	.15	.15
551	A175	20 l brn ('43)	.15	.15
551A	A175	29 l ultra ('45)	.48	.30
552	A175	30 l yel grn	.15	.15
553	A175	50 l olive blk	.22	.15
		Set value (20)	1.60	1.25

Prince Duca Type of 1941

1943 *Perf. 13½*

554	A176	3 l red org	.15	.15
555	A176	6 l dl brn	.15	.15
556	A176	12 l dl vio	.15	.15
557	A176	24 l brt bl	.22	.22
		Set value	.55	.55

Andrei Saguna — A188

Andrei Muresanu A189

Transylvanians: 4.50 l, Samuel Micu. 11 l, Gheorghe Sincai. 15 l, Michael the Brave. 31 l, Gheorghe Lazar. 35 l, Avram Jancu. 41 l, Simeon Barnutiu. 55 l, Three Heroes. 61 l, Petru Maior.

1945 Inscribed "1944" *Perf. 14*

558	A188	25b rose red	.30	.30
559	A189	50b orange	.20	.20
560	A189	4.50 l brown	.20	.20
561	A188	11 l lt ultra	.20	.20
562	A188	15 l Prus grn	.20	.20
563	A189	31 l dl vio	.20	.20
564	A188	35 l bl blk	.20	.20
565	A188	41 l olive gray	.20	.20
566	A189	55 l red brown	.20	.20
567	A189	61 l deep magenta	.20	.20
		Nos. 558-567,B251 (11)	2.60	2.60

Romania's liberation.

A198

A199

King Michael A200 A201

1945 Photo.

568	A198	50b gray blue	.15	.15
569	A199	1 l dl brn	.15	.15
570	A199	2 l violet	.15	.15
571	A198	2 l sepia	.15	.15
572	A199	4 l yel grn	.15	.15
573	A200	5 l dp mag	.15	.15
574	A198	10 l blue	.15	.15
575	A198	15 l magenta	.15	.15
576	A198	20 l dl blue	.15	.15
577	A200	25 l red org	.15	.15
578	A200	35 l brown	.15	.15
579	A200	40 l car rose	.15	.15
580	A199	50 l pale ultra	.15	.15
581	A199	55 l red	.15	.15
582	A200	75 l Prus grn	.15	.15
583	A201	80 l orange	.15	.15
584	A201	100 l dp red brn	.15	.15
585	A201	160 l yel grn	.15	.15
586	A201	200 l dk ol grn	.22	.15
587	A201	400 l dl vio	.15	.15
		Set value (20)	2.25	1.25

Nos. 571, 573, 580, 581, 585 and 587 are printed on toned paper, Nos. 576, 577, 583, 584 and 586 on both toned and white papers, others on white paper only.

See Nos. 610-624, 651-660.

Mail Carrier A202

Telegraph Operator A203

Lineman A204

Post Office, Bucharest A205

1945, July 20 Wmk. 276 *Perf. 13*

588	A202	100 l dk brn	.75	.75
589	A202	100 l gray olive	.75	.75
590	A203	150 l brown	1.25	1.25
591	A203	150 l brt rose	1.25	1.25
592	A204	250 l lt gray ol	1.50	1.50
593	A204	250 l blue	1.50	1.50
594	A205	500 l dp mag	10.50	10.50
		Nos. 588-594 (7)	17.50	17.50

Issued in sheets of 4.

I. Ionescu, G. Titeica, A. O. Idachimescu and V. Cristescu A207

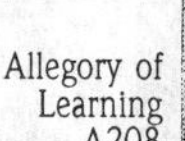

Allegory of Learning A208

1945, Sept. 5 *Perf. 13½*

596	A207	2 l sepia	.15	.15
597	A208	80 l bl blk	.15	.15
		Set value	.22	.22

50th anniversary of "Gazeta Matematica," mathematics journal.

Cernavoda Bridge, 50th Anniv. A209

1945, Sept. 26 *Perf. 14*

598	A209	80 l bl blk	.20	.15

Blacksmith and Plowman — A210

1946, Mar. 6

599	A210	80 l blue	.20	.15

Agrarian reform law of Mar. 23, 1945.

Atheneum, Bucharest — A211

Numeral in Wreath — A212

Georges Enescu — A213 Mechanic — A214

Perf. 13½

1946, Apr. 26 Photo. Wmk. 276

600	A211	10 l dk bl	.15	.15
601	A212	20 l red brn	.15	.15
602	A212	55 l pck bl	.15	.15
603	A213	80 l purple	.18	.15
a.		Tête bêche pair	.60	.60
604	A212	160 l red org	.15	.15
		Nos. 600-604,B330-B331 (7)	2.03	
		Set value		1.65

Philharmonic Society, 25th anniv.

1946, May 1 *Perf. 13½x13*

Labor Day: No. 606, Laborer. No. 607, Sower. No. 608, Reaper. 200 l, Students.

605	A214	10 l Prus grn	.38	.38
606	A214	10 l dk car rose	.15	.15
607	A214	20 l dl bl	.38	.38
608	A214	20 l dk red brn	.15	.15
609	A214	200 l brt red	.15	.15
		Set value	.95	.95

Michael Types of 1945

1946 Wmk. 276 Photo. *Perf. 14*

Toned Paper

610	A198	10 l brt red brn	.15	.15
611	A199	20 l vio brn	.15	.15
612	A201	80 l blue	.15	.15
613	A198	137 l yel grn	.15	.15
614	A201	160 l chalky bl	.15	.15
615	A201	200 l red org	.15	.15
616	A201	300 l sapphire	.15	.15

617 A201 360 l sepia .15 .15
618 A199 400 l red org .15 .15
619 A201 480 l brn red .15 .15
620 A201 600 l dk ol grn .15 .15
621 A201 1000 l Prus grn .15 .15
622 A198 1500 l Prus grn .15 .15
623 A201 2400 l magenta .15 .15
624 A201 3700 l dull bl .15 .15
Set value, #610-624, B338 (15) 2.00 1.50

See No. B339.

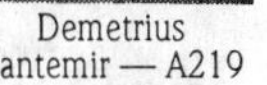

Demetrius Cantemir — A219

Soccer — A222

Designs: 100 l, "Cultural Ties." 300 l, "Economic Ties."

1946, Oct. 20 *Perf. 13½*

625 A219 80 l dk brn .15 .15
626 A219 100 l dp bl .15 .15
627 A219 300 l bl blk .15 .15
Set value .26 .26

Romania-Soviet friendship. See Nos. B338-B339.

1946, Sept. 1 *Perf. 11½, Imperf.*

Designs: 20 l, Diving. 50 l, Running. 80 l, Mountain climbing.

628 A222 10 l dp blue .35 .35
629 A222 20 l brt red .35 .35
630 A222 50 l dp violet .35 .35
631 A222 80 l chocolate .35 .35
Nos. 628-631,B340,C26,CB6 (7) 3.65 3.65

Issued in sheets of 16.

Weaving A226

Child Receiving Bread A227

Transporting Relief Supplies A228

CGM Congress Emblem A229

Wmk. 276

1946, Nov. 20 **Photo.** *Perf. 14*

636 A226 80 l dk ol brn .15 .15
Set value, #636, B342-B345 .50 .50

Democratic Women's Org. of Romania. See No. CB7.

Perf. 13½x14, 14x13½

1947, Jan. 15

637 A227 300 l dk ol brn .15 .15
638 A228 600 l magenta .15 .15
Nos. 637-638,B346-B347 (4) .60 .60

Social relief fund. See #B348.

1947, Feb. 10 *Perf. 13½*

639 A229 200 l blue .15 .15
640 A229 300 l orange .15 .15
a. Pair, #639-640 .30 .30
b. Pair, #640-641 .30 .30
641 A229 600 l crimson .15 .15
Nos. 639-641 (3) .45
Set value .24

Congress of the United Labor Unions ("CGM").
Printed in sheets of 18 comprising 3 pairs of each denomination. Sheet yields 3 each of Nos. 640a and 640b.

Peace in Chariot A230

Peace A231

Flags of US, Russia, GB & Romania A232

Dove of Peace — A233

Perf. 14x13½, 13½x14

1947, Feb. 25

642 A230 300 l dl vio .15 .15
643 A231 600 l dk org brn .15 .15
644 A232 3000 l blue .15 .15
645 A233 7200 l sage grn .15 .15
Set value .32 .32

Signing of the peace treaty of Feb. 10, 1947.

King Michael — A234

1947 *Perf. 13½*

Size: 25x30mm

646 A234 3000 l blue .15 .15
647 A234 7200 l dl vio .15 .15
648 A234 15,000 l brt bl .15 .15
649 A234 21,000 l magenta .15 .15
650 A234 36,000 l violet .25 .15
Set value .65 .50

See Nos. 661-664.

Michael Types of 1945

1947 **Wmk. 276** **Photo.** *Perf. 14*

651 A199 10 l red brn .15 .15
652 A200 20 l magenta .15 .15
653 A198 80 l blue .15 .15
654 A199 200 l brt red .15 .15
655 A198 500 l magenta .15 .15
656 A200 860 l vio brn .15 .15
657 A199 2500 l ultra .15 .15
658 A198 5000 l sl gray .20 .15
659 A198 8000 l Prus grn .35 .15
660 A201 10,000 l dk brn .25 .15

Type of 1947

Size: 18x21½mm

661 A234 1000 l gray bl .15 .15
662 A234 5500 l yel grn .15 .15
663 A234 20,000 l ol brn .15 .15
664 A234 50,000 l red org .35 .15
Nos. 651-664 (14) 2.65
Set value 1.00

For surcharge see No. B368.

Harvesting Wheat A235

Designs: 1 l, Log raft. 2 l, River steamer. 3 l, Resita. 5 l, Cathedral of Curtea de Arges. 10 l, View of Bucharest. 12 l, 36 l, Cernavoda Bridge. 15 l, 32 l, Port of Constantsa. 20 l, Petroleum field.

1947, Aug. 15 *Perf. 14½x14*

666 A235 50b red org .15 .15
667 A235 1 l red brn .15 .15
668 A235 2 l bl gray .15 .15
669 A235 3 l rose crim .20 .15
670 A235 5 l brt ultra .20 .15
671 A235 10 l brt blue .25 .15
672 A235 12 l violet .35 .15
673 A235 15 l dp ultra .55 .15
674 A235 20 l dk brown 1.00 .26
675 A235 32 l violet brn 2.00 .52
676 A235 36 l dk car rose 2.00 .26
Nos. 666-676 (11) 7.00
Set value 1.50

For overprints & surcharge see #684-694, B369.

Beehive, Savings Emblem — A236

1947, Oct. 31 *Perf. 13½*

677 A236 12 l dk car rose .30 .15

World Savings Day, Oct. 31, 1947.

People's Republic

Map, Workers and Children A237

1948, Jan. 25 *Perf. 14½x14*

678 A237 12 l brt ultra .30 .15

1948 census. For surcharge see #819A.

Government Printing Plant and Press A238

1948 *Perf. 14½x14*

679 A238 6 l magenta .90 .50
680 A238 7.50 l dk Prus grn .50 .15
b. Tête bêche pair 1.25 .90

75th anniversary of Stamp Division of Romanian State Printing Works.
Issued: No. 680, Feb. 12; No. 679, May 20.

Romanian and Bulgarian Peasants Shaking Hands A239

1948, Mar. 25 **Wmk. 276**

680A A239 32 l red brown .50 .18

Romanian-Bulgarian friendship.
For surcharge see No. 696.

Allegory of the People's Republic — A240

1948, Apr. 8 **Photo.** *Perf. 14x14½*

681 A240 1 l car rose .35 .15
682 A240 2 l dl org .35 .18
683 A240 12 l deep blue .50 .30
Nos. 681-683 (3) 1.20 .63

New constitution.
For surcharge see No. 820.

Nos. 666 to 676 Overprinted in Black

1948, Mar. *Perf. 14½x14*

684 A235 50b red org .30 .15
685 A235 1 l red brn .30 .15
686 A235 2 l bl gray .55 .15
687 A235 3 l rose crim .55 .15
688 A235 5 l brt ultra .75 .15
689 A235 10 l brt bl 1.10 .20
690 A235 12 l violet 1.25 .25
691 A235 15 l dp ultra 1.25 .30
692 A235 20 l dk brn 1.50 .50
693 A235 32 l vio brn 4.50 1.50
694 A235 36 l dk car rose 4.50 1.50
Nos. 684-694 (11) 16.55 5.00

Romanian Newspapers A241

1948, Sept. 12

695 A241 10 l red brn .28 .15
Nos. 695,B396-B398 (4) 2.78 2.65

Week of the Democratic Press, Sept. 12-19.

No. 680A Surcharged with New Value in Black

1948, Aug. 17

696 A239 31 l on 32 l red brn .55 .15

Monument to Soviet Soldier — A242

Proclamation of Islaz — A243

1948, Oct. 29 **Photo.** *Perf. 14x14½*

697 A242 10 l dk red .45 .30
Nos. 697,B399-B400,CB16 (4) 10.70 10.55

Sheets of 50 stamps and 50 labels.

1948, June 1 *Perf. 14½x14*

698 A243 11 l car rose .35 .15
Nos. 698,B409-B412 (5) 3.25 3.05

Centenary of Revolution of 1848.
For surcharge see No. 820A.

Arms of Romanian People's Republic — A243a

1948, July 8 **Wmk. 276**

698A A243a 50b red ("Lei 0.50") .40 .30
698B A243a 1 l red brn .25 .15
698C A243a 2 l dk grn .25 .15
698D A243a 3 l grnsh blk .35 .15
698E A243a 4 l chocolate .35 .15
698F A243a 5 l ultra .35 .15
698G A243a 10 l dp bl 1.10 .15

"Bani" instead of "Lei"

698H A243a 50b red ("Bani 0.50") .50 .15
Nos. 698A-698H (8) 3.55
Set value .75

See Nos. 712-717.

Nicolae Balcescu (1819-1852), Writer A244

1948, Dec. 20 **Wmk. 289**

699 A244 20 l scarlet .35 .15

Release from Bondage — A245

1948, Dec. 30 *Perf. 13½*

700	A245	5 l brt rose	.28	.15

First anniversary of the Republic.

Lenin, 25th Death Anniv. — A246

Folk Dance — A247

1949, Jan. 21

701	A246	20 l black	.35	.15

Exists imperf.

1949, Jan. 24 *Perf. 13½*

702	A247	10 l dp bl	.35	.15

90th anniv. of the union of the Danubian Principalities.

Ion C. Frimu and Revolutionary Scene A248

1949, Mar. 22 *Perf. 14½x14*

703	A248	20 l red	.35	.15

Exists imperf.

Aleksander S. Pushkin, 150th Birth Anniv. — A249

1949, May 20 *Perf. 14x14½*

704	A249	11 l car rose	.48	.15
705	A249	30 l Prus grn	.70	.28

For surcharges see Nos. 821-822.

Globe and Post Horn — A250

Evolution of Mail Transportation — A251

Perf. 13½, 14½x14

1949, June 30 Photo. Wmk. 289

706	A250	20 l org brn	1.50	.90
707	A251	30 l brt bl	1.10	.60

UPU, 75th anniv.
For surcharges see Nos. C43-C44.

Russian Army Entering Bucharest, August, 1944 A252

1949, Aug. 23 *Perf. 14½x14, Imperf.*

708	A252	50 l choc, *bl grn*	.60	.25

5th anniv. of the liberation of Romania by the Soviet army, Aug. 1944.

"Long Live Romanian-Soviet Amity" — A253

1949, Nov. 1 *Perf. 13½x14½*

709	A253	20 l dp red	.35	.20

National week of Romanian-Soviet friendship celebration, Nov. 1-7, 1949. Exists imperf.

Symbols of Transportation A254

Joseph V. Stalin A256

1949, Dec. 10 *Perf. 13½*

710	A254	11 l blue	.55	.20
711	A254	20 l crimson	.55	.20

Intl. Conference of Transportation Unions, Dec. 10, 1949.
Alternate vertical rows of stamps and labels in sheet. Exist imperf.

Arms Type of 1948

1949-50 Wmk. 289 *Perf. 14x13½*

712	A243a	50b red ("Lei 0.50")	.35	.15
713	A243a	1 l red brn	.35	.15
714	A243a	2 l dk grn	.35	.15
714A	A243a	3 l grnsh blk	.65	.15
715	A243a	5 l ultra	.50	.15
716	A243a	5 l rose vio ('50)	.70	.15
717	A243a	10 l dp blue	.90	.15
		Nos. 712-717 (7)	3.80	
		Set value		.60

1949, Dec. 21 *Perf. 13½*

718	A256	31 l olive black	.48	.18

Stalin's 70th birthday. Exists imperf.

Mihail Eminescu A257

Poem: "Life" A258

#721, "Third Letter." #722, "Angel and Demon." #723, "Emperor and Proletariat."

1950, Jan. 15 Photo. Wmk. 289

719	A257	11 l blue	.45	.18
720	A258	11 l purple	.75	.22
721	A258	11 l dk grn	.45	.45
722	A258	11 l red brn	.45	.18
723	A258	11 l rose pink	.45	.18
		Nos. 719-723 (5)	2.55	1.21

Birth cent. of Mihail Eminescu, poet.
For surcharges see Nos. 823-827.

Fair at Dragaica A259

Ion Andreescu (Self-portrait) — A260

Village Well — A261

Perf. 14½x14, 14x14½

1950, Mar. 25

724	A259	5 l dk gray grn	.45	.22
725	A260	11 l ultra	.75	.22
726	A261	20 l brown	.85	.45
		Nos. 724-726 (3)	2.05	.89

Birth cent. of Ion Andreescu, painter. No. 725 also exists imperf.
For surcharges see Nos. 827A-827B.

Graph and Factories A262

Design: 31 l, Tractor and Oil Derricks.

Inscribed: "Planul de Stat 1950."

Perf. 14½x14

1950, Apr. 23 Wmk. 289

727	A262	11 l red	.60	.18
728	A262	31 l violet	.85	.30

1950 plan for increased industrial production. No. 727 exists imperf.
For surcharges see Nos. 827C-827D.

Young Man Holding Flag A263

Arms of Republic A264

1950, May 1 *Perf. 14x14½*

729	A263	31 l orange red	.75	.15

Labor Day, May 1. Exists imperf.
For surcharge see No. 827E.

Canceled to Order

Canceled sets of new issues have long been sold by the government. Values in the second ("used") column are for these canceled-to-order stamps. Postally used copies are worth more.

1950 Photo. *Perf. 12½*

730	A264	50b black	.15	.15
731	A264	1 l red	.15	.15
732	A264	2 l ol gray	.15	.15
733	A264	3 l violet	.15	.15
734	A264	4 l rose lilac	.15	.15
735	A264	5 l red brn	.15	.15
736	A264	6 l dp grn	.15	.15
737	A264	7 l vio brn	.15	.15
738	A264	7.50 l blue	.22	.15
739	A264	10 l dk brn	.48	.15
740	A264	11 l rose car	.48	.15
741	A264	15 l dp bl	.28	.15
742	A264	20 l Prus grn	.30	.15
743	A264	31 l dl grn	.45	.15
744	A264	36 l dk org brn	.75	.28
		Set value (15)	3.65	1.00

See Nos. 947-961 which have similar design with white denomination figures.
For overprint & surcharges see #758, 828-841.

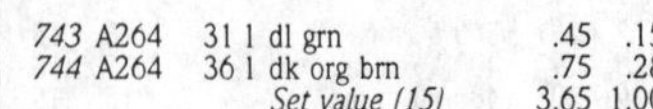

Bugler and Drummer A265

Designs: 11 l, Three school children. 31 l, Drummer, flag-bearer and bugler.

1950, May 25 *Perf. 14½x14*

745	A265	8 l blue	.45	.30
746	A265	11 l rose vio	.75	.45
747	A265	31 l org ver	1.50	.90
		Nos. 745-747 (3)	2.70	1.65

Young Pioneers, 1st anniv.
For surcharges see Nos. 841A-841C.

Factory Worker — A266

Aurel Vlaicu and his First Plane — A267

1950, July 20 Photo. *Perf. 14x14½*

748	A266	11 l red brn	.30	.15
749	A266	11 l red	.30	.15
750	A266	11 l blue	.30	.15
751	A266	11 l blk brn	.30	.15
		Nos. 748-751 (4)	1.20	.60

Nationalization of industry, 2nd anniv.

1950, July 22 Wmk. 289 *Perf. 12½*

752	A267	3 l dk grn	.35	.18
753	A267	6 l dk bl	.40	.18
754	A267	8 l ultra	.40	.18
		Nos. 752-754 (3)	1.15	.54

Aurel Vlaicu (1882-1913), pioneer of Romanian aviation.
For surcharges see Nos. 842-844.

Mother and Child — A268

Lathe and Operator — A269

1950, Sept. 9 *Perf. 13½*

755	A268	11 l rose red	.30	.15
756	A269	20 l dk ol brn	.30	.15

Congress of the Committees for the Struggle for Peace.
For surcharge see No. 844A.

Statue of Soviet Soldier — A270

1950, Oct. 6 *Perf. 14x14½*

757	A270	30 l red brn	.48	.18

Celebration of Romanian-Soviet friendship, Oct. 7-Nov. 7, 1950.

No. 741 Overprinted in Carmine **TRĂIASCĂ PRIETENIA ROMÂNO-MAGHIĂRAI**

1950, Oct. 6 *Perf. 12½*
758 A264 15 l deep blue .38 .15

Romanian-Hungarian friendship.

"Agriculture," "Manufacturing" and Sports Badge — A271

5 l, Student workers & Sports badge. 11 l, Track team & badge. 31 l, Calisthenics & badge.

1950, Oct. 30 *Perf. 14½x14*
759 A271 3 l rose car .60 .45
760 A271 5 l red brn .45 .30
761 A271 5 l brt bl .45 .30
762 A271 11 l green .45 .30
763 A271 31 l brn ol 1.10 .75
Nos. 759-763 (5) 3.05 2.10

For surcharge see No. 845.

A272

"Industry" — A273

"Agriculture" A274

1950, Nov. 2 *Perf. 13½*
764 A272 11 l blue .28 .15
765 A272 11 l red org .28 .15

3rd Soviet-Romanian Friendship Congress.

Perf. 14x14½, 14½x14
1951, Feb. 9 Photo. Wmk. 289
766 A273 11 l red brn .15 .15
767 A274 31 l deep bl .38 .16
Set value .24

Industry and Agriculture Exposition. Exist imperf.
For surcharge see No. 846.

Ski Jump — A275

Ski Descent — A276

5 l, Skating. 20 l, Hockey. 31 l, Bobsledding.

1951, Jan. 28 *Perf. 13½*
768 A275 4 l blk brn .30 .15
769 A275 5 l vermilion .45 .15
770 A276 11 l dp bl .85 .20
771 A275 20 l org brn .90 .50
772 A275 31 l dk gray grn 2.00 1.00
Nos. 768-772 (5) 4.50 2.00

9th World University Winter Games.
For surcharges see Nos. 847-848.

Medal for Work — A277

Orders: 4 l, Star of the Republic, Classes III, IV & V. 11 l, Work. 35 l, As 4 l, Classes I & II.

1951, May 1 *Perf. 13½*
773 A277 2 l ol gray .30 .15
774 A277 4 l blue .30 .15
775 A277 11 l crimson .30 .15
776 A277 35 l org brn .35 .15
Nos. 773-776 (4) 1.25 .60

Labor Day. Exist imperf.
For surcharges see Nos. 849-852.

Camp of Young Pioneers A278

Pioneers Greeting Stalin — A279

Admitting New Pioneers A280

1951, May 8 *Perf. 14x14½, 14½x14*
777 A278 1 l gray grn .90 .38
778 A279 11 l blue .90 .15
779 A280 35 l red .75 .18
Nos. 777-779 (3) 2.55 .71

Romanian Young Pioneers Organization.
For surcharge see No. 853.

Woman Orator and Flags A281

Ion Negulici A282

1951, Mar. 8 *Perf. 14x14½*
780 A281 11 l org brn .35 .15

Woman's Day, Mar. 8. Exists imperf.

1951, June 20 *Perf. 14x14½*
781 A282 35 l rose red .75 .45

Death cent. of Ion Negulici, painter.

Bicyclists A283

1951, July 9 *Perf. 14½x14*
782 A283 11 l chnt brn 1.65 .50
a. Tête bêche pair 4.00 3.25

The 1951 Bicycle Tour of Romania.

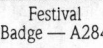

Festival Badge — A284

Boy and Girl with Flag — A285

Youths Encircling Globe — A286

1951, Aug. 1 *Perf. 13½*
783 A284 1 l scarlet .50 .22
784 A285 5 l deep blue .50 .22
785 A286 11 l deep plum .65 .50
Nos. 783-785 (3) 1.65 .94

3rd World Youth Festival, Berlin.

Filimon Sarbu A287

"Romania Raising the Masses" A288

"Revolutionary Romania" — A289

1951, July 23 *Perf. 14x14½*
786 A287 11 l dk brn .28 .15

10th death anniv. of Filimon Sarbu, patriot.

Perf. 14x14½, 14½x14
1951, July 23
787 A288 11 l yel brn 1.00 .25
788 A288 11 l rose vio 1.00 .25
789 A289 11 l dk grn 1.00 .25
790 A289 11 l org red 1.00 .25
Nos. 787-790 (4) 4.00 1.00

Death cent. of C. D. Rosenthal, painter.

Scanteia Building A290

1951, Aug. 16 *Perf. 14½x14*
791 A290 11 l blue .35 .15

20th anniv. of the newspaper Scanteia.

Miner in Dress Uniform A291

Order for National Defense A293

Design: 11 l, Miner in work clothes.

1951, Aug. 12 *Perf. 14x14½*
792 A291 5 l blue .25 .15
793 A291 11 l plum .25 .15
Set value .20

Miner's Day. For surcharge see #854.

1951, Aug. 12 *Perf. 14x14½*
794 A293 10 l crimson .50 .15

For surcharge see No. 855.

Choir — A294

Music Week Emblem — A295

Design: No. 796, Orchestra and dancers.

Perf. 13½
1951, Sept. 22 Photo. Wmk. 358
795 A294 11 l blue .35 .15
796 A294 11 l red brown .50 .30
797 A295 11 l purple .35 .15
Nos. 795-797 (3) 1.20 .60

Music Week, Sept. 22-30, 1951.

Soldier — A296

Oil Field — A297

1951, Oct. 2
798 A296 11 l blue .32 .15

Army Day, Oct. 2, 1951.

1951-52

Designs: 2 l, Coal mining. 3 l, Romanian soldier. 4 l, Smelting ore. 5 l, Agricultural machinery. 6 l, Canal construction. 7 l, Agriculture. 8 l, Self-education. 11 l, Hydroelectric production. 35 l, Manufacturing.

799 A297 1 l black brn .15 .15
800 A297 2 l chocolate .15 .15
801 A297 3 l scarlet .35 .15
802 A297 4 l yel brn ('52) .20 .15
803 A297 5 l green .35 .15
804 A297 6 l brt bl ('52) 1.25 .40
805 A297 7 l emerald .50 .40
806 A297 8 l brown ('52) .50 .40
807 A297 11 l blue .35 .15
808 A297 35 l purple 1.35 .80
Nos. 799-808,C35-C36 (12) 7.30 4.70

1951-55 Five Year Plan.
2 l and 11 l exist with wmk. 289.
For surcharges see Nos. 860-869.

Arms of Soviet Union and Romania — A298

1951, Oct. 7 **Wmk. 358**
809 A298 4 l chnt brn, *cr* .35 .15
810 A298 35 l orange red .90 .45

Month of Romanian-Soviet friendship, Oct. 7-Nov. 7.
For surcharges see Nos. 870-871.

Pavel Tcacenco A299

Railroad Conductor A300

1951, Dec. 15 *Perf. 14x14½*
811 A299 10 l ol brn & dk brn .35 .15

Revolutionary, 26th death anniv.
For surcharge see No. 872.

1952, Mar. 24 *Perf. 13½*
812 A300 55b dark brown 1.50 .45

Railroad Workers' Day, Feb. 16.

Ion L. Caragiale — A301

Announcing Caragiale Celebration A302

Designs: No. 814, Book and painting "1907." No. 815, Bust and wreath.

1952, Apr. 1 *Perf. 13¹/₂, 14¹/₂x14*
Inscribed: ". . . . I. L. Caragiale."

813 A301 55b chalky blue .85 .15
814 A302 55b scarlet .85 .15
815 A302 55b deep green .85 .15
816 A302 1 l brown 2.50 .26
Nos. 813-816 (4) 5.05
Set value .52

Birth cent. of Ion L. Caragiale, dramatist.
For surcharges see Nos. 817-819.

Types of 1952 Surcharged with New Value in Black or Carmine

1952-53
817 A302 20b on 11 l scar *(as #814)* .60 .40
818 A302 55b on 11 l dp grn *(as #815)* (C) .75 .50
819 A301 75b on 11 l chlky bl (C) 1.25 .60

Various Issues Surcharged with New Values in Carmine or Black

On No. 678, Census
Perf. 14x13¹/₂
819A A237 50b on 12 l ultra 6.75 3.75

On No. 683, New Constitution
Perf. 14
820 A240 50b on 12 l dp bl 2.50 1.25

On No. 698, Revolution
820A A243 1.75 l on 11 l car rose (Bk) 25.00 12.00

On Nos. 704-705, Pushkin
1952 **Wmk. 358**
821 A249 10b on 11 l (Bk) 2.50 1.75
822 A249 10b on 30 l 2.50 1.75

On Nos. 719-723, Eminescu
Perf. 13¹/₂x13, 13x13¹/₂
823 A257 10b on 11 l blue 2.25 1.75
824 A258 10b on 11 l pur 2.25 1.75
825 A258 10b on 11 l dk grn 2.25 1.75
826 A258 10b on 11 l red brn (Bk) 2.25 1.75
827 A258 10b on 11 l rose pink (Bk) 3.50 1.75

On Nos. 724-725, Andreescu
Perf. 14
827A A259 55b on 5 l dk gray grn 7.50 2.75
827B A260 55b on 11 l ultra 5.00 2.75

On Nos. 727-728, Production Plan
Perf. 14¹/₂x14
827C A262 20b on 11 l red (Bk) 2.00 .75
827D A262 20b on 31 l vio 2.00 .75

On No. 729, Labor Day
Perf. 14
827E A263 55b on 31 l (Bk) 3.00 2.75

On Nos. 730-739 and 741-744, National Arms
Perf. 12¹/₂
828 A264 3b on 1 l red (Bk) .70 .45
829 A264 3b on 2 l ol gray (Bk) 1.10 .55
830 A264 3b on 4 l rose lil (Bk) .70 .30
831 A264 3b on 5 l red brn (Bk) 1.10 .55
832 A264 3b on 7.50 l bl (Bk) 3.25 1.40
833 A264 3b on 10 l dk brn (Bk) 1.10 .55
834 A264 55b on 50b blk brn 3.25 .45
835 A264 55b on 3 l vio 3.25 .45
836 A264 55b on 6 l dp grn 3.25 .45
837 A264 55b on 7 l vio brn 3.25 .45
838 A264 55b on 15 l dp bl 5.00 .45
839 A264 55b on 20 l Prus grn 3.25 .45
840 A264 55b on 31 l dl grn 3.25 .45
841 A264 55b on 36 l dk org brn 5.00 .45

On Nos. 745-747, Young Pioneers
Perf. 14
841A A265 55b on 8 l 10.00 5.75
841B A265 55b on 11 l 10.00 5.75
841C A265 55b on 31 l (Bk) 10.00 5.75

On Nos. 752-754, Vlaicu
Perf. 12¹/₂
842 A267 10b on 3 l dk grn 1.50 .75
843 A267 10b on 6 l dk bl 1.50 .75
844 A267 10b on 8 l ultra 1.50 .75

Original denomination canceled with an "X."

On No. 756, Peace Congress
Perf. 13¹/₂
844A A269 20b on 20 l 2.25 1.25

On No. 759, Sports
Perf. 14¹/₂x14
845 A271 55b on 3 l (Bk) 15.00 11.50

On No. 767, Exposition
846 A274 55b on 31 l dp bl 9.00 5.75

On Nos. 771-772, Winter Games
Perf. 13¹/₂
847 A275 55b on 20 l (Bk) 25.00 8.00
848 A275 55b on 31 l 25.00 8.00

On Nos. 773-776, Labor Medals
849 A277 20b on 2 l 3.75 2.25
850 A277 20b on 4 l 3.75 2.25
851 A277 20b on 11 l (Bk) 3.75 2.25
852 A277 20b on 35 l (Bk) 3.75 2.25

On Nov. 779, Young Pioneers
Perf. 14x14¹/₂
853 A280 55b on 35 l (Bk) 15.00 9.50

On No. 792, Miners' Day
854 A291 55b on 5 l bl 11.00 7.50

On No. 794, Defense Order
855 A293 55b on 10 l (Bk) 6.00 3.75

On Nos. B409-B412, 1848 Revolution
1952 **Wmk. 276** *Perf. 13x13¹/₂*
856 SP280 1.75 l on 2 l + 2 l (Bk) 9.50 3.75
857 SP281 1.75 l on 5 l + 5 l 9.50 3.75
858 SP282 1.75 l on 10 l + 10 l 9.50 3.75
859 SP280 1.75 l on 36 l + 18 l 9.50 3.75

On Nos. 799-808, 5-Year Plan
Wmk. 358 *Perf. 13¹/₂*
860 A297 35b on 1 l blk brn 1.90 .65
861 A297 35b on 2 l choc 6.00 .70
862 A297 35b on 3 l scar (Bk) 3.00 1.25
863 A297 35b on 4 l yel brn (Bk) 3.50 1.50
a. Red surcharge 15.00 8.00
864 A297 35b on 5 l grn 3.00 2.00
865 A297 1 l on 6 l brt bl 4.75 3.00
866 A297 1 l on 7 l emer 3.50 1.50
867 A297 1 l on 8 l brn 3.50 2.25
868 A297 1 l on 11 l bl 4.75 1.75
869 A297 1 l on 35 l pur 4.75 1.50

Nos. 861, 868 exist with wmk. 289.

On Nos. 809-810, Romanian-Soviet Friendship
870 A298 10b on 4 l (Bk) 1.50 .65
871 A298 10b on 35 l (Bk) 1.50 .65

On No. 811, Tcacenco
Perf. 13¹/₂x14
872 A299 10b on 10 l 1.90 .90
Nos. 817-872 (67) 350.60 164.95

A302a

A303

Perf. 13¹/₂x13
1952, Apr. 14 **Photo.** **Wmk. 358**
873 A302a 1 l Ivan P. Pavlov 1.65 .50

Meeting of Romanian-Soviet doctors in Bucharest.

1952, May 1
874 A303 55b Hammer & sickle medal .75 .15

Labor Day.

Medal for Motherhood A304

Leonardo da Vinci A305

Medals: 55b, Maternal glory. 1.75 l, Mother-Heroine.

1952, Apr. 7 *Perf. 13x13¹/₂*
875 A304 20b plum & sl gray .30 .15
876 A304 55b henna brn .70 .18
877 A304 1.75 l rose red & brn buff 1.75 .40
Nos. 875-877 (3) 2.75 .73

International Women's Day.

1952, July 3
878 A305 55b purple 2.10 .50

500th birth anniv. of Leonardo da Vinci.

Gogol and Scene from Taras Bulba A306

Nikolai V. Gogol — A307

1952, Apr. 1 *Perf. 13¹/₂x14, 14x13¹/₂*
879 A306 55b deep blue 1.00 .15
880 A307 1.75 l olive gray 1.50 .40

Gogol, Russian writer, death cent.

Pioneers Saluting — A308

Labor Day Paraders Returning A309

Design: 55b, Pioneers studying nature.

1952, May 21 *Perf. 14*
881 A308 20b brown .45 .15
882 A308 55b dp green 1.25 .15
883 A309 1.75 l blue 2.10 .38
Nos. 881-883 (3) 3.80 .68

Third anniversary of Romanian Pioneers.

Infantry Attack, Painting by Grigorescu — A310

Miner — A311

Design: 1.10 l, Romanian and Russian soldiers.

1952, June 7 *Perf. 13x13¹/₂*
884 A310 50b rose brown .45 .15
885 A310 1.10 l blue .75 .25
Set value .30

Independence Proclamation of 1877, 75th anniv.

1952, Aug. 11 **Wmk. 358**
902 A311 20b rose red 1.25 .25
903 A311 55b purple 1.25 .15

Day of the Miner.

Book and Globe — A312

Students in Native Dress — A314

Chemistry Student A313

Design: 55b, Students playing soccer.

Perf. 13¹/₂x13, 13¹/₂x14, 13x13¹/₂
1952, Sept. 5
904 A312 10b deep blue .15 .15
905 A313 20b orange .70 .20
906 A312 55b deep green 2.00 .25
907 A314 1.75 l rose red 3.00 .50
Nos. 904-907 (4) 5.85 1.10

Intl. Student Union Congr., Bucharest, Sept.

Soldier, Sailor and Aviator — A316

1952, Oct. 2 *Perf. 14*
909 A316 55b blue .50 .20

Armed Forces Day, Oct. 2, 1952.

"Russia" Leading Peace Crusade — A317

Allegory: Romanian-Soviet Friendship — A318

1952, Oct. 7 *Perf. 13¹/₂x13, 13x13¹/₂*
910 A317 55b vermilion .65 .18
911 A318 1.75 l black brown 1.65 .65

Month of Romanian-Soviet friendship, Oct.

Rowing on Lake Snagov — A319

Nicolae Balcescu — A320

Design: 1.75 l, Athletes marching with flags.

1952, Oct. 20
912 A319 20b deep blue 3.00 .52
913 A319 1.75 l rose red 5.50 1.10

Values are for copies with poor perforations.

1952, Nov. 29

914 A320 55b gray 2.00 .50
915 A320 1.75 l lemon bister 4.00 1.25

Death cent. of Nicolae Balcescu, poet.

Arms of Republic — A321

1952, Dec. 6 **Wmk. 358**

916 A321 55b dull green .75 .25

5th anniversary of socialist constitution.

Arms and Industrial Symbols A322

1953, Jan. 8 *Perf. 12½x13½*

917 A322 55b blue, yellow & red .90 .35

5th anniv. of the proclamation of the People's Republic.

Matei Millo, Costache Caragiale and Aristita Romanescu A323

1953, Feb. **Photo.** *Perf. 13x13½*

918 A323 55b brt ultra 1.50 .35

National Theater of I. L. Caragiale, cent.

Iron Foundry Worker — A324

Worker — A325

Design: No. 921, Driving Tractor.

1953, Feb. *Perf. 13½x13, 13x13½*

919 A324 55b slate green .32 .15
920 A325 55b black brown .32 .15
921 A325 55b orange .65 .26
Nos. 919-921 (3) 1.29
Set value .46

3rd Congress of the Syndicate of the Romanian People's Republic.

"Strike at Grivita," Painted by G. Miclossy A326

Arms of Romanian People's Republic A327

1953, Feb. 16 *Perf. 13x13½*

922 A326 55b chestnut 1.25 .25

Oil industry strike, Feb. 16, 1933, 20th anniv.

1953 *Perf. 12½*

923 A327 5b crimson .28 .15
924 A327 55b purple .75 .18
Set value .26

Flags of Romania and Russia, Farm Machinery A328

1953, Mar. 24 *Perf. 14*

925 A328 55b dk brn, *bl* .95 .24

5th anniv. of the signing of a treaty of friendship and mutual assistance between Russia and Romania.

Map and Medal — A329

Rug — A330

Folk Dance A330a

1953, Mar. 24

926 A329 55b dk gray green 1.75 .38
927 A329 55b chestnut 2.25 .38

20th World Championship Table Tennis Matches, Budapest, 1953.

1953

Designs: 10b, Ceramics. 20b, Costume of Campulung (Muscel). 55b, Apuseni Mts. costume.

Inscribed: "Arta Populara Romaneasca"

928 A330 10b deep green .75 .15
929 A330 20b red brown 1.25 .15
929A A330a 35b purple 2.00 .15
930 A330 55b violet blue 3.00 .15
931 A330 1 l brt red violet 5.00 .25
Nos. 928-931 (5) 12.00
Set value .60

Romanian Folk Arts.

Karl Marx — A331

Children Planting Tree — A332

Physics Class A333

1953, May 21 *Perf. 13½x13*

932 A331 1.55 l olive brown 1.40 .45

70th death anniv. of Karl Marx.

1953, May 21 *Perf. 14*

Design: 55b, Flying model planes.

933 A332 35b deep green 1.00 .15
934 A332 55b dull blue 1.40 .18
935 A333 1.75 l brown 3.25 .45
Nos. 933-935 (3) 5.65 .78

Women and Flags A334

Discus Thrower A335

Students Offering Teacher Flowers A336

1953, June 18 *Perf. 13½x13*

936 A334 55b red brown 1.00 .20

3rd World Congress of Women, Copenhagen, 1953.

1953, Aug. 2 **Wmk. 358** *Perf. 14*

Designs: 55b, Students reaching toward dove. 1.75 l, Dance in local costumes.

937 A335 20b orange .52 .15
938 A335 55b deep blue .90 .15
939 A336 65b scarlet 1.25 .38
940 A336 1.75 l red violet 3.50 .50
Nos. 937-940 (4) 6.17 1.18

4th World Youth Festival, Bucharest, Aug. 2-16.

Waterfall — A337

Wheat Field — A338

Design: 55b, Forester holding seedling.

1953, July 29 **Photo.**

941 A337 20b violet blue .55 .15
942 A338 38b dull green 1.40 .50
943 A337 55b lt brown 1.50 .22
Nos. 941-943 (3) 3.45 .87

Month of the Forest.

Vladimir V. Mayakovsky, 60th Birth Anniv. — A339

1953, Aug. 22

944 A339 55b brown .75 .20

Miner Using Drill A340

1953, Sept. 19

945 A340 1.55 l slate black 1.40 .40

Miners' Day.

Arms of Republic — A342

1952-53 *Perf. 12½*

Size: 20x24mm

947 A342 3b deep orange .60 .20
948 A342 5b crimson .80 .15
949 A342 7b dk blue grn .80 .20
950 A342 10b chocolate 1.00 .15
951 A342 20b deep blue 1.25 .15
952 A342 35b black brn 2.75 .15
953 A342 50b dk gray grn 3.25 .15
954 A342 55b purple 7.25 .15

Size: 24x29mm

955 A342 1.10 l dk brown 6.50 .30
956 A342 1.75 l violet 24.00 .40
957 A342 2 l olive black 6.50 .50
958 A342 2.35 l orange brn 8.00 .35
959 A342 2.55 l dp orange 10.00 .40
960 A342 3 l dk gray grn 10.00 .35
961 A342 5 l deep crimson 12.00 .60
Nos. 947-961 (15) 94.70
Set value 3.75

Stamps of similar design with value figures in color are Nos. 730-744.

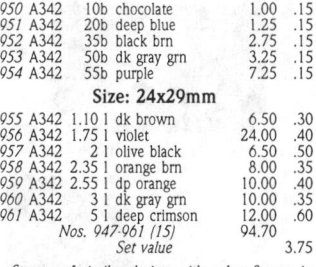

Postal Administration Building and Telephone Employees A343

Designs: 55b, Postal Adm. Bldg. and Letter carrier. 1 l, Map and communications symbols. 1.55 l, Postal Adm. Bldg. and Telegraph employees.

1953, Oct. 20 **Wmk. 358** *Perf. 14*

964 A343 20b dk red brn .18 .15
965 A343 55b olive green .30 .15
966 A343 1 l brt blue .75 .15
967 A343 1.55 l rose brown 1.10 .38
Nos. 964-967 (4) 2.33
Set value .70

50th anniv. of the construction of the Postal Administration Building.

Liberation Medal — A344

Soldier and Flag — A345

1953, Oct. 20 *Perf. 14x13½*

968 A344 55b dark brown .70 .15

9th anniv. of the liberation of Romania.

1953, Oct. 2 *Perf. 13½*

969 A345 55b olive green .70 .25

Army Day, Oct. 2.

Girl with Model Plane A346

Civil Aviation: 20b, Parachute landing. 55b, Glider and pilot. 1.75 l, Plane in flight.

1953, Oct. 20 *Perf. 14*

970 A346 10b org & dk gray grn 2.25 .30
971 A346 20b org brn & dk ol grn 4.50 .18
972 A346 55b dk scar & rose lil 7.25 .50
973 A346 1.75 l dk rose vio & brn 9.50 .75
Nos. 970-973 (4) 23.50 1.73

Workers and Flags — A347

1.55 l, Spasski Tower, lock on Volga-Don Canal.

1953, Nov. 25 *Perf. 13x13½*

974 A347 55b brown .48 .15
975 A347 1.55 l rose brown .70 .25

Month of Romanian-Soviet friendship, Oct. 7-Nov. 7.

Hemispheres and Clasped Hands — A348

Workers, Flags and Globe — A349

1953, Nov. 25 *Perf. 14*

976 A348	55b dark olive	.38	.15
977 A349	1.25 l crimson	.90	.30

World Congress of Trade Unions.

Ciprian Porumbescu A350

Harvesting Machine A351

1953, Dec. 16

978 A350	55b purple	4.00	.45

Ciprian Porumbescu (1853-1883), composer.

Perf. 13x13½

1953, Dec. 16 **Wmk. 358**

Designs: 35b, Tractor in field. 2.55 l, Cattle.

979 A351	10b sepia	.28	.15
980 A351	35b dark green	.38	.15
981 A351	2.55 l orange brown	3.50	.75
	Nos. 979-981 (3)	4.16	1.05

Aurel Vlaicu — A352

Lenin — A353

1953, Dec. 26 *Perf. 14*

982 A352	50b violet blue	.75	.18

Vlaicu, aviation pioneer, 40th death anniv.

1954, Jan. 21 *Perf. 13½*

983 A353	55b dk red brn, *buff*	.75	.18

30th death anniv. of Lenin.

Red Deer — A354

Designs: 55b, Children planting trees. 1.75 l, Mountain scene.

1954, Apr. 1

Yellow Surface-colored Paper

984 A354	20b dark brown	1.50	.15
985 A354	55b violet	1.50	.15
986 A354	1.75 l dark blue	3.25	.48
	Nos. 984-986 (3)	6.25	.78

Month of the Forest.

Calimanesti Rest Home — A355

Workers' Rest Homes: 1.55 l, Sinaia. 2 l, Predeal. 2.35 l, Tusnad. 2.55 l, Govora.

1954, Apr. 15 *Perf. 14*

987 A355	5b blk brn, *cream*	.25	.15
988 A355	1.55 l dk vio brn, *bl*	.90	.16
989 A355	2 l dk grn, *pink*	1.40	.18
990 A355	2.35 l ol blk, *grnsh*	1.40	.48
991 A355	2.55 l dk red brn, *cit*	2.00	.65
	Nos. 987-991 (5)	5.95	1.62

Octav Bancila — A356

Globe, Child, Dove and Flowers — A357

1954, May 26 *Perf. 13½*

992 A356	55b red brn & dk grn	2.75	1.00

10th death anniv. of Octav Bancila, painter.

1954, June 1 *Perf. 13x13½*

993 A357	55b brown	1.25	.25

Children's Day, June 1.

Girl Feeding Calf — A358

Designs: 55b, Girl holding sheaf of grain. 1.75 l, Young students.

1954, July 5 *Perf. 14*

994 A358	20b grnsh blk	.25	.15
995 A358	55b blue	.60	.18
996 A358	1.75 l car rose	1.75	.32
	Nos. 994-996 (3)	2.60	.65

Stephen the Great — A359

Loading Coal on Conveyor Belt — A360

1954, July 10

997 A359	55b violet brown	1.50	.38

Stephen of Moldavia (1433?-1504).

1954, Aug. 8 *Perf. 13x13½*

998 A360	1.75 l black	1.50	.38

Miners' Day.

Victor Babes — A361

Applicant Requesting Loan — A362

1954, Aug. 15 *Perf. 14*

999 A361	55b rose red	1.50	.38

Birth cent. of Victor Babes, serologist.

1954, Aug. 20

Design: 55b, Mutual aid declaration.

1000 A362	20b deep violet	.28	.15
1001 A362	55b dk redsh brn	.45	.16
	Set value		.24

5th anniv. of the Mutual Aid Organization.

Sailor and Naval Scene — A363

Monument to Soviet Soldier — A364

1954, Aug. 19 *Perf. 13x13½*

1002 A363	55b deep blue	.90	.25

Navy Day.

1954, Aug. 23 *Perf. 13½x13*

1003 A364	55b scarlet & purple	.90	.25

10th anniv. of Romania's liberation.

House of Culture A365

Academy of Music, Bucharest A366

Aviator A367

55b, Scanteia building. 1.55 l, Radio station.

1954, Sept. 6 *Perf. 14, 13½x13*

1004 A365	20b violet blue	.18	.15
1005 A366	38b violet	.40	.18
1006 A365	55b violet brown	.40	.15
1007 A366	1.55 l red brown	.75	.20
	Nos. 1004-1007 (4)	1.73	
	Set value		.52

Publicizing Romania's cultural progress during the decade following liberation.

Perf. 13½x13

1954, Sept. 13 **Wmk. 358**

1008 A367	55b blue	.90	.38

Aviation Day.

Chemical Plant and Oil Derricks — A368

Dragon Pillar, Peking — A369

1954, Sept. 21 *Perf. 13x13½*

1009 A368	55b gray	1.25	.25

Intl. Conference of chemical and petroleum workers, Bucharest, Sept. 1954.

1954, Oct. 7 *Perf. 14*

1010 A369	55b dk ol grn, *cream*	1.25	.25

Week of Chinese Culture.

Dumitri T. Neculuta A370

ARLUS Emblem A371

1954, Oct. 17 *Perf. 13½x13*

1011 A370	55b purple	1.10	.25

Neculuta, poet, 50th death anniv.

1954, Oct. 22 *Perf. 14*

65b, Romanian & Russian women embracing.

1012 A371	55b rose carmine	.45	.15
1013 A371	65b dark purple	.65	.18

Month of Romanian-Soviet Friendship.

Gheorghe Tattarescu A372

Barbu Iscovescu A373

1954, Oct. 24 *Perf. 13½x13*

1014 A372	55b cerise	1.40	.38

Gheorghe Tattarescu (1820-1894), painter.

1954, Nov. 3 *Perf. 14*

1015 A373	1.75 l red brown	2.50	.50

Death cent. of Barbu Iscovescu, painter.

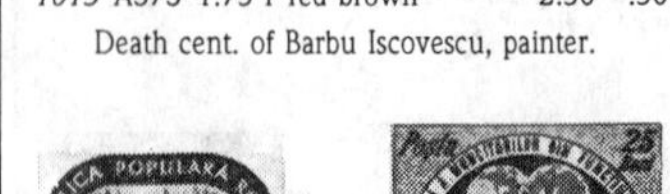

Wild Boar — A374

Globe and Clasped Hands — A375

Month of the Forest: 65b, Couple planting tree. 1.20 l, Logging.

Perf. 13½x13

1955, Mar. 15 **Wmk. 358**

1016	A374	35b brown	.52	.15
1017	A374	65b turq blue	.90	.25
1018	A374	1.20 l dark red	1.75	.75
		Nos. 1016-1018 (3)	3.17	1.15

1955, Apr. 5 **Photo.**

1019	A375	25b carmine rose	.35	.15

Intl. Conference of Universal Trade Unions (Federation Syndicale Mondiale), Vienna, Apr. 1955.

Teletype — A376 Lenin — A377

1955, Dec. 20 *Perf. 13½x13*

1020	A376	50b lilac	.45	.18

Romanian telegraph system, cent.

1955, Apr. 22 *Perf. 13½x14*

Various Portraits of Lenin.

1021	A377	20b ol bis & brn	.22	.15
1022	A377	55b copper brown	.40	.18
1023	A377	1 l vermilion	.60	.22
		Nos. 1021-1023 (3)	1.22	.55

85th anniversary of the birth of Lenin.

Chemist A378 Volleyball A379

Designs: 5b, Steelworker. 10b, Aviator. 20b, Miner. 30b, Tractor driver. 35b, Pioneer. 40b, Girl student. 55b, Mason. 1 l, Sailor. 1.55 l, Spinner. 2.35 l, Soldier. 2.55 l, Electrician.

1955-56 **Wmk. 358** *Perf. 14*

1024	A378	3b blue	.15	.15
1025	A378	5b violet	.15	.15
1026	A378	10b chocolate	.15	.15
1027	A378	20b lilac rose	.24	.15
1027A	A378	30b vio bl ('56)	.40	.15
1028	A378	35b grnsh blue	.28	.15
1028A	A378	40b slate	.70	.15
1029	A378	55b ol gray	.40	.15
1030	A378	1 l purple	.75	.15
1031	A378	1.55 l brown lake	1.40	.15
1032	A378	2.35 l bister brn	2.10	.38
1033	A378	2.55 l slate	2.25	.24
		Nos. 1024-1033 (12)	8.97	
		Set value		1.15

1955, June 17

Design: 1.75 l, Woman volleyball player.

1034	A379	55b red vio, *pink*	1.40	.50
1035	A379	1.75 l lil rose, *cr*	3.50	.50

European Volleyball Championships, Bucharest.

Globe, Flag and Dove — A379a Girls with Dove and Flag — A380

1955, May 7 **Photo.** *Perf. 13½*

1035A	A379a	55b ultra	.75	.20

Peace Congress, Helsinki.

1955, June 1 *Perf. 13½x14*

1036	A380	55b dark red brown	.70	.20

International Children's Day, June 1.

Russian War Memorial, Berlin — A381 Theodor Aman Museum — A382

1955, May 9

1037	A381	55b deep blue	.60	.18

Victory over Germany, 10th anniversary.

1955, June 28 *Perf. 13½, 14*

Bucharest Museums: 55b, Lenin and Stalin Museum. 1.20 l, Popular Arts Museum. 1.75 l, Arts Museum. 2.55 l, Simu Museum.

1038	A382	20b rose lilac	.25	.15
1039	A382	55b brown	.30	.15
1040	A382	1.20 l gray black	.45	.30
1041	A382	1.75 l slate green	.80	.30
1042	A382	2.55 l rose violet	1.50	.40
		Nos. 1038-1042 (5)	3.30	1.30

#1038, 1040, 1042 measure 29x24½mm, #1039, 1041 32½x23mm.

Sharpshooter A383

1955, Sept. 11 *Perf. 13½*

1043	A383	1 l pale brn & sepia	3.50	.45

European Sharpshooting Championship meeting, Bucharest, Sept. 11-18.

Fire Truck, Farm and Factory — A384

1955, Sept. 13 **Wmk. 358**

1044	A384	55b carmine	.55	.25

Firemen's Day, Sept. 13.

Bishop Dosoftei — A385 Mother and Child — A386

Romanian writers: #1046, Stolnicul Constantin Cantacuzino. #1047, Dimitrie Cantemir. #1048, Enachita Vacarescu. #1049, Anton Pann.

1955, Sept. 9 **Photo.**

1045	A385	55b bluish gray	.75	.30
1046	A385	55b dp vio	.75	.30
1047	A385	55b ultra	.75	.30
1048	A385	55b rose vio	.75	.30
1049	A385	55b ol gray	.75	.30
		Nos. 1045-1049 (5)	3.75	1.50

1955, July 7 *Perf. 13½x14*

1050	A386	55b ultra	.60	.18

World Congress of Mothers, Lausanne.

Pioneers and Train Set — A387 Rowing — A388

Designs: 20b, Pioneers studying nature. 55b, Home of the Pioneers.

1955 *Perf. 12½*

1051	A387	10b brt ultra	.15	.15
1052	A387	20b grnsh bl	.45	.15
1053	A387	55b dp plum	1.25	.22
		Nos. 1051-1053 (3)	1.85	
		Set value		.35

Fifth anniversary of the Pioneer headquarters, Bucharest.

1955, Aug. 22 *Perf. 13x13½*

1054	A388	55b shown	3.25	.48
1055	A388	1 l Sculling	6.00	.70

European Women's Rowing Championship on Lake Snagov, Aug. 4-7.

Insect Pest Control A389 I. V. Michurin A390

20b, Orchard. 55b, Vineyard. 1 l, Truck garden.

1955, Oct. 15 *Perf. 14x13½*

1056	A389	10b brt grn	.28	.15
1057	A389	20b lil rose	.28	.15
1058	A389	55b vio bl	.70	.20
1059	A389	1 l dp claret	1.25	.40
		Nos. 1056-1059 (4)	2.51	.90

Quality products of Romanian agriculture. See Nos. 1068-1071.

1955, Oct. 25 *Perf. 13½x14*

1060	A390	55b Prus bl	.75	.18

Birth cent. of I. V. Michurin, Russian agricultural scientist.

Congress Emblem — A391 Globes and Olive Branches — A392

1955, Oct. 20 *Perf. 13x13½*

1061	A391	20b cream & ultra	.28	.15

4th Soviet-Romanian Cong., Bucharest, Oct.

1955, Oct. 1 *Perf. 13½x13*

Design: 1 l, Three workers holding FSM banner.

1062	A392	55b dk ol grn	.28	.15
1063	A392	1 l ultra	.45	.15
		Set value		.24

Intl. Trade Union Org. (Federation Syndicale Mondiale), 10th anniv.

Sugar Beets — A393 Sheep and Shepherd — A394

20b, Cotton. 55b, Flax. 1.55l, Sunflower.

1955, Nov. 10 *Perf. 13½*

1064	A393	10b plum	.30	.15
1065	A393	20b sl grn	.42	.15
1066	A393	55b brt ultra	1.25	.25
1067	A393	1.55 l dk red brn	2.75	.38
		Nos. 1064-1067 (4)	4.72	.93

1955, Dec. 10 *Perf. 14x13½*

Stock Farming: 10b, Pigs. 35b, Cattle. 55b, Horses.

1068	A394	5b yel grn & brn	.28	.15
1069	A394	10b ol bis & dk vio	.60	.15
1070	A394	35b brick red & brn	1.25	.18
1071	A394	55b dk ol bis & brn	2.50	.38
		Nos. 1068-1071 (4)	4.63	.86

Animal husbandry.

Hans Christian Andersen — A395

Portraits: 55b, Adam Mickiewicz. 1 l, Friedrich von Schiller. 1.55 l, Baron de Montesquieu. 1.75 l, Walt Whitman. 2 l, Miguel de Cervantes.

Perf. 13½x14

1955, Dec. 17 **Engr.** **Unwmk.**

1072	A395	20b sl bl	.30	.15
1073	A395	55b dp ultra	.50	.15
1074	A395	1 l grnsh blk	.65	.15
1075	A395	1.55 l vio brn	1.75	.38
1076	A395	1.75 l dl vio	2.00	.65
1077	A395	2 l rose lake	2.00	.65
		Nos. 1072-1077 (6)	7.20	2.13

Anniversaries of famous writers.

Bank Book and Savings Bank — A396

Perf. 14x13½

1955, Dec. 29 **Photo.** **Wmk. 358**

1078	A396	55b dp vio	1.25	.50
1079	A396	55b blue	.60	.15

Advantages of systematic saving in a bank.

Census Date — A397

Design: 1.75 l, Family group.

Inscribed: "Recensamintul Populatiei"

1956, Feb. 3 *Perf. 13½*

1080	A397	55b dp org	.30	.15
1081	A397	1.75 l emer & red brn	.85	.25
a.		Center inverted	*200.00*	*200.00*

National Census, Feb. 21, 1956.

Ring-necked Pheasant A398

Great Bustard — A399 Street Fighting, Paris, 1871 — A400

Animals: No. 1082, Hare. No. 1083, Bustard. 35b, Trout. 50b, Boar. No. 1087, Brown bear. 1 l, Lynx. 1.55 l, Red squirrel. 2 l, Chamois. 3.25 l, Pintail (duck). 4.25 l, Fallow deer.

1956 Wmk. 358 *Perf. 14*

No.	Type	Description	Unused	Used
1082	A398	20b grn & blk	1.40	.32
1083	A399	20b cit & gray blk	1.40	.32
1084	A399	35b brt bl & blk	1.40	.32
1085	A398	50b dp ultra & brn blk	1.40	.52
1086	A398	55b ol bis & ind	1.65	.52
1087	A398	55b dk bl grn & dk red brn	1.65	.52
1088	A398	1 l dk grn & red brn	3.00	.90
1089	A399	1.55 l lt ultra & red brn	3.25	1.25
1090	A399	1.75 l sl grn & dk brn	3.75	1.75
1091	A398	2 l ultra & brn blk	14.00	6.50
1092	A398	3.25 l lt grn & blk brn	14.00	3.25
1093	A399	4.25 l brn org & dk brn	14.00	4.00
		Nos. 1082-1093 (12)	60.90	20.17

Exist imperf. in changed colors. Value, set $25.

1956, May 29 *Perf. 13½*

1094 A400 55b vermilion .70 .18

85th anniversary of Commune of Paris.

Globe and Child — A400a

Oak Tree — A401

1956, June 1 Photo. *Perf. 13½x14*

1095 A400a 55b dp vio .90 .22

Intl. Children's Day. The sheet of 100 contains 10 labels, each with "Peace" printed on it in one of 10 languages.

1956, June 11 Litho. Wmk. 358

Design: 55b, Logging train in timberland.

No.	Type	Description	Unused	Used
1096	A401	20b dk bl grn, *pale grn*	.52	.16
1097	A401	55b brn blk, *pale grn*	1.50	.52

Month of the Forest.

Romanian Academy A402

1956, June 19 Photo. *Perf. 14*

1098 A402 55b dk grn & dl yel .75 .20

90th anniversary of Romanian Academy.

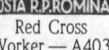

Red Cross Worker — A403

Woman Speaker and Globe — A404

1956, June 7

1099 A403 55b olive & red 1.25 .38

Romanian Red Cross Congress, June 7-9.

1956, June 14

1100 A404 55b dk bl grn .70 .20

Intl. Conference of Working Women, Budapest, June 14-17.

Traian Vuia and Planes — A405

1956, June 21 *Perf. 13x13½*

1101 A405 55b grnsh blk & brn .70 .18

1st flight by Vuia, near Paris, 50th anniv.

Ion Georgescu A406

1956, June 25 *Perf. 14x13½*

1102 A406 55b dk red brn & dk grn 1.25 .24

Ion Georgescu (1856-1898), sculptor.

White Cabbage Butterfly A407

June Bug — A408

Design: 55b, Colorado potato beetle.

Perf. 14x13½, 13½x14

1956, July 30

No.	Type	Description	Unused	Used
1103	A407	10b dp vio, pale yel & blk	3.25	.25
1104	A407	55b ol blk & yel	5.00	.35
1105	A408	1.75 l lt ol & dp plum	6.00	5.75
1106	A408	1.75 l gray ol & dk vio brn	6.00	.70
		Nos. 1103-1106 (4)	20.25	7.05

Campaign against insect pests.

Girl Holding Sheaf of Wheat — A409

Dock Workers on Strike — A410

1956 *Perf. 13½x14*

No.	Type	Description	Unused	Used
1107	A409	55b "1949-1956"	1.40	.25
a.		"1951-1956" (error)	2.75	2.00

7th anniversary of collective farming.

1956, Aug. 6

1108 A410 55b dk red brn .45 .15

Dock workers' strike at Galati, 50th anniv.

Title Page and Printer — A411

Maxim Gorki — A412

1956, Aug. 13 *Perf. 13½*

1109 A411 55b ultra .45 .15

25th anniv. of the publication of "Scanteia" (The Spark).

1956, Aug. 29 *Perf. 13½x14*

1110 A412 55b brown .45 .15

Maxim Gorki (1868-1936), Russian writer.

Theodor Aman A413

Primrose and Snowdrops A414

1956, Sept. 24 Engr.

1111 A413 55b gray blk .70 .25

Aman, painter, 125th birth anniv.

1956, Sept. 26 Photo. *Perf. 14x14½*

55b, Daffodil and violets. 1.75 l, Snapdragon and bellflowers. 3 l, Poppies and lilies of the valley.

Flowers in Natural Colors

No.	Type	Description	Unused	Used
1112	A414	5b bl, yel & red	.50	.15
1113	A414	55b blk, yel & red	1.00	.25
1114	A414	1.75 l ind, pink & yel	3.00	.40
1115	A414	3 l bl grn, dk bl grn & yel	4.00	.55
		Nos. 1112-1115 (4)	8.50	1.35

Olympic Rings and Torch — A415

Janos Hunyadi — A416

Designs: 55b, Water polo. 1 l, Gymnastics. 1.55 l, Canoeing. 1.75 l, High jump.

1956, Oct. 25 *Perf. 13½x14*

No.	Type	Description	Unused	Used
1116	A415	20b vermilion	.28	.15
1117	A415	55b ultra	.50	.15
1118	A415	1 l lil rose	.75	.15
1119	A415	1.55 l lt bl grn	1.25	.15
1120	A415	1.75 l dp pur	1.50	.40
		Nos. 1116-1120 (5)	4.28	1.00

16th Olympic Games, Melbourne, 11/22-12/8.

1956, Oct. Wmk. 358

1121 A416 55b dp vio .60 .25

Janos Hunyadi (1387-1456), national hero of Hungary. No. 1121 is found se-tenant with label showing Hunyadi Castle.

Benjamin Franklin — A417

George Enescu as a Boy — A418

Portraits: 35b, Sesshu (Toyo Oda). 40b, G. B. Shaw. 50b, Ivan Franco. 55b, Pierre Curie. 1 l, Henrik Ibsen. 1.55 l, Fedor Dostoevski. 1.75 l, Heinrich Heine. 2.55 l, Mozart. 3.25 l, Rembrandt.

1956 Unwmk.

No.	Type	Description	Unused	Used
1122	A417	20b vio bl	.20	.15
1123	A417	35b rose lake	.25	.15
1124	A417	40b chocolate	.30	.15
1125	A417	50b brn blk	.35	.15
1126	A417	55b dk ol	.35	.15
1127	A417	1 l dk bl grn	.75	.15
1128	A417	1.55 l dp pur	1.00	.15
1129	A417	1.75 l brt bl	1.50	.22
1130	A417	2.55 l rose vio	2.00	.35
1131	A417	3.25 l dk bl	2.25	.90
		Nos. 1122-1131 (10)	8.95	
		Set value		2.00

Great personalities of the world.

1956, Dec. 29 Engr.

Portrait: 1.75 l, George Enescu as an adult.

No.	Type	Description	Unused	Used
1132	A418	55b ultramarine	.45	.15
1133	A418	1.75 l deep claret	1.25	.25

75th birth anniv. of George Enescu, musician and composer.

Fighting Peasants, by Octav Bancila — A419

1957, Feb. 28 Photo. Wmk. 358

1134 A419 55b dk bl gray .75 .18

50th anniversary of Peasant Uprising.

Stephen the Great — A420

1957, Apr. 24 *Perf. 13½x14*

No.	Type	Description	Unused	Used
1147	A420	55b brown	.45	.20
1148	A420	55b ol blk	.70	.18

Enthronement of Stephen the Great, Prince of Moldavia, 500th anniv.

Dr. George Marinescu, Marinescu Institute and Congress Emblem A421

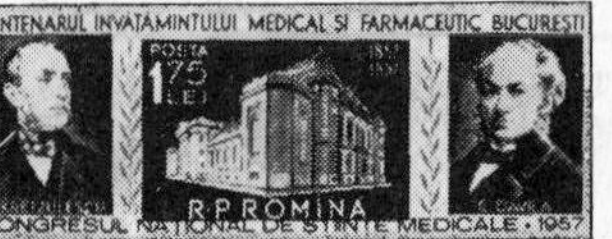

Dr. N. Kretzulescu, Medical School, Dr. C. Davila — A422

35b, Dr. I. Cantacuzino & Cantacuzino Hospital. 55b, Dr. V. Babes & Babes Institute.

1957, May 5 *Perf. 14x13½*

1149	A421	20b dp grn	.22	.15
1150	A421	35b dp red brn	.28	.15
1151	A421	55b red lil	.48	.22
1152	A422	1.75 l brt ultra & dk red	1.40	.50
		Nos. 1149-1152 (4)	2.38	1.02

National Congress of Medical Science, Bucharest, May 5-6.

No. 1152 also for centenary of medical and pharmaceutical teaching in Bucharest. It measures 66x23mm.

Dove and Handle Bars — A423

1957, May 29 *Perf. 13½x14*

1153	A423	20b shown	.18	.15
1154	A423	55b Cyclist	.48	.18

10th International Bicycle Peace Race.

Woman Watching Gymnast — A424

Woman Gymnast on Bar — A425

1957, May 21 *Perf. 13½*

1155	A424	20b shown	.18	.15
1156	A425	35b shown	.32	.15
1157	A425	55b Vaulting horse	.70	.18
1158	A424	1.75 l Acrobat	1.75	.38
		Nos. 1155-1158 (4)	2.95	.86

European Women's Gymnastic meet, Bucharest.

Slide Rule, Caliper & Atomic Symbol — A426

Rhododendron Hirsutum — A427

Wmk. 358

1957, May 29 **Photo.** *Perf. 14*

1159	A426	55b blue	.60	.15
1160	A426	55b brn red	1.00	.22

2nd Congress of the Society of Engineers and Technicians, Bucharest, May 29-31.

1957, June 22 **Litho.** **Unwmk.**

Carpathian Mountain Flowers: 10b, Daphne Blagayana. 20b, Lilium Bulbiferum L. 35b, Leontopodium Alpinum. 55b, Gentiana Acaulis L. 1 l, Dianthus Callizonus. 1.55 l, Primula Carpatica Griseb. 1.75 l, Anemone Montana Hoppe.

Light Gray Background

1161	A427	5b brt rose	.20	.15
1162	A427	10b dk grn	.30	.15
1163	A427	20b red org	.35	.15
1164	A427	35b olive	.50	.15
1165	A427	55b ultra	.60	.15
1166	A427	1 l red	1.00	.20
1167	A427	1.55 l yellow	2.00	.25
1168	A427	1.75 l dk pur	3.00	.40
		Nos. 1161-1168 (8)	7.95	
		Set value		1.30

Nos. 1161-1168 also come se-tenant with a decorative label.

"Oxcart" by Grigorescu A428

Nicolae Grigorescu A429

Painting: 1.75 l, Battle scene.

1957, June 29 **Photo.** **Wmk. 358**

1169	A428	20b dk bl grn	.40	.15
1170	A429	55b dp brn	.80	.15
1171	A428	1.75 l chlky bl	2.10	.60
		Nos. 1169-1171 (3)	3.30	.90

Grigorescu, painter, 50th death anniv.

Warship — A430

1957, Aug. 3 *Perf. 13x13½*

1172	A430	1.75 l Prus bl	1.10	.24

Navy Day.

Young Couple — A431

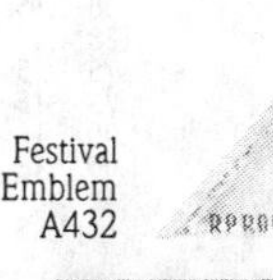

Festival Emblem A432

Folk Dance — A433

Design: 55b, Girl with flags on hoop.

Perf. 14x14½, 14x14x12½ (A432), 13½x12½ (A433)

1957, July 28

1173	A431	20b red lilac	.18	.15
1174	A431	55b emerald	.28	.15
1175	A432	1 l red orange	.70	.25
1176	A433	1.75 l ultra	1.25	.20
		Nos. 1173-1176 (4)	2.41	
		Set value		.58

Moscow 1957 Youth Festival. No. 1173 measures 23x34mm, No. 1174 22x38mm.

No. 1175 was printed in sheets of 50, alternating with 40 labels inscribed "Peace and Friendship" in 20 languages.

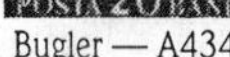

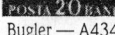

Bugler — A434

Girl Holding Dove — A435

1957, Aug. 30 **Wmk. 358** *Perf. 14*

1177	A434	20b brt pur	.65	.18

80th anniv. of the Russo-Turkish war.

1957, Sept. 3 *Perf. 13½*

1178	A435	55b Prus grn & red	.65	.18

Honoring the Red Cross.

Battle Scene — A436

1957, Aug. 31

1179	A436	1.75 l brown	.65	.24

Battle of Marasesti, 40th anniv.

Jumper and Dove — A437

55b, Javelin thrower, bison. 1.75 l, Runner, stag.

1957, Sept. 14 **Photo.** *Perf. 13½*

1180	A437	20b brt bl & blk	.28	.15
1181	A437	55b yel & blk	.60	.18
1182	A437	1.75 l brick red & blk	2.00	.50
		Nos. 1180-1182 (3)	2.88	.83

International Athletic Meet, Bucharest.

Statue of Ovid, Constanta — A438

1957, Sept. 20 **Photo.** **Wmk. 358**

1183	A438	1.75 l vio bl	1.40	.38

2000th anniv. of the birth of the Roman poet Publius Ovidius Naso.

Oil Field — A439

Design: 55b, Horse pulling drill, 1857.

1957, Oct. 5

1184	A439	20b dl red brn	.20	.15
1185	A439	20b indigo	.20	.15
1186	A439	55b vio blk	.50	.25
		Nos. 1184-1186 (3)	.90	
		Set value		.35

Centenary of Romanian oil industry.

Congress Emblem — A440

1957, Sept. 28

1187	A440	55b ultra	.42	.18

4th Intl. Trade Union Congress, Leipzig, Oct. 4-15.

Young Couple, Lenin Banner — A441

Endre Ady — A442

35b, Lenin and Flags, horiz. 55b, Lenin statue.

1957, Nov. 6 *Perf. 14x14½, 14½x14*

1188	A441	10b crimson	.15	.15
1189	A441	35b plum	.24	.15
1190	A441	55b brown	.35	.18
		Nos. 1188-1190 (3)	.74	
		Set value		.28

Russian Revolution, 40th anniversary.

1957, Dec. 5 *Perf. 14*

1191	A442	55b ol brn	.55	.18

Ady, Hungarian poet, 80th birth anniv.

Oath of Bobilna A443

Bobilna Monument A444

1957, Nov. 30

1192	A443	50b deep plum	.30	.15
1193	A444	55b slate blue	.40	.15
		Set value		.18

520th anniversary of the insurrection of the peasants of Bobilna in 1437.

Black-winged Stilt — A445

Animals: 10b, Great white egret. 20b, White spoonbill. 50b, Sturgeon. 55b, Ermine, horiz. 1.30 l, White pelican, horiz.

Perf. 13½x14, 14x13½

1957, Dec. 27 **Photo.** **Wmk. 358**

1194	A445	5b red brn & gray	.15	.15
1195	A445	10b emer & ocher	.15	.15
1196	A445	20b brt red & ocher	.20	.15
1197	A445	50b bl grn & ocher	.40	.15
1198	A445	55b dp cl & gray	.45	.16
1199	A445	1.30 l pur & org	2.00	.30
		Nos. 1194-1199,C53-C54 (8)	7.50	
		Set value		1.40

Sputnik 2 and Laika A446

1957, Dec. 20 *Perf. 14x13½*

1200	A446	1.20 l	bl & dk brn	1.25	.38
1201	A446	1.20 l	grnsh bl & choc	1.25	.38

Dog Laika, "first space traveler."

Romanian Arms, Flags — A447

Designs: 55b, Arms, "Industry and Agriculture." 1.20 l, Arms, "Art, Science and Sport (soccer)."

1957, Dec. 30 *Perf. 13½*

1202	A447	25b	ultra, red & ocher	.18	.15
1203	A447	55b	dull yellow	.35	.15
1204	A447	1.20 l	crimson rose	.55	.25
			Nos. 1202-1204 (3)	1.08	
			Set value		.38

Proclamation of the Peoples' Republic, 10th anniv.

Flag and Wreath — A448

1958, Feb. 15 **Unwmk.** *Perf. 13½*

1205	A448	1 l	dk bl & red, *buff*	.42	.15
1206	A448	1 l	brn & red, *buff*	.42	.15

Grivita Strike, 25th anniversary.

Television, Radio Antennas A449

Design: 1.75 l, Telegraph pole and wires.

1958, Mar. 21 *Perf. 14x13½*

1207	A449	55b	brt vio	.30	.15
1208	A449	1.75 l	dp mag	.80	.25

Telecommunications Conference, Moscow, Dec. 3-17, 1957.

Nicolae Balcescu — A450

Romanian Writers: 10b, Ion Creanga. 35b, Alexandru Vlahuta. 55b, Mihail Eminescu. 1.75 l, Vasile Alecsandri. 2 l, Barbu S. Delavrancea.

1958 **Wmk. 358** *Perf. 14x14½*

1209	A450	5b	bluish blk	.15	.15
1210	A450	10b	int blk	.15	.15
1211	A450	35b	dk bl	.20	.15
1212	A450	55b	dk red brn	.35	.15
1213	A450	1.75 l	blk brn	.70	.18
1214	A450	2 l	dk sl grn	1.25	.22
			Nos. 1209-1214 (6)	2.80	
			Set value		.70

See Nos. 1309-1314.

Fencer in Global Mask — A451

1958, Apr. 5 *Perf. 14½x14*

1215	A451	1.75 l	brt pink	1.10	.25

Youth Fencing World Championships, Bucharest.

Stadium and Health Symbol — A452

Globe and Dove — A453

1958, Apr. 16 *Perf. 14x14½*

1216	A452	1.20 l	lt grn & red	.85	.18

25 years of sports medicine.

1958, May 15 **Photo.**

1217	A453	55b	brt bl	.48	.15

4th Congress of the Intl. Democratic Women's Federation, June 1958.

Carl von Linné — A454

Lepiota Procera — A456

Portraits: 20b, Auguste Comte. 40b, William Blake. 55b, Mikhail I. Glinka. 1 l, Henry W. Longfellow. 1.75 l, Carlo Goldoni. 2 l, Jan A. Komensky.

Perf. 14x14½

1958, May 31 **Unwmk.**

1218	A454	10b	Prus grn	.15	.15
1219	A454	20b	brown	.18	.15
1220	A454	40b	dp lil	.28	.15
1221	A454	55b	dp bl	.40	.15
1222	A454	1 l	dp mag	.60	.15
1223	A454	1.75 l	dp vio bl	.90	.22
1224	A454	2 l	olive	1.65	.30
			Nos. 1218-1224 (7)	4.16	
			Set value		.90

Great personalities of the world.

1958, July **Litho.** **Unwmk.**

Mushrooms: 10b, Clavaria aurea. 20b, Amanita caesarea. 30b, Lactarius deliciosus. 35b, Armillaria mellea. 55b, Coprinus comatus. 1 l, Morchella conica. 1.55 l, Psalliota campestris. 1.75 l, Boletus edulis. 2 l, Cantharellus cibarius.

1225	A456	5b	gray bl & brn	.15	.15
1226	A456	10b	ol, ocher & brn	.15	.15
1227	A456	20b	gray, red & yel	.15	.15
1228	A456	30b	grn & dp org	.18	.15
1229	A456	35b	lt bl & yel brn	.20	.15
1230	A456	55b	pale grn, fawn & brn	.35	.15
1231	A456	1 l	bl grn, ocher & brn	.50	.15
1232	A456	1.55 l	gray, lt gray & pink	.85	.15
1233	A456	1.75 l	emer, brn & buff	1.00	.15
1234	A456	2 l	dl bl & org yel	1.90	.25
			Nos. 1225-1234 (10)	5.43	
			Set value		.95

Antarctic Map and Emil Racovita A457

Design: 1.20 l, Cave and Racovita.

1958, July 30 **Photo.** *Perf. 14½x14*

1235	A457	55b	indigo & lt bl	.52	.15
1236	A457	1.20 l	ol bis & dk vio	1.00	.18

90th birth anniv. of Emil Racovita, explorer and naturalist.

Armed Forces Monument — A458

Designs: 75b, Soldier guarding industry. 1.75 l, Sailor raising flag and ship.

1958, Oct. 2 *Perf. 13½x13*

1237	A458	55b	orange brown	.18	.15
1238	A458	75b	deep magenta	.22	.15
1239	A458	1.75 l	bright blue	.52	.26
			Nos. 1237-1239,C55 (4)	1.82	.98

Armed Forces Day.

Woman from Oltenia — A459

Man from Oltenia — A460

Regional Costumes: 40b, Tara Oasului. 50b, Transylvania. 55b, Muntenia. 1 l, Banat. 1.75 l, Moldavia.

1958 **Unwmk.** **Litho.** *Perf. 13½x14*

1240	A459	35b	blk & red, *dl yel*	.16	.15
1241	A460	35b	blk & red, *dl yel*	.16	.15

Designs in Dark Brown and Deep Carmine

1242	A459	40b	*pale brn*	.20	.15
1243	A460	40b	*pale brn*	.20	.15
1244	A459	50b	*lt lil*	.24	.15
1245	A460	50b	*lt lil*	.24	.15
1246	A459	55b	*gray*	.38	.15
1247	A460	55b	*gray*	.38	.15
1248	A459	1 l	*rose*	.75	.15
1249	A460	1 l	*rose*	.75	.15
1250	A459	1.75 l	*aqua*	1.00	.18
1251	A460	1.75 l	*aqua*	1.00	.18
			Nos. 1240-1251 (12)	5.46	
			Set value		1.25

Same denoms. se-tenant with label between. Exist imperf. Value, set $16.

Printer and Hand Press A461

Moldavia Stamp of 1858 A462

55b, Scissors cutting strips of 1858 stamps. 1.20 l, Postilion, mail coach. 1.30 l, Postilion blowing horn, courier on horseback. 1.75 l, 2 l, 3.30 l, Various denominations of 1858 issue.

1958, Nov. 15 **Engr.** *Perf. 14½x14*

1252	A461	35b	vio bl	.22	.15
1253	A461	55b	dk red brn	.35	.15
1254	A461	1.20 l	dull bl	.70	.15
1255	A461	1.30 l	brown vio	.90	.16
1256	A462	1.55 l	gray brn	1.00	.18
1257	A462	1.75 l	rose claret	1.10	.25
1258	A462	2 l	dull vio	1.40	.48
1259	A462	3.30 l	dull red brn	2.10	.55
			Nos. 1252-1259 (8)	7.77	
			Set value		1.80

Cent. of Romanian stamps. See No. C57. Exist imperf. Value, set $13.

Bugler A463

Runner A464

1958, Dec. 10 **Photo.** *Perf. 13½x13*

1260	A463	55b	crimson rose	.48	.18

Decade of teaching reforms.

Perf. 13½x14

1958, Dec. 9 **Wmk. 358**

1261	A464	1 l	deep brown	.90	.24

Third Youth Spartacist Sports Meet.

Building and Flag — A465

Prince Alexandru Ioan Cuza — A466

1958, Dec. 16

1262	A465	55b	dk car rose	.30	.15

Workers' Revolution, 40th anniversary.

Perf. 14x13½

1959, Jan. 27 **Unwmk.**

1263	A466	1.75 l	dk blue	.60	.24

Centenary of the Romanian Union.

Friedrich Handel — A467

Corn — A468

Sheep — A469

Portraits: No. 1265, Robert Burns. No. 1266, Charles Darwin. No. 1267, Alexander Popov. No. 1268, Shalom Aleichem.

1959, Apr. 25 **Photo.** *Perf. 13½x14*

1264	A467	55b	brown	.32	.15
1265	A467	55b	indigo	.32	.15
1266	A467	55b	slate	.32	.15
1267	A467	55b	carmine	.32	.15
1268	A467	55b	purple	.32	.15
			Nos. 1264-1268 (5)	1.60	
			Set value		.45

Various cultural anniversaries in 1959.

Perf. 13½x14, 14x13½

1959, June 1 **Photo.** **Wmk. 358**

No. 1270, Sunflower and bee. No. 1271, Sugar beet and refinery. No. 1273, Cattle. No. 1274, Rooster and hens. No. 1275, Tractor and grain. No. 276, Loaded farm wagon. No. 1277, Farm couple and "10."

1269	A468	55b	brt green	.30	.15
1270	A468	55b	red org	.30	.15
1271	A468	55b	red lilac	.30	.15
1272	A469	55b	olive grn	.30	.15
1273	A469	55b	red brown	.30	.15
1274	A469	55b	yellow brn	.30	.15
1275	A469	55b	blue	.30	.15
1276	A469	55b	brown	.30	.15

Unwmk.

1277 A469 5 l dp red lilac 3.00 .65
Nos. 1269-1277 (9) 5.40
Set value 1.00

10th anniv. of collective farming. Sizes: #1272-1276 33x23mm; #1277 38x27mm.

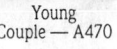

Young Couple — A470

Steel Worker and Farm Woman — A471

Design: 1.60 l, Dancer in folk costume.

Perf. 13½x14

1959, July 15 Unwmk.

1278 A470 1 l brt blue .35 .15
1279 A470 1.60 l car rose .70 .18

7th World Youth Festival, Vienna, 7/26-8/14.

1959, Aug. 23 Litho. *Perf. 13½x14*

1280 A471 55b multicolored .48 .15
a. Souvenir sheet of 1 .70 .26

15th anniv. of Romania's liberation from the Germans.

No. 1280a is ungummed and imperf. The blue, yellow and red vignette shows large "XV" and Romanian flag. Brown 1.20 l denomination and inscription in margin.

Prince Vlad Tepes and Document — A472

Designs: 40b, Nicolae Balcescu Street. No. 1283, Atheneum. No. 1284, Printing Combine. 1.55 l, Opera House. 1.75 l, Stadium.

1959, Sept. 20 Photo.

Centers in Gray

1281 A472 20b blue .60 .15
1282 A472 40b brown .90 .15
1283 A472 55b bister brn 1.00 .20
1284 A472 55b rose lilac 1.25 .25
1285 A472 1.55 l pale violet 2.75 .50
1286 A472 1.75 l bluish grn 3.00 .75
Nos. 1281-1286 (6) 9.50 2.00

500th anniversary of the founding of Bucharest. See No. C71.

No. 1261 Overprinted with Shield in Silver, inscribed: "Jocurile Bucaresti Balcanice 1959"

1959, Sept. 12 Wmk. 358

1287 A464 1 l deep brown 3.25 3.25

Balkan Games.

Soccer — A473

Motorcycle Race — A474

1959 Unwmk. Litho. *Perf. 13½*

1288 A473 20b shown .18 .15
1289 A474 35b shown .24 .15
1290 A474 40b Ice hockey .28 .15
1291 A473 55b Field ball .35 .15
1292 A473 1 l Horse race .50 .15
1293 A473 1.50 l Boxing .85 .15
1294 A474 1.55 l Rugby 1.00 .20
1295 A474 1.60 l Tennis 1.25 .28
Nos. 1288-1295,C72 (9) 6.15
Set value 1.25

Russian Icebreaker "Lenin" A475

Perf. 14½x13½

1959, Oct. 25 Photo.

1296 A475 1.75 l blue vio 1.10 .25

First atomic ice-breaker.

Stamp Album and Magnifying Glass — A476

Purple Foxglove — A477

1959, Nov. 15 Wmk. 358 *Perf. 14*

1297 A476 1.60 l + 40b label 1.10 .38

Issued for Stamp Day.

Stamp and label were printed alternately in sheet. The 40b went to the Romanian Association of Philatelists.

1959, Dec. 15 Typo. Unwmk.

Medicinal Flowers in Natural Colors

1298 A477 20b shown .15 .15
1299 A477 40b Peppermint .22 .15
1300 A477 55b Cornflower .25 .15
1301 A477 55b Daisies .32 .15
1302 A477 1 l Autumn crocus .42 .15
1303 A477 1.20 l Monkshood .48 .15
1304 A477 1.55 l Poppies .70 .18
1305 A477 1.60 l Linden .80 .24
1306 A477 1.75 l Dog rose .95 .24
1307 A477 3.20 l Buttercup 1.75 .40
Nos. 1298-1307 (10) 6.04
Set value 1.30

Cuza University, Jassy, Centenary A478

1960, Nov. 26 Photo. Wmk. 358

1308 A478 55b brown .38 .18

Romanian Writers Type of 1958

20b, Gheorghe Cosbuc. 40b, Ion Luca Caragiale. 50b, Grigore Alexandrescu. 55b, Alexandru Donici. 1 l, Costache Negruzzi. 1.55 l, Dimitrie Bolintineanu.

1960, Jan. 20 *Perf. 14*

1309 A450 20b bluish blk .15 .15
1310 A450 40b dp lilac .25 .15
1311 A450 50b brown .30 .15
1312 A450 55b violet brn .35 .15
1313 A450 1 l violet .60 .20
1314 A450 1.55 l dk blue 1.10 .30
Nos. 1309-1314 (6) 2.75
Set value .90

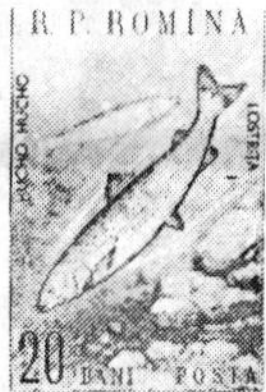

Huchen (Salmon) — A480

Woman, Dove and Globe — A481

Designs: 55b, Greek tortoise. 1.20 l, Shelduck.

1960, Feb. 1 Engr. Unwmk.

1315 A480 20b blue .18 .15
1316 A480 55b brown .30 .15
1317 A480 1.20 l dk purple .75 .15
Nos. 1315-1317,C76-C78 (6) 4.83
Set value .95

1960, Mar. 1 Photo. *Perf. 14*

1318 A481 55b violet blue .48 .18

50 years of Intl. Women's Day, Mar. 8.

A482

A483

40b, Lenin. 55b, Lenin statue, Bucharest. 1.55 l, Head of Lenin.

1960, Apr. 22 Wmk. 358 *Perf. 13½*

1319 A482 40b magenta .28 .15
1320 A482 55b violet blue .35 .15
Set value .20

Souvenir Sheet

1321 A482 1.55 l carmine 1.40 1.00

90th birth anniv. of Lenin.

1960, May 9 Wmk. 358 *Perf. 14*

1322 A483 40b Heroes Monument .35 .15
1323 A483 55b Soviet war memorial .35 .25
a. Strip of 2, #1322-1323 + label 1.65 .65

15th anniversary of the liberation.

Nos. 1322-1323 exist imperf., printed in deep magenta. Value, set $3.25; label strip, $4.50.

Swimming A484

Sports: 55b, Women's gymnastics. 1.20 l, High jump. 1.60 l, Boxing. 2.45 l, Canoeing.

1960, June Unwmk. Typo. *Perf. 14*

Gray Background

1326 A484 40b blue & yel .35 .25
1327 A484 55b blk, yel & emer .42 .30
1328 A484 1.20 l emer & brick red .95 .70
a. Strip of 3, #1326-1328 1.75
1329 A484 1.60 l blue, yel & blk 1.75 1.25
1330 A484 2.45 l blk, emer & brick red 1.75 1.25
a. Pair, #1329-1330 + 2 labels 3.50
Nos. 1326-1330 (5) 5.22 3.75

17th Olympic Games, Rome, Aug. 25-Sept. 11.

Nos. 1326-1330 were printed in one sheet, the top half containing No. 1328a, the bottom half No. 1330a, with gutter between. When the two strips are placed together, the Olympic rings join in a continuous design.

Exist imperf. (3.70 l replaced 2.45 l). Value, set $7.75.

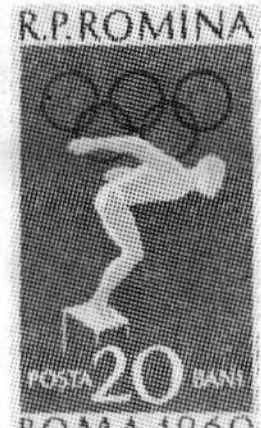

Swimming — A485

Olympic Flame, Stadium — A486

Sports: 40b, Women's gymnastics. 55b, High jump. 1 l, Boxing. 1.60 l, Canoeing. 2 l, Soccer.

1960 Photo. Wmk. 358

1331 A485 20b chalky blue .15 .15
1332 A485 40b dk brn red .30 .15
1333 A485 55b blue .45 .15
1334 A485 1 l rose red .60 .15
1335 A485 1.60 l rose lilac .75 .18
1336 A485 2 l dull violet 1.40 .32
Nos. 1331-1336 (6) 3.65
Set value .70

Souvenir Sheets

Perf. 11½

1337 A486 5 l ultra 4.50 2.25

Imperf

1338 A486 6 l dull red 7.25 3.75

17th Olympic Games.

A487

A488

Perf. 13½

1960, June 20 Unwmk. Litho.

1339 A487 55b red org & dk car .38 .18

Romanian Workers' Party, 3rd congress.

1960 Wmk. 358 Photo. *Perf. 14*

Portraits: 10b, Leo Tolstoy. 20b, Mark Twain. 35b, Hokusai. 40b, Alfred de Musset. 55b, Daniel Defoe. 1 l, Janos Bolyai. 1.20 l, Anton Chekov. 1.55 l, Robert Koch. 1.75 l, Frederick Chopin.

1340 A488 10b dull pur .15 .15
1341 A488 20b olive .15 .15
1342 A488 35b blue .15 .15
1343 A488 40b slate green .18 .15
1344 A488 55b dull brn vio .42 .15
1345 A488 1 l Prus grn .70 .18
1346 A488 1.20 l dk car rose .90 .15
1347 A488 1.55 l gray blue 1.25 .15
1348 A488 1.75 l brown 1.40 .25
Nos. 1340-1348 (9) 5.30
Set value .90

Various cultural anniversaries.

Students A489

Piano and Books A490

Designs: 5b, Diesel locomotive. 10b, Dam. 20b, Miner with drill. 30b, Ambulance and doctor. 35b, Textile worker. 50b, Nursery. 55b, Timber industry. 60b, Harvester. 75b, Feeding cattle. 1 l, Atomic reactor. 1.20 l, Oil derricks. 1.50 l, Coal mine. 1.55 l, Loading ship. 1.60 l, Athlete. 1.75 l, Bricklayer. 2 l, Steam roller. 2.40 l, Chemist. 3 l, Radio and television.

1960 Wmk. 358 Photo. *Perf. 14*

1349 A489 3b brt lil rose .15 .15
1350 A489 5b olive bis .15 .15
1351 A489 10b violet gray .15 .15
1352 A489 20b blue vio .15 .15
1353 A489 30b vermilion .15 .15
1354 A489 35b crimson .15 .15
1355 A490 40b ocher .15 .15
1356 A489 50b bluish vio .20 .15
1357 A489 55b blue .20 .15
1358 A490 60b green .20 .15

No.	Type	Denomination & Color	Unused	Used
1359	A490	75b gray ol	.30	.15
1360	A489	1 l car rose	.50	.15
1361	A489	1.20 l black	.40	.15
1362	A489	1.50 l plum	.50	.15
1363	A489	1.55 l Prus grn	.50	.15
1364	A490	1.60 l dp blue	.55	.15
1365	A489	1.75 l red brown	.65	.15
1366	A489	2 l dk ol gray	.80	.15
1367	A489	2.40 l brt lilac	1.00	.15
1368	A489	3 l grysh blue	1.50	.15
		Nos. 1349-1368,C86 (21)	9.45	
		Set value		1.20

Ovid Statue at Constanta A491

Black Sea Resorts: 35b, Constanta harbor. 40b, Vasile Rosita beach and vase. 55b, Ionian column and Mangalia beach. 1 l, Eforie at night. 1.60 l, Eforie and sailboat.

1960, Aug. 2 Litho. Unwmk.

No.	Type	Denomination & Color	Unused	Used
1369	A491	20b multicolored	.15	.15
1370	A491	35b multicolored	.16	.15
1371	A491	40b multicolored	.20	.15
1372	A491	55b multicolored	.24	.15
1373	A491	1 l multicolored	.60	.15
1374	A491	1.60 l multicolored	.90	.15
		Nos. 1369-1374,C87 (7)	3.15	
		Set value		.60

Emblem — A492

Petrushka, Russian Puppet — A493

Designs: Various Puppets.

1960, Aug. 20 Typo.

No.	Type	Denomination & Color	Unused	Used
1375	A492	20b multi	.15	.15
1376	A493	40b multi	.15	.15
1377	A493	55b multi	.18	.15
1378	A493	1 l multi	.38	.15
1379	A493	1.20 l multi	.38	.15
1380	A493	1.75 l multi	.60	.16
		Nos. 1375-1380 (6)	1.84	
		Set value		.45

International Puppet Theater Festival.

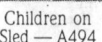

Children on Sled — A494

Globe and Peace Banner — A495

Children's Sports: 35b, Boys playing ball, horiz. 55b, Ice skating, horiz. 1 l, Running. 1.75 l, Swimming, horiz.

Unwmk.
1960, Oct. 1 Litho. *Perf. 14*

No.	Type	Denomination & Color	Unused	Used
1381	A494	20b multi	.15	.15
1382	A494	35b multi	.15	.15
1383	A494	55b multi	.28	.15
1384	A494	1 l multi	.38	.15
1385	A494	1.75 l multi	.75	.22
		Nos. 1381-1385 (5)	1.71	
		Set value		.45

Perf. 13¹/₂x14
1960, Nov. 26 Photo. Wmk. 358

No.	Type	Denomination & Color	Unused	Used
1386	A495	55b brt bl & yel	.28	.15

Intl. Youth Federation, 15th anniv.

Worker and Flags A496

Perf. 14x13
1960, Nov. 26 Litho. Unwmk.

No.	Type	Denomination & Color	Unused	Used
1387	A496	55b dk car & red org	.32	.15

40th anniversary of the general strike.

Carp A497

Fish: 20b, Pikeperch. 40b, Black Sea turbot. 55b, Allis shad. 1 l, Wels (catfish). 1.20 l, Sterlet. 1.60 l, Huchen (salmon).

1960, Dec. 5 Typo.

No.	Type	Denomination & Color	Unused	Used
1388	A497	10b multi	.15	.15
1389	A497	20b multi	.15	.15
1390	A497	40b multi	.25	.15
1391	A497	55b multi	.30	.15
1392	A497	1 l multi	.70	.15
1393	A497	1.20 l multi	.70	.20
1394	A497	1.60 l multi	1.00	.25
		Nos. 1388-1394 (7)	3.25	
		Set value		.75

Kneeling Woman and Grapes — A498

Steelworker by I. Irimescu — A499

Designs: 30b, Farmers drinking, horiz. 40b, Loading grapes into basket, horiz. 55b, Woman cutting grapes. 75b, Vintner with basket. 1 l, Woman filling basket with grapes. 1.20 l, Vintner with jug. 5 l, Antique wine jug.

1960, Dec. 20 Litho. *Perf. 14*

No.	Type	Denomination & Color	Unused	Used
1395	A498	20b brn & gray	.15	.15
1396	A498	30b red org & pale grn	.15	.15
1397	A498	40b dp ultra & gray ol	.28	.15
1398	A498	55b emer & buff	.38	.15
1399	A498	75b dk car rose & pale grn	.38	.15
1400	A498	1 l Prus grn & gray ol	.45	.16
1401	A498	1.20 l org brn & pale bl	.75	.28
		Nos. 1395-1401 (7)	2.54	
		Set value		.75

Souvenir Sheet
Imperf

No.	Type	Denomination & Color	Unused	Used
1402	A498	5 l dk car rose & bis	3.25	1.50

Each stamp represents a different wine-growing region: Dragasani, Dealul Mare, Odobesti, Cotnari, Tirnave, Minis, Murfatlar and Pietroasa.

Perf. 13¹/₂x14, 14x13¹/₂
1961, Feb. 16 Photo. Unwmk.

Modern Sculptures: 10b, G. Doja, I. Vlad. 20b, Meeting, B. Caragea. 40b, George Enescu, A. Angnel. 50b, Mihail Eminescu, C. Baraschi. 55b, Peasant Revolt, 1907, M. Constantinescu, horiz. 1 l, "Peace," I. Jalea. 1.55 l, Building Socialism, C. Medrea. 1.75 l, Birth of an Idea, A. Szobotka.

No.	Type	Denomination & Color	Unused	Used
1403	A499	5b car rose	.15	.15
1404	A499	10b violet	.15	.15
1405	A499	20b ol blk	.15	.15
1406	A499	40b ol bis	.15	.15
1407	A499	50b blk brn	.18	.15
1408	A499	55b org ver	.18	.15
1409	A499	1 l dp plum	.40	.15
1410	A499	1.55 l brt ultra	.55	.15
1411	A499	1.75 l green	.85	.25
		Nos. 1403-1411 (9)	2.76	
		Set value		.80

Peter Poni, and Chemical Apparatus — A500

Romanian Scientists: 20b, A. Saligny and Danube bridge, Cernavoda. 55b, C. Budeanu and electrical formula. 1.55 l, Gh. Titeica and geometrical symbol.

1961, Apr. 11 Litho. *Perf. 13¹/₂x13*
Portraits in Brown Black

No.	Type	Denomination & Color	Unused	Used
1412	A500	10b pink & vio bl	.15	.15
1413	A500	20b citron & mar	.15	.15
1414	A500	55b bl & red	.22	.15
1415	A500	1.55 l ocher & lil	.75	.16
		Set value	1.10	.30

Freighter "Galati" A501

Ships: 40b, Passenger ship "Oltenita." 55b, Motorboat "Tomis." 1 l, Freighter "Arad." 1.55 l, Tugboat. 1.75 l, Freighter "Dobrogea."

1961, Apr. 25 Typo. *Perf. 14x13*

No.	Type	Denomination & Color	Unused	Used
1416	A501	20b multi	.20	.15
1417	A501	40b multi	.20	.15
1418	A501	55b multi	.30	.15
1419	A501	1 l multi	.40	.15
1420	A501	1.55 l multi	.55	.20
1421	A501	1.75 l multi	.85	.25
		Nos. 1416-1421 (6)	2.50	
		Set value		.70

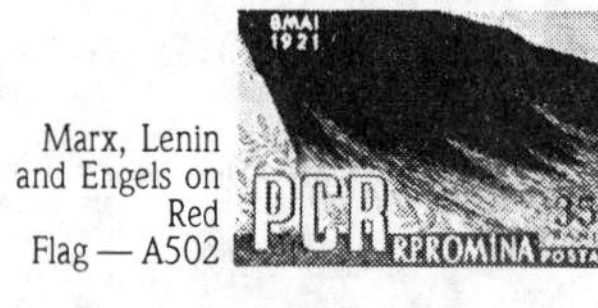

Marx, Lenin and Engels on Red Flag — A502

Designs: 55b, Workers. 1 l, "Industry and Agriculture" and Workers Party Emblem.

1961, Apr. 29 Litho.

No.	Type	Denomination & Color	Unused	Used
1422	A502	35b red, bl & ocher	.16	.15
1423	A502	55b mar, red & gray	.24	.15
		Set value		.15

Souvenir Sheet
Imperf

No.	Type	Denomination & Color	Unused	Used
1424	A502	1 l multi	1.25	.50

40th anniv. of the Romanian Communist Party. #1424 contains one 55x33mm stamp.

Roe Deer and Bronze Age Hunting Scene — A503

Lynx and Prehistoric Hunter — A504

Designs: 35b, Boar and Roman hunter. 40b, Brown bear and Roman tombstone. 55b, Red deer, 16th cent. hunter. 75b, Red fox and feudal hunter. 1 l, Black goat and modern hunter. 1.55 l, Rabbit and hunter with dog. 1.75 l, Badger and hunter. 2 l, Roebuck and hunter.

1961, July *Perf. 13x14, 14x13*

No.	Type	Denomination & Color	Unused	Used
1425	A503	10b multi	.15	.15
1426	A504	20b multi	.18	.15
1427	A504	35b multi	.24	.15
1428	A504	40b multi	.30	.15
1429	A503	55b multi	.40	.15
1430	A504	75b multi	.60	.15
1431	A503	1 l multi	.75	.15
1432	A503	1.55 l multi	.90	.15
1433	A503	1.75 l multi	1.40	.25
1434	A503	2 l multi	1.65	.35
		Nos. 1425-1434 (10)	6.57	
		Set value		1.20

Georges Enescu A505

1961, Sept. 7 Litho. *Perf. 14x13*

No.	Type	Denomination & Color	Unused	Used
1435	A505	3 l pale vio & vio brn	1.40	.25

2nd Intl. George Enescu Festival, Bucharest.

Peasant Playing Panpipe — A506

Heraclitus — A507

Peasants playing musical instruments: 20b, Alpenhorn, horiz. 40b, Flute. 55b, Guitar. 60b, Bagpipe. 1 l, Zither.

Perf. 13x14, 14x13
1961 Unwmk. Typo.
Tinted Paper

No.	Type	Denomination & Color	Unused	Used
1436	A506	10b multi	.15	.15
1437	A506	20b multi	.15	.15
1438	A506	40b multi	.20	.15
1439	A506	55b multi	.38	.15
1440	A506	60b multi	.38	.15
1441	A506	1 l multi	.55	.15
		Nos. 1436-1441 (6)	1.81	
		Set value		.44

Perf. 13¹/₂x13
1961, Oct. 25 Photo. Wmk. 358

Portraits: 20b, Francis Bacon. 40b, Rabindranath Tagore. 55b, Domingo F. Sarmiento. 1.35 l, Heinrich von Kleist. 1.75 l, Mikhail V. Lomonosov.

No.	Type	Denomination & Color	Unused	Used
1442	A507	10b maroon	.15	.15
1443	A507	20b brown	.15	.15
1444	A507	40b Prus grn	.15	.15
1445	A507	55b cerise	.18	.15
1446	A507	1.35 l brt bl	.52	.15
1447	A507	1.75 l purple	.70	.15
		Nos. 1442-1447 (6)	1.85	
		Set value		.45

Swimming — A508

Gold Medal, Boxing A509

Designs: No. 1449, Olympic torch. No. 1450, Water polo, Melbourne. No. 1451, Women's high jump, Rome.

Perf. 14x14¹/₂
1961, Oct. 30 Photo. Unwmk.

No.	Type	Denomination & Color	Unused	Used
1448	A508	20b bl gray	.18	.15
1449	A508	20b vermilion	.18	.15
1450	A508	55b ultra	.48	.22
1451	A508	55b blue	.48	.22
		Nos. 1448-1451 (4)	1.32	
		Set value		.60

Perf. 10¹/₂
Size: 33x33mm

Gold Medals: 35b, Pistol shooting, Melbourne. 40b, Sharpshooting, Rome. 55b, Wrestling. 1.35 l, Woman's high jump. 1.75 l, Three medals for canoeing.

Medals in Ocher

No.	Type	Denomination & Color	Unused	Used
1452	A509	10b Prus grn	.18	.15
1453	A509	35b brown	.35	.15
1454	A509	40b plum	.38	.15
1455	A509	55b org red	.48	.15
1456	A509	1.35 l dp ultra	.80	.18

Size: 46x32mm

No.	Type	Denomination & Color	Unused	Used
1457	A509	1.75 l dp car rose	1.50	.38
		Nos. 1452-1457 (6)	3.69	
		Set value		.88

Romania's gold medals in 1956, 1960 Olympics. #1452-1457 exist imperf. Value, set $3.75.

A souvenir sheet of one 4 l dark red & ocher was issued. Value unused $4.25, canceled $3.25.

Congress Emblem A510

Primrose A511

1961, Dec. Litho. *Perf.* $13^1/_2$x14

1458 A510 55b dk car rose .48 .24

5th World Congress of Trade Unions, Moscow, Dec. 4-16.

***Perf.* $14x13^1/_2$, $13^1/_2$x14**

1961, Sept. 15

Designs: 20b, Sweet William. 25b, Peony. 35b, Prickly pear. 40b, Iris. 55b, Buttercup. 1 l, Hepatica. 1.20 l, Poppy. 1.55 l, Gentian. 1.75 l, Carol Davilla and Dimitrie Brindza. 20b, 25b, 40b, 55b, 1.20 l, 1.55 l, are vertical.

1459 A511 10b multi .15 .15
1460 A511 20b multi .15 .15
1461 A511 25b multi .15 .15
1462 A511 35b multi .18 .15
1463 A511 40b multi .22 .15
1464 A511 55b multi .28 .15
1465 A511 1 l multi .38 .15
1466 A511 1.20 l multi .45 .15
1467 A511 1.55 l multi .90 .24
Nos. 1459-1467 (9) 2.86
Set value .75

Souvenir Sheet

Imperf

1468 A511 1.75 l car, blk & grn 3.00 2.00

Bucharest Botanical Garden, cent.
No. 1459-1467 exist imperf. Value, set $3.

United Nations Emblem — A512

Cock and Savings Book — A513

Designs: 20b, Map of Balkan peninsula and dove. 40b, Men of three races.

1961, Nov. 27 *Perf.* $13^1/_2$x14

1469 A512 20b bl, yel & pink .24 .15
1470 A512 40b multi .50 .15
1471 A512 55b org, lil & yel .65 .18
Nos. 1469-1471 (3) 1.39
Set value .32

UN, 15th anniv. Nos. 1469-1470 are each printed with alternating yellow labels.
Exist imperf. Value, set $2.75.

1962, Feb. 15 Typo. *Perf.* $13^1/_2$

Savings Day: 55b, Honeycomb, bee and savings book.

1472 A513 40b multi .24 .15
1473 A513 55b multi .24 .15
Set value .20

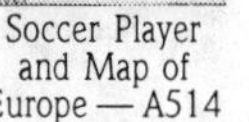

Soccer Player and Map of Europe — A514

Wheat, Map and Tractor — A515

1962, Apr. 20 Litho. *Perf.* 13x14

1474 A514 55b emer & red brn .48 .18

European Junior Soccer Championships, Bucharest. For surcharge see No. 1510.

1962, Apr. 27 *Perf.* $13^1/_2$x14

Designs: 55b, Medal honoring agriculture. 1.55Nl, Sheaf of wheat, hammer & sickle.

1475 A515 40b org & dk car .20 .15
1476 A515 55b yel, car & brn .24 .15
1477 A515 1.55 l multi .70 .18
Nos. 1475-1477 (3) 1.14
Set value .28

Collectivization of agriculture.

Canoe Race A516

Designs: 20b, Kayak. 40b, Eight-man shell. 55b, Two-man skiff. 1 l, Yachts. 1.20 l, Motorboats. 1.55 l, Sailboat. 3 l, Water slalom.

1962, May 15 Photo. *Perf.* 14x13

Vignette in Bright Blue

1478 A516 10b lil rose .15 .15
1479 A516 20b ol gray .15 .15
1480 A516 40b red brn .15 .15
1481 A516 55b ultra .22 .15
1482 A516 1 l red .28 .15
1483 A516 1.20 l dp plum .55 .15
1484 A516 1.55 l orange .75 .15
1485 A516 3 l violet 1.40 .22
Nos. 1478-1485 (8) 3.65
Set value .65

These stamps were also issued imperf. with color of denomination and inscription changed. Value, set unused $4.50, canceled $2.

Ion Luca Caragiale — A517

40b, Jean Jacques Rousseau. 1.75 l, Aleksander I. Herzen. 3.30 l, Ion Luca Caragiale (as a young man).

1962, June 9 *Perf.* $13^1/_2$x14

1486 A517 40b dk sl grn .18 .15
1487 A517 55b magenta .22 .15
1488 A517 1.75 l dp bl .75 .25
Nos. 1486-1488 (3) 1.15
Set value .38

Souvenir Sheet

***Perf.* $11^1/_2$**

1489 A517 3.30 l brown 3.00 1.75

Rousseau, French philosopher, 250th birth anniv.; Caragiale, Romanian author, 50th death anniv.; Herzen, Russian writer, 150th birth anniv. No. 1489 contains one 32x55mm stamp.

Globes Surrounded with Flags — A518

1962, July 6 Typo. *Perf.* 11

1490 A518 55b multi .40 .15

8th Youth Festival for Peace and Friendship, Helsinki, July 28-Aug. 6.

Traian Vuia — A519

Fieldball Player and Globe — A520

Portraits: 20b, Al. Davila. 35b, Vasile Pirvan. 40b, Ion Negulici. 55b, Grigore Cobilcescu. 1 l, Dr. Gheorghe Marinescu. 1.20 l, Ion Cantacuzino. 1.35 l, Victor Babes. 1.55 l, C. Levaditi.

***Perf.* $13^1/_2$x14**

1962, July 20 Photo. Wmk. 358

1491 A519 15b brown .15 .15
1492 A519 20b dl red brn .15 .15
1493 A519 35b brn mag .15 .15
1494 A519 40b bl vio .15 .15
1495 A519 55b brt bl .18 .15
1496 A519 1 l dp ultra .22 .15
1497 A519 1.20 l crimson .38 .15
1498 A519 1.35 l Prus grn .45 .15
1499 A519 1.55 l purple .90 .15
Nos. 1491-1499 (9) 2.73
Set value .65

***Perf.* 13x14**

1962, May 12 Litho. Unwmk.

1500 A520 55b yel & vio .48 .15

2nd Intl. Women's Fieldball Championships, Bucharest.

Same Surcharged in Violet Blue: "Campionana Mondiala 5 lei"

1962, July 31

1501 A520 5 l on 55b yel & vio 4.25 2.10

Romanian victory in the 2nd Intl. Women's Fieldball Championships.

Rod Fishing — A521

Various Fishing Scenes.

1962, July 25 *Perf.* 14x13

1502 A521 10b multi .15 .15
1503 A521 25b multi .15 .15
1504 A521 40b bl & brick red .15 .15
1505 A521 55b multi .20 .15
1506 A521 75b sl, gray & bl .30 .15
1507 A521 1 l multi .48 .15
1508 A521 1.75 l multi .75 .15
1509 A521 3.25 l multi 1.40 .22
Nos. 1502-1509 (8) 3.58
Set value .84

No. 1474 Surcharged in Dark Blue: "1962 Campioana Europeana 2 lei"

1962, July 31

1510 A514 2 l on 55b 1.65 1.00

Romania's victory in the European Junior Soccer Championships, Bucharest.

Child and Butterfly A522

Handicraft A523

Designs: 30b, Girl feeding bird. 40b, Boy and model sailboat. 55b, Children writing, horiz. 1.20 l, Girl at piano, and boy playing violin. 1.55 l, Pioneers camping, horiz.

***Perf.* 13x14, 14x13**

1962, Aug. 25 Litho.

1511 A522 20b lt bl, red & brn .15 .15
1512 A522 30b org, bl & red brn .15 .15
1513 A522 40b chalky bl, dp org & Prus bl .15 .15
1514 A522 55b citron, bl & red .24 .15
1515 A522 1.20 l car, brn & dk vio .38 .15
1516 A522 1.55 l bis, red & vio .70 .15
Nos. 1511-1516 (6) 1.77
Set value .45

1962, Oct. 12 *Perf.* 13x14

Designs: 10b, Food and drink. 20b, Chemical industry. 40b, Chinaware. 55b, Leather industry. 75b, Textiles. 1 l, Furniture. 1.20 l, Electrical appliances. 1.55 l, Household goods (sewing machine and pots).

1517 A523 5b multi .15 .15
1518 A523 10b multi .15 .15
1519 A523 20b multi .15 .15
1520 A523 40b multi .18 .15
1521 A523 55b multi .18 .15
1522 A523 75b multi .22 .15
1523 A523 1 l multi .30 .15
1524 A523 1.20 l multi .55 .15
1525 A523 1.55 l multi .90 .25
Nos. 1517-1525,C126 (10) 3.68
Set value .95

4th Sample Fair, Bucharest.

Lenin — A524

Bull — A525

1962, Nov. 7 *Perf.* $10^1/_2$

1526 A524 55b vio bl, red & bis .35 .15

Russian October Revolution, 45th anniv.

1962, Nov. 20 *Perf.* 14x13, 13x14

Designs: 20b, Sheep, horiz. 40b, Merino ram, horiz. 1 l, York pig. 1.35 l, Cow. 1.55 l, Heifer, horiz. 1.75 l, Pigs, horiz.

1527 A525 20b ultra & blk .15 .15
1528 A525 40b bl, yel & sep .15 .15
1529 A525 55b ocher, buff & sl grn .18 .15
1530 A525 1 l gray, yel & brn .28 .15
1531 A525 1.35 l dl grn, choc & blk .38 .15
1532 A525 1.55 l org red, dk brn & blk .60 .18
1533 A525 1.75 l dk vio bl, yel & org .75 .32
Nos. 1527-1533 (7) 2.49
Set value .85

Arms, Factory and Harvester A526

***Perf.* $14^1/_2$x$13^1/_2$**

1962, Dec. 30 Litho.

1534 A526 1.55 l multi .90 .18

Romanian People's Republic, 15th anniv.

Strikers at Grivita, 1933 — A527

1963, Feb. 16 *Perf.* $14x13^1/_2$

1535 A527 1.75 l red, vio & yel .70 .18

30th anniv. of the strike of railroad and oil industry workers at Grivita.

Tractor Driver and "FAO" Emblem A528

Tomatoes A529

55b, Farm woman, cornfield & combine. 1.55 l, Child drinking milk & milking machine. 1.75 l, Woman with basket of grapes & vineyard.

1963, Mar. 21 Photo. *Perf. 14½x13*

1536 A528 40b vio bl .15 .15
1537 A528 55b bis brn .15 .15
1538 A528 1.55 l rose red .45 .15
1539 A528 1.75 l green .75 .25
Nos. 1536-1539 (4) 1.50
Set value .46

FAO "Freedom from Hunger" campaign.

Perf. 13½x14, 14x13½
1963, Apr. 25 Litho. Unwmk.

40b, Hot peppers. 55b, Radishes. 75b, Eggplant. 1.20 l, Mild peppers. 3.25 l, Cucumbers, horiz.

1540 A529 35b multi .15 .15
1541 A529 40b multi .15 .15
1542 A529 55b multi .16 .15
1543 A529 75b multi .22 .15
1544 A529 1.20 l multi .60 .15
1545 A529 3.25 l multi 1.40 .32
Nos. 1540-1545 (6) 2.68
Set value .62

Woman Swimmer at Start — A530

Chicks — A531

Designs: 30b, Crawl, horiz. 55b, Butterfly stroke, horiz. 1 l, Backstroke, horiz. 1.35 l, Breast-stroke, horiz. 1.55 l, Woman diver. 2 l, Water polo.

1963, June 15 *Perf. 13x14, 14x13*

1546 A530 25b yel brn, emer & gray .15 .15
1547 A530 30b ol grn, gray & yel .15 .15
1548 A530 55b bl, gray & red .18 .15
1549 A530 1 l grn, gray & red .28 .15
1550 A530 1.35 l ultra, car & gray .38 .15
1551 A530 1.55 l pur, gray & org .70 .15
1552 A530 2 l car rose, gray & org .75 .35
Nos. 1546-1552 (7) 2.59
Set value .75

1963, May 23 *Perf. 10½*

Domestic poultry: 30b, Hen. 40b, Goose. 55b, White cock. 70b, Duck. 1 l, Hen. 1.35 l, Tom turkey. 3.20 l, Hen.

Fowl in Natural Colors; Inscription in Dark Blue

1553 A531 20b ultra .15 .15
1554 A531 30b tan .15 .15
1555 A531 40b org brn .15 .15
1556 A531 55b brt grn .15 .15
1557 A531 70b lilac .28 .15
1558 A531 1 l blue .38 .15
1559 A531 1.35 l ocher .55 .15
1560 A531 3.20 l yel grn 1.10 .38
Nos. 1553-1560 (8) 2.91
Set value .75

Women and Globe — A532

1963, June 15 Photo. *Perf. 14x13*

1561 A532 55b dark blue .28 .15

Intl. Women's Cong., Moscow, June 24-29.

William M. Thackeray, Writer — A533

Portraits: 50b, Eugene Delacroix, painter. 55b, Gheorghe Marinescu, physician. 1.55 l, Giuseppe Verdi, composer. 1.75 l, Stanislavski, actor and producer.

1963, July Unwmk. *Perf. 14x13*

Portrait in Black

1562 A533 40b pale vio .15 .15
1563 A533 50b bis brn .18 .15
1564 A533 55b olive .24 .15
1565 A533 1.55 l rose brn .48 .15
1566 A533 1.75 l pale vio bl .75 .15
Nos. 1562-1566 (5) 1.80
Set value .48

Walnuts A534

Designs: 20b, Plums. 40b, Peaches. 55b, Strawberries. 1 l, Grapes. 1.55 l, Apples. 1.60 l, Cherries. 1.75 l, Pears.

1963, Sept. 15 Litho. *Perf. 14x13½*

Fruits in Natural Colors

1567 A534 10b pale yel & brn ol .15 .15
1568 A534 20b pale pink & red org .15 .15
1569 A534 40b lt bl & bl .15 .15
1570 A534 55b dl yel & rose car .15 .15
1571 A534 1 l pale vio & vio .28 .15
1572 A534 1.55 l yel grn & ultra .45 .15
1573 A534 1.60 l yel & bis .75 .15
1574 A534 1.75 l lt bl & grn .75 .15
Nos. 1567-1574 (8) 2.83
Set value .58

Women Playing Volleyball and Map of Europe — A535

40b, 3 men players. 55b, 3 women players. 1.75 l, 2 men players. 3.20 l, Europa Cup.

1963, Oct. 22 *Perf. 13½x14*

1575 A535 5b gray & lil rose .15 .15
1576 A535 40b gray & vio bl .18 .15
1577 A535 55b gray & grnsh bl .30 .15
1578 A535 1.75 l gray & org brn .55 .15
1579 A535 3.20 l gray & vio 1.10 .38
Nos. 1575-1579 (5) 2.28
Set value .70

European Volleyball Championships, Oct. 22-Nov. 4.

Pine Tree, Branch and Cone — A536

Design: 1.75 l, Beech forest and branch.

Perf. 13½
1963, Dec. 5 Unwmk. Photo.

1580 A536 55b dk grn .16 .15
1581 A536 1.75 l dk bl .50 .15
Set value .23

Reforestation program.

Silkworm Moth — A537

18th Century House, Ploesti — A538

Designs: 20b, Chrysalis, moth and worm. 40b, Silkworm on leaf. 55b, Bee over mountains, horiz. 60b, 1.20 l, 1.35 l, 1.60 l, Bees pollinating various flowers, horiz.

1963, Dec. 12 Litho. *Perf. 13x14*

1582 A537 10b multi .15 .15
1583 A537 20b multi .15 .15
1584 A537 40b multi .18 .15
1585 A537 55b multi .28 .15
1586 A537 60b multi .38 .15
1587 A537 1.20 l multi .60 .15
1588 A537 1.35 l multi .75 .22
1589 A537 1.60 l multi 1.10 .25
Nos. 1582-1589 (8) 3.59
Set value .90

1963, Dec. 25 Engr. *Perf. 13*

Peasant Houses from Village Museum, Bucharest: 40b, Oltenia, 1875, horiz. 55b, Hunedoara, 19th Cent., horiz. 75b, Oltenia, 19th Cent. 1 l, Brasov, 1847. 1.20 l, Bacau, 19th Cent. 1.75 l, Arges, 19th Cent.

1590 A538 20b claret .15 .15
1591 A538 40b blue .15 .15
1592 A538 55b dl vio .18 .15
1593 A538 75b green .22 .15
1594 A538 1 l brn & mar .38 .15
1595 A538 1.20 l gray ol .45 .15
1596 A538 1.75 l dk brn & ultra .85 .18
Nos. 1590-1596 (7) 2.38
Set value .60

Ski Jump A539

20b, Speed skating. 40b, Ice hockey. 55b, Women's figure skating. 60b, Slalom. 75b, Biathlon. 1 l, Bobsledding. 1.20 l, Cross-country skiing.

1963, Nov. 25 Litho. *Perf. 14*

1597 A539 10b red & dk bl .15 .15
1598 A539 20b ultra & red brn .15 .15
1599 A539 40b emer & red brn .20 .15
1600 A539 55b vio & red brn .30 .15
1601 A539 60b org & vio bl .40 .15
1602 A539 75b lil rose & dk bl .50 .15
1603 A539 1 l bis & vio bl .85 .24
1604 A539 1.20 l grnsh bl & vio .90 .35
Nos. 1597-1604 (8) 3.45
Set value 1.05

9th Winter Olympic Games, Innsbruck, Jan. 29-Feb. 9, 1964.

Exist imperf. in changed colors. Value, set $5.50.

A souvenir sheet contains one imperf. 1.50 l ultramarine and red stamp showing the Olympic Ice Stadium at Innsbruck and the Winter Games emblem. Value $5.50.

Elena Teodorini as Carmen — A540

Munteanu Murgoci and Congress Emblem — A541

Designs: 10b, George Stephanescu, founder of Romanian opera. 35b, Ion Bajenaru as Petru Rares. 40b, D. Popovici as Alberich. 55b, Hariclea Darclée as Tosca. 75b, George Folescu as Boris Godunov. 1 l, Jean Athanasiu as Rigoletto. 1.35 l, Traian Grosavescu as Duke in Rigoletto. 1.55 l, N. Leonard as Hoffmann.

1964, Jan. 20 Photo. *Perf. 13*

Portrait in Dark Brown

1605 A540 10b olive .15 .15
1606 A540 20b ultra .15 .15
1607 A540 35b green .15 .15
1608 A540 40b grnsh bl .15 .15
1609 A540 55b car rose .18 .15
1610 A540 75b lilac .18 .15
1611 A540 1 l blue .55 .15
1612 A540 1.35 l brt vio .75 .15
1613 A540 1.55 l red org .85 .22
Nos. 1605-1613 (9) 3.11
Set value .75

1964, Feb. 5 Unwmk. *Perf. 13*

1614 A541 1.60 l brt bl, ind & bis .70 .18

8th Intl. Soil Congress, Bucharest.

Asculaphid A542

Insects: 10b, Thread-waisted wasp. 35b, Wasp. 40b, Rhyparioides metelkana moth. 55b, Tussock moth. 1.20 l, Kanetisa circe butterfly. 1.55 l, Beetle. 1.75 l, Horned beetle.

1964, Feb. 20 Litho. *Perf. 14x13*

Insects in Natural Colors

1615 A542 5b pale lilac .15 .15
1616 A542 10b lt bl & red .15 .15
1617 A542 35b pale grn .15 .15
1618 A542 40b olive green .18 .15
1619 A542 55b ultra .20 .15
1620 A542 1.20 l pale grn & red .40 .15
1621 A542 1.55 l yel & brn .60 .15
1622 A542 1.75 l orange & red .65 .18
Nos. 1615-1622 (8) 2.48
Set value .76

Tobacco Plant — A543

Jumping — A544

Garden flowers: 20b, Geranium. 40b, Fuchsia. 55b, Chrysanthemum. 75b, Dahlia. 1 l, Lily. 1.25 l, Day lily. 1.55 l, Marigold.

1964, Mar. 25 *Perf. 13x14*

1623 A543 10b dk bl, grn & bis .15 .15
1624 A543 20b gray, grn & red .15 .15
1625 A543 40b pale grn, grn & red .18 .15
1626 A543 55b grn, lt grn & lil .22 .15
1627 A543 75b cit, red & grn .24 .15
1628 A543 1 l dp cl, rose cl, grn & org .40 .15
1629 A543 1.25 l sal, vio bl & grn .42 .18
1630 A543 1.55 l red brn, yel & grn .55 .18
Nos. 1623-1630 (8) 2.31
Set value .70

Unwmk.
1964, Apr. 25 Photo. *Perf. 13*

Horse Show Events: 40b, Dressage, horiz. 1.35 l, Jumping. 1.55 l, Galloping, horiz.

1631 A544 40b lt bl, rose brn & blk .15 .15
1632 A544 55b lil, red & brn .18 .15
1633 A544 1.35 l brt grn, red & dk brn .55 .15
1634 A544 1.55 l pale yel, bl & dp claret .80 .20
Nos. 1631-1634 (4) 1.68
Set value .46

Hogfish A545

Mihail Eminescu A546

Fish (Constanta Aquarium): 10b, Peacock blenny. 20b, Mediterranean scad. 40b, Sturgeon. 50b, Sea horses. 55b, Yellow gurnard. 1 l, Beluga. 3.20 l, Stingray.

1964, May 10 Litho. *Perf. 14*

1635 A545 5b multi .15 .15
1636 A545 10b multi .15 .15
1637 A545 20b multi .15 .15
1638 A545 40b multi .15 .15
1639 A545 50b multi .18 .15
1640 A545 55b multi .18 .15
1641 A545 1 l multi .45 .15
1642 A545 3.20 l multi 1.10 .22
Set value (8) 2.20 .65

1964, June 20 Photo. *Perf. 13*

Portraits: 20b, Ion Creanga. 35b, Emil Girleanu. 55b, Michelangelo. 1.20 l, Galileo Galilei. 1.75 l, William Shakespeare.

Portraits in Dark Brown

1643 A546 5b green .15 .15
1644 A546 20b magenta .15 .15
1645 A546 35b vermilion .25 .15
1646 A546 55b bister .28 .15
1647 A546 1.20 l ultra .52 .16
1648 A546 1.75 l violet .90 .25
Nos. 1643-1648 (6) 2.25
Set value .62

50th death anniv. of Emil Girleanu, writer; the 75th death anniversaries of Ion Creanga and Mihail Eminescu, writers; the 400th anniv. of the death of Michelangelo and the births of Galileo and Shakespeare.

Road through Gorge — A547

High Jump — A548

Tourist Publicity: 55b, Lake Bilea and cottage. 1 l, Ski lift, Polana Brasov. 1.35 l, Ceahlaul peak and Lake Bicaz, horiz. 1.75 l, Hotel Alpin.

1964, June 29 Engr.

1649 A547 40b rose brn .15 .15
1650 A547 55b dk bl .18 .15
1651 A547 1 l dl pur .30 .15
1652 A547 1.35 l pale brn .45 .15
1653 A547 1.75 l green .55 .22
Nos. 1649-1653 (5) 1.63
Set value .50

1964, July 28 Photo.

1964 Balkan Games: 40b, Javelin throw. 55b, Running. 1 l, Discus throw. 1.20 l, Hurdling. 1.55 l, Map and flags of Balkan countries.

Size: 23x37½mm

1654 A548 30b ver, yel & yel grn .15 .15
1655 A548 40b grn, yel, brn & vio .15 .15
1656 A548 55b gldn brn, yel & bl grn .22 .15
1657 A548 1 l brt bl, yel, brn & red .45 .15
1658 A548 1.20 l pur, yel, brn & grn .55 .15

Litho.

Size: 23x45mm

1659 A548 1.55 l multi .90 .22
Nos. 1654-1659 (6) 2.42
Set value .60

Factory — A549

55b, Flag, Coat of Arms, vert. 75b, Combine. 1.20 l, Apartment buildings. 2 l, Flag, coat of arms, industrial & agricultural scenes. 55b, 2 l, Inscribed "A XX A aniversare a eliberarii patriei!"

1964, Aug. 23 Photo. *Perf. 13*

1660 A549 55b multi .16 .15
1661 A549 60b multi .24 .15
1662 A549 75b multi .24 .15
1663 A549 1.20 l multi .48 .15
Nos. 1660-1663 (4) 1.12
Set value .44

Souvenir Sheet

Imperf

1664 A549 2 l multi 1.25 .55

20th anniv. of Romania's liberation. No. 1664 contains one stamp 110x70mm.

High Jump A550

Sport: 30b, Wrestling. 35b, Volleyball. 40b, Canoeing. 55b, Fencing. 1.20 l, Women's gymnastics. 1.35 l, Soccer. 1.55 l, Sharpshooting.

1964, Sept. 1 Litho.

Olympic Rings in Blue, Yellow, Black, Green and Red

1665 A550 20b yel & blk .20 .15
1666 A550 30b lilac & blk .20 .15
1667 A550 35b grnsh bl & blk .20 .15
1668 A550 40b pink & blk .22 .15
1669 A550 55b lt yel grn & blk .32 .15
1670 A550 1.20 l org & blk .65 .15
1671 A550 1.35 l ocher & blk .80 .22
1672 A550 1.55 l bl & blk .90 .35
Nos. 1665-1672 (8) 3.49
Set value .95

18th Olympic Games, Tokyo, Oct. 10-25.

Nos. 1665-1669 exist imperf., in changed colors. Three other denominations exist, 1.60 l, 2 l and 2.40 l, imperf. Value, set of 8, unused $5.50, canceled $4.

An imperf. souvenir sheet contains a 3.25 l stamp showing a runner. Value unused $5.50 canceled $5.

George Enescu, Piano Keys and Neck of Violin — A551

Designs: 55b, Enescu at piano. 1.60 l, Enescu Festival medal. 1.75 l, Enescu bust by G. Anghel.

1964, Sept. 5 Engr.

1673 A551 10b bl grn .15 .15
1674 A551 55b vio blk .18 .15
1675 A551 1.60 l dk red brn .48 .20
1676 A551 1.75 l dk bl .85 .22
Nos. 1673-1676 (4) 1.66
Set value .54

3rd Intl. George Enescu Festival, Bucharest, Sept., 1964.

Black Swans A552

Designs: 5b, Indian python. 35b, Ostriches. 40b, Crowned cranes. 55b, Tigers. 1 l, Lions. 1.55 l, Grevy's zebras. 2 l, Bactrian camels.

Perf. 14x13

1964, Sept. 28 Litho. Unwmk.

1677 A552 5b multi .15 .15
1678 A552 10b multi .15 .15
1679 A552 35b multi .15 .15
1680 A552 40b multi .18 .15
1681 A552 55b multi .22 .15
1682 A552 1 l multi .38 .15
1683 A552 1.55 l multi .75 .16
1684 A552 2 l multi 1.00 .22
Nos. 1677-1684 (8) 2.98
Set value .70

Issued to publicize the Bucharest Zoo. No. 1683 inscribed "BANI."

C. Brincoveanu, Stolnicul Cantacuzino, Gheorghe Lazar and Academy A553

Designs: 40b, Alexandru Ioan Cuza, medal and University. 55b, Masks, curtain, harp, keyboard and palette, vert. 75b, Women students in laboratory and auditorium. 1 l, Savings Bank building.

Perf. 13x13½, 13½x13

1964, Oct. 14 Photo.

1685 A553 20b multi .15 .15
1686 A553 40b multi .15 .15
1687 A553 55b multi .20 .15
1688 A553 75b multi .24 .15
1689 A553 1 l dk brn, yel & org .40 .18
Nos. 1685-1689 (5) 1.14
Set value .45

No. 1685 for 250th anniv. of the Royal Academy; Nos. 1686, 1688 cent. of the University of Bucharest; No. 1687 cent. of the Academy of Art and No. 1689 cent. of the Savings Bank.

Soldier's Head and Laurel — A554

1964, Oct. 25 Litho. *Perf. 12x12½*

1690 A554 55b ultra & lt bl .28 .15

Army Day.

Canadian Kayak Singles Gold Medal, Melbourne, 1956 — A555

Romanian Olympic Gold Medals: 30b, Boxing, Melbourne, 1956. 35b, Rapid Silhouette Pistol, Melbourne, 1956. 40b, Women's High Jump, Rome, 1960. 55b, Wrestling, Rome, 1960. 1.20 l, Clay Pigeon Shooting, Rome, 1960. 1.35 l, Women's High Jump, Tokyo, 1964. 1.55 l, Javelin, Tokyo, 1964.

1964, Nov. 30 Photo. *Perf. 13½*

Medals in Gold and Brown

1691 A555 20b pink & ultra .15 .15
1692 A555 30b yel grn & ultra .20 .15
1693 A555 35b bluish grn & ultra .28 .15
1694 A555 40b lil & ultra .40 .15
1695 A555 55b org & ultra .48 .15
1696 A555 1.20 l ol grn & ultra .70 .18
1697 A555 1.35 l gldn brn & ultra .90 .26
1698 A555 1.55 l rose lil & ultra 1.25 .38
Nos. 1691-1698 (8) 4.36
Set value 1.00

Romanian athletes who won gold medals in three Olympic Games.

Nos. 1691-1695 exist imperf., in changed colors. Three other denominations exist, 1.60 l, 2 l and 2.40 l, imperf. Value, set of 8, unused $5.75, canceled $4.

A 10 l souvenir sheet shows the 1964 Olympic gold medal and world map. Value unused $5.50, canceled $4.

Strawberries — A556

Designs: 35b, Blackberries. 40b, Raspberries. 55b, Rose hips. 1.20 l, Blueberries. 1.35 l, Cornelian cherries. 1.55 l, Hazelnuts. 2.55 l, Cherries.

1964, Dec. 20 Litho. *Perf. 13½x14*

1703 A556 5b gray, red & grn .15 .15
1704 A556 35b ocher, grn & dk vio bl .15 .15
1705 A556 40b pale vio, car & grn .15 .15
1706 A556 55b yel grn, grn & red .15 .15
1707 A556 1.20 l sal pink, grn, brn & ind .38 .15
1708 A556 1.35 l lt bl, grn & red .42 .15
1709 A556 1.55 l gldn brn, grn & ocher .75 .18
1710 A556 2.55 l ultra, grn & red 1.50 .25
Nos. 1703-1710 (8) 3.65
Set value .75

Syncom 3 — A557

UN Headquarters, NY — A558

Space Satellites: 40b, Syncom 3 over TV antennas. 55b, Ranger 7 reaching moon, horiz. 1 l, Ranger 7 and moon close-up, horiz. 1.20 l, Voskhod. 5 l, Konstantin Feoktistov, Vladimir M. Komarov, Boris B. Yegorov and Voskhod.

Perf. 13x14, 14x13

1965, Jan. 5 Litho. Unwmk.

Size: 22x38mm, 38x22mm

1711 A557 30b multi .16 .15
1712 A557 40b multi .35 .15
1713 A557 55b multi .42 .15
1714 A557 1 l multi .50 .15
1715 A557 1.20 l multi, horiz. .85 .15

Perf. 13½x13

Size: 52x30mm

1716 A557 5 l multi 2.00 .52
Nos. 1711-1716 (6) 4.28
Set value .88

For surcharge see No. 1737.

1965, Jan. 25 *Perf. 12x12½*

1.60 l, Arms, flag of Romania, UN emblem.

1717 A558 55b ultra, red & gold .38 .15
1718 A558 1.60 l ultra, red, gold & yel .75 .16

20th anniv. of the UN and 10th anniv. of Romania's membership in the UN.

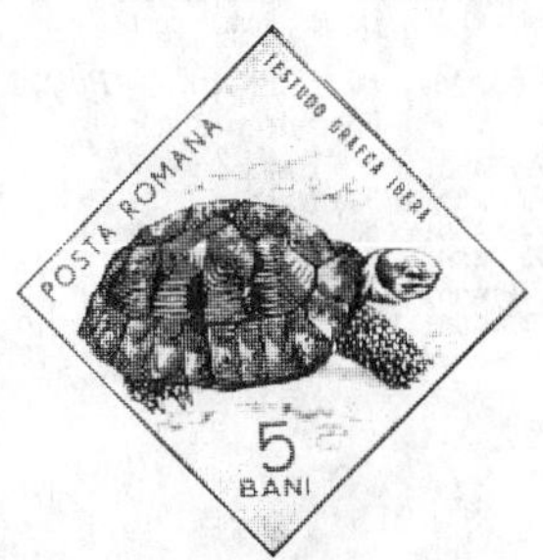

Greek Tortoise — A559

Reptiles: 10b, Bull lizard. 20b, Three-lined lizard. 40b, Sand lizard. 55b, Slow worm. 60b, Sand viper. 1 l, Desert lizard. 1.20 l, Orsini's viper. 1.35 l, Caspian whipsnake. 3.25 l, Four-lined snake.

1965, Feb. 25 Photo. *Perf. 13½*

1719 A559 5b multi .15 .15
1720 A559 10b multi .15 .15
1721 A559 20b multi .15 .15
1722 A559 40b multi .15 .15
1723 A559 55b multi .18 .15
1724 A559 60b multi .28 .15
1725 A559 1 l multi .38 .15
1726 A559 1.20 l multi .45 .15
1727 A559 1.35 l multi .60 .18
1728 A559 3.25 l multi 1.10 .25
Nos. 1719-1728 (10) 3.59
Set value .90

White Persian Cats — A560

Designs: 1.35 l, Siamese cat. Others, Various European cats. (5b, 10b, 3.25 l, horiz.)

1965, Mar. 20 **Litho.**
Size: 41x29mm, 29x41mm
Cats in Natural Colors

1729	A560	5b brn org & blk	.15	.15
1730	A560	10b brt bl & blk	.15	.15
1731	A560	40b yel grn, yel & blk	.15	.15
1732	A560	55b rose red & blk	.24	.15
1733	A560	60b yel & blk	.40	.15
1734	A560	75b lt vio & blk	.48	.15
1735	A560	1.35 l red org & blk	.85	.15

Perf. 13x13½
Size: 62x29mm

1736	A560	3.25 l blue	1.65	.35
		Nos. 1729-1736 (8)	4.07	
		Set value		.88

No. 1714 Surcharged in Violet

RANGER 9
24 - 3 - 1965

5 Lei

1965, Apr. 25 ***Perf. 14x13***

1737	A557	5 l on 1 l multi	12.50	12.50

Flight of the US rocket Ranger 9 to the moon, Mar. 24, 1965.

Dante Alighieri — A561

Portraits: 40b, Ion Bianu, philologist and historian. 55b, Anton Bacalbasa, writer. 60b, Vasile Conta, philosopher. 1 l, Jean Sibelius, Finnish composer. 1.35 l, Horace, Roman poet.

1965, May 10 **Photo.** ***Perf. 13½***
Portrait in Black

1738	A561	40b chalky blue	.15	.15
1739	A561	55b bister	.18	.15
1740	A561	60b light lilac	.22	.15
1741	A561	1 l dl red brn	.45	.15
1742	A561	1.35 l olive	.60	.18
1743	A561	1.75 l orange red	1.10	.24
		Nos. 1738-1743 (6)	2.70	
		Set value		.70

ITU Emblem, Old and New Communication Equipment — A562

1965, May 15 **Engr.**

1744	A562	1.75 l ultra	.90	.38

ITU, centenary.

Iron Gate, Danube A562a

Arms of Yugoslavia and Romania and Djerdap Dam — A562b

55b (50d), Iron Gate hydroelectric plant & dam.

Perf. 12½x12
1965, May 20 **Litho.** **Unwmk.**

1745	A562a	30b (25d) lt bl & grn	.15	.15
1746	A562a	55b (50d) lt bl & dk red	.24	.15
		Set value	.28	.15

Miniature Sheet
Perf. 13½x13

1747	A562b	Sheet of 4	2.50	2.50
a.		80b multi	.22	.15
b.		1.20 l multi	.40	.22

Issued simultaneously by Romania and Yugoslavia for the start of construction of the Iron Gate hydroelectric plant and dam. Valid for postage in both countries.

No. 1747 contains one each of Nos. 1747a, 1747b and Yugoslavia Nos. 771a and 771b. Only Nos. 1747a and 1747b were valid in Romania. Sold for 4 l. See Yugoslavia Nos. 769-771.

Small-bore Rifle Shooting, Kneeling — A563

Designs: 40b, Rifle shooting, prone. 55b, Rapid-fire pistol and map of Europe. 1 l, Free pistol and map of Europe. 1.60 l, Small-bore rifle, standing, and map of Europe. 2 l, 5 l, Marksmen in various shooting positions (all horizontal).

Perf. 12x12½, 12½x12
1965, May 30 **Litho.** **Unwmk.**
Size: 23x43mm, 43x23mm

1748	A563	20b multi	.15	.15
1749	A563	40b dl grn, pink & blk	.15	.15
1750	A563	55b multi	.18	.15
1751	A563	1 l pale grn, blk & ocher	.38	.15
1752	A563	1.60 l multi	.60	.15

Perf. 13½
Size: 51x28mm

1753	A563	2 l multi	.75	.20
		Nos. 1748-1753 (6)	2.21	
		Set value		.50

European Shooting Championships, Bucharest.

Nos. 1749-1752 were issued imperf. in changed colors. Two other denominations exist, 3.25 l and 5 l, imperf. Value, set of 6, unused $4.25, canceled $1.75.

Fat-Frumos and the Giant — A564

Fairy Tales: 40b, Fat-Frumos on horseback and Ileana Cosinzeana. 55b, Harap Alb and the Bear. 1 l, "The Moralist Wolf." 1.35 l, "The Ox and the Calif." 2 l, Wolf and bear pulling sled.

1965, June 25 **Photo.** ***Perf. 13***

1756	A564	20b multi	.18	.15
1757	A564	40b multi	.18	.15
1758	A564	55b multi	.22	.15
1759	A564	1 l multi	.40	.15
1760	A564	1.35 l multi	.60	.15
1761	A564	2 l multi	.85	.22
		Nos. 1756-1761 (6)	2.43	
		Set value		.52

Bee and Blossoms A565

Space Achievements A566

Design: 1.60 l, Exhibition Hall, horiz.

Perf. 12x12½, 12½x12
1965, July 28 **Litho.** **Unwmk.**

1762	A565	55b org, bl & pink	.28	.15
1763	A565	1.60 l multi	.50	.18

20th Congress of the Intl Federation of Beekeeping Assocs. (Apimondia), Bucharest, Aug. 26-31.

1965, Aug. 25 **Litho.** ***Perf. 12x12½***

Designs: 1.75 l, Col. Pavel Belyayev, Lt. Col. Alexei Leonov and Voskhod 2. 2.40 l, Early Bird over globe. 3.20 l, Lt. Col. Gordon Cooper and Lt. Com. Charles Conrad, Gemini 3 and globe.

1764	A566	1.75 l dk bl, bl & ver	.80	.15
1765	A566	2.40 l multi	1.10	.16
1766	A566	3.20 l dk bl, lt bl & ver	2.25	.35
		Nos. 1764-1766 (3)	4.15	.66

European Quail — A567

Birds: 10b, Eurasian woodcock. 20b, Eurasian snipe. 40b, Turtle dove. 55b, Mallard. 60b, White-fronted goose. 1 l, Eurasian crane. 1.20 l, Glossy ibis. 1.35 l, Mute swan. 3.25 l, White pelican.

1965, Sept. 10 **Photo.** ***Perf. 13½***
Size: 34x34mm
Birds in Natural Colors

1767	A567	5b red brn & rose lil	.15	.15
1768	A567	10b red brn & yel grn	.15	.15
1769	A567	20b brn & bl grn	.18	.15
1770	A567	40b lil & org brn	.22	.15
1771	A567	55b brt grn & lt brn	.25	.15
1772	A567	60b dl org & bl	.32	.15
1773	A567	1 l red & lil	.42	.15
1774	A567	1.20 l dk brn & grn	.60	.15
1775	A567	1.35 l org & ultra	.80	.15

Size: 32x73mm

1776	A567	3.25 l ultra & sep	2.10	.32
		Nos. 1767-1776 (10)	5.19	
		Set value		.85

Marx and Lenin A568

Vasile Alecsandri A569

1965, Sept. 6 **Photo.**

1777	A568	55b red, blk & yel	.38	.18

6th Conference of Postal Ministers of Communist Countries, Peking, June 21-July 15.

1965, Oct. 9 **Unwmk.** ***Perf. 13½***

1778	A569	55b red brn, dk brn & gold	.38	.18

Alecsandri (1821-1890), statesman and poet.

Bird-of-Paradise Flower — A570

Flowers from Cluj Botanical Gardens: 10b, Stanhope orchid. 20b, Paphiopedilum insigne. 30b, Zanzibar water lily, horiz. 40b, Ferocactus, horiz. 55b, Cotton blossom, horiz. 1 l, Hibiscus, horiz. 1.35 l, Gloxinia. 1.75 l, Victoria water lily, horiz. 2.30 l, Hibiscus, bird-of-paradise flower and greenhouse.

Perf. 12x12½, 12½x12
1965, Oct. 25 **Litho.**
Size: 23x43mm, 43x23mm
Flowers in Natural Colors

1779	A570	5b brown	.15	.15
1780	A570	10b green	.15	.15
1781	A570	20b dk bl	.15	.15
1782	A570	30b vio bl	.15	.15
1783	A570	40b red brn	.15	.15
1784	A570	55b dk red	.15	.15
1785	A570	1 l ol grn	.30	.15
1786	A570	1.35 l violet	.48	.15
1787	A570	1.75 l dk grn	.80	.15

Perf. 13½
Size: 52x30mm

1788	A570	2.30 l green	1.10	.35
		Set value (10)	3.15	.85

The orchid on No. 1780 is attached to the bottom of the limb.

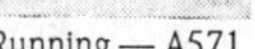

Running — A571

Pigeon and Post Horn — A572

1965, Nov. 10 **Photo.** ***Perf. 13½***

1789	A571	55b shown	.15	.15
1790	A571	1.55 l Soccer	.48	.15
1791	A571	1.75 l Woman diver	.55	.15
1792	A571	2 l Mountaineering	.60	.15
1793	A571	5 l Canoeing, horiz.	1.40	.30
		Nos. 1789-1793 (5)	3.18	
		Set value		.68

Spartacist Games. No. 1793 commemorates the Romanian victory in the European Kayak Championships.

1965, Nov. 15 **Engr.**

Designs: 1 l, Pigeon on television antenna and post horn, horiz. 1.75 l, Flying pigeon and post horn, horiz.

1794	A572	55b + 45b label	.38	.15
1795	A572	1 l green & brown	.38	.15
1796	A572	1.75 l olive grn & sepia	.85	.20
		Nos. 1794-1796 (3)	1.61	
		Set value		.38

Issued for Stamp Day. No. 1794 is printed with alternating label showing post rider and emblem of Romanian Philatelists' Association and 45b additional charge. Stamp and label are imperf. between.

Chamois and Hunting Trophy A573

Hunting Trophy and: 1 l, Brown bear. 1.60 l, Red deer. 1.75 l, Wild boar. 3.20 l, Antlers of red deer.

1965, Dec. 10 **Photo.** ***Perf. 13½***
Size: 37x22mm

1797	A573	55b rose lil, yel & brn	.15	.15
1798	A573	1 l brt grn, red & brn	.28	.15
1799	A573	1.60 l lt vio bl, org & brn	.70	.15
1800	A573	1.75 l rose, grn & blk	.90	.15

Size: 48x36½mm

1801	A573	3.20 l gray, gold, blk & org	1.40	.30
		Nos. 1797-1801 (5)	3.43	
		Set value		.58

Probe III Photographing Moon — A574

Designs: 5b, Proton I space station, vert. 15b, Molniya I telecommunication satellite, vert. 3.25 l, Mariner IV and Mars picture, vert. 5 l, Gemini 5.

Perf. 12x12½, 12½x12

1965, Dec. 25 **Litho.**

1802	A574	5b multi	.15	.15
1803	A574	10b vio bl, red & gray	.15	.15
1804	A574	15b pur, gray & org	.18	.15
1805	A574	3.25 l vio bl, blk & red	2.25	.22
1806	A574	5 l dk bl, gray & red org	3.50	.45
		Nos. 1802-1806 (5)	6.23	
		Set value		.80

Achievements in space research.

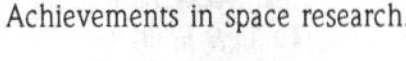

Cocker Spaniel — A575

Hunting Dogs: 5b, Dachshund (triangle). 40b, Retriever. 55b, Terrier. 60b, Red setter. 75b, White setter. 1.55 l, Pointers (rectangle). 3.25 l, Duck hunter with retriever (rectangle).

1965, Dec. 28 **Photo.** ***Perf. 13½***

Size: 30x42mm

1807	A575	5b multi	.15	.15

Size: 33½x33½mm

1808	A575	10b multi	.15	.15
1809	A575	40b multi	.24	.15
1810	A575	55b multi	.35	.15
1811	A575	60b multi	.50	.15
1812	A575	75b multi	.70	.15

Size: 43x28mm

1813	A575	1.55 l multi	1.40	.15
1814	A575	3.25 l multi	2.75	.75
		Nos. 1807-1814 (8)	6.24	
		Set value		1.20

Chessboard, Queen and Jester — A576

Chessboard and: 20b, 1.60 l, Pawn and emblem. 55b, 1 l, Rook and knight on horseback.

1966, Feb. 25 **Litho.** ***Perf. 13***

1815	A576	20b multi	.15	.15
1816	A576	40b multi	.18	.15
1817	A576	55b multi	.28	.15
1818	A576	1 l multi	.55	.15
1819	A576	1.60 l multi	1.00	.15
1820	A576	3.25 l multi	2.50	.65
		Nos. 1815-1820 (6)	4.66	
		Set value		1.05

Chess Olympics in Cuba.

Tractor, Grain and Sun — A577

1966, Mar. 5

1821	A577	55b lt grn & ocher	.24	.15

Founding congress of the National Union of Cooperative Farms.

Gheorghe Gheorghiu-Dej A578

Congress Emblem A579

1966, Mar. **Photo.** ***Perf. 13½***

1822	A578	55b gold & blk	.30	.15
a.		5 l souvenir sheet	3.75	3.75

1st death anniv. of Pres. Gheorghe Gheorghiu-Dej (1901-65). No. 1822a contains design similar to No. 1822 with signature of Gheorghiu-Dej.

1966, Mar. 21 ***Perf. 13x14½***

1823	A579	55b yel & red	.30	.15

1966 Congress of Communist Youth.

Folk Dancers of Moldavia — A580

Folk Dances: 40b, Oltenia. 55b, Maramaros. 1 l, Muntenia. 1.60 l, Banat. 2 l, Transylvania.

1966, Apr. 4 **Engr.** ***Perf. 13½***

Center in Black

1824	A580	30b lilac	.15	.15
1825	A580	40b brick red	.15	.15
1826	A580	55b brt bl grn	.18	.15
1827	A580	1 l maroon	.38	.15
1828	A580	1.60 l dk bl	.70	.15
1829	A580	2 l yel grn	1.25	.30
		Nos. 1824-1829 (6)	2.81	
		Set value		.55

Soccer Game — A581

Designs: 10b, 15b, 55b, 1.75 l, Scenes of soccer play. 4 l, Jules Rimet Cup.

1966, Apr. 25 **Litho.** **Unwmk.**

1830	A581	5b multi	.15	.15
1831	A581	10b multi	.15	.15
1832	A581	15b multi	.15	.15
1833	A581	55b multi	.45	.15
1834	A581	1.75 l multi	1.10	.15
1835	A581	4 l gold & multi	2.50	.60
a.		10 l souv. sheet	3.75	3.75
		Nos. 1830-1835 (6)	4.50	
		Set value		.90

World Cup Soccer Championship, Wembley, England, July 11-30.

No. 1835a contains one imperf. 10 l multicolored stamp in design of 4 l, but larger (32x46mm). No gum. Issued June 20.

Symbols of Industry — A582

Red-breasted Flycatcher — A583

1966, May 14 **Photo.**

1836	A582	55b multi	.24	.15

Romanian Trade Union Congress.

1966, May 25 **Photo.** ***Perf. 13½***

Song Birds: 10b, Red crossbill. 15b, Great reed warbler. 20b, European redstart. 55b, European robin. 1.20 l, White-spotted bluethroat. 1.55 l, Yellow wagtail. 3.20 l, Common penduline tit.

1837	A583	5b gold & multi	.15	.15
1838	A583	10b sil & multi	.15	.15
1839	A583	15b gold & multi	.18	.15
1840	A583	20b sil & multi	.18	.15
1841	A583	55b sil & multi	.28	.15
1842	A583	1.20 l gold & multi	.38	.15
1843	A583	1.55 l sil & multi	1.00	.30
1844	A583	3.20 l gold & multi	1.65	.45
		Nos. 1837-1844 (8)	3.97	
		Set value		1.05

Venus 3 (USSR) — A584

Urechia Nestor — A585

Designs: 20b, FR-1 (France). 1.60 l, Luna 9 (USSR). 5 l, Gemini 6 and 7 (US).

1966, June 25

1845	A584	10b dp vio, gray & red	.15	.15
1846	A584	20b ultra, blk & red	.15	.15
1847	A584	1.60 l dk bl, blk & red	.55	.15
1848	A584	5 l bl, blk, brn & red	1.50	.48
		Nos. 1845-1848 (4)	2.35	
		Set value		.66

International achievements in space.

1966, June 28

Portraits: 5b, George Cosbuc. 10b, Gheorghe Sincai. 40b, Aron Pumnul. 55b, Stefan Luchian. 1 l, Sun Yat-sen. 1.35 l, Gottfried Wilhelm Leibniz. 1.60 l, Romain Rolland. 1.75 l, Ion Ghica. 3.25 l, Constantin Cantacuzino.

1849	A585	5b grn, blk & dk bl	.15	.15
1850	A585	10b rose car, grn & blk	.15	.15
1851	A585	20b grn, plum & blk	.15	.15
1852	A585	40b vio bl, brn & blk	.15	.15
1853	A585	55b brn org, bl grn & blk	.20	.15
1854	A585	1 l ocher, vio & blk	.28	.15
1855	A585	1.35 l bl & blk	.35	.15
1856	A585	1.60 l brt grn, dl vio & blk	.55	.15
1857	A585	1.75 l org, dl vio & blk	.55	.15
1858	A585	3.25 l bl, dk car & blk	1.00	.24
		Nos. 1849-1858 (10)	3.53	
		Set value		.90

Cultural anniversaries.

Country House, by Gheorghe Petrascu — A586

Paintings: 10b, Peasant Woman, by Nicolae Grigorescu, vert. 20b, Reapers at Rest, by Camil Ressu. 55b, Man with the Blue Cap, by Van Eyck, vert. 1.55 l, Train Compartment, by Daumier. 3.25 l, Betrothal of the Virgin, by El Greco, vert.

1966, July 25 **Unwmk.**

Gold Frame

1859	A586	5b Prus grn & brn org	.18	.15
1860	A586	10b red brn & crim	.18	.15
1861	A586	20b brn & brt grn	.18	.15
1862	A586	55b vio bl & lil	.26	.15
1863	A586	1.55 l dk sl grn & org	1.25	.38
1864	A586	3.25 l vio & ultra	2.75	1.00
		Nos. 1859-1864 (6)	4.80	1.98

See Nos. 1907-1912.

Hottonia Palustris — A587

Marine Flora: 10b, Ceratophyllum submersum. 20b, Aldrovanda vesiculosa. 40b, Callitriche verna. 55b, Vallisneria spiralis. 1 l, Elodea Canadensis rich. 1.55 l, Hippuris vulgaris. 3.25 l, Myriophyllum spicatum.

1966, Aug. 25 **Litho.** ***Perf. 13½***

Size: 28x40mm

1865	A587	5b multi	.15	.15
1866	A587	10b multi	.15	.15
1867	A587	20b multi	.15	.15
1868	A587	40b multi	.15	.15
1869	A587	55b multi	.18	.15
1870	A587	1 l multi	.45	.15
1871	A587	1.55 l multi	.70	.24

Size: 28x50mm

1872	A587	3.25 l multi	1.40	.38
		Nos. 1865-1872 (8)	3.33	
		Set value		.90

Derivation of the Meter — A588

Design: 1 l, Metric system symbols.

1966, Sept. 10 **Photo.** ***Perf. 13½***

1873	A588	55b salmon & ultra	.24	.15
1874	A588	1 l lt grn & vio	.38	.15
		Set value		.18

Introduction of metric system in Romania, centenary.

Statue of Ovid and Medical School Emblem A589

Line Integral Denoting Work A590

I. H. Radulescu, M. Kogalniceanu and T. Savulescu — A591

Design: 1 l, Academy centenary medal.

1966, Sept. 30

Size: 22x27mm

1875 A589 40b lil gray, ultra, sep & gold .15 .15
1876 A590 55b gray, brn, red & gold .15 .15

Size: 22x34mm

1877 A589 1 l ultra, brn & gold .35 .15

Size: 66x28mm

1878 A591 3 l org, dk brn & gold .95 .30
Nos. 1875-1878 (4) 1.60
Set value .45

Centenary of the Romanian Academy.

Crawfish A592

Molluscs and Crustaceans: 10b, Nassa reticulata, vert. 20b, Stone crab. 40b, Campylaea trizona. 55b, Helix lucorum. 1.35 l, Mytilus galloprovincialis. 1.75 l, Lymnaea stagnalis. 3.25 l, Anodonta cygnaea. (10b, 40b, 55b, 1.75 l, are snails; 1.35 l, 3.25 l, are bivalves).

1966, Oct. 15

Animals in Natural Colors

1879 A592 5b dp org .15 .15
1880 A592 10b lt bl .15 .15
1881 A592 20b pale lil .15 .15
1882 A592 40b yel grn .15 .15
1883 A592 55b car rose .20 .15
1884 A592 1.35 l brt grn .45 .15
1885 A592 1.75 l ultra .55 .15
1886 A592 3.25 l brt org 1.40 .35
Nos. 1879-1886 (8) 3.20
Set value .85

Cave Bear — A593

Prehistoric Animals: 10b, Mammoth. 15b, Bison. 55b, Cave elephant. 1.55 l, Stags. 4 l, Dinotherium.

1966, Nov. 25

Size: 36x22mm

1887 A593 5b ultra, bl grn & red brn .15 .15
1888 A593 10b vio, emer & brn .15 .15
1889 A593 15b ol, grn & dk brn .18 .15
1890 A593 55b lil, emer & brn .30 .15
1891 A593 1.55 l ultra, grn & brn .95 .15

Size: 43x27mm

1892 A593 4 l rose car, grn & brn 1.50 .52
Nos. 1887-1892 (6) 3.23
Set value .85

Putna Monastery, 500th Anniv. — A594

1966 Photo. *Perf. 13½*

1893 A594 2 l multi .65 .15

Yuri A. Gagarin and Vostok 1 — A595

Russian Achievements in Space: 10b, Trajectory of Sputnik 1 around globe, horiz. 25b, Valentina Tereshkova and globe with trajectory of Vostok 6. 40b, Andrian G. Nikolayev, Pavel R. Popovich and globe with trajectory of Vostok 8. 55b, Alexei Leonov walking in space.

1967, Feb. 15 Photo. *Perf. 13½*

1894 A595 10b silver & multi .15 .15
1895 A595 20b silver & multi .15 .15
1896 A595 25b silver & multi .15 .15
1897 A595 40b silver & multi .18 .15
1898 A595 55b silver & multi .30 .15
Nos. 1894-1898,C163-C166 (9) 3.71
Set value .95

Ten years of space exploration.

Barn Owl — A596

Birds of Prey: 20b, Eagle owl. 40b, Saker falcon. 55b, Egyptian vulture. 75b, Osprey. 1 l, Griffon vulture. 1.20 l, Lammergeier. 1.75 l, Cinereous vulture.

1967, Mar. 20 Photo. Unwmk.

Birds in Natural Colors

1899 A596 10b vio & olive .15 .15
1900 A596 20b bl & org .24 .15
1901 A596 40b emer & org .18 .15
1902 A596 55b yel grn & ocher .24 .15
1903 A596 75b rose lil & grn .24 .15
1904 A596 1 l yel org & blk .50 .15
1905 A596 1.20 l claret & yel .85 .15
1906 A596 1.75 l sal pink & gray 1.25 .50
Nos. 1899-1906 (8) 3.65
Set value 1.00

Painting Type of 1966

10b, Woman in Fancy Dress, by Ion Andreescu. 20b, Washwomen, by J. Al. Steriadi. 40b, Women weavers, by St. Dimitrescu, vert. 1.55 l, Venus and Amor, by Lucas Cranach, vert. 3.20 l, Hercules & the Lion of Numea, by Rubens. 5 l, Haman Asking Esther's Forgiveness, by Rembrandt, vert.

1967, Mar. 30 *Perf. 13½*

Gold Frame

1907 A586 10b dp bl & rose red .15 .15
1908 A586 20b dp grn & bis .15 .15
1909 A586 40b carmine & bl .16 .15
1910 A586 1.55 l dp plum & lt ultra .52 .15
1911 A586 3.20 l brown & grn .90 .16
1912 A586 5 l ol grn & org 2.00 .45
Nos. 1907-1912 (6) 3.88
Set value .85

Mlle. Pogany, by Brancusi A597

Sculptures: 5b, Girl's head. 10b, The Sleeping Muse, horiz. 20b, The Infinite Column. 40b, The Kiss, horiz. 55b, Earth Wisdom (seated woman). 3.25 l, Gate of the Kiss.

1967, Apr. 27 Photo. *Perf. 13½*

1913 A597 5b dl yel, blk brn & ver .15 .15
1914 A597 10b bl grn, blk & lil .15 .15
1915 A597 20b lt bl, blk & rose red .15 .15
1916 A597 40b pink, sep & brt grn .18 .15
1917 A597 55b yel grn, blk & ultra .24 .15
1918 A597 1.20 l bluish lil, ol blk & org .40 .18
1919 A597 3.25 l emer, blk & cer 1.10 .50
Nos. 1913-1919 (7) 2.37
Set value 1.00

Constantin Brancusi (1876-1957), sculptor.

Coins of 1867 A598

Design: 1.20 l, Coins of 1966.

1967, May 4

1920 A598 55b multicolored .28 .15
1921 A598 1.20 l multicolored 1.10 .24

Centenary of Romanian monetary system.

Infantry Soldier, by Nicolae Grigorescu — A599

1967, May 9

1922 A599 55b multicolored .55 .18

90th anniv. of Romanian independence.

Peasants Marching, by Stefan Luchian — A600

Painting: 40b, Fighting Peasants, by Octav Bancila, vert.

1967, May 20 Unwmk. *Perf. 13½*

1923 A600 40b multicolored .28 .15
1924 A600 1.55 l multicolored 1.10 .70

60th anniversary of Peasant Uprising.

Centaury — A601

Carpathian Flora: 40b, Hedge mustard. 55b, Columbine. 1.20 l, Alpine violet. 1.75 l, Bell flower. 4 l, Dryas, horiz.

1967, June 10 Photo.

Flowers in Natural Colors

1925 A601 20b ocher .15 .15
1926 A601 40b violet .15 .15
1927 A601 55b bis & brn red .16 .15
1928 A601 1.20 l yel & red brn .32 .15
1929 A601 1.75 l bluish grn & car .45 .15
1930 A601 4 l lt ultra 1.25 .22
Nos. 1925-1930 (6) 2.48
Set value .60

Fortifications, Sibiu — A602

Map of Romania and ITY Emblem — A603

Designs: 40b, Cris Castle. 55b, Wooden Church, Plopis. 1.60 l, Ruins of Nuamtulua Fortress. 1.75 l, Mogosoaia Palace. 2.25 l, Voronet Church.

1967, June 29 Photo. *Perf. 13½*

Size: 33x33mm

1931 A602 20b ultra & multi .15 .15
1932 A602 40b vio & multi .15 .15
1933 A602 55b multi .15 .15
1934 A602 1.60 l multi .38 .15
1935 A602 1.75 l multi .45 .15

Size: 48x36mm

1936 A602 2.25 l bl & multi .75 .18
Nos. 1931-1936 (6) 2.03
Set value .50

Souvenir Sheet

Imperf

1937 A603 5 l lt bl, ultra & blk 2.50 1.40

International Tourist Year.

The Attack at Marasesti, by E. Stoica A604

1967, July 24 Unwmk. *Perf. 13½*

1938 A604 55b gray, Prus bl & brn .35 .15

Battle of Marasesti & Oituz, 50th anniv.

Dinu Lipatti, Pianist — A605

Designs: 20b, Al. Orascu, architect. 40b, Gr. Antipa, zoologist. 55b, M. Kogalniceanu, statesman. 1.20 l, Jonathan Swift, writer. 1.75 l, Marie Curie, scientist.

1967, July 29 Photo. *Perf. 13½*

1939 A605 10b ultra, blk & pur .15 .15
1940 A605 20b org brn, blk & ultra .15 .15
1941 A605 40b bl grn, blk & org brn .15 .15
1942 A605 55b dp rose, blk & dk ol grn .20 .15
1943 A605 1.20 l ol, blk & brn .35 .15
1944 A605 1.75 l dl bl, blk & bl grn .70 .22
Nos. 1939-1944 (6) 1.70
Set value .50

Cultural anniversaries.

Wrestlers A606

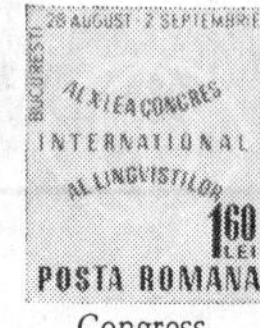

Congress Emblem A607

Designs: 20b, 55b, 1.20 l, 2 l, Various fight scenes and world map (20b, 2 l horizontal); on 2 l maps are large and wrestlers small.

1967, Aug. 28

No.	Type	Description	Unused	Used
1945	A606	10b olive & multi	.15	.15
1946	A606	20b citron & multi	.15	.15
1947	A606	55b bister & multi	.15	.15
1948	A606	1.20 l multi	.28	.15
1949	A606	2 l ultra, gold & dp car	1.00	.30
		Nos. 1945-1949 (5)	1.73	
		Set value		.60

World Greco-Roman Wrestling Championships, Bucharest.

1967, Aug. 28

No.	Type	Description	Unused	Used
1950	A607	1.60 l lt bl, ultra & dp car	.50	.15

Intl. Linguists' Congress, Bucharest, Aug. 28-Sept. 2.

Ice Skating — A608

Designs: 40b, Biathlon. 55b, 5 l, Bobsledding. 1 l, Skiing. 1.55 l, Ice Hockey. 2 l, Emblem of 10th Winter Olympic Games. 2.30 l, Ski jump.

1967, Sept. 28 Photo. *Perf. 13½x13*

No.	Type	Description	Unused	Used
1951	A608	20b lt bl & multi	.15	.15
1952	A608	40b multi	.15	.15
1953	A608	55b bl & multi	.15	.15
1954	A608	1 l lil & multi	.20	.15
1955	A608	1.55 l multi	.30	.15
1956	A608	2 l gray & multi	.50	.18
1957	A608	2.30 l multi	.85	.35
		Nos. 1951-1957 (7)	2.30	
		Set value		1.00

Souvenir Sheet

Imperf

No.	Type	Description	Unused	Used
1958	A608	5 l lt bl & multi	3.25	2.75

10th Winter Olympic Games, Grenoble, France, Feb. 6-18, 1968.

Nos. 1951-1957 issued in sheets of 10 (5x2) and 5 labels.

Curtea de Arges Monastery, 450th Anniv. — A609

1967, Nov. 1 Unwmk. *Perf. 13½*

No.	Type	Description	Unused	Used
1959	A609	55b multicolored	.30	.15

Romanian Academy Library, Bucharest, Cent. — A610

1967, Sept. 25 Litho.

No.	Type	Description	Unused	Used
1960	A610	55b ocher, gray & dk bl	.30	.15

Karl Marx and Title Page — A611

Lenin — A612

1967, Nov. 4 Photo.

No.	Type	Description	Unused	Used
1961	A611	40b rose claret, blk & yel	.24	.15

Centenary of the publication of "Das Kapital" by Karl Marx.

1967, Nov. 3

No.	Type	Description	Unused	Used
1962	A612	1.20 l red, blk & gold	.35	.15

Russian October Revolution, 50th anniv.

Monorail Leaving US EXPO Pavilion A613

Designs: 1 l, EXPO emblem and atom symbol. 1.60 l, Cup, world map and EXPO emblem. 2 l, EXPO emblem.

1967, Nov. 28 Photo.

No.	Type	Description	Unused	Used
1963	A613	55b grnsh bl, vio & blk	.15	.15
1964	A613	1 l red, blk & gray	.28	.15
1965	A613	1.60 l multicolored	.40	.16
1966	A613	2 l multicolored	.60	.18
		Nos. 1963-1966 (4)	1.43	
		Set value		.46

EXPO '67 Intl. Exhib., Montreal, Apr. 28-Oct. 27. No. 1965 also for Romania's victory in the World Fencing Championships in Montreal.

Truck — A614

Arms of the Republic — A615

Diesel Locomotive A616

Map Showing Telephone Network A617

Designs: 10b, Communications emblem, vert. 20b, Train. 35b, Plane. 50b, Telephone, vert. 60b, Small loading truck. 1.20 l, Autobus. 1.35 l, Helicopter. 1.50 l, Trolley bus. 1.55 l, Radio station and tower. 1.75 l, Highway. 2 l, Mail truck. 2.40 l, Television tower. 3.20 l, Jet plane. 3.25 l, Steamship. 4 l, Electric train. 5 l, World map and teletype.

Photo.; Engr. (type A615)

1967-68 *Perf. 13½*

No.	Type	Description	Unused	Used
1967	A614	5b lt ol grn ('68)	.15	.15
1968	A614	10b henna brn ('68)	.15	.15
1969	A614	20b gray ('68)	.15	.15
1970	A614	35b bl blk ('68)	.15	.15
1971	A615	40b violet blue	.15	.15
1972	A614	50b orange ('68)	.15	.15
1973	A615	55b dull orange	.15	.15
1974	A614	60b orange brn ('68)	.15	.15

Size: 22½x28mm, 28x22½mm

No.	Type	Description	Unused	Used
1975	A616	1 l emerald ('68)	.22	.15
1976	A617	1.20 l red lil ('68)	.28	.15
1977	A617	1.35 l brt blue ('68)	.30	.15
1978	A616	1.50 l rose red ('68)	.35	.15
1979	A616	1.55 l dk brown ('68)	.35	.15
1980	A615	1.60 l rose red	.38	.15
1981	A617	1.75 l dp green ('68)	.40	.15
1982	A617	2 l citron ('68)	.60	.15
1983	A616	2.40 l dk blue ('68)	.75	.15
1984	A617	3 l grnsh blue	.75	.15
1985	A617	3.20 l ocher ('68)	1.00	.15
1986	A616	3.25 l ultra ('68)	1.00	.15
1987	A617	4 l lil rose ('68)	1.25	.15
1988	A617	5 l violet ('68)	1.40	.15
		Nos. 1967-1988 (22)	10.23	
		Set value		1.00

40th anniv. of the first automatic telephone exchange; introduction of automatic telephone service (No. 1984).

See Nos. 2078-2079, 2269-2284 and design A792.

Coat of Arms, Symbols of Agriculture and Industry — A618

55b, Coat of arms. 1.60 l, Romanian flag. 1.75 l, Coat of arms, symbols of arts and education.

1967, Dec. 26 Photo. *Perf. 13½*

Size: 27x48mm

No.	Type	Description	Unused	Used
1989	A618	40b multicolored	.15	.15
1990	A618	55b multicolored	.15	.15

Size: 33½x48mm

No.	Type	Description	Unused	Used
1991	A618	1.60 l multicolored	.30	.18

Size: 27x48mm

No.	Type	Description	Unused	Used
1992	A618	1.75 l multicolored	.50	.24
		Nos. 1989-1992 (4)	1.10	
		Set value		.58

20th anniversary of the republic.

Souvenir Sheet

Anemones, by Stefan Luchian — A619

1968, Mar. 30 Litho. *Imperf.*

No.	Type	Description	Unused	Used
1993	A619	10 l multi	4.75	4.75

Stefan Luchian, Romanian painter, birth cent.

Portrait of a Lady, by Misu Popp — A620

Paintings: 10b, The Reveille of Romania, by Gheorghe Tattarescu. 20b, Composition, by Teodorescu Sionion, horiz. 35b, The Judgment of Paris, by Hendrick van Balen, horiz. 55b, Little Girl with Red Kerchief, by Nicolae Grigorescu. 60b, The Mystical Betrothal of St. Catherine, by Lamberto Sustris, horiz. 1 l, Old Nicolas, the Zither Player, by Stefan Luchian. 1.60 l, Man with a Skull, by Dierick Bouts (?). 1.75 l, Madonna and Child with Fruit Basket, by Jan van Bylert. 2.40 l, Medor and Angelica, by Sebastiano Ricci, horiz. 3 l, Summer, by Jacob Jordaens, horiz. 3.20 l, 5 l, Ecce Homo, by Titian.

1968 Photo. *Perf. 13½*

Gold Frame

Size: 28x49mm

No.	Type	Description	Unused	Used
1994	A620	10b multi	.15	.15

Size: 48½x36½mm, 36x48½mm

No.	Type	Description	Unused	Used
1995	A620	20b multi	.15	.15
1996	A620	35b multi	.15	.15
1997	A620	40b multi	.15	.15
1998	A620	55b multi	.15	.15
1999	A620	60b multi	.18	.15
2000	A620	1 l multi	.28	.15
2001	A620	1.60 l multi	.42	.15
2002	A620	1.75 l multi	.42	.18
2003	A620	2.40 l multi	.80	.30
2004	A620	3 l multi	.90	.50
2005	A620	3.20 l multi	1.40	.70
		Nos. 1994-2005 (12)	5.15	
		Set value		2.25

Miniature Sheet

Imperf

No.	Type	Description	Unused	Used
2006	A620	5 l multi	4.50	4.50

Issue dates: 40b, 55b, 1, 1.60, 2.40, 3.20 and 5 l, Mar. 28. Others, Sept. 9.

See Nos. 2088-2094, 2124-2130.

Human Rights Flame A621

WHO Emblem A622

1968, May 9 Unwmk. *Perf. 13½*

No.	Type	Description	Unused	Used
2007	A621	1 l multicolored	.45	.15

Intl. Human Rights Year.

1968, May 14 Photo.

No.	Type	Description	Unused	Used
2008	A622	1.60 l multi	.50	.15

WHO, 20th anniversary.

"Prince Dragos Hunting Bison," by Nicolae Grigorescu — A623

1968, May 17

No.	Type	Description	Unused	Used
2009	A623	1.60 l multi	.60	.18

15th Hunting Cong., Mamaia, May 23-29.

Pioneers and Liberation Monument — A624

Pioneers: 40b, receiving scarfs. 55b, building model planes and boat. 1 l, as radio amateurs. 1.60 l, folk dancing. 2.40 l, Girl Pioneers in camp.

1968, June 9 Photo. *Perf. 13½*

No.	Type	Description	Unused	Used
2010	A624	5b multi	.15	.15
2011	A624	40b multi	.15	.15
2012	A624	55b multi	.16	.15
2013	A624	1 l multi	.30	.15
2014	A624	1.60 l multi	.50	.15
2015	A624	2.40 l multi	.70	.16
		Nos. 2010-2015 (6)	1.96	
		Set value		.55

Foreign postal stationery (stamped envelopes, postal cards and air letter sheets) is beyond the scope of this catalogue.

Ion Ionescu de la Brad — A625

Designs: 55b, Emil Racovita. 1.60 l, Prince Mircea of Walachia.

1968

Size: 28x43mm

2016 A625 40b multicolored .20 .15
2017 A625 55b green & multi .20 .15

Size: 28x48mm

2018 A625 1.60 l gold & multi .45 .15
Nos. 2016-2018 (3) .85
Set value .20

Ion Ionescu de la Brad (1818-91); Emil Racovita (1868-1947), explorer and naturalist; 1.60 l, Prince Mircea (1386-1418). Issue dates: 40b, 55b, June 24; 1.60 l, June 22.

Geranium — A626

Designs: Various geraniums.

1968, July 20 Photo. *Perf. 13½*

2019 A626 10b multicolored .15 .15
2020 A626 20b multicolored .15 .15
2021 A626 40b multicolored .15 .15
2022 A626 55b multicolored .15 .15
2023 A626 60b multicolored .15 .15
2024 A626 1.20 l multicolored .26 .15
2025 A626 1.35 l multicolored .35 .15
2026 A626 1.60 l multicolored .75 .16
Set value (8) 1.75 .65

POSTA ROMANA 20L

Avram Iancu, by B. Iscovescu and Demonstrating Students — A627

Demonstrating Students and: 55b, Nicolae Balcescu, by Gheorghe Tattarescu. 1.60 l, Vasile Alecsandri, by N. Livaditti.

1968, July 25

2027 A627 55b gold & multi .20 .15
2028 A627 1.20 l gold & multi .45 .15
2029 A627 1.60 l gold & multi .70 .18
Nos. 2027-2029 (3) 1.35
Set value .30

120th anniversary of 1848 revolution.

Boxing — A628

Atheneum and Harp — A629

Aztec Calendar Stone and: 10b, Javelin, Women's. 20b, Woman diver. 40b, Volleyball. 60b, Wrestling. 1.20 l, Fencing. 1.35 l, Canoeing. 1.60 l, Soccer. 5 l, Running.

1968, Aug. 28

2030 A628 10b multi .15 .15
2031 A628 20b multi .15 .15
2032 A628 40b multi .15 .15
2033 A628 55b multi .15 .15
2034 A628 60b multi .15 .15
2035 A628 1.20 l multi .35 .18
2036 A628 1.35 l multi .40 .24
2037 A628 1.60 l multi .65 .28
Set value (8) 1.80 1.00

Souvenir Sheet

Imperf

2038 A628 5 l multi 2.25 1.75

19th Olympic Games, Mexico City, Oct. 12-17.

1968, Aug. 20 Litho. *Perf. 12x12½*

2039 A629 55b multicolored .24 .15

Centenary of the Philharmonic Orchestra.

Globe and Emblem — A630

1968, Oct. 4 Litho. *Perf. 13½*

2040 A630 1.60 l ultra & gold .50 .15

Intl. Fed. of Photograpic Art, 20th anniv.

Moldovita Monastery Church — A631

Historic Monuments: 10b, "The Triumph of Trajan," Roman metope, vert. 55b, Cozia monastery church. 1.20 l, Court of Tirgoviste Palace. 1.55 l, Palace of Culture, Jassy. 1.75 l, Corvinus Castle, Hunedoara.

1968, Nov. 25 Engr. *Perf. 13½*

2041 A631 10b dk bl, ol & brn .15 .15
2042 A631 40b rose car, bl & brn .15 .15
2043 A631 55b ol, brn & vio .15 .15
2044 A631 1.20 l yel, mar & gray .30 .15
2045 A631 1.55 l vio brn, dk bl & lt grn .50 .15
2046 A631 1.75 l org, blk & ol 1.00 .18
Nos. 2041-2046 (6) 2.25
Set value .50

Mute Swan — A632

Protected Birds and Animals: 20b, European stilts. 40b, Sheldrakes. 55b, Egret feeding young. 60b, Golden eagle. 1.20 l, Great bustards. 1.35 l, Chamois. 1.60 l, Bison.

1968, Dec. 20 Photo. *Perf. 13½*

2047 A632 10b pink & multi .15 .15
2048 A632 20b multicolored .15 .15
2049 A632 40b lilac & multi .15 .15
2050 A632 55b olive & multi .15 .15
2051 A632 60b multicolored .20 .15
2052 A632 1.20 l multicolored .45 .15
2053 A632 1.35 l blue & multi .50 .15
2054 A632 1.60 l multicolored .60 .16
Nos. 2047-2054 (8) 2.35
Set value .55

Michael the Brave's Entry into Alba Iulia, by D. Stoica — A633

Designs: 1 l, "The Round Dance of Union," by Theodor Aman. 1.75 l, Assembly of Alba Iulia.

1968, Dec. 1 Litho. *Perf. 13½*

2055 A633 55b gold & multi .20 .15
2056 A633 1 l gold & multi .30 .18
2057 A633 1.75 l gold & multi .40 .35
a. Souv. sheet of 3, #2055-2057, imperf. 1.50 1.50
Nos. 2055-2057 (3) .90 .68

50th anniv. of the union of Transylvania and Romania. No. 2057a sold for 4 l.

Woman from Neamt — A634

Regional Costumes: 40b, Man from Neamt. 55b, Woman from Hunedoara. 1 l, Man from Hunedoara. 1.60 l, Woman from Brasov. 2.40 l, Man from Brasov.

1968, Dec. 28 *Perf. 12x12½*

2058 A634 5b orange & multi .15 .15
2059 A634 40b blue & multi .15 .15
2060 A634 55b multi .15 .15
2061 A634 1 l brown & multi .26 .15
2062 A634 1.60 l brown & multi .52 .15
2063 A634 2.40 l multi .95 .35
Nos. 2058-2063 (6) 2.18
Set value .75

1969, Feb. 15

Regional Costumes: 5b, Woman from Dolj. 40b, Man from Dolj. 55b, Woman from Arges. 1 l, Man from Arges. 1.60 l, Woman from Timisoara. 2.40 l, Man from Timisoara.

2064 A634 5b multi .15 .15
2065 A634 40b multi .15 .15
2066 A634 55b lil & multi .15 .15
2067 A634 1 l rose & multi .28 .15
2068 A634 1.60 l multi .55 .15
2069 A634 2.40 l brn & multi 1.00 .25
Nos. 2064-2069 (6) 2.28
Set value .64

Fencing A635

Sports: 20b, Women's javelin. 40b, Canoeing. 55b, Boxing. 1 l, Volleyball. 1.20 l, Swimming. 1.60 l, Wrestling. 2.40 l, Soccer.

1969, Mar. 10 Photo. *Perf. 13½*

Denominations Black, Athletes in Gray

2070 A635 10b pale brown .15 .15
2071 A635 20b violet .15 .15
2072 A635 40b blue .15 .15
2073 A635 55b red .15 .15
2074 A635 1 l green .24 .15
2075 A635 1.20 l brt blue .28 .15
2076 A635 1.60 l cerise .48 .15
2077 A635 2.40 l dp green .85 .18
Nos. 2070-2077 (8) 2.45
Set value .65

Type of Regular Issue

1969, Jan. 10 Photo. *Perf. 13½*

2078 A614 40b Power lines, vert. .15 .15
2079 A614 55b Dam, vert. .18 .15
Set value .15

Painting Type of 1968

Paintings (Nudes): 10b, Woman Carrying Jug, by Gheorghe Tattarescu. 20b, Reclining Woman, by Theodor Pallady, horiz. 35b, Seated Woman, by Nicolae Tonitza. 60b, Venus and Amor, 17th century Flemish School. 1.75 l, 5 l, Diana and Endimion, by Marco Liberi. 3 l, The Three Graces, by Alessandro Varotari.

1969, Mar. 27 Photo. *Perf. 13½*

Gold Frame

Size: 37x49mm, 49x37mm

2088 A620 10b multi .15 .15
2089 A620 20b multi .15 .15
2090 A620 35b multi .20 .15
2091 A620 60b multi .30 .15
2092 A620 1.75 l multi .70 .26

Size: 27½x48½mm

2093 A620 3 l multi 1.50 .45
Nos. 2088-2093 (6) 3.00
Set value .92

Miniature Sheet

Imperf

2094 A620 5 l multi 3.00 3.00

No. 2094 contains one stamp 36½x48½mm. with simulated perforations.

No. 2093 is incorrectly inscribed Hans von Aachen.

ILO, 50th Anniv. — A636

Symbolic Head — A637

1969, Apr. 9 Photo. *Perf. 13½*

2095 A636 55b multicolored .40 .15

1969, Apr. 28

2096 A637 55b ultra & multi .35 .15
2097 A637 1.50 l red & multi .90 .38

Romania's cultural and economic cooperation with European countries.

Communications Symbol — A638

1969, May 12 Photo. *Perf. 13½*

2098 A638 55b vio bl & bluish gray .35 .15

7th Session of the Conference of Postal and Telecommunications Ministers, Bucharest.

Boxers, Referee and Map of Europe A639

Map of Europe and: 40b, Two boxers. 55b, Sparring. 1.75 l, Referee declaring winner.

1969, May 24

2099 A639 35b multicolored .15 .15
2100 A639 40b multicolored .15 .15
2101 A639 55b multicolored .24 .15
2102 A639 1.75 l blue & multi .60 .18
Nos. 2099-2102 (4) 1.14
Set value .35

European Boxing Championships, Bucharest, May 31-June 8.

Apatura Ilia — A640

Designs: Various butterflies and moths.

1969, June 25 Photo. *Perf. 13½*

Insects in Natural Colors

No.	Type	Denom.	Color	Unused	Used
2103	A640	5b	yellow grn	.15	.15
2104	A640	10b	rose mag	.15	.15
2105	A640	20b	violet	.15	.15
2106	A640	40b	blue grn	.15	.15
2107	A640	55b	brt blue	.15	.15
2108	A640	1 l	blue	.30	.15
2109	A640	1.20 l	violet bl	.40	.15
2110	A640	2.40 l	yellow bis	.80	.20
			Set value (8)	1.85	.65

Communist Party Flag — A641

1969, Aug. 6 Photo. *Perf. 13½*

No.	Type	Denom.	Color	Unused	Used
2111	A641	55b	multicolored	.28	.15

10th Romanian Communist Party Congress.

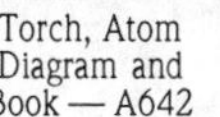

Torch, Atom Diagram and Book — A642

Broken Chain — A643

Designs: 40b, Symbols of agriculture, science and industry. 1.75 l, Pylon, smokestack and cogwheel.

1969, Aug. 10

No.	Type	Denom.	Color	Unused	Used
2112	A642	35b	multicolored	.15	.15
2113	A642	40b	green & multi	.15	.15
2114	A642	1.75 l	multicolored	.50	.18
			Nos. 2112-2114 (3)	.80	
			Set value		.28

Exhibition showing the achievements of Romanian economy during the last 25 years.

1969, Aug. 23

Designs: 55b, Construction work. 60b, Flags.

No.	Type	Denom.	Color	Unused	Used
2115	A643	10b	multicolored	.15	.15
2116	A643	55b	yellow & multi	.18	.15
2117	A643	60b	multicolored	.24	.15
			Set value	.46	.16

25th anniversary of Romania's liberation from fascist rule.

Juggler on Unicycle — A644

Masks — A645

Circus Performers: 20b, Clown. 35b, Trapeze artists. 60b, Dressage and woman trainer. 1.75 l, Woman in high wire act. 3 l, Performing tiger and trainer.

1969, Sept. 29 Photo. *Perf. 13½*

No.	Type	Denom.	Color	Unused	Used
2118	A644	10b	lt blue & multi	.15	.15
2119	A644	20b	lemon & multi	.15	.15
2120	A644	35b	lilac & multi	.15	.15
2121	A644	60b	multicolored	.16	.15
2122	A644	1.75 l	multicolored	.55	.15
2123	A644	3 l	ultra & multi	.90	.35
			Set value	1.80	.65

Painting Type of 1968

10b, Venetian Senator, Tintoretto School. 20b, Sofia Kretzulescu, by Gheorghe Tattarescu. 35b, Phillip IV, by Velazquez. 60b, Man Reading and Child, by Hans Memling. 1.75 l, Doamnei d'Aguesseau, by Madame Vigée-Lebrun. 3 l, Portrait of a Woman, by Rembrandt. 5 l, The Return of the Prodigal Son, by Bernardino Licinio, horiz.

1969

Gold Frame

Size: 36½x49mm

No.	Type	Denom.	Color	Unused	Used
2124	A620	10b	multi	.15	.15
2125	A620	20b	multi	.15	.15
2126	A620	35b	multi	.15	.15
2127	A620	60b	multi	.35	.15
2128	A620	1.75 l	multi	.70	.15
2129	A620	3 l	multi	1.25	.35
			Nos. 2124-2129 (6)	2.75	
			Set value		.65

Miniature Sheet

Imperf

No.	Type	Denom.	Color	Unused	Used
2130	A620	5 l	gold & multi	2.00	1.50

No. 2130 contains one stamp with simulated perforations.

Issue dates: 5 l, July 31. Others, Oct. 1.

1969, Nov. 24 Photo. *Perf. 13½*

No.	Type	Denom.	Color	Unused	Used
2131	A645	40b	Branesti	.15	.15
2132	A645	55b	Tudora	.15	.15
2133	A645	1.55 l	Birsesti	.50	.15
2134	A645	1.75 l	Rudaria	.60	.18
			Nos. 2131-2134 (4)	1.40	
			Set value		.42

Armed Forces Memorial A646

1969, Oct. 25

No.	Type	Denom.	Color	Unused	Used
2135	A646	55b	red, blk & gold	.20	.15

25th anniversary of the People's Army.

Locomotives of 1869 and 1969 — A647

1969, Oct. 31

No.	Type	Denom.	Color	Unused	Used
2136	A647	55b	silver & multi	.24	.15

Bucharest-Filaret-Giurgevo railroad, cent.

A648

A649

Apollo 12 landing module.

1969, Nov. 24

No.	Type	Denom.	Color	Unused	Used
2137	A648	1.50 l	multi	.55	.50

2nd landing on the moon, Nov. 19, 1969, astronauts Captains Alan Bean, Charles Conrad, Jr. and Richard Gordon.

Printed in sheets of 4 with 4 labels (one label with names of astronauts, one with Apollo 12 emblem and 2 silver labels with picture of landing module, Intrepid).

1969, Dec. 25 Photo. *Perf. 13½*

New Year: 40b, Mother Goose in Goat Disguise. 55b, Children singing and decorated tree, Sorcova. 1.50 l, Drummer, and singer, Buhaiul. 2.40 l, Singer and bell ringer, Plugusorul.

No.	Type	Denom.	Color	Unused	Used
2138	A649	40b	bister & multi	.15	.15
2139	A649	55b	lilac & multi	.15	.15
2140	A649	1.50 l	blue & multi	.50	.15
2141	A649	2.40 l	multicolored	1.00	.26
			Nos. 2138-2141 (4)	1.80	
			Set value		.52

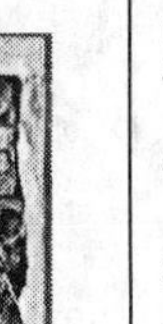

The Last Judgment (detail), Voronet Monastery — A650

North Moldavian Monastery Frescoes: 10b, Stephen the Great and family, Voronet. 20b, Three prophets, Sucevita. 60b, St. Nicholas (scene from his life), Sucevita, vert. 1.75 l, Siege of Constantinople, 7th century, Moldovita. 3 l, Plowman, Voronet, vert.

1969, Dec. 15

No.	Type	Denom.	Color	Unused	Used
2142	A650	10b	gold & multi	.15	.15
2143	A650	20b	gold & multi	.15	.15
2144	A650	35b	gold & multi	.15	.15
2145	A650	60b	gold & multi	.15	.15
2146	A650	1.75 l	gold & multi	.32	.15
2147	A650	3 l	gold & multi	1.00	.22
			Set value	1.60	.55

Ice Hockey A651

Designs: 55b, Goalkeeper. 1.20 l, Two players with puck. 2.40 l, Player and goalkeeper.

1970, Jan. 20 *Perf. 13½*

No.	Type	Denom.	Color	Unused	Used
2148	A651	20b	yellow & multi	.15	.15
2149	A651	55b	multicolored	.15	.15
2150	A651	1.20 l	pink & multi	.38	.18
2151	A651	2.40 l	lt blue & multi	1.00	.30
			Nos. 2148-2151 (4)	1.68	
			Set value		.60

World Ice Hockey Championships, Bucharest and Galati, Feb. 24-Mar. 5.

Pasqueflower — A652

Flowers: 10b, Adonis vernalis. 20b, Thistle. 40b, Almond tree blossoms. 55b, Iris. 1 l, Flax. 1.20 l, Sage. 2.40 l, Peony.

1970, Feb. 25 Photo. *Perf. 13½*

No.	Type	Denom.	Color	Unused	Used
2152	A652	5b	yellow & multi	.15	.15
2153	A652	10b	green & multi	.15	.15
2154	A652	20b	lt bl & multi	.15	.15
2155	A652	40b	violet & multi	.15	.15
2156	A652	55b	ultra & multi	.15	.15
2157	A652	1 l	multicolored	.20	.15
2158	A652	1.20 l	red & multi	.35	.15
2159	A652	2.40 l	multicolored	.70	.20
			Set value (8)	1.60	.70

Japanese Print and EXPO '70 Emblem A653

Design: 1 l, Pagoda, EXPO '70 emblem.

1970, Mar. 23

No.	Type	Denom.	Color	Unused	Used
2160	A653	20b	gold & multi	.15	.15

Size: 29x92mm

No.	Type	Denom.	Color	Unused	Used
2161	A653	1 l	gold & multi	.30	.15
			Set value		.20

EXPO '70 Intl. Exhib., Osaka, Japan, Mar. 15-Sept. 13.

A souvenir sheet exists with perforated label in pagoda design of 1 l. Issued Nov. 28, 1970. Value $1.65.

Camille, by Claude Monet (Maximum Card) — A654

1970, Apr. 19 Photo. *Perf. 13½*

No.	Type	Denom.	Color	Unused	Used
2162	A654	1.50 l	gold & multi	.45	.15

Franco-Romanian Maximafil Phil. Exhib.

Cuza, by C. Popp de Szathmary A655

Lenin (1870-1924) A656

1970, Apr. 20 *Perf. 13½*

No.	Type	Denom.	Color	Unused	Used
2163	A655	55b	gold & multi	.20	.15

Alexandru Ioan Cuza (1820-1866), prince of Romania.

1970, Apr. 21 Photo. *Perf. 13½*

No.	Type	Denom.	Color	Unused	Used
2164	A656	40b	dk red & multi	.15	.15

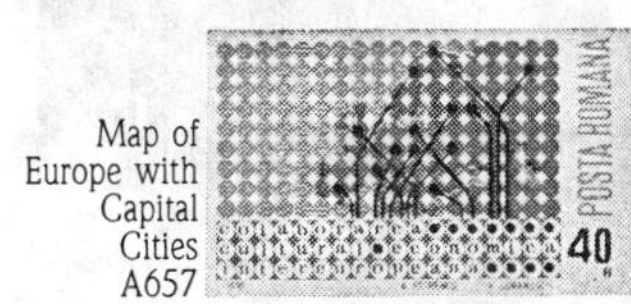

Map of Europe with Capital Cities A657

1970, Apr. 28

No.	Type	Denom.	Color	Unused	Used
2165	A657	40b	grn, brn org & blk	.50	.35
2166	A657	1.50 l	ultra, yel brn & blk	1.00	.70

Inter-European cultural and economic cooperation.

Victory Monument, Romanian and Russian Flags — A658

1970, May 9

No.	Type	Denom.	Color	Unused	Used
2167	A658	55b	red & multi	.18	.15

25th anniv. of victory over the Germans.

Greek Silver Drachm, 5th Century B.C. A659

Coins: 20b, Getic-Dacian silver didrachm, 2nd-1st centuries B.C. 35b, Emperor Trajan's copper sestertius, 106 A.D. 60b, Mircea ducat, 1400. 1.75 l, Stephen the Great's silver groschen, 1460. 3 l, Brasov klippe-taler, 1601, vert.

1970, May 15

2168 A659 10b ultra, blk & sil .15 .15
2169 A659 20b hn brn, blk & sil .15 .15
2170 A659 35b grn, dk brn & gold .15 .15
2171 A659 60b brn, blk & sil .16 .15
2172 A659 1.75 l brt bl, blk & sil .50 .18
2173 A659 3 l dk car, blk & sil 1.00 .26
Nos. 2168-2173 (6) 2.11
Set value .65

Soccer Players and Ball — A660

Soccer ball & various scenes from soccer game.

1970, May 26 *Perf. 13½*

2174 A660 40b multi .15 .15
2175 A660 55b multi .15 .15
2176 A660 1.75 l blue & multi .45 .18
2177 A660 3.30 l multi .85 .30
Nos. 2174-2177 (4) 1.60
Set value .62

Souvenir Sheet

2178 Sheet of 4 2.00 1.50
a. A660 1.20 l multi .28 .15
b. A660 1.50 l multi .35 .18
c. A660 1.55 l multi .38 .20
d. A660 1.75 l multi .38 .20

9th World Soccer Championships for the Jules Rimet Cup, Mexico City, May 30-June 21. No. 2178 contains 4 stamps similar to Nos. 2174-2177, but with only one quarter of the soccer ball on each stamp, forming one large ball in the center of the block.

Moldovita Monastery A661

Frescoes from North Moldavian Monasteries.

1970, June 29 *Perf. 13½*

Size: 36½x49mm

2179 A661 10b gold & multi .15 .15

Size: 27½x49mm

2180 A661 20b gold & multi .15 .15

Size: 36½x49mm, 48x37mm

2181 A661 40b gold & multi .15 .15
2182 A661 55b gold & multi .20 .15
2183 A661 1.75 l gold & multi .38 .22
2184 A661 3 l gold & multi 1.00 .35
Nos. 2179-2184 (6) 2.03
Set value .85

Miniature Sheet

2185 A661 5 l gold & multi 1.75 1.75

Friedrich Engels (1820-1895), German Socialist — A662

1970, July 10 **Photo.** *Perf. 13½*

2186 A662 1.50 l multi .45 .15

Aerial View of Iron Gate Power Station A663

1970, July 13

2187 A663 35b blue & multi .18 .15

Hydroelectric plant at the Iron Gate of the Danube.

Cargo Ship — A664

1970, July 17

2188 A664 55b blue & multi .18 .15

Romanian merchant marine, 75th anniv.

Exhibition Hall and Oil Derrick A665

1970, July 20

2189 A665 1.50 l multi .45 .15

International Bucharest Fair, Oct. 13-24.

Opening of UPU Headquarters, Bern — A666

1970, Aug. 17 **Photo.** *Perf. 13½*

2190 A666 1.50 l ultra & slate green .45 .15

Education Year Emblem — A667

Iceberg Rose — A668

1970, Aug. 17

2191 A667 55b black, pur & red .18 .15

International Education Year.

1970, Aug. 21

Roses: 35b, Wiener charme. 55b, Pink luster. 1 l, Piccadilly. 1.50 l, Orange Delbard. 2.40 l, Sibelius.

2192 A668 20b dk red, grn & yel .15 .15
2193 A668 35b vio, yel & grn .15 .15
2194 A668 55b blue, rose & grn .15 .15
2195 A668 1 l grn, car rose & yel .30 .15
2196 A668 1.50 l dk bl, red & grn .45 .16
2197 A668 2.40 l brt bl, dp red & grn .85 .22
Nos. 2192-2197 (6) 2.05
Set value .65

Spaniel and Pheasant, by Jean B. Oudry A669

Paintings: 10b, The Hunt, by Domenico Brandi. 35b, The Hunt, by Jan Fyt. 60b, After the Chase, by Jacob Jordaens. 1.75 l, 5 l, Game Merchant, by Frans Snyders (horiz.). 3 l, The Hunt, by Adriaen de Gryeff. Sizes: 37x49mm (10b, 35b); 35x33mm (20b, 60b, 3 l); 49x37mm (1.75 l, 3 l).

1970, Sept. 20 **Photo.** *Perf. 13½*

2198 A669 10b gold & multi .15 .15
2199 A669 20b gold & multi .15 .15
2200 A669 35b gold & multi .15 .15
2201 A669 60b gold & multi .20 .15
2202 A669 1.75 l gold & multi .60 .30
2203 A669 3 l gold & multi 1.25 .45
Nos. 2198-2203 (6) 2.50
Set value 1.00

Miniature Sheet

2204 A669 5 l gold & multi 2.00 2.00

UN Emblem A670

Mother and Child A671

1970, Sept. 29

2205 A670 1.50 l lt bl, ultra & blk .45 .15

25th anniversary of the United Nations.

1970, Sept. 25

Designs: 1.50 l, Red Cross relief trucks and tents. 1.75 l, Rebuilding houses.

2206 A671 55b bl gray, blk & ol .18 .15
2207 A671 1.50 l ol, blk & car .45 .15
a. Strip of 3, #2206-2207, C179 1.40 .55
2208 A671 1.75 l blue & multi .70 .20
Nos. 2206-2208 (3) 1.33
Set value .40

Plight of the Danube flood victims.

Arabian Thoroughbred — A672

Horses: 35b, American trotter. 55b, Ghidran (Anglo-American). 1 l, Northern Moravian. 1.50 l, Trotter thoroughbred. 2.40 l, Lippizaner.

1970, Oct. 10 **Photo.** *Perf. 13½*

2209 A672 20b blk & multi .15 .15
2210 A672 35b blk & multi .15 .15
2211 A672 55b blk & multi .15 .15
2212 A672 1 l blk & multi .28 .15
2213 A672 1.50 l blk & multi .40 .15
2214 A672 2.40 l blk & multi .95 .22
Nos. 2209-2214 (6) 2.08
Set value .62

Ludwig van Beethoven (1770-1827), Composer — A673

1970, Nov. 2

2215 A673 55b multicolored .24 .15

Abstract, by Joan Miró — A674

1970, Dec. 10 **Photo.** *Perf. 13½*

2216 A674 3 l ultra & multi .85 .70

Souvenir Sheet

Imperf

2217 A674 5 l ultra & multi 1.90 1.90

Plight of the Danube flood victims. No. 2216 issued in sheets of 5 stamps and label with signature of Miró and date of flood. No. 2217 contains one stamp with simulated perforation.

The Sense of Sight, by Gonzales Coques A675

"The Senses," paintings by Gonzales Coques (1614-1684): 20b, Hearing. 35b, Smell. 60b, Taste. 1.75 l, Touch. 3 l, Bruckenthal Museum, Sibiu. 5 l, View of Sibiu, 1808, horiz.

1970, Dec. 15 **Photo.** *Perf. 13½*

2218 A675 10b gold & multi .15 .15
2219 A675 20b gold & multi .15 .15
2220 A675 35b gold & multi .15 .15
2221 A675 60b gold & multi .18 .15
2222 A675 1.75 l gold & multi .60 .26
2223 A675 3 l gold & multi 1.00 .45
Nos. 2218-2223 (6) 2.23
Set value .92

Miniature Sheet

Imperf

2224 A675 5 l gold & multi 2.00 2.00

Men of Three Races A676

1971, Feb. 23 **Photo.** *Perf. 13½*

2225 A676 1.50 l multi .45 .15

Intl. year against racial discrimination.

Tudor Vladimirescu, by Theodor Aman — A677

1971, Feb. 20

2226 A677 1.50 l gold & multi .45 .15

Vladimirescu, patriot, 150th death anniv.

German Shepherd A677a

Dogs: 35b, Bulldog. 55b, Fox terrier. 1 l, Setter. 1.50 l, Cocker spaniel. 2.40 l, Poodle.

1971, Feb. 22

2227 A677a 20b blk & multi .15 .15
2228 A677a 35b blk & multi .15 .15
2229 A677a 55b blk & multi .20 .15
2230 A677a 1 l blk & multi .28 .15

2231 A677a 1.50 l blk & multi .40 .22
2232 A677a 2.40 l blk & multi .85 .42
Nos. 2227-2232 (6) 2.03
Set value .95

Paris Commune A678

Congress Emblem A679

1971, Mar. 15 Photo. *Perf. 13½*
2233 A678 40b multicolored .15 .15

Centenary of the Paris Commune.

1971, Mar. 23
2234 A679 55b multicolored .18 .15

Romanian Trade Unions Congress.

Rock Formation A680

Designs: 10b, Bicazului Gorge, vert. 55b, Winter resort. 1 l, Danube Delta view. 1.50 l, Lakeside resort. 2.40 l, Venus, Jupiter, Neptune Hotels on Black Sea.

1971, Apr. 15
Size: 23x38mm, 38x23mm
2235 A680 10b multi .15 .15
2236 A680 40b multi .15 .15
2237 A680 55b multi .18 .15
2238 A680 1 l multi .30 .15
2239 A680 1.50 l multi .50 .20

Size: 76½x28mm
2240 A680 2.40 l multi 1.00 .35
Nos. 2235-2240 (6) 2.28
Set value .85

Tourist publicity.

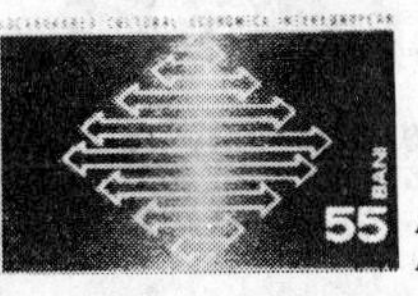

Arrow Pattern A681

Design: 1.75 l, Wave pattern.

1971, Apr. 28 Photo. *Perf. 13½*
2241 A681 55b multi .75 .60
2242 A681 1.75 l multi 1.50 1.00

Inter-European Cultural and Economic Collaboration. Sheets of 10.

Historical Museum — A682

Demonstration, by A. Anastasiu — A684

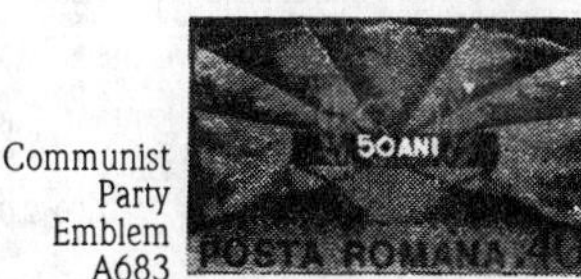

Communist Party Emblem A683

1971, May 7 Photo. *Perf. 13½*
2243 A682 55b blue & multi .15 .15

For Romania's Historical Museum.

1971, May 8

35b, Reading Proclamation, by Stefan Szonyi.

2244 A684 35b multicolored .15 .15
2245 A683 40b multicolored .15 .15
2246 A684 55b multicolored .18 .15
Set value .15

Romanian Communist Party, 50th anniv.

Souvenir Sheets

Motra Tone, by Kole Idromeno A685

Dancing the Hora, by Theodor Aman — A686

Designs: b, Maid by V. Dimitrov-Maystora. c, Rosa Botzaris, by Joseph Stieler. d, Woman in Costume, by Katarina Ivanovic. e, Argeseanca, by Carol Popp de Szathmary. f, Woman in Modern Dress, by Calli Ibrahim.

1971, May 25 Photo. *Perf. 13½*
2247 A685 Sheet of 6 3.50 3.00
a.-f. 1.20 l any single .50 .38
2248 A686 5 l multicolored 2.25 2.25

Balkanphila III Stamp Exhibition, Bucharest, June 27-July 2.

No. 2247 contains 6 stamps in 3 rows and 6 labels showing exhibition emblem and "60b."

Pomegranate Flower — A687

Flowers: 35b, Slipperwort. 55b, Lily. 1 l, Mimulus. 1.50 l, Morning-glory. 2.40 l, Leaf cactus, horiz.

1971, June 20
2249 A687 20b ultra & multi .15 .15
2250 A687 35b red & multi .15 .15
2251 A687 55b ultra & multi .15 .15
2252 A687 1 l car & multi .35 .15
2253 A687 1.50 l car & multi .60 .15
2254 A687 2.40 l ultra & multi .95 .26
Nos. 2249-2254 (6) 2.35
Set value .65

Nude, by Iosif Iser — A688

Paintings of Nudes: 20b, by Camil Ressu. 35b, by Nicolae Grigorescu. 60b, by Eugene Delacroix (odalisque). 1.75 l, by Auguste Renoir. 3 l, by Palma il Vecchio (Venus and Amor). 5 l, by Il Bronzino (Venus and Amor). 60b, 3 l, 5 l, horiz.

1971, July 25 Photo. *Perf. 13½*
Size: 38x50mm, 49x39mm, 29x50mm (20b)
2255 A688 10b gold & multi .15 .15
2256 A688 20b gold & multi .15 .15
2257 A688 35b gold & multi .15 .15
2258 A688 60b gold & multi .15 .15
2259 A688 1.75 l gold & multi .38 .18
2260 A688 3 l gold & multi 1.40 .38
Set value 2.10 .75

Miniature Sheet
Imperf
2261 A688 5 l gold & multi 2.00 2.00

Ships in Storm, by B. Peters — A689

Paintings of Ships by: 20b, Ludolf Backhuysen. 35b, Andries van Eertvelt. 60b, M. W. Arnold. 1.75 l, Ivan Konstantinovich Aivazovski. 3 l, Jean Steriadi. 5 l, N. Darascu, vert.

1971, Sept. 15 Photo. *Perf. 13½*
2262 A689 10b gold & multi .15 .15
2263 A689 20b gold & multi .15 .15
2264 A689 35b gold & multi .15 .15
2265 A689 60b gold & multi .15 .15
2266 A689 1.75 l gold & multi .45 .20
2267 A689 3 l gold & multi 1.00 .35
Set value 1.75 .75

Miniature Sheet
2268 A689 5 l gold & multi 2.00 2.00

Types of Regular Issue

Designs as Before and: 3.60 l, Mail collector. 4.80 l, Mailman. 6 l, Ministry of Posts.

1971 Photo. *Perf. 13½*
Size: 16½x23mm, 23x16½mm
2269 A616 1 l emerald .22 .15
2270 A617 1.20 l red lilac .28 .15
2271 A617 1.35 l brt blue .30 .15
2272 A616 1.50 l orange red .35 .15
2273 A616 1.55 l sepia .35 .15
2274 A617 1.75 l deep green .38 .15
2275 A617 2 l citron .45 .15
2276 A616 2.40 l dark blue .55 .15
2277 A617 3 l greenish bl .70 .15
2278 A617 3.20 l ocher .70 .15
2279 A616 3.25 l ultra .85 .15
2280 A616 3.60 l blue 1.00 .15
2281 A617 4 l lilac rose 1.25 .15
2282 A616 4.80 l grnsh blue 1.40 .15
2283 A617 5 l violet 1.40 .15
2284 A616 6 l dp magenta 1.50 .15
Nos. 2269-2284 (16) 11.68
Set value .80

Prince Neagoe Basarab — A690

Theodor Pallady (Painter) — A691

1971, Sept. 20 *Perf. 13½*
2288 A690 60b gold & multi .20 .15

450th anniversary of the death of Prince Neagoe Basarab of Walachia.

1971, Oct. 12 Photo. *Perf. 13½*

Portraits of: 55b, Benvenuto Cellini (1500-1571), sculptor. 1.50 l, Antoine Watteau (1684-1721), painter. 2.40 l, Albrecht Dürer (1471-1528), painter.

2289 A691 40b gold & multi .15 .15
2290 A691 55b gold & multi .15 .15
2291 A691 1.50 l gold & multi .50 .15
2292 A691 2.40 l gold & multi 1.00 .26
Nos. 2289-2292 (4) 1.80
Set value .52

Anniversaries of famous artists.

Proclamation of Cyrus the Great — A692

Figure Skating — A693

1971, Oct. 12
2293 A692 55b multicolored .18 .15

2500th anniversary of the founding of the Persian empire by Cyrus the Great.

1971, Oct. 25

Designs: 20b, Ice hockey. 40b, Biathlon (skier). 55b, Bobsledding. 1.75 l, Skiing. 3 l, Sapporo '72 emblem. 5 l, Olympic flame and emblem.

2294 A693 10b lt bl, blk & red .15 .15
2295 A693 20b multicolored .15 .15
2296 A693 40b multicolored .15 .15
2297 A693 55b lt bl, blk & red .15 .15
2298 A693 1.75 l lt bl, blk & red .50 .16
2299 A693 3 l lt bl, blk & red .80 .28
Set value 1.60 .60

Miniature Sheet
Imperf
2300 A693 5 l multicolored 2.00 2.00

11th Winter Olympic Games, Sapporo, Japan, Feb. 3-13, 1972. Nos. 2294-2296 printed se-tenant in sheets of 15 (5x3); Nos. 2297-2298 printed se-tenant in sheets of 10 (5x2). No. 2300 contains one stamp 37x50mm.

St. George and the Dragon A694

Frescoes from North Moldavian Monasteries: 10b, 20b, 40b, Moldovita. 55b, 1.75 l, 5 l, Voronet. 3 l, Arborea, horiz.

1971, Nov. 30 Photo. *Perf. 13½*
2301 A694 10b gold & multi .15 .15
2302 A694 20b gold & multi .15 .15
2303 A694 40b gold & multi .15 .15
2304 A694 55b gold & multi .15 .15
2305 A694 1.75 l gold & multi .60 .18
2306 A694 3 l gold & multi .90 .40
Nos. 2301-2306 (6) 2.10
Set value .75

Miniature Sheet
Imperf
2307 A694 5 l gold & multi 1.90 1.50

No. 2307 contains one stamp 44x56mm.

Ferdinand Magellan A695

Designs: 55b, Johannes Kepler and observation tower. 1 l, Yuri Gagarin and rocket orbiting earth. 1.50 l, Baron Ernest R. Rutherford, atom, nucleus and chemical apparatus.

1971, Dec. 20

2308 A695 40b grn, brt rose & dk bl .15 .15
2309 A695 55b lil, bl & gray grn .15 .15
2310 A695 1 l violet & multi .30 .15
2311 A695 1.50 l red brn, grn & bl .50 .16
Nos. 2308-2311 (4) 1.10
Set value .38

Magellan (1480?-1521), navigator; Kepler (1571-1630), astronomer; Gagarin, 1st man in space, 10th anniv.; Ernest R. Rutherford (1871-1937), British physicist.

Matei Millo — A696

Young Communists Union Emblem — A697

Design: 1 l, Nicolae Iorga.

1971, Dec.

2312 A696 55b blue & multi .15 .15
2313 A696 1 l purple & multi .28 .15
Set value .20

Millo (1814-1896), playwright; Iorga (1871-1940), historian and politician.

1972, Feb.

2314 A697 55b dk bl, red & gold .18 .15

Young Communists Union, 50th anniv.

Young Animals — A698

1972, Mar. 10 Photo. *Perf. 13½*

2315 A698 20b Lynx .15 .15
2316 A698 35b Foxes .15 .15
2317 A698 55b Roe fawns .15 .15
2318 A698 1 l Wild pigs .28 .15
2319 A698 1.50 l Wolves .40 .20
2320 A698 2.40 l Bears .85 .26
Nos. 2315-2320 (6) 1.98
Set value .75

Wrestling — A699

Olympic Rings and: 20b, Canoeing. 55b, Soccer. 1.55 l, Women's high jump. 2.90 l, Boxing. 6.70 l, Field ball.

1972, Apr. 25 Photo. *Perf. 13½*

2321 A699 10b yel & multi .15 .15
2322 A699 20b multicolored .15 .15
2323 A699 55b gray & multi .15 .15
2324 A699 1.55 l grn & multi .35 .18
2325 A699 2.90 l multicolored .80 .24
2326 A699 6.70 l lil & multi 1.25 .50
Nos. 2321-2326 (6) 2.85
Set value 1.05

20th Olympic Games, Munich, Aug. 26-Sept. 10. See Nos. C186-C187.

Stylized Map of Europe and Links A700

Design: 2.90 l, Entwined arrows and links.

1972, Apr. 28

2327 A700 1.75 l dp car, gold & blk 1.10 .75
2328 A700 2.90 l grn, gold & blk 1.50 1.00
a. Pair, #2327-2328 2.60 2.00

Inter-European Cultural and Economic Collaboration.

UIC Emblem and Trains A701

1972, May 20 Photo. *Perf. 13½*

2329 A701 55b dp car rose, blk & gold .18 .15

50th anniv., Intl. Railroad Union (UIC).

Souvenir Sheet

"Summer," by Peter Brueghel, the Younger — A702

1972, May 20 *Perf. 13x13½*

2330 A702 6 l gold & multi 2.00 2.00

Belgica 72, Intl. Phil. Exhib., Brussels, June 24-July 9.

Peony — A703

Protected Flowers: 40b, Pink. 55b, Edelweiss. 60b, Nigritella rubra. 1.35 l, Narcissus. 2.90 l, Lady's slipper.

1972, June 5 Photo. *Perf. 13*

Flowers in Natural Colors

2331 A703 20b dk vio bl .15 .15
2332 A703 40b chocolate .15 .15
2333 A703 55b dp blue .15 .15
2334 A703 60b dk green .18 .15
2335 A703 1.35 l violet .50 .18
2336 A703 2.90 l dk Prus bl .90 .40
Nos. 2331-2336 (6) 2.03
Set value .88

Saligny Bridge, Cernavoda — A704

Danube Bridges: 1.75 l, Giurgeni Bridge, Vadul. 2.75 l, Friendship Bridge, Giurgiu-Ruse.

1972, June 25 Photo. *Perf. 13½*

2337 A704 1.35 l multi .35 .15
2338 A704 1.75 l multi .50 .15
2339 A704 2.75 l multi .85 .20
Nos. 2337-2339 (3) 1.70 .50

North Railroad Station, Bucharest, Cent. A705

1972, July 4

2340 A705 55b ultra & multi .24 .15

Water Polo and Olympic Rings A706

Olympic Rings and: 20b, Pistol shoot. 55b, Discus. 1.55 l, Gymnastics, women's. 2.75 l, Canoeing. 6.40 l, Fencing.

1972, July 5 Photo. *Perf. 13½*

2341 A706 10b ol, gold & lil .15 .15
2342 A706 20b red, gold & grn .15 .15
2343 A706 55b grn, gold & brn .15 .15
2344 A706 1.55 l vio, gold & ol .25 .15
2345 A706 2.75 l bl, gold & gray .45 .18
2346 A706 6.40 l pur, gold & gray 1.10 .38
Set value 2.00 .85

20th Olympic Games, Munich, Aug. 26-Sept. 11. See No. C187.

Stamp Printing Press — A707

1972, July 25

2347 A707 55b multicolored .18 .15

Centenary of the stamp printing office.

Stefan Popescu, Self-portrait A708

1972, Aug. 10

2348 A708 55b shown .15 .15
2349 A708 1.75 l Octav Bancila .28 .15
2350 A708 2.90 l Gheorghe Petrascu .50 .16
2351 A708 6.50 l Ion Andreescu 1.25 .30
Nos. 2348-2351 (4) 2.18
Set value .65

Self-portraits by Romanian painters.

Runner with Torch, Olympic Rings — A709

City Hall Tower, Sibiu — A710

1972, Aug. 13

2352 A709 55b sil, bl & claret .18 .15

Olympic torch relay from Olympia, Greece, to Munich, Germany, passing through Romania.

1972 Photo. *Perf. 13*

Designs: 1.85 l, St. Michael's Cathedral, Cluj. 2.75 l, Sphinx Rock, Mt. Bucegi, horiz. 3.35 l, Heroes' Monument, Bucharest. 3.45 l, Sinaia Castle, horiz. 5.15 l, Hydroelectric Works, Arges, horiz. 5.60 l, Church of the Epiphany, Iasi. 6.20 l, Bran Castle. 6.40 l, Hunedoara Castle, horiz. 6.80 l, Polytechnic Institute, Bucharest, horiz. 7.05 l, Black Church, Brasov. 8.45 l, Atheneum, Bucharest. 9.05 l, Excavated Coliseum, Sarmizegetusa, horiz. 9.10 l, Hydroelectric Station, Iron Gate, horiz. 9.85 l, Monument, Cetatea. 11.90 l, Republic Palace, horiz. 12.75 l, Television Station. 13.30 l, Arch, Alba Iulia, horiz. 16.20 l, Clock Tower, Sighisoara.

Size: 23x18mm, 17x24mm

2353 A710 1.85 l brt purple .35 .15
2354 A710 2.75 l gray .50 .15
2355 A710 3.35 l magenta .60 .15
2356 A710 3.45 l green .55 .15
2357 A710 5.15 l brt blue .95 .15
2358 A710 5.60 l blue 1.00 .15
2359 A710 6.20 l cerise 1.10 .15
2360 A710 6.40 l sepia 1.25 .15
2361 A710 6.80 l rose red 1.25 .15
2362 A710 7.05 l black 1.40 .15
2363 A710 8.45 l rose red 1.50 .15
2364 A710 9.05 l dull green 1.65 .15
2365 A710 9.10 l ultra 1.65 .15
2366 A710 9.85 l green 1.65 .15

Size: 19½x29mm, 29x21mm

2367 A710 10 l dp brown 1.90 .15
2368 A710 11.90 l bluish blk 2.25 .15
2369 A710 12.75 l dk violet 2.50 .18
2370 A710 13.30 l dull red 2.50 .20
2371 A710 16.20 l olive grn 3.00 .28
Nos. 2353-2371,C193 (20) 30.30
Set value 2.00

View of Satu-Mare — A711

1972, Oct. 5

2372 A711 55b multicolored .20 .15

Millennium of Satu-Mare.

Tennis Racket and Davis Cup A712

1972, Oct. 10 *Perf. 13½*

2373 A712 2.75 l multi .75 .25

Davis Cup finals between Romania and US, Bucharest, Oct. 13-15.

Venice, by Gheorge Petrascu — A713

Paintings of Venice by: 20b, N. Darascu. 55b, Petrascu. 1.55 l, Marius Bunescu. 2.75 l, N. Darascu, vert. 6 l, Petrascu. 6.40 l, Marius Bunescu.

1972, Oct. 20

2374 A713 10b gray & multi .15 .15
2375 A713 20b gray & multi .15 .15
2376 A713 55b gray & multi .15 .15
2377 A713 1.55 l gray & multi .28 .15
2378 A713 2.75 l gray & multi .55 .18
2379 A713 6.40 l gray & multi 1.40 .38
Nos. 2374-2379 (6) 2.68
Set value .85

Souvenir Sheet

2380 A713 6 l gray & multi 2.00 2.00

Fencing, Bronze Medal — A714

Apollo 1, 2 and 3 — A715

Designs: 20b, Team handball, bronze medal. 35b, Boxing, silver medal. 1.45 l, Hurdles, women's, silver medal. 2.75 l, Pistol shoot, silver medal. 6.20 l, Wrestling, gold medal.

1972, Oct. 28

2381 A714	10b red org & multi	.15	.15
2382 A714	20b lt grn & multi	.15	.15
2383 A714	35b multicolored	.15	.15
2384 A714	1.45 l multi	.28	.18
2385 A714	2.75 l ocher & multi	.55	.24
2386 A714	6.20 l bl & multi	1.40	.48
	Nos. 2381-2386 (6)	2.68	
	Set value		1.00

Romanian medalists at 20th Olympic Games. See No. C191. For surcharge see No. 2493.

Charity Labels

Stamp day issues frequently have an attached, fully perforated, label with a face value. These are Romanian Philatelic Association charity labels. They are inscribed "AFR." The stamps are valued with label attached. When the "label" is part of the stamp, the stamp is listed in the semi-postal section. See Nos. B426-B430.

Stamp Day Semi-Postal Type of 1968

Design: Traveling Gypsies, by Emil Volkers.

1972, Nov. 15 Photo. *Perf. 13½*

2386A SP288	1.10 l + 90b label	.55	.35

Stamp Day.

1972, Dec. 27 Photo. *Perf. 13½*

2387 A715	10b shown	.15	.15
2388 A715	35b Grissom, Chaffee and White, 1967	.15	.15
2389 A715	40b Apollo 4, 5, 6	.15	.15
2390 A715	55b Apollo 7, 8	.15	.15
2391 A715	1 l Apollo 9, 10	.22	.15
2392 A715	1.20 l Apollo 11, 12	.28	.15
2393 A715	1.85 l Apollo 13, 14	.38	.15
2394 A715	2.75 l Apollo 15, 16	.60	.15
2395 A715	3.60 l Apollo 17	1.10	.30
	Nos. 2387-2395 (9)	3.18	
	Set value		.90

Highlights of US Apollo space program. See No. C192.

"25" and Flags — A716

Designs: 1.20 l, "25" and national emblem. 1.75 l, "25" and factory.

1972, Dec. 25

2396 A716	55b blue & multi	.18	.15
2397 A716	1.20 l yel & multi	.35	.15
2398 A716	1.75 l ver & multi	.60	.18
	Nos. 2396-2398 (3)	1.13	
	Set value		.38

25th anniversary of the Republic.

European Bee-eater A717

Globeflowers A718

Nature Protection: No. 2400, Red-breasted goose. No. 2401, Penduline tit. No. 2403, Garden Turk's-cap. No. 2404, Gentian.

1973, Feb. 5 Photo. *Perf. 13*

2399 A717	1.40 l gray & multi	.24	.15
2400 A717	1.85 l multi	.35	.15
2401 A717	2.75 l blue & multi	.70	.20
a.	Strip of 3, #2399-2401	1.40	.60
2402 A718	1.40 l multi	.24	.15
2403 A718	1.85 l yellow & multi	.35	.15
2404 A718	2.75 l multi	.70	.20
a.	Strip of 3, #2402-2404	1.40	.60

Nicolaus Copernicus — A719

1973, Feb. 19 Photo. *Perf. 13x13½*

2405 A719	2.75 l multi	.70	.25

Nicolaus Copernicus (1473-1543), Polish astronomer. Printed with alternating label publicizing Intl. Phil. Exhib., Poznan, Aug. 19-Sept. 2.

Suceava Woman A720

D. Paciurea (Sculptor) A721

Regional Costumes: 40b, Suceava man. 55b, Harghita woman. 1.75 l, Harghita man. 2.75 l, Gorj woman. 6.40 l, Gorj man.

1973, Mar. 15

2406 A720	10b lt bl & multi	.15	.15
2407 A720	40b multicolored	.15	.15
2408 A720	55b bis & multi	.15	.15
2409 A720	1.75 l lil & multi	.30	.15
2410 A720	2.75 l multi	.48	.15
2411 A720	6.40 l multi	1.25	.35
	Nos. 2406-2411 (6)	2.48	
	Set value		.65

1973, Mar. 26

Portraits: 40b, I. Slavici (1848-1925), writer. 55b, G. Lazar (1779-1823), writer. 6.40 l, A. Flechtenmacher (1823-1898), composer.

2412 A721	10b multi	.15	.15
2413 A721	40b multi	.15	.15
2414 A721	55b multi	.16	.15
2415 A721	6.40 l multi	1.10	.38
	Nos. 2412-2415 (4)	1.56	
	Set value		.54

Anniversaries of famous artists.

Map of Europe A722

Design: 3.60 l, Symbol of collaboration.

1973, Apr. 28 Photo. *Perf. 13½*

2416 A722	3.35 l dp bl & gold	1.10	.70
2417 A722	3.60 l brt mag & gold	1.25	1.00
a.	Pair, #2416-2417	2.35	2.00

Inter-European cultural and economic cooperation. Printed in sheets of 10 with blue marginal inscription.

Souvenir Sheet

The Rape of Proserpina, by Hans von Aachen — A723

1973, May 5

2418 A723	12 l gold & multi	2.75	2.50

IBRA Munchen 1973, Intl. Stamp Exhib., Munich, May 11-20.

Prince Alexander I. Cuza — A724

Hand with Hammer and Sickle — A725

1973, May 5 Photo. *Perf. 13½*

2419 A724	1.75 l multi	.50	.15

Alexander Ioan Cuza (1820-1873), prince of Romania, Moldavia and Walachia.

1973, May 5

2420 A725	40b gold & multi	.18	.15

Workers and Peasants Party, 25th anniv.

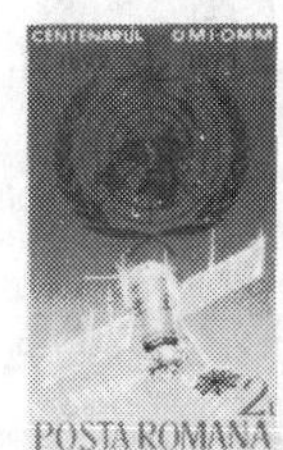

Romanian Flag, Bayonets Stabbing Swastika — A726

WMO Emblem, Weather Satellite — A727

1973, May 5

2421 A726	55b multicolored	.18	.15

Anti-fascist Front, 40th anniversary.

1973, June 15

2422 A727	2 l ultra & multi	.50	.15

Intl. meteorological cooperation, cent.

Dimitrie Ralet Holding Letter A728

Dimitrie Cantemir A729

Portraits with letters. 60b, Enachita Vacarescu, by A. Chladek. 1.55 l, Serdarul Dimitrie Aman, by C. Lecca.

1973, June 20

2423 A728	40b multi	.15	.15
2424 A728	60b multi	.18	.15
2425 A728	1.55 l multi	.50	.24
	Nos. 2423-2425,B432 (4)	2.08	
	Set value		.85

"The Letter on Romanian Portraits." Socfilex III Philatelic Exhibition, Bucharest, July 20-29. See No. B433.

1973, June 25

Design: 6 l, Portrait of Cantemir in oval frame.

2426 A729	1.75 l multi	.48	.15

Souvenir Sheet

2427 A729	6 l multi	2.00	1.40

Dimitrie Cantemir (1673-1723), Prince of Moldavia, writer. No. 2427 contains one 38x50mm stamp.

Plate — A730

Designs: 10b, Fibulae, vert. 55b, Jug, vert. 1.55 l, Necklaces and fibula. 2.75 l, Plate, vert. 6.80 l, Octagonal bowl with animal handles. 12 l, Breast-plate, vert.

1973, July 25 Photo. *Perf. 13½*

2428 A730	10b vio bl & multi	.15	.15
2429 A730	20b green & multi	.15	.15
2430 A730	55b red & multi	.18	.15
2431 A730	1.55 l multi	.35	.15
2432 A730	2.75 l plum & multi	.60	.15
2433 A730	6.80 l multi	1.50	.35
	Nos. 2428-2433 (6)	2.93	
	Set value		.75

Souvenir Sheet

2434 A730	12 l multi	2.75	2.50

Roman gold treasure of Pietroasa, 4th century.

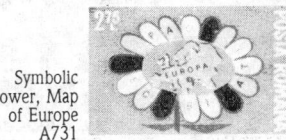

Symbolic Flower, Map of Europe A731

Design: 5 l, Map of Europe, symbolic tree.

1973, Oct. 2 Photo. *Perf. 13½*

2435 A731	2.75 l multi	1.10	.70
2436 A731	5 l multi	1.75	1.00
a.	Sheet, 2 each + 2 labels	5.50	5.50

Conference for European Security and Cooperation, Helsinki, Finland, July 1973.

Jug and Cloth, Oboga — A732

Designs: 20b, Plate and Pitcher, Vama. 55b, Bowl, Marginea. 1.55 l, Pitcher and plate, Sibiu-Saschiz. 2.75 l, Bowl and jug, Pisc. 6.80 l, Figurine (fowl), Oboga.

1973, Oct. 15 *Perf. 13*

2437 A732	10b multi	.15	.15
2438 A732	20b multi	.15	.15
2439 A732	55b multi	.18	.15
2440 A732	1.55 l multi	.35	.15
2441 A732	2.75 l multi	.60	.15
2442 A732	6.80 l multi	1.50	.35
	Nos. 2437-2442 (6)	2.93	
	Set value		.75

Pottery and cloths from various regions of Romania.

Postilion, by A. Verona — A732a

1973, Nov. 15 Photo. *Perf. 13½*

2442A A732a 1.10 l + 90b label .38 .15

Stamp Day.

Women Workers, by G. Saru A733

Paintings of Workers: 20b, Construction Site, by M. Bunescu, horiz. 55b, Shipyard Workers, by H. Catargi, horiz. 1.55 l, Worker, by Catargi. 2.75 l, Miners, by A. Phoebus. 6.80 l, Spinner, by Nicolae Grigorescu. 12 l, Farmers at Rest, by Stefan Popescu, horiz.

1973, Nov. 26 Photo. *Perf. 13½*

2443 A733	10b gold & multi	.15	.15
2444 A733	20b gold & multi	.15	.15
2445 A733	55b gold & multi	.18	.15
2446 A733	1.55 l gold & multi	.35	.15
2447 A733	2.75 l gold & multi	.60	.15
2448 A733	6.80 l gold & multi	1.50	.35
	Nos. 2443-2448 (6)	2.93	
	Set value		.75

Miniature Sheet

2449 A733 12 l gold & multi 2.50 2.25

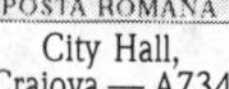

City Hall, Craiova — A734

Tugboat under Bridge — A735

Designs: 10b, Infinite Column, by Constantin Brancusi, vert. 20b, Heroes' Mausoleum, Marasesti. 35b, Risnov Citadel. 40b, Densus Church, vert. 50b, B j Church, vert. 55b, Maldaresti Fortress. 60b, National Theater, Iasi. 1 l, Curtea-de-Arges Monastery, vert. 1.20 l, Tirgu-Mures Citadel. 1.45 l, Cargoship Dimbovita. 1.50 l, Muntenia passenger ship. 1.55 l, Three-master Mircea. 1.75 l, Motorship Transilvania. 2.20 l, Ore carrier Oltul. 3.65 l, Trawler Mures. 4.70 l, Tanker Arges.

1973-74 Photo. *Perf. 13*

2450 A734	5b lake	.15	.15
2451 A734	10b brt blue	.15	.15
2452 A734	20b orange	.15	.15
2453 A734	35b green	.15	.15
2454 A734	40b dk violet	.15	.15
2455 A734	50b ultra	.15	.15
2456 A734	55b orange brn	.15	.15
2457 A734	60b carmine	.15	.15
2458 A734	1 l dp ultra	.25	.15
2459 A734	1.20 l olive grn	.30	.15
2460 A735	1.35 l gray	.35	.15
2461 A735	1.45 l dull blue	.35	.15
2462 A735	1.50 l car rose	.38	.15
2463 A735	1.55 l violet bl	.38	.15
2464 A735	1.75 l slate grn	.45	.15
2465 A735	2.20 l brt blue	.60	.15
2466 A735	3.65 l dull lilac	.95	.15
2467 A735	4.70 l violet brn	1.40	.15
	Nos. 2450-2467 (18)	6.61	
	Set value		.90

Issue dates: Nos. 2450-2459, Dec. 15, 1973. Nos. 2460-2467, Jan. 28, 1974.

Boats at Montfleur, by Claude Monet — A736

Impressionistic paintings: 40b, Church of Moret, by Alfred Sisley, vert. 55b, Orchard in Bloom, by Camille Pissarro. 1.75 l, Portrait of Jeanne, by Pissarro, vert. 2.75 l, Landscape, by Auguste Renoir. 3.60 l, Portrait of a Girl, by Paul Cezanne, vert. 10 l, Women Taking Bath, by Renoir, vert.

1974, Mar. 15 Photo. *Perf. 13½*

2468 A736	20b blue & multi	.15	.15
2469 A736	40b blue & multi	.15	.15
2470 A736	55b blue & multi	.15	.15
2471 A736	1.75 l blue & multi	.40	.15
2472 A736	2.75 l blue & multi	.60	.15
2473 A736	3.60 l blue & multi	.80	.26
	Nos. 2468-2473 (6)	2.25	
	Set value		.64

Souvenir Sheet

2474 A736 10 l blue & multi 2.25 2.00

Harness Racing A737

Designs: Various horse races.

1974, Apr. 5 Photo. *Perf. 13½*

2475 A737	40b ver & multi	.15	.15
2476 A737	55b bis & multi	.15	.15
2477 A737	60b multi	.18	.15
2478 A737	1.55 l multi	.35	.15
2479 A737	2.75 l multi	.60	.20
2480 A737	3.45 l multi	.80	.30
	Nos. 2475-2480 (6)	2.23	
	Set value		.75

Centenary of horse racing in Romania.

Nicolae Titulescu (1883-1941) — A738

1974, Apr. 16

2481 A738 1.75 l multi .50 .15

Interparliamentary Session, Bucharest, Apr. 1974. Titulescu was the first Romanian delegate to the League of Nations.

Souvenir Sheet

Roman Memorial with First Reference to Napoca (Cluj) — A739

1974, Apr. 18 Photo. *Perf. 13*

2482 A739 10 l multi 2.00 2.00

1850th anniv. of the elevation of the Roman settlement of Napoca (Cluj) to a municipality.

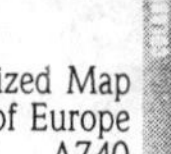

Stylized Map of Europe A740

Design: 3.45 l, Satellite over earth.

1974, Apr. 25 Photo. *Perf. 13½x13*

2483 A740	2.20 l multi	1.25	.70
2484 A740	3.45 l multi	1.50	1.00
a.	Pair, #2483-2484	2.75	2.00

Inter-European Cultural Economic Cooperation.

Young Pioneers with Banners, by Pepene Cornelia — A741

1974, Apr. 25 Photo. *Perf. 13½*

2485 A741 55b multicolored .20 .15

25th anniv. of the Romanian Pioneers Org.

Mail Motorboat, UPU Emblem A742

UPU Emblem and: 40b, Mail train. 55b, Mail-plane and truck. 1.75 l, Mail delivery by motorcycle. 2.75 l, Mailman delivering letter to little girl. 3.60 l, Young stamp collectors. 4 l, Mail collection. 6 l, Modern post office.

1974, May 11

2486 A742	20b gray & multi	.15	.15
2487 A742	40b multicolored	.15	.15
2488 A742	55b ultra & multi	.18	.15
2489 A742	1.75 l multi	.40	.15
2490 A742	2.75 l brn & multi	.60	.20
2491 A742	3.60 l org & multi	.85	.30
	Nos. 2486-2491 (6)	2.33	
	Set value		.75

Souvenir Sheet

2492	Sheet of 2	3.25	2.50
a.	A742 4 l multi	.85	
b.	A742 6 l multi	1.40	

Centenary of Universal Postal Union.

Size of stamps of No. 2492, 28x24mm.

An imperf airmail UPU souvenir sheet of one (10 l) exists. The multicolored stamp is 49x38mm. This sheet is not known to have been sold to the public at post offices.

No. 2382 Surcharged with New Value and Overprinted: "ROMÂNIA / CAMPIOANA / MONDIALĂ / 1974"

1974, May 13

2493 A714 1.75 l on 20b multi 2.50 1.75

Romania's victory in World Handball Championship, 1974.

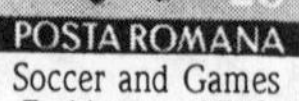

Soccer and Games Emblem — A743

"25" — A744

Designs: Games emblem and various scenes from soccer game.

1974, June 25 *Perf. 13½*

2494 A743	20b purple & multi	.15	.15
2495 A743	40b multi	.15	.15
2496 A743	55b ultra & multi	.18	.15
2497 A743	1.75 l brn & multi	.40	.15
2498 A743	2.75 l multi	.60	.20
2499 A743	3.60 l vio & multi	.85	.30
	Nos. 2494-2499 (6)	2.33	
	Set value		.80

Souvenir Sheet

2500 A743 10 l multi 2.50 2.00

World Cup Soccer Championship, Munich, June 13-July 7. No. 2500 contains one horizontal stamp 50x38mm.

An imperf. 10 l airmail souvenir sheet exists showing a globe as soccer ball and satellite. Gray blue margin showing Soccer Cup, radio tower and stadium; black control number.

1974, June 10

2501 A744 55b blue & multi .20 .15

25th anniv. of the Council for Mutual Economic Assistance (COMECON).

UN Emblem and People — A745

Hand Drawing Peace Dove — A746

1974, June 25 Photo. *Perf. 13½*

2502 A745 2 l multicolored .50 .15

World Population Year.

1974, June 28

2503 A746 2 l ultra & multi .50 .15

25 years of the National and Intl. Movement to Uphold the Cause of Peace.

Ioan, Prince of Wallachia A747

Soldier, Industry and Agriculture A748

Hunedoara Iron and Steel Works — A749

Designs: 1.10 l, Avram Iancu (1824-1872). 1.30 l, Dr. C. I. Parhon (1874-1969). 1.40 l, Bishop Dosoftei (1624-1693).

1974 Photo. *Perf. 13*

2504 A747	20b blue	.15	.15
2505 A748	55b carmine rose	.18	.15
2506 A749	1 l slate green	.28	.15
2507 A747	1.10 l dk gray ol	.28	.15
2508 A747	1.30 l dp magenta	.30	.15
2509 A747	1.40 l dk violet	.38	.15
	Nos. 2504-2509 (6)	1.57	
	Set value		.32

No. 2505 for Army Day, No. 2506 for 220th anniv. of Hunedoara Iron and Steel works; others for anniversaries of famous Romanians. Issue dates; 1l, June 17; others June 25.

Romanians and Flags — A750

Design: 40b, Romanian and Communist flags forming "XXX," vert.

1974, Aug. 20

2510	A750	40b gold, ultra & car	.15	.15
2511	A750	55b yellow & multi	.18	.15
		Set value		.15

Romania's liberation from Fascist rule, 30th anniv.

Souvenir Sheet

View, Stockholm — A751

1974, Sept. 10 **Photo.** ***Perf. 13***

2512	A751	10 l multicolored	2.00	2.00

Stockholmia 74 International Philatelic Exhibition, Stockholm, Sept. 21-29.

Thistle — A752

Nature Protection: 40b, Checkered lily. 55b, Yew. 1.75 l, Azalea. 2.75 l, Forget-me-not. 3.60 l, Pinks.

1974, Sept. 15

2513	A752	20b plum & multi	.15	.15
2514	A752	40b multi	.15	.15
2515	A752	55b multi	.18	.15
2516	A752	1.75 l multi	.40	.15
2517	A752	2.75 l brn & multi	.60	.20
2518	A752	3.60 l multi	.85	.30
		Nos. 2513-2518 (6)	2.33	
		Set value		.80

Isis, First Century A.D. — A753

Archaeological art works excavated in Romania: 40b, Serpent, by Glycon. 55b, Emperor Trajan, bronze bust. 1.75 l, Roman woman, statue, 3rd century. 2.75 l, Mithraic bas-relief. 3.60 l, Roman man, statue, 3rd century.

1974, Oct. 20 **Photo.** ***Perf. 13***

2519	A753	20b multi	.15	.15
2520	A753	40b ultra & multi	.15	.15
2521	A753	55b multi	.18	.15
2522	A753	1.75 l multi	.40	.15
2523	A753	2.75 l brn & multi	.60	.20
2524	A753	3.60 l multi	.85	.30
		Nos. 2519-2524 (6)	2.33	
		Set value		.80

Romanian Communist Party Emblem A754

Design: 1 l, similar to 55b.

1974, Nov. 20

2525	A754	55b blk, red & gold	.18	.15
2526	A754	1 l blk, red & gold	.28	.15
		Set value		.15

9th Romanian Communist Party Congress.

Discobolus and Olympic Rings A755

1974, Nov. 11

2527	A755	2 l ultra & multi	.45	.15

Romanian Olympic Committee, 60th anniv.

Skylab A756

1974, Dec. 14 **Photo.** ***Perf. 13***

2528	A756	2.50 l multi	.60	.35

Skylab, manned US space laboratory. No. 2528 printed in sheets of 4 stamps and 4 labels. A 10 l imperf. souvenir sheet exists showing Skylab.

Field Ball and Games' Emblem — A757

Designs: 1.75 l, 2.20 l, Various scenes from field ball; 1.75 l, vert.

1975, Jan. 3

2529	A757	55b ultra & multi	.18	.15
2530	A757	1.75 l yellow & multi	.40	.15
2531	A757	2.20 l multi	.50	.18
		Nos. 2529-2531 (3)	1.08	
		Set value		.36

World University Field Ball Championship.

Rocks and Birches, by Andreescu A758

Paintings by Ion Andreescu (1850-1882): 40b, Farm Woman with Green Kerchief. 55b, Winter in the Woods. 1.75 l, Winter in Barbizon, horiz. 2.75 l, Self-portrait. 3.60 l, Main Road, horiz.

1975, Jan. 24

2532	A758	20b multi	.15	.15
2533	A758	40b multi	.15	.15
2534	A758	55b multi	.18	.15
2535	A758	1.75 l multi	.40	.15
2536	A758	2.75 l multi	.60	.20
2537	A758	3.60 l multi	.85	.30
		Nos. 2532-2537 (6)	2.33	
		Set value		.80

Torch with Flame in Flag Colors and Coat of Arms — A759

1975, Feb. 1

2538	A759	40b multicolored	.15	.15

Romanian Socialist Republic, 10th anniv.

Vaslui Battle, by O. Obedeanu A760

1975, Feb. 8 **Photo.** ***Perf. 13½***

2539	A760	55b gold & multi	.18	.15

Battle at the High Bridge, Stephan the Great's victory over the Turks, 500th anniv.

Woman Spinning, by Nicolae Grigorescu A761

Michelangelo, Self-portrait A762

1975, Mar. 1

2540	A761	55b gold & multi	.18	.15

International Women's Year.

1975, Mar. 10

2541	A762	5 l multicolored	.85	.28

Michelangelo Buonarroti (1475-1564), Italian sculptor, painter and architect.

For overprint see No. 2581.

Souvenir Sheet

Escorial Palace and España 75 Emblem — A763

1975, Mar. 15 **Photo.** ***Perf. 13***

2542	A763	10 l multi	2.00	1.75

Espana 75 Intl. Phil. Exhib., Madrid, Apr. 4-13.

Letter with Postal Code, Pigeon A764

1975, Mar. 26 **Photo.** ***Perf. 13½***

2543	A764	55b blue & multi	.18	.15

Introduction of postal code system.

Children's Science Pavilion — A765

1975, Apr. 10 **Photo.** ***Perf. 13***

2544	A765	4 l multicolored	.75	.20

Oceanexpo 75, International Exhibition, Okinawa, July 20, 1975-Jan. 1976.

Peonies, by N. Tonitza A766

Design: 3.45 l, Chrysanthemums, by St. Luchian.

1975, Apr. 28

2545	A766	2.20 l gold & multi	.85	.50
2546	A766	3.45 l gold & multi	1.25	.95
a.		Pair, #2545-2546	2.10	1.75

Inter-European Cultural and Economic Cooperation. Printed checkerwise in sheets of 10 (2x5).

1875 Meter Convention Emblem A767

1975, May 10 **Photo.** ***Perf. 13***

2547	A767	1.85 l bl, blk & gold	.50	.15

Cent. of Intl. Meter Convention, Paris, 1875.

Mihail Eminescu and his Home — A768

1975, June 5

2548	A768	55b multicolored	.18	.15

Milhail Eminescu (1850-1889), poet.

Marble Plaque and Dacian Coins 1st-2nd Centuries — A769

1975, May 26

2549	A769	55b multicolored	.18	.15

2000th anniv. of the founding of Alba Iulia (Apulum).

Souvenir Sheet

"On the Bank of the Seine," by Th. Pallady — A770

1975, May 26

2550 A770 10 l multicolored 2.25 1.75

ARPHILA 75, Paris, June 6-16.

Dr. Albert Schweitzer (1875-1965), Medical Missionary — A771

1974, Dec. 20 Photo. *Perf. 13½*

2551 A771 40b black brown .15 .15

Ana Ipatescu A772

Policeman with Walkie-talkie A773

1975, June 2 Photo. *Perf. 13½*

2552 A772 55b lilac rose .18 .15

Ana Ipatescu, fighter in 1848 revolution.

1975, Sept. 1

2553 A773 55b brt blue .20 .15

Publicity for traffic rules.

Monument and Projected Reconstruction, Adam Clissi — A777

Roman Monuments: 55b, Emperor Trajan, bas-relief, vert. 1.20 l, Trajan's column, Rome, vert. 1.55 l, Governor Decibalus, bas-relief, vert. 2 l, Excavated Roman city, Turnu-Severin. 2.25 l, Trajan's Bridge, ruin and projected reconstruction. No. 2569, Roman fortifications, vert.

1975, June 26 Photo. *Perf. 13½*

2563 A777	55b	red brn & blk	.15	.15
2564 A777	1.20 l	vio bl & blk	.24	.15
2565 A777	1.55 l	green & blk	.24	.15
2566 A777	1.75 l	dl rose & multi	.35	.15
2567 A777	2 l	dl yel & blk	.40	.15
2568 A777	2.25 l	brt bl & blk	.50	.18
		Nos. 2563-2568 (6)	1.88	
		Set value		.65

Souvenir Sheet

2569 A777 10 l multicolored 2.75 2.00

European Architectural Heritage Year.

An imperf. 10 l gold and dark brown souvenir sheet exists showing the Roman wolf suckling Romulus and Remus.

A similar souvenir sheet exists with the Roman wolf 10 l imperf. It appeared in 1978, honoring the Intl. Stamp Fair, Essen, Germany.

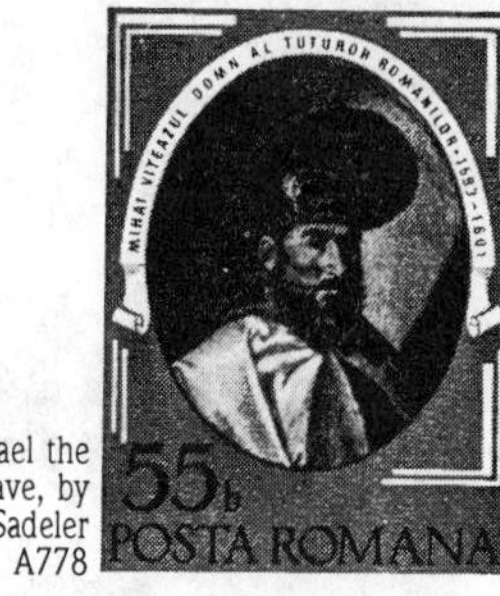

Michael the Brave, by Sadeler A778

Michael the Brave Statue — A779

Designs: 1.20 l, Ottoman Messengers Offering Gifts to Michael the Brave, by Theodor Aman, horiz. 2.75 l, Michael the Brave in Battle of Calugareni, by Aman.

1975, July 7

2571 A778	55b	gold & blk	.18	.15
2572 A778	1.20 l	gold & multi	.28	.15
2573 A778	2.75 l	gold & multi	.60	.20
		Nos. 2571-2573 (3)	1.06	
		Set value		.35

Souvenir Sheet

Imperf

2574 A779 10 l gold & multi 18.00 16.00

First political union of Romanian states under Michael the Brave, 375th anniv.

No. 2574 issued Sept. 20.

Larkspur — A780

1975, Aug. 15 Photo. *Perf. 13½*

2575 A780	20b	shown	.15	.15
2576 A780	40b	Field poppies	.15	.15
2577 A780	55b	Xeranthemum annuum	.18	.15
2578 A780	1.75 l	Rockrose	.40	.15
2579 A780	2.75 l	Meadow sage	.60	.18
2580 A780	3.60 l	Wild chicory	.85	.25
		Nos. 2575-2580 (6)	2.33	
		Set value		.68

No. 2541 Overprinted in Red:

Tîrg internaţional de mărci poştale

Riccione – Italia 23–25 august 1975

1975, Aug. 23

2581 A762 5 l multicolored 1.75 .85

Intl. Phil. Exhib., Riccione, Italy, Aug. 23-25.

Map Showing Location of Craiova, 1750 — A781

Illustration reduced.

1975, Sept. 15 Photo. *Perf. 13½*

2582 A781	Strip of 3	.55	.30
a.	20b ocher, yellow, red & black	.15	.15
b.	55b ocher, yellow, red & black	.15	.15
c.	1 l ocher, yellow, red & black	.24	.15

1750th anniv. of first documentation of Daco-Getian settlement of Pelendava and 500th anniversary of documentation of Craiova.

Size of Nos. 2582a, 2582c: 25x32mm; of No. 2582b: 80x32mm.

Muntenian Rug — A782

Romanian Peasant Rugs: 40b, Banat. 55b, Oltenia. 1.75 l, Moldavia. 2.75 l, Oltenia. 3.60 l, Maramures.

1975, Oct. 5 Photo. *Perf. 13½*

2583 A782	20b	dk bl & multi	.15	.15
2584 A782	40b	black & multi	.15	.15
2585 A782	55b	multicolored	.18	.15
2586 A782	1.75 l	black & multi	.40	.15
2587 A782	2.75 l	multicolored	.60	.18
2588 A782	3.60 l	black & multi	.80	.22
		Nos. 2583-2588 (6)	2.28	
		Set value		.65

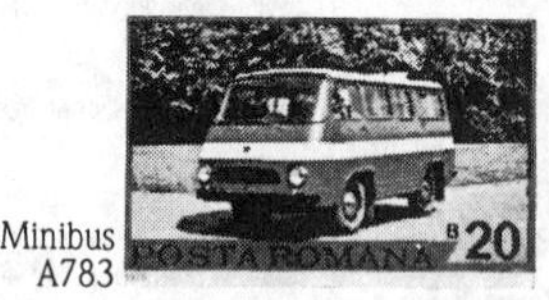

Minibus A783

1975, Nov. 5 Photo. *Perf. 13½*

2589 A783	20b	shown	.15	.15
2590 A783	40b	Gasoline truck	.15	.15
2591 A783	55b	Jeep	.18	.15
2592 A783	1.75 l	Flat-bed truck	.40	.15
2593 A783	2.75 l	Dacia automobile	.60	.18
2594 A783	3.60 l	Dump truck	.85	.22
		Nos. 2589-2594 (6)	2.33	
		Set value		.65

Souvenir Sheet

Winter, by Peter Brueghel, the Younger — A784

1975, Nov. 25 Photo. *Perf. 13½*

2595 A784 10 l multicolored 2.50 2.00

THEMABELGA Intl. Topical Phil. Exhib., Brussels, Dec. 13-21.

Luge and Olympic Games' Emblem — A785

Innsbruck Olympic Games' Emblem and: 40b, Biathlon, vert. 55b, Woman skier. 1.75 l, Ski jump. 2.75 l, Woman figure skater. 3.60 l, Ice hockey. 10 l, Two-man bobsled.

1976, Jan. 12 Photo. *Perf. 13½*

2596 A785	20b	blue & multi	.15	.15
2597 A785	40b	multicolored	.15	.15
2598 A785	55b	multicolored	.18	.15
2599 A785	1.75 l	ol & multi	.40	.15
2600 A785	2.75 l	multi	.60	.20
2601 A785	3.60 l	multi	.80	.38
		Nos. 2596-2601 (6)	2.28	
		Set value		.90

Souvenir Sheet

2602 A785 10 l multi 2.50 2.00

12th Winter Olympic Games, Innsbruck, Austria, Feb. 4-15. An imperf. 10 l souvenir sheet exists showing slalom; Romanian flag, Games' emblem.

Washington at Valley Forge, by W. T. Trego — A786

Paintings: 40b, Washington at Trenton, by John Trumbull, vert. 55b, Washington Crossing the Delaware, by Emanuel Leutze. 1.75 l, The Capture of the Hessians, by Trumbull. 2.75 l, Jefferson, by Thomas Sully, vert. 3.60 l, Surrender of Cornwallis at Yorktown, by Trumbull. 10 l, Signing of the Declaration of Independence, by Trumbull.

1976, Jan. 25 Photo. *Perf. 13½*

2603 A786	20b	gold & multi	.15	.15
2604 A786	40b	gold & multi	.15	.15
2605 A786	55b	gold & multi	.18	.15
2606 A786	1.75 l	gold & multi	.40	.15
2607 A786	2.75 l	gold & multi	.60	.28
2608 A786	3.60 l	gold & multi	.75	.35
		Nos. 2603-2608 (6)	2.23	
		Set value		.92

Souvenir Sheet

2609 A786 10 l gold & multi 2.50 2.00

American Bicentennial. No. 2609 also for Interphil 76 Intl. Phil. Exhib., Philadelphia, Pa., May 20-June 6. Printed in horizontal rows of 4 stamps with centered label showing Bicentennial emblem.

Prayer, by Brancusi
A787

Designs: 1.75 l, Architectural Assembly, by Brancusi. 3.60 l, Constantin Brancusi.

1976, Feb. 15 Photo. *Perf. 13½*

2610 A787	55b purple & multi	.18	.15
2611 A787	1.75 l blue & multi	.40	.18
2612 A787	3.60 l multicolored	.85	.35
	Nos. 2610-2612 (3)	1.43	.68

Constantin Brancusi (1876-1957), sculptor.
For surcharge see No. B440.

Anton Davidoglu — A788

Archives Museum — A789

55b, Vlad Tepes. 1.20 l, Costache Negri.

1976, Feb. 25

2613 A788	40b green & multi	.15	.15
2614 A788	55b green & multi	.18	.15
2615 A788	1.20 l green & multi	.28	.15
2616 A789	1.75 l green & multi	.40	.18
	Nos. 2613-2616 (4)	1.01	
	Set value		.46

Anniversaries: Anton Davidoglu (1876-1958), mathematician; Prince Vlad Tepes, commander in war against the Turks (d. 1476); Costache Negri (1812-1876), Moldavian freedom fighter; Romanian National Archives Museum, founded 1926.

Dr. Carol Davila — A790

Vase with King Decebalus Portrait — A791

1.75 l, Nurse with patient. 2.20 l, First aid.

1976, Apr. 20

2617 A790	55b multi	.18	.15
2618 A790	1.75 l multi	.40	.15
2619 A790	2.20 l yellow & multi	.50	.15
	Nos. 2617-2619,C199 (4)	1.78	
	Set value		.65

Romanian Red Cross cent.

1976, May 13

Design: 3.45 l, Vase with portrait of King Michael the Bold.

2620 A791	2.20 l bl & multi	1.00	.50
2621 A791	3.45 l multi	2.50	1.25

Inter-European Cultural Economic Cooperation. Nos. 2620-2621 each printed in sheets of 4 with marginal inscriptions.

Coat of Arms — A792

Spiru Haret — A793

1976, June 12

2622 A792	1.75 l multi	.40	.18

See design A615.

1976, June 25

2628 A793	20b multicolored	.15	.15

Spiru Haret (1851-1912), mathematician.

Woman Athlete — A794

Romanian Olympic Emblem and: 40b, Boxing. 55b, Team handball. 1.75 l, 2-man scull, horiz. 2.75 l, Gymnast on rings, horiz. 3.60 l, 2-man canoe, horiz. 10 l, Woman gymnast, horiz.

1976, June 25 Photo. *Perf. 13½*

2629 A794	20b org & multi	.15	.15
2630 A794	40b multi	.15	.15
2631 A794	55b multi	.18	.15
2632 A794	1.75 l multi	.40	.15
2633 A794	2.75 l vio & multi	.60	.28
2634 A794	3.60 l bl & multi	.85	.46
	Nos. 2629-2634 (6)	2.33	
	Set value		1.00

Souvenir Sheet

2635 A794	10 l rose & multi	2.50	2.00

21st Olympic Games, Montreal, Canada, July 17-Aug. 1. No. 2635 contains one stamp 49x37mm.
An imperf. airmail 10 l souvenir sheet exists showing Olympic Stadium, Montreal.

Inscribed Stone Tablets, Banat — A795

Designs: 40b, Hekate, Bacchus, bas-relief. 55b, Ceramic fragment, bowl, coins. 1.75 l, Bowl, urn and cup. 2.75 l, Sword, lance and tombstone. 3.60 l, Lances, urn. 10 l, Clay vessel and silver coins.

1976, July 25

2636 A795	20b multi	.15	.15
2637 A795	40b multi	.15	.15
2638 A795	55b org & multi	.18	.15
2639 A795	1.75 l multi	.40	.15
2640 A795	2.75 l fawn & multi	.60	.28
2641 A795	3.60 l multi	.85	.35
	Nos. 2636-2641 (6)	2.33	
	Set value		.92

Souvenir Sheet

2642 A795	10 l yel & multi	2.50	2.00

Daco-Roman archaeological treasures. No. 2642 issued Mar. 25. An imperf. 10 l souvenir sheet exists showing a silver and gold vase and silver coins.

Wolf Statue, 4th Century Map
A796

1976, Aug. 25

2643 A796	55b multi	.18	.15

Founding of Buzau, 1600th anniv.

Game
A797

1976, Sept. 20

2644 A797	20b Red deer	.15	.15
2645 A797	40b Brown bear	.15	.15
2646 A797	55b Chamois	.18	.15
2647 A797	1.75 l Boar	.40	.15
2648 A797	2.75 l Red fox	.60	.18
2649 A797	3.60 l Lynx	.85	.22
	Nos. 2644-2649 (6)	2.33	
	Set value		.65

Dan Grecu, Bronze Medal
A798

Nadia Comaneci — A799

40b, Fencing, bronze medal. 55b Gheorge Megelea (Javelin), bronze medal. 1.75 l, Handball, silver medal. 2.75 l, Boxing, 1 bronze, 2 silver medals. 3.60 l, Wrestling, silver and bronze medals. 10 l, Vasile Daba (kayak), gold and silver medals, vert.

1976, Oct. 20 Photo. *Perf. 13½*

2650 A798	20b multi	.15	.15
2651 A798	40b car & multi	.15	.15
2652 A798	55b grn & multi	.18	.15
2653 A798	1.75 l red & multi	.40	.15
2654 A798	2.75 l bl & multi	.60	.28
2655 A798	3.60 l multi	.80	.40
2656 A799	5.70 l multi	1.40	.48
	Nos. 2650-2656 (7)	3.68	
	Set value		1.40

Souvenir Sheet

2657 A798	10 l multi	2.50	2.00

Romanian Olympic medalists. No. 2657 contains one 37x50mm stamp.

Milan Cathedral — A800

1976, Oct. 20 Photo. *Perf. 13½*

2658 A800	4.75 l multi	1.10	.38

ITALIA 76 Intl. Phil. Exhib., Milan, Oct. 14-24.

Oranges and Carnations, by Luchian — A801

Paintings by Stefan Luchian (1868-1916): 40b, Flower arrangement. 55b, Vase with flowers. 1.75 l, Roses. 2.75 l, Cornflowers. 3.60 l, Carnations in vase.

1976, Nov. 5

2659 A801	20b multi	.15	.15
2660 A801	40b multi	.15	.15
2661 A801	55b multi	.18	.15
2662 A801	1.75 l multi	.40	.15
2663 A801	2.75 l multi	.60	.28
2664 A801	3.60 l multi	.85	.35
	Nos. 2659-2664 (6)	2.33	
	Set value		.92

Arms of Alba — A802

Designs: Arms of Romanian counties.

1976-77 Photo. *Perf. 13½*

2665 A802	55b shown	.25	.15
2666 A802	55b Arad	.25	.15
2667 A802	55b Arges	.25	.15
2668 A802	55b Bacau	.25	.15
2669 A802	55b Bihor	.25	.15
2670 A802	55b Bistrita-Nasaud	.25	.15
2671 A802	55b Botosani	.25	.15
2672 A802	55b Brasov	.25	.15
2673 A802	55b Braila	.25	.15
2674 A802	55b Buzau	.25	.15
2675 A802	55b Caras-Severin	.25	.15
2676 A802	55b Cluj	.25	.15
2677 A802	55b Constanta	.25	.15
2678 A802	55b Covasna	.25	.15
2679 A802	55b Dimbovita	.25	.15
2680 A802	55b Dolj	.25	.15
2681 A802	55b Galati	.25	.15
2682 A802	55b Gorj	.25	.15
2683 A802	55b Harghita	.25	.15
2684 A802	55b Hunedoara	.25	.15
2685 A802	55b Ialomita	.25	.15
2686 A802	55b Iasi	.25	.15
2687 A802	55b Ilfov	.25	.15
2688 A802	55b Maramures	.25	.15
2689 A802	55b Mehedinti	.25	.15
2690 A802	55b Mures	.25	.15
2691 A802	55b Neamt	.25	.15
2692 A802	55b Olt	.25	.15
2693 A802	55b Prahova	.25	.15
2694 A802	55b Salaj	.25	.15
2695 A802	55b Satu-Mare	.25	.15
2696 A802	55b Sibiu	.25	.15
2697 A802	55b Suceava	.25	.15
2698 A802	55b Teleorman	.25	.15
2699 A802	55b Timis	.25	.15
2700 A802	55b Tulcea	.25	.15
2701 A802	55b Vaslui	.25	.15
2702 A802	55b Vilcea	.25	.15

2703 A802 55b Vrancea .25 .15
2704 A802 55b Postal emblem .25 .15
Nos. 2665-2704 (40) 10.00
Set value 3.25

Sheets of 50 (10x5) contain 5 designs: Nos. 2665-2669; 2670-2674; 2675-2679; 2680-2684; 2685-2689; 2690-2694; 2695-2699; 2700-2704. Each row of 10 contains 5 pairs of each design.

Issue dates: Nos. 2665-2679, Dec. 20, 1976. Nos. 2680-2704, Sept. 5, 1977.

Oxcart, by Grigorescu — A803

Paintings by Nicolae Grigorescu (1838-1907): 1 l, Self-portrait, vert. 1.50 l, Shepherdess. 2.15 l, Woman Spinning with Distaff. 3.40 l, Shepherd, vert. 4.80 l, Rest at Well.

1977, Jan. 20 Photo. *Perf. 13½*

2705 A803 55b gray & multi .15 .15
2706 A803 1 l gray & multi .20 .15
2707 A803 1.50 l gray & multi .28 .15
2708 A803 2.15 l gray & multi .38 .15
2709 A803 3.40 l gray & multi .55 .30
2710 A803 4.80 l gray & multi .85 .38
Nos. 2705-2710 (6) 2.41
Set value 1.00

Cheia Telecommunications Station — A804

1977, Feb. 1

2711 A804 55b multi .15 .15

Red Deer A805

Protected Birds and Animals: 1 l, Mute swan. 1.50 l, Egyptian vulture. 2.15 l, Bison. 3.40 l, White-headed ruddy duck. 4.80 l, Kingfisher.

1977, Mar. 20 Photo. *Perf. 13½*

2712 A805 55b multi .15 .15
2713 A805 1 l multi .15 .15
2714 A805 1.50 l multi .20 .15
2715 A805 2.15 l multi .35 .15
2716 A805 3.40 l multi .50 .15
2717 A805 4.80 l multi .75 .22
Nos. 2712-2717 (6) 2.10
Set value .64

Calafat Artillery Unit, by Sava Hentia — A806

Paintings: 55b, Attacking Infantryman, by Oscar Obedeanu, vert. 1.50 l, Infantry Attack in Winter, by Stefan Luchian, vert. 2.15 l, Battle of Plevna (after etching). 3.40 l, Artillery, by Nicolae Ion Grigorescu. 10 l, Battle of Grivita, 1877.

1977

2718 A806 55b gold & multi .15 .15
2719 A806 1 l gold & multi .15 .15
2720 A806 1.50 l gold & multi .24 .15
2721 A806 2.15 l gold & multi .60 .15
2722 A806 3.40 l gold & multi .75 .15
Nos. 2718-2722,B442 (6) 3.14
Set value .70

Souvenir Sheet

2723 A806 10 l gold & multi 2.75 2.00

Centenary of Romania's independence. A 10 l imperf. souvenir sheet exists showing victorious return of army, Dobruja, 1878.

Issued: #2718-2722, May 9; #2723, Apr. 25.

Sinaia, Carpathian Mountains A807

Design: 2.40 l, Hotels, Aurora, Black Sea.

1977, May 17

2724 A807 2 l gold & multi 1.00 .85
2725 A807 2.40 l gold & multi 1.40 1.25

Inter-European Cultural and Economic Cooperation. Nos. 2724-2725 printed in sheets of 4 with marginal inscriptions.

Petru Rares A808

Ion Luca Caragiale A809

1977, June 10 Photo. *Perf. 13½*

2726 A808 40b multi .15 .15

450th anniversary of the elevation of Petru Rares to Duke of Moldavia.

1977, June 10

2727 A809 55b multi .15 .15

Ion Luca Caragiale (1852-1912), writer.

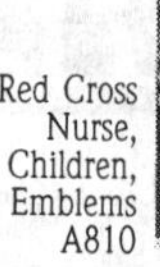

Red Cross Nurse, Children, Emblems A810

1977, June 10

2728 A810 1.50 l multi .35 .15

23rd Intl. Red Cross Conf., Bucharest.

Arch of Triumph, Bucharest A811

1977, June 10

2729 A811 2.15 l multi .50 .15

Battles of Marasesti and Oituz, 60th anniv.

Peaks of San Marino, Exhibition Emblem — A812

1977, Aug. 28 Photo. *Perf. 13½*

2730 A812 4 l brt bl & multi 1.00 .25

Centenary of San Marino stamps, and San Marino '77 Phil. Exhib., San Marino, 8/28-9/4.

Man on Pommel Horse — A813

Gymnasts: 40b, Woman dancer. 55b, Man on parallel bars. 1 l, Woman on balance beam. 2.15 l, Man on rings. 4.80 l, Woman on double bars.

1977, Sept. 25 Photo. *Perf. 13½*

2731 A813 20b multi .15 .15
2732 A813 40b multi .15 .15
2733 A813 55b multi .15 .15
2734 A813 1 l multi .20 .15
2735 A813 2.15 l multi .35 .15
2736 A813 4.80 l multi 1.25 .22
Nos. 2731-2736 (6) 2.25
Set value .50

"Carpati" near Cazane, Iron Gate — A814

Designs: 1 l, "Mircesti" at Orsova. 1.50 l, "Oltenita" at Calafat. 2.15 l, Water bus at Giurgiu. 3 l, "Herculane" at Tulcea. 3.40 l, "Muntenia" in Nature preserve, Sulina. 4.80 l, Map of Danube Delta with Sulina Canal. 10 l, Danubius, god of Danube, from Trajan's Column, Rome, vert.

1977, Dec. 28

2737 A814 55b multi .15 .15
2738 A814 1 l multi .15 .15
2739 A814 1.50 l multi .24 .15
2740 A814 2.15 l multi .40 .15
2741 A814 3 l multi .60 .20
2742 A814 3.40 l multi .65 .20
2743 A814 4.80 l multi 1.25 .30
Nos. 2737-2743 (7) 3.44
Set value 1.05

Souvenir Sheet

2744 A814 10 l multi 2.75 2.00

European Danube Commission.

A 10 l imperf. souvenir sheet exists showing map of Danube from Regensburg to the Black Sea.

Flag and Arms of Romania A815

Designs: 1.20 l, Computer production in Romania. 1.75 l, National Theater, Craiova.

1977, Dec. 30

2745 A815 55b multi .15 .15
2746 A815 1.20 l multi .18 .15
2747 A815 1.75 l multi .40 .20
Nos. 2745-2747 (3) .73
Set value .32

Proclamation of Republic, 30th anniversary.

Dancers A816

Designs: Romanian male folk dancers.

1977, Nov. 28 Photo. *Perf. 13½*

2748 A816 20b multi .15 .15
2749 A816 40b multi .15 .15
2750 A816 55b multi .15 .15
2751 A816 1 l multi .15 .15
2752 A816 2.15 l multi .38 .15
2753 A816 4.80 l multi 1.25 .20
Nos. 2748-2753 (6) 2.23
Set value .50

Souvenir Sheet

2754 A816 10 l multi 2.00 2.00

Firiza Dam A817

Hydroelectric Stations and Dams: 40b, Negovanu. 55b, Piatra Neamt. 1 l, Izvorul Muntelui-Bicaz. 2.15 l, Vidraru. 4.80 l, Iron Gate.

1978, Mar. 10 Photo. *Perf. 13½*

2755 A817 20b multi .15 .15
2756 A817 40b multi .15 .15
2757 A817 55b multi .15 .15
2758 A817 1 l multi .15 .15
2759 A817 2.15 l multi .35 .15
2760 A817 4.80 l multi 1.00 .20
Set value 1.70 .50

Soccer and Argentina '78 Emblem — A818

Various soccer scenes & Argentina '78 emblem.

1978, Apr. 15

2761 A818 55b bl & multi .15 .15
2762 A818 1 l org & multi .15 .15
2763 A818 1.50 l yel grn & multi .18 .15
2764 A818 2.15 l ver & multi .30 .15
2765 A818 3.40 l bl grn & multi .50 .15
2766 A818 4.80 l lil rose & multi 1.00 .22
Nos. 2761-2766 (6) 2.28
Set value .56

11th World Cup Soccer Championship, Argentina '78, June 1-25. See No. C222.

King Decebalus of Dacia Statue, Deva A819

Design: 3.40 l, King Mircea the Elder of Walachia statue, Tulcea, and ship.

1978, May 22 Photo. *Perf. 13½*

2767 A819 1.30 l gold & multi .90 .70
2768 A819 3.40 l gold & multi 1.65 1.25

Inter-European Cultural and Economic Cooperation. Each printed in sheet of 4.

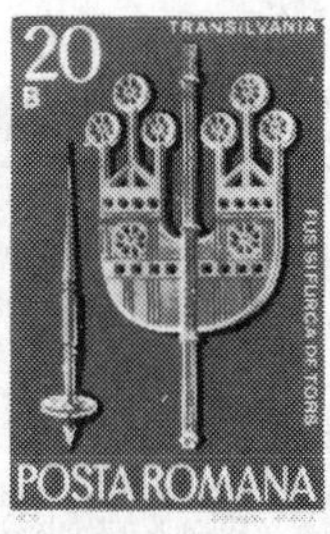

Worker, Factory, Flag — A821

Spindle and Handle, Transylvania — A822

1978, June 11 Photo. *Perf. 13½*

2770 A821 55b multi .15 .15

Nationalization of industry, 30th anniv.

1978, June 20

Wood Carvings: 40b, Cheese molds, Muntenia. 55b, Spoons, Oltenia. 1 l, Barrel, Moldavia. 2.15 l, Ladle and mug, Transylvania. 4.80 l, Water bucket, Oltenia.

2771 A822 20b multi .15 .15
2772 A822 40b multi .15 .15
2773 A822 55b multi .15 .15
2774 A822 1 l multi .15 .15
2775 A822 2.15 l multi .30 .15
2776 A822 4.80 l multi 1.00 .22
Set value 1.65 .50

Danube Delta — A823

Tourist Publicity: 1 l, Bran Castle, vert. 1.50 l, Monastery, Suceava, Moldavia. 2.15 l, Caves, Oltenia. 3.40 l, Ski lift, Brasov. 4.80 l, Mangalia, Black Sea. 10 l, Strehaia Fortress, vert.

1978, July 20 Photo. *Perf. 13½*

2777 A823 55b multi .15 .15
2778 A823 1 l multi .15 .15
2779 A823 1.50 l multi .20 .15
2780 A823 2.15 l multi .30 .15
2781 A823 3.40 l multi .50 .18
2782 A823 4.80 l multi 1.00 .35
Nos. 2777-2782 (6) 2.30
Set value .85

Miniature Sheet

2783 A823 10 l multi 2.50 2.00

No. 2783 contains one 37x51mm stamp. Issued July 30.

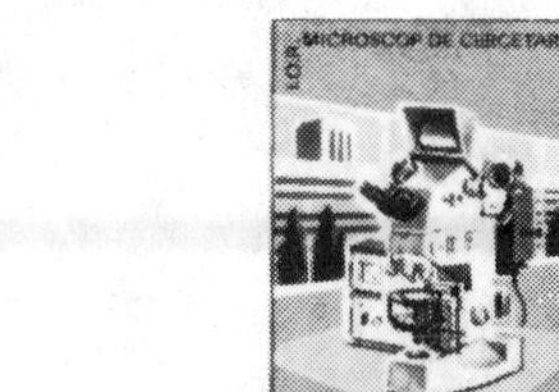

Electronic Microscope A824

Designs: 40b, Hydraulic excavator. 55b, Computer center. 1.50 l, Oil derricks. 3 l, Harvester combine, horiz. 3.40 l, Petrochemical plant.

1978, Aug. 15 Photo. *Perf. 13½*

2784 A824 20b multi .15 .15
2785 A824 40b multi .15 .15
2786 A824 55b multi .15 .15
2787 A824 1.50 l multi .24 .15
2788 A824 3 l multi .55 .15
2789 A824 3.40 l multi .70 .16
Set value 1.70 .45

Industrial development.

Polovraci Cave, Carpathians A825

"Racial Equality" A826

Caves: 1 l, Topolnita. 1.50 l, Ponoare. 2.15 l, Ratei, Mt. Bucegi. 3.40 l, Closani, Mt. Motrului. 4.80 l, Epuran. 1 l, 1.50 l, 4.80 l, Mt. Mehedinti.

1978, Aug. 25 Photo. *Perf. 13½*

2790 A825 55b multi .15 .15
2791 A825 1 l multi .15 .15
2792 A825 1.50 l multi .20 .15
2793 A825 2.15 l multi .30 .15
2794 A825 3.40 l multi .50 .15
2795 A825 4.80 l multi 1.00 .22
Nos. 2790-2795 (6) 2.30
Set value .58

1978, Sept. 28

2796 A826 3.40 l multi .50 .20

Anti-Apartheid Year.

Gold Bas-relief A827

Designs: 40b, Gold armband. 55b, Gold cameo ring. 1 l, Silver bowl. 2.15 l, Eagle from Roman standard, vert. 4.80 l, Silver armband.

1978, Sept. 25

2797 A827 20b multi .15 .15
2798 A827 40b multi .15 .15
2799 A827 55b multi .15 .15
2800 A827 1 l multi .15 .15
2801 A827 2.15 l multi .30 .15
2802 A827 4.80 l multi 1.00 .35
Set value 1.65 .70

Daco-Roman archaeological treasures. An imperf. 10 l souvenir sheet exists showing gold helmet, vert.

Woman Gymnast, Games' Emblem — A828

1 l, Running. 1.50 l, Skiing. 2.15 l, Equestrian. 3.40 l, Soccer. 4.80 l, Handball.

1978, Sept. 15

2803 A828 55b multi .15 .15
2804 A828 1 l multi .15 .15
2805 A828 1.50 l multi .20 .15
2806 A828 2.15 l multi .30 .15
2807 A828 3.40 l multi .50 .15
2808 A828 4.80 l multi 1.00 .26
Nos. 2803-2808 (6) 2.30
Set value .72

Ptolemaic Map of Dacia A829

Designs: 55b, Meeting House of Romanian National Council, Arad. 1.75 l, Pottery vases, 8th-9th centuries, found near Arad.

1978, Oct. 21 Photo. *Perf. 13½*

2809 A829 40b multi .15 .15
2810 A829 55b multi .15 .15
2811 A829 1.75 l multi .35 .15
b. Strip of 3, #2809-2811 .50 .30

2,000th anniversary of founding of Arad.

Dacian Warrior, from Trajan's Column, Rome — A829a

1978, Nov. 5 Photo. *Perf. 13x13½*

2811A A829a 6 l + 3 l label 1.65 .85

NATIONALA '78 Phil. Exhib., Bucharest. Stamp Day.

Assembly at Alba Iulia, 1919 A830

Warrior, Bas-relief A831

Design: 1 l, Open book and Romanian flag.

1978, Dec. 1

2812 A830 55b gold & multi .15 .15
2813 A830 1 l gold & multi .15 .15
Set value .24 .15

60th anniversary of national unity.

1979 Photo. *Perf. 13½*

Design: 1.50 l, Warrior on horseback, bas-relief.

2814 A831 55b multi .15 .15
2815 A831 1.50 l multi .20 .15
Set value .15

2,050 years since establishment of first centralized and independent Dacian state.

"Heroes of Vaslui" — A832

Ice Hockey, Globe, Emblem — A833

Children's Drawings: 1 l, Building houses. 1.50 l, Folk music of Tica. 2.15 l, Industrial landscape, horiz. 3.40 l, winter customs, horiz. 4.80 l, Pioneer festival, horiz.

1979, Mar. 1

2816 A832 55b multi .15 .15
2817 A832 1 l multi .15 .15
2818 A832 1.50 l multi .20 .15
2819 A832 2.15 l multi .30 .15
2820 A832 3.40 l multi .50 .15
2821 A832 4.80 l multi 1.00 .26
Nos. 2816-2821 (6) 2.30
Set value .60

International Year of the Child.

1979, Mar. 16 Photo. *Perf. 13½*

3.40 l, Ice hockey players, globe & emblem.

2822 A833 1.30 l multi .28 .15
2823 A833 3.40 l multi .55 .20
a. Pair, #2822-2823 .85 .50

European Youth Ice Hockey Championship, Miercurea-Ciuc (1.30 l) and World Ice Hockey Championship, Galati (3.40 l).

Dog's-tooth Violet — A834

Protected Flowers: 1 l, Alpine violet. 1.50 l, Linum borzaeanum. 2.15 l, Persian bindweed. 3.40 l, Primula auricula. 4.80 l, Transylvanian columbine.

1979, Apr. 25 Photo. *Perf. 13½*

2824 A834 55b multi .15 .15
2825 A834 1 l multi .15 .15
2826 A834 1.50 l multi .20 .15
2827 A834 2.15 l multi .30 .15
2828 A834 3.40 l multi .50 .15
2829 A834 4.80 l multi 1.00 .26
Nos. 2824-2829 (6) 2.30
Set value .65

Mail Coach and Post Rider, 19th Century A835

1979, May 3 Photo. *Perf. 13*

2830 A835 1.30 l multi .40 .24

Inter-European Cultural and Economic Cooperation. Printed in sheets of 4.
See No. C231.

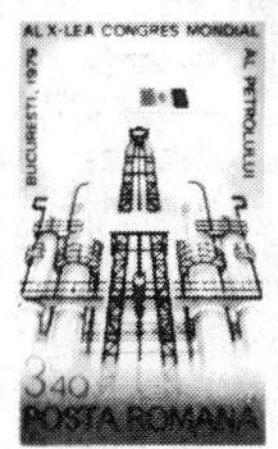

Oil Rig and Refinery — A836

Girl Pioneer — A837

1979, May 24 Photo. *Perf. 13*

2832 A836 3.40 l multi .50 .15

10th World Petroleum Congress, Bucharest.

1979, June 20

2833 A837 55b multi .15 .15

30th anniversary of Romanian Pioneers.

Children with Flowers, IYC Emblem A838

IYC Emblem and: 1 l, Kindergarten. 2 l, Pioneers with rabbit. 4.60 l, Drummer, trumpeters, flags.

1979, July 18 Photo. *Perf. 13½*

2834 A838 40b multi .15 .15
2835 A838 1 l multi .15 .15
2836 A838 2 l multi .30 .15
2837 A838 4.60 l multi .95 .18
Nos. 2834-2837 (4) 1.55
Set value .38

International Year of the Child.

Lady in a Garden, by Tattarescu A839

Stefan Gheorghiu A840

Paintings by Gheorghe Tattarescu: 40b, Mountain woman. 55b, Mountain man. 1 l, Portrait of Gh. Magheru. 2.15 l, The artist's daughter. 4.80 l, Self-portrait.

1979, June 16

2838 A839 20b multi .15 .15
2839 A839 40b multi .15 .15
2840 A839 55b multi .15 .15
2841 A839 1 l multi .15 .15
2842 A839 2.15 l multi .28 .15
2843 A839 4.80 l multi .90 .22
Set value 1.50 .50

1979, Aug.

Designs: 55b, Gheorghe Lazar monument. 2.15 l, Lupeni monument. 4.60 l, Women in front of Memorial Arch.

2844 A840 40b multi .15 .15
2845 A840 55b multi .15 .15
2846 A840 2.15 l multi .30 .15
2847 A840 4.60 l multi .95 .18
Nos. 2844-2847 (4) 1.55
Set value .35

State Theater, Tirgu-Mures — A841

Modern Architecture: 40b, University, Brasov. 55b, Political Administration Buildings, Baia Mare. 1 l, Stefan Gheorghiu Academy, Bucharest. 2.15 l, Political Administration Building, Botosani. 4.80 l, House of Culture, Tirgoviste.

1979, June 25

2848 A841 20b multi .15 .15
2849 A841 40b multi .15 .15
2850 A841 55b multi .15 .15
2851 A841 1 l multi .15 .15
2852 A841 2.15 l multi .24 .15
2853 A841 4.80 l multi .85 .22
Set value 1.35 .50

Flags of Russia and Romania — A842

Design: 1 l, Workers' Militia, by L. Suhar, horiz.

1979, Aug. 20 Photo. *Perf. 13½*

2854 A842 55b multi .15 .15
2855 A842 1 l multi .18 .15
Set value .25 .15

Liberation from Fascism, 35th anniversary.

Cargo Ship Galati — A843

Romanian Ships: 1 l, Cargo ship Bucuresti. 1.50 l, Ore carrier Resita. 2.15 l, Ore carrier Tomis. 3.40 l, Tanker Dacia. 4.80 l, Tanker Independenta.

1979, Aug. 27 Photo. *Perf. 13½*

2856 A843 55b multi .15 .15
2857 A843 1 l multi .15 .15
2858 A843 1.50 l multi .18 .15
2859 A843 2.15 l multi .28 .15
2860 A843 3.40 l multi .45 .15
2861 A843 4.80 l multi .90 .25
Nos. 2856-2861 (6) 2.11
Set value .65

Olympic Stadium, Melbourne, 1956, Moscow '80 Emblem A844

Moscow '80 Emblem and Olympic Stadiums: 1 l, Rome, 1960. 1.50 l, Tokyo, 1964. 2.15 l, Mexico City, 1968. 3.40 l, Munich, 1972. 4.80 l, Montreal, 1976. 10 l, Moscow, 1980.

1979, Oct. 23 Photo. *Perf. 13½*

2862 A844 55b multi .15 .15
2863 A844 1 l multi .15 .15
2864 A844 1.50 l multi .20 .15
2865 A844 2.15 l multi .30 .15
2866 A844 3.40 l multi .50 .15
2867 A844 4.80 l multi 1.00 .25
Nos. 2862-2867 (6) 2.30
Set value .65

Souvenir Sheet

2868 A844 10 l multi 2.50 2.00

22nd Summer Olympic Games, Moscow, July 19-Aug. 3, 1980. No. 2868 contains one 50x38mm stamp.

No. 2868 airmail.

Arms of Alba Iulia — A845

Designs: Arms of Romanian cities.

1979, Oct. 25

2869 A845 1.20 l shown .28 .15
2870 A845 1.20 l Arad .28 .15
2871 A845 1.20 l Bacau .28 .15
2872 A845 1.20 l Baia-Mare .28 .15
2873 A845 1.20 l Birlad .28 .15
2874 A845 1.20 l Botosani .28 .15
2875 A845 1.20 l Braila .28 .15
2876 A845 1.20 l Brasov .28 .15
2877 A845 1.20 l Buzau .28 .15
2878 A845 1.20 l Calarasi .28 .15
2879 A845 1.20 l Cluj .28 .15
2880 A845 1.20 l Constanta .28 .15
2881 A845 1.20 l Craiova .28 .15
2882 A845 1.20 l Dej .28 .15
2883 A845 1.20 l Deva .28 .15
2884 A845 1.20 l Turnu-Severin .28 .15
2885 A845 1.20 l Focsani .28 .15
2886 A845 1.20 l Galati .28 .15
2887 A845 1.20 l Gheorghe Gheorghiu-Dej .28 .15
2888 A845 1.20 l Giurgiu .28 .15
2889 A845 1.20 l Hunedoara .28 .15
2890 A845 1.20 l Iasi .28 .15
2891 A845 1.20 l Lugoj .28 .15
2892 A845 1.20 l Medias .28 .15
2893 A845 1.20 l Odorheiu Seguiesc .28 .15

1980, Jan. 5

2894 A845 1.20 l Oradea .28 .15
2895 A845 1.20 l Petrosani .28 .15
2896 A845 1.20 l Piatra-Neamt .28 .15
2897 A845 1.20 l Pitesti .28 .15
2898 A845 1.20 l Ploiesti .28 .15
2899 A845 1.20 l Resita .28 .15
2900 A845 1.20 l Rimnicu-Vilcea .28 .15
2901 A845 1.20 l Roman .28 .15
2902 A845 1.20 l Satu-Mare .28 .15
2903 A845 1.20 l Sibiu .28 .15
2904 A845 1.20 l Siget-Marmatiei .28 .15
2905 A845 1.20 l Sighisoara .28 .15
2906 A845 1.20 l Suceava .28 .15
2907 A845 1.20 l Tecuci .28 .15
2908 A845 1.20 l Timisoara .28 .15
2909 A845 1.20 l Tirgoviste .28 .15
2910 A845 1.20 l Tirgu-Jiu .28 .15
2911 A845 1.20 l Tirgu-Mures .28 .15
2912 A845 1.20 l Tulcea .28 .15
2913 A845 1.20 l Turda .28 .15
2914 A845 1.20 l Turnu Magurele .28 .15
2915 A845 1.20 l Bucharest .28 .15
Nos. 2869-2915 (47) 13.16
Set value 3.70

A846

A847

Regional Costumes: 20b, Maramures Woman. 40b, Maramures man. 55b, Vrancea woman. 1.50 l, Vrancea man. 3 l, Padureni woman. 3.40 l, Padureni man.

1979, Oct. 27

2916 A846 20b multi .15 .15
2917 A846 40b multi .15 .15
2918 A846 55b multi .15 .15
2919 A846 1.50 l multi .24 .15
2920 A846 3 l multi .48 .15
2921 A846 3.40 l multi .55 .15
Set value 1.45 .45

1979, July 27

Flower Paintings by Stefan Luchian: 40b, Snapdragons. 60b, Triple chrysanthemums. 1.55 l, Potted flowers on stairs.

2922 A847 40b multi .15 .15
2923 A847 60b multi .15 .15
2924 A847 1.55 l multi .24 .15
Nos. 2922-2924,B445 (4) 1.64
Set value .60

Socfilex, International Philatelic Exhibition, Bucharest. See No. B446.

Souvenir Sheet

Romanian Communist Party, 12th Congress — A848

1979, Oct.

2925 A848 5 l multi 1.25 .50

Figure Skating, Lake Placid '80 Emblem, Olympic Rings — A849

1979, Dec. 27 Photo. *Perf. 13½*

2926 A849 55b shown .15 .15
2927 A849 1 l Downhill skiing .15 .15
2928 A849 1.50 l Biathlon .20 .15
2929 A849 2.15 l Two-man bobsledding .28 .15
2930 A849 3.40 l Speed skating .50 .15
2931 A849 4.80 l Ice hockey 1.00 .22
Nos. 2926-2931 (6) 2.28
Set value .60

Souvenir Sheet

2932 A849 10 l Ice hockey, diff. 2.25 1.75

13th Winter Olympic Games, Lake Placid, NY, Feb. 12-24, 1980. No. 2932 contains one 38x50mm stamp. An imperf. 10 l air post souvenir sheet exists showing four-man bobsledding.

"Calugareni", Expo Emblem A850

1979, Dec. 29

2933 A850 55b shown .15 .15
2934 A850 1 l "Orleans" .15 .15
2935 A850 1.50 l #1059, type fawn .20 .15
2936 A850 2.15 l #15021, type 1E .30 .15
2937 A850 3.40 l "Pacific" .50 .15
2938 A850 4.80 l Electric engine 060-EA 1.00 .26
Nos. 2933-2938 (6) 2.30
Set value .65

Souvenir Sheet

2939 A850 10 l Diesel electric 2.50 2.00

Intl. Transport Expo., Hamburg, June 8-July 1. #2939 contains one 50x40mm stamp.

Dacian Warrior, Trajan's Column, Rome — A851

Design: 1.50 l, Two warriors.

1980, Feb. 9 Photo. *Perf. 13½*

2940 A851 55b multi .15 .15
2941 A851 1.50 l multi .30 .15
Set value .16

2,050 years since establishment of first centralized and independent Dacian state.

Kingfisher — A852

1980, Mar. 25 Photo. *Perf. 13½*

2942 A852 55b shown .15 .15
2943 A852 1 l Great white heron, vert. .15 .15
2944 A852 1.50 l Red-breasted goose .18 .15
2945 A852 2.15 l Red deer, vert. .26 .15
2946 A852 3.40 l Roe deer .45 .15
2947 A852 4.80 l European bison, vert. .90 .26
Nos. 2942-2947 (6) 2.09
Set value .65

European Nature Protection Year. A 10 l imperf. souvenir sheet exists showing bears; red control number. See No. C232.

Souvenir Sheets

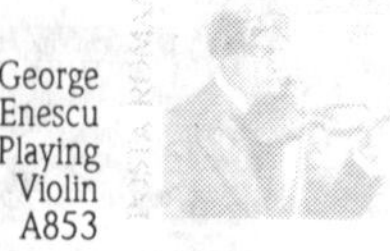

George Enescu Playing Violin A853

1980, May 6

2948 Sheet of 4 1.50 1.50
a. A853 1.30 l shown .25 .15
b. A853 1.30 l Conducting .25 .15
c. A853 1.30 l Playing piano .25 .15
d. A853 1.30 l Composing .25 .15
2949 Sheet of 4 3.25 3.25
a. A853 3.40 l Beethoven in library .70 .25
b. A853 3.40 l Portrait .70 .25
c. A853 3.40 l At piano .70 .25
d. A853 3.40 l Composing .70 .25

Inter-European Cultural and Economic Cooperation.

Vallota Purpurea
A854

Tudor Vladimirescu
A855

1980, Apr. 10 Photo. *Perf. 13½*

2950 A854 55b shown .15 .15
2951 A854 1 l Eichhornia crasipes .15 .15
2952 A854 1.50 l Sprekelia formosissima .20 .15
2953 A854 2.15 l Hypericum calycinum .30 .15
2954 A854 3.40 l Camellia japonica .50 .15
2955 A854 4.80 l Nelumbo nucifera 1.00 .25
Nos. 2950-2955 (6) 2.30
Set value .65

1980, Apr. 24

55b, Mihail Sadoveanu. 1.50 l, Battle against Hungarians. 2.15 l, Tudor Arghezi. 3 l, Horea.

2956 A855 40b multi .15 .15
2957 A855 55b multi .15 .15
2958 A855 1.50 l multi .20 .15
2959 A855 2.15 l multi .30 .15
2960 A855 3 l multi .40 .18
Set value 1.00 .52

Anniversaries: 40b, Tudor Vladimirescu (1780-1821), leader of 1821 revolution; 55b, Mihail Sadoveanu (1880-1961), author; 1.50 l, Victory of Posada; 2.15 l, Tudor Arghezi (1880-1967), poet; 3 l, Horea (1730-1785), leader of 1784 uprising.

A856

A857

Dacian fruit bowl and cup.

1980, May 8

2961 A856 1 l multicolored .18 .15

Petrodava City, 2000th anniversary.

1980, June 20 Photo. *Perf. 13½*

2962 A857 55b Javelin .15 .15
2963 A857 1 l Fencing .15 .15
2964 A857 1.50 l Shooting .20 .15
2965 A857 2.15 l Kayak .30 .15
2966 A857 3.40 l Wrestling .50 .15
2967 A857 4.80 l Rowing 1.00 .26
Nos. 2962-2967 (6) 2.30
Set value .65

Souvenir Sheet

2968 A857 10 l Handball 2.25 1.75

22nd Summer Olympic Games, Moscow, July 19-Aug. 3. No. 2968 contains one 38x50mm stamp. An imperf. 10 l air post souvenir sheet exists showing gymnast.

Congress Emblem — A858

Fireman Rescuing Child — A859

1980, Aug. 10 Photo. *Perf. 13½*

2969 A858 55b multicolored .15 .15

15th Intl. Historical Sciences Congress, Bucharest.

1980, Aug. 25

2970 A859 55b multicolored .15 .15

Firemen's Day, Sept. 13.

Chinese and Romanian Young Pioneers at Stamp Show — A860

1980, Sept. 18

2971 A860 1 l multicolored .20 .15

Romanian-Chinese Phil. Exhib., Bucharest.

Souvenir Sheet

Parliament Building, Bucharest
A861

1980, Sept. 30

2972 A861 10 l multicolored 2.00 1.65

European Security Conference, Madrid. An imperf. 10 l air post souvenir sheet exists showing Plaza Mayor, Madrid.

Knights and Chessboard
A862

1980, Oct. 1 Photo. *Perf. 13½*

2973 A862 55b shown .15 .15
2974 A862 1 l Rooks .15 .15
2975 A862 2.15 l Man .30 .15
2976 A862 4.80 l Woman 1.00 .26
Nos. 2973-2976 (4) 1.60
Set value .45

Chess Olympiad, Valletta, Malta, Nov. 20-Dec. 8.

Dacian Warrior — A863

Burebista Sculpture — A864

1980, Oct. 15

2977 A863 20b shown .15 .15
2978 A863 40b Moldavian soldier, 15th cent. .15 .15
2979 A863 55b Walachian horseman, 17th cent. .15 .15
2980 A863 1 l Flag bearer, 19th cent. .15 .15
2981 A863 1.50 l Infantryman, 19th cent. .20 .15
2982 A863 2.15 l Lancer, 19th cent. .30 .15
2983 A863 4.80 l Mounted Elite Corps Guard, 19th cent. 1.00 .35
Set value (7) 1.85 .80

1980, Nov. 5 Photo. *Perf. 13½*

2984 A864 2 l multicolored .35 .15

2050 years since establishment of first centralized and independent Dacian state.

George Oprescu (1881-1969), Art Critic — A865

National Dog Show — A866

Famous Men: 2.15 l, Marius Bunescu (1881-1971), painter. 3.40 l, Ion Georgescu (1856-1898), sculptor.

1981, Feb. 20 Photo. *Perf. 13½*

2985 A865 1.50 l multi .20 .15
2986 A865 2.15 l multi .30 .15
2987 A865 3.40 l multi .50 .25
Nos. 2985-2987 (3) 1.00
Set value .50

1981, Mar. 15

Designs: Dogs. 40b, 1 l, 1.50 l, 3.40 l horiz.

2988 A866 40b Mountain sheepdog .15 .15
2989 A866 55b Saint Bernard .15 .15
2990 A866 1 l Fox terrier .15 .15
2991 A866 1.50 l German shepherd .20 .15
2992 A866 2.15 l Boxer .30 .15
2993 A866 3.40 l Dalmatian .50 .16
2994 A866 4.80 l Poodle 1.00 .22
Nos. 2988-2994 (7) 2.45
Set value .68

River Steamer Stefan cel Mare
A867

1981, Mar. 25

2995 A867 55b shown .15 .15
2996 A867 1 l Vas de Supraveghere .15 .15
2997 A867 1.50 l Tudor Vladimirescu .24 .15
2998 A867 2.15 l Dredger Sulina .30 .15
2999 A867 3.40 l Republica Populara Romana .50 .24
3000 A867 4.80 l Sulina Canal 1.00 .35
Nos. 2995-3000 (6) 2.34
Set value .95

Souvenir Sheet

3001 A867 10 l Galati 2.50 2.00

European Danube Commission, 125th anniv. An imperf. 10 l souvenir sheet exists showing map of Danube.

Carrier Pigeon
A868

Designs: Various carrier pigeons and doves.

1981, Apr. 15 Photo. *Perf. 13½*

3002 A868 40b multi .15 .15
3003 A868 55b multi .15 .15
3004 A868 1 l multi .15 .15
3005 A868 1.50 l multi .20 .15
3006 A868 2.15 l multi .30 .15
3007 A868 3.40 l multi .50 .24
Nos. 3002-3007 (6) 1.45
Set value .65

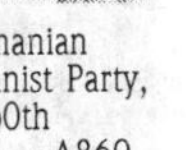

Romanian Communist Party, 60th Anniv. — A869

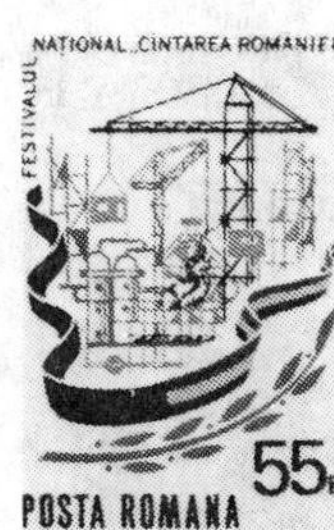

Singing Romania Festival — A871

Folkdance, Moldavia
A870

1981, Apr. 22 Photo. *Perf. 13½*

3008 A869 1 l multicolored .18 .15

1981, May 4 Photo. *Perf. 13½*

Designs: Regional folkdances.

3009 Sheet of 4 2.50 2.50
a. A870 2.50 l shown .45 .45
b. A870 2.50 l Transylvania .45 .45
c. A870 2.50 l Banat .45 .45
d. A870 2.50 l Muntenia .45 .45
3010 Sheet of 4 2.50 2.50
a. A870 2.50 l Maramures .45 .45
b. A870 2.50 l Dobruja .45 .45
c. A870 2.50 l Oltenia .45 .45
d. A870 2.50 l Crisana .45 .45

Inter-European Cultural and Economic Cooperation.

1981, July 15

3011 A871 55b Industry .15 .15
3012 A871 1.50 l Electronics .24 .15
3013 A871 2.15 l Agriculture .35 .18
3014 A871 3.40 l Culture .50 .30
Nos. 3011-3014 (4) 1.24
Set value .62

University '81 Games, Bucharest
A872

Theodor Aman, Artist, Birth Sesquicentennial
A873

1981, July 17

3015 A872 1 l Book, flag .15 .15
3016 A872 2.15 l Emblem .35 .18
3017 A872 4.80 l Stadium, horiz. 1.00 .35
Nos. 3015-3017 (3) 1.50 .68

1981, July 28

Aman Paintings: 40b, Self-portrait. 55b, Battle of Giurgiu. 1 l, The Family Picnic. 1.50 l, The Painter's Studio. 2.15 l, Woman in Interior. 3.40 l,

Aman Museum, Bucharest. 55b, 1 l, 1.50 l, 3.40 l horiz.

3018 A873 40b multi .15 .15
3019 A873 55b multi .15 .15
3020 A873 1 l multi .15 .15
3021 A873 1.50 l multi .28 .15
3022 A873 2.15 l multi .35 .18
3023 A873 3.40 l multi .60 .24
Nos. 3018-3023 (6) 1.68
Set value .68

Thinker of Cernavoda, 3rd Cent. BC — A874

1981, July 30
3024 A874 3.40 l multi .50 .24

16th Science History Congress.

Blood Donation Campaign — A875

Romanian Musicians — A877

Bucharest Central Military Hospital Sesquicentennial — A876

1981, Aug. 15 **Photo.** ***Perf. 13½***
3025 A875 55b multicolored .15 .15

1981, Sept. 1
3026 A876 55b multicolored .15 .15

1981, Sept. 20

Designs: 40b, George Enescu (1881-1955). 55b, Paul Constantinescu (1909-1963). 1 l, Dinu Lipatti (1917-1950). 1.50 l, Ionel Perlea (1900-1970). 2.15 l, Ciprian Porumbescu (1853-1883). 3.40 l, Mihail Jora (1891-1971).

3027 A877 40b multi .15 .15
3028 A877 55b multi .15 .15
3029 A877 1 l multi .15 .15
3030 A877 1.50 l multi .28 .15
3031 A877 2.15 l multi .35 .18
3032 A877 3.40 l multi .50 .24
Nos. 3027-3032 (6) 1.58
Set value .72

Stamp Day — A879

1981, Nov. 5 **Photo.** ***Perf. 13½***
3034 A879 2 l multicolored .35 .15

Children's Games — A880

Illustrations by Eugen Palade (40b, 55b, 1 l) and Norman Rockwell.

1981, Nov. 25
3035 A880 40b Hopscotch .15 .15
3036 A880 55b Soccer .15 .15
3037 A880 1 l Riding stick horse .15 .15
3038 A880 1.50 l Snagging the Big One .24 .15
3039 A880 2.15 l A Patient Friend .30 .18
3040 A880 3 l Doggone It .40 .20
3041 A880 4 l Puppy Love .48 .35
Nos. 3035-3041,C243 (8) 2.39
Set value 1.25

A881

A882

1981, Dec. 28
3042 A881 55b multi .15 .15
3043 A881 1 l multi .18 .15
3044 A881 1.50 l multi .28 .15
3045 A881 2.15 l multi .35 .18
3046 A881 3.40 l multi .50 .24
3047 A881 4.80 l multi 1.00 .38
Nos. 3042-3047 (6) 2.46
Set value 1.00

Souvenir Sheet

3048 A881 10 l multi 2.00 2.00

Espana '82 World Cup Soccer.

No. 3048 contains one 38x50mm stamp. An imperf. 10 l air post souvenir sheet exists showing game.

1982, Jan. 30 **Photo.** ***Perf. 13½***

Designs: 1 l, Prince Alexander the Good of Moldavia (ruled 1400-1432). 1.50 l, Bogdan Petriceicu Hasdeu (1838-1907), scholar. 2.15 l, Nicolae Titulescu (1882-1941), diplomat.

3049 A882 1 l multi .20 .15
3050 A882 1.50 l multi .28 .15
3051 A882 2.15 l multi .38 .20
Nos. 3049-3051 (3) .86 .50

Bucharest Subway System A883

1982, Feb. 25
3052 A883 60b Union Square station entrance .15 .15
3053 A883 2.40 l Heroes' Station platform .40 .24
Set value .32

60th Anniv. of Communist Youth Union — A884

1982
3054 A884 1 l shown .20 .15
3055 A884 1.20 l Construction worker .20 .15
3056 A884 1.50 l Farm workers .28 .15
3057 A884 2 l Research .35 .18
3058 A884 2.50 l Workers .50 .24
3059 A884 3 l Musicians, dancers .60 .28
Nos. 3054-3059 (6) 2.13
Set value .94

Dog Sled A885

1 l, 3 l, 4 l, 4.80 l, 5 l, vertical.

1982, Mar. 28 **Photo.** ***Perf. 13½***
3060 A885 55b Dog rescuing child .15 .15
3061 A885 1 l Shepherd, dog .18 .15
3062 A885 3 l Hunting dog .55 .35
3063 A885 3.40 l shown .60 .35
3064 A885 4 l Spitz, woman .70 .40
3065 A885 4.80 l Guide dog, woman .80 .45
3066 A885 5 l Dalmatian, girl .95 .48
3067 A885 6 l Saint Bernard 1.00 .40
Nos. 3060-3067 (8) 4.93 2.73

Bran Castle, Brasov, 1377 A886

1982, May 6
3068 Sheet of 4 2.50 2.50
a. A886 2.50 l shown .55 .55
b. A886 2.50 l Hunedoara, Corvinilor, 1409 .55 .55
c. A886 2.50 l Sinaia, 1873 .55 .55
d. A886 2.50 l Iasi, 1905 .55 .55
3069 Sheet of 4 2.50 2.50
a. A886 2.50 l Neuschwanstein .55 .55
b. A886 2.50 l Stolzenfels .55 .55
c. A886 2.50 l Katz-Loreley .55 .55
d. A886 2.50 l Linderhof .55 .55

Inter-European Cultural and Economic Cooperation.

Souvenir Sheet

Constantin Brancusi in Paris Studio A887

1982, June 5
3070 A887 10 l multicolored 2.00 1.65

PHILEXFRANCE '82 Intl. Stamp Exhibition, Paris, June 11-21.

Gloria C-16 Combine Harvester — A888

1982, June 29
3071 A888 50b shown .15 .15
3072 A888 1 l Dairy farm .18 .15
3073 A888 1.50 l Apple orchard .28 .15
3074 A888 2.50 l Vineyard .40 .20
3075 A888 3 l Irrigation .50 .28
Nos. 3071-3075,C250 (6) 2.11
Set value 1.00

Souvenir Sheet

3076 A888 10 l Village 2.00 1.65

Agricultural modernization. No. 3076 contains one 50x38mm stamp.

A890

A891

Resort Hotels and Beaches. 1 l, 2.50 l, 3 l, 5 l horiz.

1982, Aug. 30 **Photo.** ***Perf. 13½***
3078 A890 50b Baile Felix .15 .15
3079 A890 1 l Predeal .20 .15
3080 A890 1.50 l Baile Herculane .28 .15
3081 A890 2.50 l Eforie Nord .40 .16
3082 A890 3 l Olimp .60 .20
3083 A890 5 l Neptun .95 .32
Nos. 3078-3083 (6) 2.58
Set value .85

1982, Sept. 6

Designs: 1 l, Legend, horiz. 1.50 l, Contrasts, horiz. 3.50 l, Relay Runner, horiz. 4 l, Genesis of Romanian People, by Sabin Balasa.

3084 A891 1 l multicolored .20 .15
3085 A891 1.50 l multicolored .28 .15
3086 A891 3.50 l multicolored .60 .28
3087 A891 4 l multicolored .75 .40
Nos. 3084-3087 (4) 1.83
Set value .85

Souvenir Sheet

Merry Peasant Girl, by Nicolae Grigorescu (d. 1907) A892

1982, Sept. 30 **Photo.** ***Perf. 13½***
3088 A892 10 l multicolored 1.75 1.75

Bucharest Intl. Fair — A893

1982, Oct. 2
3089 A893 2 l Exhibition Hall, flag .35 .18

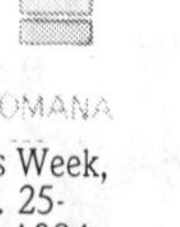

Savings Week, Oct. 25-31 — A894

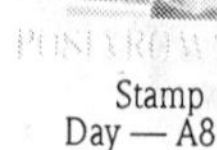
Stamp Day — A895

1982, Oct. 25
3090 A894 1 l Girl holding bank book .18 .15
3091 A894 2 l Poster .35 .18
Set value .26

1982, Nov. 10
3092 A895 1 l Woman letter carrier .18 .15
3093 A895 2 l Mailman .35 .18
Set value .26

Scene from Ileana Sinziana, by Petre Ispirescu — A896

Arms, Colors, Book — A897

Fairytales: 50b, The Youngest Child and the Golden Apples, by Petre Ispirescu. 1 l, The Bear Hoaxed by the Fox, by Ion Creanga. 1.50 l, The Prince of Tear, by Mihai Eminescu. 2.50 l, The Little Bag with Two Coins Inside, by Ion Creanga. 5 l, Danila Prepeleac, by Ion Creanga.

1982, Nov. 30

3094 A896 50b multicolored .15 .15
3095 A896 1 l multicolored .18 .15
3096 A896 1.50 l multicolored .28 .15
3097 A896 2.50 l multicolored .42 .15
3098 A896 3 l multicolored .50 .15
3099 A896 5 l multicolored .95 .30
Nos. 3094-3099 (6) 2.48
Set value .78

1982, Dec. 16

3100 A897 1 l Closed book .18 .15
3101 A897 2 l Open book .35 .18
Set value .26

Natl. Communist Party Conference, Bucharest, Dec. 16-18.

A898

50b, Wooden flask, Suceava. 1 l, Ceramic plate, Radauti. 1.50 l, Wooden scoop, Valea Mare, horiz. 2 l, Plate, jug, Vama. 3 l, Butter churn, wooden bucket, Moldavia. 3.50 l, Ceramic plates, Leheceni, horiz. 4 l, Wooden spoon, platter, Cluj. 5 l, Bowl, pitcher, Marginea. 6 l, Jug, flask, Bihor. 7 l, Spindle, shuttle, Transylvania. 7.50 l, Water buckets, Suceava. 8 l, Jug, Oboga; plate, Horezu. 10 l, Water buckets, Hunedoara, Suceava, horiz. 20 l, Wooden flask, beakers, Horezu. 30 l, Wooden spoons, Alba, horiz. 50 l, Ceramic dishes, Horezu.

1982, Dec. 22 Photo. *Perf. 13½*

3102 A898 50b red orange .15 .15
3103 A898 1 l dark blue .16 .15
3104 A898 1.50 l orange brn .25 .15
3105 A898 2 l brt blue .30 .15
3106 A898 3 l olive green .45 .15
3107 A898 3.50 l dk green .55 .15
3108 A898 4 l lt brown .60 .15
3109 A898 5 l gray blue .75 .15

Size: 23x29mm, 29x23mm

3110 A898 6 l blue .90 .15
3111 A898 7 l lake 1.10 .15
3112 A898 7.50 l red violet 1.25 .15
3113 A898 8 l brt green 1.25 .15
3114 A898 10 l red 1.50 .15
3115 A898 20 l purple 3.25 .25
3116 A898 30 l Prus blue 4.50 .38
3117 A898 50 l dark brown 8.00 .65
Nos. 3102-3117 (16) 24.96
Set value 2.10

35th Anniv. of Republic A899

Grigore Manolescu (1857-92), as Hamlet A900

1982, Dec. 27

3118 A899 1 l Symbols of development .18 .15
3119 A899 2 l Flag .35 .18
Set value .26

1983, Feb. 28

Actors or Actresses in Famous Roles: 50b, Matei Millo (1814-1896) in The Discontented. 1 l, Mihail Pascaly (1829-1882) in Director Milo. 1.50 l, Aristizza Romanescu (1854-1918), in The Dogs. 2 l, C. I. Nottara (1859-1935) in Snowstorm. 3 l, Agatha Birsescu (1857-1939) in Medea. 4 l, Ion Brezeanu (1869-1940) in The Lost Letter. 5 l, Aristide Demetriad (1872-1930) in The Despotic Prince.

3120 A900 50b multi .15 .15
3121 A900 1 l multi .18 .15
3122 A900 1.50 l multi .28 .15
3123 A900 2 l multi .35 .15
3124 A900 2.50 l multi .42 .15
3125 A900 3 l multi .50 .15
3126 A900 4 l multi .70 .26
3127 A900 5 l multi .85 .30
Nos. 3120-3127 (8) 3.43
Set value 1.15

Hugo Grotius (1583-1645), Dutch Jurist — A901

1983, Apr. 30

3128 A901 2 l brown .35 .15

Romanian-Made Vehicles — A902

1983, May 3

3129 A902 50b ARO-10 .15 .15
3130 A902 1 l Dacia, 1300 station wagon .18 .15
3131 A902 1.50 l ARO-242 jeep .25 .15
3132 A902 2.50 l ARO-244 .42 .18
3133 A902 4 l Dacia 1310 .70 .35
3134 A902 5 l OLTCIT club passenger car .85 .40
Nos. 3129-3134 (6) 2.55
Set value 1.15

Johannes Kepler (1571-1630) — A903

Famous Men: No. 3135: b, Alexander von Humboldt (1769-1859), explorer. c, Goethe (1749-1832). d, Richard Wagner (1813-1883), composer. No. 3136: a, Ioan Andreescu (1850-1882), painter. b, George Constantinescu (1881-1965), engineer. c, Tudor Arghezi (1880-1967), poet. d, C.I. Parhon (1874-1969), endocrinologist.

1983, May 16

3135 Sheet of 4 2.50 2.50
a.-d. A903 3 l multicolored .55 .55
3136 Sheet of 4 2.50 2.50
a.-d. A903 3 l multicolored .55 .55

Inter-European Cultural and Economic Cooperation.

Workers' Struggle, 50th Anniv. — A904

Birds — A905

1983, July 22 Photo. *Perf. 13½*

3137 A904 2 l silver & multi .35 .18

1983, Oct. 28 Photo. *Perf. 13½*

3138 A905 50b Luscinia svecica .15 .15
3139 A905 1 l Sturnus roseus .16 .15
3140 A905 1.50 l Coracias garrulus .22 .15
3141 A905 2.50 l Merops apiaster .38 .20
3142 A905 4 l Emberiza schoeniclus .65 .35
3143 A905 5 l Lanius minor .75 .42
Nos. 3138-3143 (6) 2.31
Set value 1.20

Water Sports A906

1983, Sept. 16 Photo. *Perf. 13½*

3144 A906 50b Kayak .15 .15
3145 A906 1 l Water polo .16 .15
3146 A906 1.50 l Canadian one-man canoes .22 .15
3147 A906 2.50 l Diving .35 .15
3148 A906 4 l Singles rowing .60 .22
3149 A906 5 l Swimming .70 .28
Nos. 3144-3149 (6) 2.18
Set value .80

Stamp Day A907

1983, Oct. 24

3150 A907 1 l Mailman on bicycle .18 .15
3151 A907 3.50 l with 3 l label, flag 1.10 .55

Souvenir Sheet

3152 A907 10 l Unloading mail plane 1.75 1.75

#3152 is airmail, contains one 38x51mm stamp.

Geum Reptans A908

Flora (No. 3154): b, Papaver dubium. c, Carlina acaulis. d, Paeonia peregrina. e, Gentiana excisa. Fauna (No. 3155): a, Sciurus vulgaria. b, Grammia quenselii. c, Dendrocopos medius. d, Lynx. e, Tichodroma muraria.

1983, Oct. 28 Photo. *Perf. 13½*

3154 Strip of 5 1.40 1.40
a.-e. A908 1 l multicolored .24 .24
3155 Strip of 5 1.40 1.40
a.-e. A908 1 l multicolored .24 .24

Issued in sheets of 15.

Lady with Feather, by Cornelius Baba — A909

1983, Nov. 3

3156 A909 1 l shown .18 .15
3157 A909 2 l Citizens .35 .15
3158 A909 3 l Farmers, horiz. .50 .18
3159 A909 4 l Resting in the Field, horiz. .70 .26
Nos. 3156-3159 (4) 1.73
Set value .64

A910

A911

1983, Nov. 30

3160 A910 1 l Banner, emblem .16 .15
3161 A910 2 l Congress building, flags .30 .18
Set value .26

Pact with Romania, 65th anniv.

1983, Dec. 17

Designs: 1 l, Flags of participating countries, post office, mailman. 2 l, Congress building, woman letter carrier. 10 l, Flags, Congress building.

3162 A911 1 l multicolored *.16 .15*
3163 A911 2 l multicolored *.30 .15*
Set value *.20*

Souvenir Sheet

3164 A911 10 l multicolored *1.65 1.65*

BALKANFILA '83 Stamp Exhibition, Bucharest. #3164 contains one 38x50mm stamp.

Souvenir Sheet

Orient Express Centenary (Paris-Istanbul) — A912

1983, Dec. 30

3165 A912 10 l Leaving Gara de Nord, Bucharest, 1883 2.50 2.50

1984 Winter Olympics A913

1984, Jan. 14

3166 A913 50b Cross-country skiing .15 .15
3167 A913 1 l Biathlon .16 .15
3168 A913 1.50 l Figure skating .22 .15
3169 A913 2 l Speed skating .30 .15
3170 A913 3 l Hockey .42 .18
3171 A913 3.50 l Bobsledding .52 .22
3172 A913 4 l Luge .60 .26
3173 A913 5 l Skiing .75 .32
Nos. 3166-3173 (8) 3.12
Set value 1.30

A 10 l imperf souvenir sheet exists showing ski jumping.

Souvenir Sheet

Prince Alexandru Ioan Cuza, Arms — A914

1984, Jan. 24 Photo. *Perf. 13½*
3174 A914 10 l multi 1.75 1.75

Union of Moldavia and Walachia Provinces, 125th anniv.

Palace of Udriste Naturel (1596-1658), Chancery Official — A915

Miron Costin (1633-91), Poet — A916

Famous Men: 1.50 l, Crisan (Marcu Giurgiu), (1733-85), peasant revolt leader. 2 l, Simion Barnutiu (1808-64), scientist. 3.50 l, Duiliu Zamfirescu (1858-1922), poet. 4 l, Nicolas Milescu (1636-1708), Court official.

1984, Feb. 8
3175 A915 50b multi .15 .15
3176 A916 1 l multi .15 .15
3177 A916 1.50 l multi .16 .15
3178 A916 2 l multi .22 .15
3179 A916 3.50 l multi .38 .15
3180 A916 4 l multi .45 .15
Nos. 3175-3180 (6) 1.51
Set value .50

See Nos. 3210-3213.

Souvenir Sheet

15th Balkan Chess Match, Herculane A917

4 successive moves culminating in checkmate.

1984, Feb. 20 Photo. *Perf. 13½*
3181 Sheet of 4 2.25 2.25
a.-d. A917 3 l, any single .55 .55

Orsova Bridge A918

Bridges: No. 3182b, Arges. c, Basarabi. d, Ohaba. No. 3183: a, Kohlbrand-Germany. b, Bosfor-Turcia. c, Europa-Austria. d, Turnului-Anglia.

1984, Apr. 24
3182 Sheet of 4 2.50 2.50
a.-d. A918 3 l multi .55 .55
3183 Sheet of 4 2.50 2.50
a.-d. A918 3 l multi .55 .55

Inter-European Cultural and Economic Cooperation.

Summer Olympics — A919

1984, May 25 Photo. *Perf. 13½*
3184 A919 50b High jump .15 .15
3185 A919 1 l Swimming .18 .15
3186 A919 1.50 l Running .26 .15
3187 A919 3 l Handball .52 .30
3188 A919 4 l Rowing .70 .40
3189 A919 5 l 2-man canoe .85 .50
Nos. 3184-3189 (6) 2.66 1.65

A 10 l imperf. airmail souvenir sheet containing a vert. stamp picturing a gymnast exists.

Environmental Protection — A920

1984, Apr. 26 Photo. *Perf. 13½*
3190 A920 1 l Sunflower .22 .15
3191 A920 2 l Stag .45 .15
3192 A920 3 l Fish .70 .22
3193 A920 4 l Bird .90 .30
Nos. 3190-3193 (4) 2.27 .82

Danube Flowers — A921

45th Anniv., Youth Anti-Fascist Committee — A922

1984, Apr. 30 Photo. *Perf. 13½*
3194 A921 50b Sagittaria sagittifolia .15 .15
3195 A921 1 l Iris pseudacorus .16 .15
3196 A921 1.50 l Butomus umbellatus .24 .16
3197 A921 3 l Nymphaea alba, horiz. .52 .25
3198 A921 4 l Nymphoides peltata, horiz. .70 .32
3199 A921 5 l Nuphar luteum, horiz. .85 .45
Nos. 3194-3199 (6) 2.62 1.48

1984, Apr. 30 Photo. *Perf. 13½*
3200 A922 2 l multicolored .40 .16

25th Congress, Ear, Nose and Throat Medicine — A923

1984, May 30 Photo. *Perf. 13½*
3201 A923 2 l Congress seal .40 .16

Souvenir Sheets

European Soccer Cup Championships — A923a

Soccer players and flags of: c, Romania. d, West Germany. e, Portugal. f, Spain. g, France. h, Belgium. i, Yugoslavia. j, Denmark.

1984, June 7 Photo. *Perf. 13½*
3201A Sheet of 4 2.50 2.50
c.-f. A923a 3 l, any single .60 .60
3201B Sheet of 4 2.50 2.50
g.-i. A923a 3 l, any single .60 .60

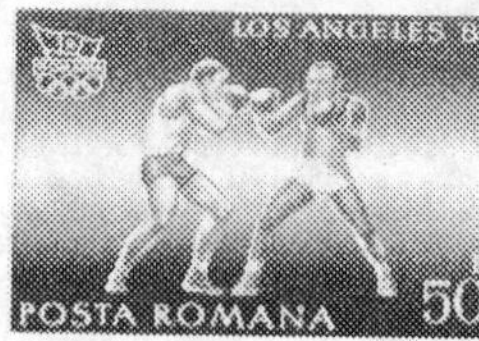

Summer Olympics — A924

1984, July 2 Photo. *Perf. 13½*
3202 A924 50b Boxing .15 .15
3203 A924 1 l Rowing .15 .15
3204 A924 1.50 l Team handball .20 .15
3205 A924 2 l Judo .25 .15
3206 A924 3 l Wrestling .40 .15
3207 A924 3.50 l Fencing .50 .20
3208 A924 4 l Kayak .55 .25
3209 A924 5 l Swimming .60 .30
Nos. 3202-3209 (8) 2.80
Set value 1.20

Two imperf. 10 l airmail souvenir sheets, showing long jumping and gymnastics exist.

Famous Romanians Type

1984, July 28 Photo. *Perf. 13½*
3210 A916 1 l Micai Ciuca .18 .15
3211 A916 2 l Petre Aurelian .35 .15
3212 A916 3 l Alexandru Vlahuta .52 .22
3213 A916 4 l Dimitrie Leonida .70 .30
Nos. 3210-3213 (4) 1.75

40th Anniv., Romanian Revolution A925

1984, Aug. 17 Photo. *Perf. 13½*
3214 A925 2 l multicolored .35 .15

Romanian Horses — A926

1984, Aug. 30 Photo. *Perf. 13½*
3215 A926 50b Lippizaner .15 .15
3216 A926 1 l Hutul .16 .15
3217 A926 1.50 l Bucovina .24 .15
3218 A926 2.50 l Nonius .40 .22
3219 A926 4 l Arabian .65 .32
3220 A926 5 l Romanian Mixed-breed .80 .40
Nos. 3215-3220 (6) 2.40 1.39

1784 Uprisings, 200th Anniv. — A927

1984, Nov. 1 Photo. *Perf. 13½*
3221 A927 2 l Monument .30 .15

Children — A928

Paintings: 50b, Portrait of Child, by T. Aman. 1 l, Shepherd, by N. Grigorescu. 2 l, Girl with Orange, by S. Luchian. 3 l, Portrait of Child, by N. Tonitza. 4 l, Portrait of Boy, by S. Popp. 5 l, Portrait of Girl, by I. Tuculescu.

1984, Nov. 10 Photo. *Perf. 13½*
3222 A928 50b multicolored .15 .15
3223 A928 1 l multicolored .16 .15
3224 A928 2 l multicolored .35 .15
3225 A928 3 l multicolored .50 .22
3226 A928 4 l multicolored .70 .30
3227 A928 5 l multicolored .85 .38
Nos. 3222-3227 (6) 2.71
Set value 1.15

Stamp Day — A929

1984, Nov. 15 Photo. *Perf. 13½*
3228 A929 2 l + 1 l label .50 .30

Souvenir Sheet

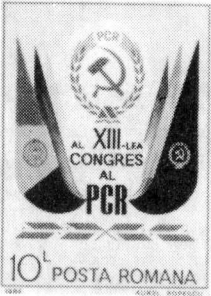

13th Party Congress A930

1984, Nov. 17 Photo. *Perf. 13½*
3229 A930 10 l Party symbols 1.75 1.75

Souvenir Sheets

Romanian Medalists, 1984 Summer Olympic Games — A931

No. 3230: a, Ecaterina Szabo, gymnastic floor exercise. b, 500-meter four-women kayak. c, Anisoara Stanciu, long jump. d, Greco-Roman wrestling. e, Mircea Fratica, half middleweight judo. f, Corneliu Ion, rapid fire pistol.

No. 3231: a, 1000-meter two-man scull. b, Weight lifting. c, Women's relays. d, Canoeing, pair oars without coxswain. e, Fencing, team foil. f, Ecaterina Szabo, all-around gymnastics.

1984, Oct. 29 Photo. *Perf. 13½*
3230 Sheet of 6 3.25 3.25
a.-f. A931 3 l, any single .52 .52
3231 Sheet of 6 3.25 3.25
a.-f. A931 3 l, any single .52 .52

A932 A933

Pelicans of the Danube Delta.

1984, Dec. 15

3232	A932 50b Flying	.15	.15
3233	A932 1 l On ground	.20	.15
3234	A932 1 l In water	.20	.15
3235	A932 2 l Nesting	.40	.15
	Nos. 3232-3235 (4)	.95	
	Set value		.35

1984, Dec. 26

Famous Men: 50b, Dr. Petru Groza (1884-1958). 1 l, Alexandru Odobescu (1834-1895). 2 l, Dr. Carol Davila (1828-1884). 3 l, Dr. Nicolae G. Lupu (1884-1966). 4 l, Dr. Daniel Danielopolu (1884-1955). 5 l, Panait Istrati (1884-1935).

3236	A933 50b multi	.15	.15
3237	A933 1 l multi	.16	.15
3238	A933 2 l multi	.35	.15
3239	A933 3 l multi	.50	.22
3240	A933 4 l multi	.70	.30
3241	A933 5 l multi	.85	.38
	Nos. 3236-3241 (6)	2.71	
	Set value		1.15

Timisoara Power Station, Electric Street Lights, Cent. A934

1984, Dec. 29

3242	A934 1 l Generator, 1884	.16	.15
3243	A934 2 l Street arc lamp, Timisoara, 1884, vert.	.35	.16
	Set value		.24

Souvenir Sheets

European Music Year A935

Composers and opera houses, No. 3244a, Moscow Theater, Tchaichovsky (1840-1893). b, Bucharest Theater, George Enescu (1881-1955). c, Dresden Opera, Wagner (1813-1883). d, Warsaw Opera, Stanislaw Moniuszko (1819-1872).

No. 3245a, Paris Opera, Gounod (1818-1893). b, Munich Opera, Strauss (1864-1949). c, Vienna Opera, Mozart (1756-1791). d, La Scala, Milan, Verdi (1813-1901).

1985, Mar. 28

3244	Sheet of 4	2.50	2.50
a.-d.	A935 3 l, any single	.58	.58
3245	Sheet of 4	2.50	2.50
a.-d.	A935 3 l, any single	.58	.58

August T. Laurian (1810-1881), Linguist and Historian — A936

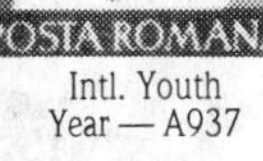

Intl. Youth Year — A937

Famous men: 1 l, Grigore Alexandrescu (1810-1885), author. 1.50 l, Gheorghe Pop de Basesti (1835-1919), politician. 2 l, Mateiu Caragiale (1885-1936), author. 3 l, Gheorghe Ionescu-Sisesti (1885-1967), scientist. 4 l, Liviu Rebreanu (1885-1944), author.

1985, Mar. 29

3246	A936 50b multi	.15	.15
3247	A936 1 l multi	.20	.15
3248	A936 1.50 l multi	.30	.16
3249	A936 2 l multi	.40	.20
3250	A936 3 l multi	.60	.30
3251	A936 4 l multi	.80	.40
	Nos. 3246-3251 (6)	2.45	1.36

1985, Apr. 15

3252	A937 1 l Scientific research	.16	.15
3253	A937 2 l Construction	.35	.16

Souvenir Sheet

3254	A937 10 l Intl. solidarity	1.75	1.75

No. 3254 contains one 54x42mm stamp.

Wildlife Conservation A938

End of World War II, 40th Anniv. A939

1985, May 6

3255	A938 50b Nyctereutes procyonoides	.15	.15
3256	A938 1 l Perdix perdix	.18	.15
3257	A938 1.50 l Nyctea scandiaca	.28	.15
3258	A938 2 l Martes martes	.35	.15
3259	A938 3 l Meles meles	.55	.22
3260	A938 3.50 l Lutra lutra	.70	.28
3261	A938 4 l Tetrao urogallus	.75	.30
3262	A938 5 l Otis tarda	.90	.38
	Nos. 3255-3262 (8)	3.86	1.78

1985, May 9

3263	A939 2 l War monument, natl. and party flags	.35	.18

Union of Communist Youth, 12th Congress — A940

1985, May 14

3264	A940 2 l Emblem	.35	.18

Danube-Black Sea Canal Opening, May 26, 1984 — A942

1985, June 7 *Perf. 13½*

3266	A942 1 l Canal, map	.18	.15
3267	A942 2 l Bridge over lock, Cernavoda	.35	.18
3268	A942 3 l Bridge over canal, Medgidea	.52	.26
3269	A942 4 l Agigea lock, bridge	.70	.35
	Nos. 3266-3269 (4)	1.75	.94

Souvenir Sheet

3270	A942 10 l Opening ceremony, Cernavoda, Ceaucescu	1.75	1.75

No. 3270 contains one 54x42mm stamp.

Audubon Birth Bicentenary — A943

No. American bird species. #3272-3275 vert.

1985, June 26

3271	A943 50b Turdus migratorius	.15	.15
3272	A943 1 l Pelecanus occidentalis	.18	.15
3273	A943 1.50 l Nyctanassa violarea	.28	.15
3274	A943 2 l Icterus galbula	.35	.18
3275	A943 3 l Podiceps grisegena	.55	.28
3276	A943 4 l Anas platyrhynchos	.70	.35
	Nos. 3271-3276 (6)	2.21	
	Set value		1.00

20th Century Paintings by Ion Tuculescu — A944

1985, July 13

3277	A944 1 l Fire, vert.	.18	.15
3278	A944 2 l Circuit, vert.	.35	.18
3279	A944 3 l Interior	.55	.28
3280	A944 4 l Sunset	.70	.35
	Nos. 3277-3280 (4)	1.78	.96

Butterflies A945

1985, July 15

3281	A945 50b Inachis io	.15	.15
3282	A945 1 l Papilio machaon	.20	.15
3283	A945 2 l Vanessa atalanta	.40	.20
3284	A945 3 l Saturnia pavonia	.60	.30
3285	A945 4 l Ammobiota festiva	.80	.40
3286	A945 5 l Smerinthus ocellatus	1.00	.50
	Nos. 3281-3286 (6)	3.15	1.70

Natl. Communist Party Achievements — A946

Natl. and party flags, and: 1 l, Transfagarasan Mountain Road. 2 l, Danube-Black Sea Canal. 3 l, Bucharest Underground Railway. 4 l, Irrigation.

1985, July 29

3287	A946 1 l multicolored	.18	.15
3288	A946 2 l multicolored	.35	.18
3289	A946 3 l multicolored	.55	.28
3290	A946 4 l multicolored	.70	.35
	Nos. 3287-3290 (4)	1.78	.96

20th annivs.: Election of Gen.-Sec. Nicolae Ceausescu; Natl. Communist Congress.

Romanian Socialist Constitution, 20th Anniv. — A947

1985, Aug. 5

3291	A947 1 l Arms, wheat, dove	.18	.15
3292	A947 2 l Arms, eternal flame	.35	.18

1986 World Cup Soccer Preliminaries — A948

Flags of participants; Great Britain, Northern Ireland, Romania, Finland, Turkey and: 50b, Sliding tackle. 1 l, Trapping the ball. 1.50 l, Heading the ball. 2 l, Dribble. 3 l, Tackle. 4 l, Scissor kick. 10 l, Dribble, diff.

1985, Oct. 15

3293	A948 50b multi	.15	.15
3294	A948 1 l multi	.18	.15
3295	A948 1.50 l multi	.28	.15
3296	A948 2 l multi	.35	.18
3297	A948 3 l multi	.55	.28
3298	A948 4 l multi	.70	.35
	Nos. 3293-3298 (6)	2.21	1.26

Souvenir Sheet

Motorcycle Centenary — A949

1985, Aug. 22 **Photo.** ***Perf. 13½***

3300	A949 10 l 1885 Daimler Einspur	1.90	.90

Retezat Natl. Park, 50th Anniv. — A950

1985, Aug. 29

3301	A950 50b Senecio glaberrimus	.15	.15
3302	A950 1 l Rupicapra rupicapra	.18	.15
3303	A950 2 l Centaurea retezatensis	.35	.18
3304	A950 3 l Viola dacica	.55	.28
3305	A950 4 l Marmota marmota	.70	.35
3306	A950 5 l Aquila chrysaetos	.90	.45
	Nos. 3301-3306 (6)	2.83	1.56

Souvenir Sheet

3307	A950 10 l Lynx lynx	1.90	.90

No. 3307 contains one 42x54mm stamp.

Tractors Manufactured by Universal — A951

1985, Sept. 10

3308	A951	50b 530 DTC	.15	.15
3309	A951	1 l 550 M HC	.16	.15
3310	A951	1.50 l 650 Super	.24	.15
3311	A951	2 l 850	.32	.16
3312	A951	3 l S 1801 IF	.48	.24
3313	A951	4 l A 3602 IF	.65	.32
		Nos. 3308-3313 (6)	2.00	1.17

Folk Costumes — A952

Women's and men's costumes from same region printed in continuous design.

1985, Sept. 28

3314	A952	50b Muscel woman	.15	.15
3315	A952	50b Muscel man	.15	.15
a.		Pair, #3314-3315	.20	.15
3316	A952	1.50 l Bistrita-Nasaud woman	.28	.15
3317	A952	1.50 l Bistrita-Nasaud man	.28	.15
a.		Pair, #3316-3317	.56	.30
3318	A952	2 l Vrancea woman	.35	.18
3319	A952	2 l Vrancea man	.35	.18
a.		Pair, #3318-3319	.70	.40
3320	A952	3 l Vilcea woman	.55	.25
3321	A952	3 l Vilcea man	.55	.25
a.		Pair, #3320-3321	1.05	.50
		Nos. 3314-3321 (8)	2.66	
		Set value		1.20

Admission to UN, 30th Anniv. — A953

1985, Oct. 21

3322	A953	2 l multicolored	.35	.18

UN, 40th Anniv. — A954 Mineral Flowers — A955

1985, Oct. 21

3323	A954	2 l multicolored	.35	.18

1985, Oct. 28

3324	A955	50b Quartz and calcite, Herja	.15	.15
3325	A955	1 l Copper, Altin Tepe	.20	.15
3326	A955	2 l Gypsum, Cavnic	.30	.20
3327	A955	3 l Quartz, Ocna de Fier	.60	.30
3328	A955	4 l Stibium, Baiut	.80	.40
3329	A955	5 l Tetrahedrite, Cavnic	1.00	.50
		Nos. 3324-3329 (6)	3.05	1.70

Stamp Day — A956

1985, Oct. 29

3330	A956	2 l + 1 l label	.35	.18

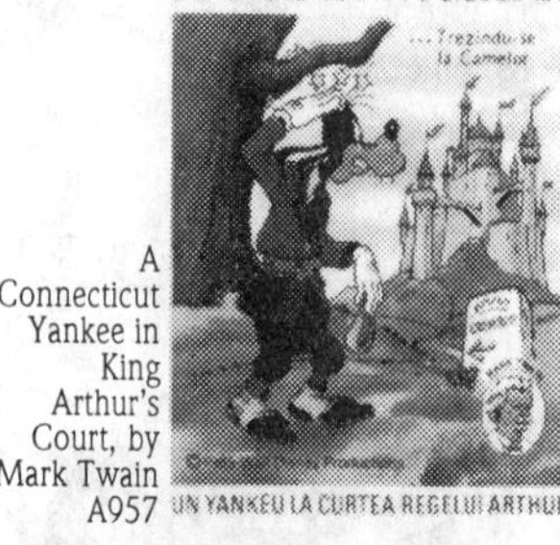

A Connecticut Yankee in King Arthur's Court, by Mark Twain A957

The Three Brothers, by Jacob and Wilhelm Grimm — A958

Disney characters in classic fairy tales.

1985, Nov. 28

3331	A957	50b Hank Morgan awakes in Camelot	.32	.15
3332	A957	50b Predicts eclipse of sun	.32	.15
3333	A957	50b Mounting horse	.32	.15
3334	A957	50b Sir Sagramor	.32	.15
3335	A958	1 l Fencing with shadow	.65	.26
3336	A958	1 l Fencing, father	.65	.26
3337	A958	1 l Shoeing a horse	.65	.26
3338	A958	1 l Barber, rabbit	.65	.26
3339	A958	1 l Father, three sons	.65	.26
		Nos. 3332-3339 (8)	4.21	1.75

Souvenir Sheets

3340	A957	5 l Tournament of knights	2.75	1.40
3341	A958	5 l Cottage	2.75	1.40

Miniature Sheets

Intereuropa 1986 A959

Fauna & flora: #3343: a, Felis silvestris. b, Mustela erminea. c, Tetrao urogallus. d, Urso arctos.
#3344: a, Dianthus callizonus. b, Pinus cembra. c, Salix sp. d, Rose pendulina.

1986, Mar. 25 Photo. *Perf. 13½*

3343		Sheet of 4	2.50	2.50
a.-d.	A959	3 l, any single	.60	.60
3344		Sheet of 4	2.50	2.50
a.-d.	A959	3 l, any single	.60	.60

Inventors and Adventurers — A960

Designs: 1 l, Orville and Wilbur Wright, Wright Flyer. 1.50 l, Jacques Cousteau, research vessel Calypso. 2 l, Amelia Earhart, Lockheed Electra. 3 l, Charles Lindbergh, Spirit of St. Louis. 3.50 l, Sir Edmund Hillary (1919-), first man to reach Mt. Everest summit. 4 l, Robert Edwin Peary, Arctic explorer. 5 l, Adm. Richard Byrd, explorer. 6 l, Neil Armstrong, first man on moon.

1985, Dec. 25 Photo. *Perf. 13½*

3345	A960	1 l multi	.20	.16
3346	A960	1.50 l multi	.30	.20
3347	A960	2 l multi	.40	.30
3348	A960	3 l multi	.60	.42
3349	A960	3.50 l multi	.65	.50
3350	A960	4 l multi	.75	.60
3351	A960	5 l multi	1.00	.70
3352	A960	6 l multi	1.25	.85
		Nos. 3345-3352 (8)	5.15	3.73

Paintings by Nicolae Tonitza — A961

1986, Mar. 12 Photo. *Perf. 13½*

3353	A961	1 l Nina in Green	.30	.16
3354	A961	2 l Irina	.60	.30
3355	A961	3 l Woodman's Daughter	.90	.45
3356	A961	4 l Woman on the Verandah	1.25	.60
		Nos. 3353-3356 (4)	3.05	1.51

Color Animated Films, 50th Anniv. — A962

Walt Disney characters in the Band Concert, 1935.

1986, Apr. 10 Photo. *Perf. 13½*

3357	A962	50b Clarabelle	.25	.15
3358	A962	50b Mickey Mouse	.25	.15
3359	A962	50b Paddy and Peter	.25	.15
3360	A962	50b Goofy	.25	.15
3361	A962	1 l Donald Duck	.50	.18
3362	A962	1 l Mickey Mouse, diff.	.50	.18
3363	A962	1 l Mickey and Donald	.50	.18
3364	A962	1 l Horace	.50	.18
3365	A962	1 l Donald and trombonist	.50	.18
		Nos. 3357-3365 (9)	3.50	
		Set value		1.20

Souvenir Sheet

3366	A962	5 l Finale	2.50	.85

1986 World Cup Soccer Championships, Mexico — A963

Various soccer plays and flags: 50b, Italy vs. Bulgaria. 1 l, Mexico vs. Belgium. 2 l, Canada vs. France. 3 l, Brazil vs. Spain. 4 l, Uruguay vs. Germany. 5 l, Morocco vs. Poland.

1986, May 9

3367	A963	50b multi	.15	.15
3368	A963	1 l multi	.25	.15
3369	A963	2 l multi	.52	.25
3370	A963	3 l multi	.75	.38
3371	A963	4 l multi	1.00	.52
3372	A963	5 l multi	1.25	.70
		Nos. 3367-3372 (6)	3.92	2.15

An imperf. 10 l airmail souvenir sheet exists picturing stadium, flags of previous winners, satellite and map.

Hotels — A964

1986, Apr. 23 Photo. *Perf. 13½*

3373	A964	50b Diana, Herculane	.15	.15
3374	A964	1 l Termal, Felix	.22	.15
3375	A964	2 l Delfin, Meduza and Steaua de Mare, Eforie Nord	.45	.22
3376	A964	3 l Caciulata, Calimanesti Caciulata	.65	.32
3377	A964	4 l Palas, Slanic Moldova	.90	.45
3378	A964	5 l Bradet, Sovata	1.10	.55
		Nos. 3373-3378 (6)	3.47	1.84

Nicolae Ceausescu, Party Flag — A965

1986, May 8 Photo. *Perf. 13½*

3379	A965	2 l multicolored	.60	.30

Natl. Communist Party, 65th anniv.

Flowers — A966

1986, June 25 Photo. *Perf. 13½*

3380	A966	50b Tulipa gesneriana	.15	.15
3381	A966	1 l Iris hispanica	.25	.15
3382	A966	2 l Rosa hybrida	.50	.25
3383	A966	3 l Anemone coronaria	.70	.35
3384	A966	4 l Freesia refracta	1.00	.50
3385	A966	5 l Chrysanthemum indicum	1.25	.60
		Nos. 3380-3385 (6)	3.85	2.00

Mircea the Great, Ruler of Wallachia, 1386-1418 — A967

1986, July 17 Photo. *Perf. 13½*

3386	A967	2 l multicolored	.60	.30

Ascent to the throne, 600th anniv.

Open Air Museum of Historic Dwellings, Bucharest, 50th Anniv. — A968

1986, July 21

3387	A968	50b Alba	.15	.15
3388	A968	1 l Arges	.22	.15
3389	A968	2 l Constantia	.45	.22
3390	A968	3 l Timis	.65	.32
3391	A968	4 l Neamt	.90	.45
3392	A968	5 l Gorj	1.10	.55
		Nos. 3387-3392 (6)	3.47	1.84

Polar Research — A969

Exploration: 50b, Julius Popper, exploration of Tierra del Fuego (1886-93). 1 l, Bazil G. Assan, exploration of Spitzbergen (1896). 2 l, Emil Racovita, Antarctic expedition (1897-99). 3 l, Constantin Dumbrava, exploration of Greenland (1927-8). 4 l, Romanians with the 17th Soviet Antarctic expedition (1971-72). 5 l, Research on krill fishing (1977-80).

1986, July 23 Photo. *Perf. 13½*

3393	A969	50b multi	.15	.15
3394	A969	1 l multi	.22	.15
3395	A969	2 l multi	.45	.22
3396	A969	3 l multi	.65	.32
3397	A969	4 l multi	.90	.45
3398	A969	5 l multi	1.10	.55
		Nos. 3393-3398 (6)	3.47	1.84

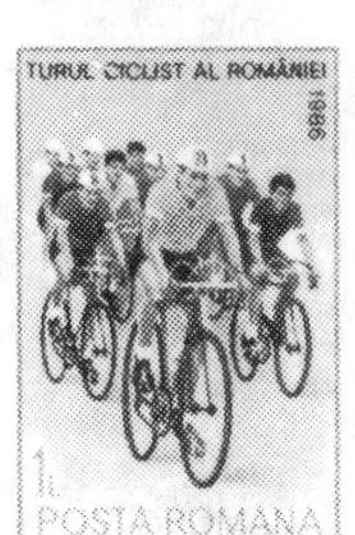

Natl. Cycling Championships A970

Various athletes.

1986, Aug. 29

3399	A970	1 l multicolored	.25	.15
3400	A970	2 l multicolored	.50	.25
3401	A970	3 l multicolored	.70	.35
3402	A970	4 l multicolored	1.00	.50
		Nos. 3399-3402 (4)	2.45	1.25

Souvenir Sheet

3403	A970	10 l multicolored	2.50	1.25

No. 3403 contains one 42x54mm stamp.

Souvenir Sheet

Intl. Peace Year — A971

1986, July 25

3404	A971	5 l multicolored	1.25	.60

Fungi — A972 A973

1986, Aug. 15

3405	A972	50b Amanita rubescens	.15	.15
3406	A972	1 l Boletus luridus	.25	.15
3407	A972	2 l Lactarius piperatus	.50	.25
3408	A972	3 l Lepiota clypeolaria	.70	.35
3409	A972	4 l Russula cyanoxantha	1.00	.50
3410	A972	5 l Tremiscus helvelloides	1.25	.60
		Nos. 3405-3410 (6)	3.85	2.00

1986, Nov. 10 Photo. *Perf. 13½*

Famous Men: 50b, Petru Maior (c. 1761-1821), historian. 1 l, George Topirceanu (1886-1937), doctor. 2 l, Henri Coanda (1886-1972), engineer. 3 l, Constantin Budeanu (1886-1959), engineer.

3411	A973	50b dl cl, gold & dk bl grn	.15	.15
3412	A973	1 l sl grn, gold & dk lil rose	.25	.15
3413	A973	2 l rose cl, gold & brt bl	.52	.25
3414	A973	3 l chlky bl, gold & choc	.70	.35
		Nos. 3411-3414 (4)	1.62	.90

UNESCO, 40th Anniv. A974

1986, Nov. 10

3415	A974	4 l multicolored	1.00	.50

Stamp Day A975

1986, Nov. 15

3416	A975	2 l + 1 l label	.75	.35

Industry A976

1986, Nov. 28

3417	A976	50b F-300 oil rigs, vert.	.15	.15
3418	A976	1 l Promex excavator	.22	.15
3419	A976	2 l Pitesti refinery, vert.	.45	.22
3420	A976	3 l 110-ton dump truck	.65	.32
3421	A976	4 l Coral computer, vert.	.90	.45
3422	A976	5 l 350-megawatt turbine	1.10	.55
		Nos. 3417-3422 (6)	3.47	1.84

Folk Costumes — A977

1986, Dec. 26

3423	A977	50b Capra	.15	.15
3424	A977	1 l Sorcova	.22	.15
3425	A977	2 l Plugusorul	.45	.22
3426	A977	3 l Buhaiul	.65	.32
3427	A977	4 l Caiutii	.90	.45
3428	A977	5 l Uratorii	1.10	.55
		Nos. 3423-3428 (6)	3.47	1.84

Recycling Campaign — A978

1986, Dec. 30

3429	A978	1 l Metal	.25	.15
3430	A978	2 l Trees	.50	.25

Young Communists' League, 65th Anniv. — A979

1987, Mar. 18 Photo. *Perf. 13½*

3431	A979	1 l Flags, youth	.26	.15
3432	A979	2 l Emblem	.52	.26
3433	A979	3 l Flags, youth, diff.	.75	.38
		Nos. 3431-3433 (3)	1.53	.79

Miniature Sheets

Intereuropa A980

Modern architecture: No. 3434a, Exposition Pavilion, Bucharest. b, Intercontinental Hotel, Bucharest. c, Europa Hotel, Black Sea coast. d, Polytechnic Institute, Bucharest.

No. 3435a, Administration Building, Satu Mare. b, House of Young Pioneers, Bucharest. c, Valahia Hotel, Tirgoviste. d, Caciulata Hotel, Caciulata.

1987, May 18 Photo. *Perf. 13½*

3434		Sheet of 4	2.50	2.50
a.-d.	A980	3 l, any single	.60	.60
3435		Sheet of 4	2.50	2.50
a.-d.	A980	3 l, any single	.60	.60

Collective Farming, 25th Anniv. — A981

1987, Apr. 25 Photo. *Perf. 13½*

3436	A981	2 l multicolored	.50	.25

Birch Trees by the Lakeside, by I. Andreescu — A982

Paintings in Romanian museums: 1 l, Young Peasant Girls Spinning, by N. Grigorescu. 2 l, Washerwoman, by S. Luchian. 3 l, Inside the Peasant's Cottage, by S. Dimitrescu. 4 l, Winter Landscape, by A. Ciucurencu. 5 l, Winter in Bucharest, by N. Tonitza, vert.

1987, Apr. 28

3437	A982	50b multicolored	.15	.15
3438	A982	1 l multicolored	.18	.15
3439	A982	2 l multicolored	.35	.18
3440	A982	3 l multicolored	.55	.28
3441	A982	4 l multicolored	.75	.38
3442	A982	5 l multicolored	1.00	.52
		Nos. 3437-3442 (6)	2.98	1.66

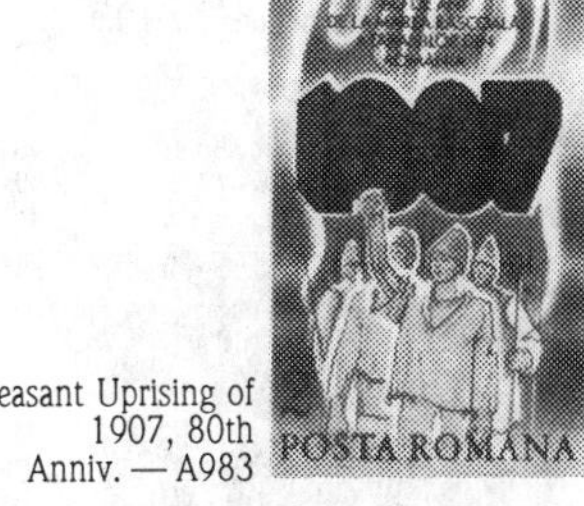

Peasant Uprising of 1907, 80th Anniv. — A983

1987, May 30

3443	A983	2 l multicolored	.50	.25

Men's World Handball Championships — A984

Various plays.

1987, July 15

3444	A984	50b multi, vert.	.15	.15
3445	A984	1 l multi	.18	.15
3446	A984	2 l multi, vert.	.38	.18
3447	A984	3 l multi	.55	.28
3448	A984	4 l multi, vert.	.75	.38
3449	A984	5 l multi	1.00	.52
		Nos. 3444-3449 (6)	3.01	1.66

A985

Natl. Currency — A986

A986 illustration reduced.

1987, July 15

3450	A985	1 l multicolored	.20	.15

Souvenir Sheet

3451	A986	10 l multicolored	2.00	2.00

Landscapes A987

1987, July 31 Photo. *Perf. 13½*

3452	A987	50b Pelicans over the Danube Delta	.15	.15
3453	A987	1 l Transfagarasan Highway	.18	.15
3454	A987	2 l Hairpin curve, Bicazului	.35	.18

3455 A987 3 l Limestone peaks, Mt. Ceahlau .52 .25
3456 A987 4 l Lake Capra, Mt. Fagaras .70 .35
3457 A987 5 l Orchard, Borsa .90 .50
Nos. 3452-3457 (6) 2.80 1.58

A988

Scenes from Fairy Tale by Peter Ispirescu (b. 1887) — A988a

A988a illustration reduced.

1987, Sept. 25 Photo. *Perf. 13½*
3458 A988 50b shown .15 .15
3459 A988 1 l multi, diff. .16 .15
3460 A988 2 l multi, diff. .35 .16
3461 A988 3 l multi, diff. .52 .25
3462 A988 4 l multi, diff. .70 .35
3463 A988 5 l multi, diff. .85 .40
Nos. 3458-3463 (6) 2.73 1.46

Souvenir Sheet

3464 A988a 10 l shown 2.00 2.00

Miniature Sheets

Flora and Fauna A989

Flora: No. 3465a, Aquilegia alpina. b, Pulsatilla vernalis. c, Aster alpinus. d, Soldanella pusilla baumg. e, Lilium bulbiferum. f, Arctostaphylos uva-ursi. g, Crocus vernus. h, Crepis aurea. i, Cypripedium calceolus. j, Centaurea nervosa. k, Dryas octopetala. l, Gentiana excisa.

Fauna: No. 3466a, Martes martes. b, Felis lynx. c, Ursus maritimus. d, Lutra lutra. e, Bison bonasus. f, Branta ruficollis. g, Phoenicopterus ruber. h, Otis tarda. i, Lyrurus tetrix. j, Gypaetus barbatus. k, Vormela peregusna. l, Oxyura leucocephala.

1987, Oct. 16

Sheets of 12

3465 A989 1 l #a.-l. 3.25 1.50
3466 A989 1 l #a.-l. 3.25 1.50

Souvenir Sheet

PHILATELIA '87, Cologne — A990

1987, Oct. 19
3467 Sheet of 2 + 2 labels 3.75 3.75
a. A990 3 l Bucharest city seal 1.90 1.90
b. A990 3 l Cologne city arms 1.90 1.90

Locomotives A991

1987, Oct. 15
3468 A991 50b L 45 H .15 .15
3469 A991 1 l LDE 125 .20 .15
3470 A991 2 l LDH 70 .42 .20
3471 A991 3 l LDE 2100 .65 .30
3472 A991 4 l LDE 3000 .90 .42
3473 A991 5 l LE 5100 1.00 .50
Nos. 3468-3473 (6) 3.32 1.72

Folk Costumes — A992

1987, Nov. 7
3474 A992 1 l Tirnave (woman) .18 .15
3475 A992 1 l Tirnave (man) .18 .15
a. Pair, #3474-3475 .36 .20
3476 A992 2 l Buzau (woman) .40 .18
3477 A992 2 l Buzau (man) .40 .18
a. Pair, #3476-3477 .80 .36
3478 A992 3 l Dobrogea (woman) .60 .30
3479 A992 3 l Dobrogea (man) .60 .30
a. Pair, #3478-3479 1.20 .60
3480 A992 4 l Ilfov (woman) .80 .40
3481 A992 4 l Ilfov (man) .80 .40
a. Pair, #3480-3481 1.60 .80
Nos. 3474-3481 (8) 3.96 2.06

Postwoman Delivering Mail A993

1987, Nov. 15 Photo. *Perf. 13½*
3482 A993 2 l + 1 l label .75 .38

Stamp Day.

Apiculture — A994

1987, Nov. 16 Photo. *Perf. 13½*
3483 A994 1 l Apis mellifica carpatica .24 .15
3484 A994 2 l Bee pollinating sunflower .50 .24
3485 A994 3 l Hives, Danube Delta .75 .38
3486 A994 4 l Apiculture complex, Bucharest 1.00 .50
Nos. 3483-3486 (4) 2.49 1.27

1988 Winter Olympics, Calgary — A995

1987, Dec. 28 Photo. *Perf. 13½*
3487 A995 50b Biathlon .15 .15
3488 A995 1 l Slalom .18 .15
3489 A995 1.50 l Ice hockey .30 .16
3490 A995 2 l Luge .40 .18
3491 A995 3 l Speed skating .60 .30
3492 A995 3.50 l Women's figure skating .65 .35
3493 A995 4 l Downhill skiing .80 .40
3494 A995 5 l Two-man bobsled 1.00 .50
Nos. 3487-3494 (8) 4.08 2.19

An imperf. 10 l souvenir sheet picturing ski jumping also exists.

Traffic Safety A996

Designs: 50b, Be aware of children riding bicycles in the road. 1 l, Young Pioneer girl as crossing guard. 2 l, Do not open car doors in path of moving traffic. 3 l, Be aware of pedestrian crossings. 4 l, Observe the speed limit; do not attempt curves at high speed. 5 l, Protect small children.

1987, Dec. 10 Photo. *Perf. 13½*
3495 A996 50b multicolored .15 .15
3496 A996 1 l multicolored .18 .15
3497 A996 2 l multicolored .40 .18
3498 A996 3 l multicolored .65 .30
3499 A996 4 l multicolored .85 .40
3500 A996 5 l multicolored 1.00 .45
Nos. 3495-3500 (6) 3.23 1.63

October Revolution, Russia, 70th Anniv. — A997

1987, Dec. 26
3501 A997 2 l multicolored .45 .22

40th Anniv. of the Romanian Republic — A998

1987, Dec. 30
3502 A998 2 l multicolored .45 .22

70th Birthday of President Nicolae Ceausescu A999

1988, Jan. 26
3503 A999 2 l multicolored .45 .22

Pottery A1000

1988, Feb. 26 Photo. *Perf. 13½*
3504 A1000 50b Marginea .15 .15
3505 A1000 1 l Oboga .18 .15
3506 A1000 2 l Horezu .40 .18
3507 A1000 3 l Curtea De Arges .65 .30
3508 A1000 4 l Birsa .85 .40
3509 A1000 5 l Vama 1.00 .45
Nos. 3504-3509 (6) 3.23 1.63

Miniature Sheets

Intereuropa A1001

Transportation and communication: No. 3510a, Mail coach. b, ECS telecommunications satellite. c, Oltcit automobile. d, ICE high-speed electric train.

No. 3511a, Santa Maria, 15th cent. b, Cheia Ground Station satellite dish receivers. c, Bucharest subway. d, Airbus-A320.

1988, Apr. 27 Photo. *Perf. 13½*
3510 Sheet of 4 2.50 2.50
a.-d. A1001 3 l any single .60 .60
3511 Sheet of 4 2.50 2.50
a.-d. A1001 3 l any single .60 .60

1988 Summer Olympics, Seoul — A1002

1988, Jun. 28
3512 A1002 50b Gymnastics .15 .15
3513 A1002 1.50 l Boxing .30 .15
3514 A1002 2 l Tennis .40 .20
3515 A1002 3 l Judo .60 .30
3516 A1002 4 l Running .80 .40
3517 A1002 5 l Rowing 1.00 .48
Nos. 3512-3517 (6) 3.25 1.68

An imperf. 10 l souvenir sheet exists.

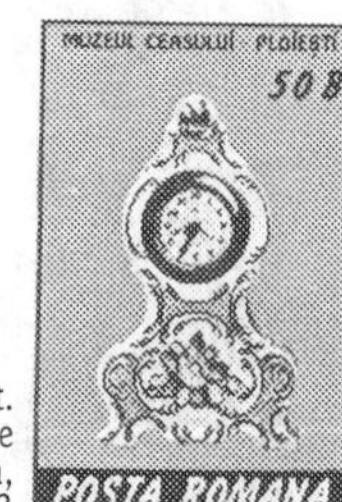
19th-20th Cent. Clocks in the Ceasului Museum, Ploesti — A1003

1988, May 20 Photo. *Perf. 13½*
3518 A1003 50b Arad Region porcelain .15 .15
3519 A1003 1.50 l French bronze .32 .15
3520 A1003 2 l French bronze, diff. .42 .20
3521 A1003 3 l Gothic bronze .65 .32
3522 A1003 4 l Saxony porcelain .85 .42
3523 A1003 5 l Bohemian porcelain 1.10 .52
Nos. 3518-3523 (6) 3.49 1.76

20th Cent. timepiece (50b); others 19th cent.

Miniature Sheets

European Soccer Championships, Germany — A1003a

Soccer players and flags of: c, Federal Republic of Germany. d, Spain. e, Italy. f, Denmark. g, England. h, Netherlands. i, Ireland. j, Soviet Union.

1988, June 9 Litho. *Perf. 13½*
3523A Sheet of 4 3.25 3.25
c.-f. A1003a 3 l any single .80 .80
3523B Sheet of 4 3.25 3.25
g.-j. A1003a 3 l any single .80 .80

Accession of Constanin Brincoveanu as Prince Regent of Wallachia, 1688-1714, 300th Anniv. — A1004

1988, June 20

3524 A1004 2 l multicolored .50 .25

1988 Summer Olympics, Seoul — A1005

1988, Sept. 1 Photo. *Perf. 13½*

3525 A1005 50b Women's running .15 .15
3526 A1005 1 l Canoeing .18 .15
3527 A1005 1.50 l Women's gymnastics .28 .15
3528 A1005 2 l Kayaking .40 .18
3529 A1005 3 l Weight lifting .55 .28
3530 A1005 3.50 l Women's swimming .60 .35
3531 A1005 4 l Fencing .70 .40
3532 A1005 5 l Women's rowing (double) .95 .45
Nos. 3525-3532 (8) 3.81 2.11

An imperf. 10 l souvenir sheet exists picturing women's gymnastics.

Romania-China Philatelic Exhibition — A1006

1988, Aug. 5 Photo. *Perf. 13½*

3533 A1006 2 l multicolored .50 .25

Souvenir Sheet

PRAGA '88 — A1007

1988, Aug. 26

3534 A1007 5 l Carnations, by Stefan Luchian 2.00 2.00

Miniature Sheets

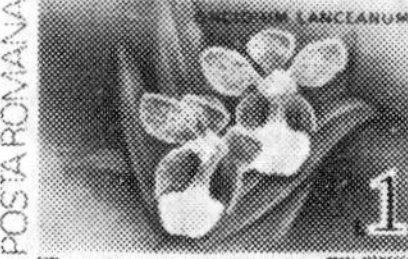

Orchids A1008

No. 3535a, Oncidium lanceanum. b, Cattleya trianae. c, Sophronitis cernua. d, Bulbophyllum lobbii. e, Lycaste cruenta. f, Mormolyce ringens. g, Phragmipedium schlimii. h, Angraecum sesquipedale. i, Laelia crispa. j, Encyclia atropurpurea. k, Dendrobium nobile. l, Oncidium splendidum.

No. 3536a, Brassavola perrinii. b, Paphiopedilum maudiae. c, Sophronitis coccinea. d, Vandopsis lissochiloides. e, Phalaenopsis lueddemanniana. f, Chysis bractescens. g, Cochleanthes discolor. h, Phalaenopsis amabilis. i, Pleione pricei. j, Sobralia macrantha. k, Aspasia lunata. l, Cattleya citrina.

1988, Oct. 24

3535 Sheet of 12 3.25 3.25
a.-l. A1008 1 l any single .24 .24
3536 Sheet of 12 3.25 3.25
a.-l. A1008 1 l any single .24 .24

Miniature Sheets

Events Won by Romanian Athletes at the 1988 Seoul Olympic Games A1009

Sporting event and medal: No. 3537a, Women's gymnastics. b, Free pistol shooting. c, Weight lifting (220 pounds). d, Featherweight boxing.

No. 3538a, Women's 1500 and 3000-meter relays. b, Women's 200 and 400-meter individual swimming medley. c, Wrestling (220 pounds). d, Rowing, coxless pairs and coxed fours.

1988, Dec. 7 Photo. *Perf. 13½*

3537 Sheet of 4 3.00 3.00
a.-d. A1009 3 l any single .75 .75
3538 Sheet of 4 3.00 3.00
a.-d. A1009 3 l any single .75 .75

Stamp Day A1010

1988, Nov. 13 Photo. *Perf. 13½*

3539 A1010 2 l + 1 l label .75 .38

Unitary Natl. Romanian State, 70th Anniv. A1011

1988, Dec. 29

3540 A1011 2 l multicolored .50 .25

Anniversaries — A1012

Designs: 50b, Athenaeum, Bucharest. 1.50 l, Trajan's Bridge, Drobeta, on a Roman bronze sestertius used in Romania from 103 to 105 A.D. 2 l, Ruins, Suceava. 3 l, Pitesti municipal coat of arms, scroll, architecture. 4 l, Trajan's Column (detail), 113 A.D. 5 l, Gold helmet discovered in Prahova County.

1988, Dec. 30

3541 A1012 50b shown .15 .15
3542 A1012 1.50 l multi .30 .15
3543 A1012 2 l multi .42 .20
3544 A1012 3 l multi .65 .30
3545 A1012 4 l multi .85 .40
3546 A1012 5 l multi 1.10 .48
Nos. 3541-3546 (6) 3.47 1.68

Athenaeum, Bucharest, cent. (50b), Suceava, capital of Moldavia from 1401-1565, 600th anniv. (2 l), & Pitesti municipal charter, 600th anniv. (3 l).

Miniature Sheets

Grand Slam Tennis Championships — A1013

No. 3547: a, Men's singles, stadium in Melbourne. b, Men's singles, scoreboard. c, Mixed doubles, spectators. d, Mixed doubles, Roland Garros stadium.

No. 3548: a, Women's singles, stadium in Wimbledon. b, Women's singles, spectators. c, Men's doubles, spectators. d, Men's doubles, stadium in Flushing Meadows.

1988, Aug. 22 Photo. *Perf. 13½*

3547 Sheet of 4 3.00 3.00
a.-d. A1013 3 l any single .75 .75
3548 Sheet of 4 3.00 3.00
a.-d. A1013 3 l any single .75 .75

Australian Open (Nos. 3547a-3547b), French Open (Nos. 3547c-3547d), Wimbledon (Nos. 3548a-3548b) and US Open (Nos. 3548c-3548d).

Architecture A1014

Designs: 50b, Zapodeni, Vaslui, 17th cent. 1.50 l, Berbesti, Maramures, 18th cent. 2 l, Voitinel, Suceava, 18th cent. 3 l, Chiojdu mic, Buzau, 18th cent. 4 l, Cimpanii de sus, Bihor, 19th cent. 5 l, Naruja, Vrancea, 19th cent.

1989, Feb. 8 Photo. *Perf. 13½*

3549 A1014 50b multi .15 .15
3550 A1014 1.50 l multi .32 .18
3551 A1014 2 l multi .42 .22
3552 A1014 3 l multi .65 .32
3553 A1014 4 l multi .85 .42
3554 A1014 5 l multi 1.10 .52
Nos. 3549-3554 (6) 3.49 1.81

Rescue and Relief Services — A1015

1989, Feb. 25

3555 A1015 50b Relief worker .15 .15
3556 A1015 1 l shown .15 .15
3557 A1015 1.50 l Fireman, child .25 .15
3558 A1015 2 l Fireman's carry .30 .15
3559 A1015 3 l Rescue team on skis .50 .25
3560 A1015 3.50 l Mountain rescue .60 .30
3561 A1015 4 l Water rescue .70 .35
3562 A1015 5 l Water safety .85 .45
Nos. 3555-3562 (8) 3.50 1.95

Nos. 3555, 3557-3558, 3560-3561 vert.

Industries — A1016

Designs: 50b, Fasca Bicaz cement factory. 1.50 l, Bridge on the Danube near Cernavoda. 2 l, MS-2-2400/450-20 synchronous motor. 3 l, Bucharest subway. 4 l, Mangalia-Constanta ferry. 5 l, *Gloria* marine platform.

1989, Apr. 10 Photo. *Perf. 13½*

3563 A1016 50b multi .15 .15
3564 A1016 1.50 l multi .30 .16
3565 A1016 2 l multi .40 .20
3566 A1016 3 l multi .60 .32
3567 A1016 4 l multi .80 .40
3568 A1016 5 l multi 1.00 .52
Nos. 3563-3568 (6) 3.25 1.75

Anti-fascist March, 50th Anniv. A1017

1989, May 1 Photo. *Perf. 13½*

3569 A1017 2 l shown .50 .25

Souvenir Sheet

3570 A1017 10 l Patriots, flag 4.75 4.75

Souvenir Sheet

BULGARIA '89, Sofia, May 22-31 — A1018

Illustration reduced.

1989, May 20

3571 A1018 10 l Roses 2.00 2.00

Miniature Sheets

Intereuropa 1989 A1019

Children's activities and games: No. 3572a, Swimming. No. 3572b, Water slide. No. 3572c, Seesaw. No. 3572d, Flying kites. No. 3573a, Playing with dolls. No. 3573b, Playing ball. No. 3573c, Playing in the sand. No. 3573d, Playing with toy cars.

1989, June 15

3572 Sheet of 4 3.00 3.00
a.-d. A1019 3 l any single .75 .75
3573 Sheet of 4 3.00 3.00
a.-d. A1019 3 l any single .75 .75

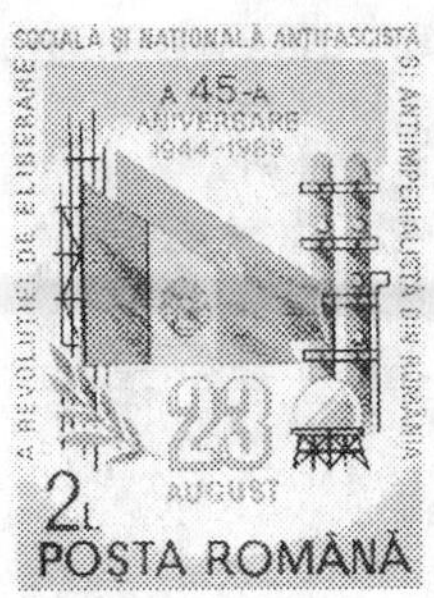

Socialist Revolution in Romania, 45th Anniv. A1020

1989, Aug. 21 Photo. *Perf. 13½*

3574 A1020 2 l multicolored .50 .25

Cartoons — A1021

1989, Sept. 25

3575	A1021	50b	Pin-pin	.15	.15
3576	A1021	1 l	Maria	.22	.15
3577	A1021	1.50 l	Gore and Grigore	.32	.16
3578	A1021	2 l	Pisoiul, Balanel, Manole and Monk	.42	.20
3579	A1021	3 l	Gruia Lui Novac	.65	.32
3580	A1021	3.50 l	Mihaela	.80	.38
3581	A1021	4 l	Harap alb	.90	.42
3582	A1021	5 l	Homo sapiens	1.00	.52
			Nos. 3575-3582 (8)	4.46	2.30

Romanian Writers — A1022

Portraits: 1 l, Ion Creanga (1837-1889). 2 l, Mihail Eminescu (1850-1889), poet. 3 l, Nicolae Teclu (1839-1916).

1989, Aug. 18 Photo. ***Perf. 13½***

3583	A1022	1 l	multicolored	.30	.15
3584	A1022	2 l	multicolored	.60	.28
3585	A1022	3 l	multicolored	.90	.45
			Nos. 3583-3585 (3)	1.80	.88

Stamp Day A1023

1989, Oct. 7

3586	A1023	2 l + 1 l label		.75	.38

No. 3586 has a second label picturing posthorn.

Storming of the Bastille, 1789 A1024

Emblems of PHILEXFRANCE '89 and the Revolution — A1025

Designs: 1.50 l, Gavroche. 2 l, Robespierre. 3 l, *La Marseillaise*, by Rouget de Lisle. 4 l, Diderot. 5 l, 1848 Uprising, Romania.

1989, Oct. 14

3587	A1024	50b	shown	.15	.15
3588	A1024	1.50 l	multicolored	.30	.16
3589	A1024	2 l	multicolored	.40	.20
3590	A1024	3 l	multicolored	.60	.30
3591	A1024	4 l	multicolored	.80	.40
3592	A1024	5 l	multicolored	1.00	.50
			Nos. 3587-3592 (6)	3.25	1.71

Souvenir Sheet

3593	A1025	10 l	shown	3.00	3.00

French revolution, bicent.

14th Romanian Communist Party Congress A1025a

1989, Nov. 20 Photo. ***Perf. 13½***

3593A	A1025a	2 l	multicolored	.50	.50

Souvenir Sheet

3593B	A1025a	10 l	multicolored	4.75	4.75

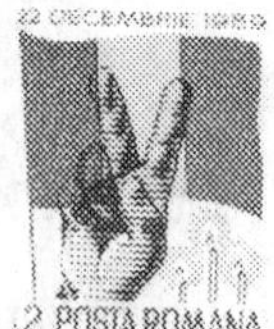

Revolution of Dec. 22, 1989 — A1026

1990, Jan. 8 Photo. ***Perf. 13½***

3594	A1026	2 l	multicolored	.40	.20

World Cup Soccer Preliminaries, Italy — A1027

Various soccer players in action.

1990, Mar. 19 Photo. ***Perf. 13½***

3595	A1027	50b	multicolored	.15	.15
3596	A1027	1.50 l	multicolored	.30	.30
3597	A1027	2 l	multicolored	.40	.40
3598	A1027	3 l	multicolored	.60	.60
3599	A1027	4 l	multicolored	.80	.80
3600	A1027	5 l	multicolored	1.00	1.00
			Nos. 3595-3600 (6)	3.25	3.25

An imperf. 10 l airmail souvenir sheet exists.

Souvenir Sheet

First Postage Stamp, 150th Anniv. — A1028

Illustration reduced.

1990, May 2 Litho. ***Perf. 13½***

3601	A1028	10 l	multicolored	2.00	2.00

Stamp World London '90.

World Cup Soccer Championships, Italy — A1029

Various soccer players in action.

1990, May 7 Photo. ***Perf. 13½***

3602	A1029	50b	multicolored	.15	.15
3603	A1029	1 l	multicolored	.15	.15
3604	A1029	1.50 l	multicolored	.15	.15
3605	A1029	2 l	multicolored	.18	.18
3606	A1029	3 l	multicolored	.28	.28
3607	A1029	3.50 l	multicolored	.30	.30
3608	A1029	4 l	multicolored	.35	.35
3609	A1029	5 l	multicolored	.45	.45
			Set Value	1.85	1.85

An imperf. 10 l airmail souvenir sheet showing Olympic Stadium, Rome exists.

Intl. Dog Show, Brno, Czechoslovakia — A1030

1990, June 6

3610	A1030	50b	German shepherd	.15	.15
3611	A1030	1 l	English setter	.22	.22
3612	A1030	1.50 l	Boxer	.32	.32
3613	A1030	2 l	Beagle	.45	.45
3614	A1030	3 l	Doberman pinscher	.65	.65
3615	A1030	3.50 l	Great Dane	.75	.75
3616	A1030	4 l	Afghan hound	.90	.90
3617	A1030	5 l	Yorkshire terrier	1.10	1.10
			Nos. 3610-3617 (8)	4.54	4.54

Riccione '90, Intl. Philatelic Exhibition A1031

1990, Aug. 24

3618	A1031	2 l	multicolored	.50	.50

See No. 3856.

Romanian-Chinese Philatelic Exhibition, Bucharest — A1032

1990, Sept. 8 Photo. ***Perf. 13½***

3619	A1032	2 l	multicolored	.18	.18

Paintings Damaged in 1989 Revolution A1033

Designs: 50b, Old Nicolas, the Zither Player, by Stefan Luchian. 1.50 l, Woman in Blue by Ion Andreescu. 2 l, The Gardener by Luchian. 3 l, Vase of Flowers by Jan Brueghel, the Elder. 4 l, Springtime by Peter Brueghel, the Elder, horiz. 5 l, Madonna and Child by G. B. Paggi.

1990. Oct. 25 Photo. ***Perf. 13½***

3620	A1033	50b	multicolored	.15	.15
3621	A1033	1.50 l	multicolored	.20	.20
3622	A1033	2 l	multicolored	.28	.28
3623	A1033	3 l	multicolored	.40	.40
3624	A1033	4 l	multicolored	.52	.52
3625	A1033	5 l	multicolored	.70	.70
			Nos. 3620-3625 (6)	2.25	2.25

Stamp Day A1033a

1990, Nov. 10 Photo. ***Perf. 13½***

3625A	A1033a	2 l + 1 l label		.25	.25

Famous Romanians A1034

Designs: 50b, Prince Constantin Cantacuzino (1640-1716). 1.50 l, Ienachita Vacarescu (c. 1740-1797), historian. 2 l, Titu Maiorescu (1840-1917), writer. 3 l, Nicolae Iorga (1871-1940), historian. 4 l, Martha Bibescu (1890-1973). 5 l, Stefan Procopiu (1890-1972), scientist.

1990, Nov. 27 Photo. ***Perf. 13½***

3626	A1034	50b	sepia & dk bl	.15	.15
3627	A1034	1.50 l	grn & brt pur	.15	.15
3628	A1034	2 l	claret & dk bl	.16	.16
3629	A1034	3 l	dk bl & brn	.24	.24
3630	A1034	4 l	brn & dk bl	.30	.30
3631	A1034	5 l	brt pur & grn	.38	.38
			Nos. 3626-3631 (6)	1.38	1.38

National Day — A1035

1990, Dec. 1 Photo. ***Perf. 13½***

3632	A1035	2 l	multicolored	.25	.25

No. 3594 Surcharged in Brown

UN AN DE LA VICTORIA REVOLUTIEI

L4

1990, Dec. 22 Photo. Perf. 13½

3633	A1026	4 l on 2 l	.50	.50

Vincent Van Gogh, Death Cent. — A1036

Paintings: 50b, Field of Irises. 2 l, Artist's Room. 3 l, Night on the Coffee Terrace, vert. 3.50 l, Blossoming Fruit Trees. 5 l, Vase with Fourteen Sunflowers, vert.

1991, Mar. 29 Photo. Perf. 13½

3634	A1036	50b	multicolored	.15	.15
3635	A1036	2 l	multicolored	.25	.25
3636	A1036	3 l	multicolored	.35	.35
3637	A1036	3.50 l	multicolored	.42	.42
3638	A1036	5 l	multicolored	.60	.60
	Nos. 3634-3638 (5)			1.77	1.77

A1037 A1038

Birds: 50b, Larus marinus. 1 l, Sterna hirundo. 1.50 l, Recurvirostra avosetta. 2 l, Stercorarius pomarinus. 3 l, Vanellus vanellus. 3.50 l, Mergus serrator. 4 l, Egretta garzetta. 5 l, Calidris alpina. 6 l, Limosa limosa. 7 l, Childonias hybrida.

1991, Apr. 3 Photo. Perf. 13½

3639	A1037	50b	ultra	.15	.15
3640	A1037	1 l	blue green	.15	.15
3641	A1037	1.50 l	bister	.18	.18
3642	A1037	2 l	dark blue	.26	.26
3643	A1037	3 l	light green	.38	.38
3644	A1037	3.50 l	dark green	.45	.45
3645	A1037	4 l	purple	.48	.48
3646	A1037	5 l	brown	.65	.65
3647	A1037	6 l	yel brown	.75	.75
3648	A1037	7 l	light blue	.90	.90
	Nos. 3639-3648 (10)			4.35	4.35

1991, Apr. 5 Photo. Perf. 13½

3649	A1038	4 l multicolored	.35	.35

Easter.

Europa A1039

1991, May 10 Photo. Perf. 13½

3650	A1039	4.50 l Eutelsat I	.58	.58

Posthorn — A1040

1991, May 24 Photo. Perf. 13½

3651	A1040	4.50 l blue	.40	.40

Gymnastics — A1041

1991, June 14

3652	A1041	1 l	Rings	.15	.15
3653	A1041	1 l	Parallel bars	.15	.15
3654	A1041	4.50 l	Vault	.50	.50
3655	A1041	4.50 l	Uneven parallel bars	.50	.50
3656	A1041	8 l	Floor exercise	.90	.90
3657	A1041	9 l	Balance beam	1.00	1.00
	Nos. 3652-3657 (6)			3.20	3.20

For surcharge on 5 l see No. 3735. For other surcharges see Nos. 3944, 3946.

Monasteries — A1042

1991, July 4 Photo. Perf. 13½

3658	A1042	1 l	Curtea de Arges, vert.	.15	.15
3659	A1042	1 l	Putna, vert.	.15	.15
3660	A1042	4.50 l	Voratec, vert.	.40	.40
3661	A1042	4.50 l	Agapia	.40	.40
3662	A1042	8 l	Golia	.70	.70
3663	A1042	9 l	Sucevita	.80	.80
	Nos. 3658-3663 (6)			2.60	2.60

Hotels, Lodges, and Resorts
A1043 A1044

Designs: 1 l, Hotel Continental, Timisoara, vert. 2 l, Valea Caprei Lodge, Fagaras. 4 l, Hotel Intercontinental, Bucharest, vert. 5 l, Lebada Hotel, Crisan. 6 l, Muntele Rosu Lodge, Ciucas. 8 l, Transylvania Hotel, Cluj-Napoca. 9 l, Hotel Orizont, Predeal. 10 l, Hotel Roman, Herculane, vert. 18 l, Rarau Lodge, Rarau, vert. 20 l, Alpine Hotel, Poiana Brasov. 25 l, Constanta Casino. 30 l, Miorija Lodge, Bucegi. 45 l, Sura Dacilor Lodge, Poiana Brasov. 60 l, Valea Draganului, Tourist Complex,. 80 l, Hotel Florica, Venus Health Resort. 120 l, International Hotel, Baile Felix, vert. 160 l, Hotel Egreta, Tulcea, vert. 250 l, Motel Valea de Pesti, Valea Jiului. 400 l, Tourist Complex, Baisoara. 500 l, Hotel Bradul, Covasna. 800 l, Hotel Gorj, Tirgu Jiu.

1991 Photo. Perf. 13½

3664	A1043	1 l	blue	.15	.15
3665	A1043	2 l	dark green	.15	.15
3666	A1043	4 l	carmine	.15	.15
3667	A1043	5 l	violet	.15	.15
3668	A1043	6 l	olive brown	.15	.15
3669	A1043	8 l	brown	.15	.15
3670	A1043	9 l	red brown	.15	.15
3671	A1043	10 l	olive green	.20	.20
3672	A1043	18 l	bright red	.30	.30
3673	A1043	20 l	brown org	.40	.40
3674	A1043	25 l	bright blue	.45	.45
3675	A1043	30 l	magenta	.55	.55
3676	A1043	45 l	dark blue	.90	.90
3677	A1044	60 l	brown olive	1.10	1.10
3678	A1044	80 l	purple	1.50	1.50

Size: 27x41mm, 41x27mm

3679	A1044	120 l	gray bl & dk bl vio	2.25	2.25
3680	A1044	160 l	lt ver & dk ver	3.00	3.00
3681	A1044	250 l	lt bl & dk bl	5.00	5.00
3682	A1044	400 l	tan & dk brn	8.00	8.00
3683	A1044	500 l	lt bl grn & dk bl grn	10.00	10.00
3684	A1044	800 l	pink & dk lil rose	16.00	16.00
	Nos. 3664-3684 (21)			50.70	50.70

Issued: 1 l, 5 l, 9 l, 10 l, Aug. 27; 2 l, 4 l, 18 l, 25 l, 30 l, Oct. 8; 6 l, 8 l, 20 l, 45 l, 60 l, 80 l, Nov. 14; 120 l, 160 l, 250 l, 400 l, 500 l, 800 l, Dec. 5.

Riccione '91, Intl. Philatelic Exhibition — A1045

1991, Aug. 27

3685	A1045	4 l multicolored	.40	.40

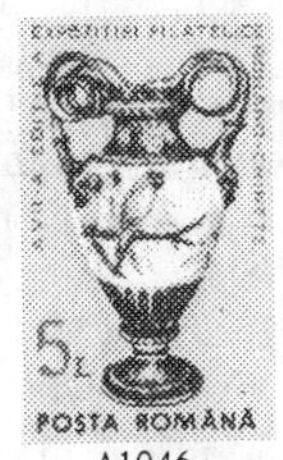

A1046 A1047

Vases: a, Decorated with birds. b, Decorated with flowers.

1991, Sept. 12

3686	A1046	5 l Pair, #a.-b.	1.00	1.00

Romanian-Chinese Philatelic Exhibition.

1991, Sept. 17

3687	A1047	1 l blue	.25	.25

Romanian Academy, 125th anniv.

A1048 A1049

Balkanfila '91 Philatelic Exhibition: 4 l, Flowers, by Nicu Enea. 5 l, Peasant Girl of Vlasca, by Georghe Tattarescu. 20 l, Sports Center, Bacau.

1991, Sept. 20

3688	A1048	4 l multicolored	.52	.52
3689	A1048	5 l multicolored	.90	.90

Souvenir Sheet

3690	A1048	20 l multicolored	2.00	2.00

No. 3689 printed se-tenant with 2 l Romanian Philatelic Assoc. label. No. 3690 contains one 54x42mm stamp.

Miniature Sheets

Birds: No. 3691a, Cissa erythrorhyncha. b, Malaconotus blanchoti. c, Sialia sialis. d, Sturnella neglecta. e, Harpactes fasciatus. f, Upupa epops. g, Malurus cyaneus. h, Brachypteracias squamigera. i, Leptopterus madagascariensis. j, Phoeniculus bollei. k, Melanerpes erythrocephalus. l, Pericrocotus flammeus.

No. 3692a, Melithreptus laetior. b, Rhynochetos jubatus. c, Turdus migratorius. d, Copsychus saularis. e, Monticola saxatilis. f, Xanthocephalus xanthocephalus. g, Scotopelia peli. h, Ptilogonys caudatus. i, Todus mexicanus. j, Copsychus malabaricus. k, Myzomela erythrocephala. l, Gymnostinops montezuma.

1991, Oct. 7 Sheets of 12

3691	A1049	2 l #a.-l.	2.50	2.50
3692	A1049	2 l #a.-l.	2.50	2.50

Natl. Census — A1050

1991, Oct. 15

3693	A1050	5 l multicolored	.30	.30

Phila Nippon '91 A1051

1991, Nov. 13 Photo. Perf. 13½

3694	A1051	10 l Sailing ship	1.00	1.00
3695	A1051	10 l Bridge building	1.00	1.00

Miniature Sheets

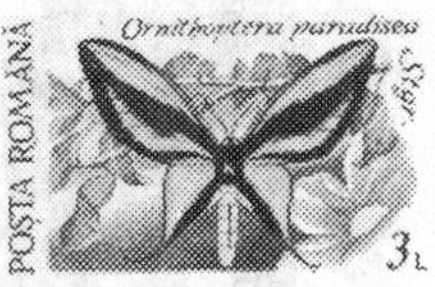

Butterflies and Moths A1052

Designs: No. 3696a, Ornithoptera paradisea. b, Bhutanitis lidderdalii. c, Morpho helena. d, Ornithoptera croesus. e, Phoebis avellaneda. f, Ornithoptera victoriae. g, Teinopalpus imperialis. h, Hypolimnas dexithea. i, Dabasa payeni. j, Morpho achilleana. k, Heliconius melpomene. l, Agrias claudina sardanapalus.

No. 3697a, Graellsia isabellae. b, Antocharis cardamines. c, Ammobiota festiva. d, Polygonia c-album. e, Catocala promisa. f, Rhyparia purpurata. g, Arctia villica. h, Polyommatus daphnis. i, Zerynthia polyxena. j, Daphnis nerii. k, Licaena dispar rutila. l, Pararge roxelana.

1991, Nov. 30 Photo. Perf. 13½
Sheets of 12

3696	A1052	3 l #a.-l.	3.00	3.00
3697	A1052	3 l #a.-l.	3.00	3.00

A1053 A1054

1991, Nov. 21 Photo. Perf. 13½

3698	A1053	1 l	Running	.15	.15
3699	A1053	4 l	Long jump	.42	.42
3700	A1053	5 l	High jump	.55	.55
3701	A1053	5 l	Runner in blocks	.55	.55
3702	A1053	9 l	Hurdles	.95	.95
3703	A1053	10 l	Javelin	1.10	1.10
	Nos. 3698-3703 (6)			3.72	3.72

World Track and Field Championships, Tokyo.

1991, Dec. 10 Photo. Perf. 13½

Famous People: 1 l, Mihail Kogalniceanu (1817-1891), politician. 4 l, Nicolae Titulescu (1882-1941), politician. No. 3706, Andrei Mureseanu (1816-1863), author. No. 3707, Aron Pumnul (1818-1866), author. 9 l, George Bacovia (1881-1957), author. 10 l, Perpessicius (1891-1971), writer.

3704	A1054	1 l	multi	.15	.15
3705	A1054	4 l	multi	.20	.20
3706	A1054	5 l	multi	.25	.25
3707	A1054	5 l	multi	.25	.25
3708	A1054	9 l	multi	.48	.48
3709	A1054	10 l	multi	.52	.52
	Nos. 3704-3709 (6)			1.85	1.85

See Nos. 3759-3761, 3776-3781.

Stamp Day
A1055

1991, Dec. 20
3710 A1055 8 l multicolored .50 .50

No. 3710 printed se-tenant with 2 l Romanian Philatelic Assoc. label.

Central University Library, Bucharest, Cent.
A1056

1991, Dec. 23
3711 A1056 8 l red brown .35 .35

Christmas
A1057

1991, Dec. 25 Photo. *Perf. 13½*
3712 A1057 8 l multicolored .50 .50

See No. 3874.

1992 Winter Olympics, Albertville
A1058

1992, Feb. 1 Photo. *Perf. 13½*
3713 A1058 4 l Biathlon .15 .15
3714 A1058 5 l Alpine skiing .15 .15
3715 A1058 8 l Cross-country skiing .16 .16
3716 A1058 10 l Two-man luge .20 .20
3717 A1058 20 l Speed skating .40 .40
3718 A1058 25 l Ski jumping .52 .52
3719 A1058 30 l Ice hockey .62 .62
3720 A1058 45 l Men's figure skating .90 .90
Nos. 3713-3720 (8) 3.10 3.10

Souvenir Sheets

3721 A1058 75 l Women's figure skating 2.50 2.50

Imperf

3722 A1058 125 l 4-Man bobsled *4.15 4.15*

No. 3721 is airmail and contains one 42x54mm stamp.

Porcelain — A1059

Designs: 4 l, Sugar and cream service. 5 l, Tea service. 8 l, Goblet and pitcher, vert. 30 l, Tea service, diff. 45 l, Vase, vert.

1992, Feb. 20 Photo. *Perf. 13½*
3723 A1059 4 l multicolored .15 .15
3724 A1059 5 l multicolored .15 .15
3725 A1059 8 l multicolored .20 .20
3726 A1059 30 l multicolored .75 .75
3727 A1059 45 l multicolored 1.15 1.15
Nos. 3723-3727 (5) 2.40 2.40

Fish
A1060

Designs: 4 l, Scomber scombrus. 5 l, Tinca tinca. 8 l, Salvelinus fontinalis. 10 l, Romanichthys valsanicola. 30 l, Chondrostoma nasus. 45 l, Mullus barbatus ponticus.

1992, Feb. 28 Photo. *Perf. 13½*
3728 A1060 4 l multicolored .16 .16
3729 A1060 5 l multicolored .20 .20
3730 A1060 8 l multicolored .30 .30
3731 A1060 10 l multicolored .40 .40
3732 A1060 30 l multicolored 1.25 1.25
3733 A1060 45 l multicolored 1.75 1.75
Nos. 3728-3733 (6) 4.06 4.06

A1060a

1992, Mar. 11 Photo. *Perf. 13½*
3734 A1060a 90 l on 5 l multi 2.25 2.25

No. 3734 not issued without surcharge.

Olympics Type of 1991 Surcharged

C.M. INDIVIDUALE DE GIMNASTICA PARIS 15-19.04.1992
90L

1992, Mar. 11 Photo. *Perf. 13½*
3735 A1041 90 l on 5 l like #3657 2.25 2.25

No. 3735 not issued without surcharge.

Horses
A1061

Various stylized drawings of horses walking, running, or jumping.

1992, Mar. 17 Photo. *Perf. 13½*
3736 A1061 6 l multi, vert. .22 .22
3737 A1061 7 l multi .28 .28
3738 A1061 10 l multi, vert. .38 .38
3739 A1061 25 l multi, vert. .95 .95
3740 A1061 30 l multi 1.15 1.15
3741 A1061 50 l multi, vert. 1.90 1.90
Nos. 3736-3741 (6) 4.88 4.88

Miniature Sheet

Discovery of America, 500th Anniv. — A1062

Columbus and ships: a, Green background. b, Violet background. c, Blue background. d, Ship approaching island.

1992, Apr. 22 Photo. *Perf. 13½*
3742 A1062 35 l Sheet of 4, #a.-d. *6.50 6.50*

Europa.

Granada '92, Philatelic Exhibition — A1063

Designs: a, 25 l, Spain No. 1 and Romania No. 1. b, 10 l, Expo emblem. c, 30 l, Building and courtyard, Granada. (Illustration reduced).

1992, Apr. 24 Photo. *Perf. 13½*
3743 A1063 Sheet of 3, #a.-c. 1.40 1.40

Icon of Christ's Descent into Hell, 1680 — A1064

1992, Apr. 24 Photo. *Perf. 13½*
3744 A1064 10 l multicolored .60 .60

Easter.

Fire Station, Bucharest, Cent. — A1065

1992, May 2
3745 A1065 10 l multicolored .60 .60

Chess Olympiad, Manila — A1066

1992, June 7 *Perf. 13½*
3746 A1066 10 l shown .35 .35
3747 A1066 10 l Building, chess board .35 .35

Souvenir Sheet

3748 A1066 75 l Shore, chess board 2.50 2.50

No. 3748 contains one 42x54mm stamp.

1992 Summer Olympics, Barcelona — A1067

1992, July 17 Photo. *Perf. 13½*
3749 A1067 6 l Shooting, vert. .15 .15
3750 A1067 7 l Weight lifting, vert. .15 .15
3751 A1067 9 l Two-man canoeing .15 .15
3752 A1067 10 l Handball, vert. .15 .15
3753 A1067 25 l Wrestling .38 .38
3754 A1067 30 l Fencing .45 .45
3755 A1067 50 l Running, vert. .75 .75
3756 A1067 55 l Boxing .82 .82
Nos. 3749-3756 (8) 3.00 3.00

Souvenir Sheets

3757 A1067 100 l Rowing 1.50 1.50

Imperf

3758 A1067 200 l Gymnastics 3.00 3.00

Nos. 3757-3758 are airmail. No. 3757 contains one 54x42mm stamp, No. 3758 one 40x53mm stamp.

Famous People Type of 1991

Designs: 10 l, Ion I. C. Bratianu (1864-1927), prime minister. 25 l, Ion Gh. Duca (1879-1933). 30 l, Grigore Gafencu (1892-1957), journalist and politician.

1992, July 27 Photo. *Perf. 13½*
3759 A1054 10 l green & violet .30 .30
3760 A1054 25 l blue & lake .75 .75
3761 A1054 30 l lake & blue .90 .90
Nos. 3759-3761 (3) 1.95 1.95

Expo '92, Seville
A1068

Designs: 6 l, The Thinker, Cernavoda. 7 l, Trajan's bridge, Drobeta. 10 l, Mill. 25 l, Railroad bridge, Cernavoda. 30 l, Trajan Vuia's flying machine. 55 l, Herman Oberth's rocket. 100 l, Prayer sculpture, by C. Brancusi.

1992, Sept. 1
3762 A1068 6 l multicolored .15 .15
3763 A1068 7 l multicolored .15 .15
3764 A1068 10 l multicolored .18 .18
3765 A1068 25 l multicolored .45 .45
3766 A1068 30 l multicolored .52 .52
3767 A1068 55 l multicolored 1.00 1.00
Nos. 3762-3767 (6) 2.45 2.45

Souvenir Sheet

3768 A1068 100 l multicolored 2.00 2.00

No. 3768 contains one 42x54mm stamp.

World Post Day — A1069

1992, Oct. 9
3769 A1069 10 l multicolored .38 .38

For surcharge see No. 3945.

Discovery of America, 500th Anniv. — A1070

Columbus and: 6 l, Santa Maria. 10 l, Nina. 25 l, Pinta. 55 l, Arrival in New World. 100 l, Sailing ship, vert.

1992, Oct. 30 Photo. *Perf. 13½*
3770 A1070 6 l multicolored .16 .16
3771 A1070 10 l multicolored .28 .28
3772 A1070 25 l multicolored .70 .70
3773 A1070 55 l multicolored 1.50 1.50
Nos. 3770-3773 (4) 2.64 2.64

Souvenir Sheet

3774 A1070 100 l multicolored 2.25 2.25

No. 3774 contains one 42x54mm stamp.

Romanian Postal Reorganization, 1st Anniv. — A1071

1992, Nov. 5 Photo. *Perf. 13½*

3775 A1071 10 l multicolored .42 .42

For surcharge see No. 4113.

Famous People Type of 1991

Designs: 6 l, Iacob Negruzzi (1842-1932), author. 7 l, Grigore Antipa (1867-1944), naturalist. 9 l, Alexe Mateevici (1888-1917), poet. 10 l, Cezar Petrescu (1892-1961), author. 25 l, Octav Onicescu (1892-1983), mathematician. 30 l, Ecaterina Teodoroiu (1894-1917), World War I soldier.

1992, Nov. 9 Photo. *Perf. 13½*

3776 A1054 6 l green & violet .15 .15
3777 A1054 7 l lilac & green .16 .16
3778 A1054 9 l gray blue & purple .22 .22
3779 A1054 10 l brown & blue .24 .24
3780 A1054 25 l blue & brown .60 .60
3781 A1054 30 l slate & blue .75 .75
Nos. 3776-3781 (6) 2.12 2.12

Wild Animals — A1072

Designs: 6 l, Haliaeetus leucocephalus, vert. 7 l, Strix occidentalis, vert. 9 l, Ursus arctos, vert. 10 l, Haematopus bachmani. 25 l, Canis lupus. 30 l, Odocoileus virginianus. 55 l, Alces alces.

1992, Nov. 16 Litho. *Perf. 13½*

3782 A1072 6 l multicolored .15 .15
3783 A1072 7 l multicolored .15 .15
3784 A1072 9 l multicolored .16 .16
3785 A1072 10 l multicolored .18 .18
3786 A1072 25 l multicolored .45 .45
3787 A1072 30 l multicolored .60 .60
3788 A1072 55 l multicolored 1.00 1.00
Nos. 3782-3788 (7) 2.69 2.69

Souvenir Sheet

3789 A1072 100 l Orcinus orca 2.00 2.00

Romanian Anniversaries and Events — A1073

7 l, Building, Galea Victoria St., 300th anniv. 9 l, Statue, School of Commerce, 600th anniv. 10 l, Curtea de Arges Monastery, 475th anniv. 25 l, School of Architecture, Bucharest, 80th anniv.

1992, Dec. 3 Photo. *Perf. 13½*

3790 A1073 7 l multicolored .20 .20
3791 A1073 9 l multicolored .25 .25
3792 A1073 10 l multicolored .30 .30
3793 A1073 25 l multicolored .75 .75
Nos. 3790-3793 (4) 1.50 1.50

Natl. Arms — A1074

1992, Dec. 7

3794 A1074 15 l multicolored .30 .30

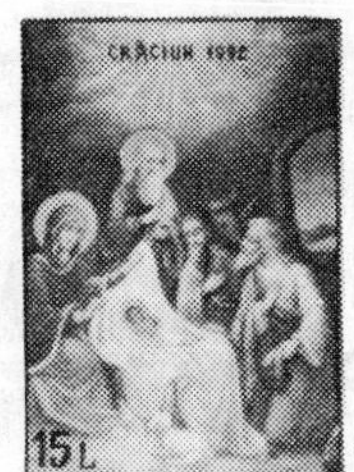

Christmas A1075

1992, Dec. 15

3795 A1075 15 l multicolored .30 .30

New Telephone Numbering System — A1076

1992, Dec. 28 Photo. *Perf. 13½*

3796 A1076 15 l blue, black & red *.35 .35*

Souvenir Sheets

1992 Summer Olympics, Barcelona A1077

Designs: No. 3797a, Shooting. b, Wrestling. c, Weight lifting. d, Boxing.
No. 3798a, Women's gymnastics. b, Four-man sculls. c, Fencing. d, High jump.

1992, Dec. 30 Photo. *Perf. 13½*

3797 A1077 35 l Sheet of 4, #a.-d. *2.50 2.50*
3798 A1077 35 l Sheet of 4, #a.-d. *2.50 2.50*

Easter — A1079

1993, Mar. 25

3803 A1079 15 l multicolored .28 .28

Historic Sites, Bucharest — A1078

Designs: 10 l, Mihai Voda Monastery. 15 l, Vacaresti Monastery. 25 l, Multi-purpose hall. 30 l, Mina Minovici Medical Institute.

1993, Feb. 11 Photo. *Perf. 13½*

3799 A1078 10 l multicolored .18 .18
3800 A1078 15 l multicolored .28 .28
3801 A1078 25 l multicolored .45 .45
3802 A1078 30 l multicolored .55 .55
Nos. 3799-3802 (4) 1.46 1.46

Medicinal Plants — A1080

1993, Mar. 30

3804 A1080 10 l Crataegus monogyna .18 .18
3805 A1080 15 l Gentiana phlogifolia .28 .28
3806 A1080 25 l Hippophae rhamnoides .48 .48
3807 A1080 30 l Vaccinium myrtillus .55 .55
3808 A1080 50 l Arnica montana .95 .95
3809 A1080 90 l Rosa canina 1.70 1.70
Nos. 3804-3809 (6) 4.14 4.14

Nichita Stanescu (1933-1983), Poet — A1081

1993, Mar. 31

3810 A1081 15 l brown and blue .28 .28

Souvenir Sheet

Polska '93 — A1082

1993, Apr. 28 Photo. *Perf. 13½*

3811 A1082 200 l multicolored 2.25 2.25

Birds — A1083

Cats — A1084

1993, Apr. 30

3812 A1083 5 l Pica pica .15 .15
3813 A1083 10 l Aquila chrysaetos .15 .15
3814 A1083 15 l Pyrrhula pyrrhula .15 .15
3815 A1083 20 l Upupa epops .15 .15
3816 A1083 25 l Dendrocopos major .15 .15
3817 A1083 50 l Oriolus oriolus .30 .30
3818 A1083 65 l Loxia leucoptera .40 .40
3819 A1083 90 l Hirundo rustica .60 .60
3820 A1083 160 l Parus cyanus 1.10 1.10
3821 A1083 250 l Sturnus roseus 1.75 1.75
Nos. 3812-3821 (10) 4.90 4.90

Nos. 3812-3813 are horiz.

1993, May 24 Photo. *Perf. 13½*

Various cats.

3822 A1084 10 l multicolored .15 .15
3823 A1084 15 l multicolored .15 .15
3824 A1084 30 l multicolored .25 .25
3825 A1084 90 l multicolored .80 .80
3826 A1084 135 l multicolored 1.10 1.10
3827 A1084 160 l multicolored 1.25 1.25
Nos. 3822-3827 (6) 3.70 3.70

Souvenir Sheet

Europa — A1085

Paintings and sculpture by: a, Pablo Picasso. b, Constantin Brancusi. c, Ion Irimescu. d, Alexandru Ciucurencu.

1993, May 31 Photo. *Perf. 13½*

3828 A1085 280 l Sheet of 4, #a.-d. 2.75 2.75

A1086

A1087

1993, June 30 Photo. *Perf. 13½*

3829 A1086 10 l Vipera berus .15 .15
3830 A1086 15 l Lynx lynx .15 .15
3831 A1086 25 l Tadorna tadorna .15 .15
3832 A1086 75 l Hucho hucho .45 .45
3833 A1086 105 l Limenitis populi .60 .60
3834 A1086 280 l Rosalia alpina 1.75 1.75
Nos. 3829-3834 (6) 3.25 3.25

Nos. 3829, 3831-3834 are horiz.

1993, June 30

3835 A1087 10 l Martes martes .15 .15
3836 A1087 15 l Oryctolagus cuniculus .15 .15
3837 A1087 20 l Sciurus vulgaris .15 .15
3838 A1087 25 l Rupicapra rupicapra .15 .15
3839 A1087 30 l Vulpes vulpes .16 .16
3840 A1087 40 l Ovis ammon .22 .22
3841 A1087 75 l Genetta genetta .45 .45
3842 A1087 105 l Eliomys quercinus .65 .65
3843 A1087 150 l Mustela ermina .85 .85
3844 A1087 280 l Herpestes ichneumon 1.75 1.75
Nos. 3835-3844 (10) 4.68 4.68

Nos. 3836, 3839, 3843-3844 are horiz.

Dinosaurs — A1088

1993, July 30 Photo. *Perf. 13½*

3845 A1088	29 l	Brontosaurus	.16	.16
3846 A1088	46 l	Plesiosaurus	.25	.25
3847 A1088	85 l	Triceratops	.48	.48
3848 A1088	171 l	Stegosaurus	.95	.95
3849 A1088	216 l	Tyrannosaurus	1.25	1.25
3850 A1088	319 l	Archaeopteryx	2.00	2.00
		Nos. 3845-3850 (6)	5.09	5.09

Souvenir Sheet

Telafila '93, Israel-Romanian Philatelic Exhibition — A1089

Woman with Eggs, by Marcel Lancu. Illustration reduced.

1993, Aug. 21

3851 A1089	535 l	multicolored	2.25	2.25

Icons — A1090

Designs: 75 l, St. Stephen. 171 l, Martyrs from Brancoveanu and Vacarescu families. 216 l, St. Anthony.

1993, Aug. 31

3852 A1090	75 l	multicolored	.45	.45
3853 A1090	171 l	multicolored	1.00	1.00
3854 A1090	216 l	multicolored	1.40	1.40
		Nos. 3852-3854 (3)	2.85	2.85

Rural Mounted Police, Cent. — A1091

1993, Sept. 1

3855 A1091	29 l	multicolored	.22	.22

Riccione '93
3–5 septembrie

171 L

No. 3618 Surcharged in Red

1993, Sept. 3

3856 A1031	171 l on 2 l		1.10	1.10

Souvenir Sheet

Bangkok '93 — A1092

Illustration reduced.

1993, Sept. 20

3857 A1092	535 l	multicolored	2.25	2.25

Famous Men — A1093

Designs: 29 l, George Baritiu (1812-93), politician. 46 l, Horia Creanga (1892-1943), architect. 85 l, Armand Calinescu (1893-1939), politician. 171 l, Dumitru Bagdasar (1893-1946), physician. 216 l, Constantin Brailoiu (1893-1958), musician. 319 l, Iuliu Maniu (1873-1953), politician.

1993, Oct. 8

3858 A1093	29 l	multicolored	.16	.16
3859 A1093	46 l	multicolored	.25	.25
3860 A1093	85 l	multicolored	.48	.48
3861 A1093	171 l	multicolored	.95	.95
3862 A1093	216 l	multicolored	1.25	1.25
3863 A1093	319 l	multicolored	2.00	2.00
		Nos. 3858-3863 (6)	5.09	5.09

Souvenir Sheet

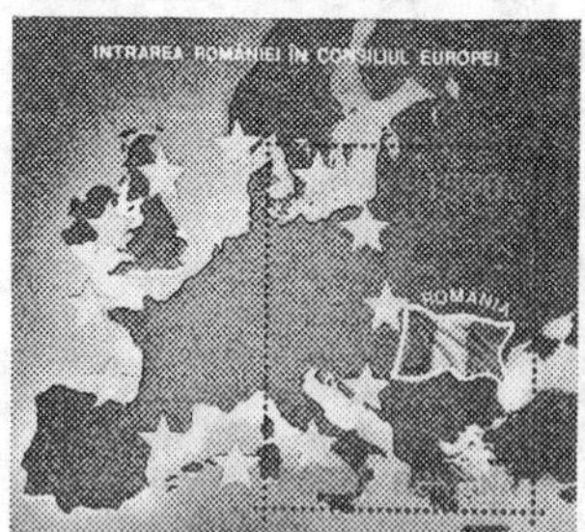

Romanian Entry into Council of Europe — A1094

1993, Nov. 26 Photo. *Perf. 13½*

3864 A1094	1590 l	multicolored	9.00	9.00

Expansion of Natl. Borders, 75th Anniv. A1095

Government leaders: 115 l, Iancu Flondor (1865-1924). 245 l, Ion I. C. Bratianu (1864-1927). 255 l, Luliu Maniu (1873-1953). 325 l, Pantelimon Halippa (1883-1979). 1060 l, King Ferdinand I (1865-1927).

1993-94

3865 A1095	115 l	multicolored	.50	.50
3866 A1095	245 l	multicolored	.85	.85
3867 A1095	255 l	multicolored	1.00	1.00
3868 A1095	325 l	multicolored	1.75	1.75
		Nos. 3865-3868 (4)	4.10	4.10

Souvenir Sheet

3869 A1095	1060 l	Romania in one color	4.00	4.00
a.		Romania in four colors	*10.00*	*10.00*

No. 3869a was redrawn because of an error in the map.

Issued: No. 3869, Feb. 1994; Nos. 3865-3868, 3869a, Dec. 1, 1993.

Anniversaries and Events — A1096

Designs: 115 l, Emblem of the Diplomatic Alliance. 245 l, Statue of Johannes Honterus, founder of first Humanitarian School. 255 l, Arms, seal of Slatina, Olt River Bridge. 325 l, Map, arms of Braila.

1993, Dec. 15

3870 A1096	115 l	multicolored	.50	.50
3871 A1096	245 l	multicolored	.85	.85
3872 A1096	255 l	multicolored	1.00	1.00
3873 A1096	325 l	multicolored	1.75	1.75
		Nos. 3870-3873 (4)	4.10	4.10

Diplomatic Alliance, 75th anniv. (#3870). Birth of Johannes Honterus, 450th anniv. (#3871). City of Slatina, 625th anniv. (#3872). County of Braila, 625th anniv. (#3873).

Christmas Type of 1991

1993, Dec. 20

3874 A1057	45 l	like #3712	.32	.32

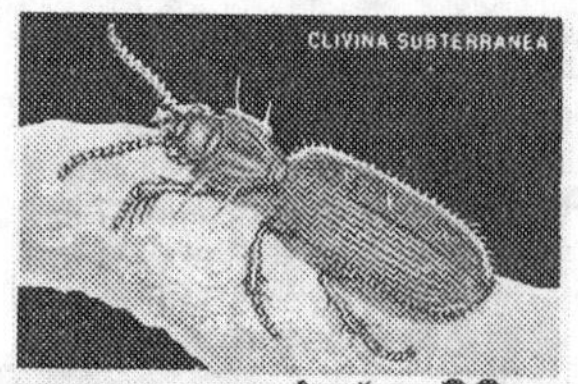

Insects, Wildlife from Movile Cavern — A1097

Designs: 29 l, Clivina subterranea. 46 l, Nepa anophthalma. 85 l, Haemopis caeca. 171 l, Lascona cristiani. 216 l, Semisalsa dobrogica. 310 l, Armadillidium tabacarui. 535 l, Exploring cavern, vert.

1993, Dec. 27

3875 A1097	29 l	multicolored	.15	.15
3876 A1097	46 l	multicolored	.24	.24
3877 A1097	85 l	multicolored	.45	.45
3878 A1097	171 l	multicolored	.85	.85
3879 A1097	216 l	multicolored	1.10	1.10
3880 A1097	310 l	multicolored	1.50	1.50
		Nos. 3875-3880 (6)	4.29	4.29

Souvenir Sheet

3881 A1097	535 l	multicolored	2.25	2.25

Alexandru Ioan Cuza — A1098

1994, Jan. 24 Photo. *Perf. 13*

3882 A1098	45 l	multicolored	.25	.25

Historic Buildings, Bucharest — A1099

Designs: 115 l, Opera House. 245 l, Vacaresti Monastery. 255 l, Church of St. Vineri. 325 l, Dominican House, Vacaresti Monastery.

1994, Feb. 7

3883 A1099	115 l	multicolored	.38	.18
3884 A1099	245 l	multicolored	.80	.40
3885 A1099	255 l	multicolored	.85	.42
3886 A1099	325 l	multicolored	1.10	.55
		Nos. 3883-3886 (4)	3.13	1.55

1994 Winter Olympics, Lillehammer A1100

1994, Feb. 12 *Perf. 13½*

3887 A1100	70 l	Speed skating	.25	.15
3888 A1100	115 l	Slalom skiing	.38	.18
3889 A1100	125 l	Bobsled	.42	.20
3890 A1100	245 l	Biathlon	.80	.40
3891 A1100	255 l	Ski jumping	.85	.42
3892 A1100	325 l	Figure skating	1.10	.55
		Nos. 3887-3892 (6)	3.80	1.90

Souvenir Sheet

3893 A1100	1590 l	Luge	5.25	5.25

No. 3893 contains one 43x54mm stamp.

Mills — A1101

1994, Mar. 31 *Perf. 13*

3894 A1101	70 l	Sarichioi	.25	.15
3895 A1101	115 l	Valea Nucarilor	.38	.18
3896 A1101	125 l	Caraorman	.42	.20
3897 A1101	245 l	Romanii de Jos	.80	.40
3898 A1101	255 l	Enisala, horiz.	.85	.42
3899 A1101	325 l	Nistoresti	1.10	.55
		Nos. 3894-3899 (6)	3.80	1.90

Dinosaurs — A1102

1994, Apr. 30 Photo. *Perf. 13½*

3900 A1102	90 l	Struthiosaurs	.30	.30
3901 A1102	130 l	Megalosaurs	.42	.42
3902 A1102	150 l	Parasaurolophus	.48	.48
3903 A1102	280 l	Stenonychosaurus	.90	.90
3904 A1102	500 l	Camarasaurus	1.60	1.60
3905 A1102	635 l	Gallimimus	2.00	2.00
		Nos. 3900-3905 (6)	5.70	5.70

Romanian Legends — A1103

Designs: 70 l, Calin the Madman. 115 l, Ileana Cosanzeana. 125 l, Ileana Cosanzeana, diff. 245 l, Ileana Cosanzeana, diff. 255 l, Agheran the Brave. 325 l, Wolf as Prince Charming, Ileana Cosanzeana.

1994, Apr. 8 Photo. *Perf. 13*

3906 A1103 70 l multicolored .25 .15
3907 A1103 115 l multicolored .38 .18
3908 A1103 125 l multicolored .42 .20
3909 A1103 245 l multicolored .80 .40
3910 A1103 255 l multicolored .85 .42
3911 A1103 325 l multicolored 1.10 .55
Nos. 3906-3911 (6) 3.80 1.90

Easter — A1104 Trees — A1105

1994, Apr. 21

3912 A1104 60 l multicolored .25 .15

Wmk. 398

1994, May 27 Photo. *Perf. 13*

3913 A1105 15 l Abies alba .15 .15
3914 A1105 35 l Pinus sylvestris .15 .15
3915 A1105 45 l Populus alba .15 .15
3916 A1105 60 l Quercus robur .15 .15
3917 A1105 70 l Larix decidua .16 .15
3918 A1105 125 l Fagus sylvatica .30 .15
3919 A1105 350 l Acer pseudoplatanus .85 .42
3920 A1105 940 l Fraxinus excelsior 2.25 1.10
3921 A1105 1440 l Picea abies 3.50 1.75
3922 A1105 3095 l Tilia platyphyllos 7.50 3.75
Nos. 3913-3922 (10) 15.16 7.92

1994 World Cup Soccer Championships, US — A1106

1994, June 17 Unwmk.

3923 A1106 90 l Group A .25 .16
3924 A1106 130 l Group B .35 .18
3925 A1106 150 l Group C .40 .20
3926 A1106 280 l Group D .75 .38
3927 A1106 500 l Group E 1.40 .70
3928 A1106 635 l Group F 1.75 .85
Nos. 3923-3928 (6) 4.90 2.47

Souvenir Sheet

3929 A1106 2075 l Action scene 5.25 5.25

No. 3929 is airmail and contains one 54x42mm stamp.

Intl. Olympic Committee, Cent. — A1107

Ancient Olympians: 150 l, Torchbearer. 280 l, Discus thrower. 500 l, Wrestlers. 635 l, Arbitrator. 2075 l, Runners, emblem of Romanian Olympic Committee.

1994, June 23

3930 A1107 150 l multicolored .40 .20
3931 A1107 280 l multicolored .75 .38
3932 A1107 500 l multicolored 1.40 .70
3933 A1107 635 l multicolored 1.75 .85
Nos. 3930-3933 (4) 4.30 2.13

Souvenir Sheet

3934 A1107 2075 l multicolored 5.25 5.25

No. 3934 contains one 54x42mm stamp. Romanian Olympic Committee, 80th anniv. (#3934).

Miniature Sheets

Mushrooms A1108

Edible: No. 3935a, 30 l, Craterellus cornucopiodes. b, 60 l, Lepista nuda. c, 150 l, Boletus edulis. d, 940 l, Lycoperdon perlatum.

Poisonous: No. 3936a, 90 l, Boletus satanas. b, 280 l, Amanita phalloides. c, 350 l, Inocybe patonillardi. d, 500 l, Amanita muscaria.

1994, Aug. 8 Photo. *Perf. 13½*

3935 A1108 Sheet of 4, #a.-d. 2.50 1.25
3936 A1108 Sheet of 4, #a.-d. 2.75 1.40
Complete booklet, #3935-3936 7.75

PHILAKOREA '94 — A1109

1994, Aug. 16 *Perf. 13½*

3937 A1109 60 l Tuning fork .18 .15

Souvenir Sheet

3938 A1109 2075 l Korean drummer 5.25 5.25

No. 3938 contains one 42x54mm stamp.

Environmental Protection in Danube River Delta — A1110

Designs: 150 l, Huso huso. 280 l, Vipera ursini. 500 l, Haliaeetus albieilla. 635 l, Mustela lutreola. 2075 l, Periploca graeca.

1994, Aug. 31

3939 A1110 150 l multicolored .35 .18
3940 A1110 280 l multicolored .65 .32
3941 A1110 500 l multicolored 1.10 .55
3942 A1110 635 l multicolored 1.50 .75
Nos. 3939-3942 (4) 3.60 1.80

Souvenir Sheet

3943 A1110 2075 l multicolored 4.75 4.75

No. 3943 contains one 54x42mm stamp.

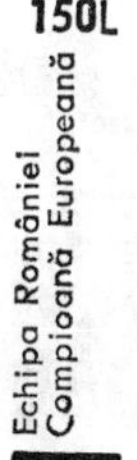

Nos. 3654-3655 Surcharged

150 LEI
1994
Posta - cea mai buna alegere

No. 3769 Surcharged

1994 *Perfs., Etc. as Before*

3944 A1041 150 l on 4.50 l #3654 .30 .20
3945 A1069 150 l on 10 l #3769 .35 .18
3946 A1041 525 l on 4.50 l #3655 1.10 .55
Nos. 3944-3946 (3) 1.75 .93

Issued: #3944, 3946 9/9/94; #3945, 10/7/94.

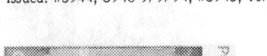

Circus Animal Acts A1111

1994, Sept. 15 Photo. *Perf. 13*

3947 A1111 90 l Elephant .22 .15
3948 A1111 130 l Bear, vert. .32 .16
3949 A1111 150 l Monkeys .38 .20
3950 A1111 280 l Tiger .70 .35
3951 A1111 500 l Lion 1.25 .60
3952 A1111 635 l Horse 1.65 .85
Nos. 3947-3952 (6) 4.52 2.31

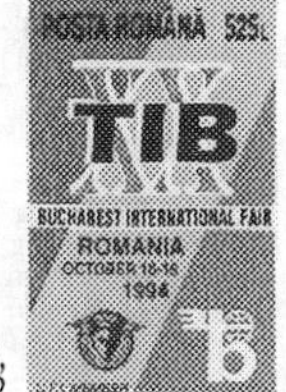

20th Intl. Fair, Bucharest — A1112

1994, Oct. 10

3953 A1112 525 l multicolored 1.25 .60

Fish A1113

World Wildlife Fund: 150 l, Acipenser ruthenus. 280 l, Acipenser guldenstaedti. 500 l, Acipenser stellatus. 635 l, Acipenser sturio.

1994, Oct. 29 Photo. *Perf. 13½*

3954 A1113 150 l multicolored .32 .16
3955 A1113 280 l multicolored .60 .30
3956 A1113 500 l multicolored 1.00 .50
3957 A1113 635 l multicolored 1.40 .70
Nos. 3954-3957 (4) 3.32 1.66

Chinese-Romanian Philatelic Exhibition — A1114

1994, Oct. 29 Photo. *Perf. 13½*

3958 A1114 150 l Serpent .38 .20
3959 A1114 1135 l Dragon 3.00 1.50
a. Pair, #3958-3959 + label 3.50 3.50

Romanian State Railway, 125th Anniv. A1115

1994, Oct. 31

3960 A1115 90 l multicolored .22 .15

Famous People — A1116

Designs: 30 l, Akex Drascu (1817-94). 60 l, Gh. Polizu (1819-86). 90 l, Gheorghe Tattarescu (1820-94), politician, prime minister. 150 l, Iulia Hasdeu (1869-88). 280 l, S. Mehedinti (1869-1962). 350 l, Camil Petrescu (1894-1957). 500 l, N. Paulescu (1869-1931). 940 l, L. Grigorescu (1894-1965).

1994 Photo. *Perf. 13½*

3961 A1116 30 l multicolored .15 .15
3962 A1116 60 l multicolored .15 .15
3962A A1116 90 l multicolored .20 .15
3963 A1116 150 l multicolored .32 .16
3964 A1116 280 l multicolored .60 .30
3965 A1116 350 l multicolored .75 .38
3966 A1116 500 l multicolored 1.00 .50
3967 A1116 940 l multicolored 2.00 1.00
Nos. 3961-3967 (8) 5.17 2.79

Issued; 90 l, 12/28/94; others, 11/30/94.

Christmas — A1117

1994, Dec. 14 *Perf. 13½*

3968 A1117 60 l multicolored .20 .15

St. Mary's Romanian Orthodox Church, Cleveland, Ohio, 90th Anniv. — A1118

1994, Dec. 21 Photo. *Perf. 13½*

3969 A1118 610 l multicolored 1.50 .75

World Tourism Organization, 20th Anniv. A1119

1994, Dec. 22

3970 A1119 525 l multicolored 1.25 .60

Miniature Sheet

Romanian Military Decorations — A1120

Year of medal: No. 3971a, 30 l, Distinguished Flying Cross, 1938. b, 60 l, Military Cross, 3rd class, 1916. c, 150 l, Distinguished Serivce Medal, 1st Class, 1880. d, 940 l, Order of the Romanian Star, 1877.

1994, Dec. 23

3971 A1120 Sheet of 4, #a.-d. 2.75 2.75

Baby Animals — A1121

1994, Dec. 27 Photo. *Perf. 13x½*

3972 A1121 90 l Kittens .25 .15
3973 A1121 130 l Puppies .40 .20
3974 A1121 150 l Kid goat .45 .25
3975 A1121 280 l Foal .80 .40
3976 A1121 500 l Bunnies 1.40 .70
3977 A1121 635 l Lambs 1.90 .95
Nos. 3972-3977 (6) 5.20 2.65

A1122 A1123

1995, Jan. 31 Photo. *Perf. 13½*

3978 A1122 60 l dark blue .22 .15

Save the Children organization.

1995, Feb. 25 Photo. *Perf. 13½*

The Young Men of Brasov (Riders representing municipal districts of Brasov): 40 l, Tanar. 60 l, Batran. 150 l, Curcan. 280 l, Dorobant. 350 l, Brasovechean. 500 l, Rosior. 635 l, Albior.

3979 A1123 40 l multicolored .15 .15
3980 A1123 60 l multicolored .20 .15
3981 A1123 150 l multicolored .45 .25
3982 A1123 280 l multicolored .80 .40
3983 A1123 350 l multicolored 1.00 .50
3984 A1123 500 l multicolored 1.40 .70
3985 A1123 635 l multicolored 1.90 .95
Nos. 3979-3985 (7) 5.90 3.10

Liberation of Concentration Camps, 50th Anniv. — A1124

1995, Mar. 24 *Perf. 13½*

3986 A1124 960 l black & red 2.75 1.40

FAO & UN, 50th Anniv. A1125

Designs: 675 l, FAO emblem, grain. 960 l, "50," UN emblem. 1615 l, Hand holding pen with flags of UN Charter countries.

1995, Apr. 12 *Perf. 13½*

3987 A1125 675 l multicolored 2.00 1.00
3988 A1125 960 l multicolored 2.75 1.40
3989 A1125 1615 l multicolored 4.75 2.25
Nos. 3987-3989 (3) 9.50 4.65

Easter — A1126

1995, Apr. 14

3990 A1126 60 l multicolored .20 .15

Romanian Fairy Tales — A1127

Designs: 90 l, King riding horse across town. 130 l, Woman feeding animals, vert. 150 l, Man riding on winged horse. 280 l, Old man, young man. 500 l, Archer aiming at apple tree, vert. 635 l, Two people riding log pulled by galloping horses.

1995, Apr. 20 *Perf. 13½*

3991 A1127 90 l multicolored .25 .15
3992 A1127 130 l multicolored .40 .20
3993 A1127 150 l multicolored .45 .25
3994 A1127 280 l multicolored .80 .40
3995 A1127 500 l multicolored 1.40 .70
3996 A1127 635 l multicolored 1.90 .95
Nos. 3991-3996 (6) 5.20 2.65

Georges Enescu (1881-1955), Composer — A1128

1995, May 5 *Perf. 13½*

3997 A1128 960 l black & dp yellow 2.75 1.40

Peace & Freedom — A1129

Europa: 150 l, Dove carryng piece of rainbow. 4370 l, Dove under rainbow with wings forming "Europa."

1995, May 8

3998 A1129 150 l multicolored .45 .25
3999 A1129 4370 l multicolored 13.00 6.50

Lucian Blaga (1895-1961), Poet — A1130

1995, May 9

4000 A1130 150 l multicolored .45 .25

See Nos. 4017-4021.

Methods of Transportation — A1131

Designs: 470 l, Bucharest Metro subway train, 1979. 675 l, Brasov aerial cable car, vert. 965 l, Sud Aviation SA 330 Puma helicopter. 2300 l, 1904 Trolleybus. 2550 l, Steam locomotive, 1869. 3410 l, Boeing 737-300.

1995, May 30 Photo. *Perf. 13½*

4001 A1131 470 l blk, gray & yel .60 .30
4002 A1131 675 l blk, gray & red .90 .45
4003 A1131 965 l bl, blk & gray 1.25 .65
4004 A1131 2300 l blk, gray & grn 3.00 1.50
4005 A1131 2550 l blk, gray & red 3.25 1.65
4006 A1131 3410 l bl, blk & gray 4.50 2.25
Nos. 4001-4006 (6) 13.50 6.80

Nos. 4003, 4006 are airmail. No. 4006, 75th anniversary of Romanian air transportation.

See Nos. 4055-4060.

Romanian Maritime Service, Cent. — A1132

Ships: 90 l, Dacia, liner, vert. 130 l, Imparatul Traian, steamer. 150 l, Romania, steamer. 280 l, Costinesti, tanker. 960 l, Caransebes, container ship. 3410 l, Tutova, car ferry.

1995, May 31 Photo. *Perf. 13½*

4007 A1132 90 l multicolored .15 .15
4008 A1132 130 l multicolored .15 .15
4009 A1132 150 l multicolored .15 .15
4010 A1132 280 l multicolored .30 .15
4011 A1132 960 l multicolored 1.00 .50
4012 A1132 3410 l multicolored 3.75 1.90
Nos. 4007-4012 (6) 5.50 3.00

A1133 A1134

European Nature Conservation Year: 150 l, Dama dama. 280 l, Otis tarda. 960 l, Cypripedium caiceolus. 1615 l, Ghetarul scarisoara (stalagmites).

1995, June 5

4013 A1133 150 l multicolored .15 .15
4014 A1133 280 l multicolored .30 .15
4015 A1133 960 l multicolored 1.00 .50
4016 A1133 1615 l multicolored 1.75 .90
Nos. 4013-4016 (4) 3.20 1.70

Famous Romanians Type of 1995

Designs: 90 l, D.D. Rosca (1895-1980). 130 l, Vasile Conta (1845-1882). 280 l, Ion Barbu (1895-1961). 960 l, Iuliu Hatieganu (1885-1959). 1650 l, Dimitrie Brandza (1846-95).

1995, June 26 Photo. *Perf. 13½*

4017 A1130 90 l multicolored .15 .15
4018 A1130 130 l multicolored .15 .15
4019 A1130 280 l multicolored .30 .15
4020 A1130 960 l multicolored 1.00 .50
4021 A1130 1650 l multicolored 1.80 .90
Nos. 4017-4021 (5) 3.40 1.85

1995, July 10 Photo. *Perf. 13½*

4022 A1134 1650 l multicolored 1.80 .90

European Youth Olympic days.

Stamp Day — A1135

Illustration reduced.

1995, July 15

4023 A1135 960 l +715 l label 1.80 .90

Cernavoda Bridge, Cent. — A1136

1995, July 27 Photo. *Perf. 13½*

4024 A1136 675 l multicolored .75 .40

A1137 A1138

Fowl: 90 l, Anas platyrhynchos. 130 l, Gallus gallus (hen). 150 l, Numida meleagris. 280 l, Meleagris gallopavo. 960 l, Anser anser. 1650 l, Gallus gallus (rooster).

1995, July 31 Photo. *Perf. 13½*

4025 A1137 90 l multicolored .15 .15
4026 A1137 130 l multicolored .15 .15
4027 A1137 150 l multicolored .15 .15
4028 A1137 280 l multicolored .30 .30

4029 A1137 960 l multicolored 1.00 1.00
4030 A1137 1650 l multicolored 1.75 1.75
Nos. 4025-4030 (6) 3.50 3.50

1995, Aug. 5 Photo. *Perf. 13½*

Institute of Air Medicine, 75th Anniv.: Gen. Dr. Victor Anastasiu (1886-1972).

4031 A1138 960 l multicolored 1.10 .55

Battle of Calugareni, 400th Anniv. — A1139

1995, Aug. 13

4032 A1139 100 l multicolored .20 .15

Romanian Buildings — A1140

Structure, year completed: 250 l, Giurgiu Castle, 1395. 500 l, Neamtului Castle, 1395, vert. 960 l, Sebes-Alba Mill, 1245. 1615 l, Dorohoi Church, 1495, vert. 1650 l, Military Observatory, Bucharest, 1895, vert.

1995, Aug. 28

4033 A1140 250 l multicolored .25 .15
4034 A1140 500 l multicolored .55 .25
4035 A1140 960 l multicolored 1.10 .55
4036 A1140 1615 l multicolored 1.75 .90
4037 A1140 1650 l multicolored 1.80 .90
Nos. 4033-4037 (5) 5.45 2.75

A1141 A1142

Buildings in Manastirea: 675 l, Moldovita Monastery. 960 l, Hurez Monastery. 1615 l, Biertan Castle, horiz.

1995, Aug. 31

4038 A1141 675 l multicolored .75 .35
4039 A1141 960 l multicolored 1.00 .50
4040 A1141 1615 l multicolored 1.75 .90
Nos. 4038-4040 (3) 3.50 1.75

1995, Sept. 8

4041 A1142 1020 l multicolored 1.10 .55

Intl. Open Tennis Tournament, Bucharest.

Magazine "Mathematics," Cent. — A1143

Design: Ion N. Ionescu, founder.

1995, Sept. 15

4042 A1143 100 l multicolored .20 .15

Plants from Bucharest Botantical Garden — A1144

Designs: 50 l, Albizia julibrissin. 100 l, Taxus baccata. 150 l, Paulownia tomentosa. 500 l, Strelitzia reginae. 960 l, Victoria amazonica. 2300 l, Rhododendron indicum.

1995, Sept. 29 Photo. *Perf. 13½*

4043 A1144 50 l multicolored .15 .15
4044 A1144 100 l multicolored .15 .15
4045 A1144 150 l multicolored .15 .15
4046 A1144 500 l multicolored .55 .30
4047 A1144 960 l multicolored 1.00 .50
4048 A1144 2300 l multicolored 2.50 1.25
Nos. 4043-4048 (6) 4.50 2.50

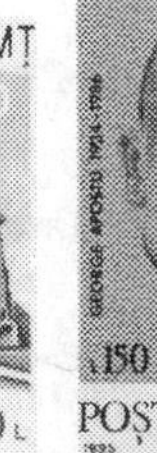

A1145 A1146

1995, Oct. 1 Photo. *Perf. 13½*

4049 A1145 250 l Church of St. John .30 .15

City of Piatra Neamt, 600th anniv.

1995, Nov. 9

Emigres: 150 l, George Apostu (1934-86), sculptor. 250 l, Emil Cioran (1911-95), philosopher. 500 l, Eugen Ionescu (1909-94), writer. 960 l, Elena Vacarescu (1866-1947), writer. 1650 l, Mircea Eliade (1907-86), philosopher.

4050 A1146 150 l grn, gray & blk .15 .15
4051 A1146 250 l bl, gray & blk .30 .15
4052 A1146 500 l tan, brn & blk .55 .30
4053 A1146 960 l lake, mag & blk 1.00 .50
4054 A1146 1650 l tan, brn & blk 1.80 .90
Nos. 4050-4054 (5) 3.80 2.00

Transportation Type of 1995

Designs: 285 l, IAR 80 fighter planes. 630 l, Training ship, Mesagerul. 715 l, IAR-316 Red Cross helicopter. 755 l, Cargo ship, Razboieni. 1575 l, IAR-818H seaplane. 1615 l, First electric tram, Bucharest, 1896, vert.

1995, Nov. 16

4055 A1131 285 l blk, gray & grn .30 .15
4056 A1131 630 l bl & red .70 .35
4057 A1131 715 l gray bl & red .80 .40
4058 A1131 755 l blk, bl & gray .85 .40
4059 A1131 1575 l blk, grn & gray 1.70 .85
4060 A1131 1615 l blk, grn & gray 1.75 .90
Nos. 4055-4060 (6) 6.10 3.05

1996 Summer Olympics, Atlanta — A1147

1995, Dec. 8

4061 A1147 50 l Track .15 .15
4062 A1147 100 l Gymnastics .15 .15
4063 A1147 150 l Two-man canoe .15 .15
4064 A1147 500 l Fencing .55 .25
4065 A1147 960 l Rowing-eights 1.10 .55
4066 A1147 2300 l Boxing 2.50 1.25
Nos. 4061-4066 (6) 4.60 2.50

Souvenir Sheet

4067 A1147 2610 l Gymnastics 2.75 1.40

No. 4067 contains one 42x54mm stamp.

Christmas A1148

1995, Dec. 15 Photo. *Perf. 13½*

4068 A1148 100 l The Holy Family .15 .15

Folk Masks & Costumes — A1149

1996, Jan. 31

4069 A1149 250 l Maramures .25 .15
4070 A1149 500 l Moldova .55 .30
4071 A1149 960 l Moldova, vert. 1.00 .50
4072 A1149 1650 l Moldova, diff., vert. 1.75 .90
Nos. 4069-4072 (4) 3.55 1.85

Tristan Tzara (1896-1963), Writer — A1151

Design: 1500 l, Anton Pann (1796-1854), writer.

1996, Mar. 27 Photo. *Perf. 13½*

4078 A1151 150 l multicolored .25 .15
4079 A1151 1500 l multicolored 1.60 .80

Easter — A1152

1996, Mar. 29

4080 A1152 150 l multicolored .25 .15

Romfilex '96, Romanian-Israeli Philatelic Exhibition A1153

Paintings from National History Museum: a, 370 l, On the Terrace at Sinaia, by Theodor Aman. b, 150 l, The Palace, by M. Stoican. c, 1500 l, Old Jerusalem, by Reuven Rubin.

1996, Apr. 5

4081 A1153 Sheet of 3, #a.-c. 2.25 1.10

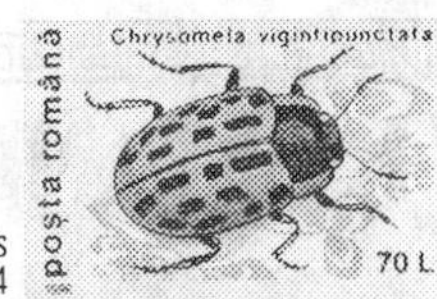

Insects A1154

Designs: 70 l, Chrysomela vigintipunctata. 220 l, Cerambyx cerdo. 370 l, Entomoscelis adonidis. 650 l, Coccinella bipunctata. 700 l, Calosoma sycophanta. 740 l, Hedobia imperialis. 960 l, Oryctes nasicornis. 1000 l, Trichius fasciatus. 1500 l, Purpuricenus kaehleri. 2500 l, Anthaxia salicis.

1996

4082 A1154 70 l multicolored .15 .15
4083 A1154 220 l multicolored .25 .15
4084 A1154 370 l multicolored .40 .20
4085 A1154 650 l multicolored .70 .35
4086 A1154 700 l multicolored .75 .35
4087 A1154 740 l multicolored .80 .40
4088 A1154 960 l multicolored 1.00 .50
4089 A1154 1000 l multicolored 1.00 .50
4090 A1154 1500 l multicolored 1.60 .80
4091 A1154 2500 l multicolored 2.60 1.30
Nos. 4082-4091 (10) 9.25 4.70

Issued: 220, 740, 960, 1000, 1500 l, 4/16/96. 70, 370, 650, 700, 2500 l, 6/10/96.

Souvenir Sheet

Dumitru Prunariu, First Romanian Cosmonaut — A1155

Illustration reduced.

1996, Apr. 22

4092 A1155 2720 l multicolored 2.90 1.45

ESPAMER '96, Aviation and Space Philatelic Exhibition, Seville, Spain.

1996 Summer Olympic Games, Atlanta — A1158

1996, July 12 Photo. *Perf. 13½*

4093 A1158 220 l Boxing .15 .15
4094 A1158 370 l Athletics .30 .15
4095 A1158 740 l Rowing .55 .30
4096 A1158 1500 l Judo 1.10 .55
4097 A1158 2550 l Gymnastics 1.90 .95
Nos. 4093-4097 (5) 4.00 2.10

Souvenir Sheet

4098 A1158 4050 l Gymnastics, diff. 3.00 1.50

No. 4098 is airmail and contains one 54x42mm stamp. Olymphilex '96 (#4098).

UNESCO World Heritage Sites — A1159

Designs: 150 l, Arbore Church. 1500 l, Voronet Monastery. 2550 l, Humor Monastery.

1996, Apr. 24 Photo. *Perf. 13½*

4099 A1159	150 l	multicolored	.15	.15
4100 A1159	1500 l	multicolored	1.60	.80
4101 A1159	2550 l	multicolored	2.70	1.30
	Nos. 4099-4101 (3)		4.45	2.25

Famous Women — A1160

Europa: 370 l, Ana Asian (1897-1988), physician. 4140 l, Lucia Bulandra (1873-1961), actress.

1996, May 6

4102 A1160	370 l	multicolored	.40	.20
4103 A1160	4140 l	multicolored	4.30	2.20
a.	Pair, #4102-4103 + 2 labels		4.70	2.40

UNICEF, 50th Anniv. — A1161

Children's paintings: 370 l, Mother and children. 740 l, Winter Scene. 1500 l, Children and Sun over House. 2550 l, House on Stilts, vert.

1996, May 25

4104 A1161	370 l	multicolored	.40	.20
4105 A1161	740 l	multicolored	.80	.40
4106 A1161	1500 l	multicolored	1.60	.80
4107 A1161	2550 l	multicolored	2.70	1.30
	Nos. 4104-4107 (4)		5.50	2.70

Habitat II (#4107).

Euro '96, European Soccer Championships, Great Britain A1162

Designs: a, 220 l, Goal keeper, ball. b, 370 l, Player with ball. c, Two players, ball. d, 1500 l, Three players, ball. e, 2550 l, Player dribbling ball. 4050 l, Two players, four balls.

1996, May 27

4108 A1162	Strip of 5, #a.-e.	5.60	2.80

Souvenir Sheet

4109 A1162	4050 l	multicolored	4.25	2.10

No. 4109 contains one 42x54mm stamp.

CAPEX '96 — A1163

Designs: 150 l, Toronto Convention Center. 4050 l, CN Tower, Skydome, Toronto skyline.

1996, May 29

4110 A1163	150 l	multicolored	.15	.15

Souvenir Sheet

4111 A1163	4050 l	multicolored	4.25	2.10

No. 4111 contains 42x54mm stamp.

Resita Factory, 225th Anniv. A1164

1996, June 20 Photo. *Perf. 13½*

4112 A1164	150 l	dark red brown	.15	.15

No. 3775 Surcharged

1996 - 5 ANI DE LA ÎNFIINTARE

L150

1996, June 22

4113 A1071	150 l on 10 l	multi	.15	.15

Stamp Day — A1165

Illustration reduced.

1996, July 15

4114 A1165	1500 l + 650 l label	1.60	.80

Conifers — A1166

1996 Aug. 1

4115 A1166	70 l	Picea glauca	.15	.15
4116 A1166	150 l	Picea omorica	.15	.15
4117 A1166	220 l	Picea pungeus	.15	.15
4118 A1166	740 l	Picea sitchensis	.55	.25
4119 A1166	1500 l	Pinus sylvestris	1.10	.55
4120 A1166	3500 l	Pinus pinaster	2.50	1.25
	Nos. 4115-4120 (6)		4.60	2.50

Wildlife A1167

Designs: 70 l, Natrix natrix, vert. 150 l, Testudo hermanni, vert. 220 l, Alauda arvensis. 740 l, Vulpes vulpes. 1500 l, Phocaena phocaena, vert. 3500 l, Aquila chrysaetos, vert.

1996, Sept. 12 Photo. *Perf. 13½*

4121 A1167	70 l	multicolored	.15	.15
4122 A1167	150 l	multicolored	.15	.15
4123 A1167	220 l	multicolored	.15	.15
4124 A1167	740 l	multicolored	.55	.25
4125 A1167	1500 l	multicolored	1.00	.50
4126 A1167	3500 l	multicolored	2.50	1.25
	Nos. 4121-4126 (6)		4.50	2.45

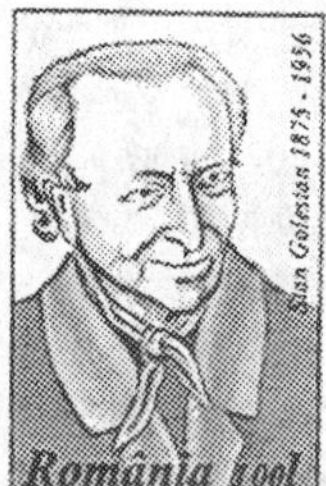

Famous Men — A1168

100 l, Stan Golestan (1875-1956). 150 l, Corneliu Coposu (1914-95). 370 l, Horia Vintila (1915-92). 1500 l, Alexandru Papana (1906-46).

1996

4127 A1168	100 l	black & rose red	.15	.15
4128 A1168	150 l	black & lake	.15	.15
4129 A1168	370 l	black & yel brown	.25	.15
4130 A1168	1500 l	black & ver	.95	.45
	Nos. 4127-4130 (4)		1.50	.90

Madonna and Child — A1169

1996

4131 A1169	150 l	multicolored	.15	.15

Antique Automobiles — A1170

No. 4132: a, 280 l, 1933 Mercedes Benz. b, 70 l, 1930 Ford Spider. c, 150 l, 1932 Citroen. d, 220 l, 1936 Rolls Royce.

No. 4133: a, 2550 l, 1936 Mercedes Benz 500k Roadster. b, 2500 l, 1934 Bugatti "Type 59." c. 2550 l, 1931 Alfa Romeo 8C. d, 120 l, 1937 Jaguar SS 100.

1996, Dec. 19 Photo. *Perf. 13½*

4132 A1170	Sheet of 4, #a.-d.	.60	.30
4133 A1170	Sheet of 4, #a.-d.	6.25	3.10

Souvenir Sheet

Deng Xiaoping, China, and Margaret Thatcher, Great Britain — A1171

1997, Jan. 20 Photo. *Perf. 13½*

4134 A1171	1500 l	multicolored	1.15	.55

Hong Kong '97.

Fur-Bearing Animals — A1172

Designs: 70 l, Mustela erminea. 150 l, Alopex lagopus. 220 l, Nyctereutes procyonoides. 740 l, Lutra lutra. 1500 l, Ondatra zibethica. 3500 l, Martes martes.

1997, Feb. 14

4135 A1172	70 l	multicolored	.15	.15
4136 A1172	150 l	multicolored	.15	.15
4137 A1172	220 l	multicolored	.15	.15
4138 A1172	740 l	multicolored	.25	.15
4139 A1172	1500 l	multicolored	.50	.25
4140 A1172	3500 l	multicolored	1.15	.55
		Nos. 4135-4140 (6)	2.35	1.40

Greenpeace, 25th Anniv. — A1173

Various views of MV Greenpeace.

1997, Mar. 6

4141 A1173	150 l	multicolored	.15	.15
4142 A1173	370 l	multicolored	.15	.15
4143 A1173	1940 l	multicolored	.55	.30
4144 A1173	2500 l	multicolored	.75	.35
		Nos. 4141-4144 (4)	1.60	.95

Souvenir Sheet

4145 A1173	4050 l	multicolored	1.50	.75

No. 4145 contains one 49x38mm stamp.

Famous People A1174

Designs: 200 l, Thomas A. Edison. 400 l, Franz Schubert. 3600 l, Miguel de Cervantes Saavedra (1547-1616), Spanish writer.

1997, Mar. 27 Photo. *Perf. 13½*

4146 A1174	200 l	multicolored	.15	.15
4147 A1174	400 l	multicolored	.15	.15
4148 A1174	3600 l	multicolored	1.00	.50
		Nos. 4146-4148 (3)	1.30	.80

Churches — A1176

A1177

1997, Apr. 21 Photo. *Perf. 13½*

4150 A1176	200 l	Surdesti	.15	.15
4151 A1176	400 l	Plopis	.15	.15
4152 A1176	450 l	Bogdan Voda	.15	.15
4153 A1176	850 l	Rogoz	.25	.15
4154 A1176	3600 l	Calinesti	1.00	.50
4155 A1176	6000 l	Birsana	1.75	.90
		Nos. 4150-4155 (6)	3.45	2.00

1997, Apr. 23 Photo. *Perf. 13½*

Shakespeare Festival, Craiova: a, 400 l, Constantin Serghe (1819-87) as Othello, 1855. b, 200 l, Al. Demetrescu Dan (1870-1948) as Hamlet, 1916. c, 3600 l, Ion Manolescu (1881-1959) as Hamlet, 1924. d, 2400 l, Gheorghe Cozorici (1933-93) as Hamlet, 1957.

4156 A1177	Sheet of 4, #a.-d. + 4 labels	2.60	1.30

Stories and Legends — A1178

Europa: 400 l, Vlad Tepes (Vlad the Impaler), prince upon which legend of Dracula said to be based. 4250 l, Dracula.

1997, May 5

4157 A1178	400 l	multicolored	.15	.15
4158 A1178	4250 l	multicolored	1.25	.65
a.		Pair, #4157-4158 + label	1.40	.70

Sports A1182

1997, Nov. 21 Photo. *Perf. 13½*

4176 A1182	500 l	Rugby	.20	.15
4177 A1182	700 l	American football, vert.	.25	.15
4178 A1182	1750 l	Baseball	.65	.35
4179 A1182	3700 l	Mountain climbing, vert.	1.40	.70
		Nos. 4176-4179 (4)	2.50	1.35

Chamber of Commerce and Industry, Bucharest, 130th Anniv. — A1185

1998 Photo. *Perf. 13½*

4189 A1185	700 l	multicolored	.25	.15

No. 4189 is printed se-tenant with label.

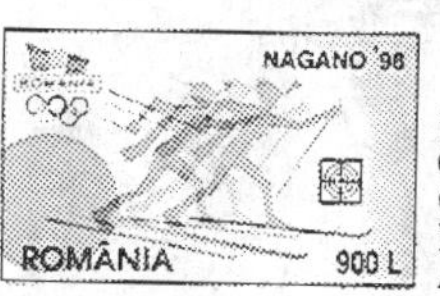

1998 Winter Olympic Games, Nagano A1186

1998

4190 A1186	900 l	Skiing	.30	.15
4191 A1186	3900 l	Figure skating	1.30	.65

SEMI-POSTAL STAMPS

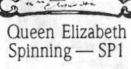

Queen Elizabeth Spinning — SP1

The Queen Weaving — SP2

Queen as War Nurse — SP3

Perf. 11½, 11½x13½

1906, Jan. 14 Typo. Unwmk.

B1	SP1	3b (+ 7b) brown		1.75	1.00
B2	SP1	5b (+ 10b) lt grn		1.75	1.00
B3	SP1	10b (+ 10b) rose red		6.00	2.50
B4	SP1	15b (+ 10b) violet		4.50	2.75
		Nos. B1-B4 (4)		14.00	7.25

1906, Mar. 18

B5	SP2	3b (+ 7b) org brn	1.75	1.00
B6	SP2	5b (+ 10b) bl grn	1.75	1.00
B7	SP2	10b (+ 10b) car	5.50	2.50
B8	SP2	15b (+ 10b) red vio	4.50	2.25
		Nos. B5-B8 (4)	13.50	6.75

Perf. 11½, 13½x11½

1906, Mar. 23

B9	SP3	3b (+ 7b) org brn	1.75	1.00
B10	SP3	5b (+ 10b) bl grn	1.75	1.00
B11	SP3	10b (+ 10b) car	5.50	2.50
B12	SP3	15b (+ 10b) red vio	4.50	2.25
		Nos. B9-B12 (4)	13.50	6.75
		Nos. B1-B12 (12)	41.00	20.75

Booklet panes of 4 exist of Nos. B1-B3, B5-B7, B9-B12.

Counterfeits of Nos. B1-B12 are plentiful. Copies of Nos. B1-B12 with smooth, even gum are counterfeits.

SP4

1906, Aug. 4 *Perf. 12*

B13	SP4	3b (+ 7b) ol brn, buff & bl	.75	.48
B14	SP4	5b (+ 10b) grn, rose & buff	.90	.48
B15	SP4	10b (+ 10b) rose red, buff & bl	1.65	1.25
B16	SP4	15b (+ 10b) vio, buff & bl	4.50	1.75
		Nos. B13-B16 (4)	7.80	3.96

Guardian Angel Bringing Poor to Crown Princess Marie — SP5

1907, Feb. Engr. *Perf. 11*

Center in Brown

B17	SP5	3b (+ 7b) org brn	1.50	1.25
B18	SP5	5b (+ 10b) dk grn	.95	.48
B19	SP5	10b (+ 10b) dk car	.95	.48
B20	SP5	15b (+ 10b) dl vio	.75	.55
		Nos. B17-B20 (4)	4.15	2.76

Nos. B1-B20 were sold for more than face value. The surtax, shown in parenthesis, was for charitable purposes.

Map of Romania — SP9

Stephen the Great — SP10

Michael the Brave SP11

Kings Carol I and Ferdinand SP12

Adam Clisi Monument — SP13

1927, Mar. 15 Typo. *Perf. 13½*

B21	SP9	1 l + 9 l lt vio	.70	.40
B22	SP10	2 l + 8 l Prus grn	.70	.40
B23	SP11	3 l + 7 l dp rose	.70	.40
B24	SP12	5 l + 5 l dp bl	.70	.40
B25	SP13	6 l + 4 l ol grn	1.90	.40
		Nos. B21-B25 (5)	4.70	2.00

50th anniv. of the Royal Geographical Society. The surtax was for the benefit of that society. The stamps were valid for postage only from 3/15-4/14.

Boy Scouts in Camp — SP15

The Rescue — SP16

Designs: 3 l+3 l, Swearing in a Tenderfoot. 4 l+4 l, Prince Nicholas Chief Scout. 6 l+6 l, King Carol II in Scout's Uniform.

1931, July 15 Photo. Wmk. 225

B26	SP15	1 l + 1 l car rose	.95	.70
B27	SP16	2 l + 2 l dp grn	1.25	.95
B28	SP15	3 l + 3 l ultra	1.65	1.25
B29	SP16	4 l + 4 l ol gray	1.65	1.50
B30	SP16	6 l + 6 l red brn	3.50	1.75
		Nos. B26-B30 (5)	9.00	6.15

The surtax was for the benefit of the Boy Scout organization.

Boy Scout Jamboree Issue

Scouts in Camp SP20

Semaphore Signaling SP21

Trailing — SP22

Camp Fire — SP23

King Carol II SP24

King Carol II and Prince Michael SP25

1932, June 8 Wmk. 230

B31	SP20	25b + 25b pck grn	2.75	1.00
B32	SP21	50b + 50b brt bl	3.50	2.00
B33	SP22	1 l + 1 l ol grn	4.00	2.75
B34	SP23	2 l + 2 l org red	6.75	4.00
B35	SP24	3 l + 3 l Prus bl	12.00	8.00
B36	SP25	6 l + 6 l blk brn	14.00	10.00
		Nos. B31-B36 (6)	43.00	27.75

For overprints see Nos. B44-B49.

Tuberculosis Sanatorium SP26

Memorial Tablet to Postal Employees Who Died in World War I — SP27

Carmen Sylva Convalescent Home SP28

1932, Nov. 1

B37	SP26	4 l + 1 l dk grn	2.10	1.25
B38	SP27	6 l + 1 l chocolate	2.10	2.00
B39	SP28	10 l + 1 l dp bl	4.25	2.50
		Nos. B37-B39 (3)	8.45	5.75

The surtax was given to a fund for the employees of the postal and telegraph services.

Philatelic Exhibition Issue

Souvenir Sheet

King Carol II — SP29

1932, Nov. 20 Unwmk. *Imperf.*

B40	SP29	6 l + 5 l dk ol grn	12.00	12.00

Intl. Phil. Exhib. at Bucharest, Nov. 20-24, 1932. Each holder of a ticket of admission to the exhibition could buy a copy of the stamp. The ticket cost 20 lei.

Roadside Shrine SP31

Woman Spinning SP33

Woman Weaving SP32

1934, Apr. 16 Wmk. 230 *Perf. 13½*

B41	SP31	1 l + 1 l dk brn	.55	.38
B42	SP32	2 l + 1 l blue	.75	.48
B43	SP33	3 l + 1 l slate grn	1.00	.65
		Nos. B41-B43 (3)	2.30	1.51

Weaving Exposition.

Boy Scout Mamaia Jamboree Issue

MAMAIA 1934

Semi-Postal Stamps of 1932 Overprinted in Black or Gold

1934, July 8

B44	SP20	25b + 25b pck grn	1.75	1.50
B45	SP21	50b + 50b brt bl (G)	2.75	1.50
B46	SP22	1 l + 1 l ol grn	3.50	2.75
B47	SP23	2 l + 2 l org red	4.00	3.50
B48	SP24	3 l + 3 l Prus bl (G)	7.75	6.75
B49	SP25	6 l + 6 l blk brn (G)	12.00	9.00
		Nos. B44-B49 (6)	31.75	25.00

Sea Scout Saluting — SP34

Scout Bugler — SP35

Sea and Land Scouts — SP36

King Carol II — SP37

Sea, Land and Girl Scouts — SP38

1935, June 8

B50	SP34	25b ol blk	.90	.70
B51	SP35	1 l violet	2.00	1.65
B52	SP36	2 l green	2.50	2.10
B53	SP37	6 l + 1 l red brn	3.75	2.25
B54	SP38	10 l + 2 l dk ultra	10.50	7.50
		Nos. B50-B54 (5)	19.65	14.20

Fifth anniversary of accession of King Carol II, and a national sports meeting held June 8. Surtax aided the Boy Scouts.

Nos. B50-B54 exist imperf.

King Carol II — SP39

1936, May

B55	SP39	6 l + 1 l rose car	.50	.35

Bucharest Exhibition and 70th anniversary of the dynasty. Exists imperf.

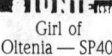

Girl of Oltenia — SP40

Girl of Saliste — SP42

Youth from Gorj — SP44

Designs: 1 l+1 l, Girl of Banat. 3 l+1 l, Girl of Hateg. 6 l+3 l, Girl of Neamt. 10 l+5 l, Youth and girl of Bucovina.

1936, June 8

B56	SP40	50b + 50b brown	.40	.25
B57	SP40	1 l + 1 l violet	.40	.25
B58	SP42	2 l + 1 l Prus grn	.40	.25
B59	SP42	3 l + 1 l car rose	.40	.25
B60	SP44	4 l + 2 l red org	.70	.52
B61	SP40	6 l + 3 l ol gray	.70	.60
B62	SP42	10 l + 5 l brt bl	1.40	1.10
		Nos. B56-B62 (7)	4.40	3.22

6th anniv. of accession of King Carol II. The surtax was for child welfare. Exist imperf.

Insignia of Boy Scouts SP47 SP48

Jamboree Emblem SP49

Submarine "Delfinul" SP50

1936, Aug. 20

B63	SP47	1 l + 1 l brt bl	1.90	1.50
B64	SP48	3 l + 3 l ol gray	2.75	1.90
B65	SP49	6 l + 6 l car rose	3.50	2.75
		Nos. B63-B65 (3)	8.15	6.15

Boy Scout Jamboree at Brasov (Kronstadt).

1936, Oct.

Designs: 3 l+2 l, Training ship "Mircea." 6 l+3 l, Steamship "S.M.R."

B66	SP50	1 l + 1 l pur	1.90	1.25
B67	SP50	3 l + 2 l ultra	1.75	1.25
B68	SP50	6 l + 3 l car rose	2.50	2.50
		Nos. B66-B68 (3)	6.15	5.00

Marine Exhibition at Bucharest. Exist imperf.

Soccer SP53

Swimming SP54

Throwing the Javelin — SP55

Skiing — SP56

King Carol II Hunting — SP57

Rowing — SP58

Horsemanship — SP59

Founding of the U.F.S.R. SP60

1937, June 8 Wmk. 230 *Perf. 13½*

B69	SP53	25b + 25b ol blk	.35	.20
B70	SP54	50b + 50b brown	.35	.20
B71	SP55	1 l + 50b violet	.35	.20
B72	SP56	2 l + 4 l slate grn	.35	.20
B73	SP57	3 l + 1 l rose lake	.45	.25
B74	SP58	4 l + 1 l red org	.70	.28
B75	SP59	6 l + 2 l dp claret	1.00	.35
B76	SP60	10 l + 4 l brt blue	1.40	1.25
		Nos. B69-B76 (8)	4.95	2.93

25th anniversary of the Federation of Romanian Sports Clubs (U.F.S.R.); 7th anniversary of the accession of King Carol II.

Exist imperf.

Start of Race — SP61

Javelin Thrower — SP62

Designs: 4 l+1 l, Hurdling. 6 l+1 l, Finish of race. 10 l+1 l, High jump.

1937, Sept. 1 Wmk. 230 *Perf. 13½*

B77	SP61	1 l + 1 l purple	.35	.35
B78	SP62	2 l + 1 l green	.45	.38
B79	SP61	4 l + 1 l vermilion	.55	.55
B80	SP62	6 l + 1 l maroon	.85	.85
B81	SP61	10 l + 1 l brt bl	2.25	1.75
		Nos. B77-B81 (5)	4.45	3.88

8th Balkan Games, Bucharest. Exist imperf.

Catalogue values for unused stamps in this section, from this point to the end of the section, are for Never Hinged items.

King Carol II — SP66

1938, May 24

B82	SP66	6 l + 1 l deep magenta	.42	.20

Bucharest Exhibition (for local products), May 19-June 19, celebrating 20th anniversary of the union of Rumanian provinces.

Exists imperf.

Dimitrie Cantemir — SP67

Maria Doamna — SP68

Mircea the Great SP69

Constantine Brancoveanu SP70

Stephen the Great — SP71

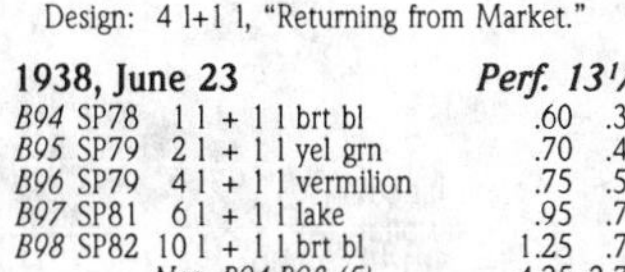
Prince Cuza — SP72

Michael the Brave — SP73

Queen Elizabeth — SP74

King Carol II — SP75

King Ferdinand I — SP76

King Carol I — SP77

1938, June 8 ***Perf. 13½***

B83	SP67	25b + 25b ol blk	.25	.25
B84	SP68	50b + 50b brn	.25	.25
B85	SP69	1 l + 1 l blk vio	.25	.25
B86	SP70	2 l + 2 l dk yel grn	.25	.25
B87	SP71	3 l + 2 l dp mag	.25	.25
B88	SP72	4 l + 2 l scarlet	.25	.25
B89	SP73	6 l + 2 l vio brn	.75	.75
B90	SP74	7.50 l gray bl	.75	.75
B91	SP75	10 l brt bl	.75	.75
B92	SP76	16 l dk slate grn	1.25	1.25
B93	SP77	20 l vermilion	1.75	1.75
		Nos. B83-B93 (11)	6.75	6.75

8th anniv. of accession of King Carol II. Surtax was for Straja Tarii, a natl. org. for boys.
Exist imperf.

"The Spring" — SP78

"Escorting Prisoners" SP79

"Rodica, the Water Carrier" SP81

Nicolae Grigorescu SP82

Design: 4 l+1 l, "Returning from Market."

1938, June 23 ***Perf. 13½***

B94	SP78	1 l + 1 l brt bl	.60	.30
B95	SP79	2 l + 1 l yel grn	.70	.42
B96	SP79	4 l + 1 l vermilion	.75	.55
B97	SP81	6 l + 1 l lake	.95	.75
B98	SP82	10 l + 1 l brt bl	1.25	.75
		Nos. B94-B98 (5)	4.25	2.77

Birth centenary of Nicolae Grigorescu, Romanian painter. Exist imperf.

St. George and the Dragon — SP83

1939, June 8 **Photo.**

B99	SP83	25b + 25b ol gray	.40	.25
B100	SP83	50b + 50b brn	.40	.25
B101	SP83	1 l + 1 l pale vio	.40	.25
B102	SP83	2 l + 2 l lt grn	.40	.25
B103	SP83	3 l + 2 l red vio	.60	.25
B104	SP83	4 l + 2 l red org	.80	.30
B105	SP83	6 l + 2 l car rose	.90	.30
B106	SP83	8 l gray vio	1.00	.40
B107	SP83	10 l brt bl	1.25	.50
B108	SP83	12 l brt ultra	1.50	.80
B109	SP83	16 l bl grn	1.75	1.00
		Nos. B99-B109 (11)	9.40	4.55

9th anniv. of accession of King Carol II. Exist imperf.

King Carol II
SP87 SP88

SP89

SP90

SP91

Perf. 13½

1940, June 8 **Photo.** **Wmk. 230**

B113	SP87	1 l + 50b dl pur	.25	.15
B114	SP88	4 l + 1 l fawn	.25	.18
B115	SP89	6 l + 1 l blue	.25	.24
B116	SP90	8 l rose brn	.38	.30
B117	SP89	16 l ultra	.50	.38
B118	SP91	32 l dk vio brn	.90	.65
		Nos. B113-B118 (6)	2.53	1.90

10th anniv. of accession of King Carol II. Exist imperf.

King Carol II
SP92 SP93

1940, June 1

B119	SP92	1 l + 50b dk grn	.15	.15
B120	SP92	2.50 l + 50b Prus grn	.18	.15
B121	SP93	3 l + 1 l rose car	.22	.15
B122	SP92	3.50 l + 50b choc	.28	.18
B123	SP93	4 l + 1 l org brn	.30	.22
B124	SP93	6 l + 1 l sapphire	.45	.15
B125	SP93	9 l + 1 l brt bl	.60	.45
B126	SP93	14 l + 1 l dk bl grn	.75	.55
		Nos. B119-B126 (8)	2.93	2.00

Surtax was for Romania's air force. Exist imperf.

View of Danube SP94

Greco-Roman Ruins — SP95

Designs: 3 l+1 l, Hotin Castle. 4 l+1 l, Hurez Monastery. 5 l+1 l, Church in Bucovina. 8 l+1 l, Tower. 12 l+2 l, Village church, Transylvania. 16 l+2 l, Arch in Bucharest.

1940, June 8 ***Perf. 14½x14, 14x14½***
Inscribed: "Straja Tarii 8 Junie 1940"

B127	SP94	1 l + 1 l dp vio	.22	.22
B128	SP95	2 l + 1 l red brn	.28	.28
B129	SP94	3 l + 1 l yel grn	.28	.28
B130	SP94	4 l + 1 l grnsh blk	.35	.35
B131	SP95	5 l + 1 l org ver	.42	.42
B132	SP95	8 l + 1 l brn car	.55	.55
B133	SP95	12 l + 2 l ultra	.80	.80
B134	SP95	16 l + 2 l dk bl gray	1.25	1.25
		Nos. B127-B134 (8)	4.15	4.15

Issued to honor Straja Tarii, a national organization for boys. Exist imperf.

King Michael SP102

Corneliu Codreanu SP103

1940-42 **Photo.** **Wmk. 230**

B138	SP102	1 l + 50b yel grn	.15	.15
B138A	SP102	2 l + 50b yel grn	.15	.15
B139	SP102	2.50 l + 50b dk bl grn	.15	.15
B140	SP102	3 l + 1 l pur	.15	.15
B141	SP102	3.50 l + 50b rose pink	.15	.15
B141A	SP102	4 l + 50b org ver	.15	.15
B142	SP102	4 l + 1 l brn	.15	.15
B142A	SP102	5 l + 1 l dp plum	.80	.80
B143	SP102	6 l + 1 l lt ultra	.15	.15
B143A	SP102	7 l + 1 l sl grn	.25	.25
B143B	SP102	8 l + 1 l dp vio	.20	.20
B143C	SP102	12 l + 1 l brn vio	.25	.25
B144	SP102	14 l + 1 l brt bl	.35	.35
B144A	SP102	19 l + 1 l lil rose	.80	.80
		Set value (14)	3.15	3.15

Issue years: #B138A, B141A, B142A, B143A, B143B, B143C, B144A, 1942; others, 1940.

1940, Nov. 8 **Unwmk.** ***Perf. 13½***

B145	SP103	7 l + 30 l dk grn	2.75	2.00

13th anniv. of the founding of the Iron Guard by Corneliu Codreanu.

Vasile Marin — SP104

Design: 15 l+15 l, Ion Mota.

1941, Jan. 13

B146	SP104	7 l + 7 l rose brn	1.10	1.10
B147	SP104	15 l + 15 l slate bl	1.65	1.65

Souvenir Sheet
Imperf

B148		Sheet of 2	26.00	26.00
a.	SP104	7 l + 7 l Prus green	6.50	6.50
b.	SP104	15 l + 15 l Prus green	6.50	6.50

Vasile Marin and Ion Mota, Iron Guardists who died in the Spanish Civil War.
No. B148 sold for 300 lei.

Crown, Leaves and Bible — SP107

Designs: 2 l+43 l, Library shelves. 7 l+38 l, Carol I Foundation, Bucharest. 10 l+35 l, King Carol I. 16 l+29 l, Kings Michael and Carol I.

Perf. 13½
1941, May 9 **Photo.** **Wmk. 230**
Inscribed: "1891 1941"

B149	SP107	1.50 l + 43.50 l pur	.35	.35
B150	SP107	2 l + 43 l rose brn	.35	.35
B151	SP107	7 l + 38 l rose	.35	.35
B152	SP107	10 l + 35 l ol blk	.35	.35
B153	SP107	16 l + 29 l brown	.35	.35
		Nos. B149-B153 (5)	1.75	1.75

50th anniv. of the Carol I Foundation, established to endow research and stimulate the arts.

Same Overprinted in Red or Black **CERNAUTI 5 Iulie 1941**

1941, Aug.

B154	SP107	1.50 l + 43.50 l (R)	1.40	1.40
B155	SP107	2 l + 43 l	1.40	1.40
B156	SP107	7 l + 38 l	1.40	1.40
B157	SP107	10 l + 35 l (R)	1.40	1.40
B158	SP107	16 l + 29 l	1.40	1.40

Occupation of Cernauti, Bucovina.

Same Overprinted in Red or Black **CHISINAU 16 Iulie 1941**

1941, Aug.

B159	SP107	1.50 l + 43.50 l (R)	1.40	1.40
B160	SP107	2 l + 43 l	1.40	1.40
B161	SP107	7 l + 38 l	1.40	1.40
B162	SP107	10 l + 35 l (R)	1.40	1.40
B163	SP107	16 l + 29 l	1.40	1.40
		Nos. B154-B163 (10)	14.00	14.00

Occupation of Chisinau, Bessarabia.

Romanian Red Cross — SP111

1941, Aug. ***Perf. 13½***

B164	SP111	1.50 l + 38.50 l	.45	.45
B165	SP111	2 l + 38 l	.45	.45
B166	SP111	5 l + 35 l	.45	.45
B167	SP111	7 l + 33 l	.45	.45
B168	SP111	10 l + 30 l	.45	.45
		Nos. B164-B168 (5)	2.25	2.25

Souvenir Sheet
Imperf
Without Gum

B169		Sheet of 2	6.50	6.50
a.	SP111	7 l + 33 l brown & red	1.25	1.40
b.	SP111	10 l + 30 l bright blue & red	1.25	1.40

The surtax on Nos. B164-B169 was for the Romanian Red Cross.
No. B169 sold for 200 l.

King Michael and Stephen the Great SP113

Hotin and Akkerman Castles SP114

Romanian and German Soldiers SP115

Soldiers SP116

SP118

1941, Oct. 11 *Perf. 14½x13½*

B170	SP113	10 l + 30 l ultra	.75	.75
B171	SP114	12 l + 28 l dl org red	.75	.75
B172	SP115	16 l + 24 l lt brn	.75	.75
B173	SP116	20 l + 20 l dk vio	.75	.75
		Nos. B170-B173 (4)	3.00	3.00

Souvenir Sheet

Imperf

Without Gum

B174	SP118	Sheet of 2	6.75	6.75
a.		16 l blue gray	.55	.55
b.		20 l brown carmine	.55	.55

No. B174 sold for 200 l. The surtax aided the Anti-Bolshevism crusade.

Nos. B170-B174 Overprinted **ODESA 16 Oct.1941**

1941, Oct. *Perf. 14½x13½*

B175	SP113	10 l + 30 l ultra	.90	.90
B176	SP114	12 l + 28 l dl org red	.90	.90
B177	SP115	16 l + 24 l lt brn	.90	.90
B178	SP116	20 l + 20 l dk vio	.90	.90
		Nos. B175-B178 (4)	3.60	3.60

Souvenir Sheet

Imperf

Without Gum

B178A	SP118	Sheet of 2	5.75	5.75

Occupation of Odessa, Russia.

Types of Regular Issue, 1941

Designs: 3 l+50b, Sucevita Monastery, Bucovina. 5.50 l+50b, Rughi Monastery, Soroca, Bessarabia. 5.50 l+1 l, Tighina Fortress, Bessarabia. 6.50 l+1 l, Soroca Fortress, Bessarabia. 8 l+1 l, St. Nicholas Monastery, Suceava, Bucovina. 9.50 l+1 l, Milisauti Monastery, Bucovina. 10.50 l+1 l, Putna Monastery, Bucovina. 16 l+1 l, Cetatea Alba Fortress, Bessarabia. 25 l+1 l, Hotin Fortress, Bessarabia.

1941, Dec. 1 **Wmk. 230** *Perf. 13½*

B179	A179	3 l + 50b rose brn	.15	.15
B180	A179	5.50 l + 50b red org	.35	.15
B181	A179	5.50 l + 1 l blk	.35	.15
B182	A179	6.50 l + 1 l dk brn	.40	.35
B183	A179	8 l + 1 l lt bl	.35	.15
B184	A177	9.50 l + 1 l gray bl	.40	.30
B185	A179	10.50 l + 1 l dk bl	.40	.15
B186	A179	16 l + 1 l vio	.50	.40
B187	A179	25 l + 1 l gray blk	.60	.45
		Nos. B179-B187 (9)	3.50	2.25

Titu Maiorescu — SP128

Statue of Miron Costin at Jassy — SP130

1942, Oct. 5

B188	SP128	9 l + 11 l dl vio	.30	.30
B189	SP128	20 l + 20 l yel brn	.75	.75
B190	SP128	20 l + 30 l blue	.75	.75
		Nos. B188-B190 (3)	1.80	1.80

Souvenir Sheet

Imperf

Without Gum

B191	SP128	Sheet of 3	3.75	3.75

The surtax aided war prisoners.

No. B191 contains one each of Nos. B188-B190, imperf. Sold for 200 l.

1942, Dec. *Perf. 13½*

B192	SP130	6 l + 44 l sepia	1.40	1.75
B193	SP130	12 l + 38 l violet	1.40	1.75
B194	SP130	24 l + 26 l blue	1.40	1.75
		Nos. B192-B194 (3)	4.20	5.25

Anniv. of the conquest of Transdniestria, and for use only in this territory which includes Odessa and land beyond the Duiester.

Michael, Antonescu, Hitler, Mussolini and Bessarabia Map SP131

Michael, Antonescu and (inset) Stephen of Moldavia SP132

Romanian Troops Crossing Pruth River to Retake Bessarabia SP133

1942 **Wmk. 230** **Photo.** *Perf. 13½*

B195	SP131	9 l + 41 l red brn	1.25	1.75
B196	SP132	18 l + 32 l ol gray	1.25	1.75
B197	SP133	20 l + 30 l brt ultra	1.25	1.75
		Nos. B195-B197 (3)	3.75	5.25

First anniversary of liberation of Bessarabia.

Bucovina Coats of Arms SP134 SP135

Design: 20 l+30 l, Bucovina arms with triple-barred cross.

1942, Nov. 1

B198	SP134	9 l + 41 l brt ver	1.25	1.75
B199	SP135	18 l + 32 l blue	1.25	1.75
B200	SP135	20 l + 30 l car rose	1.25	1.75
		Nos. B198-B200 (3)	3.75	5.25

First anniversary of liberation of Bucovina.

Andrei Muresanu — SP137

1942, Dec. 30

B201	SP137	5 l + 5 l violet	.45	.45

80th death anniv. of Andrei Muresanu, writer.

Avram Jancu, National Hero — SP138

1943, Feb. 15

B202	SP138	16 l + 4 l brown	.50	.50

Nurse Aiding Wounded Soldier SP139

1943, Mar. 1 *Perf. 14½x14*

B203	SP139	12 l + 88 l red brn & ultra	.30	.30
B204	SP139	16 l + 84 l brt ultra & red	.30	.30
B205	SP139	20 l + 80 l ol gray & red	.30	.30
		Nos. B203-B205 (3)	.90	.90

Souvenir Sheet

Imperf

B206		Sheet of 2	1.90	1.65
a.	SP139	16 l + 84 l bright ultra & red	.55	.55
b.	SP139	20 l + 80 l olive gray & red	.55	.55

Surtax on Nos. B203-B206 aided the Romanian Red Cross.

No. B206 sold for 500 l.

Sword Hilt — SP141

Sword Severing Chain — SP142

Soldier and Family, Guardian Angel — SP143

Perf. 14x14½

1943, June 22 **Wmk. 276**

B207	SP141	36 l + 164 l brn	2.25	2.25
B208	SP142	62 l + 138 l brt bl	2.25	2.25
B209	SP143	76 l + 124 l ver	2.25	2.25
		Nos. B207-B209 (3)	6.75	6.75

Souvenir Sheet

Imperf

B210		Sheet of 2	14.00	14.00
a.	SP143	62 l + 138 l deep blue	1.75	1.90
b.	SP143	76 l + 124 l red orange	1.75	1.90

2nd anniv. of Romania's entrance into WWII. No. B210 sold for 600 l.

Petru Maior — SP145

Horia, Closca and Crisan SP148

32 l+118 l, Gheorghe Sincai. 36 l+114 l, Timotei Cipariu. 91 l+109 l, Gheorghe Cosbuc.

Perf. 13½; 14½x14 (No. B214)

1943, Aug. 15 **Photo.** **Wmk. 276**

B211	SP145	16 l + 134 l red org	.30	.30
B212	SP145	32 l + 118 l lt bl	.30	.30
B213	SP145	36 l + 114 l vio	.30	.30
B214	SP148	62 l + 138 l car rose	.30	.30
B215	SP145	91 l + 109 l dk brn	.30	.30
		Nos. B211-B215 (5)	1.50	1.50

See Nos. B219-B223.

King Michael and Ion Antonescu SP150

1943, Sept. 6

B216	SP150	16 l + 24 l blue	.75	.75

3rd anniv. of the government of King Michael and Marshal Ion Antonescu.

Symbols of Sports — SP151

1943, Sept. 26 *Perf. 13½*

B217	SP151	16 l + 24 l ultra	.40	.30
B218	SP151	16 l + 24 l red brn	.40	.30

Surtax for the benefit of Romanian sports.

Portrait Type of 1943

1943, Oct. 1

Designs: 16 l+134 l, Samuel Micu. 51 l+99 l, George Lazar. 56 l+144 l, Octavian Goga. 76 l+124 l, Simeon Barnutiu. 77 l+123 l, Andrei Saguna.

B219	SP145	16 l + 134 l red vio	.25	.25
B220	SP145	51 l + 99 l orange	.25	.25
B221	SP145	56 l + 144 l rose car	.25	.25
B222	SP145	76 l + 124 l slate bl	.25	.25
B223	SP145	77 l + 123 l brown	.25	.25
		Nos. B219-B223 (5)	1.25	1.25

The surtax aided refugees.

Calafat, 1877 — SP157

Designs: 2 l +2 l, World War I scene. 3.50 l+3.50 l, Stalingrad, 1943. 4 l+4 l, Tisza, 1919. 5 l+5 l, Odessa, 1941. 6.50 l+6.50 l, Caucasus, 1942. 7 l+7 l, Sevastopol, 1942. 20 l+20 l, Prince Ribescu and King Michael.

1943, Nov. 10 **Photo.** *Perf. 13½*

B224	SP157	1 l + 1 l red brn	.15	.15
B225	SP157	2 l + 2 l dl vio	.15	.15
B226	SP157	3.50 l + 3.50 l lt ultra	.15	.15
B227	SP157	4 l + 4 l mag	.15	.15
B228	SP157	5 l + 5 l red org	.25	.25
B229	SP157	6.50 l + 6.50 l bl	.25	.25
B230	SP157	7 l + 7 l dp vio	.35	.35
B231	SP157	20 l + 20 l crim	.45	.45
		Nos. B224-B231 (8)	1.90	1.90

Centenary of Romanian Artillery.

Emblem of Romanian Engineers' Association SP165

1943, Dec. 19 *Perf. 14*

B232	SP165	21 l + 29 l sepia	.50	.40

Society of Romanian Engineers, 25th anniv.

Motorcycle, Truck and Post Horn SP166

Post Wagon SP167

Roman Post Chariot SP168

Post Rider — SP169

1944, Feb. 1 Wmk. 276 *Perf. 14*

B233	SP166	1 l + 49 l org red	1.10	1.10
B234	SP167	2 l + 48 l lil rose	1.10	1.10
B235	SP168	4 l + 46 l ultra	1.10	1.10
B236	SP169	10 l + 40 l dl vio	1.10	1.10
		Nos. B233-B236 (4)	4.40	4.40

Souvenir Sheets

Perf. 14

B237	Sheet of 3	2.75	4.00
a.	SP166 1 l + 49 l orange red	.70	.70
b.	SP167 2 l + 48 l orange red	.70	.70
c.	SP168 4 l + 46 l orange red	.70	.70

Imperf

B238	Sheet of 3	2.75	4.00
a.	SP166 1 l + 49 l dull violet	.70	.70
b.	SP167 2 l + 48 l dull violet	.70	.70
c.	SP168 4 l + 46 l dull violet	.70	.70

The surtax aided communications employees.
No. B238 is imperf. between the stamps.
Nos. B237-B238 each sold for 200 l.

Nos. B233-B238 Overprinted

1744 1944

1944, Feb. 28

B239	SP166	1 l + 49 l org red	2.75	2.75
B240	SP167	2 l + 48 l lil rose	2.75	2.75
B241	SP168	4 l + 46 l ultra	2.75	2.75
B242	SP169	10 l + 40 l dl vio	2.75	2.75
		Nos. B239-B242 (4)	11.00	11.00

Souvenir Sheets

Perf. 14

B243	Sheet of 3	4.75	5.25

Imperf

B244	Sheet of 3	4.75	5.25

Rugby Player SP171

Dr. N. Cretzulescu SP172

1944, Mar. 16 *Perf. 15*

B245 SP171 16 l + 184 l crimson 3.25 3.25

30th anniv. of the Romanian Rugby Assoc. The surtax was used to encourage the sport.

1944, Mar. 1 Photo. *Perf. 13½*

B246 SP172 35 l + 65 l brt ultra .60 .60

Centenary of medical teaching in Romania.

Queen Mother Helen — SP173

1945, Feb. 10

B247	SP173	4.50 l + 5.50 l multi	.18	.18
B248	SP173	10 l + 40 l multi	.18	.18
B249	SP173	15 l + 75 l multi	.18	.18
B250	SP173	20 l + 80 l multi	.18	.18
		Nos. B247-B250 (4)	.72	.72

The surtax aided the Romanian Red Cross.

Kings Ferdinand and Michael and Map SP174

1945, Feb. *Perf. 14*

B251 SP174 75 l + 75 l dk ol brn .50 .50

Romania's liberation.

Stefan Tomsa Church, Radaseni SP175

Municipal Home SP176

Gathering Fruit — SP177

School SP178

1944 Wmk. 276 Photo. *Perf. 14*

B252	SP175	5 l + 145 l brt bl	.50	.30
B253	SP176	12 l + 138 l car rose	.50	.30
B254	SP177	15 l + 135 l red org	.50	.30
B255	SP178	32 l + 118 l dk brn	.50	.30
		Nos. B252-B255 (4)	2.00	1.20

King Michael and Carol I Foundation, Bucharest SP179

Design: 200 l, King Carol I and Foundation.

1945, Feb. 10 *Perf. 13*

B256	SP179	20 l + 180 l dp org	.15	.15
B257	SP179	25 l + 175 l slate	.15	.15
B258	SP179	35 l + 165 l cl brn	.15	.15
B259	SP179	75 l + 125 l pale vio	.15	.15
		Nos. B256-B259 (4)	.60	
		Set value		.32

Souvenir Sheet

Imperf

Without Gum

B260 SP179 200 l blue 3.00 3.75

Surtax was to aid in rebuilding the Public Library, Bucharest.
Nos. B256-B259 were printed in sheets of 4.
No. B260 sold for 1200 l.

Ion G. Duca SP181

16 l+184 l, Virgil Madgearu. 20 l+180 l, Nikolai Jorga. 32 l+168 l, Ilie Pintilie. 35 l+165 l, Bernath Andrei. 36 l+164 l, Filimon Sarbu.

1945, Apr. 30 *Perf. 13*

B261	SP181	12 l + 188 l dk bl	.25	.25
B262	SP181	16 l + 184 l cl brn	.25	.25
B263	SP181	20 l + 180 l blk brn	.25	.25
B264	SP181	32 l + 168 l brt red	.25	.25
B265	SP181	35 l + 165 l Prus bl	.25	.25
B266	SP181	36 l + 164 l lt vio	.25	.25
		Nos. B261-B266 (6)	1.50	1.50

Souvenir Sheet

Imperf

B267	Sheet of 2	10.00	11.50
a.	SP181 32 l + 168 l magenta	2.00	2.25
b.	SP181 35 l + 165 l magenta	2.00	2.25

Honoring six victims of Nazi terrorism.
No. B267 sold for 1,000 l.

Books and Torch — SP188

Designs: #B269, Flags of Russia and Romania. #B270, Kremlin, Moscow. #B271, Tudor Vladimirescu and Alexander Nevsky.

1945, May 20 *Perf. 14*

B268	SP188	20 l + 80 l ol grn	.18	.18
B269	SP188	35 l + 165 l brt rose	.18	.18
B270	SP188	75 l + 225 l blue	.18	.18
B271	SP188	80 l + 420 l cl brn	.18	.18
		Nos. B268-B271 (4)	.72	.72

Souvenir Sheet

Imperf

Without Gum

B272	Sheet of 2	5.25	6.00
a.	SP189 35 l + 165 l bright red	1.25	1.40
b.	SP190 75 l + 225 l bright red	1.25	1.40

1st Soviet-Romanian Cong., May 20, 1945.
No. B272 sold for 900 l.

Karl Marx — SP193

120 l+380 l, Friedrich Engels. 155 l+445 l, Lenin.

1945, June 30 *Perf. 13½*

B273	SP193	75 l + 425 l car rose	1.25	1.25
B274	SP193	120 l + 380 l bl	1.25	1.25
B275	SP193	155 l + 445 l dk vio brn	1.25	1.25

Imperf

B276	SP193	75 l + 425 l bl	3.75	3.75
B277	SP193	120 l + 380 l dk vio brn	3.75	3.75
B278	SP193	155 l + 445 l car rose	3.75	3.75
		Nos. B273-B278 (6)	15.00	15.00

Nos. B276-B278 were printed in sheets of 4.

Woman Throwing Discus — SP196

Designs: 16 l+184 l, Diving. 20 l+180 l, Skiing. 32 l+168 l, Volleyball. 35 l+165 l, Worker athlete.

Wmk. 276

1945, Aug. 5 Photo. *Perf. 13*

B279	SP196	12 l +188 l ol gray	.90	.90
B280	SP196	16 l +184 l lt ultra	.90	.90
B281	SP196	20 l +180 l dp grn	.90	.90
B282	SP196	32 l +168 l mag	.90	.90
B283	SP196	35 l +165 l brt bl	.90	.90

Imperf

B284	SP196	12 l +188 l org red	.90	.90
B285	SP196	16 l +184 l vio brn	.90	.90
B286	SP196	20 l +180 l dp vio	.90	.90
B287	SP196	32 l +168 l yel grn	.90	.90
B288	SP196	35 l +165 l dk ol grn	.90	.90
		Nos. B279-B288 (10)	9.00	9.00

Printed in sheets of 9.

Mail Plane and Bird Carrying Letter SP201

1945, Aug. 5 *Perf. 13½*

B289	SP201	200 l + 1000 l bl & dk bl	3.50	3.50
a.		With label	19.00	19.00

The surtax on Nos. B279-B289 was for the Office of Popular Sports.
Issued in sheets of 30 stamps and 10 labels, arranged 10x4 with second and fourth horizontal rows each having five alternating labels.

Agriculture and Industry United SP202

King Michael SP203

1945, Aug. 23 *Perf. 14*

B290	SP202	100 l + 400 l red	.15	.15
B291	SP203	200 l + 800 l blue	.15	.15
		Set value	.20	.20

The surtax was for the Farmers' Front.
For surcharges see Nos. B318-B325.

Political Amnesty SP204

Military Amnesty SP205

Agrarian Amnesty SP206

Tudor Vladimirescu SP207

Nicolae Horia SP208

Reconstruction
SP209

1945, Aug. *Perf. 13*

B292	SP204	20 l + 580 l choc	6.00	6.00
B293	SP204	20 l + 580 l mag	6.00	6.00
B294	SP205	40 l + 560 l blue	6.00	6.00
B295	SP205	40 l + 560 l sl grn	6.00	6.00
B296	SP206	55 l + 545 l red	6.00	6.00
B297	SP206	55 l + 545 l dk vio brn	6.00	6.00
B298	SP207	60 l + 540 l ultra	6.00	6.00
B299	SP207	60 l + 540 l choc	6.00	6.00
B300	SP208	80 l + 520 l red	6.00	6.00
B301	SP208	80 l + 520 l mag	6.00	6.00
B302	SP209	100 l + 500 l sl grn	6.00	6.00
B303	SP209	100 l + 500 l red brn	6.00	6.00
		Nos. B292-B303 (12)	72.00	72.00

1st anniv. of Romania's armistice with Russia. Issued in panes of four.

Nos. B292-B303 also exist on coarse grayish paper, ungummed (same value).

Electric Train
SP210

Coats of Arms
SP211

Truck on Mountain Road
SP212

Oil Field — SP213

"Agriculture"
SP214

1945, Oct. 1 *Perf. 14*

B304	SP210	10 l + 490 l ol grn	.25	.25
B305	SP211	20 l + 480 l red brn	.25	.25
B306	SP212	25 l + 475 l brn vio	.25	.25
B307	SP213	55 l + 445 l ultra	.25	.25
B308	SP214	100 l + 400 l brn	.25	.25

Imperf

B309	SP210	10 l + 490 l blue	.25	.25
B310	SP211	20 l + 480 l violet	.25	.25
B311	SP212	25 l + 475 l bl grn	.25	.25
B312	SP213	55 l + 445 l gray	.25	.25
B313	SP214	100 l + 400 l dp mag	.25	.25
		Nos. B304-B313 (10)	2.50	2.50

16th Congress of the General Assoc. of Romanian Engineers.

"Brotherhood" — SP215

160 l+1840 l, "Peace." 320 l+1680 l, Hammer crushing Nazism. 440 l+2560 l, "World Unity."

1945, Dec. 5 *Perf. 14*

B314	SP215	80 l + 920 l mag	10.00	10.00
B315	SP215	160 l + 1840 l org brn	10.00	10.00
B316	SP215	320 l + 1680 l vio	10.00	10.00
B317	SP215	440 l + 2560 l yel grn	10.00	10.00
		Nos. B313-B317 (5)	40.25	40.25

World Trade Union Congress at Paris, Sept. 25-Oct. 10, 1945.

Nos. B290 and B291 Surcharged in Various Colors

1946, Jan. 20

B318	SP202	10 l + 90 l (Bk)	.35	.35
B319	SP203	10 l + 90 l (R)	.35	.35
B320	SP202	20 l + 80 l (G)	.35	.35
B321	SP203	20 l + 80 l (Bk)	.35	.35
B322	SP202	80 l + 120 l (Bl)	.35	.35
B323	SP203	80 l + 120 l (Bk)	.35	.35
B324	SP202	100 l + 150 l (Bk)	.35	.35
B325	SP203	100 l + 150 l (R)	.35	.35
		Nos. B318-B325 (8)	2.80	2.80

Re-distribution of Land — SP219

Sower
SP220

Ox Team Drawing Hay
SP221

Old and New Plowing Methods
SP222

1946, Mar. 6

B326	SP219	50 l + 450 l red	.15	.15
B327	SP220	100 l + 900 l red vio	.15	.15
B328	SP221	200 l + 800 l orange	.15	.15
B329	SP222	400 l + 1600 l dk grn	.15	.15
		Set value	.50	.50

Agrarian reform law of Mar. 23, 1945.

Philharmonic Types of Regular Issue

Perf. 13, 13½x13

1946, Apr. 26 Photo. Wmk. 276

B330	A211	200 l + 800 l brt red	.60	.60
a.		Sheet of 12	17.50	20.00
B331	A213	350 l + 1650 l dk bl	.65	.65
a.		Sheet of 12	17.50	20.00

Issued in sheets containing 12 stamps and 4 labels, with bars of music in the margins.

Agriculture
SP223

Dove
SP228

Designs: 10 l+200 l, Hurdling. 80 l+200 l, Research. 80 l+300 l, Industry. 200 l+400 l, Workers and flag.

Perf. 11½

1946, July 28 Photo. Wmk. 276

B332	SP223	10 l + 100 l dk org brn & red	.16	.18
B333	SP223	10 l + 200 l bl & red brn	.18	.18
B334	SP223	80 l + 200 l brn vio & brn	.18	.18
B335	SP223	80 l + 300 l dk org brn & rose lil	.18	.18
B336	SP223	200 l + 400 l Prus bl & red	.18	.28
		Nos. B332-B336 (5)	.90	1.00

Issued in panes of 4 stamps with marginal inscription.

1946, Oct. 20 ***Perf. 13½x13, Imperf.***

B338	SP228	300 l + 1200 l scar	.50	.25

Souvenir Sheet

Perf. 14x14½

B339	SP228	1000 l scarlet	1.65	2.00

Romanian-Soviet friendship. No. B339 sold for 6000 lei.

Skiing — SP230

1946, Sept. 1 ***Perf. 11½, Imperf.***

B340	SP230	160 l + 1340 l dk grn	.50	.50

Surtax for Office of Popular Sports.

Spinning
SP231

Reaping
SP232

Riding — SP233

Water Carrier — SP234

1946, Nov. 20 *Perf. 14*

B342	SP231	80 l + 320 l brt red	.15	.15
B343	SP232	140 l + 360 l dp org	.15	.15
B344	SP233	300 l + 450 l brn ol	.15	.15
B345	SP234	600 l + 900 l ultra	.15	.15
		Set value	.45	.45

Democratic Women's Org. of Romania.

Angel with Food and Clothing
SP235

Bread for Hungry Family
SP236

Care for Needy
SP237

1947, Jan. 15 ***Perf. 13½x14***

B346	SP235	1500 l + 3500 l red org	.15	.15
B347	SP236	3700 l + 5300 l dp vio	.15	.15

Miniature Sheet

Imperf

Without Gum

B348	SP237	5000 l + 5000 l ultra	1.10	1.65

Surtax helped the social relief fund.

No. B348 is miniature sheet of one.

Student Reciting
SP238

Allegory of Education — SP242

SP243

#B350, Weaving class. #B351, Young machinist. #B352, Romanian school.

Perf. 14x13½

1947, Mar. 5 Photo. Wmk. 276

B349	SP238	200 l + 200 l vio bl	.15	.15
B350	SP238	300 l + 300 l red brn	.15	.15
B351	SP238	600 l + 600 l Prus grn	.15	.15
B352	SP238	1200 l + 1200 l ultra	.15	.15
B353	SP242	1500 l + 1500 l dp rose	.15	.15
		Set value	.25	.25

Souvenir Sheet

Imperf

B354	SP243	3700 l + 3700 l dl brn & dl bl	.75	.90

Romania's vocational schools, 50th anniv.

Victor Babes — SP244

#B356, Michael Eminescu. #B357, Nicolae Grigorescu. #B358, Peter Movila. #B359, Aleksander S. Pushkin. #B360, Mikhail V. Lomonosov. #B361, Peter I. Tchaikovsky. #B362, Ilya E. Repin.

1947, Apr. 18 *Perf. 14*

B355	SP244	1500 l + 1500 l red org	.15	.15
B356	SP244	1500 l + 1500 l dk ol grn	.15	.15
B357	SP244	1500 l + 1500 l dk bl	.15	.15
B358	SP244	1500 l + 1500 l dp plum	.15	.15
B359	SP244	1500 l + 1500 l scar	.15	.15
B360	SP244	1500 l + 1500 l rose brn	.15	.15
B361	SP244	1500 l + 1500 l ultra	.15	.15
B362	SP244	1500 l + 1500 l choc	.15	.15
		Set value (8)	.95	.95

Transportation
SP252

Labor Day: No. B364, Farmer. No. B365, Farm woman. No. B366, Teacher and school. No. B367, Laborer and factory.

1947, May 1

B363	SP252	1000 l + 1000 l dk ol brn	.15	.15
B364	SP252	1500 l + 1500 l red brn	.15	.15
B365	SP252	2000 l + 2000 l blue	.15	.15
B366	SP252	2500 l + 2500 l red vio	.15	.15
B367	SP252	3000 l + 3000 l crim rose	.15	.15
		Set value	.50	.50

No. 650 Surcharged in Carmine

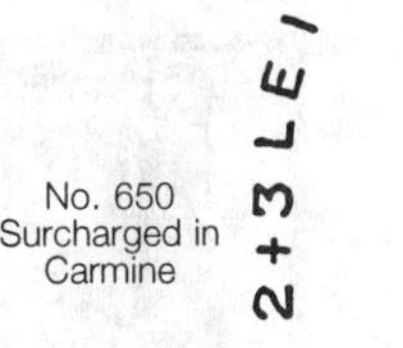

1947, Sept. 6 *Perf. 13½*
B368 A234 2 l + 3 l on 36,000 l vio .40 .40

Balkan Games of 1947, Bucharest.

Type of 1947 Surcharged in Carmine — ARLUS +5 1-7.XI-1947

Design: Cathedral of Curtea de Arges.

1947, Oct. 30 *Imperf.*
B369 A235 5 l + 5 l brt ultra .35 .35

Soviet-Romanian Congress, Nov. 1-7.

Plowing — SP257

Perf. 14x14½
1947, Oct. 5 Photo. Wmk. 276
B370 SP257 1 l + 1 l shown .15 .15
B371 SP257 2 l + 2 l Sawmill .15 .15
B372 SP257 3 l + 3 l Refinery .15 .15
B373 SP257 4 l + 4 l Steel mill .15 .15
Nos. B370-B373,CB12 (5) 1.20 .80

17th Congress of the General Assoc. of Romanian Engineers.

Allegory of Industry, Science and Agriculture SP258

Winged Man Holding Hammer and Sickle SP259

1947, Nov. 10 *Perf. 14½x14*
B374 SP258 2 l + 10 l rose lake .15 .15
B375 SP259 7 l + 10 l bluish blk .15 .15
Set value .24 .24

2nd Trade Union Conf., Nov. 10.

SP260 SP264

Designs: 1 l+1 l, Convoy of Food for Moldavia. 2 l+2 l, "Everything for the Front-Everything for Victory." 3 l+3 l, Woman, child and hospital. 4 l+4 l, "Help the Famine-stricken Regions." 5 l+5 l, "Three Years of Action."

1947, Nov. 7 *Perf. 14*
B376 SP260 1 l + 1 l dk gray bl .15 .15
B377 SP260 2 l + 2 l dk brn .15 .15
B378 SP260 3 l + 3 l rose lake .15 .15
B379 SP260 4 l + 4 l brt ultra .15 .15
B380 SP264 5 l + 5 l red .15 .15
Nos. B376-B380 (5) .75 .75

Issued in sheets of four.

Discus Thrower SP265

Labor SP266

Youths Following Filimon Sarbu Banner SP269

Balkan Games of 1947: 2 l+2 l, Runner. 5 l+5 l, Boy and girl athletes.

Perf. 13½
1948, Feb. Wmk. 276 Photo.
B381 SP265 1 l + 1 l dk brn .18 .18
B382 SP265 2 l + 2 l car lake .24 .24
B383 SP265 5 l + 5 l blue .35 .35
Nos. B381-B383,CB13-CB14 (5) 2.67 1.87

1948, Mar. 15

Designs: 3 l+3 l, Agriculture. 5 l+5 l, Education.

B384 SP266 2 l + 2 l dk sl bl .25 .16
B385 SP266 3 l + 3 l gray grn .30 .15
B386 SP266 5 l + 5 l red brn .40 .20

Imperf

B387 SP269 8 l + 8 l dk car rose .60 .28
Nos. B384-B387,CB15 (5) 2.45 1.29

No. B387 issued in triangular sheets of 4.

Gliders — SP270

Sailboat Race SP271

Designs: No. B389, Early plane. No. B390, Plane over farm. No. B391, Transport plane. B393, Training ship, Mircea. B394, Danube ferry. B395, S.S. Transylvania.

1948, July 26 *Perf. 14x14½*
B388 SP270 2 l + 2 l blue 1.25 1.25
B389 SP270 5 l + 5 l pur 1.25 1.25
B390 SP270 8 l + 8 l dk car rose 1.25 1.25
B391 SP270 10 l + 10 l choc 1.25 1.25
B392 SP271 2 l + 2 l dk grn 1.00 1.00
B393 SP271 5 l + 5 l slate 1.00 1.00
B394 SP271 8 l + 8 l brt bl 1.00 1.00
B395 SP271 10 l + 10 l ver 1.00 1.00
Nos. B388-B395 (8) 9.00 9.00

Air and Sea Communications Day.

Type of Regular Issue and

Torch, Pen, Ink and Flag SP272

Alexandru Sahia SP273

Romanian-Soviet Association Emblem SP274

Perf. 14x13½, 13½x14, Imperf.
1948, Sept. 12
B396 A241 5 l + 5 l crimson .70 .70
B397 SP272 10 l + 10 l violet .90 .90
B398 SP273 15 l + 15 l blue .90 .90
Nos. B396-B398 (3) 2.50 2.50

Week of the Democratic Press, Sept. 12-19.

1948, Oct. 29 *Perf. 14*

Design: 15 l+15 l, Spasski Tower, Kremlin.

B399 SP274 10 l + 10 l gray grn 1.25 1.25
B400 SP274 15 l + 15 l dp ultra 1.50 1.50

No. B399 was issued in sheets of 50 stamps and 50 labels.

Symbols of United Labor SP275

Agriculture SP276

Industry SP277

Automatic Riflemen SP278

Soldiers Cutting Barbed Wire — SP279

1948, May 1 *Perf. 14x13½, 13½x14*
B401 SP275 8 l + 8 l red 2.00 2.00
B402 SP276 10 l + 10 l ol grn 2.00 2.00
B403 SP277 12 l + 12 l red brn 2.00 2.00
Nos. B401-B403 (3) 6.00 6.00

Labor Day, May 1. See No. CB17.

1948, May 9
Flags and Dates:
23 Aug 1944-9 Mai 1945
B404 SP278 1.50 l + 1.50 l shown .95 .95
B405 SP279 2 l + 2 l shown .95 .95
B406 SP279 4 l + 4 l Field Artillery .95 .95
B407 SP279 7.50 l + 7.50 l Tank .95 .95
B408 SP279 8 l + 8 l Warship .95 .95
Nos. B404-B408,CB18-CB19 (7) 11.50 9.75

Honoring the Romanian Army.

Nicolae Balcescu SP280

Balcescu and Revolutionists SP281

Balcescu, Sandor Petöfi and Revolutionists SP282

Revolution of 1848: #B412, Balcescu and revolutionists.

1948, June 1 *Perf. 13x13½*
B409 SP280 2 l + 2 l car lake .60 .60
B410 SP281 5 l + 5 l dk vio .60 .60
B411 SP282 10 l + 10 l dk ol brn .60 .60
B412 SP280 36 l + 18 l dp bl 1.10 1.10
Nos. B409-B412 (4) 2.90 2.90

For surcharges see Nos. 856-859.

Loading Freighter SP283

Designs: 3 l+3 l, Lineman. 11 l+11 l, Transport plane. 15 l+15 l, Railroad train.

Wmk. 289
1948, Dec. 10 Photo. *Perf. 14*
Center in Black
B413 SP283 1 l + 1 l dk grn .30 .30
B414 SP283 3 l + 3 l redsh brn .38 .38
B415 SP283 11 l + 11 l dp bl 1.65 1.25
B416 SP283 15 l + 15 l red 2.10 1.90
a. Sheet of 4 6.00 7.00
Nos. B413-B416 (4) 4.43 3.83

No. B416a contains four imperf. stamps similar to Nos. B413-B416 in changed colors, center in brown. No gum.

Runners — SP284

Parade of Athletes SP285

Perf. 13x13½, 13½x13
1948, Dec. 31
B421 SP284 5 l + 5 l grn 1.90 1.90
B422 SP285 10 l + 10 l brn vio 3.00 3.00

Imperf

B423 SP284 5 l + 5 l grn 1.90 1.90
B424 SP285 10 l + 10 l red 3.00 3.00
Nos. B421-B424,CB20-CB21 (6) 29.30 29.30

Nos. B421-B424 were issued in sheets of 4.

Souvenir Sheet

SP286

1950, Jan. 27
B425 SP286 10 l carmine 1.10 .50

Philatelic exhib., Bucharest. Sold for 50 lei.

Crossing the Buzau, by Denis Auguste Marie Raffet — SP287

1967, Nov. 15 Engr. *Perf. 13½*
B426 SP287 55b + 45b ocher & indigo .40 .18

Stamp Day.

Old Bucharest, 18th Century Painting — SP288

1968, Nov. 15 Photo. *Perf. 13½*
B427 SP288 55b + 45b label .40 .18

Stamp Day. Label has printed perforations. See Nos. 2386A, B428-B429.

1969, Nov. 15

Design: Courtyard, by M. Bouquet.

B428 SP288 55b + 45b label .38 .15

Stamp Day. Label at right of stamp has printed perforations.

1970, Nov. 15

Mail Coach in the Winter, by Emil Volkers.

B429 SP288 55b + 45b multi .40 .15

Stamp Day.

Lady with Letter, by Sava Hentia — SP289

1971, Nov. 15 Photo. *Perf. 13½*
B430 SP289 1.10 l + 90b multi .48 .35

Stamp Day. Label portion below stamp has printed perforations and shows Romania No. 12.

Portrait Type of Regular Issue

Designs: 4 l+2 l, Barbat at his Desk, by B. Iscovescu. 6 l+2 l, The Poet Alecsandri with his Family, by N. Livaditti.

1973, June 20 Photo. *Perf. 13½*
B432 A728 4 l + 2 l multi 1.25 .50

Souvenir Sheet

B433 A728 6 l + 2 l multi 1.90 1.90

No. B433 contains one 38x50mm stamp.

Map of Europe with Emblem Marking Bucharest SP291

1974, June 25 Photo. *Perf. 13½*
B435 SP291 4 l + 3 l multi 1.40 .50

EUROMAX, European Exhibition of Maximaphily, Bucharest, Oct. 6-13.

Marketplace, Sibiu SP292

1974, Nov. 15 Photo. *Perf. 13½*
B436 SP292 2.10 l + 1.90 l multi .90 .40

Stamp Day.

No. B436 Overprinted in Red: "EXPOZITIA FILATELICA 'NATIONALA '74' / 15-24 noiembrie / Bucuresti"

1974, Nov. 15
B437 SP292 2.10 l + 1.90 l multi 2.50 .90

NATIONALA '74 Philatelic Exhibition, Bucharest, Nov. 15-24.

Post Office, Bucharest SP293

Stamp Day: 2.10 l+1.90 l, like No. B438, side view.

1975, Nov. 15 Photo. *Perf. 13½*
B438 SP293 1.50 l + 1.50 l multi .60 .30
B439 SP293 2.10 l + 1.90 l multi 1.10 .45

No. 2612 Surcharged and Overprinted: "EXPOZITIA FILATELICA / BUCURESTI / 12-19.IX.1976"

1976, Sept. 12 Photo. *Perf. 13½*
B440 A787 3.60 l + 1.80 l 2.10 1.25

Philatelic Exhibition, Bucharest, Sept. 12-19.

Elena Cuza, by Theodor Aman — SP294

Dispatch Rider Handing Letter to Officer — SP295

1976, Nov. 15 Photo. *Perf. 13½*
B441 SP294 2.10 l + 1.90 l multi .90 .45

Stamp Day.

Independence Type of 1977

Stamp Day: Battle of Rahova, after etching.

1977, May 9 Photo. *Perf. 13½*
B442 A806 4.80 l + 2 l multi 1.25 .35

1977, Nov. Photo. *Perf. 13½*
B443 SP295 2.10 l + 1.90 l multi .90 .45

Socfilex Type of 1979

Flower Paintings by Luchian: 4 l+2 l, Field flowers. 10 l+5 l, Roses.

1979, July 27 Photo. *Perf. 13½*
B445 A847 4 l + 2 l multi 1.10 .38

Souvenir Sheet

B446 A847 10 l + 5 l multi 3.00 1.25

Socfilex Intl. Phil. Exhib., Bucharest, Oct. 26-Nov. 1. #B446 contains one 50x38mm stamp.

Stamp Day SP297

1979, Dec. 12 Photo. *Perf. 13½*
B447 SP297 2.10 l + 1.90 l multi .70 .25

Souvenir Sheet

Stamp Day — SP298

1980, July 1 Photo. *Perf. 13½*
B448 SP298 5 l + 5 l multi 2.10 2.00

December 1989 Revolution — SP299

Designs: 50b+50b, Palace on fire, Bucharest. 1 l+ 1 l, Crowd, Timisoara. 1.50 l+1 l, Soldiers & crowd, Tirgu Mures. 2 l+1 l, Soldiers in Bucharest, vert. 3 l+1 l, Funeral, Timisoara. 3.50 l+1 l, Crowd celebrating, Brasov, vert. 4 l+1 l, Crowd with flags, Sibiu. No. B456, Cemetery, Bucharest. No. B457, Foreign aid.

1990, Oct. 1 Photo. *Perf. 13½*

B449	SP299	50b +50b multi	.15	.15
B450	SP299	1 l +1 l multi	.18	.18
B451	SP299	1.50 l +1 l multi	.22	.22
B452	SP299	2 l +1 l multi	.28	.28
B453	SP299	3 l +1 l multi	.35	.35
B454	SP299	3.50 l +1 l multi	.40	.40
B455	SP299	4 l +1 l multi	.45	.45
B456	SP299	5 l +2 l multi	.60	.60
		Nos. B449-B456 (8)	2.63	2.63

Souvenir Sheet

B457 SP299 5 l +2 l multi .60 .60

No. B457 contains one 54x42mm stamp.

Stamp Day — SP300

1992, July 15 Photo. *Perf. 13½*
B458 SP300 10 l +4 l multi .38 .38

For surcharge see No. B460.

Stamp Day — SP301

1993, Apr. 26 Photo. *Perf. 13½*
B459 SP301 15 l +10 l multi .15 .15

No. B458 Surcharged in Red

35 ANI DE ACTIVITATE AFR-FFR
1958–1993

70L + 45

1993, Nov. 9 Photo. *Perf. 13½*
B460 SP300 70 l + 45 l on 10 l+4 l .90 .90

National History Museum, Bucharest — SP302

1994, July 15 Photo. *Perf. 13½*
B461 SP302 90 l +60 l multi .45 .25

Stamp Day.

AIR POST STAMPS

ROMANIA
POSTA AERIANA

Capt. C. G. Craiu's Airplane AP1

Wmk. 95 Vertical

1928 Photo. *Perf. 13½*

C1	AP1	1 l red brown	1.65	1.50
C2	AP1	2 l brt blue	1.65	1.50
C3	AP1	5 l carmine rose	1.65	1.50

Wmk. 95 Horizontal

C4	AP1	1 l red brown	1.65	1.50
C5	AP1	2 l brt blue	1.65	1.50
C6	AP1	5 l carmine rose	1.65	1.50
		Nos. C1-C6 (6)	9.90	9.00

Nos. C4-C6 also come with white gum.

Nos. C4-C6 Overprinted **8 IUNIE 1930**

1930

C7	AP1	1 l red brown	4.50	4.50
C8	AP1	2 l brt blue	4.50	4.50
a.		Vert. pair, imperf. btwn.	*180.00*	
C9	AP1	5 l carmine rose	4.50	4.50
		Nos. C7-C9 (3)	13.50	13.50

Same Overprint on Nos. C1-C3

Wmk. 95 Vertical

C10	AP1	1 l red brown	32.50	32.50
C11	AP1	2 l brt blue	32.50	32.50
C12	AP1	5 l carmine rose	32.50	32.50
		Nos. C10-C12 (3)	97.50	97.50
		Nos. C7-C12 (6)	111.00	111.00

#C7-C12 for the accession of King Carol II. Excellent connterfeits are known of #C10-C12.

King Carol II — AP2

1930, Oct. 4 **Unwmk.**

Bluish Paper

C13	AP2	1 l dk violet	.70	.28
C14	AP2	2 l gray green	.85	.28
C15	AP2	5 l red brown	1.90	.55
C16	AP2	10 l brt blue	3.50	.70
		Nos. C13-C16 (4)	6.95	1.81
		Never hinged	9.00	

Junkers Monoplane AP3

Monoplanes AP7

Designs: 3 l, Monoplane with biplane behind. 5 l, Biplane. 10 l, Monoplane flying leftward.

1931, Nov. 4 **Wmk. 230**

C17	AP3	2 l dull green	.40	.15
C18	AP3	3 l carmine	.50	.20
C19	AP3	5 l red brown	.70	.20
C20	AP3	10 l blue	1.65	.38
C21	AP7	20 l dk violet	3.25	.90
		Nos. C17-C21 (5)	6.50	1.83
		Never hinged	9.00	

Exist imperforate.

Souvenir Sheets

Plane over Resita AP8

Plane over Sinaia AP9

Wmk. 276

1945, Oct. 1 **Photo.** ***Perf. 13***

Without Gum

C22	AP8	80 l slate green	5.00	5.00

Imperf

C23	AP9	80 l magenta	3.50	3.50

16th Congress of the General Assoc. of Romanian Engineers.

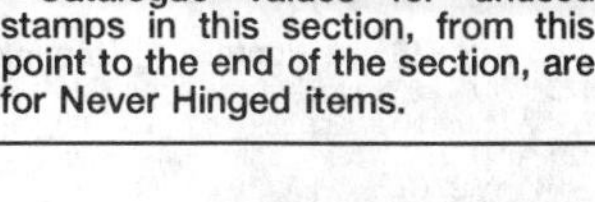
Catalogue values for unused stamps in this section, from this point to the end of the section, are for Never Hinged items.

Plane AP10

Design: 500 l, Aviator and planes.

1946, Sept. 5 ***Perf. 13½x13***

C24	AP10	200 l yel grn & bl	1.00	.75
C25	AP10	500 l org red & dl bl	1.00	.75

Printed in sheets of four with marginal inscription.

Lockheed 12 Electra AP12

CGM Congress Emblem AP13

1946, Oct. ***Perf. 11½***

C26	AP12	300 l crimson	.50	.50
a.		Pair, #C26, CB6	1.75	1.75

Sheet contains 8 each of Nos. C26 and CB6, arranged so se-tenant or normal pairs are available.

1947, Mar. **Wmk. 276** ***Perf. 13x14***

C27	AP13	1100 l blue	.28	.28

Congress of the United Labor Unions ("CGM"). Printed in sheets of 15.

"May 1" Supported by Parachutes AP14

Plane and Conference Banner AP17

Designs: No. C29, Air Force monument. No. C30, Plane over rural road.

1947, May 4 ***Perf. 11½***

C28	AP14	3000 l vermilion	.20	.15
C29	AP14	3000 l grnsh gray	.20	.15
C30	AP14	3000 l blk brown	.20	.15
		Nos. C28-C30 (3)	.60	.45

Printed in sheets of four with marginal inscriptions.

1947, Nov. 10 ***Perf. 14***

C31	AP17	11 l bl & dp car	.25	.25

2nd Trade Union Conference, Nov. 10.

Emblem of the Republic and Factories AP18

Industry and Agriculture AP19

Transportation — AP20

Perf. 14x13½

1948, Nov. 22 **Wmk. 289** **Photo.**

C32	AP18	30 l cerise	.28	.15
a.		30 l carmine ('50)	.38	.28
C33	AP19	50 l dk slate grn	.38	.20
C34	AP20	100 l ultra	1.10	.55
		Nos. C32-C34 (3)	1.76	.90

No. C32a issued May 10. For surcharges see Nos. C37-C39.

Transportation — AP21

Design: 30 l, Agriculture.

1951-52 **Wmk. 358** ***Perf. 13½***

C35	AP21	30 l dk green ('52)	1.25	1.10
C36	AP21	50 l red brown	.90	.70

1951-55 Five Year Plan.
For surcharges see Nos. C40-C41.

Nos. C32-C36 Surcharged with New Values in Blue or Carmine

1952 **Wmk. 289** ***Perf. 14x13½***

C37	AP18	3b on 30 l car (Bl)	.50	.25
a.		3b on 30 l cerise (Bl)	*7.25*	*6.50*
C38	AP19	3b on 50 l dk sl grn	.50	.25
C39	AP20	3b on 100 l ultra	.50	.25

Perf. 13½

Wmk. 358

C40	AP21	1 l on 30 l dk grn	*7.50*	*1.50*
C41	AP21	1 l on 50 l red brn	*7.50*	*1.50*
		Nos. C37-C41 (5)	*16.50*	*3.75*

Nos. 706 and 707 Surcharged in Blue or Carmine

1953 **Wmk. 289** ***Perf. 13½, 14***

C43	A250	3 l on 20 l org brn	*8.25*	*7.00*
C44	A251	5 l on 30 l brt bl (C)	*10.50*	*10.00*

Plane facing right and surcharge arranged to fit design on No. C44.

Plane over City — AP22

Sputnik 1 and Earth — AP23

Designs: 55b, Plane over Mountains. 1.75 l, over Harvest fields. 2.25 l, over Seashore.

Perf. 14½x14

1956, Dec. 15 **Photo.** **Wmk. 358**

C45	AP22	20b brt bl, org & grn	.20	.15
C46	AP22	55b brt bl, grn & ocher	.35	.15
C47	AP22	1.75 l brt bl & red org	1.25	.15
C48	AP22	2.55 l brt bl & red org	1.50	.38
		Nos. C45-C48 (4)	3.30	.83

1957, Nov. 6 ***Perf. 14***

Design: 3.75 l, Sputniks 1 and 2 circling globe.

C49	AP23	25b brt ultra	.30	.15
C50	AP23	25b dk bl grn	.30	.15
C51	AP23	3.75 l brt ultra	1.50	.38
a.		Pair, #C49, C51 + label	1.80	.50
C52	AP23	3.75 l dk bl grn	1.50	.38
a.		Pair, #C50, C52 + label	1.80	.50
		Nos. C49-C52 (4)	3.60	1.06

Each sheet contains 27 triptychs with the center rows arranged tete-beche.

In 1958 Nos. C49-C52 were overprinted: 1.) "Expozitia Universal a Bruxelles 1958" and star. 2.) Large star. 3.) Small star.

Animal Type of Regular Issue, 1957

Birds: 3.30 l, Black-headed gull, horiz. 5 l, Sea eagle, horiz.

Perf. 14x13½

1957, Dec. 27 **Wmk. 358**

C53	A445	3.30 l ultra & gray	1.65	.28
C54	A445	5 l carmine & org	2.50	.40

Armed Forces Type of Regular Issue

Design: Flier and planes.

Perf. 13½x13

1958, Oct. 2 **Unwmk.** **Photo.**

C55	A458	3.30 l brt violet	.90	.42

Day of the Armed Forces, Oct. 2.

Earth and Sputnik 3 Orbit AP24

1958, Sept. 20 ***Perf. 14x13½***

C56	AP24	3.25 l indigo & ocher	1.75	.50

Launching of Sputnik 3, May 15, 1958.

Type of Regular Issue, 1958
Souvenir Sheet

Design: Tête bêche pair of 27pa of 1858.

Perf. 11½

1958, Nov. 15 **Unwmk.** **Engr.**

C57	A462	10 l blue	10.00	10.00

A similar sheet, printed in dull red and imperf., exists.

No. C57 was overprinted in 1959 in vermilion to commemorate the 10th anniv. of the State Philatelic Trade.

Values, $25 and $50.

Lunik I Leaving Earth AP25

Frederic Joliot-Curie AP26

1959, Feb. 4 **Photo.** ***Perf. 14***

C58	AP25	3.25 l vio bl, *pnksh*	4.50	.90

Launching of the "first artificial planet of the solar system."

For surcharge see No. C70.

1959, Apr. 25 ***Perf. 13½x14***

C59	AP26	3.25 l ultra	2.50	.50

Frederic Joliot-Curie; 10th anniv. of the World Peace Movement.

Rock Thrush — AP27

Birds: 20b, European golden oriole. 35b, Lapwing. 40b, Barn swallow. No. C64, Goldfinch. No. C65, Great spotted woodpecker. No. C66, Great tit. 1 l, Bullfinch. 1.55 l, Long-tailed tit. 5 l, Wall creeper. Nos. C62-C67 vertical.

1959, June 25 **Litho.** ***Perf. 14***

Birds in Natural Colors

C60	AP27	10b gray, *cr*	.15	.15
C61	AP27	20b gray, *grysh*	.15	.15
C62	AP27	35b gray, *grysh*	.15	.15
C63	AP27	40b gray & red, *pnksh*	.15	.15
C64	AP27	55b gray, *buff*	.25	.15
C65	AP27	55b gray, *grnsh*	.25	.15
C66	AP27	55b gray & ol, *grysh*	.25	.15
C67	AP27	1 l gray and red, *cr*	.75	.15
C68	AP27	1.55 l gray & red, *pnksh*	.90	.15
C69	AP27	5 l gray, *grnsh*	3.75	.70
		Nos. C60-C69 (10)	6.75	
		Set value		1.25

No. C58 Surcharged in Red

h. 00,02,24
14-IX-1959
PRIMA RACHETA COSMICA
IN LUNA
5 LEI

1959, Sept. 14 Photo. Unwmk.

C70 AP25 5 l on 3.25 l 4.75 1.00

1st Russian rocket to reach the moon, 9/14/59.

Miniature Sheet

Prince Vlad Tepes and Document AP28

1959, Sept. 15 Engr. *Perf. 11½x11*

C71 AP28 20 l violet brn 50.00 50.00

500th anniv. of the founding of Bucharest.

Sport Type of Regular Issue, 1959

1959, Oct. 5 Litho. *Perf. 13½*

C72 A474 2.80 l Boating 1.50 .38

Soviet Rocket, Globe, Dog and Rabbit — AP29

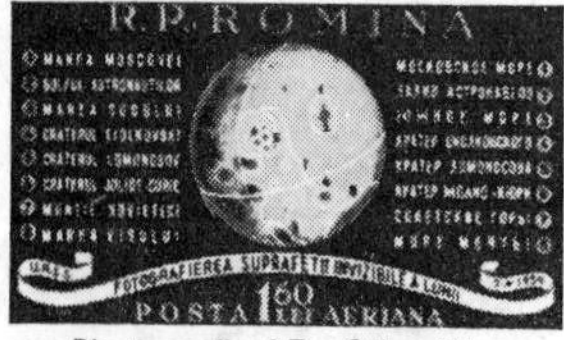

Photograph of Far Side of the Moon — AP30

Design: 1.75 l, Trajectory of Lunik 3, which hit the moon.

Perf. 14, 13½ (AP30)

1959, Dec. Photo. Wmk. 358

C73	AP29	1.55 l dk blue	1.75	.20
C74	AP30	1.60 l dk vio bl, *buff*	2.25	.25
C75	AP29	1.75 l dk blue	2.25	.25
		Nos. C73-C75 (3)	6.25	.70

Soviet conquest of space.

Animal Type of Regular Issue, 1960.

Designs: 1.30 l, Golden eagle. 1.75 l, Black grouse. 2 l, Lammergeier.

Unwmk.

1960, Mar. 3 Engr. *Perf. 14*

C76	A480	1.30 l dk blue	.85	.22
C77	A480	1.75 l olive grn	1.25	.22
C78	A480	2 l dk carmine	1.50	.26
		Nos. C76-C78 (3)	3.60	.70

Aurel Vlaicu and Plane of 1910 AP31

Bucharest Airport and Turbo-Jet — AP32

Designs: 20b, Plane and Aurel Vlaicu. 35b, Amphibian ambulance plane. 40b, Plane spraying crops. 55b, Pilot and planes, vert. 1.75 l, Parachutes at aviation sports meet.

1960, June 15 Litho. Unwmk.

C79	AP31	10b yellow & brn	.15	.15
C80	AP31	20b red org & brn	.15	.15

Photo. Wmk. 358

C81	AP31	35b crimson	.20	.15
C82	AP31	40b violet	.28	.15
C83	AP31	55b blue	.40	.15

Litho. Unwmk.

C84	AP32	1.60 l vio bl, yel & emer	.95	.20
C85	AP32	1.75 l bl, red, brn & pale grn	1.25	.35
		Nos. C79-C85 (7)	3.38	
		Set value		.80

50th anniv. of the first Romanian airplane flight by Aurel Vlaicu.

For surcharge see No. C145.

Bucharest Airport — AP33

Sputnik 4 Flying into Space — AP34

1960 Wmk. 358 Photo. *Perf. 14*

C86 AP33 3.20 l brt ultra 1.10 .15

Type of Regular Issue, 1960

Black Sea Resort: 2 l, Beach at Mamaia.

1960, Aug. 2 Litho. Unwmk.

C87 A491 2 l grn, org & lt bl .90 .18

1960, June 8 Photo. Wmk. 358

C88 AP34 55b deep blue 1.50 .25

Launching of Sputnik 4, May 15, 1960.

Saturnia Pyri — AP35

Papilio Machaon — AP36

Limenitis Populi AP37

Designs: 40b, Chrisophanus virgaureae. 1.60 l, Acherontia atropos. 1.75 l, Apatura iris, horiz.

Perf. 13, 14x12½, 14

1960, Oct. 10 Typo. Unwmk.

C89	AP35	10b multi	.15	.15
C90	AP37	20b multi	.15	.15
C91	AP37	40b multi	.15	.15
C92	AP36	55b multi	.28	.15
C93	AP36	1.60 l multi	.80	.18
C94	AP36	1.75 l multi	.90	.18
		Nos. C89-C94 (6)	2.43	
		Set value		.58

Compass Rose and Jet — AP38

Perf. 13½x14

1960, Nov. 1 Photo. Wmk. 358

C95 AP38 55b brt bl + 45b label .48 .15

Stamp Day.

Skier AP39

Slalom — AP40

Maj. Yuri A. Gagarin — AP41

Designs: 25b, Skiers going up. 40b, Bobsled. 55b, Ski jump. 1 l, Mountain climber. 1.55 l, Long-distance skier.

Perf. 14x13½, 13½x14

1961, Mar. 18 Litho. Unwmk.

C96	AP39	10b olive & gray	.15	.15
C97	AP40	20b gray & dk red	.15	.15
C98	AP40	25b gray & bl grn	.15	.15
C99	AP40	40b gray & pur	.15	.15
C100	AP39	55b gray & ultra	.20	.15
C101	AP40	1 l gray & brn lake	.42	.15
C102	AP39	1.55 l gray & brn	.75	.16
		Set value	1.70	.55

Exist imperf. with changed colors. Value, set $3.75.

Perf. 14x14½, 14½x14

1961, Apr. 19 Photo. Unwmk.

Design: 3.20 l, Gagarin in space capsule and globe with orbit, horiz.

C103	AP41	1.35 l brt blue	.60	.15
C104	AP41	3.20 l ultra	1.25	.15

No. C104 exists imperf. in dark carmine rose. Value unused $3.75, canceled $2.

Eclipse over Republic Palace Place, Bucharest AP42

1.75 l, Total Eclipse, Scinteia House, telescope.

Perf. 14x13½

1961, June 13 Wmk. 358

C106	AP42	1.60 l ultra	.70	.15
C107	AP42	1.75 l dk blue	.70	.15

Total solar eclipse of Feb. 15, 1961.

Maj. Gherman S. Titov — AP43

Globe and Stamps — AP44

55b, "Peace" and Vostok 2 rocket. 1.75 l, Yuri A. Gagarin and Gherman S. Titov, horiz.

Perf. 13½x14

1961, Sept. 11 Unwmk.

C108	AP43	55b dp blue	.38	.15
C109	AP43	1.35 l dp purple	.55	.15
C110	AP43	1.75 l dk carmine	.90	.20
		Nos. C108-C110 (3)	1.83	
		Set value		.40

Issued to honor the Russian space navigators Y. A. Gagarin and G. S. Titov.

1961, Nov. 15 Litho. *Perf. 13½x14*

C111 AP44 55b multi + 45b label .50 .18

Stamp Day.

Railroad Station, Constanta AP45

Buildings: 20b, Tower, RPR Palace place, vert. 55b, Congress hall, Bucharest. 75b, Mill, Hunedoara. 1 l, Apartment houses, Bucharest. 1.20 l, Circus, Bucharest. 1.75 l, Worker's Club, Mangalia.

Perf. 13½x14, 14x13½

1961, Nov. 20 Typo.

C112	AP45	20b multi	.15	.15
C113	AP45	40b multi	.16	.15
C114	AP45	55b multi	.16	.15
C115	AP45	75b multi	.25	.15
C116	AP45	1 l multi	.32	.15
C117	AP45	1.20 l multi	.65	.25
C118	AP45	1.75 l multi	.95	.40
		Nos. C112-C118 (7)	2.64	
		Set value		.90

Space Exploration Stamps and Dove — AP46

Design: Each stamp shows a different group of Romanian space exploration stamps.

1962, July 27 *Perf. 14x13½*

C119	AP46	35b yellow brn	.15	.15
C120	AP46	55b green	.22	.15
C121	AP46	1.35 l blue	.40	.16
C122	AP46	1.75 l rose red	.80	.28
a.		Sheet of 4	2.25	1.00
		Nos. C119-C122 (4)	1.57	
		Set value		.58

Peaceful space exploration.

No. C122a contains four imperf. stamps similar to Nos. C119-C122 in changed colors and with one dove covering all four stamps. Stamps are printed together without space between.

Andrian G. Nikolayev — AP47

Designs: 1.60 l, Globe and trajectories of Vostoks 3 and 4. 1.75 l, Pavel R. Popovich.

Perf. 13½x14

1962, Aug. 20 Photo. Unwmk.

C123	AP47	55b purple	.35	.15
C124	AP47	1.60 l dark blue	1.00	.22
C125	AP47	1.75 l rose claret	1.25	.28
		Nos. C123-C125 (3)	2.60	.65

1st Russian group space flight of Vostoks 3 and 4, Aug. 11-15, 1962.

Exhibition Hall AP48 — The Coachmen by Szatmary AP49

1962, Oct. 12 Litho. *Perf. 14x13*
C126 AP48 1.60 l bl, vio bl & org .90 .15

4th Sample Fair, Bucharest.

1962, Nov. 15 *Perf. 13½x14*
C127 AP49 55b + 45b label .75 .24

Stamp Day. Alternating label shows No. 14 on cover.

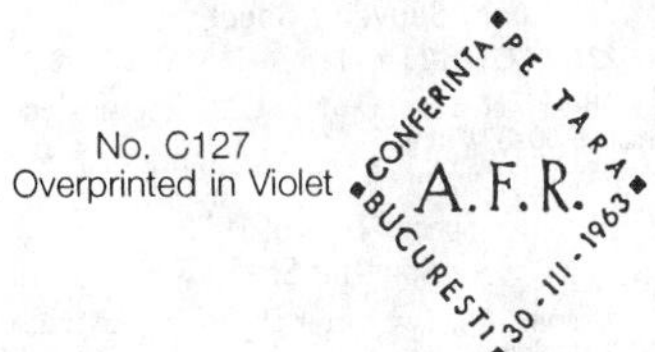

No. C127 Overprinted in Violet

1963, Mar. 30
C128 AP49 55b + 45b label 1.50 1.10

Romanian Philatelists' Assoc. meeting at Bucharest, Mar. 30. The overprint is centered on the stamp and label, about half of it on each.

Sighisoara Glass and Crockery Factory AP50

Industrial Plants: 40b, Govora soda works. 55b, Tirgul-Jiu wood processing factory. 1 l, Savinesti chemical plant (synthetic fibers). 1.55 l, Hunedoara metal factory. 1.75 l, Brazi thermal power station.

Perf. 14x13

1963, Apr. 10 Unwmk. Photo.
C129 AP50 30b dk bl & red .15 .15
C130 AP50 40b sl grn & pur .15 .15
C131 AP50 55b brn red & dp bl .15 .15
C132 AP50 1 l vio & brn .22 .15
C133 AP50 1.55 l ver & dk bl .50 .15
C134 AP50 1.75 l dk bl & mag .70 .15
Nos. C129-C134 (6) 1.87
Set value .50

Industrial achievements.

Lunik 4 Approaching Moon — AP51

1963, Apr. 29 *Perf. 13½x14*
C135 AP51 55b dk ultra & red .45 .15

Imperf

C136 AP51 1.75 l vio & red .75 .25

Moon flight of Lunik 4, Apr. 2, 1963.

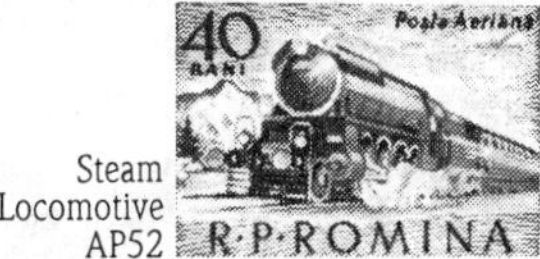

Steam Locomotive AP52

Designs: 55b, Diesel locomotive. 75b, Trolley bus. 1.35 l, Passenger ship. 1.75 l, Plane.

1963, July 10 Litho. *Perf. 14½x13*
C137 AP52 40b multi .18 .15
C138 AP52 55b multi .28 .15
C139 AP52 75b multi .38 .15
C140 AP52 1.35 l multi .70 .15
C141 AP52 1.75 l multi 1.10 .20
Nos. C137-C141 (5) 2.64
Set value .62

Valeri Bykovski AP53

Designs: 1.20 l, Bykovski, vert. 1.60 l, Tereshkova, vert. 1.75 l, Valentina Tereshkova.

1963 Photo.
C142 AP53 55b blue .16 .15
C143 AP53 1.75 l rose red .60 .18
Set value .26

Souvenir Sheet

Perf. 13

C144 Sheet of 2 1.95 .50
a. AP53 1.20 l ultra .50 .24
b. AP53 1.60 l ultra .50 .24

Space flights of Valeri Bykovski, June 14-19, and Valentina Tereshkova, first woman cosmonaut, June 16-19, 1963.

No. C79 Surcharged and Overprinted: "1913-1963 50 ani de la moarte"

Unwmk.

1963, Sept. 15 Litho. *Perf. 14*
C145 AP31 1.75 l on 10b 1.00 .38

50th death anniv. of Aurel Vlaicu, aviation pioneer.
Exists with "i" of "lei," missing.

Centenary Stamp of 1958 — AP54

Stamps on Stamps: 40b, Sputnik 2 and Laika, #1200. 55b, Yuri A. Gagarin, #C104a. 1.20 l, Nikolayev and Popovich, #C123, C125. 1.55 l, Postal Administration Bldg. and letter carrier, #965.

1963, Nov. 15 Photo. *Perf. 14x13½*
Size: 38x26mm
C146 AP54 20b lt bl & dk brn .15 .15
C147 AP54 40b brt pink & dk bl .22 .15
C148 AP54 55b lt ultra & dk car rose .28 .15
C149 AP54 1.20 l ocher & pur .55 .15
C150 AP54 1.55 l sal pink & ol gray .65 .15
Nos. C146-C150,CB22 (6) 3.25
Set value .88

15th UPU Congress, Vienna.

Pavel R. Popovich AP55

Astronauts and flag: 5b, Yuri A. Gagarin. 10b, Gherman S. Titov. 20b, John H. Glenn, Jr. 35b, M. Scott Carpenter. 40b, Andrian G. Nikolayev. 60b, Walter M. Schirra. 75b, Gordon L. Cooper. 1 l, Valeri Bykovski. 1.40 l, Valentina Tereshkova. (5b, 10b, 20b, 35b, 60b and 75b are diamond shaped).

Perf. 13½

1964, Jan. 15 Litho. Unwmk.
Light Blue Background
C151 AP55 5b red, yel & vio bl .15 .15
C152 AP55 10b red, yel & pur .15 .15
C153 AP55 20b red, ultra & ol gray .18 .15
C154 AP55 35b red, ultra & sl bl .22 .15
C155 AP55 40b red, yel & ultra .22 .15
C156 AP55 55b red, yel & ultra .38 .15
C157 AP55 60b ultra, red & sep .38 .15
C158 AP55 75b red, ultra & dk bl .45 .15
C159 AP55 1 l red, yel & mar .75 .15
C160 AP55 1.40 l red, yel & mar .90 .15
Nos. C151-C160 (10) 3.78
Set value .75

Nos. C151-C160 exist imperf. in changed colors. Value, set $6.50.
A miniature sheet contains one imperf. horizontal 2 l ultramarine and yellow stamp. Size of stamp: 59½x43mm. Value unused $7.50, canceled $3.75.

Modern and 19th Century Post Office Buildings AP56

Engr. & Typo.

1964, Nov. 15 *Perf. 13½*
C161 AP56 1.60 l ultra + 40b label .75 .25

Stamp Day. Stamp and label are imperf. between.

Plane Approaching Airport and Coach Leaving Gate — AP57

Engr. & Typo.

1966, Oct. 20 *Perf. 13½*
C162 AP57 55b + 45b label .48 .15

Stamp Day.

Space Exploration Type of Regular Issue

US Achievements in Space: 1.20 l, Early Bird satellite and globe. 1.55 l, Mariner 4 transmitting pictures of the moon. 3.25 l, Gemini 6 & 7, rendezvous in space. 5 l, Gemini 8 meeting Agena rocket, and globe.

1967, Feb. 15 Photo. *Perf. 13½*
C163 A595 1.20 l silver & multi .25 .15
C164 A595 1.55 l silver & multi .38 .15
C165 A595 3.25 l silver & multi .65 .15
C166 A595 5 l silver & multi 1.50 .50
Nos. C163-C166 (4) 2.78
Set value .70

10 years of space exploration.

Plane Spraying Crops — AP58

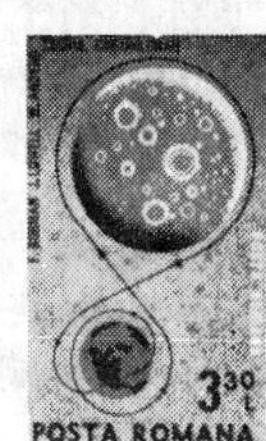

Moon, Earth and Path of Apollo 8 — AP59

Designs: 55b, Aerial ambulance over river, horiz. 1 l, Red Cross and plane. 2.40 l, Biplane and Mircea Zorileanu, aviation pioneer.

Perf. 12x12½, 12½x12

1968, Feb. 28 Litho. Unwmk.
C167 AP58 40b bl grn, blk & yel brn .15 .15
C168 AP58 55b multicolored .15 .15
C169 AP58 1 l ultra, pale grn & red org .28 .15
C170 AP58 2.40 l brt rose lil & multi .90 .30
Nos. C167-C170 (4) 1.48
Set value .48

1969 Photo. *Perf. 13½*

Design: No. C172, Soyuz 4 and 5 over globe with map of Russia.

C171 AP59 3.30 l multi 1.75 .28
C172 AP59 3.30 l multi 1.75 .28

1st manned flight around the Moon, Dec. 21-27, 1968, and the first team flights of the Russian spacecrafts Soyuz 4 and 5, Jan. 16, 1969. See note after Hungary No. C284.

Issued in sheets of 4.
Issued: #C171, Jan. 17, #C172, Mar. 28.

Apollo 9 and Lunar Landing Module over Earth AP60

Design: 2.40 l, Apollo 10 and lunar landing module over moon, vert.

1969, June 15 Photo. *Perf. 13½*
C173 AP60 60b multi .15 .15
C174 AP60 2.40 l multi .60 .25
Set value .30

US space explorations, Apollo 9 and 10.

First Man on Moon — AP61

1969, July 24 Photo. *Perf. 13½*
C175 AP61 3.30 l multi 1.10 .80

Man's first landing on the moon July 20, 1969, US astronauts Neil A. Armstrong and Col. Edwin E. Aldrin, Jr., with Lieut. Col. Michael Collins piloting Apollo 11. Printed in sheets of 4.

1970, June 29

1.50 l, Apollo 13 capsule splashing down in Pacific.

C176 AP61 1.50 l multi .48 .40

Flight and safe landing of Apollo 13, Apr. 11-17, 1970. Printed in sheets of 4.

BAC 1-11 Jet AP62

Design: 2 l, Fuselage BAC 1-11 and control tower, Bucharest airport.

1970, Apr. 6
C177 AP62 60b multi .18 .15
C178 AP62 2 l multi .55 .22
Set value .28

50th anniv. of Romanian civil aviation.

Flood Relief Type of Regular Issue

Design: 60b, Rescue by helicopter.

1970, Sept. 25 Photo. *Perf. 13½*
C179 A671 60b bl gray, blk & ol .30 .15

Publicizing the plight of victims of the Danube flood. See No. 2207a.

Henri Coanda's Model Plane AP63

1970, Dec. 1
C180 AP63 60b multicolored .25 .15

Henri Coanda's first flight, 60th anniversary.

Luna 16 on Moon AP64

#C182, Lunokhod 1, unmanned vehicle on moon. #C183, US astronaut & vehicle on moon.

1971, Mar. 5 Photo. *Perf. 13½*

C181 AP64 3.30 l silver & multi .85 .50
C182 AP64 3.30 l silver & multi .85 .50
a. Pair, #C181-C182 + 2 labels 1.75 1.00
C183 AP64 3.30 l silver & multi .85 .50
Nos. C181-C183 (3) 2.55 1.50

No. C181 commemorates Luna 16 Russian unmanned, automatic moon mission, Sept. 12-24, 1970 (labels are incorrectly inscribed Oct. 12-24). No. C182 commemorates Lunokhod 1 (Luna 17), Nov. 10-17, 1970. Nos. C181-C182 printed in sheets of 4 stamps, arranged checkerwise, and 4 labels. No. C183 commemorates Apollo 14 moon landing, Jan. 31-Feb. 9. Printed in sheets of 4 with 4 labels showing portraits of US astronauts Alan B. Shepard, Edgar D. Mitchell, Stuart A. Roosa, and Apollo 14 emblem.

Souvenir Sheet

Cosmonauts Patsayev, Dobrovolsky and Volkov — AP65

1971, July 26 Litho. *Perf. 13½*

C184 AP65 6 l black & ultra 3.75 3.75

In memory of Russian cosmonauts Viktor I. Patsayev, Georgi T. Dobrovolsky and Vladislav N. Volkov, who died during Soyuz 11 space mission, June 6-30, 1971.

No. C184 exists imperf. in black & blue green; Size: 130x90mm.

Lunar Rover on Moon AP66

1971, Aug. 26 Photo.

C185 AP66 1.50 l blue & multi .75 .60

US Apollo 15 moon mission, July 26-Aug. 7, 1971. No. C185 printed in sheets of 4 stamps and 4 labels showing astronauts David Scott, James Irwin, Alfred Worden and Apollo 15 emblem with dates.

No. C185 exists imperf. in green & multicolored. The sheet has a control number.

Olympic Souvenir Sheets

Designs: No. C186, Torchbearer and map of Romania. No. C187, Soccer.

1972 Photo. *Perf. 13½*

C186 A699 6 l pale grn & multi 3.75 3.75
C187 A699 6 l blue & multi 3.75 3.75

20th Olympic Games, Munich, Aug. 26-Sept. 11. No. C186 contains one stamp 50x38mm. No. C187 contains one stamp 48½x37mm.

Issued: No. C186, Apr. 25. No. C187, Sept. 29.

Two imperf. 6 l souvenir sheets exist, one showing equestrian, the other a satellite over globe.

Lunar Rover on Moon — AP67

1972, May 10 Photo. *Perf. 13½*

C188 AP67 3 l vio bl, rose & gray grn .90 .45

Apollo 16 US moon mission, Apr. 15-27, 1972. No. C188 printed in sheets of 4 stamps and 4 gray green and black labels showing Capt. John W. Young, Lt. Comdr. Thomas K. Mattingly 2nd, Col. Charles M. Duke, Jr., and Apollo 16 badge.

Aurel Vlaicu and Monoplane AP68

Romanian Aviation Pioneers: 3 l, Traian Vuia and his flying machine.

1972, Aug. 15

C189 AP68 60b multicolored .20 .15
C190 AP68 3 l multicolored .85 .32

Olympic Medals Type of Regular Issue
Souvenir Sheet

Design: Olympic silver and gold medals, horiz.

1972, Sept. 29 Litho. *Perf. 13½*

C191 A714 6 l multicolored 4.50 3.00

Romanian medalists at 20th Olympic Games. An imperf. 6 l souvenir sheet exists showing gold medal.

Apollo Type of Regular Issue
Souvenir Sheet

Design: 6 l, Lunar rover, landing module, rocket and astronauts on moon, horiz.

1972, Dec. 27 Photo. *Perf. 13½*

C192 A715 6 l vio bl, bis & dl grn 4.50 3.00

No. C192 contains one stamp 48½x36mm.

An imperf. 6 l souvenir sheet exists showing surface of moon with landing sites of last 6 Apollo missions and landing capsule.

Type of Regular Issue, 1972

Design: Otopeni Airport, horiz.

1972, Dec. 20 Photo. *Perf. 13*
Size: 29x21mm

C193 A710 14.60 l brt blue 2.75 .38

Apollo and Soyuz Spacecraft AP69

Design: 3.25 l, Apollo and Soyuz after link-up.

1975, July 14 Photo. *Perf. 13½*

C196 AP69 1.75 l vio bl, red & ol .45 .18
C197 AP69 3.25 l vio bl, red & ol .90 .45

Apollo Soyuz space test project (Russo-American cooperation), launching July 15; link-up, July 17. Nos. C196-C197 printed in sheets of 4 stamps, arranged checkerwise, and 4 rose lilac labels showing Apollo-Soyuz emblem.

European Security and Cooperation Conference — AP70

1975, July 30 Photo. *Perf. 13½*

C198 AP70 Sheet of 4 4.50 4.50
a. 2.75 l Map of Europe .55 .55
b. 2.75 l Peace doves .55 .55
c. 5 l Open book 1.00 1.00
d. 5 l Children playing 1.00 1.00

European Security and Cooperation Conference, Helsinki, July 30-Aug. 1. No. C198b inscribed "posta aeriana."

An imperf. 10 l souvenir sheet exists showing Helsinki on map of Europe.

Red Cross Type of 1976

Design: Blood donors, Red Cross plane.

1976, Apr. 20 Photo. *Perf. 13½*

C199 A790 3.35 l multi .70 .35

De Havilland DH-9 AP71

Airplanes: 40b, I.C.A.R. Comercial. 60b, Douglas DC-3. 1.75 l, AN-24. 2.75 l, IL-62. 3.60 l, Boeing 707.

1976, June 24 Photo. *Perf. 13½*

C200 AP71 20b blue & multi .15 .15
C201 AP71 40b blue & multi .15 .15
C202 AP71 60b multi .18 .15
C203 AP71 1.75 l multi .50 .15
C204 AP71 2.75 l blue & multi .70 .20
C205 AP71 3.60 l multi 1.00 .50
Nos. C200-C205 (6) 2.68
Set value .95

Romanian Airline, 50th anniversary.

Glider I.C.A.R.-1 — AP72

Gliders: 40b, I.S.-3d. 55b, R.G.-5. 1.50 l, I.S.-11. 3 l, I.S.-29D. 3.40 l, I.S.-28B.

1977, Feb. 20 Photo. *Perf. 13*

C206 AP72 20b multi .15 .15
C207 AP72 40b multi .15 .15
C208 AP72 55b multi .15 .15
C209 AP72 1.50 l bl & multi .25 .15
C210 AP72 3 l multi .60 .15
C211 AP72 3.40 l multi .95 .25
Nos. C206-C211 (6) 2.25
Set value .62

Souvenir Sheet

Boeing 707 over Bucharest Airport and Pioneers — AP73

1977, June 28 Photo. *Perf. 13½*

C212 AP73 10 l multi 2.50 2.50

European Security and Cooperation Conference, Belgrade.

An imperf. 10 l souvenir sheet exists showing Boeing 707, map of Europe and buildings.

Woman Letter Carrier, Mailbox AP74

30 l, Plane, newspapers, letters, packages.

1977 Photo. *Perf. 13½*

C213 AP74 20 l multicolored 4.00 1.25
C214 AP74 30 l multicolored 5.75 2.50

Issue dates: 20 l, July 25, 30 l, Sept. 10.

LZ-1 over Friedrichshafen, 1900 — AP75

Airships: 1 l, Santos Dumont's dirigible over Paris, 1901. 1.50 l, British R-34 over New York and Statue of Liberty, 1919. 2.15 l, Italia over North Pole, 1928. 3.40 l, Zeppelin LZ-127 over Brasov, 1929. 4.80 l, Zeppelin over Sibiu, 1929. 10 l, Zeppelin over Bucharest, 1929.

1978, Mar. 20 Photo. *Perf. 13½*

C215 AP75 60b multi .15 .15
C216 AP75 1 l multi .15 .15
C217 AP75 1.50 l multi .24 .15
C218 AP75 2.15 l multi .32 .15
C219 AP75 3.40 l multi .60 .15
C220 AP75 4.80 l multi 1.25 .24
Nos. C215-C220 (6) 2.71
Set value .74

Souvenir Sheet

C221 AP75 10 l multi 2.75 2.75

History of airships. No. C221 contains one stamp 50x37½mm.

Soccer Type of 1978
Souvenir Sheet

Design: 10 l, Two soccer players and Argentina '78 emblem.

1978, Apr. 15 Photo. *Perf. 13½*

C222 A818 10 l blue & multi 2.50 2.50

11th World Cup Soccer Championship, Argentina, June 1-25. No. C222 contains one stamp 37x50mm. A 10 l imperf. souvenir sheet exists showing goalkeeper.

Wilbur and Orville Wright, Flyer A AP76

Aviation History: 1 l, Louis Blériot and his plane over English Channel, 1909. 1.50 l, Anthony Fokker and Fokker F-VII trimotor, 1926. 2.15 l, Andrei N. Tupolev and ANT-25 monoplane, 1937. 3 l, Otto Lilienthal and glider, 1891-96. 3.40 l, Traian Vuia and his plane, Montesson, France, 1906. 4.80 l, Aurel Vlaicu and 1st Romanian plane, 1910. 10 l, Henri Coanda and his "jet," 1910.

1978, Dec. 18 Photo. *Perf. 13½*

C223 AP76 55b multi .15 .15
C224 AP76 1 l multi .15 .15
C225 AP76 1.50 l multi .22 .15
C226 AP76 2.15 l multi .35 .15
C227 AP76 3 l multi .50 .15
C228 AP76 3.40 l multi .60 .15
C229 AP76 4.80 l multi .75 .20
Nos. C223-C229 (7) 2.72
Set value .65

Souvenir Sheet

C230 AP76 10 l multi 2.50 2.50

No. C230 contains one stamp 50x38mm.

Inter-Europa Type of 1979

Design: 3.40 l, Jet, mail truck and motorcycle.

1979, May 3 Photo. *Perf. 13*

C231 A835 3.40 l multi .60 .18

Animal Type of 1980
Souvenir Sheet

1980, Mar. 25 Photo. *Perf. 13½*

C232 A852 10 l Pelicans 2.25 2.25

No. C232 contains one stamp 38x50mm.

Mercury — AP77

1981, June 30 Photo. *Perf. 13½*

C233 AP77 55b shown .15 .15
C234 AP77 1 l Venus, Earth, Mars .15 .15
C235 AP77 1.50 l Jupiter .18 .15
C236 AP77 2.15 l Saturn .28 .15
C237 AP77 3.40 l Uranus .45 .15
C238 AP77 4.80 l Neptune, Pluto .60 .30
Nos. C233-C238 (6) 1.81
Set value .75

Souvenir Sheet

C239 AP77 10 l Earth 2.00 2.00

No. C239 contains one stamp 37x50mm. An imperf. 10 l souvenir sheet exists showing planets in orbit.

Romanian-Russian Space Cooperation — AP78

1981 Photo. *Perf. 13½*

C240 AP78 55b Soyuz 40 .15 .15
C241 AP78 3.40 l Salyut 6, Soyuz 40 .40 .22
Set value .26

Souvenir Sheet

C242 AP78 10 l Cosmonauts, spacecraft 2.00 2.00

No. C242 contains one stamp 50x39mm. Issue dates: 55b, 3.40 l, May 14; 10 l, June 30.

Children's Games Type of 1981

1981, Nov. 25

C243 A880 4.80 l Flying model planes .52 .30

Standard Glider — AP79

1982, June 20 Photo. *Perf. 13½*

C244 AP79 50b shown .15 .15
C245 AP79 1 l Excelsior D .15 .15
C246 AP79 1.50 l Dedal I .22 .15
C247 AP79 2.50 l Enthusiast .30 .15
C248 AP79 4 l AK-22 .50 .24
C249 AP79 5 l Grifrom .70 .30
Nos. C244-C249 (6) 2.02
Set value .85

Agriculture Type of 1982

1982, June 29

C250 A888 4 l Helicopter spraying insecticide .60 .30

Vlaicu's Glider, 1909 AP80

Aurel Vlaicu (1882-19), Aviator: 1 l, Memorial, Banesti-Prahova, vert. 2.50 l, Hero Aviators Memorial, by Kotzebue and Fekete, vert. 3 l, Vlaicu-1 glider, 1910.

1982, Sept. 27 Photo. *Perf. 13½*

C251 AP80 50b multi .15 .15
C252 AP80 1 l multi .15 .15
C253 AP80 2.50 l multi .38 .15
C254 AP80 3 l multi .45 .15
Nos. C251-C254 (4) 1.13
Set value .32

25th Anniv. of Space Flight AP81

Designs: 50b, H. Coanda, reaction motor, 1910. 1 l, H. Oberth, rocket, 1923. 1.50 l, Sputnik I, 1957. 2.50 l, Vostok I, 1961. 4 l, Apollo 11, 1969. 5 l, Columbia space shuttle, 1982. 10 l, Globe.

1983, Jan. 24

C255 AP81 50b multi .15 .15
C256 AP81 1 l multi .15 .15
C257 AP81 1.50 l multi .20 .15
C258 AP81 2.50 l multi .32 .15
C259 AP81 4 l multi .50 .25
C260 AP81 5 l multi .65 .30
Nos. C255-C260 (6) 1.97
Set value .88

Souvenir Sheet

C261 AP81 10 l multi 1.90 1.90

No. C261 contains one stamp 41x53mm.

First Romanian-built Jet Airliner — AP82

1983, Jan. 25 Photo. *Perf. 13½*

C262 AP82 11 l Rombac 1-11 1.75 .70

World Communications Year — AP83

1983, July 25 Photo. *Perf. 13½*

C263 AP83 2 l Boeing 707, Postal van .45 .15

40th Anniv., Intl. Civil Aviation Organization — AP84

1984, Aug. 15 Photo. *Perf. 13½*

C265 AP84 50b Lockheed L-14 .15 .15
C266 AP84 1.50 l BN-2 Islander .24 .15
C267 AP84 3 l Rombac .45 .24
C268 AP84 6 l Boeing 707 .90 .45
Nos. C265-C268 (4) 1.74
Set value .85

Halley's Comet — AP85

1986, Jan. 27 Photo. *Perf. 13½*

C269 AP85 2 l shown .30 .15
C270 AP85 4 l Space probes .60 .30

An imperf. 10 l air post souvenir sheet exists showing comet and space probes, red control number.

Souvenir Sheet

Plane of Alexandru Papana, 1936 — AP86

1986, May 15 Photo. *Perf. 13½*

C271 AP86 10 l multi 2.75 2.75

AMERIPEX '86.

Aircraft AP87

1987, Aug. 10

C272 AP87 50b Henri Auguste glider, 1909 .15 .15
C273 AP87 1 l Sky diver, IS-28 B2 glider .18 .15
C274 AP87 2 l IS-29 D-2 glider .35 .18
C275 AP87 3 l IS-32 glider .55 .28
C276 AP87 4 l IAR-35 glider .70 .35
C277 AP87 5 l IS-28 M2, route .90 .45
Nos. C272-C277 (6) 2.83 1.56

1st Moon Landing, 20th Anniv. — AP88

Designs: 50b, C. Haas. 1.50 l, Konstantin Tsiolkovski (1857-1935), Soviet rocket science pioneer. 2 l, H. Oberth and equations. 3 l, Robert Goddard and diagram on blackboard. 4 l, Sergei Korolev (1906-66), Soviet aeronautical engineer. 5 l, Wernher von Braun (1912-77), lunar module.

1989, Oct. 25 Photo. *Perf. 13½*

C278 AP88 50b multicolored .15 .15
C279 AP88 1.50 l multicolored .35 .22
C280 AP88 2 l multicolored .50 .32
C281 AP88 3 l multicolored .80 .45
C282 AP88 4 l multicolored 1.00 .60
C283 AP88 5 l multicolored 1.10 .75
Nos. C278-C283 (6) 3.90 2.49

A 10 l souvenir sheet picturing Armstrong and *Eagle* lunar module was also issued.

Souvenir Sheet

World Stamp Expo '89, Washington, DC, Nov. 17-Dec. 3 — AP89

1989, Nov. 17 Photo. *Perf. 13½*

C284 AP89 5 l Postal coach 2.00 1.00

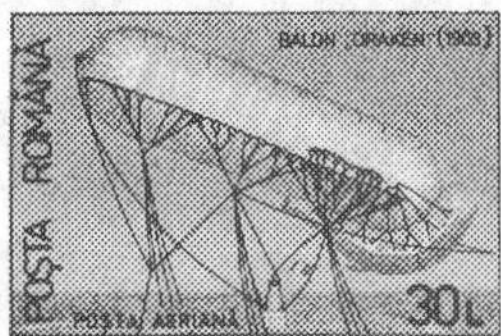

Captured Balloons — AP90

Balloons captured by Romanian army: 30 l, German balloon, Draken, 1903. 90 l, French balloon, Caquot, 1917.

1993, Feb. 26 Photo. *Perf. 13½*

C285 AP90 30 l multicolored .25 .25
C286 AP90 90 l multicolored .90 .90

Souvenir Sheet

European Inventions, Discoveries — AP91

Europa: a, 240 l, Hermann Oberth (1894-1989), rocket scientist. b, 2100 l, Henri Doanda (1886-1972), aeronautical engineer. Illustration reduced.

1994, May 25 Photo. *Perf. 13*

C287 AP91 Sheet of 2, #a.-b. + 2 labels 7.50 7.50

ICAO, 50th Anniv. AP92

Aircraft: 110 l, Traian Vuia, 1906. 350 l, Rombac 1-11. 500 l, Boeing 737-300. 635 l, Airbus A310.

1994. Aug. 12 Photo. *Perf. 13*

C288 AP92 110 l multicolored .28 .15
C289 AP92 350 l multicolored .90 .45
C290 AP92 500 l multicolored 1.25 .60
C291 AP92 635 l multicolored 1.65 .85
Nos. C288-C291 (4) 4.08 2.05

French-Romanian Aeronautical Agreement, 75th Anniv. — AP93

1995, Mar. 31 Photo. *Perf. 13x13½*

C292 AP93 60 l shown .20 .15
C293 AP93 960 l Biplane Potez IX 2.75 1.40

AIR POST SEMI-POSTAL STAMPS

Catalogue values for unused stamps in this section are for Never Hinged items.

Corneliu Codreanu SPAP1

Unwmk.

1940, Dec. 1 Photo. *Perf. 14*

CB1 SPAP1 20 l + 5 l Prus grn 1.10 1.10

Propaganda for the Rome-Berlin Axis.

No. CB1 exists with overprint "1 Mai 1941 Jamboreea Nationala."

Plane over Sinaia SPAP2

Designs: 200 l+800 l, Plane over Mountains.

1945, Oct. 1 Wmk. 276 *Imperf.*

CB2	SPAP2	80 l + 420 l gray	.70	.70
CB3	SPAP2	200 l + 800 l ultra	.70	.70

16th Congress of the General Assoc. of Romanian Engineers.

Souvenir Sheet

Re-distribution of Land — SPAP4

1946, May 4 Photo. *Perf. 14*

CB4	SPAP4	80 l blue	3.00	3.75

Agrarian reform law of Mar. 23, 1945. The sheet sold for 100 lei.

Souvenir Sheet

Plane Skywriting — SPAP5

1946, May 1 *Perf. 13*

CB5	SPAP5	200 l bl & brt red	3.75	4.50

Labor Day. The sheet sold for 10,000 lei.

Lockheed 12 Electra — SPAP6

1946, Sept. 1 *Perf. $11^1/_2$*

CB6	SPAP6	300 l + 1200 l dp bl	1.25	1.25

For se-tenant see No. C26a and note after No. C26.

The surtax was for the Office of Popular Sports.

Miniature Sheet

Women of Wallachia, Transylvania and Moldavia — SPAP7

1946, Dec. 20 Wmk. 276 *Imperf.*

CB7	SPAP7	500 l + 9500 l choc & red	1.90	2.25

Democratic Women's Org. of Romania.

SPAP8

1946, Oct. *Imperf.*

CB8	SPAP8	300 l deep plum	7.00	5.25

The surtax was for the Office of Popular Sports. Sheets of four. Stamp sold for 1300 l.

Laborer with Torch — SPAP9

1947, Mar. 1

CB9	SPAP9	3000 l + 7000 l choc	.40	.40

Sheets of four with marginal inscription.

Plane SPAP10

Plane above Shore Line SPAP11

1947, June 27 *Imperf.*

CB10	SPAP10	15,000 l + 15,000 l	.40	.40

Sheets of four with marginal inscription.

1947, May 1 *Perf. 14x13*

CB11	SPAP11	3000 l + 12,000 l bl	.30	.30

Planes over Mountains SPAP12

Plane over Athletic Field SPAP13

1947, Oct. 5 *Perf. $14x14^1/_2$*

CB12	SPAP12	5 l + 5 l blue	.60	.20

17th Congress of the General Assoc. of Romanian Engineers.

Perf. $13^1/_2$

1948, Feb. 20 Photo. Wmk. 276

CB13	SPAP13	7 l + 7 l vio	.80	.45

Imperf

CB14	SPAP13	10 l + 10 l Prus grn	1.10	.65

Balkan Games. Sheets of four with marginal inscription.

Swallow and Plane SPAP14

1948, Mar. 15 *Perf. $14x13^1/_2$*

CB15	SPAP14	12 l + 12 l blue	.90	.50

Bucharest-Moscow Passenger Plane, Douglas DC-3 Dakota — SPAP15

1948, Oct. 29 *Perf. 14*

CB16	SPAP15	20 l + 20 l dp bl	7.50	7.50

Printed in sheets of 8 stamps and 16 small, red brown labels. Sheet yields 8 triptychs, each comprising 1 stamp flanked by label with Bucharest view and label with Moscow view.

Douglas DC-4 — SPAP16

1948, May 1 *Perf. $13^1/_2x14$*

CB17	SPAP16	20 l + 20 l blue	6.75	5.75

Issued to publicize Labor Day, May 1, 1948.

Pursuit Plane and Victim SPAP17

Launching Model Plane SPAP18

1948, May 9 *Perf. 13*

CB18	SPAP17	3 l + 3 l shown	3.25	2.25
CB19	SPAP17	5 l + 5 l Bomber	3.50	2.75

Issued to honor the Romanian army.

1948, Dec. 31 *Perf. $13x13^1/_2$*

CB20	SPAP18	20 l + 20 l dp ultra	9.75	9.75

Imperf

CB21	SPAP18	20 l + 20 l Prus bl	9.75	9.75

Nos. CB20 and CB21 were issued in sheets of four stamps, with ornamental border and "1948" in contrasting color.

UPU Type of Air Post Issue, 1963

Design: 1.60 l+50b, Globe, map of Romania, planes and UPU monument.

Perf. $14x13^1/_2$

1963, Nov. 15 Litho. Unwmk.

Size: 75x27mm

CB22	AP54	1.60 l + 50b multi	1.40	.50

Surtax for the Romanian Philatelic Federation.

POSTAGE DUE STAMPS

D1

Perf. 11, $11^1/_2$, $13^1/_2$ and Compound

1881 Typo. Unwmk.

J1	D1	2b brown	4.00	1.25
J2	D1	5b brown	22.50	2.00
a.		Tête bêche pair	*190.00*	*75.00*
J3	D1	10b brown	30.00	1.25
J4	D1	30b brown	32.50	1.25
J5	D1	50b brown	26.00	2.50
J6	D1	60b brown	21.00	3.00
		Nos. J1-J6 (6)	136.00	11.25

1885

J7	D1	10b pale red brown	8.00	.50
J8	D1	30b pale red brown	8.00	.50

1887-90

J9	D1	2b gray green	4.00	.75
J10	D1	5b gray green	8.00	3.00
J11	D1	10b gray green	8.00	3.00
J12	D1	30b gray green	8.00	.75
		Nos. J9-J12 (4)	28.00	7.50

1888

J14	D1	2b green, *yellowish*	.90	.75
J15	D1	5b green, *yellowish*	2.25	2.25
J16	D1	10b green, *yellowish*	32.50	2.75
J17	D1	30b green, *yellowish*	17.50	1.25
		Nos. J14-J17 (4)	53.15	7.00

1890-96 Wmk. 163

J18	D1	2b emerald	1.65	.45
J19	D1	5b emerald	.80	.45
J20	D1	10b emerald	1.25	.45
J21	D1	30b emerald	2.00	.45
J22	D1	50b emerald	6.50	.95
J23	D1	60b emerald	8.75	3.25
		Nos. J18-J23 (6)	20.95	6.00

1898 Wmk. 200

J24	D1	2b blue green	.70	.40
J25	D1	5b blue green	.90	.30
J26	D1	10b blue green	1.40	.30
J27	D1	30b blue green	1.90	.30
J28	D1	50b blue green	4.75	.90
J29	D1	60b blue green	5.50	1.75
		Nos. J24-J29 (6)	15.15	3.95

1902-10 Unwmk.

Thin Paper, Tinted Rose on Back

J30	D1	2b green	.80	.25
J31	D1	5b green	.50	.15
J32	D1	10b green	.40	.15
J33	D1	30b green	.50	.15
J34	D1	50b green	2.50	.95
J35	D1	60b green	5.25	2.25
		Nos. J30-J35 (6)	9.95	3.90

1908-11

White Paper

J36	D1	2b green	.80	.50
J37	D1	5b green	.60	.50
a.		Tête bêche pair	12.00	12.00
J38	D1	10b green	.40	.30
a.		Tête bêche pair	12.00	12.00
J39	D1	30b green	.50	.30
a.		Tête bêche pair	12.00	12.00
J40	D1	50b green	2.00	1.25
		Nos. J36-J40 (5)	4.30	2.85

D2

1911 Wmk. 165

J41	D2	2b dark blue, *green*	.15	.15
J42	D2	5b dark blue, *green*	.15	.15
J43	D2	10b dark blue, *green*	.15	.15
J44	D2	15b dark blue, *green*	.15	.15
J45	D2	20b dark blue, *green*	.15	.15
J46	D2	30b dark blue, *green*	.25	.25
J47	D2	50b dark blue, *green*	.30	.30
J48	D2	60b dark blue, *green*	.40	.40
J49	D2	2 l dark blue, *green*	.80	.80
		Nos. J41-J49 (9)	2.50	2.50

The letters "P.R." appear to be embossed instead of watermarked. They are often faint or entirely invisible.

The 20b, type D2, has two types, differing in the width of the head of the "2." This affects Nos. J45, J54, J58, and J63.

See Nos. J52-J77, J82, J87-J88. For overprints see Nos. J78-J81, RAJ1-RAJ2, RAJ20-RAJ21, 3NJ1-3NJ7.

Regular Issue of 1908 Overprinted

TAXA
DEPLATA

1918 Unwmk.

J50	A46	5b yellow green	.75	.25
a.		Inverted overprint	5.00	5.00
J51	A46	10b rose	.75	.25
a.		Inverted overprint	3.75	3.75

Postage Due Type of 1911

1920 Wmk. 165

J52	D2	5b black, *green*	.22	.15
J53	D2	10b black, *green*	.18	.15
J54	D2	20b black, *green*	4.00	.60
J55	D2	30b black, *green*	1.10	.38
J55A	D2	50b black, *green*	3.00	.90
		Nos. J52-J55A (5)	8.50	2.18

Perf. $11^1/_2$, $13^1/_2$ and Compound

1919 Unwmk.

J56	D2	5b black, *green*	.30	.15
J57	D2	10b black, *green*	.30	.15
J58	D2	20b black, *green*	1.00	.15

J59 D2 30b black, *green* .90 .15
J60 D2 50b black, *green* 2.25 .40
Nos. J56-J60 (5) 4.75
Set value .75

1920-26

White Paper

J61 D2 5b black .15 .15
J62 D2 10b black .15 .15
J63 D2 20b black .15 .15
J64 D2 30b black .25 .25
J65 D2 50b black .40 .40
J66 D2 60b black .15 .15
J67 D2 1 l black .30 .30
J68 D2 2 l black .20 .20
J69 D2 3 l black ('26) .20 .20
J70 D2 6 l black ('26) .30 .30
Nos. J61-J70 (10) 2.25 2.25

1923-24

J74 D2 1 l black, *pale green* .24 .15
J75 D2 2 l black, *pale green* .42 .22
J76 D2 3 l black, *pale green* ('24) 1.10 .55
J77 D2 6 l blk, *pale green* ('24) 1.40 .55
Nos. J74-J77 (4) 3.16 1.47

Postage Due Stamps of 1920-26 Overprinted **8 IUNIE 1930**

1930 *Perf. 13½*

J78 D2 1 l black .15 .15
J79 D2 2 l black .18 .15
J80 D2 3 l black .30 .15
J81 D2 6 l black .45 .24
Nos. J78-J81 (4) 1.08
Set value .56

Accession of King Carol II.

Catalogue values for unused stamps in this section, from this point to the end of the section, are for Never Hinged items.

Type of 1911 Issue

1931 **Wmk. 225**

J82 D2 2 l black .70 .35

D3

1932-37 **Wmk. 230**

J83 D3 1 l black .15 .15
J84 D3 2 l black .15 .15
J85 D3 3 l black ('37) .15 .15
J86 D3 6 l black ('37) .15 .15
Set value .42 .28

See Nos. J89-J98.

Type of 1911

1942 **Typo.** *Perf. 13½*

J87 D2 50 l black .24 .18
J88 D2 100 l black .38 .24

Type of 1932

1946-47 **Unwmk.** *Perf. 14*

J89 D3 20 l black .60 .55
J90 D3 100 l black ('47) .45 .24
J91 D3 200 l black 1.10 .55
Nos. J89-J91 (3) 2.15 1.34

1946-47 **Wmk. 276**

J92 D3 20 l black .20 .15
J93 D3 50 l black .20 .15
J94 D3 80 l black .20 .15
J95 D3 100 l black .25 .20
J96 D3 200 l black .45 .35
J97 D3 500 l black .60 .50
J98 D3 5000 l black ('47) 2.50 1.25
Nos. J92-J98 (7) 4.40 2.75

Crown and King Michael D3a

Perf. 14½x13½

1947 **Typo.** **Wmk. 276**

J98A D3a 2 l carmine .40 .15
J98B D3a 4 l gray blue .75 .30
J98C D3a 5 l black 1.10 .45
J98D D3a 10 l violet brown 2.00 .75
Nos. J98A-J98D (4) 4.25 1.65

Same Overprinted  

1948

J98E D3a 2 l carmine .30 .15
J98F D3a 4 l gray blue .60 .25
J98G D3a 5 l black .75 .30
J98H D3a 10 l violet brown 1.50 .55
Nos. J98E-J98H (4) 3.15 1.25

In use, Nos. J98A-J106 and following issues were torn apart, one half being affixed to the postage due item and the other half being pasted into the postman's record book. Values are for unused and canceled-to-order pairs.

Communications Badge and Postwoman — D4

1950 **Unwmk.** **Photo.** *Perf. 14½x14*

J99 D4 2 l orange vermilion .70 .70
J100 D4 4 l deep blue .70 .70
J101 D4 5 l dark gray green .90 .90
J102 D4 10 l orange brown 1.10 1.10

Wmk. 358

J103 D4 2 l orange vermilion 1.00 .70
J104 D4 4 l deep blue 1.00 .70
J105 D4 5 l dark gray green 1.50 .90
J106 D4 10 l orange brown 2.00 1.25
Nos. J99-J106 (8) 8.90 6.95

Postage Due Stamps of 1950 Surcharged with New Values in Black or Carmine

1952 **Unwmk.**

J107 D4 4b on 2 l .24 .24
J108 D4 10b on 4 l (C) .24 .24
J109 D4 20b on 5 l (C) .45 .45
J110 D4 50b on 10 l .75 .75
Nos. J107-J110 (4) 1.68 1.68

Wmk. 358

J111 D4 4b on 2 l
J112 D4 10b on 4 l (C)
J113 D4 20b on 5 l (C) *2.50 1.25*
J114 D4 50b on 10 l *3.00 1.25*

The existence of Nos. J111-J112 has been questioned.

See note after No. J98H.

General Post Office and Post Horn — D5

1957 **Wmk. 358** *Perf. 14*

J115 D5 3b black .15 .15
J116 D5 5b red orange .15 .15
J117 D5 10b red lilac .15 .15
J118 D5 20b brt red .15 .15
J119 D5 40b lt bl grn .35 .15
J120 D5 1 l brt ultra 1.00 .16
Nos. J115-J120 (6) 1.95
Set value .45

See note after No. J98H.

General Post Office and Post Horn — D6

1967, Feb. 25 **Photo.** *Perf. 13*

J121 D6 3b brt grn .15 .15
J122 D6 5b brt bl .15 .15
J123 D6 10b lilac rose .15 .15
J124 D6 20b vermilion .15 .15
J125 D6 40b brown .20 .15
J126 D6 1 l violet .55 .15
Set value .95 .32

See note after No. J98H.

1970, Mar. 10 **Unwmk.**

J127 D6 3b brt grn .15 .15
J128 D6 5b brt bl .15 .15
J129 D6 10b lilac rose .15 .15
J130 D6 20b vermilion .15 .15
J131 D6 40b brown .18 .15
J132 D6 1 l violet .35 .15
Set value .74 .30

See note after No. J98H.

Symbols of Communications — D7

Designs: 10b, Like 5b. 20b, 40b, Pigeons, head of Mercury and post horn. 50b, 1 l, General Post Office, post horn and truck.

1974, Jan. 1 **Photo.** *Perf. 13*

J133 D7 5b brt bl .15 .15
J134 D7 10b olive .15 .15
J135 D7 20b lilac rose .15 .15
J136 D7 40b purple .15 .15
J137 D7 50b brown .18 .15
J138 D7 1 l orange .35 .15
Set value .75 .35

See note after No. J98H.

1982, Dec. 23 **Photo.** *Perf. 13½*

J139 D7 25b like #J135 .15 .15
J140 D7 50b like #J133 .15 .15
J141 D7 1 l like #J135 .18 .15
J142 D7 2 l like #J137 .35 .15
J143 D7 3 l like #J133 .52 .15
J144 D7 4 l like #J137 .70 .22
Nos. J139-J144 (6) 2.05
Set value .62

See note after No. J98H.

Post Horn — D8

1992, Feb. 3 **Photo.** *Perf. 13½*

J145 D8 4 l red .24 .15
J146 D8 8 l blue .48 .18

See note after No. J98H.

OFFICIAL STAMPS

Catalogue values for unused stamps in this section are for Never Hinged items.

Eagle Carrying National Emblem — O1

Coat of Arms — O2

1929 **Photo.** **Wmk. 95** *Perf. 13½*

O1 O1 25b red orange .25 .15
O2 O1 50b dk brown .25 .15
O3 O1 1 l dk violet .30 .15
O4 O1 2 l olive grn .30 .15
O5 O1 3 l rose car .45 .15
O6 O1 4 l dk olive .45 .15
O7 O1 6 l Prus blue 2.50 .15
O8 O1 10 l deep blue .80 .15
O9 O1 25 l carmine brn 1.65 1.25
O10 O1 50 l purple 4.75 3.50
Nos. O1-O10 (10) 11.70 5.95

Type of Official Stamps of 1929 Overprinted **8 IUNIE 1930**

1930 **Unwmk.**

O11 O1 25b red orange .20 .15
O12 O1 50b dk brown .20 .15
O13 O1 1 l dk violet .35 .15
O14 O1 3 l rose carmine .50 .15
Nos. O11-O14 (4) 1.25
Set value .35

Nos. O11-O14 were not placed in use without overprint.

Same Overprint on Nos. O1-O10

Wmk. 95

O15 O1 25b red orange .25 .15
O16 O1 50b dk brown .25 .15
O17 O1 1 l dk violet .25 .15
O18 O1 2 l dp green .25 .15
O19 O1 3 l rose carmine .60 .15
O20 O1 4 l olive black .75 .15
O21 O1 6 l Prus blue 2.00 .15
O22 O1 10 l deep blue .80 .15
O23 O1 25 l carmine brown 3.00 2.50
O24 O1 50 l purple 4.00 3.50
Nos. O15-O24 (10) 12.15 7.20

Accession of King Carol II to the throne of Romania (Nos O11-O24).

Perf. 13½, 13½x14½

1931-32 **Typo.** **Wmk. 225**

O25 O2 25b black .30 .15
O26 O2 1 l lilac .30 .20
O27 O2 2 l emerald .60 .40
O28 O2 3 l rose 1.00 .70
Nos. O25-O28 (4) 2.20 1.45

1932 **Wmk. 230** *Perf. 13½*

O29 O2 25b black .30 .25
O30 O2 1 l violet .40 .35
O31 O2 2 l emerald .65 .55
O32 O2 3 l rose .80 .65
O33 O2 6 l red brown 1.25 1.00
Nos. O29-O33 (5) 3.40 2.80

PARCEL POST STAMPS

PP1

Perf. 11½, 13½ and Compound

1895 **Wmk. 163** **Typo.**

Q1 PP1 25b brown red 12.50 2.25

1896

Q2 PP1 25b vermilion 10.00 1.25

Perf. 13½ and 11½x13½

1898 **Wmk. 200**

Q3 PP1 25b brown red 7.00 1.25
a. Tête bêche pair
Q4 PP1 25b vermilion 7.00 .90

Thin Paper
Tinted Rose on Back

1905 **Unwmk.** *Perf. 11½*

Q5 PP1 25b vermilion 6.00 1.25

1911 **White Paper**

Q6 PP1 25b pale red 6.00 1.25

No. 263 Surcharged in Carmine **FACTAJ 5 LEI**

1928 *Perf. 13½*

Q7 A54 5 l on 10b yellow green .90 .15

POSTAL TAX STAMPS

Regular Issue of 1908 Overprinted **TIMBRU DE AJUTOR**

Perf. 11½, 13½, 11½x13½

1915 **Unwmk.**

RA1 A46 5b green .18 .15
RA2 A46 10b rose .30 .15
Set value .16

The "Timbru de Ajutor" stamps represent a tax on postal matter. The money obtained from their sale was turned into a fund for the assistance of soldiers' families.

Until 1923 the only "Timbru de Ajutor" stamps used for postal purposes were the 5b and 10b. Stamps of higher values with this inscription were used to pay the taxes on railway and theater tickets and other fiscal taxes. In 1923 the postal rate was advanced to 25b.

The Queen Weaving — PT1

1916-18 **Typo.**
RA3 PT1 5b gray blk .18 .15
RA4 PT1 5b green ('18) .45 .15
RA5 PT1 10b brown .30 .15
RA6 PT1 10b gray blk ('18) .45 .15
Nos. RA3-RA6 (4) 1.38
Set value .45

For overprints see Nos. RA7-RA8, RAJ7-RAJ9, 3NRA1-3NRA8.

Stamps of 1916 Overprinted in Red or Black

1918 ***Perf. 13½***
RA7 PT1 5b gray blk (R) .38 .24
a. Double overprint 5.00
c. Black overprint 5.00
RA8 PT1 10b brn (Bk) .45 .24
a. Double overprint 5.00
b. Double overprint, one inverted 5.00
c. Inverted overprint 5.00

Same Overprint on RA1 and RA2

1919
RA11 A46 5b yel grn (R) *19.00 12.50*
RA12 A46 10b rose (Bk) *19.00 12.50*

Charity — PT3

Perf. 13½, 11½, 13½x11½
1921-24 **Typo.** **Unwmk.**
RA13 PT3 10b green .15 .15
RA14 PT3 25b blk ('24) .15 .15
Set value .20 .15

Type of 1921-24 Issue

1928 **Wmk. 95**
RA15 PT3 25b black .75 .25

Nos. RA13, RA14 and RA15 are the only stamps of type PT3 issued for postal purposes. Other denominations were used fiscally.

Catalogue values for unused stamps in this section, from this point to the end of the section, are for Never Hinged items.

Airplane PT4 — Head of Aviator PT5

1931 **Photo.** **Unwmk.**
RA16 PT4 50b Prus bl .30 .15
a. Double impression 15.00
RA17 PT4 1 l dk red brn .30 .15
RA18 PT4 2 l ultra .60 .15
Nos. RA16-RA18 (3) 1.20
Set value .20

The use of these stamps, in addition to the regular postage, was obligatory on all postal matter for the interior of the country. The money thus obtained was to augment the National Fund for Aviation. When the stamps were not used to prepay the special tax, it was collected by means of Postal Tax Due stamps Nos. RAJ20 and RAJ21.

Nos. RA17 and RA18 were also used for other than postal tax.

1932 **Wmk. 230** ***Perf. 14 x 13½***
RA19 PT5 50b Prus bl .22 .15
RA20 PT5 1 l red brn .35 .15
RA21 PT5 2 l ultra .45 .15
Nos. RA19-RA21 (3) 1.02
Set value .15

See notes after No. RA18.

After 1937 use of Nos. RA20-RA21 was limited to other than postal matter.

Nos. RA19-RA21 exist imperf.

Two stamps similar to type PT5, but inscribed "Fondul Aviatiei," were issued in 1936: 10b sepia and 20b violet.

Aviator PT6 — King Michael PT7

1937 ***Perf. 13½***
RA22 PT6 50b Prus grn .20 .15
RA23 PT6 1 l red brn .35 .15
RA24 PT6 2 l ultra .40 .15
Nos. RA22-RA24 (3) .95
Set value .15

Stamps overprinted or inscribed "Fondul Aviatiei" other than Nos. RA22, RA23 or RA24 were used to pay taxes on other than postal matters.

1943 **Wmk. 276** **Photo.** ***Perf. 14***
RA25 PT7 50b org ver .15 .15
RA26 PT7 1 l lil rose .15 .15
RA27 PT7 2 l brown .15 .15
RA28 PT7 4 l lt ultra .15 .15
RA29 PT7 5 l dull lilac .15 .15
RA30 PT7 8 l yel grn .15 .15
RA31 PT7 10 l blk brn .15 .15
Set value .60 .60

The tax was obligatory on domestic mail.

Protection of Homeless Children — PT8

1945
RA32 PT8 40 l Prus bl .24 .18

PT9 — "Hope" — PT10

1947 **Unwmk.** **Typo.** ***Perf. 14x14½***
Black Surcharge
RA33 PT9 1 l on 2 l + 2 l pink .30 .25
a. Inverted surcharge
RA34 PT9 5 l on 1 l + 1 l gray grn *4.50 3.75*

1948 ***Perf. 14***
RA35 PT10 1 l rose *1.90* .15
RA36 PT10 1 l rose violet *2.10* .15
Set value .15

A 2 lei blue and 5 lei ocher in type PT10 were issued primarily for revenue purposes.

POSTAL TAX DUE STAMPS

Catalogue values for unused stamps in this section are for Never Hinged items.

Postage Due Stamps of 1911 Overprinted **TIMBRU DE AJUTOR**

Perf. 11½, 13½, 11½x13½
1915 **Unwmk.**
RAJ1 D2 5b dk bl, *grn* .75 .15
RAJ2 D2 10b dk bl, *grn* .75 .15
a. Wmk. 165 10.00 1.00

PTD1 — PTD2

1916 **Typo.** **Unwmk.**
RAJ3 PTD1 5b brn, *grn* .40 .15
RAJ4 PTD1 10b red, *grn* .40 .15
Set value .25

See Nos. RAJ5-RAJ6, RAJ10-RAJ11. For overprint see No. 3NRAJ1.

1918
RAJ5 PTD1 5b red, *grn* .25 .15
a. Wmk. 165 1.00 .25
RAJ6 PTD1 10b brn, *grn* .25 .15
a. Wmk. 165 1.75 .25
Set value .20

Postal Tax Stamps of 1916, Overprinted in Red, Black or Blue **TAXA DE PLATA**

RAJ7 PT1 5b gray blk (R) .40 .15
a. Inverted overprint 7.50
RAJ8 PT1 10b brn (Bk) .80 .15
a. Inverted overprint 7.50
RAJ9 PT1 10b brn (Bl) *5.00 5.00*
a. Vertical overprint *20.00 15.00*

Type of 1916

1921
RAJ10 PTD1 5b red .50 .15
RAJ11 PTD1 10b brown .50 .15
Set value .25

1922-25 **Typo.**
Greenish Paper
RAJ12 PTD2 10b brown .15 .15
RAJ13 PTD2 20b brown .15 .15
RAJ14 PTD2 25b brown .15 .15
RAJ15 PTD2 50b brown .15 .15
Nos. RAJ12-RAJ15 (4) .60 .60

1923-26
RAJ16 PTD2 10b lt brn .15 .15
RAJ17 PTD2 20b lt brn .15 .15
RAJ18 PTD2 25b brown ('26) .15 .15
RAJ19 PTD2 50b brown ('26) .15 .15
Nos. RAJ16-RAJ19 (4) .60 .60

J82 and Type of 1911 Postage Due Stamps Overprinted in Red **TIMBRUL AVIATIEI**

1931 **Wmk. 225** ***Perf. 13½***
RAJ20 D2 1 l black .15 .15
RAJ21 D2 2 l black .15 .15
Set value .15

When the Postal Tax stamps for the Aviation Fund issue (Nos. RA16 to RA18) were not used to prepay the obligatory tax on letters, etc., it was collected by affixing Nos. RAJ20 and RAJ21.

OCCUPATION STAMPS

ISSUED UNDER AUSTRIAN OCCUPATION

Emperor Karl of Austria
OS1 — OS2

1917 **Unwmk.** **Engr.** ***Perf. 12½***
1N1 OS1 3b ol gray 1.10 .75
1N2 OS1 5b ol grn .80 .50
1N3 OS1 6b violet .80 .50
1N4 OS1 10b org brn .15 .15
1N5 OS1 12b dp bl 1.00 .60
1N6 OS1 15b brt rose .80 .50
1N7 OS1 20b red brn .15 .15
1N8 OS1 25b ultra .20 .15
1N9 OS1 30b slate .30 .25
1N10 OS1 40b olive bis .30 .25
a. Perf. 11½ 40.00 19.00
b. Perf. 11½x12½ 45.00 20.00
1N11 OS1 50b dp grn .30 .25
1N12 OS1 60b rose .30 .25
1N13 OS1 80b dl bl .15 .15
1N14 OS1 90b dk vio .30 .25
1N15 OS2 2 l rose, *straw* .45 .25
1N16 OS2 3 l grn, *bl* .75 .40
1N17 OS2 4 l rose, *grn* .75 .40
Nos. 1N1-1N17 (17) 8.60 5.75

Nos. 1N1-1N14 have "BANI" surcharged in red.

Nos. 1N1-1N17 also exist imperforate. Value, set $20.

OS3 — OS4

1918
1N18 OS3 3b ol gray .15 .15
1N19 OS3 5b ol grn .20 .15
1N20 OS3 6b violet .24 .24
1N21 OS3 10b org brn .26 .26
1N22 OS3 12b dp bl .20 .20
1N23 OS3 15b brt rose .15 .15
1N24 OS3 20b red brn .15 .15
1N25 OS3 25b ultra .15 .15
1N26 OS3 30b slate .15 .15
1N27 OS3 40b ol bis .20 .20
1N28 OS3 50b dp grn .24 .24
1N29 OS3 60b rose .24 .24
1N30 OS3 80b dl bl .15 .15
1N31 OS3 90b dk vio .20 .22
1N32 OS4 2 l rose, *straw* .24 .24
1N33 OS4 3 l grn, *bl* .30 .30
1N34 OS4 4 l rose, *grn* .30 .30
Nos. 1N18-1N34 (17) 3.52 3.49

Exist. imperf. Value, set $17.50.

The complete series exists with "BANI" or "LEI" inverted, also with those words and the numerals of value inverted. Neither of these sets was regularly issued.

A set of 13 stamps similar to Austria Nos. M69-M81 was prepared for use in Romania in 1918, but not placed in use there. Denominations are in bani. It is reported that they were on sale after the armistice at the Vienna post office for a few days. Value $850.

ISSUED UNDER BULGARIAN OCCUPATION

Dobruja District

Bulgarian Stamps of 1915-16 Overprinted in Red or Blue **Поща въ Ромжния 1916—1917**

1916 **Unwmk.** ***Perf. 11½, 14***
2N1 A20 1s dk blue grn (R) .20 .15
2N2 A23 5s grn & vio brn (R) 1.75 .40
2N3 A24 10s brn & brnsh blk (Bl) .25 .15
2N4 A26 25s indigo & blk (Bl) .25 .15
Nos. 2N1-2N4 (4) 2.45 .85
Set value .65

Many varieties of overprint exist.

ISSUED UNDER GERMAN OCCUPATION

German Stamps of 1905-17 Surcharged **M.V.i.R.** (Red or Black) **15 Bani** (Black)

1917 **Wmk. 125** ***Perf. 14***
3N1 A22 15b on 15pf dk vio (R) 1.00 1.00
3N2 A16 25b on 20pf ultra (Bk) 1.00 1.00
3N3 A16 40b on 30pf org & blk, *buff* (R) 17.50 17.50
Nos. 3N1-3N3 (3) 19.50 19.50

"M.V.iR." are the initials of "Militär Verwaltung in Rumänien" (Military Administration of Romania).

German Stamps of 1905-17 Surcharged **M.V.i.R. 25 Bani**

1917-18

3N4 A16 10b on 10pf car	.55	.55
3N5 A22 15b on 15pf dk vio	4.50	4.50
3N6 A16 25b on 20pf ultra	.75	.75
3N7 A16 40b on 30pf org & blk, *buff*	1.00	1.00
a. "40" omitted	50.00	67.50
Nos. 3N4-3N7 (4)	6.80	6.80

German Stamps of 1905-17 Surcharged

1918

3N8 A16 5b on 5pf grn	.20	.20
3N9 A16 10b on 10pf car	.20	.20
3N10 A22 15b on 15pf dk vio	.20	.20
3N11 A16 25b on 20pf bl vio	.20	.20
a. 25b on 20pf blue	1.50	1.50
3N12 A16 40b on 30pf org & blk, *buff*	.30	.30
Nos. 3N8-3N12 (5)	1.10	1.10

German Stamps of 1905-17 Overprinted

1918

3N13 A16 10pf carmine	7.50	*10.00*
3N14 A22 15pf dk vio	12.50	*15.00*
3N15 A16 20pf blue	1.25	*1.50*
3N16 A16 30pf org & blk, *buff*	10.00	*12.50*
Nos. 3N13-3N16 (4)	31.25	*39.00*

POSTAGE DUE STAMPS ISSUED UNDER GERMAN OCCUPATION

Postage Due Stamps and Type of Romania Overprinted in Red

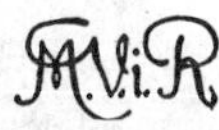

Perf. 11½, 13½ and Compound

1918 **Wmk. 165**

3NJ1 D2 5b dk bl, *grn*	19.00	24.00
3NJ2 D2 10b dk bl, *grn*	26.00	30.00

The 20b, 30b and 50b with this overprint are fraudulent.

Unwmk.

3NJ3 D2 5b dk bl, *grn*	2.50	2.25
3NJ4 D2 10b dk bl, *grn*	2.50	2.25
3NJ5 D2 20b dk bl, *grn*	2.50	2.25
3NJ6 D2 30b dk bl, *grn*	2.50	2.25
3NJ7 D2 50b dk bl, *grn*	2.50	2.25
Nos. 3NJ1-3NJ7 (7)	57.50	65.25

POSTAL TAX STAMPS ISSUED UNDER GERMAN OCCUPATION

Romanian Postal Tax Stamps and Type of 1916

Overprinted in Red or Black

Perf. 11½, 13½ and Compound

1917 **Unwmk.**

3NRA1 PT1 5b gray blk (R)	.15	.15
3NRA2 PT1 10b brown (Bk)	.20	.15

Same, Overprinted

1917-18

3NRA3 PT1 5b gray blk (R)	.40	.15
a. Black overprint	5.00	5.00
3NRA4 PT1 10b brown (Bk)	.40	.15
3NRA5 PT1 10b violet (Bk)	.35	.15
Nos. 3NRA3-3NRA5 (3)	1.15	
Set value		.28

Same, Overprinted in Red or Black

M.V.i.R.

1918

3NRA6 PT1 5b gray blk (R)	*20.00*	
3NRA7 PT1 10b brown (Bk)	*20.00*	

Same, Overprinted

1918

3NRA8 PT1 10b violet (Bk)	.18	.18

POSTAL TAX DUE STAMP ISSUED UNDER GERMAN OCCUPATION

Type of Romanian Postal Tax Due Stamp of 1916 Overprinted

M.V.i.R.

Perf. 11½, 13½, and Compound

1918 **Wmk. 165**

3NRAJ1 PTD1 10b red, *green*	2.00	2.50

ROMANIAN POST OFFICES IN THE TURKISH EMPIRE

40 Paras = 1 Piaster

King Carol I

A1 A2

Perf. 11½, 13½ and Compound

1896 **Wmk. 200**

Black Surcharge

1 A1 10pa on 5b blue	32.50	30.00
2 A2 20pa on 10b emer	24.00	22.50
3 A1 1pia on 25b violet	24.00	22.50
Nos. 1-3 (3)	80.50	75.00

Violet Surcharge

4 A1 10pa on 5b blue	17.00	15.00
5 A2 20pa on 10b emer	17.00	15.00
6 A1 1pia on 25b violet	17.00	15.00
Nos. 4-6 (3)	51.00	45.00

Romanian Stamps of 1908-18 Overprinted in Black or Red

1919 **Typo.** **Unwmk.**

7 A46 5b yellow grn	.40	.40
8 A46 10b rose	.55	.55
9 A46 15b red brown	.55	.55
10 A19 25b dp blue (R)	.70	.70
11 A19 40b gray brn (R)	1.40	1.40
Nos. 7-11 (5)	3.60	3.60

All values exist with inverted overprint.

ROMANIAN POST OFFICES IN THE TURKISH EMPIRE POSTAL TAX STAMP

Romanian Postal Tax Stamp of 1918 Overprinted

Perf. 11½, 11½x13½

1919 **Unwmk.**

RA1 PT1 5b green	1.25	1.25

ROUAD, ILE

ēl–rú–ád

(Arwad)

LOCATION — An island in the Mediterranean, off the coast of Latakia, Syria
GOVT. — French Mandate

In 1916, while a French post office was maintained on Ile Rouad, stamps were issued by France.

25 Centimes = 1 Piaster

Stamps of French Offices in the Levant, 1902-06, Overprinted

ILE ROUAD

Perf. 14x13½

1916, Jan. 12 **Unwmk.**

1	A2	5c green	350.00	175.00
2	A3	10c rose red	350.00	175.00
3	A5	1pi on 25c blue	350.00	175.00

Dangerous counterfeits exist.

Stamps of French Offices in the Levant, 1902-06, Overprinted Horizontally

ILE ROUAD

1916, Dec.

4	A2	1c gray	.60	.60
5	A2	2c violet brown	.60	.60
6	A2	3c red orange	.60	.60
a.		Double overprint	75.00	75.00
7	A2	5c green	.65	.65
8	A3	10c rose	.85	.85
9	A3	15c pale red	1.00	1.00
10	A3	20c brown violet	1.40	1.40
11	A5	1pi on 25c blue	1.40	1.40
12	A3	30c violet	1.40	1.40
13	A4	40c red & pale bl	2.75	2.75
14	A6	2pi on 50c bis brn & lavender	4.25	4.25
15	A6	4pi on 1fr cl & ol grn	7.00	7.00
16	A6	20pi on 5fr dk bl & buff	20.00	20.00
		Nos. 4-16 (13)	42.50	42.50

There is a wide space between the two words of the overprint on Nos. 13 to 16 inclusive. Nos. 4, 5 and 6 are on white and coarse, grayish (G. C.) papers.
(Note on G. C. paper follows France No. 184.)

RUANDA-URUNDI

rü-ˌän-də ü'rün-dē

(Belgian East Africa)

LOCATION — In central Africa, bounded by Congo, Uganda and Tanganyika
GOVT. — Former United Nations trusteeship administered by Belgium
AREA — 20,540 sq. mi.
POP. — 4,700,000 (est. 1958)
CAPITAL — Usumbura

See German East Africa in Vol. 3 for stamps issued under Belgian occupation.
In 1962 the two parts of the trusteeship became independent states, the Republic of Rwanda and the Kingdom of Burundi.

100 Centimes = 1 Franc

Catalogue values for unused stamps in this country are for Never Hinged items, beginning with Scott 151 in the regular postage section, and Scott B26 in the semi-postal section.

Stamps of Belgian Congo, 1923-26, Overprinted

RUANDA
URUNDI

1924-26 *Perf. 12*

6	A32	5c orange yel	.15	.15
7	A32	10c green	.15	.15
8	A32	15c olive brn	.15	.15
9	A32	20c olive grn	.15	.15
10	A44	20c green ('26)	.15	.15
11	A44	25c red brown	.20	.15
12	A44	30c rose red	.15	.15
13	A44	30c olive grn ('25)	.15	.15
14	A32	40c violet ('25)	.20	.20
15	A44	50c gray blue	.15	.15
16	A44	50c buff ('25)	.25	.15
17	A44	75c red org	.25	.25
18	A44	75c gray blue ('25)	.35	.20
19	A44	1fr bister brown	.40	.35
20	A44	1fr dull blue ('26)	.45	.20
21	A44	3fr gray brown	2.50	1.75
22	A44	5fr gray	4.50	3.75
23	A44	10fr gray black	13.00	9.00
		Nos. 6-23 (18)	23.30	17.20

Belgian Congo Nos. 112-113 Overprinted in Red or Black

RUANDA-URUNDI

1925-27 *Perf. 12½*

24	A44	45c dk vio (R) ('27)	.20	.20
25	A44	60c car rose (Bk)	.40	.30

Stamps of Belgian Congo, 1923-1927, Overprinted

RUANDA

URUNDI

1927-29

26	A32	10c green ('29)	.15	.15
27	A32	15c ol brn ('29)	.80	.60
28	A44	35c green	.15	.15
29	A44	75c salmon red	.25	.25
30	A44	1fr rose red	.40	.30
31	A32	1.25fr dull blue	.50	.35
32	A32	1.50fr dull blue	.45	.35
33	A32	1.75fr dull blue	.95	.65

No. 32 Surcharged

1.75

34	A32	1.75fr on 1.50fr dl bl	.45	.40
		Nos. 26-34 (9)	4.10	3.20

Nos. 30 and 33 Surcharged

2

1931

35	A44	1.25fr on 1fr rose red	2.25	1.25
36	A32	2fr on 1.75fr dl bl	3.00	1.75

Porter — A1

Mountain Scene — A2

Designs: 5c, 60c, Porter. 15c, Warrior. 25c, Kraal. 40c, Cattle herders. 50c, Cape buffalo. 75c, Bahutu greeting. 1fr, Barundi women. 1.25fr, Bahutu mother. 1.50fr, 2fr, Making wooden vessel. 2.50fr, 3.25fr, Preparing hides. 4fr, Watuba potter. 5fr, Mututsi dancer. 10fr, Watusi warriors. 20fr, Urundi prince.

1931-38 **Engr.** *Perf. 11½*

37	A1	5c dp lil rose ('38)	.15	.15
38	A2	10c gray	.15	.15
39	A2	15c pale red	.15	.15
40	A2	25c brown vio	.15	.15
41	A1	40c green	.20	.20
42	A2	50c gray lilac	.15	.15
43	A1	60c lilac rose	.15	.15
44	A1	75c gray black	.15	.15
45	A2	1fr rose red	.15	.15
46	A1	1.25fr red brown	.15	.15
47	A2	1.50fr brown vio ('37)	.15	.15
48	A2	2fr deep blue	.20	.15
49	A2	2.50fr dp blue ('37)	.20	.20
50	A2	3.25fr brown vio	.20	.15
51	A2	4fr rose	.25	.25
52	A1	5fr gray	.30	.30
53	A1	10fr brown violet	.50	.40
54	A1	20fr brown	1.50	1.40
		Set value	4.10	3.75

For surcharges see Nos. 56-59.

King Albert Memorial Issue

King Albert — A16

1934 **Photo.**

55	A16	1.50fr black	.45	.45

Stamps of 1931-38 Surcharged in Black

0F60 0F60

1941

56	A1	5c on 40c green	2.25	2.25
57	A2	60c on 50c gray lil	1.50	1.50
58	A2	2.50fr on 1.50fr brn vio	1.50	1.50
59	A2	3.25fr on 2fr dp bl	6.00	6.00
		Nos. 56-59 (4)	11.25	11.25

Belgian Congo No. 173 Overprinted in Black

RUANDA
URUNDI

1941 *Perf. 11*

60	A70	10c light gray	5.00	5.00

Belgian Congo Nos. 179, 181 Overprinted in Black

RUANDA
URUNDI

1941

61	A70	1.75fr orange	3.00	3.00
62	A70	2.75fr vio bl	3.00	3.00

For surcharges see Nos. 64-65.

Belgian Congo No. 168 Surcharged in Black

RUANDA
URUNDI

5 c.

1941 *Perf. 11½*

63	A66	5c on 1.50fr dp red brn & blk	.15	.15

Nos. 61-62 Surcharged with New Values and Bars in Black

1942

64	A70	75c on 1.75fr org	1.10	1.25
65	A70	2.50fr on 2.75fr vio bl	3.00	3.00

Belgian Congo Nos. 167, 183 Surcharged in Black:

RUANDA
URUNDI
75 c.

RUANDA
URUNDI
2.50

1942 *Perf. 11, 11½*

66	A65	75c on 90c car & brn	.70	.65
a.		Inverted surcharge	8.00	8.00
67	A70	2.50fr on 10fr rose red	1.10	.85
a.		Inverted surcharge	6.50	6.50

Oil Palms — A17

Oil Palms — A18

Watusi Chief — A19

Askari — A21

Leopard A20

Zebra — A22

Askari — A23

Design: 100fr, Watusi chief.

1942-43 **Engr.** *Perf. 12½*

68	A17	5c red	.15	.15
69	A18	10c ol grn	.15	.15
70	A18	15c brn car	.15	.15
71	A18	20c dp ultra	.15	.15
72	A18	25c brn vio	.15	.15
73	A18	30c dull blue	.15	.15
74	A18	50c dp grn	.80	.15
75	A18	60c chestnut	.15	.15
76	A19	75c dl lil & blk	.15	.15
77	A19	1fr dk brn & blk	.15	.15
78	A19	1.25fr rose red & blk	.18	.15
79	A20	1.75fr dk gray brn	.60	.35
80	A20	2fr ocher	.60	.28
81	A20	2.50fr carmine	.60	.15
82	A21	3.50fr dk ol grn	.35	.20
83	A21	5fr orange	.40	.25
84	A21	6fr brt ultra	.40	.25
85	A21	7fr black	.40	.32
86	A21	10fr dp brn	.60	.35
87	A21	20fr org brn & blk	1.25	.90
88	A21	50fr red & blk ('43)	1.75	1.10
89	A21	100fr grn & blk ('43)	3.50	2.75
		Nos. 68-89 (22)	12.78	8.55

Miniature sheets of Nos. 72, 76, 77 and 83 were printed in 1944 by the Belgian Government in London and given to the Belgian political review, "Message," which distributed them to its subscribers, one a month. Nos. 68-89 exist imperforate, but have no franking value. Value, set $100.
See note after Belgian Congo No. 225.
For surcharges see Nos. B17-B20.

Baluba Carving of Former King — A25

Carved Figures and Masks of Baluba Tribe: 10c, 50c, 2fr, 10fr, "Ndoha," figure of tribal king. 15c, 70c, 2.50fr, "Tshimanyi," an idol. 20c, 75c, 3.50fr, "Buangakokoma," statue of a kneeling beggar. 25c, 1fr, 5fr, "Mbuta," sacred double cup carved with two faces, Man and Woman. 40c, 1.25fr, 6fr, "Ngadimuashi," female mask. 1.50fr, 50fr, "Buadi-Muadi," mask with squared features (full face). 20fr, 100fr, "Mbowa," executioner's mask with buffalo horns.

1948-50 **Unwmk.** *Perf. 12x12½*

90	A25	10c dp org	.15	.15
91	A25	15c ultra	.15	.15
92	A25	20c brt bl	.15	.15

93 A25 25c rose car .18 .15
94 A25 40c violet .15 .15
95 A25 50c ol brn .15 .15
96 A25 70c yel grn .15 .15
97 A25 75c magenta .15 .15
98 A25 1fr yel org & dk vio .15 .15
99 A25 1.25fr lt bl grn & mag .15 .15
100 A25 1.50fr ol & mag ('50) .48 .35
101 A25 2fr org & mag .15 .15
102 A25 2.50fr brn red & bl grn .15 .15
103 A25 3.50fr lt bl & blk .20 .18
104 A25 5fr bis & mag .32 .18
105 A25 6fr brn org & ind .40 .15
106 A25 10fr pale vio & red brn .55 .20
107 A25 20fr red org & vio brn .90 .35
108 A25 50fr dp org & blk 2.50 .90
109 A25 100fr crim & blk brn 4.25 2.25
Nos. 90-109 (20) 11.43
Set value 5.45

Nos. 102 and 105 Surcharged with New Value and Bars in Black

1949

110 A25 3fr on 2.50fr .20 .15
111 A25 4fr on 6fr .15 .15
112 A25 6.50fr on 6fr .25 .22
Nos. 110-112 (3) .60 .52

St. Francis Xavier — A26

Dissotis — A27

1953 *Perf. 12½x13*

113 A26 1.50fr ultra & gray blk .35 .35

Death of St. Francis Xavier, 400th anniv.

1953 Unwmk. Photo. *Perf. 11½*

Flowers: 15c, Protea. 20c, Vellozia. 25c, Littonia. 40c, Ipomoea. 50c, Angraecum. 60c, Euphorbia. 75c, Ochna. 1fr, Hibiscus. 1.25fr, Protea. 1.50fr, Schizoglossum. 2fr, Ansellia. 3fr, Costus. 4fr, Nymphaea. 5fr, Thunbergia. 7fr, Gerbera. 8fr, Gloriosa. 10fr, Silene. 20fr, Aristolochia.

Flowers in Natural Colors

114 A27 10c plum & ocher .15 .15
115 A27 15c red & yel grn .15 .15
116 A27 20c green & gray .15 .15
117 A27 25c dk grn & dl org .15 .15
118 A27 40c grn & sal .15 .15
119 A27 50c dk car & aqua .15 .15
120 A27 60c bl grn & pink .15 .15
121 A27 75c dp plum & gray .15 .15
122 A27 1fr car & yel .18 .15
123 A27 1.25fr dk grn & bl .50 .50
124 A27 1.50fr vio & ap grn .18 .15
125 A27 2fr ol grn & buff 1.40 .15
126 A27 3fr ol grn & pink .38 .15
127 A27 4fr choc & lil .38 .15
128 A27 5fr dp plum & lt bl grn .65 .15
129 A27 7fr dk grn & fawn .75 .28
130 A27 8fr grn & lt yel .95 .32
131 A27 10fr dp plum & pale ol 1.50 .25
132 A27 20fr vio bl & dl sal 2.50 .42
Nos. 114-132 (19) 10.57
Set value 2.90

King Baudouin and Tropical Scene — A28

Designs: Various African Views.

1955 Engr. & Photo.

Portrait Photo. in Black

133 A28 1.50fr rose carmine .30 .15
134 A28 3fr green .25 .15
135 A28 4.50fr ultra .32 .18
136 A28 6.50fr deep claret .50 .25
Nos. 133-136 (4) 1.37 .73

Mountain Gorilla — A29

Cape Buffaloes — A30

Animals: 40c, 2fr, Black-and-white colobus (monkey). 50c, 6.50fr, Impalas. 3fr, 8fr, Elephants. 5fr, 10fr, Eland and Zebras. 20fr, Leopard. 50fr, Lions.

1959-61 Unwmk. Photo. *Perf. 11½*

Granite Paper

Size: 23x33mm, 33x23mm

137 A29 10c brn, crim, & blk brn .15 .15
138 A30 20c blk, gray & ap grn .15 .15
139 A29 40c mag, blk & gray grn .15 .15
140 A30 50c grn, org yel & brn .15 .15
141 A29 1fr brn, ultra & blk .15 .15
142 A30 1.50fr blk, gray & org .16 .15
143 A29 2fr grnsh bl, ind & brn .15 .15
144 A30 3fr brn, dp car & blk .15 .15
145 A30 5fr brn, dl yel, grn & blk .18 .15
146 A30 6.50fr red, org yel & brn .28 .15
147 A30 8fr bl, mag & blk .45 .30
148 A30 10fr multi .45 .20

Size: 45x26½mm

149 A30 20fr multi ('61) .55 .45
150 A30 50fr multi ('61) 1.25 1.00
Nos. 137-150 (14) 4.37
Set value 2.65

For surcharge see No. 153.

Catalogue values for unused stamps in this section, from this point to the end of the section, are for Never Hinged items.

Map of Africa and Symbolic Honeycomb A31

1960 Unwmk. *Perf. 11½*

Inscription in French

151 A31 3fr ultra & red .20 .15

Inscription in Flemish

152 A31 3fr ultra & red .20 .15

10th anniversary of the Commission for Technical Co-operation in Africa South of the Sahara (C. C. T. A.)

No. 144 Surcharged with New Value and Bars

1960

153 A30 3.50fr on 3fr .30 .15

SEMI-POSTAL STAMPS

Belgian Congo Nos. B10-B11 Overprinted **RUANDA-URUNDI**

1925 Unwmk. *Perf. 12½*

B1 SP1 25c + 25c car & blk .15 .15
B2 SP1 25c + 25c car & blk .15 .15

No. B2 inscribed "BELGISCH CONGO."
Commemorative of the Colonial Campaigns in 1914-1918. Nos. B1 and B2 alternate in the sheet.

Belgian Congo Nos. B12-B20 Overprinted in Blue or Red

RUANDA

URUNDI

1930 *Perf. 11½*

B3 SP3 10c + 5c ver .35 .35
B4 SP3 20c + 10c dk brn .70 .70
B5 SP5 35c + 15c dp grn 1.40 1.40
B6 SP5 60c + 30c dl vio 1.65 1.65
B7 SP3 1fr + 50c dk car 2.50 2.50
B8 SP5 1.75fr + 75c dp bl (R) 2.75 2.75
B9 SP5 3.50fr + 1.50fr rose lake 5.75 5.75
B10 SP5 5fr + 2.50fr red brn 4.50 4.50
B11 SP5 10fr + 5fr gray blk 5.00 5.00
Nos. B3-B11 (9) 24.60 24.60

On Nos. B3, B4 and B7 there is a space of 26mm between the two words of the overprint. The surtax was for native welfare.

Queen Astrid with Native Children — SP1

Lion of Belgium and Inscription "Belgium Shall Rise Again" — SP2

1936 **Photo.**

B12 SP1 1.25fr + 5c dk brn .65 .55
B13 SP1 1.50fr + 10c dl rose .65 .55
B14 SP1 2.50fr + 25c dk bl .75 .75
Nos. B12-B14 (3) 2.05 1.85

Issued in memory of Queen Astrid. The surtax was for the National League for Protection of Native Children.

1942 Engr. *Perf. 12½*

B15 SP2 10fr + 40fr blue 2.00 2.00
B16 SP2 10fr + 40fr dark red 2.00 2.00

Nos. 74, 78, 79 and 82 Surcharged in Red

Au profit de la Croix Rouge + 50 Fr. Ten voordeele van het Roode Kruis
a

Ten voordeele van het Roode Kruis + 100 Fr. Au profit de la Croix Rouge
b

Au profit de la Croix Rouge + 100 Fr. Ten voordeele van het Roode Kruis
c

1945 Unwmk. *Perf. 12½*

B17 A18 (a) 50c + 50fr 1.10 1.40
B18 A19 (b) 1.25fr + 100fr 1.50 1.65
B19 A20 (c) 1.75fr + 100fr 1.10 1.40
B20 A21 (b) 3.50fr + 100fr 1.50 1.65
Nos. B17-B20 (4) 5.20 6.10

Mozart at Age 7 — SP3

Queen Elizabeth and Mozart Sonata — SP4

1956 Engr. *Perf. 11½*

B21 SP3 4.50fr + 1.50fr bluish vio .90 1.00
B22 SP4 6.50fr + 2.50fr claret 2.00 2.00

200th anniv. of the birth of Wolfgang Amadeus Mozart.
Surtax for the Pro-Mozart Committee.

Nurse and Children — SP5

Designs: 4.50fr+50c, Patient receiving injection. 6.50fr+50c, Patient being bandaged.

1957 Photo. *Perf. 13x10½*

Cross in Carmine

B23 SP5 3fr + 50c dk blue .55 .55
B24 SP5 4.50fr + 50c dk grn .75 .75
B25 SP5 6.50fr + 50c red brn .90 .90
Nos. B23-B25 (3) 2.20 2.20

The surtax was for the Red Cross.

Catalogue values for unused stamps in this section, from this point to the end of the section, are for Never Hinged items.

Soccer — SP6

Sports: #B26, High Jumper. #B27, Hurdlers. #B29, Javelin thrower. #B30, Discus thrower.

1960 Unwmk. *Perf. 13½*

B26 SP6 50c + 25c int bl & maroon .15 .15
B27 SP6 1.50fr + 50c dk car & blk .20 .20
B28 SP6 2fr + 1fr blk & dk car .20 .20
B29 SP6 3fr + 1.25fr org ver & grn 1.00 1.10
B30 SP6 6.50fr + 3.50fr ol grn & red 1.00 1.10
Nos. B26-B30 (5) 2.55 2.75

17th Olympic Games, Rome, Aug. 25-Sept. 11. The surtax was for the youth of Ruanda-Urundi.

Usumbura Cathedral — SP7

Designs: 1fr+50c, 5fr+2fr, Cathedral, sideview. 1.50fr+75c, 6.50fr+3fr, Stained glass window.

1961, Dec. 18 *Perf. 11½*

B31 SP7 50c + 25c brn & buff .15 .15
B32 SP7 1fr + 50c grn & pale grn .15 .15
B33 SP7 1.50fr + 75c multi .15 .15
B34 SP7 3.50fr + 1.50fr lt bl & brt bl .15 .15
B35 SP7 5fr + 2fr car & sal .30 .30
B36 SP7 6.50fr + 3fr multi .40 .40
Set value 1.05 1.05

The surtax went for the construction and completion of the Cathedral at Usumbura.

POSTAGE DUE STAMPS

Belgian Congo Nos. J1-J7 Overprinted

RUANDA

URUNDI

1924-27 Unwmk. *Perf. 14, 14½*

J1 D1 5c black brn .15 .15
J2 D1 10c deep rose .15 .15
J3 D1 15c violet .20 .20
J4 D1 30c green .25 .25
J5 D1 50c ultra .30 .30
J6 D1 50c brt blue ('27) .30 .30
J7 D1 1fr gray .40 .40
Nos. J1-J7 (7) 1.75 1.75

Belgian Congo Nos. J8-J12 Overprinted in Carmine **RUANDA URUNDI**

1943 *Perf. 14x14½, 12½*

J8 D2 10c olive green .15 .15
J9 D2 20c dk ultra .15 .15
J10 D2 50c green .15 .15
J11 D2 1fr dark brown .20 .20
J12 D2 2fr yellow orange .22 .22
Set value .65 .65

Nos. J8-J12 values are for stamps perf. 14x14½. Those perf. 12½ sell for about three times as much.

Belgian Congo Nos. J13-J19 Overprinted **RUANDA URUNDI**

1959 Engr. *Perf. 11½*

J13	D3	10c olive brown	.15	.15
J14	D3	20c claret	.15	.15
J15	D3	50c green	.15	.15
J16	D3	1fr lt blue	.15	.15
J17	D3	2fr vermilion	.20	.20
J18	D3	4fr purple	.35	.35
J19	D3	6fr violet blue	.45	.45
		Nos. J13-J19 (7)	1.60	1.60

Both capital and lower-case U's are found in this overprint.

RUSSIA

'rəsh–ə

(Union of Soviet Socialist Republics)

LOCATION — Eastern Europe and Northern Asia
GOVT. — Republic
AREA — 8,650,000 sq. mi.
POP. — 276,300,000 (est. 1985)
CAPITAL — Moscow

An empire until 1917, the government was overthrown in that year and a socialist union of republics was formed under the name of the Union of Soviet Socialist Republics. The USSR includes the following autonomous republics which have issued their own stamps: Armenia, Azerbaijan, Georgia and Ukraine.

With the breakup of the Soviet Union on Dec. 26, 1991, eleven former Soviet republics established the Commonwealth of Independent States. Stamps inscribed "Rossija" are issued by the Russian Republic.

100 Kopecks = 1 Ruble

Catalogue values for unused stamps in this country are for Never Hinged items, beginning with Scott 1021 in the regular postage section, Scott B58 in the semi-postal section, and Scott C82 in the airpost section.

Watermarks

Wmk. 166- Colorless Numerals

Wmk. 168- Cyrillic EZGB & Wavy Lines

Initials are those of the State Printing Plant.

Wmk. 169- Lozenges

Wmk. 171- Diamonds

Wmk. 170- Greek Border and Rosettes

Wmk. 226- Diamonds Enclosing Four Dots

Wmk. 293- Hammer and Sickle, Multiple

Wmk. 383- Cyrillic Letters in Shield

Empire

Coat of Arms

A1 A2 A3

Wmk. 166

1857, Dec. 10 Typo. *Imperf.*

1	A1	10k brown & blue	*3,500.*	450.
		Pen cancellation		225.
		Penmark & postmark		350.

Genuine unused copies of No. 1 are exceedingly rare. Most of those offered are used with pen cancellation removed. The unused value is for a specimen without gum. The very few known stamps with original gum sell for much more.

See Poland for similar stamp inscribed "ZALOT KOP. 10."

1858, Jan. 10 *Perf. 14½, 15*

2	A1	10k brown & blue	1,250.	125.
3	A1	20k blue & orange	2,750.	700.
4	A1	30k carmine & green	3,500.	1,250.

1858-64 Unwmk. *Perf. 12½*

Wove Paper

5	A2	1k black & yel ('64)	35.00	20.00
a.		1k black & orange	60.00	20.00
6	A2	3k black & green ('64)	150.00	40.00
7	A2	5k black & lilac ('64)	175.00	45.00
8	A1	10k brown & blue	100.00	10.00
9	A1	20k blue & orange	350.00	85.00
a.		Half used as 10k on cover		—
10	A1	30k carmine & green	350.00	100.00
		Nos. 5-10 (6)	1,160.	300.00

1863

11	A3	5k black & blue	15.00	*150.00*

No. 11 was issued to pay local postage in St. Petersburg and Moscow. It is known to have been used in other cities. Copies canceled after July, 1864, are worth considerably less.

1865, June 2 *Perf. 14½, 15*

12	A2	1k black & yellow	32.50	15.00
a.		1k black & orange	50.00	20.00
13	A2	3k black & green	80.00	5.00
14	A2	5k black & lilac	100.00	7.50
15	A1	10k brown & blue	60.00	3.00
a.		Thick paper	115.00	7.50
17	A1	20k blue & orange	200.00	15.00
18	A1	30k carmine & green	225.00	25.00
		Nos. 12-18 (6)	697.50	70.50

1866-70 Wmk. 168

Horizontally Laid Paper

19	A2	1k black & yellow	3.00	.50
a.		1k black & orange	4.00	.75
b.		Imperf.		*1,000.*
c.		Vertically laid	175.00	25.00
d.		Groundwork inverted	*3,000.*	*1,500.*
e.		Thick paper	40.00	25.00
f.		As "c," imperf.	2,750.	2,250.
g.		As "b," "c" & "d"	*5,000.*	*5,000.*
20	A2	3k black & dp green	4.50	.50
a.		3k black & yellow green	4.50	.50
b.		Imperf.		*1,500.*
c.		Vertically laid	150.00	30.00
d.		V's in groundwork (error) ('70)	700.00	35.00
22	A2	5k black & lilac	5.50	.55
a.		5k black & gray	85.00	10.00
b.		Imperf.	2,500.	1,000.
c.		Vertically laid	700.00	125.00
d.		As "c," imperf.		*4,000.*
23	A1	10k brown & blue	22.50	1.00
a.		Vertically laid	250.00	12.50
b.		Center inverted		*7,000.*
c.		Imperf.		*4,000.*
24	A1	20k blue & orange	75.00	6.00
a.		Vertically laid	750.00	65.00
25	A1	30k carmine & green	70.00	20.00
a.		Vertically laid	500.00	40.00
		Nos. 19-25 (6)	180.50	28.55

Arms — A4

1875-79

Horizontally Laid Paper

26	A2	2k black & red	6.00	.50
a.		Vertically laid	1,250.	75.00
b.		Groundwork inverted		*7,500.*
27	A4	7k gray & rose ('79)	5.25	.25
a.		Imperf.		*4,250.*
b.		Vertically laid	450.00	50.00
c.		Wmkd. hexagons ('79)		*12,500.*
d.		Center inverted		*17,500.*
e.		Center omitted	*1,500.*	*1,500.*
28	A4	8k gray & rose	7.00	.75
a.		Vertically laid	500.00	70.00
b.		Imperf.		*1,500.*
c.		"C" instead of "B" in "Bocem"	200.00	75.00
29	A4	10k brown & blue	25.00	4.50
a.		Center inverted		*9,000.*
30	A4	20k blue & orange	50.00	6.00
a.		Cross-shaped "T" in bottom word	120.00	30.00
b.		Center inverted		*9,000.*
		Nos. 26-30 (5)	93.25	12.00

The hexagon watermark of No. 27c is that of revenue stamps. No. 27c exists with Perm and Riga postmarks.

See Finland for stamps similar to designs A4-A15, which have "dot in circle" devices or are inscribed "Markka," "Markkaa," "Pen.," or "Pennia."

Imperial Eagle and Post Horns

A5 A6

Perf. 14 to 15 and Compound

1883-88 Wmk. 168

Horizontally Laid Paper

31	A5	1k orange	2.00	.20
a.		Imperf.	600.00	600.00
b.		Groundwork inverted	*4,000.*	*4,000.*
c.		1k yellow	2.00	.25
32	A5	2k dark green	3.00	.25
a.		2k yellow green ('88)	3.00	.25
b.		Imperf.	500.00	500.00
c.		Wove paper	500.00	325.00
d.		Groundwork inverted		*4,000.*
33	A5	3k carmine	4.00	.20
a.		Imperf.	450.00	450.00
b.		Groundwork inverted		*4,000.*
c.		Wove paper	500.00	410.00
34	A5	5k red violet	4.00	.20
a.		Groundwork inverted		*4,000.*
35	A5	7k blue	4.00	.20
a.		Imperf.	400.00	450.00
b.		Groundwork inverted	800.00	800.00
c.		Double impression of frame and center		—
36	A6	14k blue & rose	5.00	.55
a.		Imperf.	800.00	800.00
b.		Center inverted	*7,000.*	*6,000.*
c.		Diagonal half surcharge "7" in red, on cover ('84)		*10,000.*
37	A6	35k violet & green	25.00	5.00
38	A6	70k brown & orange	30.00	5.00
		Nos. 31-38 (8)	77.00	11.60

Before 1882 the 1, 2, 3 and 5 kopecks had small numerals in the background; beginning with No. 31 these denominations have a background of network, like the higher values.

No. 36c is handstamped. It is known with cancellations of Tiflis and Kutais, both in Georgia. It is believed to be of philatelic origin.

A7

1884 *Perf. 13½, 13½x11½*

Vertically Laid Paper

39	A7	3.50r black & gray	475.	400.
a.		Horiz. laid	6,500.	6,500.
40	A7	7r black & orange	450.	400.

Forgeries exist, especially with forged postmarks.

Imperial Eagle and Post Horns with Thunderbolts

A8 A9

With Thunderbolts Across Post Horns

Perf. 14 to 15 and Compound

1889, May 14

Horizontally Laid Paper

41	A8	4k rose	.50	.25
a.		Groundwork inverted		*3,000.*
42	A8	10k dark blue	.50	.20
43	A8	20k blue & carmine	2.00	.30
44	A8	50k violet & green	2.25	.45

Perf. 13½

45	A9	1r lt brn, brn & org	15.00	2.00
a.		Pair, imperf. between	500.00	300.00
b.		Center omitted	500.00	500.00
		Nos. 41-45 (5)	20.25	3.20

See #57C, 60, 63, 66, 68, 82, 85, 87, 126, 129, 131. For surcharges see #216, 219, 223, 226.

A10

A11

A12

A13

With Thunderbolts Across Post Horns

1889-92 *Perf. 14½x15*

Horizontally Laid Paper

No.	Type	Description	Unused	Used
46	A10	1k orange	.20	.15
a.		Imperf.	500.00	500.00
47	A10	2k green	.20	.15
a.		Imperf.	350.00	350.00
b.		Groundwork inverted		
48	A10	3k carmine	.25	.15
a.		Imperf.	350.00	350.00
49	A10	5k red violet	.50	.15
b.		Groundwork omitted	725.00	725.00
50	A10	7k dark blue	.25	.15
a.		Imperf.	500.00	500.00
b.		Groundwork inverted		*2,000.*
c.		Groundwork omitted	200.00	200.00
51	A11	14k blue & rose	1.50	.15
a.		Center inverted	*4,500.*	*4,500.*
52	A11	35k violet & green	5.25	.60

Perf. 13½

No.	Type	Description	Unused	Used
53	A12	3.50r black & gray	22.50	7.00
54	A12	7r black & yellow	35.00	10.00
a.		Dbl. impression of black		275.00
		Nos. 46-54 (9)	65.65	18.50

Perf. 14 to 15 and Compound

1902-05

Vertically Laid Paper

No.	Type	Description	Unused	Used
55	A10	1k orange	.50	.35
a.		Imperf.	600.00	600.00
b.		Groundwork inverted	850.00	850.00
c.		Groundwork omitted	200.00	200.00
56	A10	2k yellow green	.50	.35
a.		2k deep green	7.50	.70
b.		Groundwork omitted	600.00	300.00
c.		Groundwork inverted	850.00	850.00
d.		Groundwork double	425.00	425.00
57	A10	3k rose red	.50	.35
a.		Groundwork omitted	350.00	175.00
b.		Double impression	200.00	165.00
d.		Imperf.	500.00	500.00
e.		Groundwork inverted	210.00	210.00
57C	A8	4k rose red ('04)	1.00	.50
f.		Double impression	*200.00*	*200.00*
g.		Groundwork inverted	*4,000.*	*4,000.*
58	A10	5k red violet	1.00	.35
a.		5k dull violet	4.25	2.00
b.		Groundwork inverted	*750.00*	*750.00*
c.		Imperf.	250.00	250.00
d.		Groundwork omitted	250.00	165.00
59	A10	7k dark blue	.50	.35
a.		Groundwork omitted	350.00	300.00
b.		Imperf.	375.00	375.00
c.		Groundwork inverted	350.00	350.00
60	A8	10k dark blue ('04)	.50	.35
a.		Groundwork inverted	12.50	5.00
b.		Groundwork omitted	165.00	35.00
c.		Groundwork double	165.00	35.00
61	A11	14k blue & rose	2.50	.35
a.		Center inverted	4,750.	*3,250.*
b.		Center omitted	1,100.	700.00
62	A11	15k brown vio & blue ('05)	1.90	1.00
a.		Center omitted		
b.		Center inverted	*4,000.*	*3,500.*
63	A8	20k blue & car ('04)	2.00	.75
64	A11	25k dull grn & lil ('05)	3.50	1.25
a.		Center inverted	4,000.	4,000.
b.		Center omitted	1,500.	1,500.
65	A11	35k dk vio & grn	3.75	1.00
a.		Center inverted		*4,000.*
b.		Center omitted	*1,500.*	
66	A8	50k vio & grn ('05)	10.00	1.00
67	A11	70k brown & org	10.00	1.25

Perf. 13½

No.	Type	Description	Unused	Used
68	A9	1r lt brown, brn & orange	9.00	.75
a.		Perf. 11½	450.00	50.00
b.		Perf. 13½x11½, 11½x13½	675.00	575.00
c.		Imperf.	600.00	
d.		Center inverted	250.00	250.00
e.		Center omitted	250.00	150.00
f.		Pair, imperf. btwn.	500.00	165.00
69	A12	3.50r black & gray	9.00	3.00
a.		Center inverted	*7,500.*	*7,500.*
b.		Imperf., pair	2,000.	2,000.
70	A12	7r black & yel	9.00	4.00
a.		Center inverted	*7,500.*	*7,500.*
b.		Horiz. pair, imperf. btwn.	1,600.	1,600.
c.		Imperf., pair	2,000.	2,000.

1906 *Perf. 13½*

No.	Type	Description	Unused	Used
71	A13	5r dk blue, grn & pale blue	25.00	3.75
a.		Perf. 11½	225.00	275.00
72	A13	10r car rose, yel & gray	100.00	10.00
		Nos. 55-72 (19)	190.15	30.70

The design of No. 72 differs in many details from the illustration. Nos. 71-72 were printed in sheets of 25.

See Nos. 80-81, 83-84, 86, 108-109, 125, 127-128, 130, 132-135, 137-138. For surcharges see Nos. 217-218, 220-222, 224-225, 227-229.

A14

A15

Vertical Lozenges of Varnish on Face

1909-12 Unwmk. *Perf. 14x14½*

Wove Paper

No.	Type	Description	Unused	Used
73	A14	1k dull orange yellow	.15	.15
a.		1k orange yellow ('09)	.20	.20
c.		Double impression	100.00	100.00
74	A14	2k dull green	.15	.15
a.		2k green ('09)	.20	.20
b.		Double impression	25.00	25.00
75	A14	3k carmine	.15	.15
a.		3k rose red ('09)	.20	.20
76	A15	4k carmine	.15	.15
a.		4k carmine rose ('09)	.20	.20
77	A14	5k claret	.15	.15
a.		5k lilac ('12)	.65	.65
b.		Double impressions	22.50	22.50
78	A14	7k blue	.15	.15
a.		7k light blue ('09)	1.50	.65
b.		Imperf.	175.00	175.00
79	A15	10k dark blue	.15	.15
a.		10k light blue ('09)	*500.00*	*85.00*
b.		10k pale blue	6.00	1.00
80	A11	14k dk blue & car	.15	.15
a.		14k blue & rose ('09)	.20	.20
81	A11	15k red brown & dp blue	.15	.15
a.		15k dull violet & blue ('09)	.85	.40
c.		Center omitted	115.00	85.00
d.		Center double	50.00	50.00
82	A8	20k dull bl & dk car	.15	.15
a.		20k blue & carmine ('10)	.85	.55
b.		Groundwork omitted	20.00	13.00
c.		Center double	30.00	30.00
d.		Center and value omitted	85.00	85.00
83	A11	25k dl grn & dk vio	.15	.15
a.		25k green & violet ('09)	.30	.30
b.		Center omitted	115.00	115.00
c.		Center double	25.00	25.00
84	A11	35k red brn & grn	.16	.16
a.		35k brown vio & yel green	.50	.40
b.		35k violet & green ('09)	.50	.40
c.		Center double	25.00	25.00
85	A8	50k red brn & grn	.15	.15
a.		50k violet & green ('09)	.50	.40
b.		Groundwork omitted	20.00	20.00
c.		Center double	32.50	32.50
d.		Center and value omitted	115.00	115.00
86	A11	70k brn & red org	.15	.15
a.		70k lt brown & orange ('09)	.30	.25
b.		Center double	40.00	40.00
c.		Center omitted	115.00	115.00

Perf. 13½

No.	Type	Description	Unused	Used
87	A9	1r pale brown, dk brn & orange	.15	.15
a.		1r pale brn, brn & org ('10)	.25	.20
b.		Perf. 12½	.25	.20
c.		Groundwork inverted	20.00	20.00
d.		Pair, imperf. between	22.50	22.50
e.		Center inverted	25.00	25.00
f.		Center double	16.00	16.00
		Set value (15)	1.60	1.60

See Nos. 119-124. For surcharges see Nos. 117-118, B24-B29.

No. 87a was issued in sheets of 40 stamps, while Nos. 87 and 87b came in sheets of 50. Nos. 87g-87k are listed below No. 138a.

Nearly all values of this issue are known without the lines of varnish.

The 7k has two types:

I - The scroll bearing the top inscription ends at left with three short lines of shading beside the first letter. Four pearls extend at lower left between the leaves and denomination panel.

II - Inner lines of scroll at top left end in two curls; three pearls at lower left.

Three clichés of type II (an essay) were included by mistake in the plate used for the first printing. Value of pair, type I with type II, unused $2,500.

SURCHARGES

Russian stamps of types A6-A15 with various surcharges may be found listed under Armenia, Batum, Far Eastern Republic, Georgia, Latvia, Siberia, South Russia, Transcaucasian Federated Republics, Ukraine, Russian Offices in China, Russian Offices in the Turkish Empire and Army of the Northwest.

Peter I — A16

Alexander II — A17

Alexander III — A18

Peter I — A19

Nicholas II

A20 A21

Catherine II — A22

Nicholas I — A23

Alexander I — A24

Alexis Mikhailovich A25

Paul I A26

Elizabeth Petrovna — A27

Michael Feodorovich — A28

The Kremlin — A29

Winter Palace — A30

Romanov Castle — A31

Nicholas II — A32

Without Lozenges of Varnish

1913, Jan. 2 Typo. *Perf. 13½*

No.	Type	Description	Unused	Used
88	A16	1k brown orange	.30	.15
89	A17	2k yellow green	.30	.15
90	A18	3k rose red	.30	.15
b.		Double impression	700.00	
91	A19	4k dull red	.25	.15
92	A20	7k brown	.25	.15
b.		Double impression	350.00	350.00
93	A21	10k deep blue	.50	.20
94	A22	14k blue green	.45	.20
95	A23	15k yellow brown	.80	.20
96	A24	20k olive green	1.00	.20
97	A25	25k red violet	1.00	.35
98	A26	35k gray vio & dk grn	1.00	.35
99	A27	50k brown & slate	1.25	.45
100	A28	70k yel green & brn	2.50	1.25

Engr.

No.	Type	Description	Unused	Used
101	A29	1r deep green	9.00	4.50
102	A30	2r red brown	9.00	4.50
103	A31	3r dark violet	24.00	13.50
104	A32	5r black brown	17.50	17.50
		Nos. 88-104 (17)	69.40	43.95

Imperf., Pairs

No.	Type	Description	Unused	Used
88a	A16	1k brown orange		
90a	A18	3k rose red		
92a	A20	7k brown	600.00	
93a	A21	10k deep blue	600.00	
102a	A30	2r red brown	500.00	
103b	A31	3r dark violet	600.00	

Tercentenary of the founding of the Romanov dynasty.

See #105-107, 112-116, 139-141. For surcharges see #110-111, Russian Offices in the Turkish Empire 213-227.

Arms & 5-line Inscription on Black

1915, Oct. Typo. *Perf. 13½*

Thin Cardboard

Without Gum

105 A21 10k blue .75 *3.75*
106 A23 15k brown .75 *3.75*
107 A24 20k olive green .75 *3.75*
Nos. 105-107 (3) *2.25* 11.25

Imperf

105a A21 10k 50.00
106a A23 15k 50.00 50.00
107a A24 20k 50.00

Nos. 105-107, 112-116 and 139-141 were issued for use as paper money, but contrary to regulations were often used for postal purposes. Back inscription means: "Having circulation on par with silver subsidiary coins."

Types of 1906 Issue
Vertical Lozenges of Varnish on Face

1915 *Perf. 13½, 13½x13*

108 A13 5r ind, grn & lt blue .20 .15
a. 5r dk bl, grn & pale bl ('15) 2.50 .65
b. Perf. 12½ 3.25 1.00
c. Center double 40.00
d. Pair, imperf. between 200.00
109 A13 10r car lake, yel & gray .25 .20
a. 10r carmine, yel & light gray .40 .25
b. 10r rose red, yel & gray ('15) .85 .50
c. 10r car, yel & gray blue (error) 1,500.
d. Groundwork inverted 400.00
e. Center double 50.00 50.00

Nos. 108a and 109b were issued in sheets of 25. Nos. 108, 108b, 109 and 109a came in sheets of 50. Chemical forgeries of No. 109c exist. Genuine copies usually are centered to upper right.

Nos. 92, 94 Surcharged **10** **10**

1916

110 A20 10k on 7k brown .15 .15
a. Inverted surcharge 65.00 65.00
111 A22 20k on 14k blue green .15 .15
Set value .20 .20

Types of 1913 Issue
Arms, Value & 4-line inscription on Back
Surcharged Large Numerals on Nos. 112-113

1916-17

Thin Cardboard

Without Gum

112 A16 1 on 1k brn org ('17) .60 *4.50*
113 A17 2 on 2k yel green ('17) .60 *4.50*

Without Surcharge

114 A16 1k brown orange 16.50 *32.50*
115 A17 2k yellow green 35.00 *55.00*
116 A18 3k rose red .75 *4.50*

See note after No. 107.

Nos. 78a, 80a Surcharged:

коп.10коп. a **к.20к.** b

1917 *Perf. 14x14½*

117 A14 10k on 7k lt blue .15 .15
a. Inverted surcharge 50.00 50.00
b. Double surcharge 60.00
118 A11 20k on 14k bl & rose .15 .15
a. Inverted surcharge 50.00 50.00
Set value .15 .15

Provisional Government

Civil War

Type of 1889-1912 Issues
Vertical Lozenges of Varnish on Face

Two types of 7r:
Type I - Single outer frame line.
Type II - Double outer frame line.

1917 Typo. *Imperf.*

Wove Paper

119 A14 1k orange .15 .15
120 A14 2k gray green .15 .15
121 A14 3k red .15 .15
122 A15 4k carmine .15 .20
123 A14 5k claret .15 .15
124 A15 10k dark blue 12.00 12.00
125 A11 15k red brn & dp blue .15 .15
a. Center omitted 55.00
126 A8 20k blue & car .15 .35
a. Groundwork omitted 20.00 20.00
127 A11 25k grn & gray vio .75 1.00
128 A11 35k red brn & grn .15 .35
129 A8 50k brn vio & grn .15 .25
a. Groundwork omitted 18.00 18.00
130 A11 70k brn & orange .15 .40
a. Center omitted 115.00
131 A9 1r pale brn, brn & red org .15 .15
a. Center inverted 20.00 20.00
b. Center omitted 20.00 20.00
c. Center double 20.00 20.00
d. Groundwork double 14.00 14.00
e. Groundwork inverted 20.00 20.00
f. Groundwork omitted 22.50 22.50
g. Frame double 16.00 16.00
132 A12 3.50r mar & lt green .20 .25
133 A13 5r dk blue, grn & pale blue .30 .35
a. 5r dk bl, grn & yel (error) 1,000.
b. Groundwork inverted 400.00
134 A12 7r dk green & pink (I) .75 1.00
a. Center inverted
135 A13 10r scarlet, yel & gray 25.00 27.50
a. 10r scarlet, green & gray (error) 1,250.
Nos. 119-135 (17) 40.65 44.55

Vertical Lozenges of Varnish on Face

1917 *Perf. 13½, 13½x13*

137 A12 3.50r maroon & lt grn .15 .15
138 A12 7r dark green & pink (II) .15 .15
d. Type I 2.00 2.00
Set value .15 .15

Perf. 12½

137a A12 3.50r maroon & lt grn .20 .20
138a A12 7r dk grn & pink (II) 1.00 1.00

Horizontal Lozenges of Varnish on Face

Perf. 13½x13

87g A9 1r pale brown, brn & red orange .15 .15
h. Imperf. 10.00
i. As "h," center omitted 22.50
j. As "h," center inverted 22.50
k. As "h," center double 22.50
137b A12 3.50r maroon & lt green .65 .15
d. Imperf. 250.00
138b A12 7r dk grn & pink (II) .65 .15
c. Imperf. 250.00

Nos. 87g, 137b and 138b often show the eagle with little or no embossing.

Types of 1913 Issue
Surcharge & 4-line Inscription on Back
Surcharged Large Numerals

1917

Thin Cardboard, Without Gum

139 A16 1 on 1k brown org .40 *6.00*
a. Imperf. 22.50 22.50
140 A17 2 on 2k yel green .65 *6.00*
a. Imperf. 22.50 22.50
b. Surch. omitted, imperf. 45.00 45.00

Without Surcharge

141 A18 3k rose red .40 *6.00*
a. Imperf.
Nos. 139-141 (3) 1.45 *18.00*

See note after No. 107.

Stamps overprinted with a Liberty Cap on Crossed Swords or with reduced facsimiles of pages of newspapers were a private speculation and without official sanction.

RUSSIAN TURKESTAN

25 КОП.

Russian stamps of 1917-18 surcharged as above are frauds.

Russian Soviet Federated Socialist Republic

Severing Chain of Bondage — A33

1918 Typo. *Perf. 13½*

149 A33 35k blue .15 *3.00*
a. Imperf., pair 225.00
150 A33 70k brown .15 *3.00*
a. Imperf., pair 750.00
Set value .20

In 1918-1922 various revenue stamps were permitted to be used for postal duty, sometimes surcharged with new values, more often not.

For surcharges see Nos. B18-B23, J1-J9 and note following No. B17.

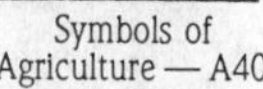

Symbols of Agriculture — A40

Symbols of Industry — A41

Soviet Symbols of Agriculture and Industry A42

Science and Arts — A43

1921 Unwmk. Litho. *Imperf.*

177 A40 1r orange 1.00 *1.25*
178 A40 2r lt brown 1.00 *1.25*
179 A41 5r dull ultra 1.00 .35
180 A42 20r blue 1.25 *3.00*
a. Pelure paper 3.25 2.75
b. Double impression 35.00
181 A40 100r orange .15 .15
a. Pelure paper .15 .15
182 A40 200r lt brown .15 .25
a. 200r olive brown 15.00 15.00
183 A43 250r dull violet .15 .15
a. Pelure paper .15 .15
b. Chalk surfaced paper .15 .20
c. Tête bêche pair 13.00 13.00
d. Double impression 35.00
184 A40 300r green .15 .25
a. Pelure paper 10.00 13.00
185 A41 500r blue .15 .35
186 A41 1000r carmine .15 .30
a. Chalk surfaced paper .15 .20
b. Thick paper .15 .20
c. Pelure paper .15 .20
Nos. 177-186 (10) 5.15 7.30

See #203, 205. For surcharges see #191-194, 196-199, 201, 210, B40, B43-B47, J10.

New Russia Triumphant A44

Type I - 37½mm by 23½mm.
Type II - 38½mm by 23¼mm.

1921, Aug. 10 Wmk. 169 Engr.

187 A44 40r slate, type II .50 .85
a. Type I 1.00 1.10

The types are caused by paper shrinkage. One type has the watermark sideways in relation to the other.

For surcharges see Nos. 195, 200.

Initials Stand for Russian Soviet Federated Socialist Republic — A45

1921 Litho. Unwmk.

188 A45 100r orange .20 .55
189 A45 250r violet .20 .55
190 A45 1000r carmine rose .75 1.40
Nos. 188-190 (3) 1.15 2.50

4th anniversary of Soviet Government.
A 200r was not regularly issued. Value $45.

Nos. 177-179 Surcharged in Black **5000 руб.**

1922

191 A40 5000r on 1r orange 1.00 .80
a. Inverted surcharge 100.00 22.50
b. Double surcharge, red & black 100.00 22.50
c. Pair, one without surcharge 125.00

192 A40 5000r on 2r lt brown 1.50 1.25
a. Inverted surcharge 75.00 15.00
b. Double surcharge 70.00
193 A41 5000r on 5r ultra 1.00 .90
a. Inverted surcharge 75.00 30.00
b. Double surcharge 75.00

No. 180 Surcharged

Р.С.Ф.С.Р.

5000 РУБЛЕЙ

194 A42 5000r on 20r blue 1.75 2.50
a. Pelure paper 1.75 2.25
b. Pair, one without surcharge 100.00

Nos. 177-180, 187-187a Surcharged in Black or Red

РСФСР

10.000 Р.

Wmk. Lozenges (169)

195 A44 10,000r on 40r, type I 2.00 3.25
a. Inverted surcharge 65.00 15.00
b. Type II 2.50 2.50
c. "1.0000" instead of "10.000" 125.00
d. Double surcharge 85.00

Red Surcharge

Unwmk.

196 A40 5000r on 1r orange 1.25 1.25
a. Inverted surcharge 75.00 15.00
197 A40 5000r on 2r lt brown 1.25 1.50
a. Inverted surcharge 75.00 30.00
198 A41 5000r on 5r ultra 1.25 1.25
199 A42 5000r on 20r blue 2.25 2.25
a. Inverted surcharge 75.00 35.00
b. Pelure paper 5.00 5.00

Wmk. Lozenges (169)

200 A44 10,000r on 40r, type I (R) .75 .75
a. Inverted surcharge 65.00 18.00
b. Double surcharge 65.00 18.00
c. With periods after Russian letters 125.00 35.00
d. Type II .75 .75
e. As "a," type II 75.00 30.00
f. As "c," type II 225.00 45.00

No. 183 Surcharged in Black or Blue Black

1922, Mar. Unwmk.

201 A43 7500r on 250r (Bk) .15 .15
a. Pelure paper .15 .15
b. Chalk surfaced paper .15 .25
c. Blue black surcharge .15 .15
Nos. 191-201 (11) 14.15 15.85

Nos. 201, 201a and 201b exist with surcharge inverted (value about $15 each), and double (about $25 each).

The horizontal surcharge was prepared but not issued.

Type of 1921 and

"Workers of the World Unite" A46

1922 Litho. Wmk. 171

202 A46 5000r dark violet .75 3.25
203 A42 7500r blue .25 .35
204 A46 10,000r blue 15.00 15.00

Unwmk.

205 A42 7500r blue, *buff* .25 .40
a. Double impression 60.00
206 A46 22,500r dk violet, *buff* .50 .60
Nos. 202-206 (5) 16.75 19.60

For surcharges see Nos. B41-B42.

No. 183 Surcharged Diagonally

100,000 РУБ.

1922 Unwmk. *Imperf.*

210 A43 100,000r on 250r .15 .15
a. Inverted surcharge 60.00 60.00
b. Pelure paper .15 .15
c. Chalk surfaced paper .15 .15
d. As "b," inverted surcharge 70.00 70.00

Marking 5th Anniversary of October Revolution — A48

1922 Typo.

211 A48 5r ocher & black .15 .15
212 A48 10r brown & black .15 .15
213 A48 25r violet & black .45 .50
214 A48 27r rose & black .85 1.00
215 A48 45r blue & black .70 .65
Nos. 211-215 (5) 2.30 2.45

Pelure Paper

213a A48 25r violet & black 60.00
214a A48 27r rose & black 60.00
215a A48 45r blue & black 65.00

5th anniv. of the October Revolution. Sold in the currency of 1922 which was valued at 10,000 times that of the preceding years.

For surcharges see Nos. B38-B39.

Nos. 81, 82a, 85-86, 125-126, 129-130 Surcharged

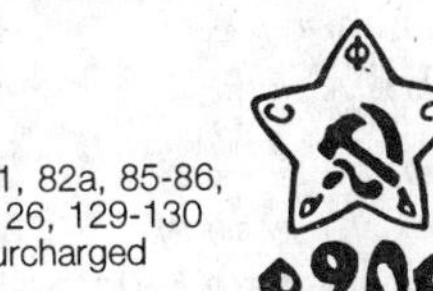

1922-23 *Perf. 14½x15*

216 A8 5r on 20k .20 2.00
a. Inverted surcharge 22.50 22.50
b. Double surcharge 35.00 35.00
217 A11 20r on 15k .35 2.00
a. Inverted surcharge 45.00 45.00
218 A11 20r on 70k .20 .35
a. Inverted surcharge 15.00 17.00
b. Double surcharge 20.00 20.00
219 A8 30r on 50k .35 .50
a. Inverted surcharge 25.00 25.00
c. Groundwork omitted 30.00 30.00
d. Double surcharge 16.00 16.00
220 A11 40r on 15k .20 .35
a. Inverted surcharge 25.00 25.00
b. Double surcharge 30.00 30.00
221 A11 100r on 15k .20 .35
a. Inverted surcharge 22.50 22.50
b. Double surcharge 30.00 30.00
222 A11 200r on 15k .20 .35
a. Inverted surcharge 20.00 20.00
b. Double surcharge 20.00 20.00

Nos. 218-220, 222 exist in pairs, one without surcharge; Nos. 221-222 with triple surcharge; No. 221 with double surcharge, one inverted. Value, each $100.

Imperf

223 A8 5r on 20k 10.00 15.00
224 A11 20r on 15k *1,500.*
225 A11 20r on 70k .50 1.00
a. Inverted surcharge 17.50 17.50
226 A8 30r on 50k brn vio & green 2.75 4.00
227 A11 40r on 15k .20 .30
a. Inverted surcharge 35.00 35.00
b. Double surcharge 27.50 27.50
228 A11 100r on 15k 1.40 1.10
a. Inverted surcharge 50.00 50.00
229 A11 200r on 15k 1.40 1.00
a. Inverted surcharge 50.00 50.00
b. Double surcharge 35.00 35.00
Nos. 216-223,225-229 (13) 17.95 28.30

Counterfeits of No. 224 exist.

Worker A49 — Soldier A50

1922-23 Typo. *Imperf.*

230 A49 10r blue .15 .15
231 A50 50r brown .15 .15
232 A50 70r brown violet .15 .15
233 A50 100r red .20 .25
Nos. 230-233 (4) .70
Set value .50

1923 *Perf. 14x14½*

234 A49 10r dp bl, perf. 13½ .15 .20
a. Perf. 14 15.00 16.00
b. Perf. 12½ 1.00 .85
235 A50 50r brown .15 .20
a. Perf. 12½ 7.50 6.00
b. Perf. 13½ 1.50 2.00
236 A50 70r brown violet .15 .20
a. Perf. 12½ 2.00 2.00
237 A50 100r red .20 .30
a. Cliché of 70r in plate of 100r 30.00 35.00
b. Corrected cliché 100.00 125.00
Nos. 234-237 (4) .65 .90

No. 237b has extra broken line at right.

Soldier- Worker- Peasant
A51 A52 A53

1923 *Perf. 14½x15*

238 A51 3r rose .15 .25
239 A52 4r brown .15 .25
240 A53 5r light blue .15 .25
a. Double impression *50.00 50.00*
241 A51 10r gray .15 .25
e. Double impression 75.00
241A A51 20r brown violet .20 .75
b. Double impression *75.00 75.00*
Nos. 238-241A (5) 1.75
Set value .60

Imperf

238a A51 3r rose 10.00 20.00
239a A52 4r brown 10.00 25.00
b. As "a," double impression *75.00*
240b A53 5r light blue 4.50 10.00
241d A51 10r gray 5.50 10.00
f. As "d," double impression 75.00
241c A51 20r brown violet 150.00 75.00

Stamps of 1r buff, type A52, and 2r green, type A53, perf. 12 and imperf. were prepared but not put in use. Value $1 each.

The imperfs of Nos. 238-241A were sold only by the philatelic bureau in Moscow.

Stamps of 20r, type A51, printed in gray black or dull violet are essays.

The stamps of this and the following issues were sold for the currency of 1923, one ruble of which was equal to 100 rubles of 1922 and 1,000,000 rubles of 1921.

Union of Soviet Socialist Republics

Reaping — A54

Sowing — A55

Fordson Tractor A56

Symbolical of the Exhibition — A57

1923, Aug. 19 Litho. *Imperf.*

242 A54 1r brown & orange 1.00 2.00
243 A55 2r dp grn & pale grn 1.00 2.00
244 A56 5r dp bl & pale blue 1.10 2.75
245 A57 7r rose & pink 1.00 3.50

Perf. 12½, 13½

246 A54 1r brown & orange 2.50 3.50
a. Perf. 12½ 20.00 35.00
247 A55 2r dp grn & pale grn, perf. 12½ 2.25 2.50
248 A56 5r dp bl & pale bl 2.50 4.25
a. Perf. 13½ 16.00 16.00
249 A57 7r rose & pink 3.25 5.00
a. Perf. 12½ 16.00 25.00
Nos. 242-249 (8) 14.60 25.50

1st Agriculture and Craftsmanship Exhibition, Moscow.

Worker- Soldier- Peasant
A58 A59 A60

1923 Unwmk. Litho. *Imperf.*

250 A58 1k orange .60 .25
251 A60 2k green .80 .40
252 A59 3k red brown .80 .40
253 A58 4k deep rose .80 .65
254 A58 5k lilac .80 .65
255 A60 6k light blue .60 .30
256 A59 10k dark blue .60 .30
257 A58 20k yellow green 2.50 .55
258 A60 50k dark brown 3.50 1.90
259 A59 1r red & brown 4.50 2.25
Nos. 250-259 (10) 15.50 7.65

1924 *Perf. 14½x15*

261 A58 4k deep rose 100.00 75.00
262 A59 10k dark blue 100.00 75.00
263 A60 30k violet 21.00 8.00
264 A59 40k slate gray 21.00 8.00
Nos. 261-264 (4) 242.00 166.00

See Nos. 273-290, 304-321. For surcharges see Nos. 349-350.

Vladimir Ilyich Ulyanov (Lenin) A61

Worker A62

1924 *Imperf.*

265 A61 3k red & black 2.50 1.50
266 A61 6k red & black 2.50 1.50
267 A61 12k red & black 2.50 1.50
268 A61 20k red & black 2.50 1.50
Nos. 265-268 (4) 10.00 6.00

Three printings of Nos. 265-268 differ in size of red frame.

Perf. 13½

269 A61 3k red & black 1.90 1.75
270 A61 6k red & black 1.90 1.75
271 A61 12k red & black 2.50 2.50
272 A61 20k red & black 3.75 3.00
Nos. 269-272 (4) 10.05 9.00
Nos. 265-272 (8) 20.05 15.00

Death of Lenin (1870-1924).

Forgeries of Nos. 265-272 exist.

Types of 1923

There are small differences between the lithographed stamps of 1923 and the typographed of 1924-25. On a few values this may be seen in the numerals.

Type A58: Lithographed. The two white lines forming the outline of the ear are continued across the cheek. Typographed. The outer lines of the ear are broken where they touch the cheek.

Type A59: Lithographed. At the top of the right shoulder a white line touches the frame at the left. Counting from the edge of the visor of the cap, lines 5, 6 and sometimes 7 touch at their upper ends. Typographed. The top line of the shoulder does not reach the frame. On the cap lines 5, 6 and 7 run together and form a white spot.

Type A60: In the angle above the first letter "C" there is a fan-shaped ornament enclosing four white dashes. On the lithographed stamps these dashes reach nearly to the point of the angle. On the typographed stamps the dashes are shorter and often only three are visible.

On unused copies of the typographed stamps the raised outlines of the designs can be seen on the backs of the stamps.

1924-25 Typo. *Imperf.*

273 A59 3k red brown 1.40 1.00
274 A58 4k deep rose 1.40 1.00
275 A59 10k dark blue 2.50 1.00
275A A60 50k brown 600.00 25.00

Other typographed and imperf. values include: 2k green, 5k lilac, 6k light blue, 20k green and 1r red and brown. Value, unused: $150, $100, $37.50, $150, and $175.

Nos. 273-275A were regularly issued. The 7k, 8k, 9k, 30k, 40k, 2r, 3r, and 5r also exist imperf. Value, set of 8, $75.

Perf. 14½x15

Typo.

276 A58 1k orange 65.00 5.50
277 A60 2k green .80 .30
278 A59 3k red brown 1.25 .40
279 A58 4k deep rose 1.00 .40
280 A58 5k lilac 10.00 2.50
281 A60 6k lt blue 1.00 .50

282	A59	7k chocolate	1.00	.50
283	A58	8k brown olive	1.10	.70
284	A60	9k orange red	1.10	1.10
285	A59	10k dark blue	1.65	.55
286	A58	14k slate blue	35.00	4.00
287	A60	15k yellow	6,000.	175.00
288	A58	20k gray green	4.00	.80
288A	A60	30k violet	175.00	7.50
288B	A59	40k slate gray	175.00	7.50
289	A60	50k brown	37.50	8.00
290	A59	1r red & brown	10.00	2.00
291	A62	2r green & rose	15.00	3.50
		Nos. 276-286,288-291 (17)	535.40	45.75

See No. 323. Forgeries of No. 287 exist.

1925 ***Perf. 12***

276a	A58	1k orange	.85	.20
277a	A60	2k green	8.00	.95
278a	A59	3k red brown	1.65	.70
279a	A58	4k deep rose	55.00	3.25
280a	A58	5k lilac	4.00	.80
282a	A59	7k chocolate	2.25	.20
283a	A58	8k brown olive	80.00	12.50
284a	A60	9k orange red	13.00	7.50
285a	A59	10k dark blue	3.00	.25
286a	A58	14k slate blue	2.75	.40
287a	A60	15k yellow	3.50	1.00
288c	A58	20k gray green	18.00	.45
288d	A60	30k violet	20.00	2.50
288e	A59	40k slate gray	15.00	2.75
289a	A60	50k brown	8.00	1.10
290a	A59	1r red & brown	650.00	150.00
		Nos. 276a-290a (16)	885.00	184.55

Soldier — A63

Worker — A64

1924-25 ***Perf. 13½***

292	A63	3r black brn & green	11.00	4.75
a.		Perf. 10	350.00	50.00
b.		Perf. 13½x10	700.00	315.00
293	A64	5r dk bl & gray brn	32.50	9.25
a.		Perf. 10½	50.00	62.50

See Nos. 324-325.

Lenin Mausoleum, Moscow — A65

1925, Jan. Photo. Wmk. 170 ***Imperf.***

294	A65	7k deep blue	3.00	3.00
295	A65	14k dark green	3.00	3.00
296	A65	20k carmine rose	3.00	3.00
297	A65	40k red brown	3.00	3.50
		Nos. 294-297 (4)	12.00	12.50

Perf. 13½x14

298	A65	7k deep blue	4.50	2.75
299	A65	14k dark green	5.00	2.75
300	A65	20k carmine rose	5.00	2.75
301	A65	40k red brown	5.50	4.00
		Nos. 298-301 (4)	20.00	12.25
		Nos. 294-301 (8)	32.00	24.75

First anniversary of Lenin's death.

Nos. 294-301 are found on both ordinary and thick paper. Those on thick paper sell for twice as much, except for No. 301, which is scarcer on ordinary paper.

Lenin — A66

Perf. 13½

1925, July Engr. Wmk. 170

302	A66	5r red brown	27.50	6.00
a.		Perf. 12½	35.00	11.00
b.		Perf. 10½ ('26)	27.50	8.00
303	A66	10r indigo	27.50	11.00
a.		Perf. 12½	190.00	90.00
b.		Perf. 10½ ('26)	22.50	11.00

Imperfs. exist. Value, set $75.
See Nos. 407-408, 621-622

Types of 1923 Issue

1925-27 Wmk. 170 Typo. ***Perf. 12***

304	A58	1k orange	.60	.35
305	A60	2k green	.60	.20
306	A59	3k red brown	.60	.35
307	A58	4k deep rose	.35	.25
308	A58	5k lilac	.50	.25
309	A60	6k lt blue	.60	.25
310	A59	7k chocolate	.60	.15
311	A58	8k brown olive	.85	.15
a.		Perf. 14½x15	100.00	20.00
312	A60	9k red	.90	.40
313	A59	10k dark blue	.90	.30
a.		10k pale blue ('27)	1.65	1.00
314	A58	14k slate blue	1.25	.35
315	A60	15k yellow	2.25	1.00
316	A59	18k violet	1.65	.25
317	A58	20k gray green	1.65	.25
318	A60	30k violet	2.00	.25
319	A59	40k slate gray	2.75	.35
320	A60	50k brown	4.25	.35
321	A59	1r red & brown	5.00	.35
a.		Perf. 14½x15	100.00	40.00
323	A62	2r green & rose red	25.00	5.50
a.		Perf. 14½x15	11.00	2.75

Perf. 13½

324	A63	3r blk brn & green	10.00	4.75
a.		Perf. 12½	40.00	14.00
325	A64	5r dark blue & gray brown	17.50	4.75
		Nos. 304-325 (21)	79.80	20.80

Nos. 304-315, 317-325 exist imperf. Value, set $75.

Mikhail V. Lomonosov and Academy of Sciences A67

1925, Sept. Photo. ***Perf. 12½, 13½***

326	A67	3k orange brown	4.25	3.00
a.		Perf. 12½x12	10.50	7.50
b.		Perf. 13½x12½	42.50	27.50
c.		Perf. 13½	17.50	10.00
327	A67	15k dk olive green	4.25	3.00
a.		Perf. 12½	17.50	7.50

Russian Academy of Sciences, 200th anniv. Exist unwatermarked, on thick paper with yellow gum, perf. 13½. These are essays, later perforated and gummed.

Prof. Aleksandr S. Popov (1859-1905), Radio Pioneer — A68

1925, Oct. ***Perf. 13½***

328	A68	7k deep blue	2.00	1.50
329	A68	14k green	3.25	1.90

For surcharge see No. 353.

Decembrist Exiles — A69

Street Rioting in St. Petersburg — A70

Revolutionist Leaders — A71

1925, Dec. 28 ***Imperf.***

330	A69	3k olive green	2.25	3.00
331	A70	7k brown	2.25	2.50
332	A71	14k carmine lake	3.50	3.75

Perf. 13½

333	A69	3k olive green	2.00	2.25
a.		Perf. 12½	60.00	50.00
334	A70	7k brown	2.00	2.25
335	A71	14k carmine lake	3.00	2.50
		Nos. 330-335 (6)	15.00	16.25

Centenary of Decembrist revolution.
For surcharges see Nos. 354, 357.

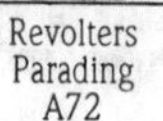
Revolters Parading A72

Speaker Haranguing Mob A73

Street Barricade, Moscow A74

1925, Dec. 20 ***Imperf.***

336	A72	3k olive green	1.25	1.50
337	A73	7k brown	1.50	1.65
338	A74	14k carmine lake	2.00	2.00

Perf. 12½, 12x12½

339	A72	3k olive green	1.25	1.25
a.		Perf. 13½	4.50	4.25
340	A73	7k brown	3.25	3.00
a.		Perf. 13½	15.00	10.50
b.		Horiz. pair, imperf. btwn.	55.00	50.00
341	A74	14k carmine lake	2.00	2.00
a.		Perf. 13½	22.50	12.00
		Nos. 336-341 (6)	11.25	11.40

20th anniversary of Revolution of 1905.
For surcharges see Nos. 355, 358.

Lenin — A75

Liberty Monument, Moscow — A76

1926 Wmk. 170 Engr. ***Perf. 10½***

342	A75	1r dark brown	4.50	2.50
343	A75	2r black violet	7.50	4.50
a.		Perf. 12½	75.00	30.00
344	A75	3r dark green	14.00	4.50
		Nos. 342-344 (3)	26.00	11.50

Nos. 342-343 exist imperf.
See Nos. 406, 620.

1926, July Litho. ***Perf. 12x12½***

347	A76	7k blue green & red	2.00	1.50
348	A76	14k blue green & violet	2.50	1.50

6th International Esperanto Congress at Leningrad. Exist perf. 11½. Value, $500.
For surcharge see No. 356.

Nos. 282, 282a and 310 Surcharged in Black

8
КОП

1927, June Unwmk. ***Perf. 14½x15***

349	A59	8k on 7k chocolate	1.40	1.00
a.		Perf. 12	8.50	7.50
b.		Inverted surcharge	125.00	105.00

Perf. 12

Wmk. 170

350	A59	8k on 7k chocolate	2.00	1.10
a.		Inverted surcharge	100.00	35.00

The surcharge on Nos. 349-350 comes in two types: With space of 2mm between lines, and with space of ¾mm. The latter is much scarcer.

Same Surcharge on Stamps of 1925-26 in Black or Red

Perf. 13½, 12½, 12x12½

353	A68	8k on 7k dp bl (R)	2.25	3.50
a.		Inverted "8"	75.00	100.00
354	A70	8k on 7k brown	6.25	7.25
355	A73	8k on 7k brown	8.25	9.50
356	A76	8k on 7k blue green & red	7.00	8.50

Imperf

357	A70	8k on 7k brown	2.75	4.00
358	A73	8k on 7k brown	2.75	4.00
		Nos. 349-350,353-358 (8)	32.65	38.85

Postage Due Stamps of 1925 Surcharged

ПОЧТОВАЯ
МАРКА
КОП. 8 КОП.

Two settings , A's aligned (shown), bottom A to left.

Lithographed or Typographed

1927, June Unwmk. ***Perf. 12***

359	D1	8k on 1k red, typo.	1.75	1.10
a.		Litho.	750.00	100.00
360	D1	8k on 2k violet	2.50	1.75

Perf. 12, 14½x14

361	D1	8k on 3k lt blue	2.25	1.65
362	D1	8k on 7k orange	2.50	1.75
363	D1	8k on 8k green	1.75	1.10
364	D1	8k on 10k dk blue	2.25	1.65
365	D1	8k on 14k brown	1.75	1.10
		Nos. 359-365 (7)	14.75	10.10

Exist with inverted surcharge. Value each, $100.

Wmk. 170

1927, June Typo. ***Perf. 12***

366	D1	8k on 1k red	1.25	1.90
367	D1	8k on 2k violet	1.25	1.90
368	D1	8k on 3k lt blue	2.00	2.25
369	D1	8k on 7k orange	2.00	2.25
370	D1	8k on 8k green	1.25	1.90
371	D1	8k on 10k dk blue	1.25	1.90
372	D1	8k on 14k brown	1.25	1.90
		Nos. 366-372 (7)	10.25	14.00

Nos. 366, 368-372 exist with inverted surcharge. Value each, $100.

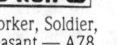

Dr. L. L. Zamenhof A77

1927 Photo. ***Perf. 10½***

373	A77	14k yel green & brown	2.00	1.90

Unwmk.

374	A77	14k yel green & brown	2.00	1.90

40th anniversary of creation of Esperanto.
No. 374 exists perf. 10, 10x10½ and imperf. Value, imperf. pair $165.

Worker, Soldier, Peasant — A78

Worker and Sailor — A81

Lenin in Car Guarded by Soldiers A79

Smolny Institute, Leningrad A80

Map of the USSR A82

Men of Various Soviet Republics A83

Workers of Different Races; Kremlin in Background A84

Typo. (3k, 8k, 18k), Engr. (7k), Litho. (14k), Photo. (5k, 28k)
Perf. 13½, 12½x12, 11

1927, Oct.			**Unwmk.**	
375	A78	3k bright rose	.90	.80
a.		Imperf., pair	300.00	
376	A79	5k deep brown	2.50	2.25
a.		Imperf.	165.00	180.00
b.		Perf. 12½	20.00	27.50
c.		Perf. 12½x10½	22.50	16.00
377	A80	7k myrtle green	2.75	2.75
a.		Perf. 11½	35.00	20.00
b.		Imperf., pair	350.00	
378	A81	8k brown & black	1.50	.95
a.		Perf. 10½x12½	*32.50*	*27.50*
379	A82	14k dull blue & red	2.50	1.65
380	A83	18k blue	1.90	1.65
a.		Imperf.	130.00	
381	A84	28k olive brown	7.25	5.75
a.		Perf. 10	37.50	32.50
		Nos. 375-381 (7)	19.30	15.80

10th anniversary of October Revolution.

The paper of No. 375 has an overprint of pale yellow wavy lines.

No. 377b exists with watermark 170. Value, $1,000.

Worker A85

Peasant A86

Lenin — A87

1927-28		**Typo.**	***Perf. 13½***	
		Chalk Surfaced Paper		
382	A85	1k orange	.30	.20
383	A86	2k apple green	.30	.15
385	A85	4k bright blue	.30	.15
386	A86	5k brown	.30	.15
388	A86	7k dark red ('28)	1.75	.60
389	A85	8k green	.90	.15
391	A85	10k light brown	.90	.15
392	A87	14k dark green ('28)	1.25	.30
393	A87	18k olive green	1.25	.30
394	A87	18k dark blue ('28)	1.75	.45
395	A86	20k dark gray green	1.25	.30
396	A85	40k rose red	2.50	.45
397	A86	50k bright blue	3.00	.85
399	A85	70k gray green	3.50	.85
400	A86	80k orange	4.75	1.40
		Nos. 382-400 (15)	24.00	6.45

The 1k, 2k and 10k exist imperf. Value, each $175.

Soldier and Kremlin A88

Sailor and Flag A89

Cavalryman A90

Aviator A91

1928, Feb. 6				
		Chalk Surfaced Paper		
402	A88	8k light brown	.70	.35
a.		Imperf.	225.00	175.00
403	A89	14k deep blue	1.50	.90
404	A90	18k carmine rose	1.65	1.75
a.		Imperf.	550.00	
405	A91	28k yellow green	2.00	2.00
		Nos. 402-405 (4)	5.85	5.00

10th anniversary of the Soviet Army.

Lenin Types of 1925-26
Perf. 10, 10½

1928-29		**Engr.**	**Wmk. 169**	
406	A75	3r dark green ('29)	5.75	2.00
407	A66	5r red brown	6.75	2.50
408	A66	10r indigo	11.50	4.50
		Nos. 406-408 (3)	24.00	9.00

No. 406 exists imperf.

Bugler Sounding Assembly
A92 A93

Perf. 12½x12

1929, Aug. 18		**Photo.**	**Wmk. 170**	
411	A92	10k olive brown	7.00	5.00
a.		Perf. 10½	35.00	25.00
b.		Perf. 12½x12x10½x12	45.00	21.00
412	A93	14k slate	3.00	2.00
a.		Perf. 12½x12x10½x12	75.00	45.00

First All-Soviet Assembly of Pioneers.

Factory Worker — A95

Peasant — A96

Farm Worker — A97

Soldier — A98

Worker, Soldier, Peasant — A100

Worker — A103

Lenin — A104

Peasant — A107

Factory Worker — A109

Farm Worker — A111

Perf. 12x12½

1929-31		**Typo.**	**Wmk. 170**	
413	A103	1k orange	.20	.15
a.		Perf. 10½	25.00	13.00
b.		Perf. 14x14½	50.00	35.00
414	A95	2k yellow green	.20	.15
415	A96	3k blue	.20	.15
a.		Perf. 14x14½	50.00	35.00
416	A97	4k claret	.30	.15
417	A98	5k orange brown	.30	.15
a.		Perf. 10½	75.00	75.00
418	A100	7k scarlet	1.10	.75
419	A103	10k olive green	.50	.15
a.		Perf. 10½	27.50	22.50
		Unwmk.		
420	A104	14k indigo	1.10	.75
a.		Perf. 10½	4.25	3.25
		Wmk. 170		
421	A100	15k dk olive green ('30)	.85	.15
422	A107	20k green	.85	.15
a.		Perf. 10½	50.00	27.50
423	A109	30k dk violet	1.40	.60
424	A111	50k dp brown	1.90	1.40
425	A98	70k dk red ('30)	2.00	1.50
426	A107	80k red brown ('31)	1.90	1.50
		Nos. 413-426 (14)	12.80	7.70

Nos. 422, 423, 424 and 426 have a background of fine wavy lines in pale shades of the colors of the stamps.

See Nos. 456-466, 613A-619A. For surcharge see No. 743.

Symbolical of Industry — A112

Tractors Issuing from Assembly Line A113

Iron Furnace (Inscription reads, "More Metal More Machines") A114

Blast Furnace and Chart of Anticipated Iron Production — A115

1929-30			***Perf. 12x12½***	
427	A112	5k orange brown	1.25	1.00
428	A113	10k olive green	1.25	1.50
		Perf. 12½x12		
429	A114	20k dull green	3.25	3.00
430	A115	28k violet black	2.00	1.75
		Nos. 427-430 (4)	7.75	7.25

Publicity for greater industrial production. No. 429 exists perf. 10½. Value *$400.*

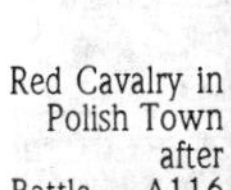

Red Cavalry in Polish Town after Battle — A116

Cavalry Charge A117

Staff Officers of 1st Cavalry Army — A118

Plan of Action for 1st Cavalry Army — A119

1930, Feb.			***Perf. 12x12½***	
431	A116	2k yellow green	1.50	1.65
432	A117	5k light brown	1.50	1.65
433	A118	10k olive gray	3.25	2.50
434	A119	14k indigo & red	1.25	1.65
		Nos. 431-434 (4)	7.50	7.45

1st Red Cavalry Army, 10th anniversary.

Students Preparing a Poster Newspaper A120

1930, Aug. 15				
435	A120	10k olive green	2.00	1.25

Educational Exhibition, Leningrad, 7/1-8/15/30.

Telegraph Office, Moscow A121

Lenin Hydroelectric Power Station on Volkhov River — A122

1930		**Photo. Wmk. 169**	***Perf. 10½***	
436	A121	1r deep blue	5.00	4.00
		Wmk. 170		
437	A122	3r yel green & blk brn	6.00	4.00

See Nos. 467, 469.

Battleship Potemkin A123

Inside Presnya Barricade — A124

Moscow Barricades in 1905 — A125

1930		**Typo.**	***Perf. 12x12½, 12½x12***	
438	A123	3k red	1.40	.55
439	A124	5k blue	1.40	.70
440	A125	10k dk green & red	2.50	1.00
1931			***Imperf.***	
452	A123	3k red	3.00	1.75
453	A124	5k deep blue	3.00	1.90
454	A125	10k dk green & red	4.00	2.25
		Nos. 438-454 (6)	15.30	8.15

Revolution of 1905, 25th anniversary.

Types of 1929-31 Regular Issue

1931-32			***Imperf.***	
456	A103	1k orange	.50	.65
457	A95	2k yellow green	.75	1.00
458	A96	3k blue	.75	1.25
459	A97	4k claret	12.50	6.50
460	A98	5k orange brown	2.00	2.75
462	A103	10k olive green	40.00	20.00
464	A100	15k dk olive green	45.00	25.00
466	A109	30k dull violet	70.00	35.00
467	A121	1r dark blue	65.00	65.00
		Nos. 456-467 (9)	236.50	157.15

Nos. 459, 462-467 were sold only by the philatelic bureau.

Type of 1930 Issue

1931		**Wmk. 170**	***Perf. 12x12½***	
469	A121	1r dark blue	1.75	.75

Maxim Gorki — A133

1932-33 **Photo.**

470 A133 15k dark brown	4.00	3.50
a. Imperf.	115.00	115.00
471 A133 35k dp ultra ('33)	15.00	10.00

40th anniversary of Gorki's literary activity.

Lenin Addressing the People
A134

Revolution in Petrograd (Leningrad)
A135

Dnieper Hydroelectric Power Station — A136

Asiatics Saluting the Soviet Flag — A139

Breaking Prison Bars — A140

Designs (dated 1917 1932): 15k, Collective farm. 20k, Magnitogorsk metallurgical plant in Urals. 30k, Radio tower and heads of 4 men.

1932-33 *Perf. 12½x12; 12½ (30k)*

472 A134 3k dark violet	1.00	.75
473 A135 5k dark brown	1.00	.75
474 A136 10k ultra	2.50	1.40
475 A136 15k dark green	1.50	.85
476 A136 20k lake ('33)	2.00	1.10
477 A136 30k dark gray ('33)	7.00	2.25
478 A139 35k gray black	70.00	57.50
Nos. 472-478 (7)	85.00	64.60

October Revolution, 15th anniversary.

1932, Nov. **Litho.** *Perf. 12½x12*

479 A140 50k dark red	7.50	6.00

Intl. Revolutionaries' Aid Assoc., 10th anniv.

Trier, Birthplace of Marx
A141

Grave, Highgate Cemetery, London
A142

35k, Portrait & signature of Karl Marx (1818-83).

Perf. 12x12½, 12½x12

1933, Mar. **Photo.**

480 A141 3k dull green	3.00	1.00
481 A142 10k black brown	5.00	2.25
482 A142 35k brown violet	10.00	5.75
Nos. 480-482 (3)	18.00	9.00

Fine Arts Museum, Moscow — A145

1932, Dec. *Perf. 12½*

485 A145 15k black brown	15.00	13.00
486 A145 35k ultra	32.50	32.50
a. Perf. 10½	50.00	30.00

Moscow Philatelic Exhibition, 1932.

Nos. 485 and 486 were also issued in imperf. sheets of 4 containing 2 of each value, on thick paper for presentation purposes. They were not valid for postage. Replicas of the sheet were made for Moscow 97 by the Canadian Society of Russian Philately.

Nos. 485 and 486a Surcharged

ЛЕНИНГРАД, 1933 г.
70
коп

1933, Mar. *Perf. 12½*

487 A145 30k on 15k black brn	30.00	20.00

Perf. 10½

488 A145 70k on 35k ultra	60.00	25.00

Leningrad Philatelic Exhibition, 1933.

Peoples of the Soviet Union

Kazaks — A146

Lezghians
A147

Tungus
A150

Crimean Tartars — A148

Jews, Birobidzhan
A149

Buryats — A151

Yakuts — A156

Chechens
A152

Abkhas — A153

Georgians
A154

Nientzians
A155

Great Russians — A157

Tadzhiks — A158

Transcaucasians — A159

Turkmen — A160

Ukrainians — A161

Uzbeks — A162

Byelorussians — A163

Koryaks — A164

Bashkirs
A165

Chuvashes
A166

Perf. 12, 12x12½, 12½x12, 11x12, 12x11

1933, Apr. **Photo.**

489 A146 1k black brown	1.40	1.00
490 A147 2k ultra	1.40	1.00
491 A148 3k gray green	1.40	1.00
492 A149 4k gray black	1.40	1.00
493 A150 5k brown violet	1.40	1.00
494 A151 6k indigo	1.40	.60
495 A152 7k black brown	1.40	.60
496 A153 8k rose red	1.40	.90
497 A154 9k ultra	2.50	1.25
498 A155 10k black brown	2.75	3.00
499 A156 14k olive green	2.25	1.25
500 A157 15k orange	2.75	1.25
501 A158 15k ultra	2.50	1.00
502 A159 15k dark brown	2.50	1.00
503 A160 15k rose red	3.75	2.75
504 A161 15k violet brown	3.25	1.25
505 A162 15k gray black	3.25	1.25
506 A163 15k dull green	3.00	1.25
507 A164 20k dull blue	9.00	2.75
508 A165 30k brown violet	9.00	2.25
509 A166 35k black	19.00	4.00
Nos. 489-509 (21)	76.70	31.35

V. V. Vorovsky
A169

3k, V. M. Volodarsky. 5k, M. S. Uritzky.

1933, Oct. *Perf. 12x12½*

514 A169 1k dull green	.75	.55
515 A169 3k blue black	1.10	.75
516 A169 5k olive brown	2.25	.90
Nos. 514-516 (3)	4.10	2.20

10th anniv, of the murder of Soviet Representative Vorovsky; 15th anniv. of the murder of the Revolutionists Volodarsky and Uritzky.

See Nos. 531-532, 580-582.

Order of the Red Banner, 15th Anniv. — A173

1933, Nov. 17 **Unwmk.** *Perf. 14*

518 A173 20k black, red & yellow	1.50	1.25

No. 518, perf. 9½, is a proof.

Commissar Schaumyan
A174

Commissar Prokofii A. Dzhaparidze
A175

Commissars Awaiting Execution — A176

Designs: 35k, Monument to the 26 Commissars. 40k, Worker, peasant and soldier dipping flags in salute.

1933, Dec. 1

519 A174 4k brown	8.75	1.65
520 A175 5k dark gray	8.75	1.65
521 A176 20k purple	5.75	1.65
522 A176 35k ultra	27.50	6.75
523 A176 40k carmine	16.50	8.25
Nos. 519-523 (5)	67.25	19.95

15th anniv. of the execution of 26 commissars at Baku. No. 521 exists imperf.

Lenin's Mausoleum
A179

1934, Feb. 7 Engr. *Perf. 14*

524 A179 5k brown 2.75 .55
a. Imperf. 150.00 125.00
525 A179 10k slate blue 4.50 2.00
a. Imperf. 150.00 125.00
526 A179 15k dk carmine 4.50 1.40
527 A179 20k green 4.50 1.40
528 A179 35k dark brown 7.50 2.25
Nos. 524-528 (5) 23.75 7.60

10th anniversary of Lenin's death.

Ivan Fedorov — A180

1934, Mar. 5

529 A180 20k carmine rose 4.50 2.50
a. Imperf. 125.00 100.00
530 A180 40k indigo 10.00 3.50
a. Imperf. 125.00 100.00

350th anniv. of the death of Ivan Fedorov, founder of printing in Russia.

Portrait Type of 1933

Designs: 10k, Yakov M. Sverdlov. 15k, Victor Pavlovich Nogin.

1934, Mar. Photo. Wmk. 170

531 A169 10k ultra 16.00 6.00
532 A169 15k red 19.00 10.00

Deaths of Yakov M. Sverdlov, chairman of the All-Russian Central Executive Committee of the Soviets, 15th anniv., Victor Pavlovich Nogin, chairman Russian State Textile Syndicate, 10th anniv.

Dmitri Ivanovich Mendeleev
A184 A185

1934, Sept. 15 Wmk. 170 *Perf. 14*

536 A184 5k emerald 9.50 3.25
537 A185 10k black brown 27.50 6.00
538 A185 15k vermilion 24.00 5.50
539 A184 20k ultra 14.00 5.50
Nos. 536-539 (4) 75.00 20.25

Prof. D. I. Mendeleev (1834-1907), chemist who discovered the Periodic Law of Classification of the Elements.

Imperfs. exist of 5k (value $100) and 15k (value $150).

Lenin as Child and Youth
A186 A187

Demonstration before Lenin Mausoleum — A190

Designs: 5k, Lenin in middle age. 10k, Lenin the orator. 30k, Lenin and Stalin.

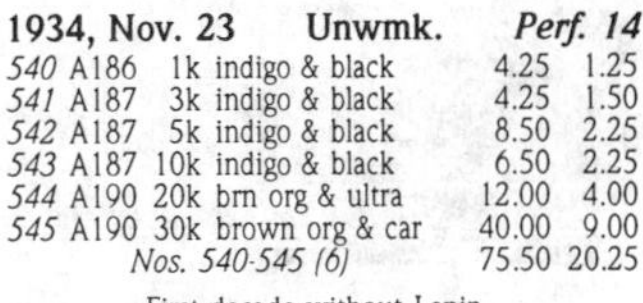

1934, Nov. 23 Unwmk. *Perf. 14*

540 A186 1k indigo & black 4.25 1.25
541 A187 3k indigo & black 4.25 1.50
542 A187 5k indigo & black 8.50 2.25
543 A187 10k indigo & black 6.50 2.25
544 A190 20k brn org & ultra 12.00 4.00
545 A190 30k brown org & car 40.00 9.00
Nos. 540-545 (6) 75.50 20.25

First decade without Lenin.
See Nos. 931-935, 937.

Bombs Falling on City
A192

"Before War and Afterwards"
A194

Designs: 10k, Refugees from burning town. 20k, "Plowing with the sword." 35k, "Comradeship."

1935, Jan. 1 Wmk. 170 *Perf. 14*

546 A192 5k violet black 6.00 3.50
547 A192 10k ultra 12.00 5.50
548 A194 15k green 14.00 5.50
549 A194 20k dark brown 12.00 5.50
550 A194 35k carmine 40.00 11.50
Nos. 546-550 (5) 84.00 31.50

Ati-war propaganda, the designs symbolize the horrors of modern warfare.

Subway Tunnel — A197

Subway Station Cross Section
A198

Subway Station — A199

Train in Station — A200

1935, Feb. 25 Wmk. 170 *Perf. 14*

551 A197 5k orange 8.50 2.00
552 A198 10k dark ultra 10.00 3.25
553 A199 15k rose carmine 40.00 14.00
554 A200 20k emerald 17.50 11.00
Nos. 551-554 (4) 76.00 30.25

Completion of Moscow subway.

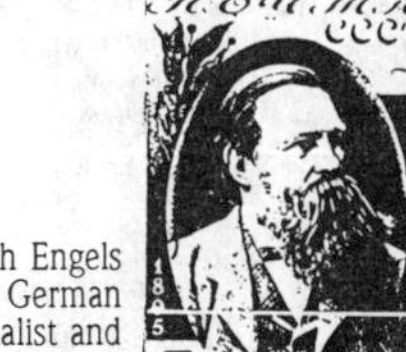
Friedrich Engels (1820-1895), German Socialist and Collaborator of Marx — A201

1935, May Wmk. 170 *Perf. 14*

555 A201 5k carmine 6.25 1.10
556 A201 10k dark green 3.25 1.65
557 A201 15k dark blue 6.25 2.00
558 A201 20k brown black 4.50 2.75
Nos. 555-558 (4) 20.25 7.50

Running — A202

Designs: 2k, Diving. 3k, Rowing. 4k, Soccer. 5k, Skiing. 10k, Bicycling. 15k, Tennis. 20k, Skating. 35k, Hurdling. 40k, Parade of athletes.

1935, Apr. 22 Unwmk. *Perf. 14*

559 A202 1k orange & ultra 1.40 .55
560 A202 2k black & ultra 1.65 .55
561 A202 3k green & blk brn 3.25 1.25
562 A202 4k rose red & ultra 2.25 .85
563 A202 5k pur & blk brn 2.25 .85
564 A202 10k rose red & vio 8.00 2.75
565 A202 15k black & blk brn 16.00 5.75
566 A202 20k blk brn & ultra 14.00 4.00
567 A202 35k ultra & blk brn 19.00 8.25
568 A202 40k black brn & car 17.50 5.75
Nos. 559-568 (10) 85.30 30.55

International Spartacist Games, Moscow. The games never took place.

Silver Plate of Sassanian Dynasty — A212

1935, Sept. 10 Wmk. 170

569 A212 5k orange red 5.25 1.50
570 A212 10k dk yellow green 5.25 1.50
571 A212 15k dark violet 6.00 2.50
572 A212 35k black brown 9.00 2.75
Nos. 569-572 (4) 25.50 8.25

3rd International Exposition of Persian Art, Leningrad, Sept. 12-18, 1935.

Kalinin, the Worker — A213

Mikhail Kalinin — A216

Kalinin as: 5k, farmer. 10k, orator.

1935, Nov. 20 Unwmk. *Perf. 14*

573 A213 3k rose lilac 1.10 .50
574 A213 5k green 1.10 .50
575 A213 10k blue slate 1.25 .80
576 A216 20k brown black 2.25 1.00
Nos. 573-576 (4) 5.70 2.80

60th birthday of Mikhail Kalinin, chairman of the Central Executive Committee of the USSR.

The 20k exists imperf. Value $110.

Leo Tolstoy
A217 A218

Design: 20k, Statue of Tolstoy.

1935, Dec. 4 *Perf. 14*

577 A217 3k ol black & vio .90 .75
578 A218 10k vio blk & blk brn 1.25 .95
579 A217 20k dk grn & blk brn 5.00 3.00
Nos. 577-579 (3) 7.15 4.70

Perf. 11

577a A217 3k 2.50 .75
578a A218 10k 4.50 1.75
579a A217 20k 10.00 2.50
Nos. 577a-579a (3) 17.00 5.00

25th anniv. of the death of Count Leo N. Tolstoy (1828-1910).

Portrait Type of 1933

Designs: 2k, Mikhail V. Frunze. 4k, N. E. Bauman. 40k, Sergei M. Kirov.

1935, Nov. Wmk. 170 *Perf. 11*

580 A169 2k purple 2.50 *2.75*
581 A169 4k brown violet 3.50 *4.50*
582 A169 40k black brown 7.00 *6.50*
Nos. 580-582 (3) 13.00 13.75

Perf. 14

580a A169 2k 7.25 .55
581a A169 4k 10.00 .55
582a A169 40k 24.00 1.65
Nos. 580a-582a (3) 41.25 2.75

Death of three revolutionary heroes.

Nos. 580-582 exist imperf. but were not regularly issued. Value, set $400.

Pioneers Preventing Theft from Mailbox — A223

Designs: 3k, 5k, Pioneers preventing destruction of property. 10k, Helping recover kite. 15k, Girl Pioneer saluting.

1936, Apr. Unwmk. *Perf. 14*

583 A223 1k yellow green .65 .35
584 A223 2k copper red 2.00 .35
585 A223 3k slate blue 1.00 .90
586 A223 5k rose lake .85 .35
587 A223 10k gray blue 2.00 1.75
588 A223 15k brown olive 10.00 6.00
Nos. 583-588 (6) 16.50 9.70

Perf. 11

583a A223 1k 1.25 .55
584a A223 2k .65 .55
585a A223 3k 3.50 .75
586a A223 5k 6.00 1.50
587a A223 10k 15.00 1.75
588a A223 15k 3.00 2.00
Nos. 583a-588a (6) 29.40 7.10

Nikolai A. Dobrolyubov, Writer and Critic, Birth Cent. — A227

1936, Aug. 13 Typo. *Perf. 11½*

589 A227 10k rose lake 2.75 2.25
a. Perf. 14 5.00 2.50

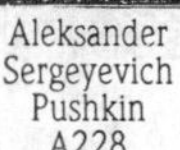

Aleksander Sergeyevich Pushkin A228

Statue of Pushkin, Moscow A229

Perf. 11 to 14 and Compound

1937, Feb. 1

Chalky or Ordinary Paper

590	A228	10k	yellow brown	.35	.35
591	A228	20k	Prus green	.50	.40
592	A228	40k	rose lake	.65	.45
593	A229	50k	blue	1.25	.55
594	A229	80k	carmine rose	1.90	.75
595	A229	1r	green	3.25	1.50
			Nos. 590-595 (6)	7.90	4.00

Souvenir Sheet

Imperf

596			Sheet of 2	4.00	*17.00*
a.	A228	10k	brown	.65	*2.25*
b.	A229	50k	brown	.65	*2.25*

Pushkin (1799-1837), writer and poet.

Tchaikovsky Concert Hall — A230

Designs: 5k, 15k, Telegraph Agency House. 10k, Tchaikovsky Concert Hall. 20k, 50k, Red Army Theater. 30k, Hotel Moscow. 40k, Palace of the Soviets.

1937, June Photo. Unwmk. ***Perf. 12***

597	A230	3k	brown violet	.65	.40
598	A230	5k	henna brown	.65	.40
599	A230	10k	dark brown	1.10	.40
600	A230	15k	black	1.10	.40
601	A230	20k	olive green	.65	.90
602	A230	30k	gray black	.65	.90
a.			Perf. 11	50.00	32.50
603	A230	40k	violet	1.25	1.25
a.			Souv. sheet of 4, imperf.	8.00	*17.00*
604	A230	50k	dark brown	1.25	1.25
			Nos. 597-604 (8)	7.30	5.90

First Congress of Soviet Architects. The 30k is watermarked Greek Border and Rosettes (170).

Nos. 597-601, 603-604 exist imperf. Value, each $225.

Feliks E. Dzerzhinski A235

Shota Rustaveli A236

1937, July 27 Typo. ***Perf. 12***

606	A235	10k	yellow brown	.40	.25
607	A235	20k	Prus green	.60	.40
608	A235	40k	rose lake	1.25	.85
609	A235	80k	carmine	1.40	1.00
			Nos. 606-609 (4)	3.65	2.50

Dzerzhinski, organizer of Soviet secret police, 10th death anniv. Exist imperf.

1938, Feb. Unwmk. Photo. ***Perf. 12***

610	A236	20k	deep green	1.00	.25

750th anniversary of the publication of the poem "Knight in the Tiger Skin," by Shota Rustaveli, Georgian poet.

Exists imperf. Value $150.

Statue Surmounting Pavilion A237

Soviet Pavilion at Paris Exposition A238

1938 **Typo.**

611	A237	5k	red	.40	.15
a.			Imperf.	100.00	
612	A238	20k	rose	.70	.25
613	A237	50k	dark blue	1.50	.50

USSR participation in the 1937 International Exposition at Paris.

Types of 1929-32 and Lenin Types of 1925-26

1937-52 Unwmk. ***Perf. 11½x12, 12***

613A	A103	1k	dull org ('40)	15.00	5.00
614	A95	2k	yel grn ('39)	5.25	2.00
615	A97	4k	claret ('40)	5.25	2.00
615A	A98	5k	org brn ('46)	100.00	12.50
616	A109	10k	blue ('38)	.50	.30
616A	A103	10k	olive ('40)	100.00	20.00
616B	A109	10k	black ('52)	.50	.35
617	A97	20k	dull green	.50	.35
617A	A107	20k	green ('39)	100.00	12.50
618	A109	30k	claret ('39)	11.50	3.50
619	A104	40k	indigo ('38)	2.00	.90
619A	A111	50k	dp brn ('40)	.85	.52

Engr.

620	A75	3r	dk green ('39)	1.50	.90
621	A66	5r	red brn ('39)	2.00	1.25
622	A66	10r	indigo ('39)	3.50	2.75
			Nos. 613A-622 (15)	348.35	64.82

#615-619 exist imperf but were not regularly issued.

No. 616B was re-issued in 1954-56 in slightly smaller format, 14½x21mm, and in gray black. See note after No. 738.

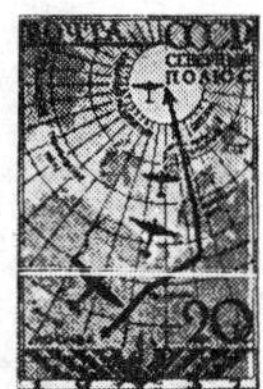

Airplane Route from Moscow to North Pole — A239

Soviet Flag and Airplanes at North Pole — A240

1938, Feb. 25 Litho. ***Perf. 12***

625	A239	10k	drab & black	1.40	.30
626	A239	20k	blue gray & blk	1.75	.60

Typo.

627	A240	40k	dull green & car	5.00	2.00
a.			Imperf.	140.00	
628	A240	80k	rose car & car	1.90	1.90
a.			Imperf.	65.00	
			Nos. 625-628 (4)	10.05	4.80

Soviet flight to the North Pole.

Infantryman A241

Soldier A242

Stalin Reviewing Cavalry — A246

Chapayev and Boy — A247

Designs: 30k, Sailor, 40k, Aviator. 50k, Antiaircraft soldier.

1938, Mar. Unwmk. Photo. ***Perf. 12***

629	A241	10k	gray blk & dk red	.50	.30
630	A242	20k	gray blk & dk red	.65	.35
631	A242	30k	gray blk & dk red	1.25	.50
632	A242	40k	gray blk & dk red	1.90	.90
633	A242	50k	gray blk & dk red	2.25	1.25
634	A246	80k	gray blk & dk red	3.50	1.25

Typo.

Perf. 12x12½

635	A247	1r	black & carmine	1.00	.60
			Nos. 629-635 (7)	11.05	5.15
			Set, never hinged	25.00	

Workers' & Peasants' Red Army, 20th anniv. No. 635 exists imperf. Value $150.

Aviators Chkalov, Baidukov, Beliakov and Flight Route — A248

Aviators Gromov, Danilin, Yumashev and Flight Route — A249

1938, Apr. 10 **Photo.**

636	A248	10k	black & red	.75	.65
637	A248	20k	brown black & red	1.00	.65
638	A248	40k	brown & red	1.50	1.10
639	A248	50k	brown vio & red	2.50	1.10
			Nos. 636-639 (4)	5.75	3.50
			Set, never hinged	15.00	

First Trans-Polar flight, June 18-20, 1937, from Moscow to Vancouver, Wash. Nos. 636-639 exist imperf. Value $150 each.

1938, Apr. 13

640	A249	10k	claret	1.50	.60
641	A249	20k	brown black	1.90	1.25
642	A249	50k	dull violet	2.00	1.50
			Nos. 640-642 (3)	5.40	3.35
			Set, never hinged	14.00	

First Trans-Polar flight, July 12-14, 1937, from Moscow to San Jacinto, Calif. Nos. 640-642 exist imperf. Value, each $150.

Arrival of the Rescuing Ice-breakers Taimyr and Murmansk A250

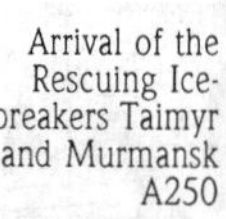

Ivan Papanin and His Men Aboard Ice-breaker Yermak — A251

1938, June 21 Typo. ***Perf. 12, 12½***

643	A250	10k	violet brown	2.25	1.00
644	A250	20k	dark blue	2.25	1.25

Photo.

645	A251	30k	olive brown	5.00	1.65
646	A251	50k	ultra	5.00	1.75
a.			Imperf.	150.00	
			Nos. 643-646 (4)	14.50	5.65
			Set, never hinged	20.00	

Rescue of Papanin's North Pole Expedition.

Arms of Uzbek — A252

Arms of USSR — A253

#650

#651

#654

#655

#656

Designs: Different arms on each stamp.

Perf. 12, 12½

1937-38 Unwmk. Typo

647	A252	20k	dp bl (Armenia)	1.00	.5
648	A252	20k	dull violet (Azerbaijan)	1.00	.5
649	A252	20k	brown orange (Byelorussia)	*5.00*	*2.5*
650	A252	20k	carmine rose (Georgia)	1.25	.7
651	A252	20k	bl grn (Kazakh)	1.25	.7
652	A252	20k	emer (Kirghiz)	1.25	.7
653	A252	20k	yel org (Uzbek)	1.25	.7
654	A252	20k	blue (R.S.F.S.R.)	1.25	.7
655	A252	20k	claret (Tadzhik)	1.25	.7
656	A252	20k	car (Turkmen)	1.25	.7
657	A252	20k	red (Ukraine)	1.25	.7

Engr.

658	A253	40k	brown red	1.90	1.9
			Nos. 647-658 (12)	18.90	11.5
			Set, never hinged	40.00	

Constitution of USSR. No. 649 has inscriptions in Yiddish, Polish, Byelorussian and Russian.

Issue dates: 40k, 1937. Others, 1938. See Nos 841-842.

Nurse Weighing Child — A264

Children at Lenin's Statue — A265

Biology Lesson — A266

Health Camp — A267

Young Model Builders A268

1938, Sept. 15 Unwmk. *Perf. 12*

No.	Type	Denom.	Color	Unused	Used
659	A264	10k	dk blue green	1.30	.35
660	A265	15k	dk blue green	1.30	.55
661	A266	20k	violet brown	1.65	.55
662	A267	30k	claret	2.00	.95
663	A266	40k	light brown	2.50	1.25
664	A268	50k	deep blue	3.50	1.75
665	A268	80k	light green	5.50	1.75
			Nos. 659-665 (7)	17.75	7.15
			Set, never hinged	40.00	

Child welfare.

View of Yalta A269

Crimean Shoreline — A272

Designs: No. 667, View along Crimean shore. No. 668, Georgian military highway. No, 670, View near Yalta. No. 671, "Swallows' Nest" Castle. 20k, Dzerzhinski Rest House for workers. 30k, Sunset in Crimea. 40k, Alupka. 50k, Gursuf. 80k, Crimean Gardens. 1r, "Swallows' Nest" Castle, horiz.

Unwmk.

1938, Sept. 21 Photo. *Perf. 12*

No.	Type	Denom.	Color	Unused	Used
666	A269	5k	brown	1.00	1.40
667	A269	5k	black brown	1.00	1.40
668	A269	10k	slate green	1.50	1.40
669	A272	10k	brown	1.50	1.40
670	A269	15k	black brown	1.50	1.40
671	A272	15k	black brown	1.50	1.40
672	A269	20k	dark brown	2.25	1.40
673	A272	30k	black brown	2.25	1.90
674	A269	40k	brown	3.25	1.90
675	A272	50k	slate green	3.25	4.00
676	A269	80k	brown	5.00	4.00
677	A269	1r	slate green	11.00	6.50
			Nos. 666-677 (12)	35.00	28.10
			Set, never hinged	55.00	

Children Flying Model Plane — A281

Glider — A282

Captive Balloon — A283

Dirigible over Kremlin — A284

Parachute Jumpers — A285

Hydroplane A286

Balloon in Flight — A287

Balloon Ascent — A288

Four-motor Plane — A289

Unwmk.

1938, Oct. 7 Typo. *Perf. 12*

No.	Type	Denom.	Color	Unused	Used
678	A281	5k	violet brown	.70	.55
679	A282	10k	olive gray	.70	.55
680	A283	15k	pink	1.25	.55
681	A284	20k	deep blue	1.25	.55
682	A285	30k	claret	1.90	.95
683	A286	40k	deep blue	2.25	.95
684	A287	50k	blue green	4.50	1.40
685	A288	80k	brown	4.00	2.50
686	A289	1r	blue green	5.25	2.00
			Nos. 678-686 (9)	21.80	10.00
			Set, never hinged	50.00	

For overprints see Nos. C76-C76D.

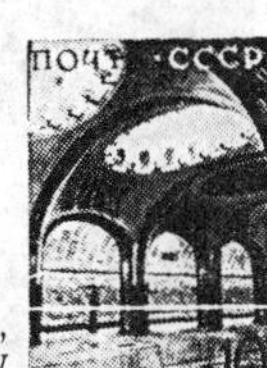

Mayakovsky Station, Moscow Subway — A290

Sokol Terminal A291

Kiev Station A292

Dynamo Station — A293

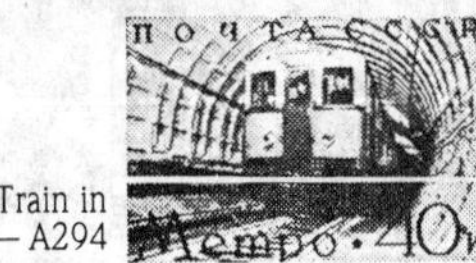

Train in Tunnel — A294

Revolution Square Station — A295

Unwmk.

1938, Nov. 7 Photo. *Perf. 12*

No.	Type	Denom.	Color	Unused	Used
687	A290	10k	deep red violet	3.00	.90
688	A291	15k	dark brown	3.00	.90
689	A292	20k	black brown	3.00	.90
690	A293	30k	dark red violet	3.00	.90
691	A294	40k	black brown	3.00	1.40
692	A295	50k	dark brown	3.00	1.90
			Nos. 687-692 (6)	18.00	6.90
			Set, never hinged	30.00	

Second line of the Moscow subway opening.

Girl with Parachute A296

Young Miner A297

Harvesting A298

Designs: 50k, Students returning from school. 80k, Aviator and sailor.

1938, Dec. 7 Typo. *Perf. 12*

No.	Type	Denom.	Color	Unused	Used
693	A296	20k	deep blue	.75	.40
694	A297	30k	deep claret	.75	.40
695	A298	40k	violet brown	.95	.40
696	A296	50k	deep rose	1.25	.75
697	A298	80k	deep blue	3.75	1.10
			Nos. 693-697 (5)	7.45	3.05
			Set, never hinged	12.50	

20th anniv. of the Young Communist League (Komsomol).

Diving A301

Discus Thrower A302

Designs: 15k, Tennis. 20k, Acrobatic motorcyclists. 30k, Skier. 40k, Runners. 50k, Soccer. 80k, Physical culture.

Unwmk.

1938, Dec. 28 Photo. *Perf. 12*

No.	Type	Denom.	Color	Unused	Used
698	A301	5k	scarlet	1.75	.55
699	A302	10k	black	1.75	.55
700	A302	15k	brown	2.00	.55
701	A302	20k	green	2.00	.90
702	A302	30k	dull violet	5.25	1.00
703	A302	40k	deep green	6.25	1.40
704	A302	50k	blue	5.25	1.00
705	A302	80k	deep blue	5.25	1.75
			Nos. 698-705 (8)	29.50	7.70
			Set, never hinged	55.00	

Gorki Street, Moscow — A309

Dynamo Subway Station A315

Foundryman A316

Moscow scenes: 20k, Council House & Hotel Moscow. 30k, Lenin Library. 40k, Crimea Bridge. 50k, Bridge over Moscow River. 80k, Khimki Station.

Paper with network as in parenthesis

1939, Mar. Typo. *Perf. 12*

No.	Type	Denom.	Color	Unused	Used
706	A309	10k	brn *(red brown)*	.70	.45
707	A309	20k	dk sl grn *(lt blue)*	.85	.45
708	A309	30k	brn vio *(red brn)*	.85	1.00
709	A309	40k	blue *(lt blue)*	1.50	1.00
710	A309	50k	rose lake *(red brn)*	2.50	1.25
711	A309	80k	gray ol *(lt blue)*	2.75	1.25
712	A315	1r	dk blue *(lt blue)*	4.50	2.00
			Nos. 706-712 (7)	13.65	7.40

"New Moscow." On 30k, denomination is at upper right.

1939, Mar.

No.	Type	Denom.	Color	Unused	Used
713	A316	15k	dark blue	1.00	.50
			Never hinged	1.25	
a.			Imperf.	80.00	
			Never hinged	100.00	

Statue on USSR Pavilion — A317

USSR Pavilion — A318

1939, May Photo.

No.	Type	Denom.	Color	Unused	Used
714	A317	30k	indigo & red	.35	.20
a.			Imperf. ('40)	.55	.35
715	A318	50k	blue & bister brn	.45	.40
a.			Imperf. ('40)	.60	.45
			Set, never hinged	2.50	
			Set, imperf., never hinged	3.50	

Russia's participation in the NY World's Fair.

Paulina Osipenko A318a

Marina Raskova A318b

Design: 60k, Valentina Grizodubova.

1939, Mar.

No.	Type	Denom.	Color	Unused	Used
718	A318a	15k	green	1.25	.60
719	A318b	30k	brown violet	1.25	.60
720	A318b	60k	red	2.75	1.10
			Nos. 718-720 (3)	5.25	2.30
			Set, never hinged	7.50	

Non-stop record flight from Moscow to the Far East.

Exist imperf. Value, each $300.

Shevchenko, Early Portrait
A319

Monument at Kharkov
A321

Design: 30k, Shevchenko portrait in later years.

1939, Mar. 9

721 A319 15k black brn & blk 1.10 .50
722 A319 30k dark red & blk 1.10 .50
723 A321 60k green & dk brn 3.00 1.75
Nos. 721-723 (3) 5.20 2.75
Set, never hinged 10.00

Taras G. Shevchenko (1814-1861), Ukrainian poet and painter.

Milkmaid with Prize Cow — A322

Tractor-plow at Work on Abundant Harvest — A323

Designs: 20k, Shepherd tending sheep. No. 727, Fair pavilion. No. 728, Fair emblem. 45k, Turkmen picking cotton. 50k, Drove of horses. 60k, Symbolizing agricultural wealth. 80k, Kolkhoz girl with sugar beets. 1r, Hunter with Polar foxes.

1939, Aug.

724 A322 10k rose pink .45 .15
725 A323 15k red brown .45 .15
726 A323 20k slate black .45 .15
727 A323 30k purple .45 .15
728 A322 30k red orange .45 .15
729 A322 45k dark green .55 .80
730 A322 50k copper red .55 .80
731 A322 60k bright purple 1.00 1.10
732 A322 80k dark violet 1.00 1.10
733 A322 1r dark blue 2.00 1.40
Nos. 724-733 (10) 7.35 5.95
Set, never hinged 17.50

Soviet Agricultural Fair.

Worker-Soldier-Aviator
A331 A332 A333

Arms of USSR
A334 A335

1939-43 Unwmk. Typo. *Perf. 12*

734 A331 5k red .15 .15
735 A332 15k dark green .25 .25
736 A333 30k deep blue .25 .25
737 A334 60k fawn ('43) .60 .25

Photo.

738 A335 60k rose carmine .50 .35
Nos. 734-738 (5) 1.75 1.25
Set, never hinged 2.00

No. 734 was re-issued in 1954-56 in slightly smaller format: 14x21½mm, instead of 14¾x22¼mm. Other values reissued in smaller format: 10k, 15k, 20k, 25k, 30k, 40k and 1r. (See notes following Nos. 622, 1260, 1347 and 1689.)

No. 416 Surcharged with New Value in Black

1939 Wmk. 170

743 A97 30k on 4k claret 7.50 7.50
Never hinged 12.50
a. Unwmkd. 100.00 30.00

M.E. Saltykov (N. Shchedrin)
A336 A337

1939, Sept. Typo. Unwmk.

745 A336 15k claret .30 .15
746 A337 30k dark green .45 .35
747 A336 45k olive gray .75 .35
748 A337 60k dark blue .95 .55
Nos. 745-748 (4) 2.45 1.40
Set, never hinged 3.50

Mikhail E. Saltykov (1826-89), writer & satirist who used pen name of N. Shchedrin.

Sanatorium of the State Bank — A338

Designs: 10k, 15k, Soviet Army sanatorium. 20k, Rest home, New Afyon. 30k, Clinical Institute. 50k, 80k, Sanatorium for workers in heavy industry. 60k, Rest home, Sukhumi.

1939, Nov. Photo. *Perf. 12*

749 A338 5k dull brown .40 .20
750 A338 10k carmine .40 .20
751 A338 15k yellow green .40 .20
752 A338 20k dk slate green .40 .20
753 A338 30k bluish black .40 .20
754 A338 50k gray black .85 .30
755 A338 60k brown violet 1.00 .45
756 A338 80k orange red 1.25 .60
Nos. 749-756 (8) 5.10 2.35
Set, never hinged 12.00

Mikhail Y. Lermontov (1814-1841), Poet and Novelist, in 1837 — A346

Portrait in 1838 — A347

Portrait in 1841 — A348

1939, Dec.

757 A346 15k indigo & sepia .80 .55
758 A347 30k dk grn & dull blk 2.00 .80
759 A348 45k brick red & indigo 1.65 1.20
Nos. 757-759 (3) 4.45 2.55
Set, never hinged 8.00

Nikolai Chernyshevski
A349

Anton Chekhov
A350

1939, Dec. Photo.

760 A349 15k dark green .60 .25
761 A349 30k dull violet .60 .45
762 A349 60k Prus green 1.25 .45
Nos. 760-762 (3) 2.45 1.15
Set, never hinged 5.00

50th anniversary of the death of Nikolai Chernyshevski, scientist and critic.

1940, Feb. Unwmk. *Perf. 12*

Design: 20k, 30k, Portrait with hat.

763 A350 10k dark yellow green .25 .25
764 A350 15k ultra .25 .25
765 A350 20k violet .50 .45
766 A350 30k copper brown 1.00 .55
Nos. 763-766 (4) 2.00 1.50
Set, never hinged 3.00

Chekhov (1860-1904), playwright.

Welcome to Red Army by Western Ukraine and Western Byelorussia
A352

Designs: 30k, Villagers welcoming tank crew. 50k, 60k, Soldier giving newspapers to crowd. 1r, Crowd waving to tank column.

1940, Apr.

767 A352 10k deep rose .60 .20
768 A352 30k myrtle green .60 .20
769 A352 50k gray black 1.10 .45
770 A352 60k indigo 1.10 .45
771 A352 1r red 1.75 .90
Nos. 767-771 (5) 5.15 2.20
Set, never hinged 10.00

Liberation of the people of Western Ukraine and Western Byelorussia.

Ice-breaker "Josef Stalin," Captain Beloussov and Chief Ivan Papanin
A356

Vadygin and Papanin
A358

Map of the Drift of the Sedov and Crew Members — A359

Design: 30k, Icebreaker Georgi Sedov, Captain Vadygin and First Mate Trofimov.

1940, Apr.

772 A356 15k dull yel green 1.40 .55
773 A356 30k dull purple 2.75 .55
774 A358 50k copper brown 2.25 .55
775 A359 1r dark ultra 4.50 1.65
Nos. 772-775 (4) 10.90 3.30
Set, never hinged 15.00

Heroism of the Sedov crew which drifted in the Polar Basin for 812 days.

Vladimir V. Mayakovsky
A360 A361

1940, June

776 A360 15k deep red .30 .15
777 A360 30k copper brown .55 .25
778 A361 60k dark gray blue .60 .35
779 A361 80k bright ultra .55 .35
Nos. 776-779 (4) 2.00 1.10
Set, never hinged 3.00

Mayakovsky, poet (1893-1930).

K.A. Timiryazev and Academy of Agricultural Sciences
A362

In the Laboratory of Moscow University
A363

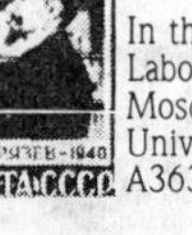

Last Portrait — A364

Monument in Moscow — A365

1940, June

780 A362 10k indigo .35 .25
781 A363 15k purple .35 .35
782 A364 30k dk violet brown .35 .35
783 A365 60k dark green 1.40 .60
Nos. 780-783 (4) 2.45 1.55
Set, never hinged 6.00

20th anniversary of the death of K. A. Timiryasev, scientist and professor of agricultural and biological sciences.

Relay Race — A366

Sportswomen Marching
A367

Children's Sport Badge — A368

Skier — A369

Throwing the Grenade
A370

1940, July 21

784 A366	15k carmine rose	.70	.25
785 A367	30k sepia	1.50	.25
786 A368	50k dk violet blue	1.65	.60
787 A369	60k dk violet blue	2.25	.60
788 A370	1r grayish green	3.75	1.25
	Nos. 784-788 (5)	9.85	2.95
	Set, never hinged	17.50	

2nd All-Union Physical Culture Day.

Tchaikovsky Museum at Klin — A371

Tchaikovsky & Passage from his Fourth Symphony — A372

Peter Ilich Tchaikovsky and Excerpt from Eugene Onegin — A373

1940, Aug. Unwmk. Typo. *Perf. 12*

789 A371	15k Prus green	1.50	.60
790 A372	20k brown	1.50	.60
791 A372	30k dark blue	1.50	.60
792 A371	50k rose lake	1.50	.80
793 A373	60k red	1.75	1.25
	Nos. 789-793 (5)	7.75	3.85
	Set, never hinged	15.00	

Tchaikovsky (1840-1893), composer.

Volga Provinces Pavilion A374

Northeast Provinces Pavilion — A376

ПАВИЛЬОН МОСКОВСКОЙ, РЯЗАНСКОЙ И ТУЛЬСКОЙ ОБЛ.
#797

ПАВИЛЬОН УКРАИНСКОЙ ССР
#798

ПАВИЛЬОН БЕЛОРУССКОЙ ССР
#799

ПАВИЛЬОН АЗЕРБАЙДЖАНСКОЙ ССР
#800

ПАВИЛЬОН ГРУЗИНСКОЙ ССР
#801

ПАВИЛЬОН АРМЯНСКОЙ ССР
#802

У ВХОДА В ПАВИЛЬОН УЗБЕКСКОЙ ССР
#803

ПАВИЛЬОН ТУРКМЕНСКОЙ ССР
#804

ПАВИЛЬОН ТАДЖИКСКОЙ ССР
#805

ПАВИЛЬОН КИРГИЗСКОЙ ССР
#806

ПАВИЛЬОН КАЗАХСКОЙ ССР
#807

ПАВИЛЬОН КАРЕЛО-ФИНСКОЙ ССР
#808

1940, Oct. Photo.

794 A374	10k shown	1.00	.45
795 A374	15k Far East Provinces	1.00	.45
796 A376	30k shown	1.00	.60
797 A376	30k Central Regions	1.00	.60
798 A376	30k Ukrainian	1.00	.60
799 A376	30k Byelorussian	1.00	.60
800 A376	30k Azerbaijan	1.00	.60
801 A374	30k Georgian	1.00	.60
802 A376	30k Armenian	1.00	.60
803 A376	30k Uzbek	1.00	.60
804 A374	30k Turkmen	1.00	.60
805 A376	30k Tadzhik	1.00	.60
806 A376	30k Kirghiz	1.50	1.25
807 A376	30k Kazakh	1.50	1.25
808 A376	30k Karelian Finnish	1.50	1.25
809 A376	50k Main building	2.00	1.25
810 A376	60k Mechanizaton Pavilion, Stalin statue	2.25	1.25
	Nos. 794-810 (17)	20.75	13.15
	Set, never hinged	40.00	

All-Union Agricultural Fair.

Nos. 796-808 printed in three sheet formats with various vertical and horizontal se-tenant combinations.

Monument to Red Army Heroes — A391

Map of War Operations and M. V. Frunze — A393

Heroic Crossing of the Sivash A394

Designs: 15k, Grenade thrower. 60k, Frunze's headquarters, Stroganovka. 1r, Victorious soldier.

1940 *Imperf.*

811 A391	10k dark green	.50	.30
812 A391	15k orange ver	.50	.30
813 A393	30k dull brown & car	.50	.30
814 A394	50k violet brn	.50	.40
815 A394	60k indigo	.50	.60
816 A391	1r gray black	1.25	.60
	Nos. 811-816 (6)	3.75	2.50
	Set, never hinged	5.00	

20th anniversary of battle of Perekop.

Also issued perf. 12. Set price about 25% more.

Coal Miners — A397

Blast Furnace — A398

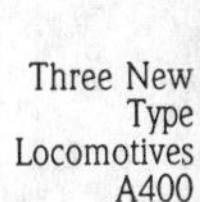

Bridge over Moscow-Volga Canal — A399

Three New Type Locomotives A400

Workers on a Collective Farm — A401

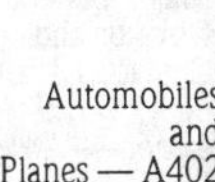

Automobiles and Planes — A402

Oil Derricks — A403

1941, Jan. *Perf. 12*

817 A397	10k deep blue	.40	.20
818 A398	15k dark violet	.40	.20
819 A399	20k deep blue	.40	.20
820 A400	30k dark brown	.55	.20
821 A401	50k olive brown	.55	.40
822 A402	60k olive brown	.80	.55
823 A403	1r dark blue green	1.50	.80
	Nos. 817-823 (7)	4.60	2.55
	Set, never hinged	8.00	

Soviet industries.

Troops on Skis — A404

Sailor — A405

Soldiers with Cannon A406

20k, Cavalry. 30k, Machine gunners. 45k, Army horsemen. 50k, Aviator. 1r, 3r, Marshal's Star.

1941-43

824 A404	5k dark violet	.50	.15
825 A405	10k deep blue	.50	.15
826 A406	15k brt yellow green	.20	.15
827 A404	20k vermilion	.20	.15
828 A404	30k dull brown	.20	.15
829 A406	45k gray green	.60	.50
830 A404	50k dull blue	.35	.65
831 A404	1r dull blue green	.50	.90
831A A404	3r myrtle grn ('43)	1.90	1.90
	Nos. 824-831A (9)	4.95	4.70
	Set, never hinged	7.50	

Army & Navy of the USSR, 23rd anniv.

Battle of Ismail A412

Field Marshal Aleksandr Suvorov A413

1941 Unwmk. *Perf. 12*

832 A412	10k dark green	.40	.30
833 A413	15k carmine rose	.55	.45
834 A413	30k blue black	.80	.65
835 A413	1r olive brown	1.65	.90
	Nos. 832-835 (4)	3.40	2.30
	Set, never hinged	5.00	

150th anniversary of the capture of the Turkish fortress, Ismail.

Kirghiz Horse Breeder A414

Kirghiz Miner — A415

1941, Mar.

836 A414	15k dull brown	.90	.45
837 A415	30k dull purple	1.25	.60
	Set, never hinged	3.50	

15th anniversary of the Kirghizian Soviet Socialist Republic.

Prof. N. E. Zhukovski A416

Zhukovski Lecturing A418

Military Air Academy A417

1941, Mar.

838 A416	15k deep blue	.45	.25
839 A417	30k carmine rose	.45	.40
840 A418	50k brown violet	.75	.50
	Nos. 838-840 (3)	1.65	1.15
	Set, never hinged	2.50	

Prof. Zhukovski, scientist (1847-1921).

Arms Type of 1938

Karelian-Finnish Soviet Socialist Republic.

1941, Mar.

841 A252	30k rose	.60	.35
842 A252	45k dark blue green	.90	.60
	Set, never hinged	2.00	

1st anniversary of the Karelian-Finnish Soviet Socialist Republic.

Spasski Tower, Kremlin A420

Kremlin and Moscow River A421

1941, May Typo. Unwmk.

843 A420	1r dull red	.45	.35
844 A421	2r brown orange	1.10	.70
	Set, never hinged	2.00	

"Suvorov's March through the Alps, 1799" A422

Vasili Ivanovich Surikov, Self-portrait A424

"Stepan Rasin on the Volga" — A423

1941, June **Photo.** ***Perf. 12***
845 A422 20k black 1.25 1.25
846 A423 30k scarlet 2.00 1.90
847 A422 50k dk violet brown 4.00 3.50
848 A423 1r gray green 6.00 3.75
849 A424 2r brown 11.00 4.50
Nos. 845-849 (5) 24.25 14.90
Set, never hinged 50.00

Surikov (1848-1916), painter.

Mikhail Y. Lermontov. Poet, Death Centenary — A425

1941, July
850 A425 15k Prus green 5.50 2.25
851 A425 30k dark violet 6.50 3.50
Set, never hinged 25.00

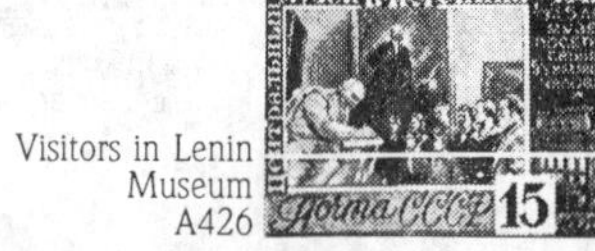
Visitors in Lenin Museum A426

Lenin Museum A427

1941-42
852 A426 15k rose red 1.25 2.00
853 A427 30k dark violet ('42) 5.00 4.00
854 A426 45k Prus green 2.25 2.25
855 A427 1r orange brn ('42) 6.50 4.00
Nos. 852-855 (4) 15.00 12.25
Set, never hinged 30.00

Fifth anniversary of Lenin Museum.

Mother's Farewell to a Soldier Son ("Be a Hero!") A428

1941, Aug.
856 A428 30k carmine 10.00 10.00
Never hinged 17.00

Alisher Navoi A429

Lenin Museum /art A427People's Militia A430

1942, Jan.
857 A429 30k brown 5.75 4.50
858 A429 1r dark violet 9.00 7.50
Set, never hinged 20.00

Alisher Navoi, Uzbekian poet, 500th birth anniv.

1941, Dec. **Typo.**
859 A430 30k dull blue 40.00 30.00
Never hinged 60.00

Junior Lieutenant Talalikhin Ramming German Plane in Midair — A431

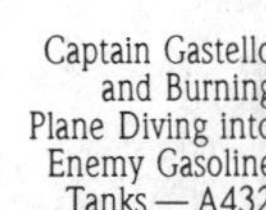

Captain Gastello and Burning Plane Diving into Enemy Gasoline Tanks — A432

Major General Dovator and Cossack Cavalry in Action — A433

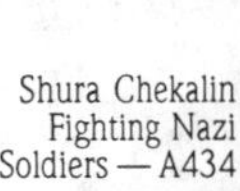

Shura Chekalin Fighting Nazi Soldiers — A434

Nazi Soldiers Leading Zoya Kosmodemjanskaja to her Death — A435

1942-44 **Unwmk.** **Photo.** ***Perf. 12***
860 A431 20k bluish black .95 .35
860A A431 30k Prus grn ('44) .95 .35
861 A432 30k bluish black .95 .35
861A A432 30k dp ultra ('44) .95 .35
862 A433 30k black .95 .35
863 A434 30k black .95 .35
863A A434 30k brt yel green ('44) .95 .35
864 A435 30k black .95 .35
864A A435 30k rose vio ('44) .95 .35
865 A434 1r slate green 4.50 3.00
866 A435 2r slate green 7.00 4.00
Nos. 860-866 (11) 20.05 10.15
Set, never hinged 30.00

Issued to honor Soviet heroes.
For surcharges see Nos. C80-C81.

Anti-tank Artillery A436

Signal Corps in Action A437

Defense of Leningrad A440

Guerrilla Fighters — A438

War Worker — A439

Red Army Scouts — A441

1942-43
867 A436 20k black .40 .40
868 A437 30k sappire .70 .50
869 A438 30k Prus green ('43) .70 .50
870 A439 30k dull red brn ('43) .70 .50
871 A440 60k blue black 1.75 1.60
872 A441 1r black brown 3.00 2.40
Nos. 867-872 (6) 7.25 5.90
Set, never hinged 10.00

Women Workers and Soldiers A442

Flaming Tank A443

Women Preparing Food Shipments A444

Sewing Equipment for Red Army — A445

Anti-Aircraft Battery in Action — A446

1942-43 **Typo.** **Unwmk.**
873 A442 20k dark blue .70 .70
874 A443 20k dull rose violet .70 .70
875 A444 30k brown violet ('43) .70 .70
876 A445 45k dull rose red 1.50 1.50
877 A446 45k deep dull blue ('43) 1.50 1.50
Nos. 873-877 (5) 5.10 5.10
Set, never hinged 6.50

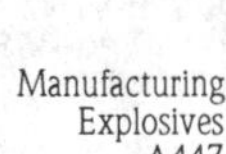

Manufacturing Explosives A447

Designs: 10k, Agriculture. 15k, Group of Fighters. 20k, Storming the Palace. 30k, Lenin and Stalin. 60k, Tanks. 1r, Lenin. 2r, Revolution scene.

Inscribed: "1917 XXV 1942"

1943, Jan. **Photo.** ***Perf. 12***
878 A447 5k black brown .20 .15
879 A447 10k black brown .20 .15
880 A447 15k blue black .20 .15
881 A447 20k blue black .30 .15
882 A447 30k black brown .30 .15
883 A447 60k black brown .60 .25
884 A447 1r dull red brown .95 .50
885 A447 2r black 2.25 .90
Nos. 878-885 (8) 5.00 2.40
Set, never hinged 10.00

25th anniversary of October Revolution.

Mount St. Elias, Alaska — A455

Bering Sea and Bering's Ship — A456

1943, Apr.
886 A455 30k chalky blue .40 .15
887 A456 60k Prus green .65 .15
888 A455 1r yellow green 1.40 .40
889 A456 2r bister brown 2.75 .65
Nos. 886-889 (4) 5.20 1.35
Set, never hinged 12.00

200th anniv. of the death of Vitus Bering, explorer (1681-1741).

Medical Corpsmen and Wounded Soldier — A457

Trench Mortar — A458

Army Scouts — A459

Repulsing Enemy Tanks — A460

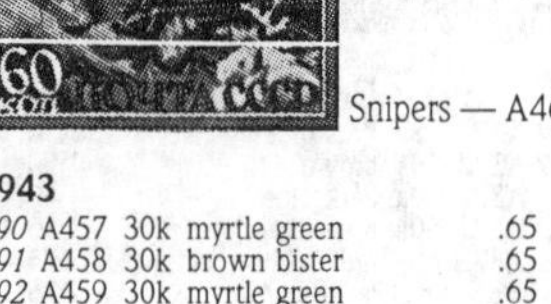
Snipers — A461

1943
890 A457 30k myrtle green .65 .55
891 A458 30k brown bister .65 .55
892 A459 30k myrtle green .65 .55
893 A460 60k myrtle green 2.00 1.90
894 A461 60k chalky blue 2.00 1.90
Nos. 890-894 (5) 5.95 5.45
Set, never hinged 9.00

Maxim Gorki (1868-1936), Writer — A462

1943, June
895 A462 30k green .35 .15
896 A462 60k slate black .45 .20
Set, never hinged 1.00

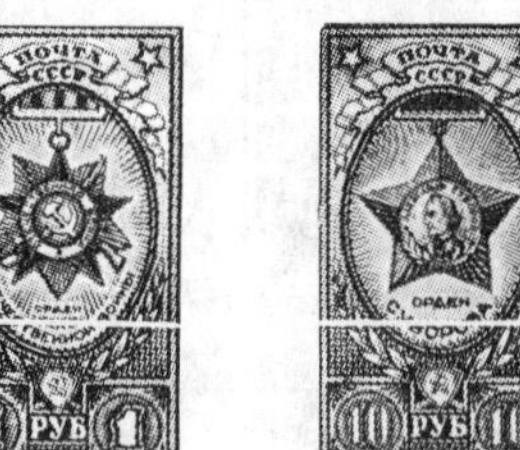

Patriotic War Medal A463

Order of Field Marshal Suvorov A464

1943, July **Engr.**
897 A463 1r black 1.00 1.00
898 A464 10r dk olive green 4.00 4.00
Set, never hinged 6.00

Sailors — A465

Designs: 30k, Navy gunner and warship. 60k, Soldiers and tank.

1943, Oct. **Photo.**
899 A465 20k golden brown .15 .15
900 A465 30k dark myrtle green .15 .15
901 A465 60k brt yellow green .30 .20
902 A465 3r chalky blue .85 .40
Nos. 899-902 (4) 1.45 .90
Set, never hinged 2.50

25th anniv. of the Red Army and Navy.

Karl Marx
A468

Vladimir V. Mayakovsky
A469

1943, Sept.

903 A468 30k blue black .40 .25
904 A468 60k dk slate green .60 .25
Set, never hinged 2.00

125th anniv. of the birth of Karl Marx.

1943, Oct.

905 A469 30k red orange .30 .25
906 A469 60k deep blue .40 .25
Set, never hinged 1.00

Mayakovsky, poet, 50th birth anniv.

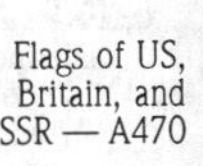

Flags of US, Britain, and USSR — A470

1943, Nov.

907 A470 30k black, dp red & dk blue .60 .30
908 A470 3r sl blue, red & lt blue 2.50 .85
Set, never hinged 3.50

The Tehran conference.

Ivan Turgenev (1818-83), Poet — A471

1943, Oct.

909 A471 30k myrtle green 3.25 3.25
910 A471 60k dull purple 4.25 4.25
Set, never hinged 12.50

Map of Stalingrad
A472

Harbor of Sevastopol and Statue of Lenin — A473

Leningrad
A474

Odessa — A475

1944, Mar. ***Perf. 12***

911 A472 30k dull brown & car .30 .15
912 A473 30k dark blue .30 .15
913 A474 30k dk slate green .30 .15
914 A475 30k yel green .30 .15
Nos. 911-914 (4) 1.20 .60
Set, never hinged 2.00

Honoring the defenders of Stalingrad, Leningrad, Sevastopol and Odessa.
See No. 959.

No. 911 measures 33x22mm and also exists in smaller size: 32x21½mm.

USSR War Heroes — A476

1944, Apr.

915 A476 30k deep ultra .35 .25
Never hinged .75

Sailor Loading Gun — A477

Tanks — A478

Soldier Bayoneting a Nazi
A479

Infantryman
A480

Soldier Throwing Hand Grenade — A481

1943-44 **Photo.**

916 A477 15k deep ultra .15 .15
917 A478 20k red orange ('44) .15 .15
918 A479 30k dull brn & dk red ('44) .25 .15
919 A480 1r brt yel green .70 .35
920 A481 2r Prus green ('44) 1.10 .70
Nos. 916-920 (5) 2.35 1.50
Set, never hinged 4.50

25th anniversary of the Young Communist League (Komsomol).

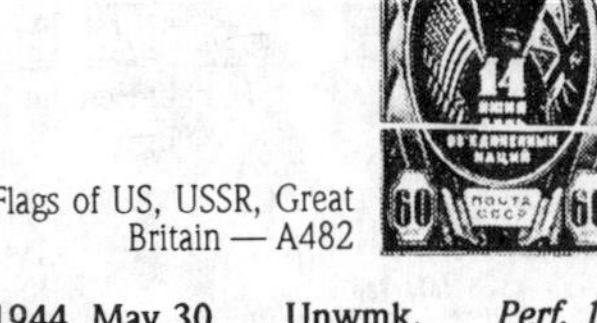

Flags of US, USSR, Great Britain — A482

1944, May 30 **Unwmk.** ***Perf. 12***

921 A482 60k black, red & blue .60 .30
922 A482 3r dk bl, red & lt bl 3.25 1.10
Set, never hinged 4.75

Day of the Nations United Against Germany, June 14, 1944.

Patriotic War Order — A483

Order of Prince Alexander Nevsky — A484

Order of Field Marshal Suvorov
A485

Order of Field Marshal Kutuzov
A486

Paper with network as in parenthesis

1944 **Typo.** ***Perf. 12, Imperf.***

923 A483 15k dull red *(rose)* .15 .15
924 A484 20k blue *(lt blue)* .20 .15
925 A485 30k green *(green)* .20 .20
926 A486 60k dull red *(rose)* .45 .35
Nos. 923-926 (4) 1.00 .85
Set, never hinged 1.75

Order of Patriotic War — A487

Order of Prince, Alexander Nevski — A488

Order of Field Marshal Kutuzov
A489

Order of Field Marshal Suvorov
A490

1944, June **Unwmk.** **Engr.** ***Perf. 12***

927 A487 1r black .25 .20
928 A488 3r blue black .55 .45
929 A489 5r dark olive green .95 .60
930 A490 10r dark red 1.65 .70
Nos. 927-930 (4) 3.40 1.95
Set, never hinged 4.00

Types of 1934, Inscribed 1924-1944 and

Lenin's Mausoleum — A491

Designs: 30k (No. 931), 3r, Lenin and Stalin. 50k, Lenin in middle age. 60k, Lenin, the orator.

1944, June **Photo.**

931 A190 30k orange & car .15 .20
932 A186 30k slate & black .15 .20
933 A187 45k slate & black .45 .30
934 A187 50k slate & black .45 .30
935 A187 60k slate & black .45 .30
936 A491 1r indigo & brown black 1.10 .40
937 A190 3r bl blk & dull org 2.75 .85
Nos. 931-937 (7) 5.50 2.55
Set, never hinged 8.25

20 years without Lenin.

Nikolai Rimski-Korsakov
A492 A493

1944, June ***Perf. 12, Imperf.***

938 A492 30k gray black .20 .15
939 A493 60k slate green .30 .15
940 A492 1r brt blue green .40 .15
941 A493 3r purple .65 .20
Nos. 938-941 (4) 1.55 .65
Set, never hinged 2.50

Rimski-Korsakov (1844-1909), composer.

N.A. Schors
A494

Sergei A. Chaplygin
A497

Heroes of the 1918 Civil War: No. 943, V.I. Chapayev. No. 944, S.G. Lazho.

1944, Sept. ***Perf. 12***

942 A494 30k gray black .30 .20
943 A494 30k dark slate green .30 .20
944 A494 30k brt yellow green .30 .20
Nos. 942-944 (3) .90 .60
Set, never hinged 1.50

See Nos. 1209-1211, 1403.

1944, Sept.

945 A497 30k gray .25 .15
946 A497 1r lt brown .85 .20
Set, never hinged 1.50

75th anniversary of the birth of Sergei A. Chaplygin, scientist and mathematician.

Khanpasha Nuradilov
A498

A. Matrosov
A499

F. Louzan — A500

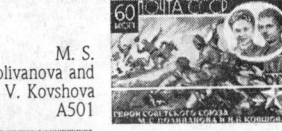

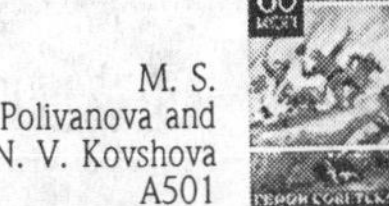
M. S. Polivanova and N. V. Kovshova
A501

Pilot B. Safonov — A502

1944, July

947 A498 30k slate green .15 .15
948 A499 60k dull purple .30 .25
949 A500 60k dull blue .30 .25
950 A501 60k bright green .30 .25
951 A502 60k slate black .45 .25
Nos. 947-951 (5) 1.50 1.15
Set, never hinged 4.50

Soviet war heroes.

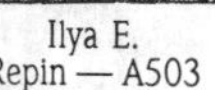

Ilya E. Repin — A503

Ivan A. Krylov — A505

"Cossacks' Reply to Sultan Mohammed IV" — A504

1944, Nov. *Perf. 12½, Imperf.*

952 A503 30k slate green .30 .20
953 A504 50k dk blue green .45 .20
954 A504 60k chalky blue .45 .20
955 A503 1r dk orange brown .60 .20
956 A504 2r dark purple 1.25 .30
Nos. 952-956 (5) 3.05 1.10
Set, never hinged 4.00

I. E. Repin (1844-1930), painter.

1944, Nov. *Perf. 12*

957 A505 30k yellow brown .15 .15
958 A505 1r dk violet blue .25 .15
Set value .25
Set, never hinged .75

Krylov, fable writer, death centenary.

Leningrad Type
Souvenir Sheet

1944, Dec. 6 *Imperf.*

959 Sheet of 4 5.00 4.75
Never hinged 7.50
a. A474 30k dark slate green .40 .40

Liberation of Leningrad, Jan. 27, 1944.

Partisan Medal — A507

Order for Bravery — A508

Order of Bogdan Chmielnicki A509

Order of Victory A510

Order of Ushakov A511

Order of Nakhimov A512

Paper with network as in parenthesis
Perf. 12½, Imperf.

1945, Jan. **Typo.** **Unwmk.**

960 A507 15k black *(green)* .15 .15
961 A508 30k dp blue *(lt blue)* .15 .15
962 A509 45k dk blue .20 .15
963 A510 60k dl rose *(pale rose)* .30 .15
964 A511 1r dull blue *(green)* .40 .20
965 A512 1r yel green *(blue)* .40 .20
Nos. 960-965 (6) 1.60 1.00
Set, never hinged 3.00

Aleksandr S. Griboedov A513

Red Army Soldier A514

1945, Jan. **Photo.** *Perf. 12½*

966 A513 30k dk slate green .30 .20
967 A513 60k gray brown .55 .30
Set, never hinged 1.25

Griboedov (1795-1829), poet & statesman.

1945, Mar.

968 A514 60k gray blk & henna .50 .55
969 A514 3r gray blk & henna 1.50 1.10
Set, never hinged 3.00

Souvenir Sheet
Imperf

970 Sheet of 4 25.00 25.00
Never hinged 40.00
a. A514 3r gray brown & henna 7.50 7.50

Second anniv. of victory at Stalingrad.

Order for Bravery A516

Order of Bogdan Chmielnicki A517

Order of Victory — A518

1945 **Engr.** *Perf. 12*

971 A516 1r indigo .35 .30
972 A517 2r black .75 .50
973 A518 3r henna 1.25 .80
Nos. 971-973 (3) 2.35 1.60
Set, never hinged 5.00

See Nos. 1341-1342. For overprints see Nos. 992, 1709.

A519

A520

A521

A522

A523

Battle Scenes — A524

1945, Apr. **Photo.** *Perf. 12½*

974 A519 20k sl grn, org red & black .40 .40
975 A520 30k blue blk & dull orange .40 .40
976 A521 30k blue black .40 .40
977 A522 60k orange red .70 .70
978 A523 1r slate green & org red 1.00 1.00
979 A524 1r slate green 1.00 1.00
Nos. 974-979 (6) 3.90 3.90
Set, never hinged 6.00

Red Army successes against Germany.

Parade in Red Square, Nov. 7, 1941 — A525

Designs: 60k, Soldiers and Moscow barricade, Dec. 1941. 1r, Air battle, 1941.

1945, June

980 A525 30k dk blue violet .25 .25
981 A525 60k olive black .40 .40
982 A525 1r black brown 1.40 1.40
Nos. 980-982 (3) 2.05 2.05
Set, never hinged 3.00

3rd anniversary of the victory over the Germans before Moscow.

Elite Guard Badge and Cannons A528

Motherhood Medal A529

Motherhood Glory Order — A530

Mother-Heroine Order — A531

1945, Apr. **Typo.**

983 A528 60k red .40 .25
Never hinged .80

1945 *Perf. 12½, Imperf.*
Paper with network as in parenthesis
Size: 22x33¼mm

984 A529 20k brown *(lt blue)* .15 .15
985 A530 30k yel brown *(green)* .25 .15
986 A531 60k dull rose *(pale rose)* .40 .15

Perf. 12½
Engr.
Size: 20x38mm

986A A529 1r blk brn *(green)* .40 .15
986B A530 2r dp bl *(lt blue)* .90 .35
986C A531 3r brn red *(lt blue)* 1.00 .60
Nos. 984-986C (6) 3.10 1.55
Set, never hinged 4.00

Academy Building, Moscow A532

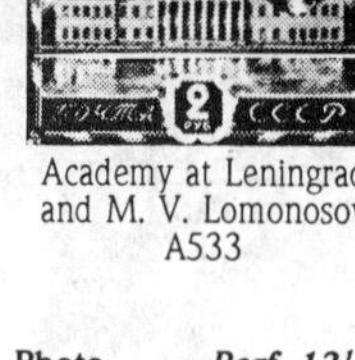

Academy at Leningrad and M. V. Lomonosov A533

1945, June **Photo.** *Perf. 12½*

987 A532 30k blue violet .35 .15
a. Horiz. pair, imperf. between 3.25
988 A533 2r grnsh black 1.25 .55
Set, never hinged 2.00

Academy of Sciences, 220th anniv.

Popov and his Invention A534

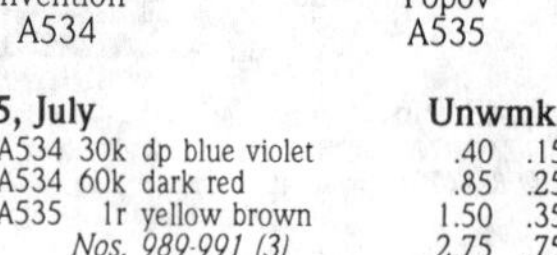

Aleksandr S. Popov A535

1945, July **Unwmk.**

989 A534 30k dp blue violet .40 .15
990 A534 60k dark red .85 .25
991 A535 1r yellow brown 1.50 .35
Nos. 989-991 (3) 2.75 .75
Set, never hinged 3.50

"Invention of radio" by A. S. Popov, 50th anniv.

No. 973 Overprinted in Blue

ПРАЗДНИК ПОБЕДЫ
9 мая 1945 года

1945, Aug. *Perf. 12*

992 A518 3r henna 1.00 .50
Never hinged 1.50

Victory of the Allied Nations in Europe.

Iakovlev Fighter — A536

Petliakov-2 Dive Bombers A537

Ilyushin-2 Bombers A538

Designs: Nos. 992A, 995, Iakovlev Fighter. Nos. 992B, 1000, Petliakov-2 dive bombers. Nos. 992C, 996, Ilyushin-2 bombers. Nos. 992D, 993, Petliakov-8 heavy bomber. Nos. 992E, 1001, Tupolev-2 bombers. Nos. 992F, 997, Ilyushin-4 bombers. Nos. 992G, 999, Polikarpov-2 biplane. Nos. 992H, 998, Lavochkin-7 fighters. Nos. 992I, 994, Iakovlev fighter in action.

1945-46 **Unwmk.** **Photo.** *Perf. 12*

992A A536 5k dk violet ('46) .30 .20
992B A537 10k henna brn ('46) .30 .20
992C A538 15k henna brn ('46) .40 .20
992D A536 15k Prus grn ('46) .40 .20
992E A538 20k gray brn ('46) .45 .25
992F A538 30k violet ('46) .45 .25
992G A538 30k brown ('46) .45 .25
992H A538 50k blue vio ('46) .95 .60
992I A536 60k dl bl vio ('46) .95 .60
993 A536 1r gray black 2.00 1.25
994 A536 1r henna brown 2.00 1.25
995 A536 1r brown 2.00 1.25
996 A538 1r deep brown 2.00 1.25

97 A538 1r intense black 2.00 1.25
98 A538 1r orange ver 2.00 1.25
99 A538 1r bright green 2.00 1.25
000 A537 1r deep brown 2.00 1.25
001 A538 1r violet blue 2.00 1.25
Nos. 992A-1001 (18) 22.65 14.00
Set, never hinged 35.00

Issued: #992A-992I, 3/26; #993-1001, 8/19.

Lenin
A545 A546
Various Lenin Portraits
Dated "1870-1945"

945, Sept. *Perf. 12½*
002 A545 30k bluish black .30 .15
003 A546 50k gray brown .40 .15
004 A546 60k orange brown .50 .20
005 A546 1r greenish black .80 .25
006 A546 3r sepia 2.50 .60
Nos. 1002-1006 (5) 4.50 1.35
Set, never hinged 8.00

75th anniversary of the birth of Lenin.

Prince M. I. Kutuzov A550 — Aleksandr Ivanovich Herzen A551

1945, Sept. 16
007 A550 30k blue violet .35 .20
008 A550 60k brown .65 .30
Set, never hinged 1.50

Field Marshal Prince Mikhail Illarionovich Kutuzov (1745-1813).

1945, Oct. 26
1009 A551 30k dark brown .35 .20
1010 A551 2r greenish black 1.10 .40
Set, never hinged 2.50

Herzen, author, revolutionist, 75th death anniv.

Ilya Mechnikov A552 — Friedrich Engels A553

1945, Nov. 27
1011 A552 30k brown .50 .20
1012 A552 1r greenish black 1.00 .40
Set, never hinged 3.00

Ilya I. Mechnikov, zoologist and bacteriologist (1845-1916).

1945, Nov. Unwmk. *Perf. 12½*
1013 A553 30k dark brown .45 .20
1014 A553 60k Prussian green .60 .30
Set, never hinged 1.25

125th anniversary of the birth of Friedrich Engels, collaborator of Karl Marx.

Tank Leaving Assembly Line — A554

Designs: 30k, Harvesting wheat. 60k, Airplane designing. 1r, Moscow fireworks.

1945, Dec. 25 **Photo.**
1015 A554 20k indigo & brown .40 .35
1016 A554 30k black & orange brn .40 .35
1017 A554 60k brown & green .75 .35
1018 A554 1r dk blue & orange 1.40 .50
Nos. 1015-1018 (4) 2.95 1.55
Set, never hinged 6.00

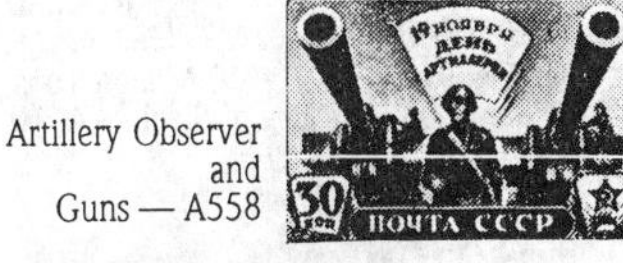

Artillery Observer and Guns — A558

Heavy Field Pieces — A559

1945, Dec.
1019 A558 30k brown .45 .35
1020 A559 60k sepia 1.00 .65
Set, never hinged 2.50

Artillery Day, Nov. 19, 1945.

Catalogue values for unused stamps in this section, from this point to the end of the section, are for Never Hinged items.

Victory Medal — A560

Soldier with Victory Flag — A561

1946, Jan. 23
1021 A560 30k dk violet .30 .20
1022 A560 30k brown .30 .20
1023 A560 60k greenish black .65 .20
1024 A560 60k henna .65 .20
1025 A561 60k black & dull red .65 .20
Nos. 1021-1025 (5) 2.55 1.00

Arms of USSR — A562

Red Square — A563

1946, Feb. 10
1026 A562 30k henna .35 .25
1027 A563 45k henna .45 .25
1028 A562 60k greenish black .95 .30
Nos. 1026-1028 (3) 1.75 .80

Elections to the Supreme Soviet of the USSR, Feb. 10, 1946.

Artillery in Victory Parade — A564

Victory Parade — A565

1946, Feb. 23
1029 A564 60k dark brown .50 .20
1030 A564 2r dull violet 1.00 .25
1031 A565 3r black & red 1.40 .45
Nos. 1029-1031 (3) 2.90 .90

Victory Parade, Moscow, June 24, 1945.

Order of Lenin — A566

Order of Red Star — A567

Medal of Hammer and Sickle A568

Order of Token of Veneration A569

Gold Star Medal — A570

Order of Red Banner — A571

Order of the Red Workers' Banner — A572

Paper with network as in parenthesis

1946 Unwmk. Typo. *Perf. 12½x12*
1032 A566 60k myrtle grn *(green)* 1.25 .80
1033 A567 60k dk vio brn *(brown)* 1.25 .80
1034 A568 60k plum *(pink)* 1.25 .80
1035 A569 60k dp blue *(green)* 1.25 .80
1036 A570 60k dk car *(salmon)* 1.25 .80
1037 A571 60k red *(salmon)* 1.25 .80
1038 A572 60k dk brn vio *(buff)* 1.25 .80
Nos. 1032-1038 (7) 8.75 5.60

See Nos. 1650-1654.

Workers' Achievement of Distinction A573

Workers' Gallantry A574

Marshal's Star — A575

Defense of Soviet Trans-Arctic Regions — A576

Meritorious Service in Battle A577

Defense of Caucasus A578

Defense of Moscow A579

Bravery A580

Paper with network as in parenthesis

1946
1039 A573 60k choc *(salmon)* 1.50 1.00
1040 A574 60k brown *(salmon)* 1.50 1.00
1041 A575 60k blue *(pale blue)* 1.50 1.00
1042 A576 60k dk green *(green)* 1.50 1.00
1043 A577 60k dk blue *(green)* 1.50 1.00
1044 A578 60k dk yel grn *(grn)* 1.50 1.00
1045 A579 60k carmine *(pink)* 1.50 1.00
1046 A580 60k dk violet *(blue)* 1.50 1.00
Nos. 1039-1046 (8) 12.00 8.00

A581

Maxim Gorki — A582

1946, June 18 **Photo.**
1047 A581 30k brown .20 .15
1048 A582 60k dark green .65 .15

10th anniversary of the death of Maxim Gorki (Alexei M. Peshkov).

Kalinin A583

Chebyshev A584

1946, June
1049 A583 20k sepia .50 .25

Mikhail Ivanovich Kalinin (1875-1946).

1946, May 25
1050 A584 30k brown .55 .20
1051 A584 60k gray brown .75 .20

Pafnuti Lvovich Chebyshev (1821-94), mathematician.

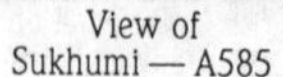

View of Sukhumi — A585

Sanatorium at Sochi — A587

Designs: #1053, Promenade at Gagri. 45k, New Afyon Sanatorium.

1946, June 18

1052	A585	15k dark brown	.35	.20
1053	A585	30k dk slate green	.45	.20
1054	A587	30k dark green	.45	.20
1055	A585	45k chestnut brown	.75	.20
		Nos. 1052-1055 (4)	2.00	.80

All-Union Parade of Physical Culturists — A589

1946, July 21

1056	A589	30k dark green	4.00	2.25

Tank Divisions in Red Square A590

1946, Sept. 8

1057	A590	30k dark green	.60	.40
1058	A590	60k brown	.95	.60

Honoring Soviet tankmen.

Belfry of Ivan the Great, Kremlin A591

Bolshoi Theater, Moscow A592

Hotel Moscow — A593

Red Square A597

Spasski Tower and Statues of Minin and Pozharski — A598

Moscow scenes: 20k, Bolshoi Theater, Sverdlov Square. 45k, View of Kremlin. 50k, Lenin Museum.

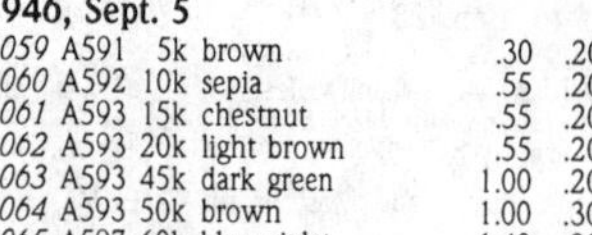

1946, Sept. 5

1059	A591	5k brown	.30	.20
1060	A592	10k sepia	.55	.20
1061	A593	15k chestnut	.55	.20
1062	A593	20k light brown	.55	.20
1063	A593	45k dark green	1.00	.20
1064	A593	50k brown	1.00	.30
1065	A597	60k blue violet	1.40	.30
1066	A598	1r chestnut brown	2.00	.30
		Nos. 1059-1066 (8)	7.35	1.90

Workers' Achievement of Distinction — A599

Workers' Gallantry — A600

Partisan of the Patriotic War — A601

Defense of Soviet Trans-Arctic Regions — A602

Meritorious Service in Battle — A603

Defense of Caucasus — A604

Defense of Moscow — A605

Bravery — A606

1946, Sept. 5 **Engr.**

1067	A599	1r dark violet brown	.85	.45
1068	A600	1r dark carmine	.85	.45
1069	A601	1r carmine	.85	.45
1070	A602	1r blue black	.85	.45
1071	A603	1r black	.85	.45
1072	A604	1r black brown	.85	.45
1073	A605	1r olive black	.85	.45
1074	A606	1r deep claret	.85	.45
		Nos. 1067-1074 (8)	6.80	3.60

See Nos. 1650-1654.

Give the Country Each Year: 127 Million Tons of Grain — A607

60 Million Tons of Oil — A608

60 Million Tons of Steel — A610

500 Million Tons of Coal — A609

50 Million Tons of Cast Iron — A611

Perf. 12½x12

1946, Oct. 6 **Photo.** **Unwmk.**

1075	A607	5k olive brown	.15	.15
1076	A608	10k dk slate green	.15	.15
1077	A609	15k brown	.15	.15
1078	A610	20k dk blue violet	.15	.15
1079	A611	30k brown	.35	.15
		Nos. 1075-1079 (5)	.95	
		Set value		.60

Symbols of Transportation, Map and Stamps — A612

Early Soviet Stamp — A613

Stamps of Soviet Russia — A614

1946, Nov. 6 ***Perf. 12½***

1080	A612	15k black & dk red	.90	.55
a.		Sheet of 4, imperf.	50.00	50.00
1081	A613	30k dk green & brn	1.40	.60
a.		Sheet of 4, imperf.	50.00	50.00
1082	A614	60k dk green & blk	1.90	.80
a.		Sheet of 4, imperf.	50.00	50.00
		Nos. 1080-1082 (3)	4.20	1.95

1st Soviet postage stamp, 25th anniv.

Lenin and Stalin — A615

1946 **Photo.** ***Perf. 12½, Imperf.***

1083	A615	30k dp brown org	1.25	1.25
a.		Sheet of 4, imperf.	25.00	17.50
1084	A615	30k dk green	1.25	1.25

29th anniversary of October Revolution.

Issue dates: Nos. 1083-1084 imperf., Nov. 6; perf., Dec. 18. No. 1083a, June, 1947.

Dnieprostroy Dam and Power Station — A616

1946, Dec. 23 ***Perf. 12½***

1085	A616	30k sepia	1.00	.4
1086	A616	60k chalky blue	1.50	.6

Aleksandr P. Karpinsky A617

Nikolai A. Nekrasov A618

1947, Jan. 17 **Unwmk.**

1087	A617	30k dark green	.65	.40
1088	A617	50k sepia	1.00	.60

Karpinsky (1847-1936), geologist.

Canceled to Order

Canceled sets of new issues have long been sold by the government. Values in the second ("used") column are for these canceled-to-order stamps. Postally used copies are worth more.

1946, Dec. 4

1089	A618	30k sepia	.40	.20
1090	A618	60k brown	.60	.30

Nikolai A. Nekrasov (1821-1878), poet.

Lenin's Mausoleum — A619

Lenin — A620

1947, Jan. 21

1091	A619	30k slate blue	.75	.40
1092	A619	30k dark green	.75	.40
1093	A620	50k dark brown	1.00	.40
		Nos. 1091-1093 (3)	2.50	1.20

23rd anniversary of the death of Lenin. See Nos. 1197-1199.

F. P. Litke and Sailing Vessel — A621

N. M. Przewalski, Mare and Foal — A622

1947, Jan. 27

1094	A621	20k blue violet	.50	.25
1095	A621	20k sepia	.50	.25
1096	A622	60k olive brown	1.00	.50
1097	A622	60k sepia	1.00	.50
		Nos. 1094-1097 (4)	3.00	1.50

Soviet Union Geographical Society, cent.

Nikolai E. Zhukovski (1847-1921), Scientist A623

1947, Jan. 17

1098 A623 30k sepia	.65	.20
1099 A623 60k blue violet	.80	.30

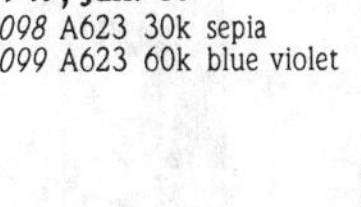

Stalin Prize Medal — A624

1946, Dec. 21 **Photo.**

1100 A624 30k black brown	2.00	.60

Russian Soldier A625

Military Instruction A626

Aviator, Sailor and Soldier — A627

Perf. 12x12½, 12½x12, Imperf.

1947, Feb. 23 **Unwmk.**

1101 A625 20k sepia	.45	.20
1102 A626 30k slate blue	.45	.20
1103 A627 30k brown	.45	.20
Nos. 1101-1103 (3)	1.35	.60

29th anniversary of the Soviet Army.

Reprints

From here through 1953 many sets exist in two distinct printings from different plates.

Arms of:

Russian Socialist Federated Soviet Republic — A628

Armenian SSR — A629

Azerbaijan SSR — A630

Byelorussian SSR — A631

Estonian SSR — A632

Georgian SSR — A633

Karelo Finnish SSR — A634

Kazakh SSR — A635

Kirghiz SSR — A636

Latvian SSR — A637

Lithuanian SSR — A638

Moldavian SSR — A639

Tadzhkistan SSR — A640

Turkmen SSR — A641

Ukrainian SSR — A642

Uzbek SSR — A643

Soviet Union — A644

1947 **Unwmk.** **Photo.** ***Perf. 12½***

1104 A628 30k henna brown	.65	.30
1105 A629 30k chestnut	.65	.30
1106 A630 30k olive brown	.65	.30
1107 A631 30k olive green	.65	.30
1108 A632 30k violet black	.65	.30
1109 A633 30k dark vio brown	.65	.30
1110 A634 30k dark violet	.65	.30
1111 A635 30k deep orange	.65	.30
1112 A636 30k dark violet	.65	.30
1113 A637 30k yellow brown	.65	.30
1114 A638 30k dark olive green	.65	.30
1115 A639 30k dark vio brown	.65	.30
1116 A640 30k dark green	.65	.30
1117 A641 30k gray black	.65	.30
1118 A642 30k blue violet	.65	.30
1119 A643 30k brown	.65	.30
Litho.		
1120 A644 1r dk brn, bl, gold & red	2.25	1.00
Nos. 1104-1120 (17)	12.65	5.80

Aleksander S. Pushkin (1799-1837), Poet — A645

1947, Feb. **Photo.** ***Perf. 12***

1121 A645 30k sepia	.60	.25
1122 A645 50k dk yellow green	.85	.30

Classroom A646

Parade of Women — A647

1947, Mar. 11

1123 A646 15k bright blue	1.00	.60
1124 A647 30k red	1.25	.90

Intl. Day of Women, Mar. 8, 1947.

Moscow Council Building A648

1947 ***Perf. 12½***

1125 A648 30k sep, gray blue & brick red	1.25	.40

30th anniversary of the Moscow Soviet. Exists imperf. The imperf. exists also with gray blue omitted.

Both perf. and imperf. stamps exist in two sizes: 40x27mm and 41x27mm.

May Day Parade in Red Square A649

1947, June 10 ***Perf. 12½***

1126 A649 30k scarlet	.55	.35
1127 A649 1r dk olive green	1.50	.55

Labor Day, May 1, 1947.

Nos. 1062, 1064-1066 Overprinted in Red

800 лет Москвы
1147 – 1947 гг.

1947, Sept. ***Perf. 12½x12***

1128 A593 20k lt brown	.75	.15
1129 A593 50k brown	.95	.50
1130 A597 60k blue violet	1.25	.60
1131 A598 1r chestnut brown	2.00	.70
Nos. 1128-1131 (4)	4.95	1.95

Overprint arranged in 4 lines on No. 1131.

Crimes Bridge, Moscow — A650

Gorki Street, Moscow A651

View of Kremlin, Moscow — A652

Designs: No. 1134, Central Telegraph Building. No. 1135, Kiev Railroad Station. No. 1136, Kazan Railroad Station. No. 1137, Kaluga St. No. 1138, Pushkin Square. 50k, View of Kremlin. No. 1141, Grand Kremlin Palace. No. 1142, "Old Moscow," by Vasnetsov. No. 1143, St. Basil Cathedral. 2r, View of Kremlin. 3r, View of Kremlin. 5r, Hotel Moscow and government building.

1947 **Photo.** ***Perf. 12½***

Various Frames, Dated 1147-1947

1132 A650 5k dk bl & dk brn	.35	.25
1133 A651 10k red brown & brn black	.35	.25
1134 A650 30k brown	.45	.25
1135 A650 30k dk Prus blue	.45	.25
1136 A650 30k ultra	.45	.25
1137 A650 30k dp yel green	.45	.25
1138 A651 30k yel green	.45	.25
1139 A650 50k dp yel green	.60	.40
1140 A652 60k red brown & brn blk	.70	.40
1141 A651 60k gray blue	.70	.40
1142 A651 1r dark violet	1.50	.95
Typo.		
Colors: Blue, Yellow and Red		
1143 A651 1r multicolored	1.50	.95
1144 A651 2r multicolored	2.75	1.90
1145 A650 3r multicolored	5.25	1.90
a. Souv. sheet of 4, imperf.	30.00	20.00
1146 A650 5r multicolored	8.75	3.25
Nos. 1132-1146 (15)	24.70	11.90

Nos. 1128-1146 for founding of Moscow, 800th anniv.

Nos. 1143-1146 were printed in a single sheet containing a row of each denomination plus a row of labels.

Karamyshevsky Dam — A653

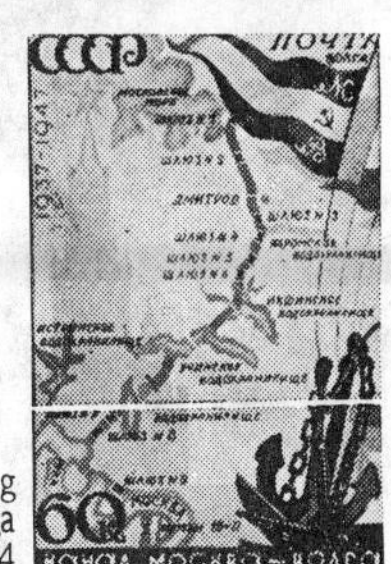

Map Showing Moscow-Volga Canal — A654

Designs: No. 1148, Direction towers, Yakromsky Lock. 45k, Yakromsky Pumping Station. 50k, Khimki Station. 1r, Lock #8.

1947, Sept. 7 **Photo.**

1147 A653 30k sepia	.65	.15
1148 A653 30k red brown	.65	.15
1149 A653 45k henna brown	.65	.15
1150 A653 50k bright ultra	.65	.15
1151 A654 60k bright rose	.65	.15
1152 A653 1r violet	.90	.35
Nos. 1147-1152 (6)	4.15	1.10

Moscow-Volga Canal, 10th anniversary.

Elektrozavodskaya Station — A655

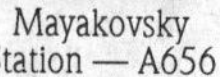
Mayakovsky Station — A656

Planes and Flag — A657

Moscow Subway scenes: No. 1154, Ismailovsky Station. No. 1155, Sokol Station. No. 1156, Stalinsky Station. No. 1158, Kiev Station.

1947, Sept.

1153 A655	30k sepia		.65	.25
1154 A655	30k blue black		.65	.25
1155 A655	45k yellow brown		.90	.25
1156 A655	45k deep violet		.90	.25
1157 A656	60k henna brown		1.50	.30
1158 A655	60k deep yellow green		1.50	.30
	Nos. 1153-1158 (6)		6.10	1.60

1947, Sept. 1

1159 A657	30k deep violet	.35	.20
1160 A657	1r bright ultra	.85	.30

Day of the Air Fleet. For overprints see Nos. 1246-1247.

Spasski Tower, Kremlin — A658

Perf. 12½

1947, Nov. Unwmk. Typo.

1161 A658 60k dark red 6.00 3.50

See No. 1260.

Agave Plant at Sukhumi A659

Gullripsh Sanatorium, Sukhumi A660

Peasants', Livadia — A661

New Riviera — A662

Russian sanatoria: No. 1166, Abkhasia, New Afyon. No. 1167, Kemeri, near Riga. No. 1168, Kirov Memorial, Kislovodsk. No. 1169, Voroshilov Memorial, Sochi. No. 1170, Riza, Gagri. No. 1171, Zapadugol, Sochi.

1947, Nov. Photo.

1162 A659	30k dark green	.50	.20
1163 A660	30k violet	.50	.20
1164 A661	30k olive	.50	.20
1165 A662	30k brown	.50	.20
1166 A660	30k red brown	.50	.20
1167 A660	30k black violet	.50	.20
1168 A660	30k bright ultra	.50	.20
1169 A660	30k dk brown violet	.50	.20
1170 A659	30k dk yel green	.50	.20
1171 A660	30k sepia	.50	.20
	Nos. 1162-1171 (10)	5.00	2.00

Blast Furnaces, Constantine A663

Tractor Plant, Kharkov — A664

Tractor Plant, Stalingrad A665

Maxim Gorki Theater, Stalingrad A666

20k, #1180, Kirov foundry, Makeevka. #1175, 1179, Agricultural machine plant, Rostov.

1947, Nov. *Perf. 12½, Imperf.*

1172 A663	15k yellow brown	.15	.15
1173 A663	20k sepia	.15	.15
1174 A663	30k violet brown	.40	.25
1175 A663	30k dark green	.40	.25
1176 A664	30k brown	.40	.25
1177 A665	30k black brown	.40	.25
1178 A666	60k violet brown	.85	.40
1179 A663	60k yellow brown	.85	.40
1180 A663	1r orange red	1.40	.45
1181 A664	1r red	1.40	.45
1182 A665	1r violet	1.40	.45
	Nos. 1172-1182 (11)	7.80	3.45

Reconstruction of war-damaged cities and factories, and as Five-Year-Plan publicity.

Revolutionists — A667

Designs: 30k, No. 1185, Revolutionists. 50k, 1r, Industry. No. 1186, 2r, Agriculture.

1947, Nov. *Perf. 12½, Imperf.*

Frame in Dark Red

1183 A667	30k greenish black	.50	.15
1184 A667	50k blue black	.75	.25
1185 A667	60k brown black	.95	.35
1186 A667	60k brown	.95	.55
1187 A667	1r black	1.60	.65
1188 A667	2r greenish black	3.00	.90
	Nos. 1183-1188 (6)	7.75	2.85

30th anniversary of October Revolution.

Palace of the Arts (Winter Palace) A668

Peter I Monument A669

Designs (Leningrad in 1947): 60k, Sts. Peter and Paul Fortress. 1r, Smolny Institute.

1948, Jan. 10 *Perf. 12½*

1189 A668	30k violet	.90	.40
1190 A669	50k dk slate green	1.65	.45
1191 A668	60k sepia	1.65	.75
1192 A669	1r dk brown violet	2.75	1.10
	Nos. 1189-1192 (4)	6.95	2.70

5th anniversary of the liberation of Leningrad from the German blockade.

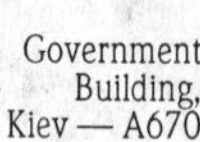

Government Building, Kiev — A670

Designs: 50k, Dnieprostroy Dam. 60k, Wheat field and granary. 1r, Steel mill and coal mine.

1948, Jan. 25 *Perf. 12½*

1193 A670	30k indigo	1.10	.40
1194 A670	50k violet	1.65	.40
1195 A670	60k golden brown	2.25	.45
1196 A670	1r sepia	3.50	1.00
	Nos. 1193-1196 (4)	8.50	2.25

Ukrainian Soviet Socialist Republic, 30th anniv.

Lenin Types of 1947
Inscribed "1924-1948"

1948, Jan. 21 Unwmk.

1197 A619	30k brown violet	.95	.55
1198 A619	60k dark gray blue	2.00	.70
1199 A620	60k deep yellow green	2.00	.70
	Nos. 1197-1199 (3)	4.95	1.95

24th anniversary of the death of Lenin.

Vasili I. Surikov — A672

Soviet Soldier and Artillery — A675

Fliers and Planes — A676

1948, Feb. 15 Photo. *Perf. 12*

1201 A672	30k red brown	1.40	.75
1202 A672	60k dark green	2.75	1.25

Vasili Ivanovich Surikov, artist, birth cent.

1948, Feb. 23

No. 1206, Soviet sailor. 60k, Military class.

1205 A675	30k brown	1.10	.55
1206 A675	30k gray	1.10	.55
1207 A676	30k violet blue	1.10	.55
1208 A676	60k red brown	1.75	.85
	Nos. 1205-1208 (4)	5.05	2.50

Hero Types of 1944

Designs: No. 1209, N.A. Schors. No. 1210, V.I. Chapayev. No. 1211, S.G. Lazho.

1948, Feb. 23

1209 A494	60k deep green	1.00	.65
1210 A494	60k yellow brown	1.00	.65
1211 A494	60k violet blue	1.00	.65
	Nos. 1209-1211 (3)	3.00	1.95

Nos. 1205-1211 for Soviet army, 30th anniv.

Karl Marx, Friedrich Engels and Communist Manifesto — A677

1948, Apr.

1212 A677	30k black	.30	.15
1213 A677	50k henna brown	.50	.20

Centenary of the Communist Manifesto.

Miner — A678

Marine — A679

Aviator — A680

Woman Farmer — A681

Arms of USSR A682

Scientist A683

Spasski Tower, Kremlin — A684

Soldier — A685

1948 Photo.

1214 A678	5k sepia	1.25	.75
1215 A679	10k violet	1.25	.75
1216 A680	15k bright blue	1.65	1.10
1217 A681	20k brown	1.75	1.25
1218 A682	30k henna brown	1.90	1.25
1219 A683	45k brown violet	2.75	1.90
1220 A684	50k bright blue	4.25	3.25
1221 A685	60k bright green	6.25	4.75
	Nos. 1214-1221 (8)	21.05	15.00

See Nos. 1306, 1343-1347, 1689.

May Day Parade in Red Square A686

1948, June 5 *Perf. 12*

1222 A686	30k deep carmine rose	1.00	.80
1223 A686	60k bright blue	2.00	1.25

Labor Day, May 1, 1948.

Vissarion G. Belinski (1811-48), Literary Critic — A687

1948, June 7 Unwmk. *Perf. 12*

1224 A687	30k brown	.80	.85
1225 A687	50k dark green	1.25	.85
1226 A687	60k purple	1.65	.85
	Nos. 1224-1226 (3)	3.70	2.55

Aleksandr N. Ostrovski
A690 A691

1948, June 10 Photo. *Perf. 12*

1227 A690	30k bright green	1.90	.85
1228 A691	60k brown	2.25	1.50
1229 A691	1r brown violet	3.75	2.50
	Nos. 1227-1229 (3)	7.90	4.85

Ostrovski (1823-1886), playwright.
Exist imperf. Value, set $100.

Ivan I. Shishkin (1832-1898), Painter — A692

"Field of Rye," by Shishkin A693

Design: 60k, "Bears in a Forest," by Shishkin.

Photo. (30k, 1r), Typo. (50k, 60k)

1948, June 12

1230 A692 30k dk grn & vio brn 2.00 .60
1231 A693 50k multicolored 2.50 .60
1232 A693 60k multicolored 4.50 .75
1233 A692 1r brown & blue blk 6.50 1.10
Nos. 1230-1233 (4) 15.50 3.05

Industrial Expansion A694

Public Gathering at Leningrad A695

Photo., Frames Litho. in Carmine

1948, June 25

1234 A694 15k red brown 2.00 1.00
1235 A695 30k slate 2.50 1.50
1236 A694 60k brown black 4.00 2.25
Nos. 1234-1236 (3) 8.50 4.75

Industrial five-year plan.

Planting Crops — A696

#1238, 1r, Gathering vegetables. 45k, #1241, Baling cotton. #1242, Harvesting grain.

1948, July 12 **Photo.**

1237 A696 30k carmine rose .25 .25
1238 A696 30k blue green .25 .25
1239 A696 45k red brown .40 .30
1240 A696 50k brown black .50 .30
1241 A696 60k dark green .50 .30
1242 A696 60k dk blue green .50 .30
1243 A696 1r purple .85 .50
Nos. 1237-1243 (7) 3.25 2.20

Agricultural five-year plan.

Arms and Citizens of USSR — A697

Soviet Miners — A698

Photo., Frames Litho. in Carmine

1948, July 25

1244 A697 30k slate 1.90 .90
1245 A697 60k greenish black 2.25 1.10

25th anniv. of the USSR.

Nos. 1159 and 1160 Overprinted in Red

ИЮЛЬ 1948 года

1948, Aug. 24 ***Perf. 12½***

1246 A657 30k deep violet 2.00 1.50
1247 A657 1r bright ultra 2.00 1.50

Air Fleet Day, 1948. On sale one day.

1948, Aug. **Photo.** ***Perf. 12½x12***

Miner's Day, Aug. 29: 60k, Scene in mine. 1r, Miner's badge.

1248 A698 30k blue .25 .15
1249 A698 60k purple .50 .20
1250 A698 1r green .80 .25
Nos. 1248-1250 (3) 1.55 .60

A. A. Zhdanov A699

Soviet Sailor A700

1948, Sept. 3

1251 A699 40k slate 1.00 .50

Andrei A. Zhdanov, statesman, 1896-1948.

1948, Sept. 12 ***Perf. 12***

1252 A700 30k blue green 1.65 1.25
1253 A700 60k bright blue 4.75 2.00

Navy Day, Sept. 12.

Slalom A701

Motorcyclist A702

Designs: No. 1254, Foot race. 30k, Soccer game. 45k, Motorboat race. 50k, Diving.

1948, Sept. 15 ***Perf. 12½x12***

1253A A701 15k dark blue 1.00 .25
1254 A702 15k violet 1.00 .25
1254A A702 20k dk slate blue 1.25 .25
1255 A701 30k brown 1.40 .25
1256 A701 45k sepia 1.65 .25
1257 A702 50k blue 2.50 .35
Nos. 1253A-1257 (6) 8.80 1.60

Tankmen Group — A703

Design: 1r, Tank parade.

1948, Sept. 25

1258 A703 30k sepia 2.00 1.25
1259 A703 1r rose 5.25 1.65

Day of the Tankmen, Sept. 25.

Spasski Tower Type of 1947

1948 **Litho.** ***Perf. 12x12½***

1260 A658 1r brown red 1.10 .30

No. 1260 was re-issued in 1954-56 in slightly smaller format: 14½x21½mm, instead of 14¾x22mm and in a paler shade. See note after No. 738.

Train — A704

Transportation 5-year plan: 60k, Auto and bus at intersection. 1r, Steamships at anchor.

1948, Sept. 30 **Photo.** ***Perf. 12½x12***

1261 A704 30k brown 3.50 1.75
1262 A704 50k dark green 5.00 2.00
1263 A704 60k blue 8.25 2.00
1264 A704 1r blue violet 10.50 3.50
Nos. 1261-1264 (4) 27.25 9.25

Horses — A705

Livestock 5-year plan: 60k, Dairy farm.

1948, Sept. 30 ***Perf. 12***

1265 A705 30k slate gray 1.50 1.10
1266 A705 60k bright green 2.50 1.75
1267 A705 1r brown 3.50 2.25
Nos. 1265-1267 (3) 7.50 5.10

Pouring Molten Metal — A706

Heavy Machinery Plant — A707

Designs: 60k, 1r, Iron pipe manufacture.

1948, Oct. 14 ***Perf. 12½***

1268 A706 30k purple 1.25 .60
1269 A706 50k brown 1.50 .80
1270 A706 60k carmine 1.75 1.25
1271 A706 1r dull blue 3.50 2.00
Nos. 1268-1271 (4) 8.00 4.65

1948, Oct. 14

Design: 60k, Pump station interior.

1272 A707 30k purple .90 .50
1273 A707 50k sepia 1.75 1.25
1274 A707 60k brown 2.50 1.40
Nos. 1272-1274 (3) 5.15 3.15

Nos. 1268-1274 publicize the 5-year plan for steel, iron and machinery industries.

Khachatur Abovian (1809-1848), Armenian Writer and Poet — A708

1948, Oct. 16 ***Perf. 12x12½***

1275 A708 40k purple 3.00 2.50
1276 A708 50k deep green 4.00 2.50

Farkhatz Hydroelectric Station — A709

Design: 60k, Zouiev Hydroelectric Station.

1948, Oct. 24 ***Perf. 12½***

1277 A709 30k green .95 .95
1278 A709 60k red 2.25 1.65
1279 A709 1r carmine rose 4.00 2.75
Nos. 1277-1279 (3) 7.20 5.35

Electrification five-year plan.

Coal Mine — A710

Designs: #1282, 1r, Oil field and tank cars.

1948, Oct. 24

1280 A710 30k sepia 1.90 .75
1281 A710 60k brown 2.00 1.10
1282 A710 60k red brown 2.00 1.10
1283 A710 1r blue green 4.00 2.50
Nos. 1280-1283 (4) 9.90 5.45

Coal mining and oil production 5-year plan.

Flying Model Planes — A712

Pioneers Saluting — A714

Marching Pioneers A713

60k, Pioneer bugler. 1r, Pioneers at campfire.

1948, Oct. 26 ***Perf. 12½***

1284 A712 30k dark blue green 4.50 2.00
1285 A713 45k dark violet 5.75 2.25
1286 A714 45k deep carmine 5.75 2.25
1287 A714 60k deep ultra 7.00 3.25
1288 A713 1r deep blue 17.50 5.50
Nos. 1284-1288 (5) 40.50 15.25

Young Pioneers, a Soviet youth organization, and governmental supervision of children's summer vacations.

Marching Youths A715

Farm Girl — A716

League Members and Flag — A717

Designs: 50k, Communist students. 1r, Flag and badges. 2r, Young worker.

1948, Oct. 29 ***Perf. 12½***

Inscribed: "1918 1948 XXX"

1289 A715 20k violet brown 1.10 .80
1290 A716 25k rose red 1.75 1.00
1291 A717 40k brown & red 2.75 1.25
1292 A715 50k blue green 4.50 1.65
1293 A717 1r multicolored 8.50 3.50
1294 A716 2r purple 16.50 7.00
Nos. 1289-1294 (6) 35.10 15.20

30th anniversary of the Young Communist League (Komsomol).

Stage of Moscow Art Theater — A719

K. S. Stanislavski, V. I. Nemirovich Danchenko — A720

1948, Nov. 1 *Perf. 12½*

1295 A719 40k gray blue 2.50 1.75
1296 A720 1r violet brown 3.50 3.25

Moscow Art Theater, 50th anniv.

Flag and Moscow Buildings — A721

1948, Nov. 7 *Perf. 12½*

1297 A721 40k red 1.50 1.25
1298 A721 1r green 2.25 1.75

31st anniversary of October Revolution.

House of Unions, Moscow A722

Player's Badge (Rook and Chessboard) A723

1948, Nov. 20 *Perf. 12½*

1299 A722 30k greenish blue .65 .35
1300 A723 40k violet 1.50 .45
1301 A722 50k orange brown 2.00 .60
Nos. 1299-1301 (3) 4.15 1.40

16th Chess Championship.

Artillery Salute — A724

1948, Nov. 19 *Perf. 12½*

1302 A724 30k blue 2.75 1.65
1303 A724 1r rose carmine 4.00 2.75

Artillery Day, Nov. 19, 1948.

Vasili Petrovich Stasov — A725

Stasov and Barracks of Paul's Regiment, Petrograd — A726

1948, Nov. 27 **Unwmk.**

1304 A725 40k brown 1.25 .70
1305 A726 1r sepia 2.50 1.00

Stasov (1769-1848), architect.

Arms Type of 1948

1948 **Litho.** *Perf. 12x12½*

1306 A682 40k brown red 5.50 .20

Y. M. Sverdlov Monument A727

Design: 40k, Lenin Street, Sverdlovsk.

1948 **Photo.** *Perf. 12½*

1307 A727 30k blue .25 .20
1308 A727 40k purple .40 .20
1309 A727 1r bright green .85 .20
Nos. 1307-1309 (3) 1.50 .60

225th anniv. of the city of Sverdlovsk (before 1924, Ekaterinburg). Exist imperf.

"Swallow's Nest," Crimea A729

Shoreline, Sukhumi A731

Tree-lined Walk, Sochi A732

Hot Spring, Piatigorsk A730

Formal Gardens, Sochi — A733

Stalin Highway, Sochi — A734

Colonnade, Kislovodsk A735

Seascape, Gagri — A736

1948, Dec. 30 *Perf. 12½*

1310 A729 40k brown .65 .15
1311 A730 40k bright red violet .65 .15
1312 A731 40k dark green .65 .15
1313 A732 40k violet .65 .15
1314 A733 40k dark purple .65 .15
1315 A734 40k dark blue green .65 .15
1316 A735 40k bright blue .65 .15
1317 A736 40k dark blue green .65 .15
Nos. 1310-1317 (8) 5.20 1.20

Byelorussian S.S.R. Arms — A737

1949, Jan. 4

1318 A737 40k henna brown 1.50 .90
1319 A737 1r blue green 3.50 1.75

Byelorussian SSR, 30th anniv.

Mikhail V. Lomonosov A738

Lomonosov Museum, Leningrad A739

1949, Jan. 10

1320 A738 40k red brown 1.10 1.00
1321 A738 50k green 1.50 1.00
1322 A739 1r deep blue 3.00 2.50
Nos. 1320-1322 (3) 5.60 4.50

Cape Dezhnev (East Cape) — A740

Design: 1r, Map and Dezhnev's ship.

1949, Jan. 30

1323 A740 40k olive green 5.50 3.25
1324 A740 1r gray 9.50 6.50

300th anniv. of the discovery of the strait between Asia and America by S. I. Dezhnev.

Souvenir Sheet

A741

1949, Dec. *Imperf.*

1325 A741 Sheet of 4 150.00 150.00
Hinged 100.00
a. 40k Stalin's birthplace, Gorki 12.00 18.00
b. 40k Lenin & Stalin, Leningrad, 1917 12.00 18.00
c. 40k Lenin & Stalin, Gorki 12.00 18.00
d. 40k Marshal Stalin 12.00 18.00

70th birthday of Joseph V. Stalin.

Lenin Mausoleum A742

1949, Jan. 21 *Perf. 12½*

1326 A742 40k ol green & org brown 2.25 2.00
1327 A742 1r gray black & org brown 5.00 3.50
a. Sheet of 4 175.00 175.00

25th anniversary of the death of Lenin. No. 1327a exists imperf. Value $600.

Admiral S. O. Makarov A743

Kirov Military Medical Academy A744

Professors Botkin, Pirogov and Sechenov A745

1949, Mar. 15

1328 A743 40k blue 1.65 1.10
1329 A743 1r red brown 2.25 1.75

Centenary of the birth of Admiral Stepan Osipovich Makarov, shipbuilder.

1949, Mar. 24

1330 A744 40k red brown 1.40 1.00
1331 A745 50k blue 2.00 1.50
1332 A744 1r blue green 3.00 2.25
Nos. 1330-1332 (3) 6.40 4.75

150th anniversary of the foundation of Kirov Military Medical Academy, Leningrad.

Soviet Soldier — A746

1949, Mar. 16 **Photo.**

1333 A746 40k rose red 6.50 4.50

31st anniversary of the Soviet army.

Textile Weaving A747

Political Leadership A748

Designs: 25k, Preschool teaching. No. 1337, School teaching. No. 1338, Farm women. 1r, Women athletes.

1949, Mar. 8 *Perf. 12½*

Inscribed: "8 МАРТА 1949г"

1334 A747 20k dark violet .15 .15
1335 A747 25k blue .30 .15
1336 A748 40k henna brown .40 .15
1337 A747 50k slate gray .70 .35
1338 A747 50k brown .70 .35
1339 A747 1r green 1.65 .50
1340 A748 2r copper red 2.50 1.50
Nos. 1334-1340 (7) 6.40 3.15

International Women's Day, Mar. 8.

Medal Types of 1945

1948-49 **Engr.**

1341 A517 2r green ('49) 1.75 .85
1341A A517 2r violet brown 8.00 6.00
1342 A518 3r brown car ('49) 2.25 .85
Nos. 1341-1342 (3) 12.00 7.70

For overprint see No. 1709.

Types of 1948

1949 **Litho.** *Perf. 12x12½*

1343 A678 15k black .40 .15
1344 A681 20k green .60 .15
1345 A680 25k dark blue .90 .15
1346 A683 30k brown .75 .20
1347 A684 50k deep blue 6.50 .55
Nos. 1343-1347 (5) 9.15 1.20

The 20k, 25k and 30k were re-issued in 1954-56 in slightly smaller format. The 20k measures 14x21mm, instead of 15x22mm; 25k, 14½x21mm, instead of 14½x21¾mm, and 30k, 14½x21mm, instead of 15x22mm.

The smaller-format 20k is olive green, the 25k, slate blue. The 15k was reissued in 1959 (?) in smaller format: 14x21mm, instead of 14½x22mm. See note after No. 738.

See No. 1709.

Vasili R. Williams (1863-1939), Agricultural Scientist — A749

1949, Apr. 18 **Photo.** *Perf. 12½*

1348 A749 25k blue green 2.00 1.25
1349 A749 50k brown 3.00 1.90

Russian Citizens and Flag — A750

A. S. Popov and Radio — A751

Popov Demonstrating Radio to Admiral Makarov A752

1949, Apr. 30 *Perf. 12½*

1350 A750	40k scarlet	1.00	.65
1351 A750	1r blue green	2.00	1.25

Labor Day, May 1, 1949.

1949, May **Unwmk.**

1352 A751	40k purple	1.25	.50
1353 A752	50k brown	2.00	.65
1354 A751	1r blue green	4.00	1.25
	Nos. 1352-1354 (3)	7.25	2.40

54th anniversary of Popov's discovery of the principles of radio.

Soviet Publications A753

Reading Pravda — A754

1949, May 4

1355 A753	40k crimson	2.10	1.65
1356 A754	1r dark violet	3.25	1.90

Soviet Press Day.

Ivan V. Michurin A755

A. S. Pushkin, 1822 A756

Pushkin Reading Poem — A757

1949, July 28

1357 A755	40k blue gray	1.75	1.00
1358 A755	1r bright green	3.50	2.25

Michurin (1855-1925), agricultural scientist.

1949, June **Unwmk.**

No. 1360, Pushkin portrait by Kiprensky, 1827. 1r, Pushkin Museum, Boldino.

1359 A756	25k indigo & sepia	.75	.55
1360 A756	40k org brn & sepia	1.75	1.25
a.	Souv. sheet of 4, 2 each #1361, 1363, imperf.	40.00	20.00
1361 A757	40k brn red & dk violet	1.75	1.40
1362 A757	1r choc & slate	4.00	3.00
1363 A757	2r brown & vio bl	6.50	5.00
	Nos. 1359-1363 (5)	14.75	11.20

150th anniversary of the birth of Aleksander S. Pushkin.

Horizontal rows of Nos. 1361 and 1363 contain alternate stamps and labels.

No. 1360a issued July 20.

River Tugboat A758

1r, Freighter, motorship "Bolshaya Volga."

1949, July, 13

1364 A758	40k slate blue	3.00	2.75
1365 A758	1r red brown	4.50	4.00

Centenary of the establishment of the Sormovo Machine and Boat Works.

VCSPS No. 3, Kislovodsk A759

State Sanatoria for Workers: No. 1367, Communications, Khosta. No. 1368, Sanatorium No. 3, Khosta. No. 1369, Electric power, Khosta. No. 1370, Sanatorium No. 1, Kislovodsk. No. 1371, State Theater, Sochi. No. 1372, Frunze Sanatorium, Sochi. No. 1373, Sanatorium at Machindzhaury. No. 1374, Clinical, Chaltubo. No. 1375, Sanatorium No. 41, Zheleznovodsk.

1949, Sept. 10 **Photo.** *Perf. 12½*

1366 A759	40k violet	.30	.15
1367 A759	40k black	.30	.15
1368 A759	40k carmine	.30	.15
1369 A759	40k blue	.30	.15
1370 A759	40k violet brown	.30	.15
1371 A759	40k red orange	.30	.15
1372 A759	40k dark brown	.30	.15
1373 A759	40k green	.30	.15
1374 A759	40k red brown	.30	.15
1375 A759	40k blue green	.30	.15
	Nos. 1366-1375 (10)	3.00	
	Set value		1.00

Regatta — A760

Sports, "1949": 25k, Kayak race. 30k, Swimming. 40k, Bicycling. No. 1380, Soccer. 50k, Mountain climbing. 1r, Parachuting. 2r, High jump.

1949, Aug. 7

1376 A760	20k bright blue	.40	.30
1377 A760	25k blue green	.50	.15
1378 A760	30k violet	.70	.15
1379 A760	40k red brown	.95	.15
1380 A760	40k green	.95	.15
1381 A760	50k dk blue gray	1.00	.15
1382 A760	1r carmine rose	1.75	.60
1383 A760	2r gray black	3.75	.80
	Nos. 1376-1383 (8)	10.00	
	Set value		1.70

V. V. Dokuchayev and Fields — A761

1949, Aug. 8

1384 A761	40k brown	.40	.30
1385 A761	1r green	.85	.50

Vasili V. Dokuchayev (1846-1903), pioneer soil scientist.

Vasili Bazhenov and Lenin Library, Moscow A762

1949, Aug. 14 **Photo.** *Perf. 12½*

1386 A762	40k violet	.90	.30
1387 A762	1r red brown	1.65	.40

Bazhenov, architect, 150th death anniv.

A. N. Radishchev A763

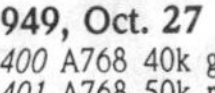
Ivan P. Pavlov A764

1949, Aug. 31

1388 A763	40k blue green	1.10	1.00
1389 A763	1r gray	2.50	2.00

200th anniversary of the birth of Aleksandr N. Radishchev, writer.

1949, Sept. 30 **Unwmk.**

1390 A764	40k deep brown	.50	.25
1391 A764	1r gray black	1.25	.35

Pavlov (1849-1936), Russian physiologist.

Globe Encircled by Letters A765

1949, Oct. *Perf. 12½*

1392 A765	40k org brn & indigo	.50	.15
a.	Imperf.	4.50	2.25
1393 A765	50k indigo & gray vio	.50	.15
a.	Imperf.	4.50	2.25

75th anniv. of the UPU.

Cultivators A766

Map of European Russia — A767

Designs: No. 1395, Peasants in grain field. 50k, Rural scene. 2r, Old man and children.

1949, Oct. 18 *Perf. 12½*

1394 A766	25k green	.65	.45
1395 A766	40k violet	1.40	.85
1396 A767	40k gray grn & blk	1.40	.85
1397 A766	50k deep blue	1.90	1.10
1398 A766	1r gray black	3.25	1.90
1399 A766	2r dark brown	7.75	4.50
	Nos. 1394-1399 (6)	16.35	9.65

Encouraging agricultural development.

Nos. 1394, 1398, 1399 measure 33x19mm. Nos. 1395, 1397 measure 33x22mm.

Maly (Little) Theater, Moscow A768

M. N. Ermolova, I. S. Mochalov, A. N. Ostrovski, M. S. Shchepkin and P. M. Sadovsky A769

1949, Oct. 27

1400 A768	40k green	.80	.25
1401 A768	50k red orange	1.00	.25
1402 A769	1r deep brown	1.90	.45
	Nos. 1400-1402 (3)	3.70	.95

125th anniversary of the Maly Theater (State Academic Little Theater).

Chapayev Type of 1944

1949, Oct. 22 **Photo.**

1403 A494	40k brown orange	4.50	3.00

30th anniversary of the death of V. I. Chapayev, a hero of the 1918 civil war.

Portrait and outer frame same as type A494. Dates "1919 1949" are in upper corners. Other details differ.

125th Anniv. of the Birth of Ivan Savvich Nikitin, Russian Poet (1824-1861) — A770

1949, Oct. 24 **Unwmk.**

1404 A770	40k brown	.80	.20
1405 A770	1r slate blue	1.25	.30

Spasski Tower and Russian Citizens A771

1949, Oct. 29 *Perf. 12½*

1406 A771	40k brown orange	2.75	1.50
1407 A771	1r deep green	4.75	2.50

October Revolution, 32nd anniversary.

Sheep, Cattle and Farm Woman A772

1949, Nov. 2

1408 A772	40k chocolate	.50	.15
1409 A772	1r violet	1.00	.30

Encouraging better cattle breeding in Russia.

Arms and Flag of USSR — A773

1949, Nov. 30 **Engr.** *Perf. 12*

1410 A773	40k carmine	9.00	5.00

Constitution Day.

Electric Trolley Car — A774

Ski Jump — A775

Designs: 40k, 1r, Diesel train. 50k, Steam train.

1949, Nov. 19 **Photo.** *Perf. 12½*

1411 A774	25k red	.90	.20
1412 A774	40k violet	1.10	.20
1413 A774	50k brown	1.75	.20
1414 A774	1r Prus green	4.00	.35
	Nos. 1411-1414 (4)	7.75	.95

1949, Nov. 12 **Unwmk.**

Designs: 40k, Girl on rings. 50k, Ice hockey. 1r, Weight lifter. 2r, Wolf hunt.

1415 A775 20k dark green .70 .15
1416 A775 40k orange red 1.25 .15
1417 A775 50k deep blue 2.00 .15
1418 A775 1r red 2.50 .25
1419 A775 2r violet 5.50 .80
Nos. 1415-1419 (5) 11.95 1.50

Textile Mills — A776

Designs: 25k, Irrigation system. 40k, 1r, Government buildings, Stalinabad. 50k, University of Medicine.

1949, Dec. 7 **Photo.** ***Perf. 12***

1420 A776 20k blue .40 .15
1421 A776 25k green .45 .15
1422 A776 40k red orange .50 .20
1423 A776 50k violet .75 .25
1424 A776 1r gray black 1.40 .50
Nos. 1420-1424 (5) 3.50 1.25

Tadzhik Republic, 20th anniv.

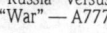

"Russia" versus "War" — A777

Byelorussians and Flag — A778

1949, Dec. 25

1425 A777 40k rose carmine .40 .15
1426 A777 50k blue .55 .25

Issued to portray Russia as the defender of world peace.

1949, Dec. 23 **Unwmk.**

Design: No. 1428, Ukrainians and flag.

Inscribed: "1939 1949"

1427 A778 40k orange red 5.00 3.00
1428 A778 40k deep orange 5.00 3.00

Return of western territories to the Byelorussian and Ukrainian Republics, 10th anniv.

Teachers College A779

Designs: 25k, State Theater. No. 1431, Government House. No. 1432, Navol Street, Tashkent. 1r, Fergana Canal. 2r, Kuigonyarsk Dam.

1950, Jan. 3

1429 A779 20k blue .35 .15
1430 A779 25k gray black .35 .15
1431 A779 40k red orange .75 .25
1432 A779 40k violet .75 .25
1433 A779 1r green 1.75 .40
1434 A779 2r brown 3.50 .50
Nos. 1429-1434 (6) 7.45 1.70

Uzbek Republic, 25th anniversary.

Lenin at Razliv — A780

Lenin's Office, Kremlin A781

Design: 1r, Lenin Museum.

1950, Jan. Unwmk. Litho. ***Perf. 12***

1435 A780 40k dk green & dk brn .55 .15
1436 A781 50k dk brn, red brn & green .90 .20
1437 A781 1r dk brn, dk grn & cream 1.65 .30
Nos. 1435-1437 (3) 3.10 .65

26th anniversary of the death of Lenin.

Textile Factory, Ashkhabad A782

Designs: 40k, 1r, Power dam and Turkmenian arms. 50k, Rug making.

1950, Jan. 7 **Photo.**

1438 A782 25k gray black 1.00 .55
1439 A782 40k brown 1.40 .85
1440 A782 50k green 2.10 1.25
1441 A782 1r purple 4.50 2.50
Nos. 1438-1441 (4) 9.00 5.15

Turkmen Republic, 25th anniversary.

Motion Picture Projection A783

1950, Feb.

1442 A783 25k brown 10.00 4.00

Soviet motion picture industry, 30th anniv.

Voter A784

Kremlin A785

1950, Mar. 8

1443 A784 40k green, *yellow* 2.00 1.50
1444 A785 1r rose carmine 3.00 2.50

Supreme Soviet elections, Mar. 12, 1950.

Morozov Monument, Moscow A786

Globes and Communication Symbols A787

1950, Mar. 16 ***Perf. 12½***

1445 A786 40k black brn & red 2.50 1.75
1446 A786 1r dk green & red 5.00 3.00

Unveiling of a monument to Pavlik Morozov, Pioneer.

1950, Apr. 1

1447 A787 40k deep green 2.25 2.00
1448 A787 50k deep blue 2.75 2.00

Meeting of the Post, Telegraph, Telephone and Radio Trade Unions.

State Polytechnic Museum A788

State Museum of Oriental Cultures A789

State University Museum — A790

Pushkin Museum A791

Museums: No. 1451, Tretiakov Gallery. No. 1452, Timiryazev Biology Museum. No. 1453, Lenin Museum. No. 1454, Museum of the Revolution. No. 1456, State History Museum.

Inscribed: "MOCKBA 1949" in Top Frame

1950, Mar. 28 Litho. ***Perf. 12½***

Multicolored Centers

1449 A788 40k dark blue 1.10 .25
1450 A789 40k dark blue 1.10 .25
1451 A789 40k green 1.10 .25
1452 A789 40k dark brown 1.10 .25
1453 A789 40k olive brown 1.10 .25
1454 A789 40k claret 1.10 .25
1455 A790 40k red 1.10 .25
1456 A790 40k chocolate 1.10 .25
1457 A791 40k brown violet 1.10 .25
Nos. 1449-1457 (9) 9.90 2.25

Soviets of Three Races A792

A. S. Shcherbakov A793

1r, 4 Russians and communist banner, horiz.

1950, May 1 **Photo.** ***Perf. 12½***

1458 A792 40k org red & gray 2.50 1.90
1459 A792 1r red & gray black 5.00 3.50

Labor Day, May 1, 1950.

1950, May **Unwmk.**

1460 A793 40k black, *pale blue* 1.00 .70
1461 A793 1r dk green, *buff* 2.00 1.75

Shcherbakov, political leader (1901-1945).

Monument A794

Victory Medal A795

Perf. 12x12½

1950 **Photo.** **Wmk. 293**

1462 A794 40k dk brown & red 3.50 2.25

Unwmk.

1463 A795 1r carmine rose 4.00 2.75

5th Intl. Victory Day, May 9, 1950.

A. V. Suvorov A796

Farmers Studying Agronomic Techniques A797

50k, Suvorov crossing Alps, 32½x47mm. 60k, Badge, flag and marchers, 24x39½mm. 2r, Suvorov facing left, 19x33½mm.

Various Designs and Sizes Dated "1800 1950"

1950 ***Perf. 12, 12½x12***

1464 A796 40k blue, *pink* 1.50 .75
1465 A796 50k brown, *pink* 1.90 .90
1466 A796 60k gray black, *pale gray* 2.25 2.00
1467 A796 1r dk brn, *lemon* 3.75 2.00
1468 A796 2r greenish blue 6.75 5.00
Nos. 1464-1468 (5) 16.15 10.65

Field Marshal Count Aleksandr V. Suvorov (1730-1800).

1950, June ***Perf. 12½***

No. 1470, 1r, Sowing on collective farm.

1469 A797 40k dk grn, *pale grn* 1.25 .65
1470 A797 40k gray black, *buff* 1.25 .65
1471 A797 1r blue, *lemon* 3.50 1.65
Nos. 1469-1471 (3) 6.00 2.95

George M. Dimitrov A798

Opera and Ballet Theater, Baku A799

1950, July 2

1472 A798 40k gray black, *citron* 1.00 .70
1473 A798 1r gray blk, *salmon* 2.50 1.40

Dimitrov (1882-1949), Bulgarian-born revolutionary leader and Comintern official.

1950, July **Photo.** ***Perf. 12½***

Designs: 40k, Azerbaijan Academy of Science. 1r, Stalin Avenue, Baku.

1474 A799 25k dp green, *citron* .65 .55
1475 A799 40k brown, *pink* 1.65 .95
1476 A799 1r gray black, *buff* 4.75 3.50
Nos. 1474-1476 (3) 7.05 5.00

Azerbaijan SSR, 30th anniversary.

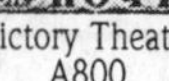

Victory Theater A800

Lenin Street A801

Designs: 50k, Gorky Theater. 1r, Monument marking Stalingrad defense line.

1950, June

1477 A800 20k dark blue .90 .40
1478 A801 40k green 1.65 .80
1479 A801 50k red orange 2.25 1.25
1480 A801 1r gray 4.75 2.50
Nos. 1477-1480 (4) 9.55 4.95

Restoration of Stalingrad.

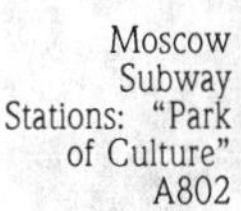

Moscow Subway Stations: "Park of Culture" A802

#1482, Kaluzskaya station. #1483, Taganskaya. #1484, Kurskaya. #1485, Paveletskaya. #1486, Park of Culture. #1487, Taganskaya.

1950, July 30

Size: 33½x23mm

1481 A802 40k deep carmine .90 .30
1482 A802 40k dark green, *buff* .90 .30
1483 A802 40k deep blue, *buff* .90 .30
1484 A802 1r dark brn, *citron* 1.90 1.00
1485 A802 1r purple 1.90 1.00
1486 A802 1r dark green, *citron* 1.90 1.00

Size: 33x18½mm

1487 A802 1r black, *pink* 1.75 .75
Nos. 1481-1487 (7) 10.15 4.65

Socialist Peoples and Flags A803

1950, Aug. 4 Unwmk. *Perf. 12½*

1488 A803 40k multicolored 1.00 .15
1489 A803 50k multicolored 2.00 .20
1490 A803 1r multicolored 2.25 .30
Nos. 1488-1490 (3) 5.25 .65

Trade Union Building, Riga — A804

Opera and Ballet Theater, Riga — A805

Designs: 40k, Latvian Cabinet building. 50k, Monument to Jan Rainis. 1r, Riga State Univ. 2r, Latvian Academy of Sciences.

1950 Photo. *Perf. 12½*

1491 A804 25k dark brown .75 .40
1492 A804 40k scarlet 1.00 1.00
1493 A804 50k dark green 2.25 1.00
1494 A805 60k deep blue 2.50 1.00
1495 A805 1r lilac 3.75 2.00
1496 A804 2r sepia 6.50 2.50
Nos. 1491-1496 (6) 16.75 7.90

Latvian SSR, 10th anniv.

Lithuanian Academy of Sciences — A806

Marite Melnik — A807

Design: 1r, Cabinet building.

1950

1497 A806 25k deep blue, *bluish* 1.40 .50
1498 A807 40k brown 2.75 1.00
1499 A806 1r scarlet 6.00 2.50
Nos. 1497-1499 (3) 10.15 4.00

Lithuanian SSR, 10th anniv.

Stalingrad Square, Tallinn A808

Victor Kingisepp A809

Designs: 40k, Government building, Tallinn. 50k, Estonia Theater, Tallinn.

1950

1500 A808 25k dark green 1.25 .80
1501 A808 40k scarlet 1.50 .95
1502 A808 50k blue, *yellow* 2.50 1.40
1503 A809 1r brown, *blue* 4.50 3.00
Nos. 1500-1503 (4) 9.75 6.15

Estonian SSR, 10th anniv.

Citizens Signing Appeal for Peace A810

Children and Governess A811

Design: 50k, Peace Demonstration.

1950, Oct. 16 Photo.

1504 A810 40k red, *salmon* .75 .70
1505 A811 40k black .75 .70
1506 A811 50k dark red 1.40 1.00
1507 A810 1r brown, *salmon* 2.25 2.00
Nos. 1504-1507 (4) 5.15 4.40

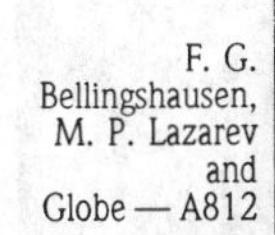

F. G. Bellingshausen, M. P. Lazarev and Globe — A812

Route of Antarctic Expedition — A813

1950, Oct. 25 Unwmk. *Perf. 12½*

Blue Paper

1508 A812 40k dark carmine 14.00 10.00
1509 A813 1r purple 26.00 10.00

130th anniversary of the Bellingshausen-Lazarev expedition to the Antarctic.

M. V. Frunze — A814

M. I. Kalinin — A815

1950, Oct. 31

1510 A814 40k blue, *buff* 2.50 1.75
1511 A814 1r brown, *blue* 6.00 4.00

Frunze, military strategist, 25th death anniv.

1950, Nov. 20 Engr.

1512 A815 40k deep green .90 .75
1513 A815 1r reddish brown 2.00 1.25
1514 A815 5r violet 4.50 2.25
Nos. 1512-1514 (3) 7.40 4.25

75th anniversary of the birth of M. I. Kalinin, Soviet Russia's first president.

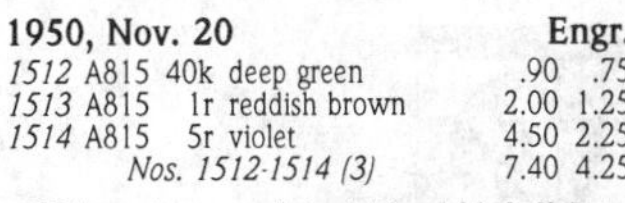

Gathering Grapes — A816

Armenian Government Building A817

G. M. Sundukian A818

1950, Nov. 29 Photo. *Perf. 12½*

1515 A816 20k dp blue, *buff* 1.50 .80
1516 A817 40k red org, *blue* 2.50 1.50
1517 A818 1r ol gray, *yellow* 6.00 3.50
Nos. 1515-1517 (3) 10.00 5.80

Armenian Republic, 30th anniv. 1r also for birth of Sundukian, playwright.

Apartment Building, Koteljnicheskaya Quay — A819

Hotel, Kalanchevkaya Square — A820

Various Buildings

Inscribed: "Mockba, 1950"

1950, Dec. 2 Unwmk.

1518 A819 1r red brown, *buff* 20.00 17.00
1519 A819 1r gray black 20.00 17.00
1520 A819 1r brown, *blue* 20.00 17.00
1521 A819 1r dk green, *blue* 20.00 17.00
1522 A820 1r dp blue, *buff* 20.00 17.00
1523 A820 1r black, *buff* 20.00 17.00
1524 A820 1r red orange 20.00 17.00
1525 A819 1r dk grn, *yellow* 20.00 17.00
Nos. 1518-1525 (8) 160.00 136.00
Set, hinged 125.00

Skyscrapers planned for Moscow.

Spasski Tower, Kremlin — A821

1950, Dec. 4

1526 A821 1r dk grn, red brn & yel brown 10.00 4.50

October Revolution, 33rd anniversary.

Golden Autumn by Levitan — A822

I. I. Levitan (1861-90), Painter — A823

1950, Dec. 6 Litho. *Perf. 12½*

1527 A822 40k multicolored 4.25 .55

Perf. 12

Photo.

1528 A823 50k red brown 5.75 .55

Black Sea by Aivazovsky — A824

Ivan K. Aivazovsky (1817-1900) Painter — A825

Design: 50k, "Ninth Surge."

1950, Dec. 6 Litho.

Multicolored Centers

1529 A824 40k chocolate 1.25 .15
1530 A824 50k chocolate 1.25 .40
1531 A825 1r indigo 1.65 .90
Nos. 1529-1531 (3) 4.15 1.45

Flags and Newspapers Iskra and Pravda — A826

Presidium of Supreme Soviet, Alma-Ata — A827

Design: 1r, Flag and profiles of Lenin and Stalin.

1950, Dec. 23 Photo.

1532 A826 40k gray blk & red 25.00 7.00
1533 A826 1r dk brn & red 35.00 11.00

1st issue of the newspaper Iskra, 50th anniv.

1950, Dec. 27

Design: 1r, Opera and Ballet Theater.

Inscribed: "ALMA-ATA" in Cyrillic

1534 A827 40k gray black, *blue* 7.25 1.50
1535 A827 1r red brn, *yellow* 7.50 2.50

Kazakh Republic, 30th anniversary. Cyrillic charcters for "ALMA-ATA" are above building in vignette on 40k, immediately below building on right on 1r.

Decembrists and Senatskaya Square, Leningrad A828

1950, Dec. 30 Unwmk.

1536 A828 1r black brn, *yellow* 7.00 4.00

Decembrist revolution of 1825.

Lenin at Razliv
A829

Design: 1r, Lenin and young communists.

1951, Jan. 21 Litho. *Perf. 12½*
Multicolored Centers

1537 A829 40k olive green 2.50 .30
1538 A829 1r indigo 4.25 .70

27th anniversary of the death of Lenin.

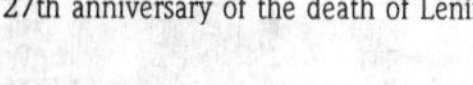

Mountain Pasture — A830

Government Building, Frunze — A831

1951, Feb. 2 Photo. *Perf. 12½*

1539 A830 25k dk brown, *blue* 3.25 1.40
1540 A831 40k dp green, *blue* 3.75 1.90

Kirghiz Republic, 25th anniv.

Government Building, Tirana — A832

1951, Jan. 6 Unwmk. *Perf. 12*

1541 A832 40k green, *bluish* 10.00 8.00

Honoring the Albanian People's Republic.

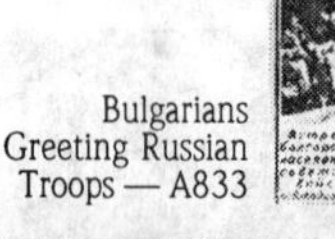
Bulgarians Greeting Russian Troops — A833

Lenin Square, Sofia — A834

Design: 60k, Monument to Soviet soldiers.

1951, Jan. 13

1542 A833 25k gray black, *bluish* 1.75 1.10
1543 A834 40k org red, *salmon* 3.25 2.25
1544 A834 60k blk brn, *salmon* 5.00 3.50
Nos. 1542-1544 (3) 10.00 6.85

Honoring the Bulgarian People's Republic.

Choibalsan State University — A835

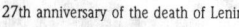

State Theater, Ulan Bator
A836

Mongolian Republic Emblem and Flag — A837

1951, Mar. 12

1545 A835 25k purple, *salmon* .55 .45
1546 A836 40k dp orange, *yellow* 1.10 .45
1547 A837 1r multicolored 2.75 1.50
Nos. 1545-1547 (3) 4.40 2.40

Honoring the Mongolian People's Republic.

D. A. Furmanov (1891-1926) Writer — A838

Furmanov at Work — A839

1951, Mar. 17 *Perf. 12½*

1548 A838 40k brown 3.00 1.25
1549 A839 1r gray black, *buff* 4.50 2.00

Russian War Memorial, Berlin — A840

1951, Mar. 21 *Perf. 12*

1550 A840 40k dk gray grn & dk red 6.00 3.00
1551 A840 1r brown blk & red 10.00 7.00

Stockholm Peace Conference.

Kirov Machine Works
A841

1951, May 19 Photo. *Perf. 12½*

1552 A841 40k brown, *cream* 4.00 2.00

Kirov Machine Works, 150th anniv.

Bolshoi Theater, Moscow — A842

Russian Composers
A843

1951, May Unwmk.

1553 A842 40k multicolored 5.00 .55
1554 A843 1r multicolored 7.00 1.25

Bolshoi Theater, Moscow, 175th anniv.

Liberty Bridge, Budapest
A844

Monument to Liberators
A845

Budapest Buildings: 40k, Parliament. 60k, National Museum.

1951, June 9 *Perf. 12*

1555 A844 25k emerald .65 .25
1556 A844 40k bright blue 1.10 .50
1557 A844 60k sepia 1.40 1.25
1558 A845 1r sepia, *salmon* 2.75 1.90
Nos. 1555-1558 (4) 5.90 3.90

Honoring the Hungarian People's Republic.

Harvesting Wheat — A846

Designs: 40k, Apiary. 1r, Gathering citrus fruits. 2r, Cotton picking.

1951, June 25

1559 A846 25k dark green .45 .30
1560 A846 40k green, *bluish* .60 .30
1561 A846 1r brown, *yellow* 1.65 .75
1562 A846 2r dk green, *salmon* 3.25 1.25
Nos. 1559-1562 (4) 5.95 2.60

Kalinin Museum, Moscow
A847

Mikhail I. Kalinin
A848

F. E. Dzerzhinski
A849

Design: 1r, Kalinin statue.

1951, Aug. 4 *Perf. 12x12½, 12½x12*

1563 A847 20k orange brn & black .40 .25
1564 A848 40k dp green & choc .75 .40
1565 A848 1r vio blue & gray 1.50 .75
Nos. 1563-1565 (3) 2.65 1.40

5th anniv. of the death of Kalinin.

1951, Aug. 4 Engr. *Perf. 12x12½*

Design: 1r, Profile of Dzerzhinski.

1566 A849 40k brown red 2.75 1.25
1567 A849 1r gray black 4.25 1.75

25th death anniv. of F. E. Dzerzhinski.

Aleksandr M. Butlerov — A850

A. Kovalevski — A850a

P. K. Kozlov — A850b

N. S. Kurnakov — A850c

P. N. Lebedev
A850d

N. I. Lobachevski
A850e

A. N. Lodygin — A850f

A. N. Svertzov — A850g

K. E. Tsiolkovsky
A850h

A. A. Aliabiev
A851

Russian Scientists: No. 1570 Sonya Kovalevskaya. No. 1572, S. P. Krasheninnikov. No. 1577, D. I. Mendeleev. No. 1578, N. N. Miklukho-Maklai. No. 1580, A. G. Stoletov. No. 1581, K. A. Timiryasev. No. 1583, P. N. Yablochkov.

1951, Aug. 15 Photo. *Perf. 12½*

1568 A850 40k org red, *bluish* 1.75 .35
1569 A850a 40k dk blue, *salmon* 1.10 .20
1570 A850 40k purple, *salmon* 1.10 .20
1571 A850b 40k orange red 1.10 .20
1572 A850 40k purple 1.10 .20
1573 A850c 40k brown, *salmon* 1.10 .20
1574 A850d 40k blue 1.10 .20
1575 A850e 40k brown 1.10 .20
1576 A850f 40k green 1.10 .20
1577 A850 40k deep blue 1.10 .20
1578 A850 40k org red, *salmon* 1.10 .20
1579 A850g 40k sepia, *salmon* 1.10 .20
1580 A850 40k green, *salmon* 1.10 .20
1581 A850 40k brown, *salmon* 1.10 .20
1582 A850h 40k gray black, *blue* 1.75 .35
1583 A850 40k sepia 1.10 .20
Nos. 1568-1583 (16) 18.90 3.50

Two printings exist in differing stamp sizes of most of this issue.

1951, Aug. 28

Design: No. 1585, V. S. Kalinnikov.

1584 A851 40k brown, *salmon* 8.00 4.00
1585 A851 40k gray, *salmon* 13.50 6.00

Russian composers.

Opera and Ballet Theater, Tbilisi — A852

Gathering Citrus Fruit — A853

40k, Principal street, Tbilisi. 1r, Picking tea.

1951 Unwmk. *Perf. 12½*

1586 A852	20k dp green, *yellow*	.65	.70
1587 A853	25k pur, org & brn	.90	.70
1588 A853	40k dk brn, *blue*	1.90	1.50
1589 A853	1r red brn & dk grn	4.50	3.50
	Nos. 1586-1589 (4)	7.95	6.40

Georgian Republic, 30th anniversary.

Emblem of Aviation Society — A854

Planes and Emblem A855

60k, Flying model planes. 1r, Parachutists.

1951, Sept. 19 Litho. *Perf. 12½*
Dated: "1951"

1590 A854	40k multicolored	.75	.15
1591 A854	60k emer, lt bl & brn	1.40	.30
1592 A854	1r blue, sal & lilac	2.00	.45
1593 A855	2r multicolored	4.50	.80
	Nos. 1590-1593 (4)	8.65	1.70

Promoting interest in aviation.

Victor M. Vasnetsov (1848-1926), Painter — A856

Three Heroes, by Vasnetsov — A857

1951, Oct. 15

1594 A856	40k dk bl, brn & buff	1.25	.25
1595 A857	1r multicolored	1.90	1.00

Hydroelectric Station, Lenin and Stalin — A858

Design: 1r, Spasski Tower, Kremlin.

1951, Nov. 6 Photo. *Perf. 12½*
Dated: "1917-1951"

1596 A858	40k blue vio & red	4.75	1.90
1597 A858	1r dk brown & red	7.25	3.25

34th anniversary of October Revolution.

Map, Dredge and Khakhovsky Hydroelectric Station — A859

Map, Volga Dam and Tugboat A860

Designs (each showing map): 40k, Stalingrad Dam. 60k, Excavating Turkmenian canal. 1r, Kuibyshev dam.

1951, Nov. 28 *Perf. 12½*

1598 A859	20k multicolored	4.00	1.65
1599 A860	30k multicolored	5.75	2.25
1600 A860	40k multicolored	8.75	3.75
1601 A860	60k multicolored	10.00	4.25
1602 A860	1r multicolored	21.50	8.50
	Nos. 1598-1602 (5)	50.00	20.40

Flag and Citizens Signing Peace Appeal A861

M. V. Ostrogradski A862

1951, Nov. 30 *Perf. 12½*

1603 A861	40k gray & red	10.00	7.00

Third All-Union Peace Conference.

1951, Dec. 10 Unwmk.

1604 A862	40k black brn, *pink*	8.00	3.50

150th anniversary of the birth of Mikhail V. Ostrogradski, mathematician.

Monument to Jan Zizka, Prague — A863

Monument to Soviet Liberators — A864

25k, Monument to Soviet Soldiers, Ostrava. 40k, Julius Fucik. 60k, Smetana Museum, Prague.

1951, Dec. 10 *Perf. 12½*

1605 A863	20k vio blue, *sal*	4.00	1.25
1606 A863	25k copper red, *yel*	5.25	1.50
1607 A863	40k red orange, *sal*	7.50	1.75
1608 A863	60k brnsh gray, *buff*	10.00	2.50
1609 A864	1r brnsh gray, *buff*	21.50	5.25
	Nos. 1605-1609 (5)	48.25	12.25

Soviet-Czechoslovakian friendship.

Volkhovski Hydroelectric Station and Lenin Statue A865

1951, Dec. 19

1610 A865	40k dk bl, gray & yel	1.75	.20
1611 A865	1r pur, gray & yel	4.00	.55

25th anniv. of the opening of the Lenin Volkhovski hydroelectric station.

Lenin as a Schoolboy — A866

Horizontal Designs: 60k, Lenin among children. 1r, Lenin and peasants.

1952, Jan. 24 Photo. *Perf. 12½*
Multicolored Centers

1612 A866	40k dk blue green	1.75	.25
1613 A866	60k violet blue	2.25	.40
1614 A866	1r orange brown	3.25	.45
	Nos. 1612-1614 (3)	7.25	1.10

28th anniversary of the death of Lenin.

Semenov A867

Kovalevski A868

1952, Feb. 1

1615 A867	1r sepia, *blue*	6.00	4.00

Petr Petrovich Semenov-Tianshanski (1827-1914), traveler and geographer who explored the Tian Shan mountains.

1952, Mar. 3 Unwmk.

1616 A868	40k sepia, *yellow*	12.00	8.00

V. O. Kovalevski (1843-1883), biologist and palaeontologist.

Skaters A869

1952, Mar. 3

1617 A869	40k shown	1.25	.25
1618 A869	60k Skiers	2.25	.35

N. V. Gogol and Characters from "Taras Bulba" — A870

Designs: 60k, Gogol and V. G. Belinski. 1r, Gogol and Ukrainian peasants.

1952, Mar. 4
Dated: "1852-1952"

1619 A870	40k sepia, *blue*	.75	.15
1620 A870	60k multicolored	1.25	.15
1621 A870	1r multicolored	1.50	.25
	Nos. 1619-1621 (3)	3.50	.55

Death centenary of N. V. Gogol, writer.

G. K. Ordzhonikidze A871

Workers and Soviet Flag A872

Workers' Rest Home A873

1952, Apr. 23 Photo. *Perf. 12½*

1622 A871	40k dp green, *pink*	2.00	1.75
1623 A871	1r sepia, *blue*	3.00	2.10

15th anniv. of the death of Grigori K. Ordzhonikidze, Georgian party worker.

1952, May 15 Unwmk.

#1626, Aged citizens. #1627, Schoolgirl.

1624 A872	40k red & blk, *cream*	4.50	3.75
1625 A873	40k red & dk grn, *pale gray*	4.50	3.75
1626 A873	40k red & brown, *pale gray*	4.50	3.75
1627 A872	40k red & black, *pale gray*	4.50	3.75
	Nos. 1624-1627 (4)	18.00	15.00

Adoption of Stalin constitution., 15th anniv

A. S. Novikov-Priboy and Ship — A874

1952, June 5

1628 A874	40k blk, pale cit & bl grn	.50	.15

Novikov-Priboy, writer, 75th birthanniv.

150th anniv. of Birth of Victor Hugo (1802-1855), French Writer — A875

1952, June 5 Unwmk. *Perf. 12½*

1629 A875	40k brn org, gray & black	.50	.15

Julaev — A876

Sedov — A877

1952, June 28
1630 A876 40k rose red, *pink* .50 .15

200th anniversary of the birth of Salavat Julaev, Bashkir hero who took part in the insurrection of 1773-1775.

1952, July 4
1631 A877 40k dk bl, dk brn & blue green 10.00 4.00

Georgi J. Sedov, Arctic explorer (1877-1914).

Arms and Flag of Romania A878

University Square, Bucharest A879

Design: 60k, Monument to Soviet soldiers.

1952, July 26
1632 A878 40k multicolored 2.25 .55
1633 A878 60k dk green, *pink* 3.50 1.25
1634 A879 1r bright ultra 4.50 2.50
Nos. 1632-1634 (3) 10.25 4.30

Zhukovski A880

Ogarev A881

Design: No. 1636, K. P. Bryulov.

1952, July 26 **Pale Blue Paper**
1635 A880 40k gray black .75 .30
1636 A880 40k brt blue green .75 .30

V. A. Zhukovski, poet, and Bryulov, painter (1799-1852).

1952, Aug. 29
1637 A881 40k deep green .50 .25

75th anniversary of the death of N. P. Ogarev, poet and revolutionary.

Uspenski — A882

Nakhimov — A883

1952, Sept. 4
1638 A882 40k indigo & dk brown .50 .25

Gleb Ivanovich Uspenski (1843-1902), writer.

1952, Sept. 9
1639 A883 40k multicolored 1.00 .75

Adm. Paul S. Nakhimov (1802-1855).

University Building, Tartu — A884

1952, Oct. 2
1640 A884 40k black brn, *salmon* 2.50 1.25

150th anniversary of the enlargement of the University of Tartu, Estonia.

Kajum Nasyri A885

A. N. Radishchev A886

1952, Nov. 5
1641 A885 40k brown, *yellow* 3.00 1.25

Nasyri (1825-1902), Tartar educator.

1952, Oct. 23
1642 A886 40k black, brn & dk red 1.75 .85

Radishchev, writer, 150th death anniv.

M.S. Joseph Stalin at Entrance to Volga-Don Canal — A887

Design: 1r, Lenin, Stalin and red banners.

1952, Nov. 6 ***Perf. 12½***
1643 A887 40k multicolored 1.90 1.25
1644 A887 1r brown, red & yel 3.50 2.75

35th anniversary of October Revolution.

Pavel Fedotov — A888

V. D. Polenov — A889

"Moscow Courtyard" — A890

1953, Nov. 26
1645 A888 40k red brn & black .50 .25

Centenary of the death of Pavel Andreievitch Fedotov (1815-1852), artist.

1952, Dec. 6
1646 A889 40k red brown & buff .75 .30
1647 A890 1r multicolored 1.75 .55

Polenov, artist, 25th death anniv.

A. I. Odoyevski (1802-39) Poet — A891

1952, Dec. 8
1648 A891 40k gray blk & red orange .80 .25

D. N. Mamin-Sibiryak A892

1952, Dec. 15
1649 A892 40k dp green, *cream* .75 .25

Centenary of the birth of Dimitrii N. Mamin-Sibiryak (1852-1912), writer.

Composite Medal Types of 1946
Frames as A599-A606
Centers as Indicated

Medals: 1r, Token of Veneration. 2r, Red Star. 3r, Red Workers' Banner. 5r, Red Banner. 10r, Lenin.

1952-59 **Engr.** ***Perf. 12½***
1650 A569 1r dark brown 7.00 7.00
1651 A567 2r red brown 1.00 .55
1652 A572 3r dp blue violet 1.50 .95
1653 A571 5r dk carmine ('53) 1.90 .95
1654 A566 10r bright rose 3.50 1.90
a. 10r dull red ('59) 3.00 2.00
Nos. 1650-1654 (5) 14.90 11.35

Vladimir M. Bekhterev (1857-1927), Neuropathologist A893

1952, Dec. 24 **Photo.**
1655 A893 40k vio bl, slate & blk .60 .30

Byelorusskaya Station — A894

Designs (Moscow Subway stations): 40k, Botanical Garden Station. 40k, Novoslobodskaya Station. 40k, Komsomolskaya Station.

1952, Dec. 30
Multicolored Centers
1656 A894 40k dull violet .60 .15
1657 A894 40k light ultra .60 .15
1658 A894 40k blue gray .60 .15
1659 A894 40k dull green .60 .15
a. Horiz. strip of 4, #1656-1659 2.50 2.00

USSR Emblem and Flags of 16 Union Republics A895

1952, Dec. 30
1660 A895 1r grn, dk red & brn 2.25 1.50

30th anniversary of the USSR.

Lenin — A896

1953, Jan. 26
1661 A896 40k multicolored 4.00 3.00

29 years without Lenin.

Stalin Peace Medal — A897

Valerian V. Kuibyshev — A898

1953, Apr. 30 ***Perf. 12½***
1662 A897 40k red brn, bl & dull yel 10.00 6.00

1953, June 6
1663 A898 40k red brn & black .95 .55

Kuibyshev (1888-1935), Bolshevik leader.

A899

A900

1953, July 21
1664 A899 40k buff & dk brown 1.50 .75

Nikolai G. Chernyshevski (1828-1889), writer and radical leader; exiled to Siberia for 24 years.

1953, July 19
1665 A900 40k ver & gray brown 2.50 1.00

60th anniv. of the birth of Vladimir V. Mayakovsky, poet.

Tsymijanskaja Dam — A901

Volga-Don Canal: No. 1666, Lock No. 9, Volga-Don Canal. No. 1667, Lock 13. No. 1668, Lock 15. No. 1669, Volga River lighthouse. No. 1671, M. S. "Joseph Stalin" in canal.

1953, Aug. 29 **Litho.**
1666 A901 40k multicolored 1.00 .15
1667 A901 40k multicolored 1.00 .15
1668 A901 40k multicolored 1.00 .15
1669 A901 40k multicolored 1.00 .15
1670 A901 40k multicolored 1.00 .15
1671 A901 1r multicolored 2.25 .50
Nos. 1666-1671 (6) 7.25
Set value 1.00

V. G. Korolenko — A902

Leo N. Tolstoy — A903

953, Aug. 29 Photo. *Perf. 12x12½*
672 A902 40k brown .75 .25

V. G. Korolenko (1853-1921), writer.

953, Sept. *Perf. 12*
673 A903 1r dark brown 5.00 3.50

125th anniversary of the birth of Count Leo N. olstoy, writer.

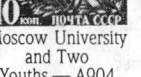

Moscow University and Two Youths — A904

Nationalities of the Soviet Union — A905

Design: 1r, Komsomol badge and four orders.

953, Oct. 29 *Perf. 12½x12*
674 A904 40k multicolored 2.50 1.40
675 A904 1r multicolored 4.50 1.90

35th anniversary of the Young Communist eague (Komsomol).

953, Nov. 6

60k, Lenin and Stalin at Smolny monastery.

676 A905 40k multicolored 4.50 3.25
677 A905 60k multicolored 10.00 6.75

36th anniversary of October Revolution.
No. 1676 measures 25½x38mm; No. 1677, 5½x42mm.

Lenin and His Writings — A906

1r, Lenin facing left and pages of "What to Do."

953
678 A906 40k multicolored 3.50 3.75
679 A906 1r dk brn, org brn & red 7.50 4.75

The 40k was issued on Nov. 12 for 50th anniv. f the formation of the Communist Party. The 1r Dec. 14 for 50th anniv. of the 2nd congress of the ussian Socialist Party.

Lenin Statue — A907

Peter I Statue, Decembrists' Square — A908

Leningrad Views: Nos. 1681 & 1683, Admiralty building. Nos. 1685 & 1687, Smolny monastery.

1953, Nov. 23
1680 A907 40k brn blk, *yellow* 2.25 1.25
1681 A907 40k vio brn, *yellow* 2.25 1.25
1682 A907 40k dk brn, *pink* 2.25 1.25
1683 A907 40k brn blk, *cream* 2.25 1.25
1684 A908 1r dk brn, *blue* 5.00 3.00
1685 A908 1r dk green, *pink* 5.00 3.00
1686 A908 1r violet, *yellow* 5.00 3.00
1687 A908 1r blk brn, *blue* 5.00 3.00
Nos. 1680-1687 (8) 29.00 17.00

See Nos. 1944-1945, 1943a.

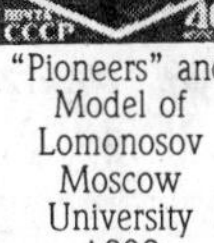

"Pioneers" and Model of Lomonosov Moscow University A909

Aleksandr S. Griboedov, Writer (1795-1829) A910

1953, Dec. 22 Litho. *Perf. 12*
1688 A909 40k dk sl grn, dk brn & red 3.50 1.50

Arms Type of 1948

1954-57
1689 A682 40k scarlet 1.00 .50
a. 8 ribbon turns on wreath at left ('54) 4.25 1.65

No. 1689 was re-issued in 1954-56 typographed in slightly smaller format: 14½x21¾mm, instead of 14¾x21¾mm, and in a lighter shade. See note after No. 738.

No. 1689 has 7 ribbon turns on left side of wreath.

1954, Mar. 4 Photo.
1690 A910 40k dp claret, *cream* .70 .20
1691 A910 1r black, *green* 1.40 .35

Kremlin View — A911

V. P. Chkalov — A912

1954, Mar. 7 Litho. *Perf. 12½x12*
1692 A911 40k red & gray 6.00 3.00

1954 elections to the Supreme Soviet.

1954, Mar. 16 *Perf. 12*
1693 A912 1r gray, vio bl & dk brown 5.00 1.00

50th anniversary of the birth of Valeri P. Chkalov (1904-1938), airplane pilot.

Lenin — A913

Lenin at Smolny A914

Designs: No. 1696, Lenin's home (later museum), Ulyanovsk. No. 1697, Lenin addressing workers. No. 1698, Lenin among students, University of Kazan.

1954, Apr. 16 Photo.
1694 A913 40k multicolored 3.50 .90

Size: 38x27½mm
1695 A914 40k multicolored 3.50 .90
1696 A914 40k multicolored 3.50 .90

Size: 48x35mm
1697 A914 40k multicolored 3.50 .90
1698 A914 40k multicolored 3.50 .90
Nos. 1694-1698 (5) 17.50 4.50

30th anniversary of the death of Lenin.
For overprint see No. 2060.

Joseph V. Stalin — A915

1954, Apr. 30 Unwmk. *Perf. 12*
1699 A915 40k dark brown 5.00 1.50

First anniversary of the death of Stalin.

Supreme Soviet Buildings in Kiev and Moscow A916

T. G. Shevchenko Statue, Kharkov — A917

Designs: No. 1701, University building, Kiev. No. 1702, Opera, Kiev. No. 1703, Ukranian Academy of Science. No. 1705, Bogdan Chmielnicki statue, Kiev. No. 1706 Flags of Soviet Russia and Ukraine. No. 1707, T. G. Shevchenko statue, Kanev. No. 1708, Chmielnicki proclaming reunion of Ukraine and Russia, 1654.

1954, May 10 Litho.
Size: 37½x26mm, 26x37½mm
1700 A916 40k red brn, sal, cream & black .95 .15
1701 A916 40k ultra, vio bl & brn .95 .15
1702 A916 40k red brn, buff, blue brown .95 .15
1703 A916 40k org brn, cream & grn .95 .20
1704 A917 40k rose red, blk, yel & brown 1.25 .20
1705 A917 60k multicolored 1.25 .30
1706 A917 1r multicolored 2.75 .50

Size: 42x28mm
1707 A916 1r multicolored 1.90 .50

Size: 45x29½mm
1708 A916 1r multicolored, *pink* 2.75 .50

300-ЛЕТИЕ

No. 1341 Overprinted in Carmine

ВОССОЕДИНЕННЯ УКРАИНЫ С РОССИЕЙ

1709 A517 2r green 6.25 1.65
Nos. 1700-1709 (10) 19.95 4.30

300th anniversary of the union between the Ukraine and Russia.

Sailboat Race — A918

Basketball — A919

Sports: No. 1711, Hurdle race. No. 1712, Swimmers. No. 1713, Cyclists. No. 1714, Track. No. 1715, Skier. No. 1716, Mountain climbing.

1954, May 29
Frames in Orange Brown
1710 A918 40k blue & black 1.25 .15
1711 A918 40k vio gray & blk 1.25 .15
1712 A918 40k dk blue & black 1.25 .15
1713 A918 40k dk brn & buff 1.25 .15
1714 A918 40k black brn & buff 1.25 .15
1715 A918 1r blue & black 2.50 .25
1716 A918 1r blue & black 2.50 .25
1717 A919 1r dk brn & brn 2.50 .25
Nos. 1710-1717 (8) 13.75 1.50

For overprint see No. 2170.

Cattle A920

Designs: No. 1719, Potato planting and cultivation. No. 1720, Kolkhoz hydroelectric station.

1954, June 8
1718 A920 40k brn, cream, ind & blue gray 1.65 .85
1719 A920 40k gray grn, buff & brown 1.65 .85
1720 A920 40k blk, bl grn & vio bl 1.65 .85
Nos. 1718-1720 (3) 4.95 2.55

Anton P. Chekhov, Writer, 50th Death Anniv. — A921

1954, July 15
1721 A921 40k green & black brn .75 .50

F. A. Bredichin, V. J. Struve, A. A. Belopolski and Observatory
A922

1954, July 26

1722	A922	40k vio bl, blk & blue	5.00	1.00

Restoration of Pulkov Observatory.

Mikhail I. Glinka, Composer, 150th Birth Anniv. — A923

Pushkin and Zhukovsky Visiting Glinka
A924

1954, July 26

1723	A923	40k dp cl, pink & blk brown	4.50	.35
1724	A924	60k multicolored	5.50	.60

Nikolai A. Ostrovsky
A925

Monument to Sunken Ships
A926

Defenders of Sevastopol
A927

1954, Sept. 29 Photo. *Perf. 12½x12*

1725	A925	40k brn, dark red & yel	1.00	.40

Ostrovsky (1904-1936), blind writer.

1954, Oct. 17 *Perf. 12½*

Design: 1r, Admiral P. S. Nakhimov.

1726	A926	40k blue grn, blk & ol brown	.50	.15
1727	A927	60k org brn, blk & brn	.65	.20
1728	A926	1r brn, blk & ol green	1.25	.35
		Nos. 1726-1728 (3)	2.40	.70

Centenary of the defense of Sevastopol during the Crimean War.

Sculpture at Exhibition Entrance — A928

Agriculture Pavilion
A929

Cattle Pavilion
A929a

Designs: No. 1732, Machinery pavilion. No. 1733, Main entrance. No. 1734, Main pavilion.

Perf. 12½, 12½x12, 12x12½

1954, Nov. 5 Litho.

Size: 26x37mm

1729	A928	40k multicolored	.50	.15

Size: 40x29mm

1730	A929	40k multicolored	.50	.15
1731	A929a	40k multicolored	.50	.15
1732	A929	40k multicolored	.50	.15

Size: 40½x33mm

1733	A929	1r multicolored	1.00	.35

Size: 28½x40½mm

1734	A928	1r multicolored	1.00	.35
		Nos. 1729-1734 (6)	4.00	1.30

1954 Agricultural Exhibition.

Marx, Engels, Lenin and Stalin — A930

1954, Nov. 6 Photo. *Perf. 12½x12*

1735	A930	1r dk brn, pale org & red	6.00	2.75

37th anniversary of October Revolution.

Kazan University Building — A931

1954, Nov. 11 *Perf. 12x12½*

1736	A931	40k deep blue	.75	.40
1737	A931	60k claret	1.00	.65

Founding of Kazan University, 150th anniv.

Salome Neris
A932

1954, Nov. 17 *Perf. 12½x12*

1738	A932	40k red org & ol gray	2.00	.50

50th anniversary of the birth of Salome Neris (1904-1945), Lithuanian poet.

Vegetables and Garden
A933

Cultivating Flax — A934

Designs: No. 1741, Tractor plowing field. No. 1742, Loading ensilage.

1954, Dec. 12 Litho. *Perf. 12x12½*

1739	A933	40k multicolored	.90	.15
1740	A934	40k multicolored	.90	.15
1741	A933	40k multicolored	.90	.15
1742	A934	60k multicolored	1.25	.25
		Nos. 1739-1742 (4)	3.95	.70

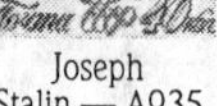

Joseph Stalin — A935

Anton G. Rubinstein — A936

1954, Dec. 21 Engr. *Perf. 12½x12*

1743	A935	40k rose brown	.65	.50
1744	A935	1r dark blue	1.40	.60

Birth of Joseph V. Stalin, 75th anniv.

1954, Dec. 30 Photo.

1745	A936	40k claret, gray & blk	5.00	.35

Rubinstein, composer, 125th birth anniv.

Vsevolod M. Garshin (1855-1888), Writer — A937

Lithographed and Photogravure

1955, Mar. 2 Unwmk. *Perf. 12*

1746	A937	40k buff, blk brn & green	.75	.25

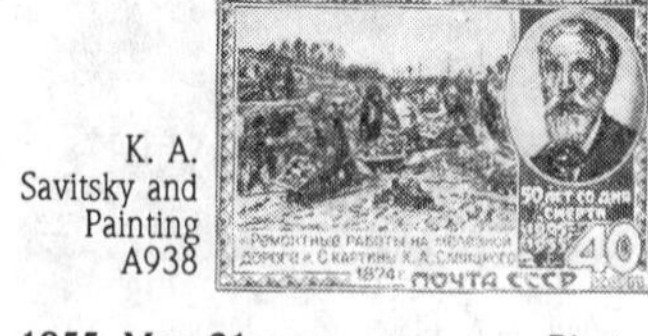

K. A. Savitsky and Painting
A938

1955, Mar. 21 Photo.

1747	A938	40k multicolored	1.00	.30
a.		Sheet of 4, black inscription	30.00	25.00
b.		As "a," red brown inscription	30.00	25.00

K. A. Savitsky (1844-1905), painter.
Size: Nos. 1747a, 1747b, 152x108mm.

Globe and Clasped Hands — A939

1955, Apr. 9 Litho.

1748	A939	40k multicolored	.50	.25

International Conference of Public Service Unions, Vienna, April 1955.

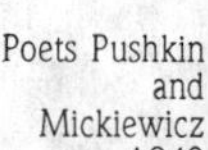

Poets Pushkin and Mickiewicz
A940

Brothers in Arms Monument, Warsaw — A941

Palace of Culture and Science, Warsaw
A942

Copernicus, Painting by Jan Matejko (in Medallion)
A943

Unwmk.

1955, Apr. 22 Photo. *Perf. 12*

1749	A940	40k chalky blue, vio & black	1.25	.25
1750	A941	40k violet black	1.25	.25
1751	A942	1r brt red & gray black	2.50	.65
1752	A943	1r multicolored	2.50	.65
		Nos. 1749-1752 (4)	7.50	1.80

Polish-USSR treaty of friendship, 10th anniv.

Lenin at Shushinskoe — A944

Lenin at Secret Printing House
A945

Friedrich von Schiller
A946

Design: 1r, Lenin and Krupskaya with peasants at Gorki, 1921.

1955, Apr. 22

Frame and Inscription in Dark Red

1753	A944	60k multicolored	1.25	.40
1754	A944	1r multicolored	2.50	.45
1755	A945	1r multicolored	2.50	.45
		Nos. 1753-1755 (3)	6.25	1.30

85th anniversary of the birth of Lenin.

1955, May 10

1756	A946	40k chocolate	1.00	.35

150th anniversary of the death of Friedrich von Schiller, German poet.

A. G. Venezianov and "Spring on the Land" — A947

1955, June 21 **Photo.**

1757 A947 1r multicolored 1.75 .60
a. Souvenir sheet of 4 20.00 15.00

Venezianov, painter, 175th birth anniv.

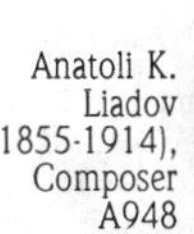

Anatoli K. Liadov (1855-1914), Composer A948

1955, July 5 **Litho.**

1758 A948 40k red brn, blk & lt brn 2.50 .40

Aleksandr Popov — A949 Lenin — A950

Storming the Winter Palace A951

1955, Nov. 5

Portraits Multicolored

1759 A949 40k light ultra 1.10 .20
1760 A949 1r gray brown 2.25 .35

60th anniv. of the construction of a coherer for detecting Hertzian electromagnetic waves by A. S. Popov, radio pioneer.

1955, Nov. 6

Design: 1r, Lenin addressing the people.

1761 A950 40k multicolored 1.25 .30
1762 A951 40k multicolored 1.25 .30
1763 A951 1r multicolored 3.00 .65
Nos. 1761-1763 (3) 5.50 1.25

38th anniversary of October Revolution.

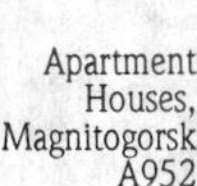

Apartment Houses, Magnitogorsk A952

1955, Nov. 29

1764 A952 40k multicolored 3.50 .25

25th anniversary of the founding of the industrial center, Magnitogorsk.

Arctic Observation Post — A953

Design: 1r, Scientist at observation post.

1955, Nov. 29 ***Perf. 12½x12***

1765 A953 40k multicolored 1.25 .20
1766 A953 60k multicolored 3.50 .30
1767 A953 1r multicolored 5.25 .45
a. Souvenir sheet of 4 ('58) 30.00 25.00
Nos. 1765-1767 (3) 10.00 .95

Publicizing the Soviet scientific drifting stations at the North Pole.

In 1962, No. 1767a was overprinted in red "1962" on each stamp and, in the lower sheet margin, a three-line Russian inscription meaning "25 years from the beginning of the work of "NP-1" station."

Sheet value, $40 unused, $35 canceled.

Fedor Ivanovich Shubin (1740-1805), Sculptor — A954

1955, Dec. 22 ***Perf. 12***

1768 A954 40k green & multi .35 .15
1769 A954 1r brown & multi .65 .20

Federal Socialist Republic Pavilion (R.S.F.S.R.) A955

ПАВИЛЬОН ТАДЖИКСКОЙ ССР
#1771

ПАВИЛЬОН БЕЛОРУССКОЙ ССР
#1772

ПАВИЛЬОН АЗЕРБАЙДЖАНСКОЙ ССР
#1773

ПАВИЛЬОН ГРУЗИНСКОЙ ССР
#1774

ПАВИЛЬОН АРМЯНСКОЙ ССР
#1775

ПАВИЛЬОН ТУРКМЕНСКОЙ ССР
#1776

ПАВИЛЬОН УЗБЕКСКОЙ ССР
#1777

ПАВИЛЬОН УКРАИНСКОЙ ССР
#1778

ПАВИЛЬОН КАЗАХСКОЙ ССР
#1779

ПАВИЛЬОН КИРГИЗСКОЙ ССР
#1780

ПАВИЛЬОН КАРЕЛО-ФИНСКОЙ ССР
#1781

ПАВИЛЬОН МОЛДАВСКОЙ ССР
#1782

ПАВИЛЬОН ЭСТОНСКОЙ ССР
#1783

ПАВИЛЬОН ЛАТВИЙСКОЙ ССР
#1784

ПАВИЛЬОН ЛИТОВСКОЙ ССР
#1785

Designs: Pavilions.

1955 **Litho.** **Unwmk.**

Centers in Natural Colors; Frames in Blue Green and Olive

1770 A955 40k shown .50 .15
a. Sheet of 4 15.00 9.50
1771 A955 40k Tadzhik .50 .15
1772 A955 40k Byelorussian .50 .15
a. Sheet of 4 15.00 9.50
1773 A955 40k Azerbaijan .50 .15
1774 A955 40k Georgian .50 .15
1775 A955 40k Armenian .50 .15
1776 A955 40k Turkmen .50 .15
1777 A955 40k Uzbek .50 .15
1778 A955 40k Ukrainian .50 .15
a. Sheet of 4 15.00 9.50
1779 A955 40k Kazakh .50 .15
1780 A955 40k Kirghiz .50 .15
1781 A955 40k Karelo-Finnish .50 .15
1782 A955 40k Moldavian .50 .15
1783 A955 40k Estonian .50 .15
1784 A955 40k Latvian .50 .15
1785 A955 40k Lithuanian .50 .15
Nos. 1770-1785 (16) 8.00
Set value 2.00

All-Union Agricultural Fair.

Nos. 1773-1785 were printed in sheets containing various stamps, providing a variety of horizontal se-tenant pairs and strips.

Lomonosov Moscow State University, 200th Anniv. A956

Design: 1r, New University buildings.

1955, June 9 ***Perf. 12***

1786 A956 40k multicolored .65 .15
a. Sheet of 4 ('56) 4.50 *4.50*
1787 A956 1r multicolored 1.40 .25
a. Sheet of 4 ('56) 9.00 *9.00*

Vladimir V. Mayakovsky A957

1955, May 31

1788 A957 40k multicolored 1.00 .25

Mayakovsky, poet, 25th death anniv.

Race Horse — A958

Trotter — A959

1956, Jan. 9

1789 A958 40k dark brown .50 .15
1790 A958 60k Prus grn & blue green .90 .20
1791 A959 1r dull pur & blue vio 1.65 .30
Nos. 1789-1791 (3) 3.05 .65

International Horse Races, Moscow, Aug. 14-Sept. 4, 1955.

Alexei N. Krylov (1863-1945), Mathematician, Naval Architect — A960

Symbol of Spartacist Games, Stadium and Factories — A961

1956, Jan. 9

1792 A960 40k gray, brown & black .40 .15

1956, Jan. 18

1793 A961 1r red vio & lt grn .55 .25

5th All-Union Spartacist Games of Soviet Trade Union sport clubs, Moscow, Aug. 12-18, 1955.

Atomic Power Station A962

Design: 60k, Atomic Reactor.

1956, Jan. 31

1794 A962 25k multicolored .50 .15
1795 A962 60k multicolored 1.65 .25
1796 A962 1r multicolored 3.00 .40
Nos. 1794-1796 (3) 5.15 .80

Establishment of the first Atomic Power Station of the USSR Academy of Science. Inscribed in Russian: "Atomic Energy in the service of the people."

Statue of Lenin, Kremlin and Flags — A963

Khachatur Abovian — A964

1956, Feb.

1797 A963 40k multicolored .60 .15
1798 A963 1r ol, buff & red org .80 .20
Set value .25

20th Congress of the Communist Party of the Soviet Union.

1956, Feb. 25 **Unwmk.** ***Perf. 12***

1799 A964 40k black brn, *bluish* 2.50 .25

Abovian, Armenian writer, 150th birth anniv.

Workers with Red Flag — A965

Nikolai A. Kasatkin — A966

1956, Mar. 14

1800 A965	40k multicolored		2.00	.25

Revolution of 1905, 50th anniversary.

1956, Apr. 30

1801 A966	40k carmine lake		.50	.25

Kasatkin (1859-1930), painter.

"On the Oka River" A967

1956, Apr. 30

Center Multicolored

1802 A967	40k bister & black	1.10	.15
1803 A967	1r ultra & black	2.00	.30

A. E. Arkhipov, painter.

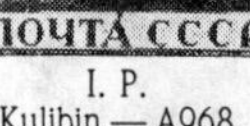

I. P. Kulibin — A968

V. G. Perov — A969

"Birdcatchers" — A970

1956, May 12

1804 A968	40k multicolored	.75	.25

Kulibin, inventor, 220th birth anniv.

1956, May 12

Painting: No. 1807, "Hunters at Rest."

Multicolored Centers

1805 A969	40k green	1.25	.15
1806 A970	1r brown	2.50	.30
1807 A970	1r orange brown	2.50	.30
	Nos. 1805-1807 (3)	6.25	.75

Vassili Grigorievitch Perov (1833-82), painter.

Ural Pavilion A971

#1809

#1810

#1811

#1812

#1813

#1814

#1815

#1816

#1817

#1818

#1819

#1820

Pavilions: No. 1809, Tatar Republic. No. 1810, Volga District. No. 1811, Central Black Earth Area. No. 1812, Northeastern District. No. 1813, Northern Caucasus. No. 1814, Bashkir Republic. No. 1815, Far East. No. 1816, Central Asia. No. 1817, Young Naturalists. No. 1818, Siberia. No. 1819, Leningrad and Northwestern District. No. 1820, Moscow, Tula, Kaluga, Ryazan and Bryansk Districts.

1956, Apr. 25

Multicolored Centers

1808 A971	1r yel green & pale yel	.95	.20
1809 A971	1r blue grn & pale yel	.95	.20
1810 A971	1r dk blue grn & pale yel	.95	.20
1811 A971	1r dk bl grn & yel grn	.95	.20
1812 A971	1r dk blue grn & buff	.95	.20
1813 A971	1r ol gray & pale yel	.95	.20
1814 A971	1r olive & yellow	.95	.20
1815 A971	1r olive grn & lemon	.95	.20
1816 A971	1r olive brn & lemon	.95	.20
1817 A971	1r olive brn & lemon	.95	.20
1818 A971	1r brown & yellow	.95	.20
1819 A971	1r redsh brown & yel	.95	.20
1820 A971	1r dk red brn & yel	.95	.20
	Nos. 1808-1820 (13)	12.35	2.60

All-Union Agricultural Fair, Moscow.

Six of the Pavilion set were printed se-tenant in one sheet of 30 (6x5), the strip containing Nos. 1809, 1816, 1817, 1813, 1818 and 1810 in that order. Two others, Nos. 1819-1820, were printed se-tenant in one sheet of 35.

Lenin A972

Lobachevski A973

1956, May 25

1821 A972	40k lilac & multi	5.00	3.50

86th anniversary of the birth of Lenin.

1956, June 4

1822 A973	40k black brown	.40	.15

Nikolai Ivanovich Lobachevski (1793-1856), mathematician.

Nurse and Textile Factory A974

Design: 40k, First aid instruction.

1956, June 4 **Unwmk.**

1823 A974	40k lt ol grn, grnsh bl & red	.40	.15
1824 A974	40k red brn, lt bl & red	.40	.15

Red Cross and Red Crescent. No. 1823 measures 37x25mm; No. 1824, 40x28mm.

V. K. Arseniev — A975

I. M. Sechenov — A976

1956, June 15 **Litho.** ***Perf. 12***

1825 A975	40k violet, black & rose	.40	.15

Arseniev (1872-1930), explorer and writer.

1956, June 15

1826 A976	40k multicolored	.40	.15

I. M. Sechenov (1829-1905), physiologist.

A. K. Savrasov, Painter — A977

1956, June 22

1827 A977	1r dull yel & brown	1.00	.20

I. V. Michurin, Scientist, Birth Centenary A978

Design: 60k, I. V. Michurin with Pioneers.

1956, June 22

Center Multicolored

1828 A978	25k dark brown	.60	.15
1829 A978	60k green & lt blue	.90	.20
1830 A978	1r light blue	2.00	.50
	Nos. 1828-1830 (3)	3.50	.85

Nos. 1828 and 1830 measure 32x25mm. No. 1829 measures 47x26mm.

Nadezhda K. Krupskaya A979

1956, June 28

1831 A979	40k brn, lt blue & pale brown	2.50	.75

Krupskaya (1869-1939), teacher and wife of Lenin.

See Nos. 1862, 1886, 1983, 2028.

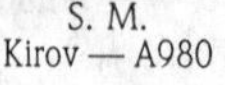

S. M. Kirov — A980

N. S. Leskov — A981

1956, June 28

1832 A980	40k red, buff & brown	.40	.15

Kirov, revolutionary (1886-1934).

1956, July 10

1833 A981	40k olive bister & brn	.15	.15
1834 A981	1r green & dk brown	.60	.40

Nikolai S. Leskov (1831-1895), novelist.

Aleksandr A. Blok (1880-1921), Poet — A982

1956, July 10

1835 A982	40k olive & brn, *cream*	.40	.15

Farm Machinery Factory A983

1956, July 23 ***Perf. 12½x12***

1836 A983	40k multicolored	.25	.15

Rostov Farm Machinery Works, 25th anniv.

A984

1956, July 23 **Unwmk.**

1837 A984	40k brown & rose violet	.75	.15

G. N. Fedotova (1846-1925), actress. See No. 2026.

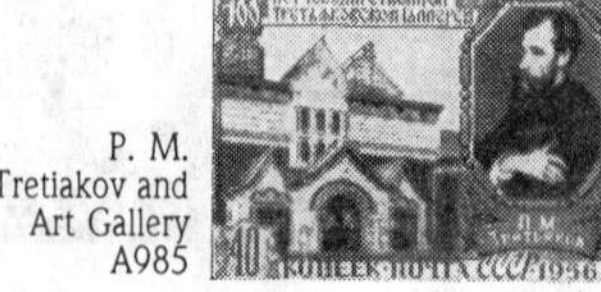

P. M. Tretiakov and Art Gallery A985

"The Rooks Have Arrived" by A. K. Savrasov — A986

1956, July 31 ***Perf. 12***

1838 A985	40k multicolored	4.00	.40
1839 A986	40k multicolored	4.00	.40

Tretiakov Art Gallery, Moscow, cent.

Relay Race — A987

Volleyball — A988

Designs: No. 1842, Rowing. No. 1843, Swimming. No. 1844, Medal with heads of man and woman. No. 1845, Tennis. No. 1846, Soccer. No. 1847, Fencing. No. 1848, Bicycle race. No. 1849, Stadium and flag. No. 1850, Diving. No. 1851, Boxing. No. 1852, Gymnast. 1r, Basketball.

1956, Aug. 5

1840 A987 10k carmine rose .20 .15
1841 A988 25k dk orange brn .35 .15
1842 A988 25k brt grnsh blue .35 .15
1843 A988 25k grn, blue & lt brn .35 .15
1844 A988 40k org, pink, bis & yellow .50 .15
1845 A988 40k orange brown .50 .15
1846 A987 40k brt yel grn & dk brown .50 .15
1847 A987 40k grn, brt grn & dk brn, *grnsh* .50 .15
1848 A987 40k blue green .50 .15
1849 A988 40k brt yel grn & red .50 .15
1850 A988 40k greenish blue .50 .15
1851 A988 60k violet .80 .15
1852 A987 60k brt violet .80 .15
1853 A987 1r red brown 1.25 .35
Nos. 1840-1853 (14) 7.60 2.30

All-Union Spartacist Games, Moscow, Aug. 5-16.

Parachute Landing A989

Building under Construction A990

1956, Aug. 5 ***Perf. 12x12½***

1854 A989 40k multicolored .50 .15

Third World Parachute Championships, Moscow, July 1956.

1956 **Photo.** ***Perf. 12***

Builders' Day: 60k, Building a factory. 1r, Building a dam.

1855 A990 40k deep orange .35 .15
1856 A990 60k brown carmine .65 .15
1857 A990 1r intense blue .95 .15
Nos. 1855-1857 (3) 1.95
Set value .30

Ivan Franko — A991

Makhmud Aivazov — A992

1956, Aug. 27

1858 A991 40k deep claret .50 .15
1859 A991 1r bright blue .90 .20

Franko, writer (1856-1916).

1956, Aug. 27

Two types:
I - Three lines in panel with "148."
II - Two lines in panel with "148."

1860 A992 40k emerald (II) 5.00 3.00
a. Type I 20.00 17.50

148th birthday of Russia's oldest man, an Azerbaijan collective farmer.

Robert Burns, Scottish Poet, 160th Death Anniv. — A993

1956-57 **Photo.**

1861 A993 40k yellow brown 4.00 2.00

Engr.

1861A A993 40k lt ultra & brn ('57) 1.90 .85

For overprint see No. 2174.

Portrait Type of 1956

Lesya Ukrainka (1871-1913), Ukrainian writer.

1956, Aug. 27 **Litho.**

1862 A979 40k olive, blk & brown 2.00 .25

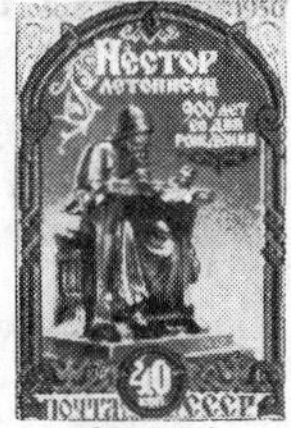
Statue of Nestor — A995

A. A. Ivanov — A996

1956, Sept. 22 ***Perf. 12x12½***

1863 A995 40k multicolored 1.25 .15
1864 A995 1r multicolored 1.25 .15

900th anniversary of the birth of Nestor, first Russian historian.

1956, Sept. 22 **Unwmk.**

1865 A996 40k gray & brown .50 .15

Aleksandr Andreevich Ivanov (1806-58), painter.

I. E. Repin and "Volga River Boatmen" — A997

"Cossacks Writing a Letter to the Turkish Sultan" — A998

1956, Aug. 21

Multicolored Centers

1866 A997 40k org brn & black 3.75 .45
1867 A998 1r chalky blue & blk 7.25 .55

Ilya E. Repin (1844-1930), painter.

Chicken Farm A999

Designs: No. 1869, Harvest. 25k, Harvesting corn. No. 1871, Women in corn field. No. 1872, Farm buildings. No. 1873, Cattle. No. 1874, Farm workers, inscriptions and silos.

1956, Oct. 7

1868 A999 10k multicolored .25 .15
1869 A999 10k multicolored .25 .15
1870 A999 25k multicolored .50 .15
1871 A999 40k multicolored .95 .15
1872 A999 40k multicolored .95 .15
1873 A999 40k multicolored .95 .15
1874 A999 40k multicolored .95 .15
Nos. 1868-1874 (7) 4.80 1.05

#1868, 1872, 1873 measure 37x25½mm; #1869-1871 37x27½mm; #1874 37x21mm.

Benjamin Franklin — A1000

G. B Shaw — A1000a

Dostoevski — A1000b

Portraits: #1876 Sesshu (Toyo Oda). #1877, Rembrandt. #1879, Mozart. #1880, Heinrich Heine. #1882, Ibsen. #1883, Pierre Curie.

1956, Oct. 17 **Photo.**

Size: 25x37mm

1875 A1000 40k copper brown 1.90 .65
1876 A1000 40k brt orange 1.50 .35
1877 A1000 40k black 1.90 .35
1878 A1000a 40k black 1.50 .35

Size: 21x32mm

1879 A1000 40k grnsh blue 1.50 .35
1880 A1000 40k violet 1.50 .35
1881 A1000b 40k green 1.50 .35
1882 A1000 40k brown 1.50 .35
1883 A1000 40k brt green 1.90 .65
Nos. 1875-1883 (9) 14.70 3.75

Great personalities of the world.

Antarctic Bases A1001

G. I. Kotovsky A1002

1956, Oct. 22 **Litho.** ***Perf. 12x12½***

1884 A1001 40k slate, grnsh bl & red 1.00 .35

Soviet Scientific Antarctic Expedition.

1956, Oct. 30

1885 A1002 40k magenta 1.00 .15

G. I. Kotovsky (1881-1925), military commander.

Portrait Type of 1956

Portrait: Julia A. Zemaite (1845-1921), Lithuanian novelist.

1956, Oct. 30 ***Perf. 12***

1886 A979 40k lt ol green & brn .50 .25

Fedor A. Bredichin (1831-1904), Astronomer A1004

1956, Oct. 30

1887 A1004 40k sepia & ultra 2.50 .75

Field Marshal Count Aleksandr V. Suvorov (1730-1800) — A1005

1956, Nov. 17 **Engr.**

1888 A1005 40k orange & maroon .30 .15
1889 A1005 1r ol & dk red brn .60 .15
1890 A1005 3r lt red brn & black 1.65 .65
Nos. 1888-1890 (3) 2.55 .95

Shatura Power Station A1006

1956 **Litho.** ***Perf. 12½x12***

1891 A1006 40k multicolored .80 .20

30th anniv. of the Shatura power station.

Kryakutni's Balloon, 1731 A1007

1956, Nov. 17

1892 A1007 40k lt brn, sepia & yel 1.00 .20

225th anniv. of the 1st balloon ascension of the Russian inventor, Kryakutni.

A1008

1956, Dec. 3 **Unwmk.** ***Perf. 12***

1893 A1008 40k ultra & brown .50 .20

Yuli M. Shokalski (1856-1940), oceanographer and geodesist.

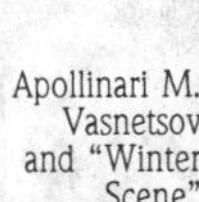

Apollinari M. Vasnetsov and "Winter Scene" A1009

1956, Dec. 30

1894 A1009 40k multicolored .80 .25

Vasnetsov (1856-1933), painter.

Indian Building and Books — A1010

Ivan Franko — A1011

1956, Dec. 26

1895 A1010 40k deep carmine .40 .20

Kalidasa, 5th century Indian poet.

1956, Dec. 26 **Engr.**

1896 A1011 40k dk slate green .40 .20

Ivan Franko, Ukrainian writer.
See Nos. 1858-1859.

Leo N. Tolstoy A1012

Portraits of Writers: No. 1898, Mikhail V. Lomonosov. No. 1899, Aleksander S. Pushkin. No. 1900, Maxim Gorki. No. 1901, Shota Rustaveli. No. 1902, Vissarion G. Belinski. No. 1903, Mikhail Y. Lermontov, poet, and Darjal Ravine in Caucasus.

1956-57 Litho. *Perf. 12½x12*

Size: 37½x27½mm

1897 A1012 40k brt grnsh blue & brown .40 .15
1898 A1012 40k dk red, ol & brn olive .40 .15

Size: 35½x25½mm

1899 A1012 40k dk gray blue & brown .40 .15
1900 A1012 40k black & brn car .40 .15
1901 A1012 40k ol, brn & ol gray .40 .15
1902 A1012 40k bis, dl vio & brn ('57) .40 .15
1903 A1012 40k indigo & ol ('57) .40 .15
Nos. 1897-1903 (7) 2.80
Set value .75

Famous Russian writers.
See Nos. 1960-1962, 2031, 2112.

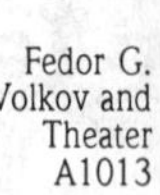

Fedor G. Volkov and Theater A1013

1956, Dec. 31 Unwmk.

1904 A1013 40k magenta, gray & yel .40 .20

200th anniversary of the founding of the St. Petersburg State Theater.

Vitus Bering and Map of Bering Strait A1016

1957, Feb. 6

1905 A1016 40k brown & blue .80 .20

275th anniversary of the birth of Vitus Bering, Danish navigator and explorer.

Dmitri I. Mendeleev A1017

Mikhail I. Glinka A1018

1957, Feb. 6 *Perf. 12x12½*

1906 A1017 40k gray & gray brn 1.00 .25

D. I. Mendeleev (1834-1907), chemist.

1957, Feb. 23 *Perf. 12*

Design: 1r, Scene from opera Ivan Susanin.

1907 A1018 40k dk red, buff & sep .40 .15
1908 A1018 1r multicolored .65 .20

Mikhail I. Glinka (1804-1857), composer.

Emblem — A1019

Emblem — A1020

1957, Feb. 23

1909 A1019 40k dk blue, red & ocher .40 .15

All-Union festival of Soviet Youth, Moscow.

1957, Feb. 24 Photo.

Designs: 40k, Player. 60k, Goalkeeper.

1910 A1020 25k deep violet .50 .15
1911 A1020 40k bright blue .50 .15
1912 A1020 60k emerald .50 .15
Nos. 1910-1912 (3) 1.50 .45

23rd Ice Hockey World Championship Games in Moscow.

Dove and Festival Emblem — A1021

Assembly Line — A1022

1957 Litho. *Perf. 12*

1913 A1021 40k multicolored .25 .15
1914 A1021 60k multicolored .35 .15

6th World Youth Festival, Moscow. Exist imperf. Value, each $30.

1957, Mar. 15

1915 A1022 40k Prus green & dp org .30 .15

Moscow Machine Works centenary.

Black Grouse A1023

Axis Deer — A1024

Animals: 10k, Gray partridge. No. 1918, Polar bear. No. 1920, Bison. No. 1921, Mallard. No. 1922, European elk. No. 1923, Sable.

1957, Mar. 28

Center in Natural Colors

1916 A1024 10k yel brown .65 .15
1917 A1023 15k brown .65 .15
1918 A1023 15k slate blue .70 .15
1919 A1024 20k red orange .70 .15
1920 A1023 30k ultra .70 .15
1921 A1023 30k dk olive grn .70 .15
1922 A1023 40k dk olive grn 1.75 .30
1923 A1024 40k violet blue 1.75 .30
Nos. 1916-1923 (8) 7.60 1.50

See Nos. 2213-2219, 2429-2431.

Wooden Products, Hohloma A1025

National Handicrafts: No. 1925, Lace maker, Vologda. No. 1926, Bone carver, North Russia. No. 1927, Woodcarver, Moscow area. No. 1928, Rug weaver, Turkmenistan. No. 1929, Painting.

1957-58 Unwmk.

1924 A1025 40k red org, yel & black 1.50 .30
1925 A1025 40k brt car, yel & brown 1.50 .30
1926 A1025 40k ultra, buff & gray 1.50 .30
1927 A1025 40k brn, pale yel & hn brown 1.50 .30
1928 A1025 40k buff, brn, bl & org ('58) 2.00 .45
1929 A1025 40k multicolored ('58) 2.00 .45
Nos. 1924-1929 (6) 10.00 2.10

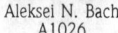

Aleksei N. Bach A1026

G. V. Plekhanov A1027

1957, Apr. 6 Litho. *Perf. 12*

1930 A1026 40k ultra, brn & buff .50 .15

Aleksei Nikolaievitch Bach, biochemist (1857-1946).

1957, Apr. 6 Engr.

1931 A1027 40k dull purple .40 .15

Georgi Valentinovich Plekhanov (1856-1918), political philosopher.

Leonhard Euler A1028

1957, Apr. 17 Litho.

1932 A1028 40k lilac & gray .55 .20

Leonhard Euler (1707-1783), Swiss mathematician and physicist.

Lenin — A1029

Youths of All Races Carrying Festival Banner — A1030

Designs: No. 1934, Lenin talking to soldier and sailor. No. 1935, Lenin building barricades.

1957, Apr. 22

Multicolored Centers

1933 A1029 40k magenta & bister .40 .15
1934 A1029 40k magenta & bister .40 .15
1935 A1029 40k magenta & bister .40 .15
Nos. 1933-1935 (3) 1.20 .45

87th anniversary of the birth of Lenin.

1957, May 27 *Perf. 12x12½*

Design: 20k, Sculptor with motherhood statu[e]. 40k, Young couples dancing. 1r, Festival banne[r] and fireworks over Moscow University.

1936 A1030 10k emerald, pur & yel .15 .1
1937 A1030 20k multicolored .15 .1
1938 A1030 25k emerald, pur & yel .20 .1
1939 A1030 40k rose, bl grn & bis brn .30 .1
1940 A1030 1r multicolored .50 .1
Nos. 1936-1940 (5) 1.30
Set value .4

6th World Youth Festival in Moscow. The 10[k] 20k, and 1r exist imperf. Value each about $25.

Marine Museum Place and Neva — A1031

Henry Fielding — A103[2]

Designs: No. 1942, Lenin monument. No. 194[3] Nevski Prospect and Admiralty.

1957, May 27 Photo. *Perf. 1*

1941 A1031 40k blue green .35 .1
1942 A1031 40k reddish brown .35 .1
1943 A1031 40k bluish violet .35 .1
a. Souv. sheet of 3, red border 7.50 6.0
Nos. 1941-1943 (3) 1.05
Set value .3

250th anniversary of Leningrad.

No. 1943a contains imperf. stamps similar t[o] #1941, 1680 (in reddish brown), 1943, and is fo[r] 40th anniv. of the October Revolution. Issued No[v] 7, 1957. A similar sheet is listed as No. 2002a.

Type of 1953 Overprinted in Red **250 лет Ленинград**

Designs: No. 1944, Peter I Statue, Decembrist[s] Square. No. 1945, Smolny Institute.

1957, May 27 *Perf. 12½x1*

1944 A908 1r black brn, *greenish* .45 .1
1945 A908 1r green, *pink* .45 .1

250th anniversary of Leningrad.
The overprint is in one line on No. 1945.

1957, June 20 Litho

1946 A1032 40k multicolored .40 .1

Fielding (1707-54), English playwright, novelist.

William Harvey — A1033

M. A. Balakirev — A103[4]

1957, May 20 Photo

1947 A1033 40k brown .40 .1

300th anniversary of the death of the Englis[h] physician William Harvey, discoverer of bloo[d] circulation.

1957, May 20 Engr

1948 A1034 40k bluish black .50 .1

Balakirev, composer (1836-1910).

A. I. Herzen and N. P. Ogarev A1035

1957, May 20 Litho

1949 A1035 40k blk vio & dk ol gray .40 .1

Centenary of newspaper Kolokol (Bell).

Kazakhstan Workers' Medal — A1036

1957, May 20

1950 A1036 40k lt blue, blk & yel .40 .15

A1037 A1037a A1037b

Portraits: No. 1951, A. M. Liapunov. No. 1952, V. Mickevicius Kapsukas, writer. No. 1953, G. Bashindchagian, Armenian painter. No. 1954, Yakub Kolas, Byelorussian poet. No. 1955, Carl von Linné, Swedish botanist.

1957 Photo.

Various Frames

1951 A1037	40k	dull red brown	3.50	2.40
1952 A1037a	40k	sepia	2.50	1.75
1953 A1037	40k	sepia	2.50	2.40
1954 A1037b	40k	gray	2.50	1.75
1955 A1037	40k	brown black	2.50	1.75
		Nos. 1951-1955 (5)	13.50	10.05

See Nos. 2036-2038, 2059.

Bicyclist A1038

1957, June 20 Litho.

1956 A1038 40k claret & vio blue .50 .15

10th Peace Bicycle Race.

Telescope — A1039

Designs: No. 1958, Comet and observatory. No. 1959, Rocket leaving earth.

1957, July 4

Size: 25½x37mm

1957 A1039 40k brn, ocher & blue 1.00 .25
1958 A1039 40k indigo, lt bl & yel 1.00 .25

Size: 14½x21mm

1959 A1039 40k blue violet 1.00 .25
Nos. 1957-1959 (3) 3.00 .75

International Geophysical Year, 1957-58. See Nos. 2089-2091.

Folksinger A1040

1957, May 20

1960 A1040 40k multicolored .40 .15

"The Song of Igor's Army," Russia's oldest literary work.

Taras G. Shevchenko, Ukrainian Poet — A1041

Design: #1962, Nikolai G. Chernyshevski, writer and politician.

1957, July 20

1961 A1041 40k green & dk red brn .25 .15
1962 A1041 40k orange brn & green .25 .15
Set value .25

Woman Gymnast — A1043

Designs: 25k, Wresting. No. 1965, Stadium. No. 1966, Youths of three races. 60k, Javelin thrower.

1957, July 15 Litho. *Perf. 12*

1963 A1043	20k	bluish vio & org brn	.20	.15
1964 A1043	25k	brt grn & claret	.20	.15
1965 A1043	40k	Prus bl, ol & red	.35	.15
1966 A1043	40k	crimson & violet	.35	.15
1967 A1043	60k	ultra & brown	.45	.15
		Nos. 1963-1967 (5)	1.55	
		Set value		.55

Third International Youth Games, Moscow.

Javelin Thrower — A1044

Designs: No. 1969, Sprinter. 25k, Somersault. No. 1971, Boxers. No. 1972, Soccer players, horiz. 60k, Weight lifter.

1957, July 20 Unwmk.

1968 A1044	20k	lt ultra & ol blk	.20	.15
1969 A1044	20k	brt grn, red vio & black	.20	.15
1970 A1044	25k	orange, ultra & blk	.20	.15
1971 A1044	40k	rose vio & blk	.45	.15
1972 A1044	40k	dp pink, bl, buff & black	.45	.15
1973 A1044	60k	lt violet & brn	.95	.15
		Nos. 1968-1973 (6)	2.45	
		Set value		.65

Success of Soviet athletes at the 16th Olympic Games, Melbourne.

Kupala A1045 Kremlin A1046

1957, July 27 Photo.

1974 A1045 40k dark gray 1.75 1.00

Yanka Kupala (1882-1942), poet.

1957, July 27 Litho.

Moscow Views: No. 1976, Stadium. No. 1977, University. No. 1978, Bolshoi Theater.

Center in Black

1975 A1046	40k	dull red brown	.25	.15
1976 A1046	40k	brown violet	.25	.15
1977 A1046	1r	red	.55	.20
1978 A1046	1r	brt violet blue	.55	.20
		Nos. 1975-1978 (4)	1.60	.70

Sixth World Youth Festival, Moscow.

Lenin Library — A1047

1957, July 27 Photo.

1979 A1047 40k brt grnsh blue .40 .15
a. Souvenir sheet of 2, light blue, imperf. 12.00 *12.00*

Intl. Phil. Exhib., Moscow, July 29-Aug. 11. No. 1979 exists imperf. Value $10.

Pierre Jean de Beranger — A1048 Globe, Dove and Olive Branch — A1049

1957, Aug. 9

1980 A1048 40k brt blue green .25 .15

Beranger (1780-1857), French song writer.

1957, Aug. 8 Litho.

1981 A1049 40k bl, grn & bis brn 1.40 .30
1982 A1049 1r violet, grn & brn 3.50 .55

Publicity for world peace.

Portrait Type of 1956

Portrait: 40k, Clara Zetkin (1857-1933), German communist.

1957, Aug. 9

1983 A979 40k gray blue, brn & blk 1.00 .20

Krenholm Factory, Narva — A1050

1957, Sept. 8 Photo.

1984 A1050 40k black brown 1.00 .15

Centenary of Krenholm textile factory, Narva, Estonia.

Carrier Pigeon and Globes — A1051

1957, Sept. 26 Unwmk. *Perf. 12*

1985 A1051 40k blue .15 .15
1986 A1051 60k lilac .25 .15
Set value .20

Intl. Letter Writing Week, Oct. 6-12.

Wyborshez Factory, Lenin Statue — A1052

1957, Sept. 23 Litho.

1987 A1052 40k dark blue .50 .15

Krasny Wyborshez factory, Leningrad, cent.

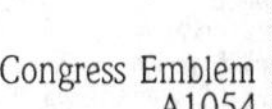

Vladimir Vasilievich Stasov (1824-1906), Art and Music Critic — A1053

1957, Sept. 23 Engr.

1988 A1053 40k brown .35 .15
1989 A1053 1r bluish black .65 .15

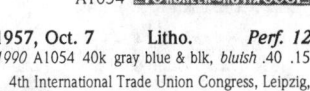

Congress Emblem A1054

1957, Oct. 7 Litho. *Perf. 12*

1990 A1054 40k gray blue & blk, *bluish* .40 .15

4th International Trade Union Congress, Leipzig, Oct. 4-15.

Konstantin E. Tsiolkovsky and Rockets — A1055

1957, Oct. 7

1991 A1055 40k dk blue & pale brown 1.50 .60

Tsiolkovsky (1857-1935), rocket and astronautics pioneer.
For overprint see No. 2021.

Sputnik 1 Circling Globe — A1056 Turbine Wheel, Kuibyshev Hydroelectric Station — A1057

1957 Photo.

1992 A1056 40k indigo, *bluish* .55 .30
1993 A1056 40k bright blue .55 .30

Launching of first artificial earth satellite, Oct. 4. Issue dates: No. 1992, Nov. 5; No. 1993, Dec. 28.

1957, Nov. 20 Litho.

1994 A1057 40k red brown .50 .15

All-Union Industrial Exhib. See #2030.

Meteor A1058 Lenin A1059

1957, Nov. 20

1995 A1058 40k multicolored .75 .15

Falling of Sihote Alinj meteor, 10th anniv.

1957, Oct. 30 Engr.

Design: 60k, Lenin reading Pravda, horiz.

1996 A1059 40k blue .40 .15
1997 A1059 60k rose red .45 .15
Set value .25

40th anniversary of October Revolution.

Students and Moscow University
A1060

Worker and Railroad
A1061

#1999, Red flag, Lenin. #2000, Lenin addressing workers and peasants. 60k, Harvester.

Perf. 12½x12, 12x12½, 12½

1957, Oct. 15 **Litho.**

1998 A1060 10k buff, sepia & red .15 .15
1999 A1060 40k buff, red, sep & yel .25 .15
2000 A1060 40k red, black & yellow .25 .15
2001 A1061 40k red, yellow & green .25 .15
2002 A1061 60k red, ocher & vio brn .35 .15
a. Souvenir sheet of 3, #2000-2002, imperf. 7.50 5.00
Nos. 1998-2002 (5) 1.25
Set value .35

40th anniv. of the October Revolution. A similar sheet is listed as No. 1943a.
Nos. 1998-2002 exist imperf.

Federal Socialist Republic
A1062

Uzbek Republic
A1063

Designs (Republic): No. 2005, Tadzhik (building and peasant girl). No. 2006, Byelorussia (truck). No. 2007, Azerbaijan (buildings). No. 2008, Georgia (valley, palm and couple). No. 2009, Armenia, (fruit, power line and mountains). No. 2010, Turkmen (couple and lambs). No. 2011, Ukraine (farmers). No. 2012, Kazakh (harvester and combine). No. 2013, Kirghiz (horseback rider and building). No. 2014, Moldavia (automatic sorting machine). No. 2015, Estonia (girl in national costume). No. 2016, Latvia (couple, sea and field). No. 2017, Lithuania (farm and farmer couple).

1957, Oct. 25

2003 A1062 40k multicolored .65 .35
2004 A1063 40k multicolored .65 .35
2005 A1062 40k multicolored .65 .35
2006 A1062 40k multicolored .65 .35
2007 A1062 40k multicolored .65 .35
2008 A1062 40k multicolored .65 .35
2009 A1062 40k multicolored .65 .35
2010 A1062 40k multicolored .65 .35
2011 A1063 40k multicolored .65 .35
2012 A1062 40k multicolored .65 .35
2013 A1062 40k multicolored .65 .35
2014 A1062 40k multicolored .65 .35
2015 A1063 40k multicolored .65 .35
2016 A1062 40k multicolored .65 .35
2017 A1062 40k multicolored .65 .35
Nos. 2003-2017 (15) 9.75 5.25

40th anniversary of the October Revolution.

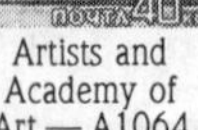
Artists and Academy of Art — A1064

Red Army Monument, Berlin — A1065

1r, Worker and Peasant monument, Moscow.

1957, Dec. 16

2018 A1064 40k black, *pale salmon* .20 .15
2019 A1065 60k black .25 .15
2020 A1065 1r black, *pink* .40 .15
Nos. 2018-2020 (3) .85
Set value .30

200th anniversary of the Academy of Arts, Leningrad. Artists on 40k are K. P. Bryulov, Ilya Repin and V. I. Surikov.

No. 1991 Overprinted in Black

4/X-57 г. Первый в мире искусств. спутник Земли

1957, Nov. 28

2021 A1055 40k 10.00 5.00

Launching of Sputnik 1.

Ukrainian Arms, Symbolic Figures
A1066

1957, Dec. 24

2022 A1066 40k yellow, red & blue .50 .15

Ukrainian Soviet Republic, 40th anniv.

Edvard Grieg
A1067

Giuseppe Garibaldi
A1068

1957, Dec. 24 **Photo.**

2023 A1067 40k black, *buff* 1.50 .20

Grieg, Norwegian composer, 50th death anniv.

1957, Dec. 24 **Litho.**

2024 A1068 40k plum, lt grn & blk .60 .15

Garibaldi, (1807-1882) Italian patriot.

V. L. Borovikovsky
A1069

Kuibyshev Hydroelectric Station and Dam
A1070

1957, Dec. 24 **Photo.**

2025 A1069 40k brown .40 .15

Vladimir Lukich Borovikovsky (1757-1825), painter.

Portrait Type of 1956

Portrait: 40k, Mariya Nikolayevna Ermolova (1853-1928), actress.

1957, Dec. 28 **Litho.**

2026 A984 40k red brn & brt violet .75 .15

1957, Dec. 28

2027 A1070 40k dark blue, *buff* .50 .15

Type of 1956

Portrait: 40k, Rosa Luxemburg (1870-1919), German socialist.

1958, Jan. 8

2028 A979 40k blue & brown .75 .60

Chi Pai-shih
A1070a

Flag and Symbols of Industry
A1070b

1958, Jan. 8 **Photo.**

2029 A1070a 40k deep violet .75 .25

Chi Pai-shih (1860-1957), Chinese painter.

1958, Jan. 8 **Litho.**

2030 A1070b 60k gray vio, red & black .50 .15

All-Union Industrial Exhib. Exists imperf.

Aleksei N. Tolstoi, Novelist & Dramatist (1883-1945)
A1071

1958, Jan. 28 **Photo.** ***Perf. 12***

2031 A1071 40k brown olive .40 .20

See Nos. 2112, 2175-2178C.

Symbolic Figure Greeting Sputnik 2 — A1072

1957-58 **Litho.**

Figure in Buff

2032 A1072 20k black & rose .25 .15
2033 A1072 40k black & grn ('58) .35 .15
2034 A1072 60k black & lt brn ('58) .55 .20
2035 A1072 1r black & blue .70 .25
Nos. 2032-2035 (4) 1.85
Set value .60

Launching of Sputnik 2, Nov. 3, 1957.

Small Portrait Type of 1957

#2036, Henry W. Longfellow, American poet. #2037, William Blake, English artist, poet, mystic. #2038, E. Sharents, Armenian poet.

1958, Mar. **Unwmk.** ***Perf. 12***

Various Frames

2036 A1037 40k gray black 2.00 .75
2037 A1037 40k gray black 2.00 .75
2038 A1037 40k sepia 2.00 .75
Nos. 2036-2038 (3) 6.00 2.25

Victory at Pskov
A1073

Soldier and Civilian
A1074

Designs: No. 2040, Airman, sailor and soldier. No. 2042, Sailor and soldier. 60k, Storming of Berlin Reichstag building.

1958, Feb. 21

2039 A1073 25k multicolored .25 .15
2040 A1073 40k multicolored .50 .15
2041 A1074 40k multicolored .50 .15
2042 A1074 40k multicolored .50 .15
2043 A1073 60k multicolored .85 .15
Nos. 2039-2043 (5) 2.60
Set value .35

40th anniversary of Red Armed Forces.

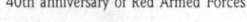

Peter Ilich Tchaikovsky — A1075

Swan Lake Ballet
A1076

Design: 1r, Tchaikovsky, pianist and violinist.

1958, Mar. 18

2044 A1075 40k grn, bl, brn & red .65 .15
2045 A1076 40k grn, ultra, red & yel .65 .15
2046 A1075 1r lake & emerald 1.65 .25
Nos. 2044-2046 (3) 2.95 .55

Honoring Tchaikovsky and for the Tchaikovsky competitions for pianists and violinists. Exist imperf. Value, set $10.

Nos. 2044-2045 were printed in sheets of 30, including 15 stamps of each value and 5 se-tenant pairs.

V. F. Rudnev — A1077

Maxim Gorki — A1078

1958, Mar. 25 **Unwmk.**

2047 A1077 40k green, blk & ocher .50 .15

Rudnev, naval commander.

1958, Apr. 3 **Litho.** ***Perf. 12***

2048 A1078 40k multicolored .40 .15

Gorki, writer, 90th birth anniv.

Spasski Tower
A1079

Russian Pavilion, Brussels
A1080

1958, Apr. 9

2049 A1079 40k dp violet, *pinkish* .25 .15
2050 A1079 60k rose red .35 .15

13th Congress of the Young Communist League (Komsomol).

1958, Apr.

2051 A1080 10k multicolored .15 .15
2052 A1080 40k multicolored .30 .15
Set value .15

Universal and International Exhibition at Brussels. Exist imperf. Value $2.

Lenin — A1081

Jan A. Komensky (Comenius) — A1082

1958, Apr. 22 **Engr.**
2053 A1081 40k dk blue gray .25 .15
2054 A1081 60k rose brown .30 .15
2055 A1081 1r brown .55 .15
Nos. 2053-2055 (3) 1.10
Set value .30

88th anniversary of the birth of Lenin.

1958, May 5

Portrait: Nos. 2056-2058, Karl Marx.

2056 A1081 40k brown .15 .15
2057 A1081 60k dark blue .30 .15
2058 A1081 1r dark red .60 .15
Nos. 2056-2058 (3) 1.05
Set value .30

140th anniversary of the birth of Marx.

1958, Apr. 17 **Photo.**
2059 A1082 40k green .30 .30

No. 1695 Overprinted in Blue **200 лет Академии художеств СССР. 1957**

1958, Apr. 22
2060 A914 40k multicolored 2.50 1.00

Academy of Arts, Moscow, 200th anniv.

Lenin Order A1083

Carlo Goldoni A1084

1958, Apr. 30 **Litho.**
2061 A1083 40k brown, yellow & red .40 .20

1958, Apr. 28 **Photo.**
2062 A1084 40k blue & dk gray .40 .20

Carlo Goldoni, Italian dramatist.

Radio Tower, Ship and Planes — A1085

1958, May 7
2063 A1085 40k blue green & red 2.00 .35

Issued for Radio Day, May 7.

Globe and Dove A1086

Ilya Chavchavadze A1087

1958, May 6 **Litho.**
2064 A1086 40k blue & black .15 .15
2065 A1086 60k ultra & black .25 .15
Set value .20

4th Congress of the Intl. Democratic Women's Federation, June, 1958, at Vienna.

1958, May 12 **Photo.**
2066 A1087 40k black & blue .40 .15

50th anniversary of the death of Ilya Chavchavadze, Georgian writer.

Flags and Communication Symbols A1088

1958-59 **Litho.**
2067 A1088 40k blue, red, yel & blk 4.00 2.00
a. Red half of Czech flag at bottom 4.00 2.00

Communist ministers' meeting on social problems in Moscow, Dec. 1957.

On No. 2067, the Czech flag (center flag in vertical row of five) is incorrectly pictured with red stripe on top. This error is corrected on No. 2067a.

Bugler — A1089

Children of Three Races — A1090

Pioneers: 25k, Boy with model plane.

1958, May 29 **Unwmk.** ***Perf. 12***
2068 A1089 10k ultra, red & red brn .20 .15
2069 A1089 25k ultra, yel & red brn .20 .15
Set value .15

1958, May 29

Design: No. 2071, Child and bomb.

2070 A1090 40k car, ultra & brn .30 .15
2071 A1090 40k carmine & brown .30 .15
Set value .20

Intl. Day for the Protection of Children.

Soccer Players and Globe A1091

Rimski-Korsakov A1092

1958, June 5
2072 A1091 40k blue, red & buff .30 .15
2073 A1091 60k blue, red & buff .70 .15
Set value .25

6th World Soccer Championships, Stockholm, June 8-29. Exist imperf. Value $4.

1958, June 5 **Photo.**
2074 A1092 40k blue & brown .75 .15

Nikolai Andreevich Rimski-Korsakov (1844-1908), composer.

Girl Gymnast — A1093

Design: No. 2076, Gymnast on rings and view.

1958, June 24 **Litho.**
2075 A1093 40k ultra, red & buff .30 .15
2076 A1093 40k blue, red buff & grn .30 .15
Set value .20

14th World Gymnastic Championships, Moscow, July 6-10.

Bomb, Globe, Atom, Sputniks, Ship A1094

1958, July 1
2077 A1094 60k dk blue, blk & org .40 .15

Conference for peaceful uses of atomic energy, held at Stockholm.

Street Fighters — A1095

Congress Emblem — A1097

Moscow State University A1096

1958, July 5
2078 A1095 40k red & violet blk .30 .15

Communist Party in the Ukraine, 40th anniv.

1958, July 8 ***Perf. 12***
2079 A1096 40k red & blue .25 .15
2080 A1097 60k lt grn, blue & red .35 .15
a. Souvenir sheet of 2 7.00 5.50

5th Congress of the International Architects' Organization, Moscow.

No. 2080a contains Nos. 2079-2080, imperf., with background design in yellow, brown, blue and red. Issued Sept. 8, 1958.

Young Couple A1098

1958, June 25
2081 A1098 40k blue & ocher .15 .15
2082 A1098 60k yel green & ocher .35 .15

Day of Soviet Youth.

Sputnik 3 Leaving Earth A1099

Sadriddin Aini A1100

1958, June 16
2083 A1099 40k vio blue, grn & rose .60 .20

Launching of Sputnik 3, May 15. Printed in sheets with alternating labels, giving details of launching.

1958, July 15
2084 A1100 40k rose, black & buff .30 .15

80th birthday of Aini, Tadzhik writer.

Emblem A1101

1958, July 21 **Typo.** ***Perf. 12***
2085 A1101 40k lilac & blue .40 .15

1st World Trade Union Conference of Working Youths, Prague, July 14-20.

Type of 1958-59 and

TU-104 and Globe — A1102

Design: 1r, Turbo-propeller liner AN-10.

1958, Aug. **Litho.**
2086 A1102 60k blue, red & bis .20 .15
2087 A1123 1r yel, red & black .40 .15

Soviet civil aviation. Exist imperf. Value, set $5.50. See Nos. 2147-2151.

L. A. Kulik — A1103

1958, Aug. 12
2088 A1103 40k sep, bl, yel & claret .60 .15

50th anniv. of the falling of the Tungus meteor and the 75th anniv. of the birth of L. A. Kulik, meteorist.

IGY Type of 1957

Designs: No. 2089, Aurora borealis and camera. No. 2090, Schooner "Zarja" exploring earth magnetism. No. 2091, Weather balloon and radar.

1958, July 29
Size: 25½x37mm
2089 A1039 40k blue & brt yel .40 .15
2090 A1039 40k blue green .40 .15
2091 A1039 40k bright ultra .40 .15
Nos. 2089-2091 (3) 1.20
Set value .30

International Geophysical Year, 1957-58.

Crimea Observatory A1104

Moscow University A1105

Design: 1r, Telescope.

1958, Aug. **Photo.**
2092 A1104 40k brn & brt grnsh bl .35 .15
2093 A1105 60k lt blue, vio & yel .50 .15
2094 A1104 1r dp blue & org brn .60 .20
Nos. 2092-2094 (3) 1.45 .50

10th Congress of the International Astronomical Union, Moscow.

Postilion, 16th Century A1106

Designs: #2095, 15th cent. letter writer. #2097, A. L. Ordyn-Natshokin and sleigh mail coach, 17th cent. No. 2098, Mail coach and post office, 18th cent. #2099, Troika, 19th cent. #2100, Lenin stamp, ship and Moscow University. #2101, Jet plane and postilion. #2102, Leningrad Communications Museum, vert. #2103, V. N. Podbielski and letter carriers. #2104, Mail train. #2105, Loading mail on plane. #2106, Ship, plane, train and globe.

1958, Aug. **Unwmk.** **Litho.** ***Perf. 12***
2095 A1106 10k red, blk, yel & lilac .15 .15
2096 A1106 10k multicolored .15 .15
2097 A1106 25k ultra & slate .25 .15
2098 A1106 25k black & ultra .25 .15
2099 A1106 40k car lake & brn black .30 .15
2100 A1106 40k black, mag & brn .30 .15
2101 A1106 40k red, org & gray .30 .15
2102 A1106 40k salmon & brown .30 .15
2103 A1106 60k grnsh blue & red lil .45 .20
2104 A1106 60k grnsh bl & lilac .45 .20
2105 A1106 1r multicolored .65 .25
2106 A1106 1r multicolored .65 .25
Nos. 2095-2106 (12) 4.20 2.10

Centenary of Russian postage stamps.

Two imperf. souvenir sheets exist, measuring 155x106mm. One contains one each of Nos. 2095-2099, with background design in red, ultramarine, yellow and brown. The other contains one each of Nos. 2100, 2103-2106, with background design in blue, gray, ocher, pink and brown. Value for both, $10 unused, $6.50 canceled.

Nos. 2096, 2100-2101 exist imperf. Value each $3.25.

M. I. Chigorin
A1107

Golden Gate, Vladimir
A1108

1958, Aug. 30 **Photo.**
2107 A1107 40k black & emerald .40 .20

50th anniversary of the death of M. I. Chigorin, chess player.

1958, Aug. 23 **Litho.**

60k, Gorki Street with trolley bus and truck.

2108 A1108 40k multicolored .15 .15
2109 A1108 60k lt violet, yel & blk .25 .15

850th anniv. of the city of Vladimir.

Nurse Bandaging Man's Leg — A1109

No. 2111, Hospital and people of various races.

1958, Sept. 15
2110 A1109 40k multicolored .20 .15
2111 A1109 40k olive, lemon & red .20 .15

40 years of Red Cross-Red Crescent work.

Portrait Type of 1958

Portrait: Mikhail E. Saltykov (Shchedrin), writer.

1958, Sept. 15
2112 A1071 40k brn black & mar .35 .15

Rudagi
A1110

V. V. Kapnist
A1111

1958, Oct. 10 **Litho.** ***Perf. 12***
2113 A1110 40k multicolored .40 .15

1100th anniversary of the birth of Rudagi, Persian poet.

1958, Sept. 30
2114 A1111 40k blue & gray .40 .15

200th anniversary of the birth of V. V. Kapnist, poet and dramatist.

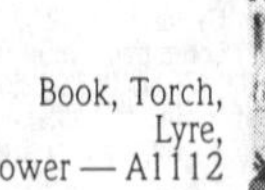

Book, Torch, Lyre, Flower — A1112

1958, Oct. 4
2115 A1112 40k red org, ol & blk .40 .15

Conf. of Asian & African Writers, Tashkent.

Chelyabinsk Tractor Factory — A1113

Designs: No. 2117, Zaporozstal foundry. No. 2118, Ural machine building plant.

1958, Oct. 20 **Photo.**
2116 A1113 40k green & yellow .30 .15
2117 A1113 40k brown red & yel .30 .15
2118 A1113 40k blue .30 .15
Nos. 2116-2118 (3) .90
Set value .25

Pioneers of Russian Industry.

Ancient Georgian on Horseback
A1114

1958, Oct. 18 **Litho.**
2119 A1114 40k ocher, ultra & red 1.25 .15

1500th anniv. of Tbilisi, capital of Georgia.

Red Square, Moscow — A1115

АЛМА-АТА · ПЛОЩАДЬ ИМ. В. И. ЛЕНИНА
#2121

ТБИЛИСИ · ПРОСПЕКТ РУСТАВЕЛИ
#2125

ФРУНЗЕ · УНИВЕРСИТЕТСКАЯ ПЛОЩАДЬ
#2127

ОБЩИЙ ВИД ГОРОДА ЕРЕВАН
#2128

МИНСК · КРУГЛАЯ ПЛОЩАДЬ
#2131

Capitals of Soviet Republics: #2121, Lenin Square, Alma Ata. #2122, Lenin statue, Ashkhabad. #2123, Lenin statue, Tashkent. #2124, Lenin Square, Stalinabad. #2125, Rustaveli Ave., Tbilisi. #2126, View from Dvina River, Riga. #2127, University Square, Frunze. #2128, View, Yerevan. #2129, Communist Street, Baku. #2130, Lenin Prospect, Kishinev. #2131, Round Square, Minsk. #2132, Viru Gate, Tallinn. #2133, Main Street, Kiev. #2134, View, Vilnius.

1958 **Engr.**
2120 A1115 40k violet .50 .15
2121 A1115 40k brt blue green .50 .15
2122 A1115 40k greenish gray .50 .15
2123 A1115 40k dark gray .50 .15
2124 A1115 40k blue .50 .15
2125 A1115 40k violet blue .50 .15
2126 A1115 40k brown red .50 .15
2127 A1115 40k dk blue gray .50 .15
2128 A1115 40k brown .50 .15
2129 A1115 40k purple .50 .15
2130 A1115 40k olive .50 .15
2131 A1115 40k gray brown .50 .15
2132 A1115 40k emerald .50 .15
2133 A1115 40k lilac rose .50 .15
2134 A1115 40k orange ver .50 .15
Nos. 2120-2134 (15) 7.50 2.25

See No. 2836.

Young Civil War Soldier, 1919 — A1116

20k, Industrial brigade. 25k, Youth in World War II. 40k, Girl farm worker. 60k, Youth building new towns. 1r, Students, fighters for culture.

1958, Oct. 25 **Litho.**
2135 A1116 10k multicolored .20 .15
2136 A1116 20k multicolored .20 .15
2137 A1116 25k multicolored .30 .15
2138 A1116 40k multicolored .35 .15
2139 A1116 60k multicolored .55 .15
2140 A1116 1r multicolored 1.25 .25
Nos. 2135-2140 (6) 2.85
Set value .60

40th anniversary of the Young Communist League (Komsomol).

Marx and Lenin — A1117

Lenin, Intellectual, Peasant and Miner — A1118

1958, Oct. 31
2141 A1117 40k multicolored .25 .15
2142 A1118 1r multicolored .55 .15

41st anniversary of Russian Revolution.

Torch, Wreath and Family
A1119

Sergei Esenin
A1120

1958, Nov. 5
2143 A1119 60k blk, beige & dull bl .40 .15

10th anniversary of the Universal Declaration of Human Rights.

1958, Nov. 29
2144 A1120 40k multicolored .40 .15

Sergei Esenin (1895-1925), poet.

G. K. Ordzhonikidze
A1121

Kuan Han-ching
A1122

1958, Dec. 12 ***Perf. 12***
2145 A1121 40k multicolored .40 .15

G. K. Ordzhonikidze (1886-1937), Georgian party worker.

1958, Dec. 5
2146 A1122 40k dk blue & gray .40 .15

700th anniversary of the theater of Kuan Han-ching, Chinese dramatist.

Airliner IL-14 and Globe — A1123

Soviet civil aviation: No. 2148, Jet liner TU-104. No. 2149, Turbo-propeller liner TU-114. 60k, Jet liner TU-110. 2r, Turbo-propeller liner IL-18.

1958-59
2147 A1123 20k ultra, black & red .15 .15
2148 A1123 40k bl grn, blk & red .25 .15
2149 A1123 40k brt bl, blk & red .25 .15
2150 A1123 60k rose car & black .25 .15
2151 A1123 2r plum, red & black ('59) .75 .20
Nos. 2147-2151 (5) 1.65 .80

Exist imperf.; value $10.
See Nos. 2086-2087.

Eleonora Duse — A1124

John Milton — A1125

1958, Dec. 26
2152 A1124 40k blue green & gray .40 .15

Duse, Italian actress, bith cent.

1958, Dec. 17
2153 A1125 40k brown .40 .15

John Milton (1608-1674), English poet.

K. F. Rulye
A1126

Fuzuli
A1127

1958, Dec. 26
2154 A1126 40k ultra & black .40 .1

Rulye, educator, death cent.

1958, Dec. 23 **Photo**
2155 A1127 40k grnsh blue & brown .40 .1

400th anniv. of the death of Fuzuli (Mehme Suleiman Oglou), Turkish poet.

Census Emblem and Family — A1128

Lunik and Sputniks over Kremlin — A1129

Design: No. 2157, Census emblem.

1958, Dec. **Litho**
2156 A1128 40k multicolored .25 .1
2157 A1128 40k yel, gray, bl & red .25 .1

1959 Soviet census.

1959, Jan. **Unwmk.** ***Perf. 1***

Designs: 40k, Lenin and view of Kremlin. 60k Workers and Lenin power plant on Volga.

2158 A1129 40k multicolored .30 .1
2159 A1129 60k multicolored .45 .2
2160 A1129 1r red, yel & vio bl 1.25 .3
Nos. 2158-2160 (3) 2.00 .7

21st Cong. of the Communist Party and "th conquest of the cosmos by the Soviet people."

Lenin Statue, Minsk Buildings — A1130

Atomic Icebreaker "Lenin" A1131

1958, Dec. 20

2161 A1130 40k red, buff & brown .40 .15

Byelorussian Republic, 40th anniv.

1958, Dec. 31

Design: 60k, Diesel Locomotive "TE-3."

2162 A1131 40k multicolored .50 .20
2163 A1131 60k multicolored .70 .25

Shalom Aleichem A1132

Evangelista Torricelli A1133

1959, Feb. 10

2164 A1132 40k chocolate .40 .15

Aleichem, Yiddish writer, birth cent.

1959, Feb.

Scientists: #2166, Charles Darwin, English biologist. #2167, N. F. Gamaleya, microbiologist.

Various Frames

2165 A1133 40k blue green & blk .50 .15
2166 A1133 40k chalky blue & brn .50 .15
2167 A1133 40k dk red & black .50 .15
Nos. 2165-2167 (3) 1.50 .45

Woman Skater A1134

Frederic Joliot-Curie A1135

1959, Feb. 5

2168 A1134 25k ultra, black & ver .20 .15
2169 A1134 40k ultra & black .35 .15

Women's International Ice Skating Championships, Sverdlovsk.

No. 1717 Overprinted in Orange Brown

Победа баскетбольной команды СССР. Чили 1959 г.

1959, Feb. 12

2170 A919 1r 5.00 5.00

"Victory of the USSR Basketball Team - Chile 1959." However, the 3rd World Basketball Championship honors went to Brazil when the Soviet team was disqualified for refusing to play Nationalist China.

1959, Mar. 3 Litho. *Perf. 12*

2171 A1135 40k turq bl & gray brn, *beige* .40 .20

Joliot-Curie (1900-58), French scientist.

Selma Lagerlöf A1136

Peter Zwirka A1137

1959, Feb. 26

2172 A1136 40k red brown & black .40 .15

Lagerlöf (1858-1940), Swedish writer.

1959, Mar. 3

2173 A1137 40k hn brn & blk, *yel* .40 .15

Zwirka (1909-1947), Lithuanian writer.

No. 1861A Overprinted in Red: "1759 1959"

1959, Feb. 26 Engr.

2174 A993 40k lt ultra & brown 10.00 7.50

200th anniversary of the birth of Robert Burns, Scottish poet.

Type of 1958

Russian Writers: No. 2175, A. S. Griboedov. No. 2176, A. N. Ostrovski. No. 2177, Anton Chekhov. No. 2178, I. A. Krylov. No. 2178A, Nikolai V. Gogol. No. 2178B, S. T. Aksakov. No. 2178C, A. V. Koltzov. poet, and reaper.

1959 Litho.

2175 A1071 40k buff, cl, blk & vio .30 .20
2176 A1071 40k vio & brown .30 .20
2177 A1071 40k slate & hn brn .30 .20
2178 A1071 40k ol bister & brn .30 .20
2178A A1071 40k ol, gray & bis .30 .20
2178B A1071 40k brn, vio & bis .30 .20
2178C A1071 40k violet & black .30 .20
Nos. 2175-2178C (7) 2.10 1.40

No. 2178A for the 150th birth anniv. of Nikolai V. Gogol, writer, No. 2178B the centenary of the death of S. T. Aksakov, writer.

A. S. Popov and Rescue from Ice Float — A1138

60k, Radio broadcasting "Peace" in 5 languages.

1959, Mar. 13

2179 A1138 40k brn, blk & dk blue .35 .15
2180 A1138 60k multicolored .55 .20

Centenary of the birth of A. S. Popov, pioneer in radio research.

M.S. Rossija at Odessa — A1139

Ships: 10k, Steamer, Vladivostok-Petropavlovsk-Kamchatka line. 20k, M.S. Feliks Dzerzhinski, Odessa-Latakia line. No. 2184, Ship, Murmansk-Tyksi line. 60k, M.S. Mikhail Kalinin at Leningrad. 1r, M.S. Baltika, Leningrad-London line.

1959 Litho. Unwmk.

2181 A1139 10k multicolored .15 .15
2182 A1139 20k red, lt grn & dk bl .15 .15
2183 A1139 40k multicolored .20 .15
2184 A1139 40k blue, buff & red .20 .15
2185 A1139 60k bl grn, red & buff .35 .15
2186 A1139 1r ultra, red & yel .50 .15
Nos. 2181-2186 (6) 1.55
Set value .50

Honoring the Russian fleet.

Globe and Luna 1 — A1140

Luna 1, launched Jan. 2, 1959: No. 2188, Globe and route of Luna 1.

1959, Apr. 13

2187 A1140 40k red brown & rose .40 .15
2188 A1140 40k ultra & blue .40 .15

Saadi and "Gulistan" A1141

1959, Mar. 20 Photo.

2189 A1141 40k dk blue & black .40 .25

Persian poet Saadi (Muslih-ud-Din) and 700th anniv. of his book, "Gulistan" (1258).

Suahan S. Orbeliani A1142

Drawing by Korin A1143

1959, Apr. 2

2190 A1142 40k dull rose & black .40 .20

Orbeliani (1658-1725), Georgian writer.

1959, Apr. 10 Litho.

2191 A1143 40k multicolored 1.00 .20

Ogata Korin (1653?-1716), Japanese artist.

Lenin A1144

Cachin A1146

1959, Apr. 17 Engr.

2192 A1144 40k sepia .40 .20

89th anniversary of the birth of Lenin.

1959, Apr. 27 Photo.

2194 A1146 60k dark brown .40 .20

Marcel Cachin (1869-1958), French Communist Party leader.

Joseph Haydn A1147

Alexander von Humboldt A1148

1959, May 8

2195 A1147 40k dk bl, gray & brn black .75 .15

Sesquicentennial of the death of Joseph Haydn, Austrian composer.

1959, May 6

2196 A1148 40k violet & brown .40 .15

Alexander von Humboldt, German naturalist and geographer, death centenary.

Three Races Carrying Flag of Peace A1149

Mountain Climber A1150

1959, Apr. 30 Litho.

2199 A1149 40k multicolored .75 .15

10th anniv. of World Peace Movement.

1959, May 15

Sports and Travel: No. 2201, Tourists reading map. No. 2202, Canoeing, horiz. No. 2203, Skiers.

2200 A1150 40k multicolored .20 .15
2201 A1150 40k multicolored .20 .15
2202 A1150 40k multicolored .20 .15
2203 A1150 40k multicolored .20 .15
Nos. 2200-2203 (4) .80
Set value .35

I. E. Repin Statue, Moscow A1151

N. Y. Coliseum and Spasski Tower A1152

Statues: No. 2205, Lenin, Ulyanovsk. 20k, V. V. Mayakovsky, Moscow. 25k, Alexander Pushkin, Leningrad. 60k, Maxim Gorki, Moscow. 1r, Tchaikovsky, Moscow.

1959 Photo. Unwmk.

2204 A1151 10k ocher & sepia .15 .15
2205 A1151 10k red & black .15 .15
2206 A1151 20k violet & sepia .15 .15
2207 A1151 25k grnsh blue & blk .15 .15
2208 A1151 60k lt green & slate .20 .15
2209 A1151 1r lt ultra & gray .35 .15
Nos. 2204-2209 (6) 1.15
Set value .50

1959, June 25 Litho. *Perf. 12*

2210 A1152 20k multicolored .20 .15
2211 A1152 40k multicolored .30 .15
a. Souv. sheet of 1, imperf. 2.50 1.00

Soviet Exhibition of Science, Technology and Culture, New York, June 20-Aug. 10.
No. 2211a issued July 20.

Animal Types of 1957

20k, Hare. #2214, Siberian horse. #2215, Tiger. #2216, Red squirrel. #2217, Pine marten. #2218, Hazel hen. #2219, Mute swan.

1959-60 Litho. *Perf. 12*

Center in Natural Colors

2213 A1023 20k vio blue ('60) .25 .15
2214 A1023 25k blue black .25 .15
2215 A1023 25k brown .25 .15
2216 A1023 40k deep green .30 .15
2217 A1023 40k dark green .30 .15
2218 A1024 60k dark green .35 .15
2219 A1023 1r bright blue .40 .30
Nos. 2213-2219 (7) 2.10
Set value 1.00

Values quoted in this catalogue are for stamps graded Very Fine and with no faults. An illustrated guide to grade is provided in the "Catalogue Information" section of the Introduction.

Louis Braille
A1153

Musa Djalil
A1154

1959, July 16
2220 A1153 60k blue grn, bis & brn .40 .15

150th anniversary of the birth of Louis Braille, French educator of the blind.

1959, July 16 **Photo.**
2221 A1154 40k violet & black .40 .15

Musa Djalil, Tatar poet.

Sturgeon — A1155

1959, July 16
2222 A1155 40k shown .40 .15
2223 A1155 60k Chum salmon .60 .15

See Nos. 2375-2377.

Gymnast
A1156

Athletes Holding Trophy
A1157

Globe and Hands
A1158

Designs: 25k, Runner. 60k, Water polo.

1959, Aug. 7
2224 A1156 15k lilac rose & gray .15 .15
2225 A1156 25k yel green & red brn .15 .15
2226 A1157 30k brt red & gray .15 .15
2227 A1156 60k blue & org yel .30 .15
Nos. 2224-2227 (4) .75
Set value .35

2nd National Spartacist Games.

1959, Aug. 12 **Litho.**
2228 A1158 40k yel, blue & red .40 .15

2nd Intl. Conf. of Public Employees Unions.

Catl.edral and Modern Building
A1159

Schoolboys in Workshop
A1160

1959, Aug. 21 **Unwmk.** ***Perf. 12***
2229 A1159 40k blue, ol, yel & red .40 .15

1100th anniv. of the city of Novgorod.

1959, Aug. 27 **Photo.**

Design: 1r, Workers in night school.

2230 A1160 40k dark purple .15 .15
2231 A1160 1r dark blue .50 .15
Set value .20

Strengthening the connection between school and life.

Glacier Survey
A1161

Rocket and Observatory
A1162

Designs: 25k, Oceanographic ship "Vityaz" and map. 40k, Plane over Antarctica, camp and emperor penguin.

1959
2232 A1161 10k blue green .15 .15
2233 A1161 25k brt blue & red .30 .15
2234 A1161 40k ultra & red .50 .15
2235 A1162 1r ultra & buff 1.40 .30
Nos. 2232-2235 (4) 2.35
Set value .50

Intl. Geophysical Year. 1st Russian rocket to reach the moon, Sept. 14, 1959 (#2235).

Workers and Farmers Holding Atom Symbol
A1163

1959, Sept. 23 **Litho.**
2236 A1163 40k red org & bister .40 .15

All-Union Economic Exhibition, Moscow.

Russian and Chinese Students
A1164

40k, Russian miner and Chinese steel worker.

1959, Sept. 25 **Litho.** ***Perf. 12***
2237 A1164 20k multicolored .40 .15
2238 A1164 40k multicolored .60 .15

People's Republic of China, 10th anniv.

Letter Carrier
A1165

Makhtumkuli
A1166

1959, Sept.
2239 A1165 40k dk car rose & black .30 .15
2240 A1165 60k blue & black .60 .15

Intl. Letter Writing Week, Oct. 4-10.

1959, Sept. 30 **Photo.**
2241 A1166 40k brown .40 .15

225th anniversary of the birth of Makhtumkuli, Turkmen writer.

East German Emblem and Workers — A1167

City Hall, East Berlin — A1168

1959, Oct. 6 **Litho.**
2242 A1167 40k multicolored .20 .15

Photo.

2243 A1168 60k dp claret & buff .35 .15

German Democratic Republic, 10th anniv.

Steel Production — A1169

7-Year Production Plan (Industries): #2244, Chemicals. #2245, Spasski Tower, hammer and sickle. #2246, Home building. #2247, Meat production, woman with farm animals. #2248, Machinery. #2249, Grain production, woman tractor driver. #2250, Oil. #2251, Textiles. #2252, Steel. #2253, Coal. #2254, Iron. #2255, Electric power.

1959-60 **Litho.**
2244 A1169 10k vio, grnsh blue & maroon .15 .15
2245 A1169 10k orange & dk car .15 .15
2246 A1169 15k brn, yel & red .15 .15
2247 A1169 15k brn, grn & mar .15 .15
2248 A1169 20k bl grn, yel & red .15 .15
2249 A1169 20k green, yel & red .15 .15
2250 A1169 30k lilac, sal & red .15 .15
2251 A1169 30k gldn brn, lil, red & green ('60) .20 .15
2252 A1169 40k vio bl, yel & org .20 .15
2253 A1169 40k dk blue, pink & dp rose .20 .15
2254 A1169 60k org red, yel, bl & maroon .30 .15
2255 A1169 60k ultra, buff & red .30 .15
Set value 2.00 1.00

Arms of Tadzhikistan
A1170

Path of Luna 3 and Electronics Laboratory
A1171

1959, Oct. 13
2258 A1170 40k red, emer, ocher & black .40 .15

Tadzhikistan statehood, 30th anniversary.

1959, Oct. 12
2259 A1171 40k violet .50 .25

Flight of Luna 3 around the moon, Oct. 4, 1959.

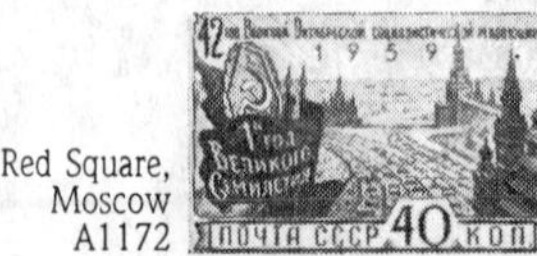
Red Square, Moscow
A1172

1959, Oct. 26 **Engr.**
2260 A1172 40k dark red .40 .15

42nd anniversary of October Revolution.

US Capitol, Globe and Kremlin
A1173

1959, Oct. 27 **Photo.**
2261 A1173 60k blue & yellow .40 .15

Visit of Premier Nikita Khrushchev to the US, Sept., 1959.

Helicopter
A1174

25k, Diver. 40k, Motorcyclist. 60k, Parachutist.

1959, Oct. 28
2262 A1174 10k vio blue & maroon .15 .15
2263 A1174 25k blue & brown .15 .15
2264 A1174 40k red brn & indigo .20 .15
2265 A1174 60k blue & ol bister .30 .15
Nos. 2262-2265 (4) .80
Set value .35

Honoring voluntary aides of the army.

Moon, Earth and Path of Rocket
A1175

Design: No. 2267, Kremlin and diagram showing rocket and positions of moon and earth.

1959, Nov. 1 **Litho.**
2266 A1175 40k bl, dk bl, red & bis .40 .15
2267 A1175 40k gray, pink & red .40 .15

Landing of the Soviet rocket on the moon, Sept. 14, 1959.

Sandor Petöfi
A1176

Victory Statue and View of Budapest
A1177

1959, Nov. 9 ***Perf. 12x12½, 12½x12***
2268 A1176 20k gray & ol bister .15 .15
2269 A1177 40k multicolored .20 .15
Set value .20

Soviet-Hungarian friendship.
For overprint see No. 2308.

Manolis Glezos and Acropolis
A1178

A. A. Voskresensky
A1179

1959, Nov. 12 **Photo.** ***Perf. 12x12½***
2270 A1178 40k ultra & brown 6.00 4.75

Manolis Glezos, Greek communist.

1959, Dec. 7 ***Perf. 12½x12***
2271 A1179 40k ultra & brown .40 .15

Voskresensky, chemist, 150th birth anniv.

Chusovaya River, Ural — A1180

Designs: No. 2273, Lake Ritza, Caucasus. No. 2274, Lena River, Siberia. No. 2275, Seashore, Far East. No. 2276, Lake Iskander, Central Asia. No. 2277, Lake Baikal, Siberia. No. 2278, Belukha Mountain, Altai range. No. 2279, Gursuf region, Crimea. No. 2280, Crimea.

1959, Dec. Engr. *Perf. 12½*

2272 A1180 10k purple .15 .15
2273 A1180 10k rose carmine .15 .15
2274 A1180 25k dark blue .15 .15
2275 A1180 25k olive .15 .15
2276 A1180 25k dark red .15 .15
2277 A1180 40k claret .25 .15
2278 A1180 60k Prus blue .30 .15
2279 A1180 1r olive green .40 .15
2280 A1180 1r deep orange .40 .15
Nos. 2272-2280 (9) 2.10
Set value 1.00

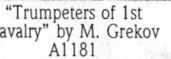

"Trumpeters of 1st Cavalry" by M. Grekov A1181

Farm Woman A1182

1959, Dec. 30 Litho. *Perf. 12½x12*

2283 A1181 40k multicolored .40 .25

40th anniversary of the 1st Cavalry.

1958-60 Engr. *Perf. 12½*

Designs: 25k, Architect. 60k, Steel worker.

2286 A1182 20k slate grn ('59) 2.00 .85
2287 A1182 25k sepia ('59) 2.00 1.00
2288 A1182 60k carmine 15.00 4.25

Perf. 12x12½

Litho.

2290 A1182 20k green ('60) .15 .15
2291 A1182 25k sepia ('60) .20 .15
2292 A1182 60k vermilion ('59) .45 .15
2293 A1182 60k blue ('60) .25 .15
Nos. 2286-2293 (7) 20.05 6.70

M. V. Frunze A1183

Gabrichevski A1184

1960, Jan. 25 Photo. *Perf. 12½*

2295 A1183 40k dark red brown .40 .15

75th anniv. of the birth of Mikhail V. Frunze (1885-1925), revolutionary leader.

Perf. 12½x12

1960, Jan. 30 Unwmk.

2296 A1184 40k brt violet & brown .40 .15

Centenary of the birth of G. N. Gabrichevski, microbiologist.

Anton Chekhov and Moscow Home — A1185

40k, Chekhov in later years, and Yalta home.

1960, Jan. 20 Litho. *Perf. 12x12½*

2297 A1185 20k red, gray & vio blue .15 .15
2298 A1185 40k dk blue, buff & brn .20 .15
Set value .20

Anton P. Chekhov (1860-1904), playwright.

Komissarzhevskaya A1186

Ice Hockey A1187

1960, Feb. 5 Photo. *Perf. 12½x12*

2299 A1186 40k chocolate .40 .15

Vera Komissarzhevskaya (1864-1910), actress.

1960, Feb. 18 Litho. *Perf. 11½*

Sports: 25k, Speed skating. 40k, Skier. 60k, Woman figure skater. 1r, Ski jumper.

2300 A1187 10k ocher & vio blue .15 .15
2301 A1187 25k multicolored .15 .15
2302 A1187 40k org, rose lil & vio blue .25 .15
2303 A1187 60k vio, green & buff .35 .15
2304 A1187 1r blue, green & brn .50 .20
Nos. 2300-2304 (5) 1.40
Set value .55

8th Olympic Winter Games, Squaw Valley, Calif., Feb. 18-29.

Sword into Plowshare Statue, UN, NY — A1188

1960 *Perf. 12x12½*

2305 A1188 40k grnsh bl, yel & brown .40 .15
a. Souvenir sheet 1.25 .45

No. 2305a for Premier Nikita Khrushchev's visit to the 15th General Assembly of the UN in NYC.

Women of Various Races — A1189

1960, Mar. 8

2306 A1189 40k multicolored .40 .15

50 years of Intl. Woman's Day, Mar. 8.

Planes in Combat and Timur Frunze A1190

1960, Feb. 23 *Perf. 12½x12*

2307 A1190 40k multicolored .40 .15

Lieut. Timur Frunze, World War II hero.

No. 2269 Overprinted in Red

15 лет освобождения Венгрии

1960, Apr. 4

2308 A1177 40k multicolored 1.40 1.00

15th anniversary of Hungary's liberation from the Nazis.

Lunik 3 Photographing Far Side of Moon — A1191

Design: 60k, Far side of the moon.

1960 Photo. *Perf. 12x12½*

2309 A1191 40k pale bl, dk bl & yel .50 .15

Litho.

2310 A1191 60k lt bl, dk bl & citron .50 .15

Photographing of the far side of the moon, Oct. 7, 1959.

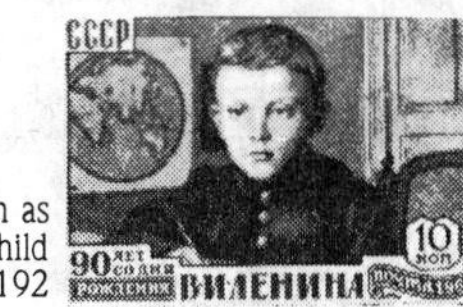

Lenin as Child A1192

Various Lenin Portraits and: 20k, Lenin with children and Christmas tree. 30k, Flag, workers and ship. 40k, Kremlin, banners and marchers. 60k, Map of Russia, buildings and ship. 1r, Peace proclamation and globe.

1960, Apr. 10 Litho. *Perf. 12½x12*

2311 A1192 10k multicolored .15 .15
2312 A1192 20k red, green & blk .15 .15
2313 A1192 30k multicolored .15 .15
2314 A1192 40k multicolored .15 .15
2315 A1192 60k multicolored .30 .15
2316 A1192 1r red, vio bl & brn .45 .15
Nos. 2311-2316 (6) 1.35
Set value .60

90th anniversary of the birth of Lenin.

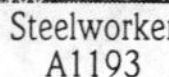

Steelworker A1193

Government House, Baku A1194

1960, Apr. 30 Photo.

2317 A1193 40k brown & red .30 .15

Industrial overproduction by 50,000,000r during the 1st year of the 7-year plan.

1960, Apr. Litho. *Perf. 12x12½*

2318 A1194 40k bister & brown .35 .20

Azerbaijan, 40th anniv.

For surcharge see #2898.

Brotherhood Monument, Prague — A1195

Design: 60k, Charles Bridge, Prague.

1960, Apr. 29 Photo. *Perf. 12½x12*

2319 A1195 40k brt blue & black .15 .15
2320 A1195 60k black brn & yellow .35 .15

Czechoslovak Republic, 15th anniv.

Radio Tower and Popov Central Museum of Communications, Leningrad — A1196

1960, May 6 Litho.

2321 A1196 40k blue, ocher & brn .40 .15

Radio Day.

Gen. I. D. Tcherniakovski and Soldiers — A1197

1960, May 4

2322 A1197 1r multicolored .60 .15

Gen. I. D. Tcherniakovski, World War II hero and his military school.

Robert Schumann A1198

Yakov M. Sverdlov A1199

1960, May 20 Photo. *Perf. 12x12½*

2323 A1198 40k ultra & black .40 .15

150th anniversary of the birth of Robert Schumann, German composer.

1960, May 24 *Perf. 12½x12*

2324 A1199 40k dk brown & org brn .40 .15

Sverdlov (1885-1919), 1st USSR Pres.

Stamp of 1957 Under Magnifying Glass — A1200

1960, May 28 Litho. *Perf. 11½*

2325 A1200 60k multicolored .40 .15

Stamp Day.

Karl Marx Avenue, Petrozavodsk, Karelian Autonomous Republic — A1201

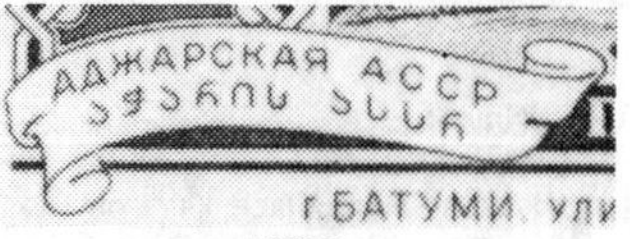

#2327

#2329

#2330

#2332

#2333

#2339

#2341

#2342

Capitals, Soviet Autonomous Republics: No. 2327, Lenin street, Batum, Adzhar. No. 2328, Cultural Palace, Izhevsk, Udmurt. No. 2329, August street, Grozny, Chechen-Ingush. No. 2330, Soviet House, Cheboksary, Chuvash. No. 2331, Buinak Street, Makhachkala, Dagestan. No. 2332, Soviet street, Ioshkar Ola, Mari. No. 2333, Chkalov street, Dzaudzhikau, North Ossetia. No. 2334, October street, Yakutsk, Yakut. No. 2335, House of Ministers, Nukus, Kara-Kalpak.

1960 Engr. *Perf. 12½*

2326 A1201 40k Prus green .35 .15
2327 A1201 40k violet blue .35 .15
2328 A1201 40k green .35 .15
2329 A1201 40k maroon .35 .15
2330 A1201 40k dull red .35 .15
2331 A1201 40k carmine .35 .15
2332 A1201 40k dark brown .35 .15
2333 A1201 40k orange brown .35 .15
2334 A1201 40k dark blue .35 .15
2335 A1201 40k brown .35 .15
Nos. 2326-2335 (10) 3.50
Set value 1.20

See Nos. 2338-2344C. For overprints see Nos. 2336-2337.

No. 2326 Overprinted in Red — 40 лет КАССР 8.VI.1960

1960, June 4

2336 A1201 40k Prus green 1.75 1.25

Karelian Autonomous Rep., 40th anniv.

No. 2328 Overprinted in Red — 40 лет Удмуртской АССР 4/XI 1960.

1960, Nov. 4

2337 A1201 40k green 2.25 1.25

Udmurt Autonomous Rep., 40th anniv.

1961-62 *Perf. 12½, 12½x12*

Capitals, Soviet Autonomous Republics: #2338, Rustaveli Street, Sukhumi, Abkhazia. #2339, House of Soviets, Nalchik, Kabardino-Balkar. #2340, Lenin Street, Ulan-Ude, Buriat. #2341, Soviet Street, Syktyvkar, Komi. #2342, Lenin Street, Nakhichevan, Nakhichevan. #2343, Elista, Kalmyk. #2344, Ufa, Bashkir. #2344A, Lobachevsky Square, Kazan, Tartar. #2344B, Kizil, Tuvinía. #2344C, Saransk, Mordovia.

2338 A1201 4k orange ver .25 .15
2339 A1201 4k dark violet .25 .15
2340 A1201 4k dark blue .25 .15
2341 A1201 4k gray .25 .15
2342 A1201 4k dk car rose .25 .15
2343 A1201 4k olive green .25 .15
2344 A1201 4k dull purple .25 .15
2344A A1201 4k grnsh blk ('62) .25 .15
2344B A1201 4k claret ('62) .25 .15
2344C A1201 4k deep green ('62) .25 .15
Nos. 2338-2344C (10) 2.50
Set value 1.00

Denominations of Nos. 2338-2344C are in the revalued currency.

Children's Friendship A1202

Drawings by Children: 20k, Collective farm, vert. 25k, Winter joys. 40k, "In the Zoo."

Perf. 12x12½, 12½x12

1960, June 1 Litho.

2345 A1202 10k multicolored .15 .15
2346 A1202 20k multicolored .15 .15
2347 A1202 25k multicolored .15 .15
2348 A1202 40k multicolored .15 .15
Set value .50 .30

Lomonosov University and Congress Emblem A1203

1960, June 17 Photo. *Perf. 12½x12*

2349 A1203 60k yellow & dk brown .40 .15

1st congress of the International Federation for Automation Control, Moscow.

Sputnik 4 and Globe — A1204

1960, June 17 *Perf. 12x12½*

2350 A1204 40k vio blue & dp org .75 .35

Launching on May 15, 1960, of Sputnik 4, which orbited the earth with a dummy cosmonaut.

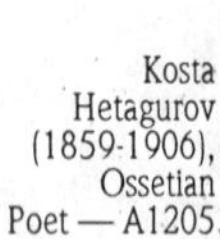

Kosta Hetagurov (1859-1906), Ossetian Poet — A1205

1960, June 20 Litho. *Perf. 12½*

2351 A1205 40k gray blue & brown .40 .15

Flag and Tallinn, Estonia — A1206

Soviet Republics, 20th Annivs.: No. 2353, Flag and Riga, Latvia. No. 2354, Flag and Vilnius, Lithuania.

Perf. 12x12½, 12½ (#2353)

1960 Photo.

2352 A1206 40k red & ultra .30 .15

Typo.

2353 A1206 40k blue, gray & red .30 .15

Litho.

2354 A1206 40k blue, red & green .30 .15
Nos. 2352-2354 (3) .90
Set value .35

Cement Factory, Belgorod A1207

Design: 40k, Factory, Novy Krivoi.

1960, June 28 *Perf. 12½x12*

2355 A1207 25k ultra & black .20 .15
2356 A1207 40k rose brown & black .20 .15

"New buildings of the 1st year of the 7-year plan."

Automatic Production Line and Roller Bearing A1208

#2358, Automatic production line and gear.

1960, June 13 *Perf. 11½*

2357 A1208 40k rose violet .20 .15
2358 A1208 40k Prus green .20 .15

Publicizing mechanization and automation of factories.

Running A1209

Sports: 10k, Wrestling. 15k, Basketball. 20k, Weight lifting. 25k, Boxing. No. 2364, Fencing. No. 2365, Diving. No. 2366, Women's gymnastics. 60k, Canoeing. 1r, Steeplechase.

1960, Aug. 1 Litho. *Perf. 11½*

2359 A1209 5k multicolored .20 .15
2360 A1209 10k brn, blue & yel .20 .15
2361 A1209 15k multicolored .20 .15
2362 A1209 20k blk, crim & sal .20 .15
2363 A1209 25k lake, sl & rose .20 .15
2364 A1209 40k vio bl, bl & bis .20 .15
2365 A1209 40k vio, gray & pink .20 .15
2366 A1209 40k multicolored .20 .15
2367 A1209 60k multicolored .30 .15
2368 A1209 1r brown, lilac & pale green .60 .25
Nos. 2359-2368 (10) 2.50
Set value 1.00

17th Olympic Games, Rome, Aug. 25-Sept. 11.

No. 2365 Overprinted in Red — Международная ярмарка в Риччоне

1960, Aug. 23

2369 A1209 40k 6.00 5.00

12th San Marino-Riccione Stamp Fair.

Kishinev, Moldavian Republic A1210

1960, Aug. 2 *Perf. 12x12½*

2370 A1210 40k multicolored .50 .15

20th anniversary of Moldavian Republic.

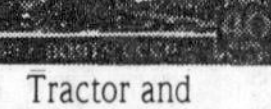

Tractor and Factory — A1211

Book Museum, Hanoi — A1212

Perf. 12x12½, 12½x12

1960, Aug. 25

2371 A1211 40k green, ocher & blk .15 .15
2372 A1212 60k blue, lilac & brn .25 .15

15th anniversary of North Viet Nam.

Gregory N. Minkh, Microbiologist, 125th Birth Anniv. — A1213

1960, Aug. 25 Photo. *Perf. 12½x12*

2373 A1213 60k bister brn & dk brn .40 .15

"March," by I. I. Levitan A1214

1960, Aug. 29

2374 A1214 40k ol bister & black .40 .15

I. I. Levitan, painter, birth cent.

Fish Type of 1959

Designs: 20k, Pikeperch. 25k, Fur seals. 40k, Ludogan whitefish.

1960, Sept. 3 *Perf. 12½*

2375 A1155 20k blue & black .15 .15
2376 A1155 25k vio gray & red brn .15 .15
2377 A1155 40k rose lilac & purple .15 .15
Nos. 2375-2377 (3) .45
Set value .25

Forest by I. I. Shishkin — A1215

1960, Aug. 29 Engr.

2378 A1215 1r red brown .80 .15

5th World Forestry Congress, Seattle, Wash., Aug. 29-Sept. 10.

Globe with USSR and Letter — A1216

1960, Sept. 10 Litho. *Perf. 12x12½*

2379 A1216 40k multicolored .15 .15
2380 A1216 60k multicolored .25 .15

Intl. Letter Writing Week, Oct. 3-9.

Farmer, Worker, Scientist A1217

1960, Oct. 4 Typo. *Perf. 12½*

2381 A1217 40k multicolored .40 .15

Kazakh SSR, 40th anniv.

Globes and Olive Branch — A1218

1960, Sept. 29 Litho. *Perf. 12½x12*

2382 A1218 60k pale vio, bl & gray .40 .15

World Federation of Trade Unions, 15th anniv.

Kremlin, Sputnik 5 and Dogs Belka and Strelka A1219

1960, Sept. 29 Photo.

2383 A1219 40k brt pur & yellow .55 .15
2384 A1219 1r blue & salmon .85 .25

Flight of Sputnik 5, Aug. 19-20, 1960.

Passenger Ship "Karl Marx" — A1220

Ships: 40k, Turbo-electric ship "Lenin." 60k, Speedboat "Raketa" (Rocket).

1960, Oct. 24 Litho. *Perf. 12x12½*

2385 A1220 25k blue, blk, red & yel .20 .15
2386 A1220 40k blue, black & red .40 .15
2387 A1220 60k blue, black & rose .45 .15
Nos. 2385-2387 (3) 1.05
Set value .35

A. N. Voronikhin and Kasansky Cathedral, Leningrad A1221

1960, Oct. 24 Photo.

2388 A1221 40k gray & brn black .40 .15

Voronikhin, architect, 200th birth anniv.

J. S. Gogebashvili A1222

1960, Oct. 29

2389 A1222 40k dk gray & magenta .40 .15

120th anniversary of the birth of J. S. Gogebashvili, Georgian teacher and publicist.

Red Flag, Electric Power Station and Factory — A1223

1960, Oct. 29 Litho.

2390 A1223 40k red, yel & brown .40 .15

43rd anniversary of October Revolution.

Leo Tolstoy — A1224

Designs: 40k, Tolstoy in Yasnaya Polyana. 60k, Portrait, vert.

Perf. 12x12½, 12½x12

1960, Nov. 14

2391 A1224 20k violet & brown .15 .15
2392 A1224 40k blue & lt brown .15 .15
2393 A1224 60k dp claret & sepia .25 .15
Nos. 2391-2393 (3) .55
Set value .25

50th anniversary of the death of Count Leo Tolstoy, writer.

Yerevan, Armenian Republic A1225

1960, Nov. 14 *Perf. 12x12½*

2394 A1225 40k bl, red, buff & brn .40 .15

Armenian Soviet Rep., 40th anniv.

Friedrich Engels A1226

Badge of Youth Federation A1227

1960, Nov. 25 Engr. *Perf. 12½*

2395 A1226 60k slate .40 .25

Friedrich Engels, 140th birth anniv.

1960, Nov. 2 Litho.

2396 A1227 60k brt pink, blk & yel .40 .15

Intl. Youth Federation, 15th anniv.

40-ton Truck MAL-530 A1228

Automotive Industry: 40k, "Volga" car. 60k, "Moskvitch 407" car. 1r, "Tourist LAS-697" Bus.

1960, Oct. 29 Photo. *Perf. 12x12½*

2397 A1228 25k ultra & gray .15 .15
2398 A1228 40k ol bister & ultra .15 .15
2399 A1228 60k Prus green & dp car .30 .15

Litho.

2400 A1228 1r multicolored .55 .15
Nos. 2397-2400 (4) 1.15
Set value .50

N. I. Pirogov A1229

Friendship University and Students A1230

1960, Dec. 13 Photo. *Perf. 12½x12*

2401 A1229 40k green & brn black .40 .15

Pirogov, surgeon, 125th birth anniv.

1960, Nov. *Perf. 12x12½*

2402 A1230 40k brown carmine .40 .15

Completion of Friendship of Nations University in Moscow.

For surcharge see No. 2462.

Mark Twain A1231

1960, Nov. 30 *Perf. 12½x12*

2403 A1231 40k dp orange & brown .70 .40

Mark Twain, 125th birth anniv.

Dove and Globe A1232

Akaki Zeretely A1233

1960, Oct. 29 Photo.

2404 A1232 60k maroon & gray .40 .15

Intl. Democratic Women's Fed, 15th anniv.

1960, Dec. 27

2405 A1233 40k violet & black brn .40 .15

Zeretely, Georgian poet, 120th birth anniv.

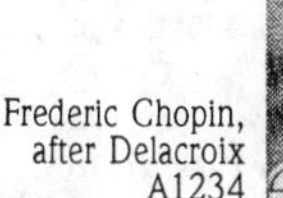

Frederic Chopin, after Delacroix A1234

1960, Dec. 24 *Perf. 12x11½*

2406 A1234 40k bister & brown .40 .15

Chopin, Polish composer, 150th birth anniv.

North Korean Flag and Flying Horse — A1235

Crocus — A1236

1960, Dec. 24 Litho. *Perf. 12½x12*

2407 A1235 40k multicolored .40 .15

15th anniversary of "the liberation of the Korean people by the Soviet army."

1960 *Perf. 12x12½*

Asiatic Flowers: No. 2409, Tulip. No. 2410, Trollius. No. 2411, Tulip. No. 2412, Ginseng. No. 2413, Iris. No. 2414, Hypericum. 1r, Dog rose.

Flowers in Natural Colors

2408 A1236 20k green & violet .25 .15
2409 A1236 20k vio blue & black .25 .15
2410 A1236 25k gray .30 .15
2411 A1236 40k ol bister & black .35 .15
2412 A1236 40k green & blk, wmkd. .35 .15
2413 A1236 60k yel, green & red .70 .15
2414 A1236 60k bluish grn & blk .70 .15
2415 A1236 1r slate green & blk 1.10 .15
Nos. 2408-2415 (8) 4.00
Set value .60

The watermark on No. 2412 consists of vertical rows of chevrons.

Lithuanian Costumes A1237

Regional Costumes: 60k, Uzbek.

Perf. 12½ (10k), 11½ (60k)

1960, Dec. 24 Typo. Unwmk.

2416 A1237 10k multicolored .25 .15
2417 A1237 60k multicolored 1.00 .15
Set value .20

Currency Revalued

1961-62 Litho. *Perf. 11½*

Regional Costumes: No. 2418, Moldavia. No. 2419, Georgia. No. 2420, Ukrainia. No. 2421, White Russia. No. 2422, Kazakhstan. No. 2422A, Latvia. 4k, Koryak. 6k, Russia. 10k, Armenia. 12k, Estonia.

2418 A1237 2k buff, brn & ver .15 .15
2419 A1237 2k red, brn, ocher & black .15 .15
2420 A1237 3k ultra, buff, red & brown .25 .15
2421 A1237 3k red org, ocher & black .25 .15
2422 A1237 3k buff, brn, grn & red .25 .15
2422A A1237 3k org red, gray ol & blk ('62) .25 .15
2423 A1237 4k multicolored .45 .15
2424 A1237 6k multicolored .55 .25
2425 A1237 10k brn, ol bis & vermilion .80 .30
2426 A1237 12k red, ultra & black 1.10 .40
Nos. 2418-2426 (10) 4.20 2.00

See Nos. 2723-2726.

Lenin and Map Showing Electrification A1238

1961 *Perf. 12½x12*

2427 A1238 4k blue, buff & brown .15 .15
2428 A1238 10k red org & blue blk .40 .25

State Electrification Plan, 40th anniv. (in 1960).

Animal Types of 1957

1961, Jan. 7 *Perf. 12½*

2429 A1024 1k Brown bear .15 .15
2430 A1023 6k Beaver .70 .35
2431 A1023 10k Roe deer .90 .55
Nos. 2429-2431 (3) 1.75 1.05

Georgian Flag and Views A1239

1961, Feb. 15 *Perf. 12½x12*

2432 A1239 4k multicolored .30 .15

40th anniv. of Georgian SSR.

Nikolai D. Zelinski A1240

N. A. Dobrolyubov A1241

1961, Feb. 6 Photo. *Perf. 12x12½*
2433 A1240 4k rose violet .30 .15

Zelinski, chemist, birth cent.

1961, Feb. 5 *Perf. 11½x12*
2434 A1241 4k brt blue & brown .50 .15

Nikolai A. Dobrolyubov, journalist and critic (1836-1861).

A1242 A1243

Designs: 3k, Cattle. 4k, Tractor in cornfield. 6k, Mechanization of Grain Harvest. 10k, Women picking apples.

1961 *Perf. 12x12½, 12x11½*

2435	A1242	3k blue & magenta	.25	.15
2436	A1242	4k green & dk gray	.25	.15
2437	A1242	6k vio blue & brn	.60	.15
2438	A1242	10k maroon & ol grn	.80	.15
		Nos. 2435-2438 (4)	1.90	
		Set value		.35

Agricultural development.

Perf. 12x12½; 12x11½ (Nos. 2439A, 2442 & 12k)

1961-65 Unwmk.

Designs: 1k, "Labor" Holding Peace Flag. 2k, Harvester and silo. 3k, Space rockets. 4k, Arms and flag of USSR. 6k, Spasski tower. 10k, Workers' monument. 12k, Minin and Pozharsky Monument and Spasski tower. 16k, Plane over power station and dam.

		Engr.		
2439	A1243	1k olive bister	1.90	.15
		Litho.		
2439A	A1243	1k olive bister	.75	.15
2440	A1243	2k green	.20	.15
2441	A1243	3k dk violet	2.50	.15
		Engr.		
2442	A1243	3k dk violet	4.25	.95
		Litho.		
2443	A1243	4k red	.75	.15
2443A	A1243	4k org brn ('65)	1.50	.35
2444	A1243	6k vermilion	6.75	.65
2445	A1243	6k dk car rose	1.90	.15
2446	A1243	10k orange	3.50	.15
		Photo.		
2447	A1243	12k brt magenta	3.50	.30
		Litho.		
2448	A1243	16k ultra	5.25	1.10
		Nos. 2439-2448 (12)	32.75	4.40

V. P. Miroshnitchenko — A1244

1961, Feb. 23 Photo. *Perf. 12½x12*
2449 A1244 4k violet brn & slate .30 .15

Soldier hero of World War II.
See Nos. 2570-2571.

Taras G. Shevchenko and Birthplace A1245

Shevchenko Statue, Kharkov A1246

Andrei Rubljov A1247

6k, Book, torch and Shevchenko with beard.

Perf. 12½, 11½x12

1961, Mar. Litho.; Photo. (4k)

2450	A1245	3k brown & violet	.30	.15
2451	A1246	4k red orange & gray	.60	.20
2452	A1245	6k black, grn & red brn	.85	.25
		Nos. 2450-2452 (3)	1.75	.60

Shevchenko, Ukrainian poet, death cent.

No. 2452 was printed with alternating green and black label, containing a quotation.

See No. 2852.

1961, Mar. 13 Litho. *Perf. 12½x12*
2453 A1247 4k ultra, bister & brn .30 .15

Rubljov, painter, 600th birth anniv.

N. V. Sklifosovsky A1248

Robert Koch A1249

1961, Mar. 26 Photo. *Perf. 11½x12*
2454 A1248 4k ultra & black .30 .15

Sklifosovsky, surgeon, 125th birth anniv.

1961, Mar. 26
2455 A1249 6k dark brown .30 .15

Koch, German microbiologist, 59th death anniv.

Globe and Sputnik 8 — A1250

Design: 10k, Space probe and its path to Venus.

1961, Apr. Litho. *Perf. 11½*
2456 A1250 6k dk & lt blue & org .60 .20

Photo.
2457 A1250 10k vio blue & yel .85 .30

Launching of the Venus space probe, 2/12/61.

Open Book and Globe A1251

1961, Apr. 7 Litho. *Perf. 12½x12*
2458 A1251 6k ultra & sepia .70 .15

Centenary of the children's magazine "Around the World."

Musician, Dancers and Singers A1252

1961, Apr. 7 Unwmk.
2459 A1252 4k yel, red & black .40 .15

Russian National Choir, 50th anniv.

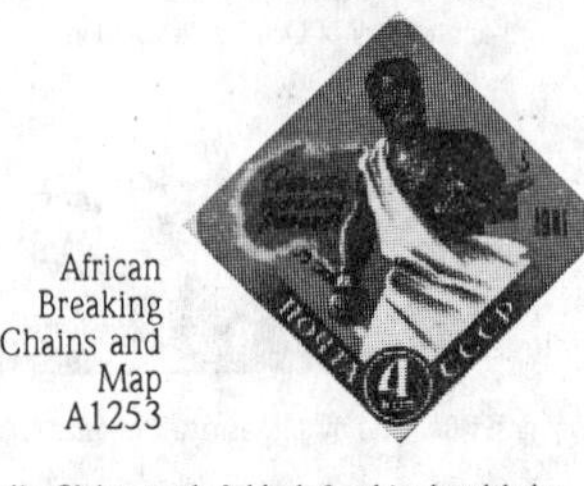

African Breaking Chains and Map A1253

6k, Globe, torch & black & white handshake.

1961, Apr. 15 *Perf. 12½*

2460	A1253	4k multicolored	.35	.15
2461	A1253	6k blue, purple & org	.35	.15

Africa Day and 3rd Conference of Independent African States, Cairo, Mar. 25-31.

No. 2402 Surcharged in Red

1961, Apr. 15 Photo. *Perf. 12x12½*
2462 A1230 4k on 40k brown car .70 .15

Naming of Friendship University, Moscow, in memory of Patrice Lumumba, Premier of Congo.

Maj. Yuri A. Gagarin A1254

6k, Kremlin, rockets and radar equipment. 10k, Rocket, Gagarin with helmet and Kremlin.

1961, Apr. *Perf. 11½ (3k), 12½x12*
2463 A1254 3k Prus blue .25 .15

Litho.

2464	A1254	6k blue, violet & red	.65	.15
2465	A1254	10k red, blue grn & brn	1.10	.35
		Nos. 2463-2465 (3)	2.00	.65

1st man in space, Yuri A. Gagarin, Apr. 12, 1961. No. 2464 printed with alternating light blue and red label.

Nos. 2463-2465 exist imperf. Value $1.75.

Lenin — A1255

Rabindranath Tagore — A1256

1961, Apr. 22 Litho. *Perf. 12x12½*
2466 A1255 4k dp car, salmon & blk .30 .15

91st anniversary of Lenin's birth.

1961, May 8 Engr. *Perf. 11½x12*
2467 A1256 6k bis, maroon & blk .60 .15

Tagore, Indian poet, birth cent.

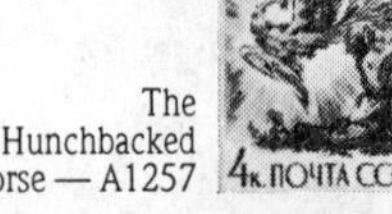

The Hunchbacked Horse — A1257

Fairy Tales: 1k, The Geese and the Swans. 3k, Fox, Hare and Cock. 6k, The Peasant and the Bear. 10k, Ruslan and Ludmilla.

1961 Litho. *Perf. 12½*

2468	A1257	1k multicolored	.15	.15
2469	A1257	3k multicolored	.50	.30
2470	A1257	4k multicolored	.15	.15
2471	A1257	6k multicolored	.55	.35
2472	A1257	10k multicolored	.65	.40
		Nos. 2468-2472 (5)	2.00	1.35

"Man Conquering Space" — A1258

Design: 6k, Giuseppe Garibaldi.

1961, May 24 Photo.

2481	A1258	4k orange brown	.25	.15
2482	A1258	6k lilac & salmon	.45	.15

International Labor Exposition, Turin.

Lenin A1259

Patrice Lumumba A1260

Various portraits of Lenin.

1961 Photo. *Perf. 12½x12*

Olive Bister Frame

2483	A1259	20k dark green	.85	.85
2484	A1259	30k dark blue	1.90	1.90
2485	A1259	50k rose red	2.75	2.75
		Nos. 2483-2485 (3)	5.50	5.50

1961, May 29 Litho.
2486 A1260 2k yellow & brown .35 .15

Lumumba (1925-61), premier of Congo.

Kindergarten A1261

Children's Day: 3k, Young Pioneers in camp. 4k, Young Pioneers, vert.

Perf. 12½x12, 12x12½

1961, May 31 Photo.

2487	A1261	2k orange & ultra	.20	.15
2488	A1261	3k ol bister & purple	.20	.15
2489	A1261	4k red & gray	.20	.15
		Nos. 2487-2489 (3)	.60	.45

Dog Zvezdochka and Sputnik 10 — A1263

Sputniks 9 and 10: 4k, Dog Chernushka and Sputnik 9, vert.

1961, June 8 Litho. *Perf. 12½, 11½*
2491 A1263 2k vio, Prus blue & blk .35 .15

Photo.
2492 A1263 4k Prus blue & brt grn .35 .15

A1265

A1266

Engraved and Photogravure

1961, June 13 *Perf. 11½x12*
2493 A1265 4k carmine & black .30 .15

150th anniversary of the birth of Vissarion G. Belinski, author and critic.

1961, June 22 Litho. *Perf. 12½*
2494 A1266 4k black, red & yel .30 .15

Lt. Gen. D. M. Karbishev, who was tortured to death in the Nazi prison camp at Mauthausen, Austria.

Hydro-meteorological Map and Instruments — A1267

1961, June 21 *Perf. 12x12½*
2495 A1267 6k ultra & green .50 .15

40th anniversary of hydro-meteorological service in Russia.

Gliders — A1268

6k, Motorboat race. 10k, Motorcycle race.

1961, July 5 Photo. *Perf. 12½*
2497 A1268 4k dk slate grn & crim .30 .15

Litho.

2498 A1268 6k slate & vermilion .40 .15
2499 A1268 10k slate & vermilion 1.25 .15
Nos. 2497-2499 (3) 1.95
Set value .30

USSR Technical Sports Spartakiad.

Javelin Thrower A1269

1961, Aug. 8 Photo. *Perf. 12½x12*
2500 A1269 6k dp carmine & pink .30 .15

7th Trade Union Spartacist Games.

S. I. Vavilov A1270

Vazha Pshavela A1271

1961, July 25
2501 A1270 4k lt green & sepia .30 .15

Vavilov, president of Academy of Science.

1961 Photo. *Perf. 11½x12*
2502 A1271 4k dk brown & cream .35 .15

Pshavela, Georgian poet, birth cent.

Scientists at Control Panel for Rocket — A1272

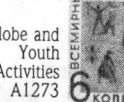

Globe and Youth Activities A1273

Design: 2k, Men pushing tank into river.

1961 Unwmk. *Perf. 11½*
2503 A1273 2k orange & sepia .15 .15
2504 A1272 4k lilac & dk green .35 .15
2505 A1273 6k ultra & citron .45 .15
Nos. 2503-2505 (3) .95
Set value .25

International Youth Forum, Moscow.

Arms of Mongolian Republic and Sukhe Bator Statue A1274

1961, July 25 Litho. *Perf. 12½x12*
2506 A1274 4k multicolored .40 .15

Mongol national revolution, 40th anniv.

Knight Kalevipoeg A1275

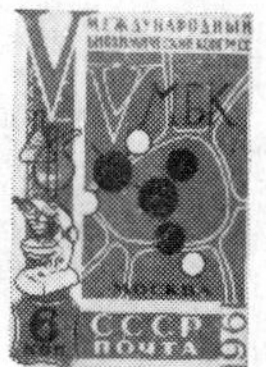

Symbols of Biochemistry A1276

1961, July 31
2507 A1275 4k black, blue & yel .30 .15

1st publication of "Kalevipoeg," Estonian national saga, recorded by R. K. Kreutzwald, Estonian writer, cent.

1961, July 31
2508 A1276 6k multicolored .35 .15

5th Intl. Biochemistry Congress, Moscow.

Major Titov and Vostok 2 — A1277

Design: 4k, Globe with orbit and cosmonaut.

1961, Aug. Photo. *Perf. 11½*
2509 A1277 4k vio blue & dp plum .25 .15
2510 A1277 6k brown, grn & org .35 .15

1st manned space flight around the world, Maj. Gherman S. Titov, Aug. 6-7, 1961. Nos. 2509-2510 exist imperf. Value, set $2.50.

A. D. Zacharov and Admiralty Building, Leningrad A1278

1961, Aug. 8 *Perf. 12x11½*
2511 A1278 4k blue, dk brn & buff .30 .15

Zacharov (1761-1811), architect.

Defense of Brest, 1941 A1279

Designs: No. 2512, Defense of Moscow. No. 2514, Defense of Odessa. No. 2514A, Defense of Sevastopol. No. 2514B, Defense of Leningrad. No. 2514C, Defense of Kiev. No. 2514D, Battle of the Volga (Stalingrad).

1961-63 Photo. *Perf. 12½x12*
2512 A1279 4k blk & red brn (Moscow) .35 .15

Litho.

2513 A1279 4k (Brest) .35 .15
2514 A1279 4k (Odessa) .35 .15
2514A A1279 4k (Sevastopol; '62) .35 .15
2514B A1279 4k brn, dl bl & bis (Leningrad; '63) .35 .15
2514C A1279 4k blk & multi (Kiev; '63) .35 .15
2514D A1279 4k dl org & multi (Volga; '63) .35 .15
Nos. 2512-2514D (7) 2.45
Set value .85

"War of Liberation," 1941-1945.
See Nos. 2757-2758.

Students' Union Emblem — A1280

1961, Aug. 8 Litho. *Perf. 12½*
2515 A1280 6k ultra & red .40 .15

15th anniversary of the founding of the International Students' Union.

Soviet Stamps A1281

Stamps and background different on each denomination.

1961, Aug. *Perf. 12½x12*
2516 A1281 2k multicolored .25 .15
2517 A1281 4k multicolored .45 .25
2518 A1281 6k multicolored .60 .30
2519 A1281 10k multicolored .85 .40
Nos. 2516-2519 (4) 2.15 1.10

40 years of Soviet postage stamps.

Nikolai A. Schors Statue, Kiev — A1282

Statue: 4k, Gregori I. Kotovski, Kishinev.

1961 Photo. *Perf. 11½x12*
2520 A1282 2k lt ultra & sepia .30 .15
2521 A1282 4k rose vio & sepia .30 .15
Set value .15

Letters and Means of Transportation A1283

1961, Sept. 15 *Perf. 11½*
2522 A1283 4k dk car & black .30 .15

International Letter Writing Week.

Angara River Bridge, Irkutsk A1284

1961, Sept. 15 Litho. *Perf. 12½x12*
2523 A1284 4k ol bis, lilac & black .30 .15

300th anniversary of Irkutsk.

Lenin, Marx, Engels and Marchers — A1285

Designs: 3k, Obelisk commemorating conquest of space and Moscow University. No. 2526, Harvester combine. No. 2527, Industrial control center. No. 2528, Worker pointing to globe.

1961 Litho.
2524 A1285 2k ver, yel & brown .55 .25
2525 A1285 3k org & deep blue .85 .25
2526 A1285 4k mar, bis & red brown .55 .25
2527 A1285 4k car rose, brn, org & blue .55 .25
2528 A1285 4k red & dk brown .55 .25
Nos. 2524-2528 (5) 3.05 1.25

22nd Congress of the Communist Party of the USSR, Oct. 17-31.

Soviet Soldier Monument, Berlin — A1286

1961, Sept. 28 Photo. *Perf. 12x12½*
2529 A1286 4k red & gray violet .40 .15

10th anniversary of the International Federation of Resistance, FIR.

Workers Studying Mathematics A1287

Designs: 2k, Communist labor team. 4k, Workers around piano.

1961, Sept. 28 Litho. *Perf. 12½x12*
2530 A1287 2k plum & red, *cream* .15 .15
2531 A1287 3k brn & red, *yellow* .20 .15
2532 A1287 4k vio blue & red, *cr* .25 .15
Nos. 2530-2532 (3) .60
Set value .30

Publicizing Communist labor teams in their efforts for labor, education and relaxation.

Rocket and Stars — A1288

Engraved on Aluminum Foil

1961, Oct. 17 *Perf. 12½*
2533 A1288 1r black & red 10.00 4.25

Soviet scientific and technical achievements in exploring outer space.

Overprinted in Red **XXII съезд КПСС**

1961, Oct. 23
2534 A1288 1r black & red 10.00 4.50

Communist Party of the USSR, 22nd cong.

Amangaldi Imanov A1289

Franz Liszt A1290

1961, Oct. 25 Photo. ***Perf. 11½x12***
2535 A1289 4k green, buff & brn .35 .15

Amangaldi Imanov (1873-1919), champion of Soviet power in Kazakhstan.

1961, Oct. 31 ***Perf. 12x11½***
2536 A1290 4k mar, dk brn & ocher .60 .15

Liszt, composer, 150th birth anniv.

Flags and Slogans A1291

1961, Nov. 4 ***Perf. 11½***
2537 A1291 4k red, yel & dark red .50 .15

44th anniversary of October Revolution.

Hand Holding Hammer A1292

Congress Emblem A1293

Designs: Nos. 2538, 2542, Congress emblem. Nos. 2539, 2543, African breaking chains. No. 2541, Three hands holding globe.

1961, Nov. ***Perf. 12, 12½, 11½***
2538 A1293 2k scarlet & bister .15 .15
2539 A1293 2k dk purple & gray .15 .15
2540 A1292 4k plum, org & blue .35 .15
2541 A1292 4k blk, lt blue & pink .40 .15
2542 A1293 6k grn, bister & red .70 .15
2543 A1293 6k ind, dull yel & red .50 .15
Nos. 2538-2543 (6) 2.25
Set value .60

Fifth World Congress of Trade Unions, Moscow, Dec. 4-16.

Lomonosov Statue A1294

Hands Holding Hammer and Sickle A1295

Designs: 6k, Lomonosov at desk. 10k, Lomonosov, his birthplace and Leningrad Academy of Science, horiz.

Perf. 11½x12, 12x11½
1961, Nov. 19 Photo. & Engr.
2544 A1294 4k Prus blue, yel grn & brown .25 .15
2545 A1294 6k green, yel & black .40 .15
2546 A1294 10k maroon, slate & brn .95 .25
Nos. 2544-2546 (3) 1.60 .55

250th anniversary of the birth of M. V. Lomonosov, scientist and poet.

1961, Nov. 27 Litho. ***Perf. 12x12½***
2547 A1295 4k red & yellow .30 .15

USSR constitution, 25th anniv.

Romeo and Juliet Ballet — A1296

Linemen — A1297

Ballets: 2k, Red Flower. 3k, Paris Flame. 10k, Swan Lake.

1961-62 ***Perf. 12x12½***
2548 A1296 2k brn, car & lt green ('62) .15 .15
2549 A1296 3k multicolored ('62) .15 .15
2550 A1296 6k dk brn, bis & vio .40 .15
2551 A1296 10k blue, pink & dk brn .60 .15
Nos. 2548-2551 (4) 1.30
Set value .50

Honoring the Russian Ballet.

1961 ***Perf. 12½***
2552 A1297 3k shown .20 .15
2553 A1297 4k Welders .25 .15
2554 A1297 6k Surveyor .35 .15
Nos. 2552-2554 (3) .80 .45

Honoring self-sacrificing work of youth in the 7-year plan.

Andrejs Pumpurs (1841-1902), Latvian Poet and Satirist — A1298

1961, Dec. 20 ***Perf. 12x11½***
2555 A1298 4k gray & claret .30 .15

Bulgarian Couple, Flag, Emblem and Building A1299

1961, Dec. 28 ***Perf. 12½x12***
2556 A1299 4k multicolored .30 .15

Bulgarian People's Republic, 15th anniv.

Fridtjof Nansen A1300

1961, Dec. 30 Photo. ***Perf. 11½***
2557 A1300 6k dk blue & brown 1.50 .55

Centenary of the birth of Fridtjof Nansen, Norwegian Polar explorer.

Mihael Ocipovich Dolivo-Dobrovolsky — A1301

1962, Jan. 25 ***Perf. 12x11½***
2558 A1301 4k bister & dark blue .30 .15

Dolivo-Dobrovolsky, scientist and electrical engineer, birth cent.

Woman and Various Activities A1302

1962, Jan. 26 ***Perf. 11½***
2559 A1302 4k bister, blk & dp org .30 .15

Honoring Soviet Women.

Aleksander S. Pushkin, 125th Death Anniv. — A1303

1962, Jan. 26 Litho. ***Perf. 12½x12***
2560 A1303 4k buff, dk brown & ver .30 .15

Dancers A1304

1962, Feb. 6 ***Perf. 12x12½***
2561 A1304 4k bister & ver .30 .15

State ensemble of folk dancers, 25th anniv.

Speed Skating, Luzhniki Stadium A1305

Perf. 11½
1962, Feb. 17 Unwmk. Photo.
2562 A1305 4k orange & ultra .45 .15

Intl. Winter Sports Championships, Moscow.

No. 2562 Overprinted **СОВЕТСКИЕ КОНЬКОБЕЖЦЫ— ЧЕМПИОНЫ МИРА**

1962, Mar. 3
2563 A1305 4k orange & ultra 1.50 .75

Victories of I. Voronina and V. Kosichkin, world speed skating champions, 1962.

Ski Jump A1305a

Design: 10k, Woman long distance skier, vert.

1962, May 31 ***Perf. 11½***
2564 A1305a 2k ultra, brown & red .25 .15
2565 A1305a 10k org, ultra & black .45 .15

Intl. Winter Sports Championships, Zakopane.

Hero Type of 1961

4k, V. S. Shalandin. 6k, Magomet Gadgiev.

1962, Feb. 22 ***Perf. 12½x12***
2570 A1244 4k dk blue & brown 1.50 .75
2571 A1244 6k brn & slate grn 1.50 .75

Soldier heroes of World War II.

Skier A1306

1962, Mar. 3 ***Perf. 11½***
2572 A1306 4k shown .30 .15
2573 A1306 6k Ice hockey .35 .15
2574 A1306 10k Ice skating .80 .15
Nos. 2572-2574 (3) 1.45 .45

First People's Winter Games, Sverdlovsk.
For overprints see Nos. 2717, 3612.

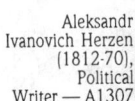

Aleksandr Ivanovich Herzen (1812-70), Political Writer — A1307

1962, Mar. 28 Litho. ***Perf. 12x12½***
2575 A1307 4k ultra, black & buff .20 .15

Lenin A1308

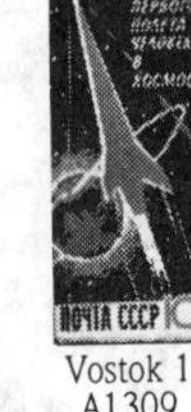
Vostok 1 A1309

Design: 6k, Lenin, horiz.

Perf. 12x12½, 12½x12
1962, Mar. 28
2576 A1308 4k brown, red & yel .30 .15
2577 A1308 6k blue, org & brn .30 .15
Set value .20

14th congress of the Young Communist League (Komsomol).

1962, Apr. Unwmk. ***Perf. 11x11½***
2578 A1309 10k multicolored 1.00 .50

1st anniv. of Yuri A. Gagarin's flight into space.
No. 2578 was printed in sheets of 20 stamps alternating with 20 labels.
No. 2578 was also issued imperf. Value $1.50.

Bust of Tchaikovsky — A1310

1962, Apr. 19 Photo. ***Perf. 11½x12***
2579 A1310 4k blue, black & bis .45 .25

Second International Tchaikovsky Competition in Moscow.

Youths of 3 Races, Broken Chain, Globe — A1311

1962, Apr. 19 ***Perf. 11½***
2580 A1311 6k black, brn & yel .30 .15

International Day of Solidarity of Youth against Colonialism.

Ulyanov (Lenin) Family Portrait A1312

Lenin — A1313

1962, Apr. 21 *Perf. 12x11½*
2581 A1312 4k gray, red & dk brn .35 .20

Typographed and Emboss
Perf. 12½

2582 A1313 10k dk red, gray & blk .65 .20
a. Souv. sheet of 2, perf. 12 4.00 2.50

92nd anniversary of the birth of Lenin.
No. 2582a for 94th anniv. of the birth of Lenin. Issued Nov. 6, 1964.

Cosmos 3 Satellite — A1314

1962, Apr. 26 Litho. *Perf. 12½x12*
2586 A1314 6k blk, lt blue & vio .50 .15

Cosmos 3 earth satellite launching, Apr. 24.

Charles Dickens A1315

Karl Marx Monument, Moscow A1316

Portrait: No. 2589, Jean Jacques Rousseau.

1962, Apr. 29
2588 A1315 6k blue, brn & pur .35 .15

Perf. 11½x12
Photo.

2589 A1315 6k gray, lilac & brn .35 .15

Charles Dickens, English writer, 150th birth anniv., and Jean Jacques Rousseau, French writer, 250th birth anniv.

1962, Apr. 29 *Perf. 12x12½*
2590 A1316 4k deep ultra & gray .30 .15

Pravda, Lenin, Revolutionists A1317

Lenin Reading Pravda A1318

Designs: No. 2592, Pravda, Lenin and rocket.

1962, May 4 **Litho.**
2591 A1317 4k black, bister & red .30 .15
2592 A1317 4k red, black & ocher .30 .15

Perf. 11½
Photo.

2593 A1318 4k ocher, dp claret & red .30 .15
Nos. 2591-2593 (3) .90 .45

50th anniversary of Pravda, Russian newspaper founded by Lenin.

Malaria Eradication Emblem and Mosquito A1319

1962
2594 A1319 4k Prus blue, red & blk .45 .15
2595 A1319 6k ol green, red & blk .45 .15

WHO drive to eradicate malaria.
Issue dates: 4k, May 6; 6k, June 23.
No. 2595 exists imperf. Value $1.

Pioneers Taking Oath before Lenin and Emblem A1320

Designs (Emblem and): 3k, Lenja Golikov and Valja Kotik. No. 2598, Pioneers building rocket model. No. 2599, Red Cross, Red Crescent and nurse giving health instruction. 6k, Pioneers of many races and globe.

1962, May 19 Litho. *Perf. 12½x12*
2596 A1320 2k green, red & brn .15 .15
2597 A1320 3k multicolored .20 .15
2598 A1320 4k multicolored .25 .15
2599 A1320 4k multicolored .25 .15
2600 A1320 6k multicolored .45 .15
Nos. 2596-2600 (5) 1.30 .75

All-Union Lenin Pioneers, 40th anniv.

Mesrob A1321

Ivan A. Goncharov A1322

1962, May 27 Photo. *Perf. 12½x12*
2601 A1321 4k yellow & dk brown .75 .15

"1600th" anniversary of the birth of Bishop Mesrob (350?-439), credited as author of the Armenian and Georgian alphabets.

1962, June 18
2602 A1322 4k gray & brown .40 .15

Ivan Aleksandrovich Goncharov (1812-91), novelist, 150th birth anniv.

Volleyball A1323

Louis Pasteur A1324

2k, Bicyclists, horiz. 10k, Eight-man shell. 12k, Goalkeeper, soccer, horiz. 16k, Steeplechase.

1962, June 27 *Perf. 11½*
2603 A1323 2k lt brn, blk & ver .20 .15
2604 A1323 4k brn org, black & buff .30 .15
2605 A1323 10k ultra, black & yel .70 .15
2606 A1323 12k lt blue, brn & yel .90 .15
2607 A1323 16k lt green, blk & red 1.10 .15
Nos. 2603-2607 (5) 3.20 .75

Intl. Summer Sports Championships, 1962.

1962, June 30 *Perf. 12½x12*
2608 A1324 6k black & brown org .30 .15

Invention of the sterilization process by Louis Pasteur, French chemist, cent.

Library, 1862 A1325

Design: No. 2610, New Lenin Library.

1962, June 30 **Photo.**
2609 A1325 4k slate & black .15 .15
2610 A1325 4k slate & black .15 .15
a. Pair, #2609-2610 .30 .15

Centenary of the Lenin Library, Moscow.

Auction Building and Ermine — A1326

1962, June 30 **Litho.**
2611 A1326 6k multicolored .50 .15

International Fur Auction, Leningrad.

Young Couple, Lenin, Kremlin — A1327

Workers of Three Races and Dove — A1328

1962, June 30 *Perf. 12x12½*
2612 A1327 2k multicolored .30 .15
2613 A1328 4k multicolored .30 .15

Program of the Communist Party of the Soviet Union for Peace and Friendship among all people.

Hands Breaking Bomb A1329

1962, July 7 *Perf. 11½*
2614 A1329 6k blue, blk & olive .30 .15

World Congress for Peace and Disarmament, Moscow, July 9-14.

Yakub Kolas and Yanka Kupala A1330

1962, July 7 Photo. *Perf. 12½x12*
2615 A1330 4k henna brn & buff .30 .15

Byelorussian poets. Kolas (1882-1956), and Kupala (1882-1942).

Alepker Sabir — A1331

Cancer Congress Emblem — A1332

1962, July 16 *Perf. 11½*
2616 A1331 4k buff, dk brn & blue .30 .15

Sabir, Azerbaijan poet & satirist, (1862-1911).
Copies inscribed "Azerbajanyn" were withdrawn before release.

1962, July 16 Litho. *Perf. 12½*
2617 A1332 6k grnsh blue, blk & red .35 .15

8th Anti-Cancer Cong., Moscow, July 1962.

N. N. Zinin, Chemist, 150th Birth Anniv. A1333

1962, July 16 Photo. *Perf. 12x11½*
2618 A1333 4k violet & dk brown .35 .15

I. M. Kramskoy, Painter A1334

I. D. Shadr, Sculptor A1335

M. V. Nesterov, Painter — A1336

Perf. 11½x12, 12x12½

1962, July 28
2619 A1334 4k gray, mar & dk brn .35 .15
2620 A1335 4k black & red brown .35 .15
2621 A1336 4k multicolored .35 .15
Nos. 2619-2621 (3) 1.05 .45

Vostok 2 Going into Space — A1337

Perf. 11½

1962, Aug. 7 Unwmk. Photo.

2622 A1337 10k blk, lilac & blue .60 .15
2623 A1337 10k blk, orange & blue .60 .15

1st anniv. of Gherman Titov's space flight. Issued imperf. on Aug. 6. Value, set $4.50.

Friendship House, Moscow A1338

1962, Aug. 15 ***Perf. 12x12½***

2624 A1338 6k ultra & gray .30 .15

Kremlin and Atom Symbol — A1339

Design: 6k, Map of Russia, atom symbol and "Peace" in 10 languages.

1962, Aug. 15 Litho. ***Perf. 12½x12***

2625 A1339 4k multicolored .35 .15
2626 A1339 6k multicolored .35 .15

Use of atomic energy for peace.

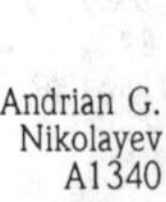

Andrian G. Nikolayev A1340

Cosmonauts in Space Helments — A1341

"To Space" Monument by G. Postnikov — A1342

Design: No. 2628, Pavel R. Popovich, with inscription at left and dated "12-15-VIII, 1962."

1962 Photo. ***Perf. 11½***

2627 A1340 4k blue, brn & red .35 .15
2628 A1340 4k blue, brn & red .35 .15

Perf. 12½x12

Litho.

2629 A1341 6k dk bl, lt bl, org & yellow .95 .15

Perf. 11½

Photo.

2630 A1342 6k brt blue & multi .90 .15
2631 A1342 10k violet & multi .95 .15
Nos. 2627-2631 (5) 3.50
Set value .55

Souvenir Sheet

Design: 1r, Monument and portraits of Gagarin, Titov, Nikolayev and Popovich.

1962, Nov. 27 Litho. ***Perf. 12½***

2631A A1342 1r brt bl, blk & sil 7.50 3.50

Nos. 2627-2631A honor the four Russian "conquerors of space," with Nos. 2627-2629 for the 1st group space flight, by Vostoks 3 and 4, Aug. 11-15, 1962. Also issued imperf.

For overprint see No. 2662.

Carp and Bream — A1343

Design: 6k, Freshwater salmon.

1962, Aug. 28 Photo. ***Perf. 11½x12***

2632 A1343 4k blue & orange .25 .15
2633 A1343 6k blue & orange .55 .15

Fish preservation in USSR.

Feliks E. Dzerzhinski A1344

1962, Sept. 6 Litho. ***Perf. 12½x12***

2634 A1344 4k ol green & dk blue .30 .15

Dzerzhinski (1877-1926), organizer of Soviet secret police, 85th birth anniv.

O. Henry and New York Skyline A1345

1962, Sept. 10 Photo. ***Perf. 12x11½***

2635 A1345 6k yel, red brn & black .30 .15

O. Henry (William Sidney Porter, 1862-1910), American writer.

Barclay de Tolly, Mikhail I. Kutuzov, Petr I. Bagration A1346

4k, Denis Davidov leading partisans. 6k, Battle of Borodino. 10k, Wasilisa Kozhina and partisans.

1962, Sept. 25 ***Perf. 12½x12***

2636 A1346 3k orange brown .25 .15
2637 A1346 4k ultra .25 .15
2638 A1346 6k blue gray .60 .15
2639 A1346 10k violet .70 .15
Nos. 2636-2639 (4) 1.80
Set value .50

War of 1812 against the French, 150th anniv.

Street in Vinnitsa A1347

1962, Sept. 25 Photo.

2640 A1347 4k yel bister & black .30 .15

Town of Vinnitsa, Ukraine, 600th anniv.

"Mail and Transportation" A1348

1962, Sept. 25 ***Perf. 11½***

2641 A1348 4k blue grn, blk & lilac .30 .15

Intl. Letter Writing Week, Oct. 7-13.

Cedar — A1349

Construction Worker — A1350

4k, Canna. 6k, Arbutus. 10k, Chrysanthemum.

1962, Sept. 27 Engr. & Photo.

2642 A1349 3k ver, black & green .25 .15
2643 A1349 4k multicolored .25 .15
2644 A1349 6k multicolored .25 .15
2645 A1349 10k multicolored .65 .15
Nos. 2642-2645 (4) 1.40
Set value .50

Nikitsky Botanical Gardens, 150th anniv.

1962, Sept. 29 Litho. ***Perf. 12x12½***

Designs: No. 2647, Hiker. No. 2648, Surgeon. No. 2649, Worker and lathe. No. 2650, Farmer's wife. No. 2651, Textile worker. No. 2652, Teacher.

2646 A1350 4k org, gray & vio blue .20 .15
2647 A1350 4k yel, gray, grn & blue .20 .15
2648 A1350 4k grn, gray & lilac rose .20 .15
2649 A1350 4k ver, gray & lilac .20 .15
2650 A1350 4k blue, gray & emer .20 .15
2651 A1350 4k brt pink, gray & vio .20 .15
2652 A1350 4k yel, gray, dp vio, red & brown .20 .15
Nos. 2646-2652 (7) 1.40 1.05

Sputnik and Stars A1351

1962, Oct. 4 ***Perf. 12½x12***

2653 A1351 10k multicolored .90 .25

5th anniversary, launching of Sputnik 1.

M. F. Ahundov, Azerbaijan Poet and Philosopher, 150th Birth Anniv. — A1352

1962, Oct. 2 Photo.

2654 A1352 4k lt green & dk brown .30 .15

Farm and Young Couple with Banner A1353

Designs: No. 2656, Tractors, map and surveyor. No. 2657, Farmer, harvester and map.

1962, Oct. 18 Litho. ***Perf. 12½x12***

2655 A1353 4k multicolored .70 .40
2656 A1353 4k multicolored .70 .40
2657 A1353 4k brown, yel & red .70 .40
Nos. 2655-2657 (3) 2.10 1.20

Honoring pioneer developers of virgin soil.

N. N. Burdenko A1354

V. P. Filatov A1355

1962, Oct. 20 ***Perf. 12½x12***

2658 A1354 4k red brn, lt brn & blk .30 .15
2659 A1355 4k multicolored .30 .15

Scientists and academicians.

Lenin Mausoleum, Red Square — A1356

1962, Oct. 26 Litho.

2660 A1356 4k multicolored .35 .15

92nd anniversary of Lenin's birth.

Worker, Flag and Factories — A1357

1962, Oct. 29 ***Perf. 12x12½***

2661 A1357 4k multicolored .35 .15

45th anniv. of the October Revolution.

No. 2631 Overprinted in Dark Violet

1.XI. ЗЕМЛЯ—МАРС

1962, Nov. 3 Photo. ***Perf. 11½***

2662 A1342 10k violet & multi 2.50 1.00

Launching of a rocket to Mars.

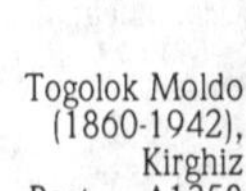

Togolok Moldo (1860-1942), Kirghiz Poet — A1358

Sajat Nova (1712-1795), Armenian Poet — A1359

1962, Nov. 17 ***Perf. 12x12½***

2663 A1358 4k brn red & black .20 .15
2664 A1359 4k ultra & black .20 .15

Arms, Hammer & Sickle and Map of USSR A1360

1962, Nov. 17 ***Perf. 11½***

2665 A1360 4k red, orange & dk red .30 .15

USSR founding, 40th anniv.

Space Rocket, Earth and Mars — A1361

1962, Nov. 17 *Perf. 12½x12*
Size: 73x27mm

2666 A1361 10k purple & org red .80 .25

Launching of a space rocket to Mars, Nov. 1, 1962.

Electric Power Industry — A1362

Designs: No. 2668, Machines. No. 2669, Chemicals and oil. No. 2670, Factory construction. No. 2671, Transportation. No. 2672, Telecommunications and space. No. 2673, Metals. No. 2674, Grain farming. No. 2675, Dairy, poultry and meat.

1962 **Litho.** *Perf. 12½x12*

2667 A1362 4k ultra, red, blk & gray .35 .15
2668 A1362 4k ultra, gray, yel & cl .35 .15
2669 A1362 4k yel, pink, blk, gray & brown .35 .15
2670 A1362 4k yel, blue, red brn & gray .35 .15
2671 A1362 4k mar, yel, red & blue .35 .15
2672 A1362 4k brt yel, blue & brn .35 .15
2673 A1362 4k lil, org, yel & dk brn .35 .15
2674 A1362 4k vio, bis, org red & dk brown .35 .15
2675 A1362 4k emer, dk brn, brn & gray .35 .15
Nos. 2667-2675 (9) 3.15
Set value .45

"Great decisions of the 22nd Communist Party Congress" and Russian people at work.
Issued: #2667-2669, 11/19; others, 12/28.

Queen, Rook and Knight — A1363

Perf. 12½
1962, Nov. 24 **Unwmk.** **Photo.**

2676 A1363 4k orange yel & black .50 .25

30th Russian Chess Championships.

Gen. Vasili Blucher A1364

1962, Nov. 27 *Perf. 11½*

2677 A1364 4k multicolored .30 .15

General Vasili Konstantinovich Blucher (1889-1938).

V. N. Podbelski (1887-1920), Minister of Posts A1365

1962, Nov. 27 *Perf. 12½x12*

2678 A1365 4k red brn, gray & black .30 .15

Makharenko A1366

Gaidar A1367

1962, Nov. 30 *Perf. 11½x12*

2679 A1366 4k multicolored .25 .15
2680 A1367 4k multicolored .25 .15

A. S. Makharenko (1888-1939) and Arkadi Gaidar (1904-1941), writers.

Dove and Globe A1368

1962, Dec. 22 **Litho.** *Perf. 12½x12*

2681 A1368 4k multicolored .30 .15

New Year 1963. Has alternating label inscribed "Happy New Year!" Issued imperf. on Dec. 20. Value $1.

D. N. Prjanishnikov A1369

Rose-colored Starlings A1370

1962, Dec. 22 *Perf. 12x12½*

2682 A1369 4k multicolored .30 .15

Prjanishnikov, founder of Russian agricultural chemistry.

1962, Dec. 26 **Photo.** *Perf. 11½*

Birds: 4k, Red-breasted geese. 6k, Snow geese. 10k, White storks. 16k, Greater flamingos.

2683 A1370 3k green, blk & pink .15 .15
2684 A1370 4k brn, blk & dp org .20 .15
2685 A1370 6k gray, black & red .25 .15
2686 A1370 10k blue, black & red .65 .15
2687 A1370 16k lt blue, rose & blk 1.10 .25
Nos. 2683-2687 (5) 2.35 .85

FIR Emblem — A1371

1962, Dec. 26 *Perf. 12x12½*

2688 A1371 4k violet & red .30 .15
2689 A1371 6k grnsh blue & red .30 .15

4th Cong. of the Intl. Federation of Resistance.

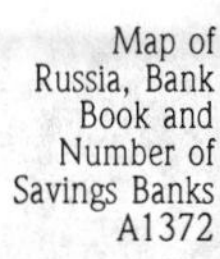

Map of Russia, Bank Book and Number of Savings Banks A1372

Design: 6k, as 4k, but with depositors.

1962, Dec. 30 **Litho.** *Perf. 12½x12*

2690 A1372 4k multicolored .30 .15
2691 A1372 6k multicolored .30 .15

40th anniv. of Russian savings banks.

Rustavsky Fertilizer Plant — A1373

Hydroelectric Power Stations: No. 2693, Bratskaya. No. 2964, Volzhskaya.

1962, Dec. 30 **Photo.** *Perf. 12½*

2692 A1373 4k ultra, lt blue & black .30 .15
2693 A1373 4k yel grn, bl grn & blk .30 .15
2694 A1373 4k gray bl, brt bl & blk .30 .15
Nos. 2692-2694 (3) .90
Set value .20

Stanislavski A1374

Serafimovich A1375

Perf. 12½
1963, Jan. 15 **Unwmk.** **Engr.**

2695 A1374 4k slate green .30 .15

Stanislavski (professional name of Konstantin Sergeevich Alekseev, 1863-1938), actor, producer and founder of the Moscow Art Theater.

1963, Jan. 19 **Photo.** *Perf. 11½*

2696 A1375 4k mag, dk brn & gray .30 .15

A. S. Serafimovich (1863-1949), writer.

Children in Nursery A1376

Designs: No. 2698, Kindergarten. No. 2699, Pioneers marching and camping. No. 2700, Young people studying and working.

1963, Jan. 31

2697 A1376 4k brn org, org red & black .35 .15
2698 A1376 4k blue, mag & orange .35 .15
2699 A1376 4k brt green, red & brn .35 .15
2700 A1376 4k multicolored .35 .15
Nos. 2697-2700 (4) 1.40 .60

Wooden Dolls and Toys, Russia — A1377

National Handicrafts: 6k, Pottery, Ukraine. 10k, Bookbinding, Estonia. 12k, Metalware, Dagestan.

1963, Jan. 31 **Litho.** *Perf. 12x12½*

2701 A1377 4k multicolored .15 .15
2702 A1377 6k multicolored .20 .15
2703 A1377 10k multicolored .50 .15
2704 A1377 12k ultra, org & black .65 .15
Nos. 2701-2704 (4) 1.50
Set value .45

Gen. Mikhail N. Tukhachevski A1378

Designs: No. 2706, U. M. Avetisian. No. 2707, A. M. Matrosov. No. 2708, J. V. Panfilov. No. 2709, Y. F. Fabriscius.

Perf. 12½x12
1963, Feb. **Photo.** **Unwmk.**

2705 A1378 4k blue grn & slate grn .30 .15
2706 A1378 4k org brown & black .30 .15
2707 A1378 4k ultra & dk brown .30 .15
2708 A1378 4k dp rose & black .30 .15
2709 A1378 4k rose lilac & vio blue .30 .15
Nos. 2705-2709 (5) 1.50
Set value .50

45th anniv. of the Soviet Army and honoring its heroes. No. 2705 for Gen. Mikhail Nikolaevich Tukhachevski (1893-1937).

M. A. Pavlov A1379

E. O. Paton and Dnieper Bridge, Kiev A1379a

Portraits: #2711, I. V. Kurchatov. #2712, V. I. Vernadski. #2713, Aleksei N. Krylov. #2714, V. A. Obrutchev, geologist.

1963 *Perf. 11½x12*
Size: 21x32mm

2710 A1379 4k gray, buff & dk bl .30 .15
2711 A1379 4k slate & brown .30 .15

Perf. 12

2712 A1379 4k lilac gray & lt brn .30 .15

Perf. 11½
Size: 23x34½mm

2713 A1379 4k dk blue, sep & red .30 .15
2714 A1379 4k brn ol, gray & red .30 .15
2715 A1379a 4k grnsh bl, blk & red .30 .15
Nos. 2710-2715 (6) 1.80 .90

Members of the Russian Academy of Science. No. 2715 for Eugene Oskarovich Paton (1870-1953), bridge building engineer.

Winter Sports A1380

1963, Feb. 28 *Perf. 11½*

2716 A1380 4k brt blue, org & blk .30 .15

5th Trade Union Spartacist Games. Printed in sheets of 50 (5x10) with every other row inverted.

No. 2573 Overprinted

Советские
хоккеисты-
чемпионы
мира
и Европы
Стокгольм
1963 г.

1963, Mar. 20

2717 A1306 6k Prus blue & plum 1.00 .40

Victory of the Soviet ice hockey team in the World Championships, Stockholm. For overprint see No. 3612.

Victor Kingisepp A1381

Blaumanis A1382

1963, Mar. 24 *Perf. 12x12½*

2718 A1381 4k blue gray & choc .30 .15

75th anniversary of the birth of Victor Kingisepp, communist party leader. Exists imperf.

1963, Mar. 24 *Perf. 12½x12*

2719 A1382 4k ultra & dk red brn .30 .15

Centenary of the birth of Rudolfs Blaumanis (1863-1908), Latvian writer.

Flower and Globe — A1383

Designs: 6k, Atom diagram and power line. 10k, Rocket in space.

1963, Mar. 26 *Perf. 11½*

2720 A1383 4k red, ultra & green .25 .15
2721 A1383 6k red, green & lilac .35 .15
2722 A1383 10k red, vio & lt blue .80 .15
Nos. 2720-2722 (3) 1.40 .45

"World without Arms and Wars."
The 10k exists imperf. Value $1.50.
For overprint see No. 2754.

Costume Type of 1960-62

Regional Costumes: 3k, Tadzhik. No. 2724, Kirghiz. No. 2725, Azerbaijan. No. 2726, Turkmen.

1963, Mar. 31 **Litho.** *Perf. 11½*

2723 A1237 3k blk, red, ocher & org .40 .15
2724 A1237 4k brown, ver, ocher & ultra .50 .15
2725 A1237 4k blk, ocher, red & grn .50 .15
2726 A1237 4k red, lil, ocher & blk .50 .15
Nos. 2723-2726 (4) 1.90 .60

Lenin — A1384

1963, Mar. 30 **Engr.** *Perf. 12*

2727 A1384 4k red & brown 1.25 .60

93rd anniversary of the birth of Lenin.

Luna 4 Approaching Moon — A1385

1963, Apr. 2 **Photo.**

2728 A1385 6k black, lt blue & red .50 .15

Soviet rocket to the moon, Apr. 2, 1963. Exists imperforate. Value, $1.25.
For overprint see No. 3160.

Woman and Beach Scene A1386

Designs: 4k, Young man's head and factory. 10k, Child's head and kindergarden.

1963, Apr. 7 **Litho.** *Perf. 12½x12*

2729 A1386 2k multicolored .30 .25
2730 A1386 4k multicolored .30 .25
2731 A1386 10k multicolored .45 .25
Nos. 2729-2731 (3) 1.05 .75

15th anniversary of World Health Day.

A1387

No. 2732: a, d, Sputnik and Earth. b, e, Vostok 1, earth and moon. c, f, Rocket and Sun.

1963, Apr. 12

2732 Block of 6 7.50 2.10
a. A1387 10k "10k" blk, blue & lil rose 1.25 .35
b. A1387 10k "10k" lil rose, blue & blk 1.25 .35
c. A1387 10k "10k" black, red & yel 1.25 .35
d. A1387 10k "10k" blue 1.25 .35
e. A1387 10k "10k" lilac rose 1.25 .35
f. A1387 10k "10k" yellow 1.25 .35

Cosmonauts' Day.

Demian Bednii (1883-1945), Poet — A1388

Soldiers on Horseback and Cuban Flag — A1389

1963, Apr. 13 **Photo.**

2735 A1388 4k brown & black .30 .15

1963, Apr. 25 *Perf. 11½*

Soviet-Cuban friendship: 6k, Cuban flag, hands with gun and book. 10k, Cuban and USSR flags and crane lifting tractor.

2736 A1389 4k black, red & ultra .25 .15
2737 A1389 6k black, red & ultra .25 .15
2738 A1389 10k red, ultra & black .50 .15
Nos. 2736-2738 (3) 1.00
Set value .30

Karl Marx A1390

Hasek A1391

1963, May 9 *Perf. 12x12½*

2739 A1390 4k dk red brn & black .30 .15

145th anniversary of the birth of Marx.

1963, Apr. 29 *Perf. 11½x12*

2740 A1391 4k black .30 .15

Jaroslav Hasek (1883-1923), Czech writer.

Moscow P.O. for Foreign Mail — A1392

1963, May 9 *Perf. 11½*

2741 A1392 6k brt violet & red brn .30 .15

5th Conference of Communications Ministers of Socialist countries, Budapest.

King and Pawn A1393

6k, Queen and bishop. 16k, Rook and knight.

1963, May 22 **Photo.**

2742 A1393 4k multicolored .25 .15
2743 A1393 6k ultra, brt pink & grnsh blue .35 .15
2744 A1393 16k brt plum, brt pink & black .90 .15
Nos. 2742-2744 (3) 1.50 .45

25th Championship Chess Match, Moscow.
Exists imperf., issued May 18. Value $3.

Richard Wagner — A1394

Boxers — A1395

Design: No. 2745A, Giuseppe Verdi.

1963 **Unwmk.** *Perf. 11½x12*

2745 A1394 4k black & red .75 .25
2745A A1394 4k red & violet brn .75 .25

150th annivs. of the births of Wagner and Verdi, German and Italian composers.

1963, May 29 **Litho.** *Perf. 12½*

Design: 6k, Referee proclaiming victor.

2746 A1395 4k multicolored .30 .15
2747 A1395 6k multicolored .30 .15

15th European Boxing Championships, Moscow.

Valeri Bykovski — A1396

Valentina Tereshkova — A1397

Designs: No. 2749, Tereshkova. No. 2751, Bykovski. No. 2752, Symbolic man and woman fliers. No. 2753, Tereshkova, vert.

Litho. (A1396); Photo. (A1397)

1963 *Perf. 12½x12, 12x12½*

2748 A1396 4k multicolored .25 .15
2749 A1396 4k multicolored .25 .15
a. Pair #2748-2749 .50 .15
2750 A1397 6k grn & dk car rose .25 .15
2751 A1397 6k purple & brown .20 .15
2752 A1397 10k blue & red .85 .15
2753 A1396 10k multicolored 1.50 .35
Nos. 2748-2753 (6) 3.30 1.10

Space flights of Valeri Bykovski, June 14-19, and Valentina Tereshkova, 1st woman cosmonaut, June 16-19, 1963, in Vostoks 5 and 6.
No. 2749a has continuous design.
Nos. 2750-2753 exist imperf. Value $3.

No. 2720 Overprinted in Red

Всемирный
конгресс
женщин.

1963, June 24 **Photo.** *Perf. 11½*

2754 A1383 4k red, ultra & green .50 .25

Intl. Women's Cong., Moscow, June 24-29.

Globe, Camera and Film — A1398

1963, July 7 **Photo.** *Perf. 11½*

2755 A1398 4k gray & ultra .40 .30

3rd International Film Festival, Moscow.

Vladimir V. Mayakovsky, Poet, 70th Birth Anniv. — A1399

1963, July 19 **Engr.** *Perf. 12½*

2756 A1399 4k red brown .30 .15

Tanks and Map A1400

Design: 6k, Soldier, tanks and flag.

1963, July **Litho.** *Perf. 12½x12*

2757 A1400 4k sepia & orange .40 .25
2758 A1400 6k org, slate green & blk .40 .25

20th anniversary of the Battle of Kursk in the "War of Liberation," 1941-1945.

Bicyclist — A1401

Sports: 4k, Long jump. 6k, Women divers, horiz. 12k, Basketball. 16k, Soccer.

Perf. 12½x12, 12x12½

1963, July 27

2759 A1401 3k multicolored .15 .15
2760 A1401 4k multicolored .15 .15
2761 A1401 6k multicolored .35 .15
2762 A1401 12k multicolored .60 .15
2763 A1401 16k multicolored .75 .15
a. Souvenir sheet of 4, imperf. 2.50 1.25
Nos. 2759-2763 (5) 2.00
Set value .45

3rd Spartacist Games.
Exist imperf. Value $2.
No. 2763a contains stamps similar to the 3k, 4k, 12k and 16k, with colors changed. Issued Dec. 22.

Ice Hockey — A1402

Lenin — A1403

1963, July 27 **Photo.**

2764 A1402 6k red & gray blue .50 .25

World Ice Hockey Championship, Stockholm.
For overprint see No. 3012.

1963, July 29

2765 A1403 4k red & black .30 .15

60th anniversary of the 2nd Congress of the Social Democratic Labor Party.

Freighter and Relief Shipment A1404

Design: 12k, Centenary emblem.

1963, Aug. 8 *Perf. 12½*

2766 A1404 6k Prus green & red .35 .15
2767 A1404 12k dark blue & red .80 .15

Centenary of International Red Cross.

Lapp Reindeer Race A1405

Designs: 4k, Pamir polo, vert. 6k, Burjat archery. 10k, Armenian wrestling, vert.

1963, Aug. 8 *Perf. 11½*

2768 A1405 3k lt vio bl, brn & red .25 .15
2769 A1405 4k bis brn, red & blk .30 .15
2770 A1405 6k yel, black & red .30 .15
2771 A1405 10k sepia, blk & dk red .45 .15
Nos. 2768-2771 (4) 1.30 .60

A. F. Mozhaisky (1825-1890), Pioneer Airplane Builder A1406

Aviation Pioneers: 10k, P. N. Nesterov (1887-1914), pioneer stunt flyer. 16k, N. E. Zhukovski (1847-1921), aerodynamics pioneer, and pressurized air tunnel.

1963, Aug. 18 **Engr. & Photo.**

2772 A1406 6k black & brt blue .25 .25
2773 A1406 10k black & brt blue .55 .25
2774 A1406 16k black & brt blue .90 .25
Nos. 2772-2774 (3) 1.70 .75

Alexander S. Dargomyzhski and Scene from "Rusalka" A1408

S. S. Gulak-Artemovsky and Scene from "Cossacks on the Danube" A1409

No. 2777, Georgi O. Eristavi and theater.

Perf. 11½x12, 12x12½

1963, Sept. 10 **Photo.**

2776 A1408 4k violet & black .30 .15
2777 A1408 4k gray violet & brn .30 .15
2778 A1409 4k red & black .30 .15
Nos. 2776-2778 (3) .90
Set value .20

Dargomyzhski, Ukrainian composer; Eristavi, Georgian writer, and Gulak-Artemovsky, Ukrainian composer, 150th birth annivs.

Map of Antarctica, Penguins, Research Ship and Southern Lights A1410

Designs: 4k, Map, southern lights and snocats (trucks). 6k, Globe, camp and various planes. 12k, Whaler and whales.

1963, Sept. 16 **Litho.** *Perf. 12½x12*

2779 A1410 3k multicolored .20 .15
2780 A1410 4k multicolored .30 .15
2781 A1410 6k violet, blue & red .45 .15
2782 A1410 12k multicolored 1.50 .15
Nos. 2779-2782 (4) 2.45 .60

"The Antarctic - Continent of Peace."

Letters, Globe, Plane, Train and Ship — A1411

1963, Sept. 20 **Photo.** *Perf. 11½*

2783 A1411 4k violet, black & org .30 .15

International Letter Writing Week.

Denis Diderot — A1412

Gleb Uspenski — A1414

1963, Oct. 10 **Unwmk.** *Perf. 11½*

2784 A1412 4k dk blue, brn & yel bister .30 .15

Denis Diderot (1713-84), French philosopher and encyclopedist.

1963, Oct. 10

Portraits: No. 2787, N. P. Ogarev. No. 2788, V. Brusov. No. 2789, F. Gladkov.

2786 A1414 4k buff, red brn & dk brown .40 .15
2787 A1414 4k black & pale green .40 .15
2788 A1414 4k car, brown & gray .40 .15
2789 A1414 4k car, ol brown & gray .40 .15
Nos. 2786-2789 (4) 1.60 .60

Gleb Ivanovich Uspenski (1843-1902), historian and writer; Ogarev, politician, 150th birth anniv.; Brusov, poet, 90th birth anniv., Fyodor Gladkov (1883-1958), writer.

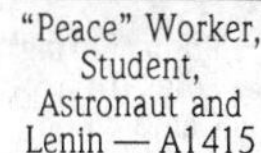

"Peace" Worker, Student, Astronaut and Lenin — A1415

Kirghiz Academy and Spasski Tower — A1416

Designs: No. 2794, "Labor," automatic controls. No. 2795, "Liberty," painter, lecturer, newspaper man. No. 2796, "Equality," elections, regional costumes. No. 2797, "Brotherhood," Recognition of achievement. No. 2798, "Happiness," Family.

1963, Oct. 15 **Litho.** *Perf. 12½x12*

2793 A1415 4k dk red, red & blk .50 .35
2794 A1415 4k red, dk red & blk .50 .35
2795 A1415 4k dk red, red & blk .50 .35
2796 A1415 4k dk red, red & blk .50 .35
2797 A1415 4k dk red, red & blk .50 .35
2798 A1415 4k dk red, red & blk .50 .35
a. Strip of 6, #2793-2798 2.75 2.25

Proclaiming Peace, Labor, Liberty, Equality, Brotherhood and Happiness.

1963, Oct. 22 *Perf. 12x12½*

2799 A1416 4k red, yel & vio blue .30 .15

Russia's annexation of Kirghizia, cent.

Lenin and Young Workers A1417

Design: No. 2801, Lenin and Palace of Congresses, the Kremlin.

1963, Oct. 24 **Photo.** *Perf. 11½*

2800 A1417 4k crimson & black .15 .15
2801 A1417 4k carmine & black .15 .15

13th Congr. of Soviet Trade Unions, Moscow.

Olga Kobylyanskaya, Ukrainian Novelist, Birth Cent. — A1418

1963, Oct. 24 *Perf. 11½x12*

2802 A1418 4k tan & dk car rose .50 .25

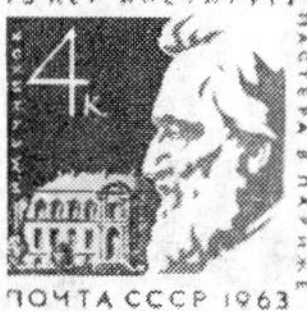

Ilya Mechnikov A1419

Cruiser Aurora and Rockets A1420

Designs: 6k, Louis Pasteur. 12k, Albert Calmette.

1963, Oct. 28 *Perf. 12*

2803 A1419 4k green & bister .20 .25
2804 A1419 6k purple & bister .30 .25
2805 A1419 12k blue & bister 1.00 .25
Nos. 2803-2805 (3) 1.50 .75

Pasteur Institute, Paris, 75th anniv; 12k for Albert Calmette (1863-1933), bacteriologist.

1963, Nov. 1

2806 A1420 4k mar, blk, gray & red orange .40 .15
2807 A1420 4k mar, blk, gray & brt rose red .40 .15
Set value .20

Development of the Armed Forces, and 46th anniv. of the October Revolution. The bright rose red ink of No. 2807 is fluorescent.

Mausoleum Gur Emi, Samarkand — A1421

Architecture in Samarkand, Uzbekistan: #2809, Shahi-Zind Mosque. 6k, Registan Square.

1963, Nov. 14 **Litho.** *Perf. 12*

Size: 27½x27½mm

2808 A1421 4k blue, yel & red brn .30 .15
2809 A1421 4k blue, yel & red brn .30 .15

Size: 55x27½mm

2810 A1421 6k blue, yel & red brn .70 .15
Nos. 2808-2810 (3) 1.30 .45

Proclamation, Spasski Tower and Globe — A1422

1963, Nov. 15 **Photo.** *Perf. 12x11½*

2811 A1422 6k purple & lt blue .50 .15

Signing of the Nuclear Test Ban Treaty between the US and the USSR.

Pushkin Monument, Kiev A1423

M. S. Shchepkin A1424

Portrait: No. 2814, V. L. Durov (1863-1934), circus clown.

1963 **Engr.** *Perf. 12x12½*

2812 A1423 4k dark brown .20 .15
2813 A1424 4k brown .20 .15
2814 A1424 4k brown black .20 .15
Nos. 2812-2814 (3) .60
Set value .20

No. 2813 for M. S. Shchepkin, actor, 75th birth anniv.

Yuri M. Steklov, 1st Editor of Izvestia, 90th Birth Anniv. A1425

1963, Nov. 17 **Photo.** *Perf. 11½*

2815 A1425 4k black & lilac rose .30 .15

Vladimir G. Shuhov and Moscow Radio Tower — A1426

1963, Nov. 17 *Perf. 12½x12*

2816 A1426 4k green & black .30 .15

Shuhov, scientist, 110th birth anniv.

USSR and Czech Flags, Kremlin and Hradcany A1427

1963, Nov. 25 *Perf. 11½*

2817 A1427 6k red, ultra & brown .40 .25

Russo-Czechoslovakian Treaty, 20th anniv.

Fyodor A. Poletaev — A1428

1963, Nov. 25 **Litho.** *Perf. 12½x12*

2818 A1428 4k multicolored .40 .30

F. A. Poletaev, Hero of the Soviet Union, National Hero of Italy, and holder of the Order of Garibaldi.

Julian Grimau and Worker Holding Flag — A1429

1963, Nov. 29 **Photo.** *Perf. 11½*

Flag and Name Panel Embossed

2819 A1429 6k vio black, red & buff .30 .15

Spanish anti-fascist fighter Julian Grimau.

Rockets, Sky and Tree — A1430

"Happy New Year!" — A1431

1963, Dec. 12 Litho. *Perf. 12x12½*
2820 A1430 6k multicolored .30 .15

Photogravure and Embossed

1963, Dec. 20 *Perf. 11½*
2821 A1431 4k grn, dk blue & red .30 .15
2822 A1431 6k grn, dk bl & fluor. rose red .30 .15
Set value .15

Nos. 2820-2822 issued for New Year 1964.

Mikas J. Petrauskas, Lithuanian Composer, 90th Birth Anniv. — A1432

1963, Dec. 20 Photo. *Perf. 11½x12*
2823 A1432 4k brt green & brown .75 .35

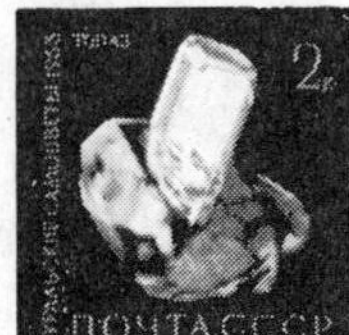

Topaz — A1433

Precious stones of the Urals: 4k, Jasper. 6k, Amethyst. 10k, Emerald. 12k, Rhodonite. 16k, Malachite.

1963, Dec. 26 Litho. *Perf. 12*
2824 A1433 2k brn, yel & blue .25 .15
2825 A1433 4k multicolored .70 .15
2826 A1433 6k red & purple .60 .15
2827 A1433 10k multicolored 1.00 .15
2828 A1433 12k multicolored 1.25 .15
2829 A1433 16k multicolored 1.40 .15
Nos. 2824-2829 (6) 5.20
Set value .75

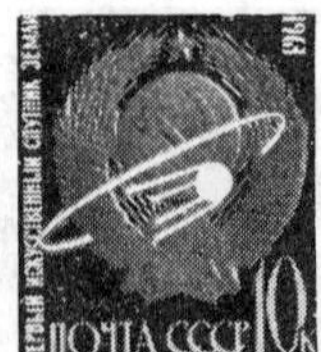

Coat of Arms and Sputnik — A1434

Rockets: No. 2831, Luna I. No. 2832, Rocket around the moon. No. 2833, Vostok I, first man in space. No. 2834, Vostok III & IV. No. 2835, Vostok VI, first woman astronaut.

1963, Dec. 27 Litho. & Embossed
2830 A1434 10k red, gold & gray .60 .20
2831 A1434 10k red, gold & gray .60 .20
2832 A1434 10k red, gold & gray .60 .20
2833 A1434 10k red, gold & gray .60 .20
2834 A1434 10k red, gold & gray .60 .20
2835 A1434 10k red, gold & gray .60 .20
a. Vert. strip of 6, #2830-2835 3.60 1.25

Soviet achievements in space.

Dyushambe, Tadzhikistan — A1435

1963, Dec. 30 Engr.
2836 A1435 4k dull blue .50 .30

No. 2836 was issued after Stalinabad was renamed Dyushambe.
For overprint see No. 2943.

Flame, Broken Chain and Rainbow — A1436

1963, Dec. 30 Litho.
2837 A1436 6k multicolored .50 .25

15th anniversary of the Universal Declaration of Human Rights.

F. A. Sergeev — A1437

1963, Dec. 30 Photo. *Perf. 12x12½*
2838 A1437 4k gray & red .35 .25

80th anniversary of the birth of the revolutionist Artjem (F. A. Sergeev).

Sun and Radar A1438

6k, Sun and Earth, vert. 10k, Earth and Sun.

1964, Jan. 1 Photo. *Perf. 11½*
2839 A1438 4k brt mag, org & black .25 .25
2840 A1438 6k org yel, red & blue .40 .25
2841 A1438 10k blue, vio & orange .45 .25
Nos. 2839-2841 (3) 1.10 .75

International Quiet Sun Year, 1964-65.

Christian Donalitius A1439

1964, Jan. 1 Unwmk. *Perf. 12*
2842 A1439 4k green & black .30 .15

Lithuanian poet Christian Donalitius (Donelaitis), 250th birth anniv.

Women's Speed Skating A1440

Designs: 4k, Women's cross country skiing. 6k, 1964 Olympic emblem and torch. 10k, Biathlon. 12k, Figure skating pair.

1964, Feb. 4 *Perf. 11½, Imperf.*
2843 A1440 2k ultra, blk & lilac rose .25 .15
2844 A1440 4k lilac rose, blk & ultra .25 .15
2845 A1440 6k dk blue, red & blk .30 .20
2846 A1440 10k green, lilac & blk .55 .25
2847 A1440 12k lilac, black & grn .75 .25
Nos. 2843-2847 (5) 2.10 1.00

9th Winter Olympic Games, Innsbruck Jan. 29-Feb. 9, 1964. See Nos. 2865, 2867-2870.

Anna S. Golubkina (1864-1927), Sculptor A1441

1964, Feb. 4 Photo.
2848 A1441 4k gray, brown & buff .30 .15

150 років з дня
народження.
1964 р.

Ovpt. on #2450 in Red

Taras G. Shevchenko — A1443

Designs: 4k, Shevchenko statue, Kiev. 10k, Shevchenko by Ilya Repin. (Portrait on 6k by I. Kremsko.)

1964 Litho. *Perf. 12*
2852 A1245 3k brown & violet .30 .15

Engr.
2853 A1443 4k magenta .30 .15
2854 A1443 4k deep green .45 .15
2855 A1443 6k red brown .45 .15
2856 A1443 6k indigo .45 .15

Photo.
2857 A1443 10k bister & brown 1.10 .15
2858 A1443 10k buff & dull violet 1.10 .15
Nos. 2852-2858 (7) 4.15 1.05

Shevchenko, Ukrainian poet, 150th birth anniv.
Issued: #2852, 2857-2858, 2/22; Others, 3/1.

K. S. Zaslonov A1444

Soviet Heroes: No. 2860, N. A. Vilkov. No. 2861, J. V. Smirnov. No. 2862, V. S. Khorujaia (heroine). No. 2862A, I. M. Sivko. No. 2862B, I. S. Polbin.

1964-65 Photo.
2859 A1444 4k hn brn & brn blk .30 .15
2860 A1444 4k Prus bl & vio blk .30 .15
2861 A1444 4k brn red & indigo .30 .15
2862 A1444 4k bluish gray & dk brown .30 .15
2862A A1444 4k lilac & black ('65) .30 .15
2862B A1444 4k blue & dk brn ('65) .30 .15
Nos. 2859-2862B (6) 1.80 .90

Printer Inking Form, 16th Century A1445

6k, Statue of Ivan Fedorov, 1st Russian printer.

1964, Mar. 1 Litho. Unwmk.
2863 A1445 4k multicolored .35 .15
2864 A1445 6k multicolored .35 .15

400th anniv. of book printing in Russia.

Nos. 2843-2847 Overprinted

Советские
женщины-
конькобежцы—
сильнейшие
в мире

and

Ice Hockey A1446

Olympic Gold Medal, "11 Gold, 8 Silver, 6 Bronze" A1447

Design: 3k, Ice hockey.

1964, Mar. 9 Photo. *Perf. 11½*
2865 A1440 2k ultra, blk & lilac rose .20 .15
2866 A1440 3k blk, bl grn & red .25 .15
2867 A1440 4k lil rose, blk & ultra .30 .15
2868 A1440 6k dk bl, red & blk .70 .15
2869 A1440 10k grn, lil & blk .80 .15
2870 A1440 12k lilac, black & grn .90 .15

Perf. 12
2871 A1447 16k org red & gldn brown 1.25 .25
Nos. 2865-2871 (7) 4.40 1.15

Soviet victories at the 9th Winter Olympic Games.
On Nos. 2865, 2867-2870 the black overprints commemorate victories in various events and are variously arranged in 3 to 6 lines, with "Innsbruck" in Russian added below "1964" on 2k, 4k, 10k and 12k.

Rubber Industry — A1448

Regular and Volunteer Militiamen — A1449

Designs: No. 2873, Textile industry. No. 2874, Cotton, wheat, corn and helicopter spraying land.

1964 Litho. *Perf. 12x12½*
2872 A1448 4k org, lilac, ultra & blk .30 .15
2873 A1448 4k org, blk, grn & ultra .30 .15
2874 A1448 4k dull yel, ol, red & bl .30 .15
Nos. 2872-2874 (3) .90 .45

Importance of the chemical industry to the Soviet economy.
Issued: #2872, Feb. 10; #2873-2874, Mar. 27.

1964, Mar. 27 Photo. *Perf. 12*
2875 A1449 4k red & deep ultra .30 .30

Day of the Militia.

Sailor and Odessa Lighthouse A1450

Liberation Monument, Minsk — A1451

Design: No. 2877, Lenin statue and Leningrad.

1964 Litho. *Perf. 12½x12*
2876 A1450 4k red, lt grn, ultra & black .30 .15
2877 A1450 4k red, yel, grn, brn & black .30 .15
2878 A1451 4k bl, gray, red & emer .30 .15
Nos. 2876-2878 (3) .90 .45

Liberation of Odessa (#2876), Leningrad (#2877), Byelorussia (#2878), 20th anniv.
Issued: #2876, 4/10; #2877, 5/9; #2878, 6/30.

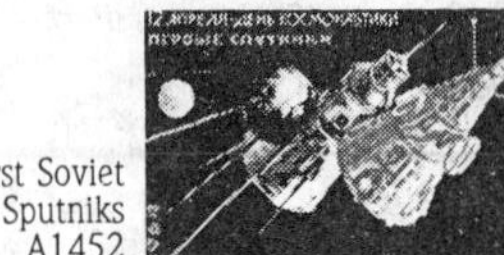
First Soviet Sputniks A1452

F. A. Tsander A1453 — Lenin A1454

Designs: 6k, Mars 1 spacecraft. No. 2886, Konstantin E. Tsiolkovsky. No. 2887, N. I. Kibaltchitch. No. 2888, Statue honoring 3 balloonists killed in 1934 accident. 12k, Gagarin and Kosmos 3.

Perf. 11½, Imperf.

1964, Apr. Photo.

2883 A1452 4k red org, blk & blue green .30 .15
2884 A1452 6k dk blue & org red .60 .15
2885 A1453 10k grn, blk & fluor. pink .75 .15
2886 A1453 10k dk bl grn, blk & fluor. pink .75 .15
2887 A1453 10k lilac, blk & lt grn .75 .15
2888 A1453 10k blue & black .75 .15
2889 A1452 12k blue grn, org brn & black .75 .25
Nos. 2883-2889 (7) 4.65
Set value 1.00

Leaders in rocket theory and technique.

Engraved and Photogravure

1964-65 *Perf. 12x11½*

2890 A1454 4k blk, buff & lilac rose 4.50 3.50
a. Re-engraved ('65) 3.50 2.00

94th anniversary of the birth of Lenin.

On No. 2890a, the portrait shading is much heavier. Lines on collar are straight and unbroken, rather than dotted.

For souvenir sheet see No. 2582a.

William Shakespeare, 400th Birth Anniv. A1455

1964, Apr. 23 *Perf. 11½*

2891 A1455 10k gray & red brown .60 .25

See Nos. 2985-2986.

"Irrigation" — A1456

1964, May 12 Litho. *Perf. 12x12½*

2892 A1456 4k multicolored .30 .15

A1457

Perf. 12½x11½

1964, May 12 Photo.

2893 A1457 4k blue & gray brown .30 .15

Y. B. Gamarnik, army commander, 70th birth anniv.

D. I. Gulia — A1458

Portraits: No. 2895, Hamza Hakim-Zade Nijazi. No. 2896, Saken Seifullin. No. 2896A, M. M. Kotsyubinsky. No. 2896B, Stepanos Nazaryan. No. 2896C, Toktogil Satyiganov.

Engraved and Photogravure

1964 Unwmk. *Perf. 12x11½*

2894 A1458 4k green, buff & blk .25 .15
2895 A1458 4k red, buff & black .25 .15
2896 A1458 4k brn, ocher, buff & black .25 .15
2896A A1458 4k brn lake, blk & buff .25 .15
2896B A1458 4k blue, pale bl, blk & buff .25 .15
2896C A1458 4k red brown & black .25 .15
Nos. 2894-2896C (6) 1.50

Abkhazian poet Gulia, 90th birth anniv.; Uzbekian writer and composer Nijazi, 75th birth anniv.; Kazakian poet Seifullin, 70th birth anniv.; Ukrainian writer Kotsyubinsky (1864-1913); Armenian writer Nazaryan (1814-1879); Kirghiz poet Satylganov (1864-1933).

Arkadi Gaidar (1904-41) A1459

Writers: No. 2897A, Nikolai Ostrovsky (1904-36) and battle scene (portrait at left).

1964 Photo. *Perf. 12*

2897 A1459 4k red orange & gray .30 .15

Engr.

2897A A1459 4k brown lake & black .30 .15
Set value .15

No. 2318 Surcharged:

**150 лет вхождения
в состав России
1964**

**4
коп.**

1964, May 27 Litho. *Perf. 12*

2898 A1194 4k on 40k bister & brn 3.00 .15

Azerbaijan's joining Russia, 150th anniv.

"Romania" A1460

Elephant A1461

No. 2900, "Poland," (map, Polish eagle, industrial and agricultural symbols). No. 2901, "Bulgaria" (flag, rose, industrial and agricultural symbols). No. 2902, Soviet and Yugoslav soldiers and embattled Belgrade. No. 2903, "Czechoslovakia" (view of Prague, arms, Russian soldier and woman). No. 2903A, Map and flag of Hungary, Liberty statue. No. 2903B, Statue of Russian Soldier and Belvedere Palace, Vienna. No. 2904, Buildings under construction, Warsaw; Polish flag and medal.

1964-65 Litho. *Perf. 12*

2899 A1460 6k gray & multi .25 .15
2900 A1460 6k ocher, red & brn .25 .15
2901 A1460 6k tan, grn & red .25 .15
2902 A1460 6k gray, blk, dl bl, ol & red .25 .15
2903 A1460 6k ultra, black & red ('65) .25 .15
2903A A1460 6k brn, red & green ('65) .25 .15
2903B A1460 6k dp org, gray bl & black ('65) .25 .15
2904 A1460 6k blue, red, yel & bister ('65) .25 .15
Nos. 2899-2904 (8) 2.00 1.20

20th anniversaries of liberation from German occupation of Romania, Poland, Bulgaria, Belgrade, Czechoslovakia, Hungary, Vienna and Warsaw.

Perf. 12x12½, 12½x12, Imperf.

1964 Photo.

Designs: 2k, Giant panda, horiz. 4k, Polar bear. 6k, European elk. 10k, Pelican. 12k, Tiger. 16k, Lammergeier.

Size: 25x36mm, 36x25mm

2905 A1461 1k red & black .15 .15
2906 A1461 2k tan & black .15 .15

Perf. 12

Size: 26x28mm

2907 A1461 4k grnsh gray, black & tan .15 .15

Perf. 12x12½

Size: 25x36mm

2908 A1461 6k ol, dk brn & tan .25 .15

Perf. 12

Size: 26x28mm

2909 A1461 10k ver, gray & black .40 .15

Perf. 12½x12, 12x12½

Size: 36x25mm, 25x36mm

2910 A1461 12k brn, ocher & blk .70 .15
2911 A1461 16k ultra, blk, bis & yellow .65 .15
Nos. 2905-2911 (7) 2.45 1.05

100th anniv. of the Moscow zoo.
Issue dates: Perf., June 18. Imperf., May.

Leningrad Post Office A1462

1964, June 30 Litho. *Perf. 12*

2912 A1462 4k citron, black & red .30 .15

Leningrad postal service, 250th anniv.

Corn A1463

Thorez A1464

1964 Photo. *Perf. 11½, Imperf.*

2913 A1463 2k shown .15 .15
2914 A1463 3k Wheat .15 .15
2915 A1463 4k Potatoes .20 .15
2916 A1463 6k Beans .25 .15
2917 A1463 10k Beets .30 .15
2918 A1463 12k Cotton .60 .15
2919 A1463 16k Flax .90 .15
Nos. 2913-2919 (7) 2.55 1.05

Issue dates: Perf., July 10. Imperf., June 25.

1964, July 31

2920 A1464 4k black & red .75 .25

Maurice Thorez, chairman of the French Communist party.

Equestrian and Russian Olympic Emblem A1465

Designs: 4k, Weight lifter. 6k, High jump. 10k, Canoeing. 12k, Girl gymnast. 16k, Fencing.

1964, July *Perf. 11½, Imperf.*

2921 A1465 3k lt yel grn, red, brn & black .15 .15
2922 A1465 4k yel, black & red .20 .15
2923 A1465 6k lt blue, blk & red .25 .15
2924 A1465 10k bl grn, red & blk .50 .15
2925 A1465 12k gray, black & red .60 .15
2926 A1465 16k lt ultra, blk & red .75 .15
Nos. 2921-2926 (6) 2.45 .90

18th Olympic Games, Tokyo, Oct. 10-25, 1964.

Two 1r imperf. souvenir sheets exist, showing emblem, woman gymnast and stadium. Size: 91x71mm.

Value, red sheet, $4.75 unused, $1.75 canceled; green sheet, $165 unused, $225 canceled.

Three Races — A1466

Jawaharlal Nehru — A1467

1964, Aug. 8 Photo. *Perf. 12*

2929 A1466 6k orange & black .40 .35

International Congress of Anthropologists and Ethnographers, Moscow.

1964, Aug. 20 *Perf. 11½*

2930 A1467 4k brown & black .40 .15

Prime Minister Nehru of India (1889-1964).

Conquest of Space

A souvenir sheet, issued Aug. 20, 1964, celebrates the Conquest of Space. It carries six perforated, multicolored 10k stamps with different, interlocking designs picturing Soviet rockets and spacecraft. Size of sheet, 141x110mm. Value, $3.75 unused, $1.50 canceled. Sheet also exists on glossy paper. Value, $10 unused, $6 canceled.

Marx and Engels A1468

A. V. Vishnevsky A1469

Designs: No. 2932 Lenin and title page of "CPSS Program." No. 2933, Worker breaking chains around the globe. No. 2934, Title pages of "Communist Manifesto" in German and Russian. No. 2935, Globe and banner inscribed "Workers of the World Unite."

1964, Aug. 27 Photo. *Perf. 11½x12*

2931 A1468 4k red, dk red & brown .30 .15
2932 A1468 4k red, brn & slate .30 .15
2933 A1468 4k blue, fluor. brt rose & black .30 .15

Perf. 12½x12

Litho.

2934 A1468 4k ol black, blk & red .30 .15
2935 A1468 4k blue, red & ol bister .30 .15
Nos. 2931-2935 (5) 1.50 .75

Centenary of First Socialist International.

1964 Photo. *Perf. 11½*

Portraits: No. 2937, N. A. Semashko. No. 2938, D. Ivanovsky.

Size: 23½x35mm

2936 A1469 4k gray & brown .30 .15
2937 A1469 4k buff, sepia & red .30 .15

Litho.

Size: 22x32½mm

2938 A1469 4k tan, gray & brown .30 .15
Nos. 2936-2938 (3) .90 .45

90th birth annivs. Vishnevsky, surgeon, and Semashko, founder of the Russian Public Health Service; Ivanovsky (1864-1920), physician.

Palmiro Togliatti (1893-1964), General Secretary of the Italian Communist Party — A1470

1964, Sept. 15 *Perf. 12½x12*

2939 A1470 4k black & red .30 .15

Letter, Aerogram and Globe A1471

1964, Sept. 20 Litho.
2940 A1471 4k tan, lilac rose & ultra .30 .15

Intl. Letter Writing Week, Oct. 5-11.

Arms of German Democratic Republic, Factories, Ship and Train — A1472

1964, Oct. 7 ***Perf. 12***
2942 A1472 6k blk, yel, red & bister .30 .15

German Democratic Republic, 15th anniv.

No. 2836 Overprinted in Red

40 лет Советскому Таджикистану
1964 год

1964, Oct. 7 Engr.
2943 A1435 4k dull blue 2.00 1.00

40th anniversary of Tadzhik Republic.

Woman Holding Bowl of Grain and Fruit A1473

Uzbek Farm Couple and Arms — A1474

Turkmen Woman Holding Arms — A1475

1964, Oct. Litho.
2944 A1473 4k red, green & brn .40 .15
2945 A1474 4k red yel & claret .40 .15
2946 A1475 4k red, black & red brn .40 .15
Nos. 2944-2946 (3) 1.20 .45

40th anniv. of the Moldavian, Uzbek and Turkmen Socialist Republics.
Issue dates: #2944, Oct. 7; others, Oct. 26.

Soldier and Flags A1476

1964, Oct. 14
2947 A1476 4k red, bis, dk brn & bl .30 .15

Liberation of the Ukraine, 20th anniv.

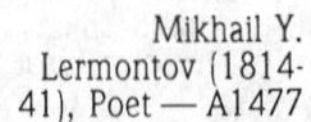

Mikhail Y. Lermontov (1814-41), Poet — A1477

Designs: 4k, Birthplace of Tarchany. 10k, Lermontov and Vissarion G. Belinski.

1964, Oct. 14 Engr.; Litho. (10k)
2948 A1477 4k violet black .15 .15
2949 A1477 6k black .25 .15
2950 A1477 10k dk red brn & buff .70 .15
Nos. 2948-2950 (3) 1.10 .45

Hammer and Sickle A1478

1964, Oct. 14 Litho.
2951 A1478 4k dk blue, red, ocher & yellow .30 .15

47th anniversary of October Revolution.

Col. Vladimir M. Komarov A1479

Komarov, Feoktistov and Yegorov — A1480

Designs: No. 2953, Boris B. Yegorov, M.D. No. 2954, Konstantin Feoktistov, scientist. 10k, Spacecraft Voskhod I and cosmonauts. 50k, Red flag with portraits of Komarov, Feoktistov and Yegorov, and trajectory around earth.

Perf. 11½ (A1479), 12½x12
1964 Photo.
2952 A1479 4k bl grn, blk & org .20 .15
2953 A1479 4k bl grn, blk & org .20 .15
2954 A1479 4k bl grn, blk & org .20 .15

Size: 73x23mm
2955 A1480 6k vio & dk brn .25 .15
2956 A1480 10k dp ultra & pur .85 .15

Imperf
Litho.
Size: 90x45½mm
2957 A1480 50k vio, red & gray 5.00 1.40
Nos. 2952-2957 (6) 6.70 2.15

3-men space flight of Komarov, Yegorov and Feoktistov, Oct. 12-13. Issued: #2952-2954, 10/19; #2955, 10/17; #2956, 10/13; #2957, 11/20.

A. I. Yelizarova-Ulyanova A1482

Portrait: #2961, Nadezhda K. Krupskaya.

1964, Nov. 6 Photo. ***Perf. 11½***
2960 A1482 4k brn, org & indigo .30 .15
2961 A1482 4k indigo, red & brn .30 .15

Yelizarova-Ulyanova, Lenin's sister, birth cent. & Krupskaya, Lenin's wife, 95th birth anniv.

Farm Woman, Sheep, Flag of Mongolia A1483

Mushrooms A1484

1964, Nov. 20 Litho. ***Perf. 12***
2962 A1483 6k multicolored .30 .15

Mongolian People's Republic, 40th anniv.

1964, Nov. 25 Litho. ***Perf. 12***

Designs: Various mushrooms.

2963 A1484 2k ol grn, red brn & yellow .15 .15
2964 A1484 4k green & yellow .15 .15
2965 A1484 6k bluish grn, brn & yellow .50 .15
2966 A1484 10k grn, org red & brn .65 .15
2967 A1484 12k ultra, yel & green 1.25 .15
Nos. 2963-2967 (5) 2.70 .75

Nos. 2963-2967 exist varnished, printed in sheets of 25 with 10 labels in outside vertical rows. Issued Nov. 30. Value, set $5.

A. P. Dovzhenko A1485

Design: 6k, Scene from "Tchapaev" (man and boy with guns).

1964, Nov. 30 Photo. ***Perf. 12***
2968 A1485 4k gray & dp ultra .45 .25
2968A A1485 6k pale olive & blk .45 .25

Dovzhenko (1894-1956), film producer, and 30th anniv. of the production of the film "Tchapaev."

"Happy New Year" A1486

V. J. Struve A1487

Photogravure and Engraved
1964, Nov. 30 ***Perf. 11½***
2969 A1486 4k multicolored .50 .30

New Year 1965. The bright rose ink is fluorescent.

1964-65 Photo. ***Perf. 12½x11½***

Portraits: No. 2971, N. P. Kravkov. No. 2971A, P. K. Sternberg. No. 2971B, Ch. Valikhanov. No. 2971C, V. A. Kistjakovski.

2970 A1487 4k slate bl & dk brn .65 .15

Litho.
2971 A1487 4k brn, red & black .35 .15

Photo.
Perf. 11½
2971A A1487 4k dk blue & dk brn .35 .15

Perf. 12
2971B A1487 4k rose vio & black .35 .15

Litho.
2971C A1487 4k brn vio, blk & cit .35 .15
Nos. 2970-2971C (5) 2.05 .75

Astronomer Struve (1793-1864), founder of Pulkov Observatory; Kravkov (1865-1924), pharmacologist; Sternberg (1865-1920), astronomer; Valikhanov (1835-1865), Kazakh scientist; Kistjakovski (1865-1952), chemist.
Issued: #2970, 11/30; #2971, 1/31/65; #2971A-2971B, 9/21/65; #2971C, 12/24.

S. V. Ivanov and Skiers A1488

1964, Dec. 22 Engr. ***Perf. 12½***
2972 A1488 4k black & brown .50 .30

S. V. Ivanov (1864-1910), painter.

Chemical Industry: Fertilizers and Pest Control — A1489

Importance of the chemical industry for the national economy: 6k, Synthetics factory.

1964, Dec. 25 Photo. ***Perf. 12***
2973 A1489 4k olive & lilac rose .30 .15
2974 A1489 6k dp ultra & black .30 .15

European Cranberries — A1490

Wild Berries: 3k, Huckleberries. 4k, Mountain ash. 10k, Blackberries. 16k, Cranberries.

1964, Dec. 25 ***Perf. 11½x12***
2975 A1490 1k pale green & car .15 .15
2976 A1490 3k gray, vio bl & grn .20 .15
2977 A1490 4k gray, org red & brown .25 .15
2978 A1490 10k lt grn, dk vio blue & claret .40 .15
2979 A1490 16k gray, brt green & car rose .50 .15
Nos. 2975-2979 (5) 1.50 .75

Academy of Science Library A1491

1964, Dec. 25 Typo. ***Perf. 12x12½***
2980 A1491 4k black, pale grn & red .30 .15

250th anniv. of the founding of the Academy of Science Library, Leningrad.

Congress Palace, Kremlin — A1492

Khan Tengri — A1493

1964, Dec. 25
2981 A1492 1r dark blue 4.50 1.00

1964, Dec. 29 Photo. ***Perf. 11½***

Mountains: 6k, Kazbek, horiz. 12k, Twin peaks of Ushba.

2982 A1493 4k grnsh bl, vio bl & buff .30 .15
2983 A1493 6k yel, dk brn & ol .30 .15
2984 A1493 12k lt yel, grn & pur .40 .15
Nos. 2982-2984 (3) 1.00 .45

Development of mountaineering in Russia.

Portrait Type of 1964

Design: 6k, Michelangelo. 12k, Galileo.

Engraved and Photogravure
1964, Dec. 30 ***Perf. 11½***
2985 A1455 6k sep, red brn & org .35 .25
2986 A1455 12k dk brown & green 1.65 .25

Michelangelo Buonarotti, artist, 400th death anniv. and Galileo Galilei, astronomer and physicist, 400th birth anniv.

Helmet
A1494

Treasures from Kremlin Treasury: 6k, Saddle. 10k, Jeweled fur crown. 12k, Gold ladle. 16k, Bowl.

1964, Dec. 30 **Litho.**

2987 A1494 4k multicolored .20 .15
2988 A1494 6k multicolored .30 .15
2989 A1494 10k multicolored .45 .15
2990 A1494 12k multicolored 1.10 .15
2991 A1494 16k multicolored 1.25 .15
Nos. 2987-2991 (5) 3.30 .75

Dante — A1495

Blood Donor — A1496

1965, Jan. 29 **Photo.** ***Perf. 11½***
2995 A1495 4k dk red brn & ol bis .35 .25

Dante Alighieri (1265-1321), Italian poet.

1965, Jan. 31 **Litho.** ***Perf. 12***

Honoring blood donors: No. 2997, Hand holding carnation, and donors' emblem.

2996 A1496 4k dk car, red, vio bl & bl .30 .15
2997 A1496 4k brt grn, red & dk grn .30 .15

Bandy — A1497

Police Dog — A1498

6k, Figure skaters and Moscow Sports Palace.

1965, Feb. **Photo.** ***Perf. 11½x12***
2998 A1497 4k blue, red & yellow .30 .15
2999 A1497 6k green, blk & red .30 .15

4k issued Feb. 21, for the victory of the Soviet team in the World Bandy Championship, Moscow, Feb. 21-27; 6k issued Feb. 12, for the European Figure Skating Championship. For overprint see No. 3017.

Perf. 12x11½, 11½x12 (Photo. stamps); 12x12½, 12½x12 (Litho.)
Photo., Litho. (1k, 10k, 12k, 16k)
1965, Feb. 26

Dogs: 1k, Russian hound. 2k, Irish setter. No. 3003, Pointer. No. 3004, Fox terrier. No. 3005, Sheepdog. No. 3006, Borzoi. 10k, Collie. 12k, Husky. 16k, Caucasian sheepdog. (1k, 2k, 4k, 12k and No. 3006 horiz.)

3000 A1498 1k black, yel & mar .20 .15
3001 A1498 2k ultra, blk & red brown .25 .15
3002 A1498 3k blk, ocher & org red .25 .15
3003 A1498 4k org, yel grn & blk .40 .15
3004 A1498 4k brn, blk & lt grn .40 .15
3005 A1498 6k chalky blue, sep & red .50 .15
3006 A1498 6k chalky bl, org brn & black .50 .15
3007 A1498 10k yel green, ocher & red .90 .15
3008 A1498 12k gray, blk & ocher 1.10 .20
3009 A1498 16k multicolored 1.25 .25
Nos. 3000-3009 (10) 5.75
Set value 1.25

Richard Sorge (1895-1944), Soviet spy and Hero of the Soviet Union — A1499

1965, Mar. 6 **Photo.** ***Perf. 12x12½***
3010 A1499 4k henna brn & black .50 .30

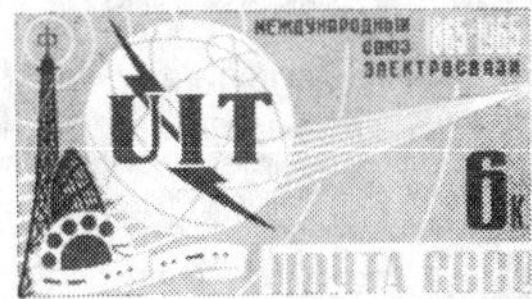

Communications Symbols — A1500

1965, Mar. 6 ***Perf. 12½x12***
3011 A1500 6k grnsh blue, vio & brt purple .50 .30

Intl. Telecommunication Union, cent.

No. 2764 Overprinted **ТАМПЕРЕ 1965 г.**

1965, Mar. 20 **Photo.** ***Perf. 12***
3012 A1402 6k red & gray blue 1.00 .30

Soviet victory in the European and World Ice Hockey Championships.

Lt. Col. Alexei Leonov Taking Movies in Space — A1501

1r, Leonov walking in space and Voskhod 2.

1965, Mar. 23 **Photo.** ***Perf. 12***
Size: 73x23mm
3015 A1501 10k brt ultra, org & gray .80 .35

First man walking in space, Lt. Col. Alexei Leonov, Mar. 17, 1965 ("18 March" on stamp).
Exists imperf. Value $1.

Souvenir Sheet

1965, Apr. 12 **Litho.**
3016 A1501 1r multicolored 5.50 2.00

Space flight of Voskhod 2. No. 3016 contains one 81x27mm stamp.

No. 2999 Overprinted **Советские фигуристы— чемпионы мира в парном катании**

1965, Mar. 26 ***Perf. 11½x12***
3017 A1497 6k green, black & red .80 .25

Soviet victory in the World Figure Skating Championships.

Flags of USSR and Poland — A1502

1965, Apr. 12 **Photo.** ***Perf. 12***
3018 A1502 6k bister & red .50 .15

20th anniversary of the signing of the Polish-Soviet treaty of friendship, mutual assistance and postwar cooperation.

Tsiolkovsky Monument, Kaluga; Globe and Rockets — A1503

Rockets, Radio Telescope, TV Antenna — A1504

Designs: 12k, Space monument, Moscow. 16k, Cosmonauts' monument, Moscow. No. 3023, Globe with trajectories, satellite and astronauts.

1965, Apr. 12 ***Perf. 11½***
3019 A1503 4k pale grn, black & brt rose .20 .15
3020 A1503 12k vio, pur & brt rose .50 .15
3021 A1503 16k multicolored .80 .15

Lithographed on Aluminum Foil
Perf. 12½x12

3022 A1504 20k black & red 5.00 3.00
3023 A1504 20k blk, blue & red 5.00 3.00
Nos. 3019-3023 (5) 11.50 6.45

National Cosmonauts' Day. On Nos. 3019-3021 the bright rose is fluorescent.

Lenin A1505

1965, Apr. 16 **Engr.** ***Perf. 12***
3024 A1505 10k tan & indigo .50 .25

95th anniversary of the birth of Lenin.

Poppies A1506

Soviet Flag, Broken Swastikas, Fighting in Berlin A1507

Flowers: 3k, Daisies. 4k, Peony. 6k, Carnation. 10k, Tulips.

1965, Apr. 23 **Photo.** ***Perf. 11***
3025 A1506 1k maroon, red & grn .20 .15
3026 A1506 3k dk brn, yel & grn .20 .15
3027 A1506 4k blk, grn & lilac .45 .15
3028 A1506 6k dk sl grn, grn & red .65 .15
3029 A1506 10k dk plum, yel & grn 1.00 .20
Nos. 3025-3029 (5) 2.50
Set value .50

1965 ***Perf. 11½***

Designs: 2k, "Fatherland Calling!" (woman with proclamation) by I. Toidze. 3k, "Attack on Moscow" by V. Bogatkin. No. 3033, "Rest after the Battle" by Y. Neprintsev. No. 3034, "Mother of Partisan" by S. Gerasimov. 6k, "Our Flag - Symbol of Victory" (soldiers with banner) by V. Ivanov. 10k, "Tribute to the Hero" (mourners at bier) by F. Bogorodsky. 12k, "Invincible Nation and Army" (worker and soldier holding shell) by V. Koretsky. 16k, "Victory celebration on Red Square" by K. Yuan. 20k, Soldier and symbols of war.

3030 A1507 1k red, black & gold .25 .15
3031 A1507 2k crim, blk & gold .25 .15
3032 A1507 3k ultra & gold .30 .15
3033 A1507 4k green & gold .45 .15
3034 A1507 4k violet & gold .45 .15
3035 A1507 6k dp claret & gold .60 .15
3036 A1507 10k plum & gold 1.25 .15
3037 A1507 12k black, red & gold 1.40 .15
3038 A1507 16k lilac rose & gold 1.50 .15
3039 A1507 20k red, black & gold 2.50 .30
Nos. 3030-3039 (10) 8.95
Set value .95

20th anniv. of the end of World War II. Issued Apr. 25-May 1.

Souvenir Sheet

From Popov's Radio to Space Telecommunications — A1508

1965, May 7 **Litho.** ***Perf. 11½***
3040 A1508 1r blue & multi 5.50 3.00

70th anniv. of Aleksandr S. Popov's radio pioneer work. No. 3040 contains 6 labels without denominations or country name.

Marx, Lenin and Crowd with Flags — A1509

1965, May 9 **Photo.** ***Perf. 12x12½***
3041 A1509 6k red & black .30 .15

6th conference of Postal Ministers of Communist Countries, Peking, June 21-July 15.

Bolshoi Theater, Moscow — A1510

1965, May 20 ***Perf. 11x11½***
3042 A1510 6k grnsh blue, bis & blk .30 .15

International Theater Day.

Col. Pavel Belyayev A1511

Design: No. 3044, Lt. Col. Alexei Leonov.

1965, May 23 ***Perf. 12x11½***
3043 A1511 6k magenta & silver .30 .15
3044 A1511 6k purple & silver .30 .15

Space flight of Voskhod 2, Mar. 18-19, 1965, and the 1st man walking in space, Lt. Col. Alexei Leonov.

Sverdlov A1512

Grothewohl A1513

Portrait: No. 3046, Juldash Akhunbabaev.

Photogravure and Engraved

1965, May 30 *Perf. $11^1/_2$x12*

3045 A1512 4k orange brn & blk .60 .30
3046 A1512 4k lt violet & blk .60 .30

Yakov M. Sverdlov, 1885-1919, 1st pres. of USSR, and J. Akhunbabaev, 1885-1943, pres. of Uzbek Republic.

1965, June 12 **Photo.** *Perf. 12*

3051 A1513 4k black & magenta .30 .15

Otto Grotewohl, prime minister of the German Democratic Republic (1894-1964).

Maurice Thorez A1514

Communication by Satellite A1515

1965, June 12

3052 A1514 6k brown & red .30 .15

Maurice Thorez (1900-1964), chairman of the French Communist party.

1965, June 15 **Litho.**

Designs: No. 3054, Pouring ladle, steel mill and map of India. No. 3055, Stars, satellites and names of international organizations.

3053 A1515 3k olive, blk & gold .25 .15
3054 A1515 6k emer, dk grn & gold .25 .15
3055 A1515 6k vio blue, gold & blk .25 .15
Nos. 3053-3055 (3) .75 .45

Emphasizing international cooperation through communication, economic cooperation and international organizations.

Symbols of Chemistry A1516

1965, June 15 **Photo.** *Perf. $11^1/_2$*

3056 A1516 4k blk, brt rose & brt bl .30 .15

20th Cong. of the Intl. Union of Pure and Applied Chemistry (IUPAC), Moscow. The bright rose ink is fluorescent.

V. A. Serov — A1517

Design: 6k, Full-length portrait of Feodor Chaliapin, the singer, by Serov.

1965, June 25 **Typo.** *Perf. $12^1/_2$*

3057 A1517 4k red brn, buff & black .30 .25
3058 A1517 6k olive bister & black .30 .25

Serov (1865-1911), historical painter.

Abay Kunanbaev, Kazakh Poet A1518

Designs (writers and poets): No. 3060, Vsevolod Ivanov (1895-1963). No. 3060A, Eduard Vilde, Estonian writer. No. 3061, Mark Kropivnitsky, Ukrainian playwright. No. 3062, Manuk Apeghyan, Armenian writer and critic. No. 3063, Musa Djalil, Tartar poet. No. 3064, Hagop Hagopian, Armenian poet. No. 3064A, Djalil Mamedkulizade, Azerbaijan writer.

1965-66 **Photo.** *Perf. $12^1/_2$x12*

3059 A1518 4k lt violet & blk .55 .30
3060 A1518 4k rose lilac & blk .55 .30
3060A A1518 4k gray & black .55 .30
3061 A1518 4k black & org brn .55 .30

Perf. $12^1/_2$

Typo.

3062 A1518 4k crim, blue grn & blk .55 .30

Perf. $11^1/_2$

Photogravure and Engraved

3063 A1518 4k black & org brn ('66) .55 .30
3064 A1518 4k green & blk ('66) .55 .30

Photo.

3064A A1518 4k Prus green & blk ('66) .55 .30
Nos. 3059-3064A (8) 4.40 2.40

Sizes: Nos. 3059-3062, 38x25mm. Nos. 3063-3064A, 35x23mm.

Jan Rainis A1518a

1965, Sept. 8 **Photo.** *Perf. $12^1/_2$x12*

3064B A1518a 4k dull blue & black .35 .25

Rainis (1865-1929), Latvian playwright. "Rainis" was pseudonym of Jan Plieksans.

Film, Screen, Globe and Star A1519

1965, July 5 **Litho.** *Perf. 12*

3065 A1519 6k brt blue, gold & blk .35 .15

4th Intl. Film Festival, Moscow: "For Humanism in Cinema Art, for Peace and Friendship among Nations."

Concert Bowl, Tallinn A1520

"Lithuania" — A1521

"Latvia" A1522

1965, July *Perf. $12x11^1/_2$, $11^1/_2$x12*

3066 A1520 4k ultra, blk, red & ocher .30 .15
3067 A1521 4k red & brown .30 .15
3068 A1522 4k yel, red & blue .30 .15
Nos. 3066-3068 (3) .90 .45

25th anniversaries of Estonia, Lithuania and Latvia as Soviet Republics. Issue dates: No. 3066, July 7; No. 3067, July 14; No. 3068, July 16.

"Keep Peace" — A1523

Protesting Women and Czarist Eagle — A1524

1965, July 10 **Photo.** *Perf. $11x11^1/_2$*

3069 A1523 6k yellow, black & blue .40 .15

1965, July 20 **Litho.** *Perf. $11^1/_2$*

Designs: No. 3071, Soldier attacking distributor of handbills. No. 3072, Fighters on barricades with red flag. No. 3073, Monument for sailors of Battleship "Potemkin," Odessa.

3070 A1524 4k black, red & ol grn .25 .15
3071 A1524 4k red, ol green & blk .25 .15
3072 A1524 4k red, black & brn .25 .15
3073 A1524 4k red & violet blue .25 .15
Nos. 3070-3073 (4) 1.00 .60

60th anniversary of the 1905 revolution.

Gheorghe Gheorghiu-Dej (1901-1965), President of Romanian State Council (1961-1965) — A1525

1965, July 26 **Photo.** *Perf. 12*

3074 A1525 4k black & red .30 .15

Relay Race A1526

Sport: No. 3076, Bicycle race. No. 3077, Gymnast on vaulting horse.

1965, Aug. 5 **Litho.** *Perf. $12^1/_2$x12*

3075 A1526 4k vio blue, bis brn & red brown .30 .15
3076 A1526 4k buff, red brn, gray & maroon .30 .15
3077 A1526 4k bl, mar, buff & lt brn .35 .15
Nos. 3075-3077 (3) .95
Set value .20

8th Trade Union Spartacist Games.

Electric Power — A1527

Designs: 2k, Metals in modern industry. 3k, Modern chemistry serving the people. 4k, Mechanization, automation and electronics. 6k, New materials for building industry. 10k, Mechanization and electrification of agriculture. 12k, Technological progress in transportation. 16k, Application of scientific discoveries to industry.

1965, Aug. 5 **Photo.** *Perf. $12x11^1/_2$*

3078 A1527 1k olive, bl & blk .15 .15
3079 A1527 2k org, blk & yel .15 .15
3080 A1527 3k yel, vio & bister .15 .15
3081 A1527 4k ultra, ind & red .25 .15
3082 A1527 6k ultra & bister .35 .15
3083 A1527 10k yel, orange & red brown .70 .15
3084 A1527 12k Prus blue & red .80 .15
3085 A1527 16k rose lilac, blk & violet blue 1.25 .30
Nos. 3078-3085 (8) 3.80
Set value 1.00

Creation of the material and technical basis of communism.

Gymnast A1528

Javelin and Running A1529

Design: 6k, Bicycling.

1965, Aug. 12 *Perf. $11^1/_2$*

3086 A1528 4k multi & red .25 .15
3087 A1528 6k grnsh bl, red & brn .25 .15

9th Spartacist Games for school children.

1965, Aug. 27

Designs: 6k, High jump and shot put. 10k, Hammer throwing and hurdling.

3088 A1529 4k brn, lilac & red .25 .15
3089 A1529 6k brn, yel green & red .25 .15
3090 A1529 10k brn, chlky bl & red .60 .15
Nos. 3088-3090 (3) 1.10 .45

US-Russian Track and Field Meet, Kiev.

Worker and Globe — A1530

Flag of North Viet Nam, Factory and Palm — A1531

Designs: No 3092, Heads of three races and torch. No. 3093, Woman with dove.

1965, Sept. 1

3091 A1530 6k dk purple & tan .30 .15
3092 A1530 6k brt bl, brn & red org .30 .15
3093 A1530 6k Prus green & tan .30 .15
Nos. 3091-3093 (3) .90 .45

Intl. Fed. of Trade Unions (#3091), Fed. of Democratic Youth (#3092), Democratic Women's Fed. (#3093), 20th annivs.

1965, Sept. 1 **Litho.** *Perf. 12*

3094 A1531 6k red, yel, brn & gray .50 .30

Republic of North Viet Nam, 20th anniv.

Scene from Film "Potemkin" A1532

Film Scenes: 6k, "Young Guard." 12k, "Ballad of a Soldier."

1965, Sept. 29 **Litho.** *Perf. $12^1/_2$x12*

3095 A1532 4k blue, blk & red .35 .25
3096 A1532 6k multicolored .35 .25
3097 A1532 12k multicolored .55 .25
Nos. 3095-3097 (3) 1.25 .75

Post Rider, 16th Century — A1533

History of the Post: No. 3099, Mail coach, 17th-18th centuries. 2k, Train, 19th century. 4k, Mail truck, 1920. 6k, Train, ship and plane. 12k, New Moscow post office, helicopter, automatic sorting and canceling machines. 16k, Lenin, airport and map of USSR.

1965 Photo. Unwmk. *Perf. 11½x12*

3098 A1533	1k org brn, dk gray & dk green	.15	.15
3099 A1533	1k gray, ocher & dk brown	.15	.15
3100 A1533	2k dl lil, brt bl & brn	.20	.15
3101 A1533	4k bis, rose lake & blk	.30	.15
3102 A1533	6k pale brn, Prus grn & black	.45	.15
3103 A1533	12k lt ultra, lt brn & blk	.65	.15
3104 A1533	16k gray, rose red & vio black	.75	.15
	Nos. 3098-3104 (7)	2.65	1.05

For overprint see No. 3175.

Atomic Icebreaker "Lenin" A1534

#3106, Icebreakers "Taimir" and "Vaigitch." 6k, Dickson Settlement. 10k, Sailing ships "Vostok" and "Mirni," Bellinghausen-Lazarev expedition & icebergs. 16k, Vostok South Pole station.

1965, Oct. 23 Litho. *Perf. 12*

Size: 37x25mm

3106 A1534	4k blue, black & org	.25	.25
3107 A1534	4k blue, black & org	.25	.25
a.	Pair #3106-3107	.60	.50
3108 A1534	6k sepia & dk violet	.65	.25

Size: 33x33mm

3109 A1534	10k red, black & buff	.80	.25

Size: 37x25mm

3110 A1534	16k vio blk & red brn	1.00	.25
	Nos. 3106-3110 (5)	2.95	1.25

Scientific conquests of the Arctic and Antarctic. No. 3107a has continuous design.

Souvenir Sheet

Basketball, Map of Europe and Flags A1535

1965, Oct. 29 Litho. *Imperf.*

3111 A1535 1r multicolored 4.00 1.00

14th European Basketball Championship, Moscow.

Timiryazev Agriculture Academy, Moscow — A1536

1965, Oct. 30 Photo. *Perf. 11*

3112 A1536 4k brt car, gray & vio bl .30 .15

Agriculture Academy, Moscow, cent.

Souvenir Sheet

Lenin A1537

Lithographed and Engraved

1965, Oct. 30 *Imperf.*

3113 A1537 10k sil, blk & dp org 2.00 .60

48th anniv. of the October Revolution.

Nicolas Poussin (1594-1665), French Painter — A1538

1965, Nov. 16 Photo. *Perf. 11½*

3114 A1538 4k gray blue, dk bl & dk brown .30 .15

Kremlin A1539

1965, Nov. 16 *Perf. 12x11½*

3115 A1539 4k black, ver & silver .30 .15

New Year 1966.

Mikhail Ivanovich Kalinin (1875-1946), USSR President (1923-1946) A1540

1965, Nov. 19 *Perf. 12½*

3116 A1540 4k dp claret & red .30 .15

Klyuchevskaya Sopka — A1541

Kamchatka Volcanoes: 12k, Karumski erupting, vert. 16k, Koryakski snowcovered.

1965, Nov. 30 Litho. *Perf. 12*

3117 A1541	4k multicolored	.20	.15
3118 A1541	12k multicolored	.45	.15
3119 A1541	16k multicolored	.75	.15
	Nos. 3117-3119 (3)	1.40	.45

October Subway Station, Moscow — A1542

Subway Stations: No. 3121, Lenin Avenue, Moscow. No. 3122, Moscow Gate, Leningrad. No. 3123, Bolshevik Factory, Kiev.

1965, Nov. 30 Engr.

3120 A1542	6k indigo	.30	.25
3121 A1542	6k brown	.30	.25
3122 A1542	6k gray brown	.30	.25
3123 A1542	6k slate green	.30	.25
	Nos. 3120-3123 (4)	1.20	1.00

Buzzard — A1543

Birds: 2k, Kestrel. 3k, Tawny eagle. 4k, Red kite. 10k, Peregrine falcon. 12k, Golden eagle, horiz. 14k, Lammergeier, horiz. 16k, Gyrfalcon.

1965 Photo. *Perf. 11½x12*

3124 A1543	1k gray grn & black	.15	.15
3125 A1543	2k pale brn & blk	.15	.15
3126 A1543	3k lt ol grn & black	.15	.15
3127 A1543	4k lt gray brn & blk	.30	.15
3128 A1543	10k lt vio brn & blk	.55	.15
3129 A1543	12k blue & black	.75	.20
3130 A1543	14k bluish gray & blk	.80	.25
3131 A1543	16k dl red brn & blk	.85	.35
	Nos. 3124-3131 (8)	3.70	
	Set value		1.25

Issued: 4k, 10k, Nov.; 1k, 2k, 12k, 14k, 12/24; 3k, 16k, 12/29.

Red Star Medal, War Scene and View of Kiev — A1544

Red Star Medal, War Scene and view of: No. 3133, Leningrad. No. 3134, Odessa. No. 3135, Moscow. No. 3136, Brest Litovsk. No.3137, Volgograd (Stalingrad). No. 3138, Sevastopol.

1965, Dec. *Perf. 11½*

Red, Gold and:

3132 A1544	10k brown	.45	.15
3133 A1544	10k dark blue	.45	.15
3134 A1544	10k Prussian blue	.45	.15
3135 A1544	10k dark violet	.45	.15
3136 A1544	10k dark brown	.45	.15
3137 A1544	10k black	.45	.15
3138 A1544	10k gray	.45	.15
	Nos. 3132-3138 (7)	3.15	1.05

Honoring the heroism of various cities during World War II.

Issued: #3136-3138, Dec. 30; others, Dec. 20.

Map and Flag of Yugoslavia, and National Assembly Building — A1545

1965, Dec. 30 Litho. *Perf. 12*

3139 A1545 6k vio blue, red & bis .40 .15

Republic of Yugoslavia, 20th anniv.

Collective Farm Watchman by S.V. Gerasimov A1547

Painting: 16k, "Major's Courtship" by Pavel Andreievitch Fedotov, horiz.

1965, Dec. 31 Engr.

3145 A1547	12k red & sepia	1.10	.25
3146 A1547	16k red & dark blue	1.40	.50

Painters: Gerasimov, 80th birth anniv; Pavel A. Fedotov (1815-52).

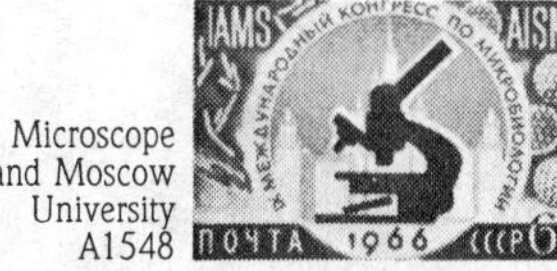

Microscope and Moscow University A1548

Congress Emblems: No. 3148, Turkeys, geese, chicken and globe. No. 3149, Crystals. No. 3150, Oceanographic instruments and ship. No. 3151, Mathematical symbols.

1966 Photo. *Perf. 11½*

3147 A1548	6k dull blue, blk & red	.25	.15
3148 A1548	6k gray, pur & black	.25	.15
3149 A1548	6k ol bister, blk & blue	.25	.15
3150 A1548	6k grnsh blue & blk	.25	.15
3151 A1548	6k dull yel, red brn & blk	.25	.15
	Nos. 3147-3151 (5)	1.25	.75

Intl. congresses to be held in Moscow: 9th Cong. of Microbiology (#3147); 13th Cong. on Poultry Raising (#3148); 7th Cong. on Crystallography (#3149); 2nd Intl. Cong. of Oceanography (#3150); Intl. Cong. of Mathematicians (#3151).

See Nos. 3309-3310.

Mailman and Milkmaid, 19th Century Figurines — A1549

1966, Jan. 28 Litho.

3152 A1549	6k shown	.25	.25
3153 A1549	10k Tea set	.35	.25

Bicentenary of Dimitrov Porcelain Works.

Romain Rolland (1866-1944), French Writer A1550

Portrait: No. 3155, Eugène Pottier (1816-1887), French poet and author of the "International."

1966 Photo. & Engr. *Perf. 11½*

3154 A1550	4k dk blue & brn org	.30	.15
3155 A1550	4k sl, red & dk red brn	.30	.15

The lack of a value for a listed item does not necessarily indicate rarity.

Horseback Rider, and Flags of Mongolia and USSR — A1551

1966, Jan. 31 Litho. *Perf. 12½x12*

3159 A1551 4k red, ultra & vio brn .35 .25

20th anniversary of the signing of the Mongolian-Soviet treaty of friendship and mutual assistance.

No. 2728 Overprinted in Silver

„ЛУНА-9" — НА ЛУНЕ!
3.2.1966

1966, Feb. 5 Photo. *Perf. 12*

3160 A1385 6k blk, lt blue & red 3.00 1.50

1st soft landing on the moon by Luna 9, Feb. 3, 1966.

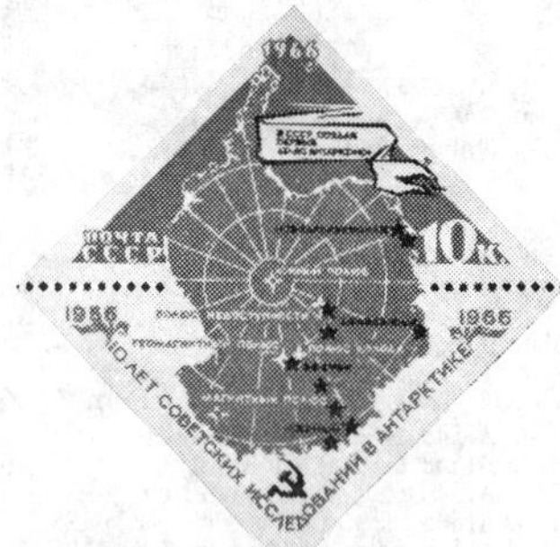

Map of Antarctica With Soviet Stations — A1552

Diesel Ship "Ob" and Emperor Penguins — A1553

#3164, Snocat tractors and aurora australis.

1966, Feb. 14 Photo. *Perf. 11*

3162 A1552 10k sky bl, sil & dk car .70 .25
3163 A1553 10k silver & dk car .70 .25
3164 A1553 10k dk car, sil & sky bl .70 .25
a. Strip of 3, #3162-3164 2.25 .75

10 years of Soviet explorations in Antarctica. No. 3162 has horizontal rows of perforation extending from either mid-side up to the map.

Lenin A1554

1966, Feb. 22 Photo. *Perf. 12x11½*

3165 A1554 10k grnsh black & gold .65 .25
3166 A1554 10k dk red & silver .65 .25

96th anniversary of the birth of Lenin.

N.Y. Iljin, Guardsman A1555

Kremlin Congress Hall A1556

Soviet Heroes: #3168, Lt. Gen. G. P. Kravchenko. #3169, Pvt. Anatoli Uglovsky.

1966 *Perf. 11½x12*

3167 A1555 4k dp org & vio black .30 .25
3168 A1555 4k grnsh blue & dk pur .30 .25
3169 A1555 4k green & brown .30 .25
Nos. 3167-3169 (3) .90 .75

1966, Feb. 28 Typo. *Perf. 12*

3172 A1556 4k gold, red & lt ultra .30 .15

23rd Communist Party Congress.

Hamlet and Queen from Film "Hamlet" A1557

Film Scene: 4k, Two soldiers from "The Quick and the Dead."

1966, Feb. 28 Litho.

3173 A1557 4k red, black & olive .35 .15
3174 A1557 10k ultra & black .35 .15

No. 3104 Overprinted

Учредительная конференция
Всесоюзного общества
филателистов. 1966

1966, Mar. 10 Photo. *Perf. 11½x12*

3175 A1533 16k multicolored 2.00 1.00

Constituent assembly of the All-Union Society of Philatelists, 1966.

Emblem and Skater — A1558

Designs: 6k, Emblem and ice hockey. 10k, Emblem and slalom skier.

1966, Mar. 11 *Perf. 11*

3176 A1558 4k ol, brt ultra & red .35 .15
3177 A1558 6k bluish lilac, red & dk brown .50 .15
3178 A1558 10k lt bl, red & dk brn .65 .15
Nos. 3176-3178 (3) 1.50 .45

Second Winter Spartacist Games, Sverdlovsk. The label-like upper halves of Nos. 3176-3178 are separated from the lower halves by a row of perforations.

Electric Locomotive A1559

Designs: 6k, Map of the Lenin Volga-Baltic Waterway, Admiralty, Leningrad, and Kremlin. 10k, Ship passing through lock in waterway, vert. 12k, M.S. Aleksander Pushkin. 16k, Passenger liner and globe.

1966 Litho. *Perf. 12½x12, 12x12½*

3179 A1559 4k multicolored .15 .15
3180 A1559 6k gray, ultra, red & black .15 .15
3181 A1559 10k Prus bl, gray brn & black .45 .15
3182 A1559 12k blue, ver & black .40 .15
3183 A1559 16k blue & multi .55 .20
Nos. 3179-3183 (5) 1.70 .80

Modern transportation.
Issued: #3179-3181, 8/6; #3182-3183, 3/25.

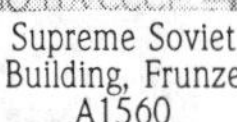

Supreme Soviet Building, Frunze A1560

Sergei M. Kirov A1561

1966, Mar. 25 Photo. *Perf. 12*

3184 A1560 4k deep red .35 .25

40th anniv. of the Kirghiz Republic.

1966 Engr. *Perf. 12*

Portraits: No. 3186, Grigori Ordzhonikidze. No. 3187, Ion Yakir.

3185 A1561 4k dk red brown .50 .25
3186 A1561 4k slate green .50 .25
3187 A1561 4k dark gray violet .50 .25
Nos. 3185-3187 (3) 1.50 .75

Kirov (1886-1934), revolutionist and Secretary of the Communist Party Central Committee; Ordzhonikidze (1886-1937), a political leader of the Red Army and government official; Yakir, military leader in October Revolution, 70th birth anniv.
Issued: #3185, 3/27; #3186, 6/22; #3187, 7/30.

Souvenir Sheet

Lenin — A1563

Embossed and Typographed

1966, Mar. 29 *Imperf.*

3188 A1563 50k red & silver 3.50 1.00

23rd Communist Party Congress.

Aleksandr E. Fersman (1883-1945), Mineralogist — A1564

Soviet Scientists: #3190, D. K. Zabolotny (1866-1929), microbiologist. #3191, M. A. Shatelen (1866-1957), physicist. #3191A, Otto Yulievich Schmidt (1891-1956), scientist and arctic explorer.

1966, Mar. 30 Litho. *Perf. 12½x12*

3189 A1564 4k vio blue & multi .50 .25
3190 A1564 4k red brown & multi .50 .25
3191 A1564 4k lilac & multi .50 .25
3191A A1564 4k Prus blue & brown .50 .25
Nos. 3189-3191A (4) 2.00 1.00

Luna 10 Automatic Moon Station — A1565

Overprinted in Red:

„Луна-10"—XXIII съезду КПСС

1966, Apr. 8 Typo. *Imperf.*

3192 A1565 10k gold, blk, brt bl & brt rose 1.75 .60

Launching of the 1st artificial moon satellite, Luna 10. The bright rose ink is fluorescent on Nos. 3192-3194.

Type A1565 Without Overprint

Design: 12k, Station on moon.

1966, Apr. 12 *Perf. 12*

3193 A1565 10k multicolored .40 .30
3194 A1565 12k multicolored .60 .30

Day of Space Research, Apr. 12, 1966.

Molniya 1 and Television Screens A1566

Ernst Thälmann A1567

1966, Apr. 12 Litho. *Perf. 12½*

3195 A1566 10k gold, blk, brt bl & red .50 .25

Launching of the communications satellite "Lightning 1," Apr. 23, 1965.

1966-67 Engr. *Perf. 12½x12*

Portraits: No. 3197, Wilhelm Pieck. No. 3198, Sun Yat-sen. No. 3199, Sen Katayama.

3196 A1567 6k rose claret .50 .25
3197 A1567 6k blue violet .50 .25
3198 A1567 6k reddish brown .50 .25

Photo.

3199 A1567 6k gray green ('67) .50 .25
Nos. 3196-3199 (4) 2.00 1.00

Thälmann (1886-1944), German Communist leader; Pieck (1876-1960), German Dem. Rep. Pres.; Sun Yat-sen (1866-1925), leader of the Chinese revolution; Katayama (1859-1933), founder of Social Democratic Party in Japan in 1901.
Issued: #3196, 4/16; #3197-3198, 6/22; #3199, 11/2/67.

Soldier, 1917, and Astronaut A1568

1966, Apr. 30 Litho. *Perf. 11½*

3200 A1568 4k brt rose & black .30 .15

15th Congress of the Young Communist League (Komsomol).

Ice Hockey Player A1569

1966, Apr. 30

3201 A1569 10k red, ultra, gold & black .40 .25

Soviet victory in the World Ice Hockey Championships. For souvenir sheet see No. 3232. For overprint see No. 3315.

Nicolai Kuznetsov — A1570

Heroes of Guerrilla Warfare during WWII (Gold Star of Hero of the Soviet Union and): No. 3203, Imant Sudmalis. No. 3204, Anya Morozova. No. 3205, Filipp Strelets. No. 3206, Tikhon Rumazhkov.

1966, May 9 Photo. *Perf. 12x12½*

3202	A1570	4k green & black	.20	.15
3203	A1570	4k ocher & black	.20	.15
3204	A1570	4k blue & black	.20	.15
3205	A1570	4k brt rose & black	.20	.15
3206	A1570	4k violet & black	.20	.15
		Nos. 3202-3206 (5)	1.00	.75

Peter I. Tchaikovsky A1571

4k, Moscow State Conservatory, Tchaikovsky monument. 16k, Tchaikovsky House, Klin.

1966, May 26 Typo. *Perf. 12½*

3207	A1571	4k red, yel & black	.25	.25
3208	A1571	6k yel, red & black	.40	.30
3209	A1571	16k red, bluish gray & black	.85	.35
		Nos. 3207-3209 (3)	1.50	.90

Third International Tchaikovsky Contest, Moscow, May 30-June 29.

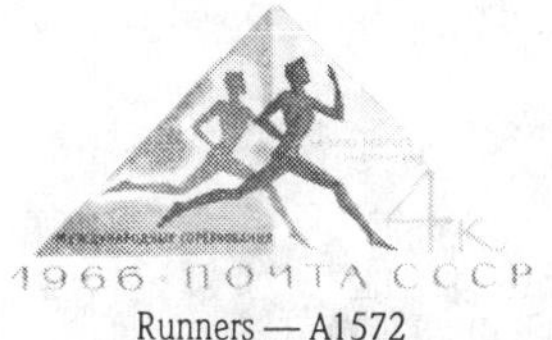

Runners — A1572

Designs: 6k, Weight lifters. 12k, Wrestlers.

1966, May 26 Photo. *Perf. 11x11½*

3210	A1572	4k emer, olive & brn	.20	.15
3211	A1572	6k org, black & lt brn	.30	.15
3212	A1572	12k grnsh bl, brn ol & black	.45	.15
		Nos. 3210-3212 (3)	.95	.45

No. 3210, Znamensky Brothers Intl. Track Competitions; No. 3211, Intl. Weightlifting Competitions; No. 3212, Intl. Wrestling Competitions for Ivan Poddubny Prize.

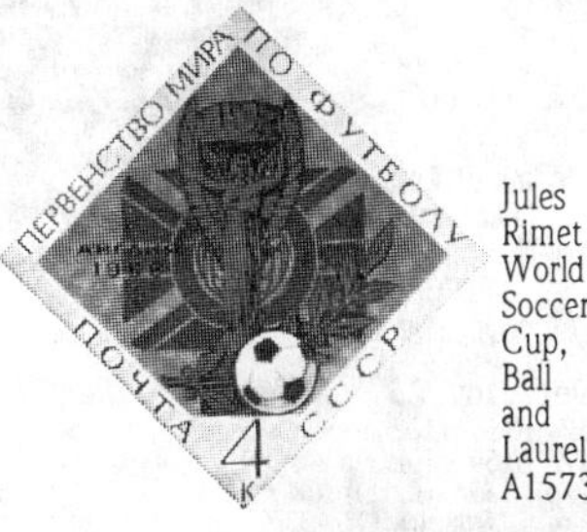

Jules Rimet World Soccer Cup, Ball and Laurel A1573

Chessboard, Gold Medal, Pawn and King — A1574

Designs: No. 3214, Soccer. 12k, Fencers. 16k, Fencer, mask, foil and laurel branch.

1966, May 31 Litho. *Perf. 11½*

3213	A1573	4k rose red, gold & black	.20	.15
3214	A1573	6k emer, tan, blk & red	.30	.15
3215	A1574	6k brn, gold, blk & white	.30	.15
3216	A1573	12k brt blue, ol & blk	.70	.15
3217	A1573	16k multicolored	.75	.15
		Nos. 3213-3217 (5)	2.25	
		Set value		.50

Nos. 3213-3214 for World Cup Soccer Championship, Wembley, England, July 11-30; No. 3215 the World Chess Title Match between Tigran Petrosian and Boris Spassky; Nos. 3216-3217 the World Fencing Championships. For souvenir sheet see No. 3232.

Sable and Lake Baikal, Map of Barguzin Game Reserve — A1575

Design: 6k, Map of Lake Baikal region and Game Reserve, brown bear on lake shore.

1966, June 25 Photo. *Perf. 12*

3218	A1575	4k steel blue & black	.35	.25
3219	A1575	6k rose lake & black	.35	.25

Barguzin Game Reserve, 50th anniv.

Pink Lotus — A1576

6k, Palms and cypresses. 12k, Victoria cruziana.

1966, June 30 *Perf. 11½*

3220	A1576	3k green, pink & yel	.15	.15
3221	A1576	6k grnsh bl, ol brn & dk brn	.30	.15
3222	A1576	12k multicolored	.50	.15
		Nos. 3220-3222 (3)	.95	.45

Sukhum Botanical Garden, 125th anniv.

Dogs Ugolek and Veterok after Space Flight — A1577

Designs: No. 3224, Diagram of Solar System, globe and medal of Venus 3 flight. No. 3225, Luna 10, earth and moon.

1966, July 15 *Perf. 12x11½*

3223	A1577	6k ocher, ind & org brn	.30	.15
3224	A1577	6k crim, blk & silver	.30	.15

Perf. 12x12½

3225	A1577	6k dk blue & bister brn	.30	.15
		Nos. 3223-3225 (3)	.90	.45

Soviet achievements in space.

Itkol Hotel, Mount Cheget and Map of USSR A1578

Arch of General Headquarters, Winter Palace and Alexander Column — A1579

Resort Areas: 4k, Ship on Volga River and Zhigul Mountain. 10k, Castle, Kislovodsk. 12k, Ismail Samani Mausoleum, Bukhara, Uzbek. 16k, Hotel Caucasus, Sochi.

Perf. 12½x12, 12½ (6k)

1966 Litho.

3226	A1578	1k multicolored	.15	.15
3227	A1578	4k multicolored	.15	.15
3228	A1579	6k multicolored	.15	.15
3229	A1578	10k multicolored	.25	.15
3230	A1578	12k multicolored	.40	.15
3231	A1578	16k multicolored	.55	.15
		Nos. 3226-3231 (6)	1.65	.90

Issue dates: 10k, Sept. 14; others, July 20.

Souvenir Sheet

A1580

1966, July 26 Litho. *Perf. 11½*

3232	A1580	Sheet of 4	10.00	1.75
a.		10k Fencers	2.00	.40
b.		10k Chess	2.00	.40
c.		10k Soccer cup	2.00	.40
d.		10k Ice hockey	2.00	.40

World fencing, chess, soccer and ice hockey championships.
See Nos. 3201, 3213-3217.

Congress Emblem, Congress Palace and Kremlin Tower — A1581

1966, Aug. 6 Photo. *Perf. 11½x12*

3233 A1581 4k brown & yellow .30 .15

Consumers' Cooperative Societies, 7th Cong.

Dove, Crane, Russian and Japanese Flags A1582

1966, Aug. 9 *Perf. 12½x11½*

3234 A1582 6k gray & red .40 .25

Soviet-Japanese friendship, and 2nd meeting of Russian and Japanese delegates at Khabarovsk.

"Knight Fighting with Tiger" by Rustaveli — A1583

Designs: 4k, Shota Rustaveli, bas-relief. 6k, "Avtandil at a Mountain Spring." 50k, Shota Rustaveli Monument and design of 3k stamp.

Perf. 11½x12½

1966, Aug. 31 Engr.

3235	A1583	3k black, *olive green*	.25	.15
3236	A1583	4k brown, *yellow*	.25	.15
3237	A1583	6k bluish black, *lt ultra*	.35	.15
		Nos. 3235-3237 (3)	.85	.45

Souvenir Sheet

Imperf

Engraved and Photogravure

3238 A1583 50k slate green & bis 3.50 1.25

800th anniv. of the birth of Shota Rustaveli, Georgian poet, author of "The Knight in the Tiger's Skin." No. 3238 contains one 32x49mm stamp; dark green margin with design of 6k stamp.

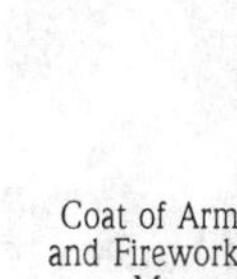

Coat of Arms and Fireworks over Moscow A1584

Lithographed (Lacquered)

1966, Sept. 14 *Perf. 11½*

3239 A1584 4k multicolored .30 .15

49th anniversary of October Revolution.

Grayling A1585

Designs (Fish and part of design of 6k stamp): 4k, Sturgeon. 6k, Trawler, net and map of Lake Baikal, vert. 10k, Two Baikal cisco. 12k, Two Baikal whitefish.

1966, Sept. 25 Photo. & Engr.

3240	A1585	2k multicolored	.15	.15
3241	A1585	4k multicolored	.15	.15
3242	A1585	6k multicolored	.30	.15
3243	A1585	10k multicolored	.60	.15
3244	A1585	12k gray, dk grn & red brown	.70	.15
		Nos. 3240-3244 (5)	1.90	.75

Fish resources of Lake Baikal.

Map of USSR and Symbols of Transportation and Communication — A1586

Designs (map of USSR and): No. 3246, Technological education. No. 3247, Agriculture and mining. No. 3248, Increased productivity through five-year plan. No. 3249, Technology and inventions.

1966, Sept. 29 Photo. *Perf. 11½x12*

3245	A1586	4k ultra & silver	.40	.15
3246	A1586	4k car & silver	.40	.15
3247	A1586	4k red brown & silver	.40	.15
3248	A1586	4k red & silver	.40	.15
3249	A1586	4k dp green & silver	.40	.15
		Nos. 3245-3249 (5)	2.00	.75

23rd Communist Party Congress decisions.

Government House, Kishinev, and Moldavian Flag A1587

1966, Oct. 8 Litho. ***Perf. 12½x12***

3250 A1587 4k multicolored .50 .30

500th anniversary of Kishinev.

Symbolic Water Cycle — A1588

1966, Oct. 12 ***Perf. 11½***

3251 A1588 6k multicolored .35 .15

Hydrological Decade (UNESCO), 1965-1974.

Nikitin Monument in Kalinin, Ship's Prow and Map — A1589

1966, Oct. 12 Photo.

3252 A1589 4k multicolored .40 .25

Afanasii Nikitin's trip to India, 500th anniv.

Scene from Opera "Nargiz" by M. Magomayev A1590

#3254, Scene from opera "Kerogli" by Y. Gadjubekov (knight on horseback and armed men).

1966, Oct. 12

3253 A1590 4k black & ocher .30 .15
3254 A1590 4k blk & blue green .30 .15
a. Pair, #3253-3254 .60 .15

Azerbaijan opera. Printed in checkerboard arrangement.

Fighters A1591

1966, Oct. 26

3255 A1591 6k red, blk & ol bister .40 .15

30th anniversary of Spanish Civil War.

National Militia A1592

Protest Rally A1592a

1966, Oct. 26 Litho. ***Perf. 12x12½***

3256 A1592 4k red & dark brown .35 .15

25th anniv. of the National Militia.

1966, Oct. 26 ***Perf. 12***

3256A A1592a 6k yel, black & red .40 .25

"Hands off Viet Nam!"

Soft Landing on Moon, Luna 9 A1593

Symbols of Agriculture and Chemistry A1594

Designs: 1k, Congress Palace, Moscow, and map of Russia. 3k, Boy, girl and Lenin banner. 4k, Flag. 6k, Plane and Ostankino Television Tower. 10k, Soldier and Soviet star. 12k, Steel worker. 16k, "Peace," woman with dove. 20k, Demonstrators in Red Square, flags, carnation and globe. 50k, Newspaper, plane, train and Communications Ministry. 1r, Lenin and industrial symbols.

1966 Litho. ***Perf. 12***

Inscribed "1966"

3257 A1593 1k dk red brown .15 .15
3258 A1593 2k violet .15 .15
3259 A1593 3k red lilac .15 .15
3260 A1593 4k bright red .15 .15
3261 A1593 6k ultra .20 .15
3262 A1593 10k olive .35 .15
3263 A1593 12k red brown .65 .15
3264 A1593 16k violet blue .70 .15

Perf. 11½

Photo.

3265 A1594 20k bis, red & dk bl 1.10 .15
3266 A1594 30k dp grn & green 1.40 .30
3267 A1594 50k blue & violet bl 3.00 .35
3268 A1594 1r black & red 4.75 .55
Nos. 3257-3268 (12) 12.75
Set value 1.75

No. 3260 was issued on fluorescent paper in 1969.

See Nos. 3470-3481.

Ostankino Television Tower, Molniya 1 Satellite and Kremlin — A1595

1966, Nov. 19 Litho. ***Perf. 12***

3273 A1595 4k multicolored .35 .15

New Year, 1967, the 50th anniversary of the October Revolution.

Diagram of Luna 9 Flight — A1596

Arms of Russia and Pennant Sent to Moon — A1597

#3276, Luna 9 & photograph of moonscape.

1966, Nov. 25 Typo. ***Perf. 12***

3274 A1596 10k black & silver .50 .25
3275 A1597 10k red & silver .50 .25
3276 A1596 10k black & silver .50 .25
a. Strip of 3, #3274-3276 1.50 .75

Soft landing on the moon by Luna 9, Jan. 31, 1966, and the television program of moon pictures on Feb. 2.

Battle of Moscow, 1941 — A1598

Details from "Defense of Moscow" Medal and Golden Star Medal — A1599

25th anniv. of Battle of Moscow: 10k, Sun rising over Kremlin. Ostankino Tower, chemical plant and rockets.

Perf. 12, 11½ (A1599)

1966, Dec. 1 Photo.

3277 A1598 4k red brown .20 .15
3278 A1599 6k bister & brown .45 .15
3279 A1598 10k dp bister & yellow .60 .15
Nos. 3277-3279 (3) 1.25 .45

Cervantes and Don Quixote A1600

1966, Dec. 15 Photo. ***Perf. 11½***

3280 A1600 6k gray & brown .30 .15

Miguel Cervantes Saavedra (1547-1616), Spanish writer.

Bering's Ship and Map of Voyage to Commander Islands — A1601

Far Eastern Territories: 2k, Medny Island and map. 4k, Petropavlosk-Kamchatski Harbor. 6k, Geyser, Kamchatka, vert. 10k, Avachinskaya Bay, Kamchatka. 12k, Fur seals, Bering Island. 16k, Guillemots in bird sanctuary, Kuril Islands.

1966, Dec. 25 Litho. ***Perf. 12***

3281 A1601 1k bister & multi .15 .15
3282 A1601 2k bister & multi .15 .15
3283 A1601 4k dp blue & multi .30 .15
3284 A1601 6k multicolored .40 .15
3285 A1601 10k dp blue & multi .60 .15
3286 A1601 12k olive & multi 1.00 .15
3287 A1601 16k lt blue & multi 1.75 .15
Nos. 3281-3287 (7) 4.35
Set value .75

Communications Satellite, Molniya 1 A1602

Design: No. 3289, Luna 11 moon probe, moon, earth and Soviet emblem.

1966, Dec. 29 Photo. ***Perf. 12x11½***

3288 A1602 6k blk, vio bl & brt rose .40 .15
3289 A1602 6k black & brt rose .40 .15
Set value .20

Space explorations. The bright rose is fluorescent.

Golden Stag, Scythia, 6th Century B.C. — A1603

Treasures from the Hermitage, Leningrad: 6k, Silver jug, Persia, 5th Century A.D. 10k, Statue of Voltaire by Jean Antoine Houdon. 12k, Malachite vase, Ural, 1840. 16k, "The Lute Player," by Michelangelo de Caravaggio. (6k, 10k, 12k are vertical).

1966, Dec. 29 Engr. ***Perf. 12***

3290 A1603 4k yellow & black .20 .15
3291 A1603 6k gray & black .30 .15
3292 A1603 10k dull vio & black .50 .20
3293 A1603 12k emer & black .75 .30
3294 A1603 16k ocher & black .85 .35
Nos. 3290-3294 (5) 2.60 1.15

Sea Water Converter and Pavilion at EXPO '67 — A1604

Designs (Pavilion and): 6k, Splitting atom, vert. 10k, "Proton" space station. 30k, Soviet pavilion.

1967, Jan. 25 Litho. ***Perf. 12***

3295 A1604 4k multicolored .25 .15
3296 A1604 6k multicolored .25 .15
3297 A1604 10k multicolored .30 .15
Nos. 3295-3297 (3) .80 .45

Souvenir Sheet

3298 A1604 30k multicolored 3.00 1.25

EXPO '67, Intl. Exhib., Montreal, 4/28-10/27.

1st Lieut. B. I. Sizov A1605

Design: No. 3300, Sailor V. V. Khodyrev.

1967, Feb. 16 Photo. ***Perf. 12x11½***

3299 A1605 4k dull yel & ocher .25 .25
3300 A1605 4k gray & dk gray .25 .25

Heroes of World War II.

Woman's Head and Pavlov Shawl — A1606

1967, Feb. 16 *Perf. 11*

3301 A1606 4k violet, red & green .30 .15

International Woman's Day, Mar. 8.

Movie Camera and Film — A1607

1967, Feb. 16 Photo. *Perf. 11½*

3302 A1607 6k multicolored .40 .25

5th Intl. Film Festival, Moscow, July 5-20.

Trawler Fish Factory and Fish — A1608

Designs: No. 3304, Refrigerationship. No. 3305, Crab canning ship. No. 3306, Fishing trawler. No. 3307, Black Sea seiner.

1967, Feb. 28 Litho. *Perf. 12x11½*

Ships in Black and Red

3303 A1608 6k blue & gray .40 .25
3304 A1608 6k blue & gray .40 .25
3305 A1608 6k blue & gray .40 .25
3306 A1608 6k blue & gray .40 .25
3307 A1608 6k blue & gray .40 .25
a. Vert. strip of 5, #3303-3307 2.00 1.25

Soviet fishing industry.

Newspaper Forming Hammer and Sickle, Red Flag — A1609

1967, Mar. 13 Litho. *Perf. 12x12½*

3308 A1609 4k cl brn, red, yel & brn .30 .15

50th anniversary of newspaper Izvestia.

Congress Type of 1966

Congress Emblems and: No. 3309, Moscow State University, construction site and star. No. 3310, Pile driver, mining excavator, crossed hammers, globe and "V."

1967, Mar. 10 Photo. *Perf. 11½*

3309 A1548 6k ultra, brt blue & blk .30 .15
3310 A1548 6k blk, org red & blue .30 .15

Intl. congresses to be held in Moscow: 7th General Assembly Session of the Intl. Standards Association (#3309); 5th Intl. Mining Cong. (#3310).

International Tourist Year Emblem and Travel Symbols — A1610

1967, Mar. 10 *Perf. 11*

3314 A1610 4k black, sky bl & silver .30 .15

International Tourist Year, 1967.

No. 3201 Overprinted **Вена - 1967**

1967, Mar. 29 Litho. *Perf. 11½*

3315 A1569 10k multicolored 1.50 .75

Victory of the Soviet team in the Ice Hockey Championships, Vienna, Mar. 18-29. Overprint reads: "Vienna-1967."

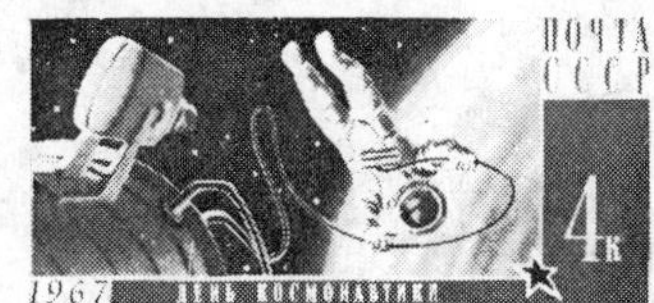

Space Walk — A1611

Designs: 10k, Rocket launching from satellite. 16k, Spaceship over moon, and earth.

1967, Mar. 30 Litho. *Perf. 12*

3316 A1611 4k bister & multi .25 .15
3317 A1611 10k black & multi .70 .15
3318 A1611 16k lilac & multi 1.00 .30
Nos. 3316-3318 (3) 1.95 .60

National Cosmonauts' Day.

Lenin as Student, by V. Tsigal A1612

Sculptures of Lenin: 3k, Monument at Ulyanovsk by M. Manizer. 4k, Lenin in Razliv, by V. Pinchuk, horiz. 6k, Head, by G. Neroda. 10k, Lenin as Leader, statue, by N. Andreyev.

1967 Photo. *Perf. 12x11½, 11½x12*

3319 A1612 2k ol grn, sepia & buff .15 .15
3320 A1612 3k maroon & brown .20 .15
3321 A1612 4k ol black & gold .30 .15
3322 A1612 6k dk bl, silver & blk .40 .15
3323 A1612 10k sil, gray bl & blk .75 .15
3323A A1612 10k gold, gray & black .75 .15
Nos. 3319-3323A (6) 2.55
Set value .40

97th anniversary of the birth of Lenin. Issued: No. 3323A, Oct. 25. Others, Apr. 22.

Lt. M. S. Kharchenko and Battle Scenes A1613

Designs: No. 3325, Maj. Gen. S. V. Rudnev. No. 3326, M. Shmyrev.

1967, Apr. 24 *Perf. 12x11½*

3324 A1613 4k brt purple & ol bis .25 .15
3325 A1613 4k ultra & ol bister .25 .15
3326 A1613 4k org brn & ol bister .25 .15
Nos. 3324-3326 (3) .75 .45

Partisan heroes of WWII.

Marshal S. S. Biryuzov, Hero of the Soviet Union — A1614

1967, May 9 Photo. *Perf. 12*

3327 A1614 4k ocher & slate green .40 .40

Driver Crossing Lake Ladoga A1615

1967, May 9 *Perf. 11½*

3328 A1615 4k plum & blue gray .30 .15

25th anniversary of siege of Leningrad.

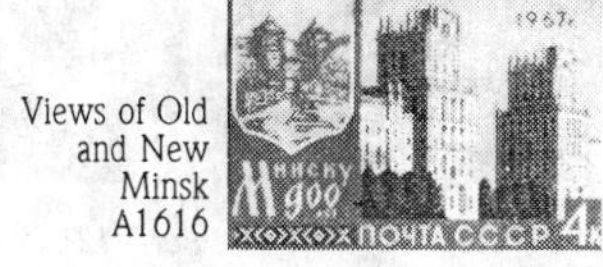

Views of Old and New Minsk A1616

1967, May 9

3329 A1616 4k slate green & black .35 .15

900th anniversary of Minsk.

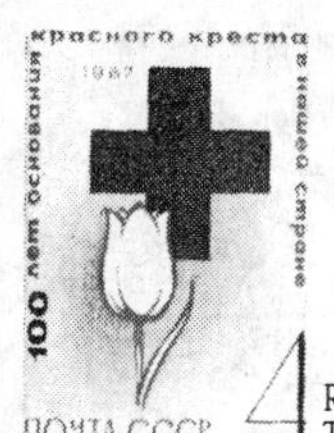

Red Cross and Tulip — A1617

1967, May 15 *Perf. 12*

3330 A1617 4k yel brown & red .30 .15

Centenary of the Russian Red Cross.

Stamps of 1918 and 1967 A1618

1967 Photo. *Perf. 11½*

3331 A1618 20k blue & black .90 .30
a. Souv. sheet of 2, imperf. 4.00 1.25

All-Union Philatelic Exhibition "50 Years of the Great October," Moscow, Oct. 1-10. Se-tenant with label showing exhibition emblem.

Issue dates: 20k, May 25. Sheet, Oct. 1.

No. 3331 was re-issued Oct. 3 with "Oct. 1-10" printed in blue on the label. Value $1.

Komsomolsk-on-Amur and Map of Amur River — A1619

1967, June 12 *Perf. 12x12½*

3332 A1619 4k red & brown .40 .15

35th anniv. of the Soviet youth town, Komsomolsk-on-Amur. Printed with label showing boy and girl of Young Communist League and tents.

Souvenir Sheet

Sputnik Orbiting Earth — A1620

1967, June 24 Litho. *Perf. 13x12*

3333 A1620 30k black & multi 3.50 1.75

10th anniv. of the launching of Sputnik 1, the 1st artificial satellite, Oct. 4, 1957.

Motorcyclist A1621

Photogravure and Engraved

1967, June 24 *Perf. 12x11½*

3334 A1621 10k multicolored .40 .15

Intl. Motor Rally, Moscow, July 19.

G. D. Gai (1887-1937), Corps Commander of the First Cavalry, 1920 — A1622

1967, June 30 Photo. *Perf. 12*

3335 A1622 4k red & black .30 .15

Children's Games Emblem and Trophy A1623

1967, July 8 *Perf. 11½*

3336 A1623 4k silver, red & black .30 .15

10th National Athletic Games of School Children, Leningrad, July, 1967.

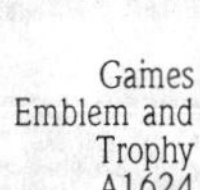

Games Emblem and Trophy A1624

Designs: No. 3338, Cup and dancer. No. 3339, Cup and bicyclists. No. 3340, Cup and diver.

1967, July 20

3337 A1624 4k silver, red & black .20 .15
3338 A1624 4k silver, red & black .20 .15
a. Pair, #3337-3338 .40 .15
3339 A1624 4k silver, red & black .20 .15
3340 A1624 4k silver, red & black .20 .15
a. Pair, #3339-3340 .40 .15
Set value .30

4th Natl. Spartacist Games, & USSR 50th anniv. Se-tenant in checkerboard arrangement.

V. G. Klochkov (1911-41), Hero of the Soviet Union A1625

1967, July 20 *Perf. 12½x12*

3341 A1625 4k red & black .40 .25

Alternating label shows citation.

Soviet Flag, Arms and Moscow Views
A1626

Arms of USSR and Laurel — A1627

АРМЯНСКАЯ ССР
ՀԱՅԿԱԿԱՆ ՍՍՀ

#3343

АЗЕРБАЙДЖАНСКАЯ ССР
АЗӘРБАЈҸАН ССР

#3344

БЕЛОРУССКАЯ ССР
БЕЛАРУСКАЯ ССР

#3345

ГРУЗИНСКАЯ ССР
ᲡᲐᲥᲐᲠᲗᲕᲔᲚᲝᲡ ᲡᲡᲠ

#3347

КИРГИЗСКАЯ ССР
КЫРГЫЗ ССР

#3349

МОЛДАВСКАЯ ССР
РСС МОЛДОВЕНЯСКЭ

#3352

ТАДЖИКСКАЯ ССР
РСС ТОҶИКИСТОН

#3353

ТУРКМЕНСКАЯ ССР
ТҮРКМЕНИСТАН ССР

#3354

УКРАИНСКАЯ ССР
УКРАЇНСЬКА РСР

#3355

УЗБЕКСКАЯ ССР
ЎЗБЕКИСТОН ССР

#3356

Flag, Crest and Capital of Republic.

1967, Aug. 4 Litho. *Perf. 12½x12*

3342 A1626 4k shown .40 .15
3343 A1626 4k Armenia .40 .15
3344 A1626 4k Azerbaijan .40 .15
3345 A1626 4k Byelorussia .40 .15
3346 A1626 4k Estonia .40 .15
3347 A1626 4k Georgia .40 .15
3348 A1626 4k Kazakhstan .40 .15
3349 A1626 4k Kirghizia .40 .15
3350 A1626 4k Latvia .40 .15
3351 A1626 4k Lithuania .40 .15
3352 A1626 4k Moldavia .40 .15
3353 A1626 4k Tadzhikistan .40 .15
3354 A1626 4k Turkmenistan .40 .15
3355 A1626 4k Ukraine .40 .15
3356 A1626 4k Uzbekistan .40 .15
3357 A1627 4k red, gold & black .40 .15
Nos. 3342-3357 (16) 6.40
Set value 1.50

50th anniversary of October Revolution.

Communication Symbols
A1628

1967, Aug. 16 Photo. *Perf. 12*

3358 A1628 4k crimson & silver 1.50 .30

Development of communications in USSR.

Flying Crane, Dove and Anniversary Emblem
A1629

1967, Aug. 20 *Perf. 12½x12*

3359 A1629 16k silver, red & blk .50 .30

Russo-Japanese Friendship Meeting, held at Khabarovsk. Emblem is for 50th anniv. of October Revolution.

Karl Marx and Title Page of "Das Kapital" — A1630

1967, Aug. 22 Engr. *Perf. 12½x12*

3360 A1630 4k sepia & dk red .40 .30

Centenary of the publication of "Das Kapital" by Karl Marx.

Russian Checkers Players — A1631

Design: 6k, Woman gymnast.

Photogravure and Engraved

1967, Sept. 9 *Perf. 12x11½*

3361 A1631 1k lt brn, dp brn & slate .30 .15
3362 A1631 6k ol bister & maroon .30 .15

World Championship of Russian Checkers (Shashki) at Moscow, and World Championship of Rhythmic Gymnastics.

Javelin — A1632

1967, Sept. 9 Engr. *Perf. 12x12½*

3363 A1632 2k shown .25 .15
3364 A1632 3k Running .25 .15
3365 A1632 4k Jumping .25 .15
Nos. 3363-3365 (3) .75
Set value .35

Europa Cup Championships, Kiev, Sept. 15-17.

Ice Skating and Olympic Emblem
A1633

Designs: 3k, Ski jump. 4k, Emblem of Winter Olympics, vert. 10k, Ice hockey. 12k, Long-distance skiing.

Photogravure and Engraved

1967, Sept. 20 *Perf. 11½*

3366 A1633 2k gray, black & blue .15 .15
3367 A1633 3k bis, ocher, blk & green .15 .15
3368 A1633 4k gray, bl, red & blk .20 .15
3369 A1633 10k bis, brn, bl & blk .50 .15
3370 A1633 12k gray, blk, lilac & green .65 .15
Nos. 3366-3370 (5) 1.65
Set value .60

10th Winter Olympic Games, Grenoble, France, Feb. 6-18, 1968.

Silver Fox
A1634

Young Guards Memorial
A1635

Fur-bearing Animals: 2k, Arctic blue fox, horiz. 6k, Red fox, horiz. 10k, Muskrat, horiz. 12k, Ermine. 16k, Sable. 20k, Mink, horiz.

1967, Sept. 20 Photo.

3371 A1634 2k brn, blk & gray blue .20 .15
3372 A1634 4k tan, dk brn & gray blue .30 .15
3373 A1634 6k gray grn, ocher & black .45 .15
3374 A1634 10k yel grn, dk brn & ocher .75 .15
3375 A1634 12k lilac, blk & bis .80 .15
3376 A1634 16k org, brn & black .90 .15
3377 A1634 20k gray blue, blk & dk brown 1.10 .30
Nos. 3371-3377 (7) 4.50
Set value .85

International Fur Auctions in Leningrad.

1967, Sept. 23

3378 A1635 4k magenta, org & blk .30 .15

25th anniv. of the fight of the Young Guards at Krasnodon against the Germans.

Map of Cedar Valley Reservation and Snow Leopard — A1636

1967, Oct. 14 *Perf. 12*

3379 A1636 10k ol bister & black .40 .15

Far Eastern Cedar Valley Reservation.

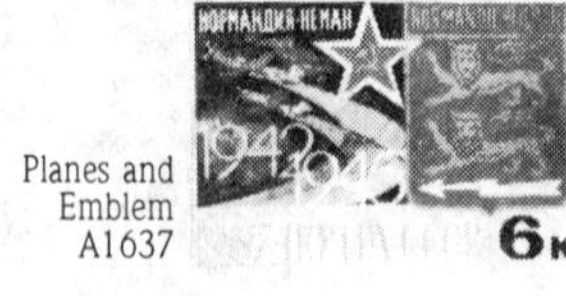

Planes and Emblem
A1637

1967, Oct. 14 *Perf. 11½*

3380 A1637 6k dp blue, red & gold .30 .15

French Normandy-Neman aviators, who fought on the Russian Front, 25th anniv.

Militiaman and Soviet Emblem
A1638

1967, Oct. 14 *Perf. 12½x12*

3381 A1638 4k ver & ultra .30 .15

50th anniversary of the Soviet Militia.

Space Station Orbiting Moon — A1639

Science Fiction: 6k, Explorers on the moon, horiz. 10k, Rocket flying to the stars. 12k, Landscape on Red Planet, horiz. 16k, Satellites from outer space.

1967 Litho. *Perf. 12x12½, 12½x12*

3382 A1639 4k multicolored .15 .15
3383 A1639 6k multicolored .35 .15
3384 A1639 10k multicolored .50 .15
3385 A1639 12k multicolored .65 .15
3386 A1639 16k multicolored .85 .20
Nos. 3382-3386 (5) 2.50
Set value .60

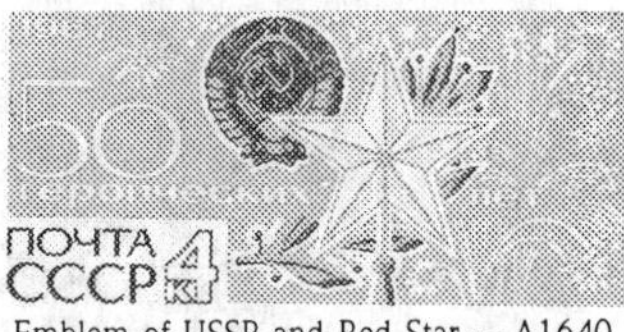

Emblem of USSR and Red Star — A1640

Lenin Addressing 2nd Congress of Soviets, by V. A. Serov — A1641

Builders of Communism, by L. M. Merpert and Y. N. Skripkov — A1641a

Paintings: #3389, Lenin pointing to Map, by L. A. Schmatjko, 1957. #3390, The First Cavalry Army, by M. B. Grekov, 1924. #3391, Working Students on the March, by B. V. Yoganson, 1928. #3392, Russian Friendship for the World, by S. M. Karpov, 1924. #3393, Five-Year Plan Morning, by Y. D. Romas, 1934. #3394, Farmers' Holiday, by S. V. Gerasimov, 1937. #3395, Victory in the Great Patriotic War, by Y. K. Korolev, 1965.

Lithographed and Embossed

1967, Oct. 25 *Perf. 11½*

3387 A1640 4k gold, yel, red & dk brown .20 .15
3388 A1641 4k gold & multi .20 .15
3389 A1641 4k gold & multi .20 .15
3390 A1641 4k gold & multi .20 .15
3391 A1641 4k gold & multi .20 .15
3392 A1641 4k gold & multi .20 .15
3393 A1641 4k gold & multi .20 .15
3394 A1641 4k gold & multi .20 .15
3395 A1641 4k gold & multi .20 .15
3396 A1641a 4k gold & multi .20 .15
a. Souvenir sheet of 2 3.00 1.00
Nos. 3387-3396 (10) 2.00
Set value .75

50th anniversary of October Revolution.

No. 3396a contains two 40k imperf. stamps similar to Nos. 3388 and 3396. Issued Nov. 5.

Souvenir Sheet

Hammer, Sickle and Sputnik — A1642

1967, Nov. 5 Engr. ***Perf. 12½x12***
3397 A1642 1r lake 5.00 2.00

50th anniv. of the October Revolution. Margin contains "50" as a watermark.

Ostankino Television Tower — A1643

1967, Nov. 5 Litho. ***Perf. 11½***
3398 A1643 16k gray, org & black .60 .25

Jurmala Resort and Hepatica A1644

Health Resorts of the Baltic Region: 6k, Narva-Joesuu and Labrador tea. 10k, Druskininkai and cranberry blossoms. 12k, Zelenogradsk and Scotch heather, vert. 16k, Svetlogorsk and club moss, vert.

Perf. 12½x12, 12x12½
1967, Nov. 30 Litho.
Flowers in Natural Colors
3399 A1644 4k blue & black .20 .15
3400 A1644 6k ocher & black .45 .15
3401 A1644 10k green & black .50 .15
3402 A1644 12k gray olive & blk .55 .15
3403 A1644 16k brown & black .75 .15
Nos. 3399-3403 (5) 2.45 .75

Emergency Commission Emblem — A1645

1967, Dec. 11 Photo. ***Perf. 11½***
3404 A1645 4k ultra & red .30 .25

50th anniversary of the All-Russia Emergency Commission (later the State Security Commission).

Hotel Russia and Kremlin A1646

1967, Dec. 14
3405 A1646 4k silver, dk brn & brt pink .30 .15

New Year 1968. The pink is fluorescent.

Soldiers, Sailors, Congress Building, Kharkov, and Monument to the Men of Arsenal — A1647

Designs: 6k, Hammer and sickle and scenes from industry and agriculture. 10k, Ukrainians offering bread and salt, monument of the Unknown Soldier, Kiev, and Lenin monument in Zaporozhye.

1967, Dec. 20 Litho. ***Perf. 12½***
3406 A1647 4k multicolored .30 .15
3407 A1647 6k multicolored .30 .15
3408 A1647 10k multicolored .35 .15
Nos. 3406-3408 (3) .95 .45

50th anniv. of the Ukrainian SSR.

Three Kremlin Towers A1648

Kremlin: 6k, Cathedral of the Annunciation, horiz. 10k, Konstantin and Elena, Nabatnaya and Spasski towers. 12k, Ivan the Great bell tower. 16k, Kutafya and Troitskaya towers.

Engraved and Photogravure
Perf. 12x11½, 11½x12
1967, Dec. 25
3409 A1648 4k dk brn & claret .15 .15
3410 A1648 6k dk brn, yel & grn .20 .15
3411 A1648 10k maroon & slate .55 .15
3412 A1648 12k sl green, yel & vio .60 .15
3413 A1648 16k brn, pink & red .80 .15
Nos. 3409-3413 (5) 2.30 .75

Coat of Arms, Lenin's Tomb and Rockets A1649

Designs: No. 3415, Agricultural Progress: Wheat, reapers and silo. No. 3416, Industrial Progress: Computer tape, atom symbol, cogwheel and factories. No. 3417, Scientific Progress: Radar, microscope, university buildings. No. 3418, Communications progress: Ostankino TV tower, railroad bridge, steamer and Aeroflot emblem, vert.

1967, Dec. 25 Engr. ***Perf. 12½***
3414 A1649 4k maroon .20 .15
3415 A1649 4k green .20 .15
3416 A1649 4k red brown .20 .15
3417 A1649 4k violet blue .20 .15
3418 A1649 4k dark blue .20 .15
Nos. 3414-3418 (5) 1.00 .75

Material and technical basis of Russian Communism.

Monument to the Unknown Soldier, Moscow — A1650

1967, Dec. 25
3419 A1650 4k carmine .35 .25

Dedication of the Monument of the Unknown Soldier of WWII in the Kremlin Wall.

Seascape by Ivan Aivazovsky — A1651

Paintings: 3k, Interrogation of Communists by B. V. Yoganson, 1933. #3422, The Lacemaker, by V. A. Tropinin, 1823, vert. #3423, Bread-makers, by T. M. Yablonskaya, 1949. #3424, Alexander Nevsky, by P. D. Korin, 1942-43, vert. #3425, The Boyar Morozov Going into Exile by V. I. Surikov, 1887. #3426, The Swan Maiden, by M. A. Vrubel, 1900, vert. #3427, The Arrest of a Propagandist by Ilya E. Repin, 1878. 16k, Moscow Suburb in February by G. G. Nissky, 1957.

Perf. 12½x12, 12x12½, 12, 11½
1967, Dec. 29 Litho.
Size: 47x33mm, 33x47mm
3420 A1651 3k multicolored .15 .15
3421 A1651 4k multicolored .15 .15
3422 A1651 4k multicolored .15 .15
Size: 60x35mm, 35x60mm
3423 A1651 6k multicolored .15 .15
3424 A1651 6k multicolored .15 .15
3425 A1651 6k multicolored .15 .15
Size: 47x33mm, 33x47mm
3426 A1651 10k multicolored .35 .15
3427 A1651 10k multicolored .35 .15
3428 A1651 16k multicolored .45 .20
Nos. 3420-3428 (9) 2.05
Set value .80

Tretiakov Art Gallery, Moscow.

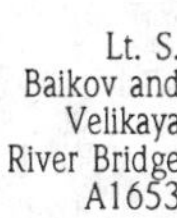

Globe, Wheel and Workers of the World — A1652

1968, Jan. 18 Photo. ***Perf. 12***
3429 A1652 6k ver & green .35 .15

14th Trade Union Congress.

Lt. S. Baikov and Velikaya River Bridge A1653

Heroes of WWII (War Memorial and): #3431. Lt. A. Pokalchuk. #3432, P. Gutchenko.

1968, Jan. 20 ***Perf. 12½x12***
3430 A1653 4k blue gray & black .30 .15
3431 A1653 4k rose & black .30 .15
3432 A1653 4k gray green & black .30 .15
Nos. 3430-3432 (3) .90 .45

Thoroughbred and Horse Race — A1654

Horses: 6k, Arab mare and dressage, vert. 10k, Orlovski trotters. 12k, Altekin horse performing, vert. 16k, Donskay race horse.

1968, Jan. 23 ***Perf. 11½***
3433 A1654 4k ultra, blk & red lil .15 .15
3434 A1654 6k crim, blk & ultra .25 .15
3435 A1654 10k grnsh blue, blk & orange .40 .15
3436 A1654 12k org brn, black & apple green .55 .15
3437 A1654 16k ol grn, blk & red .70 .15
Nos. 3433-3437 (5) 2.05
Set value .60

Horse breeding.

Maria I. Ulyanova (1878-1937), Lenin's Sister — A1655

1968, Jan. 30 ***Perf. 12x12½***
3438 A1655 4k indigo & pale green .30 .15

Soviet Star and Flags of Army, Air Force and Navy — A1656

Lenin Addressing Troops in 1919 — A1657

#3441, Dneprostroi Dam & sculpture "On Guard." #3442, 1918 poster & marching volunteers. #3443, Red Army entering Vladivostok, 1922, & soldiers' monument in Primorie. #3444, Poster "Red Army as Liberator," Western Ukraine. #3445, Poster "Westward," defeat of German army. #3446, "Battle of Stalingrad" monument & German prisoners of war. #3447, Victory parade on Red Square, May 24, 1945, & Russian War Memorial, Berlin. Nos. 3448-3449, Modern weapons and Russian flag.

1968, Feb. 20 Typo. ***Perf. 12x12½***
3439 A1656 4k gold & multi .15 .15

Photo.
Perf. 11½x12
3440 A1657 4k blk, red, pink & silver .15 .15
3441 A1657 4k gold, black & red .15 .15

Litho.
Perf. 12½x12
3442 A1657 4k yel grn, blk, red & buff .15 .15
3443 A1657 4k grn, dk brn, red & bis .15 .15
3444 A1657 4k green & multi .15 .15
3445 A1657 4k yel green & multi .15 .15

Perf. 11½x12, 12x11½
Photo.
3446 A1657 4k blk, silver & red .15 .15
3447 A1657 4k gold, blk, pink & red .15 .15
3448 A1656 4k black, red & silver .15 .15
Nos. 3439-3448 (10) 1.50
Set value 1.00

Souvenir Sheet

1968, Feb. 23 Litho. ***Imperf.***
3449 A1656 1r blk, silver & red 3.50 1.50

50th anniv. of the Armed Forces of the USSR. No. 3449 contains one 25x37½mm stamp with simulated perforations.

Maxim Gorki (1868-1936), Writer — A1658

1968, Feb. 29 Photo. ***Perf. 12***
3450 A1658 4k gray ol & dk brown .30 .15

Fireman, Fire Truck and Boat — A1659

Link-up of Cosmos 186 and 188 Satellites — A1660

1968, Mar. 30 Photo. *Perf. 12x12½*

3451 A1659 4k red & black .30 .15

50th anniversary of Soviet Fire Guards.

1968, Mar. 30 *Perf. 11½*

3452 A1660 6k blk, dp lilac rose & gold .30 .15

First link-up in space of two satellites, Cosmos 186 and Cosmos 188, Oct. 30, 1967.

N. N. Popudrenko A1661

Design: No. 3453, P. P. Vershigora.

1968, Mar. 30 *Perf. 12½x12*

3453 A1661 4k gray green & black .30 .15
3454 A1661 4k lt purple & black .30 .15
Set value .15

Partisan heroes of World War II.

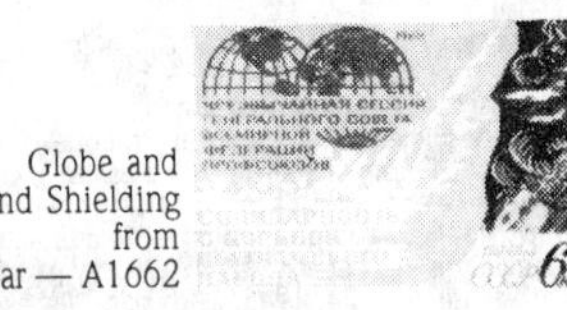

Globe and Hand Shielding from War — A1662

1968, Apr. 11 *Perf. 11½*

3455 A1662 6k sil, mar, ver & black .50 .35

Emergency session of the World Federation of Trade Unions and expressing solidarity with the people of Vietnam.

Space Walk — A1663

Designs: 6k, Docking operation of Kosmos 186 and Kosmos 188. 10k, Exploration of Venus.

1968, Apr. 12 Litho.

3456 A1663 4k multicolored .15 .15
3457 A1663 6k multicolored .15 .15
3458 A1663 10k multicolored .35 .15
a. Block of 3, #3456-3458 + 3 labels .75 .50

National Astronauts' Day.

Lenin, 1919 — A1664

Lenin Portraits: No. 3460, Addressing crowd on Red Square, Nov. 7, 1918. No. 3461, Full-face portrait, taken in Petrograd, Jan. 1918.

Engraved and Photogravure

1968, Apr. 16 *Perf. 12x11½*

3459 A1664 4k gold, brown & red .30 .15
3460 A1664 4k gold, red & black .30 .15
3461 A1664 4k gold, brn, buff & red .30 .15
Nos. 3459-3461 (3) .90
Set value .30

98th anniversary of the birth of Lenin.

Alisher Navoi, Uzbek Poet, 525th Birth Anniv. — A1665

1968, Apr. 29 Photo. *Perf. 12x12½*

3462 A1665 4k deep brown .30 .15

Karl Marx (1818-83) A1666

1968, May 5 Engr. *Perf. 11½x12*

3463 A1666 4k black & red .30 .15

Frontier Guard — A1667

Jubilee Badge — A1668

1968, May 22 Photo. *Perf. 11½*

3464 A1667 4k sl green, ocher & red .30 .15
3465 A1668 6k sl grn, blk & red brn .30 .15
Set value .25

Russian Frontier Guards, 50th anniv.

Crystal and Congress Emblem A1669

Congress Emblems and: No. 3467, Power lines and factories. No. 3468, Ground beetle. No. 3469, Roses and carbon rings.

1968, May 30

3466 A1669 6k blue, dk blue & grn .25 .15
3467 A1669 6k orange, gold & dk brn .25 .15
3468 A1669 6k red brn, gold & blk .25 .15
3469 A1669 6k lilac rose, org & blk .25 .15
Nos. 3466-3469 (4) 1.00 .60

Intl. congresses, Leningrad: 8th Cong. for Mineral Research; 7th World Power Conf.; 13th Entomological Cong.; 4th Cong. for the Study of Volatile Oils.

Types of 1966

Designs as before.

1968, June 20 Engr. *Perf. 12*

3470 A1593 1k dk red brown .15 .15
3471 A1593 2k deep violet .15 .15
3472 A1593 3k plum .20 .15
3473 A1593 4k bright red .20 .15
3474 A1593 6k blue .40 .15
3475 A1593 10k olive .60 .15
3476 A1593 12k red brown .75 .15
3477 A1593 16k violet blue .90 .15

Perf. 12½

3478 A1594 20k red 1.00 .15
3479 A1594 30k bright green 1.65 .15
3480 A1594 50k violet blue 2.75 .30

Perf. 12x12½

3481 A1594 1r gray, red brn & black 6.00 .50
Nos. 3470-3481 (12) 14.75
Set value 1.50

Sadriddin Aini A1670

1968, June 30 Photo. *Perf. 12½x12*

3482 A1670 4k olive bister & maroon .30 .15

Aini (1878-1954), Tadzhik poet.

Post Rider and C.C.E.P. Emblem A1671

Design: No. 3484, Modern means of communications (train, ship, planes and C.C.E.P. emblem).

1968, June 30

3483 A1671 6k gray & red brown .30 .15
3484 A1671 6k orange brn & bister .30 .15
Set value .20

Annual session of the Council of the Consultative Commission on Postal Investigation of the UPU (C.C.E.P.), Moscow, Sept. 20-Oct. 5.

Bolshevik Uprising, Kiev — A1672

1968, July 5 *Perf. 11½*

3485 A1672 4k gold, red & plum .30 .15

Ukrainian Communist Party, 50th anniv.

Athletes A1673

1968, July 9

3486 A1673 4k yel, dp car & bister .30 .15

1st Youth Summer Sports Games for 50th anniv. of the Leninist Young Communists League.

Field Ball — A1674

Table Tennis A1675

Designs: 6k, 20th Baltic Regatta. 10k, Soccer player and cup. 12k, Scuba divers.

Perf. 12x12½, 12½x12

1968, July 18 Litho.

3487 A1674 2k red & multi .15 .15
3488 A1675 4k purple & multi .15 .15
3489 A1674 6k blue & multi .25 .15
3490 A1674 10k multicolored .35 .15
3491 A1675 12k green & multi .45 .15
Nos. 3487-3491 (5) 1.35
Set value .50

European youth sports competitions.

Rhythmic Gymnast A1676

6k, Weight lifting. 10k, Rowing. 12k, Women's hurdling. 16k, Fencing. 40k, Running.

1968, July 31 Photo. *Perf. 11½*

Gold Background

3492 A1676 4k blue & green .20 .15
3493 A1676 6k dp rose & purple .30 .15
3494 A1676 10k yel green & green .55 .15
3495 A1676 12k orange & red brn .60 .15
3496 A1676 16k ultra & pink .70 .15
Nos. 3492-3496 (5) 2.35
Set value .50

Souvenir Sheet

Perf. 12½x12

Lithographed and Photogravure

3497 A1676 40k gold, grn, org & gray 1.75 1.00

19th Olympic Games, Mexico City, Oct. 12-27.

Gediminas Tower, Vilnius — A1677

1968, Aug. 14 Photo. *Perf. 11½*

3498 A1677 4k magenta, tan & red .30 .15

Soviet power in Lithuania, 50th anniv.

Tbilisi State University A1678

1968, Aug. 14 *Perf. 12*

3499 A1678 4k slate grn & lt brn .30 .15

Tbilisi State University, Georgia, 50th anniv.

Laocoon — A1679

1968, Aug. 16 *Perf. 11½*

3500 A1679 6k sepia, blk & maroon 3.00 2.00

"Promote solidarity with Greek democrats."

Red Army Man, Cavalry Charge and Order of the Red Banner of Battle — A1680

Designs: 3k, Young man and woman, Dneprostroi Dam and Order of the Red Banner of Labor. 4k, Soldier, storming of the Reichstag, Berlin, and

Order of Lenin. 6k, "Restoration of National Economy" (workers), and Order of Lenin. 10k, Young man and woman cultivating virgin land and Order of Lenin. 50k, like 2k.

1968, Aug. 25 Litho. *Perf.* 12½x12

3501 A1680 2k gray, red & ocher .20 .15
3502 A1680 3k multicolored .20 .15
3503 A1680 4k org, ocher & rose car .20 .15
3504 A1680 6k multicolored .20 .15
3505 A1680 10k olive & multi .20 .15
Nos. 3501-3505 (5) 1.00
Set value .50

Souvenir Sheet

Imperf

3506 A1680 50k ultra, red & bister 2.50 1.00

50th anniv. of the Lenin Young Communist League, Komsomol.

Chemistry Institute and Dimeric Molecule A1681

1968, Sept. 3 Photo. *Perf.* 11½

3507 A1681 4k vio bl, dp lil rose & black .30 .15

50th anniversary of Kurnakov Institute for General and Inorganic Chemistry.

Letter, Compass Rose, Ship and Plane A1682

Compass Rose and Stamps of 1921 and 1965 A1683

1968, Sept. 16 Photo. *Perf.* 11½

3508 A1682 4k dk car rose, brn & brt red .30 .15
3509 A1683 4k dk blue, blk & bister .30 .15
Set value .20

No. 3508 for Letter Writing Week, Oct. 7-13, and No. 3509 for Stamp Day and the Day of the Collector.

The 26 Baku Commissars, Sculpture by Merkurov A1684

1968, Sept. 20

3510 A1684 4k multicolored .40 .15

50th anniversary of the shooting of the 26 Commissars, Baku, Sept. 20, 1918.

Toyvo Antikaynen (1898-1941), Finnish Workers' Organizer — A1685

1968, Sept. 30 *Perf.* 12

3511 A1685 6k gray & sepia .60 .15

Russian Merchant Marine Emblem A1686

1968, Sept. 30 *Perf.* 12x11½

3512 A1686 6k blue, red & indigo .40 .15

Russian Merchant Marine.

Order of the October Revolution A1687

Pavel P. Postyshev A1688

Typographed and Embossed

1968, Sept. 30 *Perf.* 12x12½

3513 A1687 4k gold & multi .35 .25

51st anniv. of the October Revolution. Printed with alternating label.

1968-70 Engr. *Perf.* 12½x12

Designs: No. 3515, Stepan G. Shaumyan (1878-1918). No. 3516, Amkal Ikramov. (1898-1938). No. 3516A, N. G. Markin (1893-1918). No. 3516B, P. E. Dybenko (1889-1938). No. 3516C, S. V. Kosior (1889-1939). No. 3516D, Vasili Kikvidze (1895-1919).

Size: 21½x32½mm

3514 A1688 4k bluish black .55 .15
3515 A1688 4k bluish black .55 .15
3516 A1688 4k gray black .55 .15
3516A A1688 4k black .55 .15
3516B A1688 4k dark car ('69) .55 .15
3516C A1688 4k indigo ('69) .55 .15
3516D A1688 4k dk brown ('70) .55 .15
Nos. 3514-3516D (7) 3.85
Set value .70

Honoring outstanding workers for the Communist Party and the Soviet State.

Issued: #3514-3516, 9/30/68; #3516A, 12/31/68; #3516D, 9/24/70; others, 5/15/69.

See #3782.

American Bison and Zebra A1689

Designs: No. 3518, Purple gallinule and lotus. No. 3519, Great white egrets, vert. No. 3520, Ostrich and golden pheasant, vert. No. 3521, Eland and guanaco. No. 3522, European spoonbill and glossy ibis.

***Perf.* 12½x12, 12x12½**

1968, Oct. 16 Litho.

3517 A1689 4k ocher, brn & blk .20 .15
3518 A1689 4k ocher & multi .20 .15
3519 A1689 6k olive & black .30 .15
3520 A1689 6k gray & multi .30 .15
3521 A1689 10k dp green & multi .45 .15
3522 A1689 10k emerald & multi .45 .15
Nos. 3517-3522 (6) 1.90
Set value .60

Askania Nova and Astrakhan state reservations.

Ivan S. Turgenev (1818-83), Writer — A1690

Warrior, 1880 B.C. and Mt. Ararat — A1691

1968, Oct. 10 Engr. *Perf.* 12x12½

3523 A1690 4k green 4.50 .50

Engraved and Photogravure

1968, Oct. 18 *Perf.* 11½

Design: 12k, David Sasountsi monument, Yerevan, and Mt. Ararat.

3524 A1691 4k blk & dk blue, *gray* .25 .15
3525 A1691 12k dk brn & choc, *bis* .35 .15

Yerevan, capital of Armenia, 2,750th anniv.

First Radio Tube Generator and Laboratory A1692

1968, Oct. 26 Photo. *Perf.* 11½

3526 A1692 4k dk blue, dp bis & blk .30 .15

50th anniversary of Russia's first radio laboratory at Gorki (Nizhni Novgorod).

Prospecting Geologist and Crystals A1693

Designs: 6k, Prospecting for metals: seismographic test apparatus with shock wave diagram, plane and truck. 10k, Oil derrick in the desert.

1968, Oct. 31 Litho. *Perf.* 11½

3527 A1693 4k blue & multi .40 .15
3528 A1693 6k multicolored .20 .15
3529 A1693 10k multicolored .55 .15
Nos. 3527-3529 (3) 1.15 .45

Geology Day. Printed with alternating label.

Borovoe, Kazakhstan A1694

Landscapes: #3531, Djety-Oguz, Kirghizia, vert. #3532, Issyk-kul Lake, Kirghizia. #3533, Borovoe, Kazakhstan, vert.

***Perf.* 12½x12, 12x12½**

1968, Nov. 20 Typo.

3530 A1694 4k dk red brn & multi .20 .15
3531 A1694 4k gray & multi .20 .15
3532 A1694 6k dk red brn & multi .20 .15
3533 A1694 6k black & multi .20 .15
Nos. 3530-3533 (4) .80
Set value .40

Recreational areas in the Kazakh and Kirghiz Republics.

Medals and Cup, Riccione, 1952, 1961 and 1965 — A1695

4k, Medals, Eiffel Tower and Arc de Triomphe, Paris, 1964. 6k, Porcelain plaque, gold medal and Brandenburg Gate, Debria, Berlin, 1950, 1959. 12k, Medal and prize-winning stamp #2888, Buenos Aires. 16k, Cups and medals, Rome, 1952, 1954. 20k, Medals, awards and views, Vienna, 1961, 1965. 30k, Trophies, Prague, 1950, 1955, 1962.

1968, Nov. 27 Photo. *Perf.* 11½x12

3534 A1695 4k dp cl, sil & blk .15 .15
3535 A1695 6k dl bl, gold & blk .25 .15
3536 A1695 10k light ultra, gold & black .40 .15
3537 A1695 12k blue, silver & blk .50 .15
3538 A1695 16k red, gold & black .55 .15
3539 A1695 20k bright blue, gold & black .70 .15
3540 A1695 30k orange brown, gold & black 1.00 .30
Nos. 3534-3540 (7) 3.55
Set value .75

Awards to Soviet post office at foreign stamp exhibitions.

Worker with Banner — A1696

V. K. Lebedinsky and Radio Tower — A1697

1968, Nov. 29 *Perf.* 12x12½

3541 A1696 4k red & black .50 .35

Estonian Workers' Commune, 50th anniv.

1968, Nov. 29 *Perf.* 11½x12

3542 A1697 4k gray grn, blk & gray .50 .25

V. K. Lebedinsky (1868-1937), scientist.

Souvenir Sheet

Communication via Satellite — A1698

1968, Nov. 29 Litho. *Perf.* 12

3543 A1698 Sheet of 3 3.00 .70
a. 16k Molniya I .70 .15
b. 16k Map of Russia .70 .15
c. 16k Ground Station "Orbite" .70 .15

Television transmission throughout USSR with the aid of the earth satellite Molniya I.

Sprig, Spasski Tower, Lenin Univ. and Library — A1699

1968, Dec. 1 *Perf.* 11½

3544 A1699 4k ultra, sil, grn & red .60 .30

New Year 1969.

Maj. Gen. Georgy Beregovoi — A1700

1968, Dec. 14 Photo. *Perf.* 11½

3545 A1700 10k Prus blue, blk & red .40 .25

Flight of Soyuz 3, Oct. 26-30.

Rail-laying and Casting Machines A1701

Soviet railroad transportation: 4k, Railroad map of the Soviet Union and Train.

1968, Dec. 14 *Perf.* 12½x12

3546 A1701 4k rose mag & orange .25 .15
3547 A1701 10k brown & emerald .25 .15
Set value .20

Newspaper Banner and Monument — A1702

1968, Dec. 23 *Perf. 11½*

3548	A1702	4k tan, red & dk brn	.40	.25

Byelorussian communist party, 50th anniv.

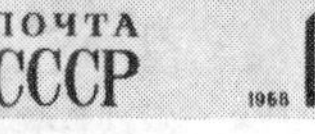

The Reapers, by A. Venetzianov A1703

Knight at the Crossroads, by Viktor M. Vasnetsov — A1704

Paintings: 2k, The Last Day of Pompeii, by Karl P. Bryullov. 4k, Capture of a Town in Winter, by Vasili I. Surikov. 6k, On the Lake, by I.I. Levitan. 10k, Alarm, 1919 (family), by K. Petrov-Vodkin. 16k, Defense of Sevastopol, 1942, by A. Deineka. 20k, Sculptor with a Bust of Homer, by G. Korzhev. 30k, Celebration on Uritsky Square, 1920, by G. Koustodiev. 50k, Duel between Peresvet and Chelubey, by Avilov.

Perf. 12x12½, 12½

1968, Dec. 25 **Litho.**

3549	A1703	1k multicolored	.15	.15
3550	A1704	2k multicolored	.15	.15
3551	A1704	3k multicolored	.20	.15
3552	A1704	4k multicolored	.25	.15
3553	A1704	6k multicolored	.35	.15
3554	A1703	10k multicolored	.55	.15
3555	A1704	16k multicolored	.60	.15
3556	A1703	20k multicolored	.65	.15
3557	A1704	30k multicolored	.85	.30
3558	A1704	50k multicolored	1.65	.40
		Nos. 3549-3558 (10)	5.40	
		Set value		1.20

Russian State Museum, Leningrad.

House, Zaoneje, 1876 — A1705

Russian Architecture: 4k, Carved doors, Gorki Oblast, 1848. 6k, Castle, Kizhi, 1714. 10k, Fortress wall, Rostov-Yaroslav, 16th-17th centuries. 12k, Gate, Tsaritsino, 1785. 16k, Architect Rossi Street, Leningrad.

1968, Dec. 27 **Engr.** *Perf. 12x12½*

3559	A1705	3k dp brown, *ocher*	.25	.15
3560	A1705	4k green, *yellow*	.25	.15
3561	A1705	6k violet, *gray violet*	.35	.15
3562	A1705	10k dl bl, *grnsh gray*	.45	.15
3563	A1705	12k car, *gray*	.55	.15
3564	A1705	16k black, *yellowish*	.70	.15
		Nos. 3559-3564 (6)	2.55	
		Set value		.60

Banners of Young Communist League, October Revolution Medal — A1707

1968, Dec. 31 **Litho.** *Perf. 12*

3566	A1707	12k red, yel & black	.40	.30

Award of Order of October Revolution to the Young Communist League on its 50th anniversary.

Soldiers on Guard — A1708

1969, Jan. 1 *Perf. 12x12½*

3567	A1708	4k orange & claret	.40	.15

Latvian Soviet Republic, 50th anniv.

Revolutionaries and Monument — A1709

Designs: 4k, Partisans and sword. 6k, Workers and Lenin Medals.

1969, Jan. **Photo.** *Perf. 11½*

3568	A1709	2k ocher & rose claret	.25	.15
3569	A1709	4k ocher & red	.25	.15
3570	A1709	6k dk olive, mag & red	.25	.15
		Nos. 3568-3570 (3)	.75	
		Set value		.30

Byelorussian Soviet Republic, 50th anniv.

Souvenir Sheet

Vladimir Shatalov, Boris Volynov, Alexei S. Elisseyev, Evgeny Khrunov — A1710

1969, Jan. 22 *Imperf.*

3571	A1710	50k dp bis & dk brn	4.00	1.25

1st team flights of Soyuz 4 and 5, Jan. 16, 1969.

Leningrad University A1711

1969, Jan. 23 **Photo.** *Perf. 12½x12*

3572	A1711	10k black & maroon	.40	.15

University of Leningrad, 150th anniv.

Ivan A. Krylov A1712

Nikolai Filchenkov A1713

1969, Feb. 13 **Litho.** *Perf. 12x12½*

3573	A1712	4k black & multi	.50	.30

Krylov (1769?-1844), fable writer.

1969 **Photo.**

Designs: No. 3575, Alexander Kosmodemiansky. No. 3575A, Otakar Yarosh, member of Czechoslovak Svoboda Battalion.

3574	A1713	4k dull rose & black	.15	.15
3575	A1713	4k emerald & dk brn	.15	.15
3575A	A1713	4k blue & black	.15	.15
		Nos. 3574-3575A (3)	.45	
		Set value		.20

Heroes of World War II. Issued: #3575A, May 9; others, Feb. 23.

"Shoulder to the Wheel," Parliament, Budapest A1714

Design: "Shoulder to the Wheel" is a sculpture by Zigmond Kisfaludi-Strobl.

1969, Mar. 21 **Typo.** *Perf. 11½*

3576	A1714	6k black, ver & lt grn	.30	.15

Hungarian Soviet Republic, 50th anniv.

Oil Refinery and Salavat Tualeyev Monument — A1715

1969, Mar. 22 **Litho.** *Perf. 12*

3577	A1715	4k multicolored	.30	.15

50th anniv. of the Bashkir Autonomous Socialist Republic.

Sergei P. Korolev, Sputnik 1, Space Monument, Moscow — A1716

Vostok on Launching Pad — A1717

Natl. Cosmonauts' Day: No. 3579, Zond 2 orbiting moon, and photograph of earth made by Zond 5. 80k, Spaceship Soyuz 3.

Perf. 12½x12, 12x12½

1969, Apr. 12 **Litho.**

3578	A1716	10k black, vio & grn	.25	.15
3579	A1716	10k dk brn, yel & brn red	.25	.15
3580	A1717	10k multicolored	.25	.15
		Nos. 3578-3580 (3)	.75	
		Set value		.30

Souvenir Sheet

Perf. 12

3581	A1716	80k vio, green & red	3.00	1.25

No. 3581 contains one 37x24mm stamp.

Lenin University, Kazan, and Kremlin A1718

Lenin House, Kuibyshev A1718a

Lenin House, Pskov A1718b

Lenin House, Shushensko A1718c

Smolny Institute, Leningrad A1718d

Places Connected with Lenin: #3586, Straw Hut, Razliv. #3587, Lenin Museum, Gorki. #3589, Lenin's room, Kremlin. #3590, Lenin Museum, Ulyanovsk. #3591, Lenin House, Ulyanovsk.

1969 **Photo.** *Perf. 11½*

3582	A1718	4k pale rose & multi	.15	.15
3583	A1718a	4k beige & multi	.15	.15
3584	A1718b	4k bister brn & multi	.15	.15
3585	A1718c	4k gray vio & multi	.15	.15
3586	A1718	4k violet & multi	.15	.15
3587	A1718	4k blue & multi	.15	.15
3588	A1718d	4k brick red & multi	.15	.15
3589	A1718	4k rose red & multi	.15	.15
3590	A1718	4k lt red brn & multi	.15	.15
3591	A1718	4k dull green & multi	.15	.15
		Nos. 3582-3591 (10)	1.50	
		Set value		1.00

99th anniv. of the birth of Lenin.

Telephone, Transistor Radio and Trademark A1719

1969, Apr. 25 *Perf. 12½x12*

3592	A1719	10k sepia & dp org	.40	.15

50th anniversary of VEF Electrical Co.

ILO Emblem and Globe — A1720

1969, May 9 ***Perf. 11***
3593 A1720 6k car rose & gold .35 .15

50th anniversary of the ILO.

Suleiman Stalsky A1721

1969, May 15 Photo. ***Perf. 12½x12***
3595 A1721 4k tan & ol green .40 .25

Stalsky (1869-1937), Dagestan poet.

Yasnaya Polyana Rose — A1722

4k, "Stroynaya" lily. 10k, Cattleya orchid. 12k, "Listopad" dahlia. 14k, "Ural Girl" gladioli.

1969, May 15 Litho. ***Perf. 11½***
3596 A1722 2k multicolored .15 .15
3597 A1722 4k multicolored .15 .15
3598 A1722 10k multicolored .25 .15
3599 A1722 12k multicolored .40 .15
3600 A1722 14k multicolored .40 .15
Nos. 3596-3600 (5) 1.35
Set value .40

Work of the Botanical Gardens of the Academy of Sciences.

Ukrainian Academy of Sciences A1723

1969, May 22 Photo. ***Perf. 12½x12***
3601 A1723 4k brown & yellow .50 .25

Ukrainian Academy of Sciences, 50th anniv.

Film, Camera and Medal — A1724

Ballet Dancers A1725

1969, June 3 Litho. ***Perf. 12x12½***
3602 A1724 6k rose car, blk & gold .30 .15
3603 A1725 6k dk brown & multi .30 .15
Set value .20

Intl. Film Festival in Moscow, and 1st Intl. Young Ballet Artists' Competitions.

Congress Emblem and Cell Division A1726

Estonian Singer and Festival Emblem A1727

1969, June 10 Photo. ***Perf. 11½***
3605 A1726 6k dp claret, lt bl & yel .50 .30

Protozoologists, 3rd Intl. Cong., Leningrad.

1969, June 14 ***Perf. 12x12½***
3606 A1727 4k ver & bister .50 .25

Centenary of the Estonian Song Festival.

СТОЛЕТИЕ ПЕРИОДИЧЕСКОГО ЗАКОНА Д.И.МЕНДЕЛЕЕВА
ПОЧТА СССР 1969 6К

Mendeleev and Formula with Author's Corrections — A1728

Design: 30k, Dmitri Ivanovich Mendeleev, vert.

Engraved and Lithographed

1969, June 20 ***Perf. 12***
3607 A1728 6k brown & rose .50 .30

Souvenir Sheet

3608 A1728 30k carmine rose 3.00 1.25

Cent. of the Periodic Law (classification of elements), formulated by Dimitri I. Mendeleev (1834-1907). No. 3608 contains one engraved 29x37mm stamp.

Hand Holding Peace Banner and World Landmarks A1729

1969, June 20 Photo. ***Perf. 11½***
3609 A1729 10k blue, dk brn & gold .40 .25

20th anniversary of the Peace Movement.

Laser Beam Guiding Moon Rocket — A1730

1969, June 20
3610 A1730 4k silver, black & red .50 .25

Soviet scientific inventions, 50th anniv.

Ivan Kotlyarevski (1769-1838), Ukrainian Writer A1731

Typographed and Photogravure

1969, June 25 ***Perf. 12½x12***
3611 A1731 4k blk, olive & lt brn .50 .25

No. 2717 Overprinted in Стокгольм. 1969 Vermilion

1969, June 25 Photo. ***Perf. 11½***
3612 A1306 6k Prus blue & plum 2.50 1.50

Soviet victory in the Ice Hockey World Championships, Stockholm, 1969.

"Hill of Glory" Monument and Minsk Battle Map — A1732

1969, July 3 Litho. ***Perf. 12x12½***
3613 A1732 4k red & olive .30 .15

25th anniv. of the liberation of Byelorussia from the Germans.

Eagle, Flag and Map of Poland — A1733

Design: No. 3615, Hands holding torch, flags of Bulgaria and USSR, and Bulgarian coat of arms.

1969, July 10 Photo. ***Perf. 12***
3614 A1733 6k red & bister .60 .15

Litho.

3615 A1733 6k bis, red, green & blk .60 .15
Set value .20

25th anniv. of the Polish Republic; liberation of Bulgaria from the Germans.

Monument to 68 Heroes A1734

1969, July 15 Photo. ***Perf. 12***
3616 A1734 4k red & maroon .50 .30

25th anniversary of the liberation of Nikolayev from the Germans.

Old Samarkand A1735

Design: 6k, Intourist Hotel, Samarkand.

1969, July 15 **Typo.**
3617 A1735 4k multicolored .30 .15
3618 A1735 6k multicolored .30 .15
Set value .20

2500th anniversary of Samarkand.

Volleyball A1736

Munkascy & "Woman Churning Butter" A1737

Design: 6k, Kayak race.

Photogravure and Engraved

1969, July 20 ***Perf. 11½***
3619 A1736 4k dp org & red brn .35 .15
3620 A1736 6k multicolored .35 .15
Set value .20

Championships: European Junior Volleyball; European Rowing.

1969, July 20 **Photo.**
3621 A1737 6k dk brn, blk & org .40 .25

Mihaly von Munkascy (1844-1900), Hungarian painter.

Miners' Monument — A1738

1969, July 30
3622 A1738 4k silver & magenta .40 .20

Centenary of the founding of the city of Donetsk, in the Donets coal basin.

Machine Gun Cart, by Mitrofan Grekov — A1739

1969, July 30 Engr. ***Perf. 12½x12***
3623 A1739 4k red brown & brn red .40 .25

First Mounted Army, 50th anniv.

Barge Pullers Along the Volga, by Repin — A1740

Ilya E. Repin (1844-1930), Self-portrait A1741

Repin Paintings: 6k, "Not Expected." 12k, Confession. 16k, Dnieper Cossacks.

Perf. 12½x12, 12x12½

1969, Aug. 5 **Litho.**
3624 A1740 4k multicolored .25 .15
3625 A1740 6k multicolored .25 .15
3626 A1741 10k bis, red brn & blk .35 .15
3627 A1740 12k multicolored .50 .15
3628 A1740 16k multicolored .65 .15
Nos. 3624-3628 (5) 2.00
Set value .50

Runner A1742

Komarov A1743

Design: 10k, Athlete on rings.

1969, Aug. 9 ***Perf. 12x12½***
3629 A1742 4k red, green & blk .25 .25
3630 A1742 10k green, lt blue & blk .25 .25

Souvenir Sheet

Imperf

3631 A1742 20k red, bister & blk 1.75 .60

9th Trade Union Spartakiad, Moscow.

1969, Aug. 22 **Photo.** ***Perf. 12x11½***
3632 A1743 4k olive & brown .30 .15

V. L. Komarov (1869-1945), botanist.

Hovannes Tumanian, Armenian Landscape A1744

1969, Sept. 1 **Typo.** ***Perf. 12½x12***
3633 A1744 10k blk & peacock blue .40 .25

Tumanian (1869-1923), Armenian poet.

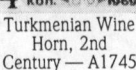

Turkmenian Wine Horn, 2nd Century — A1745

Mahatma Gandhi — A1746

Designs: 6k, Persian Simurg vessel (giant anthropomorphic bird), 13th century. 12k, Head of goddess Kannon, Korea, 8th century. 16k, Bodhisattva, Tibet, 7th century. 20k, Statue of Ebisu and fish (tai), Japan, 17th century.

1969, Sept. 3 **Litho.** ***Perf. 12x12½***
3634 A1745 4k blue & multi .25 .15
3635 A1745 6k lilac & multi .35 .15
3636 A1745 12k red & multi .60 .15
3637 A1745 16k blue vio & multi .70 .15
3638 A1745 20k pale grn & multi .95 .30
Nos. 3634-3638 (5) 2.85 .90

Treasures from the State Museum of Oriental Art.

1969, Sept. 10 **Engr.**
3639 A1746 6k deep brown .40 .35

Centenary of the birth of Mohandas K. Gandhi (1869-1948), leader in India's fight for independence.

Black Stork Feeding Young A1747

Belovezhskaya Forest reservation: 6k, Doe and fawn (red deer). 10k, Fighting bison. 12k, Lynx and cubs. 16k, Wild pig and piglets.

1969, Sept. 10 **Photo.** ***Perf. 12***

Size: 75x23mm, 10k; 35x23mm, others

3640 A1747 4k blk, yel grn & red .15 .15
3641 A1747 6k blue grn, dk brn & ocher .25 .15
3642 A1747 10k dk brn, dull org & dp org .55 .15
3643 A1747 12k dk & yel green, brn & gray .55 .15
3644 A1747 16k gray, yel grn & dk brown .65 .15
Nos. 3640-3644 (5) 2.15
Set value .50

Komitas A1748

1969, Sept. 18 **Typo.** ***Perf. 12½x12***
3645 A1748 6k blk, gray & salmon .50 .30

Komitas (S. N. Sogomonian, 1869-1935), Armenian composer.

Lisa Chaikina A1749

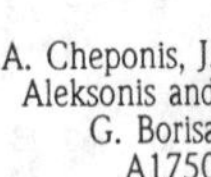

A. Cheponis, J. Aleksonis and G. Borisa A1750

#3647, Major S. I. Gritsevets & fighter planes.

1969, Sept. 20 **Photo.** ***Perf. 12½x12***
3646 A1749 4k olive & brt green .30 .15
3647 A1749 4k gray & black .30 .15

Perf. 11½

3648 A1750 4k hn brn, brn & buff .30 .20
Nos. 3646-3648 (3) .90
Set value .40

Heroes of the Soviet Union.

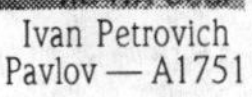

Ivan Petrovich Pavlov — A1751

East German Arms, TV Tower and Brandenburg Gate — A1752

1969, Sept. 26
3649 A1751 4k multicolored .40 .25

Pavlov (1849-1936), physiologist.

1969, Oct. 7 **Litho.**
3650 A1752 6k red, black & yel .35 .25

German Democratic Republic, 20th anniv.

Aleksei V. Koltsov — A1753

National Emblem — A1754

1969, Oct. 14 **Photo.** ***Perf. 12x12½***
3652 A1753 4k lt blue & brown .40 .25

Aleksei Vasilievich Koltsov (1809-42), poet.

1969, Oct. 14 ***Perf. 12x11½***
3653 A1754 4k gold & red .50 .30

25th anniversary of the liberation of the Ukraine from the Nazis.

Stars, Hammer and Sickle — A1755

1969, Oct. 21 **Typo.** ***Perf. 11½***
3654 A1755 4k vio blue, gold, yel & red .40 .25

52nd anniversary of October Revolution.

Georgy Shonin and Valery Kubasov A1756

Designs: No. 3656, Anatoly Filipchenko, Vladislav Volkov and Viktor Gorbatko. No. 3657, Vladimir Shatalov and Alexey Elisyev.

1969, Oct. 22 **Photo.** ***Perf. 12½x12***
3655 A1756 10k black & gold .30 .15
3656 A1756 10k black & gold .30 .15
3657 A1756 10k black & gold .30 .15
a. Strip of 3, #3655-3657 1.25 .30

Group flight of the space ships Soyuz 6, Soyuz 7 and Soyuz 8, Oct. 11-13.

Lenin as a Youth A1757

1969, Oct. 25 **Engr.** ***Perf. 11½***
3658 A1757 4k dark red, *pink* .40 .25

1st Soviet Youth Philatelic Exhibition, Kiev, dedicated to Lenin's 100th birthday.

Emblem of Communications Unit of Army — A1758

1969, Oct. 30 **Photo.**
3659 A1758 4k dk red, red & bister .40 .25

50th anniversary of the Communications Troops of Soviet Army.

Souvenir Sheet

Lenin and Quotation — A1759

Lithographed and Embossed

1969, Nov. 6 ***Imperf.***
3660 A1759 50k red, gold & pink 2.25 1.00

52nd anniv. of the October Revolution.

Cover of "Rules of the Kolkhoz" and Farm Woman's Monument A1760

1969, Nov. 18 **Photo.** ***Perf. 12½x12***
3661 A1760 4k brown & gold .40 .25

3rd All Union Collective Farmers' Congress, Moscow, Nov.-Dec.

Vasilissa, the Beauty, by Ivan Y. Bilibin — A1761

Designs (Book Illustrations by Ivan Y. Bilibin): 10k, Marya Morevna. 16k, Finist, the Fine Fellow, horiz. 20k, The Golden Cock. 50k, The Sultan and the Czar. The inscriptions on the 16k and 20k are transposed. 4k, 10k, 16k are fairy tales; 20k and 50k are tales by Pushkin.

1969, Nov. 20 **Litho.** ***Perf. 12***
3662 A1761 4k gray & multi .25 .20
3663 A1761 10k gray & multi .60 .50
3664 A1761 16k gray & multi .75 .75
3665 A1761 20k gray & multi .85 .85
3666 A1761 50k gray & multi 3.00 1.40
a. Strip of 5, #3662-3666 5.50 4.50

Illustrator and artist Ivan Y. Bilibin.

USSR Emblems Dropped on Venus, Radar Installation and Orbits — A1762

6k, Interplanetary station, space capsule, orbits.

1969, Nov. 25 Photo. *Perf. 12x11½*
3667 A1762 4k bister, black & red .25 .15
3668 A1762 6k gray, lilac rose & blk .25 .15
Set value .20

Completion of the flights of the space stations Venera 5 and Venera 6.

Flags of USSR and Afghanistan A1763

Russian State Emblem and Star A1764

1969, Nov. 30 Photo. *Perf. 11½*
3669 A1763 6k red, black & green .35 .25

50th anniversary of diplomatic relations between Russia and Afghanistan.

Coil Stamp

1969, Nov. 13 *Perf. 11x11½*
3670 A1764 4k red .60 .30

MiG Jet and First MiG Fighter Plane — A1765

1969, Dec. 12 *Perf. 11½x12*
3671 A1765 6k red, black & gray .40 .25

Soviet aircraft builders.

Lenin and Flag — A1766

Typographed and Lithographed

1969, Dec. 25 *Perf. 11½*
3672 A1766 4k gold, blue, red & blk .40 .25

Happy New Year 1970, birth cent. of Lenin.

Antonov 2 — A1767

Aircraft: 3k, PO-2. 4k, ANT-9. 6k, TsAGI 1-EA. 10k, ANT-20 "Maxim Gorki." 12k, Tupolev-104. 16k, MiG-10 helicopter. 20k, Ilyushin-62. 50k, Tupolev-144.

Photogravure and Engraved

1969 *Perf. 11½x12*
3673 A1767 2k bister & multi .15 .15
3674 A1767 3k multicolored .15 .15
3675 A1767 4k multicolored .15 .15
3676 A1767 6k multicolored .25 .15
3677 A1767 10k lt vio & multi .40 .15
3678 A1767 12k multicolored .55 .15
3679 A1767 16k multicolored .65 .15
3680 A1767 20k multicolored .70 .15
Nos. 3673-3680 (8) 3.00
Set value .80

Souvenir Sheet

Imperf

3681 A1767 50k blue & multi 2.50 1.00

History of national aeronautics and aviation. No. 3681 margin contains signs of the zodiac, partly overlapping the stamp.

Issued: #3679, 3681, 12/31; others 12/25.

Photograph of Earth by Zond 7 — A1768

Designs: No. 3683a, same as 10k. No. 3683b, Photograph of moon.

1969, Dec. 26 Photo. *Perf. 12x11½*
3682 A1768 10k black & multi .40 .30

Souvenir Sheet

Imperf

Litho.

3683 Sheet of 2 4.00 2.00
a. A1768 50k indigo & multi 1.65 .90
b. A1768 50k dark brown & multi 1.65 .90

Space explorations of the automatic stations Zond 6, Nov. 10-17, 1968, and Zond 7, Aug. 8-14, 1969. No. 3683 contains 27x40mm stamps with simulated perforations.

Model Aircraft — A1769

Technical Sports: 4k, Motorboats. 6k, Parachute jumping.

1969, Dec. 26 Engr. *Perf. 12½x12*
3684 A1769 3k bright magenta .30 .15
3685 A1769 4k dull blue green .30 .15
3686 A1769 6k red orange .30 .15
Nos. 3684-3686 (3) .90
Set value .35

Romanian Arms and Soviet War Memorial, Bucharest — A1770

1969, Dec. 31 Photo. *Perf. 11½*
3687 A1770 6k rose red & brown .60 .35

25th anniversary of Romania's liberation from fascist rule.

Ostankino Television Tower, Moscow — A1771

1969, Dec. 31 Typo. *Perf. 12*
3688 A1771 10k multicolored .60 .35

Lenin, by N. Andreyev — A1772

Paintings: No. 3690, Lenin at Marxist Meeting, St. Petersburg, by A. Moravov (behind table). No. 3691, Lenin at Second Party Day, by Y. Vinogradov (next to table). No. 3692, First Day of Soviet Power, by F. Modorov (leading crowd). No. 3693, Conversation with Lenin, by A. Shirokov (in front of red table). No. 3694, Farmers' Delegation Meeting Lenin, by Modorov (seated at desk). No. 3695, With Lenin, by V. A. Serov (with cap, in background). No. 3696, Lenin on May 1, 1920, by I. Brodsky (with cap, in foreground). No. 3697, Builder of Communism, by a group of painters (in red). No. 3698, Mastery of Space, by A. Deyneka (rockets).

1970, Jan. 1 Litho. *Perf. 12*
3689 A1772 4k multicolored .20 .15
3690 A1772 4k multicolored .20 .15
3691 A1772 4k multicolored .20 .15
3692 A1772 4k multicolored .20 .15
3693 A1772 4k multicolored .20 .15
3694 A1772 4k multicolored .20 .15
3695 A1772 4k multicolored .20 .15
3696 A1772 4k multicolored .20 .15
3697 A1772 4k multicolored .20 .15
3698 A1772 4k multicolored .20 .15
Nos. 3689-3698 (10) 2.00
Set value 1.00

Centenary of birth of Lenin (1870-1924).

Map of Antarctic, "Mirny" and "Vostok" A1773

Design: 16k, Camp and map of the Antarctic with Soviet Antarctic bases.

1970, Jan. 27 Photo. *Perf. 11½*
3699 A1773 4k multicolored .25 .25
3700 A1773 16k multicolored .70 .25

150th anniversary of the Bellingshausen-Lazarev Antarctic expedition.

F. W. Sychkov and "Tobogganing" — A1774

1970, Jan. 27 *Perf. 12½x12*
3701 A1774 4k sepia & vio blue .40 .25

F. W. Sychkov (1870-1958), painter.

Col. V. B. Borsoyev — A1775

Design: No. 3703, Sgt. V. Peshekhonov.

1970, Feb. 10 *Perf. 12x12½*
3702 A1775 4k brown olive & brn .30 .15
3703 A1775 4k dark gray & plum .30 .15
Set value .15

Heroes of the Soviet Union.

Geographical Society Emblem and Globes A1776

Torch of Peace A1777

1970, Feb. 26 Photo. *Perf. 11½*
3704 A1776 6k bis, Prus bl & dk brn .40 .30

Russian Geographical Society, 125th anniv.

1970, Mar. 3 Litho. *Perf. 12*
3705 A1777 6k blue green & tan .30 .15

Intl. Women's Solidarity Day, Mar. 8.

Symbols of Russian Arts and Crafts — A1778

Lenin — A1780

Lenin — A1779

Designs: 6k, Russian EXPO '70 pavilion. 10k, Boy holding model ship.

1970, Mar. 10 Photo. *Perf. 11½*
3706 A1778 4k dk blue grn, red & black .25 .15
3707 A1778 6k blk, silver & red .25 .15
3708 A1778 10k vio blue, sil & red .25 .15
Nos. 3706-3708 (3) .75
Set value .30

Souvenir Sheet
Engr. & Litho.
Perf. 12x12½

3709 A1779 50k dark red 2.00 1.00

EXPO '70 International Exhibition, Osaka, Japan, Mar. 15-Apr. 13.

1970, Mar. 14 **Photo.** *Perf. 11½*

3710 A1780 4k red, black & gold .40 .30

Souvenir Sheet
Photogravure and Embossed
Imperf

3711 A1780 20k red, black & gold 2.00 1.00

USSR Philatelic Exhibition dedicated to the centenary of the birth of Lenin.

Friendship Tree, Sochi — A1781

1970, Mar. 18 **Litho.** *Perf. 11½*

3712 A1781 10k multicolored .50 .30

Friendship among people. Printed with alternating label.

National Emblem, Hammer and Sickle, Oil Derricks A1782

1970, Mar. 18 **Photo.** *Perf. 11½*

3713 A1782 4k dk car rose & gold .35 .25

Azerbaijan Republic, 50th anniversary.

Ice Hockey Players A1783

1970, Mar. 18

3714 A1783 6k blue & slate green .35 .15

World Ice Hockey Championships, Sweden.

Overprinted in Upper Right Corner with Orange Cyrillic Inscription in 5 Vertical Lines

1970, Apr. 1 **Photo.** *Perf. 11½*

3715 A1783 6k blue & slate green .40 .25

Soviet hockey players as the tenfold world champions.

D. N. Medvedev A1784

Hungarian Arms, Budapest Landmarks A1786

Worker, Books, Globes and UNESCO Symbol A1785

Portrait: No. 3717, K. P. Orlovsky.

1970, Mar. 26 **Engr.** *Perf. 12x12½*

3716 A1784 4k chocolate .25 .15
3717 A1784 4k dk redsh brown .25 .15
Set value .20

Heroes of the Soviet Union.

1970, Mar. 26 **Photo.** *Perf. 12½x12*

3718 A1785 6k car lake & ocher .30 .15

UNESCO-sponsored Lenin Symposium, Tampere, Finland, Apr. 6-10.

1970, Apr. 4 **Typo.** *Perf. 11½*

3719 A1786 6k multicolored .30 .15

Liberation of Hungary, 25th anniv.
See No. 3738.

Cosmonauts' Emblem A1787

1970, Apr. 12 **Litho.** *Perf. 11½*

3720 A1787 6k buff & multi .30 .15

Cosmonauts' Day.

Lenin, 1891 — A1788

Order of Victory — A1789

Designs: Various portraits of Lenin.

Lithographed and Typographed
1970, Apr. 15 *Perf. 12x12½*

3721 A1788 2k green & gold .15 .15
3722 A1788 2k ol gray & gold .15 .15
3723 A1788 4k vio blue & gold .15 .15
3724 A1788 4k lake & gold .15 .15
3725 A1788 6k red brn & gold .15 .15
3726 A1788 6k lake & gold .15 .15
3727 A1788 10k dk brn & gold .25 .15
3728 A1788 10k dark rose brown & gold .35 .15
3729 A1788 12k blk, sil & gold .45 .15

Photo.

3730 A1788 12k red & gold .45 .15
Nos. 3721-3730 (10) 2.40
Set value 1.00

Souvenir Sheet
1970, Apr. 22 **Litho.** **Typo.**

3731 A1788 20k blk, silver & gold 2.00 .70

Cent. of the birth of Lenin. Issued in sheets of 8 stamps surrounded by 16 labels showing Lenin-connected buildings, books, coats of arms and medals. No. 3731 contains one stamp in same design as No. 3729.

1970, May 8 **Photo.** *Perf. 11½*

Designs: 2k, Monument to the Unknown Soldier, Moscow. 3k, Victory Monument, Berlin-Treptow. 4k, Order of the Great Patriotic War. 10k, Gold Star of the Order of Hero of the Soviet Union and Medal of Socialist Labor. 30k, Like 1k.

3732 A1789 1k red lilac, gold & gray .15 .15
3733 A1789 2k dark brn, gold & red .15 .15
3734 A1789 3k dark brn, gold & red .15 .15
3735 A1789 4k dark brn, gold & red .15 .15
3736 A1789 10k red lil, gold & red .35 .15
Nos. 3732-3736 (5) .95
Set value .50

Souvenir Sheet
Imperf

3737 A1789 30k dark red, gold & gray 2.00 .60

25th anniv. of victory in WWII. No. 3737 has simulated perforations.

Arms-Landmark Type of 1970

Czechoslovakia arms and view of Prague.

1970, May 8 **Typo.** *Perf. 12½*

3738 A1786 6k dk brown & multi .35 .15

25th anniversary of the liberation of Czechoslovakia from the Germans.

Young Fighters, and Youth Federation Emblem A1791

1970, May 20 **Litho.** *Perf. 12*

3739 A1791 6k blue & black .30 .15

25th anniversary of the World Federation of Democratic Youth.

Lenin A1792

1970, May 20 **Photo.** *Perf. 11½*

3740 A1792 6k red .30 .15

Intl. Youth Meeting dedicated to the cent. of the birth of Lenin, UN, NY, June 1970.

Komsomol Emblem with Lenin A1793

1970, May 20 **Litho.** *Perf. 12*

3741 A1793 4k red, yel & purple .30 .15

16th Congress of the Young Communist League, May 26-30.

Hammer and Sickle Emblem and Building of Supreme Soviet in Kazan — A1794

#3744

#3744B

#3744C

Designs (Hammer-Sickle Emblem and Supreme Soviet Building in): No. 3743, Petrozavodsk. No. 3744, Cheboksary. No. 3744A, Elista. No. 3744B, Izhevsk. No. 3744C, Yoshkar-Ola.

1970 **Engr.** *Perf. 12x12½*

3742 A1794 4k violet blue .50 .15
3743 A1794 4k green .50 .15
3744 A1794 4k dark carmine .50 .15
3744A A1794 4k red .50 .15
3744B A1794 4k dark green .50 .15
3744C A1794 4k dark carmine .50 .15
Nos. 3742-3744C (6) 3.00
Set value .60

50th annivs. of the Tatar (#3742), Karelian (#3743), Chuvash (#3744), Kalmyk (#3744A), Udmurt (#3744B) and Mari (#3744C) autonomous SSRs.

Issued: #3742, 5/27; #3743, 6/5; #3744, 6/24; #3744A-3744B, 10/22; #3744C, 11/4.

See Nos. 3814-3823, 4286, 4806.

Soccer — A1795

Sword into Plowshare Statue, UN, NY — A1796

Design: 10k, Woman athlete on balancing bar.

1970, May 31 **Photo.** *Perf. 11½*

3745 A1795 10k lt gray & brt rose .40 .15
3746 A1795 16k dk grn & org brn .65 .15
Set value .20

17th World Gymnastics Championships, Ljubljana, Oct. 22-27; 9th World Soccer Championships for the Jules Rimet Cup, Mexico City, May 29-June 21.

1970, June 1 **Litho.** *Perf. 12x12½*

3747 A1796 12k gray & lake .50 .25

25th anniversary of the United Nations.

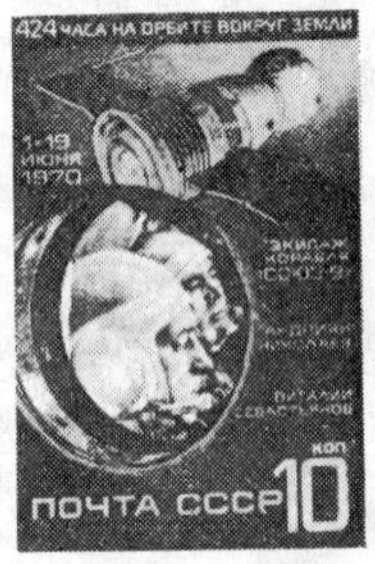

Soyuz 9, Andrian Nikolayev, Vitaly Sevastyanov A1797

1970, June 7 **Photo.** *Perf. 12x11½*

3748 A1797 10k multicolored .40 .15

424 hour space flight of Soyuz 9, June 1-19.

Friedrich Engels A1798

1970, June 16 **Engr.** *Perf. 12x12½*

3749 A1798 4k chocolate & ver .35 .15

Friedrich Engels (1820-1895), German socialist, collaborator with Karl Marx.

Armenian Woman and Symbols of Agriculture and Industry A1799

Design: No. 3751, Kazakh woman and symbols of agriculture and industry.

1970, June 16 Photo. *Perf. 11½*

3750 A1799 4k red brn & silver .30 .30
3751 A1799 4k brt rose lilac & gold .30 .30

50th anniv. of the Armenian & Kazakh Soviet Socialist Republics.

Missile Cruiser "Grozny" — A1800

Soviet Warships: 3k, Cruiser "Aurora." 10k, Cruiser "October Revolution." 12k, Missile cruiser "Varyag." 20k, Atomic submarine "Leninsky Komsomol."

1970, July 26 Photo. *Perf. 11½x12*

3752 A1800 3k lilac, pink & blk .15 .15
3753 A1800 4k yellow & black .25 .15
3754 A1800 10k rose & black .45 .15
3755 A1800 12k buff & dk brown .45 .15
3756 A1800 20k blue grn, dk brn & vio blue .90 .15
Nos. 3752-3756 (5) 2.20
Set value .50

Navy Day.

Soviet and Polish Workers and Flags A1801

"History," Petroglyphs, Sputnik and Emblem A1802

1970, July 26 *Perf. 12*

3757 A1801 6k red & slate .30 .15

25th anniversary of the Treaty of Friendship, Collaboration and Mutual Assistance between USSR and Poland.

1970, Aug. 16 *Perf. 11½*

3758 A1802 4k red brn, buff & blue .40 .25

13th International Congress of Historical Sciences in Moscow.

Mandarin Ducks A1803

Animals from the Sikhote-Alin Reserve: 6k, Pine marten. 10k, Asiatic black bear, vert. 16k, Red deer. 20k, Ussurian tiger.

Perf. 12½x12, 12x12½

1970, Aug. 19 Litho.

3759 A1803 4k multicolored .20 .15
3760 A1803 6k multicolored .25 .15
3761 A1803 10k multicolored .30 .15
3762 A1803 16k ultra & multi .45 .15
3763 A1803 20k gray & multi .60 .15
Nos. 3759-3763 (5) 1.80
Set value .50

Magnifying Glass over Stamp, and Covers — A1804

Pioneers' Badge — A1805

1970, Aug. 31 Photo. *Perf. 12x12½*

3764 A1804 4k red & silver .50 .25

2nd All-Union Philatelists' Cong., Moscow.

1970, Sept. 24 Photo. *Perf. 11½*

Soviet general education: 2k, Lenin and Children, monument. 4k, Star and scenes from play "Zarnitsa."

3765 A1805 1k gray, red & gold .25 .15
3766 A1805 2k brn red & slate grn .25 .15
3767 A1805 4k lt ol, car & gold .25 .15
Nos. 3765-3767 (3) .75
Set value .30

Yerevan University A1806

1970, Sept. 24 Photo. *Perf. 12½x12*

3768 A1806 4k ultra & salmon pink .30 .15

Yerevan State University, 50th anniv.

Library Bookplate, Vilnius University — A1807

Woman Holding Flowers — A1808

1970, Oct. Typo. *Perf. 12x12½*

3772 A1807 4k silver, gray & blk .50 .25

Vilnius University Library, 400th anniv.

1970, Oct. 30 Photo.

3773 A1808 6k blue & lt brown .30 .15

25th anniversary of the International Democratic Federation of Women.

Farm Woman, Cattle Farm — A1809

Designs: No. 3775, Farmer and mechanical farm equipment. No. 3776, Farmer, fertilization equipment and plane.

1970, Oct. 30 *Perf. 11½x12*

3774 A1809 4k olive, yellow & red .20 .15
3775 A1809 4k ocher, yellow & red .20 .15
3776 A1809 4k lt vio, yellow & red .20 .15
Nos. 3774-3776 (3) .60
Set value .30

Aims of the new agricultural 5-year plan.

Lenin — A1810

Lithographed and Embossed

1970, Nov. 3 *Perf. 12½x12*

3777 A1810 4k red & gold .30 .15

Souvenir Sheet

3778 A1810 30k red & gold 1.75 .75

53rd anniv. of the October Revolution.

No. 3389 Overprinted in Gold **50 лет ленинскому плану ГОЭЛРО • 1970**

1970, Nov. 3 *Perf. 11½*

3779 A1641 4k gold & multi .80 .75

50th anniversary of the GOELRO Plan for the electrification of Russia.

Spasski Tower and Fir Branch A1811

A. A. Baykov A1812

1970, Nov. 23 Litho. *Perf. 12x12½*

3780 A1811 6k multicolored .30 .15

New Year, 1971.

1970, Nov. 25 Photo. *Perf. 12½x12*

3781 A1812 4k sepia & golden brn .30 .15

Baykov (1870-1946), metallurgist and academician.

Portrait Type of 1968

Portrait: No. 3782, A. D. Tsyurupa.

1970, Nov. 25 Photo. *Perf. 12x12½*

3782 A1688 4k brown & salmon .35 .25

Tsyurupa (1870-1928), First Vice Chairman of the Soviet of People's Commissars.

Vasily Blazhenny Church, Red Square — A1813

Tourist publicity: 6k, Performance of Swan Lake. 10k, Two deer. 12k, Folk art. 14k, Sword into Plowshare statue, by E. Vouchetich, and museums. 16k, Automobiles and woman photographer.

Photogravure and Engraved

1970, Nov. 29 *Perf. 12x11½*

Frame in Brown Orange

3783 A1813 4k multicolored .15 .15
3784 A1813 6k multicolored .15 .15
3785 A1813 10k brn org & sl green .35 .15
3786 A1813 12k multicolored .45 .15
3787 A1813 14k multicolored .50 .20
3788 A1813 16k multicolored .65 .20
Nos. 3783-3788 (6) 2.25
Set value .75

Daisy A1814

1970, Nov. 29 Litho. *Perf. 11½*

3789 A1814 4k shown .15 .15
3790 A1814 6k Dahlia .15 .15
3791 A1814 10k Phlox .40 .15
3792 A1814 12k Aster .50 .15
3793 A1814 16k Clementis .85 .15
Nos. 3789-3793 (5) 2.05
Set value .50

UN Emblem, African Mother and Child, Broken Chain — A1815

1970, Dec. 10 Photo. *Perf. 12x12½*

3794 A1815 10k blue & dk brown .50 .15

United Nations Declaration on Colonial Independence, 10th anniversary.

Ludwig van Beethoven (1770-1827), Composer A1816

1970, Dec. 16 Engr. *Perf. 12½x12*

3795 A1816 10k deep claret, *pink* .50 .30

Skating — A1817

Luna 16 — A1818

Design: 10k, Skiing.

1970, Dec. 18 Photo. *Perf. 11½*

3796 A1817 4k light gray, ultra & dark red .20 .15
3797 A1817 10k light gray, brt green & brown .30 .15
Set value .20

1971 Trade Union Winter Games.

1970, Dec. Photo. *Perf. 11½*

Designs: No. 3799, 3801b, Luna 16 leaving moon. No. 3800, 3801c, Capsule landing on earth. No. 3801a, like No. 3798.

3798 A1818 10k gray blue .35 .15
3799 A1818 10k dk purple .35 .15
3800 A1818 10k gray blue .35 .15
Nos. 3798-3800 (3) 1.05
Set value .30

Souvenir Sheet

3801 Sheet of 3 4.00 1.00
a. A1818 20k blue .70 .25
b. A1818 20k dark purple .70 .25
c. A1818 20k blue .70 .25

Luna 16 unmanned, automatic moon mission, Sept. 12-24, 1970.

Nos. 3801a-3801c have attached labels (no perf. between vignette and label). Issue dates: No. 3801, Dec. 18; Nos. 3798-3800, Dec. 28.

The Conestabile Madonna, by Raphael A1819

Paintings: 4k, Apostles Peter and Paul, by El Greco. 10k, Perseus and Andromeda, by Rubens, horiz. 12k, The Prodigal Son, by Rembrandt. 16k, Family Portrait, by van Dyck. 20k, The Actress Jeanne Samary, by Renoir. 30k, Woman with Fruit, by Gauguin. 50k, The Litte Madonna, by da Vinci. All paintings from the Hermitage in Leningrad, except 20k from Pushkin Museum, Moscow.

Perf. 12x12½, 12½x12

1970, Dec. 23 **Litho.**

3802 A1819 3k gray & multi .15 .15
3803 A1819 4k gray & multi .20 .15
3804 A1819 10k gray & multi .50 .15
3805 A1819 12k gray & multi .50 .15
3806 A1819 16k gray & multi .60 .15
3807 A1819 20k gray & multi .85 .15
3808 A1819 30k gray & multi 1.75 .25
Nos. 3802-3808 (7) 4.55
Set value .80

Souvenir Sheet

Imperf

3809 A1819 50k gold & multi 3.00 .90

Harry Pollyt and Shipyard A1820

1970, Dec. 31 **Photo.** ***Perf. 12***

3810 A1820 10k maroon & brown .40 .30

Pollyt (1890-1960), British labor leader.

International Cooperative Alliance — A1821

1970, Dec. 31 ***Perf. 11½x12***

3811 A1821 12k yel green & red .40 .30

Intl. Cooperative Alliance, 75th anniv.

Lenin A1822

1971, Jan. 1 ***Perf. 12***

3812 A1822 4k red & gold .25 .15

Year of the 24th Congress of the Communist Party of the Soviet Union.

Georgian Republic Flag — A1823

1971, Jan. 12 **Litho.** ***Perf. 11½***

3813 A1823 4k ol bister & multi .25 .15

Georgian SSR, 50th anniversary.

Republic Anniversaries Type of 1970

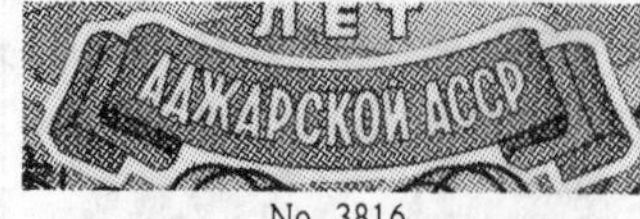

No. 3816

No. 3818

Designs (Hammer-Sickle Emblem and): No. 3814, Supreme Soviet Building, Makhachkala. No. 3815, Fruit, ship, mountain, conveyor. No. 3816, Grapes, refinery, ship. No. 3817, Supreme Soviet Building, Nalchik. No. 3818, Supreme Soviet Building, Syktyvkar, and lumber industry. No. 3819, Natural resources, dam, mining. No. 3820, Industrial installations and natural products. No. 3821, Ship, "industry." No. 3822, Grapes, pylons and mountains. No. 3823, Kazbek Mountain, industrial installations, produce.

1971-74 **Engr.** ***Perf. 12x12½***

3814 A1794 4k dk blue green .20 .15
3815 A1794 4k rose red .20 .15
3816 A1794 4k red .20 .15
3817 A1794 4k blue .20 .15
3818 A1794 4k green .20 .15
3819 A1794 4k brt bl ('72) .20 .15
3820 A1794 4k car rose ('72) .20 .15
3821 A1794 4k brt ultra ('73) .20 .15
3822 A1794 4k golden brn ('74) .20 .15

Litho.

3823 A1794 4k dark red ('74) .20 .15
Nos. 3814-3823 (10) 2.00
Set value 1.00

50th annivers. of Dagestan (#3814), Abkazian (#3815), Adzhar (#3816), Kabardino-Balkarian (#3817), Komi (#3818), Yakut (#3819), Checheno-Ingush (#3820), Buryat (#3821), Nakhichevan (#3822), and North Ossetian (#3823) autonomous SSRs.

No. 3823 also for bicentenary of Ossetia's union with Russia.

Issued: #3814, 1/20; #3815, 3/3; #3816, 6/16; #3817-3818, 8/17; #3819, 4/20; #3820, 11/22; #3821, 5/24; #3822, 2/6; #3823, 7/7.

Tower of Genoa, Cranes, Hammer and Sickle — A1824

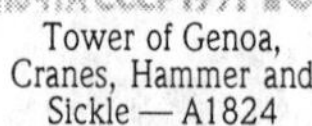

Palace of Culture, Kiev — A1825

1971, Jan. 28 **Typo.** ***Perf. 12***

3824 A1824 10k dk red, gray & yel .30 .15

Founding of Feodosiya, Crimea, 2500th anniv.

1971, Feb. 16 **Photo.** ***Perf. 11½***

3825 A1825 4k red, bister & blue .25 .15

Ukrainian Communist Party, 24th cong.

N. Gubin, I. Chernykh, S. Kosinov A1826

1971, Feb. 16 ***Perf. 12½x12***

3826 A1826 4k slate grn & vio brn .25 .15

Heroes of the Soviet Union.

"Industry and Agriculture" A1827

Lesya Ukrayinka A1828

1971, Feb. 16 ***Perf. 12x12½***

3827 A1827 6k olive bister & red .25 .15

State Planning Organization, 50th anniv.

1971, Feb. 25

3828 A1828 4k orange red & bister .25 .15

Ukrayinka (1871-1913), Ukrainian poet.

"Summer" Dance — A1829

Dancers of Russian Folk Dance Ensemble: No. 3830, "On the Skating Rink." No. 3831, Ukrainian dance "Hopak." No. 3832, Adzharian dance. No. 3833, Gypsy dance.

1971, Feb. 25 **Litho.** ***Perf. 12½x12***

3829 A1829 10k bister & multi .40 .15
3830 A1829 10k olive & multi .40 .15
3831 A1829 10k olive bis & multi .40 .15
3832 A1829 10k gray & multi .40 .15
3833 A1829 10k grnsh gray & multi .40 .15
Nos. 3829-3833 (5) 2.00
Set value .50

Luna 17 on Moon A1830

Designs: No. 3835, Ground control. No. 3836, Separation of Lunokhod 1 and carrier. 16k, Lunokhod 1 in operation.

1971, Mar. 16 **Photo.** ***Perf. 11½***

3834 A1830 10k dp violet & sepia .35 .15
3835 A1830 12k dk blue & sepia .50 .15
3836 A1830 12k dk blue & sepia .50 .15
3837 A1830 16k dp violet & sepia .60 .15
a. Souv. sheet of 4 2.50 1.00
Nos. 3834-3837 (4) 1.95
Set value .50

Luna 17 unmanned, automated moon mission, Nov. 10-17, 1970.

No. 3837a contains Nos. 3834-3837, size 32x21mm each.

Paris Commune A1831

Industry, Science, Culture A1832

1971, Mar. 18 **Litho.** ***Perf. 12***

3838 A1831 6k red & black .30 .15

Centenary of the Paris Commune.

1971, Mar. 29 ***Perf. 11½***

3839 A1832 6k bister, brn & red .25 .15

24th Communist Party Cong., Mar. 30-Apr. 3.

Yuri Gagarin Medal A1833

1971, Mar. 30 **Photo.** ***Perf. 11½***

3840 A1833 10k brown & lemon .40 .15

10th anniv. of man's first flight into space.

Space Research A1834

1971, Mar. 30

3841 A1834 12k slate blue & vio brn .40 .15

Cosmonauts' Day, Apr. 12.

E. Birznieks-Upitis A1835

Bee and Blossom A1836

1971, Apr. 1 ***Perf. 12x12½***

3842 A1835 4k red brown & gray .25 .15

Birznieks-Upitis (1871-1960), Latvian writer.

1971, Apr. 1 ***Perf. 11½***

3843 A1836 6k olive & multi .25 .15

23rd International Beekeeping Congress, Moscow, Aug. 22-Sept. 2.

Souvenir Sheet

Cosmonauts and Spacecraft — A1837

Designs: 10k, Vostok. No. 3844b, Yuri Gagarin. No. 3844c, First man walking in space. 16k, First orbital station.

1971, Apr. 12 **Litho.** ***Perf. 12***

3844 A1837 Sheet of 4 3.00 1.00
a. 10k violet brown .45 .20
b.-c. 12k Prussian green .45 .20
d. 16k violet brown .50 .20

10th anniv. of man's 1st flight into space. Size of stamps: 26x19mm.

Lenin Memorial, Ulyanovsk — A1838

1971, Apr. 16 **Photo.** ***Perf. 12***

3845 A1838 4k cop red & ol bister .25 .15

Lenin's birthday. Memorial was built for centenary celebration of his birth.

Lt. Col. Nikolai I. Vlasov — A1839

Khafiz Shirazi — A1840

1971, May 9 Photo. *Perf. 12x12½*
3846 A1839 4k gray olive & brn .30 .15

Hero of the Soviet Union.

1971, May 9 Litho.
3847 A1840 4k olive, brn & black .25 .15

650th anniversary of the birth of Khafiz Shirazi, Tadzhik-Persian poet.

GAZ-66 — A1841

Soviet Cars: 3k, BelAZ-540 truck. No. 3850, Moskvich-412. No. 3851, ZAZ-968. 10k, Volga.

1971, May 12 Photo. *Perf. 11x11½*

3848	A1841	2k yellow & multi	.20	.15
3849	A1841	3k lt blue & multi	.20	.15
3850	A1841	4k lt lilac & multi	.20	.15
3851	A1841	4k lt gray & multi	.20	.15
3852	A1841	10k lt lilac & multi	.20	.15
		Nos. 3848-3852 (5)	1.00	
		Set value		.50

Bogomolets A1842

Satellite A1843

1971, May 24 Photo. *Perf. 12*
3853 A1842 4k orange & black .25 .15

A. A. Bogomolets, physician, 90th birth anniv.

1971, June 9 *Perf. 11½*
3854 A1843 6k blue & multi .25 .15

15th General Assembly of the International Union of Geodesics and Geophysics.

Symbols of Science and History A1844

1971, June 9 *Perf. 12*
3855 A1844 6k green & gray .25 .15

13th Congress of Science History.

Oil Derrick & Symbols A1845

1971, June 9 *Perf. 11½*
3856 A1845 6k multicolored .20 .15

8th World Oil Congress.

Sukhe Bator Monument — A1846

1971, June 16 Typo. *Perf. 12*
3857 A1846 6k red, gold & black .25 .15

50th anniversary of Mongolian revolution.

Monument of Defenders of Liepaja A1847

1971, June 21 Photo.
3858 A1847 4k gray, black & brn .30 .25

30th anniversary of the defense of Liepaja (Libau) against invading Germans.

Map of Antarctica and Station A1848

Weather Map, Plane, Ship and Satellite A1849

Engraved and Photogravure

1971, June 21 *Perf. 11½*
3859 A1848 6k black, grn & ultra .50 .30

Antarctic Treaty pledging peaceful uses of & scientific co-operation in Antarctica, 10th anniv.

1971, June 21
3860 A1849 10k black, red & ultra .50 .30

50th anniversary of Soviet Hydrometeorological service.

FIR Emblem, "Homeland" by E. Vouchetich A1850

1971, June 21 Photo. *Perf. 12x12½*
3861 A1850 6k dk red & slate .25 .15

International Federation of Resistance Fighters (FIR), 20th anniversary.

Discus and Running A1851

Designs: 4k, Archery (women). 6k, Dressage. 10k, Basketball. 12k, Wrestling.

Lithographed and Engraved

1971, June 24 *Perf. 11½*

3862	A1851	3k violet blue, *rose*	.15	.15
3863	A1851	4k slate grn, *pale pink*	.20	.15
3864	A1851	6k red brn, *apple grn*	.30	.15
3865	A1851	10k dk pur, *gray blue*	.40	.15
3866	A1851	12k red brn, *yellow*	.50	.15
		Nos. 3862-3866 (5)	1.55	
		Set value		.50

5th Summer Spartakiad.

Benois Madonna, by da Vinci A1852

Paintings: 4k, Mary Magdalene, by Titian. 10k, The Washerwoman, by Jean Simeon Chardin, horiz. 12k, Portrait of a Young Man, by Frans Hals. 14k, Tancred and Arminia, by Nicolas Poussin, horiz. 16k, Girl with Fruit, by Murillo. 20k, Girl with Ball, by Picasso.

Perf. 12x12½, 12½x12

1971, July 7 Litho.

3867	A1852	2k bister & multi	.15	.15
3868	A1852	4k bister & multi	.15	.15
3869	A1852	10k bister & multi	.40	.15
3870	A1852	12k bister & multi	.45	.15
3871	A1852	14k bister & multi	.55	.15
3872	A1852	16k bister & multi	.65	.15
3873	A1852	20k bister & multi	.75	.20
		Nos. 3867-3873 (7)	3.10	
		Set value		.80

Foreign master works in Russian museums.

Kazakhstan Flag, Lenin Badge A1853

1971, July 7 Photo. *Perf. 11½*
3874 A1853 4k blue, red & brown .25 .15

50th anniversary of the Kazakh Communist Youth League.

Star Emblem and Letters A1854

1971, July 14
3875 A1854 4k oliver, blue & black .25 .15

International Letter Writing Week.

Nikolai A. Nekrasov, by Ivan N. Kramskoi A1855

Portraits: No. 3877, Aleksandr Spendiarov, by M. S. Saryan. 10k, Fedor M. Dostoevski, by Vassili G. Perov.

1971, July 14 Litho. *Perf. 12x12½*

3876	A1855	4k citron & multi	.25	.15
3877	A1855	4k gray blue & multi	.25	.15
3878	A1855	10k multicolored	.30	.15
		Nos. 3876-3878 (3)	.80	
		Set value		.30

Nikolai Alekseevitch Nekrasov (1821-1877), poet, Fedor Mikhailovich Dostoevski (1821-1881), novelist, Spendiarov (1871-1928), Armenian composer.

See Nos. 4056-4057.

Zachary Paliashvili (1871-1933), Georgian Composer and Score — A1856

1971, Aug. 3 Photo. *Perf. 12x12½*
3879 A1856 4k brown .25 .15

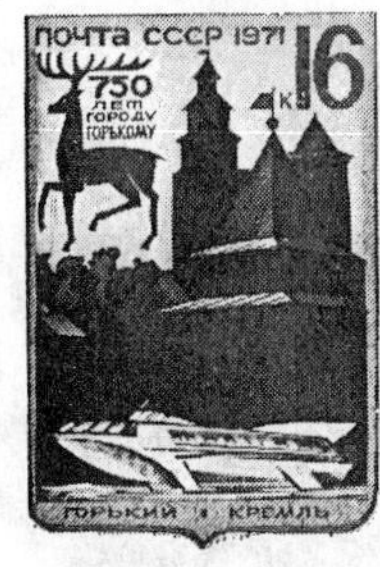

Gorki Kremlin, Stag and Hydrofoil A1857

1971, Aug. 3 Litho. *Perf. 12*
3880 A1857 16k multicolored .60 .25

Gorki (formerly Nizhni Novgorod), 750th anniv. See Nos. 3889, 3910-3914.

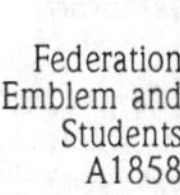

Federation Emblem and Students A1858

1971, Aug. 3 Photo. *Perf. 11½*
3881 A1858 6k ultra & multi .25 .15

Intl. Students Federation, 25th anniv.

Common Dolphins A1859

Sea Mammals: 6k, Sea otter. 10k, Narwhals. 12k, Walrus. 14k, Ribbon seals.

Photogravure and Engraved

1971, Aug. 12 *Perf. 11½*

3882	A1859	4k silver & multi	.20	.15
3883	A1859	6k silver & multi	.20	.15
3884	A1859	10k silver & multi	.30	.15
3885	A1859	12k silver & multi	.35	.15
3886	A1859	14k silver & multi	.45	.15
		Nos. 3882-3886 (5)	1.50	
		Set value		.50

Miner's Star of Valor — A1860

1971, Aug. 17 Photo. *Perf. 11½*
3887 A1860 4k bister, black & red .25 .15

250th anniversary of the discovery of coal in the Donets Basin.

Ernest Rutherford and Diagram of Movement of Atomic Particles A1861

1971, Aug. 24 Photo. *Perf. 12*
3888 A1861 6k magenta & dk ol .25 .15

Rutherford (1871-1937), British physicist.

Gorki and Gorki Statue — A1862

1971, Sept. 14 *Perf. 11½*

3889 A1862 4k steel blue & multi .25 .15

Gorki (see #3880).

Troika and Spasski Tower A1863

1971, Sept. 14

3890 A1863 10k black, red & gold .30 .15

New Year 1972.

Automatic Production Center — A1864

#3892, Agricultural development. #3893, Family in shopping center. #3894, Hydro-generators, thermoelectric station. #3895, Marchers, flags, books inscribed Marx and Lenin.

1971, Sept. 29 Photo. *Perf. 12x11½*

3891	A1864	4k purple, red & blk	.20	.15
3892	A1864	4k ocher, red & brn	.20	.15
3893	A1864	4k yel, olive & red	.20	.15
3894	A1864	4k bister, red & brn	.20	.15
3895	A1864	4k ultra, red & slate	.20	.15
		Nos. 3891-3895 (5)	1.00	
		Set value		.50

Resolutions of 24th Soviet Union Communist Party Congress.

The Meeting, by Vladimir Y. Makovsky A1865

Ivan N. Kramskoi, Self-portrait — A1866

Paintings: 4k, Woman Student, by Nikolai A. Yaroshenko. 6k, Woman Miner, by Nikolai A. Kasatkin. 10k, Harvest, by G. G. Myasoyedov, horiz. 16k, Country Road, by A. K. Savrasov. 20k, Pine Forest, by I. I. Shishkin, horiz.

Perf. 12x12½, 12½x12

1971, Oct. 14 Litho.

Frame in Light Gray

3896	A1865	2k multicolored	.15	.15
3897	A1865	4k multicolored	.20	.15
3898	A1865	6k multicolored	.30	.15
3899	A1865	10k multicolored	.60	.15
3900	A1865	16k multicolored	.65	.15
3901	A1865	20k multicolored	1.25	.15
		Nos. 3896-3901 (6)	3.15	
		Set value		.60

Souvenir Sheet

Lithographed and Gold Embossed

3902 A1866 50k dk green & multi 2.00 .60

History of Russian painting.

V. V. Vorovsky, Bolshevik Party Leader and Diplomat, Birth Cent. — A1867

1971, Oct. 14 Engr. *Perf. 12*

3903 A1867 4k red brown .25 .15

Cosmonauts Dobrovolsky, Volkov and Patsayev — A1868

1971, Oct. 20 Photo. *Perf. 11½x12*

3904 A1868 4k black, lilac & org .25 .15

In memory of cosmonauts Lt. Col. Georgi T. Dobrovolsky, Vladislav N. Volkov and Viktor I. Patsayev, who died during the Soyuz 11 space mission, June 6-30, 1971.

Order of October Revolution A1869

1971, Oct. 20 Litho. *Perf. 12*

3905 A1869 4k red, yel & black .25 .15

54th anniversary of October Revolution.

E. Vakhtangov and "Princess Turandot" A1870

Dzhambul Dzhabayev A1871

Designs: No. 3907, Boris Shchukin and scene from "Man with Rifle (Lenin)," horiz. No. 3908, Ruben Simonov and scene from "Cyrano de Bergerac," horiz.

Perf. 12x12½, 12½x12

1971, Oct. 26 Photo.

3906	A1870	10k maroon & red brn	.35	.15
3907	A1870	10k brown & dull yel	.35	.15
3908	A1870	10k red brown & ocher	.35	.15
		Nos. 3906-3908 (3)	1.05	.45

Vakhtangov Theater, Moscow, 50th anniv.

1971, Nov. 16 *Perf. 12x12½*

3909 A1871 4k orange & brown .30 .25

Dzhabayev (1846-1945), Kazakh poet.

Gorki Kremlin Type, 1971

Designs: 3k, Pskov Kremlin and Velikaya River. 4k, Novgorod Kremlin and eternal flame memorial. 6k, Smolensk Fortress and liberation monument. 10k,Kolomna Kremlin and buses. 50k, Moscow Kremlin.

1971, Nov. 16 Litho. *Perf. 12*

3910	A1857	3k multicolored	.25	.15
3911	A1857	4k multicolored	.25	.15
3912	A1857	6k gray & multi	.25	.15
3913	A1857	10k olive & multi	.25	.15
		Nos. 3910-3913 (4)	1.00	
		Set value		.40

Souvenir Sheet

Engraved and Lithographed

Perf. 11½

3914 A1857 50k yellow & multi 1.75 1.00

Historic buildings. No. 3914 contains one 21½x32mm stamp.

William Foster, View of New York — A1872

1971 Litho. *Perf. 12*

3915	A1872	10k brown & black ("-1961")	.50	.25
a.		"-1964"	10.00	7.25

William Foster (1881-1961), chairman of Communist Party of US.

No. 3915a was issued Nov. 16 with incorrect death date (1964). No. 3915, with corrected date (1961), was issued Dec. 8.

Aleksandr Fadeyev and Cavalrymen A1873

1971, Nov. 25 Photo. *Perf. 12½x12*

3916 A1873 4k slate & orange .30 .25

Aleksandr Fadeyev (1901-1956), writer.

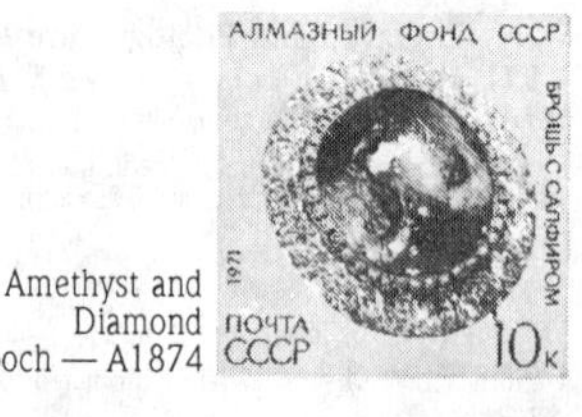

Amethyst and Diamond Brooch — A1874

Precious Jewels: #3918, Engraved Shakh diamond, India, 16th cent. #3919, Diamond daffodils, 18th cent. #3920, Amethyst & diamond pendant. #3921, Diamond rose made for centenary of Lenin's birth. 30k, Diamond & pearl pendant.

1971, Dec. 8 Litho. *Perf. 11½*

3917	A1874	10k brt blue & multi	.35	.15
3918	A1874	10k dk red & multi	.35	.15
3919	A1874	10k grnsh black & multi	.35	.15
3920	A1874	20k grnsh black & multi	.70	.25
3921	A1874	20k rose red & multi	.70	.25
3922	A1874	30k black & multi	1.10	.40
		Nos. 3917-3922 (6)	3.55	1.35

Souvenir Sheet

Workers with Banners, Congress Hall and Spasski Tower — A1875

1971, Dec. 15 Photo. *Perf. 11x11½*

3923 A1875 20k red, pale green & brown 2.00 1.00

See note after No. 3895. No. 3923 contains one partially perforated stamp.

Vanda Orchid — A1876

Flowers: 1k, #3929b, shown. 2k, Anthurium. 4k, #3929c, Flowering crab cactus. 12k, #3929a, Amaryllis. 14k, #3929d, Medinilla magnifica.

1971, Dec. 15 Litho. *Perf. 12x12½*

3924	A1876	1k olive & multi	.15	.15
3925	A1876	2k green & multi	.15	.15
3926	A1876	4k blue & multi	.15	.15
3927	A1876	12k multicolored	.50	.15
3928	A1876	14k multicolored	.55	.15
		Nos. 3924-3928 (5)	1.50	
		Set value		.50

Miniature Sheet

Perf. 12

3929		Sheet of 4	2.00	.90
a.-d.	A1876	10k any single	.40	.25

Nos. 3929a-3929d have white background, black frame line and inscription. Size of stamps 19x57mm.

Issue dates: Nos. 3924-3928, Dec. 15; No. 3929, Dec. 30.

Peter I Reviewing Fleet, 1723 — A1877

History of Russian Fleet: 4k, Oriol, first ship built in Eddinovo, 1668, vert. 10k, Battleship Poltava, 1712, vert. 12k, Armed ship Ingermanland, 1715, vert. 16k, Frigate Vladimir, 1848.

Perf. 11½x12, 12x11½

1971, Dec. 15 Engr. & Photo.

3930	A1877	1k multicolored	.30	.25
3931	A1877	4k brown & multi	.35	.25
3932	A1877	10k multicolored	.75	.35
3933	A1877	12k multicolored	.75	.35
3934	A1877	16k lt green & multi	1.50	.40
		Nos. 3930-3934 (5)	3.65	1.60

Ice Hockey A1878

1971, Dec. 15 Litho. *Perf. 12½*

3935 A1878 6k multicolored .30 .25

25th anniversary of Soviet ice hockey.

Oil Rigs and Causeway in Caspian Sea — A1879

1971, Dec. 30 *Perf. 11½*

3936 A1879 4k dp blue, org & blk .25 .15

Baku oil industry.

G. M. Krzhizhanovsky (1872-1959), Scientist and Co-worker with Lenin — A1880

1972, Jan. 5 Engr. *Perf. 12*

3937	A1880	4k yellow brown	.25	.15

Alexander Scriabin A1881

Bering's Cormorant A1882

1972, Jan. 6 Photo. *Perf. 12x12½*

3938	A1881	4k indigo & olive	.30	.25

Scriabin (1872-1915), composer.

1972, Jan. 12 *Perf. 11½*

Birds: 6k, Ross' gull, horiz. 10k, Barnacle geese. 12k, Spectacled eiders, horiz. 16k, Mediterranean gull.

3939	A1882	4k dk grn, blk & yel	.20	.15
3940	A1882	6k indigo, pink & blk	.30	.15
3941	A1882	10k grnsh blue, blk & brown	.55	.15
3942	A1882	12k multicolored	.60	.15
3943	A1882	16k ultra, gray & red	.65	.20
		Nos. 3939-3943 (5)	2.30	
		Set value		.50

Waterfowl of the USSR.

Speed Skating — A1883

Heart, Globe and Exercising Family — A1884

Designs (Olympic Rings and): 6k, Women's figure skating. 10k, Ice hockey. 12k, Ski jump. 16k, Long-distance skiing. 50k, Sapporo '72 emblem.

1972, Jan. 20 Litho. *Perf. 12x12½*

3944	A1883	4k bl grn, red & brn	.20	.15
3945	A1883	6k yel grn, blue & dp orange	.20	.15
3946	A1883	10k vio, bl & dp org	.35	.15
3947	A1883	12k light blue, blue & brick red	.40	.15
3948	A1883	16k gray, bl & brt rose	.70	.20
		Nos. 3944-3948 (5)	1.85	
		Set value		.50

Souvenir Sheet

3949	A1883	50k multicolored	1.50	.75

11th Winter Olympic Games, Sapporo, Japan, Feb. 3-13.

For overprint see No. 3961.

1972, Feb. 9 Photo.

3950	A1884	4k brt green & rose red	.25	.15

Heart Month sponsored by the WHO.

Leipzig Fair Emblem and Soviet Pavilion A1885

Hammer, Sickle and Cogwheel Emblem A1886

1972, Feb. 22 *Perf. 11½*

3951	A1885	16k red & gold	.60	.25

50th anniversary of the participation of the USSR in the Leipzig Trade Fair.

1972, Feb. 29 *Perf. 12x12½*

3952	A1886	4k rose red & lt brown	.25	.15

15th USSR Trade Union Congress, Moscow, March 1972.

Aloe A1887

Aleksandra Kollontai A1888

Medicinal Plants: 2k, Horn poppy. 4k, Groundsel. 6k, Orthosiphon stamineus. 10k, Nightshade.

1972, Mar. 14 Litho. *Perf. 12x12½*

Flowers in Natural Colors

3953	A1887	1k olive bister	.15	.15
3954	A1887	2k slate green	.15	.15
3955	A1887	4k brt purple	.15	.15
3956	A1887	6k violet blue	.20	.15
3957	A1887	10k dk brown	.40	.25
		Nos. 3953-3957 (5)	1.05	
		Set value		.70

1972, Mar. 20 Engr. *Perf. 12½x12*

Portraits: No. 3959, Georgy Chicherin. No. 3960, Kamo (pseudonym of S.A. Ter-Petrosyan).

3958	A1888	4k red brown	.20	.15
3959	A1888	4k claret	.20	.15
3960	A1888	4k olive bister	.20	.15
		Nos. 3958-3960 (3)	.60	
		Set value		.30

Outstanding workers of the Communist Party of the Soviet Union and for the State.

No. 3949 Overprinted in Margin Souvenir Sheet

СОВЕТСКИЕ СПОРТСМЕНЫ ЗАВОЕВАЛИ 8 ЗОЛОТЫХ МЕДАЛЕЙ, 5 СЕРЕБРЯНЫХ, 3 БРОНЗОВЫХ.

1972, Mar. 20 Litho. *Perf. 12x12½*

3961	A1883	50k multicolored	4.00	2.00

Victories of Soviet athletes in the 11th Winter Olympic Games (8 gold, 5 silver, 3 bronze medals).

For similar overprints see Nos. 4028, 4416.

Orbital Station Salyut and Spaceship Soyuz Docking Above Earth — A1889

Designs: No. 3963, Mars 2 approaching Mars, and emblem dropped on Mars. 16k, Mars 3, which landed on Mars, Dec. 2, 1971.

1971, Apr. 5 Photo. *Perf. 11½x12*

3962	A1889	6k vio, blue & silver	.20	.15
3963	A1889	6k purple, ocher & sil	.20	.15
3964	A1889	16k pur, blue & silver	1.00	.15
		Nos. 3962-3964 (3)	1.40	
		Set value		.30

Cosmonauts' Day.

Shield and Products of Izhory Factory A1890

1972, Apr. 20 *Perf. 12½x12*

3965	A1890	4k purple & silver	.25	.15

250th anniversary of Izhory Factory, founded by Peter the Great.

Leonid Sobinov in "Eugene Onegin," by Tchaikovsky A1891

1972, Apr. 20

3966	A1891	10k dp brown & buff	.30	.15

Sobinov (1872-1934), opera singer.

Book, Torch, Children and Globe A1892

1972, May 5 *Perf. 11½*

3967	A1892	6k brn, grnsh bl & buff	.25	.15

International Book Year 1972.

Girl in Laboratory and Pioneers A1893

Designs: 1k, Pavlik Morosov (Pioneer hero), Pioneers saluting and banner. 3k, Pioneers with wheelbarrow, Chukchi boy, and Chukotka Pioneer House. 4k, Pioneer Honor Guard and Parade. 30k, Pioneer Honor Guard, vert.

1972, May 10

3968	A1893	1k red & multi	.20	.15
3969	A1893	2k multicolored	.20	.15
3970	A1893	3k multicolored	.20	.15
3971	A1893	4k gray & multi	.20	.15
		Nos. 3968-3971 (4)	.80	
		Set value		.40

Souvenir Sheet

Perf. 12x12½

3972	A1893	30k multicolored	2.00	.75

50th anniversary of the Lenin Pioneer Organization of the USSR.

Pioneer Bugler A1894

1972, May 27 Photo. *Perf. 11½*

3973	A1894	4k red, ocher & plum	.25	.15

2nd Youth Philatelic Exhibition, Minsk, and 50th anniv. of Lenin Pioneer Org.

M. S. Ordubady (1872-1950), Azerbaijan Writer and Social Worker — A1895

1972, May 25 *Perf. 12x12½*

3974	A1895	4k orange & rose brn	.30	.15

Globe A1896

1972, May 25 *Perf. 11½*

3975	A1896	6k multicolored	.60	.30

European Safety and Cooperation Conference, Brussels.

Cossack Leader, by Ivan Nikitin — A1897

Paintings: 4k, Fedor G. Volkov (actor), by Anton Losenko. 6k, V. Majkov (poet), by Fedor Rokotov. 10k, Nikolai I. Novikov (writer), by Dimitri Levitsky. 12k, Gavriil R. Derzhavin (poet, civil servant), by Vladimir Borovikovsky. 16k, Peasants' Supper, by Mikhail Shibanov, horiz. 20k, View of Moscow, by Fedor Alexeyev, horiz.

Perf. 12x12½, 12½x12

1972, June 7 Litho.

3976	A1897	2k gray & multi	.15	.15
3977	A1897	4k gray & multi	.15	.15
3978	A1897	6k gray & multi	.25	.15
3979	A1897	10k gray & multi	.40	.15
3980	A1897	12k gray & multi	.45	.15
3981	A1897	16k gray & multi	.70	.20
3982	A1897	20k gray & multi	.95	.25
		Nos. 3976-3982 (7)	3.05	
		Set value		.80

History of Russian painting. See Nos. 4036-4042, 4074-4080, 4103-4109.

George Dimitrov A1898

Fencing, Olympic Rings A1899

1972, June 15 Photo. *Perf. 12½x12*

3983	A1898	6k brown & ol bister	.30	.15

Dimitrov (1882-1949), Bulgarian Communist Party leader and Premier.

1972, July 1 *Perf. 12x11½*

Designs (Olympic Rings and): 6k, Women's gymnastics. 10k, Canoeing. 14k, Boxing. 16k, Running. 50k, Weight lifting.

3984	A1899	4k brt mag & gold	.15	.15
3985	A1899	6k dp green & gold	.20	.15
3986	A1899	10k brt blue & gold	.55	.15
3987	A1899	14k Prus blue & gold	.60	.15
3988	A1899	16k red & gold	.85	.15
		Nos. 3984-3988 (5)	2.35	
		Set value		.50

Souvenir Sheet
Perf. 11½

3989 A1899 50k gold & multi 2.00 .80

20th Olympic Games, Munich, Aug. 26-Sept. 11. #3989 contains one 25x35mm stamp.
For overprint see No. 4028.

Congress Palace, Kiev — A1900

1972, July 1 **Photo. & Engr.**

3990 A1900 6k Prus blue & bister .25 .15

9th World Gerontology Congress, Kiev, July 2-7.

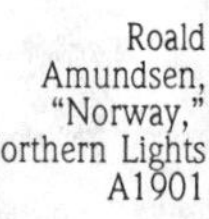

Roald Amundsen, "Norway," Northern Lights A1901

1972, July 13 **Photo.** ***Perf. 11½***

3991 A1901 6k vio blue & dp bister .40 .25

Roald Amundsen (1872-1928), Norwegian polar explorer.

17th Century House, Chernigov A1902

Designs: 4k, Market Square, Lvov, vert. 10k, Kovnirov Building, Kiev. 16k, Fortress, Kamenets-Podolski, vert.

Perf. 12x12½, 12½x12

1972, July 18 **Litho.**

3992 A1902	4k citron & multi	.15	.15
3993 A1902	6k gray & multi	.15	.15
3994 A1902	10k ocher & multi	.40	.15
3995 A1902	16k salmon & multi	.60	.15
	Nos. 3992-3995 (4)	1.30	
	Set value		.40

Historic and architectural treasures of the Ukraine.

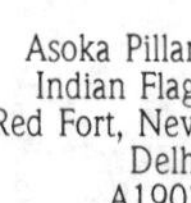

Asoka Pillar, Indian Flag, Red Fort, New Delhi A1903

1972, July 27 **Photo.** ***Perf. 11½***

3996 A1903 6k dk blue, emer & red .25 .15

25th anniversary of India's independence.

Miners' Emblem A1904

1972, Aug. 10

3997 A1904 4k violet gray & red .25 .15

25th Miners' Day.

Far East Fighters' Monument — A1905

Designs: 4k, Monument for Far East Civil War heroes, industrial view. 6k, Vladivostok rostral column, Pacific fleet ships.

1972, Aug. 10

3998 A1905	3k red org, car & black	.20	.15
3999 A1905	4k yel, sepia & blk	.20	.15
4000 A1905	6k pink, dk car & black	.20	.15
	Nos. 3998-4000 (3)	.60	
	Set value		.30

50th anniversary of the liberation of the Far Eastern provinces.

Boy with Dog, by Murillo A1906

Paintings from the Hermitage, Leningrad: 4k, Breakfast, Velazquez. 6k, Milkmaid's Family, Louis Le Nain. 16k, Sad Woman, Watteau. 20k, Moroccan Saddling Steed, Delacroix. 50k, Self-portrait, Van Dyck. 4k, 6k horiz.

Perf. 12½x12, 12x12½

1972, Aug. 15 **Litho.**

4001 A1906	4k multicolored	.15	.15
4002 A1906	6k multicolored	.25	.15
4003 A1906	10k multicolored	.35	.15
4004 A1906	16k multicolored	.50	.15
4005 A1906	20k multicolored	.75	.20
	Nos. 4001-4005 (5)	2.00	
	Set value		.50

Souvenir Sheet
Perf. 12

4006 A1906 50k multicolored 2.50 1.00

Sputnik 1 — A1907

1972, Sept. 14 **Litho.** ***Perf. 12x11½***

4007 A1907	6k shown	.20	.15
4008 A1907	6k Launching of Vostok 2	.20	.15
4009 A1907	6k Lenov floating in space	.20	.15
4010 A1907	6k Lunokhod on moon	.20	.15
4011 A1907	6k Venera 7 descending to Venus	.20	.15
4012 A1907	6k Mars & descending to Mars	.20	.15
	Nos. 4007-4012 (6)	1.20	
	Set value		.50

15 years of space era. Sheets of 6.

Konstantin Aleksandrovich Mardzhanishvili (1872-1933), Theatrical Producer — A1908

1972, Sept. 20 **Engr.** ***Perf. 12x12½***

4013 A1908 4k slate green .30 .25

Museum Emblem, Communications Symbols — A1909

1972, Sept. 20 **Photo.** ***Perf. 11½***

4014 A1909 4k slate green & multi .25 .15

Centenary of the A. S. Popov Central Museum of Communications.

"Stamp" and Topical Collecting Symbols A1910

Engraved and Lithographed

1972, Oct. 4 ***Perf. 12***

4015 A1910 4k yel, black & red .25 .15

Philatelic Exhibition in honor of 50th anniversary of the USSR.

Lenin A1911

1972, Oct. 12 **Photo.** ***Perf. 11½***

4016 A1911 4k gold & red .25 .15

55th anniversary of October Revolution.

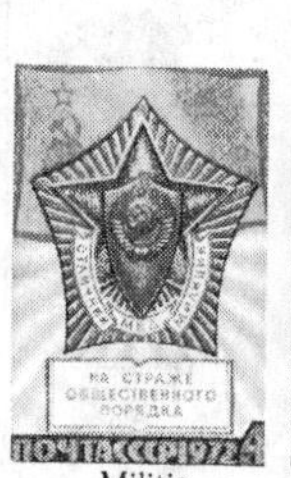

Militia Badge — A1912

Arms of USSR — A1913

1972, Oct. 12

4017 A1912 4k gold, red & dk brn .25 .15

55th anniv. of the Militia of the USSR.

1972, Oct. 28 ***Perf. 12x11½***

USSR, 50th anniv.: #4019, Arms and industrial scene. #4020, Arms, Supreme Soviet, Kremlin. #4021, Lenin. #4022, Arms, worker, book (Constitution). 30k, Coat of arms and Spasski Tower, horiz.

4018 A1913	4k multicolored	.20	.15
4019 A1913	4k multicolored	.20	.15
4020 A1913	4k multicolored	.20	.15
4021 A1913	4k multicolored	.20	.15
4022 A1913	4k multicolored	.20	.15
	Nos. 4018-4022 (5)	1.00	
	Set value		.50

Souvenir Sheet
Lithographed; Embossed
Perf. 12

4023 A1913 30k red & gold 1.50 .40

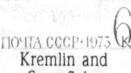

Kremlin and Snowflake A1914

Savings Bank Book A1915

Engraved and Photogravure

1972, Nov. 15 ***Perf. 11½***

4024 A1914 6k multicolored .25 .15

New Year 1973.

1972, Nov. 15 **Photo.** ***Perf. 12x12½***

4025 A1915 4k lilac & slate .25 .15

50th anniv. of savings banks in the USSR.

Soviet Olympic Emblem and Laurel — A1916

Design: 30k, Soviet Olympic emblem and obverse of gold, silver and bronze medals.

1972, Nov. 15 ***Perf. 11½***

4026 A1916	20k brn ol, red & gold	.50	.40
4027 A1916	30k dp car, gold & brn	1.00	.60

No. 3989 Overprinted in Red

СЛАВА
СОВЕТСНИМ ОЛИМПИЙЦАМ,
ЗАВОЕВАВШИМ
50 ЗОЛОТЫХ, 27 СЕРЕБРЯНЫХ
И 22 БРОНЗОВЫЕ НАГРАДЫ!

Souvenir Sheet

4028 A1899 50k gold & multi 3.00 1.25

Soviet medalists at 20th Olympic Games.

Battleship Peter the Great, 1872 — A1917

History of Russian Fleet: 3k, Cruiser Varyag, 1899. 4k, Battleship Potemkin, 1900. 6k, Cruiser Ochakov, 1902. 10k, Mine layer Amur, 1907.

Engraved and Photogravure

1972, Nov. 22 ***Perf. 11½x12***

4029 A1917	2k multicolored	.35	.15
4030 A1917	3k multicolored	.35	.15
4031 A1917	4k multicolored	.45	.15
4032 A1917	6k multicolored	.70	.15
4033 A1917	10k multicolored	1.10	.15
	Nos. 4029-4033 (5)	2.95	.75

Grigory S. Skovoroda A1918

Child Reading Traffic Rules A1919

1972, Dec. 7 **Engr.** ***Perf. 12***

4034 A1918 4k dk violet blue .30 .15

Grigory S. Skovoroda (1722-1794), Ukrainian philosopher and humanist.

1972, Dec. 7 **Photo.** ***Perf. 11½***

4035 A1919 4k Prus blue, blk & red .25 .15

Traffic safety campaign.

Russian Painting Type of 1972

Paintings: 2k, Meeting of Village Party Members, by E. M. Cheptsov, horiz. 4k, Pioneer Girl, by Nicolai A. Kasatkin. 6k, Woman Delegate, by G. G. Ryazhsky. 10k, Winter's End, by K. F. Yuon, horiz. 16k, The Partisan A. G. Lunev, by N. I. Strunnikov. 20k, Igor E. Grabar, self-portrait. 50k, Blue Space (seascape with flying geese), by Arcadi A. Rylov, horiz.

Perf. 12x12½, 12½x12

1972, Dec. 7 **Litho.**

4036 A1897	2k olive & multi	.15	.15
4037 A1897	4k olive & multi	.15	.15
4038 A1897	6k olive & multi	.15	.15
4039 A1897	10k olive & multi	.40	.15

4040 A1897 16k olive & multi .55 .15
4041 A1897 20k olive & multi .80 .25
Nos. 4036-4041 (6) 2.20
Set value .65

Souvenir Sheet
Perf. 12

4042 A1897 50k multicolored 2.00 1.25

History of Russian painting.

Symbolic of Theory and Practice — A1920

Engraved and Photogravure

1972, Dec. 7 *Perf. 11½*
4043 A1920 4k sl grn, yel & red brn .30 .15

Centenary of Polytechnic Museum, Moscow.

Venera 8 and Parachute A1921

1972, Dec. 28 **Photo.** *Perf. 11½*
4044 A1921 6k dl claret, bl & blk .30 .15

Souvenir Sheet
Imperf

4045 Sheet of 2 9.00 3.00
a. A1921 50k Venera 8 2.50 .90
b. A1921 50k Mars 3 2.50 .90

Soviet space research. No. 4045 contains 2 40x20mm stamps with simulated perforations.

Globe, Torch and Palm — A1922

1973, Jan. 5 *Perf. 11x11½*
4046 A1922 10k tan, vio blue & red .35 .30

15th anniversary of Afro-Asian Peoples' Solidarity Organization (AAPSO).

I. V. Babushkin A1923

"30," Map and Admiralty Tower, Leningrad A1924

1973, Jan. 10 **Engr.** *Perf. 12*
4047 A1923 4k greenish black .25 .15

Babushkin (1873-1906), revolutionary.

1973, Jan. 10 **Photo.** *Perf. 11½*
4048 A1924 4k pale brown, ocher & black .25 .15

30th anniversary of the breaking of the Nazi blockade of Leningrad.

TU-154 Turbojet Passenger Plane — A1925

1973, Jan. 10 **Litho.** *Perf. 12*
4049 A1925 6k multicolored .25 .15

50th anniversary of Soviet Civil Aviation.

Gediminas Tower, Flag, Modern Vilnius A1926

1973, Jan. 10 **Photo.** *Perf. 11½*
4050 A1926 10k gray, red & green .40 .30

650th anniversary of Vilnius.

Heroes' Memorial, Stalingrad — A1927

Designs (Details from Monument): 3k, Man with rifle and "Mother Russia," vert. 10k, Mourning mother and child. 12k, Arm with torch, vert. No. 4055a, Red star, hammer and sickle emblem and statuary like 3k. No. 4055b, "Mother Russia," vert.

1973, Feb. 1 **Litho.** *Perf. 11½*
4051 A1927 3k dp orange & black .25 .15
4052 A1927 4k dp yellow & black .25 .15
4053 A1927 10k olive & multi .25 .15
4054 A1927 12k dp car & black .25 .15
Nos. 4051-4054 (4) 1.00
Set value .50

Souvenir Sheet
Perf. 12x12½, 12½x12

4055 Sheet of 2 1.50 .75
a.-b. A1927 20k any single .45 .20

30th anniv. of the victory over the Germans at Stalingrad. #4055 contains 2 40x18mm stamps.

Large Portrait Type of 1971

Designs: 4k, Mikhail Prishvin (1873-1954), author. 10k, Fedor Chaliapin (1873-1938), opera singer, by K. Korovin.

1973 **Litho.** *Perf. 11½x12*
4056 A1855 4k pink & multi .20 .15
4057 A1855 10k lt blue & multi .20 .15
Set value .20

Issue dates: 4k, Feb. 1; 10k, Feb. 8.

"Mayakovsky Theater" A1928

"Mossovet Theater" A1929

1973, Feb. 1 **Photo.** *Perf. 11½*
4058 A1928 10k red, gray & indigo .30 .15
4059 A1929 10k red, mag & gray .30 .15
Set value .20

50th anniversary of the Mayakovsky and Mossovet Theaters in Moscow.

Copernicus and Solar System A1930

1973, Feb. 8 **Engr. & Photo.**
4060 A1930 10k ultra & sepia .40 .25

500th anniversary of the birth of Nicolaus Copernicus (1473-1543), Polish astronomer.

Ice Hockey A1931

Design: 50k, Two players, vert.

1973, Mar. 14 **Photo.** *Perf. 11½*
4061 A1931 10k gold, blue & sepia .40 .25

Souvenir Sheet

4062 A1931 50k bl grn, gold & sep 2.00 1.00

European and World Ice Hockey Championships, Moscow.
See No. 4082.

Athletes and Banners of Air, Land and Naval Forces — A1932

Tank, Red Star and Map of Battle of Kursk — A1933

1973, Mar. 14
4063 A1932 4k bright blue & multi .30 .15

Sports Society of Soviet Army, 50th anniv.

1973, Mar. 14
4064 A1933 4k gray, black & red .30 .15

30th anniversary of Soviet victory in the Battle of Kursk during World War II.

Nikolai E. Bauman (1873-1905), Bolshevist Revolutionary — A1934

1973, Mar. 20 **Engr.** *Perf. 12½x12*
4065 A1934 4k brown .30 .15

Red Cross and Red Crescent — A1935

Designs: 6k, Theater curtain and mask. 16k, Youth Festival emblem and young people.

1973, Mar. 20 **Photo.** *Perf. 11*
4066 A1935 4k gray green & red .20 .15
4067 A1935 6k violet blue & red .25 .15
4068 A1935 16k multicolored .80 .15
Nos. 4066-4068 (3) 1.25
Set value .30

Union of Red Cross and Red Crescent Societies of the USSR, 50th annivs.; 15th Cong. of the Intl. Theater Institute; 10th World Festival of Youth and Students, Berlin.

Aleksandr N. Ostrovsky, by V. Perov A1936

1973, Apr. 5 **Litho.** *Perf. 12x12½*
4069 A1936 4k tan & multi .30 .15

Ostrovsky (1823-1886), dramatist.

Earth Satellite "Interkosmos" A1937

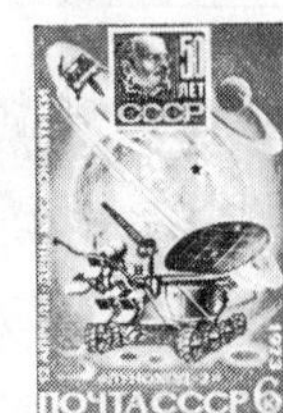

Lunokhod 2 on Moon and Lenin Moon Plaque A1938

1973, Apr. 12 **Photo.** *Perf. 11½*
4070 A1937 6k brn ol & dull claret .25 .15
4071 A1938 6k vio blue & multi .25 .15
Set value .20

Souvenir Sheets
Perf. 12x11½

4072 Sheet of 3, purple & multi 2.50 1.00
a. A1938 20k Lenin plaque .55 .30
b. A1938 20k Lunokhod 2 .55 .30
c. A1938 20k Telecommunications .55 .35
4073 Sheet of 3, slate grn & multi 2.50 1.00
a. A1938 20k Lenin plaque .55 .30
b. A1938 20k Lunokhod 2 .55 .30
c. A1938 20k Telecommunications .55 .30

Cosmonauts' Day. No. 4070 for cooperation in space research by European communist countries.

Souvenir sheets contain 3 50x21mm stamps.

Russian Painting Type of 1972

Paintings: 2k, Guitarist, V. A. Tropinin. 4k, Young Widow, by P. A. Fedotov. 6k, Self-portrait, by O. A. Kiprensky. 10k, Woman with Grapes ("An Afternoon in Italy") by K. P. Bryullov. 12k, Boy with Dog ("That was my Father's Dinner"), by A. Venetsianov. 16k, "Lower Gallery of Albano," by A. A. Ivanov. 20k, Soldiers ("Conquest of Siberia"), by V. I. Surikov, horiz.

Perf. 12x12½, 12½x12

1973, Apr. 18 **Litho.**
4074 A1897 2k gray & multi .15 .15
4075 A1897 4k gray & multi .15 .15
4076 A1897 6k gray & multi .25 .15
4077 A1897 10k gray & multi .45 .25
4078 A1897 12k gray & multi .60 .25
4079 A1897 16k gray & multi .65 .25
4080 A1897 20k gray & multi .80 .35
Nos. 4074-4080 (7) 3.05 1.55

Athlete, Ribbon of Lenin Order — A1939

1973, Apr. 18 **Photo.** *Perf. 11½*
4081 A1939 4k blue, red & ocher .25 .15

50th anniversary of Dynamo Sports Society.

No. 4062 with Blue Green Inscription and Ornaments Added in Margin

Souvenir Sheet

1973, Apr. 26 **Photo.** *Perf. 11½*
4082 A1931 50k bl grn, gold & sep 5.00 2.00

Soviet victory in European and World Ice Hockey Championships, Moscow.

"Mikhail Lermontov," Route Leningrad to New York
A1940

1973, May 20 Photo. *Perf. 11½*

4083 A1940 16k multicolored .60 .25

Inauguration of transatlantic service Leningrad to New York.

Ernest E. T. Krenkel, Polar Stations and Ship Chelyuskin
A1941

1973, May 20 Litho. & Engr.

4084 A1941 4k dull blue & olive .40 .30

Krenkel (1903-1971), polar explorer.

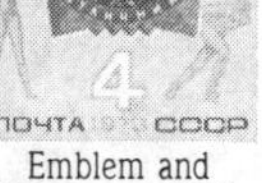

Emblem and Sports — A1942

Singers — A1943

1973, May 20 Litho. *Perf. 12x12½*

4085 A1942 4k multicolored .25 .15

Sports Association for Labor and Defense.

1973, May 24

4086 A1943 10k multicolored .35 .25

Centenary of Latvian Song Festival.

Throwing the Hammer — A1944

Designs: 3k, Athlete on rings. 4k, Woman diver. 16k, Fencing. 50k, Javelin.

1973, June 14 Litho. *Perf. 11½*

4087	A1944	2k lemon & multi	.15	.15
4088	A1944	3k blue & multi	.15	.15
4089	A1944	4k citron & multi	.15	.15
4090	A1944	16k lilac & multi	.35	.15
		Nos. 4087-4090 (4)	.80	
		Set value		.40

Souvenir Sheet

4091 A1944 50k gold & multi 1.75 1.25

Universiad, Moscow, 1973.

Souvenir Sheet

Valentina Nikolayeva-Tereshkova — A1945

1973, June 14 Photo. *Perf. 12x11½*

4092	A1945	Sheet of 3 + label	3.00	1.25
a.		20k as cosmonaut	.55	.25
b.		20k with Indian and African women	.55	.25
c.		20k with daughter	.55	.25

Flight of the 1st woman cosmonaut, 10th anniv.

European Bison — A1946

1973, July 26 Photo. *Perf. 11x11½*

4093	A1946	1k shown	.15	.15
4094	A1946	3k Ibex	.15	.15
4095	A1946	4k Caucasian snowcock	.20	.15
4096	A1946	6k Beaver	.35	.15
4097	A1946	10k Deer and fawns	.50	.15
		Nos. 4093-4097 (5)	1.35	
		Set value		.50

Caucasus and Voronezh wildlife reserves.

Party Membership Card with Lenin Portrait — A1947

1973, July 26 Litho. *Perf. 11½*

4098 A1947 4k multicolored .25 .15

70th anniversary of 2nd Congress of the Russian Social Democratic Workers' Party.

Abu-al-Rayhan al-Biruni (973-1048), Arabian (Persian) Scholar and Writer — A1948

1973, Aug. 9 Engr. *Perf. 12x12½*

4099 A1948 6k red brown .25 .15

White House, Spasski Tower, Hemispheres — A1949

#4101, Eiffel Tower, Spasski Tower, globe. #4102, Schaumburg Palace, Bonn, Spasski Tower, globe. Stamps show representative buildings of Moscow, Washington, New York, Paris & Bonn.

1973, Aug. 10 Photo. *Perf. 11½x12*

4100	A1949	10k magenta & multi	.50	.50
4101	A1949	10k brown & multi	.50	.50
4102	A1949	10k dp car & multi	.50	.50
a.		Souv. sheet of 3 + 3 labels	2.50	2.50
		Nos. 4100-4102 (3)	1.50	1.50

Visit of General Secretary Leonid I. Brezhnev to Washington, Paris and Bonn. Nos. 4100-4102 each printed with se-tenant label with different statements by Brezhnev in Russian and English, French and German, respectively.

No. 4102a contains 4k stamps similar to Nos. 4100-4102 in changed colors. Issued Nov. 26.

See Nos. 4161-4162.

Russian Painting Type of 1972

Paintings: 2k, S. T. Konenkov, sculptor, by P. D. Korin. 4k, Tractor Operators at Supper, by A. A. Plastov. 6k, Letter from the Front, by A. I. Laktionov. 10k, Mountains, by M. S. Saryan. 16k, Wedding on a Future Street, by Y. I. Pimenov. 20k, Ice Hockey, mosaic by A. A. Deineka. 50k, Lenin at 3rd Congress of Young Communist League, by B. V. Yoganson.

1973, Aug. 22 Litho. *Perf. 12x12½*

Frame in Light Gray

4103	A1897	2k multicolored	.15	.15
4104	A1897	4k multicolored	.15	.15
4105	A1897	6k multicolored	.20	.15
4106	A1897	10k multicolored	.35	.15
4107	A1897	16k multicolored	.60	.15
4108	A1897	20k multicolored	.70	.15
		Nos. 4103-4108 (6)	2.15	
		Set value		.60

Souvenir Sheet

Perf. 12

4109 A1897 50k multicolored 2.00 1.25

History of Russian Painting.

Museum, Tashkent
A1950

Y. M. Steklov
A1951

1973, Aug. 23 Photo. *Perf. 12x12½*

4110 A1950 4k multicolored .25 .15

Lenin Central Museum, Tashkent branch.

1973, Aug. 27 Photo. *Perf. 11½x12*

4111 A1951 4k multicolored .25 .15

Steklov (1873-1941), party worker, historian, writer.

Book, Pen and Torch — A1952

Echinopanax Elatum — A1953

1973, Aug. 31 *Perf. 11½*

4112 A1952 6k multicolored .25 .15

Conf. of Writers of Asia & Africa, Alma-Ata.

1973, Sept. 5 Litho. *Perf. 12x12½*

Medicinal Plants: 2k, Ginseng. 4k, Orchis maculatus. 10k, Arnica montana. 12k, Lily of the valley.

4113	A1953	1k yellow & multi	.15	.15
4114	A1953	2k lt blue & multi	.15	.15
4115	A1953	4k gray & multi	.15	.15
4116	A1953	10k sepia & multi	.30	.15
4117	A1953	12k green & multi	.55	.15
		Nos. 4113-4117 (5)	1.30	
		Set value		.50

Imadeddin Nasimi, Azerbaijani Poet, 600th Birth Anniv. — A1954

1973, Sept. 5 Engr.

4118 A1954 4k sepia .30 .15

Cruiser Kirov — A1955

Soviet Warships: 4k, Battleship October Revolution. 6k, Submarine Krasnogvardeyets. 10k, Torpedo boat Soobrazitelny. 16k, Cruiser Red Caucasus.

Engraved and Photogravure

1973, Sept. 12 *Perf. 11½x12*

4119	A1955	3k violet & multi	.15	.15
4120	A1955	4k green & multi	.15	.15
4121	A1955	6k multicolored	.20	.15
4122	A1955	10k blue grn & multi	.30	.15
4123	A1955	16k multicolored	.50	.20
		Nos. 4119-4123 (5)	1.30	
		Set value		.50

Globe and Red Flag Emblem — A1956

1973, Sept. 25 Photo. *Perf. 11½*

4124 A1956 6k gold, buff & red .25 .15

15th anniversary of the international communist review "Problems of Peace and Socialism," published in Prague.

Emelyan I. Pugachev and Peasant Army — A1957

Engraved and Photogravure

1973, Sept. 25 *Perf. 11½x12*

4125 A1957 4k brn, bister & red .25 .15

Bicentenary of peasant revolt of 1773-75 led by Emelyn Ivanovich Pugachev.

Crystal, Institute Emblem and Building
A1958

1973, Oct. 5 *Perf. 11½*

4126 A1958 4k black & multi .25 .15

Leningrad Mining Institute, 150th anniv.

Palm, Globe, Flower
A1959

Elena Stasova
A1960

1973, Oct. 5 Photo.

4127 A1959 6k red, gray & dk blue .25 .15

World Cong. of Peace-loving Forces, Moscow.

1973, Oct. 5 *Perf. 11½x12*

4128 A1960 4k deep claret .25 .15

Elena Dmitriyevna Stasova (1873-1966), communist party worker.

See Nos. 4228-4229.

Order of Friendship A1961

1973, Oct. 5 Litho. *Perf. 12*
4129 A1961 4k red & multi .25 .15

56th anniv. of the October Revolution. Printed se-tenant with coupon showing Arms of USSR and proclamation establishing Order of Friendship of People, in 1972, on the 50th anniv. of the USSR.

Marshal Malinovsky A1962

Ural Man, Red Guard, Worker A1963

1973, Oct. 5 Engr.
4130 A1962 4k slate .25 .15

Rodion Y. Malinovsky (1898-1967).
See Nos. 4203-4205.

1973, Oct. 17 Photo. *Perf. 11½*
4131 A1963 4k red, gold & black .25 .15

250th anniversary of the city of Sverdlovsk.

Dimitri Cantemir (1673-1723), Prince of Moldavia, Writer — A1964

1973, Oct. 17 Engr. *Perf. 12x12½*
4132 A1964 4k rose claret .25 .15

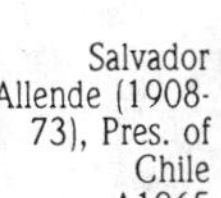

Salvador Allende (1908-73), Pres. of Chile A1965

1973, Nov. 26 Photo. *Perf. 11½*
4133 A1965 6k rose brn & black .25 .15

Spasski Tower, Kremlin A1966

Nariman Narimanov A1967

1973, Nov. 30 Litho. *Perf. 12x12½*
4134 A1966 6k brt blue & multi .25 .15

New Year 1974.

1973, Nov. 30 Engr. *Perf. 12*
4135 A1967 4k slate green .25 .15

Nariman Narimanov (1870-1925), Chairman of Executive Committee of USSR.

Russo-Balt, 1909 — A1968

Designs: 3k, AMO-F15 truck, 1924. 4k, Spartak, NAMI-1 car, 1927. 12k, Ya-6 autobus, 1929. 16k, GAZ-A car, 1932.

1973, Nov. 30 Photo. *Perf. 12x11½*
4136 A1968 2k purple & multi .15 .15
4137 A1968 3k olive & multi .15 .15
4138 A1968 4k ocher & multi .15 .15
4139 A1968 12k vio blue & multi .45 .15
4140 A1968 16k red & multi .75 .15
Nos. 4136-4140 (5) 1.65
Set value .60

Development of Russian automotive industry. See Nos. 4216-4220, 4325-4329, 4440-4444.

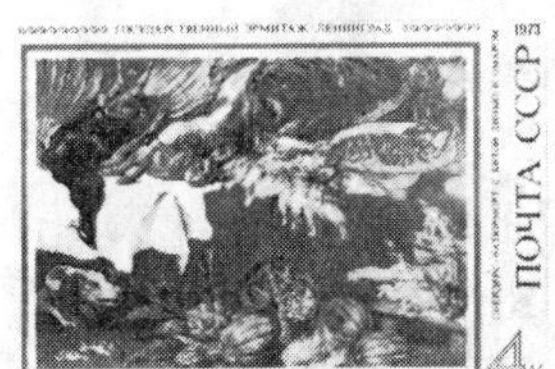
Still Life, by Frans Snyders — A1969

Paintings: 6k, Woman Trying on Earrings, by Rembrandt, vert. 10k, Sick Woman and Physician, by Jan Steen, vert. 12k, Still Life with Sculpture, by Jean-Baptiste Chardin. 14k, Lady in Garden, by Claude Monet. 16k, Young Love, by Jules Bastien-Lepage, vert. 20k Girl with Fan, by Auguste Renoir, vert. 50k, Flora, by Rembrandt, vert.

Perf. 12x11½, 11½x12
1973, Dec. 12 Litho.
4141 A1969 4k bister & multi .15 .15
4142 A1969 6k bister & multi .25 .15
4143 A1969 10k bister & multi .40 .15
4144 A1969 12k bister & multi .45 .15
4145 A1969 14k bister & multi .50 .15
4146 A1969 16k bister & multi .55 .15
4147 A1969 20k bister & multi .70 .20
Nos. 4141-4147 (7) 3.00
Set value .80

Souvenir Sheet
Perf. 12
4148 A1969 50k multicolored 2.00 1.00

Foreign paintings in Russian museums.

Pablo Picasso (1881-1973), Painter — A1970

1973, Dec. 20 Photo. *Perf. 12x11½*
4149 A1970 6k gold, slate grn & red .25 .15

Organ Pipes and Dome, Riga — A1971

#4151, Small Trakai Castle, Lithuania. #4152, Great Sea Gate, Tallinn, Estonia. 10k, Town Hall and "Old Thomas" weather vane, Tallinn.

1973, Dec. 20 Engr. *Perf. 12x12½*
4150 A1971 4k blk, red & slate grn .20 .15
4151 A1971 4k gray, red & buff .20 .15
4152 A1971 4k black, red & grn .20 .15
4153 A1971 10k sep, grn, red & blk .25 .15
Nos. 4150-4153 (4) .85
Set value .40

Architecture of the Baltic area.

I. G. Petrovsky A1972

L. A. Artsimovich A1973

#4154, I. G. Petrovsky (1901-73), mathematician, rector of Moscow State University. #4155, L. A. Artsimovich (1909-73), physician, academician. #4156, K. D. Ushinsky (1824-74), teacher. #4157, M. D. Millionschikov (1913-73), vice president of Academy of Sciences.

1973-74 Photo. *Perf. 11½*
4154 A1972 4k orange & multi .25 .15
4155 A1973 4k blk brn & olive .25 .15

Engr.
Perf. 12½x12
4156 A1973 4k multicolored .25 .15

Litho.
Perf. 12
4157 A1973 4k multicolored .25 .15
Nos. 4154-4157 (4) 1.00
Set value .40

Issued: #4154, 12/28/73; others, 2/6/74.

Flags of India and USSR, Red Fort, Taj Mahal and Kremlin — A1974

Design: No. 4162, Flags of Cuba and USSR, José Marti Monument, Moncada Barracks and Kremlin.

1973-74 Litho. *Perf. 12*
4161 A1974 4k lt ultra & multi .25 .15
4162 A1974 4k lt green & multi ('74) .25 .15
Set value .20

Visit of General Secretary Leonid I. Brezhnev to India and Cuba. Nos. 4161-4162 each printed with se-tenant label with different statements by Brezhnev in Russian and Hindi, and Russian and Spanish respectively.

Red Star, Soldier, Newspaper — A1975

1974, Jan. 1 Photo. *Perf. 11x11½*
4166 A1975 4k gold, red & black .25 .15

50th anniversary of the Red Star newspaper.

Victory Monument, Peter-Paul Fortress, Statue of Peter I — A1976

1974, Jan. 16 Litho. *Perf. 11½*
4167 A1976 4k multicolored .25 .15

30th anniversary of the victory over the Germans near Leningrad.

Oil Workers, Refinery A1977

Comecon Building A1978

1974, Jan. 16 Photo. *Perf. 11½*
4168 A1977 4k dull blue, red & blk .25 .15

10th anniversary of the Tyumen oilfields.

1974, Jan. 16 Photo. *Perf. 11½*
4169 A1978 16k red brn, olive & red .35 .25

25th anniversary of the Council for Mutual Economic Assistance.

Skaters and Rink, Medeo A1979

1974, Jan. 28
4170 A1979 6k slate, brn red & blue .25 .15

European Women's Skating Championships, Medeo, Alma-Ata.

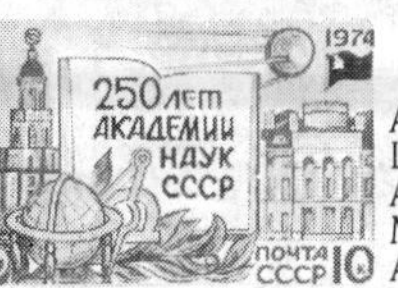
Art Palace, Leningrad, Academy, Moscow A1980

1974, Jan. 30 Photo. & Engr.
4171 A1980 10k multicolored .35 .25

25th anniversary of the Academy of Sciences of the USSR.

3rd Winter Spartiakad Emblem A1981

Young People and Emblem A1982

1974, Mar. 20 Photo. *Perf. 11½*
4172 A1981 10k gold & multi .35 .25

Third Winter Spartiakad.

1974, Mar. 20 Photo. & Engr.
4173 A1982 4k multicolored .25 .15

Youth scientific-technical work.

Azerbaijan Theater — A1983

1974, Mar. 20 Photo. *Perf. 11½*
4174 A1983 6k org, red brn & brn .30 .25

Centenary of Azerbaijan Theater.

Meteorological Satellite "Meteor" A1984

Cosmonauts V. G. Lazarev and O. G. Makarov and Soyuz 12 — A1985

Design: No. 4177, Cosmonauts P. I. Klimuk and V. V. Lebedev, and Soyuz 13.

1974, Mar. 27 *Perf. 11½*
4175 A1984 6k violet & multi .30 .15

Perf. 12x11½
4176 A1985 10k grnsh blue & multi .35 .15
4177 A1985 10k dull yel & multi .35 .15
Nos. 4175-4177 (3) 1.00
Set value .30

Cosmonauts' Day.

Odessa by Moonlight, by Aivazovski — A1986

Seascapes by Aivazovski: 4k, Battle of Chesma, 1848, vert. 6k, St. George's Monastery. 10k, Stormy Sea. 12k, Rainbow (shipwreck). 16k, Shipwreck. 50k, Portrait of Aivazovski, by Kramskoy, vert.

Perf. 12x11½, 11½x12
1974, Mar. 30 Litho.
4178 A1986 2k gray & multi .15 .15
4179 A1986 4k gray & multi .15 .15
4180 A1986 6k gray & multi .35 .15
4181 A1986 10k gray & multi .50 .15
4182 A1986 12k gray & multi .55 .15
4183 A1986 16k gray & multi .85 .25
Nos. 4178-4183 (6) 2.55
Set value .60

Souvenir Sheet
4184 A1986 50k gray & multi 1.75 .90

Ivan Konstantinovich Aivazovski (1817-1900), marine painter. Sheets of Nos. 4178-4183 each contain 2 labels with commemorative inscriptions. See Nos. 4230-4234.

Young Man and Woman, Banner A1987

1974, Mar. 30 Litho. *Perf. 12½x12*
4185 A1987 4k red, yel & brown .25 .15

17th Cong. of the Young Communist League.

Lenin, by V. E. Tsigal A1988

1974, Mar. 30
4186 A1988 4k yel, red & brown .25 .15

50th anniversary of naming the Komsomol (Young Communist League) after Lenin.

Souvenir Sheet

Lenin at the Telegraph, by Igor E. Grabar — A1989

1974, Apr. 16 Litho. *Perf. 12*
4187 A1989 50k multicolored 1.50 .90

104th anniv. of the birth of Lenin.

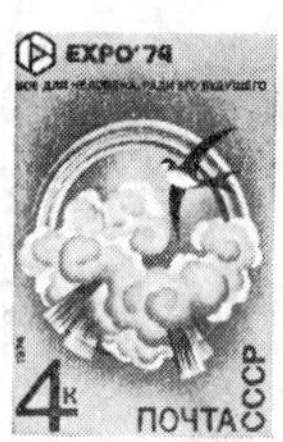

Rainbow, Swallow over Clouds — A1990

Congress Emblem and Clover — A1991

6k, Fish in water. 10k, Crystal. 16k, Rose. 20k, Fawn. 50k, Infant.

1974, Apr. 24 Photo. *Perf. 11½*
4188 A1990 4k lilac & multi .15 .15
4189 A1990 6k multicolored .20 .15
4190 A1990 10k multicolored .35 .15
4191 A1990 16k blue & multi .50 .15
4192 A1990 20k citron & multi .55 .15
Nos. 4188-4192 (5) 1.75
Set value .50

Souvenir Sheet
Litho.
Perf. 12x12½
4193 A1990 50k blue & multi 1.50 .80

EXPO '74 World's Fair, theme "Preserve the Environment," Spokane, WA, May 4-Nov. 4.

1974, May 7 Photo. *Perf. 11½*
4194 A1991 4k green & multi .25 .15

12th International Congress on Meadow Cultivation, Moscow, 1974.

"Cobblestones, Weapons of the Proletariat," by I. D. Shadra A1992

1974, May 7
4195 A1992 4k gold, red & olive .25 .15

50th anniversary of the Lenin Central Revolutionary Museum of the USSR.

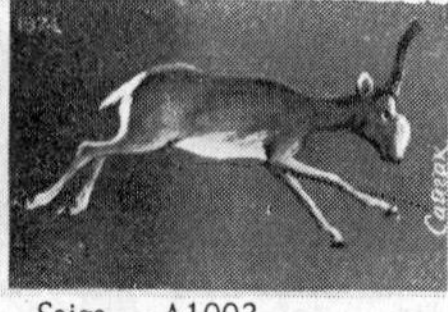

Saiga — A1993

Fauna of USSR: 3k, Koulan (wild ass). 4k, Desman. 6k, Sea lion. 10k, Greenland whale.

1974, May 22 Litho. *Perf. 11½*
4196 A1993 1k olive & multi .25 .15
4197 A1993 3k green & multi .25 .15
4198 A1993 4k multicolored .35 .15
4199 A1993 6k multicolored .60 .15
4200 A1993 10k multicolored .85 .15
Nos. 4196-4200 (5) 2.30
Set value .50

Peter Ilich Tchaikovsky A1994

1974, May 22 Photo. *Perf. 11½*
4201 A1994 6k multicolored .25 .20

5th International Tchaikovsky Competition, Moscow.

Souvenir Sheet

Aleksander S. Pushkin, by O. A. Kiprensky — A1995

1974, June 4 Litho. *Imperf.*
4202 A1995 50k multicolored 1.75 .80

Aleksander S. Pushkin (1799-1837).

Marshal Type of 1973

Designs: #4203, Marshal F. I. Tolbukhin (1894-1949); #4204, Admiral I. S. Isakov (1894-1967); #4205, Marshal S. M. Budenny (1883-1973).

1974 Engr. *Perf. 12*
4203 A1962 4k olive green .15 .15
4204 A1962 4k indigo .15 .15
4205 A1962 4k slate green .15 .15
Nos. 4203-4205 (3) .45
Set value .30

Issued: #4203, 6/5; #4204, 7/18; #4205, 8/20.

Stanislavski and Nemirovich-Danchenko — A1996

1974, June 12 Litho. *Perf. 12*
4211 A1996 10k yel, black & dk red .35 .15

75th anniv. of the Moscow Arts Theater.

Runner, Track, Open Book A1997

1974, June 12 Photo. *Perf. 11½*
4212 A1997 4k multicolored .25 .15

13th Natl. School Spartakiad, Alma-Ata.

Railroad Car — A1998

1974, June 12
4213 A1998 4k multicolored .30 .25

Egorov Railroad Car Factory, cent.

Victory Monument, Minsk — A1999

Liberation Monument, Poltava — A2000

#4215, Monument & Government House, Kiev.

1974, June 20
4214 A1999 4k violet, black & yel .25 .15
4215 A1999 4k blue, black & yel .25 .15
Set value .20

30th anniversary of liberation of Byelorussia (No. 4214), and of Ukraine (No. 4215).
Issue dates: #4214, June 20; #4215, July 18.

Automotive Type of 1973

Designs: 2k, GAZ AA truck, 1932. 3k, GAZ 03-30 bus, 1933. 4k, Zis 5 truck, 1933. 14k, Zis 8 bus, 1934. 16k, Zis 101 car, 1936.

1974, June 20 *Perf. 12x11½*
4216 A1968 2k brown & multi .15 .15
4217 A1968 3k multicolored .15 .15
4218 A1968 4k orange & multi .15 .15
4219 A1968 14k multicolored .50 .15
4220 A1968 16k multicolored .60 .15
Nos. 4216-4220 (5) 1.55
Set value .50

Soviet automotive industry.

1974, July 7 *Perf. 11½*
4221 A2000 4k dull red & sepia .25 .15

800th anniversary of city of Poltava.

Nike Monument, Warsaw and Polish Flag A2001

1974, July 7 Litho. *Perf. 12½x12*
4222 A2001 6k olive & red .25 .15

Polish People's Republic, 30th anniversary.

Mine Layer — A2002

Soviet Warships: 4k, Landing craft. 6k, Anti-submarine destroyer and helicopter. 16k, Anti-submarine cruiser.

Engraved and Photogravure

1974, July 25 *Perf. 11½x12*
4223 A2002 3k multicolored .15 .15
4224 A2002 4k multicolored .15 .15
4225 A2002 6k multicolored .40 .15
4226 A2002 16k multicolored .75 .15
Nos. 4223-4226 (4) 1.45
Set value .40

Pentathlon A2003

1974, Aug. 7 **Photo.** *Perf. 11½*
4227 A2003 16k gold, blue & brown .50 .25

World Pentathlon Championships, Moscow.

Portrait Type of 1973

Portraits: No. 4228, Dimitri Ulyanov (1874-1943). Soviet official and Lenin's brother. No. 4229, V. Menzhinsky (1874-1934), Soviet official.

1974, Aug. 7 **Engr.** *Perf. 12½x12*
4228 A1960 4k slate green .25 .20

Litho.

Perf. 12x11½

4229 A1960 4k rose lake .25 .20

Painting Type of 1974

Russian paintings: 4k, Lilac, by W. Kontchalovski. 6k, "Towards the Wind" (sailboats), by E. Kalnins. 10k, "Spring" (girl and landscape), by O. Zardarjan. 16k, Northern Harbor, G. Nissky. 20k, Kirghiz Girl, by S. Chuikov, vert.

Perf. 12x11½, 11½x12

1974, Aug. 20 **Litho.**
4230 A1986 4k gray & multi .15 .15
4231 A1986 6k gray & multi .20 .15
4232 A1986 10k gray & multi .35 .15
4233 A1986 16k gray & multi .55 .15
4234 A1986 20k gray & multi .75 .15
Nos. 4230-4234 (5) 2.00
Set value .50

Printed in sheets of 18 stamps and 2 labels.

Page of First Russian Primer — A2004

Monument, Russian and Romanian Flags — A2005

1974, Aug. 20 **Photo.** *Perf. 11½*
4235 A2004 4k black, red & gold .25 .15

1st printed Russian primer, 400th anniv.

1974, Aug. 23
4236 A2005 6k dk blue, red & yel .25 .15

Romania's liberation from Fascist rule, 30th anniversary.

Vitebsk A2006

1974, Sept. 4 **Litho.** *Perf. 12*
4237 A2006 4k dk car & olive .25 .15

Millennium of city of Vitebsk.

Kirghiz Republic A2007

50th Anniv. of Founding of Republics (Flags, industrial and agricultural themes): No. 4239, Moldavia. No. 4240, Turkmen. No. 4241, Uzbek. No. 4242, Tadzhik.

1974, Sept. 4 *Perf. 11½x11*
4238 A2007 4k vio blue & multi .20 .15
4239 A2007 4k maroon & multi .20 .15
4240 A2007 4k yellow & multi .20 .15
4241 A2007 4k green & multi .20 .15
4242 A2007 4k lt blue & multi .20 .15
Nos. 4238-4242 (5) 1.00
Set value .40

Arms and Flag of Bulgaria — A2008

Photogravure and Engraved

1974, Sept. 4 *Perf. 11½*
4243 A2008 6k gold & multi .25 .15

30th anniv. of the Bulgarian revolution.

Arms of DDR and Soviet War Memorial, Treptow A2009

1974, Sept. 4 **Photo.**
4244 A2009 6k multicolored .25 .15

German Democratic Republic, 25th anniv.

Souvenir Sheet

Soviet Stamps and Exhibition Poster — A2010

1974, Sept. 4 **Litho.** *Perf. 12x12½*
4245 A2010 50k multicolored *7.50 3.00*

3rd Cong. of the Phil. Soc. of the USSR.

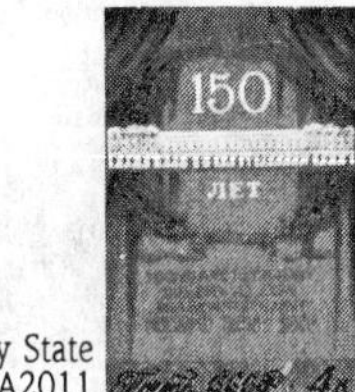
Maly State Theater — A2011

1974, Oct. 3 **Photo.** *Perf. 11x11½*
4246 A2011 4k red, black & gold .25 .15

150th anniversary of the Lenin Academic Maly State Theater, Moscow.

"Guests from Overseas," by N. K. Roerich — A2012

1974, Oct. 3 **Litho.** *Perf. 12*
4247 A2012 6k multicolored .25 .15

Nicholas Konstantin Roerich (1874-1947), painter and sponsor of Roerich Pact and Banner of Peace.

UPU Monument, Bern, and Arms of USSR — A2013

Development of Postal Service — A2014

UPU Cent.: No. 4248, Ukrainian coat of arms, letters, UPU emblem and headquarters, Bern. No. 4249, Arms of Byelorussia, UPU emblem, letters, stagecoach and rocket.

Photogravure and Engraved

1974, Oct. 9 *Perf. 12x11½*
4248 A2013 10k red & multi .35 .15
4249 A2013 10k red & multi .35 .15
4250 A2013 10k red & multi .35 .15
Nos. 4248-4250 (3) 1.05
Set value .30

Souvenir Sheet

Typo.

Perf. 11½x12

4251 A2014 Sheet of 3 7.50 3.00
a. 30k Jet and UPU emblem 2.00 .80
b. 30k Mail coach and UPU emblem 2.00 .80
c. 40k UPU emblem 2.00 .80

Order of Labor, 1st, 2nd and 3rd Grade A2015

KAMAZ Truck Leaving Kama Plant — A2016

Design: #4254, Nurek Hydroelectric Plant.

1974, Oct. 16 **Litho.** *Perf. 12½x12*
4252 A2015 4k multicolored .25 .15
4253 A2016 4k multicolored .25 .15
4254 A2016 4k multicolored .25 .15
Nos. 4252-4254 (3) .75
Set value .30

Space Stations Mars 4-7 over Mars — A2017

P. R. Popovitch, Y. P. Artyukhin and Soyuz 14 — A2018

Design: No. 4257, Cosmonauts G. V. Sarafanov and L. S. Demin, Soyuz 15, horiz.

Perf. 12x11½, 11½

1974, Oct. 28 **Photo.**
4255 A2017 6k multicolored .25 .15
4256 A2018 10k multicolored .40 .15
4257 A2018 10k multicolored .40 .15
Nos. 4255-4257 (3) 1.05
Set value .30

Russian explorations of Mars (6k); flight of Soyuz 14 (No. 4256) and of Soyuz 15, Aug. 26-28 (No. 4257).

Mongolian Flag and Arms A2019

1974, Nov. 14 **Photo.** *Perf. 11½*
4258 A2019 6k gold & multi .25 .15

Mongolian People's Republic, 50th anniv.

Guards' Ribbon, Estonian Government Building, Tower — A2020

1974, Nov. 14
4259 A2020 4k multicolored .25 .15

Liberation of Estonia, 30th anniversary.

Tanker, Passenger and Cargo Ships A2021

1974, Nov. 14 **Typo.** *Perf. 12½x12*
4260 A2021 4k multicolored .25 .15

USSR Merchant Marine, 50th anniversary.

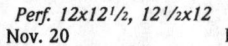

Spasski Tower Clock A2022

1974, Nov. 14 **Litho.** *Perf. 12*
4261 A2022 4k multicolored .30 .15

New Year 1975.

The Fishmonger, by Pieters A2023

Paintings: 4k, The Marketplace, by Beukelaer, 1564, horiz. 10k, A Drink of Lemonade, by Gerard Terborch. 14k, Girl at Work, by Gabriel Metsu. 16k, Saying Grace, by Jean Chardin. 20k, The Spoiled Child, by Jean Greuze. 50k, Self-portrait, by Jacques Louis David.

Perf. 12x12½, 12½x12

1974, Nov. 20 **Litho.**
4262 A2023 4k bister & multi .15 .15
4263 A2023 6k bister & multi .25 .15
4264 A2023 10k bister & multi .35 .15

4265	A2023	14k bister & multi	.50	.15
4266	A2023	16k bister & multi	.55	.20
4267	A2023	20k bister & multi	.75	.30
		Nos. 4262-4267 (6)	2.55	1.10

Souvenir Sheet

Perf. 12

4268	A2023	50k multicolored	1.50	.75

Foreign paintings in Russian museums. Printed in sheets of 16 stamps and 4 labels.

Morning Glory — A2024

Ivan Nikitin — A2025

Designs: Flora of the USSR.

1974, Nov. 20 ***Perf. 12x12½***

4269	A2024	1k red brn & multi	.15	.15
4270	A2024	2k green & multi	.15	.15
4271	A2024	4k multicolored	.15	.15
4272	A2024	10k brown & multi	.50	.15
4273	A2024	12k dk blue & multi	.55	.15
		Nos. 4269-4273 (5)	1.50	
		Set value		.50

1974, Dec. 11 Photo. ***Perf. 11½***

4274	A2025	4k gray green, grn & blk	.30	.25

Ivan S. Nikitin (1824-1861), poet.

Leningrad Mint — A2026

Photogravure and Engraved

1974, Dec. 11 ***Perf. 11***

4275	A2026	6k silver & multi	.25	.15

250th anniversary of the Leningrad Mint.

Mozhajsky Plane, 1882 — A2027

Early Russian Aircraft: No. 4277, Grizidubov-N biplane, 1910. No. 4278, Russia-A, 1910. No. 4279, Russian Vityaz (Sikorsky), 1913. No. 4280, Grigorovich flying boat, 1914.

1974, Dec. 25 Photo. ***Perf. 11½x12***

4276	A2027	6k olive & multi	.25	.15
4277	A2027	6k ultra & multi	.25	.15
4278	A2027	6k magenta & multi	.25	.15
4279	A2027	6k red & multi	.25	.15
4280	A2027	6k brown & multi	.25	.15
		Nos. 4276-4280 (5)	1.25	
		Set value		.50

Russian aircraft history, 1882-1914.

Souvenir Sheet

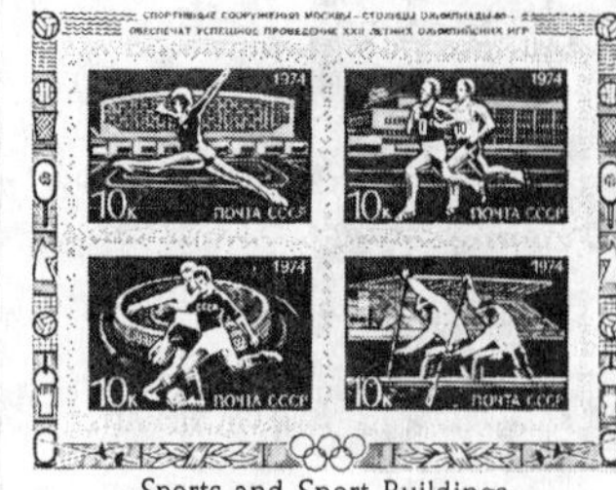
Sports and Sport Buildings, Moscow — A2028

1974, Dec. 25 ***Perf. 11½***

4281	A2028	Sheet of 4	2.50	.50
a.		10k Woman gymnast	.45	.15
b.		10k Running	.45	.15
c.		10k Soccer	.45	.15
d.		10k Canoeing	.45	.15

Moscow preparing for Summer Olympic Games, 1980.

Rotary Press, Masthead A2029

1975, Jan. 20

4282	A2029	4k multicolored	.25	.15

Komsomolskaya Pravda newspaper, 50th anniv.

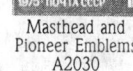

Masthead and Pioneer Emblems A2030

Spartakiad Emblem and Skiers A2031

1975, Jan. 20

4283	A2030	4k red, blk & silver	.25	.15

50th anniversary of the newspaper Pioneers' Pravda.

1975, Jan. 20

4284	A2031	4k blue & multi	.25	.15

8th Winter Spartakiad of USSR Trade Unions.

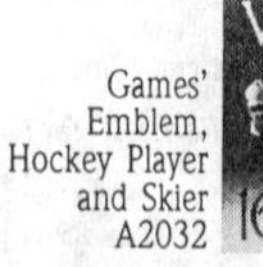

Games' Emblem, Hockey Player and Skier A2032

1975, Jan. 20

4285	A2032	16k multicolored	.50	.25

5th Winter Spartakiad of Friendly Armies, Feb. 23-Mar. 1.

Republic Anniversaries Type of 1970

Design (Hammer-Sickle Emblem and): No. 4286, Landscape and produce.

1975, Jan. 24 Engr. ***Perf. 12x12½***

4286	A1794	4k green	.30	.15

50th anniversary of Karakalpak Autonomous Soviet Socialist Republic.

David, by Michelangelo — A2033

Michelangelo, Self-portrait A2034

Designs (Works by Michelangelo): 6k, Squatting Boy. 10k, Rebellious Slave. 14k, The Creation of Adam. 20k, Staircase, Laurentian Library, Florence. 30k, The Last Judgment.

Lithographed and Engraved

1975, Feb. 27 ***Perf. 12½x12***

4296	A2033	4k slate grn & grn	.15	.15
4297	A2033	6k red brn & bister	.25	.15
4298	A2033	10k slate grn & grn	.45	.20
a.		Min. sheet, 2 each #4296-4298	1.50	.65
4299	A2033	14k red brn & bister	.65	.20
4300	A2033	20k slate grn & grn	.90	.40
4301	A2033	30k red brn & bister	1.10	.60
a.		Min. sheet, 2 each #4299-4301	5.00	2.00
		Nos. 4296-4301 (6)	3.50	1.70

Souvenir Sheet

Perf. 12x11½

4302	A2034	50k gold & multi	3.00	.80

Michelangelo Buonarroti (1475-1564), Italian sculptor, painter and architect. Issued only in the min. sheets of 6.

Mozhajski, Early Plane and Supersonic Jet TU-144 — A2035

1975, Feb. 27 Photo. ***Perf. 12x11½***

4303	A2035	6k violet blue & ocher	.25	.15

A. F. Mozhajski (1825-1890), pioneer aircraft designer, birth sesquicentennial.

"Metric System" A2036

1975, Mar. 14 ***Perf. 11½***

4304	A2036	6k blk, vio blue & org	.25	.15

Intl. Meter Convention, Paris, 1875, cent.

Spartakiad Emblem and Sports A2037

1975, Mar. 14

4305	A2037	6k red, silver & black	.25	.15

6th Summer Spartakiad.

Liberation Monument, Parliament, Arms — A2038

Charles Bridge Towers, Arms and Flags — A2039

1975, Mar. 14

4306	A2038	6k gold & multi	.25	.15
4307	A2039	6k gold & multi	.25	.15
		Set value		.20

30th anniv. of liberation from fascism, Hungary (#4306) & Czechoslovakia (#4307).

Flags of France and USSR A2040

Yuri A. Gagarin, by L. Kerbel A2041

A. V. Filipchenko, N.N. Rukavishnikov, Russo-American Space Emblem, Soyuz 16 — A2042

1975, Mar. 25 Litho. ***Perf. 12***

4308	A2040	6k lilac & multi	.25	.15

50th anniv. of the establishment of diplomatic relations between France and USSR, 1st foreign recognition of Soviet State.

Perf. 11½x12, 12x11½

1975, Mar. 28 Photo.

Cosmonauts' Day: 10k, A. A. Gubarev, G. M. Grechko aboard Soyuz 17 & orbital station Salyut 4.

4309	A2041	6k blue, silver & red	.20	.15
4310	A2042	10k black, blue & red	.40	.15
4311	A2042	16k multicolored	.50	.15
		Nos. 4309-4311 (3)	1.10	
		Set value		.30

Warsaw Treaty Members' Flags — A2043

1975, Apr. 16 Litho. ***Perf. 12***

4312	A2043	6k multicolored	.30	.15

Signing of the Warsaw Treaty (Bulgaria, Czechoslovakia, German Democratic Rep., Hungary, Poland, Romania, USSR), 20th anniv.

Lenin on Steps of Winter Palace, by V. G. Zyplakow A2044

1975, Apr. 22 ***Perf. 12x12½***

4313	A2044	4k multicolored	.30	.15

105th anniversary of the birth of Lenin.

Communications Emblem and Exhibition Pavilion — A2045

1975, Apr. 22 *Perf. 11½*

4314 A2045 6k ultra, red & silver .25 .15

International Communications Exhibition, Sokolniki Park, Moscow, May 1975.

Lenin and Red Flag A2046

War Memorial, Berlin-Treptow A2048

Order of Victory — A2047

1975, Apr. 22 **Typo.** *Perf. 12*

4315	A2046	4k shown	.25	.15
4316	A2046	4k Eternal Flame and guard	.25	.15
4317	A2046	4k Woman munitions worker	.25	.15
4318	A2046	4k Partisans	.25	.15
4319	A2046	4k Soldier destroying swastika	.25	.15
4320	A2046	4k Soldier with gun and banner	.25	.15
		Nos. 4315-4320 (6)	1.50	
		Set value		.60

Souvenir Sheet

Litho., Typo. & Photo.

Imperf

4321 A2047 50k multicolored 5.00 3.00

World War II victory, 30th anniversary.

1975, Apr. 25 **Litho.** *Perf. 12x12½*

4322 A2048 6k buff & multi .25 .15

Souvenir Sheet

4323 A2048 50k dull blue & multi 3.00 .60

Socfilex 75 Intl. Phil. Exhib. honoring 30th anniv. of WWII victory, Moscow, May 8-18.

Soyuz-Apollo Docking Emblem and Painting by Cosmonaut A. A. Leonov — A2049

1975, May 8 **Photo.** *Perf. 12x11½*

4324 A2049 20k multicolored .75 .35

Russo-American space cooperation.

Automobile Type of 1973

Designs: 2k, GAZ-M-I car, 1936. 3k, 5-ton truck, YAG-6, 1936. 4k, ZIZ-16, autobus, 1938. 12k, KIM-10 car, 1940. 16k, GAZ-67B jeep, 1943.

1975, May 23 **Photo.** *Perf. 12x11½*

4325	A1968	2k dp org & multi	.15	.15
4326	A1968	3k green & multi	.15	.15
4327	A1968	4k dk green & multi	.15	.15
4328	A1968	12k maroon & multi	.30	.15
4329	A1968	16k olive & multi	.45	.15
		Nos. 4325-4329 (5)	1.20	
		Set value		.50

Canal, Emblem, Produce — A2050

1975, May 23 *Perf. 11½*

4330 A2050 6k multicolored .25 .15

9th Intl. Congress on Irrigation and Drainage, Moscow, and International Commission on Irrigation and Drainage, 25th anniv..

Flags and Arms of Poland and USSR, Factories A2051

1975, May 23

4331 A2051 6k multicolored .25 .15

Treaty of Friendship, Cooperation and Mutual Assistance between Poland & USSR, 30th anniv.

Man in Space and Earth — A2052

1975, May 23

4332 A2052 6k multicolored .25 .15

First man walking in space, Lt. Col. Alexei Leonov, 10th anniversary.

Yakov M. Sverdlov (1885-1919), Organizer and Early Member of Communist Party — A2053

1975, June 4

4333 A2053 4k multicolored .30 .15

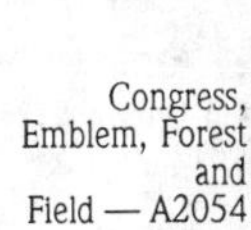

Congress, Emblem, Forest and Field — A2054

1975, June 4

4334 A2054 6k multicolored .25 .15

8th International Congress for Conservation of Plants, Moscow.

Symbolic Flower with Plants and Emblem A2055

1975, June 20 **Litho.** *Perf. 11½*

4335 A2055 6k multicolored .25 .15

12th International Botanical Congress.

Souvenir Sheet

UN Emblem A2056

1975, June 20 **Photo.** *Perf. 11½x12*

4336 A2056 50k gold & blue 2.50 1.00

30th anniversary of United Nations.

Globe and Film — A2057

1975, June 20 **Photo.** *Perf. 11½*

4337 A2057 6k multicolored .25 .15

9th Intl. Film Festival, Moscow, 1975.

Soviet and American Astronauts and Flags — A2058

Apollo and Soyuz After Link-up and Earth — A2059

Soyuz Launch — A2060

Designs: No. 4340, Spacecraft before link-up, earth and project emblem. 50k, Soviet Mission Control Center.

1975, July 15 **Litho.** *Perf. 11½*

4338	A2058	10k multicolored	.45	.15
4339	A2059	12k multicolored	.65	.20
4340	A2059	12k multicolored	.65	.20
a.		Vert. pair, #4339-4340	1.30	.40
4341	A2060	16k multicolored	.75	.40
		Nos. 4338-4341 (4)	2.50	.95

Souvenir Sheet

Photo.

Perf. 12x11½

4342 A2058 50k multicolored 2.75 1.25

Apollo-Soyuz space test project (Russo-American space cooperation), launching, July 15; link-up July 17.

No. 4342 contains one 50x21mm stamp.

See US Nos. 1569-1570.

Sturgeon, Caspian Sea, Oceanexpo 75 Emblem — A2061

Designs (Oceanexpo 75 Emblem and): 4k, Salt-water shell, Black Sea. 6k, Eel, Baltic Sea. 10k, Sea duck, Arctic Sea. 16k, Crab, Far Eastern waters. 20k, Chrisipther (fish), Pacific Ocean.

1975, July 22 **Photo.** *Perf. 11*

4343	A2061	3k multicolored	.15	.15
4344	A2061	4k multicolored	.15	.15
4345	A2061	6k green & multi	.30	.20
4346	A2061	10k dk blue & multi	.45	.30
4347	A2061	16k purple & multi	.65	.30
4348	A2061	20k multicolored	.80	.65
		Nos. 4343-4348 (6)	2.50	1.75

Souvenir Sheet

Perf. 12x11½

4349		Sheet of 2	2.50	.90
a.	A2061	30k Dolphin rising	1.00	.30
b.	A2061	30k Dolphin diving	1.00	.30

Oceanexpo 75, 1st Intl. Oceanographic Exhib., Okinawa, July 20, 1975-Jan. 1976. No. 4349 contains 55x25mm stamps.

Parade, Red Square, 1941, by K. F. Yuon — A2062

Paintings: 2k, Morning of Industrial Moscow, by Yuon. 6k, Soldiers Inspecting Captured Artillery, by Lansere. 10k, Excavating Metro Tunnel, by Lansere. 16k, Pushkin and His Wife at Court Ball, by Ulyanov, vert. 20k, De Lauriston at Kutuzov's Headquarters, by Ulyanov.

Perf. 12½x11½

1975, July 22 **Litho.**

4350	A2062	1k gray & multi	.15	.15
4351	A2062	2k gray & multi	.15	.15
4352	A2062	6k gray & multi	.25	.15
4353	A2062	10k gray & multi	.40	.15
4354	A2062	16k gray & multi	.80	.25
4355	A2062	20k gray & multi	.90	.30
		Nos. 4350-4355 (6)	2.65	
		Set value		.75

Konstantin F. Yuon (1875-1958), Yevgeni Y. Lansere (1875-1946), Nikolai P. Ulyanov (1875-1949).

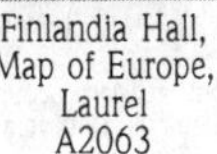

Finlandia Hall, Map of Europe, Laurel A2063

Chuyrlenis, Waves and Lighthouse A2064

1975, Aug. 18 **Photo.** *Perf. 11½*

4356 A2063 6k brt blue, gold & blk .25 .15

European Security and Cooperation Conference, Helsinki, July 30-Aug. 1. Printed se-tenant with label with quotation by Leonid I. Brezhnev, first secretary of Communist party.

1975, Aug. 20 **Photo. & Engr.**

4357 A2064 4k grn, indigo & gold .50 .15

M. K. Chuyrlenis, Lithuanian composer, birth centenary.

Avetik Isaakyan, by Martiros Saryan A2065

1975, Aug. 20 Litho. *Perf. 12x12½*
4358 A2065 4k multicolored .15 .15

Isaakyan (1875-1957), Armenian poet.

Jacques Duclos A2066

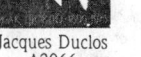

al-Farabi A2067

1975, Aug. 20 Photo. *Perf. 11½x12*
4359 A2066 6k maroon & silver .25 .15

Duclos (1896-1975), French labor leader.

1975, Aug. 20 *Perf. 11½*
4360 A2067 6k grnsh blue, brn & bis .25 .15

Nasr al-Farabi (870?-950), Arab philosopher.

Male Ruffs A2068

1975, Aug. 25 Litho. *Perf. 12½x12*

4361 A2068	1k	shown	.15	.15
4362 A2068	4k	Altai roebuck	.15	.15
4363 A2068	6k	Siberian marten	.20	.15
4364 A2068	10k	Old squaw (duck)	.40	.15
4365 A2068	16k	Badger	.55	.15
		Nos. 4361-4365 (5)	1.45	
		Set value		.50

Berezina River and Stolby wildlife reservations, 50th anniversary.

A2069

A2070

Designs: #4366, Flags of USSR, North Korea, arms of N. K., Liberation monument, Pyongyang. #4367, Flags of USSR, North Viet Nam, arms of N.V., industrial development.

1975, Aug. 28 *Perf. 12*
4366 A2069 6k multicolored .30 .15
4367 A2070 6k multicolored .30 .15
Set value .20

Liberation of North Korea from Japanese occupation (#4366); and establishment of Democratic Republic of Viet Nam (#4367), 30th annivs.

P. Klimuk and V. Sevastyanov, Soyuz 18 and Salyut 4 Docking — A2071

1975, Sept. 12 Photo. *Perf. 12x11½*
4368 A2071 10k ultra, blk & dp org .30 .15

Docking of space ship Soyuz 18 and space station Salyut 4.

S. A. Esenin and Birches A2072

Photogravure and Engraved

1975, Sept. 12 *Perf. 11½*
4369 A2072 6k brown & ocher .25 .15

Sergei A. Esenin (1895-1925), poet.

Standardization Symbols A2073

1975, Sept. 12 Photo. *Perf. 11½*
4370 A2073 4k red & multi .25 .15

USSR Committee for Standardization of Communications Ministry, 50th anniversary.

Karakul Lamb A2074

1975, Sept. 22 Photo. *Perf. 11½*
4371 A2074 6k black, yel & grn .25 .15

3rd International Symposium on astrakhan production, Samarkand, Sept. 22-27.

Dr. M. P. Konchalovsky A2075

Exhibition Emblem A2076

1975, Sept. 30 *Perf. 11½x12*
4372 A2075 4k brown & red .25 .15

Konchalovsky (1875-1942), physician.

1975, Sept. 30 *Perf. 11½*
4373 A2076 4k deep blue & red .25 .15

3rd All-Union Youth Phil. Exhib., Erevan.

IWY Emblem and Rose A2077

Yugoslavian Flag and Parliament A2078

1975, Sept. 30 Litho. *Perf. 12x11½*
4374 A2077 6k multicolored .25 .15

International Women's Year 1975.

1975, Sept. 30 Photo. *Perf. 11½*
4375 A2078 6k gold, red & blue .25 .15

Republic of Yugoslavia, 30th anniv.

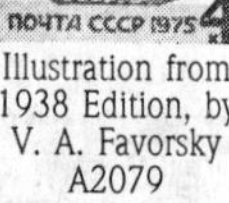

Illustration from 1938 Edition, by V. A. Favorsky A2079

Mikhail Ivanovich Kalinin A2080

1975, Oct. 20 Typo. *Perf. 12*
4376 A2079 4k buff, red & black .30 .15

175th anniversary of the 1st edition of the old Russian saga "Slovo o polku Igoreve."

1975, Oct. 20 Engr. *Perf. 12*

#4378, Anatoli Vasilievich Lunacharski.

4377 A2080 4k sepia .25 .15
4378 A2080 4k sepia .25 .15
Set value .20

Kalinin (1875-1946), chairman of Central Executive Committee and Presidium of Supreme Soviet; Lunacharski (1875-1933), writer, commissar for education.

Hand Holding Torch and Lenin Quotation — A2081

1975, Oct. 20 Engr.
4379 A2081 4k red & olive .25 .15

First Russian Revolution (1905), 70th anniv.

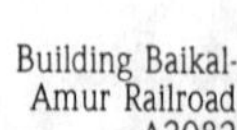

Building Baikal-Amur Railroad A2082

Novolipetsk Metallurgical Plant A2083

Nevynomyssk Chemical Plant, Fertilizer Formula A2084

1975, Oct. 30 Photo. *Perf. 11½*
4380 A2082 4k gold & multi .15 .15
4381 A2083 4k red, gray & sl green .15 .15
4382 A2084 4k red, blue & silver .15 .15
Nos. 4380-4382 (3) .45
Set value .30

58th anniversary of October Revolution.

Bas-relief of Decembrists and "Decembrists at the Senate Square," by D. N. Kardovsky — A2085

1975, Nov. 12 Litho. & Engr.
4383 A2085 4k gray & multi .25 .15

Sesquicentennial of Decembrist rising.

Star and "1976" — A2086

1975, Nov. 12 Litho. *Perf. 12x12½*
4384 A2086 4k green & multi .35 .15

New Year 1976.

Village Street, by F. A. Vasilev A2087

Paintings by Vasilev: 4k, Road in Birch Forest. 6k, After the Thunderstorm. 10k, Swamp, horiz. 12k, In the Crimean Mountains. 16k, Meadow, horiz. 50k, Self-portrait.

Perf. 12x12½, 12½x12

1975, Nov. 25

4385 A2087	2k	gray & multi	.15	.15
4386 A2087	4k	gray & multi	.15	.15
4387 A2087	6k	gray & multi	.30	.15
4388 A2087	10k	gray & multi	.45	.15
4389 A2087	12k	gray & multi	.55	.15
4390 A2087	16k	gray & multi	.70	.25
		Nos. 4385-4390 (6)	2.30	1.00

Souvenir Sheet

Perf. 12

4391 A2087 50k gray & multi 2.25 .90

Fedor Aleksandrovich Vasilev (1850-1873), landscape painter. Nos. 4385-4390 printed in sheets of 7 stamps and one label.

Landing Capsule, Venus Surface, Lenin Banner A2088

1975, Dec. 8 Photo. *Perf. 11½*
4392 A2088 10k multicolored .35 .25

Flights of Soviet interplanetary stations Venera 9 and Venera 10.

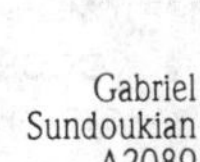

Gabriel Sundoukian A2089

1975, Dec. 8 Litho. *Perf. 12*

4393	A2089	4k multicolored	.50	.30

Sundoukian (1825-1912), Armenian playright.

Polar Poppies, Taiga — A2090

Regional Flowers: 6k, Globeflowers, tundra. 10k, Buttercups, oak forest. 12k, Wood anemones, steppe. 16k, Eminium Lehmannii, desert.

Photogravure and Engraved

1975, Dec. 25 *Perf. 12x11½*

4394	A2090	4k black & multi	.15	.15
4395	A2090	6k black & multi	.25	.15
4396	A2090	10k black & multi	.35	.15
4397	A2090	12k black & multi	.40	.15
4398	A2090	16k black & multi	.50	.25
		Nos. 4394-4398 (5)	1.65	
		Set value		.70

A. L. Mints (1895-1974), Academician — A2091

1975, Dec. 31 Photo. *Perf. 11½x12*

4399	A2091	4k dp brown & gold	.25	.15

Demon, by A. Kochupalov A2092

Paintings: 6k, Vasilisa the Beautiful, by I. Vakurov. 10k, Snow Maiden, by T. Zubkova. 16k, Summer, by K. Kukulieva. 20k, The Fisherman and the Goldfish, by I. Vakurov, horiz.

1975, Dec. 31 Litho. *Perf. 12*

4400	A2092	4k bister & multi	.20	.15
4401	A2092	6k bister & multi	.30	.15
4402	A2092	10k bister & multi	.50	.15
4403	A2092	16k bister & multi	.60	.15
4404	A2092	20k bister & multi	.80	.25
a.		Strip of 5, #4400-4404	2.40	.60

Palekh Art State Museum, Ivanov Region.

Wilhelm Pieck (1876-1960), Pres. of German Democratic Republic — A2093

1976, Jan. 3 Engr. *Perf. 12½x12*

4405	A2093	6k bluish black	.20	.15

M. E. Saltykov-Shchedrin, by I.N. Kramskoi — A2094

1976, Jan. 14 Litho. *Perf. 12x12½*

4406	A2094	4k multicolored	.25	.15

Mikhail Evgrafovich Saltykov-Shchedrin (1826-1889), writer and revolutionist.

Congress Emblem A2095

Lenin Statue, Kiev A2096

1976, Feb. 2 Photo. *Perf. 11½*

4407	A2095	4k red, gold & mar	.25	.15

Souvenir Sheet

Perf. 11½x12

4408	A2095	50k red, gold & mar	2.00	.65

25th Congress of the Communist Party of the Soviet Union.

1976, Feb. 2 *Perf. 11½*

4409	A2096	4k red, black & blue	.25	.15

Ukrainian Communist Party, 25th Congress.

Ice Hockey, Games' Emblem A2097

Designs (Winter Olympic Games' Emblem and): 4k, Cross-country skiing. 6k, Figure skating, pairs. 10k, Speed skating. 20k, Luge. 50k, Winter Olympic Games' emblem, vert.

1976, Feb. 4 Litho. *Perf. 12½x12*

4410	A2097	2k multicolored	.15	.15
4411	A2097	4k multicolored	.15	.15
4412	A2097	6k multicolored	.30	.15
4413	A2097	10k multicolored	.45	.15
4414	A2097	20k multicolored	.95	.30
		Nos. 4410-4414 (5)	2.00	
		Set value		.70

Souvenir Sheet

Perf. 12x12½

4415	A2097	50k vio bl, org & red	2.00	1.00

12th Winter Olympic Games, Innsbruck, Austria, Feb. 4-15. No. 4415 contains one stamp; silver and violet blue margin showing designs of Nos. 4410-4414. Size: 90x80mm.

No. 4415 Overprinted in Red Souvenir Sheet

СЛАВА СОВЕТСКОМУ СПОРТУ!

СПОРТСМЕНЫ СССР ЗАВОЕВАЛИ 13 ЗОЛОТЫХ, 6 СЕРЕБРЯНЫХ, 8 БРОНЗОВЫХ МЕДАЛЕЙ!

1976, Mar. 24

4416	A2097	50k multicolored	6.00	4.00

Success of Soviet athletes in 12th Winter Olympic Games. Translation of overprint: "Glory to Soviet Sport! The athletes of the USSR have won 13 gold, 6 silver and 8 bronze medals."

K.E. Voroshilov — A2098

1976, Feb. 4 Engr. *Perf. 12*

4417	A2098	4k slate green	.40	.15

Kliment Efremovich Voroshilov (1881-1969), pres. of revolutionary military council, commander of Leningrad front, USSR pres. 1953-60. See Nos. 4487-4488.

Flag over Kremlin Palace of Congresses, Troitskaya Tower — A2099

Photogravure on Gold Foil

1976, Feb. 24 *Perf. 12x11½*

4418	A2099	20k gold, green & red	4.00	2.00

25th Congress of the Communist Party of the Soviet Union (CPSU).

Lenin on Red Square, by P. Vasiliev — A2100

1976, Mar. 10 Litho. *Perf. 12½x12*

4419	A2100	4k yellow & multi	.25	.15

106th anniversary of the birth of Lenin.

Atom Symbol and Dubna Institute — A2101

1976, Mar. 10 Photo. *Perf. 11½*

4420	A2101	6k vio bl, red & silver	.25	.15

Joint Institute of Nuclear Research, Dubna, 20th anniversary.

Bolshoi Theater — A2102

1976, Mar. 24 Litho. *Perf. 11x11½*

4421	A2102	10k yel, blue & dk brn	.30	.15

Bicentenary of Bolshoi Theater.

Back from the Fair, by Konchalovsky — A2103

Paintings by P. P. Konchalovsky: 2k, The Green Glass. 6k, Peaches. 16k, Meat, Game and Vegetables. 20k, Self-portrait, 1943, vert.

1976, Apr. 6 *Perf. 12½x12, 12x12½*

4422	A2103	1k yellow & multi	.15	.15
4423	A2103	2k yellow & multi	.15	.15
4424	A2103	6k yellow & multi	.30	.15
4425	A2103	16k yellow & multi	.70	.15
4426	A2103	20k yellow & multi	.85	.30
		Nos. 4422-4426 (5)	2.15	
		Set value		.70

Birth centenary of P. P. Konchalovsky.

Vostok, Salyut-Soyuz Link-up — A2104

Yuri A. Gagarin A2105

Designs: 6k, Meteor and Molniya Satellites, Orbita Ground Communications Center. 10k, Cosmonauts on board Salyut space station and Mars planetary station. 12k, Interkosmos station and Apollo-Soyuz linking.

Lithographed and Engraved

1976, Apr. 12 *Perf. 11½*

4427	A2104	4k multicolored	.15	.15
4428	A2104	6k multicolored	.25	.15
4429	A2104	10k multicolored	.35	.15
4430	A2104	12k multicolored	.55	.20
		Nos. 4427-4430 (4)	1.30	
		Set value		.50

Souvenir Sheet

Engr. *Perf. 12*

4431	A2105	50k black	10.00	2.00

1st manned flight in space, 15th anniv.

I. A. Dzhavakhishvili A2106

Samed Vurgun and Derrick A2107

1976, Apr. 20 Photo. *Perf. 11½x12*

4432	A2106	4k multicolored	.25	.15

Dzhavakhishvili (1876-1940), scientist.

1976, Apr. 20 *Perf. 11½*

4433	A2107	4k multicolored	.25	.15

Vurgun (1906-56), natl. poet of Azerbaijan.

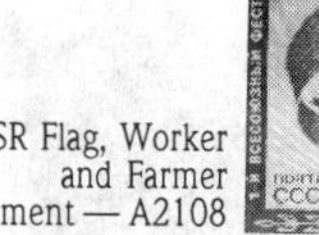

USSR Flag, Worker and Farmer Monument — A2108

1976, May 12 Litho. *Perf. 11½x12*

4434 A2108 4k multicolored .25 .15

1st All-Union Festival of Amateur Artists.

FIP Emblem — A2109

1976, May 12 Photo. *Perf. 11½*

4435 A2109 6k ultra & carmine .25 .15

Intl. Federation of Philately, 50th anniv.

Souvenir Sheet

V. A. Tropinin, Self-portrait — A2110

1976, May 12 Litho. *Perf. 12*

4436 A2110 50k multicolored 2.00 1.00

Vasily Andreevich Tropinin (1776-1857), painter.

Emblem, Dnieper Bridge A2111

Dr. N. N. Burdenko A2112

1976, May 20 Photo. *Perf. 11½*

4437 A2111 4k Prus blue, gold & blk .25 .15

Bicentenary of Dnepropetrovsk.

1976, May 20 *Perf. 11½x12*

4438 A2112 4k deep brown & red .25 .15

Burdenko (1876-1946), neurosurgeon.

K. A. Trenev (1876-1945), Playwright — A2113

1976, May 20 *Perf. 11½*

4439 A2113 4k black & multi .25 .15

Automobile Type of 1973

Designs: 2k, ZIS-110 passenger car. 3k, GAZ-51 Gorky truck. 4k, GAZ-M-20 Pobeda passenger car. 12k, ZIS-150 Moscow Motor Works truck. 16k, ZIS-154 Moscow Motor Works bus.

1976, June 15 Photo. *Perf. 12x11½*

4440 A1968 2k grnsh bl & multi .20 .15
4441 A1968 3k bister & multi .20 .15
4442 A1968 4k dk blue & multi .20 .15
4443 A1968 12k brown & multi .60 .15
4444 A1968 16k deep car & multi .80 .15
Nos. 4440-4444 (5) 2.00
Set value .50

Canoeing A2114

USSR National Olympic Committee Emblem and: 6k, Basketball, vert. 10k, Greco-Roman wrestling. 14k, Women's discus, vert. 16k, Target shooting. 50k, Olympic medal, obverse and reverse.

Perf. 12½x12, 12x12½

1976, June 23 Litho.

4445 A2114 4k red & multi .15 .15
4446 A2114 6k red & multi .20 .15
4447 A2114 10k red & multi .45 .15
4448 A2114 14k red & multi .60 .15
4449 A2114 16k red & multi .65 .25
Nos. 4445-4449 (5) 2.05
Set value .65

Souvenir Sheet

4450 A2114 50k red & multi 3.00 .75

21st Olympic Games, Montreal, Canada, July 17-Aug. 1.

For overprint see No. 4472.

Electric Trains, Overpass A2115

1976, June 23 Photo. *Perf. 11½*

4451 A2115 4k multicolored .25 .15

Electrification of USSR railroads, 50th anniversary.

L. Emilio Rekabarren A2116

1976, July 6

4452 A2116 6k gold, red & blk .25 .15

Luis Emilio Rekabarren (1876-1924), founder of Chilean Communist Party.

L. M. Pavlichenko — A2117

1976, July 6

4453 A2117 4k dp brn, silver & yel .25 .15

Ljudmilla Mikhajlovna Pavlichenko (1916-1974), WWII heroine, Komsomol, War Veterans and Women's Committee member.

New Partner, by P. A. Fedotov A2118

Paintings: 4k, The Fastidious Fiancée, horiz. 6k, Aristocrat's Breakfast. 10k, Gamblers, horiz. 16k, The Outing. 50k, Self-portrait.

Perf. 12x12½, 12½x12

1976, July 15 Litho.

4454 A2118 2k black & multi .15 .15
4455 A2118 4k black & multi .15 .15
4456 A2118 6k black & multi .20 .15
4457 A2118 10k black & multi .45 .15
4458 A2118 16k black & multi .65 .25
Nos. 4454-4458 (5) 1.60
Set value .65

Souvenir Sheet

Perf. 12

4459 A2118 50k multicolored 4.00 .75

Pavel Andreevich Fedotov (1815-1852), painter. Nos. 4454-4458 each printed in sheets of 20 stamps and center label with black commemorative inscription.

S. S. Nametkin A2119

Squacco Heron A2120

1976, July 20 Photo. *Perf. 11½x12*

4460 A2119 4k blue, black & buff .25 .15

Sergei Semenovich Nametkin (1876-1950), organic chemist.

1976, Aug. 18 Litho. *Perf. 12x12½*

Waterfowl: 3k, Arctic loon. 4k, European coot. 6k, Atlantic puffin. 10k, Slender-billed gull.

4465 A2120 1k dk green & multi .15 .15
4466 A2120 3k ol green & multi .15 .15
4467 A2120 4k orange & multi .15 .15
4468 A2120 6k purple & multi .15 .15
4469 A2120 10k brt blue & multi .20 .15
Nos. 4465-4469 (5) .80
Set value .50

Nature protection.

Peace Dove — A2121

1976, Aug. 25 Photo. *Perf. 11½*

4470 A2121 4k salmon, gold & blue .25 .15

2nd Stockholm appeal and movement to stop arms race.

Resistance Movement Emblem A2122

1976, Aug. 25

4471 A2122 6k dk blue, black & gold .25 .15

Intl. Resistance Movement Fed., 25th anniv.

No. 4450 Overprinted in Gold in Margin

Souvenir Sheet

СПОРТСМЕНЫ
СССР
ЗАВОЕВАЛИ
47 ЗОЛОТЫХ,
43 СЕРЕБРЯНЫХ
И 35 БРОНЗОВЫХ
МЕДАЛЕЙ!

СОВЕТСКОМУ
СПОРТУ
СЛАВА!

The two parts of the overprint have been moved closer together to fit the column.

1976, Aug. 25 Litho. *Perf. 12½x12*

4472 A2114 50k red & multi 4.50 .75

Victories of Soviet athletes in 21st Olympic Games (47 gold, 43 silver and 35 bronze medals).

Flags of India and USSR — A2123

UN, UNESCO Emblems, Open Book — A2124

1976, Sept. 8 *Perf. 12*

4473 A2123 4k multicolored .25 .15

Friendship and cooperation between USSR and India.

1976, Sept. 8 Engr. *Perf. 12x12½*

4474 A2124 16k multicolored .40 .30

UNESCO, 30th anniv.

B. V. Volynov, V. M. Zholobov, Star Circling Globe — A2125

1976, Sept. 8 Photo. *Perf. 12x11½*

4475 A2125 10k brn, blue & black .50 .35

Exploits of Soyuz 21 and Salyut space station.

"Industry" — A2126

1976, Sept. 17

4476 A2126 4k shown .25 .15
4477 A2126 4k Farm industry .25 .15
4478 A2126 4k Science .25 .15

4479 A2126 4k Transport & communications .25 .15
4480 A2126 4k Intl. cooperation .25 .15
Nos. 4476-4480 (5) 1.25
Set value .50

25th Congress of the Communist Party of the Soviet Union.

Au (woman), by I. V. Markichev A2127

Paintings: 2k, Plower, by I. I. Golikov, horiz. 12k, Firebird, by A. V. Kotuhin, horiz. 14k, Festival, by A. I. Vatagin. 20k, Victory, by I. I. Vakurov.

Perf. 12½x12, 12x12½

1976, Sept. 22 Litho.

4481 A2127	2k black & multi	.20	.15
4482 A2127	4k black & multi	.25	.15
4483 A2127	12k black & multi	1.10	.15
4484 A2127	14k black & multi	1.25	.15
4485 A2127	20k black & multi	1.65	.35
Nos. 4481-4485 (5)		4.45	
Set value			.75

Palekh Art State Museum, Ivanov Region.

Shostakovich, Score from 7th Symphony, Leningrad A2128

1976, Sept. 25 Engr. *Perf. 12½x12*
4486 A2128 6k dk vio blue .25 .15

Dimitri Dimitrievich Shostakovich (1906-1975), composer.

Voroshilov Type of 1976

Portraits: #4487, Zhukov. #4488, Rokossovsky.

1976, Oct. 7 Engr. *Perf. 12*
4487 A2098 4k slate green .15 .15
4488 A2098 4k brown .15 .15
Set value .20

Marshal Georgi Konstantinovich Zhukov (1896-1974), commander at Stalingrad and Leningrad and Deputy of Supreme Soviet; Marshal Konstantin K. Rokossovsky (1896-1968), commander at Stalingrad.

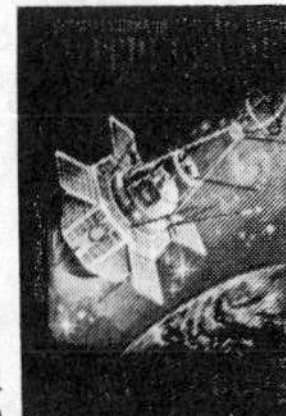
Intercosmos-14 A2129

10k, India's satellite Arryabata. 12k, Soyuz-19 and Apollo before docking. 16k, French satellite Aureole and Northern Lights. 20k, Docking of Soyuz-Apollo, Intercosmos-14 and Aureole.

1976, Oct. 15 Photo. *Perf. 11½*

4489 A2129	6k black & multi	.15	.15
4490 A2129	10k black & multi	.30	.15
4491 A2129	12k black & multi	.45	.15
4492 A2129	16k black & multi	.50	.15
4493 A2129	20k black & multi	.65	.20
Nos. 4489-4493 (5)		2.05	
Set value			.60

Interkosmos Program for Scientific and Experimental Research.

Vladimir I. Dahl — A2130

Photogravure and Engraved

1976, Oct. 15 *Perf. 11½*
4494 A2130 4k green & dk grn .25 .15

Vladimir I. Dahl (1801-1872), physician, writer, compiled Russian Dictionary.

Electric Power Industry A2131

Designs: No. 4496, Balashovo textile mill. No. 4497, Laying of drainage pipes and grain elevator.

1976, Oct. 20 Photo. *Perf. 11½*
4495 A2131 4k dk blue & multi .15 .15
4496 A2131 4k rose brn & multi .15 .15
4497 A2131 4k slate grn & multi .15 .15
Nos. 4495-4497 (3) .45
Set value .30

59th anniversary of the October Revolution.

Petrov Tumor Research Institute A2132

M. A. Novinski A2133

1976, Oct. 28
4498 A2132 4k vio blue & gold .50 .15

Perf. 11½x12
4499 A2133 4k dk brn, buff & blue .40 .15
Set value .20

Petrov Tumor Research Institute, 50th anniversary, and 135th birth anniversary of M. A. Novinski, cancer research pioneer.

Aviation Emblem, Gakkel VII, 1911 — A2134

Russian Aircraft (Russian Aviation Emblem and): 6k, Gakkel IX, 1912. 12k, I. Steglau No. 2, 1912. 14k, Dybovski's Dolphin, 1913. 16k, Iliya Muromets, 1914.

Lithographed and Engraved

1976, Nov. 4 *Perf. 12x12½*

4500 A2134	3k multicolored	.15	.15
4501 A2134	6k multicolored	.20	.15
4502 A2134	12k multicolored	.65	.35
4503 A2134	14k multicolored	.75	.35
4504 A2134	16k multicolored	.80	.50
Nos. 4500-4504 (5)		2.55	1.50

See Nos. C109-C120.

Saffron — A2135

Flowers of the Caucasus: 2k, Pasqueflowers. 3k, Gentian. 4k, Columbine. 6k, Checkered lily.

1976, Nov. 17 *Perf. 12x11½*

4505 A2135	1k multicolored	.25	.15
4506 A2135	2k multicolored	.25	.15
4507 A2135	3k multicolored	.25	.15
4508 A2135	4k multicolored	.25	.15
4509 A2135	6k multicolored	.25	.15
Nos. 4505-4509 (5)		1.25	
Set value			.50

Spasski Tower Clock, Greeting Card A2136

1976, Nov. 25 Litho. *Perf. 12½x12*
4510 A2136 4k multicolored .25 .15

New Year 1977.

Parable of the Workers in the Vineyard, by Rembrandt — A2137

Rembrandt Paintings in Hermitage: 6k, birth anniversary. 10k, 14k, Holy Family, vert. 20k, Rembrandt's brother Adrian, 1654, vert. 50k, Artaxerxes, Esther and Haman.

Perf. 12½x12, 12x12½

1976, Nov. 25 Photo.

4511 A2137	4k multicolored	.15	.15
4512 A2137	6k multicolored	.20	.15
4513 A2137	10k multicolored	.50	.15
4514 A2137	14k multicolored	.65	.15
4515 A2137	20k multicolored	.90	.30
Nos. 4511-4515 (5)		2.40	
Set value			.70

Souvenir Sheet

4516 A2137 50k multicolored 6.50 2.00

Rembrandt van Rijn (1606-69). Nos. 4511 and 4515 printed in sheets of 7 stamps and decorative label.

Armed Forces Order — A2138

Worker and Farmer, by V. I. Muhina — A2139

Marx and Lenin, by Fridman and Belostotsky A2140

Council for Mutual Economic Aid Building A2141

Lenin, 1920 Photograph A2142

Globe and Sputnik Orbits A2143

Designs: 2k, Golden Star and Hammer and Sickle medals. 4k, Coat of arms and "CCCP." 6k, TU-154 plane, globe and airmail envelope. 10k, Order of Labor. 12k, Space exploration medal with Gagarin portrait. 16k, Lenin Prize medal.

1976 Engr. *Perf. 12x12½*

4517 A2138	1k greenish black	.15	.15
4518 A2138	2k brt magenta	.15	.15
4519 A2139	3k red	.15	.15
4520 A2138	4k brick red	.15	.15
4521 A2139	6k Prus blue	.25	.15
4522 A2138	10k olive green	.45	.15
4523 A2139	12k violet blue	.50	.15
4524 A2139	16k deep green	.60	.15

Perf. 12½x12

4525 A2140	20k brown red	.80	.15
4526 A2141	30k brick red	1.10	.15
4527 A2142	50k brown	1.90	.15
4528 A2143	1r dark blue	4.00	.15
Nos. 4517-4528 (12)		10.20	
Set value			1.20

Issued: #4517-4524, 12/17; #4525-4528, 8/10. See #4596-4607. For overprint see #5720.

Luna 24 Emblem and Moon Landing A2144

1976, Dec. 17 Photo. *Perf. 11½*
4531 A2144 10k multicolored .30 .15

Moon exploration of automatic station Luna 24.

Icebreaker "Pilot" — A2145

Icebreakers: 6k, Ermak, vert. 10k, Fedor Litke. 16k, Vladimir Ilich, vert. 20k, Krassin.

Perf. 12x11½, 11½x12

1976, Dec. 22 Litho. & Engr.

4532 A2145	4k multicolored	.15	.15
4533 A2145	6k multicolored	.20	.15
4534 A2145	10k multicolored	.45	.15
4535 A2145	16k multicolored	.55	.25
4536 A2145	20k multicolored	.70	.30
Nos. 4532-4536 (5)		2.05	1.00

See Nos. 4579-4585.

Soyuz 22 Emblem, Cosmonauts V. F. Bykofsky and V. V. Aksenov — A2146

1976, Dec. 28 Photo. *Perf. 12x11½*
4537 A2146 10k multicolored .30 .25

Soyuz 22 space flight, Sept. 15-23.

Society Emblem — A2147

1977, Jan. 1 *Perf. 11½*

4538 A2147 4k multicolored .25 .15

Red Banner Voluntary Soc., supporting Red Army, Navy & Air Force, 50th anniv.

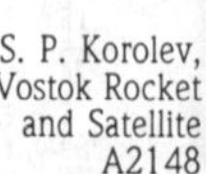

S. P. Korolev, Vostok Rocket and Satellite A2148

1977, Jan. 12

4539 A2148 4k multicolored .25 .15

Sergei Pavlovich Korolev (1907-1966), creator of first Soviet rocket space system.

Globe and Palm A2149

1977, Jan. 12

4540 A2149 4k multicolored .25 .15

World Congress of Peace Loving Forces, Moscow, Jan. 1977.

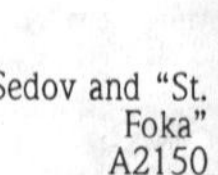

Sedov and "St. Foka" A2150

1977, Jan. 25 **Photo.** *Perf. 11½*

4541 A2150 4k multicolored .25 .15

G.Y. Sedov (1877-1914), polar explorer and hydrographer.

Worker and Farmer Monument and Izvestia Front Page — A2151

Ship Sailing Across the Oceans — A2152

1977, Jan. 25

4542 A2151 4k silver, black & red .25 .15

60th anniversary of newspaper Izvestia.

1977, Jan. 25

4543 A2152 6k deep blue & gold .30 .15

24th Intl. Navigation Cong., Leningrad.

Congress Hall and Troitskaya Tower, Kremlin A2153

Marshal Leonid A. Govorov (1897-1955) A2154

1977, Feb. 9 **Photo.** *Perf. 11½*

4544 A2153 4k red, gold & black .25 .15

16th Congress of USSR Trade Unions.

1977 **Engr.** *Perf. 12*

Marshals of the Soviet Union: No. 4546, Ivan S. Koniev. No. 4547, K. A. Merezhkov. No. 4548, W. D. Sokolovsky.

4545	A2154 4k brown		.20	.15
4546	A2154 4k slate green		.20	.15
4547	A2154 4k brown		.20	.15
4548	A2154 4k black		.20	.15
	Nos. 4545-4548 (4)		.80	
	Set value			.40

Issue dates: #4545, Feb. 9; others, June 7.

Academy, Crest, Anchor and Ribbons A2155

Photogravure and Engraved

1977, Feb. 9 *Perf. 11½*

4549 A2155 6k multicolored .25 .15

A. A. Grechko Naval Academy, Leningrad, sesquicentennial.

Jeanne Labourbe A2156

Queen and Knights A2157

1977, Feb. 25 **Photo.** *Perf. 11½*

4550 A2156 4k multicolored .25 .15

Jeanne Labourbe (1877-1919), leader of French communists in Moscow.

1977, Feb. 25

4551 A2157 6k multicolored .30 .15

4th European Chess Championships.

Cosmonauts V. D. Zudov and V. I. Rozhdestvensky — A2158

1977, Feb. 25 *Perf. 12x11½*

4552 A2158 10k multicolored .25 .15

Soyuz 23 space flight, Oct. 14-16, 1976.

A. S. Novikov-Priboy (1877-1944), Writer — A2159

1977, Mar. 16 **Photo.** *Perf. 11½*

4553 A2159 4k multicolored .25 .15

Welcome, by M. N. Soloninkin A2160

Folk Tale Paintings from Fedoskino Artists' Colony: 6k, Along the Street, by V. D. Antonov, horiz. 10k, Northern Song, by J. V. Karapaev. 12k, Tale of Czar Saltan, by A. I. Kozlov. 14k, Summer Troika, by V. A. Nalimov, horiz. 16k, Red Flower, by V. D. Lipitsky.

Perf. 12x12½, 12½x12

1977, Mar. 16 **Litho.**

4554	A2160 4k black & multi	.15	.15
4555	A2160 6k black & multi	.35	.15
4556	A2160 10k black & multi	.65	.15
4557	A2160 12k black & multi	.80	.15
4558	A2160 14k black & multi	.90	.15
4559	A2160 16k black & multi	1.00	.15
	Nos. 4554-4559 (6)	3.85	.90

Lenin on Red Square, by K.V. Filatov — A2161

1977, Apr. 12 *Perf. 12½x11½*

4560 A2161 4k multicolored .25 .15

107th anniversary of the birth of Lenin.

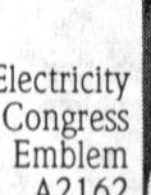

Electricity Congress Emblem A2162

1977, Apr. 12 **Photo.** *Perf. 11½*

4561 A2162 6k blue, red & gray .25 .15

World Electricity Congress, Moscow 1977.

Yuri Gagarin, Sputnik, Soyuz and Salyut — A2163

1977, Apr. 12 *Perf. 12x11½*

4562 A2163 6k multicolored .25 .15

Cosmonauts' Day.

N. I. Vavilov A2164

Feliks E. Dzerzhinski A2165

1977, Apr. 26 **Photo.** *Perf. 11½*

4563 A2164 4k multicolored .25 .15

Vavilov (1887-1943), agricultural geneticist.

1977, May 12 **Engr.** *Perf. 12½x12*

4564 A2165 4k black .30 .15

Feliks E. Dzerzhinski (1877-1926), organizer and head of secret police (OGPU).

Saxifraga Sibirica — A2166

Siberian Flowers: 3k, Dianthus repena. 4k, Novosieversia glactalis. 6k, Cerasticum maxinicem. 16k, Golden rhododendron.

1977, May 12 **Litho.** *Perf. 12x12½*

4565	A2166 2k multicolored	.15	.15
4566	A2166 3k multicolored	.20	.15
4567	A2166 4k multicolored	.20	.15
4568	A2166 6k multicolored	.30	.15
4569	A2166 16k multicolored	.80	.15
	Nos. 4565-4569 (5)	1.65	
	Set value		.50

V. V. Gorbatko, Y. N. Glazkov, Soyuz 24 Rocket A2167

1977, May 16 **Photo.** *Perf. 12x11½*

4570 A2167 10k multicolored .40 .25

Space explorations of cosmonauts on Salyut 5 orbital station, launched with Soyuz 24 rocket.

Film and Globe — A2168

1977, June 21 **Photo.** *Perf. 11½*

4571 A2168 6k multicolored .25 .15

10th Intl. Film Festival, Moscow 1977.

Lion Hunt, by Rubens — A2169

Rubens Paintings, Hermitage, Leningrad: 4k, ady in Waiting, vert. 10k, Workers in Quarry. 12k, lliance of Water and Earth, vert. 20k, Landscape ith Rainbow. 50k, Self-portrait.

Perf. 12x12½, 12½x12

977, June 24 **Litho.**

572 A2169 4k yellow & multi .15 .15
573 A2169 6k yellow & multi .20 .15
574 A2169 10k yellow & multi .40 .15
575 A2169 12k yellow & multi .50 .15
576 A2169 20k yellow & multi .75 .30
Nos. 4572-4576 (5) 2.00
Set value .70

Souvenir Sheet

577 A2169 50k yellow & multi 2.50 .80

Peter Paul Rubens (1577-1640), painter. Sheets f No. 4575 contain 2 labels with commemorative nscriptions and Atlas statue from Hermitage ntrance.

Souvenir Sheet

Judith, by Giorgione A2170

1977, July 15 **Litho.** ***Perf. 12x12½***

4578 A2170 50k multicolored 2.00 1.00

Il Giorgione (1478-1511), Venetian painter.

Icebreaker Type of 1976

Icebreakers: 4k, Aleksandr Sibiryakov. 6k, Georgi Sedov. 10k, Sadko. 12k, Dezhnev. 14k, Siberia. 16k, Lena. 20k, Amguyema.

Lithographed and Engraved

1977, July 27 ***Perf. 12x11½***

4579 A2145 4k multicolored .15 .15
4580 A2145 6k multicolored .15 .15
4581 A2145 10k multicolored .35 .15
4582 A2145 12k multicolored .40 .20
4583 A2145 14k multicolored .45 .25
4584 A2145 16k multicolored .50 .35
4585 A2145 20k multicolored .65 .45
Nos. 4579-4585 (7) 2.65 1.70

Souvenir Sheet

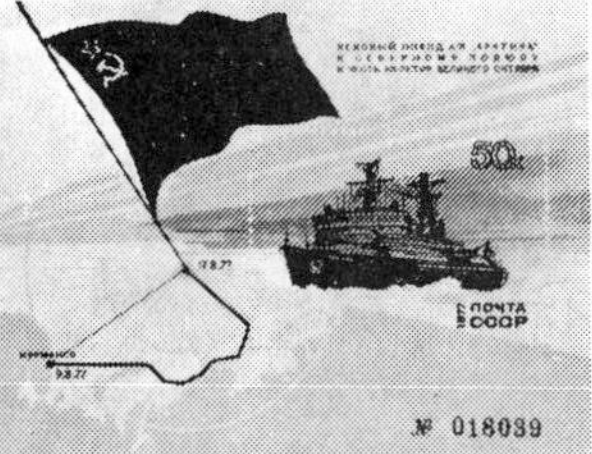

Icebreaker Arctica — A2171

Lithographed and Engraved

1977, Sept. 15 ***Perf. 12½x12***

4586 A2171 50k multicolored 9.00 5.00

Arctica, first ship to travel from Murmansk to North Pole, Aug. 9-17.

View and Arms of Stavropol A2172

Stamps and Exhibition Emblem A2173

1977, Aug. 16 **Photo.** ***Perf. 11½***

4587 A2172 6k multicolored .25 .15

200th anniversary of Stavropol.

1977, Aug. 16

4588 A2173 4k multicolored .25 .15

October Revolution Anniversary Philatelic Exhibition, Moscow.

Yuri A. Gagarin and Spacecraft — A2174

No. 4590, Alexei Leonov floating in space. No. 4591, Orbiting space station, cosmonauts at control panel.

Nos. 4592-4594, Various spacecraft: No. 4592, International cooperation for space research; No. 4593, Interplanetary flights; No. 4594, Exploring earth's atmosphere. 50k, "XX," laurel, symbolic Sputnik with Red Star.

1977, Oct. 4 **Photo.** ***Perf. 11½x12***

4589 A2174 10k sepia & multi .25 .15
4590 A2174 10k gray & multi .25 .15
4591 A2174 10k gray green & multi .25 .15
4592 A2174 20k green & multi .60 .35
4593 A2174 20k violet blue & multi .60 .35
4594 A2174 20k bister & multi .60 .35
Nos. 4589-4594 (6) 2.55 1.50

Souvenir Sheet

4595 A2174 50k claret & gold *7.50 7.50*

20th anniv. of space research. No. 4595 contains one stamp, size: 22x32mm.

Types of 1976

Designs: 15k, Communications emblem and globes; others as before.

1977-78 **Litho.** ***Perf. 12x12½***

4596 A2138 1k olive green .15 .15
4597 A2138 2k lilac rose .15 .15
4598 A2139 3k brick red .15 .15
4599 A2138 4k vermilion .15 .15
4600 A2139 6k Prus blue .20 .15
4601 A2138 10k gray green .40 .15
4602 A2139 12k vio blue .45 .15
4602A A2139 15k blue ('78) .55 .15
4603 A2139 16k slate green .60 .15

Perf. 12½x12

4604 A2140 20k brown red .75 .15
4605 A2141 30k dull brick red 1.00 .15
4606 A2142 50k brown 2.00 .15
4607 A2143 1r dark blue 3.75 .15
Nos. 4596-4607 (13) 10.30
Set value 1.30

Nos. 4596-4602A, 4604-4607 were printed on dull and shiny paper.

For overprint see No. 5720.

Souvenir Sheet

Bas-relief, 12th Century, Cathedral of St. Dimitri, Vladimir — A2175

6k, Necklace, Ryazan excavations, 12th cent. 10k, Mask, Cathedral of the Nativity, Suzdal, 13th cent. 12k, Archangel Michael, 15th cent. icon. 16k, Chalice by Ivan Fomin, 1449. 20k, St. Basil's Cathedral, Moscow, 16th cent.

1977, Oct. 12 **Litho.** ***Perf. 12***

4608 Sheet of 6 2.50 1.25
a. A2175 4k gold & black .15
b. A2175 6k gold & multi .20
c. A2175 10k gold & multi .35
d. A2175 12k gold & multi .45
e. A2175 16k gold & multi .50
f. A2175 20k gold & multi .60

Masterpieces of old Russian culture.

Fir, Snowflake, Molniya Satellite — A2176

1977, Oct. 12 ***Perf. 12x12½***

4609 A2176 4k multicolored .30 .15

New Year 1978.

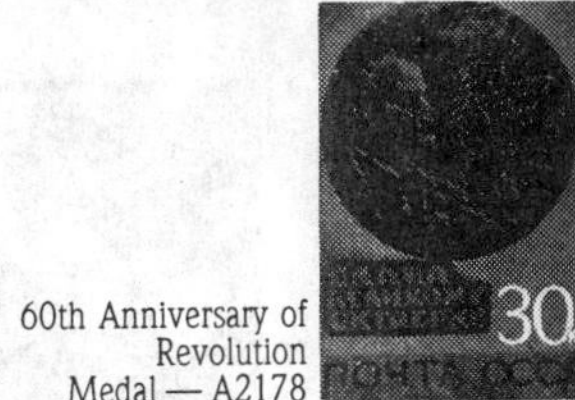

Cruiser Aurora and Torch — A2177

60th Anniversary of Revolution Medal — A2178

60th Anniv. of October Revolution: #4611, Lenin speaking at Finland Station (monument), 1917. #4612, 1917 Peace Decree, Brezhnev's book about Lenin. #4613, Kremlin tower with star and fireworks.

1977, Oct. 26 **Photo.** ***Perf. 12x11½***

4610 A2177 4k gold, red & black .20 .15
4611 A2177 4k gold, red & black .20 .15
4612 A2177 4k gold, red & black .20 .15
4613 A2177 4k gold, red & black .20 .15
Nos. 4610-4613 (4) .80
Set value .40

Souvenir Sheet

Perf. 11½

4614 A2178 30k gold, red & black 1.50 .70

Flag of USSR, Constitution (Book) with Coat of Arms — A2179

Designs: No. 4616, Red banner, people and cover of constitution. 50k, Constitution, Kremlin and olive branch.

1977, Oct. 31 **Litho.** ***Perf. 12½x12***

4615 A2179 4k red, black & yel .15 .15
4616 A2179 4k red, black & yel .15 .15
Set value .20

Souvenir Sheet

Perf. 11½x12½

Lithographed and Embossed

4617 A2179 50k red, gold & yel 1.75 1.00

Adoption of new constitution. No. 4617 contains one 70x50mm stamp.

Souvenir Sheet

Leonid Brezhnev A2180

Lithographed and Embossed

1977, Nov. 2 ***Perf. 11½x12***

4618 A2180 50k gold & multi 1.75 1.00

Adoption of new constitution, General Secretary Brezhnev, chairman of Constitution Commission.

Postal Official and Postal Code — A2181

Mail Processing (Woman Postal Official and): No. 4620, Mail collection and Moskvich 430 car. No. 4621, Automatic letter sorting machine. No. 4622, Mail transport by truck, train, ship and planes. No. 4623, Mail delivery in city and country.

Lithographed and Engraved

1977, Nov. 16 ***Perf. 12½x12***

4619 A2181 4k multicolored .20 .15
4620 A2181 4k multicolored .20 .15
4621 A2181 4k multicolored .20 .15
4622 A2181 4k multicolored .20 .15
4623 A2181 4k multicolored .20 .15
Nos. 4619-4623 (5) 1.00
Set value .50

Capital, Asoka Pillar, Red Fort — A2182

Proclamation Monument, Charkov — A2183

1977, Dec. 14 **Photo.** ***Perf. 11½***

4624 A2182 6k maroon, gold & red .25 .15

30th anniversary of India's independence.

1977, Dec. 14 **Litho.** ***Perf. 12x12½***

4625 A2183 6k multicolored .25 .15

60th anniv. of Soviet power in the Ukraine.

Lebetina Viper — A2184

Protected Fauna: 1k to 12k, Venomous snakes, useful for medicinal purposes. 16k, Polar bear and cub. 20k, Walrus and calf. 30k, Tiger and cub.

Photogravure and Engraved

1977, Dec. 16 *Perf. 11½x12*

4626 A2184 1k black & multi .15 .15
4627 A2184 4k black & multi .15 .15
4628 A2184 6k black & multi .20 .15
4629 A2184 10k black & multi .35 .15
4630 A2184 12k black & multi .45 .15
4631 A2184 16k black & multi .55 .20
4632 A2184 20k black & multi .75 .25
4633 A2184 30k black & multi 1.00 .35
Nos. 4626-4633 (8) 3.60
Set value 1.25

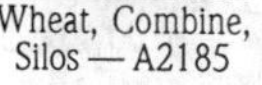

Wheat, Combine, Silos — A2185

Congress Palace, Spasski Tower — A2186

1978, Jan. 27 **Photo.** *Perf. 11½*

4634 A2185 4k multicolored .25 .15

Gigant collective grain farm, Rostov Region, 50th anniversary.

1978, Jan. 27 **Litho.** *Perf. 12x12½*

4635 A2186 4k multicolored .25 .15

Young Communist League, Lenin's Komsomol, 60th anniv. and its 25th Cong.

Liberation Obelisk, Emblem, Dove — A2187

1978, Jan. 27 **Photo.** *Perf. 11½*

4636 A2187 6k multicolored .25 .15

8th Congress of International Federation of Resistance Fighters, Minsk, Belorussia.

Soldiers Leaving for the Front — A2188

Designs: No. 4638, Defenders of Moscow Monument, Lenin banner. No. 4639, Soldier as defender of the people.

1978, Feb. 21 **Litho.** *Perf. 12½x12*

4637 A2188 4k red & multi .15 .15
4638 A2188 4k red & multi .15 .15
4639 A2188 4k red & multi .15 .15
Nos. 4637-4639 (3) .45
Set value .30

60th anniversary of USSR Military forces.

Morning, by Kustodiev — A2189

Kustodiev Paintings: 4k, Celebration in Village. 6k, Shrovetide (winter landscape). 12k, Merchant's Wife Drinking Tea. 20k, Bolshevik. 50k, Self-portrait, vert.

1978, Mar. 3 *Perf. 11½*

Size: 70x33mm

4640 A2189 4k lilac & multi .15 .15
4641 A2189 6k lilac & multi .20 .15

Size: 47x32mm

Perf. 12½x12

4642 A2189 10k lilac & multi .40 .15
4643 A2189 12k lilac & multi .50 .15
4644 A2189 20k lilac & multi .70 .25
Nos. 4640-4644 (5) 1.95
Set value .65

Souvenir Sheet

Perf. 11½x12½

4644A A2189 50k lilac & multi 1.75 .75

Boris Mikhailovich Kustodiev (1878-1927), painter. Nos. 4640-4643 have se-tenant label showing museum where painting is kept. No. 4644A has label giving short biography.

Docking in Space, Intercosmos Emblem A2190

Designs: 6k, Rocket, Soviet Cosmonaut Aleksei Gubarev and Czechoslovak Capt. Vladimir Remek on launching pad. 32k, Weather balloon, helicopter, Intercosmos emblem, USSR and Czechoslovakian flags.

1978, Mar. 10 **Litho.** *Perf. 12x12½*

4645 A2190 6k multicolored .15 .15
4646 A2190 15k multicolored .45 .15
4647 A2190 32k multicolored 1.00 .40
Nos. 4645-4647 (3) 1.60 .70

Intercosmos, Soviet-Czechoslovak cooperative space program.

Festival Emblem — A2191

1978, Mar. 17 **Litho.** *Perf. 12x12½*

4648 A2191 4k blue & multi .25 .15

11th Youth & Students' Cong., Havana.

Tulip, Bolshoi Theater A2192

Moscow Flowers: 2k, Rose "Moscow morning" and Lomonosov University. 4k, Dahlia "Red Star" and Spasski Tower. 10k, Gladiolus "Moscovite" and VDNH Building. 12k, Ilich anniversary iris and Lenin Central Museum.

1978, Mar. 17 *Perf. 12½x12*

4649 A2192 1k multicolored .15 .15
4650 A2192 2k multicolored .15 .15
4651 A2192 4k multicolored .15 .15
4652 A2192 10k multicolored .20 .15
4653 A2192 12k multicolored .25 .15
Nos. 4649-4653 (5) .90
Set value .50

IMCO Emblem and Waves — A2193

1978, Mar. 17 **Litho.** *Perf. 12x12½*

4654 A2193 6k multicolored .25 .15

Intergovernmental Maritime Consultative Org., 20th anniv., and World Maritime Day.

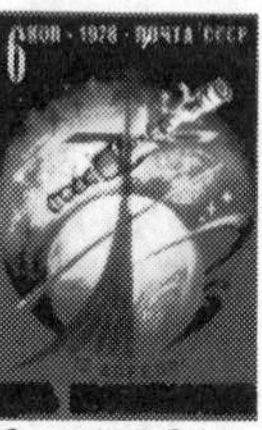

Spaceship, Orbits of Salyut 5, Soyuz 26 and 27 A2194

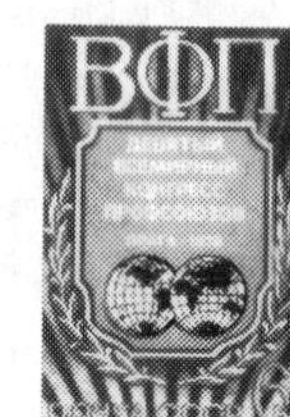

World Federation of Trade Unions Emblem A2195

1978, Apr. 12 **Photo.** *Perf. 12*

4655 A2194 6k blue, dk blue & gold .25 .15

Cosmonauts' Day, Apr. 12.

1978, Apr. 16 *Perf. 12*

4656 A2195 6k multicolored .25 .15

9th World Trade Union Congress, Prague.

2-2-0 Locomotive, 1845, Petersburg and Moscow Stations — A2196

Locomotives: 1k, 1st Russian model by E. A. and M. W. Cherepanov, vert. 2k, 1-3-0 freight, 1845. 16k, Aleksandrov 0-3-0, 1863. 20k, 2-2-0 passenger and Sergievsk Pustyn platform, 1863.

1978, Apr. 20 **Litho.** *Perf. 11½*

4657 A2196 1k orange & multi .15 .15
4658 A2196 2k ultra & multi .15 .15
4659 A2196 3k yellow & multi .15 .15
4660 A2196 16k green & multi .60 .20
4661 A2196 20k rose & multi .70 .25
Nos. 4657-4661 (5) 1.75
Set value .75

Souvenir Sheet

Lenin, by V. A. Serov A2197

1978, Apr. 22 *Perf. 12x12½*

4662 A2197 50k multicolored 1.50 .75

108th anniversary of the birth of Lenin.

Soyuz and Salyut 6 Docking in Space — A2198

Y. V. Romanenko and G. M. Grechko — A2199

1978, June 15 *Perf. 12*

4663 A2198 15k multicolored .50 .20
4664 A2199 15k multicolored .50 .20

Photographic survey and telescopic observations of stars by crews of Soyuz 26, Soyuz 27 and Soyuz 28, Dec. 10, 1977-Mar. 16, 1978. Nos. 4663-4664 printed se-tenant with label showing schematic pictures of various experiments.

Space Meteorology, Rockets, Spaceship, Earth — A2200

No. 4666, Natural resources of earth and Soyuz. No. 4667, Space communications, "Orbita" Station and Molnyia satellite. No. 4668, Man, earth and Vostok. 50k, Study of magnetosphere, Prognoz over earth.

1978, June 23 *Perf. 12x12½*

4665 A2200 10k green & multi .25 .15
4666 A2200 10k blue & multi .25 .15
4667 A2200 10k violet & multi .25 .15
4668 A2200 10k rose lilac & multi .25 .15
Nos. 4665-4668 (4) 1.00
Set value .40

Souvenir Sheet

Perf. 11½x12½

4669 A2200 50k multicolored 1.50 .75

Space explorations of the Intercosmos program. #4669 contains one 36x51mm stamp.

Soyuz Rocket on Carrier — A2201

Designs (Flags of USSR and Poland, Intercosmos Emblem): 15k, Crystal, spaceship (Sirena, experimental crystallogenesis in space). 32k, Research ship "Cosmonaut Vladimir Komarov," spaceship, world map and paths of Salyut 6, Soyuz 29-30.

1978, **Litho.** *Perf. 12½x12*

4670 A2201 6k multicolored .15 .15
4671 A2201 15k multicolored .40 .15
4672 A2201 32k multicolored .80 .40
Nos. 4670-4672 (3) 1.35 .70

Intercosmos, Soviet-Polish cooperative space program. Issued: 6k, 6/28; 15k, 6/30; 32k, 7/5.

Lenin, Awards Received by Komsomol A2202

Kamaz Car, Train, Bridge, Hammer and Sickle A2203

1978, July 5 *Perf. 12x12½*

4673 A2202 4k multicolored .15 .15
4674 A2203 4k multicolored .15 .15
Set value .20

Leninist Young Communist League (Komsomol), 60th anniv. (#4673); Komsomol's participation in 5-year plan (#4674).

For overprint see No. 4703.

M. V. Zaharov A2204

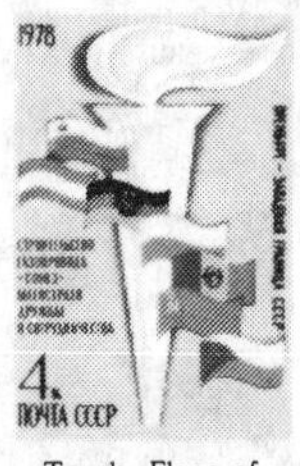

Torch, Flags of Participants A2205

1978, July 5 **Engr.** *Perf. 12*

4675 A2204 4k sepia .25 .15

M. V. Zaharov (1898-1972), Marshal of the Soviet Union.

1978, July 25 **Litho.** *Perf. 12x12½*

4676 A2205 4k multicolored .25 .15

Construction of Soyuz gas-pipeline (Friendship Line), Orenburg. Flags of participating countries shown: Bulgaria, Hungary, German Democratic Republic, Poland, Romania, USSR, Czechoslovakia.

Harvey A2206

N. G. Chernyshevsky A2207

1978, July 25 *Perf. 12*

4677 A2206 6k blue, black & dp grn .25 .15

Dr. William Harvey (1578-1657), discoverer of blood circulation.

1978, July 30 **Engr.** *Perf. 12x12½*

4678 A2207 4k brown, *yellow* .25 .15

Nikolai Gavilovich Chernyshevsky (1828-1889), revolutionary.

Whitewinged Petrel A2208

Antarctic Fauna: 1k, Crested penguin, horiz. 4k, Emperor penguin and chick. 6k, White-blooded pikes. 10k, Sea elephant, horiz.

Perf. 12x11½, 11½x12

1978, July 30 **Litho.**

4679 A2208 1k multicolored .20 .15
4680 A2208 3k multicolored .35 .15
4681 A2208 4k multicolored .35 .15
4682 A2208 6k multicolored .45 .15
4683 A2208 10k multicolored .75 .15
Nos. 4679-4683 (5) 2.10
Set value .50

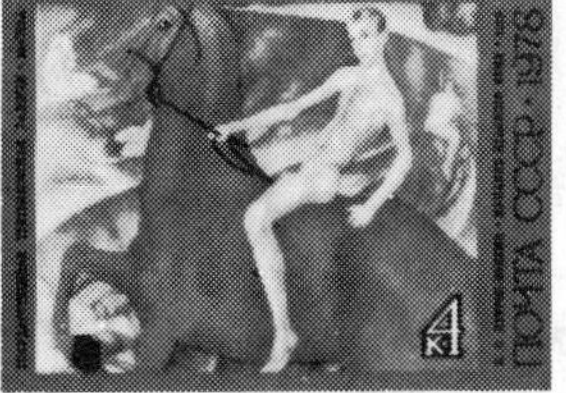

The Red Horse, by Petrov-Votkin — A2209

Paintings by Petrov-Votkin: 6k, Mother and Child, Petrograd, 1918. 10k, Death of the Commissar. 12k, Still-life with Fruit. 16k, Still-life with Teapot and Flowers. 50k, Self-portrait, 1918, vert.

1978, Aug. 16 **Litho.** *Perf. 12½x12*

4684 A2209 4k silver & multi .15 .15
4685 A2209 6k silver & multi .25 .15
4686 A2209 10k silver & multi .55 .15
4687 A2209 12k silver & multi .70 .15
4688 A2209 16k silver & multi .80 .20
Nos. 4684-4688 (5) 2.45
Set value .60

Souvenir Sheet

Perf. 11½x12

4689 A2209 50k silver & multi 1.75 1.00

Kozma Sergeevich Petrov-Votkin (1878-1939), painter. Nos. 4684-4688 have se-tenant labels. No. 4689 has label the size of stamp.

Soyuz 31 in Shop, Intercosmos Emblem, USSR and DDR Flags — A2210

Designs (Intercosmos Emblem, USSR and German Democratic Republic Flags and): 15k, Pamir Mountains photographed from space; Salyut 6, Soyuz 29 and 31 complex and spectrum. 32k, Soyuz 31 docking, photographed from Salyut 6.

1978 **Litho.** *Perf. 12x12½*

4690 A2210 6k multicolored .15 .15
4691 A2210 15k multicolored .85 .15
4692 A2210 32k multicolored 1.65 .45
Nos. 4690-4692 (3) 2.65
Set value .65

Intercosmos, Soviet-East German cooperative space program.

Issued: 6k, 8/27; 15k, 8/31; 32k, 9/3.

PRAGA '78 Emblem, Plane, Radar, Spaceship A2211

Photogravure and Engraved

1978, Aug. 29 *Perf. 11½*

4693 A2211 6k multicolored .25 .15

PRAGA '78 International Philatelic Exhibition, Prague, Sept. 8-17.

Leo Tolstoi (1828-1910), Novelist and Philosopher A2212

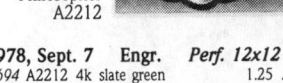

1978, Sept. 7 **Engr.** *Perf. 12x12½*

4694 A2212 4k slate green 1.25 .90

Stag, Conference Emblem — A2213

1978 **Photo.** *Perf. 11½*

4695 A2213 4k multicolored .25 .15

14th General Assembly of the Society for Wildlife Preservation, Ashkhabad.

Bronze Figure, Erebuni, 8th Century A2214

Armenian Architecture: 6k, Etchmiadzin Cathedral, 4th century. 10k, Stone crosses, Dzaghkatzor, 13th century. 12k, Library, Erevan, horiz. 16k, Lenin statue, Lenin Square, Erevan, horiz.

1978 **Litho.** *Perf. 12x12½, 12½x12*

4696 A2214 4k multicolored .15 .15
4697 A2214 6k multicolored .20 .15
4698 A2214 10k multicolored .30 .15
4699 A2214 12k multicolored .40 .15
4700 A2214 16k multicolored .50 .15
Nos. 4696-4700 (5) 1.55
Set value .50

Issued: 4k, 10k, 16k, Sept. 12; others, Oct. 14.

Memorial, Messina, Russian Warships A2215

1978, Sept. 12 **Photo.** *Perf. 11½*

4701 A2215 6k multicolored .25 .15

70th anniversary of aid given by Russian sailors during Messina earthquake.

Communications Emblem, Ostankino TV Tower — A2216

1978, Sept. 20 **Photo.** *Perf. 11½*

4702 A2216 4k multicolored .25 .15

Organization for Communication Cooperation of Socialist Countries, 20th anniv.

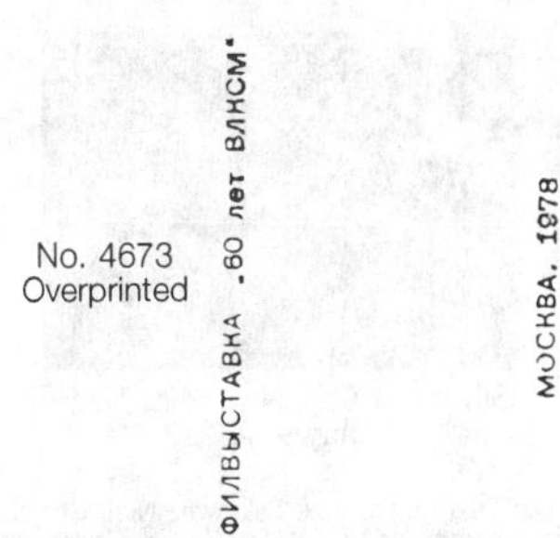

No. 4673 Overprinted

1978, Sept. 20 **Litho.** *Perf. 12x12½*

4703 A2202 4k multicolored 1.25 .70

Philatelic Exhibition for the Leninist Young Communist League.

Souvenir Sheet

Diana, by Paolo Veronese — A2217

1978, Sept. 28 **Litho.** *Perf. 12x11½*

4704 A2217 50k multicolored 1.50 1.00

Veronese (1528-88), Italian painter.

Kremlin, Moscow A2218

S. G. Shaumyan A2219

Souvenir Sheet

Lithographed and Embossed

1978, Oct. 7 *Perf. 11½x12*

4705 A2218 30k gold & multi 1.50 .65

Russian Constitution, 1st anniversary.

1978, Oct. 11 **Engr.** *Perf. 12½x12*

4706 A2219 4k slate green .25 .15

Stepan Georgevich Shaumyan (1878-1918), Communist Party functionary.

Ferry, Russian and Bulgarian Colors — A2220

Hammer and Sickle, Flags — A2221

1978, Oct. 14 **Photo.** *Perf. 11½*

4707 A2220 6k multicolored .25 .15

Opening of Ilychovsk-Varna Ferry.

1978, Oct. 26 **Photo.** *Perf. 11½*

4708 A2221 4k gold & multi .25 .15

61st anniversary of October Revolution.

Silver Gilt Cup, Novgorod, 12th Century — A2222

Old Russian Art: 10k, Pokrowna Nerli Church, 12th century, vert. 12k, St. George Slaying the Dragon, icon, Novgorod, 15th century, vert. 16k, The Czar, cannon, 1586.

Perf. 12½x12, 12x12½

1978, Nov. 28 **Litho.**

4709 A2222 6k multicolored .15 .15
4710 A2222 10k multicolored .40 .15
4711 A2222 12k multicolored .50 .15
4712 A2222 16k multicolored .60 .20
Nos. 4709-4712 (4) 1.65
Set value .50

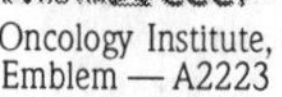

Oncology Institute, Emblem — A2223

Savior Tower, Kremlin — A2224

1978, Dec. 1 **Photo.** *Perf. 11½*

4713 A2223 4k multicolored .25 .15

P.A. Herzen Tumor Institute, 75th anniv.

1978, Dec. 20 **Litho.** *Perf. 12x12½*

4714 A2224 4k silver, blue & red .25 .15

New Year 1979.

Nestor Pechersky, Chronicler, c. 885 — A2225

History of Postal Service: 6k, Birch bark letter and stylus. 10k, Messenger with trumpet and staff, from 14th century Psalm book. 12k, Winter traffic, from 16th century book by Sigizmund Gerberstein. 16k, Prikaz post office, from 17th century icon.

Lithographed and Engraved

1978, Dec. 20 *Perf. 12½x12*

4715 A2225 4k multicolored .15 .15
4716 A2225 6k multicolored .20 .15
4717 A2225 10k multicolored .50 .15
4718 A2225 12k multicolored .55 .15
4719 A2225 16k multicolored .65 .20
Nos. 4715-4719 (5) 2.05
Set value .60

Kovalenok and Ivanchenkov, Salyut 6-Soyuz — A2226

1978, Dec. 20 **Photo.** *Perf. 11½x12*

4720 A2226 10k multicolored .30 .15

Cosmonauts V. V. Kovalenok and A. S. Ivanchenkov spent 140 days in space, June 15-Nov. 2, 1978.

Vasilii Pronchishchev — A2227

Icebreakers: 6k, Captain Belousov, 1954, vert. 10k, Moscow. 12k, Admiral Makarov, 1974. 16k, Lenin, 1959, vert. 20k, Nuclear-powered Arctica.

Perf. 11½x12, 12x11½

1978, Dec. 20 **Photo. & Engr.**

4721 A2227 4k multicolored .15 .15
4722 A2227 6k multicolored .15 .15
4723 A2227 10k multicolored .35 .15
4724 A2227 12k multicolored .40 .15
4725 A2227 16k multicolored .50 .20
4726 A2227 20k multicolored .60 .25
Nos. 4721-4726 (6) 2.15
Set value .85

Souvenir Sheet

Mastheads and Globe with Russia — A2228

1978, Dec. 28 **Litho.** *Perf. 12*

4727 A2228 30k multicolored 1.00 .35

Distribution of periodicals through the Post and Telegraph Department, 60th anniversary.

Cuban Flags Forming Star — A2229

1979, Jan. 1 **Photo.** *Perf. 11½*

4728 A2229 6k multicolored .25 .15

Cuban Revolution, 20th anniversary.

Russian and Byelorussian Flags, Government Building, Minsk A2230

1979, Jan. 1

4729 A2230 4k multicolored .25 .15

Byelorussian SSR and Byelorussian Communist Party, 60th annivs.

Ukrainian and Russian Flags, Reunion Monument — A2231

1979, Jan. 16

4730 A2231 4k multicolored .30 .15

Reunion of Ukraine & Russia, 325th anniv.

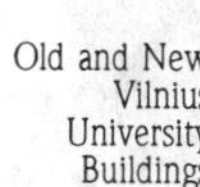

Old and New Vilnius University Buildings A2232

1979, Jan. 16 **Photo. & Engr.**

4731 A2232 4k black & salmon .25 .15

400th anniversary of University of Vilnius.

Bulgaria No. 1 and Exhibition Hall A2233

1979, Jan. 25 **Litho.** *Perf. 12½x12*

4732 A2233 15k multicolored .35 .15

Filaserdica '79 Philatelic Exhibition, Sofia, for centenary of Bulgarian postal service.

Sputniks, Soviet Radio Hams Emblem — A2234

1979, Feb. 23 **Photo.** *Perf. 11½*

4733 A2234 4k multicolored .25 .15

Sputnik satellites Radio 1 and Radio 2, launched, Oct. 1978.

1-3-0 Locomotive, 1878 — A2235

Locomotives: 3k, 1-4-0, 1912. 4k, 2-3-1, 1915. 6k, 1-3-1, 1925. 15k, 1-5-0, 1947.

1979, Feb. 23 **Litho.** *Perf. 11½*

4734 A2235 2k multicolored .15 .15
4735 A2235 3k multicolored .15 .15
4736 A2235 4k multicolored .15 .15
4737 A2235 6k multicolored .25 .15
4738 A2235 15k multicolored .65 .20
Nos. 4734-4738 (5) 1.35
Set value .60

Souvenir Sheet

Medal for Land Development A2236

1979, Mar. 14 *Perf. 11½x12½*

4739 A2236 50k multicolored 1.50 .75

25th anniv. of drive to develop virgin lands.

Venera 11 and 12 over Venus — A2237

1979, Mar. 16 **Photo.** *Perf. 11½*

4740 A2237 10k multicolored .30 .15

Interplanetary flights of Venera 11 and Venera 12, December 1978.

Albert Einstein, Equation and Signature A2238

1979, Mar. 16

4741 A2238 6k multicolored .30 .15

Einstein (1879-1955), theoretical physicist.

Congress Emblem A2239

1979, Mar. 16

4742 A2239 6k multicolored .25 .15

21st World Veterinary Congress, Moscow.

"To Arms," by R. Berens A2240

1979, Mar. 21

4743 A2240 4k multicolored .25 .15

Soviet Republic of Hungary, 60th anniv.

Salyut 6, Soyuz, Research Ship, Letters — A2241

1979, Apr. 12 **Litho.** *Perf. 11½x12*

4744 A2241 15k multicolored .50 .15

Cosmonauts' Day.

Souvenir Sheet

Ice Hockey — A2242

1979, Apr. 14 **Photo.** *Perf. 12x11½*

4745 A2242 50k multicolored 1.50 .75

World and European Ice Hockey Championships, Moscow, Apr. 14-27.

For overprint see No. 4751.

Souvenir Sheet

Lenin A2243

1979, Apr. 18
4746 A2243 50k red, gold & brown 1.50 .75

109th anniversary of the birth of Lenin.

Astronauts' Training Center — A2244

Exhibition Emblem — A2245

Design: 32k, Astronauts, landing capsule, radar, helicopter and emblem.

1979, Apr. 12 Litho. ***Perf.*** ***11½***
4747 A2244 6k multicolored .15 .15
4748 A2244 32k multicolored 1.10 .40

Joint Soviet-Bulgarian space flight.

1979, Apr. 18 Photo. ***Perf.*** ***11½***
4749 A2245 15k sil, red & vio blue .60 .15

National USSR Exhibition in the United Kingdom. Se-tenant label with commemorative inscription.

Blast Furance, Pushkin Theater, "Tent" Sculpture — A2246

1979, May 24 Photo. ***Perf.*** ***11½***
4750 A2246 4k multicolored .25 .15

50th anniversary of Magnitogorsk City.

Souvenir Sheet

No. 4745 Overprinted in Margin in Red

СОВЕТСКИЕ ХОККЕИСТЫ—
ЧЕМПИОНЫ МИРА
И ЕВРОПЫ

1979, May 24 ***Perf.*** ***12x11½***
4751 A2242 50k multicolored 3.00 .80

Victory of Soviet team in World and European Ice Hockey Championships.

Infant, Flowers, IYC Emblem — A2247

1979, June Litho. ***Perf.*** ***12x12½***
4752 A2247 4k multicolored .25 .15

International Year of the Child.

Horn Player and Bears Playing Balalaika, Bogorodsk Wood Carvings — A2248

Folk Art: 3k, Decorated wooden bowls, Khokhloma. 4k, Tray decorated with flowers, Zhestovo. 6k, Carved bone boxes, Kholmogory. 15k, Lace, Vologda.

1979, June 14 Litho. ***Perf.*** ***12½x12***
4753 A2248 2k multicolored .15 .15
4754 A2248 3k multicolored .15 .15
4755 A2248 4k multicolored .15 .15
4756 A2248 6k multicolored .20 .15
4757 A2248 15k multicolored .50 .25
Nos. 4753-4757 (5) 1.15
Set value .65

V. A. Djanibekov, O. G. Makarov, Spacecraft A2249

1979, June ***Perf.*** ***12x11½***
4758 A2249 4k multicolored .35 .15

Flights of Soyuz 26-27 and work on board of orbital complex Salyut 26-27.

COMECON Building, Members' Flags — A2250

Scene from "Potemkin" and Festival Emblem — A2251

1979, June 26 ***Perf.*** ***12***
4759 A2250 16k multicolored .50 .20

Council for Mutual Economic Aid of Socialist Countries, 30th anniversary.

Photogravure and Engraved

1979, July ***Perf.*** ***11½***
4760 A2251 15k multicolored .50 .15

11th International Film Festival, Moscow, and 60th anniversary of Soviet film industry.

Lenin Square Station, Tashkent A2252

1979, July Litho. ***Perf.*** ***12***
4761 A2252 4k multicolored .25 .15

Tashkent subway.

Souvenir Sheets

Atom Symbol, Factories, Dam — A2253

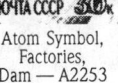

USSR Philatelic Society Emblem — A2254

1979, July 23 Photo. ***Perf.*** ***11½x12***
4762 A2253 30k multicolored 1.00 .45

50th anniversary of 1st Five-Year Plan.

1979, July 25 Litho. ***Perf.*** ***12x12½***
4763 A2254 50k gray grn & red 1.50 .70

4th Cong. of USSR Phil. Soc., Moscow.

Exhibition Hall, Scene from "Chapayev" A2255

1979, Aug. 8 Photo. ***Perf.*** ***11½***
4764 A2255 4k multicolored .25 .15

60th anniversary of Soviet Film and Exhibition of History of Soviet Film.

Roses, by P. P. Konchalovsky, 1955 — A2256

Russian Flower Paintings: 1k, Flowers and Fruit, by I. F. Khrutsky, 1830. 2k, Phlox, by I. N. Kramskoi, 1884. 3k, Lilac, by K. A. Korovin, 1915. 15k, Bluebells, by S. V. Gerasimov, 1944. 2k, 3k, 15k, vert.

Perf. 12½x12, 12x12½

1979, Aug. 16 Litho.
4765 A2256 1k multicolored .15 .15
4766 A2256 2k multicolored .15 .15
4767 A2256 3k multicolored .15 .15
4768 A2256 15k multicolored .40 .30
4769 A2256 32k multicolored .75 .55
Nos. 4765-4769 (5) 1.60
Set value 1.00

John McClean — A2257

Soviet Circus Emblem — A2258

1979, Aug. 29 Litho. ***Perf.*** ***11½***
4770 A2257 4k red & black .25 .15

John McClean (1879-1923), British Communist labor leader.

1979, Sept.
4771 A2258 4k multicolored .25 .15

Soviet Circus, 60th anniversary.

Friendship — A2259

Children's Drawings: 3k, Children and Horses. 4k, Dances. 15k, The Excursion.

1979, Sept. 10 ***Perf.*** ***12½x12***
4772 A2259 2k multicolored .15 .15
4773 A2259 3k multicolored .15 .15
4774 A2259 4k multicolored .15 .15
4775 A2259 15k multicolored .30 .20
Nos. 4772-4775 (4) .75
Set value .50

International Year of the Child.
Exist imperf.

Oriolus oriolus — A2260

Birds: 3k, Dendrocopus minor. 4k, Parus cristatus. 10k, Tyto alba. 15k, Caprimulgus europaeus.

1979, Sept. 18
4776 A2260 2k multicolored .15 .15
4777 A2260 3k multicolored .15 .15
4778 A2260 4k multicolored .15 .15
4779 A2260 10k multicolored .35 .15
4780 A2260 15k multicolored .50 .20
Nos. 4776-4780 (5) 1.30 .80

German Arms, Marx, Engels, Lenin, Berlin A2261

1979, Oct. 7 Photo. ***Perf.*** ***11½***
4781 A2261 6k multicolored .25 .15

German Democratic Republic, 30th anniv.

Valery Ryumin, Vladimir Lyakhov, Salyut 6 — A2262

Design: No. 4783, Spacecraft.

1979, Oct. 10 *Perf. 12x11½*

4782	A2262	15k	multicolored	.40	.25
4783	A2262	15k	multicolored	.40	.25
a.			Pair, #4782-4783	.80	.50

175 days in space, Feb. 25-Aug. 19. No. 4783a has continuous design.

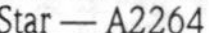

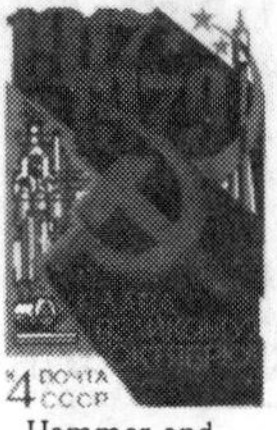

Star — A2264

Hammer and Sickle — A2265

1979, Oct. 18 *Perf. 11½*

4784	A2264	4k	multicolored	.25	.15

USSR Armed Forces, 60th anniversary.

1979, Oct. 18

4785	A2265	4k	multicolored	.25	.15

October Revolution, 62nd anniversary.

Katherina, by T. G. Shevchenko A2266

Ukrainian Paintings: 3k, Working Girl, by K.K. Kostandi. 4k, Lenin's Return to Petrograd, by A.M. Lopuhov. 10k, Soldier's Return, by N.V. Kostesky. 15k, Going to Work, by M.G. Belsky.

1979, Nov. 18 Litho. *Perf. 12x12½*

4786	A2266	2k	multicolored	.15	.15
4787	A2266	3k	multicolored	.15	.15
4788	A2266	4k	multicolored	.15	.15
4789	A2266	10k	multicolored	.20	.15
4790	A2266	15k	multicolored	.30	.20
			Nos. 4786-4790 (5)	.95	
			Set value		.60

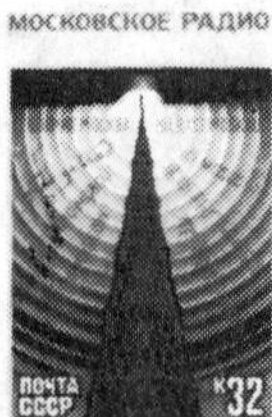

Shabolovka Radio Tower, Moscow — A2267

Mischa Holding Stamp — A2268

1979, Nov. 28 Photo. *Perf. 12*

4791	A2267	32k	multicolored	1.00	.50

Radio Moscow, 50th anniversary.

1979, Nov. 28 *Perf. 12x12½*

4792	A2268	4k	multicolored	.50	.15

New Year 1980.

Hand Holding Peace Message — A2269

Policeman, Patrol Car, Helicopter — A2270

Peace Program in Action: No. 4794, Hands holding cultural symbols. No. 4795, Hammer and sickle, flag.

1979, Dec. 5 Litho. *Perf. 12*

4793	A2269	4k	multicolored	.20	.15
4794	A2269	4k	multicolored	.20	.15
4795	A2269	4k	multicolored	.20	.15
			Nos. 4793-4795 (3)	.60	
			Set value		.30

1979, Dec. 20 *Perf. 12x12½*

Traffic Safety: 4k, Car, girl and ball. 6k, Speeding cars.

4796	A2270	3k	multicolored	.20	.15
4797	A2270	4k	multicolored	.20	.15
4798	A2270	6k	multicolored	.20	.15
			Nos. 4796-4798 (3)	.60	
			Set value		.30

Vulkanolog — A2271

Research Ships and Portraits: 2k, Professor Bogorov. 4k, Ernst Krenkel. 6k, Vladislav Volkov. 10k, Cosmonaut Yuri Gagarin. 15k, Academician E.B. Kurchatov.

Lithographed and Engraved

1979, Dec. 25 *Perf. 12x11½*

4799	A2271	1k	multicolored	.15	.15
4800	A2271	2k	multicolored	.15	.15
4801	A2271	4k	multicolored	.15	.15
4802	A2271	6k	multicolored	.20	.15
4803	A2271	10k	multicolored	.35	.15
4804	A2271	15k	multicolored	.50	.20
			Nos. 4799-4804 (6)	1.50	
			Set value		.70

See Nos. 4881-4886.

Souvenir Sheet

Explorers Raising Red Flag at North Pole — A2272

1979, Dec. 25 Photo. *Perf. 11½x12*

4805	A2272	50k	multicolored	2.00	.75

Komsomolskaya Pravda North Pole expedition.

Type of 1970

Design: 4k, Coat of arms, power line, factories.

1980, Jan. 10 Litho. *Perf. 12x12½*

4806	A1794	4k	carmine	.25	.15

Mordovian Autonomous SSR, 50th anniv.

Freestyle Skating A2273

Perf. 12x12½, 12½x12

1980, Jan. 22

4807	A2273	4k	Speed skating	.15	.15
4808	A2273	6k	shown	.15	.15
4809	A2273	10k	Ice hockey	.25	.15
4810	A2273	15k	Downhill skiing	.35	.25
4811	A2273	20k	Luge, vert.	.50	.35
			Nos. 4807-4811 (5)	1.40	
			Set value		.90

Souvenir Sheet

4812	A2273	50k	Cross-country skiing, vert.	1.75	1.00

13th Winter Olympic Games, Lake Placid, NY, Feb. 12-24.

Nos. 4808, 4809 exist imperf.

Nikolai Ilyitch Podvoiski (1880-1948), Revolutionary — A2274

1980, Feb. 16 Engr. *Perf. 12½x12*

4813	A2274	4k	claret brown	.25	.15

Rainbow, by A.K. Savrasov — A2275

#4815, Summer Harvest, by A.G. Venetsianov, vert. #4816, Old Erevan, by M.S. Saryan.

1980, Mar. 4 Litho. *Perf. 11½*

4814	A2275	6k	multicolored	.25	.15
4815	A2275	6k	multicolored	.25	.15
4816	A2275	6k	multicolored	.25	.15
			Nos. 4814-4816 (3)	.75	.45

Souvenir Sheet

Cosmonaut Alexei Leonov — A2276

1980, Mar. 18 Litho. *Perf. 12½x12*

4817	A2276	50k	multicolored	1.75	.75

Man's first walk in space (Voskhod 2, Mar. 18-19, 1965).

Georg Ots, Estonian Artist A2277

Lenin Order, 50th Anniversary A2278

1980, Mar. 21 **Engr.**

4818	A2277	4k	slate blue	.25	.15

1980, Apr. 6 Photo. *Perf. 11½*

4819	A2278	4k	multicolored	.25	.15

Souvenir Sheet

Cosmonauts, Salyut 6 and Soyuz — A2279

1980, Apr. 12 Litho. *Perf. 12*

4820	A2279	50k	multicolored	1.50	1.00

Intercosmos cooperative space program.

Flags and Arms of Azerbaijan, Government House — A2280

"Mother Russia," Fireworks over Moscow — A2282

Lenin, 110th Birth Anniversary — A2281

1980, Apr. 22 **Photo.**

4821	A2280	4k	multicolored	.25	.15

Azerbaijan Soviet Socialist Republic, Communist Party of Azerbaijan, 60th anniv.

Souvenir Sheet

1980, Apr. 22 *Perf. 12x11½*

4822	A2281	30k	multicolored	1.25	.75

1980, Apr. 25 **Litho.**

#4824, Soviet War Memorial, Berlin, raising of Red flag. #4825, Parade, Red Square, Moscow.

4823	A2282	4k	multicolored	.20	.15
4824	A2282	4k	multicolored	.20	.15
4825	A2282	4k	multicolored	.20	.15
			Nos. 4823-4825 (3)	.60	.45

35th anniv. of victory in World War II.

Nos. 4824, 4825 exist imperf.

Workers' Monument A2283

"XXV" A2284

1980, May 12 Litho. *Perf. 12*
4826 A2283 4k multicolored .25 .15

Workers' Delegates in Ivanovo-Voznesensk, 75th anniversary.

1980, May 14 Photo. *Perf. 11½*
4827 A2284 32k multicolored 1.25 .75

Signing of Warsaw Pact (Bulgaria, Czechoslovakia, German Democratic Rep., Hungary, Poland, Romania, USSR), 25th anniv.

YaK-24 Helicopter, 1953 — A2285

1980, May 15 Litho. *Perf. 12½x12*
4828 A2285 1k shown .15 .15
4829 A2285 2k MI-8, 1962 .15 .15
4830 A2285 3k KA-26, 1965 .15 .15
4831 A2285 6k MI-6, 1957 .15 .15
4832 A2285 15k MI-10 .40 .25
4833 A2285 32k V-12 .80 .55
Set value 1.50 1.05

Nos 4832-4833 exist imperf.

David Anacht, Illuminated Manuscript A2286

Emblem, Training Lab A2287

1980, May 16 *Perf. 12*
4834 A2286 4k multicolored .25 .15

David Anacht, Armenian philosopher, 1500th birth anniversary.

1980, June 4
4835 A2287 6k shown .15 .15
4836 A2287 15k Cosmonauts meeting .40 .25
4837 A2287 32k Press conference .80 .55
Nos. 4835-4837 (3) 1.35 .95

Intercosmos cooperative space program (USSR-Hungary).

Polar Fox A2288

1980, June 25 Litho. *Perf. 12x12½*
4838 A2288 2k Dark silver fox,vert. .15 .15
4839 A2288 4k shown .15 .15
4840 A2288 6k Mink .15 .15
4841 A2288 10k Azerbaijan nutria, vert. .20 .15
4842 A2288 15k Black sable .30 .20
Nos. 4838-4842 (5) .95
Set value .60

Factory, Buildings, Arms of Tatar A.S.S.R. A2289

1980, June 25 *Perf. 12*
4843 A2289 4k multicolored .25 .15

Tatar Autonomous SSR, 60th anniv.

College — A2290

Ho Chi Minh — A2291

1980, July 1 Photo. *Perf. 11½*
4844 A2290 4k multicolored .25 .15

Bauman Technological College, Moscow, 150th anniversary.

1980, July 7
4845 A2291 6k multicolored .25 .15

Red Flag, Lithuanian Arms, Flag, Red Guards Monument A2292

1980, July 12 Litho. *Perf. 12*
4846 A2292 4k multicolored .25 .15

Lithuanian SSR, 40th anniv.

Russian Flag and Arms, Latvian Flag, Monument, Buildings A2293

Design: No. 4848, Russian flag and arms, Estonian flag, monument, buildings.

1980, July 21 Litho. *Perf. 12*
4847 A2293 4k multicolored .20 .15
4848 A2293 4k multicolored .20 .15
Set value .20

Restoration of Soviet power.

Cosmonauts Boarding Soyuz — A2294

1980, July 24 *Perf. 12x12½*
4849 A2294 6k shown .15 .15
4850 A2294 15k Working aboard spacecraft .45 .25
4851 A2294 32k Return flight .80 .55
Nos. 4849-4851 (3) 1.40 .95

Center for Cosmonaut Training, 20th anniv.

Avicenna (980-1037), Philosopher and Physician — A2295

Photogravure and Engraved

1980, Aug. 16 *Perf. 11½*
4852 A2295 4k multicolored .25 .15

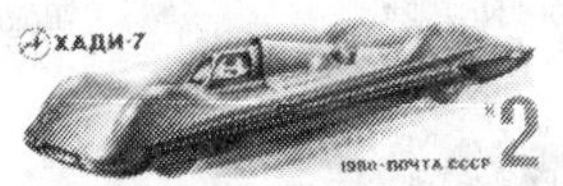

Soviet Racing Car KHADI-7 — A2296

1980, Aug. 25 Litho. *Perf. 12*
4853 A2296 2k shown .15 .15
4854 A2296 6k KHADI-10 .15 .15
4855 A2296 15k KHADI-113 .50 .30
4856 A2296 32k KHADI-133 .90 .65
Nos. 4853-4856 (4) 1.70
Set value 1.05

No. 4856 exists imperf.

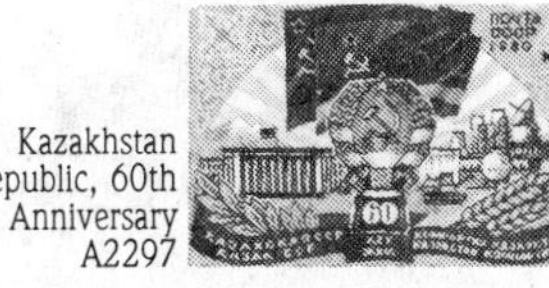

Kazakhstan Republic, 60th Anniversary A2297

1980, Aug. 26
4857 A2297 4k multicolored .50 .15

Ingres, Self-portrait, and Nymph — A2298

1980, Aug. 29 *Perf. 12x12½*
4858 A2298 32k multicolored 1.00 .50

Jean Auguste Dominique Ingres (1780-1867), French painter.
Exists imperf.

Morning on the Field of Kulikovo, by A. Bubnov — A2299

1980, Sept. 6 Litho. *Perf. 12*
4859 A2299 4k multicolored .25 .15

Battle of Kulikovo, 600th anniversary.

Town Hall, Tartu — A2300

1980, Sept. 15 Photo. *Perf. 11½*
4860 A2300 4k multicolored .25 .15

Tartu, 950th anniversary.

Y.V. Malyshev, V.V. Aksenov A2301

1980, Sept. 15 Litho. *Perf. 12x12½*
4861 A2301 10k multicolored .30 .25

Soyuz T-2 space flight.

Flight Training, Yuri Gagarin — A2302

1980, Sept. 15 Photo. *Perf. 11½x12*
4862 A2302 6k shown .15 .15
4863 A2302 15k Space walk .40 .25
4864 A2302 32K Endurance test .80 .45
Nos. 4862-4864 (3) 1.35 .85

Gagarin Cosmonaut Training Center, 20th anniversary.

Cosmonauts Training A2303

Intercosmos Emblem, Flags of USSR and Cuba and: 15k, Inside weightless cabin. 32k, Landing.

1980, Sept. 15 Litho. *Perf. 12x12½*
4865 A2303 6k multicolored .15 .15
4866 A2303 15k multicolored .40 .25
4867 A2303 32k multicolored .80 .45
Nos. 4865-4867 (3) 1.35 .85

Intercosmos cooperative space program (USSR-Cuba).

October Revolution, 63rd Anniversary A2304

1980, Sept. 20 Photo. *Perf. 11½*
4868 A2304 6k multicolored .25 .15

David Gurumishvily (1705-1792), Poet — A2305

1980, Sept. 20
4869 A2305 6k multicolored .25 .15

Family with Serfs, by N.V. Nevrev (1830-1904) — A2305a

Design: No. 4869B, Countess Tarakanova, by K.D. Flavitsky (1830-1866), vert.

1980, Sept. 25 Litho. *Perf. 11½*
4869A A2305a 6k multicolored .25 .25
4869B A2305a 6k multicolored .25 .25

A.F. Joffe (1880-1960), Physicist — A2306

1980, Sept. 29
4870 A2306 4k multicolored .25 .15

Siberian Pine A2307

1980, Sept. 29 Litho. *Perf. 12½x12*
4871 A2307 2k shown .15 .15
4872 A2307 4k Oak .15 .15
4873 A2307 6k Lime tree, vert. .15 .15
4874 A2307 10k Sea bucthorn .20 .15
4875 A2307 15k European ash .30 .20
Nos. 4871-4875 (5) .95
Set value .60

A.M. Vasilevsky (1895-1977), Soviet Marshal — A2308

1980, Sept. 30 Engr. *Perf. 12*
4876 A2308 4k dark green .25 .15

Souvenir Sheet

Mischa Holding Olympic Torch — A2309

1980, Nov. 24 *Perf. 12x12½*
4877 A2309 1r multicolored 7.50 1.75

Completion of 22nd Summer Olympic Games, Moscow, July 19-Aug. 3.

A.V. Suvorov (1730-1800), General and Military Theorist A2310

1980, Nov. 24 Engr.
4878 A2310 4k slate .25 .15

A2311

1980, Nov. 24 Litho. *Perf. 12*
4879 A2311 4k multicolored .50 .15

Armenian SSR & Armenian Communist Party, 60th annivs.

Aleksandr Blok (1880-1921), Poet — A2312

1980, Nov. 24
4880 A2312 4k multicolored .25 .15

Research Ship Type of 1979

Lithographed and Engraved

1980, Nov. 24 *Perf. 12x11½*
4881 A2271 2k Aju Dag, Fleet arms .15 .15
4882 A2271 3k Valerian Urywaev .15 .15
4883 A2271 4k Mikhail Somov .15 .15
4884 A2271 6k Sergei Korolev .15 .15
4885 A2271 10k Otto Schmidt .20 .15
4886 A2271 15k Ustislav Kelgysh .30 .20
Nos. 4881-4886 (6) 1.10
Set value .70

For overprint see No. 5499.

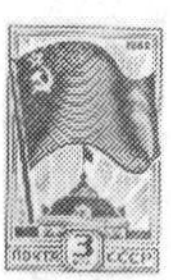

Russian Flag A2313

Soviet Medical College, 50th Anniversary A2314

1980, Dec. 1 Engr. *Perf. 12x12½*
4887 A2313 3k orange red .25 .15

1980, Dec. 1 Photo. *Perf. 11½*
4888 A2314 4k multicolored .25 .15

New Year 1981 A2315

1980, Dec. 1 Litho. *Perf. 12*
4889 A2315 4k multicolored .25 .15

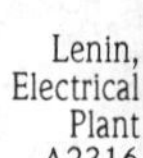

Lenin, Electrical Plant A2316

1980, Dec. 18
4890 A2316 4k multicolored .25 .15

60th anniversary of GOELRO (Lenin's electro-economic plan).

A.N. Nesmeyanov (1899-1980), Chemist — A2317

1980, Dec. 19 *Perf. 12½x12*
4891 A2317 4k multicolored .25 .15

Nagatinski Bridge, Moscow — A2318

Photogravure and Engraved

1980, Dec. 23 *Perf. 11½x12*
4892 A2318 4k shown .15 .15
4893 A2318 6k Luzhniki Bridge .15 .15
4894 A2318 15k Kalininski Bridge .30 .20
Nos. 4892-4894 (3) .60
Set value .40

S.K. Timoshenko A2319

Flags of India and USSR, Government House, New Delhi A2320

1980, Dec. 25 Engr. *Perf. 12*
4895 A2319 4k rose lake .25 .15

Timoshenko (1895-1970), Soviet marshal.

1980, Dec. 30 Litho. *Perf. 12x12½*
4896 A2320 4k multicolored .50 .35

Visit of Pres. Brezhnev to India. Printed se-tenant with inscribed label.

Mirny Base — A2321

1981, Jan. 5 *Perf. 12*
4897 A2321 4k shown .15 .15
4898 A2321 6k Earth station, rocket .15 .15
4899 A2321 15k Map, supply ship .30 .20
Nos. 4897-4899 (3) .60
Set value .40

Soviet Antarctic research, 25th anniv.

Dagestan Soviet Socialist Republic, 60th Anniversary A2322

1981, Jan. 20
4900 A2322 4k multicolored .25 .15

Bandy World Championship, Cheborovsk A2323

1981, Jan. 20
4901 A2323 6k multicolored .25 .15

26th Congress of Ukrainian Communist Party. A2324

1981, Jan. 23 Photo. *Perf. 11½*
4902 A2324 4k multicolored .25 .15

Lenin, "XXVI" A2325

Lenin and Congress Building — A2326

Banner and Kremlin — A2327

1981 Photo. *Perf. 11½*
4903 A2325 4k multicolored .25 .15

Photogravure and Embossed

1982 *Perf. 11½x12*
4904 A2326 20k multicolored 1.50 .75

Souvenir Sheet

Litho.

Perf. 12x12½
4905 A2327 50k multicolored 1.50 .75

26th Communist Party Congress. Issue dates: 4k, 20k, Jan. 22; 50k, Feb. 16.

Mstislav V. Keldysh A2328

Freighter, Flags of USSR and India A2329

Perf. 11½x12

1981, Feb. 10 Photo. Engr.

4906 A2328 4k multicolored .25 .15

Mstislav Vsevolodovich Keldysh (1911-1978), mathematician.

1981, Feb. 10 Litho. *Perf. 12*

4907 A2329 15k multicolored .50 .30

Soviet-Indian Shipping Line, 25th anniv.

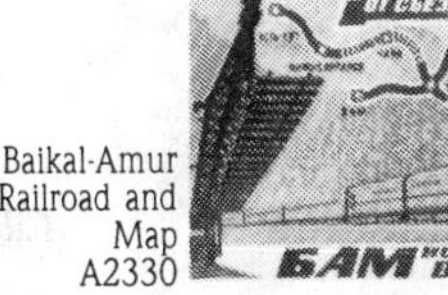

Baikal-Amur Railroad and Map A2330

10th Five-Year Plan Projects (1976-1980): No. 4909, Gas plant, Urengoi (spherical tanks). No. 4910, Enisei River power station (dam). No. 4911, Atomic power plant. No. 4912, Paper mill. No. 4913, Coal mining, Ekibstyi.

1981, Feb. 18 *Perf. 12½x12*

4908 A2330 4k multicolored .25 .15
4909 A2330 4k multicolored .25 .15
4910 A2330 4k multicolored .25 .15
4911 A2330 4k multicolored .25 .15
4912 A2330 4k multicolored .25 .15
4913 A2330 4k multicolored .25 .15
Nos. 4908-4913 (6) 1.50
Set value .60

Georgian Soviet Socialist Republic, 60th Anniv. A2331

1981, Feb. 25 *Perf. 12*

4914 A2331 4k multicolored .25 .15

Abkhazian Autonomous Soviet Socialist Republic, 60th Anniv. A2332

1981, Mar. 4

4915 A2332 4k multicolored .25 .15

Exists imperf.

Communica-tions Institute A2333

Satellite, Radio Operator A2334

1981, Mar. 12 Photo. *Perf. 11½*

4916 A2333 4k multicolored .25 .15

Moscow Electrotechnical Institute of Communications, 60th anniv.

1981, Mar. 12

4917 A2334 4k multicolored .35 .25

30th All-Union Amateur Radio Designers Exhibition.

Cosmonauts L.I. Popov and V.V. Rumin A2335

1981, Mar. 20 Litho. *Perf. 12*

4918 A2335 15k shown .40 .25
4919 A2335 15k Spacecraft complex .60 .25
a. Pair, #4918-4919 + label 1.00 .50

185-day flight of Cosmos 35-Salyut 6-Cosmos 37 complex, Apr. 9-Oct. 11, 1980. No. 4919a has a continuous design.

Cosmonauts O. Makarov, L. Kizim and G. Strekalov — A2336

1981, Mar. 20 *Perf. 12½x12*

4920 A2336 10k multicolored .25 .15

Soyuz T-3 flight, Nov. 27-Dec. 10, 1980.

Lift-Off, Baikonur Base — A2337

1981, Mar. 23

4921 A2337 6k shown .15 .15
4922 A2337 15k Mongolians watching flight on TV .40 .25
4923 A2337 32k Re-entry .80 .50
Nos. 4921-4923 (3) 1.35 .90

Intercosmos cooperative space program (USSR-Mongolia).

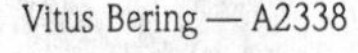

Vitus Bering — A2338

Yuri Gagarin and Earth — A2339

Yuri Gagarin — A2340

1981, Mar. 25 Engr. *Perf. 12x12½*

4924 A2338 4k dark blue .25 .15

Bering (1680-1741), Danish navigator.

1981, Apr. 12 Photo. *Perf. 11½x12*

4925 A2339 6k shown .15 .15
4926 A2339 15k S.P. Korolev (craft designer) .40 .25
4927 A2339 32k Monument .80 .50
Nos. 4925-4927 (3) 1.35 .90

Souvenir Sheet

4928 A2340 50k shown 5.00 1.00

Soviet space flights, 20th anniv. Nos. 4925-4927 each se-tenant with label.

Salyut Orbital Station, 10th Anniv. of Flight — A2341

1981, Apr. 19 Litho. *Perf. 12x12½*

4929 A2341 32k multicolored 1.00 .50

Souvenir Sheet

111th Birth Anniv. of Lenin — A2342

1981, Apr. 22 *Perf. 11½x12½*

4930 A2342 50k multicolored 1.50 .60

Sergei Prokofiev (1891-1953), Composer A2343

New Hofburg Palace, Vienna A2344

1981, Apr. 23 Engr. *Perf. 12*

4931 A2343 4k dark purple .40 .25

1981, May 5 Litho.

4932 A2344 15k multicolored .50 .20

WIPA 1981 Phil. Exhib., Vienna, May 22-31.

Adzhar Autonomous Soviet Socialist Republic, 60th Anniv. A2345

1981, May 7

4933 A2345 4k multicolored .25 .15

Centenary of Welding (Invented by N.N. Benardos) A2346

Lithographed and Engraved

1981, May 12 *Perf. 11½*

4934 A2346 6k multicolored .25 .15

Intl. Architects Union, 14th Congress, Warsaw — A2347

1981, May 12 Photo.

4935 A2347 15k multicolored .50 .25

Albanian Girl, by A.A. Ivanov A2348

#4937, Horseman, by F.A. Roubeau. #4938, The Demon, by M.A. Wrubel, horiz. #4939, Sunset over the Sea, by N.N. Ge, horiz.

1981, May 15 Litho. *Perf. 12x12½*

4936 A2348 10k multicolored .25 .15
4937 A2348 10k multicolored .25 .15
4938 A2348 10k multicolored .25 .15
4939 A2348 10k multicolored .25 .15
Nos. 4936-4939 (4) 1.00 .60

Cosmonauts in Training A2349

1981, May 15

4940 A2349 6k shown .15 .15
4941 A2349 15k In space .40 .25
4942 A2349 32k Return .80 .50
Nos. 4940-4942 (3) 1.35 .90

Intercosmos cooperative space program (USSR-Romania).

Dwarf Primrose A2350

Flowers of the Carpathian Mountains: 6k, Great carline thistle. 10k, Mountain parageum. 15k, Alpine bluebell. 32k, Rhododendron kotschyi.

1981, May 20 *Perf. 12*

4943 A2350 4k multicolored .15 .15
4944 A2350 6k multicolored .15 .15
4945 A2350 10k multicolored .25 .15
4946 A2350 15k multicolored .40 .25
4947 A2350 32k multicolored .80 .50
Nos. 4943-4947 (5) 1.75 1.20

Stamps of Russia can be mounted in the annual Scott Russia supplement.

Luigi Longo, Italian Labor Leader, 1st Death Anniv. — A2351

1981, May 24 Photo. Perf. 11½
4948 A2351 6k multicolored .25 .15

Nizami Gjanshevi (1141-1209), Azerbaijan Poet A2352

1981, May 25 Photo. & Engr.
4949 A2352 4k multicolored .25 .15

A2353

A2354

1981, June 18 Litho. Perf. 12
4950 A2353 4k Running .15 .15
4951 A2353 6k Soccer .15 .15
4952 A2353 10k Discus throwing .30 .15
4953 A2353 15k Boxing .45 .30
4954 A2353 32k Diving .85 .50
Nos. 4950-4954 (5) 1.90 1.25

1981, July 6
4955 A2354 6k multicolored .25 .15

Mongolian Revolution, 60th anniv.

12th Intl. Film Festival, Moscow — A2355

1981, July 6 Photo. Perf. 11½
4956 A2355 15k multicolored .50 .25

River Tour Boat Lenin A2356

1981, July 9 Litho. Perf. 12½
4957 A2356 4k shown .15 .15
4958 A2356 6k Cosmonaut Gagarin .15 .15
4959 A2356 15k Valerian Kuibyshev .40 .25
4960 A2356 32k Freighter Baltijski .90 .50
Nos. 4957-4960 (4) 1.60
Set value .90

Icebreaker Maligin — A2357

Photogravure and Engraved
1981, July 9 Perf. 11½x12
4961 A2357 15k multicolored .50 .25

26th Party Congress Resolutions (Intl. Cooperation) — A2358

1981, July 15 Photo. Perf. 12x11½
4962 A2358 4k shown .15 .15
4963 A2358 4k Industry .15 .15
4964 A2358 4k Energy .15 .15
4965 A2358 4k Agriculture .15 .15
4966 A2358 4k Communications .15 .15
4967 A2358 4k Arts .15 .15
Nos. 4962-4967 (6) .90
Set value .60

I.N. Ulyanov (Lenin's Father), 150th Anniv. of Birth — A2359

1981, July 25 Engr. Perf. 11½
4968 A2359 4k multicolored .25 .15

Leningrad Theater, Sesquicentennial — A2360

1981, Aug. 12 Photo. Perf. 11½
4969 A2360 6k multicolored .25 .15

A.M. Gerasimov, Artist, Birth Centenary A2361

1981, Aug. 12 Litho. Perf. 12
4970 A2361 4k multicolored .25 .15

Physical Chemistry Institute, Moscow Academy of Science, 50th Anniv. A2362

1981, Aug. 12 Photo. Perf. 11½
4971 A2362 4k multicolored .25 .15

Siberian Tit — A2363

Designs: Song birds.

Perf. 12½x12, 12x12½
1981, Aug. 20 Litho.
4972 A2363 6k shown .15 .15
4973 A2363 10k Tersiphone paradisi, vert. .35 .15
4974 A2363 15k Emberiza jankovski .45 .25
4975 A2363 20k Sutora webbiana, vert. .55 .30
4976 A2363 32k Saxicola torquata, vert. .90 .45
Nos. 4972-4976 (5) 2.40 1.30

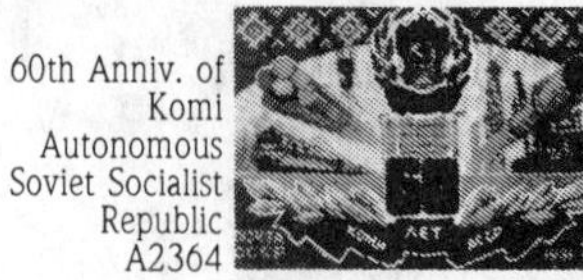
60th Anniv. of Komi Autonomous Soviet Socialist Republic A2364

1981, Aug. 22 Perf. 12
4977 A2364 4k multicolored .35 .15

Svyaz-'81 Intl. Communications Exhibition — A2365

Photogravure and Engraved
1981, Aug. 22 Perf. 11½
4978 A2365 4k multicolored .25 .15

60th Anniv. of Kabardino-Balkar Autonomous Soviet Socialist Republic — A2366

1981, Sept. 1 Litho. Perf. 12
4979 A2366 4k multicolored .25 .15

War Veterans' Committee, 25th Anniv. — A2367

Schooner Kodor — A2368

1981, Sept. 1 Photo. Perf. 11½
4980 A2367 4k multicolored .25 .15

Perf. 12½x12, 12x12½
1981, Sept. 18 Litho.

Designs: Training ships. 4k, 6k, 15k, 20k, horiz.

4981 A2368 4k 4-masted bark Tovarich I .15 .15
4982 A2368 6k Barkentine Vega I .15 .15
4983 A2368 10k shown .30 .15
4984 A2368 15k 3-masted bark Tovarich .40 .30
4985 A2368 20k 4-masted bark Kruzenstern .50 .35
4986 A2368 32k 4-masted bark Sedov .75 .50
Nos. 4981-4986 (6) 2.25 1.60

A2369

A2370

1981, Oct. 10 Perf. 12
4987 A2369 4k multicolored .25 .15

Kazakhstan's Union with Russia, 250th Anniv.

1981, Oct. 10 Photo. Perf. 11½
4988 A2370 4k multicolored .75 .50

Mikhail Alekseevich Lavrentiev (1900-80), mathematician. Exists imperf.

64th Anniv. of October Revolution — A2371

1981, Oct. 15 Litho.
4989 A2371 4k multicolored .25 .15

Ekran Satellite TV Broadcasting System A2372

1981, Oct. 15 Perf. 12
4990 A2372 4k multicolored .25 .15

A2373

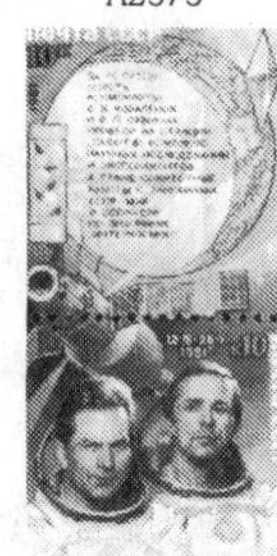
A2374

1981, Oct. 15
4991 A2373 10k multicolored .30 .15
4992 A2374 10k multicolored .30 .15
a. Pair, #4991-4992 .60 .30

Salyut 6-Soyuz flight of V.V. Kovalionok and V.P. Savinykh.

A2375

A2376

Souvenir Sheet
1981, Oct. 25 Perf. 12x12½
4993 A2375 50k multicolored 2.75 .90

Birth centenary of Pablo Picasso.

Photogravure and Engraved
1981, Nov. 5 Perf. 11½
4994 A2376 4k multicolored .25 .15

Sergei Dmitrievich Merkurov (1881-1952), artist.

Autumn, by Nino Pirosmanas, 1913 — A2377

Paintings: 6k, Guriyka, by M.G. Kokodze, 1921. 10k, Fellow Travelers, by U.M. Dzhaparidze, 1936, horiz. 15k, Shota Rustaveli, by S.S. Kobuladze, 1938. 32k, Collecting Tea, by V.D. Gudiashvili, 1964, horiz.

Perf. 12x12½, 12½x12

1981, Nov. 5 **Litho.**

4995 A2377	4k multicolored	.15	.15
4996 A2377	6k multicolored	.20	.15
4997 A2377	10k multicolored	.50	.15
4998 A2377	15k multicolored	.65	.25
4999 A2377	32k multicolored	1.40	.50
	Nos. 4995-4999 (5)	2.90	1.20

New Year 1982 — A2378

1981, Dec. 2 **Litho.** ***Perf. 12***

5000 A2378 4k multicolored .25 .15

Public Transportation 19th-20th Cent. — A2379

Photogravure and Engraved

1981, Dec. 10 ***Perf. 11½x12***

5001 A2379	4k Sled	.15	.15
5002 A2379	6k Horse-drawn trolley	.15	.15
5003 A2379	10k Coach	.30	.15
5004 A2379	15k Taxi, 1926	.40	.25
5005 A2379	20k Bus, 1926	.50	.30
5006 A2379	32k Trolley, 1912	.80	.50
	Nos. 5001-5006 (6)	2.30	1.50

Souvenir Sheet

Kremlin and New Delhi Parliament — A2380

1981, Dec. 17 **Photo.**

5007 A2380 50k multicolored 1.50 .75

1st direct telephone link with India. Labels show Brezhnev and Mrs. Gandhi talking on telephone.

A2381

A2382

1982, Jan. 11 **Litho.** ***Perf. 12***

5008 A2381	4k multicolored	.15	.15
5009 A2382	4k multicolored	.15	.15
	Set value		.20

60th anniv. of Checheno-Ingush Autonomous SSR and of Yakutsk Autonomous SSR.

1500th Anniv. of Kiev — A2383

1982, Jan. 12 **Photo.** ***Perf. 11½x12***

5010 A2383 10k multicolored .30 25

A2384 A2385

1982, Jan. 12 ***Perf. 11½***

5011 A2384 4k multicolored .25 .15

S.P. Korolev (1907-66), rocket designer.

1982, Jan. 20 **Litho.** ***Perf. 12***

5012 A2385 6k multicolored .25 .15

Nazym Khikmet (1902-1963), Turkish poet.

10th World Trade Union Congress, Havana — A2386

1982, Feb. 1 **Photo.** ***Perf. 11½***

5013 A2386 15k multicolored .50 .25

17th Soviet Trade Union Congress — A2387

1982, Feb. 10 **Litho.**

5014 A2387 4k multicolored .25 .15

Edouard Manet (1832-1883) A2388

1982, Feb. 10 ***Perf. 12x12½***

5015 A2388 32k multicolored 1.00 .45

Equestrian Sports A2389

1982, Feb. 16 **Photo.** ***Perf. 11½***

5016 A2389	4k Hurdles	.15	.15
5017 A2389	6k Riding	.15	.15
5018 A2389	15k Racing	.30	.20
	Nos. 5016-5018 (3)	.60	
	Set value		.40

No. 5016 exists imperf.

2nd Death Anniv. of Marshal Tito of Yugoslavia — A2390

1982, Feb. 25 **Litho.** ***Perf. 12***

5019 A2390 6k olive black .25 .15

350th Anniv. of State University of Tartu A2392

1982, Mar. 4 **Photo.** ***Perf. 11½***

5020 A2392 4k multicolored .25 .15

9th Intl. Cardiologists Congress, Moscow A2393

1982, Mar. 4

5021 A2393 15k multicolored .50 .20

Souvenir Sheet

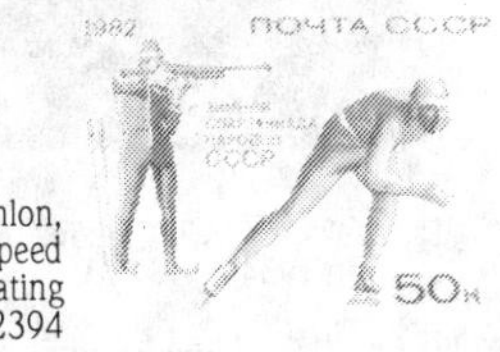

Biathlon, Speed Skating A2394

1982, Mar. 6 **Litho.** ***Perf. 12½x12***

5022 A2394 50k multicolored 1.50 .70

5th Natl. Athletic Meet.

Blueberry Bush — A2395

Venera 13 and Venera 14 Flights — A2396

1982, Mar. 10 **Litho.** ***Perf. 12x12½***

5023 A2395	4k Blackberries	.15	.15
5024 A2395	6k shown	.15	.15
5025 A2395	10k Cranberries	.35	.15
5026 A2395	15k Cherries	.45	.25
5027 A2395	32k Strawberries	1.00	.45
	Nos. 5023-5027 (5)	2.10	1.15

1982, Mar. 10 **Photo.** ***Perf. 11½***

5028 A2396 10k multicolored .30 .25

Marriage Ceremony, by W.W. Pukirev (1832-1890) A2397

Paintings: No. 5030, M.I. Lopuchino, by Vladimir Borowikowsky (1757-1825). No. 5031, E.W. Davidov, by O.A. Kiprensky (1782-1836). No. 5032, Landscape.

1982, Mar. 18 ***Perf. 12***

5029 A2397	6k multicolored	.15	.15
5030 A2397	6k multicolored	.15	.15
5031 A2397	6k multicolored	.15	.15
5032 A2397	6k multicolored	.15	.15
	Nos. 5029-5032 (4)	.60	
	Set value		.40

K.I. Tchukovsky (1882-1969), Writer — A2398

1982, Mar. 31 **Engr.**

5033 A2398 4k black .25 .15

Cosmonauts' Day — A2399

1982, Apr. 12 **Photo.** ***Perf. 12x11½***

5034 A2399 6k multicolored .25 .15

Souvenir Sheet

112th Birth Anniv. of Lenin — A2400

1982, Apr. 22 **Photo.** ***Perf. 11½x12***

5035 A2400 50k multicolored 1.50 .70

A2401 A2402

1982, Apr. 25 **Engr.** ***Perf. 12***

5036 A2401 4k brown .25 .15

V.P. Soloviev-Sedoi (1907-79), composer.

1982, Apr. 25

5037 A2402 6k green .25 .15

G. Dimitrov (1882-1949), 1st Bulgarian Prime Minister.

Kremlin Tower, Moscow A2403

70th Anniv. of Pravda Newspaper A2404

1982 Litho. *Perf. 12½x12*
5038 A2403 45k brown 1.10 .70
a. Engraved 1.10 .70

Issue dates: #5038, Apr. 25. #5038a, Oct. 12.

1982, May 5 Photo. *Perf. 12x11½*
5039 A2404 4k multicolored .25 .15

A2405

A2406

1982, May 10 *Perf. 11½*
5040 A2405 6k multicolored .25 .15

UN Conf. on Human Environment, 10th anniv.

1982, May 19
5041 A2406 4k multicolored .25 .15

Pioneers' Org., 60th anniv.

A2407

A2408

1982, May 19
5042 A2407 4k multicolored .25 .15

Communist Youth Org., 19th Cong.

1982, May 19
5043 A2408 15k multicolored .50 .25

ITU Delegates Conf., Nairobi.

TUL-80 Electric Locomotive — A2409

1982, May 20 *Perf. 12x11½*
5044 A2409 4k shown .15 .15
5045 A2409 6k TEP-75 diesel .20 .15
5046 A2409 10k TEP-7 diesel .40 .15
5047 A2409 15k WL-82m electric .60 .25
5048 A2409 32k EP-200 electric 1.25 .50
Nos. 5044-5048 (5) 2.60 1.20

1982 World Cup — A2410

1982, June 4 *Perf. 11½x12*
5049 A2410 20k olive & purple .60 .30

Grus Monacha — A2411

18th Ornithological Cong., Moscow: Rare birds.

1982, June 10 Litho. *Perf. 12x12½*
5050 A2411 2k shown .15 .15
5051 A2411 4k Haliaeetus pelagicus .15 .15
5052 A2411 6k Eurynorhynchus .15 .15
5053 A2411 10k Eulabeia indica .30 .15
5054 A2411 15k Chettusia gregaria .40 .30
5055 A2411 32k Ciconia boyciana .80 .50
Nos. 5050-5055 (6) 1.95
Set value 1.15

Komomolsk-on-Amur City, 50th Anniv. — A2412

Photogravure and Engraved

1982, June 10 *Perf. 11½*
5056 A2412 4k multicolored .25 .15

Tatchanka, by M.B. Grekov (1882-1934) — A2413

1982, June 15 Litho. *Perf. 12½x12*
5057 A2413 6k multicolored .25 .15

2nd UN Conference on Peaceful Uses of Outer Space, Vienna, Aug. 9-21 — A2414

1982, June 15 Photo. *Perf. 11½*
5058 A2414 15k multicolored .50 .20

Intercosmos Cooperative Space Program (USSR-France) — A2415

1982 Litho. *Perf. 12½x12*
5059 A2415 6k Cosmonauts .15 .15
5060 A2415 20k Rocket, globe .65 .30
5061 A2415 45k Satellites 1.40 .70
a. Miniature sheet of 8
Nos. 5059-5061 (3) 2.20 1.15

Souvenir Sheet

5062 A2415 50k Emblem, satellite 1.50 .75

#5062 contains one 41x29mm stamp. Issue dates: 6k, 50k, June 24. 20k, 45k, July 2.

The Legend of the Goldfish, by P. Sosin, 1968 — A2416

Lacquerware Paintings, Ustera: 10k, Minin's Appeal to Count Posharski, by J. Phomitchev, 1953. 15k, Two Peasants, by A. Kotjagin, 1933. 20k, The Fisherman, by N. Klykov, 1933, 32k, The Arrest of the Propagandists, by N. Shishakov, 1968.

1982, July 6 Litho. *Perf. 12½x12*
5063 A2416 6k multicolored .15 .15
5064 A2416 10k multicolored .35 .15
5065 A2416 15k multicolored .45 .25
5066 A2416 20k multicolored .65 .30
5067 A2416 32k multicolored .95 .45
Nos. 5063-5067 (5) 2.55 1.30

Telephone Centenary — A2417

1982, July 13 *Perf. 12*
5068 A2417 4k Phone, 1882 .25 .15

P. Schilling's Electro-magnetic Telegraph Sesquicentennial — A2418

Photogravure and Engraved

1982, July 16 *Perf. 11½*
5069 A2418 6k Voltaic cells .25 .15

Intervision Gymnastics Contest A2419

1982, Aug. 10 Photo.
5070 A2419 15k multicolored .50 .30

Mastjahart Glider, 1923 A2420

Gliders.

1982, Aug. 20 Litho. *Perf. 12½x12*
5071 A2420 4k shown .15 .15
5072 A2420 6k Red Star, 1930 .15 .15
5073 A2420 10k ZAGI-1, 1934 .30 .15

Size: 60x28mm

Perf. 11½x12
5074 A2420 20k Stakhanovets, 1939 .50 .15
5075 A2420 32k Troop carrier GR-29, 1941 .80 .50
Nos. 5071-5075 (5) 1.90
Set value .90

See Nos. 5118-5122.

A2421

A2422

1982, Aug. 25 Photo. *Perf. 11½*
5076 A2421 6k multicolored .25 .15

Garibaldi (1807-1882). Exists imperf.

1982, Aug. 30
5077 A2422 20k multicolored .75 .30

Intl. Atomic Energy Authority, 25th Anniv.

A2423

A2424

1982, Sept. 10 Engr. *Perf. 12*
5078 A2423 4k red brown .25 .15

Marshal B.M. Shaposhnikov (1882-1945).

1982, Sept. 10 Photo. *Perf. 11½*
5079 A2424 6k King .25 .15
5080 A2424 6k Queen .25 .15

World Chess Championship. See #5084.

A2425

A2426

1982, Sept. 10
5081 A2425 6k multicolored .25 .15

African Natl. Congress, 70th Anniv.

1982, Sept. 17 Engr. *Perf. 12½x12*
5082 A2426 4k green .25 .15

S.P. Botkin (1832-89), physician.

Souvenir Sheet

25th Anniv. of Sputnik — A2427

1982, Sept. 17 Litho. *Perf. 12x12½*
5083 A2427 50k multicolored 5.00 .85

No. 5079 Overprinted in Gold for Karpov's Victory

1982, Sept. 22 **Photo.** *Perf. 11½*
5084 A2424 6k multicolored .60 .30

World War II Warships — A2428

Photogravure and Engraved

1982, Sept. 22 *Perf. 11½x12*
5085 A2428 4k Submarine S-56 .15 .15
5086 A2428 6k Minelayer Gremjashtsky .15 .15
5087 A2428 15k Mine sweeper T-205 .50 .30
5088 A2428 20k Cruiser Red Crimea .60 .35
5089 A2428 45k Sebastopol 1.40 .70
Nos. 5085-5089 (5) 2.80 1.65

65th Anniv. of October Revolution — A2429

1982, Oct. 12 **Litho.** *Perf. 12*
5090 A2429 4k multicolored .25 .15

House of the Soviets, Moscow — A2430

60th Anniv. of USSR: No. 5092, Dnieper Dam, Komosomol Monument, Statue of worker. No. 5093, Soviet War Memorial, resistance poster. No. 5094, Worker at podium, decree text. No. 5095, Workers' Monument, Moscow, Rocket, jet. No. 5096, Arms, Kremlin.

1982, Oct. 25 **Photo.** *Perf. 11½x12*
5091 A2430 10k multicolored .25 .15
5092 A2430 10k multicolored .25 .15
5093 A2430 10k multicolored .25 .15
5094 A2430 10k multicolored .25 .15
5095 A2430 10k multicolored .25 .15
5096 A2430 10k multicolored .65 .15
Nos. 5091-5096 (6) 1.90 .90

No. 5095 Overprinted in Red for All-Union Philatelic Exhibition, 1984

Всесоюзная филателистическая выставка

1982, Nov. 10
5097 A2430 10k multicolored .75 .15

Portrait of an Actor, by Domenico Fetti — A2431

Paintings from the Hermitage: 10k, St. Sebastian, by Perugino. 20k, The Danae, by Titian, horiz. 45k, Portrait of a Woman, by Correggio. No. 5102, Portrait of a Young Man, by Capriola. No. 5103a, Portrait of a Young Woman, by Melzi.

Perf. 12x12½

1982, Nov. 25 **Litho.** **Wmk. 383**
5098 A2431 4k multicolored .15 .15
5099 A2431 10k multicolored .40 .15
5100 A2431 20k multicolored .65 .35
5101 A2431 45k multicolored 1.25 .70
5102 A2431 50k multicolored 1.25 .75
Nos. 5098-5102 (5) 3.70 2.10

Souvenir Sheet

5103 Sheet of 2 4.50 1.65
a. A2431 50k multicolored 1.00 .65

Printed in sheets of 24 stamps + label and 15 stamps + label.

See Nos. 5129-5134, 5199-5204, 5233-5238, 5310-5315, 5335-5340.

New Year 1983 — A2432

60th Anniv. of USSR — A2433

1982, Dec. 1 **Unwmk.**
5104 A2432 4k multicolored .25 .15
Exists imperf.

Souvenir Sheet

1982, Dec. 3 *Perf. 12½x12*
5105 A2433 50k multicolored 1.50 .90

Souvenir Sheet

Mountain Climbers Scaling Mt. Everest — A2434

1982, Dec. 20 **Photo.** *Perf. 11½x12*
5106 A2434 50k multicolored 2.50 1.10

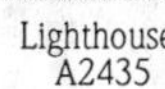

Lighthouses A2435

Mail Transport A2436

1982, Dec. 29 **Litho.** *Perf. 12*
5107 A2435 6k green & multi .15 .15
5108 A2435 6k lilac & multi .15 .15
5109 A2435 6k salmon & multi .15 .15
5110 A2435 6k lt gldn brn & multi .15 .15
5111 A2435 6k lt brown & multi .15 .15
Nos. 5107-5111 (5) .75 .75

No. 5111 exists imperf.

See Nos. 5179-5183, 5265-5269.

1982, Dec. 22 *Perf. 12*
5112 A2436 5k greenish blue .50 .15

1983, May 20 **Litho.** *Perf. 12*
5113 A2436 5k blue 1.00 .15

Iskra Newspaper Masthead A2438

Fedor P. Tolstoi A2439

1983, Jan. 5 **Litho.** *Perf. 12x12½*
5114 A2438 4k multicolored .25 .15

80th anniv. of 2nd Social-Democratic Workers' Party.

1983, Jan. 5 **Photo.** *Perf. 11½*
5115 A2439 4k multicolored .25 .15

Tolstoi (1783-1873), painter.

65th Anniv. of Armed Forces — A2440

60th Anniv. of Aeroflot Airlines — A2441

1983, Jan. 25 **Litho.** *Perf. 12*
5116 A2440 4k multicolored .25 .15
Exists imperf.

Souvenir Sheet

1983, Feb. 9 *Perf. 12x12½*
5117 A2441 50k multicolored 1.50 1.00

Glider Type of 1982

1983, Feb. 10 *Perf. 12½x12*
5118 A2420 2k A-9, 1948 .15 .15
5119 A2420 4k KAJ-12, 1957 .15 .15
5120 A2420 6k A-15, 1960 .15 .15
5121 A2420 20k SA-7, 1970 .50 .35
5122 A2420 45k LAJ-12, 1979 1.10 .70
Nos. 5118-5122 (5) 2.05
Set value 1.25

Tashkent Bimillenium — A2442

1983, Feb. 17 *Perf. 12½x12*
5123 A2442 4k View .25 .15

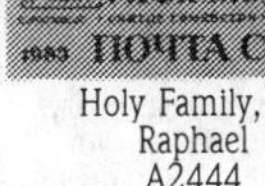

B.N. Petrov (1913-1980), Scientist A2443

Holy Family, by Raphael A2444

1983, Feb. 17
5124 A2443 4k multicolored .25 .15

1983, Feb. 17 *Perf. 12x12½*
5125 A2444 50k multicolored 1.50 1.00

Soyuz T-7-Salyut 7-Soyuz T-5 Flight A2445

1983, Mar. 10 *Perf. 12x12½*
5126 A2445 10k L. Popov, A. Serebrav, S. Savitskaya .30 .15

Souvenir Sheet

World Communications Year — A2446

1983, Mar. 10 **Photo.** *Perf. 11½*
5127 A2446 50k multicolored 1.50 1.25

A.W. Aleksandrov, Natl. Anthem Composer — A2447

1983, Mar. 22 **Litho.** *Perf. 12*
5128 A2447 4k multicolored .50 .25
Exists imperf.

Hermitage Type of 1982

Rembrandt Paintings, Hermitage, Leningrad: 4k, Portrait of an Old Woman. 10k, Portrait of a Learned Man. 20k, Old Warrior. 45k, Portrait of Mrs. B. Martens Doomer. No. 5133, Sacrifice of Abraham. No. 5134a, Portrait of an Old Man in a Red Garment.

Perf. 12x12½

1983, Mar. 25 **Wmk. 383**
5129 A2431 4k multicolored .15 .15
5130 A2431 10k multicolored .30 .15
5131 A2431 20k multicolored .60 .35
5132 A2431 45k multicolored 1.40 .90
5133 A2431 50k multicolored 1.50 .95
Nos. 5129-5133 (5) 3.95 2.50

Souvenir Sheet

Lithographed and Embossed

5134 Sheet of 2 + label 4.00 3.00
a. A2431 50k multicolored 1.65 .70

Souvenir Sheet

Cosmonauts' Day — A2449

Perf. 12½x12

1983, Apr. 12 Litho. Unwmk.
5135 A2449 50k Soyuz T *7.50* 3.50

Souvenir Sheet

113th Birth Anniv. of Lenin — A2450

Photogravure and Engraved

1983, Apr. 22 *Perf. 11½x12*
5136 A2450 50k multicolored 1.50 .80

A2451

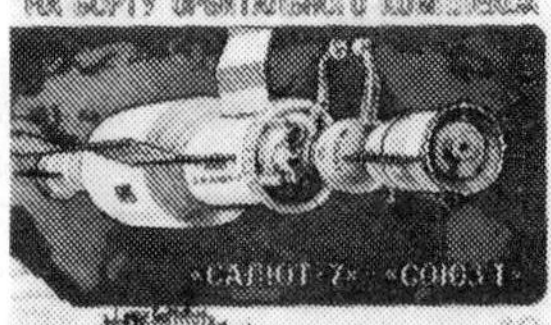

Salyut 7-Soyuz 7 211-Day Flight — A2452

1983, Apr. 25 Litho. *Perf. 12½x12*
5137 A2451 10k A. Berezovoy, V. Lebedev .30 .25
5138 A2452 10k Spacecraft .30 .25
a. Pair, #5137-5138 .60 .50

Exists se-tenant with label.

Karl Marx (1818-1883) A2453

1983, May 5 *Perf. 12x12½*
5139 A2453 4k multicolored .25 .15

View of Rostov-on-Don — A2454

1983, May 5 Photo. *Perf. 11½*
5140 A2454 4k multicolored .25 .15

Exists imperf.

Buriat Autonomous Soviet Socialist Republic, 60th Anniv. A2455

1983, May 12 Litho. *Perf. 12*
5141 A2455 4k multicolored .25 .15

Kirov Opera and Ballet Theater, Leningrad, 200th Anniv. — A2456

Photogravure and Engraved

1983, May 12 *Perf. 11½x12*
5142 A2456 4k multicolored .20 .20

Emblem of Motorcycling, Auto Racing, Shooting, Motorboating, Parachuting Organization — A2457

1983, May 20 Litho. *Perf. 11½*
5143 A2457 6k multicolored .25 .20

A.I. Khachaturian (1903-1978), Composer A2458

1983, May 25 Engr. *Perf. 12½x12*
5144 A2458 4k violet brown .50 .30

Chelyabinsk Tractor Plant, 50th Anniv. A2459

1983, June 1 Photo. *Perf. 11½*
5145 A2459 4k multicolored .25 .15

Simon Bolivar Bicentenary A2460

Photogravure and Engraved

1983, June 10 *Perf. 12*
5146 A2460 6k brown & dk brown .25 .15

City of Sevastopol, 200th Anniv. — A2461

1983, June 14 Photo. *Perf. 11½x12*
5147 A2461 5k multicolored .25 .15

Spring Flowers — A2462

1983, June 14 Litho. *Perf. 12x12½*
5148 A2462 4k multicolored .15 .15
5149 A2462 6k multicolored .15 .15
5150 A2462 10k multicolored .30 .15
5151 A2462 15k multicolored .40 .30
5152 A2462 20k multicolored .50 .35
Nos. 5148-5152 (5) 1.50 1.10

Valentina Tereshkova's Spaceflight, 20th Anniv. — A2463

1983, June 16 Litho. *Perf. 12*
5153 A2463 10k multicolored .35 .15
a. Miniature sheet of 8

A2464

A2465

Photogravure and Engraved

1983, June 20 *Perf. 11½*
5154 A2464 4k multicolored .25 .15

P.N. Pospelov (1898-1979), academician.

1983, June 21 Photo. *Perf. 11½*
5155 A2465 4k multicolored .20 .20

10th European Cong. of Rheumatologists.

13th International Film Festival, Moscow A2466

1983, July 7 Litho. *Perf. 12*
5156 A2466 20k multicolored .60 .25

Ships of the Soviet Fishing Fleet — A2467

Photogravure and Engraved

1983, July 20 *Perf. 12x11½*
5157 A2467 4k Two trawlers .15 .15
5158 A2467 6k Refrigerated trawler .20 .15
5159 A2467 10k Large trawler .55 .15
5160 A2467 15k Large refrigerated ship .60 .25
5161 A2467 20k Base ship .75 .35
Nos. 5157-5161 (5) 2.25 1.05

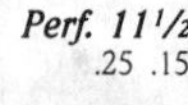
E.B. Vakhtangov (1883-1922), Actor and Producer A2468

1983, July 20 Photo. *Perf. 11½*
5162 A2468 5k multicolored .25 .15

"USSR-1" Stratospheric Flight, 50th Anniv. — A2469

1983, July 25 Photo. *Perf. 12*
5163 A2469 20k multicolored .60 .40
a. Miniature sheet of 8

Food Fish A2470

Designs 4k, Oncorhynchus nerka. 6k, Perciformes. 15k, Anarhichas minor. 20k, Neogobius fluviatilis, 45k, Platichthys stellatus.

1983, Aug. 5 Litho. *Perf. 12½x12*
5164 A2470 4k multicolored .15 .15
5165 A2470 6k multicolored .15 .15
5166 A2470 15k multicolored .55 .40
5167 A2470 20k multicolored .65 .45
5168 A2470 45k multicolored 1.40 .90
Nos. 5164-5168 (5) 2.90 2.05

A2471

Moscow Skyline — A2472

1983, Aug. 18 Photo. *Perf. 11½*
5169 A2471 6k multicolored .25 .15

Souvenir Sheet

5170 A2472 50k cobalt blue 1.50 .80

SOZPHILEX '83 Philatelic Exhibition.

Miniature Sheet

First Russian Postage Stamp, 125th Anniv. A2473

Photogravure and Engraved

1983, Aug. 25 *Perf. $11^1/_2$x12*
5171 A2473 50k pale yel & black 1.50 .70

No. 5171 Ovptd. on Margin in Red for the 5th Philatelic Society Congress

СЪЕЗД ВОФ. МОСКВА. ОКТЯБРЬ 1984 г.

1984, Oct. 1
5171A A2473 50k pale yel & black 5.00 4.50

Namibia Day
A2474

Palestinian Solidarity
A2475

1983, Aug. 26 **Photo.** *Perf. $11^1/_2$*
5172 A2474 5k multicolored .25 .15

1983, Aug. 29 **Photo.** *Perf. $11^1/_2$*
5173 A2475 5k multicolored .25 .15

1st European Championship of Radio-Telegraphy, Moscow — A2476

1983, Sept. 1 **Photo.** *Perf. $11^1/_2$*
5174 A2476 6k multicolored .25 .15

Exists imperf.

A2477

1983, Sept. 2 **Photo.** *Perf. 12x$11^1/_2$*
5175 A2477 10k multicolored .30 .15

4th UNESCO Council on Communications Development.

Muhammad Al-Khorezmi, Uzbek Mathematician, 1200th Birth Anniv. — A2478

Photogravure and Engraved

1983, Sept. 6 *Perf. $11^1/_2$*
5176 A2478 4k multicolored .25 .15

Marshal A.I. Egorov (1883-1939)
A2479

Union of Georgia and Russia, 200th Anniv.
A2480

1983, Sept. 8 **Engr.** *Perf. 12*
5177 A2479 4k brown violet .25 .15

1983, Sept. 8 **Photo.** *Perf. $11^1/_2$*
5178 A2480 6k multicolored .25 .15

Lighthouse Type of 1982

Baltic Sea lighthouses.

1983, Sept. 19 **Litho.** *Perf. 12*
5179 A2435 1k Kipu .15 .15
5180 A2435 5k Keri .15 .15
5181 A2435 10k Stirsudden .25 .15
5182 A2435 12k Tahkun .30 .15
5183 A2435 20k Tallinn .50 .25
Nos. 5179-5183 (5) 1.35
Set value .65

Early Spring, by V.K. Bjalynitzky-Birulja, 1912 — A2481

Paintings by White Russians: 4k, Portrait of the Artist's Wife with Fruit and Flowers, by J.F. Krutzky, 1838. 15k, Young Partisan, by E.A. Zaitsev, 1943. 20k, Partisan Madonna, by M.A. Savitsky, 1967. 45k, Harvest, by V.K. Tsvirko, 1972. 15k, 20k, vert.

Perf. $12^1/_2$x12, 12x$12^1/_2$

1983, Sept. 28
5184 A2481 4k multicolored .15 .15
5185 A2481 6k multicolored .15 .15
5186 A2481 15k multicolored .40 .30
5187 A2481 20k multicolored .50 .35
5188 A2481 45k multicolored 1.10 .70
Nos. 5184-5188 (5) 2.30 1.65

Hammer and Sickle Steel Mill, Moscow, Centenary
A2482

1983, Oct. 1 **Photo.** *Perf. $11^1/_2$*
5189 A2482 4k multicolored .25 .15

Natl. Food Program
A2483

1983, Oct. 10
5190 A2483 5k Wheat production .20 .15
5191 A2483 5k Cattle, dairy products .20 .15
5192 A2483 5k Produce .20 .15
Nos. 5190-5192 (3) .60 .45

A2484

A2485

1983, Oct. 12 **Litho.** *Perf. 12*
5193 A2484 4k multicolored .25 .15

October Revolution, 66th anniv.

1983, Oct. 12 **Engr.** *Perf. 12x$12^1/_2$*
5194 A2485 4k dark brown .25 .15

Ivan Fedorov, first Russian printer (Book of the Apostles), 400th death anniv.

Urengoy-Uzgorod Transcontinental Gas Pipeline Completion — A2486

1983, Oct. 12 **Photo.** *Perf. 12x$11^1/_2$*
5195 A2486 5k multicolored .25 .15

A2487

A2488

1983, Oct. 19 **Litho.** *Perf. 12*
5196 A2487 4k multicolored .25 .15

A.W. Sidorenko (1917-82), geologist.

1983, Oct. 19 **Photo.** *Perf. $11^1/_2$*
5197 A2488 5k Demonstration .25 .15

Campaign Against Nuclear Weapons.
Exists imperf.

Machtumkuli, Turkmenistan Poet, 250th Birth Anniv. — A2489

1983, Oct. 27
5198 A2489 5k multicolored .25 .15

Hermitage Painting Type of 1982

Paintings by Germans: 4k, Madonna and Child with Apple Tree, by Lucas Cranach the Elder. 10k, Self-portrait, by Anton R. Mengs. 20k, Self-portrait, by Jurgen Owen. 45k, Sailboat, by Caspar David Friedrich. No. 5203, Rape of the Sabines, by Johann Schoenfeld, horiz. No. 5204a, Portrait of a Young Man, by Hans Holbein.

Perf. 12x$12^1/_2$, $12^1/_2$x12

1983, Nov. 10 **Litho.** **Wmk. 383**
5199 A2431 4k multicolored .15 .15
5200 A2431 10k multicolored .40 .15
5201 A2431 20k multicolored .60 .35
5202 A2431 45k multicolored 1.25 .70
5203 A2431 50k multicolored 1.50 .75
Nos. 5199-5203 (5) 3.90 2.10

Souvenir Sheet

5204 Sheet of 2 4.00 2.50
a. A2431 50k multicolored 1.65 .65

Physicians Against Nuclear War Movement
A2490

Perf. $11^1/_2$

1983, Nov. 17 **Photo.** **Unwmk.**
5205 A2490 5k Baby, dove, sun .25 .15

Sukhe Bator (1893-1923), Mongolian People's Rep. Founder — A2491

1983, Nov. 17
5206 A2491 5k Portrait .25 .15

New Year 1984
A2492

1983, Dec. 1
5207 A2492 5k Star, snowflakes .25 .15

Printed in sheets of 16. No. 5207 exists imperf.

Newly Completed Buildings, Moscow — A2493

Perf. $12^1/_2$x12, 12x$12^1/_2$

1983, Dec. 15 **Engr.**
5208 A2493 3k Children's Musical Theater .15 .15
5209 A2493 4k Tourist Hotel, vert. .15 .15
5210 A2493 6k Council of Ministers .15 .15
5211 A2493 20k Ismaelovo Hotel .70 .35
5212 A2493 45k Novosti Press Agency 1.50 .70
Nos. 5208-5212 (5) 2.65
Set value 1.25

A2494

A2495

Souvenir Sheet

1983, Dec. 20 **Photo.** *Perf. $11^1/_2$*
5213 A2494 50k multicolored 5.00 5.00

Environmental Protection Campaign.

1984, Jan. 1
5214 A2495 4k multicolored .25 .15

Moscow Local Broadcasting Network, 50th anniv.

European Women's Skating Championships A2496

1984, Jan. 1 *Perf. 12x11½*
5215 A2496 5k multicolored .25 .15

Exists imperf.

Cuban Revolution, 25th Anniv. A2497

1984, Jan. 1 *Perf. 11½*
5216 A2497 5k Flag, "25" .25 .15

Exists imperf.

World War II Tanks — A2498

1984, Jan. 25 Litho. *Perf. 12½x12*
5217 A2498 10k KW .30 .15
5218 A2498 10k IS-2 .30 .15
5219 A2498 10k T-34 .30 .15
5220 A2498 10k ISU-152 .30 .15
5221 A2498 10k SU-100 .30 .15
Nos. 5217-5221 (5) 1.50 .75

No. 5220 exists imperf.

1984 Winter Olympics — A2499

1984, Feb. 8 Photo. *Perf. 11½x12*
5222 A2499 5k Biathlon .15 .15
a. Miniature sheet of 8
5223 A2499 10k Speed skating .40 .15
a. Miniature sheet of 8
5224 A2499 20k Hockey .75 .35
a. Miniature sheet of 8
5225 A2499 45k Figure skating 1.40 .70
a. Miniature sheet of 8
Nos. 5222-5225 (4) 2.70 1.35

Exist imperf.

Moscow Zoo, 120th Anniv. — A2500

1984, Feb. 16 Litho. *Perf. 12½x12*
5226 A2500 2k Mandrill .15 .15
5227 A2500 3k Gazelle .15 .15
5228 A2500 4k Snow leopard .15 .15
5229 A2500 5k Crowned crane .15 .15
5230 A2500 20k Macaw .40 .25
Nos. 5226-5230 (5) 1.00
Set value .65

Yuri Gagarin (1934-68) — A2501

1984, Mar. 9 Engr. *Perf. 12½x12*
5231 A2501 15k Portrait, Vostok .50 .35
a. Miniature sheet of 8

Souvenir Sheet

Mass Development of Virgin and Unused Land, 30th Anniv. — A2502

1984, Mar. 14 Photo. *Perf. 11½x12*
5232 A2502 50k multicolored 1.50 .75

Hermitage Painting Type of 1982

Paintings by English Artists: 4k, E.K. Vorontsova, by George Hayter. 10k, Portrait of Mrs. Greer, by George Romney. 20k, Approaching Storm, by George Morland, horiz. 45k, Portrait of an Unknown Man, by Marcus Gheeraerts Jr. No. 5237, Cupid and Venus, by Joshua Reynolds. No. 5238a, Portrait of a Lady in Blue, by Thomas Gainsborough.

Perf. 12x12½, 12½x12

1984, Mar. 20 Litho. Wmk. 383
5233 A2431 4k multicolored .15 .15
5234 A2431 10k multicolored .40 .15
5235 A2431 20k multicolored .60 .35
5236 A2431 45k multicolored 1.40 .70
5237 A2431 50k multicolored 1.65 .75
Nos. 5233-5237 (5) 4.20 2.10

Souvenir Sheet

5238 Sheet of 2 5.00 1.70
a. A2431 50k multicolored 2.00 .65

Nos. 5233-5237 each se-tenant with label showing text and embossed emblem.

S.V. Ilyushin — A2503

Andrei S. Bubnov — A2504

Perf. 11½

1984, Mar. 23 Photo. Unwmk.
5239 A2503 5k Aircraft designer, (1894-1977) .30 .15

1984, Apr. 3 *Perf. 11½x12*
5240 A2504 5k Statesman, (1884-1940) .25 .15

Intercosmos Cooperative Space Program (USSR-India) A2505

Designs: 5k, Weather Station M-100 launch. 20k, Geodesy (satellites, observatory). 45k, Rocket, satellites, dish antenna. 50k, Flags, cosmonauts.

1984 *Perf. 12x11½*
5241 A2505 5k multicolored .15 .15
5242 A2505 20k multicolored .75 .35
5243 A2505 45k multicolored 1.65 .70
Nos. 5241-5243 (3) 2.55 1.20

Souvenir Sheet

5244 A2505 50k multicolored 1.50 .75

No. 5244 contains one 25x36mm stamp. Issue dates: 50k, Apr. 5; others, Apr. 3.

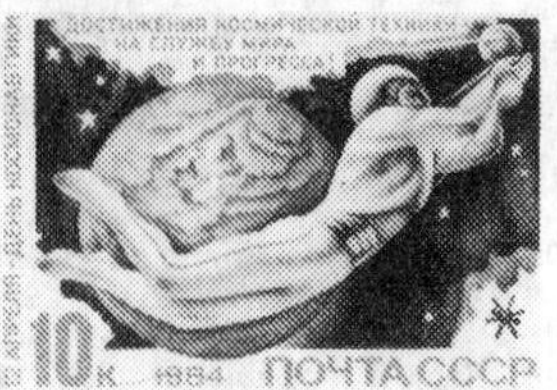

Cosmonauts' Day — A2506

1984, Apr. 12 *Perf. 11½x12*
5245 A2506 10k Futuristic spaceman .50 .30

Tchelyuskin Arctic Expedition, 50th Anniv. — A2507

Photogravure and Engraved

1984, Apr. 13 *Perf. 11½x12*
5246 A2507 6k Ship .15 .15
a. Miniature sheet of 8
5247 A2507 15k Shipwreck .50 .25
a. Miniature sheet of 8
5248 A2507 45k Rescue 1.50 .70
a. Miniature sheet of 8
Nos. 5246-5248 (3) 2.15 1.10

Souvenir Sheet

Photo.

5249 A2507 50k Hero of Soviet Union medal 1.50 .70

First HSU medal awarded to rescue crew. No. 5249 contains one 27x39mm stamp.

Souvenir Sheet

114th Birth Anniv. of Lenin A2508

Perf. 11½x12½

1984, Apr. 22 Litho.
5250 A2508 50k Portrait 1.50 .70

Aquatic Plants — A2509

Soviet Peace Policy — A2510

1984, May 5 *Perf. 12x12½, 12½x12*
5251 A2509 1k Lotus .15 .15
5252 A2509 2k Euriola .15 .15
5253 A2509 3k Water lilies, horiz. .15 .15
5254 A2509 10k White nymphaea, horiz. .20 .15
a. Miniature sheet of 8
5255 A2509 20k Marshflowers, horiz. .40 .25
Nos. 5251-5255 (5) 1.05
Set value .65

1984, May 8 Photo. *Perf. 11½*
5256 A2510 5k Marchers, banners (at left) .15 .15
5257 A2510 5k Text .15 .15
5258 A2510 5k Marchers, banners (at right) .15 .15
a. Strip of 3, #5256-5258 .45 .30

A2511

A2512

1984, May 15 Photo. *Perf. 11½*
5259 A2511 10k multicolored .30 .25

E.O. Paton Institute of Electric Welding, 50th anniv.

1984, May 21
5260 A2512 10k multicolored .30 .30

25th Conf. for Electric and Postal Communications Cooperation.

A2513

A2514

1984, May 29
5261 A2513 5k violet brown .25 .15

Maurice Bishop, Grenada Prime Minister (1944-83).

1984, May 31
5262 A2514 5k multicolored .25 .15

V.I. Lenin Central Museum, 60th anniv.

City of Archangelsk, 400th Anniv. — A2515

1984, June 1 Photo. & Engr.
5263 A2515 5k multicolored .25 .15

European Youth Soccer Championship A2516

1984, June 1 Photo. *Perf. 12x11½*
5264 A2516 15k multicolored .50 .30

Lighthouse Type of 1982

Far Eastern seas lighthouses.

1984, June 14 Litho. *Perf. 12*

5265	A2435	1k Petropavlovsk	.15	.15
5266	A2435	2k Tokarev	.15	.15
5267	A2435	4k Basargin	.15	.15
5268	A2435	5k Kronitsky	.15	.15
5269	A2435	10k Marekan	.20	.15
		Nos. 5265-5269 (5)	.80	
		Set value		.60

Salyut 7-Soyuz T-9 150-Day Flight — A2517

1984, June 27 Litho. *Perf. 12*

5270 A2517 15k multicolored .50 .30

A2518

Photogravure and Engraved

1984, July 1 *Perf. 11½*

5271 A2518 10k multicolored .30 .25

Morflot, Merchant & Transport Fleet, 60th anniv.

60th Anniv. of Awarding V.I. Lenin Name to Youth Communist League — A2519

1984, July 1 Photo. *Perf. 11½x12*

5272 A2519 5k multicolored .25 .15

Liberation of Byelorussia, 40th Anniv. — A2520

1984, July 3 Photo. *Perf. 12x11½*

5273 A2520 5k multicolored .25 .15

CMEA Conference, Moscow — A2521

1984, June 12 Photo. *Perf. 11½*

5274 A2521 5k CMEA Building & Kremlin .25 .15

A2522

A2523

1984, July 20 Photo. *Perf. 11½*

5275 A2522 5k Convention seal .25 .15

27th Intl. Geological Cong., Moscow.

1984, July 22 Photo. *Perf. 11½*

5276 A2523 5k Arms, draped flag .25 .15

People's Republic of Poland, 40th anniv.

B. V. Asafiev (1884-1949), Composer A2524

1984, July 25 Engr. *Perf. 12½x12*

5277 A2524 5k greenish black .25 .15

Relations with Mexico, 60th Anniv. A2525

1984, Aug. 4 Litho. *Perf. 12*

5278 A2525 5k USSR, Mexican flags .25 .15

Miniature Sheet

Russian Folk Tales — A2526

Designs: a, 3 archers. b, Prince and frog. c, Old man and prince. d, Crowd and swans. e, Wolf and men. f, Bird and youth. g, Youth on white horse. h, Couple with Tsar. i, Village scene. j, Man on black horse. k, Old man. l, Young woman.

1984, Aug. 10 Litho. *Perf. 12x12½*

5279	Sheet of 12	5.00	2.50
a.-l.	A2526 5k, any single	.30	.15

Friendship '84 Games A2527

1984, Aug. 15 Photo. *Perf. 11½*

5280	A2527	1k Basketball	.15	.15
5281	A2527	5k Gymnastics, vert.	.15	.15
5282	A2527	10k Weightlifting	.25	.15
5283	A2527	15k Wrestling	.40	.20
5284	A2527	20k High jump	.50	.25
		Nos. 5280-5284 (5)	1.45	
		Set value		.75

A2528

A2529

1984, Aug. 23 Litho. *Perf. 12*

5285 A2528 5k Flag, monument .25 .15

Liberation of Romania, 40th anniv.

1984, Sept. 5 Litho. *Perf. 12½x12*

Subjects: 35k, 3r, Environmental protection. 2r, Arctic development. 5r, World peace.

5286	A2529	35k Sable	.65	.50
5287	A2529	2r Ship, arctic map	3.50	2.50

Engr.

5288	A2529	3r Child and globe	5.75	3.25
5289	A2529	5r Palm frond and globe	9.00	5.75
		Nos. 5286-5289 (4)	18.90	12.00

See Nos. 6016B-6017A.

A2530

A2531

1984, Sept. 7 Photo. *Perf. 11½*

5290	A2530	15k Motherland statue, Volgograd	.50	.30
5291	A2530	15k Spasski Tower, Moscow	.50	.30

World Chess Championships.

1984, Sept. 9 Photo. *Perf. 11½*

5292 A2531 5k Bulgarian arms .25 .15

Bulgarian Revolution, 40th anniv.

Ethiopian Revolution, 10th Anniv. A2532

1984, Sept. 12 Litho. *Perf. 12*

5293 A2532 5k Ethiopian flag, seal .25 .15

Novokramatorsk Machinery Plant, 50th Anniv. — A2533

Photogravure and Engraved

1984, Sept. 20 *Perf. 11½*

5294 A2533 5k Excavator .25 .15

Nakhichevan ASSR, 60th Anniv. A2534

1984, Sept. 20 Litho. *Perf. 12*

5295 A2534 5k Arms .25 .15

Television from Space, 25th Anniv. A2535

1984, Oct. 4 Photo. *Perf. 11½*

5296	A2535	5k Luna 3	.15	.15
5297	A2535	20k Venera 9	.55	.30
5298	A2535	45k Meteor satellite	1.25	.60
		Nos. 5296-5298 (3)	1.95	1.05

Souvenir Sheet

Perf. 11½x12

5299 A2535 50k Camera, space walker, vert. 1.50 .75

No. 5299 contains one 26x37mm stamp.

German Democratic Republic, 35th Anniv. A2536

1984, Oct. 7 Photo. *Perf. 11½*

5300 A2536 5k Flag, arms .25 .15

Ukrainian Liberation, 40th Anniv. A2537

1984, Oct. 8 Photo. *Perf. 12x11½*

5301 A2537 5k Motherland statue, Kiev .25 .15

Soviet Republics and Parties, 60th Anniv. A2538

SSR Flags & Arms: #5302, Moldavian. #5303, Kirgiz. #5304, Tadzhik. #5305, Uzbek. #5306, Turkmen.

1984 Litho. *Perf. 12*

5302	A2538	5k multicolored	.20	.15
5303	A2538	5k multicolored	.20	.15
5304	A2538	5k multicolored	.20	.15
5305	A2538	5k multicolored	.20	.15
5306	A2538	5k multicolored	.20	.15
		Nos. 5302-5306 (5)	1.00	.75

Issued: #5302, 10/12; #5303-5304, 10/14; #5305-5306, 10/27.

A2539

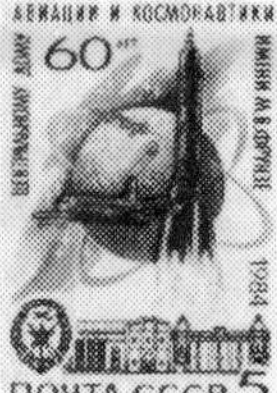

A2540

1984, Oct. 23 Photo. *Perf. 11½*

5307 A2539 5k Kremlin, 1917 flag .25 .15

October Revolution, 67th anniv.

1984, Nov. 6 Photo. *Perf. 11½*

5308 A2540 5k Aircraft, spacecraft .25 .15

M. Frunze Inst. of Aviation & Cosmonautics.

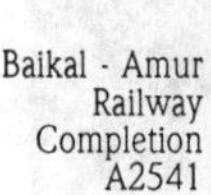

Baikal - Amur Railway Completion A2541

1984, Nov. 7 Photo. *Perf. 11½*
5309 A2541 5k Workers, map, engine .30 .15

Hermitage Type of 1982

Paintings by French Artists: 4k, Girl in a Hat, by Jean Louis Voille. 10k, A Stolen Kiss, by Jean-Honore Fragonard. 20k, Woman Combing her Hair, by Edgar Degas. 45k, Pigmalion and Galatea, by Francois Boucher. 50k, Landscape with Polyphenus, by Nicholas Poussin. No. 5315a, Child with a Whip, by Pierre-Auguste Renoir.

Perf. 12x12½, 12½x12
1984, Nov. 20 Litho. Wmk. 383
5310 A2431 4k multicolored .15 .15
5311 A2431 10k multi, horiz. .35 .15
5312 A2431 20k multicolored .55 .45
5313 A2431 45k multi, horiz. 1.25 .75
5314 A2431 50k multi, horiz. 1.40 .90
Nos. 5310-5314 (5) 3.70 2.40

Souvenir Sheet

5315 Sheet of 2 3.50 2.00
a. A2431 50k multicolored 1.00 .60

Mongolian Peoples' Republic, 60th Anniv. — A2542

Perf. 11½
1984, Nov. 26 Photo. Unwmk.
5316 A2542 5k Mongolian flag, arms .30 .15

New Year 1985 — A2543

1984, Dec. 4 Litho. *Perf. 11½*
5317 A2543 5k Kremlin, snowflakes .25 .15
a. Miniature sheet of 8

Souvenir Sheet

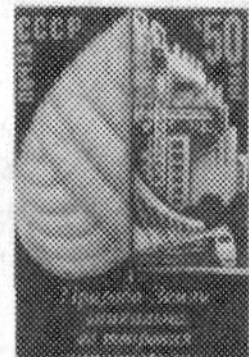

Environmental Protection — A2544

1984, Dec. 4 Litho. *Perf. 12½x12*
5318 A2544 50k Leaf, pollution sources 1.50 .75

Russian Fire Vehicles — A2545

Photogravure and Engraved
1984, Dec. 12 *Perf. 12x11½*
5319 A2545 3k Crew wagon, 19th cent. .15 .15
5320 A2545 5k Pumper, 19th cent. .15 .15
5321 A2545 10k Ladder truck, 1904 .35 .15
5322 A2545 15k Pumper, 1904 .55 .25
5323 A2545 20k Ladder truck, 1913 .65 .30
Nos. 5319-5323 (5) 1.85
Set value .85

See Nos. 5410-5414.

Intl. Venus-Halley's Comet Project — A2546

1984, Dec. 15 Photo. *Perf. 12x11½*
5324 A2546 15k Satellite, flight path .60 .35
a. Miniature sheet of 8

Indira Gandhi (1917-1984), Indian Prime Minister — A2547

1984, Dec. 28 Litho. *Perf. 12*
5325 A2547 5k Portrait 1.00 .75

1905 Revolution A2548

1985, Jan. 22 Photo. *Perf. 11½*
5326 A2548 5k Flag, Moscow memorial .25 .15

A2549

A2550

1985, Jan. 24
5327 A2549 5k multicolored .25 .15

Patrice Lumumba Peoples' Friendship University, 25th Anniv.

1985, Feb. 2
5328 A2550 5k bluish, blk & ocher .25 .15

Mikhail Vasilievich Frunze (1885-1925), party leader.

Karakalpak ASSR, 60th Anniv. A2551

1985, Feb. 16 *Perf. 12*
5329 A2551 5k Republic arms .25 .15

10th Winter Spartakiad of Friendly Armies — A2552

1985, Feb. 23 *Perf. 11½*
5330 A2552 5k Hockey player, emblem .25 .15

Kalevala, 150th Anniv. A2553

1985, Feb. 25 Litho. *Perf. 12*
5331 A2553 5k Rune singer, frontispiece .25 .15

Finnish Kalevala, collection of Karelian epic poetry compiled by Elias Lonrot.

A2554

A2555

1985, Mar. 3 Engr. *Perf. 12½x12*
5332 A2554 5k rose lake .25 .15

Yakov M. Sverdlov (1885-1919), party leader.

1985, Mar. 6 Photo. *Perf. 11½*
5333 A2555 5k Pioneer badge, awards .25 .15

Pionerskaya Pravda, All-Union children's newspaper, 60th Anniv.

Maria Alexandrovna Ulyanova (1835-1916), Lenin's Mother — A2556

1985, Mar. 6 Engr. *Perf. 12½x12*
5334 A2556 5k black .30 .15

Hermitage Type of 1982

Paintings by Spanish artists: 4k, The Young Virgin Praying, vert., by Francisco de Zurbaran (1598-1664). 10k, Still-life, by Antonio Pereda (c. 1608-1678). 20k, The Immaculate Conception, vert., by Murillo (1617-1682). 45k, The Grinder, by Antonio Puga. No. 5339, Count Olivares, vert., by Diego Velazques (1599-1660). No. 5340a, Portrait of the actress Antonia Zarate, vert., by Goya (1746-1828).

Perf. 12x12½, 12½x12
1985, Mar. 14 Litho. Wmk. 383
5335 A2431 4k multicolored .15 .15
5336 A2431 10k multicolored .30 .15
5337 A2431 20k multicolored .50 .40
5338 A2431 45k multicolored 1.25 .90
5339 A2431 50k multicolored 1.40 .95
Nos. 5335-5339 (5) 3.60 2.55

Souvenir Sheet
Lithographed and Embossed

5340 Sheet of 2 + label 3.00 2.00
a. A2431 50k multicolored 1.10 .75

EXPO '85, Tsukuba, Japan — A2557

Soviet exhibition, Expo '85 emblems and: 5k, Cosmonauts in space. 10k, Communications satellite. 20k, Alternative energy sources development. 45k, Future housing systems.

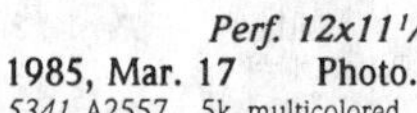

Perf. 12x11½
1985, Mar. 17 Photo. Unwmk.
5341 A2557 5k multicolored .15 .15
5342 A2557 10k multicolored .30 .20
5343 A2557 20k multicolored .55 .45
5344 A2557 45k multicolored 1.25 .90
Nos. 5341-5344 (4) 2.25 1.70

Souvenir Sheet

5345 A2557 50k Soviet exhibition emblem, globe 1.50 .90

Issued in sheets of 8.

Souvenir Sheet

Johann Sebastian Bach (1685-1750), Composer A2558

Photogravure and Engraved
1985, Mar. 21 *Perf. 12x11½*
5346 A2558 50k black 1.50 1.00

A2559

A2560

1985, Apr. 4 Litho. *Perf. 12*
5347 A2559 5k Natl. crest, Budapest memorial .25 .15

Hungary liberated from German occupation, 40th Anniv.

1985, Apr. 5 Photo. *Perf. 11½*
5348 A2560 15k Emblem .40 .30

Society for Cultural Relations with Foreign Countries, 60th anniv.

Victory over Fascism, 40th Anniv. A2561

Designs: No. 5349, Battle of Moscow, soldier, Kremlin, portrait of Lenin. No. 5350, Soldier, armed forces. No. 5351, Armaments production, worker. No. 5352, Partisan movement, cavalry. No. 5353, Berlin-Treptow war memorial, German Democratic Republic. No. 5354, Order of the Patriotic War, second class.

1985, Apr. 20 *Perf. 12x11½*
5349 A2561 5k multicolored .30 .15
5350 A2561 5k multicolored .30 .15
5351 A2561 5k multicolored .30 .15
5352 A2561 5k multicolored .30 .15
5353 A2561 5k multicolored .30 .15
Nos. 5349-5353 (5) 1.50
Set value .50

Souvenir Sheet
Perf. 11½

5354 A2561 50k multicolored 1.50 .50

No. 5354 contains one 28x40mm stamp. Issued in sheets of 8.

Всесоюзная
филатели-
стическая
выставка

No. 5353 Ovptd. in Red for 40th Year Since World War II Victory All-Union Philatelic Exhibition

„40 лет
Великой
Победы"

1985, Apr. 29 Photo. *Perf. 12x11½*

5354A A2561 5k brn lake, gold & vermilion	.50	.50

Yuri Gagarin Center for Training Cosmonauts, 25th Anniv. — A2562

Cosmonauts day: Portrait, cosmonauts, Soyuz-T spaceship.

1985, Apr. 12 Photo. *Perf. 11½x12*

5355 A2562 15k multicolored	.50	.25
a. Miniature sheet of 8		

12th World Youth Festival, Moscow A2563

1985, Apr. 15 Litho. *Perf. 12x12½*

5356 A2563 1k Three youths	.15	.15
5357 A2563 3k African girl	.15	.15
5358 A2563 5k Girl, rainbow	.20	.15
5359 A2563 20k Asian youth, camera	.95	.35
5360 A2563 45k Emblem	2.25	.75
Nos. 5356-5360 (5)	3.70	
Set value		1.30

No. 5358 issued in sheets of 8.

Souvenir Sheet

1985, July 4

5361 A2563 30k Emblem	2.00	1.00

115th Birth Anniv. of Lenin — A2564

Portrait and: No. 5362, Lenin Museum, Tampere, Finland. No. 5363, Memorial apartment, Paris, France.

1985, Apr. 22 Photo. *Perf. 11½x12*

5362 A2564 5k multicolored	.15	.15
5363 A2564 5k multicolored	.15	.15

Souvenir Sheet

Litho.

Perf. 12x12½

5364 A2564 30k Portrait	1.50	1.00

No. 5364 contains one 30x42mm stamp.

Order of Victory — A2565

Photogravure and Engraved

1985, May 9 *Perf. 11½*

5365 A2565 20k sil, royal bl, dk red & gold	.60	.35

Allied World War II victory over Germany and Japan, 40th anniv.

A2566

A2567

1985, May 9 Litho. *Perf. 12½x12*

5366 A2566 5k Arms	.25	.15

Liberation of Czechoslovakia from German occupation, 40th Anniv.

1985, May 14 Photo. *Perf. 11½*

5367 A2567 5k Flags of member nations	.25	.15

Warsaw Treaty Org., 30th anniv.

Mikhail Alexandrovich Sholokhov (1905-1984), Novelist & Nobel Laureate — A2568

Portraits and book covers: No. 5368, Tales from the Don, Quiet Flows the Don, A Human Tragedy. No. 5369, The Quiet Don, Virgin Lands Under the Plow, Thus They Have Fought for Their Homeland. No. 5370, Portrait.

1985, May 24 Litho. *Perf. 12½x12*

5368 A2568 5k reddish brn, cream & gold	.20	.15
5369 A2568 5k chest, yel brn & gold	.20	.15

Photo.

Perf. 12x11½

Size: 37x52mm

5370 A2568 5k brn, gold & black	.20	.15
Nos. 5368-5370 (3)	.60	.45

INTERCOSMOS Project Halley-Venus — A2570

1985, June 11 Litho. *Perf. 12*

5372 A2570 15k Spacecraft, satellites, Venus	.50	.25
a. Miniature sheet of 8		

Artek Pioneer Camp, 60th Anniv. A2571

1985, June 14 Photo. *Perf. 11½*

5373 A2571 4k Camp, badges, Lenin Pioneers emblem	.50	.15

Mutiny on the Battleship Potemkin, 80th Anniv. — A2572

Photogravure and Engraved

1985, June 16 *Perf. 11½x12*

5374 A2572 5k dk red, gold & black	.30	.15

Miniature Sheet

Soviet Railways Rolling Stock — A2573

Designs: a, Electric locomotive WL 80-R (grn). b, Tanker car (bl). c, Refrigerator car (bl). d, Sleeper car (brn). e, Tipper car (brn). f, Box car (brn). g, Shunting diesel locomotive (bl). h, Mail car (grn).

1985, June 15 Engr. *Perf. 12½x12*

5375 Sheet of 8	2.50	1.65
a.-h. A2573 10k any single	.25	.15

Cosmonauts L. Kizim, V. Soloviov, O. Atkov and Salyut-7 Spacecraft — A2574

1985, June 25 Litho.

5376 A2574 15k multicolored	.50	.25
a. Miniature sheet of 8		

Soyuz T-10, Salyut-7 and Soyuz T-11 flights, Feb. 8-Oct. 2, 1984.

Beating Sword into Plowshares, Sculpture Donated to UN Hdqtrs. by USSR — A2575

Photogravure and Engraved

1985, June 26 *Perf. 11½*

5377 A2575 45k multicolored	1.50	.75

UN 40th anniv.

Intl. Youth Year — A2576

1985, June 26 Photo. *Perf. 12*

5378 A2576 10k multicolored	.30	.25

Medicinal Plants from Siberia — A2577

1985, July 10 Litho. *Perf. 12½x12*

5379 A2577 2k O. dictiocarpum	.15	.15
5380 A2577 3k Thermopsis lanceolata	.15	.15
5381 A2577 5k Rosa acicularis lindi	.15	.15
5382 A2577 20k Rhaponticum carthamoides	.80	.40
a. Miniature sheet of 8		
5383 A2577 45k Bergenia crassifolia fritsch	1.65	.75
Nos. 5379-5383 (5)	2.90	
Set value		1.30

Cosmonauts V. A. Dzhanibekov, S. E. Savistskaya, and I. P. Volk, Soyuz T-12 Mission, July 17-29, 1984 — A2578

1985, July 17

5384 A2578 10k multicolored	.40	.15
a. Miniature sheet of 8		

1st woman's free flight in space.

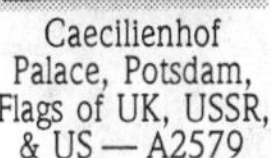

Caecilienhof Palace, Potsdam, Flags of UK, USSR, & US — A2579

Finlandia Hall, Helsinki — A2580

1985, July 17

5385 A2579 15k multicolored	.50	.25

Potsdam Conference, 40th anniv.

1985, July 25 Photo. *Perf. 11½*

5386 A2580 20k multicolored	.50	.30
a. Miniature sheet of 8		

Helsinki Conference on European security and cooperation, 10th anniv.

Flags of USSR, North Korea, Liberation Monument in Pyongyang — A2581

1985, Aug. 1

5387 A2581 5k multicolored	.25	.15

Socialist Rep. of North Korea, 40th anniv.

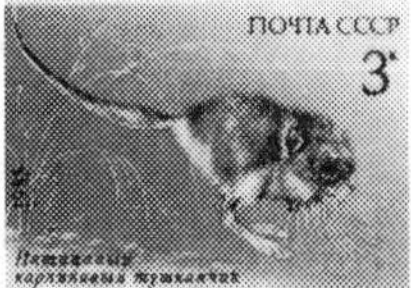

Endangered Wildlife A2582

Designs: 2k, Sorex bucharensis, vert. 3k, Cardiocranius paradoxus. 5k, Selevinia betpakdalensis, vert. 20k, Felis caracal. 45k, Gazella subgutturosa. 50k, Panthera pardus.

Perf. 12x12½, 12½x12

1985, Aug. 15 **Litho.**

5388 A2582 2k multicolored .15 .15
5389 A2582 3k multicolored .15 .15
5390 A2582 5k multicolored .15 .15

Size: 47x32mm

5391 A2582 20k multicolored .75 .35
a. Miniature sheet of 8
5392 A2582 45k multicolored 1.65 .75
Nos. 5388-5392 (5) 2.85
Set value 1.25

Souvenir Sheet

5393 A2582 50k multicolored 2.50 .75

Youth World Soccer Cup Championships, Moscow — A2583

1985, Aug. 24 *Perf. 12*

5394 A2583 5k multicolored .30 .25

Alexander G. Stakhanov, Coal Miner & Labor Leader A2584

1985, Aug. 30 **Photo.** *Perf. 11½*

5395 A2584 5k multicolored .25 .15

Stakhanovite Movement for high labor productivity, 50th anniv.

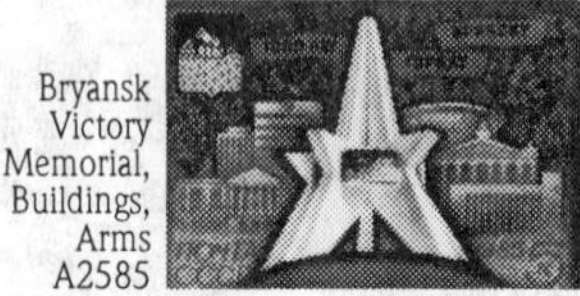

Bryansk Victory Memorial, Buildings, Arms A2585

1985, Sept. 1

5396 A2585 5k multicolored .30 .25

Millennium of Bryansk.

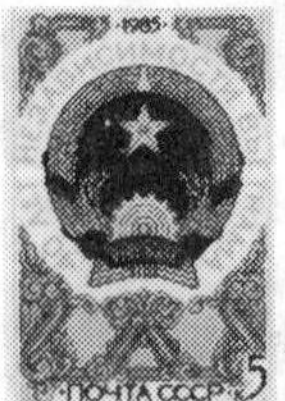

Socialist Republic of Vietnam, 40th Anniv. — A2586

1985, Sept. 2 **Litho.** *Perf. 12½x12*

5397 A2586 5k Arms .25 .15

A2587

1985, Sept. 2 **Photo.** *Perf. 11½*

5398 A2587 10k multicolored .50 .15

1985 World Chess Championship match, A. Karpov Vs. G. Kasparov, Moscow.

Lutsk City, Ukrainian SSR, 900th Anniv. — A2588

1985, Sept. 14

5399 A2588 5k Lutsk Castle .25 .15

Open Book, the Weeping Jaroslavna and Prince Igor's Army — A2589

Photogravure and Engraved

1985, Sept. 14 *Perf. 11½x12*

5400 A2589 10k multicolored .35 .15

The Song of Igor's Campaign, epic poem, 800th anniv.

Sergei Vasilievich Gerasimov (1885-1964), Painter — A2590

1985, Sept. 26 *Perf. 12x11½*

5401 A2590 5k Portrait .25 .15

October Revolution, 68th Anniv. — A2591

UN 40th Anniv. — A2592

1985, Oct. 10 **Photo.** *Perf. 11½*

5402 A2591 5k multicolored .25 .15

1985, Oct. 24

5403 A2592 15k multicolored .50 .25

Krushjanis Baron (1835-1923), Latvian Folklorist — A2593

Lithographed and Engraved

1985, Oct. 31

5404 A2593 5k beige & black .30 .15

Lenin, Laborer Breaking Chains A2594

1985, Nov. 20 **Photo.**

5405 A2594 5k multicolored .25 .15

Petersburg Union struggle for liberation of the working classes, founded by Lenin, 90th anniv.

Largest Soviet Telescope, 10th Anniv. — A2595

1985, Nov. 20 **Engr.** *Perf. 12½x12*

5406 A2595 10k dark blue .50 .25

Soviet Observatory inauguration.

A2596

A2597

1985, Nov. 25 **Photo.**

5407 A2596 5k multicolored .25 .15

Angolan Independence, 10th anniv.

1985, Nov. 29 *Perf. 11½*

5408 A2597 5k multicolored .25 .15

Socialist Federal Republic of Yugoslavia, 40th anniv.

New Year — A2598

Samantha Smith — A2599

1985, Dec. 3 **Litho.** *Perf. 12*

5409 A2598 5k multicolored .25 .15
a. Miniature sheet of 8

Vehicle Type of 1984

1985, Dec. 18 **Photo.** *Perf. 12x11½*

5410 A2545 3k AMO-F15, 1926 .15 .15
5411 A2545 5k PMZ-1, 1933 .15 .15
5412 A2545 10k AC-40, 1977 .40 .15
5413 A2545 20k AL-30, 1970 .70 .35
5414 A2545 45k AA-60, 1978 1.40 .70
Nos. 5410-5414 (5) 2.80
Set value 1.30

1985, Dec. 25 *Perf. 12*

5415 A2599 5k vio blue, choc & ver .50 .15

American student invited to meet with Soviet leaders in 1984.

A2600 A2601

1985, Dec. 30 **Litho.**

5416 A2600 5k multicolored .25 .15

N.M. Emanuel (1915-1984), chemist.

1985, Dec. 30

5417 A2601 5k Sightseeing .20 .15
5418 A2601 5k Sports .20 .15
Set value .20

Family leisure activities.

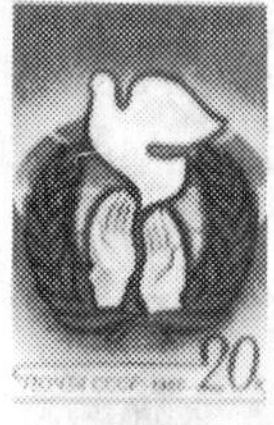

Intl. Peace Year — A2602

1986, Jan. 2 **Photo.** *Perf. 11½*

5419 A2602 20k brt blue, bluish grn & silver .60 .30

Flags, Congress Palace, Carnation A2603

Lenin, Troitskaya Tower, Congress Palace A2604

Lenin — A2605

1986, Jan. 3

5420 A2603 5k multicolored .15 .15

Photogravure and Engraved

Perf. 12x11½

5421 A2604 20k multicolored .70 .30

Souvenir Sheet

Photo.

Perf. 11½

5422 A2605 50k multicolored 1.75 .70

27th Communist Party Congress.

A2606

A2607

1986, Jan. 10 *Perf. 11½x12*
5423 A2606 15k multicolored .50 .25

Modern Olympic Games, 90th anniv.

Perf. 12½x12, 12x12½
1986, Jan. 15 **Litho.**

Flora of Russian Steppes, different.

5424 A2607 4k multicolored .15 .15
5425 A2607 5k multi, horiz. .15 .15
5426 A2607 10k multicolored .30 .15
5427 A2607 15k multicolored .40 .30
5428 A2607 20k multicolored .50 .35
a. Miniature sheet of 8
Nos. 5424-5428 (5) 1.50 1.10

A2608

A2609

Vodovzvodnaya Tower, Grand Kremlin Palace.

1986, Jan. 20 *Perf. 12½x12*
5429 A2608 50k grayish green 1.50 .70

1986, Feb. 20 *Perf. 11½*
5430 A2609 5k multicolored .30 .15

Voronezh City, 400th anniv.

A2610

A2611

1986, Feb. 20 **Engr.** *Perf. 12*
5431 A2610 10k bluish black .35 .15

Bela Kun (1886-1939), Hungarian party leader.

1986, Feb. 28 *Perf. 12½x12*
5432 A2611 5k grayish black .25 .15

Karolis Pozhela (1896-1926), Lithuanian party founder.

Intercosmos Project Halley, Final Stage — A2612

1986, Mar. 6 **Litho.** *Perf. 12*
5433 A2612 15k Vega probe, comet .50 .25
a. Miniature sheet of 8

Souvenir Sheet

Perf. 12½x12

5434 A2612 50k Vega I, comet 1.75 .75

No. 5434 contains one 42x30mm stamp.

Butterflies A2613

1986, Mar. 18 *Perf. 12x12½*
5435 A2613 4k Utetheisa pulchella .15 .15
5436 A2613 5k Allancastria caucasica .15 .15
5437 A2613 10k Zegris eupheme .40 .15
5438 A2613 15k Catocala sponsa .50 .50
5439 A2613 20k Satyrus bischoffi .65 .55
a. Miniature sheet of 8
Nos. 5435-5439 (5) 1.85 1.50

EXPO '86, Vancouver — A2614

A2615

1986, Mar. 25 **Photo.** *Perf. 12x11½*
5440 A2614 20k Globe, space station .75 .30
a. Miniature sheet of 8

1986, Mar. 27 **Engr.** *Perf. 12½x12*
5441 A2615 5k black .30 .15

S.M. Kirov (1886-1934), party leader.

Cosmonauts' Day — A2616

Designs: 5k, Konstantin E. Tsiolkovsky (1857-1935), aerodynamics innovator, and futuristic space station. 10k, Sergei P. Korolev (1906-1966), rocket scientist, and Vostok spaceship, vert. 15k, Yuri Gagarin, 1st cosmonaut, Sputnik I and Vega probe.

Perf. 12½x12, 12x12½
1986, Apr. 12 **Litho.**
5442 A2616 5k multicolored .15 .15
a. Miniature sheet of 8
5443 A2616 10k multicolored .25 .15
a. Miniature sheet of 8
5444 A2616 15k multicolored .35 .25
a. Miniature sheet of 7 + label
Nos. 5441-5444 (4) 1.05
Set value .45

No. 5444 printed se-tenant with label picturing Vostok and inscribed for the 25th anniv. of first space flight.

1986 World Ice Hockey Championships, Moscow — A2617

1986, Apr. 12 **Photo.** *Perf. 11½*
5445 A2617 15k multicolored .50 .25

Ernst Thalmann (1886-1944), German Communist Leader — A2618

1986, Apr. 16 **Engr.** *Perf. 12½x12*
5446 A2618 10k dark red brown .30 .15
5447 A2618 10k reddish brown .30 .15

Lenin, 116th Birth Anniv. — A2619

Portraits and architecture: No. 5448, Socialist-Democratic People's House, Prague. No. 5449, Lenin Museum, Leipzig. No. 5450, Lenin Museum, Poronino, Poland.

1986, Apr. 22 **Photo.** *Perf. 11½x12*
5448 A2619 5k multicolored .20 .15
5449 A2619 5k multicolored .20 .15
5450 A2619 5k multicolored .20 .15
Nos. 5448-5450 (3) .60
Set value .30

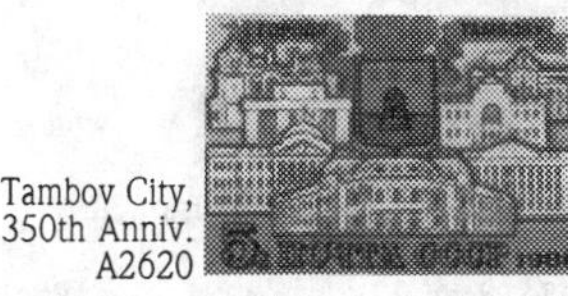
Tambov City, 350th Anniv. A2620

1986, Apr. 27 *Perf. 11½*
5451 A2620 5k Buildings, city arms .25 .15

Soviet Peace Fund, 25th Anniv. A2621

1986, Apr. 27
5452 A2621 10k lt chalky bl, gold & brt ultra .40 .15

29th World Cycle Race, May 6-22 A2622

Toadstools A2623

1986, May 6
5453 A2622 10k multicolored .40 .15

1986, May 15 **Litho.** *Perf. 12*
5454 A2623 4k Amanita phalloides .15 .15
5455 A2623 5k Amanita muscaria .15 .15
5456 A2623 10k Amanita pantherina .45 .15
5457 A2623 15k Tylopilus felleus .55 .30
5458 A2623 20k Hypholoma fasciculare .70 .35
Nos. 5454-5458 (5) 2.00
Set value .95

A2624

A2625

1986, May 19 **Photo.** *Perf. 11½*
5459 A2624 10k multicolored .35 .15

UNESCO Campaign, Man and Biosphere,

1986, May 20
5460 A2625 10k multicolored .35 .15

9th Soviet Spartakiad.

A2626

A2627

Design: Lenin's House, Eternal Glory and V. I. Chapaiev monuments, Gorky State Academic Drama Theater.

1986, May 24
5461 A2626 5k multicolored .25 .15

City of Kuibyshev, 400th anniv.

1986, May 25
5462 A2627 5k multicolored .25 .15

"COMMUNICATION '86, Moscow."

1986 World Cup Soccer Championships, Mexico — A2628

Designs: 5k, 10k, Various soccer plays. 15k, World Cup on FIFA commemorative gold medal.

1986, May 31
5463 A2628 5k multicolored .15 .15
a. Miniature sheet of 8
5464 A2628 10k multicolored .25 .15
a. Miniature sheet of 8
5465 A2628 15k multicolored .40 .25
a. Miniature sheet of 8
Nos. 5463-5465 (3) .80
Set value .45

Paintings in the Tretyakov Gallery, Moscow — A2629

Designs: 4k, Lane in Albano, 1837, by M.I. Lebedev, vert. 5k, View of the Kremlin in Foul Weather, 1851, by A.K. Savrasov. 10k, Sunlit Pine Trees, 1896, by I.I. Shishkin, vert. 15k, Return, 1896, by A.E. Arkhipov. 45k, Wedding Procession in Moscow, the 17th Century, 1901, by A.P. Ryabushkin.

Perf. 12x12½, 12½x12
1986, June 11 **Litho.**
5466 A2629 4k multicolored .15 .15
5467 A2629 5k multicolored .15 .15
5468 A2629 10k multicolored .35 .15

Size: 74x37mm

Perf. 11½

5469 A2629 15k multicolored .45 .30
5470 A2629 45k multicolored 1.25 .75
Nos. 5466-5470 (5) 2.35 1.50

Issued in sheets of 8.

Irkutsk City, 300th Anniv. — A2630

UNESCO Projects in Russia — A2632

Goodwill Games, Moscow, July 5-20 A2631

1986, June 28 Photo. *Perf. 11½*
5471 A2630 5k multicolored .25 .15

1986, July 4 Photo. *Perf. 11½*
5472 A2631 10k Prus bl, gold & blk .35 .15
5473 A2631 10k brt blue, gold & blk .35 .15

1986, July 15

Designs: 5k, Information sciences. 10k, Geological correlation. 15k, Inter-governmental oceanographic commission. 35k, Intl. hydrologic program.

5474 A2632 5k multicolored .15 .15
5475 A2632 10k multicolored .40 .15
5476 A2632 15k multicolored .50 .30
5477 A2632 35k multicolored .95 .55
Nos. 5474-5477 (4) 2.00 1.15

Tyumen, 400th Anniv. A2633

1986, July 27
5478 A2633 5k multicolored .25 .15

A2634

A2635

1986, Aug. 1 Photo. *Perf. 11½*
5479 A2634 10k multicolored .35 .15

Olof Palme (1927-86), Prime Minister of Sweden.

1986, Aug. 8
5480 A2635 15k multicolored .50 .25

10th World Women's Basketball Championships, Moscow, Aug. 15-17.

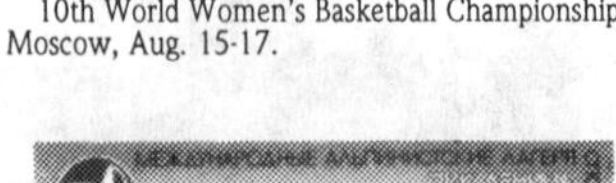

Natl. Sports Committee Intl. Alpinist Camps — A2636

1986, Sept. 5 Litho. *Perf. 12*
5481 A2636 4k Mt. Lenin .15 .15
5482 A2636 5k Mt. E. Korzhenevskaya .15 .15
a. Miniature sheet of 8
5483 A2636 10k Mt. Belukha .45 .15
5484 A2636 15k Mt. Communism .55 .30
5485 A2636 30k Mt. Elbrus 1.00 .50
Nos. 5481-5485 (5) 2.30 1.25

See Nos. 5532-5535.

Souvenir Sheet

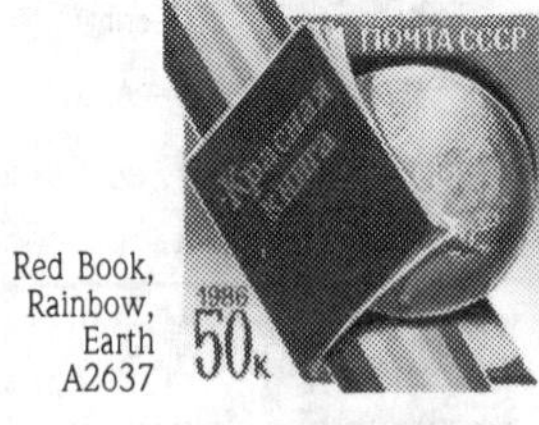

Red Book, Rainbow, Earth A2637

1986, Sept. 10 *Perf. 11½*
5486 A2637 50k multicolored 1.75 .75

Nature preservation.

A2639

A2638 A2640

1986, Sept. 13 Photo.
5487 A2638 5k multicolored .25 .15

Chelyabinsk, 250th anniv.

1986, Sept. 23
5488 A2639 15k multicolored .40 .25

Mukran, DDR to Klaipeda, Lithuania, Train Ferry, inauguration.

1986, Sept. 26
5489 A2640 5k multicolored .25 .15

Siauliai, Lithuanian SSR, 750th anniv.

Trucks — A2641

1986, Oct. 15 *Perf. 11½x12*
5490 A2641 4k Ural-375D, 1964 .20 .15
5491 A2641 5k GAZ-53A, 1965 .20 .15
5492 A2641 10k KrAZ-256B, 1966 .35 .15
a. Miniature sheet of 8
5493 A2641 15k MAZ-515B, 1974 .50 .30
5494 A2641 20k ZIL-133GY, 1979 .60 .35
Nos. 5490-5494 (5) 1.85 1.10

A2642

A2643

Design: Lenin Monument in October Square, Kremlin, Moscow.

1986, Oct. 1 Litho. *Perf. 12*
5495 A2642 5k multicolored .25 .15

October Revolution, 69th anniv.

1986, Oct. 10 Photo. *Perf. 11½*
5496 A2643 5k Icebreaker, helicopters .15 .15
5497 A2643 10k Mikhail Somov port side .20 .15
a. Pair, #5496-5497 .30 .20
b. Miniature sheet of 8, 4 each
Set value .20

Souvenir Sheet

Perf. 12½x11½

5498 A2643 50k Trapped in ice 2.25 .65

Mikhail Somov trapped in the Antarctic

No. 5497a has a continuous design. No. 5498 contains one 51½x36½mm stamp.

No. 4883 Ovptd. in Black for Rescue of the Mikhail Somov

15.III—26.VII.1985
Дрейф во льдах Антарктики

Lithographed & Engraved

1986, Oct. 10 *Perf. 12x11½*
5499 A2271 4k multicolored .75 .15

Locomotives — A2644

1986, Oct. 15 Litho. *Perf. 12*
5500 A2644 4k EU 684-37, 1929 .15 .15
5501 A2644 5k FD 21-3000, 1941 .15 .15
5502 A2644 10k OV-5109, 1907 .55 .15
a. Miniature sheet of 8
5503 A2644 20k CO17-1613, 1944 .95 .40
5504 A2644 30k FDP 20-578, 1941 1.25 .65
Nos. 5500-5504 (5) 3.05 1.50

Grigori Konstantinovich Ordzhonikidze (1886-1937), Communist Party Leader — A2645

1986, Oct. 18 Engr. *Perf. 12½x12*
5505 A2645 5k dark blue green .25 .15

A.G. Novikov (1896-1984), Composer A2646

1986, Oct. 30
5506 A2646 5k brown black .25 .15

A2647

A2648

1986, Nov. 4 Photo. *Perf. 11½*
5507 A2647 10k blue & silver .35 .15

UNESCO, 40th anniv.

1986, Nov. 12
5508 A2648 5k lt grnsh gray & black .25 .15

Sun Yat-sen (1866-1925), Chinese statesman.

Mikhail Vasilyevich Lomonosov, Scientist A2649

1986, Nov. 19 Engr. *Perf. 12x12½*
5509 A2649 5k dk violet brown .25 .15

Aircraft by A.S. Yakovlev — A2650

1986, Nov. 25 Photo. *Perf. 11½x12*
5510 A2650 4k 1927 .15 .15
5511 A2650 5k 1935 .15 .15
a. Miniature sheet of 8
5512 A2650 10k 1946 .40 .15
5513 A2650 20k 1972 .65 .35
5514 A2650 30k 1981 .95 .50
Nos. 5510-5514 (5) 2.30 1.30

New Year 1987 — A2651

A2652

1986, Dec. 4 Litho. *Perf. 11½*
5515 A2651 5k Kremlin towers .25 .15
a. Miniature sheet of 8 15.00

1986, Dec. 12 Photo. *Perf. 11½x12*

Red banner and: No. 5516, Computers. No. 5517, Engineer, computer, dish receivers. No. 5518, Aerial view of city. No. 5519, Council for Mutual Economic Assistance building, workers. No. 5520, Spasski Tower, Kremlin Palace.

5516 A2652 5k multicolored .15 .15
5517 A2652 5k multicolored .15 .15
5518 A2652 5k multicolored .15 .15
5519 A2652 5k multicolored .15 .15
5520 A2652 5k multicolored .15 .15
Nos. 5516-5520 (5) .75
Set value .35

27th Communist Party Cong., Feb. 25-Mar. 6.

A2653

A2654

1986, Dec. 24 Engr. *Perf. 12½x12*
5521 A2653 5k black .25 .15

Alexander Yakovlevich Parkhomenko (1886-1921), revolution hero.

1986, Dec. 25 Photo. *Perf. 11½*
5522 A2654 5k brown & buff .25 .15

Samora Moises Machel (1933-1986) Pres. of Mozambique.

Miniature Sheet

Palace Museums in Leningrad — A2655

1986, Dec. 25 Engr. *Perf. 12*

5523	Sheet of 5 + label	3.00	1.40
a.	A2655 5k State Museum, 1898	.15	.15
b.	A2655 10k The Hermitage, 1764	.35	.15
c.	A2655 15k Petrodvorets, 1728	.45	.30
d.	A2655 20k Yekaterininsky, 1757	.55	.35
e.	A2655 50k Pavlovsk, restored c. 1945	1.25	.75

18th Soviet Trade Unions Congress, Feb. 24-28 — A2656

1987, Jan. 7 Photo. *Perf. 11½*

5524 A2656 5k multicolored .25 .15

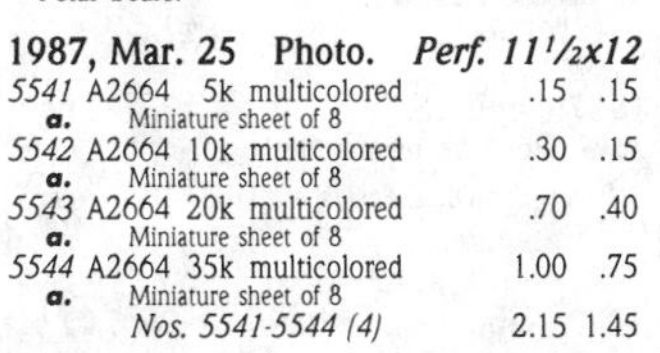

Butterflies A2657

1987, Jan. 15 Litho. *Perf. 12x12½*

5525 A2657	4k Atrophaneura alcinous	.15	.15
5526 A2657	5k Papilio machaon	.15	.15
5527 A2657	10k Papilio alexanor	.30	.15
5528 A2657	15k Papilio maackii	.40	.30
5529 A2657	30k Iphiclides podalirius	.75	.50
	Nos. 5525-5529 (5)	1.75	1.25

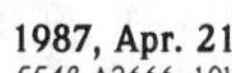

A2658 A2659

1987, Jan. 31 *Perf. 12½x12*

5530 A2658 5k multicolored .25 .15

Karlis Miyesniyek (1887-1977), Artist.

1987, Feb. 4 *Perf. 12*

5531 A2659 5k buff & lake .25 .15

Stasis Shimkus (1887-1943), composer.

Alpinist Camps Type of 1986

1987, Feb. 4

5532 A2636	4k Chimbulak Gorge	.15	.15
5533 A2636	10k Shavla Gorge	.30	.15
5534 A2636	20k Mts. Donguz-orun, Nakra-tau	.50	.35
5535 A2636	35k Mt. Kazbek	.75	.55
	Nos. 5532-5535 (4)	1.70	1.20

Vasily Ivanovich Chapayev (1887-1919), Revolution Hero — A2660

1987, Feb. 9 Engr.

5536 A2660 5k dark red brown .25 .15

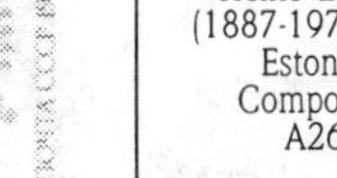

Heino Eller (1887-1970), Estonian Composer A2661

1987, Mar. 7 Litho. *Perf. 12*

5537 A2661 5k buff & brown .25 .15

A2662 A2663

1987, Mar. 8 Photo. *Perf. 11½*

5538 A2662 5k multicolored .25 .15

Souvenir Sheet

Perf. 11½x12

5539 A2662 50k "XX," and colored bands 1.75 .75

All-Union Leninist Young Communist League 20th Congress, Moscow. No. 5539 contains one 26x37mm stamp.

Photogravure and Engraved

1987, Mar. 20 *Perf. 11½*

5540 A2663 5k buff & sepia .25 .15

Iosif Abgarovich rbeli (1887-1961), first president of the Armenian Academy of Sciences.

World Wildlife Fund — A2664

Polar bears.

1987, Mar. 25 Photo. *Perf. 11½x12*

5541 A2664	5k multicolored	.15	.15
a.	Miniature sheet of 8		
5542 A2664	10k multicolored	.30	.15
a.	Miniature sheet of 8		
5543 A2664	20k multicolored	.70	.40
a.	Miniature sheet of 8		
5544 A2664	35k multicolored	1.00	.75
a.	Miniature sheet of 8		
	Nos. 5541-5544 (4)	2.15	1.45

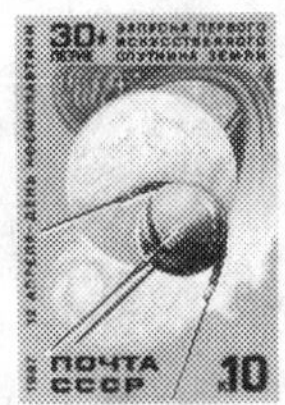

Cosmonauts' Day — A2665

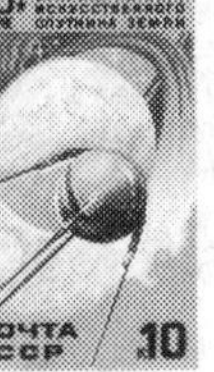

UN Emblem, ESCAP Headquarters, Bangkok — A2666

1987, Apr. 12 *Perf. 11½*

5545 A2665	10k Sputnik, 1957	.35	.15
5546 A2665	10k Vostok 3 and 4, 1962	.35	.15
5547 A2665	10k Mars 1, 1962	.35	.15
a.	Miniature sheet of 8		
	Nos. 5545-5547 (3)	1.05	.45

1987, Apr. 21

5548 A2666 10k multicolored .30 .15

UN Economic and Social Commission for Asia and the Pacific, 40th anniv.

Lenin, 117th Birth Anniv. — A2667

Paintings: No. 5549, Lenin's Birthday, by N.A. Sysoyev. No. 5550, Lenin with Delegates at the 3rd Congress of the Soviet Young Communist League, by P.O. Belousov. No. 5551a, Lenin's Underground Activity (Lenin, lamp), by D.A. Nalbandyan. No. 5551b, Before the Assault (Lenin standing at table), by S.P. Viktorov. No. 5551c, We'll Show the Earth the New Way (Lenin, soldiers, flags), by A.G. Lysenko. No. 5551d, Lenin in Smolny, October 1917 (Lenin seated), by M.G. Sokolov. No. 5551e, Lenin, by N.A. Andreyev.

1987, Apr. 22 Litho. *Perf. 12½x12*

5549 A2667	5k multicolored	.20	.15
5550 A2667	5k multicolored	.20	.15
	Set value		.20

Souvenir Sheet

Perf. 12

5551	Sheet of 5	1.75	.75
a.-e.	A2667 10k any single	.30	.15

Sizes: Nos. 5551a-5551d, 40x28mm; No. 5551e, 40x56mm.

A2668

1987, May 5 Photo. *Perf. 11½*

5552 A2668 10k multicolored .30 .15

European Gymnastics Championships, Moscow, May 18-26.

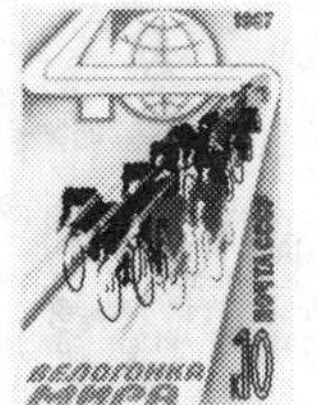

Bicycle Race — A2669

Fauna — A2670

1987, May 6

5553 A2669 10k multicolored .30 .15

40th Peace Bicycle Race, Poland-Czecholsovakia-German Democratic Republic, May.

Perf. 12½x12 (#5554), 12x12½

1987, May 15 Litho.

5554 A2670	5k Menzbira marmot	.15	.15
a.	Miniature sheet of 8	*15.00*	
5555 A2670	10k Bald badger, horiz.	.30	.15

Size: 32x47mm

5556 A2670	15k Snow leopard	.40	.25
	Nos. 5554-5556 (3)	.85	
	Set value		.45

Passenger Ships — A2671

1987, May 20 Photo. *Perf. 12x11½*

5557 A2671	5k Maxim Gorki	.15	.15
5558 A2671	10k Alexander Pushkin	.35	.15
a.	Miniature sheet of 8		
5559 A2671	30k The Soviet Union	1.10	.45
	Nos. 5557-5559 (3)	1.60	.75

Paintings by Foreign Artists in the Hermitage Museum A2672

Designs: 4k, Portrait of a Woman, by Lucas Cranach Sr. (1472-1553). 5k, St. Sebastian, by Titian. 10k, Justice, by Durer. 30k, Adoration of the Magi, by Pieter Brueghel the Younger (c. 1564-1638). 50k, Ceres, by Rubens.

Perf. 12x12½, 12½x12

1987, June 5 Litho.

5560 A2672	4k multicolored	.15	.15
5561 A2672	5k multicolored	.15	.15
a.	Miniature sheet of 8		
5562 A2672	10k multicolored	.40	.15
a.	Miniature sheet of 8		
5563 A2672	30k multicolored	.90	.50
5564 A2672	50k multicolored	1.65	.75
	Nos. 5560-5564 (5)	3.25	1.70

Tolyatti City, 250th Anniv. — A2673

Design: Zhiguli car, Volga Motors factory, Lenin Hydroelectric plant.

1987, June 6 Photo. *Perf. 11½*

5565 A2673 5k multicolored .25 .15

Aleksander Pushkin (1799-1837), Poet — A2674

1987, June 6 Litho.

5566 A2674 5k buff, yel brn & deep brown .25 .15

Printed se-tenant with label.

A2675 A2676

1987, June 7 Engr. *Perf. 12½x12*

5567 A2675 5k black .25 .15

Maj.-Gen. Sidor A. Kovpak (1887-1967), Vice-Chairman of the Ukranian SSR.

1987, June 23 Photo. *Perf. 11½*

5568 A2676 10k multicolored .30 .15

Women's World Congress on Nuclear Disarmament, Moscow, June 23-27.

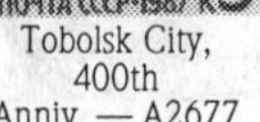

Tobolsk City, 400th Anniv. — A2677

Frelimo, 25th Anniv. — A2678

Design: Tobolsk kremlin, port, theater and Ermak Monument.

1987, June 25

5569 A2677 5k multicolored .25 .15

1987, June 25

5570 A2678 5k Flag of Congo, man .15 .15
5571 A2678 5k Flags of Frelimo, USSR .15 .15
a. Pair, #5570-5571 .30 .30

Mozambique-USSR Peace Treaty, 10th anniv. No. 5571a has continuous design.

Ferns — A2679

A2680

1987, July 2 Litho. *Perf. 12*

5572 A2679 4k Scolopendrium vulgare .15 .15
5573 A2679 5k Ceterach officinarum .15 .15
5574 A2679 10k Salvinia natans, horiz. .40 .15
5575 A2679 15k Matteuccia struthiopteris .50 .30
5576 A2679 50k Adiantum pedatum 1.40 .75
Nos. 5572-5576 (5) 2.60 1.50

1987, July 3

Designs: #5577, Kremlin and 2000 Year-old Coin of India. #5578, Red Fort, Delhi, Soviet hammer & sickle.

5577 A2680 5k shown .15 .15
5578 A2680 5k muticolored .15 .15
a. Pair, #5577-5578 .30 .30

Festivals 1987-88: India in the USSR (No. 5577) and the USSR in India (No. 5578).

15th Intl. Film Festival, July 16-17, Moscow — A2681

1987, July 6 Photo. *Perf. 11½*

5579 2681 10k multicolored .35 .15

Joint Soviet-Syrian Space Flight — A2682

Mir Space Station — A2683

Flags, Intercosmos emblem and: 5k, Cosmonaut training and launch. 10k, Mir space station, Syrian parliament and cosmonauts. 15k, Gagarin Memorial, satellite dishes and cosmonauts wearing space suits.

1987 Litho. *Perf. 12x12½*

5580 A2682 5k multicolored .15 .15
5581 A2682 10k multicolored .25 .15
5582 A2682 15k multicolored .40 .25
Nos. 5580-5582 (3) .80
Set value .45

Souvenir Sheet

5583 A2683 50k multicolored 1.75 .75

Issued: 5k, 7/22; 10k, 7/24; 15k, 50k 7/30.

Intl. Atomic Energy Agency, 30th Anniv. A2684

1987, July 29 Photo. *Perf. 11½*

5584 A2684 20k multicolored .60 .30

14th-16th Century Postrider — A2685

Designs: 5k, 17th cent. postman and 17th cent. kibitka (sled). 10k, 16th-17th cent. ship and 18th cent. packet. 30k, Railway station and 19th cent. mailcars. 35k, AMO-F-15 bus and car, 1905. 50k, Postal headquarters, Moscow, and modern postal delivery trucks.

Photo. & Engr.

1987, Aug. 25 *Perf. 11½x12*

5585 A2685 4k buff & black .15 .15
5586 A2685 5k buff & black .15 .15
5587 A2685 10k buff & black .35 .15
5588 A2685 30k buff & black 1.00 .50
5589 A2685 35k buff & black 1.10 .55
Nos. 5585-5589 (5) 2.75 1.50

Souvenir Sheet

5590 A2685 50k pale yel, dull gray grn & blk 1.75 .90

A2686

October Revolution, 70th Anniv. — A2687

Paintings by Russian artists: No. 5591, Long Live the Socialist Revolution! by V.V. Kuznetsov. No. 5592, V.I. Lenin Proclaims the Soviet Power (Lenin pointing), by V.A. Serov. No. 5593, V.I. Lenin (with pencil), by P.V. Vasiliev. No. 5594, On the Eve of the Storm (Lenin, Trotsky, Dzerzhinski), by V.V. Pimenov. No. 5595, Taking the Winter Palace by Storm, by V.A. Serov.

1987, Aug. 25 Litho. *Perf. 12½x12*

5591 A2686 5k shown .20 .15
5592 A2686 5k multicolored .20 .15
5593 A2686 5k multicolored .20 .15

Size: 70x33mm

Perf. 11½

5594 A2686 5k multicolored .20 .15
5595 A2686 5k multicolored .20 .15
Nos. 5591-5595 (5) 1.00
Set value .50

Souvenir Sheet

Photo. & Engr.

Perf. 12x11½

5596 A2687 30k gold & black 1.50 .45

For overprint see No. 5604.

Souvenir Sheet

Battle of Borodino, 175th Anniv. — A2688

1987, Sept. 7 Litho. *Perf. 12½x12*

5597 A2688 1r black, yel brn & blue gray 3.00 1.50

A2689

A2690

1987, Sept. 18 Engr.

5598 A2689 5k intense blue .25 .15

Pavel Petrovich Postyshev (1887-1939), party leader.

1987, Sept. 19 Photo. *Perf. 11½*

Design: 5k, Monument to founder Yuri Dolgoruki, by sculptor S. Orlov, A. Antropov, N. Stamm and architect V. Andreyev, in Sovetskaya Square, and buildings in Moscow.

5599 A2690 5k dark red brn, cream & dark orange .25 .15

Moscow, 840th anniv.

Scientists — A2691

Designs: No. 5600, Muhammed Taragai Ulugh Begh (1394-1449), Uzbek astronomer and mathematician. No. 5601, Sir Isaac Newton (1642-1727), English physicist and mathematician. No. 5602, Marie Curie (1867-1934), physicist, chemist, Nobel laureate.

1987, Oct. 3 Photo. & Engr.

5600 A2691 5k dk bl, org brn & blk .15 .15
5601 A2691 5k dull grn, blk & dk ultra .15 .15
5602 A2691 5k brown & deep blue .15 .15
Nos. 5600-5602 (3) .45
Set value .30

Nos. 5600-5602 each printed se-tenant with inscribed label.

Souvenir Sheet

COSPAS-SARSAT Intl. Satellite System for Tracking Disabled Planes and Ships — A2692

1987, Oct. 15 Photo.

5603 A2692 50k multicolored 2.25 .75

No. 5595 Overprinted in Gold

Всесоюзная филателистическая выставка „70 лет Великого Октября“

1987, Oct. 17 Litho.

5604 A2686 5k multicolored 1.00 .15

All-Union Philatelic Exhibition and the 70th Anniv. of the October Revolution.

Sheet of 8 No. 5595 has the overprint in the margin.

My Quiet Homeland, by V.M. Sidorov — A2693

The Sun Above Red Square, by P.P. Ossovsky — A2694

Paintings by Soviet artists exhibited at the 7th Republican Art Exhibition, Moscow, 1985: 4k, There Will be Cities in the Taiga, by A.A. Yakovlev. 5k, Mother, by V.V. Shcherbakov. 30k, On Jakutian Soil, by A.N. Osipov. 35k, Ivan's Return, by V.I. Yerofeyev.

Perf. 12x12½, 12½x12

1987, Oct. 20

5605 A2693 4k multi, vert. .15 .15
5606 A2693 5k multi, vert. .15 .15
5607 A2693 10k multicolored .40 .15
5608 A2693 30k multicolored .90 .50
5609 A2693 35k multicolored 1.00 .55
Nos. 5605-5609 (5) 2.60 1.50

Souvenir Sheet

Perf. 11½x12½

5610 A2694 50k multicolored 2.50 1.00

John Reed (1887-1920), American Journalist — A2695

1987, Oct. 22 *Perf. 11½*
5611 A2695 10k buff & dark brown .40 .15

Samuil Yakovlevich Marshak (1887-1964), Author — A2696

1987, Nov. 3 Engr. *Perf. 12½x12*
5612 A2696 5k deep claret .25 .15

A2697

1987, Nov. 8
5613 A2697 5k slate blue .50 .15

Ilja Grigorjevich Chavchavadze (1837-1907), Georgian author.

A2698

A2699

1987, Nov. 19 Photo. *Perf. 11½*
5614 A2698 5k black & brown .25 .15

Indira Gandhi (1917-1984).

1987, Nov. 25 *Perf. 12½x12*
5615 A2699 5k black .25 .15

Vadim Nikolaevich Podbelsky (1887-1920), revolution leader.

A2700

A2701

1987, Nov. 25
5616 A2700 5k dark blue gray .25 .15

Nikolai Ivanovich Vavilov (1887-1943), botantist.

Photo. & Engr.

1987, Nov. 25 *Perf. 11½*

Modern Science: 5k, TOKAMAK, a controlled thermonuclear reactor. 10k, Kola Project (Earth strata study). 20k, RATAN-600 radiotelescope.

5617 A2701 5k grnsh gray & brown .15 .15
5618 A2701 10k dull grn, lt blue gray & dark blue .35 .15
5619 A2701 20k gray olive, blk & buff .70 .30
Nos. 5617-5619 (3) 1.20
Set value .50

US and Soviet Flags, Spasski Tower and US Capitol — A2702

1987, Dec. 17 **Photo.**
5620 A2702 10k multicolored .50 .15

INF Treaty (eliminating intermediate-range nuclear missiles) signed by Gen.-Sec. Gorbachev and Pres. Reagan, Dec. 8.

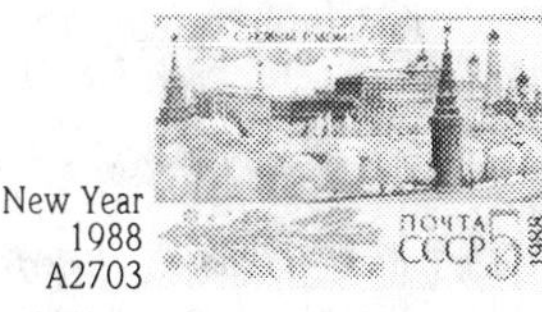

New Year 1988 A2703

1987, Dec. 2 Litho. *Perf. 12x12½*
5621 A2703 5k Kremlin .25 .15
a. Miniature sheet of 8

Marshal Ivan Khristoforovich Bagramyan (1897-1982) — A2704

1987, Dec. 2 Engr. *Perf. 12½x12*
5622 A2704 5k black .25 .15

Miniature Sheet

18th-19th Cent. Naval Commanders and War Ships — A2705

Designs: 4k, Adm. Grigori Andreyevich Spiridov (1713-1790), Battle of Chesmen. 5k, Fedor Fedorovich Ushakov (1745-1817), Storming of Corfu. 10k, Adm. Dimitiri Nikolayevich Senyavin (1763-1831) and flagship at the Battle of Afon off Mt. Athos. 25k, Mikhail Petrovich Lazarev (1788-1851), Battle of Navarin. 30k, Adm. Pavel Stepanovich Nakhimov (1802-1855), Battle of Sinop.

1987, Dec. 22
5623 Sheet of 5 + label 2.50 1.25
a. A2705 4k dark blue & indigo .15 .15
b. A2705 5k maroon & indigo .15 .15
c. A2705 10k maroon & indigo .35 .15
d. A2705 25k dark blue & indigo .80 .40
e. A2705 30k dark blue & indigo 1.00 .50

No. 5623 contains corner label (LR) picturing ensign of period Russian Navy vessels and anchor.
See No. 5850.

A2706

A2707

1987, Dec. 26 Photo. *Perf. 11½*
5624 A2706 10k multicolored .35 .15

Asia-Africa Peoples Solidarity Organization, 30th anniv.

1988, Jan. 4 Photo. *Perf. 11½*
5625 A2707 10k #149, #150 UR .50 .15
5626 A2707 10k #150, #149 UR .50 .15
a. Pair, #5625-5626 1.00 .30

1st Soviet Postage Stamp, 70th anniv. Lettering in brown on No. 5625, in blue on No. 5626.

A2708

A2709

1988, Jan. 4
5627 A2708 5k Biathlon .15 .15
a. Miniature sheet of 8
5628 A2708 10k Cross-country skiing .30 .15
a. Miniature sheet of 8
5629 A2708 15k Slalom .40 .30
a. Miniature sheet of 8
5630 A2708 20k Pairs figure skating .50 .35
a. Miniature sheet of 8
5631 A2708 30k Ski jumping .70 .50
a. Miniature sheet of 8
Nos. 5627-5631 (5) 2.05 1.45

Souvenir Sheet

5632 A2708 50k Ice hockey, horiz. 1.50 1.00

1988 Winter Olympics, Calgary.
For overprint see No. 5665.

1988, Jan. 7
5633 A2709 35k blue & gold 1.00 .65

World Health Org., 40th anniv.

Lord Byron (1788-1824), English Poet — A2710

Photo. & Engr.

1988, Jan. 22 *Perf. 12x11½*
5634 A2710 15k Prus blue, blk & grn black .50 .30

A2711

A2712

1988, Jan. 27 Photo. *Perf. 11½*
5635 A2711 20k multicolored .60 .40

Cultural, Technical and Educational Agreement with the US, 30th anniv.

1988, Feb. 5
5636 A2712 5k black & tan .25 .15

G.I. Lomov-Oppokov (1888-1938), party leader. See Nos. 5649, 5660, 5666, 5673, 5700, 5704, 5721, 5812.

Animated Soviet Cartoons — A2713

1988, Feb. 18 Litho. *Perf. 12½x12*
5637 A2713 1k Little Humpback Horse, 1947 .15 .15
5638 A2713 3k Winnie-the-Pooh, 1969 .15 .15
5639 A2713 4k Gena, the Crocodile, 1969 .15 .15
5640 A2713 5k Just you Wait! 1969 .15 .15
5641 A2713 10k Hedgehog in the Mist, 1975 .30 .20
Nos. 5637-5641 (5) .90
Set value .60

Souvenir Sheet

5642 A2713 30k Post, 1929 1.00 .60

A2714

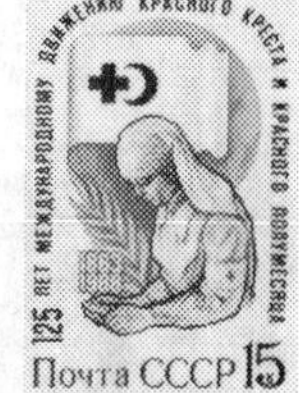

A2715

1988, Feb. 21 Photo. *Perf. 11½*
5643 A2714 10k buff & black .30 .20

Mikhail Alexandrovich Bonch-Bruevich (1888-1940), broadcast engineer.

1988, Feb. 25
5644 A2715 15k blk, brt bl & dk red .50 .30
a. Miniature sheet of 8

Intl. Red Cross and Red Crescent Organizations, 125th annivs.

World Speed Skating Championships, Mar. 5-6, Alma-Ata — A2716

1988, Mar. 13 Photo. *Perf. 11½*
5645 A2716 15k blk, vio & brt blue .45 .30

No. 5645 printed se-tenant with label picturing Alma-Ata skating rink, Medeo.

A2717

1988, Mar. 13 Litho. *Perf. 12½x12*
5646 A2717 10k dark olive green .30 .20

Anton Semenovich Makarenko (1888-1939), teacher, youth development expert.

A2718

A2719

1988, Mar. 17 Engr. *Perf. 12x12½*
5647 A2718 5k gray black .25 .15

Franzisk Skorina (b. 1488), 1st printer in Byelorussia.

1988, Mar. 22 Photo. *Perf. 11½*
5648 A2719 5k multicolored .25 .15

Labor Day.

Party Leader Type of 1988

1988, Mar. 24 Engr. *Perf. 12*

5649 A2712 5k dark green .25 .15

Victor Eduardovich Kingisepp (1888-1922).

Organized Track and Field Events in Russia, Cent. A2721

1988, Mar. 24 Photo. *Perf. 11½*

5650 A2721 15k multicolored .50 .30

Marietta Sergeyevna Shaginyan (1888-1982), Author A2722

1988, Apr. 2 Litho. *Perf. 12½x12*

5651 A2722 10k brown .30 .20

Soviet-Finnish Peace Treaty, 40th Anniv. A2723

1988, Apr. 6 Photo. *Perf. 11½*

5652 A2723 15k multicolored .50 .30

Cosmonaut's Day — A2724

Victory, 1948, Painted by P.A. Krivonogov — A2725

MIR space station, Soyuz TM transport ship, automated cargo ship *Progress* & *Quant* module.

1988, Apr. 12 *Perf. 11½x12*

5653 A2724 15k multicolored .50 .30
a. Miniature sheet of 8

1988, Apr. 20 Litho. *Perf. 12x12½*

5654 A2725 5k multicolored .25 .15

Victory Day (May 9).

Sochi City, 150th Anniv. A2726

1988, Apr. 20 Photo. *Perf. 11½*

5655 A2726 5k multicolored .25 .15

Branches of the Lenin Museum — A2727

Portrait of Lenin and: No. 5656, Central museum, Moscow, opened May 15, 1926. No. 5657, Branch, Leningrad, opened in 1937. No. 5658, Branch, Kiev, opened in 1938. No. 5659, Branch, Krasnoyarsk, opened in 1987.

1988, Apr. 22 Litho. *Perf. 12*

5656 A2727 5k vio brown & gold .20 .15
5657 A2727 5k brn vio, vio brown & gold .20 .15
5658 A2727 5k deep brown olive & gold .20 .15
5659 A2727 5k dark green & gold .20 .15
a. Block of 4, Nos. 5656-5659 .80 .40

See Nos. 5765-5767, 5885-5887.

Party Leader Type of 1988

1988, Apr. 24 Photo. *Perf. 11½*

5660 A2712 5k blue black .25 .15

Ivan Alexeyevich Akulov (1888-1939).

A2729

Karl Marx — A2730

1988, Apr. 30

5661 A2729 20k multicolored .65 .40

EXPO '88, Brisbane, Australia.

1988, May 5 Engr. *Perf. 12*

5662 A2730 5k chocolate .25 .15

Social and Economic Reforms — A2731

Designs: No. 5663, Cruiser *Aurora,* revolutionary soldiers, workers and slogans Speeding Up, Democratization, and Glasnost against Kremlin Palace. No. 5664, Worker, agriculture and industries.

1988, May 5 Photo. *Perf. 12x11½*

5663 A2731 5k multicolored .20 .15
5664 A2731 5k multicolored .20 .15
Set value .20

No. 5632 Ovptd. in Dark Red

Спортсмены СССР завоевали 11 золотых, 9 серебряных и 9 бронзовых медалей!

Souvenir Sheet

1988, May 12 Photo. *Perf. 11½*

5665 A2708 50k multicolored 2.00 1.25

Victory of Soviet athletes at the 1988 Winter Olympics, Calgary. No. 5665 overprinted below stamp on souvenir sheet margin. Soviet sportsmen won 11 gold, 9 silver and 9 bronze medals.

Party Leader Type of 1988

1988, May 19 Engr. *Perf. 12*

5666 A2712 5k black .25 .15

Nikolai Mikhailovich Shvernik (1888-1970).

Hunting Dogs — A2733

Designs: 5k, Russian borzoi, fox hunt. 10k, Kirghiz greyhound, falconry. 15k, Russian retrievers. 20k, Russian spaniel, duck hunt. 35k, East Siberian husky, bear hunt.

1988, May 20 Litho.

5667 A2733 5k multicolored .15 .15
5668 A2733 10k multicolored .35 .25
5669 A2733 15k multicolored .55 .35
5670 A2733 20k multicolored .80 .50
5671 A2733 35k multicolored 1.25 .80
Nos. 5667-5671 (5) 3.10 2.05

A2734

A2736

1988, May 29 Photo. *Perf. 11½*

5672 A2734 5k multicolored .30 .15

Soviet-US Summit Conf., May 29-June 2, Moscow.

Party Leader Type of 1988

1988, June 6 Engr. *Perf. 12*

5673 A2712 5k brown black .25 .15

Valerian Vladimirovich Kuibyshev (1888-1935).

1988, June 7 Photo. *Perf. 11½*

Design: Flags, Mir space station and Soyuz TM spacecraft.

5674 A2736 15k multicolored .50 .35

Shipka '88, USSR-Bulgarian joint space flight, June 7.

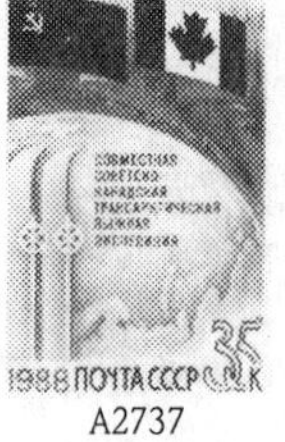

A2737

A2738

Design: Natl. & Canadian flags, skis & obe.

1988, June 16

5675 A2737 35k multicolored 1.25 .80

Soviet-Canada transarctic ski expedition, May-Aug.

1988, June 16

5676 A2738 5k multicolored .25 .15

For a world without nuclear weapons.

A2739

A2740

19th All-union Communist Party Conference, Moscow — A2741

1988, June 16 Litho. *Perf. 12*

5677 A2739 5k multicolored .20 .15

Photo.

Perf. 11½

5678 A2740 5k multicolored .20 .15
Set value .20

Souvenir Sheet

Perf. 11½x12

5679 A2741 50k multicolored 1.75 1.00

1988 Summer Olympics, Seoul A2742

1988, June 29 Litho. *Perf. 12*

5680 A2742 5k Hurdling .15 .15
a. Miniature sheet of 8
5681 A2742 10k Long jump .35 .25
a. Miniature sheet of 8
5682 A2742 15k Basketball .55 .40
a. Miniature sheet of 8
5683 A2742 20k Rhythmic gymnastics .70 .50
a. Miniature sheet of 8
5684 A2742 30k Swimming 1.00 .70
a. Miniature sheet of 8
Nos. 5680-5684 (5) 2.75 2.00

Souvenir Sheet

5685 A2742 50k Soccer 1.75 1.10

For overprint see No. 5722.

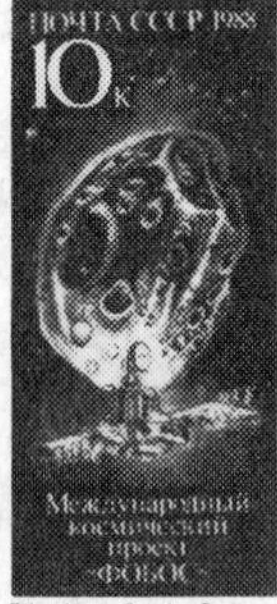

Phobos Intl. Space Project — A2743

Flowers Populating Deciduous Forests — A2744

1988, July 7 Photo. *Perf. 11½x12*

5686 A2743 10k Satellite, space probe .30 .20

For the study of Phobos, a satellite of Mars.

1988, July 7 Litho. *Perf. 12*

5687 A2744 5k Campanula latifolia .15 .15
5688 A2744 10k Orobus vernus, horiz. .35 .25
5689 A2744 15k Pulmonaria obscura .50 .35
5690 A2744 20k Lilium martagon .65 .45
5691 A2744 35k Ficaria verna 1.10 .75
Nos. 5687-5691 (5) 2.75 1.95

A2745

A2746

1988, July 14 Photo. *Perf. 11½*

5692 A2745 5k multicolored .25 .15

Leninist Young Communist League (Komsomol), 70th anniv. For overprint see No. 5699.

1988, July 18

5693 A2746 10k multicolored .30 .20

Nelson Mandela (b. 1918), South African anti-apartheid leader

Paintings in the Timiriazev Equestrian Museum of the Moscow Agricultural Academy — A2747

Paintings: 5k, *Light Gray Arabian Stallion*, by N.E. Sverchkov, 1860. 10k, *Konvoets, a Kabardian*, by M.A. Vrubel, 1882, vert. 15k, *Horsewoman Riding an Orlov-Rastopchinsky*, by N.E. Sverchkov. 20k, *Letuchya, a Gray Orlov Trotter*, by V.A. Serov, 1886, vert. 30k, *Sardar, an Akhaltekinsky Stallion*, by A.B. Villevalde, 1882.

1988, July 20 Litho. *Perf. 12½x12*
5694 A2747 5k multicolored .15 .15
5695 A2747 10k multicolored .30 .20
5696 A2747 15k multicolored .45 .30
5697 A2747 20k multicolored .60 .40
5698 A2747 30k multicolored 1.00 .70
Nos. 5694-5698 (5) 2.50 1.75

No. 5692 Ovptd. for the All-Union Philatelic Exhibition, Moscow, Aug. 10-17 **Филвыставка. Москва**

1988, Aug. 10 Photo. *Perf. 11½*
5699 A2745 5k multicolored .40 .30

Party Leader Type of 1988

1988, Aug. 13 Engr. *Perf. 12½x12*
5700 A2712 5k black .25 .15

Petr Lazarevich Voykov (1888-1927), economic and trade union plenipotentiary.

Intl. Letter-Writing Week A2749

1988, Aug. 25 Photo. *Perf. 11½*
5701 A2749 5k blue grn & dark blue green .25 .15

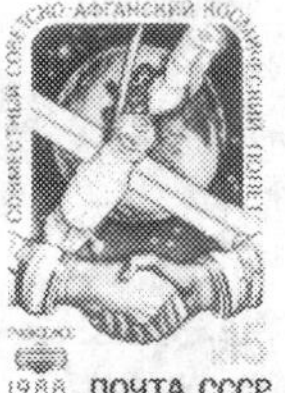

A2750

A2751

1988, Aug. 29
5702 A2750 15k Earth, Mir space station and Soyuz-TM .50 .30

Soviet-Afghan joint space flight.

1988, Sept. 1 Photo. *Perf. 11½*
5703 A2751 10k multicolored .30 .20

Problems of Peace and Socialism magazine, 30th anniv.

Party Leader Type of 1988

1988, Sept. 13 Engr. *Perf. 12*
5704 A2712 5k black .25 .15

Emmanuil Ionovich Kviring (1888-1937).

A2753

A2753a

A2753c

A2753b A2753d

Designs: No. 5705, *Ilya Muromets*, Russian lore. No. 5706, *Ballad of the Cossack Golota*, Ukrainian lore. No. 5707, *Musician-Magician*, a Byelorussian fairy tale. No. 5708, *Koblandy-batyr*, a poem from Kazakh. No. 5709, *Alpamysh*, a fairy tale from Uzbek.

Perf. 12x12½, 12½x12

1988, Sept. 22 Litho.
5705 A2753 10k multicolored .30 .20
5706 A2753a 10k multicolored .30 .20
5707 A2753b 10k multicolored .30 .20
5708 A2753c 10k multicolored .30 .20
5709 A2753d 10k multicolored .30 .20
Nos. 5705-5709 (5) 1.50 1.00

Nos. 5705-5709 each printed se-tenant with inscribed labels. See type A2795.

Appeal of the Leader, 1947, by I.M. Toidze A2754

1988, Oct. 5 *Perf. 12x12½*
5710 A2754 5k multicolored .25 .15

October Revolution, 71st anniv.

A2755 A2756

1988, Oct. 18 Engr. *Perf. 12*
5711 A2755 10k black .30 .20

Andrei Timofeyevich Bolotov (1738-1833), agricultural scientist, publisher.

1988, Oct. 18
5712 A2756 10k steel blue .30 .20

Andrei Nikolayevich Tupolev (1888-1972), aeronautical engineer.

A2757

A2758

Design: 20k, Map of expedition route, atomic icebreaker *Sibirj* and expedition members.

1988, Oct. 25 Litho.
5713 A2757 20k multicolored .60 .40

North Pole expedition (in 1987).
Exists imperf.

1988, Oct. 30 Engr.
5714 A2758 5k brown black .25 .15

Dmitry F. Ustinov (1908-84), minister of defense.

Soviet-Vietnamese Treaty, 10th Anniv. — A2759

1988, Nov. 3 Photo. *Perf. 11½*
5715 A2759 10k multicolored .30 .20

State Broadcasting and Sound Recording Institute, 50th Anniv. A2760

1988, Nov. 3
5716 A2760 10k multicolored .30 .20

UN Declaration of Human Rights, 40th Anniv. A2761

1988, Nov. 21
5717 A2761 10k multicolored .30 .20

New Year 1989 — A2762

Design: Preobrazhensky Regiment bodyguard riding to announce Peter the Great's decree to celebrate new year's eve as of January 1, 1700.

1988, Nov. 24 Litho. *Perf. 12x11½*
5718 A2762 5k multicolored .25 .15

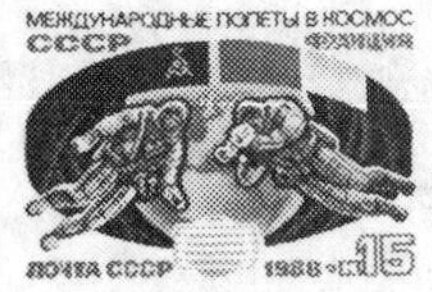

Soviet-French Joint Space Flight A2763

1988, Nov. 26 Photo. *Perf. 11½*
5719 A2763 15k Space walkers .45 .30

No. 4607 Overprinted in Red **КОСМИЧЕСКАЯ ПОЧТА**

1988, Dec. 16 Litho. *Perf. 12½x12*
5720 A2143 1r dark blue 3.50 2.25

Space mail.

Party Leader Type of 1988

1988, Dec. 16 Engr.
5721 A2712 5k slate green .25 .15

Martyn Ivanovich Latsis (1888-1938).

Souvenir Sheet

No. 5685 Overprinted in Bright Blue

СПОРТСМЕНЫ СССР ЗАВОЕВАЛИ
55 ЗОЛОТЫХ, 31 СЕРЕБРЯНУЮ
И 46 БРОНЗОВЫХ МЕДАЛЕЙ
СЕУЛ • 1988

1988, Dec. 20 Litho. *Perf. 12*
5722 A2742 50k multicolored 1.75 1.00

Victory of Soviet athletes at the 1988 Summer Olympics, Seoul. Overprint on margin of No. 5722 specifies that Soviet athletes won 55 gold, 31 silver and 46 bronze medals.

Post Rider A2765

Fountains of Petrodvorets A2766

Designs: 3k, Cruiser *Aurora*. 4k, Spasski Tower, Lenin Mausoleum. 5k, Natl. flag, crest. 10k, *The Worker and the Collective Farmer*, 1935, sculpture by V.I. Mukhina. 15k, Satellite dish. 20k, Lyre, art tools, quill pen, parchment (arts and literature). 25k, *Discobolus*, 5th cent. sculpture by Myron (c. 480-440 B.C.). 30k, Map of the Antarctic, penguins. 35k, *Mercury*, sculpture by Giambologna (1529-1608). 50k, White cranes (nature conservation). 1r, UPU emblem.

1988, Dec. 22 Engr. *Perf. 12x11½*
5723 A2765 1k dark brown .15 .15
5724 A2765 3k dark blue green .15 .15
5725 A2765 4k indigo .15 .15
5726 A2765 5k red .15 .15
5727 A2765 10k claret .30 .20
5728 A2765 15k deep blue .45 .30
5729 A2765 20k olive gray .60 .40
5730 A2765 25k dark green .75 .50
5731 A2765 30k dark blue .90 .60
5732 A2765 35k dark red brown 1.05 .70
5733 A2765 50k sapphire 1.50 1.00

Perf. 12x12½
5734 A2765 1r blue gray 3.00 2.00
Nos. 5723-5734 (12) 9.15 6.30

See Nos. 5838-5849, 5981-5987.

1988, Dec. 25 Engr. *Perf. 11½x12*

Designs: 5k, Samson Fountain, 1723, and Great Cascade. 10k, Adam Fountain, 1722, and sculptures, 1718, by D. Bonazza. 15k, Golden Mountain Cascade, by N. Miketti (1721-1723) and M.G. Zemtsov. 30k, Roman Fountains, 1763. 50k, Oak Tree Fountain, 1735.

5735 A2766 5k myrtle green .15 .15
5736 A2766 10k myrtle green .30 .20
5737 A2766 15k myrtle green .45 .30
5738 A2766 30k myrtle green .90 .60
5739 A2766 50k myrtle green 1.50 1.00
a. Pane of 5, #5735-5739 3.30 2.25

Panes have photogravure margin. Panes are printed bilaterally and separated in the center by perforations so that stamps in the 2nd pane are arranged in reverse order from the 1st pane.

19th Communist Party Congress — A2767

1988, Dec. 30 Photo. *Perf. 12x11½*
Multicolored and:
5740 A2767 5k deep car (power) .20 .15
5741 A2767 5k deep blue vio (industry) .20 .15
5742 A2767 5k green (land) .20 .15
Nos. 5740-5742 (3) .60
Set value .30

Souvenir Sheet

Inaugural Flight of the *Buran* Space Shuttle, Nov. 15 — A2768

1988, Dec. 30 *Perf. 11½x12*
5743 A2768 50k multicolored 1.50 1.00

Luna 1, 30th Anniv. — A2769

1989, Jan. 2 **Photo.** *Perf. 11½*
5744 A2769 15k multicolored .50 .30

Jalmari Virtanen (1889-1939), Karelian Poet — A2770

1989, Jan. 8
5745 A2770 5k olive brown .25 .15

Council for Mutual Economic Assistance, 40th Anniv. A2771

1989, Jan. 8
5746 A2771 10k multicolored .30 .20

Environmental Protection — A2772

1989, Jan. 18 **Litho.** *Perf. 12½x12*
5747 A2772 5k Forest .15 .15
5748 A2772 10k Arctic deer .30 .20
5749 A2772 15k Stop desert encroachment .45 .30
Nos. 5747-5749 (3) .90 .65

Nos. 5747-5749 printed se-tenant with inscribed labels picturing maps.

Samovars — A2773

Samovars in the State Museum, Leningrad: 5k, Pear-shaped urn, late 18th cent. 10k, Barrel-shaped urn by Ivan Listisin, early 19th cent. 20k, "Kabachok" urn by the Sokolov Bros., Tula, c. 1830. 30k, Vase-shaped urn by the Nikolari Malikov Studio, Tula, c. 1840.

1989, Feb. 8 **Photo.** *Perf. 11½*
5750 A2773 5k multicolored .15 .15
5751 A2773 10k multicolored .30 .20
5752 A2773 20k multicolored .60 .40
5753 A2773 30k multicolored .90 .60
Nos. 5750-5753 (4) 1.95 1.35

Modest Petrovich Mussorgsky (1839-1881), Composer — A2774

1989, Feb. 15 **Litho.** *Perf. 12½x12*
5754 A2774 10k dull vio & vio brn .30 .20

P.E. Dybenko (1889-1938), Military Commander — A2775

1989, Feb. 28 **Engr.** *Perf. 12*
5755 A2775 5k black .25 .15

T.G. Shevchenko (1814-1861), Poet A2776

1989, Mar. 6 **Litho.** *Perf. 11½*
5756 A2776 5k pale grn, blk & brn .25 .15

Exists imperf.

Cultivated Lilies — A2777

1989, Mar. 15 *Perf. 12½x12*
5757 A2777 5k Lilium speciosum .15 .15
5758 A2777 10k African queen .30 .20
5759 A2777 15k Eclat du soir .45 .30
5760 A2777 30k White tiger .90 .60
Nos. 5757-5760 (4) 1.80 1.25

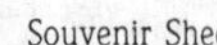

Souvenir Sheet

Labor Day, Cent. — A2778

1989, Mar. 25 *Perf. 11½x12*
5761 A2778 30k multicolored 1.00 .60

Victory Banner, by P. Loginov and V. Pamfilov A2779

1989, Apr. 5 **Litho.** *Perf. 12x12½*
5762 A2779 5k multicolored .25 .15

World War II Victory Day.

Cosmonauts' Day — A2780

Illustration reduced.

1989, Apr. 12 **Photo.** *Perf. 11x11½*
5763 A2780 15k Mir space station .45 .30

A2781

1989, Apr. 14 *Perf. 11½*
5764 A2781 10k multicolored .30 .20

Bering Bridge Soviet-American Expedition, Anadyr and Kotzebue.

Type of 1988

Portraits and branches of the Lenin Central Museum: No. 5765, Kazan. No. 5766, Kuibyshev. No. 5767, Frunze.

1989, Apr. 14 **Litho.** *Perf. 12*
5765 A2727 5k rose brown & multi .20 .15
5766 A2727 5k olive gray & multi .20 .15
5767 A2727 5k deep brown & multi .20 .15
Nos. 5765-5767 (3) .60
Set value .30

Lenin's 119th Birth Anniv.

Souvenir Sheet

Launch of Interplanetary Probe *Phobos* — A2783

1989, Apr. 24 *Perf. 11½x12*
5768 A2783 50k multicolored 1.75 1.00

A2784

A2785

1989, May 5 **Photo.** *Perf. 11½*
5769 A2784 5k multicolored .25 .15

Hungarian Soviet Republic, 70th anniv.

1989, May 5 **Photo. & Engr.**
5770 A2785 5k multicolored .25 .15

Volgograd, 400th anniv.

Honeybees — A2786

1989, May 18 **Litho.** *Perf. 12*
5771 A2786 5k Drone .15 .15
5772 A2786 10k Workers, flowers, man-made hive .30 .20
5773 A2786 20k Worker collecting pollen .65 .40
5774 A2786 35k Queen, drones, honeycomb 1.15 .80
Nos. 5771-5774 (4) 2.25 1.55

No. 5771 exists imperf.

Photography, 150th Anniv. A2787

1989, May 24 **Photo.** *Perf. 11½*
5775 A2787 5k multicolored .25 .15

I.A. Kuratov (1839-1875), Author — A2788

1989, June 26 **Litho.** *Perf. 12½x12*
5776 A2788 5k dark golden brown .25 .15

Jean Racine (1639-1699), French Dramatist A2789

Photo. & Engr.

1989, June 16 *Perf. 12x11½*
5777 A2789 15k multicolored .50 .35

Europe, Our Common Home — A2790

Mukhina, by Nesterov — A2791

Designs: 5k, Map of Europe, stylized bird. 10k, Crane, two men completing a bridge, globe. 15k, Stork's nest, globe.

1989, June 20 Photo. *Perf. 11½*

5778	A2790	5k multicolored	.15	.15
5779	A2790	10k multicolored	.35	.20
5780	A2790	15k multicolored	.50	.35
		Nos. 5778-5780 (3)	1.00	.70

1989, June 25 Litho. *Perf. 12x12½*

5781	A2791	5k chalky blue	.20	.15

Vera I. Mukhina (1889-1953), sculptor.

13th World Youth and Student Festival, Pyongyang — A2792

1989, July 1 Litho. *Perf. 12*

5782	A2792	10k multicolored	.35	.20

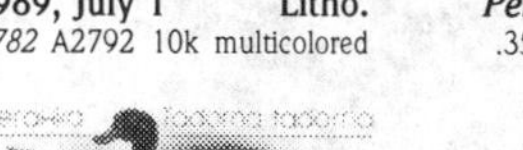

Ducks A2793

1989, July 1

5783	A2793	5k *Tadorna tadorna*	.15	.15
5784	A2793	15k *Anas crecca*	.50	.35
5785	A2793	20k *Tadorna ferruginea*	.65	.50
a.		Min. sheet, 2 5k, 4 15k, 3 20k	4.25	3.00
		Nos. 5783-5785 (3)	1.30	1.00

French Revolution, Bicent. A2794

Designs: 5k, PHILEXFRANCE '89 emblem and Storming of the Bastille. 15k, Marat, Danton, Robespierre. 20k, "La Marseillaise," from the Arc de Triomphe carved by Francois Rude (1784-1855).

Photo. & Engr., Photo. (15k)

1989, July 7 *Perf. 11½*

5786	A2794	5k multicolored	.15	.15
5787	A2794	15k multicolored	.50	.35
5788	A2794	20k multicolored	.65	.45
a.		Miniature sheet of 8	5.25	
		Nos. 5786-5788 (3)	1.30	.95

A2795 A2795a

A2795b A2795c

Folklore and Legends — A2795d

Designs: No. 5789, *Amiraniani,* Georgian lore. No. 5790, *Koroglu,* Azerbaijan lore. No. 5791, *Fir, Queen of the Grass-snakes,* Lithuanian lore. No. 5792, *Mioritsa,* Moldavian lore. No. 5793, *Lachplesis,* Latvian lore.

1989, July 12 Litho. *Perf. 12x12½*

5789	A2795	10k multicolored	.35	.20
5790	A2795a	10k multicolored	.35	.20
5791	A2795b	10k multicolored	.35	.20
5792	A2795c	10k multicolored	.35	.20
5793	A2795d	10k multicolored	.35	.20
		Nos. 5789-5793 (5)	1.75	1.00

Each printed with a se-tenant label. See types A2753-A2753d & #5890-5894.

Tallinn Zoo, 50th Anniv. — A2796

Intl. Letter Writing Week — A2797

1989, July 20 Photo. *Perf. 11½*

5794	A2796	10k Lynx	.35	.20

1989, July 20 Litho. *Perf. 12*

5795	A2797	5k multicolored	.25	.15

Exists imperf.

Pulkovskaya Observatory, 150th Anniv. — A2798

Photo. & Engr.

1989, July 20 *Perf. 11½*

5796	A2798	10k multicolored	.35	.20

Souvenir Sheet

Peter the Great and Battle Scene — A2799

1989, July 27 Photo. *Perf. 11½x12*

5797	A2799	50k dk blue & dk brn	1.75	1.15

Battle of Hango, 275th anniv.

City of Nikolaev, Bicent. A2800

1989, Aug. 3 Photo. *Perf. 11½*

5798	A2800	5k multicolored	.25	.15

80th Birth Anniv. of Kwame Nkrumah, 1st Pres. of Ghana — A2801

1989, Aug. 9

5799	A2801	10k multicolored	.35	.20

6th Congress of the All-Union Philatelic Soc., Moscow A2802

1989, Aug. 9 *Perf. 12*

5800	A2802	10k blue, blac & pink	.35	.20

Printed se-tenant with label picturing simulated stamps and congress emblem.

James Fenimore Cooper (1789-1851), American Novelist A2803

Photo. & Engr.

1989, Aug. 19 *Perf. 12x11½*

5801	A2803	15k multicolored	.50	.35

A2804

Soviet Circus Performers — A2805

Performers and scenes from their acts: 1k, V.L. Durov, clown and trainer. 3k, M.N. Rumyantsev, clown. 4k, V.I. Filatov, bear trainer. 5k, E.T. Kio, magician. 10k, V.E. Lazarenko, acrobat and clown. 30k, Moscow Circus, Tsvetnoi Boulevard.

1989, Aug. 22 Litho. *Perf. 12*

5802	A2804	1k multicolored	.15	.15
5803	A2804	3k multicolored	.15	.15
5804	A2804	4k multicolored	.15	.15
5805	A2804	5k multicolored	.15	.15
5806	A2804	10k multicolored	.35	.20
		Set value	.75	.60

Souvenir Sheet

Perf. 12x12½

5807	A2805	30k multicolored	1.05	.70

Nos. 5802-5806 exist imperf.

A2806 A2807

1989, Aug. 25 Photo. *Perf. 11½*

5808	A2806	15k multicolored	.50	.35

5th World Boxing Championships, Moscow.

1989, Oct. 5 Litho. *Perf. 12x12½*

Design: *Demonstration of the First Radio Receiver,* 1895, by N. Sysoev.

5809	A2807	10k multicolored	.35	.20

Aleksandr Popov (1859-1905), inventor of radio in Russia.

A2808 A2811

Polish People's Republic, 45th Anniv. A2809

1989, Oct. 7 Photo. *Perf. 11½*

5810	A2808	5k multicolored	.25	.15

German Democratic Republic, 40th anniv.

1989, Oct. 7

5811	A2809	5k multicolored	.25	.15

Party Leader Type of 1988

1989, Oct. 10 Engr. *Perf. 12*

5812	A2712	5k black	.25	.15

S.V. Kosior (1889-1939).

1989, Oct. 10

5813	A2811	15k dark red brown	.50	.35

Jawaharlal Nehru, 1st prime minister of independent India.

Guardsmen of October, by M.M. Chepik A2812

1989, Oct. 14 Litho. *Perf. 12½x12*

5814	A2812	5k multicolored	.25	.15

October Revolution, 72nd anniv. Exists imperf.

Kosta Khetagurov (1859-1906), Ossetic Poet A2813

1989, Oct. 14

5815 A2813 5k dark red brown .25 .15

Exists imperf.

A2814 A2815

1989, Oct. 14 Photo. *Perf. 11½*

5816 A2814 5k buff, sepia & black .25 .15

Li Dazhao (1889-1927), communist party leader of China.

1989, Oct. 20 Engr. *Perf. 12*

5817 A2815 5k black .25 .15

Jan Karlovich Berzin (1889-1938), army intelligence leader.

Russian — A2816

Musical Instruments: No. 5819, Byelorussian. No. 5820, Ukrainian. No. 5821, Uzbek.

Photo. & Engr.

1989, Oct. 20 *Perf. 12x11½*

Denomination Color

5818 A2816 10k blue .30 .20
5819 A2816 10k brown .30 .20
5820 A2816 10k lemon .30 .20
5821 A2816 10k blue green .30 .20
Nos. 5818-5821 (4) 1.20 .80

See Nos. 5929-5932, 6047-6049.

Scenes from Novels by James Fenimore Cooper A2817

Designs: No. 5822, *The Hunter,* (settlers, canoe). No. 5823, *Last of the Mohicans* (Indians, settlers). No. 5824, *The Pathfinder,* (couple near cliff). No. 5825, *The Pioneers* (women, wild animals). No. 5826, *The Prairie* (injured Indians, horse).

1989, Nov. 17 Litho. *Perf. 12x12½*

5822 A2817 20k multicolored .65 .40
5823 A2817 20k multicolored .65 .40
5824 A2817 20k multicolored .65 .40
5825 A2817 20k multicolored .65 .40
5826 A2817 20k multicolored .65 .40
a. Strip of 5, #5822-5826 3.25 2.00

Printed in a continuous design.

Monuments — A2818

#5827, Pokrovsky Cathedral, St. Basil's, statue of K. Minin and D. Pozharsky, Moscow. #5828, Petropavlovsky Cathedral, statue of Peter the Great, Leningrad. #5829, Sofiisky Cathedral, Bogdan Chmielnicki monument, Kiev. #5830, Khodzha Akhmed Yasavi Mausoleum, Turkestan. #5831, Khazret-Khyzr Mosque, Samarkand.

1989, Nov. 20 *Perf. 11½*

Color of "Sky"

5827 A2818 15k tan .50 .30
5828 A2818 15k gray green .50 .30
5829 A2818 15k blue green .50 .30
5830 A2818 15k violet blue .50 .30
5831 A2818 15k bright blue .50 .30
Nos. 5827-5831 (5) 2.50 1.50

New Year 1990 A2819

1989, Nov. 22 *Perf. 12*

5832 A2819 5k multicolored .25 .15

Space Achievements A2820

Designs: Nos. 5833, 5837a, Unmanned Soviet probe on the Moon. Nos. 5834, 5837b, American astronaut on Moon, 1969. Nos. 5835, 5837c, Soviet cosmonaut and American astronaut on Mars. Nos. 5836, 5837d, Mars, planetary body, diff.

1989, Nov. 24

5833 A2820 25k multicolored .80 .55
5834 A2820 25k multicolored .80 .55
5835 A2820 25k multicolored .80 .55
5836 A2820 25k multicolored .80 .55
a. Block of 4, #5833-5836 3.25 2.20

Souvenir Sheet

Imperf

5837 Sheet of 4 3.25 2.20
a.-d. A2820 25k any single .80 .55

World Stamp Expo '89, Washington DC, Nov. 17-Dec. 3; 20th UPU Cong.
See US No. C126.

Type of 1988
Dated 1988

1989, Dec. 25 Litho. *Perf. 12x12½*

5838 A2765 1k dark brown .15 .15
5839 A2765 3k dark blue green .15 .15
5840 A2765 4k indigo .15 .15
5841 A2765 5k red .15 .15
5842 A2765 10k claret .30 .20
5843 A2765 15k deep blue .45 .30
5844 A2765 20k olive gray .60 .40
5845 A2765 25k dark green .75 .50
5846 A2765 30k dark blue .90 .60
5847 A2765 35k dark red brown 1.05 .70
5848 A2765 50k sapphire 1.50 1.00
5849 A2765 1r blue gray 3.00 2.00
Nos. 5838-5849 (12) 9.15 6.30

Admirals Type of 1987
Miniature Sheet

Admirals and battle scenes: 5k, V.A. Kornilov (1806-1854). 10k, V.I. Istomin (1809-1855). 15k, G.I. Nevelskoi (1813-1876). 20k, G.I. Butakov (1820-1882). 30k, A.A. Popov (1821-1898). 35k, Stepan O. Makarov (1849-1904).

1989, Dec. 28 Engr. *Perf. 12½x12*

5850 Sheet of 6 3.75 2.45
a. A2705 5k brown & Prus blue .15 .15
b. A2705 10k brown & Prus blue .35 .20
c. A2705 15k dark blue & Prus blue .50 .35
d. A2705 20k dark blue & Prus blue .65 .45
e. A2705 30k brown & Prus blue .95 .65
f. A2705 35k brown & Prus blue 1.10 .75

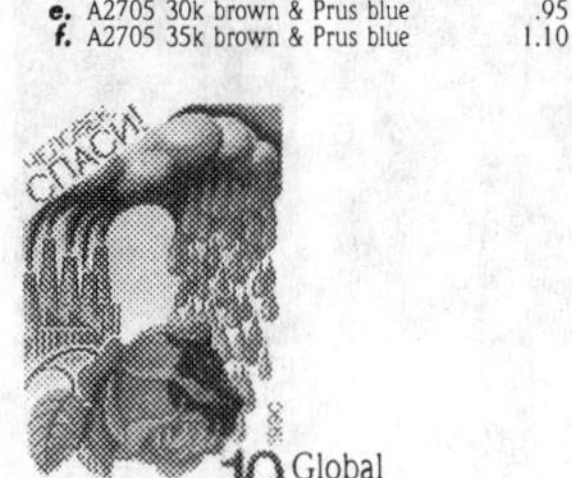

Global Ecology — A2821

Designs: 10k, Flower dying, industrial waste entering the environment. 15k, Bird caught in industrial waste, Earth. 20k, Sea of chopped trees.

1990, Jan. 5 Photo. *Perf. 11½*

5851 A2821 10k multicolored .35 .20
5852 A2821 15k multicolored .50 .35
5853 A2821 20k multicolored .65 .45
Nos. 5851-5853 (3) 1.50 1.00

Capitals of the Republics

A2822 A2822a A2822b
A2822c A2822d A2822e
A2822f A2822g A2822h
A2822i A2822j A2822k
A2822l A2822m A2822n

1990, Jan. 18 Litho. *Perf. 12x12½*

5854 A2822 5k Moscow .20 .15
5855 A2822a 5k Tallinn .20 .15
5856 A2822b 5k Riga .20 .15
5857 A2822c 5k Vilnius .20 .15
5858 A2822d 5k Minsk .20 .15
5859 A2822e 5k Kiev .20 .15
5860 A2822f 5k Kishinev .20 .15
5861 A2822g 5k Tbilisi .20 .15
5862 A2822h 5k Yerevan .20 .15
5863 A2822i 5k Baku .20 .15
5864 A2822j 5k Alma-Ata .20 .15
5865 A2822k 5k Tashkent .20 .15
5866 A2822l 5k Frunze .20 .15
5867 A2822m 5k Ashkhabad .20 .15
5868 A2822n 5k Dushanbe .20 .15
Nos. 5854-5868 (15) 3.00
Set value 1.50

A2823

A2824

1990, Feb. 3 *Perf. 11½*

5869 A2823 10k black & brown .35 .25

Ho Chi Minh (1890-1969).

1990, Feb. 3 Photo.

5870 A2824 5k multicolored .20 .15

Vietnamese Communist Party, 60th anniv.

Owls — A2825

Perf. 12x12½, 12½x12

1990, Feb. 8 Litho.

5871 A2825 10k *Nyctea scandiaca* .35 .20
5872 A2825 20k *Bubo bubo*, vert. .65 .45
5873 A2825 55k *Asio otus* 1.75 1.15
Nos. 5871-5873 (3) 2.75 1.80

Penny Black, 150th Anniv. A2826

Emblems and various Penny Blacks: No. 5875, Position TP. No. 5876, Position TF. No. 5877, Position AH. No. 5878, Position VK. No. 5879, Position AE.

1990, Feb. 15 Photo. *Perf. 11½*

5874 A2826 10k shown .35 .20
5875 A2826 20k gold & black .65 .45
5876 A2826 20k gold & black .65 .45
5877 A2826 35k multicolored 1.10 .75
5878 A2826 35k multicolored 1.10 .75
Nos. 5874-5878 (5) 3.85 2.60

Souvenir Sheet

Perf. 12x11½

5879 A2826 1r dk green & blk 3.25 2.20

Stamp World London '90 (35k).
No. 5879 contains one 37x26mm stamp.

ITU, 125th Anniv. A2827

1990, Feb. 20 Photo. *Perf. 11½*

5880 A2827 20k multicolored .70 .45

Labor Day — A2828

1990, Mar. 28 Photo. *Perf. 11½*

5881 A2828 5k multicolored .20 .15

Victory, 1945, by A. Lysenko A2829

1990, Mar. 28 Litho. *Perf. 12x12½*
5882 A2829 5k multicolored .20 .15

End of World War II, 45th anniv.

Mir Space Station, Cosmonaut A2830

1990, Apr. 12
5883 A2830 20k multicolored .65 .45

Cosmonauts' Day.

Lenin, 120th Birth Anniv. — A2831

1990, Apr. 14 Engr. *Perf. 11½*
5884 A2831 5k red brown .20 .15

LENINIANA '90 all-union philatelic exhibition.

Lenin Birthday Type of 1988

Portrait of Lenin and: No. 5885, Lenin Memorial (birthplace), Ulyanovsk. No. 5886, Branch of the Central Lenin Museum, Baku. No. 5887, Branch of the Central Lenin Museum, Tashkent.

1990, Apr. 14 Litho. *Perf. 12*
5885 A2727 5k dark car & multi .20 .15
5886 A2727 5k rose vio & multi .20 .15
5887 A2727 5k dark grn & multi .20 .15
Nos. 5885-5887 (3) .60 .45

Lenin, 120th Birth Anniv.

Tchaikovsky, Scene from *Iolanta* A2832

1990, Apr. 25 Engr. *Perf. 12½x12*
5888 A2832 15k black .45 .30

Tchaikovsky (1840-1893), composer.

Kalmyk Legend *Dzhangar*, 550th Anniv. — A2833

1990, May 22 Litho. *Perf. 12x12½*
5889 A2833 10k black & black brown .30 .25

Folklore Type of 1989

Designs: No. 5890, *Manas*, Kirghiz legend (Warrior with saber leading battle). No. 5891, *Guraguli*, Tadzhik legend (Armored warriors and elephant). No. 5892, *David Sasunsky*, Armenian legend (Men, arches, vert.). No. 5893, italGerogly, Turkmen legend (Sleeping woman, man with lute, vert.). No. 5894, *Kalevipoeg*, Estonian legend (Man with boards, vert.). Nos. 5890-5894 printed se-tenant with descriptive label.

Perf. 12½x12, 12x12½
1990, May 22
5890 A2795 10k multicolored .30 .20
5891 A2795 10k multicolored .30 .20
5892 A2795 10k multicolored .30 .20
5893 A2795 10k multicolored .30 .20
5894 A2795 10k multicolored .30 .20
Nos. 5890-5894 (5) 1.50 1.00

World Cup Soccer Championships, Italy 1990 — A2834

Various soccer players.

1990, May 25 *Perf. 12x12½*
5895 A2834 5k multicolored .20 .15
5896 A2834 10k multicolored .35 .25
5897 A2834 15k multicolored .45 .30
5898 A2834 25k multicolored .80 .55
5899 A2834 35k multicolored 1.10 .75
a. Strip of 5, #5895-5899 3.00 2.00

A2835

1990, June 5 Litho. *Perf. 11½*
5900 A2835 15k multicolored .45 .30

Final agreement, European Conference on Security and Cooperation, 15th anniv.

45th World Shooting Championships, Moscow — A2836

1990, June 5 Photo.
5901 A2836 15k multicolored .45 .30

Cooperation in Antarctic Research A2837

1990, June 13 Litho. *Perf. 12x12½*
5902 A2837 5k Scientists on ice .20 .15
5903 A2837 50k Krill 1.80 1.20
a. Souv. sheet of 2, #5902-5903 2.00

See Australia Nos. 1182-1183.

Goodwill Games A2838

1990, June 14 Litho. *Perf. 11½*
5904 A2838 10k multicolored .35 .25

Souvenir Sheet

Battle of the Neva River, 750th Anniv. — A2839

1990, June 20 Litho. *Perf. 12½x12*
5905 A2839 50k multicolored 1.75 1.25

Duck Conservation A2840

1990, July 1 Litho. *Perf. 12*
5906 A2840 5k Anas platyrhychos .20 .15
5907 A2840 15k Bucephala clangula .55 .35
5908 A2840 20k Netta rufina .75 .50
Nos. 5906-5908 (3) 1.50 1.00

Poultry A2841

1990, July 1 *Perf. 12x12½*
5909 A2841 5k Obroshinsky geese .20 .15
5910 A2841 10k Adler rooster & hen .35 .25
5911 A2841 15k North Caucasian turkeys .55 .35
Nos. 5909-5911 (3) 1.10 .75

Spaso-Efrosinievsky Monastery, Polotsk — A2842

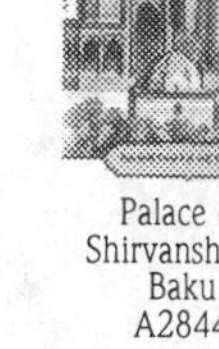

Statue of Nicholas Baratashvili and Pantheon, Mtasminda A2843

Palace of Shirvanshahs, Baku A2844

Statue of Stefan III the Great, Kishinev A2845

St. Nshan's Church, Akhpat A2846

Historic Architecture: No. 5915, Cathedral, Vilnius. No. 5917, St. Peter's Church, Riga. No. 5919, Niguliste Church, Tallinn.

1990, Aug. 1 Litho. *Perf. 11½*
5912 A2842 15k multicolored .55 .35
5913 A2843 15k multicolored .55 .35
5914 A2844 15k multicolored .55 .35
5915 A2842 15k multicolored .55 .35
5916 A2845 15k multicolored .55 .35
5917 A2842 15k multicolored .55 .35
5918 A2846 15k multicolored .55 .35
5919 A2842 15k multicolored .55 .35
Nos. 5912-5919 (8) 4.40 2.80

See Nos. 5968-5970.

Prehistoric Animals — A2847

1990, Aug. 15
5920 A2847 1k Sordes .15 .15
5921 A2847 3k Chalicotherium .15 .15
5922 A2847 5k Indricotherium .20 .15
5923 A2847 10k Saurolophus .35 .25
5924 A2847 20k Thyestes .70 .50
Nos. 5920-5924 (5) 1.55
Set value .95

Nos. 5921-5923 vert.

Indian Child's Drawing of the Kremlin A2848

No. 5926, Russian child's drawing of India.

1990, Aug. 15 *Perf. 12*
5925 A2848 10k multicolored .35 .25
5926 A2848 10k multicolored .35 .25
a. Pair, #5925-5926 .70 .50

See India Nos. 1318-1319.

A2849 A2850

1990, Sept. 12 Engr. *Perf. 12x11½*
5927 A2849 5k blue .20 .15

Letter Writing Week.

1990, Sept. 12 *Perf. 11½*
5928 A2850 5k multicolored .20 .15

Traffic safety.

Musical Instruments Type of 1989

Musical Instruments: No. 5929, Kazakh. No. 5930, Georgian. No. 5931, Azerbaijanian. No. 5932, Lithuanian.

Photo. & Engr.
1990, Sept. 20 *Perf. 12x11½*
Denomination Color
5929 A2816 10k brown .35 .25
5930 A2816 10k green .35 .25
5931 A2816 10k orange .35 .25
5932 A2816 10k blue .35 .25
Nos. 5929-5932 (4) 1.40 1.00

Killer Whales A2855

Northern Sea Lions A2856

Sea Otter A2857

Common Dolphin A2858

1990, Oct. 3 Litho. *Perf. 12x11½*

5933	A2855	25k	multicolored	.80	.55
5934	A2856	25k	multicolored	.80	.55
5935	A2857	25k	multicolored	.80	.55
5936	A2858	25k	multicolored	.80	.55
a.			Block of 4, #5933-5936	3.25	2.25

See US Nos. 2508-2511.

A2859

A2860

Design: Lenin Among the Delegates to the 2nd Congress of Soviets, by S.V. Gerasimov.

1990, Oct. 10 Litho. *Perf. 12x12½*

5937	A2859	5k	multicolored	.20	.15

October Revolution, 73rd Anniv.

1990, Oct. 22 *Perf. 12*

Nobel Laureates in Literature: #5938, Ivan A. Bunin (1870-1953). #5939, Boris Pasternak (1890-1960). #5940, Mikhail A. Sholokov (1905-1984).

5938	A2860	15k	brown olive	.55	.35
5939	A2860	15k	bluish black	.55	.35
5940	A2860	15k	black	.55	.35
			Nos. 5938-5940 (3)	1.65	1.05

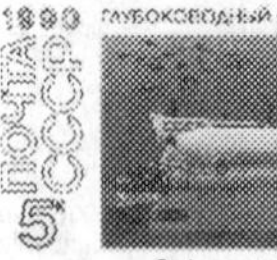

Submarines — A2861

1990, Nov. 14 Litho. *Perf. 12*

5941	A2861	5k	Sever-2	.20	.15
5942	A2861	10k	Tinro-2	.35	.25
5943	A2861	15k	Argus	.55	.35
5944	A2861	25k	Paisis	.90	.60
5945	A2861	35k	Mir	1.25	.85
			Nos. 5941-5945 (5)	3.25	2.20

A2862

A2863

Armenia-Mother Monument by E. Kochar.

1990, Nov. 27 Litho. *Perf. 11½*

5946	A2862	10k	multicolored	.35	.25

Armenia '90 Philatelic Exhibition.

1990, Nov. 29 Photo. *Perf. 11½*

Soviet Agents: #5947, Rudolf I. Abel (1903-71). #5948, Kim Philby (1912-88). #5949, Konon T. Molody (1922-70). #5950, S.A. Vaupshasov (1899-1976). #5951, I.D. Kudrya (1912-42).

5947	A2863	5k	black & brown	.20	.15
5948	A2863	5k	black & bluish blk	.20	.15
5949	A2863	5k	black & yel brown	.20	.15
5950	A2863	5k	black & yel green	.20	.15
5951	A2863	5k	black & brown	.20	.15
			Nos. 5947-5951 (5)	1.00	
			Set value		.60

Joint Soviet-Japanese Space Flight — A2864

1990, Dec. 2 Litho. *Perf. 12*

5952	A2864	20k	multicolored	.70	.50

Happy New Year — A2865

Illustration reduced.

1990, Dec. 3 *Perf. 11½*

5953	A2865	5k	multicolored	.20	.15
b.			Miniature sheet of 8		

Charter for a New Europe — A2865a

1990, Dec. 31 Litho. *Perf. 11½*

5953A	A2865a	30k	Globe, Eiffel Tower	1.10	.80

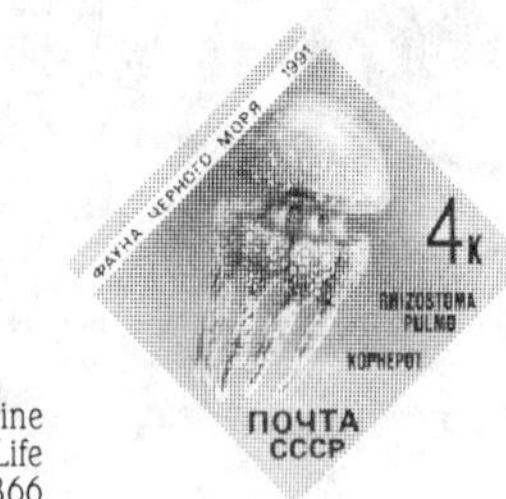

Marine Life A2866

1991, Jan. 4 Litho. *Perf. 12*

5954	A2866	4k	Rhizostoma pulmo	.15	.15
5955	A2866	5k	Anemonia sulcata	.20	.15
5956	A2866	10k	Squalus acanthias	.35	.25
5957	A2866	15k	Engraulis encrasicolus	.55	.40
5958	A2866	20k	Tursiops truncatus	.70	.50
			Nos. 5954-5958 (5)	1.95	1.45

Chernobyl Nuclear Disaster, 5th Anniv. A2867

1991, Jan. 22 *Perf. 11½*

5959	A2867	15k	multicolored	.55	.40

Sorrento Coast with View of Capri, 1826, by S.F. Shchedrin (1791-1830) A2868

Evening in the Ukraine, 1878, by A.I. Kuindzhi (1841-1910) A2869

Paintings: No. 5961, New Rome, St. Angel's Castle, 1823, by Shchedrin. No. 5963, Birch Grove, 1879, by Kuindzhi.

1991, Jan. 25 *Perf. 12½x12*

5960	A2868	10k	multicolored	.35	.25
5961	A2868	10k	multicolored	.35	.25
a.			Pair, #5960-5961+label	.70	.50
5962	A2869	10k	multicolored	.35	.25
5963	A2869	10k	multicolored	.35	.25
a.			Pair, #5962-5963+label	.70	.50
			Nos. 5960-5963 (4)	1.40	1.00

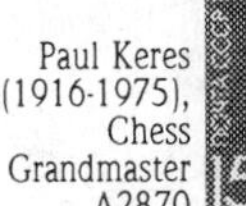

Paul Keres (1916-1975), Chess Grandmaster A2870

1991, Jan. 7 Litho. *Perf. 11½*

5964	A2870	15k	dark brown	.55	.40

Environmental Protection A2871

Designs: 10k, Bell tower near Kaliazin, Volga River region. 15k, Lake Baikal. 20k, Desert zone of former Aral Sea.

1991, Feb. 5 Litho. *Perf. 11½*

5965	A2871	10k	multicolored	.35	.25
5966	A2871	15k	multicolored	.55	.40
5967	A2871	20k	multicolored	.70	.50
			Nos. 5965-5967 (3)	1.60	1.15

Moslem Tower, Uzgen, Kirghizia A2872

Mukhammed Bashar Mausoleum, Tadzhikstan A2873

Talkhatan-baba Mosque, Turkmenistan A2874

1991, Mar. 5

5968	A2872	15k	multicolored	.20	.15
5969	A2873	15k	multicolored	.20	.15
5970	A2874	15k	multicolored	.20	.15
			Nos. 5968-5970 (3)	.60	.45

See Nos. 5912-5919.

Russian Settlements in America — A2875

Designs: 20k, G. I. Shelekhov (1747-1795), Alaska colonizer. 30k, A. A. Baranov, (1746-1819), first governor of Russian America. 50k, I. A. Kuskov, founder of Fort Ross, California.

1991, Mar. 14 *Perf. 12x11½*

5971	A2875	20k	brt blue & black	.70	.50
5972	A2875	30k	olive brn & blk	1.10	.80
5973	A2875	50k	red brn & black	1.80	1.20
			Nos. 5971-5973 (3)	3.60	2.50

Yuri A. Gagarin — A2876

МЕЖДУНАРОДНАЯ ВЫСТАВКА
«ЗВЕЗДАМ-91»
КОСМОС НА СЛУЖБЕ МИРА И ПРОГРЕССА

No. 5977c Inscription

1991, Apr. 6 *Perf. 11½x12*

5974	A2876	25k	Pilot	.90	.70
5975	A2876	25k	Cosmonaut	.90	.70
5976	A2876	25k	Pilot, wearing hat	.90	.70
5977	A2876	25k	As civilian	.90	.70
a.			Block of 4, #5974-5977	3.60	2.80
b.			Sheet of 4, #5974-5977, imperf.	3.60	2.80
c.			As "b," inscribed	3.60	2.80
d.			Sheet, 2 each, #5974-5977, Perf. 12x11½	7.20	5.50

#5977b-5977c have simulated perforations.

May 1945 by A. and S. Tkachev A2877

1991, Apr. 10 *Perf. 12*

5978	A2877	5k	multicolored	.25	.15

World War II Victory Day.

Asia and Pacific Transport Network, 10th Anniv. — A2878

1991, Apr. 15 *Perf. 11½*

5979	A2878	10k	multicolored	.25	.15

Type of 1988 Dated 1991

Designs: 2k, Early ship, train, and carriage. 7k, Airplane, helicopter, ocean liner, cable car, van. 12k, Space shuttle. 13k, Space station.

1991, Apr. 15 Litho. *Perf. 12x12½*

5984	A2765	2k	orange brown	.15	.15
5985	A2765	7k	bright blue	.25	.20
a.			Perf. 12x11½, photo.	.25	.20
5986	A2765	12k	dk lilac rose	.45	.30
5987	A2765	13k	deep violet	.50	.35
			Nos. 5984-5987 (4)	1.35	1.00

For surcharges see Tadjikistan Nos. 10-11.

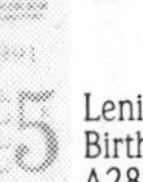

Lenin, 121st Birth Anniv. A2879

Painting: Lenin working on "Materialism and Empirical Criticism" by P.P. Belousov.

1991, Apr. 22 Litho. *Perf. 12*

5992 A2879 5k multicolored .20 .15

Sergei Prokofiev (1891-1953), Composer A2880

1991, Apr. 23 *Perf. 12½x12*

5993 A2880 15k brown .55 .40

Orchids — A2881 A2882

1991, May 7 *Perf. 12*

5994 A2881 3k Cypripedium calceolus .15 .15
5995 A2881 5k Orchis purpurea .20 .15
5996 A2881 10k Ophrys apifera .35 .25
5997 A2881 20k Calypso bulbosa .70 .50
5998 A2881 25k Epipactis palustris .90 .60
Nos. 5994-5998 (5) 2.30 1.65

1991, May 14

Nobel Prize Winners: #5999, Ivan P. Pavlov (1849-1936), 1904, Physiology. #6000, Elie Metchnikoff (1845-1916), 1908, Physiology. #6001, Andrei D. Sakharov, (1921-89), 1975, Peace.

5999 A2882 15k black .55 .40
6000 A2882 15k black .55 .40
6001 A2882 15k blue black .55 .40
Nos. 5999-6001 (3) 1.65 1.20

William Saroyan (1908-1981), American Writer A2883

1991, May 22 *Perf. 11½*

6002 A2883 1r multicolored 3.60 2.75

See US No. 2538.

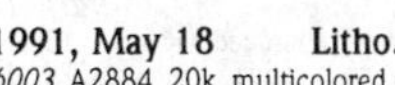

Russia-Great Britain Joint Space Mission A2884

1991, May 18 Litho. *Perf. 12*

6003 A2884 20k multicolored .70 .50

Cultural Heritage A2885

Designs: 10k, Miniature from "Ostomirov Gospel," by Sts. Cyril & Methodius, 1056-1057. 15k, "Russian Truth," manuscript, 11th-13th century by Jaroslav Mudrin. 20k, Sergei Radonezhski by Troitse Sergeiev Lavra, 1424. 25k, Trinity, icon by Andrei Rublev, c. 1411. 30k, Illustration from "Book of the Apostles," by Ivan Feodorov and Petr Mstislavetz, 1564.

1991, June 20 Litho. *Perf. 12x12½*

6004 A2885 10k multicolored .35 .25
6005 A2885 15k multicolored .55 .35
6006 A2885 20k multicolored .70 .50
6007 A2885 25k multicolored .90 .60
6008 A2885 30k multicolored 1.10 .80
a. Strip of #6004-6008 3.60 2.50

Ducks A2886

Designs: 5k, Anas acuta. 15k, Aythya marila. 20k, Oxyura leucocephala.

1991, July 1 *Perf. 12*

6009 A2886 5k multicolored .20 .15
6010 A2886 15k multicolored .55 .40
6011 A2886 20k multicolored .70 .50
a. Min. sheet of 9, 2 #6009, 4 #6010, 3 #6011 4.75 3.25
Nos. 6009-6011 (3) 1.45 1.05

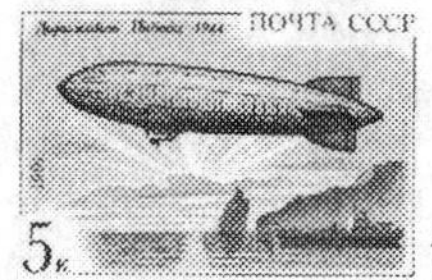

Airships A2887

Designs: 1k, Albatross, 1910, vert. 3k, GA-42, 1987, vert. 4k, Norge, 1923. 5k, Victory, 1944. 20k, Graf Zeppelin, 1928.

1991, July 18

6012 A2887 1k multicolored .15 .15
6013 A2887 3k multicolored .15 .15
6014 A2887 4k multicolored .15 .15
6015 A2887 5k multicolored .20 .15
6016 A2887 20k multicolored .70 .50
a. Miniature sheet of 8
Nos. 6012-6016 (5) 1.35
Set value .90

Types of 1984

1991-92 Litho. *Imperf.*

6016B A2529 2r Ship, Arctic map .40 .20

Perf. 12½x12

6017 A2529 3r Child & globe 1.25 .80
6017A A2529 5r Palm frond and globe 5.75 3.75
Nos. 6016B-6017A (3) 7.40 4.75

Issued: 3r, 6/25; 5r, 11/10; 2r, 4/20/92.

Conf. on Security and Cooperation in Europe — A2088

1991, July 1 Photo. *Perf. 11½*

6018 A2888 10k multicolored .25 .15

Bering & Chirikov's Voyage to Alaska, 250th Anniv. — A2889

Design: No. 6020, Sailing ship, map.

1991, July 27 *Perf. 12x11½*

6019 A2889 30k multicolored .40 .25
6020 A2889 30k multicolored .40 .25

A2890 A2891

1991, Aug. 1 *Perf. 12*

6021 A2890 30k multicolored .40 .25

Ukrainian declaration of sovereignty.

1991, Aug. 1 *Perf. 12x11½*

6022 A2891 7k brown .25 .15

Letter Writing Week.

1992 Summer Olympic Games, Barcelona A2892

1991, Sept. 4 Litho. *Perf. 12x12½*

6023 A2892 10k Canoeing .15 .15
a. Miniature sheet of 8
6024 A2892 20k Running .25 .15
a. Miniature sheet of 8
6025 A2892 30k Soccer .40 .25
a. Miniature sheet of 8
Nos. 6023-6025 (3) .80 .55

Victims of Aug. 1991 Failed Coup — A2893

Citizens Protecting Russian "White House" — A2893a

1991, Oct. 11 Litho. *Perf. 11½*

6026 A2893 7k Vladimir Usov, b. 1954 .15 .15
6027 A2893 7k Illya Krichevsky, b. 1963 .15 .15
6028 A2893 7k Dmitry Komar, b. 1968 .15 .15
Nos. 6026-6028 (3) .45
Set value .30

Souvenir Sheet

6029 A2893a 50k multicolored .75 .35

USSR-Austria Joint Space Mission A2894

1991, Oct. 2 Litho. *Perf. 11½*

6030 A2894 20k multicolored .25 .15

Folk Holidays

Ascension, Armenia A2895

New Year, Azerbaijan A2895a

Ivan Kupala Day, Byelorussia A2895b

Berikaoba, Georgia A2895d

New Year, Estonia A2895c

Kazakhstan — A2895e

Kys Kumai, Kirgizia A2895f

Ivan Kupala Day, Latvia A2895g

Palm Sunday, Lithuania A2895h

Plugushorul, Moldavia A2895i

Shrovetide, Russia A2895j

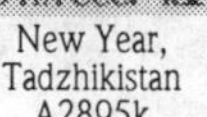

New Year, Tadzhikistan
A2895k

Spring Tulips, Uzbekistan
A2895n

Harvest, Turkmenistan — A2895l

Christmas, Ukraine — A2895m

Perf. 12x12½, 12½x12

1991, Oct. 4 **Litho.**

6031 A2895 15k multicolored .20 .15
6032 A2895a 15k multicolored .20 .15
6033 A2895b 15k multicolored .20 .15
6034 A2895c 15k multicolored .20 .15
6035 A2895d 15k multicolored .20 .15
6036 A2895e 15k multicolored .20 .15
6037 A2895f 15k multicolored .20 .15
6038 A2895g 15k multicolored .20 .15
6039 A2895h 15k multicolored .20 .15
6040 A2895i 15k multicolored .20 .15
6041 A2895j 15k multicolored .20 .15
6042 A2895k 15k multicolored .20 .15
6043 A2895l 15k multicolored .20 .15
6044 A2895m 15k multicolored .20 .15
6045 A2895n 15k multicolored .20 .15
a. Min. sheet, 2 each #6031-6045 *11.25*
Nos. 6031-6045 (15) 3.00
Set value 1.75

A2896

1991, Oct. 29 **Litho.** ***Perf. 11½***

6046 A2896 7k multicolored .25 .15

Election of Boris Yeltsin, 1st president of Russian Republic, June 12, 1991.

Musical Instruments Type of 1989

Musical Instruments: No. 6048, Moldavia. No. 6049, Latvia. No. 6050, Kirgiz.

Photo. & Engr.

1991, Nov. 19 ***Perf. 12x11½***

Denomination Color

6047 A2816 10k red .15 .15
6048 A2816 10k brt greenish blue .15 .15
6049 A2816 10k red lilac .15 .15
Nos. 6047-6049 (3) .45 .45

New Year 1992 — A2897

1991, Dec. 8 **Litho.** ***Perf. 12x12½***

6050 A2897 7k multicolored .25 .15

A2899

A2900

Russian Historians: #6052, V. N. Tatischev (1686-1750). #6053, N. M. Karamzin (1766-1826). #6054, S. M. Soloviev (1820-79). #6055, V. O. Kluchevski (1844-1911).

1991, Dec. 12 **Photo. & Engr.**

6052 A2899 10k multicolored .15 .15
6053 A2899 10k multicolored .15 .15
6054 A2899 10k multicolored .15 .15
6055 A2899 10k multicolored .15 .15
Nos. 6052-6055 (4) .60 .60

With the breakup of the Soviet Union on Dec. 26, 1991, eleven former Soviet republics established the Commonwealth of Independent States. Stamps inscribed "Rossija" are issued by the Russian Republic.

1992, Jan. 10 **Litho.** ***Perf. 11½x12***

6056 A2900 14k Cross-country skiing, ski jumping .20 .15
a. Miniature sheet of 8
6057 A2900 1r Freestyle skiing .25 .15
a. Miniature sheet of 8
6058 A2900 2r Bobsleds .55 .25
a. Miniature sheet of 8
Nos. 6056-6058 (3) 1.00
Set value .40

1992 Winter Olympics, Albertville.

Souvenir Sheet

Battle on the Ice, 750th Anniv. — A2901

1992, Feb. 20 **Litho.** ***Perf. 12½x12***

6059 A2901 50k multicolored .75 .15

A2902

Designs: 10k, Golden Portal, Vladimir. 15k, Kremlin, Pskov. 20k, Georgy the Victor. 25k, 55k, Triumph Gate, Moscow. 30k, "Millennium of Russia," by M.O. Mikeshin, Novgorod. 50k, St. George Slaying the Dragon. 60k, Minin-Posharsky Monument, Moscow. 80k, "Millenium of Russia," by M.O. Mikeshin, Novgorod. 1r, Church, Kizki. 1.50r, Monument to Peter the Great, St. Petersburg. 2r, St. Basil's Cathedral, Moscow. 3r, Tretyakov Gallery, Moscow. 5r, Morosov House, Moscow. 10r, St. Isaac's Cathedral, St. Petersburg. 25r, Monument to Yuri Dolgoruky, Moscow. 100r, Kremlin, Moscow.

Perf. 12½x12, 11½x12 (15k, 25k, 3r)

1992 **Litho.**

6060 A2902 10k salmon .15 .15
6060A A2902 15k dark brown .15 .15
6061 A2902 20k red .15 .15
6062 A2902 25k red brown .15 .15
6063 A2902 30k black .15 .15
6064 A2902 50k dark blue .15 .15
6065 A2902 55k dark blue green .15 .15
6066 A2902 60k blue green .15 .15
6066A A2902 80k lake .15 .15
6067 A2902 1r yel brown .15 .15
6067A A2902 1.50r olive .25 .15
6068 A2902 2r blue .45 .35
6068A A2902 3r red .30 .25
6069 A2902 5r dark brown .75 .55
6070 A2902 10r bright blue 1.50 1.00
6071 A2902 25r dark red 3.75 2.75
6071A A2902 100r bright olive 15.00 10.00
Nos. 6060-6071A (17) 23.50 16.55

Issued: 20k, 30k, 2/26; 10k, 60k, 2r, 4/20; 25r, 5/25; 10r, 100r, May; 1r, 1.50r, 5r, 6/25; 55k, 8/11; 50k, 80k, 8/18; 15k, 25k, 3r, 9/10.

See Nos. 6111-6121.

Victory by N. N. Baskakov — A2903

1992, Mar. 5 ***Perf. 12x12½***

6072 A2903 5k multicolored .25 .15

End of World War II, 47th anniv.

Prioksko-Terrasny Nature Reserve — A2904

1992, Mar. 12 ***Perf. 12***

6073 A2904 50k multicolored .25 .15

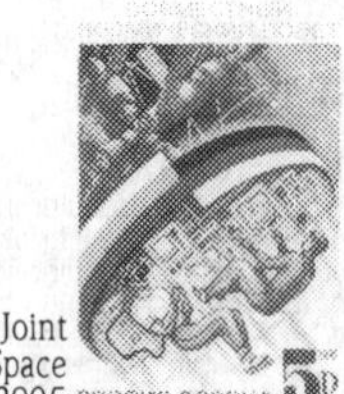

Russia-Germany Joint Space Mission — A2905

1992, Mar. 17

6074 A2905 5r multicolored 1.00 .60

Souvenir Sheet

Discovery of America, 500th Anniv. — A2906

1992, Mar. 18 ***Perf. 12x11½***

6075 A2906 3r Ship, Columbus .60 .40

Characters from Children's Books — A2907

1992, Apr. 22 **Litho.** ***Perf. 12***

6076 A2907 25k Pinocchio .15 .15
6077 A2907 30k Cipollino .15 .15
6078 A2907 35k Dunno .15 .15
6079 A2907 50k Karlson .15 .15
Nos. 6076-6079 (4) .60
Set value .40

Space Accomplishments
A2908

Designs: No. 6081, Astronaut, Russian space station and space shuttle. No. 6082, Sputnik, Vostok, Apollo Command and Lunar modules. No. 6083, Soyuz, Mercury and Gemini spacecraft.

1992, May 29 **Litho.** ***Perf. 11½x12***

6080 A2908 25r multicolored 1.00 .75
6081 A2908 25r multicolored 1.00 .75
6082 A2908 25r multicolored 1.00 .75
6083 A2908 25r multicolored 1.00 .75
a. Block of 4, #6080-6083 4.00 3.00

See US Nos. 2631-2634.

1992 Summer Olympics, Barcelona
A2909

Perf. 11½x12, 12x11½

1992, June 5 **Photo.**

6084 A2909 1r Team handball, vert. .20 .15
a. Miniature sheet of 8 .85 .65
6085 A2909 2r Fencing .25 .15
a. Miniature sheet of 8 1.70 1.30
6086 A2909 3r Judo .40 .25
a. Miniature sheet of 8 2.50 1.90
Nos. 6084-6086 (3) .85 .55

Explorers — A2910

Designs: 55r, L. A. Zagoskin, Alaska-Yukon. 70r, N. N. Miklucho-Maklai, New Guinea. 1r, G. I. Langsdorf, Brazil.

1992, June 23 **Litho.** ***Perf. 12x11½***

6087 A2910 55k multicolored .15 .15
6088 A2910 70k multicolored .15 .15
6089 A2910 1r multicolored .15 .15
Nos. 6087-6089 (3) .45
Set value .30

Ducks
A2911

1992, July 1 ***Perf. 12***

6090 A2911 1r Anas querquedula .15 .15
6091 A2911 2r Aythya ferina .20 .15
6092 A2911 3r Anas falcata .30 .25
a. Min. sheet of 9, 3 #6090, 4 #6091, 2 #6092 3.40
Nos. 6090-6092 (3) .65 .55

The Saviour, by Andrei Rublev
A2912

1992, July 3 ***Perf. 12x12½***

6093 A2912 1r multicolored .25 .15
a. Miniature sheet of 8 *2.00*

The Taj Mahal Mausoleum in Agra, by Vasili Vereshchagin (1842-1904) — A2913

Design: No. 6095, Let Me Approach (detail), by Vereshchagin.

1992, July 3 *Perf. 12½x12*

6094 A2913 1.50r multicolored .25 .15
6095 A2913 1.50r multicolored .25 .15
a. Pair, #6094-6095 + label .50 .25

Cathedral of the Assumption, Moscow — A2914

Cathedral of the Annunciation, Moscow — A2915

No. 6098, Archangel Cathedral, Moscow.

1992, Sept. 3 **Litho.** *Perf. 11½*

6096 A2914 1r multicolored .15 .15
a. Miniature sheet of 9 1.10
6097 A2915 1r multicolored .15 .15
a. Miniature sheet of 9 1.10
6098 A2915 1r multicolored .15 .15
a. Miniature sheet of 9 1.10
Nos. 6096-6098 (3) .45
Set value .30

The Nutcracker, by Tchaikovsky, Cent. A2916

Designs: No. 6099, Nutcrackers, one holding rifle. No. 6100, Nutcrackers, diff. No. 6101, Pas de deux before Christmas tree. No. 6102, Ballet scene.

1992, Nov. 4 **Litho.** *Perf. 12½x12*

6099 A2916 10r multicolored .40 .30
6100 A2916 10r multicolored .40 .30
6101 A2916 25r multicolored 1.00 .75
6102 A2916 25r multicolored 1.00 .75
a. Block of 4, #6099-6102 2.80 2.10

A2917 A2918

A2919 A2920

Christmas

Icons: No. 6103, Joachim and Anna, 16th cent. No. 6104, Madonna and Child, 14th cent. No. 6105, Archangel Gabriel, 12th cent. No. 6106, St. Nicholas, 16th cent.

1992, Nov. 27 *Perf. 11½*

6103 A2917 10r multicolored .45 .35
6104 A2918 10r multicolored .45 .35
6105 A2919 10r multicolored .45 .35
6106 A2920 10r multicolored .45 .35
a. Block of 4, #6103-6106 1.80 1.40

See Sweden Nos. 1979-1982.

New Year 1993 — A2921

1992, Dec. 2 **Litho.** *Perf. 12x12½*

6107 A2921 50k multicolored .25 .15
a. Miniature sheet of 9 2.25

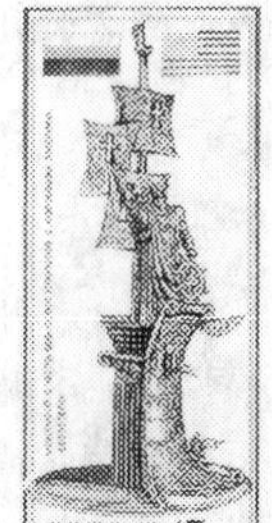

Discovery of America, 500th Anniv. — A2922

1992, Dec. 29 *Perf. 11½x12*

6108 A2922 15r Flags, sculpture .40 .30

Monuments Type of 1992

Designs: 4r, Church, Kizki. 6r, Monument to Peter the Great, St. Petersburg. 15r, 45r, The Horsebreaker, St. Petersburg. 50r, Kremlin, Rostov. 75r, Monument to Yuri Dolgoruky, Moscow. 150r, Golden Gate of Vladimir. 250r, Church, Bogolubova. 300r, Monument of Minin and Pozharsky. 500r, Lomonosov University, Moscow. 750r, State Library, Moscow. 1000r, Fortress of St. Peter and St. Paul, St. Petersburg. 1500r, Pushkin Museum, Moscow. 2500r, Admiralty, St. Petersburg. 5000r, Bolshoi Theater, Moscow.

Perf. 12½x12, 12x11½ (1000r)
Litho., Photo. (50r, 250r, 500r)
1992-95

6109 A2902 4r red brown .15 .15
6110 A2902 6r gray blue .15 .15
6111 A2902 15r brown .40 .30
a. Photo. .40 .30
6113 A2902 45r slate 1.15 .85
6114 A2902 50r purple 1.30 .95
6115 A2902 75r red brown 1.95 1.40
6118 A2902 150r blue .40 .25
6119 A2902 250r green 6.50 4.75
6120 A2902 300r red brown .75 .45
6121 A2902 500r violet 13.00 9.50
6122 A2902 750r olive green .65 .50
6123 A2902 1000r slate .65 .50
6124 A2902 1500r green 1.50 1.10
6125 A2902 2500r olive brown 2.50 1.90
6125A A2902 5000r blue green 5.00 3.75
Nos. 6109-6125A (15) 36.05 26.50

Values are as of date issued. Denominations still available may be sold at much lower prices.

Issued: #6111a, 6114, 6119, 6121, 12/25/92; #6109-6110, 6/4/93; #6113, 6115, 1/25/93; 150r, 300r, 12/30/93; 1000r, 1/27/95; 750r, 1500r, 2500r, 5000r, 2/21/95.

This is an expanding set. Numbers may change.

Marius Petipa (1818-1910), Choreographer — A2923

Ballets: No. 6126, Paquita (1847). No. 6127, Sleeping Beauty (1890). No. 6128, Swan Lake (1895). No. 6129, Raymonda (1898).

1993, Jan. 14 **Litho.** *Perf. 12½x12*

6126 A2923 25r multicolored .50 .30
6127 A2923 25r multicolored .50 .30
6128 A2923 25r multicolored .50 .30
6129 A2923 25r multicolored .50 .30
a. Block of 4, #6126-6129 2.00 1.25

A2924 A2925

Characters from Children's Books: a, 2r, Scrub and Rub. b, 3r, Big Cockroach. c, 10r, The Buzzer Fly. d, 15r, Doctor Doolittle. e, 25r, Barmalei.

1993, Feb. 25 **Litho.** *Perf. 12½x12*

6130 A2924 Strip of 5, #a.-e. .85 .65

No. 6130 printed in continuous design.

1993, Mar. 18 **Photo.** *Perf. 11½x12*

6131 A2925 10r Vyborg Castle .40 .30

City of Vyborg, 700th anniv.

Battle of Kursk, 50th Anniv. A2926

1993, Mar. 25 *Perf. 12x12½*

6132 A2926 10r multicolored .20 .15

Victory Day.

A2927 A2928

Flowers

1993, Mar. 25 *Perf. 12½x12*

6133 A2927 10r Saintpaulia ionantha .15 .15
6134 A2927 15r Hibiscus rosa-sinensis .15 .15
6135 A2927 25r Cyclamen persicum .25 .15
6136 A2927 50r Fuchsia hybrida .45 .30
6137 A2927 100r Begonia semperflorens .90 .60
Nos. 6133-6137 (5) 1.90 1.35

See Nos. 6196-6200.

1993, Apr. 12 **Photo.** *Perf. 11½*

Communications satellites.

6138 A2928 25r Molniya-3 .20 .15
6139 A2928 45r Ekran-M .35 .25
6140 A2928 50r Gorizont .40 .30
6141 A2928 75r Luch .60 .40
6142 A2928 100r Express .80 .55
Nos. 6138-6142 (5) 2.35 1.65

Souvenir Sheet

Perf. 12x11½

6143 A2928 250r Ground station, horiz. 2.10 1.40

No. 6143 contains one 37x26mm stamp.

Antique Silver — A2929

Designs: 15r, Snuff box, 1820, mug, 1849. 25r, Tea pot, 1896-1908. 45r, Vase, 1896-1908. 75r, Tray, candlestick holder, 1896-1908. 100r, Coffee pot, cream and sugar set, 1852. 250r, Sweet dish, 1896-1908, biscuit dish, 1844.

1993, May 5 **Litho.** *Perf. 11½*

6144 A2929 15r multicolored .15 .15
6145 A2929 25r multicolored .25 .15
6146 A2929 45r multicolored .45 .30
6147 A2929 75r multicolored .75 .50
6148 A2929 100r multicolored 1.00 .65
Nos. 6144-6148 (5) 2.60 1.75

Souvenir Sheet

Perf. 12½x12

6149 A2929 250r multicolored 2.50 1.65

No. 6149 contains one 52x37mm stamp.

Novgorod Kremlin
A2930 A2931

Designs: No. 6150, Kremlin towers, 14th-17th cent. No. 6151, St. Sofia's Temple, 11th cent. No. 6152, Belfry of St. Sophia's, 15th-18th cent. 250r, Icon, "Sign of the Virgin," 12th cent.

1993, June 4 **Litho.** *Perf. 12*

6150 A2930 25r multicolored .25 .15
6151 A2931 25r multicolored .25 .15
6152 A2931 25r multicolored .25 .15
Nos. 6150-6152 (3) .75

Souvenir Sheet

Perf. 12½x12

6153 A2930 250r multicolored 2.50 1.65

No. 6153 contains one 42x30mm stamp.

Russian-Danish Relations, 500th Anniv. — A2932

1993, June 17 *Perf. 11½*

6154 A2932 90r green & light green .55 .35

See Denmark No. 985.

Ducks A2933

Designs: 90r, Somateria stelleri. 100r, Somateria mollissima. 250r, Somateria spectabilis.

1993, July 1 **Litho.** *Perf. 12*

6155 A2933 90r multicolored .15 .15
6156 A2933 100r multicolored .20 .15
6157 A2933 250r multicolored .45 .30
a. Min. sheet, 4 each #6155-6156, 1 #6157 5.00
Nos. 6155-6157 (3) .80 .60

Sea Life A2934

1993, July 6

6158 A2934 50r Pusa hispida .25 .15
6159 A2934 60r Paralithodes brevipes .35 .25
6160 A2934 90r Todarodes pacificus .50 .35
6161 A2934 100r Oncorhynchus masu .55 .40
6162 A2934 250r Fulmarus glacialis 1.25 .90
Nos. 6158-6162 (5) 2.90 2.05

Natl. Museum of Applied Arts and Folk Crafts, Moscow — A2935

Designs: No. 6163, Skopino earthenware candlestick. No. 6164, Painted tray, horiz. No. 6165, Painted box, distaff. No. 6166, Enamel icon of St. Dmitry of Solun. 250r, Fedoskino lacquer miniature Easter egg depicting the Resurrection.

Perf. 12x12½, 12½x12

1993, Aug. 11 **Litho.**

6163 A2935 50r multicolored .25 .15
6164 A2935 50r multicolored .25 .15
6165 A2935 100r multicolored .55 .35

6166 A2935 100r multicolored .55 .35
6167 A2935 250r multicolored 1.25 .80
Nos. 6163-6167 (5) 2.85 1.80

Goznak (Bank Note Printer and Mint), 175th Anniv. — A2936

1993, Sept. 2 **Litho.** ***Perf. 12***

6168 A2936 100r multicolored .60 .40

Shipbuilders — A2937

Designs: No. 6169, Peter the Great (1672-1725), Goto Predestinatsia. No. 6170, K.A. Shilder (1786-1854), first all-metal submarine. No. 6171, I.A. Amosov (1800-1878), screw steamship Archimedes. No. 6172, I.G. Bubnov (1872-1919), submarine Bars. No. 6173, B.M. Malinin (1889-1949), submarine Dekabrist. No. 6174, A.I. Maslov (1894-1968), cruiser Kirov.

1993, Sept. 7

6169 A2937 100r multicolored .55 .35
6170 A2937 100r multicolored .55 .35
6171 A2937 100r multicolored .55 .35
6172 A2937 100r multicolored .55 .35
6173 A2937 100r multicolored .55 .35
6174 A2937 100r multicolored .55 .35
a. Block of 6, #6169-6174 3.30 2.25

Moscow Kremlin
A2938 A2939

Designs: No. 6175, Granovitaya Chamber (1487-91). No. 6176, Church of Rizpolozheniye (1484-88). No. 6177, Teremnoi Palace (1635-36).

1993, Oct. 28 **Litho.** ***Perf. 12***

6175 A2938 100r multicolored .40 .25
6176 A2939 100r multicolored .40 .25
6177 A2939 100r multicolored .40 .25
Nos. 6175-6177 (3) 1.20 .75

Panthera Tigris A2940

Designs: 100r, Adult in woods. 250r, Two cubs. 500r, Adult in snow.

1993, Nov. 25 **Litho.** ***Perf. 12½x12***

6178 A2940 50r multicolored .15 .15
6179 A2940 100r multicolored .25 .15
6180 A2940 250r multicolored .60 .40
6181 A2940 500r multicolored 1.25 .85
a. Block of 4, #6178-6181 2.25 1.50
b. Miniature sheet, 2 #6181a 4.50

World Wildlife Fund.

New Year 1994 — A2941

1993, Dec. 2 **Photo.** ***Perf. 11½***

6182 A2941 25r multicolored .25 .15
a. Sheet of 8 2.10

A2942 Wildlife — A2943

1993, Nov. 25 **Photo.** ***Perf. 11½x12***

6183 A2942 90r gray, black & red .35 .20

Prevention of AIDS.

1993, Dec. 30 **Litho.** ***Perf. 12½x12***

6184 A2943 250r Phascolarctos cinereus .45 .30
6185 A2943 250r Monachus schauinslandi .45 .30
6186 A2943 250r Haliaeetus leucocephalus .45 .30
6187 A2943 250r Elephas maximus .45 .30
6188 A2943 250r Grus vipio .45 .30
6189 A2943 250r Ailuropoda melanoleuca .45 .30
6190 A2943 250r Phocoenoides dalli .45 .30
6191 A2943 250r Eschrichtius robustus .45 .30
a. Miniature sheet of 8, #6184-6191 6.00
Nos. 6184-6191 (8) 3.60 2.40

Nikolai Rimsky-Korsakov (1844-1908), Scene from "Sadko" — A2944

Scenes from operas: No. 6193, "Golden Cockerel," 1907. No. 6194, "The Czar's Bride," 1898. No. 6195, "The Snow Maiden," 1881.

1994, Jan. 20 **Litho.** ***Perf. 12½x12***

6192 A2944 250r multicolored .45 .30
6193 A2944 250r multicolored .45 .30
6194 A2944 250r multicolored .45 .30
6195 A2944 250r multicolored .45 .30
a. Block of 4, #6192-6195 1.80 1.25

Flower Type of 1993

Designs: 50r, Epiphyllum peacockii. No. 6197, Mammillaria swinglei. No. 6198, Lophophora williamsii. No. 6199, Opuntia basilaris. No. 6200, Selenicereus grandiflorus.

1994, Feb. 25 **Litho.** ***Perf. 12½x12***

6196 A2927 50r multicolored .15 .15
6197 A2927 100r multicolored .20 .15
6198 A2927 100r multicolored .20 .15
6199 A2927 250r multicolored .50 .30
6200 A2927 250r multicolored .50 .30
Nos. 6196-6200 (5) 1.55 1.05

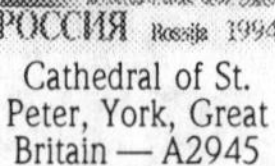

Cathedral of St. Peter, York, Great Britain — A2945

Metropolis Church, Athens — A2946

Gothic Church, Roskilde, Denmark — A2947

Notre Dame Cathedral, Paris — A2948

St. Peter's Basilica, Vatican City — A2949

Cologne Cathedral, Germany — A2950

St. Basil's Cathedral, Moscow — A2951

Seville Cathedral, Spain — A2952

#6207, St. Patrick's Cathedral, NYC, US.

1994, Mar. 24 **Litho.** ***Perf. 12x12½***

6201 A2945 150r multicolored .25 .15
6202 A2946 150r multicolored .25 .15
6203 A2947 150r multicolored .25 .15
6204 A2948 150r multicolored .25 .15
6205 A2949 150r multicolored .25 .15
6206 A2950 150r multicolored .25 .15
6207 A2950 150r multicolored .25 .15
6208 A2951 150r multicolored .25 .15
6209 A2952 150r multicolored .25 .15
a. Miniature sheet of 9, #6201-6209 *2.25*

Space Research A2953

Designs: 100r, TS-18 Centrifuge, Soyuz landing module during re-entry. 250r, Soyuz spacecraft docked at Mir space station. 500r, Training in hydrolaboratory, cosmonaut during space walk.

1994, Apr. 12 **Litho.** ***Perf. 12x11½***

6210 A2953 100r multicolored .15 .15
6211 A2953 250r multicolored .45 .30
6212 A2953 500r multicolored .85 .60
Nos. 6210-6212 (3) *1.45 1.05*

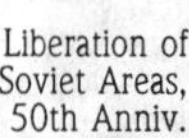

Liberation of Soviet Areas, 50th Anniv. A2954

Battle maps and: a, Katyusha rockets, liberation of Russia. b, Fighter planes, liberation of Ukraine. c, Combined offensive, liberation of Belarus.

1994, Apr. 26 ***Perf. 12***

6213 A2954 100r Block of 3 + label .60 .35

See Belarus No. 78, Ukraine No. 195.

Russian Architecture A2955

Structure, architect: 50r, Krasniye Vorota, Moscow, Prince D.V. Ukhtomsky (1719-74). 100r, Academy of Science, St. Petersburg, Giacomo Quarenghi (1744-1817). 150r, Trinity Cathedral, St. Petersburg, V.P. Stasov (1769-1848). 300r, Church of Christ the Saviour, Moscow, K.A. Ton (1794-1881).

1994, May 25 **Litho.** ***Perf. 12½x12***

6214 A2955 50r lt brown & blk .15 .15
6215 A2955 100r red brown & blk .15 .15
6216 A2955 150r olive green & blk .25 .15
6217 A2955 300r gray violet & blk .50 .35
Nos. 6214-6217 (4) 1.05 .80

Painting Type of 1992

Paintings by V. D. Polenov (1844-1927): No. 6218, Christ and the Adultress, 1886-87. No. 6219, Golden Autumn, 1893.

1994, June 1 **Litho.** ***Perf. 12½x12***

6218 A2913 150r multicolored .25 .15
6219 A2913 150r multicolored .25 .15
a. Pair, #6218-6219 + label .50 .30

Ducks A2956

1994, July 1 ***Perf. 12***

6220 A2956 150r Anas penelope .25 .15
6221 A2956 250r Aythya fuligula .40 .25
6222 A2956 300r Anas formosa .50 .35
a. Min. sheet, 3 #6220, 4 #6221, 2 #6222 3.00 2.00
b. As "a," overprinted 3.00 2.00
Nos. 6220-6222 (3) 1.15 .75

No. 6222b is overprinted in sheet margin: "World Philatelic Exhibition Moscow-97" in Cyrillic and Latin with four exhibition emblems.

A2957 A2958

1994, July 5 **Photo.** ***Perf. 11½x12***

6223 A2957 100r multicolored .25 .15

1994 Goodwill Games, St. Petersburg.

1994, July 5 **Litho.** ***Perf. 12***

Nobel Prize Winners in Physics: No. 6224, P.L. Kapitsa (1894-1984). No. 6225, P.A. Cherenkov (1904-90).

6224 A2958 150r sepia .25 .15
6225 A2958 150r sepia .25 .15

Intl. Olympic Committee, Cent. A2959

1994, July 5

6226	A2959	250r multicolored	.35	.15

Russian Postal Day — A2960

1994, July 8 *Perf. 11½x12*

6227	A2960	125r multicolored	.20	.15

Porcelain A2961

Designs: 50r, Snuff box, 1752. 100r, Candlestick, 1750-1760. 150r, Statue of watercarrier, 1818. 250r, Vase, 19th cent. 300r, Statue of lady with mask, 1910. 500r, Monogramed dinner service, 1848.

1994, Aug. 10 Litho. *Perf. 11½*

6228	A2961	50r multicolored	.15	.15
a.		Min. sheet of 9	.70	.65
b.		As "a," overprinted	.70	.65
6229	A2961	100r multicolored	.15	.15
6230	A2961	150r multicolored	.25	.15
6231	A2961	250r multicolored	.40	.25
6232	A2961	300r multicolored	.45	.30
		Nos. 6228-6232 (5)	1.40	1.00

Souvenir Sheet

6233	A2961	500r multicolored	1.00	.75

No. 6228b is overprinted in sheet margin: "World Philatelic Exhibition Moscow 97" in Cyrillic and Latin with four exhibition logos.

Integration of Tuva into Russia, 50th Anniv. — A2962

1994, Oct. 13 Photo. *Perf. 11½x12*

6234	A2962	125r multicolored	.20	.15

Russian Voyages of Exploration — A2963

Sailing ships and: No. 6235, V.M. Golovnin, Kurile Islands expedition, 1811. No. 6236, I.F. Kruzenstern, trans-global expedition, 1803-06. No. 6237, F.P. Wrangel, North American expedition, 1829-35. No. 6238, F.P. Litke, Novaya Zemlya expedition, 1821-24.

Photo. & Engr.

1994, Nov. 22 *Perf. 12x11½*

6235	A2963	250r multicolored	.20	.15
6236	A2963	250r multicolored	.20	.15
a.		Miniature sheet of 8	1.60	1.10
6237	A2963	250r multicolored	.20	.15
6238	A2963	250r multicolored	.20	.15
		Nos. 6235-6238 (4)	.80	.60

Russian Fleet, 300th anniv. (#6236a).

New Year 1995 — A2964

1994, Dec. 6 Photo. *Perf. 12x11½*

6239	A2964	125r multicolored	.20	.15
a.		Min. sheet of 8	1.60	.80

Alexander Griboedov (1795-1829), Poet, Diplomat A2965

1995, Jan. 5 Litho. *Perf. 11½*

6240	A2965	250r sepia & black	.25	.15

No. 6240 printed se-tenant with label.

A2966

Mikhail Fokine (1880-1942), Choreographer — A2967

Scenes from ballets: No. 6241, Scheherazade. No. 6242, The Fire Bird. No. 6243, Petrouchka.

1995, Jan. 18 Litho. *Perf. 12½x12*

6241	A2966	500r multicolored	.35	.25
6242	A2967	500r multicolored	.35	.25
6243	A2967	500r multicolored	.35	.25
a.		Block of 3 + label	1.05	.75

Mikhail Kutuzov (1745-1813), Field Marshal — A2968

1995, Jan. 20

6244	A2968	300r multicolored	.25	.15
a.		Miniature sheet of 8	2.00	1.25

16th-17th Cent. Architecture, Moscow A2969

Designs: 125r, English Yard, Varvarka St. 250r, Averki Kirillov's house, Bersenevskaya Embankment. 300r, Volkov's house, Kharitonievsky Lane.

1995, Feb. 15 Litho. *Perf. 12x12½*

6245	A2969	125r multicolored	.15	.15
6246	A2969	250r multicolored	.25	.15
6247	A2969	300r multicolored	.30	.15
a.		Min. sheet, 2 #6245, 4 #6246, 3 #6247	1.75	1.10
b.		Min. sheet. as "a," diff. margin	1.75	1.10
		Nos. 6245-6247 (3)	.70	.45

Sheeet margin on No. 6247b has emblems and inscriptions in Cyrillic and Latin for "World Philatelic Exhibition Moscow '97."

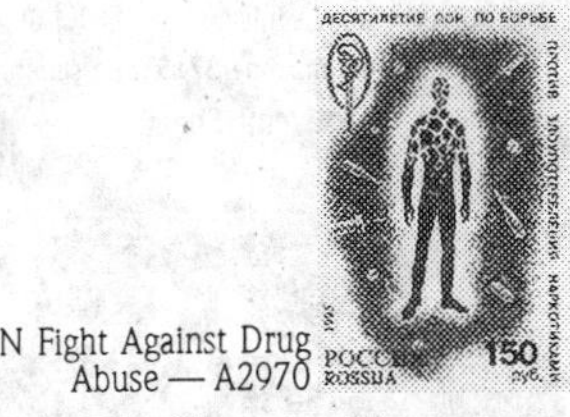

UN Fight Against Drug Abuse — A2970

1995, Mar. 1 *Perf. 12½x12*

6248	A2970	150r multicolored	.20	.15

Endangered Species A2971

a, Lake. b, Pusa hispida. c, Lynx. d, River, trees.

1995, Mar. 1 *Perf. 12x12½*

6249	A2971	250r Block of 4, #a.-d.	.75	.50

Nos. 6249a-6249b, 6249c-6249d are continuous designs. See Finland No. 960.

End of World War II, 50th Anniv. A2972

#6250, Churchill, Roosevelt, Stalin at Yalta. #6251, Ruins of Reichstag, Berlin. #6252, Monument to concentration camp victims. #6253, Tomb of the Unknown Soldier, Moscow, vert. #6254, Potsdam Conference, map of divided Germany, vert. #6255, Russian planes over Manchuria. #6256, Victory parade, Moscow, vert.

1995, Apr. 7 *Perf. 12x12½, 12½x12*

6250	A2972	250r multicolored	.25	.15
6251	A2972	250r multicolored	.25	.15
6252	A2972	250r multicolored	.25	.15
6253	A2972	250r multicolored	.25	.15
6254	A2972	250r multicolored	.25	.15
6255	A2972	250r multicolored	.25	.15

Size: 37x52mm

6256	A2972	500r multicolored	.50	.35
a.		Souv. sheet of 1, perf 11½x12	1.75	1.25
		Nos. 6250-6256 (7)	2.00	1.25

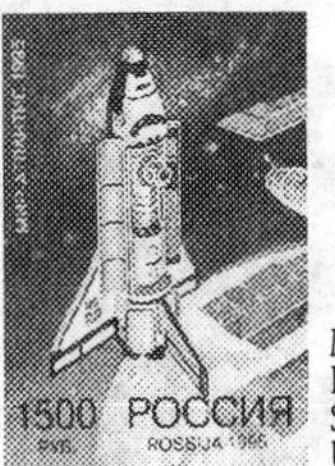

MIR-Space Shuttle Docking, Apollo-Soyuz Link-Up — A2973

a, Space shuttle Atlantis. b, MIR space station. c, Apollo command module. d, Soyuz spacecraft.

1995, June 29 Litho. *Perf. 12x12½*

6257	A2973	1500r Block of 4, #a.-d.	6.00	4.00

No. 6257 is a continuous design.

Radio, Cent. A2974

Design: 250r, Alexander Popov (1859-1905), radio-telegraph.

1995, May 3 Litho. *Perf. 11½*

6258	A2974	250r multicolored	.20	.15

Flowers — A2975

Songbirds — A2976

#6259, Campanula patula. #6260, Leucanthemum vulgare. #6261, Trifolium pratense. #6262, Centaurea jacea. 500r, Geranium pratense.

1995, May 18 Litho. *Perf. 12½x12*

6259	A2975	250r multicolored	.15	.15
6260	A2975	250r multicolored	.15	.15
6261	A2975	300r multicolored	.20	.15
a.		Min. sheet of 8	3.25	
b.		As "a," different margin	3.25	
6262	A2975	300r multicolored	.20	.15
6263	A2975	500r multicolored	.30	.20
		Nos. 6259-6263 (5)	1.00	.80

No. 6261b has emblems and inscriptions in Cyrillic and Latin for "World Philatelic Exhibition Moscow '97."

1995, June 15 Litho. *Perf. 12½x12*

6264	A2976	250r Alauda arvensis	.15	.15
6265	A2976	250r Turdus philomelos	.15	.15
6266	A2976	500r Carduelis carduelis	.35	.25
6267	A2976	500r Cyanosylvia svecica	.35	.25
6268	A2976	750r Luscinia luscinia	.50	.40
a.		Min. sheet, 2 each #6264-6265, 1 #6268 + label	1.25	.85
a.		Min. sheet, 2 each #6266-6267, 1 #6268 + label	1.75	1.40
		Nos. 6264-6268 (5)	1.50	1.20

St. Trinity, Jerusalem A2977

Sts. Peter & Paul, Karlovy Vary A2978

St. Nicholas, Vienna — A2979

St. Nicholas, New York — A2980

Russian Orthodox Churches abroad: 750r, St. Alexei, Leipzig.

1995, July 5 Litho. *Perf. 12x12½*

6269	A2977	300r multicolored	.20	.15
6270	A2978	300r multicolored	.20	.15
6271	A2979	500r multicolored	.30	.20
6272	A2980	500r multicolored	.30	.20
6273	A2980	750r multicolored	.45	.35
a.		Min. sheet, 2 each #6269-6273	3.00	2.25
		Nos. 6269-6273 (5)	1.45	1.05

Principality of Ryazan, 900th Anniv. — A2981

1995, July 20 Photo. *Perf. 11½*

6274	A2981	250r Kremlin Cathedral	.15	.15

Fabergé Jewelry in Kremlin Museums A2982

Designs: 150r, Easter egg, 1909, St. Petersburg. 250r, Goblet, 1899-1908, Moscow. 300r, Cross, 1899-1908, St. Petersburg. 600r, Ladle, 1890, Moscow. 750r, Easter egg, 1910, St. Petersburg. 1500r, Easter egg, 1904-06, St. Petersburg.

1995, Aug. 15 Litho. *Perf. 11½*

6275	A2982	150r multicolored	.15	.15
6276	A2982	250r multicolored	.20	.15
6277	A2982	300r multicolored	.20	.15
6278	A2982	500r multicolored	.35	.25
6279	A2982	750r multicolored	.50	.40
		Nos. 6275-6279 (5)	1.40	1.10

Souvenir Sheet

6280	A2982	1500r multicolored	1.00	.75

No. 6280 contains one 37x51mm stamp.

Souvenir Sheet

Singapore '95 — A2983

Illustration reduced.

1995, Sept. 1 *Perf. 12½x12*

6281	A2983	2500r multicolored	1.50	1.10

Ducks A2984

Designs: 500r, Histrionicus histrionicus. 750r, Aythya baeri. 1000r, Mergus merganser.

1995, Sept. 1 *Perf. 12*

6284	A2984	500r multicolored	.35	.25
6285	A2984	750r multicolored	.50	.40
6286	A2984	1000r multicolored	.70	.55
a.		Miniature sheet, 2 #6284, 4 #6285, 3 #6286	4.75	3.75
		Nos. 6284-6286 (3)	1.55	1.20

Russian Fleet, 300th Anniv. — A2985

Paintings: 250r, Battle of Grengam, 1720. 300r, Bay of Cesme, 1770. 500r, Battle of Revel Roadstead, 1790. 750r, Kronstadt Roadstead, 1840.

1995, Sept. 14 Litho. *Perf. 12*

6287	A2985	250r multicolored	.15	.15
6288	A2985	300r multicolored	.20	.15
6289	A2985	500r multicolored	.30	.20
6290	A2985	750r multicolored	.45	.35
		Nos. 6287-6290 (4)	1.10	.85

Arms & Flag of the Russian Federation — A2986

UN, 50th Anniv. — A2987

1995, Oct. 4 Litho. *Perf. 12x12½*

6291	A2986	500r multicolored	.30	.25

No. 6291 is printed with se-tenant label.

1995, Oct. 4

6292	A2987	500r multicolored	.30	.25

Peace and Freedom A2988

Europa: No. 6293, Storks in nest, countryside. No. 6294, Stork in flight.

1995, Nov. 15 Litho. *Perf. 12x12½*

6293	A2988	1500r multicolored	.90	.70
6294	A2988	1500r multicolored	.90	.70
a.		Pair, Nos. 6293-6294	1.80	1.40

No. 6294a is a continuous design.

Christmas A2989

1995, Dec. 1 *Perf. 12*

6295	A2989	500r multicolored	.30	.25

A2990

A2990a

A2990b

Early Russian Dukes — A2990c

Designs: No. 6296, Yuri Dolgorouki (1090-1157), Duke of Souzdal, Grand Duke of Kiev, founder of Moscow. No. 6297, Alexander Nevski (1220-63), Duke of Novgorod, Grand Duke of Vladimir. No. 6298, Michael Alexandrovitsch (1333-39), Prince of Tver. No. 6299, Dimitri Donskoi (1350-89), Duke of Moscow, Vladimir. No. 6300, Ivan III (1440-1505), Grand Duke of Moscow.

Illustrations reduced.

1995, Dec. 21 Litho. & Engr. *Perf. 12*

6296	A2990	1000r multicolored	.60	.45
6297	A2990a	1000r multicolored	.60	.45
6298	A2990b	1000r multicolored	.60	.45
6299	A2990c	1000r multicolored	.60	.45
6300	A2990c	1000r multicolored	.60	.45
		Nos. 6296-6300 (5)	3.00	2.25

A2991

A2992

1996, Jan. 31 Litho. *Perf. 12*

6301	A2991	750r dull olive black	.45	.35

Nikolai N. Semenov (1896-1986), chemist.

1996, Feb. 22 Litho. *Perf. 12*

Flowers: 500r, Viola wittrockiana. No. 6303, Dianthus barbatus. No. 6304, Lathyrus odoratus. No. 6305, Fritillaria imperialis. No. 6306, Antirrhinum majus.

6302	A2992	500r multicolored	.30	.25
6303	A2992	750r multicolored	.45	.35
6304	A2992	750r multicolored	.45	.35
6305	A2992	1000r multicolored	.60	.45
6306	A2992	1000r multicolored	.60	.45
a.		Min. sheet of 20, 4 each #6302-6306 + 4 labels	9.75	7.50
		Nos. 6302-6306 (5)	2.40	1.85

Domestic Cats — A2993

Designs: No. 6307, European tiger. No. 6308, Russian blue. No. 6309, Persian white. No. 6310, Siamese. No. 6311, Siberian.

1996, Mar. 21

Color of Background

6307	A2993	1000r orange	.60	.45
6308	A2993	1000r brown	.60	.45
6309	A2993	1000r red	.60	.45
6310	A2993	1000r blue violet	.60	.45
6311	A2993	1000r green	.60	.45
a.		Sheet of 2 each, #6307-6311	7.50	
		Nos. 6307-6311 (5)	3.00	2.25

Souvenir Sheet

Modern Olympic Games, Cent. — A2994

Illustration reduced.

1996, Mar. 27

6312	A2994	5000r multicolored	3.00	3.00

Victory Day — A2995

Design: Painting, "Plunged Down Banners," by A. S. Mikhailov. Illustration reduced.

1996, Apr. 19 Litho. *Perf. 12*

6313	A2995	1000r multicolored	.50	.35
a.		Sheet of 8 + label	5.00	

Tula, 850th Anniv. A2996

1996, May 14 *Perf. 12½x12*
6314 A2996 1500r Tula Kremlin .75 .55

Russian Trams A2997

Designs: 500r, Putilovsky plant. No. 6316, Sormovo, 1912. No. 6317, "X" series, 1928. No. 6318, "KM" series, 1931. No. 6319, LM-57, 1957. 2500r, Model 71-608 K, 1993.

1996, May 16 Photo. *Perf. 11½*
6315 A2997 500r multicolored .25 .20
6316 A2997 750r multicolored .35 .25
6317 A2997 750r multicolored .35 .25
6318 A2997 1000r multicolored .50 .35
6319 A2997 1000r multicolored .50 .35
6320 A2997 2500r multicolored 1.20 .90
a. Souvenir sheet 1.20 .90
b. Sheet of 6 7.25
Nos. 6315-6320 (6) 3.15 2.30

A2998

A2999

Europa (Famous Women): No. 6321, E.R. Daschkova (1711-1810), scientist. No. 6322, S.V. Kovalevskaya (1820-91), mathematician.

1996, May 20 Litho. *Perf. 12x12½*
6321 A2998 1500r green & black .60 .30
6322 A2998 1500r lilac & black .60 .30

1996, June 1 Litho. *Perf. 12½x12*
6323 A2999 1000r multicolored .50 .35

UNICEF, 50th anniv.

Summer, by P.P. Sokolov A3000

Post Troika, by P.N. Gruzinsky A3001

Design: No. 6326, Winter, by Sokolov.

1996, June 14
6324 A3000 1500r multicolored .75 .60
6325 A3001 1500r multicolored .75 .60
6326 A3000 1500r multicolored .75 .60
Nos. 6324-6326 (3) 2.25 1.80

Moscow, 850th Anniv. — A3002

Paintings of urban views: No. 6327, Yauza River, 1790's. No. 6328, Kremlin Palace, 1797. No. 6329, Kamenny Bridge, 1811. No. 6330, Volkhonka Steet, 1830's. No. 6331, Vorvarka St. 1830-40's. No. 6332, Petrovsky Park, troikas.

1996, June 20 Litho. *Perf. 12*
6327 A3002 500r multicolored .20 .15
6328 A3002 500r multicolored .20 .15
6329 A3002 750r multicolored .35 .25
6330 A3002 750r multicolored .35 .25
6331 A3002 1000r multicolored .40 .20
a. Sheet of 2 each, #6327, 6330-6331 2.50
6332 A3002 1000r multicolored .40 .20
a. Sheet of 2 each, #6328-6329, 6332 2.50
b. Sheet of 6, #6327-6332 2.50
Nos. 6327-6332 (6) 1.90 1.20

Traffic Police, 60th Anniv. A3003

a, Pedestrian crossing guard. b, Children receiving traffic safety education. c, Officer writing citation.

1996, July 3 Litho. *Perf. 12x12½*
6333 A3003 1500r Sheet of 3, #a.-c. 1.10 .55

1996 Summer Olympic Games, Atlanta — A3004

1996, July 10 *Perf. 12*
6334 A3004 500r Basketball .20 .15
6335 A3004 1000r Boxing .40 .20
6336 A3004 1000r Swimming .40 .20
6337 A3004 1500r Women's gymnastics .60 .30
6338 A3004 1500r Hurdles .60 .30
a. Sheet of 8 4.75
Nos. 6334-6338 (5) 2.20 1.15

A3005

Russian Navy, 300th Anniv. A3006

Ships: 750r, Yevstafy, 1762. No. 6340, Petropavlovsk, 1894. No. 6341, Novik, 1913. Nos. 6342, 6346a, Galera, 1696. Nos. 6343, 6346d, Aircraft carrier Admiral Kuznetzov, 1985. No. 6344, Tashkent, 1937. No. 6345, Submarine C-13, 1939.

No. 6346: b, Atomic submarine, 1981. c, Sailing ship Azov, 1826.

1996, July 26 Litho. & Engr. *Perf. 12*
6339 A3005 750r multicolored .25 .15
6340 A3005 1000r multicolored .35 .20
6341 A3005 1000r multicolored .35 .20
6342 A3006 1000r multicolored .35 .20
6343 A3006 1000r multicolored .35 .20
a. Sheet of 3 each, #6342-6343 2.25 1.20
6344 A3005 1500r multicolored .50 .25
6345 A3005 1500r multicolored .50 .25
Nos. 6339-6345 (7) 2.65 1.45

Souvenir Sheet

6346 A3006 1000r Sheet of 4, #a.-d. + label 1.80 .90

No. 6346 has blue background.

Aleksandr Gorsky (1871-1924), Choreographer — A3006a

Designs: a, 750r, Portrait, scenes from "The Daughter of Gudule," "Salambo". b, 1500r, Don Quixote. c, 1500r, Giselle. d, 750r, La Bayadere.

1996, Aug. 7 Litho. *Perf. 12½x12*
6347 A3006a Block of 4, #a.-d. 1.90 .95
e. Sheet of 6, #6347b 3.60 1.80

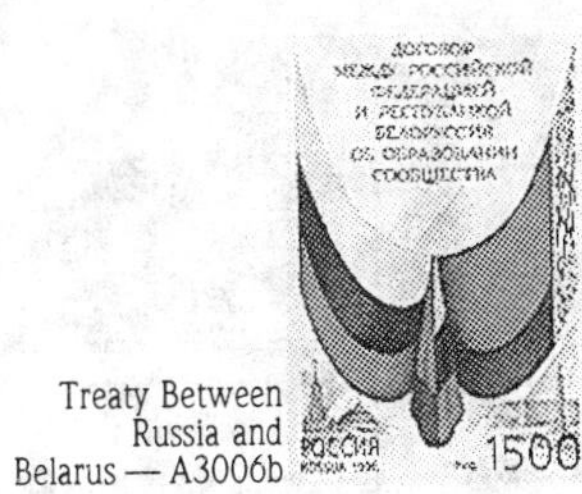
Treaty Between Russia and Belarus — A3006b

1996, Aug. 27 *Perf. 12x12½*
6348 A3006b 1500r Natl. flags .60 .30

17th-20th Cent. Enamelwork — A3007

Designs: No. 6349, Chalice, 1679. No. 6350, Aromatic bottle, 17th cent. No. 6351, Ink pot, ink set, 17th-18th cent. No. 6352, Coffee pot, 1750-1760. No. 6353, Perfume bottle, 19th-20th cent. 5000r, Icon, Our Lady of Kazan, 1894.

1996, Sept. 10 *Perf. 11½*
6349 A3007 1000r multicolored .40 .20
6350 A3007 1000r multicolored .40 .20
a. Sheet of 9 3.60
6351 A3007 1000r multicolored .40 .20
6352 A3007 1500r multicolored .60 .30
6353 A3007 1500r multicolored .60 .30
a. Sheet of 9 5.50
Nos. 6349-6353 (5) 2.40 1.20

Souvenir Sheet

6354 A3007 5000r multicolored 2.00 1.00

No. 6353a inscribed in sheet margin for Moscow '97.

No. 6354 contains one 35x50mm stamp.

UNESCO, 50th Anniv. A3008

1996, Oct. 15 *Perf. 12x12½*
6355 A3008 1000r multicolored .40 .20

No. 6355 issued in sheets of 8.

Icons, Religious Landmarks A3009

Designs: a, Icon of Our Lady of Iberia, Moscow. b, Holy Monastery of Stavrovouni, Cyprus. c, Icon of St. Nicholas, Cyprus. d, Resurrection (Iberia), Gate, Moscow.

1996, Nov. 13 *Perf. 11½*
6356 A3009 1500r Block of 4, #a.-d. 2.40 1.20

See Cyprus Nos. 893-896.

New Year 1997 — A3010

Design: Chiming Clock of Moscow, Kremlin.

1996, Dec. 5
6357 A3010 1000r multicolored .40 .20
a. Sheet of 8 3.25 1.60

Natl. Ice Hockey Team, 50th Anniv. A3011

Action scenes: a, Two players. b, Three players. c, Three players, referee.

1996, Dec. 5 *Perf. 12*
6358 A3011 1500r Strip of 3, #a.-c. 1.80 .90

Basil III — A3012

Ivan IV (the Terrible) — A3013

Feodor Ivanovich — A3014

Boris Godunov — A3015

1996, Dec. 20 Litho. & Engr. *Perf. 12*
6359 A3012 1500r multicolored .60 .30
6360 A3013 1500r multicolored .60 .30
6361 A3014 1500r multicolored .60 .30
6362 A3015 1500r multicolored .60 .30
Nos. 6359-6362 (4) 2.40 1.20

Flowers — A3016

Designs: No. 6363, Chaenomeles japonica. No. 6364, Amygdalus triloba. No. 6365, Cytisus scoparius. No. 6366, Rosa pimpinellifolia. No. 6367, Philadelphus coronarius.

1997, Jan. 21 Litho. *Perf. 12½x12*
6363 A3016 500r multicolored .25 .15
6364 A3016 500r multicolored .25 .15
6365 A3016 1000r multicolored .45 .25
6366 A3016 1000r multicolored .45 .25
6367 A3016 1000r multicolored .45 .25
Nos. 6363-6367 (5) 1.85 1.05

Souvenir Sheet

Moscow, 850th Anniv. — A3017

Illustration reduced.

1997, Feb. 20 *Perf. 12x12½*
6368 A3017 3000r Coat of arms 1.40 .70

Shostakovich Intl. Music Festival A3018

Dmitri D. Shostakovich (1906-75), composer.

1997, Feb. 26 *Perf. 12*
6369 A3018 1000r multicolored .45 .25

Souvenir Sheet

Coat of Arms of Russia, 500th Anniv. — A3019

Illustration reduced.

1997, Mar. 20
6370 A3019 3000r multicolored 1.40 .70

Post Emblem — A3020

Designs: 100r, Agriculture. 150r, Oil rig. 250r, Cranes (birds). 300r, Radio/TV tower. 500r, Russian Post emblem. 750r, St. George slaying dragon. 1000r, Natl. flag, arms. 1500r, Electric power. 2000r, Train. 2500r, Moscow Kremlin. 3000r, Satellite dish. 5000r, Fine arts.

1997 *Perf. 12x12½*
6371 A3020 100r blk & yel brn .15 .15
6372 A3020 150r blk & red lilac .15 .15
6373 A3020 250r blk & olive .15 .15
6374 A3020 300r blk & dk grn .15 .15
6375 A3020 500r blk & dark blue .20 .15
6376 A3020 750r blk & brown .30 .15
6377 A3020 1000r blue & red .40 .20
6378 A3020 1500r blk & grn bl .60 .30
6379 A3020 2000r blk & green .80 .40
6380 A3020 2500r blk & red .95 .45
6381 A3020 3000r blk & purple 1.20 .60
6382 A3020 5000r blk & brown 2.00 1.00
Nos. 6371-6382 (12) 7.05 3.85

Issued: 500r, 750r, 1000r, 1500r, 2500r, 3/31; 100r, 150r, 250r, 300r, 2000r, 3000r, 5000r, 4/30.

This is an expanding set. Numbers may change.

City of Vologda, 850th Anniv. — A3021

1997, Mar. 31 Litho. *Perf. 12*
6383 A3021 1000r multicolored .40 .20

Stories and Legends — A3022

Europa: Legend of Volga.

1997, May 5 Litho. *Perf. 12x12½*
6384 A3022 1500r multicolored .60 .30

Moscow, 850th Anniv. — A3023

Historic buildings: a, Cathedral of Christ the Savior. b, Turrets and roofs of the Kremlin. c, Grand Palace of the Kremlin, cathedral plaza. d, St. Basil's Cathedral. e, Icon, St. George slaying the Dragon. f, Text of first chronicled record of Moscow, 1147. g, Prince Aleksandr Nevski, Danilov Monastery. h, 16th cent. miniature of Moscow Kremlin. i, Miniature of coronation of Czar Ivan IV. j, 16th cent. map of Moscow.

1997, May 22
6385 A3023 1000r Sheet of 10, #a.-j. 3.75 1.90

Nos. 6385c, 6385h are 42x42mm.

Helicopters — A3024

1997, May 28 Litho. *Perf. 12½x12*
6386 A3024 500r Mi-14 .20 .15
6387 A3024 1000r Mi-24 .40 .20
6388 A3024 1500r Mi-26 .55 .55
6389 A3024 2000r Mi-28 .75 .40
a. Sheet of 6 4.50
6390 A3024 2500r Mi-34 .95 .45
Nos. 6386-6389 (4) 1.90 1.30

Fairy Tales — A3025

Designs: 500r, Man holding rope beside lake, devil running, from "Priest and Worker." 1000r, Two women, two men, from "Czar Sultan." 1500r, Man fishing in lake, fish, man, castle, from "Fisherman/Golden Fish." 2000r, Princess on steps, old woman holding apple, from "Dead Princess/Seven Knights." 3000r, Woman, King bowing while holding septor, rooster up in air, from "Golden Cockerel."

Photo. & Engr.

1997, June 6 *Perf. 12x12½*
6391 A3025 500r multicolored .20 .15
6392 A3025 1000r multicolored .40 .20
6393 A3025 1500r multicolored .60 .30
6394 A3025 2000r multicolored .80 .40
6395 A3025 3000r multicolored 1.20 .60
a. Strip of 5, #6391-6395 3.25 1.65
b. Sheet of 2 #6395a 6.40

Diplomatic Relations Between Russia and Thailand A3026

Design: St. Petersburg, Russian flag, Bangkok, Thailand flag.

1997, June 20 Litho. *Perf. 12½x12*
6396 A3026 1500r multicolored .60 .30

Wildlife A3027

Designs: a, 500r, Pteromys volans. b, 750r, Felix lynx. c, 1000r, Tetrao urogallus. d, 2000r, Lutra lutra. e, 3000r, Numenius arguata.

1997, July 10 *Perf. 12*
6397 A3027 Block of 5 + label 2.60 1.30

Russian Regions A3028

#6398, Winter scene, Archangel Oblast. #6399, Ocean, beach, Kaliningrad Oblast, vert. #6400, Ship, Krasnodarsky Krai. #6401, Mountains, Yakutia, vert. #6402, Mountain, sailing ship monument, Kamchatka Oblast.

Perf. 12½x12, 12x12½

1997, July 15

6398 A3028 1500r multicolored .55 .30
6399 A3028 1500r multicolored .55 .30
6400 A3028 1500r multicolored .55 .30
6401 A3028 1500r multicolored .55 .30
6402 A3028 1500r multicolored .55 .30
Nos. 6398-6402 (5) 2.75 1.50

Kljopa Puppets A3029

Designs: 500r, Rainbow, balloons. 1000r, Hang glider. 1500r, Troika.

1997, July 25 ***Perf. 11½***

6403 A3029 500r multicolored .20 .15
6404 A3029 1000r multicolored .35 .15

Size: 45x33mm

Perf. 12

6405 A3029 1500r multicolored .55 .30
Nos. 6403-6405 (3) 1.10 .60

World Philatelic Exhibition, Moscow 97 — A3030

Designs: a, #1, #35. b, #6061.

1997, Aug. 5 ***Perf. 11½***

6406 A3030 1500r Pair, #a.-b. 1.10 .55
c. Sheet of 6 stamps 4.25

A3031 A3032

History of Russia, Peter I: No. 6407, Planning new capital. No. 6408, Reforming the military. No. 6409, In Baltic Sea naval battle. No. 6410, Ordering administrative reform. No. 6411, Advocating cultural education.

1997, Aug. 15 ***Perf. 12x12½***

6407 A3031 2000r multicolored .75 .35
6408 A3031 2000r multicolored .75 .35
6409 A3031 2000r multicolored .75 .35
6410 A3031 2000r multicolored .75 .35
6411 A3031 2000r multicolored .75 .35
Nos. 6407-6411 (5) 3.75 1.75

1997, Aug. 15 ***Perf. 12***

6412 A3032 500r multicolored .20 .15

Indian independence, 50th anniv.

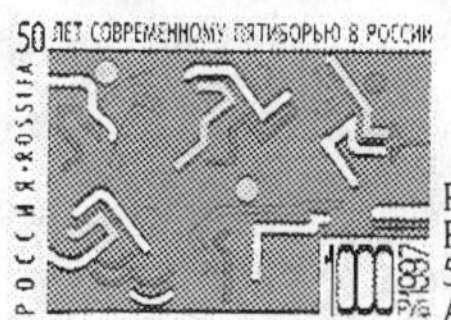

Russian Pentathlon, 50th Anniv. A3033

1997, Sept. 1 ***Perf. 12½x12***

6413 A3033 1000r multicolored .35 .20

Russian Soccer, Cent. A3034

1997, Sept. 4

6414 A3034 2000r multicolored .75 .35

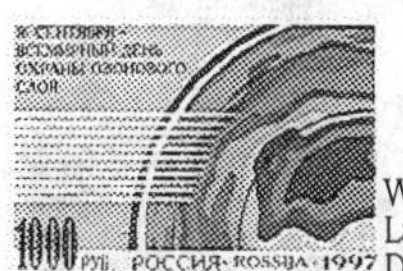

World Ozone Layer Day — A3035

1997, Sept. 16 ***Perf. 12x12½***

6415 A3035 1000r multioclored .35 .20

A3036

1997, Oct. 1

6416 A3036 1000r multicolored .35 .20

Russia's admission to European Council. No. 6416 printed with se-tenant label.

Souvenir Sheet

Pushkin's "Eugene Onegin," Translated by Abraham Shlonsky — A3038

Illustration reduced.

1997, Nov. 19 **Litho.** ***Perf. 12***

6418 A3038 3000r multicolored 1.20 .60

See Israel No. 1319.

Russian State Museum, St. Petersburg, Cent. — A3039

500r, Boris and Gleb, 14th cent. icon. 1000r, "The Volga Boatmen," by I. Repin. 1500r, "A Promenade," by Marc Chagall. 2000r, "A Merchant's Wife Having Tea," by Kustodiyev.

1997, Nov. 12 **Litho.** ***Perf. 12***

6419 A3039 500r multi, vert. .20 .15
6420 A3039 1000r multi, vert. .40 .20
6421 A3039 1500r multi .60 .30
6422 A3039 2000r multi, vert. .80 .40
Nos. 6419-6422 (4) 2.00 1.05

Nos. 6419-6422 were each issued in sheets of 8 + label.

SEMI-POSTAL STAMPS

Empire

Admiral Kornilov Monument, Sevastopol — SP1

Pozharski and Minin Monument, Moscow — SP2

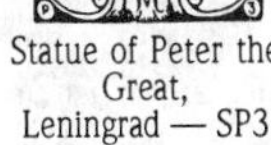

Statue of Peter the Great, Leningrad — SP3

Alexander II Memorial and Kremlin, Moscow — SP4

Perf. 11½ to 13½ and Compound

1905 **Typo.** **Unwmk.**

B1 SP1 3k red, brn & grn 3.00 2.25
a. Perf. 13½x 11½ 175.00 145.00
b. Perf. 13½ 27.50 27.50
c. Perf. 11½x13½ 200.00 165.00
B2 SP2 5k lilac, vio & straw 2.25 1.75
B3 SP3 7k lt bl, dk bl & pink 3.00 2.25
a. Perf. 13½ 42.50 42.50
B4 SP4 10k lt blue, dk bl & yel 4.50 3.25
Nos. B1-B4 (4) 12.75 9.50

These stamps were sold for 3 kopecks over face value. The surtax was donated to a fund for the orphans of soldiers killed in the Russo-Japanese war.

Ilya Murometz Legendary Russian Hero — SP5

Designs: 3k, Don Cossack Bidding Farewell to His Sweetheart. 7k, Symbolical of Charity. 10k, St. George Slaying the Dragon.

1914 ***Perf. 11½, 12½***

B5 SP5 1k red brn & dk grn, *straw* .40 .45
B6 SP5 3k mar & gray grn, *pink* .40 .45
B7 SP5 7k dk brn & dk grn, *buff* .40 .45
B8 SP5 10k dk blue & brn, *blue* 1.90 2.25
Nos. B5-B8 (4) 3.10 3.60

Perf. 13½

B5a SP5 1k .30 .45
B6a SP5 3k 35.00 32.50
B7a SP5 7k .25 .45
B8a SP5 10k 5.75 7.25
Nos. B5a-B8a (4) 41.30 40.65

1915 **White Paper**

B9 SP5 1k orange brn & gray .25 .35
B10 SP5 3k car & gray black .35 .45
B12 SP5 7k dk brown & dk green 4.75
B13 SP5 10k dk blue & brown .20 .35

These stamps were sold for 1 kopeck over face value. The surtax was donated to charities connected with the war of 1914-17.

No. B12 not regularly issued.

Nos. B5-B13 exist imperf. Value each, $150 unused, $250 canceled.

Russian Soviet Federated Socialist Republic

Volga Famine Relief Issue

Relief Work on Volga River — SP9

Administering Aid to Famine Victim — SP10

1921 **Litho.** ***Imperf.***

B14 SP9 2250r green 3.00 6.50
a. Pelure paper 100.00 55.00
B15 SP9 2250r deep red 2.50 4.50
a. Pelure paper 15.00 12.50
B16 SP9 2250r brown 2.50 11.00
B17 SP10 2250r dark blue 6.00 14.00
Nos. B14-B17 (4) 14.00 36.00

Forged cancels and counterfeits of Nos. B14-B17 are plentiful.

Stamps of type A33 with this overprint were not charity stamps nor did they pay postage in any form.

They represent taxes paid on stamps exported from or imported into Russia. In 1925 the semi-postal stamps of 1914-15 were surcharged for the same purpose. Stamps of the regular issues 1918 and 1921 have also been surcharged with inscriptions and new values, to pay the importation and exportation taxes.

Nos. 149-150 Surcharged in Black, Red, Blue or Orange

Р. С. Ф. С. Р.
ГОЛОДАЮЩИМ
250 р.+250 р

1922, Feb. ***Perf. 13½***

B18 A33 100r + 100r on 70k .60 1.65
a. "100 p. + p. 100" 55.00 65.00
B19 A33 100r + 100r on 70k (R) .60 1.65
B20 A33 100r + 100r on 70k (Bl) .30 .85
B21 A33 250r + 250r on 35k .30 .85
B22 A33 250r + 250r on 35k (R) .60 1.65
B23 A33 250r + 250r on 35k (O) 1.10 3.25
Nos. B18-B23 (6) 3.50 9.90

Issued to raise funds for Volga famine relief.

Nos. B18-B22 exist with surcharge inverted. Values $20 to $40.

Regular Issues of 1909-18 Overprinted

РСФСР
Филателия
—детям
19—8—22

1922, Aug. 19 ***Perf. 14***

B24 A14 1k orange 200.00 175.00
B25 A14 2k green 15.00 *25.00*
B26 A14 3k red 12.00 25.00
B27 A14 5k claret 15.00 25.00
B28 A15 10k dark blue 15.00 25.00

Imperf

B29 A14 1k orange 175.00 200.00
Nos. B24-B29 (6) 432.00 475.00

The overprint means "Philately for the Children". The stamps were sold at five million times their face values and 80% of the amount was devoted to child welfare. The stamps were sold only at Moscow and for one day.

Exist with overprint reading up. Counterfeits exist including those with overprint reading up. Reprints exist.

Worker and Peasant (Industry and Agriculture) — SP11

Allegory: Agriculture Will Help End Distress SP12

Star of Hope, Wheat and Worker-Peasant Handclasp — SP13

Sower — SP14

1922	**Litho.**		*Imperf.*	
	Without Gum			
B30	SP11	2t (2000r) green	8.50	20.00
B31	SP12	2t (2000r) rose	14.00	32.50
B32	SP13	4t (4000r) rose	14.00	32.50
B33	SP14	6t (6000r) green	14.00	32.50
		Nos. B30-B33 (4)	50.50	117.50

Nos. B30-B33 exist with double impression. Value, each $150.

Counterfeits of Nos. B30-B33 exist.

Miniature copies of Nos. B30-B33 exist, taken from the 1933 Soviet catalogue.

Automobile SP15

Steamship SP16

Railroad Train SP17

Airplane SP18

1922			*Imperf.*	
B34	SP15	light violet	.20	.15
B35	SP16	violet	.20	.15
B36	SP17	gray blue	.20	.15
B37	SP18	blue gray	1.50	*3.00*
		Nos. B34-B37 (4)	2.10	*3.45*

Inscribed "For the Hungry." Each stamp was sold for 200,000r postage and 50,000r charity.

Counterfeits of Nos. B34-B37 exist.

Nos. 212, 183, 202 Surcharged in Bronze, Gold or Silver

1 мая 1923 г.

Филателия — трудящимся.

2 р.+2 р.

1923			*Imperf.*	
B38	A48	1r +1r on 10r	125.00	125.00
a.		Inverted surcharge	250.00	250.00
B39	A48	1r +1r on 10r (G)	20.00	30.00
a.		Inverted surcharge	250.00	250.00
B40	A43	2r +2r on 250r	16.00	25.00
a.		Pelure paper	20.00	22.50
b.		Inverted surcharge	200.00	200.00
c.		Double surcharge		
	Wmk. 171			
B41	A46	4r +4r on 5000r	17.50	22.50
a.		Date spaced "1 923"	165.00	165.00
b.		Inverted surcharge	265.00	265.00
B42	A46	4r +4r on 5000r (S)	400.00	350.00
a.		Inverted surcharge	1,000.	850.00
b.		Date spaced "1 923"	1,000.	850.00
c.		As "b," inverted surch.	*3,500.*	
		Nos. B38-B42 (5)	578.50	552.50

The inscriptions mean "Philately's Contribution to Labor." The stamps were on sale only at Moscow and for one day. The surtax was for charitable purposes.

Counterfeits of No. B42 exist.

Leningrad Flood Issue

Nos. 181-182, 184-186 Surcharged

С.С.С.Р.

пострадавшему от наводнения Ленинграду.

7 к. + 20 к.

1924	**Unwmk.**		*Imperf.*	
B43	A40	3k + 10k on 100r	.80	1.25
a.		Pelure paper	3.00	4.00
b.		Inverted surcharge	175.00	125.00
B44	A40	7k + 20k on 200r	.80	1.25
a.		Inverted surcharge	175.00	125.00
B45	A40	14k + 30k on 300r	.90	2.50
a.		Pelure paper	250.00	215.00
	Similar Surcharge in Red or Black			
B46	A41	12k + 40k on 500r (R)	1.65	2.50
a.		Double surcharge	*115.00*	*115.00*
b.		Inverted surcharge	115.00	115.00
B47	A41	20k + 50k on 1000r	1.10	2.50
a.		Thick paper	11.50	18.00
b.		Pelure paper	20.00	25.00
c.		Chalk surface paper	10.00	12.50
		Nos. B43-B47 (5)	5.25	10.00

The surcharge on Nos. B43 to B45 reads: "S.S.S.R. For the sufferers by the inundation at Leningrad." That on Nos. B46 and B47 reads: "S.S.S.R. For the Leningrad Proletariat, 23, IX, 1924."

No. B46 is surcharged vertically, reading down, with the value as the top line.

Orphans SP19

Lenin as a Child SP20

1926	**Typo.**		*Perf. 13½*	
B48	SP19	10k brown	*3.25*	*3.00*
B49	SP20	20k deep blue	*4.00*	*4.25*
	Wmk. 170			
B50	SP19	10k brown	1.00	.90
B51	SP20	20k deep blue	1.50	1.65
		Nos. B48-B51 (4)	*9.75*	*9.80*

Two kopecks of the price of each of these stamps was donated to organizations for the care of indigent children.

Types of 1926 Issue

1927				
B52	SP19	8k + 2k yel green	1.00	.35
B53	SP20	18k + 2k deep rose	2.75	1.00

Surtax was for child welfare.

Industrial Training SP21

Agricultural Training SP22

Perf. 10, 10½, 12½

1929-30	**Photo.**		**Unwmk.**	
B54	SP21	10k +2k ol brn & org brn	2.50	2.50
a.		Perf. 10½	52.50	52.50
B55	SP21	10k +2k ol grn ('30)	1.50	1.25
B56	SP22	20k +2k blk brn & bl, perf. 10½	2.00	3.50
a.		Perf. 12½	35.00	35.00
b.		Perf. 10	10.00	10.00
B57	SP22	20k +2k bl grn ('30)	2.00	3.50
		Nos. B54-B57 (4)	8.00	10.75

Surtax was for child welfare.

Catalogue values for unused stamps in this section, from this point to the end of the section, are for Never Hinged items.

"Montreal Passing Torch to Moscow" — SP23

Moscow '80 Olympic Games Emblem — SP24

22nd Olympic Games, Moscow, 1980: 16k+6k, like 10k+5k. 60k+30k, Aerial view of Kremlin and Moscow '80 emblem.

1976, Dec. 28	**Litho.**		*Perf. 12x12½*	
B58	SP23	4k + 2k multi	.25	.15
B59	SP24	10k + 5k multi	.45	.35
B60	SP24	16k + 6k multi	.85	.40
		Nos. B58-B60 (3)	1.55	.90

Souvenir Sheet

Photo.

Perf. 11½

B61	SP23	60k + 30k multi	2.25	1.65

Greco-Roman Wrestling — SP25

Moscow '80 Emblem and: 6k+3k, Free-style wrestling. 10k+5k, Judo. 16k+6k, Boxing. 20k+10k, Weight lifting.

1977, June 21	**Litho.**		*Perf. 12½x12*	
B62	SP25	4k + 2k multi	.20	.15
B63	SP25	6k + 3k multi	.30	.20
B64	SP25	10k + 5k multi	.40	.30
B65	SP25	16k + 6k multi	.60	.35
B66	SP25	20k + 10k multi	.80	.45
		Nos. B62-B66 (5)	2.30	1.45

Perf. 12½x12, 12x12½

1977, Sept. 22

Designs: 4k+2k, Bicyclist. 6k+3k, Woman archer, vert. 10k+5k, Sharpshooting. 16k+6k, Equestrian. 20k+10k, Fencer. 50k+25k, Equestrian and fencer.

B67	SP25	4k + 2k multi	.20	.15
B68	SP25	6k + 3k multi	.25	.20
B69	SP25	10k + 5k multi	.40	.30
B70	SP25	16k + 6k multi	.55	.35
B71	SP25	20k + 10k multi	.70	.45
		Nos. B67-B71 (5)	2.10	1.45

Souvenir Sheet

Perf. 12½x12

B72	SP25	50k + 25k multi	3.00	1.65

1978, Mar. 24 *Perf. 12½x12*

Designs: 4k+2k, Swimmer at start. 6k+3k, Woman diver, vert. 10k+5k, Water polo. 16k+6k, Canoeing. 20k+10k, Canadian single. 50k+25k, Start of double scull race.

B73	SP25	4k + 2k multi	.15	.15
B74	SP25	6k + 3k multi	.25	.15
B75	SP25	10k + 5k multi	.40	.25
B76	SP25	16k + 6k multi	.55	.30
B77	SP25	20k + 10k multi	.70	.45
		Nos. B73-B77 (5)	2.05	1.30

Souvenir Sheet

B78	SP25	50k + 25k grn & blk	2.50	2.50

Star-class Yacht SP26 — Women's Gymnastics SP27

Keel Yachts and Moscow '80 Emblem: 6k+3k, Soling class. 10k+5k, Centerboarder 470. 16k+6k, Finn class. 20k+10k, Flying Dutchman class. 50k+25k, Catamaran Tornado, horiz.

1978, Oct. 26	**Litho.**		*Perf. 12x12½*	
B79	SP26	4k + 2k multi	.15	.15
B80	SP26	6k + 3k multi	.25	.15
B81	SP26	10k + 5k multi	.40	.20
B82	SP26	16k + 6k multi	.55	.30
B83	SP26	20k + 10k multi	.70	.40
		Nos. B79-B83 (5)	2.05	1.20

Souvenir Sheet

Perf. 12½x12

B84	SP26	50k + 25k multi	2.50	1.40

1979, Mar. 21 **Litho.** *Perf. 12x12½*

Designs: 6k+3k, Man on parallel bars. 10k+5k, Man on horizontal bar. 16k+6k, Woman on balance beam. 20k+10k, Woman on uneven bars. 50k+25k, Man on rings.

B85	SP27	4k + 2k multi	.15	.15
B86	SP27	6k + 3k multi	.25	.15
B87	SP27	10k + 5k multi	.40	.20
B88	SP27	16k + 6k multi	.55	.30
B89	SP27	20k + 10k multi	.70	.40
		Nos. B85-B89 (5)	2.05	1.20

Souvenir Sheet

Perf. 12½x12

B90	SP25	50k + 25k multi	2.00	1.40

1979, June *Perf. 12½x12, 12x12½*

Designs: 4k+2k, Soccer. 6k+3k, Basketball. 10k+5k, Women's volleyball. 16k+6k, Handball. 20k+10k, Field hockey.

B91	SP25	4k + 2k multi	.15	.15
B92	SP27	6k + 3k multi	.25	.15
B93	SP27	10k + 5k multi	.40	.20
B94	SP25	16k + 6k multi	.55	.30
B95	SP25	20k + 10k multi	.70	.40
		Nos. B91-B95 (5)	2.05	1.20

22nd Olympic Games, Moscow, July 19-Aug. 3, 1980.

Running, Moscow '80 Emblem SP27a

1980 Litho. *Perf. 12½x12, 12x12½*

B96	SP27a	4k + 2k shown	.15	.15
B97	SP27a	4k + 2k Pole vault	.15	.15
B98	SP27a	6k + 3k Discus	.25	.15
B99	SP27a	6k + 3k Hurdles	.25	.15
B100	SP27a	10k + 5k Javelin	.40	.20
B101	SP27a	10k + 5k Walking, vert.	.40	.20
B102	SP27a	16k + 6k Hammer throw	.70	.30
B103	SP27a	16k + 6k High jump	.70	.30
B104	SP27a	20k + 10k Shot put	.90	.40
B105	SP27a	20k + 10k Long jump	.90	.40
		Nos. B96-B105 (10)	4.80	2.40

Souvenir Sheet

B106	SP27a	50k + 25k Relay race	2.00	1.00

22nd Olympic Games, Moscow, July 19-Aug. 3. Issued: Nos. B96, B99, B101, B103, B105, Feb. 6; others, Mar. 12.

Moscow '80 Emblem, Relief from St. Dimitri's Cathedral, Arms of Vladimir — SP28

Moscow '80 Emblem and: No. B108, Bridge over Klyazma River and Vladimir Hotel. No. B109, Relief from Nativity Cathedral and coat of arms (falcon), Suzdal. No. B110, Tourist complex and Pozharski Monument, Suzdal. No. B111, Frunze Monument, Ivanovo, torch and spindle. No. B112, Museum of First Soviets, Fighters of the Revolution Monument, Ivanovo.

Photogravure and Engraved

1977, Dec. 30 *Perf. 11½x12*

B107	SP28	1r + 50k multi	2.00	.90
B108	SP28	1r + 50k multi	2.00	.90
B109	SP28	1r + 50k multi	2.00	.90
B110	SP28	1r + 50k multi	2.00	.90
B111	SP28	1r + 50k multi	2.00	.90
B112	SP28	1r + 50k multi	2.00	.90
		Nos. B107-B112 (6)	12.00	5.40

"Tourism around the Golden Ring."

Fortifications and Arms of Zagorsk — SP29

Moscow '80 Emblem and (Coat of Arms design): No. B114, Gagarin Palace of Culture and new arms of Zagorsk (building & horse). No. B115, Rostov Kremlin with St. John the Divine Church and No. B116, View of Rostov from Nero Lake (deer). No. B117, Alexander Nevski and WWII soldiers' monuments, Pereyaslav and No. B118, Peter the Great monument, Pereyaslav (lion & fish). No. B119, Tower and wall of Monastery of the Transfiguration, Jaroslaw and No. B120, Dock and monument for Soviet heroes, Jaroslaw (bear).

1978 *Perf. 12x11½*

Multicolored and:

B113	SP29	1r + 50k gold	2.00	.80
B114	SP29	1r + 50k silver	2.00	.80
B115	SP29	1r + 50k silver	2.00	.80
B116	SP29	1r + 50k gold	2.00	.80
B117	SP29	1r + 50k gold	2.00	.80
B118	SP29	1r + 50k silver	2.00	.80
B119	SP29	1r + 50k gold	2.00	.80
B120	SP29	1r + 50k silver	2.00	.80
		Nos. B113-B120 (8)	16.00	6.40

Issued: #B113-B116, 10/16; #B117-B120, 12/25.

1979 *Perf. 12x11½*

Moscow '80 Emblem and: No. B121, Narikaly Fortress, Tbilisi, 4th century. No. B122, Georgia Philharmonic Concert Hall, "Muse" sculpture, Tbilisi. No. B123, Chir-Dor Mosque, 17th century, Samarkand. No. B124, Peoples Friendship Museum, "Courage" monument, Tashkent. No. B125, Landscape, Erevan. B126, Armenian State Opera and Ballet Theater, Erevan.

Multicolored and:

B121	SP29	1r+50k sil, bl circle	2.25	1.40
B122	SP29	1r+50k gold, yel circle	2.25	1.40
B123	SP29	1r+50k sil, bl 8-point star	2.25	1.40
B124	SP29	1r+50k gold, red 8-point star	2.25	1.40
B125	SP29	1r+50k sil, bl diamond	2.25	1.40
B126	SP29	1r+50k gold, red diamond	2.25	1.40
		Nos. B121-B126 (6)	13.50	8.40

Issued: #B121-B124, Sept. 5; #B125-B126, Oct.

Kremlin SP29a

Kalinin Prospect, Moscow SP29b

Admiralteistvo, St. Isaak Cathedral, Leningrad SP29c

World War II Defense Monument, Leningrad SP29d

Bogdan Khmelnitisky Monument, St. Sophia's Monastery Kiev — SP29e

Metro Bridge, Dnieper River, Kiev — SP29f

Palace of Sports, Obelisk, Minsk — SP29g

Republican House of Cinematography, Minsk — SP29h

Vyshgorodsky Castle, Town Hall, Tallinn — SP29i

Viru Hotel, Tallinn — SP29j

1980 *Perf. 12x11½*

Moscow '80 Emblem, Coat of Arms,

B127	SP29a	1r + 50k multi	1.90	.75
B128	SP29b	1r + 50k multi	1.90	.75
B129	SP29c	1r + 50k multi	2.25	.90
B130	SP29d	1r + 50k multi	2.25	.90
B131	SP29e	1r + 50k multi	2.25	.90
B132	SP29f	1r + 50k multi	2.25	.90
B133	SP29g	1r + 50k multi	2.25	.90
B134	SP29h	1r + 50k multi	2.25	.90
B135	SP29i	1r + 50k multi	2.25	.90
B136	SP29j	1r + 50k multi	2.25	.90
		Nos. B127-B136 (10)	21.80	8.70

Tourism. Issue dates: #B127-B128, Feb. 29. #B129-B130, Mar. 25; #B131-B136, Apr. 30.

Soviet Culture Fund — SP30

Art treasures: No. B137, *Z.E. Serebriakova*, 1910, by O.K. Lansere, vert. No. B138, *Boyar's Wife Examining an Embroidery Design*, 1905, by K.V. Lebedev. No. B139, *Talent*, 1910, by N.P. Bogdanov-Belsky, vert. No. B140, *Trinity*, 15th-16th cent., Novgorod School, vert.

Perf. 12x12½, 12½x12

1988, Aug. 22 Litho.

B137	SP30	10k +5k multi	.50	.35
B138	SP30	15k +7k multi	.70	.45
B139	SP30	30k +15k multi	1.40	.95
		Nos. B137-B139 (3)	2.60	1.75

Souvenir Sheet

B140	SP30	1r +50k multi	4.50	3.00

SP31 SP33

Lenin Children's Fund SP32

1988, Oct. 20 Litho. *Perf. 12*

B141	SP31	10k +5k Bear	.45	.30
B142	SP31	10k +5k Wolf	.45	.30
B143	SP31	20k +10k Fox	.90	.60
B144	SP31	20k +10k Boar	.90	.60
B145	SP31	20k +10k Lynx	.90	.60
a.		Block of 5+label, #B141-B145	3.75	2.50

Zoo Relief Fund. See #B152-B156, B166-B168.

1988, Dec. 12 Litho. *Perf. 12*

Children's drawings and fund emblem: No. B146, Skating Rink. No. B147, Rooster. No. B148, May (girl and flowers).

B146	SP32	5k +2k multi	.25	.15
B147	SP32	5k +2k multi	.25	.15
B148	SP32	5k +2k multi	.25	.15
a.		Block of 3+label, #B146-B148	.75	.45

See Nos. B169-B171.

1988, Dec. 27 *Perf. 12½x12*

Designs: No. B149, Tigranes I (c. 140-55 B.C.), king of Armenia, gold coin. No. B150, St. Ripsime Temple, c. 618. No. B151, *Virgin and Child*, fresco (detail) by Ovnat Ovnatanyan, 18th cent., Echmiadzin Cathedral.

B149	SP33	20k +10k multi	.90	.60
B150	SP33	30k +15k multi	1.35	.90
B151	SP33	50k +25k multi	2.25	1.50
a.		Block of 3+label, #B149-B151	4.50	3.00

Armenian earthquake relief. For surcharges see Nos. B173-B175.

Zoo Relief Type of 1988

1989, Mar. 20 Litho. *Perf. 12*

B152	SP31	10k+5k Marten	.45	.30
B153	SP31	10k+5k Squirrel	.45	.30
B154	SP31	20k+10k Hare	.90	.60
B155	SP31	20k+10k Hedgehog	.90	.60
B156	SP31	20k+10k Badger	.90	.60
a.		Block of 5+label, #B152-B156	3.60	2.50

Lenin Children's Fund Type of 1988

Fund emblem and children's drawings: No. B157, Rabbit. No. B158, Cat. No. B159, Doctor. Nos. B157-B159 vert.

1989, June 14 Litho. *Perf. 12*

B157 SP32 5k +2k multi	.25	.15
B158 SP32 5k +2k multi	.25	.15
B159 SP32 5k +2k multi	.25	.15
a. Block of 3+label, #B157-B159	.75	.45

Surtax for the fund.

Soviet Culture Fund — SP34

Paintings and porcelain: No. B160, *Village Market,* by A. Makovsky. No. B161, *Lady Wearing a Hat,* by E. Zelenin. No. B162, *Portrait of the Actress Bazhenova,* by A. Sofronova. No. B163, *Two Women,* by H. Shaiber. No. B164, Popov porcelain coffee pot and plates, 19th cent.

1989 Litho. *Perf. 12x12½*

B160 SP34 4k +2k multi	.20	.15
B161 SP34 5k +2k multi	.25	.15
B162 SP34 10k +5k multi	.60	.35
B163 SP34 20k +10k multi	1.10	.65
B164 SP34 30k +15k multi	1.75	.95
Nos. B160-B164 (5)	3.90	2.25

Souvenir Sheet

Nature Conservation — SP35

1989, Dec. 14 Photo. *Perf. 11½*

B165 SP35 20k + 10k Swallow	1.25	1.25

Surtax for the Soviet Union of Philatelists.

Zoo Relief Type of 1988

1990, May 4 Litho. *Perf. 12*

B166 SP31 10k +5k *Aquila chrysaetos*	.45	.30
B167 SP31 20k +10k *Falco cherrug*	1.00	.65
B168 SP31 20k +10k *Corvus corax*	1.00	.65
a. Block of 3 + label, #B166-B168	2.50	1.65

Nos. B166-B168 horiz.

Lenin's Children Fund Type of 1988

#B169, Clown. #B170, Group of women. #B171, Group of children. #B169-B171, vert.

1990, July 3 Litho. *Perf. 12*

B169 SP32 5k +2k multi	.25	.15
B170 SP32 5k +2k multi	.25	.15
B171 SP32 5k +2k multi	.25	.15
a. Block of 3, #B169-B171 + label	.75	.45

Nature Conservation — SP36

1990, Sept. 12 Litho. *Perf. 12*

B172 SP36 20k +10k multi	1.10	1.10

Surtax for Soviet Union of Philatelists.

Nos. B149-B151 Overprinted

Филателистическая выставка „Армения-90"
#B173

Восстановление, милосердие, помощь
#B174-B175

1990, Nov. 24 Litho. *Perf. 12x12½*

B173 SP33 20k +10k multi	1.10	.75
B174 SP33 30k +15k multi	1.65	1.10
B175 SP33 50k +25k multi	2.75	1.80
a. Block of 3+label, #B173-B175	5.50	3.75

Armenia '90 Philatelic Exhibition.

Soviet Culture Fund — SP37

Paintings by N. K. Roerich: 10k+5k, Unkrada, 1909. 20k+10k, Pskovo-Pechorsky Monastery, 1907.

1990, Dec. 20 Litho. *Perf. 12½x12*

B176 SP37 10k +5k multi	.55	.35
B177 SP37 20k +10k multi	1.10	.75

Souvenir Sheet

Joys of All Those Grieving, 18th Cent. — SP38

1990, Dec. 23 *Perf. 12½x12*

B178 SP38 50k +25k multi	2.75	2.75

Surtax for Charity and Health Fund.

Ciconia Ciconia SP39

1991, Feb. 4 Litho. *Perf. 12*

B179 SP39 10k +5k multi	.55	.35

Surtax for the Zoo Relief Fund.

Souvenir Sheet

USSR Philatelic Society, 25th Anniv. — SP40

1991, Feb. 15 *Perf. 12x12½*

B180 SP40 20k +10k multi	1.10	1.10

The Universe by V. Lukianets SP41

No. B182, Another Planet by V. Lukianets.

1991, June 1 Litho. *Perf. 12½x12*

B181 SP41 10k +5k multi	.20	.15
B182 SP41 10k +5k multi	.20	.15
Set value		.20

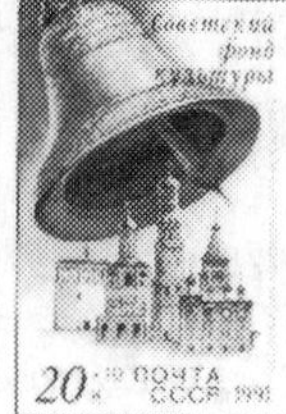

SP42

SP43

1991, July 10 *Perf. 12x12½*

B183 SP42 20k +10k multi	.35	.25

Surtax for Soviet Culture Fund.

1991, July 10 *Perf. 12*

B184 SP43 20k +10k multi	.35	.25

Surtax for Soviet Charity & Health Fund

Souvenir Sheet

SP44

1992, Jan. 22 Litho. *Perf. 12½x12*

B185 SP44 3r +50k multi	.70	.70

Surtax for Nature Preservation.

AIR POST STAMPS

AP1

Fokker F-111 — AP2

Plane Overprint in Red

1922 Unwmk. *Imperf.*

C1 AP1 45r green & black	7.50	10.00

5th anniversary of October Revolution.

No. C1 was on sale only at the Moscow General Post Office. Counterfeits exist.

1923 Photo.

C2 AP2 1r red brown	2.75
C3 AP2 3r deep blue	3.25
C4 AP2 5r green	3.25
a. Wide "5"	*500.00*
C5 AP2 10r carmine	2.25
Nos. C2-C5 (4)	11.50

Nos. C2-C5 were not placed in use.

Nos. C2-C5 Surcharged **10 КОП. ЗОЛ.**

1924

C6 AP2 5k on 3r dp blue	1.00	1.00
C7 AP2 10k on 5r green	1.00	1.00
a. Wide "5"	250.00	250.00
b. Inverted surcharge	450.00	450.00
C8 AP2 15k on 1r red brown	1.00	1.00
a. Inverted surcharge	500.00	500.00
C9 AP2 20k on 10r car	1.00	1.00
a. Inverted surcharge	500.00	500.00
Nos. C6-C9 (4)	4.00	4.00

Airplane over Map of World — AP3

1927, Septz. 1 Litho. *Perf. 13x12*

C10 AP3 10k dk bl & yel brn 5.50 3.75
C11 AP3 15k dp red & ol grn 6.75 6.75

1st Intl. Air Post Cong. at The Hague, initiated by the USSR.

Graf Zeppelin and "Call to Complete 5-Year Plan in 4 Years" — AP4

1930 Photo. Wmk. 226 *Perf. 12½*

C12 AP4 40k dk & dl blue 16.00 10.00
a. Perf. 10½ 22.50 19.00
b. Imperf. *700.00 700.00*
C13 AP4 80k dk car & rose 18.00 15.00
a. Perf. 10½ 20.00 10.00
b. Imperf. *700.00 700.00*

Flight of the Graf Zeppelin from Friedrichshafen to Moscow and return.

Symbolical of Airship Communication from the Tundra to the Steppes — AP5

Airship over Dneprostroi Dam — AP6

Airship over Lenin Mausoleum — AP7

Airship Exploring Arctic Regions — AP8

Constructing an Airship — AP9

1931-32 Wmk. 170 Photo. *Imperf.*

C15 AP5 10k dark violet 20.00 16.00

Litho.

C16 AP6 15k gray blue 20.00 22.50

Typo.

C17 AP7 20k dk carmine 20.00 22.50

Photo.

C18 AP8 50k black brown 20.00 22.50
C19 AP9 1r dark green 20.00 22.50
Nos. C15-C19 (5) 100.00 106.00

Perf. 10½, 12, 12½ and Compound

C20 AP5 10k dark violet 4.75 2.50

Litho.

C21 AP6 15k gray blue 9.00 3.75

Typo.

C22 AP7 20k dk carmine 6.50 2.00
a. 20k light red 7.50 3.00

Photo.

C23 AP8 50k black brown 4.75 2.00
a. 50k gray blue (error) 200.00 200.00
C24 AP9 1r dark green 5.50 2.00

Perf. 12½

Unwmk.

Engr.

C25 AP6 15k gray blk ('32) 1.00 .50
a. Perf. 10½ *400.00* 110.00
b. Perf. 14 57.50 37.50
c. Imperf. 325.00
Nos. C20-C25 (6) 31.50 12.75

The 11½ perforation on Nos. C20-C25 is of private origin.

North Pole Issue

Graf Zeppelin and Icebreaker "Malygin" Transferring Mail — AP10

1931 Wmk. 170 *Imperf.*

C26 AP10 30k dark violet 12.00 10.00
C27 AP10 35k dark green 12.00 10.00
C28 AP10 1r gray black 12.00 10.00
C29 AP10 2r deep ultra 15.00 12.00
Nos. C26-C29 (4) 51.00 42.00

Perf. 12x12½

C30 AP10 30k dark violet 20.00 20.00
C31 AP10 35k dark green 20.00 20.00
C32 AP10 1r gray black 20.00 20.00
C33 AP10 2r deep ultra 20.00 20.00
Nos. C30-C33 (4) 80.00 80.00

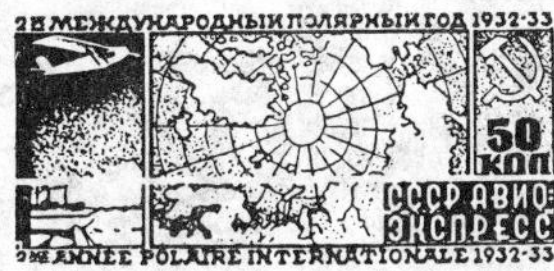

Map of Polar Region, Airplane and Icebreaker "Sibiryakov" — AP11

1932 Wmk. 170 *Perf. 12, 10½*

C34 AP11 50k carmine rose 24.00 15.00
a. Perf. 10½ 775.00 775.00
b. Perf. 10½x12 *1,200.*
C35 AP11 1r green 24.00 15.00
a. Perf. 12 125.00 40.00

2nd International Polar Year in connection with flight to Franz-Josef Land.

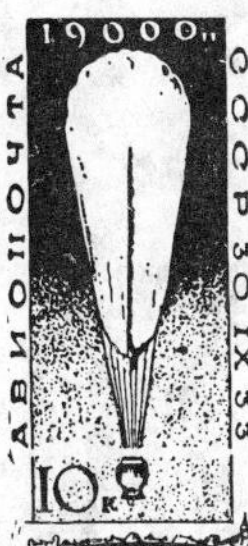

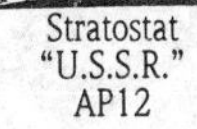

Stratostat "U.S.S.R." AP12

Furnaces of Kuznetsk AP13

1933 Photo. *Perf. 14*

C37 AP12 5k ultra 42.50 8.50
a. Vert. pair, imperf. btwn. *500.00*
C38 AP12 10k carmine 42.50 8.50
a. Horiz. pair, imperf. btwn. *500.00*
C39 AP12 20k violet 25.00 8.50
Nos. C37-C39 (3) 110.00 25.50

Ascent into the stratosphere by Soviet aeronauts, Sept. 30th, 1933.

1933 Wmk. 170 *Perf. 14*

Designs: 10k, Oil wells. 20k, Collective farm. 50k, Map of Moscow-Volga Canal project. 80k, Arctic cargo ship.

C40 AP13 5k ultra 11.00 4.75
C41 AP13 10k green 11.00 4.75
C42 AP13 20k carmine 24.00 9.00
C43 AP13 50k dull blue 30.00 9.00
C44 AP13 80k purple 24.00 9.00
Nos. C40-C44 (5) 100.00 36.50

Unwmk.

C45 AP13 5k ultra 11.00 3.25
C46 AP13 10k green 11.00 3.25
a. Horiz. pair, imperf. btwn. 450.00 350.00
C47 AP13 20k carmine 16.00 5.50
C48 AP13 50k dull blue 30.00 11.00
C49 AP13 80k purple 21.00 5.50
Nos. C45-C49 (5) 89.00 28.50

10th anniversary of Soviet civil aviation and airmail service. Counterfeits exist.

I. D. Usyskin — AP18

10k, A. B. Vasenko. 20k, P. F. Fedoseinko.

1934 Wmk. 170 *Perf. 11*

C50 AP18 5k vio brown 11.50 3.25
C51 AP18 10k brown 32.50 3.25
C52 AP18 20k ultra 32.50 3.25
Nos. C50-C52 (3) 76.50 9.75

Perf. 14

C50a AP18 5k 110.00 95.00
C51a AP18 10k 185.00 185.00
C52a AP18 20k 225.00 225.00
Nos. C50a-C52a (3) 520.00 505.00

Honoring victims of the stratosphere disaster. See Nos. C77-C79.

Airship "Pravda" — AP19

Airship Landing — AP20

Airship "Voroshilov" — AP21

Sideview of Airship — AP22

Airship "Lenin" — AP23

1934 *Perf. 14*

C53 AP19 5k red orange 12.50 2.75
C54 AP20 10k claret 12.50 4.25
C55 AP21 15k brown 12.50 5.75
C56 AP22 20k black 27.50 8.75
C57 AP23 30k ultra 50.00 8.75
Nos. C53-C57 (5) 115.00 30.25

Capt. V. Voronin and "Chelyuskin" — AP24

Prof. Otto Y. Schmidt AP25

A. V. Lapidevsky AP26

S. A. Levanevsky AP27

"Schmidt Camp" — AP28

Designs: 15k, M. G. Slepnev. 20k, I. V. Doronin. 25k, M. V. Vodopianov. 30k, V. S. Molokov. 40k, N. P. Kamanin.

1935 *Perf. 14*

C58 AP24 1k red orange 5.00 2.50
C59 AP25 3k rose carmine 6.00 2.50
C60 AP26 5k emerald 5.00 2.50
C61 AP27 10k dark brown 6.00 2.50
C62 AP27 15k black 7.25 2.50
C63 AP27 20k deep claret 10.00 4.75
C64 AP27 25k indigo 25.00 9.25
C65 AP27 30k dull green 35.00 11.00
C66 AP27 40k purple 25.00 7.00
C67 AP28 50k dark ultra 25.00 9.25
Nos. C58-C67 (10) 149.25 53.75

Aerial rescue of ice-breaker Chelyuskin crew and scientific expedition.

No. C61 Surcharged in Red

Перелет Москва— Сан-Франциско через Сев. полюс 1935 1р.

1935, Aug.

C68 AP27 1r on 10k dk brn 175.00 175.00
a. Inverted surcharge *3,200. 3,200.*
b. Small Cyrillic "f" 300.00 300.00

Moscow-San Francisco flight. Counterfeits exist.

Single-Engined Monoplane — AP34

Five-Engined Transport — AP35

20k, Twin-engined cabin plane. 30k, 4r-motored transport. 40k, Single-engined amphibian. 50k, Twin-motored transport. 80k, 8-motored transport.

1937 Unwmk. *Perf. 12*

C69 AP34 10k yel brn & blk 1.10 .75
a. Imperf. 175.00
C70 AP34 20k gray grn & blk 1.10 .75
C71 AP34 30k red brn & blk 1.40 .75
C72 AP34 40k vio brn & blk 2.00 .95
C73 AP34 50k dk vio & blk 3.25 1.50
C74 AP35 80k bl vio & brn 3.00 1.50

C75 AP35 1r black, brown & buff 8.25 3.00
a. Sheet of 4, imperf. 75.00 100.00
Nos. C69-C75 (7) 20.10 9.20
Set, never hinged 40.00

Jubilee Aviation Exhib., Moscow, Nov. 15-20.
Vertical pairs, imperf. between, exist for No. C71, value $100; No. C73, value $90.

Types of 1938 Regular Issue Overprinted in Various Colors

18 АВГУСТА
ДЕНЬ АВИАЦИИ СССР

1939 **Typo.**
C76 A282 10k red (C) 1.40 .40
C76A A285 30k blue (R) 1.40 .40
C76B A286 40k dull green (Br) 1.40 .40
C76C A287 50k dull violet (R) 2.25 .55
C76D A289 1r brown (Bl) 3.00 1.75
Nos. C76-C76D (5) 9.45 3.50
Set, never hinged 15.00

Soviet Aviation Day, Aug. 18, 1939.

Types of 1934 with "30.1.1944" Added at Lower Left

Designs: No. C77, P. F. Fedoseinko. No. C78, I. D. Usyskin. No. C79, A. B. Vasenko.

1944 **Photo.** ***Perf. 12***
C77 AP18 1r deep blue 1.75 .60
C78 AP18 1r slate green 1.75 .60
C79 AP18 1r brt yellow green 1.75 .75
Nos. C77-C79 (3) 5.25 1.95
Set, never hinged 6.50

1934 stratosphere disaster, 10th anniv.

Nos. 860A and 861A Surcharged in Red

АВИАПОЧТА
1944 г.
1 РУБЛЬ

1944, May 25
C80 A431 1r on 30k Prus green .50 .15
C81 A432 1r on 30k deep ultra .50 .15
Set, never hinged 1.25

Catalogue values for unused stamps in this section, from this point to the end of the section, are for Never Hinged items.

Planes and Soviet Air Force Flag — AP42

1948, Dec. 10 **Litho.** ***Perf. 12½***
C82 AP42 1r dark blue 3.00 1.00

Air Force Day.

Plane over Zages, Caucasus AP43

Plane over Farm Scene AP44

Map of Russian Air Routes and Transport Planes — AP45

Designs: No. C85, Sochi, Crimea. No. C86, Far East. No. C87, Leningrad. 2r, Moscow. 3r, Arctic.

Perf. 12x12½

1949, Nov. 9 **Photo.** **Unwmk.**
C83 AP43 50k red brn, *lemon* 1.65 .65
C84 AP44 60k sepia, *pale buff* 3.25 1.25
C85 AP44 1r org brn, *yelsh* 3.25 1.25
C86 AP43 1r blue, *bluish* 3.25 1.25
C87 AP43 1r red brn, *pale fawn* 3.25 1.25
C88 AP45 1r blk, ultra & red, *gray* 7.00 2.25
C89 AP43 2r org brn, *bluish* 10.00 3.25
C90 AP43 3r dk green, *bluish* 16.00 5.50
Nos. C83-C90 (8) 47.65 16.65

Plane and Mountain Stream AP46

Globe and Plane AP47

Design: 1r, Plane over river.

1955 **Litho.** ***Perf. 12½x12***
C91 AP46 1r multicolored 1.75 .55
C92 AP46 2r black & yel grn 3.50 .75

For overprints see Nos. C95-C96.

1955, May 31 **Photo.**
C93 AP47 2r chocolate 1.75 .55
C94 AP47 2r deep blue 1.75 .55

Nos. C91 and C92 Overprinted in Red

„Сев. полюс"
— Москва
1955 г.

Perf. 12x12½

1955, Nov. 22 **Litho.** **Unwmk.**
C95 AP46 1r multicolored 2.75 2.00
C96 AP46 2r black & yel grn 4.75 3.00

Issued for use at the scientific drifting stations North Pole-4 and North Pole-5. The inscription reads "North Pole-Moscow, 1955." Counterfeits exist.

Arctic Camp AP48

1956, June 8 ***Perf. 12½x12***
C97 AP48 1r blue, grn, brn, yel & red 1.50 .65

Opening of scientific drifting station North Pole-6.

Helicopter over Kremlin AP49

Air Force Emblem and Arms of Normandy AP50

1960, Mar. 5 **Photo.** ***Perf. 12***
C98 AP49 60k ultra 1.00 .30

Surcharged with New Value, Bars and "1961"

1961, Dec. 20
C99 AP49 6k on 60k ultra .80 .30

1962, Dec. 30 **Unwmk.** ***Perf. 11½***
C100 AP50 6k blue grn, ocher & car .60 .15

French Normandy-Neman Escadrille, which fought on the Russian front, 20th anniv.

Jet over Map Showing Airlines in USSR — AP51

Designs: 12k, Aeroflot emblem and globe. 16k, Jet over map showing Russian international airlines.

1963, Feb.
C101 AP51 10k red, blk & tan .60 .20
C102 AP51 12k blue, red, tan & blk .85 .25
C103 AP51 16k blue, blk & red 1.00 .35
Nos. C101-C103 (3) 2.45 .80

Aeroflot, the civil air fleet, 40th anniv.

Tupolev 134 at Sheremetyevo Airport, Moscow — AP52

Civil Aviation: 10k, An-24 (Antonov) and Vnukovo Airport, Moscow. 12k, Mi-10 (Mil helicopter) and Central Airport, Moscow. 16k, Be-10 (Beriev) and Chinki Riverport, Moscow. 20k, Antei airliner and Domodedovo Airport, Moscow.

1965, Dec. 31
C104 AP52 6k org, red & vio .30 .15
C105 AP52 10k lt green, org red & gray .45 .15
C106 AP52 12k lilac, dk sep & lt grn .45 .15
C107 AP52 16k lilac, lt brn, red & grn .70 .15
C108 AP52 20k org red, pur & gray .85 .25
Nos. C104-C108 (5) 2.75
Set value .70

Aviation Type of 1976

Aviation 1917-1930 (Aviation Emblem and): 4k, P-4 BIS biplane, 1917. 6k, AK-1 monoplane, 1924. 10k, R-3 (ANT-3) biplane, 1925. 12k, TB-1 (ANT-4) monoplane, 1925. 16k, R-5 biplane, 1929. 20k, Shcha-2 amphibian, 1930.

Lithographed and Engraved

1977, Aug. 16 ***Perf. 12x11½***
C109 A2134 4k multicolored .15 .15
C110 A2134 6k multicolored .15 .15
C111 A2134 10k multicolored .30 .15
C112 A2134 12k multicolored .30 .15
C113 A2134 16k multicolored .45 .30
C114 A2134 20k multicolored .65 .35
Nos. C109-C114 (6) 2.00 1.25

1978, Aug. 10

Designs: 4k, PO-2 biplane, 1928. 6k, K-5 passenger plane, 1929. 10k, TB-3, cantilever monoplane, 1930. 12k, Stal-2, 1931. 16k, MBR-2 hydroplane, 1932. 20k, I-16 fighter plane, 1934.

C115 A2134 4k multicolored .15 .15
C116 A2134 6k multicolored .15 .15
C117 A2134 10k multicolored .30 .15
C118 A2134 12k multicolored .35 .15
C119 A2134 16k multicolored .45 .15
C120 A2134 20k multicolored .60 .25
Nos. C115-C120 (6) 2.00
Set value .75

Aviation 1928-1934.

Jet and Compass Rose — AP53

1978, Aug. 4 **Litho.** ***Perf. 12***
C121 AP53 32k dark blue .80 .30

Aeroflot Plane AH-28 — AP54

Designs: Various Aeroflot planes.

Photogravure and Engraved

1979 ***Perf. 11½x12***
C122 AP54 2k shown .15 .15
C123 AP54 3k YAK-42 .15 .15
C124 AP54 10k T4-154 .30 .15
C125 AP54 15k IL76 transport .45 .15
C126 AP54 32k IL86 jet liner .85 .45
Nos. C122-C126 (5) 1.90
Set value .85

AIR POST OFFICIAL STAMPS

Used on mail from Russian embassy in Berlin to Moscow. Surcharged on Consular Fee stamps. Currency: the German mark.

OA1

Surcharge in Carmine

1922, July **Litho.** ***Perf. 13½***

Bicolored Burelage

CO1 OA1 12m on 2.25r 67.50
CO2 OA1 24m on 3r 67.50
CO3 OA1 120m on 2.25r 77.50
CO4 OA1 600m on 3r 97.50
CO5 OA1 1200m on 10k 135.00
CO6 OA1 1200m on 50k *10,000.*
CO7 OA1 1200m on 2.25r 850.00
CO8 OA1 1200m on 3r 1,000.

Three types of each denomination, distinguished by shape of "C" in surcharge and length of second line of surcharge. Used copies have pen or crayon cancel. Forgeries exist.

SPECIAL DELIVERY STAMPS

Motorcycle Courier — SD1

Express Truck — SD2

Design: 80k, Locomotive.

Perf. 12½x12, 12x12½

1932 **Photo.** **Wmk. 170**
E1 SD1 5k dull brown 7.50 6.25
E2 SD2 10k violet brown 9.75 6.25
E3 SD2 80k dull green 24.00 12.50
Nos. E1-E3 (3) 41.25 25.00

Used values are for c-t-o.

POSTAGE DUE STAMPS

Regular Issue of 1918 Surcharged in Red or Carmine

Доплата
3 коп.
золотом

1924-25 **Unwmk.** ***Perf. 13½***
J1 A33 1k on 35k blue .15 *.90*
J2 A33 3k on 35k blue .15 *.90*
J3 A33 5k on 35k blue .15 *.90*
a. Imperf. 60.00
J4 A33 8k on 35k blue ('25) .25 *.90*
a. Imperf. 40.00
J5 A33 10k on 35k blue .15 *1.10*
a. Pair, one without surcharge 25.00
J6 A33 12k on 70k brown .15 *.90*
J7 A33 14k on 35k blue ('25) .15 *.90*
a. Imperf. 65.00

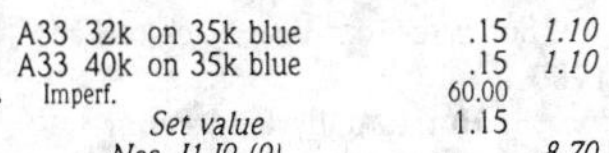

J8 A33 32k on 35k blue .15 *1.10*
J9 A33 40k on 35k blue .15 *1.10*
a. Imperf. 60.00
Set value 1.15
Nos. J1-J9 (9) *8.70*

Surcharge is found inverted on Nos. J1-J2, J4, J6-J9, value $25-$50. Double on Nos. J2, J4-J6; value, $40-$50.

Regular Issue of 1921 Surcharged in Violet — ДОПЛАТА 1 коп.

1924 *Imperf.*
J10 A40 1k on 100r orange 3.50 *6.00*
a. 1k on 100r yellow 4.00 *12.50*
b. Pelure paper 4.00 *12.50*
c. Inverted surcharge *100.00*

D1

Lithographed or Typographed

1925 *Perf. 12*
J11 D1 1k red 2.00 1.50
J12 D1 2k violet 1.00 2.25
J13 D1 3k light blue 1.00 2.25
J14 D1 7k orange 1.00 2.25
J15 D1 8k green 1.00 3.00
J16 D1 10k dark blue 1.65 4.50
J17 D1 14k brown 2.00 4.50
Nos. J11-J17 (7) 9.65 20.25

Perf. 14½x14
J13a D1 3k 4.00 6.00
J14a D1 7k 8.25 12.50
J16a D1 10k 32.50 40.00
J17a D1 14k 2.25 3.50
Nos. J13a-J17a (4) 47.00 62.00

1925 Wmk. 170 Typo. *Perf. 12*
J18 D1 1k red .45 .85
J19 D1 2k violet .45 .85
J20 D1 3k light blue .60 1.10
J21 D1 7k orange .60 1.10
J22 D1 8k green .60 1.10
J23 D1 10k dark blue .75 1.65
J24 D1 14k brown 1.10 2.25
Nos. J18-J24 (7) 4.55 8.90

For surcharges see Nos. 359-372.

WENDEN (LIVONIA)

A former district of Livonia, a province of the Russian Empire, which became part of Latvia, under the name of Vidzeme.

Used values for Nos. L2-L12 are for pen-canceled copies. Postmarked specimens sell for considerably more.

A1

1862 Unwmk. *Imperf.*
L1 A1 (2k) blue 12.50
a. Tête bêche pair *250.00*

No. L1 may have been used for a short period of time but withdrawn because of small size. Some consider it an essay.

A2

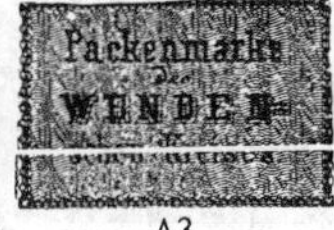
A3

1863
L2 A2 (2k) rose & black 150.00 150.00
a. Background inverted 275.00 275.00
L3 A3 (4k) blue grn & blk 70.00 70.00
a. (4k) yellow green & black 150.00 150.00
b. Half used as 2k on cover *1,800.*
c. Background inverted 150.00 150.00
d. As "a," background inverted 210.00 210.00

The official imitations of Nos. L2 and L3 have a single instead of a double hyphen after "WENDEN."

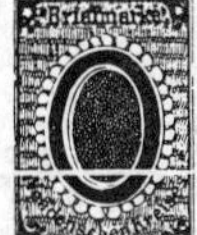

Coat of Arms
A4 A5 A6

1863-71
L4 A4 (2k) rose & green 30.00 17.50
a. Yellowish paper
b. Green frame around central oval 37.50 21.00
c. Tête bêche pair *1,800.*
L5 A5 (2k) rose & grn ('64) 70.00 57.50
L6 A6 (2k) rose & green 21.00 21.00
Nos. L4-L6 (3) 121.00 96.00

Official imitations of Nos. L4b and L5 have a rose instead of a green line around the central oval. The first official imitation of No. L6 has the central oval 5½mm instead of 6¼mm wide; the second imitation is less clearly printed than the original and the top of the "f" of "Briefmarke" is too much hooked.

Coat of Arms
A7 A8

1872-75 *Perf. 12½*
L7 A7 (2k) red & green 40.00 21.00
L8 A8 2k yel grn & red ('75) 7.00 8.00
a. Numeral in upper right corner resembles an inverted "3" 27.50 27.50

Reprints of No. L8 have no horizontal lines in the background. Those of No. L8a have the impression blurred and only traces of the horizontal lines.

A9

Wenden Castle — A10

1878-80
L9 A9 2k green & red 7.00 8.00
a. Imperf.
L10 A9 2k blk, grn & red ('80) 7.00 8.00
a. Imperf., pair 27.50

No. L9 has been reprinted in blue green and yellow green with perforation 11½ and in gray green with perforation 12½ or imperforate.

1884 *Perf. 11½*
L11 A9 2k black, green & red 10.00 2.50
a. Green arm omitted 21.00
b. Arm inverted 21.00
c. Arm double 27.50
d. Imperf., pair 21.00

1901 **Litho.**
L12 A10 2k dk green & brown 3.50 3.50
a. Tête bêche pair
b. Imperf., pair 20.00

OCCUPATION STAMPS

Issued under Finnish Occupation

Finnish Stamps of 1917-18 Overprinted — Aunus

1919 Unwmk. *Perf. 14*
N1 A19 5p green 12.50 12.50
N2 A19 10p rose 12.50 12.50
N3 A19 20p buff 12.50 12.50
N4 A19 40p red violet 12.50 12.50
N5 A19 50p orange brn 100.00 100.00
N6 A19 1m dl rose & blk 105.00 105.00
N7 A19 5m violet & blk 325.00 325.00
N8 A19 10m brown & blk 575.00 575.00
Nos. N1-N8 (8) 1,155. 1,155.

"Aunus" is the Finnish name for Olonets, a town of Russia.

Counterfeits overprints exist.

Issued under German Occupation

Germany Nos. 506 to 523 Overprinted in Black — OSTLAND

1941-43 Unwmk. Typo. *Perf. 14*
N9 A115 1pf gray black .15 .15
N10 A115 3pf light brown .15 .15
N11 A115 4pf slate .15 .15
N12 A115 5pf dp yellow green .15 .15
N13 A115 6pf purple .15 .15
N14 A115 8pf red .15 .15
N15 A115 10pf dk brown ('43) .15 *1.00*
N16 A115 12pf carmine ('43) .15 *1.00*

Engr.
N17 A115 10pf dark brown .20 .25
N18 A115 12pf brt carmine .20 .25
N19 A115 15pf brown lake .15 .15
N20 A115 16pf peacock grn .15 .15
N21 A115 20pf blue .15 .15
N22 A115 24pf orange brown .15 .15
N23 A115 25pf brt ultra .15 .15
N24 A115 30pf olive green .15 .15
N25 A115 40pf brt red violet .15 .15
N26 A115 50pf myrtle green .15 .15
N27 A115 60pf dk red brown .15 .15
N28 A115 80pf indigo .15 .15
Set value 1.50 *3.40*

Issued for use in Estonia, Latvia and Lithuania.

Same Overprinted in Black — UKRAINE

Typo.
N29 A115 1pf gray black .15 .15
N30 A115 3pf lt brown .15 .15
N31 A115 4pf slate .15 .15
N32 A115 5pf dp yel green .15 .15
N33 A115 6pf purple .15 .15
N34 A115 8pf red .15 .15
N35 A115 10pf dk brown ('43) .15 *1.00*
N36 A115 12pf carmine ('43) .15 *1.00*

Engr.
N37 A115 10pf dk brown .25 .35
N38 A115 12pf brt carmine .25 .35
N39 A115 15pf brown lake .15 .15
N40 A115 16pf peacock green .15 .15
N41 A115 20pf blue .15 .15
N42 A115 24pf orange brown .15 .15
N43 A115 25pf bright ultra .15 .15
N44 A115 30pf olive green .15 .15
N45 A115 40pf brt red violet .15 .15
N46 A115 50pf myrtle green .15 .15
N47 A115 60pf dk red brown .15 .15
N48 A115 80pf indigo .15 .15
Set value 1.50 *3.60*

ARMY OF THE NORTHWEST

(Gen. Nicolai N. Yudenich)

Russian Stamps of 1909-18 Overprinted in Black or Red — Сѣв.Зап. армія

On Stamps of 1909-12

Perf. 14 to 15 and Compound

1919, Aug. 1
1 A14 2k green 2.50 4.25
2 A14 5k claret 2.50 4.25
3 A15 10k dk blue (R) 2.75 5.00
4 A11 15k red brn & bl 2.75 5.00
5 A8 20k blue & car 5.00 7.50
6 A11 25k grn & gray violet 8.50 12.00
7 A8 50k brn vio & grn 5.00 6.25

Perf. 13½
8 A9 1r pale brn, dk brn & org 10.50 14.00
9 A13 10r scar, yel & gray 30.00 52.50

On Stamps of 1917

Imperf
10 A14 3k red 1.40 3.50
11 A12 3.50r mar & lt grn 17.50 27.50
12 A13 5r dk blue, grn & pale bl 14.00 25.00
13 A12 7r dk green & pink 77.50 125.00

No. 2 Surcharged

Perf. 14, 14½x15
14 A14 10k on 5k claret 1.75 3.75
Nos. 1-14 (14) 181.65 295.50

Nos. 1-14 exist with inverted overprint or surcharge. The 1, 3½, 5, 7 and 10 rubles with red overprint are trial printings (value $40 each). The 20k on 14k, perforated, and the 1, 2, 5, 15, 70k and 1r imperforate were overprinted but never placed in use. Value: $80, $30, $40, $40, $40, $40 and $60.

These stamps were in use from Aug. 1 to Oct. 15, 1919.

Counterfeits of Nos. 1-14 abound.

ARMY OF THE NORTH

A1

A2

A3

A4

A5

1919, Sept. Typo. *Imperf.*
1 A1 5k brown violet .40 .70
2 A2 10k blue .40 .70
3 A3 15k yellow .40 .70
4 A4 20k rose .40 .70
5 A5 50k green .40 .70
Nos. 1-5 (5) 2.00 3.50

The letters OKCA are the initials of Russian words meaning "Special Corps, Army of the North." The stamps were in use from about the end of September to the end of December, 1919.

Used values are for c-t-o stamps.

(General Miller)

A set of seven stamps of this design was prepared in 1919, but not issued. Value, set $25. Counterfeits exist.

RUSSIAN OFFICES ABROAD

For various reasons the Russian Empire maintained Post Offices to handle its correspondence in several foreign countries. These were similar to the Post Offices in foreign countries maintained by other world powers.

OFFICES IN CHINA

100 Kopecks = 1 Ruble
100 Cents = 1 Dollar (1917)

Russian Stamps Overprinted in Blue or Red

On Issues of 1889-92
Horizontally Laid Paper

1899-1904 Wmk. 168 *Perf. 14½x15*
1 A10 1k orange (Bl) .75 1.00
2 A10 2k yel green (R) .75 1.00
3 A10 3k carmine (Bl) .75 1.00
4 A10 5k red violet (Bl) .75 1.00
5 A10 7k dk blue (R) 1.50 2.50
6 A8 10k dk blue (R) 1.50 2.50
7 A8 50k vio & grn (Bl) ('04) 4.50 5.00

Perf. 13½
8 A9 1r lt brn, brn & org (Bl) ('04) 30.00 30.00
Nos. 1-8 (8) 40.50 44.00

On Issues of 1902-05
Vertically Laid Paper

Perf. 14½ to 15 and Compound

1904-08

Overprinted in Black, Red or Blue
9 A8 4k rose red (Bl) 2.00 2.50
10 A10 7k dk blue (R) 10.00 12.50
11 A8 10k dk blue (R) 1,200. 1,200.
a. Groundwork inverted *3,250.*
12 A11 14k bl & rose (R) 5.00 3.50
13 A11 15k brn vio & blue (Bl) ('08) 5.00 4.50
14 A8 20k blue & car (Bl) 1.50 2.50
15 A11 25k dull grn & lil (R) ('08) 10.00 6.50
16 A11 35k dk vio & grn (R) 2.50 3.25
17 A8 50k vio & grn (Bl) 75.00 55.00
18 A11 70k brn & org (Bl) 20.00 12.50

Perf. 13½

19 A9 1r lt brn, brn & org (Bl) 15.00 11.50
20 A12 3.50r blk & gray (R) 10.00 13.00
21 A13 5r dk bl, grn & pale bl (R) ('07) 8.00 10.00
22 A12 7r blk & yel (Bl) 12.50 10.00
23 A13 10r scar, yel & gray (Bl) ('07) 40.00 50.00
Nos. 9-10,12-23 (14) 216.50 197.25

On Issues of 1909-12
Wove Paper
Lozenges of Varnish on Face

1910-16 Unwmk. *Perf. 14x14½*

24 A14 1k orange yel (Bl) .25 .35
25 A14 1k org yel (Bl Bk) 3.50 5.00
26 A14 2k green (Bk) .25 .35
27 A14 2k green (Bl) 4.00 6.25
a. Double ovpt. (Bk and Bl)
28 A14 3k rose red (Bl) .25 .35
29 A14 3k rose red (Bk) 7.25 10.00
30 A15 4k carmine (Bl) .25 .35
31 A15 4k carmine (Bk) 5.00 7.25
32 A14 7k lt blue (Bk) .25 .35
33 A15 10k blue (Bk) .25 .35
34 A11 14k blue & rose (Bk) .55 .65
35 A11 14k blue & rose (Bl) 3.25 4.50
36 A11 15k dl vio & bl (Bk) .35 .65
37 A8 20k blue & car (Bk) .35 .65
38 A11 25k green & vio (Bl) 2.25 3.25
39 A11 25k grn & vio (Bk) .55 1.65
40 A11 35k vio & grn (Bk) .25 .35
42 A8 50k vio & grn (Bl) .25 .35
43 A8 50k brn vio & grn (Bk) 11.50 16.00
44 A11 70k lt brn & org (Bl) .25 .35

Perf. 13½

45 A9 1r pale brn, brn & org (Bl) 1.00 1.10
47 A13 5r dk bl, grn & pale bl (R) 7.25 8.25
Nos. 24-47 (22) 49.05 68.35

Russian Stamps of 1902-12 Surcharged:

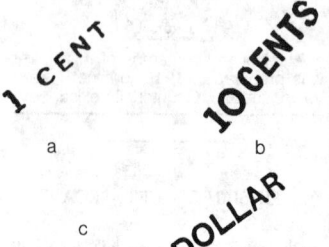

1 CENT
a

10CENTS
b

1 DOLLAR
c

On Stamps of 1909-12

1917 *Perf. 11½, 13½, 14, 14½x15*

50 A14(a) 1c on 1k dl org yel .60 5.50
51 A14(a) 2c on 2k dull grn .60 5.50
52 A14(a) 3c on 3k car .60 5.50
a. Inverted surcharge 65.00
b. Double surcharge 150.00
53 A15(a) 4c on 4k car 1.25 4.25
54 A14(a) 5c on 5k claret 1.25 15.00
55 A15(b) 10c on 10k dk blue 1.25 15.00
a. Inverted surcharge 85.00 85.00
b. Double surcharge 115.00
56 A11(b) 14c on 14k dk blue & carmine 1.25 10.00
a. Imperf. 6.00
b. Inverted surcharge 100.00
57 A11(a) 15c on 15k brn lilac & dp blue 1.25 15.00
58 A8(b) 20c on 20k bl & car 1.25 15.00
59 A11(a) 25c on 25k grn & violet 1.25 15.00
60 A11(a) 35c on 35k brn vio & green 1.50 15.00
a. Inverted surcharge 27.50
61 A8(a) 50c on 50k brn vio & green 1.25 15.00
62 A11(a) 70c on 70k brn & red orange 1.25 15.00
63 A9(c) $1 on 1r pale brn, brn & org 1.25 15.00
Nos. 50-63 (14) 15.80

On Stamps of 1902-05
Vertically Laid Paper

Perf. 11½, 13, 13½, 13½x11½
Wmk. Wavy Lines (168)

64 A12 $3.50 on 3.50r blk & gray 9.00 32.50
65 A13 $5 on 5r dk bl, grn & pale blue 9.00 32.50
66 A12 $7 on 7r blk & yel 8.50 32.50

On Stamps of 1915

Unwmk. *Perf. 13½*
Wove Paper

68 A13 $5 on 5r ind, grn & lt blue 13.00 42.50
a. Inverted surcharge 250.00
70 A13 $10 on 10r car lake, yel & gray 12.50 100.00
Nos. 64-70 (5) 52.00

The surcharge on Nos. 64-70 is in larger type than on the $1.

Russian Stamps of 1909-18 Surcharged in Black or Red

2
Cent.

On Stamps of 1909-12

1920 *Perf. 14, 14½x15*

72 A14 1c on 1k dull org yellow 32.50 37.50
73 A14 2c on 2k dull grn (R) 16.00 15.00
74 A14 3c on 3k car 16.00 15.00
75 A15 4c on 4k car 16.00 15.00
a. Inverted surcharge 130.00
76 A14 5c on 5k claret 16.00 15.00
77 A15 10c on 10k dk bl (R) 100.00 57.50
78 A14 10c on 10k on 7k blue (R) 95.00 57.50

On Stamps of 1917-18
Imperf

79 A14 1c on 1k orange 22.50 15.00
a. Inverted surcharge 45.00 75.00
80 A14 5c on 5k claret 30.00 30.00
a. Inverted surcharge 140.00
b. Double surcharge 200.00
c. Surcharged "Cent" only 95.00
Nos. 72-80 (9) 344.00

OFFICES IN THE TURKISH EMPIRE

Various powers maintained post offices in the Turkish Empire before World War I by authority of treaties which ended with the signing of the Treaty of Lausanne in 1923. The foreign post offices were closed Oct. 27, 1923.

100 Kopecks = 1 Ruble
40 Paras = 1 Piaster (1900)

Coat of Arms
A1

1863 Unwmk. Typo. *Imperf.*

1 A1 6k blue 275.00 1,000.
a. 6k light blue, thin paper 350.00 1,350.
b. 6k dark blue, chalky paper 150.00

A2

A3

1865 Litho.

2 A2 (2k) brown & blue 700.00 625.00
3 A3 (20k) blue & red 900.00 850.00

Twenty-eight varieties of each.

A4

A5

A6

1866 Horizontal Network

4 A4 (2k) rose & pale bl 35.00 52.50
5 A5 (20k) dp blue & rose 55.00 57.50

1867 Vertical Network

6 A4 (2k) rose & pale bl 70.00 87.50
7 A5 (20k) dp blue & rose 100.00 150.00

The initials inscribed on Nos. 2 to 7 are those of the Russian Company of Navigation and Trade. Stamps of Russian Offices in the Turkish Empire overprinted with these initials were used in the Ukraine and are listed under that country.

The official imitations of Nos. 2 to 7 are on yellowish white paper. The colors are usually paler than those of the originals and there are minor differences in the designs.

Horizontally Laid Paper

1868 Typo. Wmk. 168 *Perf. 11½*

8 A6 1k brown 35.00 19.00
9 A6 3k green 35.00 19.00
10 A6 5k blue 35.00 19.00
11 A6 10k car & green 35.00 19.00
Nos. 8-11 (4) 140.00 76.00

Colors of Nos. 8-11 dissolve in water.

1872-90 *Perf. 14½x15*

12 A6 1k brown 6.25 3.00
13 A6 3k green 20.00 2.00
14 A6 5k blue 3.75 1.00
15 A6 10k pale red & grn ('90) 1.00 .50
b. 10k carmine & green 11.00 3.75
Nos. 12-15 (4) 31.00 6.50

Vertically Laid Paper

12a A6 1k 37.50 12.50
13a A6 3k 37.50 12.50
14a A6 5k 37.50 12.50
15a A6 10k 87.50 30.00
Nos. 12a-15a (4) 200.00 67.50

Nos. 12-15 exist imperf.

No. 15 Surcharged in Black or Blue:

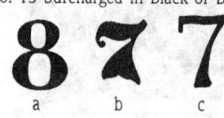

8 a
7 b
7 c

1876

16 A6(a) 8k on 10k (Bk) 60.00 45.00
a. Vertically laid
b. Inverted surcharge 375.00
17 A6(a) 8k on 10k (Bl) 85.00 65.00
a. Vertically laid
b. Inverted surcharge

1879

18 A6(b) 7k on 10k (Bk) 85.00 65.00
a. Vertically laid
b. Inverted surcharge
19 A6(b) 7k on 10k (Bl) 100.00 85.00
a. Vertically laid
b. Inverted surcharge
19C A6(c) 7k on 10k (Bl) 700.00 550.00
19D A6(c) 7k on 10k (Bk) 550.00 500.00

Nos. 16-19D have been extensively counterfeited.

1879 *Perf. 14½x15*

20 A6 1k black & yellow 3.00 1.50
a. Vertically laid 9.00 7.50
21 A6 2k black & rose 4.50 4.25
a. Vertically laid 10.00 6.00
22 A6 7k carmine & gray 6.50 1.75
a. Vertically laid 27.50 12.50
Nos. 20-22 (3) 14.00 7.50

1884

23 A6 1k orange .45 .30
24 A6 2k green .70 .40
25 A6 5k pale red violet 2.75 .95
26 A6 7k blue 1.40 .40
Nos. 23-26 (4) 5.30 2.05

Nos. 23-26 imperforate are believed to be proofs.
No. 23 surcharged "40 PARAS" is bogus, though some copies were postally used.

Russian Company of Navigation and Trade

Р. О. П. и Т.

This overprint, in two sizes, was privately applied in various colors to Russian Offices in the Turkish Empire stamps of 1900-1910.

A7

A8

A9

A10

A11

Surcharged in Blue, Black or Red

1900
Horizontally Laid Paper

27 A7 4pa on 1k orange (Bl) .15 .15
a. Inverted surcharge 30.00 30.00
28 A7 4pa on 1k orange (Bk) .15 .15
a. Inverted surcharge 30.00 30.00
29 A7 10pa on 2k green .25 .25
a. Inverted surcharge
30 A8 1pi on 10k dk blue .50 .60
a. Inverted surcharge
Nos. 27-30 (4) 1.05 1.15

1903-05
Vertically Laid Paper

31 A7 10pa on 2k yel green .30 .50
a. Inverted surcharge 70.00
32 A8 20pa on 4k rose red (Bl) .30 .50
a. Inverted surcharge 25.00
33 A8 1pi on 10k dk blue .30 .50
a. Groundwork inverted 55.00 17.50
34 A8 2pi on 20k blue & car (Bk) .70 1.00
35 A8 5pi on 50k brn vio & grn 1.75 2.00
36 A9 7pi on 70k brn & org (Bl) 2.00 3.00

Perf. 13½

37 A10 10pi on 1r lt brn, brn & org (Bl) 3.25 4.75
38 A11 35pi on 3.50r blk & gray 9.75 13.00
39 A11 70pi on 7r blk & yel 11.20 15.00
Nos. 31-39 (9) 29.55 40.25

A12

A13

A14

Wove Paper
Lozenges of Varnish on Face

1909 Unwmk. *Perf. 14½x15*

40 A12 5pa on 1k orange .25 .35
41 A12 10pa on 2k green .30 .55
a. Inverted surcharge 7.25 8.50
42 A12 20pa on 4k carmine .60 .90
43 A12 1pi on 10k blue .65 1.00
44 A12 5pi on 50k vio & grn 1.40 1.75
45 A12 7pi on 70k brn & org 2.00 2.75

Perf. 13½

46 A13 10pi on 1r brn & org 3.00 5.00
47 A14 35pi on 3.50r mar & lt grn 10.50 14.00
48 A14 70pi on 7r dk grn & pink 18.00 25.00
Nos. 40-48 (9) 36.70 51.30

50th anniv. of the establishing of the Russian Post Offices in the Levant.

Nos. 40-48 Overprinted with Names of Various Cities
Overprinted "Constantinople"
Black Overprint

1909-10 *Perf. 14½x15*

61 A12 5pa on 1k .15 .30
62 A12 10pa on 2k .15 .30
63 A12 20pa on 4k .30 .45
64 A12 1pi on 10k .30 .55
65 A12 5pi on 50k .60 .90
66 A12 7pi on 70k 1.40 2.00

"Consnantinople"

61a A12 5pa on 1k 1.65
62a A12 10pa on 2k 1.25
63a A12 20pa on 4k 2.00
64a A12 1pi on 10k 2.75
65a A12 5pi on 50k 2.75
66a A12 7pi on 70k 5.00

"Constantinopie"

61b A12 5pa on 1k 10.00
62b A12 10pa on 2k 10.00
63b A12 20pa on 4k 10.00
64b A12 1pi on 10k 10.00
65b A12 5pi on 50k 10.00
66b A12 7pi on 70k 10.00

Perf. 13½

67 A13 10pi on 1r 5.50 8.75
a. "Constantinople" 14.00
68 A14 35pi on 3.50r 16.00 27.50
69 A14 70pi on 7r 30.00 42.50

"Constautinople"

68a A14 35pi on 3.50r 32.50
69a A14 70pi on 7r 60.00

"Constantjnople"

68b A14 35pi on 3.50r 32.50

69b A14 70pi on 7r 60.00

Blue Overprint

Perf. 14½x15

70 A12 5pa on 1k 2.50 3.50
a. "Consnantinople" 8.00
Nos. 61-70 (26) 317.30 86.75

Overprinted "Jaffa"

Black Overprint

71 A12 5pa on 1k 1.40 2.50
a. Inverted overprint 11.50
72 A12 10pa on 2k 1.75 2.75
a. Inverted overprint 11.50
73 A12 20pa on 4k 2.00 3.50
a. Inverted overprint 27.50
74 A12 1pi on 10k 2.50 3.50
a. Double overprint 32.50
75 A12 5pi on 50k 6.00 7.00
76 A12 7pi on 70k 7.25 9.75

Perf. 13½

77 A13 10pi on 1r 24.00 37.50
78 A14 35pi on 3.50r 60.00 87.50
79 A14 70pi on 7r 80.00 125.00

Blue Overprint

Perf. 14½x15

80 A12 5pa on 1k 4.00 6.25
Nos. 71-80 (10) 188.90 285.25

Overprinted "Ierusalem"

Black Overprint

81 A12 5pa on 1k 1.50 2.00
a. Inverted overprint 13.00
b. "erusalem" 8.25
82 A12 10pa on 2k 2.00 3.00
a. Inverted overprint 13.00
b. "erusalem" 8.25
83 A12 20pa on 4k 3.00 4.00
a. Inverted overprint 13.00
b. "erusalem" 8.25
84 A12 1pi on 10k 3.00 4.00
a. "erusalem" 11.50
85 A12 5pi on 50k 5.00 8.00
a. "erusalem" 22.50
86 A12 7pi on 70k 10.00 13.00
a. "erusalem" 22.50

Perf. 13½

87 A13 10pi on 1r 32.50 42.50
88 A14 35pi on 3.50r 75.00 90.00
89 A14 70pi on 7r 90.00 125.00

Blue Overprint

Perf. 14½x15

90 A12 5pa on 1k 4.50 6.50
Nos. 81-90 (10) 226.50 298.00

Overprinted "Kerassunde"

Black Overprint

91 A12 5pa on 1k .30 .45
a. Inverted overprint 8.75
92 A12 10pa on 2k .30 .45
a. Inverted overprint 8.75
93 A12 20pa on 4k .45 .60
a. Inverted overprint 10.50
94 A12 1pi on 10k .55 .70
95 A12 5pi on 50k 1.00 1.25
96 A12 7pi on 70k 1.40 2.00

Perf. 13½

97 A13 10pi on 1r 5.50 7.75
98 A14 35pi on 3.50r 17.50 21.00
99 A14 70pi on 7r 25.00 30.00

Blue Overprint

Perf. 14½x15

100 A12 5pa on 1k 3.75 5.50
Nos. 91-100 (10) 55.75 69.70

Overprinted "Mont Athos"

Black Overprint

101 A12 5pa on 1k .30 .60
b. Inverted overprint 14.00
102 A12 10pa on 2k .30 .60
b. Inverted overprint 14.00
103 A12 20pa on 4k .35 .65
b. Inverted overprint 15.00
104 A12 1pi on 10k .60 .85
b. Double overprint 22.50
105 A12 5pi on 50k 2.00 2.50
106 A12 7pi on 70k 3.00 4.25
b. Pair, one without "Mont Athos" 16.00

Perf. 13½

107 A13 10pi on 1r 10.00 12.50
108 A14 35pi on 3.50r 22.50 27.50
109 A14 70pi on 7r 40.00 55.00

Blue Overprint

Perf. 14½x15

110 A12 5pa on 1k 3.50 6.25
Nos. 101-110 (10) 82.55 110.70

"Mont Atho"

101a A12 5pa on 1k 13.00
102a A12 10pa on 2k 13.00
103a A12 20pa on 4k 13.00
104a A12 1pi on 10k 20.00
c. As "a," double overprint 85.00
105a A12 5pi on 50k 27.50
106a A12 7pi on 70k 40.00
110a A12 5pa on 1k 11.50

Overprinted **С. Аѳонъ**

111 A12 5pa on 1k .35 .55
112 A12 10pa on 2k .35 .55
113 A12 20pa on 4k .45 .90
114 A12 1pi on 10k .90 1.75
115 A12 5pi on 50k 1.75 2.75
116 A12 7pi on 70k 3.00 5.00

Perf. 13½

117 A13 10pi on 1r 18.00 25.00
Nos. 111-117 (7) 24.80 36.50

The overprint is larger on No. 117.

Overprinted "Salonique"

Black Overprint

Perf. 14½x15

131 A12 5pa on 1k .30 .60
a. Inverted overprint 6.50
b. Pair, one without overprint
132 A12 10pa on 2k .45 .90
a. Inverted overprint 10.00
133 A12 20pa on 4k .60 .90
a. Inverted overprint 13.00
134 A12 1pi on 10k .60 .90
135 A12 5pi on 50k 1.25 1.75
136 A12 7pi on 70k 2.50 3.00

Perf. 13½

137 A13 10pi on 1r 15.00 15.00
138 A14 35pi on 3.50r 27.50 32.50
139 A14 70pi on 7r 50.00 50.00

Blue Overprint

Perf. 14½x15

140 A12 5pa on 1k 7.00 8.00
Nos. 131-140 (10) 105.20 113.55

Overprinted "Smyrne"

Black Overprint

141 A12 5pa on 1k .35 .60
a. Double overprint
b. Inverted overprint 5.00
142 A12 10pa on 2k .35 .60
a. Inverted overprint 8.25
143 A12 20pa on 4k .70 .80
a. Inverted overprint 10.00
144 A12 1pi on 10k .70 .90
145 A12 5pi on 50k 1.50 1.50
146 A12 7pi on 70k 2.25 3.00

Perf. 13½

147 A13 10pi on 1r 9.00 10.50
148 A14 35pi on 3.50r 18.00 21.00
149 A14 70pi on 7r 27.00 32.50

Blue Overprint

Perf. 14½x15

150 A12 5pa on 1k 3.25 4.75
Nos. 141-150 (10) 63.10 76.15

"Smyrn"

141c A12 5pa on 1k 3.50 4.00
142b A12 10pa on 2k 3.25 4.00
143b A12 20pa on 4k 3.25 4.00
144a A12 1pi on 10k 4.50 5.75
145a A12 5pi on 50k 4.50 5.25
146a A12 7pi on 70k 6.50 6.50
Nos. 141c-146a (6) 25.50 29.50

Overprinted "Trebizonde"

Black Overprint

151 A12 5pa on 1k .35 .60
a. Inverted overprint 4.50
152 A12 10pa on 2k .35 .60
a. Inverted overprint 6.50
b. Pair, one without "Trebizonde"
153 A12 20pa on 4k .45 .40
a. Inverted overprint 10.00
154 A12 1pi on 10k .45 .75
a. Pair, one without "Trebizonde" 27.50
155 A12 5pi on 50k 1.00 1.50
156 A12 7pi on 70k 1.75 3.00

Perf. 13½

157 A13 10pi on 1r 9.00 10.50
158 A14 35pi on 3.50r 18.00 21.00
159 A14 70pi on 7r 27.50 32.50

Blue Overprint

Perf. 14½x15

160 A12 5pa on 1k 3.25 4.75
Nos. 151-160 (10) 62.10 75.60

On Nos. 158 and 159 the overprint is spelled "Trebisonde".

Overprinted "Beyrouth"

Black Overprint

1910

161 A12 5pa on 1k .25 .45
162 A12 10pa on 2k .25 .45
a. Inverted overprint 20.00
163 A12 20pa on 4k .40 .60
164 A12 1pi on 10k .40 .75
165 A12 5pi on 50k .80 1.50
166 A12 7pi on 70k 1.65 3.00

Perf. 13½

167 A13 10pi on 1r 8.25 10.50
168 A14 35pi on 3.50r 16.00 21.00
169 A14 70pi on 7r 25.00 32.50
Nos. 161-169 (9) 53.00 70.75

Overprinted "Dardanelles"

Perf. 14½x15

171 A12 5pa on 1k .30 .60
172 A12 10pa on 2k .30 .60
a. Pair, one without overprint
173 A12 20pa on 4k .60 .75
a. Inverted overprint 10.00
174 A12 1pi on 10k .60 .90
175 A12 5pi on 50k 1.25 1.75
176 A12 7pi on 70k 2.50 3.00

Perf. 13½

177 A13 10pi on 1r 8.25 10.25
178 A14 35pi on 3.50r 16.00 21.00
a. Center and ovpt. inverted
179 A14 70pi on 7r 25.00 32.50
Nos. 171-179 (9) 54.80 71.35

Overprinted "Metelin"

Perf. 14½x15

181 A12 5pa on 1k .40 .75
a. Inverted overprint 10.00
182 A12 10pa on 2k .40 .75
a. Inverted overprint 13.00
183 A12 20pa on 4k .70 1.25
a. Inverted overprint 13.00
184 A12 1pi on 10k .70 1.25
185 A12 5pi on 50k 1.75 2.50
186 A12 7pi on 70k 2.25 3.50

Perf. 13½

187 A13 10pi on 1r 11.00 15.00
188 A14 35pi on 3.50r 25.00 32.50
189 A14 70pi on 7r 35.00 45.00
Nos. 181-189 (9) 77.20 102.50

Overprinted "Rizeh"

Perf. 14½x15

191 A12 5pa on 1k .35 .60
a. Inverted overprint 6.50
192 A12 10pa on 2k .35 .60
a. Inverted overprint 10.00
193 A12 20pa on 4k .60 .75
a. Inverted overprint 10.00
194 A12 1pi on 10k .60 .75
195 A12 5pi on 50k 1.00 2.00
196 A12 7pi on 70k 1.90 3.50

Perf. 13½

197 A13 10pi on 1r 10.00 12.50
198 A14 35pi on 3.50r 16.00 21.00
199 A14 70pi on 7r 25.00 32.50
Nos. 191-199 (9) 55.80 74.20

Nos. 61-199 for the establishing of Russian Post Offices in the Levant, 50th anniv.

A15 A16 A17

Vertically Laid Paper

1910 Wmk. 168 *Perf. 14½x15*

200 A15 20pa on 5k red violet (Bl) .60 .60

Wove Paper

Vertical Lozenges of Varnish on Face

1910 Unwmk. *Perf. 14x14½*

201 A16 5pa on 1k org yel (Bl) .15 .25
202 A16 10pa on 2k green (R) .15 .25
203 A17 20pa on 4k car rose (Bl) .15 .25
204 A17 1pi on 10k blue (R) .15 .25
205 A8 5pi on 50k vio & grn (Bl) .40 .60
206 A9 7pi on 70k lt brn & org (Bl) .40 .65

Perf. 13½

207 A10 10pi on 1r pale brn, brn & org (Bl) .50 .75
Nos. 201-207 (7) 1.90 3.00

Russian Stamps of 1909-12 Surcharged in Black:

20 PARA No. 208 — **1½ PIASTRE** Nos. 209-212

1912 *Perf. 14x14½*

208 A14 20pa on 5k claret .15 .20
209 A11 1½pi on 15k dl vio & blue .20 .25
210 A8 2pi on 20k bl & car .20 .30
211 A11 2½pi on 25k grn & vio .25 .45
a. Double surcharge 50.00 50.00
212 A11 3½pi on 35k vio & grn .40 .55
Nos. 208-212 (5) 1.20 1.75

Russia Nos. 88-91, 93, 95-104 Surcharged:

PARA 5 PARA c — **10 PARA 10** d

1 1 PIASTRE e — **PIAS 1½ TRE** f

g — **30 PIASTRES**

1913 *Perf. 13½*

213 A16(c) 5pa on 1k .15 .15
214 A17(d) 10pa on 2k .15 .15
215 A18(c) 15pa on 3k .15 .15
216 A19(c) 20pa on 4k .15 .15
217 A21(e) 1pi on 10k .20 .20
218 A23(f) 1½pi on 15k .45 .50
219 A24(f) 2pi on 20k .45 .50
220 A25(f) 2½pi on 25k .60 .70
221 A26(f) 3½pi on 35k 1.50 1.40
222 A27(e) 5pi on 50k 1.75 1.75
223 A28(f) 7pi on 70k 7.00 7.00
224 A29(e) 10pi on 1r 7.00 7.00
225 A30(e) 20pi on 2r 1.50 1.40
226 A31(g) 30pi on 3r 2.25 2.00
227 A32(e) 50pi on 5r 62.50 62.50
Nos. 213-227 (15) 85.80 85.55

Romanov dynasty tercentenary.
Forgeries exist of overprint on No. 227.

Russia Nos. 75, 71, 72 Surcharged:

15 PARA h — **PIAS 50 TRES** i

Perf. 14x14½

Wove Paper

228 A14(h) 15pa on 3k .15 .15

Perf. 13, 13½

230 A13(i) 50pi on 5r 5.00 10.00

Vertically Laid Paper

Wmk. Wavy Lines (168)

231 A13(i) 100pi on 10r 10.00 20.00
a. Double surcharge 24.00 40.00
Nos. 228-231 (3) 15.15 30.15

No. 228 has lozenges of varnish on face but No. 230 has not.

Wrangel Issues

For the Posts of Gen. Peter Wrangel's army and civilian refugees from South Russia, interned in Turkey, Serbia, etc.

Very few of the Wrangel overprints were actually sold to the public, and many of the covers were made up later with the original cancels. Reprints abound. Values probably are based on sales of reprints in most cases.

ПОЧТА РУССКОЙ АРМІИ 1.000 РУБЛЕЙ

Russian Stamps of 1902-18 Surcharged in Blue, Red or Black

On Russia Nos. 69-70

Vertically Laid Paper

1921 Wmk. 168 *Perf. 13½*

232 A12 10,000r on 3.50r 20.00 20.00
233 A12 10,000r on 7r 20.00 20.00
234 A12 20,000r on 3.50r 20.00 20.00
235 A12 20,000r on 7r 20.00 20.00
Nos. 232-235 (4) 80.00 80.00

On Russia Nos. 71-86, 87a, 117-118, 137-138

Wove Paper

Perf. 14x14½, 13½

Unwmk.

236 A14 1000r on 1k .60 .60
237 A14 1000r on 2k (R) .60 .60
237A A14 1000r on 2k (Bk) 9.00 9.00
238 A14 1000r on 3k .15 .15
a. Inverted surcharge 1.25 1.25
239 A15 1000r on 4k .15 .15
a. Inverted surcharge 1.25 1.25
240 A14 1000r on 5k .15 .15
a. Inverted surcharge 1.25 1.25
241 A14 1000r on 7k .15 .15
a. Inverted surcharge 1.25 1.25
242 A15 1000r on 10k .15 .15
a. Inverted surcharge 1.25 1.25
243 A14 1000r on 10k on 7k .15 .15
244 A14 5000r on 3k .15 .15
245 A11 5000r on 14k 2.00 2.00
246 A11 5000r on 15k .15 .15
a. "PYCCKIN" 3.50 3.50
247 A8 5000r on 20k .65 .65
a. "PYCCKIN" 3.50 3.50
248 A11 5000r on 20k on 14k .65 .65
249 A11 5000r on 25k .15 .15
250 A11 5000r on 35k .15 .15
a. Inverted surcharge 1.25 1.25
b. New value omitted
251 A8 5000r on 50k .20 .20
a. Inverted surcharge
252 A11 5000r on 70k .20 .20
a. Inverted surcharge 2.00 2.00
253 A9 10,000r on 1r (Bl) .20 .20
254 A9 10,000r on 1r (Bk) 1.50 1.50
255 A12 10,000r on 3.50r .60 .60
256 A13 10,000r on 5r 9.00 9.00
257 A13 10,000r on 10r .75 .75
258 A9 20,000r on 1r .45 .45
259 A12 20,000r on 3.50r .45 .45
a. Inverted surcharge 6.50 6.50
b. New value omitted 55.00 55.00

260 A12 20,000r on 7r 18.00 18.00
261 A13 20,000r on 10r .40 .40
Nos. 236-261 (27) 46.75 46.75

On Russia No. 104

261A A32 20,000r on 5r

On Russia Nos. 119-123, 125-135

Imperf

262 A14 1000r on 1k .20 .25
263 A14 1000r on 2k (R) .20 .25
263A A14 1000r on 2k (Bk) .25 .30
264 A14 1000r on 3k .20 .25
265 A15 1000r on 4k 6.50 6.50
266 A14 1000r on 5k .25 .30
267 A14 5000r on 3k .20 .25
268 A11 5000r on 15k .25 .30
268A A8 5000r on 20k 10.00
268B A11 5000r on 25k 10.00
269 A11 5000r on 35k .50 .50
270 A8 5000r on 50k .50 .50
271 A11 5000r on 70k .20 .20
272 A9 10,000r on 1r (Bl) .15 .15
a. Inverted surcharge 1.00 .65
273 A9 10,000r on 1r (Bk) .20 .25
274 A12 10,000r on 3.50r .20 .25
275 A13 10,000r on 5r .85 1.00
276 A12 10,000r on 7r 5.25 5.25
276A A13 10,000r on 10r 32.50
277 A9 20,000r on 1r (Bl) .15 .15
a. Inverted surcharge 1.00 1.00
278 A9 20,000r on 1r (Bk) .20 .25
279 A12 20,000r on 3.50r .85 1.00
280 A13 20,000r on 5r .15 .20
281 A12 20,000r on 7r 4.00 4.00
281A A13 20,000r on 10r 32.50
Nos. 262-268,269-276,277-281 (21) 21.25 22.10

A18 A19

On Postal Savings Stamps

Perf. 14½x15

Wmk. 171

282 A18 10,000r on 1k red, *buff* .15 .20
283 A19 10,000r on 5k grn, *buff* .15 .15
a. Inverted surcharge 2.75
284 A19 10,000r on 10k brn, *buff* .15 .15
a. Inverted surcharge 2.75
Set value .25 .30

On Stamps of Russian Offices in Turkey

On No. 38-39

Vertically Laid Paper

Wmk. Wavy Lines (168)

284B A11 20,000r on 35pi on 3.50r
284C A11 20,000r on 70pi on 7r

On Nos. 200-207

Vertically Laid Paper

284D A15 1000r on 20pa on 5k 1.10 1.10

Wove Paper

Unwmk.

285 A16 1000r on 5pa on 1k .35 .35
286 A16 1000r on 10pa on 2k .35 .35
287 A17 1000r on 20pa on 4k .30 .30
288 A17 1000r on 1pi on 10k .35 .35
289 A8 5000r on 5pi on 50k .40 .40
290 A9 5000r on 7pi on 70k .40 .40
291 A10 10,000r on 10pi on 1r 1.50 1.50
a. Inverted surcharge 4.75 4.75
b. Pair, one without surcharge 4.75 4.75
292 A10 20,000r on 10pi on 1r .30 .30
a. Inverted surcharge 4.75 4.75
b. Pair, one without surcharge 4.75 4.75
Nos. 284D-292 (9) 5.05 5.05

On Nos. 208-212

293 A14 1000r on 20pa on 5k .40 .40
294 A11 5000r on 1½pi on 15k .40 .40
295 A8 5000r on 2pi on 20k .40 .40
296 A11 5000r on 2½pi on 25k .40 .40
297 A11 5000r on 3½pi on 35k .50 .50
Nos. 293-297 (5) 2.10 2.10

On Nos. 228, 230-231

298 A14 1000r on 15pa on 3k .30 .30
299 A13 10,000r on 50pi on 5r 8.50 8.50
300 A13 10,000r on 100pi on 10r 10.50 10.50
301 A13 20,000r on 50pi on 5r .30 .30
302 A13 20,000r on 100pi on 10r 10.50 10.50
Nos. 298-302 (5) 30.10 30.10

On Stamps of South Russia

Denikin Issue

Imperf

303 A5 5000r on 5k org .15 .15
a. Inverted surcharge
304 A5 5000r on 10k green .15 .15
305 A5 5000r on 15k red .15 .15
306 A5 5000r on 35k lt bl .15 .15
307 A5 5000r on 70k dk blue .15 .15
307A A5 10,000r on 70k dk blue 5.25 5.25
308 A6 10,000r on 1r brn & red .15 .20
309 A6 10,000r on 2r gray vio & yel .25 .30
a. Inverted surcharge 1.25 1.25
310 A6 10,000r on 3r dull rose & grn .45 .50
311 A6 10,000r on 5r slate & vio .50 .55
312 A6 10,000r on 7r gray grn & rose 10.00 10.00
313 A6 10,000r on 10r red & gray .45 .50
314 A6 20,000r on 1r brn & red .15 .15
315 A6 20,000r on 2r gray vio & yel (Bl) 3.25 3.25
a. Inverted surcharge 5.00 5.00
315B A6 20,000r on 2r gray vio & yel (Bk) .20 .25
316 A6 20,000r on 3r dull rose & grn (Bl) 5.25 5.25
316A A6 20,000r on 3r dull rose & grn (Bk) 2.75 2.75
317 A6 20,000r on 5r slate & vio .20 .25
318 A6 20,000r on 7r gray grn & rose 6.50 6.50
319 A6 20,000r on 10r red & gray .20 .25
Nos. 303-319 (20) 36.30 36.70

Trident Stamps of Ukraine Surcharged in Blue, Red, Black or Brown

РУССКАЯ ПОЧТА 10,000 РУБЛЕЙ.

1921 ***Perf. 14, 14½x15***

320 A14 10,000r on 1k org .15 .15
321 A14 10,000r on 2k grn .65 .85
322 A14 10,000r on 3k red .15 .15
a. Inverted surcharge 1.25 1.25
323 A15 10,000r on 4k car .15 .15
324 A14 10,000r on 5k cl .20 .25
325 A14 10,000r on 7k lt bl .15 .15
a. Inverted surcharge 1.25 1.25
326 A15 10,000r on 10k dk bl .15 .15
a. Inverted surcharge 1.25 1.25
327 A14 10,000r on 10k on 7k lt bl .15 .15
a. Inverted surcharge 1.25 1.25
328 A8 20,000r on 20k bl & car (Br) .15 .15
a. Inverted surcharge 1.25 1.25
329 A8 20,000r on 20k bl & car (Bk) .15 .15
a. Inverted surcharge 1.25 1.25
330 A11 20,000r on 20k on 14k bl & rose .15 .20
331 A11 20,000r on 35k red brn & grn 10.00 10.00
332 A8 20,000r on 50k brn vio & grn .15 .15
a. Inverted surcharge 1.25 1.25
Nos. 320-332 (13) 12.35 12.65

Imperf

333 A14 10,000r on 1k org .15 .15
a. Inverted surcharge 1.65
334 A14 10,000r on 2k grn .35 .35
335 A14 10,000r on 3k red .15 .15
336 A8 20,000r on 20k bl & car .20 .20
337 A11 20,000r on 35k red brn & grn 4.00 4.00
338 A8 20,000r on 50k brn vio & grn .35 .35
Nos. 333-338 (6) 5.20 5.20

There are several varieties of the trident surcharge on Nos. 320 to 338.

Same Surcharge on Russian Stamps

On Stamps of 1909-18

Perf. 14x14½

338A A14 10,000r on 1k dl org yel .45 .25
339 A14 10,000r on 2k dl grn .45 .25
340 A14 10,000r on 3k car .15 .15
341 A15 10,000r on 4k car .15 .15
342 A14 10,000r on 5k dk cl .15 .15
343 A14 10,000r on 7k blue .20 .15
344 A15 10,000r on 10k dk bl .45 .30
344A A14 10,000r on 10k on 7k bl .90 .55
344B A11 20,000r on 14k dk bl & car 5.00 2.75
345 A11 20,000r on 15k red brn & dp bl .20 .15
346 A8 20,000r on 20k dl bl & dk car .15 .15
347 A11 20,000r on 20k on 14k dk bl & car .90 .55
348 A11 20,000r on 35k red brn & grn .35 .25
349 A8 20,000r on 50k brn vio & grn .20 .15
349A A11 20,000r on 70k brn & red org .45 .35
Nos. 338A-349A (15) 10.15 6.30

On Stamps of 1917-18

Imperf

350 A14 10,000r on 1k org .25 .20
351 A14 10,000r on 2k gray grn .25 .20
352 A14 10,000r on 3k red .25 .20
353 A15 10,000r on 4k car 7.75 5.25
354 A14 10,000r on 5k claret .25 .20
355 A11 20,000r on 15k red brn & dp bl .25 .20
356 A8 20,000r on 50k brn vio & grn .70 .55
357 A11 20,000r on 70k brn & org .35 .35
Nos. 350-357 (8) 10.05 7.15

Same Surcharge on Stamps of Russian Offices in Turkey

On Nos. 40-45

Perf. 14½x15

358 A12 10,000r on 5pa on 1k 2.50 1.65
359 A12 10,000r on 10pa on 2k 2.50 1.65
360 A12 10,000r on 20pa on 4k 2.50 1.65
361 A12 10,000r on 1pi on 10k 2.50 1.65
362 A12 20,000r on 5pi on 50k 2.50 1.65
363 A12 20,000r on 7pi on 70k 2.50 1.65
Nos. 358-363 (6) 15.00 9.90

On Nos. 201-206

364 A16 10,000r on 5pa on 1k .35 .35
365 A16 10,000r on 10pa on 2k .35 .35
366 A17 10,000r on 20pa on 4k .35 .35
367 A17 10,000r on 1pi on 10k .35 .35
368 A8 20,000r on 5pi on 50k .35 .35
369 A9 20,000r on 7pi on 70k .35 .35
Nos. 364-369 (6) 2.10 2.10

On Nos. 228, 208-212, Stamps of 1912-13

370 A14 10,000r on 15pa on 3k .20 .20
371 A14 10,000r on 20pa on 5k .35 .35
372 A11 20,000r on 1½pi on 15k .35 .35
373 A8 20,000r on 2pi on 20k .40
374 A11 20,000r on 2½pi on 25k .40
375 A11 20,000r on 3½pi on 35k .40

Same Surcharge on Stamp of South Russia, Crimea Issue

376 A8 20,000r on 5r on 20k bl & car 16.00
Nos. 370-376 (7) 18.10

RWANDA

ru-'än-də

(Rwandaise Republic)

LOCATION — Central Africa, adjoining the ex-Belgian Congo, Tanganyika, Uganda and Burundi
GOVT. — Republic
AREA — 10,169 sq. mi.
POP. — 5,650,000 (est. 1984)
CAPITAL — Kigali

Rwanda was established as an independent republic on July 1, 1962. With Burundi, it had been a UN trusteeship territory administered by Belgium.
See Ruanda-Urundi.

100 Centimes = 1 Franc

Catalogue values for all unused stamps in this country are for Never Hinged items.

Watermark

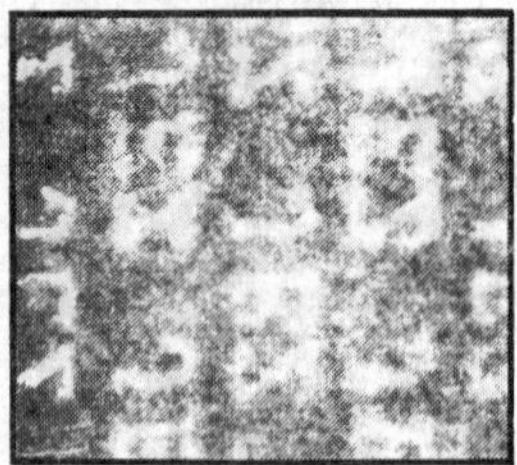

Wmk. 368- JEZ Multiple

Gregoire Kayibanda and Map of Africa — A1

Design: 40c, 1.50fr, 6.50fr, 20fr, Rwanda map spotlighted, "R" omitted.

Perf. 11½

1962, July 1 **Unwmk.** **Photo.**

1 A1 10c brown & gray grn .15 .1
2 A1 40c brown & rose lil .15 .1
3 A1 1fr brown & blue .60 .3
4 A1 1.50fr brown & lt brn .15 .1
5 A1 3.50fr brown & dp org .15 .1
6 A1 6.50fr brown & lt vio bl .18 .1
7 A1 10fr brown & citron .20 .1
8 A1 20fr brown & rose .42 .1
Set value 1.65 .8

Map of Africa and Symbolic Honeycomb A2

Ruanda-Urundi Nos. 151-152 Overprinted with Metallic Frame Obliterating Previous Inscription and Denomination. Black Commemorative Inscription and "REPUBLIQUE RWANDAISE." Surcharged with New Value.

1963, Jan. 28 **Unwmk.** ***Perf. 11½***

9 A2 3.50fr sil, blk, ultra & red .15 .15
10 A2 6.50fr brnz, blk, ultra & red .70 .70
11 A2 10fr stl bl, blk, ultra & red .20 .20
12 A2 20fr sil, blk, ultra & red .38 .38
Nos. 9-12 (4) 1.43 1.43

Rwanda's admission to UN, Sept. 18, 1962.

Stamps of Ruanda-Urundi, 1953, Overprinted

Littonia — A3

Designs as before.

1963, Mar. 21 **Unwmk.** ***Perf. 11½***

Flowers in Natural Colors; Metallic and Black Overprint

13 A3 25c dk grn & dl org .15 .15
14 A3 40c green & salmon .15 .15
15 A3 60c bl grn & pink .15 .15
16 A3 1.25fr dk green & blue .70 .70
17 A3 1.50fr violet & apple grn .55 .55
18 A3 2fr on 1.50fr vio & ap grn .80 .80
19 A3 4fr on 1.50fr vio & ap grn .80 .80
20 A3 5fr dp plum & lt bl grn .80 .80
21 A3 7fr dk green & fawn .80 .80
22 A3 10fr dp plum & pale ol .80 .80
Nos. 13-22 (10) 5.70 5.70

The overprint consists of silver panels with black lettering. The panels on No. 19 are bluish gray.

Imperforates
exist of practically every issue, starting with Nos. 23-26, except Nos. 36, 55-69, 164-169.

Wheat Emblem, Bow, Arrow, Hoe and Billhook A4

1963, July 1 **Photo.** ***Perf. 13½***

23 A4 2fr brown & green .15 .15
24 A4 4fr magenta & ultra .15 .15
25 A4 7fr red & gray .15 .15
26 A4 10fr olive grn & yel .55 .38
Set value .85 .55

FAO "Freedom from Hunger" campaign.

The 20fr leopard and 50fr lion stamps of Ruanda-Urundi, Nos. 149-150, overprinted "Republique Rwandaise" at top and "Contre la Faim" at bottom, were intended to be issued Mar. 21, 1963, but were not placed in use.

Coffee — A5

Designs: 10c, 40c, 4fr, Coffee. 20c, 1fr, 7fr, Bananas. 30c, 2fr, 10fr, Tea.

1963, July 1 *Perf. 11½*

27 A5 10c violet bl & brn .15 .15
28 A5 20c slate & yellow .15 .15
29 A5 30c vermilion & grn .15 .15
30 A5 40c dp green & brown .15 .15
31 A5 1fr maroon & yellow .15 .15
32 A5 2fr dk blue & green .65 .52
33 A5 4fr red & brown .15 .15
34 A5 7fr yellow grn & yellow .16 .15
35 A5 10fr violet & green .25 .15
Set value 1.35 1.00

First anniversary of independence.

African Postal Union Issue
Common Design Type

1963, Sept. 8 Unwmk. *Perf. 12½*

36 CD114 14fr black, ocher & red .55 .50

Post Horn and Pigeon — A6

1963, Oct. 25 Photo. *Perf. 11½*

37 A6 50c ultra & rose .15 .15
38 A6 1.50fr brown & blue .50 .40
39 A6 3fr dp plum & gray .15 .15
40 A6 20fr green & yellow .35 .18
Set value .95 .65

Rwanda's admission to the UPU, Apr. 6.

Scales, UN Emblem and Flame — A7

1963, Dec. 10 Unwmk. *Perf. 11½*

41 A7 5fr crimson .15 .15
42 A7 6fr brt purple .42 .30
43 A7 10fr brt blue .22 .15
Nos. 41-43 (3) .79
Set value .50

15th anniversary of the Universal Declaration of Human Rights.

Children's Clinic — A8

Designs: 20c, 7fr, Laboratory examination, horiz. 30c, 10fr, Physician examining infant. 40c, 20fr, Litter bearers, horiz.

1963, Dec. **Photo.**

44 A8 10c yel org, red & brn blk .15 .15
45 A8 20c grn, red & brn blk .15 .15
46 A8 30c bl, red & brn blk .15 .15
47 A8 40c red lil, red & brn .15 .15
48 A8 2fr bl grn, red brn & blk .50 .42
49 A8 7fr ultra, red & blk .15 .15
50 A8 10fr red brn, red & brn blk .20 .15
51 A8 20fr dp org, red & brn .40 .15
Set value 1.40 .95

Centenary of the International Red Cross.

Map of Rwanda and Woman at Water Pump — A9

1964, May 4 Unwmk. *Perf. 11½*

52 A9 3fr lt grn, dk brn & ultra .15 .15
53 A9 7fr pink, dk brn & ultra .30 .18
54 A9 10fr yel, dk brn & ultra .42 .30
Set value .75 .52

Souvenir Sheet
Imperf

54A A9 25fr lilac, bl, brn & blk 2.50 2.50

UN 4th World Meteorological Day, Mar. 23.

Ruanda-Urundi Nos. 138-150, 153 Overprinted "REPUBLIQUE RWANDAISE", Some Surcharged, in Silver and Black

Buffaloes — A10

Designs: 10c, 20c, 30c, Buffaloes. 40c, 2fr, Black-and-white colobus (monkey). 50c, 7.50fr, Impalas. 1fr, Mountain gorilla. 3fr, 4fr, 8fr, African elephants. 5fr, 10fr, Eland and zebras. 20fr, Leopard. 50fr, Lions. 40c, 1fr and 2fr are vertical.

1964, June 29 Photo. *Perf. 11½*
Size: 33x23mm, 23x33mm

55 A10 10c on 20c gray, ap grn & blk .15 .15
56 A10 20c blk, gray & ap grn .15 .15
57 A10 30c on 1.50fr blk, gray & org .15 .15
58 A10 40c mag, blk & gray grn .15 .15
59 A10 50c grn, org yel & brn .15 .15
60 A10 1fr ultra, blk & brn .15 .15
61 A10 2fr grnsh bl, ind & brn .15 .15
62 A10 3fr brn, dp car & blk .15 .15
63 A10 4fr on 3.50fr on 3fr brn, dp car & blk .24 .15
64 A10 5fr brn, dl yel, grn & blk .22 .15
65 A10 7.50fr on 6.50fr red, org yel & brn .45 .15
66 A10 8fr blue, mag & blk 3.00 2.50
67 A10 10fr brn, dl yel, brt pink & blk .60 .15

Size: 45x26½mm

68 A10 20fr hn brn, ocher & blk 1.00 .52
69 A10 50fr dp blue & brown 1.65 1.25
Nos. 55-69 (15) 8.36
Set value 5.00

Boy with Crutch and Gatagara Home — A11

Basketball — A12

Designs: 40c, 8fr, Girls with sewing machines, horiz. 4fr, 10fr, Girl on crutches, map of Rwanda and Gatagara Home.

1964, Nov. 10 Photo. *Perf. 11½*

70 A11 10c lilac blk brn .15 .15
71 A11 40c blue & blk brn .15 .15
72 A11 4fr org red & blk brn .15 .15
73 A11 7.50fr yel grn & blk brn .22 .18
74 A11 8fr bister & blk brn 1.10 .75
75 A11 10fr magenta & blk brn .32 .20
Nos. 70-75 (6) 2.09
Set value 1.30

Gatagara Home for handicapped children.

1964, Dec. 8 Litho. *Perf. 13½*

Sport: 10c, 4fr, Runner, horiz. 30c, 20fr, High jump, horiz. 40c, 50fr, Soccer.

Size: 26x38mm

76 A12 10c gray, sl & dk grn .15 .15
77 A12 20c pink, sl & rose red .15 .15
78 A12 30c lt grn, sl & grn .15 .15
79 A12 40c buff, sl & brn .15 .15
80 A12 4fr vio gray, sl & vio .15 .15
81 A12 5fr pale grn, sl & yel grn 1.50 1.50
82 A12 20fr pale lil, sl & red lil .38 .32
83 A12 50fr gray, sl & dk gray .90 .75
a. Souvenir sheet of 4 5.00 5.00
Set value 3.00 2.80

18th Olympic Games, Tokyo, Oct. 10-25. No. 83a contains 4 stamps (10fr, soccer; 20fr, basketball; 30fr, high jump; 40fr, runner). Size of stamps: 28x38mm.

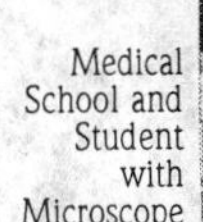

Quill, Books, Radical and Retort — A13

Medical School and Student with Microscope A14

Designs: 30c, 10fr, Scales, hand, staff of Mercury and globe. 40c, 12fr, View of University.

1965, Feb. 22 Engr. *Perf. 11½*

84 A13 10c multicolored .15 .15
85 A14 20c multicolored .15 .15
86 A13 30c multicolored .15 .15
87 A14 40c multicolored .15 .15
88 A13 5fr multicolored .15 .15
89 A14 7fr multicolored .15 .15
90 A13 10fr multicolored .80 .70
91 A14 12fr multicolored .22 .15
Set value 1.40 1.15

National University of Rwanda at Butare.

Abraham Lincoln, Death Cent. — A15

1965, Apr. 15 Photo. *Perf. 13½*

92 A15 10c emerald & dk red .15 .15
93 A15 20c red brn & dk bl .15 .15
94 A15 30c brt violet & red .15 .15
95 A15 40c brt grnsh bl & red .15 .15
96 A15 9fr orange brn & pur .16 .15
97 A15 40fr black & brt grn 1.65 .60
Set value 2.00 .90

Souvenir Sheet

98 A15 50fr red lilac & red 1.90 1.90

Marabous A16

Zebras A17

30c, Impalas. 40c, Crowned cranes, hippopotami & cattle egrets. 1fr, Cape buffalos. 3fr, Cape hunting dogs. 5fr, Yellow baboons. 10fr, Elephant & map of Rwanda with location of park. 40fr, Anhinga, great & reed cormorants. 100fr, Lions.

1965, Apr. 28 Photo. *Perf. 11½*
Size: 32x23mm

99 A16 10c multicolored .15 .15
100 A17 20c multicolored .15 .15
101 A16 30c multicolored .15 .15
102 A17 40c multicolored .15 .15
103 A16 1fr multicolored .15 .15
104 A17 3fr multicolored .15 .15
105 A16 5fr multicolored 2.50 .90
106 A17 10fr multicolored .16 .15

Size: 45x26mm

107 A17 40fr multicolored .65 .25
108 A17 100fr multicolored 1.60 .20
Nos. 99-108 (10) 5.81
Set value 1.70

Kagera National Park publicity.

Telstar and ITU Emblem A18

Designs: 40c, 50fr, Syncom satellite. 60fr, old and new communications equipment.

1965 Unwmk. *Perf. 13½*

109 A18 10c red brn, ultra & car .15 .15
110 A18 40c violet, emer & yel .15 .15
111 A18 4.50fr blk, car & dk bl 1.00 .42
112 A18 50fr dk brn, yel grn & brt grn .75 .18
Nos. 109-112 (4) 2.05
Set value .70

Souvenir Sheet

113 A18 60fr blk brn, org brn & bl 1.90 1.90

ITU, centenary. Issue dates: No. 113, July 19. Others, May 17.

Papilio Bromius Chrapkowskii Suffert — A19

Cattle, ICY Emblem and Map of Africa — A20

Various butterflies and moths in natural colors.

1965-66 Photo. *Perf. 12½*

114 A19 10c black & yellow .15 .15
115 A19 15c black & dp org ('66) .15 .15
116 A19 20c black & lilac .15 .15
117 A19 30c black & red lil .15 .15
118 A19 35c dk brn & dk bl ('66) .15 .15
119 A19 40c black & Prus bl .15 .15
120 A19 1.50fr black & grn ('66) .15 .15
121 A19 3fr dk brn & ol grn ('66) 1.40 .55
122 A19 4fr black & red brn .80 .40
123 A19 10fr black & pur ('66) .20 .15
124 A19 50fr black & brown .60 .22
125 A19 100fr dk brn & bl ('66) 1.60 .55
Set value 4.90 2.10

The 15c, 20c, 40c, 1.50fr, 10fr and 50fr are horizontal.

1965, Oct. 25 Unwmk. *Perf. 12*

Map of Africa and: 40c, Tree & lake. 4.50fr, Gazelle under tree. 45fr, Mount Ruwenzori.

126 A20 10c olive bis & bl grn .15 .15
127 A20 40c lt ultra, red brn & grn .15 .15
128 A20 4.50fr brt grn, yel & brn .80 .40
129 A20 45fr rose claret .70 .25
Nos. 126-129 (4) 1.80
Set value .75

John F. Kennedy (1917-1963) A21

1965, Nov. 22 Photo. *Perf. 11½*

130 A21 10c brt grn & dk brn .15 .15
131 A21 40c brt pink & dk brn .15 .15
132 A21 50c dk blue & dk brn .15 .15
133 A21 1fr gray ol & dk brn .15 .15
134 A21 8fr violet & dk brn 1.40 1.00
135 A21 50fr gray & dk brn 1.00 .80
Set value 2.50 2.00

Souvenir Sheet

136 Sheet of 2 6.75 6.75
a. A21 40fr orange & dark brown 3.00 3.00
b. A21 60fr ultra & dark brown 3.00 3.00

Madonna — A22

1965, Dec. 20

137 A22 10c gold & dk green .15 .15
138 A22 40c gold & dk brn red .15 .15
139 A22 50c gold & dk blue .15 .15

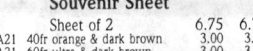

140 A22 4fr gold & slate .50 .45
141 A22 6fr gold & violet .15 .15
142 A22 30fr gold & dk brown .42 .40
Set value 1.10 1.00

Christmas.

Father Joseph Damien and Lepers — A23

Designs: 40c, 45fr, Dr. Albert Schweitzer and Hospital, Lambarene.

1966, Jan. 31 ***Perf. 11½***

143 A23 10c ultra & red brn .15 .15
144 A23 40c dk red & vio bl .15 .15
145 A23 4.50fr slate & brt grn .22 .15
146 A23 45fr brn & hn brn 1.50 .80
Nos. 143-146 (4) 2.02
Set value .95

Issued for World Leprosy Day.

Pope Paul VI, St. Peter's, UN Headquarters and Statue of Liberty — A24

Design: 40c, 50fr, Pope Paul VI, Papal arms and UN emblem.

1966, Feb. 28 **Photo.** ***Perf. 12***

147 A24 10c henna brn & slate .15 .15
148 A24 40c brt blue & slate .15 .15
149 A24 4.50fr lilac & slate 1.10 1.10
150 A24 50fr brt green & slate .90 .35
Nos. 147-150 (4) 2.30 1.75

Visit of Pope Paul VI to the UN, New York City, Oct. 4, 1965.

Globe Thistle — A25

Flowers: 20c, Blood lily. 30c, Everlasting. 40c, Natal plum. 1fr, Tulip tree. 3fr, Rendle orchid. 5fr, Aloe. 10fr, Ammocharis tinneana. 40fr, Coral tree. 100fr, Caper. (20c, 40c, 1fr, 3fr, 5fr, 10fr are vertical).

1966, Mar. 14 ***Perf. 11½***

Granite Paper

151 A25 10c lt blue & multi .15 .15
152 A25 20c orange & multi .15 .15
153 A25 30c car rose & multi .15 .15
154 A25 40c green & multi .15 .15
155 A25 1fr multicolored .15 .15
156 A25 3fr indigo & multi .15 .15
157 A25 5fr multicolored 3.00 1.90
158 A25 10fr blue grn & multi .22 .15
159 A25 40fr brown & multi .75 .38
160 A25 100fr dk bl grn & multi 1.90 1.10
a. Miniature sheet 4.00 3.00
Nos. 151-160 (10) 6.77
Set value 3.75

No. 160a contains one 100fr stamp in changed color, bright blue and multicolored.

Opening of WHO Headquarters, Geneva — A26

1966, May 1 **Litho.** ***Perf. 12½x12***

161 A26 2fr lt olive green .15 .15
162 A26 3fr vermilion .16 .16
163 A26 5fr violet blue .15 .15
Set value .28 .28

Soccer — A27

Mother and Child, Planes Dropping Bombs — A28

20c, 9fr, Basketball. 30c, 50fr, Volleyball.

1966, May 30 **Photo.** ***Perf. 15x14***

164 A27 10c dl grn, ultra & blk .15 .15
165 A27 20c crimson, grn & blk .15 .15
166 A27 30c bl, brt rose lil & blk .15 .15
167 A27 40c yel bis, grn & blk .15 .15
168 A27 9fr gray, red lil & blk .16 .15
169 A27 50fr rose lil, Prus bl & blk .90 .80
Set value 1.25 1.10

National Youth Sports Program.

1966, June 29 ***Perf. 13½***

Design and Inscription Black and Red

170 A28 20c rose lilac .15 .15
171 A28 30c yellow green .15 .15
172 A28 50c lt ultra .15 .15
173 A28 6fr yellow .15 .15
174 A28 15fr blue green .55 .20
175 A28 18fr lilac .50 .35
Set value 1.25 .75

Campaign against nuclear weapons.

A29

A30

Global soccer ball.

1966, July ***Perf. 11½***

176 A29 20c org & indigo .15 .15
177 A29 30c lilac & indigo .15 .15
178 A29 50c brt grn & indigo .15 .15
179 A29 6fr brt rose & indigo .22 .15
180 A29 12fr lt vio brn & ind .65 .25
181 A29 25fr ultra & indigo .80 .50
Set value 1.80 .95

World Soccer Cup Championship, Wembley, England, July 11-30.

1966, Oct. 24 **Engr.** ***Perf. 14***

Designs: 10c, Mikeno Volcano and crested shrike, horiz. 40c, Nyamilanga Falls. 4.50fr, Gahinga and Muhabura volcanoes and lobelias, horiz. 55fr, Rusumu Falls.

182 A30 10c green .15 .15
183 A30 40c brown carmine .15 .15
184 A30 4.50fr violet blue .45 .35
185 A30 55fr red lilac .50 .35
Set value 1.00 .75

UNESCO Emblem, African Artifacts and Musical Clef — A31

UNESCO 20th Anniv.: 30c, 10fr, Hands holding primer showing giraffe and zebra. 50c, 15fr, Atom symbol and power drill. 1fr, 50fr, Submerged sphinxes and sailboat.

1966, Nov. 4 **Photo.** ***Perf. 12***

186 A31 20c brt rose & dk bl .15 .15
187 A31 30c grnsh blue & blk .15 .15
188 A31 50c ocher & blk .15 .15
189 A31 1fr violet & blk .15 .15
190 A31 5fr yellow grn & blk .15 .15
191 A31 10fr brown & blk .16 .16
192 A31 15fr red lilac & dk bl .50 .30
193 A31 50fr dull bl & blk .55 .45
Set value 1.45 1.15

Rock Python — A32

Snakes: 20c, 20fr, Jameson's mamba. 30c, 3fr, Rock python. 50c, Gabon viper. 1fr, Black-lipped spitting cobra. 5fr, African sand snake. 70fr, Egg-eating snake. (20c, 50c, 3fr and 20fr are horizontal.)

1967, Jan. 30 **Photo.** ***Perf. 11½***

194 A32 20c red & black .15 .15
195 A32 30c bl, dk brn & yel .15 .15
196 A32 50c yel grn & multi .15 .15
197 A32 1fr lt lil, blk & bis .15 .15
198 A32 3fr lt vio, dk brn & yel .15 .15
199 A32 5fr yellow & multi .16 .15
200 A32 20fr pale pink & multi .80 .60
201 A32 70fr pale vio, brn & blk 1.20 .65
Set value 2.40 1.60

Ntaruka Hydroelectric Station and Tea Flowers — A33

Designs: 30c, 25fr, Transformer and chrysanthemums (pyrethrum). 50c, 50fr, Sluice and coffee.

1967, Mar. 6 **Photo.** ***Perf. 13½***

202 A33 20c maroon & dp bl .15 .15
203 A33 30c black & red brn .15 .15
204 A33 50c brown & violet .15 .15
205 A33 4fr dk grn & dp plum .15 .15
206 A33 25fr violet & sl grn .30 .30
207 A33 50fr dk blue & brn .90 .90
Set value 1.35 1.35

Ntaruka Hydroelectric Station.

Souvenir Sheets

Cogwheels — A34

1967, Apr. 15 **Engr.** ***Perf. 11½***

208 A34 100fr dk red brown 2.00 2.00
209 A34 100fr brt rose lilac 2.00 2.00

7th "Europa" Phil. Exhib. and the Philatelic Salon of African States, Naples, Apr. 8-16.

Souvenir Sheet

African Dancers and EXPO '67 Emblem — A35

1967, Apr. 28 ***Perf. 11½***

210 A35 180fr dark purple 3.00 3.00

EXPO '67, Intl. Exhib., Montreal, Apr. 28-Oct. 27.

A similar imperf. sheet has the stamp in violet brown.

St. Martin, by Van Dyck and Caritas Emblem — A36

Paintings: 40c, 15fr, Rebecca at the Well, by Murillo, horiz. 60c, 18fr, St. Christopher, by Dierick Bouts. 80c, 26fr, Job and his Friends, by Il Calabrese (Mattia Preti), horiz.

Perf. 13x11, 11x13

1967, May 8 **Photo.**

Black Inscription on Gold Panel

211 A36 20c dark purple .15 .15
212 A36 40c blue green .15 .15
213 A36 60c rose carmine .15 .15
214 A36 80c deep blue .15 .15
215 A36 9fr redsh brown .75 .42
216 A36 15fr orange ver .26 .15
217 A36 18fr dk olive grn .32 .15
218 A36 26fr dk carmine rose .42 .30
Set value 1.90 1.15

Issued to publicize the work of Caritas-Rwanda, Catholic welfare organization.

Round Table Emblem and Zebra — A37

Round Table Emblem and: 40c, Elephant. 60c, Cape buffalo. 80c, Antelope. 18fr, Wheat. 100fr, Palm tree.

1967, July 31 **Photo.** ***Perf. 14***

219 A37 20c gold & multi .15 .15
220 A37 40c gold & multi .15 .15
221 A37 60c gold & multi .15 .15
222 A37 80c gold & multi .15 .15
223 A37 18fr gold & multi .28 .16
224 A37 100fr gold & multi 1.60 .65
Set value 2.00 1.00

Rwanda Table No. 9 of Kigali, a member of the Intl. Round Tables Assoc.

EXPO '67 Emblem, Africa Place and Dancers and Drummers — A38

EXPO '67 Emblem, Africa Place and: 30c, 3fr, Drum and vessels. 50c, 40fr, Two dancers. 1fr, 34fr, Spears, shields and bow.

1967, Aug. 10 Photo. *Perf. 12*

225	A38	20c	brt blue & sepia	.15	.15
226	A38	30c	brt rose lil & sepia	.15	.15
227	A38	50c	orange & sepia	.15	.15
228	A38	1fr	green & sepia	.15	.15
229	A38	3fr	violet & sepia	.15	.15
230	A38	15fr	emerald & sepia	.16	.15
231	A38	34fr	rose red & sepia	.50	.35
232	A38	40fr	grnsh bl & sepia	.65	.38
			Set value	1.50	1.00

Lions Emblem, Globe and Zebra — A39

1967, Oct. 16 Photo. *Perf. 13½*

233	A39	20c	lilac, bl & blk	.15	.15
234	A39	80c	lt grn, bl & blk	.15	.15
235	A39	1fr	rose car, bl & blk	.15	.15
236	A39	8fr	bister, bl & blk	.15	.15
237	A39	10fr	ultra, bl & blk	.15	.15
238	A39	50fr	yel grn, bl & blk	.90	.65
			Set value	1.30	1.00

50th anniversary of Lions International.

Woodland Kingfisher — A40

Birds: 20c, Red bishop, vert. 60c, Red-billed quelea, vert. 80c, Double-toothed barbet. 2fr, Pin-tailed whydah, vert. 3fr, Solitary cuckoo. 18fr, Green wood hoopoe, vert. 25fr, Blue-collared bee-eater. 80fr, Regal sunbird, vert. 100fr, Red-shouldered widowbird.

1967, Dec. 18 *Perf. 11½*

239	A40	20c	multicolored	.15	.15
240	A40	40c	multicolored	.15	.15
241	A40	60c	multicolored	.15	.15
242	A40	80c	multicolored	.15	.15
243	A40	2fr	multicolored	.15	.15
244	A40	3fr	multicolored	.15	.15
245	A40	18fr	multicolored	.40	.15
246	A40	25fr	multicolored	.45	.16
247	A40	80fr	multicolored	1.20	.60
248	A40	100fr	multicolored	1.75	.70
			Set value	4.10	1.80

Souvenir Sheet

Ski Jump, Speed Skating — A41

1968, Feb. 12 Photo. *Perf. 11½*

249		Sheet of 2	2.00	2.00
a.	A41	50fr bl, blk & grn (skier)	.75	.75
b.	A41	50fr grn, blk & bl (skater)	.75	.75
c.		Souv. sheet of 2, #249a at right	2.00	2.00

10th Winter Olympic Games, Grenoble, France, Feb. 6-18.

Runner, Mexican Sculpture and Architecture — A42

Sport and Mexican Art: 40c, Hammer throw, pyramid and animal head. 60c, Hurdler and sculptures. 80c, Javelin and sculptures.

1968, May 27 Photo. *Perf. 11½*

250	A42	20c	ultra & multi	.15	.15
251	A42	40c	multicolored	.15	.15
252	A42	60c	lilac & multi	.15	.15
253	A42	80c	orange & multi	.20	.20
			Set value	.50	.50

19th Olympic Games, Mexico City, Oct. 12-27.

Souvenir Sheet

19th Olympic Games, Mexico City — A43

Designs: a, 8fr, Soccer. b, 10fr, Mexican horseman and cactus. c, 12fr, Field hockey. d, 18fr, Cathedral, Mexico City. e, 20fr, Boxing. f, 30fr, Modern buildings, musical instruments and vase.

1967, May 27 Photo. *Perf. 11½*
Granite Paper

254	A43	Sheet of 6, #a.-f.	2.75	2.75

Three sets of circular gold "medal" overprints with black inscriptions were applied to the six stamps of No. 254 to honor 18 Olympic winners. Issued Dec. 12, 1968. Value $10.

Souvenir Sheet

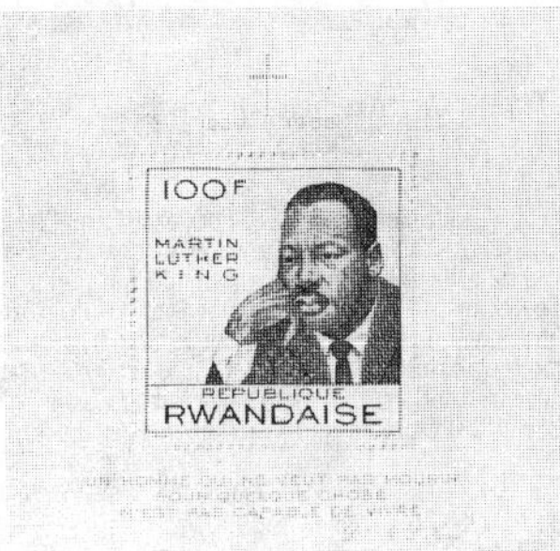

Martin Luther King, Jr. — A44

1968, July 29 Engr. *Perf. 13½*

255	A44	100fr	sepia	2.25	1.75

Rev. Dr. Martin Luther King, Jr. (1929-1968), American civil rights leader. See No. 406.

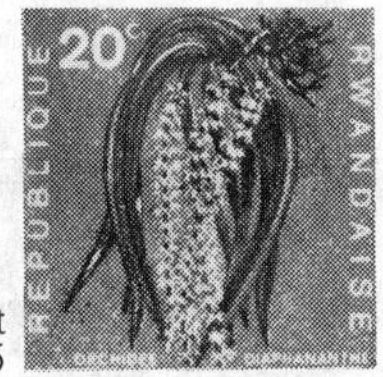

Diaphant Orchid — A45

Flowers: 40c, Pharaoh's scepter. 60c, Flower of traveler's-tree. 80c, Costus afer. 2fr, Banana tree flower. 3fr, Flower and fruit of papaw tree. 18fr, Clerodendron. 25fr, Sweet potato flowers. 80fr, Baobab tree flower. 100fr, Passion flower.

1968, Sept. 9 Litho. *Perf. 13*

256	A45	20c	lilac & multi	.15	.15
257	A45	40c	multicolored	.15	.15
258	A45	60c	bl grn & multi	.15	.15
259	A45	80c	multicolored	.15	.15
260	A45	2fr	brt yellow & multi	.15	.15
261	A45	3fr	multicolored	.15	.15
262	A45	18fr	multicolored	.25	.15
263	A45	25fr	gray & multi	.35	.16
264	A45	80fr	multicolored	1.40	.55
265	A45	100fr	multicolored	1.60	.70
			Set value	3.90	1.80

Equestrian and "Mexico 1968" — A46

Designs: 40c, Judo and "Tokyo 1964." 60c, Fencing and "Rome 1960." 80c, High jump and "Berlin 1936." 38fr, Women's diving and "London 1908 and 1948." 60fr, Weight lifting and "Paris 1900 and 1924."

1968, Oct. 24 Litho. *Perf. 14x13*

266	A46	20c	orange & sepia	.15	.15
267	A46	40c	grnsh bl & sepia	.15	.15
268	A46	60c	car rose & sepia	.15	.15
269	A46	80c	ultra & sepia	.15	.15
270	A46	38fr	red & sepia	.55	.25
271	A46	60fr	emerald & sepia	1.00	.50
			Set value	1.70	.90

19th Olympic Games, Mexico City, Oct. 12-27.

Tuareg, Algeria — A47

African National Costumes: 40c, Musicians, Upper Volta. 60c, Senegalese women. 70c, Girls of Rwanda going to market. 8fr, Young married couple from Morocco. 20fr, Nigerian officials in state dress. 40fr, Man and women from Zambia. 50fr, Man and woman from Kenya.

1968, Nov. 4 Litho. *Perf. 13*

272	A47	30c	multicolored	.15	.15
273	A47	40c	multicolored	.15	.15
274	A47	60c	multicolored	.15	.15
275	A47	70c	multicolored	.15	.15
276	A47	8fr	multicolored	.15	.15
277	A47	20fr	multicolored	.30	.16
278	A47	40fr	multicolored	.60	.35
279	A47	50fr	multicolored	.70	.50
			Set value	1.85	1.25

Souvenir Sheet

Nativity, by Giorgione — A48

1968, Dec. 16 Engr. *Perf. 11½*

280	A48	100fr	green	2.50	2.50

Christmas.

See Nos. 309, 389, 422, 494, 564, 611, 713, 787, 848, 894.

Singing Boy, by Frans Hals — A49

Paintings and Music: 20c, Angels' Concert, by van Eyck. 40c, Angels' Concert, by Matthias Grunewald. 60c, No. 283a, Singing Boy, by Frans Hals. 80c, Lute Player, by Gerard Terborch. 2fr, The Fifer, by Manet. 6fr, No. 286a, Young Girls at the Piano, by Renoir.

1969, Mar. 31 Photo. *Perf. 13*

281	A49	20c	gold & multi	.15	.15
282	A49	40c	gold & multi	.15	.15
283	A49	60c	gold & multi	.15	.15
a.			Souvenir sheet, 75fr	1.40	1.40
284	A49	80c	gold & multi	.15	.15
285	A49	2fr	gold & multi	.15	.15
286	A49	6fr	gold & multi	.15	.15
a.			Souvenir sheet, 75fr	1.40	1.40
			Set value, #281-286, C6-C7	3.00	2.25

Tuareg Men — A50

African Headdresses: 40c, Ovambo woman, South West Africa. 60c, Guinean man and Congolese woman. 80c, Dagger dancer, Guinean forest area. 8fr, Mohammedan Nigerians. 20fr, Luba dancer, Kabondo, Congo. 40fr, Senegalese and Gambian women. 80fr, Rwanda dancer.

1969, May 29 Litho. *Perf. 13*

287	A50	20c	multicolored	.15	.15
288	A50	40c	multicolored	.15	.15
289	A50	60c	multicolored	.15	.15
290	A50	80c	multicolored	.15	.15
291	A50	8fr	multicolored	.15	.15
292	A50	20fr	multicolored	.30	.16
293	A50	40fr	multicolored	.65	.35
294	A50	80fr	multicolored	1.40	.60
			Set value	2.65	1.35

See #398-405. For overprints see #550-557.

The Moneylender and his Wife, by Quentin Massys — A51

Design: 70fr, The Moneylender and his Wife, by Marinus van Reymerswaele.

1969, Sept. 10 Photo. *Perf. 13*

295	A51	30fr	silver & multi	.60	.42
296	A51	70fr	gold & multi	1.40	1.00

5th anniv. of the African Development Bank. Printed in sheets of 20 stamps and 20 labels with commemorative inscription.

For overprints see Nos. 612-613.

Souvenir Sheet

First Man on the Moon — A52

1969, Oct. 9 Engr. *Perf. 11½*
297 A52 100fr blue gray 1.60 1.60

See note after Mali No. C80. See No. 407.

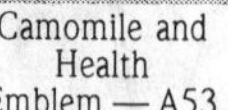

Camomile and Health Emblem — A53

Worker with Pickaxe and Flag — A54

Medicinal Plants and Health Emblem: 40c, Aloe. 60c, Cola. 80c, Coca. 3fr, Hagenia abissinica. 75fr, Cassia. 80fr, Cinchona. 100fr, Tephrosia.

1969, Nov. 24 Photo. *Perf. 13*
Flowers in Natural Colors

298 A53 20c gold, blue & blk .15 .15
299 A53 40c gold, yel grn & blk .15 .15
300 A53 60c gold, pink & blk .15 .15
301 A53 80c gold, green & blk .15 .15
302 A53 3fr gold, orange & blk .15 .15
303 A53 75fr gold, yel & blk 1.40 .55
304 A53 80fr gold, lilac & blk 1.50 .65
305 A53 100fr gold, dl yel & blk 1.75 .80
Nos. 298-305 (8) 5.40
Set value 2.20

For overprints & surcharge see #534-539, B1.

1969, Nov. Photo. *Perf. 11½*
306 A54 6fr brt pink & multi .15 .15
307 A54 18fr ultra & multi .38 .20
308 A54 40fr brown & multi .70 .42
Nos. 306-308 (3) 1.23 .77

10th anniversary of independence.
For overprints see Nos. 608-610.

Christmas Type of 1968
Souvenir Sheet

Design: "Holy Night" (detail), by Correggio.

1969, Dec. 15 Engr. *Perf. 11½*
309 A48 100fr ultra 2.75 2.75

The Cook, by Pierre Aertsen — A55

Paintings: 20c, Quarry Worker, by Oscar Bonnevalle, horiz. 40c, The Plower, by Peter Brueghel, horiz 60c, Fisherman, by Constantin Meunier. 80c, Slipway, Ostende, by Jean van Noten, horiz. 10fr, The Forge of Vulcan, by Velasquez, horiz. 50fr, "Hiercheuse" (woman shoveling coal), by Meunier. 70fr, Miner, by Pierre Paulus.

1969, Dec. 22 Photo. *Perf. 13½*
310 A55 20c gold & multi .15 .15
311 A55 40c gold & multi .15 .15
312 A55 60c gold & multi .15 .15
313 A55 80c gold & multi .15 .15
314 A55 8fr gold & multi .20 .15
315 A55 10fr gold & multi .22 .15
316 A55 50fr gold & multi 1.00 .55
317 A55 70fr gold & multi 1.40 .70
Set value 3.00 1.60

ILO, 50th anniversary.

Napoleon Crossing St. Bernard, by Jacques L. David — A56

Paintings of Napoleon Bonaparte (1769-1821): 40c, Decorating Soldier before Tilsit, by Jean Baptiste Debret. 60c, Addressing Troops at Augsburg, by Claude Gautherot. 80c, First Consul, by Jean Auguste Ingres. 8fr, Battle of Marengo, by Jacques Auguste Pajou. 20fr, Napoleon Meeting Emperor Francis II, by Antoine Jean Gros. 40fr, Gen. Bonaparte at Arcole, by Gros. 80fr Coronation, by David.

1969, Dec. 29
318 A56 20c gold & multi .15 .15
319 A56 40c gold & multi .15 .15
320 A56 60c gold & multi .15 .15
321 A56 80c gold & multi .15 .15
322 A56 8fr gold & multi .24 .15
323 A56 20fr gold & multi .50 .28
324 A56 40fr gold & multi 1.00 .55
325 A56 80fr gold & multi 2.00 1.10
Nos. 318-325 (8) 4.34
Set value 2.20

Epsom Derby, by Gericault — A57

Paintings of Horses: 40c, Horses Emerging from the Sea, by Delacroix. 60c, Charles V at Muhlberg, by Titian, vert. 80c, Amateur Jockeys, by Edgar Degas, 8fr, Horsemen at Rest, by Philips Wouwerman. 20fr, Imperial Guards Officer, by Géricault, vert. 40fr, Friends of the Desert, by Oscar Bonnevalle. 80fr, Two Horses (detail from the Prodigal Son), by Rubens.

1970, Mar. 31 Photo. *Perf. 13½*
326 A57 20c gold & multi .15 .15
327 A57 40c gold & multi .15 .15
328 A57 60c gold & multi .15 .15
329 A57 80c gold & multi .15 .15
330 A57 8fr gold & multi .15 .15
331 A57 20fr gold & multi .40 .16
332 A57 40fr gold & multi .70 .35
333 A57 80fr gold & multi 1.40 .65
Set value 2.80 1.40

Souvenir Sheet

Fleet in Bay of Naples, by Peter Brueghel, the Elder — A58

1970, May 2 Engr. *Perf. 11½*
334 A58 100fr brt rose lilac 2.00 2.00

10th Europa Phil. Exhib., Naples, Italy, May 2-10.
Copies of No. 334 were trimmed to 68x58mm and overprinted in silver or gold "NAPLES 1973" on the stamp, and "Salon Philatelique des Etats Africains / Exposition du Timbre-Poste Europa" in October, 1973.

Soccer and Mexican Decorations — A59

Tharaka Meru Woman, East Africa — A60

Designs: Various scenes from soccer game and pre-Columbian decorations.

1970, June 15 Photo. *Perf. 13*
335 A59 20c gold & multi .15 .15
336 A59 30c gold & multi .15 .15
337 A59 50c gold & multi .15 .15
338 A59 1fr gold & multi .15 .15
339 A59 6fr gold & multi .15 .15
340 A59 18fr gold & multi .40 .16
341 A59 30fr gold & multi .60 .40
342 A59 90fr gold & multi 1.75 .70
Set value 3.00 1.50

9th World Soccer Championships for the Jules Rimet Cup, Mexico City, May 30-June 21.

1970, June 1 Litho.

African National Costumes: 30c, Musician with wooden flute, Niger. 50c, Woman water carrier, Tunisia. 1fr, Ceremonial costumes, North Nigeria. 3fr, Strolling troubadour "Griot," Mali. 5fr, Quipongos women, Angola. 50fr, Man at prayer, Mauritania. 90fr, Sinehatiali dance costumes, Ivory Coast.

343 A60 20c multi .15 .15
344 A60 30c multi .15 .15
345 A60 50c multi .15 .15
346 A60 1fr multi .15 .15
347 A60 3fr multi .15 .15
348 A60 5fr multi .15 .15
349 A60 50fr multi .90 .42
350 A60 90fr multi 1.60 .70
Set value 2.75 1.40

For overprints and surcharges see Nos. 693-698, B2-B3.

Flower Arrangement, Peacock, EXPO '70 Emblem — A61

EXPO Emblem and: 30c, Torii and Camellias, by Yukihiko Yasuda. 50c, Kabuki character and Woman Playing Samisen, by Nampu Katayama. 1fr, Tower of the Sun, and Warrior Riding into Water. 3fr, Pavilion and Buddhist deity. 5fr, Pagoda and modern painting by Shuho Yamakawa. 20fr, Japanese inscription "Omatsuri" and Osaka Castle. 70fr, EXPO '70 emblem and Warrior on Horseback.

1970, Aug. 24 Photo. *Perf. 13*
351 A61 20c gold & multi .15 .15
352 A61 30c gold & multi .15 .15
353 A61 50c gold & multi .15 .15
354 A61 1fr gold & multi .15 .15
355 A61 3fr gold & multi .15 .15
356 A61 5fr gold & multi .15 .15
357 A61 20fr gold & multi .32 .25
358 A61 70fr gold & multi 1.00 .50
Set value 1.60 1.00

EXPO '70 International Exhibition, Osaka, Japan, Mar. 15-Sept. 13.

Young Mountain Gorillas — A62

Various Gorillas. 40c, 80c, 2fr, 100fr are vert.

1970, Sept. 7
359 A62 20c olive & blk .15 .15
360 A62 40c brt rose lil & blk .15 .15
361 A62 60c blue, brn & blk .15 .15
362 A62 80c org brn & blk .15 .15
363 A62 1fr dp car & blk .15 .15
364 A62 2fr black & multi .15 .15
365 A62 15fr sepia & blk .40 .20
366 A62 100fr brt bl & blk 2.50 1.50
Set value 3.10 2.00

Pierre J. Pelletier and Joseph B. Caventou — A63

Designs: 20c, Cinchona flower and bark. 80c, Quinine powder and pharmacological vessels. 1fr, Anopheles mosquito. 3fr, Malaria patient and nurse. 25fr, "Malaria" (mosquito).

1970, Oct. 27 Photo. *Perf. 13*
367 A63 20c silver & multi .15 .15
368 A63 80c silver & multi .15 .15
369 A63 1fr silver & multi .15 .15
370 A63 3fr silver & multi .15 .15
371 A63 25fr silver & multi .50 .25
372 A63 70fr silver & multi 1.40 .60
Set value 2.10 1.00

150th anniv. of the discovery of quinine by Pierre Joseph Pelletier (1788-1842) and Joseph Bienaimé Caventou (1795-1877), French pharmacologists.

Apollo Spaceship — A64

Apollo Spaceship: 30c, Second stage separation. 50c, Spaceship over moon surface. 1fr, Landing module and astronauts on moon. 3fr, Take-off from moon. 5fr, Return to earth. 10fr, Final separation of nose cone. 80fr, Splashdown.

1970, Nov. 23 Photo. *Perf. 13*
373 A64 20c silver & multi .15 .15
374 A64 30c silver & multi .15 .15
375 A64 50c silver & multi .15 .15
376 A64 1fr silver & multi .15 .15
377 A64 3fr silver & multi .15 .15
378 A64 5fr silver & multi .15 .15
379 A64 10fr silver & multi .16 .15
380 A64 80fr silver & multi 1.20 .90
Set value 1.70 1.25

Conquest of space.

Franklin D. Roosevelt and Brassocattleya Olympia Alba — A65

Portraits of Roosevelt and various orchids.

1970, Dec. 21 Photo. *Perf. 13*
381 A65 20c blue, blk & brn .15 .15
382 A65 30c car rose, blk & brn .15 .15
383 A65 50c dp org, blk & brn .15 .15
384 A65 1fr green, blk & brn .15 .15
385 A65 2fr maroon, blk & grn .15 .15
386 A65 6fr lilac & multi .15 .15
387 A65 30fr bl, blk & sl grn .60 .30
388 A65 60fr lil rose, blk & sl grn 1.25 .50
Set value 2.10 1.00

Pres. Franklin D. Roosevelt, 25th death anniv.

Christmas Type of 1968
Souvenir Sheet

Design: 100fr, Adoration of the Shepherds, by José de Ribera, vert.

1970, Dec. 24 Engr. *Perf. 11½*
389 A48 100fr Prus blue 2.00 2.00

Pope Paul VI — A66

Popes: 20c, John XXIII, 1958-1963. 30c, Pius XII, 1939-1958. 40c, Pius XI, 1922-39. 1fr, Benedict XV, 1914-22. 18fr, St. Pius X, 1903-14. 20fr, Leo XIII, 1878-1903. 60fr, Pius IX, 1846-78.

1970, Dec. 31 Photo. *Perf. 13*

390 A66 10c gold & dk brn .15 .15
391 A66 20c gold & dk grn .15 .15
392 A66 30c gold & dp claret .15 .15
393 A66 40c gold & indigo .15 .15
394 A66 1fr gold & dk pur .15 .15
395 A66 18fr gold & purple .35 .16
396 A66 20fr gold & org brn .42 .25
397 A66 60fr gold & blk brn 1.10 .60
Set value 2.00 1.20

Centenary of Vatican I, Ecumenical Council of the Roman Catholic Church, 1869-70.

Headdress Type of 1969

African Headdresses: 20c, Rendille woman. 30c, Young Toubou woman, Chad. 50c, Peul man, Niger. 1fr, Young Masai man, Kenya. 5fr, Young Peul girl, Niger. 18fr, Rwanda woman. 25fr, Man, Mauritania. 50fr, Rwanda women with pearl necklaces.

1971, Feb. 15 Litho. *Perf. 13*

398 A50 20c multi .15 .15
399 A50 30c multi .15 .15
400 A50 50c multi .15 .15
401 A50 1fr multi .15 .15
402 A50 5fr multi .15 .15
403 A50 18fr multi .30 .20
404 A50 25fr multi .45 .25
405 A50 50fr multi 1.00 .50
Set value 2.00 1.15

M. L. King Type of 1968
Souvenir Sheet

Design: 100fr, Charles de Gaulle (1890-1970), President of France.

1971, Mar. 15 Engr. *Perf. 13½*

406 A44 100fr ultra 2.00 1.50

Astronaut Type of 1969 Inscribed in Dark Violet with Emblem and: "APOLLO / 14 / SHEPARD / ROOSA / MITCHELL"

1971, Apr. 15 Engr. *Perf. 11½*
Souvenir Sheet

407 A52 100fr brown orange 4.00 3.50

Apollo 14 US moon landing, Jan. 31-Feb. 9.

Beethoven, by Christian Horneman — A67

Beethoven Portraits: 30c, Joseph Stieler. 50c, by Ferdinand Schimon. 3fr, by H. Best. 6fr, by W. Fassbender. 90fr, Beethoven's Funeral Procession, by Leopold Stöber.

1971, July 5 Photo. *Perf. 13*

408 A67 20c gold & multi .15 .15
409 A67 30c gold & multi .15 .15
410 A67 50c gold & multi .15 .15
411 A67 3fr gold & multi .15 .15
412 A67 6fr gold & multi .15 .15
413 A67 90fr gold & multi 1.90 1.00
Set value 2.25 1.20

Ludwig van Beethoven (1770-1827), composer.

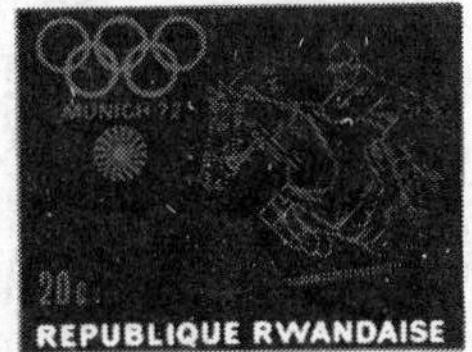

Equestrian A68

Olympic Sports: 30c, Runner at start. 50c, Basketball. 1fr, High jump. 8fr, Boxing. 10fr, Pole vault. 20fr, Wrestling. 60fr, Gymnastics (rings).

1971, Oct. 25 Photo. *Perf. 13*

414 A68 20c gold & black .15 .15
415 A68 30c gold & dp rose lil .15 .15
416 A68 50c gold & vio bl .15 .15
417 A68 1fr gold & dp grn .15 .15
418 A68 8fr gold & henna brn .16 .15
419 A68 10fr gold & purple .22 .15
420 A68 20fr gold & dp brn .40 .22
421 A68 60fr gold & Prus bl 1.20 .50
Set value 2.15 1.10

20th Summer Olympic Games, Munich, Aug. 26-Sept. 10, 1972.

Christmas Type of 1968
Souvenir Sheet

100fr, Nativity, by Anthony van Dyck, vert.

1971, Dec. 20 Engr. *Perf. 11½*

422 A48 100fr indigo 2.00 2.00

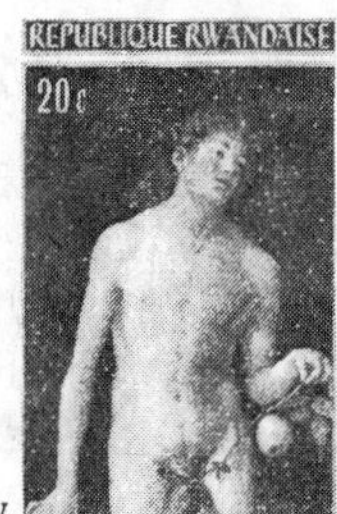

Adam by Dürer — A69

Paintings by Albrecht Dürer (1471-1528), German painter and engraver: 30c, Eve. 50c, Hieronymus Holzschuher, Portrait. 1fr, Lamentation of Christ. 3fr, Madonna with the Pear. 5fr, St. Eustace. 20fr, Sts. Paul and Mark. 70fr, Self-portrait, 1500.

1971, Dec. 31 Photo. *Perf. 13*

423 A69 20c gold & multi .15 .15
424 A69 30c gold & multi .15 .15
425 A69 50c gold & multi .15 .15
426 A69 1fr gold & multi .15 .15
427 A69 3fr gold & multi .15 .15
428 A69 5fr gold & multi .15 .15
429 A69 20fr gold & multi .42 .22
430 A69 70fr gold & multi 1.40 .90
Set value 2.10 1.35

A 600fr on gold foil honoring Apollo 15 was issued Jan. 15, 1972.

Guardsmen Exercising A70

National Guard Emblem and: 6fr, Loading supplies. 15fr, Helicopter ambulance. 25fr, Health Service for civilians. 50fr, Guardsman and map of Rwanda, vert.

1972, Feb. 7 *Perf. 13½x14, 14x13½*

431 A70 4fr dp org & multi .15 .15
432 A70 6fr yellow & multi .15 .15
433 A70 15fr lt blue & multi .22 .15
434 A70 25fr red & multi .45 .25
435 A70 50fr multicolored .90 .60
Nos. 431-435 (5) 1.87 1.30

"The National Guard serving the nation."
For overprints see Nos. 559-563.

Ice Hockey, Sapporo Olympics Emblem A71

1972, Feb. 12 *Perf. 13x13½*

436 A71 20c shown .15 .15
437 A71 30c Speed skating .15 .15
438 A71 50c Ski jump .15 .15
439 A71 1fr Men's figure skating .15 .15
440 A71 6fr Cross-country skiing .15 .15
441 A71 12fr Slalom .25 .16
442 A71 20fr Bobsledding .45 .26
443 A71 60fr Downhill skiing 1.40 .90
Set value 2.35 1.55

11th Winter Olympic Games, Sapporo, Japan, Feb. 3-13.

Antelopes and Cercopithecus — A72

1972, Mar. 20 Photo. *Perf. 13*

444 A72 20c shown .15 .15
445 A72 30c Buffaloes .15 .15
446 A72 50c Zebras .15 .15
447 A72 1fr Rhinoceroses .15 .15
448 A72 2fr Wart hogs .15 .15
449 A72 6fr Hippopotami .15 .15
450 A72 18fr Hyenas .35 .20
451 A72 32fr Guinea fowl .60 .38
452 A72 60fr Antelopes 1.20 .70
453 A72 80fr Lions 1.60 1.00
Set value 4.00 2.50

Akagera National Park.

A73 A74

Family raising flag of Rwanda.

1972, Apr. 4 *Perf. 13x12½*

454 A73 6fr dk red & multi .15 .15
455 A73 18fr green & multi .35 .20
456 A73 60fr brown & multi 1.10 .70
Nos. 454-456 (3) 1.60 1.05

10th anniversary of the Referendum establishing Republic of Rwanda.

1972, May 17 Photo. *Perf. 13*

Birds: 20c, Common Waxbills and Hibiscus. 30c, Collared sunbird. 50c, Variable sunbird. 1fr, Greater double-collared sunbird. 4fr, Ruwenzori puff-back flycatcher. 6fr, Red-billed fire finch. 10fr, Scarlet-chested sunbird. 18fr, Red-headed quelea. 60fr, Black-headed gonolek. 100fr, African golden oriole.

457 A74 20c dl grn & multi .15 .15
458 A74 30c buff & multi .15 .15
459 A74 50c yellow & multi .15 .15
460 A74 1fr lt blue & multi .15 .15
461 A74 4fr dl rose & multi .15 .15
462 A74 6fr lilac rose & multi .15 .15
463 A74 10fr pink & multi .16 .15
464 A74 18fr gray & multi .35 .20
465 A74 60fr multicolored 1.20 .70
466 A74 100fr violet & multi 1.75 1.20
Set value 3.75 2.40

Belgica '72 Emblem, King Baudouin, Queen Fabiola, Pres. and Mrs. Kayibanda — A75

1972, June 24 Photo. *Perf. 13*
Size: 37x34mm

467 A75 18fr Rwanda landscape .38 .20
468 A75 22fr Old houses, Bruges .45 .22

Size: 50x34mm

469 A75 40fr shown .80 .40
a. Strip of 3, #467-469 1.65 1.00

Belgica '72 Intl. Phil. Exhib., Brussels, June 24-July 9.

Pres. Kayibanda Addressing Meeting A76

Pres. Grégoire Kayibanda: 30c, promoting officers of National Guard. 50c, with wife and children. 6fr, casting vote. 10fr, with wife and dignitaries at Feast of Justice. 15fr, with Cabinet and members of Assembly. 18fr, taking oath of office. 50fr, Portrait, vert.

1972, July 4

470 A76 20c gold & slate grn .15 .15
471 A76 30c gold & dk pur .15 .15
472 A76 50c gold & choc .15 .15
473 A76 6fr gold & Prus bl .15 .15
474 A76 10fr gold & dk pur .20 .15
475 A76 15fr gold & dk bl .30 .15
476 A76 18fr gold & brn .42 .20
477 A76 50fr gold & Prus bl 1.00 .60
Set value 2.10 1.25

10th anniversary of independence.

Equestrian, Olympic Emblems A77

Stadium, TV Tower and: 30c, Hockey. 50c, Soccer. 1fr, Broad jump. 6fr, Bicycling. 18fr, Yachting. 30fr, Hurdles. 44fr, Gymnastics, women's.

1972, Aug. 16 Photo. *Perf. 14*

478 A77 20c dk brn & gold .15 .15
479 A77 30c vio bl & gold .15 .15
480 A77 50c dk green & gold .15 .15
481 A77 1fr dp claret & gold .15 .15
482 A77 6fr black & gold .15 .15
483 A77 18fr brown & gold .30 .20
484 A77 30fr dk vio & gold .60 .30
485 A77 44fr Prus bl & gold .80 .40
Set value 2.00 1.25

20th Olympic Games, Munich, Aug. 26-Sept. 11.

Relay (Sport) and UN Emblem — A78

1972, Oct. 23 Photo. *Perf. 13*

486 A78 20c shown .15 .15
487 A78 30c Musicians .15 .15
488 A78 50c Dancers .15 .15
489 A78 1fr Operating room .15 .15
490 A78 6fr Weaver & painter .15 .15
491 A78 18fr Classroom .16 .20
492 A78 24fr Laboratory .55 .25
493 A78 50fr Hands of 4 races reaching for equality 1.00 .60
Nos. 486-493 (8) 2.46 1.80

Fight against racism.

Christmas Type of 1968
Souvenir Sheet

Design: 100fr, Adoration of the Shepherds, by Jacob Jordaens, vert.

1972, Dec. 11 *Perf. 11½*

494 A48 100fr red brown 2.00 2.00

Phymateus Brunneri — A79

Various insects. 30c, 1fr, 6fr, 22fr, 100fr, vert.

1973, Jan. 31 Photo. *Perf. 13*

495 A79 20c multi .15 .15
496 A79 30c multi .15 .15
497 A79 50c multi .15 .15
498 A79 1fr multi .15 .15
499 A79 2fr multi .15 .15
500 A79 6fr multi .15 .15
501 A79 18fr multi .35 .20
502 A79 22fr multi .42 .20
503 A79 70fr multi 1.40 .80
504 A79 100fr multi 2.00 1.20
Nos. 495-504 (10) 5.07
Set value 2.60

Souvenir Sheet

Perf. 14

505 A79 80fr like 20c 1.75 1.75

No. 505 contains one stamp 43½x33½mm.

Emile Zola, by Edouard Manet — A80

Paintings Connected with Reading, and Book Year Emblem: 30c, Rembrandt's Mother. 50c, St. Jerome Removing Thorn from Lion's Paw, by Colantonio. 1fr, Apostles Peter and Paul, by El Greco. 2fr, Virgin and Child with Book, by Roger van der Weyden. 6fr, St. Jerome in his Cell, by Antonella de Messina. 40fr, St. Barbara, by Master of Flemalle. No. 513, Don Quixote, by Otto Bonevalle. No. 514, Pres. Kayibanda reading book.

1973, Mar. 12 Photo. *Perf. 13*

506 A80 20c gold & multi .15 .15
507 A80 30c gold & multi .15 .15
508 A80 50c gold & multi .15 .15
509 A80 1fr gold & multi .15 .15
510 A80 2fr gold & multi .15 .15
511 A80 6fr gold & multi .15 .15
512 A80 40fr gold & multi .65 .32
513 A80 100fr gold & multi 1.65 .75
Set value 2.60 1.30

Souvenir Sheet

Perf. 14

514 A80 100fr gold, bl & ind 1.65 1.25

International Book Year.

Longombe — A81

Rubens and Isabella Brandt, by Rubens — A82

Musical instruments of Central & West Africa.

1973, Apr. 9 Photo. *Perf. 13½*

515 A81 20c shown .15 .15
516 A81 30c Horn .15 .15
517 A81 50c Xylophone .15 .15
518 A81 1fr Harp .15 .15
519 A81 4fr Alur horns .15 .15
520 A81 6fr Drum, bells and horn .15 .15
521 A81 18fr Large drums (Ngoma) .30 .16
522 A81 90fr Toba 1.60 .80
Set value 2.20 1.25

1973, May 11

Paintings from Old Pinakothek, Munich (IBRA Emblem and): 30c, Young Man, by Cranach. 50c, Woman Peeling Turnips, by Chardin. 1fr, The Abduction of Leucippa's Daughters, by Rubens. 2fr, Virgin and Child, by Filippo Lippi. 6fr, Boys Eating Fruit, by Murillo. 40fr, The Lovesick Woman, by Jan Steen. No. 530, Jesus Stripped of His Garments, by El Greco. No. 531, Oswalt Krehl, by Dürer.

523 A82 20c gold & multi .15 .15
524 A82 30c gold & multi .15 .15
525 A82 50c gold & multi .15 .15
526 A82 1fr gold & multi .15 .15
527 A82 2fr gold & multi .15 .15
528 A82 6fr gold & multi .15 .15
529 A82 40fr gold & multi .70 .35
530 A82 100fr gold & multi 1.90 .80
Set value 2.90 1.40

Souvenir Sheet

531 A82 100fr gold & multi 2.00 1.60

IBRA München 1973 Intl. Phil. Exhib., Munich, May 11-20. #531 contains one 40x56mm stamp.

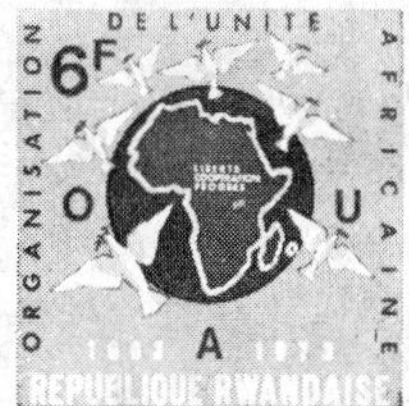

Map of Africa and Peace Doves — A83

Design: 94fr, Map of Africa and hands.

1973, July 23 Photo. *Perf. 13½*

532 A83 6fr gold & multi .16 .15
533 A83 94fr gold & multi 1.90 1.50

Org. for African Unity, 10th anniv.
For overprints see Nos. 895-896.

Nos. 298-303 Overprinted in Blue, Black, Green or Brown: "SECHERESSE / SOLIDARITE AFRICAINE"

1973, Aug. 23 Photo. *Perf. 13*

534 A53 20c multi (Bl) .15 .15
535 A53 40c multi (Bk) .15 .15
536 A53 60c multi (Bl) .15 .15
537 A53 80c multi (G) .15 .15
538 A53 3fr multi (G) .15 .15
539 A53 75fr multi (Br) 1.50 .90
Nos. 534-539,B1 (7) 4.75
Set value 3.35

African solidarity in drought emergency.

African Postal Union Issue

Common Design Type

1973, Sept. 12 Engr. *Perf. 13*

540 CD137 100fr dp brn, bl & brn 2.00 1.60

Six-lined Distichodus — A84

African Fish: 30c, Little triggerfish. 50c, Spotted upside-down catfish. 1fr, Nile mouthbreeder. 2fr, African lungfish. 6fr, Pareutropius mandevillei. 40fr, Congo characin. 100fr, Like 20c. 150fr, Julidochromis ornatus.

1973, Sept. 3 Photo. *Perf. 13*

541 A84 20c gold & multi .15 .15
542 A84 30c gold & multi .15 .15
543 A84 50c gold & multi .15 .15
544 A84 1fr gold & multi .15 .15
545 A84 2fr gold & multi .15 .15
546 A84 6fr gold & multi .15 .15
547 A84 40fr gold & multi .70 .40
548 A84 150fr gold & multi 3.00 1.50
Set value 4.00 2.15

Souvenir Sheet

549 A84 100fr gold & multi 2.00 2.00

No. 549 contains one stamp 48x29mm.

Nos. 398-405 Overprinted in Black, Silver, Green or Blue

1973, Sept. 15 Litho.

550 A50 20c multi (Bk) .15 .15
551 A50 30c multi (S) .15 .15
552 A50 50c multi (Bk) .15 .15
553 A50 1fr multi (G) .15 .15
554 A50 5fr multi (S) .15 .15
555 A50 18fr multi (Bk) .35 .20
556 A50 25fr multi (Bk) .50 .25
557 A50 50fr multi (Bl) 1.20 .55
Set value 2.35 1.20

Africa Weeks, Brussels, Sept. 15-30, 1973. On the 30c, 1fr and 25fr the text of the overprint is horizontal.

Nos. 431-435 Overprinted in Gold

Perf. 13½x14, 14x13½

1973, Oct. 31 Photo.

559 A70 4fr dp org & multi .15 .15
560 A70 6fr yellow & multi .15 .15
561 A70 15fr lt blue & multi .42 .27
562 A70 25fr red & multi .70 .40
563 A70 50fr multicolored 1.50 .80
Nos. 559-563 (5) 2.92 1.77

25th anniv. of the Universal Declaration of Human Rights.

Christmas Type of 1968

Souvenir Sheet

Adoration of the Shepherds, by Guido Reni.

1973, Dec. 15 Engr. *Perf. 11½*

564 A48 100fr brt violet 2.00 2.00

Copernicus and Astrolabe A85

Pres. Juvénal Habyarimana A86

Designs: 30c, 18fr, 100fr, Portrait. 50c, 80fr, Copernicus and heliocentric system. 1fr, like 20c.

1973, Dec. 26 Photo. *Perf. 13*

565 A85 20c silver & multi .15 .15
566 A85 30c silver & multi .15 .15
567 A85 50c silver & multi .15 .15
568 A85 1fr gold & multi .15 .15
569 A85 18fr gold & multi .22 .20
570 A85 80fr gold & multi 1.20 .80
Set value 1.60 1.10

Souvenir Sheet

571 A85 100fr gold & multi 2.00 2.00

Nicolaus Copernicus (1473-1543).

1974, Apr. 8 Photo. *Perf. 11½*

Black Inscriptions

572 A86 1fr bister & sepia .15 .15
573 A86 2fr ultra & sepia .15 .15
574 A86 5fr rose red & sep .15 .15
575 A86 6fr grnsh bl & sep .15 .15
576 A86 26fr lilac & sepia .45 .30
577 A86 60fr ol grn & sepia 1.20 .65
Set value 1.90 1.10

Souvenir Sheet

Christ Between the Thieves (Detail), by Rubens — A87

1974, Apr. 12 Engr. *Perf. 11½*

578 A87 100fr sepia 4.00 4.00

Easter.

Yugoslavia-Zaire Soccer Game — A88

Designs: Games' emblem and soccer games.

1974, July 6 Photo. *Perf. 13½*

579 A88 20c shown .15 .15
580 A88 40c Netherlands-Sweden .15 .15
581 A88 60c Germany (Fed.)-Austria .15 .15
582 A88 80c Haiti-Argentina .15 .15
583 A88 2fr Brazil-Scotland .15 .15
584 A88 6fr Bulgaria-Uruguay .15 .15
585 A88 40fr Italy-Poland .70 .40
586 A88 50fr Chile-Germany (DDR) 1.00 .65
Set value 2.00 1.30

World Cup Soccer Championship, Munich, June 13-July 7.

Marconi's Laboratory Yacht "Elletra" — A89

Designs: 30c, Marconi and steamer "Carlo Alberto." 50c, Marconi's wireless apparatus and telecommunications satellites. 4fr, Marconi and globes connected by communications waves. 35fr, Marconi's radio, and radar. 60fr, Marconi and transmitter at Poldhu, Cornwall. 50fr, like 20c.

1974, Aug. 19 Photo. *Perf. 13½*

587 A89 20c violet, blk & grn .15 .15
588 A89 30c green, blk & vio .15 .15
589 A89 50c yellow, blk & lil .15 .15
590 A89 4fr salmon, blk & bl .15 .15
591 A89 35fr lilac, blk & yel .60 .40
592 A89 60fr blue, blk & brnz 1.20 .70
Set value 2.00 1.25

Souvenir Sheet

593 A89 50fr gold, blk & lt bl 1.20 1.20

Guglielmo Marconi (1874-1937), Italian electrical engineer and inventor.

The Flute Player, by J. Leyster — A90

Messenger Monk — A91

Paintings: 20c, Diane de Poitiers, Fontainebleau school. 50c, Virgin and Child, by David. 1fr, Triumph of Venus, by Boucher. 10fr, Seated Harlequin, by Picasso. 18fr, Virgin and Child, 15th century. 20fr, Beheading of St. John, by Hans Fries. 50fr, Daughter of Andersdotter, by J. F. Höckert.

1974, Sept. 23 Photo. *Perf. 14x13*

594 A90 20c gold & multi .15 .15
595 A90 30c gold & multi .15 .15
596 A90 50c gold & multi .15 .15
597 A90 1fr gold & multi .15 .15
598 A90 10fr gold & multi .16 .15
599 A90 18fr gold & multi .30 .16
600 A90 20fr gold & multi .35 .22
601 A90 50fr gold & multi 1.00 .60
Set value 2.00 1.25

INTERNABA 74 Intl. Phil. Exhib., Basel, June 7-10, and Stockholmia 74, Intl. Phil. Exhib., Stockholm, Sept. 21-29.

Six multicolored souvenir sheets exist containing two 15fr stamps each in various combinations of designs of Nos. 594-601. One souvenir sheet of four 25fr stamps exists with designs of Nos. 595, 597, 599 and 601.

1974, Oct. 9 *Perf. 14*

UPU Emblem and Messengers: 30c, Inca. 50c, Morocco. 1fr, India. 18fr, Polynesia. 80fr, Rwanda.

602 A91 20c gold & multi .15 .15
603 A91 30c gold & multi .15 .15
604 A91 50c gold & multi .15 .15
605 A91 1fr gold & multi .15 .15
606 A91 18fr gold & multi .42 .38
607 A91 80fr gold & multi 1.65 1.60
Set value 2.25 2.10

Centenary of Universal Postal Union.

Nos. 306-308 Overprinted

1974, Dec. 16 Photo. *Perf. 11½*

608 A54 6fr brt pink & multi 3.50 3.50
609 A54 18fr ultra & multi 3.50 3.50
610 A54 40fr brn & multi 3.75 3.75
Nos. 608-610 (3) 10.75 10.75

15th anniversary of independence.

Christmas Type of 1968
Souvenir Sheet

Adoration of the Kings, by Joos van Cleve.

1974, Dec. 23 Engr. *Perf. 11½*

611 A48 100fr slate green 4.00 4.00

Nos. 295-296 Overprinted: "1974 / 10e Anniversaire"

1974, Dec. 30 Photo. *Perf. 13*

612 A51 30fr sil & multi .55 .55
613 A51 70fr gold & multi 1.10 1.10

African Development Bank, 10th anniversary.

Uganda Kob — A92

Antelopes: 30c, Bongos, horiz. 50c, Rwanda antelopes. 1fr, Young sitatungas, horiz. 4fr, Greater kudus. 10fr, Impalas, horiz. 34fr, Waterbuck. 40fr, Impalas. 60fr, Greater kudu. 100fr, Derby's elands, horiz.

1975, Mar. 17 Photo. *Perf. 13*

614 A92 20c multi .15 .15
615 A92 30c multi .15 .15
616 A92 50c multi .15 .15
617 A92 1fr multi .15 .15
618 A92 4fr multi .15 .15
619 A92 10fr multi .15 .15
620 A92 34fr multi .50 .25
621 A92 100fr multi 1.65 .75

Set value 2.50 1.30

Miniature Sheets

622 A92 40fr multi 2.75 2.75
623 A92 60fr multi 2.75 2.75

Miniature Sheets

The Burial of Jesus, by Raphael — A93

1975, Apr. 1 Photo. *Perf. 13x14*

624 A93 20fr shown 1.00 1.00
625 A93 30fr Pietá, by Cranach the Elder 1.20 1.20
626 A93 50fr by van der Weyden 1.20 1.20
627 A93 100fr by Bellini 1.20 1.20
Nos. 624-627 (4) 4.60 4.60

Easter. Size of stamps: 40x52mm.
See Nos. 681-684.

Souvenir Sheets

Prince Balthazar Charles, by Velazquez A94

Paintings: 30fr, Infanta Margaret of Austria, by Velazquez. 50fr, The Divine Shepherd, by Murillo. 100fr, Francisco Goya, by V. Lopez y Portana.

1975, Apr. 4 Photo. *Perf. 13*

628 A94 20fr multi 1.00 1.00
629 A94 30fr multi 1.20 1.20
630 A94 50fr multi 1.20 1.20
631 A94 100fr multi 1.20 1.20
Nos. 628-631 (4) 4.60 4.60

Espana 75 Intl. Phil. Exhib., Madrid, Apr. 4-13. Size of stamps: 38x48mm. See Nos. 642-643. For overprints see Nos. 844-847.

Pyrethrum (Insect Powder) — A95

1975, Apr. 14 *Perf. 13*

632 A95 20c shown .15 .15
633 A95 30c Tea .15 .15
634 A95 50c Coffee (beans and pan) .15 .15
635 A95 4fr Bananas .15 .15
636 A95 10fr Corn .16 .15
637 A95 12fr Sorghum .20 .15
638 A95 26fr Rice .45 .25
639 A95 47fr Coffee (workers and beans) 1.10 .45
Set value 2.10 1.05

Souvenir Sheets

Perf. 13½

640 A95 25fr like 50c .65 .65
641 A95 75fr like 47fr 1.60 1.60

Year of Agriculture and 10th anniversary of Office for Industrialized Cultivation.

Souvenir Sheets
Painting Type of 1975

Paintings: 75fr, Louis XIV, by Hyacinthe Rigaud. 125fr, Cavalry Officer, by Jean Gericault.

1975, June 6 Photo. *Perf. 13*

642 A94 75fr multi 1.60 1.60
643 A94 125fr multi 3.00 3.00

ARPHILA 75, Intl. Philatelic Exhibition, Paris, June 6-16. Size of stamps: 38x48mm.

Nos. 390-397 Overprinted: "1975 / ANNEE / SAINTE"

1975, June 23 Photo. *Perf. 13*

644 A66 10c gold & dk brn .15 .15
645 A66 20c gold & dk grn .15 .15
646 A66 30c gold & dp claret .15 .15
647 A66 40c gold & indigo .15 .15
648 A66 1fr gold & dk pur .15 .15
649 A66 18fr gold & purple .30 .15
650 A66 20fr gold & org brn .40 .20
651 A66 60fr gold & blk brn 1.50 .80
Set value 2.40 1.30

Holy Year 1975.

White Pelicans — A96

Designs: African birds.

1975, June 20

652 A96 20c shown .15 .15
653 A96 30c Malachite kingfisher .15 .15
654 A96 50c Goliath herons .15 .15
655 A96 1fr Saddle-billed storks .15 .15
656 A96 4fr African jacana .15 .15
657 A96 10fr African anhingas .20 .15
658 A96 34fr Sacred ibis .60 .35
659 A96 80fr Hartlaub ducks 1.60 .80
Set value 2.60 1.40

Miniature Sheets

660 A96 40fr Flamingoes 1.20 1.20
661 A96 60fr Crowned cranes 1.60 1.60

Globe Representing Races and WPY Emblem — A97

The Bath, by Mary Cassatt and IWY Emblem — A98

World Population Year: 26fr, Population graph and emblem. 34fr, Globe with open door and emblem.

1975, Sept. 1 Photo. *Perf. 13½x13*

662 A97 20fr dp bl & multi .38 .20
663 A97 26fr dl red brn & multi .50 .25
664 A97 34fr yel & multi .70 .35
Nos. 662-664 (3) 1.58 .80

1975, Sept. 15 *Perf. 13*

IWY Emblem and: 30c, Mother and Infant Son, by Julius Gari Melchers. 50c, Woman with Milk Jug, by Jan Vermeer. 1fr, Water Carrier, by Goya. 8fr, Rwanda woman cotton picker. 12fr, Scientist with microscope. 18fr, Mother and child. 25fr, Empress Josephine, by Pierre-Paul Prud'hon. 40fr, Madame Vigee-Lebrun and Daughter, self-portrait. 60fr, Woman carrying child on back and water jug on head.

665 A98 20c gold & multi .15 .15
666 A98 30c gold & multi .15 .15
667 A98 50c gold & multi .15 .15
668 A98 1fr gold & multi .15 .15
669 A98 8fr gold & multi .15 .15
670 A98 12fr gold & multi .20 .15
671 A98 18fr gold & multi .30 .18
672 A98 60fr gold & multi 1.20 .60
Set value 2.00 1.15

Souvenir Sheets

Perf. 13½

673 A98 25fr multi 6.50 6.50
674 A98 40fr multi 6.50 6.50

International Women's Year. Nos. 673-674 each contain one stamp 37x49mm.

Owl, Quill and Book — A99

Designs: 30c, Hygiene emblem. 1.50fr, Kneeling woman holding scales of Justice. 18fr, Chemist in laboratory. 26fr, Symbol of commerce and chart. 34fr, University Building.

1975, Sept. 29 *Perf. 13*

675 A99 20c pur & multi .15 .15
676 A99 30c ultra & multi .15 .15
677 A99 1.50fr lilac & multi .15 .15
678 A99 18fr blue & multi .30 .15
679 A99 26fr olive & multi .45 .25
680 A99 34fr blue & multi .70 .35
Set value 1.55 .65

National Univ. of Rwanda, 10th anniv.

Souvenir Sheets
Painting Type of 1975

Paintings by Jan Vermeer (1632-1675): 20fr, Man and Woman Drinking Wine. 30fr, Young Woman Reading Letter. 50fr, Painter in his Studio. 100fr, Young Woman Playing Virginal.

1975, Oct. 13 Photo. *Perf. 13x14*

681 A93 20fr multi .40 .40
682 A93 30fr multi .60 .60
683 A93 50fr multi 1.00 1.00
684 A93 100fr multi 2.00 2.00
Nos. 681-684 (4) 4.00 4.00

Size of stamps: 40x52mm.

Waterhole and Impatiens Stuhlmannii — A100

Designs: 30c, Antelopes, zebras, candelabra cactus. 50c, Brush fire, and tapinanthus prunifolius. 5fr, Bulera Lake and Egyptian white lotus. 8fr, Erosion prevention and protea madiensis. 10fr, Marsh and melanthera brownei. 26fr, Landscape, lobelias and senecons. 100fr, Sabyinyo Volcano and polystachya kermesina.

1975, Oct. 25 *Perf. 13*

685 A100 20c blk & multi .15 .15
686 A100 30c blk & multi .15 .15
687 A100 50c blk & multi .15 .15
688 A100 5fr blk & multi .15 .15
689 A100 8fr blk & multi .15 .15
690 A100 10fr blk & multi .16 .15
691 A100 26fr blk & multi .50 .25
692 A100 100fr blk & multi 1.90 1.00
Set value 2.90 1.60

Nature protection.
For overprints see Nos. 801-808.

SECHERESSE
SOLIDARITE
1975

Nos. 343-348 Overprinted

1975, Nov. 10 Litho. *Perf. 13*

693 A60 20c multi .15 .15
694 A60 30c multi .15 .15
695 A60 50c multi .15 .15
696 A60 1fr multi .15 .15
697 A60 3fr multi .15 .15
698 A60 5fr multi .15 .15
Set value, #693-698, B2-B3 3.80 2.75

African solidarity in drought emergency.

Fork-lift Truck on Airfield A101

Designs: 30c, Coffee packing plant. 50c, Engineering plant. 10fr, Farmer with hoe, vert. 35fr, Coffee pickers, vert. 54fr, Mechanized harvester.

Wmk. JEZ Multiple (368)

1975, Dec. 1 Photo. *Perf. 14x13½*

699 A101 20c gold & multi .15 .15
700 A101 30c gold & multi .15 .15
701 A101 50c gold & multi .15 .15
702 A101 10fr gold & multi .16 .15
703 A101 35fr gold & multi .60 .35
704 A101 54fr gold & multi 1.00 .55
Set value 1.90 1.10

Basket Carrier and Themabelga Emblem — A102

Themabelga Emblem and: 30c, Warrior with shield and spear. 50c, Woman with beads. 1fr, Indian woman. 5fr, Male dancer with painted body. 7fr, Woman carrying child on back. 35fr, Male dancer with spear. 51fr, Female dancers.

1975, Dec. 8 Unwmk. *Perf. 13½*

705 A102 20c blk & multi .15 .15
706 A102 30c blk & multi .15 .15
707 A102 50c blk & multi .15 .15
708 A102 1fr blk & multi .15 .15
709 A102 5fr blk & multi .15 .15
710 A102 7fr blk & multi .15 .15
711 A102 35fr blk & multi .60 .35
712 A102 51fr blk & multi .90 .50
Set value 1.90 1.10

THEMABELGA Intl. Topical Philatelic Exhibition, Brussels, Dec. 13-21.

Christmas Type of 1968

Adoration of the Kings, by Peter Paul Rubens.

1975, Dec. 22 Engr. *Perf. 11½*

713 A48 100fr brt rose lil 3.50 3.50

Dr. Schweitzer, Keyboard, Score — A103

Albert Schweitzer and: 30c, 5fr, Lambaréné Hospital. 50c, 10fr, Organ pipes from Strassbourg organ, and score. 1fr, 80fr, Dr. Schweitzer's house, Lambaréné. 3fr, like 20c.

1976, Jan. 30 Photo. *Perf. 13½*

714 A103 20c maroon & pur .15 .15
715 A103 30c grn & pur .15 .15
716 A103 50c brn org & pur .15 .15
717 A103 1fr red lil & pur .15 .15
718 A103 3fr vio bl & pur .15 .15
719 A103 5fr brn & pur .15 .15
720 A103 10fr bl & pur .20 .15
721 A103 80fr ver & pur 1.40 .80
Set value 1.95 1.10

World Leprosy Day.
For overprints see Nos. 788-795.

Surrender at Yorktown — A104

American Bicentennial (Paintings): 30c, Instruction at Valley Forge. 50c, Presentation of Captured Colors at Yorktown. 1fr, Washington at Fort Lee. 18fr, Washington Boarding British Warship. 26fr, Washington Studying Battle Plans at Night. 34fr, Washington Firing Cannon. 40fr, Washington Crossing the Delaware. 100fr, Sailing Ship "Bonhomme Richard," vert.

1976, Mar. 22 Photo. *Perf. 13x13½*

722 A104 20c gold & multi .15 .15
723 A104 30c gold & multi .15 .15
724 A104 50c gold & multi .15 .15
725 A104 1fr gold & multi .15 .15
726 A104 18fr gold & multi .35 .16
727 A104 26fr gold & multi .42 .22
728 A104 34fr gold & multi .60 .35
729 A104 40fr gold & multi .65 .40
Set value 2.20 1.30

Souvenir Sheet

Perf. 13½

730 A104 100fr gold & multi 2.50 2.50

Sister Yohana, First Nun — A105

Yachting — A106

30c, Abdon Sabakati, one of first converts. 50c, Father Alphonse Brard, first Superior of Save Mission. 4fr, Abbot Balthazar Gafuku, one of first priests. 10fr, Msgr. Bigirumwami, first bishop. 25fr, Save Church, horiz. 60fr, Kabgayi Cathedral, horiz.

Perf. 13x13½, 13½x13

1976, Apr. 26 Photo.

731 A105 20c multi .15 .15
732 A105 30c multi .15 .15
733 A105 50c multi .15 .15
734 A105 4fr multi .15 .15
735 A105 10fr multi .20 .15
736 A105 25fr multi .45 .25
737 A105 60fr multi 1.00 .60
Set value 1.90 1.10

50th anniv. of the Roman Catholic Church of Rwanda.

1976, May 24 Photo. *Perf. 13x13½*

Montreal Games Emblem and: 30c, Steeplechase. 50c, Long jump. 1fr, Hockey. 10fr, Swimming. 18fr, Soccer. 29fr, Boxing. 51fr, Vaulting.

738 A106 20c gray & dk car .15 .15
739 A106 30c gray & Prus bl .15 .15
740 A106 50c gray & blk .15 .15
741 A106 1fr gray & pur .15 .15
742 A106 10fr gray & ultra .25 .15
743 A106 18fr gray & dk brn .35 .16
744 A106 29fr gray & blk .60 .25
745 A106 51fr gray & slate grn .90 .50
Set value 2.25 1.15

21st Olympic Games, Montreal, Canada, July 17-Aug. 1.

First Message, Manual Switchboard — A107

Designs: 30c, Telephone, 1876 and interested crowd. 50c, Telephone c. 1900, and woman making a call. 1fr, Business telephone exchange, c. 1905. 4fr, "Candlestick" phone, globe and A. G. Bell. 8fr, Dial phone and Rwandan man making call. 26fr, Telephone, 1976, satellite and radar. 60fr, Push-button telephone, Rwandan international switchboard operator.

1976, June 21 Photo. *Perf. 14*

746 A107 20c dl red & indigo .15 .15
747 A107 30c grnsh bl & indigo .15 .15
748 A107 50c brn & indigo .15 .15
749 A107 1fr org & indigo .15 .15
750 A107 4fr lilac & indigo .15 .15
751 A107 8fr grn & indigo .20 .15
752 A107 26fr dl red & indigo .50 .25
753 A107 60fr vio & indigo 1.10 .60
Set value 2.00 1.10

Centenary of first telephone call by Alexander Graham Bell, Mar. 10, 1876.

Type of 1976 Overprinted in Silver with Bicentennial Emblem and "Independence Day"

Designs as before.

1976, July 4 *Perf. 13x13½*

754 A104 20c silver & multi .15 .15
755 A104 30c silver & multi .15 .15
756 A104 50c silver & multi .15 .15
757 A104 1fr silver & multi .15 .15
758 A104 18fr silver & multi .35 .25
759 A104 26fr silver & multi .50 .25
760 A104 34fr silver & multi .60 .35
761 A104 40fr silver & multi .65 .40
Set value 2.25 1.40

Independence Day.

Soccer, Montreal Olympic Emblem — A108

30c, Shooting. 50c, Woman canoeing. 1fr, Gymnast. 10fr, Weight lifting. 12fr, Diving. 26fr, Equestrian. 50fr, Shot put.

1976, Aug. 1 Photo. *Perf. 13½x13*

762 A108 20c multi .15 .15
763 A108 30c multi .15 .15
764 A108 50c multi .15 .15
765 A108 1fr multi .15 .15
766 A108 10fr multi .16 .15
767 A108 12fr multi .20 .15
768 A108 26fr multi .42 .25
769 A108 50fr multi 1.00 .50
Set value 1.95 1.10

Souvenir Sheet

Designs: Various phases of hurdles race, horiz.

770 Sheet of 4 3.00 3.00
a. A108 20fr Start .35 .35
b. A108 30fr Sprint .55 .55
c. A108 40fr Hurdle .70 .70
d. A108 60fr Finish 1.00 1.00

21st Olympic Games, Montreal, Canada, July 17-Aug. 1.

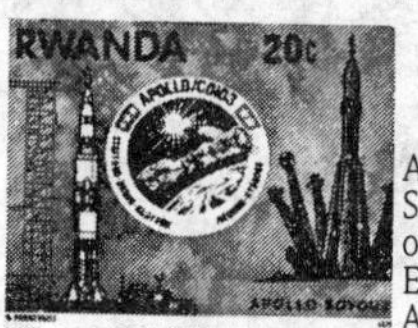

Apollo and Soyuz Take-offs, Project Emblem — A109

Designs: 30c, Soyuz in space. 50c, Apollo in space. 1fr, Apollo. 2fr, Spacecraft before docking. 12fr, Spacecraft after docking. 30fr, Astronauts visiting in docked spacecraft. 54fr, Apollo splashdown.

1976, Oct. 29 Photo. *Perf. 13½x14*

771 A109 20c multi .15 .15
772 A109 30c multi .15 .15
773 A109 50c multi .15 .15
774 A109 1fr multi .15 .15
775 A109 2fr multi .15 .15
776 A109 12fr multi .25 .15
777 A109 30fr multi .60 .30
778 A109 54fr multi .90 .55
Set value 2.00 1.15

Apollo Soyuz space test program (Russo-American cooperation), July 1975.
For overprints see Nos. 836-843.

Eulophia Cucullata — A110

Hands and Symbols of Learning — A111

Orchids: 30c, Eulophia streptopetala. 50c, Disa Stairsii. 1fr, Aerangis kotschyana. 10fr, Eulophia abyssinica. 12fr, Bonatea steudneri. 26fr, Ansellia gigantea. 50fr, Eulophia angolensis.

1976, Nov. 22 Photo. *Perf. 14x13½*

779 A110 20c multi .15 .15
780 A110 30c multi .15 .15
781 A110 50c multi .15 .15
782 A110 1fr multi .15 .15
783 A110 10fr multi .16 .15
784 A110 12fr multi .25 .15
785 A110 26fr multi .50 .25
786 A110 50fr multi 1.00 .50
Set value 2.05 1.10

Christmas Type of 1968
Souvenir Sheet

Design: Nativity, by Francois Boucher.

1976, Dec. 20 Engr. *Perf. 11½*

787 A48 100fr brt ultra 3.00 3.00

Nos. 714-721 Overprinted: "JOURNEE / MONDIALE / 1977"

1977, Jan. 29 Photo. *Perf. 13½*

788 A103 20c mar & pur .15 .15
789 A103 30c grn & pur .15 .15
790 A103 50c brn org & pur .15 .15
791 A103 1fr red lil & pur .15 .15
792 A103 3fr vio bl & pur .15 .15
793 A103 5fr brn & pur .16 .15
794 A103 10fr bl & pur .25 .15
795 A103 80fr ver & pur 1.40 .80
Set value 2.00 1.15

World Leprosy Day.

1977, Feb. 7 Litho. *Perf. 12½*

Designs: 26fr, Hands and symbols of science. 64fr, Hands and symbols of industry.

796 A111 10fr multi .20 .15
797 A111 26fr multi .52 .38
798 A111 64fr multi .90 .75
Nos. 796-798 (3) 1.62 1.28

10th Summit Conference of the African and Malagasy Union, Kigali, 1976.

Souvenir Sheets

Descent from the Cross, by Rubens — A112

Easter: 25fr, Crucifixion, by Rubens.

1977, Apr. 27 Photo. *Perf. 13*

799 A112 25fr multi .60 .60
800 A112 75fr multi 1.50 1.50

Size of stamp: 40x40mm.

Nos. 685-692 Overprinted

1977, May 2

801 A100 20c blk & multi .15 .15
802 A100 30c blk & multi .15 .15
803 A100 50c blk & multi .15 .15
804 A100 5fr blk & multi .20 .15
805 A100 8fr blk & multi .30 .15
806 A100 10fr blk & multi .30 .15
807 A100 26fr blk & multi .90 .45
808 A100 100fr blk & multi 3.00 1.90
Nos. 801-808 (8) 5.15 3.25

World Water Conference.

Roman Fire Tower, African Tom-tom — A113

ITU Emblem and: 30c, Chappe's optical telegraph and postilion. 50c, Morse telegraph and code. 1fr, Tug Goliath laying cable in English Channel. 4fr, Telephone, radio, television. 18fr, Kingsport (US space exploration ship) and Marots communications satellite. 26fr, Satellite tracking station and O.T.S. satellite. 50fr, Mariner II, Venus probe.

1977, May 23 Litho. *Perf. 12½*

809	A113	20c multi	.15	.15
810	A113	30c multi	.15	.15
811	A113	50c multi	.15	.15
812	A113	1fr multi	.15	.15
813	A113	4fr multi	.15	.15
814	A113	18fr multi	.45	.22
815	A113	26fr multi	.62	.32
816	A113	50fr multi	1.25	.62
		Set value	2.60	1.35

World Telecommunications Day.

Souvenir Sheets

Amsterdam Harbor, by Willem van de Velde, the Younger A114

Design: 40fr, The Night Watch, by Rembrandt.

1977, May 26 Photo. *Perf. 13½*

817	A114	40fr multi	.80	.80
818	A114	60fr multi	1.20	1.20

AMPHILEX '277 Intl. Philatelic Exhibition, Amsterdam, May 27-June 5. Size of stamp: 38x49mm.

Road to Calvary, by Rubens — A115

Paintings by Peter Paul Rubens (1577-1640): 30c, Judgment of Paris, horiz. 50c, Marie de Medicis. 1fr, Heads of Black Men, horiz. 4fr, 26fr, Details from St. Ildefonso triptych. 8fr, Helene Fourment and her Children, horiz. 60fr, Helene Fourment.

1977, June 13 *Perf. 14*

819	A115	20c gold & multi	.15	.15
820	A115	30c gold & multi	.15	.15
821	A115	50c gold & multi	.15	.15
822	A115	1fr gold & multi	.15	.15
823	A115	4fr gold & multi	.15	.15
824	A115	8fr gold & multi	.20	.15
825	A115	26fr gold & multi	.50	.25
826	A115	60fr gold & multi	1.20	.60
		Set value	2.15	1.10

Souvenir Sheet

Viking on Mars A116

1977, June 27 Photo. *Perf. 13*

827	A116	100fr multi	5.00	5.00

US Viking landing on Mars, first anniv.

Crested Eagle — A117

Birds of Prey: 30c, Snake eagle. 50c, Fish eagle. 1fr, Monk vulture. 3fr, Red-tailed buzzard. 5fr, Yellow-beaked kite. 20fr, Swallow-tailed kite. 100fr, Bateleur.

1977, Sept. 12 Litho. *Perf. 14*

828	A117	20c multi	.15	.15
829	A117	30c multi	.15	.15
830	A117	50c multi	.15	.15
831	A117	1fr multi	.15	.15
832	A117	3fr multi	.15	.15
833	A117	5fr multi	.15	.15
834	A117	20fr multi	.42	.22
835	A117	100fr multi	2.00	1.00
		Set value	2.75	1.45

Nos. 771-778 Overprinted: "in memoriam / WERNHER VON BRAUN / 1912-1977"

1977, Sept. 19 Photo. *Perf. 13½x14*

836	A109	20c multi	.15	.15
837	A109	30c multi	.15	.15
838	A109	50c multi	.15	.15
839	A109	1fr multi	.15	.15
840	A109	2fr multi	.15	.15
841	A109	12fr multi	.22	.15
842	A109	30fr multi	.60	.30
843	A109	54fr multi	1.20	.60
		Set value	2.25	1.20

Wernher von Braun (1912-1977), space and rocket expert.

Nos. 628-631 Gold Embossed "ESPAMER '77" and ESPAMER Emblem Souvenir Sheets

1977, Oct. 3 Photo. *Perf. 13*

844	A94	20fr multi	.50	.50
845	A94	30fr multi	.75	.75
846	A94	50fr multi	1.25	1.25
847	A94	100fr multi	2.50	2.50
		Nos. 844-847 (4)	5.00	5.00

ESPAMER '77, International Philatelic Exhibition, Barcelona, Oct. 7-13.

Christmas Type of 1968 Souvenir Sheet

Design: 100fr, Nativity, by Peter Paul Rubens.

1977, Dec. 12 Engr. *Perf. 13½*

848	A48	100fr violet blue	3.00	3.00

Marginal inscription typographed in red.

Boy Scout Playing Flute A118

Chimpanzees A119

Designs: 30c, Campfire. 50c, Bridge building. 1fr, Scouts with unit flag. 10fr, Map reading. 18fr, Boating. 26fr, Cooking. 44fr, Lord Baden-Powell.

1978, Feb. 20 Litho. *Perf. 12½*

849	A118	20c yel grn & multi	.15	.15
850	A118	30c blue & multi	.15	.15
851	A118	50c lilac & multi	.15	.15
852	A118	1fr blue & multi	.15	.15
853	A118	10fr pink & multi	.20	.15
854	A118	18fr lt grn & multi	.38	.18
855	A118	26fr orange & multi	.55	.25
856	A118	44fr salmon & multi	.90	.45
		Set value	2.20	1.15

10th anniversary of Rwanda Boy Scouts.

1978, Mar. 20 Photo. *Perf. 13½x13*

Designs: 30c, Gorilla. 50c, Colobus monkey. 3fr, Galago. 10fr, Cercopithecus monkey (mone). 26fr, Potto. 60fr, Cercopithecus monkey (griuet). 150fr, Baboon.

857	A119	20c multi	.15	.15
858	A119	30c multi	.15	.15
859	A119	50c multi	.15	.15
860	A119	3fr multi	.15	.15
861	A119	10fr multi	.20	.15
862	A119	26fr multi	.55	.25
863	A119	60fr multi	1.20	.55
864	A119	150fr multi	3.00	1.50
		Nos. 857-864 (8)	5.55	
		Set value		2.50

Euporus Strangulatus — A120

Coleoptera: 30c, Rhina afzelii, vert. 50c, Pentalobus palini. 3fr, Corynodes dejeani, vert. 10fr, Mecynorhina torquata. 15fr, Mecocerus rhombeus, vert. 20fr, Macrotoma serripes. 25fr, Neptunides stanleyi, vert. 26fr, Petrognatha gigas. 100fr, Eudicella gralli, vert.

1978, May 22 Litho. *Perf. 14*

865	A120	20c multi	.15	.15
866	A120	30c multi	.15	.15
867	A120	50c multi	.15	.15
868	A120	3fr multi	.15	.15
869	A120	10fr multi	.20	.15
870	A120	15fr multi	.30	.20
871	A120	20fr multi	.40	.25
872	A120	25fr multi	.50	.28
873	A120	26fr multi	.52	.30
874	A120	100fr multi	2.00	1.40
		Nos. 865-874 (10)	4.52	
		Set value		2.75

Crossing "River of Poverty" A121

Emblem and: 10fr, 60fr, Men poling boat, facing right. 26fr, like 4fr.

1978, May 29 *Perf. 12½*

875	A121	4fr multi	.15	.15
876	A121	10fr multi	.20	.15
877	A121	26fr multi	.52	.30
878	A121	60fr multi	1.20	.80
		Nos. 875-878 (4)	2.07	1.40

Natl. Revolutionary Development Movement (M.R.N.D.).

Soccer, Rimet Cup, Flags of Netherlands and Peru — A122

11th World cup, Argentina, June 1-25, (Various Soccer Scenes and Flags of): 30c, Sweden & Spain. 50c, Scotland & Iran. 2fr, Germany & Tunisia. 3fr, Italy & Hungary. 10fr, Brazil and Austria. 34fr, Poland & Mexico. 100fr, Argentina & France.

1978, June 19 *Perf. 13*

879	A122	20c multi	.15	.15
879A	A122	30c multi	.15	.15
879B	A122	50c multi	.15	.15
880	A122	2fr multi	.15	.15
881	A122	3fr multi	.15	.15
882	A122	10fr multi	.15	.15
883	A122	34fr multi	.50	.32
884	A122	100fr multi	1.50	1.00
		Set value	2.35	1.60

Wright Brothers, Flyer I — A123

History of Aviation: 30c, Santos Dumont and Canard 14, 1906. 50c, Henry Farman and Voisin No. 1, 1908. 1fr, Jan Olieslaegers and Bleriot, 1910. 3fr, Marshal Balbo and Savoia S-17, 1919. 10fr, Charles Lindbergh and Spirit of St. Louis, 1927. 55fr, Hugo Junkers and Junkers JU52/3, 1932. 60fr, Igor Sikorsky and Sikorsky VS 300, 1939. 130fr, Concorde over New York.

1978, Oct. 30 Litho. *Perf. 13½x14*

885	A123	20c multi	.15	.15
886	A123	30c multi	.15	.15
887	A123	50c multi	.15	.15
888	A123	1fr multi	.15	.15
889	A123	3fr multi	.15	.15
890	A123	10fr multi	.20	.15
891	A123	55fr multi	1.10	.70
892	A123	60fr multi	1.20	.80
		Set value	2.70	1.80

Souvenir Sheet

Perf. 13x13½

893	A123	130fr multi	2.25	2.25

No. 893 contains one stamp 47x35mm.

Christmas Type of 1968 Souvenir Sheet

Design: 200fr, Adoration of the Kings, by Albrecht Dürer, vert.

1978, Dec. 11 Engr. *Perf. 11½*

894	A48	200fr brown	4.00	4.00

Nos. 532-533, Overprinted "1963 1978" in Black or Blue

1978, Dec. 18 Photo. *Perf. 13½*

895	A83	6fr multi (Bk)	.16	.15
896	A83	94fr multi (Bl)	1.90	1.25

Org. for African Unity, 15th anniv.

Goats A124

Designs: 20c, Ducks, vert. 50c, Cock and chickens, vert. 4fr, Rabbits. 5fr, Pigs, vert. 15fr, Turkey. 50fr, Sheep and cattle, vert. 75fr, Bull.

1978, Dec. 28 Litho. *Perf. 14*

897	A124	20c multi	.15	.15
898	A124	30c multi	.15	.15
899	A124	50c multi	.15	.15
900	A124	4fr multi	.15	.15
901	A124	5fr multi	.15	.15
902	A124	15fr multi	.30	.20
903	A124	50fr multi	1.00	.65
904	A124	75fr multi	1.50	1.00
		Set value	3.10	2.05

Husbandry Year.

Papilio Demodocus A125

Butterflies: 30c, Precis octavia. 50c, Charaxes smaragdalis. 4fr, Charaxes guderiana. 15fr, Colotis evippe. 30fr, Danaus limniace. 50fr, Byblia acheloia. 150fr, Utetheisa pulchella.

1979, Feb. 19 Photo. *Perf. 14½*

905	A125	20c multi	.15	.15
906	A125	30c multi	.15	.15
907	A125	50c multi	.15	.15
908	A125	4fr multi	.15	.15
909	A125	15fr multi	.30	.20
910	A125	30fr multi	.60	.40
911	A125	50fr multi	1.00	.65
912	A125	150fr multi	3.00	2.00
		Nos. 905-912 (8)	5.50	3.85

Euphorbia Grantii, Weavers A126

Design: 60fr, Drummers and Intelsat IV-A.

1979, June 8 Photo. *Perf. 13*

913	A126	40fr multi	.80	.55
914	A126	60fr multi	1.20	.80

Philexafrique II, Libreville, Gabon, June 8-17.

Entandrophragma Excelsum — A127

Trees and Shrubs: 20c, Polyscias fulva. 50c, Ilex mitis. 4fr, Kigelia Africana. 15fr, Ficus thonningi. 20fr, Acacia Senegal. 50fr, Symphonia globulifera. 110fr, Acacia sieberana. 20c, 50c, 15fr, 50fr, vertical.

1979, Aug. 27 *Perf. 14*

No.	Type	Denom.	Description	Unused	Used
915	A127	20c	multi	.15	.15
916	A127	30c	multi	.15	.15
917	A127	50c	multi	.15	.15
918	A127	4 fr	multi	.15	.15
919	A127	15fr	multi	.22	.15
920	A127	20fr	multi	.30	.20
921	A127	50fr	multi	.75	.50
922	A127	110fr	multi	1.65	1.10
			Nos. 915-922 (8)	3.52	
			Set value		2.10

Black and White Boys, IYC Emblem A128

26fr, 100fr, Children of various races, diff., vert.

Perf. 13½x13, 13x13½

1979, Nov. 19 **Photo.**

No.	Type	Denom.	Description	Unused	Used
923	A128		Block of 8	4.50	3.00
a.			26fr, any single	.55	.38
924	A128	42fr	multi	.80	.55

Souvenir Sheet

No.	Type	Denom.	Description	Unused	Used
925	A128	100fr	multi	2.00	1.50

Intl. Year of the Child. No. 923 printed in sheets of 16 (4x4).

Basket Weaving A129

Perf. 12½x13, 13x12½

1979, Dec. 3 **Litho.**

No.	Type	Denom.	Description	Unused	Used
926	A129	50c	shown	.15	.15
927	A129	1.50fr	Wood carving, vert.	.15	.15
928	A129	2fr	Metal working	.15	.15
929	A129	10fr	Jewelry, vert.	.20	.15
930	A129	20fr	Straw plaiting	.40	.20
931	A129	26fr	Wall painting, vert.	.55	.25
932	A129	40fr	Pottery	.80	.40
933	A129	100fr	Smelting, vert.	2.00	1.00
			Nos. 926-933 (8)	4.40	
			Set value		2.00

Souvenir Sheet

Children of Different Races, Christmas Tree — A130

1979, Dec. 24 **Engr.** *Perf. 12*

No.	Type	Denom.	Description	Unused	Used
934	A130	200fr	ultra & dp mag	6.00	3.00

Christmas; Intl. Year of the Child.

German East Africa #N5, Hill — A131

Sir Rowland Hill (1795-1879), originator of penny postage, and Stamps of Ruanda-Urundi or: 30c, German East Africa #N23. 50c, German East Africa #NB9. 3fr, #25. 10fr, #42. 26fr, #123. 100fr, #B28.

1979, Dec. 31 **Litho.** *Perf. 14*

No.	Type	Denom.	Description	Unused	Used
935	A131	20c	multi	.15	.15
936	A131	30c	multi	.15	.15
937	A131	50c	multi	.15	.15
938	A131	3fr	multi	.15	.15
939	A131	10fr	multi	.22	.15
940	A131	26fr	multi	.65	.25
941	A131	60fr	multi	1.50	.60
942	A131	100fr	multi	2.50	1.00
			Nos. 935-942 (8)	5.47	
			Set value		2.10

Sarothrura Pulchra A132

Birds of the Nyungwe Forest: 20c Ploceus alienus, vert. 30c, Regal sunbird, vert. 3fr, Tockus alboterminatus. 10fr, Pygmy owl, vert. 26fr, Emerald cuckoo. 60fr, Finch, vert. 100fr, Stepanoaetus coronatus, vert.

Perf. 13½x13, 13x13½

1980, Jan. 7 **Photo.**

No.	Type	Denom.	Description	Unused	Used
943	A132	20c	multi	.15	.15
944	A132	30c	multi	.15	.15
945	A132	50c	multi	.15	.15
946	A132	3fr	multi	.15	.15
947	A132	10fr	multi	.22	.15
948	A132	26fr	multi	.65	.25
949	A132	60fr	multi	1.50	.60
950	A132	100fr	multi	2.50	1.00
			Nos. 943-950 (8)	5.47	
			Set value		2.10

First Footstep on Moon, Spacecraft A133

Spacecraft and Moon Exploration: 1.50fr, Descent onto lunar surface. 8fr, American flag. 30fr, Solar panels. 50fr, Gathering soil samples. 60fr, Adjusting sun screen. 200fr, Landing craft.

1980, Jan. 31 **Photo.** *Perf. 13x13½*

No.	Type	Denom.	Description	Unused	Used
951	A133	50c	multi	.15	.15
952	A133	1.50fr	multi	.15	.15
953	A133	8fr	multi	.20	.15
954	A133	30fr	multi	.70	.30
955	A133	50fr	multi	1.40	.50
956	A133	60fr	multi	1.50	.60
			Nos. 951-956 (6)	4.10	
			Set value		1.55

Souvenir Sheet

No.	Type	Denom.	Description	Unused	Used
957	A133	200fr	multi	5.00	2.00

Apollo 11 moon landing, 10th anniv. (1979).

Globe, Butare and 1905 Chicago Club Emblems — A134

Rotary Intl., 75th Anniv. (Globe, Emblems of Butare or Kigali Clubs and): 30c, San Francisco, 1908. 50c, Chicago, 1910. 4fr, Buffalo, 1911. 15fr, London, 1911. 20fr, Glasgow, 1912. 50fr, Bristol, 1917. 60fr, Rotary Intl., 1980.

1980, Feb. 23 **Litho.** *Perf. 13*

No.	Type	Denom.	Description	Unused	Used
958	A134	20c	multi	.15	.15
959	A134	30c	multi	.15	.15
960	A134	50c	multi	.15	.15
961	A134	4fr	multi	.15	.15
962	A134	15fr	multi	.30	.15
963	A134	20fr	multi	.40	.20
964	A134	50fr	multi	1.00	.50
965	A134	60fr	multi	1.20	.60
			Nos. 958-965 (8)	3.50	
			Set value		1.60

Gymnast, Moscow '80 Emblem A135

1980, Mar. 10 *Perf. 12½*

No.	Type	Denom.	Description	Unused	Used
966	A135	20c	shown	.15	.15
967	A135	30c	Basketball	.15	.15
968	A135	50c	Bicycling	.15	.15
969	A135	3fr	Boxing	.15	.15
970	A135	20fr	Archery	.50	.20
971	A135	26fr	Weight lifting	.65	.25
972	A135	50fr	Javelin	1.25	.50
973	A135	100fr	Fencing	2.50	1.00
			Nos. 966-973 (8)	5.50	
			Set value		2.10

22nd Summer Olympic Games, Moscow, July 19-Aug. 3.

Souvenir Sheet

Amalfi Coast, by Giacinto Gigante — A136

1980, Apr. 28 **Photo.** *Perf. 13½*

No.	Type	Denom.	Description	Unused	Used
974	A136	200fr	multi	5.75	2.50

20th Intl. Philatelic Exhibition, Europa '80, Naples, Apr. 26-May 4.

Geaster Mushroom A137

1980, July 21 **Photo.** *Perf. 13½*

No.	Type	Denom.	Description	Unused	Used
975	A137	20c	shown	.15	.15
976	A137	30c	Lentinus atrobrunneus	.15	.15
977	A137	50c	Gomphus stereoides	.15	.15
978	A137	4fr	Cantharellus cibarius	.15	.15
979	A137	10fr	Stilbothamnium dybowskii	.22	.15
980	A137	15fr	Xeromphalina tenuipes	.38	.15
981	A137	70fr	Podoscypha elegans	1.60	.70
982	A137	100fr	Mycena	2.25	1.00
			Nos. 975-982 (8)	5.05	
			Set value		2.10

Still Life, by Renoir A138

Impressionist Painters: 30c, 26fr, At the Theater, by Toulouse-Lautrec, vert. 50c, 10fr, Seaside Garden, by Monet. 4fr, Mother and Child, by Mary Cassatt, vert. 5fr, Starry Night, by Van Gogh. 10fr, Dancers at their Toilet, by Degas, vert. 50fr, The Card Players, by Cezanne. 70fr, Tahitian Women, by Gauguin, vert. 75fr, like 20c. 100fr, In the Park, by Seurat.

1980, Aug. 4 **Litho.** *Perf. 14*

No.	Type	Denom.	Description	Unused	Used
983	A138	20c	multi	.15	.15
984	A138	30c	multi	.15	.15
985	A138	50c	multi	.15	.15
986	A138	4fr	multi	.15	.15
a.			Sheet of 2, 4fr, 26fr	.70	.70
987	A138	5fr	multi	.15	.15
a.			Sheet of 2, 5fr, 75fr	2.00	2.00
988	A138	10fr	multi	.22	.15
a.			Sheet of 2, 10fr, 70fr	2.00	2.00
989	A138	50fr	multi	1.40	.50
a.			Sheet of 2, 50fr, 10fr	1.50	1.50
990	A138	70fr	multi	1.60	.70
991	A138	100fr	multi	2.25	1.00
			Nos. 983-991 (9)	6.22	
			Set value		2.50

Souvenir Sheet

Virgin of the Harpies, by Andrea Del Sarto — A139

Photogravure and Engraved

1980, Dec. 22 *Perf. 11½*

No.	Type	Denom.	Description	Unused	Used
992	A139	200fr	multi	5.00	3.00

Christmas.

Belgian War of Independence, Engraving — A140

Belgian Independence Sesquicentennial: Engravings of War of Independence.

1980, Dec. 29 **Litho.** *Perf. 12½*

No.	Type	Denom.	Description	Unused	Used
993	A140	20c	pale grn & brn	.15	.15
994	A140	30c	brn org & brn	.15	.15
995	A140	50c	lt bl & brn	.15	.15
996	A140	9fr	yel & brn	.18	.15
997	A140	10fr	brt lil & brn	.20	.15
998	A140	20fr	ap grn & brn	.40	.20
999	A140	70fr	pink & brn	1.40	.70
1000	A140	90fr	lem & brn	1.75	.90
			Nos. 993-1000 (8)	4.38	
			Set value		2.10

Swamp Drainage A141

1980, Dec. 31 **Photo.** *Perf. 13½*

No.	Type	Denom.	Description	Unused	Used
1001	A141	20c	shown	.15	.15
1002	A141	30c	Fertilizer shed	.15	.15
1003	A141	1.50fr	Rice fields	.15	.15
1004	A141	8fr	Tree planting	.20	.15
1005	A141	10fr	Terrace planting	.28	.15
1006	A141	40fr	Farm buildings	1.10	.55
1007	A141	90fr	Bean cultivation	2.50	1.25
1008	A141	100fr	Tea cultivation	2.75	1.40
			Nos. 1001-1008 (8)	7.28	3.95

Soil Conservation Year.

Pavetta Rwandensis A142

1981, Apr. 6 **Photo.** *Perf. 13x13½*

No.	Type	Denom.	Description	Unused	Used
1009	A142	20c	shown	.15	.15
1010	A142	30c	Cyrtorchis praetermissa	.15	.15
1011	A142	50c	Pavonia urens	.15	.15
1012	A142	4fr	Cynorkis kassnerana	.15	.15
1013	A142	5fr	Gardenia ternifolia	.15	.15
1014	A142	10fr	Leptactina platyphylla	.25	.15
1015	A142	20fr	Lobelia petiolata	.50	.25
1016	A142	40fr	Tapinanthus brunneus	1.00	.50
1017	A142	70fr	Impatiens niamniamensis	1.75	.90
1018	A142	150fr	Dissotis rwandensis	3.75	1.90
			Nos. 1009-1018 (10)	8.00	
			Set value		3.80

Girl Knitting — A143

SOS Children's Village: Various children.

1981, Apr. 27 *Perf. 13*

No.	Type	Denom.	Description	Unused	Used
1019	A143	20c	multi	.15	.15
1020	A143	30c	multi	.15	.15
1021	A143	50c	multi	.15	.15
1022	A143	1fr	multi	.15	.15
1023	A143	8fr	multi	.18	.15
1024	A143	10fr	multi	.22	.15

1025	A143	70fr	multi	1.50	.70
1026	A143	150fr	multi	3.25	1.50
			Nos. 1019-1026 (8)	5.75	
			Set value		2.50

Carolers, by Norman Rockwell A144

Designs: Saturday Evening Post covers by Norman Rockwell.

1981, May 11 Litho. Perf. 13½x14

1027	A144	20c	multi	.15	.15
1028	A144	30c	multi	.15	.15
1029	A144	50c	multi	.15	.15
1030	A144	1fr	multi	.15	.15
1031	A144	8fr	multi	.16	.15
1032	A144	20fr	multi	.40	.20
1033	A144	50fr	multi	1.00	.50
1034	A144	70fr	multi	1.40	.70
			Set value	3.10	1.60

Cerval A145

Designs: Meat-eating animals.

1981, June 29 Photo. Perf. 13½x14

1035	A145	20c	shown	.15	.15
1036	A145	30c	Jackals	.15	.15
1037	A145	2fr	Genet	.15	.15
1038	A145	2.50fr	Banded mongoose	.15	.15
1039	A145	10fr	Zorille	.20	.15
1040	A145	15fr	White-cheeked otter	.30	.15
1041	A145	70fr	Golden wild cat	1.40	.70
1042	A145	200fr	Hunting dog, vert.	4.00	2.00
			Nos. 1035-1042 (8)	6.50	
			Set value		3.10

Drummer Sending Message — A146

1981, Sept. 1 Litho. Perf. 13

1043	A146	20c	shown	.15	.15
1044	A146	30c	Map, communication waves	.15	.15
1045	A146	2fr	Jet, radar screen	.15	.15
1046	A146	2.50fr	Satellite, teletape	.15	.15
1047	A146	10fr	Dish antenna	.25	.15
1048	A146	15fr	Ship, navigation devices	.38	.18
1049	A146	70fr	Helicopter	1.75	.90
1050	A146	200fr	Satellite with solar panels	5.00	2.50
			Nos. 1043-1050 (8)	7.98	
			Set value		2.80

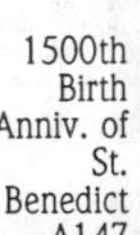

1500th Birth Anniv. of St. Benedict A147

Paintings and Frescoes of St. Benedict: 20c, Leaving his Parents, Mt. Oliveto Monastery, Maggiore. 30c, Oldest portrait, 10th cent., St. Chrisogone Church, Rome, vert. 50c, Portrait, Virgin of the Misericord polyptich, Borgo San Sepolcro. 4fr, Giving the Rules of the order to his Monks, Mt. Oliveto Monastery. 5fr, Monks at their Meal, Mt. Oliveto Monastery. 20fr, Portrait, 13th cent., Lower Chrruch of the Holy Spirit, Subiaco, vert. 70fr, Our Lady in Glory with Sts. Gregory and Benedict, San Gimigniao, vert. 100fr, Priest Carrying Easter Meal to St. Benedict, by Jan van Coninxloo, 16th cent.

Perf. 13½x13, 13x13½

1981, Nov. 30 Photo.

1051	A147	20c	multi	.15	.15
1052	A147	30c	multi	.15	.15
1053	A147	50c	multi	.15	.15
1054	A147	4fr	multi	.15	.15
1055	A147	5fr	multi	.15	.15
1056	A147	20fr	multi	.40	.20
1057	A147	70fr	multi	1.40	.65
1058	A147	100fr	multi	2.00	2.00
			Nos. 1051-1058 (8)	4.55	
			Set value		3.00

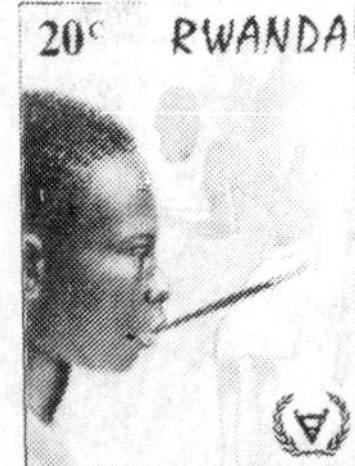

Intl. Year of the Disabled — A148

1981, Dec. 7 Litho. Perf. 13

1059	A148	20c	Painting	.15	.15
1060	A148	30c	Soccer	.15	.15
1061	A148	4.50fr	Crocheting	.15	.15
1062	A148	5fr	Painting vase	.15	.15
1063	A148	10fr	Sawing	.20	.15
1064	A148	60fr	Sign language	1.20	.65
1065	A148	70fr	Doing puzzle	1.40	.80
1066	A148	100fr	Juggling	2.00	1.10
			Nos. 1059-1066 (8)	5.40	
			Set value		2.80

Souvenir Sheet

Christmas A149

Photo. & Engr.

1981, Dec. 21 Perf. 13½

1067	A149	200fr	Adoration of the Kings, by van der Goes	4.00	2.00

Natl. Rural Water Supply Year — A150

1981, Dec. 28 Litho. Perf. 12½

1068	A150	20c	Deer drinking	.15	.15
1069	A150	30c	Women carrying water, vert.	.15	.15
1070	A150	50c	Pipeline	.15	.15
1071	A150	10fr	Filing pan, vert.	.20	.15
1072	A150	19fr	Drinking	.40	.22
1073	A150	70fr	Mother, child, vert.	1.40	.65
1074	A150	100fr	Lake pumping station, vert.	2.00	1.00
			Nos. 1068-1074 (7)	4.45	
			Set value		2.10

World Food Day, Oct. 16, 1981 A151

1982, Jan. 25 Litho. Perf. 13

1075	A151	20c	Cattle	.15	.15
1076	A151	30c	Bee	.15	.15
1077	A151	50c	Fish	.15	.15
1078	A151	1fr	Avocados	.15	.15
1079	A151	8fr	Boy eating banana	.16	.15
1080	A151	20fr	Sorghum	.40	.20
1081	A151	70fr	Vegetables	1.40	.65
1082	A151	100fr	Balanced diet	2.00	1.00
			Nos. 1075-1082 (8)	4.56	
			Set value		2.10

Hibiscus Berberidifolius A152

1982, June 14 Litho. Perf. 13

1083	A152	20c	shown	.15	.15
1084	A152	30c	Hypericum lanceolatum, vert.	.15	.15
1085	A152	50c	Canarina eminii	.15	.15
1086	A152	4fr	Polygala ruwenxoriensis	.15	.15
1087	A152	10fr	Kniphofia grantii, vert.	.20	.15
1088	A152	35fr	Euphorbia candelabrum, vert.	.70	.35
1089	A152	70fr	Disa erubescens, vert.	1.40	.65
1090	A152	80fr	Gloriosa simplex	1.60	1.00
			Nos. 1083-1090 (8)	4.50	
			Set value		2.20

20th Anniv. of Independence — A153

1982, June 28

1091	A153	10fr	Flags	.20	.15
1092	A153	20fr	Hands releasing doves	.40	.20
1093	A153	30fr	Flag, handshake	.60	.30
1094	A153	50fr	Govt. buildings	1.00	.50
			Nos. 1091-1094 (4)	2.20	1.15

1982 World Cup — A154

Designs: Various soccer players.

1982, July 6 Perf. 14x14½

1095	A154	20c	multi	.15	.15
1096	A154	30c	multi	.15	.15
1097	A154	1.50fr	multi	.15	.15
1098	A154	8fr	multi	.16	.15
1099	A154	10fr	multi	.20	.15
1100	A154	20fr	multi	.40	.20
1101	A154	70fr	multi	1.40	.65
1102	A154	90fr	multi	1.90	.90
			Nos. 1095-1102 (8)	4.51	
			Set value		2.00

TB Bacillus Centenary — A155

1982, Nov. 22 Litho. Perf. 14½

1103	A155	10fr	Microscope, slide	.20	.15
1104	A155	20fr	Serum, slide	.40	.20
1105	A155	70fr	Lungs, slide	1.40	.65
1106	A155	100fr	Koch	2.00	1.00
			Nos. 1103-1106 (4)	4.00	2.00

Souvenir Sheets

Madam Recamier, by David — A156

PHILEXFRANCE '82 Intl. Stamp Exhibition, Paris, June 11-21: No. 1108, St. Anne and Virgin and Child with Franciscan Monk, by H. van der Goes. No. 1109, Liberty Guiding the People, by Delacroix. No. 1110, Pygmalion, by P. Delvaux.

1982, Dec. 11 Perf. 13½

1107	A156	40fr	multi	.80	.42
1108	A156	40fr	multi	.80	.42
1109	A156	60fr	multi	1.20	.55
1110	A156	60fr	multi	1.20	.55
			Nos. 1107-1110 (4)	4.00	1.94

Souvenir Sheet

Rest During the Flight to Egypt, by Murillo A157

1982, Dec. 20 Photo. & Engr.

1111	A157	200fr	carmine rose	4.00	2.00

Christmas.

10th Anniv. of UN Conference on Human Environment — A158

1982, Dec. 27 Litho. Perf. 14

1112	A158	20c	Elephants	.15	.15
1113	A158	30c	Lion	.15	.15
1114	A158	50c	Flower	.15	.15
1115	A158	4fr	Bull	.15	.15
1116	A158	5fr	Deer	.15	.15
1117	A158	10fr	Flower, diff.	.20	.15
1118	A158	20fr	Zebras	.40	.20
1119	A158	40fr	Crowned cranes	.80	.40
1120	A158	50fr	Bird	1.00	.50
1121	A158	70fr	Woman pouring coffee beans	1.40	.65
			Nos. 1112-1121 (10)	4.55	
			Set value		2.00

Scouting Year A159

Perf. 13½x14½

1983, Jan. 17 Photo.

1122	A159	20c	Animal first aid	.15	.15
1123	A159	30c	Camp	.15	.15
1124	A159	1.50fr	Campfire	.15	.15
1125	A159	8fr	Scout giving sign	.16	.15
1126	A159	10fr	Knot	.20	.15
1127	A159	20fr	Camp, diff.	.40	.20
1128	A159	70fr	Chopping wood	1.40	.65
1129	A159	90fr	Sign, map	1.75	.90
			Nos. 1122-1129 (8)	4.36	
			Set value		2.00

For overprints see Nos. 1234-1241.

Nectar-sucking Birds — A160

Perf. 14x14½, 14½x14

1983, Jan. 31 **Litho.**

1130 A160 20c Angola nectar bird .15 .15
1131 A160 30c Royal nectar birds .15 .15
1132 A160 50c Johnston's nectar bird .15 .15
1133 A160 4fr Bronze nectar birds .15 .15
1134 A160 5fr Collared souimangas .15 .15
1135 A160 10fr Blue-headed nectar bird .30 .15
1136 A160 20fr Purple-bellied nectar bird .40 .20
1137 A160 40fr Copper nectar birds .80 .40
1138 A160 50fr Olive-bellied nectar birds 1.00 .50
1139 A160 70fr Red-breasted nectar bird 1.40 .65
Nos. 1130-1139 (10) 4.65
Set value 2.00

30c, 4fr, 10fr, 40fr, 70fr horiz. Inscribed 1982.

Soil Erosion Prevention A161

1983, Feb. 14 *Perf. 14½*

1140 A161 20c Driving cattle .15 .15
1141 A161 30c Pineapple field .15 .15
1142 A161 50c Interrupted ditching .15 .15
1143 A161 9fr Hedges, ditches .18 .15
1144 A161 10fr Reafforestation .20 .15
1145 A161 20fr Anti-erosion barriers .40 .20
1146 A161 30fr Contour planting .60 .30
1147 A161 50fr Terracing 1.00 .50
1148 A161 60fr Protection of river banks 1.20 .60
1149 A161 70fr Fallow, planted strips 1.40 .65
Nos. 1140-1149 (10) 5.43
Set value 2.50

For overprints & surcharges see #1247-1255.

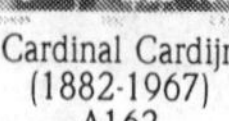

Cardinal Cardijn (1882-1967) A162

Gorilla A163

Young Catholic Workers Movement Activities. Inscribed 1982.

1983, Feb. 22 *Perf. 12½x13*

1150 A162 20c Feeding ducks .15 .15
1151 A162 30c Harvesting bananas .15 .15
1152 A162 50c Carrying melons .15 .15
1153 A162 10fr Teacher .25 .15
1154 A162 19fr Shoemakers .50 .22
1155 A162 20fr Growing millet .50 .25
1156 A162 70fr Embroidering 1.75 .80
1157 A162 80fr shown 2.00 1.00
Nos. 1150-1157 (8) 5.45 2.87

1983, Mar. 14 *Perf. 14*

Various gorillas. Nos. 1158-1163 horiz.

1158 A163 20c multi .15 .15
1159 A163 30c multi .15 .15
1160 A163 9.50fr multi .18 .15
1161 A163 10fr multi .20 .15
1162 A163 20fr multi .40 .20
1163 A163 30fr multi .60 .30
1164 A163 60fr multi 1.20 .60
1165 A163 70fr multi 1.40 .65
Nos. 1158-1165 (8) 4.28 2.35

Souvenir Sheet

The Granduca Madonna, by Raphael A164

Typo. & Engr.

1983, Dec. 19 *Perf. 11½*

1166 A164 200fr multi 2.50 1.40

Christmas.

Local Trees — A165

1984, Jan. 15 **Litho.** *Perf. 13½x13*

1167 A165 20c Hagenia abyssinica .15 .15
1168 A165 30c Dracaena steudneri .15 .15
1169 A165 50c Phoenix reclinata .15 .15
1170 A165 10fr Podocarpus milanjianus .15 .15
1171 A165 19fr Entada abyssinica .25 .15
1172 A165 70fr Parinari excelsa .90 .45
1173 A165 100fr Newtonia buchananii 1.40 .65
1174 A165 200fr Acacia gerrardi, vert. 2.50 1.40
Nos. 1167-1174 (8) 5.65
Set value 2.80

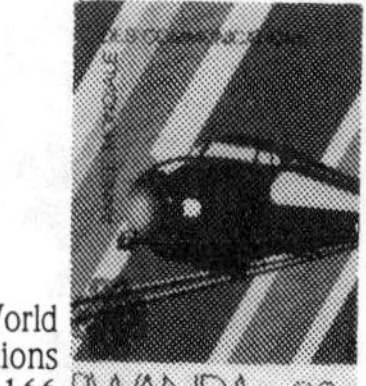

World Communications Year — A166

1984, May 21 **Litho.** *Perf. 12½*

1175 A166 20c Train .15 .15
1176 A166 30c Ship .15 .15
1177 A166 4.50fr Radio .15 .15
1178 A166 10fr Telephone .15 .15
1179 A166 15fr Mail .20 .15
1180 A166 50fr Jet .65 .35
1181 A166 70fr Satellite, TV screen .90 .45
1182 A166 100fr Satellite 1.40 .65
Nos. 1175-1182 (8) 3.75
Set value 1.75

1st Manned Flight Bicent. — A167

Historic flights: 20c, Le Martial, Sept. 19, 1783. 30c, La Montgolfiere, Nov. 21, 1783. 50c, Charles and Robert, Dec. 1, 1783, and Blanchard, Mar. 2, 1784. 9fr, Jean-Pierre Blanchard and wife in balloon. 10fr, Blanchard and Jeffries, 1785. 50fr, E. Demuyter, 1937. 80fr, Propane gas balloons. 200fr, Abruzzo, Anderson and Newman, 1978.

1984, June 4 **Litho.** *Perf. 13*

1183 A167 20c multi .15 .15
1184 A167 30c multi .15 .15
1185 A167 50c multi .15 .15
1186 A167 9fr multi .15 .15
1187 A167 10fr multi .15 .15
1188 A167 50fr multi .65 .35
1189 A167 80fr multi 1.00 .50
1190 A167 200fr multi 2.50 1.40
Nos. 1183-1190 (8) 4.90
Set value 2.50

1984 Summer Olympics A168

1984, July 16 *Perf. 14*

1191 A168 20c Equestrian .15 .15
1192 A168 30c Wind surfing .15 .15
1193 A168 50c Soccer .15 .15
1194 A168 9fr Swimming .15 .15
1195 A168 10fr Field hockey .15 .15
1196 A168 40fr Fencing .55 .25
1197 A168 80fr Running 1.10 .55
1198 A168 200fr Boxing 2.50 1.40
Nos. 1191-1198 (8) 4.90
Set value 2.45

Zebras and Buffaloes A169

1984, Nov. 26 **Litho.** *Perf. 13*

1199 A169 20c Zebra with colt .15 .15
1200 A169 30c Buffalo with calf, vert. .15 .15
1201 A169 50c Two zebras, vert. .15 .15
1202 A169 9fr Zebras fighting .15 .15
1203 A169 10fr Buffalo, vert. .15 .15
1204 A169 80fr Zebra herd 1.00 .55
1205 A169 100fr Zebra, vert. 1.25 .60
1206 A169 200fr Buffalo 2.50 1.25
Nos. 1199-1206 (8) 5.50
Set value 2.65

Souvenir Sheet

Christmas 1984 — A170

1984, Dec. 24 **Typo. & Engr.**

1207 A170 200fr Virgin and Child, by Correggio 3.50 2.25

Gorilla Gorilla Beringei — A171

1985, Mar. 25 **Litho.** *Perf. 13*

1208 A171 10fr Adults and young .15 .15
1209 A171 15fr Adults .20 .15
1210 A171 25fr Female holding young .35 .16
1211 A171 30fr Three adults .40 .20
Nos. 1208-1211 (4) 1.10
Set value .52

Souvenir Sheet

Perf. 11½x12

1212 A171 200fr Baby climbing branch, vert. 2.50 1.40

No. 1212 contains one 37x52mm stamp.

Self-Sufficiency in Food Production — A172

Designs: 20c, Raising chickens and turkeys. 30c, Pineapple harvest. 50c, Animal husbandry. 9fr, Grain products. 10fr, Education. 50fr, Sowing grain. 80fr, Food reserves. 100fr, Banana harvest.

1985, Mar. 30

1213 A172 20c multi .15 .15
1214 A172 30c multi .15 .15
1215 A172 50c multi .15 .15
1216 A172 9fr multi .15 .15
1217 A172 10fr multi .15 .15
1218 A172 50fr multi .65 .35
1219 A172 80fr multi 1.00 .50
1220 A172 100fr multi 1.40 .65
Nos. 1213-1220 (8) 3.80
Set value 1.75

Natl. Redevelopment Movement, 10th Anniv. — A173

1985, July 5

1221 A173 10fr multi .15 .15
1222 A173 30fr multi .40 .20
1223 A173 70fr multi .90 .45
Nos. 1221-1223 (3) 1.45 .80

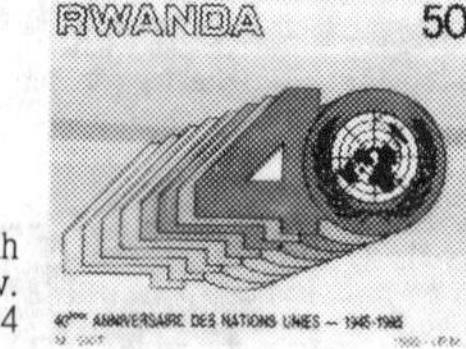

UN, 40th Anniv. A174

1985, July 25

1224 A174 50fr multi .65 .35
1225 A174 100fr multi 1.40 .65

Audubon Birth Bicent. — A175

Illustrations of North American bird species by John J. Audubon.

1985, Sept. 18

1226 A175 10fr Barn owl .15 .15
1227 A175 20fr White-faced owl .25 .15
1228 A175 40fr Red-breasted hummingbird .55 .25
1229 A175 80fr Warbler 1.00 .50
Nos. 1226-1229 (4) 1.95 1.05

Intl. Youth Year A176

985, Oct. 14
230 A176 7fr Education and agriculture .15 .15
231 A176 9fr Bicycling .15 .15
232 A176 44fr Construction .55 .28
233 A176 80fr Schoolroom 1.00 .50
Nos. 1230-1233 (4) 1.85
Set value .90

Nos. 1122-1129 Ovptd. in Green or Rose Violet with the Girl Scout Trefoil and "1910/1985"

985, Nov. 25 *Perf. 13½x14½*
234 A159 20c multi .15 .15
235 A159 30c multi (RV) .15 .15
236 A159 1.50fr multi .15 .15
237 A159 8fr multi (RV) .15 .15
238 A159 10fr multi .15 .15
239 A159 20fr multi .25 .15
240 A159 70fr multi (RV) .90 .45
241 A159 90fr multi 1.10 .60
Set value 2.60 1.40

Natl. Girl Scout Movement, 75th anniv.

Souvenir Sheet

Adoration of the Magi, by Titian — A177

Photo. & Engr.

1985, Dec. 24 *Perf. 11½*
1242 A177 200fr violet 3.00 2.00

Christmas.

Transportation and Communication — A178

1986, Jan. 27 **Litho.** *Perf. 13*
1243 A178 10fr Articulated truck .15 .15
1244 A178 30fr Hand-canceling letters .40 .20
1245 A178 40fr Kigali Satellite Station .55 .25

Size: 52x34mm

1246 A178 80fr Kayibanda Airport, Kigali 1.00 .50
Nos. 1243-1246 (4) 2.10 1.10

Nos. 1141-1149 Surcharged or Ovptd. with Silver Bar and "ANNEE 1986 / INTENSIFICATION AGRICOLE"

1986, May 5 **Litho.** *Perf. 14½*
1247 A161 9fr #1143 .18 .15
1248 A161 10fr on 30c #1141 .20 .15
1249 A161 10fr on 50c #1142 .20 .15
1250 A161 10fr #1144 .20 .15
1251 A161 20fr #1145 .40 .20
1252 A161 30fr #1146 .60 .30
1253 A161 50fr #1147 1.00 .50
1254 A161 60fr #1148 1.20 .60
1255 A161 70fr #1149 1.40 .70
Nos. 1247-1255 (9) 5.38 2.90

1986 World Cup Soccer Championships, Mexico — A179

Various soccer plays, natl. flags.

1986, June 16 *Perf. 13*
1256 A179 2fr Morocco, England .15 .15
1257 A179 4fr Paraguay, Iraq .15 .15
1258 A179 5fr Brazil, Spain .15 .15
1259 A179 10fr Italy, Argentina .20 .15
1260 A179 40fr Mexico, Belgium .80 .40
1261 A179 45fr France, USSR .90 .45
Nos. 1256-1261 (6) 2.35
Set value 1.05

For overprints see Nos. 1360-1365.

Akagera Natl. Park — A180

1986, Dec. 15 **Litho.** *Perf. 13*
1262 A180 4fr Antelopes .15 .15
1263 A180 7fr Shoebills .15 .15
1264 A180 9fr Cape elands .18 .15
1265 A180 10fr Giraffe .20 .15
1266 A180 80fr Elephants 1.60 .80
1267 A180 90fr Crocodiles 1.80 .90

Size: 48x34mm

1268 A180 100fr Weaver birds 2.00 1.00
1269 A180 100fr Pelican, zebras 2.00 1.00
Nos. 1262-1269 (8) 8.08 4.30

Nos. 1268-1269 printed se-tenant in a continuous design with label picturing map on right.

Christmas, Intl. Peace Year A181

1986, Dec. 24 **Litho.** *Perf. 13*
1270 A181 10fr shown .20 .15
1271 A181 15fr Dove, Earth .30 .15
1272 A181 30fr like 10fr .60 .30
1273 A181 70fr like 15fr 1.40 .70
Nos. 1270-1273 (4) 2.50 1.30

UN Child Survival Campaign — A182

1987, Feb. 13
1274 A182 4fr Breast feeding .15 .15
1275 A182 6fr Rehydration therapy .15 .15
1276 A182 10fr Immunization .20 .15
1277 A182 70fr Growth monitoring 1.40 .70
Nos. 1274-1277 (4) 1.90
Set value .90

Year of Natl. Self-sufficiency in Food Production — A183

1987, June 15 **Litho.** *Perf. 13*
1278 A183 5fr Farm .15 .15
1279 A183 7fr Storing produce .15 .15
1280 A183 40fr Boy carrying basket of fish, produce .80 .40
1281 A183 60fr Tropical fruit 1.20 .60
Nos. 1278-1281 (4) 2.30 1.30

Nos. 1279-1281 vert.

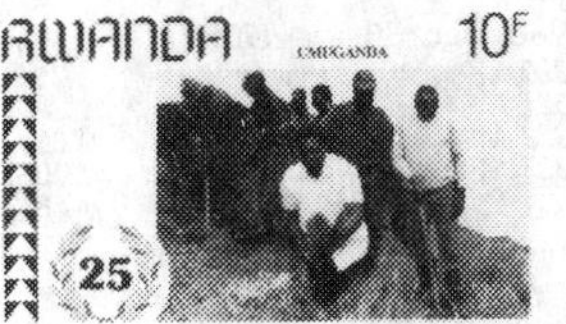

Natl. Independence, 25th Anniv. — A184

Designs: 10fr, Pres. Habyarimana, soldiers, farmers. 40fr, Pres. officiating government session. 70fr, Pres., Pope John Paul II. 100fr, Pres., vert.

1987, July 1
1283 A184 10fr multi .20 .15
1284 A184 40fr multi .80 .40
1285 A184 70fr multi 1.40 .70
1286 A184 100fr multi 2.00 1.00
Nos. 1283-1286 (4) 4.40 2.25

Fruit A185

1987, Sept. 28
1287 A185 10fr Bananas, vert. .20 .15
1288 A185 40fr Pineapples .80 .40
1289 A185 80fr Papayas 1.60 .80
1290 A185 90fr Avocados 1.80 .90
1291 A185 100fr Strawberries, vert. 2.00 1.00
Nos. 1287-1291 (5) 6.40 3.25

Leopards — A186

1987, Nov. 18 **Litho.** *Perf. 13*
1292 A186 50fr Female, cub 1.00 .50
1293 A186 50fr Three cubs playing 1.00 .50
1294 A186 50fr Adult attaching gazelle 1.00 .50
1295 A186 50fr In tree 1.00 .50
1296 A186 50fr Leaping from tree 1.00 .50
a. Strip of 5, Nos. 1292-1296 5.00 2.50

Intl. Year of the Volunteer — A187

1987, Dec. 12
1297 A187 5fr Constructing village water system .15 .15
1298 A187 12fr Education, vert. .24 .15
1299 A187 20fr Modern housing, vert. .40 .20
1300 A187 60fr Animal husbandry, vert. 1.20 .60
Nos. 1298-1300 (3) 1.84
Set value .96

Souvenir Sheet

Virgin and Child, by Fra Angelico (c. 1387-1455) A188

1987, Dec. 24 **Engr.** *Perf. 11½*
1301 A188 200fr deep mag & dull blue 4.00 2.00

Christmas.

Maintenance of the Rural Economy Year — A189

1988, June 13 **Litho.** *Perf. 13*
1302 A189 10fr Furniture store .26 .15
1303 A189 40fr Dairy farm 1.05 .52
1304 A189 60fr Produce market 1.60 .80
1305 A189 80fr Fruit market 2.10 1.05
Nos. 1302-1305 (4) 5.01 2.52

Primates, Nyungwe Forest A190

1988, Sept. 15 **Litho.** *Perf. 13*
1306 A190 2fr Chimpanzee .15 .15
1307 A190 3fr Black and white colobus .15 .15
1308 A190 10fr Pygmy galago .25 .15
1309 A190 90fr Cercopithecidae ascagne 2.35 1.20
Nos. 1306-1309 (4) 2.90
Set value 1.40

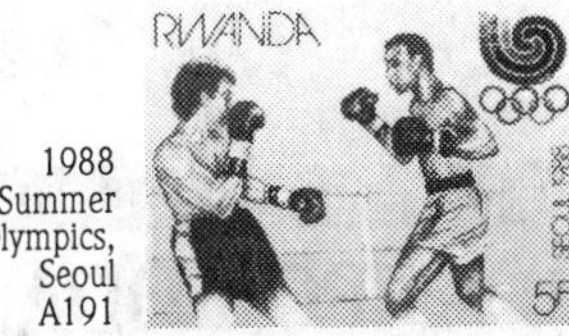

1988 Summer Olympics, Seoul A191

1988, Sept. 19
1310 A191 5fr Boxing .15 .15
1311 A191 7fr Relay .18 .15
1312 A191 8fr Table tennis .22 .15
1313 A191 10fr Women's running .28 .15
1314 A191 90fr Hurdles 2.35 1.20
Nos. 1310-1314 (5) 3.18 1.80

Organization of African Unity, 25th Anniv. — A192

1988, Nov. 30 **Litho.** *Perf. 13*
1315 A192 5fr shown .15 .15
1316 A192 7fr Handskake, map .18 .15
1317 A192 8fr "OAU" in brick, map .20 .15
1318 A192 90fr Slogan 2.35 1.20
Nos. 1315-1318 (4) 2.88 1.65

The Scott editorial staff regrettably cannot accept requests to identify, authenticate or appraise stamps and postal markings.

Souvenir Sheet

NOËL 1988

La Vierge à la soupe

VERONESE

1528 - 1588

Villa di Maser - Italie

Detail of The Virgin and the Soup, by Paolo Veronese — A193

1988, Dec. 23 Engr. *Perf. 13½*

1319 A193 200fr multicolored	5.25	5.25

Christmas. Margin is typographed.

Intl. Red Cross and Red Crescent Organizations, 125th Annivs. — A194

1988, Dec. 30 Litho. *Perf. 13*

1320 A194 10fr Refugees	.25	.15
1321 A194 30fr First aid	.78	.40
1322 A194 40fr Elderly	1.05	.52
1323 A194 100fr Travelling doctor	2.60	1.30
Nos. 1320-1323 (4)	4.68	2.37

Nos. 1322-1323 vert.

Medicinal Plants — A195

1989, Feb. 15 Litho. *Perf. 13*

1324 A195 5fr Plectranthus barbatus	.15	.15
1325 A195 10fr Tetradenia riparia	.28	.15
1326 A195 20fr Hygrophila auriculata	.55	.28
1327 A195 40fr Datura stramonium	1.10	.55
1328 A195 50fr Pavetta ternifolia	1.40	.70
Nos. 1324-1328 (5)	3.48	1.83

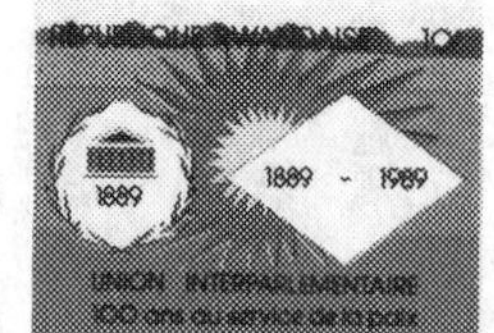

Interparliamentary Union, Cent. — A196

1989, Oct. 20 Litho. *Perf. 13*

1329 A196 10fr shown	.30	.16
1330 A196 30fr Hills, lake	.90	.50
1331 A196 70fr Hills, stream	2.10	1.15
1332 A196 90fr Sun rays, hills	2.75	1.50
Nos. 1329-1332 (4)	6.05	3.31

Souvenir Sheet

NOËL 1989

L'Adoration des Mages

P.P. RUBENS

(1577-1840)

Musées Royaux des Beaux-Arts Bruxelles

Christmas — A197

Adoration of the Magi by Rubens.

1989, Dec. 29 Engr. *Perf. 11½*

1333 A197 100fr blk, red & grn	3.40	3.40

Rural Organization Year — A198

Designs: 10fr, Making pottery. 70fr, Carrying produce to market. 90fr, Firing clay pots. 100fr, Clearing land.

1989, Dec. 29 Litho. *Perf. 13½x13*

1334 A198 10fr multi	.35	.18
1335 A198 70fr multi, vert.	2.35	1.30
1336 A198 90fr multi	3.00	1.65
1337 A198 200fr multi	6.75	3.75
Nos. 1334-1337 (4)	12.45	6.88

Revolution, 30th Anniv. (in 1989) — A199

Designs: 10fr, Improved living conditions. 60fr, Couple, farm tools. 70fr, Modernization. 100fr, Flag, map, native.

1990, Jan. 22 *Perf. 13*

1338 A199 10fr multi	.35	.18
1339 A199 60fr multi, vert.	2.05	1.10
1340 A199 70fr multi	2.35	1.30
1341 A199 100fr multi	3.35	1.85
Nos. 1338-1341 (4)	8.10	4.43

Inscribed 1989.

French Revolution, Bicent. (in 1989) — A200

Paintings of the Revolution: 10fr, Triumph of Marat by Boilly. 60fr, Rouget de Lisle singing La Marseillaise by Pils. 70fr, Oath of the Tennis Court by David. 100fr, Trial of Louis XVI by Court.

1990, Jan. 22

1342 A200 10fr multicolored	.35	.18
1343 A200 60fr multicolored	2.05	1.10
1344 A200 70fr multicolored	2.35	1.30
1345 A200 100fr multicolored	3.35	1.85
Nos. 1342-1345 (4)	8.10	4.43

Inscribed 1989.

African Development Bank, 25th Anniv. (in 1989) — A201

1990, Feb. 22 *Perf. 13½x13*

1346 A201 10fr Building construction	.35	.18
1347 A201 20fr Harvesting	.70	.40
1348 A201 40fr Cultivation	1.35	.75
1349 A201 90fr Building, truck, harvesters	3.00	1.65
Nos. 1346-1349 (4)	5.40	2.98

Belgica '90, Intl. Philatelic Exhibition — A202

Illustration reduced.

1990, May 21 Litho. *Imperf.*

1350 A202 100fr Great Britain #1	3.50	1.75
1351 A202 100fr Belgium #B1011	3.50	1.75
1352 A202 100fr Rwanda #516	3.50	1.75
Nos. 1350-1352 (3)	10.50	5.25

Visit of Pope John Paul II — A203

1990, Aug. 27 Litho. *Perf. 13½x13*

1353 A203 10fr shown	.35	.18
1354 A203 70fr Holding crucifix	2.30	1.25

Souvenir Sheet

Perf. 11½

1355 A203 100fr Hands together	3.25	1.75

No. 1355 contains one 36x51mm stamp.

Intl. Literacy Year A204

Designs: 10fr, Teacher at blackboard. 20fr, Teacher seated at desk. 50fr, Small outdoor class. 90fr, Large outdoor class.

1991, Jan. 25 Litho. *Perf. 13½x13*

1356 A204 10fr multicolored	.20	.15
1357 A204 20fr multicolored	.40	.25
1358 A204 50fr multicolored	.95	.55
1359 A204 90fr multicolored	1.75	.95
Nos. 1356-1359 (4)	3.30	1.90

Nos. 1256-1261 Ovptd. in Black on Silver

ITALIA 90

1990, May 25 Litho. *Perf. 13*

1360 A179 2fr on No. 1256	.15	.15
1361 A179 4fr on No. 1257	.15	.15
1362 A179 5fr on No. 1258	.15	.15
1363 A179 10fr on No. 1259	.28	.15
1364 A179 40fr on No. 1260	1.15	.58
1365 A179 45fr on No. 1261	1.30	.65
Nos. 1360-1365 (6)	3.18	
Set value		1.60

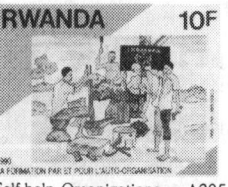

Self-help Organizations — A205

1991, Jan. 25 Litho. *Perf. 13½x13*

1366 A205 10fr Tool making	.28	.15
1367 A205 20fr Animal husbandry	.58	.30
1368 A205 50fr Textile manufacturing	1.40	.70
1369 A205 90fr Road construction	2.50	1.25
Nos. 1366-1369 (4)	4.76	2.40

Dated 1990.

World Conference on Nutrition, Rome A209

Designs: 15fr, Man fishing. 50fr, People at fruit market. 100fr, Man milking cow. 500fr, Mother breastfeeding.

1992, Dec. Litho. *Perf. 14*

1381 A209 15fr multicolored	*.20*	*.15*
1382 A209 50fr multicolored	*.70*	*.35*
1383 A209 100fr multicolored	*1.30*	*.65*
1384 A209 500fr multicolored	*6.75*	*3.40*
Nos. 1381-1384 (4)	*8.95*	*4.55*

SEMI-POSTAL STAMPS

No. 305 Surcharged in Black and Overprinted in Brown: "SECHERESSE/SOLIDARITE AFRICAINE"

1973, Aug. 23 Photo. *Perf. 13*

B1	A53	100fr + 50fr multi	2.50	2.25

African solidarity in drought emergency.

Nos. 349-350 Surcharged and Overprinted Like Nos. 693-698

1975, Nov. 10 Litho. *Perf. 13*

B2	A60	50fr + 25fr multi	1.50	1.00
B3	A60	90fr + 25fr multi	2.00	1.50

African solidarity in drought emergency.

AIR POST STAMPS

African Postal Union Issue, 1967
Common Design Type

1967, Sept. 18 Engr. *Perf. 13*

C1	CD124	6fr brown, rose cl & gray	.15	.15
C2	CD124	18fr brt lil, ol brn & plum	.40	.30
C3	CD124	30fr green, dp bl & red	.65	.55
		Nos. C1-C3 (3)	1.20	1.00

PHILEXAFRIQUE Issue

Alexandre Lenoir, by Jacques L. David — AP1

1968, Dec. 30 Photo. *Perf. 12½*

C4	AP1	100fr emerald & multi	1.90	.80

Issued to publicize PHILEXAFRIQUE, Philatelic exhibition in Abidjan, Feb. 14-23, 1969. Printed with alternating emerald label.

2nd PHILEXAFRIQUE Issue

Ruanda-Urundi No. 123, Cowherd and Lake Victoria — AP2

1969, Feb. 14 Litho. *Perf. 14*

C5	AP2	50fr multicolored	.90	.80

Issued to commemorate the opening of PHILEXAFRIQUE, Abidjan, Feb. 14.

Painting Type of Regular Issue

Paintings and Music: 50fr, The Music Lesson, by Fragonard. 100fr, Angels' Concert, by Memling, horiz.

1969, Mar. 31 Photo. *Perf. 13*

C6	A49	50fr gold & multi	.80	.38
C7	A49	100fr gold & multi	1.90	1.60

African Postal Union Issue, 1971
Common Design Type

Design: Woman and child of Rwanda and UAMPT Building, Brazzaville, Congo.

1971, Nov. 13 *Perf. 13x13½*

C8	CD135	100fr blue & multi	1.75	1.75

No. C8 Overprinted in Red

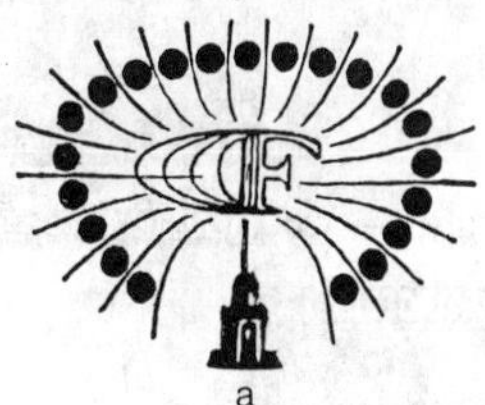

a

LIÈGE
ACCUEILLE
LES PAYS
DE LANGUE
FRANCAISE
1973

b

1973, Sept. 17 Photo. *Perf. 13x13½*

C9	CD135(a)	100fr multi	2.00	2.00
C10	CD135(b)	100fr multi	2.00	2.00
a.		Pair, #C9-C10	4.00	4.00

3rd Conference of French-speaking countries, Liège, Sept. 15-Oct. 14. Overprints alternate checkerwise in same sheet.

Sassenage Castle, Grenoble — AP3

1977, June 20 Litho. *Perf. 12½*

C11	AP3	50fr multi	1.25	1.00

10th anniversary of International French Language Council.

Philexafrique II-Essen Issue
Common Design Types

Designs: No. C12, Okapi, Rwanda #239. No. C13, Woodpecker, Oldenburg #4.

1978, Nov. 1 Litho. *Perf. 12½*

C12	CD138	30fr multi	.60	.50
C13	CD139	30fr multi	.60	.50
a.		Pair, #C12-C13	1.25	1.00

SAAR

'sär

LOCATION — On the Franco-German border southeast of Luxembourg
POP. — 1,400,000 (1959)
AREA — 991 sq. mi.
CAPITAL — Saarbrücken

A former German territory, the Saar was administered by the League of Nations 1920-35. After a January 12, 1935, plebiscite, it returned to Germany, and the use of German stamps was resumed. After World War II, France occupied the Saar and later established a protectorate. The provisional semi-independent State of Saar was established Jan. 1, 1951. France returned the Saar to the German Federal Republic Jan. 1, 1957.

Saar stamps were discontinued in 1959 and replaced by stamps of the German Federal Republic.

100 Pfennig = 1 Mark
100 Centimes = 1 Franc (1921)

Watermark

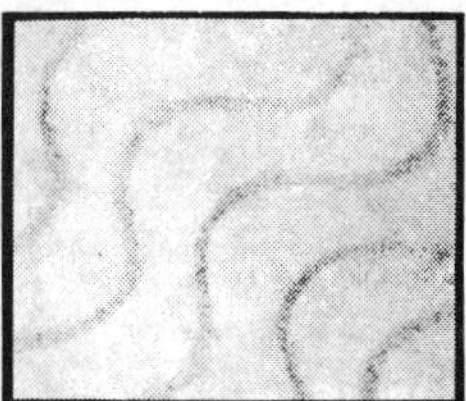

Wmk. 285- Marbleized Pattern

German Stamps of 1906-19 Overprinted

Sarre

Perf. 14, 14½

1920, Jan. 30 Wmk. 125

1	A22	2pf gray	.90	*2.75*
b.		Double overprint	*1,500.*	*2,100.*
2	A22	2½pf gray	1.75	*3.75*
3	A16	3pf brown	.70	*1.40*
4	A16	5pf green	.35	*.50*
b.		Double overprint	625.00	*900.00*
5	A22	7½pf orange	.45	*.90*
6	A16	10pf carmine	.35	*.65*
b.		Double overprint	525.00	*775.00*
7	A22	15pf dk violet	.35	.50
a.		Double overprint	525.00	*775.00*
8	A16	20pf blue violet	.35	*.65*
a.		Double overprint	450.00	*625.00*
9	A16	25pf org & blk, *yel*	9.50	10.00
10	A16	30pf org & blk, *buff*	16.00	21.00
11	A22	35pf red brown	.35	.50
12	A16	40pf lake & blk	.45	.50
13	A16	50pf pur & blk, *buff*	.35	*.50*
14	A16	60pf red violet	.40	*.65*
15	A16	75pf green & blk	.35	.50
16	A16	80pf lake & blk, *rose*	165.00	200.00

Sarre

Overprinted

17	A17	1m carmine rose	22.50	*26.00*
b.		Double overprint	525.00	*775.00*
		Nos. 1-17 (17)	220.10	270.75

Three types of overprint exist on Nos. 1-5, 12, 13; two types on Nos. 6-11, 14-16.

The 3m type A19 exists overprinted like No. 17, but was not issued.

Overprint forgeries exist.

Inverted Overprint

1a	A22	2pf gray	225.00	*325.00*
2a	A22	2½pf gray	275.00	*375.00*
3a	A16	3pf brown	225.00	*325.00*
4a	A16	5pf green	450.00	*650.00*
5a	A22	7½pf orange	325.00	*475.00*
6a	A16	10pf carmine	325.00	*475.00*
9a	A16	25pf org & blk, *yel*	575.00	850.00
11a	A22	35pf red brown	300.00	450.00
12a	A16	40pf lake & blk	300.00	450.00
13a	A16	50pf pur & blk, *buff*	350.00	*450.00*
15a	A16	75pf green & blk	165.00	250.00
17a	A17	1m carmine rose	475.00	700.00

Sarre

Bavarian Stamps of 1914-16 Overprinted

Perf. 14x14½

1920, Mar. 1 Wmk. 95

19	A10	2pf gray	*1,200.*	*4,500.*
20	A10	3pf brown	100.00	*400.00*
21	A10	5pf yellow grn	.55	*1.10*
a.		Double overprint	400.00	900.00
22	A10	7½pf green	40.00	*150.00*
23	A10	10pf carmine rose	.50	*1.10*
a.		Double overprint	165.00	*325.00*
24	A10	15pf vermilion	.65	*1.90*
a.		Double overprint	175.00	*350.00*
25	A10	15pf carmine	4.00	*12.50*
26	A10	20pf blue	.55	*1.25*
a.		Double overprint	160.00	*325.00*
27	A10	25pf gray	5.75	*11.00*
28	A10	30pf orange	5.00	*8.50*
30	A10	40pf olive green	7.00	*8.00*
31	A10	50pf red brown	.85	*1.25*
a.		Double overprint	140.00	*225.00*
32	A10	60pf dark green	2.50	*5.50*

Sarre

Overprinted

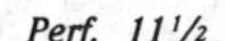

Perf. 11½

35	A11	1m brown	16.00	*35.00*
a.		1m dark brown	17.00	*37.50*
36	A11	2m violet	55.00	*140.00*
37	A11	3m scarlet	110.00	*110.00*
		Nos. 35-37 (3)	181.00	*285.00*

SARRE

Overprinted

38	A12	5m deep blue	750.00	900.00
39	A12	10m yellow green	125.00	*175.00*
a.		Double overprint	*1,750.*	*5,000.*

Nos. 19, 20 and 22 were not officially issued, but were available for postage. Examples are known legitimately used on cover. The 20m type A12 was also overprinted in small quantity.

Overprint forgeries exist.

German Stamps of 1906-20 Overprinted

SAARGEBIET

Perf. 14, 14½

1920, Mar. 26 Wmk. 125

41	A16	5pf green	.15	*.25*
42	A16	5pf red brown	.35	.35
43	A16	10pf carmine	.15	*.25*
44	A16	10pf orange	.25	.20
45	A22	15pf dk violet	.15	*.25*
46	A16	20pf blue violet	.15	*.25*
47	A16	20pf green	.35	.35
a.		Double overprint		
48	A16	30pf org & blk, *buff*	.25	.25
a.		Double overprint	55.00	
49	A16	30pf dull blue	.45	.45
50	A16	40pf lake & blk	.25	.25
51	A16	40pf carmine rose	.70	.45
52	A16	50pf pur & blk, *buff*	.25	.25
a.		Double overprint	55.00	
53	A16	60pf red violet	.40	.30
54	A16	75pf green & blk	.40	.30
a.		Double overprint	90.00	
55	A17	1.25m green	1.00	.80
56	A17	1.50m yellow brn	1.00	.70
57	A21	2.50m lilac rose	3.25	*7.50*
58	A16	4m black & rose	6.00	*16.00*
a.		Double overprint	40.00	
		Nos. 41-58 (18)	15.50	*29.15*

On No. 57 the overprint is placed vertically at each side of the stamp.

Counterfeit overprints exist.

Inverted Overprint

41a	A16	5pf green	12.50	*125.00*
43a	A16	10pf carmine	32.50	
44a	A16	10pf orange	10.50	
45a	A22	15pf dark violet	21.00	*175.00*
46a	A16	20pf blue violet	21.00	
48b	A16	30pf org & blk, *buff*		
50a	A16	40pf lake & blk		
52b	A16	50pf pur & blk, *buff*		
53a	A16	60pf red violet	57.50	*150.00*
54b	A16	75pf green & black	90.00	
55a	A17	1.25m green	72.50	
56a	A17	1.50m yellow brown	72.50	

20

SAARGEBIET

Germany No. 90 Surcharged in Black

1921, Feb.

65	A16	20pf on 75pf grn & blk	.40	*.75*
a.		Inverted surcharge	16.00	*25.00*
b.		Double surcharge	42.50	*70.00*

Mark 5 Mark

Germany No. 120 Surcharged

66	A22	5m on 15pf vio brn	3.75	*10.00*
67	A22	10m on 15pf vio brn	5.00	*11.00*
		Nos. 65-67 (3)	9.15	*21.75*

Forgeries exist of Nos. 66-67.

Saar stamps can be mounted in the Scott Germany album part 2.

Old Mill near Mettlach — A3

Miner at Work — A4

Entrance to Reden Mine — A5

Saar River Traffic — A6

Saar River near Mettlach — A7

Slag Pile at Völklingen — A8

Signal Bridge, Saarbrücken — A9

Church at Mettlach — A10

"Old Bridge," Saarbrücken — A11

Cable Railway at Ferne — A12

Colliery Shafthead — A13

Saarbrücken City Hall — A14

Pottery at Mettlach — A15

St. Ludwig's Cathedral — A16

Presidential Residence, Saarbrücken — A17

Burbach Steelworks, Dillingen A18

1921 Unwmk. Typo. *Perf. 12½*

68	A3	5pf ol grn & vio	.20	.25
a.		Tête bêche pair	3.50	*8.75*
c.		Center inverted	50.00	
69	A4	10pf orange & ultra	.20	.20
70	A5	20pf green & slate	.25	.40
a.		Tête bêche pair	5.50	*15.00*
c.		Perf. 10½	13.00	*55.00*
d.		As "c," tête bêche pair	60.00	*190.00*
71	A6	25pf brn & dk bl	.25	*.50*
a.		Tête bêche pair	6.50	*17.50*
72	A7	30pf gray grn & brn	.25	.25
a.		Tête bêche pair	5.50	*15.00*
c.		30pf ol grn & blk	1.65	*10.00*
d.		As "c," tête bêche pair	10.50	*27.50*
e.		As "c," imperf., pair	175.00	*350.00*
73	A8	40pf vermilion	.25	.20
a.		Tête bêche pair	13.00	*37.50*
74	A9	50pf gray & blk	.50	*1.10*
75	A10	60pf red & dk brn	1.10	*1.25*
76	A11	80pf deep blue	.45	.50
a.		Tête bêche pair	18.00	*50.00*
77	A12	1m lt red & blk	.45	.50
a.		1m grn & blk	*675.00*	
78	A13	1.25m lt brn & dk grn	.70	*.75*
79	A14	2m red & black	2.00	*1.90*
80	A15	3m brown & dk ol	2.50	*5.00*
a.		Center inverted	85.00	
81	A16	5m yellow & vio	6.25	*9.00*
82	A17	10m grn & red brn	8.25	*11.00*
83	A18	25m ultra, red & blk	26.00	*40.00*
		Nos. 68-83 (16)	49.60	*72.80*

Values for tête bêche are for vertical pair. Horizontal pairs sell for about twice as much.

The ultramarine ink on No. 69 appears to be brown where it overlays the orange.

Exist imperf. but were not regularly issued.

Nos. 70-83 Surcharged in Red, Blue or Black

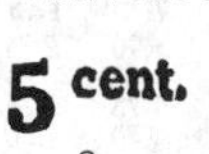

5 cent. a

1 Fr. b

c **5 FRANKEN**

1921, May 1

85	A5(a)	3c on 20pf (R)	.20	.25
a.		Tête bêche pair	3.50	*10.00*
d.		Perf. 10½	5.50	*20.00*
e.		As "d," tête bêche pair	15.00	*37.50*
86	A6(a)	5c on 25pf (R)	.15	*.45*
a.		Tête bêche pair	60.00	*190.00*
87	A7(a)	10c on 30pf (Bl)	.25	.30
a.		Tête bêche pair	3.50	*10.00*
b.		Inverted surcharge	90.00	*240.00*
88	A8(a)	15c on 40pf (Bk)	.40	.25
a.		Tête bêche pair	67.50	*190.00*
b.		Inverted surcharge	90.00	*240.00*
89	A9(a)	20c on 50pf (R)	.30	.15
90	A10(a)	25c on 60pf (Bl)	.45	.15
91	A11(a)	30c on 80pf (Bk)	1.10	.55
a.		Tête bêche pair	10.00	*25.00*
c.		Inverted surcharge	125.00	*240.00*
d.		Double surcharge	*125.00*	*250.00*
92	A12(a)	40c on 1m (Bl)	1.50	.40
a.		Inverted surcharge	125.00	*250.00*
93	A13(a)	50c on 1.25m (Bk)	2.25	.65
b.		Perf. 10½	65.00	*75.00*
94	A14(a)	75c on 2m (Bl)	2.25	.85
95	A15(b)	1fr on 3m (Bl)	3.00	1.65
96	A16(b)	2fr on 5m (Bl)	13.00	4.50
97	A17(b)	3fr on 10m (Bk)	15.00	*12.00*
b.		Double surcharge	165.00	*375.00*
98	A18(c)	5fr on 25m (Bl)	13.00	*20.00*
		Nos. 85-98 (14)	52.85	*42.15*

In these surcharges the period is occasionally missing and there are various wrong font and defective letters.

Values for tête bêche are for vertical pairs. Horizontal pairs sell for about twice as much.

Nos. 85-89, 91, 93, 97-98 exist imperf. but were not regularly issued.

Cable Railway, Ferne — A19

Miner at Work — A20

"Old Bridge," Saarbrücken A21

Saarbrücken City Hall — A22

Slag Pile at Völklingen — A23

Pottery at Mettlach — A24

Saar River Traffic — A25

St. Ludwig's Cathedral — A26

Colliery Shafthead — A27

Mettlach Church — A28

Burbach Steelworks, Dillingen A29

Perf. 12½x13½, 13½x12½

1922-23 Typo.

99	A19	3c ol grn & straw	.30	.25
100	A20	5c orange & blk	.25	.15
101	A21	10c blue green	.25	.15
102	A19	15c deep brown	.45	.15
103	A19	15c orange ('23)	2.75	.20
104	A22	20c dk bl & lem	2.25	.15
105	A22	20c brt bl & straw ('23)	3.75	.20
106	A22	25c red & yellow	3.50	1.00
107	A22	25c mag & straw ('23)	2.25	.15
108	A23	30c carmine & yel	1.25	.30
109	A24	40c brown & yel	.80	.15
110	A25	50c dk bl & straw	.75	.15
111	A24	75c dp grn & straw	9.00	*12.00*
112	A24	75c blk & straw ('23)	20.00	1.50
113	A26	1fr brown red	2.25	.30
114	A27	2fr deep violet	3.50	1.40
115	A28	3fr org & dk grn	6.50	1.50
116	A29	5fr brn & red brn	15.00	*30.00*
		Nos. 99-116 (18)	74.80	*49.70*

Nos. 99-116 exist imperforate but were not regularly issued.

For overprints see Nos. O1-O15.

Madonna of Blieskastel — A30

Perf. 13½x12½

1925, Apr. 9 Photo.

Size: 23x27mm

118	A30	45c lake brown	3.50	2.50

Size: 31½x36mm

Perf. 12

119	A30	10fr black brown	17.50	*21.00*

Nos. 118-119 exist imperf. but were not regularly issued.

For overprint see No. 154.

Market Fountain, St. Johann — A31

View of Saar Valley — A32

Colliery Shafthead A35

Burbach Steelworks A36

Designs: 15c, 75c, View of Saar Valley. 20c, 40c, 90c, Scene from Saarlouis fortifications. 25c, 50c, Tholey Abbey.

1927-32 *Perf. 13½*

120	A31	10c deep brown	.60	.15
121	A32	15c olive black	.45	*.75*
122	A32	20c brown orange	.40	.15
123	A32	25c bluish slate	.50	.25
124	A31	30c olive green	.60	.15
125	A32	40c olive brown	.50	.15
126	A32	50c magenta	.60	.15
127	A35	60c red org ('30)	2.50	.15
128	A32	75c brown violet	.60	.15
129	A35	80c red orange	2.50	*7.50*
130	A32	90c deep red ('32)	9.00	*16.00*
131	A35	1fr violet	2.00	.20
132	A36	1.50fr sapphire	3.50	.20
133	A36	2fr brown red	4.00	.35
134	A36	3fr dk olive grn	8.50	.60
135	A36	5fr deep brown	9.00	6.00
		Nos. 120-135 (16)	45.25	*32.90*

For surcharges and overprints see Nos. 136-153, O16-O26.

60 cent.

Nos. 126 and 129 Surcharged

1930-34

136	A32	40c on 50c mag ('34)	.75	.70
137	A35	60c on 80c red orange	.75	*1.25*

Plebiscite Issue

Stamps of 1925-32 Overprinted in Various Colors

VOLKSABSTIMMUNG 1935

Perf. 13½, 13½x13, 13x13½

1934, Nov. 1

139	A31	10c brown (Br)	.40	.32
140	A32	15c black grn (G)	.40	.32
141	A32	20c brown org (O)	.32	.40
142	A32	25c bluish sl (Bl)	.55	*.70*
143	A31	30c olive grn (G)	.30	.30
144	A32	40c olive brn (Br)	.32	.40
145	A32	50c magenta (R)	.70	.70
146	A35	60c red orange (O)	.32	.30
147	A32	75c brown vio (V)	.70	*.80*
148	A32	90c deep red (R)	.70	*.80*
149	A35	1fr violet (V)	.85	*.80*
150	A36	1.50fr sapphire (Bl)	1.25	*1.75*
151	A36	2fr brown red (R)	1.75	*2.25*
152	A36	3fr dk ol grn (G)	3.00	*5.00*
153	A36	5fr dp brown (Br)	14.00	*16.00*

Size: 31½x36mm

Perf. 12

154	A30	10fr black brn (Br)	18.00	*30.00*
		Nos. 139-154 (16)	43.56	*60.84*

French Administration

Miner — A37

Steel Workers — A38

Harvesting Sugar Beets — A39

Mettlach Abbey — A40

Marshal Ney — A41

Saar River near Mettlach A42

1947 Unwmk. Photo. *Perf. 14*

155	A37	2pf gray	.15	*.15*
156	A37	3pf orange	.15	*.30*
157	A37	6pf dk Prus grn	.15	*.15*
158	A37	8pf scarlet	.15	*.15*
159	A37	10pf rose violet	.15	*.15*
160	A38	15pf brown	.15	*.30*
161	A38	16pf ultra	.15	*.15*
162	A38	20pf brown rose	.15	*.15*
163	A38	24pf dp brown org	.15	*.15*
164	A39	25pf cerise	.30	*10.00*
165	A39	30pf lt olive grn	.15	*.30*
166	A39	40pf orange brn	.15	*.30*
167	A39	50pf blue violet	.30	*10.00*
168	A40	60pf violet	.30	*10.00*
169	A40	80pf dp orange	.15	*.22*
170	A41	84pf brown	.15	*.22*
171	A42	1m gray green	.15	*.30*
		Set value	1.70	
		Set, never hinged	2.00	

Nos. 155-162, 164-171 exist imperf.

Types of 1947

1947 Wmk. 285

172	A37	12pf olive green	.15	*.15*
173	A39	45pf crimson	.20	*7.50*
174	A40	75pf brt blue	.15	*.20*
		Set value	.30	
		Set, never hinged	.50	

Nos. 172-174 exist imperf.

Types of 1947 Surcharged with New Value, Bars and Ornament in Black or Red

1947, Nov. 27 Unwmk.

Printing II

175	A37	10c on 2pf gray	.15	*.25*
176	A37	60c on 3pf orange	.15	*.25*
177	A37	1fr on 10pf rose vio	.15	*.25*
178	A37	2fr on 12pf ol grn	.15	*.75*
179	A38	3fr on 15pf brown	.15	*.25*
180	A38	4fr on 16pf ultra	.15	*2.00*
181	A38	5fr on 20pf brn rose	.15	*.50*
182	A38	6fr on 24pf dp brn org	.15	*.25*
183	A39	9fr on 30pf lt ol grn	.22	*3.00*
184	A39	10fr on 50pf bl vio (R)	.28	*5.00*
185	A40	14fr on 60pf violet	.35	*2.50*
186	A41	20fr on 84pf brown	.25	*3.75*
187	A42	50fr on 1m gray grn	.95	*6.25*
		Set value	2.55	
		Set, never hinged	3.50	

Printing I

175a	A37	10c on 2pf gray	75.00	*200.00*
176a	A37	60c on 3pf orange	60.00	*525.00*
177a	A37	1fr on 10pf rose vio	5.00	*8.75*
178a	A37	2fr on 12pf ol grn, wmk. 285	.25	*.50*
179a	A38	3fr on 15pf brown	400.00	*1,200.*
180a	A38	4fr on 16pf ultra	9.00	*65.00*
181a	A38	5fr on 20pf brn rose	35.00	*2,000.*
182a	A38	6fr on 24pf dp brn org	.25	*1.00*
183a	A39	9fr on 30pf lt ol grn	37.50	*475.00*
184a	A39	10fr on 50pf bl vio (R)	380.00	*4,000.*
185a	A40	14fr on 60pf violet	90.00	*575.00*
186a	A41	20fr on 84pf brown	2.00	*3.75*
187a	A42	50fr on 1m gray grn	35.00	*275.00*
		Nos. 175a-187a (13)	1,129.	

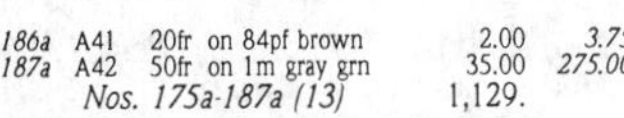

Printing I was surcharged on Nos. 155-171. The crossbar of the A's in SAAR is high on the 10c, 60c, 1fr, 2fr, 9fr and 10fr; numeral "1" has no base serif on the 3fr and 4fr; wide space between vignette and SAAR panel; 1m inscribed "1M."

Printing II was surcharged on a special printing of the basic stamps, with details of design that differ on each denomination. The "A" crossbar is low on 10c, 60c, 1fr, 2fr, 9fr, 10fr; numeral "1" has serif on 3fr and 4fr; narrow space between vignette and SAAR panel; 1m inscribed "1SM."

Inverted surcharges exist on Nos. 175-187 and 175a-187a.

French Protectorate

Clasped Hands A43

Colliery Shafthead A44

Designs: 2fr, 3fr, Worker. 4fr, 5fr, Girl gathering wheat. 6fr, 9fr, Miner. 14fr, Smelting. 20fr, Reconstruction. 50fr, Mettlach Abbey portal.

Perf. 14x13, 13

1948, Apr. 1 Engr. Unwmk.

188	A43	10c henna brn	.22	*.85*
189	A43	60c dk Prus grn	.22	*.85*
190	A43	1fr brown blk	.15	*.15*
191	A43	2fr rose car	.15	*.15*
192	A43	3fr black brn	.15	*.15*
193	A43	4fr red	.15	*.15*
194	A43	5fr red violet	.15	*.15*
195	A43	6fr henna brown	.20	*.15*
196	A43	9fr dk Prus grn	1.65	*.15*
197	A44	10fr dark blue	.90	*.18*
198	A44	14fr dk vio brn	1.25	*.45*
199	A44	20fr henna brn	2.25	*.45*
200	A44	50fr blue blk	5.00	*1.40*
		Nos. 188-200 (13)	12.44	*5.23*
		Set, never hinged	32.50	

Map of the Saar — A45

1948, Dec. 15 Photo. *Perf. 13½x13*

201	A45	10fr dark red	.85	*1.10*
202	A45	25fr deep blue	1.25	*2.50*
		Set, never hinged	4.00	

French Protectorate establishment, ist anniv.

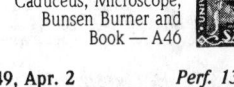

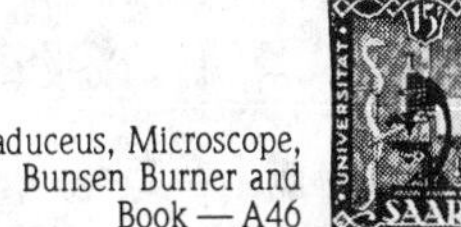
Caduceus, Microscope, Bunsen Burner and Book — A46

1949, Apr. 2 *Perf. 13x13½*

203	A46	15fr carmine	1.75	.18
		Never hinged	4.00	

Issued to honor Saar University.

Ludwig van Beethoven — A47

Laborer Using Spade — A51

Saarbrücken A52

Designs: 10c, Building trades. 1fr, 3fr, Gears, factories. 5fr, Dumping mine waste. 6fr, 15fr, Coal mine interior. 8fr, Communications symbols. 10fr, Emblem of printing. 12fr, 18fr, Pottery. 25fr, Blast furnace worker. 45fr, Rock formation "Great Boot." 60fr, Reden Colliery, Landsweiler. 100fr, View of Weibelskirchen.

1949-51 Unwmk. *Perf. 13x13½*

204	A47	10c violet brn	.15	*.85*
205	A47	60c gray ('51)	.15	*.85*
206	A47	1fr carmine lake	.60	.15
207	A47	3fr brown ('51)	2.75	.22
208	A47	5fr dp violet ('50)	.80	.15
209	A47	6fr Prus grn ('51)	4.25	.20
210	A47	8fr olive grn ('51)	.28	.20
211	A47	10fr orange ('50)	1.50	.15
212	A47	12fr dk green	5.25	.15
213	A47	15fr red ('50)	2.75	.15
214	A47	18fr brn car ('51)	1.00	*2.50*

Perf. 13½

215	A51	20fr gray ('50)	.65	.15
216	A51	25fr violet blue	6.50	.15
217	A52	30fr red brown ('51)	5.50	.30
218	A52	45fr rose lake ('51)	1.90	.32
219	A51	60fr deep green ('51)	1.90	.75
220	A51	100fr brown	2.75	1.00
		Nos. 204-220 (17)	38.68	*8.24*
		Set, never hinged	95.00	

Peter Wust — A54

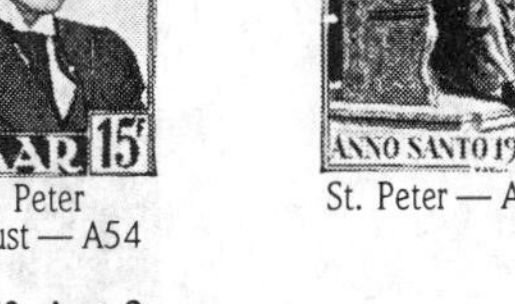
St. Peter — A55

1950, Apr. 3

221	A54	15fr carmine rose	1.75	*4.00*
		Never hinged	5.50	

Peter Wust (1884-1940), Catholic philosopher.

1950, June 29 Engr. *Perf. 13*

222	A55	12fr deep green	1.75	*4.50*
223	A55	15fr red brown	2.00	*4.50*
224	A55	25fr blue	3.75	*7.50*
		Nos. 222-224 (3)	7.50	*16.50*
		Set, never hinged	16.00	

Holy Year, 1950.

Street in Ottweiler A56

Symbols of the Council of Europe A57

1950, July 10 Photo. *Perf. 13x13½*

225	A56	10fr orange brown	1.50	*4.50*
		Never hinged	3.25	

400th anniversary of the founding of Ottweiler.

1950, Aug. 8 *Perf. 13½*

226	A57	25fr deep blue	18.00	8.00
		Never hinged	42.50	

Issued to commemorate the Saar's admission to the Council of Europe. See No. C12.

Post Rider and Guard — A62

1951, Apr. 29 Engr. *Perf. 13*

227	A62	15fr dk violet brn	3.00	*10.00*
		Never hinged	5.50	

Issued to publicize Stamp Day, 1951.

"Agriculture and Industry" and Fair Emblem — A63

Tower of Mittelbexbach and Flowers — A67

1951, May 12 Photo. *Perf. 13x13½*

228	A63	15fr dk gray grn	.85	*3.00*
		Never hinged	2.25	

1951 Fair at Saarbrücken.

1951, June 9 Engr. *Perf. 13*

229	A67	15fr dark green	.85	.60
		Never hinged	2.25	

Issued to publicize the Exhibition of Gardens and Flowers, Bexbach, 1951.

Refugees A68

Globe & Stylized Fair Building A69

1952, May 2 Unwmk. *Perf. 13*

230	A68	15fr bright red	1.00	.75
		Never hinged	1.75	

Issued to honor the Red Cross.

1952, Apr. 26

231	A69	15fr red brown	1.00	.75
		Never hinged	1.75	

1952 Fair at Saarbrücken.

Mine Shafts — A70

Ludwig's Gymnasium A71

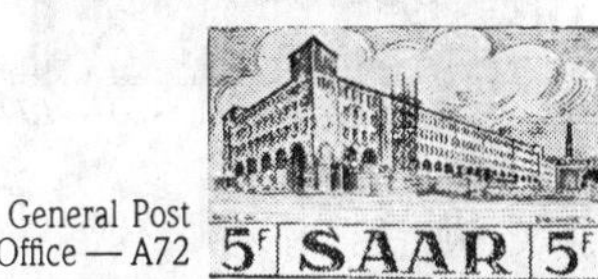
General Post Office — A72

Reconstruction of St. Ludwig's Cathedral A73

"SM" Monogram A74

3fr, 18fr, Bridge building. 6fr, Transporter bridge, Mettlach. 30fr, Saar University Library.

1952-55 Engr.

232	A70	1fr dk bl grn ('53)	.15	.15
233	A71	2fr purple ('53)	.15	.15
234	A72	3fr dk car rose ('53)	.15	.15
235	A72	5fr dk grn (no inscription)	1.90	.15

236 A72 5fr dk grn ("Hauptpostamt Saarbrücken") ('54) .15 .15
237 A72 6fr vio brn ('53) .15 .15
238 A71 10fr brn ol ('53) .20 .15
239 A72 12fr green ('53) .20 .15
240 A70 15fr blk brn (no inscription) 2.75 .15
241 A70 15fr blk brn ("Industrie-Landschaft") ('53) 1.25 .15
242 A70 15fr dp car ('55) .15 .15
243 A72 18fr dk rose brn ('55) .90 *3.00*
244 A72 30fr ultra ('53) .28 *.40*
245 A73 500fr brn car ('53) 4.75 *30.00*
Nos. 232-245 (14) 13.13 *35.05*
Set, never hinged 32.50

For overprints see Nos. 257-259.

1953, Mar. 23
246 A74 15fr dark ultra 1.00 .75
Never hinged 1.75

1953 Fair at Saarbrücken.

Bavarian and Prussian Postilions A75

1953, May 3
247 A75 15fr deep blue 1.75 *5.00*
Never hinged 2.75

Stamp Day.

Fountain and Fair Buildings — A76

1954, Apr. 10
248 A76 15fr deep green .85 .50
Never hinged 1.75

1954 International Fair at Saarbrücken.

Post Coach and Post Bus of 1920 — A77

1954, May 9 **Engr.**
249 A77 15fr red 1.65 *5.50*
Never hinged 2.75

Stamp Day, May 9, 1954.

Madonna and Child, Holbein A78

Designs: 10fr, Sistine Madonna, Raphael. 15fr, Madonna and Child with pear, Durer.

1954, Aug. 14
250 A78 5fr deep carmine .32 *1.25*
251 A78 10fr dark green .45 *1.65*
252 A78 15fr dp violet bl .70 *2.25*
Nos. 250-252 (3) 1.47 *5.15*
Set, never hinged 2.75

Centenary of the promulgation of the Dogma of the Immaculate Conception.

Cyclist and Flag — A79

Symbols of Industry and Rotary Emblem — A80

1955, Feb. 28 **Photo.** ***Perf. 13x13½***
253 A79 15fr multicolored .15 *.35*

World championship cross country bicycle race.

1955, Feb. 28
254 A80 15fr orange brown .15 *.35*
Never hinged .25

Rotary International, 50th anniversary.

Flags of Participating Nations — A81

1955, Apr. 18 **Photo.** ***Perf. 13x13½***
255 A81 15fr multicolored .15 *.35*
Never hinged .25

1955 International Fair at Saarbrücken.

Postman at Illingen A82

Unwmk.
1955, May 8 **Engr.** ***Perf. 13***
256 A82 15fr deep claret .30 *1.10*
Never hinged .60

Issued to publicize Stamp Day, 1955.

Nos. 242-244 Overprinted "VOLKSBEFRAGUNG 1955"

1955, Oct. 22
257 A70 15fr deep carmine .15 *.24*
258 A72 18fr dk rose brn .15 *.26*
259 A72 30fr ultra .15 *.50*
Set value .22
Set, never hinged .50
Nos. 257-259 (3) *1.00*

Plebiscite, Oct. 23, 1955.

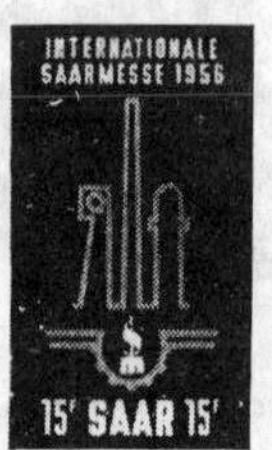

Symbols of Industry and the Fair A83

Radio Tower, Saarbrücken A84

1956, Apr. 14 **Photo.** ***Perf. 11½***
260 A83 15fr dk brn red & yel grn .15 *.25*
Never hinged .20

Intl. Fair at Saarbrücken, Apr. 14-29, 1956.

1956, May 6
Granite Paper
261 A84 15fr grn & grnsh bl .15 *.25*
Never hinged .20

Stamp Day.

German Administration

Arms of Saar — A85

Pres. Theodor Heuss — A86

Perf. 13x13½
1957, Jan. 1 **Litho.** **Wmk. 304**
262 A85 15fr brick red & blue .15 *.20*
Never hinged .15

Return of the Saar to Germany.

1957 **Typo.** ***Perf. 14***
Size: 18x22mm

263 A86 1(fr) brt green .15 .15
264 A86 2(fr) brt violet .15 .15
265 A86 3(fr) bister brown .15 .15
266 A86 4(fr) red violet .15 *.48*
267 A86 5(fr) lt olive green .15 .15
268 A86 6(fr) vermilion .15 *.38*
269 A86 10(fr) gray .15 *.22*
270 A86 12(fr) deep orange .15 .15
271 A86 15(fr) lt blue green .15 .15
272 A86 18(fr) carmine rose .28 *.95*
273 A86 25(fr) brt lilac .15 *.38*

Engr.

274 A86 30(fr) pale purple .15 *.48*
275 A86 45(fr) gray olive .48 *1.50*
276 A86 50(fr) violet brn .48 *.70*
277 A86 60(fr) dull rose .65 *1.75*
278 A86 70(fr) red orange 1.25 *2.75*
279 A86 80(fr) olive green .48 *1.75*
280 A86 90(fr) dark gray 1.10 *2.75*

Size: 24x29mm

281 A86 100(fr) dk carmine .90 *4.75*
282 A86 200(fr) violet 2.75 *13.00*
Nos. 263-282 (20) 10.02 *32.74*
Set, never hinged 18.00

See Nos. 289-308.

Steel Industry — A87

Merzig Arms and St. Peter's Church — A88

Perf. 13x13½
1957, Apr. 20 **Litho.** **Wmk. 304**
284 A87 15fr gray & magenta .15 *.20*
Never hinged .15

The 1957 Fair at Saarbrücken.

1957, May 25 ***Perf. 14***
285 A88 15fr blue .15 *.20*
Never hinged .15

Centenary of the town of Merzig.

"United Europe" — A89

Lithographed; Tree Embossed
Perf. 14x13½
1957, Sept. 16 **Unwmk.**
286 A89 20fr orange & yel .15 *.55*
287 A89 35fr violet & pink .25 *.65*
Set, never hinged .50

Europa, publicizing a united Europe for peace and prosperity.

Carrier Pigeons — A90

Wmk. 304
1957, Oct. 5 **Litho.** ***Perf. 14***
288 A90 15fr dp carmine & blk .15 .15
Never hinged .15

Intl. Letter Writing Week, Oct. 6-12.

Redrawn Type of 1957; "F" added after denomination

1957 **Wmk. 304** **Litho.** ***Perf. 14***
Size: 18x22mm

289 A86 1fr gray green .15 .15
290 A86 3fr blue .15 .15
291 A86 5fr olive .15 .15
292 A86 6fr lt brown .15 *.30*
293 A86 10fr violet .15 *.18*
294 A86 12fr brown org .15 *.18*
295 A86 15fr dull green .18 .18
296 A86 18fr gray .75 *2.25*
297 A86 20fr lt olive grn .42 *1.25*
298 A86 25fr orange brn .28 *.30*
299 A86 30fr rose lilac .35 .30
300 A86 35fr brown .85 *1.25*
301 A86 45fr lt blue grn .60 *1.75*
302 A86 50fr dk red brown .35 *.85*
303 A86 70fr brt green 1.65 *2.25*
304 A86 80fr chalky blue 1.10 *2.25*
305 A86 90fr rose carmine 1.90 *3.75*

Engr.
Size: 24x29mm

306 A86 100fr orange 1.65 *3.25*
307 A86 200fr brt green 3.25 *10.00*
308 A86 300fr blue 3.75 *12.50*
Nos. 289-308 (20) 17.98 *43.24*
Set, never hinged 37.50

"Max and Moritz" — A91

Design: 15fr, Wilhelm Busch.

Perf. 13½x13
1958, Jan. 9 **Litho.** **Wmk. 304**
309 A91 12fr lt ol grn & blk .15 *.15*
310 A91 15fr red & black .15 *.22*
Set value .18
Set, never hinged .22

Death of Wilhelm Busch, humorist, 50th anniv.

"Prevent Forest Fires" — A92

1958, Mar. 5 ***Perf. 14***
311 A92 15fr brt red & blk .15 *.20*
Never hinged .15

Issued to aid in the prevention of forest fires.

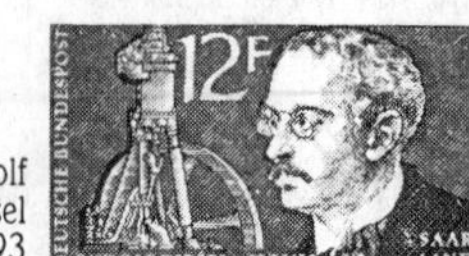

Rudolf Diesel A93

1958, Mar. 18 **Engr.**
312 A93 12fr dk blue grn .15 *.20*
Never hinged .15

Centenary of the birth of Rudolf Diesel, inventor.

Fair Emblem and City Hall, Saarbrücken A94

View of Homburg A95

1958, Apr. 10 Litho. *Perf. 14*

313	A94	15fr dull rose	.15	*.20*
		Never hinged	.15	

1958 Fair at Saarbrücken.

1958, June 14 Engr. Wmk. 304

314	A95	15fr gray green	.15	*.20*
		Never hinged	.15	

400th anniversary of Homburg.

Turner Emblem A96

Herman Schulze-Delitzsch A97

1958, July 21 Litho. *Perf. 13½x14*

315	A96	12fr gray, blk & dl grn	.15	*.20*
		Never hinged	.15	

150 years of German Turners and the 1958 Turner Festival.

1958, Aug. 29 Engr. Wmk. 304

316	A97	12fr yellow green	.15	*.20*
		Never hinged	.15	

150th anniv. of the birth of Schultze-Delitzsch, founder of German trade organizations.

Europa Issue, 1958

Common Design Type

1958, Sept. 13 Litho.

Size: 24½x30mm

317	CD1	12fr yellow grn & bl	.25	*.50*
318	CD1	30fr lt blue & red	.32	*.65*
		Set, never hinged	.95	

Issued to show the European Postal Union at the service of European integration.

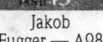

Jakob Fugger — A98

Old and New City Hall and Burbach Mill — A99

Perf. 13x13½

1959, Mar. 6 Wmk. 304

319	A98	15fr dk red & blk	.15	*.20*
		Never hinged	.15	

500th anniv. of the birth of Jakob Fugger the Rich, businessman and banker.

1959, Apr. 1 Engr. *Perf. 14x13½*

320	A99	15fr light blue	.15	*.20*
		Never hinged	.15	

Greater Saarbrucken, 50th anniversary.

Hands Holding Merchandise A100

Alexander von Humboldt A101

1959, Apr. 1 Litho.

321	A100	15fr deep rose	.15	*.20*
		Never hinged	.15	

1959 Fair at Saarbrucken.

1959, May 6 Engr. *Perf. 13½x14*

322	A101	15fr blue	.15	*.20*
		Never hinged	.15	

Cent. of the death of Alexander von Humboldt, naturalist and geographer.

SEMI-POSTAL STAMPS

Red Cross Dog Leading Blind Man — SP1

Maternity Nurse with Child — SP4

Designs: #B2, Nurse and invalid. #B3, Children getting drink at spring.

Perf. 13½

1926, Oct. 25 Photo. Unwmk.

B1	SP1	20c + 20c dk ol grn	7.00	*13.00*
B2	SP1	40c + 40c dk brn	8.00	*14.00*
B3	SP1	50c + 50c red org	8.00	*13.00*
B4	SP4	1.50fr + 1.50fr brt bl	15.00	*40.00*
		Nos. B1-B4 (4)	38.00	*80.00*

Nos. B1-B4 Overprinted **1927-28**

1927, Oct. 1

B5	SP1	20c + 20c dk ol grn	10.00	*18.00*
B6	SP1	40c + 40c dk brn	9.25	*18.00*
B7	SP1	50c + 50c red org	8.00	*15.00*
B8	SP4	1.50fr + 1.50fr brt bl	12.00	*45.00*
		Nos. B5-B8 (4)	39.25	*96.00*

"The Blind Beggar" by Dyckmans — SP5

"Almsgiving" by Schiestl — SP6

"Charity" by Raphael — SP7

1928, Dec. 23 Photo.

B9	SP5	40c (+40c) blk brn	11.00	*24.00*
B10	SP5	50c (+50c) brn rose	11.00	*24.00*
B11	SP5	1fr (+1fr) dl vio	11.00	*24.00*
B12	SP6	1.50fr (+1.50fr) cob bl	11.00	*24.00*
B13	SP6	2fr (+2fr) red brn	12.50	*30.00*
B14	SP6	3fr (+3fr) dk ol grn	12.50	*30.00*
B15	SP7	10fr (+10fr) dk brn	350.00	*3,000.*
		Nos. B9-B15 (7)	419.00	

"Orphaned" by Kaulbach — SP8

"St. Ottilia" by Feuerstein — SP9

"Madonna" by Ferruzzio — SP10

1929, Dec. 22

B16	SP8	40c (+15c) ol grn	1.75	*3.25*
B17	SP8	50c (+20c) cop red	3.50	*5.00*
B18	SP8	1fr (+50c) vio brn	3.50	*6.50*
B19	SP9	1.50fr (+75c) Prus bl	3.50	*6.50*
B20	SP9	2fr (+1fr) brn car	3.50	*6.75*
B21	SP9	3fr (+2fr) sl grn	6.00	*14.00*
B22	SP10	10fr (+8fr) blk brn	40.00	*80.00*
		Nos. B16-B22 (7)	61.75	*122.00*

"The Safety-Man" SP11

"The Good Samaritan" SP12

"In the Window" — SP13

1931, Jan. 20

B23	SP11	40c (+15c)	7.25	*20.00*
B24	SP11	60c (+20c)	7.25	*20.00*
B25	SP12	1fr (+50c)	7.25	*35.00*
B26	SP11	1.50fr (+75c)	10.00	*35.00*
B27	SP12	2fr (+1fr)	10.00	*35.00*
B28	SP12	3fr (+2fr)	14.00	*35.00*
B29	SP13	10fr (+10fr)	67.50	*225.00*
		Nos. B23-B29 (7)	123.25	*405.00*

St. Martin of Tours — SP14

#B33-B35, Charity. #B36, The Widow's Mite.

1931, Dec. 23

B30	SP14	40c (+15c)	14.00	*30.00*
B31	SP14	60c (+20c)	14.00	*30.00*
B32	SP14	1fr (+50c)	16.00	*45.00*
B33	SP14	1.50fr (+75c)	20.00	*45.00*
B34	SP14	2fr (+1fr)	21.00	*45.00*
B35	SP14	3fr (+2fr)	30.00	*90.00*
B36	SP14	5fr (+5fr)	87.50	*275.00*
		Nos. B30-B36 (7)	202.50	*560.00*

Ruins at Kirkel — SP17

Illingen Castle, Kerpen — SP23

Designs: 60c, Church at Blie. 1fr, Castle Ottweiler. 1.50fr, Church of St. Michael, Saarbrucken. 2fr, Statue of St. Wendel. 3fr, Church of St. John, Saarbrucken.

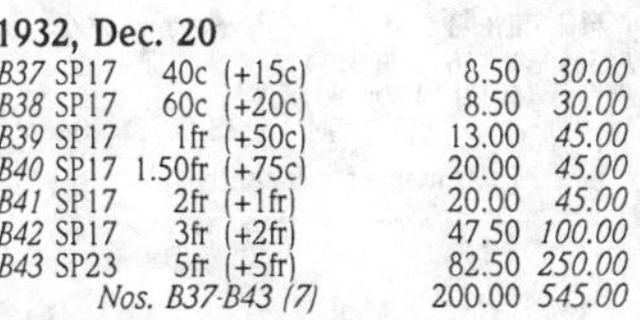

1932, Dec. 20

B37	SP17	40c (+15c)	8.50	*30.00*
B38	SP17	60c (+20c)	8.50	*30.00*
B39	SP17	1fr (+50c)	13.00	*45.00*
B40	SP17	1.50fr (+75c)	20.00	*45.00*
B41	SP17	2fr (+1fr)	20.00	*45.00*
B42	SP17	3fr (+2fr)	47.50	*100.00*
B43	SP23	5fr (+5fr)	82.50	*250.00*
		Nos. B37-B43 (7)	200.00	*545.00*

Scene of Neunkirchen Disaster SP24

1933, June 1

B44	SP24	60c (+ 60c) org red	12.50	18.00
B45	SP24	3fr (+ 3fr) ol grn	30.00	*52.50*
B46	SP24	5fr (+ 5fr) org brn	32.50	*65.00*
		Nos. B44-B46 (3)	75.00	*135.50*

The surtax was for the aid of victims of the explosion at Neunkirchen, Feb. 10.

"Love" — SP25

Designs: 60c, "Anxiety." 1fr, "Peace." 1.50fr, "Solace." 2fr, "Welfare." 3fr, "Truth." 5fr, Figure on Tomb of Duchess Elizabeth of Lorraine

1934, Mar. 15 Photo.

B47	SP25	40c (+15c) blk brn	5.00	*13.00*
B48	SP25	60c (+20c) red org	5.00	*13.00*
B49	SP25	1fr (+50c) dl vio	6.75	*17.00*
B50	SP25	1.50fr (+75c) blue	12.50	*30.00*
B51	SP25	2fr (+1fr) car rose	11.50	*30.00*
B52	SP25	3fr (+2fr) ol grn	12.50	*32.50*
B53	SP25	5fr (+5fr) red brn	27.50	*70.00*
		Nos. B47-B53 (7)	80.75	*205.50*

Nos. B47-B53 Overprinted like Nos. 139-154 in Various Colors Reading up

1934, Dec. 1 *Perf. 13x13½*

B54	SP25	40c (+15c) (Br)	3.75	*16.00*
B55	SP25	60c (+20c) (R)	3.75	*16.00*
B56	SP25	1fr (+50c) (V)	7.25	*27.50*
B57	SP25	1.50fr (+75c) (Bl)	7.25	*27.50*
B58	SP25	2fr (+1fr) (R)	9.25	*37.50*
B59	SP25	3fr (+2fr) (G)	8.50	*32.50*
B60	SP25	5fr (+5fr) (Br)	14.00	*50.00*
		Nos. B54-B60 (7)	53.75	*207.00*

French Protectorate

Various Flood Scenes SP32 SP33

Perf. 13½x13, 13x13½

1948, Oct. 12 Photo.

Inscribed "Hochwasser-Hilfe 1947-48"

B61	SP32	5fr + 5fr dl grn	1.65	*18.00*
B62	SP33	6fr + 4fr dk vio	1.65	*18.00*
B63	SP32	12fr + 8fr red	2.00	*26.00*
B64	SP33	18fr + 12fr bl	3.00	*30.00*
a.		Souv. sheet of 4, #B61-B64, imperf.	265.00	*2,000.*
		Never hinged	550.00	
		Nos. B61-B64,CB1 (5)	23.30	*187.00*
		Set, never hinged	44.50	

The surtax was for flood relief.

Hikers and Ludweiler Hostel — SP34

Designs: No. B66, Hikers approaching Weisskirchen Hostel.

1949, Jan. 11 *Perf. 13½x13*
B65 SP34 8fr + 5fr dk brn 1.25 *3.50*
B66 SP34 10fr + 7fr dk grn 1.25 *2.75*
Set, never hinged 4.50

The surtax aided youth hostels.

Mare and Foal — SP35

Design: No. B68, Jumpers.

1949, Sept. 25 *Perf. 13½*
B67 SP35 15fr + 5fr brn red 5.75 *20.00*
B68 SP35 25fr + 15fr blue 7.25 *21.00*
Set, never hinged 26.00

Day of the Horse, Sept. 25, 1949.

Detail from "Moses Striking the Rock" — SP36

#B70, "Christ at the Pool of Bethesda." #B71, "The Sick Child." #B72, "St. Thomas of Villeneuve." #B73, Madonna of Blieskastel.

1949, Dec. 20 **Engr.** *Perf. 13*
B69 SP36 8fr + 2fr indigo 4.25 *27.50*
B70 SP36 12fr + 3fr dk grn 5.00 *30.00*
B71 SP36 15fr + 5fr brn lake 7.25 *52.50*
B72 SP36 25fr + 10fr dp ultra 10.50 *80.00*
B73 SP36 50fr + 20fr choc 19.00 *110.00*
Nos. B69-B73 (5) 46.00 *300.00*
Set, never hinged 92.50

Adolph Kolping SP37

Relief for the Hungry SP38

1950, Apr. 3 **Photo.** *Perf. 13x13½*
B74 SP37 15fr + 5fr car rose 13.00 *50.00*
Never hinged 24.00

Engraved and Typographed

1950, Apr. 28 *Perf. 13*
B75 SP38 25fr + 10fr dk brn car & red 13.00 *42.50*
Never hinged 24.00

Stagecoach — SP39

1950, Apr. 22 **Engr.**
B76 SP39 15fr + 15fr brn red & dk brn 25.00 *85.00*
Never hinged 52.50

Stamp Day, Apr. 27, 1950. Sold at the exhibition and to advance subscribers.

Lutwinus Seeking Admission to Abbey SP40

Designs: 12fr+3fr, Lutwinus Building Mettlach Abbey. 15fr+5fr, Lutwinus as Abbot. 25fr+10fr, Bishop Lutwinus at Rheims. 50fr+20fr, Aid to the poor and sick.

1950, Nov. 10 **Unwmk.** *Perf. 13*
B77 SP40 8fr + 2fr dk brn 3.25 *17.00*
B78 SP40 12fr + 3fr dk grn 3.25 *17.00*
B79 SP40 15fr + 5fr red brn 4.00 *24.00*
B80 SP40 25fr + 10fr blue 6.00 *40.00*
B81 SP40 50fr + 20fr brn car 8.25 *60.00*
Nos. B77-B81 (5) 24.75 *158.00*
Set, never hinged 40.00

The surtax was for public assistance.

Mother and Child — SP41

John Calvin and Martin Luther — SP42

1951, Apr. 28
B82 SP41 25fr + 10fr dk grn & car 12.00 *35.00*
Never hinged 21.00

The surtax was for the Red Cross.

1951, Apr. 28
B83 SP42 15fr + 5fr blk brn .90 *3.50*
Never hinged 1.40

375th anniversary of the Reformation in Saar.

"Mother" SP43

Runner with Torch SP44

15fr+5fr, "Before the Theater." 18fr+7fr, "Sisters of Charity." 30fr+10fr, "The Good Samaritan." 50fr+ 20fr, "St. Martin and Beggar."

1951, Nov. 3
B84 SP43 12fr + 3fr dk grn 2.75 *10.00*
B85 SP43 15fr + 5fr pur 2.75 *10.00*
B86 SP43 18fr + 7fr dk red 3.25 *13.00*
B87 SP43 30fr + 10fr dp bl 5.25 *20.00*
B88 SP43 50fr + 20fr blk brn 12.50 *42.50*
Nos. B84-B88 (5) 26.50 *95.50*
Set, never hinged 47.50

1952, Mar. 29 **Unwmk.** *Perf. 13*

30fr+5fr, Hand with olive branch, and globe.

B89 SP44 15fr + 5fr dp grn 1.40 *6.25*
B90 SP44 30fr + 5fr dp bl 1.65 *8.75*
Set, never hinged 5.50

XV Olympic Games, Helsinki, 1952.

Postrider Delivering Mail — SP45

1952, Mar. 30
B91 SP45 30fr + 10fr dark blue 4.75 *17.50*
Never hinged 7.50

Stamp Day, Mar. 29, 1952.

Count Stroganoff as a Boy — SP46

Henri Dunant — SP47

Portraits: 18fr+7fr, The Holy Shepherd by Murillo. 30fr+10fr, Portrait of a Boy by Georg Melchior Kraus.

1952, Nov. 3
B92 SP46 15fr + 5fr dk brn 1.90 *6.75*
B93 SP46 18fr + 7fr brn lake 2.50 *9.25*
B94 SP46 30fr + 10fr dp bl 2.75 *10.50*
Nos. B92-B94 (3) 7.15 *26.50*
Set, never hinged 14.00

The surtax was for child welfare.

1953, May 3 **Cross in Red**
B95 SP47 15fr + 5fr blk brn 1.00 *4.00*
Never hinged 1.75

Clarice Strozzi by Titian — SP48

Children of Rubens SP49

Portrait: 30fr+10fr, Rubens' son.

1953, Nov. 16
B96 SP48 15fr + 5fr purple .90 *3.00*
B97 SP49 18fr + 7fr dp claret .90 *3.50*
B98 SP48 30fr + 10fr dp ol grn 1.75 *5.50*
Nos. B96-B98 (3) 3.55 *12.00*
Set, never hinged 7.00

The surtax was for child welfare.

St. Benedict Blessing St. Maurus — SP50

Child and Cross — SP51

1953, Dec. 18 **Litho.**
B99 SP50 30fr + 10fr black 1.00 *4.50*
Never hinged 1.90

The surtax was for the abbey at Tholey.

1954, May 10 **Engr.**
B100 SP51 15fr + 5fr chocolate 1.25 *4.25*
Never hinged 2.00

The surtax was for the Red Cross.

Street Urchin with Melon, Murillo — SP52

Nurse Holding Baby — SP53

Paintings: 10fr+5fr, Maria de Medici, Bronzino. 15fr+7fr, Baron Emil von Maucler, Dietrich.

1954, Nov. 15
B101 SP52 5fr + 3fr red .18 *.50*
B102 SP52 10fr + 5fr dk grn .22 *.60*
B103 SP52 15fr + 7fr purple .28 *.75*
Nos. B101-B103 (3) .68 *1.85*
Set, never hinged 1.10

The surtax was for child welfare.

Perf. 13x13½

1955, May 5 **Photo.** **Unwmk.**
B104 SP53 15fr + 5fr blk & red .15 *.45*
Never hinged .25

The surtax was for the Red Cross.

Dürer's Mother, Age 63 — SP54

Etchings by Dürer: 10fr+5fr, Praying hands. 15fr+7fr, Old man of Antwerp.

1955, Dec. 10 **Engr.** *Perf. 13*
B105 SP54 5fr + 3fr dk grn .20 *.45*
B106 SP54 10fr + 5fr ol grn .40 *.90*
B107 SP54 15fr + 7fr ol bis .50 *1.10*
Nos. B105-B107 (3) 1.10 *2.45*
Set, never hinged 1.75

The surtax was for public assistance.

First Aid Station, Saarbrücken, 1870 — SP55

1956, May 7
B108 SP55 15fr + 5fr dk brn .15 *.30*
Never hinged .20

The surtax was for the Red Cross.

"Victor of Benevent" SP56

Winterberg Monument SP57

1956, July 25 **Unwmk.** *Perf. 13*
B109 SP56 12fr + 3fr dk yel grn & bl grn .15 *.28*
B110 SP56 15fr + 5fr brn vio & brn .15 *.28*
Set value .24
Set, never hinged .50

Issued to publicize the forthcoming 16th Olympic Games at Melbourne, Nov. 22-Dec. 8, 1956.

1956, Oct. 29
B111 SP57 5fr + 2fr green .15 *.15*
B112 SP57 12fr + 3fr red lilac .15 *.28*
B113 SP57 15fr + 5fr brown .15 *.28*
Set value .22
Set, never hinged .48
Nos. B111-B113 (3) *.71*

The surtax was for the rebuilding of monuments.

"La Belle Ferronnière" by da Vinci — SP58

Designs: 10fr + 5fr, "Saskia" by Rembrandt. 15fr+7fr, "Family van Berchem," by Frans Floris. (Detail: Woman playing Spinet.)

1956, Dec. 10

B114	SP58	5fr + 3fr deep blue	.15	*.15*
B115	SP58	10fr + 5fr deep claret	.15	*.24*
B116	SP58	15fr + 7fr dark green	.15	*.40*
		Set value	.34	
		Set, never hinged	.52	
		Nos. B114-B116 (3)		*.79*

The surtax was for charitable works.

German Administration

Miner with Drill — SP59

"The Fox who Stole the Goose" — SP60

Designs: 6fr+4fr, Miner. 15fr+7fr, Miner and conveyor. 30fr+10fr, Miner and coal elevator.

Wmk. 304

1957, Oct. 1 Litho. *Perf. 14*

B117	SP59	6fr + 4fr bis brn & blk	.15	*.15*
B118	SP59	12fr + 6fr blk & yel grn	.15	*.16*
B119	SP59	15fr + 7fr blk & red	.15	*.38*
B120	SP59	30fr + 10fr blk & bl	.18	*.45*
		Set value	.46	
		Set, never hinged	.70	
		Nos. B117-B120 (4)		*1.14*

The surtax was to finance young peoples' study trip to Berlin.

1958, Apr. 1 Wmk. 304 *Perf. 14*

15fr+7fr, "A Hunter from the Palatinate."

B121	SP60	12fr + 6fr brn red, grn & blk	.15	*.18*
B122	SP60	15fr + 7fr grn, red, blk & gray	.15	*.24*
		Set value	.16	
		Set, never hinged	.28	

The surtax was to finance young peoples' study trip to Berlin.

Friedrich Wilhelm Raiffeisen SP61

Dairy Maid SP62

Designs: 15fr+7fr, Girl picking grapes. 30fr+10fr, Farmer with pitchfork.

1958, Oct. 1 Wmk. 304 *Perf. 14*

B123	SP61	6fr + 4fr gldn brn & dk brn	.15	.15
B124	SP62	12fr + 6fr grn, red & yel	.15	.15
B125	SP62	15fr + 7fr red, yel & bl	.18	*.30*
B126	SP62	30fr + 10fr bl & ocher	.22	*.40*
		Set value	.56	
		Set, never hinged	.95	
		Nos. B123-B126 (4)		*1.00*

AIR POST STAMPS

Airplane over Saarbrücken AP1

Perf. 13½

1928, Sept. 19 Unwmk. Photo.

C1	AP1	50c brown red	2.50	1.75
C2	AP1	1fr dark violet	3.00	2.25

For overprints see Nos. C5, C7.

Saarbrücken Airport and Church of St. Arnual — AP2

1932, Apr. 30

C3	AP2	60c orange red	4.00	2.50
C4	AP2	5fr dark brown	35.00	*70.00*

For overprints see Nos. C6, C8.

Nos. C1-C4 Overprinted like Nos. 139-154 in Various Colors

1934, Nov. 1 *Perf. 13½, 13½x13*

C5	AP1	50c brn red (R)	4.00	*5.25*
C6	AP2	60c org red (O)	2.75	*2.50*
C7	AP1	1fr dk vio (V)	6.00	*7.25*
C8	AP2	5fr dk brn (Br)	8.50	*9.50*
		Nos. C5-C8 (4)	21.25	*24.50*

French Protectorate

Shadow of Plane over Saar River — AP3

Unwmk.

1948, Apr. 1 Engr. *Perf. 13*

C9	AP3	25fr red	2.50	3.00
C10	AP3	50fr dk Prus grn	1.40	1.50
C11	AP3	200fr rose car	13.00	*26.00*
		Nos. C9-C11 (3)	16.90	*30.50*
		Set, never hinged	27.50	

Symbols of the Council of Europe — AP4

1950, Aug. 8 Photo. *Perf. 13½*

C12	AP4	200fr red brown	85.00	*190.00*
		Never hinged	150.00	

Saar's admission to the Council of Europe.

AIR POST SEMI-POSTAL STAMP

French Protectorate

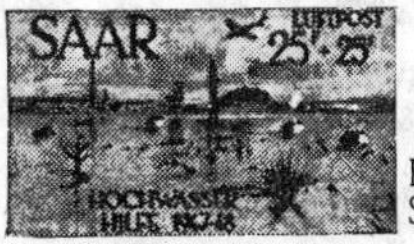

Flood Scene SPAP1

Perf. 13½x13

1948, Oct. 12 Photo. Unwmk.

CB1	SPAP1	25fr + 25fr sep	15.00	*95.00*
		Never hinged	27.50	
a.		Souvenir sheet of 1	200.00	*1,500.*
		Never hinged	450.00	

The surtax was for flood relief.

OFFICIAL STAMPS

Regular Issue of 1922-1923 Overprinted Diagonally in Red or Blue

DIENSTMARKE

Perf. 12½x13½, 13½x12½

1922-23 Unwmk.

O1	A19	3c ol grn & straw (R)	.50	*19.00*
O2	A20	5c org & blk (R)	.25	.20
O3	A21	10c bl grn (R)	.25	.15
O4	A19	15c dp brn (Bl)	.25	.15
O5	A19	15c org (Bl) ('23)	1.65	.25
O6	A22	20c dk bl & lem (R)	.25	.15
O7	A22	20c brt bl & straw (R) ('23)	1.65	.25
O8	A22	25c red & yel (Bl)	2.50	.65
O9	A22	25c mag & straw (Bl) ('23)	2.00	.25
O10	A23	30c car & yel (Bl)	.25	.15
O11	A24	40c brn & yel (Bl)	.40	.15
O12	A25	50c dk bl & straw (R)	.40	.15
O13	A24	75c dp grn & straw (R)	10.50	12.50
O14	A24	75c blk & straw (R) ('23)	3.00	1.25
O15	A26	1fr brn red (Bl)	12.00	1.40
		Nos. O1-O15 (15)	35.85	*36.65*

Inverted overprints exist on 10c, 20c, 30c, 50c, 1fr. Double overprints exist on #O4, O6, 1fr.

Regular Issue of 1927-30 Overprinted in Various Colors

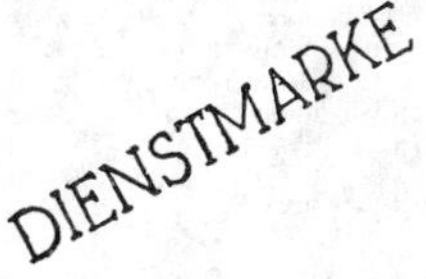

1927-34 *Perf. 13½*

O16	A31	10c dp brn (Bl) ('34)	1.10	2.00
O17	A32	15c ol blk (Bl) ('34)	1.65	*5.50*
O18	A32	20c brn org (Bk) ('31)	1.10	1.25
O19	A32	25c bluish sl (Bl)	1.65	*4.50*
O20	A31	30c ol grn (C)	1.65	.35
O21	A32	40c ol brn (C)	1.10	.20
O22	A32	50c mag (Bl)	1.10	.20
O23	A35	60c red org (Bk) ('30)	.65	.20
O24	A32	75c brn vio (C)	1.25	1.75
O25	A35	1fr vio (RO)	1.75	.15
O26	A36	2fr brn red (Bl)	1.75	.25
		Nos. O16-O26 (11)	14.75	*16.35*

The overprint listed is at a 23 to 25-degree angle. Also at 32-degree angle on Nos. O20-O22, O24-O26.

The overprint on Nos. O16 and O20 is known only inverted. Nos. O21-O26 exist with double overprint.

French Protectorate

Arms — O1

1949, Oct. 1 Engr. *Perf. 14x13*

O27	O1	10c deep carmine	.20	*11.00*
O28	O1	30c blue black	.15	*12.00*
O29	O1	1fr Prus green	.15	.15
O30	O1	2fr orange red	.85	.55
O31	O1	5fr blue	.25	.22
O32	O1	10fr black	.40	.50
O33	O1	12fr red violet	3.25	*3.75*
O34	O1	15fr indigo	.40	.20
O35	O1	20fr green	.90	.55
O36	O1	30fr violet rose	1.10	*2.00*
O37	O1	50fr purple	1.10	*1.90*
O38	O1	100fr red brown	40.00	*100.00*
		Nos. O27-O38 (12)	48.75	*132.82*
		Set, never hinged	100.00	

ST. CHRISTOPHER

sānt 'kris–tə–fər

LOCATION — Island in the West Indies, southeast of Puerto Rico

GOVT. — A Presidency of the former Leeward Islands Colony

AREA — 68 sq. mi.

POP. — 18,578 (estimated)

CAPITAL — Basseterre

Stamps of St. Christopher were discontinued in 1890 and replaced by those of Leeward Islands. For later issues, inscribed "St. Kitts-Nevis" or "St. Christopher-Nevis-Anguilla," see St. Kitts-Nevis.

12 Pence = 1 Shilling

Queen Victoria — A1

Wmk. Crown and C C (1)

1870, Apr. 1 Typo. *Perf. 12½*

1	A1	1p dull rose	55.00	40.00
2	A1	1p lilac rose	30.00	26.00
3	A1	6p green	90.00	13.00
		Nos. 1-3 (3)	175.00	79.00

1875-79 *Perf. 14*

4	A1	1p lilac rose	65.00	12.50
b.		Half used as ½p on cover		1,100.
5	A1	2½p red brown ('79)	165.00	200.00
6	A1	4p blue ('79)	150.00	15.00
7	A1	6p green	50.00	6.75
a.		Horiz. pair, imperf. vert.		
		Nos. 4-7 (4)	430.00	234.25

For surcharges see Nos. 18-20.

1882-90 Wmk. Crown and C A (2)

8	A1	½p green	.60	1.00
9	A1	1p rose	1.00	1.10
a.		Half used as ½p on cover		—
10	A1	1p lilac rose	475.00	80.00
a.		Diagonal half used as ½p on cover		—
11	A1	2½p red brown	225.00	75.00
12	A1	2½p ultra ('84)	2.00	2.50
13	A1	4p blue	350.00	37.50
14	A1	4p gray ('84)	1.25	1.25
15	A1	6p olive brn ('90)	80.00	*325.00*
16	A1	1sh violet ('87)	80.00	65.00
		Nos. 8-16 (9)	1,214.	588.35

For surcharges see Nos. 17, 21-23.

No. 9 Bisected and Handstamp Surcharged in Black

1885, Mar.

17	A1	½p on half of 1p	25.00	30.00
b.		Inverted surcharge	220.00	110.00
c.		Unsevered pair	125.00	125.00
d.		As "c," one surcharge inverted	350.00	250.00

No. 7 Surcharged in Black:

ONE
PENNY.

Nos. 18, 21

FOUR
PENCE

No. 19

4d.

No. 20

1885-86 Wmk. 1

18	A1	1p on 6p green ('86)	16.00	27.50
a.		Inverted surcharge	*6,250.*	
19	A1	4p on 6p green	50.00	*60.00*
a.		Period after "PENCE"	50.00	60.00
b.		Double surcharge	*1,750.*	
20	A1	4p on 6p green ('86)	50.00	80.00
a.		Without period after "d"	210.00	250.00
b.		Double surcharge	*1,500.*	*1,600.*
		Nos. 18-20 (3)	116.00	167.50

No. 18 with double surcharge is known only with pen cancellation or with violet handstamp (revenue cancels). Value, $1,450.

Nos. 8 and 12 Surcharged in Black Like No. 18 or:

ONE
PENNY.

No. 22

ONE
PENNY.

No. 23

1887-88 Wmk. 2

21	A1	1p on ½p green	27.50	35.00
22	A1	1p on 2½p ('88)	42.50	50.00
a.		Inverted surcharge	*7,000.*	*5,000.*
23	A1	1p on 2½p ('88)	*10,000.*	*10,000.*

Nos. 22-23 may have been printed using the same type. The bar on No. 22 is done by hand. No. 23 probably is a sheet that was missed when the bars were added.

Antigua No. 18 was used in St. Christopher in 1890. It is canceled "A12" instead of "A02." Values: used $175, on cover $750.

St. Christopher stamps can be mounted in the Scott British Leeward Islands album.

ST. HELENA

sānt 'he–lə–nə

LOCATION — Island in the Atlantic Ocean, 1,200 miles west of Angola
GOVT. — British Crown Colony
AREA — 47 sq. mi.
POP. — 5,499 (1982)
CAPITAL — Jamestown

12 Pence = 1 Shilling
20 Shillings = 1 Pound
100 Pence = 1 Pound (1971)

Catalogue values for unused stamps in this country are for Never Hinged items, beginning with Scott 128 in the regular postage section, Scott B1 in the semi-postal section and Scott J1 in the postage due section.

Values for unused stamps are for examples with original gum as defined in the catalogue introduction. Very fine examples of Nos. 2-7, 11-39a and 47-47b will have perforations touching the design on one or more sides due to the narrow spacing of the stamps on the plates. Stamps with perfs clear of the design on all four sides are scarce and will command higher prices.

Watermark

Wmk. 6- Star

Queen Victoria — A1

1856, Jan. Wmk. 6 Engr. *Imperf.*
1 A1 6p blue 550.00 175.00

For types surcharged see Nos. 8-39, 47.

1861 *Clean-Cut Perf. 14 to 15½*
2 A1 6p blue 1,500. 275.00

1863 *Rough Perf. 14 to 15½*
2B A1 6p blue 375.00 125.00

1873-74 Wmk. 1 *Perf. 12½*
3 A1 6p dull blue 550.00 90.00
4 A1 6p ultra ('74) 275.00 75.00

1879 *Perf. 14x12½*
5 A1 6p gray blue 275.00 32.50

1889 *Perf. 14*
6 A1 6p gray blue 250.00 37.50

1889 Wmk. Crown and C A (2)
7 A1 6p gray 10.00 5.50

Type of 1856 Surcharged

ONE PENNY a **ONE PENNY** b

1863 Wmk. 1 *Imperf.*
Long Bar, 16, 17, 18 or 19mm
8 A1(a) 1p on 6p brown red (surch. 17mm) 110.00 *165.00*
a. Double surcharge 5,500. 2,750.
9 A1(a) 1p on 6p brown red (surch. 19mm) 110.00 *165.00*
10 A1(b) 4p on 6p carmine 500.00 225.00
a. Surcharge omitted
b. Double surcharge *9,000.* *9,000.*

1864-73 *Perf. 12½*
11 A1(a) 1p on 6p brn red 25.00 24.00
12 A1(b) 1p on 6p brn red ('71) 60.00 17.00
a. Blue black surcharge *1,300.* *875.00*
13 A1(b) 2p on 6p yel ('73) 72.50 37.50
a. Blue black surcharge *6,750.* *4,000.*
14 A1(b) 3p on 6p dk vio ('73) 75.00 47.50
15 A1(b) 4p on 6p carmine 110.00 45.00
a. Double surcharge *9,000.* *6,250.*
16 A1(b) 1sh on 6p grn (bar 16 to 17mm) 165.00 25.00
17 A1(b) 1sh on 6p dp grn (bar 18mm) ('73) 300.00 15.00
a. Blue black surcharge

1868
Short Bar, 14 or 15mm
18 A1(a) 1p on 6p brn red ('68) 110.00 50.00
a. Imperf., pair 7,500.
b. Double surcharge
19 A1(b) 2p on 6p yel ('68) 140.00 57.50
a. Imperf., pair 17,000.
20 A1(b) 3p on 6p dk vio ('68) 75.00 47.50
a. Double surcharge 6,750.
b. Imperf., pair 2,250.
21 A1(b) 4p on 6p car (words 18mm) ('68) 77.50 47.50
a. Double surcharge *5,500.* 5,500.
b. Imperf., pair 19,000.
22 A1(b) 4p on 6p car (words 19mm) ('68) 200.00 125.00
a. Words double, 18mm and 19mm *12,500.* *12,500.*
b. Imperf.
23 A1(a) 1sh on 6p yel grn ('68) 400.00 140.00
a. Double surcharge 10,000.
b. Pair, one without surcharge 7,750.
24 A1(a) 5sh on 6p org ('68) 37.50 50.00

No. 21 exists with surcharge omitted.

1882 *Perf. 14x12½*
25 A1(a) 1p on 6p brown red 55.00 15.00
26 A1(b) 2p on 6p yellow 70.00 50.00
27 A1(b) 3p on 6p violet 165.00 70.00
28 A1(b) 4p on 6p carmine (words 16mm) 80.00 55.00

1883 *Perf. 14*
29 A1(a) 1p on 6p brown red 65.00 15.00
30 A1(b) 2p on 6p yellow 65.00 22.50
31 A1(a) 1sh on 6p yel grn 20.00 11.00

1882 *Perf. 14x12½*
Long Bar, 18mm
32 A1(b) 1sh on 6p dp green 300.00 20.00

1884-94 Wmk. 2 *Perf. 14*
Short Bar, 14 or 14½mm
33 A1(b) ½p on 6p grn (words 17mm) 3.50 3.50
a. ½p on 6p emer, blurred print (words 17mm) ('84) 5.75 7.50
b. Double surcharge 1,200.
34 A1(b) ½p on 6p grn (words 15mm) ('94) .80 1.10
35 A1(a) 1p on 6p red ('87) 2.50 1.75
36 A1(b) 2p on 6p yel ('94) 1.10 1.90
37 A1(b) 3p on 6p dp vio ('87) 2.00 2.50
a. 3p on 6p red violet 4.00 4.00
b. Double surcharge *6,750.* *6,750.*
38 A1(b) 4p on 6p dk brn ('90) 11.00 8.00
a. With thin bar below thick one

1894
Long Bar, 18mm
39 A1(b) 1sh on 6p yel grn 25.00 16.00
a. Double surcharge *4,000.*

See note after No. 47.

Queen Victoria — A3

1890-97 Typo. *Perf. 14*
40 A3 ½p green ('97) 3.00 4.00
41 A3 1p rose ('96) 7.00 1.00
42 A3 1½p red brn & grn 4.00 6.00
43 A3 2p yellow ('96) 4.00 8.00
44 A3 2½p ultra ('96) 6.00 9.00
45 A3 5p violet ('96) 10.00 22.50
46 A3 10p brown ('96) 15.00 *45.00*
Nos. 40-46 (7) 49.00 *95.50*

2½d

Type of 1856 Surcharged

1893 Engr. Wmk. 2
47 A1 2½p on 6p blue 2.00 4.00
a. Double surcharge *16,500.*
b. Double impression 7,500.

In 1905 remainders of Nos. 34-47 were sold by the postal officials. They are canceled with bars, arranged in the shape of diamonds, in purple ink. No such cancellation was ever used on the island and the stamps so canceled are of slight value. With this cancellation removed, these remainders are sometimes offered as unused. Some have been recanceled with a false dated postmark.

King Edward VII — A5

1902 Typo. Wmk. 2
48 A5 ½p green 1.50 *1.10*
49 A5 1p carmine rose 4.25 .85

Government House — A6

"The Wharf" — A7

1903, June Wmk. 1
50 A6 ½p gray green & brn 1.75 2.25
51 A7 1p carmine & blk 1.25 .50
52 A6 2p ol grn & blk 5.25 1.50
53 A7 8p brown & blk 15.00 *32.50*
54 A6 1sh org buff & brn 15.00 *35.00*
55 A7 2sh violet & blk 42.50 *75.00*
Nos. 50-55 (6) 80.75 *146.75*

A8

1908, May Wmk. 3
56 A8 2½p ultra 1.40 *1.50*
57 A8 4p black & red, *yel* 1.50 *8.00*
58 A8 6p dull violet 3.50 *15.00*
Nos. 56-58 (3) 6.40 *24.50*

Wmk. 2
60 A8 10sh grn & red, *grn* 175.00 *200.00*

Nos. 57 and 58 exist on both ordinary and chalky paper; No. 56 on ordinary and No. 60 on chalky paper.

Government House — A9

"The Wharf" — A10

1912-16 Ordinary Paper Wmk. 3
61 A9 ½p green & blk 1.25 5.00
62 A10 1p carmine & blk 1.40 1.90
a. 1p scarlet & black ('16) 22.50 *27.00*
63 A10 1½p orange & blk 2.25 4.00
64 A9 2p gray & black 2.25 1.75
65 A10 2½p ultra & blk 1.90 5.00
66 A9 3p vio & blk, *yel* 1.90 5.00
67 A10 8p dull vio & blk 5.25 40.00
68 A9 1sh black, *green* 7.50 20.00
69 A10 2sh ultra & blk, *bl* 25.00 *55.00*
70 A10 3sh violet & blk 45.00 *90.00*
Nos. 61-70 (10) 93.70 *227.65*

See Nos. 75-77.

St. Helena stamps can be mounted in the Scott British Africa album.

A11

A12

Die I

For description of dies I and II see back of this section of the Catalogue.

1912
Chalky Paper
71 A11 4p black & red, *yel* 5.25 *14.00*
72 A11 6p dull vio & red vio 2.50 *8.00*

1913
Ordinary Paper
73 A12 4p black & red, *yel* 5.25 1.75
74 A12 6p dull vio & red vio 11.00 *22.50*

1922 Wmk. 4
75 A10 1p green 1.00 *17.00*
76 A10 1½p rose red 6.00 *22.50*
77 A9 3p ultra 11.00 *35.00*
Nos. 75-77 (3) 18.00 *74.50*

Badge of the Colony — A13

1922-27 Wmk. 4
Chalky Paper
79 A13 ½p black & gray 1.00 1.50
80 A13 1p green & black 1.00 1.25
81 A13 1½p rose red 2.25 *7.00*
82 A13 2p pale gray & gray 1.90 1.90
83 A13 3p ultra 1.90 *3.75*
84 A13 5p red & grn, *emer* 2.50 *5.00*
85 A13 6p red vio & black 3.00 *8.00*
86 A13 8p violet & blk 3.00 *6.00*
87 A13 1sh dk brown & blk 5.00 *8.00*
88 A13 1sh6p grn & blk, *emer* 10.00 *40.00*
89 A13 2sh ultra & vio, *bl* 12.50 *32.50*
90 A13 2sh6p car & blk, *yel* 12.50 *45.00*
91 A13 5sh grn & blk, *yel* 32.50 *65.00*
92 A13 7sh6p orange & blk 75.00 *110.00*
93 A13 10sh ol grn & blk 100.00 *150.00*
94 A13 15sh vio & blk, *bl* 925.00 *1,250.*
Nos. 79-93 (15) 264.05 *484.90*

Nos. 88, 90, and 91 are on ordinary paper.

Wmk. 3
Chalky Paper
95 A13 4p black, *yel* 6.00 *7.00*
96 A13 1sh6p bl grn & blk, *grn* 20.00 *45.00*
97 A13 2sh6p car & blk, *yel* 24.00 *47.50*
98 A13 5sh grn & blk, *yel* 37.50 *70.00*
99 A13 £1 red vio & blk, *red* 375.00 *400.00*
Nos. 95-99 (5) 462.50 *569.50*

Issue dates: ½p, 1½p, 2p, 3p, 4p, 8p, February, 1923; 5p, Nos. 88-91, 1927; others, June 1922.

Centenary Issue

Lot and Lot's Wife — A14

Plantation; Queen Victoria and Kings William IV, Edward VII, George V — A15

Map of the Colony — A16

Quay, Jamestown A17

View of James Valley — A18

View of Jamestown A19

View of Mundens A20

St. Helena A21

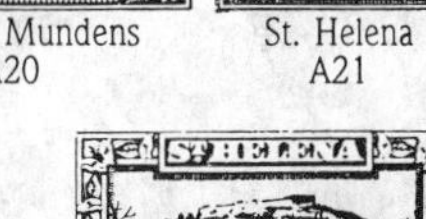

View of High Knoll — A22

Badge of the Colony — A23

Wmk. 4

1934, Apr. 23 Engr. *Perf. 12*

101 A14 ½p dk vio & black .55 .60
102 A15 1p green & blk .70 .85
103 A16 1½p red & blk 2.25 2.75
104 A17 2p orange & blk 1.75 1.90
105 A18 3p blue & blk 1.50 *5.00*
106 A19 6p lt blue & blk 3.00 *3.50*
107 A20 1sh dk brown & blk 6.50 *18.00*
108 A21 2sh6p carmine & blk 32.50 *45.00*
109 A22 5sh choc & blk 70.00 80.00
110 A23 10sh red vio & black 190.00 225.00
Nos. 101-110 (10) 308.75 382.60

Silver Jubilee Issue
Common Design Type

1935, May 6 *Perf. 13½x14*

111 CD301 1½p car & dk blue .60 *2.00*
112 CD301 2p gray blk & ultra 1.40 1.10
113 CD301 6p indigo & grn 4.75 3.75
114 CD301 1sh brt vio & indigo 6.25 *9.00*
Nos. 111-114 (4) 13.00 *15.85*
Set, never hinged 22.50

Coronation Issue
Common Design Type

1937, May 19

115 CD302 1p deep green .15 .15
116 CD302 2p deep orange .20 .20
117 CD302 3p bright ultra .30 .30
Nos. 115-117 (3) .65 .65
Set, never hinged 2.00

Badge of the Colony — A24

1938-40 *Perf. 12½*

118 A24 ½p purple .15 .15
119 A24 1p dp green 12.00 3.00
119A A24 1p org yel ('40) .15 .20
120 A24 1½p carmine .15 .20
121 A24 2p orange .15 .20
122 A24 3p ultra 55.00 27.50
122A A24 3p gray ('40) .15 .25
122B A24 4p ultra ('40) .90 .25
123 A24 6p gray blue .90 .40
123A A24 8p olive ('40) 1.75 1.10
124 A24 1sh sepia .40 .55
125 A24 2sh6p deep claret 8.00 3.00
126 A24 5sh brown 10.00 *7.00*
127 A24 10sh violet 10.00 *14.00*
Nos. 118-127 (14) 99.70 *57.80*
Set, never hinged 160.00

Issue dates: May 12, 1938, July 8, 1940.
See Nos. 136-138.

Catalogue values for unused stamps in this section, from this point to the end of the section, are for Never Hinged items.

Peace Issue
Common Design Type
Perf. 13½x14

1946, Oct. 21 Wmk. 4 Engr.

128 CD303 2p deep orange .20 .20
129 CD303 4p deep blue .25 .25

Silver Wedding Issue
Common Design Types

1948, Oct. 20 Photo. *Perf. 14x14½*

130 CD304 3p black .25 .25

Engr.; Name Typo.
Perf. 11½x11

131 CD305 10sh blue violet 19.00 *32.50*

UPU Issue
Common Design Types
Engr.; Name Typo. on 4p, 6p

1949, Oct. 10 *Perf. 13½, 11x11½*

132 CD306 3p rose carmine .30 .30
133 CD307 4p indigo .80 .80
134 CD308 6p olive 1.75 1.75
135 CD309 1sh slate 2.75 2.75
Nos. 132-135 (4) 5.60 5.60

George VI Type of 1938

1949, Nov. 1 Engr. *Perf. 12½*
Center in Black

136 A24 1p blue green .60 .60
137 A24 1½p carmine rose .80 .80
138 A24 2p carmine .80 .80
Nos. 136-138 (3) 2.20 2.20

Coronation Issue
Common Design Type

1953, June 2 *Perf. 13½x13*

139 CD312 3p purple & black 1.00 1.00

Badge of the Colony — A25

A26

A27

Designs: 1p, Flax plantation. 1½p, Heart-shaped waterfall. 2p, Lace making. 2½p, Drying flax. 3p, Wire bird. 4p, Flagstaff and barn. 6p, Donkeys carrying flax. 7p, Map. 1sh, Entrance, government offices. 2sh 6p, Cutting flax. 5sh, Jamestown. 10sh, Longwood house.

1953, Aug. 4 *Perf. 13½x14, 14x13½*
Center and Denomination in Black

140 A25 ½p emerald .15 .15
141 A25 1p dark green .15 .15
142 A26 1½p red violet .20 .15
143 A25 2p rose lake .25 .20
144 A25 2½p red .25 .20
145 A25 3p brown .35 .25
146 A25 4p deep blue .50 .30
147 A25 6p purple .70 .45
148 A25 7p gray .90 .55
149 A25 1sh dk car rose 1.25 .80
150 A25 2sh 6p violet 7.00 3.75
151 A25 5sh chocolate 15.00 8.00
152 A25 10sh orange 40.00 20.00
Nos. 140-152 (13) 66.70 34.95

Perf. 11½

1956, Jan. 3 Wmk. 4 Engr.

153 A27 3p dk car rose & blue .20 .20
154 A27 4p redsh brown & blue .35 .35
155 A27 6p purple & blue .55 .55
Nos. 153-155 (3) 1.10 1.10

Cent. of the 1st St. Helena postage stamp.

Arms of East India Company A28

Designs: 6p, Dutton's ship "London" off James Bay. 1sh, Memorial stone from fort built by Governor Dutton.

Perf. 12½x13

1959, May 5 Wmk. 314

156 A28 3p rose & black .15 .15
157 A28 6p gray & yellow green .45 .45
158 A28 1sh orange & black .65 .65
Nos. 156-158 (3) 1.25 1.25

300th anniv. of the landing of Capt. John Dutton on St. Helena and of the 1st settlement.

Cape Canary A29

Elizabeth II A30

Queen and Prince Andrew A31

Designs: 1p, Cunning fish, horiz. 2p, Brittle starfish, horiz. 4½p, Redwood flower. 6p, Red fody (Madagascar weaver). 7p, Trumpetfish, horiz. 10p, Keeled feather starfish, horiz. 1sh, Gumwood flowers. 1sh6p, Fairy tern. 2sh6p, Orange starfish, horiz. 5sh, Night-blooming cereus. 10sh, Deepwater bull's-eye, horiz.

Perf. 11½x12, 12x11½

1961, Dec. 12 Photo. Wmk. 314

159 A29 1p multicolored .15 .15
160 A29 1½p multicolored .25 .15
161 A29 2p gray & red .15 .15
162 A30 3p dk blue, rose & grnsh blue .40 .35
163 A29 4½p slate, brn & grn .50 .35
164 A29 6p cit, brn & dp car 2.00 .40
165 A29 7p vio, blk & red brn .40 .40
166 A29 10p blue & dp claret .70 .65
167 A29 1sh red brn, grn & yel .70 .65
168 A29 1sh6p gray bl & blk 5.00 1.75
169 A29 2sh6p grnsh bl, yel & red 3.75 2.75
170 A29 5sh green, brown & yel 7.50 4.25
171 A29 10sh gray bl, blk & sal 10.50 9.50

Perf. 14x14½

172 A31 £1 turq blue & choc 20.00 22.50
Nos. 159-172 (14) 52.00 44.00

For overprints see Nos. 176-179.

Freedom from Hunger Issue
Common Design Type

1963, June 4 *Perf. 14x14½*

173 CD314 1sh6p ultra 3.50 2.50

Red Cross Centenary Issue
Common Design Type
Wmk. 314

1963, Sept. 2 Litho. *Perf. 13*

174 CD315 3p black & red .30 .30
175 CD315 1sh6p ultra & red 4.00 3.00

Nos. 159, 162, 164 and 168 Overprinted: "FIRST LOCAL POST / 4th JANUARY 1965"

Perf. 11½x12, 12x11½

1965, Jan. 4 Photo. Wmk. 314

176 A29 1p multicolored .15 .15
177 A30 3p dk bl, rose & grnsh bl .15 .15
178 A29 6p cit, brn & dp car .25 .25
179 A29 1sh6p gray blue & blk .50 .50
Nos. 176-179 (4) 1.05 1.05

Establishment of the 1st internal postal service on the island.

ITU Issue
Common Design Type
Perf. 11x11½

1965, May 17 Litho. Wmk. 314

180 CD317 3p ultra & gray .30 .30
181 CD317 6p red lil & blue grn .70 .70

Intl. Cooperation Year Issue
Common Design Type

1965, Oct. 25 Litho. *Perf. 14½*

182 CD318 1p blue grn & claret .15 .15
183 CD318 6p lt violet & green 1.50 1.50

Churchill Memorial Issue
Common Design Type

1966, Jan. 24 Photo. *Perf. 14*
Design in Black, Gold and Carmine Rose

184 CD319 1p bright blue .15 .15
185 CD319 3p green .20 .20
186 CD319 6p brown .60 .60
187 CD319 1sh6p violet 2.00 2.00
Nos. 184-187 (4) 2.95 2.95

World Cup Soccer Issue
Common Design Type

1966, July 1 Litho. *Perf. 14*

188 CD321 3p multicolored .45 .45
189 CD321 6p multicolored 1.25 1.00

WHO Headquarters Issue
Common Design Type

1966, Sept. 20 Litho. *Perf. 14*

190 CD322 3p multicolored .45 .45
191 CD322 1sh6p multicolored 2.75 2.25

UNESCO Anniversary Issue
Common Design Type

1966, Dec. 1 Litho. *Perf. 14*

192 CD323 3p "Education" .80 .60
193 CD323 6p "Science" 1.25 1.00
194 CD323 1sh6p "Culture" 4.00 3.50
Nos. 192-194 (3) 6.05 5.10

Badge of St. Helena — A32

Perf. 14½x14

1967, May 5 Photo. Wmk. 314

195 A32 1sh dk green & multi .30 .30
196 A32 2sh6p blue & multi .70 .70
a. Carmine omitted 450.00

St. Helena's New Constitution.

The Great Fire of London A33

3p, Three-master Charles. 6p, Boats bringing new settlers to shore. 1sh6p, Settlers at work.

Perf. 13½x13

1967, Sept. 4 Engr. Wmk. 314

197 A33 1p black & carmine .15 .15
198 A33 3p black & vio blue .15 .15
199 A33 6p black & dull violet .20 .20
200 A33 1sh6p black & ol green .55 .55
Nos. 197-200 (4) 1.05 1.05

Tercentenary of the arrival of settlers from London after the Great Fire of Sept. 2-4, 1666.

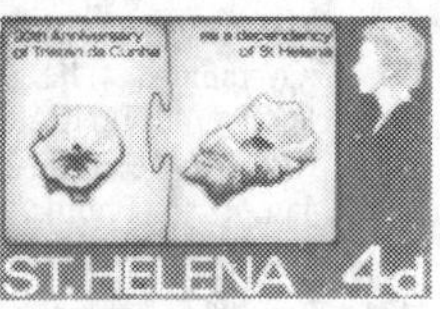

Maps of Tristan da Cunha and St. Helena A34

Designs: 8p, 2sh3p, Maps of St. Helena and Tristan da Cunha.

Perf. 14x14½

1968, June 4 Photo. Wmk. 314

Maps in Sepia

201 A34 4p dp red lilac .15 .15
202 A34 8p olive .15 .15
203 A34 1sh9p deep ultra .40 .40
204 A34 2sh3p Prus blue .60 .60
Nos. 201-204 (4) 1.30 1.30

30th anniv. of Tristan da Cunha as a Dependency of St. Helena.

Sir Hudson Lowe A35

Designs: 1sh6p, 2sh6p, Sir George Bingham.

Perf. 13½x13

1968, Sept. 4 Litho. Wmk. 314

205 A35 3p multicolored .15 .15
206 A35 9p multicolored .15 .15
207 A35 1sh6p multicolored .40 .40
208 A35 2sh6p multicolored .60 .60
Nos. 205-208 (4) 1.30 1.30

Abolition of slavery in St. Helena, 150th anniv.

Road Construction — A36

Designs: 1p, Electricity development. 1½p, Dentist. 2p, Pest control. 3p, Apartment houses in Jamestown. 4p, Pasture and livestock improvement. 6p, School children listening to broadcast. 8p, Country cottages. 10p, New school buildings. 1sh, Reforestation. 1sh6p, Heavy lift crane. 2sh6p, Playing children in Lady Field Children's Home. 5sh, Agricultural training. 10sh, Ward in New General Hospital. £1, Lifeboat "John Dutton."

Perf. 13½

1968, Nov. 4 Litho. Wmk. 314

209 A36 ½p multicolored .15 .15
210 A36 1p multicolored .15 .15
211 A36 1½p multicolored .15 .15
212 A36 2p multicolored .15 .15
213 A36 3p multicolored .15 .15
214 A36 4p multicolored .20 .20
215 A36 6p multicolored .25 .25
216 A36 8p multicolored .30 .30
217 A36 10p multicolored .35 .35
218 A36 1sh multicolored .45 .45
219 A36 1sh6p multicolored .55 .55
220 A36 2sh6p multicolored 1.10 1.10
221 A36 5sh multicolored 1.90 1.90
222 A36 10sh multicolored 3.75 3.75
223 A36 £1 multicolored 10.00 10.00
Nos. 209-223 (15) 19.60 19.60

See Nos. 244-256.

Brig Perseverance, 1819 — A37

Ships: 8p, M.S. Dane, 1857. 1sh9p, S.S. Llandovery Castle, 1925. 2sh3p, M.S. Good Hope Castle, 1969.

1969, Apr. 19 Litho. *Perf. 13½*

224 A37 4p violet & multi .15 .15
225 A37 8p ocher & multi .40 .40
226 A37 1sh9p ver & multi 1.10 1.10
227 A37 2sh3p dk blue & multi 1.25 1.25
Nos. 224-227 (4) 2.90 2.90

Issued in recognition of St. Helena's dependence on sea mail.

Surgeon and Officer (Light Company) 20th Foot, 1816 — A38

British Uniforms: 6p, Warrant Officer and Drummer, 53rd Foot, 1815. 1sh8p, Drum Major, 66th Foot, 1816, and Royal Artillery Officer, 1820. 2sh6p, Private 91st Foot and 2nd Corporal, Royal Sappers and Miners, 1832.

Perf. 14x14½

1969, Sept. 3 Litho. Wmk. 314

228 A38 6p red & multi .30 .25
229 A38 8p blue & multi .45 .30
230 A38 1sh8p green & multi 1.25 1.10
231 A38 2sh6p gray & multi 2.25 2.00
Nos. 228-231 (4) 4.25 3.65

Charles Dickens, "The Pickwick Papers" A39

Dickens and: 8p, "Oliver Twist." 1sh6p, "Martin Chuzzlewit." 2sh6p, "Bleak House."

Perf. 13½x13

1970, June 9 Litho. Wmk. 314

232 A39 4p dk brown & multi .20 .20
233 A39 8p slate & multi .50 .40
234 A39 1sh6p multicolored .80 .70
235 A39 2sh6p multicolored 1.65 1.25
Nos. 232-235 (4) 3.15 2.55

Charles Dickens (1812-70), English novelist.

Mouth to Mouth Resuscitation — A40

Centenary of British Red Cross Society: 9p, Girl in wheelchair and nurse. 1sh9p, First aid. 2sh3p, British Red Cross Society emblem.

1970, Sept. 15 *Perf. 14½*

236 A40 6p bister, red & blk .15 .15
237 A40 9p lt blue grn, red & blk .20 .20
238 A40 1sh9p gray, red & blk .55 .55
239 A40 2sh3p pale vio, red & blk .60 .60
Nos. 236-239 (4) 1.50 1.50

A41

A42

Regimental Emblems: 4p, Officer's Shako Plate, 20th Foot, 1812-16. 9p, Officer's breast plate, 66th Foot, before 1818. 1sh3p, Officer's full dress shako, 91st Foot, 1816. 2sh11p, Ensign's shako, 53rd Foot, 1815.

Perf. 14½

1970, Nov. 2 Litho. Wmk. 314

240 A41 4p multicolored .25 .20
241 A41 9p red & multi .85 .60
242 A41 1sh3p dk gray & multi 1.40 1.00
243 A41 2sh11p dk gray grn & multi 3.00 2.25
Nos. 240-243 (4) 5.50 4.05

See Nos. 263-270, 273-276.

Type of 1968
"P" instead of "d"

1971, Feb. 15 Litho. *Perf. 13½*

244 A36 ½p like #210 .15 .15
245 A36 1p like #211 .15 .15
246 A36 1½p like #212 .20 .20
247 A36 2p like #213 .30 .30
a. Perf. 14½ ('75) .55 .55
248 A36 2½p like #214 .35 .35
249 A36 3½p like #215 .45 .45
250 A36 4½p like #216 .55 .55
251 A36 5p like #217 .70 .70
252 A36 7½p like #218 .95 .95
253 A36 10p like #219 1.10 1.10
254 A36 12½p like #220 1.50 1.50
255 A36 25p like #221 3.00 3.00
256 A36 50p like #222 13.00 13.00
Nos. 244-256 (13) 22.40 22.40

The paper of Nos. 244-256 is thinner than the paper of Nos. 209-223 and No. 223 (£1) has been reprinted in slightly different colors.

Perf. 14x14½

1971, Apr. 5 Litho. Wmk. 314

St. Helena, from Italian Miniature, 1460

257 A42 2p violet blue & multi .15 .15
258 A42 5p multicolored .25 .25
259 A42 7½p multicolored .45 .45
260 A42 12½p olive & multi .70 .70
Nos. 257-260 (4) 1.55 1.55

Easter 1971.

Napoleon, after J. L. David, and Tomb in St. Helena — A43

34p, Napoleon, by Hippolyte Paul Delaroche.

1971, May 5 *Perf. 13½*

261 A43 2p multicolored .25 .15
262 A43 34p multicolored 3.75 2.75

Sesquicentennial of the death of Napoleon Bonaparte (1769-1821).

Military Type of 1970

Designs: 1½p, Sword Hilt, Artillery Private, 1815. 4p, Baker rifle and socket bayonet, c. 1816. 6p, Infantry officer's sword hilt, 1822. 22½p, Baker rifle and light sword bayonet, c. 1823.

1971, Nov. 10 *Perf. 14½*

263 A41 1½p green & multi .30 .25
264 A41 4p gray & multi .95 .75
265 A41 6p purple & multi 1.50 1.25
266 A41 22½p multicolored 4.25 3.50
Nos. 263-266 (4) 7.00 5.75

1972, June 19

Designs: 2p, Royal Sappers and Miners breastplate, 1823. 5p, Infantry sergeant's pike, 1830. 7½p, Royal Artillery officer's breastplate, 1830. 12½p, English military pistol, 1800.

267 A41 2p multicolored .25 .20
268 A41 5p plum & black .85 .70
269 A41 7½p dp blue & multi 1.40 1.10
270 A41 12½p olive & multi 2.75 2.25
Nos. 267-270 (4) 5.25 4.25

Silver Wedding Issue, 1972

Common Design Type

Design: Queen Elizabeth II, Prince Philip, St. Helena plover and white fairy tern.

1972, Nov. 20 Photo. *Perf. 14x14½*

271 CD324 2p slate green & multi .15 .15
272 CD324 16p rose brown & multi .75 .75

Military Type of 1970

Designs: 2p, Shako, 53rd Foot, 1815. 5p, Band and Drums sword hilt, 1830. 7½p, Royal Sappers and Miners officers' hat, 1830. 12½p, General's sword hilt, 1831.

1973, Sept. 20 Litho. *Perf. 14½*

273 A41 2p dull brown & multi .55 .25
274 A41 5p multicolored .75 .75
275 A41 7½p olive grn & multi 3.25 1.75
276 A41 12½p lilac & multi 4.25 3.50
Nos. 273-276 (4) 8.80 6.25

Princess Anne's Wedding Issue

Common Design Type

1973, Nov. 14 Wmk. 314 *Perf. 14*

277 CD325 2p multicolored .15 .15
278 CD325 18p multicolored .60 .60

Westminster and Claudine Beached During Storm, 1849 — A45

Designs: 4p, East Indiaman True Briton, 1790. 6p, General Goddard in action off St. Helena, 1795. 22½p, East Indiaman Kent burning in Bay of Biscay, 1825.

Perf. 14½x14

1973, Dec. 17 Litho. Wmk. 314

279 A45 1½p multicolored .30 .15
280 A45 4p multicolored .60 .50
281 A45 6p multicolored .85 .65
282 A45 22½p multicolored 2.75 2.50
Nos. 279-282 (4) 4.50 3.80

Tercentenary of the East India Company Charter.

UPU Emblem, Ships A46

Design: 25p, UPU emblem and letters.

1974, Oct. 15 *Perf. 14½x14*

283 A46 5p blue & multi .20 .20
284 A46 25p red & multi .90 .90
a. Souvenir sheet of 2, #283-284 1.25 1.25

Centenary of Universal Postal Union.

Churchill and Blenheim Palace A47

25p, Churchill, Tower Bridge & Thames.

1974, Nov. 30 Wmk. 373 *Perf. 14½*

285 A47 5p black & multi .20 .20
286 A47 25p black & multi .90 .90
a. Souvenir sheet of 2, #285-286 1.75 1.25

Sir Winston Churchill (1874-1965).

Capt. Cook and Jamestown — A48

Design: 5p, Capt. Cook and "Resolution," vert.

Perf. 14x13½, 13½x14

1975, July 14 Litho.

287 A48 5p multicolored .50 .50
288 A48 25p multicolored 2.75 2.75

Return of Capt. James Cook to St. Helena, bicent.

Mellissia Begonifolia — A49

Designs: 5p, Mellissius adumbratus (insect). 12p, Aegialitis St. Helena (bird), horiz. 25p, Scorpaenia mellissii (fish), horiz.

1975, Oct. 20 Wmk. 373 *Perf. 13*

289 A49	2p gray & multi	.15	.15
290 A49	5p gray & multi	.35	.35
291 A49	12p gray & multi	.70	.70
292 A49	25p gray & multi	1.50	1.50
	Nos. 289-292 (4)	2.70	2.70

Centenary of the publication of "St. Helena," by John Charles Melliss.

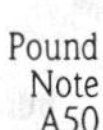

Pound Note A50

Design: 33p, 5-pound note.

1976, Apr. 15 Wmk. 314 *Perf. 13½*

293 A50	8p claret & multi	.45	.35
294 A50	33p multicolored	1.40	1.10

First issue of St. Helena bank notes.

St. Helena No. 8 — A51

Designs: 8p, St. Helena No. 80, vert. 25p, Freighter Good Hope Castle.

Perf. 13½x14, 14x13½

1976, May 4 Litho. Wmk. 373

295 A51	5p buff, brown & blk	.20	.20
296 A51	8p lt grn, grn & blk	.30	.30
297 A51	25p multicolored	1.00	1.00
	Nos. 295-297 (3)	1.50	1.50

Festival of stamps 1976. For souvenir sheet containing No. 297 see Ascension No. 214a.

High Knoll, by Capt. Barnett A52

Views on St. Helena, lithographs: 3p, Friar Rock, by G. H. Bellasis, 1815. 5p, Column Lot, by Bellasis. 6p, Sandy Bay Valley, by H. Salt, 1809. 8p, View from Castle terrace, by Bellasis. 9p, The Briars, 1815. 10p, Plantation House, by J. Wathen, 1821. 15p, Longwood House, by Wathen, 1821. 18p, St. Paul's Church, by Vincent Brooks. 26p, St. James's Valley, by Capt. Hastings, 1815. 40p, St. Matthew's Church, Longwood, by Brooks. £1, St. Helena and sailing ship, by Bellasis. £2, Sugar Loaf Hill, by Wathen, 1821.

Wmk. 373

1976, Nov. 28 Litho. *Perf. 14*

Size: 38½x25mm

298 A52	1p multicolored	.15	.15
299 A52	3p multicolored	.15	.15
300 A52	5p multicolored	.15	.15
301 A52	6p multicolored	.15	.15
302 A52	8p multicolored	.20	.20
303 A52	9p multicolored	.20	.20
304 A52	10p multicolored	.25	.25
305 A52	15p multicolored	.40	.40
306 A52	18p multicolored	.50	.50
307 A52	26p multicolored	.70	.70
308 A52	40p multicolored	.95	.95

Size: 47½x35mm

Perf. 13½

309 A52	£1 multicolored	2.50	2.50
310 A52	£2 multicolored	5.00	5.00
	Nos. 298-310 (13)	11.30	11.30

Issue dates: 1p, 3p, 5p, 8p, 10p, 18p, 26p, 40p, £1, Sept. 28; others Nov. 23.
1p, 10p and £2 reissued inscribed 1982.
For overprints see Nos. 376-377.

Royal Party Leaving St. Helena, 1947 — A53

Designs: 15p, Queen's scepter and dove. 26p, Prince Philip paying homage to the Queen.

1977, Feb. 7 Wmk. 373 *Perf. 13*

311 A53	8p multicolored	.20	.20
312 A53	15p multicolored	.35	.35
313 A53	26p multicolored	.70	.70
	Nos. 311-313 (3)	1.25	1.25

25th anniv. of the reign of Elizabeth II.

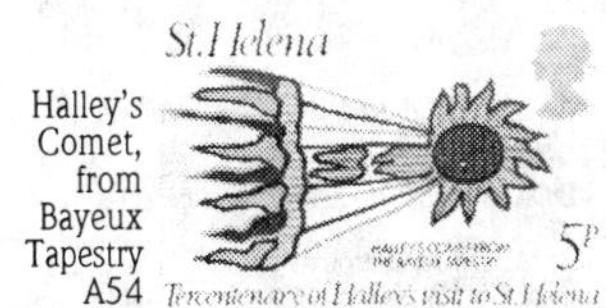

Halley's Comet, from Bayeux Tapestry A54

Designs: 8p, 17th century sextant. 27p, Edmund Halley and Halley's Mount, St. Helena.

1977, Aug. 23 Litho. *Perf. 14*

314 A54	5p multicolored	.55	.55
315 A54	8p multicolored	.80	.80
316 A54	27p multicolored	2.25	2.25
	Nos. 314-316 (3)	3.60	3.60

Edmund Halley's visit to St. Helena, 300th anniv.

Elizabeth II Coronation Anniversary Issue

Common Design Types

Souvenir Sheet

Unwmk.

1978, June 2 Litho. *Perf. 15*

317	Sheet of 6	3.00	3.00
a.	CD326 25p Black dragon of Ulster	.45	.45
b.	CD327 25p Elizabeth II	.45	.45
c.	CD328 25p Sea Lion	.45	.45

No. 317 contains 2 se-tenant strips of Nos. 317a-317c, separated by horizontal gutter.

St. Helena, 17th Century Engraving A55

Designs: 5p, 9p, 15p, Various Chinese porcelain and other utensils salvaged from wreck. 8p, Bronze cannon. 20p, Dutch East Indiaman.

Perf. 14½

1978, Aug. 14 Litho. Wmk. 373

318 A55	3p multicolored	.15	.15
319 A55	5p multicolored	.20	.20
320 A55	8p multicolored	.30	.30
321 A55	9p multicolored	.35	.35
322 A55	15p multicolored	.55	.55
323 A55	20p multicolored	.75	.75
	Nos. 318-323 (6)	2.30	2.30

Wreck of the Witte Leeuw, 1613.

"Discovery" A56

Capt. Cook's voyages: 8p, Cook's portable observatory. 12p, Pharnaceum acidum (plant), after sketch by Joseph Banks. 25p, Capt. Cook, after Flaxman/Wedgwood medallion.

1979, Feb. 19 Litho. *Perf. 11*

324 A56	3p multicolored	.15	.15
325 A56	8p multicolored	.40	.30
326 A56	12p multicolored	.55	.50

Litho.; Embossed

327 A56	25p multicolored	1.10	.95
	Nos. 324-327 (4)	2.20	1.90

St. Helena No. 176 A57

Designs: 5p, Rowland Hill and his signature, vert. 20p, St. Helena No. 8. 32p, St. Helena No. 49.

1979, Aug. 20 Litho. *Perf. 14*

328 A57	5p multicolored	.15	.15
329 A57	8p multicolored	.15	.15
330 A57	20p multicolored	.45	.45
331 A57	32p multicolored	.65	.65
	Nos. 328-331 (4)	1.40	1.40

Sir Rowland Hill (1795-1879), originator of penny postage.

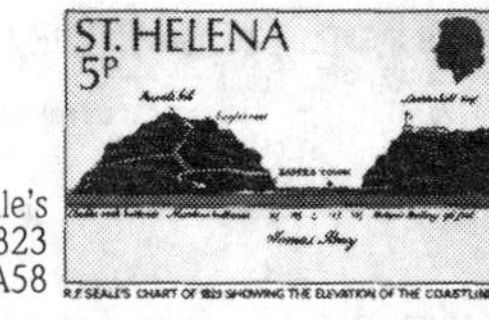

Seale's Chart, 1823 A58

Designs: 8p, Jamestown and Inclined Plane, 1829. 50p, Inclined Plane (stairs), 1979, vert.

1979, Dec. 10 Litho. *Perf. 14*

332 A58	5p multicolored	.15	.15
333 A58	8p multicolored	.15	.15
334 A58	50p multicolored	1.10	1.10
	Nos. 332-334 (3)	1.40	1.40

Inclined Plane, 150th anniversary.

Tomb of Napoleon I, 1848 — A59

Empress Eugenie: 8p, Landing at St. Helena. 62p, Visiting Napoleon's tomb.

1980, Feb. 23 Litho. *Perf. 14½*

335 A59	5p multicolored	.15	.15
336 A59	8p multicolored	.20	.20
337 A59	62p multicolored	1.65	1.65
a.	Souvenir sheet of 3, #335-337	2.00	2.00
	Nos. 335-337 (3)	2.00	2.00

Visit of Empress Eugenie (widow of Napoleon III) to St. Helena, centenary.

East Indiaman, London 1980 Emblem — A60

1980, May 6 Litho. *Perf. 14½*

338 A60	5p shown	.15	.15
339 A60	8p "Dolphin" postal stone	.20	.20
340 A60	47p Jamestown castle postal stone	1.10	1.10
a.	Souvenir sheet of 3, #338-340	1.50	1.50
	Nos. 338-340 (3)	1.45	1.45

London 1980 Intl. Stamp Exhib., May 6-14.

Queen Mother Elizabeth Birthday Issue

Common Design Type

1980, Aug. 18 Litho. *Perf. 14*

341 CD330	24p multicolored	.60	.60

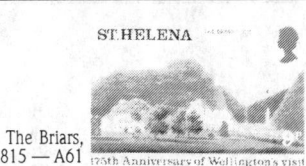

The Briars, 1815 — A61

1980, Nov. 17 Litho. *Perf. 14*

342 A61	9p shown	.25	.25
343 A61	30p Wellington, by Goya, vert.	.80	.80

Duke of Wellington's visit to St. Helena, 175th anniv. Nos. 342-343 issued in sheets of 10 with gutter giving historical background.

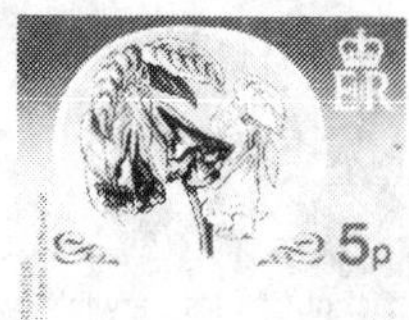

Redwood Flower — A62

1981, Jan. 5 *Perf. 13½*

344 A62	5p shown	.15	.15
345 A62	8p Old father-live-forever	.20	.20
346 A62	15p Gumwood	.40	.40
347 A62	27p Black cabbage	.70	.70
	Nos. 344-347 (4)	1.45	1.45

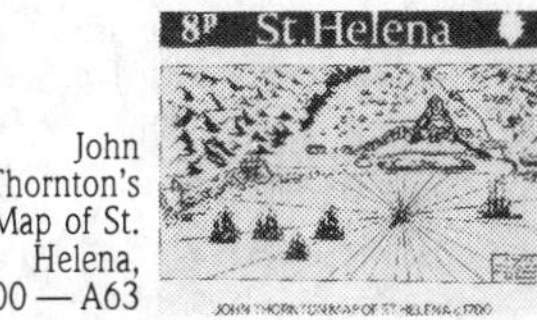

John Thornton's Map of St. Helena, 1700 — A63

1981, May 22 Litho. *Perf. 14½*

348 A63	5p Reinel Portolan Chart, 1530	.15	.15
349 A63	8p shown	.15	.15
350 A63	20p St. Helena, 1815	.40	.40
351 A63	30p St. Helena, 1817	.60	.60
	Nos. 348-351 (4)	1.30	1.30

Souvenir Sheet

352 A63	24p Gastaldi's map of Africa, 16th cent.	.75	.75

Royal Wedding Issue

Common Design Type

Wmk. 373

1981, July 22 Litho. *Perf. 14*

353 CD331	14p Bouquet	.30	.30
354 CD331	29p Charles	.65	.65
355 CD331	32p Couple	.70	.70
	Nos. 353-355 (3)	1.65	1.65

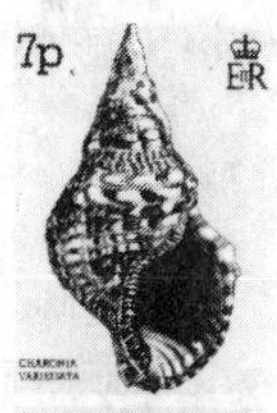

Charonia Variegata — A64

Traffic Guards Taking Oath — A65

1981, Sept. 10 Litho. *Perf. 14*

356 A64	7p shown	.20	.20
357 A64	10p Cypraea spurca sanctahelenae	.30	.30
358 A64	25p Janthina janthina	.75	.75
359 A64	53p Pinna rudis	1.65	1.65
	Nos. 356-359 (4)	2.90	2.90

1981, Nov. 5

360 A65	7p shown	.20	.20
361 A65	11p Posting signs	.30	.30
362 A65	25p Animal care	.65	.65
363 A65	50p Duke of Edinburgh	1.25	1.25
	Nos. 360-363 (4)	2.40	2.40

Duke of Edinburgh's Awards, 25th anniv.

St. Helena Dragonfly A66

1982, Jan. 4 Litho. *Perf. 14½*
364 A66 7p shown .15 .15
365 A66 10p Burchell's beetle .35 .35
366 A66 25p Cockroach wasp .85 .85
367 A66 32p Earwig 1.10 1.10
Nos. 364-367 (4) 2.45 2.45

See Nos. 386-389.

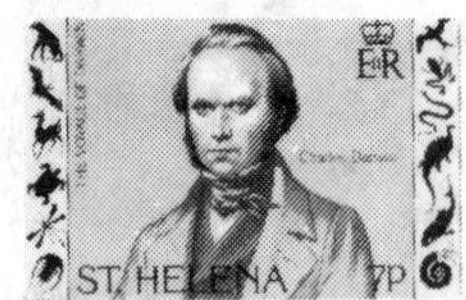

Sesquicentennial of Charles Darwin's Visit — A67

1982, Apr. 19 Litho. *Perf. 14*
368 A67 7p Portrait .20 .20
369 A67 14p Flagstaff Hill, hammer .45 .45
370 A67 25p Ring-necked pheasants .75 .75
371 A67 29p Beagle .90 .90
Nos. 368-371 (4) 2.30 2.30

Princess Diana Issue
Common Design Type

1982, July 1 Litho. *Perf. 14*
372 CD333 7p Arms .15 .15
373 CD333 11p Honeymoon .25 .25
374 CD333 29p Diana .65 .65
375 CD333 55p Portrait 1.25 1.25
Nos. 372-375 (4) 2.30 2.30

Nos. 305, 307 Overprinted: "1st PARTICIPATION / COMMONWEALTH GAMES 1982"

1982, Oct. 25 Litho. *Perf. 14*
376 A52 15p multicolored .40 .40
377 A52 26p multicolored .70 .70

Scouting Year A68

1982, Nov. 29
378 A68 3p Baden-Powell, vert. .15 .15
379 A68 11p Campfire .25 .25
380 A68 29p Canon Walcott, vert. .75 .75
381 A68 59p Thompsons Wood camp 1.50 1.50
Nos. 378-381 (4) 2.65 2.65

Coastline from Jamestown A69

1983, Jan.
382 A69 7p King and Queen Rocks, vert. .15 .15
383 A69 11p Turk's Cap, vert. .25 .25
384 A69 29p shown .75 .75
385 A69 55p Munden's Point 1.50 1.50
Nos. 382-385 (4) 2.65 2.65

Insect Type of 1982

1983, Apr. 22 Litho. *Perf. 14½*
386 A66 11p Death's-head hawk-moth .30 .30
387 A66 15p Saldid-shore bug .40 .40
388 A66 29p Click beetle .80 .80
389 A66 59p Weevil 1.50 1.50
Nos. 386-389 (4) 3.00 3.00

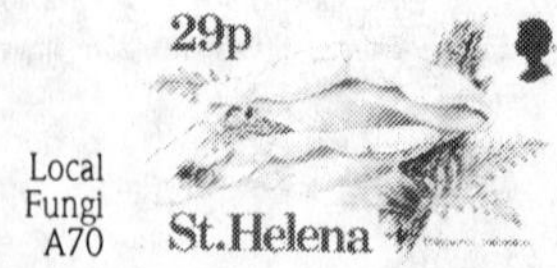

Local Fungi A70

Wmk. 373

1983, June 16 Litho. *Perf. 14*
390 A70 11p Coriolus versicolor, vert. .30 .30
391 A70 15p Pluteus brunneisucus, vert. .45 .45
392 A70 29p Polyporus induratus .85 .85
393 A70 59p Coprinus angulatus, vert. 1.65 1.65
Nos. 390-393 (4) 3.25 3.25

Local Birds — A71
Christmas 1983 — A72

1983, Sept. 12 Litho. *Perf. 14x14½*
394 A71 7p Padda oryzivora .20 .20
395 A71 15p Foudia madagascariensis .40 .40
396 A71 33p Estrilda astrild .90 .90
397 A71 59p Serinus flaviventris 1.65 1.65
Nos. 394-397 (4) 3.15 3.15

Souvenir Sheet

1983, Oct. 17 Litho. *Perf. 14x13½*

Stained Glass, Parish Church of St. Michael.

398 Sheet of 10 3.50 3.50
a. A72 10p multicolored .25 .25
b. A72 15p multicolored .40 .40

Sheet contains strips of 10p and 15p with center margin telling St. Helena story.
See Nos. 424-427, 442-445.

150th Anniv. of the Colony — A73

1984, Jan. 3 Litho. *Perf. 14*
399 A73 1p No. 101 .15 .15
400 A73 3p No. 102 .15 .15
401 A73 6p No. 103 .15 .15
402 A73 7p No. 104 .20 .20
403 A73 11p No. 105 .30 .30
404 A73 15p No. 106 .40 .40
405 A73 29p No. 107 .85 .85
406 A73 33p No. 109 .95 .95
407 A73 59p No. 110 1.65 1.65
408 A73 £1 No. 108 2.75 2.75
409 A73 £2 New coat of arms 5.75 5.75
Nos. 399-409 (11) 13.30 13.30

Visit of Prince Andrew A74

1984, Apr. 4 Litho. *Perf. 14*
410 A74 11p Andrew, Invincible .30 .30
411 A74 60p Andrew, Herald 1.65 1.65

Lloyd's List Issue
Common Design Type

1984, May *Perf. 14½x14*
412 CD335 10p St. Helena, 1814 .25 .25
413 CD335 18p Solomon's facade .40 .40
414 CD335 25p Lloyd's Coffee House .60 .60
415 CD335 50p Papanui, 1898 1.25 1.25
Nos. 412-415 (4) 2.50 2.50

New Coin Issue — A75

1984, July *Perf. 14*
416 A75 10p 2p, Donkey .30 .30
417 A75 15p 5p, Wire bird .45 .45
418 A75 29p 1p, Yellowfin tuna .90 .90
419 A75 50p 10p, Arum lily 1.50 1.50
Nos. 416-419 (4) 3.15 3.15

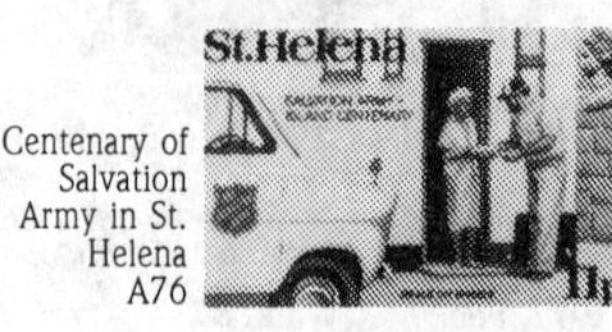

Centenary of Salvation Army in St. Helena A76

1984, Sept. Litho. Wmk. 373
420 A76 7p Secretary Rebecca Fuller, vert. .20 .20
421 A76 11p Meals on Wheels service .35 .35
422 A76 25p Jamestown SA Hall .70 .70
423 A76 60p Hymn playing, clock tower 1.75 1.75
Nos. 420-423 (4) 3.00 3.00

Stained Glass Windows Type of 1983

1984, Nov. 9
424 A72 6p St. Helena visits prisoners .15 .15
425 A72 10p Betrothal of St. Helena .30 .30
426 A72 15p Marriage of St. Helena & Constantius .40 .40
427 A72 33p Birth of Constantine .90 .90
Nos. 424-427 (4) 1.75 1.75

Queen Mother 85th Birthday Issue
Common Design Type

Perf. 14½x14

1985, June 7 Litho. Wmk. 384
428 CD336 11p Portrait, age 2 .25 .25
429 CD336 15p Queen Mother, Elizabeth II .40 .40
430 CD336 29p Attending ballet, Covent Garden .75 .75
431 CD336 55p Holding Prince Henry 1.50 1.50
Nos. 428-431 (4) 2.90 2.90

Souvenir Sheet

432 CD336 70p Queen Mother and Ford V8 Pilot 2.50 2.50

Marine Life — A78

Perf. 13x13½

1985, July 12 Litho. Wmk. 373
433 A78 7p Rock bullseye .20 .20
434 A78 11p Mackerel .30 .30
435 A78 15p Skipjack tuna .45 .45
436 A78 33p Yellowfin tuna 1.00 1.00
437 A78 50p Stump 1.40 1.40
Nos. 433-437 (5) 3.35 3.35

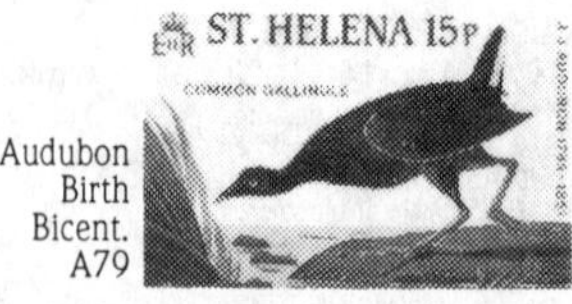

Audubon Birth Bicent. A79

Portrait of naturalist and his illustrations of American bird species.

1985, Sept. 2 *Perf. 14*
438 A79 11p John Audubon, vert. .35 .35
439 A79 15p Common gallinule .45 .45
440 A79 25p Tropic bird .80 .80
441 A79 60p Noddy tern 2.00 2.00
Nos. 438-441 (4) 3.60 3.60

Stained Glass Windows Type of 1983

Christmas: 7p, St. Helena journeys to the Holy Land. 10p, Zambres slays the bull. 15p, The bull restored to life, conversion of St. Helena. 60p, Resurrection of the corpse, the true cross identified.

1985, Oct. 14
442 A72 7p multicolored .20 .20
443 A72 10p multicolored .30 .30
444 A72 15p multicolored .50 .50
445 A72 60p multicolored 1.90 1.90
Nos. 442-445 (4) 2.90 2.90

Society Banners A80

Designs: 10p, Church Provident Society fo Women. 11p, Working Men's Christian Assoc. 25p Church Benefit Society for Children. 29p, Mechanics & Friendly Benefit Society. 33p, Ancient Orde of Foresters.

Perf. 13x13½

1986, Jan. 7 Wmk. 38
446 A80 10p multicolored .30 .3
447 A80 11p multicolored .35 .3
448 A80 25p multicolored .75 .7
449 A80 29p multicolored .85 .8
450 A80 33p multicolored 1.00 1.0
Nos. 446-450 (5) 3.25 3.2

Queen Elizabeth II 60th Birthday
Common Design Type

Designs: 10p, Making 21st birthday broadcas royal tour of South Africa, 1947. 15p, In robes o state, Throne Room, Buckingham Palace, Silve Jubilee, 1977. 20p, Onboard HMS Implacable, e route to South Africa, 1947. 50p, State visit to US 1976. 65p, Visiting Crown Agents' offices, 1983.

1986, Apr. 21 *Perf. 14½*
451 CD337 10p scarlet, blk & sil .25 .2
452 CD337 15p ultra & multi .40 .4
453 CD337 20p green, blk & sil .50 .5
454 CD337 50p violet & multi 1.40 1.4
455 CD337 65p rose vio & multi 1.75 1.7
Nos. 451-455 (5) 4.30 4.3

For overprints see Nos. 488-492.

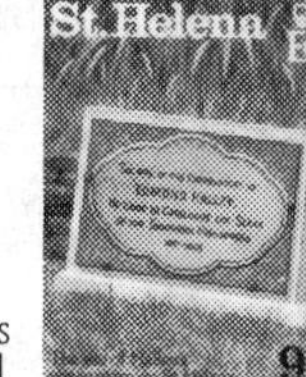

Halley's Comet — A81

Designs: 9p, Site of Halley's observatory on St Helena. 12p, Edmond Halley, astronomer. 20p Halley's planisphere of the southern stars. 65p, Voyage to St. Helena on the Unity.

1986, May 15 Wmk. 373 *Perf. 14½*
456 A81 9p multicolored .35 .3
457 A81 12p multicolored .45 .4
458 A81 20p multicolored .55 .5
459 A81 65p multicolored 1.50 1.5
Nos. 456-459 (4) 2.85 2.8

Royal Wedding Issue, 1986
Common Design Type

Designs: 10p, Informal portrait. 40p, Andrew i dress uniform at parade.

Wmk. 384

1986, July 23 Litho. *Perf. 1*
460 CD338 10p multicolored .30 .3
461 CD338 40p multicolored 1.25 1.2

Explorers and Ships A82

Designs: 1p, James Ross (1800-62), Erebus. 3p Robert FitzRoy (1805-65), Beagle. 5p, Adam Johann von Krusenstern (1770-1846), Nadezhda Russia. 9p, William Bligh (1754-1817), Resolution 10p, Otto von Kotzebue (1786-1846), Rurik, Germany. 12p, Philip Carteret (1639-82), Swallow 15p, Thomas Cavendish (c.1560-92), Desire. 20p Louis-Antoine de Bougainville (1729-1811), L Boudeuse, France. 25p, Fyodor Petrovitch Litk (1797-1882), Seniavin, Russia. 40p, Louis Isidor Duperrey (1786-1865), La Coquille, France. 60p John Byron (1723-86), Dolphin. £1, James Cook Endeavour. £2, Jules Dumont d'Urville (1790 1842), L'Astrolabe, France.

Perf. 14½

1986, Sept. 22 Litho. Wmk. 38
462 A82 1p red brown .15 .1
463 A82 3p bright ultra .15 .1
464 A82 5p olive green .15 .1
465 A82 9p deep claret .25 .2
466 A82 10p sepia .30 .3
467 A82 12p brt blue green .35 .3

468 A82 15p brown lake .45 .45
469 A82 20p sapphire .60 .60
470 A82 25p red brown .75 .75
471 A82 40p myrtle green 1.25 1.25
472 A82 60p brown 1.75 1.75
473 A82 £1 Prussian blue 3.00 3.00
474 A82 £2 bright violet 6.00 6.00
Nos. 462-474 (13) 15.15 15.15

Ships of Royal Visitors A83

Portraits and vessels: 9p, Prince Edward, HMS Repulse, 1925. 13p, King George VI, HMS Vanguard, 1947. 38p, Prince Philip, HMY Britannia, 1957. 45p, Prince Andrew, HMS Herald, 1984.

1987, Feb. 16 Wmk. 373 *Perf. 14*
475 A83 9p multicolored .40 .40
476 A83 13p multicolored .60 .60
477 A83 38p multicolored 1.75 1.75
478 A83 45p multicolored 2.00 2.00
Nos. 475-478 (4) 4.75 4.75

Rare Plants — A84

1987, Aug. 3 *Perf. 14½x14*
479 A84 9p St. Helena tea plant .45 .45
480 A84 13p Baby's toes .70 .70
481 A84 38p Salad plant 2.00 2.00
482 A84 45p Scrubwood 2.25 2.25
Nos. 479-482 (4) 5.40 5.40

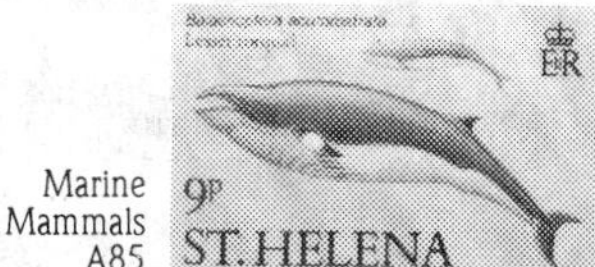

Marine Mammals A85

Wmk. 384

1987, Oct. 24 Litho. *Perf. 14*
483 A85 9p Lesser rorqual .50 .50
484 A85 13p Risso's dolphin .75 .75
485 A85 45p Sperm whale 2.75 2.75
486 A85 60p Euphrosyne dolphin 3.75 3.75
Nos. 483-486 (4) 7.75 7.75

Souvenir Sheet

487 A85 75p Humpback whale 3.75 3.75

Nos. 451-455 Ovptd. "40TH WEDDING ANNIVERSARY" in Silver.

Perf. 14½

1987, Dec. 9 Litho. Wmk. 384
488 CD337 10p scarlet, blk & sil .30 .30
489 CD337 15p ultra & multi .40 .40
490 CD337 20p green, blk & sil .55 .55
491 CD337 50p violet & multi 1.40 1.40
492 CD337 65p rose vio & multi 1.75 1.75
Nos. 488-492 (5) 4.40 4.40

Australia Bicentennial A86

Ships and signatures: 9p, HMS Defence, 1691, and William Dampier. 13p, HMS Resolution, 1775, and James Cook. 45p, HMS Providence, 1792, and William Bligh. 60p, HMS Beagle, 1836, and Charles Darwin.

Perf. 14½

1988, Mar. 1 Litho. Wmk. 384
493 A86 9p multicolored .40 .40
494 A86 13p multicolored .60 .60
495 A86 45p multicolored 2.25 2.25
496 A86 60p multicolored 2.75 2.75
Nos. 493-496 (4) 6.00 6.00

Christmas — A87

Rare Plants — A88

Religious paintings by unknown artists: 5p, The Holy Family with Child. 20p, Madonna. 38p, The Holy Family with St. John. 60p, The Holy Virgin with the Child.

Wmk. 373

1988, Oct. 11 Litho. *Perf. 14*
497 A87 5p multicolored .20 .20
498 A87 20p multicolored .65 .65
499 A87 38p multicolored 1.25 1.25
500 A87 60p multicolored 2.00 2.00
Nos. 497-500 (4) 4.10 4.10

Lloyds of London, 300th Anniv.

Common Design Type

Designs: 9p, Underwriting room, 1886. 20p, Edinburgh Castle, horiz. 45p, Bosun Bird, horiz. 60p, Spangereid on fire off St. Helena, 1920.

Wmk. 384

1988, Nov. 1 Litho. *Perf. 14*
501 CD341 9p multicolored .25 .25
502 CD341 20p multicolored .60 .60
503 CD341 45p multicolored 1.40 1.40
504 CD341 60p multicolored 1.75 1.75
Nos. 501-504 (4) 4.00 4.00

1989, Jan. 6 *Perf. 14*
505 A88 9p Ebony .30 .30
506 A88 20p St. Helena lobelia .70 .70
507 A88 45p Large bellflower 1.50 1.50
508 A88 60p She cabbage tree 2.00 2.00
Nos. 505-508 (4) 4.50 4.50

Flags and Military Uniforms, 1815 — A89

Designs: 9p, Soldier, 53rd Foot. 13p, Officer, 53rd Foot. 20p, Royal marine. 45p, Officer, 66th Foot. 60p, Soldier, 66th Foot.

1989, June 5 Litho. *Perf. 14*
509 Strip of 5 5.00 5.00
a. A89 9p multicolored .30 .30
b. A89 13p multicolored .45 .45
c. A89 20p multicolored .70 .70
d. A89 45p multicolored 1.50 1.50
e. A89 60p multicolored 2.00 2.00

Nos. 509a-509e Overprinted

1989, July 7 Litho. *Perf. 14*
510 Strip of 5 5.00 5.00
a. A89 9p multicolored .30 .30
b. A89 13p multicolored .45 .45
c. A89 20p multicolored .70 .70
d. A89 45p multicolored 1.50 1.50
e. A89 60p multicolored 2.00 2.00

PHILEXFRANCE '89.

New Central (Prince Andrew) School — A90

1989, Aug. 24 *Perf. 14½*
511 A90 13p Agriculture .50 .50
512 A90 20p Literacy .75 .75
513 A90 25p Building exterior .95 .95
514 A90 60p Campus 2.25 2.25
Nos. 511-514 (4) 4.45 4.45

Christmas — A91

10p, The Madonna with the Pear, by Durer. 20p, The Holy Family Under the Apple Tree, by Rubens. 45p, The Virgin in the Meadow, by Raphael. 60p, The Holy Family with Saint John, by Raphael.

1989, Oct. 10 Wmk. 373 *Perf. 14*
515 A91 10p multicolored .30 .30
516 A91 20p multicolored .65 .65
517 A91 45p multicolored 1.40 1.40
518 A91 60p multicolored 1.90 1.90
Nos. 515-518 (4) 4.25 4.25

Early Vehicles A92

1989, Dec. 1 Wmk. 384 *Perf. 14½*
519 A92 9p 1930 Chevrolet .30 .30
520 A92 20p 1929 Austin Seven .65 .65
521 A92 45p 1929 Morris Cowley 1.40 1.40
522 A92 60p 1932 Sunbeam 1.90 1.90
Nos. 519-522 (4) 4.25 4.25

Souvenir Sheet

523 A92 £1 Ford Model A 3.00 3.00

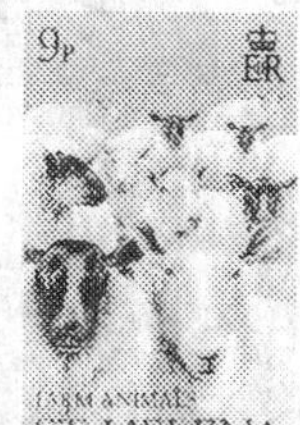

Farm Animals — A93

1990, Feb. 1 Litho. *Perf. 14*
524 A93 9p Sheep .30 .30
525 A93 13p Pigs .40 .40
526 A93 45p Cow, calf 1.40 1.40
527 A93 60p Geese 1.90 1.90
Nos. 524-527 (4) 4.00 4.00

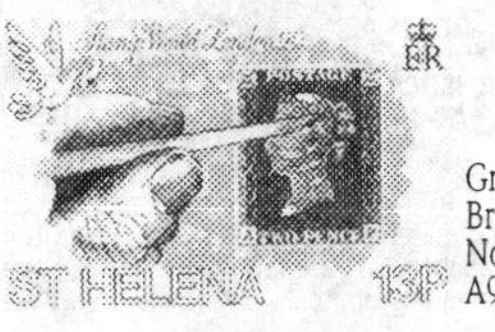

Great Britain No. 2 A94

Exhibition emblem and: 20p, Great Britain No. 1. 38p, Mail delivery to branch p.o. 45p, Main p.o., mail van.

1990, May 3 Wmk. 373
528 A94 13p shown .40 .40
529 A94 20p multicolored .70 .70
530 A94 38p multicolored 1.25 1.25
531 A94 45p multicolored 1.40 1.40
Nos. 528-531 (4) 3.75 3.75

Stamp World London '90, 150th anniv. of the Penny Black.

Queen Mother, 90th Birthday

Common Design Types

1990, Aug. 4 Wmk. 384 *Perf. 14x15*
532 CD343 25p As Duchess of York, 1923 1.00 1.00

Perf. 14½

533 CD344 £1 Visiting communal feeding center, 1940 3.75 3.75

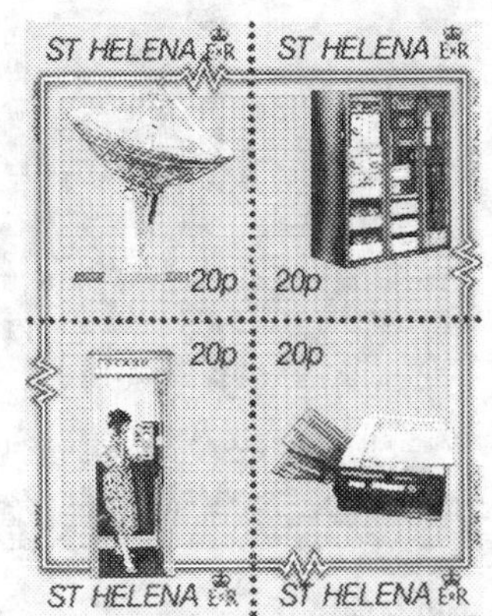

Telecommunications — A95

1990, July 28 Wmk. 373 *Perf. 14*
534 A95 Block of 4 3.50 3.50
a.-d. 20p any single .80 .80

Dane, 1857 — A96

Designs: 20p, RMS St. Helena offloading cargo. 38p, Launching new RMS St. Helena, 1989. 45p, Duke of York launching new RMS St. Helena. £1, New RMS St. Helena.

1990, Sept. 13 *Perf. 14½*
535 A96 13p multicolored .45 .45
536 A96 20p multicolored .75 .75
537 A96 38p multicolored 1.40 1.40
538 A96 45p multicolored 1.65 1.65
Nos. 535-538 (4) 4.25 4.25

Souvenir Sheet

539 A96 £1 multicolored 4.50 4.50

See Ascension Nos. 493-497, Tristan da Cunha Nos. 482-486.

Christmas A97

Parish Churches.

1990, Oct. 18 *Perf. 13*
540 A97 10p Baptist Chapel, Sandy Bay .35 .35
541 A97 13p St. Martin in the Hills .45 .45
542 A97 20p St. Helena and the Cross .65 .65
543 A97 38p St. James Church 1.40 1.40
544 A97 45p St. Paul's Church 1.65 1.65
Nos. 540-544 (5) 4.50 4.50

Removal of Napoleon's Body from St. Helena, 150th Anniv. — A98

Designs: 13p, Funeral cortege, Jamestown wharf. 20p, Moving coffin to *Belle Poule*, James Bay. 38p, Transfer of coffin from *Belle Poule* to *Normandie*, Cherbourg. 45p, Napoleon's Tomb, St. Helena.

1990, Dec. 15 Wmk. 373 *Perf. 14*
545 A98 13p green & black .45 .45
546 A98 20p blue & black .75 .75
547 A98 38p violet & black 1.40 1.40
548 A98 45p multicolored 1.65 1.65
Nos. 545-548 (4) 4.25 4.25

A99

A100

Military Uniforms 1897: 13p, Officer, Leicestershire Regiment. 15p, Officer, York and Lancaster Regiment. 20p, Color Sergeant, Leicestershire Regiment. 38p, Drummer/Flautist, York and Lancaster Regiment. 45p, Lance Corporal, York and Lancaster Regiment.

1991, May 2

549 A99 13p multicolored .55 .55
550 A99 15p multicolored .60 .60
551 A99 20p multicolored .85 .85
552 A99 38p multicolored 1.65 1.65
553 A99 45p multicolored 1.90 1.90
Nos. 549-553 (5) 5.55 5.55

Elizabeth & Philip, Birthdays
Common Design Types

1991, July 1 Wmk. 384 *Perf. 14¹/₂*

554 CD345 25p multicolored .85 .85
555 CD346 25p multicolored .85 .85
a. Pair, #554-555 + label 1.75 1.75

1991, Nov. 2 Wmk. 373 *Perf. 14*

Christmas (Paintings): 10p, Madonna and Child, Titian. 13p, Holy Family, Mengs. 20p, Madonna and Child, Dyce. 38p, Two Trinities, Murillo. 45p, Virgin and Child, Bellini.

556 A100 10p multicolored .35 .35
557 A100 13p multicolored .45 .45
558 A100 20p multicolored .65 .65
559 A100 38p multicolored 1.40 1.40
560 A100 45p multicolored 1.65 1.65
Nos. 556-560 (5) 4.50 4.50

Phila Nippon '91 — A101

Motorcycles: 13p, Matchless 346cc (ohv), 1947. 20p, Triumph Tiger 100, 500cc, 1950. 38p, Honda CD 175cc, 1967. 45p, Yamaha DTE 400, 1976. 65p, Suzuki RM 250cc, 1984.

Perf. 14x14¹/₂

1991, Nov. 16 Litho. Wmk. 384

561 A101 13p multicolored .45 .45
562 A101 20p multicolored .75 .75
563 A101 38p multicolored 1.40 1.40
564 A101 45p multicolored 1.65 1.65
Nos. 561-564 (4) 4.25 4.25

Souvenir Sheet

565 A101 65p multicolored 3.50 3.50

Discovery of America, 500th Anniv. — A102

Wmk. 373

1992, Jan. 24 Litho. *Perf. 14*

566 A102 15p STV Eye of the Wind .55 .55
567 A102 25p STV Soren Larsen .95 .95
568 A102 35p Santa Maria, Nina & Pinta 1.25 1.25
569 A102 50p Columbus, Santa Maria 1.75 1.75
Nos. 566-569 (4) 4.50 4.50

World Columbian Stamp Expo '92, Chicago and Genoa '92 Intl. Philatelic Exhibitions.

Queen Elizabeth II's Accession to the Throne, 40th Anniv.
Common Design Type

1992, Feb. 6

570 CD349 11p multicolored .45 .45
571 CD349 15p multicolored .55 .55
572 CD349 25p multicolored .95 .95
573 CD349 35p multicolored 1.40 1.40
574 CD349 50p multicolored 1.90 1.90
Nos. 570-574 (5) 5.25 5.25

Liberation of Falkland Islands, 10th Anniv. — A103

Designs: No. 579a, 13p + 3p, like No. 575. b, 20p + 4p, like No. 576. c, 38p + 8p, like No. 577. d, 45p + 8p, like No. 578.

1992, June 12

575 A103 13p HMS Ledbury .50 .50
576 A103 20p HMS Brecon .75 .75
577 A103 38p RMS St. Helena 1.50 1.50
578 A103 45p First mail drop, 1982 1.75 1.75
Nos. 575-578 (4) 4.50 4.50

Souvenir Sheet

579 A103 Sheet of 4, #a.-d. 5.00 5.00

Surtax for Soldiers', Sailors' and Airmens' Families Association.

Christmas — A104

Children in scenes from Nativity plays: 13p, Angel, shepherds. 15p, Magi, shepherds. 20p, Joseph, Mary. 45p, Nativity scene.

1992, Oct. 12 Wmk. 384

580 A104 13p multicolored .50 .50
581 A104 15p multicolored .60 .60
582 A104 20p multicolored .80 .80
583 A104 45p multicolored 1.75 1.75
Nos. 580-583 (4) 3.65 3.65

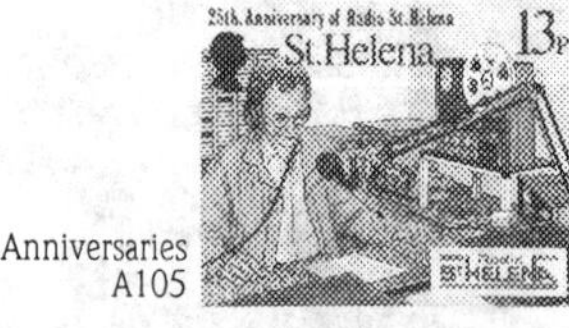

Anniversaries A105

Designs: 13p, Man broadcasting at radio station. 20p, Scouts marching in parade. 38p, Breadfruit, HMS Providence, 1792. 45p, Governor Colonel Brooke, Plantation House.

1992, Dec. 4 Wmk. 373 *Perf. 14¹/₂*

584 A105 13p multicolored .45 .45
585 A105 20p multicolored .75 .75
586 A105 38p multicolored 1.40 1.40
587 A105 45p multicolored 1.65 1.65
Nos. 584-587 (4) 4.25 4.25

Radio St. Helena, 25th anniv. (#584). Scouting on St. Helena, 75th anniv. (#585). Captain Bligh's visit, 200th anniv. (#586). Plantation House, 200th anniv. (#587).

Flowers — A106

Perf. 14¹/₂x14

1993, Mar. 19 Litho. Wmk. 384

588 A106 9p Moses in the bulrush .30 .30
589 A106 13p Periwinkle .50 .50
590 A106 20p Everlasting flower .70 .70
591 A106 38p Cigar plant 1.25 1.25
592 A106 45p Lobelia erinus 1.50 1.50
Nos. 588-592 (5) 4.25 4.25

See Nos. 635-640.

Wirebird A107

Perf. 13¹/₂

1993, Aug. 16 Litho. Wmk. 373

593 A107 3p Adult with eggs .15 .15
594 A107 5p Male, brooding female .15 .15
595 A107 12p Downy young, adult .40 .40
596 A107 25p Two immature birds .80 .80
597 A107 40p Adult in flight 1.25 1.25
598 A107 60p Immature bird 1.75 1.75
Nos. 593-598 (6) 4.50 4.50

Birds — A108

1993, Aug. 26 *Perf. 14¹/₂*

599 A108 1p Swainson's canary .15 .15
600 A108 3p Chuckar partridge .15 .15
601 A108 11p Pigeon .30 .30
602 A108 12p Waxbill .35 .35
603 A108 15p Common myna .40 .40
604 A108 18p Java sparrow .50 .50
605 A108 25p Red-billed tropicbird .70 .70
606 A108 35p Maderian storm petrel 1.00 1.00
607 A108 75p Madagascar fody 2.25 2.25
a. Souvenir sheet of 1 .95 .95
608 A108 £1 Common fairy tern 3.00 3.00
609 A108 £2 Southern giant petrel 5.75 5.75
610 A108 £5 Wirebird 15.00 15.00
Nos. 599-610 (12) 29.55 29.55

Nos. 599-604, 607, 610 are vert.
No. 607a for Hong Kong '97. Issued: 2/3/97.
See No. 691.

Christmas — A109

Toys: 12p, Teddy bear, soccer ball. 15p, Sailboat, doll. 18p, Paint palette, rocking horse. 25p, Kite, airplane. 60p, Guitar, roller skates.

1993, Oct. 1 *Perf. 13¹/₂x14*

611 A109 12p multicolored .35 .35
612 A109 15p multicolored .45 .45
613 A109 18p multicolored .50 .50
614 A109 25p multicolored .70 .70
615 A109 60p multicolored 1.75 1.75
Nos. 611-615 (5) 3.75 3.75

Flowers — A110

Photographs: No. 616a, Arum lily. No. 617a, Ebony. No. 618a, Shell ginger.
Nos. 616b-618b: Child's painting of same flower as in "a."

1994, Jan. 6 Wmk. 384 *Perf. 14*

616 A110 12p Pair, #a.-b. .65 .65
617 A110 25p Pair, #a.-b. 1.40 1.40
618 A110 35p Pair, #a.-b. 1.90 1.90

Pets — A111

Designs: 12p, Abyssinian guinea pig. 25p, Common tabby cat. 53p, Plain white, black rabbits. 60p, Golden labrador.

1994, Feb. 18 Wmk. 373 *Perf. 14¹/*

619 A111 12p multicolored .45 .4
620 A111 25p multicolored .90 .9
621 A111 53p multicolored 1.90 1.9
622 A111 60p multicolored 2.00 2.0
Nos. 619-622 (4) 5.25 5.2

Hong Kong '94.

Fish — A112

12p, Springer's blenny. 25p, Bastard five finger. 53p, Deepwater gurnard. 60p, Green fish.

1994, June 6 Wmk. 384 *Perf. 1*

623 A112 12p multicolored .35 .3
624 A112 25p multicolored .75 .7
625 A112 53p multicolored 1.65 1.6
626 A112 60p multicolored 1.75 1.7
Nos. 623-626 (4) 4.50 4.5

Butterflies A113

1994, Aug. 9 Wmk. 37

627 A113 12p Lampides boeticus .35 .3
628 A113 25p Cynthia cardui .75 .7
629 A113 53p Hypolimnas bolina 1.65 1.6
630 A113 60p Danaus chrysippus 1.75 1.7
Nos. 627-630 (4) 4.50 4.5

Christmas Carols A114

Designs: 12p, "Silent night, holy night..." 15p, "While shepherds watched..." 25p, "Away in a manger..." 38p, "We three kings..." 60p, Angels from the realms of glory.

1994, Oct. 6

631 A114 12p multicolored .50 .5
632 A114 15p multicolored .65 .6
633 A114 25p multicolored 1.00 1.0
634 A114 38p multicolored 1.65 1.6
635 A114 60p multicolored 2.50 2.5
Nos. 631-635 (5) 6.30 6.3

Flower Type of 1993

Perf. 14¹/₂

1994, Dec. 15 Litho. Wmk. 38

636 A106 12p Honeysuckle .35 .3
637 A106 15p Gobblegheer .45 .4
638 A106 25p African lily .80 .8
639 A106 38p Prince of Wales feathers 1.25 1.2
640 A106 60p St. Johns lily 1.90 1.9
Nos. 636-640 (5) 4.75 4.7

Emergency Services A115

Wmk. 384

1995, Feb. 2 Litho. *Perf. 14*

641 A115 12p Fire engine .40 .40
642 A115 25p Inshore rescue craft .80 .80
643 A115 53p Police, rural patrol 1.65 1.65
644 A115 60p Ambulance 1.90 1.90
Nos. 641-644 (4) 4.75 4.75

Harpers Earth Dam Project A116

Designs: a, Site clearance. b, Earthworks in progress. c, Laying the outlet pipe. d, Revetment block protection. e, Completed dam, June 1994.

Perf. 14½

1995, Apr. 6 Litho. Wmk. 373

645 A116 25p Strip of 5, #a.-e. 4.00 4.00

No. 645 is a continuous design.

End of World War II, 50th Anniv.

Common Design Types

Designs: No. 646, CS Lady Denison Pender. No. 647, HMS Dragon. No. 648, RFA Darkdale. No. 649, HMS Hermes. No. 650, St. Helena Rifles on parade. No. 651, Gov. Maj. W.J. Bain Gray during Victory Parade. No. 652, 6-inch gun, Ladder Hill. No. 653, Signal Station, flag hoist signalling VICTORY.

No. 654, Reverse of War Medal 1939-45.

1995, May 8 Wmk. 373 *Perf. 14*

646 CD351 5p multicolored .15 .15
647 CD351 5p multicolored .15 .15
a. Pair, #646-647 .30 .30
648 CD351 12p multicolored .40 .40
649 CD351 12p multicolored .40 .40
a. Pair, #648-649 .80 .80
650 CD351 25p multicolored .75 .75
651 CD351 25p multicolored .75 .75
a. Pair, #650-651 1.50 1.50
652 CD351 53p multicolored 1.65 1.65
653 CD351 53p multicolored 1.65 1.65
a. Pair, #652-653 3.25 3.25
Nos. 646-653 (8) 5.90 5.90

Souvenir Sheet

654 CD352 £1 multicolored 3.25 3.25

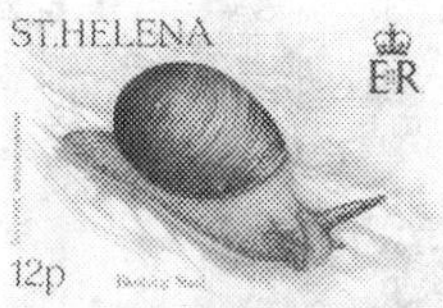

Invertebrates — A117

Designs: 12p, Blushing snail. 25p, Golden sail spider. 53p, Spiky yellow woodlouse. 60p, St. Helena shore crab. £1, Giant earwig.

1995, Aug. 29 Wmk. 373 *Perf. 14*

655 A117 12p multicolored .40 .40
656 A117 25p multicolored .80 .80
657 A117 53p multicolored 1.75 1.75
658 A117 60p multicolored 2.00 2.00
Nos. 655-658 (4) 4.95 4.95

Souvenir Sheet

659 A117 £1 multicolored 3.25 3.25

Souvenir Sheet

Orchids — A118

Designs: a, Epidendrum ibaguense. b, Vanda Miss Joquim.

Perf. 14½x14

1995, Sept. 1 Wmk. 384

660 A118 50p Sheet of 2, #a.-b. 2.00 2.00

Singapore '95.

Christmas A119

Children's drawings: 12p, Christmas Eve in Jamestown. 15p, Santa, musicians. 25p, Party at Blue Hill Community Center. 38p, Santa walking in Jamestown. 60p, RMS St. Helena.

Perf. 14x14½

1995, Oct. 17 Litho. Wmk. 373

661 A119 12p multicolored .40 .40
662 A119 15p multicolored .45 .45
663 A119 25p multicolored .75 .75
664 A119 38p multicolored 1.25 1.25
665 A119 60p multicolored 1.90 1.90
Nos. 661-665 (5) 4.75 4.75

Union Castle Mail Ships A120

Wmk. 384

1996, Jan. 8 Litho. *Perf. 14*

666 A120 12p Walmer Castle, 1915 .40 .40
667 A120 25p Llangibby Castle, 1934 .80 .80
668 A120 53p Stirling Castle, 1940 1.70 1.70
669 A120 60p Pendennis Castle, 1965 1.90 1.90
Nos. 666-669 (4) 4.80 4.80

See Nos. 707-710.

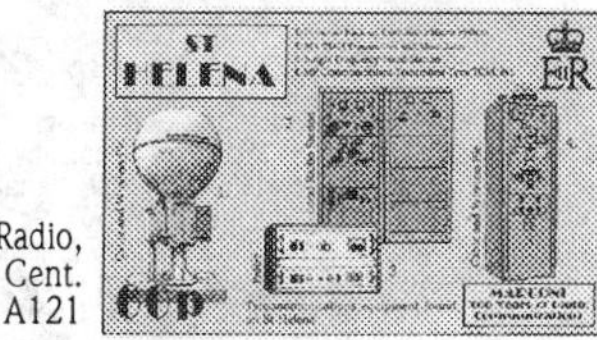

Radio, Cent. A121

Designs: 60p, Telecommunications equipment on St. Helena. £1, Marconi aboard yacht, Elettra.

Perf. 13½

1996, Mar. 28 Litho. Wmk. 373

670 A121 60p multicolored 1.80 1.80
671 A121 £1 multicolored 3.00 3.00

Queen Elizabeth II, 70th Birthday

Common Design Type

Various portraits of Queen, scenes of St. Helena: 15p, Jamestown. 25p, Prince Andrew School. 53p, Castle entrance. 60p, Plantation house.

£1.50, Queen wearing tiara, formal dress.

Perf. 14x14½

1996, Apr. 22 Litho. Wmk. 384

672 CD354 15p multicolored .50 .50
673 CD354 25p multicolored .80 .80
674 CD354 53p multicolored 1.75 1.75
675 CD354 60p multicolored 2.00 2.00
Nos. 672-675 (4) 5.05 5.05

Souvenir Sheet

676 CD354 £1.50 multicolored 4.75 4.75

CAPEX '96 A122

Postal transport: 12p, Mail airlifted to HMS Protector, 1964. 25p, First local post delivery, motorscooter, 1965. 53p, Mail unloaded at Wideawake Airfield, Ascension Island. 60p, Mail received at St. Helena.

£1, LMS Jubilee Class 4-6-0 locomotive No. 5624 "St. Helena."

Wmk. 384

1996, June 8 Litho. *Perf. 14*

677 A122 12p multicolored .40 .40
678 A122 25p multicolored .85 .85
679 A122 53p multicolored 1.75 1.75
680 A122 60p multicolored 2.00 2.00
Nos. 677-680 (4) 5.00 5.00

Souvenir Sheet

681 A122 £1 multicolored 3.30 3.30

Napoleonic Sites A123

Perf. 14½

1996, Aug. 12 Litho. Wmk. 373

682 A123 12p Mr. Porteous' House .40 .40
683 A123 25p Briars Pavillion .85 .85
684 A123 53p Longwood House 1.75 1.75
685 A123 60p Napoleon's Tomb 2.00 2.00
Nos. 682-685 (4) 5.00 5.00

Christmas — A124

Flowers: 12p, Frangipani. 15p, Bougainvillaea. 25p, Jacaranda. £1, Pink periwinkle.

Perf. 14½

1996, Oct. 1 Litho. Wmk. 373

686 A124 12p multicolored .40 .40
687 A124 15p multicolored .50 .50
688 A124 25p multicolored .80 .80
689 A124 £1 multicolored 3.25 3.25
Nos. 686-689 (4) 4.95 4.95

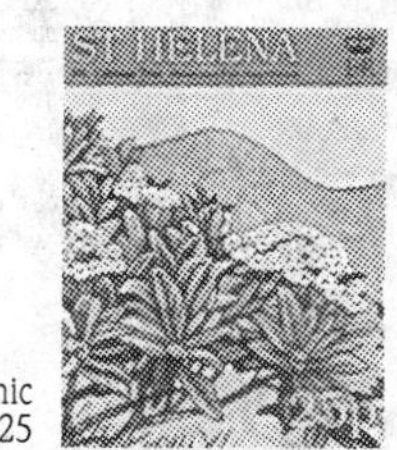

Endemic Plants — A125

Designs: a, Black cabbage tree. b, Whitewood. c, Tree fern. d, Dwarf jellico. e, Lobelia. f, Dogwood.

1997, Jan. 17 *Perf. 14½x14*

690 A125 25p Sheet of 6, #a.-f. 5.00 5.00

Bird Type of 1993

Souvenir Sheet

Perf. 14½

1997, June 20 Litho. Wmk. 373

691 A108 75p like No. 610 2.50 2.50

Return of Hong Kong to China, July 1, 1997.

Discovery of St. Helena, 500th Anniv. (in 2002) — A126

Designs: 20p, Discovery by Joao da Nova, May 21, 1502. 25p, First inhabitant, Don Fernando Lopez, 1515. 30p, Landing by Thomas Cavendish, 1588. 80p, Ship, Royal Merchant, 1591.

1997, May 29 *Perf. 14*

692 A126 20p multicolored .65 .65
693 A126 25p multicolored .85 .85
694 A126 30p multicolored 1.00 1.00
695 A126 80p multicolored 2.60 2.60
Nos. 692-695 (4) 5.10 5.10

Queen Elizabeth II and Prince Philip, 50th Wedding Anniv. — A127

#696, Queen, Prince coming down steps, royal visit, 1947. #697, Wedding portrait. #698, Wedding portrait, diff. #699, Queen receiving flowers, royal visit, 1947. #700, Royal visit, 1957. #701, Queen, Prince waving from balcony on wedding day.

£1.50, Queen, Prince riding in open carriage.

Perf. 13½

1997, July 10 Litho. Wmk. 384

696 A127 10p multicolored .35 .35
697 A127 10p multicolored .35 .35
a. Pair, #696-697 .70 .70
698 A127 15p multicolored .50 .50
699 A127 15p multicolored .50 .50
a. Pair, #698-699 1.00 1.00
700 A127 50p multicolored 1.75 1.75
701 A127 50p multicolored 1.75 1.75
a. Pair, #700-701 3.50 3.50
Nos. 696-701 (6) 5.20 5.20

Souvenir Sheet

Perf. 14x14½

702 A127 £1.50 multi, horiz. 5.00 5.00

Christmas — A128

Perf. 13½x14

1997, Sept. 29 Litho. Wmk. 384

703 A128 15p Flowers .50 .50
704 A128 20p Calligraphy .70 .70
705 A128 40p Camping 1.30 1.30
706 A128 75p Entertaining 2.50 2.50
Nos. 703-706 (4) 5.00 5.00

Duke of Edinburgh's Award in St. Helena, 25th anniv.

Union Castle Mail Ships Type of 1996

Wmk. 384

1998, Jan. 2 Litho. *Perf. 14*

707 A120 20p Avondale Castle, 1900 .65 .65
708 A120 25p Dunnottar Castle, 1936 .85 .85
709 A120 30p Llandovery Castle, 1943 1.00 1.00
710 A120 80p Good Hope Castle, 1977 2.60 2.60
Nos. 707-710 (4) 5.10 5.10

Diana, Princess of Wales (1961-97)

Common Design Type

a, Wearing hat. b, In white pin-striped suit jacket. c, In green jacket. d, Wearing choker necklace.

Perf. 14½x14

1998, Apr. 4 Litho. Wmk. 373

711 CD355 30p Sheet of 4, #a.-d. 4.75 4.75

No. 711 sold for £1.20 + 20p, with surtax from international sales being donated to Princess Diana Memorial Fund and surtax from national sales being donated to designated local charity.

SEMI-POSTAL STAMPS

Catalogue values for unused stamps in this section are for Never Hinged items.

Tristan da Cunha Nos. 46, 49-51 Overprinted "ST. HELENA / Tristan Relief" and Surcharged with New Value and "+"

Perf. 12½x13

1961, Oct. 12 Wmk. 314 Engr.

B1 A3 2½c + 3p		*425.*
B2 A3 5c + 6p		*425.*
B3 A3 7½c + 9p		*500.*
B4 A3 10c + 1sh		*600.*
Nos. B1-B4 (4)	*5,000.*	*1,950.*

Withdrawn from sale Oct. 19.

POSTAGE DUE STAMPS

Catalogue values for unused stamps in this section are for Never Hinged items.

Map — D1

Perf. 15x14

1986, June 9 Litho. Wmk. 384

Background Color

J1 D1 1p tan	.15	.15
J2 D1 2p orange	.15	.15
J3 D1 5p vermilion	.15	.15
J4 D1 7p violet	.20	.20
J5 D1 10p chalky blue	.25	.25
J6 D1 25p dull yellow grn	.65	.65
Nos. J1-J6 (6)	1.55	1.55

WAR TAX STAMPS

WAR TAX

No. 62a Surcharged

ONE PENNY

1916 Wmk. 3 *Perf. 14*

MR1 A10 1p + 1p scarlet & blk	.80	.60
a. Double surcharge		*9,500.*

WAR TAX

No. 62 Surcharged

1919

MR2 A10 1p + 1p carmine & blk	.40	.40

ST. KITTS

sānt 'kits

LOCATION — West Indies southeast of Puerto Rico
GOVT. — With Nevis, Associated State in British Commonwealth
AREA — 65 sq. mi.
POP. — 35,104 (1980)
CAPITAL — Basseterre

See St. Christopher for stamps used in St. Kitts until 1890. From 1890 until 1903, stamps of the Leeward Islands were used. From 1903 until 1956, stamps of St. Kitts-Nevis and Leeward Islands were used concurrently. See St. Kitts-Nevis for stamps used through June 22, 1980, after which St. Kitts and Nevis pursued separate postal administrations.

100 Cents = 1 Dollar

Catalogue values for all unused stamps in this country are for Never Hinged items.

Watermark

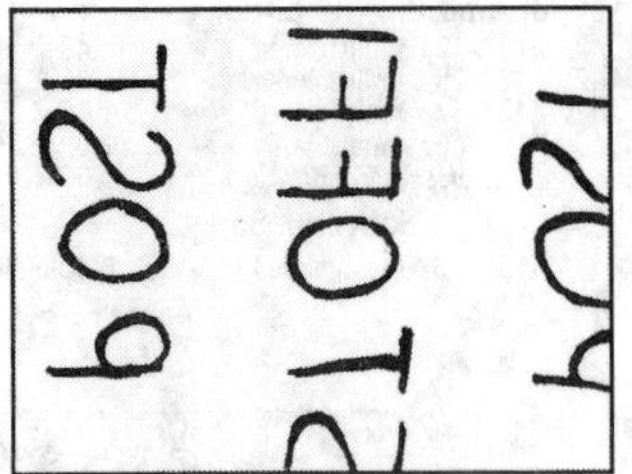

Wmk. 380- "POST OFFICE"

St. Kitts-Nevis Nos. 357-369 Ovptd.

St. Kitts

Perf. 14½x14

1980, June 23 Litho. Wmk. 373

25 A61 5c multicolored	.15	.15
26 A61 10c multicolored	.15	.15
27 A61 12c multicolored	.15	.15
28 A61 15c multicolored	.15	.15
29 A61 25c multicolored	.15	.15
30 A61 30c multicolored	.15	.15
31 A61 40c multicolored	.15	.15
32 A61 45c multicolored	.15	.15
33 A61 50c multicolored	.15	.15
34 A61 55c multicolored	.15	.15
35 A61 $1 multicolored	.25	.25
36 A61 $5 multicolored	1.25	1.25
37 A61 $10 multicolored	2.50	2.50
Set value	4.65	4.65

All but 12c, 45c, 50c, exist unwatermarked. Same values.

Ships — A2

1980, Aug. 8 *Perf. 13½*

38 A2 4c HMS *Vanguard,* 1762	.15	.15
39 A2 10c HMS *Boreas,* 1787	.15	.15
40 A2 30c HMS *Druid,* 1827	.15	.15
41 A2 55c HMS *Winchester,* 1831	.15	.15
42 A2 $1.50 *Philosopher,* 1857	.45	.45
43 A2 $2 S.S. *Contractor,* 1930	.65	.65
Nos. 38-43 (6)	1.70	1.70

Nos. 38-43 not issued without overprint. The 4c, and possibly others, exist without the overprint.

Queen Mother, 80th Birthday — A3

1980, Sept. 4 *Perf. 14*

44 A3 $2 multicolored	.45	.45

Christmas A4

1980, Nov. 10 *Perf. 14½*

45 A4 5c Magi following star	.15	.15
46 A4 15c Shepherds, star	.15	.15
47 A4 30c Bethlehem, star	.15	.15
48 A4 $4 Adoration of the Magi	.50	.50
Set value	.65	.65

Birds — A5

Military Uniforms — A6

1981 Wmk. 373 *Perf. 13½x14*

49 A5 1c Frigatebird	.15	.15
50 A5 4c Rusty-tailed flycatcher	.15	.15
51 A5 5c Purple-throated carib	.15	.15
52 A5 6c Burrowing owl	.15	.15
53 A5 8c Purple martin	.15	.15
54 A5 10c Yellow-crowned night heron	.15	.15

Perf. 14

Size: 38x25mm

55 A5 15c Bananaquit	.15	.15
56 A5 20c Scaly-breasted thrasher	.15	.15
57 A5 25c Grey kingbird	.15	.15
58 A5 30c Green-throated carib	.20	.20
59 A5 40c Ruddy turnstone	.25	.25
60 A5 45c Black-faced grassquit	.30	.30
61 A5 50c Cattle egret	.30	.30
62 A5 55c Brown pelican	.30	.30
63 A5 $1 Lesser Antillean bullfinch	.60	.60
64 A5 $2.50 Zenaida dove	1.50	1.50
65 A5 $5 Sparrow hawk	3.00	3.00
66 A5 $10 Antillean crested hummingbird	6.00	6.00
Nos. 49-66 (18)	13.80	13.80

Issued: #51, 54-66, Feb. 5; others, May 30.

Nos. 45-66 exist with "1982" imprint, issued June 8, 1982. The 1981 set has no imprint.

For overprints see Nos. 112-122.

1981-83 *Perf. 14½*

Foot Regiments: 5c, Battalion Company sergeant, 3rd Regiment, c. 1801. 15c, Light Company private, 15th Regiment, c. 1814. No. 69, Battalion Company officer, 45th Regiment, 1796-7. No. 70, Officer, 15th Regiment, c. 1780. No. 71, Officer, 9th Regiment, 1790. No. 72, Light Company officer, 5th Regiment, c. 1822. No. 73, Grenadier, 38th Regiment, 1751. No. 74, Battalion Company officer, 11th Regiment, c. 1804.

67 A6 5c multi	.15	.15
68 A6 15c multi ('83)	.15	.15
69 A6 30c multi	.15	.15
70 A6 30c multi ('83)	.15	.15
71 A6 55c multi	.15	.15
72 A6 55c multi ('83)	.30	.30
73 A6 $2.50 multi	.50	.50
74 A6 $2.50 multi ('83)	1.25	1.25
Nos. 67-74 (8)	2.80	2.80

Issued: 3/5/81; 5/25/83.

Prince Charles, Lady Diana, Royal Yacht Charlotte A6a

Prince Charles and Lady Diana — A6b

Illustration A6b is greatly reduced.

1981, June 23 *Perf. 14*

75 A6a 55c Saudadoes	.15	.15
76 A6b 55c Couple	.15	.15
a. Bklt. pane of 4, perf. 12½x12, unwmkd.	.90	
77 A6a $2.50 The Royal George	.70	.70
78 A6b $2.50 like 55c	.70	.70
a. Bklt. pane of 2, perf. 12½x12, unwmkd.	1.65	
79 A6a $4 HMY Britannia	1.10	1.10
80 A6b $4 like 55c	1.10	1.10
Nos. 75-80 (6)	3.90	3.90

Souvenir Sheet

1981, Dec. 14 *Perf. 12½x12*

81 A6b $5 like 55c	2.75	2.75

Wedding of Prince Charles and Lady Diana Spencer. Nos. 76a, 78a issued Nov. 19, 1981.

Natl. Girl Guide Movement, 50th Anniv. — A7

Christmas — A8

Designs: 5c, Miriam Pickard, 1st Guide commissioner. 30c, Lady Baden-Powell's visit, 1964. 55c, Visit of Princess Alice, 1960. $2, Thinking-Day Parade, 1980s.

1981, Sept. 21

82 A7 5c multicolored	.15	.15
83 A7 30c multicolored	.15	.15
84 A7 55c multicolored	.20	.20
85 A7 $2 multicolored	.70	.70
Nos. 82-85 (4)	1.20	1.20

1981, Nov. 30

Stained-glass windows.

86 A8 5c Annunciation	.15	.15
87 A8 30c Nativity, baptism	.15	.15
88 A8 55c Last supper, crucifixion	.15	.15
89 A8 $3 Appearance before Apostles, ascension to heaven	.80	.80
Nos. 86-89 (4)	1.25	1.25

Brimstone Hill Seige, Bicent. A9

1982, Mar. 15

90 A9 15c Adm. Samuel Hood	.15	.15
91 A9 55c Marquis de Bouille	.30	.30
Set value	.35	.35

Souvenir Sheet

92 A9 $5 Battle scene	2.00	2.00

No. 92 has multicolored margin picturing battle scene. Size: 96x71mm.

21st Birthday of Princess Diana, July 1 — A10

15c, Alexandra of Denmark, Princess of Wales 1863. 55c, Paternal arms of Alexandra. $6, Diana

1982, June 22 *Perf. 13½x14*

93 A10 15c multicolored	.15	.15
94 A10 55c multicolored	.15	.15
95 A10 $6 multicolored	.80	.80
Set value	.90	.90

Nos. 93-95 Ovptd. ROYAL BABY

1982, July 12

96 A10 15c multicolored	.15	.15
97 A10 55c multicolored	.15	.15
98 A10 $6 multicolored	.80	.90
Set value	.90	.90

Birth of Prince William of Wales.

Scouting, 75th Anniv. — A11

Merit badges.

1982, Aug. 18 *Perf. 14x13½*

99	A11	5c Nature	.15	.15
100	A11	55c Rescue	.25	.25
101	A11	$2 First aid	.90	.90
		Nos. 99-101 (3)	1.30	1.30

Christmas — A12

Children's drawings.

1982, Oct. 20

102	A12	5c shown	.15	.15
103	A12	55c Nativity	.15	.15
104	A12	$1.10 Three Kings	.15	.15
105	A12	$3 Annunciation	.50	.50
		Set value	.75	.75

A13

Commonwealth Day: 55c, Cruise ship Stella Oceanis docked. $2, RMS Queen Elizabeth 2 anchored in harbor off St. Kitts.

1983, Mar. 14 *Perf. 14*

106	A13	55c multicolored	.15	.15
107	A13	$2 multicolored	.70	.70

Boys' Brigade, Cent. — A14

Designs: 10c, Sir William Smith, founder. 45c, Brigade members outside Sandy Point Methodist Church. 50c, Drummers. $3, Badge.

1983, July 27

108	A14	10c multicolored	.15	.15
109	A14	45c multicolored	.30	.30
110	A14	50c multicolored	.30	.30
111	A14	$3 multicolored	1.90	1.90
		Nos. 108-111 (4)	2.65	2.65

Nos. 51, 55-59 and 62-66 Ovptd.

INDEPENDENCE 1983
a

INDEPENDENCE 1983
b

1983, Sept. 19

112	A5(a)	5c multicolored	.15	.15
a.		Local overprint	2.25	2.25
113	A5(b)	15c multicolored	.15	.15
114	A5(b)	20c multicolored	.15	.15
115	A5(b)	25c multicolored	.15	.15
116	A5(b)	30c multicolored	.20	.20
117	A5(b)	40c multicolored	.25	.25
118	A5(b)	55c multicolored	.35	.35
119	A5(b)	$1 multicolored	.60	.60
120	A5(b)	$2.50 multicolored	1.65	1.65
121	A5(b)	$5 multicolored	3.00	3.00
122	A5(b)	$10 multicolored	6.25	6.25
		Nos. 112-122 (11)	12.90	12.90

Nos. 113-122 have "1982" imprint. Nos. 113, 116, 118-122 exist without imprint. No. 112 is without imprint. No. 112 with imprint is twice the value.

No. 112a has serifed letters and reads down on imprinted stamp. Exists reading up and without imprint.

Manned Flight Bicent. A15

Designs: 10c, *Montgolfiere,* 1783, vert. 45c, Sikorsky *Russian Knight,* 1913. 50c, Lockheed TriStar. $2.50, Bell XS-1, 1947.

1983, Sept. 28 **Wmk. 380**

123	A15	10c multicolored	.15	.15
124	A15	45c multicolored	.15	.15
125	A15	50c multicolored	.15	.15
126	A15	$2.50 multicolored	.85	.85
a.		Souvenir sheet of 4, #123-126	1.25	1.25
		Nos. 123-126 (4)	1.30	1.30

1st Flight of a 4-engine aircraft, May 1913 (45c); 1st manned supersonic aircraft, 1947 ($2.50).

Christmas A16

1983, Nov. 7

127	A16	15c shown	.15	.15
128	A16	30c Shepherds	.15	.15
129	A16	55c Mary, Joseph	.15	.15
130	A16	$2 Nativity	.45	.45
a.		Souvenir sheet of 4, #127-130	.75	.75
		Set value	.70	.70

Batik Art A17

1984-85

131	A17	15c Country bus	.15	.15
132	A17	40c Donkey cart	.20	.20
133	A17	45c Parrot, vert.	.25	.25
134	A17	50c Man under palm tree, vert.	.25	.25
135	A17	60c Rum shop, cyclist	.30	.30
136	A17	$1.50 Fruit seller, vert.	.80	.80
137	A17	$3 Butterflies, vert.	1.50	1.50
138	A17	$3 S.V. Polynesia	1.50	1.50
		Nos. 131-138 (8)	4.95	4.95

Issued: 15c, 40c, 60c, #138, 2/6/85; others, 1/30/84.

Marine Life — A18

1984, July 4

139	A18	5c Cushion star	.15	.15
140	A18	10c Rough file shell	.15	.15
a.		Wmk. 384 ('86)	.15	.15
141	A18	15c Red-lined cleaning shrimp	.15	.15
142	A18	20c Bristleworm	.20	.15
143	A18	25c Flamingo tongue	.25	.15
144	A18	30c Christmas tree worm	.30	.30
145	A18	40c Pink-tipped anemone	.35	.35
146	A18	50c Smallmouth grunt	.45	.45
147	A18	60c Glasseye snapper	.60	.60
a.		Wmk. 384 ('88)	.80	.80
148	A18	75c Reef squirrelfish	.70	.70
149	A18	$1 Sea fans, flamefish	.90	.90
150	A18	$2.50 Reef butter-flyfish	2.25	2.25
151	A18	$5 Black soldierfish	4.50	4.50
a.		Wmk. 384 ('88)	6.25	6.25
152	A18	$10 Cocoa damselfish	9.50	9.50
a.		Wmk. 384 ('88)	13.00	13.00
		Nos. 139-152 (14)	20.45	20.30

Nos. 149-152 vert.

#140a has "1986" imprint; also exists with "1988" imprint. #147a, 151a, 152a have "1988" imprint.

4-H in St. Kitts, 25th Anniv. A19

1984, Aug. 15

153	A19	30c Agriculture	.15	.15
154	A19	55c Animal husbandry	.30	.30
155	A19	$1.10 Pledge, flag, youths	.65	.65
156	A19	$3 Parade	1.65	1.65
		Nos. 153-156 (4)	2.75	2.75

1st Anniv. of Independence — A20

Designs: 15c, Construction of Royal St. Kitts Hotel. 30c, Folk dancers. $1.10, O Land of Beauty, vert. $3, Sea, palm trees, map, vert.

1984, Sept. 18

157	A20	15c multicolored	.15	.15
158	A20	30c multicolored	.15	.15
159	A20	$1.10 multicolored	.65	.65
160	A20	$3 multicolored	1.75	1.75
		Nos. 157-160 (4)	2.70	2.70

Christmas A21

1984, Nov. 1

161	A21	15c Opening gifts	.15	.15
162	A21	60c Caroling	.45	.45
163	A21	$1 Nativity	.70	.70
164	A21	$2 Leaving church	1.40	1.40
		Nos. 161-164 (4)	2.70	2.70

Ships A22

1985, Mar. 27 *Perf. 13½x14*

165	A22	40c Tropic Jade	.45	.45
166	A22	$1.20 Atlantic Clipper	1.40	1.40
167	A22	$2 M.V. Cunard Countess	2.25	2.25
168	A22	$2 Mandalay	2.25	2.25
		Nos. 165-168 (4)	6.35	6.35

Mt. Olive Masonic Lodge, 150th Anniv. — A23

400th Anniversary of Sir Francis Drake's visit 1585
St Kitts
Christmas 1985
St.Kitts 10c

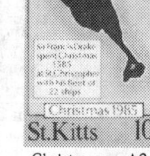

Christmas — A24

Designs: 15c, James Derrick Cardin (1871-1954). 75c, Lodge banner. $1.20, Compass, Bible, square, horiz. $3, Charter, 1835.

1985, Nov. 9 *Perf. 15*

169	A23	15c multicolored	.20	.20
170	A23	75c multicolored	.85	.85
171	A23	$1.20 multicolored	1.40	1.40
172	A23	$3 multicolored	3.50	3.50
		Nos. 169-172 (4)	5.95	5.95

1985, Nov. 27 **Unwmk.**

173	A24	10c Map of St. Kitts	.15	.15
174	A24	40c Golden Hind	.35	.35
175	A24	60c Sir Francis Drake	.55	.55
176	A24	$3 Drake's shield of arms	2.75	2.75
		Nos. 173-176 (4)	3.80	3.80

Visit of Sir Francis Drake to St. Kitts, 400th anniv.

Queen Elizabeth II, 60th Birthday — A25

Designs: 10c, With Prince Philip. 20c, Walking with government officials. 40c, Riding horse in parade. $3, Portrait.

1986, July 9 *Perf. 14*

177	A25	10c multicolored	.15	.15
178	A25	20c multicolored	.20	.20
179	A25	40c multicolored	.35	.35
180	A25	$3 multicolored	2.75	2.75
		Nos. 177-180 (4)	3.45	3.45

For overprints see Nos. 185-188.

Royal Wedding Issue, 1986
Common Design Type

Designs: 15c, Prince Andrew and Sarah Ferguson, formal engagement announcement. $2.50, Prince Andrew in military dress uniform.

Perf. 14½x14

1986, July 23 **Wmk. 384**

181	CD338	15c multicolored	.15	.15
182	CD338	$2.50 multicolored	2.00	2.00

Agriculture Exhibition — A26

Children's drawings: 15c, Family farm, by Kevin Tatem, age 14. $1.20, Striving for growth, by Alister Williams, age 19.

1986, Sept. 18 *Perf. 13½x14*

183	A26	15c multicolored	.15	.15
184	A26	$1.20 multicolored	1.40	1.40

Nos. 177-180 Ovptd. "40th ANNIVERSARY / U.N. WEEK 19-26 OCT." in Gold

1986, Oct. 22 **Unwmk.** *Perf. 14*

185	A25	10c multicolored	.15	.15
186	A25	20c multicolored	.15	.15
187	A25	40c multicolored	.30	.30
188	A25	$3 multicolored	2.25	2.25
		Nos. 185-188 (4)	2.85	2.85

World Wildlife Fund — A27

Various green monkeys, Cercopithecus aethiops sabaeus.

1986, Dec. 1

189	A27	15c multi	*.75*	*.75*
190	A27	20c multi, diff.	*1.00*	*1.00*
191	A27	60c multi, diff.	*3.00*	*3.00*
192	A27	$1 multi, diff.	*4.75*	*4.75*
		Nos. 189-192 (4)	9.50	9.50

Auguste Bartholdi — A28

Statue of Liberty, Cent. — A29

Perf. 14x14½, 14½x14

1986, Dec. 17

193 A28 40c shown .35 .35
194 A28 60c Torch, head, 1876-78 .50 .50
195 A28 $1.50 Warship Isere, France 1.25 1.25
196 A28 $3 Delivering statue, 1884 2.50 2.50
Nos. 193-196 (4) 4.60 4.60

Souvenir Sheet

197 A29 $3.50 Head 2.75 2.75

Nos. 194-195 horiz.

British and French Uniforms — A30

Sugar Cane Industry — A31

Designs: No. 198, Officer, East Norfolk Regiment, 1792. No. 199, Officer, De Neustrie Regiment, 1779. No. 200, Sergeant, Third Foot the Buffs, 1801. No. 201, Artillery officer, 1812. No. 202, Private, Light Company, 5th Foot Regiment, 1778. No. 203, Grenadier, Line Infantry, 1796.

1987, Feb. 25 *Perf. 14½*

198 A30 15c multicolored .20 .20
199 A30 15c multicolored .20 .20
200 A30 40c multicolored .55 .55
201 A30 40c multicolored .55 .55
202 A30 $2 multicolored 2.75 2.75
203 A30 $2 multicolored 2.75 2.75
a. Souvenir sheet of 6, #198-203 7.25 7.25
Nos. 198-203 (6) 7.00 7.00

1987, Apr. 15 *Perf. 14*

No. 204: a, Warehouse. b, Barns. c, Steam emitted by processing plant. d, Processing plant. e, Field hands.

No. 205a, Locomotive. b, Locomotive and tender. c, Open cars. d, Empty and loaded cars, tractor. e, Loading sugar cane.

204 Strip of 5 .60 .60
a.-e. A31 15c any single .15 .15
205 Strip of 5 3.25 3.25
a.-e. A31 75c any single .65 .65

Visiting Aircraft A32

Perf. 14x14½

1987, June 24 **Wmk. 373**

206 A32 40c L-1011-500 Tri-Star .45 .45
207 A32 60c BAe Super 748 .70 .70
208 A32 $1.20 DHC-6 Twin Otter 1.40 1.40
209 A32 $3 Aerospatiale ATR-42 3.50 3.50
Nos. 206-209 (4) 6.05 6.05

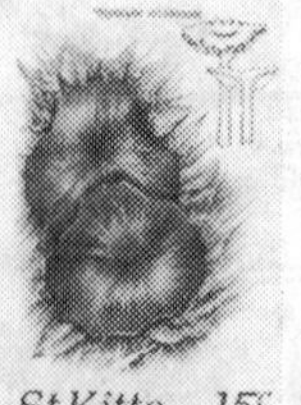

Fungi — A33

Carnival Clowns — A34

1987, Aug. 26 **Wmk. 384** *Perf. 14*

210 A33 15c Hygrocybe occidentalis .25 .25
211 A33 40c Marasmius haematocephalus .60 .60
212 A33 $1.20 Psilocybe cubensis 1.75 1.75
213 A33 $2 Hygrocybe acutoconica 3.00 3.00
214 A33 $3 Boletellus cubensis 4.50 4.50
Nos. 210-214 (5) 10.10 10.10

1987, Oct. 28 *Perf. 14½*

215 A34 15c multi .20 .20
216 A34 40c multi, diff. .50 .50
217 A34 $1 multi, diff. 1.25 1.25
218 A34 $3 multi, diff. 3.50 3.50
Nos. 215-218 (4) 5.45 5.45

Christmas 1987. See Nos. 235-238.

Flowers — A35

1988, Jan. 20

219 A35 15c Ixora .20 .20
220 A35 40c Shrimp plant .45 .45
221 A35 $1 Poinsettia 1.10 1.10
222 A35 $3 Honolulu rose 3.25 3.25
Nos. 219-222 (4) 5.00 5.00

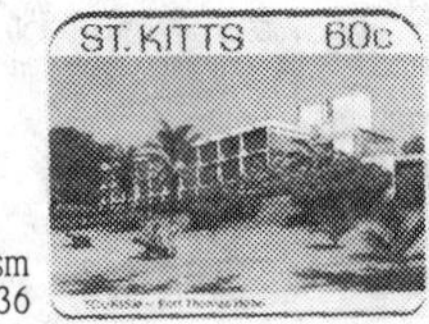

Tourism A36

1988, Apr. 20 **Wmk. 373**

223 A36 60c Ft. Thomas Hotel .45 .45
224 A36 60c Fairview Inn .45 .45
225 A36 60c Frigate Bay Beach Hotel .45 .45
226 A36 60c Ocean Terrace Inn .45 .45
227 A36 $3 The Golden Lemon 2.25 2.25
228 A36 $3 Royal St. Kitts Casino and Jack Tar Village 2.25 2.25
229 A36 $3 Rawlins Plantation Hotel and Restaurant 2.25 2.25
Nos. 223-229 (7) 8.55 8.55

See Nos. 239-244.

INDEPENDENCE
St.KITTS 15c

Leeward Islands Cricket Tournament, 75th Anniv. — A37

Independence, 5th Anniv. — A38

Designs: 40c, Leeward Islands Cricket Assoc. emblem, ball and wicket. $3, Cricket match at Warner Park.

1988, July 13 *Perf. 13x13½*

230 A37 40c multicolored .30 .30
231 A37 $3 multicolored 2.25 2.25

1988, Sept. 19 **Wmk. 384** *Perf. 14½*

Designs: 15c, Natl. flag. 60c, Natl. coat of arms. $5, Princess Margaret presenting the Nevis Constitution Order to Prime Minister Simmonds, Sept. 19, 1983.

232 A38 15c shown .15 .15
233 A38 60c multicolored .65 .65

Souvenir Sheet

234 A38 $5 multicolored 3.75 3.75

Christmas Type of 1987

Carnival clowns.

1988, Nov. 2 **Wmk. 373**

235 A34 15c multi .15 .15
236 A34 40c multi, diff. .25 .25
237 A34 80c multi, diff. .45 .45
238 A34 $3 multi, diff. 1.65 1.65
Nos. 235-238 (4) 2.50 2.50

Tourism Type of 1988

Wmk. 384

1989, Jan. 25 **Litho.** *Perf. 14*

239 A36 20c Old Colonial House .15 .15
240 A36 20c Georgian House .15 .15
241 A36 $1 Romney Manor .75 .75
242 A36 $1 Lavington Great House .75 .75
243 A36 $2 Treasury Building 1.50 1.50
244 A36 $2 Government House 1.50 1.50
Nos. 239-244 (6) 4.80 4.80

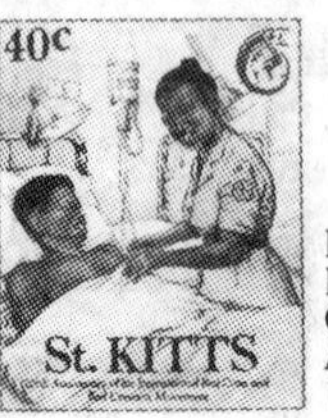

Intl. Red Cross and Red Crescent Organizations, 125th Annivs. (in 1988) — A39

Perf. 14x14½

1989, May 8 **Litho.** **Wmk. 384**

245 A39 40c shown .30 .30
246 A39 $1 Ambulance .75 .75
247 A39 $3 Anniv. emblem 2.25 2.25
Nos. 245-247 (3) 3.30 3.30

Moon Landing, 20th Anniv.

Common Design Type

Apollo 13: 10c, Lunar rover at Taurus-Littrow landing site. 20c, Fred W. Haise Jr., John L. Swigert Jr., and James A. Lovell Jr. $1, Mission emblem. $2, Splashdown in the South Pacific. $5, Buzz Aldrin disembarking from the lunar module, Apollo 11 mission.

1989, July 20 *Perf. 14*

Size of Nos. 249-250: 29x29mm

248 CD342 10c multicolored .15 .15
249 CD342 20c multicolored .15 .15
250 CD342 $1 multicolored .75 .75
251 CD342 $2 multicolored 1.50 1.50
Nos. 248-251 (4) 2.55 2.55

Souvenir Sheet

252 CD342 $5 multicolored 4.50 4.50

Souvenir Sheet

Conflict on the Champ-de-Mars — A40

1989, July 7

253 A40 $5 multicolored 3.75 3.75

PHILEXFRANCE '89, French revolution bicent.

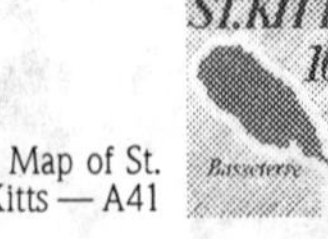

Outline Map of St. Kitts — A41

1989 *Perf. 15x14*

255 A41 10c purple & blk .15 .15
256 A41 15c red & blk .15 .15
257 A41 20c org brn & blk .15 .15
259 A41 40c bister & blk .25 .25
261 A41 60c blue & blk .35 .35
265 A41 $1 green & blk .50 .50
Nos. 255-265 (6) 1.55 1.55

This is an expanding set. Numbers will change if neccessary.

Discovery of America, 500th Anniv. (in 1992) A42

Designs: 15c, Galleon passing St. Kitts during Columbus's 2nd voyage, 1493. 80c, Coat of arms and map of 4th voyage. $1, Navigational instruments, c. 1500. $5, Exploration of Cuba and Hispaniola during Columbus's 2nd voyage, 1493-1496.

1989, Nov. 8 **Wmk. 384** *Perf. 14*

269 A42 15c multicolored .20 .20
270 A42 80c multicolored 1.10 1.10
271 A42 $1 multicolored 1.40 1.40
272 A42 $5 multicolored 6.75 6.75
Nos. 269-272 (4) 9.45 9.45

World Stamp Expo '89 — A43

Exhibition emblem, flags and: 15c, Poinciana tree. 40c, Ft. George Citadel, Brimstone Hill. $1, Light Company private, 5th Foot Regiment, 1778. $3, St. George's Anglican Church.

1989, Nov. 17 **Wmk. 373**

273 A43 15c multicolored .20 .20
274 A43 40c multicolored .55 .55
275 A43 $1 multicolored 1.40 1.40
276 A43 $3 multicolored 4.00 4.00
Nos. 273-276 (4) 6.15 6.15

Butterflies A45

15c, Junonia evarete. 40c, Anartia jatrophae. 60c, Heliconius charitonius. $3, Biblis hyperia.

Perf. 13½

1990, June 6 **Litho.** **Wmk. 373**

277 A45 15c multicolored .20 .20
278 A45 40c multicolored .45 .45
279 A45 60c multicolored .70 .70
280 A45 $3 multicolored 3.50 3.50
Nos. 277-280 (4) 4.85 4.85

Nos. 277-280 with EXPO '90 Emblem Added to Design

1990, June 6

281 A45 15c multicolored .15 .15
282 A45 40c multicolored .40 .40
283 A45 60c multicolored .60 .60
284 A45 $3 multicolored 3.25 3.25
Nos. 281-284 (4) 4.40 4.40

Expo '90, International Garden and Greenery Exposition, Osaka, Japan.

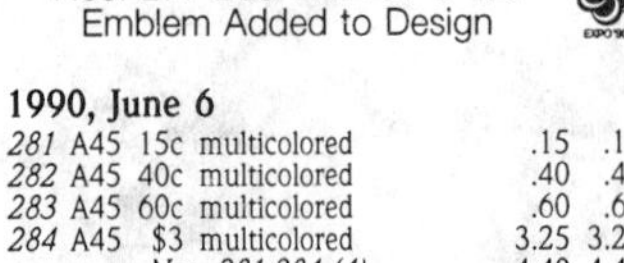

Cannon on Brimstone Hill, 300th Anniv. A46

15c, 40c, View of Brimstone Hill. 60c, Fort Charles under bombardment. $3, Men firing cannon.

1990 June 30 **Wmk. 384** *Perf. 14*

285 A46 15c multicolored .15 .15
286 A46 40c multicolored .35 .35
287 A46 60c multicolored .50 .50
288 Pair 3.00 3.00
a. A46 60c multicolored .50 .50
b. A46 $3 multicolored 2.50 2.50
Nos. 285-288 (4) 4.00 4.00

No. 288 has a continuous design.

Souvenir Sheet

Battle of Britain, 50th Anniv. — A47

1990, Sept. 15

289 Sheet of 2 7.00 7.00
a.-b. A47 $3 any single 3.50 3.50

Ships A48

1990, Oct. 10 **Wmk. 373**

294 A48 10c Romney .15 .15
a. Wmk. 384 .15 .15
295 A48 15c Baralt .15 .15
296 A48 20c Wear .15 .15
297 A48 25c Sunmount .15 .15
298 A48 40c Inanda .20 .20
299 A48 50c Alcoa Partner .25 .25
300 A48 60c Dominica .30 .30
301 A48 80c CGM Provence .45 .45
302 A48 $1 Director .50 .50
303 A48 $1.20 Typical barque, 1860-1880 .65 .65
304 A48 $2 Chignecto 1.10 1.10
305 A48 $3 Berbice 1.65 1.65
a. Souvenir sheet of 1 2.25 2.25
306 A48 $5 Vamos 2.75 2.75
307 A48 $10 Federal Maple 5.25 5.25
Nos. 294-307 (14) 13.70 13.70

No. 305a issued 2/3/97 for Hong Kong '97.

Christmas A49

Traditional games.

1990, Nov. 14 *Perf. 14*

308 A49 10c Single fork .15 .15
309 A49 15c Boulder breaking .15 .15
310 A49 40c Double fork .30 .30
311 A49 $3 Run up 2.25 2.25
Nos. 308-311 (4) 2.85 2.85

Flowers — A50 Natl. Census — A51

Perf. 14x13½, 13½x14

1991, May 8 **Litho.** **Wmk. 373**

312 A50 10c White periwinkle, horiz. .15 .15
313 A50 40c Pink oleander, horiz. .40 .40
314 A50 60c Pink periwinkle .55 .55
315 A50 $2 White oleander 1.75 1.75
Nos. 312-315 (4) 2.85 2.85

1991, May 13 **Wmk. 384** *Perf. 14*

316 A51 15c multicolored .15 .15
317 A51 $2.40 multicolored 2.25 2.25

Elizabeth & Philip, Birthdays

Common Design Types

Perf. 14½

1991, June 17 **Litho.** **Wmk. 384**

318 CD346 $1.20 multicolored 1.00 1.00
319 CD345 $1.80 multicolored 1.75 1.75
a. Pair, #318-319 + label 2.75 2.75

Fish — A52

1991, Aug. 28 **Wmk. 373** *Perf. 14*

320 A52 10c Nassau grouper .15 .15
321 A52 60c Hogfish .60 .60
322 A52 $1 Red hind .95 .95
323 A52 $3 Porkfish 2.75 2.75
Nos. 320-323 (4) 4.45 4.45

University of the West Indies A53

Designs: 15c, Chancellor Sir Shridath Ramphal, School of Continuing Studies, St. Kitts. 50c, Administration Bldg., Cave Hill Campus, Barbados. $1, Engineering Bldg., St. Augustine Campus, Trinidad & Tobago. $3, Ramphal, Mona Campus, Jamaica.

1991, Sept. 25 **Wmk. 384**

324 A53 15c multicolored .15 .15
325 A53 50c multicolored .45 .45
326 A53 $1 multicolored .95 .95
327 A53 $3 multicolored 2.75 2.75
Nos. 324-327 (4) 4.30 4.30

Christmas A54

Various scenes of traditional play, "The Bull."

1991, Nov. 6 **Wmk. 373**

328 A54 10c multicolored .15 .15
329 A54 15c multicolored .15 .15
330 A54 60c multicolored .45 .45
331 A54 $3 multicolored 2.25 2.25
Nos. 328-331 (4) 3.00 3.00

Queen Elizabeth II's Accession to the Throne, 40th Anniv.

Common Design Type

1992, Feb. 6 **Wmk. 384**

332 CD349 10c multicolored .15 .15
333 CD349 40c multicolored .35 .35
334 CD349 60c multicolored .50 .50
335 CD349 $1 multicolored .90 .90

Wmk. 373

336 CD349 $3 multicolored 2.50 2.50
Nos. 332-336 (5) 4.40 4.40

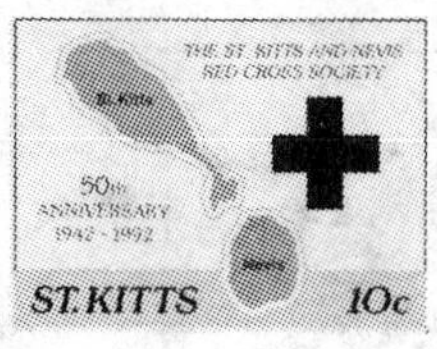

St. Kitts and Nevis Red Cross Society, 50th Anniv. A55

10c, Map of St. Kitts & Nevis. 20c, St. Kitts & Nevis flag. 50c, Red Cross House, St. Kitts. $2.40, Jean-Henri Dunant, founder of Red Cross.

Perf. 13½x14

1992, May 8 **Litho.** **Wmk. 373**

337 A55 10c multicolored .15 .15
338 A55 20c multicolored .20 .20
339 A55 50c multicolored .65 .65
340 A55 $2.40 multicolored 2.25 2.25
Nos. 337-340 (4) 3.25 3.25

Discovery of America, 500th Anniv. — A56

1992, July 6 *Perf. 13*

341 A56 $1 Coming ashore .90 .90
342 A56 $2 Natives, ships 1.75 1.75

Organization of East Caribbean States.

A57 Christmas — A58

Designs: 25c, Fountain, Independence Square. 50c, Berkeley Memorial drinking fountain and clock. 80c, Sir Thomas Warner's tomb. $2, War Memorial.

1992, Aug. 19 *Perf. 12½x13*

343 A57 25c multicolored .20 .20
344 A57 50c multicolored .40 .40
345 A57 80c multicolored .70 .70
346 A57 $2 multicolored 1.65 1.65
Nos. 343-346 (4) 2.95 2.95

1992, Oct. 28 **Wmk. 384** *Perf. 14½*

Stained glass windows: 20c, Mary and Joseph. 25c, Shepherds. 80c, Three Wise Men. $3, Mary, Joseph and Christ Child.

347 A58 20c multicolored .15 .15
348 A58 25c multicolored .20 .20
349 A58 80c multicolored .65 .65
350 A58 $3 multicolored 2.75 2.75
Nos. 347-350 (4) 3.75 3.75

Royal Air Force, 75th Anniv.

Common Design Type

Designs: 25c, Short Singapore III. 50c, Bristol Beaufort. 80c, Westland Whirlwind. $1.60, English Electric Canberra.

No. 355a, Handley Page 0/400. b, Fairey Long Range Monoplane. c, Vickers Wellesley. d, Sepecat Jaguar.

Wmk. 373

1993, Apr. 1 **Litho.** *Perf. 14*

351 CD350 25c multicolored .25 .25
352 CD350 50c multicolored .50 .50
353 CD350 80c multicolored .80 .80
354 CD350 $1.60 multicolored 1.65 1.65
Nos. 351-354 (4) 3.20 3.20

Miniature Sheet

355 CD350 $2 Sheet of 4, #a.-d. 6.00 6.00

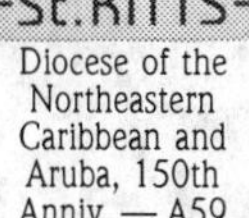

Diocese of the Northeastern Caribbean and Aruba, 150th Anniv. — A59

Coronation of Queen Elizabeth II, 40th Anniv. — A60

Designs: 25c, Diocesan Conference, Basseterre, horiz. 50c, Cathedral of St. John the Divine. 80c, Diocesan coat of arms and motto, horiz. $2, First Bishop, Right Reverend Daniel G. Davis.

Perf. 13½x14, 14x13½

1993, May 21 **Litho.** **Wmk. 384**

356 A59 25c multicolored .20 .20
357 A59 50c multicolored .45 .45
358 A59 80c multicolored .75 .75
359 A59 $2 multicolored 1.90 1.90
Nos. 356-359 (4) 3.30 3.30

1993, June 2 *Perf. 14½x14*

Royal regalia and stamps of St. Kitts-Nevis: 10c, Eagle-shaped ampulla, #119. 25c, Anointing spoon, #334. 80c, Tassels, #333. $2, Staff of Scepter with the Cross, #354a-354c.

360 A60 10c multicolored .15 .15
361 A60 25c multicolored .20 .20
362 A60 80c multicolored .75 .75
363 A60 $2 multicolored 1.90 1.90
Nos. 360-363 (4) 3.00 3.00

Girls' Brigade Intl., Cent. A61

1993, July 1 *Perf. 13½x14*

364 A61 80c Flags .55 .55
365 A61 $3 Badge, coat of arms 2.10 2.10

Independence, 10th Anniv. — A62

Designs: 20c, Flag, map of St. Kitts and Nevis, plane, ship and island scenes. 80c, Natl. arms, independence emblem. $3, Natl. arms, map.

Wmk. 373

1993, Sept. 10 **Litho.** *Perf. 14*

366 A62 20c multicolored .15 .15
367 A62 80c multicolored .55 .55
368 A62 $3 multicolored 2.00 2.00
Nos. 366-368 (3) 2.70 2.70

Christmas — A63 A64

Perf. 13½x14

1993, Nov. 16 **Litho.** **Wmk. 373**

369 A63 25c Roselle .15 .15
370 A63 50c Poinsettia .30 .30
371 A63 $1.60 Snow on the Mountain 1.00 1.00
Nos. 369-371 (3) 1.45 1.45

Wmk. 384

1994, Feb. 18 **Litho.** *Perf. 14*

Prehistoric Aquatic Reptiles: a, Mesosaurus. b, Placodus. c, Liopleurodon. d, Hydrotherosaurus. e, Caretta.

372 A64 $1.20 Strip of 5, #a.-e. 4.50 4.50
373 A64 $1.20 #372 ovptd. with Hong Kong '94 emblem 4.50 4.50

Souvenir Sheet

Treasury Building, Cent. — A65

Perf. 13½

1994, Mar. 21 **Litho.** **Wmk. 373**

374 A65 $10 multicolored 7.50 7.50

St. Kitts stamps can be mounted in the Scott British Leeward Islands album.

Order of the Caribbean Community — A66

First award recipients: Nos. 375a, 376a, Sir Shridath Ramphal, statesman, Guyana. Nos. 375b, 376b, Emblem of the Order. Nos. 375c, 376c, Derek Walcott, writer, St. Lucia. Nos. 375d, 376d, William Demas, economist, Trinidad and Tobago.

Wmk. 373

1994, July 13 Litho. ***Perf. 14***

375 A66 10c Strip of 5, #a, b, c, b, d .40 .40
376 A66 $1 Strip of 5, #a, b, c, b, d 3.75 3.75

CARICOM, 20th anniv. (#375b, 376b).

Christmas A67

1994, Oct. 31

377 A67 25c Carol singing .20 .20
378 A67 25c Opening presents .20 .20
379 A67 80c Carnival .60 .60
380 A67 $2.50 Nativity 1.90 1.90
Nos. 377-380 (4) 2.90 2.90

Intl. Year of the Family.

Green Turtle A68

Wmk. 373

1995, Feb. 27 Litho. ***Perf. 14***

381 A68 10c shown .15 .15
382 A68 40c On beach .30 .30
383 A68 50c Laying eggs .40 .40
384 A68 $1 Hatchlings .75 .75
a. Strip of 4, #381-384 1.65 1.65

World Wildlife Fund.
No. 384a issued in sheets of 16 stamps.

First St. Kitts Postage Stamp, 125th Anniv. A69

St. Christopher #1 at left and: 25c, St. Christopher #1. 80c, St. Kitts-Nevis #72. $2.50, St. Kitts-Nevis #91. $3, St. Kitts-Nevis #119.

Perf. 13½

1995, Apr. 10 Litho. Wmk. 373

385 A69 25c multicolored .20 .20
386 A69 80c multicolored .60 .60
387 A69 $2.50 multicolored 1.90 1.90
388 A69 $3 multicolored 2.25 2.25
Nos. 385-388 (4) 4.95 4.95

End of World War II, 50th Anniv.

Common Design Types

Designs: 20c, Caribbean Regiment, North Africa. 50c, TBM Avengers on anti-submarine patrol. $2, Spitfire MkVb. $8, US destroyer escort on anti-submarine duty.
$3, Reverse of War Madal 1939-45.

Perf. 13½

1995, May 8 Litho. Wmk. 373

389 CD351 20c multicolored .15 .15
390 CD351 50c multicolored .40 .40
391 CD351 $2 multicolored 1.50 1.50
392 CD351 $8 multicolored 6.00 6.00
Nos. 389-392 (4) 8.05 8.05

Souvenir Sheet

Perf. 14

393 CD352 $3 multicolored 2.25 2.25

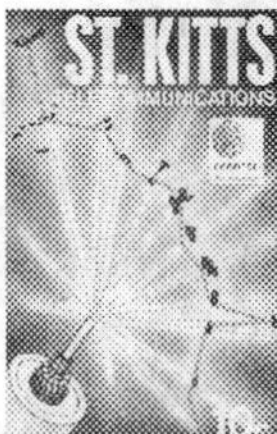

SKANTEL, 10th Anniv. — A70

Designs: 10c, Satellite transmission. 25c, Telephones, computer. $2, Transmission tower, satellite dish. $3, Satellite dish silhouetted against sun.

1995, Sept. 27 ***Perf. 13½x14***

394 A70 10c multicolored .15 .15
395 A70 25c multicolored .20 .20
396 A70 $2 multicolored 1.50 1.50
397 A70 $3 multicolored 2.25 2.25
Nos. 394-397 (4) 4.10 4.10

UN, 50th Anniv.

Common Design Type

Designs: 40c, Energy, clean environment. 50c, Coastal, ocean resources. $1.60, Solid waste management. $2.50, Forestry reserves.

1995, Oct. 24 ***Perf. 13½x13***

398 CD353 40c multicolored .30 .30
399 CD353 50c multicolored .40 .40
400 CD353 $1.60 multicolored 1.25 1.25
401 CD353 $2.50 multicolored 2.00 2.00
Nos. 398-401 (4) 3.95 3.95

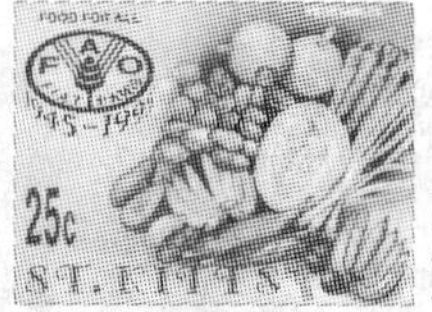

FAO, 50th Anniv. A71

Designs: 25c, Vegetables. 50c, Glazed carrots, West Indian peas & rice. 80c, Tania, Cassava plants. $1.50, Waterfall, Green Hill Mountain.

1995, Nov. 13 ***Perf. 13½***

402 A71 25c multicolored .20 .20
403 A71 50c multicolored .40 .40
404 A71 80c multicolored .60 .60
405 A71 $1.50 multicolored 1.10 1.10
Nos. 402-405 (4) 2.30 2.30

Sea Shells — A72

Designs: a, Flame helmet. b, Triton's trumpet. c, King helmet. d, True tulip. e, Queen conch.

Wmk. 373

1996, Jan. 10 Litho. ***Perf. 13***

406 A72 $1.50 Strip of 5, #a.-e. 5.50 5.50

CAPEX '96 — A73

Leeward Islands LMS Jubilee Class 4-6-0 Locomotives: 10c, No. 45614. $10, No. 5614.

Perf. 13½x14

1996, June 8 Litho. Wmk. 373

407 A73 10c multicolored .15 .15

Souvenir Sheet

Perf. 14x15

408 A73 $10 multicolored 7.50 7.50

No. 408 is 48x31mm.

A74 A75

Modern Olympic Games, Cent.: 10c, Runner, St. Kitts & Nevis flag. 25c, High jumper, US flag. 80c, Runner, Olympic flag. $3, Athens Games poster, 1896.
$6, Olympic torch.

Wmk. 384

1996, June 30 Litho. ***Perf. 14***

409 A74 10c multicolored .15 .15
410 A74 25c multicolored .20 .20
411 A74 80c multicolored .60 .60
412 A74 $3 multicolored 2.25 2.25
Nos. 409-412 (4) 3.20 3.20

Souvenir Sheet

413 A74 $6 multicolored 4.50 4.50

Olymphilex '96 (#413).

1996, Nov. 1 Wmk. 373

Defense Force, Cent.: 10c, Volunteer rifleman, 1896. 50c, Mounted infantry, 1911. $2, Bandsman, 1940-60. $2.50, Modern uniform, 1996.

414 A75 10c multicolored .15 .15
415 A75 50c multicolored .40 .40
416 A75 $2 multicolored 1.50 1.50
417 A75 $2.50 multicolored 1.90 1.90
Nos. 414-417 (4) 3.95 3.95

Christmas — A76

Paintings: 15c, Holy Virgin and Child, by Anais Colin, 1844. 25c, Holy Family, After Rubens. 50c, Madonna with the Goldfinch, by Krause on porcelain after Raphael, 1507. 80c, Madonna on Throne with Angels, by unknown Spanish, 17th cent.

1996, Dec. 9

418 A76 15c multicolored .15 .15
419 A76 25c multicolored .20 .20
420 A76 50c multicolored .40 .40
421 A76 80c multicolored .60 .60
Nos. 418-421 (4) 1.35 1.35

Fish — A77

Designs: a, Princess parrot fish. b, Yellowbelly hamlet. c, Coney. d, Clown wrasse. e, Doctor fish. f, Squirrelfish. g, Queen angelfish. h, Spanish hogfish. i, Red hind. j, Red grouper. k, Yellowtail snapper. l, Mutton hamlet.

1997, Apr. 24 ***Perf. 13½***

422 A77 $1 Sheet of 12, #a.-l. 9.00 9.00

Queen Elizabeth II and Prince Philip, 50th Wedding Anniv. — A78

Designs: No. 423, Queen. No. 424, Prince riding with Royal Guard. No. 425, Queen riding in carriage. No. 426, Prince Philip. No. 427, Early photo of Queen, Prince. No. 428, Prince riding horse.
Queen, Prince riding in open carriage, horiz.

1997 Litho. Wmk. 373 ***Perf. 13½***

423 A78 10c multicolored .15 .15
424 A78 10c multicolored .15 .15
a. Pair, #423-424 .15 .15
425 A78 25c multicolored .20 .20
426 A78 25c multicolored .20 .20
a. Pair, #425-426 .40 .40
427 A78 $3 multicolored 2.25 2.25
428 A78 $3 multicolored 2.25 2.25
a. Pair, #427-428 4.50 4.50
Nos. 423-428 (6) 5.20 5.20

Souvenir Sheet

Perf. 14x14½

429 A78 $6 multicolored 4.50 4.50

Christmas — A79

Churches: No. 430, Zion Moravian. No. 431, Wesley Methodist. $1.50, St. Georges Anglican. $15, Co-Cathedral of the Immaculate Conception.

Perf. 13½x14

1997 Litho. Wmk. 384

430 A79 10c multi .15 .15
431 A79 10c multi .15 .15
432 A79 $1.50 multi, vert. 1.15 1.15
433 A79 $15 multi, vert. 11.50 11.50
Nos. 430-433 (4) 12.95 12.95

Natl. Heroes' Day — A80

#434, Robert L. Bradshaw (1916-78), 1st premier of St. Kitts, Nevis, & Anguilla. #435, Joseph N. France, trade unionist. #436, C.A. Paul Southwell (1913-79), 1st chief minister of St. Kitts, Nevis, & Anguilla. $3, France, Bradshaw, & Southwell.

1997 ***Perf. 13½***

434 A80 25c multi, vert. .20 .20
435 A80 25c multi, vert. .20 .20
436 A80 25c multi, vert. .20 .20
437 A80 $3 multi 2.40 2.40
Nos. 434-437 (4) 3.00 3.00

Diana, Princess of Wales (1961-97)

Common Design Type

Designs: a, Wearing white hat. b, Wearing red jacket. c, Wearing white dress. d, Holding flowers.

Perf. 14½x14

1998, Mar. 31 Litho. Wmk. 373

438 CD355 $1.60 Sheet of 4, #a.-d. 5.50 5.50

No. 438 sold for $6.40 + 90c, with surtax from international sales being donated to Princess Diana Memorial Fund and surtax from national sales being donated to designated local charity.

OFFICIAL STAMPS

Nos. 28-37 Ovptd. "OFFICIAL"

Perf. 14½x14

1980, June 23 Litho. Wmk. 373

O1 A61 15c multicolored .15 .15
O2 A61 25c multicolored .15 .15
O3 A61 30c multicolored .15 .15
O4 A61 40c multicolored .15 .15
O5 A61 45c multicolored .15 .15
O6 A61 50c multicolored .15 .15
O7 A61 55c multicolored .15 .15
O8 A61 $1 multicolored .30 .30
O9 A61 $5 multicolored 1.50 1.50
O10 A61 $10 multicolored 2.75 2.75
Nos. O1-O10 (10) 5.60 5.60

Unwmk.

O2a A61 25c .15 .15
O3a A61 30c .15 .15
O4a A61 40c 20.00 20.00
O7a A61 55c .20 .20
O8a A61 $1 .40 .40
O9a A61 $5 2.00 2.00
O10a A61 $10 3.75 3.75
Nos. O2a-O10a (7) 26.65 26.65

Nos. 55-66 Ovptd. "OFFICIAL"

1981, Feb. 5 *Perf. 14*

O11 A5	15c multicolored		.15	.15
O12 A5	20c multicolored		.15	.15
O13 A5	25c multicolored		.20	.20
O14 A5	30c multicolored		.20	.20
O15 A5	40c multicolored		.25	.25
O16 A5	45c multicolored		.30	.30
O17 A5	50c multicolored		.35	.35
O18 A5	55c multicolored		.35	.35
O19 A5	$1 multicolored		.65	.65
O20 A5	$2.50 multicolored		1.65	1.65
O21 A5	$5 multicolored		3.25	3.25
O22 A5	$10 multicolored		6.50	6.50
	Nos. O11-O22 (12)		14.00	14.00

Nos. 75-80 Ovptd. or Surcharged "OFFICIAL" in Ultra or Black

1983, Feb. 2

O23 A66	45c on $2.50 No. 77	.35	.35
O24 A67	45c on $2.50 No. 78	.35	.35
O25 A66	55c No. 75	.45	.45
O26 A67	55c No. 76	.45	.45
O27 A66	$1.10 on $4 No. 79 (B)	.90	.90
O28 A67	$1.10 on $4 No. 80 (B)	.90	.90
	Nos. O23-O28 (6)	3.40	3.40

Nos. 141-152 Ovptd. "OFFICIAL"

1984, July 4 **Wmk. 380**

O29 A18	15c multicolored	.15	.15
O30 A18	20c multicolored	.20	.20
O31 A18	25c multicolored	.25	.25
O32 A18	30c multicolored	.30	.30
O33 A18	40c multicolored	.40	.40
O34 A18	50c multicolored	.50	.50
O35 A18	60c multicolored	.60	.60
O36 A18	75c multicolored	.75	.75
O37 A18	$1 multicolored	1.10	1.10
O38 A18	$2.50 multicolored	2.50	2.50
O39 A18	$5 multicolored	5.25	5.25
O40 A18	$10 multicolored	10.00	10.00
	Nos. O29-O40 (12)	22.00	22.00

ST. KITTS-NEVIS

sānt 'kits-'nē-vəs

(St. Christopher-Nevis-Anguilla)

LOCATION — West Indies southeast of Puerto Rico
GOVT. — Associated State in British Commonwealth
AREA — 153 sq. mi.
POP. — 48,000, excluding Anguilla (est. 1976)
CAPITAL — Basseterre, St. Kitts

St. Kitts-Nevis was one of the presidencies of the former Leeward Islands colony until it became a colony itself in 1956. In 1967 Britain granted internal self-government.

See "St. Christopher" for stamps used in St. Kitts before 1890. From 1890 until 1903, stamps of the Leeward Islands were used. From 1903 until 1956, stamps of St. Kitts-Nevis and Leeward Islands were used concurrently.

Starting in 1967, issues of Anguilla are listed under that heading. Starting in 1980 stamps inscribed St. Kitts or Nevis are listed under those headings.

12 Pence = 1 Shilling
20 Shillings = 1 Pound
100 Cents = 1 Dollar (1951)

Catalogue values for unused stamps in this country are for Never Hinged items, beginning with Scott 91 in the regular postage section and Scott O1 in the officials section.

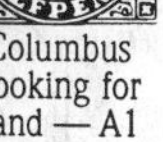

Columbus Looking for Land — A1

Medicinal Spring — A2

Wmk. Crown and C A (2)

1903 **Typo.** *Perf. 14*

1	A1	½p green & violet	2.75	2.00
2	A2	1p carmine & black	3.25	.40
3	A1	2p brown & violet	5.00	12.00
4	A1	2½p ultra & black	10.00	3.25
5	A2	3p orange & green	6.00	10.00
6	A1	6p red violet & blk	4.00	8.00
7	A1	1sh orange & green	6.50	10.00
8	A2	2sh black & green	9.00	10.00
9	A1	2sh6p violet & blk	15.00	27.50
10	A2	5sh ol grn & gray vio	32.50	47.50
		Nos. 1-10 (10)	94.00	130.65

1905-18 **Wmk. 3**

11	A1	½p green & violet	5.50	4.25
12	A1	½p green	.35	.40
13	A2	1p carmine & blk	3.25	1.10
14	A2	1p carmine	.75	.25
15	A1	2p brown & violet	.90	1.25
16	A1	2½p ultra & blk	16.00	7.00
17	A1	2½p ultra	.75	.50
18	A2	3p orange & green	1.40	2.50
19	A1	6p red vio & gray blk ('08)	3.00	10.00
a.		6p purple & gray ('08)	5.00	12.50
20	A1	1sh org & grn ('09)	4.25	14.00
21	A2	5sh ol grn & gray vio ('18)	25.00	55.00
		Nos. 11-21 (11)	61.15	96.25

Nos. 13, 19a and 21 are on chalky paper only and Nos. 15, 18 and 20 are on both ordinary and chalky paper.

For stamp and type overprinted see #MR1-MR2.

King George V — A3

A4

1920-22

Ordinary Paper

24	A3	½p green	.90	1.10
25	A4	1p carmine	1.10	.55
26	A3	1½p orange	.70	.70
27	A4	2p gray	3.00	4.25
28	A3	2½p ultramarine	1.40	3.00

Chalky Paper

29	A4	3p vio & dull vio, *yel*	1.65	4.25
30	A3	6p red vio & dull vio	2.00	5.25
31	A4	1sh blk, *gray grn*	2.25	6.00
32	A3	2sh ultra & dull vio, *blue*	9.00	18.00
33	A4	2sh 6p red & blk, *blue*	9.00	20.00
34	A3	5sh red & grn, *yel*	10.00	32.50
35	A4	10sh red & grn, *grn*	27.50	55.00
36	A3	£1 blk & vio, *red* ('22)	190.00	300.00
		Nos. 24-36 (13)	258.50	450.60

1921-29 **Wmk. 4**

Ordinary Paper

37	A3	½p green	1.00	.30
38	A4	1p rose red	.40	.30
39	A4	1p dp violet ('22)	2.75	.90
40	A3	1½p rose red ('25)	2.00	3.00
41	A3	1½p fawn ('28)	.55	.75
42	A4	2p gray	.30	1.75
43	A3	2½p ultra ('22)	1.25	.60
44	A3	2½p brown ('22)	1.40	3.00

Chalky Paper

45	A4	3p ultra ('22)	.55	3.25
46	A4	3p vio & dull vio, *yel*	.50	1.75
47	A3	6p red vio & dull vio ('24)	2.25	3.00
48	A4	1sh black, *grn* ('29)	3.00	5.50
49	A3	2sh ultra & vio, *bl* ('22)	6.50	11.00
50	A4	2sh6p red & blk, *bl* ('27)	10.50	18.00
51	A3	5sh red & grn, *yel* ('29)	30.00	35.00
		Nos. 37-51 (15)	62.95	88.10

No. 43 exists on ordinary and chalky paper.

Caravel in Old Road Bay — A5

1923 **Wmk. 4**

52	A5	½p green & blk	1.25	2.50
53	A5	1p violet & blk	1.40	1.90
54	A5	1½p carmine & blk	3.50	3.75
55	A5	2p dk gray & blk	2.50	2.75
56	A5	2½p brown & blk	3.75	5.75
57	A5	3p ultra & blk	3.75	5.75
58	A5	6p red vio & blk	6.00	10.00
59	A5	1sh ol grn & blk	10.00	16.00
60	A5	2sh ultra & blk, *bl*	22.50	45.00
61	A5	2sh6p red & blk, *blue*	40.00	62.50
62	A5	10sh red & blk, *emer*	200.00	325.00

Wmk. 3

63	A5	5sh red & blk, *yel*	87.50	175.00
64	A5	£1 vio & blk, *red*	850.00	1,500.
		Nos. 52-63 (12)	382.15	655.90

Tercentenary of the founding of the colony of St. Kitts (or St. Christopher).

Common Design Types pictured following the introduction.

Silver Jubilee Issue

Common Design Type

Inscribed "St. Christopher and Nevis"

Perf. 11x12

1935, May 6 **Engr.** **Wmk. 4**

72	CD301	1p car & dk blue	.40	.40
73	CD301	1½p gray blk & ultra	.55	.55
74	CD301	2½p ultra & brown	1.40	1.40
75	CD301	1sh brn vio & ind	4.25	4.25
		Nos. 72-75 (4)	6.60	6.60

Coronation Issue

Common Design Type

Inscribed "St. Christopher and Nevis"

1937, May 12 *Perf. 13½x14*

76	CD302	1p carmine	.20	.15
77	CD302	1½p brown	.20	.15
78	CD302	2½p bright ultra	.35	.30
		Nos. 76-78 (3)	.75	.60
		Set, never hinged	1.25	

George VI — A6

Medicinal Spring — A7

Columbus Looking for Land — A8

Map Showing Anguilla — A9

Perf. 13½x14 (A6, A9), 14 (A7, A8)

1938-48 **Typo.**

79	A6	½p green	.15	.15
80	A6	1p carmine	.15	.15
81	A6	1½p orange	.15	.15
82	A7	2p gray & car	.25	.25
83	A6	2½p ultra	.25	.25
84	A7	3p car & pale lilac	.35	.35
85	A8	6p rose lil & dull grn	1.40	1.10
86	A7	1sh green & gray blk	.90	.90
87	A7	2sh6p car & gray blk	3.00	2.50
88	A8	5sh car & dull grn	3.00	3.00

Typo., Center Litho.

Chalky Paper

89	A9	10sh brt ultra & blk	13.00	21.00
90	A9	£1 brown & blk	18.00	22.50
		Nos. 79-90 (12)	40.60	52.30
		Set, never hinged	70.00	

Issue dates: ½p, 1p, 1½p, 2½p, Aug. 15, 1938. 2p, 1941. 3p, 6p, 2sh, 5sh, 1942. 1sh, 1943. 10sh, £1, Sept. 1, 1948.

For types overprinted see Nos. 99-104.

1938, Aug. 15 *Perf. 13x11½*

82a	A7	2p	7.25	3.50
84a	A7	3p	1.40	1.40
85a	A8	6p	1.40	1.40
86a	A7	1sh	2.75	2.25
87a	A7	2sh6p	9.25	9.25
88a	A8	5sh	35.00	22.50
		Nos. 82a-88a (6)	57.05	40.30

Catalogue values for unused stamps in this section, from this point to the end of the section, are for Never Hinged items.

Peace Issue

Common Design Type

Inscribed "St. Kitts-Nevis"

1946, Nov. 1 **Engr.** *Perf. 13½x14*

91	CD303	1½p deep orange	.15	.15
92	CD303	3p carmine	.15	.15
		Set value	.25	.25

Silver Wedding Issue

Common Design Types

Inscribed: "St. Kitts-Nevis"

1949, Jan. 3 **Photo.** *Perf. 14x14½*

93	CD304	2½p bright ultra	.15	.15

Engraved; Name Typographed

Perf. 11½x11

94	CD305	5sh rose carmine	4.50	5.00

UPU Issue

Common Design Types

Inscribed: "St. Kitt's-Nevis"

Engr.; Name Typo. on 3p, 6p

1949, Oct. 10 *Perf. 13½, 11x11½*

95	CD306	2½p ultra	.15	.15
96	CD307	3p deep carmine	.20	.20
97	CD308	6p red lilac	.50	.50
98	CD309	1sh blue green	.80	.80
		Nos. 95-98 (4)	1.65	1.65

Types of 1938 Overprinted in Black or Carmine:

ANGUILLA	ANGUILLA
TERCENTENARY 1650-1950	TERCENTENARY 1650—1950
On A6	On A7-A8

Perf. 13½x14, 13x12½

1950, Nov. 10 **Wmk. 4**

99	A6	1p carmine	.15	.15
100	A6	1½p orange	.15	.15
a.		Wmk. 4a (error)	600.00	
101	A6	2½p ultra	.15	.15
102	A7	3p car & pale lilac	.15	.15
103	A8	6p rose lil & dl grn	.25	.25
104	A7	1sh grn & gray blk (C)	.40	.40
		Nos. 99-104 (6)	1.25	1.25

300th anniv. of the settlement of Anguilla.

University Issue

Common Design Types

Inscribed: "St. Kitts-Nevis"

Perf. 14x14½

1951, Feb. 16 **Engr.** **Wmk. 4**

105	CD310	3c org yel & gray blk	.20	.20
106	CD311	12c red violet & aqua	.60	.60

St. Christopher-Nevis-Anguilla

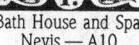

Bath House and Spa, Nevis — A10

Map — A11

Designs: 2c, Warner Park, St. Kitts. 4c, Brimstone Hill, St. Kitts. 5c, Nevis. 6c, Pinney's Beach, Nevis. 12c, Sir Thomas Warner's Tomb. 24c, Old Road Bay, St. Kitts. 48c, Picking Cotton. 60c, Treasury, St. Kitts. $1.20, Salt Pond, Anguilla. $4.80, Sugar Mill, St. Kitts.

1952, June 14 *Perf. 12½*

107	A10	1c ocher & dp grn	.15	.15
108	A10	2c emerald	.15	.15
109	A11	3c purple & red	.18	.18
110	A10	4c red	.22	.22
111	A10	5c gray & ultra	.32	.32
112	A10	6c deep ultra	.38	.38
113	A11	12c redsh brn & dp blue	.60	.60
114	A10	24c car & gray blk	.90	.70

115 A10 48c vio brn & ol bister 2.50 2.50
116 A10 60c dp green & ocher 2.50 2.50
117 A10 $1.20 dp ultra & dp green 6.00 6.00
118 A10 $4.80 car & emer 14.00 14.00
Nos. 107-118 (12) 27.90 27.70

Coronation Issue
Common Design Type

1953, June 2 *Perf. 13½x13*
119 CD312 2c brt green & blk .25 .15

Types of 1952 with Portrait of Queen Elizabeth II

½c, Salt Pond, Anguilla. 8c, Sombrero Lighthouse. $2.40, Map of Anguilla & Dependencies.

1954-57 Engr. *Perf. 12½*
120 A10 ½c gray olive ('56) .25 .15
121 A10 1c ocher & dp grn .15 .15
a. Horiz. pair, imperf. vert.
122 A10 2c emerald .35 .15
123 A11 3c purple & red .55 .15
124 A10 4c red .15 .15
125 A10 5c gray & ultra .15 .15
126 A10 6c deep ultra .40 .25
127 A11 8c dark gray ('57) 3.75 .25
128 A11 12c redsh brn & dp blue .15 .25
129 A10 24c carmine & blk .15 .45
130 A10 48c brn & ol bister .50 1.25
131 A10 60c dp grn & ocher 4.25 1.65
132 A10 $1.20 dp ultra & dp green 13.00 2.75
133 A10 $2.40 red org & blk ('57) 7.50 4.25
134 A10 $4.80 carmine & emer 10.00 11.00
Nos. 120-134 (15) 41.30 23.00

Issued: 24c-$1.20, $4.80, 12/1/54; ½c, 7/3/56; 8c, $2.40, 2/1/57; others, 3/1/54.

Alexander Hamilton and Nevis Scene — A12

1957, Jan. 11 *Perf. 12½*
135 A12 24c dp ultra & yellow grn .35 .35

Bicent. of the birth of Alexander Hamilton.

West Indies Federation
Common Design Type

Perf. 11½x11
1958, Apr. 22 Engr. Wmk. 314
136 CD313 3c green .35 .35
137 CD313 6c blue .60 .60
138 CD313 12c carmine rose 1.25 1.25
Nos. 136-138 (3) 2.20 2.20

Federation of the West Indies, Apr. 22, 1958.

Stamp of Nevis, 1861 — A13

Designs (Stamps of Nevis, 1861 issue): 8c, 4p stamp. 12c, 6p stamp. 24c, 1sh stamp.

1961, July 15 *Perf. 14*
139 A13 2c green & brown .15 .15
140 A13 8c blue & pale brown .20 .20
141 A13 12c carmine & gray .30 .30
142 A13 24c orange & green .70 .70
Nos. 139-142 (4) 1.35 1.35

Centenary of the first stamps of Nevis.

Red Cross Centenary Issue
Common Design Type

1963, Sept. 2 Litho. *Perf. 13*
143 CD315 3c black & red .15 .15
144 CD315 12c ultra & red .60 .60

New Lighthouse, Sombrero — A14

Loading Sugar Cane, St. Kitts — A15

Designs: 2c, Pall Mall Square, Basseterre. 3c, Gateway, Brimstone Hill Fort, St. Kitts. 4c, Nelson's Spring, Nevis. 5c, Grammar School, St. Kitts. 6c, Mt. Misery Crater, St. Kitts. 10c, Hibiscus. 15c, Sea Island cotton, Nevis. 20c, Boat building, Anguilla. 25c, White-crowned pigeon. 50c, St. George's Church tower, Basseterre. 60c, Alexander Hamilton. $1, Map of St. Kitts-Nevis. $2.50, Map of Anguilla. $5, Arms of St. Christopher-Nevis-Anguilla.

1963, Nov. 20 Photo. *Perf. 14*
145 A14 ½c blue & dk brn .15 .15
146 A15 1c multicolored .15 .15
147 A14 2c multicolored .15 .15
a. Yellow omitted 150.00
148 A14 3c multicolored .15 .15
149 A15 4c multicolored .15 .15
150 A15 5c multicolored .15 .15
151 A15 6c multicolored .15 .15
152 A15 10c multicolored .15 .15
153 A14 15c multicolored .20 .20
154 A15 20c multicolored .30 .30
155 A14 25c multicolored .35 .35
156 A15 50c multicolored .80 .80
157 A14 60c multicolored .90 .90
158 A14 $1 multicolored 1.65 1.65
159 A15 $2.50 multicolored 3.00 3.00
160 A14 $5 multicolored 5.00 5.00
Nos. 145-160 (16) 13.40 13.40

For overprints see Nos. 161-162.

1967-69 Wmk. 314 Sideways
145a A14 ½c ('69) .15 .15
147b A14 2c .15 .15
148a A14 3c ('68) .25 .25
153a A14 15c ('68) .60 .60
155a A14 25c ('68) 1.90 .95
158a A14 $1 ('68) 5.75 5.75
Nos. 145a-158a (6) 8.80 7.85

Nos. 148 and 155 Overprinted: "ARTS / FESTIVAL / ST. KITTS / 1964"

1964, Sept. 14
161 A14 3c multicolored .15 .15
162 A14 25c multicolored .30 .30
Set value .35 .35

ITU Issue
Common Design Type

Perf. 11x11½
1965, May 17 Litho. Wmk. 314
163 CD317 2c bister & rose red .15 .15
164 CD317 50c grnsh blue & olive .75 .75

Intl. Cooperation Year Issue
Common Design Type

1965, Oct. 25 *Perf. 14½*
165 CD318 2c blue grn & claret .15 .15
166 CD318 25c lt violet & green .55 .55

Churchill Memorial Issue
Common Design Type

1966, Jan. 24 Photo. *Perf. 14*
Design in Black, Gold and Carmine Rose
167 CD319 ½c bright blue .15 .15
168 CD319 3c green .15 .15
169 CD319 15c brown .30 .30
170 CD319 25c violet .60 .60
Set value 1.00 1.00

Royal Visit Issue
Common Design Type

1966, Feb. 14 Litho. *Perf. 11x12*
171 CD320 3c violet blue .15 .15
172 CD320 25c dk carmine rose .65 .65

World Cup Soccer Issue
Common Design Type

1966, July 1 Litho. *Perf. 14*
173 CD321 6c multicolored .15 .15
174 CD321 25c multicolored .50 .50

Festival Emblem With Dolphins — A16

Unwmk.
1966, Aug. 15 Photo. *Perf. 14*
175 A16 3c gold, grn, yel & blk .15 .15
176 A16 25c silver, grn, yel & blk .30 .30
Set value .35 .35

Arts Festival of 1966.

WHO Headquarters Issue
Common Design Type

1966, Sept. 20 Litho. *Perf. 14*
177 CD322 3c multicolored .15 .15
178 CD322 40c multicolored .55 .55

UNESCO Anniversary Issue
Common Design Type

1966, Dec. 1 Litho. *Perf. 14*
179 CD323 3c "Education" .15 .15
180 CD323 6c "Science" .15 .15
181 CD323 40c "Culture" .65 .65
Set value .80 .80

Independent State

Government Headquarters, Basseterre — A17

Designs: 10c, Flag and map of Anguilla, St. Christopher and Nevis. 25c, Coat of Arms.

Perf. 14½
1967, July 1 Wmk. 314 Photo.
182 A17 3c multicolored .15 .15
183 A17 10c multicolored .15 .15
184 A17 25c multicolored .40 .40
Set value .60 .60

Achievement of independence, Feb. 27, 1967.

Charles Wesley, Cross and Palm — A18

Designs: 3c, John Wesley. 40c, Thomas Coke.

1967, Dec. 1 Litho. *Perf. 13x13½*
185 A18 3c dp lilac, dp car & blk .15 .15
186 A18 25c ultra, grnsh blue & blk .15 .15
187 A18 40c ocher, yellow & blk .30 .30
Set value .45 .45

Attainment of autonomy by the Methodist Church in the Caribbean and the Americas, and for the opening of headquarters near St. John's, Antigua, May 1967.

Cargo Ship and Plane A19

Perf. 13½x13
1968, July 30 Litho. Wmk. 314
188 A19 25c multicolored .25 .25
189 A19 50c brt blue & multi .55 .55

Issued to publicize the organization of the Caribbean Free Trade Area, CARIFTA.

Martin Luther King, Jr. — A20

Mystical Nativity, by Botticelli — A21

Perf. 12x12½
1968, Sept. 30 Litho. Wmk. 314
190 A20 50c multicolored .35 .35

Dr. Martin Luther King, Jr. (1929-68), American civil rights leader.

Perf. 14½x14
1968, Nov. 27 Photo. Wmk. 314

Christmas (Paintings): 25c, 50c, The Adoration of the Magi, by Rubens.

191 A21 12c brt violet & multi .15 .15
192 A21 25c multicolored .15 .15
193 A21 40c gray & multi .20 .20
194 A21 50c crimson & multi .30 .30
Nos. 191-194 (4) .80 .80

Snook A22

Fish: 12c, Needlefish (gar). 40c, Horse-eye jack. 50c, Red snapper. The 6c is mis-inscribed "tarpon."

Perf. 14x14½
1969, Feb. 25 Photo. Wmk. 314
195 A22 6c brt green & multi .15 .15
196 A22 12c blue & multi .15 .15
197 A22 40c gray blue & multi .50 .50
198 A22 50c multicolored .65 .65
Nos. 195-198 (4) 1.45 1.45

Arms of Sir Thomas Warner and Map of Islands — A23

Designs: 25c, Warner's tomb in St. Kitts. 40c, Warner's commission from Charles I.

1969, Sept. 1 Litho. *Perf. 13½*
199 A23 20c multicolored .15 .15
200 A23 25c multicolored .15 .15
201 A23 40c multicolored .30 .30
Nos. 199-201 (3) .60 .60

Issued in memory of Sir Thomas Warner, first Governor of St. Kitts-Nevis, Barbados and Montserrat.

Adoration of the Kings, by Jan Mostaert — A24

Christmas (Painting): 40c, 50c, Adoration of the Kings, by Geertgen tot Sint Jans.

1969, Nov. 17 *Perf. 13½*
202 A24 10c olive & multi .15 .15
203 A24 25c violet & multi .15 .15
204 A24 40c yellow grn & multi .15 .15
205 A24 50c maroon & multi .20 .20
Set value .45 .45

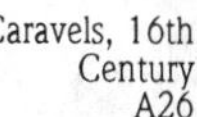

Pirates Burying Treasure, Frigate Bay — A25

Caravels, 16th Century A26

Designs: 1c, English two-decker, 1650. 2c, Flags of England, Spain, France, Holland and Portugal. 3c, Hilt of 17th cent. rapier. 5c, Henry Morgan and fire boats. 6c, The pirate L'Ollonois and a carrack (pirate vessel). 10c, Smugglers' ship. 15c, Spanish 17th cent. piece of eight and map of Caribbean. 20c, Garrison and ship cannon and map of Spanish Main. 25c, Humphrey Cole's astrolabe, 1574. 50c, Flintlock pistol and map of Spanish Main. 60c, Dutch Flute (ship). $1, Capt. Bartholomew Roberts and document with death sentence for his crew. $2.50, Railing piece (small cannon), 17th cent. and map of Spanish Main. $5, Francis Drake, John Hawkins and ships. $10, Edward Teach (Blackbeard) and his capture.

Wmk. 314 Upright (A25), Sideways (A26)

1970, Feb. 1 Litho. *Perf. 14*

206	A25	½c	multicolored	.15	.15
207	A25	1c	multicolored	.15	.15
208	A25	2c	multicolored	.15	.15
209	A25	3c	multicolored	.15	.15
210	A26	4c	multicolored	.15	.15
211	A26	5c	multicolored	.15	.15
212	A26	6c	multicolored	.15	.15
213	A26	10c	multicolored	.20	.20
214	A25	15c	*Hispanianum*	.45	.45
215	A25	15c	*Hispaniarum*	.35	.35
216	A26	20c	multicolored	.35	.35
217	A25	25c	multicolored	.35	.35
218	A26	50c	multicolored	.75	.75
219	A25	60c	multicolored	1.75	.90
220	A25	$1	multicolored	2.25	1.40
221	A26	$2.50	multicolored	3.25	2.75
222	A26	$5	multicolored	6.75	6.00
			Nos. 206-222 (17)	17.50	14.55

Coin inscription was misspelled on No. 214, corrected on No. 215 (issued Sept. 8).

Wmk. 314 Sideways (A25), Upright (A26)

1973-74

206a	A25	½c	multicolored	.15	.15
208a	A25	2c	multicolored	.15	.15
209a	A25	3c	multicolored	.15	.15
211a	A26	5c	multicolored	.20	.20
212a	A26	6c	multicolored	.30	.30
213a	A26	10c	multicolored	.45	.45
215a	A25	15c	multicolored	.55	.55
216a	A26	20c	multicolored	.85	.85
217a	A25	25c	multicolored	.60	.60
218a	A26	50c	multicolored	1.50	1.50
220a	A25	$1	multicolored	2.25	2.25
222A	A26	$10	multi ('74)	21.00	21.00
			Nos. 206a-220a,222A (12)	28.15	28.15

Issue dates: $10, Nov. 16; others, Sept. 12.

1975-77 Wmk. 373

207b	A25	1c	multi ('77)	.15	.15
209b	A25	3c	multi ('76)	.15	.15
210b	A26	4c	multi ('76)	.15	.15
211b	A26	5c	multicolored	.15	.15
212b	A26	6c	multicolored	.15	.15
213b	A26	10c	multi ('76)	.20	.15
215b	A25	15c	multi ('76)	.35	.20
216b	A26	20c	multicolored	.35	.15
219b	A25	60c	multi ('76)	1.75	1.00
220b	A25	$1	multi ('77)	2.25	1.50
			Nos. 207b-220b (10)	5.65	3.75

Pip Meeting Convict, from "Great Expectations" — A27

Designs: 20c, Miss Havisham from "Great Expectations." 25c, Dickens' birthplace, Portsmouth, vert. 40c, Charles Dickens, vert.

Perf. 13x13½, 13½x13

1970, May 1 Litho. Wmk. 314

223	A27	4c	gold, Prus blue & brn	.15	.15
224	A27	20c	gold, claret & brn	.20	.20
225	A27	25c	gold, olive & brn	.25	.25
226	A27	40c	dk blue, gold & brn	.50	.50
			Nos. 223-226 (4)	1.10	1.10

Charles Dickens (1812-70), English novelist.

Local Steel Band A28

Designs: 25c, Local string band. 40c, "A Midsummer Night's Dream," 1963 performance.

1970, Aug. 1 *Perf. 13½*

227	A28	20c	multicolored	.15	.15
228	A28	25c	multicolored	.20	.20
229	A28	40c	multicolored	.30	.30
			Nos. 227-229 (3)	.65	.65

Issued to publicize the 1970 Arts Festival.

St. Christopher No. 1 and St. Kitts Post Office, 1970 — A29

Designs: 20c, 25c, St. Christopher Nos. 1 and 3. 50c, St. Christopher No. 3 and St. Kitts postmark, Sept. 2, 1871.

Perf. 14½

1970, Sept. 14 Litho. Wmk. 314

230	A29	½c	green & rose	.15	.15
231	A29	20c	vio blue, rose & grn	.15	.15
232	A29	25c	brown, rose & grn	.20	.20
233	A29	50c	black, grn & dk red	.65	.65
			Nos. 230-233 (4)	1.15	1.15

Centenary of stamps of St. Christopher.

Holy Family, by Anthony van Dyck — A30

Christmas: 3c, 40c, Adoration of the Shepherds, by Frans Floris.

1970, Nov. 16 *Perf. 14*

234	A30	3c	multicolored	.15	.15
235	A30	20c	ocher & multi	.15	.15
236	A30	25c	dull red & multi	.20	.20
237	A30	40c	green & multi	.30	.30
			Nos. 234-237 (4)	.80	.80

Monkey Fiddle A31

Flowers: 20c, Mountain violets. 30c, Morning glory. 50c, Fringed epidendrum.

1971, Mar. 1 Litho. *Perf. 14*

238	A31	½c	multicolored	.15	.15
239	A31	20c	multicolored	.20	.20
240	A31	30c	multicolored	.35	.35
241	A31	50c	multicolored	.60	.60
			Nos. 238-241 (4)	1.30	1.30

Chateau de Poincy, St. Kitts — A32

Designs: 20c, Royal poinciana. 50c, De Poincy's coat of arms, vert.

1971, June 1 Litho. Wmk. 314

242	A32	20c	green & multi	.15	.15
243	A32	30c	dull yellow & multi	.15	.15
244	A32	50c	brown & multi	.30	.30
			Nos. 242-244 (3)	.60	.60

Philippe de Longvilliers de Poincy became first governor of French possessions in the Antilles in 1639.

East Yorks A33

Designs: 20c, Royal Artillery. 30c, French Infantry. 50c, Royal Scots.

1971, Sept. 1 *Perf. 14*

245	A33	½c	black & multi	.15	.15
246	A33	20c	black & multi	.35	.30
247	A33	30c	black & multi	.55	.45
248	A33	50c	black & multi	.90	.75
			Nos. 245-248 (4)	1.95	1.65

Siege of Brimstone Hill, 1782.

Crucifixion, by Quentin Massys — A34

Perf. 14x13½

1972, Apr. 1 Litho. Wmk. 314

249	A34	4c	brick red & multi	.15	.15
250	A34	20c	gray green & multi	.20	.20
251	A34	30c	dull blue & multi	.25	.25
252	A34	40c	lt brown & multi	.35	.35
			Nos. 249-252 (4)	.95	.95

Easter 1972.

Madonna and Child, by Bergognone — A35

Paintings: 20c, Adoration of the Kings, by Jacopo da Bassano, horiz. 25c, Adoration of the Shepherds, by Il Domenichino. 40c, Madonna and Child, by Fiorenzo di Lorenzo.

1972, Oct. 2 *Perf. 13½x14, 14x13½*

253	A35	3c	gray green & multi	.15	.15
254	A35	20c	deep plum & multi	.20	.20
255	A35	25c	sepia & multi	.25	.25
256	A35	40c	red & multi	.35	.35
			Nos. 253-256 (4)	.95	.95

Christmas 1972.

Silver Wedding Issue, 1972

Common Design Type

Queen Elizabeth II, Prince Philip, pelicans.

1972, Nov. 20 Photo. *Perf. 14x14½*

257	CD324	20c carmine rose & multi	.30	.30
258	CD324	25c ultra & multi	.40	.40

Warner Landing at St. Kitts — A36

Designs: 25c, Settlers growing tobacco. 40c, Building fort at "Old Road." $2.50, Warner's ship off St. Kitts, Jan. 28, 1623.

1973, Jan. 28 Litho. *Perf. 14x13½*

259	A36	4c	pink & multi	.15	.15
260	A36	25c	brown & multi	.15	.15
261	A36	40c	blue & multi	.25	.25
262	A36	$2.50	multicolored	1.00	1.00
			Nos. 259-262 (4)	1.55	1.55

350th anniversary of the landing of Sir Thomas Warner at St. Kitts.

For overprints see Nos. 266-269.

The Last Supper, by Juan de Juanes A37

Easter (The Last Supper, by): 4c, Titian, vert. 25c, ascribed to Roberti, vert.

Perf. 14x13½, 13½x14

1973, Apr. 16 Photo. Wmk. 314

263	A37	4c	blue black & multi	.15	.15
264	A37	25c	multicolored	.20	.20
265	A37	$2.50	purple & multi	1.25	1.25
			Nos. 263-265 (3)	1.60	1.60

Nos. 259-262 Overprinted:

VISIT OF
H. R. H. THE PRINCE OF WALES 1973

1973, May 31 Litho. *Perf. 14x13½*

266	A36	4c	pink & multi	.15	.15
267	A36	25c	brown & multi	.15	.15
268	A36	40c	blue & multi	.15	.15
269	A36	$2.50	multicolored	.65	.65
			Set value	.80	.80

Visit of Prince Charles, May 1973.

Harbor Scene and St. Kitts-Nevis No. 3 — A38

25c, Sugar mill and #2. 40c, Unloading of boat and #1. $2.50, Rock carvings and #5.

1973, Oct. 1 Litho. *Perf. 13½x14*

270	A38	4c	salmon & multi	.15	.15
271	A38	25c	lt blue & multi	.35	.35
272	A38	40c	multicolored	.70	.70
273	A38	$2.50	multicolored	2.25	2.25
a.			Souvenir sheet of 4, #270-273	3.50	3.50
			Nos. 270-273 (4)	3.45	3.45

70th anniv. of 1st St. Kitts-Nevis stamps.

Princess Anne's Wedding Issue

Common Design Type

1973, Nov. 14 *Perf. 14*

274	CD325	25c brt green & multi	.15	.15
275	CD325	40c citron & multi	.20	.20

St. Kitts-Nevis stamps can be mounted in the Scott British Leeward Islands album.

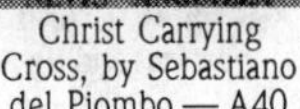

Virgin and Child, by Murillo — A39

Christ Carrying Cross, by Sebastiano del Piombo — A40

Christmas (Paintings): 40c, Holy Family, by Anton Raphael Mengs. 60c, Holy Family, by Sassoferrato. $1, Holy Family, by Filippino Lippi, horiz.

1973, Dec. 1 Litho. *Perf. 14x13½*

276	A39	4c brt blue & multi	.15	.15
277	A39	40c orange & multi	.20	.20
278	A39	60c multicolored	.30	.30
279	A39	$1 multicolored	.50	.50
		Nos. 276-279 (4)	1.15	1.15

1974, Apr. 8 *Perf. 13*

Easter: 25c, Crucifixion, by Goya. 40c, Trinity, by Diego Ribera. $2.50, Burial of Christ, by Fra Bartolomeo, horiz.

280	A40	4c olive & multi	.15	.15
281	A40	25c lt blue & multi	.15	.15
282	A40	40c purple & multi	.20	.20
283	A40	$2.50 gray & multi	1.25	1.25
		Nos. 280-283 (4)	1.75	1.75

University Center, St. Kitts, Chancellor Hugh Wooding — A41

1974, June 1 *Perf. 13½*

284	A41	10c blue & multi	.15	.15
285	A41	$1 pink & multi	.30	.30
a.		Souvenir sheet of 2, #284-285	.60	.60
		Set value	.35	.35

University of the West Indies, 25th anniv.

Nurse Explaining Family Planning — A42

Designs: 4c, Globe and hands reaching up, vert. 40c, Family, vert. $2.50, WPY emblem and scale balancing embryo and world.

Wmk. 314

1974, Aug. 5 Litho. *Perf. 14*

286	A42	4c blk, blue & brn	.15	.15
287	A42	25c multicolored	.15	.15
288	A42	40c multicolored	.15	.15
289	A42	$2.50 lilac & multi	.60	.60
		Set value	.80	.80

Family planning and World Population Week, Aug. 4-10.

Churchill as Lieutenant, 21st Lancers — A43

Knight of the Garter — A44

Designs: 25c, Churchill as Prime Minister. 60c, Churchill Statue, Parliament Square, London.

1974, Nov. 30

290	A43	4c dull violet & multi	.15	.15
291	A43	25c yellow & multi	.15	.15
292	A44	40c lt blue & multi	.20	.20
293	A44	60c lt blue & multi	.30	.30
a.		Souvenir sheet of 4, #290-293	1.25	1.25
		Nos. 290-293 (4)	.80	.80

Sir Winston Churchill (1874-1965).

Souvenir Sheets

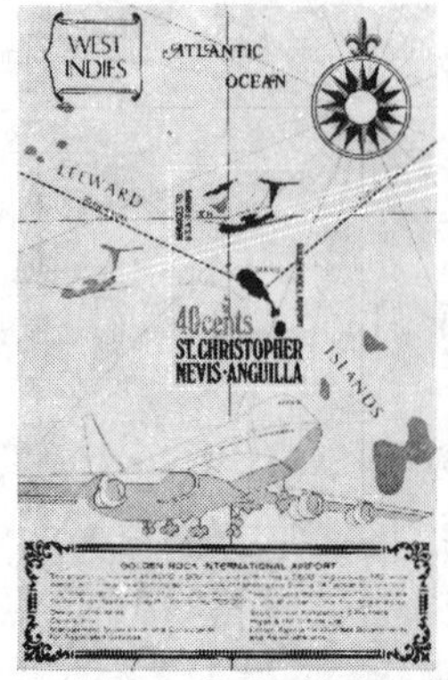

Boeing 747 over St. Kitts-Nevis — A45

1974, Dec. 16 *Perf. 14x13½*

294	A45	40c multicolored	.30	.30
295	A45	45c multicolored	.40	.40

Opening of Golden Rock Intl. Airport.

The Last Supper, by Doré — A46

Easter: 25c, Jesus mocked. 40c, Jesus falling beneath the Cross. $1, Raising the Cross. Designs based on Bible illustrations by Paul Gustave Doré (1833-1883).

1975, Mar. 24 *Perf. 14½*

296	A46	4c ultra & multi	.15	.15
297	A46	25c lt blue & multi	.15	.15
298	A46	40c bister & multi	.20	.20
299	A46	$1 salmon pink & multi	.45	.45
		Nos. 296-299 (4)	.95	.95

ECCA Headquarters, Basseterre, and Map of St. Kitts — A47

Designs: 25c, Specimen of $1 note, issued by ECCA. 40c, St. Kitts half dollar, 1801, and $4 coin, 1875. 45c, Nevis "9 dogs" coin, 1801, and 2c, 5c, coins, 1975.

Perf. 13½x14

1975, June 2 Wmk. 373

300	A47	12c orange & multi	.15	.15
301	A47	25c olive & multi	.15	.15
302	A47	40c vermilion & multi	.20	.20
303	A47	45c brt blue & multi	.25	.25
		Nos. 300-303 (4)	.75	.75

East Caribbean Currency Authority Headquarters, Basseterre, opening.

Evangeline Booth, Salvation Army — A48

Colfer Swinging Club — A49

Designs (IWY Emblem and): 25c, Sylvia Pankhurst, suffragette. 40c, Marie Curie, scientist. $2.50, Lady Annie Allen, teacher.

Perf. 14x14½

1975, Sept. 15 Litho. Wmk. 314

304	A48	4c orange brn & blk	.15	.15
305	A48	25c lilac pur & blk	.30	.30
306	A48	40c blue, vio bl & blk	.45	.45
307	A48	$2.50 yellow brn & blk	3.00	3.00
		Nos. 304-307 (4)	3.90	3.90

International Women's Year 1975.

1975, Nov. 1 *Perf. 14*

308	A49	4c rose red & blk	.15	.15
309	A49	25c yellow & blk	.75	.75
310	A49	40c emerald & blk	1.10	1.10
311	A49	$1 blue & blk	2.75	2.75
		Nos. 308-311 (4)	4.75	4.75

Opening of Frigate Bay Golf Course.

St. Paul, by Sacchi Pier Francesco — A50

Christmas (Paintings, details): 40c, St. James, by Bonifazio di Pitati. 45c, St. John, by Pier Francesco Mola. $1, Virgin Mary, by Raphael.

Wmk. 373

1975, Dec. 1 Litho. *Perf. 14*

312	A50	25c ultra & multi	.25	.25
313	A50	40c multicolored	.50	.50
314	A50	45c red brown & multi	.55	.55
315	A50	$1 gold & multi	1.25	1.25
		Nos. 312-315 (4)	2.55	2.55

Virgin Mary — A51

The Last Supper — A52

Stained Glass Windows: No. 317, Christ on the Cross. No. 318, St. John. 40c, The Last Supper (different). $1, Baptism of Christ.

Perf. 14x13½

1976, Apr. 14 Litho. Wmk. 373

316	A51	4c black & multi	.15	.15
317	A51	4c black & multi	.15	.15
318	A51	4c black & multi	.15	.15
a.		Triptych, #316-318	.15	.15

Perf. 14½

319	A52	25c black & multi	.25	.25
320	A52	40c black & multi	.40	.40
321	A52	$1 black & multi	1.00	1.00
		Set value	1.80	1.80

Easter 1976. No. 318a has continuous design.

Map of West Indies, Bats, Wicket and Ball — A52a

Prudential Cup — A52b

Unwmk.

1976, July 8 Litho. *Perf. 14*

322	A52a	12c lt blue & multi	.45	.35
323	A52b	40c lilac rose & blk	1.40	1.00
a.		Souvenir sheet of 2, #322-323	3.75	3.75

World Cricket Cup, won by West Indies Team, 1975.

Crispus Attucks and Boston Massacre — A53

Designs: 40c, Alexander Hamilton and Battle of Yorktown. 45c, Thomas Jefferson and Declaration of Independence. $1, George Washington and Crossing of the Delaware.

1976, July 26 Litho. Wmk. 373

324	A53	20c gray & multi	.15	.15
325	A53	40c gray & multi	.25	.25
326	A53	45c gray & multi	.25	.25
327	A53	$1 gray & multi	.75	.55
		Nos. 324-327 (4)	1.40	1.20

American Bicentennial.

Nativity, Sforza Book of Hours — A54

Queen Planting Tree, 1966 Visit — A55

Christmas (Paintings): 40c, Virgin and Child, by Bernardino Pintoricchio. 45c, Our Lady of Good Children, by Ford Maddox Brown. $1, Christ Child, by Margaret W. Tarrant.

1976, Nov. 1 *Perf. 14*

328	A54	20c purple & multi	.15	.15
329	A54	40c dk blue & multi	.20	.20
330	A54	45c multicolored	.20	.20
331	A54	$1 multicolored	.45	.45
		Nos. 328-331 (4)	1.00	1.00

1977, Feb. 7 Litho. *Perf. 14x13½*

Designs: 55c, The scepter. $1.50, Bishops paying homage to the Queen.

332 A55 50c multicolored .15 .15
333 A55 55c multicolored .15 .15
334 A55 $1.50 multicolored .40 .40
Nos. 332-334 (3) .70 .70

25th anniv. of the reign of Elizabeth II.

Christ on the Cross, by Niccolo di Liberatore — A56

Easter: 30c, Resurrection (Imitator of Mantegna). 50c, Resurrection, by Ugolino, horiz. $1, Christ Rising from Tomb, by Gaudenzio.

Wmk. 373

1977, Apr. 1 Litho. *Perf. 14*

335 A56 25c yellow & multi .15 .15
336 A56 30c deep blue & multi .15 .15
337 A56 50c olive green & multi .20 .20
338 A56 $1 red & multi .40 .40
Nos. 335-338 (4) .90 .90

Estridge Mission A57

20c, Mission emblem. 40c, Basseterre Mission.

1977, June 27 Litho. *Perf. 12½*

339 A57 4c blue & black .15 .15
340 A57 20c multicolored .20 .20
341 A57 40c orange yel & blk .35 .35
Nos. 339-341 (3) .70 .70

Bicentenary of Moravian Mission.

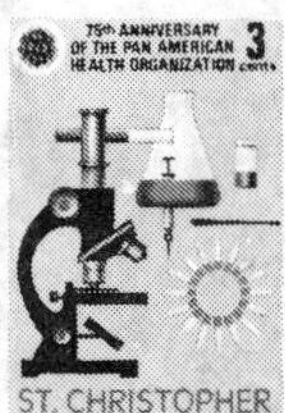

Microscope, Flask, Syringe — A58

12c, Blood, fat, nerve cells. 20c, Symbol of community participation. $1, Inoculation.

1977, Oct. 11 Litho. *Perf. 14*

342 A58 3c multicolored .15 .15
343 A58 12c multicolored .15 .15
344 A58 20c multicolored .20 .20
345 A58 $1 multicolored 1.00 1.00
Nos. 342-345 (4) 1.50 1.50

Pan American Health Organization, 75th anniversary (PAHO).

Three Kings — A59

Green Monkey and Young — A60

Christmas, Stained-glass Windows, Chartres Cathedral: 4c, Nativity, West Window. 40c, Virgin and Child. $1, Virgin and Child, Rose Window.

1977, Nov. 15 Wmk. 373

346 A59 4c multicolored .15 .15
347 A59 6c multicolored .15 .15
348 A59 40c multicolored .30 .30
349 A59 $1 multicolored .75 .75
Nos. 346-349 (4) 1.35 1.35

Perf. 14½

1978, Apr. 15 Litho. Wmk. 373

Green Monkeys: 5c, $1.50, Mother and young sitting on branch. 55c, like 4c.

350 A60 4c multicolored .15 .15
351 A60 5c multicolored .15 .15
352 A60 55c multicolored .65 .50
353 A60 $1.50 multicolored 1.75 1.40
Nos. 350-353 (4) 2.70 2.20

Elizabeth II Coronation Anniversary Issue

Common Design Types

Souvenir Sheet

Unwmk.

1978, Apr. 21 Litho. *Perf. 15*

354 Sheet of 6 1.00 1.00
a. CD326 $1 Falcon of Edward III .15 .15
b. CD327 $1 Elizabeth II .15 .15
c. CD328 $1 Pelican .15 .15

No. 354 contains 2 se-tenant strips of Nos. 354a-354c, separated by horizontal gutter with commemorative and descriptive inscriptions and showing central part of coronation procession with coach.

Tomatoes A61

Designs: 2c, Defense Force band. 5c, Radio and TV station. 10c, Technical College. 12c, TV assembly plant. 15c, Sugar cane harvest. 25c, Craft Center. 30c, Cruise ship. 40c, Sea crab and lobster. 45c, Royal St. Kitts Hotel and golf course. 50c, Pinneys Beach, Nevis. 55c, New Runway at Golden Rock. $1, Cotton pickers. $5, Brewery. $10, Pineapples and peanuts.

Perf. 14½x14

1978, Sept. 8 Wmk. 373

355 A61 1c multicolored .15 .15
356 A61 2c multicolored .15 .15
357 A61 5c multicolored .15 .15
358 A61 10c multicolored .15 .15
359 A61 12c multicolored .15 .15
360 A61 15c multicolored .15 .15
361 A61 25c multicolored .15 .15
362 A61 30c multicolored .15 .15
363 A61 40c multicolored .15 .15
364 A61 45c multicolored .15 .15
365 A61 50c multicolored .15 .15
366 A61 55c multicolored .20 .20
367 A61 $1 multicolored .30 .30
368 A61 $5 multicolored 1.50 1.50
369 A61 $10 multicolored 3.25 3.25
Set value 6.00 6.00

For overprints see Nevis #100-112, O1-O10.

Investiture — A62

King Bringing Gift — A63

Designs: 10c, Map reading. 25c, Pitching tent. 40c, Cooking. 50c, First aid. 55c, Rev. W. A. Beckett, founder of Scouting in St. Kitts.

Perf. 13½

1978, Oct. 9 Litho. Wmk. 373

370 A62 5c multicolored .15 .15
371 A62 10c multicolored .15 .15
372 A62 25c multicolored .25 .25
373 A62 40c multicolored .40 .40
374 A62 50c multicolored .50 .50
375 A62 55c multicolored .50 .50
Nos. 370-375 (6) 1.95 1.95

50th anniversary of St. Kitts-Nevis Scouting.

1978, Dec. 1 *Perf. 14x13½*

Christmas: 15c, 30c, King bringing gift, diff. $2.25, Three Kings paying homage to Infant Jesus.

376 A63 5c multicolored .15 .15
377 A63 15c multicolored .15 .15
378 A63 30c multicolored .15 .15
379 A63 $2.25 multicolored .65 .65
Set value .80 .80

Canna Coccinea — A64

Flowers: 30c, Heliconia bihai. 55c, Ruellia tuberosa. $1.50, Gesneria ventricosa.

1979, Mar. 19 *Perf. 14*

380 A64 5c multicolored .15 .15
381 A64 30c multicolored .30 .25
382 A64 55c multicolored .50 .40
383 A64 $1.50 multicolored 1.40 1.10
Nos. 380-383 (4) 2.35 1.90

See Nos. 393-396.

Rowland Hill and St. Christopher No. 1 — A65

Rowland Hill and: 15c, St. Kitts-Nevis #233. 50c, Great Britain #4. $2.50, St. Kitts-Nevis #64.

Perf. 14½

1979, July 2 Litho. Wmk. 373

384 A65 5c multicolored .15 .15
385 A65 15c multicolored .15 .15
386 A65 50c multicolored .20 .20
387 A65 $2.50 multicolored .90 .90
Nos. 384-387 (4) 1.40 1.40

Sir Rowland Hill (1795-1879), originator of penny postage.

The Woodman's Daughter, by Millais — A66

Paintings by John Everett Millais and IYC Emblem: 25c, Cherry Ripe. 30c, The Rescue, horiz. 55c, Bubbles. $1, Christ in the House of His Parents.

1979, Nov. 12 Litho. *Perf. 14*

388 A66 5c multicolored .15 .15
389 A66 25c multicolored .25 .25
390 A66 30c multicolored .30 .30
391 A66 55c multicolored .60 .60
Nos. 388-391 (4) 1.30 1.30

Souvenir Sheet

392 A66 $1 multicolored 1.10 1.10

Christmas 1979; Intl. Year of the Child.

Flower Type of 1979

Flowers: 4c, Clerodendrum aculeatum. 55c, Inga laurina. $1.50, Epidendrum difforme. $2, Salvia serontina.

1980, Feb. 4 Litho. *Perf. 14*

393 A64 4c multicolored .15 .15
394 A64 55c multicolored .30 .30
395 A64 $1.50 multicolored .80 .80
396 A64 $2 multicolored 1.10 1.10
Nos. 393-396 (4) 2.35 2.35

Nevis Lagoon, London 1980 Emblem A67

1980, May 6 Litho. *Perf. 13½*

397 A67 5c shown .15 .15
398 A67 30c Fig Tree Church, vert. .20 .20
399 A67 55c Nisbet Plantation .35 .35
400 A67 $3 Lord Nelson, by Fuger, vert. 1.90 1.90
Nos. 397-400 (4) 2.60 2.60

Souvenir Sheet

401 A67 75c Nelson Falling, by D. Dighton 1.00 .70

London 80 Intl. Phil. Exhib., May 6-14; Lord Nelson, (1758-1805).

WAR TAX STAMPS

No. 12 Overprinted **WAR TAX**

1916 Wmk. 3 *Perf. 14*

MR1 A1 ½p green .15 .15

Type of 1905-18 Issue Overprinted **WAR STAMP**

1918

MR2 A1 1½p orange .15 .15

OFFICIAL STAMPS

Catalogue values for unused stamps in this section are for Never Hinged items.

Nos. 359, 361, 363-369 Overprinted: OFFICIAL

Perf. 14½x14

1980 Litho. Wmk. 373

O1 A61 12c multicolored .15 .15
O2 A61 25c multicolored .15 .15
O3 A61 40c multicolored .25 .25
O4 A61 45c multicolored .30 .30
O5 A61 50c multicolored .30 .30
O6 A61 55c multicolored .35 .35
O7 A61 $1 multicolored .65 .65
O8 A61 $5 multicolored 3.25 3.25
O9 A61 $10 multicolored 6.75 6.75
Nos. O1-O9 (9) 12.15 12.15

ST. LUCIA

sānt 'lü-shə

LOCATION — Island in the West Indies, one of the Windward group
GOVT. — Independent state in British Commonwealth
AREA — 240 sq. mi.
POP. — 126,800 (est. 1984)
CAPITAL — Castries

The British colony of St. Lucia became an associated state March 1, 1967, and independent in 1979.

12 Pence = 1 Shilling
100 Cents = 1 Dollar (1949)

Catalogue values for unused stamps in this country are for Never Hinged items, beginning with Scott 127 in the regular postage section, Scott C1 in the air post section, Scott J3 in the postage due section, and Scott O1 in the officials section.

Watermarks

Wmk. 5- Small Star

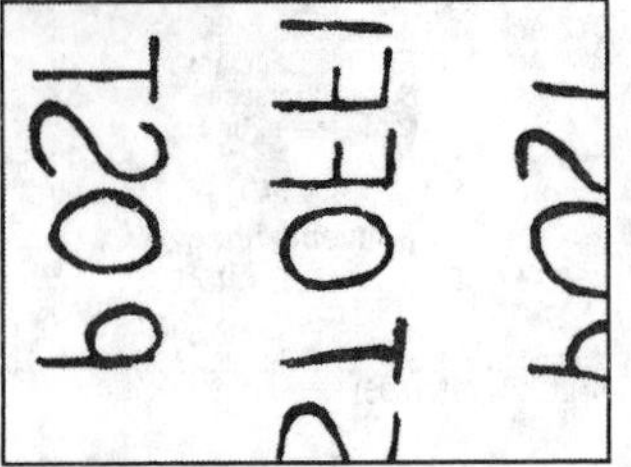
Wmk. 380- “POST OFFICE”

Values for unused stamps are for examples with original gum as defined in the catalogue introduction. Very fine examples of Nos. 1-26 will have perforations touching the design on at least one side due to the narrow spacing of the stamps on the plates. Stamps with perfs clear of the framelines on all four sides are very scarce and will command higher prices.

Queen Victoria — A1

Perf. 14 to 16

1860, Dec. 18 Engr. Wmk. 5

1 A1 (1p) rose red 110.00 82.50
a. Double impression *1,450.*
2 A1 (4p) deep blue 275.00 250.00
3 A1 (6p) green 425.00 300.00
Nos. 1-3 (3) 810.00 632.50

For types overprinted see #15, 17, 19-26.

1863 Wmk. 1 *Perf. 12½*

4 A1 (1p) lake 50.00 70.00
5 A1 (4p) slate blue 140.00 120.00
6 A1 (6p) emerald 200.00 200.00
Nos. 4-6 (3) 390.00 390.00

1864

7 A1 (1p) deep black 15.00 12.00
8 A1 (4p) yellow 120.00 50.00
a. (4p) olive yellow 250.00 70.00
9 A1 (6p) violet 65.00 30.00
a. (6p) lilac 175.00 42.50
10 A1 (1sh) red orange 225.00 42.50
a. (1sh) orange 250.00 42.50
Nos. 7-10 (4) 425.00 134.50

Perf. 14

11 A1 (1p) deep black 17.50 15.00
12 A1 (4p) yellow 75.00 25.00
a. (4p) olive yellow 175.00 80.00
13 A1 (6p) pale lilac 52.50 25.00
a. (6p) deep lilac 55.00 32.50
14 A1 (1sh) orange 150.00 30.00
Nos. 11-14 (4) 295.00 95.00

Type of 1860 Surcharged in Black or Red:

HALFPENNY a   **2½ PENCE** b

1881

15 A1(a) ½p green 50.00 60.00
17 A1(b) 2½p scarlet 20.00 17.50

1883-84 Wmk. Crown and CA (2)

19 A1(a) ½p green 12.50 20.00
20 A1(a) 1p black (R) 16.00 14.00
a. Half used as ½p on cover *2,500.*
21 A1(a) 4p yellow 200.00 27.50
22 A1(a) 6p violet 32.50 32.50
23 A1(a) 1sh orange 225.00 150.00
Nos. 19-23 (5) 486.00 244.00

1884 *Perf. 12*

24 A1(a) 4p yellow 350.00 32.50

Half penny

1885 Wmk. 1 *Perf. 12½*

25 A1 ½p emerald 60.
26 A1 6p slate blue 1,400.

Nos. 25 and 26 were prepared for use but not issued.

A5

Die B

For explanation of dies A and B see back of this section of the Catalogue.

1883-98 Typo. Wmk. 2 *Perf. 14*

27 A5 ½p green ('91) .50 .30
a. Die A ('83) 4.00 3.00
28 A5 1p rose (die A) ('83) 25.00 16.00
29 A5 1p lilac ('91) 1.00 .40
a. Die A ('86) 2.75 4.00
b. Die A, imperf., pair 725.00
30 A5 2p ultra & brn org ('98) 1.50 1.50
31 A5 2½p ultra ('91) 2.00 .60
a. Die A ('83) 21.00 2.25
32 A5 3p lilac & grn ('91) 3.00 4.50
a. Die A ('86) 70.00 16.00
33 A5 4p brown ('93) 2.50 2.50
a. Die A ('85) 20.00 3.50
b. Die A, imperf., pair 1,050.
34 A5 6p vio (die A) ('85) 275.00 275.00
a. Imperf., pair 1,800.
35 A5 6p lil & bl ('86) 3.25 5.00
a. Die B ('91) 8.50 10.50
36 A5 1sh brn org (die A) ('85) 400.00 135.00
37 A5 1sh lilac & red ('91) 2.50 *7.50*
a. Die A ('86) 70.00 30.00
38 A5 5sh lilac & org ('91) 27.50 *70.00*
39 A5 10sh lilac & blk ('91) 55.00 *80.00*
Nos. 27-39 (13) 798.75 598.30

Nos. 32, 32a, 35a and 33a Surcharged in Black:

ONE HALF PENNY — No. 40   ½d. — No. 41   ONE PENNY — No. 42

1892

40 A5 ½p on 3p lil & grn 32.50 25.00
a. Die A 65.00 65.00
b. Dbl. surch., die B 900.00 850.00
c. Invtd. surch., die B 2,000. 750.00
d. Triple surch., one on back *1,800.* *1,650.*
41 A5 ½p on half of 6p lilac & blue 15.00 10.50
a. Slanting serif 180.00 180.00
c. Without the bar of "½" 180.00 160.00
d. "2" of "½" omitted 400.00 425.00
e. Surcharged sideways 500.00
f. Double surcharge 500.00 500.00
42 A5 1p on 4p brown 5.00 5.50
b. Double surcharge 165.00
c. Inverted surcharge 1,050. 550.00
Nos. 40-42 (3) 52.50 41.00

No. 40 is found with wide or narrow "O" in "ONE," and large or small "A" in "HALF." The narrow "O" and small "A" varieties are worth about 3 times the normal No. 40.

Edward VII
A9

The Pitons
A10

Numerals of 3p, 6p, 1sh and 5sh of type A9 are in color on plain tablet.

1902-03 Typo.

43 A9 ½p violet & green .85 .55
44 A9 1p violet & car rose 2.25 .90
46 A9 2½p violet & ultra 6.00 6.50
47 A9 3p violet & yellow 6.00 6.50
48 A9 1sh green & black 10.50 10.00
Nos. 43-48 (5) 25.60 24.45

Wmk. 1 sideways

1902, Dec. 16 Engr.

49 A10 2p brown & green 6.00 6.00

Fourth centenary of the discovery of the island by Columbus.

1904-05 Typo. Wmk. 3

50 A9 ½p violet & green 1.50 .20
51 A9 1p violet & car rose 1.50 .35
52 A9 2½p violet & ultra 4.25 1.00
53 A9 3p violet & yellow 1.50 2.25
54 A9 6p vio & dp vio ('05) 8.00 5.25
55 A9 1sh green & blk ('05) 19.00 10.00
56 A9 5sh green & car ('05) 37.50 80.00
Nos. 50-56 (7) 73.25 99.05

#50, 51, 52, 54 are on both ordinary and chalky paper. #55 is on chalky paper only.

1907-10

57 A9 ½p green 1.50 .30
58 A9 1p carmine 2.50 .30
59 A9 2½p ultra 3.75 1.50

Chalky Paper

60 A9 3p violet, *yel* ('09) 1.75 *4.00*
61 A9 6p violet & red violet 4.75 *6.00*
a. 6p violet & dull vio ('10) 15.00 *13.00*
62 A9 1sh black, *grn* ('09) 3.75 *6.50*
63 A9 5sh green & red, *yel* 47.50 *50.00*
Nos. 57-63 (7) 65.50 *68.60*

King George V
A11 A12

Numerals of 3p, 6p, 1sh and 5sh of type A11 are in color on plain tablet.

For description of dies I and II see back of this section of the Catalogue.

Die I

1912-19

Ordinary Paper

64 A11 ½p deep green .40 .30
65 A11 1p scarlet .55 .40
a. 1p carmine .55 .25
66 A12 2p gray ('13) 2.00 4.25
67 A11 2½p ultra 1.25 .90

Chalky Paper

Numeral on White Tablet

68 A11 3p violet, *yel* .70 1.00
a. Die II 3.75 7.25
69 A11 6p vio & red vio 2.25 *6.00*
70 A11 1sh black, *green* 3.00 5.00
a. 1sh black, *bl grn*, ol back 3.75 6.00
71 A11 1sh fawn 3.00 6.00
72 A11 5sh green & red, *yel* 22.50 *50.00*
Nos. 64-72 (9) 35.65 *73.85*

A13

A14

1913-14

Chalky Paper

73 A13 4p scar & blk, *yel* 2.50 *4.50*
74 A14 2sh6p black & red, *bl* 14.00 *20.00*

Surface-colored Paper

75 A13 4p scarlet & blk, *yel* .90 *1.75*

Die II

1921-24 Wmk. 4

Ordinary Paper

76 A11 ½p green .50 .20
77 A11 1p carmine 2.75 *5.75*
78 A11 1p dk brn ('22) .50 .45
79 A13 1½p rose red ('22) 1.65 1.00
80 A12 2p gray .45 .45
81 A11 2½p ultra .80 *1.65*
82 A11 2½p orange ('24) 6.50 *9.25*
83 A11 3p ultra ('22) 1.40 *2.50*

Chalky Paper

84 A11 3p violet, *yel* .80 *2.25*
85 A13 4p scar & blk, *yel* ('24) .80 *1.65*
86 A11 6p vio & red vio 1.40 *4.25*
87 A11 1sh fawn 1.75 *5.00*
88 A14 2sh6p blk & red, *bl* ('24) 13.00 *19.00*
89 A11 5sh grn & red, *yel* 27.50 *40.00*
Nos. 76-89 (14) 59.80 *93.40*

Common Design Types pictured following the introduction.

Silver Jubilee Issue

Common Design Type

1935, May 6 Engr. *Perf. 13½x14*

91 CD301 ½p green & blk .15 .25
92 CD301 2p gray blk & ultra .40 .45
93 CD301 2½p blue & brn 1.00 1.25
94 CD301 1sh brt vio & indigo 3.00 3.75
Nos. 91-94 (4) 4.55 5.70

Port Castries
A15

Columbus Square, Castries
A16

Ventine Falls
A17

Soldiers' Monument
A19

Fort Rodney, Pigeon Island — A18

Government House — A20

Seal of the Colony — A21

1936, Mar. 1 *Perf. 14*

Center in Black

95 A15 ½p light green .15 .15
a. Perf. 13x12 1.00 1.50
96 A16 1p dark brown .35 .15
a. Perf. 13x12 2.00 1.40
97 A17 1½p carmine .50 .20
a. Perf. 12x13 6.00 2.75
98 A15 2p gray .40 .45
99 A16 2½p blue .40 .40
100 A17 3p dull green 1.25 .60
101 A15 4p brown .30 *.60*
102 A16 6p orange .85 .85
103 A18 1sh light blue, perf. 13x12 1.25 1.25
104 A19 2sh6p ultra 6.25 *8.50*
105 A20 5sh violet 7.75 *16.00*
106 A21 10sh carmine rose, perf. 13x12 40.00 *47.50*
Nos. 95-106 (12) 59.45 *76.65*

Nos. 95a, 96a and 97a are coils.
Issue date: Nos. 95a, 96a, Apr. 8.

Coronation Issue

Common Design Type

1937, May 12 *Perf. 11x11½*

107 CD302 1p dark purple .15 .15
108 CD302 1½p dark carmine .25 .20
109 CD302 2½p deep ultra .25 .20
Nos. 107-109 (3) .65 .55
Set, never hinged 1.40

King George VI A22

Columbus Square, Castries A23

Government House — A24

The Pitons — A25

Loading Bananas — A26

Arms of the Colony — A27

Perf. 12½ (#110-111, 1½p-3½p, 8p, 3sh, 5sh, £1), 12 (6p, 1sh, 2sh, 10sh)

1938-48

110 A22	½p	green ('43)	.15	.15
a.		Perf. 14½x14	.45	.15
111 A22	1p	deep violet	.15	.15
a.		Perf. 14½x14	.55	.55
112 A22	1p	red, Perf. 14½x14 ('47)	.15	.15
a.		Perf. 12½	.15	.15
113 A22	1½p	carmine ('43)	.15	.15
a.		Perf. 14½x14	.75	.35
114 A22	2p	gray ('43)	.15	.15
a.		Perf. 14½x14	.40	.50
115 A22	2½p	ultra ('43)	.15	.15
a.		Perf. 14½x14	.75	.15
116 A22	2½p	violet ('47)	.20	.15
117 A22	3p	red orange ('43)	.15	.15
a.		Perf. 14½x14	.15	.15
118 A22	3½p	brt ultra ('47)	.20	.15
119 A23	6p	magenta ('48)	.60	.40
a.		Perf. 13½	1.10	.30
120 A22	8p	choc ('46)	1.50	.25
121 A24	1sh	lt brn ('48)	.25	.20
a.		Perf. 13½	.35	.25
122 A25	2sh	red vio & sl bl	2.25	1.10
123 A22	3sh	brt red vio ('46)	5.00	2.50
124 A26	5sh	rose vio & blk	8.75	5.75
125 A27	10sh	black, *yel*	2.75	*8.00*
126 A22	£1	sepia ('46)	6.75	7.00
		Nos. 110-126 (17)	29.30	26.55
		Set, never hinged	45.00	

See Nos. 135-148.

Catalogue values for unused stamps in this section, from this point to the end of the section, are for Never Hinged items.

Peace Issue

Common Design Type

Perf. 13½x14

1946, Oct. 8 Wmk. 4 Engr.

127 CD303	1p	lilac	.15	.15
128 CD303	3½p	deep blue	.45	.45

Silver Wedding Issue

Common Design Types

1948, Nov. 26 Photo. *Perf. 14x14½*

129 CD304	1p	scarlet	.15	.15

Engraved; Name Typographed

Perf. 11½x11

130 CD305	£1	violet brown	18.00	30.00

UPU Issue

Common Design Types

Engr.; Name Typo. on 6c, 12c.

Perf. 13½, 11x11½

1949, Oct. 10 Wmk. 4

131 CD306	5c	violet	.15	.15
132 CD307	6c	deep orange	.20	.20
133 CD308	12c	red lilac	.50	.50
134 CD309	24c	blue green	.75	.75
		Nos. 131-134 (4)	1.60	1.60

Types of 1938

Values in Cents and Dollars

1949, Oct. 1 Engr. *Perf. 12½*

135 A22	1c	green	.15	.15
a.		Perf. 14	.60	.60
136 A22	2c	rose lilac	.20	.15
a.		Perf. 14½x14	1.75	1.75
137 A22	3c	red	.25	.15
138 A22	4c	gray	.25	.15
a.		Perf. 14½x14		*2,500.*
139 A22	5c	violet	.35	.20
140 A22	6c	red orange	.35	.20
141 A22	7c	ultra	.40	.25
142 A22	12c	rose lake	.70	.60
a.		Perf. 14½x14 ('50)	500.00	275.00
143 A22	16c	brown	.60	.55

Perf. 11½

144 A27	24c	Prus blue	.80	.70
145 A27	48c	olive green	2.00	2.00
146 A27	$1.20	purple	2.75	2.75
147 A27	$2.40	blue green	6.75	6.75
148 A27	$4.80	dark car rose	15.00	15.00
		Nos. 135-148 (14)	30.55	29.60

Nos. 144 to 148 are of a type similar to A27, but with the denomination in the top corners and "St. Lucia" at the bottom.

For overprints see Nos. 152-155.

University Issue

Common Design Types

Perf. 14x14½

1951, Feb. 16 Wmk. 4

149 CD310	3c	red & gray black	.20	.20
150 CD311	12c	brown carmine & blk	.45	.45

Phoenix Rising from Burning Buildings — A28

Perf. 13½x13

1951, June 19 Engr. & Typo.

151 A28	12c	deep blue & carmine	.35	.35

Reconstruction of Castries.

Nos. 136, 138, 139 and 142 Overprinted in Black

N 1
E 9
W 5
1
CONSTITUTION

1951, Sept. 25 *Perf. 12½*

152 A22	2c	rose lilac	.15	.15
153 A22	4c	gray	.15	.15
154 A22	5c	violet	.20	.20
155 A22	12c	rose lilac	.30	.30
		Nos. 152-155 (4)	.80	.80

Adoption of a new constitution for the Windward Islands, 1951.

Coronation Issue

Common Design Type

1953, June 2 Engr. *Perf. 13½x13*

156 CD312	3c	carmine & black	.20	.20

Queen Elizabeth II A29

Arms of St. Lucia A30

1953-54 Engr. *Perf. 14½x14*

157 A29	1c	green	.15	.15
158 A29	2c	rose lilac	.15	.15
159 A29	3c	red	.15	.15
160 A29	4c	gray	.15	.15
161 A29	5c	violet	.15	.15
162 A29	6c	orange	.15	.15
163 A29	8c	rose lake	.18	.18
164 A29	10c	ultra	.22	.20
165 A29	15c	brown	.30	.25

Perf. 11x11½

166 A30	25c	Prus blue	.55	.50
167 A30	50c	brown olive	1.25	1.00
168 A30	$1	blue green	2.75	2.50
169 A30	$2.50	dark car rose	7.25	5.75
		Nos. 157-169 (13)	13.40	11.28

Issue dates: 2c, Oct. 28. 4c, Jan. 7, 1954. 1c, 5c, Apr. 1, 1954. Others, Sept. 2, 1954.

West Indies Federation

Common Design Type

Perf. 11½x11

1958, Apr. 22 Wmk. 314

170 CD313	3c	green	.15	.15
171 CD313	6c	blue	.20	.20
172 CD313	12c	carmine rose	.40	.40
		Nos. 170-172 (3)	.75	.75

16th Century Ship and Pitons — A31

St. Lucia Stamp of 1860 — A32

1960, Jan. 1 *Perf. 12½x13*

173 A31	8c	carmine rose	.24	.24
174 A31	10c	orange	.32	.32
175 A31	25c	dark blue	.70	.70
		Nos. 173-175 (3)	1.26	1.26

Granting of new constitution.

1960, Dec. 18 Engr. *Perf. 13½*

176 A32	5c	ultra & red brown	.32	.32
177 A32	16c	yel grn & blue blk	.65	.65
178 A32	25c	carmine & green	.90	.90
		Nos. 176-178 (3)	1.87	1.87

Centenary of St. Lucia's first postage stamps.

Freedom from Hunger Issue

Common Design Type

1963, June 4 Photo. *Perf. 14x14½*

179 CD314	25c	green	.70	.70

Red Cross Centenary Issue

Common Design Type

Wmk. 314

1963, Sept. 2 Litho. *Perf. 13*

180 CD315	4c	black & red	.15	.15
181 CD315	25c	ultra & red	1.00	1.00

A33

A34

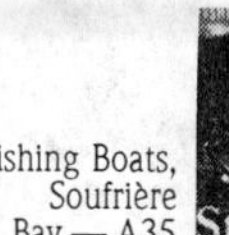
Fishing Boats, Soufrière Bay — A35

Designs: 15c, Pigeon Island. 25c, Reduit Beach. 35c, Castries Harbor. 50c, The Pitons. $1, Vigie Beach, vert. $2.50, Queen Elizabeth II, close-up.

Perf. 14½

1964, Mar. 1 Wmk. 314 Photo.

182 A33	1c	dark car rose	.15	.15
183 A33	2c	violet	.15	.15
184 A33	4c	brt blue green	.15	.15
185 A33	5c	slate blue	.15	.15
186 A33	6c	brown	.15	.15
187 A34	8c	lt blue & multi	.15	.15
188 A34	10c	multicolored	.16	.16
189 A35	12c	multicolored	.18	.18
190 A35	15c	blue & ocher	.22	.22
a.		Wmkd. sideways ('68)	.20	.20
191 A35	25c	multicolored	.38	.38
192 A35	35c	dk blue & buff	.65	.52
193 A35	50c	brt blue, blk & yel	.90	.85
194 A35	$1	multicolored	2.00	1.65
195 A34	$2.50	multicolored	4.00	3.50
		Nos. 182-195 (14)	9.39	8.36

For overprints see Nos. 215-225.

Shakespeare Issue

Common Design Type

1964, Apr. 23 *Perf. 14x14½*

196 CD316	10c	bright green	.38	.38

ITU Issue

Common Design Type

Perf. 11x11½

1965, May 17 Litho. Wmk. 314

197 CD317	2c	red lilac & brt pink	.15	.15
198 CD317	50c	lilac & yel grn	1.75	1.75

Intl. Cooperation Year Issue

Common Design Type

1965, Oct. 25 Wmk. 314 *Perf. 14½*

199 CD318	1c	blue grn & claret	.15	.15
200 CD318	25c	lt violet & grn	.50	.50

Churchill Memorial Issue

Common Design Type

1966, Jan. 24 Photo. *Perf. 14*

Design in Black, Gold and Carmine Rose

201 CD319	4c	bright blue	.15	.15
202 CD319	6c	green	.15	.15
203 CD319	25c	brown	.40	.40
204 CD319	35c	violet	.60	.60
		Nos. 201-204 (4)	1.30	1.30

Royal Visit Issue

Common Design Type

1966, Feb. 4 Litho. *Perf. 11x12*

205 CD320	4c	violet blue	.15	.15
206 CD320	25c	dk carmine rose	.75	.75

World Cup Soccer Issue

Common Design Type

1966, July 1 Litho. *Perf. 14*

207 CD321	4c	multicolored	.15	.15
208 CD321	25c	multicolored	.45	.45

WHO Headquarters Issue

Common Design Type

1966, Sept. 20 Litho. *Perf. 14*

209 CD322	4c	multicolored	.15	.15
210 CD322	25c	multicolored	.45	.45
		Set value	.50	.50

UNESCO Anniversary Issue

Common Design Type

1966, Dec. 1 Litho. *Perf. 14*

211 CD323	4c	"Education"	.15	.15
212 CD323	12c	"Science"	.30	.30
213 CD323	25c	"Culture"	.70	.70
		Nos. 211-213 (3)	1.15	1.15

Associated State

Nos. 183, 185-194 Overprinted in Red: "STATEHOOD / 1st MARCH 1967"

Perf. 14½

1967, Mar. 1 Photo. Wmk. 314

215 A33	2c	violet	.15	.15
216 A33	5c	slate blue	.15	.15
217 A33	6c	brown	.15	.15
218 A34	8c	lt blue & multi	.20	.15
219 A34	10c	multicolored	.20	.20
220 A35	12c	multicolored	.30	.25
221 A35	15c	blue & ocher	.55	.30
222 A35	25c	multicolored	.75	.45
223 A35	35c	dk blue & buff	1.10	.55
224 A35	50c	multicolored	1.10	.75
225 A35	$1	multicolored	2.25	2.00
		Nos. 215-225 (11)	6.90	5.10

The 1c and $2.50, similarly overprinted, were not sold to the public at the post office but were acknowledged belatedly (May 10) by the government and declared valid. The 1c, 6c and $2.50 overprints exist in black as well as red. No. 213 also exists with this overprint in blue and in black.

St. Lucia stamps can be mounted in the Scott British Windward Islands album.

Madonna and Child with St. John, by Raphael — A36

Cricket Batsman and Gov. Frederick Clarke — A37

1967, Oct. 16 Wmk. 314 *Perf. 14½*

227 A36 4c black, gold & multi	.15	.15
228 A36 25c multicolored	.35	.35

Christmas 1967.

Perf. 14½x14

1968, Mar. 8 Photo. Wmk. 314

229 A37 10c multicolored	.15	.15
230 A37 35c multicolored	.55	.55

Visit of the Marylebone Cricket Club to the West Indies, Jan.-Feb. 1968.

"Noli me Tangere," by Titian — A38

Martin Luther King, Jr. — A39

Easter: 10c, 25c, The Crucifixion, by Raphael.

1968, Mar. 25 *Perf. 14½*

231 A38 10c multicolored	.15	.15
232 A38 15c multicolored	.15	.15
233 A38 25c multicolored	.20	.20
234 A38 35c multicolored	.28	.28
Nos. 231-234 (4)	.78	.78

Perf. 13½x14

1968, July 4 Photo. Wmk. 314

235 A39 25c dp blue, blk & brn	.25	.25
236 A39 35c violet, blk & brn	.35	.35

Dr. Martin Luther King, Jr. (1929-68), American civil rights leader.

Virgin and Child in Glory, by Murillo — A40

Christmas: 10c, 35c, Virgin and Child, by Bartolomé E. Murillo.

Perf. 14½x14

1968, Oct. 17 Photo. Wmk. 314

237 A40 5c dark blue & multi	.15	.15
238 A40 10c multicolored	.18	.18
239 A40 25c red brown & multi	.35	.35
240 A40 35c deep blue & multi	.52	.52
Nos. 237-240 (4)	1.20	1.20

Purple-throated Carib — A41

Birds: 15c, 35c, St. Lucia parrot.

1969, Jan. 10 Litho. *Perf. 14½*

241 A41 10c multicolored	.34	.34
242 A41 15c multicolored	.38	.38
243 A41 25c multicolored	.75	.75
244 A41 35c multicolored	1.10	1.10
Nos. 241-244 (4)	2.57	2.57

Ecce Homo, by Guido Reni — A42

Painting: 15c, 35c, The Resurrection, by Il Sodoma (Giovanni Antonio de Bazzi).

Perf. 14½x14

1969, Mar. 20 Photo. Wmk. 314

245 A42 10c purple & multi	.15	.15
246 A42 15c green & multi	.16	.16
247 A42 25c black & multi	.28	.28
248 A42 35c ocher & multi	.48	.48
Nos. 245-248 (4)	1.07	1.07

Easter 1969.

Map of Caribbean A43

Design: 25c, 35c, Clasped hands and arrows with names of CARIFTA members.

1969, May 29 Wmk. 314 *Perf. 14*

249 A43 5c violet blue & multi	.15	.15
250 A43 10c deep plum & multi	.15	.15
251 A43 25c ultra & multi	.28	.28
252 A43 35c green & multi	.38	.38
Set value	.80	.80

First anniversary of CARIFTA (Caribbean Free Trade Area).

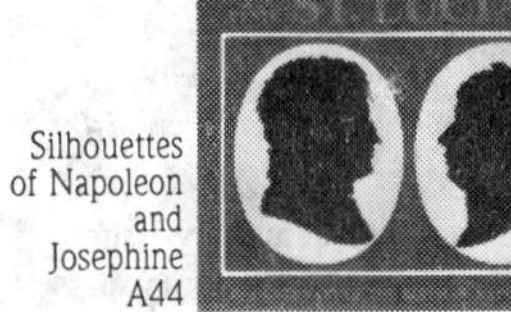

Silhouettes of Napoleon and Josephine A44

Perf. 14½x13

1969, Sept. 22 Photo. Unwmk.

Gold Inscription; Gray and Brown Medallions

253 A44 15c dull blue	.15	.15
254 A44 25c deep claret	.25	.25
255 A44 35c deep green	.38	.38
256 A44 50c yellow brown	.60	.60
Nos. 253-256 (4)	1.38	1.38

Napoleon Bonaparte, 200th birth anniv.

Madonna and Child, by Paul Delaroche — A45

Christmas: 10c, 35c, Holy Family, by Rubens.

Perf. 14½x14

1969, Oct. 27 Photo. Wmk. 314

Center Multicolored

257 A45 5c deep rose lilac & gold	.15	.15
258 A45 10c Prus blue & gold	.15	.15
259 A45 25c maroon & gold	.28	.28
260 A45 35c dp yellow grn & gold	.45	.45
Set value	.86	.86

House of Assembly A46

Queen Elizabeth II, by A. C. Davidson-Houston A47

2c, Roman Catholic Cathedral. 4c, Castries Boulevard. 5c, Castries Harbor. 6c, Sulphur springs. 10c, Vigie Airport. 12c, Reduit beach. 15c, Pigeon Island. 25c, The Pitons & sailboat. 35c, Marigot Bay. 50c, Diamond Waterfall. $1, St. Lucia flag & motto. $2.50, Coat of arms. $10, Map of St. Lucia.

Wmk. 314 Sideways, Upright (#271-274)

1970-73 Litho. *Perf. 14½*

261 A46 1c multicolored	.15	.15
262 A46 2c multicolored	.15	.15
a. Wmk. upright	.55	.55
263 A46 4c multicolored	.15	.15
a. Wmk. upright	1.00	1.00
264 A46 5c multicolored	.15	.15
265 A46 6c multicolored	.15	.15
266 A46 10c multicolored	.18	.18
267 A46 12c multicolored	.18	.18
268 A46 15c multicolored	.22	.22
269 A46 25c multicolored	.28	.28
270 A46 35c multicolored	.35	.35
271 A47 50c multicolored	.52	.52
272 A47 $1 multicolored	1.00	.90
273 A47 $2.50 multicolored	2.25	2.00
274 A47 $5 multicolored	4.75	3.75
274A A47 $10 multicolored	9.00	9.00
Nos. 261-274A (15)	19.48	18.13

Issued: #261-274, Feb. 1, 1970; #274A, Dec. 3, 1973; #262a, 263a, Mar. 15, 1974.

1975, July 28 Wmk. 373

263b A46 4c multicolored	.38	.38
264a A46 5c multicolored	.48	.48
266a A46 10c multicolored	.95	.95
268a A46 15c multicolored	1.50	1.50
Nos. 263b-268a (4)	3.31	3.31

The Three Marys at the Tomb, by Hogarth — A48

Designs: 25c, The Sealing of the Tomb. $1, The Ascension. The designs are from the altarpiece painted by William Hogarth for the Church of St. Mary Redcliffe in Bristol, 1755-56.

Roulette 8½xPerf. 12½

1970, Mar. 7 Litho. Wmk. 314

Size: 27x54mm

275 A48 25c dark brown & multi	.48	.48
276 A48 35c dark brown & multi	.65	.65

Size: 38x54mm

277 A48 $1 dark brown & multi	1.90	1.90
a. Triptych (#275-277)	3.25	3.25

Easter 1970.

Nos. 275-277 printed se-tenant in sheets of 30 (10 triptychs) with the center $1 stamp 10mm raised compared to the flanking 25c and 35c stamps.

Charles Dickens and Characters from his Works — A49

1970, June 8 Wmk. 314 *Perf. 14*

278 A49 1c brown & multi	.15	.15
279 A49 25c Prus blue & multi	.32	.32
280 A49 35c brown red & multi	.40	.40
281 A49 50c red lilac & multi	.60	.60
Nos. 278-281 (4)	1.47	1.47

Charles Dickens (1812-70), English novelist.

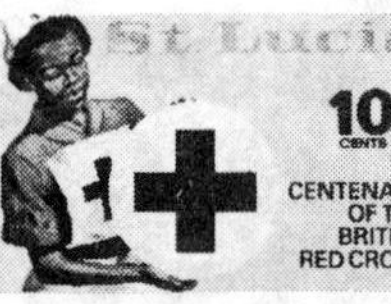

Nurse Holding Red Cross Emblem A50

15c, 35c, British, St. Lucia & Red Cross flags.

Perf. 14½x14

1970, Aug. 18 Litho. Wmk. 314

282 A50 10c multicolored	.15	.15
283 A50 15c multicolored	.18	.18
284 A50 25c buff & multi	.28	.28
285 A50 35c multicolored	.42	.42
Nos. 282-285 (4)	1.03	1.03

Centenary of British Red Cross Society.

Madonna with the Lilies, by Luca della Robbia — A51

Lithographed and Embossed

1970, Nov. 16 Unwmk. *Perf. 11*

286 A51 5c dark blue & multi	.15	.15
287 A51 10c violet blue & multi	.16	.16
288 A51 35c carmine lake & multi	.55	.55
289 A51 40c deep green & multi	.70	.70
Nos. 286-289 (4)	1.56	1.56

Christmas 1970.

Christ on the Cross, by Rubens — A52

Easter: 15c, 40c, Descent from the Cross, by Peter Paul Rubens.

Perf. 14x13½

1971, Mar. 29 Litho. Wmk. 314

290 A52 10c dull green & multi	.15	.15
291 A52 15c dull red & multi	.15	.15
292 A52 35c brt blue & multi	.36	.36
293 A52 40c multicolored	.48	.48
Nos. 290-293 (4)	1.14	1.14

Moule à Chique Lighthouse A53

Design: 25c, Beane Field Airport.

1971, Apr. 30 *Perf. 14½x14*

294 A53 5c olive & multi .15 .15
295 A53 25c bister & multi .50 .50

Opening of Beane Field Airport.

View of Morne Fortune (Old Days) — A54

Designs show for each denomination an old print and a contemporary photograph of the same view. 10c, Castries City. 25c, Pigeon Island. 50c, View from Government House. Plain frame around contemporary views.

Perf. 13½x14

1971, Aug. 10 Litho. Wmk. 314

296 A54 5c yellow & multi .15 .15
297 A54 5c lt blue & multi .15 .15
298 A54 10c yellow & multi .15 .15
299 A54 10c lt blue & multi .15 .15
300 A54 25c yellow & multi .30 .30
301 A54 25c lt blue & multi .30 .30
302 A54 50c yellow & multi .60 .60
303 A54 50c lt blue & multi .60 .60
Nos. 296-303 (8) 2.40 2.40

Stamps of the same denomination are printed se-tenant in sheets of 30.

Virgin and Child, by Verrocchio — A55

Virgin and Child painted by: 10c, Paolo Moranda. 35c, Giovanni Battista Cima. 40c, Andrea del Verrocchio.

1971, Oct. 15 *Perf. 14*

304 A55 5c green & multi .15 .15
305 A55 10c brown & multi .15 .15
306 A55 35c ultra & multi .50 .50
307 A55 40c red & multi .65 .65
Nos. 304-307 (4) 1.45 1.45

Christmas 1971.

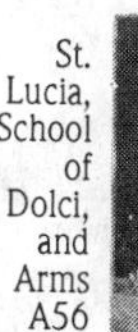

St. Lucia, School of Dolci, and Arms A56

1971, Dec. 13 *Perf. 14x14½*

308 A56 5c gray & multi .15 .15
309 A56 10c lt green & multi .18 .18
310 A56 25c tan & multi .45 .45
311 A56 50c lt blue & multi .90 .90
Nos. 308-311 (4) 1.68 1.68

National Day.

Lamentation, by Carracci A57

Easter: 25c, 50c, Angels Weeping over Body of Jesus, by Guercino.

1972, Feb. 15 Wmk. 314

312 A57 10c lt violet & multi .15 .15
313 A57 25c ocher & multi .42 .42
314 A57 35c ultra & multi .50 .50
315 A57 50c lt green & multi .85 .85
Nos. 312-315 (4) 1.92 1.92

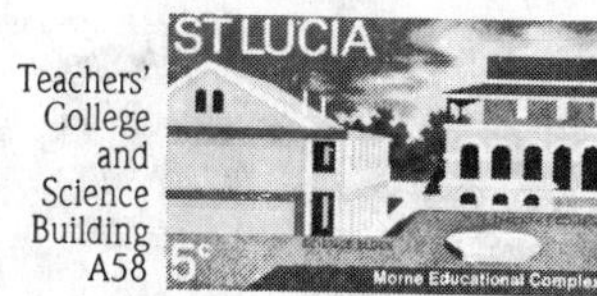

Teachers' College and Science Building A58

15c, University Center and coat of arms. 25c, Secondary School. 35c, Technical College.

1972, Apr. 18 Litho. *Perf. 14*

316 A58 5c multicolored .15 .15
317 A58 15c multicolored .16 .16
318 A58 25c multicolored .28 .28
319 A58 35c multicolored .40 .40
Nos. 316-319 (4) .99 .99

Opening of Morne Educational Complex.

Steam Conveyance Co. Stamp and Map of St. Lucia — A59

Designs: 10c, Castries Harbor and 3c stamp. 35c, Soufriere Volcano and 1c stamp. 50c, One cent, 3c, 6c stamps.

1972, June 22 *Perf. 14½*

320 A59 5c yellow & multi .15 .15
321 A59 10c violet blue & multi .15 .15
322 A59 35c car rose & multi .44 .44
323 A59 50c emerald & multi 1.00 .90
Nos. 320-323 (4) 1.74 1.64

Centenary of St. Lucia Steam Conveyance Co. Ltd. postal service.

Holy Family, by Sebastiano Ricci A60

1972, Oct. 18 *Perf. 14½x14*

324 A60 5c dk brown & multi .15 .15
325 A60 10c green & multi .16 .16
326 A60 35c carmine & multi .60 .60
327 A60 40c dk blue & multi .80 .80
Nos. 324-327 (4) 1.71 1.71

Christmas 1972.

Silver Wedding Issue, 1972

Common Design Type

Design: Queen Elizabeth II, Prince Philip, St. Lucia coat of arms and St. Lucia parrot.

1972, Nov. Photo. *Perf. 14x14½*

328 CD324 15c car rose & multi .20 .20
329 CD324 35c olive & multi .42 .42

Weekday Headdress A61

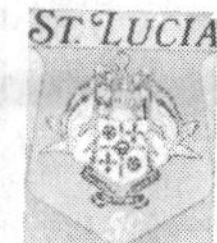

Arms of St. Lucia A62

Women's Headdresses: 10c, For church wear. 25c, Unmarried girl. 50c, Formal occasions.

1973, Feb. 1 Wmk. 314 *Perf. 13*

330 A61 5c multicolored .15 .15
331 A61 10c dark gray & multi .18 .18
332 A61 25c multicolored .45 .45
333 A61 50c slate blue & multi .90 .90
Nos. 330-333 (4) 1.68 1.68

Coil Stamps

1973, Apr. 19 Litho. *Perf. 14½x14*

334 A62 5c gray olive .30 .30
a. Watermark sideways ('76) .15 .15
335 A62 10c blue .45 .45
a. Watermark sideways ('76) .15 .15
336 A62 25c claret .45 .45

H.M.S. St. Lucia A63

Designs: Old Sailing ships.

1973, May 24 Litho. *Perf. 13½x14*

337 A63 15c shown .15 .15
338 A63 35c "Prince of Wales" .35 .35
339 A63 50c "Oliph Blossom" .45 .45
340 A63 $1 "Rose" .95 .95
a. Souv. sheet of 4, #337-340, perf. 15 1.65 1.65
Nos. 337-340 (4) 1.90 1.90

Banana Plantation and Flower A64

Designs: 15c, Aerial spraying. 35c, Washing and packing bananas. 50c, Loading.

1973, July 26 Litho. *Perf. 14*

341 A64 5c multicolored .15 .15
342 A64 15c multicolored .30 .20
343 A64 35c multicolored .70 .55
344 A64 50c multicolored 1.10 1.00
Nos. 341-344 (4) 2.25 1.90

Banana industry.

Madonna and Child, by Carlo Maratta — A65

Christmas (Paintings): 15c, Virgin in the Meadow, by Raphael. 35c, Holy Family, by Angelo Bronzino. 50c, Madonna of the Pear, by Durer.

1973, Oct. 17 Litho. *Perf. 14x13½*

345 A65 5c citron & multi .15 .15
346 A65 15c ultra & multi .18 .18
347 A65 35c dp green & multi .48 .48
348 A65 50c red & multi .80 .80
Nos. 345-348 (4) 1.61 1.61

Princess Anne's Wedding Issue

Common Design Type

1973, Nov. 14 Wmk. 314 *Perf. 14*

349 CD325 40c gray green & multi .28 .28
350 CD325 50c lilac & multi .38 .38

The Betrayal of Christ, by Ugolino A66

Easter (Paintings by Ugolino, 14th Cent.): 35c, The Way to Calvary. 80c, Descent from the Cross. $1, Resurrection.

1974, Apr. 1 *Perf. 13½x13*

351 A66 5c ocher & multi .15 .15
352 A66 35c ocher & multi .30 .30
353 A66 80c ocher & multi .70 .70
354 A66 $1 ocher & multi .80 .80
a. Souvenir sheet of 4, #351-354 2.00 2.00
Nos. 351-354 (4) 1.95 1.95

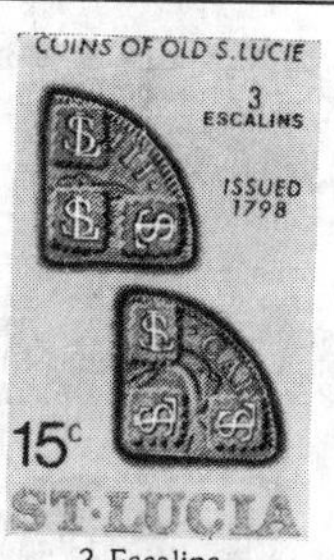

3 Escalins, 1798 — A67

Baron de Laborie, 1784 — A68

Pieces of Eight: 35c, 6 escalins, 1798. 40c, 2 livres 5 sols, 1813. $1, 6 livres 15 sols, 1813.

1974, May 20 *Perf. 13½*

355 A67 15c lt olive & multi .16 .16
356 A67 35c multicolored .35 .35
357 A67 40c green & multi .40 .40
358 A67 $1 brown & multi .95 .95
a. Souvenir sheet of 4, #355-358 2.50 2.50
Nos. 355-358 (4) 1.86 1.86

Coins of Old St. Lucia.

Perf. 14½

1974, Aug. 29 Litho. Wmk. 314

Portraits: 35c, Sir John Moore, Lieutenant Governor, 1796-97. 80c, Major General Sir Dudley St. Leger Hill, 1834-37. $1, Sir Frederick Joseph Clarke, 1967-71.

359 A68 5c ocher & multi .15 .15
360 A68 35c brt blue & multi .20 .20
361 A68 80c violet & multi .40 .40
362 A68 $1 multicolored .65 .65
a. Souvenir sheet of 4, #359-362 1.40 1.40
Nos. 359-362 (4) 1.40 1.40

Past Governors of St. Lucia.

Virgin and Child, by Verrocchio — A69

Christmas (Virgin and Child): 35c, by Andrea della Robbia. 80c, by Luca della Robbia. $1, by Antonio Rossellino.

1974, Nov. 13 Wmk. 314 *Perf. 13½*

363 A69 5c gray & multi .15 .15
364 A69 35c pink & multi .28 .28
365 A69 80c brown & multi .60 .60
366 A69 $1 olive & multi .75 .75
a. Souvenir sheet of 4, #363-366 2.25 2.25
Nos. 363-366 (4) 1.78 1.78

Churchill and Gen. Montgomery — A70

Design: $1, Churchill and Pres. Truman.

1974, Nov. 30 *Perf. 14*

367 A70 5c multicolored .15 .15
368 A70 $1 multicolored .75 .75

Sir Winston Churchill (1874-1965).

Crucifixion, by Van der Weyden — A71

Easter: 35c, "Noli me Tangere," by Julio Romano. 80c, Crucifixion, by Fernando Gallego. $1, "Noli me Tangere," by Correggio.

Perf. 14x13½

1975, Mar. 27 **Wmk. 314**
369 A71 5c brown & multi .15 .15
370 A71 35c ultra & multi .32 .32
371 A71 80c red brown & multi .70 .70
372 A71 $1 green & multi .80 .80
Nos. 369-372 (4) 1.97 1.97

Nativity — A72

Adoration of the Kings — A73

#375, Virgin & Child. #376, Adoration of the Shepherds. 40c, Nativity. $1, Virgin & Child with Sts. Catherine of Alexandria and Siena.

Perf. 14½

1975, Dec. **Litho.** **Wmk. 314**
373 A72 5c lilac rose & multi .15 .15
374 A73 10c yellow & multi .15 .15
375 A73 10c yellow & multi .15 .15
376 A73 10c yellow & multi .15 .15
a. Strip of 3, #374-376 .40 .40
377 A72 40c yellow & multi .40 .40
378 A72 $1 blue & multi 1.00 1.00
a. Souv. sheet of 3, #373, 377-378 2.00 2.00
Nos. 373-378 (6) 2.00 2.00

Christmas 1975.

"Hanna," First US Warship A74

Revolutionary Era Ships: 1c, "Prince of Orange," British packet. 2c, "Edward," British sloop. 5c, "Millern," British merchantman. 15c, "Surprise," Continental Navy lugger. 35c, "Serapis," British warship. 50c, "Randolph," first Continental Navy frigate. $1, Frigate "Alliance."

Perf. 14½

1976, Jan. 26 **Litho.** **Unwmk.**
379 A74 ½c multicolored .15 .15
380 A74 1c multicolored .15 .15
381 A74 2c multicolored .15 .15
382 A74 5c multicolored .15 .15
383 A74 15c multicolored .32 .16
384 A74 35c multicolored .85 .40
385 A74 50c multicolored 1.10 .60
386 A74 $1 multicolored 2.75 1.25
a. Souv. sheet of 4, #383-386, perf. 13 5.00 3.00
Nos. 379-386 (8) 5.62 3.01

American Bicentennial.

Laughing Gull — A75

Birds: 2c, Little blue heron. 4c, Belted kingfisher. 5c, St. Lucia parrot. 6c, St. Lucia oriole. 8c, Brown trembler. 10c, American kestrel. 12c, Red-billed tropic bird. 15c, Common gallinule. 25c, Brown noddy. 35c, Sooty tern. 50c, Osprey. $1, White-breasted thrasher. $2.50, St. Lucia black finch. $5, Rednecked pigeon. $10, Caribbean elaenia.

Wmk. 314 (1c); 373 (others)

1976, May 7 **Litho.** *Perf. 14½*
387 A75 1c gray & multi .15 .15
388 A75 2c gray & multi .15 .15
389 A75 4c gray & multi .15 .15
390 A75 5c gray & multi .15 .15
391 A75 6c gray & multi .15 .15
392 A75 8c gray & multi .15 .15
393 A75 10c gray & multi .15 .15
394 A75 12c gray & multi .15 .15
395 A75 15c gray & multi .20 .15
396 A75 25c gray & multi .30 .25
397 A75 35c gray & multi .35 .30
398 A75 50c gray & multi .55 .50
399 A75 $1 gray & multi 1.10 .95
400 A75 $2.50 gray & multi 2.75 2.50
401 A75 $5 gray & multi 5.75 5.00
402 A75 $10 gray & multi 11.00 10.00
Nos. 387-402 (16) 23.20 20.85

Map of West Indies, Bats, Wicket and Ball — A75a

Prudential Cup — A75b

1976, July 19 **Unwmk.** *Perf. 14*
403 A75a 50c lt blue & multi 1.00 1.00
404 A75b $1 lilac rose & black 2.00 2.00
a. Souvenir sheet of 2, #403-404 3.25 3.25

World Cricket Cup, won by West Indies Team, 1975.

Arms of H.M.S. Ceres — A76

Madonna and Child, by Murillo — A77

Coats of Arms of Royal Naval Ships: 20c, Pelican. 40c, Ganges. $2, Ariadne.

1976, Sept. 6 **Wmk. 373** *Perf. 14½*
405 A76 10c gold & multi .15 .15
406 A76 20c gold & multi .20 .20
407 A76 40c gold & multi .40 .40
408 A76 $2 gold & multi 1.75 1.75
Nos. 405-408 (4) 2.50 2.50

1976, Nov. 15 **Litho.** *Perf. 14½*

Paintings: 20c, Virgin and Child, by Lorenzo Costa. 50c, Madonna and Child, by Adriaea Isenbrandt. $2, Madonna and Child with St. John, by Murillo. $2.50, Like 10c.

409 A77 10c multicolored .15 .15
410 A77 20c multicolored .28 .28
411 A77 50c multicolored .60 .60
412 A77 $2 multicolored 2.25 2.25
Nos. 409-412 (4) 3.28 3.28

Souvenir Sheet

413 A77 $2.50 multicolored 3.00 3.00

Christmas.

Elizabeth II, "Palms and Water" A78

Perf. 14½

1977, Feb. 7 **Litho.** **Wmk. 373**
414 A78 10c multicolored .15 .15
415 A78 20c multicolored .15 .15
416 A78 40c multicolored .30 .30
417 A78 $2 multicolored 1.40 1.40
Nos. 414-417 (4) 2.00 2.00

Souvenir Sheet

418 A78 $2.50 multicolored 1.75 1.75

25th anniv. of the reign of Elizabeth II.

Scouts of Tapion School — A79

Nativity, by Giotto — A80

1c, Sea Scouts, St. Mary's College. 2c, Scout giving oath. 10c, Tapion School Cub Scouts. 20c, Venture Scout, Soufrière. 50c, Scout from Gros Islet Division. $1, $2.50, Boat drill, St. Mary's College.

1977, Oct. 17 **Unwmk.** *Perf. 15*
419 A79 ½c multicolored .15 .15
420 A79 1c multicolored .15 .15
421 A79 2c multicolored .15 .15
422 A79 10c multicolored .15 .15
423 A79 20c multicolored .20 .20
424 A79 50c multicolored .50 .50
425 A79 $1 multicolored 1.00 1.00
Set value 1.90 1.90

Souvenir Sheet

426 A79 $2.50 multicolored 2.00 2.00

6th Caribbean Boy Scout Jamboree, Kingston, Jamaica, Aug. 5-14.

1977, Oct. 31 **Litho.** *Perf. 14*

Christmas (Virgin and Child by): 1c, Fra Angelico. 2c, El Greco. 20c, Caravaggio. 50c, Velazquez. $1, Tiepolo. $2.50, Adoration of the Kings, by Tiepolo.

427 A80 ½c multicolored .15 .15
428 A80 1c multicolored .15 .15
429 A80 2c multicolored .15 .15
430 A80 20c multicolored .15 .15
431 A80 50c multicolored .35 .35
432 A80 $1 multicolored .70 .70
433 A80 $2.50 multicolored 1.75 1.75
Nos. 427-433 (7) 3.40 3.40

Suzanne Fourment in Velvet Hat, by Rubens — A81

Rubens Paintings: 35c, Rape of the Sabine Women (detail). 50c, Ludovicus Nonnius, portrait. $2.50, Minerva Protecting Pax from Mars (detail).

Perf. 14x14½

1977, Nov. 28 **Litho.** **Wmk. 373**
434 A81 10c multicolored .15 .15
435 A81 35c multicolored .15 .15
436 A81 50c multicolored .25 .25
437 A81 $2.50 multicolored 1.25 1.25
a. Souv. sheet of 4, #434-437, perf. 15 2.00 2.00
Nos. 434-437 (4) 1.80 1.80

Peter Paul Rubens (1577-1640).

Yeoman of the Guard and Life Guard A82

Dress Uniforms: 20c, Groom and postilion. 50c, Footman and coachman. $3, State trumpeter and herald. $5, Master of the Queen's House and Gentleman at Arms.

Unwmk.

1978, June 2 **Litho.** *Perf. 14*
438 A82 15c multicolored .15 .15
439 A82 20c multicolored .15 .15
440 A82 50c multicolored .32 .32
441 A82 $3 multicolored 2.00 2.00
Nos. 438-441 (4) 2.62 2.62

Souvenir Sheet

442 A82 $5 multicolored 3.00 3.00

25th anniv. of coronation of Elizabeth II.

Nos. 438-441 exist in miniature sheets of 3 plus label, perf. 12.

Queen Angelfish A83

Tropical Fish: 20c, Four-eyed butterflyfish. 50c, French angelfish. $2, Yellowtail damselfish. $2.50, Rock beauty.

1978, June 19 **Litho.** *Perf. 14½*
443 A83 10c multicolored .15 .15
444 A83 20c multicolored .15 .15
445 A83 50c multicolored .45 .45
446 A83 $2 multicolored 1.75 1.75
Nos. 443-446 (4) 2.50 2.50

Souvenir Sheet

447 A83 $2.50 multicolored 2.50 2.50

French Grenadier, Map of Battle A84

30c, British Grenadier & Bellin map of St. Lucia, 1762. 50c, British fleet opposing French landing & map of coast from Gros Islet to Cul-de-Sac. $2.50, Light infantrymen & Gen. James Grant.

1978, Nov. 15 **Litho.** *Perf. 14*
448 A84 10c multicolored .15 .15
449 A84 30c multicolored .24 .24
450 A84 50c multicolored .40 .40
451 A84 $2.50 multicolored 2.00 2.00
Nos. 448-451 (4) 2.79 2.79

Bicent. of Battle of St. Lucia (Cul-de-Sac).

Annunciation A85

Christmas: 55c, 80c, Adoration of the Kings.

Perf. 14x14½

1978, Dec. 4 **Wmk. 373**
452 A85 30c multicolored .22 .22
453 A85 50c multicolored .35 .35
454 A85 55c multicolored .40 .40
455 A85 80c multicolored .55 .55
Nos. 452-455 (4) 1.52 1.52

Independent State

Hewanorra Airport — A86

Independence: 30c, New coat of arms. 50c, Government house and Allen Lewis, first Governor General. $2, Map of St. Lucia, French, St. Lucia and British flags.

1979, Feb. 22 **Litho.** *Perf. 14*
456 A86 10c multicolored .15 .15
457 A86 30c multicolored .20 .20
458 A86 50c multicolored .32 .32
459 A86 $2 multicolored 1.25 1.25
a. Souvenir sheet of 4, #456-459 2.00 2.00
Nos. 456-459 (4) 1.92 1.92

Paul VI and John Paul I A87

Pope Paul VI and: 30c, Pres. Anwar Sadat of Egypt. 50c, Secretary General U Thant and UN emblem. 55c, Prime Minister Golda Meir of Israel. $2, Martin Luther King, Jr.

1979, May 7 **Litho.** *Perf. 14*
460 A87 10c multicolored .15 .15
461 A87 30c multicolored .25 .25
462 A87 50c multicolored .42 .42

463 A87 55c multicolored .45 .45
464 A87 $2 multicolored 1.75 1.75
Nos. 460-464 (5) 3.02 3.02

In memory of Popes Paul VI and John Paul I.

Jersey Cows
A88

Agricultural Diversification: 35c, Fruits and vegetables. 50c, Waterfall (water conservation). $3, Coconuts, copra industry.

1979, July 2 Litho. *Perf. 14*

465 A88 10c multicolored .15 .15
466 A88 35c multicolored .30 .30
467 A88 50c multicolored .42 .42
468 A88 $3 multicolored 2.50 2.50
Nos. 465-468 (4) 3.37 3.37

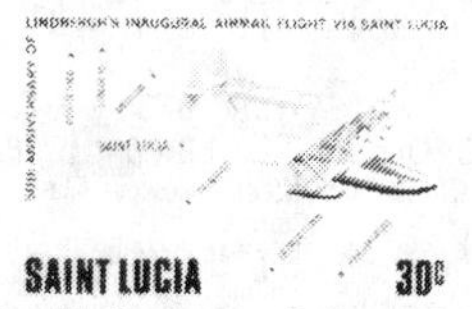

Lindbergh's Route over St. Lucia, Puerto Rico-Paramaribo — A89

1979, Nov. Litho. *Perf. 14*

469 A89 10c Lindbergh, hydroplane .15 .15
470 A89 30c shown .24 .24
471 A89 50c Landing at La Toc .40 .40
472 A89 $2 Flight covers 1.65 1.65
Nos. 469-472 (4) 2.44 2.44

Lindbergh's inaugural airmail flight (US-Guyana) via St. Lucia, 50th anniversary.

Prince of Saxony, by Cranach the Elder — A90

IYC (Emblem and): 50c, Infanta Margarita, by Velazquez. $2, Girl Playing Badminton, by Jean Baptiste Chardin. $2.50, Mary and Francis Wilcox, by Stock. $5, Two Children, by Pablo Picasso.

1979, Dec. 6 Litho. *Perf. 14*

473 A90 10c multicolored .15 .15
474 A90 50c multicolored .40 .40
475 A90 $2 multicolored 1.65 1.65
476 A90 $2.50 multicolored 2.00 2.00
Nos. 473-476 (4) 4.20 4.20

Souvenir Sheet

477 A90 $5 multicolored 3.50 3.50

A91

A92

Maltese Cross Cancels and: 10c, Penny Post notice, 1839. 50c, Hill's original stamp design. $2, St. Lucia #1. $2.50, Penny Black. $5, Hill portrait.

1979, Dec. 10

478 A91 10c multicolored .15 .15
479 A91 50c multicolored .32 .32
480 A91 $2 multicolored 1.25 1.25
481 A91 $2.50 multicolored 1.50 1.50
Nos. 478-481 (4) 3.22 3.22

Souvenir Sheet

482 A91 $5 multicolored 3.00 3.00

Sir Rowland Hill (1793-1879), originator of penny postage.

Nos. 478-481 also issued in sheets of 5 plus label, perf. 12x12½.

1980, Jan. 14

IYC Emblem, Virgin and Child Paintings by: 10c, Virgin and Child, by Bernardino Fungi, IYC emblem. 50c, Carlo Dolci. $2, Titian. $2.50, Giovanni Bellini.

483 A92 10c multicolored .15 .15
484 A92 50c multicolored .40 .40
485 A92 $2 multicolored 1.65 1.65
486 A92 $2.50 multicolored 2.00 2.00
a. Souvenir sheet of 4, #483-486 4.50 4.50
Nos. 483-486 (4) 4.20 4.20

Christmas 1979; Intl. Year of the Child.

St. Lucia Conveyance Co. Ltd. Stamp, 1873 — A92a

London 1980 Emblem and Covers: 30c, "Assistance" 1p postmark, 1879. 50c, Postage due handstamp, 1929. $2, Postmarks on 1844 cover.

Wmk. 373

1980, May 6 Litho. *Perf. 14*

487 A92a 10c multicolored .15 .15
488 A92a 30c multicolored .20 .20
489 A92a 50c multicolored .35 .35
490 A92a $2 multicolored 1.40 1.40
a. Souvenir sheet of 4, #487-490 2.50 2.50
Nos. 487-490 (4) 2.10 2.10

London 1980 Intl. Stamp Exhib., May 6-14.

Intl. Year of the Child — A93

Space scenes. 1c, 4c, 5c, 10c, $2, $2.50 horiz.

1980, May 29 Litho. *Perf. 11*

491 A93 ½c Mickey on rocket .15 .15
492 A93 1c Donald Duck spacewalking .15 .15
493 A93 2c Minnie Mouse on moon .15 .15
494 A93 3c Goofy hitch hiking .15 .15
495 A93 4c Goofy on moon .15 .15
496 A93 5c Pluto digging on moon .15 .15
497 A93 10c Donald Duck, space creature .15 .15
498 A93 $2 Donald Duck paddling satellite 2.00 2.00
499 A93 $2.50 Mickey Mouse in lunar rover 2.50 2.50
Nos. 491-499 (9) 5.55 5.55

Souvenir Sheet

500 A93 $5 Goofy on moon 4.00 4.00

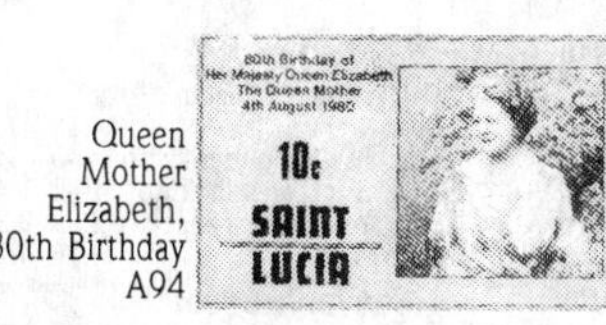

Queen Mother Elizabeth, 80th Birthday A94

1980, Aug. 4 Litho. *Perf. 14*

501 A94 10c multicolored .15 .15
502 A94 $2.50 multicolored 1.75 1.75

Souvenir Sheet

Perf. 12½x12

503 A94 $3 multicolored 2.00 2.00

HS-748 on Runway, St. Lucia Airport, Hewanorra A95

Perf. 14½

1980, Aug. 11 Litho. Wmk. 373

504 A95 5c shown .15 .15
505 A95 10c DC-10, St. Lucia Airport .15 .15
506 A95 15c Bus, Castries .15 .15
507 A95 20c Refrigerator ship .15 .15
508 A95 25c Islander plane .18 .18
509 A95 30c Pilot boat .22 .22
510 A95 50c Boeing 727 .38 .38
511 A95 75c Cruise ship .55 .55
512 A95 $1 Lockheed Tristar, Piton Mountains .75 .75
513 A95 $2 Cargo ship 1.50 1.50
514 A95 $5 Boeing 707 3.75 3.75
515 A95 $10 Queen Elizabeth 2 7.25 7.25
Nos. 504-515 (12) 15.18 15.18

For surcharges see Nos. 531-533.

1984, May 15 Wmk. 380

507a A95 20c .15 .15
508a A95 25c .18 .18
509a A95 30c .22 .22
512a A95 $1 .75 .75
513a A95 $2 1.50 1.50
515a A95 $10 7.25 7.25
Nos. 507a-515a (6) 10.05 10.05

Shot Put, Moscow '80 Emblem — A96

1980, Sept. 22 Litho. *Perf. 14*

516 A96 10c shown .15 .15
517 A96 50c Swimming .25 .25
518 A96 $2 Gymnastics 1.10 1.10
519 A96 $2.50 Weight lifting 1.40 1.40
Nos. 516-519 (4) 2.90 2.90

Souvenir Sheet

520 A96 $5 Passing the torch 2.75 2.75

22nd Summer Olympic Games, Moscow, July 19-Aug. 3.

A97

A98

1980, Sept. 30 *Perf. 14*

521 A97 10c Palms, coast at dusk .15 .15
522 A97 50c Rocky shore .25 .25
523 A97 $2 Sand beach 1.10 1.10
524 A97 $2.50 Pitons at sunset 1.40 1.40
Nos. 521-524 (4) 2.90 2.90

Souvenir Sheet

525 A97 $5 Two-master 2.75 2.75

Rotary International, 75th Anniversary.

1980, Oct. 23 Litho. *Perf. 14*

Nobel Prize Winners: 10c, Sir Arthur Lewis, Economics. 50c, Martin Luther King, Jr., peace, 1964. $2, Ralph Bunche, peace, 1950. $2.50, Albert Schweitzer, peace, 1952. $5, Albert Einstein, physics, 1921.

526 A98 10c multicolored .15 .15
527 A98 50c multicolored .32 .32
528 A98 $2 multicolored 1.25 1.25
529 A98 $2.50 multicolored 1.65 1.65
Nos. 526-529 (4) 3.37 3.37

Souvenir Sheet

530 A98 $5 multicolored 3.25 3.25

Nos. 506-507, 510 Surcharged:

1980
HURRICANE

$1.50 RELIEF

1980, Nov. 3 Litho. *Perf. 14½*

531 A95 $1.50 on 15c multi 1.50 1.50
532 A95 $1.50 on 20c multi 1.50 1.50
533 A95 $1.50 on 50c multi 1.50 1.50
Nos. 531-533 (3) 4.50 4.50

Nativity, by Battista — A99

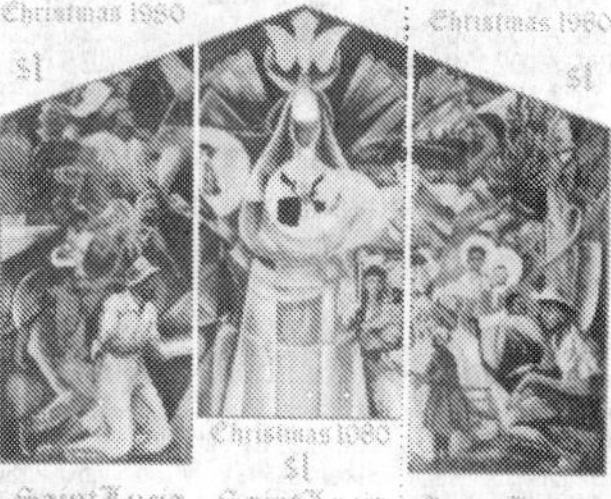

Angel and Citizens of St. Lucia — A100

Christmas: 30c, Adoration of the Kings, by Bruegel the Elder. $2, Adoration of the Shepherds, by Murillo.

1980, Dec. 1 *Perf. 14*

534 A99 10c multicolored .15 .15
535 A99 30c multicolored .22 .22
536 A99 $2 multicolored 1.50 1.50
Nos. 534-536 (3) 1.87 1.87

Souvenir Sheet

537 Sheet of 3 2.00 2.00
a. A100 $1 any single .65 .65

Agouti — A101

1981, Jan. 19 Litho. *Perf. 14*

538 A101 10c shown .15 .15
539 A101 50c St. Lucia parrot .38 .38
540 A101 $2 Purple-throated carib 1.50 1.50
541 A101 $2.50 Fiddler crab 1.90 1.90
Nos. 538-541 (4) 3.93 3.93

Souvenir Sheet

542 A101 $5 Monarch butterfly 4.00 4.00

Royal Wedding Issue
Common Design Type

1981, June 16 Litho. *Perf. 14*

543 CD331 25c Couple .16 .16
544 CD331 50c Clarence House .32 .32
545 CD331 $4 Charles 2.50 2.50
Nos. 543-545 (3) 2.98 2.98

Souvenir Sheet

546 CD331 $5 Glass coach 4.50 4.50

Nos. 543-545 also printed in sheets of 5 plus label, perf. 12, in changed colors.

549 CD331 Booklet 8.75 8.75
a. Pane of 1, $5, Couple 3.50 3.50
b. Pane of 6 (3x50c, Diana, 3x$2, Charles) 5.25 5.25

Buying Sets
It is often less expensive to purchase complete sets than individual stamps that make up the set. Set values are provided for many such sets.

Saint Lucia 30c A102 — 50c A103

Picasso Birth Centenary: 30c, The Cock. 50c, Man with Ice Cream. 55c, Woman Dressing her Hair. $3, Seated Woman. $5, Night Fishing at Antibes.

1981, May **Litho.** ***Perf. 14***

550 A102 30c multicolored .20 .20
551 A102 50c multicolored .35 .35
552 A102 55c multicolored .38 .38
553 A102 $3 multicolored 2.00 2.00
Nos. 550-553 (4) 2.93 2.93

Souvenir Sheet

554 A102 $5 multicolored 4.00 4.00

Perf. 14½

1981, Sept. 28 **Litho.** **Wmk. 373**

555 A103 10c Industry .15 .15
556 A103 35c Community service .35 .35
557 A103 50c Hikers .50 .50
558 A103 $2.50 Duke of Edinburgh 2.50 2.50
Nos. 555-558 (4) 3.50 3.50

Duke of Edinburgh's Awards, 25th anniv.

Intl. Year of the Disabled A104

1981, Oct. 30 **Litho.** ***Perf. 14***

559 A104 10c Louis Braille .15 .15
560 A104 50c Sarah Bernhardt .32 .32
561 A104 $2 Joseph Pulitzer 1.25 1.25
562 A104 $2.50 Henri de Toulouse-Lautrec 1.65 1.65
Nos. 559-562 (4) 3.37 3.37

Souvenir Sheet

563 A104 $5 Franklin D. Roosevelt 3.50 3.50

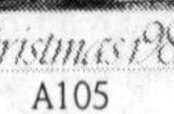

A105 — A107

A106

Christmas: Adoration of the King Paintings.

1981, Dec. 15

564 A105 10c Sfoza .15 .15
565 A105 30c Orcanga .22 .22
566 A105 $1.50 Gerard 1.10 1.10
567 A105 $2.50 Foppa 1.90 1.90
Nos. 564-567 (4) 3.37 3.37

1981, Dec. 29 **Unwmk.**

568 A106 10c No. 1 .15 .15
569 A106 30c No. 251 .34 .34
570 A106 50c No. 459 .55 .55
571 A106 $2 UPU, St. Lucia flags 2.25 2.25
Nos. 568-571 (4) 3.29 3.29

Souvenir Sheets

572 A106 $5 GPO, Castries 3.75 3.75

First anniv. of UPU membership.

Unwmk.

1981, Dec. 11 **Litho.** ***Perf. 14***

1980s Decade for Women (Paintings of Women by Women): 10c, Fanny Travis Cochran, by Cecilia Beaux. 50c, Women with Dove, by Marie Laurencin. $2, Portrait of a Young Pupil of David. $2.50, Self-portrait, by Rosalba Carriera. $5, Self-portrait, by Elisabeth Vigee-Le Brun.

573 A107 10c multicolored .15 .15
574 A107 50c multicolored .35 .35
575 A107 $2 multicolored 1.50 1.50
576 A107 $2.50 multicolored 1.75 1.75
Nos. 573-576 (4) 3.75 3.75

Souvenir Sheet

577 A107 $5 multicolored 3.50 3.50

1982 World Cup Soccer A108

Designs: Various soccer players.

1982, Feb. 15 **Litho.** ***Perf. 14½***

578 A108 10c multicolored .15 .15
579 A108 50c multicolored .38 .38
580 A108 $2 multicolored 1.50 1.50
581 A108 $2.50 multicolored 1.90 1.90
Nos. 578-581 (4) 3.93 3.93

Souvenir Sheet

582 A108 $5 multicolored 3.50 3.50

Battle of the Saints Bicentenary A109

Wmk. 373

1982, Apr. 13 **Litho.** ***Perf. 14***

583 A109 10c Pigeon Isld. .15 .15
584 A109 35c Battle .28 .28
585 A109 50c Admirals Rodney, DeGrasse .38 .38
586 A109 $2.50 Map 1.90 1.90
a. Souvenir sheet of 4, #583-586 4.50 4.50
Nos. 583-586 (4) 2.71 2.71

Scouting Year — A110 — Christmas 1982 — A111

1982, Aug. 4 **Litho.** ***Perf. 14***

587 A110 10c Map reading .15 .15
588 A110 50c First aid .40 .40
589 A110 $1.50 Camping 1.25 1.25
590 A110 $2.50 Campfire sing 2.00 2.00
Nos. 587-590 (4) 3.80 3.80

Princess Diana Issue

Common Design Type

Perf. 14½x14

1982, Sept. 1 **Unwmk.**

591 CD332 50c Leeds Castle .35 .35
592 CD332 $2 Diana 1.40 1.40
593 CD332 $4 Wedding 2.75 2.75
Nos. 591-593 (3) 4.50 4.50

Souvenir Sheet

594 CD332 $5 Diana, diff. 3.50 3.50

Wmk. 373

1982, Nov. 10 **Litho.** ***Perf. 14***

Paintings: 10c, Adoration of the Kings, by Brueghel the Elder. 30c, Nativity, by Lorenzo Costa. 50c, Virgin and Child, Fra Filippo Lippi. 80c, Adoration of the Shepherds, by Nicolas Poussin.

595 A111 10c multicolored .15 .15
596 A111 30c multicolored .22 .22
597 A111 50c multicolored .38 .38
598 A111 80c multicolored .60 .60
Nos. 595-598 (4) 1.35 1.35

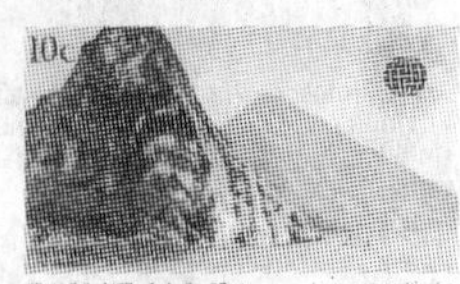

A111a

Litho.

1983, Mar. 14

599 A111a 10c Twin Peaks .15 .15
600 A111a 30c Beach .28 .28
601 A111a 50c Banana harvester .45 .45
602 A111a $2 Flag 1.75 1.75
Nos. 599-602 (4) 2.63 2.63

Commonwealth day.

Crown Agents Sesquicentennial A112

Perf. 14½

1983, Apr. 1 **Litho.** **Wmk. 373**

603 A112 10c Headquarters, London .15 .15
604 A112 15c Road construction .15 .15
605 A112 50c Map .42 .42
606 A112 $2 First stamp 1.65 1.65
Nos. 603-606 (4) 2.37 2.37

Saint Lucia 10c

World Communications Year — A113

Unwmk.

1983, July 12 **Litho.** ***Perf. 15***

607 A113 10c Shipboard intercommunication .15 .15
608 A113 50c Air-to-air .45 .45
609 A113 $1.50 Satellite 1.40 1.40
610 A113 $2.50 Computer communications 2.25 2.25
Nos. 607-610 (4) 4.25 4.25

Souvenir Sheet

611 A113 $5 Weather satellite 4.25 4.25

Coral Reef Fish A114

1983, Aug. 23

612 A114 10c Longspine squirrelfish .15 .15
613 A114 50c Banded butter-flyfish .48 .48
614 A114 $1.50 Blackbar soldierfish 1.40 1.40
615 A114 $2.50 Yellowtail snappers 2.25 2.25
Nos. 612-615 (4) 4.28 4.28

Souvenir Sheet

616 A114 $5 Red hind 4.50 4.50

For overprint see No. 800.

Locomotives A115

Perf. 12½

1983, Oct. 13 **Litho.** **Unwmk.**

Se-tenant Pairs

617 A115 35c Princess Coronation .45 .45
618 A115 35c Duke of Sutherland .45 .45
619 A115 50c Leeds United .60 .60
620 A115 50c Lord Nelson .60 .60
621 A115 $1 Bodmin 1.25 1.25
622 A115 $1 Eton 1.25 1.25
623 A115 $2 Flying Scotsman 2.50 2.50
624 A115 $2 Stephenson's Rocket 2.50 2.50
Nos. 617-624 (8) 9.60 9.60

See Nos. 674-679, 711-718, 774-777, 807-814.

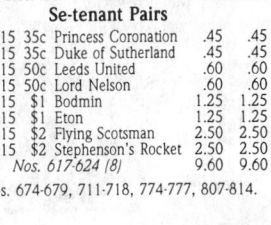

Virgin and Child Paintings by Raphael — A115a

Wmk. 373

1983, Oct. 24 **Litho.** ***Perf. 14***

629 A115a 10c Niccolini-Cowper Madonna .15 .15
630 A115a 30c Holy Family with a Palm Tree .18 .18
631 A115a 50c Sistine Madonna .32 .32
632 A115a $5 Alba Madonna 3.00 3.00
Nos. 629-632 (4) 3.65 3.65

Christmas.

Battle of Waterloo, King George III A116 — A117

Perf. 12½

1984, Mar. 13 **Litho.** **Unwmk.**

633 A116 5c shown .15 .15
634 A117 5c shown .15 .15
635 A116 10c George III, diff. .15 .15
636 A117 10c Kew Palace .15 .15
637 A116 35c Arms of Elizabeth I .18 .18
638 A117 35c Elizabeth I .18 .18
639 A116 60c Arms of George III .30 .30
640 A117 60c George III, diff. .30 .30
641 A116 $1 Elizabeth I, diff. .50 .50
642 A117 $1 Hatfield Palace .50 .50
643 A116 $2.50 Spanish Armada 1.25 1.25
644 A117 $2.50 Elizabeth, I, diff. 1.25 1.25
Nos. 633-644 (12) 5.06 5.06

Stamps of same denomination se-tenant in continuous design.

Unissued 30c, 50c, $1, $2.50 and $5 values became available with the liquidation of the printer.

Colonial Building, Late 19th Cent. A118

Local Architecture. 10c, vert.

Perf. 14x13½, 13½x14

1984, Apr. 6 **Wmk. 380**

645 A118 10c Buildings, mid-19th cent. .15 .15
646 A118 45c shown .35 .35
647 A118 65c Wooden chattel, early 20th cent. .50 .50
648 A118 $2.50 Treasury, 1906 1.90 1.90
Nos. 645-648 (4) 2.90 2.90

For overprints see Nos. 796, 801.

Logwood Tree and Blossom — A118a

Perf. 13½x14, 14x13½

1984, June 12 **Wmk. 380**

649 A118a 10c shown .15 .15
650 A118a 45c Calabash .35 .35
651 A118a 65c Gommier, vert. .50 .50
652 A118a $2.50 Rain tree 1.90 1.90
Nos. 649-652 (4) 2.90 2.90

For overprint see No. 802.

Automobiles A119

Perf. 12½

1984, June 25 **Litho.** **Unwmk.**

Se-tenant Pairs

653 A119 5c Bugatti 57SC, 1939 .15 .15
654 A119 10c Chevrolet Bel Air, 1957 .15 .15
655 A119 $1 Alfa Romeo, 1930 1.25 1.25
656 A119 $2.50 Duesenberg, 1932 3.00 3.00
Nos. 653-656 (4) 4.55 4.55

See Nos. 686-693, 739-742, 850-855.

Endangered Reptiles A120

Wmk. 380

1984, Aug. 8 **Litho.** ***Perf. 14***

661 A120 10c Pygmy gecko .15 .15
662 A120 45c Maria Isld. ground lizard .35 .35
663 A120 65c Green iguana .50 .50
664 A120 $2.50 Couresse snake 1.90 1.90
Nos. 661-664 (4) 2.90 2.90

For overprint see No. 797.

Leaders of the World, 1984 Olympics — A121

Perf. 12½

1984, Sept. 21 **Litho.** **Unwmk.**

665 A121 5c Volleyball .15 .15
666 A121 5c Volleyball, diff. .15 .15
667 A121 10c Women's hurdles .15 .15
668 A121 10c Men's hurdles .15 .15
669 A121 65c Showjumping .40 .40
670 A121 65c Dressage .40 .40
671 A121 $2.50 Women's gymnastics 1.50 1.50
672 A121 $2.50 Men's gymnastics 1.50 1.50
Nos. 665-672 (8) 4.40 4.40

Stamps of same denomination se-tenant horiz.

Locomotive Type of 1983

1984, Sept. 21 **Litho.** ***Perf. 12½***

Se-tenant Pairs

674 A115 1c TAW 2-6-2T, 1897 .15 .15
675 A115 15c Crocodile 1-C.C.-1, 1920 .15 .15
676 A115 50c The Countess 0.6.0T, 1903 .55 .55
677 A115 75c Class GE6/6C.C., 1921 .85 .85
678 A115 $1 Class P8, 4.6.0, 1906 .55 .55
679 A115 $2 Der Alder 2.2.2., 1835 2.25 2.25
Nos. 674-679 (6) 4.50 4.50

Automobile Type of 1983

1984, Dec. 19 **Litho.** ***Perf. 12½***

Se-tenant Pairs

686 A119 10c Panhard and Levassor, 1889 .15 .15
687 A119 30c N.S.U. RO-80 Saloon, 1968 .35 .35
688 A119 55c Abarth, Balbero, 1958 .65 .65
689 A119 65c TRV Vixen 2500M, 1972 .75 .75
690 A119 75c Ford Mustang Convertible, 1965 .90 .90
691 A119 $1 Ford Model T, 1914 1.25 1.25
692 A119 $2 Aston Martin DB3S, 1954 2.50 2.50
693 A119 $3 Chrysler Imperial CG, 1931 3.50 3.50
Nos. 686-693 (8) 10.05 10.05

Christmas — A122

Abolition of Slavery, 150th Anniv. — A123

Wmk. 380

1984, Oct. 31 **Litho.** ***Perf. 14***

702 A122 10c Wine glass .15 .15
703 A122 35c Altar .28 .28
704 A122 65c Creche .55 .55
705 A122 $3 Holy family, abstract 2.50 2.50
a. Souvenir sheet of 4, #702-705 3.50 3.50
Nos. 702-705 (4) 3.48 3.48

1984, Dec. 12 **Litho.** ***Perf. 14***

Engraving details, Natl. Archives, Castries: 10c, Preparing manioc. 35c, Working with cassava flour. 55c, Cooking, twisting and drying tobacco. $5, Tobacco production, diff.

706 A123 10c bright buff & blk .15 .15
707 A123 35c bright buff & blk .25 .25
708 A123 55c bright buff & blk .40 .40
709 A123 $5 bright buff & blk 3.50 3.50
Nos. 706-709 (4) 4.30 4.30

Souvenir Sheet

710 Sheet of 4 5.00 5.00
a. A123 10c like No. 706 .15 .15
b. A123 35c like No. 707 .25 .25
c. A123 55c like No. 708 .40 .40
d. A123 $5 like No. 709 3.50 3.50

#710a-710d se-tenant in continuous design.

Locomotive Type of 1983

1985, Feb. 4 **Unwmk.** ***Perf. 12½***

Se-tenant Pairs

711 A115 5c J.N.R. Class C-53, 1928, Japan .15 .15
712 A115 15c Heavy L, 1885, India .15 .15
713 A115 35c QGR Class B18¼, 1926, Australia .50 .50
714 A115 60c Owain Glyndwr, 1923, U.K. .80 .80
715 A115 75c Lion, 1838, U.K. 1.05 1.05
716 A115 $1 Coal Engine, 1873, U.K. 1.40 1.40
717 A115 $2 No. 2238 Class Q6, 1921, U.K. 2.50 2.50
718 A115 $2.50 Class H, 1920, U.K. 3.52 3.25
Nos. 711-718 (8) 10.07 9.80

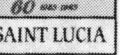

Girl Guides, 75th Anniv. — A124

Butterflies — A125

1985, Feb. 21 **Wmk. 380** ***Perf. 14***

727 A124 10c multicolored .15 .15
728 A124 35c multicolored .30 .30
729 A124 65c multicolored .60 .60
730 A124 $3 multicolored 2.75 2.75
Nos. 727-730 (4) 3.80 3.80

For overprint see No. 795.

1985, Feb. 28 **Unwmk.** ***Perf. 12½***

731 A125 15c Clossiana selene .15 .15
732 A125 15c Inachis io .15 .15
733 A125 40c Philaethria werneckei .30 .30
734 A125 40c Catagramma sorana .30 .30
735 A125 60c Kallima inachus .40 .40
736 A125 60c Hypanartia paullus .40 .40
737 A125 $2.25 Morpho rhetenor helena 1.50 1.50
738 A125 $2.25 Ornithoptera meridionalis 1.50 1.50
Nos. 731-738 (8) 4.70 4.70

Stamps of same denomination printed se-tenant.

Automobile Type of 1983

1985, Mar. 29

Se-tenant Pairs

739 A119 15c 1940 Hudson Eight, US .15 .15
740 A119 50c 1937 KdF, Germany .70 .70
741 A119 $1 1925 Kissel Goldbug, US 1.40 1.40
742 A119 $1.50 1973 Ferrari 246GTS, Italy 1.90 1.90
Nos. 739-742 (4) 4.15 4.15

Military Uniforms — A126

Designs: 5c, Grenadier, 70th Foot Reg., c. 1775. 10c, Grenadier Co. Officer, 14th Foot Reg., 1780. 20c, Battalion Co. Officer, 46th Foot Reg., 1781. 25c, Officer, Royal Artillery Reg., c. 1782. 30c, Officer, Royal Engineers Corps., 1782. 35c, Battalion Co. Officer, 54th Foot Reg., 1782. 45c, Grenadier Co. Private, 14th Foot Reg., 1782. 50c, Gunner, Royal Artillery Reg., 1796. 65c, Battalion Co. Private, 85th Foot Reg., c. 1796. 75c, Battalion Co. Private, 76th Foot Reg., 1796. 90c, Battalion Co. Private, 81st Foot Reg., c. 1796. $1, Sergeant, 74th (Highland) Foot Reg., 1796. $2.50, Private, Light Co., 93rd Foot Reg., 1803. $5, Battalion Co. Private, 1st West India Reg., 1803. $15, Officer, Royal Artillery Reg., 1850.

1985, May 7 **Wmk. 380** ***Perf. 15***

747 A126 5c multicolored .15 .15
748 A126 10c multicolored .15 .15
749 A126 20c multicolored .18 .18
750 A126 25c multicolored .20 .20
a. Wmk. 384 ('88) .25 .25
751 A126 30c multicolored .25 .25
752 A126 35c multicolored .28 .28
753 A126 45c multicolored .35 .35
754 A126 50c multicolored .40 .40
755 A126 65c multicolored .55 .55
756 A126 75c multicolored .65 .65
757 A126 90c multicolored .75 .75
758 A126 $1 multicolored .80 .80
759 A126 $2.50 multicolored 2.00 2.00
760 A126 $5 multicolored 4.00 4.00
761 A126 $15 multicolored 10.50 10.50
Nos. 747-761 (15) 21.21 21.21

Nos. 749-750 reissued inscribed 1986, Nos. 747-750, 1989.

See Nos. 876-879.

1987 **Unwmk.**

747a A126 5c .15 .15
748a A126 10c .15 .15
751a A126 30c .25 .25
753a A126 45c .35 .35
754a A126 50c .40 .40
759a A126 $2.50 2.00 2.00
760a A126 $5 4.00 4.00
Nos. 747a-760a (7) 7.30 7.30

Issued: #747a-748a, 2/24; #751a-760a, 3/16. Dated 1986.

1989 **Wmk. 384**

747b A126 5c .15 .15
748b A126 10c .15 .15
749a A126 20c .15 .15

World War II Aircraft A127

1985, May 30 **Unwmk.** ***Perf. 12½***

Se-tenant Pairs

762 A127 5c Messerschmitt 109-E .15 .15
763 A127 55c Avro 683 Lancaster Mark I Bomber .75 .75
764 A127 60c North American P.51-D Mustang .80 .80
765 A127 $2 Supermarine Spitfire Mark II 2.50 2.50
Nos. 762-765 (4) 4.20 4.20

Nature Reserves A128

Birds in habitats: 10c, Frigate bird, Frigate Island Sanctuary. 35c, Mangrove cuckoo, Savannes Bay, Scorpion Island. 65c, Yellow sandpiper, Maria Island. $3, Audubon's shearwater, Lapins Island.

1985, June 20 **Wmk. 380** ***Perf. 15***

770 A128 10c multicolored .15 .15
771 A128 35c multicolored .30 .30
772 A128 65c multicolored .55 .55
773 A128 $3 multicolored 2.75 2.75
Nos. 770-773 (4) 3.75 3.75

Locomotive Type of 1983

1985, June 26 **Unwmk.** ***Perf. 12½***

774 A115 10c No. 28 Tender engine, 1897, U.K. .15 .15
775 A115 30c No. 1621 Class M, 1893, U.K. .40 .40
776 A115 75c Class Dunalastair, 1896, U.K. .95 .95
777 A115 $2.50 Big Bertha No. 2290, 1919, U.K. 3.00 3.00
Nos. 774-777 (4) 4.50 4.50

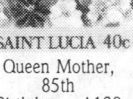

Queen Mother, 85th Birthday — A129

Intl. Youth Year — A130

Abstracts, by Lyndon Samuel — A131

1985, Aug. 16

782 A129 40c Facing right .30 .30
783 A129 40c Facing left .30 .30
784 A129 75c Facing right, diff. .55 .55
785 A129 75c Facing left, diff. .55 .55
786 A129 $1.10 Facing right, diff. .80 .80
787 A129 $1.10 Facing front .80 .80
788 A129 $1.75 Facing front, diff. 1.10 1.10
789 A129 $1.75 Facing left, diff. 1.10 1.10
Nos. 782-789 (8) 5.50 5.50

Souvenir Sheets

790 Sheet of 2 2.50 2.50
a.-b. A129 $2 any single 1.25 1.25
790C Sheet of 2 4.50 4.50
e. A129 $3 like No. 782 2.25 2.25
f. A129 $3 like No. 783 2.25 2.25
790D Sheet of 2 9.00 9.00
g. A129 $6 like No. 786 4.50 4.50
h. A129 $6 like No. 787 4.50 4.50

Stamps of same denomination printed se-tenant. For overprints see Nos. 798-799.

1985, Sept. 5 Wmk. 380 *Perf. 15*

Illustrations by local artists: 10c, Youth playing banjo, by Wayne Whitfield. 45c, Riding tricycle, by Mark D. Maragh. 75c, Youth against landscape, by Bartholemew Eugene. $3.50, Abstract, by Lyndon Samuel.

791 A130 10c multicolored .15 .15
792 A130 45c multicolored .42 .42
793 A130 75c multicolored .75 .75
794 A130 $3.50 multicolored 3.00 3.00
Nos. 791-794 (4) 4.32 4.32

Souvenir Sheet

794A A131 $5 multicolored 4.00 4.00

Intl. Youth Year.

Stamps of 1983-85 Ovptd. "CARIBBEAN ROYAL VISIT 1985" in Two or Three Lines

Wmk. as Before

1985, Nov. *Perfs. as Before*

795 A124 35c No. 728 .90 .90
796 A118 65c No. 647 1.75 1.75
797 A120 65c No. 663 1.75 1.75
798 A129 $1.10 No. 786 3.00 3.00
799 A129 $1.10 No. 787 3.00 3.00
800 A114 $2.50 No. 615 6.50 6.50
801 A118 $2.50 No. 648 6.50 6.50
802 A119 $2.50 No. 652 6.50 6.50
Nos. 795-802 (8) 29.90 29.90

Masquerade Figures — A132

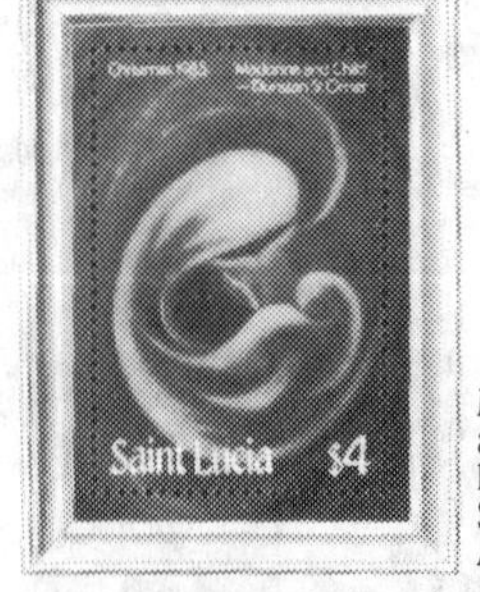

Madonna and Child, by Dunstan St. Omer A133

Unwmk.

1985, Dec. 23 Litho. *Perf. 15*

803 A132 10c Papa Jab .15 .15
804 A132 45c Paille Bananne .35 .35
805 A132 65c Cheval Bois .48 .48
Nos. 803-805 (3) .98 .98

Miniature Sheet

806 A133 $4 multi 3.00 3.00

Christmas 1985.

Locomotive Type of 1983

1986, Jan. 17 *Perf. 12½x13*

Se-tenant Pairs

Design A115

807 5c 1983 MWCR Rack Loco Tip Top, US .15 .15
808 15c 1975 BR Class 87 Stephenson Bo-Bo, UK .18 .18
809 30c 1901 Class D No. 737, UK .35 .35
810 60c 1922 No. 13 2-Co-2, UK .70 .70
811 75c 1954 BR Class EM2 Electra Co-Co, UK .85 .85
812 $1 1922 City of Newcastle, UK 1.25 1.25
813 $2.25 1930 DRG Von Kruckenberg, Propeller-driven Rail Car, Germany 2.75 2.75
814 $3 1893 JNR No. 860, Japan 3.50 3.50
Nos. 807-814 (8) 9.73 9.73

Miniature Sheets

Cook-out — A134

Designs: No. 823b, Scout sign. No. 824a, Wicker basket, weavings. No. 824b, Lady Olave Baden-Powell, Girl Guides founder.

1986, Mar. 3 Litho. *Perf. 13x12½*

823 Sheet of 2 5.50 5.50
a.-b. A134 $4 any single 2.75 2.75
824 Sheet of 2 8.00 8.00
a.-b. A134 $6 any single 4.00 4.00

Scouting anniv., Girl Guides 75th anniv. Exist with plain or decorative border.

A135

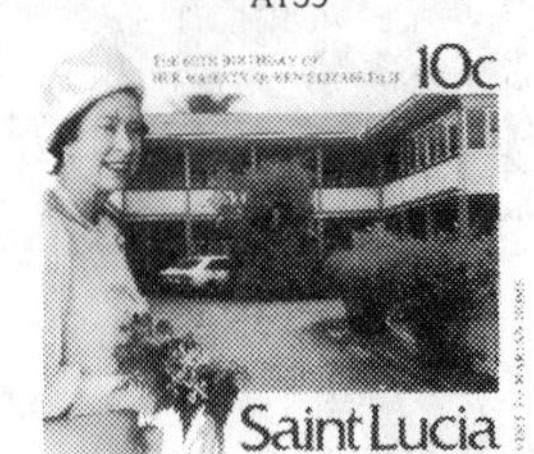

Queen Elizabeth II, 60th Birthday — A136

Various photographs.

Perf. 13x12½, 12½x13, 14x15 (A136)

1986

825 A135 5c Pink hat .15 .15
826 A136 10c Visiting Marian Home .15 .15
827 A136 45c Mindoo Phillip Park speech .30 .30
828 A136 50c Opening Leon Hess School .34 .34
829 A135 $1 Princess Elizabeth .65 .65
830 A135 $3.50 Blue hat 2.25 2.25
831 A136 $5 Government House 3.25 3.25
832 A135 $6 Canberra, 1982, vert. 3.75 3.75
Nos. 825-832 (8) 10.84 10.84

Souvenir Sheets

833 A136 $7 HMY Britannia, Castries Harbor 4.50 4.50
834 A135 $8 Straw hat 5.25 5.25

Issue dates: Nos. 825, 829-830, 832, Apr. 21. Nos. 826-828, 831, 833, June 14.

State Visit of Pope John Paul II A137

1986, July 7 *Perf. 14x15, 15x14*

835 A137 55c Kissing the ground .42 .42
836 A137 60c St. Joseph's Convent .45 .45
837 A137 80c Cathedral, Castries .60 .60
Nos. 835-837 (3) 1.47 1.47

Souvenir Sheet

838 A137 $6 Pope 4.45 4.45

Nos. 837-838 vert.

Wedding of Prince Andrew and Sarah Ferguson — A138

1986, July 23 *Perf. 12½*

839 A138 80c Sarah, vert. .60 .60
840 A138 80c Andrew, vert. .60 .60
841 A138 $2 Couple 1.50 1.50
842 A138 $2 Andrew, Nancy Reagan 1.50 1.50
Nos. 839-842 (4) 4.20 4.20

Stamps of the same denomination printed se-tenant. #841-842 show Westminster Abbey in LR.

US Peace Corps in St. Lucia, 25th Anniv. A139

1986, Sept. 25 Litho. *Perf. 14*

843 A139 80c Technical instruction .60 .60
844 A139 $2 Pres. Kennedy, vert. 1.50 1.50
845 A139 $3.50 Natl. crests, corps emblem 2.60 2.60
Nos. 843-845 (3) 4.70 4.70

Wedding of Prince Andrew and Sarah Ferguson — A140

1986, Oct. 15 *Perf. 15*

846 A140 50c Andrew .38 .38
847 A140 80c Sarah .60 .60
848 A140 $1 At altar .75 .75
849 A140 $3 In open carriage 2.25 2.25
Nos. 846-849 (4) 3.98 3.98

Souvenir Sheet

849A A140 $7 Andrew, Sarah 5.25 5.25

Automobile Type of 1983

1986, Oct. 23 Litho. *Perf. 12½x13*

Se-tenant Pairs

Design A119

850 20c 1969 AMC AMX, US .15 .15
851 50c 1912 Russo-Baltique, Russia .60 .60
852 60c 1932 Lincoln KB, US .70 .70
853 $1 1933 Rolls Royce Phantom II Continental, UK 1.25 1.25
854 $1.50 1939 Buick Century, US 1.75 1.75
855 $3 1957 Chrysler 300 C, US 3.50 3.50
Nos. 850-855 (6) 7.95 7.95

Chak-Chak Band A141

1986, Nov. 7 *Perf. 15*

862 A141 15c shown .15 .15
863 A141 45c Folk dancing .35 .35
864 A141 80c Steel band .60 .60
865 A141 $5 Limbo dancer 3.75 3.75
Nos. 862-865 (4) 4.85 4.85

Souvenir Sheet

866 A141 $10 Gros Islet 7.50 7.50

Christmas A142

Churches: 10c, St. Ann Catholic, Mon Repos. 40c, St. Joseph the Worker Catholic, Gros Islet. 80c, Holy Trinity Anglican, Castries. $4, Our Lady of the Assumption Catholic, Soufriere, vert. $7, St. Lucy Catholic, Micoud.

1986, Nov.

867 A142 10c multicolored .15 .15
868 A142 40c multicolored .30 .30
869 A142 80c multicolored .60 .60
870 A142 $4 multicolored 3.00 3.00
Nos. 867-870 (4) 4.05 4.05

Souvenir Sheet

871 A142 $7 multicolored 5.25 5.25

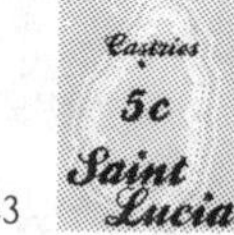

Map of St. Lucia — A143

Perf. 14x14½

1987, Feb. 24 Litho. Wmk. 373

872 A143 5c beige & blk .15 .15
a. Wmk. 384 ('89) .15 .15
873 A143 10c pale yel grn & blk .15 .15
a. Wmk. 384 ('89) .15 .15
874 A143 45c orange & blk .34 .34
875 A143 50c pale violet & blk .38 .38
Set value .85 .85

#872-873 exist inscribed 1988, #875 1989. Issued: #872a, 873a, Apr. 12. See #937.

Uniforms Type of 1985

Designs: 15c, Battalion company private, 2nd West India Regiment, 1803. 60c, Battalion company officer, 5th Regiment of Foot, 1778. 80c, Battalion company officer, 27th (or Inniskilling) Regiment of Foot, c. 1780. $20, Grenadier company private, 46th Regiment of Foot, 1778.

1987, Mar. 16 Unwmk. *Perf. 15*

876 A126 15c multicolored .15 .15
877 A126 60c multicolored .42 .42
878 A126 80c multicolored .55 .55
879 A126 $20 multicolored 13.75 13.75
Nos. 876-879 (4) 14.87 14.87

Dated 1986.

1988 Wmk. 384

876a A126 15c .15 .15
877a A126 60c .42 .42
878a A126 80c .55 .55
879a A126 $20 14.00 14.00
Nos. 876a-879a (4) 15.12 15.12

Statue of Liberty, Cent.
A144 A145

1987, Apr. 29 Wmk. 373 *Perf. 14½*

880 A144 15c Statue, flags .15 .15
881 A144 80c Statue, ship .60 .60
882 A144 $1 Statue, Concorde jet .75 .75
883 A144 $5 Statue, flying boat 3.75 3.75
Nos. 880-883 (4) 5.25 5.25

Souvenir Sheet

884 A145 $6 Statue, New York City 4.50 4.50

Maps, Surveying Instruments — A147

Wmk. 384

1987, Aug. 31 Litho. *Perf. 14*
888 A147 15c 1775 .15 .15
889 A147 60c 1814 .45 .45
890 A147 $1 1888 .75 .75
891 A147 $2.50 1987 1.90 1.90
Nos. 888-891 (4) 3.25 3.25

First cadastral survey of St. Lucia.

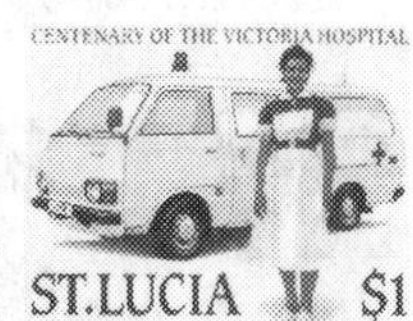

Victoria Hospital, Cent. — A148

Perf. 14½

1987, Nov. 4 Litho. Wmk. 384
892 A148 $1 Ambulance, nurse, 1987 .75 .75
893 A148 $1 Nurse, hammock, 1913 .75 .75
894 A148 $2 Hospital, 1987 1.50 1.50
895 A148 $2 Hospital, 1887 1.50 1.50
Nos. 892-895 (4) 4.50 4.50

Souvenir Sheet

896 A148 $4.50 Main gate, 1987 3.35 3.35

Stamps of the same denomination printed se-tenant.

Christmas A149

Paintings (details) by unidentified artists.

1987, Nov. 30
897 A149 15c The Holy Family .15 .15
898 A149 50c Adoration of the Shepherds .38 .38
899 A149 60c Adoration of the Magi .45 .45
900 A149 90c Madonna and Child .68 .68
Nos. 897-900 (4) 1.66 1.66

Souvenir Sheet

901 A149 $6 Holy Family 4.50 4.50

World Wildlife Fund — A150

American Indian Artifacts — A151

Amazonian parrots, Amazona versicolor.

Wmk. 384

1987, Dec. 18 Litho. *Perf. 14*
902 A150 15c multi .15 .15
903 A150 35c multi, diff. .25 .25
904 A150 50c multi, diff. .38 .38
905 A150 $1 multi, diff. .75 .75
Nos. 902-905 (4) 1.53 1.53

Perf. 14½

1988, Feb. 12 Litho. Wmk. 384
906 A151 25c Carib clay zemi .18 .18
907 A151 30c Troumassee cylinder .22 .22
908 A151 80c Three-pointer stone .60 .60
909 A151 $3.50 Dauphine petroglyph 2.60 2.60
Nos. 906-909 (4) 3.60 3.60

St. Lucia Cooperative Bank, 50th Anniv. A152

Perf. 15x14

1988, Apr. 29 Litho. Wmk. 373
910 A152 10c Coins, banknotes .15 .15
911 A152 45c Branch in Castries .35 .35
912 A152 60c like 45c .45 .45
913 A152 80c Branch in Vieux Fort .60 .60
Nos. 910-913 (4) 1.55 1.55

Cable and Wireless in St. Lucia, 50th Anniv. A153

Designs: 15c, Rural telephone exchange. 25c, Antique and modern telephones. 80c, St. Lucia Teleport (satellite dish). $2.50, Map of Eastern Caribbean microwave communications system.

Wmk. 384

1988, June 10 Litho. *Perf. 14*
914 A153 15c multicolored .15 .15
915 A153 25c multicolored .18 .18
916 A153 80c multicolored .60 .60
917 A153 $2.50 multicolored 1.90 1.90
Nos. 914-917 (4) 2.83 2.83

Cent. of the Methodist Church in St. Lucia A154

Perf. 14½

1988, Aug. 15 Litho. Wmk. 384
918 A154 15c Altar, window .15 .15
919 A154 80c Chancel .60 .60
920 A154 $3.50 Exterior 2.60 2.60
Nos. 918-920 (3) 3.35 3.35

Tourism — A155

Lagoon and: 10c, Tourists, gourmet meal. 30c, Beverage, tourists. 80c, Tropical fruit. $2.50, Fish and chef. $5.50, Market.
Illustration reduced.

Perf. 14x13½

1988, Sept. 15 Litho. Wmk. 384
921 A155 Strip of 4 2.75 2.75
a. 10c multicolored .15 .15
b. 30c multicolored .22 .22
c. 80c multicolored .60 .60
d. $2.50 multicolored 1.85 1.85

Souvenir Sheet

922 A155 $5.50 multicolored 4.00 4.00

Lloyds of London, 300th Anniv.
Common Design Type

Designs: 10c, San Francisco earthquake, 1906. 60c, Castries Harbor, horiz. 80c, *Lady Nelson*, sunk off Castries Harbor, 1942, horiz. $2.50, Castries on fire, 1948.

Wmk. 373

1988, Oct. 17 Litho. *Perf. 14*
923 CD341 10c multicolored .15 .15
924 CD341 60c multicolored .45 .45
925 CD341 80c multicolored .60 .60
926 CD341 $2.50 multicolored 1.85 1.85
Nos. 923-926 (4) 3.05 3.05

A156

A157

Christmas: Flowers.

Perf. 14½x14

1988, Nov. 22 Litho. Wmk. 384
927 A156 15c Snow on the mountain .15 .15
928 A156 45c Christmas candle .35 .35
929 A156 60c Balisier .45 .45
930 A156 80c Poinsettia .60 .60
Nos. 927-930 (4) 1.55 1.55

Souvenir Sheet

931 A156 $5.50 Flower arrangement 4.00 4.00

Perf. 13½x13

1989, Feb. 22 Wmk. 373

Natl. Independence, 10th Anniv.: 15c, Princess Alexandra presenting constitution to Prime Minister Compton. 80c, Sulfur springs geothermal well. $1, Sir Arthur Lewis Community College. $2.50, Pointe Seraphine tax-free shopping center. $5, Emblem.

932 A157 15c Nationhood .15 .15
933 A157 80c Development .60 .60
934 A157 $1 Education .75 .75
935 A157 $2.50 Progress 1.90 1.90
Nos. 932-935 (4) 3.40 3.40

Souvenir Sheet

936 A157 $5 With Confidence We Progress 3.75 3.75

Map Type of 1987

Perf. 14x14½

1989, Mar. 17 Litho. Wmk. 373
937 A143 $1 scarlet & black .75 .75

Indigenous Mushrooms — A158

Perf. 14½x14

1989, May 22 Litho. Wmk. 384
938 A158 15c Gerronema citrinum .15 .15
939 A158 25c Lepiota spiculata .18 .18
940 A158 50c Calocybe cyanocephala .38 .38
941 A158 $5 Russula puiggarii 3.75 3.75
Nos. 938-941 (4) 4.46 4.46

PHILEXFRANCE '89, French Revolution Bicent. — A159

Views of St. Lucia and text: 10c, Independence day announcement, vert. 60c, French revolutionary flag at Morne Fortune, 1791. $1, "Men are born and live free and equal in rights," vert. $3.50, Captain La Crosse's arrival at Gros Islet, 1792.

Wmk. 373

1989, July 14 Litho. *Perf. 14*
942 A159 10c multicolored .15 .15
943 A159 60c multicolored .45 .45
944 A159 $1 multicolored .75 .75
945 A159 $3.50 multicolored 2.60 2.60
Nos. 942-945 (4) 3.95 3.95

Intl. Red Cross, 125th Anniv. A160

1989, Oct. 10 Wmk. 384 *Perf. 14½*
946 A160 50c Natl. headquarters .38 .38
947 A160 80c Seminar in Castries, 1987 .60 .60
948 A160 $1 Ambulance .75 .75
Nos. 946-948 (3) 1.73 1.73

Christmas Lanterns Shaped Like Buildings A161

1989, Nov. 17 *Perf. 14x14½*
949 A161 10c multi .15 .15
950 A161 50c multi, diff. .38 .38
951 A161 90c multi, diff. .68 .68
952 A161 $1 multi, diff. .75 .75
Nos. 949-952 (4) 1.96 1.96

Trees In Danger of Extinction — A162

1990 Wmk. 384 *Perf. 14*
953 A162 10c Chinna .15 .15
954 A162 15c Latanier .15 .15
955 A162 20c Gwi gwi .15 .15
956 A162 25c L'encens .18 .18
957 A162 50c Bois lele .38 .38
958 A162 80c Bois d'amande .60 .60
959 A162 95c Mahot piman grand bois .70 .70
960 A162 $1 Balata .75 .75
961 A162 $1.50 Pencil cedar 1.10 1.10
962 A162 $2.50 Bois cendre 1.75 1.75
963 A162 $5 Lowye cannelle 3.75 3.75
964 A162 $25 Chalantier grand bois 18.50 18.50
Nos. 953-964 (12) 28.16 28.16

Issued: 20c, 25c, 50c, $25, Feb. 21; 10c, 15c, 80c, $1.50, Apr. 12; 95c, $1, $2.50, $5, June 25.
For overprints see Nos. 971, O28-O39.

1992-95 Wmk. 373 *Perf. 14*
953a A162 10c .15 .15
954a A162 15c .15 .15
955a A162 20c ('95) .15 .15
956a A162 25c ('94) .18 .18
957a A162 50c .38 .38
Nos. 953a-957a (5) 1.01 1.01

Nos. 953a, 957a exist dated 1993; Nos. 953a, 954a, 957a dated 1994; No. 955a, 1990.

Centenary of St. Mary's College, Intl. Literacy Year A163

Designs: 30c, Father Tapon, original building. 45c, Rev. Brother Collins, current building. 75c, Students in literacy class. $2, Door to knowledge, children.

1990, June 6 Wmk. 373
965 A163 30c multicolored .22 .22
966 A163 45c multicolored .34 .34
967 A163 75c multicolored .55 .55
968 A163 $2 multicolored 1.50 1.50
Nos. 965-968 (4) 2.61 2.61

Queen Mother, 90th Birthday
Common Design Types

1990, Aug. 3 Wmk. 384 *Perf. 14x15*
969 CD343 50c Coronation, 1937 .38 .38

Perf. 14½

970 CD344 $5 Arriving at theater, 1949 3.75 3.75

No. 963 Overprinted

1990, Aug. 13 *Perf. 14*
971 A162 $5 multicolored 3.75 3.75

Intl. Garden and Greenery Exposition, Osaka, Japan.

Christmas — A164

Butterflies — A166

Boats A165

Paintings: 10c, Adoration of the Magi by Rubens. 30c, Adoration of the Shepherds by Murillo. 80c, Adoration of the Magi by Rubens, diff. $5, Adoration of the Shepherds by Champaigne.

1990, Dec. 3 *Perf. 14*

972 A164 10c multicolored .15 .15
973 A164 30c multicolored .24 .24
974 A164 80c multicolored .64 .64
975 A164 $5 multicolored 3.75 3.75
Nos. 972-975 (4) 4.78 4.78

1991, Mar. 27 Wmk. 373 *Perf. 14½*

Various boats.

976 A165 50c multicolored .40 .40
977 A165 80c multicolored .65 .65
978 A165 $1 multicolored .80 .80
979 A165 $2.50 multicolored 2.00 2.00
Nos. 976-979 (4) 3.85 3.85

Souvenir Sheet

980 A165 $5 multicolored 3.75 3.75

Wmk. 373

1991, Aug. 15 Litho. *Perf. 14*

981 A166 60c Polydamas swallowtail .48 .48
982 A166 80c St. Christopher's hairstreak .65 .65
983 A166 $1 St. Lucia mestra .80 .80
984 A166 $2.50 Godman's hairstreak 2.00 2.00
Nos. 981-984 (4) 3.93 3.93

Christmas A167

Perf. 14x14½

1991, Nov. 20 Litho. Wmk. 384

985 A167 10c Jacmel Church .15 .15
986 A167 15c Red Madonna, vert. .15 .15
987 A167 80c Monchy Church .55 .55
988 A167 $5 Blue Madonna, vert. 3.45 3.45
Nos. 985-988 (4) 4.30 4.30

Atlantic Rally for Cruisers A168

Designs: 60c, Cruisers crossing Atlantic, map. 80c, Cruisers tacking.

1991, Dec. 10 Wmk. 384 *Perf. 14*

989 A168 60c multicolored .42 .42
990 A168 80c multicolored .55 .55

Discovery of America, 500th Anniv. — A169

Wmk. 373

1992, July 6 Litho. *Perf. 13*

991 A169 $1 Coming ashore .68 .68
992 A169 $2 Natives, ships 1.40 1.40

Organization of East Caribbean States.

Contact with New World A170

1992, Aug. 4 *Perf. 13½*

993 A170 15c Amerindians .15 .15
994 A170 40c Juan de la Cosa, 1499 .28 .28
995 A170 50c Columbus, 1502 .35 .35
996 A170 $5 Gimie, Dec. 13th 3.45 3.45
Nos. 993-996 (4) 4.23 4.23

Christmas A171

Paintings: 10c, Virgin and Child, by Delaroche. 15c, The Holy Family, by Rubens. 60c, Virgin and Child, by Luini. 80c, Virgin and Child, by Sassoferrato.

Perf. 14½

1992, Nov. 9 Litho. Wmk. 373

997 A171 10c multicolored .15 .15
998 A171 15c multicolored .15 .15
999 A171 60c multicolored .42 .42
1000 A171 80c multicolored .55 .55
Nos. 997-1000 (4) 1.27 1.27

Anti-Drugs Campaign — A172

Perf. 13½x14

1993, Feb. 1 Litho. Wmk. 373

1001 A172 $5 multicolored 2.80 2.80

Gros Piton from Delcer, Choiseul, by Dunstan St. Omer — A173

Paintings: 75c, Reduit Bay, by Derek Walcott. $5, Woman and Child at River, by Nancy Cole Auguste.

1993, Nov. 1 Wmk. 373 *Perf. 13*

1002 A173 20c multicolored .15 .15
1003 A173 75c multicolored .42 .42
1004 A173 $5 multicolored 2.75 2.75
Nos. 1002-1004 (3) 3.32 3.32

Christmas A174

Details of paintings: 15c, The Madonna of the Rosary, by Murillo. 60c, The Madonna and Child, by Van Dyck. 95c, The Annunciation, by Champaigne.

1993, Dec. 6 *Perf. 14*

1005 A174 15c multicolored .15 .15
1006 A174 60c multicolored .45 .45
1007 A174 95c multicolored .70 .70
Nos. 1005-1007 (3) 1.30 1.30

A175 A176

1994, July 25 *Perf. 13*

1008 A175 20c multicolored .15 .15

Souvenir Sheet

1009 A175 $5 multicolored 3.75 3.75

Abolition of Slavery on St. Lucia, bicent.

1994, Dec. 9 *Perf. 12½x13*

Christmas (Flowers): 20c, Euphorbia pulcherrima. 75c, Heliconia rostrata. 95c, Alpinia purpurata. $5.50, Anthurium andreanum.

1010 A176 20c multicolored .15 .15
1011 A176 75c multicolored .55 .55
1012 A176 95c multicolored .70 .70
1013 A176 $5.50 multicolored 4.00 4.00
Nos. 1010-1013 (4) 5.40 5.40

Battle of Rabot, Bicent. A177

1995, Apr. 28 *Perf. 13½*

1014 A177 20c Map of island .15 .15
1015 A177 75c Rebelling slaves .55 .55
1016 A177 95c Battle scene .70 .70
Nos. 1014-1016 (3) 1.40 1.40

Souvenir Sheet

Perf. 13

1017 A177 $5.50 Battle map 4.00 4.00

End of World War II, 50th Anniv.

Common Design Types

Designs: 20c, ATS women in Britain. 75c, German U-boat off St. Lucia. 95c, Caribbean regiment, North Africa. $1.10, Presentation Spitfire Mk V. $5.50, Reverse of War Medal 1939-45.

Perf. 13½

1995, May 8 Litho. Wmk. 373

1018 CD351 20c multicolored .15 .15
1019 CD351 75c multicolored .55 .55
1020 CD351 95c multicolored .70 .70
1021 CD351 $1.10 multicolored .80 .80
Nos. 1018-1021 (4) 2.20 2.20

Souvenir Sheet

Perf. 14

1022 CD352 $5.50 multicolored 4.00 4.00

UN, 50th Anniv.

Common Design Type

Designs: 10c, Puma helicopter. 65c, Renault truck. $1.35, Transall C160. $5, Douglas DC3.

Wmk. 373

1995, Oct. 24 Litho. *Perf. 14*

1023 CD353 10c multicolored .15 .15
1024 CD353 65c multicolored .50 .50
1025 CD353 $1.35 multicolored 1.00 1.00
1026 CD353 $5 multicolored 3.75 3.75
Nos. 1023-1026 (4) 5.40 5.40

Christmas — A178

Flowers: 15c, Eranthemum nervosum. 70c, Bougainvillea. $1.10, Allamanda cathartica. $3, Hibiscus rosa sinensis.

Wmk. 373

1995, Nov. 20 Litho. *Perf. 13*

1027 A178 15c multicolored .15 .15
1028 A178 70c multicolored .50 .50
1029 A178 $1.10 multicolored .80 .80
1030 A178 $3 multicolored 2.25 2.25
Nos. 1027-1030 (4) 3.70 3.70

Carnival — A179 Water — A180

Wmk. 384

1996, Feb. 16 Litho. *Perf. 14*

1031 A179 20c Calypso king .15 .15
1032 A179 65c Carnival band .50 .50
1033 A179 95c King of the band .70 .70
1034 A179 $3 Carnival queen 2.25 2.25
Nos. 1031-1034 (4) 3.60 3.60

1996, Mar. 5 Wmk. 373

1035 A180 20c Muddy stream .15 .15
1036 A180 65c Clear stream .50 .50
1037 A180 $5 Modern dam 3.75 3.75
Nos. 1035-1037 (3) 4.40 4.40

Tourism A181

Designs: 65c, Market. 75c, Riding horses on beach. 95c, Outdoor wedding ceremony. $5, Annual Intl. Jazz Festival.

Wmk. 373

1996, May 13 Litho. *Perf. 14*

1038 A181 65c multicolored .50 .50
1039 A181 75c multicolored .55 .55
1040 A181 95c multicolored .70 .70
1041 A181 $5 multicolored 3.75 3.75
Nos. 1038-1041 (4) 5.50 5.50

Modern Olympic Games, Cent. A182

Wmk. 373

1996, July 19 Litho. *Perf. 14*

1042 A182 15c Early runner .15 .15
1043 A182 15c Modern runner .15 .15
a. Pair, #1042-1043 .25 .25
1044 A182 75c Two sailboats .55 .55
1045 A182 75c Four sailboats .55 .55
a. Pair, #1044-1045 1.10 1.10

Nos. 1043a, 1045a have a continuous design.

Flags & Ships A183

Flag, ship: 10c, Spanish Royal banner, 1502, Spanish caravel. 15c, Skull & crossbones, 1550, pirate carrack. 20c, Royal Netherlands, 1660, Dutch 80-gun ship. 25c, Union flag, 1739, Royal Navy 64-gun ship. 40c, French Imperial, 1750, French 74-gun ship. 50c, Martinique & St. Lucia, 1766, French brig. 55c, British White Ensign, 1782, Royal Navy Frigate Squadron. 65c, British Red Ensign, 1782, Battle of the Saints. 75c, British Blue Ensign, 1782, RN brig. 95c, Fench Tricolor, 1792, French 38-gun frigate. $1. British Union, 1801, West Indies Grand Fleet. $2.50, Confederate, 1861, CSA steam/sail armed cruiser. $5,

Canada, 1915-19, Canadian V & W class destroyer. $10, US, 1942-48, Fletcher class destroyer. $25, National, cruise ship.

Perf. 14x15

1996-97	Litho.		Wmk. 384	
1046 A183	10c	multi	.15	.15
1047 A183	15c	multi	.15	.15
1048 A183	20c	multi	.15	.15
1049 A183	25c	multi	.20	.20
1050 A183	40c	multi	.30	.30
1051 A183	50c	multi	.40	.40
1052 A183	55c	multi	.40	.40
1053 A183	65c	multi	.50	.50
1054 A183	75c	multi	.55	.55
1055 A183	95c	multi	.70	.70
1056 A183	$1	multi	.75	.75
1057 A183	$2.50	multi	1.85	1.85
1058 A183	$5	multi	3.75	3.75
1059 A183	$10	multi	7.50	7.50
1060 A183	$25	multi	18.75	18.75
	Nos. 1056-1060 (5)		32.60	32.60

Issued: 10c, 15c, 20c, 25c, 40c, 9/16/96; 50c, 55c, 65c, 75c, 95c, 11/18/96; $1, $2.50, $5, $10, $25, 1/8/97.

Christmas — A184

Flowers: 20c, Cordia sebestena. 75c, Cryptostegia grandiflora. 95c, Hibiscus elatus. $5, Caularthron bicornutum.

Wmk. 384

1996, Dec. 1	Litho.	*Perf. 14*	
1061 A184 20c multicolored		.15	.15
1062 A184 75c multicolored		.55	.55
1063 A184 95c multicolored		.70	.70
1064 A184 $5 multicolored		3.70	3.70
Nos. 1061-1064 (4)		5.10	5.10

Queen Elizabeth II and Prince Philip, 50th Wedding Anniv. — A185

Designs: No. 1065, Queen. No. 1066, Prince with horses. No. 1067, Prince. No. 1068, Queen riding in carriage. No. 1069, Queen, Prince. No. 1070, Princess Anne riding horse.

$5, Queen, Prince riding in open carriage, horiz.

Perf. 14½x14

1997, July 10	Litho.	Wmk. 384	
1065 A185 75c multicolored		.55	.55
1066 A185 75c multicolored		.55	.55
a. Pair, #1065-1066		1.10	1.10
1067 A185 95c multicolored		.70	.70
1068 A185 95c multicolored		.70	.70
a. Pair, #1067-1068		1.40	1.40
1069 A185 $1 multicolored		.75	.75
1070 A185 $1 multicolored		.75	.75
a. Pair, #1069-1070		1.50	1.50
Nos. 1065-1070 (6)		4.00	4.00

Souvenir Sheet

Perf. 14x14½

1071 A185 $5 multicolored	3.50	3.50

Disasters — A186

20c, MV St. George capsizes, 1935. 55c, SS Belle of Bath founders. $1, SS Ethelgonda runs aground, 1897. $2.50, Hurrincane devastation, 1817.

1997, July 14	*Perf. 14x15*	
1072 A186 20c multicolored	.15	.15
1073 A186 55c multicolored	.40	.40
1074 A186 $1 multicolored	.75	.75
1075 A186 $2.50 multicolored	1.80	1.80
Nos. 1072-1075 (4)	3.10	3.10

Events of 1797 A187

Designs: 20c, Taking of Praslin. 55c, Battle of Dennery. 70c, Peace. $3, Brigands join 1st West India Regiment.

Wmk. 373

1997, Aug. 15	Litho.	*Perf. 14*	
1076 A187 20c multicolored		.15	.15
1077 A187 55c multicolored		.40	.40
1078 A187 70c multicolored		.50	.50
1079 A187 $3 multicolored		2.10	2.10
Nos. 1076-1079 (4)		3.15	3.15

Christmas — A188

Church art: 20c, Roseau Church. 60c, Altar piece, Regional Seminary, Trinidad. 95c, Our Lady of the Presentation, Trinidad. $5, The Four Days of Creation.

Perf. 14x15

1997, Dec. 1	Litho.	Wmk. 384	
1080 A188 20c multicolored		.15	.15
1081 A188 60c multicolored		.45	.45
1082 A188 95c multicolored		.70	.70
1083 A188 $5 multicolored		3.75	3.75
Nos. 1080-1083 (4)		5.05	5.05

Diana, Princess of Wales (1961-97) — A189

1998, Jan. 19	Litho.	*Perf. 14*	
1084 A189 $1 multicolored		.75	.75

No. 1084 was issued in sheets of 9.

AIR POST STAMP

> Catalogue values for unused stamps in this section are for Never Hinged items.

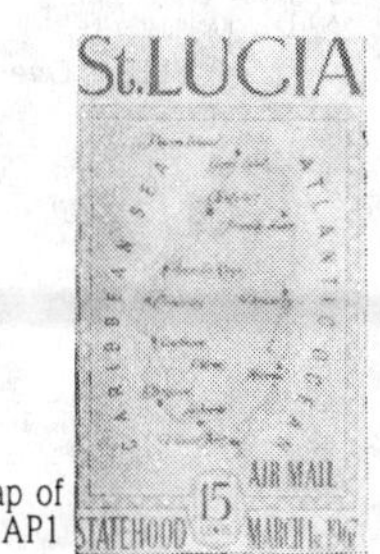

Map of St. Lucia — AP1

Perf. 14½x14

1967, Mar. 1	Photo.	Unwmk.	
C1 AP1 15c blue		.30	.30

St. Lucia's independence.
Exists imperf. and also in souvenir sheet.

POSTAGE DUE STAMPS

D1

D2

Type I - "No." 3mm wide (shown).
Type II - "No." 4mm wide.

Rough Perf. 12

1931	Unwmk.	Typeset	
J1 D1 1p blk, *gray bl*, type I		4.00	3.50
a. Type II		7.50	8.00
J2 D1 2p blk, *yel*, type I		10.00	6.00
a. Type II		15.00	16.00
b. Vertical pair, imperf. btwn.		*4,000.*	

The serial numbers are handstamped. Type II has round "o" and period. Type I has tall "o" and square period.

> Catalogue values for unused stamps in this section, from this point to the end of the section, are for Never Hinged items.

1933-47	Typo.	Wmk. 4	*Perf. 14*	
J3 D2 1p black			4.25	*3.00*
J4 D2 2p black			14.00	*5.00*
J5 D2 4p black ('47)			4.25	*6.25*
J6 D2 8p black ('47)			4.25	*7.50*
Nos. J3-J6 (4)			26.75	*21.75*

Issue date: June 28, 1947.

Values in Cents

1949, Oct. 1			
J7 D2	2c black	.25	.25
J8 D2	4c black	.50	.50
J9 D2	8c black	1.00	1.00
J10 D2	16c black	1.75	1.75
Nos. J7-J10 (4)		3.50	3.50

Values are for examples on chalky paper. Regular paper examples are worth more.

Wmk. 4a (error)

J7a D2	2c	30.00
J8a D2	4c	35.00
J9a D2	8c	67.50
J10a D2	16c	82.50
Nos. J7a-J10a (4)		215.00

1965, Mar. 9	Wmk. 314	
J11 D2 2c black	.80	*3.00*
J12 D2 4c black	.95	*5.00*

In the 2c center the "c" is heavier and the period bigger.

Nos. J9-J12 exist with overprint "Statehood/1st Mar. '67" in red.

Arms of St. Lucia — D3

1981, Aug. 4	Litho.	Wmk. 373	
J13 D3 5c red brown		.15	.15
J14 D3 15c green		.15	.15
J15 D3 25c deep orange		.15	.15
J16 D3 $1 dark blue		.55	.55
Set value		.80	.80

1990	Wmk. 384	*Perf. 15x14*	
J17 D3 5c red brown		.15	.15
J18 D3 15c green		.15	.15
J19 D3 25c deep orange		.20	.20
J20 D3 $1 dark blue		.75	.75
Set value		1.05	1.05

WAR TAX STAMPS

No. 65 Overprinted **WAR TAX**

1916	Wmk. 3	*Perf. 14*	
MR1 A11 1p scarlet		3.50	5.00
a. Double overprint		400.00	*450.00*
b. 1p carmine		27.50	30.00

Overprinted **WAR TAX**

MR2 A11 1p scarlet	.20	.20

OFFICIAL STAMPS

> Catalogue values for unused stamps in this section are for Never Hinged items.

Nos. 504-515 Overprinted "OFFICIAL"

Perf. 14½

1983, Oct. 13	Litho.	Wmk. 373	
O1 A95 5c multicolored		.15	.15
O2 A95 10c multicolored		.15	.15
O3 A95 15c multicolored		.15	.15
O4 A95 20c multicolored		.15	.15
O5 A95 25c multicolored		.20	.20
O6 A95 30c multicolored		.25	.25
O7 A95 50c multicolored		.40	.40
O8 A95 75c multicolored		.60	.60
O9 A95 $1 multicolored		.75	.75
O10 A95 $2 multicolored		1.50	1.50
O11 A95 $5 multicolored		3.75	3.75
O12 A95 $10 multicolored		7.50	7.50
Nos. O1-O12 (12)		15.55	15.55

Nos. 747-761 Ovptd. "OFFICIAL"

1985, May 7	Litho.	*Perf. 15*	
O13 A126 5c multicolored		.15	.15
O14 A126 10c multicolored		.15	.15
O15 A126 20c multicolored		.15	.15
O16 A126 25c multicolored		.15	.15
O17 A126 30c multicolored		.18	.18
O18 A126 35c multicolored		.20	.20
O19 A126 45c multicolored		.28	.28
O20 A126 50c multicolored		.30	.30
O21 A126 65c multicolored		.40	.40
O22 A126 75c multicolored		.45	.45
O23 A126 90c multicolored		.55	.55
O24 A126 $1 multicolored		.60	.60
O25 A126 $2.50 multicolored		1.50	1.50
O26 A126 $5 multicolored		3.00	3.00
O27 A126 $15 multicolored		7.50	7.50
Nos. O13-O27 (15)		15.56	15.56

Nos. 953-964 Ovptd. "OFFICIAL"

1990, Feb. 21	Wmk. 384	*Perf. 14*	
O28 A162 10c multicolored		.15	.15
O29 A162 15c multicolored		.15	.15
O30 A162 20c multicolored		.15	.15
O31 A162 25c multicolored		.18	.18
O32 A162 50c multicolored		.38	.38
O33 A162 80c multicolored		.60	.60
O34 A162 95c multicolored		.70	.70
O35 A162 $1 multicolored		.75	.75
O36 A162 $1.50 multicolored		1.10	1.10
O37 A162 $2.50 multicolored		1.75	1.75
O38 A162 $5 multicolored		3.75	3.75
O39 A162 $25 multicolored		18.50	18.50
Nos. O28-O39 (12)		28.16	28.16

Issued: 20c, 25c, 50c, $25, Feb. 21. 10c, 15c, 80c, $1.50, Apr. 12. 95c, $1, $2.50, $5, June 25.

STE.-MARIE DE MADAGASCAR

sānt–mə–rē–də–ˌmad–ə–'gas–kər

LOCATION — An island off the east coast of Madagascar
GOVT. — French Possession
AREA — 64 sq. mi.
POP. — 8,000 (approx.)

In 1896 Ste.-Marie de Madagascar was attached to the colony of Madagascar for administrative purposes.

100 Centimes = 1 Franc

Navigation and Commerce — A1

1894 Unwmk. Typo. *Perf. 14x13½*
Name of Colony in Blue or Carmine

1 A1 1c black, *lil bl* .75 .75
2 A1 2c brown, *buff* 1.00 1.00
3 A1 4c claret, *lavender* 2.75 2.50
4 A1 5c green, *grnsh* 6.00 5.00
5 A1 10c black, *lavender* 7.50 5.25
6 A1 15c blue 17.50 16.00
7 A1 20c red, *green* 15.00 11.00
8 A1 25c black, *rose* 12.50 9.00
9 A1 30c brown, *bister* 7.50 7.00
10 A1 40c red, *straw* 8.00 7.00
11 A1 50c carmine, *rose* 30.00 25.00
12 A1 75c violet, *org* 50.00 32.50
13 A1 1fr brnz grn, *straw* 30.00 20.00
Nos. 1-13 (13) 188.50 142.00

Perf. 13½x14 stamps are counterfeits.

These stamps were replaced by those of Madagascar.

ST. PIERRE & MIQUELON

sānt–'pi(ə)r and 'mik–ə–ˌlän

LOCATION — Two small groups of islands off the southern coast of Newfoundland
GOVT. — Formerly a French colony, now a Department of France
AREA — 93 sq. mi.
POP. — 6,051 (est. 1984)
CAPITAL — St. Pierre

The territory of St. Pierre and Miquelon became a Department of France in July 1976.

100 Centimes = 1 Franc

Catalogue values for unused stamps in this country are for Never Hinged items, beginning with Scott 300 in the regular postage section, Scott B13 in the semi-postal section, Scott C1 in the airpost section, and Scott J68 in the postage due section.

Stamps of French Colonies Handstamp Surcharged in Black

05
spm

1885 Unwmk. *Imperf.*

1 A8 05c on 40c ver, *straw* 75.00 32.50
2 A8 10c on 40c ver, *straw* 18.00 15.00
a. "M" inverted 160.00 125.00
3 A8 15c on 40c ver, *straw* 20.00 15.00
Nos. 1-3 (3) 113.00 62.50

Nos. 2 and 3 exist with "SPM" 17mm wide instead of 15½mm.
Nos. 1-3 exist with surcharge inverted and with it doubled.

Handstamp Surcharged in Black

05 SPM — b
25 SPM — c
25 SPM — d

1885

4 A8 (b) 05c on 35c blk, *yel* 90.00 65.00
5 A8 (b) 05c on 75c car, *rose* 225.00 150.00
6 A8 (b) 05c on 1fr brnz grn, *straw* 18.00 15.00
7 A8 (c) 25c on 1fr brnz grn, *straw* 7,500. 1,600.
8 A8 (d) 25c on 1fr brnz grn, *straw* 1,800. 1,200.

Nos. 7 and 8 exist with surcharge inverted, and with it vertical. No. 7 exists with "S P M" above "25" (the handstamping was done in two steps).

1885 *Perf. 14x13½*

9 A9 (c) 5c on 2c brn, *buff* 4,500. 1,750.
10 A9 (d) 5c on 4c cl, *lav* 325.00 200.00
11 A9 (b) 05c on 20c red, *grn* 16.00 18.00

No. 9 surcharge is always inverted. No. 10 exists with surcharge inverted.

P D
5 — A15

1886, Feb. Typo. *Imperf.*
Without Gum

12 A15 5c black 800.00
13 A15 10c black 850.00
14 A15 15c black 750.00

"P D" are the initials for "Payé a destination." Excellent forgeries exist.

Stamps of French Colonies Surcharged in Black

15 c. SPM — e
15 c. SPM — f

1891 *Perf. 14x13½*

15 A9 (e) 15c on 30c brn, *bis* 24.00 22.50
a. Inverted surcharge 150.00 110.00
16 A9 (e) 15c on 35c blk, *org* 450.00 350.00
a. Inverted surcharge 425.00 425.00
17 A9 (f) 15c on 35c blk, *org* 1,100. 700.00
a. Inverted surcharge 1,600. 1,100.
18 A9 (e) 15c on 40c red, *straw* 65.00 50.00
a. Inverted surcharge 140.00 140.00

Stamps of French Colonies Overprinted in Black or Red

ST - PIERRE M-on

1891, Oct. 15

19 A9 1c blk, *lil bl* 7.50 6.00
a. Inverted overprint 16.00 16.00
20 A9 1c blk, *lil bl* (R) 7.00 7.00
a. Inverted overprint 13.00 13.00
21 A9 2c brn, *buff* 7.50 6.00
a. Inverted overprint 18.00 18.00
22 A9 2c brn, *buff* (R) 17.50 17.50
a. Inverted overprint 45.00 45.00
23 A9 4c claret, *lav* 7.50 6.00
a. Inverted overprint 20.00 20.00
24 A9 4c claret, *lav* (R) 14.00 14.00
a. Inverted overprint 35.00 35.00
25 A9 5c grn, *grnsh* 7.50 6.00
a. Double surcharge 75.00
26 A9 10c blk, *lav* 25.00 19.00
a. Inverted overprint 50.00 50.00
27 A9 10c blk, *lav* (R) 12.00 12.00
a. Inverted overprint 35.00 35.00
28 A9 15c blk, *blue* 17.00 11.00
29 A9 20c red, *grn* 47.50 45.00
30 A9 25c blk, *rose* 19.00 15.00
31 A9 30c brn, *bis* 75.00 65.00
32 A9 35c vio, *org* 350.00 275.00
33 A9 40c red, *straw* 50.00 45.00
a. Double surcharge 150.00
34 A9 75c car, *rose* 75.00 60.00
a. Inverted overprint 125.00 125.00
35 A9 1fr brnz grn, *straw* 50.00 45.00
a. Inverted overprint 110.00 100.00
Nos. 19-35 (17) 789.00 654.50

Numerous varieties of mislettering occur in the preceding overprint: "S," "ST," "P," "M," "ON," or "-" missing; "-" instead of "ON"; "=" instead of "-". These varieties command values double or triple those of normal stamps.

Surcharged in Black

1891-92

36 A9 1c on 5c grn, *grnsh* 6.00 5.50
37 A9 1c on 10c blk, *lav* 7.00 6.00
38 A9 1c on 25c blk, *rose* ('92) 5.50 5.00
39 A9 2c on 10c blk, *lav* 5.50 5.00
a. Double surcharge 65.00
40 A9 2c on 15c bl 5.00 5.00
41 A9 2c on 25c blk, *rose* ('92) 5.00 5.00
42 A9 4c on 20c red, *grn* 5.00 5.00
43 A9 4c on 25c blk, *rose* ('92) 5.00 5.00
a. Double surcharge 65.00
44 A9 4c on 30c brn, *bis* 13.00 11.00
45 A9 4c on 40c red, *straw* 17.00 10.00
Nos. 36-45 (10) 74.00 62.50

See note after No. 35.

Surcharged

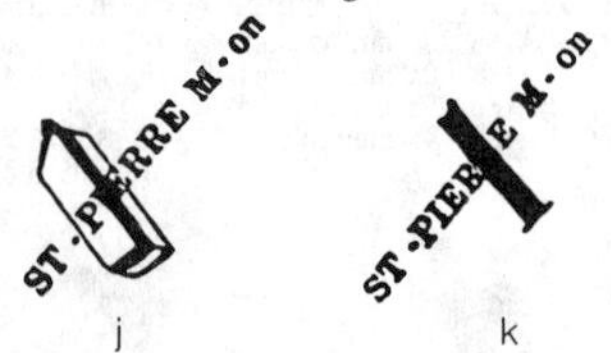

j k

1892, Nov. 4

46 A9 (j) 1c on 5c grn, *grnsh* 7.00 7.00
47 A9 (j) 2c on 5c grn, *grnsh* 7.00 7.00
48 A9 (j) 4c on 5c grn, *grnsh* 7.00 7.00
49 A9 (k) 1c on 25c blk, *rose* 4.50 4.50
50 A9 (k) 2c on 25c blk, *rose* 4.50 4.50
51 A9 (k) 4c on 25c blk, *rose* 4.50 4.50
Nos. 46-51 (6) 34.50 34.50

See note after No. 35.

Postage Due Stamps of French Colonies Overprinted in Red

T
ST - PIERRE M-on
P

1892, Dec. 1 *Imperf.*

52 D1 10c black 22.50 22.50
53 D1 20c black 16.00 16.00
54 D1 30c black 17.50 17.50
55 D1 40c black 17.50 17.50
56 D1 60c black 75.00 75.00

Black Overprint

57 D1 1fr brown 110.00 110.00
58 D1 2fr brown 175.00 175.00
59 D1 5fr brown 300.00 300.00
Nos. 52-59 (8) 733.50 733.50

See note after No. 35. "T P" stands for "Timbre Poste."

Navigation and Commerce — A16

1892-1908 Typo. *Perf. 14x13½*

60 A16 1c blk, *lil bl* .60 .60
61 A16 2c brown, *buff* .60 .60
62 A16 4c claret, *lav* 1.25 1.25
63 A16 5c green, *grnsh* 2.00 1.50
64 A16 5c yel grn ('08) 2.25 1.50
65 A16 10c black, *lav* 4.00 3.50
66 A16 10c red ('00) 3.25 1.00
67 A16 15c bl, quadrille paper 6.00 2.25
68 A16 15c gray, *lt gray* ('00) 60.00 32.50
69 A16 20c red, *grn* 16.00 12.00
70 A16 25c black, *rose* 6.00 1.25
71 A16 25c blue ('00) 10.00 6.00
72 A16 30c brown, *bis* 6.00 3.50
73 A16 35c blk, *yel* ('06) 4.50 4.00
74 A16 40c red, *straw* 5.00 3.50
75 A16 50c car, *rose* 30.00 25.00
76 A16 50c brown, *az* ('00) 20.00 18.00
77 A16 75c violet, *org* 17.00 15.00
78 A16 1fr brnz grn, *straw* 15.00 10.00
Nos. 60-78 (19) 209.45 142.95

Perf. 13½x14 stamps are counterfeits.
For surcharges and overprints see Nos. 110-120, Q1-Q2.

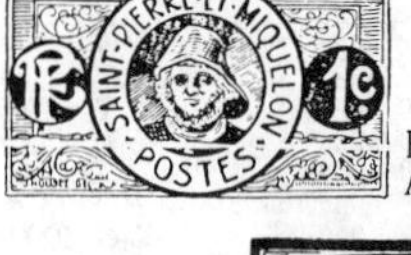

Fisherman A17

Fulmar Petrel — A18

Fishing Schooner A19

1909-30

79 A17 1c orange red & ol .15 .15
80 A17 2c olive & dp bl .15 .15
81 A17 4c violet & ol .15 .15
82 A17 5c bl grn & ol grn .30 .15
83 A17 5c blue & blk ('22) .20 .20
84 A17 10c car rose & red .30 .30
85 A17 10c bl grn & ol grn ('22) .20 .20
86 A17 10c bister & mag ('25) .30 .30
86A A17 15c dl vio & rose ('17) .30 .15
87 A17 20c bis brn & vio brn .70 .70
88 A18 25c dp blue & blue 1.65 1.10
89 A18 25c ol brn & bl grn ('22) .50 .50
90 A18 30c orange & vio brn .85 .70
91 A18 30c rose & dull red ('22) .60 .60
92 A18 30c red brn & bl ('25) .45 .45
93 A18 30c gray grn & bl grn ('26) .45 .45
94 A18 35c ol grn & vio brn .35 .30
95 A18 40c vio brn & ol grn 2.25 1.25
96 A18 45c violet & ol grn .40 .40
97 A18 50c olive & ol grn .95 .75
98 A18 50c bl & pale bl ('22) .85 .85
99 A18 50c yel brn & mag ('25) .45 .45
100 A18 60c dk bl & ver ('25) .55 .55
101 A18 65c vio & org brn ('28) 1.10 1.10
102 A18 75c brown & olive .95 .75
103 A18 90c brn red & org red ('30) 19.00 19.00
104 A19 1fr ol grn & dp bl 2.75 1.40
105 A19 1.10fr bl grn & org red ('28) 2.75 2.75
106 A19 1.50fr bl & dp bl ('30) 7.25 7.25
107 A19 2fr violet & brn 2.75 1.40
108 A19 3fr red violet ('30) 7.25 7.25
109 A19 5fr vio brn & ol grn 7.75 4.75
Nos. 79-109 (32) 64.60 56.45

For overprints and surcharges see Nos. 121-131, 206C-206D, B1-B2, Q3-Q5.

Stamps of 1892-1906 Surcharged in Carmine or Black

05 10

1912

110 A16 5c on 2c brn, *buff* 1.50 1.50
111 A16 5c on 4c claret, *lav* (C) .40 .40
112 A16 5c on 15c blue (C) .40 .40
113 A16 5c on 20c red, *grn* .40 .40
114 A16 5c on 25c blk, *rose* (C) .40 .40
115 A16 5c on 30c brn, *bis* (C) .50 .50
116 A16 5c on 35c blk, *yel* (C) 1.00 1.00
117 A16 10c on 40c red, *straw* .40 .40
118 A16 10c on 50c car, *rose* .50 .50
119 A16 10c on 75c dp vio, *org* 1.50 1.50
120 A16 10c on 1fr brnz grn, *straw* 2.00 2.00
Nos. 110-120 (11) 9.00 9.00

Two spacings between the surcharged numerals are found on Nos. 110 to 120.

Stamps and Types of 1909-17 Surcharged with New Value and Bars in Black, Blue (Bl) or Red

1924-27

No.	Type	Description	Unused	Used
121	A17	25c on 15c dl vio & rose ('25)	.30	.30
a.		Double surcharge	100.00	
b.		Triple surcharge	100.00	
122	A19	25c on 2fr vio & lt brn (Bl)	.30	.30
123	A19	25c on 5fr brn & ol grn (Bl)	.30	.30
a.		Triple surcharge	100.00	
124	A18	65c on 45c vio & ol grn ('25)	1.10	1.10
125	A18	85c on 75c brn & ol ('25)	1.10	1.10
126	A18	90c on 75c brn red & dp org ('27)	1.75	1.75
127	A19	1.25fr on 1fr dk bl & ultra (R) ('26)	1.65	1.65
128	A19	1.50fr on 1fr ultra & dk bl ('27)	2.00	2.00
129	A19	3fr on 5fr ol brn & red vio ('27)	1.90	1.90
130	A19	10fr on 5fr ver & ol grn ('27)	11.00	11.00
131	A19	20fr on 5fr vio & ver ('27)	16.00	16.00
		Nos. 121-131 (11)	37.40	37.40

Colonial Exposition Issue

Common Design Types

1931, Apr. 13 Engr. *Perf. 12½*

Name of Country in Black

No.	Type	Description	Unused	Used
132	CD70	40c deep green	2.25	2.25
133	CD71	50c violet	2.25	2.25
134	CD72	90c red orange	2.25	2.25
135	CD73	1.50fr dull blue	2.25	2.25
		Nos. 132-135 (4)	9.00	9.00

Map and Fishermen — A20

Lighthouse and Fish — A21

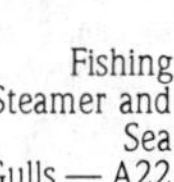

Fishing Steamer and Sea Gulls — A22

Perf. 13½x14, 14x13½

1932-33 Typo.

No.	Type	Description	Unused	Used
136	A20	1c red brn & ultra	.15	.15
137	A21	2c black & dk grn	.15	.15
138	A22	4c magenta & ol brn	.15	.15
139	A22	5c violet & dk brn	.20	.20
140	A21	10c red brn & blk	.35	.35
141	A21	15c dk blue & vio	.85	.85
142	A20	20c black & red org	.85	.85
143	A20	25c lt vio & lt grn	.85	.85
144	A22	30c ol grn & bl grn	.95	.95
145	A22	40c dp bl & dk brn	.95	.95
146	A21	45c ver & dp grn	.95	.95
147	A21	50c dk brn & dk grn	.95	.95
148	A22	65c ol brn & org	1.10	1.10
149	A20	75c grn & red org	1.10	1.10
150	A20	90c dull red & red	1.10	1.10
151	A22	1fr org brn & org red	.95	.95
152	A20	1.25fr dp bl & lake ('33)	1.25	1.25
153	A20	1.50fr dp blue & blue	1.10	1.10
154	A22	1.75fr blk & dk brn ('33)	1.40	1.40
155	A22	2fr bl blk & Prus bl	6.25	6.25
156	A21	3fr dp grn & dk brn	7.50	7.50
157	A21	5fr brn red & dk brn	18.00	18.00
158	A22	10fr dk grn & vio	47.50	47.50
159	A20	20fr ver & dp grn	47.50	47.50
		Nos. 136-159 (24)	142.10	142.10

For overprints and surcharges see Nos. 160-164, 207-221.

Nos. 147, 149, 153-154, 157 Overprinted in Black, Red or Blue

JACQUES CARTIER 1534 - 1934
p

JACQUES CARTIER 1534-1934
q

1934, Oct. 18

No.	Type	Description	Unused	Used
160	A21(p)	50c (Bk)	2.00	2.00
161	A20(q)	75c (Bk)	2.50	2.50
162	A20(p)	1.50fr (Bk)	3.00	3.00
163	A22(p)	1.75fr (R)	3.50	3.50
164	A21(p)	5fr (Bl)	19.00	19.00
		Nos. 160-164 (5)	30.00	30.00

400th anniv. of the landing of Jacques Cartier.

Paris International Exposition Issue

Common Design Types

1937 *Perf. 13*

No.	Type	Description	Unused	Used
165	CD74	20c deep violet	.95	.95
166	CD75	30c dark green	.95	.95
167	CD76	40c carmine rose	.95	.95
168	CD77	50c dk brown & blue	.95	.95
169	CD78	90c red	.95	.95
170	CD79	1.50fr ultra	.95	.95
		Nos. 165-170 (6)	5.70	5.70

Colonial Arts Exhibition Issue

Souvenir Sheet

Common Design Type

1937 *Imperf.*

No.	Type	Description	Unused	Used
171	CD78	3fr dark ultra	10.00	10.00

Dog Team — A23

Port St. Pierre — A24

Tortue Lighthouse A25

Soldiers' Bay at Langlade A26

1938-40 Photo. *Perf. 13½x13*

No.	Type	Description	Unused	Used
172	A23	2c dk blue green	.15	.15
173	A23	3c brown violet	.15	.15
174	A23	4c dk red violet	.15	.15
175	A23	5c carmine lake	.15	.15
176	A23	10c bister brown	.20	.20
177	A23	15c red violet	.25	.25
178	A23	20c blue violet	.25	.25
179	A23	25c Prus blue	1.40	1.40
180	A24	30c dk red violet	.25	.25
181	A24	35c deep green	.45	.45
182	A24	40c slate blue ('40)	.15	.15
183	A24	45c deep green ('40)	.30	.30
a.		Value omitted	55.00	
184	A24	50c carmine rose	.25	.25
185	A24	55c Prus blue	1.90	1.90
186	A24	60c violet ('39)	.35	.35
187	A24	65c brown	3.75	3.75
188	A24	70c orange yel ('39)	.45	.45
189	A25	80c violet	.75	.75
190	A25	90c ultra ('39)	.35	.35
191	A25	1fr brt pink	7.50	7.50
192	A25	1fr pale ol grn ('40)	.35	.35
193	A25	1.25fr brt rose ('39)	1.10	1.10
194	A25	1.40fr dk brown ('40)	.55	.55
195	A25	1.50fr blue green	.55	.55
196	A25	1.60fr rose violet ('40)	.55	.55
197	A25	1.75fr deep blue	1.40	1.40
198	A26	2fr rose violet	.45	.45
199	A26	2.25fr brt blue ('39)	.65	.65
200	A26	2.50fr orange yel ('40)	.80	.80
201	A26	3fr gray brown	.45	.45
202	A26	5fr henna brown	.65	.65
203	A26	10fr dk bl, *bluish*	.90	.90
204	A26	20fr slate green	1.10	1.10
		Nos. 172-204 (33)	28.65	28.65

For overprints and surcharges see Nos. 222-255, 260-299, B9-B10.

New York World's Fair Issue

Common Design Type

1939, May 10 Engr. *Perf. 12½x12*

No.	Type	Description	Unused	Used
205	CD82	1.25fr carmine lake	.75	.75
206	CD82	2.25fr ultra	.75	.75

For overprints and surcharges see Nos. 256-259.

Lighthouse on Cliff — A27

1941 Engr. *Perf. 12½x12*

No.	Type	Description	Unused	Used
206A	A27	1fr dull lilac	.55	
206B	A27	2.50fr blue	.55	

Nos. 206A-206B were issued by the Vichy government and were not placed on sale in the colony.

Stamps of types A23 and A26 without "RF" monogram were issued in 1941-1944 by the Vichy government, but were not sold in the colony.

> Free French Administration
>
> The circumstances surrounding the overprinting and distribution of these stamps were most unusual. Practically all of the stamps issued in small quantities, with the exception of Nos. 260-299, were obtained by speculators within a few days after issue. At a later date, the remainders were taken over by the Free French Agency in Ottawa, Canada, by whom they were sold at a premium for the benefit of the Syndicat des Oeuvres Sociales. Large quantities appeared on the market in 1991, including many "errors." More may exist.
>
> Excellent counterfeits of these surcharges and overprints are known.

Nos. 86 and 92 Overprinted in Black

FRANCE LIBRE
a
F. N. F. L.

1942 Unwmk. *Perf. 14x13½*

No.	Type	Description	Unused	Used
206C	A17	10c	1,000.	1,000.
206D	A18	30c	1,000.	1,000.

The letters "F. N. F. L." are the initials of "Forces Navales Francaises Libres" or "Free French Naval Forces."

Same Overprint in Black on Nos. 137-139, 145-148, 151, 154-155, 157

No.	Type	Description	Unused	Used
207	A21	2c	175.00	175.00
208	A22	4c	37.50	37.50
208A	A22	5c	600.00	600.00
209	A22	40c	10.00	10.00
210	A21	45c	125.00	125.00
211	A21	50c	8.00	8.00
212	A22	65c	24.00	24.00
213	A22	1fr	275.00	275.00
214	A22	1.75fr	6.00	6.00
215	A22	2fr	8.00	8.00
216	A22	5fr	250.00	250.00

Nos. 142, 149, 152-153 Overprinted in Black

FRANCE
LIBRE
F N F L

Perf. 13½x14

No.	Type	Description	Unused	Used
216A	A20	20c	275.00	275.00
217	A20	75c	12.00	12.00
218	A20	1.25fr	10.50	10.50
218A	A20	1.50fr	325.00	325.00

On Nos. 152, 149 Surcharged with New Value and Bars

No.	Type	Description	Unused	Used
219	A20	10fr on 1.25fr	20.00	20.00
220	A20	20fr on 75c	35.00	35.00

No. 154 Surcharged in Red

5 fr
FRANCE LIBRE
F. N. F. L.

Perf. 14x13½

No.	Type	Description	Unused	Used
221	A22	5fr on 1.75fr	7.50	7.50

Stamps of 1938-40 Overprinted type "a" in Black

Perf. 13½x13

No.	Type	Description	Unused	Used
222	A23	2c dk blue grn	275.00	275.00
223	A23	3c brown violet	75.00	75.00
224	A23	4c dk red violet	62.50	62.50
225	A23	5c carmine lake	600.00	600.00
226	A23	10c bister brown	6.25	6.25
227	A23	15c red violet	1,000.	1,000.
228	A23	20c blue violet	125.00	125.00
229	A23	25c Prus blue	6.00	6.00
230	A24	35c deep green	575.00	575.00
231	A24	40c slate blue	8.00	8.00
232	A24	45c deep green	8.00	8.00
233	A24	55c Prus blue	*6,000.*	*6,000.*
234	A24	60c violet	425.00	425.00
235	A24	65c brown	10.50	10.50
236	A24	70c orange yellow	20.00	20.00
237	A25	80c violet	250.00	250.00
238	A25	90c ultra	8.00	8.00
239	A25	1fr pale ol grn	10.50	10.50
240	A25	1.25fr brt rose	8.00	8.00
241	A25	1.40fr dark brown	6.25	6.25
242	A25	1.50fr blue green	575.00	575.00
243	A25	1.60fr rose violet	7.00	7.00
244	A26	2fr rose violet	40.00	40.00
245	A26	2.25fr brt blue	8.00	8.00
246	A26	2.50fr orange yel	10.50	10.50
247	A26	3fr gray brown	*7,000.*	*7,000.*
248	A26	5fr henna brown	*1,500.*	*1,500.*
248A	A26	20fr slate green	750.00	750.00

Nos. 176, 190 Surcharged in Black

FRANCE LIBRE
F. N. F. L.
20 c

No.	Type	Description	Unused	Used
249	A23	20c on 10c	5.25	5.25
250	A23	30c on 10c	4.00	4.00
251	A25	60c on 90c	4.25	4.25
252	A25	1.50fr on 90c	6.00	6.00
253	A23	2.50fr on 10c	8.25	8.25
254	A23	10fr on 10c	27.50	27.50
255	A25	20fr on 90c	35.00	35.00
		Nos. 249-255 (7)	90.25	90.25

New York World's Fair Issue Overprinted type "a" in Black

Perf. 12½x12

No.	Type	Description	Unused	Used
256	CD82	1.25fr carmine lake	6.50	6.50
257	CD82	2.25fr ultra	6.50	6.50

Nos. 205-206 Surcharged

2 fr 50
FRANCE LIBRE
F. N. F. L.

No.	Type	Description	Unused	Used
258	CD82	2.50fr on 1.25fr	8.25	8.25
259	CD82	3fr on 2.25fr	8.25	8.25

Stamps of 1938-40 Overprinted in Carmine

Noël 1941
FRANCE LIBRE
F. N. F. L.

1941 *Perf. 13½x13*

No.	Type	Description	Unused	Used
260	A23	10c bister brn	20.00	20.00
261	A23	20c blue violet	20.00	20.00
262	A23	25c Prus blue	20.00	20.00
263	A24	40c slate blue	20.00	20.00
264	A24	45c deep green	20.00	20.00
265	A24	65c brown	20.00	20.00
266	A24	70c orange yel	20.00	20.00
267	A25	80c violet	20.00	20.00
268	A25	90c ultra	20.00	20.00
269	A25	1fr pale ol grn	20.00	20.00
270	A25	1.25fr brt rose	20.00	20.00
271	A25	1.40fr dk brown	20.00	20.00
272	A25	1.60fr rose violet	22.50	22.50
273	A25	1.75fr brt blue	22.50	22.50
274	A26	2fr rose violet	22.50	22.50
275	A26	2.25fr brt blue	22.50	22.50
276	A26	2.50fr orange yel	22.50	22.50
277	A26	3fr gray brown	22.50	22.50

Same Surcharged in Carmine with New Values

278	A23	10fr on 10c bister brn	37.50	37.50
279	A25	20fr on 90c ultra	37.50	37.50
		Nos. 260-279 (20)	450.00	450.00

Stamps of 1938-40 Overprinted in Black

280	A23	10c	bister brn	26.00	26.00
281	A23	20c	blue violet	26.00	26.00
282	A23	25c	Prus blue	26.00	26.00
283	A24	40c	slate blue	26.00	26.00
284	A24	45c	deep green	26.00	26.00
285	A24	65c	brown	26.00	26.00
286	A24	70c	orange yel	26.00	26.00
287	A25	80c	violet	26.00	26.00
288	A25	90c	ultra	26.00	26.00
289	A25	1fr	pale ol grn	26.00	26.00
290	A25	1.25fr	brt rose	26.00	26.00
291	A25	1.40fr	dk brown	26.00	26.00
292	A25	1.60fr	rose violet	26.00	26.00
293	A25	1.75fr	brt blue	475.00	475.00
294	A26	2fr	rose vio	26.00	26.00
295	A26	2.25fr	brt blue	26.00	26.00
296	A26	2.50fr	orange yel	26.00	26.00
297	A26	3fr	gray brown	26.00	26.00

Same Surcharged in Black with New Values

298	A23	10fr on 10c bister brn	75.00	75.00
299	A25	20fr on 90c ultra	75.00	75.00
		Nos. 280-299 (20)	1,067.	1,067.

Christmas Day plebiscite ordered by Vice Admiral Emile Henri Muselier, commander of the Free French naval forces (Nos. 260-299).

Catalogue values for unused stamps in this section, from this point to the end of the section, are for Never Hinged items.

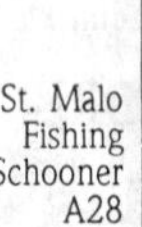

St. Malo Fishing Schooner A28

1942 Photo. *Perf. 14x14½*

300	A28	5c	dark blue	.20	.15
301	A28	10c	dull pink	.20	.15
302	A28	25c	brt green	.20	.15
303	A28	30c	slate black	.20	.15
304	A28	40c	brt grnsh blue	.20	.15
305	A28	60c	brown red	.30	.15
306	A28	1fr	dark violet	.40	.25
307	A28	1.50fr	brt red	.85	.70
308	A28	2fr	brown	.40	.35
309	A28	2.50fr	brt ultra	.85	.70
310	A28	4fr	dk orange	.45	.35
311	A28	5fr	dp plum	.45	.35
312	A28	10fr	lt ultra	.85	.70
313	A28	20fr	dark green	1.10	1.00
			Nos. 300-313 (14)	6.65	5.30

Nos. 300, 302, 309 Surcharged in Carmine or Black

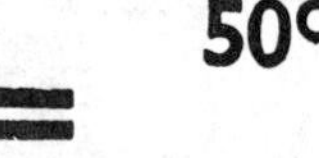

1945

314	A28	50c on 5c (C)	.15	.15
315	A28	70c on 5c (C)	.20	.20
316	A28	80c on 5c (C)	.35	.30
317	A28	1.20fr on 5c (C)	.35	.30
318	A28	2.40fr on 25c	.35	.30
319	A28	3fr on 25c	.50	.45
320	A28	4.50fr on 25c	1.00	.80
321	A28	15fr on 2.50fr (C)	1.25	1.00
		Nos. 314-321 (8)	4.15	3.50

Eboue Issue
Common Design Type

1945 Engr. *Perf. 13*

322	CD91	2fr black	.65	.35
323	CD91	25fr Prussian green	1.65	.75

Nos. 322 and 323 exist imperforate.

Soldiers' Bay — A29

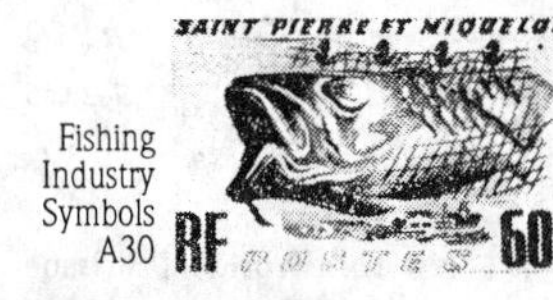

Fishing Industry Symbols A30

Fishermen A31

Weighing the Catch — A32

Fishing Boat and Dinghy A33

Storm-swept Coast — A34

1947, Oct. 6 Engr. *Perf. 12½*

324	A29	10c	chocolate	.20	.15
325	A29	30c	violet	.20	.15
326	A29	40c	rose lilac	.20	.15
327	A29	50c	intense blue	.20	.15
328	A30	60c	carmine	.20	.15
329	A30	80c	brt ultra	.60	.30
330	A30	1fr	dk green	.60	.30
331	A31	1.20fr	blue grn	.60	.30
332	A31	1.50fr	black	.60	.40
333	A31	2fr	red brown	.60	.40
334	A32	3fr	rose violet	1.75	1.25
335	A32	3.60fr	dp brown org	1.25	.80
336	A32	4fr	sepia	1.50	.80
337	A33	5fr	orange	1.50	1.25
338	A33	6fr	blue	1.50	1.25
339	A33	10fr	Prus green	2.00	1.65
340	A34	15fr	dk slate grn	3.50	2.50
341	A34	20fr	vermilion	4.50	2.75
342	A34	25fr	dark blue	5.50	3.25
			Nos. 324-342 (19)	27.00	17.95

Imperforates
Most stamps of St. Pierre and Miquelon from 1947 onward exist imperforate in issued and trial colors, and also in small presentation sheets in issued colors.

Silver Fox — A35

1952, Sept. 10 Unwmk. *Perf. 13*

343	A35	8fr dk brown	3.50	.80
344	A35	17fr blue	4.50	1.25

Military Medal Issue
Common Design Type

1952, Dec. 1 Engr. & Typo.

345	CD101	8fr multicolored	7.50 2.25

Fish Freezing Plant — A36

1955-56 Engr.

346	A36	30c ultra & dk blue	.50	.15
347	A36	50c gray, blk & sepia	.50	.15
348	A36	3fr purple	1.00	.25
349	A36	40fr Prussian blue	2.50	1.25
		Nos. 346-349 (4)	4.50	1.80

Issued: 40fr, July 4; others, Oct. 22, 1956.

FIDES Issue

Fish Freezer "Le Galantry" A37

Perf. 13x12½

1956, Mar. 15 Unwmk.

350	A37	15fr blk brn & chestnut	4.00	.60

See note in Common Design section after CD103.

Codfish A38

Design: 4fr, 10fr, Lighthouse and fishing fleet.

1957, Nov. 4 *Perf. 13*

351	A38	40c dk brn & grnsh bl	.30	.15
352	A38	1fr brown & green	.35	.15
353	A38	2fr indigo & dull blue	.55	.15
354	A38	4fr maroon, car & pur	1.40	.20
355	A38	10fr grnsh bl, dk bl & brn	1.65	.40
		Nos. 351-355 (5)	4.25	1.05

Human Rights Issue
Common Design Type

1958, Dec. 10 Engr. *Perf. 13*

356	CD105	20fr red brn & dk blue	2.50	.70

Flower Issue
Common Design Type

1959 Photo. *Perf. 12½x12*

357	CD104	5fr Spruce	2.50	.45

Ice Hockey A39

Mink — A40

1959, Sept. 14 Engr. *Perf. 13*

358	A39	20fr multicolored	2.50	.50
359	A40	25fr indigo, yel grn & brn	3.50	.70

Cypripedium Acaule — A41

Eider Ducks — A42

Flower: 50fr, Calopogon pulchellus.

1962, Apr. 24 Unwmk. *Perf. 13*

360	A41	25fr grn, org & car rose	4.00	.50
361	A41	50fr green & car lake	5.00	.90
		Nos. 360-361,C24 (3)	*17.00*	2.90

1963, Mar. 4 *Perf. 13*

Birds: 1fr, Rock ptarmigan. 2fr, Ringed plovers. 6fr, Blue-winged teal.

362	A42	50c blk, ultra & ocher	.42	.15
363	A42	1fr red brn, ultra & rose	.75	.15
364	A42	2fr blk, dk bl & bis	1.25	.25
365	A42	6fr multicolored	3.00	.60
		Nos. 362-365 (4)	5.42	1.15

Albert Calmette A43

1963, Aug. 5 Engr.

366	A43	30fr dk brn & dk blue	8.00	.90

Albert Calmette, bacteriologist, birth cent.

Red Cross Centenary Issue
Common Design Type

1963, Sept. 2 Unwmk. *Perf. 13*

367	CD113	25fr ultra, gray & car	8.00	.65

Human Rights Issue
Common Design Type

1963, Dec. 10 Unwmk. *Perf. 13*

368	CD117	20fr org, bl & dk brn	4.50	.65

Philatec Issue
Common Design Type

1964, Apr. 4 Engr.

369	CD118	60fr choc, grn & dk bl	7.00	2.25

Rabbits — A44

1964, Sept. 28 *Perf. 13*

370	A44	3fr shown	1.50	.20
371	A44	4fr Fox	1.50	.20
372	A44	5fr Roe deer	3.00	.40
373	A44	34fr Charolais bull	9.00	1.25
		Nos. 370-373 (4)	15.00	2.05

Airport and Map of St. Pierre and Miquelon A45

Designs: 40fr, Television tube and tower, and map. 48fr, Map of new harbor of St. Pierre.

1967 Engr. *Perf. 13*

374	A45	30fr ind, bl & dk red	6.00	.55
375	A45	40fr sl grn, ol & dk red	6.00	.60
376	A45	48fr dk red, brn & sl bl	8.00	.80
		Nos. 374-376 (3)	20.00	1.95

Issued: 30fr, 10/23; 40fr, 11/20; 48fr, 9/25.

WHO Anniversary Issue
Common Design Type

1968, May 4 Engr. *Perf. 13*

377	CD126	10fr multicolored	6.00	.55

René de Chateaubriand and Map of Islands — A46

Designs: 4fr, J. D. Cassini and map. 15fr, Prince de Joinville, Francois F. d'Orleans (1818-1900), ships and map. 25fr, Admiral Gauchet, World War I warship and map.

1968, May 20 Photo. *Perf. 12½x13*

378	A46	4fr multicolored	3.50	.55
379	A46	6fr multicolored	4.00	.60
380	A46	15fr multicolored	7.00	.80
381	A46	25fr multicolored	8.00	1.25
		Nos. 378-381 (4)	22.50	3.20

Human Rights Year Issue
Common Design Type

1968, Aug. 10 Engr. *Perf. 13*

382	CD127	20fr bl, ver & org yel	7.00	.45

Belle Rivière, Langlade A47

Design: 15fr, Debon Brook, Langlade.

1969, Apr. 30 Engr. *Perf. 13*
Size: 36x22mm

383 A47 5fr bl, slate grn & brn 3.00 .30
384 A47 15fr brn, bl & dl grn 4.00 .45
Nos. 383-384,C41-C42 (4) *35.50* 7.25

Treasury A48

Designs: 25fr, Scientific and Technical Institute of Maritime Fishing. 30fr, Monument to seamen lost at sea. 60fr, St. Christopher College.

1969, May 30 Engr. *Perf. 13*

385 A48 10fr brt bl, cl & blk 2.75 .25
386 A48 25fr dk bl, brt bl & brn red 6.25 .45
387 A48 30fr blue, grn & gray 6.50 .60
388 A48 60fr brt bl, brn red & blk 10.50 1.00
Nos. 385-388 (4) 26.00 2.30

Ringed Seals — A49

Designs: 3fr, Sperm whales. 4fr, Pilot whales. 6fr, Common dolphins.

1969, Oct. 6 Engr. *Perf. 13*

389 A49 1fr lil, vio brn & red brn 2.50 .40
390 A49 3fr bl grn, ind & red 2.50 .40
391 A49 4fr ol, gray grn & mar 4.25 .55
392 A49 6fr brt grn, pur & red 6.00 .60
Nos. 389-392 (4) 15.25 1.95

L'Estoile and Granville, France — A50

40fr, "La Jolie" & St. Jean de Luz, France, 1750. 48fr, "Le Juste" & La Rochelle, France, 1860.

1969, Oct. 13 Engr. *Perf. 13*

393 A50 34fr grn, mar & slate grn *11.00* .95
394 A50 40fr brn red, lem & sl grn *19.00* 1.50
395 A50 48fr multicolored *25.00* 1.60
Nos. 393-395 (3) *55.00* 4.05

Historic ships connecting St. Pierre and Miquelon with France.

ILO Issue
Common Design Type

1969, Nov. 24

396 CD131 20fr org, gray & ocher 7.00 .55

UPU Headquarters Issue
Common Design Type

1970, May 20 Engr. *Perf. 13*

397 CD133 25fr dk car, brt bl & brn 8.25 .55
398 CD133 34fr maroon, brn & gray 14.00 .70

Rowers and Globe — A51

1970, Oct. 13 Photo. *Perf. 12½x12*

399 A51 20fr lt grnsh bl & brn 13.00 .45

World Rowing Championships, St. Catherine.

Blackberries — A52

1970, Oct. 20 Engr. *Perf. 13*

400 A52 3fr shown 1.10 .15
401 A52 4fr Strawberries 1.25 .25
402 A52 5fr Raspberries 1.90 .30
403 A52 6fr Blueberries 2.75 .40
Nos. 400-403 (4) 7.00 1.10

Ewe and Lamb — A53

30fr, Animal quarantine station. 34fr, Charolais bull. 48fr, Refrigeration ship slaughterhouse.

1970 Engr. *Perf. 13*

404 A53 15fr plum, grn & olive *6.00* .45
405 A53 30fr sl, bis brn & ap grn *9.50* .45
406 A53 34fr red lil, org brn & emer *15.00* 1.25
407 A53 48fr multicolored *12.00* .80
Nos. 404-407 (4) *42.50* 2.95

Issue dates: 48fr, Nov. 10; others, Dec. 8.

Saint François d'Assise 1900 — A54

Ships: 35fr, Sainte Jehanne, 1920. 40fr, L'Aventure, 1950. 80fr, Commandant Bourdais, 1970.

1971, Aug. 25

408 A54 30fr Prus bl & hn brn *21.00* 3.00
409 A54 35fr Prus bl, lt grn & ol brn *27.50* 3.50
410 A54 40fr sl grn, bl & dk brn *37.50* 5.00
411 A54 80fr dp grn, bl & blk *47.50* 7.00
Nos. 408-411 (4) *133.50* 18.50

Deep-sea fishing fleet.

"Aconit" and Map of Islands — A55

1971, Sept. 27 Engr. *Perf. 13*

412 A55 22fr shown *20.00* .80
413 A55 25fr Alysse *25.00* 1.40
414 A55 50fr Mimosa *30.00* 1.60
Nos. 412-414 (3) *75.00* 3.80

Rallying of the Free French forces, 30th anniv.

Ship's Bell — A56

St. Pierre Museum: 45fr, Old chart and sextants, horiz.

1971, Oct. 25 Photo. *Perf. 12½x13*

415 A56 20fr gray & multi *10.00* .55
416 A56 45fr red brn & multi *20.00* .70

De Gaulle Issue
Common Design Type

Designs: 35fr, Gen. de Gaulle, 1940. Pres. de Gaulle, 1970.

1971, Nov. 9 Engr. *Perf. 13*

417 CD134 35fr vermilion & blk *15.00* 1.50
418 CD134 45fr vermilion & blk *22.50* 2.00

Haddock A57

Fish: 3fr, Hippoglossoides platessoides. 5fr, Sebastes mentella. 10fr, Codfish.

1972, Mar. 7

419 A57 2fr vio bl, ind & pink 3.25 .40
420 A57 3fr grn & gray olive 6.25 .50
421 A57 5fr Prus bl & brick red 4.50 .60
422 A57 10fr grn & slate grn 11.00 .85
Nos. 419-422 (4) 25.00 2.35

Oldsquaws — A58

Birds: 10c, 70c, Puffins. 20c, 90c, Snow owl. 40c, like 6c. Identification of birds on oldsquaw and puffin stamps transposed.

1973, Jan. 1 Engr. *Perf. 13*

423 A58 6c Prus bl, pur & brn 1.00 .15
424 A58 10c Prus bl, blk & org 1.50 .20
425 A58 20c ultra, bis & dk vio 2.00 .20
426 A58 40c pur, sl grn & brn 3.00 .40
427 A58 70c brt grn, blk & org 5.00 .55
428 A58 90c Prus bl, bis & pur 6.25 .90
Nos. 423-428 (6) 18.75 2.40

Indoor Swimming Pool — A59

Design: 1fr, Cultural Center of St. Pierre.

1973, Sept. 25 Engr. *Perf. 13*

429 A59 60c brn, brt bl & dk car 3.75 .35
430 A59 1fr bl grn, ocher & choc 5.75 .60

Opening of Cultural Center of St. Pierre.

Map of Islands, Weather Balloon and Ship, WMO Emblem A60

1974, Mar. 23 Engr. *Perf. 13*

431 A60 1.60fr multicolored 8.50 1.25

World Meteorological Day.

Gannet Holding Letter — A61

1974, Oct. 9 Engr. *Perf. 13*

432 A61 70c blue & multi 4.00 .50
433 A61 90c red & multi 5.00 .60

Centenary of Universal Postal Union.

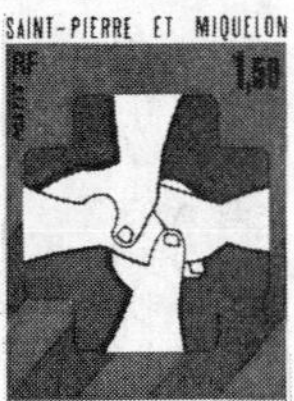

Clasped Hands over Red Cross — A62

Hands Putting Money into Fish-shaped Bank — A63

1974, Oct. 15 Photo. *Perf. 12½x13*

434 A62 1.50fr multicolored 8.50 .70

Honoring blood donors.

1974, Nov. 15 Engr. *Perf. 13*

435 A63 50c ocher & vio bl 5.00 .35

St. Pierre Savings Bank centenary.

Church of St. Pierre and Seagulls A64

Designs: 10c, Church of Miquelon and fish. 20c, Church of Our Lady of the Sailors, and fishermen.

1974, Dec. 9 Engr. *Perf. 13*

436 A64 6c multicolored 1.65 .20
437 A64 10c multicolored 2.75 .20
438 A64 20c multicolored 3.25 .35
Nos. 436-438 (3) 7.65 .75

Danaus Plexippus A65

Design: 1fr, Vanessa atalanta, vert.

1975, July 17 Litho. *Perf. 12½*

439 A65 1fr blue & multi *9.50* .60
440 A65 1.20fr green & multi *13.00* .70

Pottery — A66

Mother and Child, Wood Carving — A67

1975, Oct. 2 Engr. *Perf. 13*

441 A66 50c ol, brn & choc 3.50 .45
442 A67 60c blue & dull yel 4.50 .45

Local handicrafts.

Pointe Plate Lighthouse and Murres — A68

10c, Galantry lighthouse and Atlantic puffins. 20c, Cap Blanc lighthouse, whale and squid.

1975, Oct. 21

443 A68 6c vio bl, blk & lt grn *1.40* .15
444 A68 10c lil rose, blk & dk ol *2.50* .20
445 A68 20c blue, indigo & brn *3.50* .40
Nos. 443-445 (3) *7.40* .75

Georges Pompidou (1911-74), Pres. of France — A68a

1976, Feb. 17 Engr. *Perf. 13*
446 A68a 1.10fr brown & slate 5.50 .60

Georges Pompidou (1911-1974), President of France.

Washington and Lafayette, American Flag — A69

1976, July 12 Photo. *Perf. 13*
447 A69 1fr multicolored 5.00 .60

American Bicentennial.

Woman Swimmer and Maple Leaf — A70

Design: 70c, Basketball and maple leaf, vert.

1976, Aug. 10 Engr. *Perf. 13*
448 A70 70c multicolored *4.00* .40
449 A70 2.50fr multicolored *8.00* 1.20

21st Olympic Games, Montreal, Canada, July 17-Aug. 1.

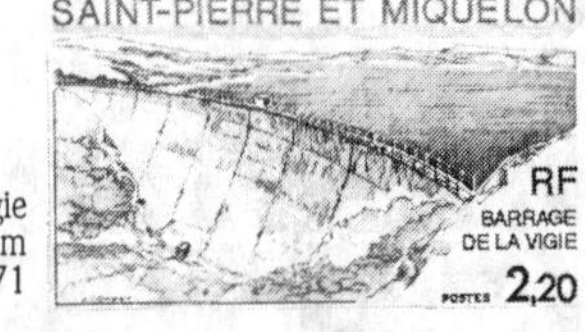

Vigie Dam A71

1976, Sept. 7 Engr. *Perf. 13*
450 A71 2.20fr multicolored 6.50 1.25

Croix de Lorraine — A72

Fishing Vessels: 1.40fr, Goelette.

1976, Oct. 5 Photo. *Perf. 13*
451 A72 1.20fr multicolored 6.50 .70
452 A72 1.40fr multicolored 8.00 1.00

France Nos. 1783-1784, 1786-1789, 1794, 1882, 1799, 1885, 1802, 1889, 1803-1804 and 1891 Ovptd. "SAINT PIERRE / ET / MIQUELON"

1986, Feb. 4 Engr. *Perf. 13*
453 A915 5c dark green .15 .15
454 A915 10c dull red .15 .15
455 A915 20c brt green .15 .15
456 A915 30c orange .15 .15
457 A915 40c brown .15 .15
458 A915 50c lilac .15 .15
459 A915 1fr olive green .25 .25
460 A915 1.80fr emerald .50 .50
461 A915 2fr brt yellow grn .50 .50
462 A915 2.20fr red .55 .55
463 A915 3fr chocolate brn .80 .80
464 A915 3.20fr sapphire .85 .85
465 A915 4fr brt carmine 1.00 1.00
466 A915 5fr gray blue 1.40 1.40
467 A915 10fr purple 2.75 2.75
Nos. 453-467 (15) 9.50 9.50

Discovery of St. Pierre & Miquelon by Jacques Cartier, 450th Anniv. — A73

1986, June 11 Engr. *Perf. 13*
476 A73 2.20fr sep, sage grn & redsh brn 1.10 .65

Statue of Liberty, Cent. — A74

1986, July 4
477 A74 2.50fr Statue, St. Pierre Harbor 1.25 .70

Fishery Resources — A75

Holy Family, Stained Glass by J. Balmet — A76

1986-89 Engr. *Perf. 13*
478 A75 1fr bright red .50 .30
479 A75 1.10fr brt orange .40 .35
480 A75 1.30fr dark red .40 .40
481 A75 1.40fr violet .70 .45
482 A75 1.40fr dark red .50 .45
483 A75 1.50fr brt ultra .60 .50
484 A75 1.60fr emerald grn .60 .50
485 A75 1.70fr green .60 .55
Nos. 478-485 (8) 4.30 3.50

Issued: 1fr, #481, 10/22; 1.10fr, 1.50fr, 10/14/87; 1.30fr, 1.60fr, 8/7/88; #482, 1.70fr, 7/14/89.

1986, Dec. 10 Litho. *Perf. 13*
486 A76 2.20fr multicolored 1.00 .70

Christmas.

Hygrophorus Pratensis A77

1987-90 Engr. *Perf. 12½*
487 A77 2.50fr shown .75 .75
488 A77 2.50fr Russula paludosa britz .85 .85
489 A77 2.50fr Tricholoma virgatum .80 .80
490 A77 2.50fr Hydnum repandum .85 .85
Nos. 487-490 (4) 3.25 3.25

Issued: #487, Feb. 14; #488, Jan. 29, 1988; #489, Jan. 28, 1989; #490, Jan. 17, 1990.

Dr. François Dunan (1884-1961), Clinic — A78

1987, Apr. 29 Engr. *Perf. 13*
491 A78 2.20fr brt bl, blk & dk red brn 1.00 .70

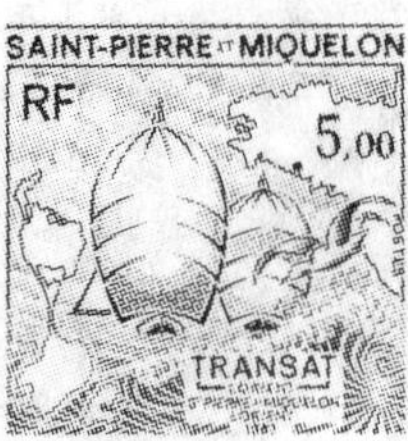

Transat Yacht Race, Lorient to St. Pierre to Lorient A79

1987, May 16
492 A79 5fr dp ultra, dk rose brn & brt bl 2.25 2.00

Visit of Pres. Mitterand A80

1987, May 29 Litho. *Perf. 12½x13*
493 A80 2.20fr dull ultra, gold & scar 1.25 .70

Marine Slip, Cent. — A81

1987, June 20 Litho. *Perf. 13*
494 A81 2.50fr pale sal & dk red brn 1.10 .65

Stern Trawler La Normande — A82

1987-91 Photo.
495 A82 3fr shown 1.40 1.25
496 A82 3fr Le Marmouset 1.00 .95
497 A82 3fr Tugboat Le Malabar 1.00 .95
498 A82 3fr St. Denis, St. Pierre 1.40 1.25
499 A82 3fr Cryos 1.25 1.10
Nos. 495-499 (5) 6.05 5.50

Issued: #495, 10/14; #496, 9/28/88; #497, 11/2/89; #498, 10/24/90; #499, 11/6/91.

This is an expanding set. Numbers will change when complete.

St. Christopher and the Christ Child, Stained Glass Window and Scout Emblem — A83

1987, Dec. 9 Litho. *Perf. 13*
503 A83 2.20fr multicolored 1.10 .80

Christmas, Scout movement in St. Pierre & Miquelon, 50th anniv.

The Great Barachoise Nature Reserve — A84

1987, Dec. 16 Engr. *Perf. 13x12½*
504 A84 3fr Horses, waterfowl 1.50 1.50
505 A84 3fr Waterfowl, seals 1.50 1.50
a. Pair, #504-505 + label 3.25 3.25

No. 505a is in continous design.

1988, Nov. 2
506 A84 2.20fr Ross Cove .75 .75
507 A84 13.70fr Caope Perce 4.75 4.75
a. Pair, #506-507 + label 5.75 5.75

No. 507a is in continous design.

1988 Winter Olympics, Calgary A86

1988, Mar. 5 Engr. *Perf. 13*
508 A86 5fr brt ultra & dark red 1.90 1.90

Louis Thomas (1887-1976), Photographer A87

1988, May 4 Engr. *Perf. 13*
509 A87 2.20fr blk, dk ol bis & Prus bl .75 .70

France No. 2105 Overprinted "ST-PIERRE ET MIQUELON"

1988, July 25 Engr. *Perf. 13*
510 A1107 2.20fr ver, blk & violet blue .85 .70

Seizure of Schooner Nellie J. Banks, 50th Anniv. A88

1988, Aug. 7
511 A88 2.50fr brn, vio blue & brt blue 1.10 .75

The Nellie J. Banks was seized by Canada for carrying prohibited alcohol in 1938.

Christmas — A89

1988, Dec. 17 Litho. *Perf. 13*
512 A89 2.20fr multicolored 1.00 .70

Judo Competitions in St. Pierre & Miquelon, 25th Anniv. A90

1989, Mar. 4 **Engr.** ***Perf. 13***
513 A90 5fr brn org, blk & yel grn 1.75 1.65

French Revolution Bicent.; 40th Anniv. of the UN Declaration of Human Rights (in 1988) — A91

1989 **Engr.** ***Perf. 12½x13***
514 A91 2.20fr Liberty .75 .75
515 A91 2.20fr Equality .75 .75
516 A91 2.20fr Fraternity .75 .75
Nos. 514-516 (3) 2.25 2.25

Issued: #514, 3/22; #515, 5/3; #516, 6/17.

Souvenir Sheet

French Revolution, Bicent. — A92

Designs: a, Bastille, liberty tree. b, Bastille, ship. :, Building, revolutionaries raising flag and liberty ree. d, Revolutionaries, building with open doors.

1989, July 14 **Engr.** ***Perf. 13***
517 A92 Sheet of 4 + 2 labels 6.50 6.50
a.-d. 5fr any single 1.60 1.60

Heritage of Ile aux Marins — A93

Designs: 2.20fr, Coastline, ships in harbor, girl in oat, fish. 13.70fr, Coastline, ships in harbor, boy lying kite from boat, map of Ile aux Marins.

1989, Sept. 9 **Engr.** ***Perf. 13x12½***
518 A93 2.20fr multi .70 .70
519 A93 13.70fr multi 4.25 4.25
a. Pair, #518-519 + label 5.00

Nos. 519a is in continuous design.

George Landry and Bank Emblem A95

1989, Nov. 8 **Engr.** ***Perf. 13***
520 A95 2.20fr bl & golden brn .75 .75

Bank of the Islands, cent.

Christmas — A96

1989, Dec. 2 **Litho.** ***Perf. 13***
521 A96 2.20fr multicolored .75 .75

France Nos. 2179-2182, 2182A-2186, 2188-2189, 2191-2194, 2204B, 2331, 2333-2334, 2336-2339, 2342 Ovptd. "ST-PIERRE / ET / MIQUELON"

1990-96 **Engr.** ***Perf. 13***
522 A1161 10c brown black .15 .15
523 A1161 20c light green .15 .15
524 A1161 50c bright violet .20 .20
525 A1161 1fr orange .35 .35
526 A1161 2fr apple grn .70 .70
527 A1161 2fr blue .75 .75
528 A1161 2.10fr green .75 .75
529 A1161 2.20fr green .80 .80
530 A1161 2.30fr red .80 .80
531 A1161 2.40fr emerald .85 .85
532 A1161 2.50fr red 1.00 1.00
533 A1161 2.70fr emerald 1.10 1.10
534 A1161 3.20fr bright blue 1.10 1.10
535 A1161 3.40fr blue 1.25 1.25
536 A1161 3.50fr apple green 1.25 1.25
537 A1161 3.80fr bright pink 1.40 1.40
538 A1161 3.80fr blue 1.60 1.60
539 A1161 4fr brt lil rose 1.50 1.50
540 A1161 4.20fr rose lilac 1.60 1.60
541 A1161 4.40fr blue 1.50 1.50
542 A1161 4.50fr magenta 1.90 1.90
543 A1161 5fr dull blue 1.75 1.75
544 A1161 10fr violet 3.50 3.50
544A A1161 (2.50fr) red .90 .90

Booklet Stamps
Self-Adhesive
Die Cut

545 A1161 2.50fr red .95 .95
a. Booklet pane of 10 9.50
Nos. 522-545 (25) 27.80 27.80

Issued: 2.30fr, 1/2/90; 2.10fr, 2/5/90; 10c, 20c, 50c, 3.20fr, #537, 4/17/90; 1fr, 5fr, #526, 10fr, 7/16/90; #532, 2.20fr, 12/21/91; 3.40fr, 4fr, 1/8/92; #545, 2/8/92; 4.20fr, 1/13/93; #544A, 7/5/93; 2.40fr, 3.50fr, 4.40fr, 10/6/93; #527, 8/17/94; #538, 4/10/96; 2.70fr, 4.50fr, 6/12/96.

A97 A98

1990, June 18 ***Perf. 13***
546 A97 2.30fr Charles de Gaulle .80 .80

De Gaulle's call for French Resistance, 50th anniv.

1990, Nov. 22
547 A98 1.70fr red, claret & blue .70 .70
548 A98 2.30fr red, claret & blue .95 .95
a. Pair, #547-548 + label 1.65 1.65

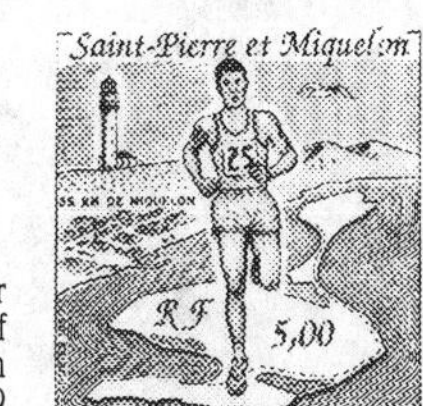

25 Kilometer Race of Miquelon A99

1990, June 23
549 A99 5fr Runner, map 1.75 1.75

Micmac Canoe, 1875 — A100

1990, Aug. 15 **Engr.** ***Perf. 13x13½***
550 A100 2.50fr multicolored .95 .95

Views of St. Pierre — A101

Harbor scene.

1990, Oct. 24 **Engr.** ***Perf. 13x12½***
551 A101 2.30fr bl, grn & brn .90 .90
552 A101 14.50fr bl, grn & brn 5.75 5.75
a. Pair, #551-552 + label 6.75 6.75

No. 552a is in continous design.

Christmas — A103

1990, Dec. 15 **Litho.**
553 A103 2.30fr multicolored .95 .95

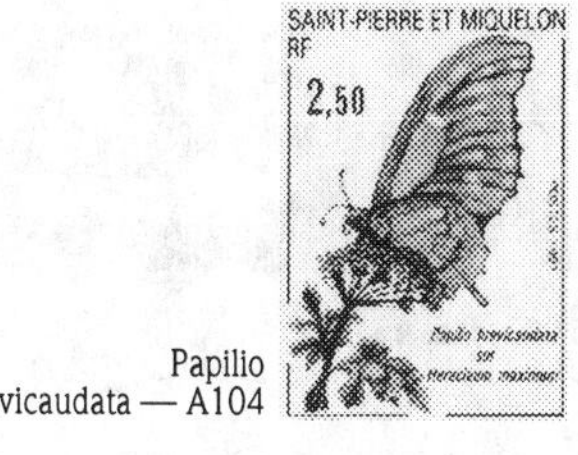

Papilio Brevicaudata — A104

1991-92 **Litho.** ***Perf. 13***
554 A104 2.50fr multicolored .95 .95

Perf. 12
555 A104 3.60fr Aeshna Eremita, Nuphar Variegatum 1.40 1.40

Issued: 2.50fr, Jan. 16; 3.60fr, Mar. 9, 1992.
This is an expanding set. Numbers will change again if necessary.

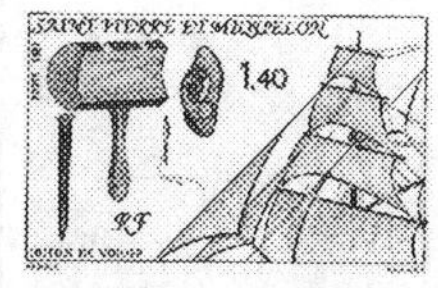

Marine Tools, Sailing Ship A105

1991, Mar. 6 **Litho. & Engr.** ***Perf. 13***
559 A105 1.40fr yellow & green .55 .55
560 A105 1.70fr yellow & red .65 .65

Scenic Views A106

Designs: Nos. 548, 552, Saint Pierre. Nos. 549, 553, Ile aux Marins. Nos. 550, 554, Langlade. Nos. 551, 555, Miquelon.

1991, Apr. 17 **Engr.** ***Perf. 13***
561 A106 1.70fr blue .65 .65
562 A106 1.70fr blue .65 .65
563 A106 1.70fr blue .65 .65
564 A106 1.70fr blue .65 .65
a. Strip of 4, #561-564 2.60 2.60
565 A106 2.50fr red .95 .95
566 A106 2.50fr red .95 .95
567 A106 2.50fr red .95 .95
568 A106 2.50fr red .95 .95
a. Strip of 4, #565-568 3.80 3.80
Nos. 561-568 (8) 6.40 6.40

Lyre Music Society, Cent. — A107

1991, June 21 **Engr.** ***Perf. 13***
569 A107 2.50fr multicolored .85 .85

Newfoundland Crossing by Rowboat "Los Gringos" — A108

1991, Aug. 3 **Engr.** ***Perf. 13x12½***
570 A108 2.50fr multicolored .85 .85

Basque Sports A109

1991, Aug. 24 ***Perf. 13***
571 A109 5fr red & green 1.75 1.75

Natural Heritage — A110

2.50fr, Fishermen. 14.50fr, Shoreline, birds.

1991, Oct. 18 **Engr.** ***Perf. 13x12½***
572 A110 2.50fr multicolored .90 .90
573 A110 14.50fr multicolored 5.00 5.00
a. Pair, #572-573 + label 6.00 6.00

No. 573a is in continuous design.

Central Economic Cooperation Bank, 50th Anniv. — A111

1991, Dec. 2 Engr. *Perf. 13x12½*
574 A111 2.50fr 1941 100fr note 1.00 1.00

Christmas — A112

1991, Dec. 21 Litho. *Perf. 13*
575 A112 2.50fr multicolored 1.00 1.00

Christmas Day Plebiscite, 50th anniv.

Vice Admiral Emile Henri Muselier (1882-1965), Commander of Free French Naval Forces A113

1992, Jan. 8 Litho. *Perf. 13*
576 A113 2.50fr multicolored 1.00 1.00

1992 Winter Olympics, Albertville A114

1992, Feb. 10 Engr. *Perf. 13*
577 A114 5fr vio bl, blue & mag 1.90 1.90

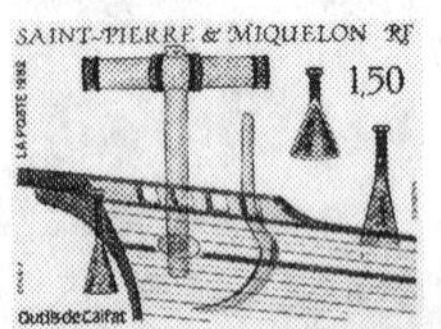

Caulking Tools, Bow of Ship A115

Perf. 13x12½
1992, Apr. 1 Litho. & Engr.
578 A115 1.50fr pale bl gray & brown .55 .55
579 A115 1.80fr pale bl gray & blue .65 .65

Lighthouses A116

Designs: a, Galantry. b, Feu Rouge. c, Pointe-Plate. d, Ile Aux Marins.

1992, July 8 Litho. *Perf. 13*
580 A116 2.50fr Strip of 4, #a.-d. 4.00 4.00

Natural Heritage — A117

1992, Sept. 9 Engr. *Perf. 13x12½*
581 A117 2.50fr Langlade 1.25 1.25
582 A117 15.10fr Doulisie Valley 7.50 7.50
a. Pair, #581-582 + label 8.75 8.75

No. 582a is in continuous design.
See Nos. 593-594, 605-606.

Discovery of America, 500th Anniv. — A118

Photo. & Engr.
1992, Oct. 12 *Perf. 13x12½*
583 A118 5.10fr multicolored 2.00 2.00

Le Baron de L'Esperance A119

1992, Nov. 18 Engr. *Perf. 13*
584 A119 2.50fr claret, brown & blue .95 .95

Christmas — A120

1992, Dec. 9 Litho. *Perf. 13*
585 A120 2.50fr multicolored .90 .90

Commander R. Birot (1906-1942) A121

1993, Jan. 13
586 A121 2.50fr multicolored .90 .90

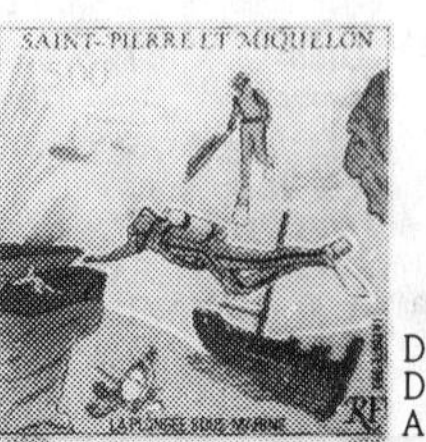

Deep Sea Diving A122

1993, Feb. 10 Engr. *Perf. 12*
587 A122 5fr multicolored 1.75 1.75

A123

A124

Monochamus Scutellatus, Cichorium Intybus.

1993, Mar. 10 Litho. *Perf. 13½x13*
588 A123 3.60fr multicolored 1.25 1.25

See No. 599.

1993, Apr. 7 Litho. *Perf. 13½x13*

Slicing cod.

589 A124 1.50fr green & multi .55 .55
590 A124 1.80fr red & multi .70 .70

Move to the Magdalen Islands, Quebec, by Miquelon Residents, Bicent. — A125

1993, June 9 Engr. *Perf. 13*
591 A125 5.10fr brown, blue & green 2.00 2.00

Fish — A126

Designs: a, Capelin. b, Ray. c, Halibut (fletan). d, Toad fish (crapaud).

1993, July 30 Photo. *Perf. 13*
592 A126 2.80fr Strip of 4, #a.-d. 3.75 3.75

Natl. Heritage Type of 1992

1993, Aug. 18 Engr. *Perf. 13x12½*
593 A117 2.80fr Miquelon 1.00 1.00
594 A117 16fr Otter pool 5.75 5.75
a. Pair, #593-594 + label 6.75 6.75

No. 594a is a continuous design.

Commissioner's Residence — A127

1993, Oct. 6 Engr. *Perf. 13*
595 A127 3.70fr multicolored 1.25 1.25

Christmas — A128

1993, Dec. 13 Litho. *Perf. 13*
596 A128 2.80fr multicolored .95 .95

Commander Louis Blaison (1906-1942), Submarine Surcouf A129

1994, Jan. 12 Litho. *Perf. 13*
597 A129 2.80fr multicolored .95 .95

Petanque World Championships — A130

1994, Feb. 9 Engr. *Perf. 12½x12*
598 A130 5.10fr multicolored 1.75 1.75

Insect and Flower Type of 1993

Cristalis tenax, taraxacum officinale, horiz.

1994, Mar. 9 Litho. *Perf. 13x13½*
599 A123 3.70fr multicolored 1.25 1.25

Drying Codfish, 1905 — A131

1994 Litho. *Perf. 13*
600 A131 1.50fr black & blue green .55 .55
601 A131 1.80fr multicolored .65 .65

Issued: 1.50fr, 5/4/94; 1.80fr, 4/6/94.

Women's Right to Vote, 50th Anniv. A132

1994, Apr. 21
602 A132 2.80fr multicolored 1.00 1.00

Hospital Ship St. Pierre, Cent. — A133

1994, July 2
603 A133 2.80fr multicolored 1.00 1.00

Souvenir Sheet

Ships A134

Designs: a, Miquelon. b, Isle of St. Pierre. c, St. George XII. d, St. Eugene IV.

1994, July 6 *Perf. 12*
604 Sheet of 4 5.00 5.00
a.-b. A134 2.80fr any single 1.00 1.00
c.-d. A134 3.70fr any single 1.50 1.50

See No. 628.

Natural Heritage Type of 1992

1994, Aug. 17 Engr. *Perf. 13*
605 A117 2.80fr Woods 1.10 1.10
606 A117 16fr "The Hat" 6.50 6.50
a. Pair, #605-606 + label 7.75 7.75

Parochial School
A135

1994, Oct. 5 **Engr.** ***Perf. 13***
607 A135 3.70fr multicolored 1.40 1.40

Stamp Show
A136

1994, Oct. 15
608 A136 3.70fr green, yellow & blue 1.40 1.40

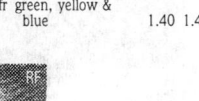

Christmas — A137

1994, Nov. 23 **Litho.** ***Perf. 13***
609 A137 2.80fr multicolored 1.10 1.10

Louis Pasteur (1822-95)
A138

1995, Jan. 11 **Litho.** ***Perf. 13***
610 A138 2.80fr multicolored 1.10 1.10

Triathlon
A139

1995, Feb. 8 **Engr.** ***Perf. 12***
611 A139 5.10fr multicolored 2.00 2.00

A140 A141

Dicranum Scoparium & Cladonia Cristatella.

1995, Mar. 8 **Litho.** ***Perf. 13***
612 A140 3.70fr multicolored 1.50 1.50

See Nos. 625, 635.

1995, Apr. 5 **Litho.** ***Perf. 13½x13***

Cooper and his tools.

613 A141 1.50fr black & multi .65 .65
614 A141 1.80fr red & multi .75 .75

Shellfish
A142

Designs: a, Snail. b, Crab. c, Scallop. d, Lobster.

1995, July 5 **Litho.** ***Perf. 13***
616 Strip of 4 4.75 4.75
a.-d. A142 2.80fr any single 1.25 1.25

Geological Mission — A143

Designs: 2.80fr, Rugged terrain along shoreline, diagram of mineral location, zircon. 16fr, Geological map, terrain.

1995, Aug. 16 **Engr.** ***Perf. 13x12½***
617 A117 2.80fr multicolored 1.25 1.25
618 A117 16fr multicolored 6.75 6.75
a. Pair, #617-618 + label 8.00 8.00

Sister Cesarine (1845-1922), St. Joseph de Cluny — A144

1995, Sept. 6 **Litho.** ***Perf. 13***
619 A144 1.80fr multicolored 1.25 1.25

The Francoforum Public Building
A145

1995, Oct. 5 **Engr.**
620 A145 3.70fr multicolored 2.50 2.50

Christmas — A146

Design: 2.80fr, Toys in store window.

1995, Nov. 22 **Litho.** ***Perf. 13***
621 A146 2.80fr multicolored 1.25 1.25

Charles de Gaulle (1890-1970)
A147

1995, Nov. 9 **Litho.** ***Perf. 13x13½***
622 A147 14fr multicolored 6.00 6.00

Commandant Jean Levasseur (1909-47)
A148

1996, Jan. 10 ***Perf. 13***
623 A148 2.80fr multicolored 1.25 1.25

Boxing
A149

1996, Feb. 7 **Engr.** ***Perf. 12x12½***
624 A149 5.10fr multicolored 2.25 2.25

Plant Type of 1995

Design: Cladonia verticillata and polytrichum juniperinum.

1996, Mar. 13 **Litho.** ***Perf. 13***
625 A140 3.70fr multicolored 1.60 1.60

Blacksmiths and Their Tools
A150

1996, Apr. 10
626 A150 1.50fr black & multi .65 .65
627 A150 1.80fr red & multi .75 .75

Ship Type of 1994

Designs: a, Radar II. b, SPM Roro. c, Pinta. d, Pascal Anne.

1996, July 15 **Litho.** ***Perf. 13***
628 Sheet of 4 5.00 5.00
a.-d. A134 3fr Any single 1.25 1.25

Aerial View of Miquelon — A151

Designs: 3fr, "Le Cap," mountains, buildings. 15.50fr, "Le Village," buildings.

1996, Aug. 14 **Engr.** ***Perf. 13x12½***
629 A151 3fr multicolored 1.25 1.25
630 A151 15.50fr multicolored 6.50 6.50
a. Pair, #629-630 + label 7.75 7.75

Customs House, Cent. — A152

1996, Oct. 9 **Engr.** ***Perf. 12½x13***
631 A152 3.80fr blue & black 1.50 1.50

Fall Stamp Show — A153

1996, Nov. 6 **Litho.** ***Perf. 13***
632 A153 1fr multicolored .40 .40

Christmas — A154

1996, Nov. 20 **Litho.** ***Perf. 13***
633 A154 3fr multicolored 1.25 1.25

Constant Colmay (1903-65)
A155

1997, Jan. 8 **Litho.** ***Perf. 13***
634 A155 3fr multicolored 1.25 1.25

Flora and Fauna Type of 1995

Design: Phalacrocorax carbo, sedum rosea.

1997, Mar. 12 **Litho.** ***Perf. 13***
635 A140 3.80fr multicolored 1.50 1.50

Maritime Heritage
A156

Designs: 1.70fr, Man in doorway of salt house. 2fr, Boat, naval architect's drawing.

1997, Apr. 9 **Litho.** ***Perf. 13***
636 A156 1.70fr multicolored .70 .70
637 A156 2fr multicolored .80 .80

Volleyball
A157

1997, Apr. 9 **Litho. & Engr.** ***Perf. 12***
638 A157 5.20fr multicolored 2.10 2.10

Fish — A158

a, Shark. b, Salmon. c, Poule d'eau. d, Mackerel.

1997, July 9 **Litho.** ***Perf. 13***
639 A158 3fr Strip of 4, #a.-d. 4.80 4.80

Bay, Headlands — A159

Designs: 3fr, Basque Cape. 15.50fr, Diamant.

1997, Aug. 13 *Perf. 13x12*
640 A159 3fr multicolored 1.00 1.00
641 A159 15.50fr multicolored 5.25 5.25
a. Pair #640-641 + label 6.25 6.25

France Nos. 2589-2603 Ovptd. "ST. PIERRE / ET / MIQUELON"

1997-98 Engr. *Perf. 13*
642 A1409 10c brown .15 .15
643 A1409 20c brt blue green .15 .15
644 A1409 50c purple .20 .20
645 A1409 1fr bright orange .35 .35
646 A1409 2fr bright blue .70 .70
647 A1409 2.70fr bright green .90 .90
648 A1409 (3fr) red 1.00 1.00
649 A1409 3.50fr apple green 1.25 1.25
650 A1409 3.80fr blue 1.25 1.25
651 A1409 4.20fr dark orange 1.50 1.50
652 A1409 4.40fr blue 1.60 1.60
653 A1409 4.50fr bright pink 1.60 1.60
654 A1409 5fr brt green blue 1.80 1.80
655 A1409 6.70fr dark green 2.40 2.40
656 A1409 10fr violet 3.60 3.60
Nos. 645-656 (12) 17.95 17.95

Issued: 2.70fr, (3fr), 3.80fr, 8/13/97; 10c, 20c, 50c, 3.50fr, 4.40fr, 10fr, 10/8/97; 1fr, 2fr, 4.20fr, 4.50fr, 5fr, 6.70fr, 1/7/98.

Post Office Building A160

1997, Oct. 8 Engr. *Perf. 13*
657 A160 3.80fr multicolored 1.40 1.40

Christmas — A161

1997, Nov. 19 Litho. *Perf. 13*
658 A161 3fr multicolored 1.10 1.10

Alain Savary (1918-88), Governor, Territorial Deputy A162

1998, Jan. 7 Litho. *Perf. 13*
659 A162 3fr multicolored 1.10 1.10

SEMI-POSTAL STAMPS

Regular Issue of 1909-17 Surcharged in Red

1915-17 Unwmk. *Perf. 14x13½*
B1 A17 10c + 5c car rose & red .80 .80
B2 A17 15c + 5c dl vio & rose ('17) .80 .80

Curie Issue
Common Design Type

1938, Oct. 24 Engr. *Perf. 13*
B3 CD80 1.75fr + 50c brt ultra 7.50 7.50

French Revolution Issue
Common Design Type

1939, July 5 Photo.
Name and Value Typo. in Black
B4 CD83 45c + 25c green 6.00 6.00
B5 CD83 70c + 30c brown 6.00 6.00
B6 CD83 90c + 35c red org 6.00 6.00
B7 CD83 1.25fr + 1fr rose pink 6.00 6.00
B8 CD83 2.25fr + 2fr blue 6.00 6.00
Nos. B4-B8 (5) 30.00 30.00

Common Design Type and

Sailor of Landing Force — SP1

Dispatch Boat "Ville d'Ys" — SP2

1941 Photo. *Perf. 13½*
B8A SP1 1fr + 1fr red 1.25
B8B CD86 1.50fr + 3fr maroon 1.25
B8C SP2 2.50fr + 1fr blue 1.25
Nos. B8A-B8C (3) 3.75

Nos. B8A-B8C were issued by the Vichy government, and were not placed on sale in the colony.

Nos. 206A-206B were surcharged "OEUVRES COLONIALES" and surtax (including change of denomination of the 2.50fr to 50c). These were issued in 1944 by the Vichy government and not placed on sale in the colony.

Nos. 239, 246 With Additional Surcharge in Carmine

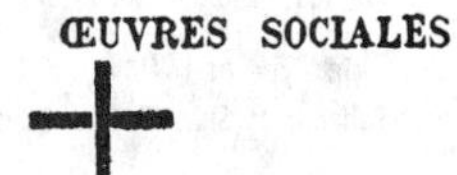

1942 Unwmk. *Perf. 13½x13*
B9 A25 1fr + 50c 25.00 25.00
B10 A26 2.50fr + 1fr 25.00 25.00

> Catalogue values for unused stamps in this section, from this point to the end of the section, are for Never Hinged items.

Red Cross Issue
Common Design Type

1944 *Perf. 14½x14*
B13 CD90 5fr + 20fr dp ultra 1.00 1.00

Surtax for the French Red Cross and national relief.

Tropical Medicine Issue
Common Design Type

1950, May 15 Engr. *Perf. 13*
B14 CD100 10fr + 2fr red brn & red 6.25 4.25

The surtax was for charitable work.

AIR POST STAMPS

> Catalogue values for unused stamps in this section are for Never Hinged items.

Common Design Type
Perf. 14½x14

1942, Aug. 17 Photo. Unwmk.
C1 CD87 1fr dark orange .40 .40
C2 CD87 1.50fr bright red .50 .50
C3 CD87 5fr brown red .70 .70
C4 CD87 10fr black .90 .90
C5 CD87 25fr ultra 1.00 1.00
C6 CD87 50fr dark green 1.50 1.50
C7 CD87 100fr plum 2.00 2.00
Nos. C1-C7 (7) 7.00 7.00

Victory Issue
Common Design Type

1946, May 8 Engr. *Perf. 12½*
C8 CD92 8fr deep claret 1.25 1.25

Chad to Rhine Issue
Common Design Types

1946, June 6
C9 CD93 5fr brown red 1.00 1.00
C10 CD94 10fr lilac rose 1.00 1.00
C11 CD95 15fr gray blk 1.50 1.50
C12 CD96 20fr violet 1.65 1.65
C13 CD97 25fr chocolate 2.25 2.25
C14 CD98 50fr grnsh blk 2.25 2.25
Nos. C9-C14 (6) 9.65 9.65

Plane, Sailing Vessel and Coast — AP2

AP3

AP4

1947, Oct. 6
C15 AP2 50fr yel grn & rose 5.75 1.50
C16 AP3 100fr dk blue grn 10.00 2.25
C17 AP4 200fr bluish blk & brt rose 13.00 3.25
Nos. C15-C17 (3) 28.75 7.00

UPU Issue
Common Design Type

1949, July 4 Engr. *Perf. 13*
C18 CD99 25fr multicolored 12.00 4.50

Liberation Issue
Common Design Type

1954, June 6
C19 CD102 15fr sepia & red 8.00 4.00

10th anniversary of the liberation of France.

Plane over St. Pierre Harbor — AP6

1956, Oct. 22
C20 AP6 500fr ultra & indigo 42.50 12.50

Dog and Village — AP7

Design: 100fr, Caravelle over archipelago.

1957, Nov. 4 Unwmk. *Perf. 13*
C21 AP7 50fr gray, brn blk & bl 35.00 9.00
C22 AP7 100fr black & gray 14.00 4.50

Anchors and Torches — AP8

1959, Sept. 14 Engr. *Perf. 13*
C23 AP8 200fr dk pur, grn & claret 11.00 3.00

Approval of the constitution and the vote which confirmed the attachment of the islands to France.

Pitcher Plant — AP9

1962, Apr. 24 Unwmk. *Perf. 13*
C24 AP9 100fr green, org & car *8.00* 1.50

Gulf of St. Lawrence and Submarine "Surcouf" — AP10

Perf. 13½x12½

1962, July 24 Photo.
C25 AP10 500fr dk red & blue 100.00 60.00

20th anniv. of St. Pierre & Miquelon's joining the Free French.

Telstar Issue
Common Design Type

1962, Nov. 22 Engr. *Perf. 13*
C26 CD111 50fr Prus grn & bister 5.00 2.25

Arrival of Governor Dangeac, 1763 — AP11

1963, Aug. 5 Unwmk. *Perf. 13*
C27 AP11 200fr dk bl, sl grn & brn 17.50 3.50

Bicentenary of the arrival of the first French governor.

Jet Plane and Map of Maritime Provinces and New England — AP12

1964, Sept. 28 Engr. *Perf. 13*
C28 AP12 100fr choc & Prus bl 11.00 3.00

Inauguration of direct airmail service between St. Pierre and New York City.

ITU Issue
Common Design Type

1965, May 17
C29 CD120 40fr org brn, dk bl & lil rose 19.00 3.50

French Satellite A-1 Issue
Common Design Type

Designs: 25fr, Diamant rocket and launching installations. 30fr, A-1 satellite.

1966, Jan. 24 Engr. *Perf. 13*
C30 CD121 25fr dk brn, dk bl & rose cl 4.75 2.00
C31 CD121 30fr dk bl, rose cl & dk brn 4.75 2.00
a. Strip of 2, #C30-C31 + label 10.00 4.50

French Satellite D-1 Issue
Common Design Type

1966, May 23 Engr. *Perf. 13*
C32 CD122 48fr brt grn, ultra & rose claret 7.00 2.25

Arrival of Settlers — AP13

1966, June 22 Photo. *Perf. 13*
C33 AP13 100fr multicolored 11.00 2.25

150th anniv. of the return of the islands of St. Pierre and Miquelon to France.

Front Page of Official Journal and Printing Presses — AP14

1966, Oct. 20 Engr. *Perf. 13*
C34 AP14 60fr dk bl, lake & dk pur 10.50 1.25

Centenary of the Government Printers and the Official Journal.

Map of Islands, Old and New Fishing Vessels — AP15

Design: 100fr, Cruiser Colbert, maps of Brest, St. Pierre and Miquelon.

1967, July 20 Engr. *Perf. 13*
C35 AP15 25fr dk bl, gray & crim 19.00 7.00
C36 AP15 100fr multicolored 35.00 15.00

Visit of President Charles de Gaulle.

Speed Skater and Olympic Emblem — AP16

60fr, Ice hockey goalkeeper.

1968, Apr. 22 Photo. *Perf. 13*
C37 AP16 50fr ultra & multi 7.50 1.25
C38 AP16 60fr green & multi 8.50 1.50

10th Winter Olympic Games, Grenoble, France, Feb. 6-18.

War Memorial, St. Pierre — AP17

1968, Nov. 11 Photo. *Perf. 12½*
C39 AP17 500fr multicolored 22.50 10.00

World War I armistice, 50th anniv.

Concorde Issue
Common Design Type

1969, Apr. 17 Engr. *Perf. 13*
C40 CD129 34fr dk brown & olive 24.00 5.00

Scenic Type of Regular Issue, 1969.

Designs: 50fr, Grazing horses, Miquelon. 100fr, Gathering driftwood on Mirande Beach, Miquelon.

1969, Apr. 30 Engr. *Perf. 13*
Size: 47½x27mm
C41 A47 50fr ultra, brn & olive 10.50 2.00
C42 A47 100fr dk brn, bl & slate 18.00 4.50

L'Esperance Leaving Saint-Malo, 1600 — AP18

1969, June 16 Engr. *Perf. 13*
C43 AP18 200fr blk, grn & dk red 37.50 3.00

Pierre Loti and Sailboats — AP19

1969, June 23
C44 AP19 300fr lemon, choc & Prus bl 45.00 6.00

Loti (1850-1923), French novelist and naval officer.

EXPO Emblem and "Mountains" by Yokoyama Taikan — AP20

34fr, Geisha, rocket and EXPO emblem, vert.

1970, Sept. 8 Engr. *Perf. 13*
C45 AP20 34fr dp claret, ol & ind 13.00 1.00
C46 AP20 85fr orange, ind & car 19.00 2.00

EXPO '70 Intl. Exposition, Osaka, Japan, Mar. 15-Sept. 13.

Etienne François Duke of Choiseul and his Ships — AP21

Designs: 50fr, Jacques Cartier, ship and landing party. 60fr, Sebastien Le Gonrad de Sourdeval, ships and map of islands.

1970, Nov. 25
Portrait in Lake
C47 AP21 25fr lilac & Prus bl 15.00 .60
C48 AP21 50fr slate grn & red lil 20.00 1.50
C49 AP21 60fr red lil & sl grn 25.00 1.50
Nos. C47-C49 (3) 60.00 3.60

De Gaulle, Cross of Lorraine, Sailor, Soldier, Coast Guard — AP22

1972, June 18 Engr. *Perf. 13*
C50 AP22 100fr lilac, brn & grn 22.50 3.00

Charles de Gaulle (1890-1970), French pres.

Louis Joseph de Montcalm — AP23

Designs: 2fr, Louis de Buade Frontenac, vert. 4fr, Robert de La Salle.

1973, Jan. 1
C51 AP23 1.60fr multicolored 6.50 .60
C52 AP23 2fr multicolored 7.50 .80
C53 AP23 4fr multicolored 14.00 1.60
Nos. C51-C53 (3) 28.00 3.00

Transall C 160 over St. Pierre — AP24

1973, Oct. 16 Engr. *Perf. 13*
C54 AP24 10fr multicolored 32.50 7.00

Arms and Map of Islands, Fish and Bird — AP25

1974, Nov. 5 Photo. *Perf. 13*
C55 AP25 2fr gold & multi 10.00 1.00

Copernicus, Kepler, Newton and Einstein — AP26

1974, Nov. 26 Engr.
C56 AP26 4fr multicolored 12.50 2.00

Nicolaus Copernicus (1473-1543), Polish astronomer.

Type of 1909, Cod and ARPHILA Emblem AP27

1975, Aug. 5 Engr. *Perf. 13*
C57 AP27 4fr ultra, red & indigo 16.00 3.00

ARPHILA 75, International Philatelic Exhibition, Paris, June 6-16.

Judo, Maple Leaf, Olympic Rings — AP28

1975, Nov. 18 Engr. *Perf. 13*
C58 AP28 1.90fr red, blue & vio 7.00 1.25

Pre-Olympic Year.

Concorde — AP29

1976, Jan. 21 Engr. *Perf. 13*
C59 AP29 10fr red, blk & slate 24.00 6.00

1st commercial flight of supersonic jet Concorde from Paris to Rio, Jan. 21.

A. G. Bell, Telephone and Satellite AP30

1976, June 22 Litho. *Perf. 12½*
C60 AP30 5fr vio bl, org & red 7.50 2.75

Centenary of first telephone call by Alexander Graham Bell, Mar. 10, 1876.

Aircraft — AP31

1987, June 30 Engr. *Perf. 13*
C61 AP31 5fr Hawker-Siddeley H. S. 748, 1987 1.90 1.90
C62 AP31 10fr Latecoere 522, 1939 3.50 3.50

Hindenburg — AP32

10fr, Douglas DC3, 1948-1988. 20fr, Piper Aztec.

1988-89 Engr. *Perf. 13*

C63 AP32	5fr multicolored		1.40	1.40
C64 AP32	10fr multicolored		3.00	3.00
C65 AP32	20fr multicolored		6.50	6.50
	Nos. C63-C65 (3)		10.90	10.90

Issued: 20fr, May 31, 1989; others, June 22.

Flying Flea, Bird — AP33

1990, May 16 Engr.

C66 AP33 5fr multicolored	1.75	1.75

Piper Tomahawk — AP34

1991, May 29 Engr. *Perf. 13*

C67 AP34 10fr multicolored	3.85	3.85

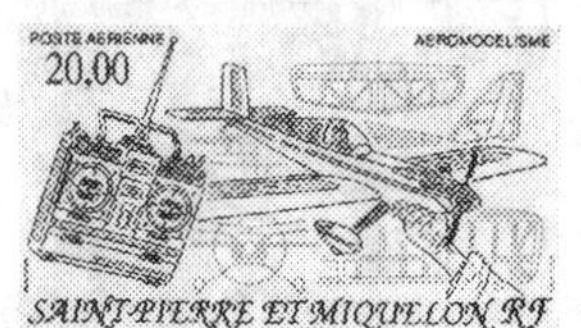
Radio-controlled Model Airplanes — AP35

1992, May 6 Engr. *Perf. 13*

C68 AP35 20fr brown, red & org	7.75	7.75

Migratory Birds — AP36

Photo. & Engr.

1993-97 *Perf. 13x12½*

C69 AP36 5fr Shearwater (Puffin)	1.85	1.85
C70 AP36 10fr Golden plover	3.70	3.70
Perf. 13x13½		
C71 AP36 10fr Arctic Tern	4.25	4.25
Perf. 13		
C72 AP36 15fr Courlis	6.30	6.30
C73 AP36 5fr Peregrine falcon, vert.	2.00	2.00
Nos. C69-C73 (5)	18.10	18.10

Issued: #C69-C70, 5/12; #C71, 5/10/95; #C72, 5/15/96; #C73, 5/28/97.

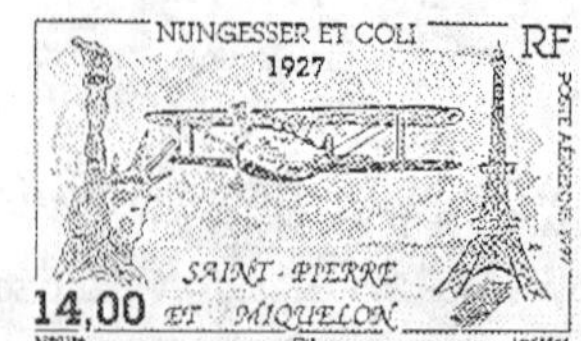
Disappearance of the Flight of Nungesser and Coli, 70th Anniv. — AP37

1997, June 11

C74 AP37 14fr blk, grn bl & brn	5.50	5.50

AIR POST SEMI-POSTAL STAMPS

V4

Stamps of the design shown above and stamp of Cameroun type V10 inscribed "St. Pierre-et-Miquelon" were issued in 1942 by the Vichy Government, but were not placed on sale in the Colony.

POSTAGE DUE STAMPS

Postage Due Stamps of French Colonies Overprinted in Red

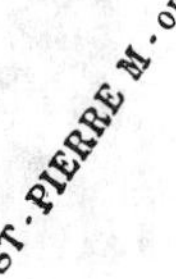

1892 Unwmk. *Imperf.*

J1 D1	5c black	40.00	40.00
J2 D1	10c black	10.00	10.00
J3 D1	15c black	10.00	10.00
J4 D1	20c black	10.00	10.00
J5 D1	30c black	10.00	10.00
J6 D1	40c black	10.00	10.00
J7 D1	60c black	32.50	32.50
Black Overprint			
J8 D1	1fr brown	90.00	90.00
J9 D1	2fr brown	90.00	90.00
	Nos. J1-J9 (9)	302.50	302.50

These stamps exist with and without hyphen. See note after No. 59.

Postage Due Stamps of France, 1893-1924, Overprinted

SAINT-PIERRE -ET- MIQUELON

1925-27 *Perf. 14x13½*

J10 D2	5c blue	.30	.30
J11 D2	10c dark brown	.30	.30
J12 D2	20c olive green	.45	.45
J13 D2	25c rose	.45	.45
J14 D2	30c red	.65	.65
J15 D2	45c blue green	.65	.65
J16 D2	50c brown vio	1.40	1.40
J17 D2	1fr red brn, *straw*	1.90	1.90
J18 D2	3fr magenta ('27)	6.25	6.25

Surcharged

SAINT-PIERRE -ET-MIQUELON 2 francs à percevoir

J19 D2	60c on 50c buff	1.40	1.40
J20 D2	2fr on 1fr red	2.25	2.25
	Nos. J10-J20 (11)	16.00	16.00

Newfoundland Dog — D3

1932, Dec. 5 Typo.

J21 D3	5c dk blue & blk	.75	.75
J22 D3	10c green & blk	.75	.75
J23 D3	20c red & blk	1.00	1.00
J24 D3	25c red vio & blk	1.00	1.00
J25 D3	30c orange & blk	2.00	2.00
J26 D3	45c lt blue & blk	2.50	2.50
J27 D3	50c blue grn & blk	4.75	4.75
J28 D3	60c brt rose & blk	6.50	6.50
J29 D3	1fr yellow brn & blk	14.00	14.00
J30 D3	2fr dp violet & blk	22.50	22.50
J31 D3	3fr dk brown & blk	27.50	27.50
	Nos. J21-J31 (11)	83.25	83.25

For overprints and surcharge see Nos. J42-J46.

Codfish — D4

1938, Nov. 17 Photo. *Perf. 13*

J32 D4	5c gray black	.15	.15
J33 D4	10c dk red violet	.15	.15
J34 D4	15c slate green	.15	.15
J35 D4	20c deep blue	.15	.15
J36 D4	30c rose carmine	.20	.20
J37 D4	50c dk blue green	.20	.20
J38 D4	60c dk blue	.35	.35
J39 D4	1fr henna brown	.65	.65
J40 D4	2fr gray brown	1.50	1.50
J41 D4	3fr dull violet	2.50	2.50
	Nos. J32-J41 (10)	6.00	6.00

For overprints see Nos. J48-J67.

Type of Postage Due Stamps of 1932 Overprinted in Black

FRANCE LIBRE F. N. F. L.

1942 Unwmk. *Perf. 14x13½*

J42 D3	25c red vio & blk	190.00	190.00
J43 D3	30c orange & blk	190.00	190.00
J44 D3	50c blue grn & blk	825.00	825.00
J45 D3	2fr dp vio & bl blk	30.00	30.00

Same Surcharged in Black

3 fr FRANCE LIBRE F. N. F. L.

J46 D3 3fr on 2fr dp vio & blk, "F.N.F.L." omitted	12.00	12.00
a. With "F.N.F.L."	7.00	7.00
Nos. J42-J46 (5)	1,247.	1,247.

Postage Due Stamps of 1938 Overprinted in Black

NOËL 1941 F N F L

1942 *Perf. 13*

J48 D4	5c gray black	14.00	14.00
J49 D4	10c dk red violet	14.00	14.00
J50 D4	15c slate green	14.00	14.00
J51 D4	20c deep blue	14.00	14.00
J52 D4	30c rose carmine	14.00	14.00
J53 D4	50c dk blue green	27.50	27.50
J54 D4	60c dark blue	60.00	60.00
J55 D4	1fr henna brown	70.00	70.00
J56 D4	2fr gray brown	75.00	75.00
J57 D4	3fr dull violet	82.50	82.50
	Nos. J48-J57 (10)	385.00	385.00

Christmas Day plebiscite ordered by Vice Admiral Emile Henri Muselier, commander of the Free French naval forces.

Postage Due Stamps of 1938 Overprinted in Black

FRANCE LIBRE F N F L

1942

J58 D4	5c gray black	30.00	30.00
J59 D4	10c dk red violet	6.00	6.00
J60 D4	15c slate green	6.00	6.00
J61 D4	20c deep blue	6.00	6.00
J62 D4	30c rose carmine	6.00	6.00
J63 D4	50c dk blue green	6.00	6.00
J64 D4	60c dark blue	7.50	7.50
J65 D4	1fr henna brown	15.00	15.00
J66 D4	2fr gray brown	17.50	17.50
J67 D4	3fr dull violet	400.00	400.00
	Nos. J58-J67 (10)	500.00	500.00

Catalogue values for unused stamps in this section, from this point to the end of the section, are for Never Hinged items.

Arms and Fishing Schooner — D5

1947, Oct. 6 Engr. *Perf. 13*

J68 D5	10c deep orange	.20	.15
J69 D5	30c deep ultra	.20	.15
J70 D5	50c dk blue green	.20	.15
J71 D5	1fr deep carmine	.30	.15
J72 D5	2fr dk green	.30	.15
J73 D5	3fr violet	1.00	.45
J74 D5	4fr chocolate	1.00	.45
J75 D5	5fr yellow green	1.00	.45
J76 D5	10fr black brown	1.25	.60
J77 D5	20fr orange red	1.65	.80
	Nos. J68-J77 (10)	7.10	3.50

Newfoundland Dog — D6

1973, Jan. 1 Engr. *Perf. 13*

J78 D6	2c brown & blk	.60	.25
J79 D6	10c purple & blk	.90	.40
J80 D6	20c grnsh bl & blk	1.50	.90
J81 D6	30c dk car & blk	3.00	2.00
J82 D6	1fr blue & blk	6.50	5.00
	Nos. J78-J82 (5)	12.50	8.55

France Nos. J106-J115 Overprinted "ST - PIERRE ET MIQUELON" Reading Up in Red

1986, Sept. 15 Engr. *Perf. 13*

J83 D8	10c multicolored	.15	.15
J84 D8	20c multicolored	.15	.15
J85 D8	30c multicolored	.15	.15
J86 D8	40c multicolored	.20	.15
J87 D8	50c multicolored	.30	.15
J88 D8	1fr multicolored	.40	.30
J89 D8	2fr multicolored	.70	.60
J90 D8	3fr multicolored	1.10	.90
J91 D8	4fr multicolored	1.40	1.25
J92 D8	5fr multicolored	1.65	1.50
	Nos. J83-J92 (10)	6.20	5.30

PARCEL POST STAMPS

No. 65 Overprinted

COLIS POSTAUX

1901 Unwmk. *Perf. 14x13½*

Q1 A16 10c black, *lavender*	80.00	60.00
a. Inverted overprint		

No. 66 Overprinted

Colis Postaux

Q2 A16 10c red	11.00	10.00

Nos. 84 and 87 Overprinted

Colis Postaux

1917-25

Q3 A17 10c	1.50	1.50
a. Double overprint		
Q4 A17 20c ('25)	1.25	1.25
a. Double overprint	*85.00*	*85.00*

No. Q4 with Additional Overprint in Black

FRANCE LIBRE F. N. F. L.

1942

Q5 A17 20c	550.00	550.00

ST. THOMAS AND PRINCE ISLANDS

sānt–'tām–əs and 'prin(t)s 'ī–lənds

Democratic Republic of Sao Tome and Principe

LOCATION — Two islands in the Gulf of Guinea, 125 miles off the west coast of Africa
GOVT. — Republic
AREA — 372 sq. mi.
POP. — 102,000 (est. 1984)
CAPITAL — Sao Tome

This colony of Portugal became a province, later an overseas territory, and achieved independence on July 12, 1975.

1000 Reis = 1 Milreis
100 Centavos = 1 Escudo (1913)
100 Cents = 1 Dobra (1977)

Catalogue values for unused stamps in this country are for Never Hinged items, beginning with Scott 353 in the regular postage section, Scott J52 in the postage due section, and Scott RA4 in the postal tax section.

Portuguese Crown — A1   King Luiz — A2

5, 25, 50 REIS:
Type I - "5" is upright.
Type II - "5" is slanting.

10 REIS:
Type I - "1" has short serif at top.
Type II - "1" has long serif at top.

40 REIS:
Type I - "4" is broad.
Type II - "4" is narrow.

Perf. 12½, 13½

1869-75 Unwmk. Typo.

No.	Type	Stamp	Unused	Used
1	A1	5r black, I	2.00	1.90
a.		Type II	2.00	1.90
2	A1	10r yellow, I	14.00	8.50
a.		Type II	17.50	10.50
3	A1	20r bister	3.50	2.75
4	A1	25r rose, I	1.25	1.10
a.		25r red	4.50	1.50
5	A1	40r blue ('75), I	4.75	3.50
a.		Type II	5.50	4.50
6	A1	50r gray grn, II	9.00	7.00
a.		Type I	15.00	14.00
7	A1	100r gray lilac	6.00	5.50
8	A1	200r red orange ('75)	8.25	6.25
9	A1	300r chocolate ('75)	8.25	7.00
		Nos. 1-9 (9)	57.00	43.50

1881-85

No.	Type	Stamp	Unused	Used
10	A1	10r gray grn, I	8.00	6.75
a.		Type II	9.50	6.00
b.		Perf. 13½, I	11.00	8.00
11	A1	20r car rose ('85)	3.50	3.00
12	A1	25r vio ('85), II	2.25	1.75
13	A1	40r yel buff, II	5.00	4.00
a.		Perf. 13½	6.00	4.50
14	A1	50r dk blue, I	2.50	2.25
a.		Type II	2.50	2.25
		Nos. 10-14 (5)	21.25	17.75

For surcharges and overprints see Nos. 63-64, 129-129B, 154.

Nos. 1-14 have been reprinted on stout white paper, ungummed, with rough perforation 13½, also on ordinary paper with shiny white gum and clean-cut perforation 13½ with large holes.

Typo., Head Embossed

1887 *Perf. 12½, 13½*

No.	Type	Stamp	Unused	Used
15	A2	5r black	3.75	2.50
16	A2	10r green	4.25	2.50
17	A2	20r brt rose	4.25	3.00
a.		Perf. 12½	55.00	55.00
18	A2	25r violet	4.25	1.65
19	A2	40r brown	4.25	2.25
20	A2	50r blue	4.25	2.50
21	A2	100r yellow brn	4.25	2.00
22	A2	200r gray lilac	15.00	10.50
23	A2	300r orange	15.00	10.50
		Nos. 15-23 (9)	59.25	37.40

For surcharges and overprints see Nos. 24-26, 62, 65-72, 130-131, 155-158, 234-237.

Nos. 15, 16, 19, 21, 22, and 23 have been reprinted in paler colors than the originals, with white gum and cleancut perforation 13½. Value $1.50 each.

Nos. 16-17, 19 Surcharged:

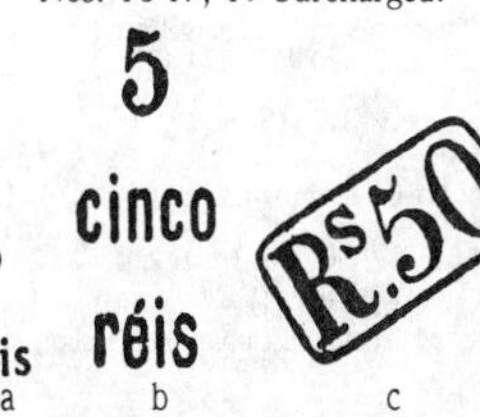

1889-91 Without Gum

No.	Type	Stamp	Unused	Used
24	A2(a)	5r on 10r	35.00	20.00
25	A2(b)	5r on 20r	25.00	20.00
26	A2(c)	50r on 40r ('91)	225.00	70.00
		Nos. 24-26 (3)	285.00	110.00

Varieties of Nos. 24-26, including inverted and double surcharges, "5" inverted, "Cinoc" and "Cinco," were deliberately made and unofficially issued.

King Carlos
A6   A7

1895 Typo. *Perf. 11½, 12½*

No.	Type	Stamp	Unused	Used
27	A6	5r yellow	.80	.60
28	A6	10r red lilac	1.25	1.00
29	A6	15r red brown	1.40	1.10
30	A6	20r lavender	1.50	1.10
31	A6	25r green	1.50	.75
32	A6	50r light blue	1.65	.70
a.		Perf. 13½	2.00	1.50
33	A6	75r rose	3.75	3.25
34	A6	80r yellow grn	8.00	6.25
35	A6	100r brn, *yel*	3.50	3.00
36	A6	150r car, *rose*	6.00	5.00
37	A6	200r dk bl, *bl*	7.75	6.50
38	A6	300r dk bl, *sal*	8.50	7.75
		Nos. 27-38 (12)	45.60	37.00

For surcharges and overprints see Nos. 73-84, 132-137, 159-165, 238-243, 262-264, 268-274.

1898-1903 *Perf. 11½*

Name and Value in Black except 500r

No.	Type	Stamp	Unused	Used
39	A7	2½r gray	.30	.25
40	A7	5r orange	.30	.25
41	A7	10r lt green	.40	.30
42	A7	15r brown	2.00	1.75
43	A7	15r gray grn ('03)	1.10	1.10
44	A7	20r gray violet	.90	.50
45	A7	25r sea green	.70	.25
46	A7	25r carmine ('03)	1.10	.30
47	A7	50r blue	.70	.50
48	A7	50r brown ('03)	4.50	4.50
49	A7	65r dull blue ('03)	11.00	9.00
50	A7	75r rose	10.00	6.50
51	A7	75r red lilac ('03)	1.75	1.40
52	A7	80r brt violet	5.00	5.00
53	A7	100r dk blue, *bl*	2.50	2.00
54	A7	115r org brn, *pink* ('03)	10.00	8.00
55	A7	130r brn, *straw* ('03)	10.00	6.00
56	A7	150r brn, *buff*	2.75	2.25
57	A7	200r red lil, *pnksh*	4.75	2.75
58	A7	300r dk blue, *rose*	5.50	5.00
59	A7	400r dull bl, *straw* ('03)	13.00	8.50
60	A7	500r blk & red, *bl* ('01)	7.25	5.00
61	A7	700r vio, *yelsh* ('01)	16.00	12.00
		Nos. 39-61 (23)	111.50	83.10

For overprints and surcharges see Nos. 86-105, 116-128, 138-153, 167-169, 244-249, 255-261, 265-267.

Stamps of 1869-95 Surcharged in Red or Black

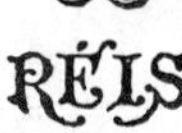

1902

On Stamp of 1887

No.	Type	Stamp	Unused	Used
62	A2	130r on 5r blk (R)	6.00	5.00
a.		Perf. 13½	32.50	32.50

On Stamps of 1869

No.	Type	Stamp	Unused	Used
63	A1	115r on 50r grn	10.00	7.50
64	A1	400r on 10r yel	25.00	12.00
a.		Double surcharge		

On Stamps of 1887

No.	Type	Stamp	Unused	Used
65	A2	65r on 20r rose	6.25	4.50
a.		Perf. 13½	8.50	7.00
66	A2	65r on 25r violet	4.50	4.00
a.		Inverted surcharge		
67	A2	65r on 100r yel brn	4.50	4.75
68	A2	115r on 10r blue grn	4.50	4.00
69	A2	115r on 300r orange	4.50	4.00
70	A2	130r on 200r gray lil	6.00	5.00
71	A2	400r on 40r brown	8.00	7.00
72	A2	400r on 50r blue	14.00	12.00
a.		Perf. 13½	110.00	90.00

On Stamps of 1895

No.	Type	Stamp	Unused	Used
73	A6	65r on 5r yellow	5.00	3.00
74	A6	65r on 10r red vio	5.00	3.00
75	A6	65r on 15r choc	5.00	3.00
76	A6	65r on 20r lav	5.00	3.00
77	A6	115r on 25r grn	5.00	3.00
78	A6	115r on 150r car, *rose*	5.00	3.00
79	A6	115r on 200r bl, *bl*	5.00	3.00
80	A6	130r on 75r rose	5.00	3.00
81	A6	130r on 100r brn, *yel*	5.00	3.50
a.		Double surcharge		
82	A6	130r on 300r bl, *sal*	5.00	3.00
83	A6	400r on 50r lt blue	1.10	.95
a.		Perf. 13½	2.00	1.65
84	A6	400r on 80r yel grn	2.00	1.50

On Newspaper Stamp No. P12

No.	Type	Stamp	Unused	Used
85	N3	400r on 2½r brown	1.10	.95
a.		Double surcharge		
		Nos. 62-85 (24)	147.45	103.65

Reprints of Nos. 63, 64, 67, 71, and 72 have shiny white gum and clean-cut perf. 13½.

Stamps of 1898 Overprinted PROVISORIO

1902

No.	Type	Stamp	Unused	Used
86	A7	15r brown	2.00	1.50
87	A7	25r sea green	2.00	1.25
88	A7	50r blue	2.25	1.25
89	A7	75r rose	5.00	3.50
		Nos. 86-89 (4)	11.25	7.50

No. 49 Surcharged in Black 50 RÉIS

1905

No.	Type	Stamp	Unused	Used
90	A7	50r on 65r dull blue	3.25	2.75

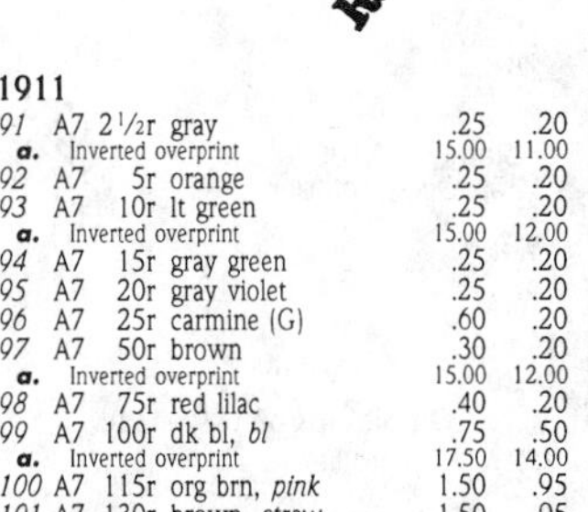

Stamps of 1898-1903 Overprinted in Carmine or Green REPUBLICA

1911

No.	Type	Stamp	Unused	Used
91	A7	2½r gray	.25	.20
a.		Inverted overprint	15.00	11.00
92	A7	5r orange	.25	.20
93	A7	10r lt green	.25	.20
a.		Inverted overprint	15.00	12.00
94	A7	15r gray green	.25	.20
95	A7	20r gray violet	.25	.20
96	A7	25r carmine (G)	.60	.20
97	A7	50r brown	.30	.20
a.		Inverted overprint	15.00	12.00
98	A7	75r red lilac	.40	.20
99	A7	100r dk bl, *bl*	.75	.50
a.		Inverted overprint	17.50	14.00
100	A7	115r org brn, *pink*	1.50	.95
101	A7	130r brown, *straw*	1.50	.95
102	A7	200r red lil, *pnksh*	6.00	4.25
103	A7	400r dull blue, *straw*	2.00	1.00
104	A7	500r blk & red, *bl*	2.00	1.00
105	A7	700r violet, *yelsh*	2.00	1.00
		Nos. 91-105 (15)	18.30	11.25

King Manuel II — A8

Overprinted in Carmine or Green

1912 *Perf. 11½, 12*

No.	Type	Stamp	Unused	Used
106	A8	2½r violet	.15	.15
a.		Double overprint	16.00	16.00
b.		Double overprint, one inverted		
107	A8	5r black	.15	.15
108	A8	10r gray green	.15	.15
a.		Double overprint	14.00	14.00
109	A8	20r carmine (G)	1.00	.75
110	A8	25r violet brn	.60	.45
111	A8	50r dk blue	.60	.55
112	A8	75r bister brn	.90	.55
113	A8	100r brn, *lt grn*	1.10	.50
114	A8	200r dk grn, *sal*	2.00	1.40
115	A8	300r black, *azure*	2.00	2.00
		Nos. 106-115 (10)	8.65	6.65

Stamps of 1898-1905 Overprinted in Black REPUBLICA

1913

On Stamps of 1898-1903

No.	Type	Stamp	Unused	Used
116	A7	2½r gray	1.00	1.00
a.		Inverted overprint	15.00	15.00
b.		Double overprint	12.00	12.00
117	A7	5r orange	1.40	1.00
118	A7	15r gray green	22.50	17.50
a.		Inverted overprint		
119	A7	20r gray violet	1.50	1.50
a.		Inverted overprint		
120	A7	25r carmine	5.75	4.50
a.		Inverted overprint		
b.		Double overprint		
121	A7	75r red lilac	5.00	5.00
122	A7	100r bl, *bluish*	8.50	7.50
123	A7	115r org brn, *pink*	37.50	35.00
a.		Double overprint	75.00	60.00
124	A7	130r brn, *straw*	13.00	13.00
125	A7	200r red lil, *pnksh*	20.00	13.00
126	A7	400r dl bl, *straw*	14.00	12.50
127	A7	500r blk & red, *gray*	35.00	42.50
128	A7	700r vio, *yelsh*	47.50	40.00
		Nos. 116-128 (13)	212.65	194.00

On Provisional Issue of 1902

No.	Type	Stamp	Unused	Used
129	A1	115r on 50r green	110.00	85.00
a.		Inverted overprint		
129B	A1	400r on 10r yellow	375.00	375.00
130	A2	115r on 10r blue grn	2.75	2.50
a.		Inverted overprint		
131	A2	400r on 50r blue	75.00	75.00
132	A6	115r on 25r green	2.00	1.75
a.		Inverted overprint		
133	A6	115r on 150r car, *rose*	42.50	40.00
a.		Inverted overprint		
134	A6	115r on 200r bl, *bl*	2.50	2.00
135	A6	130r on 75r rose	2.25	2.00
a.		Inverted overprint		
136	A6	400r on 50r lt bl	4.00	4.00
a.		Perf. 13½	7.50	7.50
137	A6	400r on 80r yel grn	5.00	4.25

Same Overprint on Nos. 86, 88, 90

No.	Type	Stamp	Unused	Used
138	A7	15r brown	2.00	1.75
139	A7	50r blue	2.25	2.00
140	A7	50r on 65r dull bl	16.00	12.00
		Nos. 138-140 (3)	20.25	15.75

No. 123-125, 130-131 and 137 were issued without gum.

Stamps of 1898-1905 Overprinted in Black REPUBLICA

On Stamps of 1898-1903

No.	Type	Stamp	Unused	Used
141	A7	2½r gray	.60	.50
a.		Inverted overprint	9.00	
b.		Double overprint	11.00	11.00
c.		Double overprint inverted		
142	A7	5r orange	27.50	22.50
143	A7	15r gray green	1.75	1.50
a.		Inverted overprint		
144	A7	20r gray violet	140.00	75.00
a.		Inverted overprint		
145	A7	25r carmine	37.50	27.50
a.		Inverted overprint		
146	A7	75r red lilac	2.75	2.25
a.		Inverted overprint		
147	A7	100r blue, *bl*	2.25	1.75
148	A7	115r org brn, *pink*	10.00	8.00
a.		Inverted overprint		
149	A7	130r brown, *straw*	8.00	7.00
a.		Inverted overprint		
150	A7	200r red lil, *pnksh*	2.50	1.75
a.		Inverted overprint		
151	A7	400r dull bl, *straw*	10.00	8.00
152	A7	500r blk & red, *gray*	9.00	8.50
153	A7	700r violet, *yelsh*	9.00	8.50

On Provisional Issue of 1902

No.	Type	Stamp	Unused	Used
154	A1	115r on 50r green	200.00	150.00
155	A2	115r on 10r bl grn	2.50	2.25
156	A2	115r on 300r orange	175.00	125.00
157	A2	130r on 5r black	175.00	125.00
158	A2	400r on 50r blue	125.00	90.00
159	A6	115r on 25r green	2.00	1.75
160	A6	115r on 150r car, *rose*	2.50	2.25
a.		"REPUBLICA" inverted		
161	A6	115r on 200r bl, *bl*	2.50	2.25
162	A6	130r on 75r rose	2.25	2.00
a.		Inverted surcharge		
163	A6	130r on 100r brn, *yel*	400.00	450.00
164	A6	400r on 50r lt bl	3.50	3.00
a.		Perf. 13½	17.50	6.00
165	A6	400r on 80r yel grn	2.50	2.25
166	N3	400r on 2½r brn	2.00	1.75

Same Overprint on Nos. 86, 88, 90

No.	Type	Stamp	Unused	Used
167	A7	15r brown	1.50	1.25
a.		Inverted overprint		
168	A7	50r blue	1.50	1.25
a.		Inverted overprint		
169	A7	50r on 65r dull bl	2.25	1.50
		Nos. 167-169 (3)	5.25	4.00

Most of Nos. 141-169 were issued without gum.

Vasco da Gama Issue of Various Portuguese Colonies Surcharged as REPUBLICA S.TOMÉ E PRINCIPE ¼ C.

On Stamps of Macao

No.	Type	Stamp	Unused	Used
170	CD20	¼c on ½a bl grn	2.00	2.00
171	CD21	½c on 1a red	2.00	2.00
172	CD22	1c on 2a red vio	2.00	2.00
173	CD23	2½c on 4a yel grn	2.00	2.00
174	CD24	5c on 8a dk bl	2.00	2.00
175	CD25	7½c on 12a vio brn	2.75	2.75
176	CD26	10c on 16a bis brn	2.00	2.00
177	CD27	15c on 24a bister	2.00	2.00
		Nos. 170-177 (8)	16.75	16.75

On Stamps of Portuguese Africa

178 CD20 ¼c on 2½r bl grn 1.40 1.40
179 CD21 ½c on 5r red 1.40 1.40
180 CD22 1c on 10r red vio 1.40 1.40
181 CD23 2½c on 25r yel grn 1.40 1.40
182 CD24 5c on 50r dk bl 1.40 1.40
183 CD25 7½c on 75r vio brn 1.75 1.75
184 CD26 10c on 100r bis brn 1.40 1.40
185 CD27 15c on 150r bister 1.40 1.40
Nos. 178-185 (8) 11.55 11.55

On Stamps of Timor

186 CD20 ¼c on ½a bl grn 1.75 1.50
187 CD21 ½c on 1a red 1.75 1.50
188 CD22 1c on 2a red vio 1.75 1.50
a. Double surcharge
189 CD23 2½c on 4a yel grn 1.75 1.50
190 CD24 5c on 8a dk bl 1.75 2.00
191 CD25 7½c on 12a vio brn 2.25 2.00
192 CD26 10c on 16a bis brn 1.75 1.50
193 CD27 15c on 24a bister 1.75 1.50
Nos. 186-193 (8) 14.50 13.00
Nos. 170-193 (24) 42.80 41.30

Ceres — A9

1914-26 Typo. *Perf. 12x11½, 15x14*
Name and Value in Black

194 A9 ¼c olive brown .15 .15
195 A9 ½c black .15 .15
196 A9 1c blue green .65 .65
197 A9 1c yellow grn ('22) .15 .15
198 A9 1½c lilac brn .15 .15
199 A9 2c carmine .15 .15
200 A9 2c gray ('26) .20 .20
201 A9 2½c lt violet .15 .15
202 A9 3c orange ('22) .20 .20
203 A9 4c rose ('22) .20 .20
204 A9 4½c gray ('22) .20 .20
205 A9 5c deep blue .45 .35
206 A9 5c brt blue ('22) .20 .20
207 A9 6c lilac ('22) .20 .20
208 A9 7c ultra ('22) .20 .20
209 A9 7½c yellow brn .20 .20
210 A9 8c slate .20 .20
211 A9 10c orange brn .25 .25
212 A9 12c blue green ('22) .50 .45
213 A9 15c plum 2.00 1.65
214 A9 15c brown rose ('22) .25 .25
215 A9 20c yellow green 1.75 1.10
216 A9 24c ultra ('26) 3.50 3.00
217 A9 25c choc ('26) 3.50 3.00
218 A9 30c brown, *grn* 2.25 1.75
219 A9 30c gray grn ('22) .50 .40
220 A9 40c brown, *pink* 2.00 1.75
221 A9 40c turq bl ('22) .55 .50
222 A9 50c orange, *sal* 4.50 3.50
223 A9 50c lt violet ('26) .75 .60
224 A9 60c dk blue ('22) 1.25 .90
225 A9 60c rose ('26) 2.00 2.00
226 A9 80c brt rose ('22) 1.65 .50
227 A9 1e green, *blue* 4.00 3.50
228 A9 1e pale rose ('22) 3.00 1.40
229 A9 1e blue ('26) 3.00 1.90
230 A9 2e dk violet ('22) 2.75 1.65
231 A9 5e buff ('26) 20.00 12.50
232 A9 10e pink ('26) 30.00 20.00
233 A9 20e pale turq ('26) 55.00 50.00
Nos. 194-233 (40) 148.75 116.25

Perforation and paper variations command a premium for some of Nos. 194-233.

For surcharges see Nos. 250-253, 281-282.

Preceding Issues Overprinted in Carmine

1915

On Provisional Issue of 1902

234 A2 115r on 10r green 2.25 2.00
235 A2 115r on 300r org 2.25 1.75
236 A2 130r on 5r black 4.00 3.00
237 A2 130r on 200r gray lil 1.50 1.25
238 A6 115r on 25r green .60 .45
239 A6 115r on 150r car, *rose* .60 .45
240 A6 115r on 200r bl, *bl* .60 .45
241 A6 130r on 75r rose .60 .45
242 A6 130r on 100r brn, *yel* 1.40 1.40
243 A6 130r on 300r bl, *sal* 1.10 .90

Same Overprint on Nos. 88 and 90

244 A7 50r blue .90 .60
245 A7 50r on 65r dull bl .90 .60
Nos. 234-245 (12) 16.70 13.30

2½ C. REPUBLICA

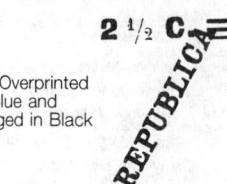

No. 86 Overprinted in Blue and Surcharged in Black

1919

246 A7 2½c on 15r brown .60 .55

No. 91 Surcharged in Black ½ C.

247 A7 ½c on 2½r gray 3.00 2.75
248 A7 1c on 2½r gray 2.25 2.00
249 A7 2½c on 2½r gray 1.10 .65

No. 194 Surcharged in Blue ½

250 A9 ½c on ¼c ol brn 2.00 1.75
251 A9 2c on ¼c ol brn 2.25 1.90
252 A9 2½c on ¼c ol brn 6.00 5.00

No. 201 Surcharged in Black $04 Centavos

253 A9 4c on 2½c lt vio .90 .75
Nos. 246-253 (8) 18.10 15.35

Nos. 246-253 were issued without gum.

Stamps of 1898-1905 Overprinted in Green or Red REPUBLICA

1920

On Stamps of 1898-1903

255 A7 75r red lilac (G) .55 .50
256 A7 100r blue, *blue* (R) .80 .75
257 A7 115r org brn, *pink* (G) 2.00 1.40
258 A7 130r brn, *straw* (G) 65.00 50.00
259 A7 200r red lil, *pnksh* (G) 2.00 1.00
260 A7 500r blk, & red, *gray* (G) 1.50 1.00
261 A7 700r vio, *yelsh* (G) 2.00 1.25

On Stamps of 1902

262 A6 115r on 25r grn (R) 1.00 .60
263 A6 115r on 200r bl, *bl* (R) 1.50 1.00
264 A6 130r on 75r rose (G) 2.00 1.50

On Nos. 88-89

265 A7 50r blue (R) 1.50 1.10
266 A7 75r rose (G) 7.50 7.00

On No. 90

267 A7 50r on 65r dl bl (R) 8.00 7.00
Nos. 255-257,259-267 (12) 30.35 24.10

Nos. 238-243 Surcharged in Blue or Red

CENTAVOS

1923 Without Gum

268 A6 10c on 115r on 25r (Bl) .70 .50
269 A6 10c on 115r on 150r (Bl) .70 .50
270 A6 10c on 115r on 200r (R) .70 .50
271 A6 10c on 130r on 75r (Bl) .70 .50
272 A6 10c on 130r on 100r (Bl) .70 .50
273 A6 10c on 130r on 300r (R) .70 .50
Nos. 268-273 (6) 4.20 3.00

Nos. 268-273 are usually stained and discolored.

República

Nos. 84-85 Surcharged

40 C.

1925

274 A6 40c on 400r on 80r yel grn .90 .45
275 N3 40c on 400r on 2½r brn .90 .45

Nos. 228 and 230 Surcharged

70 C.

1931

281 A9 70c on 1e pale rose 2.00 1.25
282 A9 1.40e on 2e dk vio 2.75 2.50

Ceres — A11

Perf. 12x11½
1934 Typo. Wmk. 232

283 A11 1c bister .20 .20
284 A11 5c olive brown .20 .20
285 A11 10c violet .20 .20
286 A11 15c black .25 .20
287 A11 20c gray .25 .20
288 A11 30c dk green .35 .30
289 A11 40c red orange .35 .30
290 A11 45c brt blue .55 .40
291 A11 50c brown .55 .30
292 A11 60c olive grn .70 .30
293 A11 70c brown org .70 .45
294 A11 80c emerald .40 .30
295 A11 85c deep rose 2.75 2.00
296 A11 1e maroon .75 .60
297 A11 1.40e dk blue 2.25 1.65
298 A11 2e dk violet 3.25 1.50
299 A11 5e apple green 7.50 4.25
300 A11 10e olive bister 17.50 10.00
301 A11 20e orange 60.00 30.00
Nos. 283-301 (19) 98.70 53.35

Common Design Types
Inscribed "S. Tomé"

1938 Unwmk. *Perf. 13½x13*
Name and Value in Black

302 CD34 1c gray green .15 .15
303 CD34 5c orange brown .20 .20
304 CD34 10c dk carmine .30 .30
305 CD34 15c dk violet brn .30 .30
306 CD34 20c slate .30 .30
307 CD35 30c rose violet .30 .30
308 CD35 35c brt green .55 .45
309 CD35 40c brown .55 .45
310 CD35 50c brt red vio .55 .45
311 CD36 60c gray black .90 .70
312 CD36 70c brown violet .90 .70
313 CD36 80c orange .90 .70
314 CD36 1e red 2.25 1.10
315 CD37 1.75e blue 1.75 1.00
316 CD37 2e brown car 11.00 6.50
317 CD37 5e olive green 11.00 6.50
318 CD38 10e blue violet 14.00 7.75
319 CD38 20e red brown 22.50 8.00
Nos. 302-319 (18) 68.40 35.85

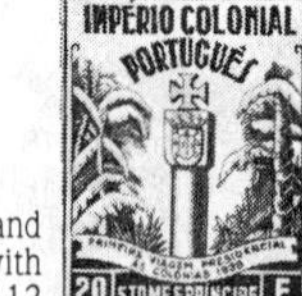

Marble Column and Portuguese Arms with Cross — A12

1938 *Perf. 12½*

320 A12 80c blue green 1.40 1.10
321 A12 1.75e deep blue 6.50 3.25
322 A12 20e brown 25.00 12.00
Nos. 320-322 (3) 32.90 16.35

Visit of the President of Portugal in 1938.

Common Design Types
Inscribed "S. Tomé e Principe"

1939 *Perf. 13½x13*
Name and Value in Black

323 CD34 1c gray grn .25 .15
324 CD34 5c orange brn .25 .15
325 CD34 10c dk carmine .25 .15
326 CD34 15c dk vio brn .25 .15
327 CD34 20c slate .25 .15
328 CD35 30c rose violet .25 .15
329 CD35 35c brt green .25 .15
330 CD35 40c brown .30 .15
331 CD35 50c brt red vio .30 .20
332 CD36 60c gray black .70 .60
333 CD36 70c brown violet .80 .70
334 CD36 80c orange .80 .70
335 CD36 1e red .75 .40
336 CD37 1.75e blue .95 .50
337 CD37 2e brown car 1.90 1.40
338 CD37 5e olive green 3.75 2.75
339 CD38 10e blue violet 8.50 3.50
340 CD38 20e red brown 11.00 5.75
Nos. 323-340 (18) 31.50 17.70

Cola Nuts — A13

UPU Symbols — A14

Designs: 10c, Breadfruit. 30c, Annona. 50c, Cacao pods. 1e, Coffee. 1.75e, Dendem. 2e, Avocado. 5e, Pineapple. 10e, Mango. 20e, Coconuts.

1948 Litho. *Perf. 14½*

341 A13 5c black & yellow .30 .30
342 A13 10c black & buff .40 .30
343 A13 30c indigo & gray 1.50 1.25
344 A13 50c brown & yellow 1.50 1.25
345 A13 1e red & rose 3.00 1.75
346 A13 1.75e blue & gray 4.00 3.25
347 A13 2e black & grn 3.00 1.50
348 A13 5e brown & lil rose 7.00 4.00
349 A13 10e black & pink 10.00 7.50
350 A13 20e black & gray 35.00 20.00
a. Sheet of 10, #341-350 90.00 90.00
Nos. 341-350 (10) 65.70 41.10

No. 350a sold for 42.50 escudos.

Lady of Fatima Issue

Common Design Type

1948, Dec. Unwmk.

351 CD40 50c purple 5.25 4.50

> Catalogue values for unused stamps in this section, from this point to the end of the section, are for Never Hinged items.

1949 Unwmk. *Perf. 14*

352 A14 3.50e black & gray 4.00 3.00

UPU, 75th anniv.

Holy Year Issue

Common Design Types

1950 *Perf. 13x13½*

353 CD41 2.50e blue 2.75 1.50
354 CD42 4e orange 4.50 3.50

Holy Year Extension Issue

Common Design Type

1951 *Perf. 14*

355 CD43 4e ind & bl gray 2.75 2.00

Medical Congress Issue

Common Design Type

1952 *Perf. 13½*

356 CD44 10c Clinic .30 .30

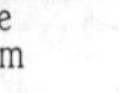

Joao de Santarem A15

Jeronymos Convent A16

Portraits: 30c, Pero Escobar. 50c, Fernao de Pole, Alvaro Esteves. 2e, Lopo Goncalves. 3.50e, Martim Fernandes.

1952 Unwmk. Litho. *Perf. 14*
Centers Multicolored

357 A15 10c cream & choc .15 .15
358 A15 30c pale grn & dk grn .15 .15
359 A15 50c gray & dk gray .15 .15
360 A15 1e gray bl & dk bl .60 .15
361 A15 2e lil gray & vio brn .45 .15
362 A15 3.50e buff & choc .60 .25
Nos. 357-362 (6) 2.10
Set value .65

For overprints and surcharges see Nos. 423, 425, 428-429, 432, 450-457, 474-481.

1953 *Perf. 13x13½*

363 A16 10c dk brown & gray .15 .15
364 A16 50c brn org & org .50 .40
365 A16 3e blue blk & gray blk 2.00 .80
Nos. 363-365 (3) 2.65 1.35

Exhib. of Sacred Missionary Art, Lisbon, 1951.

Stamp Centenary Issue

Stamp of Portugal and Arms of Colonies — A17

1953 **Photo.** ***Perf. 13***
366 A17 50c multicolored .75 .60

Centenary of Portugal's first postage stamps.

Presidential Visit Issue

Map and Plane — A18

1954 **Typo. & Litho.** ***Perf. 13½***
367 A18 15c blk, bl, red & grn .20 .15
368 A18 5e brown, green & red 1.10 .80

Visit of Pres. Francisco H. C. Lopes.

Sao Paulo Issue
Common Design Type

1954 **Litho.**
369 CD46 2.50e bl, gray bl & blk .55 .35

Fair Emblem, Globe and Arms — A19

1958 **Unwmk.** ***Perf. 12x11½***
370 A19 2.50e multicolored .60 .50

World's Fair at Brussels.

Tropical Medicine Congress Issue
Common Design Type

Design: Cassia occidentalis.

1958 ***Perf. 13½***
371 CD47 5e pale grn, brn, yel, grn & red 2.00 1.75

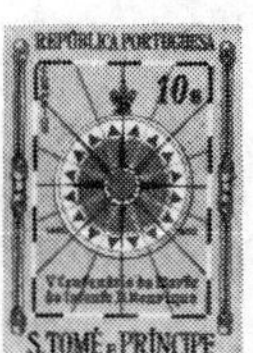
Compass Rose — A20

Going to Church — A21

1960 **Litho.** ***Perf. 13½***
372 A20 10e gray & multi 1.00 .40

500th death anniv. of Prince Henry the Navigator.

1960 ***Perf. 14½***
373 A21 1.50e multicolored .40 .30

10th anniv. of the Commission for Technical Co-operation in Africa South of the Sahara (C.C.T.A.).

Sports Issue
Common Design Type

Sports: 50c, Angling. 1e, Gymnast on rings. 1.50e, Handball. 2e, Sailing. 2.50e, Sprinting. 20e, Skin diving.

1962, Jan. 18 **Litho.** ***Perf. 13½***
Multicolored Design

374 CD48 50c gray green .15 .15
a. "$50 CORREIOS" omitted
375 CD48 1e lt lilac .60 .22
376 CD48 1.50e salmon .60 .22
377 CD48 2e blue .75 .35
378 CD48 2.50e gray green .95 .50
379 CD48 20e dark blue 2.25 1.65
Nos. 374-379 (6) 5.30 3.09

On No. 374a, the blue impression, including imprint, is missing.
For overprint see No. 449.

Anti-Malaria Issue
Common Design Type

Design: Anopheles gambiae.

1962 **Unwmk.** ***Perf. 13½***
380 CD49 2.50e multicolored 1.15 .80

Airline Anniversary Issue
Common Design Type

1963 **Unwmk.** ***Perf. 14½***
381 CD50 1.50e pale blue & multi .60 .50

National Overseas Bank Issue
Common Design Type

Design: Francisco de Oliveira Chamico.

1964, May 16 ***Perf. 13½***
382 CD51 2.50e multicolored .70 .50

ITU Issue
Common Design Type

1965, May 17 **Litho.** ***Perf. 14½***
383 CD52 2.50e tan & multi 1.50 1.00

Infantry Officer, 1788 — A22

35c, Sergeant with lance, 1788. 40c, Corporal with pike, 1788. 1e, Private with musket, 1788. 2.50e, Artillery officer, 1806. 5e, Private, 1811. 7.50e, Private, 1833. 10e, Lancer officer, 1834.

1965, Aug. 24 **Litho.** ***Perf. 13½***
384 A22 20c multicolored .16 .15
385 A22 35c multicolored .16 .15
386 A22 40c multicolored .22 .16
387 A22 1e multicolored 1.10 .50
388 A22 2.50e multicolored 1.10 .50
389 A22 5e multicolored 1.65 1.25
390 A22 7.50e multicolored 2.00 1.90
391 A22 10e multicolored 2.50 2.00
Nos. 384-391 (8) 8.89 6.61

For overprints and surcharges see Nos. 424, 426-427, 435, 458-463, 482-485, 489-490.

National Revolution Issue
Common Design Type

Design: 4e, Arts and Crafts School and Anti-Tuberculosis Dispensary.

1966, May 28 **Litho.** ***Perf. 11½***
392 CD53 4e multicolored .75 .50

Navy Club Issue
Common Design Type

Designs: 1.50e, Capt. Campos Rodrigues and ironclad corvette Vasco da Gama. 2.50e, Dr. Aires Kopke, microscope and tsetse fly.

1967, Jan. 31 **Litho.** ***Perf. 13***
393 CD54 1.50e multicolored .90 .50
394 CD54 2.50e multicolored 1.40 .75

Valinhos Shrine, Children and Apparition A23

Cabral Medal, from St. Jerome's Convent A24

1967, May 13 **Litho.** ***Perf. 12½x13***
395 A23 2.50e multicolored .30 .25

50th anniv. of the apparition of the Virgin Mary to 3 shepherd children, Lucia dos Santos, Francisco and Jacinta Marto, at Fatima.

1968, Apr. 22 **Litho.** ***Perf. 14***
396 A24 1.50e blue & multi .45 .30

500th birth anniv. of Pedro Alvares Cabral, navigator who took possession of Brazil for Portugal.

Admiral Coutinho Issue
Common Design Type

Design: 2e, Adm. Coutinho, Cago Coutinho Island and monument, vert.

1969, Feb. 17 **Litho.** ***Perf. 14***
397 CD55 2e multicolored .50 .35

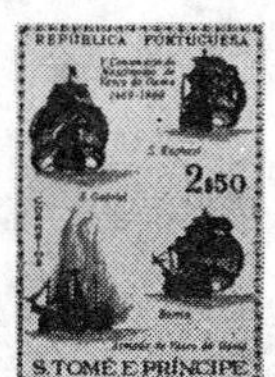
Vasco da Gama's Fleet — A25

Manuel Portal of Guarda Episcopal See — A26

1969, Aug. 29 **Litho.** ***Perf. 14***
398 A25 2.50e multicolored .75 .50

Vasco da Gama (1469-1524), navigator.

Administration Reform Issue
Common Design Type

1969, Sept. 25 **Litho.** ***Perf. 14***
399 CD56 2.50e multicolored .50 .35

For overprint see No. 430.

1969, Dec. 1 **Litho.** ***Perf. 14***
400 A26 4e multicolored .50 .35

500th birth anniv. of King Manuel I.

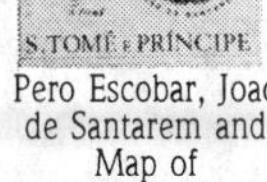
Pero Escobar, Joao de Santarem and Map of Islands — A27

Pres. Américo Rodrigues Thomaz — A28

1970, Jan. 25 **Litho.** ***Perf. 14***
401 A27 2.50e lt blue & multi .35 .30

500th anniv. of the discovery of St. Thomas and Prince Islands.

1970 **Litho.** ***Perf. 12½***
402 A28 2.50e multicolored .35 .30

Visit of Pres. Américo Rodrigues Thomaz of Portugal.

Marshal Carmona Issue
Common Design Type

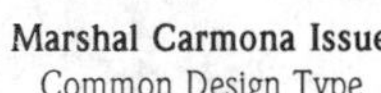

Antonio Oscar Carmona in dress uniform.

1970, Nov. 15 **Litho.** ***Perf. 14***
403 CD57 5e multicolored .75 .55

Coffee Plant and Stamps — A29

Descent from the Cross — A30

Designs: 1.50e, Postal Administration Building and stamp No. 1, horiz. 2.50e, Cathedral of St. Thomas and stamp No. 2.

1970, Dec. ***Perf. 13½***
404 A29 1e multicolored .25 .15
405 A29 1.50e multicolored .35 .15
406 A29 2.50e multicolored .60 .20
Nos. 404-406 (3) 1.20 .50

Centenary of St. Thomas and Prince Islands postage stamps.

1972, May 25 **Litho.** ***Perf. 13***
407 A30 20e lilac & multi 2.50 1.90

4th centenary of publication of The Lusiads by Luiz Camoens.

Olympic Games Issue
Common Design Type

Track and javelin, Olympic emblem.

1972, June 20 ***Perf. 14x13½***
408 CD59 1.50e multicolored .35 .25

Lisbon-Rio de Janeiro Flight Issue
Common Design Type

Design: 2.50e, "Lusitania" flying over warship at St. Peter Rocks.

1972, Sept. 20 **Litho.** ***Perf. 13½***
409 CD60 2.50e multicolored .35 .25

WMO Centenary Issue
Common Design Type

1973, Dec. 15 **Litho.** ***Perf. 13***
410 CD61 5e dull grn & multi .60 .50

For overprint see No. 434.

Republic

Flags of Portugal and St. Thomas & Prince A31

1975, July 12 **Litho.** ***Perf. 13½***
411 A31 3e gray & multi .40 .40
412 A31 10e yellow & multi 1.00 .30
413 A31 20e lt blue & multi 2.00 .50
414 A31 50e salmon & multi 3.50 2.25
Nos. 411-414 (4) 6.90 3.45

Argel Agreement, granting independence, Argel, Sept. 26, 1974.
For overprints see Nos. 675-678.

Man and Woman with St. Thomas & Prince Flag — A32

1975, Dec. 21
415 A32 1.50e pink & multi .15 .15
416 A32 4e multicolored .40 .20
417 A32 7.50e org & multi .75 .40

418 A32 20e blue & multi 1.75 1.00
419 A32 50e ocher & multi 4.00 2.00
Nos. 415-419 (5) 7.05 3.75

Proclamation of Independence, Dec. 7, 1975.

Chart and Hand — A33

1975, Dec. 21 Litho. ***Perf. 13½***

420 A33 1e ocher & multi .15 .15
421 A33 1.50e multicolored .20 .15
422 A33 2.50e orange & multi .30 .15
Nos. 420-422 (3) .65
Set value .36

National Reconstruction Fund.

****

Stamps of 1952-1973 Overprinted **Rep. Democr.**

12-7-75

1977 Litho. ***Perf. 13½, 14, 13***

423 A15 10c multi (#357)
424 A22 20c multi (#384)
425 A15 30c multi (#358)
426 A22 35c multi (#385)
427 A22 40c multi (#386)
428 A15 50c multi (#359)
429 A15 1e multi (#360)
430 CD56 2.50e multi (#399)
431 A27 2.50e multi (#401)
432 A15 3.50e multi (#362)
433 A26 4e multi (#400)
434 CD61 5e multi (#410)
435 A22 7.50e multi (#390)
436 A20 10e multi (#372)
Nos. 423-436 (14) *15.00*

The 10c, 30c, 50c, 1e, 3.50e, 10e issued with glassine interleaving stuck to back.

Pres. Manuel Pinto da Costa and Flag — A34

Designs: 3.50e, 4.50e, Portuguese Governor handing over power. 12.50e, like 2e.

1977, Jan. ***Perf. 13½***

437 A34 2e yellow & multi .20 .15
438 A34 3.50e blue & multi .25 .15
439 A34 4.50e red & multi .35 .15
440 A34 12.50e multicolored .90 .35
Nos. 437-440 (4) 1.70 .80

1st anniversary of independence.

Some of the unvalued sets that follow may not have been issued by the government.

Peter Paul Rubens (1577-1640), Painter — A35

Details from or entire paintings: 1e (60x44mm), Diana and Calixto, horiz. 5e (60x36mm), The Judgement of Paris, horiz. 10e (60x28mm), Diana and her Nymphs Surprised by Fauns, horiz. 15e (40x64mm), Andromeda and Perseus. 20e (40x64mm), The Banquet of Tereo. 50e (32x64mm) Fortuna.

No. 447a, 20e, (30x40mm) like #445. No. 447b, 75e, (40x30mm) The Banquet of Tereo, diff.

1977, June 28 Litho. ***Perf. 13½***

441 A35 1e multicolored
442 A35 5e multicolored
443 A35 10e multicolored
444 A35 15e multicolored
445 A35 20e multicolored
446 A35 50e multicolored

Souvenir Sheet

Perf. 14

447 A35 Sheet of 2, #a.-b.

See type A40 for Rubens stamps without "$" in denomination.

Ludwig van Beethoven — A36

Designs: a, 20e, Miniature, 1802, by C. Hornemann. b, 30e, Life mask, 1812, by F. Klein. c, 50e, Portrait, 1818, by Ferdinand Schimon.

1977, June 28 ***Perf. 13½***

448 A36 Strip of 3, #a.-c.

For overprint see No. 617.

No. 379 Ovptd. "Rep. Democr. / 12-7-77"

1977, July 12

449 CD48 20e multicolored

Pairs of Nos. 358-359, 357, 362, 384-386 Overprinted Alternately in Black

20 $ 20 $

a

CENTENÁRIO
1874 — 1974
UPU
MEMBRO
1877 1977

b

1977, Oct. 19 Litho. ***Perf. 14, 13½***

450 A15(a) 3e on 30c multi
451 A15(b) 3e on 30c multi
452 A15(a) 5e on 50c multi
453 A15(b) 5e on 50c multi
454 A15(a) 10e on 10c multi
455 A15(b) 10e on 10c multi
456 A15(a) 15e on 3.50e multi
457 A15(b) 15e on 3.50e multi
458 A22(a) 20e on 20c multi
459 A22(b) 20c on 20c multi
460 A22(a) 35e on 35c multi
461 A22(b) 35e on 35c multi
462 A22(a) 40e on 40c multi
463 A22(b) 40e on 40c multi

Centenary of membership in UPU. Overprints "a" and "b" alternate in sheets. Nos. 450-457 issued with glassine interleaving stuck to back.

These overprints exist in red on Nos. 452-453, 458-463 and on 1e on 10c, 3.50e and 30e on 30c.

Mao Tse-tung (1893-1976), Chairman, People's Republic of China — A37

1977, Dec. Litho. ***Perf. 13½x14***

464 A37 50d multicolored 5.50
a. Souvenir sheet 7.50

For overprint see No. 597.

Lenin — A38

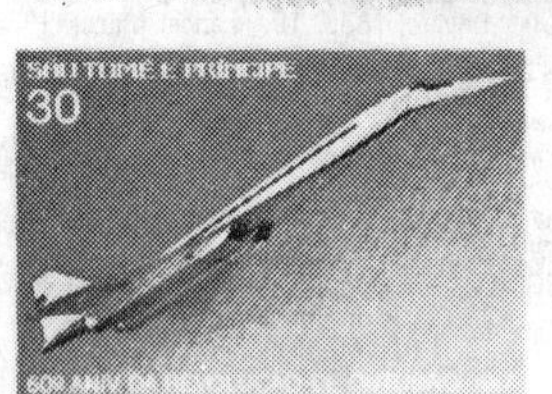

Russian Supersonic Plane — A39

Designs: 40d, Rowing crew. 50d, Cosmonaut Yuri A. Gagarin.

1977, Dec. ***Perf. 13½x14, 14x13½***

465 A38 15d multicolored .75
466 A39 30d multicolored 1.50
467 A39 40d multicolored 2.00
468 A38 50d red & black 2.50
a. Sheet of 4, #465-468
Nos. 465-468 (4) 6.75

60th anniv. of Russian October Revolution. For overprints see Nos. 592-595.

Paintings by Rubens — A40

Designs: 5d, 70d, Madonna and Standing Child. 10d, Holy Family. 25d, Holy Family, diff. 50d, Madonna and Child.

Perf. 13½, 13½x14 (50d)

1977, Dec.

Size: 31x47mm (50d)

469 A40 5d multicolored
470 A40 10d multicolored
471 A40 25d multicolored
472 A40 50d multicolored
473 A40 70d multicolored
a. Sheet of 4, #469-471, #473

Pairs of Nos. 357-359, 362, 384-385 Surcharged

3
PRÉMIO
NOBEL
DE PAZ
1954
a

3
UNHCR

#475

5
UNICEF

#477

10
OIT

#479

15
AMNESTY
INTER-
NATIONAL
#481

20
COMITE
INTERNAC.
DA CRUZ
VERMELHA
#483, 485

1978, May 25 ***Perf. 14½, 13½***

474 A15 (a) 3d on 30c #358
475 A15 3d on 30c #358
476 A15 (a) 5d on 50c #359
477 A15 5d on 50c #359
478 A15 (a) 10d on 10c #357
479 A15 10d on 10c #357
480 A15 (a) 15d on 3.50e #362
481 A15 15d on 3.50e #362
482 A22 (a) 20d on 20c #384
483 A22 20d on 20c #384
484 A22 (a) 35d on 35c #385
485 A22 35d on 35c #385

Overprints for each denomination alternate on sheet. Nos. 474-481 issued with glassine interleaving stuck to back.

Flag of St. Thomas and Prince Islands — A41

Designs: Nos. 487, 487a, Map of Islands, vert. No. 488, Coat of arms, vert.

Perf. 14x13½, 13½x14

1978, July 12

486 A41 5d multi .40
487 A41 5d multi .40
a. Souvenir sheet, 50d 4.25
488 A41 5d multi .40
a. Strip of 3, #486-488 1.25
Nos. 486-488 (3) 1.20

Third anniversary of independence. Printed in sheets of 9. No. 487a contains one imperf. stamp.

No. 386 Surcharged

40
3º
ANIV. DA
ENTRADA
NA ONU
1975/1978
#489

1975
1978
40

#490

1978, Sept. 3 Litho. ***Perf. 13½***

489 A22 40d on 40e #386
490 A22 40d on 40e #386

Membership in United Nations, 3rd anniv.

Miniature Sheets

Tahitian Women with Fan, by Paul Gauguin — A42

#491: b, Still Life, by Matisse. c, Barbaric Tales, by Gauguin. d, Portrait of Armand Roulin, by Van Gogh. e, Abstract, by Georges Braque.
#492: a, 20d, like #491c. b, 30d, Horsemen on the Beach, by Gauguin.

1978, Nov. 1 *Perf. 14*

491 A42 10d Sheet of 9, #e., 2 each #a.-d.

Imperf

492 A42 Sheet of 3, #491a, 492a-492b

Intl. Philatelic Exhibition, Essen.
No. 492 has simulated perfs and exists with green margin and without simulated perfs and stamps in different order.

Miniature Sheet

UPU, Centennial — A43

Designs: Nos. 493a, Emblem, yellow & black. b, Emblem, green & black. c, Emblem, blue & black. d, Emblem, red & black. e, Concorde, balloon. f, Sailing ship, satellite. g, Monorail, stagecoach. h, Dirigible, steam locomotive. 50d, like #487g.

1978, Nov. 1 *Perf. 14*

493 A43 Sheet of 12, #a.-d., 2 each, #e.-h.
a.-d. 5d any single
e.-h. 15d any single

Souvenir Sheet

494 A43 50d multicolored *15.00*

For overprint see No. 706.

Miniature Sheets

New Currency, 1st Anniv. A44

Obverse and reverse of bank notes: #a, 1000d. b, 50d. c, 500d. d, 100d. e, Obverse of 50c, 1d, 2d, 5d, 10d, 20d coins.

1978, Dec. 15 *Perf. 13½*

Sheet of 9

495 A44 5d #e., 2 each #a.-d.
496 A44 8d #e., 2 each #a.-d.

World Cup Soccer Championships, Argentina — A45

Various soccer plays: No. 497a, Two players in yellow shirts, one in blue. b, Two players in blue shirts, one in white. c, Six players, referee. d, Two players. No. 498a, Seven players. b, Two players at goal. c, Six players.

1978, Dec. 15 *Perf. 14*

497 A45 3d Block of 4, #a.-d.
498 A45 25d Strip of 3, #a.-c.

Souvenir sheets of one exist.

Overprinted with Names of Winning Countries

Campeão Mundial URUGUAY 1930/50

No. 499b, ITALIA, 1934/38. c, BRASIL, 1958/62/70. d, ALEMANIA 1954/74. No. 500a, INGLATERRA, 1966. b, Vencedores 1978 / 1o ARGENTINA / 2o HOLANDA / 3o BRASIL. c, ARGENTINA 1978.

1979, June 1 **Litho.** *Perf. 14*

499 A45 3d Block of 4, #a.-d.
500 A45 25d Strip of 3, #a.-c.
Nos. 499-500 *6.50*

Souvenir sheets of one exist.

Butterflies A46

Flowers — A47

Designs: 50c, Charaxes odysseus. 1d, Crinum giganteum. No. 503a, Quisqualis indicia. b, Tecoma stans. c, Nerium oleander. d, Pyrostegia venusta. 10d, Hypolimnas salmacis thomensis. No. 505a, Charaxes monteiri, male. b, Charaxes monteiri, female. c, Papillio leonidas thomasius. d, Crenis boisduvali insularis. 25d, Asystasia gangetica. No. 507, Charaxes varanes defulvata. Nos. 508, Hibiscus mutabilis.

Perf. 15, 15x14½ (#503), 14½x15 (#505)

1979, June 8

501 A46 50c multicolored
502 A47 1d multicolored
503 A47 8d Block of 4, #a.-d.
504 A46 10d multicolored
505 A46 11d Block of 4, #a.-d.
506 A47 25d multicolored
Nos. 501-506 (6) *12.00*

Souvenir Sheets

Perf. 15

507 A46 50d multicolored

Imperf

508 A47 50d multicolored *6.00*

No. 508 contains one 30x46mm stamp with simulated perforations.

Intl. Communications Day — A48

1979, July 6 *Perf. 13*

509 A48 1d shown
510 A48 11d CCIR emblem
a. Pair, #509-510 + label
511 A48 14d Syncom, 1963
512 A48 17d Symphony, 1975
a. Pair, #511-512 + label

Intl. Advisory Council on Radio Commmunications (CCIR), 50th anniv. (#510).

Intl. Year of the Child A49

Designs: 1d, Child's painting of bird. 7d, Young Pioneers. 14d, Children coloring on paper. 17d, Children eating fruit. 50d, Children from different countries joining hands.

1979, July 6

513 A49 1d multicolored
514 A49 7d multicolored
515 A49 14d multicolored
516 A49 17d multicolored

Size: 100x100mm

Imperf

517 A49 50d multicolored

Souvenir Sheets

Sir Rowland Hill, 1795-1879 — A50

1979, Sept. 15 *Perf. 15*

518 A50 25d DC-3 Dakota *15.00*

Perf. 14

519 A50 25d Graf Zeppelin, vert. *15.00*

1st Air Mail Flight, Lisbon to St. Thomas & Prince, 30th anniv. (#518), Brasiliana '79 Intl. Philatelic Exhibition and 18th UPU Congress (#519).
See Nos. 528-533 for other stamps inscribed "Historia da Aviancao."
For overprint see No. 700.

Albrecht Durer, 450th Death Anniv. — A51

Portraits: No. 520, Willibald Pirckheimer. No. 521, Portrait of a Negro. 1d, Portrait of a Young Man, facing right. 7d, Adolescent boy. 8d, The Negress Catherine. No. 525, Girl with Braided Hair. No. 526, Self-portrait as a Boy. No. 527, Feast of the Holy Family.

1979 *Perf. 14*

Background Color

520 A51 50c blue green
521 A51 50c orange
522 A51 1d blue
523 A51 7d brown
524 A51 8d red
525 A51 25d lilac

Souvenir Sheets

Perf. 13½

526 A51 25d lil, buff & blk

Perf. 13½x14

527 A51 25d blk, lil & buff

Christmas, Intl. Year of the Child (#527). No. 527 contains one 35x50mm stamp.
Issued: #520-526, Nov. 29; #527, Dec. 25.
For overprint see No. 591.

History of Aviation A52

1979, Dec. 21 *Perf. 15*

528 A52 50c Wright Flyer i
529 A52 1d Sikorsky VS 300
530 A52 5d Spirit of St. Louis
531 A52 7d Dornier DO X
532 A52 8d Santa Cruz Fairey III D
533 A52 17d Space Shuttle
Nos. 528-533 (6) *7.00*

See No. 518 for souvenir sheet inscribed "Historia da Aviancao."

History of Navigation A53

1979, Dec. 21

534 A53 50c Caravel, 1460
535 A53 1d Portuguese galleon, 1560
536 A53 3d Sao Gabriel, 1497
537 A53 5d Caravelao Navio Dos
538 A53 8d Caravel Redonda, 1512
539 A53 25d Galley Fusta, 1540
Nos. 534-539 (6) *7.00*

Size: 129x98mm

Imperf

540 A53 25d Map of St. Thomas & Prince, 1602 *5.00*

Birds — A54

1979, Dec. 21 *Perf. 14*

541 A54 50c Serinus rufobrunneus
542 A54 50c Euplectes aureus
543 A54 1d Alcedo leucogaster nais
544 A54 7d Dreptes thomensis
545 A54 8d Textor grandis
546 A54 100d Speirops lugubris
Nos. 541-546 (6) *8.50*

Souvenir Sheet

Perf. 14½

547 A54 25d Treron S. thomae *5.00*

No. 546 is airmail.

Fish A55

1979, Dec. 28 *Perf. 14*

548 A55 50c Cypselurus lineatus
549 A55 1d Canthidermis maculatus
550 A55 5d Diodon hystrix
551 A55 7d Ostracion tricornis
552 A55 8d Rhinecanthus aculeatus
553 A55 50d Chaetodon striatus
Nos. 548-553 (6) *8.50*

Souvenir Sheet

Perf. 14½

554 A55 25d Holocentrus axensionis *6.00*

No. 553 is airmail.

Balloons — A56

Designs: 50c, Blanchard, 1784. 1d, Lunardi II, 1785. 3d, Von Lutgendorf, 1786. 7d, John Wise "Atlantic," 1859. 8d, Salomon Anree "The Eagle," 1896. No. 560, Stratospheric balloon of Prof. Piccard, 1931. No. 560A, Indoor demonstration of hot air balloon, 1709, horiz.

1979, Dec. 28 *Perf. 15*

555 A56 50c multicolored
556 A56 1d multicolored
557 A56 3d multicolored
558 A56 7d multicolored
559 A56 8d multicolored
560 A56 25d multicolored
Nos. 555-560 (6) *7.50*

Souvenir Sheet

Perf. 14

560A A56 25d multicolored *6.00*

No. 560A contains one 50x38mm stamp.

Dirigibles A57

Designs: 50c, Dupuy de Lome, 1872. 1d, Paul Hanlein, 1872. 3d, Gaston brothers, 1882. 7d, Willows II, 1909. 8d, Ville de Lucerne, 1910. 17d, Mayfly, 1910.

1979, Dec. 28 *Perf. 15*

561 A57 50c multicolored
562 A57 1d multicolored
563 A57 3d multicolored
564 A57 7d multicolored
565 A57 8d multicolored
566 A57 17d multicolored
Nos. 561-566 (6) *7.50*

1980 Olympics, Lake Placid & Moscow A58

Olympic Venues: 50c, Lake Placid, 1980. Nos. 568, 572a, Mexico City, 1968. Nos. 569, 572b, Munich, 1972. Nos. 570, 572c, Montreal, 1976. Nos. 571, 572d, Moscow, 1980.

1980, June 13 **Litho.** *Perf. 15*

567 A58 50c multicolored
568 A58 11d multicolored
569 A58 11d multicolored
570 A58 11d multicolored
571 A58 11d multicolored
Nos. 567-571 (5) *5.00*

Souvenir Sheet

572 A58 7d Sheet of 4, #a.-d.

Proclamation Type of 1975 and

Sir Rowland Hill (1795-1879) A59

Sir Rowland Hill and: 50c, #1. 1d, #415. 8d, #411. No. 571, #449. No. 572, #418.

1980, June 1 *Perf. 15*

573 A59 50c multicolored
574 A59 1d multicolored
575 A59 8d multicolored
576 A59 20d multicolored
Nos. 573-576 (4) *5.00*

Souvenir Sheet

Imperf

577 A32 20d multicolored

No. 577 contains one 38x32mm stamp with simulated perforations.

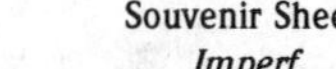

Moon Landing, 10th Anniv. (in 1979) A60

50c, Launch of Apollo 11, vert. 1d, Astronaut on lunar module ladder, vert. 14d, Setting up research experiments. 17d, Astronauts, experiment. 25d, Command module during re-entry.

1980, June 13 *Perf. 15*

578 A60 50c multicolored
579 A60 1d multicolored
580 A60 14d multicolored
581 A60 17d multicolored
Nos. 578-581 (4) *10.00*

Souvenir Sheet

582 A60 25d multicolored *7.50*

Miniature Sheet

Independence, 5th Anniv. — A61

#583: a, US #1283B. b, Venezuela #C942. c, Russia #3710. d, India #676. e, T. E. Lawrence (1888-1935). f, Ghana #106. g, Russia #2486. h, Algeria #624. i, Cuba #1318. j, Cape Verde #366. k, Mozambique #617. l, Angola #601. 25d, King Amador.

1980, July 12 *Perf. 13*

583 A61 5d Sheet of 12, #a.-l. + 13 labels

Souvenir Sheet

Perf. 14

584 A61 25d multicolored

No. 584 contains one 35x50mm stamp. For overprint see No. 596.

No. 527 Ovptd. "1980" on Stamp and Intl. Year of the Child emblem in Sheet Margin

1980, Dec. 25 *Perf. 14*

591 A51 25d on No. 527

Christmas.

Nos. 465-468a Overprinted in Black or Silver

1981, Feb. 2 *Perf. 13½x14, 14x13½*

592 A38 15d on #465 (S)
593 A39 30d on #466 (S)
594 A39 40d on #467
595 A38 50d on #468
a. on No. 468a *20.00*
Nos. 592-595 (4) *13.50*

No. 584 Ovptd. with UN and Intl. Year of the Child emblems and Three Inscriptions

1981, Feb. 2 *Perf. 14*

596 A61 25d on No. 584

Nos. 464-464a Ovptd. in Silver and Black "UNIAO / SOVIETICA / VENCEDORA / 1980" with Olympic emblem and "JOGOS OLIMPICOS DE MOSCOVO 1980"

1981, May 15 *Perf. 13½x14*

597 A37 50d on #464
a. on #464a

Mammals — A65

1981, May 22 *Perf. 14*

598 A65 50c Crocidura thomensis
599 A65 50c Mustela nivalis
600 A65 1d Viverra civetta
601 A65 7d Hipposioleros fuliginosus
602 A65 8d Rattus norvegicus
603 A65 14d Eidolon helvum
Nos. 598-603 (6) *7.50*

Souvenir Sheet

Perf. 14½

604 A65 25d Cercopithecus mona

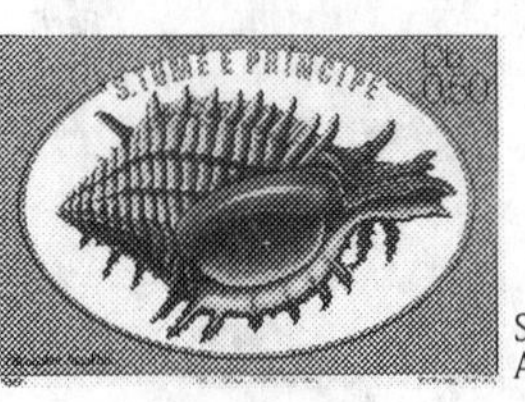

Shells A66

No. 611: a, 10d, Bolinus cornutus, diff. b, 15d, Conus genuanus.

1981, May 22 *Perf. 14*

605 A66 50c Haxaplex hoplites
606 A66 50c Bolinus cornutus
607 A66 1d Cassis tessellata
608 A66 1.50d Harpa doris
609 A66 11d Strombus latus
610 A66 17d Cymbium glans
Nos. 605-610 (6) *7.50*

Souvenir Sheet

Perf. 14½

611 A66 Sheet of 2, #a.-b.

Johann Wolfgang von Goethe (1749-1832), Poet — A67

Design: 75d, Goethe in the Roman Campagna, by Johann Heinrich W. Tischbein.

1981, Nov. 14 *Perf. 14*

612 A67 25d multicolored

Souvenir Sheet

613 A67 75d multicolored

PHILATELIA '81, Frankfurt/Main, Germany.

Tito — A68

1981, Nov. 14 *Perf. 12½x13*

614 A68 17d Wearing glasses
615 A68 17d shown
a. Sheet of 2, #614-615

Souvenir Sheet

Perf. 14x13½

616 A68 75d In uniform

Nos. 614-615 issued in sheets of 4 each plus label. For overprints see Nos. 644-646.

No. 448 Ovptd. in White

1981, Nov. 28 *Perf. 13½*

617 A36 Strip of 3, #a.-c.

Wedding of Prince Charles and Lady Diana.

On No. 617 the white overprint was applied by a thermographic process producing a shiny, raised effect.

Overprint exists in gold.

World Chess Championships A69

Chess pieces: No. 618, Egyptian. No. 619, Two Chinese, green. No. 620, Two Chinese, red. No. 621, English. No. 622, Indian. No. 623, Scandinavian. 75d, Khmer.

No. 624: a, Anatoly Karpov. b, Victor Korchnoi.

1981, Nov. 28 **Litho.** *Perf. 14*

618 A69 1.50d multicolored
619 A69 1.50d multicolored
620 A69 1.50d multicolored
621 A69 1.50d multicolored
622 A69 30d multicolored
623 A69 30d multicolored
624 A69 30d Pair, #a.-b.
Nos. 618-624 (7) *7.00*

Souvenir Sheet

625 A69 75d multicolored *7.50*

Nos. 618-623 exist in souvenir sheets of one. No. 624 exists in souvenir sheet with simulated perfs. Nos. 618-625 exist imperf.

No. 624 Ovptd. in red "ANATOLIJ KARPOV / Campeao Mundial / de Xadrez 1981"

1981, Dec. 10 *Perf. 14*

627 A69 30d Pair, #a.-b. *4.00*

Exists in souvenir sheet with simulated perfs or imperf.

Pablo Picasso — A70

Paintings: 14d, The Old and the New Year.

No. 629: a, Young Woman. b, Child with Dove. c, Paul de Pierrot with Flowers. d, Francoise, Claude, and Paloma.

No. 630: a, Girl. b, Girl with Doll. 75d, Father, Mother and Child.

1981, Dec. 10 *Perf. 14x13½*

628 A70 14d multicolored
629 A70 17d Strip of 4, #a.-d.
630 A70 20d Pair, #a.-b.

Souvenir Sheet

Perf. 13½

631 A70 75d multicolored

Intl. Year of the Child. Christmas (#628, 631). No. 630 is airmail.

Nos. 628, 629a-629d, 630a-630b exist in souvenir sheets of one. No. 631 contains one 50x60mm stamp.

See Nos. 683-685.

Intl. Year of the Child — A71

Paintings: No. 632: a, Girl with Dog, by Thomas Gainsborough. b, Miss Bowles, by Sir Joshua Reynolds. c, Sympathy, by Riviere. d, Master Simpson, by Devis. e. Two Boys with Dogs, by Gainsborough.

No. 633: a, Girl feeding cat. b, Girl wearing cat mask. c, White cat. d, Cat wearing red bonnet. e, Girl teaching cat to read.

No. 634: a, Boy and Dog, by Picasso. b, Clipper, by Picasso.

No. 635: a, Two white cats. b, Himalayan cat.

1981, Dec. 30 ***Perf. 14***

632 A71 1.50d Strip of 5, #a.-e.
633 A71 1.50d Strip of 5, #a.-e.
634 A71 50d Pair, #a.-b.
635 A71 50d Pair, #a.-b. + label

Souvenir Sheets

Perf. 13½

636 A71 75d Girl with dog
637 A71 75d Girl with cat

Nos. 636-637 contain one 30x40mm stamp.

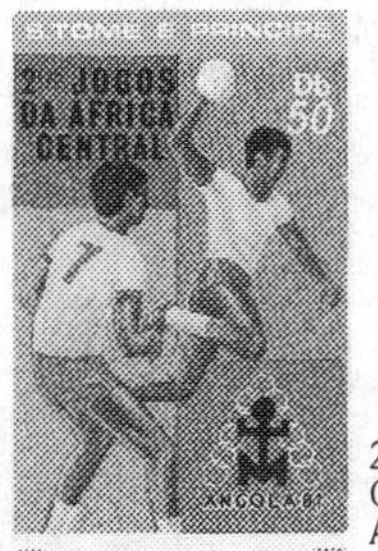

2nd Central Africa Games, Luanda, Angola — A73

No. 638: a, Shot put. b, Discus. c, High jump. d, Javelin.

50d, Team handball. 75d, Runner.

1981, Dec. 30 ***Perf. 13½x14***

638 A73 17d Strip of 4, a.-d.
639 A73 50d multicolored
Nos. 638-639 6.75

Souvenir Sheet

640 A73 75d multicolored

World Food Day — A74

No. 641: a, Ananas sativus. b, Colocasia esculenta. c, Artocarbus altilis.

No. 642: a, Mangifera indica. b, Theobroma cacao. c, Coffea arabica. 75d, Musa sapientum.

1981, Dec. 30

641 A74 11d Strip of 3, #a.-c.
642 A74 30d Strip of 3, #a.-c.
Nos. 641-642 6.00

Souvenir Sheet

643 A74 75d multicolored 4.00

Nos. 614-616 Ovptd. in Black

1982, May 25 ***Perf. 12½x13***

644 A68 17d on #614
645 A68 17d on #615
a. On #615a

Souvenir Sheet

Perf. 14

646 A68 75d on #616

World Cup Soccer Championships, Spain — A75

Emblem and: No. 647: a, Goalie in blue shirt jumping to catch ball. b, Two players, yellow, red shirts. c, Two players, black shirts. d, Goalie in green shirtcatching ball.

No. 648: a, Player dribbling. b, Goalie facing opponent.

No. 649, Goalie catching ball from emblem in front of goal. No. 650, Like #649 with continuous design.

1982, June 21 ***Perf. 13½x14***

647 A75 15d Strip of 4, #a.-d.
648 A75 25d Pair, #a.-b.
Nos. 647-648 7.50

Souvenir Sheets

649 A75 75d multicolored
650 A75 75d multicolored
Nos. 649-650 7.50

Nos. 648a-648b are airmail. Nos. 647a-647d, 648a-648b exist in souvenir sheets of one.

A76

A77

Transportation: No. 651, Steam locomotive, TGV train. No. 652, Propeller plane and Concorde.

1982, June 21 ***Perf. 12½x13***

651 A76 15d multicolored
652 A76 15d multicolored
a. Souv. sheet of 2, #651-652

PHILEXFRANCE '82.

1982, July 31

653 A77 25d multicolored

Robert Koch, discovery of tuberculosis bacillus, cent.

Goethe, 150th Anniv. of Death A78

1982, July 31 ***Perf. 13x12½***

654 A78 50d multicolored

Souvenir Sheet

655 A78 10d like #654

A79

A80

1982, July 31 ***Perf. 12½x13***

656 A79 75d multicolored

Souvenir Sheet

657 A79 10d Sheet of 1
657A A79 10d Sheet of 2, purple & multi

Princess Diana, 21st birthday. No. 657A exists with red violet inscriptions and different central flower.

1982, July 31

Boy Scouts, 75th Anniv.: 15d, Cape of Good Hope #178-179. 30d, Lord Baden-Powell, founder of Boy Scouts.

658 A80 15d multicolored
659 A80 30d multicolored
a. Souv. sheet of 2, #658-659 + label

Nos. 658-659 exits in sheets of 4 each plus label.

A81

A82

Caricatures by Picasso: No. 660a, Musicians. b, Stravinsky.

1982, July 31

660 A81 30d Pair, #a.-b.

Souvenir Sheet

661 A81 5d like #660b

Igor Stravinsky (1882-1971), composer.

1982, July 31

George Washington, 250th Anniv. of Birth: Nos. 662, 663b, Washington, by Gilbert Stuart. Nos. 663, 663c, Washington, by Roy Lichtenstein.

662 A82 30d multicolored
663 A82 30d blk & pink

Souvenir Sheet

663A A82 5d Sheet of 2, #b.-c.

Dinosaurs — A83

1982, Nov. 30 ***Perf. 14x13½***

664 A83 6d Parasaurolophus
665 A83 16d Stegosaurus
666 A83 16d Triceratops
667 A83 16d Brontosaurus
668 A83 16d Tyrannosaurus rex
669 A83 50d Dimetrodon
Nos. 664-669 (6) 7.50

Souvenir Sheet

a, 25d, Pteranodon. b, 50d, Stenopterygius.

670 A83 Sheet of 2, #a.-b. 4.00

Charles Darwin, cent. of death (#670).

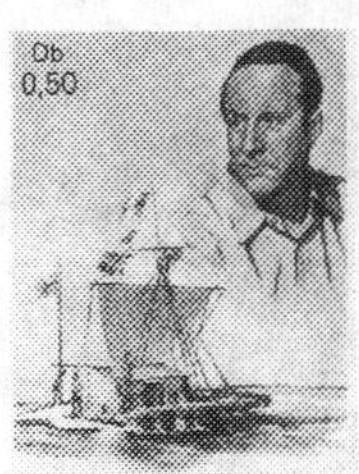

Explorers — A84

Departure of Marco Polo from Venice — A85

Explorers and their ships: 50c, Thor Heyerdahl, Kon-tiki.

No. 672: a, Magellan, Carrack. b, Drake, Golden Hind. c, Columbus, Santa Maria. d, Leif Eriksson, Viking longship.

50d, Capt. Cook, Endeavour.

1982, Dec. 21 **Litho.**

671 A84 50c multicolored
672 A84 18d Strip of 4, #a.-d.
673 A84 50d multicolored
Nos. 671-673 (3) 7.50

Souvenir Sheet

674 A85 75d multicolored 4.00

Nos. 411-414 Ovptd. with Assembly Emblem and "2o ANIVERSARIO DA 1a ASSEMBLEIA DA J.M.L.S.T.P." in Silver

1982, Dec. 24 ***Perf. 13½x14***

675 A31 3d on #411
676 A31 10d on #412
677 A31 20d on #413
678 A31 50d on #414

MLSTP 3rd Assembly — A86

1982, Dec. 24 ***Perf. 13½x14***

679 A86 8d bl & multi
680 A86 12d grn & multi
681 A86 16d brn org & multi
682 A86 30d red lilac & multi

Picasso Painting Type of 1981

Designs: No. 683a, Lola. b, Aunt Pepa. c, Mother. d, Lola with Mantilla.

No. 684a, Corina Romeu. b, The Aperitif. 75d, Holy Family in Egypt, horiz.

1982, Dec. 24

683 A70 18d Strip of 4, #a.-d.
684 A70 25d Pair, #a.-b.
Nos. 683-684 7.00

Souvenir Sheet

Perf. 14x13½

685 A70 75d multicolored

Intl. Women's Year (#683-684), Christmas (#685).

Locomotives — A87

9d, Class 231K, France, 1941.
No. 687: a, 1st steam locomotive, Great Britain, 1825. b, Class 59, Africa, 1947. c, William Mason, US, 1850. d, Mallard, Great Britain, 1938.
50d, Henschel, Portugal, 1929. 75d, Locomotive barn, Swindon, Great Britain.

1982, Dec. 31 *Perf. 14x13½*
686 A87 9d multicolored
687 A87 16d Strip of 4, #a.-d.
688 A87 50d multicolored
Nos. 686-688 (3) 7.50

Souvenir Sheet

689 A87 75d multicolored 4.00

Easter — A88

Paintings: No. 690: a, St. Catherine, by Raphael. b, St. Margaret, by Raphael.
No. 691: a, Young Man with a Pointed Beard, by Rembrandt. b, Portrait of a Young Woman, by Rembrandt.
No. 692: a, Rondo (Dance of the Italian Peasants), by Rubens, horiz. b, The Garden of Love, by Rubens, horiz.
No. 693, Samson and Delilah, by Rubens. No. 694, Descent from the Cross, by Rubens.
No. 695: a, Elevation of the Cross, by Rembrandt. b, Descent from the Cross, by Rembrandt.
Nos. 696a, 697, The Crucifixion, by Raphael. Nos. 696b, 698, The Transfiguration, by Raphael.

1983, May 9 *Perf. 13½x14, 14x13½*
690 A88 16d Pair, #a.-b.
691 A88 16d Pair, #a.-b.
692 A88 16d Pair, #a.-b.
693 A88 18d multicolored
694 A88 18d multicolored
695 A88 18d Pair, #a.-b.
696 A88 18d Pair, #a.-b.

Souvenir Sheets

697 A88 18d vio & multi
698 A88 18d multicolored

Souvenir sheets containing Nos. 690a-690b, 691a-691b, 692a-692b, 693, 694, 695a-695b exist.

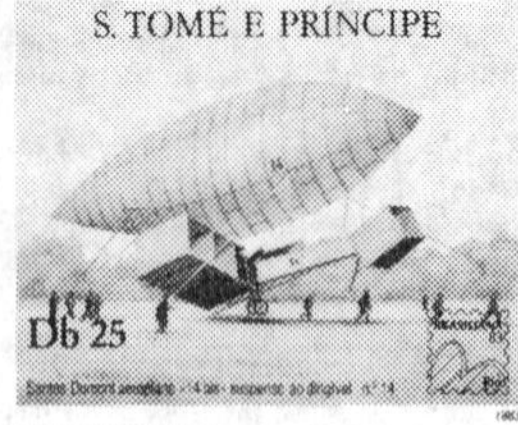

BRASILIANA '83, Rio de Janeiro — A89

Santos-Dumont dirigibles: No. 699a, #5. b, #14 with airplane.

1983, July 29 **Litho.** *Perf. 13½*
699 A89 25d Pair, #a.-b. 3.00

First manned flight, bicent.

No. 519 Overprinted with Various Designs

1983, July 29 **Litho.** *Perf. 14*

Souvenir Sheet

700 A50 25d multicolored
BRASILIANA '83.

First Manned Flight, Bicent. — A90

No. 701: a, Wright Flyer No. 1, 1903. b, Alcock & Brown Vickers Vimy, 1919.
No. 702: a, Bleriot monoplane, 1909. b, Boeing 747, 1983.
No. 703: a, Graf Zeppelin, 1929. b, Montgolfiere brother's balloon, 1783. No. 704, Pierre Testu-Brissy. 60d, Flight of Vincent Lunardi's second balloon, vert.

1983, Sept. 16 *Perf. 14x13½*
701 A90 18d Pair, #a.-b.
702 A90 18d Pair, #a.-b.
703 A90 20d Pair, #a.-b.
704 A90 20d multicolored
Nos. 701-704 (4) 7.50

Souvenir Sheet

Perf. 13½x14

705 A90 60d multicolored 4.00

Individual stamps from Nos. 701-704 exist in souvenir sheets of 1.

Nos. 493e, 493a, 493e (#706a) and 493g, 493c, 493g (#706b) Ovptd. in Gold with UPU and Philatelic Salon Emblems and:
"SALON DER PHILATELIE ZUM / XIX WELTPOSTKONGRESS / HAMBURG 1984" Across Strips of Three Stamps
Nos. 493f, 493b, 493f (#706c) 493h, 493d, 493h (#706d) Ovptd. in Gold with UPU and Philatelic Salon Emblems and:
"19TH CONGRESSO DA / UNIAO POSTAL UNIVERSAL / HAMBURGO 1984" Across Strips of Three Stamps

1983, Dec. 24 *Perf. 14*
706 A43 Sheet of 12, #a.-d.

Overprint is 91x30mm. Exists imperf with silver overprint.

Christmas — A91

Paintings: No. 707, Madonna of the Promenade, 1518, by Raphael. No. 708, Virgin of Guadalupe, 1959, by Salavador Dali.

1983, Dec. 24 *Perf. 12½x13*
707 A91 30d multicolored
708 A91 30d multicolored

Nos. 707-708 exist in souvenir sheets of 1.

Automobiles — A92

#709: a, Renault, 1912. b, Rover Phaeton, 1907.
#710: a, Morris, 1913. b, Delage, 1910.
#711: a, Mercedes Benz, 1927. b, Mercedes Coupe, 1936.
#712: a, Mercedes Cabriolet, 1924. b, Mercedes Simplex, 1902.
75d, Peugeot Daimler, 1894.

1983, Dec. 28 *Perf. 14x13½*
709 A92 12d Pair, #a.-b.
710 A92 12d Pair, #a.-b.
711 A92 20d Pair, #a.-b.
712 A92 20d Pair, #a.-b.
Nos. 709-712 (4) 9.00

Souvenir Sheet

713 A92 75d multicolored 5.00

Nos. 709-712 exist as souvenir sheets. No. 713 contains one 50x41mm stamp.

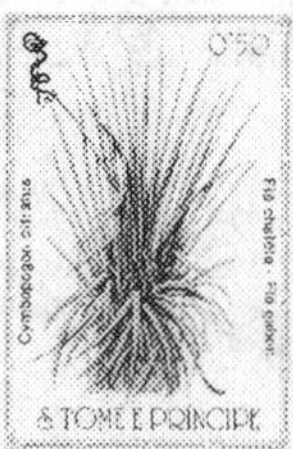

Medicinal Plants — A93

1983, Dec. 28 *Perf. 13½*
714 A93 50c Cymbopogon citratus
715 A93 1d Adenoplus breviflorus
716 A93 5.50d Bryophillum pinatum
717 A93 15.50d Buchholzia coriacea
718 A93 16d Hiliotropium indicum
719 A93 20d Mimosa pigra
720 A93 46d Piperonia pallucila
721 A93 50d Achyranthes aspera
Nos. 714-721 (8) 9.00

1984 Olympics, Sarajevo and Los Angeles — A94

#722, Pairs' figure skating.
#723: a, Downhill skiing. b, Speed skating. c, Ski jumping.
#724, Equestrian.
#725: a, Cycling. b, Rowing. c, Hurdling.
#726: a, Bobsled. b, Women's archery.

1983, Dec. 29 *Perf. 13½x14*
722 A94 16d multicolored
723 A94 16d Strip of 3, #a.-c.
724 A94 18d multicolored
725 A94 18d Strip of 3, #a.-c.
Nos. 722-725 (4) 7.50

Souvenir Sheet

726 A94 30d Sheet of 2, #a.-b. 4.00

Souvenir sheets of 2 exist containing Nos. 722 and 723b, 723a and 723c, 724 and 725b, 725a and 725c.

Birds — A95

1983, Dec. 30 *Perf. 13½*
727 A95 50c Spermestes cucullatus
728 A95 1d Xanthophilus princeps
729 A95 1.50d Thomasophantes sanctithomae
730 A95 2d Quelea erythrops
731 A95 3d Textor velatus peixotoi
732 A95 4d Anabathmis hartlaubii
733 A95 5.50d Serinus mozambicus santhome
734 A95 7d Estrilda astrild angolensis
735 A95 10d Horizorhinus dohrni

Size: 30x43mm

736 A95 11d Zosterops ficedulinus
737 A95 12d Prinia molleri
738 A95 14d Chrysococcyx cupreus insularum
739 A95 15.50d Halcyon malimhicus dryas
740 A95 16d Turdus olivaceofuscus
741 A95 17d Oriolus crassirostris
742 A95 18.50d Dicrurus modestus
743 A95 20d Columba thomensis
744 A95 25d Stigmatopelia senegalensis thome

Size: 31x47mm

Perf. 13½x14

745 A95 30d Chaetura thomensis
746 A95 42d Onychognatus fulgidus
747 A95 46d Lamprotornis ornatus
748 A95 100d Tyto alba thomenis
Nos. 727-748 (22) 25.00

Souvenir Sheet

ESPANA '84, Madrid — A96

Paintings: a, 15.50d, Paulo Riding Donkey, by Picasso. b, 16d, Abstract, by Miro. c, 18.50d, My Wife in the Nude, by Dali.

1984, Apr. 27 *Perf. 13½x14*
749 A96 Sheet of 3, #a.-c.

LUBRAPEX '84, Lisbon — A97

Children's drawings: 16d, Children watching play. 30d, Adults.

1984, May 9 *Perf. 13½*
750 A97 16d multicolored
751 A97 30d multicolored

Intl. Maritime Organization, 25th Anniv. — A98

Ships: Nos. 752a, 753a, Phoenix, 1869. 752b, 753b, Hamburg, 1893. 752c, 753c, Prince Heinrich, 1900.

No. 754: a, Leopold, 1840. b, Stadt Schaffhausen, 1851. c, Crown Prince, 1890. d, St. Gallen, 1905.

No. 755: a, Elise, 1816. b, De Zeeuw, 1824. c, Friedrich Wilhelm, 1827. d, Packet Hansa.

No. 756: a, Savannah, 1818. b, Chaperone, 1884. c, Alida, 1847. d, City of Worcester, 1881.

No. 757, Ferry, Lombard Bridge, Hamburg, c. 1900. No. 758, Train, coaches on bridge, c. 1880, vert. No. 759, Windmill, bridge, vert. No. 760, Queen of the West. No. 761, Bremen. No. 762, Union.

1984, June 19 Litho. *Perf. 14x13½*

752 A98 50c Strip of 3, #a.-c.
753 A98 50c Strip of 3, #a.-c.
754 A98 7d Piece of 4, #a.-d.
e. Souv. sheet of 2, #754a-754b
f. Souv. sheet of 2, #754c-754d
755 A98 8d Piece of 4, #a.-d.
e. Souv. sheet of 2, #755a-755b
f. Souv. sheet of 2, #755c-755d
756 A98 15.50d Piece of 4, #a.-d.
e. Souv. sheet of 2, #756a, 756d
f. Souv. sheet of 2, #756b-756c
Nos. 752-756 (5) *13.50*
Nos. 754e-754f, 755e-755f, 756e-756f (6) *55.00*

Souvenir Sheets

Perf. 14x13½, 13½x14

757 A98 10d multicolored
758 A98 10d multicolored
759 A98 10d multicolored

Perf. 13½

760 A98 15d multicolored
761 A98 15d multicolored
762 A98 15d multicolored
Nos. 757-762 (6) *45.00*

Nos. 757-759 exist imperf in different colors. Nos. 760-762 contain one 60x33mm stamp each. Nos. 753a-753c have UPU and Hamburg Philatelic Salon emblems and are additionally inscribed "PARTICIPACAO DE S. TOME E PRINCIPE / NO CONGRESSO DA U.P.U. EM HAMBURGO."

Sheets containing Nos. 754-756 contain one label.

Natl. Campaign Against Malaria A99

1984, Sept. 30 *Perf. 13½*

764 A99 8d Malaria victim
765 A99 16d Mosquito, DDT, vert.
766 A99 30d Exterminator, vert.

A100 A101

World Food Day: 8d, Emblem, animals, produce. 16d, Silhouette, animals. 46d, Plowed field, produce. 30d, Tractor, field, produce, horiz.

1984, Oct. 16

767 A100 8d multicolored
768 A100 16d multicolored
769 A100 46d multicolored

Souvenir Sheet

770 A100 30d multicolored

1984, Nov. 5

Mushrooms: 10d, Coprinus micaceus. 20d, Amanita rubescens. 30d, Armillariella mellea. 50d, Hygrophorus chrysodon, horiz.

771 A101 10d multicolored
772 A101 20d multicolored
773 A101 30d multicolored

Souvenir Sheet

774 A101 50d multicolored

Christmas — A102

Designs: 30d, Candles, offering, stable. 50d, Stable, Holy Family, Kings.

1984, Dec. 25

775 A102 30d multicolored

Souvenir Sheet

776 A102 50d multicolored

No. 776 contains one 60x40mm stamp.

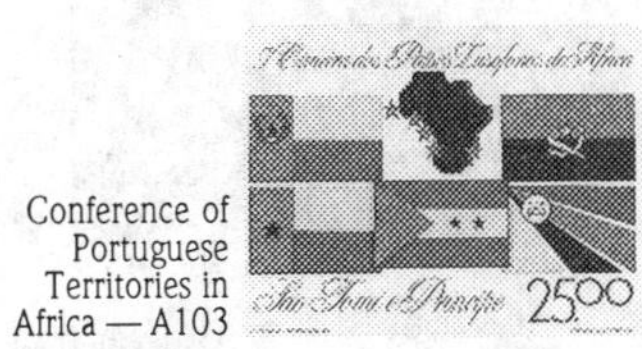

Conference of Portuguese Territories in Africa — A103

1985, Feb. 14

777 A103 25d multicolored

Reinstatement of Flights from Lisbon to St. Thomas, 1st Anniv. — A104

Designs: 25d, Douglas DC-3, map of northwest Africa. 30d, Air Portugal Douglas DC-8. 50d, Fokker Friendship.

1985, Dec. 6 Litho. *Perf. 13½*

778 A104 25d multicolored
779 A104 30d multicolored

Souvenir Sheet

779A A104 50d multicolored

Flowers A105 Mushrooms A106

1985, Dec. 30 *Perf. 11½x12*

780 A105 16d Flowering cactus
781 A105 20d Sunflower
782 A105 30d Porcelain rose

1986, Sept. 18 *Perf. 13½*

783 A106 6d Fistulina hepatica
784 A106 25d Collybia butyracea
785 A106 30d Entoloma clypeatum

Souvenir Sheet

786 A106 75d Cogumelos II

No. 786 exists with margins trimmed on four sides removing the control number.

Miniature Sheet

World Cup Soccer, Mexico A107

#787: a, Top of trophy. b, Bottom of trophy. c, Interior of stadium. d, Exterior of stadium.

1986, Oct. 1

787 A107 25d Sheet of 4, #a.-d.

For overprints see Nos. 818-818A.

Miniature Sheet

1988 Summer Olympics, Seoul A108

Seoul Olympic Games emblem, and: No. 788a, Map of North Korea. b, Torch. c, Olympic flag, map of South Korea. d, Text.

1986, Oct. 2

788 A108 25d Sheet of 4, #a.-d.

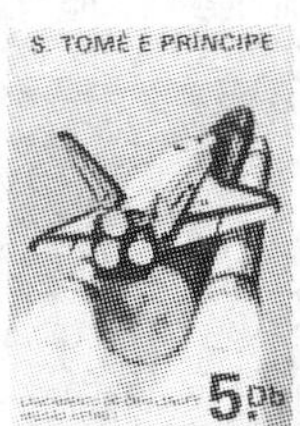

Halley's Comet — A109

Designs: No. 789a, 5d, Challenger space shuttle, 1st launch. b, 6d, Vega probe. c, 10d, Giotto probe. d, 16d, Comet over Nuremberg, A.D. 684.

90d, Comet, Giotto probe, horiz.

1986, Oct. 27

789 A109 Sheet of 4, #a.-d.+5 labels

Souvenir Sheet

790 A109 90d multicolored

Automobiles A110

Designs: No. 791a, 50c, Columbus Monument, Barcelona. b, 6d, Fire engine ladder truck, c. 1900. c, 16d, Fire engine, c. 1900. d, 30d, Fiat 18 BL Red Cross ambulance, c. 1916.

1986, Nov. 1

791 A110 Sheet of 4, #a.-d.+5 labels

Railway Stations and Signals A111

Designs: 50c, London Bridge Station, 1900. 6d, 100-300 meter warning signs. 20d, Signal lamp. 50d, St. Thomas & Prince Station.

1986, Nov. 2 *Perf. 13½*

792 A111 50c multicolored
793 A111 6d multicolored
794 A111 20d multicolored

Souvenir Sheet

795 A111 50d multicolored

LUBRAPEX '86, Brazil — A112

Exhibition emblem and: No. 796a, 1d, Line fisherman on shore. b, 1d, Line fisherman in boat. c, 2d, Net fisherman. d, 46d, Couple trap fishing, lobster.

1987, Jan. 15

796 A112 Sheet of 4, #a.-d.+2 labels

Intl. Peace Year — A113

Designs: 8d, Mahatma Gandhi. 10d, Martin Luther King, Jr. 16d, Red Cross, Intl. Peace Year, UN, UNESCO, Olympic emblems and Nobel Peace Prize medal. 20d, Albert Luthuli. 75d, Peace Dove, by Picasso.

1987, Jan. 15

797 A113 8d bl, blk & pur
798 A113 10d bl, blk & grn
799 A113 16d multicolored
800 A113 20d multicolored

Souvenir Sheet

801 A113 75d multicolored

Christmas 1986 — A114

Paintings by Albrecht Durer: No. 802a, 50c, Virgin and Child. b, 1d, Madonna of the Carnation. c, 16d, Virgin and Child, diff. d, 20d, The Nativity. 75d, Madonna of the Goldfinch.

1987, Jan. 15

802 A114 Strip of 4, #a.-d.

Souvenir Sheet

803 A114 75d multicolored

Fauna and Flora A115

Birds: a, 1d, Agapornis fischeri. b, 2d, Psittacula krameri. c, 10d, Psittacus erithacus. d, 20d, Agapornis personata psittacidae.

Flowers: e, 1d, Passiflora caerulea. f, 2d, Oncidium nubigenum. g, 10d, Heliconia wagneriana. h, 20d, Guzmania liguiata.

Butterflies: i, 1d, Aglais urticae. j, 2d, Pieris brassicae. k, 10d, Fabriciana niobe. l, 20d, Zerynthia polyxena.

Dogs: m, 1d, Sanshu. n, 2d, Hamiltonstovare. o, 10d, Gran spitz. p, 20d, Chow-chow.

1987, Oct. 15 *Perf. 14x13½*

804 A115 Sheet of 16, #a.-p.

Sports Institute, 10th Anniv. — A116

Designs: No. 805a, 50c, Three athletes. b, 20d, Map of St. Thomas and Prince, torchbearers. c, 30d, Volleyball, soccer, team handball and basketball players.
50d, Bjorn Borg.

1987, Oct. 30
805 A116 Strip of 3, #a.-c. 3.00

Souvenir Sheet
Perf. 13½x14

806 A116 50d Sheet of 1 + label 3.00

Miniature Sheet

Discovery of America, 500th Anniv. (in 1992) — A117

Emblem and: No. 807: a, 15d, Columbus with globe, map and arms. b, 20d, Battle between Spanish galleon and pirate ship. c, 20d, Columbus landing in New World. 100d, Model ship, horiz.

1987, Nov. 3 ***Perf. 13½x14***
807 A117 Sheet of 3, #a.-c. + 3 labels 3.50

Souvenir Sheet
Perf. 14x13½

808 A117 100d multicolored 5.50

Mushrooms — A118

Designs: No. 809a, 6d, Calocybe ionides. b, 25d, Hygrophorus coccineus. c, 30d, Boletus versipellis. 35d, Morchella vulgaris, vert.

1987, Nov. 10 ***Perf. 14x13½***
809 A118 Strip of 3, #a.-c.

Souvenir Sheet
Perf. 13½x14

810 A118 35d multicolored

Locomotives — A119

Designs: No. 811a, 5d, Jung, Germany. b, 10d, Mikado 2413. c, 20d, Baldwin, 1920. 50d, Pamplona Railroad Station, 1900.

1987, Dec. 1 Litho. ***Perf. 14x13½***
811 A119 Strip of 3, #a.-c. 3.00

Souvenir Sheet

812 A119 50d multicolored 3.50

Miniature Sheet

Christmas A120

Paintings of Virgin and Child by: No. 813a, 1d, Botticelli. b, 5d, Murillo. c, 15d, Raphael. d, 20d, Memling.
50d, Unkmown artist, horiz.

1987, Dec. 20 ***Perf. 13½x14***
813 A120 Sheet of 4, #a.-d. 2.50

Souvenir Sheet
Perf. 14x13½

814 A120 50d multicolored 3.50

World Boy Scout Jamboree, Australia, 1987-88 — A121

1987, Dec. 30 ***Perf. 14x13½***
815 A121 50c multicolored 3.00

Russian October Revolution, 70th Anniv. A122

1988 Litho. ***Perf. 12***
816 A122 25d Lenin addressing revolutionaries 1.20

Souvenir Sheet

Lubrapex '88 — A123

1988, May ***Perf. 14x13½***
817 A123 80d Trolley

Nos. 787a-787d Ovptd. "CAMPEONATO MUNDIAL / DE FUTEBOL MEXICO '86 / ALEMANHA / SUBCAMPIAO" in Silver (#818) or Same with "ARGENTINA / CAMPIAO" Instead in Gold (#818A) Across Four Stamps

1988, Aug. 15 ***Perf. 13½***
818 A107 25d Block of 4 (S)
818A A107 25d Block of 4 (G)

Medicinal Plants — A123a

Mushrooms A123b

Medicinal plants: No. 819a, 5d, Datura metel. b, 5d, Salaconta. c, 5d, Cassia occidentalis. d, 10d, Solanum ovigerum. e, 20d, Leonotis nepetifolia.
Mushrooms: No. 820a, 10d, Rhodopaxillus nudus. b, 10d, Volvaria volvacea. c, 10d, Psalliota bispora. d, 10d, Pleurotus ostreatus. e, 20d, Clitocybe geotropa.

1988, Oct. 26 ***Perf. 13½x14***
819 A123a Strip of 5, #a.-e. 4.50
820 A123b Strip of 5, #a.-e. 6.00

Souvenir Sheets

821 A123a 35d Hiersas durero 4.00
822 A123b 35d Mushroom on wood 4.00

Miniature Sheets

Passenger Trains — A123c

No. 823: a, Swiss Federal Class RE 6/6, left. b, Class RE 6/6, right.
No. 824: a, Japan Natl. Class EF 81, left. b, Class EF 81, right.
No. 825: a, German Electric E 18, 1930, left. b, E 18, 1930, right.
60d, Japan Natl. Class 381 Electric.

1988, Nov. 4 ***Perf. 14x13½***
823 A123c 10d Sheet of 4, 2 each #a.-b + 2 labels
824 A123c 10d Sheet of 4, 2 each #a.-b + 2 labels
825 A123c 10d Sheet of 4, 2 each #a.-b + 2 labels

Souvenir Sheet

826 A123c 60d multicolored

Butterflies A123d

Various flowers and: No. 827a, White and brown spotted butterfly. b, Dark brown and white butterfly, flower stigma pointing down. c, Brown and white butterfly, flower stigma pointing down.
50d, Brown, white and orange butterly.

1988, Nov. 25 ***Perf. 13½x14***
827 A123d 10d Strip of 3, #a.-c. 3.50

Souvenir Sheet

828 A123d 50d multicolored 5.50

Ferdinand von Zeppelin (1838-1917) — A123e

Berlin, 750th Anniv. — A123f

No. 829: a, Sailing ship, dirigible L23. b, Dirigibles flying over British merchant ships. c, Rendezvous of zeppelin with Russian ice breaker Malygin.
No. 830: a, Airship Le Jeune at mooring pad, Paris, 1903, vert. b, von Zeppelin, vert.

Perf. 14x13½, 13½x14
1988, Nov. 25
829 A123e 10d Strip of 3, #a.-c.
830 A123e 10d Pair, #a.-b.
Nos. 829-830 5.00

Souvenir Sheet

831 A123f 50d multicolored

Natl. Arms — A123g

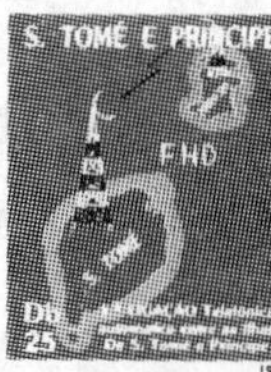

Automatic Telephone Exchange Linking the Islands, 1st Anniv. — A123h

1988, Dec. 15 ***Perf. 13½***
832 A123g 10d multicolored
833 A123h 25d multicolored

Olympics Games, Seoul, Barcelona and Albertville — A123i

World Cup Soccer Championships, Italy, 1990 — A123j

#834, View of Barcelona, Cobi. #835, Barcelona Games emblem. #836, Gold medal from 1988 Seoul games. #837, Emblems of 1988 & 1992 games. #838, Bear on skis, Albertville, 1992. #839, Soccer ball. #840, Italy '90 Championships emblem. #841, World Cup Trophy. #842, Transfer of Olympic flag during Seoul closing ceremony. #843, Olympic pins. #844, like #838. #845, Soccer balls as hemispheres of globe.

Perf. 14x13½, 13½x14
1988, Dec. 15
834 A123i 5d multi
835 A123i 5d multi, vert.
836 A123i 5d multi, vert.
837 A123i 5d multi
838 A123i 5d grn & multi
839 A123j 5d multi
840 A123j 5d multi, vert.
841 A123j 5d multi, vert.
Nos. 834-841 (8) 8.00

Souvenir Sheets
Perf. 14x13½

842 A123i 50d multi 7.50
843 A123i 50d multi 7.50
844 A123i 50d blue & multi
845 A123j 50d multi 7.50

No. 842 exists with Olympic emblems in gold or silver. No. 845 exists with marginal inscriptions in gold or silver. See Nos. 876-877 for souvenir sheets similar in design to No. 840.

Intl. Boy Scout Jamboree, Australia, 1987-88
A123k

#846: a, Campfire. b, Scout emblem, pitched tents, flag. c, Scout emblem, tent flaps, flag, axe. 110d, Trefoil center point, horiz.

1988, Dec. 15 *Perf. 13½x14*

846 A123k 10d Strip of 3, #a.-c. 5.00

Souvenir Sheet

Perf. 14x13½

847 A123k 110d multicolored 10.00

Intl. Red Cross, 125th Anniv. — A123m

No. 848: a, 50c, Patient in hospital. b, 5d, Transporting victims. c, 20d, Instructing workers. 50d, Early mail train, horiz.

1988, Dec. 15 *Perf. 13½x14*

848 A123m Strip of 3, #a.-c. 4.00

Souvenir Sheet

Perf. 14x13½

849 A123m 50d multicolored 7.50

No. 848c is airmail.

Miniature Sheet

Christmas — A123n

#850: a, 10d, Madonna and Child with St. Anthony Abbot and the Infant Baptism, by Titian. b, 10d, Madonna and Child with St. Catherine and a Rabbit, by Titian. c, 10d, Nativity Scene, by Rubens. d, 30d, Adoration of the Magi, by Rubens.
50d, The Annunciation (detail), by Titian, vert.

1988, Dec. 23 *Perf. 14x13½*

850 A123n Sheet of 4, #a.-d. 6.00

Souvenir Sheet

Perf. 13½x14

851 A123n 50d multicolored 5.00

Titian, 500th anniv. of birth. Country name does not appear on No. 850d.

French Revolution, Bicent. — A123o

Designs: No. 852, Eiffel Tower, Concorde, stylized doves, flag. No. 853 Eiffel Tower, flag, stylized doves. No. 854, Eiffel Tower, flag, stylized doves, TGV train, vert. 50d, TGV train.

Perf. 14x13½, 13½x14

1989, July 14 **Litho.**

852 A123o 10d multicolored
853 A123o 10d multicolored
854 A123o 10d multicolored
Nos. 852-854 (3) 3.00

Souvenir Sheet

855 A123o 50d multicolored 4.00

Fruit — A123p

1989, Sept. 15 *Perf. 13½x14*

856 A123p 50c Chapu-chapu
857 A123p 1d Guava
858 A123p 5d Mango
859 A123p 10d Carambola
860 A123p 25d Nona
861 A123p 50d Avacado
862 A123p 50d Cajamanga

Perf. 14x13½

863 A123p 60d Jackfruit
864 A123p 100d Cacao
865 A123p 250d Bananas
866 A123p 500d Papaya

Souvenir Sheet

Perf. 13½x14

867 A123p 1000d Pomegranate

Nos. 863-866 are horiz.

Orchids — A123q

Designs: No. 868, Dendrobium phalaenopsis. No. 869, Catteleya granulosa. 50d, Diothonea imbricata and maxillaria eburnea.

1989, Oct. 15 *Perf. 13½x14*

868 A123q 20d multicolored
869 A123q 20d multicolored
Nos. 868-869 3.00

Souvenir Sheet

870 A123q 50d multicolored 3.50

Hummingbirds — A124

Designs: No. 871, Topaza bella, sappho sparganura, vert. No. 872, Petasophores anais. No. 873, Lophornis adorabilis, chalcostigma herrani, vert. 50d, Oreotrochilus chimborazo.

Perf. 13½x14, 14x13½

1989, Oct. 15

871 A124 20d multicolored
872 A124 20d multicolored
873 A124 20d multicolored
Nos. 871-873 (3) 4.00

Souvenir Sheet

Perf. 14x13½

874 A124 50d multicolored 3.50

Miniature Sheet

1990 World Cup Soccer Championships, Italy — A125

Program covers: No. 875: a, 10d, Globe and soccer ball, 1962. b, 10d, Foot kicking ball, 1950. c, 10d, Abstract design, 1982. d, 20d, Player kicking ball, 1934.
No. 876: a, Character emblem, horiz. b, USA 94, horiz. 50d, like #876a, horiz.

1989, Oct. 24 *Perf. 13½x14*

875 A125 Block of 4, #a.-d.

Souvenir Sheets

Perf. 14x13½

876 A125 25d Sheet of 2, #a.-b.
877 A125 50d blue & multi

1992 Summer Olympics, Barcelona — A126

Perf. 13½x14, 14x13½

1989, Oct. 24

878 A126 5d Tennis, vert.
879 A126 5d Basketball, vert.
880 A126 5d Running
881 A126 35d Baseball, vert.
Nos. 878-881 (4) 4.00

Souvenir Sheet

Perf. 14x13½

882 A126 50d Sailing 8.00

Nos. 878-881 exist in souvenir sheets of one. No country name on souvenir sheet of one of No. 878.

Locomotives — A127

Perf. 14x13½, 13½x14

1989, Oct. 27

884 A127 20d Japan
885 A127 20d Philippines
886 A127 20d Spain, vert.
887 A127 20d India
888 A127 20d Asia
Nos. 884-888 (5) 7.50

Souvenir Sheets

889 A127 50d Garratt, Africa
890 A127 50d Trans-Gabon, vert.

Nos. 884-888 exist in souvenir sheets of one.

Ships
A128

#891, Merchant ships at sea, 16th cent. #892, Caravels, merchant ships in harbor, 16th cent. #893, 3 merchant ships at sea, 18th cent. #894, War ships, 18th cent. #895, 4 merchant ships, 18th cent. #896, Passenger liner, Port of Hamburg. #897, German sailing ship, 17th cent.

1989, Oct. 27 *Perf. 14x13½*

891 A128 20d multicolored
892 A128 20d multicolored
893 A128 20d multicolored
894 A128 20d multicolored
895 A128 20d multicolored
Nos. 891-895 (5) 7.00

Souvenir Sheets

896 A128 50d multicolored

Perf. 13½x14

897 A128 50d multi, vert. 4.00

Discovery of America, 500th anniv., in 1992 (#891-895) and Hamburg, 800th anniv. (#891-897).
Nos. 891-895 exist in souvenir sheets of one.

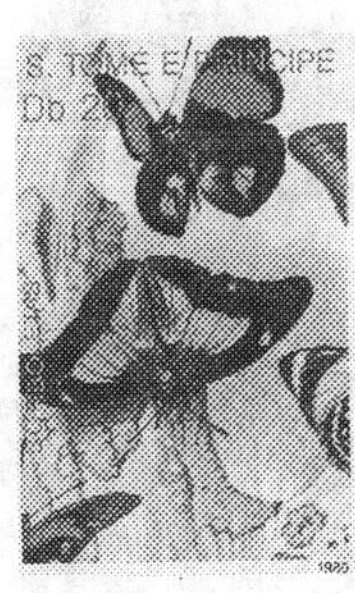

Butterflies
A129

1989, Dec. 20 *Perf. 13½x14*

898 A129 20d Tree bark
899 A129 20d Leaves
900 A129 20d Flowers
901 A129 20d Bird
902 A129 20d Blades of grass
Nos. 898-902 (5) 7.50

Souvenir Sheet

903 A129 100d yel, brn & multi 8.00

Nos. 898-902 exist in souvenir sheets of one.

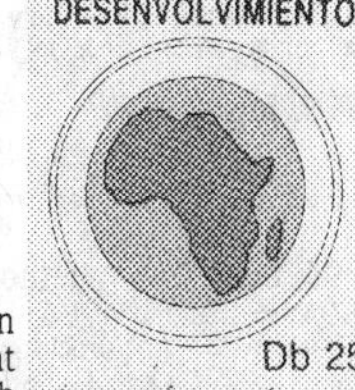

African Development Bank, 25th Anniv. — A130

1989, Dec. 20 *Perf. 13½x14*

904 A130 25d blk, lt bl & grn

World Telecommunications Day — A131

1989, Dec. 20 *Perf. 14x13½*

905 A131 60d multicolored 5.00

Souvenir Sheet

Perf. 13½x14

906 A131 100d Early Bird satellite, vert.

Christmas
A132

Paintings: No. 907, Adoration of the Magi (detail), by Durer. No. 908, Young Virgin Mary, by Titian. No. 909, Adoration of the King, by Rubens.

No. 910, Sistine Madonna, by Raphael. 100d, Madonna and Child Surrounded by Garland and Boy Angels, by Rubens.

1989, Dec. 23 *Perf. 13½x14*

907 A132 25d multicolored
908 A132 25d multicolored
909 A132 25d multicolored
910 A132 25d multicolored
Nos. 907-910 (4) *8.00*

Souvenir Sheet

911 A132 100d multicolored *8.00*

Nos. 907-910 exist in souvenir sheets of one.

Expedition of Sir Arthur Eddington to St. Thomas and Prince, 70th Anniv. A133

Designs: No. 912, Albert Einstein with Eddington. No. 913, Locomotive on Prince Island. No. 914, Roca Sundy railway station.

1990 **Litho.** *Perf. 13½*

912 A133 60d multicolored
913 A133 60d multicolored
914 A133 60d multicoloed
a. Souvenir sheet of 3, #912-914

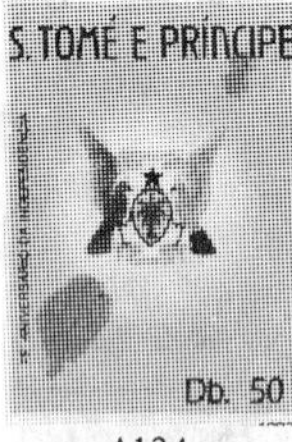

A134

Orchids — A135

Independence, 15th Anniv.: a, Map, arms. b, Map, birds carrying envelope. c, Flag.

1990, July 12 *Perf. 13½*

Souvenir Sheet

916 A134 50d Sheet of 3, #a.-c.

1990, Sept. 15 **Litho.** *Perf. 13½*

917 A135 20d Eulophia guineensis
918 A135 20d Ancistrochilus
919 A135 20d Oeceoclades maculata
920 A135 20d Vanilla imperialis
921 A135 20d Ansellia africana
Nos. 917-921 (4) *6.00*

Souvenir Sheets

Perf. 14x13½

922 A135 50d Angraecum distichum, horiz.
923 A135 50d Polystachya affinis, horiz.
Nos. 922-923 *7.00*

Expo '90, Intl. Garden and Greenery Exposition, Osaka.

Locomotives — A136

1990, Sept. 28 *Perf. 14x13½*

924 A136 5d Bohemia, 1923-41
925 A136 20d W. Germany, 1951-56
926 A136 25d Mallet, 1896-1903
927 A136 25d Russia, 1927-30
928 A136 25d England, 1927-30
Nos. 924-928 (5) *6.00*

Souvenir Sheets

929 A136 50d Camden-Amboy, 1834-38
930 A136 50d Stockton-Darlington, 1825

Souvenir Sheet

Iberoamericana '90 Philatelic Exposition — A137

1990, Oct. 7

931 A137 300d Armas Castle

1990 World Cup Soccer Championships, Italy — A138

#932, German team with World Cup Trophy. #933, 2 players with ball. #934, 3 players with ball. #935, Italian player. #936, US Soccer Federation emblem and team members. #937, World Cup Trophy.

1990, Oct. 15 *Perf. 13½*

932 A138 25d multicolored
933 A138 25d multicolored
934 A138 25d multicolored
935 A138 25d multicolored
Nos. 932-935 (4) *8.00*

Souvenir Sheets

Perf. 14x13½

936 A138 50d multi, horiz.
937 A138 50d multi, horiz.
Nos. 936-937 *8.00*

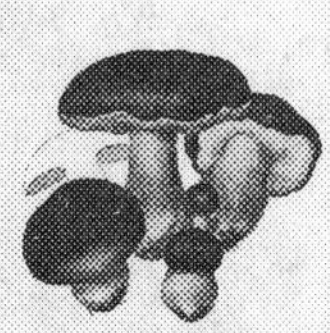

Mushrooms A139

1990, Nov. 2 *Perf. 13½x14*

938 A139 20d Boletus aereus
939 A139 20d Coprinus micaceus
940 A139 20d Pholiota spectabilis
941 A139 20d Krombholzia aurantiaca
942 A139 20d Stropharia aeruginosa

Souvenir Sheets

Perf. 14x13½

943 A139 50d Hypholoma capnoides
944 A139 50d Pleurotus ostreatus

Nos. 943-944 horiz. See Nos. 1014-1020.

Butterflies — A140

1990, Nov. 2 *Perf. 14x13½, 13½x14*

945 A140 15d Megistanis baeotus
946 A140 15d Ascia vamillae
947 A140 15d Danaus chrysippus
948 A140 15d Morpho menelaus
949 A140 15d Papilio rutulus, vert.
950 A140 25d Papilio paradiesa
Nos. 945-950 (6) *9.00*

Souvenir Sheets

951 A140 50d Parnassius clodius, vert.
952 A140 50d Papilio macmaon, vert.
Nos. 951-952 *9.00*

Presenting Gifts to the Newborn King — A141

Christmas: No. 954, Nativity scene. No. 955, Adoration of the Magi. No. 956, Flight into Egypt. No. 957, Adoration of the Magi, diff. No. 958, Portrait of Artist's Daughter Clara (detail), by Rubens, horiz.

1990, Nov. 30 *Perf. 13½x14*

953 A141 25d multicolored
954 A141 25d multicolored
955 A141 25d multicolored
956 A141 25d multicolored
Nos. 953-956 (4) *8.00*

Souvenir Sheets

957 A141 50d multicolored

Perf. 14x13½

958 A141 50d multicolored
Nos. 957-958 *8.50*

Death of Rubens, 350th anniv. (#958).

Anniversaries and Events — A142

1990, Dec. 15 *Perf. 13½x14*

959 A142 20d shown

Souvenir Sheets

Perf. 14x13½, 13½x14 (#962, 964)

960 A142 50d Oath of Confederation
961 A142 50d Pointed roof
962 A142 50d William Tell statue, vert.
963 A142 50d Brandenburg Gate
964 A142 50d Penny Black, vert.
965 A142 50d 100d bank note

Swiss Confederation, 700th anniv. (#959-962). Brandenburg Gate, 200th anniv. (#963). First postage stamp, 150th anniv. (#964). Independence of St. Thomas and Prince, 15th anniv. (#965).

Paintings — A143

#966, The Bathers, by Renoir. #967, Girl Holding Mirror for Nude, by Picasso. #968, Nude, by Rubens. #969, Descent from the Cross (detail), by Rubens. #970, Nude, by Titian. #971, Landscape, by Durer. #972, Rowboats, by Van Gogh. #973, Nymphs, by Titian. #974, Bather, by Titian. #975, Postman Joseph Roulin (detail), by Van Gogh. #976, The Abduction of the Daughters of Leucippus, by Rubens. #977, Nude, by Titian, diff.

Perf. 14x13½, 13½x14

1990, Dec. 15

966 A143 10d multi
967 A143 10d multi, vert.
968 A143 10d multi, vert.
969 A143 10d multi, vert.
970 A143 10d multi, vert.
971 A143 20d multi
972 A143 20d multi
973 A143 25d multi
974 A143 25d multi, vert.

Souvenir Sheets

Perf. 13½x14

975 A143 50d multi, vert.
976 A143 50d multi, vert.
977 A143 50d multi, vert.

Rubens, 350th anniv. of death (#968-969, 976). Titian, 500th anniv. of death (#970, 973-974, 977). Van Gogh, centennial of death (#972, 975).

See No. 958 for other souvenir sheet for Rubens death anniv.

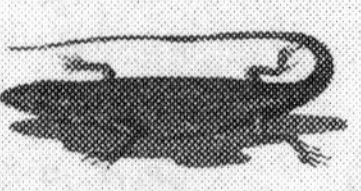

Flora and Fauna A144

Designs: 1d, Gecko. 5d, Cobra. 10d, No. 980, Sea turtle. No. 981, Fresh water turtle. No. 982, Civet. 70d, Civet in tree. No. 984, Civet with young. No. 985, Civet in den.

Psittacus erithacus: 80d, In tree, vert. 100d, On branch with wings spread, vert. 250d, Feeding young, vert. No. 989, Three in flight, vert.

1991, Feb. 2 *Perf. 14x13½*

978 A144 1d multicolored
979 A144 5d multicolored
980 A144 10d multicolored
981 A144 50d multicolored
982 A144 50d multicolored
983 A144 70d multicolored
984 A144 75d multicolored
985 A144 75d multicolored

Perf. 13½x14

986 A144 80d multicolored
987 A144 100d multicolored
988 A144 250d multicolored
989 A144 500d multicolored
Nos. 978-989 (12) *18.00*

Souvenir Sheets

990 A144 500d Orchid, vert.
991 A144 500d Rose, vert.

See Nos. 1054I-1054L.

Locomotives — A145

1991, May 7 *Perf. 14x13½, 13½x14*

992 A145 75d shown
993 A145 75d North America, vert.
994 A145 75d Germany, vert.
995 A145 75d New Delhi, vert.
996 A145 75d Brazil, vert.
997 A145 200d Two leaving terminal
Nos. 992-997 (6) *4.00*

Souvenir Sheets

998 A145 500d Engine 120, vert.
999 A145 500d Engine 151-001

Birds — A146

1991, July 8 *Perf. 13½x14*

1000 A146 75d Psittacula kuhlii
1001 A146 75d Plydolophus rosaceus
1002 A146 75d Falco tinnunculus
1003 A146 75d Platycercus palliceps

1004 A146 200d Marcrocercus ara-canga
Nos. 1000-1004 (5) 8.00

Souvenir Sheets

1005 A146 500d Ramphastos culmenatus
1006 A146 500d Strix nyctea
Nos. 1005-1006 16.00

Paintings — A147

50d, Venus and Cupid, by Titian. #1008, Horse's Head (detail), by Rubens. #1009, Child's face (detail), by Rubens. 100d, Spanish Woman, by Picasso. 200d, Man with Christian Flag, by Titian. #1012, Study of a Negro, by Rubens. #1013, Madonna and Child, by Raphael.

1991, July 31

1007 A147 50d multicolored
1008 A147 75d multicolored
1009 A147 75d multicolored
1010 A147 100d multicolored
1011 A147 200d multicolored
Nos. 1007-1011 (5) 8.00

Souvenir Sheets

1012 A147 500d multicolored
1013 A147 500d multicolored
Nos. 1012-1013 16.00

Mushroom Type of 1990

1991, Aug. 30

1014 A139 50d Clitocybe geotropa
1015 A139 50d Lepiota procera
1016 A139 75d Boletus granulatus
1017 A139 125d Coprinus comatus
1018 A139 200d Amanita rubescens
Nos. 1014-1018 (5) 8.00

Souvenir Sheets

1019 A139 500d Armillariella mellea

Perf. 14x13½

1020 A139 500d Nictalis parasitica, horiz.
Nos. 1019-1020 16.00

Flowers — A148

#1022, Zan tedeschia elliotiana. #1023, Cyrtanthes pohliana. #1024, Phalaenopsis lueddemanniana. #1025, Haemanthus katharinae. 500d, Arundina graminifolia.

1991, Sept. 9 ***Perf. 13½x14***

1021 A148 50d shown
1022 A148 50d multicolored
1023 A148 100d multicolored
1024 A148 100d multicolored
1025 A148 200d multicolored
Nos. 1021-1025 (5) 8.00

Souvenir Sheet

1026 A148 500d multicolored 8.00

Souvenir Sheet

Iberoamericano '92 Intl. Philatelic Exhibition — A149

1991, Oct. 11 Litho. ***Perf. 14x13½***

1027 A149 800d multicolored

Discovery of America, 500th Anniv. (in 1992) — A150

1991, Oct. 12 ***Perf. 13½x14***

1028 A150 50d Columbus
1029 A150 50d Sailing ship
1030 A150 75d Sailing ship, diff.
1031 A150 125d Landing in New World
1032 A150 200d Pointing the way

Souvenir Sheet

Perf. 14x13½

1033 A150 500d Columbus' fleet, horiz.

Butterflies — A151

1991, Oct. 16 ***Perf. 14x13½***

1034 A151 125d Limentis popul
1035 A151 125d Pavon inachis io
Nos. 1034-1035 5.00

Souvenir Sheet

Perf. 13½x14

1036 A151 500d Zerynthia polyxena 8.00

Phila Nippon '91.

1991, Nov. 15 ***Perf. 14x13½***

1037 A151 125d Macaon papilio machaon
1038 A151 125d Gran pavon
1039 A151 125d Pavon inachis io, diff.
1040 A151 125d Artia caja
Nos. 1037-1040 (4) 8.00

Souvenir Sheet

Perf. 13½x14

1041 A151 500d Unnamed butterfly, vert. 8.00

Christmas.

Landmarks — A152

Landmarks of France: No. 1042, Ile de France, vert. No. 1043, Chenonceau Castle. No. 1044, Azay-le-Rideau Castle. No. 1045, Chambord Castle. No. 1046, Chaumont Castle. No. 1047, Fountainebleau Palace.

Perf. 13½x14, 14x13½

1991, Nov. 15

1042-1047 A152 25d Set of 6 8.00

Souvenir Sheet

1048 A152 500d Paris map, 1615

French National Exposition.

Fauna — A153

Animals and birds: a, Weasel, monkey. b, Civet, rats. c, Goat, cow. d, Rabbits, wildcat. e, Parrot, black bird. f, White bird, multicolored bird.

1991, Nov. 15 ***Perf. 14x13½***

1049 A153 25d Sheet of 6, #a.-f.

French National Exposition.

Express Mail Service from St. Thomas and Prince — A154

1991 Litho. ***Perf. 14***

1050 A154 3000d multicolored

Souvenir Sheets

1991 Intl. Olympic Committee Session, Birmingham A154a

Designs: No. 1050A, IOC emblem, Birmingham Session. No. 1050B, 1998 Winter Olympics emblem, Nagano. No. 1050C, 1998 Winter Olympics mascot.

1992 Litho. ***Perf. 14***

1050A A154a 800d multicolored
1050B A154a 800d multicolored
1050C A154a 800d multicolored

Souvenir Sheet

IBEREX '91 — A154b

1992

1050D A154b 800d multicolored

Souvenir Sheet

1992 Winter Olympics, Albertville — A154c

1992

1050E A154c 50d Olympic medals

No. 1050E exists with pictures of different medalists in sheet margin: Blanca Fernandez, Spain; Alberto Tomba, Italy; Mark Kirchner, Germany; Torgny Mogren, Norway.

1992 Summer Olympics, Barcelona A154d

View of earth from space with: No. 1050F, High jumper. No. 1050G, Roller hockey player. No. 1050H, Equestrian. No. 1050I, Kayaker. No. 1050J, Weight lifter. No. 1050K, Archer.
No. 1050L, Michael Jordan, horiz.

1992

1050F-1050K A154d 50d Set of 6 5.00

Souvenir Sheet

1050L A154d 50d multicolored 4.00

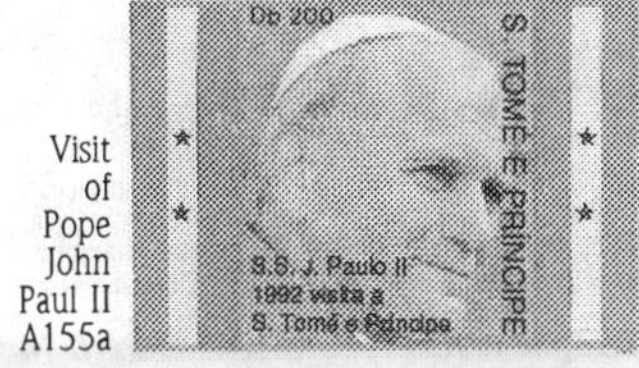

Whales — A155

Designs: No. 1051, Orcinus orca. No. 1052, Orcinus orca, two under water. No. 1053, Pseudoraca crassidens. No. 1054, Pseudoraca crassidens, three under water.

1992 Litho. ***Perf. 14***

1051-1054 A155 450d Set of 4

World Wildlife Fund.

Visit of Pope John Paul II A155a

c, Flags, Pope. d, Church with two steeples. e, Church, diff.
f, Pope, vert. g, Church, blue sky, vert. h, Church, closer view, vert.

1992, Apr. 19 Litho. ***Perf. 14***

Sheets of 4

1054A A155a 200d 2 #c, 1 each #d.-e.
1054B A155a 200d 2 #f, 1 each #g.-h.

Flora and Fauna Type of 1991

Designs: No. 1054I, 1000d, Brown & white bird, vert. No. 1054J, 1500d, Yellow flower, vert. No. 1054K, 2000d, Red flower, vert. No. 1054L, 2500d, Black bird, vert.

1992, Apr. 19

1054I-1054L A144 Set of 4

Souvenir Sheet

Olymphilex '92 — A156

Olympic athletes: a, Women's running. b, Women's gymnastics. c, Earvin "Magic" Johnson.

1992, July 29
1055 A156 300d Sheet of 3, #a.-c.

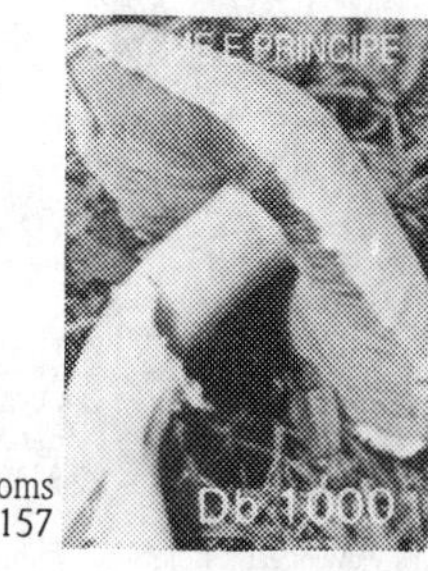

Mushrooms A157

Designs: 75d, Leccinum ocabrum. 100d, Amanita spissa, horiz. 125d, Strugilomyces floccopus. 200d, Suillus luteus. 500d, Agaricus siluaticus. No. 1061, Amanita pantherma, horiz. No. 1062, Agaricus campestre.

1992, Sept. 5 *Perf. 14*
1056 A157 75d multicolored
1057 A157 100d multicolored
1058 A157 125d multicolored
1059 A157 200d multicolored
1060 A157 500d multicolored
Nos. 1056-1060 (5) *8.00*

Souvenir Sheets

Perf. 14x13½, 13½x14

1061 A157 1000d multicolored
1062 A157 1000d multicolored
Nos. 1061-1062 *16.00*

Birds — A158

Designs: 75d, Paradisea regie, pipra rupicole. 100d, Trogon pavonis. 125d, Paradisea apoda. 200d, Pavocriotctus. 500d, Ramphatos maximus. No. 1068, Woodpecker. No. 1069, Picus major.

1992, Sept. 15 *Perf. 14*
1063 A158 75d multicolored
1064 A158 100d multicolored
1065 A158 125d multicolored
1066 A158 200d multicolored
1067 A158 500d multicolored
Nos. 1063-1067 (5) *8.00*

Souvenir Sheets

Perf. 13½x14

1068 A158 1000d multicolored
1069 A158 1000d multicolored
Nos. 1068-1069 *16.00*

Marcelo da Veiga (1892-1976), Writer A159

Designs: a, 10d. b, 40d. c, 50d. d, 100d.

1992, Oct. 3 *Perf. 13½*
1070 A159 Sheet of 4, #a.-d.

Locomotives — A160

Designs: 75d, 100d, 125d, 200d, 500d, Various locomotives. No. 1076, Steam train arriving at station. No. 1077, Engineer, stoker in locomotive cab.

1992, Oct. 3 *Perf. 14x13½*
1071 A160 75d black
1072 A160 100d black
1073 A160 125d black
1074 A160 200d black
1075 A160 500d black
Nos. 1071-1075 (5) *8.00*

Souvenir Sheets

1076 A160 1000d black
1077 A160 1000d black
Nos. 1076-1077 *16.00*

Butterflies and Moths — A161

75d, Chelonia purpurea. 100d, Hoetera philocteles. 125d, Attacus pavonia major. 200d, Ornithoptera urvilliana. 500d, Acherontia atropos. No. 1083, Peridromia amphinome, vert. No. 1084, Uramia riphacus, vert.

1992, Oct. 18 *Perf. 14x13½*
1078 A161 75d multicolored
1079 A161 100d multicolored
1080 A161 125d multicolored
1081 A161 200d multicolored
1082 A161 500d multicolored
Nos. 1078-1082 (5) *8.00*

Souvenir Sheets

Perf. 13½x14

1083 A161 1000d multicolored
1084 A161 1000d multicolored
Nos. 1083-1084 *16.00*

1992, 1996 Summer Olympics, Barcelona and Atlanta — A162

50d, Wind surfing. #1086, Wrestling. #1087, Women's 4x100 meters relay. #1088, Swimming. #1089, Equestrian, vert. #1090, Field hockey. #1091, Men's 4x100 meters relay, vert. #1092, Mascots for Barcelona and Atlanta. #1093, Opening ceremony, Barcelona.

#1094, Atlanta '96 Emblem, vert. #1095, Archer lighting Olympic Flame with flaming arrow, vert. #1096, Transfer of Olympic Flag, closing ceremony, vert. #1097, Gymnastics. #1098, Tennis players.

1992, Oct. 1 **Litho.** *Perf. 14*
1085 A162 50d multicolored
1086 A162 300d multicolored
1087 A162 300d multicolored
1088 A162 300d multicolored
1089 A162 300d multicolored
1090 A162 300d multicolored
1091 A162 300d multicolored
1092 A162 300d multicolored
1093 A162 300d multicolored

Souvenir Sheets

1094 A162 800d multicolored
1095 A162 1000d multicolored
1096 A162 1000d multicolored

Perf. 13½

1097 A162 1000d multicolored

Perf. 14

1098 A162 1000d multicolored

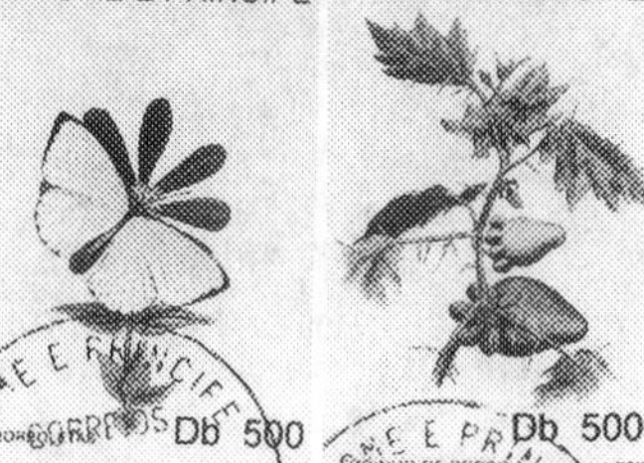

Butterflies — A163 Flowers — A164

Designs: No. 1099, White butterfly. No. 1100, Black and orange butterfly. No. 1101, Pink flower, black, white, red and blue butterfly. No. 1102, Black and white butterfly on right side of flower stem. No. 1103, Yellow and black butterfly. 2000d, Iris flower, black butterfly wing, horiz.

1993, May 26 **Litho.** *Perf. 14*
1099-1103 A163 500d Set of 5 *12.00*

Souvenir Sheet

1104 A163 2000d multicolored *15.00*

1993, June 18
1105 A164 500d Fucinho de porco
1106 A164 500d Heliconia
1107 A164 500d Gravo nacional
1108 A164 500d Tremessura
1109 A164 500d Anturius
Nos. 1105-1109 (5) *12.00*

Souvenir Sheet

1110 A164 2000d Girassol *12.00*

Miniature Sheet

Union of Portuguese Speaking Capitals — A165

Designs: a, 100d, Emblem. b, 150d, Grotto. c, 200d, Statue of Christ the Redeemer, Rio de Janeiro. d, 250d, Skyscraper. e, 250d, Monument. f, 300d, Building with pointed domed roof. g, 350d, Municipal building. h, 400d, Square tower. i, 500d, Residence, flag, truck.

1993, July 30
1111 A165 Sheet of 9, #a.-i.

Brasiliana '93.

Birds — A166

Designs: No. 1112, Cecia. No. 1113, Sui-sui. No. 1114, Falcon. No. 1115, Parrot. No. 1116, Heron.

1993, June 15 **Litho.** *Perf. 14*
1112-1116 A166 500d Set of 5 *18.50*

Souvenir Sheet

1117 A166 1000d Macaw, toucan, horiz. *7.50*

Dinosaurs — A167

#1118, Lystrosaurus. #1119, Patagosaurus. #1120, Shonisaurus ictiosaurios, vert. #1121, Dilophosaurus, vert. #1122, Dicraeosaurus, vert. #1123, Tyrannosaurus rex, vert.

1993, July 21
1118-1123 A167 500d Set of 6 *15.00*

Souvenir Sheets

1124 A167 1000d Protoavis
1125 A167 1000d Brachiosaurus
Nos. 1124-1125 *15.00*

Mushrooms A168

#1126, Agrocybe aegerita. #1127, Psalliota arvensis. #1128, Coprinus comatus. #1129, Hygrophorus psittacinus. #1130, Amanita caesarea.

#1131, Ramaria aurea. #1132, Pluteus murinus, horiz.

1993, May 25 **Litho.** *Perf. 14*
1126-1130 A168 800d Set of 5 *15.00*

Souvenir Sheets

1131-1132 A168 2000d Set of 2 *15.00*

Locomotives — A169

#1133-1137, Various views of small diesel locomotive.

#1138-1139, Various steam locomotives, vert.

1993, June 16
1133-1137 A169 800d Set of 5 *20.00*

Souvenir Sheets

1138-1139 A169 2000d Set of 2 *20.00*

1994 World Cup Soccer Championships, US — A170

Designs: No. 1140, Team photo. Nos. 1141-1147, Players in action.

No. 1148, Fans, faces painted as flags. No. 1149, Stylized player.

1993, July 6
1140-1147 A170 800d Set of 8 *20.00*

Souvenir Sheets

1148-1149 A170 2000d Set of 2 *20.00*

UPU Congress — A171

1993, Aug. 16
1150 A171 1000d shown

Souvenir Sheet

1151 A171 2000d Ship

1996 Summer Olympics, Atlanta — A172

#1152, Fencing. #1153, Women's running. #1154, Water polo. #1155, Soccer. #1156, Men's running. #1157, Boxing. #1158, Wrestling. #1159, High jump.
#1160, Shooting, vert. #1161, Sailing, vert. #1162, Equestrian, vert. #1163, Kayak, vert.

1993, Oct. 19 Litho. *Perf. 13½x14*
1152-1159 A172 800d Set of 8

Souvenir Sheets

1160-1163 A172 2000d multi

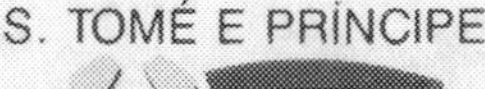

1994 World Cup Soccer Championships, US — A173

1994, Jan. 12 *Perf. 14*
1164 A173 500d black, blue & red

Issued in miniature sheets of 4.

Miniature Sheets

Movie Stars — A174

#1165a, James Dean. b, Bette Davis. c, Elvis Presley. d, Humphrey Bogart. e, John Lennon. f, Marilyn Monroe. g, Birthday cake. h, Audrey Hepburn.
#1166a-1166i, Various portraits of Elvis Presley.
#1167a-1167i, Various portraits of Marilyn Monroe.
#1168, James Dean, diff. #1169, Elvis Presley, diff. #1169A, Marilyn Monroe.

1994, Feb. 15
1165 A174 10d Sheet of 8, #a.-h.
1166-1167 A174 10d Sheets of 9, #a.-i.

Souvenir Sheets

1168-1169 A174 50d multicolored
1169A A174 2000d multicolored

Souvenir Sheet

Sydney 2000 — A175

1994, June 8
1170 A175 3000d multicolored

Signing of Argel Accord, 20th Anniv. A175a

1994 Litho. *Perf. 14*
1170A A175a 250d multicolored

Butterflies A176

Designs: No. 1171, Timeleoa maqulata-formosana. No. 1172, Morfho cypris. No. 1173, Thais polixena. No. 1174, Argema moenas. No. 1175, Leptocircus megus-ennius.
2000d, Armandia lidderdalei.

1995, May 10 Litho. *Perf. 14*
1171-1175 A176 1200d Set of 5

Souvenir Sheet

1176 A176 2000d multi

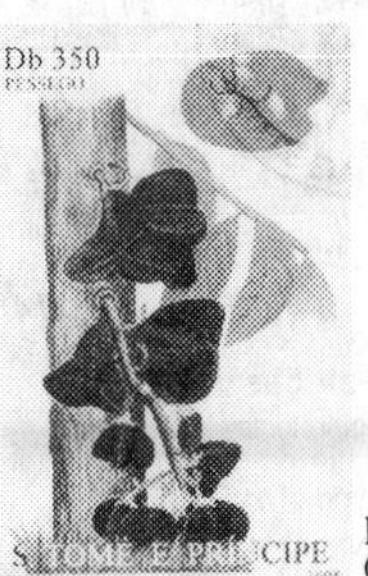

Flowering Fruits, Orchids — A177

Flowering fruits: #1177, 350d, Pessego. #1178, 370d, Untue. #1179, 380d, Pitanga. #1180, 800d, Morango. #1181, 1000d, Izaquente.
Orchids: No. 1182, Max. houtteana. No. 1183, Max. marginata.

1995, June 6
1177-1181 A177 Set of 5

Souvenir Sheets

1182-1183 A177 2000d each

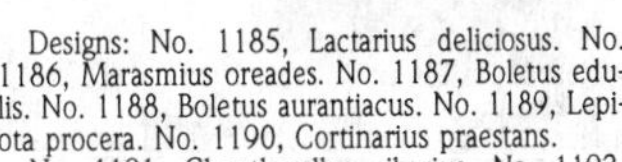

Mushrooms A179

Designs: No. 1185, Lactarius deliciosus. No. 1186, Marasmius oreades. No. 1187, Boletus edulis. No. 1188, Boletus aurantiacus. No. 1189, Lepiota procera. No. 1190, Cortinarius praestans.
No. 1191, Chantharellus cibarius. No. 1192, Lycoperdon pyriforme, horiz.

1995, Nov. 2 Litho. *Perf. 14*
1185-1190 A179 1000d Set of 6

Souvenir Sheets

1191-1192 A179 2000d each

UN, 50th Anniv. — A180

Traditional handicrafts made from palm leaves: No. 1193, 350d, Baskets. No. 1194, 350d, Brooms. No. 1195, 400d, Lamp shades. No. 1196, 500d, Klissakli, mussuá. No. 1197, 500d, Pávu. No. 1198, 1000d, Vámplêgá.

1995, June 20 Litho. *Perf. 13½x14*
1193-1198 A180 Set of 6

Trains A181

Locomotives: No. 1199, Steam, "#100." No. 1200, Steam, "#778." No. 1201, G. Thommen steam. No. 1202, Steam "#119," vert. No. 1203, Mt. Washington cog railway. No. 1204, Electric.
No. 1205, Electric train on snow-covered mountain, vert. No. 1206, Electric train car with door open, vert.

Perf. 14x13½, 13½x14

1995, July 24
1199-1204 A181 1000d Set of 6

Souvenir Sheets

1205-1206 A181 2000d multicolored

See Nos. 1280-1286.

Dogs & Cats A182

No. 1207: Various dogs. b, d, f, h, vert.
No. 1208: Various cats. b, d, f, h, vert.
No. 1209, St. Bernard, German shepherd. No. 1210, Beagle, vert. No. 1211, Cat, kittens. No. 1212, Kitten on top of mother, vert.

1995, Aug. 12 *Perf. 14*
1207-1208 A182 1000d Sheets of 9, #a.-i.

Souvenir Sheets

1209-1212 A182 2000d multicolored

New Year 1996 (Year of the Rat) — A183

Various species of rats, mice.

1995, Oct. 28
1213 A183 100d Sheet of 9, #a.-i.

Motion Pictures, Cent. — A184

Movie posters from: No. 1214: a, Gone with the Wind. b, Stagecoach. c, Tarzan and His Mate. d, Oregon Trail. e, The Oklahoma Kid. f, King Kong. g, A Lady Fights Back. h, Steamboat Around the Bend. i, Wee Willie Winkie.
No. 1215, Bring 'Em Back Alive. No. 1216 Indian chief.

1995, May 10 Litho. *Perf. 14*
1214 A184 1000d Sheet of 6, #a.-i.

Souvenir Sheets

1215-1216 A184 2000d multicolored

Horses — A185

Designs: No. 1217, Various horses.
No. 1218, Painting of Indian on horse, wild horses, horiz. No. 1219, City scene, horses, carriage, horiz.

1995, May 16
1217 A185 1000d Sheet of 9, #a.-i.

Souvenir Sheets

1218-1219 A185 2000d multicolored

Nos. 1218-1219 each contain one 50x35mm stamp.

Souvenir Sheet

Euro '96, European Soccer Championships, Great Britain — A186

Illustration reduced.

1995, July 2 *Perf. 13½x14*
1220 A186 2000d multicolored

Souvenir Sheet

Protection of World's Endangered Species — A187

Illustration reduced.

1995, July 6 *Perf. 14*
1221 A187 2000d multicolored

Mushrooms — A188

Designs: No. 1222a, Xerocomus rubellus. b, Rozites caperata. c, Cortinarius violaceus. d, Pholiota flammans. e, Lactarius volemus. f, Cortinarius (yellow). g, Cartinarius (blue). h, Higroforo. i, Boletus chrysenteron.

No. 1223, Amanita muscaria, vert. No. 1224, Russula cyanoxantha, vert.

1995, Nov. 2
1222 A188 1000d Sheet of 9, #a.-i.

Souvenir Sheets
1223-1224 A188 2000d multicolored

Details or Entire Paintings — A189

No. 1225: a, Aurora and Cefalo. b, Madonna and Child with St. John as a Boy. c, Romulus and Remus. d, Lamentation over the Dead Christ. e, Vison of All Saints Day. f, Perseus and Andromeda. g, The Scent. h, The Encounter in Lyon. i, The Art School of Rubens-Bildern.

No. 1226, Statue of Ceres. No. 1227, Flight into Egypt, horiz.

All but #1225g (Jan Brueghel the Elder) and 1221 are by Rubens.

1995, Sept. 27 **Litho.** *Perf. 14*
1225 A189 1000d Sheet of 9, #a.-i.

Souvenir Sheets
1226-1227 A189 2000d each

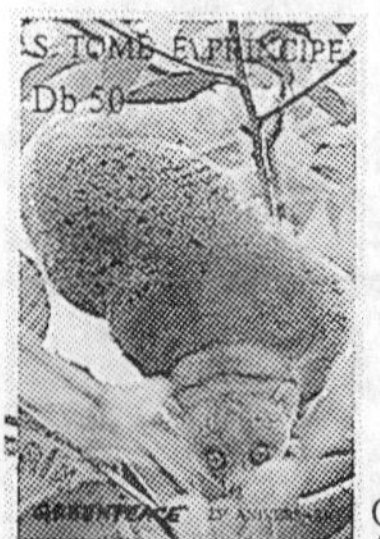

Greenpeace, 25th Anniv. — A190

Designs: No. 1237, Potto. No. 1238, Iguana. No. 1239, Tiger. No. 1240, Lion.

50d, Elephant, horiz.

1996, Aug. 5 **Litho.** *Perf. 14*
1237-1240 A190 50d Set of 4

Souvenir Sheet
1241 A190 50d multicolored

Dogs & Cats A191

Nos. 1242a-1242i: Various pictures of dogs with cats, kittens.

Nos. 1243a-1243i, vert.: Various close-up pictures of different breeds of dogs.

No. 1244, Labrador retriever. No. 1245, Bird, woman's eye, vert. No. 1246, Two kittens. No. 1247, Collie, vert. No. 1248, Poodle, vert. No. 1249, Pit bull terrier, vert. No. 1250, Brown and white terrier, vert.

1995, Aug. 12 **Litho.** *Perf. 14*

Sheets of 9
1242-1243 A191 1000d #a.-i., each

Souvenir Sheets
1244-1250 A191 2000d each

Orchids — A192

No. 1251: a, Findlayanum. b, Stan. c, Cruentum. d, Trpla suavis. e, Lowianum. f, Gratiosissimum. g, Cyrtorchis monteirae. h, Sarcanthus birmanicus. i, Loddigesii.

No. 1252, Barkeria Skinneri. No. 1253, Dendrobium nobile.

1995, Sept. 12
1251 A192 1000d Sheet of 9, #a.-i.

Souvenir Sheets
1252-1253 A192 2000d multicolored

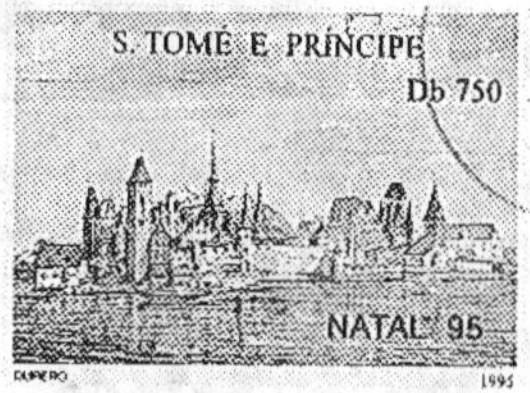

Paintings, Drawings by Durer, Rubens — A193

Designs: No. 1254, Soldier on Horseback, by Durer, vert. No. 1255, Archangel St. Michael Slaying Satan, by Rubens, vert. No. 1256, Nursing Madonna in Half Length, by Durer, vert. No. 1257, Head of a Deer, by Durer, vert. No. 1258, View of Innsbruck from the North, by Durer. No. 1259, Madonna Nursing on a Grassy Bench, by Durer, vert. No. 1260, Helene Fourment and Her Children, by Rubens, vert. No. 1261, Adam and Eve, by Durer, vert.

No. 1262, A Young Hare, by Durer, vert. No. 1263, Mills on a River Bank, by Durer. No. 1264, Holy Family with a Basket, by Rubens, vert. No. 1265, The Annunciation, by Rubens, vert.

1995, Dec. 16 **Litho.** *Perf. 14*
1254-1261 A193 750d Set of 8

Souvenir Sheets
1262-1265 A193 2000d each

Christmas.

Independence, 20th Anniv. — A194

1996, July 12 **Litho.** *Perf. 13½*
1266 A194 350d multicolored

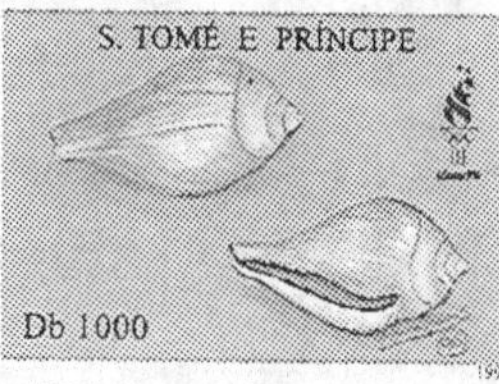

1996 Summer Olympic Games, Atlanta — A195

Various shells.

1996, Jan. 10 **Litho.** *Perf. 14*
1267-1271 A195 1000d Set of 5

Souvenir Sheet
1272 A195 2000d multicolored

Anniversaries and Events — A196

1996, Aug. 2 *Perf. 14x13½*
1273 A196 500d multicolored

UNICEF, 50th anniv., Alfred Nobel, 150th anniv. of birth, Phila-Seoul 96, KOREA 2002, 1996 Summer Olympic Games, Atlanta.

UNESCO A197

Butterflies: No. 1274, Papilio weiskei. No. 1275, Heliconius melpomene. No. 1276, Papilio arcasmylotes. No. 1277, Mesomenia cresus. No. 1278, Catagramma iyca-satrana.

No. 1279, Lemonius sudias.

1996, Sept. 10 *Perf. 13½x14*
1274-1278 A197 1000d Set of 5

Souvenir Sheet
1279 A197 2000d multicolored

Train Type of 1995

No. 1280, SNCF. No. 1281, CN. No. 1282, White locomotive. No. 1283, Green locomotive. No. 1284, Train in city.

No. 1285, Modern train. No. 1286, Old train.

1996, Oct. 7 *Perf. 14*
1280-1284 A181 1000d Set of 5

Souvenir Sheets
1285-1286 A181 2000d each

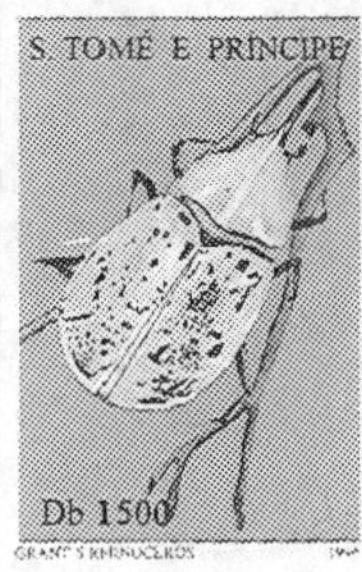

Beetles — A198

No. 1287: a, Grant's rhinoceros. b, Emerald-colored. c, California laurel borer. d, Giant stag.

No. 1288, Maple borer. No. 1289, Arizona june.

1996 *Perf. 13½x14*
1287 A198 1500d Sheet of 4, #a.-d.

Souvenir Sheets
1288-1289 A198 2000d each

Plants, Orchids — A199

No. 1290: a, Eryngium fortidum. b, Ocimum viride. c, Piper umbellatum. d, Phal. mariae. e, Odm. chiriquense. f, Phal. gigantea. g, Abutilon grandiflorum. h, Aframomium danielli. i, Chemopodium ambrosiodes.

No. 1291, Crinum jacus. No. 1292, Oncoba apinosa forsk. No. 1293, Z. mackai. No. 1294, Aspasia principissa.

1996
1290 A199 1000d Sheet of 9, #a.-i.

Souvenir Sheets
1291-1294 A199 2000d each

Nos. 857-858 Surcharged

Db. 350,00

Nos. 736-737, 744, 746, 748 Surcharged in Blue or Black

Perfs. & Printing Methods as Before

1996?
1295 A123p 350d on 1d #857
1295A A123p 400d on 5d #858
1296 A95 1000d on 11d #736 (Bl)
1297 A95 1000d on 12d #737 (Bl)
1298 A95 1000d on 42d #746
1299 A95 2500d on 25d #744 (Bl)
1300 A95 2500d on 100d #748 (Bl)

AIR POST STAMPS

Common Design Type
Inscribed "S. Tomé"

1938 *Perf. 13½x13*

Name and Value in Black

C1	CD39	10c scarlet	30.00	22.50
C2	CD39	20c purple	15.00	11.00
C3	CD39	50c orange	1.50	1.25
C4	CD39	1e ultra	2.50	2.00
C5	CD39	2e lilac brown	3.75	3.00
C6	CD39	3e dark green	5.75	4.00
C7	CD39	5e red brown	7.50	6.50
C8	CD39	9e rose carmine	8.50	6.50
C9	CD39	10e magenta	9.50	6.50
		Nos. C1-C9 (9)	84.00	63.25

Common Design Type
Inscribed "S. Tomé e Principe"

1939 **Engr.** **Unwmk.**

Name and Value Typo. in Black

C10	CD39	10c scarlet	.38	.25
C11	CD39	20c purple	.38	.25
C12	CD39	50c orange	.38	.25
C13	CD39	1e deep ultra	.38	.25

C14	CD39	2e	lilac brown	1.40	1.10
C15	CD39	3e	dark green	2.00	1.25
C16	CD39	5e	red brown	2.75	1.75
C17	CD39	9e	rose carmine	4.75	2.50
C18	CD39	10e	magenta	5.50	2.50
			Nos. C10-C18 (9)	17.92	10.10

No. C16 exists with overprint "Exposicao International de Nova York, 1939-1940" and Trylon and Perisphere.

POSTAGE DUE STAMPS

"S. Thomé" — D1

1904 Unwmk. Typo. *Perf. 12*

J1	D1	5r	yellow green	.55	.55
J2	D1	10r	slate	.65	.65
J3	D1	20r	yellow brown	.65	.65
J4	D1	30r	orange	1.00	.65
J5	D1	50r	gray brown	1.75	1.40
J6	D1	60r	red brown	2.50	1.65
J7	D1	100r	red lilac	3.00	1.75
J8	D1	130r	dull blue	4.00	3.25
J9	D1	200r	carmine	4.50	3.50
J10	D1	500r	gray violet	8.00	5.00
			Nos. J1-J10 (10)	26.60	19.05

Overprinted in Carmine or Green

1911

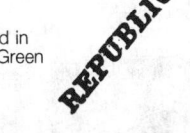

J11	D1	5r	yellow green	.25	.25
J12	D1	10r	slate	.25	.25
J13	D1	20r	yellow brown	.25	.25
J14	D1	30r	orange	.25	.25
J15	D1	50r	gray brown	.25	.25
J16	D1	60r	red brown	.60	.60
J17	D1	100r	red lilac	.70	.70
J18	D1	130r	dull blue	.70	.70
J19	D1	200r	carmine (G)	.70	.70
J20	D1	500r	gray violet	1.10	1.10
			Nos. J11-J20 (10)	5.05	5.05

Nos. J1-J10 Overprinted in Black

1913 Without Gum

J21	D1	5r	yellow green	3.75	3.75
J22	D1	10r	slate	5.00	4.50
J23	D1	20r	yellow brown	2.50	2.50
J24	D1	30r	orange	2.50	2.50
J25	D1	50r	gray brown	2.50	2.50
J26	D1	60r	red brown	3.00	3.00
J27	D1	100r	red lilac	5.00	4.00
J28	D1	130r	dull blue	21.00	21.00
a.			Inverted overprint	40.00	40.00
J29	D1	200r	carmine	37.50	32.50
J30	D1	500r	gray violet	45.00	27.50
			Nos. J21-J30 (10)	127.75	103.75

Nos. J1-J10 Overprinted in Black

1913 Without Gum

J31	D1	5r	yellow green	1.75	1.75
a.			Inverted overprint		
J32	D1	10r	slate	2.25	2.25
J33	D1	20r	yellow brown	1.75	1.75
J34	D1	30r	orange	1.75	1.75
a.			Inverted overprint		
J35	D1	50r	gray brown	1.75	1.75
J36	D1	60r	red brown	2.75	2.25
J37	D1	100r	red lilac	2.75	2.25
J38	D1	130r	dull blue	2.75	2.75
J39	D1	200r	carmine	4.50	3.50
J40	D1	500r	gray violet	13.00	13.00
			Nos. J31-J40 (10)	35.00	33.00

No. J5 Overprinted "Republica" in Italic Capitals like Regular Issue in Green

1920 Without Gum

J41	D1	50r	gray brn	40.00	35.00

"S. Tomé" — D2

1921 Typo. *Perf. 11½*

J42	D2	½c	yellow green	.20	.15
J43	D2	1c	slate	.20	.15
J44	D2	2c	orange brown	.20	.15
J45	D2	3c	orange	.20	.15
J46	D2	5c	gray brown	.20	.15
J47	D2	6c	lt brown	.20	.15
J48	D2	10c	red violet	.20	.15
J49	D2	13c	dull blue	.25	.20
J50	D2	20c	carmine	.25	.20
J51	D2	50c	gray	.35	.40
			Nos. J42-J51 (10)	2.25	1.85

In each sheet one stamp is inscribed "S. Thomé" instead of "S. Tomé." Value, set of 10, $60.

Catalogue values for unused stamps in this section, from this point to the end of the section, are for Never Hinged items.

Common Design Type
Photo. & Typo.

1952 Unwmk. *Perf. 14*

Numeral in Red, Frame Multicolored

J52	CD45	10c	chocolate	.15	.15
J53	CD45	30c	red brown	.15	.15
J54	CD45	50c	dark blue	.15	.15
J55	CD45	1e	dark blue	.25	.25
J56	CD45	2e	olive green	.60	.60
J57	CD45	5e	black brown	1.25	1.25
			Nos. J52-J57 (6)	2.55	2.55

NEWSPAPER STAMPS

N1

N2

Perf. 11½, 12½ and 13½

1892 Without Gum Unwmk.

Black Surcharge

P1	N1	2½r	on 10r green	95.00	55.00
P2	N1	2½r	on 20r rose	125.00	57.50
P3	N2	2½r	on 10r green	125.00	57.50
P4	N2	2½r	on 20r rose	125.00	57.50
			Nos. P1-P4 (4)	470.00	227.50

Green Surcharge

P5	N1	2½r	on 5r black	67.50	30.00
P6	N1	2½r	on 20r rose	125.00	57.50
P8	N2	2½r	on 5r black	125.00	60.00
P9	N2	2½r	on 10r green	125.00	62.50
P10	N2	2½r	on 20r rose	125.00	77.50
			Nos. P5-P10 (5)	567.50	287.50

Both surcharges exist on No. 18 in green.

N3

d

1893 Typo. *Perf. 11½, 13½*

P12	N3	2½r	brown	.45	.40

For surcharges and overprints see Nos. 85, 166, 275, P13.

No. P12 Overprinted Type "d" in Blue

1899

Without Gum

P13	N3	2½r	brown	25.00	16.00

POSTAL TAX STAMPS

Pombal Issue

Common Design Types

1925 Unwmk. *Perf. 12½*

RA1	CD28	15c	orange & black	.45	.45
RA2	CD29	15c	orange & black	.45	.45
RA3	CD30	15c	orange & black	.45	.45
			Nos. RA1-RA3 (3)	1.35	1.35

Certain revenue stamps (5e, 6e, 7e, 8e and other denominations) were surcharged in 1946 "Assistencia," 2 bars and new values (1e or 1.50e) and used as postal tax stamps.

Catalogue values for unused stamps in this section, from this point to the end of the section, are for Never Hinged items.

PT1

1948-58 Typo. *Perf. 12x11½*

Denomination in Black

RA4	PT1	50c	yellow grn	4.00	1.10
RA5	PT1	1e	carmine rose	4.25	1.50
RA6	PT1	1e	emerald ('58)	1.75	.75
RA7	PT1	1.50e	bister brown	2.50	1.90
			Nos. RA4-RA7 (4)	12.50	5.25

Denominations of 2e and up were used only for revenue purposes. No. RA6 lacks "Colonia de" below coat of arms.

Type of 1958 Surcharged

um escudo
1$00
m

Um escudo
1$00
n

1964-65 Typo. *Perf. 12x11½*

RA8	PT1(m)	1e	on 5e org yel	12.00	12.00
RA9	PT1(n)	1e	on 5e org yel ('65)	4.50	4.50

The basic 5e orange yellow does not carry the words "Colonia de."

No. RA6 Surcharged: "Um escudo"

1965

RA10	PT1	1e	emerald	2.00	2.00

1$00

Type of 1948 Surcharged

UM
ESCUDO

1965 Typo. *Perf. 12x11½*

RA11	PT1	1e	emerald	.40	.40

POSTAL TAX DUE STAMPS

Pombal Issue

Common Design Types

1925 Unwmk. *Perf. 12½*

RAJ1	CD28	30c	orange & black	.75	.75
RAJ2	CD29	30c	orange & black	.75	.75
RAJ3	CD30	30c	orange & black	.75	.75
			Nos. RAJ1-RAJ3 (3)	2.25	2.25

ST. VINCENT

sānt 'vin(t)-sənt

LOCATION — Island in the West Indies
GOVT. — Independent state in the British Commonwealth
AREA — 150 sq. mi.
POP. — 123,000 (est. 1984)
CAPITAL — Kingstown

The British colony of St. Vincent became an associated state in 1969 and independent in 1979.

12 Pence = 1 Shilling
20 Shillings = 1 Pound
100 Cents = 1 Dollar (1949)

Catalogue values for unused stamps in this country are for Never Hinged items, beginning with Scott 152 in the regular postage section, Scott B1 in the semi-postal section, and Scott O1 in the officials section.

Values for unused stamps are for examples with original gum as defined in the catalogue introduction. Early stamps were spaced extremely narrowly on the plates, and the perforations were applied irregularly. Therefore, very fine examples of Nos. 1-28, 30-39 will have perforations that cut into the design slightly on one or more sides. Also, very fine examples of Nos. 40-53, 55-60 will have perforations touching the design on at least one side. These stamps with perfs clear of the design on all four sides, especially Nos. 1-28, 30-39, are extremely scarce and command substantially higher prices.

Watermark

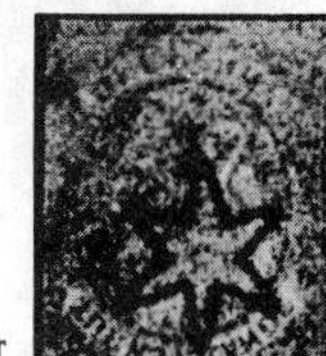

Wmk. 5- Small Star

Queen Victoria — A1

Clean-Cut Perf. 14 to 16

1861 Engr. Unwmk.

1	A1	1p	rose	*8,000.*	500.00
a.			Imperf., pair	375.00	
c.			Horiz. pair, imperf. vert.	500.00	
1B	A1	6p	yellow green	*9,000.*	300.00

1862-66 *Rough Perf. 14 to 16*

2	A1	1p	rose	35.00	12.00
a.			Horiz. pair, imperf. vert.	450.00	
3	A1	6p	dark green	65.00	17.50
a.			Imperf., pair	600.00	
b.			Horiz. pair, imperf. between	1,500.	
4	A1	1sh	slate ('66)	275.00	140.00
			Nos. 2-4 (3)	375.00	169.50

1863-69 *Perf. 11 to 13*

5	A1	1p	rose	32.50	15.00
6	A1	4p	blue ('66)	325.00	100.00
a.			Horiz. pair, imperf. vert.		
7	A1	4p	orange ('69)	300.00	150.00
8	A1	6p	deep green	250.00	60.00
8A	A1	1sh	slate ('66)	*3,000.*	1,500.
9	A1	1sh	indigo ('69)	300.00	85.00
10	A1	1sh	brown ('69)	475.00	160.00

Perf. 11 to 13x14 to 16

11	A1	1p	rose	*4,000.*	1,500.
12	A1	1sh	slate	225.00	110.00

Rough Perf. 14 to 16

1871-78 Wmk. 5

13	A1	1p	black	40.00	12.50
a.			Vert. pair, imperf. btwn.	*5,750.*	
14	A1	6p	dk blue green	300.00	75.00

Clean-Cut Perf. 14 to 16

14A	A1	1p	black	40.00	11.00
14B	A1	6p	blue green	600.00	37.50
c.			6p dull blue green	650.00	35.00
15	A1	6p	pale yel green ('78)	600.00	35.00
15A	A1	1sh	vermilion ('77)		*15,000.*

For surcharge see No. 30.

Perf. 11 to 13

16	A1	4p dark blue ('77)	400.00	100.00
17	A1	1sh deep rose ('72)	700.00	140.00
18	A1	1sh claret ('75)	600.00	225.00

Perf. 11 to 13x14 to 16

20	A1	1p black	50.00	9.00
a.		Horiz. pair, imperf. btwn.		4,250.
21	A1	6p pale yel grn ('77)	550.00	50.00
22	A1	1sh lilac rose ('72)	5,500.	400.00
23	A1	1sh vermilion ('77)	850.00	110.00
a.		Horiz. pair, imperf. vert.		

See Nos. 25-28A, 36-39, 42-53. For surcharges see Nos. 30, 32-33, 40, 55-60.

Victoria A2

Seal of Colony A3

1880-81 **Perf. 11 to 13**

24	A2	½p orange ('81)	7.00	3.50
25	A1	1p gray green	95.00	6.50
26	A1	1p drab ('81)	775.00	13.00
27	A1	4p ultra ('81)	1,100.	90.00
a.		Horiz. pair, imperf. btwn.		
28	A1	6p yellow green	450.00	55.00
28A	A1	1sh vermilion	700.00	55.00
29	A3	5sh rose	1,000.	1,250.

No. 29 is valued well centered with design well clear of the perfs.

See #35, 41, 54, 598. For surcharges see #31-33.

No. 14B Bisected and Surcharged in Red — d. 1

1880, May **Perf. 14 to 16**

30	A1	1p on half of 6p	450.	300.
a.		Unsevered pair	1,250.	900.

No. 28 Bisected and Surcharged in Red — d ½

1881, Sept. 1

31	A1	½p on half of 6p yel grn ('81)	150.	150.
a.		Unsevered pair	600.	550.
b.		"1" with straight top	900.	
c.		Without fraction bar, pair, #31, 31c	4,500.	5,500.

Nos. 28 and 28A Surcharged in Black:

ONE PENNY
c

4d
d

1881, Nov. **Perf. 11 to 13**

32	A1(c)	1p on 6p yel green	500.	300.
33	A1(d)	4p on 1sh vermilion	1,350.	800.

1883-84 **Wmk. 2** **Perf. 12**

35	A2	½p green ('84)	50.00	25.00
36	A1	4p ultra	325.00	18.00
37	A1	4p dull blue ('84)	1,250.	300.00
38	A1	6p yellow grn	350.00	325.00
39	A1	1sh orange ver	75.00	50.00
a.		Imperf., pair		

The ½p orange, 1p rose red, 1p milky blue and 5sh carmine lake were never placed in use. Some authorities believe them to be color trials.

Nos. 35-60 may be found watermarked with single straight line. This is from the frame which encloses each group of 60 watermark designs.

Type of A1 Surcharged in Black

2½ PENCE
e

1883 **Perf. 14**

40	A1	2½p on 1p lake	7.00	1.75

1883-97

41	A2	½p green ('85)	.75	.50
42	A1	1p drab	35.00	1.50
43	A1	1p rose red ('85)	1.50	.60
44	A1	1p pink ('86)	14.00	4.00
45	A1	2½p brt blue ('97)	2.50	2.50
46	A1	4p ultra	350.00	32.50
47	A1	4p red brown ('85)	900.00	24.00
48	A1	4p lake brown ('86)	30.00	2.50
a.		4p purple brown	30.00	2.50
49	A1	4p yellow ('93)	1.75	5.00
a.		4p olive yellow	350.00	350.00
50	A1	5p gray brown ('97)	5.50	15.00
a.		5p black brown	5.50	15.00
51	A1	6p violet ('88)	100.00	125.00
52	A1	6p red violet ('91)	2.00	6.00
53	A1	1sh org ver ('91)	6.00	10.00
54	A3	5sh car lake ('88)	30.00	45.00
a.		5sh brown lake	30.00	45.00

Grading footnote after No. 29 applies equally to Nos. 54-54a.

No. 40 Resurcharged in Black — 1d

1885, Mar.

55	A1	1p on 2½p on 1p lake	15.00	15.00

Copies with 3-bar cancel are proofs.

Stamps of Type A1 Surcharged in Black or Violet:

2½d.
g

5 PENCE
h

FIVE PENCE
j

1890-91

56	A1(e)	2½p on 1p brt blue	1.00	.50
a.		2½p on 1p milky blue	10.00	3.50
b.		2½p on 1p gray blue	17.50	1.75
57	A1(g)	2½p on 4p vio brn ('90)	90.00	90.00
a.		Without fraction bar	300.00	350.00

1892-93

58	A1(h)	5p on 4p lake brn (V)	10.00	22.50
59	A1(j)	5p on 6p dp lake ('93)	1.00	1.75
a.		5p on 6p carmine lake	14.00	22.50
b.		Double surcharge		5,000.

1897

60	A1(j)	3p on 1p lilac	6.00	15.00

Victoria A13

Edward VII A14

Numerals of 1sh and 5sh, type A13, and of 2p, 1sh, 5sh and £1, type A14, are in color on plain tablet.

1898 **Typo.** **Perf. 14**

62	A13	½p lilac & grn	1.90	1.00
63	A13	1p lilac & car rose	3.00	.50
64	A13	2½p lilac & ultra	3.75	2.00
65	A13	3p lilac & ol grn	3.75	8.00
66	A13	4p lilac & org	3.75	10.00
67	A13	5p lilac & blk	7.00	13.00
68	A13	6p lilac & brn	12.50	25.00
69	A13	1sh grn & car rose	14.00	42.00
70	A13	5sh green & ultra	60.00	110.00
		Nos. 62-70 (9)	109.65	211.50

1902

71	A14	½p violet & green	1.50	.45
72	A14	1p violet & car rose	2.25	.15
73	A14	2p violet & black	1.75	1.75
74	A14	2½p violet & ultra	3.00	2.50
75	A14	3p violet & ol grn	2.75	2.00
76	A14	6p violet & brn	9.50	24.00
77	A14	1sh grn & car rose	15.00	37.50
78	A14	2sh green & violet	21.00	42.50
79	A14	5sh green & ultra	52.50	80.00
		Nos. 71-79 (9)	109.25	190.85

1904-11 **Wmk. 3**

Chalky Paper

82	A14	½p vio & grn	1.10	.40
83	A14	1p vio & car rose	12.00	.35
84	A14	2½p vio & ultra	11.00	12.00
85	A14	6p vio & brn	11.00	15.00
86	A14	1sh grn & car rose	8.50	12.00
87	A14	2sh vio & bl, bl	20.00	32.50
88	A14	5sh grn & red, yel	16.00	40.00
89	A14	£1 vio & blk, red	300.00	375.00
		Nos. 82-88 (7)	79.60	112.25

#82, 83 and 86 also exist on ordinary paper.

Issued: 1p, 1904, ½p, 6p, 1905; 2½p, 1906; 1sh, 1908; 2sh, 5sh, 1909; £1, July 22, 1911.

"Peace and Justice"
A15 A16

1907 **Engr.**

Ordinary Paper

90	A15	½p yellow green	1.00	1.00
91	A15	1p carmine	2.00	.90
92	A15	2p orange	.65	4.50
93	A15	2½p ultra	13.00	10.50
94	A15	3p dark violet	3.50	15.00
		Nos. 90-94 (5)	20.15	31.90

1909

Without Dot under "d"

95	A16	1p carmine	1.10	.50
96	A16	6p red violet	5.25	25.00
97	A16	1sh black, green	3.50	8.50
		Nos. 95-97 (3)	9.85	34.00

1909-11

With Dot under "d"

98	A16	½p yellow grn ('10)	1.10	.35
99	A16	1p carmine	1.10	.20
100	A16	2p gray ('11)	2.50	4.25
101	A16	2½p ultra	5.25	2.75
102	A16	3p violet, yel	1.90	2.75
103	A16	6p red violet	3.00	8.00
		Nos. 98-103 (6)	14.85	18.30

King George V — A17

1913-14 **Perf. 14**

104	A17	½p gray green	.20	.20
105	A17	1p carmine	.20	.15
106	A17	2p gray	1.25	1.50
107	A17	2½p ultra	.50	.50
108	A17	3p violet, yellow	1.00	2.50
109	A17	4p red, yellow	.65	1.50
110	A17	5p olive green	2.00	6.50
111	A17	6p claret	1.25	2.50
112	A17	1sh black, green	1.50	2.50
113	A17	1sh bister ('14)	2.50	5.00
114	A16	2sh vio & ultra	7.00	15.00
115	A16	5sh dk grn & car	15.00	25.00
116	A16	£1 black & vio	80.00	125.00
		Nos. 104-116 (13)	113.05	187.85

Issue dates: 5p, Nov. 7, No. 113, May 1, 1914, others, Jan. 1, 1913.

For overprints see Nos. MR1-MR2.

No. 112 Surcharged in Carmine — ONE PENNY.

1915

117	A17	1p on 1sh black, grn	6.00	2.75
a.		"PENNY" & bar double	900.00	
b.		Without period	14.00	
c.		"ONE" omitted	900.00	
d.		"ONE" double	900.00	

Space between surcharge lines varies from 8 to 10mm.

1921-32 **Wmk. 4**

118	A17	½p green	.15	.15
119	A17	1p rose red	.15	.15
120	A17	1½p yel brn ('32)	.80	.20
121	A17	2p gray	.35	.25
122	A17	2½p ultra ('26)	.55	.45
123	A17	3p ultra	2.25	4.50
124	A17	3p vio, yel ('27)	.45	1.40
125	A17	4p red, yel ('30)	1.50	4.50
126	A17	5p olive green	.45	2.25
127	A17	6p claret ('27)	.55	2.25
128	A17	1sh bister	1.00	2.75
129	A16	2sh brn vio & ultra	4.50	7.50
130	A16	5sh dk grn & car	11.25	22.50
131	A16	£1 blk & vio ('28)	90.00	150.00
		Nos. 118-131 (14)	113.95	198.85

Silver Jubilee Issue

Common Design Type

1935, May 6 **Perf. 11x12**

134	CD301	1p car & dk blue	.35	.35
135	CD301	1½p gray blk & ultra	.35	.35
136	CD301	2½p ultra & brn	1.10	1.10
137	CD301	1sh brown vio & ind	3.25	3.25
		Nos. 134-137 (4)	5.05	5.05

Coronation Issue

Common Design Type

1937, May 12 **Perf. 11x11½**

138	CD302	1p dark purple	.20	.15
139	CD302	1½p dark carmine	.35	.15
140	CD302	2½p deep ultra	.50	.50
		Nos. 138-140 (3)	1.05	.80

Seal of the Colony — A18

Young's Island and Fort Duvernette — A19

Kingstown and Fort Charlotte — A20

Villa Beach — A21

Victoria Park, Kingstown — A22

1938-47 **Wmk. 4** **Perf. 12**

141	A18	½p green & brt bl	.15	.15
142	A19	1p claret & blue	.15	.15
143	A20	1½p scar & lt grn	.15	.15
144	A18	2p black & green	.15	.15
145	A21	2½p pck bl & ind	.15	.15
145A	A22	2½p choc & grn ('47)	.20	.20
146	A18	3p dk vio & org	.15	.15
146A	A21	3½p dp bl grn & ind ('47)	.60	.50
147	A18	6p claret & blk	.25	.25
148	A22	1sh green & vio	.45	.45
149	A18	2sh dk vio & brt blue	.85	.85
149A	A18	2sh6p dp bl & org brn ('47)	1.75	1.75
150	A18	5sh dk grn & car	4.00	2.50
150A	A18	10sh choc & dp vio ('47)	5.00	9.00
151	A18	£1 black & vio	10.00	12.00
		Nos. 141-151 (15)	24.00	28.40

Issue date: Mar. 11, 1938.

See Nos. 156-169, 180-184.

Catalogue values for unused stamps in this section, from this point to the end of the section, are for Never Hinged items.

Peace Issue

Common Design Type

1946, Oct. 15 **Engr.** **Perf. 13½x14**

152	CD303	1½p carmine	.20	.20
153	CD303	3½p deep blue	.30	.30

Silver Wedding Issue

Common Design Types

1948, Nov. 30 **Photo.** **Perf. 14x14½**

154	CD304	1½p scarlet	.15	.15

Engraved; Name Typographed

Perf. 11½x11

155	CD305	£1 red violet	20.00	22.50

Types of 1938

1949, Mar. 26 Engr. *Perf. 12*

156 A18 1c grn & brt bl .15 .15
157 A19 2c claret & bl .15 .15
158 A20 3c scar & lt grn .40 .30
159 A18 4c gray blk & grn .20 .15
160 A22 5c choc & grn .20 .20
161 A18 6c dk vio & org .20 .20
162 A21 7c pck blue & ind .65 .45
163 A18 12c claret & blk .60 .40
164 A22 24c green & vio 1.00 1.00
165 A18 48c dk vio & brt bl 2.00 2.00
166 A18 60c dp bl & org brn 2.25 2.25
167 A18 $1.20 dk grn & car 5.75 5.75
168 A18 $2.40 choc & dp vio 7.25 7.25
169 A18 $4.80 gray blk & vio 12.00 12.00
Nos. 156-169 (14) 32.80 32.25

For overprints see Nos. 176-179.

UPU Issue

Common Design Types

Engr.; Name Typo. on 6c, 12c

Perf. 13½, 11x11½

1949, Oct. 10 Wmk. 4

170 CD306 5c blue .20 .20
171 CD307 6c dp rose violet .25 .35
172 CD308 12c red lilac .50 .60
173 CD309 24c blue green 1.10 1.10
Nos. 170-173 (4) 2.05 2.25

University Issue

Common Design Types

1951, Feb. 16 Engr. *Perf. 14x14½*

174 CD310 3c red & blue green .25 .20
175 CD311 12c rose lilac & blk .70 .50

Nos. 158-160 and 163 Overprinted in Black

NEW CONSTITUTION 1951

1951, Sept. 21 *Perf. 12*

176 A20 3c scarlet & lt grn .15 .15
177 A18 4c gray blk & grn .15 .15
178 A22 5c chocolate & grn .15 .15
179 A18 12c claret & blk .25 .25
Nos. 176-179 (4) .70 .70

Adoption of a new constitution for the Windward Islands, 1951.

Type of 1938-47

1952

180 A18 1c gray black & green .15 .15
181 A18 3c dk violet & orange .20 .20
182 A18 4c green & brt blue .20 .20
183 A20 6c scarlet & dp green .20 .20
184 A21 10c peacock blue & indigo .35 .35
Nos. 180-184 (5) 1.10 1.10

Coronation Issue

Common Design Type

1953, June 2 *Perf. 13½x13*

185 CD312 4c dk green & blk .70 .70

Elizabeth II — A23

Seal of Colony — A24

Perf. 13x14

1955, Sept. 16 Wmk. 4 Engr.

186 A23 1c orange .15 .15
187 A23 2c violet blue .15 .15
188 A23 3c gray .15 .15
189 A23 4c dk red brown .15 .15
190 A23 5c scarlet .20 .15
191 A23 10c purple .25 .20
192 A23 15c deep blue .35 .25
193 A23 20c green .50 .25
194 A23 25c brown black .90 .65

Perf. 14

195 A24 50c chocolate 1.65 1.25
196 A24 $1 dull green 4.75 3.75
197 A24 $2.50 deep blue 16.00 9.50
Nos. 186-197 (12) 25.20 16.60

West Indies Federation

Common Design Type

Perf. 11½x11

1958, Apr. 22 Wmk. 314

198 CD313 3c green .30 .25
199 CD313 6c blue .50 .50
200 CD313 12c carmine rose 1.00 1.00
Nos. 198-200 (3) 1.80 1.75

Freedom from Hunger Issue

Common Design Type

1963, June 4 Photo. *Perf. 14x14½*

201 CD314 8c lilac 2.00 1.40

Red Cross Centenary Issue

Common Design Type

1963, Sept. 2 Litho. *Perf. 13*

202 CD315 4c black & red .50 .30
203 CD315 8c ultra & red 1.25 1.25

Types of 1955

Perf. 13x14

1964-65 Wmk. 314 Engr.

205 A23 1c orange .15 .15
206 A23 2c violet blue .25 .25
207 A23 3c gray .80 .60
208 A23 5c scarlet .45 .45
209 A23 10c purple .65 .45
a. Perf. 12½ .35 .35
210 A23 15c deep blue 1.25 .90
a. Perf. 12½ .75 .50
211 A23 20c green 1.00 .80
a. Perf. 12½ 16.00 6.50
212 A23 25c brown black 1.90 1.50
a. Perf. 12½ 1.90 1.40

Perf. 14

213 A24 50c chocolate ('65) 7.75 6.00
a. Perf. 12½ 3.25 3.00
Nos. 205-213 (9) 14.20 11.10

Scout Emblem and Merit Badges — A25

1964, Nov. 23 Litho. *Perf. 14*

216 A25 1c dk brn & brt yel grn .15 .15
217 A25 4c dk red brn & brt blue .15 .15
218 A25 20c dk violet & orange .35 .20
219 A25 50c green & red .90 .90
Nos. 216-219 (4) 1.55 1.40

Boy Scouts of St. Vincent, 50th anniv.

Breadfruit and Capt. Bligh's Ship "Providence" A26

Designs: 1c, Tropical fruit. 25c, Doric temple and pond, vert. 40c, Blooming talipot palm and Doric temple, vert.

Perf. 14½x13½, 13½x14½

1965, Mar. 23 Photo. Wmk. 314

220 A26 1c dk green & multi .15 .15
221 A26 4c lt & dk brn grn & yel .15 .15
222 A26 25c blue, grn & bister .40 .25
223 A26 40c dk blue & multi .70 .50
Nos. 220-223 (4) 1.40 1.05

Bicentenary of the Botanic Gardens.

ITU Issue

Common Design Type

1965, May 17 Litho. *Perf. 11x11½*

224 CD317 4c blue & yellow grn .30 .15
225 CD317 48c yellow & orange 3.25 2.25

Boat Building, Bequia A27

Woman Carrying Bananas — A28

Designs: 2c, Friendship Beach, Bequia. 3c, Terminal building. 5c, Crater Lake. 6c, Rock carvings, Carib Stone. 8c, Arrowroot. 10c, Owia saltpond. 12c, Ship at deep water wharf. 20c, Sea Island cotton. 25c, Map of St. Vincent and neighboring islands. 50c, Breadfruit. $1, Baleine Falls. $2.50, St. Vincent parrot. $5, Coat of arms.

Perf. 14x13½, 13½x14

1965-67 Photo. Wmk. 314

226 A27 1c multi (BEQUIA) .15 .15
226A A27 1c multi (BEQUIA) ('67) .16 .16
227 A27 2c lt ultra, grn, yel & red .15 .15
228 A27 3c red, yel & brn .15 .15
229 A28 4c brown, ultra & yel .70 .50
a. Wmkd. sideways .50 .35
230 A27 5c pur, bl, yel & grn .15 .15
231 A28 6c sl grn, yel & gray .16 .15
232 A28 8c pur, yel & grn .24 .20
233 A27 10c org brn, yel & bluish grn .28 .24
234 A27 12c grnsh bl, yel & pink .32 .32
235 A28 20c brt yel, grn, pur & brn .40 .35
236 A28 25c ultra, grn & vio blue .50 .45
237 A28 50c grn, yel & bl 1.00 .80
238 A28 $1 vio bl, lt grn & dk sl grn 2.75 2.00
239 A28 $2.50 pale lilac & multi 7.00 5.50
240 A28 $5 dull vio blue & multi 14.00 10.00
Nos. 226-240 (16) 28.11 21.27

Issued: #226A, 8/8/67; others, 8/16/65.
For overprint see No. 270.

Churchill Memorial Issue

Common Design Type

1966, Jan. 24 *Perf. 14*

Design in Black, Gold and Carmine Rose

241 CD319 1c bright blue .15 .15
242 CD319 4c green .32 .32
243 CD319 20c brown 1.90 1.25
244 CD319 40c violet 4.25 2.75
Nos. 241-244 (4) 6.62 4.47

Royal Visit Issue

Common Design Type

1966, Feb. 4 Litho. *Perf. 11x12*

Portrait in Black

245 CD320 4c violet blue .40 .25
246 CD320 25c dk carmine rose 5.00 3.00

WHO Headquarters Issue

Common Design Type

1966, Sept. 20 Litho. *Perf. 14*

247 CD322 4c multicolored .30 .20
248 CD322 25c multicolored 2.25 1.50

UNESCO Anniversary Issue

Common Design Type

1966, Dec. 1 Litho. *Perf. 14*

249 CD323 4c "Education" .25 .20
250 CD323 8c "Science" .52 .42
251 CD323 25c "Culture" 3.25 2.00
Nos. 249-251 (3) 4.02 2.62

View of Mt. Coke Area A29

Designs: 8c, Kingstown Methodist Church. 25c, First license to perform marriage, May 15, 1867. 35c, Arms of Conference of the Methodist Church in the Caribbean and the Americas.

Perf. 14x14½

1967, Dec. 1 Photo. Wmk. 314

252 A29 2c multicolored .15 .15
253 A29 8c multicolored .15 .15
254 A29 25c multicolored .50 .30
255 A29 35c multicolored .60 .40
Nos. 252-255 (4) 1.40 1.00

Attainment of autonomy by the Methodist Church in the Caribbean and the Americas, and opening of headquarters near St. John's, Antigua, May 1967.
For overprints see Nos. 268-269, 271.

Caribbean Meteorological Institute, Barbados — A30

Perf. 14x14½

1968, June 28 Photo. Wmk. 314

256 A30 4c cerise & multi .15 .15
257 A30 25c vermilion & multi .30 .20
258 A30 35c violet blue & multi .42 .30
Nos. 256-258 (3) .87 .65

Issued for World Meteorological Day.

Martin Luther King, Jr. and Cotton Pickers A31

Perf. 13½x13

1968, Aug. 28 Litho. Wmk. 314

259 A31 5c violet & multi .15 .15
260 A31 25c gray & multi .28 .25
261 A31 35c brown red & multi .35 .28
Nos. 259-261 (3) .78 .68

Dr. Martin Luther King, Jr. (1929-68), American civil rights leader.

Scales of Justice and Human Rights Flame — A32

Carnival Costume — A33

3c, Speaker addressing demonstrators, horiz.

Perf. 13x14, 14x13

1968, Nov. 1 Photo. Unwmk.

262 A32 3c orange & multi .15 .15
263 A32 35c grnsh blue & vio blue .50 .35
Set value .56 .40

International Human Rights Year.

1969, Feb. 17 Litho. *Perf. 14½*

5c, Sketch of a steel bandsman. 8c, Revelers, horiz. 25c, Queen of Bands & attendants.

264 A33 1c multicolored .15 .15
265 A33 5c red & dark brown .15 .15
266 A33 8c multicolored .18 .15
267 A33 25c multicolored .55 .35
Nos. 264-267 (4) 1.03
Set value .60

St. Vincent Carnival celebration, Feb. 17.

Nos. 252-253, 236 and 255 Overprinted: "METHODIST / CONFERENCE / MAY / 1969"

Perf. 14x14½, 13½x14

1969, May 14 Photo. Wmk. 314

268 A29 2c multicolored .15 .15
269 A29 8c multicolored .20 .15
270 A28 25c multicolored .35 .25
271 A29 35c multicolored 7.50 7.50
Nos. 268-271 (4) 8.20 8.05

1st Caribbean Methodist Conf. held outside Antigua.

"Strength in Unity" A34

Designs: 5c, 25c, Map of the Caribbean, vert.

Perf. 13½x13, 13x13½

1969, July 1 Litho.

No.	Type	Description	Unused	Used
272	A34	2c orange, yel & blk	.15	.15
273	A34	5c lilac & multi	.15	.15
274	A34	8c emerald, yel & blk	.22	.18
275	A34	25c blue & multi	.90	.50
		Nos. 272-275 (4)	1.42	
		Set value		.82

1st anniv. of CARIFTA (Caribbean Free Trade Area.)

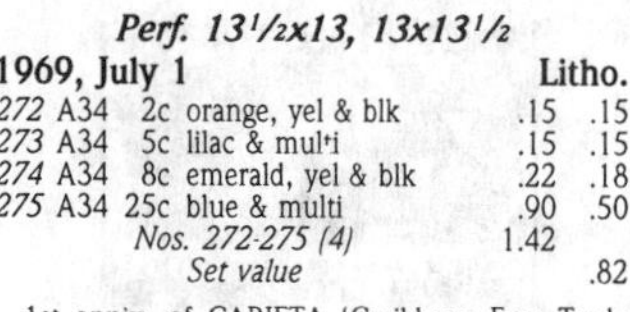

Flag and Arms of St. Vincent — A35

Designs: 10c, Uprising of 1795. 50c, Government House.

Perf. 14x14½

1969, Oct. 27 Photo. Wmk. 314

No.	Type	Description	Unused	Used
276	A35	4c deep ultra & multi	.15	.15
277	A35	10c olive & multi	.20	.18
278	A35	50c orange, gray & blk	.75	.60
		Nos. 276-278 (3)	1.10	.93

Green Heron A36

Birds: ½c, House wren, vert. 2c, Bullfinches. 3c, St. Vincent parrots. 4c, St. Vincent solitaire, vert. 5c, Scalynecked pigeon, vert. 6c, Bananaquits. 8c, Purple-throated Carib. 10c, Mangrove cuckoo, vert. 12c, Black hawk, vert. 20c, Bare-eyed thrush. 25c, Hooded tanager. 50c, Blue-hooded euphonia. $1, Barn owl, vert. $2.50, Yellow-bellied elaenia, vert. $5, Ruddy quail-dove.

Wmk. 314 Upright on ½c, 4c, 5c, 10c, 12c, 50c, $5, Sideways on Others

1970, Jan. 12 Photo. *Perf. 14*

No.	Type	Description	Unused	Used
279	A36	½c multicolored	.15	.15
280	A36	1c multicolored	.15	.15
281	A36	2c multicolored	.15	.15
282	A36	3c multicolored	.15	.15
283	A36	4c multicolored	.20	.15
284	A36	5c multicolored	1.25	.65
285	A36	6c multicolored	.38	.38
286	A36	8c multicolored	.38	.28
287	A36	10c multicolored	.45	.35
288	A36	12c multicolored	.55	.42
289	A36	20c multicolored	.80	.50
290	A36	25c multicolored	.80	.50
291	A36	50c multicolored	1.25	.80
292	A36	$1 multicolored	3.25	1.65
293	A36	$2.50 multicolored	6.50	4.00
294	A36	$5 multicolored	16.00	10.00
		Nos. 279-294 (16)	32.41	20.28

See #379-381. For surcharges see #364-366.

Wmk. 314 Upright on 2c, 3c, 6c, 20c, Sideways on Others

1973

No.	Type	Description	Unused	Used
281a	A36	2c multicolored	.25	.15
282a	A36	3c multicolored	.40	.20
283a	A36	4c multicolored	.52	.28
284a	A36	5c multicolored	.80	.40
285a	A36	6c multicolored	.80	.45
287a	A36	10c multicolored	.80	.45
288a	A36	12c multicolored	1.40	.65
289a	A36	20c multicolored	2.00	1.00
		Nos. 281a-289a (8)	6.97	3.58

DHC6 Twin Otter A37

20th anniv. of regular air services: 8c, Grumman Goose amphibian. 10c, Hawker Siddeley 748. 25c, Douglas DC-3.

Perf. 14x13

1970, Mar. 13 Litho. Wmk. 314

No.	Type	Description	Unused	Used
295	A37	5c lt blue & multi	.16	.15
296	A37	8c lt green & multi	.32	.25
297	A37	10c pink & multi	.55	.35
298	A37	25c yellow & multi	1.50	1.10
		Nos. 295-298 (4)	2.53	1.85

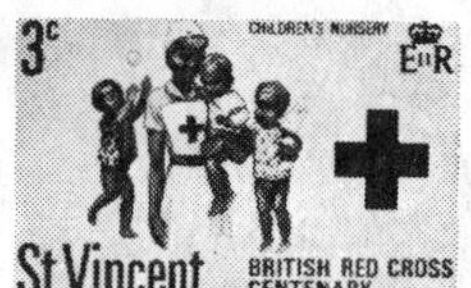

Nurse and Children A38

Red Cross and: 5c, First aid. 12c, Volunteers. 25c, Blood transfusion.

1970, June 1 Photo. *Perf. 14*

No.	Type	Description	Unused	Used
299	A38	3c blue & multi	.15	.15
300	A38	5c yellow & multi	.15	.15
301	A38	12c lt green & multi	.30	.22
302	A38	25c pale salmon & multi	.60	.55
		Nos. 299-302 (4)	1.20	
		Set value		.91

Centenary of British Red Cross Society.

St. George's Cathedral A39

Designs: ½c, 50c, Angel and Two Marys at the Tomb, stained glass window, vert. 25c, St. George's Cathedral, front view, vert. 35c, Interior with altar.

Perf. 14x14½, 14½x14

1970, Sept. 7 Litho. Wmk. 314

No.	Type	Description	Unused	Used
303	A39	½c multicolored	.15	.15
304	A39	5c multicolored	.15	.15
305	A39	25c multicolored	.32	.22
306	A39	35c multicolored	.45	.32
307	A39	50c multicolored	.60	.45
		Set value	1.45	1.05

St. George's Anglican Cathedral, 150th anniv.

Virgin and Child, by Giovanni Bellini — A40

Christmas: 25c, 50c, Adoration of the Shepherds, by Louis Le Nain, horiz.

1970, Nov. 23 Litho. Wmk. 314

No.	Type	Description	Unused	Used
308	A40	8c brt violet & multi	.15	.15
309	A40	25c crimson & multi	.28	.24
310	A40	35c yellow grn & multi	.45	.28
311	A40	50c sapphire & multi	.75	.55
		Nos. 308-311 (4)	1.63	1.22

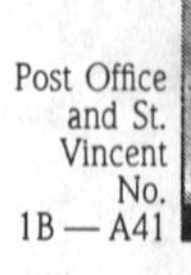

Post Office and St. Vincent No. 1B — A41

New Post Office and: 4c, $1, St. Vincent No. 1. 25c, as 2c.

1971, Mar. 29 *Perf. 14½x14*

No.	Type	Description	Unused	Used
312	A41	2c violet & multi	.15	.15
313	A41	4c olive & multi	.15	.15
314	A41	25c brown org & multi	.48	.32
315	A41	$1 lt green & multi	1.75	1.40
		Nos. 312-315 (4)	2.53	2.02

110th anniv. of 1st stamps of St. Vincent.

National Trust Emblem, Fish and Birds — A42

Designs: 30c, 45c, Cannon at Ft. Charlotte.

Perf. 13½x14

1971, Aug. 4 Litho. Wmk. 314

No.	Type	Description	Unused	Used
316	A42	12c emerald & multi	.25	.18
317	A42	30c lt blue & multi	.55	.50
318	A42	40c brt pink & multi	.90	.60
319	A42	45c black & multi	1.10	.80
		Nos. 316-319 (4)	2.80	2.08

Publicity for the National Trust (for conservation of wild life and historic buildings).

Holy Family with Angels (detail), by Pietro da Cortona A43

Christmas: 5c, 25c, Madonna Appearing to St. Anthony, by Domenico Tiepolo, vert.

1971, Oct. 6 *Perf. 14x14½, 14½x14*

No.	Type	Description	Unused	Used
320	A43	5c rose & multi	.15	.15
321	A43	10c lt green & multi	.18	.15
322	A43	25c lt blue & multi	.40	.28
323	A43	$1 yellow & multi	1.50	1.25
		Nos. 320-323 (4)	2.23	1.83

Careening — A44

Designs: 5c, 20c, Seine fishermen. 6c, 50c, Map of Grenadines. 15c, as 1c.

1971, Nov. 25 *Perf. 14x13½*

No.	Type	Description	Unused	Used
324	A44	1c dp vermilion & multi	.15	.15
325	A44	5c blue & multi	.15	.15
326	A44	6c yellow grn & multi	.20	.15
327	A44	15c orange brn & multi	.50	.38
328	A44	20c yellow & multi	.60	.45
329	A44	50c blue, blk & plum	1.50	1.25
a.		Souvenir sheet of 6, #324-329	11.00	9.25
		Nos. 324-329 (6)	3.10	2.53

The Grenadines of St. Vincent tourist issue.

Grenadier Company Private, 1764 — A45

Designs: 30c, Battalion Company officer, 1772. 50c, Grenadier Company private, 1772.

1972, Feb. 14 *Perf. 14x13½*

No.	Type	Description	Unused	Used
330	A45	12c gray violet & multi	.90	.70
331	A45	30c gray blue & multi	2.25	1.75
332	A45	50c dark gray & multi	4.00	3.25
		Nos. 330-332 (3)	7.15	5.70

Breadnut — A46

Flowers of St. Vincent — A47

1972, May 16 Litho. *Perf. 14x13½*

No.	Type	Description	Unused	Used
333	A46	3c shown	.15	.15
334	A46	5c Papaya	.25	.20
335	A46	12c Rose apples	.90	.60
336	A46	25c Mangoes	2.50	1.65
		Nos. 333-336 (4)	3.80	2.60

1972, July 31 Litho. *Perf. 13½x13*

No.	Type	Description	Unused	Used
337	A47	1c Candlestick Cassia	.15	.15
338	A47	30c Lobster claw	.70	.60
339	A47	40c White trumpet	.80	.70
340	A47	$1 Flowers, Soufriere tree	2.25	1.50
		Nos. 337-340 (4)	3.90	2.95

Sir Charles Brisbane, Arms of St. Vincent — A48

Designs: 30c, Sailing ship "Arethusa." $1, Sailing ship "Blake."

1972, Sept. 29 Wmk. 314 *Perf. 13½*

No.	Type	Description	Unused	Used
341	A48	20c yellow, brn & gold	.60	.45
342	A48	30c lilac & multi	.65	.60
343	A48	$1 multicolored	2.50	1.90
a.		Souvenir sheet of 3, #341-343	7.50	3.25
		Nos. 341-343 (3)	3.75	2.95

Bicentenary of the birth of Sir Charles Brisbane, naval hero, governor of St. Vincent.

Silver Wedding Issue, 1972

Common Design Type

Design: Queen Elizabeth II, Prince Philip, arrowroot plant, breadfruit foliage and fruit.

1972, Nov. 20 Photo. *Perf. 14x14½*

No.	Type	Description	Unused	Used
344	CD324	30c rose brown & multi	.32	.22
345	CD324	$1 multicolored	.90	.55

Columbus Sighting St. Vincent — A49

Designs: 12c, Caribs watching Columbus' ships. 30c, Christopher Columbus. 50c, Santa Maria.

1973, Jan. 18 Litho. *Perf. 13*

No.	Type	Description	Unused	Used
346	A49	5c multicolored	.30	.25
347	A49	12c multicolored	.65	.55
348	A49	30c multicolored	2.25	1.25
349	A49	50c multicolored	4.50	2.25
		Nos. 346-349 (4)	7.70	4.30

475th anniversary of Columbus's Third Voyage to the West Indies.

The Last Supper — A50

Perf. 14x13½

1973, Apr. 19 Litho. Wmk. 314

No.	Type	Description	Unused	Used
350	A50	15c red & multi	.15	.15
351	A50	60c red & multi	.60	.50
352	A50	$1 red & multi	1.25	1.00
a.		Strip of 3, #350-352	2.25	2.00
		Nos. 350-352 (3)	2.00	1.65

Easter.

William Wilberforce and Slave Auction Poster — A51

Designs: 40c, Slaves working on sugar plantation. 50c, Wilberforce and medal commemorating first anniversary of abolition of slavery.

1973, July 11 *Perf. 14x13½*

353 A51	30c multicolored		.42	.32
354 A51	40c multicolored		.50	.45
355 A51	50c multicolored		.85	.55
	Nos. 353-355 (3)		1.77	1.32

140th anniv. of the death of William Wilberforce (1759-1833), member of British Parliament who fought for abolition of slavery.

Families — A52

Design: 40c, Families and "IPPF."

1973, Oct. 3 *Perf. 14½*

356 A52	12c multicolored	.30	.20
357 A52	40c multicolored	1.00	.75

Intl. Planned Parenthood Assoc., 21st anniv.

Princess Anne's Wedding Issue

Common Design Type

1973, Nov. 14 *Perf. 14*

358 CD325	50c slate & multi	.75	.50
359 CD325	70c gray green & multi	1.00	.70

Administration Buildings, Mona University — A53

Designs: 10c, University Center, Kingstown. 30c, Mona University, aerial view. $1, Coat of arms of University of West Indies.

Perf. 14½x14, 14x14½

1973, Dec. 13

360 A53	5c multicolored	.15	.15
361 A53	10c multicolored	.16	.15
362 A53	30c multicolored	.40	.30
363 A53	$1 multicolored	.95	.60
	Nos. 360-363 (4)	1.66	1.20

University of the West Indies, 25th anniv.

Nos. 291, 286 and 292 Surcharged

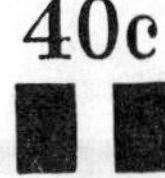

1973, Dec. 15 **Photo.** *Perf. 14*

364 A36	30c on 50c multi	.35	.35
365 A36	40c on 8c multi	.45	.45
366 A36	$10 on $1 multi	14.00	10.50
	Nos. 364-366 (3)	14.80	11.30

The position of the surcharge and shape of obliterating bars differs on each denomination.

Descent from the Cross — A54

Easter: 30c, Descent from the Cross. 40c, Pietà. $1, Resurrection. Designs are from sculptures in Victoria and Albert Museum, London, and Provincial Museum, Valladolid (40c).

1974, Apr. 10 **Litho.** *Perf. 13½x13*

367 A54	5c multicolored	.15	.15
368 A54	30c multicolored	.25	.18
369 A54	40c multicolored	.30	.22
370 A54	$1 multicolored	.65	.45
	Nos. 367-370 (4)	1.35	1.00

"Istra" A55

1974, June 28 *Perf. 14½*

371 A55	15c shown	.20	.15
372 A55	20c "Oceanic"	.26	.20
373 A55	30c "Alexander Pushkin"	.42	.32
374 A55	$1 "Europa"	1.25	.75
a.	Souvenir sheet of 4, #371-374	2.50	1.90
	Nos. 371-374 (4)	2.13	1.42

Cruise ships visiting Kingstown.

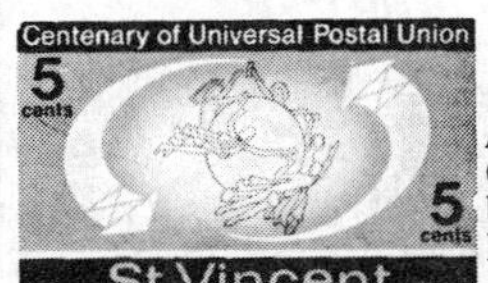

Arrows Circling UPU Emblem A56

UPU, cent.: 12c, Post horn and globe. 60c, Target over map of islands, hand canceler. 90c, Goode's map projection.

1974, July 25 *Perf. 14½*

375 A56	5c violet & multi	.15	.15
376 A56	12c ocher, green & blue	.15	.15
377 A56	60c blue green & multi	.42	.35
378 A56	90c red & multi	.65	.52
	Nos. 375-378 (4)	1.37	1.17

Bird Type of 1970

Birds: 30c, Royal tern. 40c, Brown pelican, vert. $10, Magnificent frigate bird, vert.

Wmk. 314 Sideways on 40c, $10, Upright on 30c

1974, Aug. 29 **Litho.** *Perf. 14½*

379 A36	30c multicolored	.70	.55
380 A36	40c multicolored	1.10	.80
381 A36	$10 multicolored	22.50	14.00
	Nos. 379-381 (3)	24.30	15.35

Scout Emblem and Badges — A57

Churchill as Prime Minister — A58

Perf. 13½x14

1974, Oct. 9 **Wmk. 314**

385 A57	10c lilac & multi	.15	.15
386 A57	25c bister & multi	.35	.32
387 A57	45c gray & multi	.60	.45
388 A57	$1 multicolored	1.25	.90
	Nos. 385-388 (4)	2.35	1.82

St. Vincent Boy Scouts, 60th anniversary.

1974, Nov. 28 *Perf. 14½x14*

Designs (Churchill as): 35c, Lord Warden of the Cinque Ports. 45c, First Lord of the Admiralty. $1, Royal Air Force officer.

389 A58	25c multicolored	.24	.16
390 A58	35c multicolored	.30	.20
391 A58	45c multicolored	.40	.25
392 A58	$1 multicolored	.80	.60
	Nos. 389-392 (4)	1.74	1.21

Sir Winston Churchill (1874-1965), birth centenary. Sheets of 30 in 2 panes of 15 with inscribed gutter between.

A59

A60

1974, Dec. 5 *Perf. 12x12½*

393 A59	3c like 8c	.15	.15
394 A59	3c like 35c	.15	.15
395 A60	3c like 45c	.15	.15
396 A60	3c like $1	.15	.15
a.	Strip of 4, #393-396	.25	.25
397 A59	8c Shepherds	.16	.15
398 A59	35c Virgin, Child and Star	.35	.25
399 A60	45c St. Joseph, Ass & Ox	.42	.35
400 A60	$1 Three Kings	1.10	.70
	Set value	2.25	1.55

Christmas. Nos. 396a, 397-400 have continuous picture.

Giant Mask and Dancers A61

Designs: 15c, Pineapple dancers. 25c, Giant bouquet. 35c, Girl dancers. 45c, Butterfly dancers. $1.25, Sun and moon dancers and float.

Wmk. 314

1975, Feb. 7 **Litho.** *Perf. 14*

401 A61	1c multicolored	.15	.15
a.	Bklt. pane of 2 + label	.50	
b.	Bklt. pane of 3 (#401, 403, 405)	1.25	
402 A61	15c multicolored	.16	.15
a.	Bklt. pane of 3 (#402, 404, 406)	3.00	
403 A61	25c multicolored	.20	.16
404 A61	35c multicolored	.30	.18
405 A61	45c multicolored	.38	.22
406 A61	$1.25 multicolored	1.00	.65
a.	Souvenir sheet of 6, #401-406	2.50	1.65
	Nos. 401-406 (6)	2.19	1.51

Kingstown carnival 1975.

French Angelfish A62

Designs: Fish and whales.

Two types of $2.50:
I - Line to fish's mouth.
II - Line removed (1976).

Wmk. 373

1975, Apr. 10 **Litho.** *Perf. 14*

407 A62	1c shown	.15	.15
408 A62	2c Spotfin butter-fly-fish	.15	.15
409 A62	3c Horse-eyed jack	.15	.15
410 A62	4c Mackerel	.15	.15
411 A62	5c French grunts	.15	.15
412 A62	6c Spotted goatfish	.15	.15
413 A62	8c Ballyhoos	.15	.15
414 A62	10c Sperm whale	.15	.15
415 A62	12c Humpback whale	.16	.15
416 A62	15c Cowfish	.35	.25
417 A62	20c Queen angelfish	.32	.24
418 A62	25c Princess parrotfish	.35	.25
419 A62	35c Red hind	.60	.35
420 A62	45c Atlantic flying fish	.60	.45
421 A62	50c Porkfish	.70	.60
422 A62	$1 Queen triggerfish	1.50	1.10
423 A62	$2.50 Sailfish, type I	3.25	2.25
a.	Type II	5.75	3.25
424 A62	$5 Dolphinfish	7.25	4.50
425 A62	$10 Blue marlin	13.00	9.25
	Nos. 407-425 (19)	29.28	20.59

The 4c, 10c, 20c, $1, were reissued with "1976" below design; 1c, 2c, 3c, 5c, 6c, 8c, 12c, 50c, $10, with "1977" below design; 10c with "1978" below design.

See #472-474. For surcharges and overprints see #463-464, 499-500, 502-503, 572-581, 584-586.

Cutting Bananas — A63

Banana industry: 35c, La Croix packing station. 45c, Women cleaning and packing bananas. 70c, Freighter loading bananas.

1975, June 26 **Wmk. 314** *Perf. 14*

426 A63	25c blue & multi	.25	.20
427 A63	35c blue & multi	.35	.28
428 A63	45c carmine & multi	.45	.35
429 A63	70c carmine & multi	.75	.65
	Nos. 426-429 (4)	1.80	1.48

Snorkel Diving A64

Designs: 20c, Aquaduct Golf Course. 35c, Steel band at Mariner's Inn. 45c, Sunbathing at Young Island. $1.25, Yachting marina.

Perf. 13½

1975, July 31 **Litho.** **Wmk. 373**

430 A64	15c multicolored	.15	.15
431 A64	20c multicolored	.25	.15
432 A64	35c multicolored	.40	.25
433 A64	45c multicolored	.50	.30
434 A64	$1.25 multicolored	1.25	.70
	Nos. 430-434 (5)	2.55	1.55

Tourist publicity.

Presidents Washington, John Adams, Jefferson and Madison — A65

US Presidents: 1c, Monroe, John Quincy Adams, Jackson, Van Buren. 1½c, Wm. Harrison, Tyler, Polk, Taylor. 5c, Fillmore, Pierce, Buchanan, Lincoln. 10c, Johnson, Grant, Hayes, Garfield. 25c, Arthur, Cleveland, Benjamin Harrison, McKinley. 35c, Theodore Roosevelt, Taft, Wilson, Harding. 45c, Coolidge, Hoover, Franklin D. Roosevelt, Truman. $1, Eisenhower, Kennedy, Lyndon B. Johnson, Nixon. $2, Ford and White House.

1975, Sept. 11 **Unwmk.** *Perf. 14½*

435 A65	½c violet & blk	.15	.15
436 A65	1c green & black	.15	.15
437 A65	1½c rose lilac & blk	.15	.15
438 A65	5c yellow grn & blk	.15	.15
439 A65	10c ultra & blk	.15	.15
440 A65	25c ocher & blk	.22	.22
441 A65	35c brt blue & blk	.30	.25
442 A65	45c carmine & blk	.32	.30
443 A65	$1 orange & blk	.75	.60
444 A65	$2 lt olive & blk	1.50	1.10
a.	Souvenir sheet of 10, #435-444 + 2 labels	7.00	6.50
	Set value	3.30	2.65

Bicentenary of American Independence. Issued in sheets of 10 stamps and 2 labels picturing the White House, Capitol, Mt. Vernon, etc.

A66

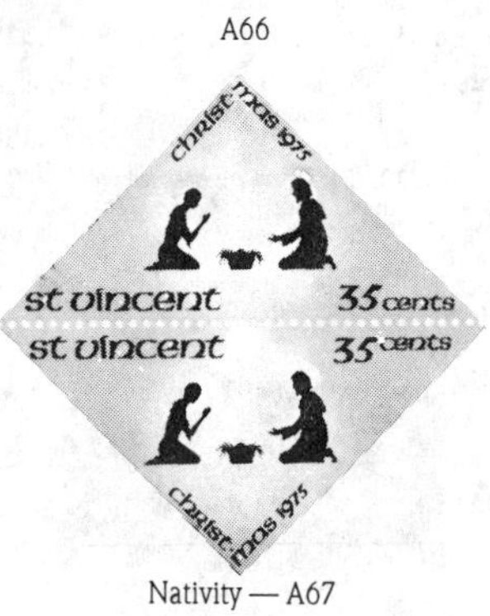

Nativity — A67

Designs: No. 445, 8c, Star of Bethlehem. No. 446, 45c, Shepherds. No. 447, $1, Kings. No. 448, 35c, Nativity.

Wmk. 314

1975, Dec. 4 Litho. *Perf. 14*

445 A66 3c deep rose & blk .15 .15
446 A66 3c deep rose & blk .15 .15
447 A66 3c deep rose & blk .15 .15
448 A67 3c deep rose & blk .15 .15
a. Triangular block of 4, #445-448 .25 .25
449 A66 8c blue & black .15 .15
450 A67 8c blue & black .15 .15
a. Pair, #449-450 .25 .25
451 A66 35c yellow & blk .25 .22
452 A67 35c yellow & blk .25 .22
a. Pair, #449-450 .50 .45
453 A66 45c yellow grn & blk .38 .28
454 A67 45c yellow grn & blk .38 .28
a. Pair, #449-450 .75 .60
455 A66 $1 violet & black .75 .65
456 A67 $1 violet & black .75 .65
a. Pair, #449-450 1.50 1.40
Set value 3.00 2.60

Christmas. No. 448a has continuous design.

Carnival Costumes — A68

Designs: 2c, Humpty-Dumpty people. 5c, Smiling faces (masks). 35c, Dragon worshippers. 45c, Duck costume. $1.25, Bumble bee dance.

Perf. 13x13½

1976, Feb. 19 Litho. Wmk. 373

457 A68 1c carmine & multi .15 .15
a. Booklet pane of 2 .20
458 A68 2c black & multi .15 .15
a. Bklt. pane of 3, #458-460 .60
459 A68 5c lt blue & multi .15 .15
460 A68 35c lt blue & multi .35 .30
a. Bklt. pane of 3, #460-462 2.25
461 A68 45c black & multi .42 .35
462 A68 $1.25 carmine & multi 1.10 .85
Set value 1.95 1.55
Nos. 457-462 (6) 2.32 1.95

Kingstown carnival 1976. No. 457a contains one each of #457-458 with inscribed gutter between.

Nos. 409 and 421 Surcharged with New Value and Bar

1976, Apr. 8 Wmk. 314 *Perf. 14*

463 A62 70c on 3c multi .75 .75
464 A62 90c on 50c multi 1.00 1.00

Yellow Hibiscus and Blue-headed Hummingbird A69

Designs: 10c, Single pink hibiscus and crested hummingbird. 35c, Single white hibiscus and purple-throated carib. 45c, Common red hibiscus and blue-headed hummingbird. $1.25, Single peach hibiscus and green-throated carib.

1976, May 20 Litho. Wmk. 373

465 A69 5c multicolored .25 .20
466 A69 10c multicolored .55 .35
467 A69 35c multicolored 1.65 1.25
468 A69 45c multicolored 2.50 2.00
469 A69 $1.25 multicolored 8.00 4.75
Nos. 465-469 (5) 12.95 8.55

Map of West Indies, Bats, Wicket and Ball — A69a

Prudential Cup — A69b

1976, Sept. 16 Unwmk. *Perf. 14*

470 A69a 15c lt blue & multi .45 .30
471 A69b 45c lilac rose & blk 1.40 .85

World Cricket Cup, won by West Indies Team, 1975.

Fish Type of 1975

1976, Oct. 14 Wmk. 373 *Perf. 14*

472 A62 15c Skipjack .15 .15
473 A62 70c Albacore .65 .65
474 A62 90c Pompano .75 .75
Nos. 472-474 (3) 1.55 1.55

The 15c was reissued with "1977" below design. For overprints see Nos. 501, 582-583.

St. Mary's R.C. Church, Kingstown A70

Christmas: 45c, Anglican Church, Georgetown. 50c, Methodist Church, Georgetown. $1.25, St. George's Anglican Cathedral, Kingstown.

1976, Nov. 18 Litho. *Perf. 14*

475 A70 35c multicolored .28 .28
476 A70 45c multicolored .35 .35
477 A70 50c multicolored .42 .42
478 A70 $1.25 multicolored 1.10 1.10
Nos. 475-478 (4) 2.15 2.15

Barrancoid Pot-stand, c. 450 A.D. — A71

Designs (National Trust Emblem and): 45c, National Museum. 70c, Carib stone head, c. 1510. $1, Ciboney petroglyph, c. 4000 B.C.

1976, Dec. 16 *Perf. 13½*

479 A71 5c multicolored .15 .15
480 A71 45c multicolored .32 .32
481 A71 70c multicolored .50 .50
482 A71 $1 multicolored .75 .75
Nos. 479-482 (4) 1.72 1.72

Carib Indian art and establishment of National Museum in Botanical Gardens, Kingstown.

Kings William I, William II, Henry I, Stephen A72

Kings and Queens of England: 1c, Henry II, Richard I, John, Henry III. 1½c, Edward I, II, III, Richard II. 2c, Henry IV, V, VI, Edward IV. 5c, Edward V, Richard III, Henry VII, VIII. 10c, Edward VI, Lady Jane Grey, Mary I, Elizabeth I. 25c, James I, Charles I, II, James II. 35c, William III, Mary II, Anne, George I. 45c, George II, III, IV. 75c, William IV, Victoria, Edward VII. $1, George V, Edward VIII, George VI. $2, Elizabeth II, coronation.

Perf. 13½

1977, Feb. 7 Litho. Wmk. 373

483 A72 ½c multicolored .15 .15
a. Bklt. pane of 4, #483-486 15.00
484 A72 1c multicolored .15 .15
485 A72 1½c multicolored .15 .15
486 A72 2c multicolored .15 .15
487 A72 5c multicolored .15 .15
a. Bklt. pane of 4, #487-490 15.00
488 A72 10c multicolored .15 .15
489 A72 25c multicolored .18 .16
490 A72 35c multicolored .25 .20
491 A72 45c multicolored .35 .28
a. Bklt. pane of 4, #491-494 17.50
492 A72 75c multicolored .45 .35
493 A72 $1 multicolored .60 .45
494 A72 $2 multicolored 1.10 .90
a. Souv. sheet of 12, #483-494, perf. 14½x14 3.50 3.50
Set value 3.15 2.60

25th anniv. of the reign of Elizabeth II. Nos. 483a, 487a and 491a are unwmkd. See No. 508.

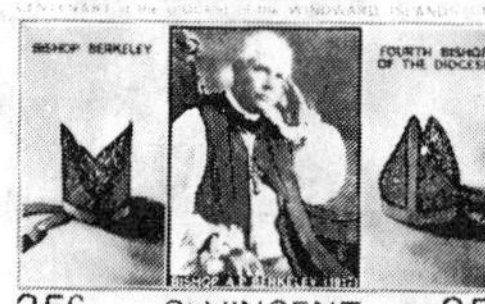

Bishop Alfred P. Berkeley, Bishop's Miters — A73

15c, Grant of Arms to Bishopric, 1951, & names of former Bishops. 45c, Coat of arms & map of Diocese. $1.25, Interior of St. George's Anglican Cathedral & Bishop G. C. M. Woodroffe.

Perf. 13½

1977, May 12 Litho. Wmk. 373

495 A73 15c multicolored .15 .15
496 A73 35c multicolored .26 .22
497 A73 45c multicolored .35 .32
498 A73 $1.25 multicolored 1.00 .80
Nos. 495-498 (4) 1.76 1.49

Diocese of the Windward Islands, centenary.

Nos. 411, 414, 472, 417, 422 Overprinted in Black or Red: "CARNIVAL 1977/ JUNE 25TH - JULY 5TH"

1977, June 2 Litho. *Perf. 14*

499 A62 5c multi .15 .15
500 A62 10c multi (R) .15 .15
501 A62 15c multi (R) .20 .15
502 A62 20c multi (R) .38 .26
503 A62 $1 multi 1.65 1.50
Nos. 499-503 (5) 2.53 2.21

St. Vincent Carnival, June 25-July 5. 5c, 15c dated "1977," 10c, 20c, $1 "1976."

Girl Guide and Emblem — A74

"While Shepherds Watched" — A75

Designs: 15c, Early Guide's uniform, Ranger, Brownie and Guide. 20c, Guide uniforms, 1917 and 1977. $2, Lady Baden-Powell, World Chief Guide, 1930-1977.

Perf. 13½

1977, Sept. 1 Litho. Wmk. 373

504 A74 5c multicolored .15 .15
505 A74 15c multicolored .15 .15
506 A74 20c multicolored .15 .15
507 A74 $2 multicolored 1.25 1.00
Nos. 504-507 (4) 1.70
Set value 1.20

St. Vincent Girl Guides, 50th anniversary.

No. 494 with Additional Inscription: "CARIBBEAN / VISIT 1977"

1977, Oct. 27

508 A72 $2 multicolored 1.25 1.25

Caribbean visit of Queen Elizabeth II.

1977, Nov. Litho. *Perf. 13x11*

Christmas: 10c, "Fear not" said He. 15c, David's Town. 25c, The Heavenly Babe. 50c, Thus Spake and Seraph. $1.25, All Glory be to God.

509 A75 5c buff & multi .15 .15
510 A75 10c buff & multi .15 .15
511 A75 15c buff & multi .15 .15
512 A75 25c buff & multi .15 .15
513 A75 50c buff & multi .32 .26
514 A75 $1.25 buff & multi .80 .65
a. Souvenir sheet of 6, #509-514, perf. 13½ 1.75 1.60
Set value 1.50 1.25

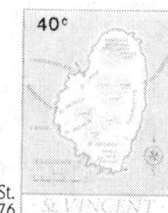

Map of St. Vincent — A76

Perf. 14½x14

1977-78 Litho. Wmk. 373

515 A76 20c dk blue & lt blue ('78) .20 .15
516 A76 40c salmon & black .40 .30
517 A76 40c car, sal & ocher ('78) .40 .30
Nos. 515-517 (3) 1.00 .75

Issued: No. 516 Nov. 30, Nos. 515, 517, Jan. 31. For types surcharged see Nos. B1-B4.

Painted Lady and Bougainvillea — A77

Butterflies and Bougainvillea: 25c, Silver spot. 40c, Red anartia. 50c, Mimic. $1.25, Giant hairstreak.

1978, Apr. 6 Litho. *Perf. 14*

523 A77 5c multicolored .15 .15
524 A77 25c multicolored .20 .18
525 A77 40c multicolored .30 .28
526 A77 50c multicolored .40 .35
527 A77 $1.25 multicolored 1.00 .90
Nos. 523-527 (5) 2.05 1.86

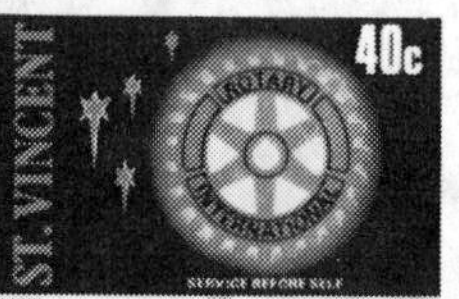

Westminster Abbey — A78

Cathedral: 50c, Gloucester. $1.25, Durham. $2.50, Exeter.

Perf. 13x13½

1978, June 2 Litho. Wmk. 373

528 A78 40c multicolored .18 .15
529 A78 50c multicolored .20 .18
530 A78 $1.25 multicolored .52 .45
531 A78 $2.50 multicolored 1.10 .90
a. Souvenir sheet of 4, #528-531, perf. 13½x14 2.00 2.00
Nos. 528-531 (4) 2.00 1.68

25th anniv. of coronation of Queen Elizabeth II. Nos. 528-531 issued in sheets of 10. #528-531 also exist in booklet panes of two.

Rotary Emblem A79

50c, Lions Intl. emblem. $1, Jaycees emblem.

Perf. 14½

978, July 13 Litho. Wmk. 373

32 A79 40c brown & multi .25 .25
33 A79 50c dark green & multi .30 .30
34 A79 $1 crimson & multi .60 .60
Nos. 532-534 (3) 1.15 1.15

Service clubs aiding in development of St. incent.

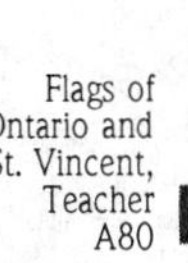

Flags of Ontario and St. Vincent, Teacher A80

Design: 40c, Flags of St. Vincent and Ontario, eacher pointing to board, vert.

978, Sept. 7 Litho. *Perf. 14*

35 A80 40c multicolored .25 .20
36 A80 $2 multicolored 1.10 1.00

School to School Project between children of ntario, Canada, and St. Vincent, 10th anniversary.

Arnos Vale Airport A81

Designs: 40c, Wilbur Wright landing Flyer I. 50c, lyer I airborne. $1.25, Orville Wright and Flyer I.

978, Oct. 19 *Perf. 14½*

537 A81 10c multicolored .15 .15
538 A81 40c multicolored .25 .25
539 A81 50c multicolored .30 .30
540 A81 $1.25 multicolored .75 .75
Nos. 537-540 (4) 1.45 1.45

75th anniversary of 1st powered flight.
For overprint see No. 568.

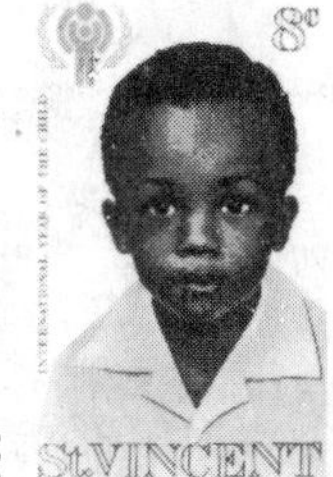

Vincentian Boy, IYC Emblem — A82

Children and IYC Emblem: 20c, Girl. 50c, Boy. 2, Girl and boy.

1979, Feb. 14 Litho. *Perf. 14x13½*

541 A82 8c multicolored .15 .15
542 A82 20c multicolored .16 .15
543 A82 50c multicolored .38 .22
544 A82 $2 multicolored 1.65 .80
Nos. 541-544 (4) 2.34 1.32

International Year of the Child.

Rowland Hill — A83

50c, Great Britain #1-2. $3, St. Vincent #1-1B.

1979, May 31 Litho. *Perf. 14*

545 A83 40c multicolored .16 .16
546 A83 50c multicolored .20 .20
547 A83 $3 multicolored 1.25 1.25
a. Souvenir sheet of 6 3.50 3.50
Nos. 545-547 (3) 1.61 1.61

Sir Rowland Hill (1795-1879), originator of penny postage.
No. 547a contains Nos. 545-547 and Nos. 560, 561 and 565.

Buccament Cancellations, Map of St. Vincent — A84

Designs: Cancellations and location of village.

1979, Sept. 1 Litho. *Perf. 14*

548 A84 1c shown .15 .15
549 A84 2c Sion Hill .15 .15
550 A84 3c Cumberland .15 .15
551 A84 4c Questelles .15 .15
552 A84 5c Layou .15 .15
553 A84 6c New Ground .15 .15
554 A84 8c Mesopotamia .15 .15
555 A84 10c Troumaca .15 .15
556 A84 12c Arnos Vale .15 .15
557 A84 15c Stubbs .15 .15
558 A84 20c Orange Hill .15 .15
559 A84 25c Calliaqua .15 .15
560 A84 40c Edinboro .20 .20
561 A84 50c Colonarie .25 .25
562 A84 80c Babou St. Vincent .40 .40
563 A84 $1 Chateaubelair .50 .50
564 A84 $2 Kingstown 1.10 1.10
565 A84 $3 Barrouallie 1.50 1.50
566 A84 $5 Georgetown 2.50 2.50
567 A84 $10 Kingstown 5.00 5.00
Nos. 548-567 (20) 13.25 13.25

See No. 547a.
The 5c, 10c, 25c reissued inscribed 1982. Singles of #562-564 from #601a are inscribed 1980.

No. 537 Overprinted in Red: "ST. VINCENT AND THE GRENADINES AIR SERVICE 1979"

1979, Aug. 6 Litho. *Perf. 14½*

568 A81 10c multicolored .15 .15

St. Vincent and Grenadines air service inauguration.

Independent State

St. Vincent Flag, Ixora Coccinea A85

Designs: 50c, House of Assembly, ixora stricta. 80c, Prime Minister R. Milton Cato.

1979, Oct. 27 *Perf. 12½x12*

569 A85 20c multicolored .15 .15
570 A85 50c multicolored .25 .25
571 A85 80c multicolored .40 .40
Nos. 569-571 (3) .80 .80

Independence of St. Vincent. Nos. 569-571 each printed se-tenant with label inscribed "Peace and Justice."

Nos. 407, 410-416, 418, 421, 473-474, 422-423, 425 Overprinted in Black: "INDEPENDENCE 1979"

1979, Oct. 27 Litho. *Perf. 14½*

572 A62 1c multicolored .15 .15
573 A62 4c multicolored .15 .15
574 A62 5c multicolored .15 .15
575 A62 6c multicolored .15 .15
576 A62 8c multicolored .15 .15
577 A62 10c multicolored .15 .15
578 A62 12c multicolored .15 .15
579 A62 15c multicolored .15 .15
580 A62 25c multicolored .15 .15
581 A62 50c multicolored .30 .30
582 A62 70c multicolored .45 .45
583 A62 90c multicolored .55 .55
584 A62 $1 multicolored .60 .60
585 A62 $2.50 multicolored 1.50 1.50
586 A62 $10 multicolored 5.50 5.50
Nos. 572-586 (15) 10.25 10.25

Silent Night Text, Virgin and Child A86

Silent Night Text and: 20c, Infant Jesus and angels. 25c, Shepherds. 40c, Angel. 50c, Angels holding Jesus. $2, Nativity.

1979, Nov. 1 *Perf. 13½x14*

587 A86 10c multicolored .15 .15
588 A86 20c multicolored .15 .15
589 A86 25c multicolored .15 .15
590 A86 40c multicolored .22 .22
591 A86 50c multicolored .30 .30
592 A86 $2 multicolored 1.10 1.10
a. Souvenir sheet of 6, #587-592 2.00 2.00
Nos. 587-592 (6) 2.07 2.07

Christmas.

Oleander and Wasp — A87

Oleander and Insects: 10c, Beetle. 25c, Praying mantis. 50c, Green guava beetle. $2, Citrus weevil.

1979, Dec. 13 Litho. *Perf. 14*

593 A87 5c multicolored .15 .15
594 A87 10c multicolored .15 .15
595 A87 25c multicolored .15 .15
596 A87 50c multicolored .32 .32
597 A87 $2 multicolored 1.25 1.25
Nos. 593-597 (5) 2.02 2.02

Type of 1880
Souvenir Sheet

1980, Feb. 28 Litho. *Perf. 14x13½*

598 Sheet of 3 2.25 2.25
a. A3 50c brown .32 .32
b. A3 $1 dark green .60 .60
c. A3 $2 dark blue 1.25 1.25

Coat of arms stamps centenary; London 1980 Intl. Stamp Exhibition, May 6-14.

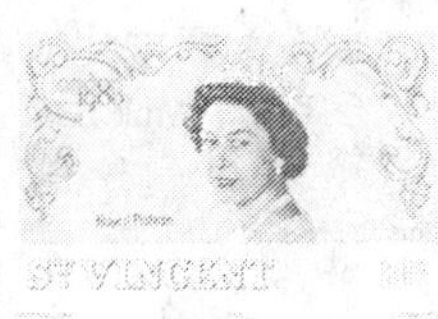

London '80 Intl. Stamp Exhibition, May 6-14 — A88

Wmk. 373

1980, Apr. 24 Litho. *Perf. 14*

599 A88 80c Queen Elizabeth II .42 .42
600 A88 $1 GB #297, SV #190 .50 .50
601 A88 $2 Unissued stamp, 1971 1.10 1.10
a. Souv. sheet of 6, #562-564, 599-601 7.75 7.75
Nos. 599-601 (3) 2.02 2.02

Steel Band A89

1980, June 12 Litho. *Perf. 14*

602 A89 20c shown .15 .15
603 A89 20c Drummers, dancers .15 .15
a. Pair, #602-603 .20 .20

Kingstown Carnival, July 7-8.

Soccer, Olympic Rings — A90

1980, Aug. 7 *Perf. 13½*

604 A90 10c shown .15 .15
605 A90 60c Bicycling .28 .28
606 A90 80c Women's basketball .40 .40
607 A90 $2.50 Boxing 1.25 1.25
Nos. 604-607 (4) 2.08 2.08

Sport for all.
For surcharges see Nos. B5-B8.

Agouti — A91

1980, Oct. 2 Litho. *Perf. 14x14½*

608 A91 25c shown .15 .15
609 A91 50c Giant toad .26 .26
610 A91 $2 Mongoose 1.10 1.10
Nos. 608-610 (3) 1.51 1.51

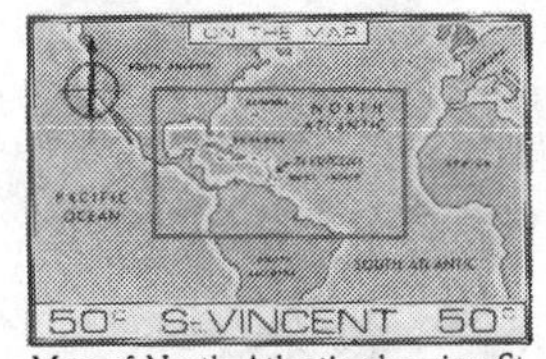

Map of North Atlantic showing St. Vincent — A92

Maps showing St. Vincent: 10c, World. $1, Caribbean. $2, St. Vincent, sail boats, plane.

1980, Dec. 4 Litho. *Perf. 13½x14*

611 A92 10c multicolored .15 .15
612 A92 50c multicolored .25 .25
613 A92 $1 multicolored .48 .48
614 A92 $2 multicolored 1.00 1.00
a. Souv. sheet of 1, perf. 14 1.00 1.00
Nos. 611-614 (4) 1.88 1.88

Ville de Paris in Battle of the Saints, 1782 — A93

Wmk. 373

1981, Feb. 19 Litho. *Perf. 14*

615 A93 50c shown .35 .35
616 A93 60c Ramillies lost in storm, 1782 .40 .40
617 A93 $1.50 Providence, 1793 1.00 1.00
618 A93 $2 Mail Packet Dee, 1840 1.40 1.40
Nos. 615-618 (4) 3.15 3.15

Arrowroot Cultivation A94

Wmk. 373

1981, May 21 Litho. *Perf. 14*

619 A94 25c Arrowroot processing .15 .15
620 A94 25c shown .15 .15
a. Pair, #619-620 .25 .25
621 A94 50c Banana packing plant .25 .25
622 A94 50c Banana cultivation .25 .25
a. Pair, #629-6220 .50 .50
623 A94 60c Copra drying frames .30 .30
624 A94 60c Coconut plantation .30 .30
a. Pair, #623-624 .60 .60
625 A94 $1 Cocoa beans .45 .45
626 A94 $1 Cocoa cultivation .45 .45
a. Pair, #625-626 .90 .90
Nos. 619-626 (8) 2.30 2.30

Prince Charles, Lady Diana, Royal Yacht Charlotte A94a

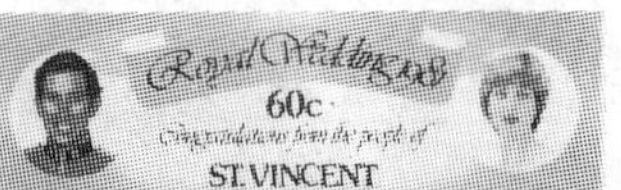

Prince Charles and Lady Diana — A94b

Illustration A94b is reduced.

Wmk. 380

1981, July 13 Litho. *Perf. 14*
627 A94a 60c Couple, Isabella .35 .35
a. Bklt. pane of 4, perf. 12 1.40
628 A94b 60c Couple .35 .35
629 A94a $2.50 Alberta 1.40 1.40
630 A94b $2.50 like #628 1.40 1.40
a. Bklt. pane of 4, perf. 12 5.75
631 A94a $4 Britannia 2.50 2.50
632 A94b $4 like #628 2.50 2.50
Nos. 627-632 (6) 8.50 8.50

Royal wedding. Each denomination issued in sheets of 7 (6 type A94a, 1 type A94b).

For surcharges and overprints see Nos. 891-892, O1-O6.

Souvenir Sheet

1981 Litho. *Perf. 12*
632A A95b $5 Couple 3.00 3.00

Kingstown General Post Office
A95 A96

Wmk. 373

1981, Sept. 1 Litho. *Perf. 14*
633 A95 $2 multicolored 1.25 1.25
634 A96 $2 multicolored 1.25 1.25
a. Pair, #633-634 2.50 2.50

UPU membership centenary.

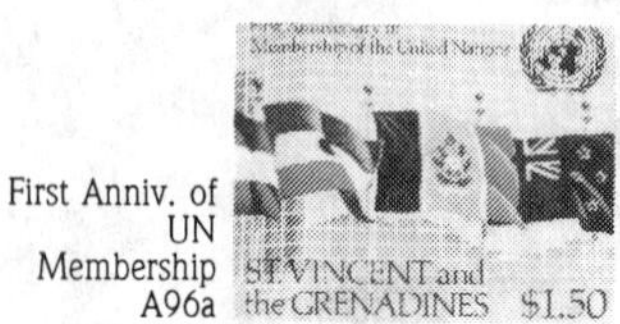

First Anniv. of UN Membership A96a

Wmk. 373

1981, Sept. 1 Litho. *Perf. 14*
634A A96a $1.50 Flags .65 .65
634B A96a $2.50 Prime Minister Cato 1.10 1.10

"The People that Walked in Darkness . . ." — A97

1981, Nov. 19 Litho. *Perf. 12*
635 A97 50c shown .22 .22
636 A97 60c Angel .28 .28
637 A97 $1 "My soul . . ." .45 .45
638 A97 $2 Flight into Egypt .90 .90
a. Souvenir sheet of 4, #635-638 1.90 1.90
Nos. 635-638 (4) 1.85 1.85

Christmas. For surcharge see No. 674.

Re-introduction of Sugar Industry, First Anniv. — A98

1982, Apr. 5 Litho. *Perf. 14*
639 A98 50c Boilers .35 .35
640 A98 60c Drying plant .40 .40
641 A98 $1.50 Gearwheels 1.00 1.00
642 A98 $2 Loading sugar cane 1.40 1.40
Nos. 639-642 (4) 3.15 3.15

50th Anniv. of Airmail Service A99

1982, July 29 Litho. *Perf. 14*
643 A99 50c DH Moth, 1932 .35 .35
644 A99 60c Grumman Goose, 1952 .40 .40
645 A99 $1.50 Hawker-Siddeley 748, 1968 1.00 1.00
646 A99 $2 Britten-Norman Islander, 1982 1.40 1.40
Nos. 643-646 (4) 3.15 3.15

21st Birthday of Princess Diana, July 1 — A99a

Wmk. 380

1982, June Litho. *Perf. 14*
647 A99a 50c Augusta of Saxe, 1736 .35 .35
648 A99a 60c Saxe arms .40 .40
649 A99a $6 Diana 4.00 4.00
Nos. 647-649 (3) 4.75 4.75

For overprints see Nos. 652-654.

Scouting Year — A100

1982, July 15 Wmk. 373
650 A100 $1.50 Emblem 1.00 1.00
651 A100 $2.50 "75" 1.75 1.75

For overprints see Nos. 890, 893.

Nos. 647-649 Overprinted: "ROYAL BABY"

1982, July Wmk. 380
652 A99a 50c multicolored .32 .32
653 A99a 60c multicolored .35 .35
654 A99a $6 multicolored 3.50 3.50
Nos. 652-654 (3) 4.17 4.17

Birth of Prince William of Wales, June 21.

Carnival A101

1982, June 10 Litho. *Perf. 13½*
655 A101 50c Butterfly float .32 .32
656 A101 60c Angel dancer, vert. .35 .35
657 A101 $1.50 Winged dancer, vert. .90 .90
658 A101 $2 Eagle float 1.25 1.25
Nos. 655-658 (4) 2.82 2.82

Cruise Ships A103

Wmk. 373

1982, Dec. 29 Litho. *Perf. 14*
662 A103 45c Geestport .30 .30
663 A103 60c Stella Oceanis .40 .40
664 A103 $1.50 Victoria 1.00 1.00
665 A103 $2 QE 2 1.40 1.40
Nos. 662-665 (4) 3.10 3.10

Pseudocorynactis Caribbeorum — A104

Sea Horses and Anemones. 60c, $1.50, $2 vert.

1983, Jan. 12 Wmk. 373 *Perf. 12*
666 A104 50c shown .35 .35
667 A104 60c Actinoporus elegans .40 .40
668 A104 $1.50 Arachnanthus nocturnus 1.00 1.00
669 A104 $2 Hippocampus reidi 1.40 1.40
Nos. 666-669 (4) 3.15 3.15

For overprint see No. 886.

Commonwealth Day — A104a

Wmk. 373

1983, Mar. 14 Litho. *Perf. 14*
670 A104a 45c Map .30 .30
671 A104a 60c Flag .40 .40
672 A104a $1.50 Prime Minister Cato 1.00 1.00
673 A104a $2 Banana industry 1.40 1.40
Nos. 670-673 (4) 3.10 3.10

No. 635 Surcharged

Wmk. 373

1983, Apr. 26 Litho. *Perf. 12*
674 A97 45c on 50c multi .45 .45

A104b

A105

Wmk. 373

1983, July 6 Litho. *Perf. 12*
675 A104b 45c Handshake .32 .32
676 A104b 60c Emblem .45 .45
677 A104b $1 Map .70 .70
678 A104b $2 Flags 1.40 1.40
Nos. 675-678 (4) 2.87 2.87

10th anniv. of Chaguaramas (Caribbean Free Trade Assoc.)

Perf. 12x11½

1983, Oct. 6 Litho. Wmk. 373
679 A105 45c Founder William A. Smith .30 .30
680 A105 60c Boy, officer .40 .40
681 A105 $1.50 Emblem 1.00 1.00
682 A105 $2 Community service 1.40 1.40
Nos. 679-682 (4) 3.10 3.10

Boys' Brigade, cent. For overprint see #887.

Christmas A106

1983, Nov. 15 Litho. *Perf. 12*
683 A106 10c Shepherds at Watch .15 .15
684 A106 50c The Angel of the Lord .40 .40
685 A106 $1.50 A Glorious Light 1.15 1.15
686 A106 $2.40 At the Manger 2.00 2.00
a. Souvenir sheet of 4, #683-686 3.75 3.75
Nos. 683-686 (4) 3.70 3.70

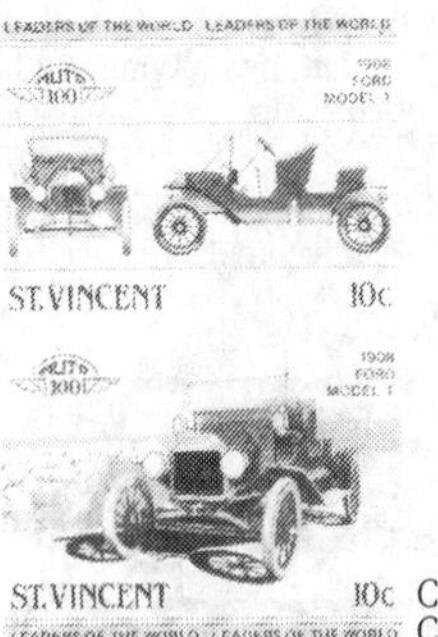

Classic Cars — A107

1983, Nov. 9 Litho. *Perf. 12½*

Se-tenant Pairs

687 A107 10c Ford Model T .15 .15
688 A107 60c Supercharged Cord .50 .50
689 A107 $1.50 Mercedes-Benz 1.40 1.40
690 A107 $1.50 Citroen Open Tourer 1.40 1.40
691 A107 $2 Ferrari Boxer 1.90 1.90
692 A107 $2 Rolls-Royce Phantom 1.90 1.90
Nos. 687-692 (6) 7.25 7.25

See #773-777, 815-822, 906-911.

Locomotives Type of 1985

1983, Dec. 8 Litho. *Perf. 12½x13*

Se-tenant Pairs

699 A120 10c King Henry VIII .15 .15
700 A120 10c Royal Scots Greys .15 .15
701 A120 25c Hagley Hall .20 .20
702 A120 50c Sir Lancelot .40 .40
703 A120 60c B12 Class .50 .50
704 A120 75c No. 1000 Deeley Compound .65 .65
705 A120 $2.50 Cheshire 2.00 2.00
706 A120 $3 Bulleid Austerity 2.50 2.50
Nos. 699-706 (8) 6.55 6.55

Fort Duvernette A108

Perf. 14x14½

1984, Feb. 13 Litho. Wmk. 380
715 A108 35c View .26 .26
716 A108 45c Wall, flag .34 .34
717 A108 $1 Canon .72 .72
718 A108 $3 Map 2.30 2.30
Nos. 715-718 (4) 3.62 3.62

Flowering Trees — A109

Perf. 13½x14

1984, Apr. 2 Litho. Wmk. 373
719 A109 5c White frangipani .15 .15
720 A109 10c Genip .15 .15
721 A109 15c Immortelle .15 .15
722 A109 20c Pink poui .15 .15
723 A109 25c Buttercup .18 .18
724 A109 35c Sandbox .26 .26
725 A109 45c Locust .34 .34
726 A109 60c Colville's glory .45 .45
727 A109 75c Lignum vitae .55 .55
728 A109 $1 Golden shower .72 .72
729 A109 $5 Angelin 3.60 3.60
730 A109 $10 Roucou 7.25 7.25
Nos. 719-730 (12) 13.95 13.95

World War I Battle Scene, King George V
A110 A111

1984, Apr. 25 Litho. *Perf. 13x12½*

731 A110 1c shown .15 .15
732 A111 1c shown .15 .15
733 A110 5c Battle of Bannockburn .15 .15
734 A111 5c Edward II .15 .15
735 A110 60c George V, diff. .45 .45
736 A111 60c York Cottage, Sandringham .45 .45
737 A110 75c Edward II, diff. .60 .60
738 A111 75c Berkeley Castle .60 .60
739 A110 $1 Arms of Edward II .75 .75
740 A111 $1 Edward II, diff. .75 .75
741 A110 $4 Arms of George V 2.75 2.75
742 A111 $4 George V, diff. 2.75 2.75
Nos. 731-742 (12) 9.70 9.70

Stamps of same denomination se-tenant in continuous design.

Carnival A112

Wmk. 380

1984, June 25 Litho. *Perf. 14*

743 A112 35c Musical fantasy .26 .26
744 A112 45c African woman .34 .34
745 A112 $1 Market woman .75 .75
746 A112 $3 Carib hieroglyph 2.25 2.25
Nos. 743-746 (4) 3.60 3.60

Locomotives Type of 1985

1984, July 27 Litho. *Perf. 12½*

Se-tenant Pairs

747 A120 1c Liberation Class 141R, 1945 .15 .15
748 A120 2c Dreadnought Class 50, 1967 .15 .15
749 A120 3c No. 242A1, 1946 .15 .15
750 A120 50c Dean Goods, 1883 .50 .50
751 A120 75c Hetton Colliery, 1822 .65 .65
752 A120 $1 Penydarren, 1804 1.00 1.00
753 A120 $2 Novelty, 1829 1.90 1.90
754 A120 $3 Class 44, 1925 3.25 3.25
Nos. 747-754 (8) 7.75 7.75

Slavery Abolition Sesquicentennial — A113

1984, Aug. 1 Litho. *Perf. 14*

761 A113 35c Hoeing .26 .26
762 A113 45c Gathering sugar cane .34 .34
763 A113 $1 Cutting sugar cane .75 .75
764 A113 $3 Abolitionist William Wilberforce 2.25 2.25
Nos. 761-764 (4) 3.60 3.60

1984 Summer Olympics — A114

Military Uniforms — A115

1984, Aug. 30 Unwmk. *Perf. 12½*

765 A114 1c Judo .15 .15
766 A114 1c Weight lifting .15 .15
767 A114 3c Bicycling (facing left) .15 .15
768 A114 3c Bicycling (facing right) .15 .15
769 A114 60c Swimming (back stroke) .30 .30
770 A114 60c Breast stroke .30 .30
771 A114 $3 Running (start) 1.50 1.50
772 A114 $3 Running (finish) 1.50 1.50
Nos. 765-772 (8) 4.20 4.20

Stamps of same denomination se-tenant.

Car Type of 1983

1984, Oct. 22 Litho. *Perf. 12½*

Se-tenant Pairs

773 A107 5c Austin-Healey Sprite, 1958 .15 .15
774 A107 20c Maserati, 1971 .15 .15
775 A107 55c Pontiac GTO, 1964 .50 .50
776 A107 $1.50 Jaguar, 1957 1.25 1.25
777 A107 $2.50 Ferrari, 1970 2.25 2.25
Nos. 773-777 (5) 4.30 4.30

1984, Nov. 12 Wmk. 380 *Perf. 14*

783 A115 45c Grenadier, 1773 .32 .32
784 A115 60c Grenadier, 1775 .45 .45
785 A115 $1.50 Grenadier, 1768 1.15 1.15
786 A115 $2 Battalion Co. Officer, 1780 1.50 1.50
Nos. 783-786 (4) 3.42 3.42

Locomotives Type of 1985

1984, Nov. 21 Litho. *Perf. 12½x13*

Se-tenant Pairs

787 A120 5c 1954 R.R. Class 20, Zimbabwe .15 .15
788 A120 40c 1928 Southern Maid, U.K. .45 .45
789 A120 75c 1911 Prince of Wales, U.K. .85 .85
790 A120 $2.50 1935 D.R.G. Class 05, Germany 2.75 2.75
Nos. 787-790 (4) 4.20 4.20

Cricket Players — A116

1985, Jan. 7 Litho. *Perf. 12½*

Se-tenant Pairs

795 A116 5c N.S. Taylor, portrait .15 .15
796 A116 35c T.W. Graveney with bat .40 .40
797 A116 50c R.G.D. Willis at wicket .60 .60
798 A116 $3 S.D. Fletcher at wicket 3.50 3.50
Nos. 795-798 (4) 4.65 4.65

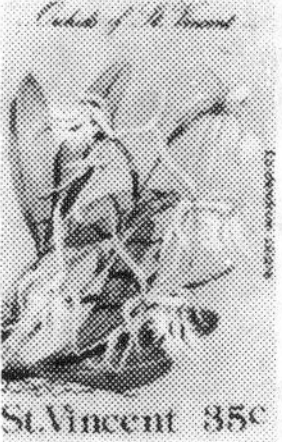

Orchids — A117

Audubon Birth Bicent. — A118

1985, Jan. 31 Litho. *Perf. 14*

803 A117 35c Epidendrum ciliare .26 .26
804 A117 45c Ionopsis utricularioides .34 .34
805 A117 $1 Epidendrum secundum .75 .75
806 A117 $3 Oncidium altissimum 2.25 2.25
Nos. 803-806 (4) 3.60 3.60

1985, Feb. 7 Litho. *Perf. 12½*

Illustrations of North American bird species by artist/naturalist John J. Audubon.

807 A118 15c Brown pelican .15 .15
808 A118 15c Green heron .15 .15
809 A118 40c Pileated woodpecker .25 .25
810 A118 40c Common flicker .25 .25
811 A118 60c Painted bunting .35 .35
812 A118 60c White-winged crossbill .35 .35
813 A118 $2.25 Red-shouldered hawk 1.40 1.40
814 A118 $2.25 Crested caracara 1.40 1.40
Nos. 807-814 (8) 4.30 4.30

Stamps of the same denomination printed se-tenant.

Car Type of 1983

1985

Se-tenant Pairs

Design A107

815 1c 1937 Lancia Aprilia, Italy .15 .15
816 25c 1922 Essex Coach, US .20 .20
817 55c 1973 Pontiac Firebird Trans Am, US .45 .45
818 60c 1950 Nash Rambler, US .55 .55
819 $1 1961 Ferrari Tipo 156, Italy .95 .95
820 $1.50 1967 Eagle-Weslake Type 58, US 1.40 1.40
821 $2 1953 Cunningham C-5R, US 2.00 2.00
Nos. 815-821 (7) 5.70 5.70

Souvenir Sheet

822 Sheet of 4 10.00 10.00
a. A107 $4 as No. 820 2.25 2.25
b. A107 $4 as No. 820, diff. 2.25 2.25
c. A107 $5 as No. 819 2.75 2.75
d. A107 $5 as No. 819, diff. 2.75 2.75

Issued: 1c, 55c, $2, Mar. 11; 25c, 60c, $1, $1.50, June 7.

Herbs and Spices — A119

1985, Apr. 22 *Perf. 14*

829 A119 25c Pepper .20 .20
830 A119 35c Sweet marjoram .28 .28
831 A119 $1 Nutmeg .75 .75
832 A119 $3 Ginger 2.25 2.25
Nos. 829-832 (4) 3.48 3.48

Locomotives of the United Kingdom A120

1985, Apr. 26 *Perf. 12½*

Se-tenant Pairs

833 A120 1c 1913 Glen Douglas .15 .15
834 A120 10c 1872 Fenchurch Terrier .15 .15
835 A120 40c 1870 No. 1 Stirling Single .35 .35
836 A120 60c 1866 No. 158A .55 .55
837 A120 $1 1893 No. 103 Class Jones Goods .90 .90
838 A120 $2.50 1908 Great Bear 2.50 2.50
Nos. 833-838 (6) 4.60 4.60

See #699-706, 747-754, 787-790, 849-860, 961-967.

Traditional Instruments A121

1985, May 16 *Perf. 15*

845 A121 25c Bamboo flute .20 .20
846 A121 35c Quatro .28 .28
847 A121 $1 Bamboo base, vert. .75 .75
848 A121 $2 Goat-skin drum, vert. 1.50 1.50
a. Sheet of 4, #845-848 2.75 2.75
Nos. 845-848 (4) 2.73 2.73

Locomotives Type of 1985

1985, June 27 *Perf. 12½*

Se-tenant Pairs

849 A120 5c 1874 Loch, U.K. .15 .15
850 A120 30c 1919 Class 47XX, U.K. .30 .30
851 A120 60c 1876 P.L.M. Class 121, France .60 .60
852 A120 75c 1927 D.R.G. Class 24, Germany .70 .70
853 A120 $1 1889 No. 1008, U.K. 1.00 1.00
854 A120 $2.50 1926 S.R. Class PS-4, US 2.50 2.50
Nos. 849-854 (6) 5.25 5.25

A122

A123

Queen Mother, 85th birthday: Photographs.

1985, Aug. 9

861 A122 35c Facing right .16 .16
862 A122 35c Facing left .16 .16
863 A122 85c Facing right, diff. .38 .38
864 A122 85c Facing left, diff. .38 .38
865 A122 $1.20 Facing right, diff. .55 .55
866 A122 $1.20 Facing left, diff. .55 .55
867 A122 $1.60 Facing front .75 .75
868 A122 $1.60 Facing left, diff. .75 .75
Nos. 861-868 (8) 3.68 3.68

Souvenir Sheet

869 Sheet of 2 2.50 2.50
a. A122 $2.10 Facing right, diff. 1.25 1.25
b. A122 $2.10 Facing front. diff. 1.25 1.25

Stamps of the same denomination printed se-tenant.

For overprints see Nos. 888-889.

1985, Dec. 19 Litho. *Perf. 12½*

869C Sheet of 2 3.75 3.75
e. A122 $3.50 like #863 1.75 1.75
f. A122 $3.50 like #864 1.75 1.75
869D Sheet of 2 6.25 6.25
g. A122 $6 like #861 3.25 3.25
h. A122 $6 like #862 3.25 3.25

1985, Aug. 16

Photographs of Elvis Presley (1935-1977), American entertainer.

870 A123 10c In concert .15 .15
871 A123 10c Facing front .15 .15
872 A123 60c In concert, diff. .35 .35
873 A123 60c Facing left .35 .35
874 A123 $1 In concert, diff. .60 .60
875 A123 $1 Facing front, diff. .60 .60
876 A123 $5 Wearing leather jacket 3.00 3.00
877 A123 $5 Facing left, diff. 3.00 3.00
Nos. 870-877 (8) 8.20 8.20

Souvenir Sheets

878 Sheet of 4 .72 .72
a. A123 30c like #870 .18 .18
b. A123 30c like #871 .18 .18
879 Sheet of 4 1.20 1.20
a. A123 50c like #872 .30 .30
b. A123 50c like #873 .30 .30
880 Sheet of 4 3.50 3.50
a. A123 $1.50 like #874 .85 .85
b. A123 $1.50 like #875 .85 .85
881 Sheet of 4 10.00 10.00
a. A123 $4.50 like #876 2.50 2.50
b. A123 $4.50 like #877 2.50 2.50

Nos. 878-881 contain two of each stamp.

Stamps of the same denomination printed se-tenant.

Two $4 "stamps" were not issued.

For other Presley souvenir sheet see No. 1567.

For overprints, see Nos. 1005-1016.

Flour Milling A124

1985, Oct. 17 Wmk. 373 *Perf. 15*

882 A124 20c Conveyor from elevators .15 .15
883 A124 30c Roller mills .22 .22
884 A124 75c Office .55 .55
885 A124 $3 Bran finishers 2.25 2.25
Nos. 882-885 (4) 3.17 3.17

Nos. 667, 680, 863-864, 650, 631-632, 651 Ovptd. "CARIBBEAN / ROYAL VISIT / -1985-" or Surcharged with 3 Black Bars and New Value in Black

1985, Oct. 27 *Perfs. as Before*

886 A104 60c multicolored *1.25 1.25*
887 A105 60c multicolored *1.25 1.25*
888 A122 85c multicolored *2.00 2.00*
889 A122 85c multicolored *2.00 2.00*
890 A100 $1.50 multicolored *3.50 3.50*
891 A94a $1.60 on $4 *3.75 3.75*
892 A94b $1.60 on $4 *3.75 3.75*
893 A100 $2.50 multicolored *5.75 5.75*
Nos. 886-893 (8) *23.25 23.25*

Michael Jackson (b. 1960), American Entertainer — A125

Photographs.

1985, Dec. 2 *Perf. 12½*

894 A125 60c Portrait .28 .28
895 A125 60c On stage .28 .28
896 A125 $1 Singing .52 .52
897 A125 $1 Portrait, diff. .52 .52
898 A125 $2 Black jacket 1.00 1.00
899 A125 $2 Red jacket 1.00 1.00
900 A125 $5 Portrait, diff. 2.75 2.75
901 A125 $5 Wearing white glove 2.75 2.75
Nos. 894-901 (8) 9.10 9.10

Stamps of same denomination printed se-tenant.

Souvenir Sheets
Perf. 13x12½

902 Sheet of 4, 2 each .90 .90
d.-e. A125 45c like #894-895 .20 .20
902A Sheet of 4, 2 each 1.90 1.90
f.-g. A125 90c like #896-897 .45 .45
902B Sheet of 4, 2 each 3.00 3.00
h.-i. A125 $1.50 like #898-899 .70 .70
902C Sheet of 4, 2 each 8.25 8.25
j.-k. A125 $4 like #900-901 2.00 2.00

Christmas A126

Children's drawings: 25c, Serenade, 75c, Poinsettia. $2.50, Jesus, Our Master.

1985, Dec. 9 Wmk. 373 *Perf. 14*

903 A126 25c multicolored .18 .18
904 A126 75c multicolored .55 .55
905 A126 $2.50 multicolored 1.90 1.90
Nos. 903-905 (3) 2.63 2.63

Car Type of 1983

1986, Jan. 27 *Perf. 12½*

Se-tenant Pairs

906 A107 30c 1916 Cadillac Type 53, US .35 .35
907 A107 45c 1939 Triumph Dolomite, UK .55 .55
908 A107 60c 1972 Panther J-72, UK .70 .70
909 A107 90c 1967 Ferrari 275 GTB/4, Italy 1.10 1.10
910 A107 $1.50 1953 Packard Caribbean, US 1.75 1.75
911 A107 $2.50 1931 Bugatti Type 41 Royale, France 3.00 3.00
Nos. 906-911 (6) 7.45 7.45

Halley's Comet A127

Wmk. 380

1986, Apr. 14 Litho. *Perf. 15*

918 A127 45c shown .35 .35
919 A127 60c Edmond Halley .45 .45
920 A127 75c Newton's reflector telescope .55 .55
921 A127 $3 Local astronomer 2.25 2.25
a. Souvenir sheet of 4, #918-921 3.60 3.60
Nos. 918-921 (4) 3.60 3.60

Souvenir Sheets

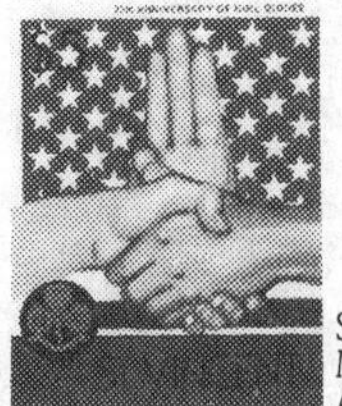

Scouting Movement, 75th Anniv. — A127a

American flag and Girl Guides or Boy Scouts emblem and: No. 922b, Scout sign, handshake. No. 922c, Paintbrushes and pallet. No. 922d, Knots. No. 922e, Lord Baden-Powell.

1986, Feb. 25 Litho. *Perf. 13x12½*

922 Sheet of 2 4.50 4.50
b.-c. A127a $5 any single 2.25 2.25
922A Sheet of 2 5.50 5.50
d.-e. A127a $6 any single 2.75 2.75

"Capex '87" overprints on this issue were not authorized.

Elizabeth II Wearing Crown Jewels — A128

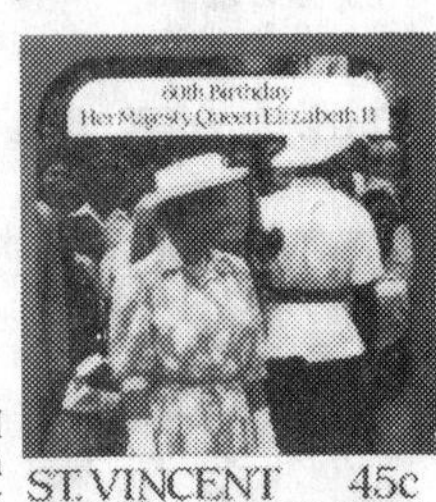

Elizabeth II at Victoria Park A129

Various portraits.

1986, Apr. 21 Wmk. 373 *Perf. 12½*

923 A128 10c multicolored .15 .15
924 A128 90c multicolored .55 .55
925 A128 $2.50 multicolored 1.50 1.50
926 A128 $8 multi, vert. 5.00 5.00
Nos. 923-926 (4) 7.20 7.20

Souvenir Sheet

927 A128 $10 multicolored 6.25 6.25

Perf. 15x14

1986, June 14 Wmk. 373

Designs: No. 928, with Prime Minister Mitchell. No. 929, Arriving at Port Elizabeth. No. 930, at Independence Day Parade.

928 A129 45c multicolored .35 .35
929 A129 60c multicolored .45 .45
930 A129 75c multicolored .55 .55
931 A129 $2.50 multicolored 1.90 1.90
Nos. 928-931 (4) 3.25 3.25

Souvenir Sheet

932 A129 $3 multicolored 2.25 2.25

Queen Elizabeth II, 60th birthday.

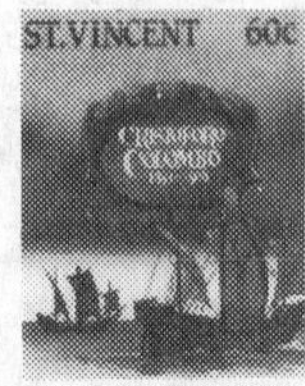

Discovery of America, 500th Anniv. (1992) — A130

1986, Jan. 23 Litho. *Perf. 12½*

933 A130 60c Fleet .45 .45
934 A130 60c Columbus .45 .45
935 A130 $1.50 At Spanish Court 1.10 1.10
936 A130 $1.50 Ferdinand, Isabella 1.10 1.10
937 A130 $2.75 Fruit, Santa Maria 2.05 2.05
938 A130 $2.75 Fruit 2.05 2.05
Nos. 933-938 (6) 7.20 7.20

Souvenir Sheet

939 A130 $6 Columbus, diff. 4.50 4.50

Stamps of same denomination printed se-tenant in continuous designs.

1986 World Cup Soccer Championships, Mexico — A131

1986, May 7 Litho. *Perf. 15*

940 A131 1c Emblem .15 .15
941 A131 2c Mexico .15 .15
942 A131 5c Mexico, diff. .15 .15
943 A131 5c Hungary vs. Scotland .15 .15
944 A131 10c Spain vs. Scotland .15 .15
945 A131 30c England vs. USSR .18 .18
946 A131 45c Spain vs. France .28 .28
947 A131 $1 England vs. Italy .60 .60

Perf. 13½

Size: 56x36mm

948 A131 75c Mexico .42 .42
949 A131 $2 Scotland 1.25 1.25
950 A131 $4 Spain 2.50 2.50
951 A131 $5 England 3.00 3.00
Nos. 940-951 (12) 8.98 8.98

1986, July 7 Souvenir Sheets

952 A131 $1.50 like #950 .65 .65
952A A131 $1.50 like #941 .65 .65
953 A131 $2.25 like #949 .95 .95
954 A131 $2.50 like #948 1.00 1.00
954A A131 $3 like #946 1.10 1.10
955 A131 $5.50 like #951 2.50 2.50
Nos. 952-955 (6) 6.85 6.85

Nos. 941-944, 946, 947, vert.

Wedding of Prince Andrew and Sarah Ferguson A132

A132a

1986 Litho. *Perf. 12½x13, 13x12½*

956 A132 60c Andrew .35 .35
957 A132 60c Sarah .35 .35
958 A132 $2 Andrew, horiz. 1.25 1.25
959 A132 $2 Andrew, Nancy Reagan, horiz. 1.25 1.25
960 A132a $10 In coach 6.00 6.00
Nos. 956-960 (5) 9.20 9.20

Stamps of the same denomination printed se-tenant.

Issued: $10, Nov.; others, July 23.

For overprints see Nos. 976-979.

A number of unissued items, imperfs., part perfs., missing color varieties, etc., were made available when the Format International inventory was liquidated.

Locomotives Type of 1985

Designs: 30c, 1926 JNR ABT Rack & Adhesion Class ED41 BZZB, Japan. 50c, 1883 Chicago RR Exposition, The Judge, 1A Type, US. $1, 1973 BM & LPRR E60C Co-Co, US. $3, 1972 GM (EMD SD40-2 Co-Co, US.

1986, July *Perf. 12½x1*

Se-tenant Pairs

961 A120 30c multi .35 .3
962 A120 50c multi .60 .6
963 A120 $1 multi 1.25 1.2
964 A120 $3 multi 3.50 3.5
Nos. 961-964 (4) 5.70 5.7

Trees — A133

1986, Sept. *Perf. 1*

968 A133 10c Acrocomia aculeata .15 .1
969 A133 60c Pithecellobium saman .45 .4
970 A133 75c Tabebuia pallida .55 .5
971 A133 $3 Andira inermis 2.25 2.2
Nos. 968-971 (4) 3.40 3.4

Anniversaries A134

1986, Sept. 30

972 A134 45c Cadet Force emblem, vert. .35 .3
973 A134 60c Grimble Building, GHS .45 .4
974 A134 $1.50 GHS class 1.10 1.1
975 A134 $2 Cadets in formation 1.50 1.5
Nos. 972-975 (4) 3.40 3.4

St. Vincent Cadet Force, 50th anniv., and Girls High School, 75th anniv.

Nos. 956-959 Overprint. "Congratulations to T.R.H. The Duke & Duchess of York" in Silver

Perf. 12½x13, 13x12½

1986, Oct. Litho

976 A132 60c No. 956 .45 .4
977 A132 60c No. 957 .45 .4
978 A132 $2 No. 958 1.50 1.5
979 A132 $2 No. 959 1.50 1.5
Nos. 976-979 (4) 3.90 3.9

Stamps of the same denomination exist printed tete-beche and se-tenant.

The Legend of King Arthur — A134a

1986, Nov. 3 *Perf. 1*

980 A134a 30c King Arthur .18 .1
980A A134a 45c Merlin raises Arthur .28 .2
980B A134a 60c Arthur pulls Excalibur from stone .38 .3
980C A134a 75c Camelot .45 .4
980D A134a $1 Lady of the Lake .60 .6
980E A134a $1.50 Knights of the Round Table .90 .9
980F A134a $2 Holy Grail 1.20 1.2
980G A134a $5 Sir Lancelot 3.00 3.0
Nos. 980-980G (8) 6.99 6.9

Statue of Liberty, Cent. — A134b

Statue of Liberty, Cent. — A135

Various views of the statue.

1986, Nov. 26 Litho. *Perf. 14*

980H A134b 15c multicolored .15 .15
980I A134b 25c multicolored .16 .16
980J A134b 40c multicolored .25 .25
980K A134b 55c multicolored .35 .35
980L A134b 75c multicolored .50 .50
980M A134b 90c multicolored .60 .60
980N A134b $1.75 multicolored 1.10 1.10
980O A134b $2 multicolored 1.25 1.25
980P A134b $2.50 multicolored 1.65 1.65
980Q A134b $3 multicolored 1.90 1.90
Nos. 980H-980Q (10) 7.91 7.91

Souvenir Sheets

981 A135 $3.50 multicolored 2.25 2.25
982 A135 $4 multicolored 2.50 2.50
983 A135 $5 multicolored 3.00 3.00

Fresh-water Fishing A136

1986, Dec. 10 *Perf. 15*

984 A136 75c Tri tri fishing .58 .58
985 A136 75c Tri tri .58 .58
986 A136 $1.50 Crayfishing 1.10 1.10
987 A136 $1.50 Crayfish 1.10 1.10
Nos. 984-987 (4) 3.36 3.36

Stamps of the same denomination printed se-tenant.

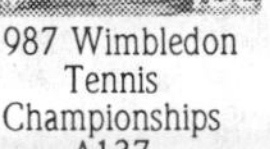

1987 Wimbledon Tennis Championships A137

Natl. Child Survival Campaign A138

1987, June 22 *Perf. 13x12½*

988 A137 40c Hana Mandlikova .24 .24
989 A137 60c Yannick Noah .35 .35
990 A137 80c Ivan Lendl .48 .48
991 A137 $1 Chris Evert Lloyd .60 .60
992 A137 $1.25 Steffi Graf .75 .75
993 A137 $1.50 John McEnroe .95 .95
994 A137 $1.75 Martina Navratilova 1.10 1.10
995 A137 $2 Boris Becker 1.25 1.25
Nos. 988-995 (8) 5.72 5.72

Souvenir Sheet

996 Sheet of 2 3.50 3.50
a. A137 $2.25 like $2 1.75 1.75
b. A137 $2.25 like $1.75 1.75 1.75

1987, June 10 *Perf. 14x14½*

997 A138 10c Growth monitoring .15 .15
998 A138 50c Oral rehydration therapy .38 .38
999 A138 75c Breast-feeding .58 .58
1000 A138 $1 Universal immunization .75 .75
Nos. 997-1000 (4) 1.86 1.86

For overprints see Nos. 1040-1043.

Carnival, 10th Anniv. — A139

Designs: 20c, Queen of the Bands, Miss Prima Donna 1986. 45c, Donna Young, Miss Carival 1985. 55c, M. Haydock, Miss. St. Vincent and the Grenadines 1986.

1987, June 29 *Perf. 12½x13*

1001 A139 20c multicolored .15 .15
1002 A139 45c multicolored .35 .35
1003 A139 55c multicolored .42 .42
1004 A139 $3.70 multicolored 2.75 2.75
Nos. 1001-1004 (4) 3.67 3.67

Nos. 870-881 Overprinted "THE KING OF ROCK AND ROLL LIVES FOREVER . AUGUST 16TH" and "1977-1987" (Nos. 1005-1012) or "TENTH ANNIVERSARY" (Nos. 1013-1016)

1987, Aug. 26 Litho. *Perf. 12½*

1005 A123 10c like No. 870 .15 .15
1006 A123 10c like No. 871 .15 .15
1007 A123 60c like No. 872 .40 .40
1008 A123 60c like No. 873 .40 .40
1009 A123 $1 like No. 874 .65 .65
1010 A123 $1 like No. 875 .65 .65
1011 A123 $5 like No. 876 3.25 3.25
1012 A123 $5 like No. 877 3.25 3.25
Nos. 1005-1012 (8) 8.90 8.90

Souvenir Sheets

1013 Sheet of 4 .90 .90
a. A123 30c like No. 870 .22 .22
b. A123 30c like No. 871 .22 .22
1014 Sheet of 4 1.50 1.50
a. A123 50c like No. 872 .35 .35
b. A123 50c like No. 873 .35 .35
1015 Sheet of 4 4.50 4.50
a. A123 $1.50 like No. 874 1.10 1.10
b. A123 $1.50 like No. 875 1.10 1.10
1016 Sheet of 4 13.00 13.00
a. A123 $4.50 like No. 876 3.25 3.25
b. A123 $4.50 like No. 877 3.25 3.25

Stamps of the same denomination printed se-tenant. Nos. 1013-1016 contain two of each stamp.

Portrait of Queen Victoria, 1841, by R. Thorburn A140

Portraits and photographs: 75c, Elizabeth and Charles, 1948. $1, Coronation, 1953. $2.50, Duke of Edinburgh, 1948. $5, Elizabeth, c. 1980. $6, Elizabeth and Charles, 1948, diff.

1987, Nov. 20 Litho. *Perf. 12½x13*

1017 A140 15c multicolored .15 .15
1018 A140 75c multicolored .45 .45
1019 A140 $1 multicolored .60 .60
1020 A140 $2.50 multicolored 1.50 1.50
1021 A140 $5 multicolored 3.00 3.00
Nos. 1017-1021 (5) 5.70 5.70

Souvenir Sheet

1022 A140 $6 multicolored 4.50 4.50

Sesquicentennial of Queen Victoria's accession to the throne, wedding of Queen Elizabeth II and Prince Philip, 40th anniv.

Nos. 997-1000 Ovptd. "WORLD POPULATION / 5 BILLION / 11TH JULY 1987"

1987, July 11 Litho. *Perf. 14x14½*

1040 A138 10c on No. 997 .15 .15
1041 A138 50c on No. 998 .38 .38
1042 A138 75c on No. 999 .58 .58
1043 A138 $1 on No. 1000 .75 .75
Nos. 1040-1043 (4) 1.86 1.86

Automobile Centenary — A143

Automotive pioneers and vehicles: $1, $3, Carl Benz (1844-1929) and the Velocipede, patented 1886. $2, No. 1049, Enzo Ferrari (b. 1898) and 1966 Ferrari Dino 206SP. $4, $6, Charles Rolls (1877-1910), Sir Henry Royce (1863-1933) and 1907 Rolls Royce Silver Ghost. No. 1047, $8, Henry Ford (1863-1947) and Model T Ford.

1987, Dec. 4 *Perf. 13x12½*

1044 A143 $1 multicolored .60 .60
1045 A143 $2 multicolored 1.10 1.10
1046 A143 $4 multicolored 2.25 2.25
1047 A143 $5 multicolored 3.00 3.00
Nos. 1044-1047 (4) 6.95 6.95

Souvenir Sheets

1048 A143 $3 like No. 1044 2.25 2.25
1049 A143 $5 like No. 1045 3.75 3.75
1050 A143 $6 like No. 1046 4.50 4.50
1051 A143 $8 like No. 1047 6.00 6.00
Nos. 1048-1051 (4) 16.50 16.50

Soccer Teams — A144

1987, Dec. 4

1052 A144 $2 Derby County 1.10 1.10
1053 A144 $2 Leeds United 1.10 1.10
1054 A144 $2 Tottenham Hotspur 1.10 1.10
1055 A144 $2 Manchester United 1.10 1.10
1056 A144 $2 Everton 1.10 1.10
1057 A144 $2 Liverpool 1.10 1.10
1058 A144 $2 Portsmouth 1.10 1.10
1059 A144 $2 Arsenal 1.10 1.10
Nos. 1052-1059 (8) 8.80 8.80

A145 A146

A Christmas Carol, by Charles Dickens (1812-1870) — A147

Portrait of Dickens as left page of book and various scenes from novels as right page of book.

1987, Dec. 17 *Perf. 14x14½*

Se-tenant Pair, Types A145-A146

1061 6c Mr. Fezziwig's Ball .15 .15
1062 25c Ghost of Christmases to Come .40 .40
1063 50c The Cratchits .75 .75
1064 75c Carolers 1.10 1.10
Nos. 1061-1064 (4) 2.40 2.40

Souvenir Sheet

1065 A147 $5 Reading book to children 3.75 3.75

Eastern Caribbean Currency — A148

Various Eastern Caribbean coins (Nos. 1069-1081) and banknotes (Nos. 1082-1086) in denominations equaling that of the stamp on which they are pictured.

1987-89 Litho. *Perf. 15*

1069 A148 5c multicolored .15 .15
1070 A148 6c multicolored .15 .15
1071 A148 10c multicolored .15 .15
1072 A148 12c multicolored .15 .15
1073 A148 15c multicolored .15 .15
1074 A148 20c multicolored .15 .15
1075 A148 25c multicolored .20 .20
1076 A148 30c multicolored .24 .24
1077 A148 35c multicolored .28 .28
1078 A148 45c multicolored .35 .35
1079 A148 50c multicolored .38 .38
1080 A148 65c multicolored .50 .50
1081 A148 75c multicolored .58 .58
1082 A148 $1 multi, horiz. .75 .75
1083 A148 $2 multi, horiz. 1.50 1.50
1084 A148 $3 multi, horiz. 2.25 2.25
1085 A148 $5 multi, horiz. 3.75 3.75
1086 A148 $10 multi, horiz. 7.50 7.50
1086A A148 $20 multi, horiz. 15.00 15.00
Nos. 1069-1086A (19) 34.18 34.18

Issue dates: $20, Nov. 7, 1989. Others, Dec. 11.

1991 *Perf. 12*

1071a A148 10c .15 .15
1073a A148 15c .15 .15
1074a A148 20c .15 .15
1075a A148 25c .18 .18
1078a A148 45c .32 .32
1079a A148 50c .35 .35
1080a A148 65c .45 .45
1081a A148 75c .55 .55
1082a A148 $1 .70 .70
1083a A148 $2 1.40 1.40
1085a A148 $5 3.50 3.50
Nos. 1071a-1085a (11) 7.90 7.90

1991 *Perf. 16*

1071b A148 10c .15 .15
1073b A148 15c .15 .15
1074b A148 20c .15 .15
1075b A148 25c .18 .18
1078b A148 45c .32 .32
1079b A148 50c .35 .35
1080b A148 65c .44 .45
1081b A148 75c .55 .55
1082b A148 $1 .70 .70
1083b A148 $2 1.40 1.40
1085b A148 $5 3.50 3.50
Nos. 1071b-1085b (11) 7.89 7.90

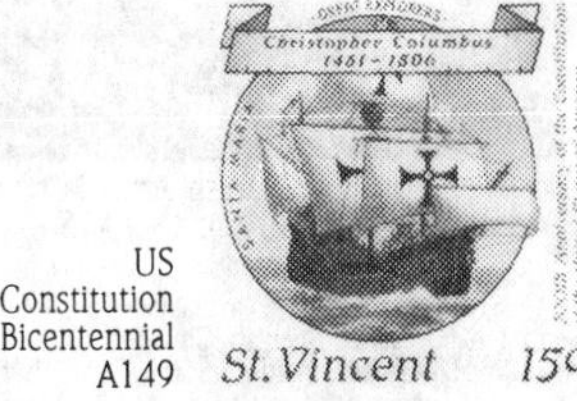

US Constitution Bicentennial A149

Christopher Columbus's fleet: 15c, Santa Maria. 75c, Nina and Pinta. $1, Hour glass, compass. $1.50, Columbus planting flag of Spain on American soil. $3, Arawak natives. $4, Parrot, hummingbird, corn, pineapple, eggs. $5, $6, Columbus, Spanish royal coat of arms and caravel.

1988, Jan. 11 *Perf. 14½x14*

1087 A149 15c multicolored .15 .15
1088 A149 75c multicolored .58 .58
1089 A149 $1 multicolored .75 .75
1090 A149 $1.50 multicolored 1.15 1.15
1091 A149 $3 multicolored 2.25 2.25
1092 A149 $4 multicolored 3.00 3.00
Nos. 1087-1092 (6) 7.88 7.88

Souvenir Sheets

Perf. 14x14½, 14½x14

1093 A149 $5 multicolored 3.75 3.75
1093A A149 $6 multicolored 4.50 4.50

US Constitution, bicent.; 500th anniv. of the discovery of America (in 1992).

Brown Pelican — A150

1988, Feb. 15 *Perf. 14*

1094 A150 45c multicolored	.35	.35

See No. 1298.

A151

Tourism — A152

1988, Feb. 22 **Litho.** *Perf. 15*

1095 A151 10c Windsurfing, diff., vert.	.15	.15
1096 A151 45c Scuba diving, vert.	.35	.35
1097 A151 65c shown	.50	.50
1098 A151 $5 Chartered ship	3.75	3.75
Nos. 1095-1098 (4)	4.75	4.75

Souvenir Sheet

Perf. 13x12¹/₂

1099 A152 $10 shown	7.50	7.50

A153

Destruction of the Spanish Armada by the English, 400th Anniv. — A154

16th cent. ships and artifacts: 15c, Nuestra Senora del Rosario, Spanish Chivalric Cross. 75c, Ark Royal, Armada medal. $1.50, English fleet, 16th cent. navigational instrument. $2, Dismasted galleon, cannon balls. $3.50, English fireships among the Armada, firebomb. $5, Revenge, Drake's drum. $8, Shoreline sentries awaiting the outcome of the battle.

1988, July 29 **Litho.** *Perf. 12¹/₂*

1100 A153 15c multicolored	.15	.15
1101 A153 75c multicolored	.45	.45
1102 A153 $1.50 multicolored	1.00	1.00
1103 A153 $2 multicolored	1.25	1.25
1104 A153 $3.50 multicolored	2.00	2.00
1105 A153 $5 multicolored	3.00	3.00
Nos. 1100-1105 (6)	7.85	7.85

Souvenir Sheet

1106 A154 $8 multicolored	5.00	5.00

Cricket Players A156

1988, July 29 **Litho.** *Perf. 14¹/₂x14*

1108 A156 15c D.K. Lillee	.15	.15
1109 A156 50c G.A. Gooch	.38	.38
1110 A156 75c R.N. Kapil Dev	.58	.58
1111 A156 $1 S.M. Gavaskar	.75	.75
1112 A156 $1.50 M.W. Gatting	1.15	1.15
1113 A156 $2.50 Imran Khan	1.90	1.90
1114 A156 $3 I.T. Botham	2.25	2.25
1115 A156 $4 I.V.A. Richards	3.00	3.00
Nos. 1108-1115 (8)	10.16	10.16

A souvenir sheet containing a $2 stamp like No. 1115 and a $3.50 stamp like No. 1114 was not issued by the post office.

1988 Summer Olympics, Seoul A158

1988, Dec. 7 **Litho.** *Perf. 14*

1116 A158 10c Running	.15	.15
1117 A158 50c Long jump, vert.	.38	.38
1118 A158 $1 Triple jump	.75	.75
1119 A158 $5 Boxing, vert.	3.75	3.75
Nos. 1116-1119 (4)	5.03	5.03

Souvenir Sheet

1120 A158 $10 Torch	7.50	7.50

1st Participation of St. Vincent athletes in the Olympics.

For overprints see Nos. 1346-1351.

Christmas — A159

Walt Disney characters: 1c, Minnie Mouse in freight car. 2c, Morty and Ferdy in open rail car. 3c, Chip 'n Dale in open boxcar. 4c, Huey, Dewey, Louie and reindeer. 5c, Donald and Daisy Duck aboard dining car. 10c, Gramma Duck conducting chorus including Scrooge McDuck, Goofy and Clarabelle Cow. No. 1127, Mickey Mouse in locomotive. $6, Santa Claus in caboose. No. 1129, Mickey, Minnie Mouse and nephews in train station, vert. No. 1130, Characters riding carousel, vert.

Perf. 14x13¹/₂, 13¹/₂x14

1988, Dec. 23 **Litho.**

1121 A159 1c multicolored	.15	.15
1122 A159 2c multicolored	.15	.15
1123 A159 3c multicolored	.15	.15
1124 A159 4c multicolored	.15	.15
1125 A159 5c multicolored	.15	.15
1126 A159 10c multicolored	.15	.15
1127 A159 $5 multicolored	3.75	3.75
1128 A159 $6 multicolored	4.50	4.50
Nos. 1121-1128 (8)	9.15	9.15

Souvenir Sheets

1129 A159 $5 multicolored	3.75	3.75
1130 A159 $5 multicolored	3.75	3.75

Babe Ruth (1895-1948), American Baseball Star — A160

1988, Dec. 7 **Litho.** *Perf. 14*

1131 A160 $2 multicolored	1.50	1.50

India '89, Jan. 20-29, New Delhi — A161

Exhibition emblem and Walt Disney characters: 1c, Mickey Mouse as snake charmer, Minnie Mouse as dancer. 2c, Goofy tossing rings at a chowsingha antelope. 3c, Mickey, Minnie, blue peacock. 5c, Goofy and Mickey as miners, Briolette diamond. 10c, Goofy as count presenting Orloff Diamond to Catherine the Great of Russia (Clarabelle Cow). 25c, Regent Diamond and Donald Duck as Napoleon (portrait) in the Louvre. $4, Minnie as Queen Victoria, Mickey as King Albert, crown bearing the Kohinoor Diamond. $5, Mickey and Goofy on safari. No. 1140, Mickey as Nehru, riding an elephant. No. 1141, Mickey as postman delivering Hope Diamond to the Smithsonian Institute.

1989, Feb. 7 **Litho.** *Perf. 14*

1132 A161 1c multicolored	.15	.15
1133 A161 2c multicolored	.15	.15
1134 A161 3c multicolored	.15	.15
1135 A161 5c multicolored	.15	.15
1136 A161 10c multicolored	.15	.15
1137 A161 25c multicolored	.20	.20
1138 A161 $4 multicolored	3.00	3.00
1139 A161 $5 multicolored	3.75	3.75
Nos. 1132-1139 (8)	7.70	7.70

Souvenir Sheets

1140 A161 $6 multicolored	4.50	4.50
1141 A161 $6 multicolored	4.50	4.50

Entertainers of the Jazz and Big Band Eras A162

Designs: 10c, Harry James (1916-83). 15c, Sidney Bechet (1897-1959). 25c, Benny Goodman (1909-86). 35c, Django Reinhardt (1910-53). 50c, Lester Young (1909-59). 90c, Gene Krupa (1909-73). $3, Louis Armstrong (1900-71). $4, Duke Ellington (1899-1974). No. 1150, Charlie Parker, Jr. (1920-55). No. 1151, Billie Holiday (1915-59).

1989, Apr. 3 **Litho.** *Perf. 14*

1142 A162 10c multicolored	.15	.15
1143 A162 15c multicolored	.15	.15
1144 A162 25c multicolored	.18	.18
1145 A162 35c multicolored	.26	.26
1146 A162 50c multicolored	.38	.38
1147 A162 90c multicolored	.68	.68
1148 A162 $3 multicolored	2.25	2.25
1149 A162 $4 multicolored	3.00	3.00
Nos. 1142-1149 (8)	7.05	7.05

Souvenir Sheets

1150 A162 $5 multicolored	3.75	3.75
1151 A162 $5 multicolored	3.75	3.75

Holiday misspelled "Holliday" on No. 1151.

Miniature Sheet

Noah's Ark — A163

Designs: a, Clouds, 2 birds at right. b, Rainbow, 4 clouds. c, Ark. d, Rainbow, 3 clouds. e, Clouds, 2 birds at left. f, African elephant facing right. g, Elephant facing forward. h, Leaves on tree branch. i, Kangaroos. j, Hummingbird facing left, flower. k, Lions. l, White-tailed deer. m, Koala at right. n, Koala at left. o, Hummingbird facing right, flower. p, Flower, toucan facing left. q, Toucan facing right. r, Camels. s, Giraffes. t, Sheep. u, Ladybugs. v, Butterfly (UR). w, Butterfly (LL). x, Snakes. y, Dragonflies.

1989, Apr. 10 *Perf. 1*

1152 A163 Sheet of 25	7.50	7.50
a.-y. 40c any single	.30	.30

Easter — A164

Paintings by Titian: 5c, Baptism of Christ. 30c, Temptation of Christ. 45c, Ecce Homo. 65c, Noli Me Tangere. 75c, Christ Carrying the Cross. $1, Christ Crowned with Thorns. $4, Lamentation Over Christ. $5, The Entombment. No. 1161, Pieta. No. 1162, The Deposition.

1989, Apr. 17 *Perf. 13¹/₂x14*

1153 A164 5c multicolored	.15	.15
1154 A164 30c multicolored	.22	.22
1155 A164 45c multicolored	.35	.35
1156 A164 65c multicolored	.48	.48
1157 A164 75c multicolored	.56	.56
1158 A164 $1 multicolored	.75	.75
1159 A164 $4 multicolored	3.00	3.00
1160 A164 $5 multicolored	3.75	3.75
Nos. 1153-1160 (8)	9.26	9.26

Souvenir Sheets

1161 A164 $6 multicolored	4.50	4.50
1162 A164 $6 multicolored	4.50	4.50

Telstar II and Cooperation in Space — A165

Designs: 15c, Recovery of astronaut L. Gordon Cooper, Mercury 9/Faith 7 mission. 35c, Satellite transmission of Martin Luther King's civil rights march address, 1963. 40c, US shuttle STS-7, first use of Canadarm, deployment and recovery of a W. German free-flying experiment platform. 50c, Satellite transmission of the 1964 Olympics, Innsbruck (speed skater). 60c, Vladimir Remek of Czechoslovakia, 1st non-Soviet cosmonaut, 1978. $1, CNES Hermes space plane, France, ESA emblem and Columbus space station. $3, Satellite transmission of Pope John XXIII (1881-1963) blessing crowd at the Vatican. $4, Ulf Merbold, W. Germany, 1st non-American astronaut, 1983. No. 1171, Launch of Telstar II, May 7, 1963. No. 1172, 1975 Apollo-Soyuz mission members shaking hands.

1989, Apr. 26 **Litho.** *Perf. 14*

1163 A165 15c multicolored	.15	.15
1164 A165 35c multicolored	.28	.28
1165 A165 40c multicolored	.30	.30
1166 A165 50c multicolored	.38	.38
1167 A165 60c multicolored	.45	.45
1168 A165 $1 multicolored	.75	.75
1169 A165 $3 multicolored	2.25	2.25
1170 A165 $4 multicolored	3.00	3.00
Nos. 1163-1170 (8)	7.56	7.56

Souvenir Sheets

1171 A165 $5 multicolored	3.75	3.75
1172 A165 $5 multicolored	3.75	3.75

Cruise Ships A166

1989, Apr. 21 **Litho.** *Perf. 14*

1173 A166 10c Ile de France	.15	.15
1174 A166 40c Liberte	.30	.30
1175 A166 50c Mauretania	.38	.38
1176 A166 75c France	.55	.55
1177 A166 $1 Aquitania	.75	.75
1178 A166 $2 United States	1.50	1.50

1179 A166 $3 Olympic 2.25 2.25
1180 A166 $4 Queen Elizabeth 3.00 3.00
Nos. 1173-1180 (8) 8.88 8.88

Souvenir Sheets

1181 A166 $6 Queen Mary 4.50 4.50
1182 A166 $6 QE 2 4.50 4.50

Nos. 1181-1182 contain 84x28mm stamps.
For overprints see Nos. 1352-1361.

Souvenir Sheet

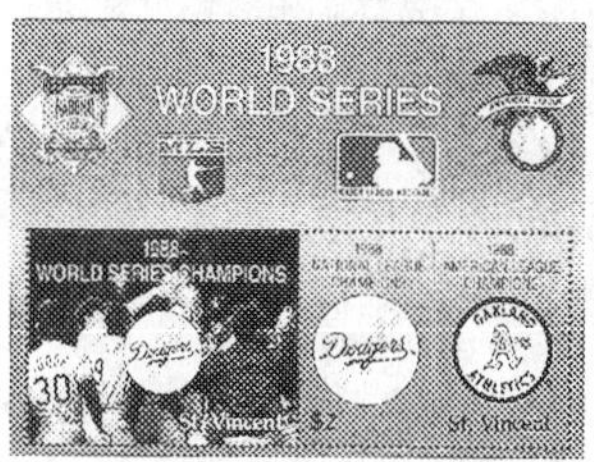

1988 World Series — A167

Designs: a, Dodgers emblem and players celebrating victory. b, Emblems of the Dodgers and the Oakland Athletics.

1989, May 3 Litho. ***Perf. 14x13½***

1183 Sheet of 2 3.00 3.00
a.-b. A167 $2 any single 1.50 1.50

World Wildlife Fund, St. Vincent Parrots A168

Indigenous Birds — A169

1989, Apr. 5 ***Perf. 14***

1184 A168 10c Parrot's head .15 .15
1185 A168 20c Parrot's wing span .15 .15
1186 A169 25c Mistletoe bird .18 .18
1187 A168 40c Parrot feeding, vert. .30 .30
1188 A168 70c Parrot on rock, vert. .52 .52
1189 A169 75c Crab hawk .58 .58
1190 A169 $2 Coucou 1.50 1.50
1191 A169 $3 Prince bird 2.25 2.25
Nos. 1184-1191 (8) 5.63 5.63

Souvenir Sheets

1192 A169 $5 Doctor bird 3.75 3.75
1193 A169 $5 Soufrieres, vert. 3.75 3.75

Fan Paintings — A170

By Hiroshige unless otherwise stated: 10c, Autumn Flowers in Front of the Full Moon. 40c, Hibiscus. 50c, Iris. 75c, Morning Glories. $1, Dancing Swallows. $2, Sparrow and Bamboo. $3, Yellow Bird and Cotton Rose. $4, Judos Chrysanthemums in a deep ravine in China. No. 1202, Rural Cottages in Spring, by Sotatsu. No. 1203, The Six Immortal Poets Portrayed as Cats, by Kuniyoshi.

1989, July 6 Litho. ***Perf. 14x13½***

1194 A170 10c multicolored .15 .15
1195 A170 40c multicolored .30 .30
1196 A170 50c multicolored .38 .38
1197 A170 75c multicolored .58 .58
1198 A170 $1 multicolored .75 .75
1199 A170 $2 multicolored 1.50 1.50
1200 A170 $3 multicolored 2.25 2.25
1201 A170 $4 multicolored 3.00 3.00
Nos. 1194-1201 (8) 8.91 8.91

Souvenir Sheets

1202 A170 $6 multicolored 4.50 4.50
1203 A170 $6 multicolored 4.50 4.50

Hirohito (1901-89) and enthronement of Akihito as emperor of Japan.

First Moon Landing, 20th Anniv. A171

Apollo 11 Mission: 35c, Columbia command module. 75c, Lunar module Eagle landing. $1, Rocket launch. No. 1207a, Buzz Aldrin conducting solar wind experiments. No. 1207b, Lunar module on plain. No. 1207c, Earthrise. No. 1207d, Neil Armstrong. No. 1208, Separation of lunar and command modules. No. 1209a, Command module. No. 1209b, Lunar module. $6, Armstrong preparing to take man's 1st step onto the Moon.

1989, Sept. 11 ***Perf. 14***

1204 A171 35c multicolored .28 .28
1205 A171 75c multicolored .58 .58
1206 A171 $1 multicolored .75 .75
1207 Strip of 4 6.00 6.00
a.-d. A171 $2 any single 1.50 1.50
1208 A171 $3 multicolored 2.25 2.25
Nos. 1204-1208 (5) 9.86 9.86

Souvenir Sheets

1209 Sheet of 2 4.50 4.50
a.-b. A171 $3 any single 2.25 2.25
1210 A171 $6 multicolored 4.50 4.50

No. 1207 has continuous design.

Players Elected to the Baseball Hall of Fame — A172

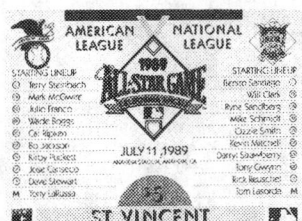

1989 All-Star Game, July 11, Anaheim, California — A173

Rookies and Team Emblems A174

Rookies of the Year, Most Valuable Players and Cy Young Award Winners A175

1989, July 23 Litho. ***Perf. 14***

1211 A172 $2 Cobb, 1936 1.50 1.50
1212 A172 $2 Mays, 1979 1.50 1.50
1213 A172 $2 Musial, 1969 1.50 1.50
1214 A172 $2 Bench, 1989 1.50 1.50
1215 A172 $2 Banks, 1977 1.50 1.50
1216 A172 $2 Schoendienst, 1989 1.50 1.50
1217 A172 $2 Gehrig, 1939 1.50 1.50
1218 A172 $2 Robinson, 1962 1.50 1.50
1219 A172 $2 Feller, 1962 1.50 1.50
1220 A172 $2 Williams, 1966 1.50 1.50
1221 A172 $2 Yastrzemski, 1989 1.50 1.50
1222 A172 $2 Kaline, 1980 1.50 1.50
Nos. 1211-1222 (12) 18.00 18.00

"Yastrzemski" is misspelled on No. 1221.

Size: 116x82mm

Imperf

1223 A173 $5 multicolored 3.75 3.75

Miniature Sheets

No. 1224: a, Dante Bichette, 1989. b, Carl Yastrzemski, 1961. c, Randy Johnson, 1989. d, Jerome Walton, 1989. e, Ramon Martinez, 1989. f, Ken Hill, 1989. g, Tom McCarthy, 1989. h, Gaylord Perry, 1963. i, John Smoltz, 1989.

No. 1225: a, Bob Milacki, 1989. b, Babe Ruth, 1915. c, Jim Abbott, 1989. d, Gary Sheffield, 1989. e, Gregg Jeffries, 1989. f, Kevin Brown, 1989. g, Cris Carpenter, 1989. h, Johnny Bench, 1968. i, Ken Griffey Jr., 1989.

No. 1226: a, Chris Sabo, 1988 Natl. League Rookie of the Year. b, Walt Weiss, 1988 American League Rookie of the Year. c, Willie Mays, 1951 Rookie of the Year. d, Kirk Gibson, 1988 Natl. League Most Valuable Player. e, Ted Williams, Most Valuable Player of 1946 and 1949. f, Jose Canseco, 1988 American League Most Valuable Player. g, Gaylord Perry, Cy Young winner for 1972 and 1978. h, Orel Hershiser, 1988 National League Cy Young winner. i, Frank Viola, 1988 American League Cy Young winner.

Perf. 13½

1224 Sheet of 9 4.00 4.00
a.-i. A174 60c any single .44 .44
1225 Sheet of 9 4.00 4.00
a.-i. A174 60c any single .44 .44
1226 Sheet of 9 4.00 4.00
a.-i. A175 60c any single .44 .44

For surcharges see Nos. B9-B11.

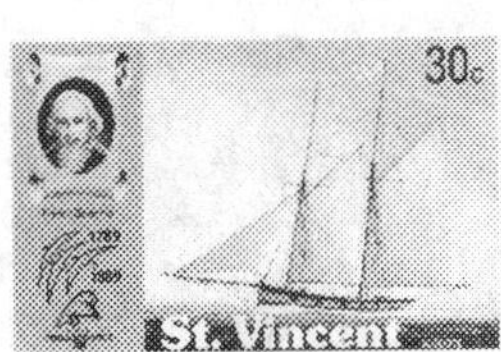

French Revolution Bicent., PHILEXFRANCE '89 — A176

French governors and ships.

1989, July 7 Litho. ***Perf. 13½x14***

1227 A176 30c Goelette .22 .22
1228 A176 55c Corvette .42 .42
1229 A176 75c Fregate 36 .58 .58
1230 A176 $1 Vaisseau 74 .75 .75
1231 A176 $3 Ville de Paris 2.25 2.25
Nos. 1227-1231 (5) 4.22 4.22

Souvenir Sheet

1232 A176 $6 Map 4.50 4.50

Miniature Sheet

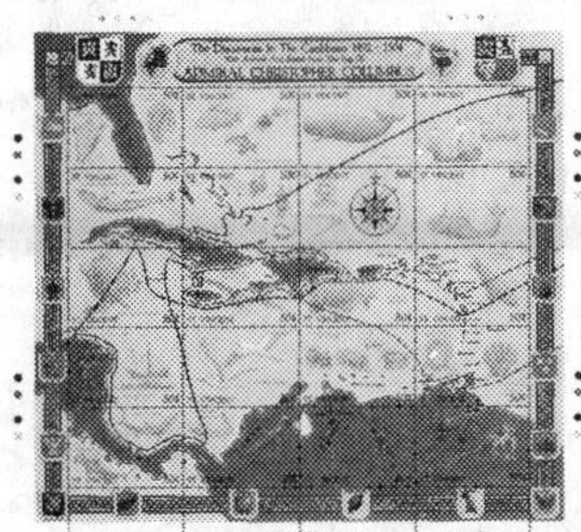

Discovery of the New World, 500th Anniv. (in 1992) — A177

Designs: a, Map of Florida, queen conch and West Indian purpura. b, Caribbean reef fish. c, Sperm whale. d, Columbus's fleet. e, Cuba, Isle of Pines, remora. f, The Bahamas, Turks & Caicos Isls., Columbus raising Spanish flag. g, Navigational instruments. h, Sea monster. i, Kemp's Ridley turtle, Cayman Isls. j, Jamaica, parts of Cuba and Hispaniola, magnificent frigatebird. k, Caribbean manatee, Hispaniola, Puerto Rico, Virgin Isls. l, Caribbean Monk seal, Anguilla and Caribbean isls. m, Mayan chief, galleon, dugout canoe. n, Masked boobies. o, Venezuelan village on pilings and the Netherlands Antilles. p, Atlantic wing oyster, lion's paw scallop, St. Vincent, Grenada, Trinidad & Tobago, Barbados. q, Panama, great hammerhead and mako sharks. r, Brown pelican, Colombia, Hyacinthine macaw. s, Venezuela, Indian bow and spear hunters. t, Capuchin and squirrel monkeys.

1989, Aug. 31 ***Perf. 14***

1233 A177 Sheet of 20 9.50 9.50
a.-t. 50c any single .47 .47

Major League Baseball: Los Angeles Dodgers — A178

No. 1234: a, Jay Howell, Alejandro Pena. b, Mike Davis, Kirk Gibson. c, Fernando Valenzuela, John Shelby. d, Jeff Hamilton, Franklin Stubbs. e, Dodger Stadium. f, Ray Searage, John Tudor. g, Mike Sharperson, Mickey Hatcher. h, Coaches Amalfitano, Cresse, Ferguson, Hines, Mota, Perranoski, Russell. i, John Wetteland, Ramon Martinez.

No. 1235: a, Tim Belcher, Tim Crews. b, Orel Hershiser, Mike Morgan. c, Mike Scioscia, Rick Dempsey. d, Dave Anderson, Alfredo Griffin. e, Team emblem. f, Kal Daniels, Mike Marshall. g, Eddie Murray, Willie Randolph. h, Manager Tom Lasorda, Jose Gonzalez. i, Lenny Harris, Chris Gwynn, Billy Bean.

1989, Sept. 23 ***Perf. 12½***

1234 Sheet of 9 4.00 4.00
a.-i. A178 60c any single .44 .44
1235 Sheet of 9 4.00 4.00
a.-i. A178 60c any single .44 .44

See Nos. 1344-1345.

1990 World Cup Soccer Championships, Italy — A179

1989, Oct. 16 Litho. ***Perf. 14***

1236 A179 10c shown .15 .15
1237 A179 55c Youth soccer teams .42 .42
1238 A179 $1 Natl. team .75 .75
1239 A179 $5 Trophy winners 3.75 3.75
Nos. 1236-1239 (4) 5.07 5.07

Souvenir Sheets

1240 A179 $6 Youth soccer team 4.50 4.50
1241 A179 $6 Natl. team, diff. 4.50 4.50

Fauna and Flora A180

1989, Nov. 1

1242 A180 65c St. Vincent parrot .50 .50
1243 A180 75c Whistling warbler .58 .58
1244 A180 $5 Black snake 3.75 3.75
Nos. 1242-1244 (3) 4.83 4.83

Souvenir Sheet

1245 A180 $6 Volcano plant, vert. 4.50 4.50

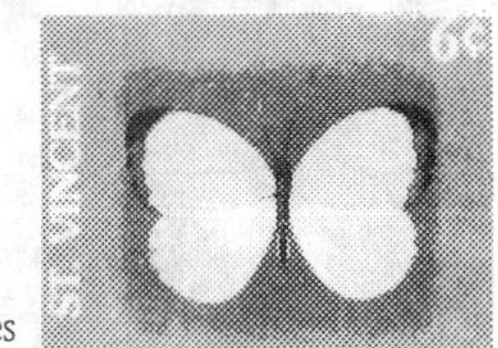

Butterflies A181

Perf. 14x14½, 14½x14

1989, Oct. 16

1246 A181 6c Little yellow .15 .15
1247 A181 10c Orion .15 .15
1248 A181 15c American painted lady .15 .15

1249	A181	75c Cassius blue	.58	.58
1250	A181	$1 Polydamus swallow-tail	.75	.75
1251	A181	$2 Guaraguao skipper	1.50	1.50
1252	A181	$3 The Queen	2.25	2.25
1253	A181	$5 Royal blue	3.75	3.75
		Nos. 1246-1253 (8)	9.28	9.28

Souvenir Sheets

1254	A181	$6 Monarch	4.50	4.50
1255	A181	$6 Lesser whirlabout, barred sulphur	4.50	4.50

Exhibition Emblem, Disney Characters and US Natl. Monuments A182

Designs: 1c, Seagull Monument, UT. 2c, Lincoln Memorial, Washington, DC. 3c, Crazy Horse Memorial, SD. 4c, Uncle Sam Wilson, Troy, NY. 5c, Benjamin Franklin Natl. Memorial, Philadelphia, PA. 10c, Statue of George Washington, Federal Hall, NY. $3, John F. Kennedy's birthplace, Brookline, MA. $6, George Washington's home, Mount Vernon, VA. No. 1264, Mt. Rushmore, SD. No. 1265, Stone Mountain, GA.

1989, Nov. 17 *Perf. 13½x14*

1256	A182	1c multicolored	.15	.15
1257	A182	2c multicolored	.15	.15
1258	A182	3c multicolored	.15	.15
1259	A182	4c multicolored	.15	.15
1260	A182	5c multicolored	.15	.15
1261	A182	10c multicolored	.15	.15
1262	A182	$3 multicolored	2.25	2.25
1263	A182	$6 multicolored	4.50	4.50
		Nos. 1256-1263 (8)	7.65	7.65

Souvenir Sheets

1264	A182	$5 multicolored	3.75	3.75
1265	A182	$5 multicolored	3.75	3.75

World Stamp Expo '89.

Souvenir Sheet

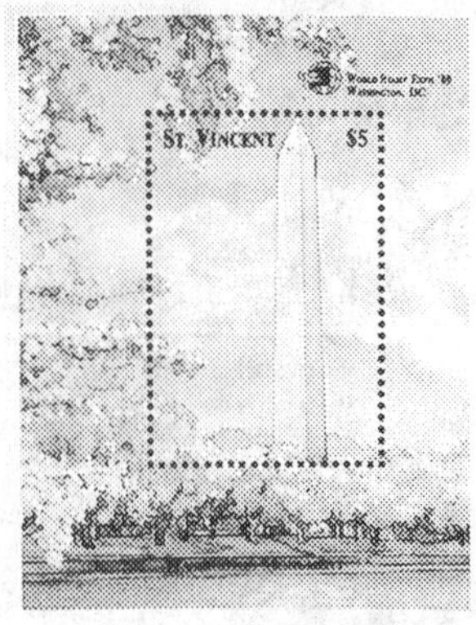

The Washington Monument, Washington, DC — A183

1989, Nov. 17 Litho. *Perf. 14*

1266	A183	$5 multicolored	3.75	3.75

World Stamp Expo '89.

Miniature Sheets

Major League Baseball — A184

Players, owners and commissioner.

No. 1267: a, Early Wynn. b, Cecil Cooper. c, Joe DiMaggio. d, Kevin Mitchell. e, Tom Browning. f, Bobby Witt. g, Tim Wallach. h, Bob Gibson. i, Steve Garvey.

No. 1268: a, Rick Sutcliffe. b, A. Bartlett Giamatti, commissioner. c, Cory Snyder. d, Rollie Fingers. e, Willie Hernandez. f, Sandy Koufax. g, Carl Yastrzemski. h, Ron Darling. i, Gerald Perry.

No. 1269: a, Mike Marshall. b, Tom Seaver. c, Bob Milacki. d, Dave Smith. e, Robin Roberts. f, Kent Hrbek. g, Bill Veeck, owner. h, Carmelo Martinez. i, Rogers Hornsby.

No. 1270: a, Barry Bonds. b, Jim Palmer. c, Lou Boudreau. d, Ernie Whitt. e, Jose Canseco. f, Ken Griffey, Jr. g, Johnny Vander Meer. h, Kevin Seitzer. i, Dave Dravecky.

No. 1271: a, Glenn Davis. b, Nolan Ryan. c, Hank Greenberg. d, Richie Allen. e, Dave Righetti. f, Jim Abbott. g, Harold Reynolds. h, Dennis Martinez. i, Rod Carew.

No. 1272: a, Joe Morgan. b, Tony Fernandez. c, Ozzie Guillen. d, Mike Greenwell. e, Bobby Valentine. f, Doug DeCinces. g, Mickey Cochrane. h, Willie McGee. i, Von Hayes.

No. 1273: a, Frank White. b, Brook Jacoby. c, Boog Powell. d, Will Clark. e, Ray Kroc, owner. f, Fred McGriff. g, Willie Stargell. h, John Smoltz. i, B. J. Surhoff.

No. 1274: a, Keith Hernandez. b, Eddie Mathews. c, Tom Paciorek. d, Alan Trammell. e, Greg Maddux. f, Ruben Sierra. g, Tony Oliva. h, Chris Bosio. i, Orel Hershiser.

No. 1275: a, Casey Stengel. b, Jim Rice. c, Reggie Jackson. d, Jerome Walton. e, Bob Knepper. f, Andres Galarraga. g, Christy Mathewson. h, Willie Wilson. i, Ralph Kiner.

1989, Nov. 30 *Perf. 12½*

1267	Sheet of 9	2.00	2.00
a.-i.	A184 30c any single	.22	.22
1268	Sheet of 9	2.00	2.00
a.-i.	A184 30c any single	.22	.22
1269	Sheet of 9	2.00	2.00
a.-i.	A184 30c any single	.22	.22
1270	Sheet of 9	2.00	2.00
a.-i.	A184 30c any single	.22	.22
1271	Sheet of 9	2.00	2.00
a.-i.	A184 30c any single	.22	.22
1272	Sheet of 9	2.00	2.00
a.-i.	A184 30c any single	.22	.22
1273	Sheet of 9	2.00	2.00
a.-i.	A184 30c any single	.22	.22
1274	Sheet of 9	2.00	2.00
a.-i.	A184 30c any single	.22	.22
1275	Sheet of 9	2.00	2.00
a.-i.	A184 30c any single	.22	.22

No. 1268 is incorrectly inscribed "Finger." Cochrane is misspelled "Cochpane" on No. 1272g.

See No. 1277.

Miniature Sheet

Achievements of Nolan Ryan, American Baseball Player — A185

Portrait and inscriptions: a, 383 League-leading strikeouts, 1973. b, No hitter, Kansas City Royals, May 15, 1973. c, No hitter, Detroit Tigers, July 15, 1973. d, No hitter, Minnesota Twins, Sept. 28, 1974. e, No hitter, Baltimore Orioles, June 1, 1975. f, No hitter, Los Angeles Dodgers, Sept. 26, 1981. g, Won 100+ games in both leagues. h, Struck out 200+ batters in 13 seasons. i, 5000th Strikeout, Aug. 22, 1989, Arlington, Texas.

1989, Nov. 30 Litho. *Perf. 12½*

1276	Sheet of 9	13.50	13.50
a.-i.	A185 $2 any single	1.50	1.50

For overprints see Nos. 1336-1337.

1989, Nov. 30 Litho. *Perf. 12½*

1277	A184	30c Mike Greenwell, Boston Red Sox	.22	.22

No. 1277 issued in sheets of 9.

Coat of Arms, No. 570 — A186

Boy Scouts and Girl Guides — A187

1989, Dec. 20 *Perf. 14*

1278	A186	65c multicolored	.50	.50

Souvenir Sheet

1279	A186	$10 multicolored	7.50	7.50

Independence, 10th anniv.

1989, Dec. 20 *Perf. 14*

Lord or Lady Baden-Powell and various scouts or girl guides.

1280	A187	35c Boy's modern uniform	.28	.28
1281	A187	35c Guide, ranger, brownie	.28	.28
1282	A187	55c Boy's old uniform	.42	.42
1283	A187	55c Mrs. Jackson	.42	.42
1284	A187	$2 75th anniv. emblem	1.50	1.50
1285	A187	$2 Mrs. Russell	1.50	1.50
		Nos. 1280-1285 (6)	4.40	4.40

Souvenir Sheets

1286	A187	$5 Canoeing, merit badges	3.75	3.75
1287	A187	$5 Flag-raising, Camp Yourumei, 1985	3.75	3.75

Christmas — A188

Paintings by Da Vinci and Botticelli: 10c, The Adoration of the Magi (holy family), by Botticelli. 25c, The Adoration of the Magi (witnesses). 30c, The Madonna of the Magnificat, by Botticelli. 40c, The Virgin and Child with St. Anne and St. John the Baptist, by Da Vinci. 55c, The Annunciation (angel), by Da Vinci. 75c, The Annunciation (Madonna). No. 1294, Madonna of the Carnation, by Da Vinci. $6, The Annunciation, by Botticelli. No. 1296, The Virgin of the Rocks, by Da Vinci. No. 1297, The Adoration of the Magi, by Botticelli.

1989, Dec. 20 *Perf. 14*

1288	A188	10c multicolored	.15	.15
1289	A188	25c multicolored	.18	.18
1290	A188	30c multicolored	.22	.22
1291	A188	40c multicolored	.30	.30
1292	A188	55c multicolored	.42	.42
1293	A188	75c multicolored	.58	.58
1294	A188	$5 multicolored	3.75	3.75
1295	A188	$6 multicolored	4.50	4.50
		Nos. 1288-1295 (8)	10.10	10.10

Souvenir Sheets

1296	A188	$5 multicolored	3.75	3.75
1297	A188	$5 multicolored	3.75	3.75

Bird Type of 1988

1989, July 31 Litho. *Perf. 15x14*

1298	A150	55c St. Vincent parrot	.42	.42

Lions Intl. of St. Vincent, 25th Anniv. (in 1989) A189

Services: 10c, Scholarships for the blind, vert. 65c, Free textbooks. 75c, Health education (diabetes). $2, Blood sugar testing machines. $4, Publishing and distribution of pamphlets on drug abuse.

1990, Mar. 5 Litho. *Perf. 14*

1303	A189	10c multicolored	.15	.15
1304	A189	65c multicolored	.48	.48
1305	A189	75c multicolored	.58	.58
1306	A189	$2 multicolored	1.50	1.50
1307	A189	$4 multicolored	3.00	3.00
		Nos. 1303-1307 (5)	5.71	5.71

World War II A190

Historic events: 5c, Defeat of the Graf Spee, Dec. 13-17, 1939. 10c, Charles De Gaulle calls the French Resistance to arms, June 18, 1940. 15c, The British drive the Italian army out of Egypt, Dec. 15, 1940. 25c, US destroyer Reuben James torpedoed off Iceland, Oct. 31, 1941. 30c, MacArthur becomes allied supreme commander of the southwest Pacific, Apr. 18, 1942. 40c, US forces attack Corregidor, Feb. 16, 1945. 55c, HMS King George V engages the Bismarck, May 27, 1941. 75c, U.S. fleet enters Tokyo Harbor, Aug. 27, 1945. $5, Russian takeover of Berlin completed, May 2, 1945. No. 1317, Battle of the Philippine Sea, June 18, 1944. No. 1318, Battle of the Java Sea, Feb. 28, 1942.

1990, Apr. 2 *Perf. 14x13½*

1308	A190	5c multicolored	.15	.15
1309	A190	10c multicolored	.15	.15
1310	A190	15c multicolored	.15	.15
1311	A190	25c multicolored	.18	.18
1312	A190	30c multicolored	.22	.22
1313	A190	40c multicolored	.30	.30
1314	A190	55c multicolored	.42	.42
1315	A190	75c multicolored	.58	.58
1316	A190	$5 multicolored	3.75	3.75
1317	A190	$6 multicolored	4.50	4.50
		Nos. 1308-1317 (10)	10.40	10.40

Souvenir Sheet

1318	A190	$6 multicolored	4.50	4.50

Penny Black, 150th Anniv. — A191

Great Britain No. 1 (various plate positions).

1990, May 3 Litho. *Perf. 14x15*

1319	A191	$2 "NK"	1.50	1.50
1320	A191	$4 "AB"	3.00	3.00

Souvenir Sheet

1321	A191	$6 Simulated #1, "SV"	4.50	4.50

Stamp World London '90 — A192

Walt Disney characters in British military uniforms: 5c, Donald Duck as 18th cent. Admiral. 10c, Huey as Bugler, 68th Light Infantry, 1854. 15c, Minnie Mouse as Drummer, 1st Irish Guards, 1900. 25c, Goofy as Lance Corporal, Seaforth Highlanders, 1944. $1, Mickey Mouse as officer, 58th Regiment, 1879, 1881. $2, Donald Duck as officer, Royal Engineers, 1813. $4, Mickey Mouse as Drum Major, 1914. $5, Goofy as Pipe Sergeant, 1918. No. 1330, Scrooge as Company Clerk and Goofy as King's Lifeguard of Foot. No. 1331, Mickey Mouse as British Grenadier.

1990, May Litho. *Perf. 13½x14*

1322	A192	5c multicolored	.15	.15
1323	A192	10c multicolored	.15	.15
1324	A192	15c multicolored	.15	.15
1325	A192	25c multicolored	.18	.18
1326	A192	$1 multicolored	.75	.75
1327	A192	$2 multicolored	1.50	1.50
1328	A192	$4 multicolored	3.00	3.00
1329	A192	$5 multicolored	3.75	3.75
		Nos. 1322-1329 (8)	9.63	9.63

Souvenir Sheets

1330	A192	$6 multicolored	4.50	4.50
1331	A192	$6 multicolored	4.50	4.50

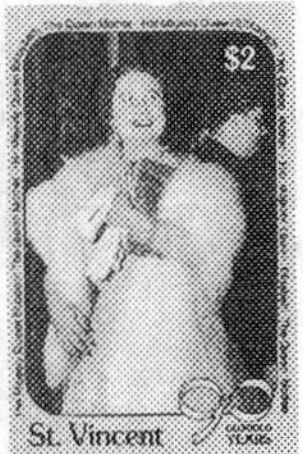

Queen Mother 90th Birthday
A193 A194

1990, July 5 *Perf. 14*

1332 A193 $2 shown	1.55	1.55
1333 A193 $2 Queen Mother signing book	1.55	1.55
1334 A194 $2 shown	1.55	1.55
Nos. 1332-1334 (3)	4.65	4.65

Souvenir Sheet

1335 A194 $6 Like No. 1334	4.75	4.75

No. 1276 Overprinted
Miniature Sheets

a Sixth No-Hitter
11 June 90
Oakland Athletics

b 300th Win
Milwaukee Brewers
July 31, 1990

1990, July 23 Litho. *Perf. 12½*

Sheets of 9

1336 A185(a) $2 #1336a-1336i	13.50	13.50
1337 A185(b) $2 #1337a-1337i	13.50	13.50

World Cup Soccer Championships, Italy — A195

Players from participating countries.

1990, Sept. 24 Litho. *Perf. 14*

1338 A195 10c Argentina	.15	.15
1339 A195 75c Colombia	.55	.55
1340 A195 $1 Uruguay	.75	.75
1341 A195 $5 Belgium	3.75	3.75
Nos. 1338-1341 (4)	5.20	5.20

Souvenir Sheets

1342 A195 $6 Brazil	4.50	4.50
1343 A195 $6 West Germany	4.50	4.50

Dodger Baseball Type of 1989

No. 1344: a, Hubie Brooks, Orel Hershiser. b, Manager Tom Lasorda, Tim Crews. c, Fernando Valenzuela, Eddie Murray. d, Kal Daniels, Jose Gonzalez. e, Dodger centennial emblem. f, Chris Gwynn, Jeff Hamilton. g, Kirk Gibson, Rick Dempsey. h, Jim Gott, Alfredo Griffin. i, Coaches, Ron Perranoski, Bill Russell, Joe Ferguson, Joe Amalfitano, Mark Cresse, Ben Hines, Manny Mota.

No. 1345: a, Mickey Hatcher, Jay Howell. b, Juan Samuel, Mike Scioscia. c, Lenny Harris, Mike Hartley. d, Ramon Martinez, Mike Morgan. e, Dodger Stadium. f, Stan Javier, Don Aase. g, Ray Searage, Mike Sharperson. h, Tim Belcher, Pat Perry. i, Dave Walsh, Jose Vizcaino, Jim Neidlinger, Jose Offerman, Carlos Hernandez.

Hyphen-hole roulette 7

1990, Sept. 21

1344 Sheet of 9	4.00	4.00
a.-i. A178 60c any single	.44	.44
1345 Sheet of 9	4.00	4.00
a.-i. A178 60c any single	.44	.44

Nos. 1116-1120 Ovptd. or Similarly — JOE DELOACH U.S.A. / STEVE LEWIS U.S.A. / PAUL ERANG KENYA

1990, Oct. 18 *Perf. 14*

1346 A158 10c shown	.15	.15
1347 A158 50c "CARL / LEWIS / U.S.A."	.38	.38
1348 A158 $1 "HRISTO / MARKOV / BULGARIA"	.75	.75
1349 A158 $5 "HENRY / MASKE / E. GERMANY"	3.75	3.75
Nos. 1346-1349 (4)	5.03	5.03

Souvenir Sheets

1350 A158 $10 USSR, US medals	7.50	7.50
1351 A158 $10 South Korea, Spain medals	7.50	7.50

Overprint on No. 1350 reads "FINAL MEDAL STANDINGS / USSR / GOLD 55 / SILVER 31 / BRONZE 46 and USA / GOLD 36 / SILVER 31 / BRONZE 27."

Overprint on No. 1351 reads "FINAL MEDAL STANDINGS / S. KOREA / GOLD 12 / SILVER 10 / BRONZE 11 and SPAIN / GOLD 1 / SILVER 1 / BRONZE 2."

Nos. 1173-1182 Overprinted

1990, Oct. 18 Litho. *Perf. 14*

1352 A166 10c *Ile de France*	.15	.15
1353 A166 40c *Liberte*	.30	.30
1354 A166 50c *Mauretania*	.38	.38
1355 A166 75c *France*	.55	.55
1356 A166 $1 *Aquitania*	.75	.75
1357 A166 $2 *United States*	1.50	1.50
1358 A166 $3 *Olympic*	2.25	2.25
1359 A166 $4 *Queen Elizabeth*	3.00	3.00
Nos. 1352-1359 (8)	8.88	8.88

Souvenir Sheets

1360 A166 $6 *Queen Mary*	4.50	4.50
1361 A166 $6 *QE 2*	4.50	4.50

Overprint on #1360-1361 is 12mm in diameter.

Orchids — A196

Designs: 10c, Dendrophylax funalis, Dimeranda emarginata. 15c, Epidendrum elongatum. 45c, Comparettia falcata. 60c, Brassia maculata. $1, Encyclia cochleata, Encyclia cordigera. $2, Cyrtopodium punctatum. $4, Cattelya labiata. $5, Bletia purpurea. No. 1370, Ionopsis utricularioides. No. 1371, Vanilla planifolia.

1990, Nov. 23

1362 A196 10c multicolored	.15	.15
1363 A196 15c multicolored	.15	.15
1364 A196 45c multicolored	.35	.35
1365 A196 60c multicolored	.45	.45
1366 A196 $1 multicolored	.75	.75
1367 A196 $2 multicolored	1.50	1.50
1368 A196 $4 multicolored	3.00	3.00
1369 A196 $5 multicolored	3.75	3.75
Nos. 1362-1369 (8)	10.10	10.10

Souvenir Sheets

1370 A196 $6 multicolored	4.50	4.50
1371 A196 $6 multicolored	4.50	4.50

Christmas A197

Details from paintings by Rubens: 10c, Miraculous Draught of Fishes. 45c, $2, Crowning of Holy Katherine. 50c, St. Ives of Treguier. 65c, Allegory of Eternity. $1, $4, St. Bavo Receives Monastic Habit of Ghent. $5, Communion of St. Francis. No. 1380, St. Ives of Treguier (entire). No. 1381, Allegory of Eternity. No. 1382, St. Bavo Receives Monastic Habit of Ghent. No. 1383, The Miraculous Draft of Fishes.

1990, Dec. 3 Litho. *Perf. 14*

1372 A197 10c multicolored	.15	.15
1373 A197 45c multicolored	.35	.35
1374 A197 50c multicolored	.38	.38
1375 A197 65c multicolored	.48	.48
1376 A197 $1 multicolored	.75	.75
1377 A197 $2 multicolored	1.50	1.50
1378 A197 $4 multicolored	3.00	3.00
1379 A197 $5 multicolored	3.75	3.75
Nos. 1372-1379 (8)	10.36	10.36

Souvenir Sheets

1380 A197 $6 multicolored	4.50	4.50
1381 A197 $6 multicolored	4.50	4.50
1382 A197 $6 multi, horiz.	4.50	4.50
1383 A197 $6 multi, horiz.	4.50	4.50

Miniature Sheet

Intl. Literacy Year A198

Canterbury Tales: a, Geoffrey Chaucer (1342-1400), author. b, "When April with his showers sweet..." c, "When Zephyr also has,..." d. "And many little birds make melody..." e, "And palmers to go seeking out strange strands..." f, Quill pen, open book. g, Bluebird in tree. h, Trees, rider's head with white hair. i, Banner on staff. j, Town. k, Rider's head, diff. l, Blackbird in tree. m, Old monk. n, Horse, rider. o, Nun, monk carrying banner. p, Monks. q, White horse, rider. r, Black horse, rider. s, Squirrel. t, Rooster. u, Chickens. v, Rabbit. w, Butterfly. x, Mouse.

1990, Dec. 12 *Perf. 13½*

1384 Sheet of 24	7.20	7.20
a.-x. A198 40c any single	.30	.30

Vincent Van Gogh (1853-1890), Painter A198a

Self-Portraits.

1990, Dec. 17 Litho. *Perf. 13*

1385 A198a 1c 1889	.15	.15
1386 A198a 5c 1886	.15	.15
1387 A198a 10c 1888, with hat & pipe	.15	.15
1388 A198a 15c 1888, painting	.15	.15
a. Strip of 4, #1385-1388	.30	.30
1389 A198a 20c 1887	.15	.15
1390 A198a 45c 1889, diff.	.35	.35
1391 A198a $5 1889, with bandaged ear	3.75	3.75
1392 A198a $6 1887, with straw hat	4.50	4.50
a. Strip of 4, #1389-1392	8.75	8.75
Nos. 1385-1392 (8)	9.35	9.35

Hummel Figurines — A199

1990, Dec. 30 Litho. *Perf. 14*

1393 A199 10c Photographer	.15	.15
1394 A199 15c Boy with ladder & rope	.15	.15
1395 A199 40c Pharmacist	.30	.30
1396 A199 60c Boy answering telephone	.45	.45
1396A A199 $1 Bootmaker	.75	.75
1396B A199 $2 Artist	1.50	1.50
1397 A199 $4 Waiter	3.00	3.00
a. Sheet of 4, 15c, 40c, $2, $4	5.00	5.00
1398 A199 $5 Mailman	3.75	3.75
a. Sheet of 4, 10c, 60c, $1, $5	5.00	5.00
Nos. 1393-1398 (8)	10.05	10.05

Souvenir Sheets

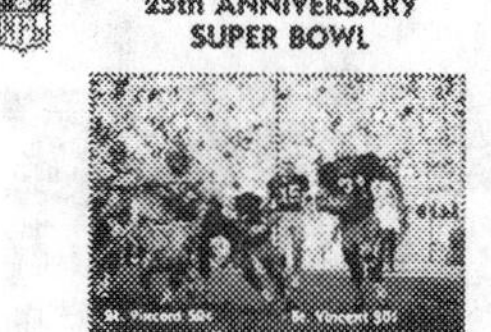

Super Bowl Highlights — A200

Designs: Nos. 1400-1424, 1425-1449, Super Bowl I (1967) through Super Bowl XXV (1991). Nos. 1425-1449 picture Super Bowl Program Covers. Nos. 1443, 1449 horiz.

1991, Jan. 15 Litho. *Perf. 13½x14*

1400-1424 A200 Set of 25	18.00	18.00

Size: 99x125mm

Imperf

1425-1449 A200 $2 Set of 25	37.50	37.50

Nos. 1400-1423 contain two 50c stamps printed with continuous design showing game highlights. No. 1424 contains three 50c stamps showing AFC and NFC team helmets and the Vince Lombardi Trophy.

Miniature Sheets

Discovery of America, 500th Anniv. (in 1992) A201

No. 1450: a, 1c, US #230. b, 2c, US #231. c, 3c, US #232. d, 4c, US #233. e, $10, Sailing ship, parrot. f, 5c, US #234. g, 6c, US #235. h, 8c, US #236. i, 10c, US #237.

No. 1451: a, 15c, US #238. b, 30c, US #239. c, 50c, US #240. d, $1, US #241. e, $10, Compass rose, sailing ship. f, $2, US #242. g, $3, US #243. h, $4, US #244. i, $5, US #245.

No. 1452, Bow of sailing ship. No. 1453, Ship's figurehead.

1991, Mar. 18 Litho. *Perf. 14*

Sheets of 9

1450 A201 #1450a-1450i	7.35	7.35
1451 A201 #1451a-1451i	18.00	18.00

Souvenir Sheets

1452 A201 $6 multicolored	4.50	4.50
1453 A201 $6 multicolored	4.50	4.50

Nos. 1452-1453 each contain one 38x31mm stamp.

Jetsons, The Movie — A202

Hanna-Barbera characters: 5c, Cosmo Spacely, vert. 20c, Elroy, Judy, Astro, Jane & George Jetson, vert. 45c, Judy, Apollo Blue, vert. 50c, Mr. Spacely, George, vert. 60c, George, sprocket factory. $1, Apollo Blue, Judy, Elroy and Grungees. $2, Jane and George in Grungee cavern. $4, George, Elroy, Jane and Little Grungee, vert. $5, Jetsons leaving for Earth, vert. No. 1463, Jetsons in sprocket factory. No. 1464, Jetsons traveling to Orbiting Ore Asteroid.

1991, Mar. 25 Litho. *Perf. 13½*

1454 A202 5c multicolored	.15	.15
1455 A202 20c multicolored	.15	.15
1456 A202 45c multicolored	.35	.35
1457 A202 50c multicolored	.38	.38
1458 A202 60c multicolored	.45	.45
1459 A202 $1 multicolored	.75	.75
1460 A202 $2 multicolored	1.50	1.50
1461 A202 $4 multicolored	3.00	3.00
1462 A202 $5 multicolored	3.75	3.75
Nos. 1454-1462 (9)	10.48	10.48

Souvenir Sheets

1463 A202 $6 multicolored 4.50 4.50
1464 A202 $6 multicolored 4.50 4.50

The Flintstones Enjoy Sports — A203

1991, Mar. 25

1465 A203 10c Boxing .15 .15
1466 A203 15c Soccer .15 .15
1467 A203 45c Rowing .35 .35
1468 A203 55c Dinosaur riding .42 .42
1469 A203 $1 Basketball .75 .75
1470 A203 $2 Wrestling 1.50 1.50
1471 A203 $4 Tennis 3.00 3.00
1472 A203 $5 Cycling 3.75 3.75
Nos. 1465-1472 (8) 10.07 10.07

Souvenir Sheets

1473 A203 $6 Baseball, batting 4.50 4.50
1474 A203 $6 Baseball, sliding home 4.50 4.50

Voyages of Discovery A204

5c, Sanger 2. 10c, Magellan probe, 1990. 25c, Buran space shuttle. 75c, American space station. $1, Mars mission, 21st century. $2, Hubble space telescope, 1990. $4, Sailship to Mars. $5, Craf satellite, 2000. #1483, Sailing ship, island hopping. #1484, Sailing ship returning home.

1991, May 13

1475 A204 5c multicolored .15 .15
1476 A204 10c multicolored .15 .15
1477 A204 25c multicolored .18 .18
1478 A204 75c multicolored .55 .55
1479 A204 $1 multicolored .75 .75
1480 A204 $2 multicolored 1.50 1.50
1481 A204 $4 multicolored 3.00 3.00
1482 A204 $5 multicolored 3.75 3.75
Nos. 1475-1482 (8) 10.03 10.03

Souvenir Sheets

1483 A204 $6 multicolored 4.50 4.50
1484 A204 $6 multicolored 4.50 4.50

Discovery of America, 500th anniv. (in 1992).

Royal Family Birthday, Anniversary
Common Design Type

1991, July Litho. *Perf. 14*

1485 CD347 5c multicolored .15 .15
1486 CD347 20c multicolored .15 .15
1487 CD347 25c multicolored .18 .18
1488 CD347 60c multicolored .45 .45
1489 CD347 $1 multicolored .75 .75
1490 CD347 $2 multicolored 1.50 1.50
1491 CD347 $4 multicolored 3.00 3.00
1492 CD347 $5 multicolored 3.75 3.75
Nos. 1485-1492 (8) 9.93 9.93

Souvenir Sheets

1493 CD347 $5 Elizabeth, Philip 3.75 3.75
1494 CD347 $5 Charles, Diana, sons 3.75 3.75

20c, 25c, $1, Nos. 1492, 1494, Charles and Diana, 10th wedding anniversary. Others, Queen Elizabeth II, 65th birthday.

Miniature Sheets

Japanese Trains A205

Designs: No. 1495a, D51 steam locomotive. b, 9600 steam locomotive. c, Chrysanthemum emblem. d, Passenger coach. e, C57 steam locomotive. f, Oil tank car. g, C53 steam locomotive. h, First steam locomotive. i, C11 steam locomotive.

No. 1496a, Class 181 electric train. b, EH-10 electric locomotive. c, Special Express emblem. d, Sendai City Class 1 trolley. e, Class 485 electric train. f, Sendai City trolley street cleaner. g, Hakari bullet train. h, ED-11 electric locomotive. i, EF-66 electric locomotive.

No. 1497, C55 steam locomotive, vert. No. 1498, Series 400 electric train. No. 1499, C62 steam locomotive, vert. No. 1500, Super Hitachi electric train, vert.

1991, Aug. 12 Litho. *Perf. 14x13½*

1495 A205 75c Sheet of 9, #a.-i. 5.00 5.00
1496 A205 $1 Sheet of 9, #a.-i. 6.75 6.75

Souvenir Sheets

Perf. 13x13½

1497 A205 $6 multicolored 4.50 4.50
1498 A205 $6 multicolored 4.50 4.50
1499 A205 $6 multicolored 4.50 4.50
1500 A205 $6 multicolored 4.50 4.50

Phila Nippon '91. Nos. 1497-1500 each contain 27x44mm or 44x27mm stamps.

Miniature Sheets

Entertainers — A206

#1501a-1501i, Various portraits of Madonna.
Italian entertainers: #1502a, Marcello Mastroianni. b, Sophia Loren. c, Mario Lanza (1921-59). d, Federico Fellini. e, Arturo Toscanini (1867-1957). f, Anna Magnani (1908-73). g, Giancarlo Giannini. h, Gina Lollobrigida. i, Enrico Caruso (1873-1921).
#1503a-1503i, Various portraits of John Lennon.

1991, Aug. 22 *Perf. 13*

1501 A206 $1 Sheet of 9, #a.-i. 6.75 6.75
1502 A206 $1 Sheet of 9, #a.-i. 6.75 6.75
1503 A206 $1 +2c, Sheet of 9, #a.-i. 6.90 6.90

Souvenir Sheets

Perf. 12x13

1504 A206 $6 Madonna 4.50 4.50

Perf. 13

1505 A206 $6 Luciano Pavarotti, horiz. 4.50 4.50

No. 1503 is semi-postal with surtax going to the Spirit Foundation.

No. 1504 contains one 28x42mm stamp. Compare with No. 1566. See Nos. 1642-1643, 1729, 2055.

Intl. Literacy Year — A207

Walt Disney characters in "The Prince and the Pauper": 5c, Pauper pals. 10c, Princely boredom. 15c, The valet. 25c, Look alikes. 60c, Trading places. 75c, How to be a prince. 80c, Food for the populace. $1, Captain's plot. $2, Doomed in the dungeon. $3, Looking for a way out. $4, A Goofy jailbreak. $5, Long live the real prince. No. 1518, Crowning the wrong guy. No. 1519, Mickey meets the captain of the guard. No. 1520, Real prince arrives. No. 1521, Seize the guard.

1991, Nov. 18 *Perf. 14x13½*

1506 A207 5c multicolored .15 .15
1507 A207 10c multicolored .15 .15
1508 A207 15c multicolored .15 .15
1509 A207 25c multicolored .18 .18
1510 A207 60c multicolored .45 .45
1511 A207 75c multicolored .55 .55
1512 A207 80c multicolored .60 .60
1513 A207 $1 multicolored .75 .75
1514 A207 $2 multicolored 1.50 1.50
1515 A207 $3 multicolored 2.25 2.25
1516 A207 $4 multicolored 3.00 3.00
1517 A207 $5 multicolored 3.75 3.75
Nos. 1506-1517 (12) 13.48 13.48

Souvenir Sheets

1518 A207 $6 multicolored 4.50 4.50
1519 A207 $6 multicolored 4.50 4.50
1520 A207 $6 multicolored 4.50 4.50
1521 A207 $6 multicolored 4.50 4.50

1991, Nov. 18

Walt Disney's "The Rescuers Down Under": 5c, Miss Bianca, Heroine. 10c, Bernard, Shy Hero. 15c, Maitre d'Francois. 25c, Wilbur, the Albatross. 60c, Jake, the Aussie kangaroo mouse. 75c, Bernard, Bianca and Jake in the outback. 80c, Bianca and Bernard. $1, Marahute, the magnificent rare eagle. $2, Cody and Marahute. $3, McLeach and his pet Goanna, Joanna. $4, Frank, the frill-necked lizard. $5, Endangered animals: Red Kangaroo, Krebbs Koala, and Polly Platypus. No. 1534, Cody with the rescuers. No. 1535, Delegates of Intl. Rescue Aid Society. No. 1536, Wilbur's painful touchdown "down under." No. 1537, Wilbur transports Miss Bianca and Bernard to Australia.

1522 A207 5c multicolored .15 .15
1523 A207 10c multicolored .15 .15
1524 A207 15c multicolored .15 .15
1525 A207 25c multicolored .18 .18
1526 A207 60c multicolored .45 .45
1527 A207 75c multicolored .55 .55
1528 A207 80c multicolored .60 .60
1529 A207 $1 multicolored .75 .75
1530 A207 $2 multicolored 1.50 1.50
1531 A207 $3 multicolored 2.25 2.25
1532 A207 $4 multicolored 3.00 3.00
1533 A207 $5 multicolored 3.75 3.75
Nos. 1522-1533 (12) 13.48 13.48

Souvenir Sheets

1534 A207 $6 multicolored 4.50 4.50
1535 A207 $6 multicolored 4.50 4.50
1536 A207 $6 multicolored 4.50 4.50
1537 A207 $6 multicolored 4.50 4.50

Brandenburg Gate, Bicent. — A209

Designs: 50c, Demonstrator with sign. 75c, Soldiers at Berlin Wall. 90c, German flag, shadows on wall. $1, Pres. Gorbachev and Pres. Bush shaking hands. $4, Coat of Arms of Berlin.

1991, Nov. 18 Litho. *Perf. 14*

1538 A209 50c multicolored .38 .38
1539 A209 75c multicolored .55 .55
1540 A209 90c multicolored .70 .70
1541 A209 $1 multicolored .75 .75
Nos. 1538-1541 (4) 2.38 2.38

Souvenir Sheet

1542 A209 $4 multicolored 3.00 3.00

Wolfgang Amadeus Mozart, Death Bicent. A210

Designs: $1, Scene from "Marriage of Figaro." $3, Scene from "The Clemency of Titus." $4, Portrait of Mozart, vert.

1991, Nov. 18

1543 A210 $1 multicolored .75 .75
1544 A210 $3 multicolored 2.25 2.25

Souvenir Sheet

1545 A210 $4 multicolored 3.00 3.00

17th World Scout Jamboree, Korea — A211

Designs: 65c, Adventure tales around camp fire, vert. $1.50, British defenses at Mafeking, 1900, Cape of Good Hope #179. $3.50, Scouts scuba diving, queen angelfish.

1991, Nov. 18 Litho. *Perf. 14*

1546 A211 65c multicolored .48 .48
1547 A211 $1.50 multicolored 1.15 1.15
1548 A211 $3.50 multicolored 2.65 2.65
Nos. 1546-1548 (3) 4.28 4.28

Souvenir Sheet

1549 A211 $5 multicolored 3.75 3.75

Charles de Gaulle, Birth Cent. A212

De Gaulle and: 10c, Free French Forces, 1944. 45c, Churchill, 1944. 75c, Liberation of Paris, 1944.

1991, Nov. 18 Litho. *Perf. 14*

1550 A212 10c multicolored .15 .15
1551 A212 45c multicolored .35 .35
1552 A212 75c multicolored .55 .55
Nos. 1550-1552 (3) 1.05 1.05

Souvenir Sheet

1553 A212 $5 Portrait 3.75 3.75

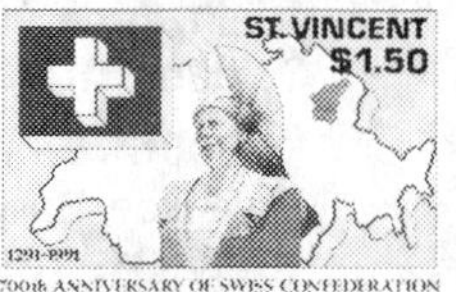

Anniversaries and Events — A213

Designs: No. 1554, Woman, flag, map. No. 1555, Steam locomotive. $1.65, Otto Lilienthal, glider in flight. No. 1557, Gottfried Wilhelm Liebniz, mathematician. No. 1558, Street warfare.

1991, Nov. 18

1554 A213 $1.50 multicolored 1.15 1.15
1555 A213 $1.50 multicolored 1.15 1.15
1556 A213 $1.65 multicolored 1.25 1.25
1557 A213 $2 multicolored 1.50 1.50
1558 A213 $2 multicolored 1.50 1.50
Nos. 1554-1558 (5) 6.55 6.55

Swiss Confedration, 700th anniv. (#1554) Trans-Siberian Railway, 100th anniv. (#1555). First glider flight, cent. (#1556). City of Hanover, 750th anniv. (#1557). Fall of Kiev, Sept. 19, 1941 (#1558).

Miniature Sheet

Heroes of Pearl Harbor A214

Congressional Medal of Honor recipients: a, Myrvyn S. Bennion. b, George H. Cannon. c, John W. Finn. d, Francis C. Flaherty. e, Samuel G. Fuqua. f, Edwin J. Hill. g, Herbert C. Jones. h, Isaac C. Kidd. i, Jackson C. Pharris. j, Thomas J. Reeves. k, Donald K. Ross. l, Robert R. Scott. m, Franklin Van Valkenburgh. n, James R. Ward. o, Cassin Young.

1991, Nov. 18 *Perf. 14½x15*

1559 A214 $1 Sheet of 15, #a.-o. 11.25 11.25

Miniature Sheets

Famous People — A215

Golfers: No. 1560a, Player. b, Faldo. c, Ballesteros. d, Hogan. e, Nicklaus. f, Norman. g, Olazabal. h, Bobby Jones.

Statesmen and historical events: No. 1561a, Hans-Dietrich Genscher, German Foreign Minister, winged victory symbol. b, Destruction of Berlin Wall. c, Charles de Gaulle delivering radio appeal, Winston Churchill, de Gaulle. d, Dwight D. Eisenhower, de Gaulle, Normandy invasion. e, Brandenburg Gate. f, German Chancellor Helmut Kohl mayors of East, West Berlin. g, De Gaulle and Konrad Adenauer. h, George Washington and Lafayette, De Gaulle and John F. Kennedy.

Chess masters: No. 1562a, Francois Andre Danican Philidor. b, Adolph Anderssen. c, Wilhelm Steinitz. d, Alexander Alekhine. e, Boris Spassky. f, Bobby Fischer. g, Anatoly Karpov. h, Garri Kasparov.

Nobel Prize winners: No. 1563a, Einstein, physics. b, Roentgen, physics. c, William Shockley, physics. d, Charles Townes, physics. e, Lev Landau, physics. f, Marconi, physics. g, Willard Libby, chemistry. h, Ernest Lawrence, physics.

Entertainers: No. 1564a, Michael Jackson. b, Madonna. c, Elvis Presley. d, David Bowie. e, Prince. f, Frank Sinatra. g, George Michael. h, Mick Jagger.

No. 1565, Roosevelt, de Gaulle, Churchill at Morocco Conf., 1943. No. 1566, Madonna. No. 1567, Elvis Presley.

1991, Nov. 25 Litho. *Perf. 14½*

1560 A215 $1 Sheet of 8, #a.-h. 6.00 6.00
1561 A215 $1 Sheet of 8, #a.-h. 6.00 6.00
1562 A215 $1 Sheet of 8, #a.-h. 6.00 6.00
1563 A215 $1 Sheet of 8, #a.-h. 6.00 6.00
1564 A215 $2 Sheet of 8, #a.-h. 12.00 12.00

Souvenir Sheets

Perf. 14

1565 A215 $6 multicolored 4.50 4.50
1566 A215 $6 multicolored 4.50 4.50
1567 A215 $6 multicolored 4.50 4.50

Nos. 1565-1567 each contain one 27x43mm stamp.

See Nos. 1642-1643, 1729-1730 for more Elvis Presley stamps.

Walt Disney Christmas Cards — A216

Designs and year of issue: 10c, Goofy, Mickey and Pluto decorating Christmas tree, 1982. 45c, Mickey, reindeer, 1980. 55c, Christmas tree ornament, 1970. 75c, Baby duck holding 1944 sign, 1943. $1.50, Characters papering globe with greetings, 1941. $2, Lady and the Tramp beside Christmas tree, 1986. $4, Donald, Goofy, Mickey and Pluto reciting "Night Before Christmas," 1977. $5, Mickey in doorway of Snow White's Castle, 1965. No. 1576, People from around the world, 1966. No. 1577, Mickey in balloon basket with people of different countries, 1966.

1991, Dec. 23 *Perf. 13½x14*

1568 A216 10c multicolored .15 .15
1569 A216 45c multicolored .35 .35
1570 A216 55c multicolored .42 .42
1571 A216 75c multicolored .55 .55
1572 A216 $1.50 multicolored 1.15 1.15
1573 A216 $2 multicolored 1.50 1.50
1574 A216 $4 multicolored 3.00 3.00
1575 A216 $5 multicolored 3.75 3.75
Nos. 1568-1575 (8) 10.87 10.87

Souvenir Sheets

1576 A216 $6 multicolored 4.50 4.50
1577 A216 $6 multicolored 4.50 4.50

Environmental Preservation — A217

1992, Jan. Litho. *Perf. 14*

1578 A217 10c Kings Hill .15 .15
1579 A217 55c Tree planting .42 .42
1580 A217 75c Botanical Gardens .58 .58
1581 A217 $2 Kings Hill Project 1.50 1.50
Nos. 1578-1581 (4) 2.65 2.65

Queen Elizabeth II's Accession to the Throne, 40th Anniv.

Common Design Type

1992, Feb. 6

1582 CD348 10c multicolored .15 .15
1583 CD348 20c multicolored .15 .15
1584 CD348 $1 multicolored .75 .75
1585 CD348 $5 multicolored 3.75 3.75
Nos. 1582-1585 (4) 4.80 4.80

Souvenir Sheets

1586 CD348 $6 Queen, beach 4.50 4.50
1587 CD348 $6 Queen, harbor 4.50 4.50

Queen Elizabeth II's Acession to the Throne, 40th Anniv. A217a

Designs: No. 1587A, Queen Elizabeth II. No. 1587B, King George VI.

1993, Mar. 2 Embossed *Perf. 12*

Without Gum

1587A A217a $5 gold
1587B A217a $5 gold

1992 Winter Olympics, Albertville — A218

1992 Summer Olympics, Barcelona — A219

1992, Apr. 21 Litho. *Perf. 14*

1588 A218 10c Women's luge, horiz. .15 .15
1589 A218 15c Women's figure skating .15 .15
1590 A218 25c Two-man bobsled, horiz. .18 .18
1591 A218 30c Mogul skiing .24 .24
1592 A218 45c Nordic combined, horiz. .35 .35
1593 A218 55c Ski jump, horiz. .42 .42
1594 A218 75c Giant slalom, horiz. .58 .58
1595 A218 $1.50 Women's slalom 1.15 1.15
1596 A218 $5 Ice hockey, horiz. 3.75 3.75
1597 A218 $8 Biathlon 6.00 6.00
Nos. 1588-1597 (10) 12.97 12.97

Souvenir Sheets

1598 A218 $6 Downhill skiing 4.50 4.50
1599 A218 $6 Speed skating 4.50 4.50

1992, Apr. 21

10c, Women's synchronized swimming duet, horiz. 15c, High jump. 25c, Small-bore rifle, horiz. 30c, 200-meter run. 45c, Judo. 55c. 200-meter freestyle swimming, horiz. 75c, Javelin. $1.50, Pursuit cycling. $5, Boxing. $8, Women's basketball. #1610, Tennis. #1611, Board sailing.

1600 A219 10c multicolored .15 .15
1601 A219 15c multicolored .15 .15
1602 A219 25c multicolored .18 .18
1603 A219 30c multicolored .22 .22
1604 A219 45c multicolored .35 .35
1605 A219 55c multicolored .42 .42
1606 A219 75c multicolored .55 .55
1607 A219 $1.50 multicolored 1.15 1.15
1608 A219 $5 multicolored 3.75 3.75
1609 A219 $8 multicolored 6.00 6.00
Nos. 1600-1609 (10) 12.92 12.92

Souvenir Sheets

1610 A219 $15 multicolored 11.25 11.25
1611 A219 $15 multicolored 11.25 11.25

World Columbian Stamp Expo '92, Chicago — A220

Walt Disney characters visiting Chicago area landmarks: 10c, Mickey, Pluto at Picasso Sulpture. 50c, Mickey, Donald admiring Frank Lloyd Wright's Robie House. $1, Gus Gander at Calder Sculpture in Sears Tower. $5, Pluto in Buckingham Memorial Fountain. No. 1616, Mickey painting Minnie at Chicago Art Institute, vert.

1992, Apr. Litho. *Perf. 14x13½*

1612 A220 10c multicolored .15 .15
1613 A220 50c multicolored .38 .38
1614 A220 $1 multicolored .75 .75
1615 A220 $5 multicolored 3.75 3.75
Nos. 1612-1615 (4) 5.03 5.03

Souvenir Sheet

Perf. 13½x14

1616 A220 $6 multicolored 4.50 4.50

Nos. 1617-1621 have not been assigned.

Granada '92 — A221

Walt Disney characters from "The Three Little Pigs" in Spanish military uniforms: 15c, Big Bad Wolf as General of Spanish Moors. 40c, Pig as Captain of Spanish infantry. $2, Pig in Spanish armor, c. 1580. $4, Pig as Spaniard of rank, c. 1550. $6, Little Pig resisting wolf from castle built of stone.

1992, Apr. 28 *Perf. 13½x14*

1622 A221 15c multicolored .15 .15
1623 A221 40c multicolored .30 .30
1624 A221 $2 multicolored 1.50 1.50
1625 A221 $4 multicolored 3.00 3.00
Nos. 1622-1625 (4) 4.95 4.95

Souvenir Sheet

1626 A221 $6 multicolored 4.25 4.25

Nos. 1627-1631 have not been assigned.

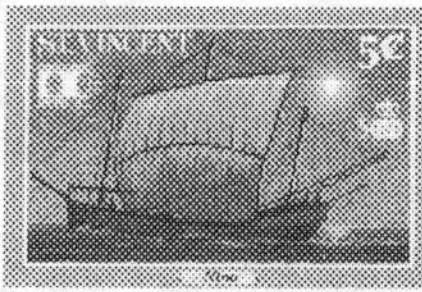

Discovery of America, 500th Anniv. A222

1992, May 22 *Perf. 14*

1632 A222 5c Nina .15 .15
1633 A222 10c Pinta .15 .15
1634 A222 45c Santa Maria .35 .35
1635 A222 55c Leaving Palos, Spain .42 .42
1636 A222 $4 Columbus, vert. 3.00 3.00
1637 A222 $5 Columbus' arms, vert. 3.75 3.75
Nos. 1632-1637 (6) 7.82 7.82

Souvenir Sheet

1638 A222 $6 Map, vert. 4.50 4.50
1639 A222 $6 Sailing ship, vert. 4.50 4.50

World Columbian Stamp Expo '92, Chicago. Nos. 1638-1639 contain one 42x57mm stamp.

Bonnie Blair, US Olympic Speed Skating Champion — A223

Designs: No. 1641a, Skating around corner. b, Portrait holding skates. c, On straightaway.

1992, May 25 *Perf. 13½*

1640 A223 $3 multicolored 2.25 2.25

Souvenir Sheet

1641 A223 $2 Sheet of 3, #a.-c. 4.50 4.50

World Columbian Stamp Expo '92. No. 1641b is 48x60mm.

Entertainers Type of 1991

Miniature Sheet

Various portraits of Elvis Presley.

1992, May 25 *Perf. 13½x14*

1642 A206 $1 Sheet of 9, #a.-i. 6.75 6.75

Souvenir Sheet

Perf. 14

1643 A206 $6 multicolored 4.50 4.50

No. 1643 contains one 28x43mm stamp.

See Nos. 1729-1730.

Hummingbirds A224

1992, June 15 *Perf. 14*

1644 A224 5c Rufous-breasted hermit .15 .15
1645 A224 15c Hispaniolan emerald .15 .15
1646 A224 45c Green-throated carib .35 .35
1647 A224 55c Jamaican mango .42 .42
1648 A224 65c Vervain .50 .50
1649 A224 75c Purple-throated carib .58 .58
1650 A224 90c Green mango .70 .70
1651 A224 $1 Bee .78 .78
1652 A224 $2 Cuban emerald 1.55 1.55
1653 A224 $3 Puerto Rican emerald 2.30 2.30
1654 A224 $4 Antillean mango 3.00 3.00
1655 A224 $5 Streamertail 3.75 3.75
Nos. 1644-1655 (12) 14.23 14.23

Souvenir Sheets

1656 A224 $6 Antillean crested 4.50 4.50
1657 A224 $6 Bahama woodstar 4.50 4.50
1658 A224 $6 Blue-headed 4.50 4.50

Genoa '92 Intl. Philatelic Exhibition.

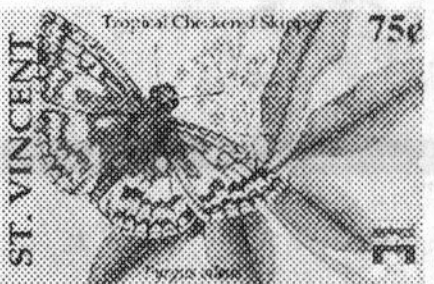

Butterflies A225

Designs: 5c, Dull astraptes, vert. 10c, White peacock. 35c, Tropic queen, vert. 45c, Polydamas swallowtail, vert. 55c, West Indian buckeye. 65c, Longtailed skipper, vert. 75c, Tropical checkered skipper. $1, Crimson-banded black, vert. $2, Barred sulphur, vert. $3, Cassius blue. $4, Florida duskywing. $5, Malachite, vert. No. 1671, Cloudless giant sulphur, vert. No. 1672, Julia. No. 1673, Zebra longwing.

1992, June 15 Litho. *Perf. 14*

1659 A225 5c multicolored .15 .15
1660 A225 10c multicolored .15 .15
1661 A225 35c multicolored .28 .28
1662 A225 45c multicolored .35 .35
1663 A225 55c multicolored .42 .42
1664 A225 65c multicolored .48 .48
1665 A225 75c multicolored .58 .58
1666 A225 $1 multicolored .75 .75

1667 A225 $2 multicolored 1.50 1.50
1668 A225 $3 multicolored 2.25 2.25
1669 A225 $4 multicolored 3.00 3.00
1670 A225 $5 multicolored 3.75 3.75
Nos. 1659-1670 (12) 13.66 13.66

Souvenir Sheets

1671 A225 $6 multicolored 4.50 4.50
1672 A225 $6 multicolored 4.50 4.50
1673 A225 $6 multicolored 4.50 4.50

Genoa '92.

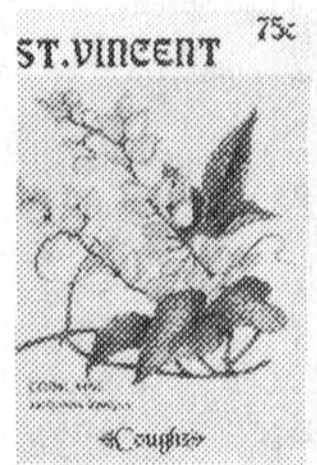

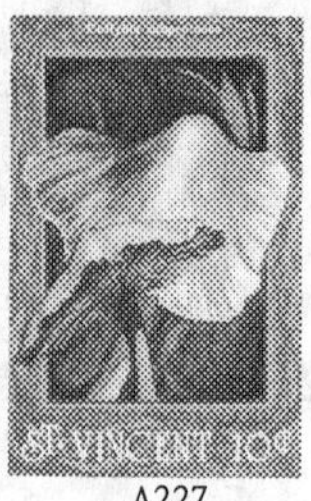

A226 A227

Medicinal Plants: No. 1674a, Coral vine. b, Cocoplum. c, Angel's trumpet. d, Lime. e, White ginger. f, Pussley. g, Sea grape. h, Indian mulberry. i, Plantain. j, Lignum vitae. k, Periwinkle. l, Guava.

1992, July 22 Litho. *Perf. 14*

Miniature Sheet

1674 A226 75c Sheet of 12, #a.-l. 6.75 6.75

Souvenir Sheets

1675 A226 $6 Aloe 4.50 4.50
1676 A226 $6 Clove tree 4.50 4.50
1677 A226 $6 Wild sage 4.50 4.50

1992, July 2 Litho. *Perf. 14*

Mushrooms: 10c, Collybia subpruinosa. 15c, Gerronema citrinum. 20c, Amanita antillana. 45c, Dermoloma atrobrunneum. 50c, Inopilus maculosus. 65c, Pulveroboletus brachyspermus. 75c, Mycena violacella. $1, Xerocomus brasiliensis. $2, Amanita ingrata. $3, Leptonia caeruleocaptata. $4, Limacella myochroa. $5, Inopilus magnificus. No. 1690, Limacella guttata. No. 1691, Amanita agglutinata. No. 1692, Trogia buccinalis.

1678 A227 10c multicolored .15 .15
1679 A227 15c multicolored .15 .15
1680 A227 20c multicolored .15 .15
1681 A227 45c multicolored .35 .35
1682 A227 50c multicolored .38 .38
1683 A227 65c multicolored .48 .48
1684 A227 75c multicolored .58 .58
1685 A227 $1 multicolored .75 .75
1686 A227 $2 multicolored 1.50 1.50
1687 A227 $3 multicolored 2.25 2.25
1688 A227 $4 multicolored 3.00 3.00
1689 A227 $5 multicolored 3.75 3.75
Nos. 1678-1689 (12) 13.49 13.49

Souvenir Sheets

1690 A227 $6 multicolored 4.50 4.50
1691 A227 $6 multicolored 4.50 4.50
1692 A227 $6 multicolored 4.50 4.50

Baseball Players — A228

Designs: #1693, Ty Cobb. #1694, Dizzy Dean. #1695, Bob Feller. #1696, Whitey Ford. #1697, Lou Gehrig. #1698, Rogers Hornsby. #1699, Mel Ott. #1700, Satchel Paige. #1701, Babe Ruth. #1702, Casey Stengel. #1703, Honus Wagner. #1704, Cy Young.

1992, Aug. 5 Litho. *Imperf.*

Self-Adhesive

Size: 64x89mm

1693-1704 A228 $4 Set of 12 36.00

Nos. 1693-1704 printed on thin card and distributed in boxed sets. To affix stamps, backing containing player's statistics must be removed.

A229 A230

1992 Winter Olympic Gold Medalists, Albertville: No. 1705a, Alberto Tomba, Italy, giant slalom. b, Fabrice Guy, France, Nordic combined. c, Patrick Ortlieb, Austria, men's downhill. d, Vegard Ulvang, Norway, cross country. e, Edgar Grospiron, France, freestyle Mogul skiing. f, Kjetil-Andre Aamodt, Norway, super giant slalom. g, Viktor Petrenko, Russia, men's figure skating.

No. 1706a, Kristi Yamaguchi, US, women's figure skating. b, Pernilla Wiberg, Sweden, women's giant slalom. c, Lyubov Yegorova, Unified Team, women's 10-kilometer cross country. d, Josef Polig, Italy, combined Alpine skiing. e, Finn Christian-Jagge, Norway, slalom. f, Kerrin Lee-Gartner, Canada, women's downhill. g, Steffania Belmondo, Italy, women's 30-kilometer cross country.

No. 1707, Alberto Tomba, diff. No. 1708, Kristi Yamaguchi, diff.

1992, Aug. 10 Litho. *Perf. 14*

Sheets of 7

1705 A229 $1 #a.-g. + label 5.25 5.25
1706 A229 $1 #a.-g. + label 5.25 5.25

Souvenir Sheets

1707 A229 $6 multicolored 4.50 4.50
1708 A229 $6 multicolored 4.50 4.50

1992 Litho. *Perf. 14½*

1709 A230 $1 Coming ashore .75 .75
1710 A230 $2 Natives, ships 1.50 1.50

Discovery of America, 500th anniv. Organization of East Caribbean States.

Miniature Sheet

Opening of Euro Disney — A231

Walt Disney movies: #1711a, Pinocchio. b, Alice in Wonderland. c, Bambi. d, Cinderella. e, Snow White and the Seven Dwarfs. f, Peter Pan.

1992 Litho. *Perf. 13*

1711 A231 $1 Sheet of 6, #a.-f. 4.50 4.50

Souvenir Sheet

Perf. 12½

1712 A231 $5 Mickey Mouse 3.75 3.75

Christmas A232

Details or entire paintings of The Nativity by: 10c, Hospitality Refused to the Virgin Mary and Joseph, by Jan Metsys. 40c, Albrecht Durer. 45c, The Nativity, by Geertgen Tot Sint Jans. 50c, The Nativity, by Tintoretto. 55c, Follower of Jan Joest Calcar. 65c, Workshop of Fra Angelico. 75c, Master of the Louvre Nativity. $1, Filippino Lippi. $2, Petrus Christus. $3, Edward Burne-Jones. $4, Giotto. $5, The Birth of Christ, by Domenico Ghirlandaio. No. 1725, Nativity, by Jean Fouquet. No. 1726, Sandro Botticelli. No. 1727, Gerard Horenbout.

1992, Nov. Litho. *Perf. 13½x14*

1713 A232 10c multicolored .15 .15
1714 A232 40c multicolored .30 .30
1715 A232 45c multicolored .35 .35
1716 A232 50c multicolored .38 .38
1717 A232 55c multicolored .42 .42
1718 A232 65c multicolored .48 .48
1719 A232 75c multicolored .58 .58
1720 A232 $1 multicolored .75 .75
1721 A232 $2 multicolored 1.50 1.50
1722 A232 $3 multicolored 2.25 2.25
1723 A232 $4 multicolored 3.00 3.00
1724 A232 $5 multicolored 3.75 3.75
Nos. 1714-1724 (11) 13.76 13.76

Souvenir Sheets

1725 A232 $6 multicolored 4.50 4.50
1726 A232 $6 multicolored 4.50 4.50
1727 A232 $6 multicolored 4.50 4.50

Souvenir Sheet

Jacob Javits Convention Center, NYC — A233

1992, Oct. 28 Litho. *Perf. 14*

1728 A233 $6 multicolored 4.50 4.50

Postage Stamp Mega Event '92, NYC.

No. 1642 Inscribed Vertically "15th Anniversary"

Nos. 1564, 1567 (in margin) Inscribed or Ovptd. "15th Anniversary" and "Elvis Presley's Death / August 16, 1977"

1992, Dec. 15 *Perf. 13½x14*

1729 A206 $1 Sheet of 9, #a.-i. 6.75 6.75

Perf. 14½

1729J A215 $2 Sheet of 8, #k.-r. 12.00 12.00

Perf. 14

1730 A215 $6 Souvenir sheet 4.50 4.50

Baseball Players — A234

Members of Baseball Hall Fame — A235

1992, Nov. 9 Litho. *Perf. 14*

1731 A234 $5 Howard Johnson 3.75 3.75
1732 A234 $5 Don Mattingly 3.75 3.75

1992 Summer Olympics, Barcelona.

1992, Dec. 21

Player, year inducted: No. 1733, Roberto Clemente, 1973. No. 1734, Hank Aaron, 1982. No. 1735, Tom Seaver, 1992.

1733 A235 $2 multicolored 1.50 1.50
1734 A235 $2 multicolored 1.50 1.50
1735 A235 $2 multicolored 1.50 1.50
Nos. 1733-1735 (3) 4.50 4.50

Fishing Industry A236

1992, Nov.

1736 A236 5c Fishing with rods .15 .15
1737 A236 10c Inside fishing complex .15 .15
1738 A236 50c Landing the catch .38 .38
1739 A236 $5 Fishing with nets 3.75 3.75
Nos. 1736-1739 (4) 4.43 4.43

Uniting the Windward Islands A237

Children's paintings: 10c, Island coastline. 40c, Four people standing on islands. 45c, Four people standing on beach.

1992, Nov. Litho. *Perf. 14*

1740 A237 10c multicolored .15 .15
1741 A237 40c multicolored .30 .30
1742 A237 45c multicolored .35 .35
Nos. 1740-1742 (3) .80 .80

Miniature Sheets

US Olympic Basketball "Dream Team" — A238

Designs: No. 1744a, Scottie Pippen. b, Earvin "Magic" Johnson. c, Larry Bird. d, Christian Laettner. e, Karl Malone. f, David Robinson.

No. 1745a, Michael Jordan. b, Charles Barkley. c, John Stockton. d, Chris Mullin. e, Clyde Drexler. f, Patrick Ewing.

1992, Dec. 22 Litho. *Perf. 14*

1744 A238 $2 Sheet of 6, #a.-f. 9.00 9.00
1745 A238 $2 Sheet of 6, #a.-f. 9.00 9.00

1992 Summer Olympics, Barcelona.

A239

A240

A241

A242

Anniversaries and Events: 10c, Globe and UN emblem. 45c, Zeppelin Viktoria Luise over Kiel Regatta, 1912, vert. 65c, Food products. No. 1749, America's Cup Trophy and Bill Koch, skipper of America 3. No. 1750, Konrad Adenauer, German flag. No. 1751, Adenauer, diff. No. 1752, Snow leopard. $1.50, Caribbean manatee. $2, Humpback whale. No. 1755, Adenauer, John F. Kennedy. No. 1756, Lions Intl. emblem, patient having eye exam. No. 1757, Space shuttle Discovery, vert. No. 1758, Adenauer, Pope John XXIII. $5, Michael Schumacher, race car. $6, Count Zeppelin's first airship over Lake Constance, 1900. No. 1761, Gondola of Graf Zeppelin. No. 1762, Formula I race car. No. 1763, Sailing ship, steam packet. No. 1764, denauer at podium. No. 1765, Woolly spider ionkey. No. 1765A, People waving to plane during Berlin airlift.

992-93 Litho. *Perf. 14*

746	A239	10c	multicolored	.15	.15
747	A239	45c	multicolored	.35	.35
748	A242	65c	multicolored	.48	.48
749	A239	75c	multicolored	.58	.58
750	A239	75c	multicolored	.58	.58
751	A239	$1	multicolored	.75	.75
752	A239	$1	multicolored	.75	.75
753	A239	$1.50	multicolored	1.15	1.15
754	A239	$2	multicolored	1.50	1.50
755	A239	$3	multicolored	2.25	2.25
756	A239	$3	multicolored	2.25	2.25
757	A239	$4	multicolored	3.00	3.00
758	A239	$4	multicolored	3.00	3.00
759	A240	$5	multicolored	3.75	3.75
760	A239	$6	multicolored	4.50	4.50
	Nos. 1746-1760 (15)			25.04	25.04

Souvenir Sheets

761	A239	$6	multicolored	4.50	4.50
762	A240	$6	multicolored	4.50	4.50
763	A241	$6	multicolored	4.50	4.50
764	A239	$6	multicolored	4.50	4.50
765	A239	$6	multicolored	4.50	4.50
765A	A239	$6	multicolored	4.50	4.50

UN Intl. Space Year (#1746, 1757). Count eppelin, 75th anniv. of death (#1747, 1760-761). Intl. Conference on Nutrition, Rome #1748). America's Cup yacht race (#1749). Konad Adenauer, 25th death anniv. (#1750-1751, 755, 1758, 1764). Earth Summit, Rio de Janeiro #1752-1754, 1765). Lions Intl., 75th anniv. #1756). Belgian Grand Prix (#1759, 1762). Disovery of America, 500th anniv. (#1763). Konrad denauer, 75th death anniv. (#1765A).

Issued: #1747, 1759-1762, Dec; #1763, 0/28/92; #1746, 1749, 1750-1751, 1755-1758, 764, Dec; #1752-1754, 1765, Dec. 15; #1765A, /30/93.

A243

A244

Care Bears Promote Conservation: 75c, Bear, tork. $2, Bear riding in hot air balloon, horiz.

992, Dec. Litho. *Perf. 14*

766 A243 75c multicolored .58 .58

Souvenir Sheet

767 A243 $2 multicolored 1.50 1.50

993 Litho. *Perf. 14*

Elvis Presley (1935-1977): b, Portrait. c, With uitar. d, With microphone.

767A A244 $1 Strip of 3, #b.-d. 2.25 2.25

Printed in sheets of 9 stamps.

Walt Disney's Beauty and the Beast — A245

Designs: 2c, Gaston. 3c, Belle and her father, Maurice. 5c, Lumiere, Mrs. Potts and Cogsworth. 0c, Philippe. 15c, Beast and Lumiere. 20c, umiere and Feather Duster.

No. 1774a, Belle and Gaston. b, Maurice. c, The Beast. d, Mrs. Potts. e, Belle and the Enchanted Vase. f, Belle discovers an Enchanted Rose. g, Belle with wounded Beast. h, Belle. i, Household objects larmed.

No. 1774k, Belle and Chip. l, Lumiere. m, Cogworth. n, Armoire. o, Belle and Beast. p, Feather Duster. q, Footstool. r, Belle. All vert.

No. 1775, Belle reading, vert. No. 1776, umiere, diff., vert. No. 1776A, Lumiere, Mrs. Potts. No. 1776B, Belle, lake and castle, vert. No. 776C, The Beast, vert.

Perf. 14x13½, 13½x14

1992, Dec. 15 Litho.

1768	A245	2c	multicolored	.15	.15
1769	A245	3c	multicolored	.15	.15
1770	A245	5c	multicolored	.15	.15
1771	A245	10c	multicolored	.15	.15
1772	A245	15c	multicolored	.15	.15
1773	A245	20c	multicolored	.15	.15
			Set Value	.42	.42

Miniature Sheets

1774	A245	60c	Sheet of 9, #a.-i.	4.00	4.00
1774J	A245	60c	Sheet of 8, #k.-r.	4.00	4.00

Souvenir Sheets

1775	A245	$6	multicolored	4.50	4.50
1776	A245	$6	multicolored	4.50	4.50
1776A	A245	$6	multicolored	4.50	4.50
1776B	A245	$6	multicolored	4.50	4.50
1776C	A245	$6	multicolored	4.50	4.50

Louvre Museum, Bicent. A246

Details or entire paintings by Jean-Auguste-Dominique Ingres: No. 1777a, Louis-Francois Bertin. b, The Apotheosis of Homer. c, Joan of Arc. d, The Composer Cherubini with the Muse of Lyric Poetry. e, Mlle Caroline Riviere. f, Oedipus Answers the Sphinx's Riddle. g, Madame Marcotte. h, Mademoiselle Caroline Riviere.

Details or entire paintings by Jean Louis Andre Theodore Gericault (1791-1824): No. 1778a, The Woman with Gambling Mania. b, Head of a White Horse. c, Wounded Cuirassier. d, An Officer of the Cavalry. e, The Vendean. f, The Raft of the Medusa. g-h, The Horse Market (left, right).

Details or entire paintings by Nicolas Poussin (1594-1665): No. 1779a-1779b, The Arcadian Shepherds (left, right). c, Ecstasy of Paul. d-e, The Inspiration of the Poet (left, right). f-g, St. John Baptizing (left, right). h, The Miracle of St. Francis Xavier.

Details or entire paintings by Eustache Le Sueur (1616-1655): No. 1780a-1780b, Melpomene, Erato & Polyhymnia (left, right). By Poussin: c, Christ and Woman Taken in Adultery. d, Spring. e, Autumn. f-h, The Plague of Asdod (left, center, right).

No. 1781a, The Beggars, by Pieter Brueghel, the Elder (1520-1569). b, The Luncheon, by Francois Boucher (1703-1770). c, Louis Guene, Royal Violinist, by Francois Dumont (1751-1831). d, The Virgin of Chancellor Rolin, by Jan Van Eyck. e, Conversation in the Park, by Thomas Gainsborough. f, Lady Alston, by Gainsborough. g, Mariana Waldstein, by Francisco de Goya. h, Ferdinand Guillemardet, by Goya.

No. 1782, The Grand Odalisque, horiz. No. 1783, The Dressing Room of Esther, by Theodore Chasseriau (1819-1856). No. 1784, Liberty Guiding the People, by Eugene Delecroix (1798-1863), horiz.

1993, Apr. 19 *Perf. 12x12½*

Sheets of 8

1777	A246	$1	#a.-h. + label	6.00	6.00
1778	A246	$1	#a.-h. + label	6.00	6.00
1779	A246	$1	#a.-h. + label	6.00	6.00
1780	A246	$1	#a.-h. + label	6.00	6.00
1781	A246	$1	#a.-h. + label	6.00	6.00

Souvenir Sheet

Perf. 14½

1782	A246	$6	multicolored	4.50	4.50
1783	A246	$6	multicolored	4.50	4.50
1784	A246	$6	multicolored	4.50	4.50

Nos. 1783-1784 each contain a 55x88mm or 88x55mm stamp.

Paintings on Nos. 1777d and 1777h were switched.

Numbers have been reserved for two additional souvenir sheets in this set.

Miniature Sheets

A247

A247a

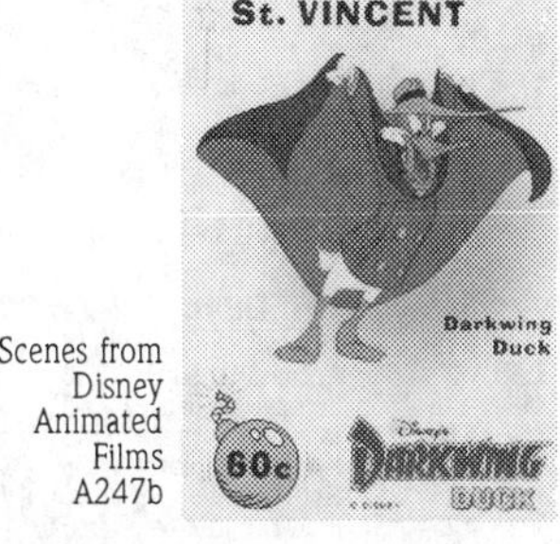

Scenes from Disney Animated Films A247b

Symphony Hour (1942): No. 1787a, Maestro Mickey. b, Goofy plays a mean horn. c, On first bass with Clara Cluck. d, Stringing along with Clarabelle. e, Donald on drums. f, Clarabelle all fiddled out. g, Donald drumming up trouble. h, Goofy's sour notes. i, Mickey's moment.

No. 1794, Bird's-eye-view of Goofy. No. 1795, Mickey and Macaroni enjoying applause.

The Small One: No. 1791k, Morning comes in Nazareth. l, Good morning, small one. m, Too old to keep. n, Heatbroken. o, Nazareth markplace. p, Auction mockery. q, Off the auction block. r, Lonely and dejected. s, Happy and useful again.

No. 1804, Hard Work in Nazareth. No. 1805, Finding a buyer in Nazareth.

The Three Little Pigs (1933): No. 1792a, Fifer Pig building house of straw. b, Fiddler Pig building house of sticks. c, Practical Pig building house of bricks. d, The Big Bad Wolf. e, Wolf scaring two lazy pigs. f, Wolf blowing down staw house. g, Wolf in sheep's clothing. h, Wolf blowing down twig house. i, Wolf huffs and puffs at brick house.

No. 1806, Animator's sketch of little pig and brick house. No. 1807, Little pigs playing and singing at piano, vert.

How to Play Football (1944): No. 1792k, Cheerleaders. l, Here comes the team. m, In the huddle. n, Who's got the ball? o, Who, me coach? p, Halftime pep talk. q, Another down, and out. r, Only a little injury. s, Up and at 'em.

No. 1807A, Goofy demonstrating how to score touchdown. No. 1807B, Goofy shouting "Hooray for the team," vert.

Rescue Rangers: No. 1793a, Special agents. b, Chip 'n Dale, ready for action. c, Chip 'n Dale on stakeout. d, Gadget in gear. e, Gadget and Monterey Jack rescue Zipper. f, Zipper confers with Monterey Jack. g, Zipper zaps fat cat. h, Team work. i, Innovative Gadget.

No. 1807C, Gadget at controls of Ranger plane, vert. No. 1807D, Dale, vert.

Darkwing Duck: No. 1793k, Darkwing Duck. l, Launchpad McQuack. m, Gosalyn. n, Honker Muddlefoot. o, Tank Muddlefoot. p, Herb & Binkie Muddlefoot. q, Drake Mallard, aka Darkwing Duck. r, Darkwing Duck logo.

No. 1807E, Quarterjack. No. 1807F, Darkwing Duck and Launchpad to the rescue in Ratcatcher.

Clock Cleaners (1937): No. 1788a, Goofy gets in gear. b, Donald on the mainspring. c, Donald in the works. d, Mickey's fine-feathered friend. e, Stork with bundle of joy. f, Father Time. g, Goofy, Mickey leaping upward. h, Donald, Goofy, Mickey out of gear. i, Donald, Goofy, Mickey with headaches.

No. 1796, On the edge of Goofyness. No. 1797, Gonged-out Goofy.

The Art of Skiing (1941): No. 1789a, The ultimate back scratcher. b, Striking a pose. c, And we're off. d, Divided he stands. e, A real twister. f, Hangin' in there. g, Over the hill. h, At the peak of his form. i, Up a tree.

No. 1798, Film poster for Art of Skiing with Goofy slaloming down mountain. No. 1799, Goofy home in bed at last.

Orphan's Benefit (1941): No. 1790a, Mickey introduces Donald. b, Donald recites "Little Boy Blue." c, Orphan mischief. d, Clara Cluck, singing sensation. e, Goofy's debut with Clarabelle. f, Encore for Clara and Mickey. g, A Bronx cheer. h, Donald blows his stack. i, Donald's final bow.

No. 1800, Caveman ballet. No. 1801, Mickey tickles the ivories.

Thru the Mirror (1936): No. 1791a, Mickey steps thru the looking glass. b, Mickey finds a tasty treat. c, Mickey's nutty effect. d, Hats off to Mickey. e, What a card, Mickey. f, Mickey dancing with the Queen Hearts. g, A real two-faced opponent. h, Mickey with a pen mightier than a sword. i, Mickey awake at last.

No. 1802, Mickey's true reflection. No. 1803, Mickey hopping home.

Perf. 14x13½, 13½x14

1992, Dec. 15 Litho.

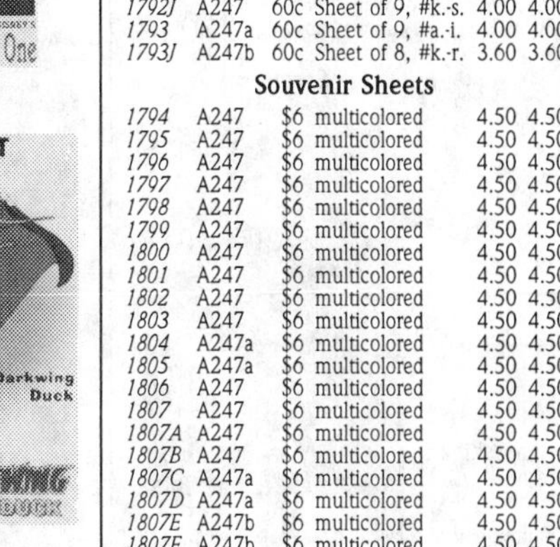

1787	A247	60c	Sheet of 9, #a.-i.	4.00	4.00
1788	A247	60c	Sheet of 9, #a.-i.	4.00	4.00
1789	A247	60c	Sheet of 9, #a.-i.	4.00	4.00
1790	A247	60c	Sheet of 9, #a.-i.	4.00	4.00
1791	A247	60c	Sheet of 9, #a.-i.	4.00	4.00
1791J	A247a	60c	Sheet of 9, #k.-s.	4.00	4.00
1792	A247	60c	Sheet of 9, #a.-i.	4.00	4.00
1792J	A247	60c	Sheet of 9, #k.-s.	4.00	4.00
1793	A247a	60c	Sheet of 9, #a.-i.	4.00	4.00
1793J	A247b	60c	Sheet of 8, #k.-r.	3.60	3.60

Souvenir Sheets

1794	A247	$6	multicolored	4.50	4.50
1795	A247	$6	multicolored	4.50	4.50
1796	A247	$6	multicolored	4.50	4.50
1797	A247	$6	multicolored	4.50	4.50
1798	A247	$6	multicolored	4.50	4.50
1799	A247	$6	multicolored	4.50	4.50
1800	A247	$6	multicolored	4.50	4.50
1801	A247	$6	multicolored	4.50	4.50
1802	A247	$6	multicolored	4.50	4.50
1803	A247	$6	multicolored	4.50	4.50
1804	A247a	$6	multicolored	4.50	4.50
1805	A247a	$6	multicolored	4.50	4.50
1806	A247	$6	multicolored	4.50	4.50
1807	A247	$6	multicolored	4.50	4.50
1807A	A247	$6	multicolored	4.50	4.50
1807B	A247	$6	multicolored	4.50	4.50
1807C	A247a	$6	multicolored	4.50	4.50
1807D	A247a	$6	multicolored	4.50	4.50
1807E	A247b	$6	multicolored	4.50	4.50
1807F	A247b	$6	multicolored	4.50	4.50

See Nos. 2144-2146 for 30c & $3 stamps.

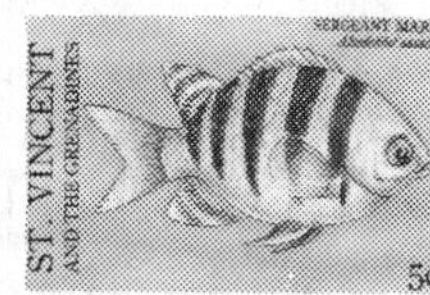

Fish A248

1993, Apr. 1 Litho. *Perf. 14*

1808	A248	5c	Sergeant major	.15	.15
1809	A248	10c	Rainbow parrotfish	.15	.15
1810	A248	55c	Hogfish	.42	.42
1811	A248	75c	Porkfish	.58	.58
1812	A248	$1	Spotfin butterflyfish	.75	.75
1813	A248	$2	Trunkfish	1.50	1.50
1814	A248	$4	Queen triggerfish	3.00	3.00
1815	A248	$5	Queen angelfish	3.75	3.75
	Nos. 1808-1815 (8)			10.30	10.30

Souvenir Sheets

1816	A248	$6	Bigeye, vert.	4.50	4.50
1817	A248	$6	Smallmouth grunt, vert.	4.50	4.50

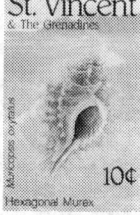

Birds — A249 Seashells — A250

Designs: 10c, Brown pelican. 25c, Red-necked grebe, horiz. 45c, Belted kingfisher, horiz. 55c, Yellow-bellied sapsucker. $1, Great blue heron. $2, Crab hawk, horiz. $4, Yellow warbler. $5, Northern oriole, horiz. No. 1826, White ibises, map, horiz. No. 1827, Blue-winged teal, map, horiz.

1993, Apr. 1 Litho. *Perf. 14*

1818	A249	10c	multicolored	15	.15
1819	A249	25c	multicolored	.18	.18
1820	A249	45c	multicolored	.35	.35
1821	A249	55c	multicolored	.42	.42
1822	A249	$1	multicolored	.75	.75
1823	A249	$2	multicolored	1.50	1.50
1824	A249	$4	multicolored	3.00	3.00
1825	A249	$5	multicolored	3.75	3.75
	Nos. 1818-1825 (8)			10.10	10.10

Souvenir Sheets

1826	A249	$6	multicolored	4.50	4.50
1827	A249	$6	multicolored	4.50	4.50

1993, May 24 Litho. *Perf. 14*

1828	A250	10c	Hexagonal murex	.15	.15
1829	A250	15c	Caribbean vase	.15	.15
1830	A250	30c	Measled cowrie	.22	.22
1831	A250	45c	Dyson's keyhole limpet	.35	.35
1832	A250	50c	Atlantic hairy triton	.38	.38
1833	A250	65c	Orange-banded marginella	.48	.48
1834	A250	75c	Bleeding tooth	.55	.55
1835	A250	$1	Pink conch	.75	.75
1836	A250	$2	Hawk-wing conch	1.50	1.50

1837 A250 $3 Music volute 2.25 2.25
1838 A250 $4 Alphabet cone 3.00 3.00
1839 A250 $5 Antillean cone 3.75 3.75
Nos. 1828-1839 (12) 13.53 13.53

Souvenir Sheets

1840 A250 $6 Flame auger, horiz. 4.50 4.50
1841 A250 $6 Netted olive, horiz. 4.50 4.50
1842 A250 $6 Wide-mouthed purpura, horiz. 4.50 4.50

Miniature Sheet

Yujiro Ishihara, Actor — A251

Various portraits: No. 1843a, $1. b, 55c. c, $1. d, 55c. e, 55c. f, 55c. g, $1. h, 55c. i, $1.
No. 1844a, 55c. b, $1. c, $2. d, $2.
No. 1845a, 55c. b, $2. c, $1. d, $2.
No. 1846a, 55c. b, $2. c, $4.
No. 1847a, 55c. b, $4. c, $4.

1993, May 24 Litho. *Perf. 13½x14*

1843 A251 Sheet of 9, #a.-i. 5.25 5.25

Souvenir Sheets

1844 A251 Sheet of 4, #a.-d. 4.25 4.25

Stamp Size: 32x41mm

Perf. 14½

1845 A251 Sheet of 4, #a.-d. 4.25 4.25

Stamp Size: 60x41mm

Perf. 14x14½

1846 A251 Sheet of 3, #a.-c. 5.00 5.00
1847 A251 Sheet of 3, #a.-c. 6.50 6.50

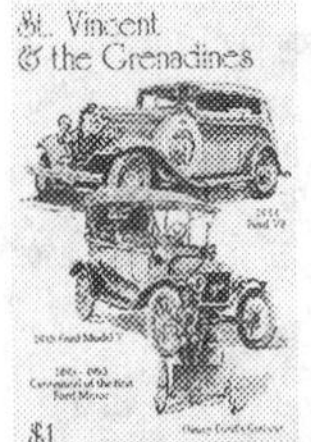

Automobiles — A252

$1, 1932 Ford V8, 1915 Ford Model T, Henry Ford's 1st car. $2, Benz 540K, 1928 Benz Stuttgart, 1908 Benz Racer. $3, 1911 Blitzen Benz, 1905 Benz Tourenwagen, 1894 Benz. $4, 1935 Ford, 1903 Ford A Runabout, 1913 Ford Model T Tourer. #1852, Karl Benz. #1853, Henry Ford.

1993, May Litho. *Perf. 14*

1848 A252 $1 multicolored .75 .75
1849 A252 $2 multicolored 1.50 1.50
1850 A252 $3 multicolored 2.25 2.25
1851 A252 $4 multicolored 3.00 3.00
Nos. 1848-1851 (4) 7.50 7.50

Souvenir Sheets

1852 A252 $6 multicolored 4.50 4.50
1853 A252 $6 multicolored 4.50 4.50

First Ford motor, cent. (#1848, 1851, 1853). First Benz motor car, cent. (#1849-1850, 1852).

Miniature Sheet

Coronation of Queen Elizabeth II, 40th Anniv. — A253

a, 45c, Official coronation photograph. b, 65c, Opening Parliament, 1980s. c, $2, Coronation ceremony, 1953. d, $4, Queen with her dog, 1970s.
No. 1855, Portrait of Queen as a child.

1993, June 2 Litho. *Perf. 13½x14*

1854 A253 Sheet, 2 each #a.-d. 11.00 11.00

Souvenir Sheet

Perf. 14

1855 A253 $6 multicolored 4.50 4.50

No. 1855 contains one 28x42mm stamp.

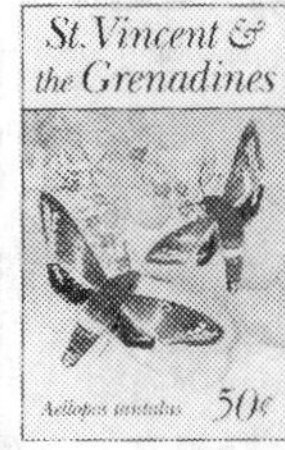

Moths — A254

1993, June 14 Litho. *Perf. 14*

1856 A254 10c Erynnyis ello .15 .15
1857 A254 50c Aellopos tantalus .38 .38
1858 A254 65c Erynnyis alope .48 .48
1859 A254 75c Manduca rustica .55 .55
1860 A254 $1 Xylophanes pluto .75 .75
1861 A254 $2 Hyles lineata 1.50 1.50
1862 A254 $4 Pseudosphinx tetrio 3.00 3.00
1863 A254 $5 Protambulyx strigilis 3.75 3.75
Nos. 1856-1863 (8) 10.56 10.56

Souvenir Sheets

1864 A254 $6 Xylophanes tersa 4.50 4.50
1864A A254 $6 Utetheisa ornatrix 4.50 4.50

A255

A256

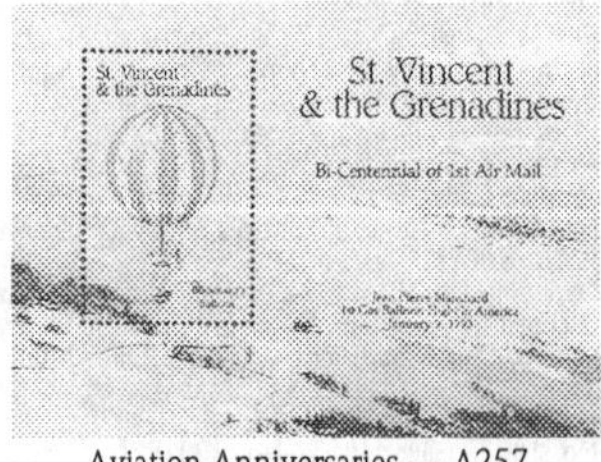

Aviation Anniversaries — A257

Designs: 50c, Supermarine Spitfire. No. 1866, Graf Zeppelin over Egypt, 1931, Hugo Eckener. No. 1867, Jean Pierre Blanchard, balloon, George Washington. No. 1868, De Havilland Mosquito. No. 1869, Eckener, Graf Zeppelin over New York, 1928. $3, Eckener, Graf Zeppelin over Tokyo, 1929. $4, Philadelphia's Walnut State Prison, balloon lifting off. No. 1872, Hawker Hurricane. No. 1873, Hugo Eckener, vert. No. 1874, Blanchard's Balloon, vert.

1993, June Litho. *Perf. 14*

1865 A255 50c multicolored .38 .38
1866 A256 $1 multicolored .75 .75
1867 A257 $1 multicolored .75 .75
1868 A255 $2 multicolored 1.50 1.50
1869 A256 $2 multicolored 1.50 1.50
1870 A256 $3 multicolored 2.25 2.25
1871 A257 $4 multicolored 3.00 3.00
Nos. 1865-1871 (7) 10.13 10.13

Souvenir Sheets

1872 A255 $6 multicolored 4.50 4.50
1873 A256 $6 multicolored 4.50 4.50
1874 A257 $6 multicolored 4.50 4.50

Royal Air Force, 75th anniv. (#1865, 1868, 1872). Dr. Hugo Eckener, 125th anniv. of birth (#1866, 1869-1870, 1873). First US balloon flight, bicent. (#1867, 1871). Tokyo spelled incorrectly on No. 1870.

Two values and a souvenir sheet commemorating the Wedding of Japan's Crown Prince Naruhito and Masako Owada were printed in 1993 but not accepted by the St. Vincent post office.

1994 Winter Olympics, Lillehammer, Norway — A259

Designs: 45c, Marc Girardelli, silver medalist, giant slalom, 1992. $5, Paul Accola, downhill, 1992. $6, Thommy Moe, downhill, 1992.

1993, June 30 Litho. *Perf. 14*

1878 A259 45c multicolored .35 .35
1879 A259 $5 multicolored 3.75 3.75

Souvenir Sheet

1880 A259 $6 multicolored 4.50 4.50

Picasso (1881-1973) — A260

Paintings: 45c, Massacre in Korea, 1951. $1, Family of Saltimbanques, 1905. $4, La Joie de Vivre, 1946. $6, Woman Eating a Melon and Boy Writing, 1965, vert.

1993, June 30

1881 A260 45c multicolored .35 .35
1882 A260 $1 multicolored .75 .75
1883 A260 $4 multicolored 3.00 3.00
Nos. 1881-1883 (3) 4.10 4.10

Souvenir Sheet

1884 A260 $6 multicolored 4.50 4.50

Willy Brandt (1913-1992), German Chancellor — A261

Designs: 45c, Brandt, Richard Nixon, 1971. $5, Brandt, Robert Kennedy, 1967. $6, Brandt at signing of "Common Declaration," 1973.

1993, June 30

1885 A261 45c multicolored .35 .35
1886 A261 $5 multicolored 3.75 3.75

Souvenir Sheet

1887 A261 $6 multicolored 4.50 4.50

A262

A263

Copernicus: 45c, Astronomical instrument. $4, Space shuttle lift-off. $6, Copernicus.

1993, June 30

1888 A262 45c multicolored .35 .35
1889 A262 $4 multicolored 3.00 3.00

Souvenir Sheet

1890 A262 $6 multicolored 4.50 4.50

1993, June 30

European Royalty: 45c, Johannes, Gloria Thurn & Taxis. 65c, Thurn & Taxis family, horiz. $1, Princess Stephanie of Monaco. $2, Gloria Thurn & Taxis.

1891 A263 45c multicolored .35 .35
1892 A263 65c multicolored .48 .48
1893 A263 $1 multicolored .75 .75
1894 A263 $2 multicolored 1.50 1.50
Nos. 1891-1894 (4) 3.08 3.08

Inauguration of Pres. William J. Clinton — A264

Designs: $5, Bill Clinton, children. $6, Clinton wearing cowboy hat, vert.

1993, June 30

1895 A264 $5 multicolored 3.75 3.75

Souvenir Sheet

1896 A264 $6 multicolored 4.50 4.50

Polska '93 — A265

#1897, Bogusz Church, Gozlin. #1898a, $1, Deux Tetes (Man), by S.I. Witkiewicz, 1920, vert. #1898b, $3, Deux Tetes (Woman), vert. No. 1899, Dancing, by Wladyslaw Roguski, vert.

1993, June 30

1897 A265 $6 multicolored 4.50 4.50
1898 A265 Pair, #a.-b. 3.00 3.00

Souvenir Sheet

1899 A265 $6 multicolored 4.50 4.50

1994 World Cup Soccer Qualifying A266

St. Vincent vs: 5c, Mexico. 10c, Honduras. 65c, Costa Rica. $5, St. Vincent goalkeeper.

1993, Sept. 2

1900-1903 A266 Set of 4 4.25 4.25

Cooperation with Japan — A267

Designs: 10c, Fish delivery van. 50c, Fish aggregation device, vert. 75c, Trawler. $5, Fish complex.

1993, Sept. 2

1904-1907 A267 Set of 4 4.75 4.75

Pope John Paul II's Visit to Denver, CO A268

Design: $6, Pope, Denver skyline, diff.

1993, Aug. 13

1908 A268	$1 multicolored		.75	.75

Souvenir Sheet

1909 A268	$6 multicolored		4.50	4.50

No. 1908 issued in sheets of 9.

Miniature Sheet

Corvette, 40th Anniv. — A269

Corvettes: a, 1953. b, 1993, c, 1958, d, 1960. e, "40," Corvette emblem (no car). f, 1961. g, 1963. h, 1968, i, 1973. j, 1975. k, 1982. l, 1984.

1993, Aug. 13 *Perf. 14x13½*

1910 A269	$1 Sheet of 12, #a.-l.	9.00	9.00

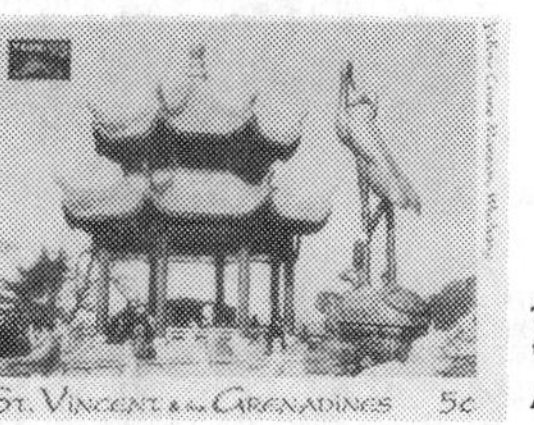

Taipei '93 A270

Designs: 5c, Yellow Crane Mansion, Wuchang. 10c, Front gate, Chung Cheng Ceremonial Arch, Taiwan. 20c, Marble Peifang, Ming 13 Tombs, Beijing. 45c, Jinxing Den, Beijing. 55c, Forbidden City, Beijing. 75c, Tachih, the Martyr's Shrine, Taiwan. No. 1917, Praying Hall, Xinjiang, Gaochang. No. 1918, Chih Kan Tower, Taiwan. $2, Taihu Lake, Jiangsu. $4, Chengde, Hebei, Pula Si. No. 1921, Kaohsiung, Cheng Ching Lake, Taiwan. No. 1922, Great Wall.

Chinese paintings: No. 1923a, Street in Macao, China, by George Chinnery. b, Pair of Birds on Cherry Branch. c, Yellow Dragon Cave, by Patrick Procktor. d, Great Wall of China, by William Simpson. e, Dutch Folly Fort Off Conton, by Chinnery. f, Forbidden City, by Procktor.

Chinese silk paintings: No. 1924a, Rhododendron. b, Irises and bees. c, Easter lily. d, Poinsettia. e, Peach and cherry blossoms. f, Weeping cherry and yellow bird.

Chinese kites: No. 1925a, Dragon and tiger fighting. b, Two immortals. c, Five boys playing round a general. d, Zheng Chenggong. e, Nezha stirs up the sea. f, Immortal maiden He.

No. 1926, Giant Buddha, Longmen Caves, Luoyang, Hunan. No. 1927, Guardian and Celestial King, Longmen Caves, Hunan, vert. No. 1928, Giant Buddha, Yungang Caves, Datong, Shanxi, vert.

1993, Aug. 16 Litho. *Perf. 14x13½*

1911 A270	5c multicolored	.15	.15
1912 A270	10c multicolored	.15	.15
1913 A270	20c multicolored	.15	.15
1914 A270	45c multicolored	.35	.35
1915 A270	55c multicolored	.42	.42
1916 A270	75c multicolored	.55	.55
1917 A270	$1 multicolored	.75	.75
1918 A270	$1 multicolored	.75	.75
1919 A270	$2 multicolored	1.50	1.50
1920 A270	$4 multicolored	3.00	3.00
1921 A270	$5 multicolored	3.75	3.75
1922 A270	$5 multicolored	3.75	3.75
	Nos. 1911-1922 (12)	15.27	15.27

Miniature Sheets

1923 A270	$1.50 Sheet of 6, #a.-f.	6.75	6.75
1924 A270	$1.50 Sheet of 6, #a.-f.	6.75	6.75
1925 A270	$1.50 Sheet of 6, #a.-f.	6.75	6.75

Souvenir Sheets

1926 A270	$6 multicolored	4.50	4.50

Perf. 13½x14

1927 A270	$6 multicolored	4.50	4.50
1928 A270	$6 multicolored	4.50	4.50

No. 1925e issued missing "St." in country name. Some sheets of No. 1925 may have been withdrawn from sale after discovery of error.

With Bangkok '93 Emblem

Designs: 5c, Phra Nakhon Khiri (Rama V's Palace), vert. 10c, Grand Palace, Bangkok. 20c, Rama IX Park, Bangkok. 45c, Phra Prang Sam Yot, Lop Buri. 55c, Dusit Maha Prasad, vert. 75c, Phimai Khmer architecture, Pak Tong Chai. No. 1935, Burmese style Chedi, Mae Hong Son. No. 1936, Antechamber, Central Prang, Prasat Hin Phimai. $2, Brick chedi on laterite base, Si Thep, vert. $4, Isan's Phanom Rung, Korat, vert. No. 1939, Phu Khau Thong, the Golden Mount, Bangkok. No. 1940, Islands, Ang Thong.

Thai Buddha sculpture: No. 1941a, Interior of Wat Hua Kuang Lampang, vert. b, Wat Yai Suwannaram, vert. c, Phra Buddha Sihing, City Hall Chapel, vert. d, Wat Ko Keo Suttharam, vert. e, U Thong B image, Wat Ratburana crypt, vert. f, Sri Sakyamuni Wat Suthat, vert.

No. 1942a-1942f: Various details from Mural at Buddhaisawan Chapel.

Thai painting: No. 1943a, Untitled, by Arunothai Somsakul. b, Mural at Wat Rajapradit. c, Mural at Wat Phumin (detail). d, Serenity, by Surasit Souakong. e, Scenes of early Bangkok mural (detail). f, Ramayana.

No. 1944, Roof detail of Dusit Mahaprasad, vert. No. 1945, Standing Buddha, Hua Hin, vert. No. 1946, Masked dance.

Perf. 13½x14, 14x13½

1993, Aug. 16 **Litho.**

1929 A270	5c multicolored	.15	.15
1930 A270	10c multicolored	.15	.15
1931 A270	20c multicolored	.15	.15
1932 A270	45c multicolored	.35	.35
1933 A270	55c multicolored	.42	.42
1934 A270	75c multicolored	.55	.55
1935 A270	$1 multicolored	.75	.75
1936 A270	$1 multicolored	.75	.75
1937 A270	$2 multicolored	1.50	1.50
1938 A270	$4 multicolored	3.00	3.00
1939 A270	$5 multicolored	3.75	3.75
1940 A270	$5 multicolored	3.75	3.75
	Nos. 1929-1940 (12)	15.27	15.27

Miniature Sheets

1941 A270	$1.50 Sheet of 6, #a.-f.	6.75	6.75
1942 A270	$1.50 Sheet of 6, #a.-f.	6.75	6.75
1943 A270	$1.50 Sheet of 6, #a.-f.	6.75	6.75

Souvenir Sheets

1944 A270	$6 multicolored	4.50	4.50
1945 A270	$6 multicolored	4.50	4.50
1946 A270	$6 multicolored	4.50	4.50

With Indopex '93 Emblem

Indopex '93 emblem with designs: 5c, Local landmark, Gedung site, 1920. 10c, Masjid Jamik Mosque, Sumenep. 20c, Bromo Caldera, seen from Penanjakan. 45c, Kudus Mosque, Java. 55c, Kampung Naga. 75c, Lower level of Borobudur. No. 1953, Dieng Temple, Dieng Plateau. No. 1954, Temple 1, Gedung Songo group, Semarang. $2, Istana Bogor, 1856. $4, Taman Sari complex, Yogyakarta. No. 1957, Landscape near Mt. Sumbing, Central Java. No. 1958, King Adityawarman's Palace, Batusangar.

Paintings: No. 1959a, Female Coolies, by Djoko Pekik. b, Family Outing, by Sudjana Kerton. c, My Family, by Pekik. d, Javanese Dancers, by Arthur Melville. e, Leisure Time, by Kerton. f, In the Garden of Eden, by Agus Djaja.

No. 1960a, Tayubon, by Pekik. b, Three Dancers, by Nyoman Gunarsa. c, Nursing Neighbor's Baby, by Hendra Gunawan. d, Imagining within a Dialogue, by Sagito. e, Three Balinese Mask Dancers, by Anton H. f, Three Prostitutes, by Gunawan.

Masks: No. 1961a, Hanuman. b, Subali/Sugnwa. c, Kumbakarna. d, Sangut. e, Jatayu. f, Rawana.

No. 1962, Relief of Sudamala story, Mt. Lawu. No. 1963, Plaque, 9th Cent., Banyumas, Central Java. No. 1964, Panel from Ramayana reliefs, vert.

1993, Aug. 16 Litho. *Perf. 14x13½*

1947 A270	5c multicolored	.15	.15
1948 A270	10c multicolored	.15	.15
1949 A270	20c multicolored	.15	.15
1950 A270	45c multicolored	.35	.35
1951 A270	55c multicolored	.42	.42
1952 A270	75c multicolored	.55	.55
1953 A270	$1 multicolored	.75	.75
1954 A270	$1 multicolored	.75	.75
1955 A270	$2 multicolored	1.50	1.50
1956 A270	$4 multicolored	3.00	3.00
1957 A270	$5 multicolored	3.75	3.75
1958 A270	$5 multicolored	3.75	3.75
	Nos. 1947-1958 (12)	15.27	15.27

Minature Sheets

1959 A270	$1.50 Sheet of 6, #a.-f.	6.75	6.75
1960 A270	$1.50 Sheet of 6, #a.-f.	6.75	6.75
1961 A270	$1.50 Sheet of 6, #a.-f.	6.75	6.75

Souvenir Sheets

1962 A270	$6 multicolored	4.50	4.50
1963 A270	$6 multicolored	4.50	4.50

Perf. 13½x14

1964 A270	$6 multicolored	4.50	4.50

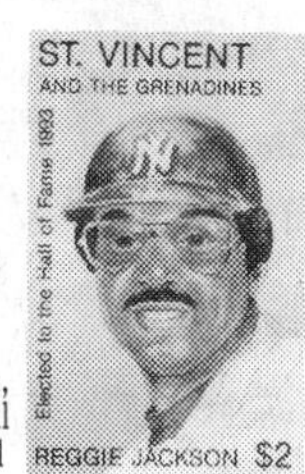

Reggie Jackson, Selection to Baseball Hall of Fame — A271

1993, Oct. 4 *Perf. 14*

1965 A271	$2 multicolored	1.50	1.50

Christmas A272

Details or entire woodcut, The Adoration of the Magi, by Durer: 10c, 35c, 40c, $5.

Details or entire paintings by Rubens: 50c, Holy Family with Saint Francis. 55c, 65c, Adoration of the Shepherds. $1, Holy Family.

No. 1974, The Adoration of the Magi, by Durer, horiz. No. 1975, Holy Family with St. Elizabeth & St. John, by Rubens.

Perf. 13½x14, 14x13½

1993, Nov. 18

1966-1973 A272	Set of 8	7.00	7.00

Souvenir Sheets

1974-1975 A272	$6 each	4.50	4.50

Miniature Sheet

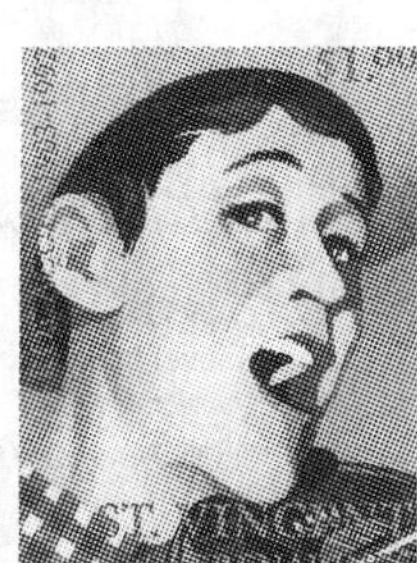

Legends of Country Music A273

Various portraits of: a, f, l, Roy Acuff. b, g, j, Patsy Cline. c, h, i, Jim Reeves. d, e, k, Hank Williams, Sr.

1994, Jan. 17 Litho. *Perf. 13½x14*

1976 A273	$1 Sheet of 12, #a.-l.	9.00	9.00

Mickey's Portrait Gallery A274

Mickey Mouse as: 5c, Aviator. 10c, Foreign Legionnaire. 15c, Frontiersman. 20c, Best Pals, Mickey, Goofy, Donald. 35c, Horace, Clarabelle. 50c, Minnie, Frankie, Figuro. 75c, Donald, Pluto today. 80c, Party boy Mickey. 85c, Best Friends, Minnie, Daisy. 95c, Mickey's Girl, Minnie. $1, Cool forties Mickey. $1.50, Mickey, "Howdy!", 1950. $2, Totally Mickey. $3, Minnie, Mickey. $4, Congratulations Mickey, birthday cake. $5, Uncle Sam.

No. 1993, Donald Duck, early photo of Mickey, horiz. No. 1994, Minnie disco dancing, horiz. No. 1995, Mickey photographing nephews, horiz. No. 1996, Pluto, Mickey looking at wall of photos.

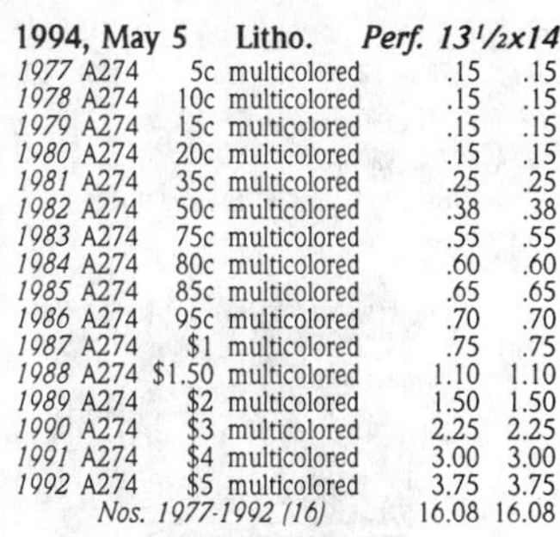

1994, May 5 Litho. *Perf. 13½x14*

1977 A274	5c multicolored	.15	.15
1978 A274	10c multicolored	.15	.15
1979 A274	15c multicolored	.15	.15
1980 A274	20c multicolored	.15	.15
1981 A274	35c multicolored	.25	.25
1982 A274	50c multicolored	.38	.38
1983 A274	75c multicolored	.55	.55
1984 A274	80c multicolored	.60	.60
1985 A274	85c multicolored	.65	.65
1986 A274	95c multicolored	.70	.70
1987 A274	$1 multicolored	.75	.75
1988 A274	$1.50 multicolored	1.10	1.10
1989 A274	$2 multicolored	1.50	1.50
1990 A274	$3 multicolored	2.25	2.25
1991 A274	$4 multicolored	3.00	3.00
1992 A274	$5 multicolored	3.75	3.75
	Nos. 1977-1992 (16)	16.08	16.08

Souvenir Sheets

Perf. 14x13½

1993 A274	$6 multicolored	4.50	4.50
1994 A274	$6 multicolored	4.50	4.50
1995 A274	$6 multicolored	4.50	4.50
1996 A274	$6 multicolored	4.50	4.50

Breadfruit A275

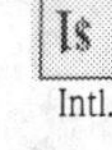

Intl. Year of the Family A276

1994, Jan. Litho. *Perf. 13½x14*

1997 A275	10c Planting	.15	.15
1998 A275	45c Captain Bligh, plant	.35	.35
1999 A275	65c Fruit sliced	.50	.50
2000 A275	$5 Fruit on branch	3.75	3.75
	Nos. 1997-2000 (4)	4.75	4.75

1994, Jan. *Perf. 14x13½, 13½x14*

2001 A276	10c Outing	.15	.15
2002 A276	50c Praying in church	.38	.38
2003 A276	65c Working in garden	.50	.50
2004 A276	75c Jogging	.55	.55
2005 A276	$1 Portrait	.75	.75
2006 A276	$2 Running on beach	1.50	1.50
	Nos. 2001-2006 (6)	3.83	3.83

Nos. 2001-2004, 2006 are horiz.

Library Service, Cent. A277

1994, Jan. *Perf. 14x13½*

2007 A277	5c Mobile library	.15	.15
2008 A277	10c Old public library	.15	.15
2009 A277	$1 Family education	.75	.75
2010 A277	$1 Younger, older men	.75	.75
	Nos. 2007-2010 (4)	1.80	1.80

Barbra Streisand, 1993 MGM Grand Garden Concert — A278

A278a

Illustration A278a reduced.

1994, Jan.

2011 A278 $2 multicolored 1.50 1.50

Embossed ***Perf. 12***

2011A A278a $20 gold

No. 2011 issued in sheets of 9.

A279

A280

Hong Kong '94 — A281

Hong Kong '94 — A282

Stamps, 19th cent. painting of Hong Kong Harbor: No. 2012, Hong Kong #626, ship under sail. No. 2013, Ship at anchor, #1548.

Porcelain ware, Qing Dynasty: No. 2014a, Bowl with bamboo & sparrows. b, Bowl with flowers of four seasons. c, Bowl with lotus pool & dragon. d, Bowl with landscape. e, Shar-Pei puppies in bowl (not antiquity). f, Covered bowl with dragon & pearls.

Chinese dragon boat races: No. 2015a, Dragon boats. b, Tapestry of dragon races. c, Dragon race. d, Dragon boats, diff. e, Chinese crested dog. f, Dragon boats, 4 banners above boats.

Chinese junks: No. 2016a, Junk, Hong Kong Island. b, Junk with white sails in harbor. c, Junk with inscription on stern, Hong Kong Island. d, Junk KLN B/G. e, Chow dog, junk. f, Junk with red, white sails, Hong Kong Island.

Chinese seed stitch purses: No. 2017a, Vases, fruit on pink purse. b, Peonies, butterflies. c, Vase, fruit on dark blue purse. d, Vases, fruit on light blue purse. e, Fu-dog. f, Flowers.

Chineses pottery: No. 2018a, Plate, bird on flowering spray, Qianlong. b, Large dish, Kangxi. c, Egshell plate, cocks on rocky ground, Yongzheng. d, Gladen dish decorated with Qilin curicorn, Yuan. e, Porcelain pug dog. f, Dish with Dutch ship, Uryburg, Qianlong.

Ceramic figures, Qing Dynasty, vert: No. 2018h, Waterdropper. i, Two women playing chess. j, Liu-Hai. k, Laughing twins. l, Seated hound. m, Louhan (Ma Ming).

No. 2019: Dr. Sun Yat-sen. No. 2020: Chiang Kai-shek.

Dinosaurs: No. 2021a, Triceratops. b, Unidentified, vert. c, Apatosaurus (d). d, Stegosaurus, vert.

1994, Feb. 18 ***Perf. 14***

2012 A279 40c multicolored .30 .30
2013 A279 40c multicolored .30 .30
a. Pair, #2012-2013 .60 .60

Miniature Sheets

2014 A280 40c Sheet of 6, #a.-f. 1.90 1.90
2015 A280 40c Sheet of 6, #a.-f. 1.90 1.90
2016 A280 45c Sheet of 6, #a.-f. 2.00 2.00
2017 A280 45c Sheet of 6, #a.-f. 2.00 2.00
2018 A281 50c Sheet of 6, #a.-f. 2.25 2.25

Perf. 13

2018G A280 50c Sheet of 6, #h.-m. 2.25 2.25

Souvenir Sheets

2019 A281 $2 multicolored 1.50 1.50
2020 A281 $2 multicolored 1.50 1.50
2021 A282 $1.50 Sheet of 4, #a.-d. 4.50 4.50

Nos. 2012-2013 issued in sheets of 5 pairs. No. 2013a is a continuous design.

Portions of the design on No. 2021 have been applied by a thermographic process producing a shiny, raised effect.

New Year 1994 (Year of the Dog) (#2014e, 2015e, 2016e, 2017e, 2018e, 2018 l). Hong Kong '94 (#2018G, 2021).

Miniature Sheet

Hong Kong '94 — A283

Butterflies: a, Blue flasher. b, Tiger swallowtail. c, Lustrous copper. d, Tailed copper. e, Blue copper. f, Ruddy copper. g, Viceroy. h, California sister. i, Mourning cloak. j, Red passion flower. k, Small flambeau. l, Blue wave. m, Chiricahua metalmark. n, Monarch. o, Anise swallowtail. p, Buckeye.

1994, Feb. 18 Litho. ***Perf. 14½***

2022 A283 50c Sheet of 16, #a.-p. 6.00 6.00

A284

A285

Players: No. 2023, Causio. No. 2024, Tardelli. No. 2025, Rossi. No. 2026, Bettega. No. 2027, Platini, Baggio. No. 2028, Cabrini. No. 2029, Scirea. No. 2030, Furino. No. 2031, Kohler. No. 2032, Zoff. No. 2033, Gentile.

$6, Three European Cups won by team, horiz.

1994, Mar. 22 Litho. ***Perf. 14***

2023-2033 A284 $1 Set of 11 8.25 8.25

Souvenir Sheet

2034 A284 $6 multicolored 4.50 4.50

Juventus football (soccer) club of Turin.

1994, Apr. 6 Litho. ***Perf. 14***

Orchids: 10c, Epidendrum ibaguense. 25c, Ionopsis utricularioides. 50c, Brassavola cucullata. 65c, Enclyclia cochleata. $1, Liparis nervosa. $2, Vanilla phaeantha. $4, Elleanthus cephalotus. $5, Isochilus linearis.

No. 2043, Rodriguezia lanceolata. No. 2044, Eulophia alta.

2035-2042 A285 Set of 8 10.00 10.00

Souvenir Sheets

2043-2044 A285 $6 each 4.50 4.50

A286

Dinosaurs — A287

Designs: No. 2045a, Protoavis (e). b, Pteranodon. c, Quetzalcoatlus (b). d, Lesothosaurus (a, c, e-h). e, Hetrodontosaurus. f, Archaeopteryx (b, e). g, Cearadactylus (f). h, Anchisaurus.

No. 2046a, Dimorphodon (e). b, Camarasaurus (e, f). c, Spinosaurus (b). d, Allosaurus (a-c, e-h). e, Rhamphorhynchus (a). f, Pteranodon (b). g, Eudimorphodon (c). h, Ornithomimus.

No. 2047a, Dimorphodon (b). b, Pterodactylus (a). c, Rhamphorhynchus (b). d, Pteranodon. e, Gallimimus. f, Setgosaurus. g, Acanthopholis. h, Trachodon (g). i, Thecodonti (j). j, Ankylosaurus (i). k, Compsognathus. l, Protoceratops.

No. 2048a, Hesperonis. b, Mesosaurus. c, Plesiosaurus. d, Squalicorax (a). e, Tylosaurus (d, g). f, Plesiosoar. g, Stenopterygius ichthyosaurus (j). h, Stenosaurus (f). i, Eurhinosaurus longirostris (e, f, h, l). j, Cryptocleidus oxoniensis. k, Caturus (h, i, j, l). l, Protostega (k).

No. 2049a, Quetzalcoatlus. b, Diplodocus (a). c, Spinosaurus (f, g). d, Apatosaurus (c). e, Ornitholestes. f, Lesothosaurus (e). g, Trachodon. h, Protoavis. i, Oviraptor. j, Coelophysis (i). k, Ornitholestes (j). l, Archaeopteryx.

No. 2050, horiz: a, Albertosaurus. b, Chasmosaurus (c). c, Brachiosaurus. d, Coelophysis (e). e, Deinonychus (d). f, Anatosaurus. g, Iguanodon. h, Baryonyx. i, Steneosaurus. j, Nanotyrannus. k, Camptosaurus (j). l, Camarasaurus.

No. 2051, Tyrannosaurus rex. No. 2052: Triceratops, horiz. No. 2053, Pteranodon, diplodocus carnegii, horiz. No. 2054, Styracosaurus.

1994, Apr. 20 Litho. ***Perf. 14***

2045 A286 75c Sheet of 8, #a.-h. 4.50 4.50
2046 A286 75c Sheet of 8, #a.-h. 4.50 4.50

Miniature Sheets of 12

2047-2050 A287 75c #a.-l, each 6.75 6.75

Souvenir Sheets

2051 A286 $6 multi 4.50 4.50
2052-2054 A287 $6 each 4.50 4.50

No. 2048 is horiz.

Entertainers Type of 1991
Miniature Sheet

Various portraits of Marilyn Monroe.

1994, May 16 ***Perf. 13½***

2055 A206 $1 Sheet of 9, #a.-i. 6.75 6.75

1994 World Cup Soccer Championships, US — A288

Team photos: No. 2056, Colombia. No. 2057, Romania. No. 2058, Switzerland. No. 2059, US. No. 2060, Brazil. No. 2061, Cameroon. No. 2062, Russia. No. 2063, Sweden. No. 2064, Bolivia. No. 2065, Germany. No. 2066, South Korea. No. 2067, Spain. No. 2068, Argentina. No. 2069, Bulgaria. No. 2070, Greece. No. 2071, Nigeria. No. 2072, Ireland. No. 2073, Italy. No. 2074, Mexico. No. 2075, Norway. No. 2076, Belgium. No. 2077, Holland. No. 2078, Morocco. No. 2079, Saudi Arabia.

1994 ***Perf. 13½***

2056-2079 A288 50c Set of 24 9.00 9.00

Miniature Sheets of 9

First Manned Moon Landing, 25th Anniv. A289

Famous men, aviation & space scenes: No. 2080a, Fred L. Whipple, Halley's Comet. b, Robert G. Gilruth, Gemini 12. c, George E. Mueller, Ed White walking in space during Gemini 4. d, Charles A. Berry, Johnsville Centrifuge. e, Christopher C. Kraft, Jr., Apollo 4 re-entry. f, James A. Van Allen, Explorer I, Van Allen Radiation Belts. g, Robert H. Goddard, Goddard Liquid Fuel Rocket, 1926. h, James E. Webb, Spirit of '76 flight. i, Rocco A. Patrone, Apollo 8 coming home.

No. 2081: a, Walter R. Dornberger, missile launch, 1942. b, Alexander Lippisch, Wolfgang Spate's ME-163B. c, Kurt H. Debus, A4b Launch, 1945. d, Hermann Oberth, Oberth's Spaceship, 1923. e, Hanna Reitsch, Reichenberg (type 2) Piloted Bomb. f, Ernst Stuhlinger, Explorer I, 2nd stage ignition. g, Werner von Braun, Rocket Powered He112. h, Arthur Rudolph, Rudolph Rocket Motor, 1934. i, Willy Ley, Rocket Airplane, Greenwood Lake NY.

No. 2082, Hogler N. Toftoy. No. 2083, Eberhardt Rees.

1994, July 12 ***Perf. 14***

2080-2081 A289 $1 #a.-i, each 6.75 6.75

Souvenir Sheets

2082-2083 A289 $6 each 4.50 4.50

Nos. 2082-2083 each contain one 50x38mm stamp.

D-Day, 50th Anniv. A290

Designs: 40c, Supply armada. $5, Beached cargo ship unloads supplies.

$6, Liberty ship.

1994, July 19 Litho. ***Perf. 14***

2084 A290 40c multicolored .30 .30
2085 A290 $5 multicolored 3.75 3.75

Souvenir Sheet

2086 A290 $6 multicolored 4.50 4.50

New Year 1994 (Year of the Dog) — A291

Designs: 10c, Yorkshire terrier. 25c, Yorkshire terrier, diff. 50c, Golden retriever. 65c, Bernese mountain dog. $1, Vorstehhund. $2, Tibetan terrier. $4, West highland terrier. $5, Shih tzu.

No. 2095a, Pomeranian. b, English springer spaniel. c, Bearded collie. d, Irish wolfhound. e, Pekingese. f, Irish setter. g, Old English sheepdog. h, Basset hound. i, Cavalier King Charles spaniel. j, Kleiner munsterlander. k, Shetland sheepdog. l, Dachshund.

No. 2096, Afghan hound. No. 2097, German shepherd.

1994, July 21

2087-2094 A291 Set of 8 10.00 10.00

Miniature Sheet of 12

2095 A291 50c #a.-l. 4.50 4.50

Souvenir Sheets

2096-2097 A291 $6 each 4.50 4.50

English Touring Cricket, Cent. A292

Designs: 10c, M.R. Ramprakash, England. 30c, P.V. Simmons, W. Indies. $2, Sir. G. St. A. Sobers, W. Indies, vert.

$3, Firsh English team, 1895.

1994, July 25

2098-2100 A292 Set of 3 1.90 1.90

Souvenir Sheet

2101 A293 $3 multicolored 2.25 2.25

A293

Intl. Olympic Committee, Cent. — A294

Designs: 45c, Peter Frennel, German Democratic Republic, 20k walk, 1972. 50c, Kijung Son, Japan, marathon, 1936. 75c, Jesse Owens, US, 100-, 200-meters, 1936. $1, Greg Louganis, US, diving, 1984, 1988.

$6, Katja Seizinger, Germany, Picabo Street, US, Isolde Kastner, Italy, women's downhill, 1994.

1994, July 25

2102-2105 A293 Set of 4 2.00 2.00

Souvenir Sheet

2106 A294 $6 multicolored 4.50 4.50

PHILAKOREA '94

A295 A296

Designs: 10c, Oryon Waterfall. 45c, Outside P'yongyang Indoor Sports Stadium, horiz. 65c, Pombong, Ch'onhwadae. 75c, Uisangdae, Naksansa. $1, Buddha of the Sokkuram Grotto, Kyangju, horiz. $2, Moksogwon, horiz.

Nos. 2113a-2113h, Various letter pictures, eight panel screen, 18th cent. Choson Dynasty.

Letter pictures, 19th cent. Choson Dynasty: No. 2114a, Fish. No. 2114b, Birds. Nos. 2114c-2114d, 2114h, Various bookshelf pictures. Nos. 2114e-2114g, Various designs from six-panel screen.

No. 2115, Hunting scene, embroidery on silk, Choson Dynasty, horiz. No. 2116, Chongdong Mirukbul.

1994, July 25 ***Perf. 14***

2107-2112 A295 Set of 6 3.75 3.75

Miniature Sheets of 8

Perf. 13½

2113-2114 A296 50c #a.-h. 3.00 3.00

Souvenir Sheets

Perf. 14

2115-2116 A295 $4 each 3.00 3.00

Miniature Sheet of 9

Star Trek, The Next Generation, 7th Anniv. — A297

A297a

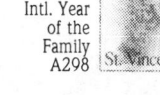

Designs: No. 2117a, Capt. Picard. b, Cmdr. Riker. c, Lt. Cmdr. Data. d, Lt. Worf. e, Cast members. f, Dr. Crusher. g, Lt. Yar, Lt. Worf. h, Q. i, Counselor Troi.

$10, Cast members, horiz.

$20, Starship Enterprise, Capt. Picard.

Illustration A297a reduced.

1994, June 27 Litho. ***Perf. 14x13½***

2117 A297 $2 #a.-i. 14.00 14.00

Souvenir Sheet

Perf. 14x14½

2118 A297 $10 multicolored 5.75 5.75

No. 2117e exists in sheets of 9. No. 2118 contains one 60x40mm stamp.

Litho. & Embossed

1994, May ***Perf. 9***

2118A A297a $20 gold & multi

Intl. Year of the Family A298

1994 ***Perf. 14***

2119 A298 75c multicolored .55 .55

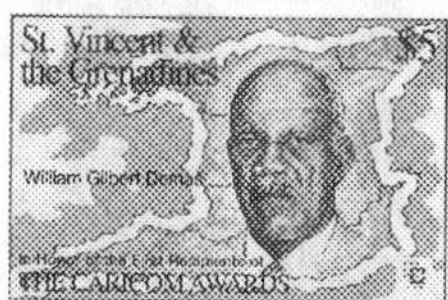

Order of the Caribbean Community — A299

First award recipients: $1, Sir Shridath Ramphal, statesman, Guyana, vert. $2, Derek Walcott, writer, St. Lucia, vert. $5, William Demas, economist, Trinidad and Tobago.

1994, Sept. 1

2120-2122 A299 Set of 3 6.00 6.00

Miniature Sheets of 6 or 12

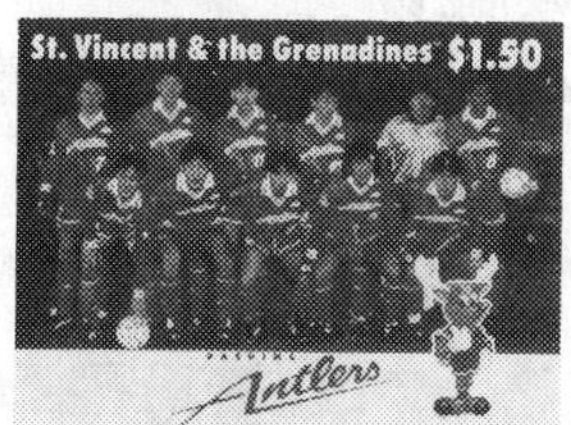

Japanese Soccer — A300

Team photos: No. 2123a, Kahsima Antlers. b, JEF United. c, Red Diamonds. d, Verdy Yomiuri. e, Nissan FC Yokohama Marinos. f, AS Flugels. g, Bellmare. h, Shimizu S-pulse. i, Jubilo Iwata. j, Nogoya Grampus Eight. k, Panasonic Gamba Osaka. l, Sanfrecce Hiroshima FC.

Jubilo Iwata, action scenes: Nos. 2124a, c-d, 55c. b, e, $1.50. f, $3, Team picture.

Red Diamonds, action scenes: Nos. 2125a, c-d, 55c. b, e, $1.50. f, $3, Team picture.

Nissan FC Yokohama Marinos, action scenes: Nos. 2126a, c-d, 55c. b, e, $1.50. f, $3, Team picture.

Verdy Yomiuri, action scenes: Nos. 2127a, c-d, 55c. b, e, $1.50. f, $3, Team picture.

Nagoya Grampus eight, action scenes: Nos. 2128a, c-d, 55c. b, e, $1.50. f, $3, Team picture.

Kashima Antlers, action scenes: Nos. 2129a, c-d, 55c. b, e, $1.50. f, $3, Team picture.

JEF United, action scenes: Nos. 2130a, c-d, 55c. b, e, $1.50. f, $3, Team picture.

AS Flugels, action scenes: Nos. 2131a, c-d, 55c. b, e, $1.50. f, $3, Team picture.

Bellmare, action scenes: Noa. 2132a, c-d, 55c. b, e, $1.50. f, $3, Team picture.

Sanfrecce Hiroshima FC, action scenes: Nos. 2133a, c-d, 55c. b, e, $1.50. f, $3, Team picture.

Shimizu S-pulse, action scenes: Nos. 2134a, c-d, 55c. b, e, $1.50. f, $3, Team picture.

Panasonic Gamba Isajam, action scenes: Nos. 2135a, c-d, 55c. b, e, $1.50. f, $3, Team picture.

League All-Stars: No. 2136a, $1.50, League emblem. b, 55c, Shigetatsu Matsunaga. c, 55c, Masami Ihara. d, $1.50, Takumi Horiike. e, 55c, Shunzoh Ohno. f, 55c, Luiz Carlos Pereira. g, 55c, Tetsuji Hashiratani. h, 55c, Carlos Alberto Souza Dos Santos. i, $1.50, Rui Ramos. j, 55c, Yasuto Honda. k, 55c, Kazuyoshi Miura. l, $1.50, Ramon Angel Diaz.

1994, July 1 ***Perf. 14x13½***

2123 A300 #a.-l. 7.75 7.75

2124-2135 A300 #a.-f., each 5.75 5.75

Perf. 13½x14

2136 A300 #a.-l., vert. 7.75 7.75

Christmas A301

Illustrations from Book of Hours, by Jean de Berry: 10c, The Annunciation, angel kneeling. 45c, The Visitation. 50c, The Nativity, Madonna seeing infant. 65c, The Purification of the Virgin. 75c, Presentation of Jesus in the Temple. $5, Flight into Egypt.

$6, Adoration of the Magi.

1994 Litho. ***Perf. 13½x14***

2137-2142 A301 Set of 6 5.75 5.75

Souvenir Sheet

2143 A301 $6 multicolored 4.50 4.50

Miniature Sheet

Nos. 1792, 1806-1807 with New Denominations and Added Inscription

1995, Jan. 24 ***Perf. 14x13½***

2144 A247 30c Sheet of 9, #a.-i. 2.00 2.00

Souvenir Sheets

2145 A247 $3 multi (#1806) 2.25 2.25

2146 A247 $3 multi (#1807) 2.25 2.25

Nos. 2144-2146 are inscribed with emblem for "New Year 1995, Year of the Pig."

ICAO, 50th Anniv. A302

Designs: 10c, Bequia Airport. 65c, Union Island. 75c, Liat 8-100, E.T. Joshua Airport. No. 2150, $1, Airplanes, ICAO emblem. No. 2151, $1, J.F. Mitchell Airport, Bequia.

1994, Dec. 1 Litho. ***Perf. 14***

2147-2151 A302 Set of 5 2.75 2.75

Miniature Sheets of 9

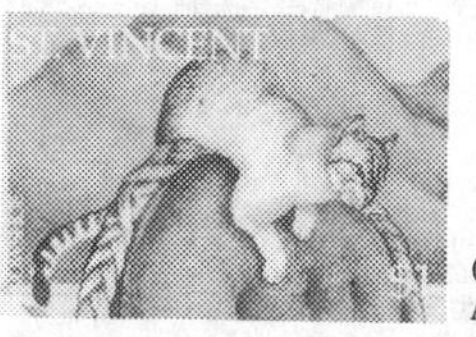

Cats A303

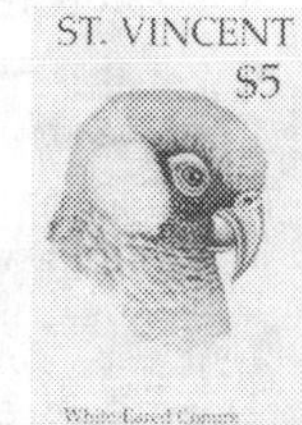

Parrots — A304

Cats: No. 2152a, Snowshoe. b, Abyssinian. c, Ocicat. d, Tiffany (e, h). e, Russian blue. f, Siamese. g, Bi-color. h, Malayan. i, Manx.

Parrots: No. 2153a, Mealy Amazon. b, Nanday conure. c, Black-headed caique. d, Scarlet macaw (g). e, Red-masked conure. f, Blue-headed parrot. g, Hyacinth macaw. h, Sun conure. i, Blue & yellow macaw.

#2154, White-eared conure. #2155, Birman.

1995, Apr. 25 Litho. ***Perf. 14***

2152-2153 A303 $1 #a.-i., each 6.75 6.75

Souvenir Sheets

2154 A304 $5 multicolored 3.75 3.75

2155 A304 $6 multicolored 4.50 4.50

A305

Birds A306

World Wildlife Fund, masked booby: No. 2156: a, One standing. b, Two birds. c, One nesting. d, One stretching wings.

No. 2157: a, Greater egret. b, Roseate spoonbill. c, Ring-billed gull. d, Ruddy quail-dove. e, Royal tern. f, Killdeer. g, Osprey. h, Frigatebird. i, Masked booby. j, Green-backed heron. k, Cormorant. l, Brown pelican.

No. 2158, Flamingo, vert. No. 2159, Purple gallinule, vert.

1995, May 2

2156 A305 75c Strip of 4, #a.-d. 2.25 2.25

Miniature Sheet of 12

2157 A306 75c #a.-l. 6.75 6.75

Souvenir Sheets

2158 A306 $5 multicolored 3.75 3.75

2159 A306 $6 multicolored 4.50 4.50

No. 2156 is a continuous design and was issued in sheets of 3.

Miniature Sheets of 6 and 8

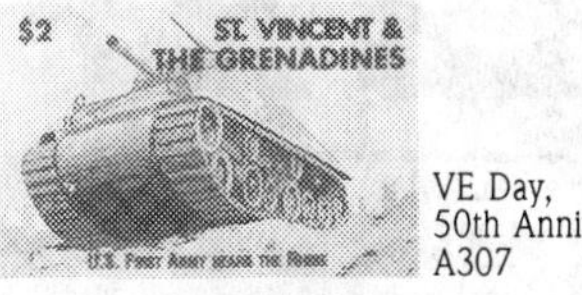

VE Day, 50th Anniv. A307

No. 2159A: b, Douglas Devastator. c, Doolittle's B25 leads raid on Tokyo. d, Curtis Helldiver. e, USS Yorktown. f, USS Wasp. g, USS Lexington sinks.

No. 2160: a, US First Army nears the Rhine. b, Last V2 rocket fired at London, Mar. 1945. c, 8th Air Force B24 Liberators devastate industrial Germany. d, French Army advances on Strasbourg. e, Gloster Meteor, first jet aircraft to enter squadron service. f, Berlin burns from both air and ground bombardments. g, Soviet tanks on Unter Den Linden near Brandenburg Gate. h, European war is won.

No. 2161, Pilot in cockpit of Allied bomber.

No. 2161A, Ships in Pacific, sunset.

1995, May 8 Litho. ***Perf. 14***

2159A A307 $2 #b.-g. + label 9.25 9.25

2160 A307 $2 #a.-h. + label 12.00 12.00

Souvenir Sheets

2161-2161A A307 $6 each 4.50 4.50

No. 2161 contains one 57x43mm stamp.

A308 A309

UN, 50th anniv.: a, Globe, dove. b, Lady Liberty. c, UN Headquarters. $6, Child.

1995

2162 A308 $2 Strip of 3, #a.-c. 4.50 4.50

Souvenir Sheet

2163 A308 $6 multicolored 4.50 4.50

No. 2162 is a continuous design and was issued in miniature sheets of 3.

1995

18th World Scout Jamboree, Holland: $1, Natl. Scout flag. $4, Lord Baden Powell. $5, Scout handshake.

No. 2167, Scout sign. No. 2168, Scout salute.

1995

2164-2166 A309 Set of 3 7.50 7.50

Souvenir Sheets

2167-2168 A309 $6 each 4.50 4.50

Yalta Conference, 50th Anniv. A310

Design: $50, like #2169. Illustration reduced.

1995, May 8 **Litho.** ***Perf. 14***

2169 A310 $1 multicolored .75 .75

Litho. & Embossed

Perf. 9

2169A A310 $50 gold & multi

No. 2169 was issued in sheets of 9.

New Year 1995 (Year of the Boar) — A311

FAO, 50th Anniv. — A312

Stylized boars: a, blue green & multi. b, brown & multi. c, red & multi. $2, Two boars, horiz.

1995, May 8

2170 A311 75c Strip of 3, #a.-c. 1.75 1.75

Souvenir Sheet

2171 A311 $2 multicolored 1.50 1.50

No. 2170 was issued in sheets of 3.

1995, May 8

Designs: a, Girl holding plate, woman with bowl. b, Stirring pot of food. c, Working in fields of grain. $6, Infant.

1995, May 8

2172 A312 $2 Strip of 3, #a.-c. 4.50 4.50

Souvenir Sheet

2173 A312 $6 multicolored 4.50 4.50

No. 2172 is a continuous design and was issued in sheets of 3.

Rotary Intl., 90th Anniv. A313

Designs: $5, Paul Harris, Rotary emblem. $6, St. Vincent flag, Rotary emblem.

1995, May 8

2174 A313 $5 multicolored 3.75 3.75

Souvenir Sheet

2175 A313 $6 multicolored 4.50 4.50

Queen Mother, 95th Birthday A314

Designs: a, Drawing. b, Wearing blue hat. c, Formal portrait. d, Wearing lavender outfit. $6, Wearing crown jewels, yellow dress.

1995, May 8 ***Perf. 13½x14***

2176 A314 $1.50 Block or strip of 4, #a.-d. 4.50 4.50

Souvenir Sheet

2177 A314 $6 multicolored 4.50 4.50

No. 2176 was issued in sheet of 2.

Miniature Sheets

Marine Life A315

No. 2178, vert: a, Humpback whale (b, d, e, f, i). b, Green turtle (c). c, Bottlenosed dolphin (f). d, Monk seal (e). e, Krill. f, Blue shark. g, Striped pork fish. h, Chaelodon sedentarius (e, g). i, Ship wreck, bottom of sea.

No. 2179: a, Pomacentrus leucostictus (b). b, Pomacanthus arcuatus (d). c, Microspathodon chrysurus (d). d, Chaetodon capistratus.

No. 2180, Physalia physalis, vert. No. 2181, Sea anemones, vert.

1995, May 23 ***Perf. 14***

2178 A315 90c Sheet of 9, #a.-i. 6.25 6.25

2179 A315 $1 Sheet of 4, #a.-d. 4.25 4.25

Souvenir Sheets

2180-2181 A315 $6 each 4.50 4.50

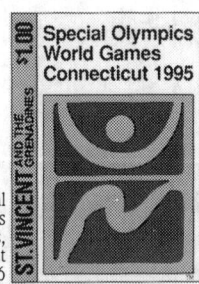

1995 Special Olympics World Games, Connecticut A316

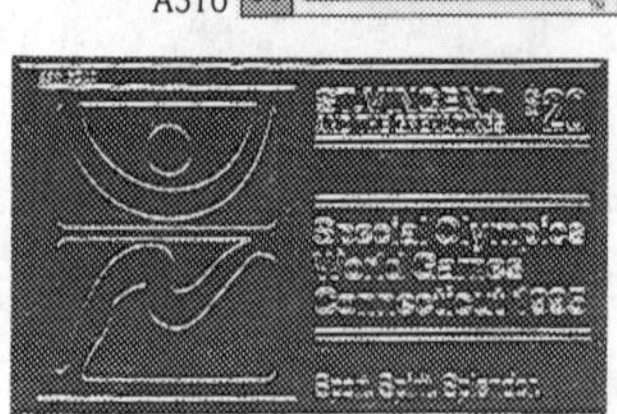

A316a

Illustration A316a reduced.

1995, July 6

2182 A316 $1 black, yellow & blue .75 .75

Embossed

Perf. 9

2182A A316a $20 gold

No. 2182 issued in sheets of 9.

Miniature Sheet of 6

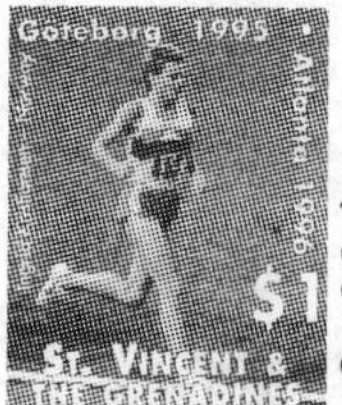

1995 IAAF World Track & Field Championships, Gothenburg & 1996 Summer Olympics, Atlanta — A317

No. 2183: a, Ingrid Kristiansen, Norway. b, Trine Hattestad, Norway. c, Grete Waitz, Norway. d, Vebjorn Rodal, Norway. e, Geir Moen, Norway. f, Steinar Hoen, Norway, horiz.

1995, July 31 **Litho.** ***Perf. 14***

2183 A317 $1 #a.-f. 4.50 4.50

A318

A319

Designs: 15c, Breast, bowl of food, horiz. 20c, Expressing milk, cup, spoon. 90c, Drawing of mother breastfeeding child, by Picasso. $5, Mother, child, olive wreath.

1995, Aug. 4

2184-2187 A318 Set of 4 4.75 4.75

WHO, UNICEF Baby Friendly Program.

1995, Aug. 8

Designs: 10c, Leeward Coast, horiz. 15c, Feeder roads project, horiz. 25c, Anthurium andraeanum, horiz. 50c, Coconut palm. 65c, Housing scene, Fairhall, horiz.

2188-2192 A319 Set of 5 1.25 1.25

Caribbean Development Bank, 25th anniv.

Fudo Myoou (God of Fire), Woodprint, by Shunichi Kadowaki — A320

1995, July 1 **Litho.** ***Perf. 14***

2193 A320 $1.40 multicolored 1.10 1.10

A321

Nolan Ryan, Baseball Player — A322

Designs: No. 2194, Nolan Ryan Foundation emblem. No. 2195, Emblem of major league All Star Game, Arlington,TX.

Portraits of Ryan: No. 2196a, In NY Mets uniform. b, With western hat, dog. c, In Texas Rangers' cap. d, Throwing football. e, With son. f, Laughing, without hat. g, With family. h, Wearing Houston Astros cap.

Ryan in Rangers' uniform: No. 2197a, Blue outfit. b, "34" on front. c, Looking left. d, After pitch looking forward. e, After pitch looking left. f, With bloody lip. g, Ready to pitch ball. h, Holding up cap.

$6, Being carried by team mates.

$30, Ready to pitch (illustration reduced).

1995, Aug. 1 ***Perf. 13½x14***

2194 A321 $1 multicolored .75 .75

2195 A321 $1 multicolored .75 .75

a. Pair, #2194-2195 1.50 1.50

Miniature Sheets of 9

2196 A321 $1 #a.-h. + #2194 6.75 6.75

2197 A321 $1 #a.-h. + #2195 6.75 6.75

Souvenir Sheet

2198 A321 $6 multicolored 4.50 4.50

Litho. & Embossed

Perf. 9

2199 A322 $30 gold & multi

Nos. 2194-2195 were issued in sheets containing 5 #2194, 4 #2195.

Miniature Sheets of 6 or 8

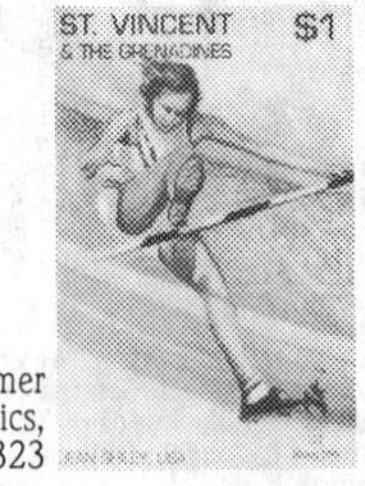

1996 Summer Olympics, Atlanta — A323

No. 2200: a, Jean Shiley, US. b, Ruth Fuchs, Germany. c, Alessandro Andrei, Italy. d, Dorando Pietri, Italy. e, Heide Rosendahl, Germany. f, Mitsuoki Watanabe, Japan. g, Yasuhiro Yamashita, Japan. h, Dick Fosbury, US.

No. 2201: a, Long jump. b, Hurdles. c, Sprint. d, Marathon. e, Gymnastics. f, Rowing.

No. 2202, Magic Johnson. No. 2203, Swimmer's hand, horiz.

1995, Aug. 24 **Litho.** ***Perf. 14***

2200 A323 $1 #a.-h. 6.00 6.00

2201 A323 $2 #a.-f. 9.00 9.00

Souvenir Sheets

2202-2203 A323 $5 each 3.75 3.75

Miniature Sheet

Stars of American League Baseball A324

A324a

#2204, Different portraits of: a, e, i, Frank Thomas, Chicago White Sox. b, f-g, Cal Ripken, Jr., Baltimore Orioles. c-d, h, Ken Griffey, Jr., Seattle Mariners.

No. 2204J, Ken Griffey, Jr. No. 2204K, Cal Ripken, Jr. No. 2204L, Frank Thomas.

Illustration A324a reduced.

1995, Sept. 6 **Litho.** ***Perf. 14***

2204 A324 $1 Sheet of 9, #a.-i. 6.75 6.75

Litho. & Embossed

Perf. 9

2204J-2204L A324a $30 Set of 3, gold & multi

Miniature Sheets of 6 or 9

Entertainers A325

#2205-2206: Portraits of Elvis Presley.
#2207: Portraits of John Lennon.
#2208-2210: Portraits of Marilyn Monroe.
#2211, Presley, diff. #2212, Lennon, diff. #2213, Monroe, in black. #2214, Monroe, in red.

1995, Sept. 18 *Perf. $13^1/_2$x14*

2205 A325 $1 #a.-f. 4.50 4.50
2206-2210 A325 $1 #a.-i., each 6.75 6.75

Souvenir Sheets

2211-2214 A325 $6 each 4.50 4.50

No. 2208 has serifs in lettering. No. 2209 has pink lettering.

Elvis Presley — A325a

$30, Marilyn Monroe. Illustration reduced. Illustration reduced.

1995 **Litho. & Embossed** *Perf. 9*

2214A A325a $20 gold & multi
2214B A325a $30 gold & multi

Miniature Sheet

Passenger Trains A326

Designs: No. 2215a, German Federal Railway ET4-03, high speed four car electric. b, Tres Grande Vitesse (TGV), France. c, British Railways Class 87 electric. d, Beijing locomotive, Railways of the People's Republic of China. e, American Amtrak turbo. f, Swedish State Railways class RC4 electric.
$6, Eurostar.

1995, Oct. 3 *Perf. 14*

2215 A326 $1.50 Sheet of 6, #a.-f. 5.25 5.25

Souvenir Sheet

2216 A326 $6 multicolored 4.50 4.50

No. 2216 contains one 85x28mm stamp.

Miniature Sheets of 12

Nobel Prize Fund Established, Cent. — A327

Recipients: No. 2217a, Heinrich Böll, literature, 1972. b, Walther Bothe, physics, 1954. c, Richard Kuhn, chemistry, 1938. d, Hermann Hesse, literature, 1946. e, Knut Hamsun, literature, 1920. f, Konrad Lorenz, medicine, 1973. g, Thomas Mann, literature, 1929. h, Fridtjof Nansen, peace, 1922. i, Fritz Pregl, chemistry, 1923. j, Christian Lange, peace, 1921. k, Otto Loewi, medicine, 1936. l, Erwin Schrodinger, physics, 1933.

No. 2218: a, Giosue Carducci, literature, 1906. b, Wladyslaw Reymont, literature, 1924. c, Ivan Bunin, literature, 1933. d, Pavel Cherenkov, physics, 1958. e, Ivan Pavlov, medicine, 1904. f, Pyotr Kapitza, physics, 1978. g, Lev Landau, physics, 1962. h, Daniel Bovet, medicine, 1957. i, Henryk Sienkiewicz, literature, 1905. j, Aleksandr Prokhorov, physics, 1964. k, Julius Wagner von Jauregg, medicine, 1927. l, Grazia Deledda, literature, 1926.

No. 2219: a, Bjornstjerne Bjornson, literature, 1903. b, Frank Kellogg, peace, 1929. c, Gustav Hertz, physics, 1925. d, Har Gobind Khorana, medicine, 1968. e, Kenichi Fukui, chemistry, 1981. f, Henry Kissinger, peace, 1973. g, Martin Luther King, Jr., peace, 1964. h, Odd Hassel, chemistry, 1969. i, Polykarp Kusch, physics, 1955. j, Ragnar Frisch, economics, 1969. k, Willis E. Lamb, Jr., physics, 1955. l, Sigrid Undset, literature, 1928.

No. 2220: a, Robert Barany, medicine, 1914. b, Ernest Walton, physics, 1951. c, Alfred Fried, peace, 1911. d, James Franck, physics, 1925. e, Werner Forssmann, medicine, 1956. f, Yasunari Kawabata, literature, 1968. g, Wolfgang Pauli, physics, 1945. h, Jean-Paul Sartre, literature, 1964. i, Aleksandr Solzhenitsyn, literature, 1970. j, Hermann Staudinger, chemistry, 1953. k, Igor Tamm, physics, 1958. l, Samuel Beckett, literature, 1969.

No. 2221, Adolf Windaus, chemistry, 1928. No. 2222, Hideki Yukawa, physics, 1949. No. 2223, Bertha von Suttner, peace, 1905. No. 2224, Karl Landsteiner, medicine, 1930.

1995, Oct. 2 **Litho.** *Perf. 14*

2217-2220 A327 $1 #a.-l., each 9.00 9.00

Souvenir Sheets

2221-2224 A327 $6 each 4.50 4.50

Miniature Sheet

Classic Cars A328

No. 2225: a, 1931 Duesenberg Model J. b, 1913 Sleeve-valve Minerva. c, 1933 Delage D.8. SS. d, 1931-32 Bugatti Royale, Coupe De Ville chassis 41111. e, 1926 Rolls Royce 7668CC Phantom 1 Landauette. f, 1927 Mercedes Benz S26/120/180 PS.
$5, Hispano-Suiza Type H6B tulipwood-bodied roadster by Neuport.

1995, Oct. 3

2225 A328 $1.50 Sheet of 6, #a.-f. 6.75 6.75

Souvenir Sheet

2226 A328 $5 multicolored 3.75 3.75

Singapore '95 (#2225). No. 2226 contains one 85x28mm stamp.

Miniature Sheet

Sierra Club, Cent. — A329

#2227: a, Gray wolf in front of trees. b. Gray wolf pup. c, Gray wolf up close. d, Hawaiian goose. e, Two Hawaiian geese. f, Jaguar. g, Lion-tailed macaque. h, Sand cat. i, Three sand cats.

#2228, horiz.: a, Orangutan swinging from tree. b, Orangutan facing forward. c, Orangutan looking left. d, Jaguar on rock. e, Jaguar up close. f, Sand cats. g, Hawaiian goose. h, Three lion-tailed macaques. i, Lion-tailed macaque.

1995, Dec. 1 **Litho.** *Perf. 14*

2227 A329 $1 Sheet of 9, #a.-i. 6.75 6.75
2228 A329 $1 Sheet of 9, #a.-i. 6.75 6.75

Miniature Sheet

Natural Wonders of the World A330

No. 2229: a, Nile River. b, Yangtze River. c, Niagara Falls. d, Victoria Falls. e, Grand Canyon, US. f, Sahara Desert, Algeria. g, Kilimanjaro, Tanzania. h, Amazon river.
No. 2230, Haleakala Crater, Hawaii.

1995, Dec. 1

2229 A330 $1.10 Sheet of 8, #a.-h. 6.75 6.75

Souvenir Sheet

2230 A330 $6 multicolored 4.50 4.50

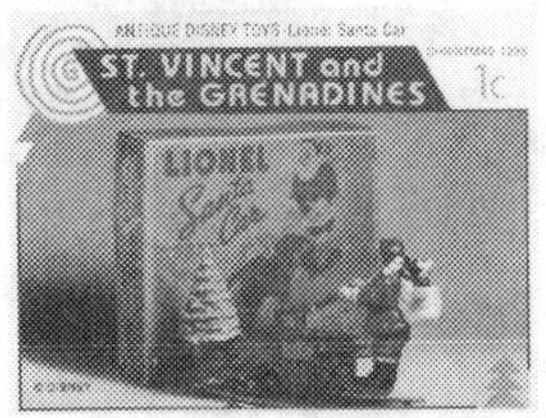

Disney Christmas — A331

Antique Disney toys: 1c, Lionel Santa car. 2c, Mickey Mouse "Choo Choo." 3c, Minnie Mouse pram. 5c, Mickey Mouse circus pull toy. 10c, Mickey, Pluto wind-up cart. 25c, Mickey Mouse mechanical motorcycle. $3, Lionel's Mickey Mouse handcar. $5, Casey Jr. Disneyland Express.
No. 2239, Silver Link, Mickey the Stoker. No. 2240, Mickey, Streamliner Engine.

1995, Dec. 7 *Perf. $13^1/_2$x14*

2231-2238 A331 Set of 8 6.50 6.50

Souvenir Sheets

2239-2240 A331 $6 each 4.50 4.50

New Year 1996 (Year of the Rat) — A332

Stylized rats, Chinese inscriptions within checkered squares, #2241-2242: a, lilac & multi. b, orange & multi. c, pink & multi.
$2, orange, green & black.

1996, Jan. 2 **Litho.** *Perf. $14^1/_2$*

2241 A332 75c Strip of 3, #a.-c. 1.75 1.75

Miniature Sheet

2242 A332 $1 Sheet of 3, #a.-c. 2.25 2.25

Souvenir Sheet

2243 A332 $2 multicolored 1.50 1.50

No. 2241 was issued in sheets of 9 stamps.

Miniature Sheets of 9

A333

Star Trek, 30th Anniv. — A333a

#2244: a, Spock. b, Kirk. c, Uhura. d, Sulu. e, Starship Enterprise. f, McCoy. g, Scott. h, Kirk, McCoy, Spock. i, Chekov.

#2245: a, Spock holding up hand in Vulcan greeting. b, Kirk, Spock in "A Piece of the Action." c, Kirk, "The Trouble with Tribbles." d, Crew, "City on the Edge of Forever." e, Uhura, Sulu, "Mirror, Mirror." f, Romulans, "Balance of Terror." g, Building exterior. h, Khan, "Space Seed."
$6, Spock, Uhura.
$30, Spock, Kirk, McCoy, Scott, Starship Enterprise.
Illustration A333a reduced.

1996, Jan. 4 *Perf. $13^1/_2$x14*

2244-2245 A333 $1 #a-i., each 6.75 6.75

Souvenir Sheet

2246 A333 $6 multicolored 4.50 4.50

2246A A333a $30 gold & multi

Miniature Sheets

Disney Characters in Various Occupations — A334

Merchants: No. 2247: a, Stamp dealer. b, At supermarket. d, Car salesman. e, Florist. f, Fast food carhop. g, Street vendor. h, Gift shop. i, Hobby shop owner. j, Bakery.

Transport workers: No. 2248: a, Delivery service. b, Truck driver. c, Airplane crew. d, Railroad men. e, Bus driver. f, Tour guide. g, Messenger service. h, Trolley conductor. i, Air traffice controller.

Law & order: No. 2249: a, Postal inspector. b, Traffic cop. c, Private detectives. d, Highway patrol. e, Justice of the peace. f, Security guard. g, Judge and lawyer. h, Sheriff. i, Court stenographer.

Sports professionals: No. 2250: a, Basketball player. b, Referee. c, Track coach. d, Ice skater. e, Golfer and caddy. f, Sportscaster. g, Tennis champs. h, Football coach. i, Race car driver.

Scientists: No. 2251: a, Paleontologist. b, Archaeologist. c, Inventor. d, Astronaut. e, Chemist. f, Engineer. g, Computer graphics. h, Astronomer. i, Zoologist.

School of education, vert: No. 2252: a, Classroom teacher. b, Nursery school teacher. c, Band teacher. d, Electronic teacher. e, School psychologist. f, School principal. g, Professor. h, Graduate.

Sea & shore workers: No. 2253: a, Ship builders. b, Fisherman. c, Pearl diver. d, Underwater photographer. e, Bait & tackle shop owner. f, Bathing suit covergirls. g, Marine life painter. h, Lifeguard. i, Lighthouse keeper.

No. 2254, Donald in ice cream parlor. No. 2255, Goofy as an oceanographer. No. 2256, Grandma, Grandpa, Daisy Duck as jury, vert. No. 2257, Donald as deep sea treasure hunter, vert. No. 2258, Minnie as librarian, vert. No. 2259, Mickey, ducks, as cheerleaders, vert. No. 2260, Mickey as seaman, vert.

1996, Jan. 8 *Perf. 14x$13^1/_2$, $13^1/_2$x14*

2247 A334 10c Sheet of 9, #a.-i. .70 .70
2248 A334 50c Sheet of 9, #a.-i. 3.50 3.50
2249 A334 75c Sheet of 9, #a.-i. 5.00 5.00
2250 A334 90c Sheet of 9, #a.-i. 6.00 6.00
2251 A334 95c Sheet of 9, #a.-i. 6.50 6.50
2252 A334 $1.10 Sheet of 8, #a.-h. 6.75 6.75
2253 A334 $1.20 Sheet of 9, #a.-i. 8.25 8.25

Souvenir Sheets

2254-2260 A334 $6 each 4.50 4.50

#2248-2253 exist in sheets of 7 or 8 10c stamps + label. The label replaces the following stamps: #2248e, 2249e, 2250e, 2251e, 2252d, 2253e. The sheets had limited release on Dec. 3, 1996.

Miniature Sheets

Paintings from Metropolitan Museum of Art — A335

Details or entire paintings, artist: No. 2261a, Moses Striking Rock, by Bloemaert. b, The Last Communion, by Botticelli. c, The Musicians, by Caravaggio. d, Francesco Sassetti & Son, by Ghirlandaio. e, Pepito Costa y Bunells, by Goya. f, Saint Andrew, by Martini. g, The Nativity, by the Netherlands School. h, Christ Blessing, by Solario.

By Cézanne: No. 2262a, Madame Cézanne. b, Still Life with Apples and Pears. c, Man in a Straw Hat. d, Still Life with a Ginger Jar. e, Madame Cézanne in a Red Dress. f, Still Life. g, Dominique Aubert. h, Still Life, diff. i, The Card Players.

No. 2263a, Bullfight, by Goya. b, Portrait of a Man, by Frans Hals. c, Mother and Son, by Sully. d, Portrait of a Young Man, by Memling. e, Maltilde Stoughton de Jaudenes, by Stuart. f, Josef de Jaudenes y Nebot, by Stuart. g, Mont Sainte-Victore, by Cézanne. h, Gardanne, by Cézanne. i, The Empress Eugenie, by Winterhalter.

No. 2264a, The Dissolute Household, by Steen. b, Portrait of Gerard de Lairesse, by Rembrandt. c, Juan de Pareja, by Velázquez. d, Curiosity, by G. Ter Borch. e, The Companions of Rinaldo, by Poussin. f, Don Gaspar de Guzman, by Velázquez. g, Merry Company on a Terrace, by Steen. h, Pilate Washing Hands, by Rembrandt. i, Portrait of a Man, by Van Dyck.

No. 2265, Hagar in Wilderness, by Corot. No. 2266, Young Ladies from the Village, by Courbet. No. 2267, Two Young Peasant Women, by Pissaro. No. 2268, Allegory of the Planets and Continents, by Tiepolo.

1996, Feb. 1 Litho. *Perf. 14*

2261 A335 75c Sheet of 8, #a.-h. + label 4.50 4.50
2262 A335 90c Sheet of 9, #a.-i. 6.00 6.00
2263 A335 $1 Sheet of 9, #a.-i. 6.75 6.75
2264 A335 $1.10 Sheet of 9, #a.-i. 7.50 7.50

Souvenir Sheets

2265-2268 A335 $6 each 4.50 4.50

Nos. 2265-2268 each contain one 81x53mm stamp.

Michael Jordan, Basketball Player, Baseball Player — A335a

Design: No. 2268B, Jordan as basketball player. Illustration reduced.

1996 Litho. & Embossed *Perf. 9*

2268A A335a $30 gold & multi
2268B A325a $30 gold & multi

Joe Montana, Football Player — A335b

Designs: d, In red jersey. e, In white jersey.

1996

Sheet of 2

2268C A335b $15 #d.-e., gold & multi

Lou Gehrig and Cal Ripken, Jr., Baseball Ironmen — A336

Illustration reduced.

1995 Litho. & Embossed *Perf. 9*

2269 A336 $30 gold & multi

A336a

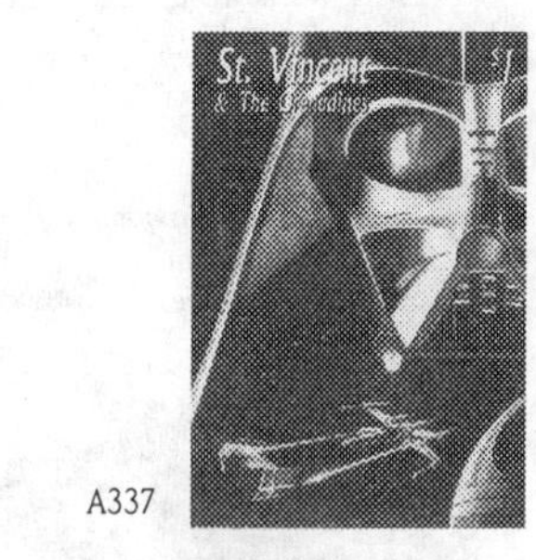

A337

Star Wars Trilogy — A338

#2269: b, In Space Bar. c, Luke, Emperor. d, X-Wing Fighter. e, Star Destroyers. f, Cloud City. g, Speeders on Forest Moon.

Nos. 2270, 2273a, Darth Vader, "Star Wars," 1977. Nos. 2271, 2273c, Yoda, "Return of the Jedi," 1983. Nos. 2272, 2273b, Storm troopers, "The Empire Strikes Back," 1980.

No. 2274, Darth Vader, "Star Wars," 1977. No. 2275, Yoda, "Return of the Jedi," 1983. No. 2276, Storm Trooper, "The Empire Strikes Back," 1980.

Illustration A338 reduced.

1996, Mar. 19 Litho. *Perf. 14*

2269A A336a 35c Sheet of 6, #b.-g. 1.60 1.60

Self-Adhesive

Serpentine Die Cut 6

2270 A337 $1 silver & multi .75 .75
2271 A337 $1 silver & multi .75 .75
2272 A337 $1 silver & multi .75 .75

Souvenir Sheet

Serpentine Die Cut 9

2273 A338 $2 Sheet of 3, #a.-c. 4.50 4.50

Litho. & Embossed

Perf. 9

2274-2276 A337 $30 gold & multi

Nos. 2270-2272 were issued in sheets of 3 each arranged in alternating order.

Nos. 2274-2276 also exist in silver & multi.

Issued: Nos. 2274-2276, 11/18/95; others 3/19/96.

Butterflies — A339

70c, Anteos menippe. $1, Eunica alcmena. $1.10, Doxocopa lavinia. $2, Tithorea tarricina.

No. 2281: a, Papilio lycophron. b, Prepona buckleyana. c, Parides agavus. d, Papilio cacicus. e, Euryades duponchelli. f, Diaethria dymena. g, Orimba jansoni. h, Polystichtis siaka. i, Papilio machaonides.

$5, Adelpha abia. $6, Themone pais.

1996, Apr. 15 Litho. *Perf. 14*

2277-2280 A339 Set of 4 3.60 3.60
2281 A339 90c Sheet of 9, #a.-i. 6.00 6.00

Souvenir Sheets

2282 A339 $5 multicolored 3.75 3.75
2283 A339 $6 multicolored 4.50 4.50

Queen Elizabeth II, 70th Birthday A340

Designs: a, Portrait. b, In robes of Order of the Garter. c, Wearing red coat, hat.

$6, Waving from balcony, horiz.

1996, June 12 Litho. *Perf. 13½x14*

2284 A340 $2 Strip of 3, #a.-c. 4.50 4.50

Souvenir Sheet

Perf. 14x13½

2285 A340 $6 multicolored 4.50 4.50

No. 2284 was issued in sheets of 9 stamps.

Birds A341

Designs: 60c, Coereba flaveola. $1, Myadestes genibarbis. $1.10, Tangara cucullata. $2, Eulampis jugularis.

No. 2290: a, Progne subis. b, Buteo platypterus. c, Phaethon lepturus. d, Himantopus himantopus. e, Sterna anaethetus. f, Euphonia musica. g, Arenaria interpres. h, Sericotes holosericeus. i, Nyctanassa violacea.

$5, Dendrocygna autumnalis, vert.. $6, Amazona guildingii.

1996, July 11 *Perf. 14*

2286-2289 A341 Set of 4, vert. 3.50 3.50

Miniature Sheet

2290 A341 $1 Sheet of 9, #a.-i. 6.80 6.80

Souvenir Sheets

2291 A341 $5 multi, vert. 3.80 3.80
2292 A341 $6 multi, vert. 4.50 4.50

Radio, Cent. — A342

Entertainers: 90c, Walter Winchell. $1, Fred Allen. $1.10, Hedda Hopper. $2, Eve Arden.

$6, Major Bowes.

1996, July 11 *Perf. 13½x14*

2293-2296 A342 Set of 4 3.75 3.75

Souvenir Sheet

2297 A342 $6 multicolored 4.50 4.50

UNICEF, 50th Anniv. A343

Designs: $1, Boy raising arm. $1.10, Children reading. $2, Girl, microscope. $5, Boy.

1996, July 11 *Perf. 14*

2298-2300 A343 Set of 3 3.25 3.25

Souvenir Sheet

2301 A343 $5 multicolored 3.80 3.80

Chinese Animated Films — A344

Nos. 2302, 2304: Various characters from "Uproar in Heaven."

Nos. 2303, 2305: Various characters from "Nezha Conquers the Dragon King."

1996, May 10 Litho. *Perf. 12*

Strips of 5

2302-2303 A344 15c #a.-e., each .55 .55

Souvenir Sheets

2304-2305 A344 75c vert., each .55 .55

Nos. 2302-2303 each were issued in a sheet of 10 stamps. CHINA '96, 9th Asian Intl. Philatelic Exhibition.

Jerusalem, 3000th Anniv. — A345

Designs: $1, Knesset. $1.10, Montefiore Windmill. $2, Shrine of the Book. $5, Jerusalem of Gold.

1996, July 11 Litho. *Perf. 14*

2306-2308 A345 Set of 3 3.25 3.25

Souvenir Sheet

2309 A345 $5 multicolored 3.75 3.75

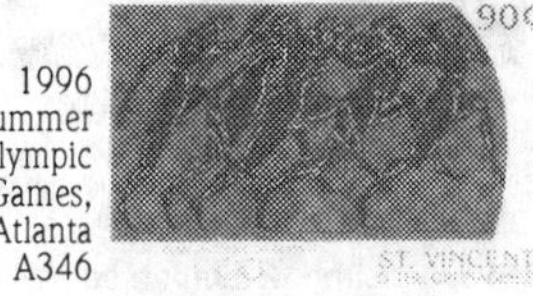

1996 Summer Olympic Games, Atlanta A346

20c, Maurice King, weight lifter, vert. 70c, Eswort Coombs, 400-meter relay, vert. No. 2312, 90c, Runners, Olympia, 530BC. No. 2313, 90c, Pamenos Ballantyne, Benedict Ballantyne, runners, vert. $1, London landmarks, 1908 Olympics, Great Britain. No. 2315, $1.10, Rodney "Chang" Jack, soccer player, vert. No. 2316, $1.10, Dorando Pietri, marathon runner, London, 1908, vert. $2, Yachting.

Past winners, event: No. 2318, vert: a, Vitaly Shcherbo, gymnastics. b, Fu Mingxia, diving. c, Wilma Rudolph, track & field. d, Rafer Johnson, decathlon. e, Teofilo Stevenson, boxing. f, Babe Didrikson, track & field. g, Kyoko Iwasaki, swimming. h, Yoo Namkyu, table tennis. i, Michael Gross, swimming.

No. 2319: a, Chuhei Nambu, triple jump. b, Duncan McNaughton, high jump. c, Jack Kelly, single sculls. d, Jackie Joyner-Kersee, heptathlon. e, Tyrell Biggs, boxing. f, Larisa Latynina, gymnastics. g, Bob Garrett, discus. h, Paavo Nurmi, 5000-meters. i, Eric Lemming, javelin.

No. 2320: a, Yasuhiro Yamashita, judo. b, Peter Rono, 1500-meters. c, Aleksandr Kourlovitch, weight lifting. d, Juha Tiainen, hammer throw. e, Sergei Bubka, pole vault. f, O. F. Newall, women's archery. g, Nadia Comaneci, gymnastics. h, Carl Lewis, long jump. i, Bob Mathias, decathlon.

Sporting events, vert.: No. 2321a, Women's archery. b, Gymnastics. c, Basketball. d, Soccer. e, Water polo. f, Baseball. g, Kayak. h, Fencing. i, Cycling.

No. 2322, Olympic Flag. No. 2323, Carl Lewis, runner, vert. No. 2324, Alexander Ditiatin, gymnastics, 1980. No. 2325, Hannes Kolehmainen, marathon runner.

1996, July 19

2310-2317 A346 Set of 8 6.00 6.00

Sheets of 9

2318-2321 A346 $1 #a.-i., each 6.75 6.75

Souvenir Sheets

2322-2325 A346 $5 each 3.75 3.75

St. Vincent Olympic Committee (#2310-2311, 2313, 2315).

Disney's "The Hunchback of Notre Dame" A347

No. 2326: a, Quasimodo. b, Phoebus. c, Laverne, Hugo. d, Clopin. e, Frollo. f, Esmeralda. g, Victor. h, Djali.
No. 2327, Esmeralda, Quasimodo, horiz. No. 2328, Esmeralda, Phoebus, horiz.

1996, July 25 *Perf. 13½x14*
2326 A347 $1 Sheet of 8, #a.-h. 6.00 6.00

Souvenir Sheets
Perf. 14X13½
2327-2328 A347 $6 each 4.50 4.50

Fish A348

Designs: 70c, French angelfish. 90c, Redspotted hawkfish. $1.10, Spiny puffer. $2, Gray triggerfish.
No. 2333: a, Barred hamlet. b, Flamefish. c, Longsnout butterflyfish. d, Fairy basslet. e, Redtail parrotfish. f, Blackbar soldierfish. g, Threespot damselfish. h, Candy basslet. i, Spotfin hogfish.
No. 2334: a, Equetus lanceolatus. b, Acanthurus coeruleus. c, Lutjanus analis. d, Hippocampus hudsonius. e, Serranus annularis. f, Squatina dumerili. g, Muraena miliaris. h, Bolbometopon bicolor. i, Tritonium nodiferum.
$5, Queen triggerfish. $6, Blue marlin.

1996, Aug. 10 *Perf. 14*
2329-2332 A348 Set of 4 3.60 3.60

Sheets of 9
2333-2334 A348 $1 #a.-i., each 6.75 6.75

Souvenir Sheets
2335 A348 $5 multicolored 3.75 3.75
2336 A348 $6 multicolored 4.50 4.50

Flowers A349

70c, Beloperone guttata. $1, Epidendrum elongatum. $1.10, Pettrea volubilis. $2, Oncidium altrissimum.
No. 2341: a, Datura candida. b, Amherstia nobilis. c, Ipomoea acuminata. d, Bougainvillea glabra. e, Cassia alata. f, Cordia sebestena. g, Opuntia dilenii. h, Cryptostegia grandiflora. i, Rodriguezia lanceolata.
No. 2342, Acalypha hispida. No. 2343, Hibiscus rosa-sinensis.

1996, Aug. 15
2337-2340 A349 Set of 4 3.60 3.60
2341 A349 90c Sheet of 9, #a.-i. 6.00 6.00

Souvenir Sheets
2342 A349 $5 multicolored 3.75 3.75

Perf. 14x13½
2343 A349 $5 multicolored 3.75 3.75

John F. Kennedy (1917-63) — A350

No. 2344a: , As young boy. b, Proclamation to send man to the moon. c, With Caroline, Jackie. d, Inauguration. e, Giving speech. f, On PT 109. g, With Jackie. h, Funeral procession, portrait. i, Guard, Eternal Flame.
No. 2345: a, With family on yacht. b, On yacht. c, On yacht holding sail. d, "JFK," portrait. e, Talking to astronauts in space. f, Younger picture in uniform. g, Portrait. h, Riding in motorcade. i, Giving speech, US flag.
No. 2346: a, Up close picture. b, In front of house at Hyannis Port. c, Memorial plaque, picture. d, Photograph among crowd. e, Portrait, flag. f, Rocket, portrait. g, Signing document. h, Martin Luther King, John F. Kennedy, Robert F. Kennedy. i, Painting looking down toward microphones.
No. 2347: a, Photograph with Jacqueline greeting people. b, Formal oval-shaped portrait. c, Photograph. d, With family. e, Space capsule, painting. f, Addressing UN. g, In rocking chair. h, Seated at desk, dignitaries. i, Holding telephone, map.

1996, Aug. *Perf. 14x13½*

Sheets of 9
2344-2347 A350 $1 #a.-i., each 6.75 6.75

Ships A351

No. 2348: a, SS Doric, 1923, Great Britain. b, SS Nerissa, 1926, Great Britain. c, SS Howick Hall, 1910, Great Britain. d, SS Jervis Bay, 1922, Great Britain. e, SS Vauban, 1912, Great Britain. f, MV Orinoco, 1928, Germany.
No. 2349: a, SS Lady Rodney, 1929, Canada. b, SS Empress of Russia, 1913, Canada. c, SS Providence, 1914, France. d, SS Reina Victori-Eugenia, 1913, Spain. e, SS Balmoral Castle, 1910, Great Britain. f, SS Tivives, 1911, US.
No. 2350, SS Imperator, 1913, Germany. No. 2351, SS Aquitania, 1914, Great Britain.

1996, Sept. 5 *Perf. 14*

Sheets of 6
2348-2349 A351 $1.10 #a.-f., each 5.00 5.00

Souvenir Sheets
2350-2351 A351 $6 each 4.50 4.50

Elvis Presley's 1st "Hit" Year, 40th Anniv. — A352

Various portraits.

1996, Sept. 8 *Perf. 13½x14*
2352 A352 $2 Sheet of 6, #a.-f. 9.00 9.00

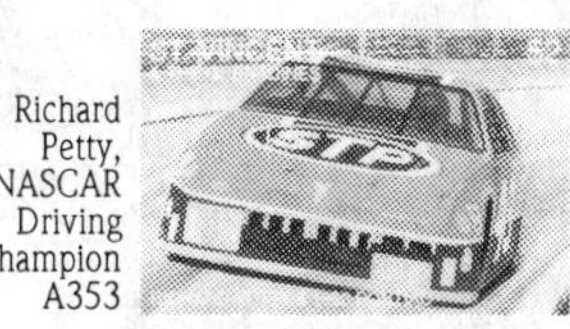
Richard Petty, NASCAR Driving Champion A353

a, 1990 Pontiac. b, Richard Petty. c, 1972 Plymouth. d, 1974 Dodge.
$5, 1970 Plymouth Superbird. $6, 1996 STP 25th Anniversary Pontiac.

1996, Sept. 26 *Perf. 14*
2353 A353 $2 Sheet of 4, #a.-d. 6.00 6.00

Souvenir Sheets
2354 A353 $5 multicolored 3.75 3.75
2355 A353 $6 multicolored 4.50 4.50

No. 2354 contains one 85x28mm stamp.

Sandy Koufax, Baseball Pitcher — A354

A354a

No. 2356: a.-c., Various action shots.
Illustration A354a reduced.

Perf. 14, Imperf. (#2356d)

1996, Sept. 26
2356 Sheet of 17 28.50 28.50
a.-c. A354 $2 each 1.50 1.50
d. A354 $6 Portrait 4.50 4.50

Litho. & Embossed
Perf. 9
2356E A354a $30 gold & multi

No. 2356 contains 6 #2356a, 5 each #2356b, 2356c and 1 #2356d. No. 2356d is 70x103mm and has simulated perforations.

Cadet Force, 60th Anniv. — A355

Insignia and: 70c, 2nd Lt. D.S. Cozier, founder. 90c, Cozier, first 12 cadets, 1936.

1996, Oct. 23 Litho. *Perf. 14x13½*
2357 A355 70c multicolored .55 .55
2358 A355 90c multicolored .70 .70

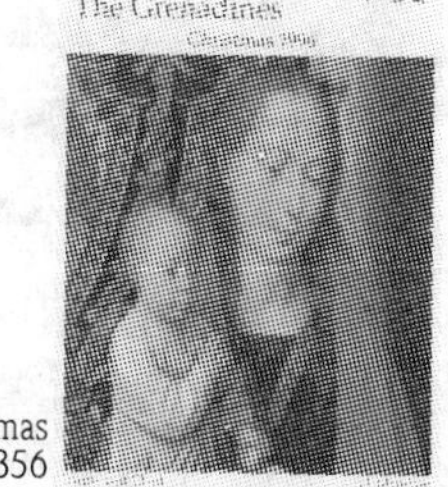
Christmas A356

Details or entire paintings: 70c, Virgin and Child, by Memling. 90c, St. Anthony, by Memling. $1, Madonna and Child, by Bouts. $1.10, Virgin and Child, by Lorenzo Lotto. $2, St. Roch, by Lotto. $5, St. Sebastian, by Lotto.
No. 2365, Virgin and Child with St. Roch and St. Sebastian, by Lotto. No. 2366, Virgin and Child with St. Anthony and a Donor, by Memling.

1996, Nov. 14 *Perf. 13½x14*
2359-2364 A356 Set of 6 8.00 8.00

Souvenir Sheets
2365-2366 A356 $5 each 3.75 3.75

Disney's "The Hunchback of Notre Dame" — A357

Designs: Various scenes from film.
No. 2370, Quasimodo, Phoebus, Esmeralda. No. 2371, Esmeralda, vert. No. 2372, Quasimodo, citizens, vert.

1996, Dec. 12 Litho. *Perf. 13½x14*
2367 A357 10c Sheet of 6, #a.-f., vert. .45 .45

Perf. 14x13½
2368 A357 30c Sheet of 9, #a.-i. 2.00 2.00
2369 A357 $1 Sheet of 9, #a.-i. 6.75 6.75

Souvenir Sheets
2370-2372 A357 $6 each 4.50 4.50

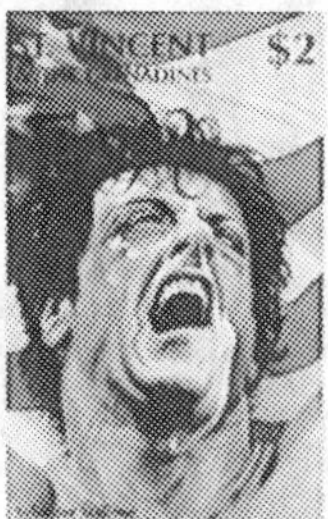
Sylvester Stallone in Movie "Rocky IV" — A358

1996 Litho. *Perf. 14*
2373 A358 $2 Sheet of 3 4.50 4.50

A359

New Year 1997 (Year of the Ox) — A359a

Stylized oxen, Chinese inscriptions within checkered squares: Nos. 2374a, 2375a, pale orange, pale lilac & black. Nos. 2374b, 2375b, green, violet & black. Nos. 2374c, 2375c, tan, pink & black.
Illustration A359a reduced.

1997, Jan. 2 *Perf. 14½*
2374 A359 75c Strip of 3, #a.-c. 1.70 1.70
2375 A359 $1 Sheet of 3, #a.-c. 2.25 2.25

Souvenir Sheet
2376 A359 $2 orange, yellow & blk 1.50 1.50

Litho. & Embossed
Perf. 9
2376A A359a $30 gold & multi

No. 2374 was issued in sheets of 9 stamps.

Star Trek Voyager — A360

No. 2377: a, Lt. Tuvak. b, Kes. c, Lt. Paris. d, The Doctor. e, Capt. Janeway. f, Lt. Torres. g, Neelix. h, Ens. Kim. i, Cdr. Chakotay.
$6, Cast of characters.

1997, Jan. 23 Litho. *Perf. 14*
2377 A360 $2 Sheet of 9, #a.-i. 13.50 13.50

Souvenir Sheet

2378 A360 $2 multicolored 4.50 4.50

No. 2378 contains one 29x47mm stamp.

A361

A362

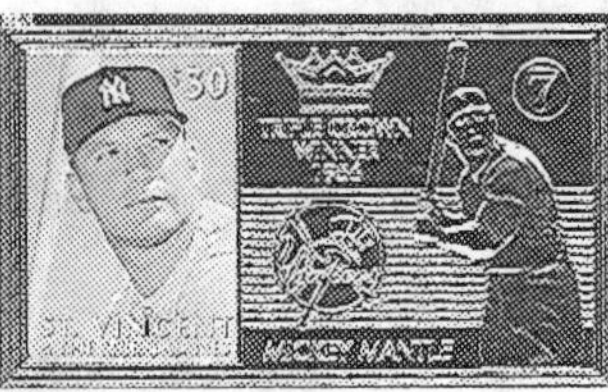
A361a

Mickey Mantle (1931-95), baseball player.
Illustration A361a reduced.

Perf. 14, Imperf. (#2379b)

1997, Jan. 23

2379 Sheet of 17, 16 #2379a, 1 #2379b 28.50 28.50
a. A361 $2 shown 1.50 1.50
b. A361 $6 Portrait holding bat 4.50 4.50

Litho. & Embossed

Perf. 9

2379C A361a $30 gold & multi

No. 2379b is 70x100mm.

Perf. 14x14¹/₂, Imperf. (#2380q)

1997, Jan. 23

Black Baseball Players: a, Frank Robinson. b, Satchel Paige. c, Billy Williams. d, Reggie Jackson. e, Roberto Clemente. f, Ernie Banks. g, Hank Aaron. h, Roy Campanella. i, Willie McCovey. j, Monte Irvin. k, Willie Stargell. l, Rod Carew. m, Ferguson Jenkins. n, Bob Gibson. o, Lou Brock. p, Joe Morgan. q, Jackie Robinson.

2380 Sheet of 17 16.50 16.50
a.-p. A362 $1 each .75 .75
q. A362 $6 Portrait 4.50 4.50

No. 2380q is 66x100mm and has simulated perforations.

Souvenir Sheet

Chongqing Dazu Stone Carving — A363

Illustration reduced.

1996, May 20 Litho. *Perf. 12*
2381 A363 $2 multicolored 1.50 1.50

China '96.
No. 2381 was not available until March 1997.

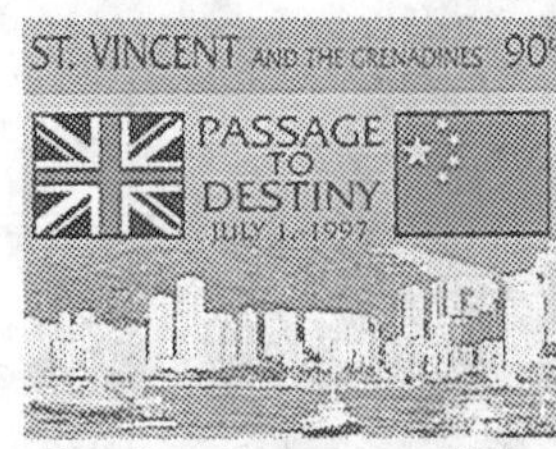

Hong Kong Changeover — A364

A364a

Flags of Great Britain, Peoples' Republic of China and panoramic view of Hong Kong: Nos. 2382a-2382e, In daytime. Nos. 2382f-2382j, At night.
Market scene: No. 2383: a, Vendors, corner of building. b, People strolling. c, Man choosing items to purchase.
Buddhist religious ceremony: No. 2384a, Fruit, incense pot, torch. b, Monk at fire. c, Flower.
Lantern ceremony: No. 2385: a, Boy, girl. b, Couple on bridge. c, Girls with lanterns.
Illustration A364a reduced.

1997, Feb. 12 *Perf. 14*
2382 A364 90c Sheet of 10, #a.-j. 6.75 6.75

Sheets of 3

Perf. 13

2383-2385 A364 $2 #a.-c., each 4.50 4.50

Litho. & Embossed

Perf. 9

2385A A364a $30 gold & multi

Hong Kong '97.
Nos. 2383-2385 each contain 3 35x26mm stamps.

UNESCO, 50th Anniv. — A365

World Heritage Sites: 70c, Lord Howe Islands, Australia, vert. 90c, Uluru-Kata Tjuta Natl. Park, Australia, vert. $1, Kakadu Natl. Park, Australia, vert. $1.10, Te Wahipounamu, New Zealand, vert. $2, $5, vert., Tongariro Natl. Park, New Zealand.
Various sites in Greece, vert: No. 2392: a, Monastery of Rossanou, Meteora. b, f, h, Painted ceiling, interior, Mount Athos Monastery. c, Monastery Osios Varlaam, Meteora. d, Ruins in Athens. e, Museum of the Acropolis. g, Mount Athos.
Various sites in Japan, vert: No. 2393: a, Himeji-Jo. b, Temple Lake, Gardens, Kyoto. c, Kyoto. d, Buddhist Temple of Ninna-Ji. e, View of city of Himeji-Jo. f, Forest, Shirakami-Sanchi. g, h, Forest, Yakushima.
No. 2394, vert: a, City of San Gimignano, Italy. b, Cathedral of Santa Maria Asunta, Pisa, Italy. c, Cathedral of Santa Maria Fiore, Florence, Italy. d, Archaeological site, Valley of the Boyne, Ireland. e, Church of Saint-Savin-Sur-Gartempe, France. f, g, h, City of Bath, England.
No. 2395a, Trinidad, Valley de los Ingenios, Cuba. b, City of Zacatecas, Mexico. c, Lima, Peru. d, Ruins of Monastery, Paraguay. e, Mayan Ruins, Copan, Honduras.
Various sites in China: No. 2396: a, Palace, Wudang Mountains, Hubei Province. b, Cave Sanctuaries, Mogao. c, House, Desert of Taklamakan. d, e, Great Wall.
Nos. 2397a-2397e: Various sites in Quedlinberg, Germany.
No. 2398, Monastery of Meteora, Greece. No. 2399, Wailing Wall, Jerusalem. No. 2400, Quedlinburg, Germany. No. 2401, Oasis, Dunbuang, China. No. 2402, Himeji-Jo, Japan. No. 2403, Great Wall, China. No. 2404, City of Venice, Italy.

Perf. 13¹/₂x14, 14x13¹/₂

1997, Mar. 24 Litho.
2386-2391 A365 Set of 6 8.00 8.00

Sheets of 8 + Label

2392-2394 A365 $1.10 #a.-h., each 6.60 6.60

Sheets of 5 + Label

2395-2397 A365 $1.50 #a.-e., each 5.75 5.75

Souvenir Sheets

2398-2404 A365 $5 each 3.75 3.75

Telecommunications in St. Vincent, 125th Anniv. — A366

Designs: 5c, Microwave radio relay tower, Dorsetshire Hill. 10c, Cable & wireless headquarters, Kingstown. 20c, Microwave relay tower, vert. 35c, Cable & wireless complex, Arnos Vale. 50c, Cable & wireless tower, Mt. St. Andrew. 70c, Cable ship. 90c, Eastern telecommunication network, 1872. $1.10, Telegraph map of world, 1876.

Perf. 14x14¹/₂, 14¹/₂x14

1997, Apr. 3 Litho.
2405-2412 A366 Set of 8 3.00 3.00

Birds of the World — A367

Water Birds — A368

Designs: 60c, Smooth-billed ani. 70c, Belted kingfisher. 90c, Blackburnian warbler. $1.10, Blue tit. $2, Chaffinch. $5, Ruddy turnstone.
No. 2419: a, Blue grosbeak. b, Bananaquit. c, Cedar waxwing. d, Ovenbird. e, Hooded warbler. f, Flicker.
No. 2420: a, Song thrush. b, Robin. c, Blackbird. d, Great spotted woodpecker. e, Wren. f, Kingfisher.
No. 2421, St. Vincent parrot. No. 2422, Tawny owl.

1997, Apr. 7 *Perf. 14*
2413-2418 A367 Set of 6 7.75 7.75
2419 A367 $1 Sheet of 6, #a.-f. 4.50 4.50
2420 A367 $2 Sheet of 6, #a.-f. 9.00 9.00

Souvenir Sheets

2421-2422 A367 $5 each 3.75 3.75

1997, Apr. 7 *Perf. 15*

Designs: 70c, Mandarin duck, horiz. 90c, Green heron, horiz. $1, Drake ringed teal, horiz. $1.10, Blue-footed boobies, horiz. $2, Australian jacana. $5, Reddish egret.
No. 2429: a, Crested auklet. b, Whiskered auklet. c, Pigeon guillemot. d, Adelie penguins. e, Rockhopper penguin. f, Emperor penguin.
No. 2430, Snowy egrets, horiz. No. 2431, Flamingos, horiz.

2423-2428 A368 Set of 6 8.00 8.00
2429 A368 $1.10 Sheet of 6, #a.-f. 5.00 5.00

Souvenir Sheet

2430-2431 A368 $5 each 3.75 3.75

Jackie Robinson (1919-72) A369

A369a

Illustration A369a reduced.

Serpentine Die Cut 7

1997, Jan. 23 Litho.

Self-Adhesive

2432 A369 $1 multicolored .75 .75

Litho. & Embossed

Perf. 9

2432A A369a $30 gold & multi

No. 2432 was issued in sheets of 3 and was not available until June 1997.

Queen Elizabeth II, Prince Philip, 50th Wedding Anniv. A370

No. 2433: a, Queen. b, Royal arms. c, Portrait of Queen, Prince. d, Queen, Prince, crowd. e, Buckingham Palace. f, Prince.
$5, Queen seated in wedding gown, crown.

1997, June 3 Litho. *Perf. 14*
2433 A370 $1.10 Sheet of 6, #a.-f. 5.00 5.00

Souvenir Sheet

2434 A370 $5 multicolored 3.75 3.75

Paintings by Hiroshige (1797-1858) A371

No. 2435: a, Furukawa River, Hiroo. b, Chiyogaike Pond, Meguro. c, New Fuji, Meguro. d, Moon-Viewing Point. e, Ushimachi, Takanawa. f, Original Fuji, Meguro.
No. 2436, Gotenyama, Shinagawa. No. 2437, Shinagawa Susaki.

1997, June 3 *Perf. 13¹/₂x14*
2435 A371 $1.50 Sheet of 6, #a.-f. 6.75 6.75

Souvenir Sheets

2436-2437 A371 $5 each 4.50 4.50

Paul Harris (1868-1947), Founder of Rotary Intl. — A372

Designs: $2, World Community Service, blankets from Japan donated to Thai children, Harris.
$5, Rotary Intl. Pres. Luis Vincente Giay, US Pres. Jimmy Carter, Rotary award recipient.

1997, June 3 *Perf. 14*
2438 A372 $2 multicolored 1.50 1.50

Souvenir Sheet

2439 A372 $5 multicolored 3.75 3.75

Heinrich von Stephan (1831-97) A373

Portraits of Von Stephan and: a, Bicycle postman, India, 1800's. b, UPU emblem. c, Zebu-drawn post carriage, Indochina.
$5, Post rider, Indochina.

1997, June 3

2440 A373 $2 Sheet of 3, #a.-c. 4.50 4.50

Souvenir Sheet

2441 A373 $5 gray brown 3.75 3.75

PACIFIC 97.

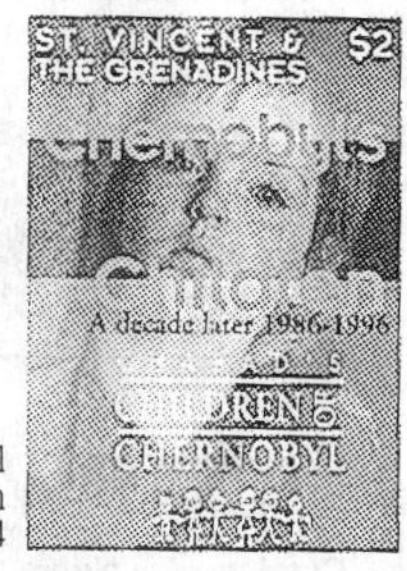

Chernobyl Disaster, 10th Anniv. — A374

Designs: No. 2442, Chabad's Children of Chernobyl. No. 2443, UNESCO.

1997, June 3 Litho. *Perf. 13½x14*

2442 A374 $2 multicolored 1.50 1.50
2443 A374 $2 multicolored 1.50 1.50

Grimm's Fairy Tales A375

Mother Goose A376

Scenes showing "Old Sultan:" No. 2444: a, With woman, man. b, On hillside. c, With wolf. No. 2446, Man, Old Sultan, girl.
Scenes from "The Cobbler and the Elves:" No. 2445: a, Cobbler. b, Elves. c, Cobbler holding elf. No. 2447, Elf.
No. 2448, Curly-Locks sewing.

1997, June 3 *Perf. 13½x14*

Sheets of 3

2444-2445 A375 $2 #a.-c., each 4.50 4.50

Souvenir Sheets

2446-2447 A375 $5 each 3.75 3.75

Perf. 14

2448 A376 $5 multicolored 3.75 3.75

Numbers have been reserved for two additional souvenir sheets with this set.

Inaugural Cricket Test, Arnos Vale — A377

Designs: 90c, Alphonso Theodore Roberts (1937-96), vert. $5, Arnos Vale Playing field.

Perf. 13½x14, 14x13½

1997, June 20 Litho.

2451 A377 90c multicolored .70 .70
2452 A377 $5 multicolored 3.75 3.75

1998 World Cup Soccer Championships, France — A378

Players: 70c, Beckenbauer, W. Germany. 90c, Moore, England. $1, Lato, Poland. $1.10, Pele, Brazil. $2, Maier, W. Germany. $10, Eusebio, Portugal.
Scenes from England's victory, 1966: No. 2459: a, Stadium. b, c, d, e, f, h, Various action scenes. g, Coming from field, holding trophy.
Action scenes from various finals: No 2460: a, c, Argentina, W. Germany, 1986. b, e, England, W. Germany, 1966. d, Italy, W. Germany, 1982. f, g, Argentina, Holland, 1978. h, W. Germany, Holland, 1974.
Players, vert.: No. 2461: a, Bergkamp, Holland. b, Seaman, England. c, Schmeichel, Denmark. d, Ince, England. e, Futre, Portugal. f, Ravanelli, Italy. g, Keane, Ireland. h, Gascoigne, England.
Action scenes from Argentina v. Holland, 1978, vert.: No. 2462a-2462h.
No. 2463, Ally McCoist, Scotland, vert. No. 2464, Salvatori Schillaci, Italy, vert. No. 2465, Mario Kempes, Argentina, vert. No. 2466, Paulao, Angola.

Perf. 14x13½, 13½x14

1997, Aug. 26 Litho.

2453-2458 A378 Set of 6 4.25 4.25

Sheets of 8 + Label

2459-2462 A378 $1 #a.-h., each 6.00 6.00

Souvenir Sheets

2463-2466 A378 $5 each 3.75 3.75

Vincy Mas Carnival, 20th Anniv. A379

10c, Mardi Gras Band, "Cinemas." 20c, Queen of the Bands, J. Ballantyne. 50c, Queen of the Bands, vert. 70c, King of the Bands, "Conquistadore." 90c, Starlift Steel Orchestra, Panorama Champs. $2, Frankie McIntosh, musical arranger, vert.

Perf. 14½x14, 14x14½

1997, July 24

2467-2472 A379 Set of 6 3.30 3.30

Sierra Club, Cent. A380

No. 2473: a, Snow leopard. b, Polar bear. c, d, Isle Royale Natl. Park. e, f, Denali Natl. Park. g, h, i, Joshua Tree Natl. Park.
No. 2474, vert: a, b, c, Mountain gorilla. d, e, Snow leopard. f, g, Polar bear. h, Denali Natl. Park. i, Isle Royale Nat. Park.
No. 2475, vert: a, b, c, Sifaka. d, e, Peregrine falcon. f, Galapagos tortoise. g, h, African Rain Forest. i, China's Yellow Mountains.
No. 2476: a, b, c, Red panda. d, Peregrine falcon. e, f, Galapagos tortoise. g, African Rain Forest. h, i, China's Yellow Mountains.
No. 2477: a, Mountain lion. b, c, Siberian tiger. d, Red wolf. e, Black bear. f, i, Wolong Natl. Reserve. g, h, Belize Rain Forest.
No. 2478, vert: a, Siberian tiger. b, c, Mountain lion. d, e, Black bear. f, g, Red wolf. h, Belize Rain Forest. i, Wolong Natl. Reserve.
No. 2479, vert: a, b, c, Indri. d, e, Gopher tortoise. f, g, Black-footed ferret. h, Haleakala Natl. Park. i, Grand Teton Natl. Park.
No. 2480: a, Black-footed ferret. b, Gopher tortoise. c, d, Grand Teton Natl. Park. e, f. Haleakala Natl. Park. g, h, i, Madagascar Rain Forest.

Scenes in Olympic Natl. Park: No. 2481, Lake, trees. No. 2482, Mountain summit. No. 2483, Snow-topped mountains.

1997, Sept. 18 *Perf. 14*

2473 A380 20c Sheet of 9, #a.-i. 1.40 1.40
2474 A380 40c Sheet of 9, #a.-i. 2.75 2.75
2475 A380 50c Sheet of 9, #a.-i. 3.40 3.40
2476 A380 60c Sheet of 9, #a.-i. 4.00 4.00
2477 A380 70c Sheet of 9, #a.-i. 4.75 4.75
2478 A390 90c Sheet of 9, #a.-i. 6.00 6.00
2479 A380 $1 Sheet of 9, #a.-i. 6.75 6.75
2480 A380 $1.10 Sheet of 9, #a.-i. 7.50 7.50

Souvenir Sheets

2481-2483 A380 $5 each 3.75 3.75

Deng Xiaoping (1904-97), Chinese Leader — A381

Various portraits: No. 2484, Dark brown. No. 2485, Dark blue. No. 2486, Black.
No. 2487, Deng Xiaoping, Zhuo Lin, horiz.

1997, June 3 Litho. *Perf. 14*

Sheets of 4

2484-2486 A381 $2 #a.-d., each 6.00 6.00

Souvenir Sheet

2487 A381 $5 multicolored 3.75 3.75

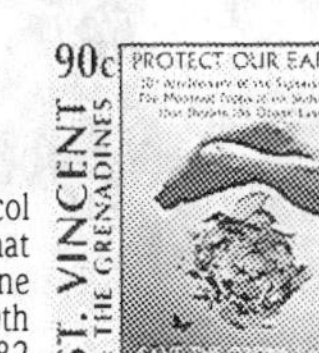

Montreal Protocol on Substances that Deplete Ozone Layer, 10th Anniv. — A382

1997, Sept. 16

2488 A382 90c multicolored .70 .70

A383

A384

Orchids: 90c, Rhyncholaelia digbyana. $1, Laeliocattleya. $1.10, Doritis pulcherrima. $2, Phalaenopsis.
No. 2493: a, Eulophia speciosa. b, Aerangis rhodosticta. c, Angraecum infundibularea. d, Calanthe sylvatica. e, Phalaenopsis mariae. f, Paphiopedilum insigne. g, Dendrobium nobile. h, Aerangis kotschyana. i, Cyrtorchis chailluana.
No. 2494, Brassavola nodosa. No. 2495, Sanguine broughtonia.

1997, Sept. 18

2489-2492 A383 Set of 4 3.75 3.75
2493 A383 $1 Sheet of 9, #a.-i. 6.75 6.75

Souvenir Sheets

2494-2495 A383 $5 each 3.75 3.75

Nos. 2494-2495 each contain one 51x38mm stamp.

1997

Close-up portraits: No. 2496: a, Wearing tiara. b, Black dress. c, Blue dress. d, Denomination in black.
No. 2497: a, White collar. b, Sleeveless. c, Black dress, holding flowers. d, Blue collar, flowers.
No. 2498, Blue dress. No. 2499, White collar.

Sheets of 4

2496-2497 A384 $2 #a.-d., each 6.00 6.00

Souvenir Sheets

2498-2499 A384 $6 each 3.75 3.75

Diana, Princess of Wales (1961-97).

Sinking of RMS Titanic, 85th Anniv. — A385

Sections of the ship: a, 1st funnel. b, 2nd, 3rd funnels. c, 4th funnel. d, Upper decks. e, Stern.

1997, Nov. 5 Litho. *Perf. 14*

2500 A385 $1 Sheet of 5, #a.-e. 3.75 3.75

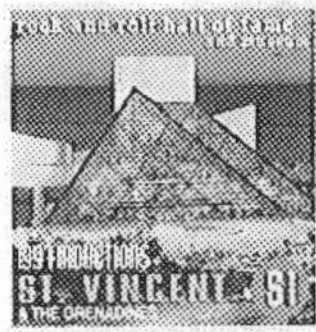

A386

A387

1997 Inductions, Rock & Roll Hall of Fame, Cleveland, OH: $1, Exterior view. $1.50, Stylized guitar, "the house that rock built."

1997, Nov. 5

2501 A386 $1 multicolored .75 .75
2502 A386 $1.50 multicolored 1.15 1.15

Nos. 2501-2502 were each issued in sheets of 8.

1997, Nov. 5

"The Doors" album covers: 90c, Morrison Hotel, 1970. 95c, Waiting for the Sun, 1968. $1, L.A. Woman, 1971. $1.10, The Soft Parade, 1969. $1.20, Strange Days, 1967. $1.50, The Doors, 1967.

2503-2508 A387 Set of 6 5.00 5.00

Nos. 2503-2508 were each issued in sheets of 8.

20th Cent. Artists — A388

Opera singers: No. 2509: a, Lily Pons (1904-76). b, Donizetti's "Lucia Di Lammermoor," Lily Pons. c, Bellini's "I Puritani," Maria Callas. d, Callas (1923-77). e, Beverly Sills (b. 1929). f, Donizetti's "Daughter of the Regiment," Sills. g, Schoenberg's "Erwartung," Jessye Norman. h, Norman (b.1945).
No. 2510: a, Enrico Caruso (1873-1921). b, Verdi's "Rigoletto," Caruso. c, "The Seven Hills of Rome," Mario Lanza. d, Lanza (1921-59). e, Luciano Pavarotti (b. 1935). f, Donizetti's "Elixer of Love," Pavarotti. g, Puccini's "Tosca," Placido Domingo. h, Domingo (b. 1941).
Artists, sculptures: No. 2511: a, Constantin Brancusi (1876-1957). b, "The New Born," Brancusi, 1920. c, "Four Elements," Alexander Calder, 1962. d, Calder (1898-1976). e, Isamu Noguchi (1904-88). f, "Dodge Fountain," Noguchi, 1975. g, "The Shuttlecock," Claes Oldenburg, 1994. h, Oldenburg (b. 1929).

1997, Nov. 5

Sheets of 8

2509-2511 A388 $1.10 #a.-h., each 6.50 6.50

Size: Nos. 2509b-2509c, 2509f-2509g, 2510b-2510c, 2510f-2510g, 2511b-2511c, 2511f-2511g, 53x38mm.

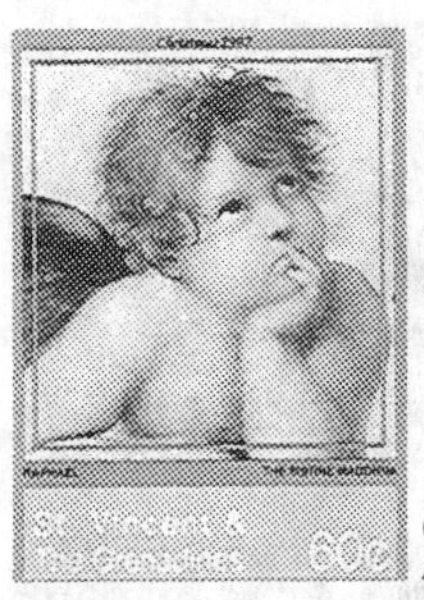

Christmas A389

Paintings (entire or details), or sculptures: 60c, The Sistine Madonna, by Raphael. 70c, Angel, by Edward Burne-Jones. 90c, Cupid, by Etienne-Maurice Flaconet. $1, Saint Michael, by Hubert Gerhard. $1.10, Apollo and the Horae, by Tiepolo. $2, Madonna in a Garland of Flowers, by Rubens and Bruegel the Elder.

No. 2518, The Sacrifice of Isaac, by Tiepolo, horiz. No. 2519, Madonna in a Garland of Flowers, by Rubens and Bruegel the Elder.

1997, Nov. 26
2512-2517 A389 Set of 6 6.25 6.25

Souvenir Sheets
2518-2519 A389 $5 each 3.75 3.75

New Year 1998 (Year of the Tiger) — A390

Stylized tigers, Chinese inscriptions within checkered squares: No. 2520: a, light brown & pale olive. b, tan & gray. c, pink & pale violet.
$2, yellow orange & pink.

1998 *Perf. 14½*
2520 A390 $1 Sheet of 3, #a.-c. 2.25 2.25

Souvenir Sheet
2521 A390 $2 multicolored 1.50 1.50

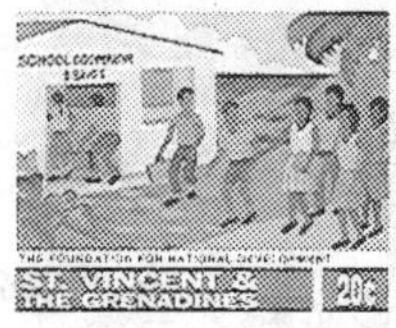

Cooperative Foundation for Natl. Development A391

Designs: 20c, Children going to shcool. 90c, People working in field, Credit Union office, vert. $1.10, Industry, ship at dock.

1998, Jan. 5 Litho. *Perf. 13½*
2522-2524 A391 Set of 3 2.10 2.10

Jazz Entertainers — A392

Designs: a, King Oliver. b, Louis Armstrong. c, Sidney Bechet. d, Nick Larocca. e, Louis Prima. f, Buddy Bolden.

1998, Feb. 2 *Perf. 14x13½*
2525 A392 $1 Sheet of 6, #a.-f. 4.50 4.50

1998 Winter Olympic Games, Nagano
A393 A394

Designs, horiz: 70c, Ice hockey. $1.10, Bobsled. $2, Pairs figure skating. $2, Skier, vert.

Medalists: No. 2530: a, Bjorn Daehlie. b, Gillis Grafstrom. c, Sonja Henie. d, Ingemar Stenmark. e, Christian Jagge. f, Tomas Gustafson. g, Johann Olav Koss. h, Thomas Wassberg.

Olympic rings in background: No. 2531: a, Downhill skier. b, Woman figure skater. c, Ski jumper. d, Speed skater. e, 4-Man bobsled team. f, Cross country country skier.

Olympic flame in background: No. 2532: a, Downhill skier. b, Bobsled. c, Ski jumper. d, Slalom skier. e, Luge. f, Biathlon.

No. 2533, Slalom skiing. No. 2534, Hockey player, horiz.

1998, Feb. 2 *Perf. 14*
2526-2529 A393 Set of 4 4.50 4.50
2530 A394 $1.50 Sheet of 8, #a.-h. 6.75 6.75

Sheets of 6
2531-2532 A393 $1.50 #a.-f., each 6.75 6.75

Souvenir Sheets
2533-2534 A393 $5 each 3.75 3.75

Butterflies A395

20c, Amarynthis meneria. 50c, Papillo polyxenes. 70c, Emesis fatima, vert. $1, Anartia amathea.

No. 2539, vert: a, Heliconius erato. b, Danaus plexippus. c, Papillo phorcas. d, Morpho pelaides. e, Pandoriana pandora. f, Basilarchia astyanax. g, Vanessa cardui. h, Colobura dirce. i, Heraclides cresphontes.

No. 2540, Colias eurytheme. No. 2541, Everes comyntas.

1998, Feb, 23 *Perf. 13½*
2535-2538 A395 Set of 4 1.80 1.80
2539 A395 $1 Sheet of 9, #a.-i. 6.75 6.75

Souvenir Sheets
2540-2541 A395 $6 each 4.50 4.50

Endangered Fauna — A396

50c, Anegada rock iguana. 70c, Jamaican swallowtail. 90c, Blossom bat. $1, Solenodon. $1.10, Hawksbill turtle. $2, West Indian whistling duck.

No. 2548: a, Roseate spoonbill. b, Golden swallow. c, Short-snouted spinner dolphin. d, Queen conch. e, West Indian manatee. f, Loggerhead turtle.

No. 2549: a, Magnificent frigatebird. b, Humpback whale. c, Southern dagger-tail. d, St. Lucia whiptail e, St. Lucia oriole. f, Green turtle.

No. 2550, St. Vincent parrot. No. 2551, Antiguan racer.

1998, Feb. 23 *Perf. 13*
2542-2547 A396 Set of 6 4.75 4.75

Sheets of 6
2548-2549 A396 $1.10 #a.-f., each 5.00 5.00

Souvenir Sheets
2550-2551 A396 $5 each 3.75 3.75

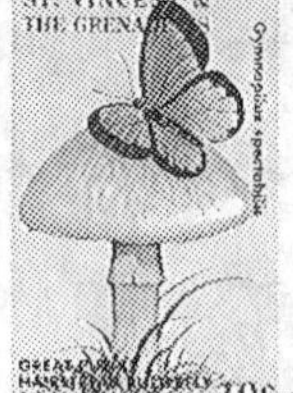

Mushrooms — A397

Designs: 10c, Gymnopilus spectabilis. 20c, Entoloma lividium. 70c, Pholiota flammans. 90c, Panaeolus semiovatus. $1, Stropharia rugosoannulata. $1.10, Tricholoma sulphureum.

No. 2558: a, Amanita caesarea. b, Amanita muscaria. c, Aminita ovoidea. d, Amanita phalloides. e, Amanitopsis inaurata. f, Amanitopsis vaginata. g, Psalliota campestris, alfalfa butterfly. h, Psalliota arvenis. i, Coprinus comatus.

No. 2559: a, Coprinus picaceus. b, Stropharia umbonatescens. c, Hebeloma crustuliniforme, figure-of-eight butterfly. d, Cortinarius collinitus. e, Cortinarius violaceus, common dotted butterfly. f, Cortinarius armillatus. g, Tricholoma aurantium. h, Russula virescens. i, Clitocybe infundibuliformis.

No. 2560, Hygrocybe conica. No. 2561, Amanita caesarea.

1998, Feb. 23 Litho. *Perf. 13½*
2552-2557 A397 Set of 6 3.00 3.00
2558 A397 $1 Sheet of 9, #a.-i. 6.75 6.75
2559 A397 $1.10 Sheet of 9, #a.-i. 7.50 7.50

Souvenir Sheets
2560-2561 A397 $6 each 4.50 4.50

Mickey Mouse, 70th Birthday — A398

Designs: 2c, Wake up, Mickey. 3c, Morning run. 4c, Getting ready. 5c, Eating breakfast. 10c, School "daze." 65c, Time out for play. $3, Volunteer worker. $4, A date with Minnie. $5, Ready for bed.

Weekly hi-lites from "Mickey Mouse Club," vert: a, The opening march. b, Monday, fun with music day. c, Tuesday, guest star day. d, Wednesday, anything can happen day. e, Thursday, circus day. f, Friday, talent round up day.

Mickey Mouse: No. 2572, Reading, vert. No. 2573, Playing piano, vert. No. 2574, Blowing trumpet. No. 2575, On the Internet, vert.

Perf. 14x13½, 13½x14

1998, Mar. 23 Litho.
2562-2570 A398 Set of 9 9.75 9.75
2571 A398 $1.10 Sheet of 6, #a.-f. 5.00 5.00

Souvenir Sheets
2572 A398 $5 multicolored 3.75 3.75
2573-2575 A398 $6 each 4.50 4.50

Winnie the Pooh — A399

Scenes from animated films: a, Pooh looking out open window. b, Eeyore, Kanga, Roo. c, Pooh getting honey from tree. d, Rabbit, Pooh stuck in entrance to Rabbit's house. e, Christopher Robin pulling Pooh from Rabbit's house, Owl. f, Piglet sweeping leaves. g, Pooh sleeping. h, Eeyore. i, Tigger on top of Pooh.

No. 2577, Tigger, Pooh, Piglet.

1998, Mar. 23 *Perf. 14x13½*
2576 A399 $1 Sheet of 9, #a.-i. 6.75 6.75

Souvenir Sheet
2577 A399 $6 multicolored 4.50 4.50

Dogs — A400

Designs: 70c, Australian terrier. 90c, Bull mastiff. $1.10, Pomeranian. $2, Dandie dinmont terrier.

No. 2582, horiz: a, Tyrolean hunting dog. b, Papillon. c, Fox terriers. d, Bernese mountain dog. e, King Charles spaniel. f, German shepherd.

No. 2583, horiz: a, Beagle. b, German shepherd. c, Pointer. d, Vizsla. e, Bulldog. f, Shetland sheepdogs.

No. 2584, Scottish terrier, wooden deck, grass. No. 2585, Scottish terrier, grass, trees.

1998, Apr. 21 *Perf. 14*
2578-2581 A400 Set of 4 3.50 3.50

Sheets of 6
2582-2583 A400 $1.10 #a.-f., each 5.00 5.00

Souvenir Sheets
2584-2585 A400 $6 each 4.50 4.50

SEMI-POSTAL STAMPS

Catalogue values for unused stamps in this section are for Never Hinged items.

Map Type of 1977-78 Overprinted: "SOUFRIERE / RELIEF / FUND 1979" and New Values, "10c+5c" etc.

Litho. and Typo.

1979 Wmk. 373 *Perf. 14½x14*
B1 A76 10c + 5c multi .15 .15
B2 A76 50c + 25c multi .35 .35
B3 A76 $1 + 50c multi .70 .70
B4 A76 $2 + $1 multi 1.40 1.40
Nos. B1-B4 (4) 2.60 2.60

The surtax was for victims of the eruption of Mt. Soufrière.

Nos. 604-607 Surcharged: "HURRICANE / RELIEF / 50c"

1980, Aug. 7 Litho. *Perf. 13½*
B5 A90 10c + 50c multi .30 .30
B6 A90 60c + 50c multi .52 .52
B7 A90 80c + 50c multi .65 .65
B8 A90 $2.50 + 50c multi 1.50 1.50
Nos. B5-B8 (4) 2.97 2.97

Surtax was for victims of Hurricane Allen.

Nos. 1224-1226 Surcharged "CALIF EARTHQUAKE RELIEF" on 1 or 2 Lines and "+10c"

1989, Nov. 17 Litho. *Perf. 13½x14*
B9 Sheet of 9 4.50 4.50
a.-i. A174 60c +10c #1224a-1224i .50 .50
B10 Sheet of 9 4.50 4.50
a.-i. A174 60c +10c #1225a-1225i .50 .50
B11 Sheet of 9 4.50 4.50
a.-i. A175 60c +10c #1226a-1226i .50 .50

WAR TAX STAMPS

No. 105 Overprinted **WAR STAMP.**

Type I - Words 2 to 2½mm apart.
Type II - Words 1½mm apart.
Type III - Words 3½mm apart.

1916 Wmk. 3 *Perf. 14*
MR1 A17 1p car, type III 2.00 3.00
a. Double ovpt., type III 175.00 200.00
b. 1p carmine, type I 2.25 1.75
c. Comma after "STAMP", type I 7.50 10.00
d. Double overprint, type I 150.00 150.00
e. 1p carmine, type II 80.00 80.00

Overprinted **WAR STAMP**

MR2 A17 1p carmine .25 .25

OFFICIAL STAMPS

Catalogue values for unused stamps in this section are for Never Hinged items.

Nos. 627-632 Ovptd. "OFFICIAL"

1982, Nov. Litho. *Perf. 14*

O1	A94a	60c Couple, Isabella	.30	.30
O2	A94b	60c Couple	.30	.30
O3	A94a	$2.50 Couple, Alberta	.80	.80
O4	A94b	$2.50 Couple	1.25	1.25
O5	A94a	$4 Couple, Britannia	1.50	1.50
O6	A94b	$4 Couple	1.75	1.75
		Nos. O1-O6 (6)	5.90	5.90

ST. VINCENT GRENADINES

sānt 'vin(t)-sənt grə-'nā-də

LOCATION — Group of islands south of St. Vincent
CAPITAL — None

St. Vincent's portion of the Grenadines includes Bequia, Canouan, Mustique, Union and a number of smaller islands.

Catalogue values for unused stamps in this area are for Never Hinged items.

All stamps are a type of St. Vincent unless otherwise noted or illustrated.

See St. Vincent Nos. 324-329a for six stamps and a souvenir sheet issued in 1971 inscribed "The Grenadines of St. Vincent."

Princess Anne's Wedding Issue

Common Design Type

1973, Nov. 14 Litho. *Perf. 14*

1	CD325	25c green & multi	.15	.15
2	CD325	$1 orange brn & multi	.50	.50

Bird Type of 1970 and St. Vincent Nos. 281a-285a, 287a-289a Overprinted

GRENADINES OF
a

GRENADINES OF
b

1974 Photo. Wmk. 314 *Perf. 14*

3	A36(a)	1c multicolored	.15	.15
4	A36(a)	2c multicolored	.15	.15
5	A36(b)	2c multicolored	.60	.60
6	A36(a)	3c multicolored	.15	.15
7	A36(b)	3c multicolored	.90	.90
8	A36(a)	4c multicolored	.15	.15
9	A36(a)	5c multicolored	.15	.15
10	A36(a)	6c multicolored	.15	.15
11	A36(a)	8c multicolored	.15	.15
12	A36(a)	10c multicolored	.15	.15
13	A36(a)	12c multicolored	.15	.15
14	A36(a)	20c multicolored	.25	.25
15	A36(a)	25c multicolored	.25	.25
16	A36(a)	50c multicolored	.50	.50
17	A36(a)	$1 multicolored	1.00	1.00
18	A36(a)	$2.50 multicolored	2.50	2.50
19	A36(a)	$5 multicolored	6.00	6.00
		Nos. 3-19 (17)	13.35	13.35

Nos. 8-9, 12-13, 17-18 vert.
Issue dates: #5, 7, June 7. Others, Apr. 24.

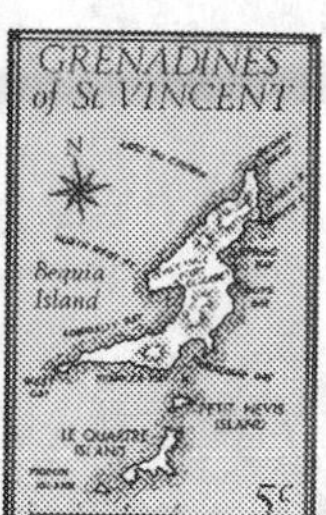

Maps of Islands — G1

Perf. 13x12½

1974, May 9 Litho. Wmk. 314

20	G1	5c Bequia	.15	.15
21	G1	15c Prune	.15	.15
22	G1	20c Mayreau	.15	.15
23	G1	30c Mustique	.15	.15
24	G1	40c Union	.15	.15
24A	G1	$1 Canouan	.30	.30
		Set value	.75	.75

No. 20 has no inscription at bottom. No. 84 is dated "1976."

See Nos. 84-111.

UPU Type of 1974

2c, Arrows circling UPU emblem. 15c, Post horn, globe. 40c, Target over map of islands, hand canceler. $1, Goode's map projection.

1974, July 25 Litho. *Perf. 14½*

25	A56	2c multicolored	.15	.15
26	A56	15c multicolored	.15	.15
27	A56	40c multicolored	.15	.15
28	A56	$1 multicolored	.40	.40
		Set value	.60	.60

Bequia Island G2

Designs: 5c, Boat building. 30c, Careening at Port Elizabeth. 35c, Admiralty Bay. $1, Fishing Boat Race.

1974

29	G2	5c multicolored	.15	.15
30	G2	30c multicolored	.15	.15
31	G2	35c multicolored	.15	.15
32	G2	$1 multicolored	.35	.35
		Set value	.65	.65

Shells — G3

Designs: 1c, Atlantic thorny oyster. 2c, Zigzag scallop. 3c, Reticulated helmet. 4c, Music volute. 5c, Amber pen shell. 6c, Angular triton. 8c, Flame helmet. 10c, Caribbean olive. 12c, Common sundial. 15c, Glory of the atlantic cone. 20c, Flame auger. 25c King venus. 35c. Long-spined star-shell. 45c, Speckled tellin. 50c, Rooster tail conch. $1, Green star-shell. $2.50, Incomparable cone. $5, Rough file clam. $10, Measled cowrie.

1974-76 Wmk. 373

33	G3	1c multicolored	.15	.15
34	G3	2c multicolored	.15	.15
35	G3	3c multicolored	.15	.15
36	G3	4c multicolored	.15	.15
37	G3	5c multicolored	.15	.15
38	G3	6c multicolored	.15	.15
39	G3	8c multicolored	.15	.15
40	G3	10c multicolored	.15	.15
41	G3	12c multicolored	.15	.15
42	G3	15c multicolored	.15	.15
43	G3	20c multicolored	.20	.20
44	G3	25c multicolored	.25	.25
45	G3	35c multicolored	.35	.35
46	G3	45c multicolored	.45	.45
47	G3	50c multicolored	.50	.50
48	G3	$1 multicolored	1.00	1.00
49	G3	$2.50 multicolored	2.50	2.50
50	G3	$5 multicolored	5.00	5.00
51	G3	$10 multicolored	10.00	10.00
		Nos. 33-51 (19)	21.75	21.75

Issued: #33-50, 11/27/74; #51, 7/12/76.
#36-40, 43, 45, 47-48, exist dated "1976," #40, 42-45, 49-50 dated "1977."

Churchill Type

Designs (Churchill as): 5c, Prime Minister. 40c, Lord Warden of the Cinque Ports. 50c, First Lord of the Admiralty. $1, Royal Air Force officer.

1974, Nov. 28

52	A58	5c multicolored	.15	.15
53	A58	40c multicolored	.15	.15
54	A58	50c multicolored	.15	.15
55	A58	$1 multicolored	.30	.30
		Set value	.60	.60

Mustique Island G4

1975, Feb. 27 Wmk. 373

56	G4	5c Cotton House	.15	.15
57	G4	35c Blue Waters, Endeavour	.15	.15
58	G4	45c Endeavour Bay	.15	.15
59	G4	$1 Gelliceaux Bay	.35	.35
		Set value	.65	.65

Butterflies G5

1975, May 15 *Perf. 14*

60	G5	3c Soldier martinique	.15	.15
61	G5	5c Silver-spotted flambeau	.15	.15
62	G5	35c Gold rim	.90	.90
63	G5	45c Bright blue, Donkey's eye	1.10	1.10
64	G5	$1 Biscuit	2.50	2.50
		Nos. 60-64 (5)	4.80	4.80

Views of Petit St. Vincent G6

1975, July 24 *Perf. 14½*

65	G6	5c Resort pavilion	.15	.15
66	G6	35c Harbor	.15	.15
67	G6	45c Jetty	.15	.15
68	G6	$1 Sailing in coral lagoon	.35	.35
		Set value	.65	.65

Christmas G7

Island churches: 5c, Ecumenical Church, Mustique. 25c, Catholic Church, Union. 50c, Catholic Church, Bequia. $1, Anglican Church, Bequia.

1975, Nov. 20 Wmk. 314

69	G7	5c multicolored	.15	.15
70	G7	25c multicolored	.15	.15
71	G7	50c multicolored	.15	.15
72	G7	$1 multicolored	.30	.30
		Set value	.55	.55

Union Island G8

1976, Feb. 26 Wmk. 373 *Perf. 13½*

73	G8	5c Sunset	.15	.15
74	G8	35c Customs and post office	.15	.15
75	G8	45c Anglican Church	.15	.15
76	G8	$1 Mail boat	.30	.30
		Set value	.55	.55

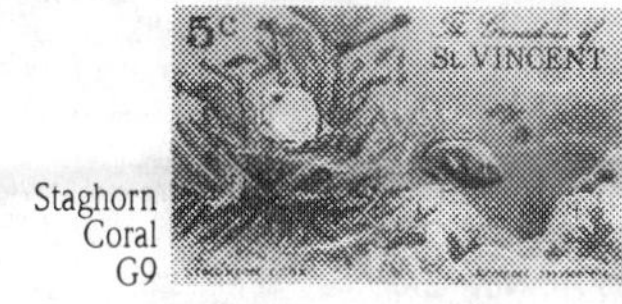

Staghorn Coral G9

1976, May 13 *Perf. 14½*

77	G9	5c shown	.15	.15
78	G9	35c Elkhorn coral	.25	.25
79	G9	45c Pillar coral	.30	.30
80	G9	$1 Brain coral	.70	.70
		Nos. 77-80 (4)	1.40	1.40

US Bicentennial Coins — G10

1976, July 15 *Perf. 13½*

81	G10	25c Washington quarter	.15	.15
82	G10	50c Kennedy half dollar	.15	.15
83	G10	$1 Eisenhower dollar	.30	.30
		Nos. 81-83 (3)	.60	.60

St. Vincent Grenadines Map Type of 1974

Bequia Island

1976, Sept. 23 Litho. *Perf. 14*

84	G1	5c grn, brt grn & blk	.15	.15
85	G1	10c multicolored	.15	.15
	a.	Bklt. pane of 3 (2 #84, 85)	.15	.15
86	G1	35c multicolored	.20	.20
	a.	Bklt. pane of 3 (2 #85, 86)	.35	.35
87	G1	45c multicolored	.25	.25
	a.	Bklt. pane of 3 (#84, 85, 87)	.40	.40
	b.	Bklt. pane of 3 (2 #86, 87)	.75	.75
		Set value	.60	.60

For previous 5c see No. 20.

Canouan Island

1976, Sept. 23

88	G1	5c multicolored	.15	.15
89	G1	10c multicolored	.15	.15
	a.	Bklt. pane of 3 (2 #88, 89)	.15	.15
90	G1	35c multicolored	.20	.20
	a.	Bklt. pane of 3 (2 #89, 90)	.35	.35
91	G1	45c multicolored	.25	.25
	a.	Bklt. pane of 3 (#88-89, 91)	.40	.40
	b.	Bklt. pane of 3 (2 #90, 91)	.75	.75
		Set value	.60	.60

Mayreau Island

1976, Sept. 23

92	G1	5c multicolored	.15	.15
93	G1	10c multicolored	.15	.15
	a.	Bklt. pane of 3 (2 #92, 93)	.15	.15
94	G1	35c multicolored	.20	.20
	a.	Bklt. pane of 3 (2 #93, 94)	.35	.35
95	G1	45c multicolored	.25	.25
	a.	Bklt. pane of 3 (#92-93, 95)	.40	.40
	b.	Bklt. pane of 3 (2 #94, 95)	.75	.75
		Set value	.60	.60

Mustique Island

1976, Sept. 23

96	G1	5c multicolored	.15	.15
97	G1	10c multicolored	.15	.15
	a.	Bklt. pane of 3 (2 #96, 97)	.15	.15
98	G1	35c multicolored	.20	.20
	a.	Bklt. pane of 3 (2 #97, 98)	.35	.35
99	G1	45c multicolored	.25	.25
	a.	Bklt. pane of 3 (#96-97, 99)	.40	.40
	b.	Bklt. pane of 3 (2 #98, 99)	.75	.75
		Set value	.60	.60

Petit St. Vincent

1976, Sept. 23

100	G1	5c multicolored	.15	.15
101	G1	10c multicolored	.15	.15
	a.	Bklt. pane of 3 (2 #100, 101)	.15	.15
102	G1	35c multicolored	.20	.20
	a.	Bklt. pane of 3 (2 #101, 102)	.35	.35
103	G1	45c multicolored	.25	.25
	a.	Bklt. pane of 3 (#100-101, 103)	.40	.40
	b.	Bklt. pane of 3 (2 #102, 103)	.75	.75
		Set value	.60	.60

Prune Island

1976, Sept. 23

104	G1	5c multicolored	.15	.15
105	G1	10c multicolored	.15	.15
	a.	Bklt. pane of 3 (2 #104, 105)	.15	.15
106	G1	35c multicolored	.20	.20
	a.	Bklt. pane of 3 (2 #105, 106)	.35	.35
107	G1	45c multicolored	.25	.25
	a.	Bklt. pane of 3 (#104-105, 107)	.40	.40
	b.	Bklt. pane of 3 (2 #106, 107)	.75	.75
		Set value	.60	.60

Union Island

1976, Sept. 23

108	G1	5c multicolored	.15	.15
109	G1	10c multicolored	.15	.15
	a.	Bklt. pane of 3 (2 #108, 109)	.15	.15
110	G1	35c multicolored	.20	.20
	a.	Bklt. pane of 3 (2 #109, 110)	.35	.35
111	G1	45c multicolored	.25	.25
	a.	Bklt. pane of 3 (#108-109, 111)	.40	.40
	b.	Bklt. pane of 3 (2 #110, 111)	.75	.75
		Set value	.60	.60

Mayreau Island G11

Designs: 5c, Station Hill school, post office. 35c, Church at Old Wall. 45c, Cruiser at anchor, La Souciere. $1, Saline Bay.

1976, Dec. 2 *Perf. 14½*

112 G11 5c multicolored .15 .15
113 G11 35c multicolored .15 .15
114 G11 45c multicolored .15 .15
115 G11 $1 multicolored .30 .30
Set value .55 .55

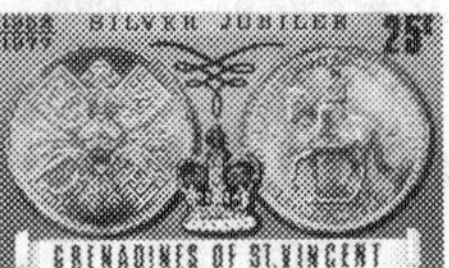

Queen Elizabeth II, Silver Jubilee G12

Coins: 25c, Coronation Crown. 50c, Silver Wedding Crown. $1, Silver Jubilee Crown.

1977, Mar. 3

116 G12 25c multicolored .15 .15
117 G12 50c multicolored .15 .15
118 G12 $1 multicolored .25 .25
Set value .45 .45

Fiddler Crab G13

1977, May 19

119 G13 5c shown .15 .15
120 G13 35c Ghost crab .20 .20
121 G13 50c Blue crab .30 .30
122 G13 $1.25 Spiny lobster .70 .70
Nos. 119-122 (4) 1.35 1.35

Prune Island G14

1977, Aug. 25

123 G14 5c Snorkel diving .15 .15
124 G14 35c Palm Island Resort .15 .15
125 G14 45c Casuarina Beach .15 .15
126 G14 $1 Palm Island Beach Club .30 .30
Set value .55 .55

Map Type of 1977 Overprinted

SILVER JUBILEE 1952-1977

ROYAL VISIT MUSTIQUE

30TH OCTOBER 1977

Perf. 14½x14

1977, Oct. 31 **Wmk. 314**

127 A76 40c multicolored (R) .15 .15
128 A76 $2 multicolored (B) .60 .60

Canouan Island G15

1977, Dec. 8 **Wmk. 373** *Perf. 14½*

129 G15 5c Clinic, Charlestown .15 .15
130 G15 35c Town jetty, Charlestown .15 .15
131 G15 45c Mailboat, Charlestown .15 .15
132 G15 $1 Grand Bay .35 .35
Set value .65 .65

Birds and Eggs G16

1978, May 11 *Perf. 13x12*

133 G16 1c Tropical Mockingbird .15 .15
134 G16 2c Mangrove cuckoo .15 .15
135 G16 3c Osprey .15 .15
136 G16 4c Smooth bellied ani .15 .15
137 G16 5c House wren .15 .15
138 G16 6c Bananaquit .15 .15
139 G16 8c Carib grackle .15 .15
140 G16 10c Yellow bellied elaenia .15 .15
141 G16 12c Collared plover .15 .15
142 G16 15c Cattle egret .15 .15
143 G16 20c Red footed booby .15 .15
144 G16 25c Red-billed tropic bird .15 .15
145 G16 40c Royal tern .25 .25
146 G16 50c Rusty tailed flycatcher .35 .35
147 G16 80c Purple gallinule .55 .55
148 G16 $1 Broad winged hawk .70 .70
149 G16 $2 Common ground dove 1.40 1.40
150 G16 $3 Laughing gull 2.00 2.00
151 G16 $5 Brown noddy 3.50 3.50
152 G16 $10 Grey kingbird 7.25 7.25
Nos. 133-152 (20) 17.80 17.80

#139, 143, 149 exist imprinted "1979," #137-138, 140, 142, 144 imprinted "1980."

Nos. 147-148 imprinted "1979" are from No. 175a. Nos. 145-146, 150 imprinted "1980" are from No. 189a.

For surcharge see No. 266.

Elizabeth II Coronation Anniv. Type

Cathedrals.

1978, June 2 *Perf. 13½*

153 A78 5c Worcester .15 .15
154 A78 40c Coventry .15 .15
155 A78 $1 Winchester .15 .15
156 A78 $3 Chester .40 .40
a. Souv. sheet of 4, #153-156, perf. 14 .70 .70
Set value .60 .60

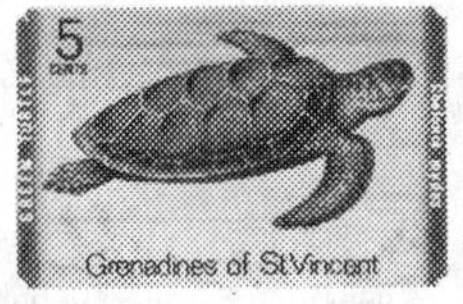

Turtles G17

1978, July 20 *Perf. 14*

157 G17 5c Green turtle .15 .15
158 G17 40c Hawksbill turtle .15 .15
159 G17 50c Leatherback turtle .25 .25
160 G17 $1.25 Loggerhead turtle .65 .65
Nos. 157-160 (4) 1.20 1.20

Christmas G18

Christmas scenes and verses from the carol "We Three Kings of Orient Are".

1978, Nov. 2

161 G18 5c Three kings following star .15 .15
162 G18 10c Gold .15 .15
163 G18 25c Frankincense .15 .15
164 G18 50c Myrrh .15 .15
165 G18 $2 With infant Jesus .35 .35
a. Souvenir sheet of 5 + label, #161-165 .80 .80
Set value .55 .55

Sailing Yachts — G19

1979

166 G19 5c multicolored .15 .15
167 G19 40c multi, diff. .15 .15
168 G19 50c multi, diff. .20 .20
169 G19 $2 multi, diff. .75 .75
Nos. 166-169 (4) 1.25 1.25

Wildlife Type of 1980

1979, Mar. 8 *Perf. 14½*

170 A91 20c Green iguana .15 .15
171 A91 40c Manicou .15 .15
172 A91 $2 Red-legged tortoise .85 .85
Nos. 170-172 (3) 1.15 1.15

Sir Rowland Hill Type of 1979

Designs: 80c, Sir Rowland Hill. $1, Great Britain Types A1 and A5 with "A10" (Kingstown, St. Vincent) cancel. $2, St. Vincent #41 & 43 with Bequia cancel.

1979, May 21 *Perf. 13x12*

173 A83 80c multicolored .15 .15
174 A83 $1 multicolored .25 .25
175 A83 $2 multicolored .40 .40
a. Souv. sheet of 6, #173-175, 147-149 1.50 1.50
Nos. 173-175 (3) .80 .80

IYC Type of 1979

Children and IYC emblem: 6c, Boy. 40c, Girl. $1, Boy, diff. $3, Girl and boy.

1979, Oct. 24 *Perf. 14x13½*

176 A82 6c multicolored .15 .15
177 A82 40c multicolored .15 .15
178 A82 $1 multitolored .15 .15
179 A82 $3 multicolored .50 .50
Set value .75 .75

Independence Type of 1979

Designs: 5c, National flag, Ixora salici-folia. 40c, House of Assembly, Ixora odorata. $1, Prime Minister R. Milton Cato, Ixora jayanica.

1979, Oct. 27 *Perf. 12½x12*

180 A85 5c multicolored .15 .15
181 A85 40c multicolored .15 .15
182 A85 $1 multicolored .35 .35
Set value .50 .50

Printed se-tenant with label inscribed "Independence of St. Vincent and the Grenadines."

False Killer Whale G20

1979, Jan. 25 *Perf. 14*

183 G20 10c shown .15 .15
184 G20 50c Spinner dolphin .45 .45
185 G20 90c Bottle nosed dolphin .75 .75
186 G20 $2 Blackfish 1.75 1.75
Nos. 183-186 (4) 3.10 3.10

London '80 Type

1980, Apr. 24 *Perf. 13x12*

187 A88 40c Queen Elizabeth II .15 .15
188 A88 50c St. Vincent #227 .15 .15
189 A88 $3 #1-2 .60 .60
a. Souvenir sheet of 6, #187-189, 145-146, 150 2.75 2.75
Set value .75 .75

Olympics Type of 1980

1980, Aug. 7 *Perf. 13½*

190 A90 25c Running .15 .15
191 A90 50c Sailing .15 .15
192 A90 $1 Long jump .20 .20
193 A90 $2 Swimming .40 .40
Nos. 190-193 (4) .90 .90

Christmas — G21

Scenes and verse from the carol "De Borning Day."

1980, Nov. 13 *Perf. 14*

194 G21 5c multicolored .15 .15
195 G21 50c multicolored .15 .15
196 G21 60c multicolored .15 .15
197 G21 $1 multicolored .15 .15
198 G21 $2 multicolored .30 .30
a. Souvenir sheet of 5 + label, #194-198 1.00 1.00
Set value .65 .65

Bequia Island G22

1981, Feb. 19 *Perf. 14½*

199 G22 50c P.O., Port Elizabeth .15 .15
200 G22 60c Moonhole .15 .15
201 G22 $1.50 Fishing boats, Admiralty Bay .35 .35
202 G22 $2 Friendship Rose at jetty .45 .45
Nos. 199-202 (4) 1.10 1.10

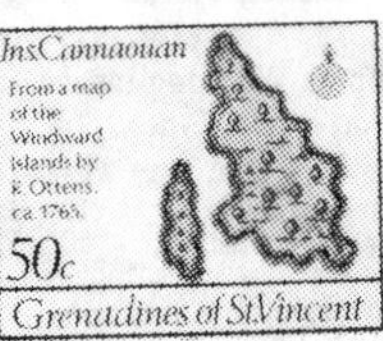

Map by R. Ottens, c. 1765 — G23

Maps: Nos. 204, 206 by J. Parsons, 1861. No. 208, by T. Jefferys, 1763.

1981, Apr. 2 *Perf. 14*

203 G23 50c Ins. Cannaouan .20 .20
204 G23 50c Cannouan Island .20 .20
a. Pair, #203-204 .40 .40
205 G23 60c Ins. Moustiques .30 .30
206 G23 60c Mustique Island .30 .30
a. Pair, #205-206 .60 .60
207 G23 $2 Ins. Bequia .85 .85
208 G23 $2 Bequia Island .85 .85
a. Pair, #207-208 1.75 1.75
Nos. 203-208 (6) 2.70 2.70

Royal Wedding Types

1981, July 17 **Wmk. 380**

209 A94a 50c Couple, the Mary .15 .15
a. Booklet pane of 4, perf. 12 .60 .60
210 A94b 50c Couple .15 .15
211 A94a $3 Couple, the Alexandra .90 .90
212 A94b $3 like #210 .90 .90
a. Booklet pane of 2, perf. 12 2.00 2.00
213 A94a $3.50 Couple, the Brittania 1.10 1.10
214 A94b $3.50 like #210 1.10 1.10
Nos. 209-214 (6) 4.30 4.30

Each denomination issued in sheets of 7 (6 type A94a, 1 type A94b).

For surcharges see Nos. 507-508.

Souvenir Sheet

1981 *Perf. 12*

215 A94b $5 like #210 1.10 1.10

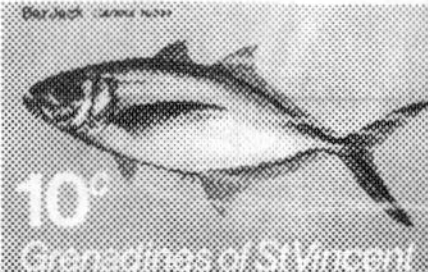

Bar Jack G25

1981, Oct. 9 Wmk. 373 *Perf. 14*
218 G25 10c shown .15 .15
219 G25 50c Tarpon .30 .30
220 G25 60c Cobia .40 .40
221 G25 $2 Blue marlin 1.50 1.50
Nos. 218-221 (4) 2.35 2.35

Ships G26

1982, Jan. 28 *Perf. 14x13½*
222 G26 1c Experiment .15 .15
223 G26 3c Lady Nelson .15 .15
224 G26 5c Daisy .15 .15
225 G26 6c Carib canoe .15 .15
226 G26 10c Hairoun Star .15 .15
227 G26 15c Jupiter .15 .15
228 G26 20c Christina .15 .15
229 G26 25c Orinoco .15 .15
230 G26 30c Lively .20 .20
231 G26 50c Alabama .30 .30
232 G26 60c Denmark .40 .40
233 G26 75c Santa Maria .50 .50
234 G26 $1 Baffin .70 .70
235 G26 $2 QE 2 1.40 1.40
236 G26 $3 Britannia 2.00 2.00
237 G26 $5 Geeststar 3.50 3.50
238 G26 $10 Grenadines Star 6.75 6.75
Nos. 222-238 (17) 16.95 16.95

For overprint see No. 509.

G27 G29

1982, Apr. 5 *Perf. 14*
239 G27 10c Prickly pear fruit .15 .15
240 G27 50c Flower buds .35 .35
241 G27 $1 Flower .65 .65
242 G27 $2 Cactus 1.40 1.40
Nos. 239-242 (4) 2.55 2.55

Princess Diana Type of Kiribati

1982, July 1 Wmk. 380 *Perf. 14*
243 A99a 50c Anne Neville .15 .15
244 A99a 60c Arms of Anne Neville .15 .15
245 A99a $6 Diana, Princess of Wales .85 .85
Nos. 243-245 (3) 1.15 1.15

For overprints see Nos. 248-262.

1982, July 1 Wmk. 373 *Perf. 14½*
246 G29 $1.50 Old, new uniforms .60 .60
247 G29 $2.50 Lord Baden-Powell 1.00 1.00

75th anniversary of Boy Scouts.

Nos. 243-245 Ovptd. "ROYAL BABY / BEQUIA"

1982, July 19 Wmk. 380 *Perf. 14*
248 A99a 50c multicolored .15 .15
249 A99a 60c multicolored .15 .15
250 A99a $6 multicolored .85 .85
Nos. 248-250 (3) 1.15 1.15

"ROYAL BABY / CANOUAN"

1982, July 19
251 A99a 50c multicolored .15 .15
252 A99a 60c multicolored .15 .15
253 A99a $6 multicolored .85 .85
Nos. 251-253 (3) 1.15 1.15

"ROYAL BABY / MAYREAU"

1982, July 19
254 A99a 50c multicolored .15 .15
255 A99a 60c multicolored .15 .15
256 A99a $6 multicolored .85 .85
Nos. 254-256 (3) 1.15 1.15

"ROYAL BABY / MUSTIQUE"

1982, July 19
257 A99a 50c multicolored .15 .15
258 A99a 60c multicolored .15 .15
259 A99a $6 multicolored .85 .85
Nos. 257-259 (3) 1.15 1.15

"ROYAL BABY / UNION"

1982, July 19
260 A99a 50c multicolored .15 .15
261 A99a 60c multicolored .15 .15
262 A99a $6 multicolored .85 .85
Nos. 260-262 (3) 1.15 1.15

Christmas Type of 1981

1982, Nov. 18 *Perf. 13½*
263 A97 10c Mary and Joseph at inn .15 .15
264 A97 $1.50 Animals of stable .45 .45
265 A97 $2.50 Nativity .75 .75
a. Souvenir sheet of 3, #263-265 1.40 1.40
Nos. 263-265 (3) 1.35 1.35

No. 146 Surcharged

45¢

1983, Apr. 26 Wmk. 373 *Perf. 13x12*
266 G16 45c on 50c multicolored .35 .35

Union Island G30

1983, May 12 *Perf. 13½*
267 G30 50c Power Station, Clifton .15 .15
268 G30 60c Sunrise, Clifton Harbor .20 .20
269 G30 $1.50 School, Ashton .45 .45
270 G30 $2 Frigate Rock, Conch Shell Beach .65 .65
Nos. 267-270 (4) 1.45 1.45

Treaty of Versailles, Bicent. — G31

1983, Sept. 15 *Perf. 14½x14*
271 G31 45c British warship .20 .20
272 G31 60c American warship .30 .30
273 G31 $1.50 US troops, flag .65 .65
274 G31 $2 British troops in battle .95 .95
Nos. 271-274 (4) 2.10 2.10

200 Years of Manned Flight G32

Designs: 45c, Montgolfier balloon 1783, vert. 60c, Ayres Turbo-thrush Commander. $1.50, Lebaudy "1" dirigible. $2, Space shuttle Columbia.

1983, Sept. 15 *Perf. 14*
275 G32 45c multicolored .15 .15
276 G32 60c multicolored .20 .20
277 G32 $1.50 multicolored .45 .45
278 G32 $2 multicolored .65 .65
a. Souvenir sheet of 4, #275-278 1.75 1.75
Nos. 275-278 (4) 1.45 1.45

British Monarch Types of 1984

1983, Oct. 25 Unwmk. *Perf. 12½*
279 A110 60c Arms of Henry VIII .15 .15
280 A111 60c Henry VIII .15 .15
281 A110 60c Arms of James I .15 .15
282 A111 60c James I .15 .15
283 A110 75c Henry VIII .20 .20
284 A111 75c Hampton Court .20 .20
285 A110 75c James I .20 .20
286 A111 75c Edinburgh Castle .20 .20
287 A110 $2.50 Mary Rose .60 .60
288 A111 $2.50 Henry VIII, Portsmouth harbor .60 .60
289 A110 $2.50 Gunpowder Plot .60 .60
290 A111 $2.50 James I & Gunpowder Plot .60 .60
Nos. 279-290 (12) 3.80 3.80

Stamps of same denomination se-tenant.

Old Coinage — G33

1983, Dec. 1 Wmk. 373 *Perf. 14*
291 G33 20c Quarter and half dollar, 1797 .15 .15
292 G33 45c Nine bitts, 1811-14 .20 .20
293 G33 75c Six and twelve bitts, 1811-14 .30 .30
294 G33 $3 Sixty six shillings, 1798 1.10 1.10
Nos. 291-294 (4) 1.75 1.75

Locomotives Type of 1985

1984-87 Litho. Unwmk. *Perf. 12½*
Pairs, Type A120
295 1c 1948 Class C62, Japan .15 .15
296 1c 1898 P.L.M. Grosse C, France .15 .15
297 5c 1892 Class D13, US .15 .15
298 5c 1903 Class V, UK .15 .15
299 10c 1980 Class 253, UK .15 .15
300 10c 1968 Class 581, Japan .15 .15
301 10c 1874 1001 Class, UK .15 .15
302 10c 1977 Class 142, East Germany .15 .15
303 15c 1899 T-9 Class, UK .15 .15
304 15c 1932 Class C12, Japan .15 .15
305 15c 1897 Class T15, Germany .15 .15
306 20c 1808 Catch-me-who-can, UK .15 .15
307 35c 1900 Claud Hamilton Class, UK .25 .25
308 35c 1948 Class E10, Japan .25 .25
309 35c 1937 Coronation Class, UK .25 .25
310 40c 1936 Class 231, Algeria .30 .30
311 40c 1927 Class 4P, UK .30 .30
312 40c 1979 Class 120, West Germany .30 .30
313 45c 1941 Class J, US .30 .30
314 45c 1900 Class 13, UK .30 .30
315 50c 1913 Slieve Gullion Class S, UK .35 .35
316 50c 1929 Class A3, UK .35 .35
317 50c 1954 Class X, Australia .35 .35
318 60c 1895 Class D16, US .45 .45
319 60c 1904 J. B. Earle, UK .45 .45
320 60c 1879 Halesworth, UK .45 .45
321 60c 1930 Class V1, UK .45 .45
322 60c 1986 Class 59, UK .45 .45
323 70c 1935 Class E18, Germany .55 .55
324 75c 1923 Class D50, Japan .60 .60
325 75c 1859 Problem Class, UK .60 .60
326 75c 1958 Class 40, UK .60 .60
327 75c 1875 Class A, US .60 .60
328 $1 1907 Star Class, British .85 .85
329 $1 1898 Lyn, UK .85 .85
330 $1 1961 Western Class, UK .85 .85
331 $1 1958 Warship Class 42, UK .85 .85
332 $1 1831 Samson Type, US .85 .85
333 $1.20 1854 Hayes, US .90 .90
334 $1.25 1902 Class P-69, US .95 .95
335 $1.50 1865 Talyllyn, UK 1.25 1.25
336 $1.50 1899 Drummond's Bug, UK 1.25 1.25
337 $1.50 1913 Class 60-3 Shay, US 1.25 1.25
338 $1.50 1938 Class H1-d, Canada 1.25 1.25
339 $2 1890 Class 2120, Japan 1.60 1.60
340 $2 1951 Clan Class, UK 1.60 1.60
341 $2 1934 Pioneer Zephyr, US 1.60 1.60
342 $2.50 1948 Blue Peter, UK 2.00 2.00
343 $2.50 1874 Class Beattie Well Tank, UK 2.00 2.00
344 $3 1906 Cardean, UK 2.25 2.25
345 $3 1840 Fire Fly, UK 2.25 2.25
a. Souvenir sheet of 4, #324, 345 4.50
346 $3 1884 Class 1800, Japan 2.25 2.25
Nos. 295-346 (52) 36.95 36.95

Issued: #297, 299, 303, 307, 313, 318, 328, 342, 3/15/84; #295, 298, 296, 308, 319, 329, 335, 344, 10/9/84; #296, 304, 324, 345, 1/31/85; #300, 310, 315, 343, 5/17/85; #309, 323, 333, 339, 9/16/85; #305, 314, 320, 325, 330, 336, 340, 346, 3/14/86; #301, 311, 316, 321, 326, 331, 334, 337, 5/5/87; #302, 312, 3317, 322, 327, 332, 338, 341, 8/26/87.

Spotted Eagle Ray — G34

Wmk. 380
1984, Apr. 26 Litho. *Perf. 14*
399 G34 45c shown .15 .15
400 G34 60c Queen trigger fish .20 .20
401 G34 $1.50 White spotted file fish .50 .50
402 G34 $2 Schoolmaster .70 .70
Nos. 399-402 (4) 1.55 1.55

For overprint see No. 504.

Cricket Players Type of 1985

1984-85 Unwmk. *Perf. 12½*
Pairs, Type A116
403 1c R. A. Woolmer, portrait .15 .15
404 3c K. S. Ranjitsinhji, portrait .15 .15
405 5c W. R. Hammond, in action .15 .15
406 5c S. F. Barnes, portrait .15 .15
407 30c D. L. Underwood, in action .15 .15
408 30c R. Peel, in action .15 .15
409 55c M. D. Moxon, in action .20 .20
410 60c W. G. Grace, portrait .20 .20
411 60c L. Potter, portrait .20 .20
412 $1 E. A. E. Baptiste, portrait .40 .40
413 $1 H. Larwood, in action .40 .40
414 $2 A. P. E. Knott, portrait .80 .80
415 $2 Yorkshire & Kent county cricket clubs .80 .80
416 $2.50 Sir John Berry Hobbs, portrait 1.00 1.00
417 $3 L. E. G. Ames, in action 1.10 1.10
Nos. 403-417 (15) 6.00 6.00

Size of stamps in No. 415: 58x38mm.
Issued: #403, 407, 410, 412, 414, 417, 8/16/84; #406, 408, 413, 416, 11/2/84; #409, 411, 415, 2/22/85.

Canouan Island G35

1984, Sept. 3 Wmk. 380
433 G35 35c Junior secondary school .15 .15
434 G35 45c Police station .20 .20
435 G35 $1 Post office .45 .45
436 G35 $3 Anglican church 1.25 1.25
Nos. 433-436 (4) 2.05 2.05

Night-blooming Flowers — G36

1984, Oct. 15
437 G36 35c Lady of the night .25 .25
438 G36 45c Four o'clock .30 .30
439 G36 75c Mother-in-law's tongue .50 .50
440 G36 $3 Queen of the night 2.00 2.00
Nos. 437-440 (4) 3.05 3.05

Car Type of 1983

1984-86 Unwmk. *Perf. 12½*
Pairs, Type A107
441 5c 1959 Facel Vega, France .15 .15
442 5c 1903 Winton, Britain .15 .15
443 15c 1914 Mercedes-Benz, Germany .15 .15
444 25c 1936 BMW, Germany .15 .15
445 45c 1954 Rolls Royce, Britain .15 .15
446 50c 1934 Frazer Nash, Britain .20 .20
447 60c 1931 Invicta, Britain .20 .20
448 60c 1974 Lamborghini, Italy .20 .20

449 $1 1959 Daimler, Britain .35 .35
450 $1 1932 Marmon, US .35 .35
451 $1.50 1966 Brabham Repco, Britain .60 .60
452 $1.75 1968 Lotus Ford .70 .70
453 $3 1949 Buick, US 1.25 1.25
454 $3 1927 Delage, France 1.25 1.25
Nos. 441-454 (14) 5.85 5.85

Issued: #441, 444, 446, 457, 11/28/84; #442, 447, 449, 452, 4/9/85; #443, 445, 448, 450, 452, 454, 2/20/86.
Stamps issued 2/20/86 not inscribed "Leaders of the World."

Christmas Type of 1983

Perf. 14½

1984, Dec. 3 Litho. Wmk. 380

469 A106 20c Three wise men, star .15 .15
470 A106 45c Journeying to Bethlehem .15 .15
471 A106 $3 Presenting gifts 1.00 1.00
a. Souvenir sheet of 3, #469-471 1.40 1.40
Nos. 469-471 (3) 1.30 1.30

Shellfish G37

1985, Feb. 11 ***Perf. 14***

472 G37 25c Caribbean king crab .15 .15
473 G37 60c Queen conch .30 .30
474 G37 $1 White sea urchin .50 .50
475 G37 $3 West Indian top shell 1.40 1.40
Nos. 472-475 (4) 2.35 2.35

Flowers — G38

1985, Mar. 13 Unwmk. ***Perf. 12½***

476 G38 5c Cypripedium calceolus .15 .15
477 G38 5c Gentiana asclepiadea .15 .15
478 G38 55c Clianthus formosus .15 .15
479 G38 55c Celmisia coriacea .15 .15
480 G38 60c Erythronium americanum .15 .15
481 G38 60c Laelia anceps .15 .15
482 G38 $2 Leucadendron discolor .55 .55
483 G38 $2 Meconopsis horridula .55 .55
Nos. 476-483 (8) 2.00 2.00

Stamps of same denomination printed se-tenant.

Water Sports G39

1985, May 9 Wmk. 380 ***Perf. 14***

484 G39 35c Windsurfing .15 .15
485 G39 45c Water skiing .15 .15
486 G39 75c Scuba diving .25 .25
487 G39 $3 Deep sea fishing 1.00 1.00
Nos. 484-487 (4) 1.55 1.55

Tourism.

Fruits and Blossoms G40

1985, June 24 ***Perf. 15***

488 G40 30c Passion fruit .15 .15
489 G40 75c Guava .40 .40
490 G40 $1 Sapodilla .60 .60
491 G40 $2 Mango 1.10 1.10
a. Souvenir sheet of 4, #488-491, perf. 14½x15 2.75 2.75
Nos. 488-491 (4) 2.25 2.25

For overprint see No. 503.

Queen Mother Type of 1985

1985, July 31 Unwmk. ***Perf. 12½***

492 A122 40c Facing right .15 .15
493 A122 40c Facing forward .15 .15
494 A122 75c Facing right, diff. .15 .15
495 A122 75c Facing left, diff. .15 .15
496 A122 $1.10 Facing right, diff. .20 .20
497 A122 $1.10 Facing forward, diff. .20 .20
498 A122 $1.75 Facing right, diff. .35 .35
499 A122 $1.75 Facing left, diff. .35 .35
Nos. 492-499 (8) 1.70 1.70

Souvenir Sheet

500 Sheet of 2 1.00 1.00
a. A122 $2 As girl facing forward .50 .50
b. A122 $2 Facing left .50 .50

Stamps of same denomination printed se-tenant.
Souvenir sheets containing two $4 or two $5 stamps exist.

Nos. 213-214, 236, 399, 488, and 496-497 Overprinted or Surcharged "CARIBBEAN ROYAL VISIT 1985" in 1, 2 or 3 Lines

1985, Oct. 27 ***Perfs., Wmks. as Before***

503 G40 30c On #488 *.85 .85*
504 G37 45c On #399 *1.40 1.40*
505 A122 $1.10 On #496 *3.25 3.25*
506 A122 $1.10 On #497 *3.25 3.25*
507 A94a $1.50 On $3.50, #213 *4.75 4.75*
508 A94b $1.50 On $3.50, #214 *4.75 4.75*
509 G26 $3 On #236 *9.25 9.25*
Nos. 503-509 (7) 27.50 27.50

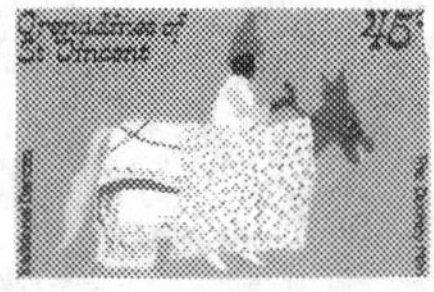

Traditional Dances G41

1985, Dec. 16 Unwmk. ***Perf. 15***

510 G41 45c Donkey man .15 .15
511 G41 75c Cake dance, vert. .30 .30
512 G41 $1 Bois-bois man, vert. .45 .45
513 G41 $2 Maypole dance .85 .85
Nos. 510-513 (4) 1.75 1.75

Queen Elizabeth II 60th Birthday Type

Designs: 5c, Elizabeth II. $1, At Princess Anne's christening. $4, As Princess. $6, In Canberra, 1982. $8, Elizabeth II with crown.

1986, Apr. 21 ***Perf. 12½***

514 A128 5c multicolored .15 .15
515 A128 $1 multicolored .25 .25
516 A128 $4 multicolored .95 .95
517 A128 $6 multi, vert. 1.40 1.40
Nos. 514-517 (4) 2.75 2.75

Souvenir Sheet

518 A128 $8 multicolored 3.25 3.25

Handicrafts — G41a

Wmk. 380

1986, Apr. 22 Litho. ***Perf. 15***

519 G41a 10c Dolls .15 .15
520 G41a 60c Basketwork .20 .20
521 G41a $1 Scrimshaw .35 .35
522 G41a $3 Model boat 1.10 1.10
Nos. 519-522 (4) 1.80 1.80

World Cup Soccer Championship, Mexico — G42

Perf. 12½, 15 (#525-528)

1986, May 7 Unwmk.

523 G42 1c Uruguayan team .15 .15
524 G42 10c Polish team .15 .15
525 G42 45c Bulgarian player .20 .20
526 G42 75c Iraqi player .30 .30
527 G42 $1.50 S. Korean player .60 .60
528 G42 $2 N. Ireland player .80 .80
529 G42 $4 Portuguese team 1.65 1.65
530 G42 $5 Canadian team 1.90 1.90
Nos. 523-530 (8) 5.75 5.75

Souvenir Sheets

531 G42 $1 like #529 .40 .40
532 G42 $3 like #523 1.25 1.25

Size: Nos. 525-528, 25x40mm.

Fungi — G43

Wmk. 380

1986, May 23 Litho. ***Perf. 14***

533 G43 45c Marasmius pallescens *.60 .60*
534 G43 60c Leucocoprinus fragilissimus *.80 .80*
535 G43 75c Hygrocybe occidentalis *1.00 1.00*
536 G43 $3 Xerocomus hypoxanthus *4.00 4.00*
Nos. 533-536 (4) 6.40 6.40

Royal Wedding Type of 1986

1986 Unwmk. ***Perf. 12½***

537 A132 60c Sarah, Diana .20 .20
538 A132 60c Andrew .20 .20
539 A132 $2 Anne, Andrew, Charles, Margaret, horiz. .65 .65
540 A132 $2 Sarah, Andrew, horiz. .65 .65
Nos. 537-540 (4) 1.70 1.70

Souvenir Sheet

541 A132a $8 Andrew, Sarah, in coach 3.50 3.50

Issued: #537-540, July 18; #541, Oct. 15.
Stamps of same denomination printed se-tenant.

Nos. 537-540 Ovptd. in Silver "Congratulations to TRH The Duke & Duchess of York" in 3 Lines

1986, Oct. 15

542 A132 60c on #537 .30 .30
543 A132 60c on #538 .30 .30
544 A132 $2 on #539 1.10 1.10
545 A132 $2 on #540 1.10 1.10
Nos. 542-545 (4) 2.80 2.80

Dragonflies G44

1986, Nov. 19 ***Perf. 15***

546 G44 45c Brachymesia furcata .20 .20
547 G44 60c Lepthemis vesiculosa .25 .25
548 G44 75c Perithemis domitta .30 .30
549 G44 $2.50 Tramea abdominalis, vert. .95 .95
Nos. 546-549 (4) 1.70 1.70

Statue of Liberty Type Souvenir Sheets

Each stamp shows different views of Statue of Liberty and a different US president in the margin.

1986, Nov. 26 ***Perf. 14***

550 A135 $1.50 multicolored .60 .60
551 A135 $1.75 multicolored .70 .70
552 A135 $2 multicolored .80 .80
553 A135 $2.50 multicolored 1.00 1.00
554 A135 $3 multicolored 1.10 1.10
555 A135 $3.50 multicolored 1.40 1.40
556 A135 $5 multicolored 1.90 1.90
557 A135 $6 multicolored 2.25 2.25
558 A135 $8 multicolored 3.25 3.25
Nos. 550-558 (9) 13.00 13.00

Birds of Prey — G45

Grenadines of St. Vincent
45c
Christmas — G46

1986, Nov. 26 Litho.

560 G45 10c Sparrow hawk .15 .15
561 G45 45c Black hawk .30 .30
562 G45 60c Duck hawk .35 .35
563 G45 $4 Fish hawk 2.50 2.50
Nos. 560-563 (4) 3.30 3.30

1986, Nov. 26

564 G46 45c Santa playing drums .25 .25
565 G46 60c Santa wind surfing .30 .30
566 G46 $1.25 Santa water skiing .80 .80
567 G46 $2 Santa limbo dancing 1.25 1.25
a. Souvenir sheet of 4, #564-567 2.75 2.75
Nos. 564-567 (4) 2.60 2.60

Queen Elizabeth II, 40th Wedding Anniv. Type of 1987

1987, Oct. 15 ***Perf. 12½***

568 A140 15c Elizabeth, Charles .15 .15
569 A140 45c Victoria, Albert .20 .20
570 A140 $1.50 Elizabeth, Philip .55 .55
571 A140 $3 Elizabeth, Philip, diff. 1.10 1.10
572 A140 $4 Elizabeth, portrait 1.50 1.50
Nos. 568-572 (5) 3.50 3.50

Souvenir Sheet

573 A140 $6 Elizabeth as Princess 2.50 2.50

Victoria's accession to the throne, 150th anniv.

Marine Life G48

1987, Dec. 17 ***Perf. 15***

574 G48 45c Banded coral shrimp .25 .25
575 G48 50c Arrow crab, flamingo tongue .30 .30
576 G48 65c Cardinal fish .40 .40
577 G48 $5 Moray eel 3.25 3.25
Nos. 574-577 (4) 4.20 4.20

Souvenir Sheet

578 G48 $5 Puffer fish 3.25 3.25

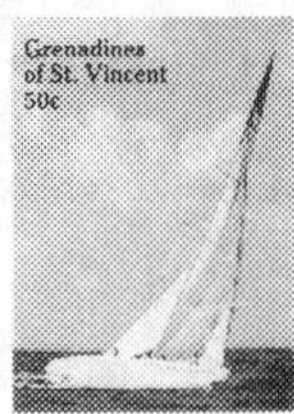

America's Cup Yachts — G49

1988, Mar. 31 ***Perf. 12½***

579 G49 50c Australia IV .20 .20
580 G49 65c Crusader II .25 .25
581 G49 75c New Zealand K27 .30 .30
582 G49 $2 Italia .85 .85
583 G49 $4 White Crusader 1.75 1.75
584 G49 $5 Stars and Stripes 2.25 2.25
Nos. 579-584 (6) 5.60 5.60

Souvenir Sheet

585 G49 $1 Champosa V .80 .80

Bequia Regatta G50

1988, Mar. 31 *Perf. 15*
586 G50 5c Seine boats .15 .15
587 G50 50c Friendship Rose .20 .20
588 G50 75c Fishing boats .30 .30
589 G50 $3.50 Yacht racing 1.50 1.50
Nos. 586-589 (4) 2.15 2.15

Souvenir Sheet

Perf. 12½
590 G50 $8 Port Elizabeth 5.25 5.25

Tourism — G51

Aircraft of Mustique Airways, Genadine Tours.

1988, May 26 *Perf. 14x13½*
591 G51 15c multicolored .15 .15
592 G51 65c multi, diff. .25 .25
593 G51 75c multi, diff. .30 .30
594 G51 $5 multi, diff. 2.00 2.00
Nos. 591-594 (4) 2.70 2.70

Souvenir Sheet

595 G51 $10 Waterfall, vert. 6.00 6.00

No. 595 contains one 35x56mm stamp.

Great Explorers G52

Designs: 15c, Vitus Bering and the St. Peter. 75c, Bering and pancake ice. $1, David Livingstone and the Ma-Robert. $2, Livingstone meeting Henry M. Stanley. $3, John Speke (1827-1864) and Sir Richard Burton (1821-1890) welcomed at Tabori. $3.50, Speke, Burton at Lake Victoria. $4, Crewman of Christopher Columbus spotting land. $4.50, Columbus, exchange of gifts. $5, Sextant. $6, Columbus' ship landing in Bahamas, 1492.

1988, July 29 *Perf. 14*
596 G52 15c multicolored .15 .15
597 G52 75c multicolored .15 .15
598 G52 $1 multicolored .25 .25
599 G52 $2 multicolored .45 .45
600 G52 $3 multicolored .70 .70
601 G52 $3.50 multicolored .80 .80
602 G52 $4 multicolored .90 .90
603 G52 $4.50 multicolored 1.00 1.00
Nos. 596-603 (8) 4.40 4.40

Souvenir Sheets

604 G52 $5 multicolored 2.00 2.00
605 G52 $6 multicolored 2.25 2.25

Nos. 602-603, 605 picture 500th anniversary discovery of America emblem.

A number of unissued items, imperfs., part perfs., missing color varieties, etc., were made available when the Format International inventory was liquidated.

Cricketers — G53

1988, July 29 *Perf. 15*
606 G53 20c A. I. Razvi .15 .15
607 G53 45c R. J. Hadlee .25 .25
608 G53 75c M. D. Crowe .50 .50
609 G53 $1.25 C. H. Lloyd .80 .80
610 G53 $1.50 A. R. Boarder .95 .95
611 G53 $2 M. D. Marshall 1.25 1.25
612 G53 $2.50 G. A. Hick 1.50 1.50
613 G53 $3.50 C. G. Greenidge, horiz. 2.25 2.25
Nos. 606-613 (8) 7.65 7.65

A $3 souvenir sheet in the design of the $2 stamp was not a postal issue according to the St. Vincent P.O.

Tennis Type of 1987

1988, July 29 *Perf. 12½*
614 A137 15c Pam Shriver, horiz. .15 .15
615 A137 50c Kevin Curran .20 .20
616 A137 75c Wendy Turnbull .30 .30
617 A137 $1 Evonne Cawley .40 .40
618 A137 $1.50 Ilie Nastase, horiz. .60 .60
619 A137 $2 Billie Jean King .80 .80
620 A137 $3 Bjorn Borg 1.25 1.25
621 A137 $3.50 Virginia Wade 1.40 1.40
Nos. 614-621 (8) 5.10 5.10

Souvenir Sheet

622 Sheet of 2 2.75 2.75
a. A137 $2.25 Stefan Edberg 1.25 1.25
b. A137 $2.25 Steffi Graf 1.25 1.25

No. 616 inscribed "Turnball" in error.

India '89, International Stamp Exhibition, New Dehli — G54

Disney characters and sites in India.

1989, Feb. 7 *Perf. 14x13½*
623 G54 1c Fatehpur Sikri .15 .15
624 G54 2c Palace on Wheels .15 .15
625 G54 3c Old fort, Delhi .15 .15
626 G54 5c Pinjore Gardens .15 .15
627 G54 10c Taj Mahal .15 .15
628 G54 25c Chandni Chowk .15 .15
629 G54 $4 Agra Fort, Jaipur 2.50 2.50
630 G54 $5 Gandhi Memorial 3.50 3.50
Nos. 623-630 (8) 6.90 6.90

Souvenir Sheets

631 G54 $6 Qutab Minar, vert. 4.00 4.00
632 G54 $6 Palace of the Winds 4.00 4.00

Japanese Art Type

Paintings: 5c, The View at Yotsuya, by Hokusai. 30c, Landscape at Ochanomizu, by Hokuju. 45c, Itabashi, by Eisen. 65c, Early Summer Rain, by Kunisada. 75c, High Noon at Kasumigaseki, by Kuniyoshi. $1, The Yoshiwara Embankment by Moonlight, by Kuniyoshi. $4, The Bridge of Boats at Sano, by Hokusai. $5, Lingering Snow on Mount Hira, by Kunitora. No. 641, Colossus of Rhodes, by Kunitora. No. 642, Shinobazu Pond, by Kokan.

1989, July 6 *Perf. 14x13½*
633 A170 5c multicolored .15 .15
634 A170 30c multicolored .22 .22
635 A170 45c multicolored .35 .35
636 A170 65c multicolored .50 .50
637 A170 75c multicolored .58 .58
638 A170 $1 multicolored .75 .75
639 A170 $4 multicolored 3.00 3.00
640 A170 $5 multicolored 3.75 3.75
Nos. 633-640 (8) 9.30 9.30

Souvenir Sheets

641 A170 $6 multicolored 4.50 4.50
642 A170 $6 multicolored 4.50 4.50

Miniature Sheet

1990 World Cup Soccer Championships, Italy — G55

Soccer players and landmarks: a, Mt. Vesuvius. b, The Colosseum. c, Venice. d, Roman Forum. e, Leaning Tower of Pisa. f, Florence. g, The Vatican. h, The Pantheon.

1989, July 10 *Perf. 14*
643 Sheet of 8 9.00 9.00
a.-h. G55 $1.50 any single 1.10 1.10

Discovery of America 500th Anniv. Type of Antigua & Barbuda

UPAE emblem and American Indians: 25c, Smoking tobacco. 75c, Rolling tobacco. $1, Body painting. No. 647a, Starting campfire. No. 647b, Woman drinking from bowl. No. 647c, Woman frying grain or corn patties. No. 647d, Adult resting in hammock using stone mortar and pestle. $4, Smoothing wood. No. 649, Chief. No. 650, Fishing with bow and arrow.

1989, Oct. 2 **Litho.** *Perf. 14*
644 A196 25c multicolored .18 .18
645 A196 75c multicolored .58 .58
646 A196 $1 multicolored .75 .75
647 Strip of 4 4.50 4.50
a.-d. A196 $1.50 any single 1.10 1.10
648 A196 $4 multicolored 3.00 3.00
Nos. 644-648 (5) 9.01 9.01

Souvenir Sheets

649 A196 $6 multicolored 4.50 4.50
650 A196 $6 multicolored 4.50 4.50

No. 647 has continuous design.

1st Moon Landing Type

Designs: 5c *Columbia* command module. 40c, Neil Armstrong saluting flag on the Moon. 55c. Command module over Moon. 65c, *Eagle* liftoff from Moon. 70c, *Eagle* on the Moon. $1, Command module re-entering Earth's atmosphere. $3, Apollo 11 mission emblem. $5, Armstrong and Buzz Aldrin walking on the Moon. No. 659, Apollo 11 launch, vert. No. 660, Splashdown.

1989, Oct. 2 *Perf. 14*
651 A171 5c multicolored .15 .15
652 A171 40c multicolored .30 .30
653 A171 55c multicolored .42 .42
654 A171 65c multicolored .50 .50
655 A171 70c multicolored .52 .52
656 A171 $1 multicolored .75 .75
657 A171 $3 multicolored 2.25 2.25
658 A171 $5 multicolored 3.75 3.75
Nos. 651-658 (8) 8.64 8.64

Souvenir Sheets

659 A171 $6 multi, vert. 4.50 4.50
660 A171 $6 multicolored 4.50 4.50

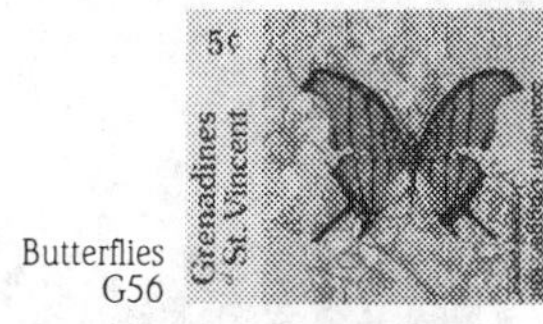

Butterflies G56

1989, Oct. 16 **Litho.** *Perf. 14x14½*
661 G56 5c Southern dagger tail .15 .15
662 G56 30c Androgeus swallowtail .22 .22
663 G56 45c Clench's hairstreak .35 .35
664 G56 65c Buckeye .48 .48
665 G56 75c Venezuelan sulphur .58 .58
666 G56 $1 Mimic .75 .75
667 G56 $4 Common longtail skipper 3.00 3.00
668 G56 $5 Carribean buckeye 3.75 3.75
Nos. 661-668 (8) 9.28 9.28

Souvenir Sheets

669 G56 $6 Flambeau 4.50 4.50
670 G56 $6 Queen, large orange sulphur, Ramsden's giant white 4.50 4.50

Flora — G57

1989, Nov. 1 **Litho.** *Perf. 14*
671 G57 80c Solanum urens .60 .60
672 G57 $1.25 Passiflora andersonii .95 .95
673 G57 $1.65 Miconia andersonii 1.25 1.25
674 G57 $1.85 Pitcairnia sulphurea 1.40 1.40
Nos. 671-674 (4) 4.20 4.20

Christmas — G58

Walt Disney characters and classic automobiles.

Perf. 14x13½, 13½x14

1989, Dec. 20
675 G58 5c 1907 Rolls-Royce .15 .15
676 G58 10c 1897 Stanley Steamer .15 .15
677 G58 15c 1904 Darracq Genevieve .15 .15
678 G58 45c 1914 Detroit Electric Coupe .35 .35
679 G58 55c 1896 Ford .42 .42
680 G58 $2 1904 REO Runabout 1.50 1.50
681 G58 $3 1899 Winton Mail Truck 2.25 2.25
682 G58 $5 1893 Duryea Car 3.75 3.75
Nos. 675-682 (8) 8.72 8.72

Souvenir Sheets

683 G58 $6 1912 Pope-Hartford 4.50 4.50
684 G58 $6 1908 Buick Model 10 4.50 4.50

Nos. 683-684 vert.

Battles of World War II G59

Designs: 10c, 1st Battle of Narvik, Apr. 10, 1940. 15c, Allies land at Anzio, Jan. 22, 1944. 20c, Battle of Midway, June 4, 1942. 45c, Allies launch offensive on Gustav Line, May 11, 1944. 55c, Allies take over zones in Berlin, July 3, 1945. 65c, Battle of the Atlantic, Mar. 1-20, 1943. 90c, Allies launch final phase of North African Campaign, Apr. 22, 1943. $3, US forces land on Guam, July 21, 1944. $5, US 7th Army meets the 3rd Army across the Rhine, Mar. 26, 1945. No. 694, Battle of Leyte Gulf, Oct. 23, 1944. No. 695, The Dambusters Raid, May 16, 1943.

1990, Apr. 2 **Litho.** *Perf. 14*
685 G59 10c multicolored .15 .15
686 G59 15c multicolored .15 .15
687 G59 20c multicolored .15 .15
688 G59 45c multicolored .35 .35
689 G59 55c multicolored .42 .42
690 G59 65c multicolored .50 .50
691 G59 90c multicolored .68 .68
692 G59 $3 multicolored 2.25 2.25
693 G59 $5 multicolored 3.75 3.75
694 G59 $6 multicolored 4.50 4.50
Nos. 685-694 (10) 12.90 12.90

Souvenir Sheet

695 G59 $6 multicolored 4.50 4.50

Penny Black, 150th Anniv. — G60

Designs: $1, Stamp World London '90 emblem. $5, Negative image of the Penny Black. $6, Penny Black with non-existent letters.

1990, May 3 *Perf. 14x15*
696 G60 $1 pale rose & blk .75 .75
697 G60 $5 pale violet & blk 3.50 3.50

Souvenir Sheet

698 G60 $6 dull blue & blk 4.50 4.50

Stamp World London '90.

Disney Characters Portraying Shakespearian Roles — G61

Designs: 20c, Goofy as Marc Antony in "Julius Caesar." 30c, Clarabelle Cow as nurse in "Romeo and Juliet." 45c, Pete as Falstaff in "Henry IV." 50c, Minnie Mouse as Portia in "The Merchant of Venice." $1, Donald Duck holding head of Yorick in "Hamlet." $2, Daisy Duck as Ophelia in "Hamlet." $4, Donald and Daisy Duck as Benedick and Beatrice in "Much Ado About Nothing." $5, Minnie Mouse and Donald Duck as Katherine and Petruchio in "The Taming of the Shrew." No. 707, Mickey and Minnie Mouse portraying Romeo and Juliet. No. 708, Clarabelle Cow as Titania in "A Midsummer Night's Dream."

1990, May *Perf. 14x13½*

699 G61 20c multicolored .15 .15
700 G61 30c multicolored .22 .22
701 G61 45c multicolored .34 .34
702 G61 50c multicolored .38 .38
703 G61 $1 multicolored .75 .75
704 G61 $2 multicolored 1.50 1.50
705 G61 $4 multicolored 3.00 3.00
706 G61 $5 multicolored 3.75 3.75
Nos. 699-706 (8) 10.09 10.09

Souvenir Sheets

707 G61 $6 multicolored 4.50 4.50
708 G61 $6 multicolored 4.50 4.50

World Cup Soccer Championships, Italy — G62

World Cup Trophy and players from participating countries.

1990, Sept. 24 Litho. *Perf. 14*

709 G62 25c Scotland .18 .18
710 G62 50c Egypt .38 .38
711 G62 $2 Austria 1.50 1.50
712 G62 $4 United States 3.00 3.00
Nos. 709-712 (4) 5.06 5.06

Souvenir Sheets

713 G62 $6 Holland 4.50 4.50
714 G62 $6 England 4.50 4.50

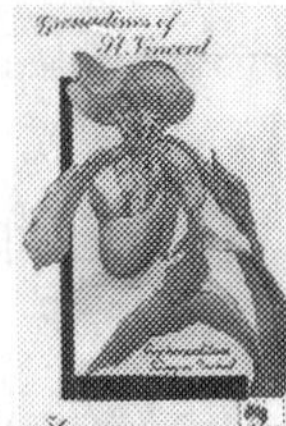

Orchids — G63

Designs: 5c, Paphiopedilum. 25c, Dendrobium phalaenopsis, Cymbidium. 30c, Miltonia candida. 50c, Epidendrum ibaguense, Cymbidium Elliot Rogers. $1, Rossioglassum grande. $2, Phalaenopsis Elisa Chang Lou, Masdevallia coccinea. $4, Cypripedium accale, Cypripedium calceolus. $5, Orchis spectabilis. No. 723, Epidendrum ibaguense, Phalaenopsis. No. 724, Dendrobium anosmum.

1990, Nov. 23 Litho. *Perf. 14*

715 G63 5c multicolored .15 .15
716 G63 25c multicolored .18 .18
717 G63 30c multicolored .22 .22
718 G63 50c multicolored .38 .38
719 G63 $1 multicolored .75 .75
720 G63 $2 multicolored 1.50 1.50
721 G63 $4 multicolored 3.00 3.00
722 G63 $5 multicolored 3.75 3.75
Nos. 715-722 (8) 9.93 9.93

Souvenir Sheets

723 G63 $6 multicolored 4.50 4.50
724 G63 $6 multicolored 4.50 4.50

Expo '90, Intl. Garden and Greenery Exposition, Osaka, Japan.

Birds G64

1990, Nov. 26

725 G64 5c Common ground dove .15 .15
726 G64 25c Purple martin .18 .18
727 G64 45c Painted bunting .35 .35
728 G64 55c Blue-hooded euphonia .42 .42
729 G64 75c Blue-gray tanager .55 .55
730 G64 $1 Red-eyed vireo .75 .75
731 G64 $2 Palm chat 1.50 1.50
732 G64 $3 North American jacana 2.25 2.25
733 G64 $4 Green-throated carib 3.00 3.00
734 G64 $5 St. Vincent parrot 3.75 3.75
Nos. 725-734 (10) 12.90 12.90

Souvenir Sheets

735 Sheet of 2 4.50 4.50
a. G64 $3 Bananaquit 2.25 2.25
b. G64 $3 Magnificent frigatebird 2.25 2.25
736 G64 $6 Red-legged honey-creeper 4.50 4.50

Queen Mother 90th Birthday Type

Photographs: Nos. 737a-737i, From 1900-1929. Nos. 738a-738i, From 1930-1959. Nos. 739a-739i, From 1960-1989. Nos. 740-748, Enlarged photographs used for Nos. 737-739.

1991, Feb. 14 Litho. *Perf. 14*

Miniature Sheets of 9, #a.-i.

737 A193 $2 blue & multi 13.50 13.50
738 A193 $2 pink & multi 13.50 13.50
739 A193 $2 green & multi 13.50 13.50

Souvenir Sheets

740 A193 $5 like #737a 3.75 3.75
741 A193 $5 like #737f 3.75 3.75
742 A193 $5 like #737h 3.75 3.75
743 A193 $5 like #738b 3.75 3.75
744 A193 $5 like #738f 3.75 3.75
745 A193 $5 like #738g 3.75 3.75
746 A193 $5 like #739b 3.75 3.75
747 A193 $5 like #739d 3.75 3.75
748 A193 $5 like #739h 3.75 3.75

Paintings by Vincent Van Gogh — G65

Designs: 5c, View of Arles with Irises in the Foreground. 10c, View of Saintes-Maries, vert. 15c, An Old Woman of Arles, vert. 20c, Orchard in Blossom, Bordered by Cypresses. 25c, Three White Cottages in Saintes-Maries. 35c, Boats at Saintes-Maries-De-La-Mer. 40c, Interior of a Restaurant in Arles. 45c, Peasant Woman, vert. 55c, Self-Portrait, Sept. 1888, vert. 60c, A Pork Butcher's Shop Seen From a Window, vert. 75c, The Night Cafe in Arles. $1, Portrait of Milliet, Second Lieutenant of the Zouaves, vert. $2, The Cafe Terrace on the Place Du Forum Arles, at Night, vert. $3, The Zouave, vert. $4, Two Lovers (Fragment), vert. No. 764, Still Life: Blue Enamel Coffeepot, Earthenware and Fruit. No. 765, Street in Saintes-Maries. No. 766, A Lane Near Arles. No. 767, Harvest at La Crau, with Montmajour in the Background. No. 768, The Sower.

1991, June 10 Litho. *Perf. 13½*

749 G65 5c multicolored .15 .15
750 G65 10c multicolored .15 .15
751 G65 15c multicolored .15 .15
752 G65 20c multicolored .15 .15
753 G65 25c multicolored .18 .18
754 G65 35c multicolored .28 .28
755 G65 40c multicolored .30 .30
756 G65 45c multicolored .35 .35
757 G65 55c multicolored .42 .42
758 G65 60c multicolored .45 .45
759 G65 75c multicolored .58 .58
760 G65 $1 multicolored .75 .75
761 G65 $2 multicolored 1.50 1.50
762 G65 $3 multicolored 2.25 2.25
763 G65 $4 multicolored 3.00 3.00
764 G65 $5 multicolored 3.75 3.75

Size: 102x76mm

Imperf

765 G65 $5 multicolored 3.75 3.75
766 G65 $5 multicolored 3.75 3.75
767 G65 $6 multicolored 4.50 4.50
768 G65 $6 multicolored 4.50 4.50
Nos. 749-768 (20) 30.91 30.91

Royal Family Birthday, Anniversary

Common Design Type

1991, July 5 Litho. *Perf. 14*

769 CD347 10c multicolored .15 .15
770 CD347 15c multicolored .15 .15
771 CD347 40c multicolored .30 .30
772 CD347 50c multicolored .38 .38
773 CD347 $1 multicolored .75 .75
774 CD347 $2 multicolored 1.50 1.50
775 CD347 $4 multicolored 3.00 3.00
776 CD347 $5 multicolored 3.75 3.75
Nos. 769-776 (8) 9.98 9.98

Souvenir Sheets

777 CD347 $5 Henry, William, Charles, Diana 3.75 3.75
778 CD347 $5 Elizabeth, Andrew, Philip 3.75 3.75

10c, 50c, $1, Nos. 776-777, Charles and Diana, 10th wedding anniversary. Others, Queen Elizabeth II, 65th birthday.

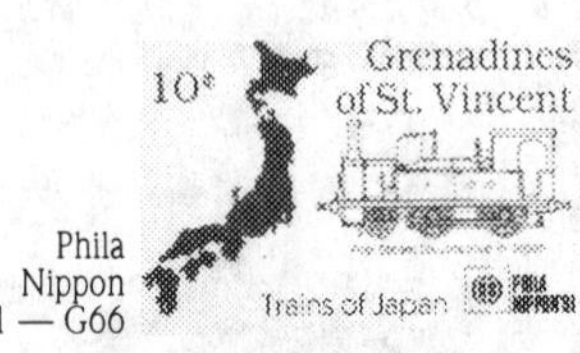

Phila Nippon '91 — G66

Japanese locomotives: 10c, First Japanese steam. 25c, First American steam locomotive in Japan. 35c, Class 8620 steam. 50c, C53 steam. $1, DD-51 diesel. $2, RF 22327 electric. $4, EF-55 electric. $5, EF-58 electric. No. 787, Class 9600 steam, vert. No. 788, Class 4100 steam, vert. No. 789, C57 steam, vert. No. 790, C62 steam, vert.

1991, Aug. 12 Litho. *Perf. 14x13½*

779 G66 10c red, green & black .15 .15
780 G66 25c red, green & black .18 .18
781 G66 35c red, green & black .26 .26
782 G66 50c red, green & black .38 .38
783 G66 $1 red, green & black .75 .75
784 G66 $2 red, green & black 1.50 1.50
785 G66 $4 red, green & black 3.00 3.00
786 G66 $5 red, green & black 3.75 3.75
Nos. 779-786 (8) 9.97 9.97

Souvenir Sheets

Perf. 12x13

787 G66 $6 red, black & green 4.50 4.50
788 G66 $6 red, black & green 4.50 4.50
789 G66 $6 red, black & green 4.50 4.50
790 G66 $6 red, black & green 4.50 4.50

Brandenburg Gate Type

Designs: 45c, Brandenburg Gate and Soviet Pres. Mikhail Gorbachev. 65c, Sign. 80c, Statue, soldier escaping through barbed wire. No. 794, Berlin police insignia. No. 795, Berlin coat of arms.

1991, Nov. 18 Litho. *Perf. 14*

791 A209 45c multicolored .35 .35
792 A209 65c multicolored .48 .48
793 A209 80c multicolored .60 .60
Nos. 791-793 (3) 1.43 1.43

Souvenir Sheets

794 A209 $5 multicolored 3.75 3.75
795 A209 $5 multicolored 3.75 3.75

Wolfgang Amadeus Mozart Type

Portrait of Mozart and: $1, Scene from "Abduction from the Seraglio." $3, Dresden, 1749. No. 799, Portrait, vert. No. 800, Bust, vert.

1991, Nov. 18 Litho. *Perf. 14*

797 A210 $1 multicolored .75 .75
798 A210 $3 multicolored 2.25 2.25

Souvenir Sheets

799 A210 $5 multicolored 3.75 3.75
800 A210 $5 multicolored 3.75 3.75

Boy Scout Type

Designs: $2, Scout delivering mail and Czechoslovakian (local) scout stamp. $4, Cog train, Boy Scouts on Mt. Snowdon, Wales, vert. Nos. 803-804, Emblem of World Scout Jamboree, Korea.

1991, Nov. 18 Litho. *Perf. 14*

801 A211 $2 multicolored 1.50 1.50
802 A211 $4 multicolored 3.00 3.00

Souvenir Sheets

803 A211 $5 tan & multi 3.75 3.75
804 A211 $5 violet blue & multi 3.75 3.75

Lord Robert Baden-Powell, 50th death anniv. and 17th World Scout Jamboree, Korea.

De Gaulle Type

Designs: 60c, De Gaulle in Djibouti, 1959. No. 807, In military uniform, vert. No. 808, Portrait as President.

1991, Nov. 18 Litho. *Perf. 14*

806 A212 60c .45 .45

Souvenir Sheets

807 A212 $5 multicolored 3.75 3.75
808 A212 $5 multicolored 3.75 3.75

A number has been reserved for additional value in this set.

Anniversaries and Events Type of 1991

Designs: $1.50, Otto Lilienthal, aviation pioneer. No. 810, Train in winter, vert. No. 811, Trans-Siberian Express Sign. No. 812, Man and woman celebrating. No. 813, Woman and man wearing hats. No. 814, Georg Ludwig Friedrich Laves, architect of Hoftheater, Hanover. No. 815, Locomotive, Trans-Siberian Railway, vert. No. 816, Cantonal arms of Appenzell and Thurgau. No. 817, Hanover, 750th anniv.

1991, Nov. 18 Litho. *Perf. 14*

809 A213 $1.50 multicolored 1.15 1.15
810 A213 $1.75 multicolored 1.30 1.30
811 A213 $1.75 multicolored 1.30 1.30
812 A213 $2 multicolored 1.50 1.50
813 A213 $2 multicolored 1.50 1.50
814 A213 $2 multicolored 1.50 1.50
Nos. 809-814 (6) 8.25 8.25

Souvenir Sheets

815 A213 $5 multicolored 3.75 3.75
816 A213 $5 multicolored 3.75 3.75
817 A213 $5 multicolored 3.75 3.75

First glider flight, cent. (#809). Trans-Siberian Railway, cent. (#810-811, 815). Swiss Confederation, 700th anniv. (#812-813, 816). City of Hanover, 750th anniv. (#814, 817). No. 815 contains one 42x58mm stamp.

Miniature Sheet

Pearl Harbor Type of 1991

Designs: a, Japanese submarines and aircraft leave Truk to attack Pearl Harbor. b, Japanese flagship, Akagi. c, Nakajima B5N2 Kate, attack leader. d, Torpedo bombers attack battleship row. e, Ford Island Naval Air Station. f, Doris Miller earns Navy Cross. g, USS West Virginia and USS Tennessee ablaze. h, USS Arizona destroyed. i, USS New Orleans. j, Pres. Roosevelt declares war.

1991, Nov. 18 *Perf. 14½x15*

818 A214 $1 Sheet of 10, #a.-j. 7.50 7.50

Disney Christmas Card Type

Card design and year of issue: 10c, Mickey in sleigh pulled by Pluto, 1974. 55c, Donald, Pluto, and Mickey watching marching band, 1961. 65c, Greeting with stars, 1942. 75c, Mickey, Donald watch Merlin create a snowman, 1963. $1.50, Mickey placing wreath on door, 1958. $2, Mickey as Santa beside fireplace, 1957. $4, Mickey manipulating "Pinnochio" for friends. $5, Prince Charming and Cinderella dancing beside Christmas tree, 1987. No. 827, Snow White, 1957, vert. No. 828, Santa riding World War II bomber, 1942, vert.

Perf. 14x13½, 13½x14

1991, Nov. 18

819 A216 10c multicolored .15 .15
820 A216 55c multicolored .42 .42
821 A216 65c multicolored .48 .48
822 A216 75c multicolored .58 .58
823 A216 $1.50 multicolored 1.15 1.15
824 A216 $2 multicolored 1.50 1.50
825 A216 $4 multicolored 3.00 3.00
826 A216 $5 multicolored 3.75 3.75
Nos. 819-826 (8) 11.03 11.03

Souvenir Sheets

827 A216 $6 multicolored 4.50 4.50
828 A216 $6 multicolored 4.50 4.50

Nos. 819-826 are horiz.

Queen Elizabeth II's Accession to the Throne, 40th Anniv.

Common Design Type

1992, Feb. 6 Litho. *Perf. 14*

829 CD348 15c multicolored .15 .15
830 CD348 45c multicolored .35 .35
831 CD348 $2 multicolored 1.50 1.50
832 CD348 $4 multicolored 3.00 3.00
Nos. 829-832 (4) 5.00 5.00

Souvenir Sheets

833 CD348 $6 Queen at left, beach 4.50 4.50
834 CD348 $6 Queen at right, building 4.50 4.50

World Columbian Stamp Expo Type

Walt Disney characters as famous Chicagoans: 10c, Mickey as Walt Disney walking past birthplace. 50c, Donald Duck and nephews sleeping in George Pullman's railway cars. $1, Daisy Duck as Jane Addams in front of Hull House. $5, Mickey as Carl Sandburg. No. 839, Grandma McDuck as Mrs. O'Leary with her cow, vert.

1992, Apr. Litho. *Perf. 14x13½*
835 A220 10c multicolored .15 .15
836 A220 50c multicolored .38 .38
837 A220 $1 multicolored .75 .75
838 A220 $5 multicolored 3.75 3.75
Nos. 835-838 (4) 5.03 5.03

Souvenir Sheet
Perf. 13½x14
839 A220 $6 multicolored 4.50 4.50

Nos. 840-844 have not been used.

Granada '92 Type

Walt Disney characters as Spanish explorers in New World: 15c, Aztec King Goofy giving treasure to Big Pete as Hernando Cortes. 40c, Mickey as Hernando de Soto discovering Mississippi River. $2, Goofy as Vasco Nunez de Balboa discovering Pacific Ocean. $4, Donald Duck as Francisco Coronado discovering Rio Grande. $6, Mickey as Ponce de Leon discovering Fountain of Youth.

1992, Apr. *Perf. 14x13½*
845 A221 15c multicolored .15 .15
846 A221 40c multicolored .30 .30
847 A221 $2 multicolored 1.50 1.50
848 A221 $4 multicolored 3.00 3.00
Nos. 845-848 (4) 4.95 4.95

Souvenir Sheet
Perf. 13½x14
849 A221 $6 multicolored 4.50 4.50

Nos. 850-854 have not been used.

Discovery of America, 500th Anniv. Type

10c, King Ferdinand & Queen Isabella. 45c, Santa Maria & Nina in Acul Bay, Haiti. 55c, Santa Maria, vert. $2, Columbus' fleet departing Canary Islands, vert. $4, Sinking of Santa Maria off Hispanola. $5, Nina and Pinta returning to Spain. #861, Columbus' fleet during night storm. #862, Columbus landing on San Salvador.

1992, May 22 Litho. *Perf. 14*
855 A222 10c multicolored .15 .15
856 A222 45c multicolored .35 .35
857 A222 55c multicolored .42 .42
858 A222 $2 multicolored 1.50 1.50
859 A222 $4 multicolored 3.00 3.00
860 A222 $5 multicolored 3.75 3.75
Nos. 855-860 (6) 9.17 9.17

Souvenir Sheets
861 A222 $6 multicolored 4.50 4.50
862 A222 $6 multicolored 4.50 4.50

World Columbian Stamp Expo '92, Chicago.
Nos. 863-866 have not been used.

Mushrooms — G67

Designs: 10c, Entoloma bakeri. 15c, Hydropus paraensis. 20c, Leucopaxillus gracillimus. 45c, Hygrotrama dennisianum. 50c, Leucoagaricus hortensis. 65c, Pyrrhoglossum pyrrhum. 75c, Amanita craeoderma. $1, Lentinus bertieri. $2, Dennisiomyces griseus. $3, Xerulina asprata. $4, Hygrocybe acutoconica. $5, Lepiota spiculata. No. 879, Pluteus crysophlebius. No. 880, Lepiota volvatua. No. 881, Amanita lilloi.

1992, July 2
867-878 G67 Set of 12 13.00 13.00

Souvenir Sheets
879-881 G67 $6 each 4.50 4.50

Butterfly Type of 1992

Designs: 15c, Nymphalidae paulogramma 20c, Heliconius cydno. 30c, Ithomiidae eutresis hypereia. 45c, Eurytides Columbus koll, vert. 55c, Papilio ascolius. 75c, Anaea pasibula. 80c, Heliconius doris. $1, Nymphalidae persisama pitheas. $2, Nymphalidae batesia hypochlora. $3, Heliconius erato. $4, Elzunia cassandrina. $5, Ithomiidae sais. No. 894, Pieridae dismorphia orise. No. 895, Nymphalidae podotricha. No. 896, Oleria tigilla.

1992, June 15 Litho. *Perf. 14*
882 A225 15c multicolored .15 .15
883 A225 20c multicolored .15 .15
884 A225 30c multicolored .22 .22
885 A225 45c multicolored .35 .35
886 A225 55c multicolored .42 .42
887 A225 75c multicolored .58 .58
888 A225 80c multicolored .60 .60
889 A225 $1 multicolored .75 .75
890 A225 $2 multicolored 1.50 1.50
891 A225 $3 multicolored 2.25 2.25
892 A225 $4 multicolored 3.00 3.00
893 A225 $5 multicolored 3.75 3.75
Nos. 882-893 (12) 13.72 13.72

Souvenir Sheets
894 A225 $6 multicolored 4.50 4.50
895 A225 $6 multicolored 4.50 4.50
896 A225 $6 multicolored 4.50 4.50

Genoa '92.

Hummingbirds Type of 1992

Designs: 5c, Antillean crested, female, horiz. 10c, Blue-tailed emerald, female. 35c, Antillean mango, male, horiz. 45c, Antillean mango, female, horiz. 55c, Green-throated carib, horiz. 65c, Green violet-ear. 75c, Blue-tailed emerald, male, horiz. $1, Purple throated carib. $2, Copper-rumped, horiz. $3, Rufous-breasted hermit. $4, Antillean crested, male. $5, Green breasted mango, male. No. 909, Blue-tailed emerald. No. 910, Antillean mango, diff. No. 911, Antillean crested, male, diff.

1992, July 7 Litho. *Perf. 14*
897 A224 5c multicolored .15 .15
898 A224 10c multicolored .15 .15
899 A224 35c multicolored .28 .28
900 A224 45c multicolored .35 .35
901 A224 55c multicolored .42 .42
902 A224 65c multicolored .48 .48
903 A224 75c multicolored .58 .58
904 A224 $1 multicolored .75 .75
905 A224 $2 multicolored 1.50 1.50
906 A224 $3 multicolored 2.25 2.25
907 A224 $4 multicolored 3.00 3.00
908 A224 $5 multicolored 4.00 4.00
Nos. 897-908 (12) 13.91 13.91

Souvenir Sheets
909 A224 $6 multicolored 4.50 4.50
910 A224 $6 multicolored 4.50 4.50
911 A224 $6 multicolored 4.50 4.50

Genoa '92.

Discovery of America Type

1992 Litho. *Perf. 14½*
912 A230 $1 Coming ashore .75 .75
913 A230 $2 Natives, ships 1.50 1.50

Organization of East Caribbean States.

Summer Olympics Type of 1992

Designs: 10c, Volleyball, vert. 15c, Men's floor exercise. 25c, Cross-country skiing, vert. 30c, 110-meter hurdles. 45c, 120-meter ski jump. 55c, Women's 4x100-meter relay, vert. 75c, Triple jump, vert. 80c, Mogul skiing, vert. $1, 100-meter butterfly. $2, Tornado class yachting. $3, Decathlon. $5, Equestrian jumping. No. 926, Ice hockey. No. 927, Single luge. No. 928, Soccer.

1992, Apr. 21 Litho. *Perf. 14*
914 A219 10c multicolored .15 .15
915 A219 15c multicolored .15 .15
916 A218 25c multicolored .18 .18
917 A219 30c multicolored .22 .22
918 A218 45c multicolored .35 .35
919 A219 55c multicolored .42 .42
920 A219 75c multicolored .58 .58
921 A218 80c multicolored .60 .60
922 A219 $1 multicolored .75 .75
923 A219 $2 multicolored 1.50 1.50
924 A219 $3 multicolored 2.25 2.25
925 A219 $5 multicolored 3.75 3.75
Nos. 914-925 (12) 10.90 10.90

Souvenir Sheets
926 A218 $6 multicolored 4.50 4.50
927 A218 $6 multicolored 4.50 4.50
928 A219 $6 multicolored 4.50 4.50

Christmas Art Type of 1992

Details or entire paintings: 10c, Our Lady with St. Roch and St. Anthony of Padua, by Giorgione. 40c, St. Anthony of Padua, by Master of the Embroidered Leaf. 45c, Madonna and Child in a Landscape, by Orazio Gentileschi. 50c, Madonna and Child with St. Anne, by Leonardo da Vinci. 55c, The Holy Family, by Giuseppe Maria Crespi. 65c, Madonna and Child, by Andrea Del Sarto. 75c, Madonna and Child with Sts. Lawrence and Julian, by Gentile da Fabriano. $1, Virgin and Child, by School of Parma. $2, Madonna with the Iris in the style of Durer. $3, Virgin and Child with St. Jerome and St. Dominic, by Filippino Lippi. $4, Rapolano Madonna, by Ambrogio Lorenzetti. $5, The Virgin and Child with Angels in a Garden with a Rose Hedge, by Stefano da Verona. No. 941, Virgin and Child with St. John the Baptist, by Botticelli. No. 942, Madonna and Child with St. Anne, by Leonardo da Vinci. No. 943, Madonna and Child with Grapes, by Lucas Cranach the Elder.

1992, Nov. Litho. *Perf. 13½x14*
929 A232 10c multicolored .15 .15
930 A232 40c multicolored .30 .30
931 A232 45c multicolored .35 .35
932 A232 50c multicolored .38 .38
933 A232 55c multicolored .42 .42
934 A232 65c multicolored .48 .48
935 A232 75c multicolored .58 .58
936 A232 $1 multicolored .75 .75
937 A232 $2 multicolored 1.50 1.50
938 A232 $3 multicolored 2.25 2.25
939 A232 $4 multicolored 3.00 3.00
940 A232 $5 multicolored 3.75 3.75
Nos. 929-940 (12) 13.91 13.91

Souvenir Sheets
941 A232 $6 multicolored 4.50 4.50
942 A232 $6 multicolored 4.50 4.50
943 A232 $6 multicolored 4.50 4.50

Anniversaries and Events — G68

Designs: 10c, Nina in the harbor of Baracoa. No. 948, Columbus' fleet at sea. No. 949, America 3, US and Il Moro, Italy. No. 945, Zeppelin LZ3, 1907. No. 946, Blind man with guide dog, vert. No. 947, Guide dog. No. 950, German flag, natl. arms, Konrad Adenauer. No. 951, Hands breaking bread, vert. $2, Mars, Voyager 2. $3, Berlin airlift, Adenauer. No. 954, Wolfgang Amadeus Mozart, Constanze, vert. No. 955, Adenauer, Cologne after World War II. No. 956, Zeppelin LZ 37 shot down over England, World War I. $5, Buildings in Germany, Adenauer. No. 958, Scene from "Don Giovanni," vert. No. 959, Columbus looking through telescope. No. 960, Count Ferdinand von Zeppelin, facing right. No. 960A, Count Ferdinand von Zeppelin, facing left. No. 961, Mars Observer. No. 962, Adenauer with hand on face, vert. No. 963, Adenauer, diff.

1992, Dec. *Perf. 14*
944 G68 10c multicolored .15 .15
945 G68 75c multicolored .58 .58
946 G68 75c multicolored .58 .58
947 G68 75c multicolored .58 .58
948 G68 $1 multicolored .75 .75
949 G68 $1 multicolored .75 .75
950 G68 $1 multicolored .75 .75
951 G68 $1 multicolored .75 .75
952 G68 $2 multicolored 1.50 1.50
953 G68 $3 multicolored 2.25 2.25
954 G68 $4 multicolored 3.00 3.00
955 G68 $4 multicolored 3.00 3.00
956 G68 $4 multicolored 3.00 3.00
957 G68 $5 multicolored 3.75 3.75
Nos. 944-957 (14) 21.39 21.39

Souvenir Sheets
958-963 G68 $6 each 4.50 4.50

Discovery of America, 500th anniv. (#944, 948, 959). Count Zeppelin, 75th death anniv. (#945, 956, 960-960A). Lions Intl., 75th anniv. (#946-947). Konrad Adenauer, 25th death anniv. (#950, 953, 955, 957, 962-963).America's Cup yacht race (#949). Intl. Conference on Nutrition, Rome (#951). Intl. Space Year (#952, 961). Wolfgang Amadeus Mozart, bicent. of death (in 1991) (#954, 958).

Issued: #945, 956, 960-960A, 12/15; others, Dec.

Miniature Sheets

Walt Disney's Tales of Uncle Scrooge — G69

Goldilocks (Daisy Duck) and the Three Bears: No. 964a, Comes upon the house. b, Finds three bowls of soup. c, Finds three chairs. d, Ventures upstairs. e, Tries Papa Bear's bed. f, Falls asleep in Baby Bear's bed. g, The Three Bears return home. h, Baby Bear finds Goldilocks in his bed. i, Goldilocks awakens.

No. 970, The Three Bears in the forest, vert. No. 971, Goldilocks runs home.

The Princess (Minnie Mouse) and the Pea: No. 965a, Prince Mickey in search of a bride. b, Princess Minnie caught in a storm. c, Queen Clarbelle meets the princess. d, Royal family entertains Princess Minnie. e, Queen places a pea on the mattress. f, Mattresses upon mattresses. g, Princess Minnie at her bed-chamber. h, Princess Minnie very tired the next morning. i, A true princess for a real prince.

No. 972, Prince Mickey's useless search for a true princess. No. 973, Mickey's royal family lived happily ever after.

Little Red Riding Hood (Minnie Mouse): No. 966a, Off to Grandmother's. b, Stopping for flowers. c, Followed by the wolf. d, Frightened by the wolf. e, Wolf charges into Grandmother's house. f, Little Red Riding Hood at Grandmother's door. g, "What big teeth you have." h, Calling woodsman for help. i, Woodsman to the rescue.

No. 974, Little Riding Hood on the way to Grandmother's, vert. No. 975, A happy ending.

Hop O'-My-Thumb (Mickey, Minnie, family): No. 967a, Poor woodcutter without food for his children. b, Pebbles to find way back. c, Sadly leaving children's forest. d, Surveying from tree top. e, Ogress sends boys to bed. f, Ogre and his magic seven-league boots. g, Ogre chasing boys. h, Taking the magic seven-league boots. i, Running to Royal Palace.

No. 976, Boy of woodcutter with bag over shoulder. No. 977, Woodcutter's family reunited.

Pied Piper of Hamelin (Donald, Mickey and friends): No. 968a, Mayor (Donald) offers reward. b, Piper Mickey accepts the challenge. c, Piper leads rats to the river. d, Piper promises revenge. Children follow Piper outside village gates. f, Mayor and townspeople watch from above. g, Children follow Piper through countryside. h, Children pass through the cavern. i, All closed off from Hamelin, except for one.

No. 978, Pied Piper leading rats past town square. No. 979, Piper Mickey encouraging children in land of sweets, vert.

Puss in Boots (Goofy, Donald and friends): No. 969a, Gift for the king. b, Puss brings Marquis of Carabas to bathe in river. c, Puss calls for king's help. d, King introduces his daughter (Daisy Duck). e, Puss and reapers. f, Puss received by the Ogre. g, Ogre changed into a lion. h, Ogre changed into a mouse. i, Puss shows off Marquis' castle.

No. 980, Miller's estate, Donald with cat, Puss, donkey. No. 981, Marriage of Marquis of Carabis to daughter of the king, vert.

Perf. 14x13½, 13½x14
1992, Dec. 15 Litho.
964 G69 60c Sheet of 9, #a.-i. 4.25 4.25
965 G69 60c Sheet of 9, #a.-i. 4.25 4.25
966 G69 60c Sheet of 9, #a.-i. 4.25 4.25
967 G69 60c Sheet of 9, #a.-i. 4.25 4.25
968 G69 60c Sheet of 9, #a.-i. 4.25 4.25
969 G69 60c Sheet of 9, #a.-i. 4.25 4.25

Souvenir Sheets
Perf. 13½x14, 14x13½
970-981 G69 $6 each 4.50 4.50

Disney Animated Films Type
Miniature Sheets

Duck Tales (Donald Duck and family): No. 982: a, Scrooge McDuck, Launchpad. b, Scrooge reads treasure map. c, Collie Baba's treasure revealed. d, Webby finds magic lamp. e, Genie and new masters. f, Webby gets her wish. g, Scrooge McDuck, Genie. h, Retrieving the magic lamp. i, Villain Merlock, Genie.

No. 984, Webby's tea party, vert. No. 985, Treasure of the lost lamp, vert.

Darkwing Duck: No. 983: a, Darkwing Duck. b, Tuskerninni. c, Megavolt. d, Bushroot. e, Steelbeak. f, Eggman. g, Agent Gryzlikoff. h, Director J. Gander Hooter.

No. 985A, Gosalyn. No. 985B, Honker, horiz.

Perf. 14x13½, 13½x14
1992, Dec. 15 Litho.
982 A247a 60c Sheet of 9, #a.-i. 4.00 4.00
983 A247b 60c Sheet of 8, #a.-h. 3.60 3.60

Souvenir Sheets
984 A247a $6 multicolored 4.50 4.50
985 A247a $6 multicolored 4.50 4.50
985A A247b $6 multicolored 4.50 4.50
985B A247b $6 multicolored 4.50 4.50

Miniature Sheets

G71

Disney Animated Films — G72

The Great Mouse Detective: No. 986: a, Olivia and Flaversham. b, Olivia's mechanical mouse. c, Ratigan's evil scheme. d, Ratigan and Mechanical Mouse Queen. e, Fidget pens ransom note. f, Basil studies clues. g, Fidget holds Olivia captive. h, Ratigan in disguise. i, Basil and Dr. Dawson, crime stoppers.

Oliver & Company: No. 987: a, Dodger. b, Oliver. c, Dodger and Oliver. d, Oliver introduced to the Company. e, Oliver meets Fagin. f, Fagin's bed-time story hour. g, Oliver sleeping with Dodger. h, Fagin's trike. i, Georgette and Tito.

The Legend of Sleepy Hollow: No. 988: a, Ichabod Crane comes to town. b, Ichabod meets Katrina Van Tassel. c, Schoolmaster Ichabod Crane. d, Ichabod and rival, Brom Bones. e, Ichabod and Katrina at Halloween dance. f, Ichabod is scared of ghosts. g, Ichabod in Sleepy Hollow. h, Ichabod and his horse. i, Meeting the Headless Horseman.

No. 989, Detective Basil holding pipe. No. 990, Detective Basil holding magnifying glass. No. 991, Oliver. No. 992, Oliver and kittens. No. 993, Ichabod Crane, children praying, vert. No. 994, Headless Horseman.

Perf. 14x13½, 13½x14

1992, Dec. 15 **Litho.**

986 G71 60c Sheet of 9, #a.-i. 4.00 4.00
987 G71 60c Sheet of 9, #a.-i. 4.00 4.00
988 G72 60c Sheet of 9, #a.-i. 4.00 4.00

Souvenir Sheets

989-994 G71 $6 each 4.50 4.50

Elvis Presley Type of 1993

Designs: a, Portrait. b, With guitar. c, With microphone.

1993 **Litho.** *Perf. 14*

1001 A244 $1 Strip of 3, #a.-c. 2.25 2.25

Printed in sheets of 9 stamps.

Medicinal Plants — G73

Designs: 5c, Oleander. 10c, Beach morning glory. 30c, Calabash. 45c, Porita tree. 55c, Cashew. 75c, Prickly pear. $1, Shell ginger. $1.50, Avocado. $2, Mango. $3, Blood flower. $4, Sugar apple. $5, Barbados lily.

1994, May 20 **Litho.** *Perf. 13½x13*

1002-1013 G73 Set of 12 14.00 14.00

SEMI-POSTAL STAMPS

Nos. 190-193 Surcharged **HURRICANE RELIEF 50¢**

1980, Aug. 7 **Litho.** *Perf. 13½*

B1 A90 25c + 50c Running .15 .15
B2 A90 50c + 50c Sailing .15 .15
B3 A90 $1 + 50c Long jump .20 .20
B4 A90 $2 + 50c Swimming .35 .35
Nos. B1-B4 (4) .85 .85

OFFICIAL STAMPS

Nos. 209-214 Ovptd. "OFFICIAL"

1982, Oct. 11

O1 A66 50c on No. 209 .15 .15
O2 A67 50c on No. 210 .15 .15
O3 A66 $3 on No. 211 .90 .90
O4 A67 $3 on No. 212 .90 .90
O5 A66 $3.50 on No. 213 1.10 1.10
O6 A67 $3.50 on No. 214 1.10 1.10
Nos. O1-O6 (6) 4.30 4.30

BEQUIA

All stamps are types of St. Vincent ("A" illustration letter), St. Vincent Grenadines ("G" illustration letter) or Bequia ("B" illustration letter).

"Island" issues are listed separately beginning in 1984. See St. Vincent Grenadines Nos. 84-111, 248-262 for earlier issues.

Locomotive Type of 1985

1984-87 **Litho.** **Unwmk.** *Perf. 12½*

Pairs, Type A120

1 1c 1942 Challenger Class, US .15 .15
2 1c 1908 S3/6, Germany .15 .15
3 5c 1944 2900 Class, US .15 .15
4 5c 1903 Jersey Lily, UK .15 .15
5 10c 1882 Gladstone Class, UK .15 .15
6 10c 1909 Thundersley, UK .15 .15
7 15c 1860 Ser Class 118, UK .15 .15
8 25c 1893 No. 999 NY Central & Hudson River, US .15 .15
9 25c 1921 Class G2, UK .15 .15
10 25c 1902 Jr. Class 6400, Japan .15 .15
11 25c 1877 Class G3, Germany .15 .15
12 35c 1945 Niagara Class, US .25 .25
13 35c 1938 Manor Class, UK .25 .25
14 40c 1880 Class D VI, Germany .25 .25
15 45c 1914 K4 Class, US .30 .30
16 50c 1960 Class U25B, US .35 .35
17 55c 1921 Stephenson, UK .40 .40
18 55c 1909 Class H4, US .40 .40
19 60c 1922 Baltic, UK .40 .40
20 60c 1903 J.R. 4500, Japan .40 .40
21 60c 1915 Class LS .40 .40
22 75c 1841 Borsig, Germany .50 .50
23 75c 1943 Royal Scot, UK .50 .50
24 75c 1961 Krauss-Maffei, US .50 .50
25 $1 1928 River IRT, UK .70 .70
26 $1 1890 Electric, UK .70 .70
27 $1 1934 A.E.C., UK .70 .70
28 $1.50 1929 No. 10000, UK 1.00 1.00
29 $2 1904 City Class, UK 1.40 1.40
30 $2 1901 No. 737, UK 1.40 1.40
31 $2 1847 Cornwall, UK 1.40 1.40
32 $2.50 1938 Duke Dog Class, UK 1.75 1.75
33 $2.50 1881 Ella, UK 1.75 1.75
34 $3 1910 George V Class, UK 2.00 2.00
Nos. 1-34 (34) 19.35 19.35

Issued: #1, 3, 5, 8, 12, 15, 28-29, 2/22/84; #2, 4, 6, 13, 22, 25, 32, 34, 11/26/84; #9, 17, 19, 30, 2/1/85; #10, 18, 20, 23, 26, 33, 8/14/85; #7, 11, 14, 16, 21, 24, 27, 31, 11/16/87.

Stamps issued 11/16/87 are not inscribed "Leaders of the World."

St. Vincent Grenadines Nos. 222-238 Ovptd. "BEQUIA"

Perf. 14x13½

1984, Aug. 23 **Wmk. 373**

69 G26 1c on No. 222 .15 .15
70 G26 3c on No. 223 .15 .15
71 G26 5c on No. 224 .15 .15
72 G26 6c on No. 225 .15 .15
73 G26 10c on No. 226 .15 .15
74 G26 15c on No. 227 .15 .15
75 G26 20c on No. 228 .15 .15
76 G26 25c on No. 229 .15 .15
77 G26 30c on No. 230 .20 .20
78 G26 50c on No. 231 .30 .30
79 G26 60c on No. 232 .40 .40
80 G26 75c on No. 233 .50 .50
81 G26 $1 on No. 234 .65 .65
82 G26 $2 on No. 235 1.25 1.25
83 G26 $3 on No. 236 2.00 2.00
84 G26 $5 on No. 237 3.25 3.25
85 G26 $10 on No. 238 6.75 6.75
Nos. 69-85 (17) 16.50 16.50

Car Type of 1983

1984-87 **Unwmk.** *Perf. 12½*

Pairs, Type A107

86 5c 1953 Cadillac, US .15 .15
87 5c 1932 Fiat, Italy .15 .15
88 5c 1968 Excalibur, US .15 .15
89 5c 1952 Hudson, US .15 .15
90 10c 1924 Leyand, UK .15 .15
91 20c 1911 Marmon, US .15 .15
92 20c 1950 Alfa Romeo, Italy .15 .15
93 20c 1968 Ford Escort, UK .15 .15
94 20c 1939 Maserati 8 CTF, Italy .15 .15
95 25c 1963 Ford, UK .15 .15
96 25c 1958 Vanwall, UK .15 .15
97 25c 1910 Stanley, US .15 .15
98 35c 1948 Ford Wagon, US .25 .25
99 40c 1936 Auto Union, Germany .30 .30
100 45c 1907 Chadwick, US .35 .35
101 50c 1924 Lanchester, UK .40 .40
102 50c 1957 Austin-Healy, UK .40 .40
103 60c 1935 Brewster-Ford, US .45 .45
104 60c 1942 Willys Jeep, US .45 .45
104 65c 1929 Isotta, Italy .50 .50
106 75c 1940 Lincoln, US .60 .60
107 75c 1964 Bluebird II, UK .60 .60
108 75c 1948 Moore-Offenhauser, US .60 .60
109 75c 1936 Ford, UK .60 .60
110 80c 1936 Mercedes Benz, Germany .65 .65
111 90c 1928 Mercedes Benz SSK, Germany .70 .70
112 $1 1907 Rolls Royce, UK .75 .75
113 $1 1955 Citroen, France .75 .75
114 $1 1936 Fiat, Italy .75 .75
115 $1 1922 Dusenberg, US .75 .75
116 $1 1957 Pontiac Bonneville, US .75 .75
117 $1.25 1916 Hudson Super Six, US 1.00 1.00
118 $1.25 1977 Coyote Ford, US 1.00 1.00
119 $1.50 1960 Porsche, Germany 1.25 1.25
120 $1.50 1970 Plymouth, US 1.25 1.25
121 $1.75 1933 Stutz, US 1.35 1.35
122 $2 1910 Benz-Blitzen, Germany 1.60 1.60
123 $2 1933 Napier Railton, UK 1.60 1.60
124 $2.50 1978 BMW, Germany 2.00 2.00
125 $3 1912 Hispano Suiza, Spain 2.40 2.40
126 $3 1954 Mercedes Benz, Germany 2.40 2.40
127 $3 1927 Stutz Black Hawk, US 2.40 2.40
Nos. 86-127 (42) 30.65 30.65

Issued: #86, 99, 112, 119, 9/14; #87, 90-91, 95, 106, 113, 124-125, 12/19; #88, 96, 101, 114, 117, 122, 6/25/85; #92, 100, 120, 123, 9/26/85. #97, 102, 105, 107, 115, 126, 1/29/86; #93, 103, 108, 111, 116, 127, 12/23/86. #89, 94, 98, 104, 109-110, 118, 121, 7/22/87.

Beginning on Sept. 26, 1985, this issue is not inscribed "Leaders of the World."

1984 Summer Olympics — B1

Dogs — B2

1984, Sept. 14 *Perf. 12½*

170 B1 1c Men's gymnastics .15 .15
171 B1 1c Women's gymnastics .15 .15
172 B1 10c Men's javelin .15 .15
173 B1 10c Women's javelin .15 .15
174 B1 60c Women's basketball .25 .25
175 B1 60c Men's basketball .25 .25
176 B1 $3 Women's long jump 1.10 1.10
177 B1 $3 Men's long jump 1.10 1.10
Nos. 170-177 (8) 3.30 3.30

Stamps of same denomination printed se-tenant.

1985, Mar. 14 *Perf. 12½*

178 B2 25c Hungarian Kuvasz .15 .15
179 B2 25c Afghan .15 .15
180 B2 35c Whippet .15 .15
181 B2 35c Bloodhound .15 .15
182 B2 55c Cavalier King Charles Spaniel .25 .25
183 B2 55c German Shepherd .25 .25
184 B2 $2 Pekinese .80 .80
185 B2 $2 Golden Retriever .80 .80
Nos. 178-185 (8) 2.70 2.70

Stamps of same denomination printed se-tenant.

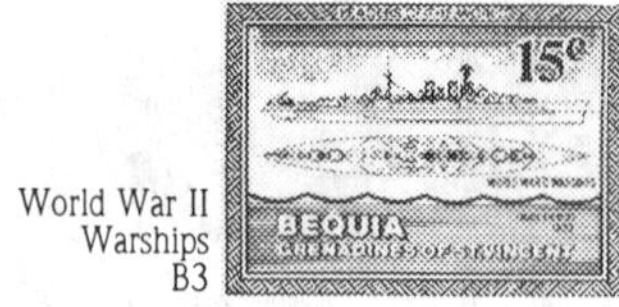

World War II Warships B3

1985, Apr. 29 *Perf. 12½*

Pairs, Design B3

186 B3 15c HMS Hood .15 .15
187 B3 50c HMS Duke of York .25 .25
188 B3 $1 KM Admiral Graf Spee .35 .35
189 B3 $1.50 USS Nevada .55 .55
Nos. 186-189 (4) 1.30 1.30

St. Vincent Grenadines Flower Type

1985, May 31 *Perf. 12½*

194 G38 10c Primula veris .15 .15
195 G38 10c Pulsatilla vulgaris .15 .15
196 G38 20c Lapageria rosea .15 .15
197 G38 20c Romneya coulteri .15 .15
198 G38 70c Anigozanthos manglesii .25 .25
199 G38 70c Metrosideros collina .25 .25
200 G38 $2.50 Protea laurifolia .90 .90
201 G38 $2.50 Thunbergia grandiflora .90 .90
Nos. 194-201 (8) 2.90 2.90

Stamps of same denomination printed se-tenant.

Queen Mother Type of 1985

Various Portraits of Queen Mother

1985, Aug. 29 *Perf. 12½*

202 A122 20c Blue hat .15 .15
203 A122 20c Violet hat .15 .15
204 A122 65c Blue hat, diff. .25 .25
205 A122 65c Tiara .25 .25
206 A122 $1.35 Blue hat, diff. .52 .52
207 A122 $1.35 White hat .52 .52
208 A122 $1.80 Blue hat, diff. .70 .70
209 A122 $1.80 Pink hat .70 .70
Nos. 202-209 (8) 3.24 3.24

Souvenir Sheets

210 Sheet of 2 1.65 1.65
a. A122 $2.05 Hat .80 .80
b. A122 $2.05 Tiara .80 .80
211 Sheet of 2 2.75 2.75
a. A122 $3.50 like #204 1.25 1.25
b. A122 $3.50 like #205 1.25 1.25
212 Sheet of 2 4.75 4.75
a. A122 $6 like #202 2.25 2.25
b. A122 $6 like #203 2.25 2.25

Stamps of same denomination printed se-tenant.

Queen Elizabeth II Type of 1986

Various portraits.

1986, Apr. 21

213 A128 5c multicolored .15 .15
214 A128 75c multicolored .30 .30
215 A128 $2 multicolored .80 .80
216 A128 $8 multicolored, vert. 3.25 3.25
Nos. 213-216 (4) 4.50 4.50

Souvenir Sheet

217 A128 $10 multicolored 4.00 4.00

B4

World Cup Soccer Championships, Mexico, 1986 — B5

1986 July 3 *Perf. 12½, 15 (B5)*

218 B4 1c South Korean team .15 .15
219 B4 2c Iraqi team .15 .15
220 B4 5c Algerian team .15 .15
221 B4 10c Bulgaria vs. France .15 .15
222 B5 45c Belgium .22 .22
223 B4 60c Danish team .28 .28
224 B4 75c Italy vs. W. Germany .35 .35
225 B4 $1.50 USSR vs. England .65 .65
226 B5 $1.50 Italy, 1982 champions .65 .65
227 B5 $2 W. Germany .95 .95
228 B5 $3.50 N. Ireland 1.65 1.65
229 B4 $6 England 2.75 2.75
Nos. 218-229 (12) 8.10 8.10

Souvenir Sheets

230 B4 $1 like No. 219 .45 .45
231 B4 $1.75 like No. 221 .85 .85

Royal Wedding Type of 1986

Perf. 12½x13, 13x12½

1986, July 15

232 A132 60c Andrew .24 .24
233 A132 60c Andrew in helicopter .24 .24
234 A132 $2 Andrew in crowd .75 .75
235 A132 $2 Andrew, Sarah .75 .75
Nos. 232-235 (4) 1.98 1.98

Souvenir Sheet

236 A132a $8 Andrew, Sarah in coach 3.25 3.25

Nos. 234-235 horiz.

Railway Engineers and Locomotives — B6

Designs: $1, Sir Daniel Gooch, Fire Fly Class, 1840. $2.50, Sir Nigel Gresley, A4 Class, 1938. $3, Sir William Stanier, Coronation Class, 1937. $4, Oliver V. S. Bulleid, Battle of Britain Class, 1946.

1986, Sept. 30 *Perf. 13x12½*

237 B6 $1 multicolored .48 .48
238 B6 $2.50 multicolored 1.25 1.25
239 B6 $3 multicolored 1.40 1.40
240 B6 $4 multicolored 1.90 1.90
Nos. 237-240 (4) 5.03 5.03

Nos. 232-235 Ovptd. "Congratulations to TRH The Duke & Duchess of York" in 3 Lines

1986 *Perf. 12½x13, 13x12½*

241 A132 60c on No. 232 .22 .22
242 A132 60c on No. 233 .22 .22
243 A132 $2 on No. 234 .75 .75
244 A132 $2 on No. 235 .75 .75
Nos. 241-244 (4) 1.94 1.94

Royalty Portrait Type

Portraits and photographs: 15c, Queen Victoria, 1841. 75c, Elizabeth, Charles, 1948. $1, Coronation, 1953. $2.50, Duke of Edinburgh, 1948. $5, Elizabeth c. 1980. $6, Elizabeth, Charles, 1948, diff.

1987, Oct. 15 *Perf. 12½x13*

245 A140 15c multicolored .15 .15
246 A140 75c multicolored .35 .35
247 A140 $1 multicolored .48 .48
248 A140 $2.50 multicolored 1.25 1.25
249 A140 $5 multicolored 2.50 2.50
Nos. 245-249 (5) 4.73 4.73

Souvenir Sheet

250 A140 $6 multicolored 3.00 3.00

Great Explorers Type of St. Vincent Grenadines

Designs: 15c, Gokstad, ship of Leif Eriksson (c. 1000). 50c, Eriksson and bearing dial. $1.75, The Mathew, ship of John Cabot. $2, Cabot, quadrant. $2.50, The Trinidad, ship of Ferdinand Magellan. $3, Arms, portrait of Christopher Columbus. $3.50, Columbus' ship Santa Maria. $4, Magellan, globe. $5, Anchor, long boat, ship.

1988, July 11 **Litho.** *Perf. 14*

251 G52 15c multicolored .15 .15
252 G52 50c multicolored .35 .35
253 G52 $1.75 multicolored .90 .90
254 G52 $2.00 multicolored 1.40 1.40
255 G52 $2.50 multicolored 1.75 1.75
256 G52 $3.00 multicolored 2.00 2.00
257 G52 $3.50 multicolored 2.50 2.50
258 G52 $4.00 multicolored 2.75 2.75
Nos. 251-258 (8) 11.80 11.80

Souvenir Sheet

259 G52 $5.00 multicolored 3.50 3.50

Tennis Type of 1987

1988, July 29 *Perf. 13x13½*

260 A137 15c Anders Jarryd .15 .15
261 A137 45c Anne Hobbs .25 .25
262 A137 80c Jimmy Connors .50 .50
263 A137 $1.25 Carling Bassett .75 .75
264 A137 $1.75 Stefan Edberg, horiz. 1.00 1.00
265 A137 $2.00 Gabriela Sabatini, horiz. 1.20 1.20
266 A137 $2.50 Mats Wilander 1.50 1.50
267 A137 $3.00 Pat Cash 1.80 1.80
Nos. 260-267 (8) 7.15 7.15

No. 263 inscribed "Carlene Basset" instead of "Carling Bassett."
An unissued souvenir sheet exists.

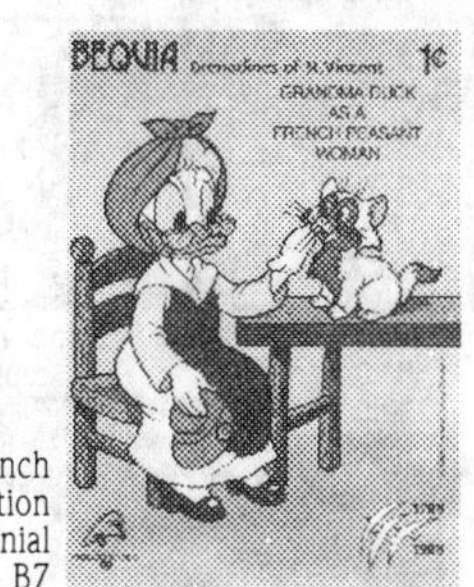

French Revolution Bicentennial B7

Designs: 1c, Grandma Duck as French peasant woman. 2c, Donald and Daisy celebrating liberty. 3c, Minnie as Marie Antoinette. 4c, Clarabelle and patriotic chair. 5c, Goofy in Republican citizen's costume. 10c, Mickey and Donald planting liberty tree. No. 274, Horace taking Tennis Court Oath. $6, Grand Master Mason McDuck. No. 276, Dancing the Carmagnole. No. 277, Philosophers at Cafe La Procope.

1989, July 7 *Perf. 13½x14*

268 B7 1c multicolored .15 .15
269 B7 2c multicolored .15 .15
270 B7 3c multicolored .15 .15
271 B7 4c multicolored .15 .15
272 B7 5c multicolored .15 .15
273 B7 10c multicolored .15 .15
274 B7 $5 multicolored 3.00 3.00
275 B7 $6 multicolored 3.50 3.50
Nos. 268-275 (8) 7.40 7.40

Souvenir Sheets

276 B7 $5 multicolored 3.00 3.00
277 B7 $5 multicolored 3.00 3.00

Anniversaries and Events Type

Design: $5, Otto Lililienthal, aviation pioneer.

1991, Nov. 18 **Litho.** *Perf. 14*

278 A213 $5 multicolored 3.75 3.75

Japanese Attack on Pearl Harbor, 50th Anniv. B8

Designs: 50c, Kate from second-wave over Hickam Field. $1, B17 sights Zeros in Pearl Harbor attack. $5, Firefighters rescue sailors from blazing USS Tennessee.

1991, Nov. 18

287 B8 50c multicolored .38 .38
288 B8 $1 multicolored .75 .75

Souvenir Sheet

289 B8 $5 multicolored 3.75 3.75

Wolfgang Amadeus Mozart, Death Bicentennial B9

Mozart and: 10c, Piccolo. 75c, Piano. $4, Violotta.

No. 293, Mozart's last composition, Lacrimosa from the Requiem Mass. No. 294, Bronze of Mozart by Adrien-Etienne Gaudez, vert. No. 295, Score of opening of the "Paris" symphony, K297.

1991 **Litho.** *Perf. 14*

290 B9 10c multicolored .15 .15
291 B9 75c multicolored .58 .58
292 B9 $4 multicolored 3.00 3.00
Nos. 290-292 (3) 3.73 3.73

Souvenir Sheets

293 B9 $6 multicolored 4.50 4.50
294 B9 $6 multicolored 4.50 4.50
295 B9 $6 multicolored 4.50 4.50

Nos. 293-295 each contain one 57x42mm or 42x57mm stamp.

Boy Scout Type

Designs: 50c, Lord Baden-Powell and killick hitch knot. $1, Baden-Powell and clove hitch knot. $2, Drawing of Boy Scout by Baden-Powell, vert. $3, American First Class Scout badge, vert. $6, Baden-Powell and Lark's head knot.

1991

296 A211 50c multicolored .38 .38
297 A211 $1 multicolored .75 .75
298 A211 $2 multicolored 1.50 1.50
299 A211 $3 multicolored 2.25 2.25
Nos. 296-299 (4) 4.88 4.88

Souvenir Sheet

300 A211 $6 multicolored 4.50 4.50

UNION ISLAND

All stamps are types of St. Vincent ("A" illustration letter), St. Vincent Grenadines ("G" illustration letter) or Union ("U" illustration letter).

"Island" issues are listed separately beginning in 1984. See St. Vincent Grenadines Nos. 84-111, 248-262 for earlier issues.

British Monarch Type of 1984

Perf. 12½

1984, Mar. 29 **Litho.** **Unwmk.**

1 A110 1c Battle of Hastings .15 .15
2 A111 1c William the Conqueror .15 .15
3 A110 5c William the Conqueror, diff. .15 .15
4 A111 5c Abbaye Aux Dames .15 .15
5 A110 10c Skirmish at Dunbar .15 .15
6 A111 10c Charles II .15 .15
7 A110 20c Arms of Willian the Conqueror .15 .15
8 A111 20c William the Conqueror, diff. .15 .15
9 A111 60c Charles II .22 .22
10 A110 60c St. James Palace .22 .22
11 A110 $3 Arms of Charles II 1.10 1.10
12 A111 $3 Charles II, Great Fire of London 1.10 1.10
Set value 3.00 3.00

Stamps of same denomination printed se-tenant.

Locomotives Type of 1985

1984-87 *Perf. 12½*

Pairs, Type A120

13 5c 1813 Puffing Billy, UK .15 .15
14 5c 1911 Class 9N, UK .15 .15
15 5c 1882 Class Skye Bogie, UK .15 .15
16 10c 1912 Class G8, Germany .15 .15
17 15c 1954 Class 65.10, Germany .15 .15
18 15c 1900 Castle Class, UK .15 .15
19 15c 1887 Spinner Class 25, UK .15 .15
20 15c 1951 Fell #10100, UK .15 .15
21 20c 1942 Class 42, Germany .15 .15
22 20c 1951 Class 5MT, UK .15 .15
23 25c 1929 P.O. Rebuilt Class 3500, France .18 .18
24 25c 1886 Class 123, UK .18 .18
25 30c 1976 Class 56, UK .22 .22
26 30c 1897 Class G5, US .22 .22
27 40c 1947 9400 Class, UK .30 .30
28 45c 1888 Sir Theodore, UK .35 .35
29 45c 1929 Class Z, UK .35 .35
30 45c 1896 Atlantic City RR, US .35 .35
31 50c 1906 45xx Class, UK .38 .38
32 50c 1912 Class D15, UK .38 .38
33 50c 1938 Class U4-b, Canada .38 .38
34 60c 1812 Prince Regent, UK .45 .45
35 60c 1920 Butler Henderson, UK .45 .45
36 60c 1889 Elidir, UK .45 .45
37 60c 1934 7200 Class, UK .45 .45
38 60c 1911 Class Z, UK .45 .45
39 75c 1938 Class C, Australia .58 .58
40 75c 1879 Sir Haydn, UK .58 .58
41 75c 1850 Aberdeen No. 26, UK .58 .58
42 75c 1883 Class Y14, UK .58 .58
43 75c 1915 River Class, UK .58 .58
44 $1 1936 D51 Class, Japan .75 .75
45 $1 1837 L&B Bury, UK .75 .75
46 $1 1903 Class 900, US .75 .75
47 $1 1904 Class H-20, US .75 .75
48 $1 1905 Class L, UK .75 .75
49 $1.50 1952 Class 4, UK 1.10 1.10
50 $1.50 1837 Campbell's 8-Wheeler, US 1.10 1.10
51 $1.50 1934 Class GG1, US 1.10 1.10
52 $2 1924 Class 01, Germany 1.50 1.50
53 $2 1920 Gordon Highlander, UK 1.50 1.50
54 $2 1969 Metroliner Railcar, US 1.50 1.50
55 $2 1951 Class GP7, US 1.50 1.50
56 $2.50 1873 Hardwicke Precedent Class, UK 1.75 1.75
57 $2.50 1899 Highflyer Class, UK 1.75 1.75
58 $3 1925 Class U1, UK 2.25 2.25
59 $3 1880 Class 7100, Japan 2.25 2.25
60 $3 1972 Gas Turbine Prototype, France 2.25 2.25
Nos. 13-60 (48) 33.24 33.24

Issued: #13, 34, 44, 52, 8/9/84; #14, 16, 21, 23, 39, 45, 56, 58, 12/18/84; #15, 31, 35, 53, 3/25/85; #17, 25, 28, 36, 40, 49, 57, 59, 1/31/86; #18, 29, 37, 41, 46, 50, 54, 60, 12/23/86; #19, 24, 27, 32, 38, 42, 47, 55, 9/87; #20, 22, 26, 308, 33, 43, 48, 51, 12/4/87.

Beginning on Jan. 31, 1986, this issue is not inscribed "Leaders of the World."

St. Vincent Grenadines Nos. 222-238 Overprinted "UNION ISLAND"

Perf. 14x13½

1984, Aug. 23 **Wmk. 373**

109 G26 1c on No. 222 .15 .15
110 G26 3c on No. 223 .15 .15
111 G26 5c on No. 224 .15 .15
112 G26 6c on No. 225 .15 .15
113 G26 10c on No. 226 .15 .15
114 G26 15c on No. 227 .15 .15
115 G26 20c on No. 228 .15 .15
116 G26 25c on No. 229 .16 .16
117 G26 30c on No. 230 .20 .20
118 G26 50c on No. 231 .35 .35
119 G26 60c on No. 232 .40 .40
120 G26 75c on No. 233 .45 .45
121 G26 $1 on No. 234 .70 .70
122 G26 $2 on No. 235 1.40 1.40
123 G26 $3 on No. 236 2.00 2.00
124 G26 $5 on No. 237 3.40 3.40
125 G26 $10 on No. 238 6.50 6.50
Nos. 109-125 (17) 16.61 16.61

Cricket Players Type of 1985

1984, Nov. **Unwmk.** *Perf. 12½*

Pairs, Type A116

126 1c S. N. Hartley .15 .15
127 10c G. W. Johnson .15 .15
128 15c R. M. Ellison .15 .15
129 55c C. S. Cowdrey .40 .40
130 60c K. Sharp .48 .48
131 75c M. C. Cowdrey, in action .60 .60
132 $1.50 G. R. Dilley, in action 1.25 1.25
133 $3 R. Illingworth, in action 2.25 2.25
Nos. 126-133 (8) 5.43 5.43

Classic Car Type of 1983

1985-86 *Perf. 12½*

Pairs, Type A107

142 1c 1963 Lancia, Italy .15 .15
143 5c 1895 Duryea, US .15 .15
144 10c 1970 Datsun, Japan .15 .15
145 10c 1962 BRM, UK .15 .15
146 50c 1927 Amilcar, France .35 .35
147 55c 1929 Duesenberg, US .40 .40
148 60c 1913 Peugeot, France .48 .48
149 60c 1938 Lagonda, UK .48 .48
150 60c 1924 Fiat, Italy .48 .48
151 75c 1957 Alfa Romeo, Italy .60 .60
152 75c 1957 Panhard, France .60 .60
153 75c 1954 Porsche, Germany .60 .60
154 90c 1904 Darraco, France .70 .70
155 $1 1927 Daimler, UK .85 .85
156 $1 1949 Oldsmobile, US .85 .85
157 $1 1934 Chrysler, US .85 .85
158 $1.50 1965 MG, UK 1.25 1.25
159 $1.50 1922 Fiat, Italy 1.25 1.25
160 $1.50 1934 Bugatti, France 1.25 1.25
161 $2 1963 Watson/Meyer-Drake, US 1.60 1.60
162 $2.50 1917 Locomobile, US 2.00 2.00
163 $3 1928 Ford, US 2.50 2.50
Nos. 142-163 (22) 17.69 17.69

Issued: #142, 146, 151, 162, 1/4/85; #143, 148, 155, 158, 5/20/85; #144, 147, 149, 152, 154, 156, 159, 161, 7/15/85; #145, 150, 153, 157, 160, 163, 7/30/86.

Beginning on 7/30/86, this issue is not inscribed "Leaders of the World."

Birds — U1

Butterflies — U2

1985, Feb. *Perf. 12½*

186 U1 15c Hooded warbler .15 .15
187 U1 15c Carolina wren .15 .15
188 U1 50c Song sparrow .20 .20
189 U1 50c Black-headed grosbeak .20 .20
190 U1 $1 Scarlet tanager .40 .40
191 U1 $1 Lazuli bunting .40 .40
192 U1 $1.50 Sharp-shinned hawk .60 .60
193 U1 $1.50 Merlin .60 .60
Nos. 186-193 (8) 2.70 2.70

Stamps of same denomination printed se-tenant.

1985, Apr. 15

194 U2 15c Cynthia cardui .15 .15
195 U2 15c Zerynthia rumina .15 .15
196 U2 25c Byblia ilithyia .15 .15
197 U2 25c Papilio machaon .15 .15
198 U2 75c Carterocephalus palaemon .30 .30
199 U2 75c Acraea anacreon .30 .30
200 U2 $2 Anartia amathea .80 .80
201 U2 $2 Salamis temora .80 .80
Nos. 194-201 (8) 2.80 2.80

Stamps of same denomination printed se-tenant.

Queen Mother Type of 1985

Various portraits of Queen Mother honoring 85th birthday.

1985, Aug. 19

202 A122 55c Mortarboard .18 .18
203 A122 55c Blue hat .18 .18
204 A122 70c Turquoise hat .24 .24
205 A122 70c Blue hat, diff. .24 .24
206 A122 $1.05 Without hat .35 .35
207 A122 $1.05 White hat .35 .35
208 A122 $1.70 White hat, violet feathers .65 .65
209 A122 $1.70 Blue hat, diff. .65 .65
Nos. 202-209 (8) 2.84 2.84

Souvenir Sheets

210 Sheet of 2 1.50 1.50
a. A122 $1.95 Crown .75 .75
b. A122 $1.95 Hat, diff. .75 .75
211 Sheet of 2 1.65 1.65
a. A122 $2.25 Like No. 208 .80 .80
b. A122 $2.25 Like No. 209 .80 .80
212 Sheet of 2 5.00 5.00
a. A122 $7 Like No. 206 2.50 2.50
b. A122 $7 Like No. 207 2.50 2.50

Stamps of same denomination printed se-tenant.

Elizabeth II 60th Birthday Type of 1986

Designs: 10c, Wearing scarf. 60c, Riding clothes. $2, Wearing crown and jewels. $8, In Canberra, vert. $10, Holding flowers.

1986, Apr. 21

213 A128 10c multicolored .15 .15
214 A128 60c multicolored .24 .24
215 A128 $2 multicolored .75 .75
216 A128 $8 multicolored 3.25 3.25
Nos. 213-216 (4) 4.39 4.39

Souvenir Sheet

217 A128 $10 multicolored 4.00 4.00

U3

World Cup Soccer Championships, Mexico — U4

Perf. 12½ (U3), 15 (U4)

1986, May 7

218 U3 1c Moroccan team .15 .15
219 U3 10c Argentinian team .15 .15
220 U4 30c Algerian player .15 .15
221 U3 75c Hungarian team .32 .32
222 U3 $1 Russian team .45 .45
223 U4 $2.50 Belgian player 1.10 1.10
224 U4 $3 French player 1.25 1.25
225 U4 $6 W. German player 2.50 2.50
Nos. 218-225 (8) 6.07 6.07

Souvenir Sheets

226 U3 $1.85 like No. 222 .85 .85
227 U3 $2 like No. 219 .85 .85

Souvenir sheets contain one 60x40mm stamp.

Prince Andrew Royal Wedding Type

Perf. 12½x13, 13x12½

1986, July 15

228 A132 60c Andrew with cap .25 .25
229 A132 60c Andrew, diff. .25 .25
230 A132 $2 Sarah Ferguson .75 .75
231 A132 $2 Sarah, Andrew .75 .75
Nos. 228-231 (4) 2.00 2.00

Nos. 228-231 Overprinted in Silver "CONGRATULATIONS TO T.R.H. THE DUKE & DUCHESS OF YORK" in 3 Lines

1986, Oct.

232 A132 60c on No. 228 .25 .25
233 A132 60c on No. 229 .25 .25
234 A132 $2 on No. 230 .75 .75
235 A132 $2 on No. 231 .75 .75
Nos. 232-235 (4) 2.00 2.00

Queen Elizabeth II Wedding Anniv. Type of St. Vincent Grenadines

1987, Oct. 15 *Perf. 12½*

236 G47 15c like No. 568 .15 .15
237 G47 45c like No. 569 .22 .22
238 G47 $1.50 like No. 570 .70 .70
239 G47 $3 like No. 571 1.40 1.40
240 G47 $4 like No. 572 1.75 1.75
Nos. 236-240 (5) 4.22 4.22

U5

Disney characters in various French vehicles: 1c, 1893 Peugeot. 2c, 1890-91Panhard-Levassor. 3c, 1910 Renault. 4c, 1919 Citroen. 5c, 1878 La Mancelle. 10c, 1891 De Dion Bouton Quadricycle. $5, 1896 Leon Bollee Trike. No. 248, 1911 Brasier Coupe. No. 249, French road race. No. 250, 1769, Cugnot's artillery tractor.

1989, July 7 *Perf. 14x13½*

241 U5 1c multicolored .15 .15
242 U5 2c multicolored .15 .15
243 U5 3c multicolored .15 .15
244 U5 4c multicolored .15 .15
245 U5 5c multicolored .15 .15
246 U5 10c multicolored .15 .15
247 U5 $5 multicolored 3.75 3.75
248 U5 $6 multicolored 4.50 4.50
249 U5 $6 multicolored 4.50 4.50
250 U5 $6 multicolored 4.50 4.50
Nos. 241-250 (10) 18.15 18.15

PHILEXFRANCE '89.

EL SALVADOR

'el–sal–və–,dȯr

LOCATION — On the Pacific coast of Central America, between Guatemala, Honduras and the Gulf of Fonseca
GOVT. — Republic
AREA — 8,236 sq. mi.
POP. — 5,300,000 (est. 1984)
CAPITAL — San Salvador

8 Reales = 100 Centavos = 1 Peso
100 Centavos = 1 Colón

Catalogue values for unused stamps in this country are for Never Hinged items, beginning with Scott 589 in the regular postage section, Scott C85 in the airpost section, and Scott O362 in the official section.

Watermarks

Wmk. 117- Liberty Cap

Position of wmk. on reprints

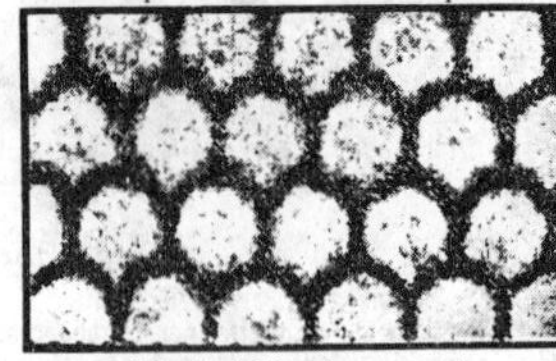

Wmk. 172- Honeycomb

Wmk. 173- S

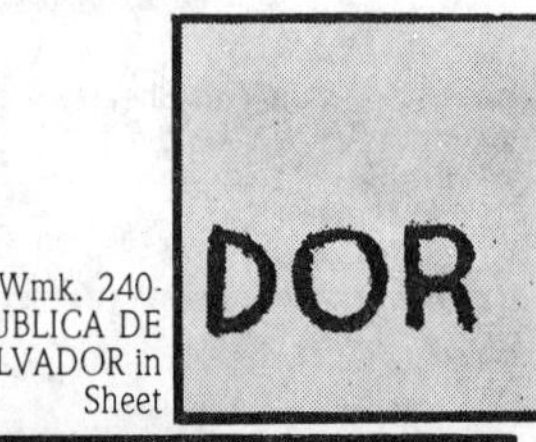

Wmk. 240- REPUBLICA DE EL SALVADOR in Sheet

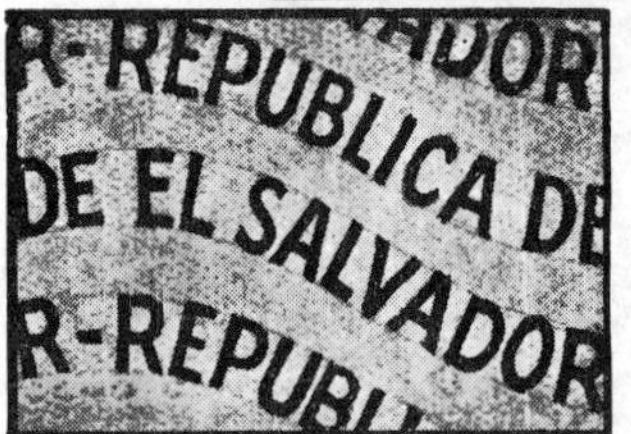

Wmk. 269- REPUBLICA DE EL SALVADOR

Volcano San Miguel — A1

1867 Unwmk. Engr. *Perf. 12*

1 A1 ½r blue .65 .75
2 A1 1r red .65 .65
3 A1 2r green 1.50 2.00
4 A1 4r bister 3.50 3.00
Nos. 1-4 (4) 6.30 6.40

Nos. 1-4 when overprinted "Contra Sello" and shield with 14 stars, are telegraph stamps. For similar overprint see Nos. 5-12.

Counterfeits exist.

Nos. 1-4 Handstamped

1874

5 A1 ½r blue 6.50 3.50
6 A1 1r red 6.50 3.50
7 A1 2r green 6.50 3.50
8 A1 4r bister 19.00 17.50
Nos. 5-8 (4) 38.50 28.00

Nos. 1-4 Handstamped

9 A1 ½r blue 3.75 2.00
10 A1 1r red 3.75 2.00
11 A1 2r green 3.75 2.00
12 A1 4r bister 7.50 5.00
Nos. 9-12 (4) 18.75 11.00

The overprints on Nos. 5-12 exist double. Counterfeits are plentiful.

Coat of Arms
A2 A3

A4 A5

A6

1879 Litho. *Perf. 12½*

13 A2 1c green 2.00 .90
a. Invtd. "V" for 2nd "A" in "SALVADOR" 4.00 2.00
b. Invtd. "V" for "A" in "REPUBLICA" 4.00 2.00
c. Invtd. "V" for "A" in "UNIVERSAL" 4.00 2.00
14 A3 2c rose 2.75 1.50
a. Invtd. scroll in upper left corner 8.00 5.00
15 A4 5c blue 5.00 1.25
a. 5c ultra 8.00 4.00
16 A5 10c black 10.00 3.50
17 A6 20c violet 16.00 10.00
Nos. 13-17 (5) 35.75 17.15

There are fifteen varieties of the 1c and 2c, twenty-five of the 5c and five each of the 10 and 20c.

In 1881 the 1c, 2c and 5c were redrawn, the 1c in fifteen varieties and the 2c and 5c in five varieties each.

No. 15 comes in a number of shades from light to dark blue.

These stamps, when overprinted "Contra sello" and arms, are telegraph stamps.

Counterfeits of No. 14 exist.

For overprints see Nos. 25D-25E, 28A-28C.

Allegorical Figure of El Salvador — A7

Volcano — A8

1887 Engr. *Perf. 12*

18 A7 3c brown .38 .18
a. Imperf., pair 2.50 2.50
19 A8 10c orange 3.00 .90

For surcharges and overprints see Nos. 25, 26C-28, 30-32.

A9

A10

1888 ***Rouletted***

20 A9 5c deep blue .30 .25

For overprints see Nos. 35-36.

1889 *Perf. 12*

21 A10 1c green .15
22 A10 2c scarlet .15

Same Overprinted with Heavy Bar Obliterating "UNION POSTAL DEL"

23 A10 1c green .30 .25
24 A10 2c scarlet .30

Nos. 21, 22 and 24 were never placed in use.
For overprints see Nos. 26, 29.

No. 18 Surcharged **1 centavo**

Type I - thick numerals, heavy serifs.
Type II - thin numerals, straight serifs.

25 A7 1c on 3c brn, type II .65 .50
a. Double surcharge 1.50
b. Triple surcharge 3.50
c. Type I .65

The 1c on 2c scarlet is bogus.

Handstamped **1889.**

1889

Violet Handstamp

25D A2 1c green 12.50 12.50
25E A6 20c violet 30.00 30.00
26 A10 1c green, #23 1.00 .90
26C A7 1c on 3c, #27 20.00 20.00
27 A7 3c brown 1.00 .90
28 A8 10c orange 5.00 4.00

Black Handstamp

28A A2 1c green 15.00 14.00
28B A3 2c rose 17.50 17.50
28C A6 20c violet 30.00 30.00
29 A10 1c green, #23 1.25 1.00
30 A7 3c brown 1.25 1.00
31 A7 1c on 3c, #27 17.50 17.50
32 A8 10c orange 4.50 3.50

Rouletted

Black Handstamp

35 A9 5c deep blue 1.25 .75

Violet Handstamp

36 A9 5c deep blue 1.25 .75

The 1889 handstamps as usual, are found double, inverted, etc. Counterfeits are plentiful.

A13 A14

1890 **Engr.** *Perf. 12*

38 A13 1c green .15 .15
39 A13 2c bis brn .15 .15
40 A13 3c yellow .15 .15
41 A13 5c blue .15 .15
42 A13 10c violet .15 .15
43 A13 20c orange .15 .20
44 A13 25c red .50 *1.00*
45 A13 50c claret .15 *.65*
46 A13 1p carmine .15 *1.50*
Set value (9) 1.08
Nos. 38-46 (9) *4.10*

The issues of 1890 to 1898 inclusive were printed by the Hamilton Bank Note Co., New York, to the order of N. F. Seebeck, who held a contract for stamps with the government of El Salvador. This contract gave the right to make reprints of the stamps and such were subsequently made in some instances, as will be found noted in italic type.

Used values of 1890-1898 issues are for stamps with genuine cancellations applied while the stamps were valid. Various counterfeit cancellations exist.

1891

47 A14 1c vermilion .15 .15
48 A14 2c yellow green .15 .15
49 A14 3c violet .15 .15
50 A14 5c carmine lake .15 .15
51 A14 10c blue .15 .15
52 A14 11c violet .15 .15
53 A14 20c green .15 *.32*
54 A14 25c yellow brown .15 *.38*
55 A14 50c dark blue .15 *.90*
56 A14 1p dark brown .15 *1.50*
Set value (10) 1.20
Nos. 47-56 (10) *4.00*

For surcharges see Nos. 57-59.

Nos. 47 and 56 have been reprinted in thick toned paper with dark gum.

A15

Nos. 48, 49 Surcharged in Black or Violet:

UN CENTAVO 5 CENTAVOS
b c

1891

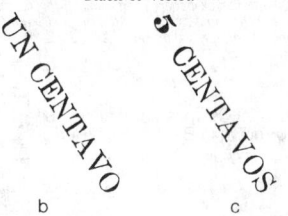

57 A15 1c on 2c yellow grn 2.25 2.00
a. Inverted surcharge 4.00
58 A14 (b) 1c on 2c yellow grn 1.65 1.40
59 A14 (c) 5c on 3c violet 4.00 3.25
Nos. 57-59 (3) 7.90 6.65

Landing of Columbus — A18

1892 **Engr.**

60 A18 1c blue green .15 .15
61 A18 2c orange brown .15 .15
62 A18 3c ultra .15 .15
63 A18 5c gray .15 .15
64 A18 10c vermilion .15 .15
65 A18 11c brown .15 *.38*
66 A18 20c orange .15 *.38*
67 A18 25c maroon .15 *.45*
68 A18 50c yellow .15 *.90*
69 A18 1p carmine lake .15 *1.25*
Set value (10) 1.20
Nos. 60-69 (10) *4.11*

400th anniversary of the discovery of America by Columbus.

Nos. 63, 66-67 Surcharged

UN CENTAVO **UN CENTAVO**
Nos. 70, 72 Nos. 73-75

Surcharged in Black, Red or Yellow

1892

70 A18 1c on 5c gray (Bk) (down) 1.00 .65
a. Surcharge reading up 1.75 1.10
72 A18 1c on 5c gray (R) (up) 1.00 .80
a. Surcharge reading down
73 A18 1c on 20c org (Bk) 1.25 .75
a. Inverted surcharge 3.50 2.50
b. "V" of "CENTAVO" inverted 3.50 2.50
Nos. 70-73 (3) 3.25 2.20

Similar Surcharge in Yellow or Blue, "centavo" in lower case letters

74 A18 1c on 25c mar (Y) 1.50 1.25
a. Inverted surcharge 2.50 2.50
75 A18 1c on 25c mar (Bl) *200.00 200.00*
a. Double surcharge (Bl + Bk) *225.00 225.00*

Counterfeits exist of Nos. 75 and 75a. Nos. 75, 75a have been questioned.

Pres. Carlos Ezeta — A21

1893 **Engr.**

76 A21 1c blue .15 .15
77 A21 2c brown red .15 .15
78 A21 3c purple .15 .15
79 A21 5c deep brown .15 .15
80 A21 10c orange brown .15 .15
81 A21 11c vermilion .15 *.25*
82 A21 20c green .15 *.30*
83 A21 25c dk olive gray .15 *.40*
84 A21 50c red orange .15 *.50*
85 A21 1p black .15 *.75*
Set value (10) 1.20
Nos. 76-85 (10) *2.95*

For surcharge see No. 89.

Founding City of Isabela — A22 Columbus Statue, Genoa — A23

Departure from Palos — A24

1893

86 A22 2p green .75 —
87 A23 5p violet .75
88 A24 10p orange .75
Nos. 86-88 (3) 2.25

Discoveries by Columbus. No. 86 is known on cover, but experts are not positive that Nos. 87 and 88 were postally used.

No. 77 Surcharged "UN CENTAVO"

1893

89 A21 1c on 2c brown red .50 .42
a. "CENTNVO" 3.00 3.00

Liberty A26 Columbus before Council of Salamanca A27

Columbus Protecting Indian Hostages — A28

Columbus Received by Ferdinand and Isabella — A29

1894, Jan.

91 A26 1c brown .15 .15
92 A26 2c blue .15 .15
93 A26 3c maroon .15 .15
94 A26 5c orange brn .15 .15
95 A26 10c violet .15 .15
96 A26 11c vermilion .15 *.25*
97 A26 20c dark blue .15 *.32*
98 A26 25c orange .15 *.38*
99 A26 50c black .15 *.65*
100 A26 1p slate blue .15 *.90*
101 A27 2p deep blue .75
102 A28 5p carmine lake .75
103 A29 10p deep brown .75
Nos. 91-103 (13) 3.75
Nos. 91-100 (10) *3.25*

Nos. 101-103 for the discoveries by Columbus. Experts are not positive that these were postally used.

No. 96 Surcharged **1 Centavo**

1894, Dec.

104 A26 1c on 11c vermilion 1.50 .65
a. "Ccntavo" *20.00 20.00*
b. Double surcharge

Coat of Arms
A31 A32

Arms Overprint in Second Color
Various Frames

1895, Jan. 1

105 A31 1c olive & green .20 .20
106 A31 2c dk green & bl .20 .20
a. 2c dark green & green 1.00 .85
107 A31 3c brown & brown .20 .20
108 A31 5c blue & brown .20 .20
109 A31 10c orange & brn .20 *.25*
110 A31 12c magenta & brn .20 *.30*
111 A31 15c ver & ver .20 *.35*
112 A31 20c yellow & brn .20 *.42*
a. Inverted overprint 2.00
113 A31 24c violet & brn .20 *.45*
114 A31 30c dp blue & blue .20 *.50*
115 A31 50c carmine & brn .20 *.65*
116 A31 1p black & brn .20 *.90*
Nos. 105-116 (12) 2.40 *4.62*

As printed, Nos. 105-116 portrayed Gen. Antonio Ezeta, brother of Pres. Carlos Ezeta. Before issuance, Ezeta's overthrow caused the government to obliterate his features with the national arms overprint. The 3c, 10c, 30c exist without overprint. Value $1 each.

Reprints of 2c are in dark yellow green on thick paper. Value 15 cents.

1895 **Engr.** *Perf. 12*

117 A32 1c olive .60 .50
118 A32 2c dk blue grn .15 .15
119 A32 3c brown .15 .15
120 A32 5c blue .15 .15
121 A32 10c orange .65 .30
122 A32 12c claret .65 .30
123 A32 15c vermilion .15 *.30*
124 A32 20c deep green .18 *.50*
125 A32 24c violet .18 *.50*
126 A32 30c deep blue .15 *.45*
127 A32 50c carmine lake 1.00 *1.25*
128 A32 1p gray black 1.25 *1.75*
Nos. 117-128 (12) 5.26 *6.30*

The reprints are on thicker paper than the originals, and many of the shades differ. Value 15c each.

Nos. 122, 124-126 Surcharged in Black or Red: **UN centavo**

1895

129 A32 1c on 12c claret (Bk) 1.00 .90
130 A32 1c on 24c violet 1.00 .90
131 A32 1c on 30c dp blue 1.00 .90
132 A32 2c on 20c dp green 1.00 .90
133 A32 3c on 30c dp blue 1.25 1.10
a. Double surcharge 4.50
Nos. 129-133 (5) 5.25 4.70

"Peace" — A45

1896, Jan. 1 **Engr.** **Unwmk.**

134 A45 1c blue .15 .15
135 A45 2c dark brown .15 .15
136 A45 3c blue green .15 .15
137 A45 5c brown olive .15 .15
138 A45 10c yellow .15 .20
139 A45 12c dark blue .75 .90
140 A45 15c brt ultra .15 *.20*
a. 15c light violet 1.00 *2.00*
141 A45 20c magenta .65 .50
142 A45 24c vermilion .15 *.25*
143 A45 30c orange .15 *.42*
144 A45 50c black brn .15 *.50*
145 A45 1p rose lake .15 *.90*
Nos. 134-145 (12) 2.90 *4.47*

The frames of Nos. 134-145 differ slightly on each denomination.

For overprints see Nos. O1-O12, O37-O48.

Wmk. 117

145B A45 2c dark brown .20 .20

The 1c, 2c, 12c, 20c, 30c, 50c and 1p on unwatermarked paper and the 2c on watermarked have been reprinted. The paper is thicker than that of the originals and the shades are different. The watermark is always upright on original stamps of Salvador, sideways on the reprints. Value 15c each.

Coat of Arms — A46

"White House" — A47

Locomotive — A48

Mt. San Miguel — A49

Ocean Steamship
A50 A51

Post Office — A52

Lake Ilopango — A53

Atehausillas Waterfall — A54

Coat of Arms — A55

Coat of Arms — A56

Columbus — A57

1896

No.	Type	Description	Unused	Used
146	A46	1c emerald	.18	.18
147	A47	2c lake	.18	.18
148	A48	3c yellow brn	.18	.18
149	A49	5c deep blue	.18	.18
150	A50	10c brown	.18	.18
151	A51	12c slate	.18	*.18*
152	A52	15c blue green	.18	*.25*
153	A53	20c carmine rose	.18	*.30*
154	A54	24c violet	*.18*	*.38*
155	A55	30c deep green	.18	*.38*
156	A56	50c orange	.18	*.38*
157	A57	100c dark blue	.18	*.90*
		Nos. 146-157 (12)	2.16	*3.67*

Nos. 146-157 exist imperf.

Unwmk.

No.	Type	Description	Unused	Used
157B	A46	1c emerald	.15	.15
157C	A47	2c lake	.15	.15
157D	A48	3c yellow brn	.15	.15
157E	A49	5c deep blue	.15	.15
157F	A50	10c brown	.18	.18
157G	A51	12c slate	.15	*.18*
157I	A52	15c blue green	.22	*.25*
157J	A53	20c carmine rose	.15	*.38*
157K	A54	24c violet	.50	*.90*
157M	A55	30c deep green	.15	*.65*
157N	A56	50c orange	.15	*.65*
157O	A57	100c dark blue	.15	*1.10*
		Nos. 157B-157O (12)	2.25	*4.89*

See Nos. 159-170L. For surcharges and overprints see Nos. 158, 158D, 171-174C, O13-O36, O49-O72, O79-O126.

The 15c, 30c, 50c and 100c have been reprinted on watermarked and the 1c, 2c, 3c, 5c, 12c, 20c, 24c and 100c on unwatermarked paper. The papers of the reprints are thicker than those of the originals and the shades are different. Value, set of 12, $1.20.

Black Surcharge on Nos. 154, 157K **Quince centavos**

1896				Wmk. 117
158	A54	15c on 24c violet	4.00	4.00
a.		Double surcharge		
b.		Inverted surcharge	8.50	

Unwmk.

No.	Type	Description	Unused	Used
158D	A54	15c on 24c violet	4.00	3.00

Exist spelled "Qnince."

Types of 1896

1897		Engr.		Wmk. 117
159	A46	1c scarlet	*.15*	*.15*
160	A47	2c yellow grn	.15	.15
161	A48	3c bister brn	.15	.15
162	A49	5c orange	.15	.15
163	A50	10c blue grn	.15	.15
164	A51	12c blue	.42	.30
165	A52	15c black	2.50	2.00
166	A53	20c slate	.15	.15
167	A54	24c yellow	.15	.25
168	A55	30c rose	.15	.20
169	A56	50c violet	.18	.50
170	A57	100c brown lake	2.50	2.00
		Nos. 159-170 (12)	6.80	6.15

Unwmk.

No.	Type	Description	Unused	Used
170A	A46	1c scarlet	.15	.15
170B	A47	2c yellow grn	.15	.15
170C	A48	3c bister brn	.15	.15
170D	A49	5c orange	.15	.15
170E	A50	10c blue grn	.75	.50
170F	A51	12c blue	.75	.75
170G	A52	15c black	2.00	2.00
170H	A53	20c slate	.15	*.25*
170I	A54	24c yellow	.15	*.50*
170J	A55	30c rose	1.90	1.25
170K	A56	50c violet	.90	.90
170L	A57	100c brown lake	6.25	6.25
		Nos. 170A-170L (12)	13.45	13.00

The 1c, 2c, 3c, 5c, 12c, 15c, 50c and 100c have been reprinted on watermarked and the entire issue on unwatermarked paper. The papers of the reprints are thicker than those of the originals. Value, set of 20, $2.

Surcharged in Red or Black **TRECE centavos**

1897				Wmk. 117
171	A54	13c on 24c yel (R)	2.50	2.50
172	A55	13c on 30c rose (Bk)	2.50	2.50
173	A56	13c on 50c vio (Bk)	2.50	2.50
174	A57	13c on 100c brn lake (Bk)	2.50	2.50

Unwmk.

No.	Type	Description	Unused	Used
174A	A54	13c on 24c yel (R)	2.50	2.50
174B	A55	13c on 30c rose (Bk)	2.50	2.50
174C	A56	13c on 50c vio (Bk)	2.50	2.50
		Nos. 171-174C (7)	17.50	17.50

Coat of Arms of "Republic of Central America" — A59

ONE CENTAVO:

Originals: The mountains are outlined in red and blue. The sea is represented by short red and dark blue lines on a light blue background.

Reprints: The mountains are outlined in red only. The sea is printed in green and dark blue, much blurred.

FIVE CENTAVOS:

Originals: The sea is represented by horizontal and diagonal lines of dark blue on a light blue background.

Reprints: The sea is printed in green and dark blue, much blurred. The inscription in gold is in thicker letters.

1897				Litho.
175	A59	1c bl, gold, rose & grn	.50	*1.00*
176	A59	5c rose, gold, bl & grn	.50	*1.50*

Forming of the "Republic of Central America."

For overprints see Nos. O73-O76.

Stamps of type A59 formerly listed as "Type II" are now known to be reprints.

Allegory of Central American Union — A60

1898		Engr.		Wmk. 117
177	A60	1c orange ver	.18	.15
178	A60	2c rose	.18	.18
179	A60	3c pale yel grn	.18	.18
180	A60	5c blue green	.18	.15
181	A60	10c gray blue	.18	.18
182	A60	12c violet	.18	.25
183	A60	13c brown lake	.18	.18
184	A60	20c deep blue	.18	*.30*
185	A60	24c deep ultra	.18	*.35*
186	A60	26c bister brn	.18	*.40*
187	A60	50c orange	.18	*.75*
188	A60	1p yellow	.18	*1.00*
		Nos. 177-188 (12)	2.16	*4.07*

For overprints and surcharges see Nos. 189-198A, 224-241, 269A-269B, O129-O142.

The entire set has been reprinted on unwatermarked paper and all but the 12c and 20c on watermarked paper. The shades of the reprints are not the same as those of the originals, and the paper is thicker. Value, set of 22, $2.25.

No. 180 Overprinted Vertically, up or down in Black, Violet, Red, Magenta and Yellow **Transito Territorial**

1899				
189	A60	5c blue grn (Bk)	7.50	6.25
a.		Italic 3rd "r" in "Territorial"	12.50	12.50
b.		Double ovpt. (Bk + Y)	37.50	37.50
190	A60	5c blue grn (V)	*82.50*	*82.50*
191	A60	5c blue grn (R)	*70.00*	*70.00*
191A	A60	5c blue grn (M)	*70.00*	*70.00*
191B	A60	5c blue grn (Y)	*75.00*	*75.00*
		Nos. 189-191B (5)	*305.00*	*303.75*

Counterfeits exist.

Nos. 177-184 Overprinted in Black

1899				
192	A60	1c orange ver	1.00	.50
193	A60	2c rose	1.25	1.00
194	A60	3c pale yel grn	1.25	.50
195	A60	5c blue green	1.25	.50
196	A60	10c gray blue	2.00	1.25
197	A60	12c violet	3.25	2.50
198	A60	13c brown lake	3.25	2.00
198A	A60	20c deep blue	100.00	100.00
		Nos. 192-198A (8)	113.25	108.25

Counterfeits exist of the "wheel" overprint used in 1899-1900.

Ceres ("Estado") — A61

Inscribed: "Estado de El Salvador"

1899	Unwmk.	Litho.		*Perf. 12*
199	A61	1c brown	.15	
200	A61	2c gray green	.15	
201	A61	3c blue	.15	
202	A61	5c brown org	.15	
203	A61	10c chocolate	.15	
204	A61	12c dark green	.15	
205	A61	13c deep rose	.15	
206	A61	24c light blue	.15	
207	A61	26c carmine rose	.15	
208	A61	50c orange red	.15	
209	A61	100c violet	.15	
		Set value (11)	1.10	

#208-209 were probably not placed in use.

For overprints and surcharges see Nos. 210-223, 242-252D, O143-O185.

Same, Overprinted

Red Overprint

No.	Type	Description	Unused	Used
210	A61	1c brown	50.00	32.50

Blue Overprint

No.	Type	Description	Unused	Used
211	A61	1c brown	.50	.15
212	A61	5c brown org	.50	.20
212A	A61	10c chocolate	5.00	3.50

Black Overprint

No.	Type	Description	Unused	Used
213	A61	1c brown	.50	.15
214	A61	2c gray grn	.75	.15
215	A61	3c blue	.75	.25
216	A61	5c brown org	.35	.15
217	A61	10c chocolate	.50	.15
218	A61	12c dark green	1.25	.50
219	A61	13c deep rose	1.10	.65
220	A61	24c light blue	12.50	10.00
221	A61	26c car rose	3.25	2.00
222	A61	50c orange red	3.25	2.75
223	A61	100c violet	3.25	3.25
		Nos. 213-223 (11)	27.45	20.00

"Wheel" overprint exists double and triple.

No. 177 Handstamped **1900**

1900				Wmk. 117
224	A60	1c orange ver	1.00	1.00

No. 177 Overprinted **1900**

No.	Type	Description	Unused	Used
225	A60	1c orange ver	12.50	12.50

Stamps of 1898 Surcharged in Black **1900 1 centavo**

1900				
226	A60	1c on 10c gray blue	5.00	4.25
a.		Inverted surcharge	7.50	6.50
227	A60	1c on 13c brn lake	*275.00*	
228	A60	2c on 12c vio	17.50	12.50
a.		"eentavo"		
b.		Inverted surcharge		
c.		"centavos"	30.00	
d.		As "c," double surcharge		
e.		Vertical surcharge		
229	A60	2c on 13c brn lake	2.00	1.75
a.		"eentavo"	3.25	2.75
b.		Inverted surcharge	5.00	4.00
c.		"1900" omitted		
230	A60	2c on 20c dp blue	2.00	2.00
a.		Inverted surcharge	3.25	3.25
230B	A60	2c on 26c bis brn	*175.00*	*175.00*
231	A60	3c on 12c vio	*37.50*	*37.50*
a.		"eentavo"		
b.		Inverted surcharge	*35.00*	*35.00*
c.		Double surcharge		
232	A60	3c on 50c org	10.00	10.00
a.		Inverted surcharge	10.00	10.00
233	A60	5c on 12c vio		
234	A60	5c on 24c ultra	11.00	11.00
a.		"eentavo"		
b.		"centavos"	11.00	
235	A60	5c on 26c bis brn	*37.50*	*37.50*
a.		Inverted surcharge	*35.00*	*35.00*
236	A60	5c on 1p yel	15.00	15.00
a.		Inverted surcharge	15.00	15.00

With Additional Overprint in Black

No.	Type	Description	Unused	Used
237	A60	2c on 12c vio	2.50	2.50
a.		Inverted surcharge	2.50	2.50
b.		"eentavo"	8.00	
c.		"centavos" (plural)	75.00	
d.		"1900" omitted		
237H	A60	2c on 13c brn lake		
238	A60	3c on 12c vio	42.50	42.50
a.		"eentavo"	35.00	35.00
239	A60	5c on 26c bis brn	67.50	67.50
a.		Inverted surcharge		

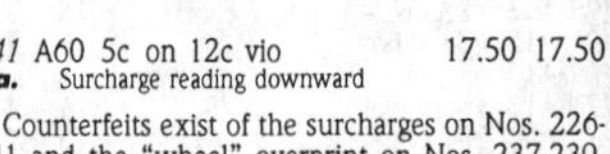

Vertical Surcharge "Centavos" in the Plural

No.	Type	Description	Unused	Used
240	A60	2c on 12c vio	95.00	95.00
b.		Without wheel		
240A	A60	5c on 24c dp ultra	95.00	95.00

With Additional Overprint in Black

No.	Type	Description	Unused	Used
241	A60	5c on 12c vio	17.50	17.50
a.		Surcharge reading downward		

Counterfeits exist of the surcharges on Nos. 226-241 and the "wheel" overprint on Nos. 237-239, 241.

Same Surcharge on Stamps of 1898 Without Wheel

1900				Unwmk.
242	A61	1c on 13c dp rose	.40	.40
a.		Inverted surcharge	.75	.75
b.		"eentavo"	.75	.75
c.		"ecntavo"	1.25	.75
d.		"1 centavo 1"	4.00	3.00
e.		Double surcharge		
243	A61	2c on 12c dk grn	1.75	1.25
a.		Inverted surcharge	2.50	2.50
b.		"eentavo"		
244	A61	2c on 13c dp rose	1.00	.75
a.		"eentavo"	1.25	1.25
b.		"ecntavo"	1.40	1.40
c.		Inverted surcharge		
245	A61	3c on 12c dk grn	1.00	.85
a.		Inverted surcharge	2.00	1.50
b.		"eentavo"	4.00	4.00
c.		Double surcharge	2.00	
		Nos. 242-245 (4)	4.15	3.25

With Additional Overprint in Black

No.	Type	Description	Unused	Used
246	A61	1c on 2c gray grn	.25	.15
a.		"eentavo"	.90	.65
b.		Inverted surcharge	4.00	3.00
247	A61	1c on 13c dp rose	1.00	.85
a.		"eentavo"	4.00	
b.		"1 centavo 1"		
248	A61	2c on 12c dk grn	1.40	1.00
a.		"eentavo"	4.00	
b.		Inverted surcharge	1.25	1.25
c.		Double surcharge	2.00	
249	A61	2c on 13c dp rose	42.50	
a.		"eentavo"		
b.		Double surcharge	75.00	75.00

250 A61 3c on 12c dk grn 1.40 .90
a. Inverted surcharge 1.50 1.25
b. "eentavo" 2.50 2.25
c. Date double 4.00
251 A61 5c on 24c lt bl 2.50 1.25
a. "eentavo" 4.00 4.00
252 A61 5c on 26c car rose 1.10 1.00
a. Inverted surcharge 4.00 2.50
b. "eentavo" 1.75 1.50
252D A61 5c on 1c on 26c car rose
Nos. 246-248,250-252 (6) 7.65 5.15

Counterfeits exist of the surcharges on Nos. 242-252D and the "wheel" overprint on Nos. 246-252D.

Ceres ("Republica") — A63

There are two varieties of the 1c, type A63, one with the word "centavo" in the middle of the label (#253, 263, 270, 299, 305, 326), the other with "centavo" nearer the left end than the right (#270, 299, 305, 326).

The stamps of type A63 are found in a great variety of shades. Stamps of type A63 without handstamp were not regularly issued.

Handstamped in Violet or Black

Inscribed: "Republica de El Salvador"

1900

253 A63 1c blue green .20 .20
a. 1c yellow green .20 .20
254 A63 2c rose .30 .20
255 A63 3c gray black .20 .20
256 A63 5c pale blue .50 .35
a. 5c deep blue .50 .35
257 A63 10c deep blue .60 .45
258 A63 12c yel green .60 .45
259 A63 13c yel brown .50 .45
260 A63 24c gray 4.00 4.00
261 A63 26c yel brown 1.75 1.75
262 A63 50c rose red 1.75 1.50
Nos. 253-262 (10) 10.40 9.55

For overprints and surcharges see Nos. 263-269, 270-282, 293A-311B, 317, 326-335, O223-O242, O258-O262, O305-O312.

Handstamped in Violet or Black

263 A63 1c lt green 1.75 1.75
264 A63 2c pale rose 1.75 1.75
265 A63 3c gray black 1.75 .75
266 A63 5c slate blue 1.75 .50
267 A63 10c deep blue 50.00 42.50
268 A63 13c yellow brn 12.50 8.75
269 A63 50c dull rose 1.75 1.75
Nos. 263-269 (7) 71.25 57.75

Handstamped on 1898 Stamps

Wmk. 117

269A A60 2c rose 30.00 30.00
269B A60 10c gray blue 30.00 30.00

The overprints on Nos. 253 to 269B are handstamped and, as usual with that style of overprint, are to be found double, inverted, omitted, etc.

Stamps of Type A63 Overprinted in Black

1900 **Unwmk.**

270 A63 1c light green .20 .15
271 A63 2c rose .20 .15
272 A63 3c gray black .20 .15
273 A63 5c pale blue .20 .15
a. 5c dark blue .20 .15
274 A63 10c deep blue .40 .15
a. 10c pale blue .30 .15
275 A63 12c light green .40 .30
276 A63 13c yellow brown .20 .15
277 A63 24c gray .40 .40
278 A63 26c yellow brown .50 .50
Nos. 270-278 (9) 2.70 2.10

This overprint is known double, inverted, etc.

Nos. 271-273 Surcharged in Black

1902

280 A63 1c on 2c rose 2.75 2.25
281 A63 1c on 3c black 2.00 1.40
282 A63 1c on 5c blue 1.25 1.00
Nos. 280-282 (3) 6.00 4.65

Morazán Monument — A64

Perf. 14, 14½

1903 **Engr.** **Wmk. 173**

283 A64 1c green .35 .15
284 A64 2c carmine .35 .15
285 A64 3c orange .80 .50
286 A64 5c dark blue .35 .15
287 A64 10c dull violet .35 .15
288 A64 12c slate .40 .15
289 A64 13c red brown .40 .18
290 A64 24c scarlet 2.50 1.25
291 A64 26c yellow brn 2.50 1.25
292 A64 50c bister 1.25 .75
293 A64 100c grnsh blue 3.75 2.50
Nos. 283-293 (11) 13.00 7.18

For surcharges and overprint see Nos. 312-316, 318-325, O253.

Stamps of 1900 with Shield in Black Overprinted:

1905 (5¾x13½mm) a
1905 (5x14¾mm) b
1905 (4½x16mm) c
1905 (4½x13½mm) d
(5x14½mm) — e 1905

1905-06 **Unwmk.** ***Perf. 12***

Blue Overprint

293A A63 (a) 2c rose
294 A63 (a) 3c gray blk 4.00 3.00
a. Without shield
295 A63 (a) 5c blue 4.50 3.00

Purple Overprint

296 A63 (b) 3c gray blk (Shield in purple) 4.50 4.00
296A A63 (b) 5c bl (Shield in purple) 3.25 3.00
297 A63 (b) 3c gray blk 6.00 4.50
298 A63 (b) 5c blue 4.00 3.00

Black Overprint

298A A63 (b) 5c blue

Blue Overprint

299 A63 (c) 1c green 4.50 3.00
299B A63 (c) 2c rose .40 .35
c. "1905" vert. .80
300 A63 (c) 5c blue 1.25 .60
301 A63 (c) 10c deep blue .75 .60

Black Overprint

302 A63 (c) 2c rose 3.00 1.50
303 A63 (c) 5c blue 12.50 12.50
304 A63 (c) 10c deep blue 4.00 3.50

Blue Overprint

305 A63 (d) 1c green 5.00 3.50
306 A63 (d) 2c rose (ovpt. vert.) 3.00 1.50
a. Overprint horiz.
306B A63 (d) 3c gray black 5.00 1.75
307 A63 (d) 5c blue 2.50 1.00

Blue Overprint

311 A63 (e) 2c rose 2.50 2.00
a. Without shield 4.00 3.00

Black Overprint

311B A63 (e) 5c blue 20.00 19.00
Nos. 293-311B (20) 94.40 73.80

These overprints are found double, inverted, omitted, etc. Counterfeits exist.

Regular Issue of 1903 Surcharged with New Values:

UN CENTAVO f
5 CENTAVOS g

1 1

1 CENTAVO 1
h

1905-06 **Wmk. 173** ***Perf. 14, 14½***

Black Surcharge

312 A64 (f) 1c on 2c car .40 .25
a. Double surcharge 3.00 3.00

Red Surcharge

312B A64 (g) 5c on 12c slate .75 .50
c. Double surcharge
d. Black surcharge 3.50 3.50
e. As "d," double surcharge

Blue Handstamped Surcharge

313 A64 (h) 1c on 2c car .25 .15
314 A64 (h) 1c on 10c vio .20 .15
315 A64 (h) 1c on 12c sl ('06) 1.00 .50
316 A64 (h) 1c on 13c red brn 4.00 3.25

No. 271 with Handstamped Surcharge in Blue

Unwmk.

317 A63 (h) 1c on 2c rose 42.50 37.50
Nos. 312-317 (7) 49.10 42.30

The "h" is handstamped in strips of four stamps each differing from the others in the size of the upper figures of value and in the letters of the word "CENTAVO," particularly in the size of the "N" and the "O" of that word. The surcharge is known inverted, double, etc.

Regular Issue of 1903 with Handstamped Surcharge:

5 5
i
5 5
5 5
5 5 5 5
j k

Wmk. 173

Red Handstamped Surcharge

318 A64 (i) 5c on 12c slate 2.25 1.50
319 A64 (j) 5c on 12c slate 2.25 1.75
a. Blue surcharge

Blue Handstamped Surcharge

320 A64 (k) 5c on 12c slate 2.00 1.75
Nos. 318-320 (3) 6.50 5.00

One or more of the numerals in the handstamped surcharges on Nos. 318, 319 and 320 are frequently omitted, inverted, etc.

Surcharged:

6 6 1 1
6 CENTAVOS 6
l m

Blue Handstamped Surcharge

321 A64 (l) 6c on 12c slate .50 .30
322 A64 (l) 6c on 13c red brn 1.00 .42

Red Handstamped Surcharge

323 A64 (l) 6c on 12c slate 17.50 12.00

Type "l" is handstamped in strips of four varieties, differing in the size of the numerals and letters. The surcharge is known double and inverted.

Black Surcharge

324 A64 (m) 1c on 13c red brn 1.50 1.00
a. Double surcharge 4.00 3.00
b. Right "1" & dot omitted
c. Both numerals omitted
325 A64 (m) 3c on 13c red brn .50 .38

Stamps of 1900, with Shield in Black, Overprinted — n
01905

1905 **Unwmk.** ***Perf. 12***

Blue Overprint

326 A63 (n) 1c green 4.50 3.25
a. Inverted overprint
327 A63 (n) 2c rose 3.25 3.25
a. Vertical overprint 6.00 5.00
327B A63 (n) 3c black 30.00 27.50
327C A63 (n) 5c blue 12.50 10.00
328 A63 (n) 10c deep blue 6.00 4.50

Black Overprint

328A A63 (n) 10c deep blue 7.50 4.50
Nos. 326-328A (6) 63.75 53.00

Counterfeits of Nos. 326-335 abound.

Stamps of 1900, with Shield in Black Surcharged or Overprinted:

1906

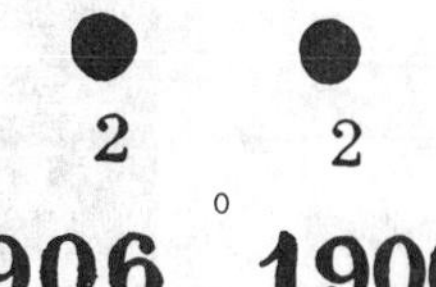

2 2
o

1906 p
1906 q

1906

Blue and Black Surcharge

329 A63 (o) 2c on 26c brn org .50 .40
a. "2" & dot double 7.50 7.50
330 A63 (o) 3c on 26c brn org 4.00 3.25
a. "3" & dot double

Black Surcharge or Overprint

331 A63 (o) 3c on 26c brn org 3.00 2.50
a. Disks & numerals omitted
b. "3" and disks double
c. "1906" omitted
333 A63 (p) 10c deep blue 1.75 1.40
334 A63 (q) 10c deep blue 1.25 1.25
334A A63 (q) 26c brown org 22.50 20.00
b. "1906" in blue

No. 257 Overprinted in Black

335 A63 (q) 10c dp bl (Shield in violet) 17.50 15.00
a. Overprint type "p"
Nos. 329-335 (7) 50.50 43.80

There are numerous varieties of these surcharges and overprints.

Pres. Pedro José Escalón — A65

1906 **Engr.** ***Perf. 11½***

Glazed Paper

336 A65 1c green & blk .15 .15
a. Thin paper .75 .15
337 A65 2c red & blk .15 .15
338 A65 3c yellow & blk .15 .15
339 A65 5c ultra & blk .15 .15
a. 5c dark blue & black .15 .15
340 A65 6c carmine & blk .15 .15
341 A65 10c violet & blk .15 .15
342 A65 12c violet & blk .15 .15
343 A65 13c dk brn & blk .15 .15
345 A65 24c carmine & blk .35 .35
346 A65 26c choc & blk .35 .35
347 A65 50c yellow & blk .35 .45
348 A65 100c blue & blk *3.00 3.00*
Nos. 336-348 (12) *5.25 5.35*

All values of this set are known imperforate but are not believed to have been issued in this condition.

See Nos. O263-O272. For overprints and surcharges see Nos. 349-354.

The entire set has been reprinted. The shades of the reprints differ from those of the originals, the paper is thicker and the perforation 12. Value, set of 12, $1.20.

Nos. 336-338 Overprinted in Black

1907

349 A65 1c green & blk .25 .25
a. Shield in red 3.50
350 A65 2c red & blk .25 .25
a. Shield in red 3.50
351 A65 3c yellow & blk .25 .25
Nos. 349-351 (3) .75 .75

Reprints of Nos. 349 to 351 have the same characteristics as the reprints of the preceding issue. Value, set of 3, 15c.

Stamps of 1906 Surcharged with Shield and **1**

352	A65	1c on 5c ultra & blk	.15	.15
a.		1c on 5c dark blue & black	.15	.15
b.		Inverted surcharge		
c.		Double surcharge		
352D	A65	1c on 6c rose & blk	.20	.20
e.		Double surcharge	1.25	1.25
353	A65	2c on 6c rose & blk	2.00	1.00
354	A65	10c on 6c rose & blk	.50	.35
		Nos. 352-354 (4)	2.85	1.70

The above surcharges are frequently found with the shield double, inverted, or otherwise misplaced.

National Palace — A66

Overprinted with Shield in Black

1907 Engr. Unwmk.

Paper with or without colored dots

355	A66	1c green & blk	.15	.15
356	A66	2c red & blk	.15	.15
357	A66	3c yellow & blk	.15	.15
358	A66	5c blue & blk	.15	.15
a.		5c ultramarine & black	.15	.15
359	A66	6c ver & blk	.15	.15
a.		Shield in red	3.75	
360	A66	10c violet & blk	.15	.15
361	A66	12c violet & blk	.15	.15
362	A66	13c sepia & blk	.15	.15
363	A66	24c rose & blk	.15	.15
364	A66	26c yel brn & blk	.30	.20
365	A66	50c orange & blk	.50	.35
a.		50c yellow & black	3.50	
366	A66	100c turq bl & blk	1.00	.50
		Nos. 355-366 (12)	3.15	
		Set value		1.70

Most values exist without shield, also with shield inverted, double, and otherwise misprinted. Many of these were never sold to the public.

See 2nd footnote following No. 421.

See Nos. 369-373, 397-401. For surcharges and overprints see Nos. 367-368A, 374-77, 414-421, 443-444, J71-J74, J76-J80, O329-O331.

No. 356 With Additional Surcharge in Black **UN CENTAVO**

1908

367	A66	1c on 2c red & blk	.25	.25
a.		Double surcharge	1.00	1.00
b.		Inverted surcharge	.50	.50
c.		Double surcharge, one inverted	.50	.50
d.		Red surcharge		

Same Surcharged in Black or Red **UN CENTAVO**

368	A66	1c on 2c	*19.00*	*17.50*
368A	A66	1c on 2c (R)	*27.50*	*25.00*

Counterfeits exist of the surcharges on Nos. 368-368A.

Type of 1907

1909 Engr. Wmk. 172

369	A66	1c green & blk	.15	.15
370	A66	2c rose & blk	.15	.15
371	A66	3c yellow & blk	.25	.15
372	A66	5c blue & blk	.25	.15
373	A66	10c violet & blk	.30	.20
		Nos. 369-373 (5)	1.10	
		Set value		.70

The note after No. 366 will apply here also.

Nos. 355, 369 Overprinted in Red **1821 15 septiembre 1909**

1909, Sept. Unwmk.

374	A66	1c green & blk	2.25	1.10
a.		Inverted overprint	10.00	

Wmk. 172

375	A66	1c green & blk	1.75	1.40
a.		Inverted overprint		

88th anniv. of El Salvador's independence.

Nos. 362, 364 Surcharged **2 CENTAVOS 1909**

1909 Unwmk.

376	A66	2c on 13c sep & blk	1.50	1.25
a.		Inverted surcharge		
377	A66	3c on 26c yel brn & blk	1.75	1.40
a.		Inverted surcharge		

A67 A68

Design: Pres. Fernando Figueroa.

1910 Engr. Wmk. 172

378	A67	1c sepia & blk	.15	.15
379	A67	2c dk grn & blk	.15	.15
380	A67	3c orange & blk	.15	.15
381	A67	4c carmine & blk	.15	.15
a.		4c scarlet & black	.15	.15
382	A67	5c purple & blk	.15	.15
383	A67	6c scarlet & blk	.15	.15
384	A67	10c purple & blk	.15	.15
385	A67	12c dp bl & blk	.15	.15
386	A67	17c ol grn & blk	.15	.15
387	A67	19c brn red & blk	.15	.15
388	A67	29c choc & blk	.15	.15
389	A67	50c yellow & blk	.15	.15
390	A67	100c turq bl & blk	.15	.15
		Set value (13)	1.60	1.45

1911 Unwmk.

Designs: 5c, José Matías Delgado. 6c, Manuel José Arce. 12c, Centenary Monument.

Paper with colored dots

391	A68	5c dp blue & brn	.15	.15
392	A68	6c orange & brn	.15	.15
393	A68	12c violet & brn	.15	.15

Wmk. 172

394	A68	5c dp blue & brn	.15	.15
395	A68	6c orange & brn	.15	.15
396	A68	12c violet & brn	.15	.15
		Set value	.54	.60

Centenary of the insurrection of 1811.

Palace Type of 1907 without Shield

1911

Paper without colored dots

397	A66	1c scarlet	.15	.15
398	A66	2c chocolate	.25	.25
a.		Paper with brown dots		
399	A66	13c deep green	.15	.15
400	A66	24c yellow	.15	.15
401	A66	50c dark brown	.15	.15
		Set value	.70	.70

José Matías Delgado A71

Manuel José Arce A72

Francisco Morazán A73

Rafael Campo A74

Trinidad Cabañas A75

Monument of Gerardo Barrios A76

Centenary Monument A77

National Palace A78

Rosales Hospital — A79

Coat of Arms — A80

1912 Unwmk. *Perf. 12*

402	A71	1c dp bl & blk	.20	.15
403	A72	2c bis brn & blk	.25	.15
404	A73	5c scarlet & blk	.25	.15
405	A74	6c dk grn & blk	.20	.15
406	A75	12c ol grn & blk	1.00	.18
407	A76	17c violet & slate	.60	.15
408	A77	19c scar & slate	1.25	.20
409	A78	29c org & slate	1.50	.20
410	A79	50c blue & slate	1.75	.38
411	A80	1col black & slate	2.50	.75
		Nos. 402-411 (10)	9.50	2.46

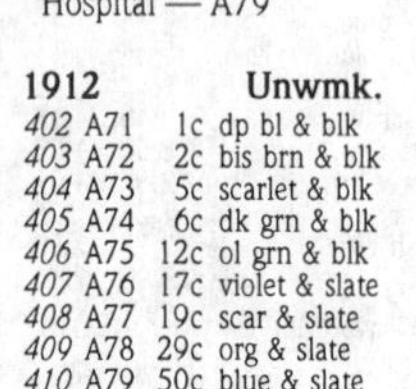

Juan Manuel Rodríguez A81

Pres. Manuel E. Araujo A82

1914 *Perf. 11½*

412	A81	10c orange & brn	2.50	.75
413	A82	25c purple & brn	2.50	.75

Type of 1907 without Shield Overprinted in Black **1915**

1915

Paper overlaid with colored dots

414	A66	1c gray green	.15	.15
415	A66	2c red	.15	.15
416	A66	5c ultra	.15	.15
417	A66	6c pale blue	.15	.15
418	A66	10c yellow	.60	.30
419	A66	12c brown	.50	.15
420	A66	50c violet	.15	.15
421	A66	100c black brn	1.40	1.40
		Nos. 414-421 (8)	3.25	
		Set value		2.25

Varieties such as center omitted, center double, center inverted, imperforate exist with or without date, date inverted, date double, etc., but are believed to be entirely unofficial.

Preceding the stamps with the "1915" overprint a quantity of stamps of this type was overprinted with the letter "S." Evidence is lacking that they were ever placed in use. The issue was demonetized in 1916.

National Theater — A83

Various frames.

1916 Engr. *Perf. 12*

431	A83	1c deep green	.15	.15
432	A83	2c vermilion	.15	.15
433	A83	5c deep blue	.15	.15
434	A83	6c gray violet	.25	.15
435	A83	10c black brn	.25	.15
436	A83	12c violet	2.50	.50
437	A83	17c orange	.35	.15
438	A83	25c dk brown	.80	.20
439	A83	29c black	5.00	.75
440	A83	50c slate	2.50	1.50
		Nos. 431-440 (10)	12.10	
		Set value		3.40

Watermarked letters which occasionally appear are from the papermaker's name.

For surcharges and overprints see Nos. 450-455, 457-466, O332-O341.

Nos. O324-O325 with "OFICIAL" Barred out in Black

1917

441	O3	2c red	.45	.45
a.		Double bar		
442	O3	5c ultramarine	.50	.35
a.		Double bar		

Regular Issue of 1915 Overprinted "OFICIAL" and Re-overprinted In Red

CORRIENTE

443	A66	6c pale blue	.65	.50
a.		Double bar		
444	A66	12c brown	.85	.65
a.		Double bar		
b.		"CORRIENTE" inverted		

Same Overprint in Red On Nos. O323-O327

445	O3	1c gray green	1.75	1.25
a.		"CORRIENTE" inverted		
b.		Double bar		
c.		"CORRIENTE" omitted		
446	O3	2c red	1.75	1.25
a.		Double bar		
447	O3	5c ultra	9.00	6.00
a.		Double bar, both in black		
448	O3	10c yellow	1.00	.50
a.		Double bar		
b.		"OFICIAL" and bar omitted		
449	O3	50c violet	.50	.50
a.		Double bar		
		Nos. 443-449 (7)	15.50	10.65

Nos. O334-O335 Overprinted or Surcharged in Red:

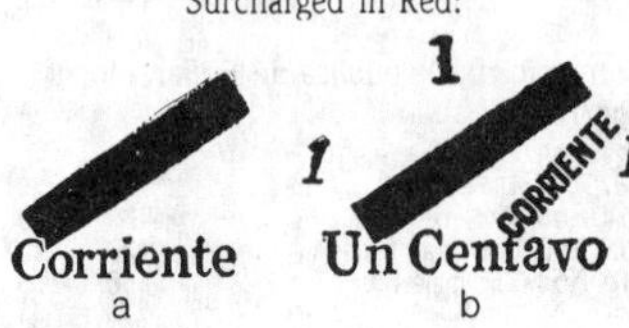

a b

450	A83 (a)	5c deep blue	1.50	1.00
a.		"CORRIENTE" double		
451	A83 (b)	1c on 6c gray vio	1.00	.75
a.		"CORRIENTE"		
b.		"CORRIENRE"	5.00	
c.		"CORRIENTE" double		

No. 434 Surcharged in Black

1918

452	A83	1c on 6c gray vio	1.75	1.00
a.		Double surcharge		
b.		Inverted surcharge		

No. 434 Surcharged in Black

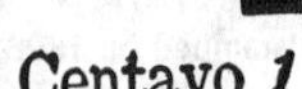

1918

453	A83	1c on 6c gray vio	1.50	.75
a.		"Centado"	2.25	1.50
b.		Double surcharge	2.50	1.75
c.		Inverted surcharge		

No. 434 Surcharged in Black or Red

454	A83	1c on 6c gray vio	4.00	3.25
a.		Double surcharge		
b.		Inverted surcharge	5.00	5.00
455	A83	1c on 6c gray vio (R)	4.00	3.25
a.		Double surcharge		
b.		Inverted surcharge	5.00	5.00
		Nos. 454-455 (2)	8.00	6.50

Counterfeits exist of Nos. 454-455.

Pres. Carlos Meléndez — A85

1919 **Engr.**

456 A85 1col dk blue & blk .50 .50

For surcharge see No. 467.

No. 437 Surcharged in Black

1

1 Centavo 1

1919

457 A83 1c on 17c orange .20 .15
- *a.* Inverted surcharge .75 .75
- *b.* Double surcharge .75 .75

Nos. 435-436, 438, 440 Surcharged in Black or Blue

1

1 Centavo 1

2

2 centavos 2

VALE
5 Centavos

6

SEIS

1920-21

458 A83 1c on 12c violet .20 .15
- *a.* Double surcharge 1.00 1.00

459 A83 2c on 10c dk brn .25 .15

460 A83 5c on 50c slate ('21) .40 .15

461 A83 6c on 25c dk brn (Bl) ('21) .40 .20

Same Surch. in Black on No. O337

462 A83 1c on 12c violet 1.00 1.00
- *a.* Double surcharge

Nos. 458-462 (5) 2.25 1.65

No. 460 surcharged in yellow and 461 surcharged in red are essays.

No. 462 is due to some sheets of Official Stamps being mixed with the ordinary 12c stamps at the time of surcharging. The error stamps were sold to the public and used for ordinary postage.

Surcharged in Red:

Types:

15 15 15 15
I II III IV

463 A83 15c on 29c blk (III) ('21) 1.00 .38
- *a.* Double surcharge 2.00
- *b.* Type I 1.50 1.00
- *c.* Type II 1.00 .75
- *d.* Type IV 2.50

35
Treinta y cinco

Surcharged in Blue or Black

464 A83 26c on 29c blk (Bl) 1.00 .60
- *a.* Double surcharge

466 A83 35c on 50c slate (Bk) 1.00 .60

One stamp in each row of ten of No. 464 has the "t" of "cts" inverted and one stamp in each row of No. 466 has the letters "c" in "cinco" larger than the normal.

No. 464 surcharged in green or yellow and the 35c on 29c black are essays.

No. 456 Surcharged in Red

60
CENTAVOS

467 A85 60c on 1col dk bl & blk .30 .25

Setting includes three types of numerals and "CENTAVOS" measuring from 16mm to 20mm wide.

A93

1921

468 A93 1c on 1c ol grn .15 .15
- *a.* Double surcharge .75

469 A93 1c on 5c yellow .15 .15
- *a.* Inverted surcharge
- *b.* Double surcharge

470 A93 1c on 10c blue .15 .15
- *a.* Double surcharge .50

471 A93 1c on 25c green .15 .15
- *a.* Double surcharge

472 A93 1c on 50c olive .15 .15
- *a.* Double surcharge

473 A93 1c on 1p gray blk .18 .18
- *a.* Double surcharge

Set value .50 .50

The frame of No. 473 differs slightly from the illustration.

Setting includes many wrong font letters and numerals.

Francisco Menéndez A94

Manuel José Arce A95

Confederation Coin — A96

Delgado Addressing Crowd — A97

Coat of Arms of Confederation A98

Francisco Morazán A99

Independence Monument A100

Columbus A101

1921 **Engr.** ***Perf. 12***

474 A94 1c green .25 .15

475 A95 2c black .25 .15

476 A96 5c orange 1.00 .15

477 A97 6c carmine rose .50 .15

478 A98 10c deep blue .50 .15

479 A99 25c olive grn 2.50 .15

480 A100 60c violet 6.00 .50

481 A101 1col black brn 10.00 .75

Nos. 474-481 (8) 21.00

Set value 1.70

For overprints and surcharges see Nos. 481A-485, 487-494, 506, O342-O349.

Nos. 474-477 Overprinted in Red, Black or Blue

CENTENARIO CENTENARIO
a b

1921

481A A94 (a) 1c green (R) 5.00 4.00

481B A95 (a) 2c black (R) 5.00 4.00

481C A96 (b) 5c orange (Bk) 5.00 4.00

481D A97 (b) 6c car rose (Bl) 5.00 4.00

Nos. 481A-481D (4) 20.00 16.00

Centenary of independence.

No. 477 Surcharged:

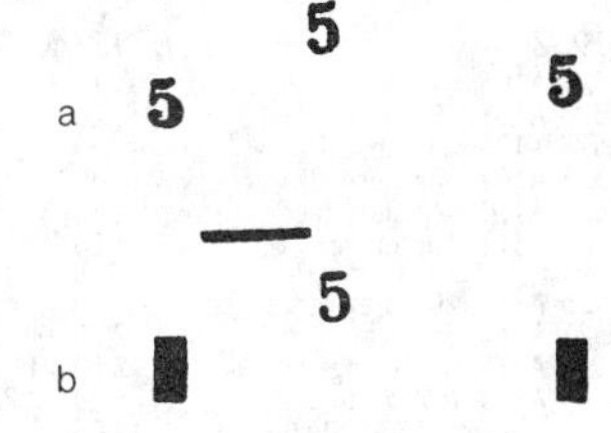

1923

482 A97 (a) 5c on 6c .35 .15

483 A97 (b) 5c on 6c .30 .15

484 A97 (b) 20c on 6c .35 .25

Nos. 482-484 (3) 1.00 .55

Nos. 482-484 exist with double surcharge.

No. 475 Surcharged in Red

10

1923

485 A95 10c on 2c black .50 .15

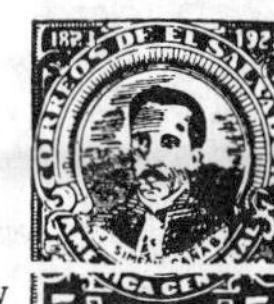

José Simeón Cañas y Villacorta — A102

1923 **Engr.** ***Perf. 11½***

486 A102 5c blue .50 .25

Centenary of abolition of slavery.

For surcharge see No. 571.

Nos. 479, 481 Surcharged in Red or Black

6 6

Seis centavos

1924 ***Perf. 12***

487 A99 1c on 25c ol grn (R) .15 .15
- *a.* Numeral at right inverted
- *b.* Double surcharge

488 A99 6c on 25c ol grn (R) .20 .15

489 A99 20c on 25c ol grn (R) .50 .25

490 A101 20c on 1col blk brn (Bk) .65 .38

Nos. 487-490 (4) 1.50 .93

Nos. 476, 478 Surcharged:

1 6 6

centavo Centavos

1924

491 A96 1c on 5c orange (Bk) .35 .20

492 A98 6c on 10c dp bl (R) .35 .20

Nos. 491-492 exist with double surcharge.

A stamp similar to No. 492 but with surcharge "6 centavos 6" is an essay.

No. 476 Surcharged

2
Dos centavos

493 A96 2c on 5c orange .35 .25
- *a.* Top ornament omitted 2.00 2.00

Nos. 491-493 (3) 1.05 .65

No. 480 Surcharged:

15 Sept.
1874 — 1924
5 5
U. P. U.
CINCO CENTAVOS

1924

Red Surcharge

494 A100 5c on 60c violet 4.25 3.25
- *a.* "1781" for "1874" 10.00 8.75
- *b.* "1934" for "1924" 10.00 8.75

Universal Postal Union, 50th anniversary.

This stamp with black surcharge is an essay. Copies have been passed through the post.

Daniel Hernández Monument A106

National Gymnasium A107

Atlacatl — A108

Conspiracy of 1811 — A109

Bridge over Lempa River — A110

Map of Central America — A111

Balsam Tree — A112

Tulla Serra — A114

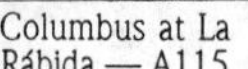
Columbus at La Rábida — A115

Coat of Arms — A116

Photogravure; Engraved (35c, 1col)

1924-25 *Perf. 12½; 14 (35c, 1col)*

495 A106 1c red violet .15 .15
496 A107 2c dark red .25 .15
497 A108 3c chocolate .15 .15
498 A109 5c olive blk .15 .15
499 A110 6c grnsh blue .25 .15
500 A111 10c orange .60 .15
a. "ATLANT CO" 5.25 5.25
501 A112 20c deep green 1.00 .25
502 A114 35c scar & grn 2.50 .38
503 A115 50c orange brown 2.00 .30
504 A116 1col grn & vio ('25) 3.00 .30
Nos. 495-504 (10) 10.05
Set value 1.70

For overprints and surcharges see Nos. 510-511, 520-534, 585, C1-C10, C19, O350-O361, RA1-RA4.

No. 480 Surcharged in Red

*1525
2 2
1925*
Dos centavos

1925, Aug. *Perf. 12*

506 A100 2c on 60c violet 1.25 1.25

City of San Salvador, 400th anniv.
The variety with dates in black is an essay.

View of San Salvador — A118

1925 **Photo.** *Perf. 12½*

507 A118 1c blue .65 .65
508 A118 2c deep green .65 .65
509 A118 3c Mahogany red .65 .65
Nos. 507-509 (3) 1.95 1.95

#506-509 for the 4th centenary of the founding of the City of San Salvador.

Black Surcharge

Exposición Santaneca
Julio de 1928

3 """ 3

1928, July 17

510 A111 3c on 10c orange .65 .50
a. "ATLANT CO" 12.50 12.50

Industrial Exhibition, Santa Ana, July 1928.

Red Surcharge

1928

511 A109 1c on 5c olive black .25 .20
a. Bar instead of top left "1" .38 .25

Pres. Pío Romero Bosque, Salvador, and Pres. Lázaro Chacón, Guatemala A121

1929 **Litho.** *Perf. 11½*

Portraits in Dark Brown

512 A121 1c dull violet .25 .25
a. Center inverted 12.50 12.50
513 A121 3c bister brn .25 .25
a. Center inverted 37.50 37.50
514 A121 5c gray grn .25 .25
515 A121 10c orange .25 .25
Nos. 512-515 (4) 1.00 1.00

Opening of the international railroad connecting El Salvador and Guatemala.

Nos. 512-515 exist imperforate. No. 512 in the colors of No. 515.

Tomb of Menéndez A122

1930, Dec. 3

516 A122 1c violet 2.50 2.25
517 A122 3c brown 2.50 2.25
518 A122 5c dark green 2.50 2.25
519 A122 10c yellow brn 2.50 2.25
Nos. 516-519 (4) 10.00 9.00

Centenary of the birth of General Francisco Menéndez.

Stamps of 1924-25 Issue Overprinted **1932**

1932 *Perf. 12½, 14*

520 A106 1c deep violet .15 .15
521 A107 2c dark red .20 .15
522 A108 3c chocolate .30 .15
523 A109 5c olive blk .30 .15
524 A110 6c deep blue .35 .15
525 A111 10c orange 1.00 .15
a. "ATLANT CO" 7.50 6.25
526 A112 20c deep green 1.50 .45
527 A114 35c scar & grn 2.25 .75
528 A115 50c orange brown 3.00 1.00
529 A116 1col green & vio 5.00 2.25
Nos. 520-529 (10) 14.05 5.35

Values are for the overprint measuring 7½x3mm. It is found in two other sizes: 7½x3¼mm and 8x3mm.

Types of 1924-25 Surcharged with New Values in Red or Black

1934 *Perf. 12½*

530 A109 2(c) on 5c grnsh blk .15 .15
a. Double surcharge
531 A111 3(c) on 10c org (Bk) .15 .15
a. "ATLANT CO" 4.00 4.00

Nos. 503, 504, 502 Surcharged with New Values in Black

Perf. 12½, 14½

532 A115 2(c) on 50c .30 .15
a. Double surcharge 3.00
533 A116 8(c) on 1col .15 .15
534 A114 15(c) on 35c .30 .18
Nos. 530-534 (5) 1.05
Set value .55

Police Barracks — A123

Two types of the 2c:

Type I - The clouds have heavy lines of shading.

Type II - The lines of shading have been removed from the clouds.

Perf. 12½

1934-35 **Wmk. 240** **Litho.**

535 A123 2c gray brn, type I .20 .15
a. 2c brown, type II .20 .15
536 A123 5c car, type II .20 .15
537 A123 8c lt ultra, type II .20 .15
Nos. 535-537,C33-C35 (6) 3.10
Set value 1.35

Discus Thrower A124

1935, Mar. 16 **Engr.** **Unwmk.**

538 A124 5c carmine 2.00 1.65
539 A124 8c blue 2.25 1.90
540 A124 10c orange yel 2.75 2.00
541 A124 15c bister 3.25 2.25
542 A124 37c green 4.00 3.25
Nos. 538-542,C36-C40 (10) 47.75 36.55

3rd Central American Games.

Same Overprinted in Black **HABILITADO**

1935, June 27

543 A124 5c carmine 2.75 2.00
544 A124 8c blue 4.00 2.00
545 A124 10c orange yel 4.00 2.50
546 A124 15c bister 4.00 2.50
547 A124 37c green 6.50 4.00
Nos. 543-547,C41-C45 (10) 62.75 39.75

Flag of El Salvador A125

Tree of San Vicente A126

1935, Oct. 26 **Litho.** **Wmk. 240**

548 A125 1c gray blue .15 .15
549 A125 2c black brn .15 .15
550 A125 3c plum .16 .15
551 A125 5c rose carmine .25 .15
552 A125 8c ultra .30 .15
553 A125 15c fawn .40 .25
Nos. 548-553,C46 (7) 1.91
Set value .75

1935, Dec. 26

Numerals in Black, Tree in Yellow Green

554 A126 2c black brn .50 .25
555 A126 3c dk blue grn .50 .30
556 A126 5c rose red .50 .35
557 A126 8c dark blue .50 .40
558 A126 15c brown .50 .50
Nos. 554-558,C47-C51 (10) 6.50 5.30

Tercentenary of San Vicente.

Volcano of Izalco — A127

Wharf at Cutuco — A128

Doroteo Vasconcelos A129

Parade Ground A130

Dr. Tomás G. Palomo — A131

Sugar Mill — A132

Coffee at Pier — A133

Gathering Balsam — A134

Pres. Manuel E. Araujo — A135

1935, Dec. **Engr.** **Unwmk.**

559 A127 1c deep violet .15 .15
560 A128 2c chestnut .15 .15
561 A129 3c green .15 .15
562 A130 5c carmine .40 .15
563 A131 8c dull blue .15 .15
564 A132 10c orange .25 .15
565 A133 15c dk olive bis .40 .15
566 A134 50c indigo 2.00 1.25
567 A135 1col black 5.00 3.00
Nos. 559-567 (9) 8.65
Set value 4.70

Paper has faint imprint "El Salvador" on face.

For surcharges and overprint see Nos. 568-570, 573, 583-584, C52.

Stamps of 1935 Surcharged with New Value in Black

1938 *Perf. 12½*

568 A130 1c on 5c carmine .15 .15
569 A132 3c on 10c orange .15 .15
570 A133 8c on 15c dk ol bis .18 .15
Nos. 568-570 (3) .48
Set value .26

No. 486 Surcharged with New Value in Red

1938 *Perf. 11½*

571 A102 3c on 5c blue .18 .18

Centenary of the death of José Simeón Cañas, liberator of slaves in Latin America.

Map of Flags of US and El Salvador — A136

Engraved and Lithographed

1938, Apr. 21 *Perf. 12*

572 A136 8c multicolored .38 .30

150th anniv. of US Constitution. See No. C61.

No. 560 Surcharged with New Value in Black

1938 *Perf. 12½*

573 A128 1c on 2c chestnut .15 .15

Indian Sugar Mill — A137

Designs: 2c, Indian women washing. 3c, Indian girl at spring. 5c, Indian plowing. 8c, Izote flower. 10c, Champion cow. 20c, Extracting balsam. 50c, Maquilishuat in bloom. 1col, Post Office, San Salvador.

1938-39 **Engr.** *Perf. 12*

574 A137 1c dark violet .15 .15
575 A137 2c dark green .15 .15
576 A137 3c dark brown .25 .15
577 A137 5c scarlet .25 .15
578 A137 8c dark blue 1.25 .15
579 A137 10c yel org ('39) 2.00 .15
580 A137 20c bis brn ('39) 1.75 .20

581 A137 50c dull blk ('39) 2.25 .45
582 A137 1col black ('39) 2.00 .75
Nos. 574-582 (9) 10.05
Set value 1.85

For surcharges & overprints see #591-592, C96.

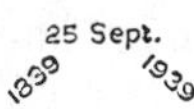

Nos. 566-567, 504 Surcharged in Red

BATALLA
SAN PEDRO PERULAPAN
₡ 0.50

1939, Sept. 25 *Perf. 12½, 14*

583 A134 8c on 50c indigo .25 .15
584 A135 10c on 1col blk .38 .15
585 A116 50c on 1col grn & vio 2.50 2.50
Nos. 583-585 (3) 3.13 2.80

Battle of San Pedro Perulapán, 100th anniv.

Sir Rowland Hill — A146

1940, Mar. 1 *Perf. 12½*

586 A146 8c dk bl, lt bl & blk 2.50 .50

Postage stamp centenary. See #C69-C70.

Statue of Christ and San Salvador Cathedral A147

A148

Wmk. 269

1942, Nov. 23 **Engr.** *Perf. 14*

587 A147 8c deep blue .50 .20

Souvenir Sheet

Imperf

Without Gum

Lilac Tinted Paper

588 A148 Sheet of 4 12.00 12.00
a. 8c deep blue 3.50 3.50
b. 30c red orange 3.50 3.50

Nos. 587-588 were issued to commemorate the first Eucharistic Congress of Salvador. See No. C85.

No. 588 contains two No. 587 and two No. C85, imperf.

Catalogue values for unused stamps in this section, from this point to the end of the section, are for Never Hinged items.

Cuscatlán Bridge, Pan-American Highway — A149

Arms Overprint at Right in Carmine

Perf. 12½

1944, Nov. 24 **Unwmk.** **Engr.**

589 A149 8c dk bl & blk .16 .15

See No. C92.

Gen. Juan José Canas — A150

1945, June 9

590 A150 8c blue .15 .15

No. 575 Surcharged in Black 1 1
a *b*

1944-46

591 A137(a) 1(c) on 2c dk grn .15 .15
592 A137(b) 1(c) on 2c dk grn ('46) .15 .15
Set value .24 .15

Lake of Ilopango A151

Ceiba Tree A152

Water Carriers — A153

1946-47 **Litho.** **Wmk. 240**

593 A151 1c bl ('47) .15 .15
594 A152 2c lt bl grn ('47) .20 .15
595 A153 5c carmine .15 .15
Set value .40 .18

Isidro Menéndez — A154

Designs: 2c, Cristano Salazar. 3c, Juan Bertis.5c, Francisco Duenas, 8c, Ramon Belloso. 10c, Jose Presentacion Trigueros. 20c, Salvador Rodriguez Gonzalez. 50c, Francisco Castaneda. 1col, David Castro.

1947 **Unwmk.** **Engr.** *Perf. 12*

596 A154 1c car rose .15 .15
597 A154 2c dp org .15 .15
598 A154 3c violet .15 .15
599 A154 5c slate gray .15 .15
600 A154 8c dp bl .15 .15
601 A154 10c bis brn .16 .15
602 A154 20c green .28 .15
603 A154 50c black .65 .30
604 A154 1col scarlet 1.40 .40
Set value (9) 2.80 1.10

For surcharges and overprints see Nos. 621-626, 634, C118-C120, O362-O368.

Manuel José Arce — A163

1948, Feb. 25 *Perf. 12½*

605 A163 8c deep blue .28 .15
Nos. 605,C108-C110 (4) 2.93 1.85

President Roosevelt Presenting Awards for Distinguished Service — A164

President Franklin D. Roosevelt — A165

A166

Designs: 8c, Pres. and Mrs. Roosevelt. 15c, Mackenzie King, Roosevelt and Winston Churchill. 20c, Roosevelt and Cordell Hull. 50c, Funeral of Pres. Roosevelt.

1948, Apr. 12

Various Frames; Center in Black

606 A164 5c dk bl .15 .15
607 A164 8c green .15 .15
608 A165 12c violet .20 .15
609 A164 15c vermilion .24 .18
610 A164 20c car lake .28 .20
611 A164 50c gray .70 .45
Nos. 606-611,C111-C117 (13) 10.60 7.28

Souvenir Sheet

Perf. 13½

612 A166 1col ol grn & brn 1.90 1.40

3rd anniv. of the death of F. D. Roosevelt.

Torch and Winged Letter — A167

Perf. 12½

1949, Oct. 9 **Unwmk.** **Engr.**

613 A167 8c blue .42 .15
Nos. 613,C122-C124 (4) 5.98 5.70

75th anniv. of the UPU.

Workman and Soldier Holding Torch — A168

Wreath and Open Book — A169

1949, Dec. 15 **Litho.** *Perf. 10½*

614 A168 8c blue .30 .15
Nos. 614,C125-C129 (6) 6.53 4.75

Revolution of Dec. 14, 1948, 1st anniv.

Perf. 11½

1952, Feb. 14 **Photo.** **Unwmk.**

Wreath in Dark Green

615 A169 1c yel grn .15 .15
616 A169 2c magenta .15 .15
617 A169 5c brn red .15 .15
618 A169 10c yellow .15 .15
619 A169 20c gray grn .20 .15
620 A169 1col dp car 1.00 .75
Nos. 615-620,C134-C141 (14) 7.90 5.33

Constitution of 1950.

Nos. 598, 600 and 603 Surcharged with New Values in Various Colors

1952-53 *Perf. 12½*

621 A154 2c on 3c vio (C) .15 .15
622 A154 2c on 8c dp bl (C) .15 .15
623 A154 3c on 8c dp bl (G) .15 .15
624 A154 5c on 8c dp bl (O) .15 .15
625 A154 7c on 8c dp bl (Bk) .15 .15
626 A154 10c on 50c blk (O) ('53) .20 .15
Set value .78 .50

Nos. C106 and C107 Surcharged and "AEREO" Obliterated in Various Colors

1952-53 **Wmk. 240**

627 AP31 2c on 12c choc (Bl) .15 .15
628 AP32 2c on 14c dk bl (R) ('53) .15 .15
629 AP31 5c on 12c choc (Bl) .15 .15
630 AP32 10c on 14c dk bl (C) .15 .15
Set value .48 .40

José Marti — A170

Perf. 10½

1953, Feb. 27 **Litho.** **Unwmk.**

631 A170 1c rose red .15 .15
632 A170 2c bl grn .15 .15
633 A170 10c dk vio .16 .15
Nos. 631-633,C142-C144 (6) 1.43
Set value .75

Cent. of the birth of José Marti, Cuban patriot.

No. 598 Overprinted in Carmine "IV Congreso Médico Social Panamericano 15 / 19 Abril, 1953"

1953, June 19 *Perf. 12½*

634 A154 3c violet .20 .15

4th Pan-American Congress of Social Medicine, San Salvador, April 16-19, 1953. See #C146.

Signing of Act of Independence A171

Capt. Gen. Gerardo Barrios A172

1953, Sept. 15 **Litho.** *Perf. 11½*

635 A171 1c rose pink .15 .15
636 A171 2c dp bl grn .15 .15
637 A171 3c purple .15 .15
638 A171 5c dp bl .15 .15
639 A171 7c lt brn .15 .15
640 A171 10c ocher .20 .15
641 A171 20c dp org .28 .15
642 A171 50c green .60 .30
643 A171 1col gray 1.25 .90
Set value, #635-643, C147-C150 3.60 2.45

132nd anniversary of the Act of Independence, Sept. 15, 1821.

1953, Dec. 1 *Perf. 11½*

Portrait: 3c, 7c, 10c, 22c, Francisco Morazan, (facing left).

Black Overprint ("C de C")

644 A172 1c green .15 .15
645 A172 2c blue .15 .15
646 A172 3c green .15 .15
647 A172 5c carmine .15 .15
648 A172 7c blue .15 .15
649 A172 10c carmine .16 .15
650 A172 20c violet .20 .15
651 A172 22c violet .28 .20
Set value (8) 1.00 .65

The overprint "C de C" is a control indicating "Tribunal of Accounts." A double entry of this overprint occurs twice in each sheet of each denomination.

For overprint see No. 729.

Coastal Bridge — A173

Motherland and Liberty A174

Census Allegory A175

Balboa Park A176

Designs: Nos. 654, 655, National Palace. Nos. 659, 665, Izalco Volcano. Nos. 660, 661, Guayabo dam. No. 666, Lake Ilopango. No. 669, Housing development. Nos. 670, 673, Coast guard boat. No. 671, Modern highway.

Perf. 11½

1954, June 1 Unwmk. Photo.

652 A173 1c car rose & brn .15 .15
653 AP43 1c ol & bl gray .15 .15
654 A173 1c pur & pale lil .15 .15
655 A173 2c yel grn & lt gray .15 .15
656 A174 2c car lake .15 .15
657 A175 2c org red .15 .15
658 AP44 3c maroon .15 .15
659 A173 3c bl grn & bl .16 .15
660 A174 3c dk gray & vio .15 .15
661 A174 5c red vio & vio .15 .15
662 AP44 5c emerald .15 .15
663 A176 7c magenta & buff .16 .15
664 AP43 7c bl grn & gray bl .16 .15
665 A173 7c org brn & org .16 .15
666 A173 10c car lake .16 .15
667 AP46 10c red, dk brn & bl .16 .15
668 A174 10c dk bl grn .16 .15
669 A174 20c org & cr .32 .15
670 A173 22c gray vio .32 .25
671 A176 50c dk gray & brn .65 .28
672 AP46 1col brn org, dk brn & bl 1.25 .75
673 A173 1col brt bl 1.25 .50
Nos. 652-673 (22) 6.41
Set value 3.00
Nos. 652-673,C151-C165 (37) 16.44 9.08
Set value 6.75

For surcharges & overprints see #692-693, 736, C193.

Capt. Gen. Gerardo Barrios — A177

Coffee Picker — A178

Perf. 12½

1955, Dec. 20 Wmk. 269 Engr.

674 A177 1c red .15 .15
675 A177 2c yel grn .15 .15
676 A177 3c vio bl .16 .15
677 A177 20c violet .20 .15
Nos. 674-677,C166-C167 (6) 1.06
Set value .60

Perf. 13½

1956, June 20 Litho. Unwmk.

678 A178 3c bis brn .15 .15
679 A178 5c red org .15 .15
680 A178 10c dk bl .16 .15
681 A178 2col dk red 1.65 1.00
Nos. 678-681,C168-C172 (9) 6.50
Set value 3.50

Centenary of Santa Ana Department.
For overprint see No. C187.

Map of Chalatenango — A179

1956, Sept. 14

682 A179 2c blue .15 .15
683 A179 7c rose red .28 .25
684 A179 50c yel brn .48 .30
Nos. 682-684,C173-C178 (9) 3.07
Set value 2.00

Centenary of Chalatenango Department (in 1955).
For surcharge see No. 694.

Coat of Arms of Nueva San Salvador — A180

Perf. 12½

1957, Jan. 3 Wmk. 269 Engr.

685 A180 1c rose red .15 .15
686 A180 2c green .15 .15
687 A180 3c violet .15 .15
688 A180 7c red org .32 .25
689 A180 10c ultra .15 .15
690 A180 50c pale brn .40 .30
691 A180 1col dl red .85 .65
Nos. 685-691,C179-C183 (12) 5.69
Set value 3.40

Centenary of the founding of the city of Nueva San Salvador (Santa Tecla).
For surcharges and overprints see Nos. 695-696, 706, 713, C194-C195, C197-C199.

Nos. 664-665, 683 and 688 Surcharged with New Value in Black

1957 Unwmk. Photo. *Perf. 11½*

692 A173 6c on 7c bl grn & gray bl .30 .30
693 A173 6c on 7c org brn & org .30 .30

1957 Litho. *Perf. 13½*

694 A179 6c on 7c rose red .20 .15

Perf. 12½

1957-58 Wmk. 269 Engr.

695 A180 5c on 7c red org ('58) .25 .15
696 A180 6c on 7c red org .30 .16
Nos. 692-696 (5) 1.35 1.06

El Salvador Intercontinental Hotel — A181

Perf. 11½

1958, June 28 Unwmk. Photo.

Granite Paper

Vignette in Green, Dark Blue & Red

697 A181 3c brown .15 .15
698 A181 6c crim rose .15 .15
699 A181 10c brt bl .15 .15
700 A181 15c brt grn .18 .15
701 A181 20c lilac .30 .16
702 A181 30c brt yel grn .42 .22
Set value 1.18 .68

Presidents Eisenhower and Lemus and Flags A182

1959, Dec. 14 Granite Paper

Design in Ultramarine, Dark Brown, Light Brown and Red

703 A182 3c pink .18 .15
704 A182 6c green .18 .15
705 A182 10c crimson .28 .15
Nos. 703-705,C184-C186 (6) 1.38
Set value .60

Visit of Pres. José M. Lemus of El Salvador to the US, Mar. 9-21.

No. 686 Overprinted: "5 Enero 1960 XX Aniversario Fundacion Sociedad Filatelica de El Salvador"

1960 Wmk. 269 Engr. *Perf. 12½*

706 A180 2c green .15 .15

Philatelic Association of El Salvador, 20th anniv.

Apartment Houses A183

1960 Unwmk. Photo. *Perf. 11½*

Multicolored Centers; Granite Paper

707 A183 10c scarlet .15 .15
708 A183 15c brt pur .15 .15
709 A183 25c brt yel grn .24 .15
710 A183 30c Prus bl .26 .16
711 A183 40c olive .42 .25
712 A183 80c dk bl .75 .75
Nos. 707-712 (6) 1.97 1.61

Issued to publicize the erection of multifamily housing projects in 1958.
For surcharges see Nos. 730, 733.

No. 686 Surcharged with New Value

1960 Wmk. 269 Engr. *Perf. 12½*

713 A180 1c on 2c grn .15 .15

Poinsettia — A184

Perf. 11½

1960, Dec. Unwmk. Photo.

Granite Paper

Design in Slate Green, Red and Yellow

714 A184 3c yellow .15 .15
715 A184 6c salmon .20 .15
716 A184 10c grnsh bl .28 .15
717 A184 15c pale vio bl .32 .15
Nos. 714-717,C188-C191 (8) 2.42 1.50

Miniature Sheet

718 A184 40c silver .65 .50

Nos. 718 and C192 exist with overprints for: 1- 1st Central American Philatelic Cong., July, 1961. 2- Death of General Barrios, 96th anniv. 3- Cent. of city of Ahuachapan. 4- Football (soccer) games. 5- 4th Latin American Cong. of Pathological Anatomy and 10th Central American Medical Cong., Dec., 1963. 6- Alliance for Progress, 2nd anniv.
For surcharge see No. C196.

Fathers Nicolas, Vicente and Manuel Aguilar A185

Parish Church, San Salvador, 1808 A186

Designs: 5c, 6c, Manuel José Arce, José Matias Delgado and Juan Manuel Rodriguez. 10c, 20c, Pedro Pablo Castillo, Domingo Antonio de Lara and Santiago José Celis. 50c, 80c, Monument to the Fathers, Plaza Libertad.

Perf. 11½

1961, Nov. 5 Unwmk. Photo.

719 A185 1c gray & dk brn .15 .15
720 A185 2c rose & dk brn .15 .15
721 A185 5c pale brn & dk ol grn .18 .15
722 A185 6c brt pink & dk brn .20 .15
723 A185 10c bl & dk brn .20 .15
724 A185 20c vio & dk brn .28 .15
725 A186 30c brt bl & vio .40 .16
726 A186 40c brn org & sep .55 .20
727 A186 50c bl grn & sep .75 .40
728 A186 80c gray & ultra 1.25 .75
Nos. 719-728 (10) 4.11
Set value 1.95

Sesquicentennial of the first cry for Independence in Central America.

For surcharges and overprints see Nos. 731-732, 734-735, 737, 760, 769, 776.

No. 651 Overprinted: "III Exposición Industrial Centroamericana Diciembre de 1962"

1962, Dec. 21 Litho. *Perf. 11½*

729 A172 22c violet .28 .20

Issued to publicize the 3rd Central American Industrial Exposition. See Nos. C193-C195.

Nos. 708, 726-728 and 673 Surcharged

1962-63 Photo.

730 A183 6c on 15c ('63) .28 .15
731 A186 6c on 40c ('63) .28 .15
732 A186 6c on 50c ('63) .28 .15
733 A183 10c on 15c .28 .15
734 A186 10c on 50c ('63) .28 .15
735 A186 10c on 80c ('63) .28 .15
736 A173 10c on 1col ('63) .28 .15
Nos. 730-736 (7) 1.96
Set value .88

Surcharge includes bars on Nos. 731-734, 736; dot on Nos. 730, 735.

No. 726 Overprinted in Arc: "CAMPAÑA MUNDIAL CONTRA EL HAMBRE"

1963, Mar. 21

737 A186 40c brn org & sepia .70 .40

FAO "Freedom from Hunger" campaign.

Coyote — A187

Christ on Globe — A188

2c, Spider monkey, vert. 3c, Raccoon. 5c, King vulture, vert. 6c, Brown coati. 10c, Kinkajou.

1963 Photo. *Perf. 11½*

738 A187 1c lil, blk, ocher & brn .15 .15
739 A187 2c lt grn & blk .15 .15
740 A187 3c fawn, dk brn & buff .15 .15
741 A187 5c gray grn, ind, red & buff .15 .15
742 A187 6c rose lil, blk, brn & buff .15 .15
743 A187 10c lt bl, brn & buff .15 .15
Set value .45 .30

See Nos. C200-C207.

1964-65 *Perf. 12x11½*

744 A188 6c bl & brn .15 .15
745 A188 10c bl & bis .15 .15
Set value, #744-745, C208-C209 .50 .30

Miniature Sheets

Imperf

746 A188 60c bl & brt pur .60 .60
a. Marginal ovpt. La Union 1.25 1.25
b. Marginal ovpt. Usulutan 1.25 1.25
c. Marginal ovpt. La Libertad 1.25 1.25

2nd Natl. Eucharistic Cong., San Salvador, Apr. 16-19.
Nos. 746a, 746b and 746c commemorate the centenaries of the Departments of La Union, Usulután and La Libertad.
Issued: #744-746, Apr. 16, 1964; #746a-746b, June 22, 1965; #746c, Jan. 28, 1965.
See No. C210. For overprints see Nos. C232, C238.

Pres. John F. Kennedy A189

Perf. 11½x12

1964, Nov. 22 Unwmk.

747 A189 6c buff & blk .15 .15
748 A189 10c tan & blk .16 .15
749 A189 50c pink & blk .50 .22
Nos. 747-749,C211-C213 (6) 1.61
Set value .80

Miniature Sheet

Imperf

750 A189 70c dp grn & blk .65 .50

President John F. Kennedy (1917-1963).
For overprints & surcharge see #798, 843, C259.

Water Lily — A190

1965, Jan. 6 Photo. *Perf. 12x11½*

751 A190	3c shown	.15	.15
752 A190	5c Maquilishuat	.15	.15
753 A190	6c Cinco negritos	.15	.15
754 A190	30c Hortensia	.20	.15
755 A190	50c Maguey	.60	.18
756 A190	60c Geranium	.65	.20
	Set value	1.60	.60

See Nos. C215-C220. For overprints and surcharges see Nos. 779, C243, C348-C349.

ICY Emblem — A191

1965, Apr. 27 Photo. *Perf. 11½x12*
Design in Brown and Gold

757 A191	5c dp yel	.15	.15
758 A191	6c dp rose	.15	.15
759 A191	10c gray	.15	.15
	Set value, #757-759, C221-C223	.80	.50

International Cooperation Year.
For overprints see #764, 780, C227, C244, C312.

No. 728 Overprinted in Red: "ler. Centenario Muerte / Cap. Gral. Gerardo Barrios / 1865 1965 / 29 de Agosto"

1965 Unwmk. *Perf. 11½*

760 A186	80c gray & ultra	.65	.50
a.	"Garl." instead of "Gral."	1.00	1.00

Cent. of the death of Capt. Gen. Gerardo Barrios.

Gavidia A192

Fair Emblem A193

Perf. 11½x12
1965, Sept. 24 Photo. Unwmk.
Portrait in Natural Colors

761 A192	2c blk & rose vio	.15	.15
762 A192	3c blk & org	.16	.15
763 A192	6c blk & lt ultra	.16	.15
	Nos. 761-763,C224-C226 (6)	2.16	
	Set value		1.00

Francisco Antonio Gavidia, philosopher.
For surcharges see Nos. 852-853.

No. 759 Overprinted in Carmine: "1865 / 12 de Octubre / 1965 / Dr. Manuel Enrique Araujo"

1965, Oct. 12

764 A191	10c brn, gray & gold	.15	.15

Centenary of the birth of Manuel Enrique Araujo, president of Salvador, 1911-1913. See No. C227.

1965, Nov. 5 Photo. *Perf. 12x11½*

765 A193	6c yel & multi	.15	.15
766 A193	10c multi	.15	.15
767 A193	20c pink & multi	.20	.15
	Nos. 765-767,C228-C230 (6)	4.56	3.27

Intl. Fair of El Salvador, Nov. 5-Dec. 4.
For overprints and surcharge see Nos. 784, C246, C311, C323.

WHO Headquarters, Geneva A194

1966, May 20 Photo. Unwmk.

768 A194	15c beige & multi	.16	.15

Inauguration of WHO Headquarters, Geneva. See No. C231. For overprints and surcharges see Nos. 778, 783, 864, C242, C245, C322.

No. 728 Overprinted in Red: "Mes de Conmemoracion / Civica de la Independencia / Centroamericana / 19 Sept. / 1821 1966"

1966, Sept. 19 Photo. *Perf. 11½*

769 A186	80c gray & ultra	.52	.50

Issued to publicize the month of civic commemoration of Central American independence.

UNESCO Emblem A195

1966, Nov. 4 Unwmk. *Perf. 12*

770 A195	20c gray, blk & vio bl	.16	.15
771 A195	1col emer, blk & vio bl	.85	.40
	Nos. 770-771,C233-C234 (4)	2.98	1.70

20th anniv. of UNESCO.
For surcharges see Nos. 853A, C352.

Map of Central America, Flags and Cogwheels A196

1966, Nov. 27 Litho. *Perf. 12*

772 A196	6c multi	.15	.15
773 A196	10c multi	.15	.15
	Nos. 772-773,C235-C237 (5)	1.16	
	Set value		.82

2nd Intl. Fair of El Salvador, Nov. 5-27.

José Simeon Cañas Pleading for Indian Slaves — A197

1967, Feb. 18 Litho. *Perf. 11½*

774 A197	6c yel & multi	.15	.15
775 A197	10c lil rose & multi	.15	.15
	Set value	.22	.15

Father José Simeon Cañas y Villacorta, D.D. (1767-1838), emancipator of the Central American slaves.
See Nos. C239-C240. For surcharges see Nos. 841A-842, 891, C403-C405.

No. 726 Overprinted in Red: "XV Convención de Clubes / de Leones, Región de / El Salvador-11 y 12 / de Marzo de 1967"

1967 Photo.

776 A186	40c brn org & sepia	.48	.25

Issued to publicize the 15th Convention of Lions Clubs of El Salvador, March 11-12.

Volcano San Miguel A198

1967, Apr. 14 Photo. *Perf. 13*

777 A198	70c lt rose lil & brn	1.00	.60

Centenary of stamps of El Salvador.
See No. C241. For surcharges see Nos. 841, C320, C350.

No. 768 Overprinted in Red: "VIII CONGRESO / CENTROAMERICANO DE / FARMACIA Y BIOQUIMICA / 5 di 11 Noviembre de 1967"

1967, Oct. 26 Photo. *Perf. 12x11½*

778 A194	15c multi	.16	.15

8th Central American Congress for Pharmacy and Biochemistry. See No. C242.

No. 751 Overprinted in Red: "I Juegos / Centroamericanos y del / Caribe de Basquetbol / 25 Nov. al 3 Dic. 1967"

1967, Nov. 15

779 A190	3c dl grn, brn, yel & org	.15	.15

First Central American and Caribbean Basketball Games, Nov. 25-Dec. 3. See No. C243.

No. 757 Overprinted in Carmine: "1968 / AÑO INTERNACIONAL DE / LOS DERECHOS HUMANOS"

1968, Jan. 2 Photo. *Perf. 11½x12*

780 A191	5c dp yel, brn & gold	.15	.15

Intl. Human Rights Year. See #C244.

Weather Map, Satellite and WMO Emblem — A199

1968, Mar. 25 Photo. *Perf. 11½x12*

781 A199	1c multi	.15	.15
782 A199	30c multi	.30	.15
	Set value		.16

World Meteorological Day, Mar. 25.

No. 768 Overprinted in Red: "1968 / XX ANIVERSARIO DE LA / ORGANIZACION MUNDIAL / DE LA SALUD"

1968, Apr. 7 *Perf. 12x11½*

783 A194	15c multi	.20	.20

20th anniv. of WHO. See No. C245.

No. 765 Overprinted in Red: "1968 / Año / del Sistema / del Crédito / Rural"

1968, May 6 Photo. *Perf. 12x11½*

784 A193	6c yellow & multi	.15	.15

Rural credit system. See No. C246.

Alberto Masferrer — A200

Scouts Helping to Build — A201

1968, June 22 Litho. *Perf. 12x11½*

785 A200	2c multi	.15	.15
786 A200	6c multi	.15	.15
787 A200	25c vio & multi	.32	.15
	Set value, #785-787, C247-C248	.68	.38

Issued to commemorate the centenary of the birth of Alberto Masferrer, philosopher and scholar.

For surcharges and overprints see Nos. 819, 843A, 890, C297.

1968, July 26 Litho. *Perf. 12*

788 A201	25c multi	.24	.15

Issued to publicize the 7th Inter-American Boy Scout Conference, July-Aug., 1968.
See No. C249.

Map of Central America, Flags and Presidents of US, Costa Rica, Salvador, Guatemala, Honduras and Nicaragua — A202

1968, Dec. 5 Litho. *Perf. 14½*

789 A202	10c tan & multi	.15	.15
790 A202	15c multi	.16	.15
	Nos. 789-790,C250-C251 (4)	1.21	
	Set value		.75

Meeting of Pres. Lyndon B. Johnson with the presidents of the Central American republics (J. J. Trejos, Costa Rica; Fidel Sanchez Hernandez, Salvador; J. C. Mendez Montenegro, Guatemala; Osvaldo López Arellano, Honduras; Anastasio Somoza Debayle, Nicaragua), San Salvador, July 5-8, 1968.

Heliconius Charithonius A203

Various Butterflies.

1969 Litho. *Perf. 12*

791 A203	5c bluish lil, blk & yel	.15	.15
792 A203	10c beige & multi	.15	.15
793 A203	30c lt grn & multi	.24	.15
794 A203	50c tan & multi	.40	.18
	Nos. 791-794,C252-C255 (8)	11.40	7.13

For surcharge see No. C353.

Red Cross Activities A204

1969 Litho. *Perf. 12*

795 A204	10c lt bl & multi	.15	.15
796 A204	20c pink & multi	.15	.15
797 A204	40c lil & multi	.28	.15
	Nos. 795-797,C256-C258 (6)	4.92	3.60

50th anniv. of the League of Red Cross Societies.

No. 749 Overprinted in Green: "Alunizaje / Apolo-11 / 21 Julio / 1969"

1969, Sept. Photo. *Perf. 11½x12*

798 A189	50c pink & blk	.40	.30

Man's first landing on the moon, July 20, 1969. See note after US No. C76.
The same overprint in red brown and pictures of the landing module and the astronauts on the moon were applied to the margin of No. 750.
See No. C259.

Social Security Hospital A205

1969, Oct. 24 Litho. *Perf. 11½*

799 A205	6c multi	.15	.15
800 A205	10c multi, diff.	.15	.15
801 A205	30c multi, diff.	.28	.15
	Nos. 799-801,C260-C262 (6)	7.33	4.45

For surcharges see Nos. 857, C355.

ILO Emblem — A206

1969 Litho. Perf. 13
802 A206 10c yel & multi .15 .15

50th anniv. of the ILO. See No. C263.

Chorros Spa A207

Views: 40c, Jaltepeque Bay. 80c, Fountains, Amapulapa Spa.

1969, Dec. 19 Photo. Perf. 12x11½
803 A207 10c blk & multi .15 .15
804 A207 40c blk & multi .32 .25
805 A207 80c blk & multi .65 .50
Nos. 803-805,C264-C266 (6) 2.06 1.65

Tourism.

Euchroma Gigantea — A208

Insects: 25c, Grasshopper. 30c, Digger wasp.

1970, Feb. 24 Litho. Perf. 11½x11
806 A208 5c lt bl & multi .15 .15
807 A208 25c dl yel & multi .20 .15
808 A208 30c dl rose & multi .28 .15
Nos. 806-808,C267-C269 (6) 8.03 4.95

For surcharges see Nos. C371-C373.

Map and Arms of Salvador, National Unity Emblem A209

1970, Apr. 14 Litho. Perf. 14
809 A209 10c yel & multi .15 .15
810 A209 40c pink & multi .48 .15
Nos. 809-810,C270-C271 (4) 1.59
Set value .65

Salvador's support of universal human rights. For overprints and surcharge see Nos. 823, C301, C402.

Soldiers with Flag — A210

Design: 30c, Anti-aircraft gun.

1970, May 7 Perf. 12
811 A210 10c green & multi .15 .15
812 A210 30c lemon & multi .30 .15
Nos. 811-812,C272-C274 (5) 1.38
Set value .58

Issued for Army Day, May 7.
For overprints see Nos. 836, C310.

National Lottery Headquarters — A211

1970, July 15 Litho. Perf. 12
813 A211 20c lt vio & multi .16 .15

National Lottery centenary. See No. C291.

UN and Education Year Emblems A212

1970, Sept. 11 Litho. Perf. 12
814 A212 50c multi .40 .15
815 A212 1col multi .85 .45
Nos. 814-815,C292-C293 (4) 3.06 1.75

Issued for International Education Year.

Map of Salvador, Globe and Cogwheels A213

1970, Oct. 28 Litho. Perf. 12
816 A213 5c pink & multi .15 .15
817 A213 10c buff & multi .15 .15
Set value, #816-817, C294-C295 .80 .25

4th International Fair, San Salvador.

Beethoven — A214

1971, Feb. 22 Litho. Perf. 13½
818 A214 50c ol, brn & yel .50 .20

Second International Music Festival. See No. C296. For overprint see No. 833.

No. 787 Overprinted: "Año / del Centenario de la / Biblioteca Nacional / 1970"

1970, Nov. 25 Perf. 12x11½
819 A200 25c vio & multi .20 .18

Cent. of the National Library. See No. C297.

Maria Elena Sol — A215

Pietà, by Michelangelo — A216

1971, Apr. 1 Litho. Perf. 14
820 A215 10c lt grn & multi .15 .15
821 A215 30c multi .20 .15
Nos. 820-821,C298-C299 (4) .95 .75

Maria Elena Sol, Miss World Tourism, 1970-71. For overprint see No. 832.

1971, May 10
822 A216 10c sal & vio brn .15 .15

Mother's Day, 1971. See No. C300.

No. 810 Overprinted in Red

1867
CIV Aniversario*
Fundación de la
Policía Nacional
6-Julio
1971

1971, July 6 Litho. Perf. 14
823 A209 40c pink & multi .35 .18

104th anniv. of National Police. See No. C301.

Tiger Sharks A217

1971, July 28
824 A217 10c shown .15 .15
825 A217 40c Swordfish .20 .20
Nos. 824-825,C302-C303 (4) 1.18 1.10

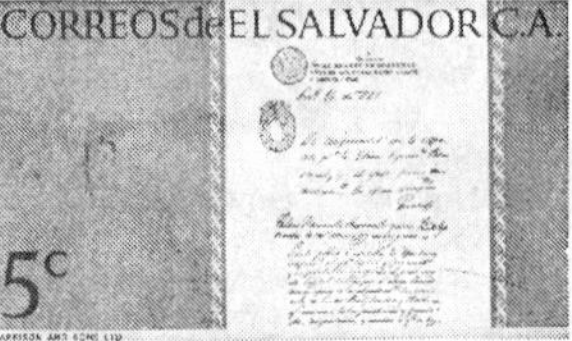

Declaration of Independence — A218

Designs: Various sections of Declaration of Independence of Central America.

1971 Perf. 13½x13
826 A218 5c yel grn & blk .15 .15
827 A218 10c brt rose & blk .15 .15
828 A218 15c dp org & blk .15 .15
829 A218 20c dp red lil & blk .15 .15
Set value, #826-829, C304-C307 1.70 1.30

Sesquicentennial of independence of Central America.
For overprints see Nos. C321, C347.

Izalco Church A219

Design: 30c, Sonsonate Church.

1971, Aug. 21 Litho. Perf. 13x13½
830 A219 20c blk & multi .20 .15
831 A219 30c pur & multi .30 .15
Nos. 830-831,C308-C309 (4) 1.20 .80

No. 821 Overprinted in Carmine: "1972 Año de Turismo / de las Américas"

1972, Nov. 15 Litho. Perf. 14
832 A215 30c multi .20 .15

Tourist Year of the Americas, 1972.

No. 818 Overprinted in Red

III Festival
Internacional de
Música 9-25-
Febrero - 1973.

1973, Feb. 5 Litho. Perf. 13½
833 A214 50c ol, brn & yel .25 .20

3rd Intl. Music Festival, Feb. 9-25. See No. C313.

Lions International Emblem — A220

1973, Feb. 20 Litho. Perf. 13
834 A220 10c pink & multi .15 .15
835 A220 25c lt bl & multi .15 .15
Set value, #834-835, C314-C315 .60 .45

31st Lions International District "D" Convention, San Salvador, May 1972.

No. 812 Overprinted: "1923 1973 / 50 AÑOS FUNDACION / FUERZA AEREA"

1973, Mar. 20 Litho. Perf. 12
836 A210 30c lem & multi .18 .18

50th anniversary of Salvadorian Air Force.

Hurdling A221

1973, May 21 Litho. Perf. 13
837 A221 5c shown .15 .15
838 A221 10c High jump .15 .15
839 A221 25c Running .15 .15
840 A221 60c Pole vault .28 .25
Nos. 837-840,C316-C319 (8) 3.48
Set value 2.25

20th Olympic Games, Munich, Aug. 26-Sept. 11, 1972.

No. 777 Surcharged:

10
CTS.

1973, Dec. Photo. Perf. 13
841 A198 10c on 70c multi .15 .15

See No. C320.

Nos. 774, C240 Surcharged with New Value and Overprinted "1823-1973 / 150 Aniversario Liberación / Esclavos en Centroamérica"

1973-74 Litho. Perf. 11½
841A A197 5c on 6c multi ('74) .15 .15
842 A197 10c on 45c multi .15 .15
Set value .15 .15

Sesquicentennial of the liberation of the slaves in Central America. On No. 841A two bars cover old denomination. On No. 842 "Aereo" is obliterated with a bar and old denomination with two bars.

Nos. 747 and 786 Surcharged:

5
CTS.

1974 Photo. Perf. 11½x12
843 A189 5c on 6c buff & blk .15 .15

Litho. Perf. 12x11½
843A A200 5c on 6c multi .15 .15
Set value .16 .15

No. 843A has one obliterating rectangle and sans-serif "5."
Issued: No. 843, Apr. 22. No. 843A, June 21.

Rehabilitation Institute Emblem — A222

1974, Apr. 30 Litho. Perf. 13
844 A222 10c multi .15 .15

10th anniversary of the Salvador Rehabilitation Institute. See No. C324.

INTERPOL Headquarters, Saint-Cloud, France — A223

1974, Sept. 2 Litho. *Perf. 12½*

845 A223 10c multi .15 .15

50th anniv. of Intl. Criminal Police Organization (INTERPOL). See No. C341.

UN and FAO Emblems — A224

1974, Sept. 2 Litho. *Perf. 12½*

846 A224 10c bl, dk bl & gold .15 .15

World Food Program, 10th anniv. See #C342.

25c Silver Coin, 1914 — A225

1974, Nov. 19 Litho. *Perf. 12½x13*

848 A225 10c shown .15 .15
849 A225 15c 50c silver, 1953 .15 .15
850 A225 25c 25c silver, 1943 .15 .15
851 A225 30c 1c copper, 1892 .15 .15
Set value, #848-851, C343-C346 1.80 1.25

No. 763 Surcharged

XII Serie Ajedrez de Centro America y del Caribe Oct. 1974 5 cts.

1974, Oct. 14 Photo. *Perf. 11½x12*

852 A192 5c on 6c multi .15 .15

12th Central American and Caribbean Chess Tournament, Oct. 1974.

₵ 0.10

No. 762 and 771 Surcharged

1974-75 *Perf. 11½x12, 12*

853 A192 10c on 3c multi .15 .15
853A A195 25c on 1col multi ('75) .15 .15
Set value .16 .15

Bar and surcharge on one line on No. 853A. Issued: #853, Dec. 19; #853A, Jan. 13.

UPU Emblem — A226

1975, Jan. 22 Litho. *Perf. 13*

854 A226 10c bl & multi .15 .15
855 A226 60c bl & multi .24 .30
Nos. 854-855,C356-C357 (4) .83 .80

Cent. of UPU.

Acajutla Harbor — A227

1975, Feb. 17

856 A227 10c blue & multi .15 .15

See No. C358.

₵ 0.05

No. 799 Surcharged

1975 Litho. *Perf. 11½*

857 A205 5c on 6c multi .15 .15

Central Post Office, San Salvador A228

1975, Apr. 25 Litho. *Perf. 13*

858 A228 10c bl & multi .15 .15

See No. C359.

Map of Americas and El Salvador, Trophy A229

1975, June 25 Litho. *Perf. 12½*

859 A229 10c red org & multi .15 .15
860 A229 40c yel & multi .25 .25
Set value .32
Nos. 859-860,C360-C361 (4) 1.10 .95

El Salvador, site of 1975 Miss Universe Contest.

Claudia Lars, Poet, and IWY Emblem — A230

1975, Sept. 4 Litho. *Perf. 12½*

861 A230 10c yel & bl blk .15 .15
Set value, #861, C362-C363 .40 .25

Intl. Women's Year 1975.

Nurses Attending Patient — A231

1975, Oct. 24 Litho. *Perf. 12½*

862 A231 10c lt grn & multi .15 .15

Nurses' Day. See No. C364. For overprint see No. 868.

Congress Emblem — A232

1975, Nov. 19 Litho. *Perf. 12½*

863 A232 10c yel & multi .15 .15

15th Conference of Inter-American Federation of Securities Enterprises, San Salvador, Nov. 16-20. See No. C365.

No. 768 Overprinted in Red: "XVI / CONGRESO MEDICO / CENTROAMERICANO / SAN SALVADOR, / EL SALVADOR, / DIC. 10-13, 1975"

1975, Nov. 26 Photo. *Perf. 12x11½*

864 A194 15c beige & multi .15 .15

16th Central American Medical Congress, San Salvador, Dec. 10-13.

Flags of Participants, Arms of Salvador — A233

1975, Nov. 28 Litho. *Perf. 12½*

865 A233 15c blk & multi .15 .15
866 A233 50c brn & multi .20 .20
Nos. 865-866,C366-C367 (4) .75
Set value .24

8th Ibero-Latin-American Dermatological Congress, San Salvador, Nov. 28-Dec. 3.

Jesus and Caritas Emblem — A234

1975, Dec. 18 Litho. *Perf. 13½*

867 A234 10c dl red & mar .15 .15

7th Latin American Charity Congress, San Salvador, Nov. 1971. See No. C368.

No. 862 Overprinted: "III CONGRESO / ENFERMERIA / CENCAMEX 76"

1976, May 10 Litho. *Perf. 12½*

868 A231 10c lt grn & multi .15 .15

CENCAMEX 76, 3rd Nurses' Congress.

Map of El Salvador — A235

1976, May 18

869 A235 10c vio bl & multi .15 .15

10th Congress of Revenue Collectors (Centro Interamericano de Administradores Tributarios, CIAT), San Salvador, May 16-22. See No. C382.

Flags of Salvador and US, Torch, Map of Americas A236

The Spirit of '76, by Archibald M. Willard — A237

1976, June 30 Litho. *Perf. 12½*

870 A236 10c yel & multi .15 .15
871 A237 40c multi .16 .15
Nos. 870-871,C383-C384 (4) 4.26 2.95

American Bicentennial.

American Crocodile — A238

1976, Sept. 23 Litho. *Perf. 12½*

872 A238 10c shown .18 .15
873 A238 20c Green iguana .15 .15
874 A238 30c Iguana .25 .25
Nos. 872-874,C385-C387 (6) 1.41 1.38

Post-classical Vase, San Salvador — A239

Pre-Columbian Art: 15c, Brazier with classical head, Tazumal. 40c, Vase with classical head, Tazumal.

1976, Oct. 11 Litho. *Perf. 12½*

875 A239 10c multi .15 .15
876 A239 15c multi .15 .15
877 A239 40c multi .32 .32
Nos. 875-877,C388-C390 (6) 1.77 1.42

For overprint see No. C429.

Fair Emblem — A240

1976, Oct. 25 Litho. *Perf. 12½*

878 A240 10c multi .15 .15
879 A240 30c gray & multi .24 .24
Nos. 878-879,C391-C392 (4) 1.14 .94

7th Intl. Fair, Nov. 5-22.

Child under Christmas Tree — A241

1976, Dec. 16 Litho. *Perf. 11*

880 A241 10c yel & multi .15 .15
881 A241 15c buff & multi .15 .15
882 A241 30c vio & multi .24 .24
883 A241 40c pink & multi .32 .32
Nos. 880-883,C393-C396 (8) 2.56 1.96

Christmas 1976.

Rotary Emblem, Map of Salvador — A242

1977, June 20 **Litho.** *Perf. 11*

884 A242 10c multi .15 .15
885 A242 15c multi .15 .15
Nos. 884-885,C397-C398 (4) 1.30 .95

San Salvador Rotary Club, 50th anniversary.

Cerron Grande Hydroelectric Station A243

Designs: No. 887, 15c, Central sugar refinery, Jiboa. 30c, Radar station, Izalco, vert.

1977, June 29 *Perf. 12½*

886 A243 10c multi .15 .15
887 A243 10c multi .15 .15
888 A243 15c multi .15 .15
889 A243 30c multi .24 .15
Nos. 886-889,C399-C401 (7) 1.89
Set value 1.00

Industrial development. Nos. 886-889 have colorless overprint in multiple rows: GOBIERNO DEL SALVADOR.

Nos. 785 and 774 Surcharged with New Value and Bar

1977, June 30 *Perf. 12x11½, 11½*

890 A200 15c on 2c multi .15 .15
891 A197 25c on 6c multi .20 .15
Set value .15

Microphone, ASDER Emblem A244

1977, Sept. 14 **Litho.** *Perf. 14*

892 A244 10c multi .15 .15
893 A244 15c multi .15 .15
Set value, #892-893, C406-C407 .50 .40

Broadcasting in El Salvador, 50th anniversary (Asociacion Salvadoreño de Empresa Radio).

Wooden Drum A245

Design: 10c, Flute and recorder.

1978, Aug. 29 **Litho.** *Perf. 12½*

894 A245 5c multi .15 .15
895 A245 10c multi .15 .15
Nos. 894-895,C433-C435 (5) 1.50
Set value .80

For surcharge see No. C492.

The index in each volume of the Scott Catalogue contains many listings that help identify stamps.

"Man and Engineering" A246

1978, Sept. 12 **Litho.** *Perf. 13½*

896 A246 10c multi .15 .15

4th National Engineers' Congress, San Salvador, Sept. 18-23. See No. C436.

Izalco Station — A247

1978, Sept. 14 *Perf. 12½*

897 A247 10c multi .15 .15

Inauguration of Izalco satellite earth station, Sept. 15, 1978. See No. C437.

Fair Emblem — A248

1978, Oct. 30 **Litho.** *Perf. 12½*

898 A248 10c multi .15 .15
899 A248 20c multi .16 .16
Set value, #898-899, C440-C441 .55 .45

8th Intl. Fair, Nov. 3-20.

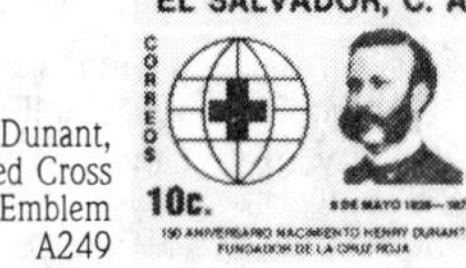

Henri Dunant, Red Cross Emblem A249

1978, Oct. 30 *Perf. 11*

900 A249 10c multi .15 .15

Henri Dunant (1828-1910), founder of the Red Cross. See No. C442.

World Map and Cotton Boll — A250

1978, Nov. 22 *Perf. 12½*

901 A250 15c multi .15 .15

International Cotton Consulting Committee, 37th Meeting, San Salvador, Nov. 27-Dec. 2. See No. C443.

Nativity, Stained-glass Window A251

1978, Dec. 5 **Litho.** *Perf. 12½*

902 A251 10c multi .15 .15
903 A251 15c multi .15 .15
Nos. 902-903,C444-C445 (4) 1.30
Set value .75

Christmas 1978.

Athenaeum Coat of Arms — A252

1978, Dec. 20 **Litho.** *Perf. 14*

904 A252 5c multi .15 .15

Millennium of Castilian language. See No. C446.

Postal Service and UPU Emblems A253

1979, Apr. 2 **Litho.** *Perf. 14*

905 A253 10c multi .15 .15

Centenary of Salvador's membership in Universal Postal Union. See No. C447.

"75," Health Organization and WHO Emblems A254

1979, Apr. 7 *Perf. 14x14½*

906 A254 10c multi .15 .15

Pan-American Health Organization, 75th anniversary. See No. C448.

Flame and Pillars — A255

1979, May 25 **Litho.** *Perf. 12½*

907 A255 10c multi .15 .15
908 A255 15c multi .15 .15
Nos. 907-908,C449-C450 (4) 1.30
Set value .80

Social Security 5-year plan, 1978-1982.

Pope John Paul II, Map of Americas — A256

1979, July 12 **Litho.** *Perf. 14½x14*

909 A256 10c multi .15 .15
910 A256 20c multi .16 .15
Nos. 909-910,C454-C455 (4) 4.81 3.10

Mastodon A257

1979, Sept. 7 **Litho.** *Perf. 14*

911 A257 10c shown .15 .15
912 A257 20c Saber-toothed tiger .16 .16
913 A257 30c Toxodon .24 .24
Nos. 911-913,C458-C460 (6) 2.55 1.85

Salvador Flag, José Aberiz and Proclamation — A258

1979, Sept. 14 *Perf. 14½x14*

914 A258 10c multi .15 .15

National anthem centenary. See No. C461.

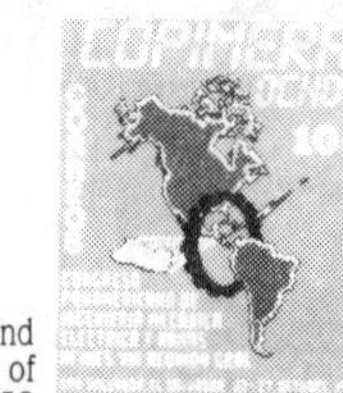

Cogwheel around Map of Americas — A259

1979, Oct. 19 **Litho.** *Perf. 14½x14*

915 A259 10c multi .15 .15

8th COPIMERA Congress (Mechanical, Electrical and Allied Trade Engineers), San Salvador, Oct. 22-27. See No. C462.

Children of Various Races, IYC Emblem A260

Children and Nurses, IYC Emblem — A261

Perf. 14x14½, 14½x14

1979, Oct. 29

916 A260 10c multi .15 .15
917 A261 15c multi .15 .15
Set value .20 .20

International Year of the Child.

Map of Central and South America, Congress Emblem — A262

1979, Nov. 1 Litho. *Perf. 14½x14*

918 A262 10c multi .15 .15

5th Latin American Clinical Biochemistry Congress, San Salvador, Nov. 5-10. See No. C465.

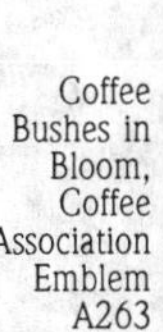

Coffee Bushes in Bloom, Coffee Association Emblem A263

Salvador Coffee Assoc., 50th Anniv.: 30c, Planting coffee bushes, vert. 40c, Coffee berries.

Perf. 14x14½, 14½x14

1979, Dec. 18

919 A263 10c multi .15 .15
920 A263 30c multi .24 .24
921 A263 40c multi .32 .32
Nos. 919-921,C466-C468 (6) 2.51 1.91

Children, Dove and Star — A264

1979, Dec. 18 *Perf. 14½x14*

922 A264 10c multi .15 .15

Christmas 1979.

Hoof and Mouth Disease Prevention A265

1980, June 3 Litho. *Perf. 14½x14*

923 A265 10c multi .15 .15

See No. C469.

Anadara Grandis A266

1980, Aug. 12 *Perf. 14x14½*

924 A266 10c *shown* .15 .15
925 A266 30c *Ostrea iridescens* .24 .24
926 A266 40c *Turitello leucostoma* .32 .32
Nos. 924-926,C470-C473 (7) 2.36 1.96

Quetzal (Pharomachrus mocino) — A267

1980, Sept. 10 Litho. *Perf. 14x14½*

927 A267 10c shown .15 .15
928 A267 20c Penelopina nigra .16 .16
Nos. 927-928,C474-C476 (5) 1.51 1.11

Local Snakes A268

1980, Nov. 12 Litho. *Perf. 14x14½*

929 A268 10c Tree snake .15 .15
930 A268 20c Water snake .16 .16
Nos. 929-930,C477-C478 (4) .91 .71

A269

A270

1980, Nov. 26 Litho. *Perf. 14*

931 A269 15c multi .15 .15
932 A269 20c multi .16 .16
Nos. 931-932,C479-C480 (4) 1.31 .96

Corporation of Auditors, 50th anniv.

1980, Dec. 5 Litho. *Perf. 14*

933 A270 5c multi .15 .15
934 A270 10c multi .15 .15
Nos. 933-934,C481-C482 (4) 1.00
Set value .60

Christmas. See Nos. C481-C482.

A271

A272

Dental association emblems.

1981, June 18 Litho. *Perf. 14*

935 A271 15c lt yel grn & blk .15 .15

Dental Society of Salvador, 50th anniv.; Odontological Federation of Central America and Panama, 25th anniv. See No. C494.

1981, Aug. 14 Litho. *Perf. 14x14½*

Design: Hands reading braille book.

936 A272 10c multi .15 .15
Nos. 936,C495-C498 (5) 2.15 1.50

Intl. Year of the Disabled.

A273

A274

1981, Aug. 28 Litho. *Perf. 14x14½*

937 A273 10c multi .15 .15

Roberto Quinonez Natl. Agriculture College, 25th anniv. See No. C499.

1981, Sept. 16 Litho. *Perf. 14x14½*

938 A274 10c multi .15 .15

World Food Day. See No. C500.

1981 World Cup Preliminaries A275

1981, Nov. 27 Litho. *Perf. 14x14½*

939 A275 10c shown .15 .15
940 A275 40c Cup soccer ball, flags .32 .25
Nos. 939-940,C505-C506 (4) 1.27 .95

Salvador Lyceum (High School), 100th Anniv. — A276

1981, Dec. 17 Litho. *Perf. 14*

941 A276 10c multi .15 .15

See No. C507.

Pre-Columbian Stone Sculptures — A277

1982, Jan. 22 Litho. *Perf. 14*

942 A277 10c Axe with bird's head .15 .15
943 A277 20c Sun disc .16 .16
944 A277 40c Stele Carving with effigy .32 .32
Nos. 942-944,C508-C510 (6) 1.73 1.43

Scouting Year — A278

1982, Mar. 17 Litho. *Perf. 14½x14*

945 A278 10c shown .15 .15
946 A278 30c Girl Scout helping woman .24 .24
Nos. 945-946,C511-C512 (4) .99 .79

Armed Forces A279

1982, May 7 Litho. *Perf. 14x13½*

947 A279 10c multi .15 .15

See No. C514.

1982 World Cup A280

1982, July 14 *Perf. 14x14½*

948 A280 10c Team, emblem .15 .15
Nos. 948,C518-C520 (4) 2.50 1.65

10th International Fair — A281

1982, Oct. 14 Litho. *Perf. 14*

949 A281 10c multi .15 .15

See No. C524.

Christmas 1982 — A282

1982, Dec. 14 Litho. *Perf. 14*

950 A282 5c multi .15 .15

See No. C528.

Dancers, Pre-Colombian Ceramic Design — A283

1983, Feb. 18 Litho. *Perf. 14*

951 A283 10c shown .15 .15
952 A283 20c Sower .16 .16
953 A283 25c Flying Man .20 .20
954 A283 60c Hunters .50 .50
955 A283 60c Hunters, diff. .50 .50
956 A283 1col Procession .80 .80
957 A283 1col Procession, diff. .80 .80
Nos. 951-957 (7) 3.11 3.11

Nos. 953-957 airmail. Stamps of same denomination se-tenant.

Visit of Pope John Paul II — A284

1983, Mar. 4 Litho. *Perf. 14*

958 A284 25c shown .20 .20
959 A284 60c Monument to the Divine Savior, Pope .50 .40

Salvadoran Air Force, 50th Anniv. A285

1983, Mar. 24 Litho. *Perf. 14*

960 A285 10c Ricardo Aberle .15 .15
961 A285 10c Air Force Emblem .15 .15
962 A285 10c Enrico Massi .15 .15
a. Strip of 3, #960-962 .24 .24
963 A285 10c Juan Ramon Munes .15 .15
964 A285 10c American Air Force Cooperation Emblem .15 .15
965 A285 10c Belisario Salazar .15 .15
a. Strip of 3, #963-965 .24 .24
Set value .48 .48

Arranged se-tenant horizontally with two Nos. 960 or 963 at left and two Nos. 962 or 965 at right.

A286 A287

Local butterflies.

1983, May 31 Litho. *Perf. 14*

966 Pair .15 .15
a. A286 5c Papilio torquatus .15 .15
b. A286 5c Metamorpha steneles .15 .15
967 Pair .16 .16
a. A286 10c Papilio torquatus, diff. .15 .15
b. A286 10c Anaea marthesia .15 .15
968 Pair .24 .24
a. A286 15c Prepona brooksiana .15 .15
b. A286 15c Caligo atreus .15 .15
969 Pair .40 .40
a. A286 25c Morpho peleides .20 .20
b. A286 25c Dismorphia praxinoe .20 .20
970 Pair .80 .80
a. A286 50c Morpho polyphemus .40 .40
b. A286 50c Metamorphia epaphus .40 .40
Nos. 966-970 (5) 1.75 1.75

1983, June 23 Litho. *Perf. 14*

971 A287 75c multi .60 .50

Simon Bolivar, 200th birth anniv.

A288 A289

1983, July 21 Litho. *Perf. 14*

972 A288 10c Dr. Jose Mendoza, college emblem .15 .15

Salvador Medical College, 40th anniv.

Perf. 13½x14, 14x13½

1983, Oct. 30 Litho.

973 A289 10c multi .15 .15
974 A289 50c multi, horiz. .40 .40

Centenary of David J. Guzman national museum. 50c airmail.

World Communications Year — A290

Designs: 10c, Gen. Juan Jose Canas, Francisco Duenas (organizers of First natl. telegraph service), Morse key, 1870. 25c, Mailman delivering letters, vert. 50c, Post Office sorting center, San Salvador. 25c, 50c airmail.

Perf. 14x13½, 13½x14

1983, Nov. 23 Litho.

975 A290 10c multi .15 .15
976 A290 25c multi .20 .20
977 A290 50c multi .40 .30
Nos. 975-977 (3) .75 .65

A291 A292

Perf. 13½x14, 14x13½

1983, Nov. 30

978 A291 10c Dove over globe .15 .15
979 A291 25c Creche figures, horiz. .20 .20
Set value .28 .28

Christmas. 25c is airmail.

1983, Dec. 13

980 A292 10c Vehicle exhaust .15 .15
981 A292 15c Fig tree .15 .15
982 A292 25c Rodent .20 .20
Set value .40 .40

Environmental protection. 15c, 25c airmail.

Philatelists' Day — A293 Corn — A294

1984, Jan. 5 *Perf. 14x13½*

983 A293 10c No. 1 .15 .15

1984, Feb. 21 Litho. *Perf. 14½x14*

984 A294 10c shown .15 .15
985 A294 15c Cotton .15 .15
986 A294 25c Coffee beans .15 .15
987 A294 50c Sugar cane .20 .15
988 A294 75c Beans .30 .22
989 A294 1col Agave .40 .30
990 A294 5col Balsam 2.00 1.50
Nos. 984-990 (7) 3.35 2.62

See Nos. 1047-1051.

Caluco Church, Sonsonate A295

1984, Mar. 30 *Perf. 14x13½*

991 A295 5c shown .15 .15
992 A295 10c Salcoatitan, Sonsonate .15 .15
993 A295 15c Huizucar, La Libertad .15 .15
994 A295 25c Santo Domingo, Sonsonate .15 .15
995 A295 50c Pilar, Sonsonate .20 .15
996 A295 75c Nahuizalco, Sonsonate .30 .22
Set value .75 .60

Nos. 993-996 airmail.

Central Reserve Bank of Salvador, 50th Anniv. A296

1984, July 17 Litho. *Perf. 14x14½*

997 A296 10c First reserve note .15 .15
998 A296 25c Bank, 1959 .15 .15
Set value .15 .15

25c airmail.

1984 Summer Olympics A297

Perf. 14x13½, 13½x14

1984, July 20

999 A297 10c Boxing .15 .15
1000 A297 25c Running, vert. .15 .15
1001 A297 40c Bicycling .16 .15
1002 A297 50c Swimming .20 .15
1003 A297 75c Judo, vert. .30 .22
1004 A297 1col Pierre de Coubertin .40 .30
Set value 1.20 .90

Nos. 1000-1004 airmail.
For surcharge see No. C536A.

Govt. Printing Office Building Opening A298

1984, July 27 *Perf. 14x13½*

1005 A298 10c multi .15 .15

5th of November Hydroelectric Plant — A299

Designs: 55c, Cerron Grande Plant. 70c, Ahuachapan Geothermal Plant. 90c, Mural. 2col, 15th of September Plant. 7c, 90c, 2 col airmail.

1984, Sept. 13 Litho. *Perf. 14x14½*

1006 A299 20c multi .15 .15
1007 A299 55c multi .22 .18
1008 A299 70c multi .28 .22
1009 A299 90c multi .36 .28
1010 A299 2col multi .80 .60
Nos. 1006-1010 (5) 1.81 1.43

Boys Playing Marbles — A300

1984, Oct. 16 *Perf. 14½x14*

1011 A300 55c shown .22 .18
1012 A300 70c Spinning top .28 .22
1013 A300 90c Flying kite .36 .28
1014 A300 2col Top, diff. .80 .60
Nos. 1011-1014 (4) 1.66 1.28

11th International Fair — A301

1984, Oct. 31 Litho. *Perf. 14x14½*

1015 A301 25c shown .15 .15
1016 A301 70c Fairgrounds .28 .22
Set value .30

70c airmail.

Los Chorros Tourist Center A302

1984, Nov. 23 Litho. *Perf. 14x14½*

1017 A302 15c shown .15 .15
1018 A302 25c Plaza las Americas .15 .15
1019 A302 70c El Salvador International Airport .28 .22
1020 A302 90c El Tunco Beach .36 .28
1021 A302 2col Sihuatehuacan Tourist Center .80 .60
Nos. 1017-1021 (5) 1.74
Set value 1.20

The Paper of Papers, 1979, by Roberto A. Galicia (b. 1945) A302a

Paintings by natl. artists: 20c, The White Nun 1939, by Salvador Salazar Arrue (b. 1899), vert 70c, Supreme Elegy to Masferrer, 1968, by Antonic G. Ponce (b. 1938), vert. 90c, Transmutation 1979, by Armando Solis (b. 1940). 2 col, Figures a Theater, 1959, by Carlos Canas (b. 1924), vert.

1984, Dec. 10 Litho. *Perf. 14*

1021A A302a 20c multi .15 .15
1021B A302a 55c multi .22 .16
1021C A302a 70c multi .28 .22
1021D A302a 90c multi .35 .26
1021E A302a 2col multi .75 .60
Nos. 1021A-1021E (5) 1.75 1.39

Nos. 1021B-1021E are airmail. 70c and 2col issued with overprinted silver bar and corrected inscription in black; copies exist without overprint

Christmas 1984 — A303

1984, Dec. 19 Litho

1022 A303 25c Glass ornament .15 .15
1023 A303 70c Ornaments, dove .28 .22
Set value .30

No. 1023 airmail.

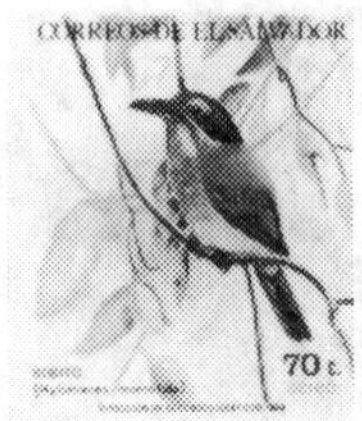

Birds — A304

1984, Dec. 21 Litho. *Perf. 14½x14*

1024 A304 15c Lepidocolaptes affinis .15 .15
1025 A304 25c Spodiornis rusticus barriliensis .15 .15
1026 A304 55c Claravis mondetoura .22 .18
1027 A304 70c Hylomanes momotula .28 .22
1028 A304 90c Xenotriccus calizonus .36 .28
1029 A304 1col Cardellina rubrifrons .45 .35
Nos. 1024-1029 (6) 1.61
Set value 1.15

Nos. 1026-1029 airmail.

Salvador Bank Centenary A305

1985, Feb. 6 Litho. *Perf. 14*

1030 A305 25c Stock certificate .15 .15

Mortgage Bank, 50th Anniv. — A306

1985, Feb. 20 Litho. *Perf. 14*

1031 A306 25c Mortgage .15 .15

Intl. Youth Year — A307

1985, Feb. 28 Litho. *Perf. 14*

1032	A307	25c	IYY emblem	.15	.15
1033	A307	55c	Woodcrafting	.22	.18
1034	A307	70c	Professions symbolized	.28	.22
1035	A307	1.50col	Youths marching	.60	.45
			Nos. 1032-1035 (4)	1.25	1.00

Nos. 1033-1035 airmail.

Archaeology A308

1985, Mar. 6 Litho. *Perf. 14½x14*

1036	A308	15c	Pre-classical figure	.15	.15
1037	A308	20c	Engraved vase	.15	.15
1038	A308	25c	Post-classical ceramic	.15	.15
1039	A308	55c	Post-classical figure	.22	.18
1040	A308	70c	Late post-classical deity	.28	.22
1041	A308	1col	Late post-classical figure	.40	.30
			Set value	1.12	.88

Souvenir Sheet

Rouletted 13½

1042	A308	2col	Tazumal ruins, horiz.	.80	.60

Nos. 1039-1041 airmail. No. 1042 has enlargement of stamp design in margin.

Natl. Red Cross, Cent. — A309

1985, Mar. 13 Litho. *Perf. 14*

1043	A309	25c	Anniv. emblem vert.	.15	.15
1044	A309	55c	Sea rescue	.20	.15
1045	A309	70c	Blood donation service	.25	.20
1046	A309	90c	First aid, ambulance, vert.	.35	.26
			Nos. 1043-1046 (4)	.95	.76

Nos. 1044-1046 are airmail.

Agriculture Type of 1984

1985 *Perf. 14½x14*

1047	A294	55c	Cotton	.20	.15
1048	A294	70c	Corn	.25	.20
1049	A294	90c	Sugar cane	.35	.26
1050	A294	2col	Beans	.75	.60
1051	A294	10col	Agave	4.00	3.00
			Nos. 1047-1051 (5)	5.55	4.21

Issued: 55c, 70c, 90c, 4/4; 2col, 10col, 9/4.

Child Survival A310

Children's drawings.

1985, May 3 Litho. *Perf. 14x14½*

1052	A310	25c	Hand, houses	.15	.15
1053	A310	55c	House, children	.20	.15
1054	A310	70c	Boy, girl holding hands	.25	.20
1055	A310	90c	Oral vaccination	.35	.28
			Nos. 1052-1055 (4)	.95	.78

Nos. 1053-1055 are airmail.

Salvador Army A311

1985, May 17 *Perf. 14*

1056	A311	25c	Map	.15	.15
1057	A311	70c	Recruit, natl. flag	.25	.20
			Set value		.26

No. 1057 is airmail.

Inauguration of Pres. Duarte, 1st Anniv. — A312

1985, June 28 *Perf. 14½x14*

1058	A312	25c	Flag, laurel, book	.15	.15
1059	A312	70c	Article I, Constitution	.25	.20

Inter-American Development Bank, 25th Anniv. — A313

25c, Central Hydro-electric Dam, power station. 70c, Map of Salvador. 1col, Natl. arms.

1985, July 5 *Perf. 14x13½*

1060	A313	25c	multi	.15	.15
1061	A313	70c	multi	.25	.20
1062	A313	1col	multi	.38	.30
			Nos. 1060-1062 (3)	.78	.65

Nos. 1061-1062 are airmail.

Fish — A314

1985, Sept. 30 *Perf. 14x14½*

1064	A314	25c	Cichlasoma trimaculatum	.15	.15
1065	A314	55c	Rhamdia guatemalenis	.20	.15
1066	A314	70c	Poecilia sphenops	.25	.20
1067	A314	90c	Cichlasoma nigrofasciatum	.35	.28
1068	A314	1col	Astyanax fasciatus	.38	.30
1069	A314	1.50col	Dormitator latifrons	.60	.42
			Nos. 1064-1069 (6)	1.93	1.50

Nos. 1065-1069 are airmail.

UNFAO, 40th Anniv. — A315

1985, Oct. 16 *Perf. 14½x14*

1070	A315	20c	Cornucopia	.15	.15
1071	A315	40c	Centeotl, Nahuat god of corn	.15	.15
			Set value	.22	.18

Dragonflies A316

Designs: 25c, Cordulegaster godmani mclachlan. 55c, Libellula herculea karsch. 70c, Cora marina selys. 90c, Aeshna cornigera braver. 1col, Mecistogaster ornata rambur. 1.50col, Hetaerina smaragdalis de marmels.

1985, Dec. 9 *Perf. 14x14½*

1072	A316	25c	multi	.15	.15
1073	A316	55c	multi	.20	.15
1074	A316	70c	multi	.25	.20
1075	A316	90c	multi	.35	.28
1076	A316	1col	multi	.38	.30
1077	A316	1.50col	multi	.60	.42
			Nos. 1072-1077 (6)	1.93	1.50

Nos. 1073-1077 are airmail.
For surcharge see No. C544.

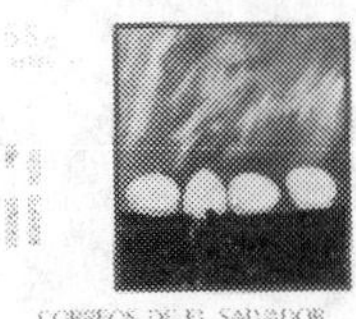

Summer, 1984, by Roberto Huezo (b.1947) A317

Paintings by natl. artists: 25c, Profiles, 1978, by Rosa Mena Valenzuela (b. 1924), vert. 70c, The Deliverance, 1984, by Fernando Llort (b. 1949). 90c, Making Tamale, 1975, by Pedro A. Garcia (b. 1930). 1col, Warm Presence, 1984, by Miguel A. Orellana (b. 1929), vert. Nos. 1079-1082 are airmail.

1985, Dec. 18 *Perf. 14*

1078	A317	25c	multi	.15	.15
1079	A317	55c	multi	.20	.15
1080	A317	70c	multi	.25	.20
1081	A317	90c	multi	.35	.26
1082	A317	1col	multi	.38	.30
			Nos. 1078-1082 (5)	1.33	1.06

San Vincente de Austria y Lorenzana City, 350th Anniv. A318

1985, Dec. 20

1083	A318	15c	Tower, vert.	.15	.15
1084	A318	20c	Cathedral	.15	.15
			Set value	.15	.15

Intl. Peace Year 1986 — A319

1986, Feb. 21 Litho. *Perf. 14*

1085	A319	15c	multi	.15	.15
1086	A319	70c	multi	.50	.38

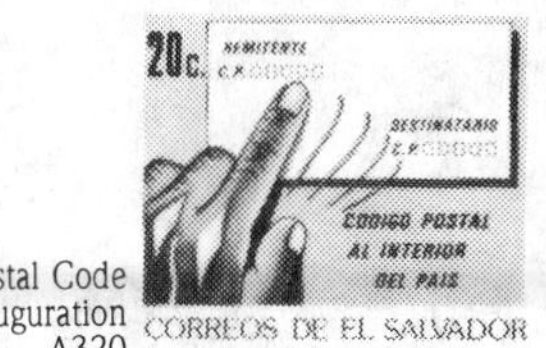

Postal Code Inauguration A320

1986, Mar. 14 Litho. *Perf. 14x14½*

1087	A320	20c	Domestic mail	.16	.15
1088	A320	25c	Intl. mail	.18	.15

Radio El Salvador, 60th Anniv. A321

1986, Mar. 21

1089	A321	25c	Microphone	.18	.15
1090	A321	70c	Map	.50	.38

No. 1090 is airmail.

Mammals A322

1986, May 30 Litho. *Perf. 14x14½*

1091	A322	15c	Felis wiedii	.15	.15
1092	A322	20c	Tamandua tetradactyla	.16	.15
1093	A322	1col	Dasypus novemcinctus	.80	.60
1094	A322	2col	Pecarii tajacu	1.60	1.20
			Nos. 1091-1094 (4)	2.71	2.10

Nos. 1093-1094 are airmail.

1986 World Cup Soccer Championships, Mexico — A323

Designs: 70c, Flags, mascot. 1col, Players, Soccer Cup, vert. 2col, Natl. flag, player dribbling, vert. 5col, Goal, emblem.

1986, June 6 *Perf. 14x14½, 14½x14*

1095	A323	70c	multi	.55	.42
1096	A323	1col	multi	.80	.60
1097	A323	2col	multi	1.60	1.20
1098	A323	5col	multi	4.00	3.00
			Nos. 1095-1098 (4)	6.95	5.22

Teachers — A324

1986, June 30 Litho. *Perf. 14½x14*

1099	A324	20c	Dario Gonzalez	.15	.15
1100	A324	20c	Valero Lecha	.15	.15
a.			Pair, #1099-1100	.20	.20
1101	A324	40c	Marcelino G. Flamenco	.20	.15
1102	A324	40c	Camilo Campos	.20	.15
a.			Pair, #1101-1102	.40	.30
1103	A324	70c	Saul Flores	.32	.25
1104	A324	70c	Jorge Larde	.32	.25
a.			Pair, #1103-1104	.65	.50
1105	A324	1col	Francisco Moran	.50	.35
1106	A324	1col	Mercedes M. De Luarca	.50	.35
a.			Pair, #1105-1106	1.00	.70
			Nos. 1099-1106 (8)	2.34	1.80

Nos. 1103-1106 are airmail.

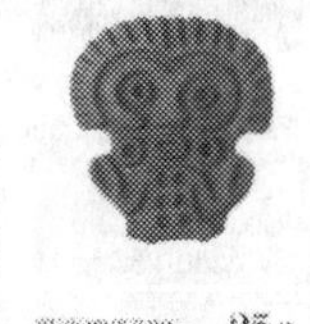

Pre-Hispanic Ceramic Seal, Cara Sucia, Ahuachapan, Tlaloc Culture (300 B.C.-A.D. 1200) — A325

1986, July 23 Litho. *Perf. 13½*

1107	A325	25c	org & brn	.15	.15
1108	A325	55c	grn, org & brn	.25	.18
1109	A325	70c	pale gray, org & brn	.32	.24
1110	A325	90c	pale yel, org & brn	.45	.32
1111	A325	1col	pale grn, org & brn	.48	.35

1112 A325 1.50col pale pink, org & brn .70 .52
Nos. 1107-1112 (6) 2.35 1.76

Nos. 1108-1112 are airmail.

World Food Day — A326

1986, Oct. 30 Litho. *Perf. 14x14½*
1113 A326 20c multi .16 .15

Flowers A327

1986, Sept. 30 *Perf. 14*
1114 A327 20c Spathiphyllum phrynifolium, vert. .15 .15
1115 A327 25c Asclepias curassavica .15 .15
1116 A327 70c Tagetes tenuifolia .32 .24
1117 A327 1col Ipomoea tiliacea, vert. .48 .35
Nos. 1115-1117 (3) .95
Set value .76

Nos. 1116-1117 are airmail.

Christmas A328

Perf. 14x14½, 14½x14
1986, Dec. 10 Litho.
1118 A328 25c Candles, vert. .15 .15
1119 A328 70c Doves .32 .24

No. 1119 is airmail.

Crafts — A329

1986, Dec. 18
1120 A329 25c Basket-making .15 .15
1121 A329 55c Ceramicware .25 .18
1122 A329 70c Guitars, vert. .32 .24
1123 A329 1col Baskets, diff. .48 .35
Nos. 1120-1123 (4) 1.20 .92

Christmas A330

Paintings: 25c, Church, by Mario Araujo Rajo, vert. 70c, Landscape, by Francisco Reyes.

1986, Dec. 22
1124 A330 25c multi .15 .15
1125 A330 70c multi .32 .24

No. 1125 is airmail.

Promotion of Philately A331

1987, Mar. 10 Litho. *Perf. 14½x14*
1126 A331 25c multi .15 .15

Intl. Aid Following Earthquake, Oct. 10, 1986 — A332

1987, Mar. 25
1127 A332 15c multi .15 .15
1128 A332 70c multi .32 .24
1129 A332 1.50col multi .70 .52
1130 A332 5col multi 2.40 1.80
Nos. 1127-1130 (4) 3.57 2.71

Orchids — A333

1987, June 8 Litho. *Perf. 14½x14*
1131 A333 20c Maxillaria tenuifolia .15 .15
1132 A333 20c Ponthieva maculata .15 .15
a. Pair, #1131-1132 .20 .15
1133 A333 25c Meiracyllium trinasutum .15 .15
1134 A333 25c Encyclia vagans .15 .15
a. Pair, #1133-1134 .25 .20
1135 A333 70c Encyclia cochleata .32 .25
1136 A333 70c Maxillaria atrata .32 .25
a. Pair, #1135-1136 .65 .50
1137 A333 1.50col Sobrialia xantholeuca .70 .52
1138 A333 1.50col Encyclia microcharis .70 .52
a. Pair, #1137-1138 1.40 1.05
Nos. 1131-1138 (8) 2.64
Set value 1.85

#1133-1138 horiz. #1135-1138 are airmail.

Teachers — A334

Designs: No. 1139, C. de Jesus Alas, music. No. 1140, Luis Edmundo Vasquez, medicine. No. 1141, David Rosales, law. No. 1142, Guillermo Trigueros, medicine. No. 1143, Manuel Farfan Castro, history. No. 1144, Iri Sol, voice. No. 1145, Carlos Arturo Imendia, primary education. No. 1146, Benjamin Orozco, chemistry.

1987, June 30 Litho. *Perf. 14½x14*
1139 A334 15c greenish blue & blk .15 .15
1140 A334 15c greenish blue & blk .15 .15
a. Pair, #1139-1140 .15 .15
1141 A334 20c beige & blk .15 .15
1142 A334 20c beige & blk .15 .15
a. Pair, #1141-1142 .20 .15
1143 A334 70c yel org & blk .32 .25
1144 A334 70c yel org & blk .32 .25
a. Pair, #1143-1144 .65 .50
1145 A334 1.50col lt blue grn & blk .70 .52
1146 A334 1.50col lt blue grn & blk .70 .52
a. Pair, #1145-1146 1.40 1.05
Nos. 1139-1146 (8) 2.64
Set value 1.80

Nos. 1143-1146 are airmail.

10th Pan American Games, Indianapolis A335

Perf. 14½x14, 14x14½
1987, July 31
1147 A335 20c Emblem, vert. .15 .15
1148 A335 20c Table tennis, vert. .15 .15
a. Pair, #1147-1148 .20 .15
1149 A335 25c Wrestling .15 .15
1150 A335 25c Fencing .15 .15
a. Pair, #1149-1150 .25 .20
1151 A335 70c Softball .32 .25
1152 A335 70c Equestrian .32 .25
a. Pair, #1151-1152 .65 .50
1153 A335 5col Weight lifting, vert. 2.35 1.75
1154 A335 5col Hurdling, vert. 2.35 1.75
a. Pair, #1153-1154 2.75 3.50
Nos. 1147-1154 (8) 5.94 4.60

Nos. 1151-1154 are airmail.

Prior Nicolas Aguilar (1742-1818) A336

Famous men: 20c, Domingo Antonio de Lara (1783-1814), aviation pioneer. 70c, Juan Manuel Rodrigues (1771-1837), president who abolished slavery. 1.50col, Pedro Pablo Castillo (1780-1814), patriot.

1987, Sept. 11 Litho. *Perf. 14½x14*
1155 A336 15c multi .15 .15
1156 A336 20c multi .15 .15
1157 A336 70c multi .32 .24
1158 A336 1.50col multi .70 .52
Nos. 1155-1158 (4) 1.32
Set value .90

Nos. 1157-1158 are airmail.

World Food Day A337

1987, Oct. 16 *Perf. 14x14½*
1159 A337 50c multi .24 .18

Paintings by Salarrue — A338

Perf. 14½x14, 14x14½
1987, Nov. 30
1160 A338 25c Self-portrait .15 .15
1161 A338 70c Lake .32 .24

#1161 is airmail. See #1186-1189.

Christmas 1987 — A339

25c, Virgin of Perpetual Sorrow, stained-glas window. 70c, The Three Magi, figurines.

1987, Nov. 18 *Perf. 14x14½*
1162 A339 25c multi .15 .1
1163 A339 70c multi .32 .2

No. 1163 is airmail.

Pre-Columbian Musical Instruments A340

Designs: 20c, Pottery drum worn around neck No. 1165, Frieze picturing pre-Columbian musicians, from a Salua culture ceramic vase, c. 700 800 A.D. (left side), vert. No. 1166, Frieze (right side), vert. 1.50col, Conch shell trumpet.

Perf. 14x14½, 14½x14
1987, Dec. 14 Litho.
1164 A340 20c multi .15 .1
1165 A340 70c multi .32 .2
1166 A340 70c multi .32 .2
a. Pair, #1165-1166 .65 .5
1167 A340 1.50col multi .70 .5
Nos. 1164-1167 (4) 1.49 1.1

Nos. 1165-1167 are airmail. No. 1166a has a continuous design.

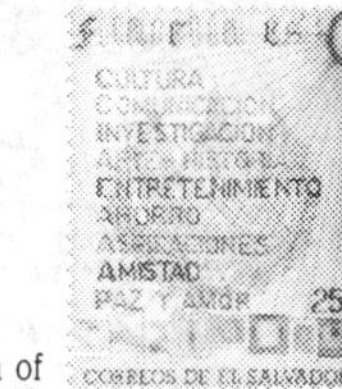

Promotion of Philately — A341

1988, Jan. 20 Litho. *Perf. 1*
1168 A341 25c multi .15 .1

Young Entrepreneurs of El Salvador A342

1988 *Perf. 14x14½*
1169 A342 25c multi .15 .1

St. John Bosco (1815-88) A343

1988, Mar. 15 Litho. *Perf. 14x14½*
1170 A343 20c multi .15 .1

Environmental Protection A344

988, June 3 Litho. *Perf. 14x14½*

171 A344 20c Forests .15 .15
172 A344 70c Forests and rivers .35 .28
Set value .35

No. 1172 is airmail.

1988-1992 Summer Olympics, Seoul and Barcelona A345

988, Aug. 31 Litho. *Perf. 13½*

173 A345 1col High jump
174 A345 1col Javelin
175 A345 1col Shooting
176 A345 1col Wrestling
177 A345 1col Basketball
a. Strip of 5, Nos. 1173-1177
b. Min. sheets of 5 + 5 labels

Souvenir Sheets

178 A345 2col Torch

Printed in sheets of 10 containing 2 each Nos. 173-1177.

No. 1177b exists in 2 forms: 1st contains labels icturing 1988 Summer Games emblem or charac- er trademark; 2nd contains labels picturing the 992 Summer Games emblem or character rademark.

No. 1178 exists in 2 forms: 1st contains 1988 ames emblem; 2nd 1992 Games emblem.

Some, or all, of this issue seem not to have been vailable to the public.

World Food Day — A346

988, Oct. 11 Litho. *Perf. 14x14½*

179 A346 20c multi .15 .15

13th Intl. Fair, Nov. 23-Dec. 11 — A347

988, Oct. 25 *Perf. 14½x14*

180 A347 70c multi .35 .28

Child Protection A348

988, Nov. 10

181 A348 15c Flying kite .15 .15
182 A348 20c Child hugging adult's leg .15 .15
Set value .18 .15

Christmas A349

Paintings by Titian: 25c, *Virgin and Child with the Young St. John and St. Anthony.* 70c, *Virgin and Child in Glory with St. Francis and St. Alvise,* vert.

Perf. 14x14½, 14½x14

1988, Nov. 15

1183 A349 25c multi .15 .15
1184 A349 70c multi .35 .28
Set value .36

70c is airmail.

Return to Moral Values — A350

1988, Nov. 22 *Perf. 14½x14*

1185 A350 25c multi .15 .15

Art Type of 1987

Paintings by Salvadoran artists: 40c, *Esperanza de los Soles,* by Victor Rodriguez Preza. 1col, *Shepherd's Song,* by Luis Angel Salinas, horiz. 2col, *Children,* by Julio Hernandez Aleman, horiz. 5col, *El Nino de Las Alcancias,* by Camilo Minero. Nos. 1187-1189 are airmail.

Perf. 14½x14, 14x14½

1988, Nov. 30

1186 A338 40c multi .20 .15
1187 A338 1col multi .50 .38
1188 A338 2col multi 1.00 .75
1189 A338 5col multi 2.50 1.90
Nos. 1186-1189 (4) 4.20 3.18

A351

Discovery of America, 500th Anniv. (in 1992) — A352

Ruins and artifacts: a, El Tazumul. b, Multicolored footed bowl. c, San Andres. d, Two-color censer. e, Sihuatan. f, Carved head of the God of Lluvia. g, Cara Sucia. h, Man-shaped vase. i, San Lorenzo. j, Multicolored pear-shaped vase. 2col, Christopher Columbus.

1988, Dec. 21 *Perf. 14x14½*

1190 Sheet of 10 5.00 3.80
a.-j. A351 1col any single .50 .38

Souvenir Sheet

Roulette 13½

1191 A352 2col vermilion 1.00 .75

UN Declaration of Human Rights, 40th Anniv. A353

1988, Dec. 9 *Perf. 14½x14, 14x14½*

1192 A353 25c Family, map, emblem, vert. .15 .15
1193 A353 70c shown .35 .28
Set value .36

70c is airmail.

World Wildlife Fund — A354

Felines: a, *Felis wiedii* laying on tree branch. b, *Felis wiedii* sitting on branch. c, *Felis pardalis* laying in brush. d, *Felis pardalis* standing on tree branch.

1988 *Perf. 14½x14*

1194 Strip of 4 .82 .60
a.-b. A354 25c any single .15 .15
c.-d. A354 55c any single .28 .21

World Meteorological Organization, 40th Anniv. — A355

1989, Feb. 3 Litho. *Perf. 14½x14*

1195 A355 15c shown .15 .15
1196 A355 20c Wind gauge .15 .15
Set value .18 .15

Meteorology in El Salvador, cent.

Promotion of Philately A356

1989, Mar. 15 Litho. *Perf. 14½x14*

1197 A356 25c Philatelic Soc. emblem .15 .15

See No. 1230.

Natl. Fire Brigade, 106th Anniv. A357

1989, June 19 Litho. *Perf. 14x14½*

1198 A357 25c Fire truck .15 .15
1199 A357 70c Firemen .35 .28
Set value .36

French Revolution, Bicent. A358

1989, July 12

1200 A358 90c Anniv. emblem .45 .35
1201 A358 1col Storming of the Bastille .48 .38

Souvenir Sheets

Stamps on Stamps A359

Statues of Queen Isabella and Christopher Columbus A360

Designs: a, #88. b, #101. c, #86. d, #102. e, #87. f, #103.

1989, May 31 Litho. *Perf. 14x14½*

Miniature Sheet

1202 Sheet of 6 1.20 .90
a.-f. A359 50c any single .20 .15

Souvenir Sheet

Rouletted 13½

1203 A360 2col shown .78 .58

Discovery of America, 500th anniv. (in 1992).

No. 1203 exists in two forms: margin pictures Natl. Palace with either 500th anniv. emblem or anniv. emblem and "92" at lower right.

Signing Act of Independence A361

1989, Sept. 1 *Perf. 14x14½*

1204 A361 25c shown .15 .15
1205 A361 70c Flag, natl. seal, heroes .28 .20
Set value .28

Natl. independence, 168th anniv. No. 1205 is airmail.

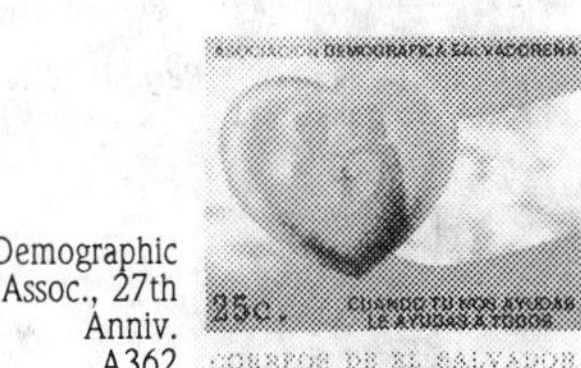

Demographic Assoc., 27th Anniv. A362

1989, July 26

1206 A362 25c multi .15 .15

1990 World Cup Soccer Championships, Italy — A363

Soccer ball, flags of Salvador and: No. 1207, US No. 1208, Guatemala. No. 1209, Costa Rica. No. 1210, Trinidad & Tobago. 55c, Trinidad & Tobago, Guatemala, US, Costa Rica. 1col, Soccer ball, Cuscatlan Stadium.

1989, Sept. 1 Litho. *Perf. 14x14½*

1207 A363 20c shown .15 .15
1208 A363 20c multicolored .15 .15
a. Pair, #1207-1208 .20 .20
1209 A363 25c multicolored .15 .15
1210 A363 25c multicolored .15 .15
a. Pair, #1209-1210 .25 .25
1211 A363 55c multicolored .25 .18
1212 A363 1col multicolored .48 .36
Set value 1.15 .86

Beatification of Marcellin Champagnat, Founder of the Marist Brothers Order A364

1989, Sept. 28

1213 A364 20c multicolored .16 .15

America Issue — A365

UPAE emblem and pre-Columbian artifacts: 25c, *The Cultivator*, rock painting. 70c, Ceramic urn.

1989, Oct. 12

1214 A365 25c multicolored .15 .15
1215 A365 70c multicolored .35 .28

World Food Day — A366

Perf. 14x14½, 14½x14

1989, Oct. 16 **Litho.**

1216 A366 15c shown .15 .15
1217 A366 55c Aspects of agriculture, vert. .28 .20
Set value .36 .26

Children's Rights — A367

1989, Oct. 26 Litho. ***Perf. 14½x14***

1218 A367 25c multicolored .18 .15

Creche Figures — A368

1989, Dec. 1

1219 A368 25c shown .15 .15
1220 A368 70c Holy Family, diff. .35 .28

Christmas.

Birds of Prey — A369

Perf. 14½x14, 14x14½

1989, Dec. 20

1221 A369 70c *Sarcoramphus papa* .35 .28
1222 A369 1col *Polyborus plancus* .50 .38
1223 A369 2col *Accipiter striatus* 1.00 .75
1224 A369 10col *Glaucidium brasilianum* 5.00 3.75
Nos. 1221-1224 (4) 6.85 5.16

Nos. 1221 and 1223 vert.

Tax Court, 50th Aniv. A370

1990, Jan. 12 Litho. ***Perf. 14x14½***

1225 A370 50c multicolored .20 .16

Lord Baden-Powell, 133rd Birth Anniv. — A371

1990, Feb. 23 ***Perf. 14½x14***

1226 A371 25c multicolored .18 .15

Intl. Women's Day — A372

1990, Mar. 8 Litho. ***Perf. 14½x14***

1227 A372 25c multicolored .15 .15

Type of 1989 and

Hour Glass — A373

1990 ***Perf. 14½x14***

1228 A373 25c multicolored .15 .15
1229 A373 55c multicolored .22 .16
Set value .24

Souvenir Sheet

Rouletted 13½ with Simulated Perfs.

1230 A356 2col blk & pale blue .78 .58

Philatelic Soc., 50th anniv. Nos. 1229-1230 are airmail.

Fight Against Addictions A375

1990, Apr. 26 Litho. ***Perf. 14x14½***

1231 A375 20c Alcohol .15 .15
1232 A375 25c Smoking .15 .15
1233 A375 1.50col Drugs .55 .42
Set value .68 .52

No. 1233 is airmail.

La Prensa, 75th Anniv. — A376

1990, May 14 Litho. ***Perf. 14½x14***

1234 A376 15c multicolored .15 .15
1235 A376 25c "75," newspaper .15 .15
Set value .20

A377

World Cup Soccer Championships, Italy — A378

Soccer player and flags of: No. 1236, Argentina, USSR, Cameroun, Romania. No. 1237, Italy, US, Austria, Czechoslovakia. No. 1238, Brazil, Costa Rica, Sweden, Scotland. No. 1239, Germany, United Arab Emirates, Yugoslavia, Colombia. No. 1240, Belgium, Spain, Korea, Uruguay. No. 1241, England, Netherlands, Ireland, Egypt.

1990, June 15 ***Perf. 14x14½***

1236 A377 55c multicolored .25 .18
1237 A377 55c multicolored .25 .18
1238 A377 70c multicolored .35 .25
1239 A377 70c multicolored .35 .25
1240 A377 1col multicolored .50 .38
1241 A377 1col multicolored .50 .38
1242 A378 1.50col multicolored .75 .58
Nos. 1236-1242 (7) 2.95 2.20

For surcharge see No. 1245.

Christopher Columbus A379

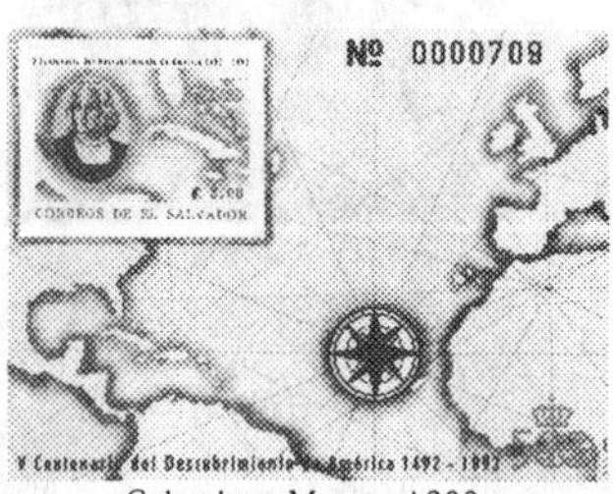

Columbus, Map — A380

Stained glass window: b, Queen Isabella. c, Columbus' Arms. d, Discovery of America 500th anniv. emblem. e, One boat of Columbus' fleet. f, Two boats.

1990, July 30 Litho. ***Perf. 14***

Miniature Sheet

1243 Sheet of 6 3.00 2.30
a.-f. A379 1col any single .50 .38

Souvenir Sheet

Rouletted 13 1/2

1244 A380 2col multicolored 1.10 .82

See Nos. 1283-1284.

No. 1239 Surcharged in Black

90c.

1991, Feb. Litho. ***Perf. 14x14½***

1245 A377 90c on 70c multi .45 .25

World Summit for Children — A381

1990, Sept. 25 ***Perf. 14½x14***

1246 A381 5col blk, gold & dk bl 2.75 2.00

First Postage Stamps, 150th Anniv. A382

Designs: a, Sir Rowland Hill. b, Penny Black. c, No. 21. d, Central Post Office. e, No. C124.

1990, Oct. 5 Litho. ***Perf. 14***

1247 Sheet of 5 + label 4.65 3.50
a.-e. A382 2col any single .95 .70

World Food Day — A383

1990, Oct. 16 Litho. ***Perf. 14***

1248 A383 5col multicolored 2.35 1.75

San Salvador Electric Light Co., Cent. — A384

1990, Oct. 30

1249 A384 20c shown .15 .15
1250 A384 90c Lineman, power lines .45 .35

America Issue A385

1990, Oct. 11 Litho. ***Perf. 14x14½***

1251 A385 25c Chichontepec Volcano .15 .15
1252 A385 70c Lake Coatepeque .35 .25

Chamber of Commerce, 75th Anniv. A386

1990, Nov. 22

1253 A386 1 col blk, gold & bl .48 .35

Traffic Safety — A387

Design: 40c, Intersection, horiz.

Perf. 14½x14, 14x14½

1990, Nov. 13

1254 A387 25c multicolored .15 .15
1255 A387 40c multicolored .20 .15

Butterflies A388

Perf. 14x14½, 14½x14

1990, Nov. 28

1256 A388 15c Eurytides calliste .15 .15
1257 A388 20c Papilio garamas amerias .15 .15
1258 A388 25c Papilio garamas .15 .15
1259 A388 55c Hypanartia godmani .28 .20
1260 A388 70c Anaea excellens .35 .30
1261 A388 1col Papilio pilumnus .50 .38
Nos. 1256-1261 (6) 1.58
Set value 1.10

Souvenir Sheet

Roulette 13½

1262 A388 2col Anaea proserpina 1.00 .78

Nos. 1259-1261 are vert.

University of El Salvador, 150th Anniv. — A389

1991, Feb. 27 Litho. ***Perf. 14½x14***

1263 A389 25c shown .15 .15
1264 A389 70c Sun, footprints, hand .35 .30
1265 A389 1.50col Dove, globe .75 .65
Nos. 1263-1265 (3) 1.25 1.10

Christmas A390

Perf. 14x14½, 14½x14

1990, Dec. 7 Litho.

1266 A390 25c shown .15 .15
1267 A390 70c Nativity, vert. .35 .30

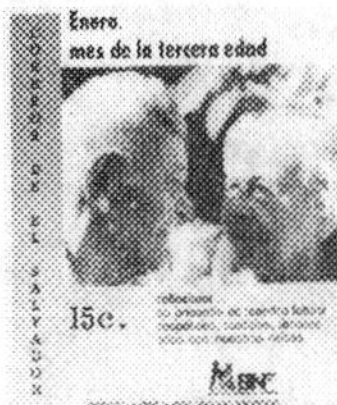

Month of the Elderly — A391

1991, Jan. 31 ***Perf. 14½x14***

1268 A391 15c purple & blk .15 .15

Restoration of Santa Ana Theater A392

1991, Apr. 12 ***Perf. 14***

1269 A392 20c Interior .15 .15
1270 A392 70c Exterior .35 .30
Set value .35

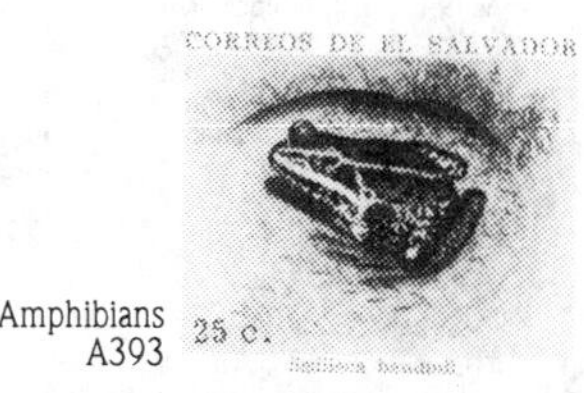

Amphibians A393

Designs: 25c, Smilisca baudinii. 70c, Eleutherodactylus rugulosus. 1col, Plectrohyla guatemalensis. 1.50col, Agalychnis moreletii.

1991, May 29 Litho. ***Perf. 14x14½***

1271 A393 25c multicolored .15 .15
1272 A393 70c multicolored .35 .30
1273 A393 1col multicolored .50 .38
1274 A393 1.50col multicolored .75 .65
Nos. 1271-1274 (4) 1.75 1.48

Aid for Children's Village A394

Designs: 90c, Children playing outdoors.

1991, June 21 Litho. ***Perf. 14x14½***

1275 A394 20c multicolored .15 .15
1276 A394 90c multicolored .42 .35

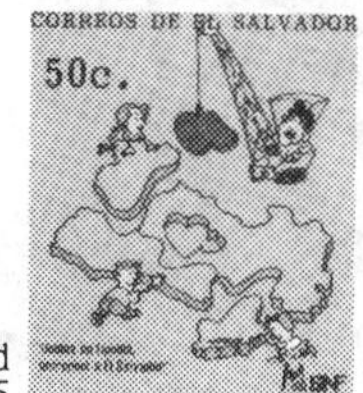

United Family — A395

1991, June 28 Litho. ***Perf. 14½x14***

1277 A395 50c multicolored .25 .15

Birds — A396

1991, Aug. 30

1278 A396 20c Melanotis hypoleucus .15 .15
1279 A396 25c Agelaius phoeniceus .15 .15
1280 A396 70c Campylorhynchus rufinucha .35 .30
1281 A396 1col Cissilopha melanocyanea .50 .38
1282 A396 5col Chiroxiphia linearis 2.35 1.75
Nos. 1278-1282 (5) 3.50 2.73

Discovery of America, 500th Anniv. Type of 1990

No. 1283: a, Hourglass, chart. b, Chart, ship's sails. c, Sailing ship near Florida. d, Corner of chart, ships. e, Compass rose, Cuba, Yucatan Peninsula. f, South America, "500" emblem. No. 1284, Sail, landfall.

1991, Sept. 16 Litho. ***Perf. 14***

Miniature Sheet

1283 A379 1col Sheet of 6, #a.-f. 3.00 1.50

Souvenir Sheet

Rouletted 6½

1284 A380 2col multicolored 1.00 .50

America Issue — A397

Designs: 25c, Battle of Acaxual. 70c, First missionaries in Cuzcatlan.

1991, Oct. 11 Litho. ***Perf. 14x14½***

1285 A397 25c multicolored .15 .15
1286 A397 70c multicolored .35 .30

World Food Day — A398

1991, Oct. 16 ***Perf. 14½x14***

1287 A398 50c multicolored .25 .15

Wolfgang Amadeus Mozart, Death Bicent. A399

1991, Oct. 23 ***Perf. 14x14½***

1288 A399 1col multicolored .50 .38

Christmas A400

Perf. 14½x14, 14x14½

1991, Nov. 13 Litho.

1289 A400 25c Nativity scene, vert. .15 .15
1290 A400 70c Children singing .38 .30

Total Solar Eclipse, July 11 — A401

1991, Dec. 17 ***Perf. 14x14½***

1291 A401 70c shown .38 .30
1292 A401 70c Eastern El Salvador .38 .30
a. Pair, #1291-1292 .76 .60

No. 1292a has continous design.

Red Cross Life Guards A402

1992, Feb. 28 Litho. ***Perf. 14x14½***

1293 A402 3col Rescue 1.50 1.15
1294 A402 4.50col Swimming competition 2.25 1.70

Lions Clubs in El Salvador, 50th Anniv. — A403

1992, Mar. 13 ***Perf. 14½x14***

1295 A403 90c multicolored .45 .35

Protect the Environment — A404

Designs: 60c, Man riding bicycle. 80c, Children walking outdoors. 1.60col, Sower in field. 3col, Clean water. 2.20col, Natural foods. 5col, Recycling center. 10col, Conservation of trees and nature. 25col, Wildlife protection.

1992, Apr. 6 Litho. ***Perf. 14x14½***

1298 A404 60c multi .30 .22
1299 A404 80c multi .40 .30
1300 A404 1.60col multi .80 .60
1302 A404 2.20col multi 1.10 .85
1303 A404 3col multi 1.50 1.15
1304 A404 5col multi 2.50 1.90
1305 A404 10col multi 5.00 3.75
1307 A404 25col multi 12.50 9.40
Nos. 1298-1307 (8) 24.10 18.17

This is an expanding set. Numbers may change.

Physicians A405

Designs: 80c, Dr. Roberto Orellana Valdes. 1col, Dr. Carlos Gonzalez Bonilla. 1.60col, Dr. Andres Gonzalo Funes. 2.20col, Dr. Joaquin Coto.

1992, Apr. 30 ***Perf. 14½x14***

1308 A405 80c multicolored .40 .30
1309 A405 1col multicolored .50 .38
1310 A405 1.60col multicolored .80 .60
1311 A405 2.20col multicolored 1.10 .85
Nos. 1308-1311 (4) 2.80 2.13

Women's Auxiliary of St. Vincent de Paul Society, Cent. — A406

1992, Mar. 10 Litho. ***Perf. 14½x14***

1312 A406 80c multicolored .45 .38

CORREOS DE EL SALVADOR
CENSO
60c.

Population and Housing Census — A407

80c, Globe showing location of El Salvador.

1992, June 29 Litho. ***Perf. 14½x14***

1313 A407 60c multicolored .35 .30
1314 A407 80c multicolored .45 .38

1992 Summer Olympics, Barcelona — A408

1992, July 17 Litho. *Perf. 14½x14*

1315 A408 60c Hammer throw .35 .30
1316 A408 80c Volleyball .45 .38
1317 A408 90c Shot put .75 .58
1318 A408 2.20col Long jump 1.30 .65
1319 A408 3col Vault 1.75 .85
1320 A408 5col Balance beam 3.00 1.50
Nos. 1315-1320 (6) 7.60 4.26

Simon Bolivar — A409

1992, July 24

1321 A409 2.20col multicolored 1.30 .65

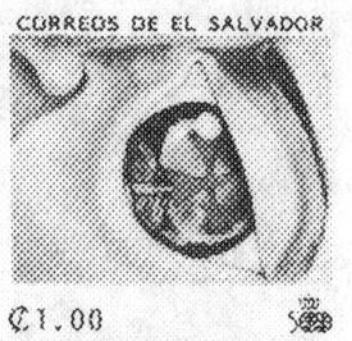

A410

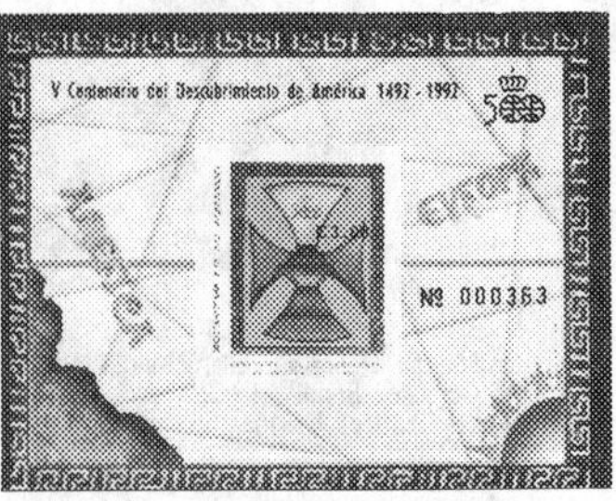

Discovery of America, 500th Anniv. — A411

Designs: No. 1322, European and Amerindian faces. No. 1323, Ship in person's eye. No. 1324, Ship at sea. No. 1325, Ship, satellite over Earth. 3col, Cross, Indian pyramid.

1992, Aug. 28 Litho. *Perf. 14x14½*

1322 A410 1col multicolored .58 .30
1323 A410 1col multicolored .58 .30

Perf. 14½x14

1324 A410 1col multicolored .58 .30
1325 A410 1col multicolored .58 .30
a. Min. sheet, 2 each #1322-1325 4.65 2.40
Nos. 1322-1325 (4) 2.32 1.20

Souvenir Sheet

Rouletted 13½

1326 A411 3col multicolored 1.75 .85

Immigrants to El Salvador A412

Designs: No. 1327, Feet walking over map. No. 1328, Footprints leading to map.

1992, Sept. 16 Litho. *Perf. 14x14½*

1327 A412 2.20col multicolored 1.15 .58
1328 A412 2.20col multicolored 1.15 .58
a. Pair, #1327-1328 2.30 1.15

General Francisco Morazan (1792-1842) A413

1992, Sept. 28 *Perf. 14½x14*

1329 A413 1col multicolored .58 .30

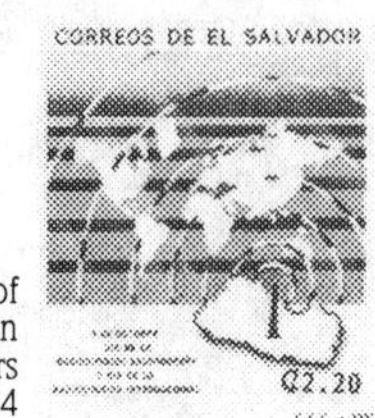

Association of Salvadoran Broadcasters A414

1992, Oct. 3

1330 A414 2.20col multicolored 1.15 .58

Salvadoran Radio Day, Intl. Radio Day.

Discovery of America, 500th Anniv. A415

1992, Oct. 13 Litho. *Perf. 14x14½*

1331 A415 80c Indian artifacts .45 .22
1332 A415 2.20col Map, ship 1.25 .62

Exfilna '92 — A416

1992, Oct. 22 *Perf. 14x14½*

1333 A416 5col multicolored 2.75 1.38

Discovery of America, 500th Anniv.

Peace in El Salvador A417

1992, Oct. 30

1334 A417 50c black, blue & yellow .28 .15

Christmas A418

Perf. 14x14½, 14½x14

1992, Nov. 23 Litho.

1335 A418 80c shown .45 .22
1336 A418 2.20col Nativity, vert. 1.25 .62

Wildlife A419

Designs: 50c, Tapirus bairdii. 70c, Chironectes minimus. 1col, Eira barbara. 3col, Felis yagouaroundi. 4.50col, Odocoileus virginianus.

1993, Jan. 15 Litho. *Perf. 14x14½*

1337 A419 50c multicolored .28 .15
1338 A419 70c multicolored .40 .20
1339 A419 1col multicolored .58 .30
1340 A419 3col multicolored 1.70 .85
1341 A419 4.50col multicolored 2.50 1.25
Nos. 1337-1341 (5) 5.46 2.75

Month of the Elderly A420

Design: 2.20col, Boy, old man holding tree.

1993, Jan. 27

1342 A420 80c black .45 .22
1343 A420 2.20col multicolored 1.25 .62

Agape Social Welfare Organization A421

Designs: a, Divine Providence Church. b, People, symbols of love and peace.

1993, Mar. 4 Litho. *Perf. 14x14½*

1344 A421 1col Pair, #a.-b. .45 .22

Secretary's Day — A422

1993, Apr. 26 Litho. *Perf. 14x14½*

1345 A422 1col multicolored .45 .22

Benjamin Bloom Children's Hospital A423

1993, June 18 Litho. *Perf. 14x14½*

1346 A423 5col multicolored 2.25 1.15

Visit by Mexican President Carlos Salinas de Gortari A424

1993, July 14

1347 A424 2.20col multicolored 1.00 .50

Aquatic Birds — A425

1993, Sept. 28 Litho. *Perf. 14x14½*

1348 A425 80c Casmerodius albus .18 .15
1349 A425 1col Mycteria americana .22 .15
1350 A425 2.20col Ardea herodias .50 .25
1351 A425 5col Ajaja ajaja 1.10 .58
Nos. 1348-1351 (4) 2.00 1.13

Pharmacy Review Commission, Cent. — A426

1993, Oct. 6

1352 A426 80c multicolored .18 .15

America Issue — A427

Endangered species: 80c, Dasyprocta punctata. 2.20col, Procyon lotor.

1993, Oct. 11 Litho. *Perf. 14x14½*

1353 A427 80c multicolored .18 .15
1354 A427 2.20col multicolored .50 .25

Fifth Central America Games — A428

Designs: 50c, Mascot, torch. 1.60col, Emblem. 2.20col, Mascot, map of Central America, horiz. 4.50col, Map of El Salvador, mascot, horiz.

Perf. 14½x14, 14x14½

1993, Oct. 29 Litho.

1355 A428 50c multicolored .15 .15
1356 A428 1.60col multicolored .38 .18
1357 A428 2.20col multicolored .50 .25
1358 A428 4.50col multicolored 1.00 .50
Nos. 1355-1358 (4) 2.03 1.08

Miniature Sheet

Medicinal Plants — A429

Designs: a, Solanum mammosum. b, Hamelia patens. c, Tridex procumbens. d, Calea urticifolia. e, Ageratum conyzoides. f, Pluchea odorata.

1993, Dec. 10 Litho. *Perf. 14½x14*

1359 A429 1col Sheet of 6, #a.-f. 1.25 .65

Christmas A430

993, Nov. 23 *Perf. 14x14½*

360 A430 80c Holy Family .30 .15
361 A430 2.20col Nativity Scene .85 .42

Alberto Masferrer (1868-1932), Writer — A431

993, Nov. 30

362 A431 2.20col multicolored .85 .42

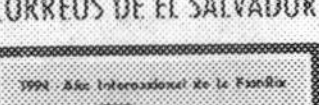

Intl. Year of the Family — A432

994, Feb. 28 Litho. *Perf. 14½x14*

1363 A432 2.20col multicolored .85 .42

Military Hospital, Cent. — A433

1994, Apr. 27 Litho. *Perf. 14*

1364 A433 1col shown .22 .15
1365 A433 1col Hospital building .22 .15

CORREOS DE EL SALVADOR
CENTENARIO GESTA DE LOS 44

City of Santa Ana, Cent. — A434

Designs: 60c, Arms of Department of Santa Ana. 80c, Inscription honoring heroic deeds of 44 patriots.

1994, Apr. 29 Litho. *Perf. 14*

1366 A434 60c multicolored .15 .15
1367 A434 80c multicolored .18 .15

1994 World Cup Soccer Championships, US — A435

Soccer plays, flags from: 60c, Romania, Colombia, Switzerland, US. 80c, Sweden, Cameroun, Russia, Brazil. 1col, South Korea, Spain, Bolivia, Germany. 2.20col, Bulgaria, Nigeria, Greece, Argentina. 4.50col, Mexico, Norway, Ireland, Italy. 5col, Saudi Arabia, Netherlands, Morocco, Belgium.

1994, June 6 Litho. *Perf. 14*

1368 A435 60c multicolored .15 .15
1369 A435 80c multicolored .18 .15
1370 A435 1col multicolored .22 .15
1371 A435 2.20col multicolored .48 .24
1372 A435 4.50col multicolored 1.00 .50
1373 A435 5col multicolored 1.10 .55
Nos. 1368-1373 (6) 3.13 1.74

Plaza of Sovereign Military Order of Malta A436

1994, June 24 Litho. *Perf. 14*

1374 A436 2.20col multicolored .48 .24

Traditions A437

Designs: 1col, Tiger and deer dance. 2.20col, Spotted bull dance.

1994, June 30

1375 A437 1col multicolored .22 .15
1376 A437 2.20col multicolored .48 .24

Nutritional Plants — A438

1994, Aug. 29 Litho. *Perf. 14*

1377 A438 70c Capsicum annuum .15 .15
1378 A438 80c Theobroma cacao .18 .15
1379 A438 1col Ipomoea batatas .22 .15
1380 A438 5col Chamaedorea tepejilote 1.10 .55
Nos. 1377-1380 (4) 1.65 1.00

Postal Transport Vehicles A439

1994, Oct. 11 Litho. *Perf. 14*

1381 A439 80c Jeep .40 .20
1382 A439 2.20col Train 1.10 .55

America issue.

22nd Bicycle Race of El Salvador A440

1994, Oct. 26

1383 A440 80c multicolored .40 .20

16th Intl. Fair of El Salvador A441

1994, Oct. 31

1384 A441 5col multicolored 2.50 1.25

Christmas A442

1994, Nov. 16

1385 A442 80c shown .40 .20
1386 A442 2.20col Magi, Christ child 1.10 .55

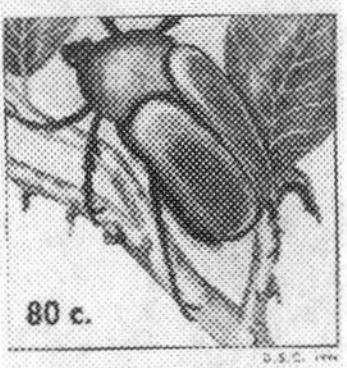

Beetles — A443

1994, Dec. 16 Litho. *Perf. 14*

1387 A443 80c Cotinis mutabilis .18 .15
1388 A443 1col Phyllophaga .22 .15
1389 A443 2.20col Galofa .50 .25
1390 A443 5col Callipogon barbatus 1.10 .55
Nos. 1387-1390 (4) 2.00 1.10

Salvadoran Culture Center, 40th Anniv. — A444

1995, Mar. 24 Litho. *Perf. 14½x14*

1391 A444 70c shown .16 .15
1392 A444 1col "40" emblem .22 .15

CORREOS DE
El Salvador

Ceramic Treasures Archeological Site — A445

Designs: 60c, Cup. 70c, Three-footed earthen dish. 80c, Two-handled jar. 2.20col, Long-necked jar. 4.50col, Excavation structure #3. 5col, Excavation structure #4.

1995, Apr. 26 Litho. *Perf. 14½x14*

1393 A445 60c multicolored .32 .16
1394 A445 70c multicolored .38 .18
1395 A445 80c multicolored .42 .22
1396 A445 2.20col multicolored 1.10 .55
1397 A445 4.50col multicolored 2.50 1.25
1398 A445 5col multicolored 2.75 1.25
Nos. 1393-1398 (6) 7.47 3.61

Fr. Isidro Menendez (1795-1858), Physician — A446

1995, May 19

1399 A446 80c multicolored .42 .22

Central America, SA, 80th Anniv. — A447

Designs: 80c, Insuring the future of children. 2.20col, Child wearing costume.

1995, July 7 Litho. *Perf. 14*

1400 A447 80c multicolored .40 .20
1401 A447 2.20col multicolored 1.10 .55

Sared Heart College, Cent. — A448

1995, July 26 *Perf. 14x14½*

1402 A448 80c multicolored .40 .20

FAO, 50th Anniv. — A449

1995, Aug. 16 Litho. *Perf. 14½x14*

1403 A449 2.20col multicolored 1.10 .55

Tourism A450

Designs: 50c, Los Almendros Beach, Sonsonate. 60c, Green Lagoon, Apaneca. 2.20col, Guerrero Beach, La Union. 5col, Usulutan Volcano.

1995, Aug. 30 *Perf. 14x14½*

1404 A450 50c multicolored .25 .15
1405 A450 60c multicolored .30 .15
1406 A450 2.20col multicolored 1.10 .55
1407 A450 5col multicolored 2.75 1.25
Nos. 1404-1407 (4) 4.40 2.10

Orchids — A451

#1408, Pleurothallis glandulosa. #1409, Pleurothallis grobyi. #1410, Pleurothallis fuegii. #1411, Lemboglossum stellatum. #1412, Lepanthes inaequalis. #1413, Pleurothallis hirsuta.

#1414, Hexadesmia micrantha. #1415, Pleurothallis segoviense. #1416, Stelis aprica. #1417, Platystele stenostachya. #1418, Stelis barbata. #1419, Pleurothallis schiedeii.

1995, Sept. 28 Litho. *Perf. 14½x14*

1408 A451	60c multicolored	.30	.15
1409 A451	60c multicolored	.30	.15
a.	Pair, #1408-1409	.60	.30
1410 A451	70c multicolored	.40	.20
1411 A451	70c multicolored	.40	.20
1412 A451	1col multicolored	.55	.30
1413 A451	1col multicolored	.55	.30
1414 A451	3col multicolored	1.65	.80
1415 A451	3col multicolored	1.65	.80
1416 A451	4.50col multicolored	2.50	1.25
1417 A451	4.50col multicolored	2.50	1.25
a.	Pair, #1416-1417	5.00	2.50
1418 A451	5col multicolored	2.75	1.40
1419 A451	5col multicolored	2.75	1.40
	Nos. 1408-1419 (12)	16.30	8.20

America Issue — A452

Martins: 80c, Chloroceryle aenea. 2.20col, Chloroceryle americana.

1995, Oct. 11

1420 A452	80c multicolored	.40	.20
1421 A452	2.20col multicolored	1.25	.60

UN, 50th Anniv. — A453

Design: 2.20col, Hands of different races holding UN emblem, "50."

1995, Oct. 23

1422 A453	80c multicolored	.40	.20
1423 A453	2.20col multicolored	1.25	.60

Christmas A454

1995, Nov. 17 Litho. *Perf. 14½x14*

1424 A454	80c shown	.40	.20
1425 A454	2.20col Families, clock tower	1.25	.60

Miniature Sheet

Fauna A455

Designs: a, Bubo virginianus. b, Potos flavus. c, Porthidium godmani. d, Felis pardalis (f). e, Dellathis bifurcata. f, Felis concolor (h). g, Mazama americana. h, Leptophobia aripa. i, Bolitoglossa salvinii. j, Eugenes fulgens (h, i).

1995, Nov. 24 *Perf. 14x14½*

1426 A455	80c Sheet of 10, #a.-j.	4.00	2.00

Independence, 174th Anniv. — A456

Designs: 80c, Natl. arms, export products, money, textile workers, pharmaceuticals. 25col, Crates of products leaving El Salvador.

1995, Sept. 14 *Perf. 14½x14*

1427 A456	80c shown	.40	.20
1428 A456	25col multicolored	13.00	7.50

2nd Visit of Pope John Paul II — A457

5.40col, Pope John Paul II, Metropolitan Cathedral.

1996, Feb. 8 Litho. *Perf. 14½x14*

1429 A457	1.50col multicolored	.90	.45
1430 A457	5.40col multicolored	3.25	1.65

ANTEL, Telecommunications Workers' Day — A458

1.50col, Satellite dish, hand holding cable fibers. 5col, Three globes, telephone receiver, vert.

Perf. 14x14½, 14½x14

1996, Apr. 27 Litho.

1431 A458	1.50col multicolored	.90	.45
1432 A458	5col multicolored	2.90	1.45

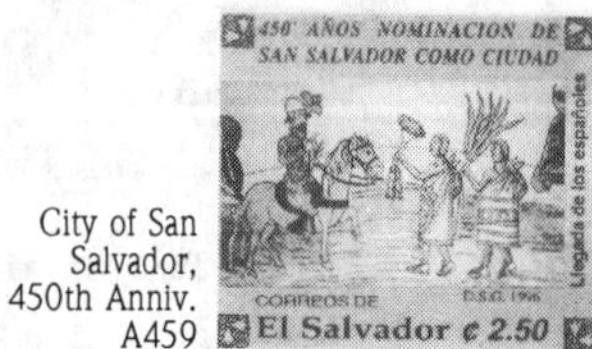

City of San Salvador, 450th Anniv. A459

Designs: 2.50col, Spanish meeting natives. 2.70col, Diego de Holguin, first mayor, mission. 3.30col, Old National Palace. 4col, Heroe's Boulevard, modern view of city.

1996, Mar. 27 *Perf. 14x14½*

1433 A459	2.50col multicolored	1.55	.80
1434 A459	2.70col multicolored	1.70	.85
1435 A459	3.30col multicolored	2.00	1.00
1436 A459	4col multicolored	2.50	1.25
	Nos. 1433-1436 (4)	7.75	3.90

Natl. Artists, Entertainers A460

Designs: 1col, Rey Avila (1929-95). 1.50col, María Teresa Moreira (1934-95). 2.70col, Francisco Antonio Lara (1900-89). 4col, Carlos Alverez Pineda (1928-93).

1996, May 17 Litho. *Perf. 14½x14*

1437 A460	1col multicolored	.60	.30
1438 A460	1.50col multicolored	.90	.45
1439 A460	2.70col multicolored	1.50	.75
1440 A460	4col multicolored	2.30	1.10
	Nos. 1437-1440 (4)	5.30	2.60

YSKL Radio, 40th Anniv. A461

1996, May 24 *Perf. 14x14½*

1441 A461	1.40col multicolored	.85	.40

1996 Summer Olympic Games, Atlanta A462

Early Greek athletes: 1.50col, Discus thrower. 3col, Jumper. 4col, Wrestlers. 5col, Javelin thrower.

1996, July 3 Litho. *Perf. 14*

1442 A462	1.50col multicolored	.90	.45
1443 A462	3col multicolored	1.80	.90
1444 A462	4col multicolored	2.40	1.20
1445 A462	5col multicolored	3.00	1.50
	Nos. 1442-1445 (4)	8.10	4.05

Birds — A463

Designs: a, Pheucticus ludovicianus. b, Tyrannus forficatus. c, Dendroica petechia. d, Falco sparverius. e, Icterus galbula.

1996, Aug. 9 Litho. *Perf. 14x14½*

1446 A463	1.50col Strip of 5, #a.-e.	4.60	2.30

Diaro de Hoy Newspaper, 60th Anniv. A464

1996, Sept. 20

1447 A464	5.20col multicolored	3.00	1.50

Channel 2 Television Station, 30th Anniv. — A465

1996, Sept. 27 *Perf. 14½x14*

1448 A465	10col multicolored	5.75	2.90

UNICEF, 50th Anniv. A466

1996, Oct. 4 *Perf. 14x14½*

1449 A466	1col multicolored	.60	.30

Traditional Costumes — A467

America issue: 1.50col, Blouse, short flannel skirt, Nahuizalco. 4col, Blouse, long skirt, Panchimalco.

1996, Oct. 11 *Perf. 14½x14*

1450 A467	1.50col multicolored	.90	.45
1451 A467	4col multicolored	2.30	1.15

Christmas A468

Designs: 2.50col, Night scene of homes, Christmas tree, church. 4col, Day scene of people celebrating outside homes, church.

1996, Nov. 28 Litho. *Perf. 14½x14*

1452 A468	2.50col multicolored	1.50	.75
1453 A468	4col multicolored	2.25	1.10

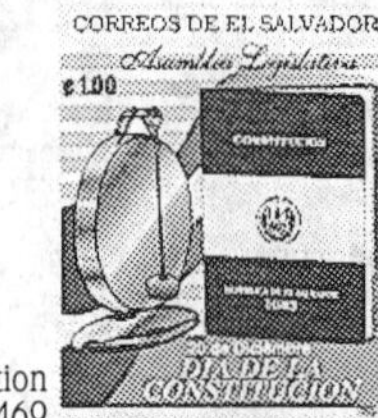

Constitution Day — A469

1996, Dec. 19 Litho. *Perf. 14½x14*

1454 A469	1col multicolored	.60	.30

Marine Life — A470

a, Nasolamia velox. b, Scomberomorus sierra. c, Delphinus delphis. d, Eretmochelys imbricata. e, Epinephelus labriformis. f, Pomacanthus zonipectus. g, Scarus perrico. h, Hippocampus ingens.

1996, Dec. 17

1455 A470	1col Sheet of 8, #a.-h.	4.60	2.30

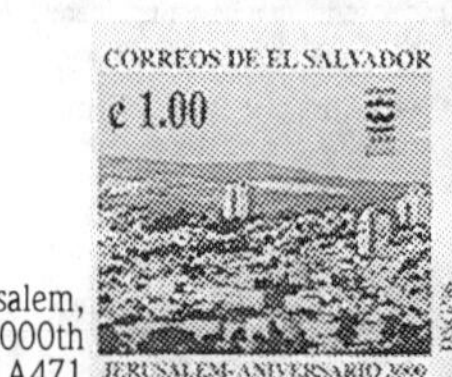

Jerusalem, 3000th Anniv. — A471

1996, Dec. 5 Litho. *Perf. 14x14½*

1456 A471	1col multicolored	.60	.30

El Mundo Newspaper, 30th Anniv. — A472

1997, Feb. 6 Litho. *Perf. 14x14½*

1457 A472	10col multicolored	5.75	2.90

Exfilna '97 — A473

997, Feb. 21
458 A473 4col Baldwin 58441, 1925 2.30 1.20

Carmelite Order of San Jose, 80th Anniv. A474

Design: Mother Clara Maria of Jesus Quiros.

1997, Mar. 19
1459 A474 1col multicolored .60 .30

American School, 50th Anniv. — A475

1997, Apr. 10 *Perf. 14½x14*
1460 A475 25col multicolored 14.50 7.25

Tropical Fruit — A476

No. 1461: a, Annona diversifolia. b, Anacardium occidentale. c, Cucumis melo. d, Pouteria mammosa.
4col, Carica papaya.

1997, May 28 Litho. *Perf. 14x14½*
1461 A476 1.50col Sheet of 4, #a.-d. 3.50 3.50

Souvenir Sheet
Rouletted 13½

1462 A476 4col multicolored 2.30 2.30

Lions Club in El Salvador, 55th Anniv. A476a

1997, Aug. 15 Litho. *Perf. 14*
1463 A476a 4col multicolored 2.25 1.10

Montreal Protocol on Substances that Deplete Ozone Layer, 10th Anniv. — A477

1997, Aug. 28 Litho. *Perf. 14*
1464 A477 1.50col shown .90 .45
1465 A477 4col Boy drinking water 2.30 1.20

Inter-American Water Day (#1465).

Miguel de Cervantes Saavedra (1547-1616), Writer A478

1997, Sept. 26 Litho. *Perf. 14*
1466 A478 4col multicolored 2.25 1.10

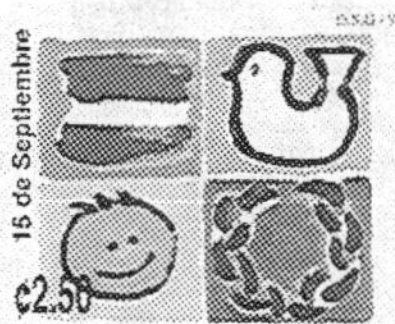

Independence Day — A479

1997, Sept. 10 Litho. *Perf. 14x14½*
1467 A479 2.50col shown 1.40 .70
1468 A479 5.20col Flag, children, dove 2.80 1.40

Scouting in El Salvador, 75th Anniv. — A480

1997, Oct. 3 *Perf. 14½x14*
1469 A480 1.50col multicolored .90 .45

Life of a Postman — A481

America issue: 1col, Postman delivering mail. 4col, Postman on motor scooter, dog.

1997, Oct. 10 Litho. *Perf. 14½x14*
1470 A481 1col multicolored .60 .30
1471 A481 4col multicolored 2.40 1.20

ACES (Automobile Club of El Salvador), 26th Anniv. — A482

1997, Oct. 28 *Perf. 14x14½*
1472 A482 10col multicolored 5.75 2.90

Christmas A483

Children's paintings: No. 1473, Outdoor scene. No. 1474, Indoor scene.

1997, Nov. 20 Litho. *Perf. 14*
1473 A483 1.50col multicolored .90 .45
1474 A483 1.50col multicolored .90 .45
a. Pair, #1473-1474 1.80 .90

Salesian Order in El Salvador, Cent. — A484

Designs: a, Map, St. John Bosco (1715-88). b, St. Cecilia College. c, San Jose College, priest. d, Ricaldone, students working with machinery. e, Maria Auxiliadora Church. f, City of St. John Bosco, students working with computers.

1997, Dec. 6
1475 A484 1.50col Sheet of 6, #a.-f. 2.75 1.40

Antique Automobiles A485

Designs: a, 1946 Standard. b, 1936 Chrysler. c, 1954 Jaguar. d, 1930 Ford. e, 1953 Mercedes Benz. f, 1956 Porsche.

1997, Dec. 17
1476 A485 2.50col Sheet of 6, #a.-f. 4.50 2.25

St. Joseph Missionaries, 125th Anniv. A486

1col, Image, Church of St. Joseph, Ahuachapan. 4col, Jose M. Vilaseca, Cesarea Esparza.

1997 Litho. *Perf. 14*
1477 A486 1col multicolored .30 .15
1478 A486 4col multicolored 1.25 .60

AIR POST STAMPS

Regular Issue of 1924-25 Overprinted in Black or Red **Servicio Aéreo**

First Printing.
15c on 10c: "15 QUINCE 15" measures 22½mm.
20c: Shows on the back of the stamp an albino impression of the 50c surcharge.
25c on 35c: Original value canceled by a long and short bar.
40c on 50c: Only one printing.
50c on 1col: Surcharge in dull orange red.

Perf. 12½, 14

1929, Dec. 28 Unwmk.
C1 A112 20c dp green (Bk) 3.25 3.25
a. Red overprint 600.00 600.00

Counterfeits exist of No. C1a.

With Additional Surcharge of New Values and Bars in Black or Red

C3 A111 15c on 10c orange .50 .50
a. "ATLANT CO" 14.00 14.00
C4 A114 25c on 35c scar & grn 1.25 1.25
a. Bars inverted 7.50 7.50
C5 A115 40c on 50c org brn .50 .35
C6 A116 50c on 1col grn & vio (R) 8.00 6.50
Nos. C1-C6 (5) 13.50 11.85

Second Printing.
15c on 10d: "15 QUINCE 15" measures 20½mm.
20c: Has not the albino impression on the back of the stamp.
25c on 35c: Original value cancelled by two bars of equal length.
50c on 1col: Surcharge in carmine rose.

1930, Jan. 10
C7 A112 20c deep green .45 .45
C8 A111 15c on 10c org .45 .45
a. "ATLANT CO" 17.50
b. Double surcharge 10.00
c. As "a," double surcharge 75.00
d. Pair, one without surcharge *175.00*

C9 A114 25c on 35c scar & grn .38 .38
C10 A116 50c on 1col grn & vio (C) .90 .90
a. Without bars over "UN COLON" 2.50
b. As "a," without block over "1" 2.50
Nos. C7-C10 (4) 2.18 2.18

Numerous wrong font and defective letters exist in both printings of the surcharges.
No. C10 with black surcharge is bogus.

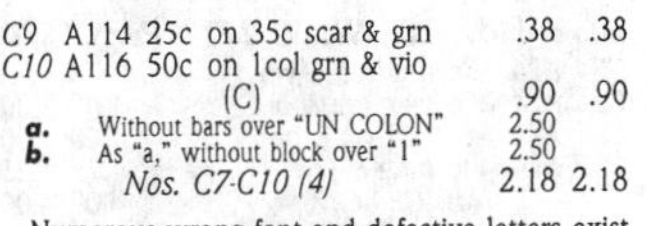

Mail Plane over San Salvador — AP1

1930, Sept. 15 Engr. *Perf. 12½*
C11 AP1 15c deep red .15 .15
C12 AP1 20c emerald .18 .15
C13 AP1 25c brown violet .18 .15
C14 AP1 40c ultra .32 .15
Nos. C11-C14 (4) .83
Set value .32

Simón Bolivar — AP2

1930, Dec. 17 Litho. *Perf. 11½*
C15 AP2 15c deep red 3.75 3.50
a. "15" double 82.50
C16 AP2 20c emerald 3.75 3.50
C17 AP2 25c brown violet 3.75 3.50
a. Vert. pair, imperf. btwn. 110.00
b. Imperf., pair
C18 AP2 40c dp ultra 3.75 3.50
Nos. C15-C18 (4) 15.00 14.00

Centenary of death of Simón Bolivar. Counterfeits of Nos. C15-C18 exist.

No. 504 Overprinted in Red 

1931, June 29 Engr. *Perf. 14*
C19 A116 1col green & vio 2.50 2.00

Tower of La Merced Church — AP3

1931, Nov. 5 Litho. *Perf. 11½*
C20 AP3 15c dark red 2.50 2.00
a. Imperf., pair 50.00
C21 AP3 20c blue green 2.50 2.00
C22 AP3 25c dull violet 2.50 2.00
a. Vert. pair, imperf. btwn. 110.00
C23 AP3 40c ultra 2.50 2.00
a. Imperf., pair 60.00
Nos. C20-C23 (4) 10.00 8.00

120th anniv. of the 1st movement toward the political independence of El Salvador. In the tower of La Merced Church (AP3) hangs the bell which José Matias Delgado-called the Father of his Country-rang to initiate the movement for liberty.

José Matias Delgado AP4

Airplane and Caravels of Columbus AP5

1932, Nov. 12 Wmk. 271 *Perf. 12½*
C24 AP4 15c dull red & vio .75 .75
C25 AP4 20c blue grn & bl 1.00 1.00
C26 AP4 25c dull vio & brn 1.00 1.00
C27 AP4 40c ultra & grn 1.25 1.25
Nos. C24-C27 (4) 4.00 4.00

1st centenary of the death of Father José Matías Delgado, who is known as the Father of El Salvadoran Political Emancipation.
Nos. C24-C27 show cheek without shading in the 72nd stamp of each sheet.

1933, Oct. 12 Wmk. 240 *Perf. 13*
C28 AP5 15c red orange 2.00 1.40
C29 AP5 20c blue green 2.00 1.40
C30 AP5 25c lilac 2.00 1.40
C31 AP5 40c ultra 2.00 1.40
C32 AP5 1col black 2.00 1.40
Nos. C28-C32 (5) 10.00 7.00

441st anniversary of the sailing of Chistopher Columbus from Palos, Spain, for the New World.

Police Barracks Type

1934, Dec. 16 *Perf. 12½*
C33 A123 25c lilac .40 .15
C34 A123 30c brown .60 .30
a. Imperf., pair 42.50
C35 A123 1col black 1.50 .65
Nos. C33-C35 (3) 2.50 1.10

Runner AP7

1935, Mar. 16 Engr. Unwmk.
C36 AP7 15c carmine 3.00 2.75
C37 AP7 25c violet 3.00 2.75
C38 AP7 30c brown 2.50 2.00
C39 AP7 55c blue 15.00 10.00
C40 AP7 1col black 10.00 8.00
Nos. C36-C40 (5) 33.50 25.50

Third Central American Games.
For overprints and surcharge see Nos. C41-C45, C53.

Same Overprinted in Black HABILITADO

1935, June 27
C41 AP7 15c carmine 3.00 1.25
C42 AP7 25c violet 3.00 1.25
C43 AP7 30c brown 3.00 1.25
C44 AP7 55c blue 22.50 15.00
C45 AP7 1col black 10.00 8.00
Nos. C41-C45 (5) 41.50 26.75

Flag of El Salvador Type

1935, Oct. 26 Litho. Wmk. 240
C46 A125 30c black brown .50 .15

Tree of San Vicente Type

1935, Dec. 26 *Perf. 12½*
Numerals in Black, Tree in Yellow Green
C47 A126 10c orange .80 .70
C48 A126 15c brown .80 .70
C49 A126 20c dk blue grn .80 .70
C50 A126 25c dark purple .80 .70
C51 A126 30c black brown .80 .70
Nos. C47-C51 (5) 4.00 3.50

Tercentenary of San Vicente.

No. 565 Overprinted in Red AEREO

1937 Engr. Unwmk.
C52 A133 15c dk olive bis .20 .15
a. Double overprint 25.00

No. C44 Surcharged in Red 30

C53 AP7 30c on 55c blue 1.75 .75

Panchimalco Church AP10

1937, Dec. 3 Engr. *Perf. 12*
C54 AP10 15c orange yel .20 .15
C55 AP10 20c green .20 .15
C56 AP10 25c violet .20 .15
C57 AP10 30c brown .20 .15
C58 AP10 40c blue .20 .20
C59 AP10 1col black .90 .25
C60 AP10 5col rose carmine 3.00 2.00
Nos. C54-C60 (7) 4.90 3.05

US Constitution Type of Regular Issue

1938, Apr. 22 Engr. & Litho.
C61 A136 30c multicolored .60 .50

José Simeón Cañas y Villacorta — AP12

1938, Aug. 18 Engr.
C62 AP12 15c orange .75 .75
C63 AP12 20c brt green .90 .75
C64 AP12 30c redsh brown .90 .75
C65 AP12 1col black 3.00 2.50
Nos. C62-C65 (4) 5.55 4.75

José Simeón Cañas y Villacorta (1767-1838), liberator of slaves in Central America.

Golden Gate Bridge, San Francisco Bay AP13

1939, Apr. 14 *Perf. 12½*
C66 AP13 15c dull yel & blk .20 .15
C67 AP13 30c dk brown & blk .25 .15
C68 AP13 40c dk blue & blk .38 .20
Nos. C66-C68 (3) .83
Set value .40

Golden Gate Intl. Exposition, San Francisco.
For surcharges see Nos. C86-C91.

Sir Rowland Hill Type

1940, Mar. 1 Engr.
C69 A146 30c dk brn, buff & blk 3.25 1.25
C70 A146 80c org red & blk 8.00 6.00

Centenary of the postage stamp. Covers postmarked Feb. 29 were predated. Actual first day was Mar. 1.

Map of the Americas, Figure of Peace, Plane — AP15

1940, May 22 *Perf. 12*
C71 AP15 30c brown & blue .25 .20
C72 AP15 80c dk rose & blk .50 .42

Pan American Union, 50th anniversary.

Coffee Tree in Bloom — AP16

Coffee Tree with Ripe Berries — AP17

1940, Nov. 27
C73 AP16 15c yellow orange 1.00 .20
C74 AP16 20c deep green 1.25 .15
C75 AP16 25c dark violet 1.50 .40
C76 AP17 30c copper brown 2.00 .20
C77 AP17 1col black 6.00 .45
Nos. C73-C77 (5) 11.75 1.40

Juan Lindo, Gen. Francisco Mallespin and New National University of El Salvador — AP18

Designs (portraits changed): 40c, 80c, Narciso Monterey and Antonio José Canas. 60c, 1col, Isidro Menéndez and Chrisanto Salazar.

1941, Feb. 16 *Perf. 12½*
C78 AP18 20c dk grn & rose lake .80 .52
C79 AP18 40c ind & brn org .80 .52
C80 AP18 60c dl pur & brn .80 .52
C81 AP18 80c hn brn & dk bl grn 2.00 1.40
C82 AP18 1col black & org 2.00 1.40
C83 AP18 2col yel org & rose vio 2.00 1.40
a. Min. sheet of 6, #C78-C83, perf. 11½ 9.25 9.25
Nos. C78-C83 (6) 8.40 5.76

Centenary of University of El Salvador.
Stamps from No. C83a, perf. 11½, sell for about the same values as the perf. 12½ stamps.

Catalogue values for unused stamps in this section, from this point to the end of the section, are for Never Hinged items.

Map of El Salvador AP20

Wmk. 269
1942, Nov. 25 Engr. *Perf. 14*
C85 AP20 30c red orange .50 .30
a. Horiz. pair, imperf. between 100.00

1st Eucharistic Cong. of El Salvador. See #588.

Nos. C66 to C68 Surcharged with New Values in Dark Carmine 15

1943 Unwmk. *Perf. 12½*
C86 AP13 15c on 15c dl yel & blk .28 .20
C87 AP13 20c on 30c dk brn & blk .40 .30
C88 AP13 25c on 40c dk bl & blk .65 .50
Nos. C86-C88 (3) 1.33 1.00

Nos. C66 to C68 Surcharged with New Values in Dark Carmine 15

1944
C89 AP13 15c on 15c dl yel & blk .32 .22
C90 AP13 20c on 30c dk brn & blk .52 .30
C91 AP13 25c on 40c dk bl & blk .65 .30
Nos. C89-C91 (3) 1.49 .82

Bridge Type of Regular Issue Arms Overprint at Right in Blue Violet

1944, Nov. 24 Engr.
C92 A149 30c crim rose & blk .32 .15

No. C92 exists without overprint, but was not issued in that form.

Presidential Palace AP22

National Theater AP23

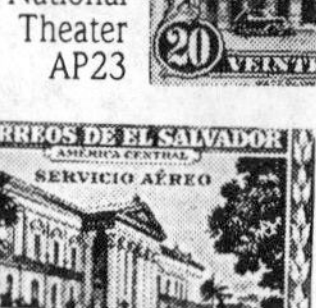
National Palace AP24

1944, Dec. 22 *Perf. 12½*
C93 AP22 15c red violet .15 .15
C94 AP23 20c dk blue grn .16 .15
C95 AP24 25c dull violet .20 .15
Nos. C93-C95 (3) .51
Set value .24

For surcharge and overprint see Nos. C145-C146.

No. 582 Overprinted in Red **Aéreo**

1945, Aug. 23 *Perf. 12*
C96 A137 1col black .60 .22

Juan Ramon Uriarte — AP25

Perf. 12½
1946, Jan. 1 Wmk. 240 Typo.
C97 AP25 12c dark blue .16 .15
C98 AP25 14c deep orange .16 .15
Set value .15

Mayan Pyramid, St. Andrés Plantation AP26

Municipal Children's Garden, San Salvador AP27

Civil Aeronautics School, Ilopango Airport AP28

1946, May 1 Unwmk.
C99 AP26 30c rose carmine .16 .15
C100 AP27 40c deep ultra .16 .15
C101 AP28 1col black .85 .30
Nos. C99-C101 (3) 1.17
Set value .45

For surcharge see No. C121.

Alberto Masferrer — AP29

1946, July 19 Litho. Wmk. 240
C102 AP29 12c carmine .20 .15
C103 AP29 14c dull green .20 .15
a. Imperf., pair 10.00
Set value .18

Souvenir Sheets

AP30

Designs: 40c, Charles I of Spain. 60c, Juan Manuel Rodriguez. 1col, Arms of San Salvador. 2col, Flag of El Salvador.

Perf. 12, Imperf.

1946, Nov. 8 Engr. Unwmk.

C104 AP30 Sheet of 4 2.50 2.50
- **a.** 40c brown .42 .42
- **b.** 60c carmine .42 .42
- **c.** 1col green .42 .42
- **d.** 2col ultramarine .42 .42

4th cent. of San Salvador's city charter. The imperf. sheets are without gum.

Felipe Soto — AP31

Alfredo Espino — AP32

Perf. 12½

1947, Sept. 11 Wmk. 240 Litho.

C106 AP31 12c chocolate .20 .15
C107 AP32 14c dark blue .16 .15
Set value .18

For surcharges see Nos. 627-630.

Arce Type of Regular Issue

1948, Feb. 26 Engr. Unwmk.

C108 A163 12c green .16 .15
C109 A163 14c rose carmine .24 .15
C110 A163 1col violet 2.25 1.40
Nos. C108-C110 (3) 2.65 1.70

Cent. of the death of Manuel José Arce (1783-1847). "Father of Independence" and 1st pres. of the Federation of Central America.

Roosevelt Types of Regular Issue

Designs: 12c, Pres. Franklin D. Roosevelt. 14c, Pres. Roosevelt presenting awards for distinguished service. 20c, Roosevelt and Cordell Hull. 25c, Pres. and Mrs. Roosevelt. 1col, Mackenzie King, Roosevelt and Winston Churchill. 2col, Funeral of Pres. Roosevelt. 4col, Pres. and Mrs. Roosevelt.

1948, Apr. 12 Engr. *Perf. 12½*

Various Frames, Center in Black

C111 A165 12c green .32 .25
C112 A164 14c olive .32 .25
C113 A164 20c chocolate .32 .25
C114 A164 25c carmine .32 .25
C115 A164 1col violet brn 1.35 .75
C116 A164 2col blue violet 2.25 1.25
Nos. C111-C116 (6) 4.88 3.00

Souvenir Sheet

Perf. 13½

C117 A166 4col gray & brn 4.00 3.00

Nos. 599, 601 and 604 Overprinted in Carmine or Black **Aéreo**

1948, Sept. 7 *Perf. 12½*

C118 A154 5c slate gray .15 .15
C119 A154 10c bister brown .15 .15
C120 A154 1col scarlet (Bk) 1.20 .50
Nos. C118-C120 (3) 1.50
Set value .60

No. C99 Surcharged in Black

1949, July 23

C121 AP26 10(c) on 30c rose car .16 .15

UPU Type of Regular Issue

1949, Oct. 9 Engr. *Perf. 12½*

C122 A167 5c brown .15 .15
C123 A167 10c black .16 .15
C124 A167 1col purple 5.25 5.25
Nos. C122-C124 (3) 5.56 5.55

Flag and Arms of El Salvador — AP38

1949, Dec. 15 *Perf. 10½*

Flag and Arms in Blue, Yellow and Green

C125 AP38 5c ocher .15 .15
C126 AP38 10c dk green .20 .15
- **a.** Yellow omitted 20.00

C127 AP38 15c violet .28 .15
C128 AP38 1col rose .60 .40
C129 AP38 5col red violet 5.00 3.75
Nos. C125-C129 (5) 6.23 4.60

1st anniv. of the Revolution of Dec. 14, 1948.

Isabella I of Spain — AP39

Flag, Torch and Scroll — AP40

1951, Apr. 28 Litho. Unwmk.

Background in Ultramarine, Red and Yellow

C130 AP39 10c green .32 .15
C131 AP39 20c purple .32 .15
- **a.** Horiz. pair, imperf. between 25.00

C132 AP39 40c rose carmine .32 .15
C133 AP39 1col black brown 1.25 .50
Nos. C130-C133 (4) 2.21 .95

500th anniv. of the birth of Queen Isabella I of Spain. Nos. C130-C133 exist imperforate.

1952, Feb. 14 Photo. *Perf. 11½*

Flag in Blue

C134 AP40 10c brt blue .15 .15
C135 AP40 15c chocolate .16 .15
C136 AP40 20c deep blue .16 .15
C137 AP40 25c gray .16 .15
C138 AP40 40c purple .32 .20
C139 AP40 1col red orange .65 .38
C140 AP40 2col orange brn 2.25 1.75
C141 AP40 5col violet blue 2.25 .90
Nos. C134-C141 (8) 6.10 3.83

Constitution of 1950.

Marti Type of Regular Issue Inscribed "Aereo"

1953, Feb. 27 Litho. *Perf. 10½*

C142 A170 10c dk purple .16 .15
C143 A170 20c dull brown .16 .15
C144 A170 1col dull orange .65 .38
Nos. C142-C144 (3) .97
Set value .58

No. C95 Surcharged "C 0.20" and Obliterations in Red

1953, Mar. 20 *Perf. 12½*

C145 AP24 20c on 25c dl vio .28 .15

No. C95 Overprinted in Carmine **"IV Congreso Medico Social Panamericano 16 / 19 Abril, 1953"**

1953, June 19

C146 AP24 25c dull violet .40 .18

See note after No. 634.

Bell Tower, La Merced Church — AP42

1953, Sept. 15 *Perf. 11½*

C147 AP42 5c rose pink .15 .15
C148 AP42 10c dp blue grn .15 .15
C149 AP42 20c blue .20 .15
C150 AP42 1col purple .65 .50
Set value 1.00 .74

132nd anniv. of the Act of Independence, Sept. 15, 1821.

Postage Types and

Fishing Boats — AP43

Gen. Manuel José Arce — AP44

ODECA Officials and Flag — AP46

#C155, National Palace. #C157, Coast guard boat. #C158, Lake Ilopango. #C160, Guayabo dam. #C161, Housing development. #C162, Modern highway. #C164, Izalco volcano.

Perf. 11½

1954, June 1 Unwmk. Photo.

C151 AP43 5c org brn & cr .20 .15
C152 A175 5c brt carmine .20 .15
C153 AP44 10c gray blue .24 .15
C154 A178 10c pur & lt brn .24 .15
C155 AP43 10c ol & bl gray .24 .15
C156 AP46 10c bl grn, dk grn & bl .24 .15
C157 AP43 10c rose carmine .30 .15
C158 AP43 15c dk gray .35 .15
C159 A173 20c pur & gray .42 .15
C160 AP46 25c bl grn & bl .42 .15
C161 AP46 30c mag & sal .48 .15
C162 A176 40c brt org & brn .65 .25
C163 A174 80c red brown 1.40 .90
C164 AP43 1col magenta & sal 1.65 .90
C165 A174 2col orange 3.00 .90
Nos. C151-C165 (15) 10.03
Set value 3.75

Barrios Type of Regular Issue, 1955

Perf. 12½

1955, Dec. 20 Wmk. 269 Engr.

C166 A177 20c brown .16 .15
C167 A177 30c dp red lilac .24 .15

Santa Ana Type of Regular Issue, 1956

Perf. 13½

1956, June 20 Unwmk. Litho.

C168 A178 5c orange brown .15 .15
C169 A178 10c green .15 .15
C170 A178 40c red lilac .24 .15
C171 A178 80c emerald .60 .38
C172 A178 5col gray blue 3.25 1.75
Nos. C168-C172 (5) 4.39 2.58

For overprint see No. C187.

Chalatenango Type of Regular Issue, 1956

1956, Sept. 14

C173 A179 10c brt rose .15 .15
C174 A179 15c orange .16 .15
C175 A179 20c lt olive grn .16 .15
C176 A179 25c dull purple .32 .18
C177 A179 50c orange brn .52 .40
C178 A179 1col brt vio bl .85 .65
Nos. C173-C178 (6) 2.16
Set value 1.45

Nueva San Salvador Type of Regular Issue, 1957

Perf. 12½

1957, Jan. 3 Wmk. 269 Engr.

C179 A180 10c pink .15 .15
C180 A180 20c dull red .20 .15
C181 A180 50c pale org red .32 .22
C182 A180 1col lt green .85 .45
C183 A180 2col orange red 2.00 1.25
Nos. C179-C183 (5) 3.52 2.22

For overprints see Nos. C195, C198.

Lemus' Visit Type of Regular Issue, 1959

Perf. 11½

1959, Dec. 14 Unwmk. Photo.

Granite Paper

Design in Ultramarine, Dark Brown Light Brown and Red

C184 A182 15c red .20 .15
C185 A182 20c green .24 .15
C186 A182 30c carmine .30 .18
Nos. C184-C186 (3) .74
Set value .38

No. C169 Overprinted in Red: "ANO MUNDIAL DE LOS REFUGIADOS 1959-1960"

1960, Apr. 7 Litho. *Perf. 13½*

C187 A178 10c green .24 .15

World Refugee Year, 7/1/59-6/30/60.

Type of Regular Issue, 1960
Poinsettia

Perf. 11½

1960, Dec. 17 Unwmk. Photo.

Granite Paper

Design in Slate Green, Red and Yellow

C188 A184 20c rose lilac .28 .15
C189 A184 30c gray .32 .20
C190 A184 40c light gray .32 .20
C191 A184 50c salmon pink .55 .35
Nos. C188-C191 (4) 1.47 .90

Miniature Sheet

Imperf

C192 A184 60c gold .65 .35

See note after No. 718.
For surcharge see No. C196.

Nos. 672, 691 and C183 Overprinted: "III Exposición Industrial Centroamericana Diciembre de 1962" with "AEREO" Added on Nos. 672, 691

1962, Dec. 21 *Perf. 11½, 12½*

C193 A174 1col brn org, dk brn & bl 1.00 .75
C194 A180 1col dull red .50 .32
C195 A180 2col orange red 1.00 .65
Nos. C193-C195 (3) 2.50 1.72

3rd Central American Industrial Exposition.
For surcharges see Nos. C197, C199.

Nos. C189, C194, C182 and C195 Surcharged

1963

C196 A184 10c on 30c multi .16 .15
C197 A180 10c on 1col dl red .16 .15
C198 A180 10c on 1col lt grn 1.10 .25
C199 A180 10c on 2col org red 1.10 .25
Nos. C196-C199 (4) 2.52
Set value .70

Surcharges include: "X" on No. C196; two dots and bar at bottom on No. C197. Heavy bar at bottom on No. C198. On No. C199, the four-line "Exposition" overprint is lower than on No. C195.

Turquoise-browed Motmot — AP49

Birds: 5c, King vulture (vert., like No. 741). 6c, Yellow-headed parrot, vert. 10c, Spotted-breasted oriole. 30c, Greattailed grackle. 40c, Great curassow, vert. 50c, Magpie-jay. 80c, Golden-fronted woodpecker, vert.

1963 Unwmk. Photo. *Perf. 11½*

Birds in Natural Colors

C200 AP49 5c gray grn & blk .15 .15
C201 AP49 6c tan & blue .15 .15
C202 AP49 10c lt bl & blk .15 .15
C203 AP49 20c gray & brn .24 .15
C204 AP49 30c ol bis & blk .38 .15
C205 AP49 40c pale & dk vio .50 .20
C206 AP49 50c lt grn & blk .55 .25
C207 AP49 80c vio bl & blk 1.00 .60
Nos. C200-C207 (8) 3.12
Set value 1.45

Eucharistic Congress Type of Regular Issue, 1964

1964-65 *Perf. 12x11½*

C208 A188 10c slate grn & bl .15 .15
C209 A188 25c red & blue .20 .15
Set value .16

Miniature Sheets

Imperf

C210 A188 80c blue & green .65 .65
a. Marginal ovpt. La Union .85 .85
b. Marginal ovpt. Usulutan .85 .85
c. Marginal ovpt. La Libertad .85 .85

See note after No. 746.
Issued: #C208-C210, Apr. 16, 1964; #C210a-C210b, June 22, 1965; #210c, Jan. 28, 1965.
For overprints see Nos. C232, C238.

Kennedy Type of Regular Issue

1964, Nov. 22 ***Perf. 11½x12***

C211 A189 15c gray & blk .16 .15
C212 A189 20c sage grn & blk .24 .15
C213 A189 40c yellow & blk .40 .22
Nos. C211-C213 (3) .80
Set value .44

Miniature Sheet

Imperf

C214 A189 80c grnsh bl & blk 1.00 .75

For overprint see No. C259.

Flower Type of Regular Issue

1965, Jan. 6 Photo. ***Perf. 12x11½***

C215 A190 10c Rose .15 .15
C216 A190 15c Platanillo .15 .15
C217 A190 25c San Jose .20 .15
C218 A190 40c Hibiscus .28 .18
C219 A190 45c Veranera .40 .20
C220 A190 70c Fire flower .55 .32
Nos. C215-C220 (6) 1.73
Set value .95

For overprint and surcharges see Nos. C243, C348-C349.

ICY Type of Regular Issue

Perf. 11½x12

1965, Apr. 27 Photo. Unwmk.

Design in Brown and Gold

C221 A191 15c light blue .15 .15
C222 A191 30c dull lilac .20 .15
C223 A191 50c ocher .32 .22
Nos. C221-C223 (3) .67
Set value .38

For overprints see Nos. C227, C244, C312.

Gavidia Type of Regular Issue

1965, Sept. 24 Photo. Unwmk.

Portraits in Natural Colors

C224 A192 10c black & green .16 .15
C225 A192 20c black & bister .28 .15
C226 A192 1col black & rose 1.25 .50
Nos. C224-C226 (3) 1.69
Set value .70

No. C223 Overprinted in Green: "1865 / 12 de Octubre / 1965 / Dr. Manuel Enrique Araujo"

1965, Oct. 12 ***Perf. 11½x12***

C227 A191 50c brn, ocher & gold .42 .40

See note after No. 764.

Fair Type of Regular Issue, 1965

1965, Nov. 5 ***Perf. 12x11½***

C228 A193 20c blue & multi .16 .15
C229 A193 80c multi .65 .42
C230 A193 5col multi 3.25 2.25
Nos. C228-C230 (3) 4.06 2.82

For overprint see No. C311.

WHO Type of Regular Issue

1966, May 20 Photo. Unwmk.

C231 A194 50c multicolored .42 .22

For overprints see Nos. C242, C245.

No. C209 Overprinted in Dark Green: "1816 1966 / 150 años / Nacimiento / San Juan Bosco"

1966, Sept. 3 Photo. ***Perf. 12x11½***

C232 A188 25c red & blue .32 .25

150th anniv. of the birth of St. John Bosco (1815-88), Italian priest, founder of the Salesian Fathers and Daughters of Mary.

UNESCO Type of Regular Issue

1966, Nov. 4 Photo. ***Perf. 12***

C233 A195 30c tan, blk & vio bl .32 .15
C234 A195 2col emer, blk & vio bl 1.65 1.00

For surcharge see No. C352.

Fair Type of Regular Issue, 1966

1966, Nov. 27 Litho. ***Perf. 12***

C235 A196 15c multicolored .16 .15
C236 A196 20c multicolored .20 .15
C237 A196 60c multicolored .50 .38
Nos. C235-C237 (3) .86 .68

No. C209 Overprinted: "IX-Congreso / Interamericano / de Educacion / Católica / 4 Enero 1967"

1967, Jan. 4 Photo. ***Perf. 12x11½***

C238 A188 25c red & blue .32 .25

Issued to publicize the 9th Inter-American Congress for Catholic Education.

Cañas Type of Regular Issue

1967, Feb. 18 Litho. ***Perf. 11½***

C239 A197 5c multicolored .15 .15
C240 A197 45c lt bl & multi .55 .35
Set value .40

For surcharges see Nos. C403-C405.

Volcano Type of Regular Issue

1967, Apr. 14 Photo. ***Perf. 13***

C241 A198 50c ol gray & brn .50 .22

For surcharges see Nos. C320, C350

No. C231 Overprinted in Red: "VIII CONGRESO / CENTROAMERICANO DE / FARMACIA & B10QUIMICA / 5 di 11 Noviembre de 1967"

1967, Oct. 26 Photo. ***Perf. 12x11½***

C242 A194 50c multicolored .42 .40

Issued to publicize the 8th Central American Congress for Pharmacy and Biochemistry.

No. C217 Overprinted in Red: "I Juegos / Centroamericanos y del / Caribe de Basquetbol / 25 Nov. al 3 Dic. 1967"

1967, Nov. 15

C243 A190 25c bl, yel & grn .25 .25

First Central American and Caribbean Basketball Games, Nov. 25-Dec. 3.

No. C222 Overprinted in Carmine: "1968 / AÑO INTERNACIONAL DE / LOS DERECHOS HUMANOS"

1968, Jan. 2 Photo. ***Perf. 11½x12***

C244 A191 30c dl lil, brn & gold .40 .30

International Human Rights Year 1968.

No. C231 Overprinted in Red: "1968 / XX ANIVERSARIO DE LA / ORGANIZACION MUNDIAL / DE LA SALUD"

1968, Apr. 7 ***Perf. 12x11½***

C245 A194 50c multicolored .50 .50

20th anniv. of WHO.

No. C229 Overprinted in Red: "1968 / Año / del Sistema / del Crédito / Rural"

1968, May 6 Photo. ***Perf. 12x11½***

C246 A193 80c multicolored .65 .50

Rural credit system.

Masferrer Type of Regular Issue

1968, June 22 Litho. ***Perf. 12x11½***

C247 A200 5c brown & multi .15 .15
C248 A200 15c green & multi .15 .15
Set value .22 .15

For overprint see No. C297.

Scouts Hiking AP50

1968, July 26 Litho. ***Perf. 12***

C249 AP50 10c multicolored .15 .15

Issued to publicize the 7th Inter-American Boy Scout Conference, July-Aug., 1968.

Presidents' Meeting Type of Regular Issue

1968, Dec. 5 Litho. ***Perf. 14½***

C250 A202 20c salmon & multi .15 .15
C251 A202 1col lt blue & multi .75 .50
Set value .56

Butterfly Type of Regular Issue

Designs: Various butterflies.

1969 Litho. ***Perf. 12***

C252 A203 20c multi .16 .15
C253 A203 1col multi .65 .35
C254 A203 2col multi 1.65 1.00
C255 A203 10col gray & multi 8.00 5.00
Nos. C252-C255 (4) 10.46 6.50

For surcharge see No. C353.

Red Cross, Crescent and Lion and Sun Emblems — AP51

1969 Litho. ***Perf. 11***

C256 AP51 30c yellow & multi .24 .15
C257 AP51 1col multicolored .85 .50
C258 AP51 4col multicolored 3.25 2.50
Nos. C256-C258 (3) 4.34 3.15

50th anniv. of the League of Red Cross Societies.
For surcharges see Nos. C351, C354.

No. C213 Overprinted in Green: "Alunizaje / Apolo-11 / 21 Julio / 1969"

1969, Sept. Photo. ***Perf. 11½x12***

C259 A189 40c yellow & blk .30 .30

Man's 1st landing on the moon, July 20, 1969. See note after US No. C76.
The same overprint in red brown and pictures of the landing module and the astronauts on the moon were applied to the margin of No. C214.

Hospital Type of Regular Issue

Design: Benjamin Bloom Children's Hospital.

1969, Oct. 24 Litho. ***Perf. 11½***

C260 A205 1col multi .85 .50
C261 A205 2col multi 1.65 1.00
C262 A205 5col multi 4.25 2.50
Nos. C260-C262 (3) 6.75 4.00

For surcharge see No. C355.

ILO Type of Regular Issue

1969 Litho. ***Perf. 13***

C263 A206 50c lt bl & multi .40 .18

Tourist Type of Regular Issue

Views: 20c, Devil's Gate. 35c, Ichanmichen Spa. 60c, Aerial view of Acajutla Harbor.

1969, Dec. 19 Photo. ***Perf. 12x11½***

C264 A207 20c black & multi .16 .15
C265 A207 35c black & multi .28 .20
C266 A207 60c black & multi .50 .40
Nos. C264-C266 (3) .94 .75

Insect Type of Regular Issue, 1970

1970, Feb. 24 Litho. ***Perf. 11½x11***

C267 A208 2col Bee 1.65 1.00
C268 A208 3col Elaterida 2.50 1.50
C269 A208 4col Praying mantis 3.25 2.00

For surcharges see Nos. C371-C373.

Human Rights Type of Regular Issue

20c, 80c, Map and arms of Salvador and National Unity emblem similar to A209, but vert.

1970, Apr. 14 Litho. ***Perf. 14***

C270 A209 20c blue & multi .16 .15
C271 A209 80c blue & multi .80 .40
Set value .45

For overprint & surcharge see #C301, C402.

Army Type of Regular Issue

Designs: 20c, Fighter plane. 40c, Gun and crew. 50c, Patrol boat.

1970, May 7 ***Perf. 12***

C272 A210 20c gray & multi .16 .15
C273 A210 40c green & multi .35 .15
C274 A210 50c blue & multi .42 .15
Nos. C272-C274 (3) .93
Set value .32

For overprint see No. C310.

Brazilian Team, Jules Rimet Cup — AP52

Designs: Soccer teams and Jules Rimet Cup.

1970, May 25 Litho. ***Perf. 12***

C275 AP52 1col Belgium 1.00 .65
C276 AP52 1col Brazil 1.00 .65
C277 AP52 1col Bulgaria 2.00 1.00
C278 AP52 1col Czechoslovakia 1.00 .65
C279 AP52 1col Germany (Fed. Rep.) 1.00 .65
C280 AP52 1col Britain 1.00 .65
C281 AP52 1col Israel 1.00 .65
C282 AP52 1col Italy 1.00 .65
C283 AP52 1col Mexico 1.00 .65
C284 AP52 1col Morocco 1.00 .65
C285 AP52 1col Peru 1.00 .65
C286 AP52 1col Romania 1.00 .65
C287 AP52 1col Russia 1.00 .65
C288 AP52 1col Salvador 1.00 .65
C289 AP52 1col Sweden 1.00 .65
C290 AP52 1col Uruguay 1.00 .65
Nos. C275-C290 (16) 17.00 10.75

9th World Soccer Championships for the Jules Rimet Cup, Mexico City, May 30-June 21, 1970.
For overprints see Nos. C325-C340.

Lottery Type of Regular Issue

1970, July 15 Litho. ***Perf. 12***

C291 A211 80c multi .65 .25

Education Year Type of Regular Issue

1970, Sept. 11 Litho. ***Perf. 12***

C292 A212 20c pink & multi .16 .15
C293 A212 2col buff & multi 1.65 1.00

Fair Type of Regular Issue

1970, Oct. 28 Litho. ***Perf. 12***

C294 A213 20c multi .24 .15
C295 A213 30c yel & multi .32 .15
Set value .15

Music Type of Regular Issue

Johann Sebastian Bach, harp, horn, music.

1971, Feb. 22 Litho. ***Perf. 13½***

C296 A214 40c gray & multi .38 .18

For overprint see No. C313.

No. C247 Overprinted: "Año / del Centenario de la / Biblioteca Nacional / 1970"

1970, Nov. 25 ***Perf. 12x11½***

C297 A200 5c brn & multi .15 .15

Miss Tourism Type of Regular Issue

1971, Apr. 1 Litho. ***Perf. 14***

C298 A215 20c lil & multi .15 .15
C299 A215 60c gray & multi .45 .30
Set value .38

Pietà Type of Regular Issue

1971, May 10

C300 A216 40c lt yel grn & vio brn .32 .20

No. C270 Overprinted in Red Like No. 823

1971, July 6 Litho. ***Perf. 14***

C301 A209 20c bl & multi .18 .25

Fish Type of Regular Issue

30c, Smalltooth sawfish. 1col, Atlantic sailfish.

1971, July 28

C302 A217 30c lilac & multi .18 .25
C303 A217 1col multi .65 .50

Independence Type of Regular Issue

Designs: Various sections of Declaration of Independence of Central America.

1971 Litho. ***Perf. 13½x13***

C304 A218 30c bl & blk .20 .15
C305 A218 40c brn & blk .30 .20
C306 A218 50c yel & blk .38 .25
C307 A218 60c gray & blk .50 .35
a. Souvenir sheet of 8 1.75 1.65
Nos. C304-C307 (4) 1.38 .95

No. C307a contains 8 stamps with simulated perforations similar to Nos. 826-829, C304-C307.
For overprints see Nos. C311, C347.

Church Type of Regular Issue

15c, Metapan Church. 70c, Panchimalco Church.

1971, Aug. 21 Litho. *Perf. 13x13½*

C308 A219 15c ol & multi .15 .15
C309 A219 70c multi .55 .35

No. C274 Overprinted in Red

1951-12 Octubre-1971
XX Aniversario
MARINA NACIONAL

1971, Oct. 12 Litho. *Perf. 12*

C310 A210 50c bl & multi .38 .30

National Navy, 20th anniversary.

No. C229 Overprinted: "V Feria / Internacional / 3-20 Noviembre / de 1972"

1972, Nov. 3 Photo. *Perf. 12x11½*

C311 A193 80c multi .90 .50

5th Intl. Fair, El Salvador, Nov. 3-20.

No. C223 Overprinted in Red

1972 - XXX Aniversario
Creacion Instituto
Interamericano de
Clencias Agricolas

1972, Nov. 30 Photo. *Perf. 11½x12*

C312 A191 50c ocher, brn & gold .42 .30

30th anniversary of the Inter-American institute for Agricultural Sciences.

No. C296 Overprinted

III Festival
Internacional de
Música 9 - 25-
Febrero - 1973.

1973, Feb. 5 Litho. *Perf. 13½*

C313 A214 40c gray & multi .30 .25

3rd International Music Festival, Feb. 9-29.

Lions Type of Regular Issue

Designs: 20c, 40c, Map of El Salvador and Lions International Emblem.

1973, Feb. 20 Litho. *Perf. 13*

C314 A220 20c gray & multi .15 .15
C315 A220 40c multi .30 .20

Olympic Type of Regular Issue

Designs: 20c, Javelin, women's. 80c, Discus, women's. 1col, Hammer throw. 2col, Shot put.

1973, May 21 Litho. *Perf. 13*

C316 A221 20c lt grn & multi .15 .15
C317 A221 80c sal & multi .55 .35
C318 A221 1col ultra & multi .65 .50
C319 A221 2col multi 1.40 .90
Nos. C316-C319 (4) 2.75 1.90

No. C241 Surcharged Like No. 841

1973, Dec. Photo. *Perf. 13*

C320 A198 25c on 50c multi .15 .15

No. C307a Overprinted: "Centenario / Cuidad / Santiago de Maria / 1874 1974"

Souvenir Sheet

1974, Mar. 7 Litho. *Imperf.*

C321 A218 Sheet of 8 1.00 1.00

Centenary of the City Santiago de Maria. The overprint is so arranged that each line appears on a different pair of stamps.

No. C231 Surcharged in Red

25 cts.

1974, Apr. 22 Photo. *Perf. 12x11½*

C322 A194 25c on 50c multi .15 .15

No. C229 Surcharged

10 CTS.

1974, Apr. 24

C323 A193 10c on 80c multi .15 .15

Rehabilitation Type of 1974

1974, Apr. 30 Litho. *Perf. 13*

C324 A222 25c multi .20 .15

Nos. C275-C290 Overprinted

ALEMANIA 1974

1974, June 4 Litho. *Perf. 12*

C325 AP52 1col Belgium .65 .50
C326 AP52 1col Brazil .65 .50
C327 AP52 1col Bulgaria .65 .50
C328 AP52 1col Czech. .65 .50
C329 AP52 1col Germany .65 .50
C330 AP52 1col Britain .65 .50
C331 AP52 1col Israel .65 .50
C332 AP52 1col Italy .65 .50
C333 AP52 1col Mexico .65 .50
C334 AP52 1col Morocco .65 .50
C335 AP52 1col Peru .65 .50
C336 AP52 1col Romania .65 .50
C337 AP52 1col Russia .65 .50
C338 AP52 1col Salvador .65 .50
C339 AP52 1col Sweden .65 .50
C340 AP52 1col Uruguay .65 .50
Nos. C325-C340 (16) 10.40 8.00

World Cup Soccer Championship, Munich, June 13-July 7.

INTERPOL Type of 1974

1974, Sept. 2 Litho. *Perf. 12½*

C341 A223 25c multi .20 .20

FAO Type of 1974

1974, Sept. 2 Litho. *Perf. 12½*

C342 A224 25c bl, dk bl & gold .20 .15

Coin Type of 1974

1974, Nov. 19 Litho. *Perf. 12½x13*

C343 A225 20c 1p silver, 1892 .16 .15
C344 A225 40c 20c silver, 1828 .32 .20
C345 A225 50c 20p gold, 1892 .50 .25
C346 A225 60c 20col gold, 1925 .50 .30
Nos. C343-C346 (4) 1.48 .90

No. C307a Overprinted: "X ASAMBLEA GENERAL DE LA CONFERENCIA / INTERAMERICANA DE SEGURIDAD SOCIAL Y XX / REUNION DEL COMITE PERMANENTE INTERAMERICANO / DE SEGURIDAD SOCIAL, 24 -- 30 NOVIEMBRE 1974"

1974, Nov. 18 Litho. *Imperf.*

Souvenir Sheet

C347 A218 Sheet of 8 1.75 1.75

Social Security Conference, El Salvador, Nov. 24-30. The overprint is so arranged that each line appears on a different pair of stamps.

Issues of 1965-69 Surcharged

₡0.10 a

₡0.10 b

c ₡0.25

₡0.25 d

1974-75

C348 A190(a) 10c on 45c #C219 .15 .15
C349 A190(a) 10c on 70c #C220 .15 .15
C350 A198(b) 10c on 50c #C241 .15 .15
C351 AP51(d) 25c on 1col #C257 .20 .20
C352 A195(c) 25c on 2col #C234 ('75) .32 .18
C353 A203(d) 25c on 2col #C254 ('75) .20 .20
C354 AP51(d) 25c on 4col #C258 .20 .20
C355 A205(d) 25c on 5col #C262 .20 .20
Set value (8) 1.35 1.20

No. C353 has new value at left and 6 vertical bars. No. C355 has 7 vertical bars.

UPU Type of 1975

1975, Jan. 22 Litho. *Perf. 13*

C356 A226 25c bl & multi .20 .15
C357 A226 30c bl & multi .24 .20

Acajutla Harbor Type of 1975

1975, Feb. 17

C358 A227 15c bl & multi .15 .15

Post Office Type of 1975

1975, Apr. 25 Litho. *Perf. 13*

C359 A228 25c bl & multi .20 .15

Miss Universe Type of 1975

1975, June 25 *Perf. 12½*

C360 A229 25c multi .20 .15
C361 A229 60c lil & multi .50 .40

Women's Year Type and

IWY Emblem — AP53

1975, Sept. 4 Litho. *Perf. 12½*

C362 A230 15c bl & bl blk .15 .15
C363 AP53 25c yel grn & blk .20 .15
Set value .20

International Women's Year 1975.

Nurse Type of 1975

1975, Oct. 24 Litho. *Perf. 12½*

C364 A231 25c lt blue & multi .20 .15

Printers' Congress Type of 1975

1975, Nov. 19 Litho. *Perf. 12½*

C365 A232 30c green & multi .24 .24

Dermatologists' Congress Type, 1975

1975, Nov. 28

C366 A233 20c blue & multi .16 .15
C367 A233 30c red & multi .24 .15

Caritas Type of 1975

1975, Dec. 18 Litho. *Perf. 13½*

C368 A234 20c bl & vio bl .16 .15

UNICEF Emblem — AP54

1975, Dec. 18

C369 AP54 15c lt grn & sil .15 .15
C370 AP54 20c dl rose & sil .16 .15

UNICEF, 25th anniv. (in 1971).

Nos. C267-C269 Surcharged

25c.

1976, Jan. 14 *Perf. 11½x11*

C371 A208 25c on 2col multi .20 .15
C372 A208 25c on 3col multi .20 .15
C373 A208 25c on 4col multi .20 .15
Nos. C371-C373 (3) .60 .45

Caularthron Bilamellatum AP55

Designs: Orchids.

1976, Feb. 19 Litho. *Perf. 12½*

C374 AP55 25c *shown* .20 .20
C375 AP55 25c *Oncidium oliganthum* .20 .20
C376 AP55 25c *Epidendrum radicans* .20 .20
C377 AP55 25c *Epidendrum vitellinum* .20 .20
C378 AP55 25c *Cyrtopodium punctatum* .20 .20
C379 AP55 25c *Pleurothallis schiedei* .20 .20
C380 AP55 25c *Lycaste cruenta* .20 .20
C381 AP55 25c *Spiranthes speciosa* .20 .20
Nos. C374-C381 (8) 1.60 1.60

CIAT Type of 1976

1976, May 18 Litho. *Perf. 12½*

C382 A235 50c org & multi .40 .15

Bicentennial Types of 1976

1976, June 30 Litho. *Perf. 12½*

C383 A236 25c multi .20 .15
C384 A237 5col multi 3.75 2.50

Reptile Type of 1976

Reptiles: 15c, Green fence lizard. 25c, Basilisk. 60c, Star lizard.

1976, Sept. 23 Litho. *Perf. 12½*

C385 A238 15c multi .15 .15
C386 A238 25c multi .20 .20
C387 A238 60c multi .48 .48
Nos. C385-C387 (3) .83 .83

Archaeology Type of 1976

Pre-Columbian Art: 25c, Brazier with pre-classical head, El Trapiche. 50c, Kettle with pre-classical head, Atiquizaya. 70c, Classical whistling vase, Tazumal.

1976, Oct. 11 Litho. *Perf. 12½*

C388 A239 25c multi .20 .15
C389 A239 50c multi .40 .25
C390 A239 70c multi .55 .40
Nos. C388-C390 (3) 1.15 .80

For overprint see No. C429.

Fair Type of 1976

1976, Oct. 25 Litho. *Perf. 12½*

C391 A240 25c multi .20 .15
C392 A240 70c yel & multi .55 .40

Christmas Type of 1976

1976, Dec. 16 Litho. *Perf. 11*

C393 A241 25c bl & multi .20 .15
C394 A241 50c multi .40 .25
C395 A241 60c multi .50 .30
C396 A241 75c red & multi .60 .40
Nos. C393-C396 (4) 1.70 1.10

Rotary Type of 1977

1977, June 20 Litho. *Perf. 11*

C397 A242 25c multi .20 .15
C398 A242 1col multi .80 .50

Industrial Type of 1977

Designs: 25c, Radar station, Izalco (vert.). 50c, Central sugar refinery, Jiboa. 75c, Cerron Grande hydroelectric station.

1977, June 29 *Perf. 12½*

C399 A243 25c multi .20 .15
C400 A243 50c multi .40 .15
C401 A243 75c multi .60 .40
Nos. C399-C401 (3) 1.20 .70

Nos. C399-C401 have colorless overprint in multiple rows: GOBIERNO DEL SALVADOR.

Nos. C271 and C239 Surcharged with New Value and Bar

1977 *Perf. 14, 11½*

C402 A209 25c on 80c multi .22 .15
C403 A197 30c on 5c multi .25 .15
C404 A197 40c on 5c multi .30 .20
C405 A197 50c on 5c multi .40 .25
Nos. C402-C405 (4) 1.17 .75

Broadcasting Type of 1977

1977, Sept. 14 Litho. *Perf. 14*

C406 A244 20c multi .15 .15
C407 A244 25c multi .20 .15

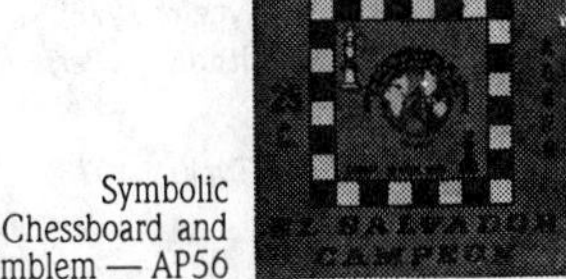

Symbolic Chessboard and Emblem — AP56

1977, Oct. 20 Litho. *Perf. 11*
C408 AP56 25c multi .20 .15
C409 AP56 50c multi .40 .25

El Salvador's victory in International Chess Olympiad, Tripoli, Libya, Oct. 24-Nov. 15, 1976.

Soccer — AP57

Boxing AP58

1977, Nov. 16 Litho. *Perf. 16*
C410 AP57 10c shown .15 .15
C411 AP57 10c Basketball .15 .15
C412 AP57 15c Javelin .15 .15
C413 AP57 15c Weight lifting .15 .15
C414 AP57 20c Volleyball .16 .15
C415 AP58 20c shown .16 .15
C416 AP57 25c Baseball .20 .15
C417 AP58 25c Softball .20 .15
C418 AP58 30c Swimming .24 .20
C419 AP58 30c Fencing .24 .20
C420 AP58 40c Bicycling .32 .25
C421 AP58 50c Rifle shooting .40 .30
C422 AP58 50c Women's tennis .40 .30
C423 AP57 60c Judo .48 .35
C424 AP58 75c Wrestling .60 .40
C425 AP58 1col Equestrian hurdles .80 .50
C426 AP58 1col Woman gymnast .80 .50
C427 AP58 2col Table tennis 1.65 1.00
Nos. C410-C427 (18) 7.25 5.20

Size: 100x119mm

C428 AP57 5col Games' poster 4.00 4.00

2nd Central American Olympic Games, San Salvador, Nov. 25-Dec. 4.

No. C390 Overprinted in Red: "CENTENARIO / CIUDAD DE / CHALCHUAPA / 1878-1978"

1978, Feb. 13 Litho. *Perf. 12¹/₂*
C429 A239 70c multi .55 .55

Centenary of Chalchuapa.

Map of South America, Argentina '78 Emblem — AP59

1978, Aug. 15 Litho. *Perf. 11*
C430 AP59 25c multi .20 .15
C431 AP59 60c multi .50 .40
C432 AP59 5col multi 4.00 3.00
Nos. C430-C432 (3) 4.70 3.55

11th World Cup Soccer Championship, Argentina, June 1-25.

Musical Instrument Type of 1978

Designs: 25c, Drum, vert. 50c, Hollow rattles. 80c, Xylophone.

1978, Aug. 29 *Perf. 12¹/₂*
C433 A245 25c multi .20 .15
C434 A245 50c multi .40 .15
C435 A245 80c multi .60 .40
Nos. C433-C435 (3) 1.20 .70

For surcharge see No. C492.

Engineering Type of 1978

1978, Sept. 12 Litho. *Perf. 13¹/₂*
C436 A246 25c multi .15 .15

Izalco Station Type of 1978

1978, Sept. 14 *Perf. 12¹/₂*
C437 A247 75c multi .60 .40

Softball, Bat and Globes AP60

1978, Oct. 17 Litho. *Perf. 12¹/₂*
C438 AP60 25c pink & multi .20 .15
C439 AP60 1col yel & multi .80 .50

4th World Softball Championship for Women, San Salvador, Oct. 13-22.

Fair Type, 1978

1978, Oct. 30 Litho. *Perf. 12¹/₂*
C440 A248 15c multi .15 .15
C441 A248 25c multi .20 .15

Red Cross Type, 1978

1978, Oct. 30 Litho. *Perf. 11*
C442 A249 25c multi .20 .15

Cotton Conference Type, 1978

1978, Nov. 22 *Perf. 12¹/₂*
C443 A250 40c multi .32 .20

Christmas Type, 1978

1978, Dec. 5 Litho. *Perf. 12¹/₂*
C444 A251 25c multi .20 .15
C445 A251 1col multi .80 .50

Athenaeum Type 1978

1978, Dec. 20 Litho. *Perf. 14*
C446 A252 25c multi .20 .15

UPU Type of 1979

1979, Apr. 2 Litho. *Perf. 14*
C447 A253 75c multi .60 .40

Health Organization Type of 1979

1979, Apr. 7 *Perf. 14x14¹/₂*
C448 A254 25c multi .20 .15

Social Security Type of 1979

1979, May 25 Litho. *Perf. 12¹/₂*
C449 A255 25c multi .20 .15
C450 A255 1col multi .80 .50

Games Emblem — AP61

1979, July 12 Litho. *Perf. 14¹/₂x14*
C451 AP61 25c multi .20 .15
C452 AP61 40c multi .30 .20
C453 AP61 70c multi .55 .40
Nos. C451-C453 (3) 1.05 .75

8th Pan American Games, Puerto Rico, July 1-15.
For surcharge see No. C493.

Pope John Paul II Type of 1979

60c, 5col, Pope John Paul II & pyramid, horiz.

1979, July 12
C454 A256 60c multi .50 .30
C455 A256 5col multi 4.00 2.50

"25," Family and Map of Salvador — AP62

1979, May 14 Litho. *Perf. 14x14¹/₂*
C456 AP62 25c blk & bl .20 .15
C457 AP62 60c blk & lil rose .50 .35

Social Security, 25th anniversary.

Pre-Historic Animal Type, 1979

1979, Sept. 7 Litho. *Perf. 14*
C458 A257 15c Mammoth .15 .15
C459 A257 25c Giant anteater, vert. .20 .15
C460 A257 2 col Hyenas 1.65 1.00
Nos. C458-C460 (3) 2.00 1.30

National Anthem Type, 1979

1979, Sept. 14 *Perf. 14¹/₂x14*
C461 A258 40c Jose Aberiz, score .30 .20

COPIMERA Type, 1979

1979, Oct. 19 Litho. *Perf. 14¹/₂x14*
C462 A259 50c multi .40 .25

Circle Dance, IYC Emblem — AP63

Children's Village and IYC Emblems AP64

Perf. 14¹/₂x14, 14x14¹/₂
1979, Oct. 29
C463 AP63 25c multi .20 .15
C464 AP64 30c vio & blk .24 .20

International Year of the Child.

Biochemistry Type of 1979

1979, Nov. 1 Litho. *Perf. 14¹/₂x14*
C465 A262 25c multi .20 .15

Coffee Type of 1979

Designs: 50c, Picking coffee. 75, Drying coffee beans. 1col, Coffee export.

Perf. 14x14¹/₂, 14¹/₂x14
1979, Dec. 18
C466 A263 50c multi .40 .25
C467 A263 75c multi .60 .40
C468 A263 1 col multi .80 .55
Nos. C466-C468 (3) 1.80 1.20

Hoof and Mouth Disease Type of 1980

1980, June 3 Litho. *Perf. 14¹/₂x14*
C469 A265 60c multi .50 .30

Shell Type of 1980

1980, Aug. 12 *Perf. 14x14¹/₂*
C470 A266 15c *Hexaplex regius* .15 .15
C471 A266 25c *Polinices helicoides* .20 .15
C472 A266 75c *Jenneria pustulata* .50 .40
C473 A266 1 col *Pitar lupanaria* .80 .55
Nos. C470-C473 (4) 1.65 1.25

Birds Type

1980, Sept. 10 Litho. *Perf. 14x14¹/₂*
C474 A267 25c Aulacorhynchus prasinus .20 .15
C475 A267 50c Strix varia fulvescens .40 .25
C476 A267 75c Myadestes unicolor .60 .40
Nos. C474-C476 (3) 1.20 .80

Snake Type of 1980

1980, Nov. 12 Litho. *Perf. 14x14¹/₂*
C477 A268 25c Rattlesnake .20 .15
C478 A268 50c Coral snake .40 .25

Auditors Type

1980, Nov. 26 Litho. *Perf. 14*
C479 A269 50c multi .40 .25
C480 A269 75c multi .60 .40

Christmas Type

1980, Dec. 5 Litho. *Perf. 14*
C481 A270 25c multi .20 .15
C482 A270 60c multi .50 .30

Intl. Women's Decade, 1976-85 — AP65

1981, Jan. 30 *Perf. 14¹/₂x1*
C483 AP65 25c olive green & blk .20 .1
C484 AP65 1 col orange & black .80 .5

Protected Animals AP66

1981, Mar. 20 Litho. *Perf. 14x14¹/₂*
C485 AP66 25c Ateles geoffroyi .20 .1
C486 AP66 40c Lepisosteus tropicus .30 .2
C487 AP66 50c Iguana iguana .40 .2
C488 AP66 60c Eretmochelys imbricata .50 .3
C489 AP66 75c Spizaetus ornatus .60 .4
Nos. C485-C489 (5) 2.00 1.37

Heinrich von Stephan, 150th Birth Anniv. — AP67

1981, May 18 Litho. *Perf. 14¹/₂x14*
C490 AP67 15c multi .15 .15
C491 AP67 2 col multi 1.65 1.00

Nos. C435, C453 Surcharged

Perf. 12¹/₂, 14¹/₂x14
1981, May 18 Litho.
C492 A245 50c on 80c, #C435 .40 .25
C493 AP61 1 col on 70c, #C453 .80 .55

Dental Associations Type

1981, June 18 Litho. *Perf. 14*
C494 A271 5 col bl & blk 4.00 3.00

IYD Type of 1981

1981, Aug. 14 Litho. *Perf. 14x14¹/₂*
C495 A272 25c like #936 .20 .15
C496 A272 50c Emblem .40 .25
C497 A272 75c like #936 .60 .40
C498 A272 1 col like # C496 .80 .55
Nos. C495-C498 (4) 2.00 1.35

Quinonez Type

1981, Aug. 28 Litho. *Perf. 14x14¹/₂*
C499 A273 50c multi .40 .25

World Food Day Type

1981, Sept. 16 Litho. *Perf. 14x14¹/₂*
C500 A274 25c multi .20 .15

Land Registry Office, 100th Anniv. — AP68

1981, Oct. 30 Litho. *Perf. 14x14¹/₂*
C501 AP68 1 col multi .80 .55

TACA Airlines, 50th Anniv. AP69

1981, Nov. 10 Litho. *Perf. 14*
C502 AP69 15c multi .15 .15
C503 AP69 25c multi .20 .15
C504 AP69 75c multi .60 .40
Nos. C502-C504 (3) .95 .70

World Cup Preliminaries Type

1981, Nov. 27 Litho. *Perf. 14x14½*

C505 A275 25c Like No. 939 .20 .15
C506 A275 75c Like No. 940 .60 .40

Lyceum Type

1981, Dec. 17 Litho. *Perf. 14*

C507 A276 25c multi .20 .15

Sculptures Type

1982, Jan. 22 Litho. *Perf. 14*

C508 A277 25c Palm leaf with effigy .20 .15
C509 A277 30c Jaguar mask .25 .20
C510 A277 80c Mayan flint carving .65 .45
Nos. C508-C510 (3) 1.10 .80

Scouting Year Type of 1982

1982, Mar. 17 Litho. *Perf. 14½x14*

C511 A278 25c Baden-Powell .20 .15
C512 A278 50c Girl Scout, emblem .40 .25

TB Bacillus Cent. — AP70

Symbolic Design — AP71

1982, Mar. 24 *Perf. 14*

C513 AP70 50c multi .40 .25

Armed Forces Type of 1982

1982, May 7 Litho. *Perf. 14x13½*

C514 A279 25c multi .20 .15

1982, May 14 *Perf. 14*

C515 AP71 75c multi .60 .40

25th anniv. of Latin-American Tourist Org. Confederation (COTAL).

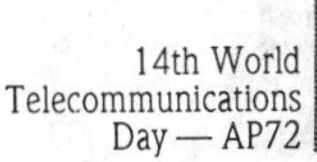

14th World Telecommunications Day — AP72

1982, May 17 *Perf. 14x14½*

C516 AP72 15c multi .15 .15
C517 AP72 2col multi 1.65 1.00

World Cup Type of 1982

1982, July 14

C518 A280 25c Team, emblem .20 .15
C519 A280 60c Map, cup .50 .35

Size: 67x47mm

Perf. 11½

C520 A280 2col Team, emblem, diff. 1.65 1.00

1982 World Cup — AP73

Flags or Arms of Participating Countries; #C521a, C522a, Italy. #C521b, C522c, Germany. #C521c, C522e, Argentina. #C521d, C522m, England. #C521e, C522o, Spain. #C521f, C522q, Brazil. #C521g, C522b, Poland. #C521h, C522d, Algeria. #C521i, C522f, Belgium. #C521j, C522n, France. #C521k, C522p, Honduras. #C521l, C522r, Russia. #C521m, C522g, Peru. #C521n, C522i, Chile. #C521o, C522k, Hungary. #C521p, C522s, Czechoslovakia. #C521q, C522u, Yugoslavia. #C521r, C522w, Scotland. #C521s, C522h, Cameroun. #C521t, C522j, Austria. #C521u, C522l, Salvador. #C521v, C522t, Kuwait. #C521w, C522v, Ireland. #C521x, C522x, New Zealand.

1982, Aug. 26

C521 Sheet of 24 3.00
a.-x. AP73 15c Flags .15 .15
C522 Sheet of 24 5.00
a.-x. AP73 25c Arms .20 .15

Salvador Team, Cup, Flags — AP74

1982, Aug. 26 Litho. *Perf. 11½*

C523 AP74 5col multi 4.00 2.50

International Fair Type

1982, Oct. 14 Litho. *Perf. 14*

C524 A281 15c multi .15 .15

World Food Day — AP75

1982, Oct. 21 Litho. *Perf. 14*

C525 AP75 25c multi .20 .15

St. Francis of Assisi, 800th Birth Anniv. AP76

Natl. Labor Campaign AP77

1982, Nov. 10 Litho. *Perf. 14*

C526 AP76 1col multi .80 .60

1982, Nov. 30 Litho. *Perf. 14x14½*

C527 AP77 50c multi .40 .25

Christmas Type

1982, Dec. 14 Litho. *Perf. 14*

C528 A282 25c multi, horiz. .20 .15

Salvadoran Paintings AP78

#C529, The Pottery of Paleca, by Miguel Ortiz Villacorta. #C530, The Rural School, by Luis Caceres Madrid. #C531, To the Wash, by Julia Diaz. #C532, "La Pancha" by Jose Mejia Vides. #C533, Boats Near The Beach, by Raul Elas Reyes. #C534, The Muleteers, by Canjura.

Perf. 14x13½, 13½x14

1983, Oct. 18 Litho.

C529 AP78 25c multi .20 .15
C530 AP78 25c multi .20 .15
a. Pair, #C529-C530 .40 .30
C531 AP78 75c multi, vert. .60 .40
C532 AP78 75c multi, vert. .60 .40
a. Pair, #C531-C532 1.20 .80
C533 AP78 1col multi, vert. .80 .55
C534 AP78 1col multi, vert. .80 .55
a. Pair, #C533-C534 1.60 1.10
Nos. C529-C534 (6) 3.20 2.20

Fishing Industry — AP79

1983, Dec. 20 Litho. *Perf. 14½x14*

C535 AP79 25c Fisherman .20 .15
C536 AP79 75c Feeding fish .60 .40

No. 999 Surcharged

1985, Apr. 10 Litho. *Perf. 14*

C536A A297 1col on 10c multi .80 .50

Natl. Constitution, Cent. — AP80

1986, Aug. 29 Litho. *Perf. 14*

C537 AP80 1col multi .48 .35

Hugo Lindo (1917-1985), Writer — AP81

1986, Nov. 10 Litho. *Perf. 14½x14*

C538 AP81 1col multi .48 .35

Central American Economic Integration Bank, 25th Anniv. — AP82

1986, Nov. 20

C539 AP82 1.50col multi .70 .52

12th Intl. Fair, Feb. 14-Mar. 1 AP83

1987, Jan. 20 Litho. *Perf. 14½x14*

C540 AP83 70c multi .32 .24

Intl. Year of Shelter for the Homeless AP84

Perf. 14x14½, 14½x14

1987, July 15 Litho.

C541 AP84 70c shown .32 .24
C542 AP84 1col Emblem, vert. .45 .35

Miniature Sheet

Discovery of America, 500th Anniv. (in 1992) AP85

15th cent. map of the Americas (details) and: a, Ferdinand. b, Isabella. c, Caribbean. d, Ships, coat of arms. e, Base of flagstaff. f, Ships. g, Pre-Columbian statue. h, Compass. i, Anniv. emblem. j, Columbus rose.

1987, Dec. 21 Litho. *Perf. 14*

C543 Sheet of 10 4.50 3.50
a.-j. AP85 1col any single .45 .35

No. 1075 Surcharged

₡ 5.00

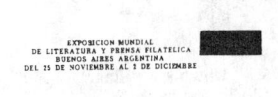

PRENFIL 88

EXPOSICION MUNDIAL DE LITERATURA Y PRENSA FILATELICA BUENOS AIRES ARGENTINA DEL 25 DE NOVIEMBRE AL 2 DE DICIEMBRE

1988, Oct. 28 Litho. *Perf. 14x14½*

C544 A316 5col on 90c multi 2.35 1.75

PRENFIL '88, Nov. 25-Dec. 2, Buenos Aire.

Organization of American States 18th General Assembiy, Nov. 14-19 — AP86

1988, Nov. 19

C545 AP86 70c multi .38 .28

Handicapped Soccer Championships AP87

1990, May 2 Litho. *Perf. 14½x14*

C546 AP87 70c multicolored .34 .25

REGISTRATION STAMPS

Gen. Rafael Antonio Gutiérrez — R1

1897 Engr. Wmk. 117 *Perf. 12*

F1 R1 10c dark blue *125.00*
F2 R1 10c brown lake .15

Unwmk.

F3 R1 10c dark blue .20
F4 R1 10c brown lake .15

Nos. F1 and F3 were probably not placed in use without the overprint "FRANQUEO OFICIAL" (Nos. O127-O128).

The reprints are on thick unwatermarked paper. Value, set of 2, 16c.

ACKNOWLEDGMENT OF RECEIPT STAMPS

AR1

1897 Engr. Wmk. 117 *Perf. 12*

H1 AR1 5c dark green .15

Unwmk.

H2 AR1 5c dark green .15
Set value .18

#H2 has been reprinted on thick paper. Value 15c.

POSTAGE DUE STAMPS

D1

1895 Unwmk. Engr. *Perf. 12*

J1 D1 1c olive green .15 .15
J2 D1 2c olive green .15 .15
J3 D1 3c olive green .15 .15
J4 D1 5c olive green .15 .15
J5 D1 10c olive green .15 .15
J6 D1 15c olive green .15 .15
J7 D1 25c olive green .15 .18
J8 D1 50c olive green .15 .25
Set value (8) .85 1.05

See Nos. J9-J56. For overprints see Nos. J57-J64, O186-O214.

1896 Wmk. 117

J9 D1 1c red .20 .20
J10 D1 2c red .20 .20
J11 D1 3c red .20 .25
J12 D1 5c red .20 .25
J13 D1 10c red .20 .25
J14 D1 15c red .20 .30
J15 D1 25c red .20 .30
J16 D1 50c red .20 .35
Nos. J9-J16 (8) 1.60 2.10

Unwmk.

J17 D1 1c red .15 .15
J18 D1 2c red .15 .15
J19 D1 3c red .15 .15
J20 D1 5c red .15 .15
J21 D1 10c red .15 .15
J22 D1 15c red .15 .15
J23 D1 25c red .15 .15
J24 D1 50c red .15 .18
Set value (8) .80 1.00

Nos. J17 to J24 exist imperforate.

1897

J25 D1 1c deep blue .15 .15
J26 D1 2c deep blue .15 .15
J27 D1 3c deep blue .15 .15
J28 D1 5c deep blue .15 .15
J29 D1 10c deep blue .15 .15
J30 D1 15c deep blue .15 .15
J31 D1 25c deep blue .15 .15
J32 D1 50c deep blue .15 .20
Set value (8) .80 1.00

1898

J33 D1 1c violet .20
J34 D1 2c violet .20
J35 D1 3c violet .20
J36 D1 2c violet .20
J37 D1 10c violet .20
J38 D1 15c violet .20
J39 D1 25c violet .20
J40 D1 50c violet .20
Nos. J33-J40 (8) 1.60

Reprints of Nos. J1 to J40 are on thick paper, often in the wrong shades and usually with the impression somewhat blurred. Value, set of 40, $2, watermarked or unwatermarked.

1899 Wmk. 117 Sideways

J41 D1 1c orange .15
J42 D1 2c orange .15
J43 D1 3c orange .15
J44 D1 5c orange .15
J45 D1 10c orange .15
J46 D1 15c orange .15
J47 D1 25c orange .15
J48 D1 50c orange .15
Set value (8) .80

Unwmk.
Thick Porous Paper

J49 D1 1c orange .15
J50 D1 2c orange .15
J51 D1 3c orange .15
J52 D1 5c orange .15
J53 D1 10c orange .15
J54 D1 15c orange .15
J55 D1 25c orange .15
J56 D1 50c orange .15
Set value (8) .80

Nos. J41-J56 were probably not put in use without the wheel overprint.

Nos. J49-J56 Overprinted in Black

1900

J57 D1 1c orange .50
J58 D1 2c orange .50
J59 D1 3c orange .50
J60 D1 5c orange .75
J61 D1 10c orange 1.00
J62 D1 15c orange 1.00
J63 D1 25c orange 1.25
J64 D1 50c orange 1.50
Nos. J57-J64 (8) 7.00

See note after No. 198A.

Morazán Monument — D2

Perf. 14, 14½

1903 Engr. Wmk. 173

J65 D2 1c yellow green 1.25 1.00
J66 D2 2c carmine 2.00 1.50
J67 D2 3c orange 2.00 1.50
J68 D2 5c dark blue 2.00 1.50
J69 D2 10c dull violet 2.00 1.50
J70 D2 25c blue green 2.00 1.50
Nos. J65-J70 (6) 11.25 8.50

Nos. 355, 356, 358 and 360 Overprinted **DEFICIENCIA DE FRANQUEO**

1908 Unwmk. *Perf. 11½*

J71 A66 1c green & blk .38 .35
J72 A66 2c red & blk .30 .25
J73 A66 5c blue & blk .75 .50
J74 A66 10c violet & blk 1.10 1.00

Same Overprint on No. O275

J75 O3 3c yellow & blk .75 .65
Nos. J71-J75 (5) 3.28 2.75

Nos. 355-358, 360 Overprinted **Deficiencia de franqueo**

J76 A66 1c green & blk .25 .25
J77 A66 2c red & blk .30 .30
J78 A66 3c yellow & blk .35 .35
J79 A66 5c blue & blk .50 .50
J80 A66 10c violet & blk 1.00 1.00
Nos. J76-J80 (5) 2.40 2.40

It is now believed that stamps of type A66, on paper with Honeycomb watermark, do not exist with genuine overprints of the types used for Nos. J71-J80.

Pres. Fernando Figueroa — D3

1910 Engr. Wmk. 172

J81 D3 1c sepia & blk .15 .15
J82 D3 2c dk grn & blk .15 .15
J83 D3 3c orange & blk .15 .15
J84 D3 4c scarlet & blk .15 .15
J85 D3 5c purple & blk .15 .15
J86 D3 12c deep blue & blk .15 .15
J87 D3 24c brown red & blk .15 .15
Set value (7) .62 .62

OFFICIAL STAMPS

Overprint Types

a

b

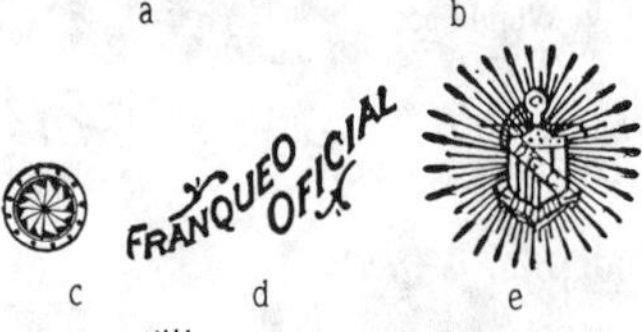

c d e

f

g

Punch with 12 small holes

Type "c" is called the "wheel" overprint.

Nos. 134-157O Overprinted Type a

1896 Unwmk. *Perf. 12*

O1 A45 1c blue .15
O2 A45 2c dk brown .15
a. Double overprint
O3 A45 3c blue grn .30
O4 A45 5c brown ol .15
O5 A45 10c yellow .15
O6 A45 12c dk blue .15
O7 A45 15c blue vio .15
O8 A45 20c magenta .30
O9 A45 24c vermilion .15
O10 A45 30c orange .30
O11 A45 50c black brn .15
O12 A45 1p rose lake .15
Nos. O1-O12 (12) 2.25

The 1c has been reprinted on thick unwatermarked paper. Value 15c.

Wmk. 117

O13 A46 1c emerald .15
O14 A47 2c lake .15
O15 A48 3c yellow brn .15
a. Inverted overprint 1.00
O16 A49 5c dp blue .15
O17 A50 10c brown .15
a. Inverted overprint 1.25
O18 A51 12c slate .15
O19 A52 15c blue grn .15
O20 A53 20c car rose .15
a. Inverted overprint
O21 A54 24c violet .15
O22 A55 30c dp green .15
O23 A56 50c orange .15
O24 A57 100c dk blue .20
Nos. O13-O24 (12) 1.85

Unwmk.

O25 A46 1c emerald .15
a. Double overprint
O26 A47 2c lake .15
O27 A48 3c yellow brn .15
O28 A49 5c dp blue .85
O29 A50 10c brown .15
a. Inverted overprint
O30 A51 12c slate .15
O31 A52 15c blue grn .22
O32 A53 20c car rose .15
a. Inverted overprint
O33 A54 24c violet .42
O34 A55 30c dp green .15
O35 A56 50c orange .85
O36 A57 100c dk blue 1.10
Nos. O25-O36 (12) 4.49

The 3, 5, 10, 12, 15, 20, 24, 30 and 100c have been reprinted on thick unwatermarked paper and the 15c, 50c and 100c on thick watermarked paper. Value, set of 12, $1.20.

Nos. 134-145 Handstamped Type b in Black or Violet

1896

O37 A45 1c blue 7.50
O38 A45 2c dk brown 7.50
O39 A45 3c blue green 7.50
O40 A45 5c brown olive 7.50
O41 A45 10c yellow 8.75
O42 A45 12c dk blue 11.50
O43 A45 15c blue violet 11.50
O44 A45 20c magenta 11.50
O45 A45 24c vermilion 11.50
O46 A45 30c orange 11.50
O47 A45 50c black brown 15.00
O48 A45 1p rose lake 15.00
Nos. O37-O48 (12) 126.25

Reprints of the 1c and 2c on thick paper exist with this handstamp. Value, set of 2, 20c.

Forged overprints exist of Nos. O37-O78, O103-O126 and of the higher valued stamps of O141-O214.

Nos. 146-157F, 157I-157O, 158D Handstamped Type b in Black or Violet

1896 Wmk. 117

O49 A46 1c emerald 6.25
O50 A47 2c lake 6.25
O51 A48 3c yellow brn 6.25
O52 A49 5c deep blue 6.25
O53 A50 10c brown 6.25
O54 A51 12c slate 10.00
O55 A52 15c blue green 11.50
O56 A53 20c carmine rose 11.50
O57 A54 24c violet 11.50
O58 A55 30c deep green 11.50
O59 A56 50c orange 11.50
O60 A57 100c dark blue 11.50
Nos. O49-O60 (12) 110.25

Unwmk.

O61 A46 1c emerald 6.25
O62 A47 2c lake 6.25
O63 A48 3c yellow brn 6.25
O64 A49 5c deep blue 6.25
O65 A50 10c brown 8.75
O66 A52 15c blue green 11.50
O67 A58 15c on 24c vio 11.50
O68 A53 20c carmine rose 11.50
O69 A54 24c violet 11.50
O70 A55 30c deep green 11.50
O71 A56 50c orange 12.50
O72 A57 100c dark blue 12.50
Nos. O61-O72 (12) 116.25

Nos. 175-176 Overprinted Type a in Black

1897

O73 A59 1c bl, gold, rose & grn .25
O74 A59 5c rose, gold, bl & grn .25

These stamps were probably not officially issued.

Nos. 175-176 Handstamped Type b in Black or Violet

1900

O75 A59 1c bl, gold, rose & grn 17.50
O76 A59 5c rose, gold, bl & grn 17.50

Nos. 159-170L Overprinted Type a in Black

1897 Wmk. 117

O79 A46 1c scarlet .15
O80 A47 2c yellow green 1.25
O81 A48 3c bister brown .50
O82 A49 5c orange .15 .15
O83 A50 10c blue green .15
O84 A51 12c blue .25
O85 A52 15c black .25 .50
O86 A53 20c slate .15
O87 A54 24c yellow .18
a. Inverted overprint
O88 A55 30c rose .50
O89 A56 50c violet 1.25 1.00
O90 A57 100c brown lake 1.75
Nos. O79-O90 (12) 6.53

Unwmk.

O91 A46 1c scarlet .15
O92 A47 2c yellow green .30
O93 A48 3c bister brown .20
O94 A49 5c orange .15 .18
O95 A50 10c blue green .65
O96 A51 12c blue .65
O97 A52 15c black .75
O98 A53 20c slate .15 .38
O99 A54 24c yellow .15 .38
O100 A55 30c rose .15 .38

O101 A56 50c violet .65
O102 A57 100c brown lake .38 1.00
Nos. O91-O102 (12) 4.33

All values have been reprinted on thick paper ithout watermark and the 1c, 12c, 15c and 100c n thick paper with watermark. Value, set of 16, 1.60.

Nos. 159-170L Handstamped Type b in Violet or Black

897 Wmk. 117
O103 A46 1c scarlet 7.50
O104 A47 2c yellow green 7.50
O105 A48 3c bister brown 7.50
O106 A49 5c orange 7.50
O107 A50 10c blue green 8.75
O108 A51 12c blue
O109 A52 15c black
O110 A53 20c slate 15.00
O111 A54 24c yellow 17.50
O112 A55 30c rose
O113 A56 50c violet
O114 A57 100c brown lake

Unwmk.
O115 A46 1c scarlet 7.50
O116 A47 2c yellow grn 7.50
O117 A48 3c bister brn 7.50
O118 A49 5c orange 7.50
O119 A50 10c blue green 7.50
O120 A51 12c blue
O121 A52 15c black
O122 A53 20c slate
O123 A54 24c yellow
O124 A55 30c rose 15.00
O125 A56 50c violet
O126 A57 100c brown lake 17.50

Reprints of the 1 and 15c on thick watermarked paper and the 12, 30, 50 and 100c on thick unwatermarked paper are known with this overprint. Value, set of 6, 60c.

Nos. F1, F3 Overprinted Type a in Red

Wmk. 117
O127 R1 10c dark blue .15

Unwmk.
O128 R1 10c dark blue .20

The reprints are on thick paper. Value 15c.
Originals of the 10c brown lake Registration Stamp and the 5c Acknowledgment of Receipt stamp are believed not to have been issued with the "FRANQUEO OFICIAL" overprint. They are believed to exist only as reprints.

Nos. 177-188 Overprinted Type a

1898 Wmk. 117
O129 A60 1c orange ver .15
O130 A60 2c rose .15
O131 A60 3c pale yel grn 1.40
O132 A60 5c blue green .15
O133 A60 10c gray blue .15
O134 A60 12c violet 1.40
O135 A60 13c brown lake .20
O136 A60 20c deep blue .15
O137 A60 24c ultra .15
O138 A60 26c bister brn .20
O139 A60 50c orange .15
O140 A60 1p yellow .20
Nos. O129-O140 (12) 4.45

Reprints of the above set are on thick paper. Value, set of 12, $1.20, with or without watermark.

No. 177 Handstamped Type b in Violet

O141 A60 1c orange ver 30.00

No. O141 with Additional Overprint Type c in Black

O142 A60 1c orange ver

Counterfeits exist of the "wheel" overprint.

Nos. 204-205, 207 and 209 Overprinted Type a

1899 Unwmk.
O143 A61 12c dark green
O144 A61 13c deep rose
O145 A61 26c carmine rose
O146 A61 100c violet

Nos. O143-O144 Punched With Twelve Small Holes

O147 A61 12c dark green
O148 A61 13c deep rose

Official stamps punched with twelve small holes were issued and used for ordinary postage.

Nos. 199-209 Overprinted Type d

1899

Blue Overprint
O149 A61 1c brown .15
O150 A61 2c gray green .15
O151 A61 3c blue .15
O152 A61 5c brown orange .15
O153 A61 10c chocolate .15
O154 A61 13c deep rose .15
O155 A61 26c carmine rose .15
O156 A61 50c orange red .15
O157 A61 100c violet .15

Black Overprint
O158 A61 3c blue .15
O159 A61 12c dark green .15
O160 A61 24c lt blue .15
Set value (12) 1.20

#O149-O160 were probably not placed in use.

With Additional Overprint Type c in Black

O161 A61 1c brown .40 .35
O162 A61 2c gray green .60 .50
O163 A61 3c blue .40 .35
O164 A61 5c brown org .40 .35
O165 A61 10c chocolate .50 .40
O166 A61 12c dark green
O167 A61 13c deep rose 1.00 .85
O168 A61 24c lt blue 15.00 15.00
O169 A61 26c carmine rose 1.00 .60
O170 A61 50c orange red 1.00 .85
O171 A61 100c violet 1.25 .85
Nos. O161-O165,O167-O171 (10) 21.55 20.10

Nos. O149-O155, O159-O160 Punched With Twelve Small Holes

Blue Overprint
O172 A61 1c brown .90 .30
O173 A61 2c gray green 1.10 .30
O174 A61 3c blue 1.50 1.25
O175 A61 5c brown org 2.00 1.00
O176 A61 10c chocolate 2.50 1.75
O177 A61 13c deep rose 2.50 1.25
O177A A61 24c lt blue
O178 A61 26c carmine rose 25.00 12.00

Black Overprint
O179 A61 12c dark green 2.00 1.50
Nos. O172-O177,O178-O179 (8) 37.50 19.35

It is stated that Nos. O172-O214 inclusive were issued for ordinary postage and not for use as official stamps.

Nos. O161-O167, O169 Overprinted Type c in Black

O180 A61 1c brown 1.25 1.10
O180A A61 2c gray green
O181 A61 3c blue
O182 A61 5c brown orange 1.25
O182A A61 10c chocolate
O182B A61 12c dark green
O183 A61 13c deep rose 4.00 2.00
O184 A61 26c carmine rose

Overprinted Types a and e in Black

O185 A61 100c violet

Nos. J49-J56 Overprinted Type a in Black

1900
O186 D1 1c orange 22.50
O187 D1 2c orange 22.50
O188 D1 3c orange 22.50
O189 D1 5c orange 22.50
O190 D1 10c orange 22.50
O191 D1 15c orange 50.00
O192 D1 25c orange 50.00
O193 D1 50c orange 50.00
Nos. O186-O193 (8) 262.50

Nos. O194-O189, O191-O193 Overprinted Type c in Black

O194 D1 1c orange
O195 D1 2c orange 12.50
O196 D1 3c orange
O197 D1 5c orange
O198 D1 15c orange 12.50
O199 D1 25c orange 15.00
O200 D1 50c orange 135.00

Nos. O186-O189 Punched With Twelve Small Holes

O201 D1 1c orange 25.00
O202 D1 2c orange 25.00
O203 D1 3c orange 25.00
O204 D1 5c orange 25.00
Nos. O201-O204 (4) 100.00 .00

Nos. O201-O204 Overprinted Type c in Black

O205 D1 1c orange 9.00 6.50
O206 D1 2c orange 6.50
O207 D1 3c orange 6.50
O208 D1 5c orange 9.00 6.50

Overprinted Type a in Violet and Type c in Black

O209 D1 2c orange 12.50
a. Inverted overprint
O210 D1 3c orange
O211 D1 10c orange 3.00

Nos. O186-O188 Handstamped Type e in Violet

O212 D1 1c orange 9.00 7.50
O213 D1 2c orange 9.00 7.50
O214 D1 3c orange 9.00 9.00
Nos. O212-O214 (3) 27.00 24.00

See note after No. O48.

Type of Regular Issue of 1900 Overprinted Type a in Black

O223 A63 1c lt green .35 .35
a. Inverted overprint
O224 A63 2c rose .40 .35
a. Inverted overprint 1.75
O225 A63 3c gray black .25 .25
a. Overprint vertical
O226 A63 5c blue .25 .25
O227 A63 10c blue .70 .70
a. Inverted overprint
O228 A63 12c yellow grn .70 .70
O229 A63 13c yellow brn .70 .70
O230 A63 24c gray black .50 .70
O231 A63 26c yellow brn 25.00 20.00
a. Inverted overprint
O232 A63 50c dull rose
a. Inverted overprint
Nos. O223-O231 (9) 28.85 24.00

Nos. O223-O224, O231-O232 Overprinted Type f in Violet

O233 A63 1c lt green 4.75 4.00
O234 A63 2c rose 25.00
a. "FRANQUEO OFICIAL" inverted
O235 A63 26c yellow brown .50 .50
O236 A63 50c dull rose .75 .55

Nos. O223, O225-O228, O232 Overprinted Type g in Black

O237 A63 1c lt green 5.00 5.00
O238 A63 3c gray black
O239 A63 5c blue
O240 A63 10c blue
O241 A63 12c yellow green

Violet Overprint
O242 A63 50c dull rose 10.00

The shield overprinted on No. O242 is of the type on No. O212.

O1

1903 Wmk. 173 Perf. 14, 14½
O243 O1 1c yellow green .35 .25
O244 O1 2c carmine .35 .20
O245 O1 3c orange 1.00 .85
O246 O1 5c dark blue .35 .20
O247 O1 10c dull violet .50 .35
O248 O1 13c red brown .50 .35
O249 O1 15c yellow brown 3.25 1.75
O250 O1 24c scarlet .35 .35
O251 O1 50c bister .50 .35
O252 O1 100c grnsh blue .50 .75
Nos. O243-O252 (10) 7.65 5.40

For surcharges see Nos. O254-O257.

No. 285 Handstamped Type b in Black

1904
O253 A64 3c orange 35.00

2 2

Nos. O246-O248 Surcharged in Black

1905
O254 O1 2c on 5c dk bl 3.25 2.75
O255 O1 3c on 5c dk bl
a. Double surcharge
O256 O1 3c on 10c dl vio 9.00 6.00
O257 O1 3c on 13c red brn .85 .70

A 2c surcharge of this type exists on No. O247.

No. O225 Overprinted in Blue

1905 a
1905 b

1905 Unwmk.
O258 A63(a) 3c gray black 2.00 1.75
O259 A63(b) 3c gray black 1.75 1.50

Nos. O224-O225 Overprinted in Blue

1906 c
1906 d

1906
O260 A63(c) 2c rose 11.25 10.00
O261 A63(c) 3c gray black 1.25 1.00
a. Overprint "1906" in blk
O262 A63(d) 3c gray black 1.40 1.25
Nos. O260-O262 (3) 13.90 12.25

Escalón — O2

National Palace — O3

1906 Engr. Perf. 11½
O263 O2 1c green & blk .15 .15
O264 O2 2c carmine & blk .15 .15
O265 O2 3c yellow & blk .15 .15
O266 O2 5c blue & blk .15 .32
O267 O2 10c violet & blk .15 .15
O268 O2 13c dk brown & blk .15 .15
O269 O2 15c red org & blk .20 .15
O270 O2 24c carmine & blk .25 .20
O271 O2 50c orange & blk .25 .65
O272 O2 100c dk blue & blk .25 2.00
Nos. O263-O272 (10) 1.85 4.07

The centers of these stamps are also found in blue black.
Nos. O263 to O272 have been reprinted. The shades differ, the paper is thicker and the perforation 12. Value, set of 10, 50c.

1908
O273 O3 1c green & blk .15 .15
O274 O3 2c red & blk .15 .15
O275 O3 3c yellow & blk .15 .15
O276 O3 5c blue & blk .15 .15
O277 O3 10c violet & blk .15 .15
O278 O3 13c violet & blk .20 .15
O279 O3 15c pale brn & blk .15 .15
O280 O3 24c rose & blk .15 .15
O281 O3 50c yellow & blk .15 .15
O282 O3 100c turq blue & blk .20 .15
Set value (10) 1.10 .90

For overprints see Nos. 441-442, 445-449, J75, O283-O292, O323-O328.

Nos. O273-O282 Overprinted Type g in Black

O283 O3 1c green & blk .85
O284 O3 2c red & blk 1.00
O285 O3 3c yellow & blk 1.00
O286 O3 5c blue & blk 1.25
O287 O3 10c violet & blk 1.25
O288 O3 13c violet & blk 1.50
O289 O3 15c pale brn & blk 1.50
O290 O3 24c rose & blk 2.00
O291 O3 50c yellow & blk 2.50
O292 O3 100c turq & blk 3.00
Nos. O283-O292 (10) 15.85

Pres. Figueroa — O4

1910 Engr. Wmk. 172
O293 O4 2c dk green & blk .15 .15
O294 O4 3c orange & blk .15 .15
O295 O4 4c scarlet & blk .15 .15
a. 4c carmine & black
O296 O4 5c purple & blk .15 .15
O297 O4 6c scarlet & blk .15 .15
O298 O4 10c purple & blk .15 .15
O299 O4 12c dp blue & blk .15 .15
O300 O4 17c olive grn & blk .15 .15
O301 O4 19c brn red & blk .15 .15
O302 O4 29c choc & blk .15 .15
O303 O4 50c yellow & blk .15 .15
O304 O4 100c turq & blk .15 .15
Set value (12) 1.00 1.00

Regular Issue, Type A63, Overprinted or Surcharged:

OFICIAL
a

OFICIAL 3
b

OFICIAL UN COLON
c

1911 Unwmk.
O305 A63(a) 1c lt green .15 .15
O306 A63(b) 3c on 13c yel brn .15 .15
O307 A63(b) 5c on 10c dp bl .15 .15
O308 A63(a) 10c deep blue .15 .15
O309 A63(a) 12c lt green .15 .15
O310 A63(a) 13c yellow brn .15 .15

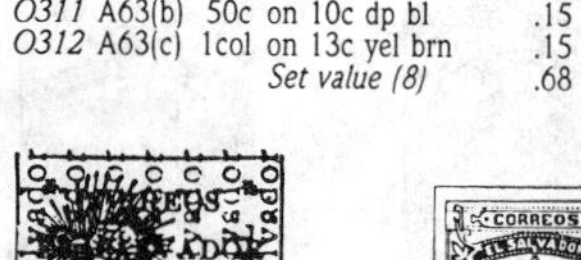

O311 A63(b) 50c on 10c dp bl .15 .15
O312 A63(c) 1col on 13c yel brn .15 .15
Set value (8) .68 .68

O5

O6

1914 Typo. *Perf. 12*
Background in Green, Shield and "Provisional" in Black

O313 O5 2c yellow brn .15 .15
O314 O5 3c yellow .15 .15
O315 O5 5c dark blue .15 .15
O316 O5 10c red .15 .15
O317 O5 12c green .15 .15
O318 O5 17c violet .15 .15
O319 O5 50c brown .15 .15
O320 O5 100c dull rose .15 .15
Set value (8) .64 .64

Stamps of this issue are known imperforate or with parts of the design omitted or misplaced. These varieties were not regularly issued.

1914 Typo.
O321 O6 2c blue green .15 .15
O322 O6 3c orange .15 .15
Set value .16 .16

Type of Official Stamps of 1908 With Two Overprints

1915

1915
O323 O3 1c gray green .30 .25
a. "1915" double
b. "OFICIAL" inverted
O324 O3 2c red .30 .25
O325 O3 5c ultra .30 .25
O326 O3 10c yellow .30 .25
a. Date omitted
O327 O3 50c violet .60 .50
O328 O3 100c black brown 1.25 1.00
Nos. O323-O328 (6) 3.05 2.50

Same Overprint on #414, 417, 429
O329 A66 1c gray green 1.65 1.65
O330 A66 6c pale blue .50 .40
a. 6c ultramarine
O331 A66 12c brown .60 .60
Nos. O329-O330 (2) 2.15 2.05

Nos. O323-O327, O329-O331 exist imperforate.
Nos. O329-O331 exist with "OFICIAL" inverted and double. See note after No. 421.

Nos. 431-440 Overprinted in Blue or Red

1916
O332 A83 1c deep green .15 .15
O333 A83 2c vermilion .35 .15
O334 A83 5c dp blue (R) .25 .15
O335 A83 6c gray vio (R) .15 .15
O336 A83 10c black brown .15 .15
O337 A83 12c violet .40 .25
O338 A83 17c orange .15 .15
O339 A83 25c dark brown .15 .15
O340 A83 29c black (R) .15 .15
O341 A83 50c slate (R) .15 .15
Set value (10) 1.60 1.00

Nos. 474-481 Overprinted

OFICIAL
a

OFICIAL
b

1921
O342 A94(a) 1c green .15 .15
O343 A95(a) 2c black .15 .15
a. Inverted overprint
O344 A96(b) 5c orange .20 .15
O345 A97(a) 6c carmine rose .15 .15
O346 A98(a) 10c deep blue .20 .15
O347 A99(a) 25c olive green .50 .25
O348 A100(a) 60c violet .62 .50
O349 A101(a) 1col black brown .65 .65
Nos. O342-O349 (8) 2.62
Set value 1.90

Nos. 498 and 500 Overprinted in Black or Red **OFICIAL**

1925
O350 A109 5c olive black .35 .15
O351 A111 10c orange (R) .50 .15
a. "ATLANT CO" 7.50 6.25
Set value .22

Inverted overprints exist.

Regular Issue of 1924-25 Overprinted in Black or Red OFICIAL

1927
O352 A106 1c red violet .20 .15
O353 A107 2c dark red .40 .25
O354 A109 5c olive blk (R) .40 .25
O355 A110 6c dp blue (R) 3.00 2.50
O356 A111 10c orange .50 .30
a. "ATLANT CO" 12.50 11.50
O357 A116 1col grn & vio (R) 1.50 1.00
Nos. O352-O357 (6) 6.00 4.45

Inverted overprints exist on 1c, 2c, 5c, 10c.

Regular Issue of 1924-25 Overprinted in Black **OFICIAL**

1932 *Perf. 12½*
O358 A106 1c deep violet .20 .15
O359 A107 2c dark red .40 .15
O360 A109 5c olive black .20 .15
O361 A111 10c orange .70 .30
a. "ATLANT CO" 14.00 12.50
Nos. O358-O361 (4) 1.50 .75

Catalogue values for unused stamps in this section, from this point to the end of the section, are for Never Hinged items.

Regular Issue of 1947 Overprinted in Black or Red **OFICIAL**

1948 Unwmk. Engr. *Perf. 12*
O362 A154 1c carmine rose 42.50 22.50
O363 A154 2c deep orange 42.50 22.50
O364 A154 5c slate gray (R) 42.50 22.50
O365 A154 10c bister brn (R) 42.50 22.50
O366 A154 20c green (R) 42.50 22.50
O367 A154 50c black (R) 42.50 22.50
Nos. O362-O367 (6) 255.00 135.00

No. 602 Surcharged in Carmine and Black

1 CTS

X X

1964(?)
O368 A154 1c on 20c green

The X's are black, the rest carmine.

PARCEL POST STAMPS

Mercury — PP1

1895 Unwmk. Engr. *Perf. 12*
Q1 PP1 5c brown orange .25
Q2 PP1 10c dark blue .25
Q3 PP1 15c red .25
Q4 PP1 20c orange .25
Q5 PP1 50c blue green .25
Nos. Q1-Q5 (5) 1.25

POSTAL TAX STAMPS

Nos. 503, 501 Surcharged **EDIFICIOS POSTALES 1**

1931 Unwmk. *Perf. 12½*
RA1 A115 1c on 50c org brn .20 .15
a. Double surcharge 2.00 2.00
RA2 A112 2c on 20c dp grn .20 .15
Set value .20

Nos. 501, 503 Surcharged **EDIFICIOS POSTALES ₡ 0.01**

RA3 A112 1c on 20c dp grn .20 .15
RA4 A115 2c on 50c org brn .20 .15
a. Without period in "0.02" 1.25
Set value .20

The use of these stamps was obligatory, in addition to the regular postage, on letters and other postal matter. The money obtained from their sale was to be used to erect a new post office in San Salvador.

SAMOA

sə-'mō-ə

(Western Samoa)

LOCATION — Archipelago in the south Pacific Ocean, east of Fiji
GOVT. — Independent state; former territory mandated by New Zealand
AREA — 1,093 sq. mi.
POP. — 156,349 (1981)
CAPITAL — Apia

In 1861-99, Samoa was an independent kingdom under the influence of the US, to which the harbor of Pago Pago had been ceded, and that of Great Britain and Germany. In 1898 a disturbance arose, resulting in the withdrawal of Great Britain, and the partitioning of the islands between Germany and the US. Early in World War I the islands under German domination were occupied by New Zealand troops and in 1920 the League of Nations declared them a mandate to New Zealand. Western Samoa became independent Jan. 1, 1962.

12 Pence = 1 Shilling
20 Shillings = 1 Pound
100 Pfennig = 1 Mark (1900)
100 Sene (Cents) = 1 Tala (Dollar) (1967)

Catalogue values for unused stamps in this country are for Never Hinged items, beginning with Scott 191 in the regular postage section, Scott B1 in the semi-postal section and Scott C1 in the air post section.

Watermarks

Wmk. 62- NZ and Star Wide Apart

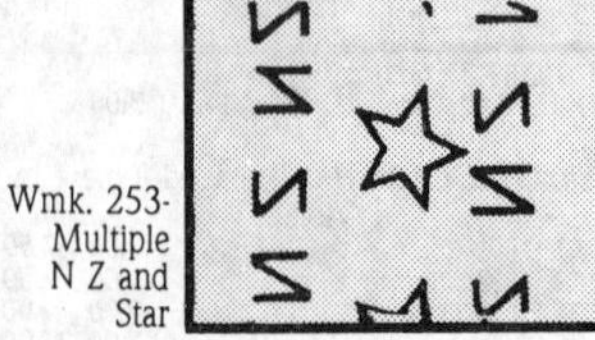
Wmk. 253- Multiple N Z and Star

Wmk. 355- Kava Bowl and WS, Multiple

Issues of the Kingdom

A1

Type I - Line above "X" is usually unbroken. Dots over "SAMOA" are uniform and evenly spaced. Upper right serif of "M" is horizontal.
Type II - Line above "X" is usually broken. Small dot near upper right serif of "M."
Type III - Line above "X" roughly retouched. Upper right serif of "M" bends down.
Type IV - Speck of color on curved line below center of "M."

Perf. 12, 12½
1877-82 Litho. Unwmk.
1 A1 1p blue (III) ('79) 25.00 40.00
a. 1p ultra (III) ('79) 30.00 40.00
b. 1p ultra (II) ('78) 90.00 90.00
c. 1p ultra (I) ('77) 250.00 100.00
2 A1 2p lil rose (IV) ('82) 25.00
3 A1 3p ver (III) ('79) 50.00 70.00
a. 3p brt scarlet (III) 50.00 70.00
b. 3p scarlet (II) ('77) 250.00 125.00
c. 3p deep scarlet (I) ('77) 250.00 125.00
4 A1 6p violet (III) ('79) 42.50 50.00
a. 6p violet (II) ('78) 165.00 85.00
b. 6p violet (I) ('77) 300.00 100.00
5 A1 9p yel brn (IV) ('80) 62.50 *125.00*
a. 9p orange brown (IV) ('80) 62.50 *125.00*
6 A1 1sh org yel (II) ('78) 90.00 95.00
a. 1sh dull yellow (I) ('77) *150.00* *100.00*
7 A1 2sh dp brn (III) ('79) 140.00 225.00
a. 2sh red brown (II) ('78) 275.00 190.00
b. 2sh brown (II) ('78) 275.00 350.00
8 A1 5sh deep green (III) ('79) 425.00 550.00
a. 5sh yel grn (III) ('79) 425.00 600.00
b. 5sh gray green (II) ('78) *1,500.* *1,250.*

The 1p often has a period after "PENNY." The 2p was never placed in use since the Samoa Express service was discontinued late in 1881.

Imperforates of this issue are proofs.

Sheets of the first issue were not perforated around the outer sides. All values except the 2p were printed in sheets of 10 (2x5). The 1p, 3p and 6p type I and the 1p type III were also printed in sheets of 20 (4x5), and six stamps on each of these sheets were perforated all around. The 2p was printed in sheets of 21 (3x7) and five stamps in the second row were perforated all around. These are the only varieties of the original stamps which have not one or two imperforate edges.

Reprints are of type IV and nearly always perforated on all sides. They have a spot of color at the edge of the panel below the "M." This spot is not on any originals except the 2p, which may be distinguished by its color, and the 9p which may be distinguished by having a rough blind perf. 12.

Forgeries exist.

Palms — A2

King Malietoa Laupera — A3

1895-99 Typo. Wmk. 62 *Perf. 11*
9 A2 ½p brown vio .65 1.75
10 A2 ½p green ('99) .65 1.40
11 A2 1p green 1.25 1.75
12 A2 1p red brown ('99) .55 1.25
13 A2 2p brt yellow 5.00 1.00
14 A3 2½p rose .80 *4.50*
15 A3 2½p blk, perf. 10x11 ('96) .90 *3.00*
a. Perf. 11 75.00 *65.00*
16 A2 4p blue 1.00 2.00
17 A2 6p maroon 1.75 3.00
18 A2 1sh rose 1.50 3.75
19 A2 2sh6p red violet 4.75 *7.50*
c. Vert. pair, imperf. btwn. 400.00
Nos. 9-19 (11) 18.80 30.90

1886-92 *Perf. 12½*
9a A2 ½p brown violet 17.00 *35.00*
11a A2 1p green 6.50 12.00
13a A2 2p orange 14.00 8.50
14a A3 2½p rose ('92) *22.50* *4.75*
16a A2 4p blue 25.00 8.50

17a A2 6p maroon 750.00
18a A2 1sh rose 65.00 8.00
c. Diagonal half used as 6p on cover 350.00
19a A2 2sh6p purple 60.00 60.00
Nos. 9a-16a,18a-19a (7) 210.00 136.75

1887-92 *Perf. 12x11½*
9b A2 ½p brown violet 2.50 2.50
11b A2 1p green 15.00 1.40
13b A2 2p brown orange 18.00 1.75
14b A3 2½p rose ('92) 75.00 3.50
16b A2 4p blue 125.00 5.00
17b A2 6p maroon 22.50 8.00
18b A2 1sh rose *250.00* *4.00*
19b A2 2sh6p red violet 325.00 *8.50*
Nos. 9b-19b (8) 833.00 34.65

Three forms of watermark 62 are found on stamps of type A2:
1 - Wide "N Z" and wide star, 6mm apart (used 1886-87).
2 - Wide "N Z" and narrow star, 4mm apart (1890).
3 - Narrow "NZ" and narrow star, 7mm apart (1890-1900). The 2½p has only the 3rd form.
For surcharges or overprints on stamps or types of design A2 see Nos. 20-22, 24-38.

No. 16b Handstamp Surcharged in Black or Red:

FIVE PENCE

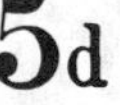

5d

a b c

1893 *Perf. 12x11½*
20 A2(a) 5p on 4p blue 45.00 45.00
21 A2(b) 5p on 4p blue 80.00 *100.00*
22 A2(c) 5p on 4p blue (R) 15.00 22.50
Nos. 20-22 (3) 140.00 *167.50*

As the surcharges on Nos. 20-21 were handstamped in two steps and on No. 22 in three steps, various varieties exist.

Flag Design — A7

1894-95 **Typo.** *Perf. 11½x12*
23 A7 5p vermilion 18.00 2.50
a. Perf. 11 ('95) 10.00 7.00

Types of 1887-1895 Surcharged in Blue, Black, Red or Green:

Surcharged 1½d. — 1½p, 2½p

R 3d. — 3p

1895 *Perf. 11*
24 A2 1½p on 2p orange (Bl) 1.50 *3.75*
a. 1½p on 2p brn org, perf 12x11½ (bl) 7.50 5.50
b. 1½p on 2p yellow, "2" ends with vertical stroke 2.50 *22.50*
25 A2 3p on 2p orange (Bk) 6.00 *8.00*
a. 3p on 2p brn org, perf. 12x11½ (Bk) 25.00 8.50
b. 3p on 2p yel, perf. 11 (Bk) 75.00 60.00
c. Vert. pair, imperf. btwn. 425.00

1898-1900 *Perf. 11*
26 A2 2½p on 1sh rose (Bk) 3.50 *9.00*
a. Double surcharge 425.00
27 A2 2½p on 2sh6p vio (Bk) 5.25 *12.00*
28 A2 2½p on 1p bl grn (R) .55 *2.25*
a. Inverted surcharge *425.00*
29 A2 2½p on 1sh rose (R) 3.50 *9.00*
30 A2 3p on 2p orange (G) 1.50
Nos. 26-30 (5) 14.30

No. 30 was a reissue, available for postage.

Stamps of 1886-99 Overprinted in Red or Blue

PROVISIONAL GOVT.

1899
31 A2 ½p green (R) .30 *1.40*
32 A2 1p red brown (Bl) 1.00 *3.00*
33 A2 2p orange (R) .90 *3.50*
a. 2p yellow .80 *3.50*
34 A2 4p blue (R) .45 *3.25*
35 A7 5p scarlet (Bl) .90 *4.75*
36 A2 6p maroon (Bl) 1.00 *4.00*
37 A2 1sh rose (Bl) 1.40 *12.00*
38 A2 2sh6p violet (R) 4.50 *18.00*
Nos. 31-38 (8) 10.45 *49.90*

In 1900 the Samoan islands were partitioned between the US and Germany. The part which became American has since used US stamps.

Issued under German Dominion

Stamps of Germany Overprinted

1900 **Unwmk.** *Perf. 13½x14½*
51 A9 3pf dark brown 10.00 12.00
52 A9 5pf green 14.00 15.00
53 A9 10pf carmine 10.00 *15.00*
54 A10 20pf ultra 20.00 *17.00*
55 A10 25pf orange 47.50 *72.50*
56 A10 50pf red brown 47.50 *72.50*
Nos. 51-56 (6) 149.00 *204.00*

Kaiser's Yacht "Hohenzollern"
A12 A13

1900 **Typo.** *Perf. 14*
57 A12 3pf brown 1.00 .75
58 A12 5pf green 1.25 .75
59 A12 10pf carmine 1.25 .75
60 A12 20pf ultra 1.00 *1.25*
61 A12 25pf org & blk, *yel* 1.50 *11.00*
62 A12 30pf org & blk, *sal* 1.40 *11.00*
63 A12 40pf lake & blk 1.40 *11.00*
64 A12 50pf pur & blk, *sal* 1.75 *11.00*
65 A12 80pf lake & blk, *rose* 3.50 *27.50*

Perf. 14½x14
Engr.
66 A13 1m carmine 4.25 *50.00*
67 A13 2m blue 5.25 *70.00*
68 A13 3m black vio 7.50 *100.00*
69 A13 5m slate & car 160.00 *425.00*
Nos. 57-69 (13) 191.05

1915 **Wmk. 125** **Typo.** *Perf. 14*
70 A12 3pf brown 1.25
71 A12 5pf green 1.50
72 A12 10pf carmine 1.50

Perf. 14½x14
Engr.
73 A13 5m slate & car 22.50

Nos. 70-73 were never put in use.

Issued under British Dominion

#57-69 Surcharged:

G.R.I. 2½ d. — On A12

G.R.I. 1 Shillings. — On A13

1914 **Unwmk.** *Perf. 14*
101 A12 ½p on 3pf brown 20.00 9.00
a. Double surcharge 500.00 400.00
b. Fraction bar omitted 50.00 30.00
c. Comma after "I" 435.00 360.00
102 A12 ½p on 5pf green 42.50 10.00
a. Double surcharge 450.00 325.00
b. Fraction bar omitted 125.00 55.00
d. Comma after "I" 360.00 300.00
103 A12 1p on 10pf car 100.00 40.00
a. Double surcharge 375.00 375.00
104 A12 2½p on 20pf ultra 30.00 10.00
a. Fraction bar omitted 65.00 37.50
b. Inverted surcharge 725.00 650.00
c. Double surcharge 650.00 600.00
d. Commas after "I" 375.00 310.00
105 A12 3p on 25pf org & blk, *yel* 50.00 40.00
a. Double surcharge 425.00 360.00
b. Comma after "I" 4,000. 800.00
106 A12 4p on 30pf org & blk, *sal* 110.00 57.50
107 A12 5p on 40pf lake & blk 110.00 70.00
108 A12 6p on 50pf pur & blk, *sal* 55.00 35.00
a. Inverted "9" for "6" 165.00 110.00
b. Double surcharge 500.00 500.00
109 A12 9p on 80pf lake & blk, *rose* 200.00 82.50

Perf. 14½x14
110 A13 1sh on 1m car ("1 Shillings.") 3,000. 2,000.
a. "1 Shilling." *9,500.* *7,000.*
111 A13 2sh on 2m blue 3,500. 3,500.
112 A13 3sh on 3m blk vio 1,200. 750.00
a. Double surcharge *7,500.* *7,500.*
113 A13 5sh on 5m slate & car 850.00 800.00

G.R.I. stands for Georgius Rex Imperator.
The 3d on 30pf and 4d on 40pf were produced at a later time.

Stamps of New Zealand Overprinted in Red or Blue:

SAMOA. — k SAMOA. — m

Perf. 14, 14x13½, 14x14½
1914, Sept. 29 **Wmk. 61**
114 A41(k) ½p yellow grn (R) .30 .30
115 A42(k) 1p carmine .30 .15
116 A41(k) 2p mauve (R) .60 .95
117 A22(m) 2½p blue (R) 1.50 1.75
118 A41(k) 6p car rose, perf. 14x14½ 1.50 1.75
a. Perf. 14x13½ 17.00 20.00
119 A41(k) 1sh vermilion 3.50 *10.00*
Nos. 114-119 (6) 7.70 *14.90*

Overprinted Type "m"

1914-25 *Perf. 14, 14½x14*
120 PF1 2sh blue (R) 4.00 *5.50*
121 PF1 2sh6p brown (Bl) 4.50 *8.50*
122 PF1 3sh vio (R) ('22) 12.00 *32.50*
123 PF1 5sh green (R) 9.00 *11.00*
124 PF1 10sh red brown (Bl) 20.00 *27.50*
125 PF2 £1 rose (Bl) 52.50 *45.00*
126 PF2 £2 vio (R) ('25) 350.00
Nos. 120-126 (7) 452.00
Nos. 120-125 (6) *130.00*

Postal use of the £2 is questioned.

Overprinted Type "k"

Perf. 14x13½, 14x14½
1916-19 **Typo.**
127 A43 ½p yellow grn (R) .15 .15
128 A47 1½p gray blk (R) ('17) .25 .25
129 A47 1½p brn org (R) ('19) .20 .25
130 A43 2p yellow (R) ('18) .35 .30
131 A43 3p chocolate (Bl) 1.25 3.00

Engr.
132 A44 2½p dull blue (R) .50 .55
133 A45 3p violet brn (Bl) .50 .65
134 A45 6p carmine rose (Bl) 1.40 1.50
135 A45 1sh vermilion (Bl) 1.75 1.75
Nos. 127-135 (9) 6.35 8.40

Overprinted Type "k" On New Zealand Victory Issue of 1919

1920, June *Perf. 14*
136 A48 ½p yellow grn (R) 1.75 .40
137 A49 1p carmine (Bl) 1.50 .50
138 A50 1½p brown org (R) 1.25 1.10
139 A51 3p black brn (Bl) 4.75 4.25
140 A52 6p purple (R) 3.50 5.00
141 A53 1sh vermilion (Bl) 11.00 10.00
Nos. 136-141 (6) 23.75 21.25

British Flag and Samoan House — A22

1921, Dec. 23 **Engr.** *Perf. 14x13½*
142 A22 ½p green .60 *1.40*
a. Perf. 14x14½ .50 *4.00*
143 A22 1p lake .30 .15
a. Perf. 14x14½ .30 .15
144 A22 1½p orange brn, perf. 14x14½ .50 *5.00*
a. Perf. 14x13½ 3.00 *7.00*
145 A22 2p yel, perf. 14x14½ .50 .30
a. Perf. 14x13½ 4.00 .50
146 A22 2½p dull blue .75 *4.00*
147 A22 3p dark brown 1.65 *2.75*
148 A22 4p violet 1.50 *2.50*
149 A22 5p brt blue 1.50 *4.00*
150 A22 6p carmine rose 2.25 *3.25*
151 A22 8p red brown 3.00 *7.50*
152 A22 9p olive green 3.00 *11.00*
153 A22 1sh vermilion 3.00 *12.50*
Nos. 142-153 (12) 18.55 *54.35*

For overprints see Nos. 163-165.

New Zealand Nos. 182-183 Overprinted Type "m" in Red

1926-27 *Perf. 14½x14*
154 A56 2sh dark blue 4.50 *8.75*
a. 2sh blue ('27) 10.00 *25.00*
155 A56 3sh deep violet 10.00 *20.00*
a. 3sh violet ('27) 42.50 *55.00*

Issued: 2sh, Nov.; 3sh, Oct.; #154a, 155a, 11/10.

New Zealand Postal-Fiscal Stamps, Overprinted Type "m" in Blue or Red

1932, Aug. *Perf. 14*
156 PF5 2sh6p brown 15.00 *25.00*
157 PF5 5sh green (R) 20.00 *32.50*
158 PF5 10sh lake 40.00 70.00
159 PF5 £1 pink 55.00 *80.00*
160 PF5 £2 violet (R) *700.00*
161 PF5 £5 dark blue (R) *1,800.*
Nos. 156-159 (4) 130.00 *207.50*

See Nos. 175-180, 195-202, 216-219.

Silver Jubilee Issue

Stamps of 1921 Overprinted in Black

SILVER JUBILEE OF KING GEORGE V 1910 - 1935.

1935, May 7 *Perf. 14x13½*
163 A22 1p lake .30 .30
a. Perf. 14x14½ *75.00* *110.00*
164 A22 2½p dull blue .80 .95
165 A22 6p carmine rose 3.00 3.00
Nos. 163-165 (3) 4.10 4.25

25th anniv. of the reign of George V.

Western Samoa

Samoan Girl and Kava Bowl — A23

View of Apia — A24

River Scene — A25

Samoan Chief and Wife — A26

Samoan Canoe and House — A27

"Vailima," Stevenson's Home — A28

Stevenson's Tomb — A29

Lake Lanuto'o — A30

Falefa Falls — A31

Perf. 14x13½, 13½x14
1935, Aug. 7 **Engr.** **Wmk. 61**
166 A23 ½p yellow grn .15 .15
167 A24 1p car lake & blk .15 .15
168 A25 2p red org & blk, perf. 14 .40 .40
a. Perf. 13½x14 1.40 2.75
169 A26 2½p dp blue & blk .25 .25
170 A27 4p blk brn & dk gray .50 .50
171 A28 6p plum .50 .50
172 A29 1sh brown & violet .80 .80
173 A30 2sh red brn & yel grn 1.25 1.25
174 A31 3sh org brn & brt bl 2.00 2.00
Nos. 166-174 (9) 6.00 6.00

See Nos. 186-188.

Postal-Fiscal Stamps of New Zealand Overprinted in Blue or Carmine

WESTERN SAMOA.

1935 *Perf. 14*

175 PF5 2sh6p brown 5.00 12.50
176 PF5 5sh green 10.00 15.00
177 PF5 10sh dp carmine 40.00 55.00
178 PF5 £1 pink 55.00 80.00
179 PF5 £2 violet (C) 125.00 250.00
180 PF5 £5 dark blue (C) 300.00 500.00
Nos. 175-180 (6) 535.00 912.50

See Nos. 195-202, 216-219.

Samoan Coastal Village — A32

Map of Western Samoa — A33

Samoan Dancing Party A34

Robert Louis Stevenson A35

Perf. 13½x14

1939, Aug. 29 Engr. Wmk. 253

181 A32 1p scar & olive .20 .25
182 A33 1½p copper brn & bl .40 .50
183 A34 2½p dk blue & brn .75 1.00

Perf. 14x13½

184 A35 7p dp sl grn & vio 4.50 2.00
Nos. 181-184 (4) 5.85 3.75
Set, never hinged 7.75

25th anniv. of New Zealand's control of the mandated territory of Western Samoa.

Samoan Chief — A36

1940, Sept. 2 *Perf. 14x13½*

185 A36 3p on 1½p brown .15 .15
Never hinged .30

Issued only with surcharge. Examples without surcharge are from printer's archives.

Types of 1935 and A37

Apia Post Office — A37

1944-49 Wmk. 253 *Perf. 14*

186 A23 ½p yellow green .40 .40
187 A25 2p red orange & blk .50 .50
188 A26 2½p dp blue & blk ('48) 1.25 1.25

Perf. 13½x14

189 A37 5p dp ultra & ol brn ('49) .25 .25
Nos. 186-189 (4) 2.40 2.40
Set, never hinged 6.75

Issue date: 5p, June 8.

Catalogue values for unused stamps in this section, from this point to the end of the section, are for Never Hinged items.

Peace Issue

New Zealand Nos. 248, 250, 254, and 255 Overprinted in Black or Blue

WESTERN SAMOA
p

WESTERN SAMOA
q

1946, June 1 *Perf. 13x13½, 13½x13*

191 A94(p) 1p emerald .15 .15
192 A96(q) 2p rose violet (Bl) .15 .15
193 A100(p) 6p org red & red brn .25 .25
194 A101(p) 8p brn lake & blk (Bl) .30 .30
Nos. 191-194 (4) .85 .85

Stamps and Type of New Zealand, 1931-50 Overprinted Like Nos. 175-180 in Blue or Carmine

1945-50 Wmk. 253 *Perf. 14*

195 PF5 2sh6p brown 1.10 2.25
196 PF5 5sh green 4.25 5.25
197 PF5 10sh carmine ('48) 13.00 13.00
198 PF5 £1 pink ('48) 47.50 50.00
199 PF5 30sh choc ('48) 125.00 150.00
200 PF5 £2 violet (C) 140.00 150.00
201 PF5 £3 lt green ('50) 175.00 225.00
202 PF5 £5 dk bl (C) ('50) 300.00 350.00

Making Siapo Cloth — A38

Thatching Hut — A40

Western Samoa and New Zealand Flags, Village A39

Samoan Chieftainess — A41

Designs: 2p, Western Samoa seal. 3p, Aleisa Falls (actually Malifa Falls). 5p, Manumea (tooth-billed pigeon). 6p, Fishing canoe. 8p, Harvesting cacao. 2sh, Preparing copra.

Perf. 13, 13½x13

1952, Mar. 10 Engr. Wmk. 253

203 A38 ½p org brn & claret .15 .15
204 A39 1p green & olive .15 .15
205 A38 2p deep carmine .25 .20
206 A39 3p indigo & blue .40 .30
207 A38 5p dk grn & org brn .55 .45
208 A39 6p dp rose pink & bl .60 .50
209 A39 8p rose carmine .90 .70
210 A40 1sh blue & brown 1.10 .90
211 A39 2sh yellow brown 2.75 2.25
212 A41 3sh ol gray & vio brn 4.75 3.75
Nos. 203-212 (10) 11.60 9.35

Coronation Issue

Types of New Zealand 1953

1953, May 25 Photo. *Perf. 14x14½*

214 A113 2p brown .35 .35
215 A114 6p slate black 1.10 1.10

Type of New Zealand 1944-52 Overprinted in Blue or Carmine

WESTERN SAMOA

Wmk. 253

1955, Nov. 14 Typo. *Perf. 14*

216 PF5 5sh yellow green 9.50 15.00
217 PF5 10sh carmine rose 12.00 19.00
218 PF5 £1 dull rose 26.00 35.00
219 PF5 £2 violet (C) 62.50 115.00
Nos. 216-219 (4) 110.00 184.00

Redrawn Types of 1952 and

Map of Western Samoa and Mace — A42

Designs: 4p, as 1p. 6p, as 2p.

Inscribed: "Fono Fou 1958" and "Samoa I Sisifo"

Perf. 13½x13, 13

1958, Mar. 21 Engr. Wmk. 253

220 A39 4p rose carmine .15 .15
221 A38 6p dull purple .20 .20
222 A42 1sh light violet blue .30 .30
Nos. 220-222 (3) .65 .65

INDEPENDENT STATE

Samoa College A43

Designs: 1p, Woman holding ceremonial mat, vert. 3p, Public Library. 4p, Fono House (Parliament). 6p, Map of Western Samoa, ship and plane. 8p, Faleolo airport. 1sh, Talking chief with fly whisk, vert. 1sh3p, Government House, Vailima. 2sh6p, Flag of Western Samoa. 5sh, State Seal.

Perf. 13½

1962, July 2 Wmk. 253 Litho.

223 A43 1p carmine & brown .15 .15
224 A43 2p org, lt grn, red & brown .15 .15
225 A43 3p blue, grn & brn .20 .20
226 A43 4p dk grn, bl & car .35 .35
227 A43 6p yel, grn & ultra .45 .45
228 A43 8p blue & emerald .55 .55
229 A43 1sh brt grn & brn .85 .85
230 A43 1sh3p blue & emerald 1.10 1.10
231 A43 2sh6p vio blue & red 1.65 1.65
232 A43 5sh olive gray, red & dk blue 4.00 4.00
Nos. 223-232 (10) 9.45 9.45

Western Samoa's independence. See #242-247.

Tupua Tamasese Mea'ole, Malietoa Tanumafili II and Seal — A44

1963, Oct. 1 Photo. *Perf. 14*

233 A44 1p green & blk .15 .15
234 A44 4p dull blue & blk .15 .15
235 A44 8p carmine rose & blk .15 .15
236 A44 2sh orange & blk .45 .45
Set value .70 .70

First anniversary of independence.

Signing of Western Samoa-New Zealand Friendship Treaty — A45

1964, Sept. 1 Unwmk. *Perf. 13½*

237 A45 1p multicolored .15 .15
238 A45 8p multicolored .15 .15
239 A45 2sh multicolored .35 .35
240 A45 3sh multicolored .45 .45
Nos. 237-240 (4) 1.10 1.10

2nd anniv. of the signing of the Treaty of Friendship between Western Samoa and New Zealand. Signers: J. B. Wright, N. Z. High Commissioner for Western Pacific, and Fiame Mata'afa, Prime Minister of Western Samoa.

Type of 1962

Perf. 13½

1965, Oct. 4 Litho. Wmk. 355

242 A43 1p carmine & brn .40 .40
243 A43 3p blue, grn & brn 35.00 14.00
244 A43 4p dk green, bl & car .40 .40
245 A43 6p yellow, grn & ultra .45 .45
246 A43 8p blue & emerald .55 .55
247 A43 1sh brt green & brn .70 .70
Nos. 242-247 (6) 37.50 16.50

For surcharge see No. B1.

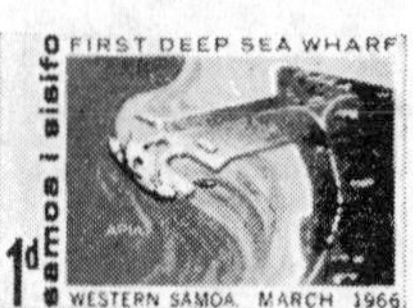

Aerial View of Deep-Sea Wharf A46

8p, 2sh, View of Apia harbor & deep-sea wharf.

1966, Mar. 2 Photo. *Perf. 13½*

251 A46 1p multicolored .15 .15
252 A46 8p multicolored .15 .15
253 A46 2sh multicolored .30 .30
254 A46 3sh multicolored .50 .50
Nos. 251-254 (4) 1.10 1.10

Opening of Western Samoa's first deep-sea wharf at Apia.

Inauguration of WHO Headquarters, Geneva — A47

Design: 4p, 1sh, WHO building and flag.

1966, July 4 Photo. Wmk. 355

255 A47 3p gray, ultra & bister .20 .20
256 A47 4p multicolored .30 .30
257 A47 6p lt olive grn, pur & grn .40 .40
258 A47 1sh multicolored .85 .85
Nos. 255-258 (4) 1.75 1.75

Tuatagaloa L.S., Minister of Justice A48

Designs: 8p, F.C.F. Nelson, Minister of Works, Marine and Civil Aviation. 2sh, To'omata T. L., Minister of Lands. 3sh, Fa'alava'au Galu, Minister of Post Office, Radio and Broadcasting.

Perf. 14½x14

1967, Jan. 16 Photo. Wmk. 355

259 A48 3p violet & sepia .15 .15
260 A48 8p blue & sepia .16 .16
261 A48 2sh lt olive grn & sepia .30 .30
262 A48 3sh lilac rose & sepia .48 .48
Nos. 259-262 (4) 1.09 1.09

Fifth anniversary of Independence.

Samoan Fales, 1900, and Fly Whisk A49

Design: 1sh, Fono House (Parliament) and mace.

1967, May 16 *Perf. 14½*

263 A49 8p multicolored .20 .20
264 A49 1sh multicolored .30 .30

Centenary of Mulinu'u as Government Seat.

Wattled Honey-Eater A50

Birds of Western Samoa: 2s, Pacific pigeon. 3s, Samoan starling. 5s, Samoan broadbill. 7s, Red-headed parrot finch. 10s, Purple swamp hen. 20s, Barn owl. 25s, Tooth-billed pigeon. 50s, Island thrush. $1, Samoan fantail. $2, Mao (gymnomyza samoensis). $4, Samoan white-eye (zosterops samoensis).

Perf. 14x14½

1967, July 10 Photo. Wmk. 355

Birds in Natural Colors

Size: 37x24mm

265 A50 1s black & lt brown .15 .15
266 A50 2s lt ultra, blk & brn org .15 .15
267 A50 3s black, lt brn & emer .15 .15
268 A50 5s lilac, blk & vio bl .20 .15
269 A50 7s blk, vio bl & gray .30 .25
270 A50 10s Prus blue & blk .45 .35
271 A50 20s dk gray & blue .95 .75
272 A50 25s pink, blk & dk grn 1.10 .95
273 A50 50s brn, blk & lt ol grn 2.25 1.90
274 A50 $1 yellow & black 4.50 3.75

1969 Size: 43x28mm *Perf. 13½*

274A A50 $2 blk & lt grnsh bl 11.00 9.25
274B A50 $4 dp orange & blk 37.50 40.00
Nos. 265-274B (12) 58.70 57.80

For surcharge see No. 294.

Child Care A51

Designs: 7s, Leprosarium. 20s, Mobile X-ray unit. 25s, Apia Hospital.

1967, Dec. 1 Litho. *Perf. 14*

275 A51	3s multicolored	.15	.15
276 A51	7s multicolored	.15	.15
277 A51	20s multicolored	.40	.40
278 A51	25s multicolored	.50	.50
	Nos. 275-278 (4)	1.20	1.20

South Pacific Health Service.

Thomas Trood A52

Portraits: 7s, Dr. Wilhelm Solf. 20s, John C. Williams. 25s, Fritz Marquardt.

1968, Jan. 1 Unwmk. *Perf. 13½*

279 A52	2s multicolored	.15	.15
280 A52	7s multicolored	.15	.15
281 A52	20s multicolored	.30	.30
282 A52	25s multicolored	.40	.40
	Nos. 279-282 (4)	1.00	1.00

Sixth anniversary of independence.

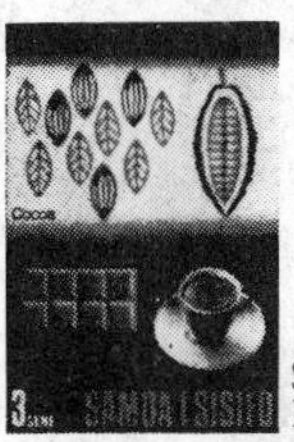

Samoan Agricultural Development — A53

Perf. 13x12½

1968, Feb. 15 Photo. Wmk. 355

283 A53	3s Cocoa	.15	.15
284 A53	5s Breadfruit	.15	.15
285 A53	10s Copra	.20	.20
286 A53	20s Bananas	.45	.45
	Nos. 283-286 (4)	.95	.95

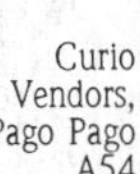

Curio Vendors, Pago Pago A54

20s, Palm trees at the shore. 25s, A'Umi Beach.

Perf. 14½x14

1968, Apr. 22 Photo. Wmk. 355

287 A54	7s multicolored	.15	.15
288 A54	20s multicolored	.35	.35
289 A54	25s multicolored	.40	.40
	Nos. 287-289 (3)	.90	.90

South Pacific Commission, 21st anniv.

Bougainville and Compass Rose — A55

Designs: 3s, Map showing Western Samoa Archipelago and Bougainville's route. 20s, Bougainvillea. 25s, Bougainville's ships La Boudeuse and L'Etoile.

1968, June 10 Litho. *Perf. 14*

290 A55	3s brt blue & blk	.15	.15
291 A55	7s ocher & blk	.15	.15
292 A55	20s grnsh blk, brt rose & grn	.50	.50
293 A55	25s brt lil, vio, blk & org	.65	.65
	Nos. 290-293 (4)	1.45	1.45

200th anniv. of the visit of Louis Antoine de Bougainville (1729-1811) to Samoa.

No. 270 Surcharged with New Value, Three Bars and: "1928-1968 / KINGSFORD-SMITH / TRANSPACIFIC FLIGHT"

1968, June 13 Photo. *Perf. 14x14½*

294 A50	20s on 10s multicolored	.35	.35

40th anniv. of the 1st Transpacific flight under Capt. Charles Kingsford-Smith (Oakland, CA to Brisbane, Australia, via Honolulu and Fiji).

Human Rights Flame and Globe A56

Perf. 14½x14

1968, Aug. 26 Photo. Wmk. 355

295 A56	7s multicolored	.15	.15
296 A56	20s multicolored	.35	.35
297 A56	25s multicolored	.40	.40
	Nos. 295-297 (3)	.90	.90

International Human Rights Year, 1968.

Martin Luther King, Jr. — A57

Polynesian Madonna — A58

1968, Sept. 23 Litho. *Perf. 14*

298 A57	7s green & black	.15	.15
299 A57	20s brt rose lilac & black	.40	.40

Rev. Dr. Martin Luther King, Jr. (1929-68), American civil rights leader.

1968, Oct. 12 Wmk. 355

300 A58	1s olive & multi	.15	.15
301 A58	3s multicolored	.15	.15
302 A58	20s crimson & multi	.40	.40
303 A58	30s dp orange & multi	.50	.50
	Nos. 300-303 (4)	1.20	1.20

Christmas 1968.

Frangipani A59

Flowers: 7s, Chinese hibiscus, vert. 20s, Red ginger, vert. 30s, Canangium odoratum.

1969, Jan. 20 Unwmk. *Perf. 14*

304 A59	2s brt blue & multi	.15	.15
305 A59	7s multicolored	.25	.25
306 A59	20s yellow & multi	.70	.70
307 A59	30s multicolored	1.00	1.00
	Nos. 304-307 (4)	2.10	2.10

Seventh anniversary of independence.

R. L. Stevenson and Silver from "Treasure Island" A60

Perf. 14x13½

1969, Apr. 21 Litho. Wmk. 355

308 A60	3s gray & multi	.15	.15
309 A60	7s gray & multi	.15	.15
310 A60	20s gray & multi	.50	.50
311 A60	22s gray & multi	.60	.60
	Nos. 308-311 (4)	1.40	1.40

Robert Louis Stevenson and: 7s, Stewart and Balfour on the moor from "Kidnapped," 20s, "Doctor Jekyll and Mr. Hyde." 22s, Archie Weir and Christiana Elliot from "Weir of Hermiston."

75th anniv. of the death of Robert Louis Stevenson, who is buried in Samoa.

Weight Lifting — A61

Perf. 13½x13

1969, July 21 Photo. Unwmk.

312 A61	3s shown	.15	.15
313 A61	20s Sailing	.40	.40
314 A61	22s Boxing	.45	.45
	Nos. 312-314 (3)	1.00	1.00

3rd Pacific Games, Port Moresby, Papua and New Guinea, Aug. 13-23.

American Astronaut on Moon, Splashdown and Map of Samoan Islands — A62

1969, July 24 Photo.

315 A62	7s red, blk, silver & grn	.15	.15
316 A62	20s car, blk, silver & ultra	.40	.40

US astronauts. See note after US No. C76.

Holy Family by El Greco — A63

Christmas (Paintings): 1s, Virgin and Child, by Murillo. 20s, Nativity, by El Greco. 30s, Virgin and Child (from Adoration of the Kings), by Velazquez.

1969, Oct. 13 Unwmk. *Perf. 14*

317 A63	1s gold, red & multi	.15	.15
318 A63	3s gold, red & multi	.15	.15
319 A63	20s gold, red & multi	.35	.35
320 A63	30s gold, red & multi	.55	.55
a.	Souvenir sheet of 4, #317-320	1.25	1.25
	Nos. 317-320 (4)	1.20	1.20

Seventh Day Adventists' Sanatorium, Apia — A64

7s, Father Louis Violette, R. C. Cathedral, Apia. 20s, Church of Latter Day Saints (Mormon), Tuasivi, Safotulafai, vert. 22s, John Williams, London Missionary Soc. Church, Sapapali'i.

1970, Jan. 19 Litho. Wmk. 355

321 A64	2s brown, blk & gray	.15	.15
322 A64	7s violet, blk & bister	.15	.15
323 A64	20s rose, blk & lt violet	.35	.35
324 A64	22s olive, blk & bister	.40	.40
	Nos. 321-324 (4)	1.05	1.05

Eighth anniversary of independence.

U.S.S. Nipsic A65

Designs: 5s, Wreck of German ship Adler. 10s, British ship Calliope in storm. 20s, Apia after hurricane.

1970, Apr. 27 *Perf. 13½x14*

325 A65	5s multicolored	.40	.40
326 A65	7s multicolored	.50	.50
327 A65	10s multicolored	.85	.85
328 A65	20s multicolored	1.65	1.65
	Nos. 325-328 (4)	3.40	3.40

The great Apia hurricane of 1889.

Cook Statue, Whitby, England — A66

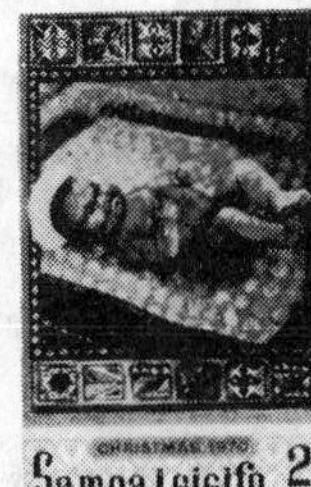

"Peace for the World" by Frances B. Eccles — A67

Designs: 1s, Kendal's chronometer and Cook's sextant. 20s, Capt. Cook bust, in profile. 30s, Capt. Cook, island scene and "Endeavour," horiz.

Perf. 14x14½

1970, Sept. 14 Litho. Wmk. 355

Size: 25x41mm

329 A66	1s silver, dp car & blk	.15	.15
330 A66	2s multicolored	.25	.15
331 A66	20s gold, black & ultra	2.25	1.50

Perf. 14½x14

Size: 83x25mm

332 A66	30s multicolored	3.25	2.25
	Nos. 329-332 (4)	5.90	4.05

Bicentenary of Capt. James Cook's exploration of South Pacific.

Perf. 13½

1970, Oct. 26 Photo. Unwmk.

Christmas: 3s, Samoan coat of arms and Holy Family, by Werner Erich Jahnke. 20s, Samoan Mother and Child, by F. B. Eccles. 30s, Prince of Peace, by Sister Melane Fe'ao.

333 A67	2s gold & multi	.15	.15
334 A67	3s gold & multi	.15	.15
335 A67	20s gold & multi	.50	.50
336 A67	30s gold & multi	.70	.70
a.	Souvenir sheet of 4, #333-336	1.75	1.75
	Nos. 333-336 (4)	1.50	1.50

Pope Paul VI — A68

Lumberjack — A69

Wmk. 355

1970, Nov. 29 Litho. *Perf. 14*

337 A68	8s Prus blue & black	.20	.20
338 A68	20s deep plum & black	.45	.45

Visit of Pope Paul VI, Nov. 29, 1970.

Perf. 14x13½, 13½x14

1971, Feb. 1 Litho. Unwmk.

8s, Woman and tractor in clearing, horiz. 20s, Log and saw carrier, horiz. 22s, Logging and ship.

339 A69	3s multicolored	.15	.15
340 A69	8s multicolored	.15	.15
341 A69	20s multicolored	.35	.35
342 A69	22s multicolored	.45	.45
	Nos. 339-342 (4)	1.10	1.10

Development of the timber industry on Savaii Island by the American Timber Company of Potlatch.

Souvenir Sheet

Longboat in Apia Harbor; Samoa #3 and US #3 — A70

1971, Mar. 12 Photo. *Perf. 11½*
Granite Paper

343	A70	70s blue & multi	2.00	2.00

INTERPEX, 13th Intl. Stamp Exhib., NYC, Mar. 12-14.

Siva Dance A71

Tourist Publicity: 7s, Samoan cricket game. 8s, Hideaway Resort Hotel. 10s, Aggie Grey and Aggie's Hotel.

Wmk. 355
1971, Aug. 9 Litho. *Perf. 14*

344	A71	5s orange brn & multi	.45	.45
345	A71	7s orange brn & multi	.60	.60
346	A71	8s orange brn & multi	.75	.75
347	A71	10s orange brn & multi	.90	.90
		Nos. 344-347 (4)	2.70	2.70

A72

A73

Samoan Legends, carved by Sven Ortquist: 3s, Queen Salamasina. 8s, Lu and his sacred hens (Samoa). 10s, God Tagaloa fishing Samoan islands of Upolu and Savaii from the sea. 22s, Mt. Vaea and Pool of Tears.

1971, Sept. 20

348	A72	3s dark violet & multi	.15	.15
349	A72	8s multicolored	.20	.20
350	A72	10s dark blue & multi	.25	.25
351	A72	22s dark blue & multi	.65	.65
		Nos. 348-351 (4)	1.25	1.25

See Nos. 399-402.

1971, Oct. 4 *Perf. 14x13½*

Christmas: 2s, 3s, Virgin and Child, by Giovanni Bellini. 20c, 30c, Virgin and Child with St. Anne and St. John the Baptist, by Leonardo da Vinci.

352	A73	2s blue & multi	.15	.15
353	A73	3s black & multi	.15	.15
354	A73	20s yellow & multi	.55	.55
355	A73	30s dark red & multi	.80	.80
		Nos. 352-355 (4)	1.65	1.65

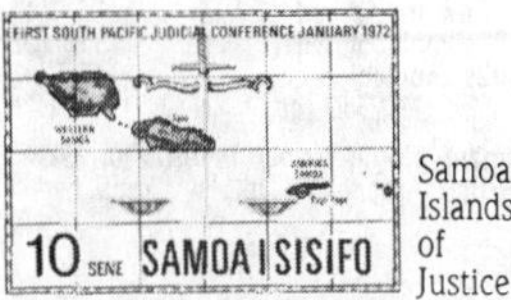

Samoan Islands, Scales of Justice — A74

1972, Jan. 10 Photo. *Perf. 11½x12*

356	A74	10s light blue & multi	.35	.35

1st So. Pacific Judicial Conf., Samoa, Jan. 1972.

Asau Wharf, Savaii A75

Designs: 8s, Parliament Building. 10s, Mothers' Center. 22s, Portraits of Tupua Tamasese Mea'ole and Malietoa Tanumafili II, and view of Vailima.

Perf. 13x13½
1972, Jan. 10 Litho. Wmk. 355

357	A75	1s bright pink & multi	.15	.15
358	A75	8s lilac & multi	.20	.20
359	A75	10s green & multi	.25	.25
360	A75	22s multicolored	.60	.60
		Nos. 357-360 (4)	1.20	1.20

10th anniversary of independence.

Commission Members' Flags — A76

Sunset and Ships — A77

Designs: 7s, Afoafouvale Misimoa, Secretary-General, 1970-71 and Commission flag. 8s, Headquarters Building, Noumea, New Caledonia, horiz. 10s, Flag of Samoa, flag and map of South Pacific Commission area, horiz.

Perf. 14x13½, 13½x14
1972, Mar. 17

361	A76	3s ultra & multi	.15	.15
362	A76	7s yellow, black & ultra	.25	.25
363	A76	8s multicolored	.30	.30
364	A76	10s lt green & multi	.35	.35
		Nos. 361-364 (4)	1.05	1.05

South Pacific Commission, 25th anniv.

1972, June 14 *Perf. 14½*

Designs: 8s, Sailing ships Arend, Thienhoven and Africaansche Galey in storm. 10s, Outrigger canoe and Roggeveen's ships. 30s, Hemispheres with exploration route and map of Samoan Islands. All horiz.

365	A77	2s carmine rose & multi	.15	.15
366	A77	8s violet blue & multi	.40	.30
367	A77	10s ultra & multi	.45	.40

Size: 85x25mm

368	A77	30s ocher & multi	2.00	1.10
		Nos. 365-368 (4)	3.00	1.95

250th anniv. of Jacob Roggeveen's Pacific voyage and discovery of Samoa in June 1722.

Bull Conch A78

1972-75 Litho. *Perf. 14½*
Size: 41x24mm

369	A78	1s shown	.15	.15
370	A78	2s Rhinoceros beetle	.15	.15
371	A78	3s Skipjack (fish)	.15	.15
372	A78	4s Painted crab	.15	.15
373	A78	5s Butterflyfish	.15	.15
374	A78	7s Samoan monarch	.15	.15
375	A78	10s Triton shell	.20	.20
376	A78	20s Jewel beetle	.45	.45
377	A78	50s Spiny lobster	1.25	1.25

Perf. 14x13½
Size: 29x45mm

378	A78	$1 Hawk moth	2.25	2.25
378A	A78	$2 Green turtle	4.50	4.50
378B	A78	$4 Black marlin	9.25	9.25
378C	A78	$5 Green tree lizard	12.00	12.00
		Nos. 369-378C (13)	30.80	30.80

Issued: 1s-$1, Oct. 18, 1972; $2, June 18, 1973; $4, Mar. 27, 1974; $5, June 30, 1975.

Ascension, Stained Glass Window — A79

Stained Glass Windows in Apia Churches: 4s, Virgin and Child. 10s, St. Andrew blessing Samoan canoe. 30s, The Good Shepherd.

Perf. 14x14½
1972, Nov. 1 Wmk. 355

379	A79	1s ocher & multi	.15	.15
380	A79	4s gray & multi	.15	.15
381	A79	10s dull green & multi	.30	.30
382	A79	30s blue & multi	.90	.90
a.		Souvenir sheet of 4, #379-382	1.65	1.65
		Nos. 379-382 (4)	1.50	1.50

Christmas.

Scouts Saluting Flag, Emblems A80

1973, Jan. 29 *Perf. 14*

383	A80	2s shown	.15	.15
384	A80	3s First aid	.15	.15
385	A80	8s Pitching tent	.40	.40
386	A80	20s Action song	1.00	1.00
		Nos. 383-386 (4)	1.70	1.70

Boy Scouts of Samoa.

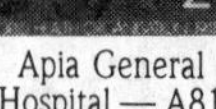

Apia General Hospital — A81

"A Prince is Born," by Jahnke — A82

WHO, 25th anniv.: 8s, Baby clinic. 20s, Filariasis research. 22s, Family welfare.

1973, Aug. 20 Wmk. 355

387	A81	2s green & multi	.15	.15
388	A81	8s multicolored	.25	.25
389	A81	20s brown & multi	.55	.55
390	A81	22s vermilion & multi	.65	.65
		Nos. 387-390 (4)	1.60	1.60

1973, Oct. 15 Litho. *Perf. 14*

Christmas: 4s, "Star of Hope," by Fiasili Keil. 10s, "Mother and Child," by Ernesto Coter. 30s, "The Light of the World," by Coter.

391	A82	3s blue & multi	.15	.15
392	A82	4s purple & multi	.15	.15
393	A82	10s red & multi	.30	.30
394	A82	30s blue & multi	.95	.95
a.		Souvenir sheet of 4, #391-394	2.00	2.00
		Nos. 391-394 (4)	1.55	1.55

Boxing and Games' Emblem A83

1974, Jan. 24

395	A83	8s shown	.20	.2
396	A83	10s Weight lifting	.30	.3
397	A83	20s Lawn bowling	.65	.6
398	A83	30s Stadium	.90	.9
		Nos. 395-398 (4)	2.05	2.0

10th British Commonwealth Games, Christchurch, New Zealand, Jan. 24-Feb. 2.

Legends Type of 1971

Samoan Legends, Wood Carvings by Sven Ortquist: 2s, Tigilau and dove. 8s, Pili with his sons and famous fish net. 20s, The girl Sina and the eel which became the coconut tree. 30s, Nafanua who returned from the spirit world to free her village.

1974, Aug. 13 Wmk. 355 *Perf. 14*

399	A72	2s lemon & multi	.15	.15
400	A72	8s rose red & multi	.20	.20
401	A72	20s yellow grn & multi	.65	.65
402	A72	30s lt violet & multi	.95	.95
		Nos. 399-402 (4)	1.95	1.95

Faleolo Airport A84

Designs: 20s, Apia Wharf. 22s, Early post office, Apia. 50s, William Willis, raft "Age Unlimited" and route from Callao, Peru, to Tully, Western Samoa.

1974, Sept. 4 Unwmk. *Perf. 13½*
Size: 47x29mm

403	A84	8s multicolored	.20	.20
404	A84	20s multicolored	.45	.45
405	A84	22s multicolored	.60	.60

Size: 86x29mm

406	A84	50s multicolored	1.25	1.25
a.		Souvenir sheet of 1, perf. 13	1.75	1.75
		Nos. 403-406 (4)	2.50	2.50

Cent. of UPU. The 8s is inscribed "Air Mail"; 20s, "Sea Mail"; 22s, "Raft Mail."

Holy Family, by Sebastiano A85

Christmas: 4s, Virgin and Child with Saints, by Lotto. 10s, Virgin and Child with St. John, by Titian. 30s, Adoration of the Shepherds, by Rubens.

1974, Nov. 18 Litho. *Perf. 13x13½*

407	A85	3s ocher & multi	.15	.15
408	A85	4s fawn & multi	.15	.15
409	A85	10s dull green & multi	.25	.25
410	A85	30s blue & multi	.80	.80
a.		Souvenir sheet of 4, #407-410	1.40	1.40
		Nos. 407-410 (4)	1.35	1.35

Winged Passion Flower A86

20s, Gardenias, vert. 22s, Lecythidaceae, vert. 30s, Malay apple.

Perf. 14½
1975, Jan. 17 Litho. Wmk. 355

411	A86	8s dull yellow & multi	.25	.25
412	A86	20s pale pink & multi	.55	.55
413	A86	22s pink & multi	.60	.60
414	A86	30s lt green & multi	.85	.85
		Nos. 411-414 (4)	2.25	2.25

Joyita Loading at Apia — A87

Designs: 8s, Joyita, Samoa and Tokelau Islands. 20s, Joyita sinking, Oct. 1955. 22s, Rafts in storm. 50s, Plane discovering wreck.

1975, Mar. 14 Photo. *Perf. 13*

415 A87	1s multicolored	.15 .15
416 A87	8s multicolored	.15 .15
417 A87	20s multicolored	.45 .45
418 A87	22s multicolored	.55 .55
419 A87	50s multicolored	1.25 1.25
a.	Souvenir sheet of 5, #415-419	2.75 2.75
	Nos. 415-419 (5)	2.55 2.55

17th INTERPEX Phil. Exhib., NYC, Mar. 14-16.

Pate Drum — A88

Mother and Child, by Meleane Fe'ao — A89

1975, Sept. 30 Litho. *Perf. 14½x14*

420 A88	8s shown	.20 .20
421 A88	20s Lali drum	.50 .50
422 A88	22s Logo drum	.55 .55
423 A88	30s Pu shell horn	.75 .75
	Nos. 420-423 (4)	2.00 2.00

1975, Nov. 25 Litho. Wmk. 355

Christmas (Paintings): 4s, Christ Child and Samoan flag, by Polataia Tuigamala. 10s, "A Star is Born," by Iosua Toafa. 30s, Mother and Child, by Ernesto Coter.

424 A89	3s multicolored	.15 .15
425 A89	4s multicolored	.15 .15
426 A89	10s multicolored	.25 .25
427 A89	30s multicolored	.75 .75
a.	Souvenir sheet of 4, #424-427	1.40 1.40
	Nos. 424-427 (4)	1.30 1.30

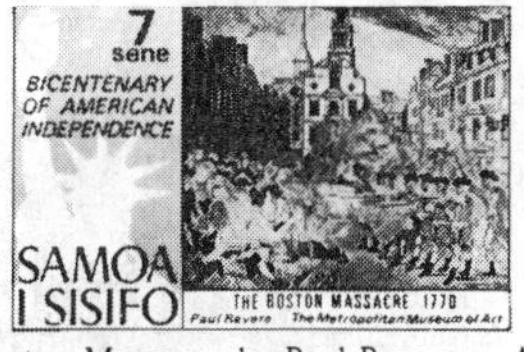

Boston Massacre, by Paul Revere — A90

8s, Declaration of Independence, by John Trumbull. 20s, The Sinking of the Bonhomme Richard, by J. L. G. Ferris. 22s, Wm. Pitt Addressing House of Commons, by R. A. Hickel. 50s, Battle of Princeton, by William Mercer.

Perf. 13½x14

1976, Jan. 20 Litho. Wmk. 355

428 A90	7s salmon & multi	.20 .20
429 A90	8s green & multi	.25 .25
430 A90	20s lilac & multi	.60 .60
431 A90	22s blue & multi	.65 .65
432 A90	50s yellow & multi	1.50 1.50
a.	Souvenir sheet of 5, #428-432 + label	5.50 5.50
	Nos. 428-432 (5)	3.20 3.20

Bicentenary of American Independence.

Mullet Fishing A91

1976, Apr. 27 Litho. *Perf. 14½*

433 A91	10s shown	.20 .20
434 A91	12s Fish traps	.25 .25
435 A91	22s Fishermen	.45 .45
436 A91	50s Net fishing	1.00 1.00
	Nos. 433-436 (4)	1.90 1.90

Souvenir Sheet

Samoan $100 Gold Coin with Paul Revere and US Map — A92

Unwmk.

1976, May 29 Photo. *Perf. 13*

437 A92	$1 green & gold	3.00 3.00

American Bicentennial and Interphil 76 Intl. Phil. Exhib., Philadelphia, PA, May 29-June 6.

Boxing A93

12s, Wrestling. 22s, Javelin. 50s, Weight lifting.

Perf. 14½x14

1976, June 21 Litho. Wmk. 355

438 A93	10s black & multi	.20 .20
439 A93	12s dark brown & multi	.25 .25
440 A93	22s dark purple & multi	.45 .45
441 A93	50s dark blue & multi	1.10 1.10
	Nos. 438-441 (4)	2.00 2.00

21st Olympic Games, Montreal, Canada, July 17-Aug. 1.

Mary and Joseph on Road to Bethlehem — A94

Christmas: 5s, Adoration of the Shepherds. 22s, Nativity. 50s, Adoration of the Kings.

1976, Oct. 18 Litho. *Perf. 14x13½*

442 A94	3s multicolored	.15 .15
443 A94	5s multicolored	.15 .15
444 A94	22s multicolored	.45 .45
445 A94	50s multicolored	1.25 1.25
a.	Souvenir sheet of 4, #442-445	2.50 2.50
	Nos. 442-445 (4)	2.00 2.00

Presentation of the Spurs of Chivalry — A95

Designs: 12s, Queen and view of Apia. 32s, Royal Yacht Britannia and Queen. 50s, Queen leaving Westminster Abbey.

Perf. 13½x14

1977, Feb. 11 Wmk. 355

446 A95	12s multicolored	.15 .15
447 A95	26s multicolored	.35 .35
448 A95	32s multicolored	.55 .55
449 A95	50s multicolored	.85 .85
	Nos. 446-449 (4)	1.90 1.90

25th anniv. of the reign of Elizabeth II.

Lindbergh and Spirit of St. Louis A96

Designs: 22s, Map of transatlantic route and plane. 24s, Spirit of St. Louis in flight. 26s, Spirit of St. Louis taking off.

1977, May 20 Litho. *Perf. 14*

450 A96	22s multicolored	.35 .35
451 A96	24s multicolored	.40 .40
452 A96	26s multicolored	.45 .45
453 A96	50s multicolored	.85 .85
a.	Souvenir sheet of 4, #450-453	2.50 2.50
	Nos. 450-453 (4)	2.05 2.05

Charles A. Lindbergh's solo transatlantic flight from New York to Paris, 50th anniv.

Apia Automatic Telephone Exchange A97

Designs: 13s, Mulinuu radio terminal. 26s, Old wall and new dial telephones. 50s, Global communications (2 telephones and globe).

1977, July 11 Litho. *Perf. 14*

454 A97	12s multicolored	.15 .15
455 A97	13s multicolored	.20 .20
456 A97	26s multicolored	.45 .45
457 A97	50s multicolored	.80 .80
	Nos. 454-457 (4)	1.60 1.60

Telecommunications.

Samoa No. 3 and First Mail Notice A98

13s, Samoa #4 & 1881 cover. 26s, Samoa #1 & Chief Post Office, Apia. 50s, Samoa #4 7 schooner "Energy," which carried 1st mail.

1977, Aug. 29 Wmk. 355 *Perf. 13½*

458 A98	12s multicolored	.15 .15
459 A98	13s multicolored	.20 .20
460 A98	26s multicolored	.40 .40
461 A98	50s multicolored	.80 .80
	Nos. 458-461 (4)	1.55 1.55

Samoan postage stamp centenary.

Nativity — A99

Christmas: 6s, People bringing gifts to Holy Family in Samoan hut. 26s, Virgin and Child. 50s, Stars over Christ Child.

1977, Oct. 11 Litho. *Perf. 14*

462 A99	4s multicolored	.15 .15
463 A99	6s multicolored	.15 .15
464 A99	26s multicolored	.35 .35
465 A99	50s multicolored	1.25 1.25
a.	Souvenir sheet of 4, #462-465	2.00 2.00
	Nos. 462-465 (4)	1.90 1.90

Polynesian Airlines' Boeing 737 — A100

Aviation Progress: 24s, Kitty Hawk. 26s, Kingsford-Smith Fokker. 50s, Concorde.

Unwmk.

1978, Mar. 21 Litho. *Perf. 14*

466 A100	12s multicolored	.20 .20
467 A100	24s multicolored	.45 .45
468 A100	26s multicolored	.50 .50
469 A100	50s multicolored	.95 .95
a.	Souvenir sheet of 4, #466-469, perf. 13½	3.00 3.00
	Nos. 466-469 (4)	2.10 2.10

Turtle Hatchery, Aleipata A101

$1, Hawksbill turtle & Wildlife Fund emblem.

1978, Apr. 14 Wmk. 355 *Perf. 14½*

470 A101	24s multicolored	*1.00 1.00*
471 A101	$1 multicolored	*4.25 4.25*

Project to replenish endangered hawksbill turtles.

Elizabeth II Coronation Anniversary Issue

Souvenir Sheet

Common Design Types

1978, Apr. 21 Unwmk. *Perf. 15*

472	Sheet of 6	3.00 3.00
a.	CD326 26s King's lion	.45 .45
b.	CD327 26s Elizabeth II	.45 .45
c.	CD328 26s Pacific pigeon	.45 .45

No. 472 contains 2 se-tenant strips of Nos. 472a-472c, separated by horizontal gutter with commemorative and descriptive inscriptions and showing central part of coronation procession with coach.

Souvenir Sheet

Canadian and Samoan Flags A102

Perf. 14½

1978, June 9 Wmk. 355 Litho.

473 A102	$1 multicolored	2.25 2.25

CAPEX Canadian Intl. Phil. Exhib., Toronto, June 9-18.

Capt. James Cook — A103

Designs: 24s, Cook's cottage, now in Melbourne, Australia. 26s, Old drawbridge over River Esk, Whitby, 1766-1833. 50s, Resolution and map of Hawaiian Islands.

1978, Aug. 28 Litho. *Perf. 14½x14*

474 A103	12s multicolored	.25 .25
475 A103	24s multicolored	.55 .55
476 A103	26s multicolored	.70 .70
477 A103	50s multicolored	1.40 1.40
	Nos. 474-477 (4)	2.90 2.90

A104 A105

Cowrie Shells: 1s, Thick-edged Cowrie. 2s, Isabella cowrie. 3s, Money cowrie. 4s, Eroded cowrie. 6s, Honey cowrie. 7s, Banded cowrie. 10s, Globe cowrie. 11s, Mole cowrie. 12s, Children's cowrie. 13s, Flag cone. 14s, Soldier cone. 24s, Cloth-of-gold cone. 26s, Lettered cone. 50s, Tiled cone. $1, Black marble cone. $2, Marlin-spike auger. $3, Scorpion spider conch. $5, Common harp.

1978-80 Photo. Unwmk. *Perf. 12½*
Size: 31x24mm
Granite Paper

478 A104 1s multicolored .15 .15
479 A104 2s multicolored .15 .15
480 A104 3s multicolored .15 .15
481 A104 4s multicolored .15 .15
482 A104 6s multicolored .15 .15
483 A104 7s multicolored .15 .15
484 A104 10s multicolored .15 .15
485 A104 11s multicolored .15 .15
486 A104 12s multicolored .15 .15
487 A104 13s multicolored .15 .15
488 A104 14s multicolored .15 .15
489 A104 24s multicolored .25 .25
490 A104 26s multicolored .25 .25
491 A104 50s multicolored .45 .45
492 A104 $1 multicolored .90 .90

Perf. 11½
Size: 36x26mm

493 A104 $2 multi ('79) 1.75 1.75
494 A104 $3 multi ('79) 3.00 3.00
494A A104 $5 multi ('80) 7.50 7.50
Nos. 478-494A (18) 15.75 15.75

Issue dates: 1s-12s, Sept. 15. 13s-$1, Nov. 20. $2, $3, July 18. $5, Aug. 26.

Wmk. 355
1978, Nov. 6 Litho. *Perf. 14*

Works by Dürer: 4s, The Virgin in Glory. 6s, Nativity. 26s, Adoration of the Kings. 50s, Annunciation.

495 A105 4s lt brown & blk .15 .15
496 A105 6s grnsh blue & blk .15 .15
497 A105 26s violet blue & blk .40 .40
498 A105 50s purple & blk .80 .80
a. Souvenir sheet of 4, #495-498 1.75 1.75
Nos. 495-498 (4) 1.50 1.50

Christmas and for 450th death anniv. of Albrecht Dürer.

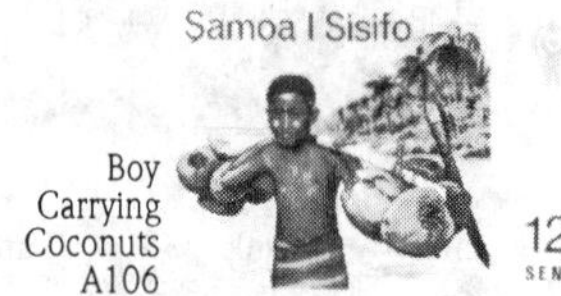

Boy Carrying Coconuts A106

Designs: 24s, Children leaving church on White Sunday. 26s, Children pumping water. 50s, Girl playing ukulele.

1979, Apr. 10 Litho. *Perf. 14*

499 A106 12s multicolored .20 .20
500 A106 24s multicolored .40 .40
501 A106 26s multicolored .45 .45
502 A106 50s multicolored .95 .95
Nos. 499-502 (4) 2.00 2.00

International Year of the Child.

Charles W. Morgan A107

1979, May 29 Litho. *Perf. 13½*

503 A107 12s multicolored .30 .30
504 A107 14s Lagoda .40 .40
505 A107 24s James T. Arnold .65 .65
506 A107 50s Splendid 1.40 1.40
Nos. 503-506 (4) 2.75 2.75

See Nos. 521-524, 543-546.

Saturn V Launch — A108

Penny Black, Hill Statue — A109

Designs: 14s, Landing module and astronaut on moon, horiz. 24s, Earth seen from moon. 26s, Astronaut on moon, horiz. 50s, Lunar and command modules. $1, Command module after splashdown, horiz.

Perf. 14½x14, 14x14½
1979, June 20 Litho. Wmk. 355

507 A108 12s multicolored .15 .15
508 A108 14s multicolored .15 .15
509 A108 24s multicolored .30 .30
510 A108 26s multicolored .35 .35
511 A108 50s multicolored .65 .65
512 A108 $1 multicolored 1.40 1.40
a. Souvenir sheet 1.75 1.75
Nos. 507-512 (6) 3.00 3.00

1st moon landing, 10th anniv.

1979, Aug. 27 *Perf. 14*

Designs: 24s, Great Britain No. 2 with Maltese Cross postmark. 26s, Penny Black and Rowland Hill. $1, Great Britain No. 2 and Hill statue.

513 A109 12s multicolored .15 .15
514 A109 24s multicolored .25 .25
515 A109 26s multicolored .30 .30
516 A109 $1 multicolored 1.10 1.10
a. Souvenir sheet of 4, #513-516 1.90 1.90
Nos. 513-516 (4) 1.80 1.80

Sir Rowland Hill (1795-1879), originator of penny postage.

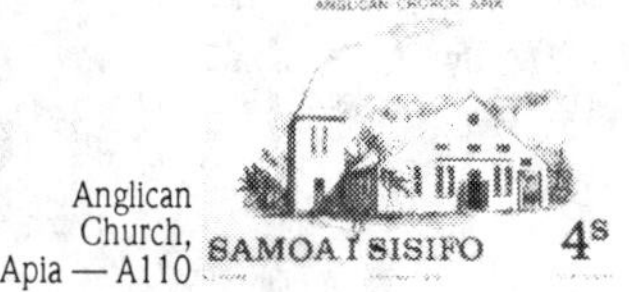

Anglican Church, Apia — A110

Samoan Churches: 6s, Congregational Christian Church, Leulumoega. 26s, Methodist Church, Piula. 50s, Protestant Church, Apia.

1979, Oct. 22 Photo. *Perf. 12x11½*

517 A110 4s lt blue & blk .15 .15
518 A110 6s lt yellow grn & blk .15 .15
519 A110 26s dull yellow & blk .40 .40
520 A110 50s lt lilac & blk .75 .75
a. Souvenir sheet of 4, #517-520 1.40 1.40
Nos. 517-520 (4) 1.45 1.45

Christmas.

Ship Type of 1979
Wmk. 355
1980, Jan. 22 Litho. *Perf. 14*

521 A107 12s William Hamilton .25 .25
522 A107 14s California .30 .30
523 A107 24s Liverpool II .55 .55
524 A107 50s Two Brothers 1.10 1.10
Nos. 521-524 (4) 2.20 2.20

Map of Samoan Islands, Rotary Emblem A111

Missionary Flag, John Williams, Plaque A112

Flag-raising Memorial A113

1980, Mar. 26 Photo. *Perf. 14*

525 A111 12s shown .15 .15
526 A112 13s shown .20 .20
527 A112 14s German flag, Dr. Wilhelm Solf, plaque .20 .20
528 A113 24s shown .35 .35
529 A113 26s Williams Memorial, Savai'i .40 .40
530 A111 50s Emblem, Paul P. Harris, founder .70 .70
Nos. 525-530 (6) 2.00 2.00

Rotary Intl., 75th anniv. (A111); arrival of Williams, missionary in Samoa, 150th anniv. (13s, 26s); raising of the German flag, 80th anniv. (14s, 24s).

Souvenir Sheet

Village and Long Boat — A114

Wmk. 355
1980, May 6 Litho. *Perf. 14*

531 A114 $1 multicolored 2.00 2.00

London 80 Intl. Phil. Exhib., May 6-14.

Queen Mother Elizabeth Birthday Issue
Common Design Type
1980, Aug. 4 Litho.

532 CD330 50s multicolored .70 .70

Souvenir Sheet

Samoa No. 239, ZEAPEX Emblem — A115

Unwmk.
1980, Aug. 23 Litho. *Perf. 14*

533 A115 $1 multicolored 2.00 2.00

ZEAPEX '80, New Zealand International Stamp Exhibition, Auckland, Aug. 23-31.

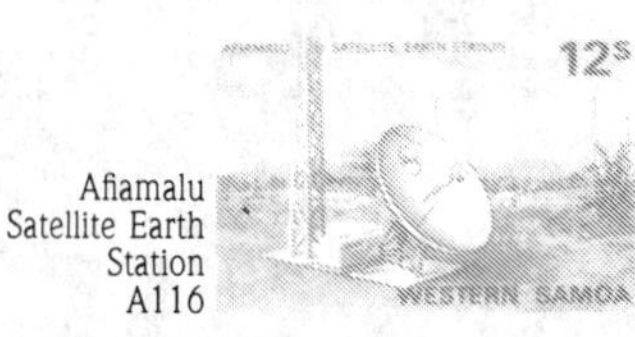

Afiamalu Satellite Earth Station A116

Designs: 14s, Station, diff. 24s, Station, map of Samoa. 50s, Satellite sending waves to earth. $2, Samoa No. 536, Sydpex '80 emblem.

1980, Sept. 17 Litho. *Perf. 11½*
Granite Paper

534 A116 12s multicolored .15 .15
535 A116 14s multicolored .20 .20
536 A116 24s multicolored .30 .30
537 A116 50s multicolored .70 .70
Nos. 534-537 (4) 1.35 1.35

Souvenir Sheet
1980, Sept. 29 *Imperf.*

538 A116 $2 multicolored 2.25 2.25

Sydpex '80 Natl. Phil. Exhib., Sydney.

The Savior, by John Poynton — A117

Christmas (Paintings by Local Artists): 14s, Madonna and Child, by Lealofi F. Siaopo. 27s, Nativity, by Pasila Feata. 50s, Yuletide, by R.P. Aiono.

Wmk. 355
1980, Oct. 28 Litho. *Perf. 14*

539 A117 8s multicolored .15 .15
540 A117 14s multicolored .15 .15
541 A117 27s multicolored .30 .30
542 A117 50s multicolored .50 .50
a. Souvenir sheet of 4, #539-542 1.40 1.40
Nos. 539-542 (4) 1.10 1.10

Ship Type of 1979
1981, Jan. 26 Litho. *Perf. 13½*

543 A107 12s Ocean .25 .25
544 A107 18s Horatio .40 .40
545 A107 27s Calliope .60 .60
546 A107 32s Calypso .70 .70
Nos. 543-546 (4) 1.95 1.95

Pres. Franklin Roosevelt and Hyde Park Home A118

IYD: Scenes of Franklin D. Roosevelt.

Wmk. 355
1981, Apr. 29 Litho. *Perf. 1*

547 A118 12s shown .15 .1
548 A118 18s Inauguration .20 .2
549 A118 27s Pres. & Mrs. Roosevelt .25 .2
550 A118 32s Atlantic convoy (Lend Lease Bill) .30 .3
551 A118 38s With stamp collection .35 .3
552 A118 $1 Campobello House .85 .8
Nos. 547-552 (6) 2.10 2.1

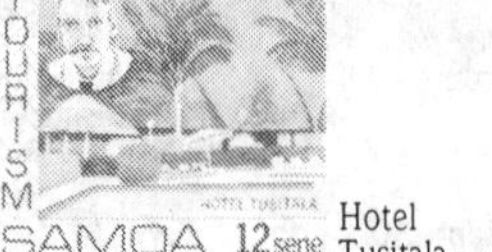

Hotel Tusitala — A119

Perf. 14½x14
1981, June 29 Litho. Wmk. 35

553 A119 12s shown .15 .1
554 A119 18s Apia Harbor .20 .2
555 A119 27s Aggie Grey's Hotel .30 .3
556 A119 32s Ceremonial kava preparation .35 .3
557 A119 54s Piula Pool .60 .6
Nos. 553-557 (5) 1.60 1.6

Royal Wedding Issue
Common Design Type
Wmk. 355
1981, July 22 Litho. *Perf. 1*

558 CD331 18s Bouquet .15 .1
559 CD331 32s Charles .20 .2
560 CD331 $1 Couple .65 .6
Nos. 558-560 (3) 1.00 1.0

Tattooing Instruments A120

1981, Sept. 29 Litho. *Perf. 13½x1*

561 Strip of 4 1.75 1.7
a. A120 12s shown .15 .1
b. A120 18s 1st stage .20 .2
c. A120 27s Later stage .30 .3
d. A120 $1 Tattooed man 1.10 1.1

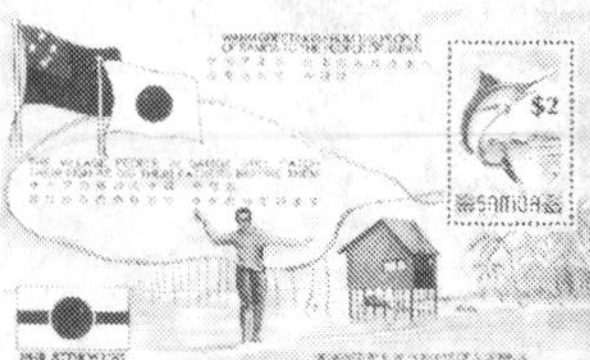

Christmas — A121

1981, Nov. 30 Litho. *Perf. 13¹/*

562 A121 11s Milo tree blossom .15 .1
563 A121 15s Copper leaf .15 .1
564 A121 23s Yellow allamanda .25 .2
565 A121 $1 Mango blossom 1.10 1.1
a. Souvenir sheet of 4, #562-565 2.25 2.2
Nos. 562-565 (4) 1.65 1.6

Souvenir Sheet

Philatokyo '81 Intl. Stamp Exhibition — A122

1981, Oct. 9 Litho. *Perf. 14x13¹/*

566 A122 $2 multicolored 2.25 2.2

250th Birth Anniv. of George Washington A123

1982, Feb. 26 Litho. *Perf. 14*

567 A123 23s Pistol .25 .25
568 A123 25s Mt. Vernon .30 .30
569 A123 34s Portrait .45 .45
Nos. 567-569 (3) 1.00 1.00

Souvenir Sheet

570 A123 $1 Taking oath 1.25 1.25

20th Anniv. of Independence A124

1982, May 24 Litho. *Perf. 13½x14*

571 A124 18s Freighter Forum Samoa .25 .25
572 A124 23s Jet, routes .30 .30
573 A124 25s Natl. Provident Fund building .35 .35
574 A124 $1 Intl. subscriber dialing system 1.25 1.25
Nos. 571-574 (4) 2.15 2.15

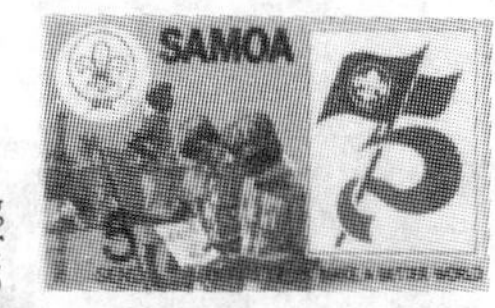

Scouting Year A125

1982, July 20 Wmk. 355 *Perf. 14½*

575 A125 5s Map reading .15 .15
576 A125 38s Salute .50 .50
577 A125 44s Rope bridge .60 .60
578 A125 $1 Troop 1.10 1.10
a. Souvenir sheet 1.50 1.50
Nos. 575-578 (4) 2.35 2.35

No. 578a contains one stamp similar to No. 578, 48x36mm.

12th Commonwealth Games, Brisbane, Australia, Sept. 30-Oct. 9 — A126

Perf. 14x14½

1982, Sept. 20 Wmk. 373

579 A126 23s Boxing .25 .25
580 A126 25s Hurdles .30 .30
581 A126 34s Weightlifting .40 .40
582 A126 $1 Lawn bowling 1.00 1.00
Nos. 579-582 (4) 1.95 1.95

Christmas A127

Children's Drawings: 11s, 15s, Flight into Egypt diff. 38s, $1, Virgin and Child, diff.

1982, Nov. 15 Litho. Wmk. 355

583 A127 11s multicolored .15 .15
584 A127 15s multicolored .20 .20
585 A127 38s multicolored .50 .50
586 A127 $1 multicolored 1.10 1.10
a. Souvenir sheet of 4, #583-586 2.00 2.00
Nos. 583-586 (4) 1.95 1.95

Commonwealth Day — A128

Perf. 13½x14

1983, Feb. 23 Litho. Wmk. 373

587 A128 14s Map .15 .15
588 A128 29s Flag .35 .35
589 A128 43s Harvesting copra .50 .50
590 A128 $1 Malietoa Tanumafili II 1.10 1.10
Nos. 587-590 (4) 2.10 2.10

Manned Flight Bicentenary and 50th Anniv. of Douglas Aircraft A129

Designs: a, DC-1. b, DC-2. c, DC-3. d, DC-4. e, DC-5. f, DC-6. g, DC-7. h, DC-8. i, DC-9. j, DC-10.

Wmk. 373

1983, June 7 Litho. *Perf. 14*

591 Sheet of 10 4.00 4.00
a.-j. A129 32s any single .40 .40

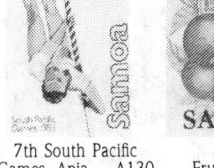

7th South Pacific Games, Apia — A130

Local Fruit — A131

1983, Aug. 29 Litho. *Perf. 14x14½*

592 A130 8s Pole vault .15 .15
593 A130 15s Basketball .15 .15
594 A130 25c Tennis .25 .25
595 A130 32s Weightlifting .35 .35
596 A130 35s Boxing .35 .35
597 A130 46s Soccer .50 .50
598 A130 48s Golf .55 .55
599 A130 56s Rugby .60 .60
Nos. 592-599 (8) 2.90 2.90

Perf. 14x13½

1983-84 Litho. Wmk. 373

600 A131 1s Limes .15 .15
601 A131 2s Star fruit .15 .15
602 A131 3s Mangosteen .15 .15
603 A131 4s Lychee .15 .15
604 A131 7s Passion fruit .15 .15
605 A131 8s Mangoes .15 .15
606 A131 11s Papaya .15 .15
607 A131 13s Pineapple .15 .15
608 A131 14s Breadfruit .15 .15
609 A131 15s Bananas .20 .20
610 A131 21s Cashew nut .25 .25
611 A131 25s Guava .30 .30
612 A131 32s Water Melon .35 .35
613 A131 48s Sasalapa .55 .55
614 A131 56s Avocado .65 .65
615 A131 $1 Coconut 1.10 1.10

Perf. 13½

616 A131 $2 Apples ('84) 2.25 2.25
617 A131 $4 Grapefruit ('84) 4.50 4.50
618 A131 $5 Oranges ('84) 5.50 5.50
Nos. 600-618 (19) 17.00 17.00

Issued: 1s-15s, 9/28; 21s-$1, 11/30; $2-$5, 4/11.

For overprint see No. 628.

Miniature Sheet

Boys' Brigade Centenary — A132

1983, Oct. 10 *Perf. 14½*

619 A132 $1 multicolored 1.00 1.00

Togitogiga Falls, Upolu A133

Wmk. 373

1984, Feb. 15 Litho. *Perf. 14*

620 A133 25s shown .25 .25
621 A133 32s Lano Beach, Savai'i .30 .30
622 A133 48s Mulinu'u Point, Upolu .45 .45
623 A133 56s Nu'utele Isld. .50 .50
Nos. 620-623 (4) 1.50 1.50

Lloyd's List Issue

Common Design Type

Perf. 14½x14

1984, May 24 Litho. Wmk. 373

624 CD335 32s Apia Harbor .30 .30
625 CD335 48s Apia hurricane, 1889 .50 .50
626 CD335 60s Forum Samoa .60 .60
627 CD335 $1 Matua 1.00 1.00
Nos. 624-627 (4) 2.40 2.40

No. 615 Overprinted: "19th U.P.U. CONGRESS / HAMBURG 1984"

1984, June 7 *Perf. 14x13½*

628 A131 $1 multicolored 1.25 1.25

Los Angeles Coliseum A134

1984, June 26 Litho. *Perf. 14½*

629 A134 25s shown .25 .25
630 A134 32s Weightlifting .35 .35
631 A134 48s Boxing .55 .55
632 A134 $1 Running 1.10 1.10
a. Souvenir sheet of 4, #629-632 2.25 2.25
Nos. 629-632 (4) 2.25 2.25

1984 Summer Olympics and Samoa's first Olympic participation.

Souvenir Sheet

Ausipex '84 A135

1984, Sept. 21 Litho. *Perf. 14*

633 A135 $2.50 Nomad N24 3.25 3.25

Christmas — A136

The Three Virtues, by Raphael.

1984, Nov. 7 *Perf. 14½x14*

634 A136 25s Faith .25 .25
635 A136 35s Hope .30 .30
636 A136 $1 Charity .95 .95
a. Souvenir sheet of 3, #634-636 1.50 1.50
Nos. 634-636 (3) 1.50 1.50

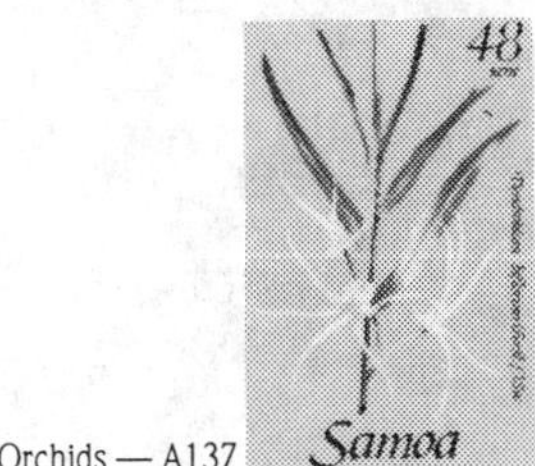

Orchids — A137

Unwmk.

1985, Jan. 23 Litho. *Perf. 14*

637 A137 48s Dendrobium biflorum .75 .45
638 A137 56s Dendrobium vaupelianum kraenzl .90 .90
639 A137 67s Glomera montana 1.10 1.10
640 A137 $1 Spathoglottis plicata 1.65 1.65
Nos. 637-640 (4) 4.40 4.10

Vintage Automobiles — A138

Wmk. 373

1985, Mar. 26 Litho. *Perf. 14*

641 A138 48s Ford Model A, 1903 .65 .65
642 A138 56s Chevrolet Tourer, 1912 .75 .75
643 A138 67s Morris Oxford, 1913 .85 .85
644 A138 $1 Austin Seven, 1923 1.40 .95
Nos. 641-644 (4) 3.65 3.20

Fungi — A139

1985, Apr. 17 Litho. *Perf. 14½*

645 A139 48s Dictyophora indusiata .70 .70
646 A139 56s Ganoderma tornatum .85 .85
647 A139 67s Mycena chlorophos .95 .95
648 A139 $1 Mycobonia flava 1.50 1.50
Nos. 645-648 (4) 4.00 4.00

Queen Mother 85th Birthday

Common Design Type

Perf. 14½x14

1985, June 7 Litho. Wmk. 384

649 CD336 32s Photo., age 9 .30 .30
650 CD336 48s With Prince William at christening of Prince Henry .50 .50
651 CD336 56s At Liverpool street station .60 .60
652 CD336 $1 Holding Prince Henry 1.00 1.00
Nos. 649-652 (4) 2.40 2.40

Souvenir Sheet

653 CD336 $2 Arriving at Tattenham corner station 2.00 2.00

Souvenir Sheet

EXPO '85, Tsukuba, Japan — A140

Unwmk.

1985, Aug. 26 Litho. *Perf. 14*

654 A140 $2 Emblem, elevation map 1.75 1.75

Intl. Youth Year — A141

Christmas 1985 — A142

Portions of world map and: a, Emblem, map of No. America, Europe and Africa. b, Hands reaching high. c, Arms reaching, hands limp. d, Hands clenched. e, Emblem and map of Africa, Asia and Europe.

1985, Sept. 18 **Wmk. 373**

655 Strip of 5 2.75 2.75
a.-e. A141 60s any single .55 .55

1985, Nov. 5 Unwmk. *Perf. 14x14½*

Illustrations by Millicent Sowerby from A Child's Garden of Verses, by Robert Louis Stevenson.

656 A142 32s System .30 .30
657 A142 48s Time to Rise .40 .40
658 A142 56s Auntie's skirts .50 .50
659 A142 $1 Good Children .90 .90
a. Souvenir sheet of 4, #656-659 2.10 2.10
Nos. 656-659 (4) 2.10 2.10

Butterflies — A143

1986, Feb. 13 Wmk. 384 *Perf. 14½*

660 A143 25s Hypolimnas bolina inconstans .40 .40
661 A143 32s Anapheis java sparrman .50 .50
662 A143 48s Deudorix epijarbas doris .70 .70
663 A143 56s Badamia exclamationis .85 .85
664 A143 60s Tirumala hamata mellitula 1.00 1.00
665 A143 $1 Catochrysops taitensis 1.75 1.75
Nos. 660-665 (6) 5.20 5.20

Halley's Comet A144

Designs: 32s, Comet over Apia. 48s, Edmond Halley, astronomer. 60s, Comet orbiting the Earth. $2, Giotto space probe under construction at British Aerospace.

1986, Mar. 24

666 A144 32s multicolored .30 .30
667 A144 48s multicolored .40 .40
668 A144 60s multicolored .55 .55
669 A144 $2 multicolored 1.75 1.75
Nos. 666-669 (4) 3.00 3.00

Queen Elizabeth II 60th Birthday
Common Design Type

Designs: 32s, Engagement to the Duke of Edinburgh, 1947. 48s, State visit to US, 1976. 56s, Attending outdoor ceremony, Apia, 1977. 67s, At Badminton Horse Trials, 1978. $2, Visiting Crown Agents' offices, 1983.

1986, Apr. 21

670 CD337 32s scarlet, blk & sil .30 .30
671 CD337 48s ultra & multi .40 .40
672 CD337 56s green & multi .50 .50
673 CD337 67s violet & multi .60 .60
674 CD337 $2 rose violet & multi 1.75 1.75
Nos. 670-674 (5) 3.55 3.55

AMERIPEX '86, Chicago, May 22-June 1 — A145

1986, May 22 **Unwmk.**

675 A145 48s USS Vincennes .40 .40
676 A145 56s Sikorsky S-42 .50 .50
677 A145 60s USS Swan .55 .55
678 A145 $2 Apollo 10 splashdown 1.75 1.75
Nos. 675-678 (4) 3.20 3.20

Souvenir Sheet

Vailima, Estate of Novelist Robert Louis Stevenson, Upolu Is. — A146

1986, Aug. 4 Litho. *Perf. 13½*

679 A146 $3 multicolored 3.25 3.25

STAMPEX '86, Adelaide, Aug. 4-10.

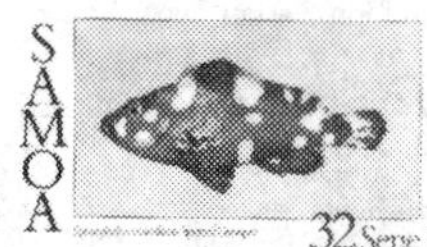

Fish — A147

Unwmk.
1986, Aug. 13 Litho. *Perf. 14*

680 A147 32s Spotted grouper .30 .30
681 A147 48s Sabel squirrelfish .45 .45
682 A147 60s Lunartail grouper .55 .55
683 A147 67s Longtail snapper .70 .70
684 A147 $1 Berndt's soldierfish 1.10 1.10
Nos. 680-684 (5) 3.10 3.10

US Peace Corps in Samoa, 25th Anniv. A148

Statesmen: Vaai Kolone of Samoa, Ronald Reagan of US and: 45s, Fiame Mata'afa, John F. Kennedy (1961) and Parliament House. 60s, Jules Grevy, Grover Cleveland (1886) and the Statue of Liberty.

1986, Dec. 1 *Perf. 14½*

685 A148 45s multicolored .40 .40
686 A148 60s multicolored .55 .55
a. Souvenir sheet of 2, #685-686 2.00 2.00

Christmas, Statue of Liberty, cent.

Natl. Independence, 25th Anniv. — A149

Perf. 14x14½
1987, Feb. 16 Litho. Unwmk.

687 A149 15s Map, hibiscus .15 .15
688 A149 45s Parliament .60 .60
689 A149 60s Rowing race, 1987 .80 .80
690 A149 70s Dove .90 .90
691 A149 $2 Prime minister, flag 2.50 2.50
Nos. 687-691 (5) 4.95 4.95

Nos. 687-690 vert.

Marine Life A150

1987, Mar. 31

692 A150 45s Gulper .45 .45
693 A150 60s Hatchet-fish .60 .60
694 A150 70s Angler .70 .70
695 A150 $2 Gulper, diff. 1.90 1.90
Nos. 692-695 (4) 3.65 3.65

Souvenir Sheet

CAPEX '87 — A151

1987, June 13 *Perf. 14½*

696 A151 $3 Logger, construction workers 2.75 2.75

Landscapes A152

1987, July 29 *Perf. 14*

697 A152 45s Lefaga Beach, Upolu .40 .40
698 A152 60s Vaisala Beach, Savaii .55 .55
699 A152 70s Solosolo Beach, Upolu .65 .65
700 A152 $2 Neiafu Beach, Savaii 1.90 1.90
Nos. 697-700 (4) 3.50 3.50

Australia Bicentennial A153

Explorers of the Pacific: 40s, Abel Tasman (c. 1603-1659), Dutch navigator, discovered Tasmania, 1642. 45s, James Cook. 80s, Count Louis-Antoine de Bougainville (1729-1811), French navigator, discovered Bougainvelle Is., largest of the Solomon Isls., 1768. $2, Comte de La Perouse (1741-1788), French navigator, discovered La Perouse Strait.

1987, Sept. 30 Litho. *Perf. 14½*

701 A153 40s multicolored .35 .35
702 A153 45s multicolored .45 .45
703 A153 80s multicolored .80 .80
704 A153 $2 multicolored 1.90 1.90
a. Souvenir sheet of 1 1.90 1.90
Nos. 701-704 (4) 3.50 3.50

No. 704a Ovptd. with HAFNIA '87 Emblem in Scarlet

1987, Oct. 16

705 A153 $2 multicolored 2.00 2.00

Christmas 1987 — A154

1987, Nov. 30 *Perf. 14*

706 A154 40s Christmas tree .35 .35
707 A154 45s Going to church .45 .45
708 A154 50s Bamboo fire-gun .50 .50
709 A154 80s Going home .75 .75
Nos. 706-709 (4) 2.05 2.05

Australia Bicentennial A155

a, Samoan natl. crest, Australia Post emblem. b, Two jets, postal van. c, Loading airmail. d, Jet, van, postman. e, Congratulatory aerogramme.

1988, Jan. 27 *Perf. 14½*

710 Strip of 5 3.00 3.00
a.-e. A155 45s any single .60 .60

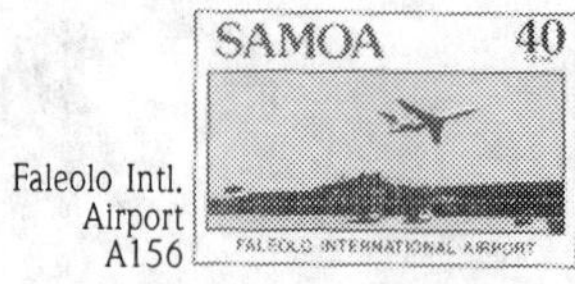

Faleolo Intl. Airport A156

Perf. 13x13½
1988, Mar. 24 Litho. Unwmk

711 A156 40s Terminal, Boeing 727 .40 .4
712 A156 45s Boeing 727, Fuatino .45 .4
713 A156 60s So. Pacific Is. N43SP, terminal .60 .6
714 A156 70s Air New Zealand Boeing 737 .70 .7
715 A156 80s Tower, jet .80 .8
716 A156 $1 Hawaiian Air DC-9, VIP house 1.00 1.0
Nos. 711-716 (6) 3.95 3.9

EXPO '88, Brisbane, Australia A157

1988, Apr. 27 *Perf. 14½*

717 A157 45s Island village display .45 .4
718 A157 70s EXPO complex, monorail and flags .70 .7
719 A157 $2 Map 2.00 2.0
Nos. 717-719 (3) 3.15 3.1

Souvenir Sheet

Arrival of the Latter Day Saints in Samoa, Cent. — A158

1988, June 9 Litho. *Perf. 13½*

720 A158 $3 The Temple, Apia 3.00 3.0

1988 Summer Olympics, Seoul — A159

Birds — A160

1988, Aug. 10 Litho. *Perf. 14*

721 A159 15s Running .15 .1
722 A159 60s Weight lifting .60 .6
723 A159 80s Boxing .80 .8
724 A159 $2 Olympic Stadium 2.00 2.0
a. Souvenir sheet of 4, #721-724 3.55 3.5
Nos. 721-724 (4) 3.55 3.5

1988-89 Unwmk. *Perf. 13½*

725 A160 10s Polynesian triller .15 .1
726 A160 15s Samoan wood rail .15 .1
727 A160 20s Flat-billed kingfisher .20 .2
728 A160 25s Samoan fantail .25 .2
729 A160 35s Scarlet robin .35 .3
730 A160 40s Mao .40 .4
731 A160 50s Cardinal honeyeater .50 .5
732 A160 65s Samoan whistler .60 .6
733 A160 75s Many-colored fruit dove .75 .7
734 A160 85s White-throated pigeon .80 .8

Perf. 14
Size:45x39mm

735 A160 75s Silver gull .75 .7
736 A160 85s Great frigatebird .80 .8
737 A160 90s Eastern reef heron .85 .8
738 A160 $3 Short-tailed albatross 3.00 3.0

739 A160 $10 Common fairy tern 9.25 9.25
740 A160 $20 Shy albatross 19.00 19.00
Nos. 725-740 (16) 37.80 37.80

Issue dates: #725-734, 8/17/88; #735-738, 2/28/89; #739-740, 7/31/89.

Conservation — A161

1988, Oct. 25 *Perf. 14*
741 A161 15s Forests, vert. .15 .15
742 A161 40s Culture, vert. .40 .40
743 A161 45s Wildlife, vert. .45 .45
744 A161 50s Water .50 .50
745 A161 60s Marine resources .60 .60
746 A161 $1 Land and soil .95 .95
Nos. 741-746 (6) 3.05 3.05

Christmas — A162 Orchids — A163

Designs: 15s, 40s, Congregational Church of Jesus, Apia. 40s, Roman Catholic Church, Leauvaa. 45s, Congregational Christian Church, Moataa. $2, Baha'i Temple, Vailima.

Perf. 14x14½
1988, Nov. 14 Litho. Unwmk.
747 A162 15s multicolored .15 .15
748 A162 40s multicolored .40 .40
749 A162 45s multicolored .45 .45
750 A162 $2 multicolored 2.00 2.00
a. Souvenir sheet of 4, #747-750 3.00 3.00
Nos. 747-750 (4) 3.00 3.00

1989, Jan. 31 Litho. *Perf. 14*
751 A163 15s Phaius flavus .20 .20
752 A163 45s Calanthe triplicata .65 .65
753 A163 60s Luisia teretifolia .85 .85
754 A163 $3 Dendrobium mohlianum 4.50 4.50
Nos. 751-754 (4) 6.20 6.20

Apia Hurricane, 1889 — A164

1989, Mar. 16 Litho. Unwmk.
755 Strip of 4 4.50 4.50
a. A164 50s SMS Eber .55 .55
b. A164 65s SMS Olga .70 .70
c. A164 85s SMS Calliope .95 .95
d. A164 $2 SMS Vandalia 2.25 2.25
e. Souv. sheet of 2, #c.-d., imperf. 4.00 4.00

World Stamp Expo '89.
#755e, issued Nov. 17, is wmk. 355.

Intl. Red Cross and Red Crescent Organizations, 125th Annivs. — A165

1989, May 15 *Perf. 14½x14*
756 A165 50s Youths in parade .45 .45
757 A165 65s Blood donation .60 .60
758 A165 75s First Aid .70 .70
759 A165 $3 Volunteers 2.75 2.75
Nos. 756-759 (4) 4.50 4.50

Moon Landing, 20th Anniv.
Common Design Type

Apollo 14: 18s, Saturn-Apollo vehicle and mobile launcher. 50s, Alan Shepard, Stuart Roosa and Edgar Mitchell. 65s, Mission emblem. $2, Tracks of the modularised equipment transporter. $3, Buzz Aldrin and American flag raised on the Moon, Apollo 11 mission.

1989, July 20 Wmk. 384 *Perf. 14*
Size of Nos. 761-762: 29x29mm
760 CD342 18s multicolored .15 .15
761 CD342 50s multicolored .45 .45
762 CD342 65s multicolored .60 .60
763 CD342 $2 multicolored 1.75 1.75
Nos. 760-763 (4) 2.95 2.95

Souvenir Sheet
764 CD342 $3 multicolored 2.75 2.75

"Roosa" is misspelled on No. 761.

Christmas A166

Perf. 13½x13
1989, Nov. 1 Litho. Unwmk.
765 A166 18s Joseph and Mary .15 .15
766 A166 50s Shepherds .45 .45
767 A166 55s Animals .50 .50
768 A166 $2 Three kings 1.75 1.75
Nos. 765-768 (4) 2.85 2.85

Local Transport — A167

Designs: 18s, Pao pao (outrigger canoe). 55s, Fautasi (longboat). 60s, Polynesian Airlines propeller plane. $3, Lady Samoa ferry.

1990, Jan. 31 Unwmk. *Perf. 14x15*
769 A167 18s multicolored .15 .15
770 A167 55s multicolored .45 .45
771 A167 60s multicolored .55 .55
772 A167 $3 multicolored 2.60 2.60
Nos. 769-772 (4) 3.75 3.75

Otto von Bismarck, Brandenburg Gate — A168

1990, May 3 *Perf. 14x13½*
773 A168 75s shown .65 .65
774 A168 $3 SMS Adler 2.50 2.50
a. Pair, #773-774 3.25 3.25

Opening of the Berlin Wall, 1989, and cent. of the Treaty of Berlin (in 1989). No. 774a has a continuous design.

Great Britain No. 1 and Alexandra Palace — A169

Illustration reduced.

1990, May 3
775 A169 $3 multicolored 2.50 2.50

Stamp World London '90 and 150th anniv. of the Penny Black.

Tourism A170

1990, July 30 Litho. *Perf. 14*
776 A170 18s Visitors Bureau .16 .16
777 A170 50s Samoa Village Resorts .45 .45
778 A170 65s Aggies Hotel .60 .60
779 A170 $3 Tusitala Hotel 2.75 2.75
Nos. 776-779 (4) 3.96 3.96

Souvenir Sheet

No. 240, Exhibition Emblem — A171

1990, Aug. 24 Litho. *Perf. 13*
780 A171 $3 multicolored 2.30 2.30

World Stamp Exhib., New Zealand 1990.

Christmas — A172

Paintings of Madonna and Child.

1990, Oct. 31 *Perf. 12½*
781 A172 18s Bellini .15 .15
782 A172 50s Bouts .45 .45
783 A172 55s Correggio .50 .50
784 A172 $3 Cima 2.75 2.75
Nos. 781-784 (4) 3.85 3.85

The 55s is "The School of Love," not "Madonna of the Basket."

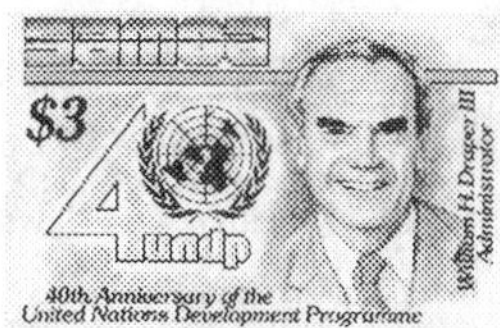

UN Development Program, 40th Anniv. — A173

1990, Nov. 26 *Perf. 13½*
785 A173 $3 multicolored 2.75 2.75

Parrots — A174

1991, Apr. 8 Litho. *Perf. 13½*
786 A174 18s Black-capped lory .20 .20
787 A174 50s Eclectus parrot .55 .55
788 A174 65s Scarlet macaw .70 .70
789 A174 $3 Palm cockatoo 3.25 3.25
Nos. 786-789 (4) 4.70 4.70

Elizabeth & Philip, Birthdays
Common Design Types
Perf. 14½
1991, June 17 Litho. Wmk. 384
790 CD346 75s multicolored .60 .60
791 CD345 $2 multicolored 1.65 1.65
a. Pair, #790-791 + label 2.25 2.25

Souvenir Sheet

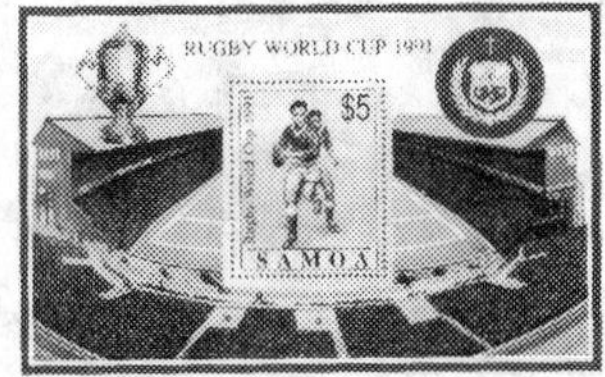

1991 Rugby World Cup — A175

1991, Oct. 12 Litho. *Perf. 14½*
792 A175 $5 multicolored 5.00 5.00

Christmas A176

Orchids and Christmas carols: 20s, O Come All Ye Faithful. 60s, Joy to the World. 75s, Hark! the Herald Angels Sing. $4, We Wish You a Merry Christmas.

1991, Oct. 31 Litho. *Perf. 14½*
793 A176 20s multicolored .20 .20
794 A176 60s multicolored .55 .50
795 A176 75s multicolored .70 .70
796 A176 $4 multicolored 3.50 3.50
Nos. 793-796 (4) 4.95 4.90

See Nos. 815-818, 836-840.

Phila Nippon '91 A177

Samoan hawkmoths: 60s, Herse convolvuli. 75s, Gnathothlibus erotus. 75s, Hippotion celerio. $3, Cephonodes armatus.

1991, Nov. 16 *Perf. 13½x14*
797 A177 60s multicolored .60 .60
798 A177 75s multicolored .75 .75
799 A177 85s multicolored .90 .90
800 A177 $3 multicolored 3.00 3.00
Nos. 797-800 (4) 5.25 5.25

Independence, 30th Anniv. — A178

1992, Jan. 8 Litho. *Perf. 14*
801 A178 50s Honor guard .40 .40
802 A178 65s Siva scene .50 .50
803 A178 $1 Parade float .80 .80
804 A178 $3 Raising flag 2.50 2.50
Nos. 801-804 (4) 4.20 4.20

Queen Elizabeth II's Accession to the Throne, 40th Anniv.
Common Design Type
1992, Feb. 6 Wmk. 384
805 CD349 20s multicolored .15 .15
806 CD349 60s multicolored .50 .50
807 CD349 75s multicolored .60 .60
808 CD349 85s multicolored .70 .70

Wmk. 373
809 CD349 $3 multicolored 2.50 2.50
Nos. 805-809 (5) 4.45 4.45

Souvenir Sheet

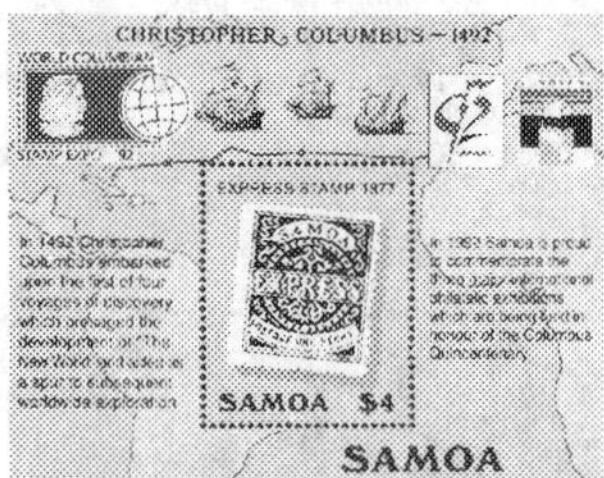

Discovery of America, 500th Anniv. — A179

1992, Apr. 17 Unwmk. *Perf. 14½*
810 A179 $4 No. 1 3.25 3.25

World Columbian Stamp Expo '92, Granada '92 and Genoa '92 Philatelic Exhibitions.

1992 Summer Olympics, Barcelona — A180

1992, July 28 Wmk. 373 *Perf. 14*
811 A180 60s Weight lifting .50 .50
812 A180 75s Boxing .65 .65
813 A180 85s Running .75 .75
814 A180 $3 Stadium, statue 2.60 2.60
Nos. 811-814 (4) 4.50 4.50

Christmas Type of 1991

Christmas carol, orchid: 50s, "God rest you, merry gentlemen...," liparis layardii. 60s, "While shepherds watched...," corymborkis veratrifolia. 75s, "Away in a manger...," phaius flavus. $4, "O little town...," bulbophyllum longifolium.

1992, Oct. 28 Litho. *Perf. 14½*
815 A176 50s multicolored .45 .45
816 A176 60s multicolored .50 .50
817 A176 75s multicolored .65 .65
818 A176 $4 multicolored 3.50 3.50
Nos. 815-818 (4) 5.10 5.10

Fish A182

1993, Mar. 17 Litho. *Perf. 14*
819 A182 60s Batfish .55 .55
820 A182 75s Lined surgeonfish .65 .65
821 A182 $1 Red-tail snapper .90 .90
822 A182 $3 Long-nosed emperor 2.75 2.75
Nos. 819-822 (4) 4.85 4.85

World Cup Seven-a-Side Rugby Championships, Scotland — A183

60s, Team performing traditional dance. 75c, Two players. 85c, Player. $3, Edinburgh Castle.

1993, May 12 *Perf. 13½x14*
823 A183 60s multi .50 .50
824 A183 75s multi, vert. .60 .60
825 A183 85s multi, vert. .70 .70
826 A183 $3 multi 2.25 2.25
Nos. 823-826 (4) 4.05 4.05

Bats A184

1993, June 10 *Perf. 14x14½*
827 A184 20s Two hanging .15 .15
828 A184 50s Two flying .40 .40
829 A184 60s Three flying .50 .50
830 A184 75s One on flower .55 .55
Nos. 827-830 (4) 1.60 1.60

World Wildlife Fund.

Souvenir Sheet

Taipei '93, Asian Intl. Invitation Stamp Exhibition — A185

Illustration reduced.

1993, Aug. 16 Litho. *Perf. 14*
831 A185 $5 multicolored 4.00 4.00

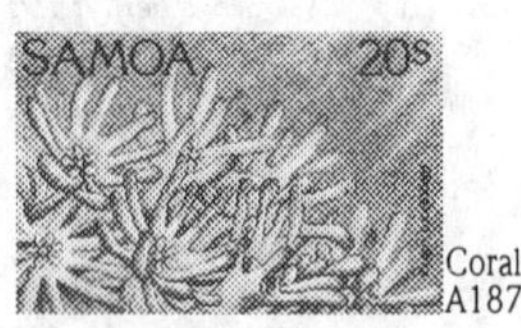

World Post Day A186

Designs: 60s, Globe, letter, flowers. 75s, Customers at Post Office. 85s, Black, white hands exchanging letter. $4, Globe, national flags, letter.

1993, Oct. 8 Litho. *Perf. 14*
832 A186 60s multicolored .45 .45
833 A186 75s multicolored .55 .55
834 A186 85s multicolored .65 .65
835 A186 $4 multicolored 3.00 3.00
Nos. 832-835 (4) 4.65 4.65

Christmas Type of 1991

Flowers, Christmas carol: 20s, "Silent Night! Holy Night!..." 60s, "As with gladness men of old..." 75s, "Mary had a Baby, Yes Lord..." $1.50, "Once in Royal David's City..." $3, "Angels, from the realms of Glory..."

Perf. 14½
1993, Nov. 1 Litho. Unwmk.
836 A176 20s multicolored .15 .15
837 A176 60s multicolored .45 .45
838 A176 75s multicolored .55 .55
839 A176 $1.50 multicolored 1.10 1.10
840 A176 $3 multicolored 2.25 2.25
Nos. 836-840 (5) 4.50 4.50

Corals A187

1994, Feb. 18 Litho. *Perf. 14*
841 A187 20s Alveropora allingi .15 .15
842 A187 60s Acropora polystoma .45 .45
843 A187 90s Acropora listeri .70 .70
844 A187 $4 Acropora grandis 3.00 3.00
Nos. 841-844 (4) 4.30 4.30

Ovptd. with Hong Kong '94 Emblem

1994, Feb. 18
845 A187 20s on #841 .15 .15
846 A187 60s on #842 .45 .45
847 A187 90s on #843 .70 .70
848 A187 $4 on #844 3.00 3.00
Nos. 845-848 (4) 4.30 4.30

Manu Samoa Rugby Team A188

Designs: 70s, Management. 90s, Test match with Wales. 95s, Test match with New Zealand. $4, Apia Park Stadium.

1994, Apr. 11 Litho. *Perf. 14*
849 A188 70s multicolored .50 .50
850 A188 90s multicolored .65 .65
851 A188 95s multicolored .70 .70
852 A188 $4 multicolored 3.00 3.00
Nos. 849-852 (4) 4.85 4.85

Souvenir Sheet

PHILAKOREA '94 — A189

Butterflies: $5, White caper, glasswing. Illustration reduced.

1994, Aug. 16 Litho. *Perf. 13*
853 A189 $5 multicolored 4.00 4.00

Teuila Tourism Festival A190

1994, Sept. 22 Litho. *Perf. 13½*
854 A190 70s Singers .55 .55
855 A190 90s Fire dancer .70 .70
856 A190 95s Parade float .75 .75
857 A190 $4 Police band 3.25 3.25
Nos. 854-857 (4) 5.25 5.25

A191 A192

1994, Nov. 21 *Perf. 14*
858 A191 70s Schooner Equator .55 .55
859 A191 90s Portrait .70 .70
860 A191 $1.20 Tomb, Mount Vaea .95 .95
861 A191 $4 Vailima House, horiz. 3.25 3.25
Nos. 858-861 (4) 5.45 5.45

Robert Louis Stevenson (1850-94), writer.

1994, Nov. 30

Children's Christmas paintings: 70s, Father Christmas. 95s, Nativity. $1.20, Picnic. $4, Greetings.

862 A192 70s multicolored .55 .55
863 A192 95s multicolored .75 .75
864 A192 $1.20 multicolored .95 .95
865 A192 $4 multicolored 3.25 3.25
Nos. 862-865 (4) 5.50 5.50

Scenic Views A193

Designs: 5s, Lotofaga Beach, Aleipata. 10s, Nuutele Island. 30s, Satuiatua, Savaii. 50s, Sinalele, Aleipata. 60s, Paradise Beach, Lefaga. 70s, Houses, Piula Cave. 80s, Taga blowholes. 90s, View from east coast road. 95s, Canoes, Leulumoega. $1, Parliament Building.

1995 Litho. *Perf. 14½x13*
866 A193 5s multicolored .15 .15
867 A193 10s multicolored .15 .15
871 A193 30s multicolored .25 .25
874 A193 50s multicolored .40 .40
875 A193 60s multicolored .50 .50
876 A193 70s multicolored .55 .55
877 A193 80s multicolored .65 .65
878 A193 90s multicolored .70 .70
879 A193 95s multicolored .75 .75
880 A193 $1 multicolored .80 .80
Nos. 866-880 (10) 4.90 4.90

Issued: Nos. 866-867, 871, 874-880, 3/29/95. This is an expanding set. Numbers may change.

1995 World Rugby Cup Championships, South Africa — A194

Designs: 70s, Players under age 12. 90s, Secondary Schools' rugby teams. $1, Manu Samoa test match with New Zealand. $4, Ellis Park Stadium, Johannesburg.

1995, May 25 Litho. *Perf. 14x13½*
886 A194 70s multicolored .55 .55
887 A194 90s multicolored .70 .70
888 A194 $1 multicolored .80 .80
889 A194 $4 multicolored 3.25 3.25
Nos. 886-889 (4) 5.30 5.30

End of World War II, 50th Anniv.
Common Design Types

Designs: 70s, OS2U Kingfisher over Faleolo Air Base. 90s, F4U Corsair, Faleolo Air Base. 95s, US troops in landing craft. $3, US Marines landing on Samoan beach. $4, Reverse of War Medal 1939-45.

1995, May 31 Litho. *Perf. 13½*
890 CD351 70s multicolored .55 .55
891 CD351 90s multicolored .70 .70
892 CD351 95s multicolored .75 .75
893 CD351 $3 multicolored 2.50 2.50
Nos. 890-893 (4) 4.50 4.50

Souvenir Sheet
Perf. 14
894 CD352 $4 multicolored 3.25 3.25

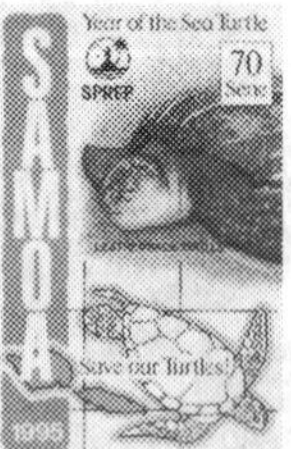

Year of the Sea Turtle — A195

1995, Aug. 24 Litho. *Perf. 13x13½*
895 A195 70s Leatherback .55 .55
896 A195 90s Loggerhead .70 .70
897 A195 $1 Green turtle .80 .80
898 A195 $4 Pacific Ridley 3.25 3.25
Nos. 895-898 (4) 5.30 5.30

Souvenir Sheet

Singapore '95 — A196

1995, Sept. 1 *Perf. 14*
899 A196 $5 Phaius tankervilleae 4.00 4.00

See No. 935.

UN, 50th Anniv.
Common Design Type

70s, Mobile hospital. 90s, Bell Sioux helicopter. $1, Bell 212 helicopter. $4, RNZAF Andover.

Unwmk.
1995, Oct. 24 Litho. *Perf. 14*
900 CD353 70s multicolored .55 .55
901 CD353 90s multicolored .70 .70
902 CD353 $1 multicolored .80 .80
903 CD353 $4 multicolored 3.25 3.25
Nos. 900-903 (4) 5.30 5.30

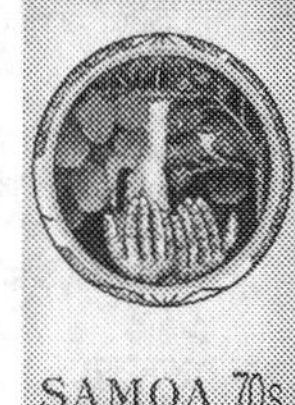

A197 A198

1995, Nov. 15 *Perf. 14½*
904 A197 25s Madonna & Child .20 .20
905 A197 70s Wise Man .55 .55
906 A197 90s Wise Man, diff. .70 .70
907 A197 $5 Wise Man, diff. 4.00 4.00
Nos. 904-907 (4) 5.45 5.45

Christmas.

1996, Jan. 26 Litho. *Perf. 14*

Importance of Water: 70s, Waterfall, bird, woman, hands. 90s, Girl standing under fountain, "WATER FOR LIFE." $2, Outline of person's head containing tree, birds, waterfall, girl. $4, Community receiving water from protected watersheds.

908 A198 70s multicolored .55 .55
909 A198 90s multicolored .70 .70
910 A198 $2 multicolored 1.50 1.50
911 A198 $4 multicolored 3.00 3.00
Nos. 908-911 (4) 5.75 5.75

Queen Elizabeth II, 70th Birthday
Common Design Type

Various portraits of Queen, Samoan scenes: 70s, Apia, Main Street. 90s, Neiafu beach. $1, Official residence of Head of State. $3, Parliament Building. $5, Queen wearing tiara, formal dress.

Perf. 14½
1996, Apr. 22 Litho. Unwmk.
912 CD354 70s multicolored .55 .55
913 CD354 90s multicolored .75 .75
914 CD354 $1 multicolored .80 .80
915 CD354 $3 multicolored 2.50 2.50
Nos. 912-915 (4) 4.60 4.60

Souvenir Sheet
916 CD354 $5 multicolored 4.25 4.25

Souvenir Sheet

Moon Festival — A199

Illustration reduced.

1996, May 18 Litho. *Perf. 14*
917 A199 $2.50 multicolored 2.00 2.00

CHINA '96.

Souvenir Sheet

63rd Session of African-Carribean-Pacific-European Union Council of Ministers — A200

Illustration reduced.

1996, June 19 Litho. *Perf. 13½*
918 A200 $5 multicolored 4.00 4.00

A201 A202

1996, July 15 Litho. *Perf. 13½*
919 A201 70s Boxing .60 .60
920 A201 90s Running .75 .75
921 A201 $1 Weight lifting .80 .80
922 A201 $4 Javelin 3.25 3.25
Nos. 919-922 (4) 5.40 5.40

1996 Summer Olympic Games, Atlanta.

1996, Sept. 13 Litho. *Perf. 14*
923 A202 60s Logo .50 .50
924 A202 70s Pottery .60 .60
925 A202 80s Stained glass .65 .65
926 A202 90s Dancing .75 .75
927 A202 $1 Wood carving .80 .80
928 A202 $4 Samoan chief 3.25 3.25
Nos. 923-928 (6) 6.55 6.55

7th Pacific Festival of Arts, Apia.

UNICEF, 50th Anniv. — A203

70s, Children in doctor's waiting room. 90s, Children in hospital undergoing treatment. $1, Child receiving injection. $4, Mothers, children playing.

1996, Oct. 24 Litho. *Perf. 14*
929 A203 70s multicolored .60 .60
930 A203 90s multicolored .75 .75
931 A203 $1 multicolored .80 .80
932 A203 $4 multicolored 3.25 3.25
Nos. 929-932 (4) 5.40 5.40

Souvenir Sheet

Many-Colored Fruit Dove — A204

Illustration reduced.

1997, Feb. 3 Litho. *Perf. 14*
933 A204 $3 multicolored 2.50 2.50

Hong Kong '97.

Souvenir Sheet

1st US Postage Stamps, 150th Anniv., 1st Samoan Postage Stamps, 120th Anniv. — A205

1997, May 29 Litho. *Perf. 14½*
934 A205 $5 US #2, Samoa #1 4.25 4.25

PACIFIC 97.

Phaius Tankervilleae Type of 1995
Souvenir Sheet
Perf. 14½
1997, June 20 Litho. Wmk. 373
935 A196 $2.50 multicolored 2.00 2.00

Return of Hong Kong to China, July 1, 1997.

Queen Elizabeth II & Prince Philip, 50th Wedding Anniv. — A206

#936, Queen. #937, Prince at reins of team, Royal Windsor Horse Show, 1996. #938, Queen, horse. #939, Prince laughing, horse show, 1995. #940, Zara Philips, Balmoral 1993, Prince Philip. #941, Queen, Prince William.
$5, Queen, Prince, Royal Ascot 1988.

1997, July 10 Unwmk. *Perf. 13*
936 A206 70s multicolored .60 .60
937 A206 70s multicolored .60 .60
a. Pair, #936-937 1.20 1.20
938 A206 90s multicolored .75 .75
939 A206 90s multicolored .75 .75
a. Pair, #938-939 1.50 1.50
940 A206 $1 multicolored .80 .80
941 A206 $1 multicolored .80 .80
a. Pair, #940-941 1.60 1.60
Nos. 936-941 (6) 4.30 4.30

Souvenir Sheet
942 A206 $5 multicolored 4.00 4.00

Greenpeace, 26th Anniv. — A207

Dolphins: 50s, #947a, Jumping out of water. 60s, #947b, Two swimming right. 70s, #947c, Two facing front. $1, #947d, With mouth open out of water.

1997, Sept. 17 Litho. *Perf. 13½x14*
943 A207 50s multicolored .40 .40
944 A207 60s multicolored .50 .50
945 A207 70s multicolored .60 .60
946 A207 $1 multicolored .80 .80
Nos. 943-946 (4) 2.30 2.30

Miniature Sheet
947 A207 $1.25 Sheet of 4, #a.-d. 4.00 4.00

Christmas A208

1997, Nov. 26 Litho. *Perf. 14*
948 A208 70s Bells .60 .60
949 A208 80s Ornament .65 .65
950 A208 $2 Candle 1.65 1.65
951 A208 $3 Star 2.50 2.50
Nos. 948-951 (4) 5.40 5.40

Mangroves — A209

Bruguiera gymnorrhiza: 70s, Fruit on trees. 80s, Saplings. $2, Roots. $4, Tree at water's edge.

1998, Feb. 26 Litho. *Perf. 13½*
952 A209 70s multicolored .60 .60
953 A209 80s multicolored .65 .65
954 A209 $2 multicolored 1.60 1.60
955 A209 $4 multicolored 3.20 3.20
Nos. 952-955 (4) 6.05 6.05

Diana, Princess of Wales (1961-97)
Common Design Type

Designs: a, Up close portrait. b, Wearing checkered jacket. c, In red dress. d, Holding flowers.

Perf. 14½x14
1997, Mar. 31 Litho. Unwmk.
956 CD355 $1.40 Sheet of 4, #a.-d. 12.75 12.75

No. 956 sold for $5.60 + 75c, with surtax from international sales being donated to the Princess Diana Memorial Fund and surtax from national sales being donated to designated local charity.

Royal Air Force, 80th Anniversary
Common Design Type of 1993
Re-Inscribed

Designs: 70s, Westland Wallace. 80s, Hawker Fury. $2, Vickers Varsity. $5, BAC Jet Provost.
No. 961: a, Norman-Thompson N.T.2b. b, Nieuport 27 Scout. c, Miles Magister. d, Bristol Bombay.

1998, Apr. 1 *Perf. 13½*
957 CD350 70s multicolored .60 .60
958 CD350 80s multicolored .65 .65
959 CD350 $2 multicolored 1.60 1.60
960 CD350 $5 multicolored 4.00 4.00
Nos. 957-960 (4) 6.85 6.85

Miniature Sheet
961 CD350 $2 Sheet of 4, #a.-d. 6.50 6.50

SEMI-POSTAL STAMP

Catalogue values for unused stamps in this section are for Never Hinged items.

No. 246 Surcharged: "HURRICANE RELIEF / 6d"
Perf. 13½
1966, Sept. 1 Wmk. 355 Litho.
B1 A43 8p + 6p blue & emerald .25 .25

Surtax for aid to plantations destroyed by the hurricane of Jan. 29, 1966.

AIR POST STAMPS

Catalogue values for unused stamps in this section are for Never Hinged items.

Red-tailed Tropic Bird — AP1

Perf. 14½

1965, Dec. 29 Wmk. 355 Photo.

C1	AP1	8p shown	.25	.25
C2	AP1	2sh Flying fish	.65	.65

Sir Gordon Taylor's Bermuda Flying Boat "Frigate Bird III" — AP2

Designs: 7s, Polynesian Airlines DC-3. 20s, Pan American Airways "Samoan Clipper." 30s, Air Samoa Britten-Norman "Islander."

Perf. 13½x13

1970, July 27 Photo. Unwmk.

C3	AP2	3s multicolored	.15	.15
C4	AP2	7s multicolored	.30	.30
C5	AP2	20s multicolored	.90	.90
C6	AP2	30s multicolored	1.40	1.40
		Nos. C3-C6 (4)	2.75	2.75

Hawker Siddeley 748 — AP3

Planes at Faleolo Airport: 10s, Hawker Siddeley 748 in the air. 12s, Hawker Siddeley 748 on ground. 22s, BAC 1-11 planes on ground.

1973, Mar. 9 *Perf. 11½*

Granite Paper

C7	AP3	8s multicolored	.30	.30
C8	AP3	10s multicolored	.40	.40
C9	AP3	12s multicolored	.45	.45
C10	AP3	22s multicolored	.85	.85
		Nos. C7-C10 (4)	2.00	2.00

SAN MARINO

ˌsan mə-ˈrē-(ˌ)nō

LOCATION — Eastern Italy, about 20 miles inland from the Adriatic Sea
GOVT. — Republic
AREA — 24.1 sq. mi.
POP. — 21,622 (1981)
CAPITAL — San Marino

100 Centesimi = 1 Lira

Catalogue values for unused stamps in this country are for Never Hinged items, beginning with Scott 412 in the regular postage section, Scott B39 in the semi-postal section, Scott C97 in the airpost section, Scott E26 in the special delivery section, and Scott Q40 in the parcel post section.

Watermarks

Wmk. 140- Crown

Wmk. 174- Coat of Arms

Wmk. 217- Three Plumes

Wmk. 277- Winged Wheel

Wmk. 303- Multiple Stars

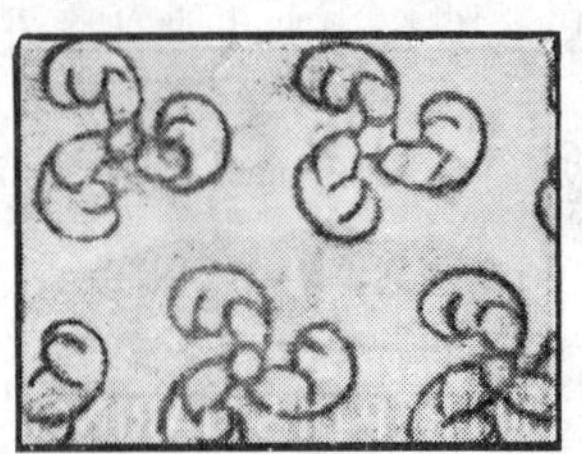
Wmk. 339- Triskelion

Numeral — A1

Coat of Arms — A2

1877-99 Typo. Wmk. 140 *Perf. 14*

1	A1	2c green	5.50	1.90
2	A1	2c blue ('94)	3.00	1.90
3	A1	2c claret ('95)	2.50	1.75
4	A2	5c orange ('90)	50.00	5.50
5	A2	5c olive grn ('92)	1.50	.85
6	A2	5c green ('99)	1.50	.70
7	A2	10c ultra	55.00	5.50
a.		10c blue ('90)	175.00	22.50
8	A2	10c dk green ('92)	1.90	1.00
9	A2	10c claret ('99)	1.50	.90
10	A2	15c claret ('94)	100.00	21.00
11	A2	20c vermilion	7.50	1.90
12	A2	20c lilac ('95)	1.90	1.50
13	A2	25c maroon ('90)	60.00	5.50
14	A2	25c blue ('99)	1.75	1.40
15	A2	30c brown	500.00	24.00
16	A2	30c org yel ('92)	3.00	1.75
17	A2	40c violet	475.00	25.00
18	A2	40c dk brown ('92)	2.25	1.75
19	A2	45c gray grn ('92)	2.25	1.75
20	A2	65c red brown ('92)	2.25	1.75
21	A2	1 l car & yel ('92)	1,100.	275.00
22	A2	1 l lt blue ('95)	1,000.	250.00
23	A2	2 l brn & yel ('94)	30.00	26.00
24	A2	5 l vio & grn ('94)	80.00	70.00

See Nos. 911-915.

Nos. 7a, 15, 11 Surcharged in Black **Cmi. 5**

1892

25	A2	5c on 10c blue	32.50	6.25
a.		Inverted surcharge	32.50	6.25
b.		5c on 10c ultramarine	*20,000.*	*2,750.*
c.		As "b," inverted surcharge	*20,000.*	*2,750.*
26	A2	5c on 30c brown	225.00	40.00
a.		Inverted surcharge	225.00	40.00
b.		Double surch., one inverted	225.00	85.00
c.		Double invtd. surcharge	225.00	85.00
27	A2	10c on 20c ver	20.00	2.25
a.		Inverted surcharge	22.50	4.00
b.		Double surch., one inverted	20.00	7.00
c.		Double surcharge	20.00	7.00
		Nos. 25-27 (3)	277.50	48.50

Ten to twelve varieties of each surcharge.

No. 11 Surcharged **10 10**

28	A2	10c on 20c ver	175.00	3.00

Government Palace and Portraits of Regents, Tonnini and Marcucci
A6 A7

Portraits of Regents and View of Interior of Palace — A8

Perf. 15½

1894, Sept. 30 Litho. Wmk. 174

29	A6	25c blue & dk brn	2.00	.75
30	A7	50c dull red & dk brn	13.00	1.50
31	A8	1 l green & dk brown	13.00	1.75
		Nos. 29-31 (3)	28.00	4.00

Opening of the new Government Palace and the installation of the new Regents.

Statue of Liberty — A9

Wmk. 140

1899-1922 Typo. *Perf. 14*

32	A9	2c brown	.70	.45
33	A9	2c claret ('22)	.15	.15
34	A9	5c brown org	1.00	.90
35	A9	5c olive grn ('22)	.15	.15
36	A9	10c brown org ('22)	.15	.15
37	A9	20c dp brown ('22)	.15	.15
38	A9	25c ultra ('22)	.20	.20
39	A9	45c red brown ('22)	.60	.60
		Nos. 32-39 (8)	3.10	2.75

Numeral of Value — A10

Mt. Titano — A11

1903-25 *Perf. 14, 14½x14*

40	A10	2c violet	5.25	.70
41	A10	2c orange brn ('21)	.15	.15
42	A11	5c blue grn	1.50	.30
43	A11	5c olive grn ('21)	.15	.15
44	A11	5c red brn ('25)	.15	.15
45	A11	10c claret	1.50	.30
46	A11	10c brown org ('21)	.15	.15
47	A11	10c olive grn ('25)	.15	.15
48	A11	15c blue grn ('22)	.15	.15
49	A11	15c brown vio ('25)	.15	.15
50	A11	20c brown orange	40.00	7.25
51	A11	20c brown ('21)	.15	.15
52	A11	20c blue grn ('25)	.15	.15
53	A11	25c blue	5.50	1.25
54	A11	25c gray ('21)	.15	.15
55	A11	25c violet ('25)	.15	.15
56	A11	30c brown red	2.75	2.75
57	A11	30c claret ('21)	.15	.15
58	A11	30c orange ('25)	3.75	.45
59	A11	40c orange red	3.50	3.00
60	A11	40c dp rose ('21)	.20	.20
61	A11	40c brown ('25)	.15	.15
62	A11	45c yellow	3.50	3.00
63	A11	50c brown vio ('23)	.30	.30
64	A11	50c gray blk ('25)	.15	.15
65	A11	60c brown red ('25)	.20	.20
66	A11	65c chocolate	3.50	3.00
67	A11	80c blue ('21)	.30	.30
68	A11	90c brown ('23)	.30	.30
69	A11	1 l olive green	10.00	5.50
70	A11	1 l ultra ('21)	.30	.30
71	A11	1 l lt blue ('25)	.20	.20
72	A11	2 l violet	450.00	140.00
73	A11	2 l orange ('21)	8.00	8.00
74	A11	2 l lt green ('25)	2.00	1.40
75	A11	5 l slate	70.00	70.00
76	A11	5 l ultra ('25)	7.25	7.00
		Nos. 40-76 (37)	621.90	257.80

For overprints and surcharges see Nos. 77, 93-96, 103, 107, 188-189, B1-B2, E2, E4.

No. 50 Surcharged **1905 15**

1905, Sept. 1

77	A11	15c on 20c brown org	4.50	1.50
a.		Large 5 in 1905 on level with 9	30.00	19.00

Coat of Arms
A12 A13

Two types:
I - Width 18½mm.
II - Width 19mm.

1907-10 Unwmk. Engr. *Perf. 12*

78	A12	1c brown, II ('10)	1.10	.55
a.		Type I	2.00	.80
79	A13	15c gray, I	9.00	1.40
a.		Type II ('10)	110.00	7.25

No. 79a Surcharged in Brown **Cent. 20 1918**

1918, Mar. 15

80	A13	20c on 15c gray	1.40	1.25

St. Marinus — A14

Perf. 14½x14, 14x14½

1923, Aug. 11 Typo. Wmk. 140

81	A14	30c dark brown	.30	.30

San Marino Intl. Exhib. of 1923. Proceeds from the sale of this stamp went to a mutual aid society.

Italian Flag and Views of Arbe and Mt. Titano A15

1923, Aug. 6

82	A15	50c olive green	.30	.30

Presentation to San Marino of the Italian flag which had flown over the island of Arbe, the birthplace of the founder of San Marino. Inscribed on back: "V. Moraldi dis. Blasi inc. Petiti impr.-Roma."

Mt. Titano and Sword — A16

1923, Sept. 29 *Perf. 14x14½*

83 A16 1 l dark brown 4.50 4.50

In honor of the San Marino Volunteers who were killed or wounded in WWI.

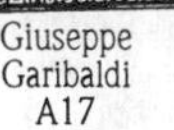
Giuseppe Garibaldi A17

Allegory-San Marino Sheltering Garibaldi A18

1924, Sept. 25 *Perf. 14*

84 A17 30c dark violet .60 .60
85 A17 50c olive brown .60 .60
86 A17 60c dull red 1.65 1.65
87 A18 1 l deep blue 2.50 2.50
88 A18 2 l gray green 3.25 3.25
Nos. 84-88 (5) 8.60 8.60

75th anniv. of Garibaldi's taking refuge in San Marino.

Semi-Postal Stamps of 1918 Surcharged with New Values and Bars

Cmi 30

1924, Oct. 9

89 SP1 30c on 45c yel brn & blk .30 .30

Surcharged

LIRE UNA

90 SP2 60c on 1 l bl grn & blk 3.25 2.50
91 SP2 1 l on 2 l vio & blk 7.75 7.25
92 SP2 2 l on 3 l red brn & blk 5.75 5.00
Nos. 89-92 (4) 17.05 15.05

Nos. 67 and 68 Surcharged in Black or Red — Lire 1,20

1926, July 1

93 A11 75c on 80c blue .35 .35
94 A11 1.20 l on 90c brown .35 .35
95 A11 1.25 l on 90c brn (R) 1.65 1.25
96 A11 2.50 l on 80c blue (R) 2.75 2.75
Nos. 93-96 (4) 5.10 4.70

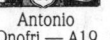

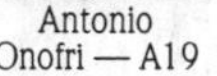
Antonio Onofri — A19

A20

Unwmk.

1926, July 29 **Engr.** *Perf. 11*

97 A19 10c dk blue & blk .15 .15
98 A19 20c olive grn & blk .55 .40
99 A19 45c dk vio & blk .35 .35
100 A19 65c green & blk .35 .35
101 A19 1 l orange & blk 1.50 1.00
102 A19 2 l red vio & blk 2.50 1.50
Nos. 97-102 (6) 5.40 3.75

For surcharges see Nos. 104-106, 181-182.

Special Delivery Stamp No. E2 surcharged with New Value and Bars

Perf. 14½x14

1926, Nov. 25 **Wmk. 140**

103 A20 1.85 l on 60c violet .40 .40

Nos. 101 and 102 Surcharged 1,25

1927, Mar. 10 **Unwmk.** *Perf. 11*

104 A19 1.25 l on 1 l 1.10 1.10
105 A19 2.50 l on 2 l 3.00 3.00
106 A19 5 l on 2 l 21.00 21.00
Nos. 104-106 (3) 25.10 25.10

Type of Special Delivery Stamp of 1923 Surcharged — L. 1,75

1927, Sept. 15 **Wmk. 140** *Perf. 14*

107 A11 1.75 l on 50c on 25c vio .45 .45

The 50c on 25c violet was not issued without 1.75-lire surcharge.

War Memorial A21

Unwmk.

1927, Sept. 28 **Engr.** *Perf. 12*

108 A21 50c brown violet .65 .65
109 A21 1.25 l blue 1.10 1.10
110 A21 10 l gray 9.00 9.00
Nos. 108-110 (3) 10.75 10.75

Erection of a cenotaph in memory of the San Marino volunteers in WWI.

Capuchin Church and Convent A22

Design: 2.50 l, 5 l, Death of St. Francis.

1928, Jan. 2

111 A22 50c red 10.50 1.10
112 A22 1.25 l dp blue 1.75 1.10
113 A22 2.50 l dk brown 1.75 1.10
114 A22 5 l dull violet 12.00 10.50
Nos. 111-114 (4) 26.00 13.80

7th centenary of the death of St. Francis of Assisi.
For surcharges see Nos. 183-184.

The Rocca (State Prison) — A24

Government Palace — A25

Statue of Liberty — A26

1929-35 **Wmk. 217**

115 A24 5c vio brn & ultra .15 .15
116 A24 10c bl gray & red vio .15 .15
117 A24 15c dp org & emer .15 .15
118 A24 20c dk bl & org red .15 .15
119 A24 25c grn & gray blk .15 .15
120 A24 30c gray brn & red .15 .15
121 A24 50c red vio & ol gray .15 .15
122 A24 75c dp red & gray blk .15 .15
123 A25 1 l dk brn & emer .15 .15
124 A25 1.25 l dk blue & blk .15 .15
125 A25 1.75 l green & org .15 .15
126 A25 2 l bl gray & red .15 .15
127 A25 2.50 l car rose & ultra .15 .15
128 A25 3 l dp org & bl .15 .15
129 A25 3.70 l ol blk & red brn ('35) .18 .18
130 A26 5 l dk vio & dk grn .20 .20
131 A26 10 l bis brn & dk bl 3.50 3.50
132 A26 15 l green & red vio 35.00 35.00
133 A26 20 l dk blue & red 190.00 165.00
Nos. 115-133 (19) 230.98 205.98

General Post Office — A27

San Marino-Rimini Electric Railway — A28

1932, Feb. 4

134 A27 20c blue green 2.00 .85
135 A27 50c dark red 3.50 1.75
136 A27 1.25 l dark blue 125.00 55.00
137 A27 1.75 l dark brown 52.50 27.50
138 A27 2.75 l dark violet 15.00 10.00
Nos. 134-138 (5) 198.00 95.10

Opening of new General Post Office.
For surcharges see Nos. 151-160.

1932, June 11

139 A28 20c deep green .55 .55
140 A28 50c dark red .80 .80
141 A28 1.25 l dark blue 1.50 1.50
142 A28 5 l deep brown 27.50 22.50
Nos. 139-142 (4) 30.35 25.35

Opening of the new electric railway between San Marino and Rimini.

Giuseppe Garibaldi A29

Garibaldi's Arrival at San Marino A30

1932, July 30

143 A29 10c violet brown .60 .60
144 A29 20c violet .30 .30
145 A29 25c green .55 .55
146 A29 50c yellow brn 2.00 1.75
147 A30 75c dark red 2.00 1.75
148 A30 1.25 l dark blue 4.00 4.00
149 A30 2.75 l brown orange 15.00 15.00
150 A30 5 l olive green 200.00 200.00
Nos. 143-150 (8) 224.45 223.95

Garibaldi (1807-1882), Italian patriot.

Nos. 138 and 137 Surcharged — 50 CENT 28 MAGGIO 1933 CONVEGNO FILATELICO

1933, May 27

151 A27 25c on 2.75 l .75 .55
152 A27 50c on 1.75 l 2.00 1.75
153 A27 75c on 2.75 l 11.00 11.00
154 A27 1.25 l on 1.75 l 200.00 200.00
Nos. 151-154 (4) 213.75 213.30

Convention of philatelists, San Marino, May 28.

Nos. 134-137 Surcharged in Black — 0,50 12-27 APRILE 1934 MOSTRA FILATELICA

1934, Apr. 12

155 A27 25c on 1.25 l .48 .48
156 A27 50c on 1.75 l .70 .70
157 A27 75c on 50c 2.00 2.00
158 A27 1.25 l on 20c 13.00 13.00
Nos. 155-158 (4) 16.18 16.18

San Marino's participation (with a philatelic pavilion) in the 15th annual Trade Fair at Milan, Apr. 12-27.

Nos. 136 and 138 Surcharged Wheel and New Value

1934, Apr. 12

159 A27 3.70 l on 1.25 l 50.00 50.00
160 A27 3.70 l on 2.75 l 50.00 50.00

Ascent to Mt. Titano A31

Unwmk.

1935, Feb. 7 **Engr.** *Perf. 14*

161 A31 5c choc & blk .15 .15
162 A31 10c dk vio & blk .15 .15
163 A31 20c orange & blk .15 .15
164 A31 25c green & blk .15 .15
165 A31 50c olive bis & blk .20 .20
166 A31 75c brown red & blk 1.25 1.25
167 A31 1.25 l blue & blk 2.50 2.50
Nos. 161-167 (7) 4.55 4.55

12th anniv. of the founding of the Fascist Movement.

Melchiorre Delfico — A32

Statue of Delfico — A33

1935, Apr. 15 **Wmk. 217** *Perf. 12*

Center in Black

169 A32 5c brown lake .15 .15
170 A32 7½c lt brown .15 .15
171 A32 10c dk blue grn .15 .15
172 A32 15c rose carmine 4.00 1.00
173 A32 20c orange .15 .15
174 A32 25c green .15 .15
175 A33 30c dull violet .15 .15
176 A33 50c olive green 1.40 .55
177 A33 75c red 4.00 4.00
178 A33 1.25 l dark blue 1.25 .95
179 A33 1.50 l dk brown 20.00 18.00
180 A33 1.75 l brown org 26.00 25.00
Nos. 169-180 (12) 57.55 50.40

Melchiorre Delfico (1744-1835), historian.
For surcharges see Nos. 202, 277.

Nos. 99-100 Surcharged in Black

80

Nos. 112-113 Surcharged in Black

L. 2,05

1936 **Unwmk.** *Perf. 11*

181 A19 80c on 45c dk vio & blk 1.50 1.50
182 A19 80c on 65c grn & blk 1.50 1.50

Perf. 12

183 A22 2.05 l on 1.25 l 4.00 4.00
184 A22 2.75 l on 2.50 l 14.00 14.00
Nos. 181-184 (4) 21.00 21.00

Issued: #181-182, 4/14; #183-184, 8/23.

San Marino stamps can be mounted in the annual Scott San Marino supplement.

Souvenir Sheet

Design from Base of Roman Column A34

1937, Aug. 23 Engr. Wmk. 217

185 A34 5 l steel blue 8.50 8.50

Unveiling of the Roman Column at San Marino. The date "1636 d. F. R." means the 1,636th year since the founding of the republic.

No. 185 was privately surcharged "+ 10 L 1941."

Souvenir Sheets

Abraham Lincoln — A35

1938, Apr. 7 Wmk. 217 *Perf. 13*

186 A35 3 l dark blue .85 .85
187 A35 5 l rose red 9.50 9.50

Dedication of a Lincoln bust, Sept. 3, 1937.

No. 49 and Type of 1925 Surcharged with New Value in Black

1941 Wmk. 140 *Perf. 14*

188 A11 10c on 15c brown vio .15 .15
189 A11 10c on 30c brown org .55 .40

Flags of Italy and San Marino — A36

Harbor of Arbe — A37

1942 Photo.

190 A36 10c yel brn & brn org .15 .15
191 A36 15c brn & red brn .15 .15
192 A36 20c gray grn & gray blk .15 .15
193 A36 25c green & blue .15 .15
194 A36 50c brn red & brn .15 .15
195 A36 75c red & gray blk .15 .15
196 A37 1.25 l bl & gray bl .15 .15
197 A37 1.75 l brn & grnsh blk .22 .22
198 A37 2.75 l bis brn & gray bl .38 .38
199 A37 5 l green & brown 2.25 2.25
Set value 3.35 3.45

Return of the Italian flag to Arbe.

No. 190 Surcharged in Black

GIORNATA FILATELICA
3 AGOSTO 1942
(1641 d. F. R.)
RIMINI • SAN MARINO
C.——30

1942, July 30

200 A36 30c on 10c .28 .28

Rimini-San Marino Stamp Day, Aug. 3.

No. 192 Surcharged with New Value and Bars in Black

1942, Sept. 14

201 A36 30c on 20c .20 .20

No. 177 Surcharged with New Value in Black

1942, Sept. 28 Wmk. 217 *Perf. 12*

202 A33 20 l on 75c red & blk 6.75 6.75

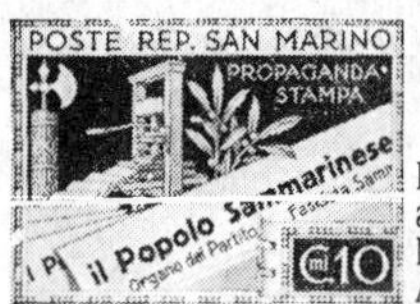

Printing Press and Newspaper A38

Newspapers — A39

Wmk. 140

1943, Apr. 12 Photo. *Perf. 14*

203 A38 10c deep green .15 .15
204 A38 15c bister .15 .15
205 A38 20c dk orange brn .15 .15
206 A38 30c dk rose vio .15 .15
207 A38 50c blue black .15 .15
208 A38 75c red orange .15 .15
209 A39 1.25 l blue .15 .15
210 A39 1.75 l deep violet .15 .15
211 A39 5 l slate .18 .18
212 A39 10 l dark brown 1.75 1.75
Set value 2.45 2.60

Nos. 206 and 207 Overprinted in Red

GIORNATA FILATELICA
RIMINI - SAN MARINO
5 LUGLIO 1943
(1642 d. F. R.)

1943, July 1

213 A38 30c dk rose vio .15 .15
214 A38 50c blue black .15 .15
Set value .20 .20

Rimini-San Marino Stamp Day, July 5.

A40

A41

Overprinted in Black: "28 LVGLIO 1943 1642 F. R."

1943, Aug. 27

215 A40 5c brown .15 .15
216 A40 10c orange red .15 .15
217 A40 20c ultra .15 .15
218 A40 25c deep green .15 .15
219 A40 30c brown carmine .15 .15
220 A40 50c deep violet .15 .15
221 A40 75c car rose .15 .15
222 A41 1.25 l sapphire .15 .15
223 A41 1.75 l red org .15 .15
224 A41 2.75 l dk red brn .18 .18
225 A41 5 l green .45 .45
226 A41 10 l violet .75 .75
227 A41 20 l slate blue 1.90 1.90
Nos. 215-227,C26-C33 (21) 8.66 9.16

This series was prepared for the 20th anniv. of fascism, but as Mussolini was overthrown July 25, 1943, it was overprinted for the downfall of fascism.

Overprint on Nos. 222-227 adds "d." before "F.R."

Exist without overprint. Value of set $45.

A42

A43

Overprinted "Governo Provvisorio" in Black

1943, Aug. 27

228 A42 5c brown .15 .15
229 A42 10c orange red .15 .15
230 A42 20c ultra .15 .15
231 A42 25c deep green .15 .15
232 A42 30c brown carmine .15 .15
233 A42 50c deep violet .15 .15
234 A42 75c carmine rose .15 .15
235 A43 1.25 l sapphire .15 .15
236 A43 1.75 l red orange .30 .30
237 A43 5 l green .55 .55
238 A43 20 l slate blue 1.90 1.90
Nos. 228-238,C34-C39 (17) 6.83 6.83

Souvenir Sheets

A44

Perf. 14, Imperf.

1945, Mar. 15 Photo. Unwmk.

239 A44 Sheet of 3 27.50 27.50
a. 10 l dull blue 6.00 6.00
b. 15 l dull green 6.00 6.00
c. 25 l dull red brown 6.00 6.00

Sheets contain a papermaker's watermark, "Hammermill Bond, Made in U.S.A."

Nos. 239, 241 and C40 were issued to commemorate the 50th anniv. of the reconstruction of the Government Palace.

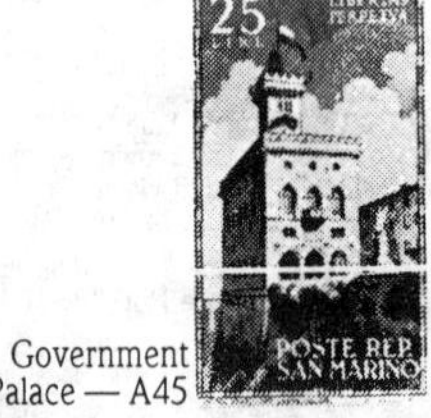

Government Palace — A45

1945, Mar. 15 Wmk. 140 *Perf. 14*

241 A45 25 l brown violet 3.00 3.00

Coat of Arms of Faetano — A46

Coats of Arms: 20c, 60c, 25 l, Montegiardino. 40c, 5 l, 50 l, San Marino. 80c, 2 l-4 l, Fiorentino. 10 l, Borgomaggiore. 20 l, Serravalle.

1945-46 Wmk. 277

242 A46 10c dark blue .15 .15
243 A46 20c vermilion .15 .15
244 A46 40c deep orange .15 .15
245 A46 60c slate black .15 .15
246 A46 80c dark green .15 .15
247 A46 1 l dk car rose .15 .15
248 A46 1.20 l deep violet .15 .15
249 A46 2 l chestnut .15 .15
250 A46 3 l dp blue ('46) .15 .15
250A A46 4 l red org ('46) .15 .15
251 A46 5 l dark brown .15 .15
251A A46 15 l dp blue ('46) .65 1.10

Lithographed and Engraved

252 A46 10 l brt red & brown 1.50 1.10
253 A46 20 l brt red & ultra 2.75 1.65
254 A46 20 l org brn & ultra ('46) 2.75 1.65
a. Vert. pair, imperf. btwn. 175.00
255 A46 25 l hn brn & ultra ('46) 2.75 1.90

Size: 22x27mm

256 A46 50 l ol brn & ultra ('46) 3.00 5.75
Nos. 242-256 (17) 15.05 14.80

Nos. 252-256 are in sheets of 10 (2x5). Values: Nos. 252, 254-255, $60 each. No. 253, $90, No. 256, $200.

For surcharges see Nos. 258-259, B26.

"Dawn of New Hope" — A52

Engr. & Litho.

1946 Unwmk. *Perf. 14*

257 A52 100 l dull yel & brn vio 3.25 3.25
j. Vert. pair, imperf. btwn. 175.00

UN Relief and Rehabilitation Administration. Sheets of 10 with blue coat of arms in top margin.

Franklin D. Roosevelt and Flags of San Marino and US — A52a

Designs: 1 l, 50 l, Quotation on Liberty, from Franklin D. Roosevelt. 2 l, 100 l, Roosevelt portrait, vert. 5 l, 15 l, Roosevelt and flags (as shown).

Wmk. 277

1947, May 3 Photo. *Perf. 14*

257A A52a 1 l bister & brn .15 .15
257B A52a 2 l blue & sepia .15 .15
257C A52a 5 l violet & multi .15 .15
257D A52a 15 l green & multi .15 .15
257E A52a 50 l vermilion & brn .45 .45
257F A52a 100 l violet & sepia .65 .65
Nos. 257A-257F,C51A-C51H (14) 13.03 10.33

For surcharges see #257G-257I, C51I-C51K.

Nos. 257A-257C Surcharged with New Value

1947, June 16

257G A52a 3 l on 1 l .25 .25
257H A52a 4 l on 2 l .25 .25
257I A52a 6 l on 5 l .25 .25
Nos. 257G-257I,C51I-C51K (6) 1.59 1.59

No. 250A Surcharged with New Value in Black

1947, June 16 Wmk. 277

258 A46 6(l) on 4 l red org .15 .15

No. 250A Surcharged in Black

21

259 A46 21 l on 4 l red org .50 .60

"St. Marinus Raising the Republic" by Girolamo Batoni — A53

Wmk. 217

1947, July 18 Engr. *Perf. 12*

260 A53 1 l brt grn & vio .15 .15
261 A53 2 l purple & olive .15 .15
262 A53 4 l vio brn & dk bl grn .15 .15
263 A53 10 l org & bl blk .15 .15

264	A53	25 l carmine & purple	.40	.55
265	A53	50 l dk bl grn & brn	9.00	8.25
		Nos. 260-265,C52-C53 (8)	13.00	12.40

For overprints and surcharges see Nos. 294-295, B27-B38, C56.

United States 1847 Stamp — A54

United States Stamps of 1847 and 1869 — A55

A56

Wmk. 277

1947, Dec. 24 Photo. *Perf. 14*

266	A54	2 l red vio & dk brn	.15	.15
267	A55	3 l sl gray, dp ultra & car	.15	.15
268	A54	6 l dp bl & dk gray grn	.15	.15
269	A56	15 l vio, dp ultra & car	.18	.22
270	A55	35 l dk brn, dp ultra & car	.60	.60
271	A56	50 l sl grn, dp ultra & car	.85	.90
		Nos. 266-271,C55 (7)	6.08	6.17

1st United States postage stamps, cent.

Laborer and San Marino Flag — A57

1948, June 3

272	A57	5 l brown	.15	.15
273	A57	8 l green	.15	.18
274	A57	30 l crimson	.20	.24
275	A57	50 l red brn & rose lil	1.40	1.40

Engr.

276	A57	100 l dk bl & dp vio	19.00	19.00
		Nos. 272-276 (5)	20.90	20.97

See Nos. 373-374.

No. 172 Surcharged with New Value and Ornaments in Black

1948 Wmk. 217 *Perf. 12*

277	A32	100 l on 15c	21.00	21.00

Government Palace — A58

Mt. Titano, Distant View — A59

Various Views of San Marino.

1949-50 Wmk. 277 Photo. *Perf. 14*

278	A58	1 l black & blue	.15	.15
279	A58	2 l violet & car	.15	.15
280	A58	3 l violet & ultra	.15	.15
281	A58	4 l black & vio	.15	.15
282	A58	5 l violet & brn	.15	.15
283	A58	6 l dp blue & sep	.15	.18
284	A59	8 l blk brn & yel brn	.15	.24
285	A59	10 l brn blk & bl	.15	.15
286	A58	12 l brt rose & vio	.35	.52
287	A58	15 l vio & brt rose	.52	.75
288	A58	20 l dp bl & brn ('50)	3.25	1.00
289	A58	35 l green & violet	1.90	1.90
290	A58	50 l brt rose & yel brn	.75	1.00
291	A58	55 l dp bl & dl grn ('50)	10.50	11.00

Perf. 14x13½

Engr.

292	A59	100 l blk brn & dk grn	42.50	22.50
293	A59	200 l dp blue & brn	47.50	32.50
		Nos. 278-293 (16)	108.47	72.49

Nos. 260 and 261 Overprinted in Black

Giornata Filatelica
San Marino-Riccione
28-6-1949

1949, June 28 Wmk. 217

294	A53	1 l brt green & vio	.15	.15
295	A53	2 l purple & olive	.15	.15
		Set value	.20	.18

San Marino-Riccione Stamp Day, June 28.

Francesco Nullo — A60

1 l, 20 l, Francesco Nullo. 2 l, 5 l, Anita Garibaldi. 3 l, 50 l, Giuseppe Garibaldi. 4 l, 15 l, Ugo Bassi.

Wmk. 277

1949, July 31 Photo. *Perf. 14*

Size: 22x28mm

296	A60	1 l blk & car lake	.15	.15
297	A60	2 l red brn & blue	.15	.15
298	A60	3 l car lake & dk grn	.15	.15
299	A60	4 l violet & dk brn	.15	.15

Size: 26½x36½mm

300	A60	5 l purple & dk brn	.15	.15
301	A60	15 l car lake & gray bl	.70	.70
302	A60	20 l violet & car lake	1.10	1.10
303	A60	50 l red brn & violet	12.00	12.00
		Nos. 296-303 (8)	14.55	14.55

Centenary of Garibaldi's escape to San Marino. See Nos. C57-C61, 404-410.

Stagecoach on Road from San Marino A61

1949, Dec. 29 Engr.

304	A61	100 l blue & gray vio	5.00	5.00
		Sheet of 6	100.00	100.00

UPU, 75th anniversary.

A62

A63a

A63

Perf. 13½x14, 14x13½

1951, Mar. 15 Engr. Wmk. 277

Sky and Cross in Carmine

305	A62	25 l dk brn & red vio	3.00	3.00
306	A63	75 l org brn & dk brn	3.75	3.75
307	A63a	100 l dk brn & gray blk	5.50	5.50
		Nos. 305-307 (3)	12.25	12.25

Issued to honor the San Marino Red Cross.

Christopher Columbus A64

Designs: 2 l, 25 l, Columbus on his ship. 3 l, 10 l, 20 l, Landing of Columbus. 4 l, 15 l, 80 l, Pioneers trading with Indians. 5 l, 200 l, Columbus and map of Americas.

1952, Jan. 28 Photo. *Perf. 14*

308	A64	1 l brn org & dk grn	.15	.15
309	A64	2 l dk brown & vio	.15	.15
310	A64	3 l violet & dk brn	.15	.15
311	A64	4 l blue & org brn	.15	.15
312	A64	5 l grn & dk bl grn	.15	.15
313	A64	10 l dk brown & blk	.15	.20
314	A64	15 l carmine & blk	.18	.18

Engr.

315	A64	20 l dp bl & dk bl grn	.30	.35
316	A64	25 l vio brn & blk brn	1.25	1.00
317	A64	60 l choc & vio bl	3.00	3.00
318	A64	80 l gray & blk	6.00	6.00
319	A64	200 l Prus grn & dp ultra	14.00	14.00
		Nos. 308-319,C80 (13)	39.63	39.48

Issued to honor Christopher Columbus.

Type of 1952 in New Colors Overprinted in Black or Red

FIERA DI TRIESTE
1952

1952, June 29 Photo.

320	A64	1 l vio & dk brn	.15	.15
321	A64	2 l carmine & blk	.15	.15
322	A64	3 l grn & dk bl grn (R)	.15	.15
323	A64	4 l dk brn & blk	.15	.15
324	A64	5 l purple & vio	.15	.20
325	A64	10 l bl & org brn (R)	1.00	1.00
326	A64	15 l org brn & blue	2.75	2.75
		Nos. 320-326,C81 (8)	16.50	16.55

4th Intl. Sample Fair of Trieste.

Discobolus — A65

Tennis A66

Model Airplane — A67

Designs: 3 l, Runner. 4 l, Cyclist. 5 l, Soccer. 25 l, Shooting. 100 l, Roller skating.

1953, Apr. 20 Wmk. 277 *Perf. 14*

327	A65	1 l dk brn & blk	.15	.15
328	A66	2 l black & brown	.15	.15
329	A65	3 l blk & grnsh bl	.15	.15
330	A66	4 l blk & brt bl	.15	.15
331	A66	5 l dk brn & sl grn	.15	.15
332	A67	10 l dp blue & crim	.15	.28
333	A67	25 l blk & dk brn	1.10	1.10
334	A66	100 l dk brn & slate	2.75	2.75
		Nos. 327-334,C90 (9)	44.75	44.88

See No. 438.

Type of 1953 Overprinted in Black

GIORNATA FILATELICA
S. MARINO • RICCIONE
24 AGOSTO 1953

1953, Aug. 24

335	A66	100 l grn & dk bl grn	12.00	12.00

San Marino-Riccione Stamp Day, Aug. 24.

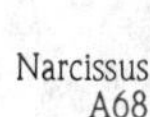

Narcissus A68

Flowers: 2 l, Tulips. 3 l, Oleanders. 4 l, Cornflowers. 5 l, Carnations. 10 l, Irises. 25 l, Cyclamen. 80 l, Geraniums. 100 l, Roses.

1953, Dec. 28 Photo.

336	A68	1 l multicolored	.15	.15
337	A68	2 l multicolored	.15	.15
338	A68	3 l multicolored	.15	.15
339	A68	4 l multicolored	.15	.15
340	A68	5 l multicolored	.15	.15
341	A68	10 l multicolored	.15	.24
342	A68	25 l multicolored	1.75	1.75
343	A68	80 l multicolored	8.75	8.75
344	A68	100 l multicolored	11.00	11.00
		Nos. 336-344 (9)	22.40	22.49

Walking Racer — A69

Fencing A70

Sports: 3 l, Boxing. 4 l, 200 l, 250 l, Gymnastics. 5 l, Motorcycling. 8 l, Javelin-throwing. 12 l, Automobiling. 25 l, Wrestling. 80 l, Walk racer.

1954-55 Photo. Wmk. 277

345	A69	1 l violet & cer	.15	.15
346	A70	2 l dk green & vio	.15	.15
347	A70	3 l brn & brn org	.15	.15
348	A69	4 l dk bl & brt bl	.15	.15
349	A70	5 l dk grn & dk brn	.15	.15
350	A70	8 l lilac rose & pur	.15	.20
351	A70	12 l black & crim	.15	.20
352	A69	25 l bl & dk bl grn	.20	.20
353	A69	80 l dk bl & bl grn	.38	.38
354	A69	200 l violet & brn	2.25	2.25

Perf. 12½x13

Engr.

355	A69	250 l multi ('55)	27.50	27.50
		Sheet of 4 (#355)	180.00	180.00
		Nos. 345-355 (11)	31.38	31.48

A71

A72

Liberty statue and Government palace.

1954, Dec. 16 *Perf. 13x13½*

356	A71	20 l choc & blue	.20	.22
357	A71	60 l car & dk grn	.75	.75

See No. C92.

1955, Aug. 27 Wmk. 303 *Perf. 14*

358	A72	100 l gray blk & bl	2.50	2.50
		Never hinged	3.75	

7th San Marino-Riccione Stamp Fair. See No. 385.

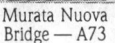

Murata Nuova Bridge — A73

View of La Rocca — A74

Design: 15 l, Government Palace.

1955, Nov. 15 *Perf. 14*

Size: 22x27½mm; 27½x22mm

359 A73	5 l blue & brown	.15	.15
360 A74	10 l org & bl grn	.15	.15
361 A74	15 l Prus grn & car	.15	.15
362 A73	25 l dk brn & vio	.15	.15
363 A74	35 l vio & red car	.15	.15
	Set value	.46	.46
	Set, never hinged	1.00	

See Nos. 386-388, 636-638.

Ice Skater — A75

Skier — A76

3 l, 50 l, Tobogganing. 4 l, Skier going downhill. 5 l, 100 l, Ice Hockey player. 10 l, Girl ice skater.

1955, Dec. 15 **Wmk. 303** *Perf. 14*

364 A75	1 l brown & yellow	.15	.15
365 A76	2 l brt blue & red	.15	.15
366 A76	3 l blk brn & lt brn	.15	.15
367 A75	4 l brown & green	.15	.15
368 A76	5 l ultra & sal pink	.15	.15
369 A75	10 l ultra & pink	.15	.15
370 A76	25 l gray blk & red	.60	.60
371 A76	50 l brown & indigo	1.40	1.40
372 A76	100 l blk & Prus grn	3.25	3.25
	Nos. 364-372,C95 (10)	15.65	15.65
	Set, never hinged	35.00	

7th Winter Olympic Games at Cortina d'Ampezzo, Jan. 26-Feb. 5, 1956.

For surcharge see No. C96.

Type of 1948 Inscribed: "50th Anniversario Arengo 25 Marzo 1906"

1956, Mar. 24 **Wmk. 303** *Perf. 14*

373 A57	50 l sapphire	4.00	5.00
	Never hinged	5.00	

50th anniv. of the meeting of the heads of families (Arengo), the beginning of the democratic era in San Marino.

Type of 1948 inscribed: "Assistenza Invernale"

1956, Mar. 24 **Photo.**

374 A57	50 l dark green	4.00	5.00
	Never hinged	5.00	

Issued to publicize the Winterhelp charity.

Pointer and Arms — A77

Dogs: 2 l, Russian greyhound. 3 l, Sheep dog. 4 l, English greyhound. 5 l, Boxer. 10 l, Great Dane. 25 l, Irish setter. 60 l, German shepherd. 80 l, Scotch collie. 100 l, Hunting hound.

1956, June 8 **Wmk. 303** *Perf. 14*

375 A77	1 l ultra & brown	.15	.15
376 A77	2 l car lake & bl gray	.15	.15
377 A77	3 l ultra & brown	.15	.15
378 A77	4 l grnsh bl & gray vio	.15	.15
379 A77	5 l car lake & dk brn	.15	.15
380 A77	10 l ultra & brown	.15	.15
381 A77	25 l dk blue & multi	.18	.18
382 A77	60 l car lake & multi	1.40	1.40
383 A77	80 l dk blue & multi	1.75	1.75
384 A77	100 l car lake & multi	2.75	2.75
	Nos. 375-384 (10)	6.98	6.98
	Set, never hinged	17.50	

Sailboat Type of 1955

1956 **Wmk. 303** *Perf. 14*

385 A72	100 l brown & bl grn	1.50	1.75
	Never hinged	2.00	

8th San Marino-Riccione Stamp Fair.

Types of 1955 with added inscription: "Congresso Internaz. Periti Filatelici San Marino-Salsomaggiore 6-8 Ottobre 1956."

Designs: 20 l, La Rocca. 80 l, Murata Nuova Bridge. 100 l, Government palace.

1956, Oct. 6 *Perf. 14*

Size: 26x36mm; 36x26mm

386 A74	20 l blue & brown	.38	.28
387 A73	80 l vio & red car	1.50	1.40
388 A74	100 l org & bl grn	1.65	1.65
	Nos. 386-388 (3)	3.53	3.33
	Set, never hinged	4.25	

Intl. Philatelic Congress, San Marino, Oct. 6-8.

Street and Borgo Maggiore Church — A78

Hospital Street — A79

Views: 3 l, Gate tower. 20 l, Covered Market of Borgo Maggiore. 125 l, View from South Bastion.

1957, May 9 **Photo.** **Wmk. 303**

389 A78	2 l dk grn & rose red	.15	.15
390 A78	3 l blue & brown	.15	.15
391 A78	20 l dk blue green	.18	.15
392 A79	60 l brn & blue vio	.75	.65

Engr.

393 A78	125 l dk blue & blk	.32	.28
	Nos. 389-393 (5)	1.55	1.38
	Set, never hinged	2.00	

See Nos. 473-476, 633-635.

Daisies and View of San Marino — A80

Flowers: 2 l, Primrose. 3 l, Lily. 4 l Orchid. 5 l, Lily of the Valley. 10 l, Poppy. 25 l, Pansy. 60 l, Gladiolus. 80 l, Wild Rose. 100 l, Anemone.

Wmk. 303

1957, Aug. 31 **Photo.** *Perf. 14*

Flowers in Natural Colors

394 A80	1 l dk vio blue	.15	.15
395 A80	2 l dk vio blue	.15	.15
396 A80	3 l dk vio blue	.15	.15
397 A80	4 l dk vio blue	.15	.15
398 A80	5 l dk vio blue	.15	.15
399 A80	10 l blue, buff & lilac	.15	.15
400 A80	25 l blue, yel & lilac	.15	.15
401 A80	60 l blue, yel & dl red brn	.28	.24
402 A80	80 l blue & dl red brn	.40	.35
403 A80	100 l bl, yel & dl red brn	.90	.90
	Set value	2.15	2.05
	Set, never hinged	3.25	

Type of 1949 Inscribed: "Commemorazione 150 Nascita G. Garibaldi."

Portraits: 2 l, 50 l, Anita Garibaldi. 3 l, 25 l, Francesco Nullo. 5 l, 100 l, Giuseppe Garibaldi. 15 l, Ugo Bassi.

1957, Dec. 12 **Wmk. 303** *Perf. 14*

Size: 22x28mm

404 A60	2 l vio & dull bl	.15	.15
405 A60	3 l lake & dk grn	.15	.15
406 A60	5 l brn & ol gray	.15	.15

Size: 26½x37mm

407 A60	15 l blue & vio	.15	.15
408 A60	25 l green & dk gray	.15	.30
409 A60	50 l violet & brn	.85	1.50
410 A60	100 l brown & vio	.85	1.50
	Set value	2.00	
	Set, never hinged	3.50	

Nos. 409-410 are printed se-tenant.

Birth of Giuseppe Garibaldi, 150th anniv.

Panoramic View — A81

1958, Feb. 27 **Engr.** *Perf. 14*

411 A81	500 l green & blk	37.50	37.50
	Never hinged	85.00	
	Sheet of 6	300.00	275.00

Catalogue values for unused stamps in this section, from this point to the end of the section, are for Never Hinged items.

Fair Emblem and San Marino Peaks — A82

1958, Apr. 12 **Photo.** *Perf. 14*

412 A82	40 l yel green & brn	.22	.15
413 A82	60 l brt blue & mar	.30	.28

World's Fair, Brussels, Apr. 17-Oct. 19.

Madonna and Fair Entrance A83

Design: 60 l, View of Fair Grounds.

1958, Apr. 12

414 A83	15 l yellow, grn & bl	.20	.15
415 A83	60 l green & rose red	.70	.60
	Nos. 414-415,C97 (3)	2.90	2.75

San Marino's 10th participation in the Milan Fair.

Wheat — A84

Designs: 2 l, 125 l, Corn. 3 l, 80 l, Grapes. 4 l, 25 l, Peaches. 5 l, 40 l, Plums.

1958, Aug. 30 **Wmk. 303** *Perf. 14*

416 A84	1 l dk blue & yel org	.15	.15
417 A84	2 l dk green & red org	.15	.15
418 A84	3 l blue & ocher	.15	.15
419 A84	4 l green & rose car	.15	.15
420 A84	5 l blue, yel & grn	.15	.15
421 A84	15 l ultra & brn org	.15	.15
422 A84	25 l multicolored	.15	.15
423 A84	40 l multicolored	.32	.22
424 A84	80 l multicolored	.65	.45
425 A84	125 l bl, grn & org ver	2.75	1.75
	Set value	4.20	2.90

Bay and Stamp of Naples A85

1958, Oct. 8 **Photo.**

426 A85	25 l lilac & red brn	.32	.30

Cent. of the stamps of Naples. See No. C100.

Pierre de Coubertin — A86

Portraits: 3 l, Count Alberto Bonacossa. 5 l, Avery Brundage. 30 l, Gen. Carlo Montu. 60 l, J. Sigfrid Edstrom. 80 l, Henri de Baillet Latour.

1959, May 19 **Wmk. 303** *Perf. 14*

427 A86	2 l brn org & blk	.15	.15
428 A86	3 l lilac & gray brn	.15	.15
429 A86	5 l blue & dk grn	.15	.15
430 A86	30 l violet & blk	.15	.15
431 A86	60 l dk grn & gray brn	.22	.18
432 A86	80 l car rose & dp grn	.22	.18
	Set value, #427-432, C106	1.65	1.45

Leaders of the Olympic movement; 1960 Olympic Games, Rome.

See Nos. 1060-1062.

Lincoln and his Praise of San Marino, May 7, 1861 — A87

Lincoln Portraits and: 10 l, Map of San Marino. 15 l, Government palace. 70 l, San Marino peaks, vert.

1959, July 1 *Perf. 14*

433 A87	5 l brown & blk	.15	.15
434 A87	10 l blue grn & ultra	.15	.15
435 A87	15 l gray & green	.15	.15

Perf. 13x13½

Engr.

436 A87	70 l violet	.95	.75
	Nos. 433-436,C108 (5)	4.90	3.70

Birth sesquicentennial of Abraham Lincoln.

Arch of Augustus, Rimini, and Romagna ½b Stamp A88

1959, Aug. 29 **Photo.** *Perf. 14*

437 A88	30 l black & brown	.22	.16

Centenary of the first stamps of Romagna. See No. C109.

Type of 1953 Inscribed: "Universiade Torino"

1959, Aug. 29 **Wmk. 303** *Perf. 14*

438 A65	30 l red orange	.60	.40

Turin University Sports Meet, Aug. 27-Sept. 6.

Messina Cathedral Portal and Stamp of Sicily 1859 — A89

Stamp of Sicily and: 2 l, Greek temple, Selinus. 3 l, Erice Church. 4 l, Temple of Concordia, Agrigento. 5 l, Ruins of Castor and Pollux Temple,

Agrigento. 25 l, San Giovanni degli Eremiti Church. 60 l, Greek theater, Taormina, horiz.

1959, Oct. 16

439 A89	1 l	ocher & dk brn	.15	.15
440 A89	2 l	olive & dk red	.15	.15
441 A89	3 l	blue & slate	.15	.15
442 A89	4 l	red & brown	.15	.15
443 A89	5 l	dull bl & rose lil	.15	.15
444 A89	25 l	multicolored	.22	.18
445 A89	60 l	multicolored	.25	.22
		Set value, #439-445, C110	1.95	1.45

Centenary of stamps of Sicily.

Golden Oriole — A90

Nightingale — A91

Shot Put — A92

Birds: 3 l, Woodcock. 4 l, Hoopoe. 5 l, Red-legged partridge. 10 l, Goldfinch. 25 l, European Kingfisher. 60 l, Ringnecked pheasant. 80 l, Green woodpecker. 110 l, Red-breasted flycatcher.

1960, Jan. 28 Photo. *Perf. 14*

Centers in Natural Colors

446 A90	1 l	blue	.15	.15
447 A91	2 l	green & red	.15	.15
448 A90	3 l	green & red	.15	.15
449 A91	4 l	dk green & red	.15	.15
450 A90	5 l	dark green	.15	.15
451 A91	10 l	blue & red	.15	.15
452 A91	25 l	grnsh blue	.26	.20
453 A90	60 l	blue & red	1.40	1.00
454 A91	80 l	Prus blue & red	2.25	1.90
455 A91	110 l	blue & red	2.75	2.25
		Nos. 446-455 (10)	7.56	6.25

1960, May 23 Wmk. 303 *Perf. 14*

Sports: 2 l, Gymnastics. 3 l, Walking. 4 l, Boxing. 5 l, Fencing, horiz. 10 l, Bicycling. 15 l, Hockey, horiz. 25 l, Rowing, horiz. 60 l, Soccer. 110 l, Equestrian, horiz.

456 A92	1 l	car rose & vio	.15	.15
457 A92	2 l	gray & org	.15	.15
458 A92	3 l	brn ol & pur	.15	.15
459 A92	4 l	rose red & brn	.15	.15
460 A92	5 l	brown & blue	.15	.15
461 A92	10 l	red brn & bl	.15	.15
462 A92	15 l	emer & lilac	.15	.15
463 A92	25 l	bl grn & org	.15	.15
464 A92	60 l	dp grn & org	.15	.15
465 A92	110 l	emer, red & blk	.15	.15
		Set of 3 souvenir sheets	8.00	8.00
		Set value, #456-465, C111-C114	1.65	1.45

17th Olympic Games, Rome, Aug. 25-Sept. 11.

Souvenir sheets are: (1.) Sheet of 4, one each of 1 l, 2 l, 3 l and 60 l, all printed in deep green and brown. (2.) Sheet of 4, one each of 4 l and 10 l plus a 20 l and 40 l in designs of Nos. C111-C112 but without "Posta Aerea" inscribed-all 4 printed in rose red and brown. (3.) Sheet of 6, one each of 5 l, 15 l, 25 l and 110 l plus an 80 l and 125 l in designs of Nos. C113-C114 but without "Posta Aerea"- all 6 printed in emerald and brown.

Mt. Titano — A93

Founder Melvin Jones and Lions Headquarters A94

60 l, Government Palace and statue of Liberty. 115 l, Clarence L. Sturm, president. 150 l, Finis E. Davis, vice president.

1960, July 1 Photo. Wmk. 303

466 A93	30 l	red brn & dk bl	.15	.15
467 A94	45 l	bl vio & bis brn	.50	.50
468 A93	60 l	dull rose & bl	.15	.15
469 A94	115 l	green & blk	.50	.50
470 A94	150 l	brn & dk bl	3.50	2.75
		Nos. 466-470,C115 (6)	9.80	8.05

Lions Intl.; founding of the Lions Club of San Marino.

Beach of Riccione and San Marino Peaks — A95

1960, Aug. 27 *Perf. 14*

471 A95	30 l	multicolored	.45	.32

12th San Marino-Riccione Stamp Day, Aug. 27. See No. C116.

Boy with Basket of Fruit, by Caravaggio — A96

1960, Dec. 29 Wmk. 303 *Perf. 14*

472 A96	200 l	multicolored	6.50	4.75

350th anniversary of the death of Michelangelo da Caravaggio (Merisi), painter.

Types of 1957

Views: 1 l, Hospital street. 4 l, Government building. 80 l, Gate tower. 115 l, Covered market of Borgo Maggiore.

1961, Feb. 16 *Perf. 14*

473 A79	1 l	dk blue grn	.15	.15
474 A78	4 l	dk blue & blk	.15	.15
475 A78	30 l	brt vio & brn	.70	.28
476 A78	115 l	brown & blue	.42	.35
		Set value	1.25	.75

Hunting Roebuck A97

Hunting Scenes (16th-18th century): 2 l, Falconer, vert. 3 l, Wild boar hunt. 4 l, Duck shooting with crossbow. 5 l, Stag hunt. 10 l, Mounted falconer, vert. 30 l, Hunter with horn and dogs. 60 l, Hunter with rifle and dog, vert. 70 l, Hunter and beater. 115 l, Duck hunt.

Wmk. 303

1961, May 4 Photo. *Perf. 14*

477 A97	1 l	lil rose & vio bl	.15	.15
478 A97	2 l	gray, dk red & blk	.15	.15
479 A97	3 l	red org, brn & blk	.15	.15
480 A97	4 l	lt bl, red & blk	.15	.15
481 A97	5 l	yellow grn & brn	.15	.15
482 A97	10 l	org, blk, brn & vio	.15	.15
483 A97	30 l	yel, bl & dk grn	.15	.15
484 A97	60 l	ocher, brn, blk & red	.16	.16
485 A97	70 l	green, blk & car	.24	.24
486 A97	115 l	brt pink, blk & dk bl	.42	.42
		Set value	1.25	1.25

Mt. Titano and Cancelled Stamp of Sardinia, 1862 A98

Photogravure and Embossed

1961, Sept. 5 Wmk. 303 *Perf. 13*

487 A98	30 l	multicolored	.60	.60
488 A98	70 l	multicolored	1.25	1.25
489 A98	200 l	multicolored	.65	.65
		Nos. 487-489 (3)	2.50	2.50

Cent. of Independence Phil. Exhib., Turin, 1961.

Europa Issue, 1961

View of San Marino — A99

Wmk. 339

1961, Oct. 20 Photo. *Perf. 13*

490 A99	500 l	brn & blue grn	9.75	9.75
		Sheet of 6	55.00	55.00

King Enzo's Palace and Neptune Fountain, Bologna — A100

Views of Bologna: 70 l, Loggia dei Mercanti. 100 l, Two Towers.

1961, Nov. 25 Wmk. 339 *Perf. 14*

491 A100	30 l	grnsh bl & blk	.15	.15
492 A100	70 l	dk ol grn & blk	.15	.15
493 A100	100 l	red brown & blk	.18	.18
		Set value	.40	.40

Bophilex, philatelic exhibition, Bologna.

Duryea, 1892 — A101

Automobiles (pre-1910): 2 l, Panhard-Levassor. 3 l, Peugeot. 4 l, Daimler. 5 l, Fiat, vert. 10 l, Decauville. 15 l, Wolseley. 20 l, Benz. 25 l, Napier. 30 l, White, vert. 50 l, Oldsmobile. 70 l, Renault, vert. 100 l, Isotta Fraschini. 115 l, Bianchi. 150 l, Alfa.

1962, Jan. 23 Wmk. 303 *Perf. 14*

494 A101	1 l	red brn & bl	.15	.15
495 A101	2 l	ultra & org brn	.15	.15
496 A101	3 l	black, brn & org	.15	.15
497 A101	4 l	gray & dk red	.15	.15
498 A101	5 l	violet & org	.15	.15
499 A101	10 l	black & org	.15	.15
500 A101	15 l	black & ver	.15	.15
501 A101	20 l	black & ultra	.15	.15
502 A101	25 l	gray & org	.15	.15
503 A101	30 l	black & ocher	.15	.15
504 A101	50 l	black & brt pink	.18	.18
505 A101	70 l	black, gray & grn	.18	.18
506 A101	100 l	black, yel & car	.18	.18
507 A101	115 l	blk, org & bl grn	.18	.18
508 A101	150 l	multicolored	.45	.45
		Set value	2.00	2.00

Wright Plane, 1904 — A102

Historic Planes (1907-1910): 2 l, Ernest Archdeacon. 3 l, Albert and Emile Bonnet-Labranche. 4 l, Glenn Curtiss. 5 l, Farman. 10 l, Louis Bleriot. 30 l, Hubert Latham. 60 l, Alberto Santos Dumont. 70 l, Alliott Verdon Roe. 115 l, Faccioli.

Wmk. 339

1962, Apr. 4 Photo. *Perf. 14*

509 A102	1 l	blk & dull yel	.15	.15
510 A102	2 l	red brn & grn	.15	.15
511 A102	3 l	red brn & gray grn	.15	.15
512 A102	4 l	brown & blk	.15	.15
513 A102	5 l	magenta & blue	.15	.15
514 A102	10 l	ocher & bl grn	.15	.15
515 A102	30 l	ocher & ultra	.15	.15
516 A102	60 l	black & ocher	.22	.22
517 A102	70 l	dp orange & blk	.30	.30
518 A102	115 l	blk, grn & ocher	.75	.75
		Set value	1.75	1.75

Mountaineer Descending — A103

Designs: 2 l, View of Sassolungo. 3 l, Mt. Titano. 4 l, Three Peaks of Javaredo. 5 l, Matterhorn. 15 l, Skier on downhill run. 30 l, Climbing an overhang. 40 l, Cutting steps in ice. 85 l, Giant's Tooth. 115 l, Mt. Titano.

1962, June 14 Wmk. 339 *Perf. 14*

519 A103	1 l	bis brn & blk	.15	.15
520 A103	2 l	Prus grn & blk	.15	.15
521 A103	3 l	lilac & blk	.15	.15
522 A103	4 l	brt bl & blk	.15	.15
523 A103	5 l	dp org & blk	.15	.15
524 A103	15 l	org yel & blk	.15	.15
525 A103	30 l	carmine & blk	.15	.15
526 A103	40 l	grnsh bl & blk	.15	.15
527 A103	85 l	lt green & blk	.18	.18
528 A103	115 l	vio bl & blk	.28	.28
		Set value	1.00	1.00

Hunter with Dog — A104

Modern Hunting Scenes: 2 l, Hound master on horseback, vert. 3 l, Duck hunt. 4 l, Stag hunt. 5 l, Partridge hunt. 15 l, Lapwing (hunt). 50 l, Wild duck hunt. 70 l, Duck hunt from boat. 100 l, Boar hunt. 150 l, Pheasant hunt, vert.

1962, Aug. 25 Photo. *Perf. 14*

529 A104	1 l	brown & yel grn	.15	.15
530 A104	2 l	dk bl & org	.15	.15
531 A104	3 l	blk & Prus bl	.15	.15
532 A104	4 l	black & brown	.15	.15
533 A104	5 l	brn & yel grn	.15	.15
534 A104	15 l	blk & org brn	.15	.15
535 A104	50 l	brn, dp grn & blk	.15	.15
536 A104	70 l	grn, sal pink & blk	.15	.15
537 A104	100 l	blk, brick red & sep	.18	.18
538 A104	150 l	grn, lil & blk	.22	.22
		Set value	1.00	1.00

Europa Issue, 1962

Mt. Titano and "Europa" A105

1962, Oct. 25 Wmk. 339

539 A105	200 l	gray & car	1.75	1.75
		Sheet of 6	12.50	12.50

Egyptian Cargo Ship — A106

Ancient Ships: 2 l, Greece, 2nd Cent. B.C. 3 l, Roman galley. 4 l, Vikings, 10th Cent. 5 l, "Santa Maria," 1492. 10 l, Cypriote galleon, vert. 30 l, Galley, 1600. 60 l, "Sovereign of the Seas," 1637, vert. 70 l, Danish ship, 1750, vert. 115 l, Frigate, 1850.

1963, Jan. 10

540 A106	1 l	blue & org yel	.15	.15
541 A106	2 l	mag, tan & brn	.15	.15
542 A106	3 l	brown & lil rose	.15	.15
543 A106	4 l	vio brn & gray	.15	.15
544 A106	5 l	brown & yellow	.15	.15
545 A106	10 l	brn & brt yel grn	.15	.15
546 A106	30 l	blk, bl & sep	.60	.45
547 A106	60 l	lt vio bl & yel grn	.45	.45

548 A106 70 l blk, gray & dl red .45 .45
549 A106 115 l blk, brn & gray bl 1.25 1.40
Set value 3.20 3.20

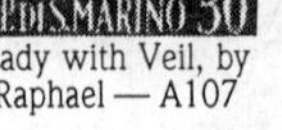
Lady with Veil, by Raphael — A107

Jousting with "Saracen," Arezzo — A108

Paintings by Raphael: 70 l, Self-portrait. 100 l, St. Barbara from Sistine Madonna. 200 l, Portrait of a Young Woman (Maddalena Strozzi).

Wmk. 339

1963, Mar. 28 Photo. *Perf. 14*

Size: 26½x37mm

550 A107 30 l multicolored .32 .32
551 A107 70 l multicolored .15 .15
552 A107 100 l multicolored .20 .20

Size: 26½x44mm

553 A107 200 l multicolored .38 .38
Nos. 550-553 (4) 1.05 1.05

1963, June 22 Wmk. 339 *Perf. 14*

Medieval "Knightly Games": 2 l, French knights, horiz. 3 l, Crossbow contest. 4 l, English knight receiving lance, horiz. 5 l, Tournament, Florence. 10 l, Jousting with "Quintana," Ascoli Piceno. 30 l, "Quintana," Foligno, horiz. 60 l, Race through Siena. 70 l, Tournament, Malpaga, horiz. 115 l, Knights challenging.

554 A108 1 l lilac rose .15 .15
555 A108 2 l slate .15 .15
556 A108 3 l black .15 .15
557 A108 4 l violet .15 .15
558 A108 5 l rose violet .15 .15
559 A108 10 l dull green .15 .15
560 A108 30 l red brown .15 .15
561 A108 60 l Prus green .15 .15
562 A108 70 l brown .15 .15
563 A108 115 l black .15 .15
Set value .75 .75

Butterfly — A109

St. Marinus Statue, Government Palace — A110

Designs: Various butterflies. 70 l, 115 l, horiz.

Wmk. 339

1963, Aug. 31 Photo. *Perf. 14*

564 A109 25 l multicolored .16 .16
565 A109 30 l multicolored .16 .16
566 A109 60 l multicolored .18 .18
567 A109 70 l multicolored .20 .20
568 A109 115 l multicolored .32 .32
Nos. 564-568 (5) 1.02 1.02

1963, Aug. 31

569 A110 100 l shown .25 .25
570 A110 100 l Modern fountain .25 .25

San Marino-Riccione Stamp Fair.

Europa Issue, 1963

Flag and "E" — A111

1963, Sept. 21 Wmk. 339 *Perf. 14*

571 A111 200 l blue & brn org .40 .40

Women's Hurdles A112

Sports: 2 l, Pole vaulting, vert. 3 l, Women's relay race. 4 l, Men's high jump. 5 l, Soccer. 10 l, Women's high jump. 30 l, Women's discus throw, vert. 60 l, Women's javelin throw. 70 l, Water polo. 115 l, Hammer throw.

1963, Sept. 21

572 A112 1 l org & red brn .15 .15
573 A112 2 l lt grn & dk brn .15 .15
574 A112 3 l bl & dk brn .15 .15
575 A112 4 l dp bl & dk brn .15 .15
576 A112 5 l red & dk brn .15 .15
577 A112 10 l lil rose & claret .15 .15
578 A112 30 l gray & red brn .15 .15
579 A112 60 l brt yel & dk brn .15 .15
580 A112 70 l brt bl & dk brn .15 .15
581 A112 115 l grn & dk brn .15 .15
Set value .55 .55

Publicity for 1964 Olympic Games.

Modern Pentathlon A113

Designs: 1 l, Runner, vert. 2 l, Woman gymnast, vert. 3 l, Basketball, vert. 5 l, Dual rowing. 15 l, Broad jumper. 30 l, Swimmer in racing dive. 70 l, Woman sprinter. 120 l, Bicycle racers, vert. 150 l, Fencers, vert.

Inscribed "Tokio, 1964"

1964, June 25 Wmk. 339 *Perf. 14*

582 A113 1 l brn & yel grn .15 .15
583 A113 2 l blk & red brn .15 .15
584 A113 3 l blk & brown .15 .15
585 A113 4 l blk & org red .15 .15
586 A113 5 l blk & brt bl .15 .15
587 A113 15 l dk brn & org .15 .15
588 A113 30 l dk vio & bl .15 .15
589 A113 70 l red brn & grn .15 .15
590 A113 120 l brn & brt bl .15 .15
591 A113 150 l blk & crimson .15 .15
Set value .85 .85

18th Olympic Games, Tokyo, Oct. 10-25.

Same Inscribed "Verso Tokio"

1964, June 25 Photo.

592 A113 30 l indigo & lilac .15 .15
593 A113 70 l brn & Prus grn .16 .16
Set value .25 .25

"Verso Tokyo" Stamp Exhibition at Rimini, Italy, June 25-July 6.

Murray-Blenkinsop Locomotive, 1812 — A114

History of Locomotive: 2 l, Puffing Billy, 1813. 3 l, Locomotion I, 1825. 4 l, Rocket, 1829. 5 l, Lion, 1838. 15 l, Bayard, 1839. 20 l, Crampton, 1849. 50 l, Little England, 1851. 90 l, Spitfire, c. 1860. 110 l, Rogers, c. 1865.

1964, Aug. 29 Wmk. 339 *Perf. 14*

594 A114 1 l blk & buff .15 .15
595 A114 2 l blk & green .15 .15
596 A114 3 l blk & rose lilac .15 .15
597 A114 4 l blk & yellow .15 .15
598 A114 5 l blk & salmon .15 .15
599 A114 15 l blk & yel grn .15 .15
600 A114 20 l blk & dp pink .15 .15
601 A114 50 l blk & pale bl .15 .15
602 A114 90 l blk & yel org .35 .35
603 A114 110 l blk & brt bl .60 .60
Set value 1.50 1.50

Baseball Players A115

1964, Aug. 29 Photo.

604 A115 30 l shown .16 .16
605 A115 70 l Pitcher .16 .16

8th European Baseball Championship, Milan.

Europa Issue, 1964

"E" and Globe A116

1964, Oct. 15 Wmk. 339 *Perf. 14*

606 A116 200 l dk blue & red .55 .55

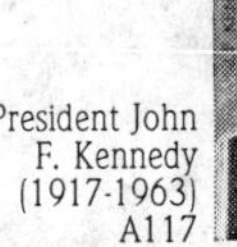

President John F. Kennedy (1917-1963) A117

Design: 130 l, John F. Kennedy and American flag, vert.

1964, Nov. 22 Photo. *Perf. 14*

607 A117 70 l multicolored .16 .16
608 A117 130 l multicolored .24 .24

Start of Bicycle Race from Government Palace — A118

Rooks on Chessboard — A120

Brontosaurus A119

Designs: 70 l, Cyclists (going right) and view of San Marino. 200 l, Cyclists (going left) and view of San Marino.

1965, May 15 Photo. Wmk. 339

609 A118 30 l sepia .15 .15
610 A118 70 l deep claret .15 .15
611 A118 200 l rose red .22 .22
Set value .40 .40

48th Bicycle Tour of Italy.

1965, June 30 Wmk. 339 *Perf. 14*

Dinosaurs: 2 l, Brachiosaurus, vert. 3 l, Pteranodon. 4 l, Elasmosaurus. 5 l, Tyrannosaurus. 10 l, Stegosaurus. 75 l, Thaumatosaurus victor. 100 l, Iguanodon. 200 l, Triceratops.

612 A119 1 l dk brn & emer .15 .15
613 A119 2 l blk & sl bl .15 .15
614 A119 3 l sl grn, ol grn & yel .15 .15
615 A119 4 l brn & slate bl .15 .15
616 A119 5 l claret & grn .15 .15
617 A119 10 l claret & grn .15 .15
618 A119 75 l dk bl & bl grn .30 .30
619 A119 100 l green & claret .30 .30
620 A119 200 l brown & grn .45 .45
Set value 1.50 1.50

Europa Issue, 1965

1965, Aug. 28 Photo. *Perf. 14*

621 A120 200 l brown & multi .28 .28

Dante by Gustave Doré A121

Doré's Illustrations for Divina Commedia: 90 l, Charon ferrying boat across Acheron. 130 l, Eagle carrying Dante from Purgatory to Paradise. 140 l, Dante with Beatrice examined by Sts. Peter, James and John on faith.

Perf. 14x14½

1965, Nov. 20 Engr. Wmk. 339

Center in Brown Black

622 A121 40 l indigo .15 .15
623 A121 90 l car rose .15 .15
624 A121 130 l red brown .15 .15
625 A121 140 l ultra .18 .18
Set value .55 .55

Dante Alighieri (1265-1321), poet.

Stylized Peaks, Flags of Italy and San Marino A122

1965, Nov. 25 Photo. *Perf. 14*

626 A122 115 l grn, red, ocher & bl .18 .18

Visit of Giuseppe Saragat, president of Italy.

Trotter A123

Horses: 20 l, Cross Country, vert. 40 l, Hurdling. 70 l, Gallop. 90 l, Steeplechase. 170 l, Polo, vert.

Perf. 14x13, 13x14

1966, Feb. 28 Photo. Wmk. 339

627 A123 10 l multicolored .15 .15
628 A123 20 l multicolored .15 .15
629 A123 40 l multicolored .15 .15
630 A123 70 l multicolored .15 .15
631 A123 90 l multicolored .15 .15
632 A123 170 l multicolored .18 .18
Set value .64 .64

Scenic Types of 1955-57

5 l, Hospital Street. 10 l, Gate tower. 15 l, View from South Bastion. 40l, Murata Nuova Bridge. 90 l, View of La Rocca. 140 l, Government Palace.

1966, Mar. 29 Wmk. 339 *Perf. 14*

633 A79 5 l blue & brn .15 .15
634 A78 10 l dk sl grn & bl grn .15 .15
635 A78 15 l dk brn & vio .15 .15
636 A73 40 l dk pur & brick red .15 .15
637 A74 90 l blk & dull bl .15 .15
638 A74 140 l violet & org .15 .15
Set value .45 .45

"Bella" by Titian A124

Titian Paintings: 90 l, 100 l, Details from "The Education of Love." 170 l, Detail from "Sacred and Profane Love."

1966, June 16 Wmk. 339 *Perf. 14*

639	A124	40 l	multicolored	.15	.15
640	A124	90 l	multicolored	.15	.15
641	A124	100 l	multicolored	.15	.15
642	A124	170 l	multicolored	.22	.22
			Set value	.54	.54

Stone Bass — A125

Fish: 2 l, Cuckoo wrasse. 3 l, Dolphin. 4 l, John Dory. 5 l, Octopus, vert. 10 l, Orange scorpionfish. 40 l, Electric ray, vert. 90 l, Jellyfish, vert. 115 l, Sea Horse, vert. 130 l, Dentex.

Perf. 14x13½, 13½x14

1966, Aug. 27 Photo. Wmk. 339

643	A125	1 l	multicolored	.15	.15
644	A125	2 l	multicolored	.15	.15
645	A125	3 l	multicolored	.15	.15
646	A125	4 l	multicolored	.15	.15
647	A125	5 l	multicolored	.15	.15
648	A125	10 l	multicolored	.15	.15
649	A125	40 l	multicolored	.15	.15
650	A125	90 l	multicolored	.15	.15
651	A125	115 l	multicolored	.15	.15
652	A125	130 l	multicolored	.15	.15
			Set value	.85	.85

Europa Issue, 1966

Our Lady of Europe A126

1966, Sept. 24 Wmk. 339 *Perf. 14*

653	A126	200 l	multicolored	.25	.25

Peony and Mt. Titano — A127

Flowers and Various Views of Mt. Titano: 10 l, Bell flowers. 15 l, Pyrenean poppy. 20 l, Purple nettle. 40 l, Day lily. 140 l, Gentian. 170 l, Thistle.

Wmk. 339

1967, Jan. 12 Photo. *Perf. 14*

654	A127	5 l	multicolored	.15	.15
655	A127	10 l	multicolored	.15	.15
656	A127	15 l	multicolored	.15	.15
657	A127	20 l	multicolored	.15	.15
658	A127	40 l	multicolored	.15	.15
659	A127	140 l	multicolored	.15	.15
660	A127	170 l	multicolored	.15	.15
			Set value	.70	.70

St. Marinus — A128

The Return of the Prodigal Son — A129

Design: 170 l, St. Francis. The paintings are by Giovanni Francesco Barbieri (1591-1666).

Wmk. 339

1967, Mar. 16 Photo. *Perf. 14*

661	A128	40 l	multicolored	.15	.15
662	A128	170 l	multicolored	.20	.20
663	A129	190 l	multicolored	.22	.22
a.			Strip of 3, #661-663	.55	.55

Map Showing Members of CEPT — A130

Amanita Caesarea — A131

Europa Issue, 1967

1967, May 5 Wmk. 339 *Perf. 14*

664	A130	200 l	sl grn & brn org	.25	.20

1967, June 15 Photo. *Perf. 14*

Various Mushrooms.

665	A131	5 l	multicolored	.15	.15
666	A131	15 l	multicolored	.15	.15
667	A131	20 l	multicolored	.15	.15
668	A131	40 l	multicolored	.15	.15
669	A131	50 l	multicolored	.15	.15
670	A131	170 l	multicolored	.15	.15
			Set value	.55	.55

Amiens Cathedral A132

Designs: 40 l, Siena Cathedral. 80 l, Toledo Cathedral. 90 l, Salisbury Cathedral. 170 l, Cologne Cathedral.

Wmk. 339

1967, Sept. 21 Engr. *Perf. 14*

671	A132	20 l	dk vio, *bister*	.15	.15
672	A132	40 l	slate grn, *bis*	.15	.15
673	A132	80 l	slate bl, *bis*	.15	.15
674	A132	90 l	sepia, *bis*	.15	.15
675	A132	170 l	deep plum, *bis*	.16	.16
			Set value	.55	.55

Crucifix of Santa Croce, by Cimabue A133

1967, Dec. 5 Wmk. 339 *Perf. 15*

676	A133	300 l	brn & vio blue	.40	.40

The Crucifix of Santa Croce, by Giovanni Cimabue (1240-1302), was severely damaged in the Florentine flood of Nov. 1966.

Coat of Arms — A134

Coats of Arms: 3 l, Penna Rossa. 5 l, Fiorentino. 10 l, Montecerreto. 25 l, Serravalle. 35 l, Montegiardino. 50 l, Faetano. 90 l, Borgo Maggiore. 180 l, Montelupo. 500 l, State arms of San Marino.

Perf. 13x13½

1968, Mar. 14 Litho. Wmk. 339

677	A134	2 l	multi	.15	.15
678	A134	3 l	multi	.15	.15
679	A134	5 l	multi	.15	.15
680	A134	10 l	multi	.15	.15
681	A134	25 l	multi	.15	.15
682	A134	35 l	multi	.15	.15
683	A134	50 l	multi	.15	.15
684	A134	90 l	multi	.15	.15
685	A134	180 l	multi	.15	.15
686	A134	500 l	multi	.48	.48
			Set value	1.15	1.15

Europa Issue, 1968

Common Design Type

1968, Apr. 29 Engr. *Perf. 14x13½*

Size: 37x27½mm

687	CD11	250 l	cl brn	.38	.38

"Battle of San Romano" (Detail), by Paolo Uccello — A135

Designs: Details from "The Battle of San Romano," by Paolo Uccello (1397-1475).

Photogravure and Engraved

1968, June 14 Wmk. 339 *Perf. 14*

688	A135	50 l	pale lil & blk	.15	.15
689	A135	90 l	pale lil & blk, vert.	.15	.15
690	A135	130 l	pale lil & blk	.15	.15
691	A135	230 l	pale pink & blk	.30	.30
			Set value	.60	.60

The Mystic Nativity, by Botticelli, Detail A136

Wmk. 339

1968, Dec. 5 Engr. *Perf. 14*

692	A136	50 l	dark blue	.15	.15
693	A136	90 l	deep claret	.15	.15
694	A136	180 l	sepia	.25	.25
			Set value	.45	.45

Christmas.

"Peace" by Lorenzetti A137

Designs: 80 l, "Justice." 90 l, "Moderation." 180 l, View of Siena, 14th century, horiz. All designs are from the "Good Government" frescoes by Ambrogio Lorenzetti in the Town Hall of Siena.

Wmk. 339

1969, Feb. 13 Engr. *Perf. 14*

695	A137	50 l	dark blue	.15	.15
696	A137	80 l	brown	.15	.15
697	A137	90 l	dk blue vio	.15	.15
698	A137	180 l	magenta	.22	.22
			Set value	.48	.48

Young Soldier, by Bramante — A138

Designs: 90 l, Old Soldier, by Bramante. Designs are from murals in the Pinakotheke of Brear, Milan.

1969, Apr. 28 Photo. *Perf. 14*

699	A138	50 l	multicolored	.15	.15
700	A138	90 l	multicolored	.15	.15
			Set value	.22	.22

Bramante (1444-1514), Italian architect and painter.

Europa Issue, 1969

Common Design Type

1969, Apr. 28 Engr. *Perf. 14x13*

Size: 37x27mm

701	CD12	50 l	dull green	.15	.15
702	CD12	180 l	rose claret	.15	.18

Charabanc A139

Coaches, 19th Century: 10 l, Barouche. 25 l, Private drag. 40 l, Hansom cab. 50 l, Curricle. 90 l, Wagonette. 180 l, Spider phaeton.

Perf. 14½x14

1969, June 25 Photo. Unwmk.

703	A139	5 l	blk, ocher & dk bl	.15	.15
704	A139	10 l	blk, grn & pur	.15	.15
705	A139	25 l	dk grn, pink & brn	.15	.15
706	A139	40 l	ind, lil & lt brn	.15	.15
707	A139	50 l	blk, dl yel & dk bl	.15	.15
708	A139	90 l	blk, yel grn & brn	.15	.15
709	A139	180 l	multi	.15	.15
			Set value	.60	.60

Pier at Rimini A140

Paintings by R. Viola: 20 l, Mt. Titano. 200 l, Pier at Riccione, horiz.

1969, Sept. 17 Unwmk. *Perf. 14*

710	A140	20 l multicolored	.15	.15
711	A140	180 l multicolored	.20	.20
712	A140	200 l multicolored	.24	.24
		Nos. 710-712 (3)	.59	.59

"Faith" by Raphael — A141

Designs: 180 l, "Hope" by Raphael. 200 l, "Charity" by Raphael.

Perf. 13½x14

1969, Dec. 10 Engr. Wmk. 339

713	A141	20 l dl pur & sal	.15	.15
714	A141	180 l dl pur & lt grn	.20	.20
715	A141	200 l dp pur & bis	.24	.24
		Nos. 713-715 (3)	.59	.59

Signs of the Zodiac A142

Perf. 14x13½

1970, Feb. 18 Photo. Unwmk.

716	A142	1 l Aries	.15	.15
717	A142	2 l Taurus	.15	.15
718	A142	3 l Gemini	.15	.15
719	A142	4 l Cancer	.15	.15
720	A142	5 l Leo	.15	.15
721	A142	10 l Virgo	.15	.15
722	A142	15 l Libra	.15	.15
723	A142	20 l Scorpio	.15	.15
724	A142	70 l Sagittarius	.15	.15
725	A142	90 l Capricorn	.15	.15
726	A142	100 l Aquraius	.15	.15
727	A142	180 l Pisces	.24	.24
		Set value	1.10	1.10

Fleet in Bay of Naples, by Peter Brueghel, the Elder — A143

Unwmk.

1970, Apr. 30 Photo. *Perf. 14*

728	A143	230 l multi	.40	.40

10th Europa Phil. Exhib., Naples, May 2-10.

Europa Issue, 1970

Common Design Type

1970, Apr. 30 *Perf. 14x13½*

Size: 36x27mm

729	CD13	90 l brt yel grn & red	.15	.15
730	CD13	180 l ocher & red	.20	.20

St. Francis' Gate and Rotary Emblem — A144

Woman with Mandolin, by Tiepolo — A145

220 l, Rocca (State Prison) and Rotary emblem.

1970, June 25 Photo. *Perf. 13½x14*

731	A144	180 l multi	.25	.25
732	A144	220 l multi	.30	.30

65th anniv. of Rotary Intl.; 10th anniv. of the San Marino Rotary Club.

1970, Sept. 10 Unwmk. *Perf. 14*

Paintings by Tiepolo: 180 l, Woman with Parrot. 220 l, Rinaldo and Armida Surprised, horiz.

Size: 26½x37½mm

733	A145	50 l multi	.15	.15
734	A145	180 l multi	.22	.22

Size: 56x37½mm

735	A145	220 l multi	.30	.30
a.		Strip of 3, #733-735	.70	.70

Giambattista Tiepolo (1696-1770), Venetian painter.

Black Pete — A146

Walt Disney and Jungle Book Scene A147

Disney Characters: 2 l, Gyro Gearloose. 3 l, Pluto. 4 l, Minnie Mouse. 5 l, Donald Duck. 10 l, Goofy. 15 l, Scrooge McDuck. 50 l, Huey, Louey and Dewey. 90 l, Mickey Mouse.

Perf. 13x14, 14x13

1970, Dec. 22 Photo.

736	A146	1 l multi	.15	.15
737	A146	2 l multi	.15	.15
738	A146	3 l multi	.15	.15
739	A146	4 l multi	.15	.15
740	A146	5 l multi	.15	.15
741	A146	10 l multi	.15	.15
742	A146	15 l multi	.15	.15
743	A146	50 l multi	.20	.20
744	A146	90 l multi	.38	.38
745	A147	220 l multi	4.50	4.50
		Nos. 736-745 (10)	6.13	6.13

Walt Disney (1901-66), cartoonist & film maker.

Customhouse Dock, by Canaletto — A148

Paintings by Canaletto: 180 l, Grand Canal between Balbi Palace and Rialto Bridge. 200 l, St. Mark's and Doges' Palace.

1971, Mar. 23 Unwmk. *Perf. 14*

746	A148	20 l multi	.15	.15
747	A148	180 l multi	.30	.30
748	A148	200 l multi	.32	.32
		Nos. 746-748 (3)	.77	.77

Save Venice campaign.

Europa Issue, 1971

Common Design Type

1971, May 29 *Perf. 13½x14*

Size: 27½x23mm

749	CD14	50 l org & blue	.15	.15
750	CD14	90 l blue & org	.18	.18

Congress Emblem and Hall, San Marino Flag — A149

Design: 90 l, Detail from Government Palace door, Congress and San Marino emblems, vert.

1971, May 29 Photo. *Perf. 12*

751	A149	20 l vio & multi	.15	.15
752	A149	90 l ol & multi	.15	.15
753	A149	180 l multi	.22	.22
		Set value	.42	.42

Italian Philatelic Press Union Congress, San Marino, May 29-30.

Duck-shaped Jug with Flying Lasa — A150

Etruscan Art, 6th-3rd Centuries B.C.: 80 l, Head of Mercury, vert. 90 l, Sarcophagus of a married couple, vert. 180 l, Chimera.

Photo. & Engr.

1971, Sept. 16 *Perf. 14*

754	A150	50 l blk & org	.15	.15
755	A150	80 l blk & lt grn	.15	.15
756	A150	90 l blk & lt bl	.15	.15
757	A150	180 l blk & org	.22	.22
		Set value	.58	.58

Tiger Lily A151

Venus, by Botticelli A152

1971, Dec. 2 Photo. *Perf. 11½*

758	A151	1 l shown	.15	.15
759	A151	2 l Phlox	.15	.15
760	A151	3 l Carnations	.15	.15
761	A151	4 l Globe flowers	.15	.15
762	A151	5 l Thistles	.15	.15
763	A151	10 l Peonies	.15	.15
764	A151	15 l Hellebore	.15	.15
765	A151	50 l Anemones	.15	.15
766	A151	90 l Gaillardia	.15	.15
767	A151	220 l Asters	.20	.20
		Set value	.70	.70

1972, Feb. 23 *Perf. 14, 13x14 (180 l)*

Details from La Primavera, by Sandro Botticelli: 180 l, Three Graces. 220 l, Spring.

Sizes: 50 l, 220 l, 21x37mm; 180 l, 27x37mm

768	A152	50 l gold & multi	.15	.15
769	A152	180 l gold & multi	.22	.22
770	A152	220 l gold & multi	.30	.30
		Nos. 768-770 (3)	.67	.67

Europa Issue 1972

Common Design Type

1972, Apr. 27 *Perf. 11½*

Granite Paper

Size: 22½x33mm

771	CD15	50 l org & multi	.15	.15
772	CD15	90 l lt bl & multi	.15	.15
		Set value	.25	.25

St. Marinus Taming Bear — A153

Designs: 55 l, Donna Felicissima asking St. Marinus for mercy for her sons. 100 l, St. Marinus turning archers to stone. 130 l, Felicissima giving mountains to St. Marinus to establish Republic.

Photo. & Engr.

1972, Apr. 27 *Perf. 14*

773	A153	25 l dl yel & blk	.15	.15
774	A153	55 l sal pink & blk	.15	.15
775	A153	100 l dl bl & blk	.15	.15
776	A153	130 l citron & blk	.15	.15
		Set value	.38	.38

Allegories of San Marino after 16th century paintings.

Italian House Sparrow — A154

1972, June 30 Photo. *Perf. 11½*

Granite Paper

777	A154	1 l shown	.15	.15
778	A154	2 l Firecrest	.15	.15
779	A154	3 l Blue tit	.15	.15
780	A154	4 l Ortolan bunting	.15	.15
781	A154	5 l White-spotted bluethroat	.15	.15
782	A154	10 l Bullfinch	.15	.15
783	A154	25 l Linnet	.15	.15
784	A154	50 l Black-eared wheater	.15	.15
785	A154	90 l Sardinian warbler	.15	.15
786	A154	220 l Greenfinch	.24	.24
		Set value	.80	.80

Young Man, Heart, Emblem — A155

Italian Philatelic Federation Emblem — A156

Design: 90 l, Heart disease victim, horiz.

Perf. 13½x14, 14x13½

1972, Aug. 26

787	A155	50 l lt bl & multi	.15	.15
788	A155	90 l ocher & multi	.16	.16

World Heart Month.

1972, Aug. 26 *Perf. 13½x14*

789	A156	25 l gold & ultra	.15	.15

Honoring veterans of Philately.

5c Coin, 1864 A157

Coins: 10 l, 10c coin, 1935. 15 l, 1 lira, 1906. 20 l, 5 lire, 1898. 25 l, 5 lire, 1937. 50 l, 10 lire, 1932. 55 l, 20 lire, 1938. 220 l, 20 lire, 1925.

1972, Dec. 15 Litho. *Perf. 12½x13*

No.	Type	Value	Description	Unused	Used
790	A157	5 l	gray, blk & brn	.15	.15
791	A157	10 l	org, blk & sil	.15	.15
792	A157	15 l	brt rose, blk & sil	.15	.15
793	A157	20 l	lil, blk & sil	.15	.15
794	A157	25 l	vio, blk & sil	.15	.15
795	A157	50 l	brt bl, blk & sil	.15	.15
796	A157	55 l	ocher, blk & sil	.15	.15
797	A157	220 l	emer, blk & gold	.22	.22
			Set value	.74	.74

New York, 1673 A158

300 l, View of New York from East River, 1973.

1973, Mar. 9 Photo. *Perf. 11½*
Granite Paper

No.	Type	Value	Description	Unused	Used
798	A158	200 l	bis, ocher & ol grn	.32	.32
799	A158	300 l	bl, lil & blk	.40	.40
a.			Pair, #798-799	.80	.80

New York, 300th anniv. Printed checkerwise.

Rotary Press, San Marino Towers — A159

Gymnasts and Olympic Rings — A160

1973, May 10 Photo. *Perf. 13x14*

No.	Type	Value	Description	Unused	Used
800	A159	50 l	multi	.15	.15

Tourist Press Congress, San Marino.

1973, May 10 Unwmk.

No.	Type	Value	Description	Unused	Used
801	A160	100 l	grn & multi	.18	.18

5th Youth Games.

Europa Issue 1973
Common Design Type

1973, May 10 *Perf. 11½*
Size: 32½x23mm

No.	Type	Value	Description	Unused	Used
802	CD16	20 l	salmon & multi	.16	.16
803	CD16	180 l	lt bl & multi	.85	.85

Grapes — A161

1973, July 11 Photo. *Perf. 11½*

No.	Type	Value	Description	Unused	Used
804	A161	1 l	shown	.15	.15
805	A161	2 l	Tangerines	.15	.15
806	A161	3 l	Apples	.15	.15
807	A161	4 l	Plums	.15	.15
808	A161	5 l	Strawberries	.15	.15
809	A161	10 l	Pears	.15	.15
810	A161	25 l	Cherries	.15	.15
811	A161	50 l	Pomegranate	.15	.15
812	A161	90 l	Apricots	.15	.15
813	A161	220 l	Peaches	.15	.15
			Set value	.70	.70

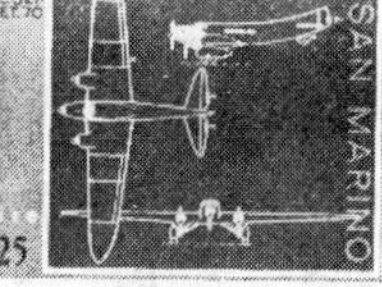

Arc-en-Ciel, France A162

Famous Aircraft: 55 l, Macchi Castoldi, Italy. 60 l, Antonov, USSR. 90 l, Spirit of St. Louis, US. 220 l, Handley Page, Great Britain.

1973, Aug. 31 Photo. *Perf. 14x13½*

No.	Type	Value	Description	Unused	Used
814	A162	25 l	ocher, vio bl & gold	.15	.15
815	A162	55 l	gray, vio bl & gold	.15	.15
816	A162	60 l	rose, vio bl & gold	.15	.15
817	A162	90 l	lem, vio bl & gold	.15	.15
818	A162	220 l	org, vio bl & gold	.22	.22
			Set value	.55	.55

Crossbowman, Serravalle Castle — A163

Attendants, by Gentile Fabriano — A164

1973, Nov. 7 Photo. *Perf. 13½*

Designs: 10 l, Crossbowman, Pennarossa Castle. 15 l, Drummer, Montegiardino Castle. 20 l, Trumpeter, Fiorentino Castle. 30 l, Crossbowman, Borga Maggiore Castle. 50 l, Trumpeter, Guaita Castle. 80 l, Crossbowman, Faetano Castle. 200 l, Crossbowman, Montelupo Castle.

No.	Type	Value	Description	Unused	Used
819	A163	5 l	black & multi	.15	.15
820	A163	10 l	black & multi	.15	.15
821	A163	15 l	black & multi	.15	.15
822	A163	20 l	black & multi	.15	.15
823	A163	30 l	black & multi	.15	.15
824	A163	40 l	black & multi	.15	.15
825	A163	50 l	black & multi	.15	.15
826	A163	80 l	black & multi	.15	.15
827	A163	200 l	black & multi	.20	.20
			Set value	.88	.88

San Marino victories in the Crossbow Tournament, Massa Marittima, July 15, 1973.

1973, Dec. 19 Photo. *Perf. 11½*

Christmas: Details from Adoration of the Kings, by Gentile Fabriano (1370-1427).

No.	Type	Value	Description	Unused	Used
828	A164	5 l	shown	.15	.15
829	A164	30 l	King	.15	.15
830	A164	115 l	King	.15	.15
831	A164	250 l	Horses	.22	.22
			Set value	.52	.52

Shield, 16th Century — A165

16th Century Armor: 5 l, Round shield. 10 l, German full armor. 15 l, Helmet with intricate etching. 20 l, Horse's head armor "Massimiliano." 30 l, Decorated helmet with Sphinx statuette on top. 50 l, Pommeled sword and gauntlets. 80 l, Sparrow-beaked helmet. 250 l, Sforza round shield.

Engr. & Litho.

1974, Mar. 12 *Perf. 13*

No.	Type	Value	Description	Unused	Used
832	A165	5 l	blk, lt grn & buff	.15	.15
833	A165	10 l	blk, buff & bl	.15	.15
834	A165	15 l	blk, bl & ultra	.15	.15
835	A165	20 l	blk, tan & ultra	.15	.15
836	A165	30 l	blk & lt bl	.15	.15
837	A165	50 l	blk, rose & ultra	.15	.15
838	A165	80 l	blk, gray & grn	.15	.15
839	A165	250 l	blk & yel	.22	.22
			Set value	.78	.78

Head of Woman, by Emilio Greco — A166

Europa: 200 l, Nude, by Emilio Greco (head shown on 100 l).

Engr. & Litho.

1974, May 9 *Perf. 13x14*

No.	Type	Value	Description	Unused	Used
840	A166	100 l	buff & blk	.16	.16
841	A166	200 l	pale grn & blk	.32	.32

Yachts at Riccione and San Marino Peaks — A167

1974, July 18 Photo. *Perf. 11½*
Granite Paper

No.	Type	Value	Description	Unused	Used
842	A167	50 l	ultra & multi	.18	.18

26th San Marino-Riccione Stamp Day.

Arms of San Sepolcro — A168

Designs: Coats of arms of participating cities.

1974, July 18 *Perf. 12*

No.	Type	Value	Description	Unused	Used
843	A168	15 l	shown	.60	.60
844	A168	20 l	Massa Marittima	.60	.60
845	A168	50 l	San Marino	.60	.60
846	A168	115 l	Gubbio	.60	.60
847	A168	300 l	Lucca	.60	.60
a.			Strip of 5, #843-847	3.00	3.00
			Nos. 843-847 (5)	3.00	3.00

9th Crossbow Tournament, San Marino.

UPU Emblem A169

1974, Oct. 9 Photo. *Perf. 11½*
Granite Paper

No.	Type	Value	Description	Unused	Used
848	A169	50 l	multi	.15	.15
849	A169	90 l	grn & multi	.15	.15
			Set value	.22	.22

Centenary of Universal Postal Union.

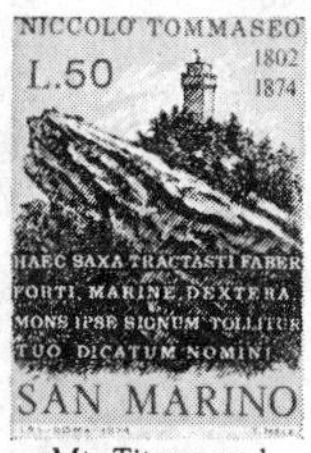

Mt. Titano and Hymn by Tommaseo — A170

Niccolo Tommaseo — A171

1974, Dec. 12 Photo. *Perf. 13½x14*

No.	Type	Value	Description	Unused	Used
850	A170	50 l	lt grn, blk & red	.15	.15
851	A171	150 l	yel, grn & blk	.18	.18
			Set value	.24	.24

Tommaseo (1802-1874), Italian writer.

Virgin and Child, 14th Century Wood Panel — A172

1974, Dec. 12 *Perf. 11½*

No.	Type	Value	Description	Unused	Used
852	A172	250 l	gold & multi	.35	.35

Christmas.

"Refuge in San Marino" — A173

1975, Feb. 20 Photo. *Perf. 13½x14*

No.	Type	Value	Description	Unused	Used
853	A173	50 l	multi	.15	.15

Flight of 100,000 refugees from Romagna to San Marino, 30th anniversary.

Musicians, from Leopard Tomb, Tarquinia — A174

Etruscan Art: 30 l, Chariot race, from Tomb on the Hill, Chiusi. 180 l, Achilles and Troilus, from Bulls' Tomb, Tarquinia. 220 l, Dancers, from Triclinium Tomb, Tarquinia.

Litho. & Engr.

1975, Feb. 20 *Perf. 14*

No.	Type	Value	Description	Unused	Used
854	A174	20 l	multi	.15	.15
855	A174	30 l	multi	.15	.15
856	A174	180 l	multi	.15	.15
857	A174	220 l	multi	.28	.28
			Set value	.60	.60

Europa Issue 1975

St. Marinus, by Guercino (Francesco Barbieri)
A175 A176

1975, May 14 Photo. *Perf. 11½*
Granite Paper

No.	Type	Value	Description	Unused	Used
858	A175	100 l	multi	.15	.15
859	A176	200 l	multi	.25	.25

The Lamentation, by Giotto — A177

Frescoes by Giotto (details): 40 l, Mary and Jesus (Flight into Egypt). 50 l, Heads of four angels (Flight into Egypt). 100 l, Mary Magdalene (Noli Me Tangere), horiz. 500 l, Angel and the elect (Last Judgment), horiz.

1975, July 10 Photo. *Perf. 11½*
Granite Paper

No.	Type	Value	Description	Unused	Used
860	A177	10 l	gold & multi	.15	.15
861	A177	40 l	gold & multi	.15	.15
862	A177	50 l	gold & multi	.15	.15
863	A177	100 l	gold & multi	.15	.15
864	A177	500 l	gold & multi	.52	.52
			Set value	.95	.95

Holy Year.

Tokyo, 1835, Woodcut by Hiroshige — A178

Design: 300 l, Tokyo, Business District, 1975.

1975, Sept. 5 Photo. *Perf. 11½*

Granite Paper

865 A178 200 l multi .28 .28
866 A178 300 l multi .42 .42
a. Pair, #865-866 .70 .70

Printed checkerwise.

Aphrodite A179

1975, Sept. 19 Photo. *Perf. 11½*

867 A179 50 l vio, blk & gray .20 .20

Europa '75 Philatelic Exhibition, Naples.

Multiple Crosses — A180

1975, Sept. 19

868 A180 100 l blk, dp org & vio .15 .15

EUROCOPHAR Intl. Pharmaceutical Cong.

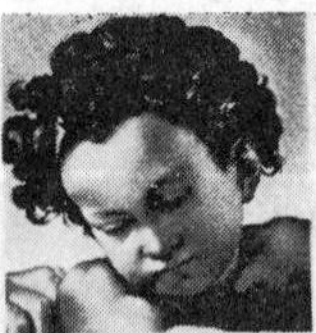

Angel — A181

Doni Madonna — A182

Christmas: 100 l, Head of Virgin, from Doni Madonna by Michelangelo.

1975, Dec. 3 Photo. *Perf. 11½*

Granite Paper

869 A181 50 l multi .15 .15
870 A181 100 l multi .15 .15
871 A182 250 l multi .60 .60
a. Strip of 3, #869-871 .80 .80

Woman on Balcony, by Gentilini — A183

Two Women, by Gentilini A184

Design: 230 l, Woman (same as right head on 150 l) and IWY emblem, by Franco Gentilini.

1975, Dec. 3

Granite Paper

872 A183 70 l bl & multi .15 .15
873 A184 150 l multi .15 .15
874 A183 230 l multi .25 .25
Nos. 872-874 (3) .55 .55

International Women's Year.

Modesty, by Emilio Greco — A185

Capitol, Washington, D.C. — A186

"Civic Virtues": 20 l, Temperance. 50 l, Fortitude. 100 l, Altruism. 150 l, Hope. 220 l, Prudence. 250 l, Justice. 300 l, Faith. 500 l, Honesty. 1000 l, Industry. Designs show drawings of women's heads by Emilio Greco.

1976, Mar. 4 Photo. *Perf. 11½*

Granite Paper

875 A185 10 l buff & blk .15 .15
876 A185 20 l pink & blk .15 .15
877 A185 50 l grnsh & blk .15 .15
878 A185 100 l salmon & blk .15 .15
879 A185 150 l lilac & blk .16 .16
880 A185 220 l gray & blk .25 .25
881 A185 250 l yel & multi .35 .35
882 A185 300 l gray & blk .38 .38
883 A185 500 l yel & blk .60 .60
884 A185 1000 l gray & blk 1.25 1.25
Nos. 875-884 (10) 3.59 3.59

See Nos. 900-905, 931-933.

1976, May 29 Photo. *Perf. 11½*

Arms of San Marino and: 150 l, Statue of Liberty. 180 l, Independence Hall, Philadelphia.

885 A186 70 l multi .15 .15
886 A186 150 l multi .16 .16
887 A186 180 l multi .22 .22
Nos. 885-887 (3) .53 .53

American Bicentennial.

Montreal Olympic Games Emblem A187

1976, May 29

888 A187 150 l crimson & blk .20 .20

21st Olympic Games, Montreal, Canada, 7/17-8/1.

Decorated Plate — A188

Europa: 180 l, Seal of San Marino.

1976, July 8 Photo. *Perf. 11½*

Granite Paper

889 A188 150 l multi .22 .22
890 A188 180 l bl, sil & blk .22 .22

"Unity" — A189

"Peaks of San Marino" — A190

1976, July 8 *Perf. 13½x14*

891 A189 150 l vio blk, yel & red .22 .22

United Mutual Aid Society, centenary.

1976, Oct. 14 Photo. *Perf. 13x14*

892 A190 150 l blk & multi .22 .22

ITALIA 76 Intl. Phil. Exhib., Milan, Oct. 14-24.

Children and UNESCO Emblem A191

1976, Oct. 14 *Perf. 11½*

Granite Paper

893 A191 180 l multi .22 .22
894 A191 220 l multi .25 .25

UNESCO, 30th anniv.

Annunciation (detail), by Titian — A192

Design: 300 l, Virgin and Child, by Titian.

Litho. & Engr.

1976, Dec. 15 *Perf. 13x14*

895 A192 150 l multi .15 .15
896 A192 300 l multi .42 .42
a. Pair, #895-896 .65 .65

Christmas.

Exhibition Emblem A193

1977, Jan. 28 Photo. *Perf. 11½*

Granite Paper

897 A193 80 l multi .15 .15
898 A193 170 l multi .15 .15
899 A193 200 l multi .24 .24
Nos. 897-899,C133 (4) .76 .76

San Marino 77 Phil. Exhib.

Civic Virtues Type of 1976

70 l, Fortitude. 90 l, Prudence. 120 l, Altruism. 160 l, Temperance. 170 l, Hope. 320 l, Faith.

1977, Apr. 14 Photo. *Perf. 11½*

Granite Paper

900 A185 70 l pink & blk .15 .15
901 A185 90 l buff & blk .15 .15
902 A185 120 l lt bl & blk .15 .15
903 A185 160 l lt grn & blk .22 .22
904 A185 170 l cream & blk .22 .22
905 A185 320 l lil & blk .40 .40
Set value 1.12 1.12

San Marino, after Ghirlandaio A194

Europa: 200 l, San Marino, detail from painting by Guercino.

1977, Apr. 14

Granite Paper

906 A194 170 l multi .24 .24
907 A194 200 l multi .28 .28

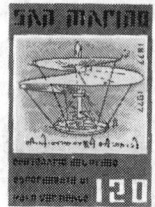

Vertical Flying Machine, by da Vinci — A195

Litho. & Engr.

1977, June 6 *Perf. 13x14*

908 A195 120 l multi .18 .18

Centenary of Enrico Forlanini's experiments with vertical flight.

University Square, Bucharest, 1877 — A196

Design: 400 l, National Theater and Intercontinental Hotel, 1977.

1977, June 6 Photo. *Perf. 11½*

Granite Paper

909 A196 200 l bis & multi .28 .28
910 A196 400 l lt bl & multi .40 .40
a. Pair, #909-910 .68 .58

Centenary of Romanian independence. Printed checkerwise.

Type A2 of 1877 — A197

1977, June 15 Engr. *Perf. 15x14½*

911 A197 40 l slate grn .15 .15
912 A197 70 l deep blue .15 .15
913 A197 170 l red .30 .30
914 A197 500 l brown .52 .52
915 A197 1000 l purple 1.00 1.00
Nos. 911-915 (5) 2.12 2.12

Centenary of San Marino stamps.

SAN MARINO

St. Marinus, by Retrosi — A198

Medicinal Plants — A199

Souvenir Sheet

1977, Aug. 28 Photo. *Perf. 11½*
Granite Paper

916 A198 Sheet of 5 8.50 8.50
a. 1000 l single stamp 1.65 1.65

Centenary of San Marino stamps; San Marino '77 Phil. Exhib., Aug. 28-Sept. 4.

1977, Oct. 19 Photo. *Perf. 11½*
917 A199 170 l multi .22 .22

Congress of Italian Pharmacists' Union.

Design shows high mallow, tilia, camomile, borage, centaury and juniper.

Woman Attacked by Octopus, Emblem A200

1977, Oct. 19
918 A200 200 l multi .25 .25

World Rheumatism Year.

Virgin Mary — A201

San Francisco Gate — A202

Christmas: 230 l, Palm, olive and star. 300 l, Angel.

1977, Dec. 5 Photo. *Perf. 11½*
919 A201 170 l sil, gray & blk .20 .20
920 A201 230 l sil, gray & blk .25 .25
921 A201 300 l sil, gray & blk .30 .30
a. Strip of 3, #919-921 .75 .75

1978, May 30 Photo. *Perf. 11½*

Europa: 200 l, Ripa Gate.

922 A202 170 l lt bl & dk bl .20 .20
923 A202 200 l buff & brn .28 .28

Baseball Player and Diamond — A203

Feather, WHO Emblem — A204

1978, May 30
924 A203 90 l multi .15 .15
925 A203 120 l multi .18 .18

World Baseball Championships.

1978, May 30
926 A204 320 l multi .38 .38

Fight against hypertension.

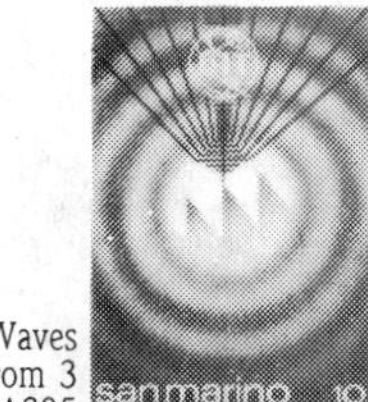

ITU Emblem, Waves Coming from 3 Peaks — A205

1978, July 26 Photo. *Perf. 11½*
927 A205 10 l car & yel .15 .15
928 A205 200 l vio bl & lt bl .30 .30
Set value .35 .35

Membership in ITU.

Seagull and Falcon, 3 Peaks A206

1978, July 26
929 A206 120 l multi .15 .15
930 A206 170 l multi .22 .22

30th San Marino-Riccione Stamp Day.

Civic Virtues Type of 1976

Drawings by Emilio Greco: 5 l, Wisdom. 35 l, Love. 2000 l, Faithfulness.

1978, Sept. 28 Photo. *Perf. 11½*
Granite Paper

931 A185 5 l lt vio & blk .15 .15
932 A185 35 l gray & blk .15 .15
933 A185 2000 l yel & blk 2.25 2.25
Nos. 931-933 (3) 2.55 2.55

Christmas A207

1978, Dec. 6 Photo. *Perf. 14x13½*
941 A207 10 l Holly leaves .15 .15
942 A207 120 l Stars .15 .15
943 A207 170 l Snowflakes .24 .24
Set value .40 .40

Globe and Woman Holding Torch — A208

1978, Dec. 6 *Perf. 11½x12*
944 A208 200 l multi .22 .22

Universal Declaration of Human Rights, 30th anniversary.

First San Marino Autobus, 1915 — A209

Europa: 220 l, Mail coach, 1895.

1979, Mar. 29 Photo. *Perf. 11½x12*
945 A209 170 l multi .28 .28
946 A209 220 l multi .35 .35

Albert Einstein (1879-1955), Theoretical Physicist A210

1979, Mar. 29 *Perf. 11½*
947 A210 120 l gray, lt & dk brn .20 .20

San Marino Crossbow Federation Emblem — A211

Maigret — A212

1979, July 12 Litho. *Perf. 14x13*
948 A211 120 l multi .20 .20

14th Crossbow Tournament.

Litho. & Engr.

1979, July 12 *Perf. 13x14*

Fictional Detectives: 80 l, Perry Mason. 150 l, Nero Wolfe. 170 l, Ellery Queen. 220 l, Sherlock Holmes.

949 A212 10 l multi .15 .15
950 A212 80 l multi .15 .15
951 A212 150 l multi .20 .20
952 A212 170 l multi .20 .20
953 A212 220 l multi .32 .32
Nos. 949-953 (5) 1.02 1.02

Girl Holding Bird — A213

IYC Emblem, Paintings by Marina Busignani: 120 l, 170 l, 220 l, Children and birds, diff. 350 l, Mother nursing child.

1979, Sept. 6 Litho. *Perf. 11½*
954 A213 20 l multi .15 .15
955 A213 120 l multi .15 .15
956 A213 170 l multi .20 .20
957 A213 220 l multi .24 .24
958 A213 350 l multi .35 .35
Set value .95 .95

St. Apollonia, 15th Century Woodcut — A214

Chestnut Tree, Deer — A216

Waterskier A215

1979, Sept. 6 Photo.
959 A214 170 l multi .20 .20

13th Biennial Intl. Congress of Stomatology.

1979, Sept. 6
960 A215 150 l multi .20 .20

European Waterskiing Championship.

1979, Oct. 25 Photo. *Perf. 11½*

Protected Trees and Animals or Birds: 10 l, Cedar of Lebanon, falcon. 35 l, Dogwood, racoon. 50 l, Banyan, tiger. 70 l, Umbrella pine, hoopoe. 90 l, Siberian spruce, marten. 100 l, Eucalyptus, koala bear. 120 l, Date palm, camel. 150 l, Sugar maple, beaver. 170 l, Adansonia, elephant.

961 A216 5 l multi .15 .15
962 A216 10 l multi .15 .15
963 A216 35 l multi .15 .15
964 A216 50 l multi .15 .15
965 A216 70 l multi .15 .15
966 A216 90 l multi .15 .15
967 A216 100 l multi .15 .15
968 A216 120 l multi .15 .15
969 A216 150 l multi .18 .18
970 A216 170 l multi .22 .22
Set value 1.05 1.05

Holy Family, by Antonio Alberto de Ferrara, 15th Century Fresco — A217

Christmas (de Ferrara Fresco): 80 l, St. Joseph. 170 l, Infant Jesus. 220 l, One of the Three Kings.

1979, Dec. 6 Photo. *Perf. 12*
971 A217 80 l multi .15 .15
972 A217 170 l multi .24 .24
973 A217 220 l multi .28 .28
974 A217 320 l multi .32 .32
Nos. 971-974 (4) .99 .99

Disturbing Muses, by Giorgio de Chirico — A218

1979, Dec.
975 A218 40 l shown .15 .15
976 A218 150 l Ancient horses .18 .18
977 A218 170 l Self-portrait .22 .22
Nos. 975-977 (3) .55 .55

Giorgio de Chirico, Italian surrealist painter.

St. Benedict, 15th Century Fresco — A219

SAN MARINO 220

Fight Against Cigarette Smoking — A220

1980, Mar. 27 Photo. *Perf. 12x11½*
Granite Paper

978 A219 170 l multi .22 .22

St. Benedict of Nursia, 1500th birth anniversary.

1980, Mar. 27

Designs: Sketches of smokers and cigarettes by Giuliana Consilivio.

979 A220 120 l multi .15 .15
980 A220 220 l multi .40 .40
981 A220 520 l multi .65 .65
Nos. 979-981 (3) 1.20 1.20

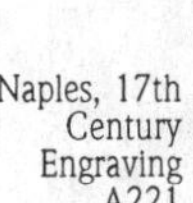
Naples, 17th Century Engraving A221

1980, Mar. 27 *Perf. 14x13½*

982 A221 170 l multi .25 .25

20th Intl. Phil. Exhib., Europa '80, Naples, Apr. 26-May 4.

View of London, 1850 — A222

1980, May 8 *Perf. 11½x12*

983 A222 200 l shown .24 .24
984 A222 400 l London, 1980 .55 .55
a. Pair, #983-984 .80 .80

London 1980 Intl. Stamp Exhib., May 6-14. Printed checkerwise.

See Nos. 1001-1002, 1032-1033, 1054-1055, 1069-1070, 1098-1099, 1110-1111, 1141-1142, 1339-1340.

A223 A224

Europa: 170 l, Giovanbattista Belluzzi (1506-54), military architect. 220 l, Antonio Orafo (1460-1552), goldsmith and jeweler.

1980, May 8 *Perf. 11½*

985 A223 170 l multi .22 .22
986 A223 220 l multi .30 .30

1980, July 7 **Photo.** *Perf. 11½*

Granite Paper

987 A224 70 l Bicycling .15 .15
988 A224 90 l Basketball .15 .15
989 A224 170 l Running .28 .28
990 A224 350 l Gymnast .42 .42
991 A224 450 l High jump .55 .55
Nos. 987-991 (5) 1.55 1.55

22nd Summer Olympic Games, Moscow, July 19-Aug. 3.

Ancient Fortifications A225 Weight Lifting A226

Photogravure and Engraved

1980, Sept. 18 *Perf. 13½x14*

992 A225 220 l multi .32 .32

World Tourism Conf., Manila, Sept. 27.

1980, Sept. 18 **Photo.** *Perf. 14x13½*

993 A226 170 l multi .22 .22

European Junior Weight Lifting Championship, Sept.

Robert Stolz, "Philatelic Waltz" Score A227

Photo. & Engr.

1980, Sept. 18 *Perf. 14*

994 A227 120 l lt bl & blk .22 .22

Robert Stolz (1880-1975) composer.

Madonna of the Harpies, by Andrea Del Sarto — A228

Annunciation by Del Sarto (Details): 250 l, Virgin Mary. 500 l Angel.

1980, Dec. 11 *Perf. 13½*

995 A228 180 l multi .25 .25
996 A228 250 l multi .38 .38
997 A228 500 l multi .75 .75
Nos. 995-997 (3) 1.38 1.38

Christmas; 450th death anniv. of Del Sarto.

St. Joseph's Eve Bonfire — A229 Intl. Year of the Disabled — A230

Europa Issue 1981

1981, Mar. 24 **Photo.** *Perf. 12*

Granite Paper

998 A229 200 l shown .24 .24
999 A229 300 l San Marino Day fireworks .40 .40

1981, May 15 **Photo.** *Perf. 11½*

Granite Paper

1000 A230 300 l multi .38 .38

Exhibition Type of 1980

St. Charles' Square, Vienna, by Jakob Alt, 1817.

1981, May 15

Granite Paper

1001 A222 200 l shown .28 .28
1002 A222 300 l Vienna, 1981 .38 .38
a. Pair, #1001-1002 .70 .70

WIPA '81 Intl. Phil. Exhib., Vienna, May 22-31.

Woman Playing Flute — A232 Grand Prix Motorcycle Race — A233

Designs: Drawings based on Roman sculptures.

1981, July 10 **Photo.** *Perf. 11½*

Granite Paper

1003 A232 300 l shown .48 .48
1004 A232 550 l Soldier .80 .80
1005 A232 1500 l Shepherd 1.40 1.40
a. Souv. sheet of 3, #1003-1005 3.00 3.00

Virgil's birth bimillennium. No. 1005a has continuous design.

1981, July 10 **Litho.** *Perf. 14x15*

1006 A233 200 l multi .22 .22

Natl. Urban Development Plan (Housing) — A234

1981, Sept. 22 **Photo.**

Granite Paper

1007 A234 20 l shown .15 .15
1008 A234 80 l Parks .15 .15
1009 A234 400 l Energy plants .45 .45
Set value .60 .60

European Junior Judo Championship, Oct. 30-Nov. 1 — A235

1981, Sept. 22 **Photo.** *Perf. 11½*

Granite Paper

1010 A235 300 l multi .42 .42

World Food Day — A236

1981, Oct. 23

Granite Paper

1011 A236 300 l multi .42 .42

A237 A238

Designs: 150 l, Child Holding a Dove, by Pablo Picasso (1881-1973). 200 l, Homage to Picasso, by Renato Guttuso.

1981, Oct. 23

Granite Paper

1012 A237 150 l multi .20 .20
1013 A237 200 l multi .28 .24

Photo. & Engr.

1981, Dec. 15 *Perf. 13½*

Christmas; 500th Birth Anniv. of Benvenuto Tisi da Garafalo Adoration of the Kings and St. Bartholomew): 200 l, One of the Three Kings with Goblet, by Garafalo. 300 l, King with a Jar. 600 l, Virgin and Child.

1014 A238 200 l multi .24 .24
1015 A238 300 l multi .35 .35
1016 A238 600 l multi .75 .75
Nos. 1014-1016 (3) 1.34 1.34

Postal Stationery Centenary A239

1982, Feb. 19 **Photo.** *Perf. 12*

1017 A239 200 l multi .22 .22

Savings Bank Centenary A240

1982, Feb. 19

1018 A240 300 l multi .38 .38

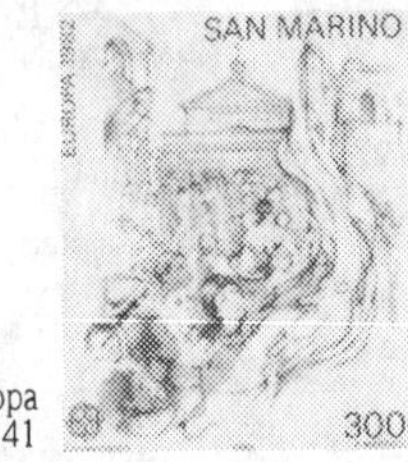

Europa 1982 — A241

Designs: 300 l, Convocation of the Assembly of Heads of Families, 1906. 450 l, Napoleons's Treaty of Friendship offer, 1797.

1982, Apr. 21 **Photo.** *Perf. 11½*

Granite Paper

1019 A241 300 l multi .48 .48
1020 A241 450 l multi .75 .75

Archimedes A242 800th Birth Anniv. of St. Francis of Assisi A243

1982, Apr. 21 **Photo.** *Perf. 14x13½*

1021 A242 20 l shown .15 .15
1022 A242 30 l Copernicus .15 .15
1023 A242 40 l Newton .15 .15
1024 A242 50 l Lavoisier .15 .15
1025 A242 60 l Marie Curie .15 .15
1026 A242 100 l Robert Koch .15 .15

Litho. & Engr.

1027 A242 200 l Thomas Edison .16 .16
1028 A242 300 l Guglielmo Marconi .38 .38
1029 A242 450 l Hippocrates .75 .75

Engr.

1030 A242 5000 l Galileo 6.00 6.00
Nos. 1021-1030 (10) 8.19 8.19

See Nos. 1041-1046.

1982, June 10 **Photo.**

1031 A243 200 l multi .25 .25

Exhibition Type of 1980

1982, June 10

1032 A222 300 l Notre Dame, 1806 .35 .35
1033 A222 450 l 1982 .55 .55
a. Pair, #1032-1033 .90 .90

PHILEXFRANCE '82 Stamp Exhibition, Paris, June 11-21.

Visit of Pope John Paul II — A245

Natl. Flags of ASCAT Members — A246

1982, Aug. 29 Litho. ***Perf. 13½x14***
1034 A245 900 l multi 1.00 1.00

1982, Sept. 1 Photo. ***Perf. 11½***
Granite Paper
1035 A246 300 l multi .40 .40

Inaugural Meeting of ASCAT (Assoc. of Editors of Philatelic Catalogues), 1977.

15th Amnesty Intl. Congress, Rimini, Italy, Sept. 9-15 — A247

Christmas — A248

1982, Sept. 1 **Unwmk.**
1036 A247 700 l blk & red .80 .80

Photo. & Engr.
1982, Dec. 15 ***Perf. 13½***

Paintings by Gregorio Sciltian (b. 1900).

1037 A248 200 l Angel .25 .25
1038 A248 300 l Virgin and Child .38 .38
1039 A248 450 l Angel, diff. .55 .55
Nos. 1037-1039 (3) 1.18 1.18

Secondary School Centenary — A249

Auguste Piccard — A251

3rd Formula One Grand Prix — A250

1983, Feb. 24 Photo. ***Perf. 13½x14***
1040 A249 300 l Begni Building .35 .35

Scientist Type of 1982

1983, Apr. 21 ***Perf. 14x13½***
1041 A242 150 l Alexander Fleming .15 .15
1042 A242 250 l Alessandro Volta .35 .35
1043 A242 350 l Evangelista Torricelli .52 .52
1044 A242 400 l Carolus Linnaeus .55 .55
1045 A242 1000 l Pythagoras 1.00 1.00
1046 A242 1400 l Leonardo da Vinci 1.50 1.50
Nos. 1041-1046 (6) 4.07 4.07

1983, Apr. 20 Photo. ***Perf. 14x13½***
1047 A250 50 l multi .15 .15
1048 A250 350 l multi .40 .40

Perf. 12x11½
1983, Apr. 20 **Granite Paper**
1049 A251 400 l Aerostat .90 .90
1050 A251 500 l Bathyscaph 1.10 1.10

Europa. Piccard (1884-1962), Swiss scientist.

World Communications Year — A252

1983, Apr. 28 Engr. ***Perf. 14x13***
1051 A252 400 l Ham radio operator .50 .50
1052 A252 500 l Mailman .60 .60

Manned Flight Bicentenary — A253

Lithographed and Engraved
1983, May 22 ***Perf. 13½x14***
1053 A253 500 l Montgolfiere, 1783 .60 .60

Exhibition Type of 1980

Designs: Botafogo Bay and Monte Corcovado, Rio de Janeiro.

1983, July 29 Photo. ***Perf. 11½x12***
Granite Paper
1054 A222 400 l 1845 .50 .50
1055 A222 1400 l 1983 1.65 1.65

Se-tenant. BRASILIANA '83 Intl. Stamp Show, Rio de Janeiro, July 29-Aug. 7.

20th Anniv. of World Food Program A255

1983, Sept. 29 Photo. ***Perf. 14x13½***
1056 A255 500 l multi .60 .60

Christmas — A256

Flag-wavers Group, 2nd Anniv. — A257

Paintings, Raphael (1483-1520): 300 l, Our Lady of the Grand Duke. 400 l, Our Lady of the Goldfinch. 500 l, Our Lady of the Chair.

Photo. & Engr.
1983, Dec. 1 ***Perf. 13½***
1057 A256 300 l multi .38 .38
1058 A256 400 l multi .45 .45
1059 A256 500 l multi .55 .55
a. Strip of 3, #1057-1059 1.40 1.40

Olympic Type of 1959

IOC Presidents: 300 l, Demetrius Vikelas, 1894-96. 400 l, Lord Killanin. 550 l, Antonio Samaranch, 1984.

1984, Feb. 8 Photo. ***Perf. 14x13½***
1060 A86 300 l multi .35 .35
1061 A86 400 l multi .48 .48
1062 A86 550 l multi .65 .65
Nos. 1060-1062 (3) 1.48 1.48

Litho. & Engr.
1984, Apr. 27 ***Perf. 13x14***
1063 A257 300 l Flag .35 .35
1064 A257 400 l Flags .48 .48

Europa (1959-1984) A258

1984, Apr. 27 Photo. ***Perf. 11½***
Granite Paper
1065 A258 400 l multi .80 .80
1066 A258 550 l multi .95 .95

A259

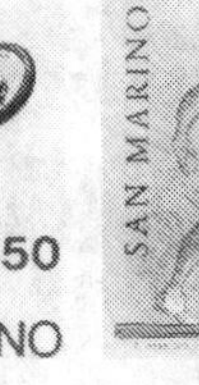

A260

1984, June 14 Photo. ***Perf. 13½x14***
1067 A259 450 l multi .55 .55

Motorcross Grand Prix, Baldasserona.

Souvenir Sheet

1984, June 14 Litho. ***Perf. 13x14***
1068 Sheet of 2 2.00 2.00
a. A260 550 l Man .70 .70
b. A260 1000 l Woman 1.25 1.25

1984 Summer Olympics.

Exhibition Type of 1980

Ausipex '84: Views of Melbourne. Se-tenant.

1984, Sept. 21 Photo. ***Perf. 11½***
Granite Paper
1069 A222 1500 l 1839 2.00 2.00
1070 A222 2000 l 1984 2.75 2.75

Visit of Italian Pres. Pertini A262

1984, Oct. 20 Photo. ***Perf. 14x13½***
1071 A262 1950 l multi 3.00 2.75

School and Philately — A263

Christmas — A264

Sketches by Jacovitti.

1984, Oct. 30 ***Perf. 13½x14***
1072 A263 50 l Universe .15 .15
1073 A263 100 l Evolution .15 .15
1074 A263 150 l Environment .24 .24
1075 A263 200 l Mankind .25 .25
1076 A263 450 l Science .60 .60
1077 A263 550 l Philosophy .70 .70
Nos. 1072-1077 (6) 2.09 2.09

1984, Dec. 5 Litho. ***Perf. 13½x14***

Details of Madonna of San Girolamo by Correggio, 1527.

1078 A264 400 l multi .55 .55
1079 A264 450 l multi .60 .60
1080 A264 550 l multi .80 .80
a. Strip of 3, #1078-1080 2.00 2.00

Composers and Music — A265

Olympiad of the Small States, May 23-26 — A266

Europa: 450 l, Johann Sebastian Bach (1685-1750), Toccata and Fugue. 600 l, Vincenzo Bellini (1801-1835), Norma.

1985, Mar. 18 Photo. ***Perf. 12***
1081 A265 450 l ocher & gray blk 1.00 1.00
1082 A265 600 l yel grn & gray blk 1.25 1.25

1985, May 16 Litho. ***Perf. 13½x14***

Sportphilex '85: Natl. Olympic Committee and Sportphilex '85 emblems, flags of Andorra, Cyprus, Iceland, Liechtenstein, Luxembourg, Malta, Monaco, San Marino.

1083 A266 50 l Diving .15 .15
1084 A266 350 l Running .45 .45
1085 A266 400 l Rifle shooting .52 .52
1086 A266 450 l Cycling .60 .60
1087 A266 600 l Handball .80 .80
Nos. 1083-1087 (5) 2.52 2.52

Emigration — A267

Intl. Youth Year — A268

1985, May 16
1088 A267 600 l Birds migrating .80 .80

1985, June 24 Photo. ***Perf. 12***
Granite Paper
1089 A268 400 l Boy, dove .55 .55
1090 A268 600 l Girl, dove, horse .85 .85

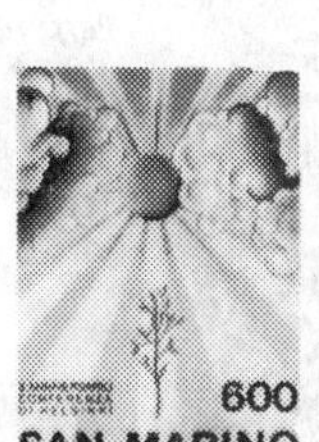

Helsinki Conference, 10th Anniv. — A269

City Hall, by Renzo Bonelli, Camera Lens. — A270

1985, June 24 ***Perf. 13½x14***
1091 A269 600 l Sapling, sunburst, clouds .80 .80

1985, June 24 ***Perf. 13½x14½***
1092 A270 450 l multi .60 .60

Intl. Fed. of Photographic Art, 18th Congress.

World Angling Championships, Arno River, Florence, Sept. 14-15 — A271

1985, Sept. 11 Photo. ***Perf. 14½x15***
1093 A271 600 l Hooked fish .80 .80

Alessandro Manzoni (1785-1873), Novelist & Poet — A272

19th century engravings from Manzoni's I Promessi Sposi (1825-27): 400 l, Don Abbondio encounters Don Rodrigo's henchmen. 450 l, The attempt to force the curate to perform a dubious marriage ceremony. 600 l, The Plague at Milan.

1985, Sept. 11 Engr. *Perf. 14x13½*

1094 A272 400 l multi	.55	.55
1095 A272 450 l multi	.60	.60
1096 A272 600 l multi	.85	.85
Nos. 1094-1096 (3)	2.00	2.00

Intl. Feline Fed. Congress A273

Mosaic detail: Cat, Natl. Museum, Naples.

1985, Oct. 25 Photo. *Perf. 12*
Granite Paper

1097 A273 600 l multi	.85	.85

Exhibition Type of 1980

ITALIA '85: Views of the Colosseum, Rome.

1985, Oct. 25 *Perf. 11½x12*
Granite Paper

1098 A222 1000 l multi	1.25	1.25
1099 A222 1500 l multi	1.90	1.90
a. Pair, #1098-1099	3.25	3.25

Christmas A275

Photo. & Engr.
1985, Dec. 3 *Perf. 14*

1100 A275 400 l Angel	.60	.60
1101 A275 450 l Mother and Child	.70	.70
1102 A275 600 l Angel, diff.	.90	.90
a. Strip of 3, #1100-1102	2.25	2.25

Hospital, Cailungo A276

1986, Mar. 6 Photo. *Perf. 12x11½*

1103 A276 450 l multi	.60	.60
1104 A276 650 l multi	.85	.85

Natl. social security org., ISS, 30th anniv., and World Health Day.

Halley's Comet — A277

Designs: 550 l, Giotto space probe. 1000 l, Adoration of the Magi, by Giotto (1276-1337).

1986, Mar. 6 *Perf. 11½x12*

1105 A277 550 l multi	.75	.75
1106 A277 1000 l multi	1.35	1.35

Deer A278

3rd Veterans World Table Tennis Championships A279

Europa Issue 1986
1986, May 22 Photo. *Perf. 13½x14*

1107 A278 550 l shown	*3.25*	*3.25*
1108 A278 650 l Falcon	*3.75*	*3.75*

1986, May 22 Engr.

1109 A279 450 l multicolored	.62	.62

AMERIPEX '86, Chicago, May 22-June 1 — A280

Views of Old Water Tower, Chicago: 2000 l, Lithograph, 1870, by Charles Shober. 3000 l, Photograph, 1986.

Perf. 11½x12
1986, May 22 Photo. Unwmk.

1110 A280 2000 l multi	2.75	2.75
1111 A280 3000 l multi	4.25	4.25
a. Pair, #1110-1111	7.00	7.00

Intl. Peace Year — A281

1986, July 10 Photo. *Perf. 11½x12*

1112 A281 550 l multi	.75	.75

Souvenir Sheet

Terra Cotta Statuary, Tomb of Emperor Qin Shi Huang Di (259-210 B.C.) — A282

Litho. & Engr.
1986, July 10 *Perf. 13½*

1113 Sheet of 3	4.50	4.50
a. A282 550 l Bearded man	.75	.75
b. A282 650 l Horse, horiz.	.88	.88
c. A282 2000 l Bearded man, diff.	2.75	2.75

Normalization of diplomatic relations with the People's Republic of China, 15th anniv.

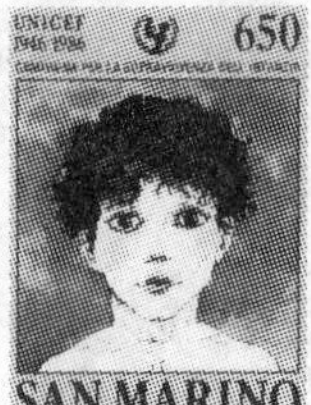

UNICEF, 40th Anniv. A283

European Boccie Championships A284

1986, Sept 16 Photo. *Perf. 12*

1114 A283 650 l multi	.95	.95

1986, Sept. 16 *Perf. 14x15*

1115 A284 550 l multi	.80	.80

Choral Society, 25th Anniv. — A285

Christmas — A286

Painting (detail): Apollo Dancing with the Muses, by Giulio Romano (1492-1546).

1986, Sept. 16

1116 A285 450 l multi	.75	.75

Photo. & Engr.
1986, Nov. 26 *Perf. 14*

Design: Oil on wood triptych, 15th cent., by Hans Memling (1435-1494), Kunsthistorisches Museum, Vienna.

1117 A286 450 l St. John the Baptist	.75	.75
1118 A286 550 l Virgin and Child	.90	.90
1119 A286 650 l St. John the Evangelist	1.10	1.10
a. Strip of 3, #1117-1119	2.75	2.75

Europa Issue 1987

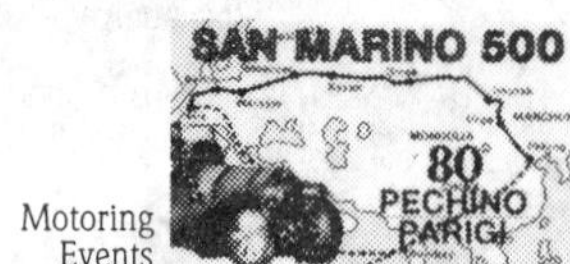

Motoring Events A288

Our Lady of Consolation Church, Borgomaggiore A287

Church designed by Giovanni Michelucci, architect: 600 l, Architect's sketch of interior. 700 l, Actual interior.

1987, Mar. 12 Photo. *Perf. 12*

1120 A287 600 l multi	*3.25*	*3.25*
1121 A287 700 l multi	*3.75*	*3.75*

Designs: 500 l, 80th anniv., Peking-Paris Race. 600 l, 15th San Marino Rally. 700 l, Mille Miglia Race, 60th anniv.

1987, Mar. 12 *Perf. 11½*

1122 A288 500 l multi	.80	.80
1123 A288 600 l multi	.95	.95
1124 A288 700 l multi	1.10	1.10
Nos. 1122-1124 (3)	2.85	2.85

Sculptures, Open-air Museum A289

Seventh Natl. Art Biennale A290

Perf. 14½x13½
1987, June 13 Photo.

1125 A289 50 l Reffi Busignani	.15	.15
1126 A289 100 l Bini	.16	.16
1127 A289 200 l Guguianu	.32	.32
1128 A289 300 l Berti	.48	.48
1129 A289 400 l Crocetti	.62	.62
1130 A289 500 l Berti, diff.	.78	.78
1131 A289 600 l Messina	.90	.90
1132 A289 1000 l Minguzzi	1.50	1.50
1133 A289 2200 l Greco	3.50	3.50
1134 A289 10000 l Sassu	15.50	15.50
Nos. 1125-1134 (10)	23.91	23.91

1987, June 13 *Perf. 11½*

Abstract works: 500 l, Dal Diario del Brasileforesta Vergine, by Emilio Vedova. 600 l, Invenzione Cromatica con Brio, by Corrado Cagli.

Granite Paper

1135 A290 500 l multi	.78	.78
1136 A290 600 l multi	.90	.90

Air Club of San Marino Ultra-lightweight Aircraft — A291

1987, June 13
Granite Paper

1137 A291 600 l multi	.90	.90

Mahatma Gandhi A292

1987, Aug. 2 Photo. *Perf. 14x13½*

1138 A292 500 l Gandhi Square, bust	.78	.78

A293

A294

1987, Aug. 29 *Perf. 12*
Granite Paper

1139 A293 600 l Olympic emblem, athlete	.90	.90

OLYMPHILEX '87, Rome.

1987, Aug. 29 Granite Paper

1140 A294 700 l ultra, blk & red	1.00	1.00

First Representation of San Marino at the Mediterranean Games, Syria, Sept. 11-15.

Exhibition Type of 1980

HAFNIA '87: Views of Copenhagen (1836-1986), as seen from the Round Tower.

1987, Oct. 16 Photo. *Perf. 11½x12*
Granite Paper

1141 A222 1200 l multi	1.90	1.90
1142 A222 2200 l multi, diff.	3.50	3.50
a. Pair, #1141-1142	5.50	5.50

Christmas — A296 High Speed Train — A297

Details from Triptych of Cortona and The Annunciation, by Fra Angelico (c. 1400-1455), Diocesan Museum of Cortona: No. 1143, Angel. No. 1144, Madonna and child. No. 1145, Saint. Printed se-tenant.

Photo. & Engr.

1987, Nov. 12 *Perf. 13½*

1143 A296 600 l multi .98 .98
1144 A296 600 l multi .98 .98
1145 A296 600 l multi .98 .98
a. Strip of 3, #1143-1145 3.00 3.00

Europa Issue 1988

1988, Mar. 17 Photo. *Perf. 12*

Granite Paper

1146 A297 600 l shown *2.25 2.25*
1147 A297 700 l Fiber optics *2.75 2.75*

Promote Stamp Collecting A298

Stamps, cancellations, covers: 50 l, Nos. 81, B25 and 859. 150 l, No. C11. 300 l, Nos. 349 and 1006. 350 l, Nos. 944 and 1031. 1000 l, Nos. 303, 1081 and 308.

1988, Mar. 17 *Perf. 11½*

Granite Paper

1148 A298 50 l multi .15 .15
1149 A298 150 l multi .24 .24
1150 A298 300 l multi .50 .50
1151 A298 350 l multi .58 .58
1152 A298 1000 l multi 1.60 1.60
Nos. 1148-1152 (5) 3.07 3.07

See Nos. 1179-1183, 1225-1229.

A299 A300

Historic sites and distinguished professors: 550 l, Carlo Malagola. 650 l, Pietro Ellero. 1300 l, Giosue Carducci (1835-1907), professor of literary history, 1861-1904, and Nobel Prize winner for literature, 1906. 1700 l, Giovanni Pascoli (1855-1912), lyric poet, Pascoli's successor as professor at Bologna.

1988, May 7 Photo. *Perf. 13½x14*

1153 A299 550 l multi .85 .85
1154 A299 650 l multi 1.00 1.00
1155 A299 1300 l multi 1.90 1.90
1156 A299 1700 l multi 2.50 2.50
Nos. 1153-1156 (4) 6.25 6.25

Bologna University, 900th anniv.

1988, July 8 Photo. *Perf. 13½x14*

Posters from Fellini Films: 300 l, La Strada. 900 l, La Dolce Vita. 1200 l, Amarcord.

1157 A300 300 l multi .45 .45
1158 A300 900 l multi 1.35 1.35
1159 A300 1200 l multi 1.80 1.80
Nos. 1157-1159 (3) 3.60 3.60

Federico Fellini, Italian film director and winner of the 1988 San Marino Prize.

See Nos. 1187-1190, 1202-1204.

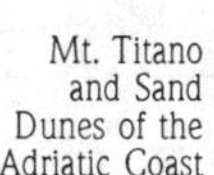

Mt. Titano and Sand Dunes of the Adriatic Coast A301

1988, July 8 *Perf. 14x13½*

1160 A301 750 l multi 1.10 1.10

40th Stamp Fair, Riccione.

Souvenir Sheet

1988 Summer Olympics, Seoul — A302

1988, Sept. 19 Photo. *Perf. 13½x14*

1161 A302 Sheet of 3 4.00 4.00
a. 650 l Running .95 .95
b. 750 l Hurdles 1.10 1.10
c. 1300 l Gymnastics 1.90 1.90

Intl. AIDS Congress, San Marino, Oct. 10-14 A303

1988, Sept. 19 *Perf. 14x13½*

1162 A303 250 l shown .38 .38
1163 A303 350 l "AIDS" .52 .52
1164 A303 650 l Virus, knot .95 .95
1165 A303 1000 l Newspaper 1.50 1.50
Nos. 1162-1165 (4) 3.35 3.35

Kurhaus Scheveningen, The Hague — A304

Perf. 11½x12

1988, Oct. 18 Photo. Granite Paper

1166 A304 1600 l Lithograph, c. 1885 2.35 2.35
1167 A304 3000 l 1988 4.40 4.40
a. Pair, #1166-1167 6.75 6.75

FILACEPT '88, Holland.

See Nos. 1190-1191.

Christmas A305

Paintings by Melozzo da Forli (1438-1494): No. 1168, Angel with Violin, Vatican Art Gallery. No. 1169, Angel of the Annunciation, Uffizi Gallery, Florence. No. 1170, Angel with Mandolin, Vatican Art Gallery.

1988, Dec. 9 Photo. *Perf. 13½*

Size of No. 1169: 21x40mm

1168 A305 650 l multi 1.05 1.05
1169 A305 650 l multi 1.05 1.05
1170 A305 650 l multi 1.05 1.05
a. Strip of 3, #1168-1168 3.25 3.25

Europa Issue 1989

Souvenir Sheet

Children's Games — A306

1989, Mar. 31 Photo. *Perf. 13½x14*

1171 Sheet of 2 *7.00 7.00*
a. A306 650 l Sledding *3.25 3.25*
b. A306 750 l Hopscotch *3.75 3.75*

Nature Conservation A307

Illustrations by contest-winning youth: 200 l, Federica Sparagna. 500 l, Giovanni Monteduro. 650 l, Rosa Mannarino.

1989, Mar. 31 *Perf. 14x13½*

1172 A307 200 l multi .30 .30
1173 A307 500 l multi .75 .75
1174 A307 650 l multi .95 .95
Nos. 1172-1174 (3) 2.00 2.00

Sporting Anniversaries and Events — A308

1989, May 13 Photo. *Perf. 12*

Granite Paper

1175 A308 650 l Olympics .98 .98
1176 A308 750 l Soccer 1.15 1.15
1177 A308 850 l Tennis 1.25 1.25
1178 A308 1300 l Car racing 1.95 1.95
Nos. 1175-1178 (4) 5.33 5.33

Natl. Olympic Committee, 30th anniv. (650 l); admission of San Marino Soccer Federation to the UEFA and FIFA (750 l); San Marino '89, the tennis grand prix (850 l); Grand Prix of San Marino, Imola (1300 l).

Stamp Collecting Type of 1988

Covers and canceled stamps (postal history): 100 l, No. 916a with Iserravalle cancel, Sept. 1, 1977. 200 l, No. 1151 with Montegiardino cancel, May 3, 1986. 400 l, Italy No. 47 canceled on San Marino parcel card #422, 1895. 500 l, Type SP3 essay proposed by Martin Riester di Parigi, March 1865. 1000 l, Stampless cover, 1862.

1989, May 13 Granite Paper *Perf. 12*

1179 A298 100 l multi .15 .15
1180 A298 200 l multi .30 .30
1181 A298 400 l multi .60 .60
1182 A298 500 l multi .75 .75
1183 A298 1000 l multi 1.50 1.50
Nos. 1179-1183 (5) 3.30 3.30

French Revolution, Bicent. — A309

1989, July 7 Litho. *Perf. 12½x13*

1184 A309 700 l The Tennis Court Oath 1.00 1.00
1185 A309 1000 l Arrest of Louis XVI 1.50 1.50
1186 A309 1800 l Napoleon 2.75 2.75
Nos. 1184-1186 (3) 5.25 5.25

Show Business Type of 1988

Scenes from: 1200 l, *Marguerite et Armand.* 1500 l, *Apollon Musagete.* 1700 l, *Valentino.*

1989, Sept. 18 Photo. *Perf. 13½x14*

1187 A300 1200 l multi 1.80 1.80
1188 A300 1500 l multi 2.25 2.25
1189 A300 1700 l multi 2.55 2.55
Nos. 1187-1189 (3) 6.60 6.60

Rudolf Nureyev, Russian ballet dancer and winner of the 1989 San Marino Prize.

See Nos. 1187-1189, 1202-1204.

Exhibition Type of 1988

Views of The Capitol, Washington, DC.: 2000 l, In 1850. 2500 l, In 1989.

1989, Nov. 17 Photo. *Perf. 11½*

Granite Paper

1190 A304 2000 l multi 3.00 3.00
1191 A304 2500 l multi 3.75 3.75
a. Pair, #1190-1191 6.75 6.75

World Stamp Expo '89.

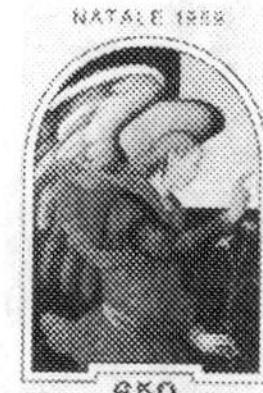

A310 A311

Christmas: Panels from a Polyptych, c. 1540, by Coda Studio of Rimini, in the Church of the Servants of Mary, Valdragone.

1989, Nov. 17

Size of No. 1193: 50x40mm

Granite Paper

1192 A310 650 l Angel .95 .95
1193 A310 650 l Holy family .95 .95
1194 A310 650 l Praying Madonna .95 .95
a. Strip of 3, #1192-1194 3.00 3.00

1990, Feb. 22 Photo. *Perf. 13½x14*

Europa: Post offices.

1195 A311 700 l Palazzeto delle Poste, 1842 1.10 1.10
1196 A311 800 l Dogana 1.30 1.30

SAN MARINO Siamo qui We are here Wir sind hier 600

A312 A313

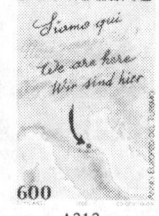

Design: *The Martyrdom of Saint Agatha,* by Giambattista Tiepolo, and occupation force departing by the Porta del Loco.

1990, Feb. 22 Granite Paper *Perf. 12*

1197 A312 3500 l multicolored 5.50 5.50

Liberation from Cardinal Alberoni's occupation force, 250th anniv.

Perf. 11½x12

1990, Mar. 23 Photo.

Granite Paper

European Tourism Year: No. 1198, The republic pinpointed on a map of Italy. No. 1199, San Marino atop Mt. Titano in proximity to other cities in the region. No. 1200, Rocca Guaita, San Marino.

1198 A313 600 l shown .95 .95
1199 A313 600 l multicolored .95 .95
1200 A313 600 l multicolored .95 .95
Nos. 1198-1200 (3) 2.85 2.85

See Nos. 1209a, 1260-1262.

Souvenir Sheet

1990 World Cup Soccer Championships, Italy — A314

Various athletes: a, Germany. b, Italy. c, Great Britain. d, Uruguay. e, Brazil. f, Argentina.

1990, Mar. 23 *Perf. 13½x14*

1201 Sheet of 6 6.25 6.25
a.-f. A314 700 l any single 1.00 1.00

Show Business Type of 1988

Scenes from: 600 l, *Hamlet*. 700 l, *Richard III*. 1500 l, *Marathon Man*.

1990, May 3 Photo. *Perf. 13½x14*

1202 A300 600 l multi .98 .98
1203 A300 700 l multi 1.15 1.15
1204 A300 1500 l multi 2.45 2.45
Nos. 1202-1204 (3) 4.58 4.58

Sir Laurence Olivier (1907-1989), British actor, winner of the 1990 San Marino Prize. Name misspelled "Lawrence" on the stamps.

President of Italy, State Visit — A315

1990, June 11 Litho. *Perf. 13x12½*

1205 A315 600 l multicolored .98 .98

Statue of Saint Marinus — A316

Designs: No. 1207, Liberty statue. No. 1208, Government Palace. No. 1209, Flag of San Marino.

1990, June 11 Photo. *Perf. 11½*
Granite Paper
Booklet Stamps

1206 A316 50 l multicolored .15 .15
1207 A316 50 l multicolored .15 .15
1208 A316 50 l multicolored .15 .15
1209 A316 50 l multicolored .15 .15
a. Bklt. pane of 7, #1198-1200, perf. 11½ vert., #1206-1209 3.20
Set value .32 .32

See Nos. 1256-1259.

Discovery of America, 500th Anniv. (in 1992) A317

1990, Sept. 6 Litho. *Perf. 13x12½*

1210 A317 1500 l Artifacts, map 1.90 1.90
1211 A317 2000 l Native plants, map 2.50 2.50

See Nos. 1230-1231.

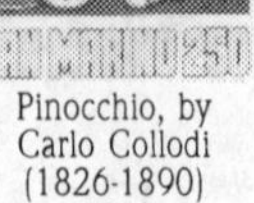

Pinocchio, by Carlo Collodi (1826-1890) A318

Flora and Fauna A319

1990, Sept. 6 Photo. *Perf. 11½x12*
Granite Paper

Cartoon style drawings from Pinocchio.

1212 A318 250 l shown .40 .40
1213 A318 400 l Geppetto .65 .65
1214 A318 450 l Blue fairy .75 .75
1215 A318 600 l Cat & wolf .95 .95
Nos. 1212-1215 (4) 2.75 2.75

1990, Oct. 31 Photo. *Perf. 14x13½*

Designs: 200 l, Papilio machaon, Ephedra major. 300 l, Apoderus coryli, Corylus avellana. 500 l, Eliomys quercinus, Quercus ilex. 1000 l, Lacerta viridis, Ophrys bertolonii. 2000 l, Regulus ignicapillus, Pinus nigra.

1216 A319 200 l multicolored .30 .30
1217 A319 300 l multicolored .45 .45
1218 A319 500 l multicolored .75 .75
1219 A319 1000 l multicolored 1.50 1.50
1220 A319 2000 l multicolored 3.00 3.00
Nos. 1216-1220 (5) 6.00 6.00

A320 A321

Christmas: Cuciniello Crib, San Martino Museum of Naples.

1990, Oct. 31 *Perf. 11½*
Granite Paper

1221 A320 750 l shown 1.25 1.25
1222 A320 750 l Nativity, diff. 1.25 1.25
a. Pair, #1221-1222 2.50 2.50

1991, Feb. 12 Photo. *Perf. 13½x14*

1223 A321 750 l Ariane 4 rocket 3.50 3.50
1224 A321 800 l ERS-1 satellite 3.75 3.75

Europa.

Stamp Collecting Type of 1988

Areas of philately: 100 l, Stamp store. 150 l, Clubs. 200 l, Exhibitions. 450 l, Albums, catalogues. 1500 l, Magazines, books.

1991, Feb. 12 *Perf. 12*
Granite Paper

1225 A298 100 l multicolored .16 .16
1226 A298 150 l multicolored .24 .24
1227 A298 200 l multicolored .32 .32
1228 A298 450 l multicolored .75 .75
1229 A298 1500 l multicolored 2.25 2.25
Nos. 1225-1229 (5) 3.72 3.72

Italian Philatelic Press Union, 25th anniv. (No. 1229).

Discovery of America Type

1991, Mar. 22 Litho. *Perf. 13x12½*

1230 A317 750 l Map, instruments 1.10 1.10
1231 A317 3000 l Columbus' fleet 4.50 4.50

1992 Summer Olympics, Barcelona A323

Olympic torch relay.

1991, Mar. 22 *Perf. 15x14*

1232 A323 400 l Athens .60 .60
1233 A323 600 l San Marino .90 .90
1234 A323 2000 l Barcelona 3.00 3.00
Nos. 1232-1234 (3) 4.50 4.50

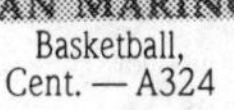

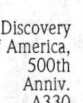

Basketball, Cent. — A324

Fauna — A325

Designs: 750 l, James Naismith (1861-1939), creator of basketball, players.

1991, June 4 Photo. *Perf. 13½x14*

1235 A324 650 l multicolored 1.05 1.05
1236 A324 750 l multicolored 1.20 1.20

1991, June 4 *Perf. 14x13½*

1237 A325 500 l House cat .75 .75
1238 A325 550 l Hamster on wheel .85 .85
1239 A325 750 l Great Dane, poodle 1.10 1.10
1240 A325 1000 l Tropical fish 1.50 1.50
1241 A325 1200 l Birds in cage 1.75 1.75
Nos. 1237-1241 (5) 5.95 5.95

Children's Day.
See Nos. 1251-1255.

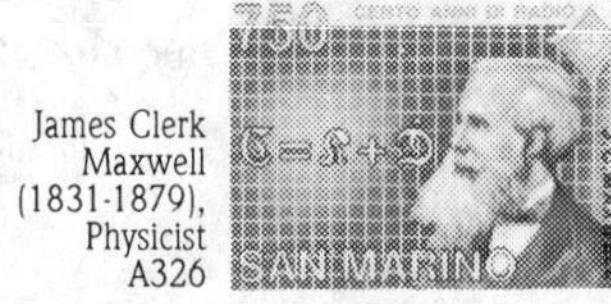

James Clerk Maxwell (1831-1879), Physicist A326

1991, Sept. 24 Photo. *Perf. 14x13½*

1242 A326 750 l multicolored 1.20 1.20

Radio, cent. (in 1995).
See Nos. 1263, 1279, 1300.

Souvenir Sheet

Birth of New Europe — A327

Designs: No. 1243a, Dove, broken chains, Brandenburg Gate. b, Pres. Gorbachev, rainbow, Pres. Bush. c, Flower, broken barbed wire, map.

1991, Sept. 24 **Litho.**

1243 A327 1500 l Sheet of 3, #a.-c. 7.20 7.20

La Rocca fortress — A328

Christmas: Diff. winter views of 10th cent.

1991, Nov. 13 Litho. *Perf. 14½*

1244 A328 600 l multicolored .95 .95
1245 A328 750 l multicolored 1.10 1.10
1246 A328 1200 l multicolored 1.90 1.90
Nos. 1244-1246 (3) 3.95 3.95

No. 1246 is airmail.

Gioacchino Rossini (1792-1868), Composer — A329

Designs: 750 l, Bianca e Falliero, Rossini opera festival 1989. 1200 l, The Barber of Seville, La Scala 1982-83.

1992, Feb. 3 Photo. *Perf. 14x13½*

1247 A329 750 l multicolored 1.20 1.20
1248 A329 1200 l multicolored 2.00 2.00

Discovery of America, 500th Anniv. A330

Designs: 1500 l, Columbus, ships at anchor, natives. 2000 l, Map of voyages.

1992, Feb. 3 Litho. *Perf. 12*

1249 A330 1500 l multicolored 2.50 2.50
1250 A330 2000 l multicolored 3.35 3.35

Fauna Type of 1991

Flora.

1992, Mar. 26 Litho. *Perf. 13½*

1251 A325 50 l Roses .15 .15
1252 A325 200 l House plant .32 .32
1253 A325 300 l Orchids .50 .50
1254 A325 450 l Cacti .75 .75
1255 A325 5000 l Geraniums 8.25 8.25
Nos. 1251-1255 (5) 9.97 9.97

Tourism Types of 1990

Designs: No. 1256, Crossbowman. No. 1257, Tennis player. No. 1258, Motorcyclist. No. 1259, Race car. No. 1260, Couple in moonlight. No. 1261, Man in restaurant. No. 1262, Woman reading beneath umbrella.

1992, Mar. 26 *Perf. 14½x13½*
Booklet Stamps

1256 A316 50 l multicolored .15 .15
1257 A316 50 l multicolored .15 .15
1258 A316 50 l multicolored .15 .15
1259 A316 50 l multicolored .15 .15

Perf. 13½ Vert.

1260 A313 600 l multicolored .95 .95
1261 A313 600 l multicolored .95 .95
1262 A313 600 l multicolored .95 .95
a. Bklt. pane of 7, #1256-1262+label 3.35

Physicist Type of 1991

Design: Heinrich Rudolf Hertz (1857-94).

1992, Mar. 26 Photo. *Perf. 14x13½*

1263 A326 750 l multicolored 1.20 1.20

Radio, cent. (in 1995).

Discovery of America, 500th Anniv. — A331

1992, May 22 Photo. *Perf. 12x11½*
Granite Paper

1264 A331 750 l Globe, ship at sea 1.20 1.20
1265 A331 850 l Ship in egg 1.40 1.40

Europa.

Souvenir Sheet

1992 Summer Olympics, Barcelona — A332

a, Soccer. b, Shooting. c, Swimming. d, Running.

1992, May 22 Litho. *Perf. 14*

1266 A332 1250 l Sheet of 4, #a.-d. 8.00 8.00

Mushrooms — A333

Designs: Nos. 1267, Poisonous mushrooms. No. 1268a, Edible mushrooms in bowl. No. 1268b, Edible mushrooms on table.

1992, Sept. 18 Photo. *Perf. 11½x12*
Granite Paper

1267 A333 Pair .80 .80
a.-b. 250 l any single .40 .40
1268 A333 Pair 1.15 1.15
a.-b. 350 l any single .56 .56

Admission to the UN — A334

Designs: a, Arms of San Marino, buildings. b, UN emblem, buildings.

1992, Sept. 18 Litho. *Perf. 12x12½*

1269 A334 Pair 3.20 3.20
a.-b. 1000 l any single 1.60 1.60

The Sacred Conversation, by Piero della Francesca (1420-1492)
A335

Christmas: a, Entire painting. b, Detail of faces. c, Detail of dome.

1992, Nov. 16 Litho. *Perf. 14½*

1270 Triptych 3.60 3.60
a.-c. A335 750 l any single 1.20 1.20

Contemporary Art — A336

Paintings: 750 l, Stars, by Nicola de Maria. 850 l, Abstract face, by Mimmo Paladino.

1993, Jan. 29 Litho. *Perf. 11½*

1271 A336 750 l multicolored 1.20 1.20
1272 A336 850 l multicolored 1.40 1.40

Europa.

1993 Sporting Events — A337

1993, Jan. 29 *Perf. 13½x14*

1273 A337 300 l Tennis .48 .48
1274 A337 400 l Cross-country skiing .65 .65
1275 A337 550 l Women running .90 .90
1276 A337 600 l Fisherman 1.00 1.00
1277 A337 700 l Men running 1.15 1.15
1278 A337 1300 l Sailboat, runners 2.10 2.10
Nos. 1273-1278 (6) 6.28 6.28

No. 1273, Youth Games. No. 1274-1275, European Youth Olympic Days. No. 1276, World Championships for Freshwater Angling Clubs, Ostellato, Italy. No. 1277, Games of Small European Countries, Malta. No. 1278, Mediterranean Games, Roussillon, France.

Physicists Type of 1991

Design: 750 l, Edouard Branly (1844-1940).

1993, Mar. 26 Photo. *Perf. 14x13½*

1279 A326 750 l multicolored .95 .95

Radio, cent. (in 1995).

Souvenir Sheet

Inauguration of State Television — A338

Designs: a, 100-meter finals, World Track Championships, Tokyo, 1991. b, San Marino. c, Neil Armstrong on moon, 1969.

1993, Mar. 26 Litho. *Perf. 13½*

1280 Sheet of 3 7.50 7.50
a.-c. A338 2000 l any single 2.50 2.50

Soaking may affect the hologram on #1280b.

Butterflies — A339

1993, May 26 Litho. *Perf. 14x15*

1281 A339 250 l Iphiclides podalirius .38 .38
1282 A339 250 l Colias crocea .38 .38
1283 A339 250 l Nymphalis antiopa .38 .38
1284 A339 250 l Melitaea cinxia .38 .38
a. Block or strip of 4, #1281-1284 1.55 1.55

World Wildlife Fund.

Miniature Sheet

United Europe — A340

Village of Europe: No. 1285a, Denmark. b, England. c, Ireland. d, Luxembourg. e, Germany. f, Netherlands. g, Belgium. h, Portugal. i, Italy. j, Spain. k, France. l, Greece.

1993, May 26 *Perf. 13½x14*

1285 A340 750 l Sheet of 12 13.00 13.00
a. Any single, #a.-l. 1.00 1.00

Famous Men — A341

Designs: 550 l, Carlo Goldoni (1707-93), playwright, vert. 650 l, Horace (65-8 BC), poet and satrist, vert. 850 l, Claudio Monteverdi (1567-1643), composer. 1850 l, Guy de Maupassant (1850-93), writer.

1993, Sept. 17 Litho. *Perf. 13½x14*

1286 A341 550 l multicolored .85 .85
1287 A341 650 l multicolored 1.00 1.00
1288 A341 850 l multicolored 1.25 1.25
1289 A341 1850 l multicolored 2.75 2.75
Nos. 1286-1289 (4) 5.85 5.85

Christmas
A342

Designs: 600 l, San Marino in winter, vert. Paintings by Gerard van Honthorst: 750 l, Adoration of the Child. 850 l, Adoration of the Shepherds, vert.

1993, Nov. 12 Litho. *Perf. 14½*

1290 A342 600 l multicolored .70 .70
1291 A342 750 l multicolored .90 .90
1292 A342 850 l multicolored 1.00 1.00
Nos. 1290-1292 (3) 2.60 2.60

10th Intl. Dog Show
A343

Designs: 350 l, Dachshund. 400 l, Afghan hound. 450 l, Belgian tervueren shepherd dog. 500 l, Boston terrier. 550 l, Mastiff. 600 l, Alaskan malamute.

1994, Jan. 31 Litho. *Perf. 15x14*

1293 A343 350 l multicolored .42 .42
1294 A343 400 l multicolored .48 .48
1295 A343 450 l multicolored .55 .55
1296 A343 500 l multicolored .60 .60
1297 A343 550 l multicolored .65 .65
1298 A343 600 l multicolored .70 .70
Nos. 1293-1298 (6) 3.40 3.40

Souvenir Sheet

1994 Winter Olympics, Lillehammer
A344

Designs: a, 90-meter ski jump. b, Downhill skiing. c, Giant slalom skiing. d, Pairs figure skating.

1994, Jan. 31 *Perf. 13½*

1299 A344 750 l 2 each #a.-d. 7.25 7.25

Physicists Type of 1991

Aleksandr Stepanovich Popov (1859-1905).

1994, Mar. 11 Photo. *Perf. 14x13½*

1300 A326 750 l multicolored .90 .90

Radio cent. (in 1995).

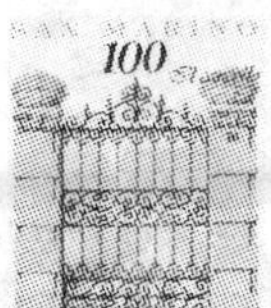

Gardens — A345

1994, Mar. 11 Litho. *Perf. 13*

1301 A345 100 l Gate .15 .15
1302 A345 200 l Grape arbor .25 .25
1303 A345 300 l Well .35 .35
1304 A345 450 l Gazebo .55 .55
1305 A345 1850 l Pond 2.25 2.25
Nos. 1301-1305 (5) 3.55 3.55

Intl. Olympic Committee, Cent. — A346

1994, Mar. 11 Photo. *Perf. 14x13½*

1306 A346 600 l multicolored .70 .70

A347 A348

Various soccer plays: a, Two players, one with #8 on shirt. b, Player in blue shirt kicking ball upward. c, Player heading ball. d, Players, one with #6 on shirt. e, Goal keeper.

1994, May 23 Litho. *Perf. 14*

1307 A347 600 l Strip of 5, #a.-e. 3.50 3.50

1994 World Cup Soccer Championships, US. No. 1307 has a continuous design.

1994, May 23

Europa (Ulysses spacecraft and: 750 l, Flight path around Sun and Jupiter. 850 l, Sun.

1308 A348 750 l multicolored 1.00 1.00
1309 A348 850 l multicolored 1.25 1.25

Inauguration of Government Building, Cent.
A349

Designs: 150 l, Exterior in shade, vert. 600 l, Exterior in sunshine, vert. 650 l, Clock tower. 1000 l, Interior.

Perf. 13½x13, 13x13½

1994, Sept. 30 Litho.

1310 A349 150 l multicolored .20 .20
1311 A349 600 l multicolored .75 .75
1312 A349 650 l multicolored .85 .85
1313 A349 1000 l multicolored 1.25 1.25
Nos. 1310-1313 (4) 3.05 3.05

Dedication of St. Mark's Basilica, 900th Anniv.
A350

1994, Oct. 8 Photo. *Perf. 13½x13*

1314 A350 750 l multicolored 1.10 1.10
a. Souvenir sheet of 2, tete beche 2.25 2.25

No. 1314 printed with se-tenant label. No. 1314a contains No. 1314 and Italy No. 2003. Only No. 1314 was valid for postage in San Marino.

Touring Club of Italy, Cent. — A351

Vehicles traveling on road in middle of flower field: a, Traffic cop, bus. b, Tandem tanker truck. c, Sailboat, volcano. d, Truck loaded with animals, camper, fish in lake.

1994, Nov. 18 Litho. *Perf. 14x13½*

1315	Block of 4	5.00	5.00
a.-d.	A351 1000 l any single	1.25	1.25

No. 1315 is a continuous design.

A352

A353

The Enthroned Madonna and Child with Saints, by Giovanni Santi (1440-1494) (Christmas): 600 l, Drummer, piper. 750 l, Madonna and Child. 850 l, Piper, harpist.

1994, Nov. 18 *Perf. 14x15*

1316	A352	600 l multicolored	.75	.75
1317	A352	750 l multicolored	.90	.90
1318	A352	850 l multicolored	1.00	1.00
		Nos. 1316-1318 (3)	2.65	2.65

1995, Feb. 10 Photo. *Perf. 13x14*

1319	A353	100 l Cycling	.15	.15
1320	A353	500 l Volleyball	.65	.65
1321	A353	650 l Speed skater	.80	.80
1322	A353	850 l Runner	1.10	1.10
		Nos. 1319-1322 (4)	2.70	2.70

Sporting Events of 1995: Junior World Cycling Championships, Forli, San Marino (#1319). Volleyball, cent. (#1320). Men's Speed Skating World Championships, Baselga di Pine, Italy (#1321). World Track & Field Championships, Goteborg, Sweden (#1322).

European Nature Conservation Year — A354

Nature scenes with flowers, water: a, Snails, dragonfly, fish. b, Frog, snake. c, Ladybugs, butterfly. d, Ducklings, frog. e, Ducks, snail.

1995, Feb. 10

1323	A354	600 l Strip of 5, #a.-e.	3.75	3.75

No. 1323 is a continuous design.

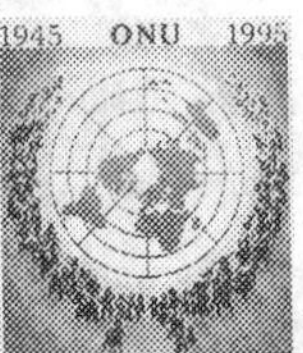

UN, 50th Anniv. — A355

Designs: 550 l, UN emblem surrounded by people. 600 l, Emblem in center of rose. 650 l, Hourglass shaped from halves of globe. 1200 l, "50," Emblem, rainbow.

1995, Mar. 24 Litho. *Perf. 14x15*

1324	A355	550 l multicolored	.65	.65
1325	A355	600 l multicolored	.70	.70
1326	A355	650 l multicolored	.75	.75
1327	A355	1200 l multicolored	1.40	1.40
		Nos. 1324-1327 (4)	3.50	3.50

Peace & Freedom A356

1995, Mar. 24 *Perf. 15x14*

1328	A356	750 l shown	.90	.90
1329	A356	850 l Sheep, meadow	1.00	1.00

Europa.

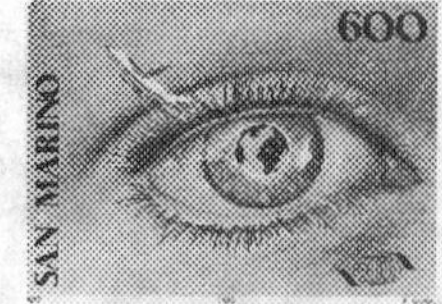

World Tourism Organization, 20th Anniv. — A357

Designs: 750 l, Mt. Titano encircled by five colored lines symbolizing continents. 850 l, Airplane over globe. 1200 l, Five lines encircling earth.

1995, May 5 Litho. *Perf. 15x14*

1330	A357	600 l multicolored	.75	.75
1331	A357	750 l multicolored	.90	.90
1332	A357	850 l multicolored	1.00	1.00
1333	A357	1200 l multicolored	1.50	1.50
		Nos. 1330-1333 (4)	4.15	4.15

Santa Croce Basilica, Florence, 700th Anniv. A358

Designs: 1200 l, Detail from fresco, The Legend of the True Cross, by Agnolo Gaddi, facade of the basilica. 1250 l, Painting, The Madonna and Child with Saints, by Andrea della Robbia, Santa Croce Cloister, Pazzi Chapel.

1995, May 5

1334	A358	1200 l multicolored	1.50	1.50
1335	A358	1250 l multicolored	1.50	1.50

Radio, Cent. A359

Designs: No. 1336, Stations on radio dial. No. 1337, Guglielmo Marconi (1874-1937), transmitting equipment.

1995, June 8 Litho. *Perf. 14*

1336	A359	850 l multicolored	1.00	1.00
1337	A359	850 l multicolored	1.00	1.00
a.		Pair, #1336-1337	2.00	2.00

Printed in sheets of 10 stamps.

See Germany #1900, Ireland #973-974, Italy #2038-2039, Vatican City #978-979.

Miniature Sheet

Motion Picture, Cent. A360

Different frames from films:
The General: a, 1. b, 2. c, 3. d, 4.
Il Gattopardo: e, 1. f, 2. g, 3. h, 4.
Allegro Non Troppo: i, 1. j, 2. k, 3. l, 4.
Braveheart: m, 1. n, 2. o, 3. p, 4.

1995, Sept. 14 Litho. *Perf. 15x14*

1338	Sheet of 16	5.00	5.00
a.-p.	A360 250 l any single	.30	.30

Exhibition Type of 1980

Qianmen complex of Zhengyangmen Rostrum, Embrasured Watchtower, Beijing: No. 1339, In 1914. No. 1340, In 1995.

1995, Sept. 14 *Perf. 14*

1339	A222	1500 l multicolored	1.90	1.90
1340	A222	1500 l multicolored	1.90	1.90
a.		Pair, #1339-1340	3.75	3.75

Beijing '95.

Neri of Rimini, 14th Cent. Artist — A361

Designs: 650 l, The Annunciation.

1995, Nov. 6 Litho. *Perf. 14x15*

1341	A361	650 l multicolored	.85	.85

Christmas — A362

Designs: a, Santa, sleigh, reindeer. b, Children, Christmas tree. c, Nativity, star.

1995, Nov. 6 Litho. *Perf. 14x15*

1342	Strip of 3	2.85	2.85
a.-c.	A362 750 l any single	.95	.95

No. 1342 is a continuous design.

Express Mail Service A363

1995, Nov. 6 *Perf. 15x14*

1343	A363	6000 l multicolored	7.50	7.50

A364 A365

1996, Feb. 12 Litho. *Perf. 14x15*

1344	A364	100 l Discus	.15	.15
1345	A364	500 l Wrestling	.65	.65
1346	A364	650 l Athletics	.85	.85
1347	A364	1500 l Javelin	1.90	1.90
1348	A364	2500 l Running	3.20	3.20
		Nos. 1344-1348 (5)	6.75	6.75

1996 Summer Olympics, Atlanta.

1996, Mar. 22 Photo. *Perf. 12*

Portrait of Mother Teresa of Calcutta, by Gina Lollobrigida.

Granite Paper

1349	A365	750 l multicolored	1.10	1.10

Europa.

China '96 Philatelic Exhibition, Beijing A366

1996, Mar. 22 *Perf. 14x13½*

1350	A366	1250 l multicolored	1.75	1.75

Marco Polo's return from China, 700th anniv. (in 1995).

See Italy No. 2070.

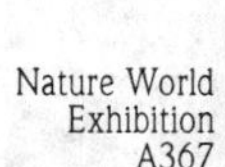

Nature World Exhibition A367

Photographs of wildlife: 50 l, Dolphin. 100 l, Frog. 150 l, Penguins. 1000 l, Butterfly. 3000 l, Ducks.

1996, Mar. 22 *Perf. 12*

Granite Paper

1351	A367	50 l multicolored	.15	.15
1352	A367	100 l multicolored	.15	.15
1353	A367	150 l multicolored	.20	.20
1354	A367	1000 l multicolored	1.40	1.40
1355	A367	3000 l multicolored	4.30	4.30
		Nos. 1351-1355 (5)	6.20	6.20

China-San Marino Relations, 25th Anniv. A82

Designs: No. 1356, Great Wall of China. No. 1357, Wall surrounding Mount Titano, San Marino.

1996, May 6 Litho. *Perf. 12*

1356	A368	750 l multicolored	1.00	1.00
1357	A368	750 l multicolored	1.00	1.00
a.		Pair, Nos. 1356-1357	2.00	2.00
b.		Souvenir sheet, No. 1357a	2.00	2.00

No. 1357a is a continuous design.

See People's Republic of China Nos. 2675-2676.

Medieval Days Celebration A369

Festival activities: No. 1358, Woman weaving yarn, vert. No. 1359, Potter, vert. No. 1360, Woman making brushes, vert. No. 1361, Man playing checkers, vert. No. 1362, Group blowing trumpets. No. 1363, Group holding banners. No. 1364, Men seated with crossbows. No. 1365, Street performers.

Perf. 14 on 2 Sides

1996, May 6 Litho. & Photo.

Booklet Stamps

1358	A369	750 l multicolored	1.00	1.00
1359	A369	750 l multicolored	1.00	1.00
1360	A369	750 l multicolored	1.00	1.00
1361	A369	750 l multicolored	1.00	1.00
1362	A369	750 l multicolored	1.00	1.00
1363	A369	750 l multicolored	1.00	1.00
1364	A369	750 l multicolored	1.00	1.00
1365	A369	750 l multicolored	1.00	1.00
a.		Booklet pane, #1358-1365	8.00	
		Complete booklet, #1365a	8.00	

Festival Bar — A370

History of Italian Songs A371

Singer, allegory of song: a, Enrico Caruso, "O Sole Mio." b, Armando Gill, "Come Pioveva." c, Ettore Petrolini, "Gastone." d, Vittorio de Sica, "Parlami D'Amore Mariu." e, Odoardo Spadaro, "La Porti un Bacione a Firenze." f, Alberto Rabagliati, "O Mia Bela Madonina." g, Beniamino Gigli, "Mamma." h, Claudio Villa, "Luna Rossa." i, Secondo Casadei, "Romagna Mia." j, Renato Rascel, "Arrivederci Roma." k, Fred Buscaglione, "Guarda Che Luna." l, Domenico Modugno, "Nel Blu Dipinto di Blu."

1996, May 25 Litho. *Perf. 14x13½*

1366	A370	2000 l shown	2.70	2.70

Granite Paper
Photo.
Perf. 12x11½

1367 A371 750 l Sheet of 12, #a.-l. 12.00 12.00

Gazzetta Dello Sport, Cent. — A372

1996, May 25 ***Perf. 12***
Granite Paper

1368 A372 1850 l multicolored 2.50 2.50

UNICEF, 50th Anniv. A373

1996, Sept. 20 Photo. ***Perf. 12***
Granite Paper

1369 A373 550 l Hen, chicks .75 .75
1370 A373 1000 l Baby birds 1.30 1.30

UNESCO, 50th Anniv. A374

World Heritage Sites: 450 l, Yellowstone Natl. Park, US. 500 l, Prehistoric caves, Vézère Valley, France. 650 l, Old town center, San Gimignano, Italy. 1450 l, Church of the Wies Pilgrimage, Germany.

1996, Sept. 20
Granite Paper

1371 A374 450 l multicolored .60 .60
1372 A374 500 l multicolored .65 .65
1373 A374 650 l multicolored .85 .85
1374 A374 1450 l multicolored 1.90 1.90
Nos. 1371-1374 (4) 4.00 4.00

Christmas — A375

Scenes looking through windows of a home: a, Playing game underneath Christmas tree. b, Tags draped from holly branch. c, Girl reading book, Santa in sleigh. d, Christmas tree. e, Fruits, candles, nuts. f, Streaking star, snowflakes. g, Toys. h, Presents. i, Santa Claus puppet. j, Nativity. k, Mistletoe. l, Stocking hung by fireplace. m, Family eating, drinking. n, Christmas tree, silhouettes of mother, father, wreath. o, Wreath, silhouettes of children & grandmother, snowman. p, Calendar, champaigne bottle popping cork.

1996, Nov. 8 Photo. ***Perf. 14½***

1375 A375 750 l Sheet of 16, #a.-p. 16.00 16.00

Souvenir Sheet

Hong Kong A376

View from harbor: a, 1897. b, 1997.

1997, Feb. 12 Litho. ***Perf. 12½***

1376 A376 750 l Sheet of 2, #a.-b. 1.80 1.80

World Alpine Skiing Championships, Sestrière, Italy — A377

Scene of people skiing on mountain: a, Skier jumping left, birds. b, Ski lift, bird in sky. c, Coming down mountain, sleigh. d, Coming down mountain, Sestrière sign.

1997, Feb. 12 ***Perf. 12***
Granite Paper

1377 A377 1000 l Block of 4, #a.-d. 4.80 4.80

No. 1377 is a continuous design.

San Marino Townships (Castelli) A378

1997, Mar. 21 Photo. ***Perf. 12***
Granite Paper

1378 A378 100 l Acquaviva .15 .15
1379 A378 200 l Borgomaggiore .25 .25
1380 A378 250 l Chiesanuova .30 .30
1381 A378 400 l Domagnano .50 .50
1382 A378 500 l Faetano .60 .60
1383 A378 550 l Fiorentino .65 .65
1384 A378 650 l Montegiardino .80 .80
1385 A378 750 l Serravalle .90 .90
1386 A378 5000 l San Marino 6.00 6.00
Nos. 1378-1386 (9) 10.15 10.15

Stories and Legends — A379

St. Marinus, Mt. Titano: 650 l, St. Marinus talking to bear that killed the mule. 750 l, Mother begging St. Marinus to forgive her son for trying to kill him.

1997, Mar. 21
Granite Paper

1387 A379 650 l multicolored .80 .80
1388 A379 750 l multicolored .90 .90

Europa.

Sporting Events A380

500 l, Giro d'Italia cycling event. 550 l, 10th Tennis Intl. 750 l, Formula 1 San Marino Grand Prix. 850 l, Republic of San Marino (Soccer) Trophy. 1000 l, Bowls (pétanque) World Championship. 1250 l, Motorcross 250cc World Championship. 1500 l, Mille Miglia classic car spectacle.

1997, May 19 Photo. ***Perf. 12***
Granite Paper

1389 A380 500 l multicolored .60 .60
1390 A380 550 l multicolored .65 .65
1391 A380 750 l multicolored .90 .90
1392 A380 850 l multicolored 1.00 1.00
1393 A380 1000 l multicolored 1.20 1.20
1394 A380 1250 l multicolored 1.50 1.50
1395 A380 1500 l multicolored 1.75 1.75
Nos. 1389-1395 (7) 7.60 7.60

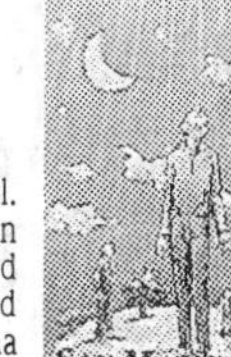
5th Intl. Symposium on UFO's and Associated Phenomena A381

1997, May 19
Granite Paper

1396 A381 750 l multicolored .90 .90

Trees — A382

50 l, Pinus pinea. 800 l, Quercus pubescens. 1800 l, Juglans regia. 2000 l, Pirus communis.

1997, June 27 Photo. ***Perf. 12***
Granite Paper

1397 A382 50 l multicolored .15 .15
1398 A382 800 l multicolored .90 .90
1399 A382 1800 l multicolored 2.00 2.00
1400 A382 2000 l multicolored 2.20 2.20
Nos. 1397-1400 (4) 5.25 5.25

First Stamps of San Marino, 120th Anniv. — A383

Designs: No. 1401, G. Battista Barbavara di Gravellona, director general of Sardinian Post Office. No. 1402, Enrico Repettati, chief engraver for Officina Carte Valori, Turin. No. 1403, Otto Bickel, German stamp dealer, promoter of San Marino-Philatelist. No. 1404, Alfredo Reffi, San Marino stamp dealer, publisher of post cards, stamp catalogue.

1997, June 27 ***Perf. 11½***
Granite Paper

1401 A383 800 l multicolored .90 .90
1402 A383 800 l multicolored .90 .90
1403 A383 800 l multicolored .90 .90
1404 A383 800 l multicolored .90 .90
a. Strip of 4, #1401-1404 3.60 3.60

Beatification of Bartolomeo Maria Dal Monte (1726-78) A384

1997, Sept. 18 Photo. ***Perf. 12***
Granite Paper

1405 A384 800 l multicolored .95 .95

Italian Comic Book Characters A385

Designs: a, "Quadratino," by Antonio Rubino. b, "Signor Bonaventura," by Sergio Tofano. c, "Kit Carson," by Rino Albertarelli. d, "Cocco Bill," by Benito Jacovitti. e, "Tex Willer," by Gian Luigi Bonelli and Arelio Galleppini. f, "Diabolik," by Angela and Luciana Giussani and Franco Paludetti. g, "Valentina," by Guido Crepax. h, "Corto Maltese," by Hugo Pratt. i, "Sturmtruppen," by Franco Bonvicini. j, "Alan Ford," by Max Bunker. k, "Lupo Alberto," by Guido Silvestri. l, "Pimpa," by Francesco Tullio Altan. m, "Bobo," by Sergio Staino. n, "Zanardi," by Andrea Pazienza. o, "Martin Mystère," by Alfredo Castelli and Giancarlo Alessandrini. p, "Dylan Dog," by Tiziano Sclavi and Angelo Stano.

1997, Sept. 18 Granite Paper
Sheet of 16

1406 A385 800 l #a.-p. 15.00 15.00

Adoration of the Magi, by Georgio Vasari (1511-74) — A386

1997, Nov. 14 Photo. ***Perf. 12***
Granite Paper

1407 A386 800 l multicolored 1.00 1.00

Volunteer Service, Solidarity A387

Designs: 550 l, St. Francis of Assisi, doves. 650 l, Mariele Ventre, children. 800 l, Children circling hands around world, Zecchino d'Oro song festival.

1997, Nov. 14
Granite Paper

1408 A387 550 l multicolored .70 .70
1409 A387 650 l multicolored .85 .85
1410 A387 800 l multicolored 1.00 1.00
Nos. 1408-1410 (3) 2.55 2.55

Volkswagen Beetle A388

Designs: a, Maggiolino (old Beetle). b, Golf I. c, New Beetle. d, Golf IV.

1997, Nov. 14

Granite Paper

1411	A388	800 l Sheet of 4, #a.-d.	4.25	4.25

No. 1411 was issued with attached entry form for drawing to win a new Beetle car. Entry form is rouletted at top to separate from bottom of sheet.

Ferrari's Formula 1 Race Cars, 50th Anniv. A389

Model number, year: a, 125S, 1947. b, 500F2, 1952. c, 801, 1956. d, 246 Dino, 1958. e, 156, 1961. f, 158, 1964. g, 312T, 1975. h, 312T4, 1979. i, 126C, 1981. j, 156/85, 1985. k, 639, 1989. l, F310, 1996.

1998, Feb. 11 Litho. *Perf. 13*

1412	A389	800 l Sheet of 12, #a.-l.	11.00	11.00

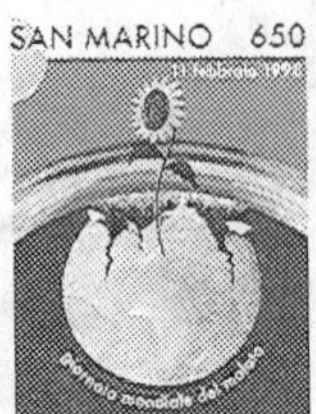

A390

A391

6th World Day of the Sick: 1500 l, Rainbow pulled over earth by dove.

1998, Feb. 11 *Perf. 14x14½*

1413	A390	650 l shown	.75	.75
1414	A390	1500 l multicolored	1.70	1.70

1998, Mar. 31 Litho. *Perf. 14x15*

Europa (Natl. Feasts and Festivals): 650 l, Installation of the Captains Regent. 1200 l, Feast Day of the Republic's Patron Saint.

1415	A391	650 l multicolored	.75	.75
1416	A391	1200 l multicolored	1.30	1.30

Giacomo Leopardi (1798-1837), Poet — A392

Words from poem, illustration: 550 l, "The Infinite," 1819, hedges, hill. 650 l, "A Village Saturday," 1829, woman walking. 900 l, "Nocturne of a Wandering Asian Shepherd," 1822-30, man looking at moon. 2000 l, "To Sylvia," woman's face.

1998, Mar. 31 *Perf. 15x14*

1417	A392	550 l multicolored	.60	.60
1418	A392	650 l multicolored	.75	.75
1419	A392	900 l multicolored	1.00	1.00
1420	A392	2000 l multicolored	2.25	2.25
		Nos. 1417-1420 (4)	4.60	4.60

SEMI-POSTAL STAMPS

Regular Issue of 1903 Surcharged:

1917 **Pro combattenti** = 25 — a

1917 **Pro combattenti** **Cent. 50** — b

1917, Dec. 15 Wmk. 140 *Perf. 14*

B1	A10(a)	25c on 2c vio	1.25	1.25
B2	A11(b)	50c on 2 l vio	16.00	16.00

Statue of Liberty — SP1

View of San Marino SP2

1918, June 1 Typo.

B3	SP1	2c dl vio & blk	.15	.15
B4	SP1	5c bl grn & blk	.15	.15
B5	SP1	10c lake & blk	.15	.15
B6	SP1	20c brn org & blk	.15	.15
B7	SP1	25c ultra & blk	.30	.30
B8	SP1	45c yel brn & blk	.30	.30
B9	SP2	1 l bl grn & blk	7.00	7.00
B10	SP2	2 l vio & blk	5.50	5.50
B11	SP2	3 l claret & blk	5.50	5.50
		Nos. B3-B11 (9)	19.20	19.20

These stamps were sold at an advance of 5c each over face value, the receipts from that source being devoted to the support of a hospital for Italian soldiers.

For surcharges see Nos. 89-92.

Nos. B6-B8 Overprinted

3
Novembre
1918

1918, Dec. 12

B12	SP1	20c brn org & blk	.90	.90
B13	SP1	25c ultra & blk	.90	.90
B14	SP1	45c yel brn & blk	.90	.90

Overprinted **3 Novembre 1918**

B15	SP2	1 l blue grn & blk	.90	.90
B16	SP2	2 l violet & blk	4.75	4.75
B17	SP2	3 l claret & blk	4.75	4.75
		Nos. B12-B17 (6)	13.10	13.10

Celebration of Italian Victory over Austria. Inverted overprints were privately produced.

Coat of Arms SP3

Liberty SP4

1923, Sept. 20 Engr.

B18	SP3	5c + 5c olive grn	.15	.15
B19	SP3	10c + 5c orange	.15	.15
B20	SP3	15c + 5c dk green	.15	.15
B21	SP3	25c + 5c brn lake	.40	.40
B22	SP3	40c + 5c vio brn	.80	.80
B23	SP3	50c + 5c gray	.60	.25
B24	SP4	1 l + 5c blk & bl	1.90	1.90
		Nos. B18-B24 (7)	4.15	3.80

St. Marinus — SP5

Wmk. 140

1944, Apr. 25 Photo. *Perf. 14*

B25	SP5	20 l + 10 l gldn brn	.90	.50
		Sheet of 8	27.50	27.50

The surtax was used for workers' houses. See No. CB1.

No. 256 Surcharged in Red "L. 10"

1946, Aug. 24 Unwmk.

B26	A46	50 l + 10 l	5.00	5.00
		Sheet of 10	*575.00*	*575.00*

Third Philatelic Day, Rimini. The surtax was for the exhibition.

Air Post Types of 1946 Surcharged "CONVEGNO FILATELICO / 30 NOVEMBRE 1946 / + LIRE 25" (or "LIRE 50") in Red or Violet

1946, Nov. 30 Wmk. 277

B26A	AP7	3 l + 25 l dk brn (R)	.25	.18
B26B	AP8	5 l + 25 l red org (V)	.25	.18
B26C	AP6	10 l + 50 l ultra (R)	2.75	2.50
		Nos. B26A-B26C (3)	3.25	2.86

Inscription "Posta Aerea" does not appear on these stamps.

No. 260 Surcharged in Black + 1

1947, Nov. 13 Wmk. 217 *Perf. 12*

B27	A53	1 l + 1 l brt grn & vio	.15	.15
B28	A53	1 l + 2 l brt grn & vio	.15	.15
B29	A53	1 l + 3 l brt grn & vio	.15	.15
B30	A53	1 l + 4 l brt grn & vio	.15	.15
B31	A53	1 l + 5 l brt grn & vio	.15	.15
a.		Strip of 5, #B27-B31	1.00	1.00

Surcharged on No. 261

B32	A53	2 l + 1 l pur & olive	.15	.15
B33	A53	2 l + 2 l pur & olive	.15	.15
B34	A53	2 l + 3 l pur & olive	.15	.15
B35	A53	2 l + 4 l pur & olive	.15	.15
B36	A53	2 l + 5 l pur & olive	.15	.15
a.		Strip of 5, #B32-B36	1.00	1.00

Surcharged on No. 262

B37	A53	4 l + 1 l	3.00	3.25
B38	A53	4 l + 2 l	3.00	3.25
a.		Pair, #B37-B38	12.00	12.00
		Set value	6.60	7.25

Surcharges on Nos. B27-B38 are arranged consecutively, changing from ascending to descending order of denomination on alternate rows in the sheet.

Catalogue values for unused stamps in this section, from this point to the end of the section, are for Never Hinged items.

Refugee Boy — SP6

1982, Dec. 15 Photo. *Perf. 11½*

B39	SP6	300 l + 100 l multi	.48	.48

Surcharge was for refugee support.

AIR POST STAMPS

View of San Marino AP1

Wmk. 217

1931, June 11 Engr. *Perf. 12*

C1	AP1	50c blue grn	1.10	1.10
C2	AP1	80c red	1.90	1.90
C3	AP1	1 l bister brn	1.10	1.10
C4	AP1	2 l brt violet	1.10	1.10
C5	AP1	2.60 l Prus bl	12.50	12.50
C6	AP1	3 l dk gray	12.50	12.50
C7	AP1	5 l olive grn	1.75	1.75
C8	AP1	7.70 l dk brown	2.25	2.25
C9	AP1	9 l dp orange	2.75	2.75
C10	AP1	10 l dk blue	165.00	165.00
		Nos. C1-C10 (10)	201.95	201.95

Exist imperf.

Graf Zeppelin Issue

Stamps of Type AP1 Surcharged in Blue or Black

ZEPPELIN 1933

L. 3.

1933, Apr. 28

C11	AP1	3 l on 50c org	1.25	*45.00*
C12	AP1	5 l on 80c ol grn	21.00	*45.00*
C13	AP1	10 l on 1 l dk bl (Bk)	21.00	*57.50*
C14	AP1	12 l on 2 l yel brn	21.00	*70.00*
C15	AP1	15 l on 2.60 l dl red (Bk)	21.00	*80.00*
C16	AP1	20 l on 3 l bl grn (Bk)	21.00	*90.00*
		Nos. C11-C16 (6)	106.25	*387.50*

Exist imperf.

Nos. C1 and C2 Surcharged

C. 75

1936, Apr. 14

C17	AP1	75c on 50c blue grn	2.75	2.75
C18	AP1	75c on 80c red	7.75	7.75

Nos. C5 and C6 Surcharged with New Value and Bars

1941, Jan. 12

C19	AP1	10 l on 2.60 l	100.00	100.00
C20	AP1	10 l on 3 l	24.00	24.00

View of Arbe — AP2

Wmk. 140

1942, Mar. 16 Photo. *Perf. 14*

C21	AP2	25c brn & gray blk	.15	.15
C22	AP2	50c grn & brn	.15	.15
C23	AP2	75c gray bl & red brn	.16	.16
C24	AP2	1 l ocher & brn	.28	.28
C25	AP2	5 l bis brn & bl	3.50	3.50
		Nos. C21-C25 (5)	4.24	4.24

Return of the Italian flag to Arbe.

San Marino Map, Fasces and Wing
AP3 AP4

Overprinted "28 LVGLIO 1943 1642 d. F. R." in Black

1943, Aug. 27

C26 AP3 25c yellow org .15 .15
C27 AP3 50c car rose .15 .15
C28 AP3 75c dark brown .15 .15
C29 AP3 1 l dk rose vio .15 .15
C30 AP3 2 l sapphire .15 .15
C31 AP3 5 l orange red .28 .28
C32 AP3 10 l deep green .75 .75
C33 AP3 20 l black 2.25 2.75
Nos. C26-C33 (8) 4.03 4.53

See footnote after No. 227. Nos. C26-C33 exist without overprint (not regularly issued). Value $2,250.

Overprinted "GOVERNO PROVVISORIO"

1943, Aug. 27

C34 AP4 25c yellow org .15 .15
C35 AP4 50c car rose .15 .15
C36 AP4 75c dark brown .15 .15
C37 AP4 1 l dk rose vio .15 .15
C38 AP4 5 l orange red .38 .38
C39 AP4 20 l black 1.90 1.90
Nos. C34-C39 (6) 2.88 2.88

Government Palace — AP5

Planes over Mt. Titano — AP8

Gulls and San Marino Skyline AP6

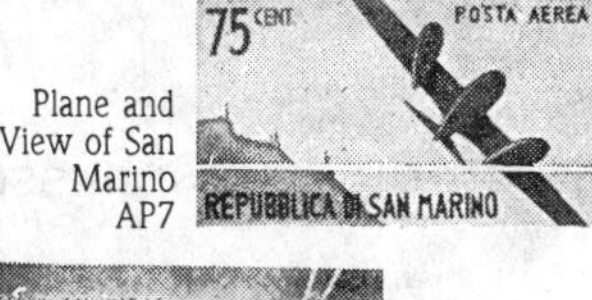

Plane and View of San Marino AP7

Plane over Globe — AP9

1945, Mar. 15 **Photo.**

C40 AP5 25 l bister brn 2.50 2.50

See note after No. 239.

Photo., Engr. (20 l, 50 l)

1946-47 **Unwmk.** ***Perf. 14***

C41 AP6 25c blue blk .15 .15
C42 AP7 75c red org .15 .15
C43 AP6 1 l brown .15 .15
C44 AP7 2 l dull green .15 .15
C45 AP7 3 l violet .15 .15
C46 AP8 5 l violet blue .15 .15
C47 AP6 10 l crimson .15 .16
C48 AP8 20 l brown lake 1.50 1.75
C49 AP8 35 l orange red 3.50 3.25
C50 AP8 50 l dk yellow grn 3.50 3.25
C51 AP9 100 l sepia ('47) 1.25 1.25
Nos. C41-C51 (11) 10.80 10.56

Some values exist imperforate.

Issue dates: 35 l, Nov. 3, 1946; 100 l, Mar. 27, 1947; others, Aug. 8, 1946.

For surcharges and overprint see Nos. B26A-B26C, C54.

Roosevelt Type of Regular Issue, 1947

F. D. Roosevelt and: 1 l, 31 l, 50 l, Eagle. 2 l, 20 l, 100 l, San Marino arms. 5 l, 200 l, Flags of San Marino and US, vert.

Wmk. 277

1947, May 3 **Photo.** ***Perf. 14***

C51A A52a 1 l dp ultra & sep .15 .15
C51B A52a 2 l org red & sep .15 .15
C51C A52a 5 l multicolored .15 .15
C51D A52a 20 l choc & sepia .15 .15
C51E A52a 31 l orange & sepia .28 .28
C51F A52a 50 l dk car & sepia .35 .40
C51G A52a 100 l blue & sepia .60 .85
C51H A52a 200 l multicolored 9.50 6.50
Nos. C51A-C51H (8) 11.33 8.63

Nos. C51A-C51E, C51H exist imperf. Value, set $105.

Nos. C51A-C51C Surcharged

1947, June 16

C51I A52a 3 l on 1 l dp ultra & sep .28 .28
C51J A52a 4 l on 2 l org red & sep .28 .28
C51K A52a 6 l on 5 l multicolored .28 .28
Nos. C51I-C51K (3) .84 .84

St. Marinus Type of Regular Issue, 1947

Wmk. 217

1947, July 18 **Engr.** ***Perf. 12***

Center in Bright Blue

C52 A53 25 l deep orange 1.00 1.00
C53 A53 50 l red brown 2.00 2.00

No. C51 Overprinted in Red

Giornata Filatelica
Rimini - San Marino
18 Luglio 1947

1947, July 18 **Unwmk.** ***Perf. 14***

C54 AP9 100 l sepia .70 .70
 a. Double overprint 22.50
 b. Inverted overprint 65.00

Rimini Phil. Exhib., July 18-20.

US No. 1 and Mt. Titano AP11

Wmk. 277

1947, Dec. 24 **Engr.** ***Perf. 14***

C55 AP11 100 l dk pur & dk brn 4.00 4.00
 a. Imperf. 47.50
 Sheet of 10 *1,250.*

1st US postage stamps, cent.

No. 264 Surcharged "POSTA AEREA" and New Value in Black

1948, Oct. 9 **Wmk. 217** ***Perf. 12***

C56 A53 200 l on 25 l 12.00 12.00

Giuseppe and Anita Garibaldi Entering San Marino — AP12

Wmk. 277

1949, June 28 **Photo.** ***Perf. 14***

Size: 27½x22mm

C57 AP12 2 l brn red & ultra .15 .15
C58 AP12 3 l dk green & sepia .15 .15
C59 AP12 5 l dk bl grn & ultra .15 .20

Size: 37x22mm

C60 AP12 25 l dk green & vio 1.00 1.00
C61 AP12 65 l grnsh blk & gray blk 5.00 5.00
Nos. C57-C61 (5) 6.45 6.50

Garibaldi's escape to San Marino, cent.

Stagecoach on Road from San Marino AP13

1950, Feb. 9 **Engr.** ***Perf. 14***

C62 AP13 200 l deep blue 1.40 1.40
 a. Perf. 13½x14 ('51) 2.75 2.75
 As "a," sheet of 6 22.50 22.50
 b. Imperf ('51) 11.50 11.50
 As "b," sheet of 6 90.00 90.00

UPU, 75th anniv. #C62 was issued in sheets of 25; #C62a & C62b in sheets of 6. See #C75.

AP14

AP15

AP16

Various Views of San Marino.

1950, Apr. 12 **Photo.** ***Perf. 14***

Size: 27½x21½mm, 21½x27½mm

C63 AP14 2 l vio & dp grn .15 .15
C64 AP14 3 l blue & brown .15 .15
C65 AP15 5 l brn blk & rose red .15 .15
C66 AP14 10 l grnsh blk & bl .20 .24
C67 AP14 15 l grnsh blk & vio .22 .30

Size: 36x26½mm, 26½x36mm

C68 AP15 55 l dp bl & dp grn 8.75 7.25
C69 AP14 100 l car & gray 2.25 2.25
C70 AP15 250 l violet & brn 8.75 7.25

Engr.

C71 AP16 500 l bl, dk grn & vio brn 55.00 55.00
Nos. C63-C71 (9) 75.62 72.74

See No. C78. For overprints and surcharges see Nos. C72-C74, C76, C79.

Types of 1950 Overprinted in Black, Blue or Brown

XXVIII FIERA
INTERNAZIO-
NALE DI
MILANO
APRILE
1950

1950, Apr. 12 **Photo.**

New Colors; Sizes as Before

C72 AP15 5 l dp bl & dp grn .15 .15
C73 AP14 15 l car & gray (Bl) .60 .55
C74 AP15 55 l vio & brn (Br) 2.50 2.50
Nos. C72-C74 (3) 3.25 3.20

The overprint is arranged differently on each denomination.

San Marino's participation in the 28th Intl. Fair of Milan, Apr., 1950.

Stagecoach Type of 1950

1951, Jan. 31 **Engr.** ***Perf. 13½x14***

C75 AP13 300 l multi 11.00 11.00
 Sheet of 6 100.00 100.00
 a. Imperf. 350.00

No. C71 Surcharged in Black "Giornata Filatelica San Marino-Riccione 20-8-1951," New Value and Bars

1951, Aug. 20 ***Perf. 14***

C76 AP16 300 l on 500 l 22.50 22.50

Flag and Plane — AP17

Perf. 13½x14

1951, Nov. 22 **Engr.** **Wmk. 277**

C77 AP17 1000 l multi 275.00 275.00
 Sheet of 6 *5,250.* *4,250.*

Type of 1950

1951, Apr. 28 **Photo.** ***Perf. 14***

Size: 36x26½mm

C78 AP16 500 l dk grn & brn 75.00 75.00
 Sheet of 6 1,000. 1,000.

No. C70 Surcharged in Black

Pro-alluvionati
italiani
1951
100

1951, Dec. 6

C79 AP15 100 l on 250 l 3.75 3.75

Issued to raise funds for flood victims in northern Italy.

Columbus, Globe, Statue of Liberty and Buildings AP18

1952, Jan. 28 **Engr.**

C80 AP18 200 l dk bl & blk 14.00 14.00

Issued to honor Christopher Columbus.

Type of 1952 Overprinted in Red

FIERA DI TRIESTE
1952

1952, June 29

C81 AP18 200 l blk brn & choc 12.00 12.00

4th Intl. Sample Fair of Trieste.

Cyclamen — AP19

Flowers and Seacoast — AP20

2 l, As #C85-C87 with flowers omitted. 3 l, Rose.

1952, Aug. 25 **Photo.** ***Perf. 10x14***

C82 AP19 1 l pur & lil rose .15 .15
C83 AP19 2 l blue & bl grn .15 .15
C84 AP19 3 l dk brn & red .15 .15

Perf. 14

C85 AP20 5 l rose lil & brn .15 .15
C86 AP20 25 l vio & bl grn .22 .30

Perf. 13

Engr.

C87 AP20 200 l multicolored 22.50 22.50
 Sheet of 6, #C87 300.00 300.00
Nos. C82-C87 (6) 23.32 23.40

Riccione Phil. Exhib., Aug. 25, 1952.

Plane Making Photographic Survey AP21

75 l, Aerial survey, seen through window.

1952, Nov. 17 **Photo.** ***Perf. 14***

C88 AP21 25 l olive green .90 .90
C89 AP21 75 l red brn & pur 3.50 3.50

Aerial photographic survey of San Marino, 1952.

Skier AP22

1953, Apr. 20 **Engr.**

C90	AP22	200 l	bl grn & dk grn	40.00	40.00
			Sheet of 6	600.00	600.00

Plane and Arms of San Marino AP23

1954, Apr. 5

C91	AP23	1000 l	dk blue & brn	65.00	65.00
			Sheet of 6	575.00	575.00

Type of Regular Issue, 1954

1954, Dec. 16 **Photo.** ***Perf. 13***

C92	A71	120 l	dp bl & red brn	1.10	1.10

Hurdler AP25

1955, June 26 **Wmk. 303** ***Perf. 14***

C93	AP25	80 l	shown	.85	.65
C94	AP25	120 l	Relay	.85	.90
			Set, never hinged	2.75	

San Marino's first Intl. Exhib. of Olympic Stamps, June.

Ski Jumper AP26

1955, Dec. 15

C95	AP26	200 l	blk & red org	9.50	9.50

7th Winter Olympic Games at Cortina d'Ampezzo, Jan. 26-Feb. 5, 1956.

No. 372 Overprinted in Upper Right Corner with Plane and "Posta Aerea"

1956, Dec. 10

C96	A76	100 l	blk & Prus grn	.95	1.25
			Never hinged	1.25	

Catalogue values for unused stamps in this section, from this point to the end of the section, are for Never Hinged items.

Helicopter, Plane and Modernistic Building — AP27

Wmk. 303

1958, Apr. 12 **Photo.** ***Perf. 14***

C97	AP27	125 l	lt blue & brn	2.00	2.00

10th participation in Milan Fair.
See Nos. 414-415.

View of San Marino AP28

Design: 300 l, Road from Mt. Titano.

Wmk. 303

1958, June 23 **Engr.** ***Perf. 13***

C98	AP28	200 l	brn & dk blue	2.00	2.00
C99	AP28	300 l	magenta & vio	2.00	2.00
a.			Strip, Nos. C98, C99 + label	5.00	5.00

Printed in sheets containing 20 each of Nos. C98 and C99 flanking a center label with San Marino coat of arms. Nos. C98 and C99 also come se-tenant in sheet.

Naples Stamps Type of Regular Issue

Design: Bay of Naples and 50g stamp of Naples.

1958, Oct. 8 **Photo.** ***Perf. 14***

C100	A85	125 l	brn & red brn	1.65	1.65

Sea Gull — AP29

Birds: 10 l, Falcon. 15 l, Mallard. 120 l, Stock dove. 250 l, Barn swallow.

1959, Feb. 12 ***Perf. 14***

C101	AP29	5 l	green & gray	.15	.15
C102	AP29	10 l	blue & org brn	.15	.15
C103	AP29	15 l	red & multi	.15	.15
C104	AP29	120 l	rose red, yel & gray blk	.45	.35
C105	AP29	250 l	dp grn, yel & blk	1.25	1.10
			Set value	1.90	1.70

Pierre de Coubertin AP30

Wmk. 303

1959, May 19 **Engr.** ***Perf. 13***

C106	AP30	120 l	sepia	1.00	.85

Pierre de Coubertin; 1960 Olympic Games in Rome.

Alitalia Viscount Over San Marino AP31

1959, June 3 **Photo.** ***Perf. 14***

C107	AP31	120 l	bright violet	1.75	1.10

First flight San Marino-Rimini-London.

Lincoln Type of Regular Issue, 1959

Design: Abraham Lincoln and San Marino peaks.

1959, July 1 **Engr.** ***Perf. 14x13***

C108	A87	200 l	dark blue	3.50	2.50

Romagna Stamps Type

Design: Bologna view, 3b Romagna stamp.

Wmk. 303

1959, Aug. 29 **Photo.** ***Perf. 14***

C109	A88	120 l	blk & blue grn	2.25	1.65

Sicily Stamps Type

Design: Fishing boats, Monte Pellegrino and 50g stamp of Sicily, horiz.

1959, Oct. 16

C110	A89	200 l	multicolored	1.25	.75

Olympic Games Type

Sports: 20 l, Basketball. 40 l, Sprint race. 80 l, Swimming, horiz. 125 l, Target shooting, horiz.

1960, May 23 **Wmk. 303** ***Perf. 14***

C111	A92	20 l	lilac	.15	.15
C112	A92	40 l	bis brn & dk red	.22	.22
C113	A92	80 l	ultra & buff	.32	.30
C114	A92	125 l	ver & dk brn	.40	.22
			Nos. C111-C114 (4)	1.09	.89

Souvenir sheets are valued and described below No. 465.

Lions Intl. Type

Design: 200 l, Globe and Lions emblem.

1960, July 1 **Photo.**

C115	A94	200 l	ol grn, brn & ultra	5.00	4.00

12th Stamp Fair Type

1960, Aug. 27 **Wmk. 303** ***Perf. 14***

C116	A95	125 l	multicolored	1.40	1.25

Helicopter and Mt. Titano AP32

1961, July 6 **Engr.** ***Perf. 14***

C117	AP32	1000 l	rose carmine	37.50	27.50
			Sheet of 6	240.00	175.00

Tupolev TU-104A AP33

Planes: 10 l, Boeing 707, vert. 15 l, Douglas DC-8. 25 l, Boeing 707. 50 l, Vickers Viscount 837. 75 l, Caravelle, vert. 120 l, Vickers VC10. 200 l, D. H. Comet 4C. 300 l, Boeing 727. 500 l, Rolls Royce Dart turbo-prop. 1000 l, Boeing 707.

1963-65 **Wmk. 339** **Photo.** ***Perf. 14***

C118	AP33	5 l	blue & vio brn	.15	.15
C119	AP33	10 l	org & dk bl	.15	.15
C120	AP33	15 l	violet & red	.15	.15
C121	AP33	25 l	violet & car	.15	.15
C122	AP33	50 l	grnsh bl & red	.15	.15
C123	AP33	75 l	emer & dp org	.15	.15
C124	AP33	120 l	vio bl & red	.28	.28
C125	AP33	200 l	brt yel & blk	.22	.22
C126	AP33	300 l	orange & blk	.25	.25

Perf. 13

C127	AP33	500 l	multicolored	3.50	3.50
			Sheet of 4	14.00	14.00
C128	AP33	1000 l	lil rose, ultra & yel	2.50	2.50
			Sheet of 4	21.00	21.00
			Nos. C118-C128 (11)	7.65	7.65

Issued: Nos. C118-C126, Dec. 5, 1963. No. C127, Mar. 4, 1965. No. C128, Mar. 12, 1964.

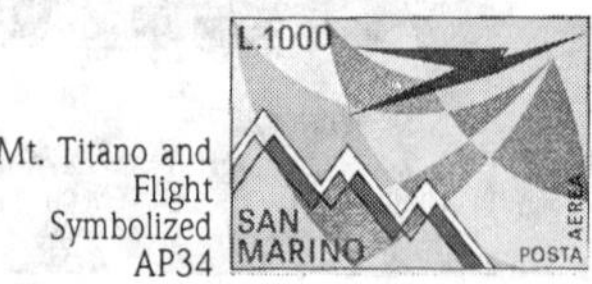
Mt. Titano and Flight Symbolized AP34

1972, Oct. 25 **Unwmk.** ***Perf. 11½***
Granite Paper

C129	AP34	1000 l	multi	1.00	.90

Glider AP35

Designs: Each stamp shows a different type of air current in background.

1974, Oct. 9 **Photo.** ***Perf. 11½***
Granite Paper

C130	AP35	40 l	multicolored	.15	.15
C131	AP35	120 l	multicolored	.15	.15
C132	AP35	500 l	multicolored	.50	.50
			Nos. C130-C132 (3)	.80	.80

50th anniversary of gliding in Italy.

San Marino 77 Type of 1977

1977, Jan. 28 **Photo.** ***Perf. 11½***

C133	A193	200 l	multicolored	.22	.22

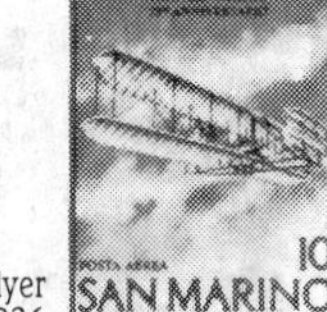
Wright Brothers' Flyer A — AP36

1978, Sept. 28 **Photo.** ***Perf. 11½***

C134	AP36	10 l	multicolored	.15	.15
C135	AP36	50 l	multicolored	.15	.15
C136	AP36	200 l	multicolored	.22	.22
			Set value	.35	.35

75th anniversary of first powered flight.

AIR POST SEMI-POSTAL STAMP

View of San Marino APSP1

Wmk. 140

1944, Apr. 25 **Photo.** ***Perf. 14***

CB1	APSP1	20 l + 10 l	ol grn	.90	.90
			Sheet of 8	22.50	22.50

The surtax was used for workers' houses.

SPECIAL DELIVERY STAMPS

SD1

Unwmk.

1907, Apr. 25 **Engr.** ***Perf. 12***

E1	SD1	25c	carmine	9.00	4.50

For surcharges see Nos. E3, E5.

Type of Regular Issue of 1903 Overprinted **ESPRESSO**

Perf. 14½x14

1923, May 30 **Wmk. 140**

E2	A11	60c	violet	.30	.30

For surcharge see No. 103.

Type of 1907 Issue Surcharged

Cent. 60

1923, July 26 ***Perf. 14***

E3	SD1	60c on 25c	carmine	.30	.30
a.			Vert. pair, imperf. between	125.00	

No. E2 Surcharged **Lire 1,25**

1926, Nov. 25 ***Perf. 14½x14***

E4	A11	1.25 l on 60c	violet	.45	.45

No. E3 Surcharged

L. 1,25

1927, Sept. 15

E5 SD1 1.25 l on 60c on 25c .55 .55
a. Inverted surcharge 57.50
b. Vert. pair, imperf. between 300.00
c. Double surcharge 225.00

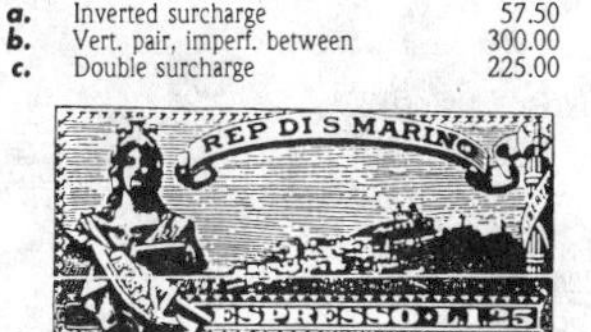

Statue of Liberty and View of San Marino
SD2

Wmk. 217

1929, Aug. 29 Engr. *Perf. 12*

E6 SD2 1.25 l green .15 .15

Overprinted in Red UNION POSTALE UNIVERSELLE

E7 SD2 2.50 l deep blue .55 .55

Arms of San Marino
SD3

Wmk. 140

1943, Sept. Photo. *Perf. 14*

E8 SD3 1.25 l green .15 .15
E9 SD3 2.50 l reddish orange .15 .15
Set value .22 .22

View of San Marino
SD4

Pegasus
SD5

1945-46 Photo. Wmk. 140

E12 SD4 2.50 l deep green .15 .15
E13 SD4 5 l deep orange .15 .15

Unwmk.

E14 SD4 5 l carmine rose .70 .50

Wmk. 277

E15 SD4 10 l sapphire ('46) 1.75 1.25

Engr.

Unwmk.

E16 SD5 30 l deep ultra ('46) 4.00 4.00
Nos. E12-E16 (5) 6.75 6.05

See Nos. E22-E23. For surcharges see Nos. E17-E21, E24-E25.

Nos. E14 and E15 Surcharged in Black

L. 15

1947 Unwmk. *Perf. 14*

E17 SD4 15 l on 5 l car rose .25 .20

Wmk. 277

E18 SD4 15 l on 10 l saph .25 .20

No. E16 Surcharged with New Value and Bars in Carmine

1947-48 Unwmk.

E19 SD5 35 l on 30 l ('48) 18.00 18.00
E20 SD5 60 l on 30 l 3.00 3.00
E21 SD5 80 l on 30 l ('48) 8.50 10.00
Nos. E19-E21 (3) 29.50 31.00

Types of 1945-46

1950, Dec. 11 Photo. Wmk. 277

E22 SD4 60 l rose brown 3.50 3.50
E23 SD5 80 l deep blue 3.50 3.50
Set, never hinged 25.00

Nos. E22-E23 Surcharged with New Value and Three Bars

1957, Dec. 12 *Perf. 14*

E24 SD4 75 l on 60 l rose brn 1.50 1.50
E25 SD5 100 l on 80 l dp blue 1.50 1.50
Set, never hinged 7.00

Catalogue values for unused stamps in this section, from this point to the end of the section, are for Never Hinged items.

Crossbow
SD6

Design: No. E27, "Espresso" at left; crossbow casts two shadows.

1965, Aug. 28 Photo. Wmk. 339

E26 SD6 120 l on 75 l blk, gray & yel .15 .15
E27 SD6 135 l on 100 l blk & org .20 .20

Without Surcharge

Design: 80 l, 100 l, "Espresso" at left; crossbow casts two shadows.

1966, Mar. 29

E28 SD6 75 l blk, gray & yel .15 .15
E29 SD6 80 l blk & lilac .15 .15
E30 SD6 100 l blk & orange .20 .20
Nos. E28-E30 (3) .50 .50

SEMI-POSTAL SPECIAL DELIVERY STAMP

SPSD1

Wmk. 140

1923, Sept. 20 Engr. *Perf. 14*

EB1 SPSD1 60c + 5c brown red .75 .75

POSTAGE DUE STAMPS

D1

Wmk. 140

1897-1920 Typo. *Perf. 14*

J1 D1 5c bl grn & dk brn .15 .15
J2 D1 10c bl grn & dk brn .15 .15
a. Numerals inverted 100.00 100.00
J3 D1 30c bl grn & dk brn .60 .40
J4 D1 50c bl grn & dk brn 1.40 .80
a. Numerals inverted 100.00 100.00
J5 D1 60c bl grn & dk brn 3.00 1.65
J6 D1 1 l claret & dk brn 2.75 .80
J7 D1 3 l claret & brn ('20) 8.00 7.25
J8 D1 5 l claret & dk brn 37.50 21.00
J9 D1 10 l claret & dk brn 12.00 14.00
Nos. J1-J9 (9) 65.55 46.20

See Nos. J10-J36. For surcharges see Nos. J37-J60, J64.

1924

J10 D1 5c rose & brown .15 .15
J11 D1 10c rose & brown .15 .15
J12 D1 30c rose & brown .15 .15
J13 D1 50c rose & brown .15 .15
J14 D1 60c rose & brown 2.75 2.75
J15 D1 1 l green & brown 4.00 4.00
J16 D1 3 l green & brown 12.00 12.00
J17 D1 5 l green & brown 13.00 13.00
J18 D1 10 l green & brown 165.00 165.00
Nos. J10-J18 (9) 197.35 197.35

1925-39 *Perf. 14*

J19 D1 5c blue & brn .15 .15
a. Numerals inverted 42.50 42.50
J20 D1 10c blue & brn .15 .15
a. Numerals inverted 42.50 42.50
J21 D1 15c blue & brn ('39) .15 .15
J22 D1 20c blue & brn ('39) .15 .15
J23 D1 25c blue & brn ('39) .15 .15
J24 D1 30c blue & brn .15 .15
J25 D1 40c blue & brn ('39) 1.50 1.40
J26 D1 50c blue & brn .15 .15
a. Numerals inverted 42.50 42.50
J27 D1 60c blue & brn 1.00 .75
J28 D1 1 l buff & brn 2.00 .70
J29 D1 2 l buff & brn ('39) .75 .75
J30 D1 3 l buff & brn 37.50 13.00
J31 D1 5 l buff & brn 11.00 2.50
J32 D1 10 l buff & brn 15.00 4.00
J33 D1 15 l buff & brn ('28) .85 .52
J34 D1 25 l buff & brn ('28) 22.50 10.50
J35 D1 30 l buff & brn ('28) 4.25 5.00
J36 D1 50 l buff & brn ('28) 5.75 5.75
Nos. J19-J36 (18) 103.15 45.92

Postage Due Stamps of 1925 Surcharged in Black and Silver

1931, May 18

J37 D1 15c on 5c bl & brn .15 .15
J38 D1 15c on 10c bl & brn .15 .15
J39 D1 15c on 30c bl & brn .15 .15
J40 D1 20c on 5c bl & brn .15 .15
J41 D1 20c on 10c bl & brn .15 .15
J42 D1 20c on 30c bl & brn .15 .15
J43 D1 25c on 5c bl & brn .50 .50
J44 D1 25c on 10c bl & brn .50 .50
J45 D1 25c on 30c bl & brn 7.00 3.25
J46 D1 40c on 5c bl & brn .40 .15
J47 D1 40c on 10c bl & brn .50 .15
J48 D1 40c on 30c bl & brn .50 .15
J49 D1 2 l on 5c bl & brn 27.50 16.00
J50 D1 2 l on 10c bl & brn 47.50 27.50
J51 D1 2 l on 30c bl & brn 40.00 22.50
Nos. J37-J51 (15) 125.30 71.60

Nos. J19, J24-J25, J30, J34, J33, J22 Surcharged in Black

Lire 1

Perf. 14, 14½x14

1936-40 Wmk. 140

J52 D1 10c on 5c ('38) .55 .55
J53 D1 25c on 30c ('38) 4.25 4.25
J54 D1 50c on 5c ('37) 4.25 4.00
J55 D1 1 l on 30c 13.00 3.25
J56 D1 1 l on 40c ('40) 4.25 3.00
J57 D1 1 l on 3 l ('37) 11.00 1.10
J58 D1 1 l on 25 l ('39) 27.50 6.75
J59 D1 2 l on 15 l ('38) 13.00 8.00
J60 D1 3 l on 20c ('40) 15.00 13.00
Nos. J52-J60 (9) 92.80 43.90

Coat of Arms — D6

1939 Typo. *Perf. 14*

J61 D6 5c blue & brown .15 .15

Nos. J61 and J36 Surcharged with New Values and Bars

1940-43

J62 D6 10c on 5c .38 .38
J63 D6 50c on 5c 1.50 .75
J64 D1 25 l on 50 l ('43) 1.75 1.75
Nos. J62-J64 (3) 3.63 2.88

Coat of Arms — D7

Unwmk.

1945, June 7 Photo. *Perf. 14*

J65 D7 5c dk green .15 .15
J66 D7 10c orange brn .15 .15
J67 D7 15c rose red .15 .15
J68 D7 20c dp ultra .15 .15
J69 D7 25c dk purple .15 .15
J70 D7 30c rose lake .15 .15
J71 D7 40c bister .15 .15
J72 D7 50c slate blk .15 .15
J73 D7 60c chestnut .15 .15
J74 D7 1 l dp orange .15 .15
J75 D7 2 l carmine .15 .15
J76 D7 5 l dull violet .15 .15
J77 D7 10 l dark blue .15 .22
J78 D7 20 l dark green 4.50 4.00
J79 D7 25 l red orange 4.50 4.00
J80 D7 50 l dark brown 4.50 4.00
Nos. J65-J80 (16) 15.45 14.02

PARCEL POST STAMPS

These stamps were used by affixing them to the way bill so that one half remained on it following the parcel, the other half staying on the receipt given the sender. Most used halves are right halves. Complete stamps were and are obtainable canceled, probably to order. Both unused and used values are for complete stamps.

PP1

Engraved, Typographed

1928, Nov. 22 Unwmk. *Perf. 12*

Pairs are imperforate between

Q1 PP1 5c blk brn & bl .15 .15
a. Imperf. 16.00
Q2 PP1 10c dk bl & bl .15 .15
Q3 PP1 20c gray blk & bl .15 .15
a. Imperf. 16.00
Q4 PP1 25c car & blue .15 .15
Q5 PP1 30c ultra & blue .15 .15
Q6 PP1 50c orange & bl .15 .15
Q7 PP1 60c rose & blue .15 .15
Q8 PP1 1 l violet & brn .15 .15
a. Imperf. 16.00
Q9 PP1 2 l green & brn .25 .25
Q10 PP1 3 l bister & brn .35 .35
Q11 PP1 4 l gray & brn .50 .50
Q12 PP1 10 l rose lilac & brn 1.65 1.65
Q13 PP1 12 l red brn & brn 4.00 4.00
Q14 PP1 15 l olive grn & brn 7.25 7.25
a. Imperf. 16.00
Q15 PP1 20 l brn vio & brn 10.00 10.00
Nos. Q1-Q15 (15) 25.20 25.20

Halves Used

Q1-Q8 .15
Q9-Q10 .15
Q11 .15
Q12 .35
Q13 .65
Q14 2.75
Q15 3.00

1945-46 Wmk. 140 *Perf. 14*

Pairs are perforated between

Q16 PP1 5c rose vio & red org .15 .15
Q17 PP1 10c red org & blk .15 .15
Q18 PP1 20c dark red & grn .15 .15
Q19 PP1 25c yel & blk .15 .15
Q20 PP1 30c red vio & org red .15 .15
Q21 PP1 50c dull pur & blk .15 .15
Q22 PP1 60c rose lake & blk .15 .15
Q23 PP1 1 l brown & dp bl .15 .15
Q24 PP1 2 l dk brn & dk bl .15 .15
Q25 PP1 3 l olive brn & brn .15 .15
Q26 PP1 4 l blue grn & brn .15 .15
Q27 PP1 10 l bl blk & brt pur .15 .15
Q28 PP1 12 l myr grn & dl bl 1.90 1.25
Q29 PP1 15 l green & purple 1.75 1.10
Q30 PP1 20 l rose lil & brn 1.25 .85
Q31 PP1 25 l dp car & ultra ('46) 24.00 22.50
Q32 PP1 50 l yel & dp org ('46) 27.50 27.50
Nos. Q16-Q32 (17) 58.20 55.00

Halves Used

Q16-Q27 .15
Q28 .15
Q29 .15
Q30 .15
Q31 .25
Q32 .50

Nos. Q32 and Q31 Surcharged with New Value and Wavy Lines in Black

1948-50

Q33 PP1 100 l on 50 l 35.00 37.50
Half, used 1.00
Q34 PP1 200 l on 25 l ('50) 72.50 77.50
Half, used 1.00

1953, Mar. 5 Wmk. 277 *Perf. 13½*

Pairs Perforated Between

Q35 PP1 10 l dk grn & rose lil 17.00 6.25
Half, used 1.00
Q36 PP1 300 l purple & lake 110.00 110.00
Half, used 1.00

1956 Wmk. 303 *Perf. 13½*

Q37 PP1 10 l gray & brt pur .35 .30
Half, used .15
Q38 PP1 50 l yel & dp org 1.10 1.00
Half, used .15

No. Q38 Surcharged with New Value and Wavy Lines In Black

Q39 PP1 100 l on 50 l 1.25 1.10
Half, used .25

Catalogue values for unused stamps in this section, from this point to the end of the section, are for Never Hinged items.

1960-61

Q40 PP1 300 l violet & brn 75.00 75.00
Half, used .50
Q41 PP1 500 l dk brn & car ('61) 4.50 4.00
Half, used .15

1965-72 Wmk. 339 *Perf. 13½*

Pairs Perforated Between

No.	Type	Description	Unused	Used
Q42	PP1	10 l gray & brt pur	.15	.15
Q43	PP1	50 l yellow & red org	.15	.15
Q44	PP1	100 l on 50 l yel & red org	1.40	1.40
Q45	PP1	300 l violet & brown	.45	.45
Q46	PP1	500 l brn & red ('72)	8.25	8.25
Q47	PP1	1000 l bl grn & lt red brn ('67)	.90	.90
		Nos. Q42-Q47 (6)	11.30	11.30

Halves Used

Q42-Q43	.15
Q44-Q45	.15
Q46	.20
Q47	.45

SARAWAK

sə-'rä-(,)wä(k)

LOCATION — Northwestern part of the island of Borneo, bordering on the South China Sea

GOVT. — Former British Crown Colony

AREA — 48,250 sq. mi. (approx.)

POP. — 975,918 (1970)

CAPITAL — Kuching

The last ruling Raja, who retired in 1946 when he ceded Sarawak to the British Crown, was Sir Charles Vyner Brooke, an Englishman. He inherited the title from his father, Sir Charles Johnson Brooke, who in turn received it from his uncle, Sir James Brooke. The title of Raja was conferred on Sir James by Raja Muda Hassim after Sir James had aided him in subduing a rebellion. The title and right of succession were duly recognized by the Sultan of Brunei and by Great Britain.

Sarawak joined the Federation of Malaysia in 1963.

100 Cents = 1 Dollar

Catalogue values for unused stamps in this country are for Never Hinged items, beginning with Scott 155.

Watermarks

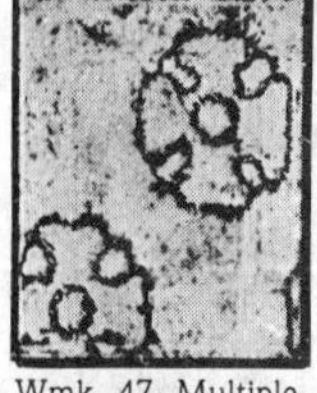

Wmk. 47- Multiple Rosettes

Wmk. 71- Rosette

Wmk. 231- Oriental Crown

Unused examples of Nos. 1-7, 25 and 32-35 are valued without gum. Stamps with original gum are worth more.

Sir James Brooke — A1

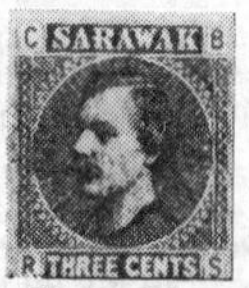

Sir Charles Johnson Brooke — A2

Unwmk.

1869, Mar. 1 Litho. *Perf. 11*

No.	Type	Description	Unused	Used
1	A1	3c brown, *yellow*	35.00	*225.00*

1871, Jan.

No.	Type	Description	Unused	Used
2	A2	3c brown, *yellow*	1.00	*3.00*

No. 2 surcharged "TWO CENTS" is believed to be bogus.

There are a number of varieties including narrow A, "period" after THREE, etc.

Imperfs. of Nos. 1, 2 are proofs.

For surcharges see Nos. 25, 32.

1875, Jan. 1 *Perf. 12*

No.	Type	Description	Unused	Used
3	A2	2c gray lilac, *lilac*	3.25	*10.00*
4	A2	4c brown, *yellow*	2.00	*2.50*
b.		Vertical pair, imperf between	*525.00*	
5	A2	6c green, *green*	3.00	*2.50*
6	A2	8c blue, *blue*	3.50	*4.00*
c.		Laid paper		
7	A2	12c red, *rose*	5.00	*6.00*
		Nos. 3-7 (5)	16.75	*25.00*

Nos. 3-7 have each five varieties of the words of value.

For surcharges see Nos. 33-35.

Imperfs are proofs.

Sir Charles Johnson Brooke — A4

1888-97 Typo. *Perf. 14*

No.	Type	Description	Unused	Used
8	A4	1c lilac & black ('92)	1.00	.45
9	A4	2c lilac & rose	1.25	.80
10	A4	3c lilac & blue	1.10	.75
11	A4	4c lilac & yellow	9.00	*16.00*
12	A4	5c lilac & green ('91)	6.00	4.00
13	A4	6c lilac & brown	10.00	*30.00*
14	A4	8c green & rose	4.00	2.00
a.		8c green & carmine	10.00	4.25
15	A4	10c green & vio ('93)	21.00	12.50
16	A4	12c green & blue	3.00	*6.00*
17	A4	16c gray grn & org ('97)	27.50	*40.00*
18	A4	25c green & brown	22.50	*27.50*
19	A4	32c gray grn & blk ('97)	20.00	*30.00*
20	A4	50c gray green ('97)	22.50	*60.00*
21	A4	$1 gray grn & blk ('97)	42.50	*60.00*
		Nos. 8-21 (14)	191.35	*290.00*

No. 21 shows the numeral on white tablet.

Three higher values —$2, $5, $10— were prepared but not issued. Value $300 each.

For surcharges see Nos. 22-24, 26-27.

Nos. 14 and 16 Surcharged in Black:

2c. (a) — 5c. (No. 23) — 5c. (No. 24)

1889-91

No.	Type	Description	Unused	Used
22	A4	2c on 8c	2.25	4.50
a.		Double surcharge	300.00	
b.		Pair, one without surcharge	2,000.	
c.		Inverted surcharge	2,000.	
23	A4	5c on 12c ('91)	15.00	20.00
a.		Double surcharge	1,100.	*1,100.*
b.		Pair, one without surcharge	—	
c.		No period after "C"	18.00	21.00
d.		Without "C"	250.00	—
e.		Double surch., one vert.	1,750.	
24	A4	5c on 12c ('91)	40.00	*105.00*
a.		No period after "C"	45.00	*100.00*
b.		Double surcharge	750.00	
c.		"C" omitted	375.00	300.00

No. 2 Surcharged in Black

ONE CENT

1892, May 23 *Perf. 11*

No.	Type	Description	Unused	Used
25	A2	1c on 3c brown, *yel*	.70	2.00
b.		Without bar	2.75	
c.		Period after "THREE"	13.00	18.00
d.		Double surcharge	375.00	

No. 10 Surcharged in Black:

one cent. (e) — One Cent. (f)

1892 *Perf. 14*

No.	Type	Description	Unused	Used
26	A4(e)	1c on 3c lilac & blue	2.75	4.25
a.		No period after "cent"	100.00	100.00
27	A4(f)	1c on 3c lilac & blue	26.00	24.00
b.		Double surcharge	375.00	275.00

Issued: #26, Feb.; #27, Jan. 12.

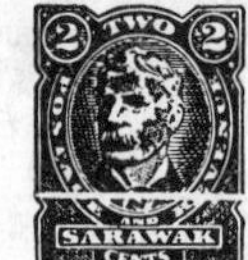

Sir Charles Johnson Brooke

A11 A12

A13

A14

1895, Jan. 1 Engr. *Perf. 11½, 12*

No.	Type	Description	Unused	Used
28	A11	2c red brn	4.00	4.25
a.		Perf. 12½	5.00	5.00
29	A12	4c black	3.00	2.50
30	A13	6c violet	3.00	6.00
31	A14	8c deep green	12.50	6.00
		Nos. 28-31 (4)	22.50	18.75

The 2c and 8c imperf are proofs. Perforated stamps of these designs in other colors are color trials.

Stamps of 1871-75 Surcharged in Black or Red

2 CENTS.

1899 *Perf. 11*

No.	Type	Description	Unused	Used
32	A2	2c on 3c brown, *yel*	1.00	1.50
a.		Period after "THREE"	50.00	

Perf. 12

No.	Type	Description	Unused	Used
33	A2	2c on 12c red, *rose*	2.25	*2.75*
a.		Inverted surcharge	900.00	*1,050.*
34	A2	4c on 6c green, *grn* (R)	14.00	*35.00*
a.		Inverted surcharge		
35	A2	4c on 8c blue, *bl* (R)	3.25	6.50
		Nos. 32-35 (4)	20.50	*45.75*

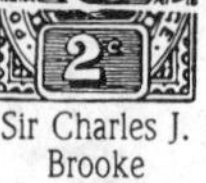

Sir Charles J. Brooke

A16

Sir Charles Vyner Brooke

A17

1899-1908 Typo. *Perf. 14*

No.	Type	Description	Unused	Used
36	A16	1c blue & car ('01)	.40	.65
37	A16	2c gray green	.75	.40
38	A16	3c dull violet ('08)	2.25	.35
39	A16	4c rose	1.25	2.00
40	A16	8c yellow & black	1.25	1.00
41	A16	10c ultra	1.25	.50
42	A16	12c light violet	1.90	1.75
43	A16	16c org brn & grn	1.25	1.75
44	A16	20c brn ol & vio ('00)	3.00	2.25
45	A16	25c brown & ultra	2.00	4.00
46	A16	50c ol grn & rose	10.00	*15.00*
47	A16	$1 rose & green	22.50	*45.00*
		Nos. 36-47 (12)	47.80	*74.65*

A 5c was prepared but not issued. Value $11.

1901 Wmk. 71

No.	Type	Description	Unused	Used
48	A16	2c gray green	15.00	10.00

1918-23 Unwmk.

No.	Type	Description	Unused	Used
50	A17	1c slate blue & rose	.60	.15
51	A17	2c deep green	1.10	.20
52	A17	2c violet ('23)	1.10	.30
53	A17	3c violet brown	2.25	1.00
54	A17	3c deep green ('22)	.75	.30
55	A17	4c carmine rose	2.00	.40
56	A17	4c purple brn ('23)	.75	.15
57	A17	5c orange ('23)	.90	.20
58	A17	6c lake brown ('22)	.75	1.00
59	A17	8c yellow & blk	4.75	*30.00*
60	A17	8c carmine rose ('22)	1.75	.65
61	A17	10c ultra	1.75	1.50
a.		10c blue	1.75	1.50
62	A17	10c black ('23)	1.50	2.00
63	A17	12c violet	5.50	8.00
64	A17	12c ultra ('22)	5.75	*10.00*
65	A17	16c brn & blue grn	3.75	4.00
66	A17	20c olive bis & vio	3.00	4.00
a.		20c olive green & violet	3.00	4.00
67	A17	25c brown & blue	3.00	*5.00*
68	A17	30c bis & gray ('22)	2.75	*2.50*
69	A17	50c olive grn & rose	4.75	6.00
70	A17	$1 car rose & grn	9.50	*12.00*
		Nos. 50-70 (21)	57.95	*89.35*

In 1918 a supply of the 1c (No. 50) had the value tablet printed, by error, in slate blue instead of rose. It is officially stated that this stamp was never issued and had no franking power. Value $20.

The $1 denomination shows numeral of value in color on white tablet.

Nos. 61 and 63 Surcharged

ONE cent

1st Printing - bars 1¼mm apart.

2nd Printing - Bars ¾mm apart.

1923, Jan.

No.	Type	Description	Unused	Used
77	A17	1c on 10c ultra	11.00	*42.50*
a.		"cnet"	300.00	*600.00*
b.		Bars ¾mm apart	75.00	
78	A17	2c on 12c violet	5.00	*15.00*
a.		Bars ¾mm apart	45.00	

Type of 1918 Issue

1928-29 Typo. Wmk. 47

No.	Type	Description	Unused	Used
79	A17	1c slate blue & rose	.50	.30
80	A17	2c dull violet	.75	.25
81	A17	3c deep green	.50	*1.00*
82	A17	4c purple brown	1.25	.20
83	A17	5c orange ('29)	4.00	*4.00*
84	A17	6c brown lake	.90	.40
85	A17	8c carmine	1.90	*6.00*
86	A17	10c black	1.50	1.00
87	A17	12c ultra	2.25	*7.50*
88	A17	16c dp brn & bl grn	1.90	*2.00*
89	A17	20c dp olive & vio	1.50	1.40
90	A17	25c dk brown & ultra	3.00	*3.00*
91	A17	30c olive bis & gray	3.00	2.50
92	A17	50c olive grn & rose	3.50	*3.00*
93	A17	$1 car rose & grn	12.50	*20.00*
		Nos. 79-93 (15)	38.95	*52.55*

Sir Charles Vyner Brooke

A18 A19

Perf. 12½

1932, Jan. 1 Engr. Wmk. 231

No.	Type	Description	Unused	Used
94	A18	1c indigo	.60	.40
95	A18	2c dark green	.60	.40
96	A18	3c deep violet	2.50	.65
97	A18	4c deep orange	.90	.25
98	A18	5c brown lake	2.50	.65
99	A18	6c deep red	3.50	*4.00*
100	A18	8c orange yel	2.50	*5.00*
101	A18	10c black	2.50	*5.00*
102	A18	12c violet blue	2.50	*4.00*
103	A18	15c orange brown	3.75	*4.00*
104	A18	20c violet & org	2.50	*4.00*
105	A18	25c org brn & yel	5.00	*7.00*
106	A18	30c org red & ol brn	4.00	*10.00*
107	A18	50c olive grn & red	5.00	*8.75*
108	A18	$1 car & green	8.00	*17.50*
		Nos. 94-108 (15)	46.35	*71.60*

1934-41 Unwmk. *Perf. 12*

No.	Type	Description	Unused	Used
109	A19	1c brown violet	.15	.15
110	A19	2c blue green	.15	.15
111	A19	2c black ('41)	.70	*1.25*
112	A19	3c black	.20	.15
113	A19	3c blue grn ('41)	1.00	2.00
114	A19	4c magenta	.45	.15
115	A19	5c violet	.20	.15
116	A19	6c deep rose	.20	.40
117	A19	6c red brn ('41)	2.50	*6.00*
118	A19	8c red brown	.20	.20
119	A19	8c deep rose ('41)	2.00	.25
120	A19	10c red	.90	.45
121	A19	12c deep ultra	.45	.50
122	A19	12c orange ('41)	.70	*5.25*
123	A19	15c orange	.80	*4.00*
124	A19	15c deep blue ('41)	2.50	*5.25*
125	A19	20c dp rose & olive	1.00	.60
126	A19	25c orange & vio	1.00	*.70*
127	A19	30c violet & red brn	1.00	1.00
128	A19	50c red & violet	1.00	.50
129	A19	$1 dk brown & red	1.00	1.00
130	A19	$2 violet & mag	2.75	*5.50*
131	A19	$3 blue grn & rose	15.00	*16.00*
132	A19	$4 red & ultra	16.00	*17.00*
133	A19	$5 red brn & red	18.00	*22.50*
134	A19	$10 orange & blk	20.00	*37.50*
		Nos. 109-134 (26)	89.85	*128.60*

Issue dates: May 1, 1934, Mar. 1, 1941.

For overprints see #135-154, 159-173, N1-N22.

Stamps of 1934-41 Overprinted in Black or Red

B M A

1945, Dec. 17

No.	Type	Description	Unused	Used
135	A19	1c brown violet	.15	.20
136	A19	2c black (R)	.15	.20
137	A19	3c blue green	.15	.20
138	A19	4c magenta	.15	.20
139	A19	5c violet (R)	.20	.45
140	A19	6c red brown	.20	.45
141	A19	8c deep rose	6.00	7.00
142	A19	10c red	.25	.45
143	A19	12c orange	.40	*2.75*
144	A19	15c deep blue	.60	.25

145 A19 20c dp rose & ol 1.00 1.00
146 A19 25c org & vio (R) 1.00 1.50
147 A19 30c vio & red brn 1.00 2.00
148 A19 50c red & violet .85 .25
149 A19 $1 dk brown & red 2.00 .95
150 A19 $2 violet & mag 5.00 3.50
151 A19 $3 blue grn & rose 10.50 19.00
152 A19 $4 red & ultra 15.00 19.00
153 A19 $5 red brn & red 60.00 70.00
154 A19 $10 org & blk (R) 60.00 85.00
Nos. 135-154 (20) 164.60 214.35
Set, never hinged 275.00

Catalogue values for unused stamps in this section, from this point to the end of the section, are for Never Hinged items.

Sir James Brooke, Sir Charles V. Brooke and Sir Charles J. Brooke A20

1946, May 18
155 A20 8c dark carmine .30 .15
156 A20 15c dark blue .30 .35
157 A20 50c red & black .60 1.25
158 A20 $1 sepia & black 2.25 6.25
Nos. 155-158 (4) 3.45 8.00

Type of 1934-41 Overprinted in Blue or Red

1947, Apr. 16 Wmk. 4 *Perf. 12*
159 A19 1c brown violet .15 .15
160 A19 2c black (R) .15 .15
161 A19 3c blue green (R) .15 .15
162 A19 4c magenta .15 .15
163 A19 6c red brown .15 .15
164 A19 8c deep rose .15 .15
165 A19 10c red .15 .15
166 A19 12c orange .15 .15
167 A19 15c deep blue (R) .20 .20
168 A19 20c dp rose & ol (R) .25 .25
169 A19 25c orange & vio (R) .25 .25
170 A19 50c red & vio (R) .40 .40
171 A19 $1 dk brown & red 1.10 1.10
172 A19 $2 violet & mag 1.90 1.90
173 A19 $5 red brown & red 4.25 4.25
Nos. 159-173 (15) 9.55 9.55

Silver Wedding Issue
Common Design Types

1948, Oct. 25 Photo. *Perf. 14x14½*
174 CD304 8c scarlet .15 .15

Engraved; Name Typographed
Perf. 11½x11
175 CD305 $5 light brown 24.00 25.00

UPU Issue
Common Design Types
Engr.; Name Typo. on 15c, 25c
Perf. 13½, 11x11½

1949, Oct. 10 Wmk. 4
176 CD306 8c rose carmine .55 .55
177 CD307 15c indigo .75 .75
178 CD308 25c green 1.40 1.40
179 CD309 50c violet 3.50 3.50
Nos. 176-179 (4) 6.20 6.20

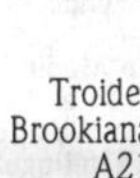

Troides Brookiana A21

Western Tarsier — A22

Designs: 3c, Kayan tomb. 4c, Kayan girl and boy. 6c, Bead work. 8c, Dyak dancer. 10c, Scaly anteater. 12c, Kenyah boys. 15c, Fire making. 20c, Kelemantan rice barn. 25c, Pepper vines. 50c, Iban woman. $1, Kelabit smithy. $2, Map of Sarawak. $5, Arms of Sarawak.

Perf. 11½x11, 11x11½

1950, Jan. 3 Engr.
180 A21 1c black .20 .15
181 A22 2c orange red .20 .15
182 A22 3c green .25 .20
183 A22 4c brown .25 .20
184 A22 6c aquamarine .30 .20
185 A21 8c red .45 .30
186 A21 10c orange .50 2.25
187 A21 12c purple 1.65 1.25
188 A21 15c deep blue .50 .25
189 A21 20c red org & brn .85 .50
190 A21 25c carmine & grn .90 .60
191 A22 50c purple & brn 1.40 .20
192 A21 $1 dk brn & bl grn 4.75 1.50
193 A21 $2 rose car & blue 19.00 6.50

Engr. and Typo.
194 A21 $5 dp vio, blk, red & yel 19.00 8.75
Nos. 180-194 (15) 50.20 23.00

1952, Feb. 1
195 A21 10c orange *(Map)* .90 .40

Coronation Issue
Common Design Type

1953, June 3 Engr. *Perf. 13½x13*
196 CD312 10c ultra & black .75 .60

Logging — A23

Hornbill — A24

Elizabeth II — A25

Designs: 2c, Young Orangutan. 4c, Kayan Dancing. 8c, Shield with spears. 10c, Kenyah ceremonial carving. 12c, Barong Panau (sailboat). 15c, Turtles. 20c, Melanau basket making. 25c, Astana, Kuching (Governor's Residence). $1, $2, Queen Elizabeth II (Portrait like Fiji A39). $5, Arms.

Perf. 11x11½, 11½x11, 12x12½ (A25)

1955-57 Wmk. 4 Engr.
197 A23 1c green .15 .15
198 A23 2c red orange .15 .25
199 A23 4c brown carmine .15 .15
200 A24 6c greenish blue 2.50 .40
201 A24 8c rose red .15 .15
202 A24 10c dark green .25 .15
203 A24 12c purple 2.50 .50
204 A24 15c ultra .95 .15
205 A24 20c brown & olive .95 .25
206 A24 25c brt green & brn 6.00 .25
207 A25 30c violet & red brn 1.50 .15
208 A25 50c car rose & blk 1.50 .30
209 A25 $1 orange brn & grn 2.50 .50
210 A25 $2 green & violet 8.00 2.25

Engr. and Typo.
211 A24 $5 dp vio, blk, red & yel 17.00 6.00
Nos. 197-211 (15) 44.25 11.60

Issued: 30c, June 1, 1955; others, Oct. 1, 1957.
See Nos. 215-222.

Freedom from Hunger Issue
Common Design Type
Perf. 14x14½

1963, June 4 Photo. Wmk. 314
212 CD314 12c sepia 1.50 .20

STATE OF MALAYSIA
Types of 1955-57
Perf. 11x11½, 11½x11

1964-65 Engr. Wmk. 314
215 A23 1c green .15 .30
216 A23 2c red orange .60 5.00
217 A24 6c green blue 3.75 2.25
218 A24 10c dark green .95 .60
219 A24 12c purple 1.40 4.50
220 A24 15c ultra 1.10 8.00
221 A24 20c brown & olive .40 1.25
222 A24 25c brt green & brown 1.90 2.25
Nos. 215-222 (8) 10.25 24.15

Issued: 20c, 6/9/64; 2c, 15c, 8/17/65; others, 9/9/64.

Orchid Type of Johore (Malaysia), 1965, with State Crest
Perf. 14½

1965, Nov. 15 Wmk. 338 Photo.
Flowers in Natural Colors
228 A14 1c black & lt grnsh bl .15 .15
229 A14 2c black, red & gray .15 .15
230 A14 5c black & Prus blue .40 .15
231 A14 6c black & lt lilac .55 .20
232 A14 10c black & lt ultra .70 .30
233 A14 15c black, lil rose & grn 1.40 .30
234 A14 20c black & brown 1.75 .50
Nos. 228-234 (7) 5.10
Set value 1.45

Clipper and State Crest — A26

Perf. 13½x13

1971, Feb. 1 Litho. Unwmk.
235 A26 1c Delias ninus .15 .15
236 A26 2c Danaus melanippus .35 .15
237 A26 5c Parthenos sylvia .70 .15
a. Booklet pane of 4 ('73) 2.25
238 A26 6c Papilio demoleus .90 .15
239 A26 10c Hebomnia glaucippe .90 .15
a. Booklet pane of 4 ('73) 3.00
240 A26 15c Precis orithya 1.25 .25
a. Booklet pane of 4 ('73) 4.50
241 A26 20c Valeria valeria 1.50 .40
Nos. 235-241 (7) 5.75
Set value .95

Clipper and New State Crest — A27

Changed Colors, Designs as Before

1977-78 Photo. Unwmk.
242 A27 1c multi ('78) 7.00 4.00
243 A27 2c multi ('78) 5.00 2.00
244 A27 5c multicolored 1.00 .15
245 A27 10c multicolored .65 .20
246 A27 15c multicolored 1.50 .30
247 A27 20c multi ('78) 2.75 .40
Nos. 242-247 (6) 17.90 7.05

Flower Type of Johore, 1979, with State Crest

1979, Apr. 30 Wmk. 47 *Perf. 14½*
248 A16 1c multicolored .15 .15
249 A16 2c multicolored .15 .15
250 A16 5c multicolored .15 .15
251 A16 10c multicolored .15 .15
252 A16 15c multicolored .15 .15
253 A16 20c multicolored .20 .15
254 A16 25c multicolored .45 .15
Set value 1.20 .45

1984-86 Unwmk.
250a A16 5c ('86) 1.00 1.25
251a A16 10c ('85) 1.00 1.10
253a A16 20c 1.00 1.10
Nos. 250a-253a (3) 3.00 3.45

Agriculture and State Arms Type of Johore
Wmk. 388

1986, Oct. 25 Litho. *Perf. 12*
255 A19 1c multicolored .15 .15
256 A19 2c multicolored .15 .15
257 A19 5c multicolored .15 .15
258 A19 10c multicolored .15 .15
259 A19 15c multicolored .15 .15
260 A19 20c multicolored .15 .15
261 A19 30c multicolored .25 .15
Set value .75 .45

OCCUPATION STAMPS

Issued under Japanese Occupation
Stamps of 1934-41 Handstamped in Violet
府政国帝本日大

1942 Unwmk. *Perf. 12*
N1 A19 1c brown violet 40.00 60.00
N2 A19 2c blue green 80.00 150.00
N3 A19 2c black 80.00 110.00
N3A A19 3c black 225.00 250.00
N4 A19 3c blue green 55.00 80.00
N5 A19 4c magenta 50.00 50.00
N6 A19 5c violet 60.00 60.00
N7 A19 6c deep rose 100.00 110.00
N8 A19 6c red brown 60.00 80.00
N8A A19 8c red brown 225.00 250.00
N9 A19 8c deep rose 110.00 165.00
N10 A19 10c red 60.00 80.00
N11 A19 12c deep ultra 125.00 125.00
N12 A19 12c orange 125.00 125.00
N12A A19 15c orange 275.00 275.00
N13 A19 15c deep blue 100.00 100.00
N14 A19 20c dp rose & ol 60.00 80.00
N15 A19 25c orange & vio 80.00 80.00
N16 A19 30c violet & red brn 50.00 80.00
N17 A19 50c red & violet 60.00 80.00
N18 A19 $1 dk brown & red 90.00 110.00
N19 A19 $2 violet & mag 190.00 225.00
N19A A19 $3 blue grn & rose 800.00 1,000.
N20 A19 $4 red & ultra 200.00 250.00
N21 A19 $5 red brown & red 200.00 250.00
N22 A19 $10 orange & blk 200.00 250.00
Nos. N1-N22 (26) 3,700. 4,475.

Stamps overprinted with Japanese characters in oval frame or between 2 vertical black lines were not for paying postage.

SASENO

'sə–'zä–(,)nō

LOCATION — An island in the Adriatic Sea, lying at the entrance of Valona Bay, Albania.
GOVT. — Italian possession
AREA — 2 sq. mi.

Italy occupied this Albanian islet in 1914, and returned it to Albania in 1947.

100 Centesimi = 1 Lira

Used values in italics are for postally used stamps. CTO's or stamps with fake cancels sell for about the same as unused, hinged stamps.

Italian Stamps of 1901-22 Overprinted **SASENO**

1923 Wmk. 140 *Perf. 14*
1 A48 10c claret 2.50 8.25
2 A48 15c slate 2.50 8.25
3 A50 20c brown orange 2.50 8.25
4 A49 25c blue 2.50 8.25
5 A49 30c yellow brown 2.50 8.25
6 A49 50c violet 2.50 8.25
7 A49 60c carmine 2.50 8.25
8 A46 1 l brown & green 2.50 8.25
a. Double overprint 70.00
Nos. 1-8 (8) 20.00

Superseded by postage stamps of Italy.

SAUDI ARABIA

'saú–dē ə–'rā–bē–ə

LOCATION — Southwestern Asia, on the Arabian Peninsula between the Red Sea and the Persian Gulf
GOVT. — Kingdom
AREA — 927,000 sq. mi.
POP. — 8,400,000 (est. 1984)
CAPITAL — Riyadh

In 1916 the Grand Sherif of Mecca declared the Sanjak of Hejaz independent of Turkish rule. In 1925, Ibn Saud, then Sultan of the Nejd, captured the Hejaz after a prolonged siege of Jedda, the last Hejaz stronghold.

The resulting Kingdom of the Hejaz and Nejd was renamed Saudi Arabia in 1932.

40 Paras = 1 Piaster = 1 Guerche (Garch, Qirsh)
11 Guerche = 1 Riyal (1928)
110 Guerche = 1 Sovereign (1931)
440 Guerche = 1 Sovereign (1952)
20 Piasters (Guerche) = 1 Riyal (1960)
100 Halalas = 1 Riyal (1976)

Catalogue values for unused stamps in this country are for Never Hinged items, beginning with Scott 178 in the regular postage section, Scott C1 in the airpost section, Scott J28 in the postage due section, Scott O7 in official section, and Scott RA6 in the postal tax section.

Watermarks

Wmk. 337- Crossed Swords and Palm Tree

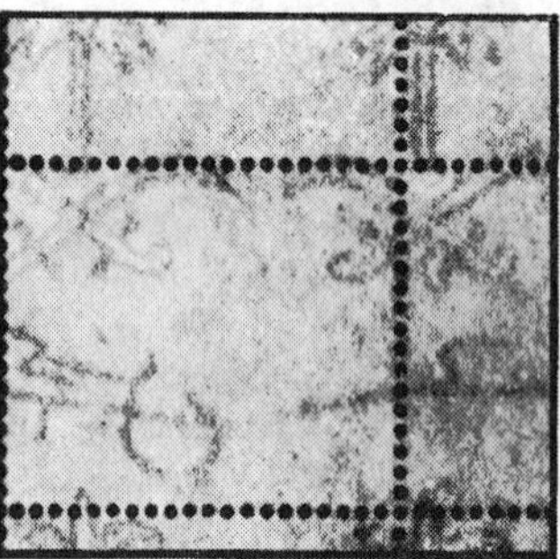

Wmk. 361- Crossed Swords, Palm Tree and Arabic Inscription

HEJAZ

Sherifate of Mecca

Adapted from Carved Door Panels of Mosque El Salih Talay, Cairo — A1

Taken from Page of Koran in Mosque of El Sultan Barquq, Cairo — A2

Taken from Details of an Ancient Prayer Niche in the Mosque of El Amri at Qus in Upper Egypt — A3

Perf. 10, 12

1916, Oct. Unwmk. Typo.

No.	Type	Description	Unused	Used
L1	A1	1/4pi green	40.00	32.50
L2	A2	1/2pi red	40.00	30.00
a.		Perf. 10	110.00	90.00
L3	A3	1pi blue	11.00	11.00
a.		Perf. 12	140.00	140.00
b.		Perf. 10x12		775.00
		Nos. L1-L3 (3)	91.00	73.50

Exist imperf. Forged perf. exist.

See Nos. L5-L7, L10-L12. For overprints see Nos. L16-L18, L26-L28, L52-L54, L57-L59, L61-L66, L67, L70-L72, L77-L81, 37.

Central Design Adapted from a Koran Design for a Tomb. Background is from Stone Carving on Entrance Arch to the Ministry of Wakfs — A4

1916-17 *Roulette 20*

No.	Type	Description	Unused	Used
L4	A4	1/8pi orange ('17)	3.50	1.40
L5	A1	1/4pi green	4.50	1.40
L6	A2	1/2pi red	5.50	1.40
L7	A3	1pi blue	5.50	1.40

See No. L9. For overprints and surcharge see Nos. L15a, L16c, L17b, L18d, L25, L51, L56, L69, 33.

Adapted from Stucco Work above Entrance to Cairo R. R. Station — A5

Adapted from First Page of the Koran of Sultan Farag — A6

1917 *Serrate Roulette 13*

No.	Type	Description	Unused	Used
L8	A5	1pa lilac brown	2.75	1.40
L9	A4	1/8pi orange	2.75	1.40
L10	A1	1/4pi green	2.75	1.40
L11	A2	1/2pi red	2.75	1.40
L12	A3	1pi blue	2.75	1.40
L13	A6	2pi magenta	18.00	9.00
		Nos. L8-L13 (6)	31.75	16.00

Designs A1-A6 are inscribed "Hejaz Postage."

For overprints and surcharge see Nos. L14-L24, L29-L31, L55, L60, L66B, L73-L75, 32, 38.

Kingdom of the Hejaz

Stamps of 1917-18 Overprinted in Black, Red or Brown:

الحكومة العربية الهاشمية ١٣٤٠ ١٣٤٠

1921, Dec. 21 *Serrate Roulette 13*

No.	Type	Description	Unused	Used
L14	A5	1pa lilac brown	27.50	14.00
L15	A4	1/8pi orange	55.00	16.00
a.		Inverted overprint	90.00	
b.		Double overprint	175.00	
c.		Roulette 20	550.00	
d.		As "c," invtd. overprint		*1,400.*
L16	A1	1/4pi green	11.00	5.50
a.		Inverted overprint	90.00	
b.		Double overprint	175.00	
c.		Roulette 20	550.00	
d.		As "c," invtd. overprint		
L17	A2	1/2pi red	14.00	6.75
a.		Inverted overprint	140.00	77.50
b.		Roulette 20	550.00	
L18	A3	1pi blue (R)	11.00	6.25
a.		Brown overprint	25.00	18.00
b.		Black overprint	32.50	27.50
c.		As "b," invtd. overprint	350.00	
d.		Roulette 20	625.00	
L19	A6	2pi magenta	16.00	9.00
		Nos. L14-L19 (6)	134.50	57.50

Nos. L15-L17, L18b and L19 exist with date (1340) omitted at left or right side.

Some values exist with gold overprint.

Forgeries of Nos. L14-L23 abound.

No. L14 With Additional Surcharge:

نصف قرش — a
قرش واحد — b

No.	Type	Description	Unused	Used
L22	A5(a)	1/2pi on 1pa	275.00	125.00
L23	A5(b)	1pi on 1pa	275.00	125.00

Stamps of 1917-18 Overprinted in Black

1922, Jan. 7

No.	Type	Description	Unused	Used
L24	A5	1pa lilac brown	3.00	2.75
a.		Inverted overprint	140.00	
b.		Double overprint	90.00	
c.		Double ovpt., one inverted	175.00	
L25	A4	1/8pi orange	9.00	6.25
a.		Inverted overprint	90.00	
b.		Double ovpt., one inverted	175.00	
L26	A1	1/4pi green	3.00	2.75
a.		Inverted overprint	90.00	
b.		Double ovpt., one inverted	175.00	
L27	A2	1/2pi red	2.25	1.75
a.		Inverted overprint	90.00	
b.		Double ovpt., one inverted	175.00	
L28	A3	1pi blue	2.25	.80
a.		Double overprint	80.00	
b.		Inverted overprint	140.00	
L29	A6	2pi magenta	6.50	5.50
a.		Double overprint	140.00	

With Additional Surcharge of New Value

No.	Type	Description	Unused	Used
L30	A5(a)	1/2pi on 1pa lilac brn	20.00	14.00
L31	A5(b)	1pi on 1pa lilac brn	2.25	.90
a.		Inverted surcharge	90.00	
b.		Double surcharge	80.00	
c.		Dbl. surch., one invtd., ovpt. invtd.		
		Nos. L24-L31 (8)	48.25	34.70

The 1921 and 1922 overprints read: "The Government of Hashemite Arabia, 1340."

The overprint on No. L28 in red is bogus.

Forgeries abound.

Types A7 and A8

Very fine examples will be somewhat off center but perforations will be clear of the framelines.

Arms of Sherif of Mecca — A7

1922, Feb. Typo. *Perf. 11 1/2*

No.	Type	Description	Unused	Used
L32	A7	1/8pi red brown	1.75	.45
L34	A7	1/2pi red	1.75	.45
L35	A7	1pi dark blue	1.75	.45
L36	A7	1 1/2pi violet	1.75	.45
L37	A7	2pi orange	1.75	.45
L38	A7	3pi olive brown	1.75	.45
L39	A7	5pi olive green	1.75	.55
		Nos. L32-L39 (7)	12.25	3.25

Numerous shades exist. Some values were printed in other colors in 1925 for handstamping by the Nedji authorities in Mecca. These exist without handstamps.

Exist imperf.

Forgeries exist, usually perf. 11.

Reprints of Nos. L32, L35 exist; paper and shades differ.

See Nos. L48A-L49. For surcharges and overprints see Nos. L40-L48, L76, L82-L159, 7-20, 38A-48, 55A-58A, LJ11-LJ16, LJ26-LJ39, J1-J8, J10-J11, P1-P3, Jordan 64-72, 91, 103-120, J1-J17, O1.

Stamps of 1922 Surcharged with New Values in Arabic:

c d

1923

No.	Type	Description	Unused	Used
L40	A7(c)	1/4pi on 1/8pi org brn	32.50	32.50
a.		Double surcharge		
b.		Double inverted surcharge		
c.		Double surch., one invtd.		
L41	A7(d)	10pi on 5pi ol grn	27.50	27.50
a.		Double surch., one invtd.		
b.		Inverted surcharge		

Forgeries exist.

Caliphate Issue

Stamps of 1922 Overprinted in Gold

تذكار الخلافة شعبان ١٣٤٢

1924

No.	Type	Description	Unused	Used
L42	A7	1/8pi orange brown	3.25	
L43	A7	1/2pi red	3.25	
L44	A7	1pi dark blue	3.25	
L45	A7	1 1/2pi violet	3.25	
L46	A7	2pi orange	3.25	
L47	A7	3pi olive brown	3.50	
L48	A7	5pi olive green	3.50	
		Nos. L42-L48 (7)	23.25	

Assumption of the Caliphate by King Hussein in Mar., 1924. The overprint reads "In commemoration of the Caliphate, Shaaban, 1342."

The overprint was typographed in black and dusted with "gold" powder while wet. It exists inverted on the 1pi, 2pi and 5pi. Inverted overprints on other values are forgeries.

The overprint is 18-20mm wide. The 1st setting of the 1/2p is 16mm.

Forgeries exist.

Nos. L43-L44, L46 exist with postage due overprint as on Nos. LJ11-LJ13.

Type of 1922 and

Arms of Sherif of Mecca — A8

1924 *Perf. 11 1/2*

No.	Type	Description	Unused	Used
L48A	A7	1/4pi yellow green	5.75	5.75
b.		Tête bêche pair	*27.50*	
L49	A7	3pi brown red	9.00	9.00
a.		3pi dull red	4.50	4.50
L50	A8	10pi vio & dk brn	4.50	4.50
a.		Center inverted	*55.00*	55.00
b.		Center omitted	67.50	
c.		10pi purple & sepia	4.50	4.50
		Nos. L48A-L50 (3)	19.25	19.25

Nos. L48A, L50, L50a exist imperf.

Reprints, official and unofficial, of Nos. L48A-L50 exist; paper and shades differ.

Forgeries exist, usually perf. 11.

For overprint see Nos. L76A, Jordan 121.

Jedda Issues

Stamps of 1916-17 Overprinted

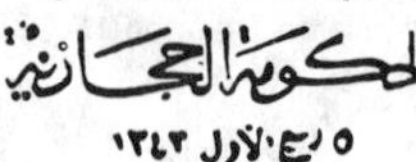

The control overprints on Nos. L51-L159 read: "Hukumat al Hejaziyeh, 5 Rabi al'awwal 1343" (The Hejaz Government, October 4, 1924). This is the date of the accession of King Ali.

Counterfeits exist of all Jedda overprints.

Jedda issues were also used in Medina and Yambo. Used values for #L51-L186 and LJ17-LJ39 are for genuine cancels. Privately applied cancels exist for "Mekke" (Mecca, bilingual or all Arabic), Khartoum, Cairo, as well as for Jeddah. Many private cancels have wrong dates, some as early as 1916. These are worth half the used values.

Red Overprint

1925, Jan. *Roulette 20*

No.	Type	Description	Unused	Used
L51	A4	1/8pi orange	14.00	*14.00*
a.		Inverted overprint	90.00	
b.		Ovptd. on face and back	175.00	
L52	A1	1/4pi green	14.00	*14.00*
a.		Inverted overprint	60.00	
b.		Double overprint	55.00	
c.		Double overprint, one invtd.	140.00	
L53	A2	1/2pi red	67.50	*67.50*
a.		Inverted overprint	150.00	
L54	A3	1pi blue	32.50	*32.50*
a.		Inverted overprint	*140.00*	
b.		Double ovpt., one invtd.	125.00	
		Nos. L51-L53 (3)	95.50	*95.50*

Serrate Roulette 13

No.	Type	Description	Unused	Used
L55	A5	1pa lilac brown	12.50	*12.50*
a.		Inverted overprint	67.50	
b.		Double overprint	60.00	
c.		Ovptd. on face and back	*175.00*	

L56 A4 1/8pi orange 35.00 35.00
a. Inverted overprint 80.00
L57 A1 1/4pi green 20.00 20.00
a. Pair, one without overprint 1,600.
b. Inverted overprint 45.00
c. Double ovpt., one inverted 275.00
L58 A2 1/2pi red 27.50 27.50
a. Inverted overprint 140.00
L59 A3 1pi blue 32.50 32.50
a. Inverted overprint 100.00
L60 A6 2pi magenta 35.00 35.00
a. Inverted overprint 140.00
Nos. L55-L60 (6) 162.50 162.50

Gold Overprint
Roulette 20

L61 A1 1/4pi green 2,250. 2,250.

Serrate Roulette 13

L62 A1 1/4pi green 22.50 22.50
a. Inverted overprint 100.00

The overprint on No. L61 was typographed in red or blue (No. L62 only in red) and dusted with "gold" powder while wet.

Blue Overprint
Roulette 20

L63 A1 1/4pi green 22.50 22.50
a. Inverted overprint 80.00
b. Ovptd. on face and back 80.00
L64 A2 1/2pi red, invtd. ovpt. 80.00 80.00
a. Upright overprint 140.00

Serrate Roulette 13

L65 A1 1/4pi green 16.00 16.00
a. Inverted overprint 67.50
b. Vertical overprint 900.00
L66 A2 1/2pi red 27.50 27.50
a. Inverted overprint 90.00
L66B A6 2pi mag, invtd. ovpt. 1,400.

Blue overprint on Nos. L4, L8, L9 are bogus.

Same Overprint in Blue on Provisional Stamps of 1922
Overprinted on No. L17

L67 A2 1/2pi red 2,500.

Overprinted on Nos. L24-L29

L68 A5 1pa lilac brn 165.00 165.00
L69 A4 1/8pi orange 1,800. 1,800.
a. Inverted overprint
L70 A1 1/4pi green 65.00 65.00
a. Inverted overprint 725.00
L71 A2 1/2pi red 85.00 85.00
a. Inverted overprint 800.00
L72 A3 1pi blue 110.00 110.00
L73 A6 2pi magenta 165.00 165.00
a. Inverted overprint 1,400.

Same Overprint on Nos. L30 and L31

L74 A5(a) 1/2pi on 1pa 90.00 90.00
L75 A5(b) 1pi on 1pa 75.00 75.00
a. Inverted overprint 575.00

Same Overprint in Blue Vertically, Reading Up or Down, on Stamps of 1922-24
Perf. 11 1/2

L76 A7 1/2pi red 900.00 900.00
L76A A8 10pi vio & dk brn 1,800. 1,800.

Nos. L5, L10 Overprinted in Blue or Red

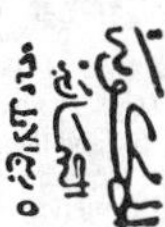

Roulette 20

L77 A1 1/4pi green (Bl) 175.00 175.00
L78 A1 1/4pi green (R) 450.00 450.00

Serrate Roulette 13

L79 A1 1/4pi green (Bl) 90.00 90.00
L80 A1 1/4pi green (R) 60.00 60.00

Nos. L77, L79-L80 exist with overprint reading up or down. It reads up in illustration.

Nos. L10, L32-L39, L48A, L49a, L50 Overprinted

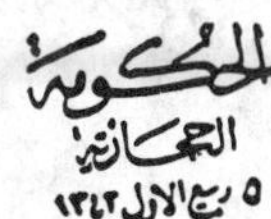

Serrate Roulette 13
Red Overprint (vertical)

L81 A1 1/4pi green 900.00

Overprint on No. L81 also exists horizontal and inverted.

Perf. 11 1/2
Blue Overprint

L82 A7 1/8pi red brown 5.50 5.50
a. Inverted overprint 45.00
L83 A7 1/2pi red 7.25 7.25
a. Double overprint 67.50
b. Inverted overprint 45.00 45.00
c. Double ovpt., one invtd. 67.50
d. Overprint reading up
L84 A7 1pi dark blue 350.00
a. Inverted overprint 350.00
L85 A7 1 1/2pi violet 11.00 11.00
a. Inverted overprint 45.00 45.00
L86 A7 2pi orange 11.00 11.00
a. Double ovpt., one invtd. 67.50
b. Inverted overprint 45.00
c. Double overprint 67.50
L87 A7 3pi olive brown 9.00 9.00
a. Inverted overprint 45.00
b. Double ovpt., one invtd. 67.50
c. Overprint reading up 165.00
d. Dbl. ovpt., both invtd. 90.00
L88 A7 3pi dull red 11.00 11.00
a. Inverted overprint 45.00
b. Double ovpt., one invtd. 67.50
L89 A7 5pi olive green 11.00 11.00
a. Inverted overprint 45.00

Some values exist in pairs, one without overprint.

Black Overprint

L90 A7 1/8pi red brown 45.00
a. Inverted overprint 140.00
L91 A7 1/2pi red 4.50 4.50
a. Inverted overprint 60.00
L92 A7 1pi dark blue 350.00
a. Inverted overprint 350.00
L93 A7 1 1/2pi violet 12.00 12.00
a. Inverted overprint 67.50
L94 A7 2pi orange 7.25 7.25
a. Inverted overprint 45.00
L95 A7 3pi olive brown 5.50 5.50
a. Inverted overprint 67.50 67.50
L96 A7 3pi dull red 7.25 7.25
a. Inverted overprint 45.00
L97 A7 5pi olive green 9.00 9.00
a. Inverted overprint 45.00

Red Overprint

L98 A7 1/8pi red brn, invtd. 725.00
L99 A7 1/4pi yellow grn 16.00 16.00
a. Tête bêche pair 62.50
b. Inverted overprint 45.00
L100 A7 1/2pi red
a. Inverted overprint
L101 A7 1pi dark blue 8.00 8.00
a. Inverted overprint 45.00
b. Double ovpt., one invtd. 32.50
L102 A7 1 1/2pi violet 4.50 4.50
a. Inverted overprint 45.00
L103 A7 2pi orange 12.00 12.00
a. Inverted overprint 45.00
b. Overprint reading up 165.00
L104 A7 3pi olive brown 12.00 12.00
a. Inverted overprint 45.00
L105 A7 3pi dull red, invtd. 725.00
L106 A7 5pi olive green 7.25 7.25
a. Inverted overprint 45.00
b. Overprint reading up
c. Overprint reading down
L107 A8 10pi vio & dk brn 16.00 16.00
a. Inverted overprint 45.00
b. Center inverted 90.00
c. As "b," invtd. ovpt. 140.00

Nos. L98, L105 with normal overprint are fakes.

Gold Overprint

L108 A7 1/8pi red brown 27.50 27.50
L109 A7 1/2pi red 27.50 27.50
L110 A7 1pi dark blue 27.50 27.50
L111 A7 1 1/2pi violet 110.00 110.00
L112 A7 2pi orange 90.00 90.00
L113 A7 3pi olive brown 35.00 35.00
L114 A7 3pi dull red 100.00 100.00
L115 A7 5pi olive green 85.00 85.00
Nos. L108-L115 (8) 502.50 502.50

Inverted overprints are forgeries.

Same Overprint on Nos. L42-L48
Blue Overprint

L116 A7 1/8pi red brown 42.50 42.50
a. Double ovpt., one invtd. 275.00
L117 A7 1/2pi red 80.00 80.00
L118 A7 1pi dark blue 55.00 55.00
L119 A7 1 1/2pi violet 65.00 65.00
L120 A7 2pi orange 275.00 275.00
a. Inverted overprint 425.00
L121 A7 3pi olive brown 110.00 110.00
a. Inverted overprint 175.00
L122 A7 5pi olive green 37.50 37.50
a. Inverted overprint 200.00
Nos. L116-L122 (7) 665.00 665.00

Black Overprint

L123 A7 1/8pi red brown 42.50 42.50
a. Inverted overprint 225.00
L125 A7 1 1/2pi violet 140.00 140.00
a. Inverted overprint 225.00
L127 A7 3pi olive brown 110.00 110.00
a. Inverted overprint 225.00
L128 A7 5pi olive green 140.00 140.00
a. Inverted overprint 225.00
Nos. L123-L128 (4) 432.50 432.50

Red Overprint

L129 A7 1pi dark blue 90.00 90.00
L130 A7 1 1/2pi violet 110.00 110.00
L131 A7 2pi orange 90.00 90.00
Nos. L129-L131 (3) 290.00 290.00

Overprints on stamps or in colors other than those listed are forgeries.

Stamps of 1922-24 Surcharged

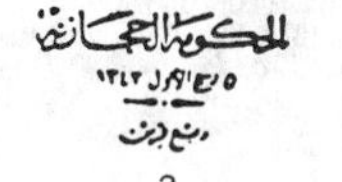

a

and Handstamped

b

1pi 10pi

1925 Litho. *Perf. 11 1/2*

L135 A7 1/4pi on 1/8pi red brn 47.50 47.50
b. 1pi on 1/4pi on 1/8pi red brown
L136 A7 1/4pi on 1/4pi on 1/2pi red 30.00 30.00
c. 1pi on 1/4pi on 1/2pi 55.00 55.00
L138 A7 1pi on 1pi on 2pi orange 30.00 30.00
a. 1/4pi on 1/4pi on 2pi org
b. 10pi on 1pi on 2pi org 90.00
c. 1/4pi on 1pi on 2pi org 45.00
d. 1pi on 1/4pi on 2pi org 90.00
L139 A7 1pi on 1pi on 3pi ol brn 22.50 22.50
L140 A7 1pi on 1pi on 3pi dl red 35.00 35.00
b. 1/4pi on 1pi on 3pi dl red
L141 A7 10pi on 10pi on 5pi ol grn 16.00 16.00
b. 1pi on 10 pi on 5 pi
Nos. L135-L141 (6) 181.00 181.00

The printed surcharge (a) reads "The Hejaz Government. October 4, 1924." with new denomination in third line. This surcharge alone was used for the first issue (Nos. L135a-L141a). The new denomination was so small and indistinct that its equivalent in larger characters was soon added by handstamp (b) at bottom of each stamp for the second issue (Nos. L135-L141).

The handstamped surcharge (b) is found double, inverted, etc. It is also known in dark violet.

Without Handstamp "b"

L135a A7 1/4pi on 1/8pi red brn 90.00
L136b A7 1/4pi on 1/2pi red 90.00
L138e A7 1pi on 2pi orange 90.00
L139a A7 1pi on 3pi olive brn 90.00
L140a A7 1pi on 3pi dull red 90.00
L141a A7 10pi on 5pi olive grn 90.00
Nos. L135a-L141a (6) 540.00

Stamps of 1922-24 Surcharged

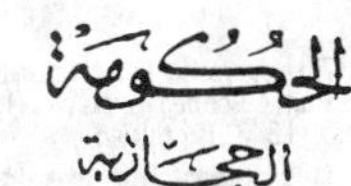

Black Surcharge

L142 A7 1/8pi on 1/2pi red 7.25 7.25
a. Inverted surcharge 35.00
L143 A7 1/4pi on 1/2pi red 7.25 7.25
a. Inverted surcharge 35.00
L144 A7 1pi on 1/2pi red 7.25 7.25
a. Inverted surcharge 22.50
L145 A7 1pi on 1 1/2pi violet 7.25 7.25
a. Inverted surcharge 32.50
L146 A7 1pi on 2pi orange 7.25 7.25
a. "10pi" 77.50
b. Inverted surcharge 35.00
L147 A7 1pi on 3pi olive brn 7.25 7.25
a. "10pi" 67.50
b. Inverted surcharge 45.00
L148 A7 10pi on 5pi olive grn 14.00 14.00
a. Inverted surcharge 60.00
Nos. L142-L148 (7) 57.50 57.50

Blue Surcharge

L149 A7 1/8pi on 1/2pi red 11.00 11.00
a. Inverted surcharge 60.00
L150 A7 1/4pi on 1/2pi red 11.00 11.00
a. Inverted surcharge 45.00
L151 A7 1pi on 1/2pi red 11.00 11.00
a. Inverted surcharge 45.00
b. Double surcharge
L152 A7 1pi on 1 1/2pi violet 11.00 11.00
a. Inverted surcharge 60.00
L153 A7 1pi on 2pi orange 11.00 11.00
a. "10pi" 62.50
b. Inverted surcharge 60.00
L154 A7 1pi on 3pi olive brn 22.50 22.50
a. "10pi" 77.50
b. Inverted surcharge 62.50
L155 A7 10pi on 5pi olive grn 25.00 25.00
a. Inverted surcharge 55.00
Nos. L149-L155 (7) 102.50 102.50

Red Surcharge

L156 A7 1pi on 1 1/2pi violet 22.50 22.50
a. Inverted surcharge 72.50
L157 A7 1pi on 2pi orange 22.50 22.50
a. "10pi" 72.50
b. Inverted surcharge 72.50
L158 A7 1pi on 3pi olive brn 22.50 22.50
a. "10pi" 90.00
b. Inverted surcharge 72.50
L159 A7 10pi on 5pi olive grn 22.50 22.50
a. Inverted surcharge 72.50
Nos. L156-L159 (4) 90.00 90.00
Nos. L142-L159 (18) 250.00 250.00

The "10pi" surcharge is found inverted on Nos. L146a, L147a. The existence of genuine inverted "10pi" surcharges on Nos. L153a, L154a, L157a and L158a is in doubt.

King Ali Issue

A9

A10

A11

A12

1925, May-June *Perf. 11 1/2*
Black Overprint

L160 A9 1/8pi chocolate 1.50 1.50
L161 A9 1/4pi ultra 1.50 1.50
L162 A9 1/2pi car rose 1.50 1.50
L163 A10 1pi yellow green 1.75 1.75
L164 A10 1 1/2pi orange 1.75 1.75
L165 A10 2pi blue 2.25 2.25
L166 A11 3pi dark green 2.25 2.25
L167 A11 5pi orange brn 2.25 2.25
L168 A12 10pi red & green 4.50 4.50
a. Center inverted 67.50
Nos. L160-L168 (9) 19.25 19.25

Red Overprint

L169 A9 1/8pi chocolate 2.75 2.75
L170 A9 1/4pi ultra 1.65 1.65
L171 A10 1pi yellow green 2.00 2.00
L172 A10 1 1/2pi orange 2.00 2.00
L173 A10 2pi deep blue 2.50 2.50
L174 A11 3pi dark green 2.75 2.75
a. Horiz. pair, imperf. vert.
L175 A11 5pi orange brown 2.75 2.75
L176 A12 10pi red & green 5.50 5.50
Nos. L169-L176 (8) 21.90 21.90

Blue Overprint

L177 A9 1/8pi chocolate 1.75 1.75
L179 A9 1/2pi car rose 1.75 1.75
L180 A10 1pi yellow green 1.75 1.75
L181 A10 1 1/2pi orange 1.75 1.75
L182 A11 3pi dark green 1.75 1.75
L183 A11 5pi orange brn 5.50 5.50
L184 A12 10pi red & green 7.25 7.25
L185 A12 10pi red & org 275.00
Nos. L177-L184 (7) 21.50 21.50

Without Overprint

L186 A12 10pi red & green 6.75 6.75
a. Dbl. impression of center 90.00

The overprint in the tablets on Nos. L160-L185 reads: "5 Rabi al'awwal, 1343" (Oct. 5, 1924), the date of the accession of King Ali.

The tablet overprints vary slightly in size. Each is found reading upward or downward and at either side of the stamp. These control overprints were first applied in Jedda by the government press. They were later made from new plates by the stamp printer in Cairo. In the Jedda overprint, the bar over the "0" figure extends to the left. Some values exist with 13m or 15mm instead of 18mm between tablets. They sell for more. The lines of the Cairo overprinting are generally wider, but more lightly printed, usually appearing slightly grayish and the bar is at center right. The Cairo overprints are believed not to have been placed in use.

Imperforates exist.

Nos. L160-L168 are known with the overprints spaced as on type D3 and aligned horizontally.

Copies of these stamps (perforated or imperforate) without the overprint, except No. L186 were not regularly issued and not available for postage.

No. L185 exists only with Cairo overprint. Imperfs of No. L185 sell for much less than No. L185. Fake perfs have been added to the imperfs.

The 1/4pi with blue overprint is bogus.

No. L186 in other colors are color trials.

For overprints see #58B-58C, Jordan 122-129.

NEJDI ADMINISTRATION OF HEJAZ

Handstamped in Blue, Red, Black or Violet

The overprint reads: "1343. Barid al Sultanat at Nejdia" (1925. Post of the Sultanate of Nejd).

The overprints on this and succeeding issues are handstamped and, as usual, are found double, inverted, etc. These variations are scarce.

1925, Mar.-Apr. Unwmk. *Perf. 12*

On Stamp of Turkey, 1915, With Crescent and Star in Red

1 A22 5pa ocher (Bl) 35.00 27.50
2 A22 5pa ocher (R) 22.50 20.00
3 A22 5pa ocher (Bk) 27.50 22.50
4 A22 5pa ocher (V) 22.50 18.00

On Stamp of Turkey, 1913

5 A28 10pa green (Bl) 20.00 16.00
6 A28 10pa green (R) 16.00 12.50

On Stamps of Hejaz, 1922-24
Perf. 11½

7 A7 ⅛pi red brn (R) 22.50 22.50
8 A7 ⅛pi red brn (Bk) 32.50 32.50
9 A7 ⅛pi red brn (V) 22.50 22.50
10 A7 ⅛pi car (R) 27.50 27.50
11 A7 ⅛pi car (Bk) 32.50 32.50
12 A7 ⅛pi car (V) *25.00 25.00*
13 A7 ½pi red (Bl) 20.00 20.00
14 A7 ½pi red (V) 16.00 16.00
15 A7 1½pi vio (R) 22.50 22.50
16 A7 2pi yel buff (R) 55.00 55.00
a. 2pi orange (R) 35.00
17 A7 2pi yel buff (V) 55.00 55.00
a. 2pi orange (V) 32.50 32.50
18 A7 3pi brn red (Bl) 27.50 27.50
19 A7 3pi brn red (R) 20.00 20.00
20 A7 3pi brn red (V) 22.50 22.50

Many Hejaz stamps of the 1922 type were especially printed for this and following issues. The reimpressions are usually more clearly printed, in lighter shades than the 1922 stamps, and some are in new colors.

Counterfeits exist.

Arabic Inscriptions
R1 R2

On Hejaz Bill Stamp

22 R1 1pi violet (R) 14.00 14.00

On Hejaz Notarial Stamps

23 R2 1pi violet (R) 18.00 18.00
24 R2 2pi blue (R) 27.50 27.50
25 R2 2pi blue (V) 25.00 25.00

For overprint see No. 49.

Locomotive — R3

On Hejaz Railway Tax Stamps

26 R3 1pi blue (R) 35.00 9.00
27 R3 2pi ocher (R) 42.50 14.00
28 R3 2pi ocher (V) 35.00 14.00
29 R3 3pi lilac (R) 35.00 20.00
Nos. 1-20,22-29 (28) 776.50 659.00

There are two types of the basic stamps. The difference is in the locomotive.

For overprints and surcharges see Nos. 34, 50-54, 55, 59-68, J12-J15.

Pilgrimage Issue

Various Stamps Handstamp Surcharged in Blue and Red in Types "a" and "b" and with Tablets with New Values

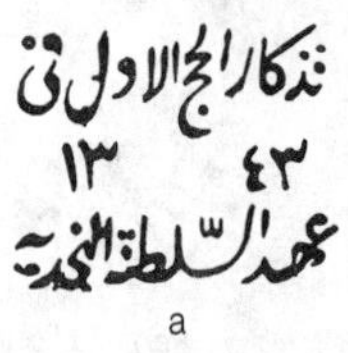
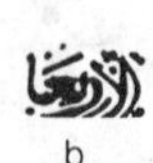

a b

Surcharge "a" reads: "Tezkar al Hajj al Awwal Fi 'ahd al Sultanat al Nejdia, 1343" (Commemorating the first pilgrimage under the Nejdi Sultanate, 1925).

"b" reads: "Al Arba" (Wednesday.)

1925, July 1 *Perf. 12*

On Stamps of Turkey, 1913

30 A28 1pi on 10pa grn (Bl & R) 67.50 55.00
31 A30 5pi on 1pi bl (Bl & R) 67.50 55.00

On Stamps of Hejaz, 1917-18
Serrate Roulette 13

32 A5 2pi on 1pa lil brn (R & Bl) 85.00 67.50
33 A4 4pi on ⅛pi org (R & Bl) 325.00 325.00

On Hejaz Railway Tax Stamp
Perf. 11½

34 R3 3pi lilac (Bl & R) 67.50 35.00
Nos. 30-34 (5) 612.50 537.50

No. 30 with handstamp "a" in black was a favor item.

Handstamped in Blue, Red, Black or Violet

This overprint has practically the same meaning as that described over No. 1. The Mohammedan year (1343) is omitted.

This handstamp is said to be in private hands at this time. Extreme caution is advised before buying rare items.

1925, July-Aug. *Perf. 12*

On Stamp of Turkey, 1915, with Crescent and Star in Red

35 A22 5pa ocher (Bl) 22.50 22.50

On Stamps of Turkey, 1913

36 A28 10pa green (Bl) 18.00 18.00
a. Black overprint 72.50

On Stamps of Hejaz, 1922 (Nos. L28-L29)
Serrate Roulette 13

37 A3 1pi blue (R) 55.00 *67.50*
38 A6 2pi magenta (Bl) 55.00 *67.50*

On Stamps of Hejaz, 1922-24
Perf. 11½

38A A7 ⅛pi red brn (Bk) *4,250.*
38B A7 ⅛pi red brn (Bl) *3,500.*
39 A7 ½pi red (Bl) 9.00 9.00
a. Imperf., pair 22.50 22.50
39B A7 ½pi red (Bk) 18.00 18.00
c. Imperf., pair 37.50 37.50
40 A7 1pi gray vio (R) 27.50 27.50
a. 1pi black violet (R) *40.00*
41 A7 1½pi dk red (Bk) 27.50 27.50
a. 1½pi brick red (Bk) 45.00
42 A7 2pi yel buff (Bl) 45.00 45.00
a. 2pi orange (Bl) 55.00 55.00
43 A7 2pi deep vio (Bl) 50.00 50.00
44 A7 3pi brown red (Bl) 27.50 27.50
45 A7 5pi scarlet (Bl) 35.00 35.00
Nos. 35-38,39-45 (12) 390.00 *415.00*

Overprint on Nos. 38A, 39B, 39C is blue-black.

See note above No. 35.

With Additional Surcharge of New Value Typo. in Black:

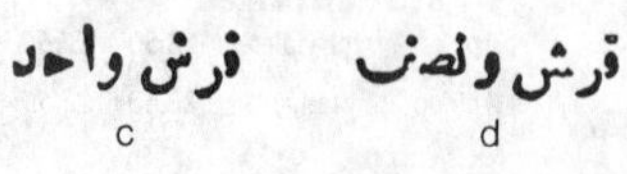

c d

e

Color in parenthesis is that of overprint on basic stamp.

46 A7(c) 1pi on ½pi (Bl) 9.00 1.75
a. Imperf, pair 27.50
b. Ovpt. & surch. inverted
47 A7(d) 1½pi on ½pi (Bl) 13.00 7.25
a. Imperf., pair 27.50
b. Black overprint 18.00
48 A7(e) 2pi on 3pi (Bl) 13.00 13.00
Nos. 46-48 (3) 35.00 22.00

Several variations in type settings of "c," "d" and "e" exist, including inverted letters and values.

On Hejaz Notarial Stamp

49 R2 2pi blue (Bk) 18.00 18.00

On Hejaz Railway Tax Stamps

50 R3 1pi blue (R) 22.50 22.50
51 R3 1pi blue (Bk) 27.50 9.00
52 R3 2pi ocher (Bl) 25.00 9.00
53 R3 3pi lilac (Bl) 20.00 20.00
54 R3 5pi green (Bl) 18.00 18.00
Nos. 49-54 (6) 131.00 96.50

Hejaz Railway Tax Stamp Handstamped in Black

السعوديه

السلطنه النجديه

This overprint reads: "Al Saudia. - Al Sultanat al Nejdia." (The Saudi Sultanate of Nejd.)

1925-26

55 R3 1pi blue *165.00*

On Nos. L34, L36-L37, L41

55A A7 ½ pi red *325.00*
56 A7 1½pi violet *325.00*
a. Violet overprint *325.00*
57 A7 2pi orange *325.00*
57A A7 10pi on 5pi ol grn *325.00*

On Nos. L95 and L97
Color in parentheses is that of rectangular overprint on basic stamp

58 A7 3pi olive brn (Bk) *325.00*
58A A7 5pi olive grn (Bk) *325.00*

On Nos. L162-L163, L173
Perf. 11½

58B A9 ½pi car rose (Bk) *325.00*
58C A10 1pi yellow grn (Bk) *190.00*
58D A10 2pi blue (R) *325.00*

Nos. 55-58D were provisionally issued at Medina after its capitulation.

Specialists question the status of unused examples of Nos. 55-58D.

This overprint exists on Nos. L160-L161, L164-L172, L174-L175, L180-L183. These 17 are known as bogus items, but may exist genuine.

No. L161 (¼pi) is known with a similar but larger overprint. It is a forgery.

Lithographed overprints are forgeries.

The illustrated overprint is not genuine.

Medina Issue

Hejaz Railway Tax Stamps Handstamped

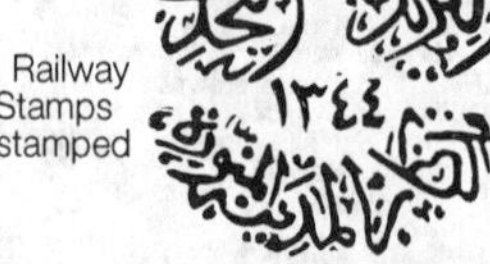

and Handstamp Surcharged in Various Colors

The large overprint reads: "The Nejdi Posts - 1344 - Commemorating Medina, the Illustrious." The tablet shows the new value.

1925

59 R3 1pi on 10pi vio (Bk & V) 45.00 55.00
60 R3 2pi on 50pi lt bl (R & Bl) 45.00 55.00
61 R3 3pi on 100pi red brn (Bl & Bk) 45.00 55.00
62 R3 4pi on 500pi dull red (Bl & Bk) 45.00 55.00
63 R3 5pi on 1000pi dp red (Bl & Bk) 45.00 55.00
Nos. 59-63 (5) 225.00 275.00

Jedda Issue

Hejaz Railway Tax Stamps Handstamped and Tablet with New Value in Various Colors

This handstamp reads: "Commemorating Jedda - 1344 - The Nejdi Posts."

1925

64 R3 1pi on 10pi vio (Bk & Bl) 55.00 55.00
65 R3 2pi on 50pi lt bl (R & Bk) 55.00 55.00
66 R3 3pi on 100pi red brn (R & Bl) 55.00 55.00
67 R3 4pi on 500pi dl red (Bk & Bl) 55.00 55.00
68 R3 5pi on 1000pi dp red (Bk & Bl) 55.00 55.00
Nos. 64-68 (5) 275.00 275.00

Nos. 59-63 and 64-68 were prepared in anticipation of the surrender of Medina and Jedda.

Kingdom of Hejaz-Nejd

Arabic Inscriptions and Value — A1

A2

Inscriptions in upper tablets: "Barid al Hejaz wa Nejd" (Posts of the Hejaz and Nejd)

1926, Feb. Typo. Unwmk. *Perf. 11*

69 A1 ¼pi violet 11.00 8.25
70 A1 ½pi gray 11.00 8.25
71 A1 1pi deep blue 14.00 10.00
72 A2 2pi blue green 12.00 8.25
73 A2 3pi carmine 14.00 9.00
74 A2 5pi maroon 7.50 5.75
Nos. 69-74 (6) 69.50 49.50

Nos. 69-71, 74 exist imperf. Value, each $30.

Used values are for favor cancels.

1926, Mar. *Perf. 11*

75 A1 ¼pi orange 5.75 3.25
76 A1 ½pi blue green 2.25 1.40
77 A1 1pi carmine 1.75 1.10
78 A2 2pi violet 2.25 1.40
79 A2 3pi dark blue 2.25 1.40
80 A2 5pi lt brown 5.75 3.25
a. 5pi olive brown
Nos. 75-80 (6) 20.00 11.80

Nos. 75-80 also exist with perf. 14, 14x11, 11x14 and imperf. All of these sell for 10 times the values quoted.

Counterfeits of types A1 and A2 are perf. 11½. They exist with and without overprints.

Types A1 and A2 in colors other than listed are proofs.

Pan-Islamic Congress Issue

Stamps of 1926 Handstamped

1926 *Perf. 11*

92 A1 ¼pi orange 4.75 2.75
93 A1 ½pi blue green 4.75 2.75
94 A1 1pi carmine 4.75 2.75
95 A2 2pi violet 4.75 2.75
96 A2 3pi dark blue 4.75 2.75
97 A2 5pi light brown 4.75 2.75
Nos. 92-97 (6) 28.50 16.50

The overprint reads: "al Mootamar al Islami 20 Zilkada, Sanat 1344." (The Islamic Congress, June 1, 1926.)

See counterfeit note after No. 80.

Tughra of King Abdul Aziz — A3

1926-27 Typo. *Perf. 11 1/2*

No.	Type	Description	Unused	Used
98	A3	1/8pi ocher	3.25	.45
99	A3	1/4pi gray green	3.50	1.10
100	A3	1/2pi dull red	3.50	1.10
101	A3	1pi deep violet	3.50	1.10
102	A3	1 1/2pi gray blue	11.00	1.75
103	A3	3pi olive green	9.00	3.50
104	A3	5pi brown orange	18.00	4.00
105	A3	10pi dark brown	55.00	5.50
		Nos. 98-105 (8)	106.75	18.50

Inscription at top reads: "Al Hukumat al Arabia" (The Arabian Government). Inscription below tughra reads: "Barid al Hejaz wa Nejd" (Post of the Hejaz and Nejd).

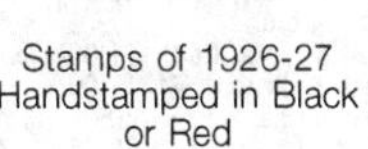

Stamps of 1926-27 Handstamped in Black or Red

1927

No.	Type	Description	Unused	Used
107	A3	1/8pi ocher	11.00	4.50
108	A3	1/4pi gray grn	11.00	4.50
109	A3	1/2pi dull red	11.00	4.50
110	A3	1pi deep violet	11.00	4.50
111	A3	1 1/2pi gray bl (R)	11.00	4.50
112	A3	3pi olive green	11.00	4.50
113	A3	5pi brown orange	11.00	4.50
114	A3	10pi dark brown	11.00	4.50
		Nos. 107-114 (8)	88.00	36.00

The overprint reads: "In commemoration of the Kingdom of Nejd and Dependencies, 25th Rajab 1345."

Turkey No. 258 Surcharged in Violet قرش واحد

1927 (?) *Perf. 12*

No.	Type	Description	Unused	Used
115	A28	1g on 10pa green		

The authenticity of this stamp has been questioned. Similar surcharges of 6g and 20g were made in red, but were not known to have been issued.

A4 A5

1929-30 Typo. *Perf. 11 1/2*

No.	Type	Description	Unused	Used
117	A4	1 3/4g gray blue	18.00	2.25
119	A4	20g violet	22.50	5.00
120	A4	30g green	35.00	11.00

1930 *Perf. 11, 11 1/2*

No.	Type	Description	Unused	Used
125	A5	1/2g rose	14.00	2.75
126	A5	1 1/2g violet	14.00	1.75
127	A5	1 3/4g ultra	14.00	2.25
128	A5	3 1/2g emerald	14.00	3.50
		Perf. 11		
129	A5	5g black brown	22.50	5.50
		Nos. 125-129 (5)	78.50	16.25

Anniversary of King Ibn Saud's accession to the throne of the Hejaz, January 8, 1926.

A6

A7

1931-32 *Perf. 11 1/2*

No.	Type	Description	Unused	Used
130	A6	1/8g ocher ('32)	12.50	2.25
131	A6	1/4g blue green	12.50	1.75
133	A6	1 3/4g ultra	16.00	2.25
		Nos. 130-133 (3)	41.00	6.25

1932 *Perf. 11 1/2*

No.	Type	Description	Unused	Used
135	A7	1/4g blue green	5.50	1.75
a.		Perf 11		
136	A7	1/2g scarlet	16.00	2.75
a.		Perf 11		
137	A7	2 1/4g ultra	37.50	4.50
a.		Perf 11		
		Nos. 135-137 (3)	59.00	9.00

Kingdom of Saudi Arabia

A8

1934, Jan. *Perf. 11 1/2, Imperf.*

No.	Type	Description	Unused	Used
138	A8	1/4g yellow green	7.25	7.25
139	A8	1/2g red	7.25	7.25
140	A8	1 1/2g light blue	14.00	14.00
141	A8	3g blue green	14.00	14.00
142	A8	3 1/2g ultra	25.00	5.50
143	A8	5g yellow	32.50	27.50
144	A8	10g red orange	60.00	
145	A8	20g bright violet	77.50	
146	A8	1/4s claret	150.00	
147	A8	30g dull violet	90.00	
148	A8	1/2s chocolate	325.00	
149	A8	1s violet brown	675.00	
		Nos. 138-149 (12)	1,477.	

Proclamation of Emir Saud as Heir Apparent of Arabia. Perf. and imperf. stamps were issued in equal quantities.

Favor cancels exist on Nos. 144-149.

Tughra of King Abdul Aziz — A9

1934-57 *Perf. 11, 11 1/2*

No.	Type	Description	Unused	Used
159	A9	1/8g yellow	3.25	.35
160	A9	1/4g yellow grn	3.25	.35
161	A9	1/2g rose red ('43)	2.50	.15
a.		1/2g dark carmine	12.00	1.40
162	A9	7/8g lt blue ('56)	4.00	.45
163	A9	1g blue green	3.25	.35
164	A9	2g olive grn ('57)	6.50	1.75
a.		2g olive bister ('57)	25.00	7.25
165	A9	2 7/8g violet ('57)	4.00	.45
166	A9	3g ultra ('38)	4.00	.20
a.		3g light blue	20.00	1.75
167	A9	3 1/2g lt ultra	16.00	1.75
168	A9	5g orange	4.00	.45
169	A9	10g violet	14.00	1.40
170	A9	20g purple brn	20.00	.90
a.		20g purple black	20.00	2.25
171	A9	100g red vio ('42)	65.00	4.00
172	A9	200g vio brn ('42)	80.00	5.50
		Nos. 159-172 (14)	229.75	18.05

The 1/2g has two types differing in position of the tughra.

No. 162 measures 31x22mm. No. 164 30 1/2x21 1/2mm. No. 165, 30 1/2x22mm. No. 166 30x21mm. No. 171, 31x22mm. No. 172, 30 1/2x21 1/2mm. Rest of set, 29x20 1/2mm. Grayish paper was used in 1946-49 printings.

No. 168 exists with pin-perf 6.

For overprint see No. J24.

Yanbu Harbor near Radwa — A10

1945 Typo. *Perf. 11 1/2*

No.	Type	Description	Unused	Used
173	A10	1/2g brt carmine	5.75	.25
174	A10	3g lt ultra	7.50	.90
175	A10	5g purple	22.50	1.10
176	A10	10g dk brown vio	50.00	2.75
		Nos. 173-176 (4)	85.75	5.00

Meeting of King Abdul Aziz and King Farouk of Egypt at Jebal Radwa, Saudi Arabia, Jan. 24, 1945.

Catalogue values for unused stamps in this section, from this point to the end of the section, are for Never Hinged items.

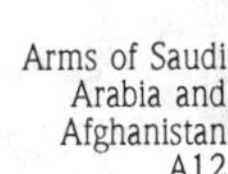

Arms of Saudi Arabia and Afghanistan A12

1950, Mar. *Perf. 11*

No.	Type	Description	Unused	Used
178	A12	1/2g carmine	6.75	.90
179	A12	3g violet blue	11.00	.90

Visit of Zahir Shah of Afghanistan, March 1950. One 3g in each sheet inscribed POSTFS, value $45.

Old City Walls, Riyadh — A13

1950

Center in Red Brown

No.	Type	Description	Unused	Used
180	A13	1/2g magenta	3.50	.15
181	A13	1g lt blue	6.75	.15
182	A13	3g violet	10.00	.45
183	A13	5g vermilion	22.50	.90
184	A13	10g green	40.00	2.25
a.		Singular "guerche" in Arabic	300.00	35.00
		Nos. 180-184 (5)	82.75	3.90

50th lunar anniversary of King Ibn Saud's capture of Riyadh, Jan. 16, 1902.

No. 184a: On the 3g, 5g and 10g the currency is expressed in the plural in both French (grouche) and Arabic. One stamp in each sheet of 20 (4x5), position 11, of the 10g shows the Arabic characters in the singular form of "guerche," as on the 1/2g and 1g.

Arms of Saudi Arabia and Jordan — A14

1951, Nov. *Perf. 11*

No.	Type	Description	Unused	Used
185	A14	1/2g carmine	4.75	.90
a.		"BOYAUME"	200.00	
186	A14	3g violet blue	15.00	1.40
a.		"BOYAUME"	200.00	

Visit of King Tallal of Jordan, Nov. 1951.

Bedouins and Train — A15

1952, June Engr. *Perf. 12*

No.	Type	Description	Unused	Used
187	A15	1/2q redsh brown	4.25	.65
188	A15	1q deep green	4.25	.65
189	A15	3q violet	8.50	.45
190	A15	10q rose pink	17.00	3.25
191	A15	20q blue	35.00	6.75
		Nos. 187-191 (5)	69.00	11.75

Inaugural trip over the Saudi Government Railroad between Riyadh and Dammam.

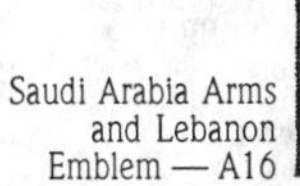

Saudi Arabia Arms and Lebanon Emblem — A16

1953, Feb. Typo. *Perf. 11*

No.	Type	Description	Unused	Used
192	A16	1/2g carmine	4.75	.90
193	A16	3g violet blue	9.50	1.40

Visit of President Camille Chamoun of Lebanon.

Arms of Saudi Arabia and Emblem of Pakistan — A17

1953, Mar.

No.	Type	Description	Unused	Used
194	A17	1/2g dark carmine	6.00	.90
195	A17	3g violet blue	12.50	1.40

Visit of Gov.-Gen. Ghulam Mohammed of Pakistan.

Arms of Saudi Arabia and Jordan — A18

Globe — A18a

1953, July **Unwmk.**

196	A18	½g carmine	4.50	.90
a.		"GOERCHE"	110.00	
197	A18	3g violet blue	14.00	1.40

Visit of King Hussein of Jordan, July, 1953.

1955, July **Litho.**

198	A18a	½g emerald	2.50	.45
199	A18a	3g violet	7.00	.90
200	A18a	4g orange	10.00	2.25
		Nos. 198-200 (3)	19.50	3.60

Founding of the Arab Postal Union, July 1, 1954.

Ministry of Communications Building, Riyadh — A19

1960, Apr. 12 **Photo.** ***Perf. 13***

201	A19	2p bright blue	.65	.15
202	A19	5p deep claret	1.40	.20
203	A19	10p dark green	3.50	.45
		Nos. 201-203 (3)	5.55	.80

Arab Postal Union Conference, at Riyadh, Apr. 11. Imperfs. exist.

Arab League Center, Cairo A20

1960, Mar. 22 ***Perf. 13x13½***

204	A20	2p dull grn & blk	1.75	.20

Opening of the Arab League Center and the Arab Postal Museum in Cairo. Exists imperf.

Radio Tower and Waves A21

1960, June 4

205	A21	2p red & black	1.75	.25
206	A21	5p brown blk & mar	2.75	.30
207	A21	10p bluish blk & ultra	4.50	.65
		Nos. 205-207 (3)	9.00	1.20

1st international radio station in Saudi Arabia. Imperfs. exist.

Map of Palestine, Refugee Camp and WRY Emblem — A22

1960, Oct. 30 **Litho.** ***Perf. 13***

208	A22	2p dark blue	.35	.15
209	A22	8p lilac	.35	.15
210	A22	10p green	1.10	.20
		Nos. 208-210 (3)	1.80	
		Set value		.40

World Refugee Year, July 1, 1959-June 30, 1960. Imperfs. exist.

Wadi Hanifa Dam, near Riyadh — A23

Gas-Oil Separating Plant, Buqqa — A24

Type I (Saud Cartouche) (Illustrated over No. 286)

1960-62 **Unwmk.** **Photo.** ***Perf. 14***

Size: 27½x22mm

211	A23	½p bis brn & org	1.25	.15
212	A23	1p ol bis & pur	1.25	.15
213	A23	2p blue & sepia	1.25	.15
214	A23	3p sepia & blue	1.25	.15
215	A23	4p sepia & ocher	1.25	.15
216	A23	5p blk & dk violet	1.25	.15
217	A23	6p brn blk & car rose ('62)	1.25	.20
a.		6p black & carmine rose	1.50	.35
218	A23	7p red & gray ol	1.25	.15
219	A23	8p dk bl & brn blk	1.25	.30
220	A23	9p org brn & scar	1.25	.30
c.		9p yel brn & metallic red	1.50	.45
221	A23	10p emer grn & mar ('62)	1.50	.35
a.		10p blue green & maroon	1.75	.70
222	A23	20p brown & green	3.50	.35
223	A23	50p black & brown	20.00	1.75
224	A23	75p brown & gray	55.00	2.00
225	A23	100p dk bl & grn bl	50.00	2.25
226	A23	200p lilac & green	77.50	5.75
		Nos. 211-226 (16)	220.00	14.30

1960-61

227	A24	½p maroon & org	1.10	.15
228	A24	1p blue & red org	1.10	.15
229	A24	2p vermilion & blue	1.10	.15
230	A24	3p lilac & brt grn	1.10	.15
231	A24	4p yel grn & lilac	1.10	.15
232	A24	5p dk gray & brn red	1.10	.15
233	A24	6p brn org & dk vio	1.10	.15
234	A24	7p vio & dull grn	1.10	.15
235	A24	8p blue grn & gray	1.10	.20
236	A24	9p ultra & sepia	3.25	.20
237	A24	10p dk blue & rose	1.75	.35
238	A24	20p org brn & blk	6.25	.45
239	A24	50p red & brn grn	18.00	1.40
240	A24	75p red & blk brn	27.50	2.75
241	A24	100p dk bl & red brn	42.50	2.50
242	A24	200p dk gray & ol grn	72.50	5.75
		Nos. 227-242 (16)	181.65	14.80

Nearly all of Nos. 211-242 exist imperf; probably not regularly issued.

See Nos. 258-273, 286-341, 393-450, 461-483.

Dammam Port — A25

Wmk. 337

1961, Aug. 16 **Litho.** ***Perf. 13***

243	A25	3p lilac	1.65	.20
244	A25	6p light blue	2.25	.30
245	A25	8p dark green	3.75	.35
		Nos. 243-245 (3)	7.65	.85

Expansion of the port of Dammam. Imperf min. sheets of 4 were for presentation purposes and have wmk. sideways. Value, set $200.

Globe, Radio and Telegraph A26

Perf. 13x13½

1961, Aug. 7 **Photo.** **Unwmk.**

246	A26	3p dull purple	1.40	.15
247	A26	6p gray black	2.25	.30
248	A26	8p brown	3.50	.45
		Nos. 246-248 (3)	7.15	.90

Arab Union of Telecommunications. Imperfs. exist.

Arab League Building, Cairo — A27

Malaria Eradication Emblem — A28

1962, Apr. 22 **Wmk. 337** ***Perf. 13***

249	A27	3p olive green	1.10	.20
250	A27	6p carmine rose	2.25	.30
251	A27	8p slate blue	3.50	.35
		Nos. 249-251 (3)	6.85	.85

Arab League Week, Mar. 22-28.

Imperforate or missing-color varieties of Nos. 249-285 and 344-353 were not regularly issued.

1962, May 7 **Litho.** **Wmk. 337**

252	A28	3p red org & blue	.75	.15
253	A28	6p emerald & Prus bl	1.10	.25
254	A28	8p black & lil rose	1.75	.40
a.		Souv. sheet of 3, #252-254, imperf.	14.00	14.00
		Nos. 252-254 (3)	3.60	.80

WHO drive to eradicate malaria.

Nos. 252-254 are known unofficially overprinted with new dates only or with "AIR MAIL" and two plane silhouettes.

A 4p exists as an essay.

Koran — A29

1963, Mar. 12 **Wmk. 337** ***Perf. 11***

255	A29	2½p lilac rose & pink	.90	.15
256	A29	7½p blue & pale grn	1.75	.35
257	A29	9½p green & gray	2.75	.35
		Nos. 255-257 (3)	5.40	.85

First anniversary of the Islamic Institute, Medina. A 3p exists as an essay. Copies of the 2½p exist with virtually all the pink background omitted. No copies are known with the pink completely omitted.

Dam Type of 1960 Redrawn
Type I (Saud Cartouche)

Perf. 13½x13

1963-65 **Wmk. 337** **Litho.**

Size: 28½x23mm

258	A23	½p bis brn & org	9.00	.65

Nos. 258, 264-265 are widely spaced in the sheet, producing large margins.

Perf. 14

Photo.

Size: 27½x22mm

259	A23	½p bis brn & org ('65)	20.00	1.40
260	A23	3p sepia & blue	7.75	.55
261	A23	4p sepia & ocher ('64)	11.00	.70
262	A23	5p black & dk vio	11.00	.70
263	A23	20p dk carmine & grn	20.00	1.40
		Nos. 258-263 (6)	78.75	5.40

A 1p was prepared but not issued. It is known only imperf.

Gas-Oil Plant Type of 1960 Redrawn
Type I (Saud Cartouche)

Perf. 13½x13

1963-65 **Wmk. 337** **Litho.**

Size: 28½x23mm

264	A24	½p maroon & orange	9.50	.90
265	A24	1p blue & red org ('64)	4.50	.30

Photo.

Perf. 14

Size: 27½x22mm

266	A24	½p mar & org ('64)	9.00	.45
267	A24	1p blue & red org	7.75	.30
268	A24	3p lilac & brt grn	18.00	.90
269	A24	4p yel grn & lilac	11.00	.45
270	A24	5p dk gray & brn red	11.00	.45
271	A24	6p brn org & dk vio ('65)	16.00	.60
272	A24	8p dull grn & blk	27.50	1.10
273	A24	9p blue & sepia	27.50	1.40
		Nos. 264-273 (10)	141.75	6.85

The 3p, 4p and 6p exist imperf.

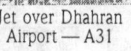

Hands Holding Wheat Emblem A30

1963, Mar. 21 **Litho.** ***Perf. 11***

274	A30	2½p lilac rose & rose	1.10	.15
275	A30	7½p brt lilac & pink	1.10	.30
276	A30	9p red brn & lt blue	2.25	.35
		Nos. 274-276 (3)	4.45	.80

FAO "Freedom from Hunger" campaign. The 3p imperf in various colors are essays.

Jet over Dhahran Airport — A31

Flame — A32

1963, July 27 **Litho.** ***Perf. 13***

277	A31	1p blue gray & ocher	1.10	.15
278	A31	3½p ultra & emer	2.25	.20
279	A31	6p emerald & rose	3.75	.25
a.		"Thahran" for "Dharan" in Arabic	5.50	
280	A31	7½p lilac rose & lt bl	3.75	.30
281	A31	9½p ver & dull vio	5.50	.35
		Nos. 277-281 (5)	16.35	1.25

Opening of the US-financed terminal of the Dhahran Airport and inauguration of international jet service.

On No. 279a the misspelling consists of an omitted dot over character near top left in one horiz. row of five.

1964, Apr. Wmk. 337 *Perf. 13x13½*

282	A32	3p lil, pink & Prus bl	3.00	.15
283	A32	6p yel grn, lt bl & Prus bl	3.75	.25
284	A32	9p brn, buff & Prus bl	7.75	.35
		Nos. 282-284 (3)	14.50	.75

15th anniv. of the signing of the Universal Declaration of Human Rights.

The 3p in other colors is an essay.

King Faisal and Arms of Saudi Arabia A33

1964, Nov. Litho. *Perf. 13*

285	A33	4p dk blue & emerald	4.00	.15

Installation of Prince Faisal ibn Abdul Aziz as King, Nov. 2, 1964.

King Saud's Cartouche — Type I

King Faisal's Cartouche — Type II

Redrawn Dam Type of 1960
Type I (Saud Cartouche)

1965-70 Litho. Unwmk. *Perf. 14*
Size: 27x22mm

286	A23	1p olive bis & pur	18.00	.90
287	A23	2p dk blue & sep	3.50	.25
288	A23	3p sepia & blue	3.50	.30
289	A23	4p sepia & ocher	6.25	.30
290	A23	5p black & dk vio	4.50	.30
291	A23	6p black & car rose	11.00	.55
292	A23	7p brown & gray	11.00	.30
293	A23	8p dk blue & gray	*60.00*	4.50
294	A23	9p org brn & scar	*55.00*	4.50
295	A23	10p blue grn & mar	*60.00*	2.75
296	A23	11p red & yel grn	4.75	1.75
297	A23	12p orange & dk bl	4.75	.30
298	A23	13p dk olive & rose	4.75	.35
299	A23	14p org brn & yel grn	4.75	.35
300	A23	15p sepia & gray grn	4.75	1.75
301	A23	16p dk red & dl vio	6.00	.40
302	A23	17p rose lil & dk bl	6.00	2.00
303	A23	18p green & brt bl	6.00	.40
304	A23	19p black & bister	8.00	.45
305	A23	20p brown & green	10.00	.90
306	A23	23p mar & lilac	8.00	1.75
307	A23	24p ver & blue	8.00	.55
308	A23	26p olive & yel	10.00	.65
309	A23	27p ultra & red brn	10.00	.65
310	A23	31p gray & dull bl	10.00	.70
311	A23	33p ol grn & lilac	10.00	.70
312	A23	100p dk bl & grnsh bl	*300.00*	*45.00*
313	A23	200p dull lilac & grn	*300.00*	*45.00*
		Nos. 286-313 (28)	*948.50*	*118.30*

A 50p exists but was never placed in use.

Issue years: 1966, 2p, 4p, 10p-20p, 1968, 6p-9p. 1970, 100p-200p.

Redrawn Gas-Oil Plant Type of 1960
Type I (Saud Cartouche)

1964-70 Litho. Unwmk.
Size: 27x22mm

314	A24	1p blue & red org	7.25	.20
315	A24	2p vermilion & bl	11.00	.20
316	A24	3p lilac & brt grn	4.50	.15
317	A24	4p yel grn & lilac	6.50	.20
318	A24	5p dl gray vio & dk red brn	24.00	1.75
319	A24	6p brn org & dk vio	50.00	4.50
320	A24	7p vio & dull grn	27.50	1.75
321	A24	8p blue grn & gray	6.00	.30
322	A24	9p ultra & sepia	12.50	.70
323	A24	10p dk blue & rose	*325.00*	32.50
324	A24	11p olive & orange	4.00	.30
325	A24	12p bister & green	4.00	.30
326	A24	13p rose red & dk bl	4.00	.35
327	A24	14p vio & lt brown	5.50	.35
328	A24	15p rose red & sep	6.00	.45
329	A24	16p green & rose red	8.00	.45
330	A24	17p car rose & red brn	12.50	1.40
331	A24	18p gray & ultra	8.00	.55
332	A24	19p brown & yellow	8.00	.55
333	A24	20p dull org & dk gray	27.50	1.75
334	A24	23p orange & car	7.25	.65
335	A24	24p emer & org yel	8.00	.70
336	A24	26p lilac & red brn	11.00	.70
337	A24	27p ver & dk gray	11.00	.70
338	A24	31p dull grn & car	19.00	1.40
339	A24	33p red brn & gray	17.00	1.40
340	A24	50p red brn & dull grn	*325.00*	*45.00*
341	A24	200p dk gray & ol gray	*325.00*	*45.00*
		Nos. 314-341 (28)	*1,285.*	*144.25*

A 100p exists but was never placed in use.

Issue years: 1965, 4p, 8p, 9p, 23p-33p. 1966, 1p, 2p, 5p, 11p-14p, 16p-20p. 1967, 15p. 1968, 6p, 7p. 1969, 50p. 1970, 200p. Others, 1964.

Holy Ka'aba, Mecca — A34

1965, Apr. 17 Wmk. 337 *Perf. 13*

344	A34	4p salmon & blk	3.25	.20
345	A34	6p brt pink & blk	5.00	.25
346	A34	10p yel grn & blk	7.00	.35
		Nos. 344-346 (3)	15.25	.80

Mecca Conf. of the Moslem World League.

Arms of Saudi Arabia and Tunisia A35

1965, Apr. Litho.

347	A35	4p car rose & silver	2.75	.20
348	A35	8p red lilac & silver	3.50	.35
349	A35	10p ultra & silver	5.00	.35
		Nos. 347-349 (3)	11.25	.90

Visit of Pres. Habib Bourguiba of Tunisia, Feb. 22-26.

Highway, Hejaz Mountains — A36

1965, June 2 Wmk. 337 *Perf. 13*

350	A36	2p red & blk	1.65	.30
351	A36	4p blue & blk	2.50	.35
352	A36	6p lilac & blk	3.50	.45
353	A36	8p brt green & blk	5.00	.55
		Nos. 350-353 (4)	12.65	1.65

Opening of highway from Mecca to Tayif.

ICY Emblem A37

1965, Nov. 13 Unwmk. *Perf. 13*

354	A37	1p yellow & dk brn	1.40	.15
355	A37	2p orange & ol grn	1.40	.15
356	A37	3p lt blue & gray	1.40	.15
357	A37	4p yel grn & dk sl grn	1.40	.20
358	A37	10p orange & magenta	3.50	.45
		Nos. 354-358 (5)	9.10	
		Set value		.85

International Cooperation Year, 1965.

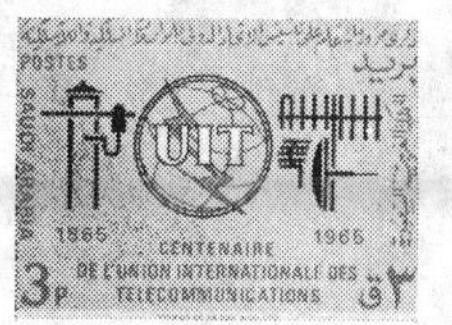

ITU Emblem, Old and New Communication Equipment — A38

1965, Dec. 22 Litho. *Perf. 13*

359	A38	3p blue & blk	2.00	.15
360	A38	4p lilac & dk grn	2.00	.15
361	A38	8p emerald & dk brn	2.00	.35
362	A38	10p dull org & dk grn	2.00	.35
		Nos. 359-362 (4)	8.00	1.00

Centenary of the ITU.

Library Aflame and Lamp A39

1966, Jan. Litho. *Perf. 12x12½*

363	A39	1p orange	1.40	.15
364	A39	2p dark red	1.40	.15
365	A39	3p red violet	2.00	.15
366	A39	4p violet	2.25	.20
367	A39	5p lilac rose	4.75	.35
368	A39	6p vermilion	8.00	.45
		Nos. 363-368 (6)	19.80	1.45

Burning of the Library of Algiers, June 2, 1962. Nos. 363-368 were withdrawn from sale Jan. 26, 1966, due to incorrect Arabic inscriptions. Later some values were inadvertently again placed in use.

Arab Postal Union Emblem — A40

Dagger in Map of Palestine — A41

1966, Mar. 15 Litho. *Perf. 14*

369	A40	3p dull pur & olive	1.00	.15
370	A40	4p deep blue & olive	1.00	.15
371	A40	6p maroon & olive	4.00	.25
372	A40	7p deep green & olive	4.00	.35
		Nos. 369-372 (4)	10.00	.90

10th anniv. (in 1964) of the APU. Printed in sheets of two panes, so horizontal gutter pairs exist.

1966, Mar. 19 Litho. *Perf. 13*

373	A41	2p yel grn & blk	1.65	.15
374	A41	4p lt brown & blk	3.00	.15
375	A41	6p dull blue & blk	4.50	.25
376	A41	8p ocher & blk	6.25	.35
		Nos. 373-376 (4)	15.40	.90

Deir Yassin massacre, Apr. 9, 1948.

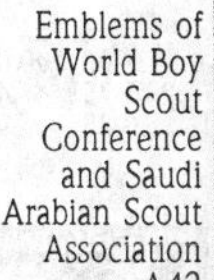

Emblems of World Boy Scout Conference and Saudi Arabian Scout Association A42

1966, Mar. 23 Unwmk.

377	A42	4p yel, blk, grn & gray	4.50	.45
378	A42	8p yel, blk, org & lt bl	4.50	.45
379	A42	10p yel, blk, sal & bl	9.00	.65
		Nos. 377-379 (3)	18.00	1.55

Arab League Rover Moot (Boy Scout Jamboree).

WHO Headquarters, Geneva, and Flag — A43

1966, May Litho. *Perf. 13*

380	A43	4p aqua & multi	1.40	.15
381	A43	6p yel brn & multi	2.75	.25
382	A43	10p pink & multi	5.50	.35
		Nos. 380-382 (3)	9.65	.75

Opening of the WHO Headquarters, Geneva.

UNESCO Emblem — A44

1966, Sept. Unwmk. *Perf. 12*

383	A44	1p apple grn & multi	1.25	.15
384	A44	2p dull org & multi	1.25	.15
385	A44	3p lilac rose & multi	1.75	.15
386	A44	4p pale green & multi	1.75	.15
387	A44	10p gray & multi	2.50	.35
		Nos. 383-387 (5)	8.50	
		Set value		.70

20th anniv. of UNESCO.

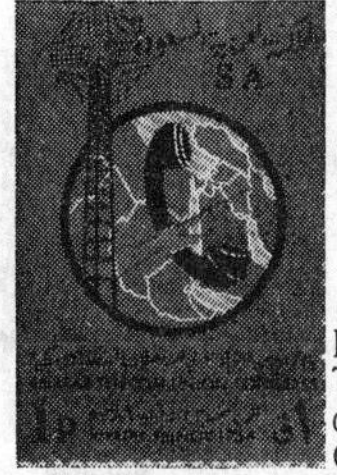

Radio Tower, Telephone and Map of Arab Countries — A45

1966, Nov. 7 Litho. *Perf. 12½*
Design in Black, Carmine & Yellow

388	A45	1p vio blue	1.65	.15
389	A45	2p bluish lilac	1.65	.15
390	A45	4p rose lilac	3.25	.15
391	A45	6p lt olive grn	3.25	.30
392	A45	7p gray green	4.00	.40
		Nos. 388-392 (5)	13.80	1.15

Issued to publicize the 8th Congress of the Arab Telecommunications Union, Riyadh.

Redrawn Dam Type of 1960
Type II (Faisal Cartouche)
(Illustrated over No. 286)

1966-76 Litho. Unwmk. *Perf. 14*
Size: 27x22mm

393	A23	1p ol bis & pur	*165.00*	*22.50*
394	A23	2p dk blue & sep	19.00	1.50
395	A23	3p blk & dk bl	11.00	.80
396	A23	4p sepia & ocher	15.00	.40
397	A23	5p blk & dk vio	40.00	7.50
398	A23	6p blk & car rose	32.50	6.75
399	A23	7p sepia & gray	18.00	1.75
400	A23	8p dk blue & gray	11.00	.45
401	A23	9p org brn & scar	7.50	.80
402	A23	10p blue grn & mar	15.00	1.40
403	A23	11p red & yel grn	11.00	1.40
404	A23	12p orange & dk bl	6.50	1.40
405	A23	13p blk & rose	22.50	1.40
406	A23	14p org brn & yel grn	19.00	1.40
407	A23	15p sep & gray grn	19.00	1.75
408	A23	16p dk red & dl vio	27.50	3.25
409	A23	17p rose lil & dk bl	32.50	1.75
410	A23	18p green & brt bl	22.50	2.50
411	A23	19p black & bister	7.25	.80
412	A23	20p brown & grn	72.50	*2.25*
413	A23	23p maroon & lil	275.00	*4.50*
414	A23	24p ver & blue	52.50	5.50
415	A23	26p olive & yel	8.25	.70
416	A23	27p ultra & red brn	7.75	.70
417	A23	33p ol grn & lilac	42.50	2.25
419	A23	50p black & brown	175.00	*35.00*
420	A23	100p dk bl & grnsh bl	275.00	*45.00*
421	A23	200p dull lilac & grn	275.00	*72.50*
		Nos. 393-421 (28)	*1,685.*	227.90

A 31p has been reported.

Issue years: 1966, 1p. 1967, 2p, 10p. 1968, 3p, 4p, 6p, 7p, 20p; 1969, 5p, 8p. 1970, 9p, 23p; 1972, 12p, 15p, 16p. 1973, 11p; 1974, 17p, 50p-200p; 1975, 13p, 14p, 19p, 24p-33p; 1976, 18p.

Redrawn Gas-Oil Plant Type of 1960
Type II (Faisal Cartouche)

1966-78 Unwmk.
Size: 27x22mm

422	A24	1p bl & red org	35.00	*2.75*
423	A24	2p ver & dull bl	7.00	.30
424	A24	3p lilac & brt grn	14.00	.55
425	A24	4p grn & dull lil	8.00	.30
426	A24	5p dl gray vio & dk red brn	37.50	1.75
427	A24	6p brn org & dull pur	24.00	3.50
428	A24	7p vio & dull grn	32.50	1.75
429	A24	8p bl grn & grnsh gray	5.50	.30
430	A24	9p ultra & sep	4.50	.30
431	A24	10p dk blue & rose	4.50	.55
432	A24	11p olive & orange	72.50	7.25
433	A24	12p bister & grn	4.50	.70
434	A24	13p rose red & dk bl	42.50	.30
435	A24	14p vio & lt brn	40.00	2.25
436	A24	15p car & sepia	14.00	.60
437	A24	16p grn & rose red	14.00	.70
438	A24	17p car rose & red brn	10.00	.55
439	A24	18p gray & ultra	14.00	1.50
440	A24	19p brown & yellow	16.00	1.50
441	A24	20p brn org & gray	12.00	1.50
442	A24	23p orange & car	27.50	1.75
443	A24	24p emer & org yel	9.00	.70
444	A24	26p lilac & red brn	*175.00*	
445	A24	27p ver & dk gray	35.00	3.50

446	A24	31p green & rose car	11.00	.70
447	A24	33p brown & gray	20.00	1.10
448	A24	50p red brn & dl grn	350.00	*140.00*
449	A24	100p dk bl & red brn	300.00	*40.00*
450	A24	200p dk gray & ol gray	350.00	*57.50*
		Nos. 422-450 (29)	1,690.	

Issue years: 1967, 20p; 1968, 3p, 5p-9p, 15p, 16p; 1969, 100p; 1970, 11p, 14p, 200p; 1973, 13p, 18p, 24p; 1974, 19p, 50p; 1975, 12p, 17p, 27p-33p; 1978, 26p; others, 1966.

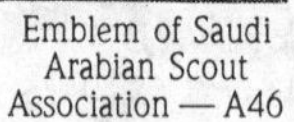

Emblem of Saudi Arabian Scout Association — A46

Meteorological Instruments and WMO Emblem — A47

1967, Mar. 28 Litho. *Perf. 13½*
Emblem in Green, Red, Yellow & Black

451	A46	1p dk blue & blk	2.00	.15
452	A46	2p blue grn & blk	2.00	.15
453	A46	3p lt blue & blk	3.00	.15
454	A46	4p rose brn & blk	3.75	.15
455	A46	10p brown & blk	8.50	.45
		Nos. 451-455 (5)	19.25	1.05

2nd Arabic League Rover Moot, Mecca, March 13-28.

1967, July Unwmk. *Perf. 13*

456	A47	1p brt magenta	1.25	.15
457	A47	2p violet	2.25	.15
458	A47	3p olive	2.25	.15
459	A47	4p blue green	7.25	.15
460	A47	10p blue	10.00	.35
		Nos. 456-460 (5)	23.00	
		Set value		.60

Issued for World Meteorological Day.

Redrawn Dam Type of 1960
Type II (Faisal Cartouche)

1968-76 Wmk. 361 Litho. *Perf. 14*

461	A23	1p ol bis & pur ('71)	*1,100.*	*275.00*
462	A23	2p dk blue & sep	30.00	*1.75*
463	A23	3p blk & dk bl	20.00	.90
464	A23	4p sepia & ocher	175.00	*30.00*
465	A23	5p blk & dk vio	25.00	*1.75*
466	A23	6p blk & car rose	24.00	*1.40*
467	A23	7p sepia & gray	35.00	*2.75*
468	A23	8p dk bl & gray	18.00	.90
469	A23	9p org brn & ver	65.00	*6.25*
470	A23	10p bl grn & mar	45.00	*3.50*
471	A23	11p red & yel grn	55.00	*5.50*
472	A23	12p org & sl bl	50.00	*4.50*
473	A23	13p black & rose	67.50	*6.75*
		Nos. 462-473 (12)	609.50	*65.95*

Issue years: 1968, 2p, 10p; 1969, 3p; 1970, 8p; 1971, 1p, 5p; 1972, 6p, 9p, 11p, 12p; 1973, 4p; 1974, 13p; 1976, 9p.

Redrawn Gas-Oil Plant Type of 1960
Type II (Faisal Cartouche)

1968-76 *Perf. 14*

474	A24	1p bl & red org	9.50	.90
475	A24	2p ver & dl bl	5.75	.45
476	A24	4p grn & dl lil	72.50	*7.25*
477	A24	5p dk brn & red brn ('73)	20.00	1.40
478	A24	6p brn org & dk vio ('73)	25.00	1.75
479	A24	9p dk bl & sep ('76)	40.00	3.50
480	A24	10p dk bl & rose	8.50	.60
481	A24	11p ol & org ('72)	30.00	1.75
482	A24	12p bis & grn ('72)	32.50	2.75
483	A24	23p org & car ('74)	55.00	2.75
		Nos. 474-483 (10)	298.75	23.10

Map Showing Dammam to Jedda Road, and Dates — A48

Wmk. 361
1968, Aug. Litho. *Perf. 14*

484	A48	1p yellow & multi	1.40	.15
485	A48	2p orange & multi	1.40	.15
486	A48	3p multicolored	2.75	.15
487	A48	4p multicolored	2.75	.15
488	A48	10p multicolored	8.00	.35
		Nos. 484-488 (5)	16.30	
		Set value		.70

Issued to commemorate the completion of the trans-Saudi Arabia highway in 1967.

Several positions in the sheet have the dots representing Dammam and Riyadh omitted. Most had the dots added by pen before issuance.

Prophet's Mosque, Medina — A49

New Arcade, Mecca Mosque — A50

Perf. 13½x14
1968-76 Litho. Wmk. 361

489	A49	1p org & grn, wmk. 337 ('70)	2.75	.30
490	A49	2p red brn & grn, redrawn ('72)	4.25	.35
a.		Wmk. 337 ('71)	6.25	.30
b.		As "a," redrawn	*175.00*	
491	A49	3p vio & grn ('72)	3.75	.35
a.		Wmk. 337 ('70)	2.75	.30
492	A49	4p ocher & green	4.25	.35
a.		Redrawn, wmk. 361 ('71)	5.50	.45
b.		Redrawn, wmk. 337	6.25	
493	A49	5p dp lil rose & grn, wmk. 337 ('71)	9.00	.90
494	A49	6p blk & grn ('73)	11.00	.90
a.		6p gray & green ('76)	18.00	.90
495	A49	10p brown & green	14.00	.90
a.		Redrawn	9.00	
496	A49	20p dk brn & grn ('70)	18.00	1.75
a.		Redrawn	18.00	
497	A49	50p sepia & grn ('75)	22.50	5.75
498	A49	100p dk bl & grn ('75)	18.00	4.50
499	A49	200p red & grn ('75)	22.50	6.25
		Nos. 489-499 (11)	130.00	22.30

See redrawn note following design A55. No. 494 exists imperf.

1968-69

500	A50	3p dp org & gray ('69)	350.00	90.00
501	A50	4p green & gray	5.75	.45
502	A50	10p magenta & gray	8.25	.90

Expansion of Prophet's Mosque — A51

Madayin Saleh — A52

1968-76

503	A51	1p org & grn ('72)	4.50	.25
504	A51	2p brn & grn ('72)	7.25	.25
505	A51	3p blk & grn ('69)	6.25	.35
b.		3p gray & green ('76)	18.00	1.75
c.		As No. 505, redrawn	4.50	
506	A51	4p org & grn ('70)	6.25	.45
507	A51	5p red & grn ('74)	6.75	.75
508	A51	6p Prus bl & grn ('72)	9.00	.90
509	A51	8p rose red & grn ('76)	22.50	1.75
510	A51	10p brn red & grn ('70)	8.25	.55
b.		10p orange & green ('76)	18.00	.90
511	A51	20p vio & grn ('74)	18.00	2.25
		Nos. 503-511 (9)	88.75	7.50

Wmk. 337

503a	A51	1p	5.00	.35
504a	A51	2p ('70)	6.75	.35
b.		As "a," redrawn	35.00	
505a	A51	3p ('71)	7.25	.70
d.		As "a," redrawn	9.00	
506a	A51	4p ('72)	4.50	.45
b.		As "a," redrawn	9.00	
507a	A51	5p ('70)	4.50	.45
508a	A51	6p ('72)	6.25	.55
510a	A51	10p ('70)	11.00	.60
c.		As "a," redrawn	18.00	
511a	A51	20p ('72)	8.25	.70
		Nos. 503a-511a (8)	53.50	4.15

See redrawn note following design A55.

1968-75

512	A52	2p ultra & bis brn ('70)	20.00	3.50
513	A52	4p dk & lt brown	5.00	.70
514	A52	7p org & lt brn ('75)	50.00	*9.00*
515	A52	10p sl grn & lt brn	12.50	1.75
516	A52	20p lil rose & brn ('71)	14.00	1.40
		Nos. 512-516 (5)	101.50	*16.35*

Arabian Stallion — A53

Camels and Oil Derrick — A54

517	A53	4p mag & org brn	5.00	.70
518	A53	10p blk & org brn	14.00	2.75
519	A53	14p bl & ocher ('71)	22.50	5.50
520	A53	20p ol grn & ocher ('71)	9.50	1.75
		Nos. 517-520 (4)	51.00	10.70

1969-71

521	A54	4p dk pur & redsh brn ('71)	27.50	3.50
522	A54	10p ultra & hn brn	19.00	2.75

Holy Ka'aba, Mecca — A55

Original

Redrawn

On the original stamps the knob-shaped Arabic letter, located under the two square dots in the middle of the top panel, has a small central dot. The dot often is missing.

On the redrawn stamps the dot has been enlarged into a conspicuous irregular oval. The 3p also has a period added after the value and the 4p has the "4" under the "T" instead of the "S." There are other small differences.

Numeral & "Postage" on Gray Background, 8p on White

1969-75

523	A55	4p dp grn & blk ('70)	7.75	.70
a.		Redrawn, value corner white ('74)	16.00	1.75
b.		Redrawn ('75)	14.00	
524	A55	6p dp lil rose & blk ('71)	4.50	.35
a.		Value corner white ('74)	22.50	2.75
525	A55	8p red & blk ('75)	27.50	2.75
526	A55	10p org & blk ('69)	16.00	1.40
a.		Redrawn, value corner white ('74)	14.00	1.75
b.		Redrawn ('75)	18.00	
		Nos. 523-526 (4)	55.75	5.20

Rover Moot Badge — A56

Perf. 13½x14
1969, Feb. 19 Litho. Wmk. 337

607	A56	1p orange & multi	1.50	.15
608	A56	4p dull purple & multi	4.50	.20
609	A56	10p orange brn & multi	12.50	.55
		Nos. 607-609 (3)	18.50	.90

3rd Arab League Rover Moot, Mecca, Feb. 19-Mar. 3.

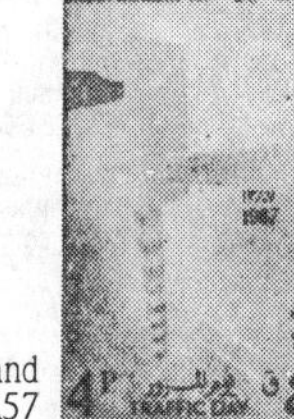

Traffic Light and Intersection — A57

1969, Feb. Wmk. 361 *Perf. 13½*

610	A57	3p dl bl, red & brt bl grn	2.00	.15
a.		3p dull blue, red & gray green	6.00	.90
611	A57	4p org brn, red & gray grn	2.00	.15
612	A57	10p dl pur, red & gray grn	4.00	.45
		Nos. 610-612 (3)	8.00	.75

Issued for Traffic Day.

WHO Emblem — A58

1969, Oct. 20 Wmk. 337 *Perf. 14*

613	A58	4p lt bl, vio bl & yel	11.00	.15

20th anniv. (in 1968) of WHO.

Islamic Conference Emblem A59

1970, Mar. 23 Litho. Wmk. 361

614	A59	4p blue & black	2.75	.15
615	A59	10p yellow bis & blk	4.25	.40

Islamic Conference of Foreign Ministers, Jedda, March 1970.

Open Book and Satellite Earth Receiving Station — A60

Perf. 14x13½
1970, Aug. 1 Litho. Wmk. 337

616	A60	4p violet bl & multi	4.25	.15
617	A60	10p green & multi	8.50	.45

World Telecommunications Day.

Steel Rolling Mill, Jedda — A61

1970, Oct. 26 Wmk. 337 *Perf. 13½*

618 A61 3p yellow org & multi 2.50 .15
619 A61 4p violet & multi 3.75 .15
620 A61 10p brt green & multi 6.50 .45
Nos. 618-620 (3) 12.75 .75

Inauguration of 1st steel mill in Saudi Arabia.

Rover Moot Emblem — A62

1971, Feb. Litho. *Perf. 14*

621 A62 10p brt blue & multi 8.00 .65

4th Arab League Rover Moot, 1971.

Telecommunications Symbol — A63

1971, May 17 Wmk. 337 *Perf. 14*

622 A63 4p blue & blk 2.00 .15
623 A63 10p lilac & blk 4.25 .35

World Telecommunications Day.

University Minaret — A64

Arab League Emblem — A65

Wmk. 337; Wmk. 361 (4p)

1971, Aug. Litho. *Perf. 14*

624 A64 3p brt green & black 1.65 .15
625 A64 4p brown & black 3.00 .15
626 A64 10p blue & black 5.75 .45
Nos. 624-626 (3) 10.40 .75

King Abdul Aziz National University.

1971, Nov. Wmk. 337 *Perf. 13½*

627 A65 10p multicolored 5.75 .35

Arab League Week.

Education Year Emblem — A66

OPEC Emblem — A67

1971, Nov. Litho.

628 A66 4p apple grn & brn red 5.75 .15

International Education Year 1970.

1971, Dec. *Perf. 14*

629 A67 4p light blue 6.25 .15

10th anniversary of OPEC (Organization of Petroleum Exporting Countries).

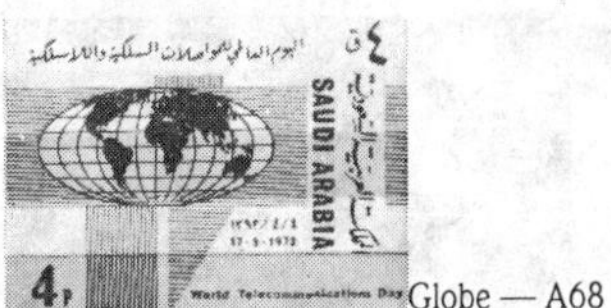

Globe — A68

1972, Aug. Wmk. 361 *Perf. 14*

630 A68 4p multicolored 5.75 .15

4th World Telecommunications Day.

Telephone — A69

1972, Oct. Wmk. 337, 361 (5p)

631 A69 1p red, blk & grn 2.00 .15
632 A69 4p dk grn, blk & grn 2.00 .15
633 A69 5p lil, blk & grn 3.75 .20
634 A69 10p tan, blk & grn 8.00 .45
Nos. 631-634 (4) 15.75 .95

Inauguration of automatic telephone system (1969).

Writing Hand — A70

1972, Sept. 8 Litho. Wmk. 361

635 A70 10p multicolored 8.00 .35

World Literacy Day, Sept. 8.

Holy Ka'aba and Grand Mosque, Mecca — A71

Designs (Rover Moot Emblem and): 4p, Prophet's Mosque, Medina. 10p, Plains of Arafat.

1973

636 A71 4p lt blue & multi 3.00 .20
637 A71 6p lilac & multi 5.75 .30
638 A71 10p salmon & multi 9.00 .55
Nos. 636-638 (3) 17.75 1.05

5th Arab League Rover Moot.

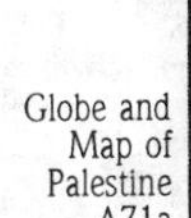

Globe and Map of Palestine A71a

1973 Litho. Wmk. 361 *Perf. 14*

639 A71a 4p black, yel & red 3.00 .15
640 A71a 10p blue, yel & red 6.00 .35

Palestine Week.

Leaf and Emblem — A72

1973

641 A72 4p yellow & multi 5.50 .25

International Hydrological Decade 1965-74.

Arab Postal Union Emblem — A73

1973, Dec. Litho. *Perf. 14*

642 A73 4p sepia & multi 4.25 .25
643 A73 10p purple & multi 9.00 .45

25th anniversary (in 1971) of the Conference of Sofar, Lebanon, establishing the Arab Postal Union.

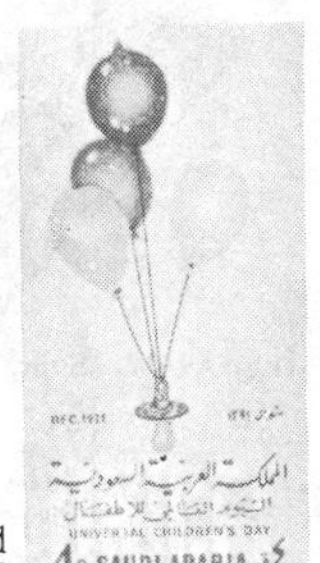

Balloons and Pacifier — A74

1973, Dec.

644 A74 4p lt blue & multi 6.75 .15

Universal Children's Day (stamp dated 1971).

Arab Postal and UPU Emblems A75

1974, July 7 Wmk. 361 *Perf. 14*

645 A75 3p yellow & multi *45.00* 2.25
646 A75 4p rose & multi *45.00* 4.50
647 A75 10p lt green & multi *45.00* 6.75
Nos. 645-647 (3) *135.00* 13.50

Centenary of the Universal Postal Union.

Handshake and UNESCO Emblem — A76

1974, May 21 *Perf. 13½*

648 A76 4p orange & multi 2.75 .25
649 A76 10p green & multi 11.00 .65

International Book Year, 1972.

Desalination Plant — A77

1974, Sept. 3 Wmk. 361 *Perf. 14*

650 A77 4p dp orange & bl 2.00 .15
651 A77 6p emerald & vio 4.25 .25
652 A77 10p rose red & blk 6.50 .45
Nos. 650-652 (3) 12.75 .85

Opening (in 1971) of sea water desalination plant, Jedda.

A78

A79

Design: INTERPOL emblem.

1974, Nov. 1

653 A78 4p ocher & ultra 7.00 .20
654 A78 10p emerald & ultra 14.00 .45

50th anniversary (in 1973) of International Criminal Police Organization.

1974, Oct. 26 Litho. Wmk. 361

APU emblem, tower and letter.

655 A79 4p multicolored 9.00 .15

Arab Consultative Council for Postal Studies, 3rd session.

UPU Headquarters, Bern — A80

1974, Nov. 15 *Perf. 13½*

656 A80 3p orange & multi 2.75 .25
657 A80 4p lilac & multi 5.75 .45
658 A80 10p blue & multi 8.00 1.10
Nos. 656-658 (3) 16.50 1.80

Opening of new Universal Postal Union Headquarters, Bern, May 1970.

Tank, Planes, Rockets and Flame — A81

1974, Dec. 15 *Perf. 14*

659 A81 3p slate & multi 2.25 .15
660 A81 4p brown & multi 4.50 .25
661 A81 10p lilac & multi 12.50 .65
Nos. 659-661 (3) 19.25 1.05

King Faisal Military Cantonment, 1971.

A82

A84

A83

Red Crescent flower.

1974, Dec. 17 *Perf. 14x14½*

662 A82 4p gray & multi 1.75 .25
663 A82 6p lt green & multi 4.50 .45
664 A82 10p lt blue & multi 9.00 .90
Nos. 662-664 (3) 15.25 1.60

Saudi Arabian Red Crescent Society, 10th anniversary (in 1973).

1974, Dec. 23 Wmk. 361 *Perf. 14*

Saudi Arabian scout emblem and minarets.

665 A83 4p brown & multi 4.25 .20
666 A83 6p blue blk & multi 8.25 .30
667 A83 10p purple & multi 12.50 .55
Nos. 665-667 (3) 25.00 1.05

6th Arab League Rover Moot, Mecca.

1975, Mar. 31 *Perf. 14x13½*

Design: Reading braille.

668 A84 4p multicolored 3.50 .25
669 A84 10p multicolored 8.50 .45

Day of the Blind.

Anemometer and Weather Balloon with UN Emblem — A85

Perf. 13½x14

1975, May 8 Litho. Wmk. 361

670 A85 4p multicolored 8.00 .25

Centenary (in 1973) of International Meteorological Cooperation.

King Faisal — A86

Conference Emblem — A87

1975, July 6 Unwmk. *Perf. 14*

671 A86 4p green & rose brn 2.75 .25
672 A86 16p violet & green 3.50 .65
673 A86 23p dk green & vio 7.25 1.10
Nos. 671-673 (3) 13.50 2.00

Miniature Sheet

Imperf

674 A86 40p Prus bl & ocher *400.00*

King Faisal ibn Abdul-Aziz Al Saud (1906-1975). Size of No. 674: 71x80mm.

1975, July 11 *Perf. 14*

675 A87 10p rose brn & blk 5.50 .45

6th Islamic Conference of Foreign Ministers, Jedda, July 12.

Wheat and Sun — A88

1975, Sept. 17 Litho. Wmk. 361

676 A88 4p lilac & multi 2.75 .20
677 A88 10p blue & multi 8.00 .35

Charity Society, 20th anniversary.

Holy Ka'aba, Globe, Clasped Hands — A89

1975, Sept. 17 *Perf. 14*

678 A89 4p olive bis & multi *6.25* .15
679 A89 10p orange & multi *12.50* .35

Conference of Moslem Organizations, Mecca, Apr. 6-10, 1974.

Saudia Tri-Star and DC-3 — A90

1975, Sept. Litho. Unwmk.

680 A90 4p buff & multi *6.25* .25
681 A90 10p lt blue & multi *12.50* .45

Saudia, Saudi Arabian Airline, 30th anniversary.

Conference Centers in Mecca and Riyadh — A91

1975, Sept. *Perf. 14*

682 A91 10p multicolored *9.00* .45

Friday Mosque, Medina, and Juwatha Mosque, al-Hasa — A92

1975, Oct. 26 Litho. Unwmk.

683 A92 4p green & multi *5.25* .25
684 A92 10p vermilion & multi *7.25* .45

Ancient Islamic holy places.

FAO Emblem — A93

1975, Oct. 26

685 A93 4p gray & multi 3.50 .20
686 A93 10p buff & multi 11.00 .45

World Food Program, 10th anniversary (in 1973). Stamps are dated 1973.

Conference Emblem — A94

1976, Mar. 20 Unwmk. *Perf. 14*

687 A94 4p multicolored 12.50 .25

Islamic Solidarity Conference of Science and Technology.

Saudi Arabia Map, Transmission Tower, TV Screen — A95

1976, May 26 Litho. *Perf. 14*

688 A95 4p multicolored 16.00 .25

Saudi Arabian television, 10th anniversary.

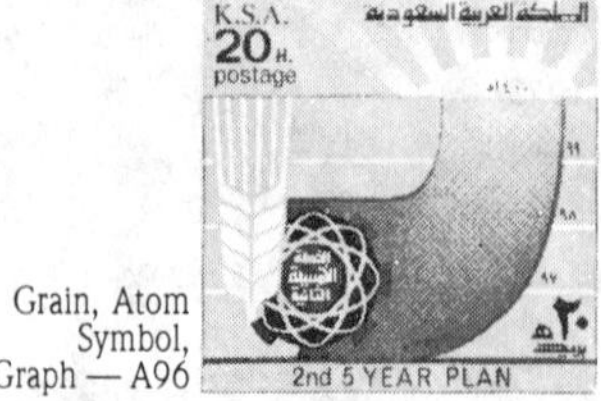

Grain, Atom Symbol, Graph — A96

1976, June 28 Litho. *Perf. 14*

689 A96 20h yellow & multi 3.25 .25
690 A96 50h yellow & multi 5.50 .45

Second Five-year Plan.

Holy Ka'aba — A97

Two types:
I - "White" minarets. Gray vignette.
II - Black minarets and vignette. Design redrawn, strengthened, darkened, clarified.

1976-79 Litho. Wmk. 361 *Perf. 14*

Type II

691 A97 5h lilac & blk .20 .15
692 A97 10h lt violet & blk .25 .15
693 A97 15h salmon & blk .35 .15
 a. Type I 4.25 .20
694 A97 20h lt bl & blk, II 3.75 .20
 a. Type I 5.00 .20
695 A97 25h yellow & blk 1.00 .15
696 A97 30h gray grn & blk 1.40 .15
697 A97 35h bister & blk .80 .15
698 A97 40h lt green & blk 3.25 .20
 a. Type I ('77) 6.00 .30
 b. Imperf., pair, II *110.00*
699 A97 45h dull rose & blk 1.10 .15
700 A97 50h pink & blk 1.00 .15
703 A97 65h gray blue & blk 1.25 .15
710 A97 1r lt yel grn & blk 1.75 .20
711 A97 2r green & black 6.50 .35
Nos. 691-711 (13) 22.60
Set value 2.00

Imperfs of Nos. 691-711 other than No. 698b were not regularly issued.

Issue years: 20h, 1977; 5h-15h, 25h-50h, 1r, 1978; 65h, 2r, 1979.

See Nos. 872-882, 961-968.

Quba Mosque, Medina, built 622 — A98

1976-77

719 A98 20h orange & blk 2.00 .15
720 A98 50h emer & lilac ('77) 3.75 .20
 a. Imperf., pair

Reissued in 1978 in different shades.

Globe, Telephones 1876 and 1976 A100

1976, July 17 Unwmk. *Perf. 13½*

721 A100 50h multicolored *7.25* .30

Centenary of first telephone call by Alexander Graham Bell, Mar. 10, 1876.

Arab Leaders A101

1976, Oct. 30 Litho. *Perf. 14*

722 A101 20h ultra & emerald *5.25* .25

Arab Summit Conference, Riyadh, October. Leaders pictured: Pres. Elias Sarkis, Lebanon; Pres. Anwar Sadat, Egypt; Pres. Hafez al Assad, Syria; King Khalid, Saudi Arabia; Amir Sabah, Kuwait; Yasir Arafat, Palestine Liberation Organization chairman.

WHO Emblem and Eye — A102

1976, Nov. 28 Litho. *Perf. 14*

723 A102 20h multicolored *11.00* .15

World Health Day; Prevention of Blindness.

Holy Ka'aba — A103

1976, Nov. 28 **Unwmk.**
724 A103 20h multicolored *6.75* .20

50th anniversary of installation of new covering of Holy Ka'aba, Mecca.

Conference Emblem A104

Unwmk.
1977, Feb. 18 **Litho.** ***Perf. 14***
725 A104 20h multicolored *7.00* .15

Islamic Jurisprudence Conference, Riyadh, Oct. 24-Nov. 2, 1976.

A105

A106

Design: Sharia College emblem.

1977, Feb. 25 ***Perf. 14***
726 A105 4p multicolored *6.25* .15

25th anniversary (in 1974) of the founding of Sharia (Islamic Law) College, Mecca.

1977

727	A106 20h dk brn & brt grn	1.75	.15
a.	Incorrect date	15.00	
728	A106 80h bl blk & brt grn	3.50	.50
a.	Incorrect date	15.00	

2nd anniversary of installation of King Khalid ibn Abdul-Aziz. Nos. 727a-728a (illustrated), issued Mar. 3, have incorrect Arabic date in bottom panel, last characters of 2nd and 3rd rows identical "ir." Stamps withdrawn after a few days and replaced Aug. 14 with corrected date, last characters in 3rd row changed to "ro."

Diesel Train and Map of Route — A107

1977, May 23 **Litho.** ***Perf. 14***
729 A107 20h multicolored *22.50* .15

Dammam-Riyadh railroad, 25th anniversary.

Arabic Ornament and Names — A108

Designs (Names from Left to Right): UL, Malik Ben Anas (715-795). UR, Mohammad Ben Idris Al-Shafi'i (767-820). LL, Abu Hanifa an-Nu'man (699-767). LR, Ahmed Ben Hanbal (780-855).

1977, Aug. 15 **Litho.** ***Perf. 14***

730	A108 Block of 4	*35.00*	2.00
a.-d.	20h, single stamp	*3.25*	.25

Famous Imams (7th-9th centuries), founders of traditional schools of Islamic jurisprudence. Sheets of 60.

Al Khafji Oil Rig — A109

1976-80 **Wmk. 361**

731	A109 5h vio blue & org	.15	.15
732	A109 10h yellow grn & org	.15	.15
733	A109 15h brown & orange	.15	.15
734	A109 20h green & orange	.20	.15
735	A109 25h dk purple & org	.20	.15
736	A109 30h blue & orange	.25	.15
737	A109 35h sepia & orange	.30	.15
a.	Imperf., pair	*275.00*	
738	A109 40h magenta & orange	.30	.15
a.	40h dull purple & org	*175.00*	
739	A109 45h violet & orange	.35	.20
740	A109 50h rose & orange	.40	.20
a.	50h dull org & org (error)	*67.50*	*6.75*
741	A109 55h grnsh bl & org	20.00	3.50
743	A109 65h sepia & orange	1.10	.35
750	A109 1r gray & orange	1.40	.55
751	A109 2r dk vio & org ('80)	3.00	.90
	Nos. 731-751 (14)	27.95	6.90

All values exist with extra dot in Arabic "Al Khafji." The 20h, 25h, 50h, 65h and 1r were retouched to remove the dot.

Color of flame varies from light orange to vermilion. See Nos. 885-892.

Imperfs of other values are believed not to have been regularly issued.

Mohenjo-Daro Ruins — A110

1977, Oct. 23 **Litho.** **Unwmk.**
761 A110 50h multicolored 7.25 .30

UNESCO campaign to save Mohenjo-Daro excavations in Pakistan.

Idrisi's World Map, 1154 — A111

1977, Nov. 1 **Litho.** ***Perf. 14***

762	A111 20h multicolored	1.75	.15
763	A111 50h multicolored	3.50	.35

First International Symposium on Studies in the History of Arabia at the University of Riyadh, Apr. 23-26, 1977.

King Faisal Specialist Hospital, Riyadh — A112

1977, Nov. 13 **Litho.** **Unwmk.**

764	A112 20h multicolored	3.00	.20
765	A112 50h multicolored	4.75	.35

Conference Emblem — A113

1978, Jan. 24 **Litho.** ***Perf. 14***
766 A113 20h vio blue & yel 4.00 .15

1st World Conf. on Moslem Education.

APU Emblem, Members' Flags — A114

1978, Jan. 21

767	A114 20h multicolored	1.65	.15
768	A114 80h multicolored	3.50	.45

25th anniversary of Arab Postal Union.

Taif-Abha-Gizan Highway — A115

1978, Oct. 15 **Litho.** ***Perf. 14***

769	A115 20h multicolored	1.75	.15
770	A115 80h multicolored	3.50	.35

Inauguration of Taif-Abha-Gizan highway.

Pilgrims, Mt. Arafat and Holy Ka'aba — A116

Unwmk.
1978, Nov. 6 **Litho.** ***Perf. 14***

771	A116 20h multicolored	1.75	.15
772	A116 80h multicolored	3.50	.35

Pilgrimage to Mecca.

Gulf Postal Organization Emblem — A117

1979, Feb. 6 **Litho.** ***Perf. 14***

773	A117 20h multicolored	1.50	.15
774	A117 50h multicolored	3.00	.25

First Conference of Gulf Postal Organization, Baghdad.

Saudi Arabia No. 129, King Abdul Aziz ibn Saud A118

Unwmk.
1979, June 4 **Litho.** ***Perf. 14***

775	A118 20h multicolored	1.40	.15
776	A118 50h multicolored	3.00	.25
777	A118 115h multicolored	4.75	.50
	Nos. 775-777 (3)	9.15	.90

Souvenir Sheet
Imperf
778 A118 100h multicolored *90.00*

1st commemorative stamp, 50th anniv. No. 778 contains one stamp with simulated perforations. Size: 101x76mm.

Crown Prince Fahd — A119

1979, June 25 ***Perf. 14***

779	A119 20h multicolored	1.75	.15
780	A119 50h multicolored	3.50	.25

Crown Prince Fahd ibn Abdul Aziz.

Dome of the Rock, Jerusalem A120

1979, July 2 **Wmk. 361**
781 A120 20h multi (shades) 1.65 .25

Imperfs. exist. See No. 866.

Gold Door, Holy Ka'aba — A121

1979, Oct. 13 **Litho.** ***Perf. 14***

782	A121 20h multicolored	1.65	.15
783	A121 80h multicolored	3.50	.35

Installation of new gold doors. Imperfs. exist.

Pilgrims at Holy Ka'aba, Mecca Mosque — A122

1979, Oct. 27

784	A122 20h multicolored	1.10	.15
785	A122 50h multicolored	2.75	.25

Pilgrimage to Mecca. Imperfs. exist.

Birds in Trees, IYC Emblem — A123

IYC Emblem and: 50h, Child's drawing.

1980, Feb. 17 Litho. *Perf. 14*

786 A123 20h multicolored	*10.00*	.15
787 A123 50h multicolored	*16.00*	.25

Intl. Year of the Child (1979). Imperfs. exist.

King Abdul Aziz ibn Saud on Horseback, Saudi Flag — A124

1980, Apr. 5 Litho. *Perf. 14*

788 A124 20h multicolored	1.40	.15
789 A124 80h multicolored	3.25	.35

Saudi Arabian Army, 80th anniv. (1979). Imperfs. exist.

Arab League, 35th Anniversary A125

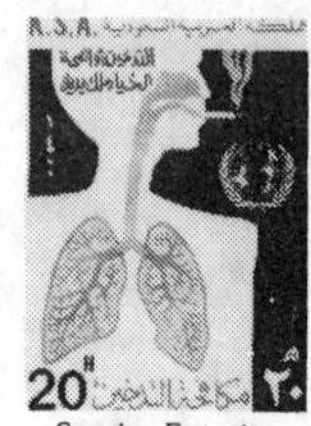
Smoke Entering Lungs, WHO Emblem A127

International Bureau of Education, 50th Anniversary A126

1980, Apr. 27 Litho. *Perf. 14*

790 A125 20h multicolored	1.75	.15

Imperfs. exist.

1980, May 4

791 A126 50h multicolored	*2.25*	.25

Imperfs. exist.

1980, May 20

792 A127 20h shown	*1.40*	.15
793 A127 50h Cigarette, horiz.	*3.25*	.25

Anti-smoking campaign. Imperfs. exist.

20th Anniversary of OPEC — A128

Design: 50h, Workers holding OPEC emblem (Organization of Petroleum Exporting Countries).

1980, Sept. 1 Litho. *Perf. 14*

794 A128 20h multicolored	1.40	.15
795 A128 50h multi, vert.	2.75	.25

Pilgrims Arriving at Jedda Airport A129

1980, Oct. 18

796 A129 20h multicolored	.90	.15
797 A129 50h multicolored	1.75	.25

Pilgrimage to Mecca.

Conference Emblem A130

Holy Ka'aba, Mecca Mosque — A131

1981, Jan. 25 Litho. *Perf. 14*

798 A130 20h shown	1.00	.15
799 A131 20h shown	1.00	.15
800 A131 20h Prophet's Mosque, Medina	1.00	.15
801 A131 20h Dome of the Rock, Jerusalem	1.00	.15
Nos. 798-801 (4)	4.00	
Set value		.35

Third Islamic Summit Conference, Mecca.

Hegira, 1500th Anniv. A132

1981, Jan. 26

802 A132 20h multicolored	.75	.15
803 A132 50h multicolored	1.50	.25
804 A132 80h multicolored	3.00	.35
Nos. 802-804 (3)	5.25	.75

Souvenir Sheet

805 A132 300h multicolored

Industry Week — A133

1981, Feb. 21

806 A133 20h multicolored	.70	.15
807 A133 80h multicolored	2.25	.35

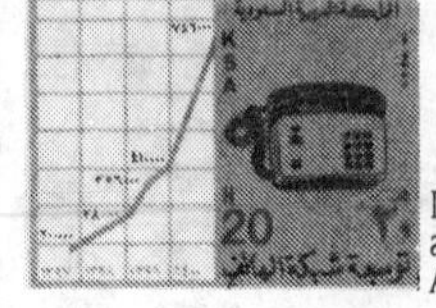
Line Graph and Telephone A134

Map of Saudi Arabia, Microwave Tower A135

1981, Feb. 28

808 A134 20h shown	.30	.15
809 A135 80h shown	2.25	.35
810 A134 115h Earth satellite station	2.50	.50
Nos. 808-810 (3)	5.05	1.00

Souvenir Sheets

811 A134 100h like #808
812 A135 100h like #809
813 A134 100h like #810

Ministry of Posts and Telecommunications achievements.

Arab City Day — A135a

1981, Apr. 2 Litho. *Perf. 14*

814 A135a 20h multicolored	.35	.15
815 A135a 65h multicolored	1.10	.35
816 A135a 80h multicolored	1.50	.35
817 A135a 115d multicolored	2.00	.55
Nos. 814-817 (4)	4.95	1.40

Jedda Airport Opening A136

1981, Apr. 12

818 A136 20h shown	.60	.15
819 A136 80h Plane over airport, diff.	2.50	.35

1982 World Cup Soccer Preliminary Games — A137

Intl. Year of the Disabled — A138

1981, July 26 Litho. *Perf. 14*

820 A137 20h multicolored	*1.75*	.15
821 A137 80h multicolored	*3.25*	.35

1981, Aug. 5

822 A138 20h Reading braille	*1.65*	.15
823 A138 50h Man weaving rug	*2.50*	.25

3rd Five-year Plan (1981-1985) A139

1981, Sept. 5

824 A139 20h multicolored	1.40	.15

King Abdul Aziz, Map of Saudi Arabia A140

1981, Sept. 23 Litho. *Perf. 14*

825 A140 5h multicolored	.15	.15
826 A140 10h multicolored	.15	.15
827 A140 15h multicolored	.15	.15
828 A140 20h multicolored	.30	.15
829 A140 50h multicolored	.65	.25
830 A140 65h multicolored	1.00	.35
831 A140 80h multicolored	2.50	.35
832 A140 115h multicolored	3.00	.50
Nos. 825-832 (8)	7.90	
Set value		1.65

Souvenir Sheet

Imperf

833 A140 10r multicolored	*72.50*	

50th anniv. of kingdom. No. 833 shows king, map, document. Size: 100x75mm.

Pilgrimage to Mecca A141

1981, Oct. 7

834 A141 20h multicolored	*1.65*	.15
835 A141 65h multicolored	*3.25*	.35

World Food Day — A142

1981, Oct. 16

836 A142 20h multicolored	1.25	.15

2nd Session of the Gulf Cooperative Council Summit Conference, Riyadh, Nov. 10 — A143

1981, Nov. 10 Litho. *Perf. 14*

837 A143 20h multicolored	.70	.15
838 A143 80h multicolored	2.25	.40

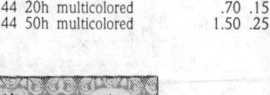

King Saud University, 25th Anniv. A144

1982, Mar. 10 Litho. *Perf. 14*

839 A144 20h multicolored	.70	.15
840 A144 50h multicolored	1.50	.25

New Regional Postal Centers A145

1982, July 14 Litho. *Perf. 14*

841 A145 20h Riyadh P.O. .35 .15
842 A145 65h Jedda 1.10 .35
843 A145 80h Dammam 1.50 .35
844 A145 115h Automated sorting 1.75 .50
Nos. 841-844 (4) 4.70 1.35

Four 300h souvenir sheets exist in same designs as Nos. 841-844 respectively.

Riyadh Television Center — A146

1982, Sept. 4

845 A146 20h multicolored 1.25 .15

25th Anniv. of King's Soccer Cup — A147

1982, Sept. 8

846 A147 20h multicolored .85 .15
847 A147 65h multicolored 1.75 .30

30th Anniv. of Arab Postal Union — A148

1982, Sept. 8

848 A148 20h Emblem .70 .15
849 A148 65h Map, vert. 1.75 .35

Pilgrimage to Mecca A149

1982, Sept. 26

850 A149 20h multicolored .80 .15
851 A149 50h multicolored 1.75 .25

World Standards Day — A150

1982, Oct. 14

852 A150 20h multicolored 1.25 .15

World Food Day — A151

1982, Oct. 16

853 A151 20h multicolored 1.25 .15

Coronation of King Fahd, June 14, 1982 A152

Installation of Crown Prince Abdullah, June 14, 1982 A153

1983, Feb. 12 Litho. *Perf. 14*

854 A152 20h multicolored .30 .15
855 A153 20h multicolored .30 .15
856 A152 50h multicolored .60 .25
857 A153 50h multicolored .60 .25
858 A152 65h multicolored .90 .30
859 A153 65h multicolored .90 .30
860 A152 80h multicolored 1.10 .35
861 A153 80h multicolored 1.10 .35
862 A152 115h multicolored 1.65 .55
863 A153 115h multicolored 1.65 .55
Nos. 854-863 (10) 9.10 3.20

Two one-stamp souvenir sheets contain Nos. 862-863, perf. 12½.

6th Anniv. of United Arab Shipping Co. — A154

Various freighters.

1983, Aug. 9 Litho. *Perf. 14*

864 A154 20h multicolored .50 .15
865 A154 65h multicolored 2.00 .20
Set value .25

Dome of the Rock, Jerusalem A155

1983, Sept. Wmk. 361 *Perf. 12*

866 A155 20h multicolored .65 .15

See No. 781.

Pilgrimage to Mecca A156

1983, Sept. 16 Litho. *Perf. 14*

867 A156 20h brt blue & multi .45 .15
868 A156 65h dk black & multi 1.65 .20
Set value .25

World Communications Year — A157

1983, Oct. 8 Litho. *Perf. 14*

869 A157 20h Post and UPU emblems .30 .15
870 A157 80h Telephone and ITU emblems 1.40 .25
Set value .30

Holy Ka'ba Type of 1976
Type II

Perf. 14x13½

1982-86 Litho. Wmk. 361

Size: 26x21mm

872 A97 10h lt vio & blk ('83) .15 .15
a. Perf. 12, unwmkd. ('87) .15 .15
873 A97 15h sal & blk, perf. 12 ('85) .15 .15
874 A97 20h lt blue & blk .20 .15
a. Perf. 12 ('84) .20 .15
b. Perf. 12, unwmkd. .15 .15
c. Perf. 13½ .25 .15
880 A97 50h pink & blk ('83) .45 .15
a. Perf. 13½ .45 .15
b. Perf. 12 ('86) .30 .15
881 A97 65h gray bl & blk .60 .15
a. Perf. 13½ .60 .15
b. Perf. 12 ('84) .60 .15
c. Perf. 12, unwmkd. ('84) .60 .15
882 A97 1r lt yel grn & blk 1.40 .20
a. Perf. 13½ 1.40 .20
b. Perf. 12 ('83) 1.40 .20
c. Perf. 12, unwmkd. ('85) 1.40 .20
Nos. 872-882 (6) 2.95
Set value .60

Counterfeits of the 1r are perf. 11.

Al Khafji Oil Rig Type of 1976

Perf. 14x13½

1982-84 Litho. Wmk. 361

Size: 26x21mm

885 A109 5h vio bl & org .15 .15
886 A109 10h yel grn & org .15 .15
887 A109 15h bis brn & org .15 .15
888 A109 20h green & org .15 .15
890 A109 50h rose & org .30 .15
891a A109 65h sepia & orange 2.75 1.40
892 A109 1r gray & org .60 .30

Perf. 13½

885a A109 5h .15 .15
886a A109 10h .15 .15
887a A109 15h .15 .15
888a A109 20h .15 .15
890a A109 50h .30 .15
891 A109 65h sepia & org ('84) .35 .20
892a A109 1r .55 .30

1983 *Perf. 12*

886b A109 10h .15 .15
887b A109 15h .15 .15
888b A109 20h .15 .15
889 A109 25h dk pur & org .15 .15
890b A109 50h .30 .15
891b A109 65h .35 .20
892b A109 1r .45 .30
Set value, #885-892 1.40 .70

Opening of King Khalid International Airport — A158

1983, Nov. 16 Litho. *Perf. 13½x14*

893 A158 20h shown .45 .15
894 A158 65h blue & multi 1.40 .20
Set value .25

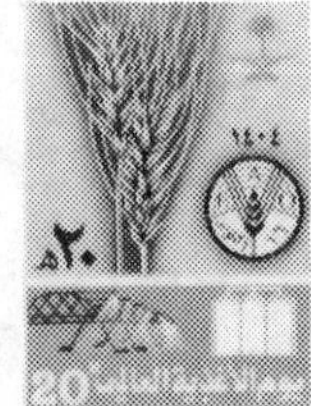

World Food Day — A159

1983, Nov. 29 Litho. *Perf. 14*

895 A159 20h Wheat, Irrigation, Silos .45 .15

Aqsa Mosque, Jerusalem A160

1983, Dec. 13 Litho. *Perf. 14*

896 A160 20h multicolored .45 .15

Old and Modern Riyadh — A161

Shobra Palace, Taif — A162

Old and New Jedda (Waterfront) — A163

Damman — A164

1984-95 Litho. Wmk. 361 *Perf. 12*

897 A161 20h lilac rose & multi .15 .15
898 A162 20h Prus grn & multi .15 .15
899 A161 50h black & multi .30 .15
900 A162 50h brown & multi .65 .35

Unwmk.

901 A161 50h multicolored .45 .25
902 A162 50h multicolored .65 .35
903 A163 50h multicolored .90 .45
904 A164 50h green & multi .40 .25
905 A161 75h green & multi .65 .35
906 A162 75h multicolored .65 .35
907 A163 75h pink & multi .90 .45
908 A164 75h blue & multi .60 .35
909 A161 150h pink & multi 1.50 .75
910 A162 150h green & multi 1.50 .75
911 A163 150h green & multi 1.65 .75
911A A164 150h red lilac & multi 1.25 .60
Nos. 897-911A (16) 12.35 6.45

Issued: #897, 6/27/84; #898, 10/13/84; #899, 8/29/84; #900, 3/10/87; #910, 9/3/87; #902, 11/3/87; #909, 5/4/88; #903, 911, 1/31/89; #906, 1990; #901, 907, 1991; #905, 1992; #904, 908, 911A, 1995.

Estate Development Fund, 10th Anniv. A165

1984, July 28 Unwmk.

912 A165 20h multicolored .45 .15

Opening of Solar Village, near Al-Eyenah A166

1984, Aug. 14 Litho. *Perf. 12*

913 A166 20h multicolored	.45	.15
914 A166 80h Stylized sun, solar panels	1.40	.25
Set value		.30

Imperf

Size: 81x81mm

915 A166 100h like 20h	*11.00*	
916 A166 100h like 80h	*11.00*	

Pilgrimage to Mecca — A167

1984, Sept. 4 Litho. *Perf. 14*

917 A167 20h brown & multi	.45	.15

Perf. 12

918 A167 65h olive gray & multi	1.40	.20
Set value		.25

Participation of Saudi Arabian Soccer Team in 1984 Olympics — A168

1984, Sept. 25 Litho. *Perf. 12*

919 A168 20h blue & multi	.45	.15
920 A168 115h green & multi	1.40	.35
Set value		.40

"Games" and "Olympiad" are misspelled on both stamps.

World Food Day — A169

1984, Oct. 16 Litho. *Perf. 12*

921 A169 20h multicolored	.40	.15

Beginning with Nos. 922-923 some issues are printed in sheets that have labels inscribed in Arabic. Generally there are from 2 to 6 labels per sheet. Stamps with label attached command a premium.

90th Anniv. International Olympic Committee A170

1984, Dec. 23 Litho. *Perf. 12*

922 A170 20h multicolored	.30	.15
923 A170 50h multicolored	1.65	.15
Set value		.15

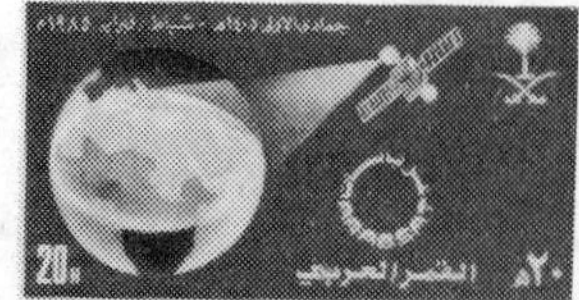

Launch of ARABSAT — A171

1985, Feb. 9 Litho. *Perf. 12*

924 A171 20h ARABSAT, view of Earth	1.75	.15

7th Holy Koran Competition A172

1985, Feb. 10 Litho. *Perf. 12*

925 A172 20h multicolored	.35	.15
926 A172 65h multicolored	1.00	.20
Set value		.25

4th Five-Year Development Plan, 1985-1990 A173

Portrait of King Fahd, industry emblems and: 20h, Dhahran Harbor, Jubail. 50h, Television tower, earth receiver, microwave tower. 65h, Agriculture. 80h, Harbor, Yanbu.

1985, Mar. 23 Litho. *Perf. 13x12*

927 A173 20h multicolored	.40	.15
928 A173 50h multicolored	1.10	.15
929 A173 65h multicolored	1.25	.20
930 A173 80h multicolored	1.75	.25
a. Block of 4, #927-930	5.00	.75

Intl. Youth Year — A174

1985, May 4 *Perf. 12*

931 A174 20h multicolored	.30	.15
932 A174 80h multicolored	1.10	.25
Set value		.30

Self-sufficiency in Wheat Production — A175

1985, May 4

933 A175 20h multicolored	.45	.15

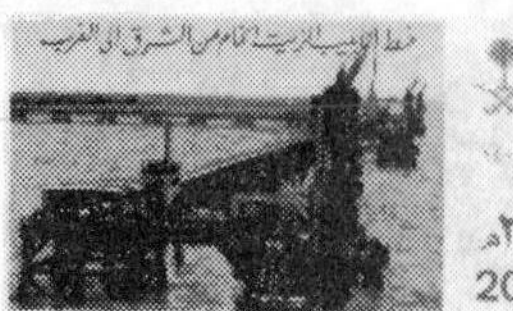

East-West Pipeline — A176

1985, June 9

934 A176 20h Tanker loading berth, Yanbu	.45	.15
935 A176 65h Pipeline, map	1.40	.20
Set value		.25

Shuttle Launch — A177

Shuttle, Missions Emblem — A178

1985, July 7

936 A177 20h multicolored	.45	.15
937 A178 115h multicolored	2.25	.35
Set value		.40

Prince Sultan Ibn Salman Al-Saud, 1st Arab-Moslem astronaut, on Discovery 51-G.

UN, 40th Anniv. A179

1985, July 15

938 A179 20h multicolored	.55	.15

Highway, Map, Holy Ka'aba in Mecca to Prophet's Mosque in Medina — A180

1985, July 22

939 A180 20h multicolored	.35	.15
940 A180 65h multicolored	1.00	.20
Set value		.25

Mecca-Medina Highway opening, Oct. 11, 1984.

Post Code Inauguration — A181

1985, July 24

941 A181 20h Covers	.45	.15

1984 Asian Soccer Cup Victory A182

1985, July 30

942 A182 20h multicolored	.30	.15
943 A182 65h multicolored	.75	.20
944 A182 115h multicolored	1.75	.35
Nos. 942-944 (3)	2.80	
Set value		.60

Pilgrimage to Mecca — A183

1985, Aug. 25 Litho. *Perf. 12*

945 A183 10h multicolored	.15	.15
946 A183 15h multicolored	.25	.15
947 A183 20h multicolored	.35	.15
948 A183 65h multicolored	.90	.20
Nos. 945-948 (4)	1.65	
Set value		.35

1st Gulf Olympics Day, Riyadh, May 2 A184

1985, Sept. 8

949 A184 20h multicolored	.35	.15
950 A184 115h multicolored	1.75	.35
Set value		.40

World Food Day — A185

1985, Oct. 16

951 A185 20h multicolored	.45	.15
952 A185 65h multicolored	1.50	.20
Set value		.25

King Abdul Aziz, Masmak Fort and Horsemen — A186

1985, Dec. 1

953 A186 15h multicolored	.25	.15
954 A186 20h multicolored	.25	.15
955 A186 65h multicolored	.90	.20
956 A186 80h multicolored	1.10	.25
Nos. 953-956 (4)	2.50	
Set value		.55

Intl. Conference on the History of King Abdul Aziz Al-Sa'ud, Riyadh. An imperf. souvenir sheet showing smaller versions of Nos. 953-956 and the conference emblem exists. Sold for 10r.

King Fahd Koran Publishing Center, Medina — A187

1985, Dec. 18

957 A187 20h multicolored	.20	.15
958 A187 65h multicolored	1.10	.20
Set value		.25

OPEC, 25th Anniv. A188

1985, Dec. 24

959 A188 20h multicolored	.25	.15
960 A188 65h multicolored	1.40	.20
Set value		.25

Holy Ka'aba Type of 1976

Type II

Booklet Stamps

1986, Feb. 17 Litho. *Perf. 12*

Size: 29x19mm

961 A97 10h lt vio & blk		
a. Booklet pane of 4	*22.50*	

65 A97 20h bluish grn & blk
68 A97 50h pink & black
a. Bklt. pane of 4, #961, 2 #965, #968 *35.00*

Due to vending machine breakdowns, distribu-on of this set has been very limited. The govern-ient does have stocks of these stamps but they are ot currently being sold.

A189 A191

A190

1986, Jan. 8 Litho. *Perf. 12*

971 A189 20h multicolored .90 .15

Intl. Peace Year.

1986, Mar. 24 *Perf. 14, 12 (65h)*

972 A190 20h multicolored .45 .15
a. Perf. 12 .45 .15
973 A190 65h multicolored .90 .20
Set value .25

Riyadh Municipality, 50th aAnniv.

1986, Apr. 21 *Perf. 12*

974 A191 20h multicolored .45 .15
975 A191 50h multicolored .90 .15
Set value .20

UN child survival campaign.

General Establishment for Electric Power, 10th Anniv. A192

1986, Apr. 26

976 A192 20h multicolored .25 .15
977 A192 65h multicolored .90 .20
Set value .25

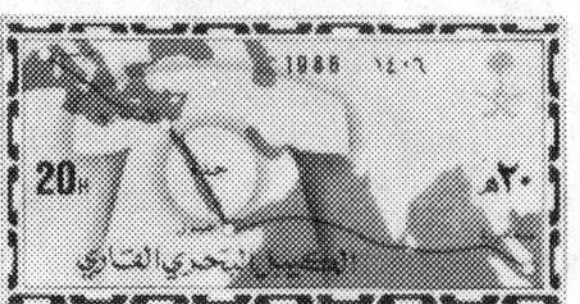

Continental Maritime Cable Inauguration — A193

1986, June 1 Litho. *Perf. 12*

978 A193 20h multicolored .45 .15
979 A193 50h multicolored .90 .15
Set value .20

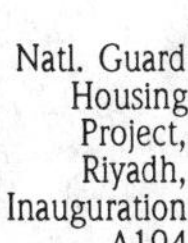

Natl. Guard Housing Project, Riyadh, Inauguration A194

1986, July 19

980 A194 20h multicolored .35 .15
981 A194 65h multicolored 1.10 .20
Set value .25

Islamic Arch, Holy Ka'aba — A195

1986-92 Litho. *Perf. 12*

984 A195 30h black & bluish grn .20 .15
985 A195 40h black & lilac rose .25 .15
986 A195 50h black & brt green .65 .35
987 A195 75h black & Prus bl .80 .40
a. Perf. 13½x14 .65 .35
989 A195 150h black & rose lilac 1.65 .80
a. Perf. 13½x14 1.40 .70
Nos. 984-989 (5) 3.55 1.85

Issued: 30h, 40h, 8/5; 75h, 150h, 7/30/90; 50h, 10/9/90; #987a, 6/13/92; #989a, 6/6/92.

Pilgrimage to Mecca — A196

Designs of: a, A116. b, A129. c, A156. d, A149. e, A141. f, A122. g, A183. h, A167.

1986, Aug. 13 Litho. *Perf. 12*

1002 Block of 8 *11.00 11.00*
a.-h. A196 20h, any single

Discovery of Oil, 50th Anniv. — A197

World Food Day — A198

1986, Sept. 16

1003 A197 20h Well, refinery .45 .15
1004 A197 65h Well, map 1.40 .20
Set value .25

Because of difficulty in separation most copies have damaged perfs.

1986, Oct. 18

1005 A198 20h shown .20 .15
1006 A198 115h Stylized plant 1.00 .35
Set value .40

Massacre of Palestinian Refugees, Sept. 17, 1982 — A199

1986, Nov. 1 Litho. *Perf. 12*

1007 A199 80h multicolored .70 .35
1008 A199 115h multicolored 1.10 .55

Definitive stamps generally do not have an official date of issue. Any dates shown probably reflect sales at the Riyadh or Dammam post offices only.

Saudi Universities

Imam Mohammed ibn Saud — A200

Umm al-Qura — A201

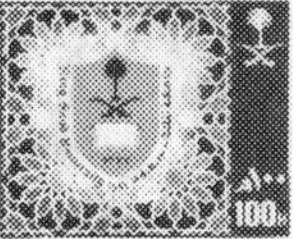

King Saud — A202

King Fahd Petroleum and Minerals — A203

King Faisal — A204

King Abdul Aziz — A205

Medina Islamic — A206

1986-91

1009	A200	15h	sage grn & blk	.15	.15
1010	A200	20h	ultra & black	.15	.15
1010A	A200	50h	ultra & black	.40	.25
1011	A200	65h	brt blue & blk	.50	.25
1011A	A200	75h	brt blue & blk	.65	.35
1012	A200	100h	rose & black	.70	.35
1013	A200	150h	rose claret & blk	1.25	.60
1014	A201	50h	ultra & black	.50	.30
1015	A201	65h	brt blue & blk	.65	.25
1016	A201	75h	brt blue & blk	.65	.35
1017	A201	100h	dull rose & blk	1.00	.50
1018	A201	150h	rose claret & blk	1.50	.75
1020	A202	50h	ultra & black	.55	.30
1021	A202	75h	brt blue & blk	.65	.35
1022	A202	100h	dull rose & blk	1.00	.50
1023	A202	150h	rose claret & blk	1.40	.65
1025	A203	50h	ultra & black	.40	.25
1026	A203	75h	brt blue & blk	.65	.35
1027	A203	150h	rose claret & blk	1.25	.60
1029	A204	50h	ultra & black	.40	.25
1029A	A204	75h	brt blue & blk	.65	.35
1030	A204	150h	rose claret & blk	1.40	.45
1033	A205	50h	ultra & black	.40	.25
1033A	A205	75h	brt blue & blk	.65	.40
1034	A205	150h	rose claret & blk	1.40	.65
1036	A206	50h	ultra & black	.45	.20
1036A	A206	75h	brt blue & blk	.65	.35
1037	A206	150h	rose claret & blk	1.25	.25
			Nos. 1009-1037 (28)	21.25	10.40

Issued: #1009-1012, 11/26; #1017, 3/29; #1022, 7/22; #1014, 1018, 8/8; #1013, 1027, 1037, 1/31/89; #1025, 1029, 1033, 2/25/89; #1015, 3/89; #1030, 4/29/89; #1036, 7/4/89; #1023, 1034, 4/29/89; #1010A, 2/25/89; #1020, 1989; #1011A, 1016, 1026, 1990; #1021, 1029A, 1033A, 1036A, 1991.

This is an expanding set. Numbers will change if necessary.

Saudi-Bahrain Highway Inauguration — A207

1986, Nov. 26 *Perf. 14*

1039 Strip of 2 1.40 .20
a.-b. A207 20h any single .65 .15

Printed se-tenant in a continuous design.

1st Modern Olympic Games, Athens, 90th Anniv. A208

1986, Dec. 27

1040 A208 20h multicolored .40 .15
1041 A208 100h multicolored 2.25 .35

General Petroleum and Minerals Organization (Petromin), 25th Anniv. A209

Unwmk.

1987, Feb. 23 Litho. *Perf. 12*

1042 A209 50h multicolored .50 .25
1043 A209 100h multicolored 1.00 .50

Restoration and Expansion of Quba Mosque, Medina — A210

Design: View of mosque and model of expanded mosque.

1987, Mar. 21

1044 A210 50h multicolored .65 .25
1045 A210 75h multicolored 1.00 .35

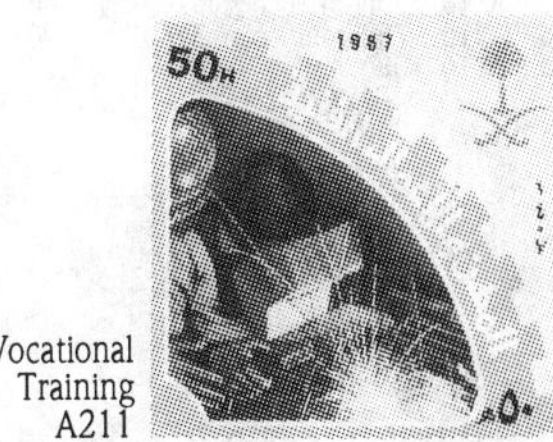

Vocational Training A211

Designs: a, Welding. b, Drill press operation. c, Lathe operation. d, Electrician.

Unwmk.

1987, Apr. 8 Litho. *Perf. 12*

1046 Block of 4 5.00 2.50
a.-d. A211 50h any single 1.25 .60

Cairo Exhibition — A212

Design: Desert fortifications in silhouette, Riyadh television tower, King Khalid Intl. Airport hangars and pyramid of Giza.

Unwmk.

1987, June 17 Litho. *Perf. 12*

1047 A212 50h multicolored .70 .30
1048 A212 75h multicolored 1.10 .40

A213

Inauguration of King Fahd Telecommunications Center, Jedda — A214

1987, July 21

1049 A213 50h multicolored .70 .30
1050 A214 75h multicolored 1.10 .40

Afghan Resistance Movement — A215

1987, July 25

1051 A215 50h multicolored .60 .30
1052 A215 100h multicolored 1.10 .50

Pilgrimage to Mecca — A216

Design: View of Ihram and Meqat Wadi Muhrim Mosque from Wadi Muhrim Meqat.

1987, Aug. 3

1053 A216 50h multicolored .60 .30
1054 A216 75h multicolored .90 .40
1055 A216 100h multicolored 1.10 .55
Nos. 1053-1055 (3) 2.60 1.25

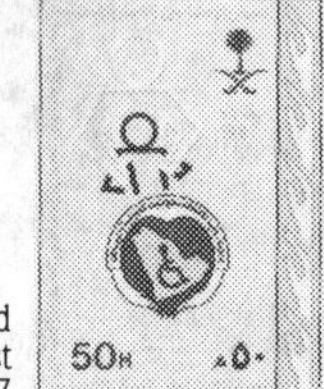

Home for Disabled Children, 1st Anniv. — A217

1987, Oct. 3

1056 A217 50h multicolored .60 .25
1057 A217 75h multicolored .90 .35

World Post Day — A218

1987, Oct. 10

1058 A218 50h multicolored .60 .30
1059 A218 150h multicolored 1.65 .70

World Food Day — A219

1987, Oct. 17

1060 A219 50h multicolored .70 .25
1061 A219 75h multicolored 1.10 .35

Social Welfare Society, 25th Anniv. — A220

Dome of the Rock — A221

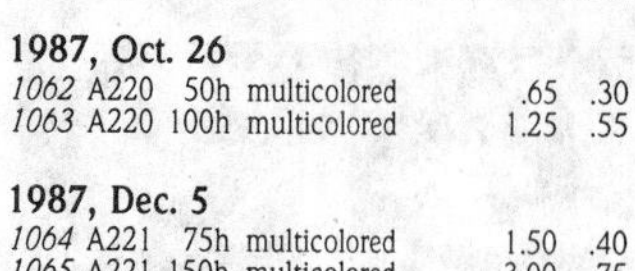

1987, Oct. 26

1062 A220 50h multicolored .65 .30
1063 A220 100h multicolored 1.25 .55

1987, Dec. 5

1064 A221 75h multicolored 1.50 .40
1065 A221 150h multicolored 3.00 .75

Restoration and Expansion of the Prophet's Mosque, Medina — A222

1987, Dec. 15 *Perf. 14*

1066 A222 50h multicolored .60 .25
1067 A222 75h multicolored .90 .35
1068 A222 150h multicolored 1.75 .70
Nos. 1066-1068 (3) 3.25 1.30

An imperf. 300h souvenir sheet exists.

Battle of Hattin, 800th Anniv. A223

Warriors in silhouette and Dome of the Rock.

1987, Dec. 21 *Perf. 12*

1069 A223 75h multicolored 1.50 .35
1070 A223 150h multicolored 3.00 .75

Saladin's conquest of Jerusalem.

A224

A225

1987, Dec. 26

1071 A224 50h multicolored .70 .30
1072 A224 75h multicolored 1.10 .40

8th session of the Supreme Council of the Gulf Cooperation Council.

1988, Feb. 13 **Litho.** *Perf. 12*

1073 A225 50h multicolored .90 .45
1074 A225 75h multicolored 1.40 .65

3rd Regional Highways Conf. of the Middle East.

A226

Inauguration of King Fahd Intl. Stadium — A227

1988, Mar. 2

1075 A226 50h multicolored .65 .30
1076 A227 150h multicolored 2.00 .85

Blood Donation — A228

1988, Apr. 13 **Litho.** *Perf. 12*

1077 A228 50h multicolored .65 .30
1078 A228 75h multicolored .90 .40

WHO, 40th Anniv. — A229

1988, Apr. 7

1079 A229 50h multicolored .85 .30
1080 A229 75h multicolored .90 .40

King Fahd, Custodian of the Holy Mosques — A230

King Fahd and mosques at Medina and Mecca.

1988, Apr. 23 **Litho.** *Perf. 12*

1081 A230 50h multicolored .45 .25
1082 A230 75h multicolored .65 .35
1083 A230 150h multicolored 1.40 .65
Nos. 1081-1083 (3) 2.50 1.25

A 75h souvenir sheet exists containing an enlarged version of No. 1082. Sold for 3r.

Environmental Protection — A231

1988, June 5

1084 A231 50h multicolored .70 .25
1085 A231 75h multicolored 1.10 .35

Palestinian Uprising, Gaza and the West Bank A232

1988, July 10

1086 A232 75h multicolored 1.10 .40
1087 A232 150h multicolored 2.00 .75

Pilgrimage to Mecca — A233

1988, July 23 **Litho.** *Perf. 12*

1088 A233 50h multicolored .85 .30
1089 A233 75h multicolored 1.25 .45

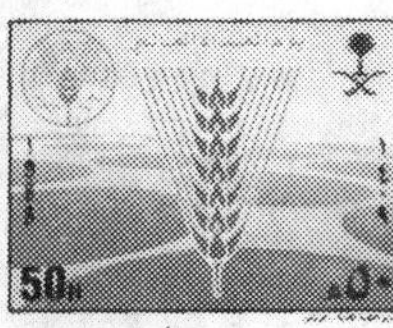

World Food Day — A234

1988, Oct. 16 **Litho.** *Perf. 1*

1090 A234 50h multicolored .70 .2
1091 A234 75h multicolored 1.10 .4

Qiblatain Mosque Expansion — A235

1988, Nov. 9

1092 A235 50h multicolored .70 .25
1093 A235 75h multicolored 1.10 .40

5th World Youth Soccer Championships, Riyadh, Dammam, Jedda and Taif — A250

1989, Feb. 16 **Litho.** *Perf. 12*

1094 A250 75h multicolored .75 .25
1095 A250 150h multicolored 1.50 .50

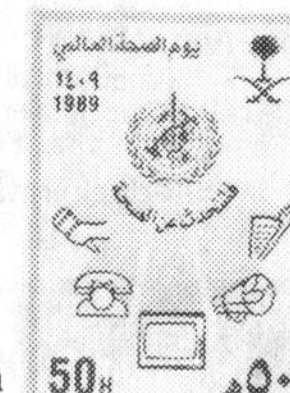

World Health Day — A251

1989, Apr. 8 **Litho.** *Perf. 12*

1096 A251 50h multicolored .80 .25
1097 A251 75h multicolored 1.25 .40

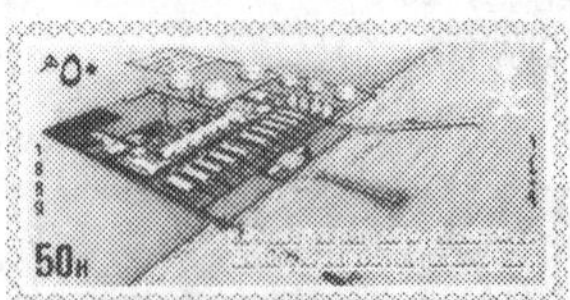

Sea Water Desalination Plant — A252

1989, May 30 **Litho.** *Perf. 12*

1098 A252 50h multicolored .65 .30
1099 A252 75h multicolored 1.00 .45

Proclamation of the State of Palestine, Nov. 15, 1988 A253

1989, June 6 **Litho.** *Perf. 12*

1100 A253 50h multicolored .65 .20
1101 A253 75h multicolored 1.00 .25

Pilgrimage to Mecca — A254

Design: Al-Tan'eem Mosque, Mecca.

1989, July 12 Litho. *Perf. 12*
1102 A254 50h multicolored .60 .20
1103 A254 75h multicolored .95 .25

World Food Day — A255

1989, Oct. 16 Litho. *Perf. 12*
1104 A255 75h multicolored .70 .35
1105 A255 150h multicolored 1.40 .70

Holy Mosque Expansion — A256

1989, Dec. 30 Litho. *Perf. 12*
1106 A256 50h multicolored .55 .25
1107 A256 75h multicolored .80 .40
1108 A256 150h multicolored 1.55 .80
Nos. 1106-1108 (3) 2.90 1.45

An imperf souvenir sheet containing an enlarged version of design A256 exists. Sold for 5r.

Youth Soccer Cup Championships A257

UNESCO World Literacy Year A258

1989, Dec. 20
1109 A257 75h multicolored .80 .35
1110 A257 150h multicolored 1.65 .75

1990, Jan. 9
1111 A258 50h multicolored .70 .30
1112 A258 75h multicolored 1.00 .40

World Health Day — A259

Unwmk.
1990, Apr. 7 Litho. *Perf. 12*
1113 A259 75h multicolored .80 .35
1114 A259 150h multicolored 1.65 .70

Flowers — A262

1990
1115 Block of 21 8.50
a.-u. A262 50h any single .40 .20
1116 Block of 21 12.50
a.-u. A262 75h any single .55 .30
1117 Block of 21 24.00
a.-u. A262 150h any single 1.10 .60
Nos. 1115-1117 (3) 45.00

21 Different species pictured on the sheets. Issue dates: 50h, 75h, Feb, 6; 150h, Jan. 17.

Islamic Conference, 20th Anniv. A263

1990, Feb. 7 Litho. *Perf. 12*
1118 A263 75h blue & multi .50 .25
1119 A263 150h gray & multi 1.00 .50

Islamic Heritage A264

Designs: b, Arabic script in rectangle. c, Circular design. d, Mosque and minaret.

1990, July 29
1120 Block of 4 3.75 1.90
a.-d. A264 75h any single .90 .45

Horses A265

1990, Apr. 14

Color of Horse

1121 Block of 4 3.50 1.20
a. A265 50h white, red tassels on bridle .85 .30
b. A265 50h black .85 .30
c. A265 50h white, brown bridle .85 .30
d. A265 50h chestnut .85 .30
1122 A265 50h like #1121d .60 .30
1123 A265 75h like #1121b .90 .45
1124 A265 100h like #1121a 1.25 .60
1125 A265 150h like #1121c 1.75 .90
Nos. 1121-1125 (5) 8.00 3.45

No. 1121 has white border on two sides. Nos. 1122-1125 have white border on four sides.

Pilgrimage to Mecca — A266

1990, June 28
1126 A266 75h multicolored .80 .40
1127 A266 150h multicolored 1.65 .80

Television Tower — A267

1990, July 21
1128 A267 75h multicolored .80 .40
1129 A267 150h multicolored 1.65 .80

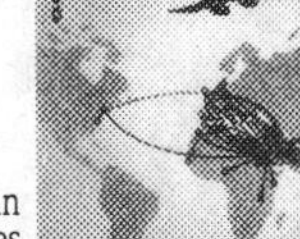

Saudi Arabian Airlines Route Map — A268

1990, Sept. 3
1130 A268 75h Global routes .75 .35
1131 A268 75h Domestic routes .75 .35
a. Pair, #1130-1131 1.50 .75
1132 A268 150h like #1130 1.50 .75
1133 A268 150h like #1131 1.50 .75
a. Pair, #1132-1133 3.00 1.50
Nos. 1130-1133 (4) 4.50 2.20

World Food Day — A269

1990, Oct. 16 Litho. *Perf. 12*
1134 A269 75h multicolored .75 .40
1135 A269 150h multicolored 1.50 .75

Organization of Petroleum Exporting Countries (OPEC), 30th Anniv. A270

1990, Sept. 26
1136 A270 75h multicolored 1.00 .40
1137 A270 150h multicolored 2.00 .75

Fifth Five Year Development Plan — A271

Designs: a, Oil refinery, irrigation, and oil storage tanks. b, Radio tower, highway, and mine. c, Monument, sports stadium, and vocational training. d, Television tower, environmental protection, and modern architecture.

1990, Oct. 30
1138 A271 75h Block of 4, #a.-d. 4.00 1.50

Battle of Badr, 624 — A272

1991, Apr. 3 Litho. *Perf. 12*
1139 A272 75h org, dk grn & grn .70 .35
1140 A272 150h lt bl, dk bl & grn 1.40 .70

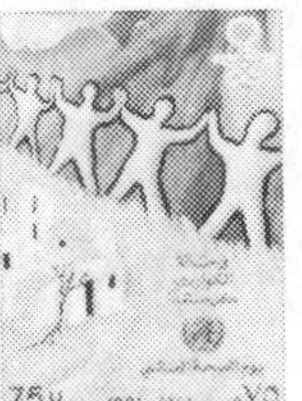
A273

A274

1991, Apr. 9
1141 A273 75h multicolored .70 .35
1142 A273 150h multicolored 1.40 .70

World Health Day.

1991 Litho. *Perf. 12*

Animals: a, k, Impala. b, l, Ibex. c, m, Oryx. d, n, Fox. e, o, Bat. f, p, Hyena. g, q, Cat. h, r, Dugong. i, s, Leopard.

Blocks of 9

1143 A274 25h Block, #a.-i. 2.50 1.25
1144 A274 50h Block, #a.-i. 4.75 2.50
1145 A274 75h Block, #a.-i. 7.25 3.75
1146 A274 100h Block, #a.-i. 9.50 4.75
1146J A274 150h Block, #k.-s. 15.00 11.00
t. Perf 14x13½ 15.00 11.00
Nos. 1143-1146J (5) 39.00 23.25

Issued: #1143-1146, May 1; #1146J, Dec. 1. No. 1146J exists imperf.

Pilgrimage to Mecca — A275

1991, June 20 Litho. *Perf. 14*
1147 A275 75h blue & multi .70 .35
1148 A275 150h green & multi 1.40 .70

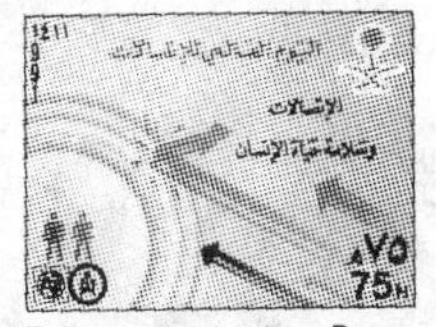
World Telecommunications Day — A276

1991, June 3 *Perf. 12*
1149 A276 75h multicolored .70 .35
1150 A276 150h multicolored 1.40 .70

A277

A278

1991, May 11
1151 A277 75h multicolored 1.00 .50
1152 A277 150h multicolored 2.00 1.00

Liberation of Kuwait.

1991, Sept. 8 Litho. *Perf. 12*
1153 A278 75h blue & multi 1.00 .50
1154 A278 150h buff & multi 2.00 1.00

Literacy Day.

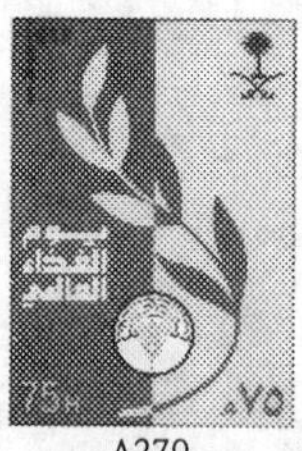
A279

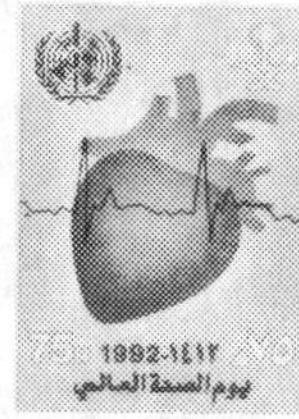
A281

A280

1991, Oct. 16 Litho. *Perf. 12*

1155 A279	75h	green & multi	.80	.40
1156 A279	150h	orange & multi	1.60	.80

World Food Day.

1991, Dec. 7

1157 A280	75h	green & multi	.80	.40
1158 A280	150h	dk blue & multi	1.60	.80

Childrens' Day.

1992, Apr. 8 Litho. *Perf. 12*

1159 A281	75h	lt blue & multi	.75	.40
1160 A281	150h	lt orange & multi	1.50	.75

World Health Day.

War Between the Arabs of Medina and Mecca, 624-630
A282

1992, Apr. 18

1161 A282	75h	lt orange & green	.75	.40
1162 A282	150h	lt bl, dk bl & grn	1.50	.75

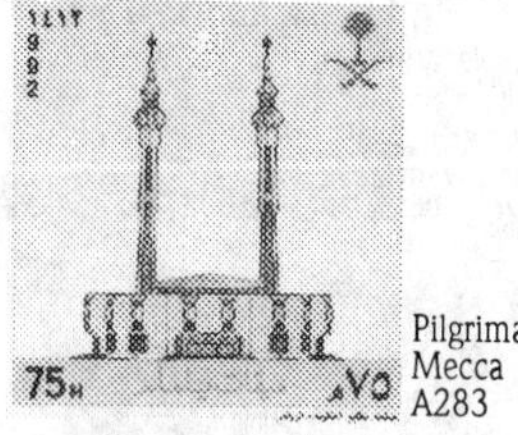
Pilgrimage to Mecca
A283

Unwmk.

1992, June 9 Litho. *Perf. 12*

1163 A283	75h	lt blue & multi	.75	.40
1164 A283	150h	lt orange & multi	1.50	.75

Population and Housing Census — A284

1992, Sept. 26 Litho. *Perf. 14*

1165 A284	75h	blue & multi	.70	.35
1166 A284	150h	org yellow & multi	1.40	.70

World Food Day — A285

1992, Oct. 17 *Perf. 12*

1167 A285	75h	Vegetables	.70	.35
1168 A285	150h	Fruits	1.40	.70

Consultative Council — A286

Document: d, g, 12 lines. e, h, 13 lines. f, i, 11 lines. 5r, Scrolls of 12, 11, & 13 lines.

1992, Dec. 12 Litho. *Perf. 12*

1168A A286	75h	Strip of 3, #d.-f.	2.00	1.00
1168B A286	150h	Strip of 3, #g.-i.	4.00	2.00

Imperf

Size: 120x79mm

1168C A286	5r	multicolored	17.00	8.50

Birds — A287

a, k, Woodpecker. b, l, Arabian bustard. c, m, Lark. d, n, Turtle dove. e, o, Heron. f, p, Partridge. g, q, Hoopoe. h, r, Falcon. i, s, Houbara bustard. Illustration reduced.

1992-94 *Perf. 14x13½*

Blocks of 9

1169 A287	25h	#a.-i.	2.25	2.25
1170 A287	50h	Block of 9, #a.-i.		
1171 A287	75h	#a.-i.	6.65	3.30
j.		Perf. 12, #k.-r.		
1172 A287	100h	#a.-i.	8.00	4.00
j.		Perf. 12, #k.-r.	8.00	4.00
1173 A287	150h	#a.-i.	13.00	6.50
j.		Perf. 12, #k.-r.	13.00	6.50
		Nos. 1169-1173 (4)	29.90	16.05

Issued: 150h, 3/18/92; 75h, 7/14/92; 100h, 3/1/93; 25h, 11/6/94; #1171j, 1173j, 8/94; 50h, 11/6/94.

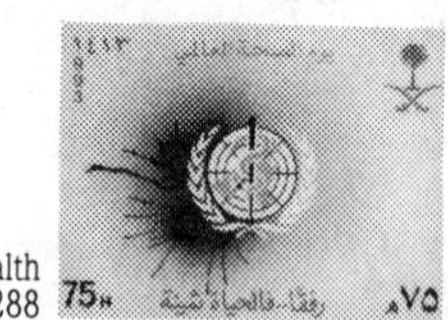
World Health Day — A288

1993, Apr. 7 Litho. *Perf. 12*

1175 A288	75h	red & multi	.70	.35
1175A A288	150h	blue & multi	1.40	.70

King Fahd Championship Soccer Cup — A289

1993, Mar. 15

1176 A289	75h	green & multi	.70	.35
1176A A289	150h	rose red & multi	1.40	.70

Pilgrimage to Mecca — A290

1993, May 30 Litho. *Perf. 12*

1177 A290	75h	green & multi	.70	.35
1178 A290	150h	blue & multi	1.40	.70

Intl. Telecommunications Day — A291

1993, May 17

Inscription Color

1179 A291	75h	dark blue	.70	.35
1180 A291	150h	red lilac	1.40	.70

Battle of Alkandk
A292

1993, May 15

1181 A292	75h	light orange & grn	.70	.35
1182 A292	150h	lt bl, dk bl & grn	1.40	.70

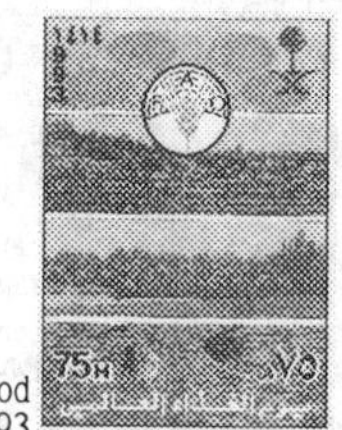
World Food Day — A293

1993, Dec. 14 Litho. *Perf. 12*

1183 A293	75h	black & multi	.70	.35
1184 A293	150h	red & multi	1.40	.70

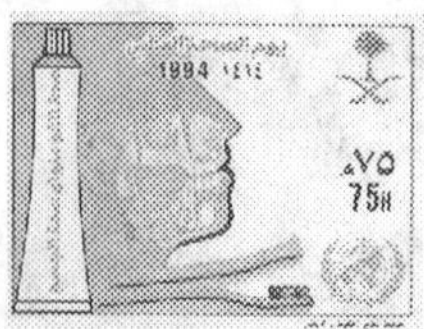
World Dental Health Day — A294

1994, Apr. 9 Litho. *Perf. 12*

1185 A294	75h	multicolored	.70	.35
1186 A294	150h	multicolored	1.40	.70

Intl. Olympic Committee, Cent. — A295

1994, Apr. 23 Litho. *Perf. 12*

1187 A295	75h	blue & multi	.70	.35
1188 A295	150h	red & multi	1.40	.70

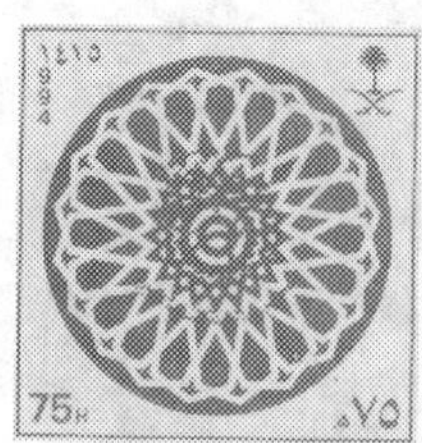
Battle of Kaben
A296

1994, June 14 Litho. *Perf. 12*

1189 A296	75h	bister & green	.70	.35
1190 A296	150h	silver, blue & green	1.40	.70

Pilgrimage to Mecca — A297

1994, May 14

1191 A297	75h	green & multi	.70	.35
1192 A297	150h	red & multi	1.40	.70

Consultative Council — A298

Design: 150h, Different view of building, inscription tablet at right.

1994, July 12 Litho. *Perf. 12*

1193 A298	75h	multicolored	.70	.35
1194 A298	150h	multicolored	1.40	.70
a.		Souv. sheet of 2, #1193-1194, imperf.		

No. 1194a sold for 5r.

A299

1994 World Soccer Cup Championships, US — A300

1994, June 18

1195 A299	75h	multicolored	.70	.35
1196 A300	150h	multicolored	1.40	.70

King Abdul Aziz Port, Dammam — A301

1994-95 Litho. *Perf. 12*

1196A A301	25h	multicolored	.50	.25
1196B A301	50h	multicolored	.45	.25
1197 A301	75h	multicolored	.70	.35
1201 A301	100h	like #1197	.90	.45
1204 A301	150h	multicolored	1.40	.70
		Nos. 1196A-1204 (5)	3.95	2.00

Issued: 75h, 8/21/94; 100h, 2/18/95; 150h, 11/12/94; 25h, 11/28/95; 50h, 11/28/95.
This is an expanding set. Numbers may change.

A304

World Food Day — A305

1994, Oct. 16 **Litho.** *Perf. 12*
1212 A304 75h Green house .70 .35
1213 A305 150h Foods 1.40 .70

A306

Arab League, 50th Anniv. A307

1995, Mar. 25 **Litho.** *Perf. 12*
1214 A306 75h multicolored .70 .35
1215 A307 150h multicolored 1.40 .70

UN, 50th Anniv.
A308 A309

1995, Feb. 19
1216 A308 75h multicolored .70 .35
1217 A309 150h multicolored 1.40 .70

Refugee Care — A310

1995, Apr. 9 **Litho.** *Perf. 12*
1218 A310 75h green & multi .70 .35
1219 A310 150h tan & multi 1.40 .70

Pilgrimage to Mecca A311

1995, May 3 **Litho.** *Perf. 12*
1220 A311 75h blue & multi .70 .35
1221 A311 150h tan & multi 1.40 .70

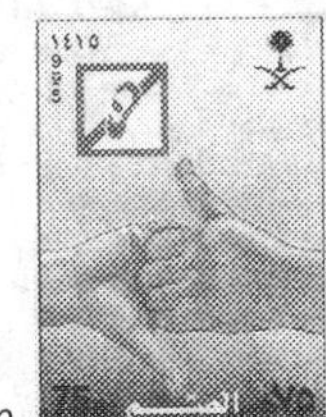
Deaf Week — A312

1995, May 3 **Litho.** *Perf. 12*
1222 A312 75h shown .70 .35
1223 A312 150h Hand sign, ear 1.40 .70

Saudi Arabian Airlines, 50th Anniv. A313

1995, Aug. 21
1224 A313 75h Anniv. emblem, vert. .70 .35
1225 A313 150h shown 1.40 .70

FAO, 50th Anniv. — A314

1995, Oct. 16 **Litho.** *Perf. 12*
1226 A314 75h shown .70 .35
1227 A314 150h Emblem over globe 1.40 .70

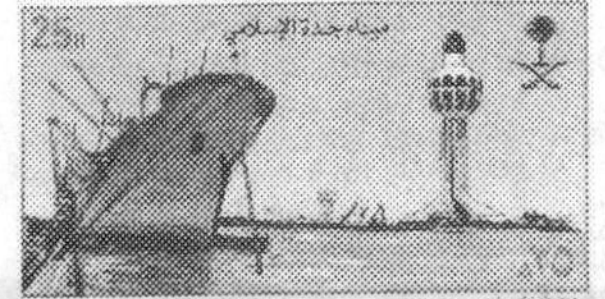
Jeddah Port — A315

1996, Jan. 27 **Litho.** *Perf. 12*
1228 A315 25h multicolored .25 .15
1229 A315 50h multicolored .50 .25
1230 A315 75h multicolored .75 .40
1230A A315 100h multicolored 1.25 1.25
Nos. 1228-1230A (4) 2.75 2.05

1996 Summer Olympics, Atlanta A316

1996
1231 A316 150h orange & multi 1.50 .75
1232 A316 2r blue & multi 2.00 1.00

Pilgrimage to Mecca — A317

1996, Apr. 21
1233 A317 150h black & multi 1.50 .75
1234 A317 2r rose red & multi 2.00 1.00
1235 A317 3r green & multi 3.00 1.50
Nos. 1233-1235 (3) 6.50 3.25

World Health Organization A318

1996 **Litho.** *Perf. 12*
1236 A318 2r green & multi 1.80 .90
1237 A318 3r red & multi 2.75 1.40

FAO, 50th Anniv. A319

1996 **Litho.** *Perf. 12*
1238 A319 2r blue & multi 1.85 .90
1239 A319 3r red & multi 2.75 1.40

UNICEF, 50th Anniv. A320

1996
1240 A320 150h buff & multi 1.40 .70
1241 A320 2r blue & multi 1.85 .90

King Abdul Aziz Research Center, 25th Anniv. A321

1996 **Litho.** *Perf. 12*
1242 A321 150h brown & multi 1.40 .70
1243 A321 2r green & multi 1.90 .95

Rabigh Steam Power Plant — A322

Designs: 150h, Power plant. 2r, Power plant, electrical power lines.

1996
1244 A322 150h multicolored 1.40 .70

Size: 51x26mm

1245 A322 2r multicolored 1.90 .95

Yanbu Port — A323

1997 **Litho.** *Perf. 12*
1246 A323 2r multicolored 1.90 .95

Opening Mecca A324

1997
1247 A324 1r brt grn & multi .95 .45
1248 A324 2r lt yel grn & multi 1.90 .95

King Fahd, Birthday A325

1997, Feb. 26
1249 A325 100h green & multi .95 .45
1250 A325 150h pink & multi 1.40 .70
1251 A325 2r tan & multi 1.90 .95
Nos. 1249-1251 (3) 4.25 2.10

An imperf souvenir sheet containing an enlarged version of design A325 exists. Sold for 5r.

Jubail Port — A326

1997
1252 A326 50h multicolored .55 .30
1252A A326 2r multicolored 1.90 .95

Campaign Against Use of Illegal Drugs A327

1997
1253 A327 150h blue & multi 1.40 .70
1254 A327 2r red & multi 1.90 .95

Battle of Kayban A328

1997 **Litho.** *Perf. 12*
1255 A328 150h multicolored 1.40 .70
1256 A328 2r multicolored 1.85 .95

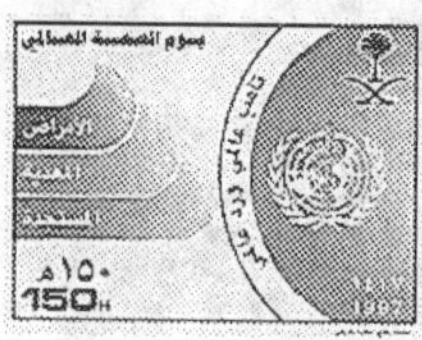

World Health Day — A329

1997, May 9 **Litho.** ***Perf. 14***

1257	A329	150h multicolored	1.40	.70
1258	A329	2r multicolored	1.90	.95

A330

Al-Hijjah A331

1997, Apr. 29

1259	A330	1r multicolored	.95	.45
1260	A331	2r multicolored	1.90	.95

King Fahd Natl. Library A332

1997 **Litho.** ***Perf. 12***

1261	A332	1r shown	.95	.45
1262	A332	2r Open book	1.90	.95

A333

A334

1997

1263	A333	150h Emblem, rays	1.40	.70
1264	A333	2r shown	1.90	.95

King Abdul Aziz Public Library.

1997 **Litho.** ***Perf. 12***

1265	A334	1r red & multi	.95	.50
1266	A334	2r green & multi	1.85	.95

Montreal Protocol on Substances that Deplete Ozone Layer, 10th anniv.

3rd GCC Stamp Exhibition, Riyadh A335

1997 **Litho.** ***Perf. 12***

1267	A335	1r multicolored	1.00	.50

Prince Salman Center — A336

1997 **Litho.** ***Perf. 12***

1268	A336	1r multicolored	1.00	.50

Battle of Tabuk A337

1997 **Litho.** ***Perf. 12***

1269	A337	1r multicolored	.95	.50

World Food Day — A338

1997

1270	A338	2r multicolored	1.90	1.00

AIR POST STAMPS

Catalogue values for unused stamps in this section are for Never Hinged items.

Airspeed Ambassador Airliner — AP1

1949-58 **Unwmk.** **Typo.** ***Perf. 11***

C1	AP1	1g blue green	2.00	.15
C2	AP1	3g ultra	2.50	.15
a.		3g blue ('58)	10.50	.90
C3	AP1	4g orange	2.50	.15
C4	AP1	10g purple	7.00	.15
C5	AP1	20g brn vio ('58+)	6.25	.20
a.		20g chocolate ('49)	12.50	.45
C6	AP1	100g violet rose	62.50	6.25
		Nos. C1-C6 (6)	82.75	7.05

Imperfs. exist, not regularly issued.

The 1st printings are on grayish paper and sell for more.

No. C3 exists with pin-perf 6.

+ The date for No. C5 is not definite.

Saudi Airlines Convair 440 — AP2

Type I (Saud Cartouche)
(Illustrated over No. 286)

1960-61 **Photo.** ***Perf. 14***

C7	AP2	1p dull pur & grn	.55	.15
C8	AP2	2p grn & dull pur	.55	.15
C9	AP2	3p brn red & bl	.55	.15
C10	AP2	4p bl & dull pur	.55	.15
C11	AP2	5p grn & rose red	.55	.15
C12	AP2	6p ocher & slate	.90	.20
C13	AP2	8p rose & gray ol	1.10	.20
C14	AP2	9p purple & red brn	1.65	.20
C15	AP2	10p blk & dl red brn	4.50	.40
C16	AP2	15p bl & bis brn	4.50	.20
C17	AP2	20p bis brn & emer	4.50	.35
C18	AP2	30p sep & Prus grn	11.00	.90
C19	AP2	50p green & indigo	22.50	.65
C20	AP2	100p gray & dk brn	45.00	1.75
C21	AP2	200p dk vio & black	67.50	2.75
		Nos. C7-C21 (15)	165.90	8.35

Nos. C7-C18 exist imperf., probably not regularly issued.

1963-64 **Photo.** **Wmk. 337**

Size: 27½x22mm

C24	AP2	1p lilac & green	2.25	.15
C25	AP2	2p green & dull pur	8.50	.20
C26	AP2	4p blue & dull pur	3.25	.15
C27	AP2	6p ocher & slate	8.50	.70
C28	AP2	8p rose & gray olive	16.00	1.40
C29	AP2	9p pur & red brn ('64)	11.00	.90
		Nos. C24-C29 (6)	49.50	3.50

Redrawn

Perf. 13½x13

1964 **Wmk. 337** **Litho.**

Size: 28½x23mm

C30	AP2	3p brn red & dull bl	4.75	.45
C31	AP2	10p blk & dk red brn	7.50	.70
C32	AP2	20p bis brn & emer	16.00	1.65
		Nos. C30-C32 (3)	28.25	2.80

Nos. C30-C32 are widely spaced in the sheet, producing large margins.

Saudi Airline Boeing 720-B Jet — AP3

Type I (Saud Cartouche)
(Illustrated over No. 286)

1965-70 **Unwmk.** **Litho.** ***Perf. 14***

C33	AP3	1p lilac & green	80.00	2.75
C34	AP3	2p grn & dull pur	2,250.	90.00
C35	AP3	3p rose lil & dull bl	9.50	.15
C36	AP3	4p blue & dull pur	5.50	.15
C37	AP3	5p ol & rose red	1,800.	400.00
C38	AP3	6p ocher & slate	100.00	1.75
C39	AP3	7p rose & ol gray	6.25	.35
C40	AP3	8p rose & gray ol	80.00	1.75
C41	AP3	9p purple & red brn	6.75	.30
C42	AP3	10p blk & dk red brn	80.00	5.50
C43	AP3	11p green & bister	80.00	18.00
C44	AP3	12p orange & gray	5.50	.30
C45	AP3	13p dk green & yel grn	5.50	.30
C46	AP3	14p dk blue & org	5.50	.35
C47	AP3	15p blue & bis brn	75.00	5.50
C48	AP3	16p black & ultra	8.00	.45
C49	AP3	17p bister & sepia	6.75	.35
C50	AP3	18p dk bl & yel grn	6.75	.35
C51	AP3	19p car & dp org	8.00	.45
C52	AP3	20p bis brn & emer	140.00	6.25
C53	AP3	23p olive & bister	150.00	11.00
C54	AP3	24p dk blue & sep	6.75	.45
C55	AP3	26p ver & blue grn	6.75	.45
C56	AP3	27p ol brn & ap grn	7.00	.45
C57	AP3	31p car rose & rose red	7.25	.55
C58	AP3	33p red & dull pur	12.00	.55

The 50p, 100p and 200p exist but were not placed in use.

Issue years: 1966, 1p, 3p, 7p, 10p, 12p-14p, 16p-19p. 1969, 5p, 11p. 1970, 2p, 6p, 8p, 15p, 20p. Others, 1965.

Type II (Faisal Cartouche)

1966-78 **Unwmk.** **Litho.** ***Perf. 14***

C59	AP3	1p dull pur & grn	20.00	.90
C60	AP3	2p green & dull pur	20.00	1.40
C61	AP3	3p brn red & dull bl	20.00	.45
C62	AP3	4p blue & dull pur	10.00	.25
C63	AP3	5p ol & rose red	1,800.	450.00
C64	AP3	6p ocher & slate	125.00	9.00
C65	AP3	7p rose & ol gray	57.50	6.25
C66	AP3	8p rose & gray ol	77.50	11.00
C67	AP3	9p purple & red brn	6.00	.55
C68	AP3	10p blk & dull red brn	16.00	.90
C69	AP3	11p green & bister	12.00	.45
C70	AP3	12p orange & gray	45.00	3.50
C71	AP3	13p dk grn & yel grn	14.00	.90
C72	AP3	14p dk blue & org	16.00	1.50
C73	AP3	15p blue & bis brn	11.00	.70
C74	AP3	16p black & ultra	16.00	2.75
C75	AP3	17p bister & sepia	14.00	1.40
C76	AP3	18p dk bl & yel grn	16.00	2.25
C77	AP3	19p carmine & org	18.00	.90
C78	AP3	20p brn & brt grn	175.00	12.50
C79	AP3	23p olive & bister	22.50	2.75
C80	AP3	24p dk blue & blk	27.50	2.75
C83	AP3	31p car rose & rose red	675.00	
C84	AP3	33p red & dull pur	11.00	.45
C85	AP3	50p emer & ind	575.00	175.00
C86	AP3	100p gray & dk brn	775.00	275.00
C87	AP3	200p dk vio & blk	900.00	175.00

The existence of 26p and 27p denominations has been reported.

The status of the 31p has been questioned. If it exists it may not have been issued.

Issue years: 1968, 4p, 33p. 1969, 7p. 1970, 8p, 9p, 20p. 1971, 13p, 16p. 1974, 50p, 200p. 1975, 12p, 14p, 15p, 17p, 19p, 24p. 1976, 18p. 1978, 31p, 100p. Others, 1966.

1968-71 **Wmk. 361** **Litho.** ***Perf. 14***

C88	AP3	1p lilac & green	7.50	.20
C89	AP3	2p green & lilac	7.50	.20
C90	AP3	3p rose lil & dull bl	35.00	1.75
C91	AP3	4p blue & dull pur	12.00	1.10
C92	AP3	7p rose & gray	12.00	1.50
C93	AP3	8p red & gray ol	37.50	6.00
C94	AP3	9p pur & red brn	52.50	7.25
C95	AP3	10p blk & dull red brn	35.00	3.50
		Nos. C88-C95 (8)	199.00	21.50

Issue years: 1969, 3p, 10p. 1970, 4p. 1971, 7p-9p. Others, 1968.

Falcon — AP4

Perf. 13½x14

1968-71 **Litho.** **Wmk. 361**

C96	AP4	1p green & red brn	12.50	.15
C97	AP4	4p dk red & red brn	82.50	11.00
C98	AP4	10p blue & red brn	18.00	2.75
C99	AP4	20p green & red brn ('71)	32.50	5.50
		Nos. C96-C99 (4)	145.50	19.40

Nine other denominations were printed but are not known to have been issued.

HEJAZ POSTAGE DUE STAMPS

From Old Door at El Ashraf Barsbai in Shari el Ashrafiya, Cairo — D1

Serrate Roulette 13

1917, June 27 **Typo.** **Unwmk.**

LJ1	D1	20pa red	2.75	2.00
LJ2	D1	1pi blue	2.75	2.00
LJ3	D1	2pi magenta	2.75	2.00
		Nos. LJ1-LJ3 (3)	8.25	6.00

For overprints see Nos. LJ4-LJ10, LJ17-LJ25, J9,

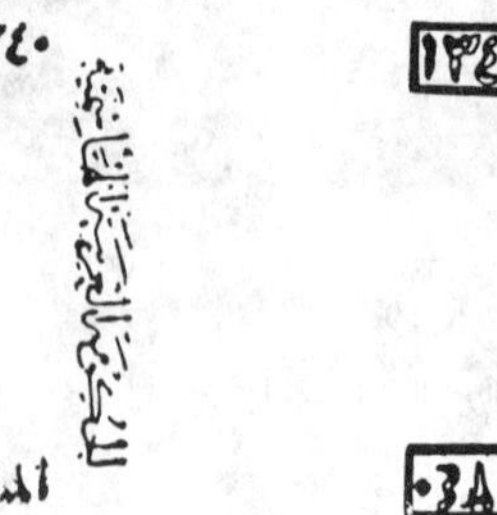

a b

Nos. LJ1-LJ3 Overprinted Type "a" in Black or Red

1921, Dec.

LJ4	D1	20pa red	18.00	2.75
a.		Double overprint, one at left	140.00	
b.		Overprint at left	30.00	20.00
LJ5	D1	1pi blue (R)	5.50	3.50
LJ6	D1	1pi bl, ovpt. at left	27.50	18.00
a.		Overprint at right	27.50	32.50
LJ7	D1	2pi magenta	10.00	7.25
a.		Double overprint, one at left	62.50	
b.		Overprint at left	27.50	
		Nos. LJ4-LJ7 (4)	61.00	31.50

Nos. LJ1-LJ3 Overprinted Type "b" in Black

1922, Jan.

LJ8	D1	20pa red	22.50	27.50
a.		Overprint at left	35.00	
LJ9	D1	1pi blue	3.25	3.25
a.		Overprint at left	45.00	
LJ10	D1	2pi magenta	3.25	3.25
a.		Overprint at left	32.50	
		Nos. LJ8-LJ10 (3)	29.00	34.00

Regular issue of 1922 Overprinted

Black Overprint

1923 *Perf. 11 1/2*

No.	Type	Value	Color	Unused	Used
LJ11	A7	1/2pi	red	3.50	1.40
LJ12	A7	1pi	dark blue	6.50	1.40
LJ13	A7	2pi	orange	3.50	1.75
			Nos. LJ11-LJ13 (3)	13.50	4.55

1924

Blue Overprint

No.	Type	Value	Color	Unused	Used
LJ14	A7	1/2pi	red	16.00	2.75
LJ15	A7	1pi	dark blue	35.00	2.75
LJ16	A7	2pi	orange	27.50	4.50
			Nos. LJ14-LJ16 (3)	78.50	10.00

This overprint reads "Mustahaq" (Due).

Jedda Issues

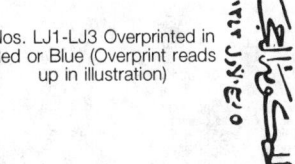

Nos. LJ1-LJ3 Overprinted in Red or Blue (Overprint reads up in illustration)

Jedda issues were also used in Medina and Yambo. Used values for #L51-L186 and LJ17-LJ39 are for genuine cancels. Privately applied cancels exist for "Mekke" (Mecca, bilingual or all Arabic), Khartoum, Cairo, as well as for Jeddah. Many private cancels have wrong dates, some as early as 1916. These are worth half the used values.

1925, Jan. *Serrate Roulette 13*

No.	Type	Value	Color	Unused	Used
LJ17	D1	20pa	red (R)	350.00	*350.00*
LJ19	D1	1pi	blue (R)	18.00	*18.00*
LJ20	D1	1pi	blue (Bl)	25.00	*25.00*
LJ21	D1	2pi	magenta (Bl)	14.00	*14.00*

Overprint Reading Down

No.	Type	Value	Color	Unused	Used
LJ17a	D1	20pa		*550.00*	*550.00*
LJ18	D1	20pa	red (Bl)	*450.00*	
LJ19a	D1	1pi		18.00	*18.00*
LJ20a	D1	1pi		67.50	*80.00*
LJ21a	D1	2pi		60.00	*60.00*

Nos. LJ1-LJ3 Overprinted in Blue or Red

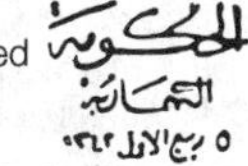

1925

No.	Type	Value	Color	Unused	Used
LJ22	D1	20pa	red (Bl)	425.00	*425.00*
a.			Inverted overprint	325.00	*325.00*
LJ24	D1	1pi	blue (R)	22.50	*27.50*
a.			Inverted overprint	32.50	*32.50*
LJ25	D1	2pi	magenta (Bl)	18.00	*18.00*
a.			Inverted overprint	35.00	*45.00*
b.			Double overprint	350.00	

No. LJ2 with this overprint in blue is bogus.

Regular Issues of 1922-24 Overprinted

a

and Handstamped

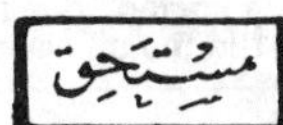

b

1925 *Perf. 11 1/2*

No.	Type	Value	Color	Unused	Used
LJ26	A7	1/8pi	red brown	18.00	*18.00*
LJ27	A7	1/2pi	red	25.00	*25.00*
LJ28	A7	1pi	dark blue	18.00	*18.00*
LJ29	A7	1 1/2pi	violet	18.00	*18.00*
LJ30	A7	2pi	orange	20.00	*20.00*
LJ31	A7	3pi	olive brown	20.00	*20.00*
LJ32	A7	3pi	dull red	45.00	*45.00*
LJ33	A7	5pi	olive green	25.00	*20.00*
LJ34	A7	10pi	vio & dk brn	25.00	*25.00*
			Nos. LJ26-LJ34 (9)	209.00	209.00

The printed overprint *(a)*, consisting of the three top lines of Arabic, was used alone for the first issue (Nos. LJ26a-LJ34a). The "postage due" box was so small and indistinct that its equivalent in larger characters was added by boxed handstamp *(b)* at bottom of each stamp for the second issue (Nos. LJ26-LJ34).

The handstamped overprint *(b)* is found double, inverted, etc. It is also known in dark violet.

Counterfeits exist of both overprint and handstamp.

Without Boxed Handstamp "b"

No.	Type	Value	Color	Unused
LJ26a	A7	1/8pi	red brown	42.50
LJ27a	A7	1/2pi	red	42.50
LJ28a	A7	1pi	dark blue	42.50
LJ29a	A7	1 1/2pi	violet	42.50
LJ30a	A7	2pi	orange	42.50
LJ31a	A7	3pi	olive brown	42.50
LJ32a	A7	3pi	dull red	42.50
LJ33a	A7	5pi	olive green	55.00
LJ34a	A7	10pi	vio & dk brn	55.00
			Nos. LJ26a-LJ34a (9)	407.50

Regular Issue of 1922 Overprinted

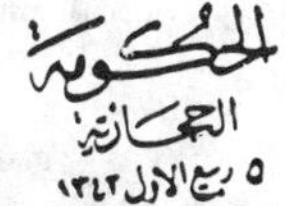

and Handstamped

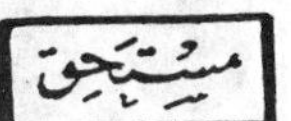

No.	Type	Value	Color	Unused	Used
LJ35	A7	1/2pi	red	*140.00*	*140.00*
LJ36	A7	1 1/2pi	violet	*140.00*	*140.00*
a.			Overprint in red, boxed handstamp violet		*1,400.*
LJ37	A7	2pi	orange	*175.00*	*175.00*
LJ38	A7	3pi	olive brown	*140.00*	*140.00*
LJ39	A7	5pi	olive green	*140.00*	*140.00*
			Nos. LJ35-LJ39 (5)	*735.00*	*735.00*

Counterfeits exist of Nos. LJ4-LJ39.

Arabic Numeral of Value

D2 D3

1925, May-June *Perf. 11 1/2*

No.	Type	Value	Color	Unused
LJ40	D2	1/2pi	light blue	2.75
LJ41	D2	1pi	orange	2.75
LJ42	D2	2pi	lt brown	2.75
LJ43	D2	3pi	pink	2.75
			Nos. LJ40-LJ43 (4)	11.00

Nos. LJ40-LJ43 exist imperforate. Impressions in colors other than issued are trial color proofs.

Black Overprint

1925

No.	Type	Value	Color	Unused
LJ44	D3	1/2pi	light blue	2.75
LJ45	D3	1pi	orange	2.75
LJ46	D3	2pi	light brown	2.75
LJ47	D3	3pi	pink	3.50
			Nos. LJ44-LJ47 (4)	11.75

Nos. LJ44-LJ47 exist with either Jedda or Cairo overprints and the tablets normally read upward. Values are for Cairo overprints; Jedda overprints sell for more.

Red Overprint

No.	Type	Value	Color	Unused
LJ48	D3	1/2pi	light blue	3.50
LJ49	D3	1pi	orange	3.50
LJ50	D3	2pi	light brown	3.50
LJ51	D3	3pi	pink	3.50

Blue Overprint

No.	Type	Value	Color	Unused
LJ52	D3	1/2pi	light blue	3.50
LJ53	D3	1pi	orange	3.50
LJ54	D3	2pi	light brown	3.50
LJ55	D3	3pi	pink	3.50
			Nos. LJ40-LJ55 (16)	50.75

Red and blue overprints are from Cairo. Nos. LJ44-LJ55 exist imperf.

NEJD POSTAGE DUE STAMPS

Handstamped in Blue, Red or Black

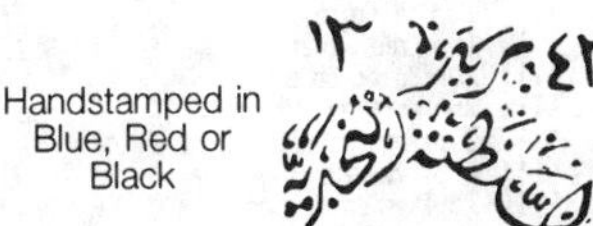

On Hejaz Postage Due Stamps Typographed or Handstamped in Black

1925, Apr.-June Unwmk. *Perf. 11 1/2*

No.	Type	Value	Color	Unused	Used
J1	A7	1/2pi	red (Bl)	27.50	27.50
J2	A7	1pi	lt blue (R)	55.00	55.00
a.		1pi	dark blue (R)	35.00	35.00
J3	A7	2pi	yel buff (Bl)	55.00	55.00
a.		2pi	orange (Bl)	47.50	47.50
			Nos. J1-J3 (3)	137.50	137.50

Same, with Postage Due Overprint in Blue

No.	Type	Value	Color	Unused
J4	A7	1/2pi	red (Bl)	*140.00*
J6	A7	2pi	orange (Bl)	*175.00*

Genuine copies of the 1pi dark blue with postage due overprint in blue, are not known.

On Hejaz Stamps of 1922-24

Handstamped in Blue

No.	Type	Value	Color	Unused	Used
J7	A7	1/2pi	red (Bl & Bl)	16.00	16.00
J8	A7	3pi	brn red (Bl & Bl)	19.00	19.00

Handstamped in Blue, Black or Violet

See note before No. 35.

On Hejaz No. LJ9

Serrate Roulette 13 1/2

No.	Type	Value	Color	Unused	Used
J9	D1	1pi	blue (V)	60.00	27.50

Same Overprint on Hejaz Stamps of 1924 with additional Handstamp in Black, Blue or Red

Perf. 11 1/2

No.	Type	Value	Color	Unused	Used
J10	A7	3pi	brn red (Bl & Bk)	11.00	11.00
J11	A7	3pi	brn red (Bk & Bl)	11.00	11.00

Same Handstamps on Hejaz Railway Tax Stamps

No.	Type	Value	Color	Unused	Used
J12	R3	1pi	blue (Bk & R)	12.00	12.00
J13	R3	2pi	ocher (Bl & Bk)	12.00	12.00
J14	R3	5pi	green (Bk & R)	20.00	20.00
J15	R3	5pi	green (V & BK)	20.00	9.00
			Nos. J10-J15 (6)	86.00	75.00

The second handstamp, which is struck on the lower part of the Postage Due Stamps, is the word Mustahaq (Due) in various forms.

No. J13 exists with second handstamp in blue.

Hejaz-Nejd

D1

1926 Typo. *Perf. 11*

No.	Type	Value	Color	Unused	Used
J16	D1	1/2pi	carmine	4.00	.65
J17	D1	2pi	orange	4.00	.65
J18	D1	6pi	light brown	4.00	.65
			Nos. J16-J18 (3)	12.00	1.95

Nos. J16-J18 exist with perf. 14, 14x11 and 11x14, and imperf. These sell for six times the values quoted.

Nos. J16-J18 in colors other than listed (both perf. and imperf.) are proofs.

Counterfeit note after No. 80 also applies to Nos. J16-J21.

Pan-Islamic Congress Issue

Postage Due Stamps of 1926 Handstamped like Regular Issue

No.	Type	Value	Color	Unused	Used
J19	D1	1/2pi	carmine	5.50	4.50
J20	D1	2pi	orange	5.50	4.50
J21	D1	6pi	light brown	5.50	4.50
			Nos. J19-J21 (3)	16.50	13.50

D2

1927 *Perf. 11 1/2*

No.	Type	Value	Color	Unused	Used
J22	D2	1pi	slate	18.00	.45
a.			Inscription reads "2 piastres" in upper right circle	175.00	100.00
J23	D2	2pi	dark violet	5.75	.45

Saudi Arabia

Saudi Arabia No. 161 Handstamped in Black

1935

No.	Type	Value	Color	Unused
J24	A9	1/2g	dark carmine	175.00

Two types of overprint.

D3

1937-39 **Unwmk.**

No.	Type	Value	Color	Unused	Used
J25	D3	1/2g	org brn ('39)	12.00	12.00
J26	D3	1g	light blue	12.00	12.00
J27	D3	2g	rose vio ('39)	17.00	8.00
			Nos. J25-J27 (3)	41.00	32.00

Catalogue values for unused stamps in this section, from this point to the end of the section, are for Never Hinged items.

D4

1961 Litho. *Perf. 13x13 1/2*

No.	Type	Value	Color	Unused	Used
J28	D4	1p	purple	5.00	5.00
J29	D4	2p	green	8.50	4.00
J30	D4	4p	rose red	10.00	10.00
			Nos. J28-J30 (3)	23.50	19.00

The use of Postage Due stamps ceased in 1963.

OFFICIAL STAMPS

Official stamps were normally used only on external correspondence.

O1

O2

1939 Unwmk. Typo. *Perf. 11 1/2*

No.	Type	Value	Color	Unused	Used
O1	O1	3g	deep ultra	3.00	1.40

Perf. 11, 11 1/2

No.	Type	Value	Color	Unused	Used
O2	O1	5g	red violet	3.75	1.75

Perf. 11

No.	Type	Value	Color	Unused	Used
O3	O1	20g	brown	8.00	3.50
O4	O1	50g	blue green	15.00	7.25
O5	O1	100g	olive grn	62.50	32.50
O6	O1	200g	purple	50.00	22.50
			Nos. O1-O6 (6)	142.25	68.90

Catalogue values for unused stamps in this section, from this point to the end of the section, are for Never Hinged items.

1961 Litho. *Perf. 13x13½*
Size: 18x22-22½mm

O7 O2	1p	black	.90	.20
O8 O2	2p	dark green	1.50	.30
O9 O2	3p	bister	1.75	.35
O10 O2	4p	dark blue	2.25	.45
O11 O2	5p	rose red	2.75	.55
O12 O2	10p	maroon	4.75	1.75
O13 O2	20p	violet blue	8.25	3.25
O14 O2	50p	dull brown	22.50	9.00
O15 O2	100p	dull green	40.00	16.00
		Nos. O7-O15 (9)	84.65	31.85

Nos. O8, O10-O15 exist imperf., probably not regularly issued.

1964-65 Wmk. 337 *Perf. 13½x13*
Size: 21x26mm

O16 O2	1p	black	.90	.35
O17 O2	2p	green ('65)	1.75	.70
O18 O2	3p	bister	6.25	2.50
O19 O2	4p	dark blue	4.50	1.75
O20 O2	5p	rose red	5.50	1.10
		Nos. O16-O20 (5)	18.90	6.40

1965-70 Wmk. 337 Typo. *Perf. 11*

O21 O2	1p	dark brown	3.50	1.40
O22 O2	2p	green	3.50	1.40
O23 O2	3p	bister	3.50	1.40
O24 O2	4p	dark blue	3.50	1.40
O25 O2	5p	deep orange	6.75	1.75
O26 O2	6p	red lilac	6.75	1.75
O27 O2	7p	emerald	6.75	1.75
O28 O2	8p	car rose	6.75	1.75
O29 O2	9p	red	27.50	
O30 O2	10p	red brown	27.50	1.75
O31 O2	11p	pale green	*55.00*	
O32 O2	12p	violet	*275.00*	
O33 O2	13p	blue	9.00	2.75
O34 O2	14p	purple	9.00	2.75
O35 O2	15p	orange	*90.00*	
O36 O2	16p	black	*90.00*	
a.		"19" instead of "16"	*450.00*	
O37 O2	17p	gray green	*90.00*	
O38 O2	18p	yellow	*90.00*	
O39 O2	19p	dp red lilac	*90.00*	
O39A O2	20p	lt blue green		
O40 O2	23p	ultra	*225.00*	
O41 O2	24p	yellow green	*90.00*	
O42 O2	26p	bister	*90.00*	
O43 O2	27p	pale lilac	*90.00*	
O44 O2	31p	pale salmon	*140.00*	
O45 O2	33p	yellow green	*90.00*	
O46 O2	50p	olive bister	*350.00*	
O47 O2	100p	ol gray ('70)	*800.00*	
		Nos. O21-O39,O40-O47 (27)	*2,769.*	

Nos. O21-O28, O30 and O33-O34 were released to the philatelic trade in 1964. Nos. O21-O47 were printed from new plates; lines of the design are heavier. The numerals have been enlarged and the P's are smaller. Head of "P" 2mm wide on 1964-65 issue, 1mm wide on 1965-70 issue.

O3

Wmk. 361, 337 (7p, 8p, 9p, 11p, 12p, 23p)
1970-72 Litho. *Perf. 13½x14*

O48 O3	1p	red brown	2.75	.90
O49 O3	2p	deep green	2.75	.90
O50 O3	3p	rose red	3.50	1.40
O51 O3	4p	bright blue	4.50	1.75
O52 O3	5p	brick red	4.50	1.75
O53 O3	6p	orange	4.50	1.75
a.		Wmk. 337	*175.00*	*45.00*
O54 O3	7p	deep salmon	*175.00*	
O55 O3	8p	violet		
O56 O3	9p	dk blue green		
O57 O3	10p	blue	6.25	2.75
a.		Wmk. 337		
O58 O3	11p	olive green		
O58A O3	12p	black brown		
O59 O3	20p	gray violet	14.00	4.50
a.		Wmk. 337	*175.00*	*90.00*
O59B O3	23p	ocher ('72)	*375.00*	
O60 O3	31p	deep plum	*45.00*	*18.00*
O61 O3	50p	light brown		
O62 O3	100p	green		

Use of official stamps ceased in 1974.

NEWSPAPER STAMPS

Nos. 8, 9 and 14 with Additional Overprint in Black

1925 Unwmk. *Perf. 11½*

P1 A7	⅛pi	red brown (Bk)	*1,800.*	*1,800.*
P2 A7	⅛pi	red brown (V)	*1,400.*	*900.*
P3 A7	½pi	red (V)	*2,750.*	*1,800.*

Overprint reads: "Matbu'a" (Newspaper), but these stamps were normally used for regular postage. Counterfeits exist.

The status of this set in question. The government may have declared it to be unauthorized.

POSTAL TAX STAMPS

PT1

1934, May 15 Unwmk. *Perf. 11½*

RA1 PT1	½g	scarlet	*175.00*	4.50

No. RA1 collected a "war tax" to aid wounded of the 1934 Saudi-Yemen war.

Nos. RA2-RA8 raised funds for the Medical Aid Society.

General Hospital, Mecca — PT2

1936, Oct.
Size: 37x20mm

RA2 PT2	⅛g	scarlet	*550.00*	9.00

Type of 1936, Redrawn

1937-42
Size: 30½x18mm

RA3 PT2	⅛g	scarlet	60.00	.90
a.		⅛g rose ('39)	*110.00*	*1.75*
b.		⅛g rose car, perf. 11 ('42)	*175.00*	*6.75*

General Hospital, Mecca — PT3

1943 Typo. *Perf. 11½, 11*
Grayish Paper

RA4 PT3	⅛g	car rose	*35.00*	.15
a.		⅛g scarlet	*35.00*	.15

The 1g green and 5g indigo were not for postal use.

See Nos. RA5-RA8.

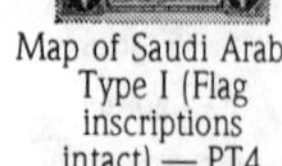

Map of Saudi Arabia Type I (Flag inscriptions intact) — PT4

Type II (Flag inscriptions scratched out)

1946 Unwmk. *Perf. 11½*

RA4B PT4	½g	magenta (II)	16.00	.90
c.		Type I	55.00	.90
d.		Type I, perf. 11	45.00	9.00
e.		Type II, perf. 11	67.50	

Return of King Ibn Saud from Egypt.

This stamp was required on all mail during Jan.-July.

Type of 1943, Redrawn

1948-53 Litho. *Perf. 10*

RA5 PT3	⅛g	rose brn ('53)	*20.00*	.20
c.		Perf. 11x10	*27.50*	*2.75*

Catalogue values for unused stamps in this section, from this point to the end of the section, are for Never Hinged items.

1950 *Rouletted*

RA6 PT3	⅛g	red brown	5.50	.15
a.		⅛g rose	7.25	.20
b.		⅛g carmine	9.00	.25

All lines in lithographed design considerably finer; some shading in center eliminated.

Type of 1943

1955-56 Photo. *Perf. 11*

RA7 PT3	⅛g	rose car	8.00	.15
RA8 PT3	¼g	car rose ('56)	4.75	.15
		Set value		.20

The tax on postal matter was discontinued in May, 1964.

Coat of Arms, Waves and View — PT5

Wmk. 361
1974, Oct. Litho. *Perf. 14*

RA9 PT5	1r	blue & multi	*110.00*	

Obligatory on all mailed entries in a government television contest during month of Ramadan in 1974 and 1975. The tax aided a benevolent society.

SCHLESWIG

'shles-(,)wig

LOCATION — In the northern part of the former Schleswig-Holstein Province, in northern Germany.

Schleswig was divided into North and South Schleswig after the Versailles Treaty, and plebiscites were held in 1920. North Schleswig (Zone 1) voted to join Denmark, South Schleswig to stay German.

100 Pfennig = 1 Mark
100 Ore = 1 Krone

Watermark

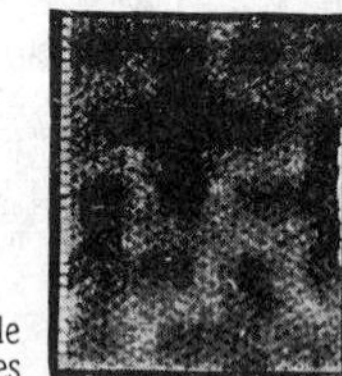

Wmk. 114- Multiple Crosses

Plebiscite Issue

Arms — A11

View of Schleswig — A12

Perf. 14x15
1920, Jan. 25 Typo. Wmk. 114

1 A11	2½pf	gray	.15	*.15*
2 A11	5pf	green	.15	*.15*
3 A11	7½pf	yellow brown	.15	*.15*
4 A11	10pf	deep rose	.25	*.15*
5 A11	15pf	red violet	.15	*.15*
6 A11	20pf	deep blue	.25	*.20*
7 A11	25pf	orange	.40	*.30*
8 A11	35pf	brown	.60	*.45*
9 A11	40pf	violet	.35	*.25*
10 A11	75pf	greenish blue	.60	*.45*
11 A12	1m	dark brown	.60	*.45*
12 A12	2m	deep blue	.80	*.65*
13 A12	5m	green	1.40	*1.25*
14 A12	10m	red	2.50	*2.50*
		Nos. 1-14 (14)	8.35	*7.25*

The colored portions of type A11 are white, and the white portions are colored, on Nos. 7-10.

Types of 1920 Overprinted in Blue **1. ZONE**

1920, May 20

15 A11	1o	dark gray	.15	*1.00*
16 A11	5o	green	.15	*.50*
17 A11	7o	yellow brn	.15	*.70*
18 A11	10o	rose red	.15	*1.00*
19 A11	15o	lilac rose	.15	*1.00*
20 A11	20o	dark blue	.15	*1.25*
21 A11	25o	orange	.25	*5.00*
22 A11	35o	brown	1.10	*9.00*
23 A11	40o	violet	.35	*2.75*
24 A11	75o	greenish blue	.50	*5.25*
25 A12	1k	dark brown	.65	*8.00*
26 A12	2k	deep blue	5.25	*30.00*
27 A12	5k	green	3.50	*30.00*
28 A12	10k	red	7.25	*60.00*
		Nos. 15-28 (14)	19.75	*155.45*

OFFICIAL STAMPS

Nos. 1-14 Overprinted **C·I·S**

1920 Wmk. 114 *Perf. 14x15*

O1 A11	2½pf	gray	70.00	*90.00*
O2 A11	5pf	green	70.00	*100.00*
O3 A11	7½pf	yellow brn	70.00	*90.00*
O4 A11	10pf	deep rose	70.00	*110.00*
O5 A11	15pf	red violet	45.00	*60.00*
O6 A11	20pf	dp blue	65.00	*70.00*
O7 A11	25pf	orange	140.00	*150.00*
a.		Inverted overprint	*1,250.*	
O8 A11	35pf	brown	125.00	*165.00*
O9 A11	40pf	violet	100.00	100.00
O10 A11	75pf	grnsh blue	125.00	*225.00*
O11 A12	1m	dark brown	125.00	*225.00*
O12 A12	2m	deep blue	200.00	*275.00*
O13 A12	5m	green	250.00	*400.00*
O14 A12	10m	red	500.00	*600.00*
		Nos. O1-O14 (14)	1,955.	*2,660.*

The letters "C.I.S." are the initials of "Commission Interalliée Slesvig," under whose auspices the plebiscites took place.

Counterfeit overprints exist.

SENEGAL

,se-ni-'gäl

LOCATION — West coast of Africa, bordering on the Atlantic Ocean
GOVT. — Republic
AREA — 76,000 sq. mi.
POP. — 6,300,000 (est. 1984)
CAPITAL — Dakar

The former French colony of Senegal became part of French West Africa in 1943. The Republic of Senegal was established Nov. 25, 1958. From Apr. 4, 1959, to June 20, 1960, the Republic of Senegal and the Sudanese Republic together formed the Mali Federation. After its breakup, Senegal resumed issuing its own stamps in 1960.

100 Centimes = 1 Franc

Catalogue values for unused stamps in this country are for Never Hinged items, beginning with Scott 195 in the regular postage section, Scott B16 in the in the semi-postal section, Scott C26 in the airpost section, Scott CB2 in the airpost semi-postal section, Scott J32 in the postage due section, and Scott O1 in the official section.

French Colonies Nos. 48, 49, 51, 52, 55, Type A9, Surcharged:

5 *a* **5** *b* **5** *c* **5** *d* **5** *e*

1887 Unwmk. *Perf. 14x13½*
Black Surcharge

1	(a) 5c	on 20c red, *grn*	125.00	125.00
a.		Double surcharge		
2	(b) 5c	on 20c red, *grn*	200.00	200.00
3	(c) 5c	on 20c red, *grn*	650.00	650.00
4	(d) 5c	on 20c red, *grn*	175.00	175.00
5	(e) 5c	on 20c red, *grn*	275.00	275.00
6	(a) 5c	on 30c brn, *bis*	200.00	200.00

7 (b) 5c on 30c brn, *bis* 850.00 850.00
8 (d) 5c on 30c brn, *bis* 300.00 300.00
Nos. 1-8 (8) 2,775. 2,775.

See Madagascar #6-7 for stamps with surcharge like "d" on 10c and 25c stamps.

10 10 10 10
f g h i
10 10 10 10
j k l m

9 (f) 10c on 4c cl, *lav* 75.00 75.00
10 (g) 10c on 4c cl, *lav* 110.00 110.00
11 (h) 10c on 4c cl, *lav* 50.00 50.00
12 (i) 10c on 4c cl, *lav* 57.50 57.50
a. "1" without top stroke
13 (f) 10c on 20c red, *grn* 400.00 400.00
14 (g) 10c on 20c red, *grn* 475.00 475.00
15 (h) 10c on 20c red, *grn* 375.00 375.00
16 (i) 10c on 20c red, *grn* *2,500. 2,500.*
17 (j) 10c on 20c red, *grn* 475.00 475.00
18 (k) 10c on 20c red, *grn* 1,400. 1,400.
19 (l) 10c on 20c red, *grn* 425.00 425.00
20 (m) 10c on 20c red, *grn* 425.00 425.00

15 15 15 15 15
n o p q r
15 15 15 15
s t u v
15
w

21 (n) 15c on 20c red, *grn* 57.50 57.50
22 (o) 15c on 20c red, *grn* 50.00 50.00
23 (p) 15c on 20c red, *grn* 50.00 40.00
24 (q) 15c on 20c red, *grn* 70.00 70.00
25 (r) 15c on 20c red, *grn* 45.00 45.00
26 (s) 15c on 20c red, *grn* 45.00 45.00
27 (t) 15c on 20c red, *grn* 125.00 125.00
28 (u) 15c on 20c red, *grn* 42.50 42.50
29 (v) 15c on 20c red, *grn* 55.00 55.00
30 (w) 15c on 20c red, *grn* 250.00 250.00
Nos. 21-30 (10) 790.00 780.00

Counterfeits exist of Nos. 1-34.

Surcharged:

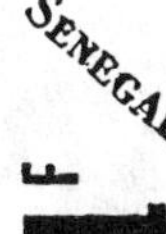

1892

Black Surcharge

31 A9 75c on 15c blue 350. 125.
32 A9 1fr on 5c grn, *grnsh* 350. 140.

"SENEGAL" in Red

33 A9 75c on 15c blue *8,000. 3,250.*
34 A9 1fr on 5c grn, *grnsh* *3,750. 850.*

Navigation and Commerce — A24

1892-1900 Typo. *Perf. 14x13½*

Name of Colony in Blue or Carmine

35 A24 1c blk, *lil bl* .50 .45
36 A24 2c brn, *buff* 1.25 1.00
37 A24 4c claret, *lav* 1.00 .85
38 A24 5c grn, *grnsh* 1.25 .85
39 A24 5c yel grn ('00) .90 .60
40 A24 10c blk, *lav* 4.50 3.75
41 A24 10c red ('00) 2.00 .65
42 A24 15c bl, quadrille paper 6.00 .90
43 A24 15c gray ('00) 2.00 1.25
44 A24 20c red, *grn* 6.00 4.00
45 A24 25c blk, *rose* 12.00 3.75
46 A24 25c blue ('00) 22.50 20.00
47 A24 30c brn, *bis* 9.00 3.75
48 A24 40c red, *straw* 12.50 10.50
49 A24 50c car, *rose* 24.00 17.50
50 A24 50c brn, *az* ('00) 27.50 26.00
51 A24 75c vio, *org* 12.50 8.75
52 A24 1fr brnz grn, *straw* 10.50 8.75
Nos. 35-52 (18) 155.90 113.30

Perf. 13½x14 stamps are counterfeits.
For surcharges see Nos. 53-56, 73-78.

Stamps of 1892 Surcharged:

5 10

1903

53 A24 5c on 40c red, *straw* 7.50 7.50
54 A24 10c on 50c car, *rose* 11.00 11.00
55 A24 10c on 75c vio, *org* 10.00 10.00
56 A24 10c on 1fr brnz grn, *straw* 55.00 50.00
Nos. 53-56 (4) 83.50 78.50

General Louis Faidherbe — A25

Oil Palms — A26

Dr. Noel Eugène Ballay — A27

1906 Typo.

"SÉNÉGAL" in Red or Blue

57 A25 1c slate .45 .45
a. "SENEGAL" omitted 80.00 80.00
58 A25 2c choc (R) .60 .55
58A A25 2c choc (Bl) 1.25 1.10
59 A25 4c choc, *gray bl* .80 .80
60 A25 5c green 1.50 .45
61 A25 10c car (Bl) 5.00 .45
a. "SENEGAL" omitted 300.00 300.00
62 A25 15c violet 4.00 2.25
63 A26 20c blk, *az* 4.25 2.25
64 A26 25c bl, *pnksh* 1.40 1.00
65 A26 30c choc, *pnksh* 3.50 3.00
66 A26 35c blk, *yellow* 15.00 1.50
67 A26 40c car, *az* (Bl) 5.25 4.50
67A A26 45c choc, *grnsh* 13.00 8.50
68 A26 50c dp violet 5.00 4.25
69 A26 75c bl, *org* 4.25 2.25
70 A27 1fr blk, *azure* 16.00 11.00
71 A27 2fr blue, *pink* 22.50 16.00
72 A27 5fr car, *straw* (Bl) 42.50 40.00
Nos. 57-72 (18) 146.25 100.30

Stamps of 1892-1900 Surcharged in Carmine or Black

05 10

1912

73 A24 5c on 15c gray (C) .50 .50
74 A24 5c on 20c red, *grn* .60 .60
75 A24 5c on 30c brn, *bis* (C) .60 .60
76 A24 10c on 40c red, *straw* .70 .70
77 A24 10c on 50c car, *rose* 1.75 1.75
78 A24 10c on 75c vio, *org* 3.25 3.25
Nos. 73-78 (6) 7.40 7.40

Two spacings between the surcharged numerals found on Nos. 73 to 78.

Senegalese Preparing Food — A28

1914-33 Typo.

79 A28 1c ol brn & vio .15 .15
80 A28 2c black & blue .15 .15
81 A28 4c gray & brn .15 .15
82 A28 5c yel grn & bl grn .20 .15
83 A28 5c blk & rose ('22) .15 .15
84 A28 10c org red & rose .30 .15
85 A28 10c yel grn & bl grn ('22) .20 .20
86 A28 10c red brn & bl ('25) .15 .15
87 A28 15c red org & brn vio ('17) .15 .15
88 A28 20c choc & blk .15 .15
89 A28 20c grn & bl grn ('26) .15 .15
90 A28 20c db & lt bl ('27) .20 .20
91 A28 25c ultra & bl .15 .15
92 A28 25c red & blk ('22) .20 .15
93 A28 30c black & rose .20 .15
94 A28 30c red org & rose ('22) .20 .20
95 A28 30c gray & bl ('26) .20 .20
96 A28 30c dl grn & dp grn ('28) .25 .20
97 A28 35c orange & vio .20 .15
98 A28 40c violet & grn .45 .15
99 A28 45c bl & ol brn .75 .75
100 A28 45c rose & bl ('22) .30 .20
101 A28 45c rose & ver ('25) .30 .20
102 A28 45c ol brn & org ('28) 2.25 1.75
103 A28 50c vio brn & bl .60 .40
104 A28 50c ultra & bl ('22) 1.25 .95
105 A28 50c red org & grn ('26) .20 .20
106 A28 60c vio, *pnksh* ('26) .25 .20
107 A28 65c rose red & dp grn ('28) .80 .70
108 A28 75c gray & rose .50 .35
109 A28 75c dk bl & lt bl ('25) .35 .20
110 A28 75c rose & gray bl ('26) 1.00 .30
111 A28 90c brn red & rose ('30) 3.50 3.00
112 A28 1fr violet & blk .55 .25
113 A28 1fr blue ('26) .35 .20
114 A28 1fr blk & gray bl ('26) .95 .20
115 A28 1.10fr bl grn & blk ('28) 1.75 1.75
116 A28 1.25fr dp grn & dp org ('33) .55 .40
117 A28 1.50fr dk bl & bl ('30) 1.25 1.25
118 A28 1.75fr dk grn & Prus bl ('33) 4.75 .50
119 A28 2fr carmine & bl 2.00 1.50
120 A28 2fr lt bl & brn ('22) 1.50 .35
121 A28 3fr red vio ('30) 2.75 1.25
122 A28 5fr green & vio 2.75 .65
Nos. 79-122 (44) 35.15 20.75

Nos. 79, 82, 84 and 97 are on both ordinary and chalky paper.
For surcharges see Nos. 123-137, B1-B2.

No. 108 and Type of 1914 Surcharged:

60 60

1922-25

123 A28 60c on 75c vio, *pnksh* .45 .45
124 A28 65c on 15c red org & dl vio ('25) .60 .60
125 A28 85c on 15c red org & dl vio ('25) .60 .60
126 A28 85c on 75c ('25) .65 .65

No. 87 Surcharged in Various Colors

0,01 0,01

1922

127 A28 1c on 15c (Bk) .25 .25
128 A28 2c on 15c (Bl) .25 .25
129 A28 4c on 15c (G) .25 .25
130 A28 5c on 15c (R) .25 .25
Nos. 123-130 (8) 3.30 3.30

Stamps and Type of 1914 Surcharged with New Value and Bars in Black or Red

1924-27

131 A28 25c on 5fr grn & vio .35 .30
132 A28 90c on 75c brn red & cer ('27) .60 .55
a. Double surcharge 80.00 80.00
133 A28 1.25fr on 1fr bl & lt bl (R) ('26) .35 .30
134 A28 1.50fr on 1fr dk bl & ultra ('27) .50 .35
135 A28 3fr on 5fr mag & ol brn ('27) 1.25 .50
136 A28 10fr on 5fr dk bl & red org ('27) 4.50 1.50
137 A28 20fr on 5fr vio & ol bis ('27) 5.50 4.50
Nos. 131-137 (7) 13.05 8.00

Common Design Types pictured following the introduction

Colonial Exposition Issue

Common Design Types
Name of Country Typographed in Black

1931 Engr. *Perf. 12½*

138 CD70 40c deep green 1.25 1.25
139 CD71 50c violet 1.25 1.25
140 CD72 90c red orange 1.25 1.25
a. "SENEGAL" double 70.00
141 CD73 1.50fr dull blue 1.25 1.25
Nos. 138-141 (4) 5.00 5.00

Faidherbe Bridge, St. Louis — A29

Diourbel Mosque A30

1935-40 *Perf. 12½x12*

142 A29 1c violet blue .15 .15
143 A29 2c brown .15 .15
144 A29 3c violet ('40) .15 .15
145 A29 4c gray blue .15 .15
146 A29 5c orange red .15 .15
147 A29 10c violet .15 .15
148 A29 15c black .15 .15
149 A29 20c dk carmine .15 .15
150 A29 25c black brn .15 .15
151 A29 30c green .15 .15
152 A29 40c rose lake .15 .15
153 A29 45c dk blue grn .20 .15
154 A30 50c red orange .15 .15
155 A30 60c violet ('40) .20 .20
156 A30 65c dk violet .20 .20
157 A30 70c red brn ('40) .30 .30
158 A30 75c brown .40 .40
159 A30 90c rose car 1.50 .95
160 A30 1fr violet 6.25 1.25
161 A30 1.25fr redsh brn .70 .40
162 A30 1.25fr rose car ('39) .50 .50
163 A30 1.40fr dk bl grn ('40) .40 .40
164 A30 1.50fr dk blue .20 .20
165 A30 1.60fr pck bl ('40) .40 .40
166 A30 1.75fr dk blue grn .20 .20
167 A30 2fr blue .30 .20
168 A30 3fr green .30 .20
169 A30 5fr black brn .50 .30
170 A30 10fr rose lake .80 .50
171 A30 20fr grnsh slate .80 .50
Nos. 142-171 (30) 15.95
Set value 7.50

Nos. 143, 148 and 156 surcharged with new values are listed under French West Africa.
For surcharges see Nos. B9, B11-B12.

Paris International Exposition Issue

Common Design Types

1937 *Perf. 13*

172 CD74 20c deep violet .50 .50
173 CD75 30c dark green .50 .50
174 CD76 40c car rose .55 .55
175 CD77 50c dark brown .65 .65
176 CD78 90c red .65 .65
177 CD79 1.50fr ultra 1.10 1.10
Nos. 172-177 (6) 3.95 3.95

Colonial Arts Exhibition Issue

Souvenir Sheet
Common Design Type

1937 Unwmk. *Imperf.*

178 CD76 3fr rose violet 3.50 3.50

Senegalese Woman — A31

1938-40 *Perf. 12x12½, 12½x12*

179 A31 35c green .40 .25
180 A31 55c chocolate .40 .35
181 A31 80c violet .70 .25
182 A31 90c lt rose vio ('39) .30 .30
183 A31 1fr car lake 1.50 .65
184 A31 1fr cop brn ('40) .20 .20
185 A31 1.75fr ultra .50 .25
186 A31 2.25fr ultra ('39) .40 .40
187 A31 2.50fr black ('40) .70 .70
Nos. 179-187 (9) 5.10 3.35

For surcharge see No. B10.

Caillié Issue

Common Design Type

1939 Engr. *Perf. 12½x12*

188 CD81 90c org brn & org .35 .35
189 CD81 2fr brt vio .50 .50
190 CD81 2.25fr ultra & dk bl .50 .50
Nos. 188-190 (3) 1.35 1.35

For No. 188 surcharged 20fr and 50fr, see French West Africa.

New York World's Fair Issue

Common Design Type

1939 *Perf. 12½x12*

191 CD82 1.25fr car lake .35 .35
192 CD82 2.25fr ultra .35 .35

Diourbel Mosque and Marshal Pétain
A32

1941 **Engr.**

193 A32 1fr green .30
194 A32 2.50fr blue .30

Nos. 193-194 were issued by the Vichy government, but it is doubtful whether they were placed on sale in Senegal.

Stamps of types A29, A30 and A31, without "RF," were issued in 1943 by the Vichy Government, but were not placed on sale in the colony.

See French West Africa No. 69 for additional stamp inscribed "Senegal" and "Afrique Occidentale Francaise."

Catalogue values for unused stamps in this section, from this point to the end of the section, are for Never Hinged items.

Republic

Roan Antelope — A33

Animals: 10fr, Savannah buffalo, horiz. 15fr, Wart hog. 20fr, Giant eland. 25fr, Bushbuck, horiz. 85fr, Defassa waterbuck.

1960 **Unwmk.** **Engr.** ***Perf. 13***

195 A33 5fr brn, grn & claret .15 .15
196 A33 10fr grn & brn .16 .15
197 A33 15fr blk, claret & org brn .20 .15
198 A33 20fr brn, grn, ocher & sal .25 .15
199 A33 25fr brn, lt grn & org .35 .16
200 A33 85fr brn, grn, olive & bis 1.10 .50
Nos. 195-200 (6) 2.21
Set value .98

Imperforates
Most Senegal stamps from 1960 onward exist imperforate in issued and trial colors, and also in small presentation sheets in issued colors.

Allegory of Independent State — A34

1961, Apr. 4

201 A34 25fr bl, choc & grn .22 .15

Independence Day, Apr. 4.

Wrestling
A35

Designs: 1fr, Pirogues racing. 2fr, Horse race. 30fr, Male tribal dance. 45fr, Lion game.

1961, Sept. 30 ***Perf. 13***

202 A35 50c ol, bl & choc .15 .15
203 A35 1fr grn, bl & maroon .15 .15
204 A35 2fr ultra, bis & sepia .15 .15
205 A35 30fr carmine & claret .30 .18
206 A35 45fr indigo & brn org .40 .25
Set value .80 .55

UN Headquarters, New York and Flag — A36

1962, Jan. 6 **Engr.** ***Perf. 13***

207 A36 10fr grn, ocher & car .15 .15
208 A36 30fr car, ocher & grn .30 .20
209 A36 85fr grn, ocher & car .70 .42
Nos. 207-209 (3) 1.15 .77

1st anniv. of Senegal's admission to the United Nations, Sept. 28, 1960.

Map of Africa, ITU Emblem and Man with Telephone
A37

1962, Jan. 22 **Photo.** ***Perf. 12½x12***

210 A37 25fr blk, grn, red & ocher .25 .20

Meeting of the Commission for the Africa Plan of the ITU, Dakar.

African and Malgache Union Issue
Common Design Type

1962, Sept. 8 **Unwmk.**

211 CD110 30fr grn, bluish grn, red & gold .40 .35

Boxing — A38

Charaxes Varanes — A40

UPU Monument, Bern — A39

15fr, Diving, horiz. 20fr, High jump, horiz. 25fr, Soccer. 30fr, Basketball. 85fr, Running.

1963, Apr. 11 **Engr.** ***Perf. 13***
Athletes in Dark Brown

212 A38 10fr ver & emer .15 .15
213 A38 15fr dk bl & bis .16 .15
214 A38 20fr ver & dk bl .22 .15
215 A38 25fr grn & dk bl .25 .16
216 A38 30fr ver & grn .35 .20
217 A38 85fr vio bl .90 .60
Nos. 212-217 (6) 2.03 1.41

Friendship Games, Dakar, Apr. 11-21.

1963, June 14 **Unwmk.** ***Perf. 13***

218 A39 10fr grn & ver .16 .15
219 A39 15fr dk bl & red brn .20 .16
220 A39 30fr red brn & dk bl .35 .22
Nos. 218-220 (3) .71 .53

2nd anniv. of Senegal's admission to the UPU.

1963, July 20 **Photo.** ***Perf. 12½x13***

Butterflies: 45fr, Papilio nireus. 50fr, Colotis danae. 85fr, Epiphora bauhiniae. 100fr, Junonia hierta. 500fr, Danaus chrysippus.

Butterflies in Natural Colors

221 A40 30fr bl gray & blk .60 .16
222 A40 45fr org & blk .80 .22
223 A40 50fr brt yel & blk .90 .30
224 A40 85fr red & blk 1.40 .55
225 A40 100fr bl & blk 1.65 .65
226 A40 500fr emer & blk 6.25 2.25
Nos. 221-226 (6) 11.60 4.13

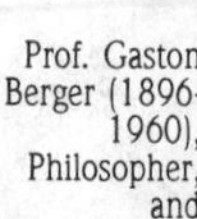

Prof. Gaston Berger (1896-1960), Philosopher, and Owl — A41

1963, Nov. 13 ***Perf. 12½x12***

227 A41 25fr multi .22 .15

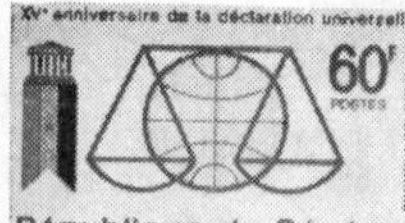

Scales, Globe, Flag and UNESCO Emblem
A42

1963, Dec. 10

228 A42 60fr multi .55 .30

15th anniv. of the Universal Declaration of Human Rights.

Flag, Mother and Child — A43

1963, Dec. 21 ***Perf. 12x12½***

229 A43 25fr multi .30 .22

Issued for the Senegalese Red Cross.

Dredging of Titanium-bearing Sand — A44

Designs: 10fr, Titanium extraction works. 15fr, Cement works at Rufisque. 20fr, Phosphate quarry at Pallo. 25fr, Extraction of phosphate ore at Taiba. 85fr, Mineral dock, Dakar.

1964, July 4 **Engr.** ***Perf. 13***

230 A44 5fr grnsh bl, car & dk brn .15 .15
231 A44 10fr ocher, grn & ind .15 .15
232 A44 15fr dk bl, brt grn & dk brn .15 .15
233 A44 20fr ultra, ol & pur .16 .15
234 A44 25fr dk bl, yel & blk .25 .15
235 A44 85fr bl, red & brn .80 .42
Nos. 230-235 (6) 1.66
Set value .72

Cooperation Issue
Common Design Type

1964, Nov. 7 **Engr.** ***Perf. 13***

236 CD119 100fr dk grn, dk brn & car .90 .60

St. Theresa's Church, Dakar — A45

10fr, Mosque, Touba. 15fr, Mosque, Dakar, vert.

1964, Nov. 28 **Unwmk.** ***Perf. 13***

237 A45 5fr bl, grn & red brn .15 .15
238 A45 10fr dk bl, ocher & blk .15 .15
239 A45 15fr brn, bl & sl grn .16 .15
Set value .35 .26

Leprosy Examination A46

Leprosarium, Peycouk Village — A47

1965, Jan. 30 **Engr.** ***Perf. 13***

240 A46 20fr brn red, grn & blk .22 .20
241 A47 65fr org, dk bl & grn .65 .40

Issued to publicize the fight against leprosy.

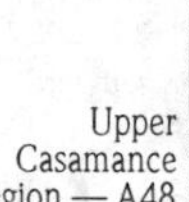

Upper Casamance Region — A48

Views: 30fr, Sangalkam. 45fr, Forest along Senegal River.

1965, Feb. 27 **Unwmk.** ***Perf. 13***

242 A48 25fr red brn, sl bl & grn .22 .15
243 A48 30fr indigo & lt brn .25 .15
244 A48 45fr yel grn, red brn & dk brn .40 .22
Nos. 242-244,C41 (4) 1.87 .94

Abdoulaye Seck
A49

Berthon-Ader Telephone
A51

General Post Office, Dakar — A50

1965, Apr. 24 **Unwmk.** ***Perf. 13***

245 A49 10fr dk brn & blk .15 .15
246 A50 15fr brn & dk sl grn .16 .15
Set value .16

1965, May 17 **Engr.**

Designs: 60fr, Cable laying ship "Alsace." 85fr, Picard's cable relay for submarine telegraph.

247 A51 50fr bl grn & org brn .50 .30
248 A51 60fr mag & dk bl .60 .38
249 A51 85fr ver, bl & red brn .90 .50
Nos. 247-249 (3) 2.00 1.18

ITU, centenary.

Plowing with Ox Team — A52

Designs: 60fr, Harvesting millet, vert. 85fr, Men working in rice field.

1965, July 3 **Unwmk.** ***Perf. 13***

250 A52 25fr dk ol grn, brn & pur .25 .15
251 A52 60fr ind, sl grn & dk brn .55 .22
252 A52 85fr dp car, sl grn & brt grn .80 .38
Nos. 250-252 (3) 1.60 .75

Gorée Sailboat
A53

Cashew
A54

Designs: 20fr, Large Seumbediou canoe. 30fr, Fadiouth one-man canoe. 45fr, One-man canoe on Senegal River.

1965, Aug. 7 **Photo.** ***Perf. 12½x13***

253 A53 10fr multi .15 .15
254 A53 20fr multi .16 .15
255 A53 30fr multi .30 .16
256 A53 45fr multi .42 .25
Nos. 253-256 (4) 1.03
Set value .58

1965 **Photo.** ***Perf. 12½***

257 A54 10fr shown .15 .15
258 A54 15fr Papaya .16 .15
259 A54 20fr Mango .20 .15
260 A54 30fr Peanuts .30 .15
Nos. 257-260 (4) .81
Set value .36

Issued: 10fr, 15fr, 20fr, Nov. 6. 30fr, Dec. 18.

"Elegant Man" — A55

Drummer and Map of Africa — A56

Dolls of Gorée: 2fr, "Elegant Woman." 3fr, Woman peddling fruit. 4fr, Woman pounding grain.

1966, Jan. 22 — Engr. — *Perf. 13*

261 A55 1fr brn, rose car & ultra .15 .15
262 A55 2fr brn, bl & org .15 .15
263 A55 3fr brn, red & bl .15 .15
264 A55 4fr brn, lil & emer .15 .15
Set value .22 .22

1966

15fr, Sculpture; mother & child. #267, Music; stringed instrument. 75fr, Dance; carved antelope headpiece (Bambara). 90fr, Ideogram.

265 A56 15fr dk red brn, bl & ocher .15 .15
266 A56 30fr brn, red & grn .30 .18
267 A56 30fr dk red brn, bl & yel .30 .18
268 A56 75fr dk red brn, bl & blk .70 .42
269 A56 90fr dk red brn, org & sl grn .90 .55
a. Souv. sheet of 4, #265, 267-269 2.50 2.50
Nos. 265-269 (5) 2.35 1.48

Intl. Negro Arts Festival, Dakar, Apr. 1-24.
Issued: #266, Feb. 5; others, Apr. 2. See #364.

Fish — A57

1966, Feb. 26 — Photo. — *Perf. 12½x13*

270 A57 20fr Tuna .22 .15
271 A57 30fr Merou .35 .16
272 A57 50fr Girella .55 .30
273 A57 100fr Parrot fish 1.10 .50
Nos. 270-273 (4) 2.22 1.11

Arms of Senegal — A58

Flowers — A59

1966, July 2 — Litho. — *Perf. 13x12½*

274 A58 30fr multi .25 .15

1966, Nov. 19 — Photo. — *Perf. 11½*

275 A59 45fr Mexican poppy .42 .18
276 A59 55fr Mimosa .50 .20
277 A59 60fr Haemanthus .60 .22
278 A59 90fr Baobab .80 .38
Nos. 275-278 (4) 2.32 .98

Harbor, Gorée Island — A60

Designs: 25fr, S.S. France in roadstead, Dakar and seagulls. 30fr, Hotel and tourist village, N'Gor. 50fr, Hotel and bay, N'Gor.

1966, Dec. 25 — Engr. — *Perf. 13*

279 A60 20fr mar & vio bl .20 .15
280 A60 25fr red, grn & blk .22 .15
281 A60 30fr dk red & dp bl .25 .16
282 A60 50fr brn, sl grn & emer .45 .20
Nos. 279-282 (4) 1.12 .66

Laying Urban Water Pipes — A61

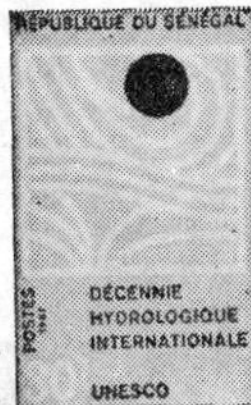

Symbolic Water Cycle — A62

20fr, Cattle at water trough. 50fr, Village well.

1967, Mar. 25 — Engr. — *Perf. 13*

283 A61 10fr org brn, grn & dk bl .15 .15
284 A61 20fr grn, brt bl & org brn .25 .20

Typo.
Perf. 13x14

285 A62 30fr sky bl, blk & org .35 .15

Engr.
Perf. 13

286 A62 50fr brn red, brt bl & bis .55 .20
Nos. 283-286 (4) 1.30
Set value .60

Intl. Hydrological Decade (UNESCO), 1965-74.

Lions Emblem A63

1967, May 27 — Photo. — *Perf. 12½x13*

287 A63 30fr lt ultra & multi .30 .16

50th anniversary of Lions International.

Blaise Diagne A64

1967, June 10 — Engr. — *Perf. 13*

288 A64 30fr ocher, sl grn & dk red brn .30 .20

Blaise Diagne (1872-1934), member of French Chamber of Deputies and Colonial Minister.
For surcharge see No. 380.

City Hall and Arms, Dakar — A65

1967, June 10

289 A65 90fr bl, dk grn & blk .80 .38

Eagle and Antelope Carvings — A66

150fr, Flags, maple leaf and EXPO '67 emblem.

1967, Sept. 2 — Photo. — *Perf. 13x12½*

290 A66 90fr red & blk .60 .30
291 A66 150fr red & multi 1.00 .50

EXPO '67 Intl. Exhib., Montreal, Apr. 28-Oct. 27.

International Tourist Year Emblem A67

Tourist Photographing Hippopotamus and Siminti Hotel — A68

1967, Oct. 7 — Typo. — *Perf. 14x13*

292 A67 50fr blk & bl .55 .38

Perf. 13
Engr.

293 A68 100fr blk, sl grn & ocher 1.10 .50

International Tourist Year.

Monetary Union Issue
Common Design Type

1967, Nov. 4 — Engr. — *Perf. 13*

294 CD125 30fr multi .25 .15

5th anniv. of the West African Monetary Union.

Lyre-shaped Megalith, Kaffrine A69

Design: 70fr, Ancient covered bowl, Bandiala.

1967, Dec. 2 — Engr. — *Perf. 13*

295 A69 30fr grn, grnsh bl & red brn .25 .15
296 A69 70fr red brn, ocher & brt bl .60 .25

Nurse Feeding Child — A70

Human Rights Flame — A71

1967, Dec. 23

297 A70 50fr bl grn, red & red brn .45 .22

Issued for the Senegalese Red Cross.

1968, Jan. 20 — Photo. — *Perf. 13x12½*

298 A71 30fr brt grn & gold .30 .15

International Human Rights Year.

Parliament, Dakar — A72

1968, Apr. 16 — Photo. — *Perf. 12½x13*

299 A72 30fr car rose .25 .15

Inter-Parliamentary Union Meeting, Dakar.

Pied Kingfisher A73

Goose Barnacles A74

10fr, Green lobster. 15fr, African jacana. 20fr, Sea cicada. 35fr, Shrimp. 70fr, African anhinga.

1968-69 — Photo. — *Perf. 11½*
Dated "1968" or (70fr) "1969"
Granite Paper

300 A73 5fr brn & multi .15 .15
301 A74 10fr red & multi .15 .15
302 A73 15fr yel & multi .16 .15
303 A74 20fr ultra & multi .20 .15
304 A74 35fr car rose & ol grn .30 .20
305 A73 70fr Prus bl & multi .65 .35
306 A74 100fr yel grn & multi .90 .50
Nos. 300-306 (7) 2.51
Set value 1.35

Issued: 5fr, 7/13/68; 15fr, 12/21/68; 70fr, 4/26/69; others 5/18/68. See #C53-C57.

Steer and Hypodermic Syringe A75

1968, Aug. 17 — Engr. — *Perf. 13*

307 A75 30fr dk grn, dp bl & brn red .22 .16

Campaign against cattle plague.

Boy and WHO Emblem — A76

Bambara Antelope Symbol — A77

1968, Nov. 16 — Engr. — *Perf. 13*

308 A76 30fr blk, grn & car .25 .15
309 A76 45fr red brn, grn & blk .40 .20

WHO, 20th anniversary.

1969, Jan. 13 — Engr. — *Perf. 13*

Design: 30fr, School of Medicine and Pharmacology, Dakar, horiz.

310 A77 30fr emer, brt bl & ind .25 .16
311 A77 50fr red, gray ol & bl grn .40 .20

6th Medical Meeting, Dakar, Jan. 13-18.

Panet, Camels and Mogador-St. Louis Route — A78

1969, Feb. 15 — Engr. — *Perf. 13*

312 A78 75fr ultra, Prus bl & brn .60 .25

Leopold Panet (1819-1859), first explorer of the Mauritanian Sahara.

ILO Emblem A79

1969, May 3 — Photo. — *Perf. 12½x13*

313 A79 30fr blk & grnsh bl .22 .15
314 A79 45fr blk & dp car .40 .18

ILO, 50th anniversary.

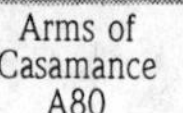

Arms of Casamance
A80

Mahatma Gandhi
A81

Design: 20fr, Arms of Gorée Island.

1969, July 26 Litho. *Perf. 13½*

315 A80 15fr rose & multi	.15	.15
316 A80 20fr bl & multi	.15	.15
Set value	.24	.15

Development Bank Issue
Common Design Type

1969, Sept. 10 Engr. *Perf. 13*

317 CD130 30fr gray, grn & ocher	.25	.16
318 CD130 45fr brn, grn & ocher	.40	.20

1969, Oct. 2 Engr. *Perf. 13*

319 A81 50fr multi	.52	.52
a. Miniature sheet of 4	2.25	2.25

Mohandas K. Gandhi (1869-1948), leader in India's fight for independence.

Rotary Emblem and Symbolic Ship — A82

1969, Nov. 29 Photo. *Perf. 12½x13*

320 A82 30fr ultra, yel & blk	.35	.20

Dakar Rotary Club, 30th anniversary.

ASECNA Issue
Common Design Type

1969, Dec. 12 Engr. *Perf. 13*

321 CD132 100fr dark gray	.65	.35

Niokolo-Koba Campsite
A83

Tourism: 20fr, Cape Skiring, Casamance. 35fr, Elephants at Niokolo-Koba National Park. 45fr, Millet granaries, pigs and boats, Fadiouth Island.

1969, Dec. 27

322 A83 20fr bl, red brn & ol	.16	.15
323 A83 30fr bl, red brn & ocher	.25	.15
324 A83 35fr grnsh bl, blk & ocher	.30	.16
325 A83 45fr vio bl & hn brn	.35	.16
Nos. 322-325 (4)	1.06	
Set value		.52

Bottle-nosed Dolphins
A84

Lenin (1870-1924)
A85

1970, Feb. 21 Photo. *Perf. 12x12½*

326 A84 50fr dl bl, blk & red	.40	.20

1970, Apr. 22 Photo. *Perf. 11½*

327 A85 30fr brn, buff & ver	.22	.16

Souvenir Sheet
Perf. 12x11½

327A A85 50fr brn, buff & ver	.40	.20

No. 327A contains one 32x48mm stamp.

UPU Headquarters Issue
Common Design Type

1970, May 20 Engr. *Perf. 13*

328 CD133 30fr dk red, ind & dp cl	.22	.15
329 CD133 45fr dl brn, dk car & bl grn	.40	.18

Textile Plant, Thies — A86

Design: 45fr, Fertilizer plant, Dakar.

1970, Nov. 21 Engr. *Perf. 13*

330 A86 30fr grn, brt bl & brn red	.25	.15
331 A86 45fr brn red & brt bl	.40	.18

Industrialization of Senegal.

Boy Scouts — A87

Three Heads and Sun — A88

Design: 100fr, Lord Baden-Powell, map of Africa with Dakar, and fleur-de-lis.

1970, Dec. 11 Photo. *Perf. 11½*

332 A87 30fr multi	.22	.15
333 A87 100fr multi	.80	.38

1st African Boy Scout Conf., Dakar, Dec. 11-14.

1970, Dec. 19 Engr. *Perf. 13*

Design: 40fr, African man and woman, globe with map of Africa.

334 A88 25fr ultra, org & vio brn	.25	.15
335 A88 40fr brn ol, dk brn & org	.45	.20

International Education Year.

Senegal Arms — A89

Refugees and UN Emblem — A90

1970-76 Photo. *Perf. 12*

336 A89 30fr yel grn & multi	.20	.15
336A A89 35fr brt pink & multi ('71)	.22	.15
b. Bklt. pane of 10 ('72)	2.50	
336C A89 50fr bl & multi ('75)	.25	.15
336D A89 65fr lil rose & multi ('76)	.35	.15
Nos. 336-336D (4)	1.02	
Set value		.40

The booklet pane has a control number in the margin.

See No. 654.

1971, Jan. 16 *Perf. 12½x12*

337 A90 40fr ver, blk, yel & grn	.35	.16

High Commissioner for Refugees, 20th anniversary. See No. C94.

Mare "Mbayang"
A91

Horses: 25fr, Mare Madjiguene. 100fr, Stallion Pass. 125fr, Stallion Pepe.

1971 Photo. *Perf. 11½*

338 A91 25fr multi	.20	.15
339 A91 40fr multi	.35	.16
340 A91 100fr multi	.70	.40
341 A91 125fr multi	.90	.40
Nos. 338-341 (4)	2.15	1.11

Improvements in horse breeding.

For surcharge see No. 392.

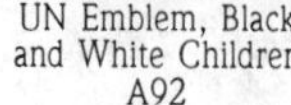

UN Emblem, Black and White Children
A92

Globe and Telephone
A94

UN Emblem, Four Races — A93

Perf. 13x12½, 12½x11

1971, Mar. 21 Litho.

342 A92 30fr multi	.22	.15
343 A93 50fr multi	.40	.20

Intl. Year against Racial Discrimination.

1971, May 17 Engr. *Perf. 13*

Design: 40fr, Radar, satellite, orbits.

344 A94 30fr pur, grn & brn	.22	.15
345 A94 40fr Prus bl, dk brn & red brn	.30	.15

3rd World Telecommunications Day.

Drummer (Hayashida) — A95

50fr, Dwarf Japanese quince and grape hyacinth. 65fr, Judo. 75fr, Mt. Fuji.

1971, Aug. 7 Photo. *Perf. 13½*

346 A95 35fr lt ultra & multi	.32	.15
347 A95 50fr yel & multi	.52	.20
348 A95 65fr dp org & multi	.65	.22
349 A95 75fr grn & multi	.80	.35
Nos. 346-349 (4)	2.29	.92

13th Boy Scout World Jamboree, Asagiri Plain, Japan, Aug. 2-10.

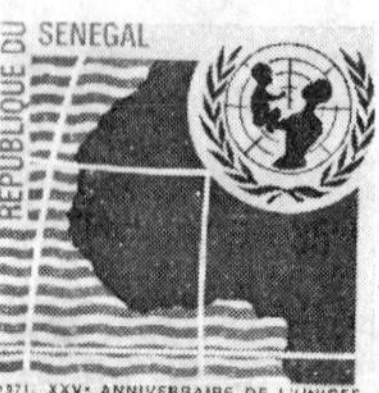

Map of West Africa with Senegal, UNICEF Emblem — A97

100fr, Nurse, children and UNICEF emblem.

1971, Oct. 30 *Perf. 12½*

352 A97 35fr dl bl, org & blk	.25	.15
353 A97 100fr multi	.80	.38

UNICEF, 25th anniv.

Basketball and Games' Emblem — A98

40fr, Basketball. 75fr, Emblem.

1971, Dec. 24 Photo. *Perf. 13½x13*

354 A98 35fr lt vio & multi	.30	.16
355 A98 40fr emer & multi	.35	.18
356 A98 75fr ocher & multi	.65	.38
Nos. 354-356 (3)	1.30	.72

6th African Basketball Championships, Dakar, Dec. 25, 1971-Jan. 2, 1972.

"The Exile of Albouri" — A99

Design: 40fr, "The Merchant of Venice."

1972, Mar. 25 *Perf. 13x12½*

357 A99 35fr dk red & multi	.30	.16
358 A99 40fr dk red & multi	.38	.20

Intl. Theater Day. See No. C112.

WHO Emblem and Heart
A100

Design: 40fr, Physician with patient, WHO emblem and electrocardiogram.

1972, Apr. 7 Engr. *Perf. 13*

359 A100 35fr brt bl & red brn	.25	.15
360 A100 40fr slate grn & brn	.30	.16

"Your heart is your health," World Health Month.

Containment of the Desert, Environment Emblem — A101

1972, June 3 Photo. *Perf. 13x12½*

361 A101 35fr multi	.30	.16

UN Conference on Human Environment, Stockholm, June 5-16. See No. C113.

Tartarin Shooting the Lion — A102

Design: 100fr, Alphonse Daudet.

1972, June 24 Engr. *Perf. 13*

362 A102 40fr brt grn, rose car & brn	.35	.15
363 A102 100fr Prus bl, bl & brn	.80	.35

Alphonse Daudet (1840-1897), French novelist, and centenary of the publication of his "Tartarin de Tarascon."

Souvenir Sheet

Stringed Instrument — A103

1972, July 1 **Engr.** ***Perf. 11½***
364 A103 150fr rose red 1.25 1.00

Belgica 72, Intl. Phil. Exhib., Brussels, June 24-July 9. No. 364 contains one stamp in design similar to No. 267.

Wrestling, Olympic Rings — A104

1972, July 22 **Photo.** ***Perf. 14x13½***
365 A104 15fr shown .15 .15
366 A104 20fr 100-meter dash .16 .15
367 A104 100fr Basketball .65 .35
368 A104 125fr Judo .80 .40
Nos. 365-368 (4) 1.76
Set value .92

Souvenir Sheet

Perf. 13½x14½

369 A104 240fr Torchbearer and Munich 1.90 1.60

20th Olympic Games, Munich, Aug. 26-Sept. 11.

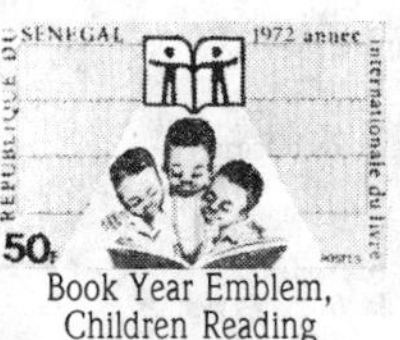

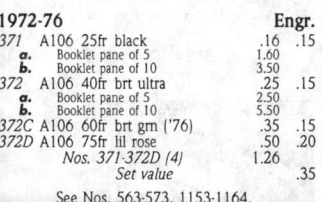

Book Year Emblem, Children Reading A105

Senegalese Fashion A106

1972, Sept. 16 **Photo.** ***Perf. 13***
370 A105 50fr gray & multi .38 .16

International Book Year.

1972-76 **Engr.**
371 A106 25fr black .16 .15
a. Booklet pane of 5 1.60
b. Booklet pane of 10 3.50
372 A106 40fr brt ultra .25 .15
a. Booklet pane of 5 2.50
b. Booklet pane of 10 5.50
372C A106 60fr brt grn ('76) .35 .15
372D A106 75fr lil rose .50 .20
Nos. 371-372D (4) 1.26
Set value .35

See Nos. 563-573, 1153-1164.

Aleksander Pushkin — A107

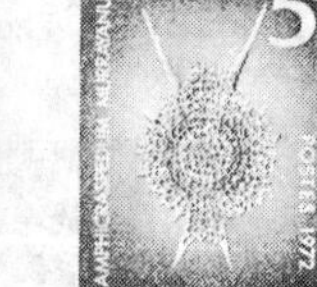

Amphicrasphedum Murrayanum — A108

1972, Oct. 28 **Photo.** ***Perf. 11½***
373 A107 100fr salmon & purple .80 .40

Aleksander Pushkin (1799-1837), Russian writer.

West African Monetary Union Issue

Common Design Type

Design: 40fr, African couple, city, village and commemorative coin.

1972, Nov. 2 **Engr.** ***Perf. 13***
374 CD136 40fr ol brn, bl & gray .30 .16

1972-73 **Photo.** ***Perf. 11½***

Marine Life: 10fr, Pterocanium tricolpum. 15fr, Ceratospyris polygona. 20fr, Cortiniscus typicus. 30fr, Theopera cortina.

375 A108 5fr multi .15 .15
376 A108 10fr multi .15 .15
377 A108 15fr multi .15 .15
378 A108 20fr multi .15 .15
379 A108 30fr multi .16 .15
Nos. 375-379,C115-C118 (9) 2.86
Set value 1.30

Issued: #375-377, 11/25/72; #378-379, 7/28/73.

1872-1972

100F

No. 288 Surcharged in Vermilion

1972, Dec. 9 **Engr.** ***Perf. 13***
380 A64 100fr on 30fr multi .60 .30

Blaise Diagne (1872-1934).

Melchior — A109

Black and White Men Carrying Emblem — A110

1972, Dec. 23 **Photo.** ***Perf. 13x13½***
381 A109 10fr shown .15 .15
382 A109 15fr Caspar .15 .15
383 A109 40fr Balthasar .22 .15
384 A109 60fr Joseph .30 .20
385 A109 100fr Virgin and Child .50 .32
a. Strip of 5, #381-385 1.30 1.00
Set value .72

Christmas. No. 385a has continuous design, showing traditional Gorée dolls.

Europafrica Issue

1973, Jan. 20 **Engr.** ***Perf. 13***
386 A110 65fr blk & grn .42 .22

Radar Station, Gandoul A111

1973, May 17 **Engr.** ***Perf. 13***
387 A111 40fr multi .25 .16

Phases of Solar Eclipse A112

Designs: 65fr, Moon between earth and sun casting shadow on earth. 150fr, Diagram of areas of partial and total eclipse, satellite in space.

1973, June 30 **Photo.** ***Perf. 13x14***
388 A112 35fr dk bl & multi .22 .15
389 A112 65fr dk bl & multi .38 .25
390 A112 150fr dk bl & multi .90 .60
Nos. 388-390 (3) 1.50 1.00

Total solar eclipse over Africa, June 30.

Men Holding Torch over Africa — A113

1973, July 7 ***Perf. 12½x13***
391 A113 75fr multi .42 .30

Org. for African Unity, 10th anniv.

No. 338 Surcharged with New Value, 2 Bars, and Overprinted in Ultramarine: "SECHERESSE / SOLIDARITE AFRICAINE"

1973, July 21 **Photo.** ***Perf. 11½***
392 A91 100fr on 25fr multi .60 .40

African solidarity in drought emergency.

African Postal Union Issue

Common Design Type

1973, Sept. 12 **Engr.** ***Perf. 13***
393 CD137 100fr dk grn, vio & dk red .60 .30

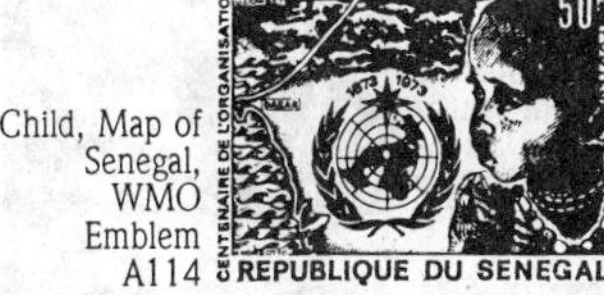

Child, Map of Senegal, WMO Emblem A114

1973, Sept. 22
394 A114 50fr multi .30 .15

Intl. meteorological cooperation, cent.

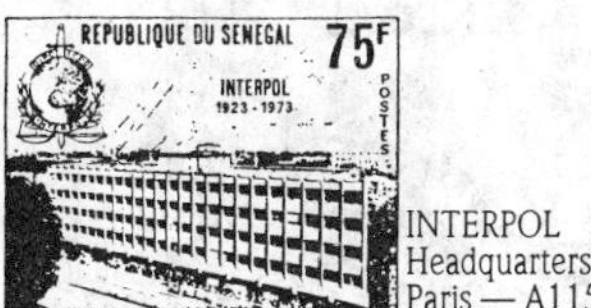

INTERPOL Headquarters, Paris — A115

1973, Oct. 6 **Engr.** ***Perf. 13***
395 A115 75fr ultra, bis & slate grn .42 .25

50th anniv. of Intl. Criminal Police Org.

Souvenir Sheet

John F. Kennedy (1917-1963) A116

1973, Nov. 22 **Engr.** ***Perf. 13***
396 A116 150fr ultra 1.00 1.00

Amilcar Cabral — A117

Victorious Athletes and Flag — A118

1973, Dec. 15 **Photo.** ***Perf. 12½x13***
397 A117 75fr multi .42 .35

Cabral (1924-1973), leader of anti-Portuguese guerrilla movement in Portuguese Guinea.

1974, Apr. 6 **Photo.** ***Perf. 12½x13***
398 A118 35fr shown .22 .15
399 A118 40fr Folk theater .30 .20

National Youth Week.

Soccer Cup, Yugoslavia-Brazil Game, Our Lady's Church, Munich — A119

Soccer Cup and Games: 40fr, Australia-Germany (Fed. Rep.) and Belltower, Hamburg. 65fr, Netherlands-Uruguay and Tower, Hanover. 70fr, Zaire-Italy and Church, Stuttgart.

1974, June 29 **Photo.** ***Perf. 13x14***
400 A119 25fr car & multi .16 .15
401 A119 40fr car & multi .25 .16
402 A119 65fr car & multi .40 .16
403 A119 70fr car & multi .42 .18
Nos. 400-403 (4) 1.23 .65

World Cup Soccer Championship, Munich, June 13-July 7.

For surcharge see No. 406.

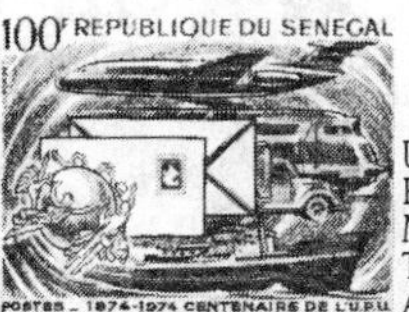

UPU Emblem, Envelopes and Means of Transportation A120

1974, Oct. 9 **Engr.** ***Perf. 13***
404 A120 100fr multi .60 .40

Centenary of Universal Postal Union.

Fair Emblem — A121

1974, Nov. 28 **Engr.** ***Perf. 12½x13***
405 A121 100fr bl, org & dk brn .55 .35

Dakar International Fair.

200F

ALLEMAGNE RFA—HOLLANDE 2-1

No. 401 Surcharged in Black on Gold

1975, Feb. 1 **Photo.** ***Perf. 13x14***
406 A119 200fr on 40fr multi 1.10 .65

World Cup Soccer Championships, 1974, victory of German Federal Republic.

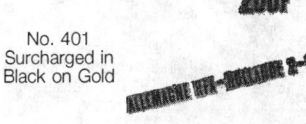

Pres. Senghor and King Baudouin A122

1975, Feb. 28 **Photo.** ***Perf. 13x13½***
407 A122 65fr lil & dk bl .35 .20
408 A122 100fr org & grn .55 .35

Visit of King Baudouin of Belgium.

ILO Emblem — A123

1975, Apr. 30 **Photo.** ***Perf. 13½x13***
409 A123 125fr multi .65 .38

International Labor Festival.

Globe, Stamp, Letters, España 75 Emblem — A124

1975, June 6 Engr. *Perf. 13*
410 A124 55fr indigo, grn & red .30 .20

Espana 75 Intl. Phil. Exhib., Madrid, Apr. 4-13.

Apollo of Belvedere, Arphila 75 Emblem, Stamps — A125

1975, June 6
411 A125 95fr dk brn, brn & bis .50 .35

Arphila 75 International Philatelic Exhibition, Paris, June 6-16.

Professional Instruction — A126

1975, June 28 Engr. *Perf. 13*
412 A126 85fr multi .45 .25

Dr. Albert Schweitzer (1875-1965), Medical Missionary, Lambarene Hospital — A127

1975, July 5
413 A127 85fr grn & vio brn .45 .25

Senegalese Soldier, Batallion Flag, Map of Sinai — A128

1975, July 10 Litho. *Perf. 12½*
414 A128 100fr multi .75 .35

Senegalese Battalion of the UN' Sinai Service, 1973-74.

Women and Child — A129

55fr, Women pounding grain, vert.

1975, Oct. 18 Photo. *Perf. 13½*
415 A129 55fr silver & multi .30 .15
416 A129 75fr silver & multi .40 .20

International Women's Year.

Staff of Aesculapius and African Mask — A130

1975, Dec. 1 Photo. *Perf. 12½x13*
417 A130 50fr multi .25 .15

40th French Medical Cong., Dakar, Dec. 1-3.

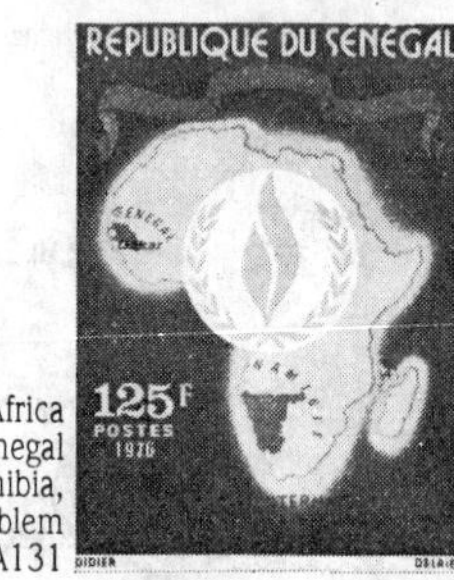

Map of Africa with Senegal and Namibia, UN Emblem A131

1976, Jan. 5 Photo. *Perf. 13*
418 A131 125fr vio bl & multi .65 .35

International Human Rights and Namibia Conference, Dakar, Jan. 5-8.

Sailfish Fishing A132

200fr, Racing yachts & Oceanexpo 75 emblem.

1976, Jan. 28 Photo. *Perf. 13½x13*
419 A132 140fr multi .70 .38
420 A132 200fr multi 1.10 .55

Oceanexpo 75, 1st Intl. Oceanographic Exhib., Okinawa, July 20, 1975-Jan. 1976.

Servals — A133

Designs: 3fr, Black-tailed godwits. 4fr, River hogs. 5fr, African fish eagles. No. 425, Okapis. No. 426, Sitatungas.

1976, Feb. 26 Photo. *Perf. 13*
421 A133 2fr gold & multi .15 .15
422 A133 3fr gold & multi .15 .15
423 A133 4fr gold & multi .15 .15
424 A133 5fr gold & multi .15 .15
425 A133 250fr gold & multi 1.40 .65
426 A133 250fr gold & multi 1.40 .65
a. Strip of 2, #425-426 + label 3.00
Set value 3.00 1.50

Basse Casamance National Park.
See Nos. 473-478.

A. G. Bell, Telephone, ITU Emblem — A134

1976, Mar. 31 Litho. *Perf. 12½x13*
427 A134 175fr multi .90 .42

Centenary of first telephone call by Alexander Graham Bell, Mar. 10, 1876.

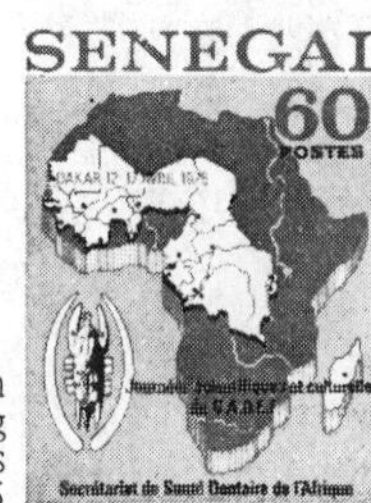

Map of African French-speaking Countries A135

1976, Apr. 12 Litho. *Perf. 13½*
428 A135 60fr yel grn & multi .35 .20

Scientific and Cultural Meeting of the African Dental Association, Dakar, Apr. 12-17.

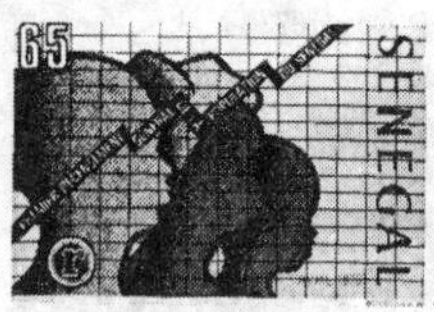

Family and Graph A136

1976, Apr. 26
429 A136 65fr multi .35 .20

1st population census in Senegal, Apr. 1976.

Thomas Jefferson and 13-star Flag — A137

1976, June 19 Engr. *Perf. 13*
430 A137 50fr bl, red & blk .25 .15

American Bicentennial.

Planting Seedlings — A138

1976, Aug. 21 Litho. *Perf. 12*
431 A138 60fr yel & multi .35 .16

Reclamation of Sahel region.

Campfire A139

Jamboree Emblem, Map of Africa — A140

1976, Aug. 30 Litho. *Perf. 12½*
432 A139 80fr multi .42 .35
433 A140 100fr multi .55 .40

1st All Africa Scout Jamboree, Sherehills, Jos, Nigeria, Apr. 2-8, 1977.

A140a

1976 Summer Olympics, Montreal — A140b

1976, Sept. 11 Litho. *Perf. 13½*
433A A140a 5fr Swimming
433B A140a 10fr Weightlifting
433C A140a 15fr Hurdles, horiz.
433D A140a 20fr Equestrian, horiz.
433E A140a 25fr Steeplechase, horiz.
433F A140a 50fr Wrestling
433G A140a 60fr Field hockey
433H A140a 65fr Track
433I A140a 70fr Women's gymnastics
433J A140a 100fr Cycling, horiz.
433K A140a 400fr Boxing
433L A140a 500fr Judo

Litho. & Embossed

433M A140b 1000fr Basketball

Souvenir Sheet

433Q A140b 1000fr Boxers, city skyline

Nos. 433K-433Q are airmail.

Mechanized Tomato Harvest A141

1976, Oct. 23 Photo. *Perf. 13*
434 A141 180fr multi 1.00 .42

Map of Dakar and Gorée A142

Designs: 60fr, Star over Africa. 70fr, Students in laboratory and library. 200fr, Handshake over world map, Pres. Senghor.

1976, Oct. 9 Litho. *Perf. 13½x14*

435 A142 40fr multi .15 .15
436 A142 60fr multi .20 .16
437 A142 70fr multi .20 .20
438 A142 200fr multi .58 .55
Nos. 435-438 (4) 1.13 1.06

70th birthday of Pres. Leopold Sedar Senghor.

Scroll with Map of Africa, Senegalese People — A143

1977, Jan. 8 *Perf. 12½*

439 A143 60fr multi .35 .16

Day of the Black People.

Joe Frazier and Muhammad Ali — A144

Design: 60fr, Ali and Frazier in ring, vert.

1977, Jan. 7 Photo. *Perf. 13x13½*

440 A144 60fr blue & blk .65 .16
441 A144 150fr emerald & blk 1.20 .40

World boxing champion Muhammad Ali.

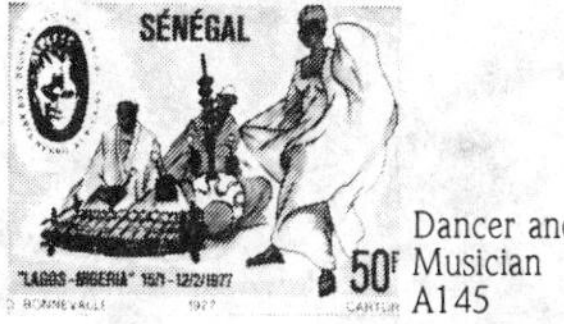

Dancer and Musician A145

Festival Emblem and: 75fr, Wood carving and masks. 100fr, Dancers and ancestor statuette.

1977, Feb. 10 Litho. *Perf. 12½*

442 A145 50fr yellow & multi .25 .15
443 A145 75fr green & multi .40 .20
444 A145 100fr rose & multi .55 .25
Nos. 442-444 (3) 1.20 .60

2nd World Black and African Festival, Lagos, Nigeria, Jan. 15-Feb. 12.

Cogwheels and Symbols of Industry — A146

1977, Mar. 28 Engr. *Perf. 13*

445 A146 70fr yel grn & ocher .38 .18

Dakar Industrial Zone, 1st anniversary.

Burning Match and Burnt Trees — A147

60fr, Burnt trees and house, fire-truck, horiz.

1977, Apr. 30 Litho. *Perf. 12½*

446 A147 40fr green & multi .20 .15
447 A147 60fr slate & multi .35 .16

Prevention of forest fires.

Drummer, Telephone, Agriculture and Industry — A148

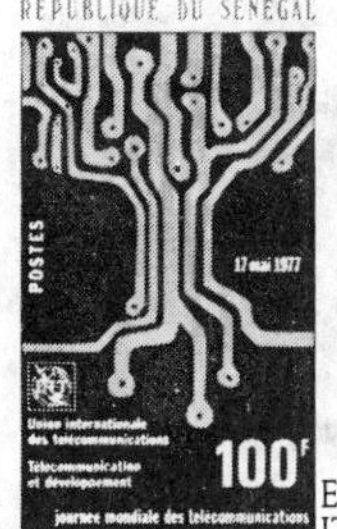

Electronic Tree and ITU Emblem — A149

1977, May 17 Litho. *Perf. 13*

448 A148 80fr multi .35 .22
449 A149 100fr multi .40 .25

World Telecommunications Day.

Symbol of Language Studies — A150

Sassenage Castle, Grenoble — A151

Perf. 12x12½, 12½

1977, May 21 Litho.

450 A150 65fr multi 22 .18
451 A151 250fr multi 1.00 .65

10th anniv. of Intl. French Language Council.

Woman in Boat, Wooden Shoe A152

Design: 125fr, Senegalese woman, symbolic tulip and stamp, vert.

1977, June 4 *Perf. 13½x14, 14x13½*

452 A152 50fr blue grn & multi .25 .15
453 A152 125fr ocher & multi .65 .35

Amphilex '77 International Philatelic Exhibition, Amsterdam, May 26-June 5.

Adult Reading Class — A153

Design: 65fr, Man learning to read.

1977, Sept. 10 Litho. *Perf. 12½*

454 A153 60fr multi .35 .16
455 A153 65fr multi .38 .16

National Literacy Week, Sept. 8-14.

A154 A155

Paintings: 20fr, Mercury, by Rubens. 25fr, Daniel in the Lions' Den, by Peter Paul Rubens (1577-1640). 40fr, The Empress, by Titian (1477-1576). 60fr, Flora, by Titian. 65fr, Jo, the Beautiful Irish Woman, by Gustave Courbet (1819-1877). 100fr, The Painter's Studio, by Courbet.

1977, Nov. Photo. *Perf. 13x13½*

456 A154 20fr multi .15 .15
457 A154 25fr multi .15 .15
458 A154 40fr multi .20 .15
459 A154 60fr multi .30 .16
460 A154 65fr multi .35 .18
461 A154 100fr multi .55 .25
Nos. 456-461 (6) 1.70
Set value .80

1977, Dec. 22 Litho. *Perf. 12½*

Christmas: 20fr, Adoration by People of Various Races. 25fr, Decorated arch and procession. 40fr, Christmas tree, mother and child. 100fr, Adoration of the Kings, horiz.

462 A155 20fr multi .15 .15
463 A155 25fr multi .15 .15
464 A155 40fr multi .20 .15
465 A155 100fr multi .55 .25
Nos. 462-465 (4) 1.05
Set value .46

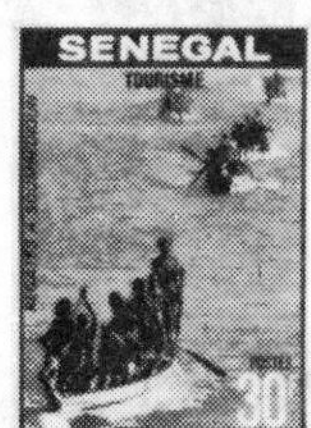

Regatta at Soumbedioun A156

Tourism: 10fr, Senegalese wrestlers. 65fr, Regatta at Soumbedioun. 100fr, Dancers.

1978, Jan. 7 Litho. *Perf. 12½*

466 A156 10fr multi .15 .15
467 A156 30fr multi .16 .15
468 A156 65fr multi, horiz. .35 .18
469 A156 100fr multi, horiz. .55 .25
Nos. 466-469 (4) 1.21
Set value .55

Acropolis, Athens, and African Buildings A157

1978, Jan. 30

470 A157 75fr multi .40 .20

UNESCO campaign to save world's cultural heritage.

Solar-powered Pump, Field and Sheep — A158

Energy in Senegal: 95fr, Pylon bringing electricity to villages and factories.

1978, Feb. 25

471 A158 50fr multi .25 .15
472 A158 95fr multi .50 .25

Park Type of 1976

5fr, Caspian terns in flight, royal terns on ground. 10fr, Pink-backed pelicans. 15fr, Wart hog & gray heron. 20fr, Greater flamingoes, nests, eggs & young. #477, Gray heron & royal terns. #478, Abyssinian ground hornbill & wart hog.

1978, Apr. 22 Photo. *Perf. 13*

473 A133 5fr gold & multi .15 .15
474 A133 10fr gold & multi .15 .15
475 A133 15fr gold & multi .15 .15
476 A133 20fr gold & multi .15 .15
477 A133 150fr gold & multi 1.00 .65
478 A133 150fr gold & multi 1.00 .65
a. Strip of 2, #477-478 + label 2.00
Nos. 473-478 (6) 2.60
Set value 1.50

Salum Delta National Park.

Dome of the Rock, Jerusalem — A159

1978, May 15 Litho. *Perf. 12½*

479 A159 60fr multi .40 .15

Palestinian fighters and their families.

Vaccination, Dr. Jenner, WHO Emblem A160

1978, June 3

480 A160 60fr multi .40 .15

Eradication of smallpox.

Soccer, Flags: Argentina, Hungary, France, Italy — A161

Mahatma Gandhi — A162

Soccer, Cup, Argentina '78 Emblem and Flags of: 40fr, No. 486a, Poland, German Democratic Rep., Tunisia, Mexico. 65fr, 125fr, Austria, Spain, Sweden, Brazil. 75fr, No. 484, Netherlands, Iran, Peru, Scotland. 150fr, like 25fr.

1978, June 24 Photo. *Perf. 13*

481 A161 25fr multi .15 .15
482 A161 40fr multi .20 .15
483 A161 65fr multi .32 .15
484 A161 100fr multi .50 .22
Nos. 481-484 (4) 1.17
Set value .48

Souvenir Sheets

485 Sheet of 2 1.10
a. A161 75fr multi .38
b. A161 125fr multi .65
486 Sheet of 2 1.40
a. A161 100fr multi .50
b. A161 150fr multi .75

11th World Cup Soccer Championship, Argentina, June 1-25.

1978, June 27 *Perf. 12*

Design: 150fr, No. 489a, Martin Luther King. No. 489b, like 125fr.

487 A162 125fr multi .95 .35
488 A162 150fr multi 1.25 .40

Souvenir Sheet

489	Sheet of 2	3.50	
a.	A162 200fr multi	1.65	
b.	A162 200fr multi	1.65	

Mahatma Gandhi and Martin Luther King, advocates of non-violence.

Homes and Industry — A163

1978, Aug. 5 Litho. *Perf. 12½*

490 A163 110fr multi		.70	.30

3rd Intl. Fair, Dakar, Nov. 28-Dec. 10.

Wright Brothers and Flyer — A164

Designs: 150fr, like 75fr. 100fr, 250fr, Yuri Gagarin and spacecraft. 200fr, 300fr, US astronauts Frank Borman, William Anders, James Lovell Jr. and spacecraft.

1978, Sept. 25 Litho. *Perf. 13½x14*

491 A164	75fr multi	.50	.20
492 A164	100fr multi	.65	.28
493 A164	200fr multi	1.40	.55
	Nos. 491-493 (3)	2.55	1.03

Souvenir Sheet

494	Sheet of 3	4.00	
a.	A164 150fr multi	.60	
b.	A164 250fr multi	1.40	
c.	A164 300fr multi	2.00	

75th anniv. of 1st powered flight; 10th anniv. of the death of Yuri Gagarin, first man in space; 10th anniv. of Apollo 8 flight around moon.

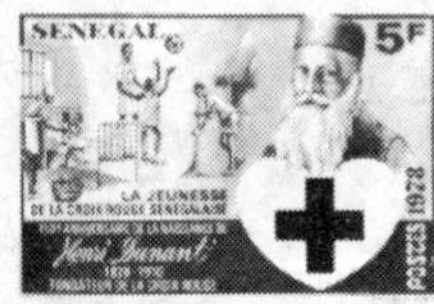

Henri Dunant (1828-1910), Founder of Red Cross, and Patients A165

Design: 20fr, Henri Dunant, First Aid station, Red Cross flag.

1978, Oct. 28 Photo. *Perf. 11½*

495 A165	5fr brt blue & red	.15	.15
496 A165	20fr multi	.15	.15
	Set value	.18	.15

Bedside Lecture and Emblem — A166

100fr, Pollution, fish and mercury bottles.

1979, Jan. 15 Litho. *Perf. 13½x13*

497 A166	50fr multi	.35	.15
498 A166	100fr multi	.65	.25

9th Medical Days, Dakar, Jan. 15-20.

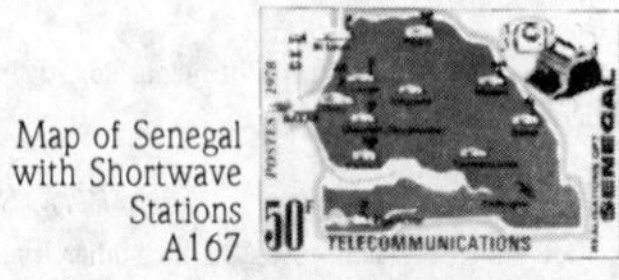

Map of Senegal with Shortwave Stations A167

Designs: 60fr, Children on vacation, ambulance, soccer player. 65fr, Rural mobile post office.

1978, Dec. 27 Litho. *Perf. 13½x13*

499 A167	50fr multi	.35	.15
500 A167	60fr multi	.40	.16
501 A167	65fr multi	.42	.18
	Nos. 499-501 (3)	1.17	.49

Achievements of postal service.

Farmer A168

Design: 150fr, Factories, communication, transportation, fish, physician and worker.

1979, Feb. 17 Litho. *Perf. 12½*

502 A168	30fr multi	.20	.15
503 A168	150fr multi	1.00	.40

Pride in workmanship.

Children's Village and Children — A169

Design: 60fr, Different view of village.

1979, Mar. 30 *Perf. 12x12½*

504 A169	40fr multi	.25	.15
505 A169	60fr multi	.40	.16

Children's SOS villages.

Infant, Physician Vaccinating Child, IYC Emblem — A170

65fr, Boys with book and globe, IYC emblem.

1979, Apr. 24 Litho. *Perf. 13½x13*

506 A170	60fr multi	.40	.16
507 A170	65fr multi	.42	.18

International Year of the Child.

Drum, Carrier Pigeon, Satellite A171

Design: 60fr, Baobab tree and flower, Independence monument with lion, vert.

1979, June 8 *Perf. 12½x13*

Size: 36x48mm

508 A171	60fr multi	.40	.16

Perf. 12½

Size: 36x36mm

509 A171	150fr multi	1.00	.40

Philexafrique II, Libreville, Gabon, June 8-17. Nos. 508, 509 each printed with labels showing UAPT '79 emblem.

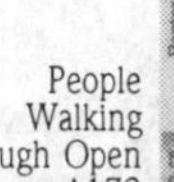

People Walking through Open Book — A172

1979, Sept. 15 Photo. *Perf. 11½x12*

510 A172	250fr multi	1.90	.65

Intl. Bureau of Education, Geneva, 50th anniv.

Sir Rowland Hill (1795-1879), Originator of Penny Postage, Type AP3 with Exhibition Cancel — A173

1979, Oct. 9 *Perf. 11½*

511 A173	500fr multi	3.50	1.40

Black Trees, by Hundertwasser A174

Perf. 13½x14

1979, Dec. 10 Litho. & Engr.

512 A174	60fr shown	.40	.16
a.	Souvenir sheet of 4	1.90	.80
513 A174	100fr Head of a man	.65	.25
a.	Souvenir sheet of 4	3.00	1.20
514 A174	200fr Rainbow windows	1.40	.55
a.	Souvenir sheet of 4	5.75	2.25
	Nos. 512-514 (3)	2.45	.96

Paintings by Friedensreich Hundertwasser, pseudonym of Friedrich Stowasser (b. 1928).

Running, Championship Emblem — A175

1980, Jan. 14 Litho. *Perf. 13*

515 A175	20fr shown	.15	.15
516 A175	25fr Javelin	.16	.15
517 A175	50fr Relay race	.35	.15
518 A175	100fr Discus	.80	.25
	Nos. 515-518 (4)	1.46	
	Set value		.50

1st African Athletic Championships.

Mudra Afrique Arts Festival A176

1980, Mar. 22 Photo. *Perf. 14*

519 A176	50fr Musicians	.35	.15
520 A176	100fr Dancers, festival building	.65	.25
521 A176	200fr Drummer, dancers	1.40	.55
	Nos. 519-521 (3)	2.40	.95

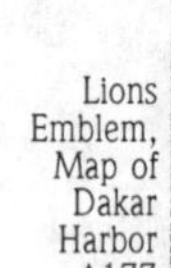

Lions Emblem, Map of Dakar Harbor A177

1980, May 17 Litho. *Perf. 13*

522 A177	100fr multi	.80	.25

22nd Congress, Lions Intl. District 403, Dakar.

Chimpanzees — A178

1980, June 2 Photo. *Perf. 13½*

523 A178	40fr shown	.25	.15
524 A178	60fr Elephants	.40	.16
525 A178	65fr Derby's elands	.42	.18
526 A178	100fr Hyenas	.65	.25
527	Pair	2.50	1.10
a.	A178 200fr Herd	1.25	.55
b.	A178 200fr Guest house	1.25	.55
	Nos. 523-527 (5)	4.22	1.84

Souvenir Sheet

528	Sheet of 4	4.00	1.40
a.	A178 125fr like #523	1.00	.35
b.	A178 125fr like #524	1.00	.35
c.	A178 125fr like #525	1.00	.35
d.	A178 125fr like #526	1.00	.35

Niokolo Koba National Park. No. 527 printed in continuous design with label showing location of park.

Tree Planting Year — A179

1980, June 27 Litho. *Perf. 13*

529 A179	60fr multi	.40	.16
530 A179	65fr multi	.42	.18

Rural Women Workers — A180

Rural women workers. 50fr, 200fr, horiz.

1980, July 19

531 A180	50fr multi	.35	.15
532 A180	100fr multi	.65	.25
533 A180	200fr multi	1.40	.55
	Nos. 531-533 (3)	2.40	.95

Wrestling, Moscow '80 Emblem — A181

1980, Aug. 21 *Perf. 14½*
534 A181 60fr shown .40 .16
535 A181 65fr Running .42 .18
536 A181 70fr Sports, map showing Moscow .45 .20
537 A181 100fr Judo .80 .25
538 A181 200fr Basketball 1.60 .55
Nos. 534-538 (5) 3.67 1.34

Souvenir Sheet

539 Sheet of 2 1.50
a. A181 75fr like #534 .50 .22
b. A181 125fr like #535 .80 .35
540 Sheet of 2 1.50
a. A181 75fr like #527 .50 .22
b. A181 125fr like #538 .80 .35

22nd Summer Olympic Games, Moscow, July 19-Aug. 3.

Caspian Tern and Sea Gulls, Kalissaye Bird Sanctuary A182

National Park Wildlife: 70fr, Laughing gulls and Hansel's tern, Barbarie Spit. 85fr, Turtle and crab, Madeleine Islands. 150fr, Cormorant, Madeleine Islands.

1981, Jan. 31 **Litho.** *Perf. 14½x14*
541 A182 50fr multi .50 .15
542 A182 70fr multi .65 .20
543 A182 85fr multi .75 .22
544 A182 150fr multi 1.20 .40
Nos. 541-544 (4) 3.10 .97

Souvenir Sheet

545 Sheet of 4 4.00 1.40
a. A182 125fr like #541 1.00 .35
b. A182 125fr like #542 1.00 .35
c. A182 125fr like #543 1.00 .35
d. A182 125fr like #544 1.00 .35

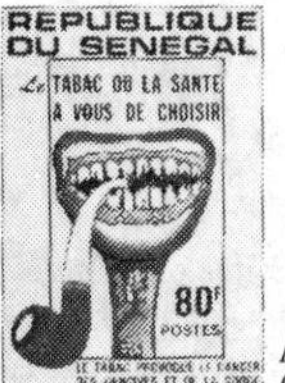

Anti-Tobacco Campaign — A183

1981, June 20 **Litho.** *Perf. 13*
546 A183 75fr Healthy people .50 .20
547 A183 80fr shown .55 .22

4th Intl. Dakar Fair, Nov. 25-Dec. 7 A184

1981, Sept. 19 **Litho.** *Perf. 12½*
548 A184 80fr multi .55 .22

Natl. Hero Lat Dior A185

1982, Jan. 11 **Photo.** *Perf. 14*
549 A185 80fr Portrait, vert. .55 .22
550 A185 500fr Battle 3.50 1.40

Local Flora — A186

1982, Feb. 1 *Perf. 11½*
551 A186 50fr Nymphaea lotus .35 .15
552 A186 75fr Strophanthus sarmentosus .50 .20
553 A186 200fr Crinum moorei 1.40 .55
554 A186 225fr Cochlospermum tinctorium 1.50 .60
Nos. 551-554 (4) 3.75 1.50

Inscribed 1981.

Euryphrene Senegalensis A187

1982, Feb. 27 **Litho.** *Perf. 14*
555 A187 45fr shown .30 .15
556 A187 55fr Hypolimnas salmacis .38 .15
557 A187 75fr Cymothoe caenis .50 .20
558 A187 80fr Precis cebrene .55 .22
Nos. 555-558 (4) 1.73 .72

Souvenir Sheet

Perf. 14½

559 Sheet of 4 6.00 2.00
a. A187 100fr like 45fr .65 .25
b. A187 150fr like 55fr 1.00 .40
c. A187 200fr like 75fr 1.40 .55
d. A187 250fr like 80fr 1.60 .65

Destructive Insects — A188

Banner and Stamp — A189

Various insects. 80fr, 100fr horiz.

1982, Apr. 7 **Litho.** *Perf. 14*
560 A188 75fr multi .50 .20
561 A188 80fr multi .55 .22
562 A188 100fr multi .65 .25
Nos. 560-562 (3) 1.70 .67

Fashion Type of 1972

1982-93 **Engr.** *Perf. 13*
563 A106 5fr Prus blue .15 .15
564 A106 10fr dull red .15 .15
565 A106 15fr orange .15 .15
566 A106 20fr dk purple .15 .15
567 A106 30fr henna brn .20 .15
568 A106 45fr orange yellow .35 .18
569 A106 50fr bright magenta .38 .20
570 A106 90fr brt carmine .25 .15
571 A106 125fr ultramarine .95 .48
572 A106 145fr orange .75 .35
573 A106 180fr gray blue 1.40 .70
Nos. 563-573 (11) 4.88 2.81

Issued: 5fr, 10fr, 15fr, 20fr, 30fr, Apr. 30; 90fr, Dec., 1984; 180fr, 1991; 45fr, 50fr, 125fr, 1993; 145fr, 1995.

1982, Dec. 30 **Photo.** *Perf. 13*
575 A189 100fr shown .50 .25
576 A189 500fr Stamp, arrows 3.00 1.40

PHILEXFRANCE Intl. Stamp Exhibition, Paris, June 11-21.

Senegambia Confederation, Feb. 1 — A190

1982, Nov. 15 **Litho.** *Perf. 12½*
577 A190 225fr Map, flags 1.00 .65
578 A190 350fr Arms 1.60 1.00

Local Birds — A191

1982 World Cup — A192

1982, Dec. 1 **Photo.** *Perf. 11½*

Granite Paper

579 A191 45fr Godwit .30 .15
580 A191 75fr Jabiru .50 .20
581 A191 80fr Francolin .55 .22
582 A191 500fr Eagle 3.50 1.40
Nos. 579-582 (4) 4.85 1.97

1982, Dec. 11 **Litho.** *Perf. 12½x13*
583 A192 30fr Player .20 .15
584 A192 50fr Player, diff. .35 .15
585 A192 75fr Ball .50 .20
586 A192 80fr Cup .55 .22
Nos. 583-586 (4) 1.60 .72

Souvenir Sheets

Perf. 12½

587 A192 75fr like 30fr .50 .25
588 A192 100fr like 50fr .65 .35
589 A192 150fr like 75fr 1.00 .50
590 A192 200fr like 80fr 1.40 .65
Nos. 587-590 (4) 3.55 1.75

A193

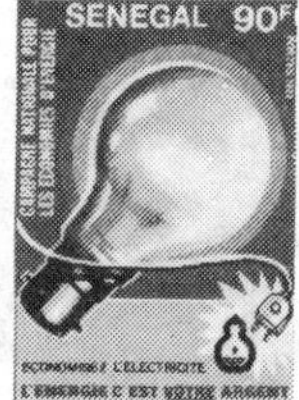

A194

Designs: 60fr, Exhibition poster, viewers, horiz. 70fr, Simulated butterfly stamps. 90fr, Simulated stamps under magnifying glass. 95fr, Coat of Arms over Exhibition Building.

1983, Aug. 6 **Litho.** *Perf. 12½*
591 A193 60fr multi .20 .15
592 A193 70fr multi .22 .15
593 A193 90fr multi .30 .15
594 A193 95fr multi .32 .16
Nos. 591-594 (4) 1.04
Set value .52

Dakar '82 Stamp Exhibition.

1983, Oct. 25 **Litho.** *Perf. 12½x13*
595 A194 90fr Electricity .30 .15
596 A194 95fr Gasoline .32 .16
597 A194 260fr Coal, wood .90 .42
Nos. 595-597 (3) 1.52 .73

Energy conservation.

Namibia Day — A195

1983, Nov. 14 **Litho.** *Perf. 13½x13*
598 A195 90fr Torch .30 .15
599 A195 95fr Chain, fist .32 .16
600 A195 260fr Woman bearing torch .90 .42
Nos. 598-600 (3) 1.52 .73

West African Monetary Union, 20th Anniv. — A196

Dakar Alizes Rotary Club, First Anniv. — A197

Designs: 60fr, Mask emblem, Ziguinchor Agency building, Dakar, horiz. 65fr, Monetary Union headquarters, emblem.

Perf. 13½x13, 13x13½

1983, Nov. 28
601 A196 60fr multi .20 .15
602 A196 65fr multi .20 .15
Set value .22

1983, Dec. 5 *Perf. 13x13½*
603 A197 70fr green & multi .22 .15
604 A197 500fr blue & multi 1.60 .80

Customs Cooperation Council, 30th Anniv. — A198

Economic Comm. for Africa, 25th Anniv. — A199

1983, Dec. 23 *Perf. 12½x13*
605 A198 90fr multi .30 .15
606 A198 300fr multi 1.00 .50

1984, Jan. 10 *Perf. 12½*
607 A199 90fr multi .30 .15
608 A199 95fr multi .32 .16

SOS Children's Village — A200

Perf. 13½x13, 13x13½

1984, Mar. 29
609 A200 90fr Village .30 .15
610 A200 95fr Mother & child, vert. .32 .16
611 A200 115fr Brothers & sisters .40 .20
612 A200 260fr House, vert. .90 .42
Nos. 609-612 (4) 1.92 .93

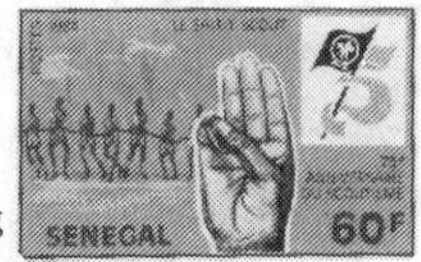

Scouting Year — A201

1984, May 28 **Litho.** *Perf. 13*
613 A201 60fr Sign .20 .15
614 A201 70fr Emblem .22 .15
615 A201 90fr Scouts .30 .15
616 A201 95fr Baden-Powell .32 .16
Nos. 613-617 (5) 1.34 .76

1984 Olympic Games — A202

1984, July 28 **Litho.** *Perf. 13*
617 A202 90fr Javelin .30 .15
618 A202 95fr Hurdles .35 .16
619 A202 165fr Soccer .55 .30
Nos. 617-619 (3) 1.20 .61

Souvenir Sheet

Perf. 13x12½

620 Sheet of 3 1.90 1.00
a. A202 125fr like 90fr .40 .20
b. A202 175fr like 95fr .60 .30
c. A202 250fr like 165fr .80 .45

World Food Day — A203

Perf. 13x12½, 12½x13

1984, Dec. 16 **Litho.**

621 A203 65fr Food production .18 .15
622 A203 70fr Cooking, vert. .18 .15
623 A203 225fr Dining .60 .30
Nos. 621-623 (3) .96
Set value .50

No. 612 Overprinted "AIDE AU SAHEL 84"

1984, Dec. *Perf. 13x13½*

624 A200 260fr multi .70 .35

Drought relief.

UNESCO World Heritage Campaign — A204

Water Emergency Plan — A205

1984, Dec. 6 **Litho.** *Perf. 13½*

625 A204 90fr William Ponty School .25 .15
626 A204 95fr Island map, horiz. .25 .15
627 A204 250fr History Museum .65 .35
628 A204 500fr Slave Prison, horiz. 1.40 .65
Nos. 625-628 (4) 2.55 1.30

Souvenir Sheet

Perf. 13x12½, 12½x13

629 Sheet of 4 3.50 1.90
a. A204 125fr like No. 625 .30 .16
b. A204 150fr like No. 626 .40 .20
c. A204 325fr like No. 627 .90 .40
d. A204 675fr like No. 628 1.90 .90

Restoration of historic sites, Goree Island.

Perf. 13x12½, 12½x13

1985, Mar. 28

630 A205 40fr Well and pump .15 .15
631 A205 50fr Spigot and crops .15 .15
632 A205 90fr Water tanks, livestock .25 .15
633 A205 250fr Women at well .65 .35
Nos. 630-633 (4) 1.20
Set value .60

Nos. 631-633 horiz.

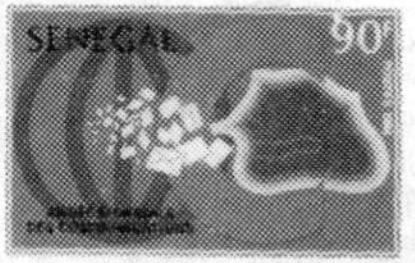

World Communications Year — A206

Designs: 95fr, Maps of Africa and Senegal, transmission tower. 350fr, Globe, pigeon with letter.

1985, Apr. 13 **Litho.** *Perf. 13*

634 A206 90fr multi .25 .15
635 A206 95fr multi .25 .15
636 A206 350fr multi .90 .45
Nos. 634-636 (3) 1.40 .75

Traditional Musical Instruments A207

Designs: 50fr, Gourd fiddle and bamboo flute. 85fr, Drums and stringed instrument. 125fr, Musician playing balaphone, drums. 250fr, Rabab, shawm and single-string fiddles.

1985, May 4 *Perf. 12½x13, 13x12½*

637 A207 50fr multi .15 .15
638 A207 85fr multi .22 .15
639 A207 125fr multi .35 .16
640 A207 250fr multi .65 .35
Nos. 637-640 (4) 1.37
Set value .70

Nos. 638-640 vert. For surcharge see No. 676.

PHILEXAFRICA '85, Lome, Togo, Nov. 16-24 — A208

1985, Oct. 21 *Perf. 13*

641 A208 100fr Political and civic education .35 .16
642 A208 125fr Vocational training .42 .20
643 A208 150fr Culture, space exploration .55 .25
644 A208 175fr Self-sufficiency in food production .60 .30
Nos. 641-644 (4) 1.92 .91

Intl. Youth Year A209

1985, Nov. 30 *Perf. 14*

645 A209 40fr Vocational training .15 .15
646 A209 50fr Communications .16 .15
647 A209 90fr World peace .30 .15
648 A209 125fr Cultural exchange .42 .20
Nos. 645-648 (4) 1.03 .65
Set value .50

Senegal Arms Type of 1970

1985, Dec. **Litho.** *Perf. 13*

Background Color

654 A89 95fr bright orange .35 .16

Fishing at Kayar A210

1986, Jan. 28 **Litho.** *Perf. 14*

659 A210 40fr Hauling boat .20 .15
660 A210 50fr Women on beach .25 .15
661 A210 100fr Fisherman, catch .52 .25
662 A210 125fr Women buying fish .68 .35
663 A210 150fr Unloading fish .80 .40
Nos. 659-663 (5) 2.45 1.30

Nos. 661-662 vert.

Folk Costumes — A211

1985, Dec. 28 **Litho.** *Perf. 13½*

664 A211 40fr multi .15 .15
665 A211 95fr multi, vert., diff. .35 .16
666 A211 100fr multi, vert., diff. .38 .18
667 A211 150fr multi, vert., diff. .55 .28
Nos. 664-667 (4) 1.43 .77

Coiffures A212

1986 Africa Soccer Cup, Cairo A213

1986, Mar. 3 *Perf. 13*

668 A212 90fr Perruque, Ceeli .50 .25
669 A212 125fr Ndungu, Kearly, Rasta .68 .35
670 A212 250fr Jamono Kura, Kooraa 1.35 .68
671 A212 300fr Mbaram, Jeere 1.65 .82
Nos. 668-671 (4) 4.18 2.10

1986, Mar. 7 *Perf. 13½*

672 A213 115fr Soccer ball, flags .62 .32
673 A213 125fr Athlete, map .68 .35
674 A213 135fr Pyramid, heraldic lion .75 .38
675 A213 165fr Flag, lions, map .90 .45
Nos. 672-675 (4) 2.95 1.50

No. 638 Surcharged with Lions Intl. Emblem, Two Bars, and "Ve CONVENTION / MULTI-DISTRICT / 403 / 8-10 / MAI / 1986" in Dark Ultramarine

1986, May 8 **Litho.** *Perf. 13x12½*

676 A207 165fr on 85fr multi 1.00 .50

World Wildlife Fund — A214

Ndama gazelles.

1986, June 30 *Perf. 13*

677 A214 15fr multi .15 .15
678 A214 45fr multi .25 .15
679 A214 85fr multi .48 .24
680 A214 125fr multi .70 .35
Nos. 677-680 (4) 1.58
Set value .75

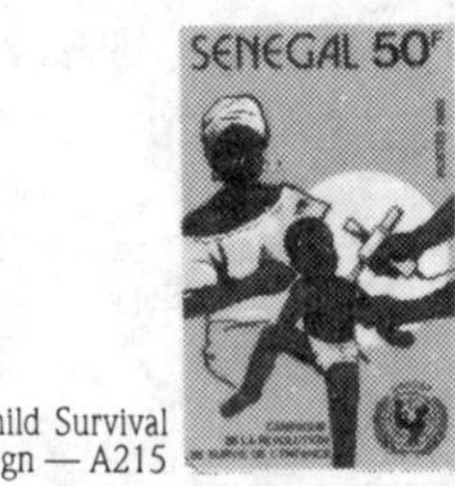

UN Child Survival Campaign — A215

1986, Sept. 5 **Litho.** *Perf. 14*

681 A215 50fr Immunization .32 .16
682 A215 85fr Nutrition .50 .25

1986 World Cup Soccer Championships, Mexico — A216

Various plays, world cup and artifacts: 125fr, Ceremonial vase. 135fr, Mayan mask, Palenque. 165fr, Gold breastplate. 340fr, Porcelain mask, Teofihuacan, 7th cent. B.C.

1986, Nov. 17 *Perf. 12½x12*

683 A216 125fr multi .80 .40
684 A216 135fr multi .85 .42
685 A216 165fr multi 1.10 .55
686 A216 340fr multi 2.25 1.10
Nos. 683-686 (4) 5.00 2.47

Nos. 683-686 Overprinted "ARGENTINE 3 / R.F.A. 2" in Scarlet

1986, Nov. 17

687 A216 125fr multi .80 .40
688 A216 135fr multi .85 .42
689 A216 165fr multi 1.10 .55
690 A216 340fr multi 2.25 1.10
Nos. 687-690 (4) 5.00 2.47

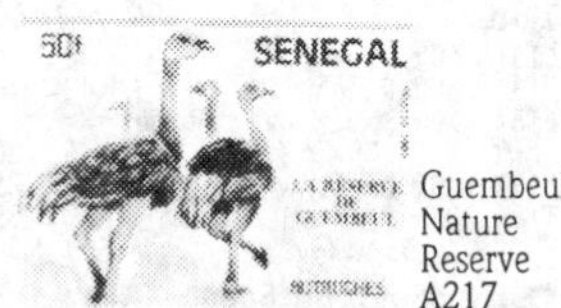

Guembeul Nature Reserve A217

1986, Dec. 4 **Litho.** *Perf. 13¹/*

691 A217 50fr Ostriches .28 .1
692 A217 65fr Kob antelopes .38 .2
693 A217 85fr Giraffes .48 .2
694 A217 100fr Ostrich, buffalo, kob, giraffe .55 .2
695 A217 150fr Buffaloes .85 .4
Nos. 691-695 (5) 2.54 1.2

Christmas A218

1986, Dec. 22 **Litho.** *Perf. 1*

696 A218 70fr Puppet, vert. .40 .2
697 A218 85fr Folk musicians .48 .2
698 A218 150fr Outdoor celebration, vert. .82 .4
699 A218 250fr Boy praying, creche 1.40 .7
Nos. 696-699 (4) 3.10 1.5

Inscribed 1985.

Statue of Liberty, Cent. — A219

1986, Dec. 30 **Litho.** *Perf. 12¹/*

700 A219 225fr multi 1.30 .6

Marine Life A220

1987, Jan. 2 *Perf. 1*

701 A220 50fr Jellyfish, coral .28 .1
702 A220 85fr Sea urchin, starfish .48 .2
703 A220 100fr Spiny lobster .55 .2
704 A220 150fr Dolphin .85 .4
705 A220 200fr Octopus 1.15 .5
Nos. 701-705 (5) 3.31 1.6

Senegal Stamp Cent. — A221

1987, Apr. 8 *Perf. 1.*

706 A221 100fr Intl. express mail .55 .2
707 A221 130fr #37 .75 .3
708 A221 140fr Similar to #201 .80 .4
709 A221 145fr #151, similar to #154 .82 .4
710 A221 320fr #27 1.80 .9
Nos. 706-710 (5) 4.72 2.3

Designs of Nos. 37, 151 and 27 same as originally released but perfs simulated.
For overprint see No. 784.

Paris-Dakar Rally A222

1987, Jan. 22 *Perf. 14*

711 A222 115fr Motorcycle, truck, vert. .65 .32
712 A222 125fr Official, race .72 .35
713 A222 135fr Sabine, truck .78 .40
714 A222 340fr Eiffel Tower, Dakar huts, vert. 1.95 .95
Nos. 711-714 (4) 4.10 2.02

Homage to Thierry Sabine. Inscribed 1986.

Ferlo Nature Reserve — A223

1987, Feb. 5 *Perf. 13½*

715 A223 55fr Antelope .30 .15
716 A223 70fr Ostrich .40 .20
717 A223 85fr Warthog .48 .24
718 A223 90fr Elephant .52 .25
Nos. 715-718 (4) 1.70 .84

Inscribed 1986.

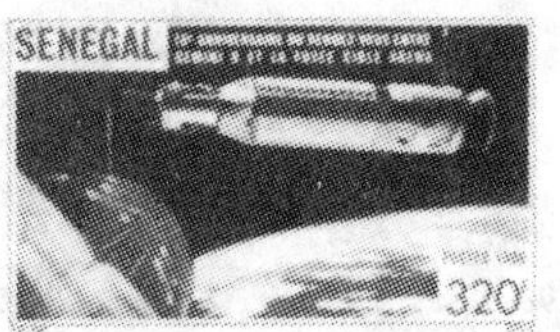

Agena-Gemini 8 Link-up in Outer Space, 20th Anniv. — A224

1987, Feb. 27 **Litho.** *Perf. 13*

719 A224 320fr multi 1.75 .90

Souvenir Sheet

Perf. 12½

720 A224 500fr multi 2.75 1.40

Nos. 719-720 inscribed 1986 and have erroneous "10e Anniversaire" inscription.

Solidarity Against South African Apartheid — A225

1987, July 31 **Litho.** *Perf. 13*

721 A225 130fr shown .85 .42
722 A225 140fr Mandela, hand, broken chain, vert. .92 .45
723 A225 145fr Mandela, dove, death .95 .48
Nos. 721-723 (3) 2.72 1.35

Inscribed 1986.

Intelsat, 20th Anniv. A226

1987, Aug. 31 *Perf. 14*

724 A226 50fr Emblem .32 .16
725 A226 125fr Satellite 85 .42
726 A226 150fr Emblem, globe 1.00 .50
727 A226 200fr Earth, satellite in space 1.35 .68
Nos. 724-727 (4) 3.52 1.76

Inscribed 1985. Nos. 726-727 vert.

West African Union, 10th Anniv. — A227

Dakar Rotary Club, 45th Anniv. — A228

1987, Sept. 7

728 A227 40fr shown .30 .15
729 A227 125fr Emblem, handshake .90 .45

Inscribed 1985.

1987, Sept. 29 *Perf. 13*

730 A228 500fr multi 3.60 1.80

Inscribed 1985.

United Nations, 40th Anniv. — A229

1987, Oct. 8 *Perf. 14*

731 A229 85fr Emblem, NYC office .62 .30
732 A229 95fr Emblem .70 .35
733 A229 150fr Hands, emblem 1.10 .55
Nos. 731-733 (3) 2.42 1.20

Inscribed 1985.

Cathedral of African Memory, 50th Anniv. A230

130fr, Statue of saint, Fr. Daniel Brottier, vert.

Perf. 12½x13, 13x12½

1987, Oct. 16

734 A230 130fr multi .95 .48
735 A230 140fr multi 1.00 .50

Inscribed 1986.

Lat Dior, King of Cayor (d. 1887) A231

1987, Oct. 27 **Litho.** *Perf. 14*

736 A231 130fr Battle of Dekhele .95 .48
737 A231 160fr Lat Dior 1.20 .60

World Food Day — A232

1987, Oct. 30 **Litho.** *Perf. 12½*

738 A232 130fr Earth storing grain, vert. .90 .45
739 A232 140fr shown .98 .48
740 A232 145fr Emblem, vert. 1.00 .50

Inscribed 1986.

A233 SENEGAL

Fauna, Bassa Casamance Natl. Park — A234

1987, Nov. 9 *Perf. 13*

741 A233 115fr Felis servaline .85 .40
742 A233 135fr Galagoides demidovii .95 .50
743 A233 150fr Potamochoerus porcus 1.10 .55
744 A233 250fr Panthera pardus 1.80 .90
745 A234 300fr Aigrette 2.15 1.10
746 A234 300fr Guepier 2.15 1.10
a. Pair, #745-746 + label 4.30 2.25
Nos. 741-746 (6) 9.00 4.55

Inscribed 1986. No. 745-746 has continuous design with corner label picturing map of Senegal with park highlighted.

Traditional Wrestling — A235

Birds in Djoudj Natl. Park — A236

Various moves.

1987, Nov. 30 **Litho.** *Perf. 14*

747 A235 115fr multi, horiz. .82 .40
748 A235 125fr multi, diff., horiz. .90 .45
749 A235 135fr multi, diff. .95 .48
750 A235 165fr multi, diff. 1.20 .60
Nos. 747-750 (4) 3.87 1.93

1987, Dec. 4

751 A236 115fr Stork .82 .40
752 A236 125fr Pink flamingos, horiz. .90 .45
753 A236 135fr White pelicans, horiz. .95 .48
754 A236 300fr Pelicans in water 2.15 1.10
755 A236 350fr like 125fr, horiz. 2.50 1.25
756 A236 350fr like 135fr, horiz. 2.50 1.25
a. Pair, #755-756 + label 5.00 2.50
Nos. 751-756 (6) 9.82 4.93

Christmas A237

Designs: 145fr, Youth dreaming of presents. 150fr, Madonna and child. 180fr, Holy Family, congregation praying. 200fr, Holy Family, candle and Christmas tree.

1987, Dec. 24 *Perf. 12½x13*

757 A237 145fr multi 1.05 .52
758 A237 150fr multi 1.10 .55
759 A237 180fr multi 1.30 .65
760 A237 200fr multi 1.45 .72
Nos. 757-760 (4) 4.90 2.44

Dakar Intl. Fair, 10th Anniv. (in 1985) — A238

1988, Feb. 27 **Litho.** *Perf. 13*

761 A238 125fr multi .90 .45

Inscribed 1985.

Fish A239

1988, Feb. 29 **Litho.** *Perf. 13*

762 A239 5fr Amelurus nebulosus .15 .15
763 A239 100fr Heniochus acuminatus .72 .35
764 A239 145fr Anthias anthias 1.05 .52
765 A239 180fr Cyprinus carpio 1.30 .65
Nos. 762-765 (4) 3.22 1.67

World Meteorology Day — A240

1988, Mar. 15 *Perf. 13½*

766 A240 145fr multi 1.05 .52

Paris-Dakar Rally, 10th Anniv. (in 1987) — A241

Various motorcycle and automobile entries in desert settings.

1988 *Perf. 13*

767 A241 145fr Motorcycle 1.05 .52
768 A241 180fr Race car 1.30 .65
769 A241 200fr Race car, truck 1.45 .72
770 A241 410fr Thierry Sabine 2.90 1.45
Nos. 767-770 (4) 6.70 3.34

Inscribed 1987. For surcharge see No. 1051.

Mollusks A242

1988, Apr. 20 *Perf. 12½*

771 A242 10fr Squid .15 .15
772 A242 20fr Donax trunculus .15 .15
773 A242 145fr Achatina fulica, vert. 1.05 .52
774 A242 165fr Helix nemoralis 1.20 .60
Nos. 771-774 (4) 2.55
Set value 1.25

1988 African Soccer Cup Championships, Rabat — A243

1988, May 10 Litho. *Perf. 13*

775 A243 80fr Cameroun (winner) .55 .28
776 A243 100fr Kick, CAF emblem .70 .35
777 A243 145fr Map, players, final score 1.00 .50
778 A243 180fr Trophy 1.25 .62
Nos. 775-778 (4) 3.50 1.75

Nos. 776-778 vert.

US Peace Corps in Senegal, 25th Anniv. — A244

1988, May 11 Litho. *Perf. 13*

779 A244 190fr multi 1.25 .62

Marine Flora — A245

1988, June 13 Litho. *Perf. 12½*

780 A245 10fr Dictyota atomaria .15 .15
781 A245 65fr Agarum gmelini .45 .22
782 A245 145fr Saccorrhiza bulbosa .95 .48
783 A245 180fr Rhodymenia palmetta 1.20 .60
Nos. 780-783 (4) 2.75 1.45

Inscribed 1987.

No. 710 Overprinted

RICCIONE 88 27-29-08-89

1988, Aug. 27 Litho. *Perf. 13*

784 A221 320fr multi 2.20 1.10

Stamp Fair, Riccione, Aug. 27-29, 1988. Stamp incorrectly overprinted "89," instead of "88."

ENDA — A246

1988 Litho. *Perf. 13*

785 A246 125fr Thierno Saidou Nourou Tall Center .80 .40

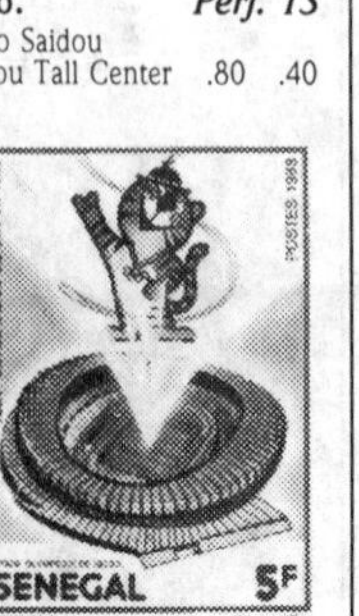

1988 Summer Olympics, Seoul — A247

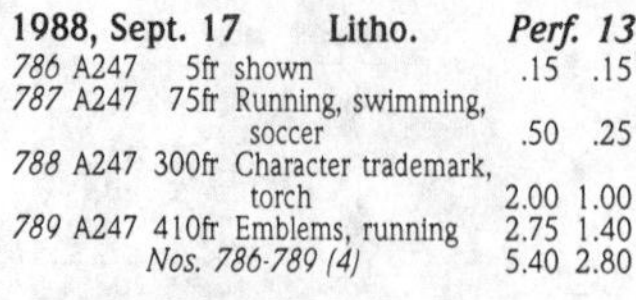

1988, Sept. 17 Litho. *Perf. 13*

786 A247 5fr shown .15 .15
787 A247 75fr Running, swimming, soccer .50 .25
788 A247 300fr Character trademark, torch 2.00 1.00
789 A247 410fr Emblems, running 2.75 1.40
Nos. 786-789 (4) 5.40 2.80

Industries — A248

Indigenous Flowers — A250

Postcards, c. 1900 — A249

1988, Nov. 7 Litho. *Perf. 13*

790 A248 5fr Phosphate, Thies .15 .15
791 A248 20fr I.C.S. .15 .15
792 A248 145fr Seib Mill, Diourbel .92 .45
793 A248 410fr Mbao refinery 2.60 1.30
Nos. 790-793 (4) 3.82 2.05

1988, Nov. 26

20fr, Boys, Government Palace. 145fr, Wrestlers, St. Louis Great Mosque. 180fr, Dakar Depot, young woman in folk costume. 200fr, Governor's Residence, housewife using mortar & pestle.

794 A249 20fr red brn & blk .15 .15
795 A249 145fr red brn & blk .92 .45
796 A249 180fr red brn & blk 1.15 .58
797 A249 200fr red brn & blk 1.30 .65
Nos. 794-797 (4) 3.52 1.83

1988, Dec. 4 *Perf. 13x12½*

798 A250 20fr Packia biglobosa .15 .15
799 A250 60fr Eurphorbia pulcherrima .38 .20
800 A250 65fr Cyrtosperma senegalense .42 .20
801 A250 410fr Bombax costatum 2.60 1.30
Nos. 798-801 (4) 3.55 1.85

11th Paris-Dakar Rally — A251

1989, Jan. 13 Litho. *Perf. 13½*

802 A251 10fr Mask, vehicle, Eiffel Tower .15 .15
803 A251 145fr Helmet, desert scene .95 .48
804 A251 180fr Turban, rallyist in desert 1.20 .60
805 A251 220fr Thierry Sabine 1.45 .72
Nos. 802-805 (4) 3.75 1.95

For surcharge see No. 1050.

Tourism — A252

1989, Feb. 15 *Perf. 13*

806 A252 10fr Teranga .15 .15
807 A252 80fr Campement .52 .25
808 A252 100fr Saly .65 .32
809 A252 350fr Dior 2.25 1.15
Nos. 806-809 (4) 3.57 1.87

Inscribed 1988.

Tourism — A253

1989, Mar. 11

810 A253 130fr Natl. tourism emblem, vert. .85 .42
811 A253 140fr Visiting rural community .92 .45
812 A253 145fr Sport fishing .95 .48
813 A253 180fr Water skiing, polo 1.20 .60
Nos. 810-813 (4) 3.92 1.95

Inscribed 1987.

French Revolution, Bicent. — A254

Designs: 180fr, Governor's Palace, St. Louis. 220fr, Declaration of Human Rights and Citizenship, vert. 300fr, Flag, revolutionaries.

1989, May 24 Litho. *Perf. 13*

814 A254 180fr shown 1.10 .55
815 A254 220fr multi 1.30 .65
816 A254 300fr multi 1.80 .90
Nos. 814-816 (3) 4.20 2.10

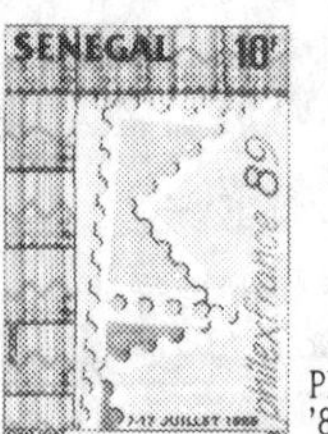

PHILEXFRANCE '89 — A255

1989, July 7 Litho. *Perf. 13x12½*

817 A255 10fr shown .15 .15
818 A255 25fr Simulated stamp, map of France .15 .15
819 A255 75fr Exhibit .45 .22
820 A255 145fr Affixing stamp .85 .42
Nos. 817-820 (4) 1.60
Set value .75

Antoine de Saint-Exupery (1900-1944), French Aviator and Writer — A256

Scenes from novels: 180fr, *Southern Courier*, 1929. 220fr, *Night flier*, 1931. 410fr, *Bomber pilot*, 1942.

1989, Aug. 30 Litho. *Perf. 13*

821 A256 180fr multi 1.15 .58
822 A256 220fr multi 1.40 .70
823 A256 410fr multi 2.65 1.35
Nos. 821-823 (3) 5.20 2.63

No. 785 Surcharged in Bright Green

1989 Litho. *Perf. 13*

824 A246 555fr on 125fr multi 4.00 2.00

3rd Francophone Summit on the Arts and Culture — A257

Designs: 5fr, Palette, quill pen in ink pot, dancer, vert. 30fr, Children reading. 100fr, Architecture, women, Earth. 200fr, Artist sketching, easel, gear wheels, chemist, computer operator.

1989 *Perf. 13x13½, 13½x13*

825 A257 5fr multicolored .15 .15
826 A257 30fr multicolored .22 .15
827 A257 100fr multicolored .70 .35
828 A257 200fr multicolored 1.40 .70
Nos. 825-828 (4) 2.47 1.35

Pottery — A258

1989, Nov. 1 *Perf. 13*

829 A258 15fr shown .15 .15
830 A258 30fr Potter, three-handled urn .22 .15
831 A258 75fr Vases .52 .25
832 A258 145fr Woman carrying pottery 1.05 .52
Nos. 829-832 (4) 1.94
Set value .90

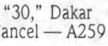

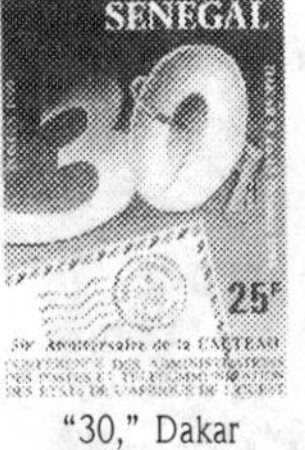

"30," Dakar Cancel — A259

Natl. Archives, 75th Anniv. — A260

Designs: 30fr, Telephone handset, map. 180fr, Map, simulated stamp, phone handset. 220fr, Telecommunications satellite, globe, map.

1989, Oct. 9 *Perf. 13½*

833 A259 25fr multicolored .18 .15
834 A259 30fr multicolored .22 .15
835 A259 180fr multicolored 1.25 .62
836 A259 220fr multicolored 1.55 .78
Nos. 833-836 (4) 3.20 1.70

Conference of Postal and Telecommunication Administrations of West African Nations (CAPTEAO), 30th anniv.

1989, Oct. 23 *Perf. 11½*

Designs: 15fr, Stacks, postal card of 1922. 40fr, Document, 1825. 145fr, Document, Archives building. 180fr, Tome.

837 A260 15fr multicolored .15 .15
838 A260 40fr multicolored .28 .15
839 A260 145fr multicolored 1.05 .52
840 A260 180fr multicolored 1.25 .62
Nos. 837-840 (4) 2.73 1.44

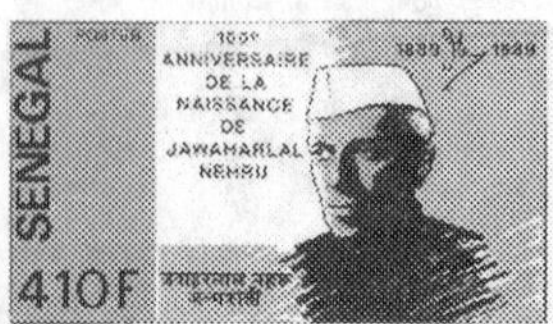

Jawarharlal Nehru, 1st Prime Minister of Independent India — A261

1989, Nov. 14 *Perf. 13*

841 A261 220fr Portrait, vert. 1.55 .78
842 A261 410fr shown 2.90 1.45

Marine Life
A262

1989, Nov. 27

843 A262 10fr *Grapsus grapsus* .15 .15
844 A262 60fr *Hippocampus guttulatus* .45 .22
845 A262 145fr *Lepas anatifera* 1.00 .50
846 A262 220fr Beach flea 1.55 .78
Nos. 843-846 (4) 3.15 1.65

Children's March to the Sanctuary — A263

1989, Dec. 9 Litho. *Perf. 13½*

847 A263 145fr shown 1.05 .52
848 A263 180fr Church 1.25 .62

Pilgrimage to Notre Dame de Popenguine, cent.

Birds
A263a

Designs: 10fr, *Phalacrocovax carbolucidus, Anhinga rufa.* 45fr, *Lavius cirrocephalus.* 100fr, Dwarf bee-eater, *Lophogetus occipitalis.* 180fr, *Egretta gularis.*

1989, Dec. 11 *Perf. 13*

849 A263a 10fr multicolored .15 .15
850 A263a 45fr multicolored .32 .16
851 A263a 100fr multicolored .72 .35
852 A263a 180fr multicolored 1.30 .65
Nos. 849-852 (4) 2.49 1.31

Natl. parks: Djoudj (10fr), Langue de Barbarie (45fr), Basse Casamance (100fr) and Saloum (180fr).

Christmas
A264

Joan of Arc Institute, 50th Anniv.
A265

1989, Dec. 22 Litho. *Perf. 13*

853 A264 10fr shown .15 .15
854 A264 25fr Teddy bear .18 .15
855 A264 30fr Manger .22 .15
856 A264 200fr Mother and child 1.40 .70
Nos. 853-856 (4) 1.95
Set value .95

1989, Dec. 26 *Perf. 13½*

857 A265 20fr shown .15 .15
858 A265 500fr Institute 3.50 3.50

Flight of the 1st Seaplane, Mar. 28, 1910 — A266

Perf. 13x12½, 12½x13

1989, Dec. 30 Litho.

859 A266 125fr shown .90 .45
860 A266 130fr Seaplane, Fabre .92 .46
861 A266 475fr Fabre, schematic of aircraft, vert. 3.40 1.70
Nos. 859-861 (3) 5.22 2.61

Souvneir Sheet

862 A266 700fr like 475fr, vert. 5.00 2.50

Henri Fabre (1882-1984), aviator.

1992 Summer Olympics, Barcelona — A267

Various athletes and monuments or architecture.

1990, Jan. 8 *Perf. 12½*

863 A267 10fr Basketball .15 .15
864 A267 130fr High jump .92 .45
865 A267 180fr Discus 1.25 .62
866 A267 190fr Running 1.35 .68
867 A267 315fr Tennis 2.25 1.10
868 A267 475fr Equestrian 3.35 1.65
Nos. 863-868 (6) 9.27 4.65

Souvenir Sheet

869 A267 600fr Soccer 4.25 2.10

Fight AIDS Worldwide — A268

1989, Dec. 1 Litho. *Perf. 13½*

870 A268 5fr shown .15 .15
871 A268 100fr Umbrella .72 .35
872 A268 145fr Fist crushing virus 1.05 .52
873 A268 180fr Hammering away at virus 1.30 .65
Nos. 870-873 (4) 3.22 1.67

12th Paris-Dakar Rally — A269

1990, Jan. 16 *Perf. 13*

874 A269 20fr shown .15 .15
875 A269 25fr Motorcycle .18 .15
876 A269 180fr Trophy winner, crowd 1.25 .62
877 A269 200fr Thierry Sabine 1.40 .70
Nos. 874-877 (4) 2.98 1.62

1990 World Cup Soccer Championships, Italy — A270

Various athletes and: 45fr, Trophy, the Piazza Della Signoria, Florence. 140fr, Piazza Navona, Rome. 180fr, *The Virgin with St. Anne and the Infant Jesus,* by Leonardo da Vinci. 220fr, Portrait of Giuseppe Garibaldi (1807-1882), Risorgimento Museum, Turin. 300fr, *The Sistine Madonna,* by Raphael. 415fr, *The Virgin and Child,* by Daniele da Volterra. 700fr, Columbus Monument, Milan.

1990, Jan. 31 Litho. *Perf. 13x12½*

878 A270 45fr multicolored .32 .16
879 A270 140fr multicolored 1.00 .50
880 A270 180fr multicolored 1.30 .65
881 A270 220fr multicolored 1.60 .80
882 A270 300fr multicolored 2.15 1.10
883 A270 415fr multicolored 3.00 1.50
Nos. 878-883 (6) 9.37 4.71

Souvenir Sheet

884 A270 700fr multicolored 5.00 2.50

1990 African Soccer Cup Championships, Algeria — A271

1990, Mar. 2 Litho. *Perf. 13*

885 A271 20f shown .15 .15
886 A271 60f Goalie .45 .22
887 A271 100f Exchange of flags .75 .38
888 A271 500f Ball, trophy 3.75 1.90
Nos. 885-888 (4) 5.10 2.65

Postal Services
A272

1990, Apr. 30 Litho. *Perf. 13*

889 A272 5fr Facsimile transmission .15 .15
890 A272 15fr Express mail .15 .15
891 A272 100fr Postal money orders .75 .38
892 A272 180fr CNE 1.30 .65
Nos. 889-892 (4) 2.35
Set value 1.10

A273 A274

1990, May 31 *Perf. 13½*

893 A273 145fr shown 1.00 .50
894 A273 180fr Hand, wreath, envelope 1.30 .65

Multinational Postal School, 20th anniv.

1990, May 31

895 A274 5fr shown .15 .15
896 A274 500fr Family 3.75 1.50

S.O.S. Children's Village appeal for aid.

Boy Scouts
A275

Scouting emblems and: 30fr, Camping. 100fr, Hiking at lakeshore. 145fr, Following trail. 200fr, Scout, vert.

1990, Nov. 5 Litho. *Perf. 11½*

897 A275 30fr multicolored .25 .15
898 A275 100fr multicolored .90 .45
899 A275 145fr multicolored 1.25 .65
900 A275 200fr multicolored 1.75 .85
Nos. 897-900 (4) 4.15 2.10

Medicinal Plants — A276

1990, Nov. 30 *Perf. 13x13½*

901 A276 95fr Cassia tora .85 .42
902 A276 105fr Tamarindus indica .95 .45
903 A276 125fr Cassia occidentalis 1.10 .55
904 A276 175fr Leptadenia hastata 1.50 .75
Nos. 901-904 (4) 4.40 2.17

A277

A278

1990, Dec. 24 Litho. *Perf. 13½*

905 A277 25fr shown .20 .15
906 A277 145fr Angel, stars, people 1.25 .65
907 A277 180fr Adoration of the Magi 1.60 .80
908 A277 200fr Animals, baby in manger 1.75 .85
Nos. 905-908 (4) 4.80 2.45

Christmas.

1991, Jan. 2 Litho. *Perf. 13x12½*

909 A278 180fr multicolored 1.55 .80

Intl. Red Cross, 125th Anniv., Senegalese Red Cross, 25th anniv. No. 909 inscribed 1988.

Paris-Dakar Rally — A279

1991, Jan. 17

910 A279 15fr shown .15 .15
911 A279 125fr Car, motorcycle 1.10 .55
912 A279 180fr Car racing in water 1.55 .80
913 A279 220fr Two motorcycles, beach 1.90 .95
Nos. 910-913 (4) 4.70 2.45

Reptiles
A280

1991, Jan. 31 *Perf. 13½x13*

914 A280 15fr Python sebae .15 .15
915 A280 60fr Chelonia mydas .55 .28
916 A280 100fr Crocolylus niloticus .90 .45

917 A280 180fr Chameleo senegalensis 1.55 .80
Nos. 914-917 (4) 3.15 1.68

Inscribed 1990.

African Film Festival — A281

Designs: 30fr, Sphinx, slave house, cave paintings, tomb of Mohammed. 60fr, Dogon mask, mosque of Dioulasso, drawing of Osiris, man on camel. 100fr, Ruins, drum, statue of scribe, camels. 180fr, mask, mosque of Djenne, pyramids, Moroccan architecture.

1991, Feb. 23 ***Perf. 11½***

918 A281 30fr org & multi .25 .15
919 A281 60fr org & multi .50 .25
920 A281 100fr org & multi .90 .45
921 A281 180fr org & multi 1.55 .80
Nos. 918-921 (4) 3.20 1.65

Alfred Nobel (1833-1896), Industrialist A282

Designs: 145fr, Drawing of Nobel.

1991, Mar. 29 Litho. ***Die Cut***

Self-adhesive

922 A282 145fr multi, vert. 1.10 .55
923 A282 180fr shown 1.35 .65

Antelope A283

1991, Apr. 24 Litho. ***Perf. 13½x13***

924 A283 5fr Ouerbia ourebi .15 .15
925 A283 10fr Gazella dorcas .15 .15
926 A283 180fr Kobos kob kob 1.35 .70
927 A283 555fr Alcelaphus buselaphus major 4.10 2.05
Nos. 924-927 (4) 5.75 3.05

Trees A284

Perf. 13½x13, 13x13½

1991, May 30

928 A284 90fr Ancardium occidentalus .65 .35
929 A284 100fr Mangifera indica .75 .38
930 A284 125fr Borassus flabellifer, vert. .95 .48
931 A284 145fr Elaeis guineensis, vert. 1.10 .55
Nos. 928-931 (4) 3.45 1.76

Christopher Columbus — A285

100fr, Meeting Haitian natives. 145fr, Columbus' personal coat of arms, vert. 180fr, Santa Maria, Columbus. 200fr, 220fr, Columbus, ships. 500fr, Details of voyages. 625fr, Columbus at chart table.

1991, July 8 Litho. ***Perf. 13***

932 A285 100fr multicolored .75 .38
a. Sheet of 1, perf. 12½ .75 .38
933 A285 145fr multicolored 1.10 .55
a. Sheet of 1, perf. 12½ 1.10 .55
934 A285 180fr multicolored 1.35 .65
a. Sheet of 1, perf. 12½ 1.35 .65
935 A285 200fr multicolored 1.50 .75
a. Sheet of 1, perf. 12½ 1.50 .75
936 A285 220fr multicolored 1.65 .80
a. Sheet of 1, perf. 12½ 1.65 .80
937 A285 500fr multicolored 3.70 1.85
a. Sheet of 1, perf. 12½ 3.70 1.85
938 A285 625fr multicolored 4.65 2.30
a. Sheet of 1, perf. 12½ 4.65 2.30
Nos. 932-938 (7) 14.70 7.28

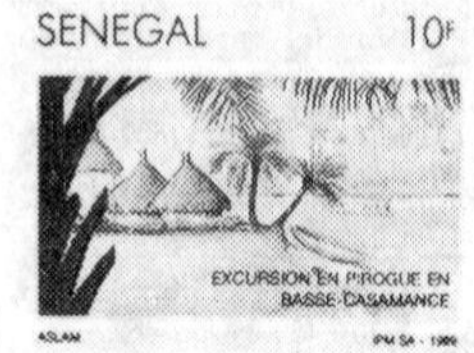

Tourism A286

Designs: 10fr, Canoe excursion, Basse-Casamance. 25fr, Shore at Boufflers Hotel, Goree Island. 30fr, Huts built on stilts, Fadiouth Island. 40fr, Salt collecting on lake.

1991, July 30 Litho. ***Perf. 13***

939 A286 10fr multicolored .15 .15
940 A286 25fr multicolored .18 .15
941 A286 30fr multicolored .22 .15
942 A286 40fr multicolored .30 .15
Nos. 939-942 (4) .85 .60

Dated 1989.

Louis Armstrong, Jazz Musician, 20th Death Anniv. A287

1991, Oct. 7 ***Perf. 13½***

943 A287 10fr shown .15 .15
944 A287 145fr Singing 1.20 .60
945 A287 180fr With trumpets 1.50 .75
946 A287 220fr Playing trumpet 1.80 .90
Nos. 943-946 (4) 4.65 2.40

Yuri Gagarin, First Man in Space, 30th Anniv. — A288

Various portraits of Gagarin with Vostok I in Earth orbit.

1991, Nov. 25 Litho. ***Perf. 13½***

947 A288 15fr multicolored .15 .15
948 A288 145fr multicolored 1.20 .60
949 A288 180fr multicolored 1.50 .75
950 A288 220fr multicolored 1.80 .90
Nos. 947-950 (4) 4.65 2.40

Rural Water Supply Project — A289

6th Islamic Summit — A290

1991, Dec. 2 Litho. ***Perf. 13½***

951 A289 30fr Bowl of water .25 .15
952 A289 145fr Water faucet, huts 1.25 .65
953 A289 180fr Dripping faucet, flags 1.60 .80
954 A289 220fr Water tower, huts 1.90 .95
Nos. 951-954 (4) 5.00 2.55

1991, Dec. 9

955 A290 15fr shown .15 .15
956 A290 145fr Upraised hands 1.25 .65
957 A290 180fr Congress Center, Dakar 1.60 .80
958 A290 220fr Grand Mosque, Dakar 1.90 .95
Nos. 955-958 (4) 4.90 2.55

A291

A292

Basketball, Cent.: 145fr, Player dribbling ball. 180fr, Couple holding trophy. 220fr, Lion, basketball, trophies.

1991, Dec. 21 Litho. ***Perf. 13½***

959 A291 125fr multicolored 1.00 .50
960 A291 145fr multicolored 1.20 .60
961 A291 180fr multicolored 1.50 .75
962 A291 220fr multicolored 1.80 .90
Nos. 959-962 (4) 5.50 2.75

1991, Dec. 24 Litho. ***Perf. 13½***

963 A292 5fr Jesus .15 .15
964 A292 145fr Madonna and Child 1.25 .62
965 A292 160fr Angels 1.40 .70
966 A292 220fr Christ Child, animals 1.90 .95
Nos. 963-966 (4) 4.70 2.42

Christmas. For surcharge see No. 975.

A293

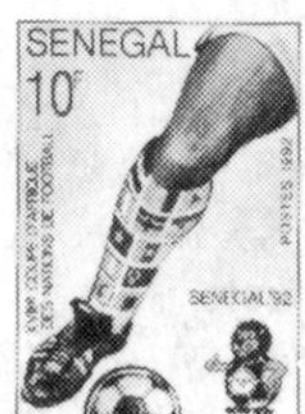

A294

A293a

Musical score and: 5fr, Bust of Mozart. 150fr, Mozart conducting. 180fr, Mozart at piano. 220fr, Portrait.

1991, Dec. 31

967 A293 5fr multicolored .15 .15
968 A293 150fr multicolored 1.30 .65
969 A293 180fr multicolored 1.60 .80
970 A293 220fr multicolored 1.90 .95
Nos. 967-970 (4) 4.95 2.55

Wolfgang Amadeus Mozart, death bicent.

1991 Litho. ***Perf. 13½***

970A A293a 15fr multicolored

Jean Mermoz (1901-36), pilot. This is one of two stamps released on this subject. The editors would like to examine the other stamp.

1992, Jan. 12 Litho. ***Perf. 13½***

971 A294 10fr shown .15 .15
972 A294 145fr Map, soccer balls 1.20 .60
973 A294 200fr Lion, trophy 1.65 .82
974 A294 220fr Players 1.80 .90
Nos. 971-974 (4) 4.80 2.47

18th African Soccer Cup Championships.

No. 965 Surcharged

VISITE DU
PAPE JEAN PAUL II
AU SENEGAL
19 - 23 / 02 / 92

180F

1992, Feb. 19 Litho. ***Perf. 13½***

975 A292 180fr on 160fr 1.50 .75

Natl. Parks A295

1992, Mar. 20 ***Perf. 13½x13***

976 A295 10fr Delta Du Saloum .15 .15
977 A295 125fr Djoudj 1.05 .50
978 A295 145fr Niokolo-Koba 1.20 .60
979 A295 220fr Basse Casamance 1.80 .90
Nos. 976-979 (4) 4.20 2.15

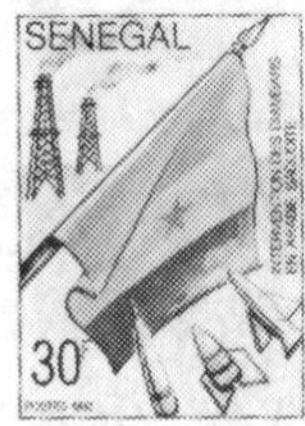

Senegal's Participation in Gulf War — A296

Designs: 30fr, Oil wells, flag and missiles. 145fr, Oil wells, soldier. 180fr, Holy Ka'aba, soldier with gun. 220fr, Peace dove with flag, map.

1992, Apr. 4 ***Perf. 13½***

980 A296 30fr multicolored .25 .15
981 A296 145fr multicolored 1.20 .60
982 A296 180fr multicolored 1.50 .75
983 A296 220fr multicolored 1.80 .90
Nos. 980-983 (4) 4.75 2.40

Fish Industry A297

Stylized designs: 5fr, Catching fish. 60fr, Retail outlets. 100fr, Processing plant. 150fr, Packaging.

1992, Apr. 6 Litho. ***Perf. 13½***

984 A297 5fr multicolored .15 .15
985 A297 60fr multicolored .55 .28
986 A297 100fr multicolored .90 .45
987 A297 150fr multicolored 1.30 .65
Nos. 984-987 (4) 2.90 1.53

Tourism — A298

1992, May 5 ***Perf. 13½x13***

988 A298 5fr Niokolo complex .15 .15
989 A298 10fr Casamance River .15 .15
990 A298 150fr Dakar region 1.30 .65
991 A298 200fr Saint-Louis excursion 1.75 .90
Nos. 988-991 (4) 3.35 1.85

Planting Trees — A299

Various designs showing children planting trees.

Perf. 13½x13, 13x13½

1992, May 29

992 A299 145fr multi 1.25 .65
993 A299 180fr multi 1.60 .80
994 A299 200fr multi 1.75 .90
995 A299 220fr multi, vert. 1.90 .95
Nos. 992-995 (4) 6.50 3.30

Public Works Projects A300

Various scenes of people cleaning and repairing public walkways.

Perf. 13½x13, 13x13½

1992, June 1 **Litho.**

996 A300 25fr multi .22 .15
997 A300 145fr multi 1.25 .65
998 A300 180fr multi, vert. 1.60 .80
999 A300 220fr multi, vert. 1.95 1.00
Nos. 996-999 (4) 5.02 2.60

Children's Rights — A301

1992, June 12 *Perf. 13*

1000 A301 20fr Education .18 .15
1001 A301 45fr Guidance .40 .20
1002 A301 165fr Instruction 1.45 .70
1003 A301 180fr Health care 1.60 .80
Nos. 1000-1003 (4) 3.63 1.85

African Integration A302

1992, June 29 **Litho.** *Perf. 13*

1004 A302 10fr Free trade .15 .15
1005 A302 30fr Youth activities .25 .15
1006 A302 145fr Communications 1.25 .65
1007 A302 220fr Women's movements 1.95 1.00
Nos. 1004-1007 (4) 3.60 1.95

1992 Summer Olympics, Barcelona — A303

Blue Train — A304

1992, July 25 **Litho.** *Perf. 13½*

1008 A303 145fr Map, horiz. 1.10 .55
1009 A303 180fr Runner 1.40 .70
1010 A303 200fr Sprinter, horiz. 1.50 .75
1011 A303 300fr Torch bearer 2.25 1.15
Nos. 1008-1011 (4) 6.25 3.15

1992, Aug. 3

1012 A304 70fr shown .55 .28
1013 A304 145fr Train yard 1.10 .55
1014 A304 200fr Train, passengers 1.50 .75
1015 A304 220fr Station 1.65 .85
Nos. 1012-1015 (4) 4.80 2.43

Intl. Maritime Heritage Year — A305

Designs: 25fr, Map of Antarctica, horiz. 100fr, Ocean, sea life. 180fr, Man addressing UN. 220fr, Hands holding globe, flags, ship, fish.

1992, Sept. 4

1016 A305 25fr multicolored .18 .15
1017 A305 100fr multicolored .75 .38
1018 A305 180fr multicolored 1.40 .70
1019 A305 220fr multicolored 1.65 .85
Nos. 1016-1019 (4) 3.98 2.08

Corals A306

Various coral formations.

Perf. 13½x13, 13x13½

1992, Sept. 18 **Litho.**

1020 A306 50fr multicolored .42 .20
1021 A306 100fr multicolored .85 .42
1022 A306 145fr multi, vert. 1.20 .60
1023 A306 220fr multicolored 1.80 .90
Nos. 1020-1023 (4) 4.27 2.12

Konrad Adenauer (1876-1967) — A307

Designs: 5fr, Portrait, vert. 145fr, Schaumburg Palace, Bonn. 180fr, Hands clasped. 220fr, Map of West Germany.

Perf. 13x13½, 13½x13

1992, Sept. 30 **Litho.**

1024 A307 5fr multicolored .15 .15
1025 A307 145fr multicolored 1.20 .60
1026 A307 180fr multicolored 1.50 .75
1027 A307 220fr multicolored 1.80 .90
Nos. 1024-1027 (4) 4.65 2.40

Shellfish — A308

1992, Oct. 1 **Litho.** *Perf. 13½*

1028 A308 20fr Crab .15 .15
1029 A308 30fr Spider crab .22 .15
1030 A308 180fr Lobster 1.40 .70
1031 A308 200fr Shrimp 1.50 .75
Nos. 1028-1031 (4) 3.27 1.75

Fruit-bearing Plants — A309

1992, Oct. 16 **Litho.** *Perf. 13x13½*

1032 A309 10fr Parkia biglobosa .15 .15
1033 A309 50fr Balanites aegyptiaca .42 .20
1034 A309 200fr Parinari macrophylla 1.60 .80
1035 A309 220fr Opuntiatuna 1.80 .90
Nos. 1032-1035 (4) 3.97 2.05

John Glenn's Orbital Flight, 30th Anniv. — A310

15fr, Astronaut in spacesuit, flag, map, spacecraft, horiz. 145fr, American flag, Glenn, horiz. 180fr, Flag, lift-off of rocket, Glenn in spacesuit, horiz. 200fr, Astronaut in spacesuit, spacecraft.

1992, Nov. 30 **Litho.** *Perf. 13½*

1036 A310 15fr multicolored .15 .15
1037 A310 145fr multicolored 1.15 .58
1038 A310 180fr multicolored 1.40 .70
1039 A310 200fr multicolored 1.60 .80
Nos. 1036-1039 (4) 4.30 2.23

Maps Featuring Bakari II — A311

100fr, Map from Spanish Atlas, 1375. 145fr, Stone head, Vera Cruz, Mexico, world map, 1413.

1992, Dec. 2 *Perf. 13*

1040 A311 100fr multicolored .82 .40
1041 A311 145fr multicolored 1.20 .60

No. 1041 issued only with black bar obliterating "Mecades."

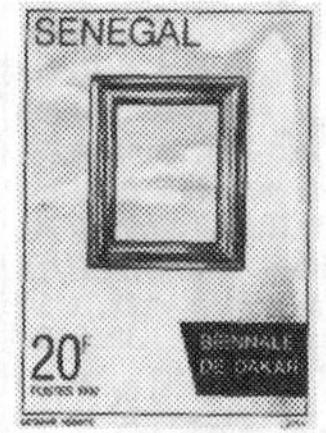

Biennial of Dakar — A312

Christmas — A313

20fr, Picture frame. 50fr, Puppet head, stage. 145fr, Open book. 220fr, Musical instrument.

1992, Dec. 14 *Perf. 13½*

1042 A312 20fr multicolored .15 .15
1043 A312 50fr multicolored .40 .20
1044 A312 145fr multicolored 1.15 .58
1045 A312 220fr multicolored 1.75 .88
Nos. 1042-1045 (4) 3.45 1.81

1992, Dec. 24 *Perf. 13½*

Designs: 15fr, Children dancing around large ornament, horiz. 145fr, Christmas tree. 180fr, Jesus Christ. 200fr, Santa Claus.

1046 A313 15fr multicolored .15 .15
1047 A313 145fr multicolored 1.15 .58
1048 A313 180fr multicolored 1.40 .70
1049 A313 200fr multicolored 1.60 .80
Nos. 1046-1049 (4) 4.30 2.23

Nos. 770, 804 Surcharged in Red

145 F

Dakar le 17-01-93

15e

1993, Jan. 17 **Litho.** *Perf. 13½*

1050 A251 145fr on 180fr #804 1.15 .58

Perf. 13

1051 A241 220fr on 410fr #770 1.75 .88

Size and location of surcharge varies.

Environmental Protection — A314

Accident Prevention A315

Designs: 20fr, Medical clinic. 25fr, Preventing industrial accidents. 145fr, Preventing chemical spills. 200fr, Red Cross helicopter, airline crash.

Perf. 13 (#1052, 1055), 13½

1993, Mar. 22 **Litho.**

1052 A314 20fr multicolored .16 .15
1053 A315 25fr multicolored .20 .15
1054 A315 145fr multicolored 1.15 .58
1055 A314 200fr multicolored 1.60 .80
Nos. 1052-1055 (4) 3.11 1.68

Abdoulaye Seck Marie Parsine (1873-1931), PTT Director — A316

1993, Apr. 21 **Litho.** *Perf. 13½*

1056 A316 220fr multicolored 1.75 .88

Wild Animals A317

Designs: 30fr, Crocuta crocuta. 50fr, Panthera leo. 70fr, Panthera pardus. 150fr, Giraffa camelopardalis peratta, vert. 180fr, Cervus.

1993, Nov. 26 **Litho.** *Perf. 13½*

1057 A317 30fr multicolored .15 .15
1058 A317 50fr multicolored .20 .15
1059 A317 70fr multicolored .25 .15
1060 A317 150fr multicolored .55 .28
1061 A317 180fr multicolored .70 .35
Nos. 1057-1061 (5) 1.85 1.08

Christmas A318

Designs: 80fr, Two children seated by Christmas tree. 145fr, Santa holding presents, three children. 150fr, Girl, Santa with present.

1993, Dec. 24 **Litho.** *Perf. 13x13½*

1062 A318 5fr multicolored .15 .15
1063 A318 80fr multicolored .32 .16
1064 A318 145fr multicolored .55 .28
1065 A318 150fr multicolored .60 .30
Nos. 1062-1065 (4) 1.62 .89

Paris-Dakar Rally, 16th Anniv.
A319

Designs: 145fr, Truck, car, motorcycle racing by tree. 180fr, Racing through desert, men with camel. 220fr, Car, truck, village.

1994, Jan. 5 *Perf. 13½*

1066 A319 145fr multicolored .55 .28
1067 A319 180fr multicolored .70 .35
1068 A319 220fr multicolored .90 .45
Nos. 1066-1068 (3) 2.15 1.08

Assassination of John F. Kennedy, 30th Anniv. — A320

1993, Dec. 31 **Litho.** *Perf. 13*

1069 A320 80fr shown .32 .16
1070 A320 555fr Kennedy, White House 2.25 1.10

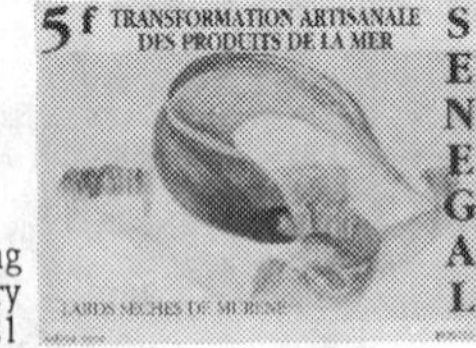

Fishing Industry
A321

Designs: 5fr, Drying eels. 90fr, Sifting for shellfish. 100fr, Salting fish. 200fr, Cooking fish.

1994, Feb. 28

1071 A321 5fr multicolored .15 .15
1072 A321 90fr multicolored .35 .18
1073 A321 100fr multicolored .40 .20
1074 A321 200fr multicolored .80 .40
Nos. 1071-1074 (4) 1.70 .93

Conservation of the Seashore — A322

Stylized designs: 5fr, Halting removal of sand. 75fr, Fight against drifting sand dunes. 100fr, Dams, dikes against beach erosion. 200fr, Healthy, aesthetic environment.

1994, Mar. 7

1075 A322 5fr multicolored .15 .15
1076 A322 75fr multicolored .30 .15
1077 A322 100fr multicolored .40 .20
1078 A322 200fr multicolored .80 .40
Nos. 1075-1078 (4) 1.65 .90

Save the Elephant
A323

1994, Apr. 18

1079 A323 30fr shown .15 .15
1080 A323 60fr Elephant in "SOS" .25 .15
1081 A323 90fr Elephants forming "SOS" .35 .18
1082 A323 145fr Elephant, tusks .60 .30
Nos. 1079-1082 (4) 1.35 .78

Arrival of Portuguese in Senegal, 550th Anniv.
A324

1994, Nov. 17 **Litho.** *Perf. 12*

1083 A324 175fr multicolored .80 .40

See Portugal No. 2036.

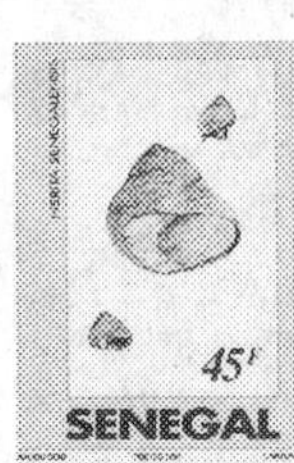

A325 A326

Shells: 20fr, Murex saxatilis, horiz. 45fr, Nerita senegalensis. 75fr, Polymita picea, horiz. 175fr, Scalaria pretiosa. 215fr, Conus gloria maris.

1994, Oct. 3 **Litho.** *Perf. 13½*

1084 A325 20fr multicolored .15 .15
1085 A325 45fr multicolored .20 .15
1086 A325 75fr multicolored .32 .16
1087 A325 175fr multicolored .75 .38
1088 A325 215fr multicolored .95 .48
Nos. 1084-1088 (5) 2.37 1.32

1994, Nov. 4

1089 A326 175fr multi, horiz. .75 .38
1090 A326 215fr multi, horiz. .95 .48
1091 A326 275fr multicolored 1.25 .60
1092 A326 290fr multi, diff. 1.25 .65
Nos. 1089-1092 (4) 4.20 2.11

Intl. Olympic Committee, Cent.

Wild Animals
A327

1994, Oct. 28 **Litho.** *Perf. 13½*

1093 A327 60fr Canis aureus .28 .15
1094 A327 70fr Aonyx capensis .30 .15
1095 A327 100fr Herpestes ichneumon .45 .22
1096 A327 175fr Manis gigantea .75 .38
1097 A327 215fr Varanus niloticus .95 .48
Nos. 1093-1097 (5) 2.73 1.38

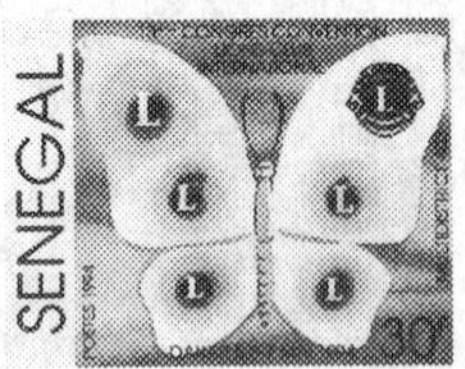

Lions Club Intl., 13th Multidistrict Convention, Dakar — A328

1994, May 5 **Litho.** *Perf. 13½x13*

1098 A328 30fr shown .15 .15
1099 A328 60fr Emblem, butterfly .30 .15
1100 A328 175fr Emblem, "L's" .85 .40
1101 A328 215fr Colors, emblem 1.00 .50
Nos. 1098-1101 (4) 2.30 1.20

African Children's Day — A329

UNICEF emblem and: 175fr, Children playing. 215fr, Family, huts.

1994, June 16 **Litho.** *Perf. 13½*

1102 A329 175fr multicolored .80 .40
1103 A329 215fr multicolored 1.00 .50

1994 World Cup Soccer Championships, US — A330

Designs: 45fr, Flags of participants, soccer ball, vert. 175fr, Top of globe, bottom of soccer ball, vert. 215fr, Player. 665fr, Two players.

1994, June 17

1104 A330 45fr multicolored .20 .15
1105 A330 175fr multicolored .80 .40
1106 A330 215fr multicolored 1.00 .50
1107 A330 665fr multicolored 3.00 1.50
Nos. 1104-1107 (4) 5.00 2.55

Intl. Year of the Family
A333

UN emblem and: 5fr, People of different races, national flags, peace dove, globe, sun. 175fr, Globe, flags, people. 215fr, Globe, mother & child. 290fr, Buildings, family, dove, sun, globe.

1994, Aug. 19 *Perf. 13½x13*

1113 A333 5fr multicolored .15 .15
1114 A333 175fr multicolored .80 .40
1115 A333 215fr multicolored 1.00 .50
1116 A333 290fr multicolored 1.40 .70
Nos. 1113-1116 (4) 3.35 1.75

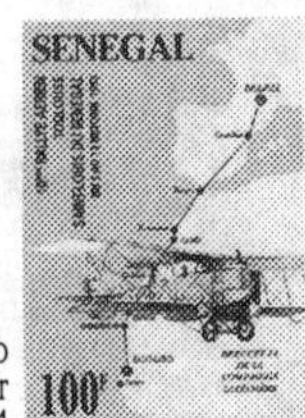

10th Toulouse to Saint-Louis Air Rally — A334

1994, Apr. 10 *Perf. 13½*

1117 A334 100fr Breguet 14 .45 .22
1118 A334 145fr Guillaumet .65 .32
1119 A334 180fr Jean Mermoz .85 .42
1120 A334 220fr Saint-Exupery 1.00 .50
Nos. 1117-1120 (4) 2.95 1.46

Dated 1993.

Christmas
A335

175fr, Santa Claus, Christ, children, presents. 215fr, Christmas trees, religious scenes. 275fr, Magi, Christ Child. 290fr, Madonna & Child.

Perf. 13x13½, 13½x13

1994, Nov. 24

1121 A335 175fr multi, vert. .80 .40
1122 A335 215fr multi, vert. 1.00 .50
1123 A335 275fr multi 1.25 .65
1124 A335 290fr multi, vert. 1.40 .70
Nos. 1121-1124 (4) 4.45 2.25

Historical Sites
A336

Designs: 100fr, Goree Chateau. 175fr, Soudan Mansion. 215fr, Goree Island. 275fr, Pinet Laprade fort, Sedhiou.

1994, Mar. 20 **Litho.** *Perf. 13½x13*

1125 A336 100fr multicolored .45 .20
1126 A336 175fr multicolored .80 .40
1127 A336 215fr multicolored 1.00 .50
1128 A336 275fr multicolored 1.25 .65
Nos. 1125-1128 (4) 3.50 1.75

Kallisaye Natl. Park — A337

Water birds: 100fr, Ardea melanocephala, vert. 275fr, Sterna caspia, vert. 290fr, Egretta gularis, vert. 380fr, Pelecanus rufescens.

1995, Feb. 2 *Perf. 13½*

1129 A337 100fr multicolored .45 .20
1130 A337 275fr multicolored 1.25 .65
1131 A337 290fr multicolored 1.40 .70
1132 A337 380fr multicolored 1.75 .85
Nos. 1129-1132 (4) 4.85 2.40

Dinosaurs
A338

1995, Jan. 27

1133 A338 100fr Diplodocus .45 .20
1134 A338 175fr Brontosaurus .80 .40
1135 A338 215fr Triceratops 1.00 .50
1136 A338 290fr Stegosaurus 1.40 .70
1137 A338 300fr Tyrannosaurus 1.40 .70
Nos. 1133-1137 (5) 5.05 2.50

House of Slaves, Goree
A339

1994 **Litho.** *Perf. 13½*

1138 A339 500fr multicolored 2.50 1.25

Flowers — A340

Designs: 30fr, Bombax costatum. 75fr, Allamanda cathartica. 100fr, Catharantus roseus. 1000fr, Clerodendron speciossimum.

1995, Apr. 9

1139 A340 30fr multicolored .15 .15
1140 A340 75fr multicolored .40 .20
1141 A340 100fr multicolored .50 .25
1142 A340 1000fr multicolored 5.00 2.50
Nos. 1139-1142 (4) 6.05 3.10

A341 A342

1995, May 11 **Litho.** *Perf. 11½*

1143 A341 260fr shown 1.35 .65
1144 A341 275fr Emblem, dove 1.40 .70

District 9100 Conference of Rotary, Intl.

1995, June 17

Map of Africa with countries highlighted, native item or animal: 10fr, Sudan, musical instrument. 15fr, Dahomey (Benin), huts, canoes. 30fr, Ivory

Coast, elephant. 70fr, Mauritania, camel. 175fr, Guinea, string instrument, bananas. 180fr, Upper Volta (Burkina Faso), ox, vegetables, drum. 215fr, Niger, Cross of Agadès. 225fr, Senegal, lions.

1145 A342 10fr multicolored .15 .15
1146 A342 15fr multicolored .15 .15
1147 A342 30fr multicolored .15 .15
1148 A342 70fr multicolored .35 .20
1149 A342 175fr multicolored .90 .45
1150 A342 180fr multicolored .90 .45
1151 A342 215fr multicolored 1.10 .55
1152 A342 225fr multicolored 1.25 .60
Nos. 1145-1152 (8) 4.95 2.70

Fashion Type of 1972

1995, June 30 *Perf. 13½x13*

Size: 21x26mm

1153 A106 5fr light brown .15 .15
1154 A106 10fr bright green .15 .15
1155 A106 20fr henna brown .15 .15
1156 A106 25fr olive .15 .15
1157 A106 30fr light olive .15 .15
1158 A106 40fr yellow green .20 .15
1159 A106 100fr slate blue .50 .25
1160 A106 150fr deep blue .75 .35
1161 A106 175fr dull brown .90 .45
1162 A106 200fr black 1.00 .50
1163 A106 250fr red 1.25 .60
1164 A106 275fr rose carmine 1.40 .80
Nos. 1153-1164 (12) 6.75 3.85

Economic Community of West African States (ECOWAS), 20th Anniv. A343

Designs: 175fr, Satellite dish, telephone, computer, map, dam, vert. 215fr, Flags of member nations, fruits, vegetables.

1995, Sept. 11 **Litho.** *Perf. 13½*

1165 A343 175fr multicolored .90 .45
1166 A343 215fr multicolored 1.10 .55

Louis Pasteur (1822-95) — A345

275fr, Holding vial. 500fr, In laboratory.

1995, Sept. 28 **Litho.** *Perf. 11½*

1168 A345 275fr multicolored 1.25 .60
1169 A345 500fr multicolored 2.25 1.25

Motion Pictures, Cent. — A346

Early developments by Lumiere Brothers: 100fr, Scene from "The Water Sprinkler." 200fr, First pulbic showing of motion picture. 250fr, Auguste, Louis Lumiere watching picture of train arriving at station. 275fr, Demonstrating cinematography.

1995, Oct. 2 *Perf. 13½*

1170 A346 100fr multicolored .45 .20
1171 A346 200fr multicolored .90 .45
1172 A346 250fr multicolored 1.10 .55
1173 A346 275fr multicolored 1.25 .60
Nos. 1170-1173 (4) 3.70 1.80

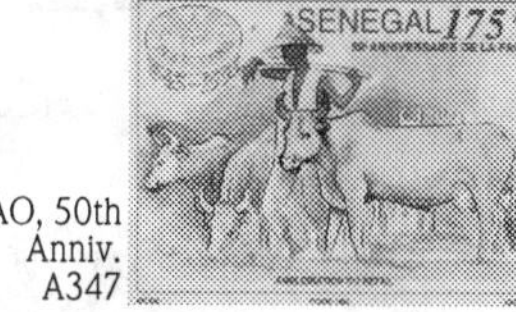

FAO, 50th Anniv. A347

Designs: 175fr, Farmer, oxen. 215fr, Technician, bringing water to arid regions. 260fr, Gathering fish. 275fr, Nutrition of infants.

1995, Oct. 16

1174 A347 175fr multicolored .80 .40
1175 A347 215fr multicolored .95 .50
1176 A347 260fr multicolored 1.10 .55
1177 A347 275fr multicolored 1.25 .60
Nos. 1174-1177 (4) 4.10 2.05

A348 A349

1995, Oct. 24 *Perf. 11½*

1178 A348 275fr shown 1.25 .60
1179 A348 1000fr Building 4.25 2.00

UN, 50th anniv.

1995, Nov. 2

1180 A349 150fr shown .70 .35
1181 A349 500fr Contestants 2.25 1.10

La Francophonie, 25th anniv.

Wild Animals A350

Designs: a, 90fr, Syncerus nanus savanensis. b, 150fr, Phacochoerus aethiopicus. c, 175fr, Tragelaphus scriptus. d, 275fr, Goechelone sulcata. e, 300fr, Hystrix cristata.

1995, Nov. 13 *Perf. 13½*

1182 A350 Strip of 5, #a.-e. 4.50 2.25

Endangered Birds — A351

1995, Nov. 30 *Perf. 13½x13*

1183 A351 90fr Hydroprogne caspia .40 .20
1184 A351 145fr Gelochelidon nilotica .65 .30
1185 A351 150fr Sterna maxima .70 .35
1186 A351 180fr Sterna hirunda .80 .40
Nos. 1183-1186 (4) 2.55 1.25

Butterflies A352

Designs: 45fr, Meganostoma eurydice. 100fr, Luehdorfia japonica. 200fr, Hebomoia glaucippe. 220fr, Aglais urticae.

1995, Dec. 4 *Perf. 13*

1187 A352 45fr multicolored .20 .15
1188 A352 100fr multicolored .45 .20
1189 A352 200fr multicolored .90 .45
1190 A352 220fr multicolored 1.00 .50
Nos. 1187-1190 (4) 2.55 1.30

Tourism A353

1995, Dec. 28 *Perf. 13½*

1191 A353 100fr Bassari Festival .45 .20
1192 A353 175fr Baawnaan, vert. .80 .40
1193 A353 220fr Traditional huts 1.00 .50
1194 A353 500fr Turu 2.25 1.10
Nos. 1191-1194 (4) 4.50 2.20

A354 A355

Paris-Granada-Dakar Rally, 17th Anniv.: 215fr, Car, silhouettes of three people. 275fr, Man racing on motorcycle, vert. 290fr, Car under Eiffel Tower, car racing toward finish line. 665fr, Two cars going over hill.

1996, Jan. 16 **Litho.** *Perf. 11½*

1195 A354 215fr multicolored 1.15 .60
1196 A354 275fr multicolored 1.50 .75
1197 A354 290fr multicolored 1.60 .80
1198 A354 665fr multicolored 3.50 1.75
Nos. 1195-1198 (4) 7.75 3.90

1996, Feb.2

Flowers: 175fr, Gossypium barbadense. 275fr, Hibiscus sabdariffa. 290fr, Hibiscus asper. 500fr, Nymphaea lotus.

1199 A355 175fr multicolored .95 .45
1200 A355 275fr multicolored 1.50 .75
1201 A355 290fr multicolored 1.60 .80
1202 A355 500fr multicolored 2.70 1.35
Nos. 1199-1202 (4) 6.75 3.35

Sports — A356

1996, Mar. 29 **Litho.** *Perf. 11½*

1203 A356 125fr Boxing .70 .35
1204 A356 215fr Judo 1.15 .60
1205 A356 275fr Javelin 1.50 .75
1206 A356 320fr Discus 1.75 .90
Nos. 1203-1206 (4) 5.10 2.60

Art by Serge Correa, Hall of Pearls — A357

1996,Apr. 18

1207 A357 260fr Corridor 1 1.35 .70
1208 A357 320fr Symphony 1 1.75 .85

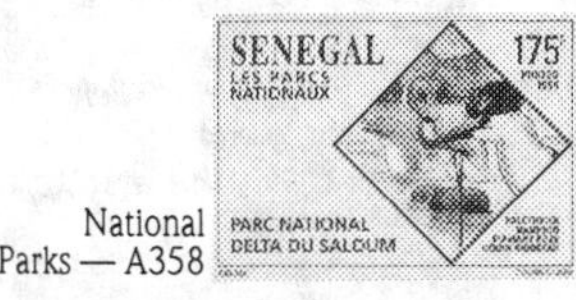

National Parks — A358

Designs: 175fr, Dolphin, flamingo, heron, Saloum Delta. 200fr, Chimpanzee, giraffe, elephant, Niokolo-Koba. 220fr, Crustaceans, bird in cave, Madeleine Island. 275fr, Abyssinia hornbill, crocodile, hippopotamus, Basse Casamance.

1996, Mar. 4

1209 A358 175fr multicolored .95 .50
1210 A358 200fr multicolored 1.10 .55
1211 A358 220fr multicolored 1.20 .60
1212 A358 275fr multicolored 1.50 .75
Nos. 1209-1212 (4) 4.75 2.40

Intl. Olympic Committee, Cent. A359

1996, July 1 **Litho.** *Perf. 12½*

1213 A359 215fr multicolored 1.25 .60

1996 Summer Olympic Games, Atlanta A360

1996, July 15 *Perf. 13*

1214 A360 10fr Swimming .15 .15
1215 A360 80fr Gymnastics .45 .20
1216 A360 175fr Running .95 .50
1217 A360 260fr Hurdles 1.40 .70
Nos. 1214-1217 (4) 2.95 1.55

Decade of UN Against Illegal Drug Abuse and Trafficking A361

215fr, UN emblem, hand holding red stop sign, drug paraphernalia.

1996, June 21 *Perf. 13½*

1218 A361 175fr multicolored .95 .50
1219 A361 215fr multicolored 1.15 .60

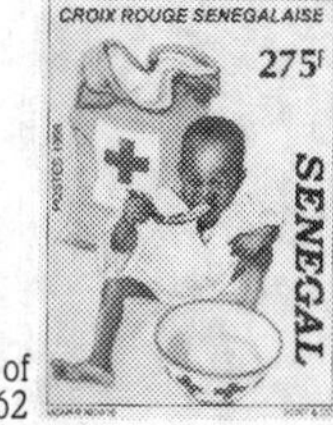

Red Cross of Senegal — A362

1996, Oct. 21 *Perf. 12½*

1220 A362 275fr multicolored 1.50 .75

Primates — A363

Designs: 10fr, Cercopithecus aethiops. 30fr, Erthrocebus patas. 90fr, Cercopithecus campbelli. 215fr, Pantroglodytes verus. 260fr, Papio papio.

1996, Nov. 29 **Litho.** *Perf. 13x13½*

1221 A363 10fr multicolored .15 .15
1222 A363 30fr multicolored .15 .15
1223 A363 90fr multicolored .35 .15
1224 A363 215fr multicolored .85 .45
1225 A363 260fr multicolored 1.00 .50
a. Strip of 5, #1221-1225 2.40 1.20

UNICEF, 50th Anniv. A364

1996, Dec. 11 *Perf. 13½x13*

1226 A364 75fr shown .30 .15
1227 A364 275fr Child, diff. 1.20 .60

19th Dakar-Agades-Dakar Rally — A365

25fr, Semi-truck. 75fr, Man pushing car, figure of man. 215fr, Race car. 300fr, Man on motorcycle.

1996 Litho. *Perf. 13x13½*

1228 A365 25fr multicolored .15 .15
1229 A365 75fr multicolored .30 .15
1230 A365 215fr multicolored .90 .45
1231 A365 300fr multicolored 1.25 .65
Nos. 1228-1231 (4) 2.60 1.40

Trees — A366

Designs: 80fr, Faidherbia albida. 175fr, Eucalyptus. 220fr, Khaya senegalensis. 260fr, Casuarina equisetifolia.

1996

1232 A366 80fr multicolored .35 .20
1233 A366 175fr multicolored .70 .35
1234 A366 220fr multicolored .90 .45
1235 A366 260fr multicolored 1.00 .50
Nos. 1232-1235 (4) 2.95 1.50

Birds — A367

25fr, Platalea leucorodia. 70fr, Leptilos crumeniferus. 175fr, Balcarica pavonina. 215fr, Ephippiarhychus senegalensis. 220fr, Numenius arquata.

1996

1236 A367 25fr multicolored .15 .15
1237 A367 70fr multicolored .30 .15
1238 A367 175fr multicolored .75 .35
1239 A367 215fr multicolored .90 .45
1240 A367 220fr multicolored .95 .50
a. Strip of 5, #1236-1240 3.00 1.50

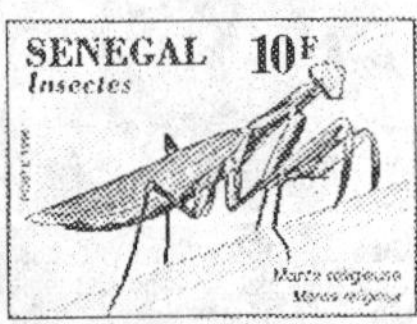

Insects A368

Designs: 10fr, Mantis religiosa. 50fr, Forficula auricularia. 75fr, Schistocerca gregaria. 215fr, Cicindela lunulata. 220fr, Gryllus campestris.

1996 *Perf. 13½x13*

1241 A368 10fr multicolored .15 .15
1243 A368 50fr multicolored .20 .15
1244 A368 75fr multicolored .30 .15
1245 A368 215fr multicolored .90 .45
1246 A368 220fr multicolored .95 .45
a. Strip of 5, #1241-1246 2.40 1.20

Third World — A370

Design: 500fr, Hot air balloon in flight.

1996, Apr. 13 Litho. *Perf. 13½*

1258 A370 215fr shown .75 .40
1259 A370 500fr multicolored 1.75 .90

See Mali Nos. 812-813.

Niokolo-Badiar Natl. Park — A372

Designs: 30fr, Haliaetus vacifer. 90fr, Hippopotamus amphibius. 240fr, Loxindonta africana oxyotis. 300fr, Taurotragus derbianus.

1997 Litho. *Perf. 13½x13*

1262 A372 30fr multicolored .15 .15
1263 A372 90fr multicolored .40 .20
1264 A372 240fr multicolored 1.00 .50
1265 A372 300fr multicolored 1.25 .65
Nos. 1262-1265 (4) 2.80 1.50

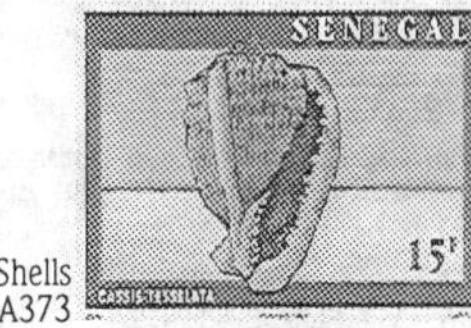

Shells A373

Designs: a, 15fr, Cassis tesselata. b, 40fr, Pugilina meria. c, 190fr, Cyprea mappa. d, 200fr, Natica adansoni. e, 300fr, Bullia miran.

1997 *Perf. 13x13½*

1266 A373 Strip of 5, #a.-e. 3.10 1.60

Wild Animals A374

a, 25fr, African buffaloes. b, 90fr, Gazelles. c, 100fr, Gnu. d, 200fr, Wild dogs. e, 240fr, Cheetah.

1997

1267 A374 Strip of 5, #a.-e. 2.75 1.40

Goree Island A375

1997 *Perf. 13½*

1268 A375 180fr multicolored .75 .40

No. 1268 is dated 1992 and has word "almadies" obliterated.

Dakar-Dakar Rally, 20th Anniv. — A376

Designs: 20fr, Truck traveling across Sahel. 45fr, Motorcycle arriving at Lake Rose. 190fr, Sports utility vehicle crossing Mauritanian Desert. 240fr, Car at Senegal River.

1997 Litho. *Perf. 13½x13*

1269 A376 20fr multicolored .15 .15
1270 A376 45fr multicolored .20 .15
1271 A376 190fr multicolored .80 .40
1272 A376 240fr multicolored 1.00 .50
Nos. 1269-1272 (4) 2.15 1.20

Food Day A377

Designs: 190fr, Receiving grain through cereal bank. 200fr, Proper nutrition for women.

1997

1273 A377 190fr multicolored .80 .40
1274 A377 200fr multicolored .85 .45

A378 A379

Masks: 45fr, Planche, Burkina Faso. 90fr, Kpeliyehe, Ivory Coast. 200fr, Nimba, Guinea Bissau. 240fr, Walu, Mali. 300fr, Dogon, Mali.

1997

1275 A378 45fr multicolored .20 .15
1276 A378 90fr multicolored .45 .20
1277 A378 200fr multicolored .85 .40
1278 A378 240fr multicolored 1.00 .50
1279 A378 300fr multicolored 1.25 .65
a. Strip of 5, #1275-1279 3.75 1.90

1997 *Perf. 11½*

1280 A379 310fr multicolored 1.30 .65

Heinrich von Stephan (1831-97).

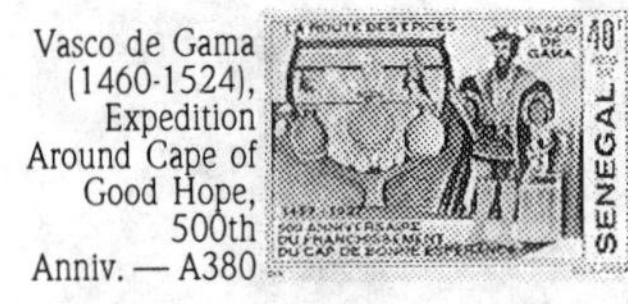

Vasco de Gama (1460-1524), Expedition Around Cape of Good Hope, 500th Anniv. — A380

De Gama and: 40fr, Route of spices. 75fr, Port of Zanzibar. 190fr, Caravel revolution. 200fr, Maps being printed.

1997

1281 A380 40fr multicolored .20 .15
1282 A380 75fr multicolored .30 .15
1283 A380 190fr multicolored .80 .40
1284 A380 200fr multicolored .85 .40
Nos. 1281-1284 (4) 2.15 1.10

Trains A381

Designs: 15fr, CC2400. 90fr, Loco-tractor. 100fr, Mountain train. 240fr, Maquinista. 310fr, Freight train, series 151-A.

1997 *Perf. 13x13½*

1285 A381 15fr multicolored .15 .15
1286 A381 90fr multicolored .40 .20
1287 A381 100fr multicolored .45 .25
1288 A381 240fr multicolored 1.00 .50
1289 A381 310fr multicolored 1.30 .65
a. Strip of 5, #1285-1289 3.25 1.65

Musical Instruments A382

1997 *Perf. 13x13½*

1290 A382 125fr Riiti .55 .25
1291 A382 190fr Kora .80 .40
1292 A382 200fr Fama .85 .45
1293 A382 240fr Dioung dioung 1.00 .50
Nos. 1290-1293 (4) 3.20 1.60

World Wildlife Fund A383

Profelis aurata: 100fr, Climbing on tree limb. 240fr, Lying on tree limb. 300fr, Two cubs.

1997, Dec. 24 Litho. *Perf. 11½*

1294 A383 45fr multicolored .20 .15
1295 A383 100fr multicolored .40 .20
1296 A383 240fr multicolored 1.00 .50
1297 A383 300fr multicolored 1.25 .65
Nos. 1294-1297 (4) 2.85 1.50

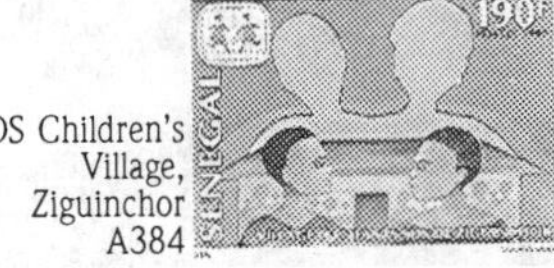

SOS Children's Village, Ziguinchor A384

1997 Litho. *Perf. 11½*

1298 A384 190fr shown .80 .40
1299 A384 240fr Child, buildings 1.00 .50

Club Aldiana, 25th Anniv. — A385

Designs: 290fr, Hut, people at market, mother and baby. 320fr, People on boats, woman in traditional dress, fish in basket.

1998 *Perf. 13½*

1300 A385 290fr multicolored 1.20 .60
1301 A385 320fr multicolored 1.30 .65

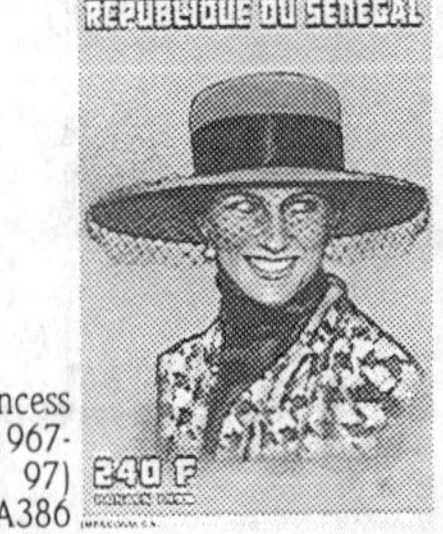

Diana, Princess of Wales (1967-97) A386

Various portraits.

1998

1302 A386 240fr like #1304g 1.00 .50

Sheets of 9

1303 A386 200fr #a.-i. 7.50 3.75
1304 A386 250fr #a.-i. 9.50 4.75

Nos. 1303-1304 are continuous designs.

Souvenir Sheets

1305 A386 1000fr Portrait 4.20 2.10
1306 A386 1500fr With her sons 6.25 3.25
1307 A386 2000fr Wearing tiara 8.25 4.25

SEMI-POSTAL STAMPS

No. 84 Surcharged in Red 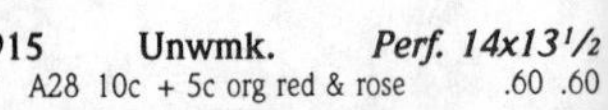

1915 Unwmk. *Perf. 14x13½*

B1 A28 10c + 5c org red & rose .60 .60

No. B1 is on both ordinary and chalky paper.

Same Surcharge on No. 87

1918

32 A28 15c + 5c red org & brn vio .70 .70

Curie Issue
Common Design Type

1938 **Engr.** *Perf. 13*

33 CD80 1.75fr + 50c brt ultra 6.50 6.50

French Revolution Issue
Common Design Type

Photo., Name & Value Typo. in Black

1939

34 CD83 45c + 25c green 4.50 4.50
35 CD83 70c + 30c brown 4.50 4.50
36 CD83 90c + 35c red org 4.50 4.50
37 CD83 1.25fr + 1fr rose pink 4.50 4.50
38 CD83 2.25fr + 2fr blue 4.50 4.50
Nos. B4-B8 (5) 22.50 22.50

Stamps of 1935-38 Surcharged in Red or Black

SECOURS + 1 fr. NATIONAL

1941 *Perf. 12x12½, 12*

39 A30 50c + 1fr red org .60
310 A31 80c + 2fr vio (R) 2.25
311 A30 1.50fr + 2fr dk bl 3.00
312 A30 2fr + 3fr blue 3.00
Nos. B9-B12 (4) 8.85

Common Design Type and

Bambara Sharpshooter SP1

Colonial Soldier SP2

1941 **Photo.** *Perf. 13½*

313 SP1 1fr + 1fr red .55
314 CD86 1.50fr + 3fr maroon .55
315 SP2 2.50fr + 1fr blue .55
Nos. B13-B15 (3) 1.65

The surtax was for the defense of the colonies.
Nos. B13-B15 were issued by the Vichy government, but it is doubtful whether they were placed in use in Senegal.
Stamps of type A32 surcharged "OEUVRES COLONIALES" and new values were issued in 1944 by the Vichy Government, but were not placed on sale in the colony.

Catalogue values for unused stamps in this section, from this point to the end of the section, are for Never Hinged items.

Republic
Anti-Malaria Issue
Common Design Type

Perf. 12½x12

962, Apr. 7 **Engr.** **Unwmk.**

16 CD108 25fr + 5fr brt grn .40 .40

Freedom from Hunger Issue
Common Design Type

963, Mar. 21 *Perf. 13*

17 CD112 25fr + 5fr dp vio, grn & brn .35 .35

AIR POST STAMPS

Landscape AP1

Caravan AP2

Perf. 12½x12, 12x12½

1935 **Engr.** **Unwmk.**

C1 AP1 25c dk brown .20 .15
C2 AP1 50c red orange .40 .30
C3 AP1 1fr rose lilac .20 .15
C4 AP1 1.25fr yellow grn .20 .15
C5 AP1 2fr blue .20 .15
C6 AP1 3fr olive grn .20 .15
C7 AP2 3.50fr violet .20 .15
C8 AP2 4.75fr orange .50 .30
C9 AP2 6.50fr dk blue .60 .45
C10 AP2 8fr black 1.25 .85
C11 AP2 15fr rose lake .75 .45
Nos. C1-C11 (11) 4.70 3.25

No. C8 surcharged "ENTR' AIDE FRANCAIS + 95f 25" in green, red violet or blue, was never issued in this colony.

Common Design Type

1940 **Engr.** *Perf. 12½x12*

C12 CD85 1.90fr ultra .25 .25
C13 CD85 2.90fr dk red .25 .25
C14 CD85 4.50fr dk gray grn .35 .35
C15 CD85 4.90fr yellow bis .40 .40
C16 CD85 6.90fr dp orange .40 .40
Nos. C12-C16 (5) 1.65 1.65

Common Design Types

1942

C17 CD88 50c car & bl .15
C18 CD88 1fr brn & blk .25
C19 CD88 2fr dk grn & red brn .25
C20 CD88 3fr dk bl & scar .60
C21 CD88 5fr vio & brn red .35

Frame Engr., Center Typo.

C22 CD89 10fr ultra, ind & hn .35
C23 CD89 20fr rose car, mag & choc .45
C24 CD89 50fr yel grn, dl grn & yel .90 1.25

Engr. & Photo.

Size: 47x26mm

C25 CD88 100fr dk red & bl 1.50 2.50
Nos. C17-C25 (9) 4.80

There is doubt whether Nos. C17 to C23 were officially placed in use.

Catalogue values for unused stamps in this section, from this point to the end of the section, are for Never Hinged items.

Republic

Abyssinian Roller — AP3

Designs: 50fr, Carmine bee-eater, vert. 200fr, Violet touraco, vert. 250fr, Red bishop, vert. 500fr, Fish eagle, vert.

Perf. 12½x13, 13x12½

1960-63 **Photo.** **Unwmk.**

Birds in Natural Colors

C26 AP3 50fr blk & gray bl ('61) .65 .20
C27 AP3 100fr blk, yel & lil 1.40 .45
C28 AP3 200fr blk, grn & bl ('61) 2.50 1.50
C29 AP3 250fr blk & pale grn ('63) 3.50 1.90
C30 AP3 500fr blk & bl 8.50 2.50
Nos. C26-C30 (5) 16.55 6.55

Air Afrique Issue
Common Design Type

1962, Feb. 17 **Engr.** *Perf. 13*

C31 CD107 25fr vio brn, sl grn & ocher .30 .16

African Postal Union Issue
Common Design Type

1963, Sept. 8 **Photo.** *Perf. 12½*

C32 CD114 85fr choc, ocher & red .65 .42

Air Afrique Issue, 1963
Common Design Type

1963, Nov. 19 **Unwmk.** *Perf. 13x12*

C33 CD115 50fr multicolored .70 .50

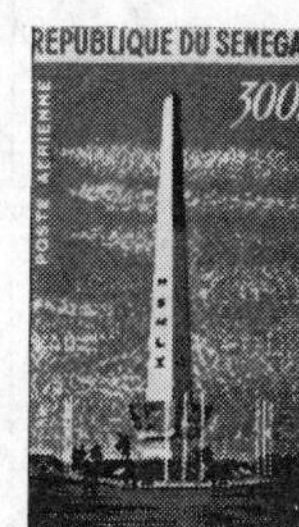

Independence Monument — AP4

1964, Apr. 4 **Photo.** *Perf. 12x13*

C34 AP4 300fr ultra, tan, ocher & grn 2.00 1.00

Symbolic European and African Cities — AP5

1964, Apr. 18 **Engr.** *Perf. 13*

C35 AP5 150fr grn, brn red & blk 1.60 1.00

Congress of the Intl. Federation of Twin Cities, Dakar.

Europafrica Issue, 1964

Peanuts, Globe, Factory, Figures of "Africa," and "Europe" — AP6

1964, July 20 **Photo.** *Perf. 13x12*

C36 AP6 50fr multicolored .65 .50

See note after Madagascar No. 357.

Basketball — AP7 Launching of Syncom 2 — AP8

1964, Aug. 22 **Engr.** *Perf. 13*

C37 AP7 85fr shown .65 .42
C38 AP7 100fr Pole vault .90 .50

18th Olympic Games, Tokyo, Oct. 10-25.

1964, Oct. 24 **Unwmk.** *Perf. 13*

C39 AP8 150fr grn, red brn & ultra 1.10 .55

Communication through space.

Pres. John F. Kennedy (1917-1963) AP9

Mother and Child, Globe and Emblems AP10

1964, Dec. 5 **Photo.** *Perf. 13*

C40 AP9 100fr brt yel, dk grn & brn red .90 .75
a. Souvenir sheet of 4 4.00 4.00

Scenic Type of Regular Issue, 1965

View: 100fr, Shore of Gambia River in Eastern Senegal.

1965, Feb. 27 **Engr.** *Perf. 13*

Size: 48x27mm

C41 A48 100fr brn blk, grn & bis 1.00 .42

1965, Sept. 25 **Unwmk.** *Perf. 13*

C42 AP10 50fr choc, brt bl & grn .45 .25

International Cooperation Year.

A-1 Satellite and Earth — AP11

Designs: No. C44, Diamant rocket. 90fr, Scout rocket and FR-1 satellite.

1966, Feb. 19 **Engr.** *Perf. 13*

C43 AP11 50fr yel brn, dk grn & blk .38 .20
C44 AP11 50fr Prus bl, lt red brn & car rose .38 .20
C45 AP11 90fr dk red brn, dk gray & Prus bl .80 .42
Nos. C43-C45 (3) 1.56 .82

French achievements in space.

D-1 Satellite over Globe — AP12

1966, June 11 **Engr.** *Perf. 13*

C46 AP12 100fr dk car, sl & vio 1.00 .55

Launching of the D-1 satellite at Hammaguir, Algeria, Feb. 17, 1966.

Air Afrique Issue, 1966
Common Design Type

1966, Aug. 31 **Photo.** *Perf. 13*

C47 CD123 30fr red brn, blk & lem .30 .15

Mermoz Plane "Arc-en-Ciel" — AP13

Jean Mermoz — AP14

Designs: 35fr, Latecoère 300 "Croix du Sud." 100fr, Map showing last flight from Dakar to Brazil.

1966, Dec. 7 Engr. *Perf. 13*

C48 AP13	20fr bl, rose lil & indigo	.22	.16
C49 AP13	35fr slate, brn & grn	.38	.20
C50 AP13	100fr grn, lt grn & mar	1.00	.42
C51 AP14	150fr blk, ultra & mar	1.50	.70
	Nos. C48-C51 (4)	3.10	1.48

Jean Mermoz (1901-36), French aviator, on the 30th anniv. of his last flight.

Dakar-Yoff Airport — AP15

1967, Apr. 22 Engr. *Perf. 13*

C52 AP15	200fr red brn, ind & brt bl	1.10	.38

Knob-billed Goose — AP16

Flowers and Birds: 100fr, Mimosa. 150fr, Flowering cactus. 250fr, Village weaver. 500fr, Bateleur.

1967-69 Photo. *Perf. 11½*

Granite Paper

Dated "1967"

C53 AP16	100fr gray, yel & grn	1.10	.45
C54 AP16	150fr multicolored	1.60	.65

Dated "1969"

C55 AP16	250fr gray & multi	2.00	1.00

Dated "1968"

C56 AP16	300fr brt bl & multi	3.00	1.25
C57 AP16	500fr orange & multi	4.25	1.90
	Nos. C53-C57 (5)	11.95	5.25

Issued: 100fr, 150fr, 6/24/67; 500fr, 7/13/68; 300fr, 12/21/68; 250fr, 4/26/69.

The Girls from Avignon, by Picasso AP17

1967, July 22 *Perf. 12x13*

C59 AP17	100fr multicolored	1.20	.80

African Postal Union Issue, 1967

Common Design Type

1967, Sept. 9 Engr. *Perf. 13*

C60 CD124	100fr brt grn, vio & car lake	.90	.45

Konrad Adenauer — AP18

Weather Balloon, Vegetation and WMO Emblem — AP19

1968, Feb. 17 Photo. *Perf. 12½*

C61 AP18	100fr dk red, ol & blk	1.10	.55
a.	Souvenir sheet of 4	4.50	4.50

Konrad Adenauer (1876-1967), chancellor of West Germany (1949-63).

1968, Mar. 23 Engr. *Perf. 13*

C62 AP19	50fr blk, ultra & bl grn	.45	.22

8th World Meteorological Day, Mar. 23.

19th Olympic Games, Mexico City, Oct. 12-27 — AP20

1968, Oct. 12 Engr. *Perf. 13*

C63 AP20	20fr Hurdling	.20	.15
C64 AP20	30fr Javelin	.22	.16
C65 AP20	50fr Judo	.42	.18
C66 AP20	75fr Basketball	.60	.22
	Nos. C63-C66 (4)	1.44	.71

PHILEXAFRIQUE Issue

Young Woman Reading Letter, by Jean Raoux AP21

1968, Oct. 26 Photo. *Perf. 12½*

C67 AP21	100fr buff & multi	1.10	1.00

PHILEXAFRIQUE, Phil. Exhib. in Abidjan, Feb. 14-23, 1969. Printed with alternating buff label.

2nd PHILEXAFRIQUE Issue

Common Design Type

50fr, Senegal No. 160 and Boulevard, Dakar.

1969, Feb. 14 Engr. *Perf. 13*

C68 CD128	50fr grn, gray & pur	.60	.50

Tourist Emblem with Map of Africa and Dove — AP22

1969 Photo. *Perf. 13*

C69 AP22	100fr red, lt grn & lt bl	.70	.35

Year of African Tourism, 1969.

Pres. Lamine Gueye (1891-1968) — AP23

Design: 45fr, Pres. Gueye wearing fez.

1969, June 10 Photo. *Perf. 12½*

C70 AP23	30fr brn, org & blk	.22	.15
C71 AP23	45fr brn, lt grnsh bl & blk	.35	.16
a.	Min. sheet of 4, 2 #C70, 2 #C71	1.25	1.25

"Transmission of Thought" Tapestry by Ousmane Faye — AP24

Fari, Tapestry by Allaye N'Diaye — AP25

1969, Oct. 25 Photo. *Perf. 12½*

C72 AP24	25fr multicolored	.22	.15

Perf. 12x12½

C73 AP25	50fr multicolored	.45	.22

Europafrica Issue

Baila Bridge — AP26

1969, Nov. 15 Photo. *Perf. 13x12*

C74 AP26	100fr multicolored	.70	.38

Emile Lécrivain, Plane and Toulouse-Dakar Route — AP27

1970, Jan. 31 Engr. *Perf. 13*

C75 AP27	50fr grn, slate & rose brn	.40	.22

40th anniv. of the disappearance of the aviator Emile Lécrivain (1897-1929).

René Maran, Martinique — AP28

Portraits: 45fr, Marcus Garvey, Jamaica. 50fr, Dr. Price Mars, Haiti.

1970, Mar. 21 Photo. *Perf. 12½*

C76 AP28	30fr red brn, lt grn & blk	.25	.15
C77 AP28	45fr blue, pink & blk	.42	.16
C78 AP28	50fr grn, buff & blk	.48	.16
	Nos. C76-C78 (3)	1.15	.47

Issued to honor prominent Negro leaders.

"One People, One Purpose, One Faith" — AP29

1970, Apr. 3 Photo. *Perf. 11½*

C79 AP29	500fr gold & multi	4.00	1.90
a.	Souvenir sheet	4.50	4.50

10th anniv. of independence. No. C79 sold for 600fr.

Bay of Naples and Dakar Post Office — AP30

1970, May 2 Photo. *Perf. 13x12½*

C80 AP30	100fr multicolored	.80	.55

10th Europa Phil. Exhib., Naples, May 2-10.

Blue Cock, by Mamadou Niang AP31

Tapestries: 45fr, Fairy. 75fr, "Lunaris," by Jean Lurçat.

1970, June 20 Photo. *Perf. 12½x12*

C81 AP31	30fr black & multi	.20	.15
C82 AP31	45fr dk red brn & multi	.35	.15
C83 AP31	75fr yellow & multi	.50	.30
	Nos. C81-C83 (3)	1.05	.60

Head of the Courtesan Nagakawa, by Chobunsai Yeishi, and Mt. Fuji, by Hokusai — AP32

EXPO Emblem and: 25fr, Woman Playing Guitar, by Hokusai, and Sun Tower, vert. 150fr, "One of the Present-day Beauties of Nanboku" by Katsukawa Shuncho, vert.

1970, July 18 Engr. *Perf. 13*

C84 AP32 25fr red & green .20 .15
C85 AP32 75fr yel grn, dk bl & red brn .55 .22
C86 AP32 150fr bl, red brn & ocher 1.10 .55
Nos. C84-C86 (3) 1.85 .92

EXPO '70 Intl. Exhib., Osaka, Japan, Mar. 15-Sept. 13.

Tuna, Processing Plant and Ship — AP33

Urban Development in Dakar — AP34

1970, Aug. 22 Engr. *Perf. 13*

C87 AP33 30fr dl red, blk & brt bl .22 .15
C88 AP34 100fr chocolate & grn .70 .40

Progress in industrialization and urbanization in Dakar.

Beethoven; Napoleon and Allegory of Eroica Symphony — AP35

Design: 100fr, Beethoven holding quill.

1970, Sept. 26 Engr. *Perf. 13*

C89 AP35 50fr ol, brn & ocher .52 .22
C90 AP35 100fr Prus grn & dp claret 1.00 .50

Ludwig van Beethoven (1770-1827), composer.

Globe, Scales and Women of Four Races — AP36

1970, Oct. 24 Engr. *Perf. 13*

C91 AP36 100fr grn, ocher & red .90 .55

25th anniversary of United Nations.

De Gaulle, Map of Africa, Symbols — AP37

Phillis Wheatley, American Poet — AP39

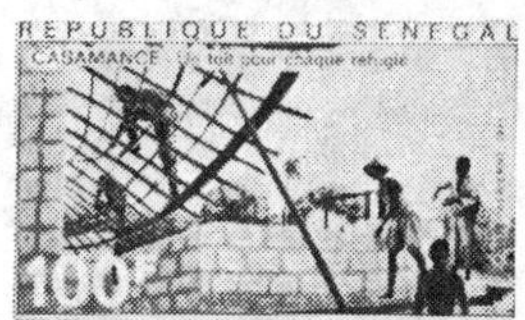

"A Roof for Every Refugee" — AP38

100fr, Charles de Gaulle & map of Senegal.

1970, Dec. 31 Photo. *Perf. 12½*

C92 AP37 50fr multicolored .45 .35
C93 AP37 100fr blue & multi 1.00 .65

Honoring Pres. Charles de Gaulle as liberator of the colonies.

1971, Jan. 16

C94 AP38 100fr multicolored .80 .42

High Commissioner for Refugees, 20th anniv.

1971, Apr. 10 Photo. *Perf. 12½*

Prominent Blacks: 40fr, James E. K. Aggrey, Methodist missionary, Ghana. 60fr, Alain Le Roy Locke, American educator. 100fr, Booker T. Washington, American educator.

C95 AP39 25fr multicolored .16 .15
C96 AP39 40fr blk, bl & bis .30 .16
C97 AP39 60fr blk, bl & emer .45 .18
C98 AP39 100fr blk, bl & red .70 .38
Nos. C95-C98 (4) 1.61 .87

Napoleon as First Consul, by Ingres — AP40

Designs: 25fr, Napoleon in 1809, by Robert Lefevre. 35fr, Napoleon on his death bed, by Georges Rouget. 50fr, Awakening into Immortality, sculpture by Francois Rude.

1971, June 19 Photo. *Perf. 13*

C99 AP40 15fr gold & multi .25 .20
C100 AP40 25fr gold & multi .40 .25
C101 AP40 35fr gold & multi .45 .35
C102 AP40 50fr gold & multi .65 .60
Nos. C99-C102 (4) 1.75 1.40

Napoleon Bonaparte (1769-1821).

Gamal Abdel Nasser — AP41

Alfred Nobel — AP41a

1971, July 17 *Perf. 12½*

C103 AP41 50fr multicolored .40 .20

Nasser (1918-1970), President of Egypt.

1971, Sept. 25 Photo. *Perf. 13½x13*

C103A AP41a 100fr multicolored .80 .45

Alfred Nobel (1833-1896), inventor of dynamite who established the Nobel Prizes.

Iranian Flag and Senegal Coat of Arms — AP42

1971, Oct. 15 *Perf. 13x12½*

C104 AP42 200fr multicolored 1.50 .65

2500th anniversary of the founding of the Persian empire by Cyrus the Great.

African Postal Union Issue, 1971

Common Design Type

Design: 100fr, Arms of Senegal and UAMPT Building, Brazzaville, Congo.

1971, Nov. 13 *Perf. 13x13½*

C105 CD135 100fr blue & multi .70 .30

Louis Armstrong (1900-1971), American Jazz Musician AP43

1971, Nov. 27 Photo. *Perf. 12½*

C106 AP43 150fr gold & dk brn 1.20 .80

Sapporo Olympic Emblem and Speed Skating — AP44

Sapporo '72 Emblem and: 10fr, Bobsledding. 125fr, Skiing.

1972, Jan. 22 *Perf. 13*

C107 AP44 5fr multicolored .15 .15
C108 AP44 10fr multicolored .15 .15
C109 AP44 125fr multicolored .90 .40
Set value 1.00 .50

11th Winter Olympic Games, Sapporo, Japan, Feb. 3-13.

Fonteghetto della Farina, by Canaletto — AP45

Design: 100fr, San Giorgio Maggiore, by Giovanni Antonio Guardi, vert.

1972, Feb. 26

C110 AP45 50fr gold & multi .40 .20
C111 AP45 100fr gold & multi .80 .40

UNESCO campaign to save Venice.

Theater Type of Regular Issue

Design: 150fr, Daniel Sorano as Shylock, vert.

1972, Mar. 25 Photo. *Perf. 12½x13*

C112 A99 150fr multicolored 1.40 .70

Environment Type of Regular Issue

Design: 100fr, Protection of the ocean (oil slick).

1972, June 3 Photo. *Perf. 13x12½*

C113 A101 100fr multicolored .80 .45

Emperor Haile Selassie, Ethiopian and Senegalese Flags — AP46

1972, July 23 Photo. *Perf. 13½x13*

C114 AP46 100fr gold & multi .80 .40

80th birthday of Emperor Haile Selassie of Ethiopia.

Swordfish — AP47

Designs: 65fr, Killer whale. 75fr, Rhincodon. 125fr, Common rorqual (whale).

1972-73 Photo. *Perf. 11½*

C115 AP47 50fr multi .35 .15
C116 AP47 65fr multi .40 .18
C117 AP47 75fr multi .45 .22
C118 AP47 125fr multi .90 .55

Issued: #C115, C118, 11/25/72; #C116-C117, 7/28/73.

Palace of the Republic — AP48

1973, Apr. 3 Photo. *Perf. 13*

C119 AP48 100fr multi .60 .35

Hotel Teranga, Dakar — AP49

1973, May 26 **Photo.** ***Perf. 13***
C120 AP49 100fr multi .60 .35

Emblem of African Lions Club AP50

1973, June 2
C121 AP50 150fr multi 1.00 .65

15th Congress of Lions Intl., District 403, Dakar, June 1-2.

"Couple with Mimosa," by Marc Chagall AP51

1973, Aug. 11 **Photo.** ***Perf. 13***
C122 AP51 200fr multi 1.90 .90

Map of Italy with Riccione — AP52

Human Rights Flame and People — AP54

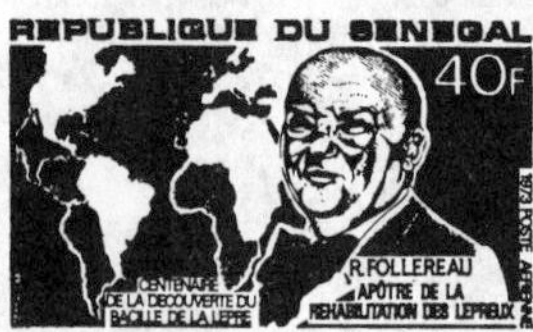
Raoul Follereau and World Map — AP53

1973, Aug. 25 **Engr.**
C123 AP52 100fr dk grn, red & pur .60 .38

Intl. Phil. Exhib., Riccione 1973.

1973, Dec. 22 **Engr.** ***Perf. 13***

100fr, Dr. Armauer G. Hansen & leprosy bacilli.

C124 AP53 40fr sl grn, pur & red brn .25 .15
C125 AP53 100fr sl grn, mag & plum .65 .40

Centenary of the discovery of the Hansen bacillus, the cause of leprosy.

1973, Dec. 15 **Photo.** ***Perf. 13½***

65fr, Human Rights flame and drummer.

C126 AP54 35fr grn & multi .20 .15
C127 AP54 65fr org & multi .25 .22

25th anniv. of the Universal Declaration of Human Rights.

Men of Four Races, Arms of Dakar, Congress Emblem — AP55

50fr, Key joining twin cities & emblem, vert.

1973, Dec. 26 **Photo.**
C128 AP55 50fr org & multi .35 .20
C129 AP55 125fr red & multi .80 .45

8th Congress of the World Federation of Twin Cities, Dakar, Dec. 26-29.

Finfoots — AP56

1974, Feb. 9 **Photo.** ***Perf. 13***
C130 AP56 1fr shown .15 .15
C131 AP56 2fr Spoonbills .15 .15
C132 AP56 3fr Crested cranes .15 .15
C133 AP56 4fr Egrets .15 .15
C134 AP56 250fr Flamingos 1.40 .90
C135 AP56 250fr Flamingos 1.40 .90
a. Strip of 2 + label 3.00
Set value 3.00 2.00

Djoudj Park bird sanctuary. Denomination in gold on No. C134, in black on No. C135.

Tiger Attacking Wild Horse, by Delacroix — AP57

Design: 200fr, Tiger Hunt, by Eugéne Delacroix (1798-1863).

1974, Mar. 23 **Photo.** ***Perf. 13***
C136 AP57 150fr gold & multi .90 .60
C137 AP57 200fr gold & multi 1.20 .65

Intl. Fair, Dakar — AP57a

1974, Nov. 28 **Embossed** ***Perf. 10½***
C137A AP57a 350fr silver
C137B AP57a 1500fr gold

Soyuz and Apollo, Space Docking Emblem — AP58

1975, May 23 **Engr.** ***Perf. 13***
C138 AP58 125fr multi .50 .35

US-USSR space cooperation.
For overprint see No. C140.

Senegal Type D6, Tuscany Type A1, Map of Italy — AP59

1975, Aug. 23 **Engr.** ***Perf. 13***
C139 AP59 125fr org, vio & dk red .65 .35

Intl. Phil. Exhib., Riccione 1975.

No. C138 Overprinted: "JONCTION / 17 Juil. 1975"

1975, Oct. 21 **Engr.** ***Perf. 13***
C140 AP58 125fr multi .50 .35

Apollo-Soyuz link-up in space, July 17, 1975.

Boston Massacre — AP60

Design: 500fr, Lafayette, Washington, Rochambeau and Battle of Yorktown.

1975, Dec. 20 **Engr.** ***Perf. 13***
C141 AP60 250fr ultra, red & brn 1.40 .65
C142 AP60 500fr bl & ver 2.50 1.40

American Bicentennial.

Concorde and Map — AP61

1976, Jan. 21 **Litho.** ***Perf. 13***
C143 AP61 300fr multi 1.60 .80

First commercial flight of supersonic jet Concorde, Paris to Rio de Janeiro, Jan. 21.
For overprint see No. C145.

2nd Intl. Fair, Dakar — AP61a

1976, Dec. 3 **Embossed** ***Perf. 10½***
C143A AP61a 500fr silver
C143B AP61a 1500fr gold

Spaceship and Control Room — AP62

1977, June 25 **Litho.** ***Perf. 12½***
C144 AP62 300fr multi 1.60 .80

Viking space mission to Mars.

No. C143 Overprinted in Red: "22.11.77 / PARIS NEW-YORK"

1977, Nov. 22 ***Perf. 13***
C145 AP61 300fr multi 1.60 .80

Concorde, 1st commercial flight, Paris-New York.

Philexafrique II-Essen Issue
Common Design Types

Designs: No. C146, Lion & Senegal #C28. No. C147, Capercaillie & Schleswig-Holstein #1.

1978, Nov. 1 **Litho.** ***Perf. 12½***
C146 CD138 100fr multi .65 .28
C147 CD139 100fr multi .65 .28
a. Pair, #C146-C147 1.30 .60

J. Dabry, L. Gimie, and J. Mermoz, Airplane, Map of Route (St. Louis-Natal) — AP63

1980, Dec. **Photo.** ***Perf. 13***
C148 AP63 300fr multi 2.25 .80

1st airmail crossing of So. Atlantic, 50th anniv.

1st Transatlantic Commercial Airmail Flight, 55th Anniv. — AP64

1985, May 12 **Litho.** ***Perf. 13***
C149 AP64 250fr multi .65 .35

Clement Ader (1841-1926), Engineer and Aviation Pioneer — AP65

Ader and: 145fr, Automobile, microphone. 180fr, 615fr, 940fr, Bat-winged steam powered airplane.

1991, June 7 **Litho.** ***Perf. 13***
C150 AP65 145fr multicolored 1.10 .55
C151 AP65 180fr multicolored 1.35 .65
C152 AP65 615fr multi, vert. 4.50 2.25
Nos. C150-C152 (3) 6.95 3.45

Souvenir Sheet

C153 AP65 940fr multi, vert. 7.00 3.50

AIR POST SEMI-POSTAL STAMPS

French Revolution Issue
Common Design Type

1939 **Unwmk.** **Photo.** ***Perf. 13***
Name and Value Typo. in Orange
CB1 CD83 4.75 + 4fr brn blk 7.50 7.50

Surtax used for the defense of the colonies.

Stamps of types of Dahomey V1, V2, V3, and V4 inscribed "Sénégal" were issued in 1942 by the Vichy Government, but were not placed on sale in the colony.

Catalogue values for unused stamps in this section, from this point to the end of the section, are for Never Hinged items.

Republic

Nile Gods Uniting Upper and Lower Egypt (Abu Simbel) — SPAP1

1964, Mar. 7 Engr. *Perf. 13*
CB2 SPAP1 25fr + 5fr Prus bl, red brn & sl grn .80 .60

UNESCO campaign to save historic monuments in Nubia.

POSTAGE DUE STAMPS

Postage Due Stamps of French Colonies Surcharged **10**

1903 Unwmk. *Imperf.*
J1 D1 10c on 50c lilac 55.00 55.00
J2 D1 10c on 60c brn, *buff* 55.00 55.00
J3 D1 10c on 1fr rose, *buff* 300.00 300.00
Nos. J1-J3 (3) 410.00 410.00

D2

D3

1906 Typo. *Perf. 14x13½*
J4 D2 5c grn, *grnsh* 3.00 3.00
J5 D2 10c red brown 3.50 3.50
J6 D2 15c dark blue 4.25 4.00
J7 D2 20c blk, *yellow* 4.75 4.00
J8 D2 30c red, *straw* 5.50 4.75
J9 D2 50c violet 6.00 4.75
J10 D2 60c blk, *buff* 7.50 7.50
J11 D2 1fr blk, *pinkish* 12.50 12.50
Nos. J4-J11 (8) 47.00 44.00

1914
J12 D3 5c green .15 .15
J13 D3 10c rose .25 .20
J14 D3 15c gray .25 .25
J15 D3 20c brown .50 .30
J16 D3 30c blue .85 .60
J17 D3 50c black 1.10 .80
J18 D3 60c orange 1.25 1.10
J19 D3 1fr violet 1.40 1.10
Nos. J12-J19 (8) 5.75 4.50

Type of 1914 Issue Surcharged **2F.**

1927
J20 D3 2fr on 1fr lil rose 3.25 3.25
J21 D3 3fr on 1fr org brn 3.25 3.25

D4

1935 Engr. *Perf. 12½x12*
J22 D4 5c yellow green .15 .15
J23 D4 10c red orange .15 .15
J24 D4 15c violet .15 .15
J25 D4 20c olive green .15 .15
J26 D4 30c reddish brown .15 .15
J27 D4 50c rose lilac .40 .40
J28 D4 60c orange .80 .80
J29 D4 1fr black .60 .60
J30 D4 2fr dark blue .60 .60
J31 D4 3fr dark carmine .60 .60
Nos. J22-J31 (10) 3.75 3.75

Catalogue values for unused stamps in this section, from this point to the end of the section, are for Never Hinged items.

Republic

D5

Lion — D6

1961, Feb. 20 Typo. *Perf. 14x13½*
J32 D5 1fr orange & red .15 .15
J33 D5 2fr ultra & red .15 .15
J34 D5 5fr brown & red .15 .15
J35 D5 20fr green & red .50 .50
J36 D5 25fr red lilac & red .55 .55
Nos. J32-J36 (5) 1.50 1.50

1966-83 Typo. *Perf. 14x13*
Lion in Gold
J37 D6 1fr red & black .15 .15
J38 D6 2fr yel brn & blk .15 .15
J39 D6 5fr red lil & blk .15 .15
J40 D6 10fr brt bl & blk .20 .20
J41 D6 20fr emer & blk .32 .32
J42 D6 30fr gray & blk .55 .55
J43 D6 60fr blue & blk .28 .28
J44 D6 90fr rose & blk .42 .42
Nos. J37-J44 (8) 2.22 2.22

Issued: 1fr-30fr, Dec. 1, 1966; others, Oct. 1983.

OFFICIAL STAMPS

Catalogue values for unused stamps in this section are for Never Hinged items.

Arms — O1

Baobab Tree — O2

Perf. 14x13½
1961, Sept. 18 Typo. Unwmk.
Denominations in Black
O1 O1 1fr sepia & bl .15 .15
O2 O1 2fr dk bl & org .15 .15
O3 O1 5fr maroon & grn .15 .15
O4 O1 10fr ver & bl .15 .15
O5 O1 25fr vio bl & ver .35 .15
O6 O1 50fr ver & gray .65 .35
O7 O1 85fr lilac & org 1.20 .62
O8 O1 100fr ver & yel grn 1.60 .90
Nos. O1-O8 (8) 4.40 2.62

1966-77 Typo. *Perf. 14x13*
O9 O2 1fr yel & blk .15 .15
O10 O2 5fr org & blk .15 .15
O11 O2 10fr red & blk .15 .15
O12 O2 20fr dp red lil & blk .15 .15
O13 O2 25fr dp lil & blk ('75) .15 .15
O14 O2 30fr bl & blk .28 .15
O15 O2 35fr bl & blk ('73) .40 .15
O16 O2 40fr grnsh bl & blk ('75) .25 .15
O17 O2 55fr emer & blk .65 .45
O18 O2 60fr emer & blk ('77) .32 .15
O19 O2 90fr dk bl grn & blk 1.00 .22
O20 O2 100fr brn & blk 1.20 .22
Nos. O9-O20 (12) 4.85
Set value 1.55

See Nos. O22-O25.

No. O17 Surcharged with New Value and Two Bars

1969
O21 O2 60fr on 55fr emer & blk 1.00 .15

1983, Oct. Typo. *Perf. 14x13*
O22 O2 90fr dk grn & blk .42 .15

"90F" is shorter and wider than on Nos. O9-O22.

1991 Litho. *Perf. 13*
O23 O2 50fr red & blk .40 .20
O24 O2 145fr brt grn & blk 1.25 .62
O25 O2 180fr org yel & blk 1.50 .75
Nos. O23-O25 (3) 3.15 1.57

This is an expanding set. Numbers will change if necessary.

SENEGAMBIA & NIGER

ˌse–nə–ˈgam–bē–ə and ˈnī–jər

A French Administrative unit for the Senegal and Niger possessions in Africa during the period when the French possessions in Africa were being definitely divided into colonies and protectorates. The name was dropped in 1904 when this territory was consolidated with part of French Sudan, under the name Upper Senegal and Niger.

100 Centimes = 1 Franc

Navigation and Commerce — A1

1903 Unwmk. Typo. *Perf. 14x13½*
Name of Colony in Blue or Carmine
1 A1 1c black, *lil bl* .90 .90
2 A1 2c brown, *buff* 1.10 1.10
3 A1 4c claret, *lav* 2.00 2.00
4 A1 5c yel grn 3.00 3.00
5 A1 10c red 3.00 3.00
6 A1 15c gray 6.00 6.00
7 A1 20c red, *green* 6.00 6.00
8 A1 25c blue 8.00 8.00
9 A1 30c brn, *bister* 8.00 8.00
10 A1 40c red, *straw* 11.00 11.00
11 A1 50c brn, *azure* 25.00 25.00
12 A1 75c deep vio, *org* 32.50 32.50
13 A1 1fr brnz grn, *straw* 45.00 45.00
Nos. 1-13 (13) 151.50 151.50

Perf. 13½x14 stamps are counterfeits.

SERBIA

ˈsər–bē–ə

LOCATION — In southeastern Europe, bounded by Romania and Bulgaria on the east, the former Austro-Hungarian Empire on the north, Greece on the south, and Albania and Montenegro on the west
GOVT. — Kingdom
AREA — 18,650 sq. mi.
POP. — 2,911,701 (1910)
CAPITAL — Belgrade

Following World War I, Serbia united with Montenegro, Bosnia and Herzegovina, Croatia, Dalmatia and Slovenia to form the kingdom (later republic) of Yugoslavia.

100 Paras = 1 Dinar

Coat of Arms — A1

Prince Michael (Obrenovich III) — A2

1866 Unwmk. Typo. *Imperf.*
Paper colored Through
1 A1 1p dk green, *dk vio rose* 45.00

Surface Colored Paper, Thin or Thick
2 A1 1p dk green, *lil rose* 50.00
a. 1p olive green, *rose* 50.00
b. 1p yel grn, *pale rose* (thick paper) 300.00
3 A1 2p red brown, *lilac* 60.00
a. 2p red brn, *lil gray* (thick paper) 250.00
b. 2p dl grn, *lil gray* (thick paper) 800.00
Nos. 1-3 (3) 155.00

Vienna Printing
Perf. 12
4 A2 10p orange 750.00 500.00
5 A2 20p rose 425.00 17.50
6 A2 40p blue 475.00 125.00
a. Half used as 20p on cover
Nos. 4-6 (3) 1,650. 642.50

Belgrade Printing
Perf. 9½
7 A2 1p green 15.00
8 A2 2p bister brn 22.50
9 A2 20p rose 15.00 15.00
a. Pair, imperf. between
10 A2 40p ultra 165.00 175.00
a. Half used as 20p on cover
Nos. 7-10 (4) 217.50

Pelure Paper
11 A2 10p orange 65.00 70.00
12 A2 20p rose 60.00 8.75
a. Pair, imperf. between
13 A2 40p ultra 35.00 25.00
a. Pair, imperf. between
b. Half used as 20p on cover
Nos. 11-13 (3) 160.00 103.75

Nos. 1-3, 7-8, 14-16, 25-26 were used only as newspaper tax stamps.

1868-69 Ordinary Paper *Imperf.*
14 A2 1p green 35.00
a. 1p olive green ('69) *2,000.*
15 A2 2p brown 50.00
a. 2p bister brown ('69) 165.00

Counterfeits of type A2 are common.

Prince Milan (Obrenovich IV)
A3 A4

Perf. 9½, 12 and Compound
1869-78
16 A3 1p yellow 3.75 *95.00*
17 A3 10p red brown 7.50 3.75
a. 10p yellow brown *350.00* 35.00
18 A3 10p orange ('78) 1.25 3.25
19 A3 15p orange 85.00 15.00
20 A3 20p gray blue 1.50 2.50
a. 20p ultramarine 3.25 2.00
b. Half used as 10p on cover
21 A3 25p rose 1.50 5.75
22 A3 35p lt green 3.00 3.50
23 A3 40p violet 1.50 2.75
a. Half used as 20p on cover
24 A3 50p blue green 5.00 3.75
Nos. 16-24 (9) 110.00 *135.25*

The first setting, which included all values except No. 18, had the stamps 2-2½mm apart. A new setting, introduced in 1878, had the stamps 3-4mm apart, providing wider margins. Only Nos. 17, 18, 20 and 21 exist in this new setting, which differs also in shades from the earlier setting. The narrow-spaced Nos. 17, 20 and 21 are rarer, especially unused, as are the early shades of Nos. 23 and 24. All values except Nos. 19 and 24 are known in various partly perforated varieties.

Counterfeits exist.

See No. 25.

1872-79 *Imperf.*
25 A3 1p yellow 4.50 8.75
a. Tête bêche pair
26 A4 2p blk, thin paper ('79) .50 .50
a. Thick paper ('73) 1.50 *10.00*

Used value of No. 26 is for canceled-to-order.

King Milan I — A5

King Alexander (Obrenovich V) — A6

1880 *Perf. 13x13½*
27 A5 5p green .50 .15
a. 5p olive green 475.00 2.00
28 A5 10p rose 1.50 .15
29 A5 20p orange .50 .20
a. 20p yellow 3.00 1.25
30 A5 25p ultra 1.00 .75
a. 25p blue 1.25 .75
31 A5 50p brown 1.00 *3.75*
a. 50p brown violet 140.00 3.00
32 A5 1d violet 6.75 6.00
Nos. 27-32 (6) 11.25 11.00

1890
33 A6 5p green .15 .15
34 A6 10p rose red .50 .15
35 A6 15p red violet .50 .15
36 A6 20p orange .35 .15
37 A6 25p blue .60 .25
38 A6 50p brown 2.00 2.00
39 A6 1d dull lilac 7.50 6.25
Nos. 33-39 (7) 11.60 9.10

King Alexander — A7

1894-96 *Perf. 13x13½*

Granite Paper

40 A7 5p green 3.25 .15
a. Perf. 11½ 3.50 .40
41 A7 10p car rose 3.50 .15
b. Perf. 11½ 45.00 .75
42 A7 15p violet 5.00 .15
43 A7 20p orange 52.50 .50
a. Half used as 10p on cover 375.00
44 A7 25p blue 10.50 .20
45 A7 50p brown 11.00 .45
46 A7 1d dk green 1.50 2.50
47 A7 1d red brn, *bl* ('96) 11.00 3.75
Nos. 40-47 (8) 98.25 7.85

1898-1900 *Perf. 13x13½, 11½*

Ordinary Paper

48 A7 1p dull red .15 .25
49 A7 5p green 1.50 .20
50 A7 10p rose 42.50 .20
51 A7 15p violet 7.00 .20
52 A7 20p orange 6.25 .25
53 A7 25p deep blue 7.00 .30
54 A7 50p brown 12.50 3.00
Nos. 48-54 (7) 76.90 4.40

Nos. 49-54 exist imperf.

Nos. 49-51, 53 and 56-57 exist with perf. 13x13½x11½x13½.

Type of 1900 Stamp Surcharged **10 ПАРА**

1900

56 A7 10p on 20p rose 2.50 .15

Same, Surcharged **10 ПАРА**

1901

57 A7 10p on 20p rose 1.75 .15
58 A7 15p on 1d red brn, *bl* 3.75 1.00
a. Inverted surcharge 100.00 110.00

King Alexander (Obrenovich V)
A8 A9

1901-03 **Typo.** *Perf. 11½*

59 A8 5p green .15 .15
60 A8 10p rose .15 .15
61 A8 15p red violet .15 .15
62 A8 20p orange .15 .15
63 A8 25p ultra .15 .15
64 A8 50p bister .15 .15
65 A9 1d brown .70 .60
66 A9 3d brt rose 6.75 5.75
67 A9 5d deep violet 5.25 5.75
Nos. 59-67 (9) 13.60 13.00

Counterfeits of Nos. 66-67 exist. Nos. 59-67 imperf. value of set of pairs, $100.

Arms of Serbia on Head of King Alexander — A10

Two Types of the Overprint

Type I - Overprint 12mm wide. Bottom of mantle defined by a single line. Wide crown above shield.

Type II - Overprint 10mm wide. Double line at bottom of mantle. Smaller crown above shield.

Arms Overprinted in Blue, Black, Red and Red Brown

1903-04 **Type I** *Perf. 13½*

68 A10 1p red lil & blk (Bl) .50 .50
a. Inverted overprint 10.00
69 A10 5p yel grn & blk (Bl) .35 .15
70 A10 10p car & blk (Bk) .15 .15
a. Double overprint 8.75
71 A10 15p ol gray & blk (Bk) .15 .15
a. Double overprint 8.75
72 A10 20p org & blk (Bk) .25 .15
73 A10 25p bl & blk (Bk) .25 .15
a. Double overprint 10.00
74 A10 50p gray & blk (R) 2.50 .65

There were two printings of the type I overprint on Nos. 68-74, one typographed and one lithographed.

Type II

75 A10 1d bl grn & blk (Bk) 7.50 2.50

#68-75 with overprint omitted, value, set $75.

Perf. 11½

Type I

75A A10 5p (Bl) .15 .35
75B A10 50p (R) .75 2.00
75C A10 1d (Bk) 1.50 4.00

Type II

76 A10 3d vio & blk (R Br) 1.50 1.75
a. Perf. 13½ 100.00 100.00
77 A10 5d lt brn & blk (Bl) 1.50 2.00

Type I With Additional Surcharge **1 ПАРА 1**

78 A10 1p on 5d (R) .75 2.75
a. Perf. 13½ 265.00 265.00
Nos. 68-78 (14) 17.80 17.25

Karageorge and Peter I — A11

Insurgents, 1804 — A12

1904 **Typo.**

79 A11 5p yellow green .15 .15
80 A11 10p rose red .15 .15
81 A11 15p red violet .35 .30
82 A11 25p blue .50 .35
83 A11 50p gray brown .60 .60
84 A12 1d bister 1.00 1.25
85 A12 3d blue green 2.00 3.50
86 A12 5d violet 2.50 4.00
Nos. 79-86 (8) 7.25 10.30

Centenary of the Karageorgevich dynasty and the coronation of King Peter. Counterfeits of Nos. 79-86 exist.

King Peter I Karageorgevich
A13 A14

Perf. 11½, 12x11½

1905 **Wove Paper**

87 A13 1p gray & blk .15 .15
88 A13 5p yel grn & blk .50 .15
89 A13 10p red & blk 1.50 .15
90 A13 15p red lil & blk 1.75 .15
91 A13 20p yellow & blk 3.00 .15
92 A13 25p ultra & blk 4.25 .15
93 A13 30p sl grn & blk 2.50 .15
94 A13 50p dk brown & blk 3.00 .20
95 A13 1d bister & blk .60 .25
96 A13 3d blue grn & blk .60 .60
97 A13 5d violet & blk 2.50 1.90
Nos. 87-97 (11) 20.35 4.00

Counterfeits of Nos. 87-97 abound.

The stamps of this issue may be found on both thick and thin paper.

1908 **Laid Paper**

98 A13 1p gray & blk .28 .15
99 A13 5p yel grn & blk 2.25 .15
100 A13 10p red & blk 6.75 .15
101 A13 15p red lilac & blk 6.75 .20
102 A13 20p yellow & blk 7.25 .20
103 A13 25p ultra & blk 6.75 .20
104 A13 30p gray grn & blk 10.00 .20
105 A13 50p dk brn & blk 13.00 .60
Nos. 98-105 (8) 53.03 1.85

Nos. 90, 98-100, 102-104 are known imperforate but are not believed to have been issued in this condition.

Values of Nos. 98-105 are for horizontally laid paper. Four values also exist on vertically laid paper (1p, 5p, 10p, 30p).

1911-14

Thick Wove Paper

108 A14 1p slate green .15 .15
109 A14 2p dark violet .15 .15
110 A14 5p green .15 .15
111 A14 5p pale yel grn ('14) .15 .15
112 A14 10p carmine .15 .15
113 A14 10p red ('14) .15 .15
114 A14 15p red violet .15 .15
115 A14 15p slate blk ('14) .15 .15
a. 15p red (error)
116 A14 20p yellow .20 .15
117 A14 20p brown ('14) .35 .20
118 A14 25p deep blue .30 .15
119 A14 25p indigo ('14) .15 .15
120 A14 30p blue green .15 .15
121 A14 30p olive grn ('14) .15 .15
122 A14 50p dk brown .15 .15
123 A14 50p brown red ('14) .15 .15
124 A14 1d orange 15.00 25.00
125 A14 1d slate ('14) 2.00 2.75
126 A14 3d lake 27.50 77.50
127 A14 3d olive yel ('14) 77.50 475.00
128 A14 5d violet 27.50 42.50
129 A14 5d dk violet ('14) 2.00 14.00
Nos. 108-129 (22) 154.30

Counterfeits exist.

King Peter and Military Staff — A15

1915 *Perf. 11½*

132 A15 5p yellow green .15 —
133 A15 10p scarlet .15 —
134 A15 15p slate 3.75
135 A15 20p brown .60
136 A15 25p blue 7.50
137 A15 30p olive green 5.00
138 A15 50p orange brown 20.00
Nos. 132-138 (7) 37.15

Nos. 134-138 were prepared but not issued for postal use. Instead they were permitted to be used as wartime emergency currency. Some are known imperf. The 15p also exists in blue; value $250.

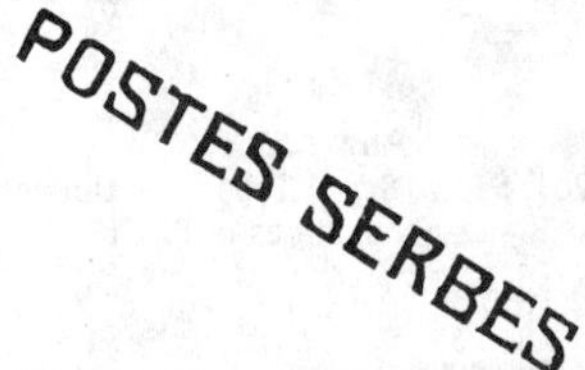

Stamps of France, 1900-1907, with this handstamped control were issued in 1916-1918 by the Serbian Postal Bureau, in the Island of Corfu, during a temporary shortage of Serbian stamps. On the 1c to 35c, the handstamp covers 2 or 3 stamps. It was applied after the stamps were on the cover, and frequently no further cancellation was used.

King Peter and Prince Alexander — A16

1918-20 **Typo.** *Perf. 11, 11½*

155 A16 1p black .15 .15
156 A16 2p olive brown .15 .15
157 A16 5p apple green .15 .15
158 A16 10p red .15 .15
159 A16 15p black brown .15 .15
160 A16 20p red brown .15 .15
161 A16 20p violet ('20) 1.10 .60
162 A16 25p deep blue .15 .15
163 A16 30p olive green .15 .15
164 A16 50p violet .15 .15
165 A16 1d violet brown .25 .15
166 A16 3d slate green .75 .60
167 A16 5d red brown 1.25 .75
Set value 4.00 2.90

#157-160, 164 exist imperf. Value each $6.

1920 **Pelure Paper** *Perf. 11½*

169 A16 1p black .15 .15
170 A16 2p olive brown .15 .15
Set value .20

POSTAGE DUE STAMPS

Coat of Arms
D1 D2

1895 **Unwmk.** **Typo.** *Perf. 13x13½*

Granite Paper

J1 D1 5p red lilac 2.50 .80
J2 D1 10p blue 2.50 .20
J3 D1 20p orange brown 30.00 5.00
J4 D1 30p green .20 .35
J5 D1 50p rose .30 .40
a. Cliché of 5p in plate of 50p 75.00 95.00
Nos. J1-J5 (5) 35.50 6.75

No. J1 exists imperf. Value $35.

1898-1904

Ordinary Paper

J6 D1 5p magenta ('04) .70 .70
J7 D1 20p brown 3.00 .70
a. Tête bêche pair 150.00 150.00
J8 D1 20p dp brn ('04) 3.00 .70
Nos. J6-J8 (3) 6.70 2.10

1906 **Granite Paper** *Perf. 11½*

J9 D1 5p magenta 5.25 1.00

1909

Laid Paper

J10 D1 5p magenta .65 .65
J11 D1 10p pale blue 3.00 1.65
J12 D1 20p pale brown .40 .40
Nos. J10-J12 (3) 4.05 2.70

1914

White Wove Paper

J13 D1 5p rose .25 .50
J14 D1 10p deep blue 3.75 6.25

1918-20 *Perf. 11*

J15 D2 5p red .40 .85
J16 D2 5p red brown ('20) .40 .85
J17 D2 10p yellow green .40 .85
J18 D2 20p olive brown .40 .85
J19 D2 30p slate green .40 .85
J20 D2 50p chocolate .80 1.25
Nos. J15-J20 (6) 2.80 5.50

NEWSPAPER STAMPS

N1

Overprinted with Crown-topped Shield in Black

1911 **Unwmk.** **Typo.** *Perf. 11½*

P1 N1 1p gray .45 .45
P2 N1 5p green .45 .45
P3 N1 10p orange .45 .45
a. Cliché of 1p in plate of 10p 200.00
P4 N1 15p violet .45 .45
P5 N1 20p yellow .45 .45
a. Cliché of 50p in plate of 20p 75.00 125.00
P6 N1 25p blue .45 .45
P7 N1 30p slate 5.25 5.25
P8 N1 50p brown 4.50 4.50
P9 N1 1d bister 4.50 4.50
P10 N1 3d rose red 4.50 4.50
P11 N1 5d gray vio 4.50 4.50
Nos. P1-P11 (11) 25.95 25.95

ISSUED UNDER AUSTRIAN OCCUPATION

100 Heller = 1 Krone

Stamps of Bosnia, 1912-14, Overprinted

1916 **Unwmk.** *Perf. 12½*

1N1 A23 1h olive green 1.65 2.25
1N2 A23 2h brt blue 1.65 2.25
1N3 A23 3h claret 1.65 1.75
1N4 A23 5h green .40 .45

1N5 A23 6h dk gray .80 1.50
1N6 A23 10h rose carmine .40 .40
1N7 A23 12h dp olive grn .80 1.50
1N8 A23 20h orange brown .50 .90
1N9 A23 25h ultra .50 .80
1N10 A23 30h orange red .50 .80
1N11 A24 35h myrtle grn .50 .80
1N12 A24 40h dk violet .50 .80
1N13 A24 45h olive brown .50 .80
1N14 A24 50h slate blue .50 .80
1N15 A24 60h brown violet .50 .80
1N16 A24 72h dark blue .50 .80
1N17 A25 1k brn vio, *straw* .70 1.00
1N18 A25 2k dk gray, *bl* .70 1.00
1N19 A26 3k carmine, *grn* .70 1.00
1N20 A26 5k dk vio, *gray* .70 1.00
1N21 A25 10k dk ultra, *gray* 10.00 19.00
Nos. 1N1-1N21 (21) 24.65 40.40

Stamps of Bosnia, 1912-14, Overprinted "SERBIEN" Horizontally at Bottom

1916

1N22 A23 1h olive green 6.75 8.00
1N23 A23 2h bright blue 6.75 8.00
1N24 A23 3h claret 6.75 8.00
1N25 A23 5h green .50 .65
1N26 A23 6h dark gray 6.75 8.00
1N27 A23 10h rose carmine .50 .65
1N28 A23 12h dp olive grn 6.75 8.00
1N29 A23 20h orange brown 6.75 8.00
1N30 A23 25h ultra 6.75 8.00
1N31 A23 30h orange red 6.75 8.00
1N32 A24 35h myrtle green 6.75 8.00
1N33 A24 40h dark violet 6.75 8.00
1N34 A24 45h olive brown 6.75 8.00
1N35 A24 50h slate blue 6.75 8.00
1N36 A24 60h brown violet 6.75 8.00
1N37 A24 72h dark blue 6.75 8.00
1N38 A25 1k brn vio, *straw* 14.00 19.00
1N39 A25 2k dk gray, *bl* 16.00 19.00
1N40 A26 3k carmine, *grn* 18.00 19.00
1N41 A26 5k dk vio, *gray* 27.50 30.00
1N42 A25 10k dk ultra, *gray* 42.50 45.00
Nos. 1N22-1N42 (21) 213.50 245.30

Nos. 1N22-1N42 were prepared in 1914, at the time of the 1st Austrian occupation of Serbia. They were not issued at that time because of the retreat. The stamps were put on sale in 1916, at the same time as Nos. 1N1-1N21.

ISSUED UNDER GERMAN OCCUPATION

In occupied Serbia, authority was ostensibly in the hands of a government created by the former Yugoslav General, Milan Nedich, supported by the Chetniks, a nationalist organization which turned fascist. Actually the German military ran the country.

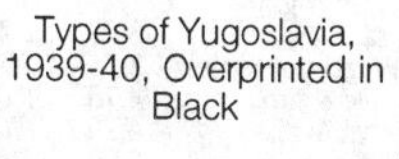
Types of Yugoslavia, 1939-40, Overprinted in Black

1941 Unwmk. Typo. *Perf. 12½*
Paper with colored network

2N1 A16 25p blk *(lt grn)* .15 1.25
2N2 A16 50p orange *(pink)* .15 .25
2N3 A16 1d yel grn *(lt grn)* .15 .25
2N4 A16 1.50d red *(pink)* .15 .25
2N5 A16 2d dp mag *(pink)* .15 .25
2N6 A16 3d dl red brn *(pink)* .90 5.00
2N7 A16 4d ultra *(lt grn)* .15 .75
2N8 A16 5d dk bl *(lt grn)* .50 2.00
2N9 A16 5.50d dk vio brn *(pink)* .50 2.00
2N10 A16 6d sl bl *(pink)* .50 2.00
2N11 A16 8d sep *(lt grn)* .70 3.00
2N12 A16 12d brt vio *(lt grn)* .70 3.00
2N13 A16 16d dl vio *(pink)* 1.10 10.00
2N14 A16 20d bl *(lt grn)* 1.10 12.50
2N15 A16 30d brt pink *(lt grn)* 5.75 75.00
Nos. 2N1-2N15 (15) 12.65 117.50

Double overprints exist on 50p, 1d, 5d, 5.50d and 12d. Value, each $125 to $250.

Stamps of Yugoslavia, 1939-40, Overprinted in Black

Paper with colored network

2N16 A16 25p blk *(lt grn)* .15 3.75
2N17 A16 50p org *(pink)* .15 .75
2N18 A16 1d yel grn *(lt grn)* .15 .50
2N19 A16 1.50d red *(pink)* .15 .75
2N20 A16 2d dp mag *(pink)* .15 .50
2N21 A16 3d dl red brn *(pink)* .30 3.00
2N22 A16 4d ultra *(lt grn)* .20 .50
2N23 A16 5d dk bl *(lt grn)* .20 1.25
2N24 A16 5.50d dk vio brn *(pink)* .45 3.00
2N25 A16 6d sl bl *(pink)* .45 3.00
2N26 A16 8d sep *(lt grn)* .65 3.75
2N27 A16 12d brt vio *(lt grn)* 1.10 3.75
2N28 A16 16d dl vio *(pink)* 1.10 12.50
2N29 A16 20d bl *(lt grn)* 1.10 20.00
2N30 A16 30d brt pink *(lt grn)* 5.75 65.00
Nos. 2N16-2N30 (15) 12.05 122.00

Lazaritza Monastery — OS1

Ruins of Manassia Monastery OS4

Designs: 1d, Kalenica Monastery. 1.50d, Ravanica Monastery. 3d, Ljubostinja Monastery. 4d, Sopocane Monastery. 7d, Tsitsa Monastery. 12d, Goriak Monastery. 16d, Studenica Monastery.

1942-43 Typo. *Perf. 11½*

2N31 OS1 50p brt violet .15 .15
2N32 OS1 1d red .15 .15
2N33 OS1 1.50d red brn .75 2.00
2N34 OS1 1.50d green ('43) .15 .20
2N35 OS4 2d dl rose violet .15 .15
2N36 OS4 3d brt blue .75 2.00
2N37 OS4 3d rose pink ('43) .15 .15
2N38 OS4 4d ultra .15 .20
2N39 OS4 7d dk slate grn .15 .20
2N40 OS1 12d lake .20 1.25
2N41 OS1 16d grnsh blk 1.00 1.50
Set value 3.25
Nos. 2N31-2N41 (11) 7.95

For surcharges see Nos. 2NB29-2NB37.

Post Rider — OS10

Post Wagon — OS11

9d, Mail train. 30d, Mail truck. 50d, Mail plane.

1943, Oct. 15 Photo. *Perf. 12½*

2N42 OS10 3d copper red & gray lilac .40 1.00
2N43 OS11 8d vio rose & gray .40 1.00
2N44 OS10 9d dk bl grn & sep .40 1.00
2N45 OS10 30d chnt & sl grn .40 1.00
2N46 OS10 50d dp bl & red brn .40 1.00
Nos. 2N42-2N46 (5) 2.00 5.00

Centenary of postal service in Serbia. Printed in sheets of 24 containing 4 of each stamp and 4 labels.

OCCUPATION SEMI-POSTAL STAMPS

Smederevo Fortress on the Danube OSP1

Refugees OSP2

Perf. 11½x12½
1941, Sept. 22 Typo. Unwmk.

2NB1 OSP1 50p + 1d dk brn .35 .65
2NB2 OSP2 1d + 2d dk gray grn .35 .85
2NB3 OSP2 1.50d + 3d dp cl .65 1.50
a. Perf. 12½ 4.00 6.25
2NB4 OSP1 2d + 4d dk bl .95 2.00
Nos. 2NB1-2NB4 (4) 2.30 5.00

Souvenir Sheets

2NB5 Sheet of 2 40.00 100.00
a. OSP2 1d + 49d rose lake 6.75 17.50
b. OSP1 2d + 48d gray 6.75 17.50

Imperf

2NB6 Sheet of 2 40.00 100.00
a. OSP2 1d + 49d gray 6.75 17.50
b. OSP1 2d + 48d rose lake 6.75 17.50

The surtax aided the victims of an explosion at Smederevo and was used for the reconstruction of the town.

Christ and Virgin Mary — OSP4

a b

1941, Dec. 5 Photo. *Perf. 11½*
With Rose Burelage

2NB7 OSP4 50p + 1.50d brn red .35 3.75
2NB8 OSP4 1d + 3d sl grn .35 3.75
2NB9 OSP4 2d + 6d dp red .35 3.75
2NB10 OSP4 4d + 12d dp bl .35 3.75
Nos. 2NB7-2NB10 (4) 1.40 15.00

With Symbol "a" Outlined in Cerise

2NB7a OSP4 50p 10.00 37.50
2NB8a OSP4 1d 10.00 37.50
2NB9a OSP4 2d 10.00 37.50
2NB10a OSP4 4d 10.00 37.50
Nos. 2NB7a-2NB10a (4) 40.00 150.00

With Symbol "b" Outlined in Cerise

2NB7b OSP4 50p 10.00 37.50
2NB8b OSP4 1d 10.00 37.50
2NB9b OSP4 2d 10.00 37.50
2NB10b OSP4 4d 10.00 37.50
Nos. 2NB7b-2NB10b (4) 40.00 150.00

Without Burelage

2NB7c OSP4 50p 1.50 12.00
2NB8c OSP4 1d 1.50 12.50
2NB9c OSP4 2d 1.50 12.50
2NB10c OSP4 4d 1.50 12.50
Nos. 2NB7c-2NB10c (4) 6.00 49.50

These stamps were printed in sheets of 50, in 2 panes of 25. In the panes, #8, 12, 13, 14, 18, forming a cross, are without burelage. #7, 17 are type "a," #9, 19 type "b." 16 of the 25 stamps have overall burelage.
Surtax aided prisoners of war.

1942, Mar. 26
Thicker Paper, Without Burelage

2NB11 OSP4 50p + 1.50d brn .60 2.75
2NB12 OSP4 1d + 3d bl grn .60 2.75
2NB13 OSP4 2d + 6d magenta .60 2.75
2NB14 OSP4 4d + 12d ultra .60 3.00
Nos. 2NB11-2NB14 (4) 2.40 11.25

OSP5

OSP6

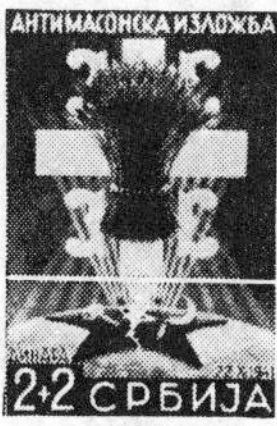
OSP7

OSP8

Designs: Anti-Masonic symbolisms.

1942, Jan. 1

2NB15 OSP5 50p + 50p yel brn .25 .65
2NB16 OSP6 1d + 1d dk grn .25 .65
2NB17 OSP7 2d + 2d rose car .45 1.25
2NB18 OSP8 4d + 4d indigo .45 1.25
Nos. 2NB15-2NB18 (4) 1.40 3.80

Anti-Masonic Exposition of Oct. 22, 1941. The surtax was used for anti-Masonic propaganda.

Mother and Children — OSP9

1942

2NB19 OSP9 2d + 6d brt pur 1.10 2.50
2NB20 OSP9 4d + 8d dp bl 1.10 2.50
2NB21 OSP9 7d + 13d dk bl grn 1.10 2.50
2NB22 OSP9 20d + 40d dp rose lake 1.10 2.50
Nos. 2NB19-2NB22 (4) 4.40 10.00

Nos. 2NB19-2NB22 were issued in sheets of 16 consisting of a block of four of each denomination. The surtax aided war orphans.

Broken Sword — OSP10

Wounded Flag-bearer OSP11

Designs: 1.50d+48.50d, Broken sword. 3d+5d, 2d+48d, Wounded soldier. 3d+47d, Wounded flag-bearer. 4d+10d, 4d+46d, Tending casualty.

1943

2NB23 OSP10 1.50d + 1.50d dk brn .55 1.25
2NB24 OSP11 2d + 3d dk bl grn .55 1.25
2NB25 OSP11 3d + 5d dp rose vio .80 2.00
2NB26 OSP10 4d + 10d dp bl 1.25 3.00
Nos. 2NB23-2NB26 (4) 3.15 7.50

Souvenir Sheets
Thick Paper

2NB27 Sheet of 2 27.50 550.00
a. OSP10 1.50d + 48.50d dk brn 10.00 225.00
b. OSP10 4d + 46d dp bl 10.00 225.00
2NB28 Sheet of 2 27.50 550.00
a. OSP11 2d + 48d dk bl grn 10.00 225.00
b. OSP11 3d + 47d dp rose vio 10.00 225.00

The sheets measure 150x110mm. The surtax aided war victims.

Stamps of 1942-43 Surcharged in Black

За пострадале од англо-америчког терор. бомбардовања Ниша — 20-X-1943

+ 9

1943, Dec. 11

Pale Green Burelage

No.	Type	Description	Unused	Used
2NB29	OS1	50p + 2d brt vio	.15	2.50
2NB30	OS1	1d + 3d red	.15	2.50
2NB31	OS1	1.50d + 4d dp grn	.15	2.50
2NB32	OS4	2d + 5d dl rose vio	.20	2.50
2NB33	OS4	3d + 7d rose pink	.20	2.50
2NB34	OS4	4d + 9d ultra	.20	2.50
2NB35	OS4	7d + 15d dk sl grn	.55	2.50
2NB36	OS1	12d + 25d lake	.55	12.50
2NB37	OS1	16d + 33d grnsh blk	.95	12.50
		Nos. 2NB29-2NB37 (9)	3.10	42.50

The surtax aided victims of the bombing of Nisch.

OCCUPATION AIR POST STAMPS

Types of Yugoslavia, 1937-40, Overprinted in Carmine or Maroon

Nos. 2NC1-2NC3, 2NC5-2NC7, 2NC9

Nos. 2NC4, 2NC8, 2NC10

1941 Unwmk. *Perf. 12½*

Paper with colored network

No.	Type	Description	Unused	Used
2NC1	AP6	50p brown	3.00	25.00
2NC2	AP7	1d yellow grn	3.00	25.00
2NC3	AP8	2d blue gray	3.00	25.00
2NC4	AP9	2.50d rose red (M)	3.00	25.00
2NC5	AP6	5d brown vio	3.00	25.00
2NC6	AP7	10d brown lake (M)	3.00	25.00
2NC7	AP8	20d dk green	3.00	25.00
2NC8	AP9	30d ultra	3.00	25.00
2NC9	AP10	40d Prus grn & pale grn (C)	6.75	125.00
2NC10	AP11	50d sl bl & gray bl (C)	8.50	190.00
		Nos. 2NC1-2NC10 (10)	39.25	515.00

Nos. 2NC1-2NC2 exist without network.

Same Surcharged in Maroon or Carmine with New Values and Bars

Without colored network

No.	Type	Description	Unused	Used
2NC11	AP7	1d on 10d brn lake (M)	2.25	15.00
2NC12	AP8	3d on 20d dk grn	2.25	15.00
2NC13	AP9	6d on 30d ultra	2.25	15.00
2NC14	AP10	8d on 40d Prus grn & pale grn	2.50	30.00
2NC15	AP11	12d on 50d sl bl & gray bl	5.00	75.00
		Nos. 2NC11-2NC15 (5)	14.25	150.00

Regular Issue of Yugoslavia, 1939-40, Surcharged in Black

14 СРБИЈА

1942

Green Network

No.	Type	Description	Unused	Used
2NC16	A16	2d on 2d dp mag	.15	1.25
2NC17	A16	4d on 4d ultra	.15	1.25
2NC18	A16	10d on 12d brt vio	.15	2.00
2NC19	A16	14d on 20d blue	.15	2.00
2NC20	A16	20d on 30d brt pink	.45	10.00
		Nos. 2NC16-2NC20 (5)	1.05	16.50

German Occupation stamps of Serbia can be mounted in the Scott Germany album part 2.

OCCUPATION POSTAGE DUE STAMPS

Types of Yugoslavia Similar to OD3-OD4 Overprinted

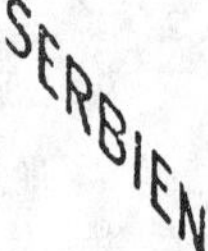

1941 Unwmk. Typo. *Perf. 12½*

No.	Type	Description	Unused	Used
2NJ1	OD3	50p violet	.65	3.75
2NJ2	OD3	1d lake	.65	3.75
2NJ3	OD3	2d dark blue	.65	3.75
2NJ4	OD3	3d red	.95	5.00
2NJ5	OD4	4d lt blue	1.25	12.50
2NJ6	OD4	5d orange	1.25	12.50
2NJ7	OD4	10d violet	2.75	25.00
2NJ8	OD4	20d green	8.00	75.00
		Nos. 2NJ1-2NJ8 (8)	16.15	141.25

OD3

OD4

1942 *Perf. 12½*

No.	Type	Description	Unused	Used
2NJ9	OD3	1d maroon & grn	.30	1.25
2NJ10	OD3	2d dk blue & red	.30	1.25
2NJ11	OD3	3d vermilion & bl	.55	2.50
2NJ12	OD4	4d blue & red	.55	2.50
2NJ13	OD4	5d orange & bl	.60	3.00
2NJ14	OD4	10d violet & red	.70	7.50
2NJ15	OD4	20d green & red	3.00	22.50
		Nos. 2NJ9-2NJ15 (7)	6.00	40.50

OD5

No.	Type	Description	Unused	Used
2NJ16	OD5	50p black	.20	1.25
2NJ17	OD5	3d violet	.20	1.25
2NJ18	OD5	4d blue	.20	1.25
2NJ19	OD5	5d dark slate green	.20	1.25
2NJ20	OD5	6d orange	.35	3.75
2NJ21	OD5	10d red	.60	6.25
2NJ22	OD5	20d ultra	1.75	15.00
		Nos. 2NJ16-2NJ22 (7)	3.50	30.00

OCCUPATION OFFICIAL STAMP

OOS1

1943 Unwmk. Typo. *Perf. 12½*

No.	Type	Description	Unused	Used
2NO1	OOS1	3d red lilac	1.00	1.50

SEYCHELLES

sā-'shel(z)

LOCATION — A group of islands in the Indian Ocean, off the coast of Africa north of Madagascar.

GOVT. — Republic

AREA — 156 sq. mi.

POP. — 64,718 (est. 1984)

CAPITAL — Victoria

The islands were attached to the British colony of Mauritius from 1810 to 1903, when they became a separate colony. Seychelles achieved internal self-government in October 1975 and independence on June 29, 1976.

100 Cents = 1 Rupee

Catalogue values for unused stamps in this country are for Never Hinged items, beginning with Scott 149 in the regular postage section and Scott J1 in the postage due section.

Watermark

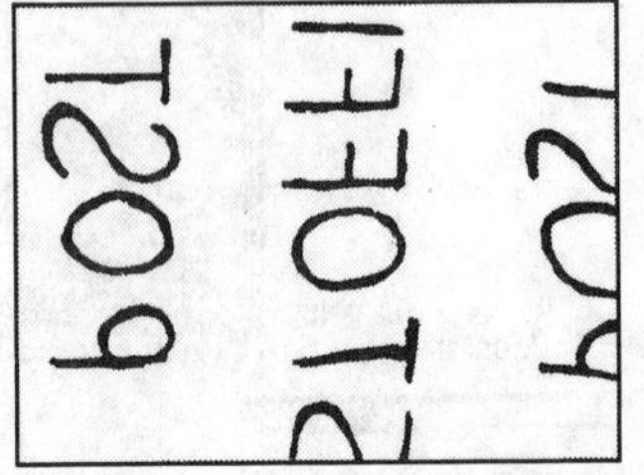

Wmk. 380- "POST OFFICE"

Queen Victoria — A1

Two dies of 2c, 4c, 8c, 10c, 13c, 16c:

Die I - Shading lines at right of diamond in tiara band.

Die II - No shading lines in this rectangle.

1890-1900 Typo. Wmk. 2 *Perf. 14*

No.	Type	Description	Unused	Used
1	A1	2c green & rose (II)	.65	.85
a.		Die I	1.10	7.00
2	A1	2c org brn & grn ('00)	.55	.40
3	A1	3c dk vio & org ('93)	.70	.35
4	A1	4c car rose & grn (II)	.75	.75
a.		Die I	13.00	9.00
5	A1	6c car rose ('00)	2.00	.50
6	A1	8c brn vio & ultra (II)	3.00	1.50
a.		8c brn vio & bl (I)	3.75	3.00
7	A1	10c ultra & brn (II)	3.25	3.00
a.		10c bl & brn (I)	4.50	10.00
8	A1	12c ol gray & grn ('93)	.85	.60
9	A1	13c slate & blk (II)	.85	1.75
a.		Die I	4.50	8.50
10	A1	15c ol grn & vio ('93)	3.00	2.25
11	A1	15c ultra ('00)	2.25	2.75
12	A1	16c org brn & bl (I)	1.65	3.00
a.		16c org brn & ultra (II)	32.50	6.50
13	A1	18c ultra ('97)	1.65	1.00
14	A1	36c brn & rose ('97)	13.00	4.00
15	A1	45c brn & rose ('93)	20.00	27.50
16	A1	48c ocher & green	15.00	15.00
17	A1	75c yel & pur ('00)	35.00	60.00
18	A1	96c violet & car	35.00	45.00
19	A1	1r vio & red ('97)	7.75	4.00
20	A1	1.50r blk & rose ('00)	45.00	70.00
21	A1	2.25r vio & grn ('00)	60.00	70.00
		Nos. 1-21 (21)	251.90	314.20

Numerals of 75c, 1r, 1.50r and 2.25r of type A1 are in color on plain tablet.

For surcharges see Nos. 22-37.

Surcharged in Black **3 cents**

1893

No.	Type	Description	Unused	Used
22	A1	3c on 4c car rose & green (II)	1.00	1.10
a.		Inverted surcharge	300.00	325.00
b.		Double surcharge	600.00	
d.		Pair, one without surcharge	4,750.	
23	A1	12c on 16c org brown & ultra (II)	4.00	1.10
a.		12c on 16c org brn & bl (I)	1.50	1.35
b.		Inverted surcharge (I)	325.00	325.00
d.		Double surcharge (I)	4,250.	5,000.
e.		Double surcharge (II)		
24	A1	15c on 16c org brn & ultra (II)	6.75	2.25
a.		15c on 16c org brn & bl (I)	8.00	10.00
b.		Inverted surcharge (I)	375.00	375.00
c.		Inverted surcharge (II)	650.00	650.00
d.		Double surcharge (I)	650.00	650.00
e.		Double surcharge (II)	1,000.	1,000.
f.		Triple surcharge (II)	3,250.	
25	A1	45c on 48c ocher & grn	12.00	5.00
26	A1	90c on 96c vio & car	27.50	24.00
		Nos. 22-26 (5)	51.25	33.45

No. 15 Surcharged in Black **18 CENTS**

1896

No.	Type	Description	Unused	Used
27	A1	18c on 45c brn & rose	7.50	3.00
a.		Double surcharge	1,100.	1,100.
b.		Triple surcharge	1,500.	
28	A1	36c on 45c brn & rose	10.00	40.00
a.		Double surcharge	1,100.	

Surcharged in Black:

3 cents

6 cents

1901

No.	Type	Description	Unused	Used
29	A1	3c on 10c bl & brn (II)	.60	.70
a.		Double surcharge	825.00	
30	A1	3c on 16c org brn & ultra (II)	.60	1.75
a.		"3 cents" omitted (II)	500.00	500.00
b.		Inverted surcharge (II)	700.00	700.00
c.		Double surcharge (II)	650.00	
31	A1	3c on 36c brn & rose	.60	.95
a.		Without bars		
b.		Double surcharge	700.00	825.00
c.		"3 cents" omitted	550.00	600.00
32	A1	6c on 8c brn vio & ultra (II)	.60	1.40
a.		Inverted surcharge	775.00	700.00
		Nos. 29-32 (4)	2.40	4.80

Stamps of 1890-1900 Surcharged **2 cents**

1902, June

No.	Type	Description	Unused	Used
33	A1	2c on 4c car rose & grn (II)	2.50	2.50
34	A1	30c on 75c yel & pur	2.50	7.75
a.		Narrow "0" in "30"	25.00	50.00
35	A1	30c on 1r vio & red	5.25	15.00
a.		Narrow "0" in "30"	40.00	87.50
b.		Double surcharge	850.00	
36	A1	45c on 1r vio & red	5.25	13.00
37	A1	45c on 2.25r vio & grn	17.50	32.50
a.		Narrow "5" in "45"	150.00	165.00
		Nos. 33-37 (5)	33.00	70.75

King Edward VII — A6

Numerals of 75c, 1.50r and 2.25r of type A6 are in color on plain tablet.

1903, May 26 Typo. Wmk. 2

No.	Type	Description	Unused	Used
38	A6	2c red brn & grn	.90	.40
39	A6	3c green	.90	1.10
40	A6	6c carmine rose	1.50	.30
41	A6	12c ol gray & grn	1.75	1.25
42	A6	15c ultra	3.25	1.75
43	A6	18c pale yel grn & rose	2.75	5.75
44	A6	30c purple & grn	4.75	8.00
45	A6	45c brown & rose	6.25	10.00
46	A6	75c yel & pur	8.00	18.00
47	A6	1.50r black & rose	30.00	50.00
48	A6	2.25r red vio & grn	21.00	60.00
		Nos. 38-48 (11)	81.05	156.55

Nos. 42-43, 45 Surcharged

1903

No.	Type	Description	Unused	Used
49	A6	3c on 15c	1.00	1.50
50	A6	3c on 18c	2.00	22.00
51	A6	3c on 45c	1.25	1.75
		Nos. 49-51 (3)	4.25	25.25

Type of 1903

1906 Wmk. 3

No.	Type	Description	Unused	Used
52	A6	2c red brn & grn	.75	2.00
53	A6	3c green	.75	.40
54	A6	6c car rose	1.40	.24
55	A6	12c ol gray & grn	2.75	1.25
56	A6	15c ultra	1.75	2.75
57	A6	18c pale yel grn & rose	3.00	5.00
58	A6	30c purple & grn	5.50	7.50
59	A6	45c brown & rose	2.75	5.25
60	A6	75c yellow & pur	8.00	35.00
61	A6	1.50r black & rose	40.00	35.00
62	A6	2.25r red vio & grn	27.50	42.50
		Nos. 52-62 (11)	94.15	136.89

King George V

A7 A8

Numerals of 75c, 1.50r and 2.25r of type A7 are in color on plain tablet.

1912 *Perf. 14*

No.	Type	Description	Unused	Used
63	A7	2c org brn & grn	.35	.75
64	A7	3c green	.40	.35
65	A7	6c car rose	5.00	3.00
66	A7	12c ol gray & grn	.90	2.75
67	A7	15c ultra	1.40	1.40
68	A7	18c pale yel grn & rose	1.25	2.75
69	A7	30c purple & grn	4.50	1.75
70	A7	45c brown & rose	2.25	12.50
71	A7	75c yellow & pur	3.50	5.00
72	A7	1.50r black & rose	15.00	1.75
73	A7	2.25r violet & grn	27.50	3.50
		Nos. 63-73 (11)	62.05	35.50

Die I

For description of dies I and II see back of this section of the Catalogue.

The 5c of type A8 has a colorless numeral on solid-color tablet. Numerals of 9c, 20c, 25c, 50c, 75c, and 1r to 5r of type A8 are in color on plain tablet.

1917-20

No.	Type	Description	Unused	Used
74	A8	2c org brn & grn	.20	.75
75	A8	3c green	.75	.50
76	A8	5c brown ('20)	.90	2.50
77	A8	6c carmine rose	.50	.40
78	A8	12c gray	.40	1.50
79	A8	15c ultra	.50	1.10
80	A8	18c violet, *yel*	2.00	12.50
a.		Die II ('20)	1.00	10.00
81	A8	25c blk & red, *yel* ('20)	1.90	12.50
a.		Die II ('20)	1.90	5.00
82	A8	30c dull vio & ol grn	1.90	5.50
83	A8	45c dull vio & org	2.50	15.00
84	A8	50c dull vio & blk ('20)	2.50	10.00
85	A8	75c blk, *bl grn, ol back*	2.75	6.75
a.		75c blk, *emer* (Die II) ('20)	3.50	10.00
86	A8	1r dl vio & red ('20)	13.00	20.00
87	A8	1.50r vio & bl, *bl*	12.50	32.50
a.		Die II ('20)	9.25	18.00
88	A8	2.25r gray grn & dp vio	27.50	75.00
89	A8	5r gray grn & ultra ('20)	65.00	140.00
		Nos. 74-89 (16)	134.80	336.50

Die II

1921-32 **Wmk. 4**

Ordinary Paper

No.	Type	Description	Unused	Used
91	A8	2c org brn & grn	.15	.20
92	A8	3c green	.15	.20
93	A8	3c black ('22)	.30	.30
94	A8	4c green ('22)	.50	.80
95	A8	4c ol grn & rose red ('28)	2.50	9.00
96	A8	5c dk brown	1.25	2.50
97	A8	6c car rose	1.25	4.50
98	A8	6c violet ('22)	.30	.20
99	A8	9c rose red ('27)	1.00	2.00
100	A8	12c gray	.50	.20
a.		Die I ('32)	2.25	.65
101	A8	12c carmine ('22)	.35	.30
102	A8	15c ultra	5.00	32.50
103	A8	15c yellow ('22)	.80	1.75
104	A8	18c violet, *yel*	1.50	5.00
105	A8	20c ultra ('22)	.90	.65

Chalky Paper

No.	Type	Description	Unused	Used
106	A8	25c blk & red, *yel* ('22)	1.50	5.00
107	A8	30c dull vio & ol grn	1.25	7.50
108	A8	45c dull vio & org	.95	6.25
109	A8	50c dull vio & blk	.95	3.75
110	A8	75c blk, *emerald*	7.75	14.00
111	A8	1r dull vio & red	10.00	21.00
a.		Die I ('32)	14.00	27.50
112	A8	1.50r vio & bl, *bl*	10.00	16.00
113	A8	2.25r green & vio	12.50	25.00
114	A8	5r green & ultra	65.00	90.00
		Nos. 91-114 (24)	126.35	248.60

Silver Jubilee Issue

Common Design Type

1935, May 6 **Engr.** *Perf. 11x12*

No.	Type	Description	Unused	Used
118	CD301	6c black & ultra	.25	.40
119	CD301	12c indigo & green	.60	.45
120	CD301	20c ultra & brown	.95	.50
121	CD301	1r brn vio & indigo	3.50	7.50
		Nos. 118-121 (4)	5.30	8.85

Coronation Issue

Common Design Type

1937, May 12 *Perf. 11x11½*

No.	Type	Description	Unused	Used
122	CD302	6c olive green	.15	.15
123	CD302	12c deep orange	.15	.15
124	CD302	20c deep ultra	.30	.30
		Nos. 122-124 (3)	.60	.60

Coco-de-mer Palm — A9

Seychelles Giant Tortoise — A10

Fishing Canoe — A11

Perf. 13½x14½, 14½x13½

1938-41 **Photo.** **Wmk. 4**

No.	Type	Description	Unused	Used
125	A9	2c violet brown	.15	.15
126	A10	3c green	2.50	1.00
127	A10	3c orange	.25	.25
128	A11	6c orange	2.50	2.00
129	A11	6c green	.25	.25
130	A9	9c rose red	4.75	1.65
131	A9	9c peacock blue	1.50	.30
132	A10	12c violet	18.00	1.00
133	A10	15c copper red	1.25	.20
134	A9	18c rose lake	1.40	.45
135	A11	20c bright blue	18.00	4.00
136	A11	20c ocher	.95	.35
137	A9	25c ocher	27.50	11.00
138	A10	30c rose lake	27.50	7.25
139	A9	30c bright blue	.65	.40
140	A11	45c brown	.60	.60
141	A9	50c dull violet	.30	.30
142	A10	75c gray blue	40.00	30.00
143	A10	75c dull violet	.45	.45
144	A11	1r yellow green	47.50	37.50
145	A11	1r gray	.60	.60
146	A9	1.50r ultra	1.75	1.10
147	A10	2.25r olive bister	4.00	3.00
148	A11	5r copper red	2.75	2.50
		Nos. 125-148 (24)	205.10	106.30

Issued: #126, 128, 132, 135, 137, 1/1; #125, 130, 138, 140-142, 144, 146-148, 2/10; others, 8/8/41.

See Nos. 158-169, 174-188.

Catalogue values for unused stamps in this section, from this point to the end of the section, are for Never Hinged items.

Peace Issue

Common Design Type

Perf. 13½x14

1946, Sept. 23 **Engr.** **Wmk. 4**

No.	Type	Description	Unused	Used
149	CD303	9c light blue	.15	.15
150	CD303	30c dark blue	.15	.15
		Set value	.25	.25

Silver Wedding Issue

Common Design Types

1948, Nov. 11 **Photo.** *Perf. 14x14½*

No.	Type	Description	Unused	Used
151	CD304	9c bright ultra	.20	.20

Engraved; Name Typographed

Perf. 11½x11

No.	Type	Description	Unused	Used
152	CD305	5r rose carmine	7.00	10.00

UPU Issue

Common Design Types

Perf. 13½, 11x11½

1949, Oct. 10 **Engr.**

No.	Type	Description	Unused	Used
153	CD306	18c red violet	.15	.15
154	CD307	50c dp rose violet	.35	.35
155	CD308	1r gray	.55	.55
156	CD309	2.25r olive	1.00	1.00
		Nos. 153-156 (4)	2.05	2.05

Types of 1938-41 Redrawn and

Sailfish — A12

Map — A13

Perf. 14½x13½, 13½x14½

1952, Mar. 3 **Photo.** **Wmk. 4**

No.	Type	Description	Unused	Used
157	A12	2c violet	.15	.15
158	A10	3c orange	.35	.35
159	A9	9c peacock blue	.60	.60
160	A11	15c yellow green	.60	.60
161	A13	18c rose lake	.60	.60
162	A11	20c ocher	.60	.60
163	A10	25c bright red	.70	.70
164	A12	40c ultra	1.50	1.50
165	A11	45c violet brown	1.25	1.25
166	A9	50c brt violet	1.25	1.25
167	A13	1r gray	1.50	1.50
168	A9	1.50r brt blue	2.75	2.75
169	A10	2.25r olive bister	4.25	4.25
170	A13	5r copper red	9.00	9.00
171	A12	10r green	13.00	13.00
		Nos. 157-171 (15)	38.10	38.10

The redrawn design shows a new portrait of King George VI surmounted by crown, as on type A12.

Nos. 157-170 exist with watermark 4a.

Coronation Issue

Common Design Type

1953, June 2 **Engr.** *Perf. 13½x13*

No.	Type	Description	Unused	Used
172	CD312	9c dark blue & blk	.30	.30

Types of 1938-52 with Portrait of Queen Elizabeth II

Perf. 14½x13½, 13½x14½

1954-56 **Photo.**

No.	Type	Description	Unused	Used
173	A12	2c violet	.22	.22
174	A10	3c orange	.26	.26
175	A9	9c peacock blue	.26	.26
176	A9	10c blue ('56)	.35	.35
177	A11	15c yellow grn	.15	.15
178	A13	18c rose lake	.45	.45
179	A11	20c ocher	.18	.18
180	A10	25c bright red	.22	.22
181	A13	35c mag ('56)	.55	.55
182	A12	40c ultra	.42	.42
183	A11	45c violet brn	.75	.75
184	A9	50c brt violet	.35	.35
185	A11	70c vio brn ('56)	1.00	1.00
186	A13	1r gray	.70	.70
187	A9	1.50r brt blue	1.50	1.50
188	A10	2.25r olive bister	3.50	3.00
189	A13	5r copper red	10.00	5.25
190	A12	10r green	19.00	11.00
		Nos. 173-190 (18)	39.86	26.61

Issued: 10c, 35c, 70c, 9/15/56; others, 2/1/54.

For surcharge see No. 193.

"Stone of Possession" A14

Flying Fox A15

Perf. 14½x14

1956, Nov. 15 **Wmk. 4**

No.	Type	Description	Unused	Used
191	A14	40c ultra	.38	.38
192	A14	1r gray black	.65	.65

Bicentenary of French colonization.

No. 183 Surcharged "5 cents" and Bars

1957, Sept. 16 *Perf. 13½x14½*

No.	Type	Description	Unused	Used
193	A11	5c on 45c violet brn	.30	.30
a.		Double surcharge	200.00	
b.		Thick bars omitted	450.00	

The "c," "e" or "s" of surcharge may be found in italic.

1957, Oct. 25 *Perf. 14½x13½*

No.	Type	Description	Unused	Used
194	A15	5c light violet	.15	.15

Mauritius Stamp of 1859 with Seychelles "B64" Cancellation A16

Perf. 11½x11

Engr. & Typo.

1961, Dec. 11 **Wmk. 314**

Stamp in Dull Blue & Black

No.	Type	Description	Unused	Used
195	A16	10c lilac	.15	.15
196	A16	35c dull green	.30	.30
197	A16	2.25r orange brown	1.10	1.10
		Nos. 195-197 (3)	1.55	1.55

1st post office in Victoria, Seychelles, cent.

Black Parrot — A17

Anse Royal Bay — A18

Designs: 10c, Vanilla. 15c, Fisherman. 20c, Denis Island Lighthouse. 25c, Clock Tower, Victoria. 30c, 35c, Anse Royal Bay. 40c, Government House. 45c, Fishing boat. 50c, Cascade Church. 60c, Flying fox. 70c, 85c, Sailfish. 75c, Coco-de-mer palm. 1r, Cinnamon. 1.50r, Copra. 2.25r, Map of Indian Ocean. 3.50r, Settlers' homes. 5r, Regina Mundi Convent. 10r, Badge of Seychelles.

Perf. 14½x13½, 13½x14½

1962-69 **Photo.** **Wmk. 314**

Size: 24x31mm, 31x24mm

No.	Type	Description	Unused	Used
198	A17	5c yel grn, brn & crimson	.15	.15
a.		Wmkd. sideways ('67)	.16	.15
199	A17	10c ocher, grn & dk bl	.15	.15
a.		Wmkd. sideways ('68)	.20	.16
200	A17	15c multicolored	.15	.15
201	A17	20c brt bl, blk & grn	.15	.15
202	A17	25c Prus bl, org brn & grn	.15	.15
202A	A18	30c multi ('68)	.80	.80
203	A18	35c bl, grn & dk brn	1.00	1.00
204	A18	40c bl, dk grn & yel grn	.24	.24
204A	A18	45c brt bl & yel ('66)	1.00	.65
205	A17	50c multicolored	.35	.35
b.		Wmkd. sideways ('69)	.80	.80
205A	A17	60c bl, rose & blk ('68)	.80	.80
206	A17	70c grnsh bl & vio bl	2.25	2.25
206A	A17	75c multi ('66)	1.00	1.00
206B	A17	85c grnsh bl & vio bl ('68)	1.00	1.00
207	A18	1r yel brn, emer & yel	.65	.65
208	A18	1.50r dk grn, choc & yel	1.40	1.40
209	A18	2.25r ocher, bl grn & crimson	2.25	2.25
210	A18	3.50r multicolored	3.50	3.50
211	A18	5r multicolored	4.75	4.75

Perf. 13x14

Size: 22½x39mm

No.	Type	Description	Unused	Used
212	A17	10r multicolored	14.00	14.00
		Nos. 198-212 (20)	35.74	35.39

Issue dates: 45c and 75c, Aug. 1, 1966. No. 198a, Feb. 7, 1967. The 30c, 60c, 85c, July 15, 1968. Others, Feb. 21, 1962.

The 60c and 85c have watermark sideways.

For surcharges see Nos. 216-217, 241-243. For overprints see Nos. 233-236.

Freedom from Hunger Issue

Common Design Type

1963, June 4 *Perf. 14x14½*

No.	Type	Description	Unused	Used
213	CD314	70c lilac	.75	.60

Red Cross Centenary Issue

Common Design Type

1963, Sept. 2 **Litho.** *Perf. 13*

No.	Type	Description	Unused	Used
214	CD315	10c black & red	.16	.15
215	CD315	75c ultra & red	.85	.60

Nos. 203 and 206 Surcharged with New Value and Bars

Perf. 14x14½, 14½x14

1965, Apr. **Photo.** **Wmk. 314**

No.	Type	Description	Unused	Used
216	A18	45c on 35c	.20	.20
217	A17	75c on 70c	.30	.30

ITU Issue

Common Design Type

Perf. 11x11½

1965, June 1 **Litho.** **Wmk. 314**

No.	Type	Description	Unused	Used
218	CD317	5c orange & vio bl	.15	.15
219	CD317	1.50r red lil & apple grn	.90	.80

Intl. Cooperation Year Issue

Common Design Type

1965, Oct. 25 *Perf. 14½*

No.	Type	Description	Unused	Used
220	CD318	5c blue green & claret	.15	.15
221	CD318	40c lt violet & green	.48	.48

Churchill Memorial Issue
Common Design Type

1966, Jan. 24 Photo. *Perf. 14*
Design in Black, Gold and Carmine Rose

222 CD319 5c bright blue .15 .15
223 CD319 15c green .16 .15
224 CD319 75c brown .80 .55
225 CD319 1.50r violet 1.50 1.10
Nos. 222-225 (4) 2.61 1.95

World Cup Soccer Issue
Common Design Type

1966, July 1 Litho. *Perf. 14*
226 CD321 15c multicolored .15 .15
227 CD321 1r multicolored .45 .45

WHO Headquarters Issue
Common Design Type

1966, Sept. 20 Litho. *Perf. 14*
228 CD322 20c multicolored .15 .15
229 CD322 50c multicolored .55 .55

UNESCO Anniversary Issue
Common Design Type

1966, Dec. 1 Litho. *Perf. 14*
230 CD323 15c "Education" .15 .15
231 CD323 1r "Science" .40 .40
232 CD323 5r "Culture" 2.25 2.25
Nos. 230-232 (3) 2.80 2.80

Nos. 200, 204A, 206A and 210 Overprinted: "UNIVERSAL / ADULT / SUFFRAGE / 1967"

Perf. 14½x14, 14x14½
1967, Sept. 18 Photo. Wmk. 314
233 A17 15c multicolored .15 .15
234 A18 45c brt blue & yel .16 .16
235 A17 75c multicolored .24 .24
236 A18 3.50r multicolored .90 .90
Nos. 233-236 (4) 1.45 1.45

Cowries: Tiger, Mole, Money A19

Sea Shells (ITY Emblem and): 40c, Textile, betulinus and virgin cones. 1r, Arthritic spider conch. 2.25r, Triton and subulate auger.

Perf. 14x13½
1967, Dec. 4 Photo. Wmk. 314
237 A19 15c multicolored .15 .15
238 A19 40c multicolored .26 .26
239 A19 1r multicolored .60 .60
240 A19 2.25r multicolored 1.25 1.25
Nos. 237-240 (4) 2.26 2.26

Issued for International Tourist Year, 1967.

Nos. 204, 204A and 206A Surcharged

Perf. 14x14½, 14½x14
1968, Apr. 16 Photo. Wmk. 314
241 A18 30c on 40c multicolored .15 .15
242 A18 60c on 45c blue & yel .16 .16
243 A17 85c on 75c multicolored .26 .26
Nos. 241-243 (3) .57 .57

The surcharge on No. 241 includes 2 bars; on Nos. 242-243 it includes 3 bars and "CENTS."

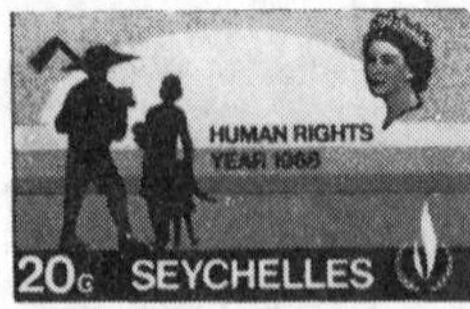

Family, Rising Sun and Human Rights Flame A20

Perf. 14½x14
1968, Sept. 2 Litho. Wmk. 314
244 A20 20c chocolate & multi .15 .15
245 A20 50c vio blue & multi .15 .15
246 A20 85c black & multi .22 .22
247 A20 2.25r brown & multi .65 .65
Nos. 244-247 (4) 1.17 1.17

International Human Rights Year.

First Landing on Praslin Island — A21

Designs: 50c, La Digue and La Curieuse at anchor, vert. 85c, Coco-de-mer and black parrot, vert. 2.25r, La Digue and La Curieuse under sail.

Litho.; Head Embossed in Gold
Perf. 14x14½
1968, Dec. 30 Wmk. 314
248 A21 20c multicolored .15 .15
249 A21 50c dk blue, blk & red .24 .24
250 A21 85c rose red & multi .40 .40
251 A21 2.25r ultra & multi 1.90 1.90
Nos. 248-251 (4) 2.69 2.69

Landing on Praslin Island of the Chevalier Marion Dufresne expedition, 200th anniv.

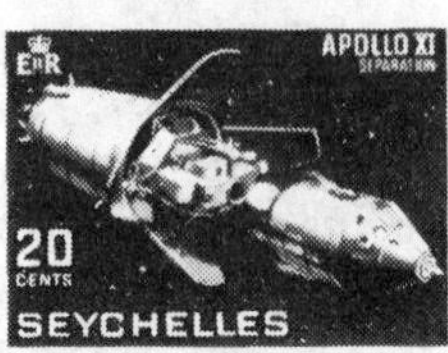

Separation of Rocket and Spacecraft — A22

5c, Launching of Apollo XI, vert. 50c, Landing module & men on the moon. 85c, Seychelles tracking station. 2.25r, Moonscape & earth.

1969, Sept. 9 Litho. *Perf. 13½*
252 A22 5c multicolored .15 .15
253 A22 20c multicolored .15 .15
254 A22 50c multicolored .22 .22
255 A22 85c multicolored .35 .35
256 A22 2.25r multicolored 1.10 1.10
Nos. 252-256 (5) 1.97 1.97

See note after US No. C76.

Lazare Picault Landing in 1741 — A23

History of Seychelles: 10c, US satellite tracking station. 15c, German cruiser Königsberg at Aldabra, 1915. 20c, British fleet refueling, St. Anne, 1939-45. 25c, Ashanti King Prempeh in exile, 1896. 30c, 40c, Stone of Possession placed, 1756. 50c, 65c, Pirates. 60c, Corsairs. 85c, 95c, Jet and airport. 1r, First capitulation of the French to the British, 1794. 1.50r, Battle between the sailing vessels Sybille and Chiffone, 1801. 3.50r, Visit of Duke of Edinburgh, 1956. 5r, Chevalier Queau de Quincy. 10r, Map of Indian Ocean, 1574. 15r, Seychelles coat of arms.

Perf. 13x12½
1969-72 Litho. Wmk. 314
257 A23 5c multicolored .15 .15
258 A23 10c multicolored .15 .15
259 A23 15c multicolored .15 .15
260 A23 20c multicolored .15 .15
261 A23 25c multicolored .15 .15
262 A23 30c multicolored .65 .65
262A A23 40c multicolored .32 .32
263 A23 50c multicolored .22 .22
264 A23 60c multicolored .95 .95
264A A23 65c multicolored .48 .48
265 A23 85c multicolored 1.00 1.00
265A A23 95c multicolored .48 .48
266 A23 1r multicolored .42 .42
267 A23 1.50r multicolored .65 .65
268 A23 3.50r multicolored 1.65 1.65
269 A23 5r multicolored 2.25 2.25
270 A23 10r multicolored 4.50 4.50
271 A23 15r multicolored 7.25 7.25
Nos. 257-271 (18) 21.57 21.57

Issued: 40, 65, 95c, 12/11/72; others, 11/3/69.
For overprints & surcharges see Nos. 294-298, 323-330, 361-369.

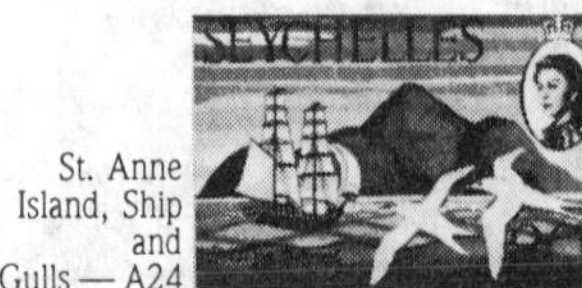

St. Anne Island, Ship and Gulls — A24

Designs: 50c, Flying fish, island and ship. 85c, Map of Seychelles and compass rose. 3.50r, Anchor, chain on sea bottom.

1970, Apr. 27 *Perf. 14*
272 A24 20c multicolored .15 .15
273 A24 50c multicolored .32 .32
274 A24 85c multicolored .50 .50
275 A24 3.50r multicolored 1.50 1.50
Nos. 272-275 (4) 2.47 2.47

Bicentenary of first settlement on St. Anne.

Girl and Eye Chart A25

Designs: 50c, Infant on scales and milk bottles. 85c, Mother and child, vert. 3.50r, Red Cross branch headquarters.

1970, Aug. 4 Litho. Wmk. 314
276 A25 20c lt blue & multi .15 .15
277 A25 50c multicolored .32 .32
278 A25 85c multicolored .52 .52
279 A25 3.50r multicolored 1.50 1.50
Nos. 276-279 (4) 2.49 2.49

Centenary of British Red Cross Society.

Pitcher Plant — A26

Flowers: 50c, Wild vanilla. 85c, Tropic-bird flower. 3.50r, Vare hibiscus.

1970, Dec. 29 *Perf. 14½*
280 A26 20c multicolored .20 .20
281 A26 50c multicolored .55 .55
282 A26 85c multicolored 1.00 1.00
283 A26 3.50r multicolored 5.25 5.25
a. Souvenir sheet of 4, #280-283 16.00 13.00
Nos. 280-283 (4) 7.00 7.00

Souvenir Sheet

Map Showing Location of Seychelles — A27

Perf. 13½x14
1971, Apr. 20 Litho. Wmk. 314
284 A27 5r yellow grn & multi 10.00 10.00

Issued to publicize Seychelles' location.

Consolidated Catalina Amphibian — A28

Designs: 5c, Piper Navajo, vert. 20c, Westland Wessex, vert. 60c, Grumman Albatross amphibian, vert. 85c, "G" class Short Brothers flying boat. 3.50r, Vickers supermarine "Walrus" amphibian.

Perf. 14x14½, 14½x14
1971, June 28 Litho. Wmk. 314
285 A28 5c orange & multi .15 .15
286 A28 20c purple & multi .18 .15
287 A28 50c olive & multi .35 .18
288 A28 60c sepia & multi .45 .22
289 A28 85c brown & multi .60 .35
290 A28 3.50r blue & multi 5.00 1.90
Nos. 285-290 (6) 6.73 2.95

Completion of Seychelles Airport.

Santa Claus, by Jean-Claude Waye Hive — A29

Christmas (Children's Drawings): 15c, Santa Claus riding a tortoise, by Edison Thérésine. 3.50r, Santa Claus on the seashore, by Isabelle Tirant.

1971, Oct. 12 *Perf. 13½*
291 A29 10c dark blue & multi .15 .15
292 A29 15c dark green & multi .15 .15
293 A29 3.50r violet & multi 1.50 1.50
Nos. 291-293 (3) 1.80 1.80

Nos. 262, 264-265 Surcharged with New Value and 5 Bars

1971, Dec. 21 *Perf. 13x12½*
294 A23 40c on 30c multicolored .28 .28
295 A23 65c on 60c multicolored .42 .42
296 A23 95c on 85c multicolored .60 .60
Nos. 294-296 (3) 1.30 1.30

Nos. 260, 269 Overprinted in Black or Gold: "ROYAL VISIT 1972"

1972, Mar. 21 Litho. Wmk. 314
297 A23 20c multicolored .15 .15
298 A23 5r multicolored (G) 2.50 2.50

Visit of Elizabeth II and Prince Philip.

Brush Warbler — A30 Fireworks — A31

1972, July 15 *Perf. 14x13½*
299 A30 5c shown .15 .15
300 A30 20c Scops owl .32 .22
301 A30 50c Blue pigeons .90 .45
302 A30 65c Magpie robin 1.25 .70
303 A30 95c Paradise flycatchers 2.25 1.25
304 A30 3.50r Kestrel 9.00 4.50
a. Souvenir sheet of 6, #299-304 24.00 19.00
Nos. 299-304 (6) 13.87 7.27

1972, Sept. 18 Litho. *Perf. 14*
305 A31 10c shown .15 .15
306 A31 15c Canoe race, horiz. .15 .15
307 A31 25c Women in local costumes .15 .15
308 A31 5r Water-skiing, horiz. 1.65 1.65
Nos. 305-308 (4) 2.10 2.10

Seychelles Festival 1972.

Silver Wedding Issue, 1972
Common Design Type

Design: Queen Elizabeth II, Prince Philip, giant tortoise and leaping sailfish.

1972, Nov. 20 Photo. *Perf. 14x14½*
309 CD324 95c multicolored .35 .35
310 CD324 1.50r multicolored .55 .55

Princess Anne's Wedding Issue
Common Design Type

1973, Nov. 14 Litho. *Perf. 14*
311 CD325 95c ocher & multi .25 .25
312 CD325 1.50r slate & multi .40 .40

Soldierfish A32

Wmk. 314
1974, Mar. 5 Litho. *Perf. 14*
313 A32 20c shown .20 .20
314 A32 50c Filefish .42 .42
315 A32 95c Butterflyfish .80 .80
316 A32 1.50r Gaterin 1.75 1.75
Nos. 313-316 (4) 3.17 3.17

Envelope and Globe A33

UPU, cent.: 50c, Globe with location of Seychelles and radio tower. 95c, Cancellation and globe. 1.50r, "UPU" with emblems.

Perf. 12½x12

1974, Oct. 9 Wmk. 314

317 A33 20c multicolored .15 .15
318 A33 50c multicolored .22 .22
319 A33 95c multicolored .42 .42
320 A33 1.50r multicolored .65 .65
Nos. 317-320 (4) 1.44 1.44

Winston Churchill A34

Design: 1.50r, Churchill, different portrait.

1974, Nov. 30 Litho. *Perf. 14½*

321 A34 95c lt blue & multi .40 .40
322 A34 1.50r lt green & multi .60 .60
a. Souvenir sheet of 2, #321-322 1.10 1.10

Sir Winston Churchill (1874-1965).

Nos. 260, 263, 265A and 267 Overprinted in Black or Silver

VISIT OF
Q.E.II

Perf. 13x12½

1975, Feb. 8 Wmk. 314

323 A23 20c multi (B) .15 .15
324 A23 50c multi (B) .22 .22
325 A23 95c multi (S) .35 .35
326 A23 1.50r multi (B) .55 .55
Nos. 323-326 (4) 1.27 1.27

Visit of cruise ship Queen Elizabeth II, Mahe, Seychelles.

Nos. 260, 264A, 266, 268 Overprinted in Gold

INTERNAL
SELF-GOVERNMENT
OCTOBER
1975

1975, Oct. 1 Litho. Wmk. 314

327 A23 20c multicolored .15 .15
328 A23 65c multicolored .24 .24
329 A23 1r multicolored .32 .32
330 A23 3.50r multicolored 1.10 1.10
Nos. 327-330 (4) 1.81 1.81

Queen Elizabeth I — A35

Portraits: 15c, Gladys Aylward. 20c, Elizabeth Fry. 25c, Emmeline Pankhurst. 65c, Florence Nightingale. 1r, Amy Johnson. 1.50r, Joan of Arc. 3.50r, Eleanor Roosevelt.

Perf. 13½

1975, Dec. 15 Litho. Wmk. 314

331 A35 10c dp brown & multi .15 .15
332 A35 15c dk brown & multi .15 .15
333 A35 20c dk green & multi .15 .15
334 A35 25c purple & multi .15 .15
335 A35 65c dk blue & multi .30 .30
336 A35 1r Prus blue & multi .42 .42
337 A35 1.50r dp violet & multi .65 .65
338 A35 3.50r dk olive & multi 1.75 1.75
Nos. 331-338 (8) 3.72 3.72

International Women's Year.

Praslin Map and Grand Anse Postmark, 1907 — A36

First Landing, 1609, and James Mancham — A37

Designs: 65c, La Digue map and postmark, 1916. 1r, Partial map of Mahé and Victoria postmark, 1917. 1.50r, Southern part of Mahé and Anse Royale postmark, 1938.

1976, Mar. 30 Wmk. 373 *Perf. 14*

339 A36 20c lt blue & multi .15 .15
340 A36 65c lt blue & multi .32 .32
341 A36 1r lt blue & multi .50 .50
342 A36 1.50r lt blue & multi .75 .75
a. Souvenir sheet of 4, #339-342 2.50 2.50
Nos. 339-342 (4) 1.72 1.72

Rural posts of Seychelles.

1976, June 29 *Perf. 14*

Designs: 25c, Stone of Possession. 40c, Arrival of 1st settlers, 1770 (ship). 75c, Le Chevalier Quéau de Quincy. 1r, Sir Bickham Sweet-Escott. 1.25r, Government House. 1.50r, Coat of arms of Internal Self-government. 3.50r, Seychelles flag.

343 A37 20c rose & multi .15 .15
344 A37 25c yellow & multi .15 .15
345 A37 40c lilac & multi .16 .16
346 A37 75c green & multi .24 .24
347 A37 1r salmon & multi .35 .35
348 A37 1.25r multicolored .40 .40
349 A37 1.50r ocher & multi .48 .48
350 A37 3.50r blue & multi 1.10 1.10
Nos. 343-350 (8) 3.03 3.03

Seychelles' independence, June 29, 1976.

Flags of Seychelles and US — A38

US bicent.: 10r, State House, Seychelles, and Independence Hall, Philadelphia.

1976, July 12 Litho.

351 A38 1r blue & multi .25 .25
352 A38 10r red & multi 2.50 2.50

Swimming A39

Designs (Olympic Rings and): 65c, Hockey. 1r, Basketball. 3.50r, Soccer.

1976, July 26 *Perf. 14½*

353 A39 20c vio blue & blk .15 .15
354 A39 65c dk grn, yel grn & blk .25 .25
355 A39 1r brown, grn & blk .35 .35
356 A39 3.50r car rose & blk 1.25 1.25
Nos. 353-356 (4) 2.00 2.00

21st Olympic Games, Montreal, Canada, July 17-Aug. 1.

Seychelles Sunbird — A40

Seychelles Birds (James R. Mancham, Congress Emblem and): 20c, Paradise flycatcher, vert. 1.50r, Gray white-eye. 5r, Black parrot, vert.

Perf. 14½

1976, Nov. 8 Litho. Wmk. 373

357 A40 20c multicolored .15 .15
358 A40 1.25r multicolored .80 .65
359 A40 1.50r multicolored .95 .85
360 A40 5r multicolored 2.75 2.50
a. Souvenir sheet of 4, #357-360 6.00 6.00
Nos. 357-360 (4) 4.65 4.15

4th Pan-African Ornithological Cong., Mahe Beach Hotel, Nov. 6-13.

Nos. 260, 263, 265A-266, 268-271, 264A Overprinted or Surcharged: "Independence / 1976"

Perf. 13x12½

1976, Nov. 22 Litho. Wmk. 314

361 A23 20c multicolored .15 .15
362 A23 50c multicolored .28 .24
363 A23 95c multicolored .48 .40
364 A23 1r multicolored .48 .40
365 A23 3.50r multicolored 2.00 1.75
366 A23 5r multicolored 2.50 2.00
367 A23 10r multicolored 4.75 4.00
368 A23 15r multicolored 6.75 6.00
369 A23 25r on 65c multi 12.00 10.00
Nos. 361-369 (9) 29.39 24.94

Washington's Inauguration — A41

American Bicentennial: 2c, Jefferson and map of Louisiana Purchase. 3c, Seward and map of Alaska Purchase. 4c, Pony Express, 1860. 5c, Lincoln's Emancipation Proclamation, 1863. 1.50r, Completion of Transcontinental Railroad, 1869. 3.50r, Wright Brothers' 1st flight, 1903. 5r, Ford assembly line, 1913. 10r, Kennedy and Apollo 11 moon landing, 1969. 25r, Declaration of Independence, 1776.

Perf. 14x13½

1976, Dec. 21 Wmk. 373

370 A41 1c rose & plum .15 .15
371 A41 2c lilac & vio .15 .15
372 A41 3c blue & vio bl .15 .15
373 A41 4c yellow & brn .15 .15
374 A41 5c brt yel & grn .15 .15
375 A41 1.50r yel brn & brn .35 .35
376 A41 3.50r brt grn & bl grn .80 .80
377 A41 5r yellow & brn 1.25 1.25
378 A41 10r dull bl & dk bl 2.50 2.50
Nos. 370-378 (9) 5.65 5.65

Souvenir Sheet

379 A41 25r lilac rose & pur 6.00 6.00

Seychelles Islands and Arms — A42

The Orb — A43

Designs: 40c, 5r, 10r, similar to 20c. 1r, St. Edward's Crown. 1.25r, Ampulla and Spoon. 1.50r, Scepter with Cross.

1977, Sept. 5 Litho. *Perf. 14*

380 A42 20c multicolored .15 .15
381 A42 40c multicolored .15 .15
382 A43 50c multicolored .15 .15
383 A43 1r multicolored .20 .20
384 A43 1.25r multicolored .25 .25
385 A43 1.50r multicolored .30 .30
386 A42 5r multicolored 1.00 1.00
387 A42 10r multicolored 2.00 2.00
a. Souv. sheet of 4, #380, 382, 383, 387 3.00 3.00
Nos. 380-387 (8) 4.20 4.20

25th anniv. of reign of Elizabeth II.

Coral Reef — A44

Perf. 14, 14x14½ (40c, 1, 1.25, 1.50r)

1977-78 Litho. Wmk. 373

Sizes: 40c, 1, 1.25, 1.50r, 30x25mm, Others 28x23mm

388 A44 5c Reef fish .15 .15
389 A44 10c Hawksbill turtle .15 .15
390 A44 15c Coco de mer .15 .15
391 A44 20c Wild vanilla .15 .15
392 A44 25c Butterfly .15 .15
393 A44 40c Coral reef .15 .15
394 A44 50c Giant tortoise .20 .20
a. Wmk. 384, perf. 14x14½ .30 .30
395 A44 75c Crayfish .20 .20
396 A44 1r Madagascar cardinal .30 .30
397 A44 1.25r Fairy tern .40 .40
398 A44 1.50r Flying fox .45 .45
398A A44 3r like #399, wmk. 384 1.65 1.65
399 A44 3.50r Green gecko 1.00 1.00

Perf. 13

Size: 27x35mm

400 A44 5r Octopus, vert. 1.50 1.50
401 A44 10r Tiger cowrie, vert. 3.00 3.00
402 A44 15r Pitcher plant, vert. 4.50 4.50
403 A44 20r Arms, vert. 6.25 6.25
Nos. 388-403 (17) 20.35 20.35

Issue dates: 40c, 1r, 1.25r, 1.50r, Oct. 31, 1977. No. 394a and 398A, Nov., 1991. Others, 1978.

Reissued dated "1979" below design: 10, 15, 25, 40, 50, 75c, 1r, 1.50r. Dated "1981": 40c. Dated "1982": 40c.

See No. 446. For surcharge and overprint see Nos. 446, 605.

Denomination "R" Instead of "Re." or "Rs."

Perf. 14x14½, 14 (1.10r)

1981, Jan. 6 Litho.

Sizes: 1.10r, 28x23mm, Others, 30x25mm

403A A44 1r like No. 396 .30 .30
403B A44 1.10r like No. 399 .35 .35
403C A44 1.25r like No. 397 .38 .38
i. Wmk. 384 ('89) .45 .45
403D A44 1.50r like No. 398 .45 .45

Perf. 13

403E A44 5r like No. 400 1.50 1.50
j. Perf. 14x14½, Wmk 384 ('90) 1.85 1.85
403F A44 10r like No. 401 3.00 3.00
403G A44 15r like No. 402 4.50 4.50
403H A44 20r like No. 403 6.00 6.00
Nos. 403A-403H (8) 16.48 16.48

Reissued dated "1981" below design: 1.50r. Dated "1982": 1r, 1.50r. Dated "1985": 5r, Dated "1986": 1r, Dated "1990": 1r, Dated "1991": 1r, 1.50r.

See No. 576 for No. 403C with commemorative inscription.

Cruiser Aurora, Star and Flag — A45

1977, Nov. 7 Unwmk. *Perf. 12*

404 A45 1.50r red, black & gold .45 .45
a. Souvenir sheet .55 .55

60th anniv. of Russian Oct. Revolution.

St. Roch Roman Catholic Church, Bel Ombre — A46

Christmas: 1r, Anglican Cathedral, Victoria. 1.50r, R. C. Cathedral, Victoria. 5r, St. Mark's Anglican Church, Praslin.

Perf. 13½x14

1977, Dec. 5 Wmk. 373

405 A46 20c multicolored .15 .15
406 A46 1r multicolored .18 .18
407 A46 1.50r multicolored .28 .28
408 A46 5r multicolored .90 .90
Nos. 405-408 (4) 1.51 1.51

Calendar Page, June 5, 1977 — A47

Edward VII, George V, George VI — A48

Designs: 1.25r, Hands holding rifle, torch and Seychelles flag. 1.50r, Fisherman and farmer holding hands. 5r, Soldiers and waving children.

Perf. 14x13½

1978, June 5 Litho. Wmk. 373

409 A47 40c multicolored .15 .15
410 A47 1.25r multicolored .16 .16
411 A47 1.50r multicolored .24 .24
412 A47 5r multicolored .85 .85
Nos. 409-412 (4) 1.40 1.40

First anniversary of Liberation Day.

1978, Aug. 21 Litho. *Perf. 14*

Designs: 1.50r, Queens Victoria and Elizabeth II. 3r, Queen Victoria Monument, Seychelles. 5r, Queen's Building, Victoria, Seychelles.

413 A48 40c multicolored .15 .15
414 A48 1.50r multicolored .26 .26
415 A48 3r multicolored .55 .55
416 A48 5r multicolored .90 .90
a. Souvenir sheet of 4, #413-416 2.50 2.50
Nos. 413-416 (4) 1.86 1.86

25th anniv. of coronation of Elizabeth II.

Gardenia from Aride Island — A49

Designs (Coat of Arms and): 1.25r, Magpie robin of Fregate Island. 1.50r, Seychelles paradise flycatchers. 5r, Green turtle.

Perf. 13½x14

1978, Oct. 16 Litho. Wmk. 373

417 A49 40c multicolored .16 .16
418 A49 1.25r multicolored .42 .42
419 A49 1.50r multicolored .50 .50
420 A49 5r multicolored 1.90 1.90
Nos. 417-420 (4) 2.98 2.98

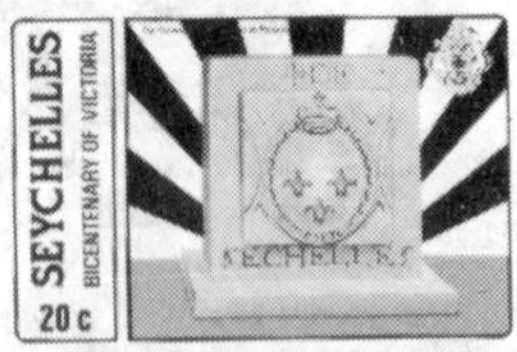

"Stone of Possession" — A50

1978, Dec. 15 Litho. *Perf. 13½*

421 A50 20c shown .15 .15
422 A50 1.25r Map, 1782 .24 .24
423 A50 1.50r Clock tower .30 .30
424 A50 5r Pierre Poivre .90 .90
Nos. 421-424 (4) 1.59 1.59

Bicentennary of the founding of Victoria.

Seychelles Fody — A51

Patrice Lumumba — A52

Birds: No. 426, Green-backed heron. No. 427, Seychelles bulbul. No. 428, Seychelles cave swiftlets. No. 429, Grayheaded lovebirds.

1979, Feb. 27 Litho. *Perf. 14*

425 A51 2r multicolored .70 .70
426 A51 2r multicolored .70 .70
427 A51 2r multicolored .70 .70
428 A51 2r multicolored .70 .70
429 A51 2r multicolored .70 .70
a. Strip of 5, #425-429 3.50 3.50
Nos. 425-429 (5) 3.50 3.50

1979, June 5 Litho. *Perf. 14½*

African Liberation Heroes: 2r, Kwame Nkrumah. 2.25r, Dr. Eduardo Mondlane. 5r, Amilcar Cabral.

430 A52 40c violet & blk .15 .15
431 A52 2r dark blue & blk .32 .32
432 A52 2.25r orange brn & blk .35 .35
433 A52 5r olive grn & blk .75 .75
Nos. 430-433 (4) 1.57 1.57

Coat of Arms, Rowland Hill, Seychelles No. 412 — A53

Coat of Arms, Hill, Seychelles stamps: 2.25r, No. 301. 3r, No. 205. 5r, No. 4.

1979, Aug. Litho. *Perf. 14x14½*

434 A53 40c multicolored .15 .15
435 A53 2.25r multicolored .45 .45
436 A53 3r multicolored .60 .60
Nos. 434-436 (3) 1.20 1.20

Souvenir Sheet

437 A53 5r multicolored 1.25 1.25

Sir Rowland Hill (1795-1879), originator of penny postage.

Schoolboy, IYC Emblem A54

IYC Emblem and: 2.25r, Children. 3r, Boy with ball, vert. 5r, Girl with puppet, vert.

Perf. 14½x14, 14x14½

1979, Oct. 25 Litho.

438 A54 40c multicolored .15 .15
439 A54 2.25r multicolored .35 .35
440 A54 3r multicolored .45 .45
441 A54 5r multicolored .75 .75
Nos. 438-441 (4) 1.70 1.70

International Year of the Child.

Three Kings Bearing Gifts A55

Christmas (Stained Glass Windows): 20c, Angel, vert. 2.25r, Virgin and Child, vert. 5r, Flight into Egypt.

1979, Dec. 3 Litho. *Perf. 14½*

442 A55 20c multicolored .15 .15
443 A55 2.25r multicolored .55 .55
444 A55 3r multicolored .75 .75
Nos. 442-444 (3) 1.45 1.45

Souvenir Sheet

445 A55 5r multicolored 1.40 1.40

No. 399 Surcharged

Wmk. 373

1979, Dec. 7 Litho. *Perf. 14*

446 A44 1.10r on 3.50r multicolored .35 .35

Seychelles Kestrel — A56

Seychelles Kestrel: a, shown. b, Pair. c, Female, eggs. d, Mother and chick. e, Chicks nesting.

1980, Feb. 29 Litho. *Perf. 14*

447 Strip of 5 3.50 3.50
a.-e. A56 2r any single .70 .70

See Nos. 468, 483.

50-Rupee Bank Note, London 1980 Emblem — A57

Sprinting, Moscow '80 Emblem — A58

New Currency: 40c, 1.50r, horiz.

1980, Apr. 18 Litho. *Perf. 14*

448 A57 40c multicolored .15 .15
449 A57 1.50r multicolored .28 .28
450 A57 2.25r multicolored .42 .42
451 A57 5r multicolored .90 .90
a. Souvenir sheet of 4, #448-451 1.90 1.90
Nos. 448-451 (4) 1.75 1.75

London 1980 Intl. Stamp Exhib., May 6-14.

1980, June 13 *Perf. 14½*

452 A58 40c shown .15 .15
453 A58 2.25r Weight lifting .32 .32
454 A58 3r Boxing .42 .42
455 A58 5r Yachting 1.50 1.50
a. Souvenir sheet of 4, #452-455 2.75 2.75
Nos. 452-455 (4) 2.39 2.39

22nd Summer Olympic Games, Moscow, July 19-Aug. 3.

Boeing 747 — A59

1980, Aug. 22 Litho. *Perf. 14*

456 A59 40c shown .15 .15
457 A59 2.25r Tour bus .45 .45
458 A59 3r Ocean liner, pirogue .65 .65
459 A59 5r Tour motor boat 1.10 1.10
Nos. 456-459 (4) 2.35 2.35

World Tourism Conf., Manila, Sept. 27.

Female Coco-de-Mer Palm Tree — A60

1980, Oct. 31 Litho. *Perf. 14*

460 A60 40c shown .15 .15
461 A60 2.25r Male tree .42 .42
462 A60 3r Bowls .55 .55
463 A60 5r Gourds, canoes .95 .95
a. Souvenir sheet of 4, #460-463 2.25 2.25
Nos. 460-463 (4) 2.07 2.07

Vasco da Gama's San Gabriel, 1497 A61

Perf. 14½

1981, Feb. Litho. Wmk. 373

464 A61 40c shown .15 .15
465 A61 2.25r Mascarenhas' Caravel, 1505 .48 .48
466 A61 3.50r Darwin's Beagle, 1831 .75 .75
467 A61 5r Queen Elizabeth 2, 1968 1.00 1.00
a. Souvenir sheet of 4, #464-467 2.50 2.50
Nos. 464-467 (4) 2.38 2.38

Bird Type of 1980

1981, Apr. 10 Litho. *Perf. 14*

468 Strip of 5, multi 5.00 5.00
a. A56 2r Male fairy tern 1.00 1.00
b. A56 2r Pair 1.00 1.00
c. A56 2r Female 1.00 1.00
d. A56 2r Female, diff. 1.00 1.00
e. A56 2r Adult bird, chick 1.00 1.00

Prince Charles, Lady Diana, Royal Yacht Charlotte A61a

Prince Charles and Lady Diana — A61b

Illustration A61b is reduced.

Wmk. 380

1981, June 23 Litho. *Perf. 14*

469 A61a 1.50r Couple, Victoria & Albert I .48 .48
a. Bklt. pane of 4, perf. 12 1.50
470 A61b 1.50r Couple .48 .48
471 A61a 5r Cleveland 1.50 1.50
472 A61b 5r like #470 1.50 1.50
a. Bklt. pane of 2, perf. 12 2.50
473 A61a 10r Britannia 3.25 3.25
474 A61b 10r like #470 3.25 3.25
Nos. 469-474 (6) 10.46 10.46

Each denomination issued in sheets of 7 (6 type A61a, 1 type A61b).

For surcharges see Nos. 528-533.

Souvenir Sheet

1981 Litho. *Perf. 12*

474A A61b 7.50r Couple 2.25 2.25

Seychelles Intl. Airport, 10th Anniv. A62

Perf. 14½

1981, July 27 Litho. Wmk. 373

475 A62 40c Britten-Norman Islander .15 .15
476 A62 2.25r Britten-Norman Trislander .55 .55

477 A62 3.50r Vickers VC-10 .80 .80
478 A62 5r Boeing 747 1.10 1.10
Nos. 475-478 (4) 2.60 2.60

A63

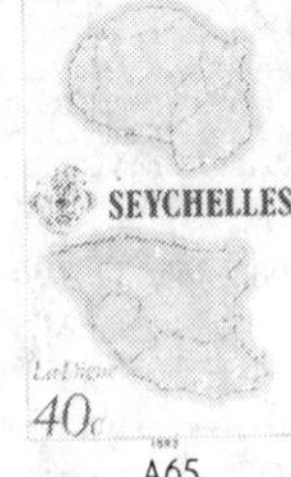

A65

Designs: Various flying foxes.

1981, Oct. 9 Litho. *Perf. 14*
479 A63 40c multicolored .15 .15
480 A63 2.25r multicolored .75 .75
481 A63 3r multicolored .95 .95
482 A63 5r multicolored 1.65 1.65
a. Souvenir sheet, #479-482 4.75 4.75
Nos. 479-482 (4) 3.50 3.50

Bird Type of 1980

Designs: a, Male Chinese bittern. b, Female. c, Hen on nest. d, Nest, eggs. e, Hen, chicks.

Wmk. 373

1982, Feb. 4 Litho. *Perf. 14*
483 Strip of 5 8.50 8.50
a.-e. A56 3r any single 1.65 1.65

1982, Apr. 22 Litho. *Perf. 14½*
487 A65 40c Map of Silhouette Island and La Digue .15 .15
488 A65 1.50r Denis & Bird Islds. .30 .30
489 A65 2.75r Curieuse Isld., Praslin .60 .60
490 A65 7r Mahe 1.40 1.40
a. Souvenir sheet of 4, #487-490 3.25 3.25
Nos. 487-490 (4) 2.45 2.45

5th Anniv. of Liberation A66

1982, June 5 *Perf. 14*
491 A66 40c Bookmobile .15 .15
492 A66 1.75r Mobile dental clinic .35 .35
493 A66 2.75r Farming .52 .52
494 A66 7r Construction site 1.40 1.40
a. Souvenir sheet of 4, #491-494 4.25 4.25
Nos. 491-494 (4) 2.42 2.42

Tourist Board Emblem A67

Tourism: Hotels.

1982, Sept. 1
495 A67 1.75r Northolme .40 .40
496 A67 1.75r Reef .40 .40
497 A67 1.75r Barbarons Beach .40 .40
498 A67 1.75r Coral Strand .40 .40
499 A67 1.75r Beau Vallon Bay .40 .40
500 A67 1.75r Fisherman's Cove .40 .40
501 A67 1.75r Mahe Beach, shown .40 .40
502 A67 1.75r Island scene .40 .40
Nos. 495-502 (8) 3.20 3.20

Tata Bus — A68

Wmk. 373

1982, Nov. 18 Litho. *Perf. 14*
503 A68 20c shown .15 .15
504 A68 1.75r Mini moke .35 .35
505 A68 2.75r Ox cart .55 .55
506 A68 7r Truck 1.40 1.40
Nos. 503-506 (4) 2.45 2.45

World Communications Year — A69

1983, Feb. 25
507 A69 40c Radio control room .15 .15
508 A69 2.75r Satellite earth station .60 .60
509 A69 3.50r TV control room .75 .75
510 A69 5r Postal services 1.10 1.10
Nos. 507-510 (4) 2.60 2.60

Commonwealth Day — A70

1983, Mar. 14
511 A70 40c Agricultural research .15 .15
512 A70 2.75r Food processing plant .60 .60
513 A70 3.50r Fishing industry .80 .80
514 A70 7r Flag 1.65 1.65
Nos. 511-514 (4) 3.20 3.20

Denis Isld. Lighthouse, 1910 — A71

1983, July 14 *Perf. 14x13½*
515 A71 40c shown .15 .15
516 A71 2.75r Seychelles Hospital, 1924 .75 .75
517 A71 3.50r Supreme Court, 1894 1.00 1.00
518 A71 7r State House, 1911 2.00 2.00
a. Souvenir sheet of 4, #515-518 4.50 4.50
Nos. 515-518 (4) 3.90 3.90

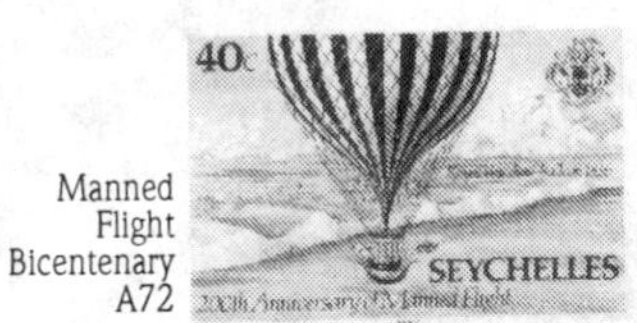

Manned Flight Bicentenary A72

1983, Sept. 15 *Perf. 14*
519 A72 40c Royal Vauxhall balloon, 1836 .15 .15
520 A72 1.75r DeHavilland D.H.-50j .50 .50
521 A72 2.75r Grumman Albatross .80 .80
522 A72 7r Sweavingen Merlin 2.00 2.00
Nos. 519-522 (4) 3.45 3.45

First Intl. Air Seychelles Flight A73

1983, Oct. 26 Litho.
523 A73 2r DC10 aircraft .65 .65

Paintings, Marianne North — A74

1983, Nov. 17 Litho. *Perf. 14*
524 A74 40c Swamp Plant and Moorhen .15 .15
525 A74 1.75r Wormia flagellaria .50 .50
526 A74 2.75r Asiatic Pancratium .80 .80
527 A74 7r Pitcher Plant 2.00 2.00
a. Souvenir sheet of 4, #524-527 4.50 4.50
Nos. 524-527 (4) 3.45 3.45

Nos. 469-474 Surcharged

Wmk. 380

1983, Dec. 28 Litho. *Perf. 14*
528 A61a 50c on 1.50r multi .16 .16
529 A61b 50c on 1.50r multi .16 .16
530 A61a 2.25r on 5r multi .75 .75
531 A61b 2.25r on 5r multi .75 .75
532 A61a 3.75r on 10r multi 1.25 1.25
533 A61b 3.75r on 10r multi 1.25 1.25
Nos. 528-533 (6) 4.32 4.32

Handicrafts A75

Wmk. 373

1984, Feb. 29 Litho. *Perf. 14*
534 A75 50c Coconut kettle .15 .15
535 A75 2r Scarf, doll .60 .60
536 A75 3r Coconut-fiber roses .90 .90
537 A75 10r Carved fishing boat, doll 2.75 2.75
Nos. 534-537 (4) 4.40 4.40

Lloyd's List Issue

Common Design Type

1984, May 21 Litho. *Perf. 14½x14*
538 CD335 50c Port Victoria .15 .15
539 CD335 2r Steamship, 1930s .60 .60
540 CD335 3r Cruise liner .90 .90
541 CD335 10r Ennerdale 2.75 2.75
Nos. 538-541 (4) 4.40 4.40

People's United Party, 20th Anniv. A76

1984, June 2 Litho. *Perf. 14*
542 A76 50c Original headquarters .15 .15
543 A76 2r Liberation statue, vert. .60 .60
544 A76 3r New headquarters .90 .90
545 A76 10r Pres. Rene, vert. 2.75 2.75
Nos. 542-545 (4) 4.40 4.40

Souvenir Sheet

UPU Congress A77

1984, June 18 *Perf. 14½*
546 A77 5r No. 156 1.50 1.50

1984 Summer Olympics A78

1984, July 28 *Perf. 14*
547 A78 50c Long jump .15 .15
548 A78 2r Boxing .55 .55
549 A78 3r Diving .80 .80
550 A78 10r Weight lifting 2.75 2.75
a. Souvenir sheet of 4, #547-550 4.25 4.25
Nos. 547-550 (4) 4.25 4.25

Scuba Diving A79

1984, Sept. 24
551 A79 50c shown .18 .18
552 A79 2r Paragliding .70 .70
553 A79 3r Sailing 1.00 1.00
554 A79 10r Water skiing 3.25 3.25
Nos. 551-554 (4) 5.13 5.13

Whale Conservation — A80

1984, Nov. Litho.
555 A80 50c Humpback whale .30 .30
556 A80 2r Sperm whale 1.00 1.00
557 A80 3r Right whale 1.50 1.50
558 A80 10r Blue whale 5.25 5.25
Nos. 555-558 (4) 8.05 8.05

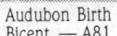

Audubon Birth Bicent. — A81

EXPO '85, Tsukuba — A82

Bare-legged scops owls.

1985, Mar. 11 Litho. *Perf. 14*
559 A81 50c multicolored .18 .18
560 A81 2r multicolored .70 .70
561 A81 3r multicolored 1.00 1.00
562 A81 10r multicolored 3.50 3.50
Nos. 559-562 (4) 5.38 5.38

Wmk. 373

1985, Mar. 15 Litho. *Perf. 14*
563 A82 50c Giant tortoise .15 .15
564 A82 2r Fairy tern .55 .55
565 A82 3r Wind surfing .80 .80
566 A82 5r Coco de mer 1.40 1.40
a. Souvenir sheet of 4, #563-566 3.00 3.00
Nos. 563-566 (4) 2.90 2.90

See No. 604.

Queen Mother 85th Birthday

Common Design Type

Perf. 14½x14

1985, June 7 Litho. Wmk. 384
567 CD336 50c Queen Elizabeth, 1930 .15 .15
568 CD336 2r With grandchildren, 1970 .60 .60
569 CD336 3r 75th birthday celebration .90 .90
570 CD336 5r Holding Prince Henry 1.50 1.50
Nos. 567-570 (4) 3.15 3.15

Souvenir Sheet

571 CD336 10r Exiting from helicopter 3.00 3.00

2nd Indian Ocean Islands Games A83

1985, Aug. 24
572 A83 50c Boxing .15 .15
573 A83 2r Soccer .55 .55
574 A83 3r Swimming .80 .80
575 A83 10r Wind surfing 2.75 2.75
Nos. 572-575 (4) 4.25 4.25

A83a

A84

1985, Nov. 1 Wmk. 384
576 A83a 1.25r Fairy tern .35 .35

Air Seychelles 1st Airbus.

1985, Nov. 28

577 A84 50c Agriculture .15 .15
578 A84 2r Construction .55 .55
579 A84 3r Carpentry .80 .80
580 A84 10r Science education 2.75 2.75
Nos. 577-580 (4) 4.25 4.25

Intl. Youth Year.

Vintage Cars — A85

1985, Dec. 18

581 A85 50c 1919 Ford Model T .15 .15
582 A85 2r 1922 Austin Seven .60 .60
583 A85 3r 1924 Morris Bullnose Oxford .85 .85
584 A85 10r 1929 Humber Coupe 3.00 3.00
Nos. 581-584 (4) 4.60 4.60

Halley's Comet — A86

1986, Feb. Wmk. 384 *Perf. 14x14½*

585 A86 50c Transit instrument .15 .15
586 A86 2r Quadrant .60 .60
587 A86 3r Trajectory diagram .85 .85
588 A86 10r Edmond Halley 3.00 3.00
Nos. 585-588 (4) 4.60 4.60

Giselle, Performed by the Ballet Louvre, Apr. 4-8 — A87

Wmk. 384

1986, Apr. 4 Litho. *Perf. 14*

589 A87 2r Heroine .60 .60
590 A87 3r Hero .90 .90

Souvenir Sheet

591 A87 10r United 3.00 3.00

First ballet performed in the Seychelles.

Queen Elizabeth II 60th Birthday

Common Design Type

Designs: 50c, Marrying the Duke of Edinburgh, 1947. 1.25r, Silver Jubilee celebration. 2r, Greeting child aboard the Britannia, Qatar Harbor. 3r, State opening of Parliament, 1982. 5r, Visiting Crown Agents' offices, 1983.

1986, Apr. 21 *Perf. 14½*

592 CD337 50c scarlet, blk & sil .15 .15
593 CD337 1.25r ultra & multi .38 .38
594 CD337 2r green & multi .60 .60
595 CD337 3r violet & multi .90 .90
596 CD337 5r rose vio & multi 1.50 1.50
Nos. 592-596 (5) 3.53 3.53

For overprints see Nos. 625-629.

AMERIPEX '86, Inter-island Communications — A88

Wmk. 384

1986, May 22 Litho. *Perf. 14*

597 A88 50c La Digue Ferry .16 .16
598 A88 2r Phone booth, vert. .62 .62
599 A88 3r Victoria P.O., vert. .90 .90
600 A88 7r Air Seychelles trislander 2.25 2.25
Nos. 597-600 (4) 3.93 3.93

Coptic Catholic Knights of Malta Celebration Day — A89

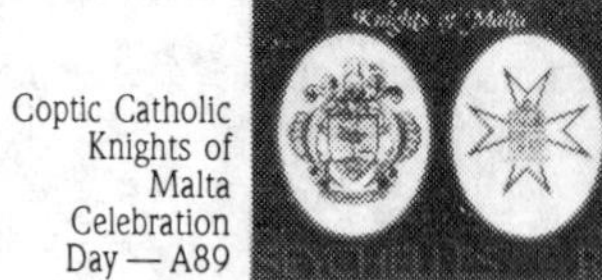

Perf. 14½x14

1986, June 7 Litho. Wmk. 384

601 A89 5r Natl. arms, assoc. emblem 1.50 1.50
a. Souvenir sheet of 1 1.65 1.65

Royal Wedding Issue, 1986

Common Design Type

2r, Informal portrait. 10r, Andrew, helicopter.

1986, July 23 Litho. *Perf. 14*

602 CD338 2r multicolored .60 .60
603 CD338 10r multicolored 3.00 3.00

Tsukuba Expo Type of 1985

Souvenir Sheet

Wmk. 384

1986, July 12 Litho. *Perf. 14*

604 Sheet of 4 3.00 3.00
a. A82 50c multicolored .15 .15
b. A82 2r multicolored .55 .55
c. A82 3r multicolored .80 .80
d. A82 5r multicolored 1.40 1.40

No. 604 inscribed "Seychelles Philatelic Exhibition-Tokyo-1986" and printed without EXPO '85 emblem on margin or on individual stamps. Nos. 604a-604d inscribed "1986."

No. 396 Overprinted

LAZOURNEN ENTERNASYONAL KREOL

Perf. 14½x14

1986, Oct. 28 Wmk. 373

605 A44 1r multicolored .30 .30

Intl. Creole Day.

State Visit of Pope John Paul II — A90

Pope and: 50c, Seychelles Airport. 2r, Cathedral. 3r, Baie Lazare parish church. 10r, People's Stadium.

1986, Dec. 1 Wmk. 384 *Perf. 14½*

606 A90 50c multicolored .18 .18
607 A90 2r multicolored .70 .70
608 A90 3r multicolored 1.00 1.00
609 A90 10r multicolored 3.25 3.25
a. Souvenir sheet of 4, #606-609 5.00 5.00
Nos. 606-609 (4) 5.13 5.13

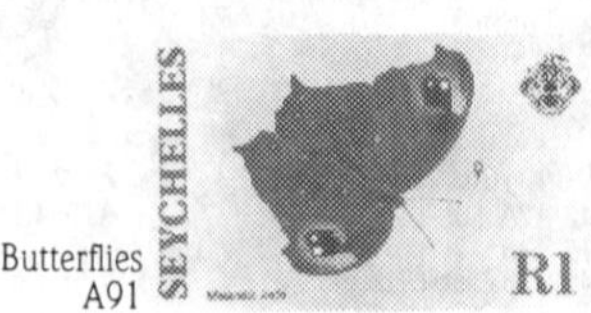

Butterflies A91

Perf. 14½

1987, Feb. 18 Litho. Wmk. 384

610 A91 1r Melanitis leda .38 .38
611 A91 2r Phalanta philiberti .75 .75
612 A91 3r Danaus chrysippus 1.10 1.10
613 A91 10r Euploea mitra 3.50 3.50
Nos. 610-613 (4) 5.73 5.73

Seashells — A92

Liberation, 10th Anniv. — A93

1987, May 7 Wmk. 373

614 A92 1r Gloripallium pallium .38 .38
615 A92 2r Spondylus aurantius .70 .70
616 A92 3r Harpa ventricosa, Lioconcha ornata 1.10 1.10
617 A92 10r Strombus lentiginosus 3.50 3.50
Nos. 614-617 (4) 5.68 5.68

Perf. 14x14½, 14½x14

1987, June 5 Wmk. 384

618 A93 1r Liberation monument .32 .32
619 A93 2r Hospital, horiz. .62 .62
620 A93 3r Orphanage, horiz. .92 .92
621 A93 10r Fish monument 3.00 3.00
Nos. 618-621 (4) 4.86 4.86

Natl. Banking Cent. — A94

1987, June 25 *Perf. 14½x14*

622 A94 1r Savings Bank, Praslin .32 .32
623 A94 2r Development Bank .60 .60
624 A94 10r Central Bank 3.00 3.00
Nos. 622-624 (3) 3.92 3.92

Nos. 592-596 Ovptd. in Silver

40TH WEDDING ANNIVERSARY

Perf. 14½

1987, Dec. 9 Litho. Wmk. 384

625 CD337 50c scarlet, blk & sil .16 .16
626 CD337 1.25r ultra & multi .42 .42
627 CD337 2r green & multi .70 .70
628 CD337 3r violet & multi 1.00 1.00
629 CD337 5r rose vio & multi 1.75 1.75
Nos. 625-629 (5) 4.03 4.03

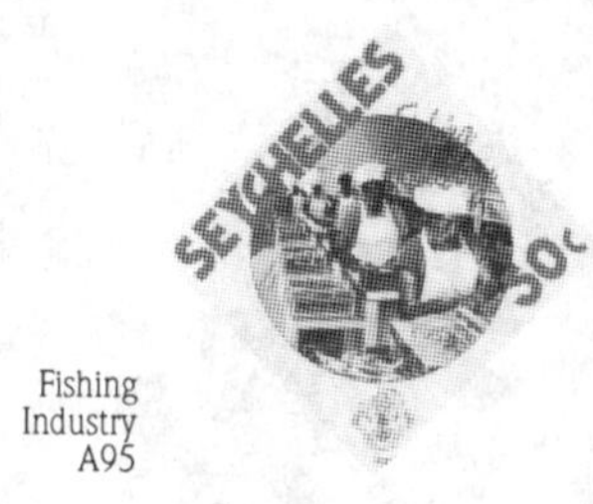

Fishing Industry A95

Wmk. 384

1987, Dec. 11 Litho. *Perf. 14*

630 A95 50c Tuna cannery .16 .16
631 A95 2r Fishing trawler .65 .65
632 A95 3r Weighing fish 1.00 1.00
633 A95 10r Hauling catch from net 3.50 3.50
Nos. 630-633 (4) 5.31 5.31

Beach Scenes A96

Perf. 14½

1988, Feb. 9 Litho. Wmk. 384

634 A96 1r Para-sailing, windsurfing, kayaks .32 .32
635 A96 2r Boating .65 .65
636 A96 3r Yacht at anchor .95 .95
637 A96 10r Hotel, cabanas 3.00 3.00
Nos. 634-637 (4) 4.92 4.92

Green Turtles — A97

A98

No. 638, Newly hatched turtles headed toward ocean. No. 639, Offspring hatching. No. 640, Female emerging from ocean. No. 641, Female laying eggs in sand. Stamps of same denomination printed se-tenant in a continuous design.

1988, Apr. 22 Wmk. 373

638 A97 2r multicolored .75 .75
639 A97 2r multicolored .75 .75
640 A97 3r multicolored 1.15 1.15
641 A97 3r multicolored 1.15 1.15
Nos. 638-641 (4) 3.80 3.80

1988, July 29 Wmk. 384 *Perf. 14½*

Designs: 1r, No. 647a, Shot put. Nos. 643, 647b, High jump. 3r, No. 647c, Medal winner, grandstand and flags. 4r, No. 647d, Running. 5r, No. 647e, Javelin. 10r, Tennis.

642 A98 1r multicolored .30 .30
643 A98 2r multicolored .60 .60
644 A98 3r multicolored .90 .90
645 A98 4r multicolored 1.25 1.25
646 A98 5r multicolored 1.40 1.40
647 Strip of 5 3.00 3.00
a.-e. A98 2r any single .60 .60
Nos. 642-647 (6) 7.45 7.45

Souvenir Sheet

Wmk. 373

648 A98 10r multicolored 3.75 3.75

No. 647 has a continuous design.

1988 Summer Olympics, Seoul, (1r-5r). Intl. Tennis Fed., 75th anniv. (10r). No. 648 contains one stamp, size: 28x39mm.

Lloyds of London, 300th Anniv.

Common Design Type

Designs: 1r, Leadenhall Street, London, 1928. 2r, Cinq Juin, horiz. 3r, Queen Elizabeth II, horiz. 10r, Explosion of the Hindenburg, Lakehurst, New Jersey, 1937.

Wmk. 384

1988, Sept. 30 Litho. *Perf. 14*

649 CD341 1r multicolored .38 .38
650 CD341 2r multicolored .72 .72
651 CD341 3r multicolored 1.05 1.05
652 CD341 10r multicolored 3.50 3.50
Nos. 649-652 (4) 5.65 5.65

Defense Forces Day, 1st Anniv. A99

1988, Nov. 25 Litho. Wmk. 373

653 A99 1r Motorcycle police .38 .38
654 A99 2r Air force helicopter .72 .72
655 A99 3r Navy patrol boat 1.05 1.05
656 A99 10r Tank 3.50 3.50
Nos. 653-656 (4) 5.65 5.65

Christmas — A100

Illustrations by local artists.

1988, Dec. 1 Litho. Wmk. 373

657 A100 50c Selwyn Hoareau .15 .15
658 A100 2r Robin Leste .72 .72
659 A100 3r France Anacoura 1.10 1.10
660 A100 10r Andre McGaw 3.65 3.65
Nos. 657-660 (4) 5.62 5.62

Orchids A101

Wmk. 384

1988, Dec. 21 Litho. *Perf. 14*

661 A101 1r Dendrobium, vert. .38 .38
662 A101 2r Arachnis hybrid .75 .75
663 A101 3r Vanda caerulea, vert. 1.15 1.15
664 A101 10r Dendrobium phalaenopsis 3.75 3.75
Nos. 661-664 (4) 6.03 6.03

Jawaharlal Nehru (1889-1964), 1st Prime Minister of Independent India — A102

1989, Mar. 30 *Perf. 13½*

665 A102 2r India Type A409 .75 .75
666 A102 10r Portrait 3.75 3.75

People's United Party (SPUP), 25th Anniv. — A103

1989, June 5 *Perf. 14*

667 A103 1r Rally, old office .38 .38
668 A103 2r Maison Du Peuple .75 .75
669 A103 3r Pres. Rene, banner, torch 1.10 1.10
670 A103 10r Torch, flag, Rene 3.65 3.65
Nos. 667-670 (4) 5.88 5.88

Moon Landing, 20th Anniv.
Common Design Type

Apollo 15: 1r, Saturn 5 lift-off. 2r, David R. Scott, Alfred M. Worden and James B. Irwin. 3r, Mission emblem. 5r, Irwin salutes flag in front of the Hadley Delta. 10r, Buzz Aldrin about to step onto the Moon, Apollo 11 mission.

1989, July 20
Size of Nos. 677-678: 29x29mm

676 CD342 1r multicolored .35 .35
677 CD342 2r multicolored .72 .72
678 CD342 3r multicolored 1.10 1.10
679 CD342 5r multicolored 1.80 1.80
Nos. 676-679 (4) 3.97 3.97

Souvenir Sheet

680 CD342 10r multicolored 3.65 3.65

Intl. Red Cross and Red Crescent Organizations, 125th Annivs. — A104

1989, Sept. 12 *Perf. 14½*

681 A104 1r Ambulance, 1870 .40 .40
682 A104 2r H.M. Hospital Ship Liberty, 1914-18 .78 .78
683 A104 3r Sunbeam Standard Army Ambulance, 1914-18 1.20 1.20
684 A104 10r The White Train, 1899-1902 4.00 4.00
Nos. 681-684 (4) 6.38 6.38

Island Birds — A105

1989, Oct. 16 *Perf. 14½x14*

685 A105 50c Black parrot .25 .25
686 A105 2r Sooty tern .85 .85
687 A105 3r Magpie robin 1.40 1.40
688 A105 5r Roseate tern 2.25 2.25
a. Souvenir sheet of 4, #685-688 4.75 4.75
Nos. 685-688 (4) 4.75 4.75

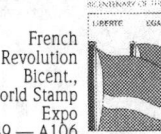

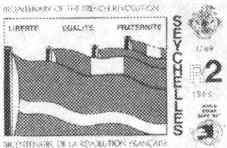

French Revolution Bicent., World Stamp Expo '89 — A106

1989, Nov. 17 *Perf. 14*

689 A106 2r Flags .70 .70
690 A106 5r Storming of the Bastille 1.75 1.75

Souvenir Sheet

691 A106 10r Raising French flag, Seychelles, 1791 3.50 3.50

African Development Bank, 25th Anniv. — A107

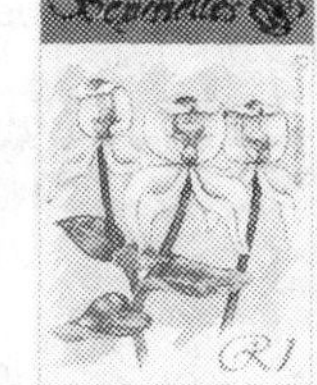

Orchids — A108

1r, Beau Vallon School, horiz. 2r, Fishing Authority headquarters, horiz. 3r, Variola. 10r, Deneb.

1989, Dec. 29 **Wmk. 384**

692 A107 1r multicolored .35 .35
693 A107 2r multicolored .70 .70
694 A107 3r multicolored 1.05 1.05
695 A107 10r multicolored 3.50 3.50
Nos. 692-695 (4) 5.60 5.60

1990, Jan. 26

696 A108 1r Disperis tripetaloides .35 .35
697 A108 2r Vanilla phalaenopsis .70 .70
698 A108 3r Angraecum eburneum superbum 1.05 1.05
699 A108 10r Polystachya concreta 3.50 3.50
Nos. 696-699 (4) 5.60 5.60

Expo '90 (International Garden & Greenery Exposition), Japan — A109

Designs: 2r, Fumiyo Sako. 3r, Coco-de-mer, male and female plants. 5r, Pitcher plant, Aldabra lily. 7r, Gardenia, Arms of Seychelles.

1990, June 8 **Litho.** **Wmk. 373**

700 A109 2r multicolored .70 .70
701 A109 3r multicolored 1.05 1.05
702 A109 5r multicolored 1.75 1.75
703 A109 7r multicolored 2.50 2.50
a. Souvenir sheet of 4, #700-703 6.00 6.00
Nos. 700-703 (4) 6.00 6.00

Penny Black 150th Anniv., Stamp World London '90
A110

Exhibition emblem and stamps on stamps: 1r, Seychelles #38, Great Britain #80 canceled. 2r, Seychelles #81, Great Britain #64 canceled. 3r, Seychelles #74, Great Britain #62 canceled. 5r, Seychelles #2, Great Britain #3 canceled. 10r, Seychelles #197, Great Britain #1 canceled.

1990, May 3 *Perf. 12½*

704 A110 1r multicolored .35 .35
705 A110 2r multicolored .70 .70
706 A110 3r multicolored 1.05 1.05
707 A110 5r multicolored 1.75 1.75
Nos. 704-707 (4) 3.85 3.85

Souvenir Sheet

708 A110 10r multicolored 3.50 3.50

Boeing 767-200ER
A111

Perf. 14½x14½

1990, July 27 **Litho.** **Wmk. 384**

709 A111 3r multicolored 1.05 1.05

Printed in panes of 10 (2 strips of 5 separated by pictorial gutter).

Queen Mother, 90th Birthday
Common Design Types

1990, Aug. 4 **Wmk. 384** *Perf. 14x15*

710 CD343 2r Queen Elizabeth in coronation robes, 1937 .70 .70

Perf. 14½

711 CD344 10r Visiting workshops, 1947 3.50 3.50

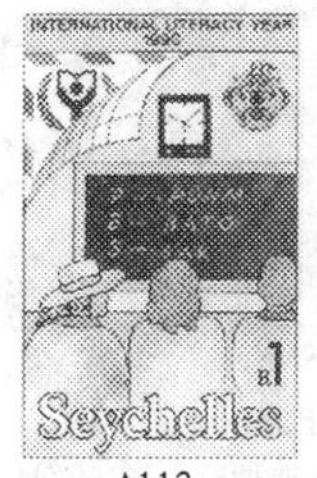

A112

A113

1990, Sept. 8 **Wmk. 373** *Perf. 14*

712 A112 1r Blackboard .36 .36
713 A112 2r Reading mail .72 .72
714 A112 3r Reading directions 1.10 1.10
715 A112 10r Crossword puzzle 3.60 3.60
Nos. 712-715 (4) 5.78 5.78

Intl. Literacy Year.

1990, Oct. 27 *Perf. 13½x14*

Various Sega Dancers: a, Pink and white skirt, white blouse. b, Yellow dress. c, Blue, sky blue and pink dress. d, Yellow, green and pink dress. e, White and pink skirt, green blouse.

716 Strip of 5 3.60 3.60
a.-e. A113 2r any single .72 .72

Festival Kreol 1990.

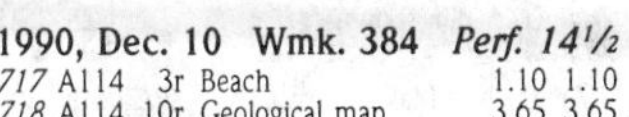

First Regional Seminar, Indian Ocean Petroleum Exploration
A114

1990, Dec. 10 **Wmk. 384** *Perf. 14½*

717 A114 3r Beach 1.10 1.10
718 A114 10r Geological map 3.65 3.65

Orchids — A115

1991, Feb. 1 *Perf. 14*

719 A115 1r Bulbophyllum intertextum .36 .36
720 A115 2r Agrostophyllum occidentale .72 .72
721 A115 3r Vanilla planifolia 1.10 1.10
722 A115 10r Malaxis seychellarum 3.60 3.60
Nos. 719-722 (4) 5.78 5.78

Elizabeth & Philip, Birthdays
Common Design Types

1991, June 17 *Perf. 14½*

723 CD345 4r multicolored 1.40 1.40
724 CD346 4r multicolored 1.40 1.40
a. Pair, #723-724 + label 2.80 2.80

Butterflies
A116

Perf. 14½x14

1991, Nov. 15 **Litho.** **Wmk. 373**

725 A116 1.50r Precis rhadama .58 .58
726 A116 3r Lampides boeticus 1.15 1.15
727 A116 3.50r Zizeeria knysna 1.35 1.35
728 A116 10r Phalanta phalanta aethiopica 4.00 4.00
Nos. 725-728 (4) 7.08 7.08

Souvenir Sheet

729 A116 10r Eagris sabadius 4.00 4.00

Phila Nippon '91.

Christmas — A117

Woodcuts: 50c, The Holy Virgin, Joseph, the Holy Child and St. John by Raphael, engraved by S. Vouillemont. 1r, The Holy Virgin, the Child and an Angel by Van Dyck, engraved by A. Blooting. 2r, The Holy Family, St. John and St. Anna by Rubens, engraved by Lucas Vorsterman. 7r, The Holy Family, an Angel and St. Catherine, painting and engraving by Cornelius Bloemaert.

1991, Dec. 2 **Wmk. 384** *Perf. 14*

730 A117 50c multicolored .18 .18
731 A117 1r multicolored .40 .40
732 A117 2r multicolored .80 .80
733 A117 7r multicolored 2.75 2.75
Nos. 730-733 (4) 4.13 4.13

Queen Elizabeth II's Accession to the Throne, 40th Anniv.
Common Design Type

1992, Feb. 6 **Wmk. 373**

734 CD349 1r multicolored .38 .38
735 CD349 1.50r multicolored .55 .55
736 CD349 3r multicolored 1.15 1.15
737 CD349 3.50r multicolored 1.30 1.30
738 CD349 5r multicolored 1.85 1.85
Nos. 734-738 (5) 5.23 5.23

Flora and Fauna — A118

Designs: 10c, Brush warbler. 25c, Bronze gecko, vert. 50c, Seychelles tree frog. 1r, Seychelles splendid palm, vert. 1.50r, Seychelles skink, vert. 2r, Giant tenebrionid beetle. 3r, Seychelles sunbird. 3.50r, Seychelles killifish. 4r, Magpie robin. 5r, Seychelles vanilla, vert. 10r, Tiger chameleon. 15r, Coco-de-mer, vert. 25r, Paradise flycatcher, vert. 50r, Giant tortoise.

Perf. 13½

1993, Mar. 1 **Litho.** **Wmk. 373**

739 A118 10c multicolored .15 .15
740 A118 25c multicolored .15 .15
741 A118 50c multicolored .20 .20
742 A118 1r multicolored .38 .38
743 A118 1.50r multicolored .58 .58
744 A118 2r multicolored .80 .80
745 A118 3r multicolored 1.15 1.15

746 A118 3.50r multicolored 1.35 1.35
747 A118 4r multicolored 1.55 1.55
748 A118 5r multicolored 1.95 1.95
749 A118 10r multicolored 3.85 3.85
750 A118 15r multicolored 5.75 5.75
751 A118 25r multicolored 9.50 9.50
752 A118 50r multicolored 19.00 19.00
Nos. 739-752 (14) 46.36 46.36

#742, 748-749, 751-752 exist inscribed "1994": #739-741, 744, 750 "1996."

First Visit to Seychelles by Archbishop of Canterbury — A119

Archbishop and: 3r, Anglican Cathedral, Victoria. 10r, Air France, Air Seychelles airplanes.

1993, June 8 ***Perf. 13½***
753 A119 3r multicolored 1.15 1.15
754 A119 10r multicolored 3.85 3.85

4th Indian Ocean Island Games — A120

1993, Aug. 21 ***Perf. 14½***
755 A120 1.50r Running .58 .58
756 A120 3r Soccer 1.10 1.10
757 A120 3.50r Cycling 1.40 1.40
758 A120 10r Sailing 3.75 3.75
Nos. 755-758 (4) 6.83 6.83

Telecommunications, Cent. — A121

Designs: 1r, Cable ship Scotia, Victoria, 1893. 3r, Eastern Telegraph Company's Office, Victoria, 1904. 4r, HF Transmitting Station, operational 1971. 10r, New Telecoms House, Victoria, 1993.

1993, Nov. 12 ***Perf. 13***
759 A121 1r multicolored .40 .40
760 A121 3r multicolored 1.25 1.25
761 A121 4r multicolored 1.65 1.65
762 A121 10r multicolored 4.00 4.00
Nos. 759-762 (4) 7.30 7.30

Zil Elwannyen Sesel Nos. 59, 61, 63, 64 Surcharged

R1

1994, Feb. 18 ***Perf. 14x14½***
763 A9 1r on 2.10r #59 .38 .38
764 A9 1.50r on 2.75r #61 .55 .55
765 A9 3.50r on 7r #63 1.40 1.40
766 A9 10r on 15r #64 3.75 3.75
Nos. 763-766 (4) 6.08 6.08

Hong Kong '94. Size and location of surcharge varies.

Butterflies A122

1994, Aug. 16 Wmk. 384 ***Perf. 14***
767 A122 1.50r Eurema floricola .60 .60
768 A122 3r Coeliades forestan 1.25 1.25
769 A122 3.50r Borbo borbonica 1.40 1.40
770 A122 10r Zizula hylax 4.00 4.00
Nos. 767-770 (4) 7.25 7.25

A123

A124

1995, Sept. 26 Wmk. 373
771 A123 1.50r Age 9 .65 .65
772 A123 3r Wedding day 1.25 1.25
773 A123 3.50r 1936 Portrait 1.50 1.50
774 A123 10r 1975 Photograph 4.25 4.25
Nos. 771-774 (4) 7.65 7.65

Queen Mother, 95th birthday.

Wmk. 384

1996, July 12 Litho. ***Perf. 14***

Black Paradise Flycatcher.

775 A124 1r Female on branch .40 .40
776 A124 1r Male in flight .40 .40
777 A124 1r Male on branch .40 .40
778 A124 1r Female, young .40 .40
a. Strip of 4, #775-778 1.60 1.60

Souvenir Sheet

779 A124 10r Female, male birds 4.00 4.00

World Wildlife Fund.

Stamps in No. 778a may be out of Scott number sequence.

A125

A126

1996, July 15
780 A125 50c Swimming .20 .20
781 A125 1.50r Running .60 .60
782 A125 3r Sailing 1.20 1.20
783 A125 5r Boxing 2.00 2.00
Nos. 780-783 (4) 4.00 4.00

Modern Olympic Games, cent.

Wmk. 373

1996, Aug. 19 Litho. ***Perf. 14***
784 A126 3r shown 1.25 1.25
785 A126 10r Portrait up close 4.00 4.00

Archbishop Makarios of Cyprus, Exiled in Seychelles, 40th anniv.

Birds — A127

#786, Aldabra souimanga sunbird. #787, Seychelles sunbird. #788, Aldabra blue pigeon. #789, Seychelles blue pigeon. #790, Aldabra red headed fody. #791, Seychelles fody. #792, Aldabra white-eye. #793, Seychelles white-eye.

Perf. 14½

1996, Nov. 11 Litho. Wmk. 373
786 A127 3r multicolored 1.20 1.20
787 A127 3r multicolored 1.20 1.20
a. Pair, #786-787 2.40 2.40
788 A127 3r multicolored 1.20 1.20
789 A127 3r multicolored 1.20 1.20
a. Pair, #788-789 2.40 2.40
790 A127 3r multicolored 1.20 1.20
791 A127 3r multicolored 1.20 1.20
a. Pair, #790-791 2.40 2.40
792 A127 3r multicolored 1.20 1.20
793 A127 3r multicolored 1.20 1.20
a. Pair, #792-793 2.40 2.40
Nos. 786-793 (8) 9.60 9.60

Zil Elwannyen Sesel No. 58 Surcharged

SEYCHELLES

R1.50

1997, Feb. 12 ***Perf. 14x14½***
794 A9 1.50r on 2r .60 .60

Hong Kong '97.

Queen Elizabeth II and Prince Philip, 50th Wedding Anniv. — A128

Designs: No. 795, Queen in red & white dress. No. 796, Prince driving four-in-hand team. No. 797, Prince in business suit. No. 798, Queen, horse. No. 799, Prince Charles, Princess Anne. No. 800, Prince, Queen.

10r, Queen and Prince in open carriage, horiz.

Wmk. 373

1997, Nov. 20 Litho. ***Perf. 13***
795 A128 1r multicolored .40 .40
796 A128 1r multicolored .40 .40
a. Pair, #795-796 .80 .80
797 A128 1.50r multicolored .60 .60
798 A128 1.50r multicolored .60 .60
a. Pair, #797-798 1.20 1.20
799 A128 3r multicolored 1.25 1.25
800 A128 3r multicolored 1.25 1.25
a. Pair, #799-800 2.50 2.50
Nos. 795-800 (6) 4.50 4.50

Souvenir Sheet

801 A128 10r multicolored 4.00 4.00

Diana, Princess of Wales (1961-97)

Common Design Type

Designs: a, In red dress. b, Wearing white blouse, printed vest. c, In blue dress, flowers. d, Wearing white dress.

Perf. 14½x14

1998, Mar. 31 Litho. Wmk. 373
802 CD355 3r Sheet of 4, #a.-d. 5.50 5.50

No. 802 sold for 12r + 3r, with surtax from international sales being donated to the Princess Diana Memorial Fund and surtax from national sales being donated to designated local charity.

POSTAGE DUE STAMPS

Catalogue values for unused stamps in this section are for Never Hinged items.

D1

Engr.; Denomination Typo. in Carmine

1951, Mar. 1 Wmk. 4 ***Perf. 11½***
J1 D1 2c carmine 1.50 *3.25*
J2 D1 3c blue green 1.50 *3.25*
J3 D1 6c ocher 1.00 *1.65*
J4 D1 9c brown orange 1.25 *5.00*
J5 D1 15c purple 1.50 *6.25*
J6 D1 18c deep blue 1.90 *7.00*
J7 D1 20c black brown 2.00 *8.25*
J8 D1 30c red brown 2.50 *10.50*
Nos. J1-J8 (8) 13.15 *45.15*

Engr.; Denomination Typo.

1964-65 Wmk. 314
J9 D1 2c carmine .80 .80
J10 D1 3c green & red ('65) 2.50 2.50

Issue dates: July 7, 1964, Sept. 14, 1965.

Dated "1980"

1980 Litho. ***Perf. 14***
J11 D1 5c lilac rose & red .15 .15
J12 D1 10c dk green & red .15 .15
J13 D1 15c bister & red .15 .15
J14 D1 20c brown org & red .15 .15
J15 D1 25c violet & red .15 .15
J16 D1 75c dk red brown & red .25 .25
J17 D1 80c dk blue & red .28 .28
J18 D1 1r claret & red .30 .30
Set value 1.10 1.10

ZIL ELWANNYEN SESEL

LOCATION — South of Seychelles

The islands of Aldabra, Farquhar and Des Roches. Formerly part of the British Indian Ocean Territory.

Catalogue values for unused stamps in this country are for Never Hinged items.

Type of Seychelles, 1977-78

Perf. 14, 14½x14 (40c, 1r, 1.25r, 1.50r)

1980-81 Litho. Wmk. 373

Size: 30x26mm (40c, 1r, 1.25r, 1.50r)
1 A44 5c Reef fish .15 .15
2 A44 10c Hawksbill turtle .15 .15
3 A44 15c Coco-de-mer .15 .15
4 A44 20c Wild vanilla .15 .15
5 A44 25c Butterfly .15 .15
6 A44 40c Coral reef .15 .15
7 A44 50c Giant tortoise .15 .15
8 A44 75c Crayfish .20 .20
9 A44 1r Madagascar fody .25 .25
10 A44 1.10r Green gecko .28 .28
11 A44 1.25r Fairy tern .32 .32
12 A44 1.50r Flying fox .40 .40

Size: 27x35mm
13 A44 5r Octopus, vert. 1.25 1.25
a. Perf. 13 ('81) 1.25 1.25
14 A44 10r Giant tiger cowrie, vert. 2.50 2.50
a. Perf. 13 ('81) 2.50 2.50
15 A44 15r Pitcher plant, vert. 4.00 4.00
a. Perf. 13 ('81) 4.00 4.00
16 A44 20r Natl. arms, vert. 5.00 5.00
a. Perf. 13 ('81) 5.00 5.00
Nos. 1-16 (16) 15.25 15.25

Nos. 1-12 exist with 1981 imprint.

Traveling Post Office A1

1980, Oct. 24 ***Perf. 14***
17 A1 1.50r Cinq Juin .38 .38
18 A1 2.10r Canceling letters .55 .55
19 A1 5r Map 1.25 1.25
Nos. 17-19 (3) 2.18 2.18

The 5r showing Agalega as part of the Seychelles was not issued.

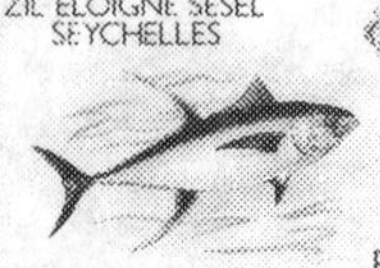

Yellowfin Tuna — A2

1980, Nov. 28
20 A2 1.50r shown .38 .38
21 A2 2.10r Blue marlin .55 .55
22 A2 5r Sperm whale 1.25 1.25
Nos. 20-22 (3) 2.18 2.18

Royal Wedding Types of Seychelles

1981, June 23 Wmk. 380 Perf. 14
23 A61a 40c Royal Escape .15 .15
a. Bklt. pane of 4, perf. 12½x12, unwmkd. .45 .45
24 A61b 40c Couple .15 .15
25 A61a 5r Victoria & Albert II 1.25 1.25
26 A61b 5r like #24 1.25 1.25
a. Bklt pane of 2, perf. 12½x12, unwmkd. 2.50 2.50
27 A61a 10r Britannia 2.50 2.50
28 A61b 10r like #24 2.50 2.50
Nos. 23-28 (6) 7.80 7.80

Souvenir Sheet

Perf. 12½x12

29 A61b 7.50r like #24 2.00 2.00

Each denomination issued in sheets of 7 (6 type A61a, 1 type A61b).

For surcharges see Nos. 70-75.

Wildlife A3

1981, Dec. 11 Wmk. 373 Perf. 14
30 A3 1.40r Wright's skink .35 .35
31 A3 2.25r Tree frog .60 .60
32 A3 5r Robber crab 1.25 1.25
Nos. 30-32 (3) 2.20 2.20

Workboats A4

1982, Mar. 11 Perf. 14x14½
33 A4 1.75r Cinq Juin .45 .45
34 A4 2.10r Junon .55 .55
35 A4 5r Diamond M. Dragon 1.25 1.25
Nos. 33-35 (3) 2.25 2.25

Mailboats A5

1982, July 22 Wmk. 373 Perf. 14
36 A5 40c Paulette .15 .15
37 A5 1.75r Janette .45 .45
38 A5 2.75r Lady Esme .70 .70
39 A5 3.50r Cinq Juin .90 .90
Nos. 36-39 (4) 2.20 2.20

Aldabra, World Heritage Site — A6

1982, Nov. 19
40 A6 40c Birds flying over island .15 .15
41 A6 2.75r Map .70 .70
42 A6 7r Giant tortoises 1.90 1.90
Nos. 40-42 (3) 2.75 2.75

Wildlife — A7

1983, Feb. 25 Perf. 14x14½
43 A7 1.75r Red land crab .55 .55
44 A7 2.75r Black terrapin .90 .90
45 A7 7r Madagascar green gecko 2.25 2.25
Nos. 43-45 (3) 3.70 3.70

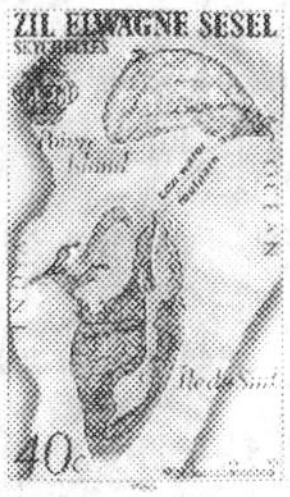

Maps — A8

1983, Apr. 27 Perf. 14½
46 A8 40c Poivre Island, Ile du Sud .15 .15
47 A8 1.50r Ile des Roches .50 .50
48 A8 2.75r Astove Island .90 .90
49 A8 7r Coetivy Island 2.25 2.25
a. Souvenir sheet of 4, #46-49 4.00 4.00
Nos. 46-49 (4) 3.80 3.80

Birds — A9

Perf. 14x14½

1983, July 13 Wmk. 373
50 A9 5c Aldabra brush warbler .15 .15
51 A9 10c Barred ground dove .15 .15
52 A9 15c Aldabra nightjar .15 .15
53 A9 20c Malagasy grass warbler .15 .15
54 A9 25c Aldabra white-eye .15 .15
55 A9 40c Aldabra fody .15 .15
56 A9 50c Aldabra rail .16 .16
57 A9 75c Aldabra bulbul .25 .25
58 A9 2r Dimorphic little egret .60 .60
59 A9 2.10r Aldabra sunbird .65 .65
60 A9 2.50r Aldabra turtle dove .80 .80
61 A9 2.75r Aldabra sacred ibis .90 .90

Perf. 14½x14

62 A9 3.50r Aldabra coucal 1.10 1.10
63 A9 7r Aldabra kestrel 2.25 2.25
64 A9 15r Aldabra blue pigeon 5.00 5.00
65 A9 20r Greater flamingo 6.25 6.25
Nos. 50-65 (16) 18.86 18.86

Nos. 62-65 vert. See Nos. 96-100. For surcharges see Seychelles Nos. 763-766.

World Tourism Day — A10

1983, Sept. 27 Perf. 14
66 A10 50c Windsurfing .16 .16
67 A10 2r Hotel .60 .60
68 A10 3r Beach .95 .95
69 A10 10r Sunset 3.25 3.25
Nos. 66-69 (4) 4.96 4.96

Nos. 23-28 Surcharged

1983 Wmk. 380 Perf. 14
70 A61a 30c on 40c multi .15 .15
71 A61b 30c on 40c multi .15 .15
72 A61a 2r on 5r multi .65 .65
73 A61b 2r on 5r multi .65 .65
74 A61a 3r on 10r multi .95 .95
75 A61b 3r on 10r multi .95 .95
Nos. 70-75 (6) 3.50 3.50

Each denomination issued in sheets of 7 (6 type A61a, 1 type A61b).

Aldabra Post Office, Reopening A11

1984, Mar. 30 Wmk. 373 Perf. 14
76 A11 50c Map, postmark .16 .16
77 A11 2.75r Aldabra rail .85 .85
78 A11 3r Giant tortoise .95 .95
79 A11 10r Red-footed booby 3.25 3.25
Nos. 76-79 (4) 5.21 5.21

Game Fishing A12

1984, May 31
80 A12 50c Fishing boat .16 .16
81 A12 2r Hooked fish, vert. .65 .65
82 A12 3r Weighing catch, vert. .95 .95
83 A12 10r Fishing boat, stern view 3.25 3.25
Nos. 80-83 (4) 5.01 5.01

Crabs A13

1984, Aug. 24 Perf. 14½
84 A13 50c Giant hermit crab .16 .16
85 A13 2r Fiddler crabs .65 .65
86 A13 3r Ghost crab .95 .95
87 A13 10r Spotted pebble crab 3.25 3.25
Nos. 84-87 (4) 5.01 5.01

Constellations A14

Mushrooms A15

1984, Oct. 16 Perf. 14
88 A14 50c Orion .16 .16
89 A14 2r Cygnus .65 .65
90 A14 3r Virgo .95 .95
91 A14 10r Scorpio 3.25 3.25
Nos. 88-91 (4) 5.01 5.01

Wmk. 373

1985, Jan. 31 Litho. Perf. 14
92 A15 50c Lenzites elegans .15 .15
93 A15 2r Xylaria telfairei .55 .55
94 A15 3r Lentinus sajor-caju .80 .80
95 A15 10r Hexagonia tenuis 2.75 2.75
Nos. 92-95 (4) 4.25 4.25

Bird Type of 1983

Inscribed "Zil Elwannyen Sesel"

Wmk. 373, 384 (5c)

1985-88 Perf. 14x14½
96 A9 5c Like #50 ('88) .15 .15
97 A9 10c Like #51 .15 .15
a. Wmk. 384 ('88) .15 .15
98 A9 25c Like #54 .15 .15
99 A9 50c Like #56 ('87) .15 .15
a. Wmk. 384 ('88) .15 .15
100 A9 2r Like #58 .55 .55
a. Wmk. 384 ('88) .55 .55
Set value .78 .78

No. 97 exists with 1987 imprint, No. 100a with 1990 imprint.

Queen Mother 85th Birthday

Common Design Type

Perf. 14½x14

1985, June 1 Wmk. 384
101 CD336 1r Coronation portrait .28 .28
102 CD336 2r With Princess Anne .55 .55
103 CD336 3r Wearing tiara .80 .80
104 CD336 5r Holding Prince Henry 1.40 1.40
Nos. 101-104 (4) 3.03 3.03

Souvenir Sheet

105 CD336 10r In river taxi, Venice 2.75 2.75

Giant Tortoise A16

1985, Sept. 27 Perf. 14
106 A16 50c shown .15 .15
107 A16 75c Tortoises crossing stream .20 .20
108 A16 1r Three tortoises .28 .28
109 A16 2r Tortoise facing right .55 .55
Nos. 106-109 (4) 1.18 1.18

Souvenir Sheet

Perf. 13x13½

110 A16 10r Two tortoises 2.75 2.75

World Wildlife Fund. See Nos. 131-134.

Famous Visitors A17

Visitors and their ships: 50c, Phoenician trader, 600 B.C. 2r, Sir Hugh Scott, HMS Sealark, 1908. 10r, Vasco de Gama, Sao Gabriel, 1502.

1985, Oct. 25 Wmk. 373 Perf. 14
111 A17 50c multicolored .15 .15
112 A17 2r multicolored .55 .55
113 A17 10r multicolored 2.75 2.75
Nos. 111-113 (3) 3.45 3.45

Queen Elizabeth II, 60th Birthday

Common Design Type

Designs: 75c, As princess. 1r, With Prince Philip. 1.50r, Wearing blue cape. 3.75r, Portrait. 5r, Wearing red hat.

Perf. 14½x14

1986, Apr. 21 Wmk. 384
114 CD337 75c scar, blk & sil .20 .20
115 CD337 1r blue & multi .28 .28
116 CD337 1.50r grn & multi .40 .40
117 CD337 3.75r vio & multi 1.00 1.00
118 CD337 5r rose vio & multi 1.40 1.40
Nos. 114-118 (5) 3.28 3.28

For overprints see Nos. 135-139.

Royal Wedding

Common Design Type

3r, Sarah Ferguson, Prince Andrew. 7r, Andrew.

1986, July 23 Perf. 14
119 CD338 3r multicolored .80 .80
120 CD338 7r multicolored 1.90 1.90

Coral — A18

Flowers — A19

Continuous design: a, Acropora palifera, Tubastraea coccinea. b, Echinopora lamellosa, Favia pallida. c, Sarcophyton sp, Porites lutea. d, Goniopora sp, Goniastrea retiformis. e, Tubipora musica, Fungia fungites.

1986, Sept. 17
121 A18 2r Strip of 5, #a.-e. 2.75 2.75

1986, Nov. 12
122 A19 50c Hibiscus tiliaceus .15 .15
123 A19 2r Crinum angustum .55 .55
124 A19 3r Phaius tetragonus .80 .80
125 A19 10r Rothmannia annae 2.75 2.75
Nos. 122-125 (4) 4.25 4.25

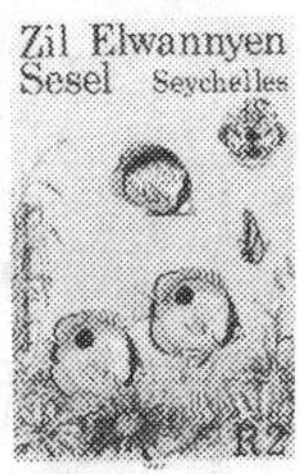

Fish — A20

Trees — A21

Continuous design: a, Chaetodon unimaculatus. b, Ostorhincus fleurieu. c, Platax orbicularis. d, abudefduf annulatus. e, Chaetodon lineolatus.

1987, Mar. 26

126 A20 2r Strip of #126a-126e 2.75 2.75

1987, Aug. 26 ***Perf. 14½***

127 A21 1r Coconut .28 .28
128 A21 2r Mangrove .55 .55
129 A21 3r Pandanus palm .80 .80
130 A21 5r Indian almond 1.40 1.40
Nos. 127-130 (4) 3.03 3.03

Nos. 106-110 Redrawn
World Wildlife Fund Emblem without Circle

1987, Sept. 9 Wmk. 384 ***Perf. 14***

131 A16 50c multicolored .15 .15
132 A16 75c multicolored .20 .20
133 A16 1r multicolored .28 .28
134 A16 2r multicolored .55 .55
Nos. 131-134 (4) 1.18 1.18

Nos. 114-118 Ovptd. in Silver
"40TH WEDDING ANNIVERSARY"

1987, Dec. 9 ***Perf. 14½x14***

135 CD337 75c scar, blk & sil .22 .22
136 CD337 1r blue & multi .30 .30
137 CD337 1.50r grn & multi .45 .45
138 CD337 3.75r vio & multi 1.10 1.10
139 CD337 5r rose vio & multi 1.50 1.50
Nos. 135-139 (5) 3.57 3.57

Mai Valley Tropical Forest — A22

Continuous design: b, Trunk of palm tree at right. c, Bamboo.

1987, Dec. 16 ***Perf. 14***

140 A22 3r Strip of 3, #a.-c. 2.75 2.75

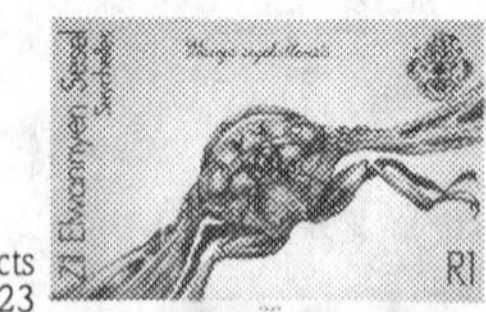

Insects A23

1988, July 28 Wmk. 373

141 A23 1r Yanga seychellensis .30 .30
142 A23 2r Belenois aldabraensis .60 .60
143 A23 3r Polyspilota seychelliana .90 .90
144 A23 5r Polposipus herculeanus 1.50 1.50
Nos. 141-144 (4) 3.30 3.30

Souvenir Sheet

1988 Summer Olympics, Seoul — A24

1988, Aug. 31 Wmk. 384

145 A24 10r multicolored 3.00 3.00

Lloyds' of London, 300th Anniv.

Common Design Type

Designs: 1r, Lloyd's building, 1988. 2r, Cable ship Retriever, horiz. 3r, Chantel, horiz. 5r, Torrey Canyon aground off Cornwall, 1967.

1988, Oct. 28 Wmk. 373

146 CD341 1r multicolored .30 .30
147 CD341 2r multicolored .60 .60
148 CD341 3r multicolored .90 .90
149 CD341 5r multicolored 1.50 1.50
Nos. 146-149 (4) 3.30 3.30

Christmas — A25

Perf. 13½x14, 14x13½

1988, Nov. 18 Wmk. 384

150 A25 1r Santa, toys in canoe .30 .30
151 A25 2r Church, vert. .60 .60
152 A25 3r Santa riding bird, vert. .90 .90
153 A25 5r Sleigh over island 1.50 1.50
Nos. 150-153 (4) 3.30 3.30

Moon Landing, 20th Anniv.

Common Design Type

Apollo 18: 1r, Firing room, Launch Control Center. 2r, Astronauts Slayton, Stafford, Brand and cosmonauts Leonov and Kubasov. 3r, Mission emblem. 5r, Apollo and Soyuz docking in space. 10r, Apollo 11 lifted aboard USS Hornet.

Perf. 14x13½, 14 (#155-156)

1989, July 20

Size of Nos. 155-156: 29x29mm

154 CD342 1r multicolored .38 .38
155 CD342 2r multicolored .75 .75
156 CD342 3r multicolored 1.10 1.10
157 CD342 5r multicolored 1.75 1.75
Nos. 154-157 (4) 3.98 3.98

Souvenir Sheet

158 CD342 10r multicolored 3.75 3.75

Poisonous Plants A26

1989, Oct. 9 ***Perf. 14***

159 A26 1r Dumb cane .38 .38
160 A26 2r Star of Bethlehem .75 .75
161 A26 3r Indian licorice 1.10 1.10
162 A26 5r Black nightshade 1.75 1.75
Nos. 159-162 (4) 3.98 3.98

See Nos. 173-176.

Creole Cooking — A27

1989, Dec. 18

163 A27 1r Tec-tec broth .38 .38
164 A27 2r Pilaf a la Seychelloise .75 .75
165 A27 3r Mullet grilled in banana leaves 1.10 1.10
166 A27 5r Daube 1.75 1.75
a. Souvenir sheet of 4, #163-166 4.00 4.00
Nos. 163-166 (4) 3.98 3.98

No. 166a has continuous design.

Stamp World London '90 — A28

Designs: 1r, #22. 2r, #13. 3r, #61. 5r, #32.

Perf. 12½

1990, May 3 Litho. Wmk. 373

167 A28 1r multicolored .35 .35
168 A28 2r multicolored .70 .70
169 A28 3r multicolored 1.05 1.05
170 A28 5r multicolored 1.75 1.75
a. Souvenir sheet of 4, #167-170 4.00 4.00
Nos. 167-170 (4) 3.85 3.85

Queen Mother 90th Birthday

Common Design Types

Designs: 2r, As Duchess of York with infant Elizabeth. 10r, With King George VI viewing bomb-damaged London, 1940.

1990, Aug. 4 Wmk. 384 ***Perf. 14x15***

171 CD343 2r multi .70 .70

Perf. 14½

172 CD344 10r yel brn & blk 3.50 3.50

Poisonous Plants Type of 1989

Perf. 12½

1990, Nov. 5 Litho. Wmk. 373

173 A26 1r Ordeal plant .35 .35
174 A26 2r Thorn apple .70 .70
175 A26 3r Strychnine tree 1.05 1.05
176 A26 5r Bwa zasmen 1.75 1.75
Nos. 173-176 (4) 3.85 3.85

Elizabeth & Philip, Birthdays

Common Design Types

Perf. 14½

1991, June 17 Litho. Wmk. 384

177 CD345 4r multicolored 1.40 1.40
178 CD346 4r multicolored 1.40 1.40
a. Pair, #177-178 + label 2.80 2.80

Shipwrecks A29

Wmk. 373

1991, Oct. 28 Litho. ***Perf. 14***

179 A29 1.50r St. Abbs, 1860 .55 .55
180 A29 3r Norden, 1862 1.05 1.05
181 A29 3.50r Clan Mackay, 1894 1.25 1.25
182 A29 10r Glenlyon, 1905 3.50 3.50
Nos. 179-182 (4) 6.35 6.35

Queen Elizabeth II's Accession to the Throne, 40th Anniv.

Common Design Type

1992, Feb. 6

183 CD349 1r multicolored .38 .38
184 CD349 1.50r multicolored .55 .55
185 CD349 3r multicolored 1.15 1.15
186 CD349 3.50r multicolored 1.30 1.30
187 CD349 5r multicolored 1.85 1.85
Nos. 183-187 (5) 5.23 5.23

Aldabra World Heritage Site, 10th Anniv. — A30

Designs: 1.50r, Lomatopyllum aldabrense. 3r, Dryolimnas cuvieri aldabranus. 3.50r, Birgus latro. 10r, Dicrurus aldabranus.

1992, Nov. 19 ***Perf. 14½***

188 A30 1.50r multicolored .60 .60
189 A30 3r multicolored 1.25 1.25
190 A30 3.50r multicolored 1.45 1.45
191 A30 10r multicolored 4.10 4.10
Nos. 188-191 (4) 7.40 7.40

SHANGHAI

shaŋ-'hī

LOCATION — A city on the Whangpoo River, Kiangsu Province, China
POP. — 3,489,998

A British settlement was founded there in 1843 and by agreement with China settlements were established by France and the United States. Special areas were set aside for the foreign settlements and a postal system independent of China was organized which was continued until 1898.

16 Cash = 1 Candareen
100 Candareens = 1 Tael
100 Cents = 1 Dollar (1890)

Watermark

Wmk. 175- Kung Pu (Municipal Council)

Dragon — A1

1865-66 Unwmk. Typo. ***Imperf.***

Antique Numerals

Roman "I" in "16"

"Candareens" in the Plural

Wove Paper

1 A1 2ca black 200.00
a. Pelure paper 275.00
2 A1 4ca yellow 150.00
a. Pelure paper 425.00
b. Double impression
3 A1 8ca green 200.00
a. 8ca yellow green 225.00
4 A1 16ca scarlet 225.00
a. 16ca vermilion 225.00
b. Pelure paper 300.00
Nos. 1-4 (4) 775.00

No. 1: top character of three in left panel as illustrated. No. 5: top character is two horiz. lines.

Nos. 2, 3: center character of three in left panel as illustrated. Nos. 6, 7: center character much more complex.

Antique Numerals

"Candareens" in the Plural

Pelure Paper

5 A1 2ca black 275.00
a. Wove paper 190.00
6 A1 4ca yellow 200.00
7 A1 8ca deep green 200.00
Nos. 5-7 (3) 675.00

Antique Numerals

"Candareen" in the Singular

Laid Paper

8 A1 1ca blue 165.00
9 A1 2ca black 2,000.
10 A1 4ca yellow 500.00
Nos. 8-10 (3) 2,665.

Wove Paper

11 A1 1ca blue 275.00
12 A1 2ca black 300.00
13 A1 4ca yellow 225.00
14 A1 8ca olive green 200.00
15 A1 16ca vermilion 165.00
a. "1" of "16" omitted
Nos. 11-15 (5) 1,165.

Only one copy of No. 15a is known.

Antique Numerals

Roman "I"

"Candareens" in the Plural Except on 1ca

Wove Paper

16 A1 1ca blue 450.00
17 A1 12ca fawn 225.00
18 A1 12ca chocolate 200.00
Nos. 16-18 (3) 875.00

Antique Numerals

"Candareens" in the Plural Except on 1ca

Wove Paper

19 A1 1ca indigo, pelure paper 150.00
20 A1 3ca orange brown 165.00
a. Pelure paper 225.00
21 A1 6ca red brown 140.00
22 A1 6ca fawn 400.00

23 A1 6ca vermilion 175.00
24 A1 12ca orange brown 110.00
25 A1 16ca vermilion 150.00
a. "1" of "16" omitted 350.00
Nos. 19-25 (7) 1,290.

Antique Numerals
Roman "I"
"Candareens" in the Plural Except on 1ca
Laid Paper

26 A1 1ca blue *14,000.*
27 A1 2ca black 2,000.
28 A1 3ca red brown *9,000.*

Modern Numerals
"Candareen" in the Singular

29 A1 1ca dark blue 125.00
a. 1ca slate blue 90.00
30 A1 3ca red brown 100.00

"Candareens" in the Plural Except the 1c

31 A1 2ca black 125.00
32 A1 3ca red brown 90.00

Coarse Porous Wove Paper

33a A1 1ca blue 90.00
34a A1 2ca black 165.00
b. Grayish paper 165.00
35a A1 3ca red brown 80.00
36a A1 4ca yellow 80.00
37a A1 6ca olive green 90.00
38a A1 8ca emerald 90.00
39a A1 12ca orange vermilion 75.00
40a A1 16ca red 85.00
41a A1 16ca red brown 95.00
Nos. 33a-41a (9) 850.00

Chinese characters change on same denomination stamps.

Nos. 1, 2, 11 and 32 exist on thicker paper, usually toned. Most authorities consider these four stamps and Nos. 33a-41a to be official reprints made to present sample sets to other post offices. The tone in this paper is an acquired characteristic, due to various causes. Many shades and minor varieties exist of Nos. 1-41a.

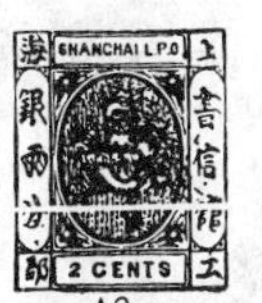
A2

A3

A4

A5

1866 **Litho.** *Perf. 12*
42 A2 2c rose 8.50 11.00
43 A3 4c lilac 19.00 21.00
44 A4 8c gray blue 19.00 21.00
45 A5 16c green 55.00 70.00
Nos. 42-45 (4) 101.50

Nos. 42-45 imperf. are proofs. See No. 50. For surcharges see Nos. 51-61, 67.

A6

A7

A8

A9

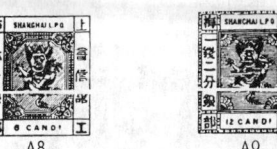

1866 *Perf. 15*
46 A6 1ca brown 6.00 5.50
a. "CANDS" 45.00 50.00
47 A7 3ca orange 22.50 27.50
48 A8 6ca slate 22.50 27.50
49 A9 12ca olive gray 50.00 60.00
Nos. 46-49 (4) 101.00

See Nos. 69-77. For surcharges see Nos. 62-66, 68, 78-83.

1872
50 A2 2c rose 70.00 95.00

Handstamp Surcharged in Blue, Red or Black

a

1873 *Perf. 12*
51 A2 1ca on 2c rose 25.00 30.00
52 A3 1ca on 4c lil 15.00 18.00
53 A3 1ca on 4c lil (R) *1,500.* *1,500.*
54 A3 1ca on 4c lil (Bk) 20.00 25.00
55 A4 1ca on 8c gray bl 20.00 25.00
56 A4 1ca on 8c gray bl (R) *3,250.* *3,250.*
57 A5 1ca on 16c grn *2,500.* *2,500.*
58 A5 1ca on 16c grn (R) *3,500.* *3,500.*

Perf. 15
59 A2 1ca on 2c rose 30.00 35.00

1875 *Perf. 12*
60 A2 3ca on 2c rose 60. 60.
61 A5 3ca on 16c grn *1,100.* *1,100.*

Perf. 15
62 A7 1ca on 3ca org *3,500.* *3,500.*
63 A8 1ca on 6ca sl 225. 225.
64 A8 1ca on 6ca sl (R) *2,300.* *2,300.*
65 A9 1ca on 12ca ol gray 200. 200.
66 A9 1ca on 12ca ol gray (R) *2,250.* *2,250.*
67 A2 3ca on 2c rose 200. 200.
68 A9 3ca on 12ca ol gray *5,500.* *5,500.*

Counterfeits exist of Nos. 51-68.

Types of 1866

1875 *Perf. 15*
69 A6 1ca yel, *yel* 20.00 22.50
70 A7 3ca rose, *rose* 20.00 22.50

Perf. 11½
71 A6 1ca yel, *yel* 225.00 250.00

1876 *Perf. 15*
72 A6 1ca yellow 5.50 6.50
73 A7 3ca rose 35.00 40.00
74 A8 6ca green 65.00 65.00
75 A9 9ca blue 75.00 75.00
76 A9 12ca light brown 100.00 100.00
Nos. 72-76 (5) 280.50

1877 **Engr.** *Perf. 12½*
77 A6 1ca rose 800.00 800.00

Stamps of 1875-76 Surcharged type "a" in Blue or Red

1877 **Litho.** *Perf. 15*
78 A7 1ca on 3ca rose, *rose* 200. 200.
79 A7 1ca on 3ca rose 40. 40.
80 A8 1ca on 6ca green 50. 50.
81 A9 1ca on 9ca blue 175. 175.
82 A9 1ca on 12ca lt brn 800. 800.
83 A9 1ca on 12ca lt brn (R) *3,000.* *3,000.*

Counterfeits exist of Nos. 78-83.

A11

A12

A13

A14

1877 *Perf. 15*
84 A11 20 cash violet 8.00 9.00
a. 20 cash blue violet 5.50 5.50
85 A12 40 cash rose 10.00 9.00
86 A13 60 cash green 10.00 11.00
87 A14 80 cash blue 17.00 17.00
88 A14 100 cash brown 16.00 22.50
Nos. 84-88 (5) 61.00

Handstamp Surcharged in Blue

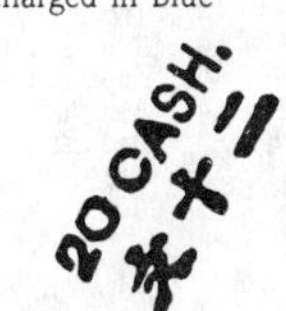
b

1879 *Perf. 15*
89 A12 20 cash on 40c rose 17.00 17.00
90 A14 60 cash on 80c blue 24.00 30.00
91 A14 60 cash on 100c brn 24.00 30.00
Nos. 89-91 (3) 65.00 77.00

Types of 1877

1880 *Perf. 11½*
92 A11 20 cash violet 5.00 5.50
93 A12 40 cash rose 7.50 6.50
94 A13 60 cash green 2.75 2.75
95 A14 80 cash blue 8.00 9.50
96 A14 100 cash brown 9.50 10.50

Perf. 15x11½
97 A11 20 cash lilac 30.00 30.00
Nos. 92-97 (6) 62.75

Surcharged type "b" in Blue

1884 *Perf. 11½*
98 A12 20 cash on 40c rose 7.00 8.50
99 A14 60 cash on 80c blue 15.00 17.00
100 A14 60 cash on 100c brn 17.00 17.00
Nos. 98-100 (3) 39.00

Types of 1877

1884
101 A11 20 cash green 5.00 6.00

1885 *Perf. 15*
102 A11 20 cash green 2.75 2.75
103 A12 40 cash brown 3.50 3.50
104 A13 60 cash violet 7.00 8.00
a. 60 cash red violet 11.00 17.00
105 A14 80 cash buff 7.00 6.00
106 A14 100 cash yellow 8.00 9.00

Perf. 11½x15
107 A11 20 cash green 3.50 6.00
108 A13 60 cash red vio 7.00 7.00
Nos. 102-108 (7) 38.75

Surcharged type "b" in Blue

1886 *Perf. 15*
109 A14 40 cash on 80c buff 4.25 3.75
110 A14 60 cash on 100c yel 5.75 5.00

Types of 1877

1888 *Perf. 15*
111 A11 20 cash gray 3.25 3.25
112 A12 40 cash black 3.25 4.25
113 A13 60 cash rose 4.50 4.25
a. Third character at left lacks dot at top 6.25 7.00
114 A14 80 cash green 4.50 5.00
115 A14 100 cash lt blue 6.50 7.00
Nos. 111-115 (5) 22.00

Handstamp Surcharged in Blue or Red Type "b" or:

20 CASH.
文十二
c

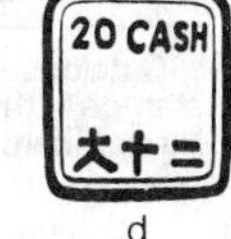
d

1888 *Perf. 15*
116 A14(b) 40 cash on 100c yel 4.50 6.00
117 A14(b) 40 cash on 100c yel (R) 5.00 6.00
118 A12(c) 20 cash on 40c brn 10.00 10.00
119 A14(c) 20 cash on 80c buff 2.50 2.50
120 A12(d) 20 cash on 40c brn 11.00 11.00
Nos. 116-120 (5) 33.00

Inverted surcharges exist on Nos. 116-120; double on Nos. 116, 119, 120; omitted surcharges paired with normal stamp on Nos. 116, 119.

Handstamp Surcharged in Black and Red (100 cash) or Red (20 cash)

e

1889 **Unwmk.**
121 A14(e) 100 cash on 20c on 100c yel 27.50 27.50
a. Without the surcharge "100 cash" 275.00
b. Blue & red surcharge
122 A14(c) 20 cash on 80c grn 6.00 6.00
123 A14(c) 20 cash on 100c bl 5.00 6.00
Nos. 121-123 (3) 38.50

Counterfeits exist of Nos. 116-123.

1889 **Wmk. 175** *Perf. 15*
124 A11 20 cash gray 1.65 1.65
125 A12 40 cash black 3.00 3.00
126 A13 60 cash rose 3.50 4.00
a. Third character at left lacks dot at top 6.50 7.00

Perf. 12
127 A14 80 cash green 3.25 4.00
128 A14 100 cash dk bl 9.00 8.00
Nos. 124-128 (5) 20.40

Nos. 124-126 are sometimes found without watermark. This is caused by the sheet being misplaced in the printing press, so that the stamps are printed on the unwatermarked margin of the sheet.

Shield with Dragon Supporters — A20

1890 **Unwmk.** **Litho.** *Perf. 15*
129 A20 2c brown 1.75 2.25
130 A20 5c rose 4.00 4.00
131 A20 15c blue 4.50 4.50

Nos. 129-131 imperforate are proofs.

Wmk. 175
132 A20 10c black 5.50 5.50
133 A20 15c blue 11.00 11.00
134 A20 20c violet 4.50 4.50
Nos. 129-134 (6) 31.25

See Nos. 135-141. For surcharges and overprints see Nos. 142-152, J1-J13.

1891 *Perf. 12*
135 A20 2c brown 2.00 2.00
136 A20 5c rose 3.50 3.50

1892
137 A20 2c green 1.25 1.10
138 A20 5c red 3.00 2.75
139 A20 10c orange 8.50 10.00
140 A20 15c violet 5.00 6.00
141 A20 20c brown 6.00 6.00
Nos. 137-141 (5) 23.75 25.85

No. 130 Handstamp Surcharged in Blue

2 Cts.
時先式
f

1892 **Unwmk.** *Perf. 15*
142 A20 2c on 5c rose 35.00 22.50

Counterfeits exist of Nos. 142-152.

Stamps of 1892 Handstamp Surcharged in Blue:

銀分半
HALF CENT.
g

銀分壹
ONE CENT.
h

1893 **Wmk. 175** *Perf. 12*
143 A20 ½c on 15c violet 5.00 5.00
144 A20 1c on 20c brown 5.00 5.00
a. ½c on 20c brown (error) *4,000.*

Surcharged in Blue or Red (#152) on Halves of #136 (#145-147), #138 (#148-150), #135 (#151), #137 (#152):

½Ct. ½Ct. ½Ct. 1Ct.
i j k m

145 A20(i) ½c on half of 5c 5.00 4.00
146 A20(j) ½c on half of 5c 7.00 5.50
147 A20(k) ½c on half of 5c 70.00 60.00
148 A20(i) ½c on half of 5c 5.00 3.50
149 A20(j) ½c on half of 5c 7.00 5.50
150 A20(k) ½c on half of 5c 70.00 60.00
151 A20(m) 1c on half of 2c 2.00 2.00
c. Dbl. surch., one in green *325.00*
d. Dbl. surch., one in black *325.00*
152 A20(m) 1c on half of 2c 11.00 10.00
Nos. 145-152 (8) 177.00 150.50

The ½c surcharge setting of 20 (2x10) covers a vertical strip of 10 unsevered stamps, with horizontal gutter midway. This setting has 11 of type "i," 8 of type "j" and 1 of type "k." Nos. 145-152 are perforated vertically down the middle.

Inverted surcharges exist on Nos. 145-151. Double surcharges, one inverted, are also found in this issue.

Handstamped provisionals somewhat similar to Nos. 145-152 were issued in Foochow by the Shanghai Agency.

Coat of Arms — A24

Mercury — A26

1893 Litho. *Perf. 13½x14*

Frame Inscriptions in Black

No.	Type	Description	Unused	Used
153	A24	½c orange, typo.	.30	.25
a.		½c orange, litho.	5.00	5.00
154	A24	1c brown, typo.	.30	.25
a.		1c brown, litho.	5.00	5.00
155	A24	2c vermilion	9.00	8.00
a.		Imperf.		
156	A24	5c blue	.30	.25
a.		Black inscriptions inverted	650.00	
157	A24	10c grn, typo. & litho.	3.25	4.00
a.		10c green, litho.	8.00	9.00
158	A24	15c yellow	.45	.40
159	A24	20c lil, typo. & litho.	2.75	3.50
a.		20c lilac, litho.	4.50	4.50
		Nos. 153-159 (7)	16.35	16.65

On Nos. 157 and 159, frame inscriptions are lithographed, rest of design typographed.

See Nos. 170-172. For overprints and surcharges see Nos. 160-166, 168-169.

Stamps of 1893 Overprinted in Black

1893, Dec. 14

No.	Type	Description	Unused	Used
160	A24	½c orange & blk	.30	.30
161	A24	1c brown & blk	.35	.35
a.		Double overprint	25.00	25.00
162	A24	2c vermilion & blk	.75	.75
a.		Inverted overprint	55.00	
163	A24	5c blue & black	3.00	3.50
a.		Inverted overprint	110.00	
164	A24	10c green & blk	5.50	6.50
165	A24	15c yellow & blk	3.50	3.50
166	A24	20c lilac & blk	6.00	6.50
		Nos. 160-166 (7)	19.40	21.40

50th anniv. of the first foreign settlement in Shanghai.

1893, Nov. 11 Litho. *Perf. 13½*

No.	Type	Description	Unused	Used
167	A26	2c vermilion & black	.40	.60

Nos. 158 and 159 Handstamp Surcharged in Black

FOUR CENTS.
分 四

1896 *Perf. 13½x14*

No.	Type	Description	Unused	Used
168	A24	4c on 15c yellow & blk	5.50	5.50
169	A24	6c on 20c lilac & blk	5.50	5.50

Surcharge occurs inverted or double on Nos. 168-169.

Arms Type of 1893

1896

No.	Type	Description	Unused	Used
170	A24	2c scarlet & blk	.30	1.25
a.		Black inscriptions inverted	140.00	
171	A24	4c orange & blk, *yel*	2.00	3.00
172	A24	6c car & blk, *rose*	1.25	3.50
		Nos. 170-172 (3)	3.55	7.75

POSTAGE DUE STAMPS

Postage Stamps of 1890-92 Handstamped in Black, Red or Blue

Postage
Due.

1892 Unwmk. *Perf. 15*

No.	Type	Description	Unused	Used
J1	A20	2c brown (Bk)	200.00	275.00
J2	A20	5c rose (Bk)	3.50	5.00
J3	A20	15c blue (Bk)	22.50	22.50

Wmk. 175

No.	Type	Description	Unused	Used
J4	A20	10c black (R)	7.50	7.50
J5	A20	15c blue (Bk)	8.00	10.00
J6	A20	20c violet (Bk)	4.00	5.00

1892-93 *Perf. 12*

No.	Type	Description	Unused	Used
J7	A20	2c brown (Bk)	1.75	1.75
J8	A20	2c brown (Bl)	1.40	2.00
J9	A20	5c rose (Bl)	2.75	3.00
J10	A20	10c orange (Bk)	65.00	65.00
J11	A20	10c orange (Bl)	3.50	*8.00*
J12	A20	15c violet (R)	10.00	10.00
J13	A20	20c brown (R)	9.00	9.00
		Nos. J7-J13 (7)	93.40	98.75

D2

1893 Litho. *Perf. 13½*

No.	Type	Description	Unused	Used
J14	D2	½c orange & blk	.55	.55

Perf. 14x13½

No.	Type	Description	Unused	Used
J15	D2	1c brown & black	.55	.55
J16	D2	2c vermilion & black	.55	.55
J17	D2	5c blue & black	.90	.90
J18	D2	10c green & black	1.25	1.25
J19	D2	15c yellow & black	1.25	1.25
J20	D2	20c violet & black	1.25	1.25
		Nos. J14-J20 (7)	6.30	6.30

Stamps of Shanghai were discontinued in 1898.

SHARJAH & DEPENDENCIES

'shär-jə

LOCATION — Oman Peninsula, Arabia, on Persian Gulf

GOVT. — Sheikdom under British protection

POP. — 5,000 (estimated)

CAPITAL — Sharjah

The dependencies on the Gulf of Oman are Dhiba, Khor Fakkan, and Kalba.

Sharjah is one of six Persian Gulf sheikdoms to join the United Arab Emirates which proclaimed independence Dec. 2, 1971. See United Arab Emirates.

100 Naye Paise = 1 Rupee

Catalogue values for all unused stamps in this country are for Never Hinged items.

Sheik Sagr bin Sultan al Qasimi, Flag and Map — A1

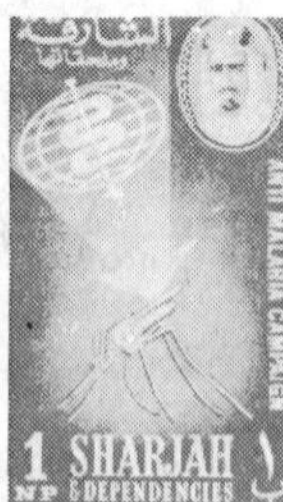

Malaria Eradication Emblem — A2

Perf. 14½x14

1963, July 10 Photo. Unwmk.

Black Portrait and Inscriptions; Lilac Rose Flag

No.	Type	Description	Unused	Used
1	A1	1np lt bl grn & pink	.15	.15
2	A1	2np grnsh bl & sal	.15	.15
3	A1	3np violet & yel	.15	.15
4	A1	4np emerald & gray	.15	.15
5	A1	5np aqua & lt grn	.15	.15
6	A1	6np dl grn & brt yel	.15	.15
7	A1	8np Prus bl & bis	.15	.15
8	A1	10np aqua & tan	.15	.15
9	A1	16np ultra & bis	.15	.15
10	A1	20np lt vio & lem	.15	.15
11	A1	30np rose lil & brt yel grn	.25	.25
12	A1	40np dk bl & yel grn	.30	.30
13	A1	50np green & fawn	.42	.42
14	A1	75np ultra & fawn	.60	.60
15	A1	100np ol bis & rose	.75	.75
		Set value	3.10	3.10

1963, Aug. 8

No.	Type	Description	Unused	Used
16	A2	1np grnsh blue	.15	.15
17	A2	2np dull blue	.15	.15
18	A2	3np violet blue	.15	.15
19	A2	4np emerald	.15	.15
20	A2	90np yellow brown	.50	.50
		Set value	.78	.70

Miniature Sheet

Imperf

No.	Type	Description	Unused	Used
21	A2	100np bright blue	.80	.80

WHO drive to eradicate malaria. No. 21 contains one 39x67mm stamp.

See Nos. C1-C6. For surcharge and overprints see Nos. 35, C7-C12, O1-O9.

Red Crescent and Sheik — A3

1963, Aug. 25 *Perf. 14x14½*

No.	Type	Description	Unused	Used
22	A3	1np purple & red	.15	.15
23	A3	2np brt green & red	.15	.15
24	A3	3np dark blue & red	.15	.15
25	A3	4np dark green & red	.15	.15
26	A3	5np dark brown & red	.15	.15
27	A3	85np green & red	.40	.40
		Set value	.65	.65

Miniature Sheet

Imperf

No.	Type	Description	Unused	Used
28	A3	100np plum & red	1.00	1.00

Cent. of the Intl. Red Cross. Imperfs. exist. No. 28 contains one 67x39m stamp.

Nos. 36-40 and No. 20 Surcharged

Nos. 29-34

1RP. اروبية

No. 35

1963, Oct. 6 Photo. *Perf. 14½x14*

No.	Type	Description	Unused	Used
29	A4	10np on 1np brt grn	.15	.15
30	A4	20np on 2np red brn	.30	.30
31	A4	30np on 3np ol grn	.45	.45
32	A4	40np on 4np dp ultra	.60	.60
33	A4	75np on 90np carmine	1.00	1.00
34	A4	80np on 90np carmine	1.25	1.25
35	A2	1r on 90np yel brn	1.65	1.65
		Nos. 29-35 (7)	5.40	5.40

Due to a stamp shortage the surcharged set appeared before the commemorative issue.

Wheat Emblem and Hands with Broken Chains — A4

1963, Oct. 15 *Perf. 14½x14*

No.	Type	Description	Unused	Used
36	A4	1np brt green	.15	.15
37	A4	2np red brown	.15	.15
38	A4	3np olive green	.15	.15
39	A4	4np deep ultra	.15	.15
40	A4	90np carmine	.40	.40
		Set value	.60	.60

Miniature Sheet

Imperf

No.	Type	Description	Unused	Used
41	A4	100np purple	.50	.50

"Freedom from Hunger" campaign of the FAO. Imperfs. exist. No. 41 contains one 39x67mm stamp.

For surcharges see Nos. 29-34.

Orbiting Astronomical Observatory — A5

Satellites: 2np, Nimbus weather satellite. 3np, Pioneer V space probe. 4np, Explorer XIII. 5np, Explorer XII. 35np, Relay satellite. 50np, Orbiting Solar Observatory.

1964, Feb. 5 Photo. *Perf. 14*

No.	Type	Description	Unused	Used
42	A5	1np blue	.15	.15
43	A5	2np red brn & yel grn	.15	.15
44	A5	3np blk & grnsh bl	.15	.15
45	A5	4np lemon & blk	.15	.15
46	A5	5np brt pur & lem	.15	.15
47	A5	35np grnsh bl & pur	.50	.50
48	A5	50np ol grn & redsh brn	.70	.70
		Set value	1.50	1.50

Issued to publicize space research. A 100np imperf. souvenir sheet shows various satellites, the Earth and stars. Colors: dark blue, gold, green & pink. Size: 112x80mm.

Runner — A6

1964, Mar. 3 Unwmk.

No.	Type	Description	Unused	Used
49	A6	1np shown	.15	.15
50	A6	2np Discus	.15	.15
51	A6	3np Hurdler	.15	.15
52	A6	4np Shot put	.15	.15
53	A6	20np High jump	.15	.15
54	A6	30np Weight lifting	.20	.20
55	A6	40np Javelin	.28	.28
56	A6	1r Diving	.65	.65
		Set value	1.45	1.45

18th Olympic Games, Tokyo, Oct. 10-25, 1964. An imperf. souvenir sheet contains one 1r stamp similar to No. 56. Size of stamp: 67x67mm, size of sheet: 102x102mm.

Girl Scouts A7

1964, June 30 *Perf. 14x14½*

No.	Type	Description	Unused	Used
57	A7	1np grnsh gray	.15	.15
58	A7	2np emerald	.15	.15
59	A7	3np brt blue	.15	.15
60	A7	4np brt violet	.15	.15
61	A7	5np carmine rose	.15	.15
62	A7	2r dark red brown	2.00	2.00
		Set value	2.25	2.25

An imperf. souvenir sheet contains one 2r bright red stamp. Size of stamp: 67x40mm. Size of sheet: 102½x76mm.

Sharjah Boy Scout — A8

Marching Scouts With Drummers — A9

Designs: 3np, 2r, Boy Scout portrait.

Perf. 14½x14, 14x14½

1964, June 30 Photo. Unwmk.

63 A8 1np gray green .15 .15
64 A9 2np emerald .15 .15
65 A8 3np brt blue .15 .15
66 A8 4np brt violet .15 .15
67 A9 5np brt carmine rose .15 .15
68 A8 2r dk red brown 2.00 2.00
Nos. 63-68 (6) 2.75 2.75

Issued to honor the Sharjah Boy Scouts. An imperf. souvenir sheet exists with one 2r bright red stamp in design of No. 68. Size of stamp: 39½x67mm. Size of sheet: 77x103mm.

Olympic Torch and Rings — A10

1964, Oct. 15 Litho. *Perf. 14*

69 A10 1np olive green .15 .15
70 A10 2np ultra .15 .15
71 A10 3np orange brown .15 .15
72 A10 4np blue green .15 .15
73 A10 5np dark violet .15 .15
74 A10 40np brt blue .35 .35
75 A10 50np dark red brown .40 .40
76 A10 2r bister 1.60 1.60
Set value 2.50 2.50

18th Olympic Games, Tokyo, Oct. 10-25. An imperf. souvenir sheet exists with one 2r yellow green stamp. Size of stamp: 82mm at base. Size of sheet: 107x76mm.

Early Telephone — A11

Designs: No. 78, Modern telewriter. No. 79, 1895 car. No. 80, American automobile, 1964. No. 81, Early X-ray. No. 82, Modern X-ray. No. 83, Mail coach. No. 84, Telstar and Delta rocket. No. 85, Sailing vessel. No. 86, Nuclear ship "Savannah." No. 87, Early astronomers. No. 88, Jodrell Bank telescope. No. 89, Greek messengers. No. 90, Relay satellite, Delta rocket and globe. No. 91, Early flying machine. No. 92, Caravelle plane. No. 93, Persian water wheel. No. 94, Hydroelectric dam. No. 95, Old steam locomotive. No. 96, Diesel locomotive.

Unwmk.

1965, Apr. 23 Litho. *Perf. 14*

77 A11 1np rose red & blk .15 .15
78 A11 1np rose red & blk .15 .15
79 A11 2np orange & indigo .15 .15
80 A11 2np orange & indigo .15 .15
81 A11 3np dk brn & emer .15 .15
82 A11 3np emer & dk brn .15 .15
83 A11 4np yel grn & dk vio .15 .15
84 A11 4np dk vio & yel grn .15 .15
85 A11 5np bl grn & brn .15 .15
86 A11 5np bl grn & brn .15 .15
87 A11 30np gray & bl .20 .15
88 A11 30np blue & gray .20 .15
89 A11 40np vio bl & yel .30 .15
90 A11 40np vio bl & yel .30 .15
91 A11 50np blue & sepia .42 .20
92 A11 50np blue & sepia .42 .20
93 A11 75np brt grn & dk brn .60 .30
94 A11 75np brt grn & dk brn .60 .30
95 A11 1r yellow & vio bl .75 .38
96 A11 1r yellow & vio bl .75 .38
Nos. 77-96 (20) 6.04
Set value 3.20

Issued to show progress in science, transport and communications. Each two stamps of same denomination are printed se tenant. Two imperf. souvenir sheets exist. One contains one each of Nos. 89-90 and the other, of Nos. 95-96. Size: 102x75mm.

Stamps of Sharjah & Dependencies were replaced in 1972 by those of United Arab Emirates.

AIR POST STAMPS

Type of Regular Issue, 1963 with Flying Hawk and "Air Mail" in English and Arabic Added

Perf. 14½x14

1963, July 10 Photo. Unwmk.

Black Portrait and Inscriptions; Lilac Rose Flag

C1 A1 1r ultra & fawn .40 .40
C2 A1 2r lt violet & lemon .70 .70
C3 A1 3r dl grn & brt yel 1.00 1.00
C4 A1 4r grnsh bl & sal 1.40 1.40
C5 A1 5r emerald & gray 1.60 1.60
C6 A1 10r olive bis & rose 3.50 3.50
Nos. C1-C6 (6) 8.60 8.60

Nos. C1-C6 Overprinted

ذكرى جون ف. كنيدي ١٩١٧-١٩٦٣

In Memoriam

John F Kennedy 1917-1963

1964, Apr. 7

Black Portrait and Inscriptions; Lilac Rose Flag

C7 A1 1r ultra & fawn
C8 A1 2r lt violet & lem
C9 A1 3r dull grn & brt yel
C10 A1 4r grnsh blue & sal
C11 A1 5r emerald & gray
C12 A1 10r olive bis & rose
Nos. C7-C12 35.00 27.50

Pres. John F. Kennedy (1917-63).

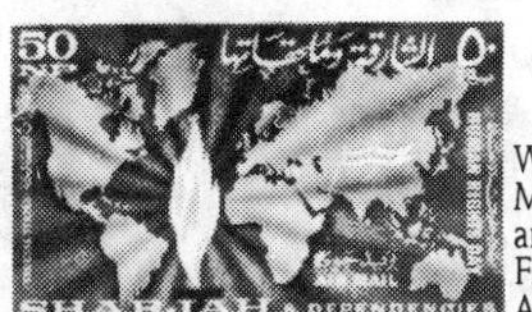

World Map and Flame AP1

1964, Apr. 15 *Perf. 14x14½*

C13 AP1 50np red brown .20 .20
C14 AP1 1r purple .40 .40
C15 AP1 150np Prus green .60 .60
Nos. C13-C15 (3) 1.20 1.20

Issued for Human Rights Day. An imperf. souvenir sheet contains one 3r carmine rose stamp. Size of stamp: 67x40mm. Size of sheet: 89x64mm.

View of Khor Fakkan AP2

Designs: 20np, Beni Qatab Bedouin camp near Dhaid. 30np, Oasis of Dhaid. 40np, Kalba Castle. 75np, Sharjah street with wind tower. 100np, Sharjah Fortress.

1964, Aug. 13 Photo. Unwmk.

C16 AP2 10np multi .15 .15
C17 AP2 20np multi .15 .15
C18 AP2 30np multi .15 .15
C19 AP2 40np multi .15 .15
C20 AP2 75np multi .28 .18
C21 AP2 100np multi .40 .22
Set value 1.05 .65

Unisphere and Sheik Saqr — AP3

J. F. Kennedy, Statue of Liberty — AP4

20np, Offshore oil rig. 1r, New York skyline.

Perf. 14½x14

1964, Sept. 5 Photo. Unwmk.

Size: 26x45mm

C22 AP3 20np multi .15 .15
C23 AP3 40np multi .15 .15

Size: 86x45mm

C24 AP3 1r multi, horiz. .40 .40
a. Strip of 3, Nos. C22-C24 .60 .60

New York World's Fair, 1964-65.

An imperf. souvenir sheet exists with one 40np stamp in AP3 design. Size of stamp: 40x68mm. Size of sheet: 76x108mm.

1964, Nov. 22 *Perf. 14x13½*

C25 AP4 40np multicolored .75 .75
C26 AP4 60np multicolored 1.25 1.25
C27 AP4 100np multicolored 2.00 2.00
Nos. C25-C27 (3) 4.00 4.00

Pres. John F. Kennedy. A souvenir sheet contains one each of Nos. C25-C27, imperf. Size: 107x76mm.

Rock Dove AP5

Birds: 40np, 2r, Red jungle fowl. 75np, 3r, Hoopoe.

Perf. 14x14½

1965, Feb. 20 Photo. Unwmk.

C28 AP5 30np gray & multi .15 .15
C29 AP5 40np multicolored .15 .15
C30 AP5 75np brt blue & multi .28 .15
C31 AP5 150np blue & multi .60 .20
C32 AP5 2r multicolored .65 .28
C33 AP5 3r red & multi 1.00 .40
Nos. C28-C33 (6) 2.83
Set value 1.10

OFFICIAL STAMPS

Nos. 7-15 Overprinted

ON STATE SERVICE

Perf. 14½x14

1965, Jan. 13 Photo. Unwmk.

O1 A1 8np multi .15 .15
O2 A1 10np multi .15 .15
O3 A1 16np multi .15 .15
O4 A1 20np multi .15 .15
O5 A1 30np multi .16 .16
O6 A1 40np multi .20 .20
O7 A1 50np multi .22 .22
O8 A1 75np multi .35 .35
O9 A1 100np multi .50 .50
Set value 1.75 1.75

SIBERIA

sī-'bir-ē-ə

LOCATION — A vast territory of Russia lying between the Ural Mountains and the Pacific Ocean.

The anti-Bolshevist provisional government set up at Omsk by Adm. Aleksandr V. Kolchak issued Nos. 1-10 in 1919. The monarchist, anti-Soviet government in Priamur province issued Nos. 51-118 in 1921-22.

(Stamps of the Czechoslovak Legion are listed under Czechoslovakia.)

100 Kopecks = 1 Ruble

Russian Stamps of 1909-18 Surcharged

35 — a

1 рубль — b

On Stamps of 1909-12

1919 Unwmk. *Perf. 14x14½*

Wove Paper

Lozenges of Varnish on Face

1 A14(a) 35k on 2k dull grn .45 1.10
a. Inverted surcharge 27.50
2 A14(a) 50k on 3k carmine .45 1.25
a. Inverted surcharge 35.00
3 A14(a) 70k on 1k dl org yel .90 3.00
a. Inverted surcharge 27.50
4 A15(b) 1r on 4k carmine .90 1.75
a. Dbl. surch., one inverted 45.00
b. Inverted surcharge 50.00
5 A14(b) 3r on 7k blue 1.50 3.50
a. Double surcharge 22.50
b. Inverted surcharge 20.00
6 A11(b) 5r on 14k dk bl & car 2.50 5.50
a. Double surcharge 22.50
b. Inverted surcharge 22.50

On Stamps of 1917

Imperf

7 A14(a) 35k on 2k gray grn .90 1.75
8 A14(a) 50k on 3k red .90 1.75
a. Inverted surcharge 100.00
9 A14(a) 70k on 1k orange .75 1.65
a. Inverted surcharge 25.00
10 A15(b) 1r on 4k carmine 4.50 7.75
Nos. 1-10 (10) 13.75 29.00

Nos. 1-10, were first issued in Omsk during the regime of Admiral Kolchak. Later they were used along the line of the Trans-Siberian railway to Vladivostok.

Some experts question the postal use of most off-cover canceled copies of Nos. 1-10.

25 P 1-

Similar surcharges, handstamped as above are bogus.

Priamur Government Issues

Nikolaevsk Issue

A5

A6

A7

Russian Stamps Handstamp Surcharged or Overprinted

On Stamps of 1909-17

1921 Unwmk. *Perf. 14x14½, 13½*

51 A5 10k on 4k carmine
52 A5 10k on 10k dark blue
53 A6 15k on 14k dk blue & car
54 A6 15k on 15k red brn & dp bl
55 A6 15k on 35k red brn & grn
56 A6 15k on 50k brn vio & grn
57 A6 15k on 70k brn & red org
58 A7 15k on 1r brn & orange
59 A5 on 20k dl bl & dk car
60 A5 on 20k on 14k dk bl & car (No. 118)
a. 15k on 20k on 14k dk bl & car (error)

61	A7	20k on 3½r mar & lt grn		
62	A7	20k on 5r ind, grn & lt bl		
63	A7	20k on 7r dk grn & pink		

Nos. 59-60 are overprinted with initials but original denominations remain.

A 10k on 5k claret (Russia No. 77) and a 15k on 20k blue & carmine (Russia No. 82a) were not officially issued. Some authorities consider them bogus.

No evidence found of genuine usage of #51-72.

Reprints exist.

On Semi-Postal Stamp of 1914

64	SP6	20k on 3k mar & gray grn, *pink*		

On Stamps of 1917

Imperf

65	A5	10k on 1k orange		
66	A5	10k on 2k gray green		
67	A5	10k on 3k red		
68	A5	10k on 5k claret		
69	A6	15k on 1r pale brn, brn & red org		
70	A7	20k on 1r pale brn, brn & red org		
71	A7	20k on 3½r mar & lt grn		
72	A7	20k on 7r dk grn & pink		

The letters of the overprint are the initials of the Russian words for "Nikolaevsk on Amur Priamur Provisional Government."

As the surcharges on Nos. 51-72 are handstamped, a number exist inverted or double.

A 20k blue & carmine (Russia No. 126) with Priamur overprint and a 15k on 20k (Russia No. 126) were not officially issued. Some authorities consider them bogus.

No evidence found of genuine usage of #51-72.

Stamps of Far Eastern Republic Overprinted

1922

78	A2	2k gray green	25.00	25.00
a.		Inverted overprint	125.00	
79	A2a	4k rose	25.00	25.00
a.		Inverted overprint	*115.00*	
80	A2	5k claret	25.00	25.00
81	A2a	10k blue	25.00	25.00
		Nos. 78-81 (4)	100.00	100.00

Anniv. of the overthrow of the Bolshevik power in the Priamur district.

The letters of the overprint are the initials of "Vremeno Priamurski Pravitel'stvo" i.e. Provisional Priamur Government, 26th May.

Russian Stamps of 1909-21 Overprinted in Dark Blue or Vermilion

Приам.
Земскій
Край

On Stamps of 1909-18

1922 *Perf. 14x14½*

85	A14	1k dull org yel	45.00	50.00
86	A14	2k dull green	80.00	65.00
87	A14	3k carmine	25.00	30.00
88	A15	4k carmine	12.50	15.00
89	A14	5k dk claret	25.00	27.50
90	A14	7k blue (V)	25.00	27.50
91	A15	10k dark blue (V)	35.00	40.00
92	A11	14k dk bl & car	45.00	55.00
93	A11	15k red brn & dp bl	12.50	15.00
94	A8	20k dl bl & dk car	12.50	15.00
95	A11	20k on 14k dk bl & car	100.00	100.00
96	A11	25k dl grn & dk vio (V)	25.00	30.00
97	A11	35k red brn & grn	7.50	10.00
a.		Inverted overprint	80.00	
98	A8	50k brn vio & grn	12.50	15.00
99	A11	70k brn & red org	25.00	30.00
		Nos. 85-99 (15)	487.50	525.00

On Stamps of 1917

Imperf

100	A14	1k orange	4.25	5.00
a.		Inverted overprint	65.00	85.00
101	A14	2k gray green	9.00	9.00
102	A14	3k red	12.00	12.00
103	A15	4k carmine	65.00	65.00
104	A14	5k claret	19.00	15.00
105	A11	15k red brn & dp bl	110.00	100.00
106	A8	20k blue & car	47.50	40.00
107	A9	1r pale brn, brn & red org	14.00	15.00
		Nos. 100-107 (8)	280.75	261.00

On Stamps of Siberia, 1919

Perf. 14½x15

108	A14	35k on 2k green	60.00	60.00

Imperf

109	A14	70k on 1k orange	85.00	85.00

On Stamps of Far Eastern Republic, 1921

110	A2	2k gray green	6.00	5.50
111	A2a	4k rose	6.00	5.50
112	A2	5k claret	6.00	5.50
a.		Inverted overprint	100.00	
113	A2a	10k blue (R)	4.00	3.50
		Nos. 109-113 (5)	107.00	105.00

Same, Surcharged with New Values

114	A2	1k on 2k gray grn	4.00	3.50
115	A2a	3k on 4k rose	4.00	3.50

The overprint is in a rectangular frame on stamps of 1k to 10k and 1r; on the other values the frame is omitted. It is larger on the 1 ruble than on the smaller stamps.

The overprint reads "Priamurski Zemski Krai," Priamur Rural Province.

Far Eastern Republic Nos. 30-32 Overprinted in Blue

Perf. 14½x15

116	A14	35k on 2k green	5.00	6.50

Imperf

117	A14	35k on 2k green	90.00	110.00
118	A14	70k on 1k orange	8.25	11.50
		Nos. 116-118 (3)	103.25	128.00

Counterfeits of Nos. 51-118 abound.

SIERRA LEONE

sē-ˌer-ə lē-ˈōn

LOCATION — West coast of Africa, between Guinea and Liberia
GOVT. — Republic in British Commonwealth
AREA — 27,925 sq. mi.
POP. — 3,354,000 (est. 1982)
CAPITAL — Freetown

Sierra Leone was a British colony and protectorate. In 1961 it became fully independent, remaining within the Commonwealth. It became a republic April 19, 1971.

12 Pence = 1 Shilling
20 Shillings = 1 Pound
100 Cents = 1 Leone (1964)

Catalogue values for unused stamps in this country are for Never Hinged items, beginning with Scott 186 in the regular postage section and Scott C1 in the air post section.

Watermark

Wmk. 336- St. Edwards Crown & SL, Multiple

Queen Victoria
A1 A2

1859 Unwmk. Typo. *Perf. 14*

3	A1	6p bright violet	37.50	25.00
a.		6p dull violet	200.00	40.00

1872 *Perf. 12½*

5	A1	6p violet	300.00	50.00

1872 Wmk. 1 Sideways *Perf. 12½*

6	A2	1p rose	65.00	27.50
8	A2	3p yellow buff	100.00	30.00
9	A2	4p blue	140.00	35.00
10	A2	1sh yellow green	225.00	45.00

1873 Wmk. 1 Upright

6a	A2	1p	50.00	27.50
7	A2	2p magenta	100.00	45.00
8a	A2	3p	500.00	75.00
9a	A2	4p	250.00	45.00
10a	A2	1sh	350.00	85.00

1876-96 Wmk. 1 Upright *Perf. 14*

11	A2	½p bister	1.90	4.50
12	A2	1p rose	40.00	9.50
13	A2	1½p violet ('77)	40.00	6.00
14	A2	2p magenta	45.00	3.50
15	A2	3p yellow buff	45.00	3.50
16	A2	4p blue	100.00	6.00
17	A1	6p brt violet ('85)	50.00	20.00
a.		Half used as 3p on cover		3,000.
18	A1	6p violet brn ('90)	12.50	13.00
19	A1	6p brown vio ('96)	2.00	5.50
20	A2	1sh green	47.50	5.00
		Nos. 11-20 (10)	383.90	76.50

For surcharge see No. 32.

1883-93 Wmk. Crown and C A (2)

21	A2	½p bister	19.00	35.00
22	A2	½p dull green ('84)	.35	.45
23	A2	1p carmine ('84)	1.75	.45
a.		1p rose carmine	27.50	8.00
b.		1p rose	190.00	30.00
24	A2	1½p violet ('93)	1.50	4.00
25	A2	2p magenta	35.00	6.00
26	A2	2p slate ('84)	18.00	1.50
27	A2	2½p ultra ('91)	6.00	.65
28	A2	3p org yel ('92)	1.50	4.25
29	A2	4p blue	825.00	25.00
30	A2	4p bister ('84)	1.25	.90
31	A2	1sh org brn ('88)	11.00	10.00
		Nos. 21-28,30-31 (10)	95.35	63.20

For surcharge see No. 33.

Nos. 13 and 24 Surcharged in Black

HALF
PENNY

1893 Wmk. 1

32	A2	½p on 1½p violet	400.00	*425.00*
a.		"PFNNY"	2,000.	*2,500.*

Wmk. 2

33	A2	½p on 1½p violet	2.50	2.75
a.		"PFNNY"	65.00	*65.00*
b.		Inverted surcharge	100.00	100.00
c.		Same as "a," inverted	1,500.	
d.		Double surcharge	*900.00*	

A4

1896-97

34	A4	½p lilac & grn ('97)	.75	1.00
35	A4	1p lilac & car	.75	1.00
36	A4	1½p lilac & blk ('97)	2.50	7.00
37	A4	2p lilac & org	2.00	4.50
38	A4	2½p lilac & ultra	1.25	.75
39	A4	3p lilac & sl ('97)	6.50	6.50
40	A4	4p lilac & car ('97)	6.00	11.00
41	A4	5p lilac & blk	7.00	11.00
42	A4	6p lilac ('97)	6.50	13.00
43	A4	1sh green & blk	5.50	14.00
44	A4	2sh green & ultra	22.50	27.50
45	A4	5sh green & car	35.00	75.00
46	A4	£1 violet, *red*	140.00	275.00
		Nos. 34-46 (13)	236.25	447.25

Numerals of Nos. 39-46 of type A4 are in color on plain tablet.

A5

A6

2½d. 2½d. 2½d.
a b c

2½d. 2½d. 2½d.
d e f

1897 Wmk. C A over Crown (46)

47	A5	1p lilac & grn	1.65	1.75
48	A6(a)	2½p on 3p lil & grn	12.00	14.00
49	A6(b)	2½p on 3p	60.00	67.50
50	A6(c)	2½p on 3p	140.00	150.00
51	A6(d)	2½p on 3p	275.00	325.00
52	A6(a)	2½p on 6p lil & grn	10.00	12.50
53	A6(b)	2½p on 6p	42.50	47.50
54	A6(c)	2½p on 6p	110.00	125.00
55	A6(d)	2½p on 6p	225.00	240.00
56	A6(a)	2½p on 1sh lilac	85.00	65.00
57	A6(b)	2½p on 1sh lilac	1,100.	1,100.
58	A6(c)	2½p on 1sh lilac	400.00	400.00
59	A6(e)	2½p on 1sh lilac	1,750.	2,000.
59A	A6(f)	2½p on 1sh lilac	1,300.	1,300.
60	A6(a)	2½p on 2sh lilac	1,200.	1,450.
61	A6(b)	2½p on 2sh lilac	*10,000.*	
62	A6(c)	2½p on 2sh lilac	7,500.	
63	A6(e)	2½p on 2sh lilac	*30,000.*	
63A	A6(f)	2½p on 2sh lilac	*30,000.*	

The words "POSTAGE AND REVENUE" on Nos. 56-63A are set in two lines and overprinted below instead of above "2½d."

The "d" in type "f" is 3½mm wide; that in type "a" is 3mm.

Very fine examples of Nos. 47-63A will have perforations touching the frameline on one or more sides.

Nos. 56-59A are often found discolored. Such copies sell for about half the values quoted.

King Edward VII — A7

Numerals of 3p to £1 of type A7 are in color on plain tablet.

1903 Wmk. Crown and C A (2)

64	A7	½p violet & grn	2.75	2.75
65	A7	1p violet & car	1.10	.20
66	A7	1½p violet & blk	1.10	4.00
67	A7	2p violet & brn org	3.50	9.00
68	A7	2½p violet & ultra	4.00	4.50
69	A7	3p violet & gray	6.00	8.00
70	A7	4p violet & car	6.50	8.00
71	A7	5p violet & blk	6.50	15.00
72	A7	6p violet & dull vio	10.00	10.00
73	A7	1sh green & blk	11.00	27.50
74	A7	2sh green & ultra	32.50	45.00
75	A7	5sh green & car	45.00	70.00
76	A7	£1 violet, *red*	200.00	215.00
		Nos. 64-76 (13)	329.95	418.95

1904-05 Wmk. 3

Chalky Paper

77	A7	½p violet & grn	4.50	2.25
78	A7	1p violet & car	.75	.25
79	A7	1½p violet & blk	2.50	*7.50*
80	A7	2p violet & brn org	4.00	3.00
81	A7	2½p violet & ultra	4.00	1.75
82	A7	3p violet & gray	19.00	3.00
83	A7	4p violet & car	5.00	5.50
84	A7	5p violet & blk	10.00	*16.00*
85	A7	6p violet & dl vio	4.50	*3.00*
86	A7	1sh green & blk	7.00	*8.00*
87	A7	2sh green & ultra	12.00	18.00
88	A7	5sh green & car	30.00	45.00
89	A7	£1 violet, *red*	200.00	200.00
		Nos. 77-89 (13)	303.25	313.25

The 1p also exists on ordinary paper.

1907-10

Ordinary Paper

90	A7	½p green	.40	.25
91	A7	1p carmine	6.00	.25
92	A7	1½p orange ('10)	.48	1.25
93	A7	2p gray	.70	1.25
94	A7	2½p ultra	1.75	1.10

Chalky Paper

95	A7	3p violet, *yel*	5.00	*2.50*
96	A7	4p blk & red, *yel*	2.00	1.00
97	A7	5p vio & ol grn	5.00	3.50
98	A7	6p vio & red vio	3.00	4.50
99	A7	1sh black, *green*	5.00	4.00
100	A7	2sh vio & bl, *bl*	14.00	12.00
101	A7	5sh grn & red, *yel*	25.00	35.00
102	A7	£1 vio & blk, *red*	150.00	160.00
		Nos. 90-102 (13)	218.33	226.60

The 3p also exists on ordinary paper.

King George V and Seal of the Colony
A8 A9
Die I

For description of dies I and II see back of this volume.

Numerals of 3p, 4p, 5p, 6p and 10p of type A8 are in color on plain tablet. Numerals of 7p and 9p are on solid-color tablet.

1912-24 Ordinary Paper Wmk. 3

103 A8 ½p green 1.00 .65
104 A8 1p scarlet 1.00 .50
a. 1p carmine 1.00 .15
105 A8 1½p orange 1.00 .75
106 A8 2p gray .90 .18
107 A8 2½p ultra 6.50 2.00

Chalky Paper

108 A9 3p violet, *yel* 2.50 2.00
109 A8 4p blk & red, *yel* 1.25 5.00
a. Die II ('24) 3.00 *3.00*
110 A8 5p violet & ol grn .85 2.75
111 A8 6p vio & red vio 3.00 3.50
112 A8 7p violet & org 1.40 4.00
113 A8 9p violet & blk 4.50 *6.00*
114 A8 10p violet & red 3.00 *12.00*
115 A9 1sh black, *green* 3.50 3.00
a. 1sh black, *emerald* *165.00*
116 A9 2sh vio & ultra, *bl* 7.50 3.75
117 A9 5sh grn & red, *yel* 9.00 *17.00*
118 A9 10sh grn & red, *grn* 42.50 70.00
119 A9 £1 vio & blk, *red* 110.00 140.00
120 A9 £2 violet & ultra 500.00 *600.00*
121 A9 £5 gray grn & org *1,250.* —
Nos. 103-119 (17) 199.40 273.08

The status of No. 115a has been questioned.

Die II

1921-27 Wmk. 4

Ordinary Paper

122 A8 ½p green .75 .15
123 A8 1p violet ('26) 1.00 .65
a. Die I ('24) 1.00 .15
124 A8 1½p scarlet .70 .25
125 A8 2p gray ('22) .50 .15
126 A8 2½p ultra .50 2.00
127 A8 3p ultra ('22) .55 .28
128 A8 4p blk & red, *yel* 2.00 2.00
129 A8 5p vio & ol grn .48 .75

Chalky Paper

130 A8 6p dp vio & red vio 1.40 1.75
131 A8 7p vio & org ('27) 2.00 11.00
132 A8 9p dl vio & blk ('22) 2.25 8.00
133 A8 10p violet & red 1.75 14.00
134 A9 1sh blk, *emerald* 4.00 4.00
135 A9 2sh vio & ultra, *bl* 8.00 8.00
136 A9 5sh grn & red, *yel* 8.00 30.00
137 A9 10sh grn & red, *grn* 55.00 100.00
138 A9 £2 violet & ultra 450.00 *525.00*
139 A9 £5 gray grn & org *1,000. 1,500.*
Nos. 122-137 (16) 88.88 182.98

Rice Field — A10

Palms and Kola Tree — A11

1932, Mar. 1 Engr. *Perf. 12½*

140 A10 ½p green .15 .15
141 A10 1p dk violet .15 .15
142 A10 1½p rose car .30 1.00
143 A10 2p yellow brn .30 .15
144 A10 3p ultra .70 1.00
145 A10 4p orange .70 2.25
146 A10 5p olive green .70 1.25
147 A10 6p light blue .70 *1.25*
148 A10 1sh red brown 2.50 *3.00*

Perf. 12

149 A11 2sh dk brown 6.00 *8.25*
150 A11 5sh indigo 10.00 *14.00*
151 A11 10sh deep green 40.00 85.00
152 A11 £1 deep violet 77.50 125.00
Nos. 140-152 (13) 139.70 242.45

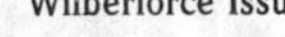

Wilberforce Issue

Arms of Sierra Leone — A12

Slave Throwing Off Shackles — A13

Map of Sierra Leone — A14

Old Slave Market, Freetown — A15

Fruit Seller A16

Government Sanatorium A17

Bullom Canoe — A18

Punting near Banana Islands — A19

Government Buildings, Freetown — A20

Old Slavers' Resort, Bunce Island — A21

African Elephant — A22

George V — A23

Freetown Harbor — A24

1933, Oct. 2

153 A12 ½p deep green .45 .75
154 A13 1p brown & blk .45 .40
155 A14 1½p orange brn 4.00 4.50
156 A15 2p violet 2.50 .40
157 A16 3p ultra 2.00 1.25
158 A17 4p dk brown 6.50 *10.00*
159 A18 5p red brn & sl grn 6.50 *15.00*
160 A19 6p dp org & blk 6.50 *7.00*
161 A20 1sh dk violet 5.25 *14.00*
162 A21 2sh bl & dk brn 21.00 *30.00*
163 A22 5sh red vio & blk 125.00 *175.00*
164 A23 10sh green & blk 140.00 *225.00*
165 A24 £1 yel & dk vio 350.00 *375.00*
Nos. 153-165 (13) 670.15 *858.30*

Abolition of slavery in the British colonies and cent. of the death of William Wilberforce, English philanthropist and agitator against the slave trade.

Silver Jubilee Issue
Common Design Type

1935, May 6 *Perf. 11x12*

166 CD301 1p black & ultra .20 .20
167 CD301 3p ultra & brown 1.00 1.00
168 CD301 5p indigo & green 1.50 *2.50*
169 CD301 1sh brown vio & ind 3.25 3.25
Nos. 166-169 (4) 5.95 6.95

Coronation Issue
Common Design Type

1937, May 12 *Perf. 11x11½*

170 CD302 1p deep orange .25 .25
171 CD302 2p dark violet .30 .30
172 CD302 3p deep ultra .40 .40
Nos. 170-172 (3) .95 .95

Freetown Harbor A25

Rice Harvesting A26

1938-44 *Perf. 12½*

173 A25 ½p green & blk .15 .15
174 A25 1p dp claret & blk .20 .15
175 A26 1½p rose red 12.00 .35
175A A26 1½p red vio ('41) .15 .15
176 A26 2p red violet 24.00 1.25
176A A26 2p dark red ('41) .15 .40
177 A25 3p ultra & blk .20 .15
178 A25 4p red brn & blk .45 .70
179 A26 5p olive green 3.00 2.50
180 A26 6p gray .45 .25
181 A25 1sh ol grn & blk .90 .30
181A A26 1sh3p org yel ('44) .20 .25
182 A25 2sh sepia & blk 2.50 1.25
183 A26 5sh red brown 5.75 3.00
184 A26 10sh emerald 9.50 6.00
185 A25 £1 dk blue 10.00 10.00
Nos. 173-185 (16) 69.60 26.85

Catalogue values for unused stamps in this section, from this point to the end of the section, are for Never Hinged items.

Peace Issue
Common Design Type
Perf. 13½x14

1946, Oct. 1 Engr. Wmk. 4

186 CD303 1½p lilac .15 .15
187 CD303 3p bright ultra .15 .15

Silver Wedding Issue
Common Design Types

1948, Dec. 1 Photo. *Perf. 14x14½*

188 CD304 1½p brt red violet .15 .15

Engraved; Name Typographed
Perf. 11½x11

189 CD305 £1 dark blue 16.00 17.00

UPU Issue
Common Design Types

Engr.; Name Typo. on 3p, 6p

1949, Oct. 10 *Perf. 13½, 11x11½*

190 CD306 1½p rose violet .20 .25
191 CD307 3p indigo .35 .35
192 CD308 6p gray .60 .60
193 CD309 1sh olive 1.25 1.25
Nos. 190-193 (4) 2.40 2.45

Coronation Issue
Common Design Type

1953, June 2 Engr. *Perf. 13½x13*

194 CD312 1½p purple & black .15 .15

Cape Lighthouse A27

Cotton Tree, Freetown — A28

1p, Queen Elizabeth II Quay. 1½d, Piassava workers. 3p, Rice harvesting. 4p, Iron ore production, Marampa. 6p, Whale Bay, York Village. 1sh, Bullom boat. 1sh3p, Map of Sierra Leone & plane. 2sh6p, Orugu Bridge. 5sh, Kuranko chief. 10sh, Law Courts, Freetown. £1, Government House.

Perf. 13 (A27), 13½ (A28)

1956, Jan. 2 Engr. Wmk. 4

Center in Black

195 A27 ½p lt violet .55 .75
196 A27 1p reseda .55 .15
197 A27 1½p ultra 1.10 2.00
198 A28 2p lt brown .35 .15
199 A28 3p ultra .85 .15
a. Perf 13x13½ 1.40 5.00
200 A27 4p gray blue 2.25 .65
201 A27 6p violet .65 .15
202 A28 1sh carmine .65 .20
203 A27 1sh3p gray brown 5.50 .20
204 A28 2sh6p brown org 6.50 2.50
205 A28 5sh green 1.10 .75
206 A27 10sh red violet 2.75 1.90
207 A27 £1 orange 7.75 12.00
Nos. 195-207 (13) 30.55 21.55

For surcharges and overprints see Nos. 242-247, 251-253, 255-256, 319, 322, C1-C7, C13.

Independent State

Carrying Oil Palm Fruit — A29

Diamond Miner and Badge — A30

Badge and: 1½p, 5sh, Bundu mask. 2p, 10sh, Bishop Crowther and Old Fourah Bay College. 3p, 6p, Sir Milton Margai. 4p, 1sh3p, Lumley Beach, Freetown. £1, Bugler.

Perf. 13x13½, 13½x13

1961, Apr. 27 Engr. Wmk. 336

208 A29 ½p blue grn & dk brn .15 .15
209 A30 1p gray grn & brn org .15 .15
210 A29 1½p green & blk .15 .15
211 A29 2p vio blue & blk .15 .15
212 A30 3p brn org & ultra .15 .15
213 A30 4p rose red & grnsh bl .15 .15
214 A30 6p lilac & gray .16 .15
215 A29 1sh org & dk brn .30 .30
216 A30 1sh3p vio & grnsh bl .30 .22
217 A30 2sh6p black & grn .65 .60
218 A29 5sh rose red & blk 1.25 1.10
219 A29 10sh emerald & blk 2.50 2.50
220 A29 £1 carmine & yel 4.50 4.50
Nos. 208-220 (13) 10.56 10.27

Sierra Leone's Independence.

For surcharges see Nos. 254, 274, 279-280, 285-286, 290-291, 294, 296, 299, C10, C29-C31, C132-C133.

Royal Charter, 1799 — A31

House of Representatives, Freetown, 1924 — A32

Designs: 4p, King's Yard Gate, Freetown, 1817. 1sh3p, Yacht "Britannia."

1961, Nov. 25 Engr. Wmk. 336

221	A31	3p vermilion & blk	.15	.15
222	A31	4p violet & blk	.22	.22
223	A32	6p orange & blk	.30	.30
224	A32	1sh3p blue & blk	.60	.60
		Nos. 221-224 (4)	1.27	1.27

Visit of Elizabeth II to Sierra Leone, Nov., 1961.
For overprints and surcharges see Nos. 272, 278, C8-C9, C11-C12.

Malaria Eradication Emblem — A33

1962, Apr. 7 ***Perf. 11x11½***

225	A33	3p crimson	.15	.15
226	A33	1sh3p green	.38	.38
		Set value	.45	.45

WHO drive to eradicate malaria.

Fireball Lily — A34

Jina Gbo — A35

Plants: 1½p, Stereospermum. 2p, Black-eyed Susan. 3p, Beniseed. 4p, Blushing hibiscus. 6p, Climbing lily. 1sh, Beautiful crinum. 1sh3p, Bluebells. 2sh6p, Broken hearts. 5sh, Ra-ponthi. 12sh, Blue plumbago. £1, African tulip tree.

1963, Jan. 1 Photo. ***Perf. 14***

Flowers in Natural Colors

227	A34	½p olive brown	.15	.15
228	A35	1p org ver & dk red	.15	.15
229	A34	1½p green	.15	.15
230	A35	2p lemon	.15	.15
231	A34	3p dark green	.15	.15
232	A34	4p lt violet blue	.15	.15
233	A35	6p indigo	.16	.15
234	A34	1sh brt yel grn & red	.40	.24
235	A35	1sh3p dk yellow grn	.48	.24
236	A34	2sh6p dk gray	1.00	.70
237	A34	5sh deep violet	1.50	1.25
238	A34	10sh red lilac	3.25	2.75
239	A35	£1 bright blue	8.50	6.75
		Nos. 227-239 (13)	16.19	12.98

For surcharges see Nos. 271, 273, 276-277, 283-284, 289, 295, 300-305, 317-318, 320-321, 329-332, C37-C41, C57-C60, C134.

Wheat Emblem, Grain Bin and Threshing Machine A36

1sh3p, Bullom woman examining onion crop.

Perf. 11½x11

1963, Mar. 21 Engr. Wmk. 336

240	A36	3p orange yel & blk	.15	.15
241	A36	1sh3p green & brown	.40	.40

FAO "Freedom from Hunger" campaign.
For surcharges see Nos. 275, C28.

Nos. 195, 197 and 199 Surcharged in Red, Brown, Orange, Violet or Blue:

2nd Year of Independence 19 Progress 63 Development
3d.
on A27

2nd Year Independence Progress Development 1963
10d.
on A28

Perf. 13, 13½

1963, Apr. 27 Wmk. 4

Center in Black

242	A27	3p on ½p lt vio (R)	.15	.15
243	A27	4p on 1½p ultra (Br)	.15	.15
244	A27	6p on ½p lt vio (O)	.15	.15
245	A28	10p on 3p ultra (R)	.28	.28
246	A28	1sh6p on 3p ultra (V)	.38	.38
247	A28	3sh6p on 3p ultra (Bl)	.85	.85
		Nos. 242-247 (6)	1.96	1.96

Type "a" exists in two settings, varying in the width of the line "19 Progress 63." In each sheet of 60, this line measures 19½-21mm on 55 stamps, and 17½-18mm on 5 stamps. See Nos. C1-C7.

Centenary Emblem — A37

Design: 6p, Red Cross. 1sh3p, Centenary Emblem with curved-lines background.

Perf. 11x11½

1963, Nov. 1 Engr. Wmk. 336

248	A37	3p purple & red	.15	.15
249	A37	6p black & red	.15	.15
250	A37	1sh3p dark green & red	.32	.32
		Nos. 248-250 (3)	.62	.62

Centenary of International Red Cross.
For surcharge see No. C56.

Nos. 199, 197, 216 and 195 Overprinted or Surcharged in Pink, Red, Violet or Brown

1853–1859–1963
Oldest Postal Service
Newest G.P.O.
in West Africa

4d.

Perf. 13, 13½, 13½x13

1963, Nov. 4 Engr. Wmk. 4

Center in Black except No. 254

251	A28	3p (P)	.15	.15
252	A27	4p on 1½p (R)	.15	.15
253	A27	9p on 1½p (V)	.18	.18
254	A30	1sh on 1sh3p (R)	.20	.20
255	A27	1sh6p on ½p (P)	.28	.28
256	A28	2sh on 3p (Br)	.35	.35
		Nos. 251-256,C8-C13 (12)	12.58	12.58

Oldest postal service (1st stamps in 1859) and the newest GPO in West Africa. Overprint in 5 lines on Nos. 251 and 256. A number of surcharge varieties and errors exist.

Map and Lion of Sierra Leone — A38

Engraved and Lithographed

1964, Feb. 10 Unwmk. ***Imperf.***

Self-adhesive

257	A38	1p multicolored	.15	.15
258	A38	3p multicolored	.15	.15
259	A38	4p multicolored	.15	.15
260	A38	6p multicolored	.15	.15
261	A38	1sh multicolored	.16	.16
262	A38	2sh multicolored	.30	.30
263	A38	5sh multicolored	.80	.80
		Nos. 257-263,C14-C20 (14)	5.49	5.49

New York World's Fair, 1964-65.
For surcharges see Nos. 288, 297, 335 and note under No. 299.

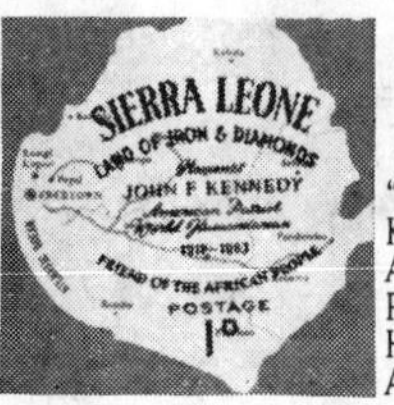

"John F. Kennedy, American Patriot, World Humanitarian" A39

1964, May 11

Self-adhesive

264	A39	1p multicolored	.15	.15
265	A39	3p multicolored	.15	.15
266	A39	4p multicolored	.15	.15
267	A39	6p multicolored	.15	.15
268	A39	1sh multicolored	.18	.18
269	A39	2sh multicolored	.35	.35
270	A39	5sh multicolored	.95	.95
		Nos. 264-270,C21-C27 (14)	6.47	6.47

For surcharges see Nos. 281-282, 287, 292-293, 298, 333, 336, and note under No. 299.

Issues of 1961-63 Surcharged in Red, Black, Dark Blue, Violet or Orange

1964, Aug. 4

271	A35	1c on 6p (#233) (R)	.15	.15
272	A31	2c on 3p (#221)	.15	.15
273	A34	3c on 3p (#231)	.15	.15
274	A29	5c on ½p (#208) (DB)	.15	.15
275	A36	8c on 3p (#240) (R)	.20	.20
276	A35	10c on 1sh3p (#235) (R)	.28	.25
277	A34	15c on 1sh (#234)	.40	.40
278	A32	25c on 6p (#223) (V)	.60	.60
279	A30	50c on 2sh6p (#217) (O)	1.20	1.20
		Nos. 271-279,C28-C31 (13)	5.47	5.44

Issues of 1961-64 Surcharged in Black or Gold

1965, Jan. 20

280	A30	1c on 3p (#212)	.15	.15
281	A39	2c on 1p (#264)	.15	.15
282	A39	4c on 3p (#265)	.15	.15
283	A35	5c on 2p (#230)	.15	.15
284	A34	1 le on 5sh (#237) (G)	2.50	2.50
285	A29	2 le on £1 (#220)	5.25	5.25
		Nos. 280-285 (6)	8.35	8.35

The surcharges on Nos. 284-285 are given in numerals and spelled out in two lines; numeral on Nos. 280-283.

Issues of 1961-64 Surcharged in Red, Black, Orange, Blue or Pink

1965, Apr.

286	A29	1c on 1½p (#210) (R)	.15	.15
287	A39	2c on 3p (#265)	.15	.15
288	A38	2c on 4p (#259)	.15	.15
289	A35	3c on 1p (#228)	.15	.15
290	A29	3c on 2p (#211) (O)	.15	.15
291	A30	5c on 1sh3p (#216) (O)	.15	.15
292	A39	15c on 6p (#267)	.95	.95
293	A39	15c on 1sh (#268) (O)	1.65	1.65
294	A30	20c on 6p (#214) (O)	.40	.40
295	A35	25c on 6p (#233) (R)	.55	.55
296	A30	50c on 3p (#212) (R)	1.10	1.10
297	A38	60c on 5sh(#263) (Bl)	2.50	2.50
298	A39	1 le on 4p (#266) (P)	3.25	3.25
299	A29	2 le on £1 (#220) (Bl)	6.00	6.00
		Nos. 286-299 (14)	17.30	17.30

Additional surcharges exist: "1c" on Nos. 260, 262, 269-270. See note after No. C41 for airmails. Value $4 each.
For surcharges see Nos. 333, 335-336.

Nos. 228, 231, 234, 235, 232, 237 Surcharged

Designs of Surcharge: Nos. 301, 304, Sir Milton Margai. Nos. 302, 305, Sir Winston Churchill.

Wmk. 336

1965, May 19 Photo. ***Perf. 14***

300	A35	2c on 1p multi	.15	.15
301	A34	3c on 3p multi	.15	.15
302	A34	10c on 1sh multi	.30	.30
303	A35	20c on 1sh3p multi	.55	.55
304	A34	50c on 4p multi	1.25	1.25
305	A34	75c on 5sh multi	2.25	2.25
		Nos. 300-305,C37-C41 (11)	14.20	14.20

For surcharges see Nos. 329-332.

Cola Nut and Plant — A40

Coat of Arms — A41

Typographed; Embossed on Silver Foil

1965 Unwmk. ***Imperf.***

Self-adhesive

310	A40	1c multicolored	.15	.15
311	A40	2c multicolored	.20	.20
312	A40	3c multicolored	.20	.20
313	A40	4c multicolored	.30	.30
314	A40	5c multicolored	.30	.30

Engr.; Embossed on Paper

315	A41	20c multi, *cream*	.75	.60
316	A41	50c multi, *cream*	2.00	1.75
		Nos. 310-316,C53-C55 (10)	6.75	6.35

Various advertisements printed on peelable paper backing. Nos. 310-316 have side tabs for handling and come packed in boxes of 100. Nos. 310-312 and 314 were released during November due to a stamp shortage; official release date for set, Dec. 17, 1965. See #338-356, C67, C97. For surcharges see #334, 337, 364-368.

Nos. 197-198, and 232-234, 236 Surcharged with New Value in Black or Ultramarine and Overprinted: "FIVE YEARS / INDEPENDENCE / 1961-1966"

1966, Apr. 27 Wmk. 4, 336

317	A35	1c on 6p multi	.15	.15
318	A34	2c on 4p multi	.15	.15
319	A27	3c on 1½p ultra & blk (U)	.15	.15
320	A34	8c on 1sh multi (U)	.16	.16
321	A34	10c on 2sh6p multi (U)	.20	.20
322	A28	20c on 2p lt brown (U)	.42	.42
		Nos. 317-322,C56-C60 (11)	5.88	5.88

5th anniv. of independence. The surcharge on No. 317 includes an "X" over old denomination.

Lion's Head Coin — A42

Designs: 2c, 3c, ¼ Golde coin. 5c, 8c, ½ Golde coin. 25c, 1 le, 1 Golde coin. (3c, 8c, 1 le, Map of Sierra Leone.)

Litho.; Embossed on Gilt Foil

1966, Nov. 12 Unwmk. *Imperf.*

Self-adhesive

Diameter: 2c, 3c, 38mm; 5c, 8c, 54mm; 25c, 1 le, 82mm

323	A42	2c	orange & dp plum	.15	.15
324	A42	3c	red lilac & emerald	.15	.15
325	A42	5c	vio blue & red org	.15	.15
326	A42	8c	black & Prus blue	.15	.15
327	A42	25c	emerald & violet	.38	.38
328	A42	1 le	red & orange	1.75	1.75
			Nos. 323-328,C61-C66 (12)	8.13	8.13

1st gold coinage of Sierra Leone. Advertising printed on paper backing.

Nos. 297-298, 303-305 and 316 Surcharged in Red, Silver, Violet, Green, Blue or Black:

12½ on A34, A35

17½ on A38, A39

=17½ on A41

1967, Dec. 2

329	A34	6½c	on 75c on 5sh (R)	.30	.30
330	A34	7½c	on 75c on 5sh (S)	.30	.30
331	A34	9½c	on 50c on 4p (G)	.40	.40
332	A35	12½c	on 20c on 1sh3p (V)	.50	.50
333	A39	17½c	on 1 le on 4p (Bl)	3.50	3.50
334	A41	17½c	on 50c	3.50	3.50
335	A38	18½c	on 60c on 5sh	10.00	10.00
336	A39	18½c	on 1 le on 4p	3.50	3.50
337	A41	25c	on 50c	1.00	1.00
			Nos. 329-337,C67-C69 (12)	24.90	24.90

Self-adhesive & Imperf.

Nos. 338-421 are self-adhesive and imperforate.

Cola Nut Type of 1965

Typographed; Embossed on White Paper

1967-68 Unwmk.

White Numeral Tablet

338	A40	½c	brt car, grn & yel	.15	.15
339	A40	1c	brt car, grn & yel	.15	.15
340	A40	1½c	orange, grn & yel	.15	.15
341	A40	2c	brt car, grn & yel	.25	.25
342	A40	2½c	emer, bl grn & yel	.40	.40
343	A40	3c	brt car, grn & yel	.25	.25
344	A40	3½c	olive, rose & ultra	.25	.25
345	A40	4½c	gray ol, grn & yel	.40	.40
346	A40	5c	brt car, grn & yel	.40	.40
347	A40	5½c	red brn, grn & yel	.40	.40
			Nos. 338-347 (10)	2.80	2.80

Advertisements printed on peelable backing except on the 2c, 3c, 3½c and 5c.

Colored Numeral Tablet

348	A40	½c	brt car, grn & yel	.15	.15
349	A40	1c	brt car, grn & yel	.15	.15
350	A40	2c	pink, brn & car	.20	.20
351	A40	2c	brt car, grn & yel	.75	.60
352	A40	2½c	bl grn, vio & org	1.00	.75
353	A40	2½c	emer, bl grn & yel	.30	.20
354	A40	3c	brt car, grn & yel	.20	.20
355	A40	3½c	lilac rose, grn & yel	.30	.30
356	A40	4c	brt car, grn & yel	.25	.25
			Nos. 348-356 (9)	3.30	2.80

Nos. 344, 348-354 issued in 1968.

Advertisements printed on peelable backing on the 3½c and 4c.

Map of Africa Showing Rhodesia A43

Each denomination shows map of Africa with map of one of the following countries—Portuguese Guinea, South Africa, Mozambique, Rhodesia, South West Africa or Angola.

1968, Sept. 25 Unwmk. Litho.

357	A43	½c	multicolored	.15	.15
358	A43	2c	multicolored	.15	.15
359	A43	2½c	multicolored	.15	.15
360	A43	3½c	multicolored	.20	.20
361	A43	10c	multicolored	.40	.40
362	A43	11½c	multicolored	.45	.45
363	A43	15c	multicolored	.60	.60
			Nos. 357-363 (7)	2.10	2.10
			7 Strips of 6 (1 of each design) (42)	11.40	

Intl. Human Rights Year. Sheets of 30 have 5 horizontal rows containing one stamp of each design. Advertisements printed on peelable backing.

See #C72-C78. For surcharges see #C106-C111.

No. 316 Surcharged

1968 OLYMPIC PARTICIPATION

*6½

Engraved; Embossed on Paper

1968, Nov. 30

364	A41	6½c	on 50c multi	.15	.15
365	A41	17½c	on 50c multi	.28	.28
366	A41	22½c	on 50c multi	.38	.38
367	A41	28½c	on 50c multi	.52	.52
368	A41	50c	on 50c multi	.85	.85
			Nos. 364-368,C79-C83 (10)	4.49	4.49

19th Olympic Games, Mexico City, Oct. 12-27.

Sierra Leone Type A1, 1859 A44

Designs: 2c, Type A40, 2c, 1965. 3½c, #220. 5c, #315. 12½c, #189. 1 le, Type A9, #2, 1912.

1969, Mar. 1 Litho.

369	A44	1c	multicolored	.15	.15
370	A44	2c	multicolored	.15	.15
371	A44	3½c	multicolored	.15	.15
372	A44	5c	multicolored	.15	.15
373	A44	12½c	multicolored	.38	.38
374	A44	1 le	multicolored	4.75	4.75
			Nos. 369-374,C84-C89 (12)	25.00	25.00

5th anniv. of free-form self-adhesive postage stamps. Various advertisements printed on peelable paper backing. No. 369 has side tab for handling and comes packed in boxes of 50. Nos. 370-374 are without side tabs and come 20 stamps attached to one sheet.

Globe, Freighter, Flags of Sierra Leone and Japan — A45

Map of Europe and Africa, Freighter, Flags of Sierra Leone and Netherlands — A46

Anvil Shape with Flags of Sierra Leone and: 3½c, Union Jack. 10c, 50c, West Germany. 18½c, Netherlands.

1969, July 10

375	A45	1c	multicolored	.15	.15
376	A46	2c	multicolored	.15	.15
377	A46	3½c	multicolored	.15	.15
378	A46	10c	multicolored	.16	.16
379	A46	18½c	multicolored	.30	.30
380	A46	50c	multicolored	.80	.80
			Nos. 375-380,C90-C95 (12)	7.58	7.58

Completion of the Pepel Port iron ore carrier terminal. Various advertisements printed on peelable paper backing. No. 375 has side tab for handling and comes packed in boxes of 50. Nos. 376-380 are without side tabs and come 20 stamps attached to one sheet.

African Development Bank Emblem — A47

Lithographed; Gold Impressed

1969, Sept. 10

381	A47	3½c	lt blue, grn & gold	.30	.30

5th anniv. of the African Development Bank. Advertising printed on peelable paper backing, 20 imperf. stamps to a sheet of backing, roulette 10.

See No. C96.

Diamond and Boy Scout Emblem A48

1969, Dec. 6 Litho.

382	A48	1c	multicolored	.15	.15
383	A48	2c	multicolored	.15	.15
384	A48	3½c	multicolored	.20	.16
385	A48	4½c	multicolored	.24	.20
386	A48	5c	multicolored	.32	.28
387	A48	75c	multicolored	10.00	8.00
			Nos. 382-387,C100-C105 (12)	123.39	91.02

60th anniv. of the Sierra Leone Boy Scouts. Various advertising printed on peelable paper backing. No. 382 has side tab for handling and comes packed in boxes of 100. Nos. 383-387 are without side tabs and come 20 stamps attached to one sheet.

EXPO '70 Emblems, Torii, Maps of Sierra Leone and Japan — A49

1970, June 22

388	A49	2c	multicolored	.15	.15
389	A49	3½c	multicolored	.15	.15
390	A49	10c	multicolored	.20	.20
391	A49	12½c	multicolored	.28	.28
392	A49	20c	multicolored	.45	.45
393	A49	45c	multicolored	1.00	1.00
			Nos. 388-393,C112-C117 (12)	12.89	12.89

EXPO '70 Intl. Exhib., Osaka, Japan, Mar. 15-Sept. 13. Various advertising printed on peelable paper backing.

Diamond A50

Palm Kernel — A51

Lithographed and Embossed

1970, Oct. 3 Unwmk.

Light Blue Background

394	A50	1c	carmine & blk	.15	.15
395	A50	1½c	brt green & car	.15	.15
396	A50	2c	lilac & yel grn	.15	.15
397	A50	2½c	ocher & dk blue	.15	.15
398	A50	3c	vio bl & org red	.22	.22
399	A50	3½c	dk blue & grn	.28	.28
400	A50	4c	olive & ultra	.28	.28
401	A50	5c	black & lilac	.32	.32

Orange Brown Background

402	A51	6c	bright green	.32	.32
403	A51	7c	rose lilac	.45	.45
404	A51	8½c	orange	.50	.50
405	A51	9c	lilac	.50	.50
406	A51	10c	dark blue	.55	.55
407	A51	11½c	blue	.75	.75
408	A51	18½c	yellow green	1.10	1.10
			Nos. 394-408,C118-C124 (22)	28.37	24.57

Advertisements printed on peelable paper backing. Packed in boxes of 500.

Sewa Diadem in Jewelry Box — A52

1970, Dec. 30

409	A52	2c	multicolored	.15	.15
410	A52	3½c	multicolored	.15	.15
411	A52	10c	multicolored	.35	.35

412 A52 12½c multicolored .45 .45
413 A52 40c multicolored 1.50 1.35
414 A52 1 le multicolored 7.50 5.00
Nos. 409-414,C125-C130 (12) 39.15 30.50

Diamond industry. Advertisement printed on peelable paper backing. Sheets of 20.

Traffic Pattern — A53

1971, Mar. 1 **Litho.**
415 A53 3½c orange & vio blue .25 .25

Right hand traffic change-over. See No. C131. Advertisements printed on peelable paper backing.

Flag and Lion's Head — A54

Litho.; Embossed in Silver
1971, Apr. 27
416 A54 2c multicolored .15 .15
417 A54 3½c multicolored .15 .15
418 A54 10c multicolored .18 .18
419 A54 12½c multicolored .20 .20
420 A54 40c multicolored .80 .80
421 A54 1 le multicolored 1.75 1.75
Nos. 416-421,C137-C142 (12) 12.03 12.03

10th anniversary of independence. Advertisements printed on peelable paper backing. Stamps are in shape of Sierra Leone map.

Pres. Siaka Stevens — A55

1972 **Litho.** *Perf. 13*
422 A55 1c pink & multi .15 .15
423 A55 2c violet & multi .15 .15
424 A55 4c lt ultra & multi .15 .15
425 A55 5c buff & multi .15 .15
426 A55 7c rose & multi .15 .15
427 A55 10c olive & multi .18 .18
428 A55 15c emerald & multi .24 .24
429 A55 18c yellow & multi .30 .30
430 A55 20c lt blue & multi .35 .35
431 A55 25c orange & multi .42 .42
432 A55 50c brt green & multi .90 .90
433 A55 1 le multicolored 1.65 1.65
434 A55 2 le red org & multi 3.25 3.25
435 A55 5 le multicolored 8.50 8.50
Nos. 422-435 (14) 16.54 16.54

Shades from later printings are found on several denominations including 1c, 2c, 7c, 10c, 1 le, 2 le.

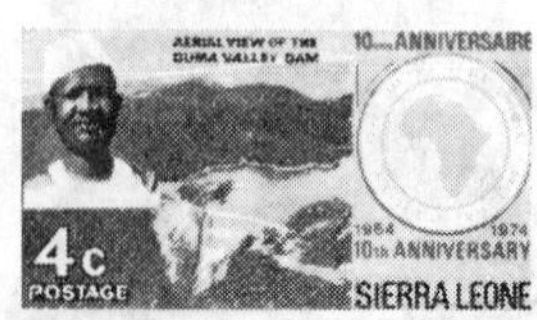

Guma Valley Dam and Bank Emblem — A56

1975, Jan. 14 **Litho.** *Perf. 13½*
436 A56 4c multicolored *125.00 82.50*

African Development Bank, 10th anniversary. See No. C143.

Pres. Siaka Stevens and Opening of Congo Bridge — A57

1975, Aug. 24 **Litho.** *Perf. 13x13½*
437 A57 5c multicolored *11.00 11.00*

Congo Bridge opening and Pres. Siaka Stevens' 70th birthday. See No. C144.

Pres. Tolbert and Stevens, Hands across Mano River — A58

1975, Oct. 3 **Litho.** *Perf. 13x13½*
438 A58 4c multicolored 1.40 1.40

Mano River Union Agreement between Liberia and Sierra Leone, signed Oct. 3, 1973. See No. C145.

Mohammed Ali Jinnah, Flags of Sierra Leone and Pakistan
A59

Elizabeth II
A60

1977, Jan. 28 **Litho.** *Perf. 13 rough*
439 A59 30c multicolored .80 .80

Mohammed Ali Jinnah (1876-1948), First Governor General of Pakistan.

1977, Nov. 28 **Litho.** *Perf. 12½x12*
440 A60 5c multicolored .15 .15
441 A60 1 le multicolored 1.40 1.40

25th anniv. of the reign of Elizabeth II.

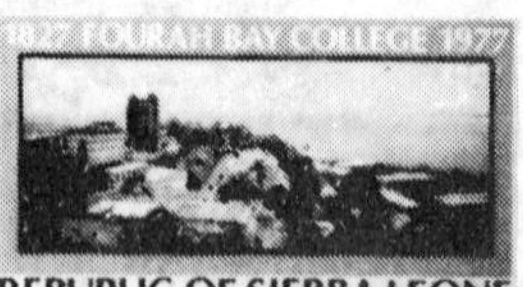

Fourah Bay College — A61

Design: 20c, Old College, vert.

Perf. 12x12½, 12½x12
1977, Dec. 19 **Litho.**
442 A61 5c multicolored .15 .15
443 A61 20c multicolored .35 .35

Fourah Bay College, Mt. Aureol, Freetown, founded 1827.

St. Edward's Crown and Scepters — A62

Designs: 50c, Elizabeth II in coronation coach. 1 le, Elizabeth II and Prince Philip on coronation day.

1978, Sept. 14 **Litho.** *Perf. 14½x14*
444 A62 5c multicolored .15 .15
445 A62 50c multicolored .60 .60
446 A62 1 le multicolored 1.10 1.10
Nos. 444-446 (3) 1.85 1.85

25th anniv. of coronation of Elizabeth II.

Fig Tree Blue
A63

Butterflies: 15c, Narrow blue-banded swallowtail. 25c, Pirate. 1 le, African giant swallowtail.

1979, Apr. 9 **Litho.** *Perf. 14½*
447 A63 5c multicolored .15 .15
448 A63 15c multicolored .35 .35
449 A63 25c multicolored .60 .60
450 A63 1 le multicolored 2.50 2.50
Nos. 447-450 (4) 3.60 3.60

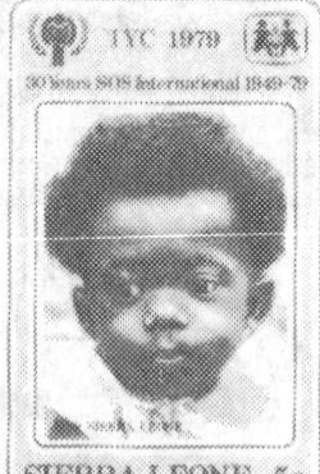

Child, IYC and SOS Emblems — A64

Designs (Emblems and): 27c, Girl and infant. 1 le, Mother and infant.

Perf. 14x13½
1979, Aug. 13 **Litho.** **Wmk. 373**
451 A64 5c multicolored .15 .15
452 A64 27c multicolored .55 .55
453 A64 1 le multicolored 2.25 2.25
a. Souvenir sheet of 1 2.50 2.50
Nos. 451-453 (3) 2.95 2.95

Intl. Year of the Child and 30th anniv. of SOS villages (villages for homeless children).

Presidents Stevens and Tolbert, Pigeon Post, Mano River
A65

1979, Oct. 3 *Perf. 13½*
454 A65 5c multicolored .15 .15
455 A65 22c multicolored .30 .30
456 A65 27c multicolored .38 .38
457 A65 35c multicolored .45 .45
458 A65 1 le multicolored 1.40 1.40
a. Souvenir sheet of 1 1.40 1.40
Nos. 454-458 (5) 2.68 2.68

Mano River Union, 5th anniv.; Postal Union, 1st anniv.

Sierra Leone No. 9, Hill — A66

1979, Dec. 19 **Litho.** *Perf. 14½x14*
459 A66 10c Grt. Britain #6 .18 .18
460 A66 15c shown .25 .25
461 A66 50c Sierra Leone #220 .90 .90
Nos. 459-461 (3) 1.33 1.33

Souvenir Sheet
462 A66 1 le Sierra Leone #119 1.25 1.25

Sir Rowland Hill (1795-1879), originator.

Touraco
A67

1980, Jan. 29 *Perf. 14*
463 A67 1c shown .15 .15
464 A67 2c Olive-bellied sunbird .15 .15
465 A67 3c Black-headed oriole .15 .15
466 A67 5c Spur-winged goose .15 .15
467 A67 7c White-bellied didric cuckoo .15 .15
468 A67 10c Gray parrot, vert. .20 .20
469 A67 15c African blue quail, vert. .30 .30
470 A67 20c West African wood owl, vert. .40 .40
471 A67 30c Blue plantain eater, vert. .60 .60
472 A67 40c Nigerian blue-breasted kingfisher, vert. .75 .75
473 A67 50c Black crake, vert. 1.10 1.10
474 A67 1 le Hartlaub's duck 2.00 2.00
475 A67 2 le Black bee-eater 4.00 4.00
476 A67 5 le Denham's bustard 10.00 10.00
Nos. 463-476 (14) 20.10 20.10

Reissues: Nos. 464-476 inscribed 1982. Nos. 463-464, 466, 468-473, 475-476 inscribed 1983.

For surcharges see Nos. 632-636. For overprints see Nos. 637-638.

Rotary Intl., 75th Anniv.
A68

1980, Feb. 23 *Perf. 14*
477 A68 5c orange & multi .15 .15
478 A68 27c red & multi .35 .35
479 A68 50c green & multi .70 .70
480 A68 1 le blue & multi 1.40 1.40
Nos. 477-480 (4) 2.60 2.60

Mail Ship "Maria," 1884, London '80 Emblem
A69

1980, May 6 **Litho.** *Perf. 14*
481 A69 6c shown .15 .15
482 A69 31c "Tarquah," 1902 .45 .45
483 A69 50c "Aureol," 1951 .75 .75
484 A69 1 le "Africa Palm," 1974 1.50 1.50
Nos. 481-484 (4) 2.85 2.85

London 80 Intl. Stamp Exhib., May 6-14.

Conf. Emblem — A70

Small Striped Swordtail — A71

1980, July 1 **Litho.** *Perf. 14½*
485 A70 20c multicolored .25 .25
486 A70 1 le multicolored 1.25 1.25

17th African Summit Conf., Freetown, July 1-4.

1980, Oct. 6 **Litho.** *Perf. 14*
487 A71 5c shown .15 .15
488 A71 27c Pearl charaxes .45 .45
489 A71 35c White barred charaxes .55 .55
490 A71 1 le Zaddach's forester 1.65 1.65
Nos. 487-490 (4) 2.80 2.80

Freetown Airport — A72

1980, Dec. 5 Litho. *Perf. 13½*

491 A72 6c shown .15 .15
492 A72 26c Mammy Yoko Hotel .30 .30
493 A72 31c Freetown Cotton Tree .35 .35
494 A72 40c Beindomgo Falls .50 .50
495 A72 50c Water skiing .60 .60
496 A72 1 le Elephant 1.25 1.25
Nos. 491-496 (6) 3.15 3.15

Servals A73

Cats and Kittens: No. 498, Serval kittens. No. 500a, African golden cats. No. 502a, Leopards. No. 504a, Lions. Pairs have continuous design.

1981, Feb. 23 Litho. *Perf. 14*

497 A73 6c multicolored .15 .15
498 A73 6c multicolored .15 .15
a. Pair, #497-498 .18 .18
499 A73 31c multicolored .45 .45
500 A73 31c multicolored .45 .45
a. Pair, #499-500 .90 .90
501 A73 50c multicolored .75 .75
502 A73 50c multicolored .75 .75
a. Pair, #501-502 1.50 1.50
503 A73 1 le multicolored 1.50 1.50
504 A73 1 le multicolored 1.50 1.50
a. Pair, #503-504 3.00 3.00
Nos. 497-504 (8) 5.70 5.70

Ambulance Clinic — A74

Perf. 14½

1981, Apr. 18 Litho. Wmk. 373

505 A74 6c Soldiers, vert. .15 .15
506 A74 31c shown .50 .50
507 A74 40c Traffic policeman, vert. .65 .65
508 A74 1 le Coast Guard ship 1.65 1.65
Nos. 505-508 (4) 2.95 2.95

Anniv.: independence, 20th; republic, 10th.

Royal Wedding Issue
Common Design Type

1981 Litho. *Perf. 12, 14*

509 CD331 31c Bouquet .60 .60
510 CD331 35c Sandringham .70 .70
511 CD331 45c Charles .95 .95
512 CD331 60c Charles 1.25 1.25
513 CD331 70c like 35c 1.50 1.50
514 CD331 1 le Couple 2.00 2.00
515 CD331 1.30 le Charles 2.50 2.50
516 CD331 1.50 le Couple 3.00 3.00
517 CD331 2 le Couple 4.00 4.00
Nos. 509-517 (9) 16.50 16.50

Souvenir Sheet

518 CD331 3 le Royal landau 5.00 5.00

31c, 45c, 1 le, 3 le issued July 22, perf. 14. 35c, 60c, 1.50 le issued in sheets of 5 plus label; perf. 12, Sept. 9. 70c, 1.30 le, 2 le issued in booklets only, perf. 14.

For surcharges see #540-546, 714, 716, 721.

Soccer Player — A75

Wmk. 373

1981, Sept. 30 Litho. *Perf. 14*

519 A75 6c shown .15 .15
520 A75 31c Boys planting trees .45 .45
521 A75 1 le Duke of Edinburgh 1.50 1.50
522 A75 1 le Pres. Stevens 1.50 1.50
Nos. 519-522 (4) 3.60 3.60

Duke of Edinburgh's Awards and Pres. Steven's Awards, 25th anniv.

Pineapples — A76

Woman Tending Rice Plants A77

Perf. 14, 14½ (A77)

1981 Litho. Wmk. 373

523 A76 6c shown .15 .15
524 A77 6c Peanuts for export .15 .15
525 A76 31c Peanuts .50 .50
526 A77 31c Crushing, eating cassava .50 .50
527 A76 50c Cassava fruits .85 .85
528 A77 50c shown .85 .85
529 A76 1 le Rice plants 1.65 1.65
530 A77 1 le Men tending pineapple plants 1.65 1.65
Nos. 523-530 (8) 6.30 6.30

World Food Day. Issue dates: Nos. 523, 525, 527, 529, Oct. 16; others, Nov. 2.

Princess Diana Issue
Common Design Type

1982, July Litho. *Perf. 14½*

531 CD332 31c Caernarvon Castle .50 .50
532 CD332 50c Honeymoon .85 .85
533 CD332 2 le Wedding 3.00 3.00
Nos. 531-533 (3) 4.35 4.35

Souvenir Sheet

534 CD332 3 le Diana 4.75 4.75

Also issued in sheetlets of 5 + label.

For overprints and surcharges see Nos. 552-555, 713, 715, 717-720, 722-723.

Scouting Year — A78

1982, Aug. 23 *Perf. 14*

535 A78 20c Studying animal husbandry .32 .32
536 A78 50c Botanical study .85 .85
537 A78 1 le Baden-Powell 1.65 1.65
538 A78 2 le Fishing at campsite 3.00 3.00
Nos. 535-538 (4) 5.82 5.82

Souvenir Sheet

539 A78 3 le Raising flag 4.75 4.75

For surcharges see Nos. 694-698.

Nos. 509-512, 514, 516, 518 Surcharged

1982, Aug. 30 Wmk. 373

540 CD331 50c on 31c 1.65 1.65
541 CD331 50c on 35c 1.65 1.65
542 CD331 50c on 45c 1.65 1.65
543 CD331 50c on 60c 1.65 1.65
544 CD331 90c on 1 le 2.75 2.75
545 CD331 2 le on 1.50 le 6.00 6.00
Nos. 540-545 (6) 15.35 15.35

Souvenir Sheet

546 CD331 3.50 le on 3 le 6.00 6.00

1982 World Cup — A79

Designs: Various soccer players.

1982, Sept. 7

547 A79 20c multicolored .35 .35
548 A79 30c multicolored .50 .50
549 A79 1 le multicolored 1.75 1.75
550 A79 2 le multicolored 3.25 3.25
Nos. 547-550 (4) 5.85 5.85

Souvenir Sheet

551 A79 3 le multicolored 4.75 4.75

For overprints see Nos. 561-565.

Nos. 531-534 Overprinted: "ROYAL BABY/ 21.6.82"

1982, Oct. 15 Litho. *Perf. 14½*

552 CD332 31c multicolored .50 .50
553 CD332 50c multicolored .85 .85
554 CD332 2 le multicolored 3.00 3.00
Nos. 552-554 (3) 4.35 4.35

Souvenir Sheet

555 CD332 3 le multicolored 4.75 4.75

Birth of Prince William of Wales, June 21.

Also issued in sheetlets of 5 + label.

For surcharges see Nos. 715, 719-720, 723.

George Washington A80

Various paintings of Washington. 31c, 1 le, vert.

1982, Oct. 30 Litho. *Perf. 14*

556 A80 6c multicolored .15 .15
557 A80 31c multicolored .45 .45
558 A80 50c multicolored .75 .75
559 A80 1 le multicolored 1.50 1.50
Nos. 556-559 (4) 2.85 2.85

Souvenir Sheet

560 A80 2 le multicolored 3.00 3.00

Nos. 547-551 Overprinted with Finalists and Score

1982, Nov. 9 *Perf. 14*

561 A79 20c multicolored .30 .30
562 A79 30c multicolored .42 .42
563 A79 1 le multicolored 1.50 1.50
564 A79 2 le multicolored 2.75 2.75
Nos. 561-564 (4) 4.97 4.97

Souvenir Sheet

565 A79 3 le multicolored 4.25 4.25

Italy's victory in 1982 World Cup.

Christmas — A81 Christmas 1982

Stained-glass Windows, St. George's Cathedral, Freetown.

1982, Nov. 18 *Perf. 14*

566 A81 6c Temptation of Christ .15 .15
567 A81 31c Baptism of Christ .45 .45
568 A81 50c Annunciation .75 .75
569 A81 1 le Nativity 1.50 1.50
Nos. 566-569 (4) 2.85 2.85

Souvenir Sheet

570 A81 2 le Mary and Joseph 3.00 3.00

Charles Darwin (1809-82) A82

1982, Dec. 10

571 A82 6c Long-snouted crocodile .18 .18
572 A82 31c Rainbow lizard .50 .50
573 A82 50c River turtle .90 .90
574 A82 1 le Chameleon 1.75 1.75
Nos. 571-574 (4) 3.33 3.33

Souvenir Sheet

575 A82 2 le Royal python, vert. 3.25 3.25

500th Birth Anniv. of Raphael — A83

School of Athens, Fresco, Vatican. Nos. 576-579 show details.

1983, Jan. 28 Litho. *Perf. 14*

576 A83 6c Diogenes .15 .15
577 A83 31c Euclid, Ptolemy .45 .45
578 A83 50c Euclid and his Students .75 .75
579 A83 2 le Pythagoras, Heraclitus 3.00 3.00
Nos. 576-579 (4) 4.35 4.35

Souvenir Sheet

580 A83 3 le Entire painting 4.50 4.50

A83a

1983, Mar. 14 Litho. *Perf. 14*

581 A83a 6c Agricultural training .15 .15
582 A83a 10c Tourism development .15 .15
583 A83a 50c Broadcast training .75 .75
584 A83a 1 le Airport services 1.50 1.50
Nos. 581-584 (4) 2.55 2.55

Commonwealth Day.

25th Anniv. of Economic Commission for Africa — A84

1983, Apr. 29 Litho. *Perf. 13½x13*

585 A84 1 le multicolored 1.40 1.40

Endangered Chimpanzees, World Wildlife Fund Emblem — A85

Various chimpanzees from Outamba-Kilimi Natl. Park. 10c, 31c, vert.

1983, May Litho. *Perf. 14*

586 A85 6c multicolored .15 .15
587 A85 10c multicolored .24 .24
588 A85 31c multicolored .70 .70
589 A85 60c multicolored 1.50 1.50
Nos. 586-589 (4) 2.59 2.59

Souvenir Sheet

590 A85 3 le Elephants 4.00 4.00

World Communications Year — A86

1983, July 14 *Perf. 14*
591 A86 6c Traditional communications .15 .15
592 A86 10c Mano River mail .15 .15
593 A86 20c Satellite ground station .30 .30
594 A86 1 le English packet, 1805 1.50 1.50
Nos. 591-594 (4) 2.10 2.10

Souvenir Sheet

595 A86 2 le Map, phone, envelope 3.00 3.00

Manned Flight Bicentenary A87

1983, Aug. 31 **Litho.** *Perf. 14*
596 A87 6c Montgolfiere, 1783, vert. .15 .15
597 A87 20c Deutschland blimp, 1897 .32 .32
598 A87 50c Norge I blimp, North Pole, 1926 .80 .80
599 A87 1 le Cape Sierra sport balloon, Freetown, 1983, vert. 1.65 1.65
Nos. 596-599 (4) 2.92 2.92

Souvenir Sheet

600 A87 2 le Futuristic airship 2.75 2.75

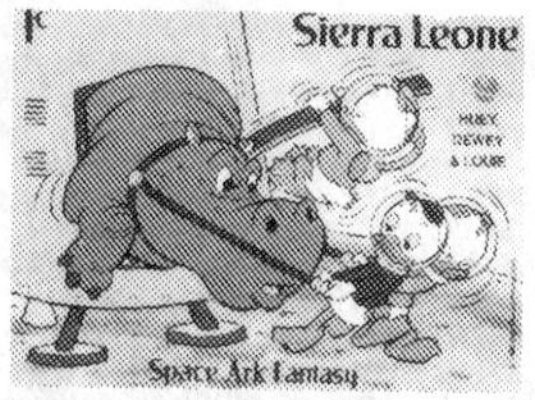

Walt Disney, Space Ark Fantasy — A88

1983, Nov.
601 A88 1c Hippopotamus, Huey, Dewey and Louie .15 .15
602 A88 1c Mickey Mouse and Snake .15 .15
603 A88 3c Elephant and Donald Duck .15 .15
604 A88 3c Zebra and Goofy .15 .15
605 A88 10c Lion and Ludwig von Drake .15 .15
606 A88 10c Rhinoceros and Goofy .15 .15
607 A88 2 le Giraffe and Mickey Mouse 1.75 1.75
608 A88 3 le Monkey and Donald Duck 2.50 2.50
Nos. 601-608 (8) 5.15 5.15

Souvenir Sheet

609 A88 5 le Mickey Mouse and animals 4.50 4.50

10th Anniv. of Mano River Union A89

1984, Feb. 8 **Litho.** *Perf. 15*
610 A89 6c Teaching Program graduates .15 .15
611 A89 25c Emblem .20 .20
612 A89 31c Map, presidents .25 .25
613 A89 41c Guinea Accession signing .35 .35
a. Souvenir sheet of 1 .50 .50
Nos. 610-613 (4) .95 .95

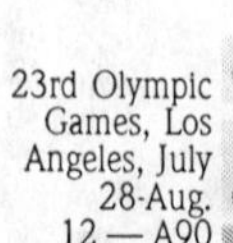

23rd Olympic Games, Los Angeles, July 28-Aug. 12 — A90

1984, Mar. 15 *Perf. 14*
614 A90 90c Gymnastics .65 .65
615 A90 1 le Hurdles .70 .70
616 A90 3 le Javelin 2.25 2.25
Nos. 614-616 (3) 3.60 3.60

Souvenir Sheet

617 A90 7 le Boxing 5.25 5.25

For surcharges see Nos. 699-702.

Apollo 11, 15th Anniv. — A91

1984, May 14 **Litho.** *Perf. 14*
618 A91 50c Lift off .40 .40
619 A91 75c Lunar landing .60 .60
620 A91 1.25 le 1st step on moon 1.00 1.00
621 A91 2.50 le Walking on moon 2.00 2.00
Nos. 618-621 (4) 4.00 4.00

Souvenir Sheet

622 A91 5 le TV transmission, horiz. 4.00 4.00

UPU Congress A92

1984, June 19
623 A92 4 le Concorde 2.75 2.75

Souvenir Sheet

624 A92 4 le UPU emblem, von Stephan 2.75 2.75

UN Decade for African Transportation — A93

Various cars.

1984, July 16 *Perf. 14½x15*
625 A93 12c Citroen .15 .15
626 A93 60c Locomobile .50 .50
627 A93 90c AC Ace .70 .70
628 A93 1 le Vauxhall Prince Henry .80 .80
629 A93 1.50 le Delahaye-185 1.25 1.25
630 A93 2 le Mazda 1.65 1.65
Nos. 625-630 (6) 5.05 5.05

Souvenir Sheet

Perf. 15

631 A93 6 le Volkswagon Beetle 5.00 5.00

Nos. 466, 468, 475 Surcharged

Wmk. 373

1984, Aug. 3 **Litho.** *Perf. 14*
632 A67 25c on 10c multi .20 .20
633 A67 40c on 10c multi .32 .32
634 A67 50c on 2 le multi .50 .50
635 A67 70c on 5c multi .56 .56
636 A67 10 le on 5c multi 8.00 8.00
Nos. 632-636 (5) 9.58 9.58

#473, 476 Ovptd.: "AUSIPEX 84"

Wmk. 373

1984, Aug. 22 **Litho.** *Perf. 14*
637 A67 50c multicolored .40 .40
638 A67 5 le multicolored 4.00 4.00

Portuguese Caravel Da Sintra A94

1984
639 A94 2c shown .15 .15
640 A94 5c Merlin of Bristol .15 .15
641 A94 10c Golden Hind .15 .15
642 A94 15c Interloper Morduant .15 .15
643 A94 20c Navy Board Transport Atlantic .15 .15
644 A94 25c Navy Vessel Lapwing .16 .16
645 A94 30c Brig Traveller .20 .20
646 A94 40c Schooner Amistad .25 .25
647 A94 50c Teazer .32 .32
648 A94 70c Cable Ship Scotia .45 .45
649 A94 1 le Alecto .65 .65
650 A94 2 le Blonde 1.25 1.25
651 A94 5 le Fox 3.25 3.25
652 A94 10 le Mail ship Accra 6.50 6.50
Nos. 639-652 (14) 13.78 13.78

Issued: #639-649, 9/5; #650-651, 10/9; 10 le, 11/7.
See #739-740. For surcharges see #809-812.

1985 *Perf. 12½x12*
639a A94 2c .15 .15
640a A94 5c .15 .15
641a A94 10c .15 .15
643a A94 20c .15 .15
644a A94 25c .15 .15
645a A94 30c .15 .15
646a A94 40c .15 .15
647a A94 50c .15 .15
648a A94 70c .18 .18
649a A94 1 le .25 .25
650a A94 2 le .50 .50
651a A94 5 le 1.25 1.25
652a A94 10 le 2.50 2.50
Nos. 639a-652a (13) 5.88 5.88

125th Anniv. of Sierra Leone Postage Stamps A95

1984, Oct. 9
653 A95 50c Mail messenger, No. 2 .32 .32
654 A95 2 le Post Master receiving letters, No. 2 1.25 1.25
655 A95 3 le Cover 2.00 2.00
Nos. 653-655 (3) 3.57 3.57

Souvenir Sheet

656 A95 5 le Penny Black, No. 2 3.25 3.25

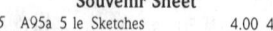

50th Anniv. of Donald Duck — A95a

1984, Nov. **Litho.** *Perf. 14x13½*
657 A95a 1c Wise Little Hen .15 .15
658 A95a 2c Boat Builders .15 .15
659 A95a 3c Three Caballeros .15 .15
660 A95a 4c Mathematic Land .15 .15
661 A95a 5c Mickey Mouse Club .15 .15
662 A95a 10c On Parade .15 .15
663 A95a 1 le Don Donald .80 .80
663A A95a 2 le Donald gets drafted, p. 12½x12 1.60 1.60
664 A95a 4 le Tokyo Disneyland 3.25 3.25
Nos. 657-664 (9) 6.55 6.55

Souvenir Sheet

665 A95a 5 le Sketches 4.00 4.00

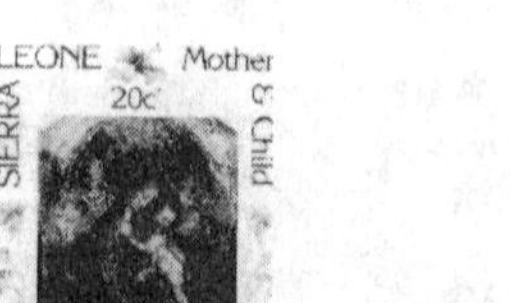

Christmas — A96

Mother and Child paintings.

1984, Nov. 28 *Perf. 14*
666 A96 20c Pisanello .15 .15
667 A96 1 le Memling .70 .70
668 A96 2 le Raphael 1.40 1.40
669 A96 3 le van der Werff 2.00 2.00
Nos. 666-669 (4) 4.25 4.25

Souvenir Sheet

670 A96 6 le Picasso 4.25 4.25

Songbirds A97

1985, Jan. 31 **Litho.**
671 A97 40c Straw-tailed whydah .40 .40
672 A97 90c Spotted flycatcher .95 .95
673 A97 1.30 le Garden warbler 1.40 1.40
674 A97 3 le Speke's weaver 3.00 3.00
Nos. 671-674 (4) 5.75 5.75

Souvenir Sheet

675 A97 5 le Great gray shrike 5.00 5.00

International Youth Year — A98

1985, Feb. 14 **Litho.**
676 A98 1.15 le Fishing 1.10 1.10
677 A98 1.50 le Timber 1.40 1.40
678 A98 2.15 le Rice farming 2.00 2.00
Nos. 676-678 (3) 4.50 4.50

Souvenir Sheet

679 A98 5 le Diamond polishing 4.50 4.50

Intl. Civil Aviation Org., 40th Anniv. A100

Early aviators and their aircraft: 70c, Eddie Rickenbacker, Spad XIII (1918). 1.25 le, Samuel P. Langley, Aerodrome No. 5. 1.30 le, Orville and Wilbur Wright, Flyer 1. 2 le, Charles Lindbergh, Spirit of St. Louis.

1985, Feb. 28 **Litho.** *Perf. 14*
680 A100 70c multicolored .60 .60
681 A100 1.25 le multicolored 1.10 1.10
682 A100 1.30 le multicolored 1.10 1.10
683 A100 2 le multicolored 1.90 1.90
Nos. 680-683 (4) 4.70 4.70

Souvenir Sheet

684 A100 5 le Jet over Freetown 4.50 4.50

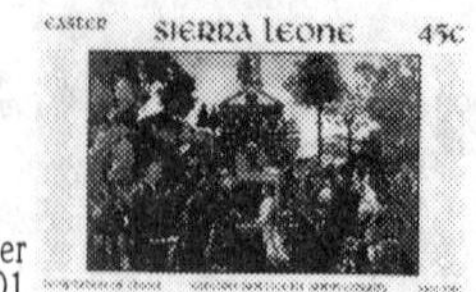

Easter A101

Religious paintings: Nos. 685, 687, 689 by Botticelli (1445-1510). Nos. 686, 688 by Velazquez (1599-1660).

1985, Apr. 29
685 A101 45c The Temptation of Christ .15 .15
686 A101 70c Christ at the Column .25 .25
687 A101 1.55 le Pieta .55 .55
688 A101 10 le Christ on the Cross 4.00 4.00
Nos. 685-688 (4) 4.95 4.95

Souvenir Sheet

689 A101 12 le Man of Sorrows 4.75 4.75

Queen Mother, 85th Birthday — A102

Designs: 1 le, Queen Mother at St. Peter's Cathedral, London, vert. 1.70 le, With Double Star at Sandown Racetrack. 10 le, Attending the gala ballet at Covent Garden, 1971, vert. 12 le, With Princess Anne at Ascot, vert.

1985, July 8 Litho. *Perf. 14*

690 A102 1 le multicolored .32 .32
691 A102 1.70 le multicolored .60 .60
692 A102 10 le multicolored 3.25 3.25
Nos. 690-692 (3) 4.17 4.17

Souvenir Sheet

693 A102 12 le multicolored 4.00 4.00

Nos. 535-539 Surcharged "75th Anniversary / of Girl Guides," Black Bar and New Value

1985, July 25

694 A78 70c on 20c multi .60 .60
695 A78 1.30 le on 50c multi 1.25 1.25
696 A78 5 le on 1 le multi .90 .90
697 A78 7 le on 2 le multi 1.75 1.75
Nos. 694-697 (4) 4.50 4.50

Souvenir Sheet

698 A78 15 le on 3 le multi 5.00 5.00

Nos. 614-617 Surcharged with Winners Names, Country, "Gold Medal," Black Bar and New Value

1985, July 25

699 A90 2 le on 90c Ma Yanhonjg, China .65 .65
700 A90 4 le on 1 le E. Moses, USA 1.25 1.25
701 A90 8 le on 3 le A. Haerkoenen, Finland 2.50 2.50
Nos. 699-701 (3) 4.40 4.40

Souvenir Sheet

702 A90 15 le on 7 le M. Taylor, USA 4.75 4.75

1905 Chater-Lea, Hill Station House A103

Designs: 2 le, Honda XR 350 R, QE II Quay. 4 le, Kawasaki Vulcan, Bo Clock Tower. 5 le, Harley-Davidson Electra-Glide, Makeni. 12 le, 1893 Millet.

1985, Aug. 15

703 A103 1.40 le multicolored .45 .45
704 A103 2 le multicolored .65 .65
705 A103 4 le multicolored 1.25 1.25
706 A103 5 le multicolored 1.65 1.65
Nos. 703-706 (4) 4.00 4.00

Souvenir Sheet

707 A103 12 le multicolored 4.00 4.00

Motorcycle cent., Decade for African Transport.

A104 Christmas — A105

1985, Sept. 3

708 A104 70c Viola pomposa .24 .24
709 A104 3 le Spinet 1.00 1.00
710 A104 4 le Lute 1.25 1.25
711 A104 5 le Oboe 1.65 1.65
Nos. 708-711 (4) 4.14 4.14

Souvenir Sheet

712 A104 12 le Portrait 4.00 4.00

Johann Sebastian Bach (1685-1750), composer. Nos. 708-712 show music from "Clavier Ubang."

Nos. 510, 512, 516, 531-534, 552-555 Surcharged

1985, Sept. 30 *Perfs. as Before*

Designs CD331-CD332

713 70c on 31c #531 .48 .48
714 1.30 le on 60c #512 .90 .90
715 1.30 le on 31c #552 .90 .90
716 2 le on 35c #510 1.25 1.25
717 4 le on 50c #532 2.75 2.75
718 5 le on 2 le #533 3.25 3.25
719 5 le on 50c #553 3.25 3.25
720 7 le on 2 le #554 4.50 4.50
721 8 le on 1.50 le #516 5.50 5.50
Nos. 713-721 (9) 22.78 22.78

Souvenir Sheets

722 15 le on 3 le #534 7.00 7.00
723 15 le on 3 le #555 7.00 7.00

1985, Oct. 18 Litho. *Perf. 14*

Madonna and child paintings by: 70c, Carlo Crivelli (c. 1430-1494). 3 le, Dirk Bouts (c. 1400-1475). 4 le, Antonello de Messina (c. 1430-1479). 5 le, Stefan Lochner (c. 1400-1451). 12 le, Miniature from the Book of Kells, 9th cent., Ireland.

724 A105 70c multicolored .25 .25
725 A105 3 le multicolored 1.00 1.00
726 A105 4 le multicolored 1.35 1.35
727 A105 5 le multicolored 1.65 1.65
Nos. 724-727 (4) 4.25 4.25

Miniature Sheet

728 A105 12 le multicolored 4.00 4.00

Jacob and Wilhelm Grimm, Fabulists — A106

Mark Twain, American Humorist A107

Walt Disney characters acting out Twain quotes (A107) or in Rumpelstiltskin (A106).

1985, Oct. 30 Litho. *Perf. 14*

729 A106 70c multicolored .22 .22
730 A106 1.30 le multicolored .38 .38
731 A107 1.50 le multicolored .42 .42
732 A106 2 le multicolored .55 .55
733 A107 3 le multicolored .85 .85
734 A107 4 le multicolored 1.25 1.25
735 A107 5 le multicolored 1.40 1.40
736 A106 10 le multicolored 2.75 2.75
Nos. 729-736 (8) 7.82 7.82

Souvenir Sheets

737 A106 15 le multicolored 4.25 4.25
738 A107 15 le multicolored 4.25 4.25

Nos. 731, 733-735 bear the Intl. Youth Year emblem.

Ship Type of 1984

1985, Nov. 15

739 A94 15 le Favourite 4.50 4.50
740 A94 25 le Euryalus 7.50 7.50

UN, 40th Anniv. A108

Stamps of UN and famous men: 2 le, No. 30, Kennedy. 4 le, No. 59, Einstein. 7 le, No. 44, Maimonides (1135-1204), medieval Judaic scholar. 12 le, Martin Luther King, Jr. (1929-1968), civil rights leader, vert.

1985, Nov. 28 Litho. *Perf. 14½*

741 A108 2 le multicolored .65 .65
742 A108 4 le multicolored 1.35 1.35
743 A108 7 le multicolored 2.30 2.30
Nos. 741-743 (3) 4.30 4.30

Souvenir Sheet

744 A108 12 le multicolored 4.00 4.00

1986 World Cup Soccer Championships A109

Statue of Liberty, Cent. A110

Various soccer plays.

1986, Mar. 3 *Perf. 14*

745 A109 70c multicolored .28 .28
746 A109 3 le multicolored 1.10 1.10
747 A109 4 le multicolored 1.50 1.50
748 A109 5 le multicolored 1.90 1.90
Nos. 745-748 (4) 4.78 4.78

Souvenir Sheet

749 A109 12 le multicolored 4.50 4.50

For overprints and surcharges see Nos. 788-792.

1986, Mar. 11

New York City: 40c, Times Square, 1905. 70c, Times Square, 1986. 1 le, Tally Ho Coach, c. 1880, horiz. 10 le, Liberty Lines express bus, 1986. 12 le, Statue of Liberty.

750 A110 40c multicolored .16 .16
751 A110 70c multicolored .28 .28
752 A110 1 le multicolored .42 .42
753 A110 10 le multicolored 4.00 4.00
Nos. 750-753 (4) 4.86 4.86

Souvenir Sheet

754 A110 12 le multicolored 4.00 4.00

A111

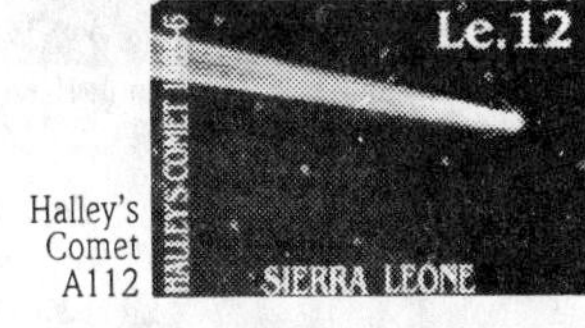

Halley's Comet A112

15c, Johannes Kepler (1571-1630), German astronomer, & Paris Observatory. 50c, US space shuttle landing, 1985. 70c, Bayeux Tapestry (detail), 1066 sighting. 10 le, Arthurian magician, Merlin, sights comet, 530. 12 le, Comet over Sierra Leone.

1986, Apr. 1

755 A111 15c multicolored .15 .15
756 A111 50c multicolored .16 .16
757 A111 70c multicolored .24 .24
758 A111 10 le multicolored 3.35 3.35
Nos. 755-758 (4) 3.90 3.90

Souvenir Sheet

759 A112 12 le multicolored 4.00 4.00

For overprints and surcharges see Nos. 813-817.

Queen Elizabeth II, 60th Birthday

Common Design Type

1986, Apr. 21

760 CD339 10c Cranwell, 1951 .15 .15
761 CD339 1.70 le Garter Ceremony .55 .55
762 CD339 10 le Braemar Games, 1970 3.35 3.35
Nos. 760-762 (3) 4.05 4.05

Souvenir Sheet

763 CD339 12 le Windsor Castle, 1943 4.00 4.00

For surcharges see Nos. 793-795.

AMERIPEX '86 — A113

Locomotives.

1986, May 22

764 A113 50c Hiawatha, Milwaukee .16 .16
765 A113 2 le The Rocket, Rock Is. .65 .65
766 A113 4 le Prospector, Rio Grande 1.35 1.35
767 A113 7 le Daylight, So. Pacific 2.35 2.35
Nos. 764-767 (4) 4.51 4.51

Souvenir Sheet

768 A113 12 le Broadway, Pennsylvania 4.00 4.00

Royal Wedding Issue, 1986

Common Design Type

Designs: 10c, Prince Andrew and Sarah Ferguson. 1.70 le, Andrew with shotgun. 10 le, Andrew saluting. 12 le, Couple, diff.

1986, July 23

769 CD340 10c multi .15 .15
770 CD340 1.70 le multi .55 .55
771 CD340 10 le multi 3.35 3.35
Nos. 769-771 (3) 4.05 4.05

Souvenir Sheet

772 CD340 12 le multi 4.00 4.00

For surcharges see Nos. 796-798.

Indigenous Flowers — A114

1986, Aug. 25 Litho. *Perf. 15*

773 A114 70c Monodora myristica .15 .15
774 A114 1.50 le Gloriosa simplex .15 .15
775 A114 4 le Mussaenda erythrophylla .35 .35
776 A114 6 le Crinum ornatum .52 .52
777 A114 8 le Bauhinia purpurea .75 .75
778 A114 10 le Bombax costatum .90 .90
779 A114 20 le Hibiscus rosa-sinensis 1.75 1.75
780 A114 30 le Cassia fistula 2.75 2.75
Nos. 773-780 (8) 7.32 7.32

Souvenir Sheets

781 A114 40 le Clitoria ternatea 3.50 3.50
782 A114 40 le Plumbago auriculata 3.50 3.50

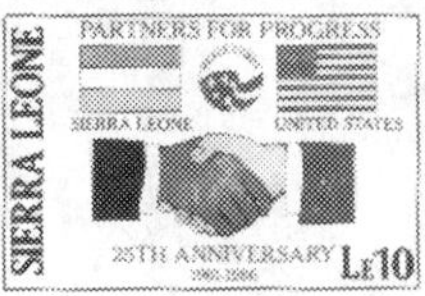

US Peace Corps in Sierra Leone, 25th Anniv. A115

1986, Aug. 26 Litho. *Perf. 14*

783 A115 10 le multi 1.25 1.25

Intl. Peace Year — A116

1986, Sept. 1

784 A116 1 le Transportation .15 .15
785 A116 2 le Education .24 .24
786 A116 5 le Communications .60 .60
787 A116 10 le Fishing 1.25 1.25
Nos. 784-787 (4) 2.24 2.24

Nos. 745-749 Ovptd. or Surcharged "WINNERS / Argentina 3 / West Germany 2" in Gold

1986, Sept. 15 *Perf. 14*

788 A109 70c multi .15 .15
789 A109 3 le multi .24 .24
790 A109 4 le multi .32 .32
791 A109 40 le on 5 le multi 3.20 3.20
Nos. 788-791 (4) 3.91 3.91

Souvenir Sheet

792 A109 40 le on 12 le multi 3.20 3.20

Nos. 760, 762-763 Surcharged in Silver or Black

1986, Sept. 15

793 CD339 70c on 10c multi .15 .15
794 CD339 45 le on 10 le multi 3.60 3.60

Souvenir Sheet

795 CD339 50 le on 12 le (B) 4.00 4.00

Nos. 769, 771-772 Surcharged in Silver

1986, Sept. 15

796 CD340 70c on 10c multi .15 .15
797 CD340 45 le on 10 le multi 3.60 3.60

Souvenir Sheet

798 CD340 50 le on 12 le multi 4.00 4.00

STOCKHOLMIA '86 — A117

Disney characters in Mother Goose fairy tales.

1986, Sept. 22 *Perf. 11*

799 A117 70c Jack and Jill .15 .15
800 A117 1 le Wee Willie Winkie .15 .15
801 A117 2 le Little Miss Muffet .16 .16
802 A117 4 le Old King Cole .32 .32
803 A117 5 le Mary Quite Contrary .40 .40
804 A117 10 le Little Bo Peep .80 .80
805 A117 25 le Polly Put the Kettle On 2.00 2.00
806 A117 35 le Rub-a-Dub-Dub 2.80 2.80
Nos. 799-806 (8) 6.78 6.78

Souvenir Sheets

807 A117 40 le Old Woman in the Shoe 3.20 3.20
808 A117 40 le Simple Simon 3.20 3.20

Nos. 639, 645-646 and 648 Surcharged

1986, Oct. 15

809 A94 30 le on 2c multi 2.75 2.75
810 A94 40 le on 30c multi 3.75 3.75
811 A94 45 le on 40c multi 4.25 4.25
812 A94 50 le on 70c multi 4.75 4.75
Nos. 809-812 (4) 15.50 15.50

Nos. 755-759 Ovptd. or Surcharged with Halley's Comet Emblem in Black or Silver

1986, Oct. 15

813 A111 50c multi .15 .15
814 A111 70c multi .15 .15
815 A111 1.50 le on 15c multi .15 .15
816 A111 45 le on 10 le multi 4.25 4.25
Nos. 813-816 (4) 4.70 4.70

Souvenir Sheet

817 A112 50 le on 12 le multi (S) 4.75 4.75

Christmas A118

Paintings by Titian: 70c, Virgin and Child with St. Dorothy. $1.50 le, The Gypsy Madonna, vert. 20 le, The Holy Family. 30 le, Virgin and Child in an Evening Landscape, vert. 40 le, Madonna with the Pesaro Family.

1986, Nov. 17 **Litho.** *Perf. 14*

818 A118 70c multi .15 .15
819 A118 1.50 le multi .15 .15
820 A118 20 le multi 1.60 1.60
821 A118 30 le multi 2.40 2.40
Nos. 818-821 (4) 4.30 4.30

Souvenir Sheet

822 A118 40 le multi 3.25 3.25

Statue of Liberty, Cent. A119

Pictures of the statue by Peter B. Kaplan before and after renovation. Nos. 823, 825-826, 828-829, 831, vert.

1987, Jan. 2 *Perf. 14*

823 A119 70c Torch assembly .15 .15
824 A119 1.50 le Liberty holding torch .15 .15
825 A119 2 le Torch assembly, diff. .16 .16
826 A119 3 le Man, torch .24 .24
827 A119 4 le Crown .32 .32
828 A119 5 le Lighting of the statue .40 .40
829 A119 10 le Lighting, diff. .80 .80
830 A119 25 le Liberty Is. 2.00 2.00
831 A119 30 le Face 2.40 2.40
Nos. 823-831 (9) 6.62 6.62

UNICEF, 40th Anniv. A120

1987, Mar. 18 **Litho.** *Perf. 14*

832 A120 10 le multi .80 .80

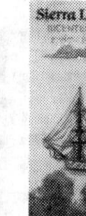

Nomoli Soapstone Sculpture — A121

Tall Ship in Harbor, Freetown — A122

1987, Jan. 2 *Perf. 15*

833 A121 2 le shown .15 .15
834 A121 5 le King's Yard Gate, 1817 .35 .35

Souvenir Sheet

835 A122 60 le shown 4.00 4.00

First settlement of liberated slaves returned to the African continent by the British, Freetown, bicent.

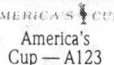

America's Cup — A123

Constellation, 1964 — A124

1987, June 15 **Litho.** *Perf. 14*

836 A123 1 le USA, 1987 .15 .15
837 A123 1.50 le New Zealand, 1987 .15 .15
838 A123 2.50 le French Kiss, 1987 .15 .15
839 A123 10 le Stars & Stripes, 1987 .60 .60
840 A123 15 le Australia II, 1983 .90 .90
841 A123 25 le Freedom, 1980 1.50 1.50
842 A123 30 le Kookaburra III, 1987 1.75 1.75
Nos. 836-842 (7) 5.20 5.20

Souvenir Sheet

843 A124 50 le shown 3.00 3.00

Nos. 837, 839 and 842 horiz.

For overprint see No. 964.

CAPEX '87 — A125

Disney characters, Canadian sights.

1987, June 15 *Perf. 11*

849 A125 2 le Parliament .15 .15
850 A125 5 le Totem poles .25 .25
851 A125 10 le Perce Rock .52 .52
852 A125 20 le Canadian Rockies 1.00 1.00
853 A125 25 le Old Quebec City 1.40 1.40
854 A125 45 le Aurora Borealis 2.25 2.25
855 A125 50 le Yukon P.O. 2.75 2.75
856 A125 75 le Niagara Falls 4.00 4.00
Nos. 849-856 (8) 12.32 12.32

Souvenir Sheets

857 A125 100 le Exploring Newfoundland 5.25 5.25
858 A125 100 le Calgary Exhibition and Stampede 5.25 5.25

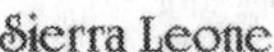

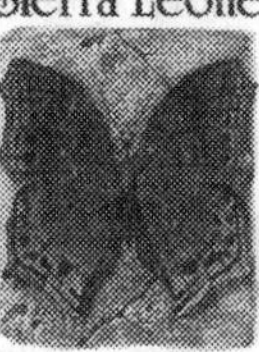

Butterflies — A126

1988 Summer Olympics, Seoul — A127

1987, Aug. 4 *Perf. 14*

859 A126 10c Blue salamis .15 .15
860 A126 20c Pale-tailed blue .15 .15
861 A126 40c Acraea swallowtail .15 .15
862 A126 1 le Broad blue-banded swallowtail .15 .15
863 A126 2 le Giant blue swallowtail .15 .15
864 A126 3 le Blood-red cymothoe .15 .15
865 A126 5 le Green-spotted swallowtail .20 .20
866 A126 10 le Small-striped swordtail .40 .40
867 A126 20 le Congo long-tailed blue .80 .80
868 A126 25 le Blue monarch 1.00 1.00
869 A126 30 le Black and yellow swallowtail 1.20 1.20
870 A126 45 le Western blue charaxes 1.75 1.75
871 A126 60 le Violet-washed charaxes 2.40 2.40
872 A126 75 le Orange admiral 3.00 3.00
873 A126 100 le Blue-patched judy 4.00 4.00
Nos. 859-873 (15) 15.65 15.65

Nos. 859-864 exist with 1989 date, No. 871 with 1990.

See Nos. 1257-1260, 1332A-1332I.

1988-89 *Perf. 12x12½*

859a A126 10c .15 .15
860a A126 20c .15 .15
861a A126 40c .15 .15
862a A126 1 le .15 .15
863a A126 2 le .15 .15
864a A126 3 le .15 .15
865a A126 5 le .20 .20
866a A126 10 le .40 .40
867a A126 20 le .80 .80
868a A126 25 le 1.00 1.00
869a A126 30 le 1.20 1.20
870a A126 45 le 1.75 1.75
873a A126 100 le 5.00 5.00
Nos. 859a-873a (13) 11.25 11.25

1987, Aug. 10

874 A127 5 le Cycling .25 .2
875 A127 10 le Equestrian .50 .5
876 A127 45 le Running 2.25 2.2
877 A127 50 le Tennis 2.50 2.5
Nos. 874-877 (4) 5.50 5.5

Souvenir Sheet

878 A127 100 le Gold medal, map 5.50 5.5

Works of Art by Marc Chagall, (1887-1985) A128

1987, Aug. 17 *Perf. 14*

879 A128 3 le The Quarrel, 1911-1912 .15 .15
880 A128 5 le Rebecca Giving Abraham's Servant a Drink .22 .22
881 A128 10 le The Village .45 .45
882 A128 20 le Ida at the Window, 1924 .45 .45
883 A128 25 le Promenade, 1913 1.10 1.10
884 A128 45 le Peasants 2.00 2.00
885 A128 50 le Turquoise Plate 2.25 2.25
886 A128 75 le Cemetery Gate, 1917 3.25 3.25
Nos. 879-886 (8) 9.87 9.87

Size: 111x95mm

Imperf

887 A128 100 le Wedding Feast, Stravinsky's Ballet, 1945 4.50 4.50
888 A128 100 le The Falling Angel 4.50 4.50

Nos. 879-886 printed in sheets of 10 (5x2). Stamp selvage inscribed with name of painting.

Transportation Innovations — A129

1987, Aug. 28 *Perf. 15*

889 A129 3 le Apollo 8, 1968, vert. .15 .15
890 A129 5 le Blanchard's Balloon, 1793 .20 .20
891 A129 10 le Lockheed Vega, 1932 .40 .40
892 A129 15 le Vicker's Vimy, 1919 .60 .60
893 A129 20 le Tank Mk1, c. 1918 .80 .80
894 A129 25 le Sikorsky VS-300, 1939 1.00 1.00
895 A129 30 le Flyer 1, 1903 1.20 1.20
896 A129 35 le Bleriot XI, 1909 1.40 1.40
897 A129 40 le Paraplane, 1983, vert. 1.60 1.60
898 A129 50 le Daimler's motorcycle, 1885 2.00 2.00
Nos. 889-898 (10) 9.35 9.35

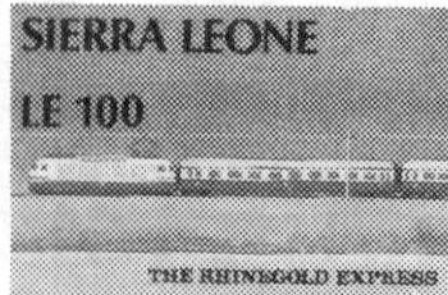

Rhinegold Express, Ireland (1st Electric Railroad, 1884) A129a

1987, Aug. 28 **Litho.** *Perf. 15*

898A A129a 100 le multi 4.00 4.00

Wimbledon Tennis Champions A130

1987, Sept. 4 *Perf. 14*

899 A130 2 le Evonne Goolagong, Australia .15 .15
900 A130 5 le Martina Navratilova, US-Czechoslovakia .30 .30
901 A130 10 le Jimmy Connors, US .60 .60
902 A130 15 le Bjorn Borg, Sweden .90 .90
903 A130 30 le Boris Becker, West Germany 1.90 1.90
904 A130 40 le John McEnroe, US 2.50 2.50
905 A130 50 le Chris Evert Lloyd, US 3.00 3.00
906 A130 75 le Virgina Wade, Great Britain 4.75 4.75
Nos. 899-906 (8) 14.10 14.10

Souvenir Sheets

907 A130 100 le Steffi Graf, German Open 1986 6.25 6.25
908 A130 100 le Boris Becker 6.25 6.25

For overprints see Nos. 965, 1023-1024.

Discovery of America, 500th Anniv. (in 1992) A131

5 le, Ducats, Santa Maria, Issac Abravanel (1437-1508), fund raiser. 10 le, Astrolabe, Pinta, Abraham Zacuto (1452-1515), astronomer. 45 le, Maravedis (coins), Nina, Luis de Santangel (1448-1498), fund raiser. 50 le, Tobacco leaves, plant, Luis de Torres (1453-1522), translator.

1987, Sept. 11

909 A131 5 le multicolored .22 .22
910 A131 10 le multicolored .45 .45
911 A131 45 le multicolored 2.00 2.00
912 A131 50 le multicolored 2.25 2.25
Nos. 909-912 (4) 4.92 4.92

Souvenir Sheet

913 A131 100 le Columbus, map 4.50 4.50

For overprint see No. 966.

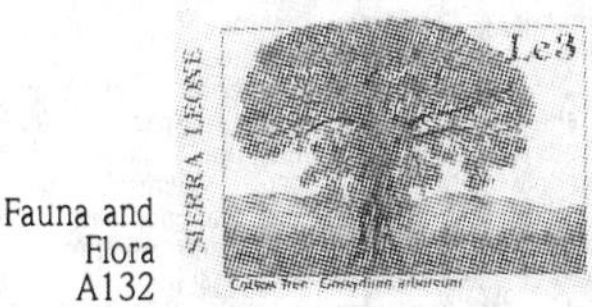

Fauna and Flora A132

1987, Sept. 15

914 A132 3 le Cotton tree .15 .15
915 A132 5 le Dwarf crocodile .20 .20
916 A132 10 le Kudu .40 .40
917 A132 20 le Yellowbells .80 .80
918 A132 25 le Hippopotamus 1.00 1.00
919 A132 45 le Comet orchid 1.80 1.80
920 A132 50 le Baobab tree 2.00 2.00
921 A132 75 le Elephant 3.00 3.00
Nos. 914-921 (8) 9.35 9.35

Souvenir Sheets

922 A132 100 le Banana, papaya, coconut, pineapple 4.00 4.00
923 A132 100 le Leopard 4.00 4.00

16th World Scout Jamboree, Australia, 1987-88 A133

Scouts, jamboree emblem, map of Australia and: 5 le, Ayers Rock. 15 le, Sailing. 40 le, Sydney skyline. 50 le, Sydney harbor bridge, opera house. 100 le, Flags of Sierra Leone, Australia and Scouts.

1987, Oct. 5 **Litho.** *Perf. 15*

924 A133 5 le multicolored .45 .45
925 A133 15 le multicolored 1.35 1.35
926 A133 40 le multicolored 3.60 3.60
927 A133 50 le multicolored 4.50 4.50
Nos. 924-927 (4) 9.90 9.90

Souvenir Sheet

928 A133 100 le multicolored 9.00 9.00

1.50 le stamps like the 50 le were printed but not issued.

US Constitution Bicentennial A134

Designs: 5 le, White House. 10 le, George Washington. 30 le, Patrick Henry. 65 le, New Hampshire state flag. 100 le, John Jay.

1987, Nov. 9 *Perf. 14*

929 A134 5 le multi .45 .45
930 A134 10 le multi, vert. .90 .90
931 A134 30 le multi, vert. 2.70 2.70
932 A134 65 le multi 5.85 5.85
Nos. 929-932 (4) 9.90 9.90

Souvenir Sheet

933 A134 100 le multi, vert. 9.00 9.00

Tokyo Disneyland, 5th Anniv. — A135

Disney animated characters and attractions at Tokyo Disneyland.

1987, Dec. 9 **Litho.** *Perf. 14*

934 A135 20c Space Mountain .15 .15
935 A135 40c Country Bear Jamboree .15 .15
936 A135 80c Mickey Mouse Review .15 .15
937 A135 1 le Mark Twain's River Boat .15 .15
938 A135 2 le Western River Railroad .18 .18
939 A135 3 le Pirates of the Caribbean .28 .28
940 A135 10 le Big Thunder Mountain train .90 .90
941 A135 20 le It's a Small World 1.80 1.80
942 A135 30 le Park entrance 2.70 2.70
Nos. 934-942 (9) 6.46 6.46

Souvenir Sheet

943 A135 65 le Cinderella's Castle 5.85 5.85

Mickey Mouse, 60th anniv.

Christmas A136

Paintings by Titian: 2 le, The Annunciation. 10 le, Madonna and Child with Saints. 20 le, Madonna and Child with Saints Ulfus and Brigid. 35 le, Madonna of the Cherries. 65 le, Pesaro Altarpiece, vert.

1987, Dec. 21

944 A136 2 le multicolored .18 .18
945 A136 10 le multicolored .90 .90
946 A136 20 le multicolored 1.80 1.80
947 A136 35 le multicolored 3.20 3.20
Nos. 944-947 (4) 6.08 6.08

Souvenir Sheet

948 A136 65 le multicolored 5.85 5.85

40th Wedding Anniv. of Queen Elizabeth II and Prince Philip A137

Mushrooms A138

1988, Feb. 15 **Litho.** *Perf. 14*

949 A137 2 le Ceremony, 1947 .18 .18
950 A137 3 le Elizabeth, Charles, 1948 .28 .28
951 A137 10 le Elizabeth, Anne, Charles, c. 1950 .90 .90
952 A137 50 le Elizabeth, c. 1970 4.50 4.50
Nos. 949-952 (4) 5.86 5.86

Souvenir Sheet

953 A137 65 le Wedding portrait 5.85 5.85

1988, Feb. 29

954 A138 3 le Russula cyanoxantha .18 .18
955 A138 10 le Lycoperdon perlatum .90 .90
956 A138 20 le Lactarius deliciosus 1.80 1.80
957 A138 30 le Boletus edulis 2.70 2.70
Nos. 954-957 (4) 5.58 5.58

Miniature Sheet

958 A138 65 le Amanita muscaria 5.80 5.80

Fish A139

1988, Apr. 13 *Perf. 15*

959 A139 3 le Golden pheasant .28 .28
960 A139 10 le Banded toothcarp .90 .90
961 A139 20 le Jewel fish 1.80 1.80
962 A139 35 le Butterfly fish 3.20 3.20
Nos. 959-962 (4) 6.18 6.18

Miniature Sheet

963 A139 65 le African longfin 5.90 5.90

Nos. 841, 903 and 911 Ovptd. for Philatelic Exhibitions in Black

a INDEPENDENCE 40

b

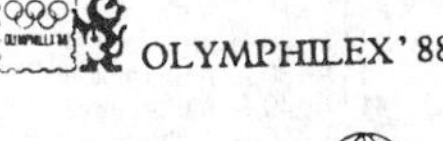

c Praga '88

1988, Apr. 19 **Litho.** *Perf. 14*

964 A123(a) 25 le multicolored 2.00 2.00
965 A130(b) 30 le multicolored 2.40 2.40
966 A131(c) 45 le multicolored 3.60 3.60
Nos. 964-966 (3) 8.00 8.00

Intl. Fund for Agricultural Development (IFAD), 10th Anniv. A140

1988, May 3 **Litho.** *Perf. 14*

967 A140 3 le Cocoa, coffee .28 .28
968 A140 15 le Tropical fruit 1.35 1.35
969 A140 25 le Rice harvest 2.25 2.25
Nos. 967-969 (3) 3.88 3.88

1988 Summer Olympics, Seoul — A141

Birds — A142

1988, June 15

970 A141 3 le Basketball .24 .24
971 A141 10 le Judo .80 .80
972 A141 15 le Gymnastics 1.20 1.20
973 A141 40 le Synchronized swimming 3.20 3.20
Nos. 970-973 (4) 5.44 5.44

Souvenir Sheet

974 A141 65 le Torch-bearer 5.25 5.25

1988, June 25

975 A142 3 le Swallow-tailed bee-eater .24 .24
976 A142 5 le Tooth-billed barbet .40 .40
977 A142 8 le African golden oriole .65 .65
978 A142 10 le Red bishop .80 .80
979 A142 12 le Red-billed shrike .95 .95
980 A142 20 le European bee-eater 1.60 1.60
981 A142 35 le Barbary shrike 2.80 2.80
982 A142 40 le Black-headed oriole 3.20 3.20
Nos. 975-982 (8) 10.64 10.64

Souvenir Sheets

983 A142 65 le Saddlebill stork 5.25 5.25
984 A142 65 le Purple heron 5.25 5.25

Merchant Marine A143

1988, July 1

985 A143 3 le Aureol .24 .24
986 A143 10 le Dunkwa .80 .80
987 A143 15 le Melampus 1.20 1.20
988 A143 30 le Dumbaia 2.40 2.40
Nos. 985-988 (4) 4.64 4.64

Souvenir Sheet

989 A143 65 le Loading containers 5.25 5.25

Paintings by Titian — A144

Designs: 1 le, The Concert, 1512. 2 le, Philip II of Spain, c. 1550-51. 3 le, St. Sebastian, c. 1520-22. 5 le, Martyrdom of St. Peter Martyr, c. 1528-30. 15 le, St. Jerome, 1560. 20 le, St. Mark Enthroned with Saints Cosmas and Damian, Roch and Sebastian, c. 1508-09. 25 le, Portrait of a Young Man, 1506. 30 le, St. Jerome in Penitence, 1555. No. 998, Self-portrait, 1567. No. 999, Orpheus and Eurydice, 1508.

1988, Aug. 22 **Litho.** *Perf. 13½x14*

990 A144 1 le multicolored .15 .15
991 A144 2 le multicolored .16 .16
992 A144 3 le multicolored .24 .24
993 A144 5 le multicolored .40 .40
994 A144 15 le multicolored 1.20 1.20
995 A144 20 le multicolored 1.60 1.60
996 A144 25 le multicolored 2.00 2.00
997 A144 30 le multicolored 2.40 2.40
Nos. 990-997 (8) 8.15 8.15

Souvenir Sheets

998 A144 50 le multicolored 4.00 4.00
999 A144 50 le multicolored 4.00 4.00

John F. Kennedy A145

Kennedy half-dollar and space achievements: 3 le, Recovery of a Mercury capsule by the US Navy. 5 le, Splashdown and recovery of Liberty Bell 7, July 21, 1961, piloted by Virgil "Gus" Grissom, vert. 15 le, Launch of Freedom 7, piloted by Alan B. Shepherd, May 5, 1961, vert. 40 le, Friendship 7 in orbit, piloted by John Glenn, Feb. 20, 1962. 65 le, Kennedy, speech excerpt.

1988, Sept. 26 **Litho.** *Perf. 14*

1000 A145 3 le multicolored .25 .25
1001 A145 5 le multicolored .40 .40
1002 A145 15 le multicolored 1.20 1.20
1003 A145 40 le multicolored 1.60 1.60
Nos. 1000-1003 (4) 3.45 3.45

Souvenir Sheet

1004 A145 65 le multicolored 5.25 5.25

Intl. Red Cross and Red Crescent Organizations, 125th Annivs. — A146

1988, Nov. 1

1005 A146	3 le	Africa food relief	.25	.25
1006 A146	10 le	Battle of Solferino	.80	.80
1007 A146	20 le	WWII Pacific	1.60	1.60
1008 A146	40 le	WWI Europe	3.20	3.20
		Nos. 1005-1008 (4)	5.85	5.85

Souvenir Sheet

Size: 41x28mm

1009 A146	65 le	Alfred Nobel, Dunant, horiz.	5.25	5.25

Miniature Sheet

Christmas, Mickey Mouse 60th Anniv. — A147

Walt Disney characters dancing: No. 1010a, Huey, Dewey and Louie. No. 1010b, Clarabelle Cow. No. 1010c, Goofy. No. 1010d, Scrooge McDuck and Grandma Duck. No. 1010e, Donald Duck. No. 1010f, Daisy Duck. No. 1010g, Minnie Mouse. No. 1010h, Mickey Mouse. No. 1011, Dance, c. 1920. No. 1012, Dance, c. 1950.

1988, Dec. 1 *Perf. 13½x14*

1010 A147	Sheet of 8	5.50	5.50
a.-h.	10 le any single	.70	.70

Souvenir Sheets

1011 A147	70 le	multicolored	4.50	4.50
1012 A147	70 le	multicolored	4.50	4.50

Sierra Leone Le3

Christmas A148

Paintings by Rubens (details): 3 le, Adoration of the Magi (Virgin and Child). 3.60 le, Adoration of the Shepherds (shepherds and child). 5 le, Adoration of the Magi (Magi). 10 le, Adoration of the Shepherds (Virgin and Child). 20 le, Virgin and Child Surrounded by Flowers. 40 le, St. Gregory the Great and Other Saints (Virgin and Child). 60 le, Adoration of the Magi, (Virgin, Child and Magi), diff. 80 le, Madonna and Child with Saints. No. 1021, St. Gregory the Great and Other Saints. No. 1022, Virgin and Child Enthroned with Saints.

1988, Dec. 15 Litho. *Perf. 13½x14*

1013 A148	3 le	multicolored	.18	.18
1014 A148	3.60 le	multicolored	.22	.22
1015 A148	5 le	multicolored	.30	.30
1016 A148	10 le	multicolored	.60	.60
1017 A148	20 le	multicolored	1.20	1.20
1018 A148	40 le	multicolored	2.40	2.40
1019 A148	60 le	multicolored	3.60	3.60
1020 A148	80 le	multicolored	4.80	4.80
		Nos. 1013-1020 (8)	13.30	13.30

Souvenir Sheets

1021 A148	100 le	multicolored	6.00	6.00
1022 A148	100 le	multicolored	6.00	6.00

No. 907 Ovptd. "GRAND SLAM WINNER" in Gold

1989, Jan. 16 *Perf. 14*

Souvenir Sheets

1023 A130	100 le	multicolored	5.20	5.20

No. 1023 exists with four diff. gold marginal overprints: "AUSTRALIAN OPEN / JANUARY 11-24, 1988 / GRAF v EVERET / 6-1 / 7-6," "FRENCH OPEN / MAY 23-JUNE 5, 1988 / GRAF v ZVEREVA / 6-0 / 6-0," "WIMBLEDON / JUNE 20-JULY 4, 1988 / GRAF v NAVRATILOVA / 5-7 / 6-2 / 6-1," or "U.S. OPEN / AUGUST 29-SEPTEMBER 11, 1988 / GRAF v SABATINI / 6-3 / 3-6 / 6-1."

No. 907 Ovptd. "GOLD MEDALIST" in Gold

1989, Jan. 16 Litho. *Perf. 14*

1024 A130	100 le	multi	5.20	5.20

Marginal overprint: "SEOUL OLYMPICS 1988 / GRAF v SABATINI / 6-3 / 6-3."

Medalists of the 1988 Summer Olympics, Seoul A149

Designs: 3 le, Christian Schenk, German Democratic Republic, decathlon. 6 le, Hitoshi Saito, Japan, heavyweight judo. 10 le, Jutta Niehaus, Federal Republic of Germany, women's road race. 15 le, Tomas Lange, German Democratic Republic, single sculls. 20 le, Matthew Biondi, US, 50m and 100m freestyle. 30 le, Carl Lewis, US, 100m sprint. 40 le, Nicole Uphoff, Federal Republic of Germany, individual dressage. 50 le, Andras Sike, Hungary, 126-pound Greco-Roman wrestling. No. 1033, Gold medal, five-ring emblem. No. 1034, Torch, five-ring emblem.

1989, Apr. 28 Litho. *Perf. 14*

1025 A149	3 le	multicolored	.15	.15
1026 A149	6 le	multicolored	.30	.30
1027 A149	10 le	multicolored	.50	.50
1028 A149	15 le	multicolored	.75	.75
1029 A149	20 le	multicolored	1.00	1.00
1030 A149	30 le	multicolored	1.50	1.50
1031 A149	40 le	multicolored	2.00	2.00
1032 A149	50 le	multicolored	2.50	2.50
		Nos. 1025-1032 (8)	8.70	8.70

Souvenir Sheets

1033 A149	100 le	multicolored	5.00	5.00
1034 A149	100 le	multicolored	5.00	5.00

Name of athlete not inscribed on No. 1031.

1990 World Cup Soccer Championships, Italy — A150

1989, May 8

1035 A150	3 le	Brazil vs. Sweden	.15	.15
1036 A150	6 le	Germany vs. Hungary	.30	.30
1037 A150	8 le	England vs. Germany	.40	.40
1038 A150	10 le	Argentina vs. The Netherlands	.50	.50
1039 A150	12 le	Brazil vs. Czechoslovakia	.60	.60
1040 A150	20 le	Germany vs. The Netherlands	1.00	1.00
1041 A150	30 le	Italy vs. Germany	1.50	1.50
1042 A150	40 le	Brazil vs. Italy	2.00	2.00
		Nos. 1035-1042 (8)	6.45	6.45

Souvenir Sheets

1043 A150	100 le	Uruguay vs. Brazil	5.00	5.00
1044 A150	100 le	Argentina vs. Germany	5.00	5.00

Mano River Union, 15th Anniv. A151

Designs: 1 le, Sierra Leone-Guinea postal service. 3 le, Presidents Momoh, Conte of Guinea and Doe of Liberia. 10 le, Freetown-Monrovia Highway under construction. 15 le, Presidents signing the Communique at a 1988 summit.

1989, May 19 *Perf. 14*

1045 A151	1 le	multicolored	.15	.15
1046 A151	3 le	multicolored	.24	.24
1047 A151	10 le	multicolored	.80	.80
		Nos. 1045-1047 (3)	1.19	1.19

Souvenir Sheet

1048 A151	15 le	multicolored	1.20	1.20

SIERRA LEONE

Le3

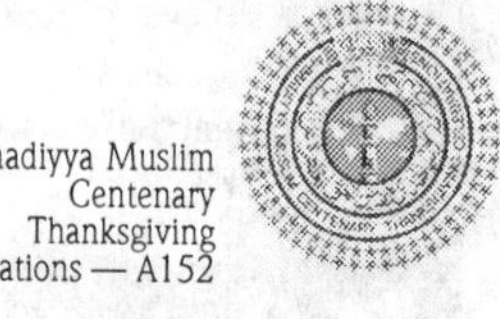

Ahmadiyya Muslim Centenary Thanksgiving Celebrations — A152

1989, June 8

1049 A152	3 le	black & brt blue	.24	.24

Miniature Sheets

Shakespeare's 425th Birth Anniv. — A153

Scenes from the playwright's works.

No. 1050: a, Richard III. b, Othello (Desdemona and two men). c, The Two Gentlemen of Verona. d, Macbeth (chamber). e, Hamlet. f, Taming of the Shrew (scene with dog). g, The Merry Wives of Windsor. h, Henry IV (assembly room).

No. 1051: a, Macbeth (horsemen). b, Romeo and Juliet. c, Merchant of Venice. d, As You Like It. e, Taming of the Shrew (ruined meal). f, King Lear. g, Othello (death scene). h, Henry IV (street scene).

1989, May 30 *Perf. 13*

1050	Sheet of 8 + label	6.00	6.00
a.-h.	A153 15 le any single	.75	.75
1051	Sheet of 8 + label	6.00	6.00
a.-h.	A153 15 le any single	.75	.75

Souvenir Sheets

1052 A153	100 le	Portrait	5.00	5.00
1053 A153	100 le	Portrait, coat of arms	5.00	5.00

Nos. 1050-1051 contain center label picturing Shakespeare's portrait (No. 1050) or his birthplace in Stratford (No. 1051).

Paintings by Takeuchi Seiho (1864-1942) — A154

Designs: 3 le, Lapping Waves. 6 le, Hazy Moon, vert. 8 le, Passing Spring, vert. 10 le, Mackerels. 12 le, Calico Cat. 30 le, The First Time To Be a Model, vert. 40 le, Kingly Lion. 75 le, After a Shower, vert. No. 1062, Domesticated Monkeys and Rabbits. No. 1063, Dozing in the Midst of All the Chirping, vert.

Perf. 14x13½, 13½x14

1989, July 3 Litho.

1054 A154	3 le	multicolored	.15	.15
1055 A154	6 le	multicolored	.22	.22
1056 A154	8 le	multicolored	.28	.28
1057 A154	10 le	multicolored	.35	.35
1058 A154	12 le	multicolored	.42	.42
1059 A154	30 le	multicolored	1.05	1.05
1060 A154	40 le	multicolored	1.45	1.45
1061 A154	75 le	multicolored	2.65	2.65
		Nos. 1054-1061 (8)	6.57	6.57

Souvenir Sheets

1062 A154	150 le	multicolored	4.50	4.50
1063 A154	150 le	multicolored	4.50	4.50

Hirohito (1901-89) and enthronement of Akihito as emperor of Japan.

See Nos. 1098-1129.

PHILEXFRANCE '89, French Revolution Bicent. — A155

Famous people, sites, exhibition and anniv. emblems: 6 le, Robespierre (1758-94), the Bastille. 20 le, Georges Jacques Danton (1759-94), the Louvre. 45 le, Marie Antoinette (1755-93), Notre Dame Cathedral interior. 80 le, Louis XVI (1754-93), Palace of Versailles. 150 le, Revolutionaries in Paris, vert.

1989, July 14 Litho. *Perf. 14*

1064 A155	6 le	multicolored	.30	.30
1065 A155	20 le	multicolored	1.00	1.00
1066 A155	45 le	multicolored	2.25	2.25
1067 A155	80 le	multicolored	4.00	4.00
		Nos. 1064-1067 (4)	7.55	7.55

Souvenir Sheet

1068 A155	150 le	multicolored	7.50	7.50

Miniature Sheets

Space Exploration — A156

Satellites, probes and spacecraft.

No. 1069: a, Sputnik, 1957. b, Telstar, 1962. c, Rendezvous of Gemini 6 and 7, 1965. d, Yuri Gagarin, 1st man in space, 1961. e, Mariner, 1964. f, Surveyor on Mars, 1966. g, US-Canadian Alouette satellite, 1962. h, Edward White, 1st American to walk in space, 1965. i, OGO-4 satellite, 1967.

No. 1070: a, Buzz Aldrin on the Moon, Apollo 11 mission, 1969. b, Apollo 15 mission lunar rover. c, Apollo 15 crew member. d, Conducting experiments on the lunar surface. e, Splitrock, Valley of Taurus-Littrow. f, Saluting the flag, Apollo 15 lunar module. g, Solar wind experiment. h, Lunar rover, diff. i, Apollo command module.

No. 1071: a, Module separation. b, Docking maneuvers. c, Lunar module in space. d, Second stage separation. e, Module transposition. f, Lunar module controlled descent, Moon's surface. g, Apollo 11 liftoff, 1969. h, Lunar module separates from command module. i, Neil Armstrong's first step on the Moon.

No. 1072: a, Mariner-Mars, 1971. b, Mariner 10, 1973. c, Viking, 1975. d, Skylab, 1974. e, Soyuz-Salyut, 1974. f, Viking robot craft, 1974. g, Pioneer 2, 1973. h, Apollo-Soyuz, 1975. i, Pioneer-Venus, 1978.

No. 1073: a, Apollo 17 lunar module, 1972. b, Command module jettison of service module before reentry. c, Soyuz 11, 1971. d, Lunar module liftoff. e, U.S. Navy recovery operation. f, Mars 2, 1971. g, Command module in docking position. h, Luna 17, 1970. i, Mars 3, 1971.

No. 1074: a, Voyager 1 and 2, 1977. b, Columbia space shuttle, 1981. c, Mir space station, 1986. d, IUE-Ultraviolet Explorer, US, U.K. and the European Space Agency, 1978. e, Astronaut operating out of shuttle cargo bay, 1983. f, Magellan, 1989. g, Soyuz-Salyut, 1978. h, STS-10, 1984. i, Shuttle, space telescope, 1989.

No. 1075, Spacelab. No. 1076, Future space station. No. 1077, Voyager.

1989, July 20 Litho. *Perf. 14*

1069	Sheet of 9	2.75	2.75
a.-i.	A156 10 le any single	.30	.30
1070	Sheet of 9	2.75	2.75
a.-i.	A156 10 le any single	.30	.30
1071	Sheet of 9	2.75	2.75
a.-i.	A156 10 le any single	.30	.30
1072	Sheet of 9	4.05	4.05
a.-i.	A156 15 le any single	.45	.45
1073	Sheet of 9	4.05	4.05
a.-i.	A156 15 le any single	.45	.45
1074	Sheet of 9	4.05	4.05
a.-i.	A156 15 le any single	.45	.45

Souvenir Sheets

1075 A156	100 le	multicolored	3.00	3.00
1076 A156	100 le	multicolored	3.00	3.00
1077 A156	100 le	multicolored	3.00	3.00

Nos. 1069f is incorrectly inscribed "Mars" instead of "Moon."

Orchids — A157 Butterflies — A158

1989, Sept. 8 Litho. *Perf. 14*

1078 A157 3 le Bulbophyllum barbigerum .15 .15
1079 A157 6 le Bulbophyllum falcatum .20 .20
1080 A157 12 le Habenaria macrara .38 .38
1081 A157 20 le Eurychone rothchildiana .60 .60
1082 A157 50 le Calyptrochilum christyanum 1.50 1.50
1083 A157 60 le Bulbophyllum distans 1.80 1.80
1084 A157 70 le Eulophia guineensis 2.10 2.10
1085 A157 80 le Diaphananthe pellucida 2.40 2.40
Nos. 1078-1085 (8) 9.13 9.13

Souvenir Sheets

1086 A157 100 le Cyrtorchis arcuata 3.00 3.00
1087 A157 100 le Butterflies, Eulophia cucullata 3.00 3.00

1989, Sept. 11

1088 A158 6 le Salamis temora .20 .20
1089 A158 12 le Pseudacraea lucretia .38 .38
1090 A158 18 le Charaxes boueti .55 .55
1091 A158 30 le Graphium antheus .90 .90
1092 A158 40 le Colotis protomedia 1.20 1.20
1093 A158 60 le Asterope pechueli 1.80 1.80
1094 A158 72 le Coenura aurantiaca 2.15 2.15
1095 A158 80 le Precis octavia 2.40 2.40
Nos. 1088-1095 (8) 9.58 9.58

Souvenir Sheets

1096 A158 100 le Charaxes cithaeron 3.00 3.00
1097 A158 100 le Euphaedra themis 3.00 3.00

Nos. 1088-1090, 1095 and 1097 horiz.

Art Type of 1989

Paintings by Hiroshige in the series Fifty-three Stations on the Tokaido: No. 1098, Coolies Warming Themselves at Hamamatsu. No. 1099, Imakiri Ford at Maisaka. No. 1100, Pacific Ocean Seen from Shirasuka. No. 1101, Futakawa Street Singers. No. 1102, Repairing Yoshida Castle. No. 1103, The Inn at Akasaka. No. 1104, The Bridge to Okazaki. No. 1105, Samurai's Wife Entering Narumi. No. 1106, Harbour at Kuwana. No. 1107, Autumn in Ishiyakushi. No. 1108, Snowfall at Kameyama. No. 1109, The Frontier Station of Seki. No. 1110, Teahouse at Sakanoshita. No. 1111, Kansai Houses at Minakushi. No. 1112, Kusatsu Station. No. 1113, Ferry to Kawasaki. No. 1114, The Hilly Town of Hodogaya. No. 1115, Lute Players at Fujisawa. No. 1116, Mild Rainstorm at Oiso. No. 1117, Lake Ashi and Mountains of Hakone. No. 1118, Twilight at Numazu. No. 1119, Mount Fuji From Hara. No. 1120, Samurai's Children Riding Through Yoshiwara. No. 1121, Mountain Pass at Yui. No. 1122, Harbour at Ejiri. No. 1123, Stopping at Fujieda. No. 1124, Misty Kanaya on the Oi River. No. 1125, The Bridge to Kakegawa. No. 1126, Teahouse at Fukuroi. No. 1127, The Ford at Mistuke. No. 1128, Sanjo Bridge in Kyoto. No. 1129, Nibonbashi Bridge in Edo.

1989, Nov. 13 Litho. *Perf. 14x13½*

1098-1127 A154 25 le Set of 30 22.50 22.50

Souvenir sheets

1128-1129 A154 120 le each 4.00 4.00

Hirohito (1901-1989) and enthronement of Akihito as emperor of Japan.

Souvenir Sheet

Jefferson Memorial, Washington, DC — A159

1989, Nov. 17 Litho. *Perf. 14*

1136 A159 100 le multicolored 3.00 3.00

World Stamp Expo '89.

Endangered Species — A160

1989, Nov. 29 *Perf. 14*

1137 A160 6 le Humpback whale .18 .18
1138 A160 9 le Formosan sika deer .28 .28
1139 A160 16 le Spanish lynx .48 .48
1140 A160 20 le Goitered gazelle .60 .60
1141 A160 30 le Japanese sea lion .90 .90
1142 A160 50 le Long-eared owl 1.50 1.50
1143 A160 70 le Chinese copper pheasant 2.10 2.10
1144 A160 100 le Siberian tiger 3.00 3.00
Nos. 1137-1144 (8) 9.04 9.04

Souvenir Sheets

1145 A160 150 le Mauritius kestrel falcon 4.50 4.50
1146 A160 150 le Crested ibis 4.50 4.50

World Stamp Expo '89.

Christmas — A161

Disney characters and classic automobiles: 3 le, 1934 Phantom II Rolls-Royce Roadstar. 6 le, 1935 Mercedes-Benz 500K. 10 le, 1938 Jaguar SS-100. 12 le, 1941 Jeep. 20 le, 1937 Buick Roadmaster Sedan Model 91. 30 le, 1948 Tucker. 40 le, 1933 Alfa Romeo. 50 le, 1937 Cord. No. 1155, 1938 Fiat Topolino. No. 1156, 1931 Pontiac Model 401, 1929 Pontiac Landau.

1989, Dec. 18 *Perf. 14x13½*

1147 A161 3 le multicolored .15 .15
1148 A161 6 le multicolored .20 .20
1149 A161 10 le multicolored .32 .32
1150 A161 12 le multicolored .38 .38
1151 A161 20 le multicolored .65 .65
1152 A161 30 le multicolored .98 .98
1153 A161 40 le multicolored 1.30 1.30
1154 A161 50 le multicolored 1.60 1.60
Nos. 1147-1154 (8) 5.58 5.58

Souvenir Sheets

1155 A161 100 le multicolored 3.25 3.25
1156 A161 100 le multicolored 3.25 3.25

Christmas — A162

Religious paintings by Rembrandt: 3 le, Adoration of the Magi. 6 le, The Holy Family with a Cat. 10 le, The Holy Family with Angels. 15 le, Simeon in the Temple. 30 le, The Circumcision. 90 le, The Holy Family. 100 le, The Visitation. 120 le, The Flight into Egypt. No. 1165, The Adoration of the Shepherds. No. 1166, The Presentation of Jesus in the Temple.

1989, Dec. 22 *Perf. 14*

1157 A162 3 le multicolored .15 .15
1158 A162 6 le multicolored .20 .20
1159 A162 10 le multicolored .32 .32
1160 A162 15 le multicolored .48 .48
1161 A162 30 le multicolored .98 .98
1162 A162 90 le multicolored 2.90 2.90
1163 A162 100 le multicolored 3.25 3.25
1164 A162 120 le multicolored 4.00 4.00
Nos. 1157-1164 (8) 12.28 12.28

Souvenir Sheets

1165 A162 150 le multicolored 4.75 4.75
1166 A162 150 le multicolored 4.75 4.75

Miniature Sheets

Exploration of Mars — A163

No. 1167: a, Kepler. b, Galileo. c, Drawings by Huygens in 1672 and Schiaparelli in 1886. d, Sir W. Herschel. e, Percival Lowell in Arizona, 1896-1907. f, Mars. g, Mariner 4, 1965. h, Mars 2, 1971. i, Mars 3, 1971.

No. 1168: a, Mariner 9, 1971. b, Mariner 9, Phobos. c, Cydonia Region. d, South polar cap. e, Profile of Mars. f, Polar cap, diff. g, Nix Olympica. h, Grand Canyon of Mars. i, North Pole.

No. 1169: a, Olympus Mons. b, Viking 1, July 1976. c, Viking 2 releases Lander, Sept. 1976. d, Lander entering Mars's atmosphere. e, Parachute deployed. f, Terminal descent. g, Viking Lander on Mars. h, Soil sampler (robotic arm). i, Soil Sampler (US flag, machine).

No. 1170: a, Martian dusk. b, Project Deimos. c, Exploration of Mars (astronauts surveying land). d, Return to Rombus. e, US rocket bound for Mars. f, Spacecraft bound for Mars. g, Spacecraft in Martian orbit. h, Mission to Mars (astronauts weightless in spacecraft cabin). i, Space station.

No. 1171, "The Face," Mars.

1990 Litho. *Perf. 14*

1167 Sheet of 9 25.00 25.00
a.-i. A163 175 le any single 2.75 2.75
1168 Sheet of 9 25.00 25.00
a.-i. A163 175 le any single 2.75 2.75
1169 Sheet of 9 25.00 25.00
a.-i. A163 175 le any single 2.75 2.75
1170 Sheet of 9 25.00 25.00
a.-i. A163 175 le any single 2.75 2.75

Souvenir Sheet

1171 A163 150 le multicolored 2.50 2.50
1171A A163 150 le Space station 2.50 2.50

Issued: No. 1171A, Dec. 24; others, Jan. 15.

Extreme speculation has occured with this issue, centered around No. 1171, the face on Mars stamp.

World War II — A164

USAF aircraft.

1990, Feb. 5 Litho. *Perf. 14*

1172 A164 1 le Doolittle Raid B-25 .15 .15
1173 A164 2 le B-24 Liberator .15 .15
1174 A164 3 le A-20 Boston .15 .15
1175 A164 9 le P-38 Lightning .28 .28
1176 A164 12 le B-26 .35 .35
1177 A164 16 le B-17 F .48 .48
1178 A164 50 le B-25 D Mitchell 1.50 1.50
1179 A164 80 le Boeing B-29 2.40 2.40
1180 A164 90 le B-17 G 2.70 2.70
1181 A164 100 le The Enola Gay 3.00 3.00
Nos. 1172-1181 (10) 11.16 11.16

Souvenir Sheets

1182 A164 150 le B-25, USS Hornet 4.50 4.50
1183 A164 150 le B-17 G 4.50 4.50

Stage and Screen Roles Played by Sir Laurence Olivier (1907-1989) — A165

1990, Apr. 27

1184 A165 3 le Antony & Cleopatra, 1951 .15 .15
1185 A165 9 le Henry V, 1943 .18 .18
1186 A165 16 le Oedipus, 1945 .32 .32
1187 A165 20 le Wuthering Heights, 1939 .40 .40
1188 A165 30 le Marathon Man, 1976 .60 .60
1189 A165 70 le Othello, 1964 1.40 1.40
1190 A165 175 le Beau Geste, 1929 3.50 3.50
1191 A165 200 le Richard III, 1956 4.00 4.00
Nos. 1184-1191 (8) 10.55 10.55

Souvenir Sheets

1192 A165 250 le The Battle of Britain, 1969 5.00 5.00
1193 A165 250 le Hamlet, 1947 5.00 5.00

Walt Disney Characters, Settings in Sierra Leone — A166

1990, Apr. 23

1194 A166 3 le Bauxite mine .15 .15
1195 A166 6 le Panning for gold .15 .15
1196 A166 10 le Lungi Intl. Airport .24 .24
1197 A166 12 le Old Fourah Bay College .30 .30
1198 A166 16 le Mining bauxite .42 .42
1199 A166 20 le Rice harvest .48 .48
1200 A166 30 le The Cotton Tree .75 .75
1201 A166 100 le Rutile Mine 2.50 2.50
1202 A166 200 le Fishing at Goderich 5.00 5.00
1203 A166 225 le Bintumani Hotel 5.50 5.50
Nos. 1194-1203 (10) 15.49 15.49

Souvenir Sheets

1204 A166 250 le Market Place, King Jimmy 5.00 5.00
1205 A166 250 le Diamond mining 5.00 5.00

Penny Black, 150th Anniv. — A167

1990, May 3 *Perf. 14*

1206 A167 50 le deep ultra 1.00 1.00
1207 A167 100 le violet brown 2.50 2.50

Souvenir Sheet

1208 A167 250 le black 5.00 5.00

Market value for a particular scarce stamp may remain relatively low if few collectors want it.

World Cup Soccer Championships, Italy — A168

Team photographs.

1990, May 11 Litho. *Perf. 14*

1209 A168 15 le Colombia .25 .25
1210 A168 15 le United Arab Emirates .25 .25
1211 A168 15 le South Korea .25 .25
1212 A168 15 le Cameroun .25 .25
1213 A168 15 le Costa Rica .25 .25
1214 A168 15 le Romania .25 .25
1215 A168 15 le Yugoslavia .25 .25
1216 A168 15 le Egypt .25 .25
1217 A168 30 le Netherlands .50 .50
1218 A168 30 le Uruguay .50 .50
1219 A168 30 le USSR .50 .50
1220 A168 30 le Czechoslovakia .50 .50
1221 A168 30 le Scotland .50 .50
1222 A168 30 le Belgium .50 .50
1223 A168 30 le Austria .50 .50
1224 A168 30 le Sweden .50 .50
1225 A168 45 le West Germany .75 .75
1226 A168 45 le England .75 .75
1227 A168 45 le United States .75 .75
1228 A168 45 le Ireland .75 .75
1229 A168 45 le Spain .75 .75
1230 A168 45 le Brazil .75 .75
1231 A168 45 le Italy .75 .75
1232 A168 45 le Argentina .75 .75
Nos. 1209-1232 (24) 12.00 12.00

No. 1209 spelled "Columbia," No. 1218 "Uraguay," No. 1220 "Czecheslovakia" on stamps.

Great Crested Grebe A169

1990, June 4

1233 A169 3 le shown .15 .15
1234 A169 6 le Green woodhoopoe .15 .15
1235 A169 10 le African jacana .18 .18
1236 A169 12 le Avocet .20 .20
1237 A169 20 le African finfoot .35 .35
1238 A169 80 le Glossy ibis 1.40 1.40
1239 A169 150 le Hamerkop 2.50 2.50
1240 A169 200 le Greater honey guide 3.40 3.40
Nos. 1233-1240 (8) 8.33 8.33

Souvenir Sheets

1241 A169 250 le Painted snipe 4.25 4.25
1242 A169 250 le Palm swift 4.25 4.25

Mickey as Yeoman Warder A170

Disney characters: 6 le, Scrooge as lamplighter. 12 le, Knight Goofy. 15 le, Clarabell as Anne Boleyn. 75 le, Minnie Mouse as Queen Elizabeth I. 100 le, Donald Duck as chimmey sweep. 125 le, Pete as King Henry VIII. 150 le, May dancers in Salisbury. No. 1251, Boadicea, Queen of the Iceni. No. 1252, Lawyers at Parliament House.

1990, June 6 *Perf. 13½x14*

1243 A170 3 le multicolored .15 .15
1244 A170 6 le multicolored .15 .15
1245 A170 12 le multicolored .20 .20
1246 A170 15 le multicolored .25 .25
1247 A170 75 le multicolored 1.25 1.25
1248 A170 100 le multicolored 1.75 1.75
1249 A170 125 le multicolored 2.25 2.25
1250 A170 150 le multicolored 2.50 2.50
Nos. 1243-1250 (8) 8.50 8.50

Souvenir Sheets

1251 A170 250 le multicolored 4.50 4.50
1252 A170 250 le multicolored 4.50 4.50

Queen Mother, 90th Birthday — A171

1990, July 5 *Perf. 14*

1253 A171 75 le shown 1.25 1.25
1254 A171 75 le Wearing black hat 1.25 1.25
1255 A171 75 le Wearing yellow hat 1.25 1.25
Nos. 1253-1255 (3) 3.75 3.75

Souvenir Sheet

1256 A171 250 le Like No. 1252 4.50 4.50

Butterfly Type of 1987

1990 *Perf. 12½x11½*

1257 A126 3 le like No. 861 .15 .15
1258 A126 9 le like No. 864 .15 .15
1259 A126 12 le like No. 859 .20 .20
1260 A126 16 le like No. 860 .28 .28
Nos. 1257-1260 (4) .78 .78

Inscribed 1989.

Miniature Sheet

Wildlife A172

Designs: No. 1261a, Golden cat. b, White-backed night heron. c, Bateleur eagle. d, Marabou stork. e, White-faced whistling duck. f, Aardvark. g, Royal antelope. h, Pygmy hippopotamus. i, Leopard. j, Sacred ibis. k, Mona monkey. l, Darter. m, Chimpanzee. n, African elephant. o, Potto. p, African manatee. q, African fish eagle. r, African spoonbill.

1990, Sept. 24 Litho. *Perf. 14*

1261 Sheet of 18 7.60 7.60
a.-r. A172 25 le any single .42 .42

Souvenir Sheet

1262 A172 150 le Crowned eagle, vert. 2.50 2.50

No. 1261 printed in continuous design showing map of Sierra Leone in background.

A173 A174

Carousel animals.

1990, Oct. 22 Litho. *Perf. 14*

1263 A173 5 le Rabbit .15 .15
1264 A173 10 le Horse with panther saddle .16 .16
1265 A173 20 le Ostrich .32 .32
1266 A173 30 le Zebra .48 .48
1267 A173 50 le White horse .80 .80
1268 A173 80 le Sea monster 1.30 1.30
1269 A173 100 le Giraffe 1.60 1.60
1270 A173 150 le Armored horse 2.40 2.40
1271 A173 200 le Camel 3.20 3.20
Nos. 1263-1271 (9) 10.41 10.41

Souvenir Sheets

1272 A173 300 le Centaur, Lord Baden-Powell 4.75 4.75
1273 A173 300 le Horse head 4.75 4.75

1990, Nov. 12 Litho. *Perf. 14*

1274 A174 5 le Men's 100-meter race .15 .15
1275 A174 10 le Men's 4x400-meter relay .16 .16
1276 A174 20 le Men's 100-meter race, diff. .32 .32
1277 A174 30 le Weight lifting .48 .48
1278 A174 40 le Freestyle wrestling .65 .65
1279 A174 80 le Water polo 1.30 1.30
1280 A174 150 le Women's gymnastics 2.40 2.40
1281 A174 200 le Cycling 3.20 3.20
Nos. 1274-1281 (8) 8.66 8.66

Souvenir Sheets

1282 A174 400 le Boxing 6.40 6.40
1283 A174 400 le Olympic flag 6.40 6.40

1992 Summer Olympics, Barcelona.

Christmas A175

Paintings: 10 le, The Holy Family Resting by Rembrandt. 20 le, The Holy Family with St. Elizabeth by Andrea Mantegna. 30 le, Virgin and Child with an Angel by Correggio. 50 le, The Annunciation by Bernardo Strozzi. 100 le, Madonna and Child Appearing to St. Anthony by Filippino Lippi. 175 le, Virgin and Child by Giovanni Boltraffio. 200 le, The Esterhazy Madonna by Raphael. 300 le, Coronation of Mary by Orcagna. No. 1292, Adoration of the Shepherds by Bronzino. No. 1293, Adoration of the Shepherds by Gerard David.

1990, Dec. 17 *Perf. 13*

1284 A175 10 le multicolored .16 .16
1285 A175 20 le multicolored .32 .32
1286 A175 30 le multicolored .48 .48
1287 A175 50 le multicolored .80 .80
1288 A175 100 le multicolored 1.60 1.60
1289 A175 175 le multicolored 2.80 2.80
1290 A175 200 le multicolored 3.20 3.20
1291 A175 300 le multicolored 4.80 4.80
Nos. 1284-1291 (8) 14.16 14.16

Souvenir Sheets

1292 A175 400 le multicolored 6.40 6.40
1293 A175 400 le multicolored 6.40 6.40

Christmas A176

Walt Disney characters in "The Night Before Christmas."

No. 1294a, 'Twas the night. . . b, Not a creature. . . c, The stockings were hung. . . d, And Mama in her kerchief. . . e, When out on the lawn. . . f, I sprang from my bed. . . g, Away to the window. . . h, Tore open the shutter. . .

No. 1295a, The moon on the breast. . . b, When what to my wondering. . . c, With a little old driver. . . d, More rapid than eagles. . . e, To the top of the porch. . . f, And then in a twinkling. . . g, As I drew in my head. . . h, He was dressed. . .

No. 1296a, A bundle of toys. . . b, The stump of a pipe. . . c, He had a broad face. . . d, He was chubby and plump. . . e, A wink of his eye. . . f, Then turned with a jerk. . . g, And giving a nod. . . h, He sprang to his sleigh. . .

No. 1297, The children were nestled. . . No. 1298, His eyes, how they twinkled. . . No. 1299, He spoke not a word. . . No. 1300, And he whistled. . . No. 1301, As dry leaves. . . No. 1302, But I heard him exclaim. . .

1990, Dec. 17 Litho. *Perf. 13*

Miniature Sheets of 8

1294 A176 50 le #a.-h. 4.50 4.50
1295 A176 75 le #a.-h. 6.75 6.75
1296 A176 100 le #a.-h. 9.00 9.00

Souvenir Sheets

1297 A176 400 le multi 4.50 4.50
1298 A176 400 le multi, horiz. 4.50 4.50
1299 A176 400 le multi 4.50 4.50
1300 A176 400 le multi, horiz. 4.50 4.50
1301 A176 400 le multi, horiz. 4.50 4.50
1302 A176 400 le multi 4.50 4.50

Peter Paul Rubens (1577-1640), Painter A177

Entire paintings or different details from: 5 le, Helena Fourment as Hagar in the Wilderness. 10 le, Isabella Brant. 20 le, 60 le, Countess of Arundel and Her Party. 80 le, Nicolaas Rockox. 100 le, Adriana Perez. 150 le, George Villiers, Duke of Buckingham. 300 le, Countess of Buckingham. No. 1311, Veronica Spinola Dorio. No. 1312, Giovanni Carlo Dorio.

1990, Dec. 24 *Perf. 14*

1303 A177 5 le multicolored .15 .15
1304 A177 10 le multicolored .16 .16
1305 A177 20 le multicolored .32 .32
1306 A177 60 le multicolored .95 .95
1307 A177 80 le multicolored 1.30 1.30
1308 A177 100 le multicolored 1.60 1.60
1309 A177 150 le multicolored 2.40 2.40
1310 A177 300 le multicolored 4.80 4.80
Nos. 1303-1310 (8) 11.68 11.68

Souvenir Sheets

1311 A177 350 le multicolored 5.60 5.60
1312 A177 350 le multicolored 5.60 5.60

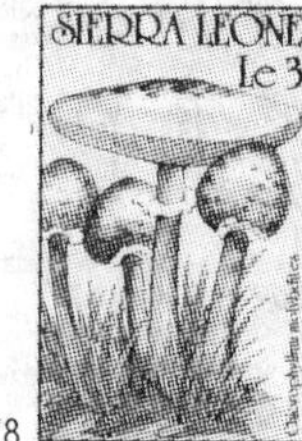

Mushrooms — A178

Designs: 3 le, Chlorophyllum molybdites. 5 le, Lepista nuda. 10 le, Clitocybe nebularis. 15 le, Cyathus striatus. 20 le, Bolbitius vitellinus. 25 le, Leucoagaricus naucinus. 30 le, Suillus luteus. 40 le, Podaxis pistillaris. 50 le, Oudemansiella radicata. 60 le, Phallus indusiatus. 80 le, Macrolepiota rhacodes. 100 le, Mycena pura. 150 le, Volvariella volvacea. 175 le, Omphalotus olearius. 200 le, Sphaerobolus stellatus. 250 le, Schizophyllum commune. No. 1329, Agaricus campestris. No. 1330, Hypholama fasciculare. No. 1331, Suillus granulatus. No. 1332, Psilocybe coprophila.

1990, Dec. 31 *Perf. 14*

1313 A178 3 le multicolored .15 .15
1314 A178 5 le multicolored .15 .15
1315 A178 10 le multicolored .16 .16
1316 A178 15 le multicolored .24 .24
1317 A178 20 le multicolored .32 .32
1318 A178 25 le multicolored .40 .40
1319 A178 30 le multicolored .48 .48
1320 A178 40 le multicolored .65 .65
1321 A178 50 le multicolored .80 .80
1322 A178 60 le multicolored .95 .95
1323 A178 80 le multicolored 1.30 1.30
1324 A178 100 le multicolored 1.60 1.60
1325 A178 150 le multicolored 2.40 2.40
1326 A178 175 le multicolored 2.80 2.80
1327 A178 200 le multicolored 3.20 3.20
1328 A178 250 le multicolored 4.00 4.00
Nos. 1313-1328 (16) 19.60 19.60

Souvenir Sheets

1329-1332 A178 350 le each 5.60 5.60

Butterfly Type of 1987
"Sierra Leone" in Blue

1990(?) Litho.

1332A A126 50c like #861 .15 .15
1332B A126 2 le like #863
1332C A126 5 le like #865
1332D A126 10 le like #866
1332E A126 30 le like #864
1332F A126 50 le like No. 859
1332G A126 60 le like #871
1332H A126 80 le like No. 860
1332I A126 300 le like No. 869

Issued: 2, 5, 10, 30, 60 le, 1990(?), perf. 14; 50c, 50, 80, 300 le, Aug, 1991, perf. 12½x11½; Nos. 1332A, 1332F, 1332H-1332I inscribed 1990.

Easter — A179

Entire works or details from paintings by Rubens: 10 le, Flight of St. Barbara. 20 le, No. 1341, The Last Judgement. 30 le, St. Gregory of Nazianzus. 50 le, Doubting Thomas. 80 le, No. 1342, The Way to Calvary. 100 le, St. Gregory with Sts. Domitilla, Maurus and Papianus. 175 le, Sts. Gregory, Maurus and Papianus. 300 le, Christ and the Penitent Sinners.

1991, Apr. 8 Litho. *Perf. 13½x14*

1333 A179 10 le multicolored .16 .16
1334 A179 20 le multicolored .32 .32
1335 A179 30 le multicolored .48 .48
1336 A179 50 le multicolored .80 .80
1337 A179 80 le multicolored 1.30 1.30
1338 A179 100 le multicolored 1.60 1.60
1339 A179 175 le multicolored 2.80 2.80
1340 A179 300 le multicolored 4.80 4.80
Nos. 1333-1340 (8) 12.26 12.26

Souvenir Sheets

1341-1342 A179 400 le each 6.40 6.40

Phila Nippon '91 A180

Japanese locomotives: 10 le, Class 1400 steam. 20 le, Streamlined C55 steam. 30 le, ED17 electric. 60 le, EF13 electric. 100 le, Baldwin Mikado steam. 150 le, C62 steam. 200 le, KiHa 81 class diesel. 300 le, Class 8550 steam. No. 1351, Hikari bullet train. No. 1352, Class 7000 electric. No. 1353, D51 steam. No. 1354, Class 9600 steam.

1991, May 13 Litho. *Perf. 14*

1343 A180 10 le multicolored .16 .16
1344 A180 20 le multicolored .32 .32
1345 A180 30 le multicolored .48 .48
1346 A180 60 le multicolored .95 .95
1347 A180 100 le multicolored 1.60 1.60
1348 A180 150 le multicolored 2.40 2.40
1349 A180 200 le multicolored 3.20 3.20
1350 A180 300 le multicolored 4.80 4.80
Nos. 1343-1350 (8) 13.91 13.91

Souvenir Sheets

1351-1354 A180 400 le each 6.40 6.40

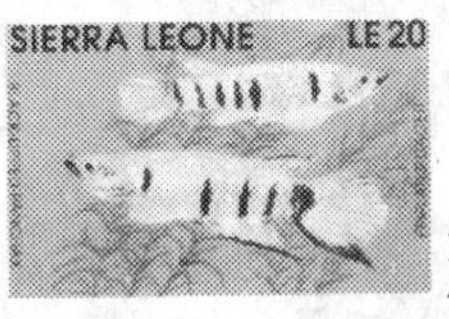

Fish A181

1991, June 3 Litho. *Perf. 14*

1355 A181 10 le Aphyosemion ghana .15 .15
1356 A181 20 le Black-lipped panchax .24 .24
1357 A181 30 le Peter's killie .36 .36
1358 A181 60 le Micro-walkeri killie .72 .72
1359 A181 100 le Butterfly fish 1.20 1.20
1360 A181 150 le Green panchax 1.80 1.80
1361 A181 200 le Six-barred panchax 2.40 2.40
1362 A181 300 le Banded puffer 3.60 3.60
Nos. 1355-1362 (8) 10.47 10.47

Souvenir Sheets

1363 A181 400 le Spotfin synodontis 4.80 4.80
1364 A181 400 le Two-striped panchax 4.80 4.80

Paintings by Vincent Van Gogh — A182

Designs: 10c, The Langlois Bridge at Arles. 50c, Trees in the Garden of Saint-Paul Hospital, vert. 1 le, Wild Flowers and Thistles in a Vase, vert. 2 le, Still Life: Vase with Oleanders and Books. 5 le, Farmhouses in a Wheat Field Near Arles. 10 le, Self-Portrait, Sept. 1889, vert. 20 le, Portrait of Patience Escalier, vert. 30 le, Portrait of Doctor Felix Rey, vert. 50 le, The Iris, vert. 60 le, The Shepherdess, vert. 80 le, Vincent's House in Arles (The Yellow House). 100 le, The Road Menders. 150 le, The Garden of Saint-Paul Hospital, vert. 200 le, View of the Church of Saint-Paul-De-Mausole. 250 le, Seascape at Saintes- Maries. 300 le, Pieta, vert. No. 1381, Church at Auvers Sur Dise, vert. No. 1382, Vineyards with a View of Auvers. No. 1383, The Trinquetaille Bridge. No. 1384, Two Poplars on a Road Through the Hills, vert. No. 1385, Haystacks in Provence. No. 1386, The Garden of Saint-Paul Hospital, diff.

1991, June 28 Litho. *Perf. 13½*

1365 A182 10c multicolored .15 .15
1366 A182 50c multicolored .15 .15
1367 A182 1 le multicolored .15 .15
1368 A182 2 le multicolored .15 .15
1369 A182 5 le multicolored .15 .15
1370 A182 10 le multicolored .15 .15
1371 A182 20 le multicolored .24 .24
1372 A182 30 le multicolored .35 .35
1373 A182 50 le multicolored .60 .60
1374 A182 60 le multicolored .72 .72
1375 A182 80 le multicolored .95 .95
1376 A182 100 le multicolored 1.20 1.20
1377 A182 150 le multicolored 1.80 1.80
1378 A182 200 le multicolored 2.40 2.40
1379 A182 250 le multicolored 3.00 3.00
1380 A182 300 le multicolored 3.60 3.60
Nos. 1365-1380 (16) 15.76 15.76

Size: 102x76mm

Imperf

1381-1386 A182 400 le each 4.80 4.80

Royal Family Birthday, Anniversary

Common Design Type

1991, July 5 Litho. *Perf. 14*

1387 CD347 10 le multi .16 .16
1388 CD347 20 le multi .32 .32
1389 CD347 30 le multi .48 .48
1390 CD347 80 le multi 1.30 1.30
1391 CD347 100 le multi 1.60 1.60
1392 CD347 200 le multi 3.20 3.20
1393 CD347 250 le multi 4.00 4.00
1394 CD347 300 le multi 4.80 4.80
Nos. 1387-1394 (8) 15.86 15.86

Souvenir Sheets

1395 CD347 400 le Elizabeth, Philip 6.40 6.40
1396 CD347 400 le Charles, Diana, sons 6.40 6.40

10 le, 30 le, 200 le, 250 le, No. 1395, Queen Elizabeth II, 65th birthday. Others, Charles and Diana, 10th wedding anniversary.

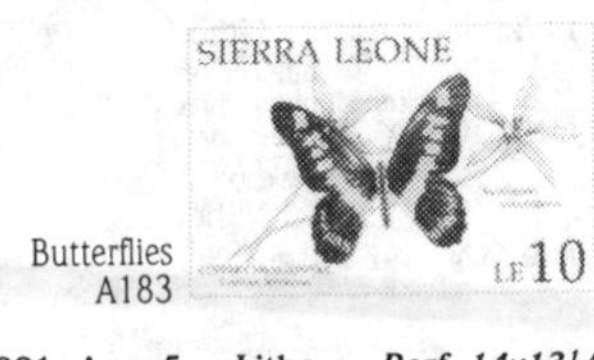

Butterflies A183

1991, Aug. 5 Litho. *Perf. 14x13½*

1397 A183 10 le Coppery swallowtail .15 .15
1398 A183 30 le Orange forester .35 .35
1399 A183 50 le Large striped swordtail .60 .60
1400 A183 60 le Lilac beauty .75 .75
1401 A183 80 le African leaf .95 .95
1402 A183 100 le Blue diadem 1.20 1.20
1403 A183 200 le Beautiful monarch 2.40 2.40
1404 A183 300 le Veined swallowtail 3.60 3.60
Nos. 1397-1404 (8) 10.00 10.00

Souvenir Sheets

Perf. 13x12

1405 A183 400 le Blue banded nymph 4.80 4.80
1406 A183 400 le Western red charaxes 2.75 2.75
1407 A183 400 le Broad-bordered grass yellow 2.75 2.75
1408 A183 400 le African clouded yellow 3.25 3.25

A number has been reserved for additional value in this set. While numbers 1406-1407 have the same issue date as Nos. 1397-1405, the dollar value of Nos. 1406-1407 was lower when they were released. While No. 1408 has the same issue date as Nos. 1397-1407, the value of No. 1408 was different when released.

World War II Motion Pictures A184

Designs: 2 le, To Hell and Back, Audie Murphy. 5 le, Attack, Jack Palance. 10 le, Mrs. Miniver, Greer Garson and Walter Pidgeon. 20 le, The Guns of Navarone. 30 le, The Great Dictator, Paulette Goddard and Charlie Chaplin. 50 le, The Train. 60 le, The Diary of Anne Frank. 80 le, The Bridge on the River Kwai, William Holden. 100 le, Lifeboat, Alfred Hitchcock, Tallulah Bankhead. 200 le, Sands of Iwo Jima, John Wayne. 300 le, Thirty Seconds Over Tokyo, Van Johnson and Spencer Tracy. 350 le, Casablanca, Humphrey Bogart and Ingrid Bergman. No. 1421, Twelve O'Clock High, Gregory Peck. No. 1422, Tora! Tora! Tora!. No. 1423, Patton, George C. Scott.

1991, Oct. 14 Litho. *Perf. 14*

1409 A184 2 le multicolored .15 .15
1410 A184 5 le multicolored .15 .15
1411 A184 10 le multicolored .15 .15
1412 A184 20 le multicolored .24 .24
1413 A184 30 le multicolored .35 .35
1414 A184 50 le multicolored .60 .60
1415 A184 60 le multicolored .72 .72
1416 A184 80 le multicolored .95 .95
1417 A184 100 le multicolored 1.20 1.20
1418 A184 200 le multicolored 2.40 2.40
1419 A184 300 le multicolored 3.60 3.60
1420 A184 350 le multicolored 4.25 4.25
Nos. 1409-1420 (12) 14.76 14.76

Souvenir Sheets

1421 A184 450 le multicolored 5.40 5.40
1422 A184 450 le multicolored 5.40 5.40
1423 A184 450 le multicolored 5.40 5.40

Miniature Sheets

Botanic Gardens — A185

Munich Botanic Garden: No. 1424a, Meissen China ornament. b, Masdevallia. c, White Egyptian lotus. d, French marigold. e, Pitcher plant. f, The Palm House. g, Dog's tooth violet. h, Passion flower. i, Hedge rose. j, Sensitive plant. k, Pitcher plant, diff. l, Trillium. m, Wild plantain. n, German primrose. o, Tulip. p, Spring walk.

Kyoto Botanic Garden: No. 1425a, Flowering cherry. b, Gardenia. c, The Domed Conservatory. d, Chrysanthemums. e, Bleeding heart. f, Hibiscus. g, Hiryu azalea. h, Sweet honeysuckle. i, Goldband lily. j, Non-traditional garden art. k, Viburnum. l, Japanese iris. m, Orchid. n, Hydrangea. o, View of Kyoto Botanic Garden. p, Camelia.

Brooklyn Botanic Garden: No. 1426a, The Palm House. b, Kurume azalea. c, Southern magnolia. d, Oleander. e, Chinese wisteria. f, Sourwood tree. g, Cattleya orchid. h, Gingko tree. i, Japanese Hill and Pond Garden. j, Rose. k, German iris. l, East Indian lotus. m, Speciosum lily. n, Lilac. o, Rose bay. p, Cranford Rose Garden.

No. 1427, Rhododendron, Munich, horiz. No. 1428, Chrysanthemum, Kyoto, horiz. No. 1429, Magnolia soulangeana, Brooklyn, horiz.

1991, Oct. 28

Sheets of 16

1424 A185 60 le #a.-p. 11.50 11.50
1425 A185 60 le #a.-p. 11.50 11.50
1426 A185 60 le #a.-p. 11.50 11.50

Souvenir Sheets

1427-1429 A185 600 le each 7.25 7.25

Christmas A186

Details from paintings or engravings by Albrecht Durer: 6 le, Mary being Crowned by Two Angels. 60 le, St. Christopher. 80 le, Virgin and Child. 100 le, Madonna and Child (Virgin with the Pear). 200 le, Madonna and Child. 300 le, The Virgin in Half-Length. 700 le, The Madonna with the Siskin. No. 1437, The Feast of the Rose Garlands. No. 1438, Virgin and Child with St. Anne.

1991, Dec. 9 Litho. *Perf. 12*

1430 A186 6 le pink & black .15 .15
1431 A186 60 le blue & black .48 .48
1432 A186 80 le multicolored .65 .65
1433 A186 100 le multicolored .80 .80
1434 A186 200 le multicolored 1.60 1.60
1435 A186 300 le multicolored 2.40 2.40
1436 A186 700 le multicolored 5.60 5.60
Nos. 1430-1436 (7) 11.68 11.68

Souvenir Sheets

Perf. 14½

1437-1438 A186 600 le each 4.75 4.75

Wolfgang Amadeus Mozart, Death Bicent. A187

Mozart and: 50 le, National Theatre, Prague. 100 le, St. Peter's Abbey, Salzburg. 500 le, Scene from opera, "Idomeneo."

1991, Dec. 20 *Perf. 14*

1439 A187 50 le multicolored .40 .40
1440 A187 100 le multicolored .80 .80
1441 A187 500 le multicolored 4.00 4.00
Nos. 1439-1441 (3) 5.20 5.20

Souvenir Sheet

1442 A187 600 le Bust, vert. 4.75 4.75

17th World Scout Jamboree, Korea A188

Designs: 250 le, Scouts learning to sail. 300 le, Lord Robert Baden-Powell, founder. 400 le, Scouts playing baseball. 750 le, Jamboree emblem, vert.

1991, Dec. 20

1443 A188 250 le multicolored 2.00 2.00
1444 A188 300 le multicolored 2.40 2.40
1445 A188 400 le multicolored 3.20 3.20
Nos. 1443-1445 (3) 7.60 7.60

Souvenir Sheet

1446 A188 750 le multicolored 6.00 6.00

Miniature Sheet

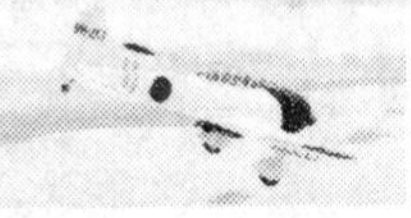

Attack on Pearl Harbor, 50th Anniv. A189

Designs: a, Japanese D3A1 Val dive bomber. b, Plane amid rising smoke over Ford Island. c, Battleships ablaze. d, Naval station, three planes. e, Drydock ablaze, tank farm. f, Two Vals over water, ships. g, USS Utah and Ford Island installations ablaze, ship underway. h, Installations on Ford Island ablaze. i, US P-40 Warhawk fighter plane. j, Two Japanese torpedo bombers, plane on fire falling from sky. k, Three Japanese bombers over Pearl City. l, Two Japanese bombers diving on four ships, one burning ship. m, Japanese plane on fire. n, Two

Japanese planes. o, One Japanese plane over Waipio Peninsula.

1991, Dec. 20 *Perf. 14½x15*

1447	A189 75 le Sheet of 15, #a.-o.	9.00	9.00

Walt Disney Christmas Cards — A190

Designs and year of issue: 12 le, Mickey and Donald decorating tree, 1952. 30 le, Characters surrounding book with "Alice in Wonderland", 1950. 60 le, Dwarf asleep with hare and tortoise, 1938. 75 le, Minnie, Donald, Mickey and Pluto mailing Christmas card, 1936. 100 le, Costumed characters in front of Magic Kingdom, 1984. 125 le, Mickey singing, Donald's nephews and Pluto reading 20,000 Leagues Under the Sea, 1954. 150 le, 101 Dalmations with season's greetings, 1960. 200 le, Donald and Mickey among gifts, 1948. 300 le, Mickey, Minnie at home for Christmas, 1983. 400 le, Donald and ducks preparing for Christmas watching Mickey Mouse Club, 1956. Characters on parade with Christmas cheer. 500 le, Disney characters, 50th birthday of Walt Disney Productions, 1972. No. 1460, Map of Magic Kingdom, 1955, vert. No. 1461, Seven dwarfs in bobsled, 1959, vert. No. 1462, Alice in Wonderland at tea party, 1950, vert.

1991, Dec. 24 Litho. *Perf. 14x13½*

1448	A190	12 le multicolored	.15	.15
1449	A190	30 le multicolored	.20	.20
1450	A190	60 le multicolored	.35	.35
1451	A190	75 le multicolored	.40	.40
1452	A190	100 le multicolored	.55	.55
1453	A190	125 le multicolored	.75	.75
1454	A190	150 le multicolored	.85	.85
1455	A190	200 le multicolored	1.25	1.25
1456	A190	300 le multicolored	1.75	1.75
1457	A190	400 le multicolored	2.25	2.25
1458	A190	500 le multicolored	2.75	2.75
1459	A190	600 le multicolored	3.25	3.25
		Nos. 1448-1459 (12)	14.50	14.50

Souvenir Sheets

Perf. 13½x14

1460-1462 A190 900 le each	5.25	5.25

Disney Characters on World Tour — A192

Designs: 6 le, Chiquita Minnie in Central America. 10 le, Gold Medal Goofy in Ancient Greece. 20 le, Donald, Daisy having Flamenco Fun in Spain. 30 le, Goofy guarding Donald at London's Buckingham Palace. 50 le, Mickey and Minnie dressed in Paris originals. 100 le, Goofy with mountain goat in Switzerland. 200 le, Daisy, Minnie as luau ladies in Hawaii. 350 le, Mickey, Donald and Goofy as ancient Egyptian comic strips, horiz. 500 le, Daisy and Minnie as can-can dancers in Paris, horiz. No. 1479, Mickey playing bagpipes in Scotland. No. 1480, Goofy fishes from Donald's gondola in Venice, Italy. No. 1481, Mickey and Goofy taking crash course in Greek.

Perf. 13x13½, 13½x13

1992, Feb. Litho.

1470	A192	6 le multicolored	.15	.15
1471	A192	10 le multicolored	.15	.15
1472	A192	20 le multicolored	.16	.16
1473	A192	30 le multicolored	.24	.24
1474	A192	50 le multicolored	.40	.40
1475	A192	100 le multicolored	.80	.80
1476	A192	200 le multicolored	1.60	1.60
1477	A192	350 le multicolored	2.80	2.80
1478	A192	500 le multicolored	4.00	4.00
		Nos. 1470-1478 (9)	10.30	10.30

Souvenir Sheets

1479-1481 A192 700 le each	5.60	5.60

Queen Elizabeth II's Accession to the Throne, 40th Anniv.

Common Design Type

1992, Feb. 6 Litho. *Perf. 14*

1482	CD348	60 le multicolored	.48	.48
1483	CD348	100 le multicolored	.80	.80
1484	CD348	300 le multicolored	2.40	2.40
1485	CD348	400 le multicolored	3.20	3.20
		Nos. 1482-1485 (4)	6.88	6.88

Souvenir Sheets

1486	CD348	700 le Queen, hillside	5.60	5.60
1487	CD348	700 le Queen, houses	5.60	5.60

Spanish Art — A193

Paintings by Francisco de Zurbaran: 1 le, The Visit of St. Thomas Aquinas to St. Bonaventure. 10 le, St. Gregory. 30 le, St. Andrew. 50 le, St. Gabriel the Archangel. 60 le, The Blessed Henry Suso. 100 le, St. Lucy. 300 le, St. Casilda. 400 le, St. Margaret of Antioch. 500 le, St. Apollonia. 600 le, St. Bonaventure at the Council of Lyons. 700 le, St. Bonaventure on His Bier. 800 le, The Martyrdom of St. James (detail). No. 1496, St. Hugh in the Refectory, horiz. No. 1497, The Martyrdom of St. James. No. 1497A, The Young Virgin.

1992, May 25 Litho. *Perf. 13*

1487A	A193	1 le multi	.15	.15
1488	A193	10 le multi	.15	.15
1489	A193	30 le multi	.22	.22
1490	A193	50 le multi	.38	.38
1491	A193	60 le multi	.48	.48
1491A	A193	100 le multi	.50	.50
1491B	A193	300 le multi	1.50	1.50
1492	A193	400 le multi	3.00	3.00
1493	A193	500 le multi	4.00	4.00
1494	A193	600 le multi	4.80	4.80
1495	A193	700 le multi	3.50	3.50
1495A	A193	800 le multi	4.00	4.00

Size: 120x95mm

Imperf

1496	A193	900 le multi	7.20	7.20
1497	A193	900 le multi	6.85	6.85
1497A	A193	900 le multi	4.65	4.65
		Nos. 1487A-1497A (15)	41.38	41.38

Granada '92.

While Nos. 1487A-1497A all have the same issue date, the dollar value of Nos. 1487A, 1489-1490, 1491A-1491B, 1492, 1495, 1497-1497A was lower when they were released.

Prehistoric Animals — A194

Designs: No. 1498a, Rhamphorhynchus. b, Pteranodon. c, Dimorphodon. d, Pterodactyl. e, Archaeopteryx. f, Iguanodon. g, Hypsilophodon. h, Nothosaurus. i, Brachiosaurus. j, Kentrosaurus. k, Plesiosaurus. l, Trachodon. m, Hesperornis. n, Henodus. o, Steneosaurus. p, Stenopterygius. q, Eurhinosaurus r, Placodus. s, Mosasaurus. t, Mixosaurus. No. 1499, Herperornis, diff.

1992, June 8 *Perf. 14*

1498	A194 50 le Sheet of 20, #a.-t.	8.00	8.00

Souvenir Sheet

1499	A194 50 le multicolored	.40	.40

"Sierra Leone" is 22mm wide on No. 1499.

A195 A196

Tropical Birds: 30 le, Greater flamingo. 50 le, White-crested hornbill. 100 le, Verreaux's touraco. 170 le, Yellow-spotted barbet. 200 le, African spoonbill. 250 le, Saddlebill stork. 300 le, Red-headed lovebird. 600 le, Yellow-billed barbet. No. 1508, Fire-bellied woodpecker. No. 1509, Swallow-tailed bee-eater.

1992, July 20 Litho. *Perf. 14*

1500	A195	30 le multicolored	.25	.25
1501	A195	50 le multicolored	.38	.38
1502	A195	100 le multicolored	.52	.52
1503	A195	170 le multicolored	.90	.90
1504	A195	200 le multicolored	1.55	1.55
1505	A195	250 le multicolored	1.30	1.30
1506	A195	300 le multicolored	1.60	1.60
1507	A195	600 le multicolored	4.65	4.65
		Nos. 1500-1507 (8)	11.15	11.15

Souvenir Sheets

1508	A195	1000 le multicolored	7.60	7.60
1509	A195	1000 le multicolored	5.25	5.25

While Nos. 1500-1509 all have the same release date, the value of Nos. 1502-1503, 1505-1506, 1509 was lower when they were released.

1992 Litho. *Perf. 14*

1992 Summer Olympics, Barcelona: 10 le, Marathon. 20 le, Gymnastics, parallel bars. 30 le, Discus. 50 le, 110-meter hurdles, horiz. 60 le, Women's long jump. 100 le, Gymnastics, floor exercise, horiz. 200 le, Windsurfing. 300 le, Road race cycling. 400 le, Weight lifting. 900 le, Soccer, horiz.

1510	A196	10 le multicolored	.15	.15
1511	A196	20 le multicolored	.15	.15
1512	A196	30 le multicolored	.22	.22
1513	A196	50 le multicolored	.38	.38
1514	A196	60 le multicolored	.45	.45
1515	A196	100 le multicolored	.75	.75
1516	A196	200 le multicolored	1.55	1.55
1517	A196	300 le multicolored	2.30	2.30
1518	A196	400 le multicolored	3.00	3.00
		Nos. 1510-1518 (9)	8.95	8.95

Souvenir Sheet

1519	A196	900 le multicolored	6.75	6.75

1992 Winter Olympics, Albertville A197

Designs: 250 le, Women's biathlon, vert. 500 le, Speed skating, vert. 600 le, Men's downhill skiing. No. 1523, Men's single luge. No. 1524, Ice dancing, vert.

1992, Sept. 8 Litho. *Perf. 14*

1520	A197	250 le multicolored	1.30	1.30
1521	A197	500 le multicolored	2.60	2.60
1522	A197	600 le multicolored	3.10	3.10
		Nos. 1520-1522 (3)	7.00	7.00

Souvenir Sheets

1523-1524 A197 900 le each	4.65	4.65

Discovery of America, 500th Anniv. A198

Designs: 300 le, Ferdinand, Isabella, Columbus. 500 le, Landing in New World. 900 le, Columbus, vert.

1992, Oct. Litho. *Perf. 14*

1525	A198	300 le multicolored	1.60	1.60
1526	A198	500 le multicolored	2.60	2.60

Souvenir Sheet

1527	A198	900 le multicolored	4.65	4.65

Birds — A199

Designs: 50c, Pygmy goose. 1 le, Spotted eagle owl. 2 le, Verreaux's touraco. 5 le, Saddlebill stork. 10 le, African golden oriole. 20 le, Malachite king fisher. 30 le, Fire-crowned bishop. 40 le, Fire-bellied woodpecker. 50 le, Red-billed fire-finch. 80 le, Blue fairy flycatcher. 100 le, Crested malimbe. 150 le, Vitelline masked weaver. 170 le, Blue plantain-eater. 200 le, Superb sunbird. 250 le, Swallow-tailed bee-eater. 300 le, Cabani's yellow bunting. 500 le, Crocodile bird. 750 le, White-faced owl. 1000 le, Blue cuckoo-shrike. 2000 le, Bare-headed rock-fowl. 3000 le, Red-tailed buzzard.

1992-93 Litho. *Perf. 14x15*

1528	A199	50c multi	.15	.15
1529	A199	1 le multi	.15	.15
1530	A199	2 le multi	.15	.15
1531	A199	5 le multi	.15	.15
1532	A199	10 le multi	.15	.15
1533	A199	20 le multi	.15	.15
1534	A199	30 le multi	.16	.16
1535	A199	40 le multi	.20	.20
1536	A199	50 le multi	.26	.26
1537	A199	80 le multi	.42	.42
1538	A199	100 le multi	.52	.52
1539	A199	150 le multi	.80	.80
1540	A199	170 le multi	.90	.90
1541	A199	200 le multi	1.05	1.05
1542	A199	250 le multi	1.30	1.30
1543	A199	300 le multi	1.60	1.60
1544	A199	500 le multi	2.65	2.65
1545	A199	750 le multi	4.00	4.00
1546	A199	1000 le multi	5.25	5.25
1546A	A199	2000 le multi	10.50	10.50
1546B	A199	3000 le multi	15.75	15.75
		Nos. 1528-1546B (21)	46.26	46.26

#1536, 1538-1539, 1541, 1543 exist inscribed 1994; #1538, 1541, 1543-1544, 1546, 1546B inscribed 1996.

Issue dates: Nos. 1528-1546, Sept. 1992. Nos. 1546A-1546B, 1993.

Model Trains A200

Lionel models: No. 1547a, Pennsylvannia RR GG-1 electric #6-18306, O gauge, 1992. b, Wabash RR Hudson #8610, O gauge, 1985. c, Locomotive #1911, standard gauge, 1911. d, Chesapeake & Ohio 4-4-2 #6-18627, O gauge, 1992. e, Gang car #50, O gauge, 1954. f, #8004, 1980 model of Rock Island & Peoria RR engine built for Columbian Exposition of 1893, O gauge. g, Western Maryland RR Shay #6-18023, O gauge, 1992. h, (Kenner-Parker) Boston & Albany Hudson #784, O gauge, 1986. i, Locomotive #6, standard gauge, 1906.

No. 1548a, Pennsylvania RR Torpedo #238EW, O gauge, 1936. b, Denver & Rio Grande Western Alco Pa No. 6-18107, O gauge, 1992. c, #408E Locomotive, standard gauge, 1930. d, Mickey Mouse 60th birthday boxcar No. 19241, O gauge, 1991. e, Polished brass locomotive, No. 54, standard gauge, 1913. f, Broadway limited #392E, standard gauge, 1936. g, Great Northern RR EP-5 #18302, O gauge, 1988. h, 4-4-0 Locomotive #6, standard gauge, 1918. i, 4-4-4 Locomotive No. 400E, standard gauge, 1933.

No. 1549a, Special F-3 diesel engine, O gauge, 1947. b, Pennsylvannia RR GE 44-ton switcher #6-18905, O gauge, 1992. c, #1 trolley, standard gauge, 1913. d, Seaboard RR freight diesel, O gauge, 1958. e, Pennsylvania S-2 turbine, O gauge, 1991. f, Western Pacific RR GP-9 diesel #6-18822, O gauge, 1992. g, #10 with Ives plates transition model, standrad gauge, 1929. h, 4-4-4 locomotive #400E, standard gauge, 1931. i, #384E, standard gauge, 1928.

No. 1550, Hudson No. 8210 Special, O gauge. No. 1551, #381E, standard gauge, 1928. No. 1552, 2-Rail electric model #300 trolley with converse body, 2⅞-inch gauge.

1992, Nov. 23 Litho. *Perf. 14*

1547	A200 150 le Sheet of 9, #a.-i.	7.00	7.00
1548	A200 170 le Sheet of 9, #a.-i.	8.00	8.00
1549	A200 170 le Sheet of 9, #a.-i.	8.00	8.00

Souvenir Sheets

Perf. 13

1550-1552 A200 1000 le each	5.25	5.25

Genoa '92 (#1547-1549). Nos. 1550-1552 contains one 51x39mm stamp.

Walt Disney Characters in Christmas Scenes
A201

1992, Nov. 16 *Perf. 13½x14*

1553 A201 10 le Minnie & Chip .15 .15
1554 A201 20 le Goofy as Santa .15 .15
1555 A201 30 le Daisy, Minnie .15 .15
1556 A201 50 le Mickey, Goofy .26 .26
1557 A201 80 le Pete .42 .42
1558 A201 100 le Donald Duck .52 .52
1559 A201 150 le Morty & Ferdie .78 .78
1560 A201 200 le Mickey 1.05 1.05
1561 A201 300 le Goofy with ornament 1.60 1.60
1562 A201 500 le Chip & Dale 2.60 2.60
1563 A201 600 le Donald & Dale 3.20 3.20
1564 A201 800 le Huey, Dewey & Louie 4.15 4.15
Nos. 1553-1564 (12) 15.03 15.03

Souvenir Sheets

1565 A201 900 le Mickey Mouse 4.75 4.75

Perf. 14x13½

1566 A201 900 le Angel with Chip, horiz. 4.75 4.75
1567 A201 900 le Mickey & Minnie, horiz. 4.75 4.75

Mickey Mouse Magazines and Books — A202

10 le, Magazine cover, Mar. 1936, v. 1, #6. 20 le, Magazine cover, June 1936, v. 1, #9. 30 le, Magazine cover, Nov. 1936, v. 2, #2. 40 le, Magazine cover, Aug. 1937, v. 2, #11. 50 le, Magazine cover, Oct. 1937, v. 2, #13. 60 le, Magazine cover, Dec. 1937, v. 3, #3. 70 le, Magazine cover, Jan. 1938, v. 3, #4. 150 le, Cover, Big Book #4062, 1935. 170 le, Story book cover, 1936. 200 le, Comic book cover, unnumbered. 300 le, Comic book cover, No. 181. 400 le, Comic book cover #194. 500 le, Story book cover, Book 1, 1931. No. 1581, Boys' and Girls' March of Comics cover, 1948. No. 1582, First Mickey Mouse Magazine cover for June-Aug. 1935, v. 1, #1, horiz. No. 1583, Cover of early Mickey Mouse story book published in England, 1933, horiz.

1992 *Perf. 13½x14*

1568 A202 10 le multicolored .15 .15
1569 A202 20 le multicolored .15 .15
1570 A202 30 le multicolored .15 .15
1571 A202 40 le multicolored .20 .20
1572 A202 50 le multicolored .28 .28
1573 A202 60 le multicolored .32 .32
1574 A202 70 le multicolored .38 .38
1575 A202 150 le multicolored .78 .78
1576 A202 170 le multicolored .90 .90
1577 A202 200 le multicolored 1.05 1.05
1578 A202 300 le multicolored 1.60 1.60
1579 A202 400 le multicolored 2.05 2.05
1580 A202 500 le multicolored 2.60 2.60
Nos. 1568-1580 (13) 10.61 10.61

Souvenir Sheets

1581 A202 900 le multicolored 4.65 4.65

Perf. 14x13½

1582 A202 900 le multicolored 4.65 4.65
1583 A202 900 le multicolored 4.65 4.65

Christmas
A203

Details or entire paintings: 1 le, Virgin and Child, by Fiorenzo di Lorenzo. 10 le, Madonna and Child on a Wall, by Circle of Dirk Bouts. 20 le, Virgin and Child with the Flight into Egypt, by Master of Hoogstraeten. 30 le, Madonna and Child before Firescreen, by Master of Flemalle. 50 le, Mary in a Rose Garden, by Hans Memling. 100 le, Virgin Mary and Child, by Lucas Cranach the Elder. 170 le, Virgin and Child, by Rogier van der Weyden. 200 le, Madonna and Saints, by Perugino. 250 le, Madonna Enthroned with Saints Catherine and Barbara, by Master of Hoogstraeten. 300 le, The Virgin in a Rose Arbor, by Stefan Lochner. 500 le, Madonna and Child with Angels, by Sandro Botticelli. 1000 le, Madonna and Child with Young St. John the Baptist, by Fra Bartolemmeo. No. 1596, The Virgin with the Green Cushion, by Andrea Solario. No. 1597, The Virgin and Child, by Jan Gossaert. No. 1598, The Virgin and Child, by Lucas Cranach the Younger.

1992, Dec. 7 **Litho.** *Perf. 13½x14*

1584 A203 1 le multicolored .15 .15
1585 A203 10 le multicolored .15 .15
1586 A203 20 le multicolored .15 .15
1587 A203 30 le multicolored .15 .15
1588 A203 50 le multicolored .28 .28
1589 A203 100 le multicolored .52 .52
1590 A203 170 le multicolored .90 .90
1591 A203 200 le multicolored 1.05 1.05
1592 A203 250 le multicolored 1.30 1.30
1593 A203 300 le multicolored 1.60 1.60
1594 A203 500 le multicolored 2.60 2.60
1595 A203 1000 le multicolored 5.20 5.20
Nos. 1584-1595 (12) 14.05 14.05

Souvenir Sheets

1596-1598 A203 900 le each 4.75 4.75

Anniversaries and Events — A204

150 le, Emblems of FAO, ICN, WHO. #1600, Graf Zeppelin. #1601, Cow, emblems, grain stalk. 200 le, Starving child. #1603, Lions Intl. emblem, map. #1604, Cottonwood tree. 300 le, African elephant. 600 le, Space Shuttle. 700 le, Graf Zeppelin LZ 127, specifications. #1608, Astronaut. #1609, Count Zeppelin.

1992, Dec. **Litho.** *Perf. 14*

1599 A204 150 le multicolored .78 .78
1600 A204 170 le multicolored .90 .90
1601 A204 170 le multicolored .90 .90
1602 A204 200 le multicolored 1.05 1.05
1603 A204 250 le multicolored 1.30 1.30
1604 A204 250 le multicolored 1.30 1.30
1605 A204 300 le multicolored 1.60 1.60
1606 A204 600 le multicolored 3.25 3.25
1607 A204 700 le multicolored 3.65 3.65
Nos. 1599-1607 (9) 14.73 14.73

Souvenir Sheets

1608-1609 A204 900 le each 4.75 4.75

Intl. Conference on Nutrition, Rome (#1599, 1601). Count Zeppelin, 75th anniv. of death (#1600, 1607, 1609). World Health Organization (#1602). Lions Intl., 75th anniv. (#1603). Earth Summit, Rio de Janeiro (#1604-1605). Intl. Space Year (#1606, 1608).

Miniature Sheet

Boxing
A205

Boxing movies, stars: No. 1610a, The Champ, Wallace Beery. b, Golden Boy, William Holden. c, Body and Soul, John Garfield. d, Champion, Kirk Douglas. e, The Set-Up, Robert Ryan. f. Requiem for a Heavyweight, Anthony Quinn. g, Kid Galahad, Elvis Presley. h, Fat City, Jeff Bridges.

No. 1612, Gentlemen Jim, Errol Flynn. No. 1614, Rocky III, Sylvester Stallone.

Boxing champions: No. 1611a, Joe Louis. b, Archie Moore. c, Muhammad Ali. d, George Foreman. e, Joe Frazier. f, Marvin Hagler. g, Sugar Ray Leonard. h, Evander Holyfield.

No. 1613, Muhammad Ali, diff.

1993, Feb. 8 **Litho.** *Perf. 13½x14*

1610 A205 200 le Sheet of 8, #a.-h. 8.50 8.50
1611 A205 200 le Sheet of 8, #a.-h. 8.50 8.50

Souvenir Sheets

1612-1614 A205 1000 le each 5.20 5.20

Miniature Sheets

Louvre Museum, Bicent.
A206

Details or entire paintings by Eugene Delacroix (1798-1863): Nos. 1615a-1615b, Entry of the Crusaders into Constantinople (left, right). c-d, Jews Purchasing Brides in Morocco (left, right). e-f, The Death of Sardanapalus (left, right). g-h, Liberty Guiding the People (left, right).

No. 1616a, An Orphan at the Cemetery. b-c, Women of Algiers in their Apartment (left, right). d, Dante and Virgil in the Infernal Regions. e, Self-Portrait. f-g, Massacre at Chios (left, right). h, Frederic Chopin.

No. 1617, Rape of the Sabine Women, by Jacques-Louis David (1748-1825).

1993, Mar. 8 **Litho.** *Perf. 12x12½*

1615 A206 70 le Sheet of 8, #a.-h. + label 3.00 3.00
1616 A206 70 le Sheet of 8, #a.-h. + label 3.00 3.00

Souvenir Sheet

Perf. 14½

1617 A206 900 le multicolored 4.75 4.75

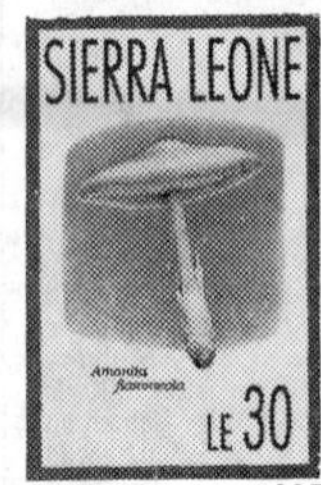

Mushrooms — A207 Butterflies — A208

Designs: 30 le, Amanita flammeola. 50 le, Cantharellus pseudocbarius. 100 le, Volvariella volvacea. 200 le, Termitomyces microcarpus. 300 le, Auricularia auricula. 400 le, Pleurotus tuberregium. 500 le, Schizophyllum commune. 600 le, Termitomyces robustus. No. 1626, Phallus rubicundus. No. 1627, Daldina concentrica.

1993, May 5 *Perf. 14*

1618 A207 30 le multicolored .15 .15
1619 A207 50 le multicolored .28 .28
1620 A207 100 le multicolored .52 .52
1621 A207 200 le multicolored 1.05 1.05
1622 A207 300 le multicolored 1.55 1.55
1623 A207 400 le multicolored 2.10 2.10
1624 A207 500 le multicolored 2.60 2.60
1625 A207 600 le multicolored 3.20 3.20
Nos. 1618-1625 (8) 11.45 11.45

Souvenir Sheets

1626-1627 A207 1000 le each 5.25 5.25

1993, May 5

1628 A208 20 le False acraea .15 .15
1629 A208 30 le Blue temora .15 .15
1630 A208 50 le Foxy charaxes .28 .28
1631 A208 100 le Leaf blue .52 .52
1632 A208 150 le Blue-banded swallowtail .78 .78
1633 A208 170 le African monarch .90 .90
1634 A208 200 le Mountain beauty 1.05 1.05
1635 A208 250 le Gaudy commodore 1.30 1.30
1636 A208 300 le Palla butterfly 1.60 1.60
1637 A208 500 le Pirate butterfly 2.60 2.60
1638 A208 600 le Painted lady 3.25 3.25
1639 A208 700 le Gold-banded forester 3.75 3.75
Nos. 1628-1639 (12) 16.33 16.33

Souvenir Sheets

1640 A208 1000 le Blue diadem 5.25 5.25
1641 A208 1000 le Blue swallowtail 5.25 5.25
1642 A208 1000 le African leaf butterfly 5.25 5.25

Miniature Sheets

Cats — A209

Designs: No. 1643a, Somali. b, Egyptian Mau smoke. c, Chocolate-point Siamese. d, Mi-Ke Japanese bobtail. e, Chinchilla. f, Red Burmese. g, British shorthair brown tabby. h, Blue Persian. i, British silver classic tabby. j, Oriental ebony. k, Red Persian. l, British calico shorthair.

No. 1644a, Black Persian. b, Blue-point Siamese. c, American wirehair. d, Birman. e, Scottish fold (silver tabby). f, American shorthair red tabby. g, Blue & white Persian bicolor. h, Havana brown. i, Norwegian forest cat. j, Brown tortie Burmese. k. Angora. l, Exotic shorthair.

No. 1645, American shorthair blue tabby, horiz. No. 1646, Seal-point colorpoint, horiz.

1993, May 17 **Litho.** *Perf. 14*

1643 A209 150 le Sheet of 12, #a.-l. 9.50 9.50
1644 A209 150 le Sheet of 12, #a.-l. 9.50 9.50

Souvenir Sheets

1645-1646 A209 1000 le each 5.25 5.25

Nos. 1643-1646 Ovptd. with Hong Kong '94 Emblem

1994 **Litho.** *Perf. 14*

1643m On #1643b & in sheet margin 9.50 9.50
1644m On #1644b & in sheet margin 9.50 9.50
1645a Ovptd. in sheet margin 5.25 5.25
1646a Ovptd. in sheet margin 5.25 5.25

Wild Animals
A210

1993, June 17

1647 A210 30 le Gorilla .16 .16
1648 A210 100 le Bongo .52 .52
1649 A210 150 le Potto .78 .78
1650 A210 170 le Chimpanzee .90 .90
1651 A210 200 le Dwarf galago 1.05 1.05
1652 A210 300 le African linsang 1.60 1.60
1653 A210 500 le Banded duiker 2.65 2.65
1654 A210 750 le Diana monkey 4.00 4.00
Nos. 1647-1654 (8) 11.66 11.66

Souvenir Sheets

1655 A210 1200 le Leopard 6.25 6.25
1656 A210 1200 le Elephant 6.25 6.25

Flowers
A211

30 le, Bleeding-heart vine. 40 le, Passion vine. 50 le, Hydrangea. 60 le, Wax begonia. 100 le, Hibiscus. 150 le, Crape-myrtle. 170 le, Bougainvillea. 200 le, Leadwort. 250 le, Gerbera daisy. 300 le, Black-eyed susan. 500 le, Gloriosa lily. 900 le, Sweet violet. #1669, Gloriosa lily, diff. #1670, Passion vine, diff. #1671, Hibiscus, diff.

1993, July 15 Litho. *Perf. 14*

1657 A211 30 le multicolored .15 .15
1658 A211 40 le multicolored .20 .20
1659 A211 50 le multicolored .25 .25
1660 A211 60 le multicolored .30 .30
1661 A211 100 le multicolored .52 .52
1662 A211 150 le multicolored .80 .80
1663 A211 170 le multicolored .90 .90
1664 A211 200 le multicolored 1.00 1.00
1665 A211 250 le multicolored 1.25 1.25
1666 A211 300 le multicolored 1.50 1.50
1667 A211 500 le multicolored 2.50 2.50
1668 A211 900 le multicolored 3.00 3.00
Nos. 1657-1668 (12) 12.37 12.37

Souvenir Sheets

1669-1671 A211 1200 le each 6.25 6.25

Coronation of Queen Elizabeth II, 40th Anniv. — A212

100 le, Queen, Princess Anne. 200 le, Coronation procession. 600 le, Official coronation photograph. 1500 le, Portrait, by Pietro Annigoni, 1954-55.

1993, Oct. Litho. *Perf. 14*

1672 A212 100 le multicolored .52 .52
1673 A212 200 le black 1.00 1.00
1674 A212 600 le multicolored 3.25 3.25
Nos. 1672-1674 (3) 4.77 4.77

Souvenir Sheet

1675 A212 1500 le multicolored 7.75 7.75

Copernicus (1473-1543)
A213

Picasso (1881-1973)
A214

250 le, Early telescope. 800 le, Moon's surface.

1993, Oct.

1676 A213 250 le multicolored 1.25 1.25
1677 A213 800 le multicolored 4.25 4.25

1993, Oct.

Sculpture: 170 le, Woman with Hat, 1961.
Paintings: 200 le, Buste de Femme, 1958. 800 le, Maya with a Doll, 1938. 1000 le, Women of Algiers (after Delacroix), 1955.

1678 A214 170 le multicolored .90 .90
1679 A214 200 le multicolored 1.00 1.00
1680 A214 800 le multicolored 4.25 4.25
Nos. 1678-1680 (3) 6.15 6.15

Souvenir Sheet

1681 A214 1000 le multicolored 5.25 5.25

Christmas
A215

Details or entire paintings, by Raphael: 50 le, 100 le, No. 1690, Madonna of the Fish. 150 le, Madonna & Child Enthroned with Five Saints. 800 le, The Holy Family with the Lamb.

Details or entire woodcuts, by Durer: 200 le, 250 le, 300 le, The Circumcision. 500 le, No. 1691, Holy Clan with Saints and Two Angels Playing Music.

1993, Dec. *Perf. 13½x14*

1682 A215 50 le multicolored .25 .25
1683 A215 100 le multicolored .52 .52
1684 A215 150 le multicolored .80 .80
1685 A215 200 le multicolored 1.00 1.00
1686 A215 250 le multicolored 1.25 1.25
1687 A215 300 le multicolored 1.50 1.50
1688 A215 500 le multicolored 2.50 2.50
1689 A215 800 le multicolored 4.25 4.25
Nos. 1682-1689 (8) 12.07 12.07

Souvenir Sheets

1690-1691 A215 1200 le each 6.25 6.25

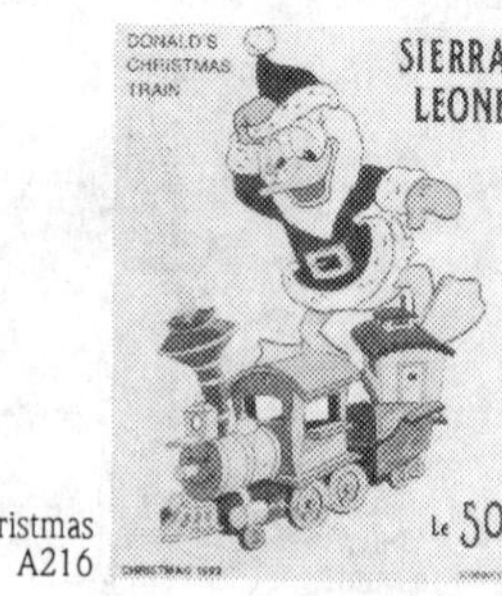

Christmas
A216

Disney characters celebrate Christmas: different.
No. 1700, Santa. No. 1701, Elves, horiz. No. 1702, Santa, horiz. No. 1703, Mickey, Minnie, horiz.

1993, Dec. 17 *Perf. 13½x14*

1692 A216 50 le multicolored .25 .25
1693 A216 100 le multicolored .52 .52
1694 A216 170 le multicolored .90 .90
1695 A216 200 le multicolored 1.00 1.00
1696 A216 250 le multicolored 1.25 1.25
1697 A216 500 le multicolored 2.50 2.50
1698 A216 600 le multicolored 3.00 3.00
1699 A216 800 le multicolored 4.25 4.25
Nos. 1692-1699 (8) 13.67 13.67

Souvenir Sheets

Perf. 13½x14, 14x13½

1700-1703 A216 1200 le each 6.25 6.25

1994 World Cup Soccer Championships, US — A217

Players, country: 30 le, Jose Luis Brown (R), Argentina. 50 le, Gary Lineker, England. 100 le, Carlos Valderrama, Colombia. 250 le, Skuhravy, Czechoslovakia; Marchena, Costa Rica. 300 le, Butragueno, Spain. 400 le, Roger Milla, Cameroun. 500 le, Roberto Donadoni, Italy. 700 le, Enzo Scifo, Belgium.

No. 1712, 1200 le, Socrates, Brazil. No. 1713, 1200 le, Wright, England; Demol, Belgium.

1993 *Perf. 13½x14*

1704-1711 A217 Set of 8 10.00 10.00

Souvenir Sheets

1712-1713 A217 1200 le Set of 2 12.50 12.50

A218

Hong Kong '94
A219

Stamps and: No. 1714, Hong Kong #455, pagoda, Tiger Baum Garden. No. 1715, Ai Par Garden, #1084.

Carved lacquer, Qing Dynasty: No. 1716a, Bowl with "Wan-Sui-Ch'ang-Chun." b, Four-wheeled box. c, Flower container. d, Box with human figure design. e, Shishi dog (not lacquer). f, Persimmon.

1994, Feb. 18 Litho. *Perf. 14*

1714 A218 200 le multicolored 1.00 1.00
1715 A218 200 le multicolored 1.00 1.00
a. Pair, #1714-1715 2.00 2.00

Miniature Sheet

1716 A219 100 le Sheet of 6, #a.-f. 3.25 3.25

Nos. 1714-1715 issued in sheets of 5 pairs. No. 1715a is a continuous design.

New Year 1994 (Year of the Dog) (#1716e).

Miniature Sheet

New Year 1994 (Year of the Dog)
A220

a, 100 le, Pekingese. b, 150 le, Doberman pinscher. c, 200 le, Tibetan terrier. d, 250 le, Weimaraner. e, 400 le, Rottweiler. f, 500 le, Akita. g, 600 le, Schnauzer. h, 1000 le, Tibetan spaniel.

No. 1718, Wire-haired pointing Griffon. No. 1719, Shih Tzu.

1994, June 20 Litho. *Perf. 14*

1717 A220 Sheet of 8, #a.-h. 13.00 13.00

Souvenir Sheets

1718-1719 A220 1200 le each 4.75 4.75

D-Day, 50th Anniv.
A221

Designs: 500 le, British paratroops drop behind enemy lines. 750 le, US paratrooper jumps from C47 transport.

1000 le, C47 Douglas Dakota, paratroops.

1994, July 11 Litho. *Perf. 14*

1720 A221 500 le multicolored 2.00 2.00
1721 A221 750 le multicolored 3.00 3.00

Souvenir Sheet

1722 A221 1000 le multicolored 4.00 4.00

A222

PHILAKOREA '94 — A223

100 le, Traditional wedding, Korea House, Seoul. 400 le, Royal tombs, Koryo Dynasty, Kaesong. 600 le, Terraced farm land, near Chungmu.

Tiger paintings, Choson Dynasty: No. 1726: a, Tiger, cubs, 19th cent. b, Munsa-pasal seated on lion. c, Extinct Korean tiger. d, Tiger, bamboo. e, Tiger guarding 3 cubs, 4 magpies. f, Tiger, 19th cent. g, Mountain Spirit. h, Tiger, bird in tree.

No. 1727, Wall painting of mounted hunters from Tomb of the Dancers of Kungnaesong, Koguryo period.

Perf. 14, 13½ (#1726)

1994, July 11 Litho.

1723-1725 A222 Set of 3 4.50 4.50

Miniature Sheet of 8

1726 A223 200 le #a.-h. 6.50 6.50

Souvenir Sheet

1727 A222 1200 le multicolored 4.75 4.75

Miniature Sheets of 6

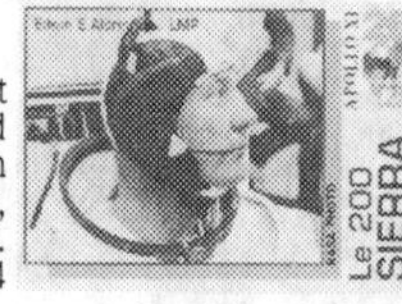

First Manned Moon Landing, 25th Anniv.
A224

No. 1728: a, Edwin E. Aldrin, Jr. b, Michael Collins. c, Neil A. Armstrong. d, Apollo 11 liftoff. e, Aldrin descending to lunar surface. f, Armstrong, lunar module Eagle reflected in Aldrin's face shield.

No. 1729: a, Aldrin gathering soil samples. b, Eagle with Aldrin deploying solar wind experiment. c, Aldrin, ALSEP & Eagle at Tranquility Base. d, US flag, Aldrin, Tranquility Base. e, Plaque on moon. f, Apollo 11 crew, stamp ceremony.

1000 le, First footprint on moon.

1994, July 11 *Perf. 14*

1728-1729 A224 200 le #a.-f, each 4.75 4.75

Souvenir Sheet

1730 A224 1000 le multicolored 4.00 4.00

Miniature Sheet of 6

A225

1994 World Cup Soccer Championships, US — A226

Players: No. 1731a, Kim Ho, South Korea. b, Cobi Jones, US. c, Claudio Suarez, Mexico. d, Tomas Brolin, Sweden. e, Ruud Gullit, Netherlands. f, Andreas Herzog, Austria.

No. 1732, Sierra Leone team. No. 1733, Giants Stadium, New Jersey.

1994, July 15

1731 A225 250 le #a.-f. 6.00 6.00

Souvenir Sheets

1732-1733 A226 1500 le each 6.00 6.00

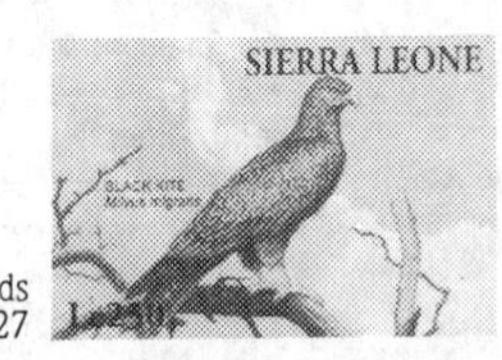

Birds
A227

Designs: 250 le, Black kite. 300 le, Superb sun-ird. 500 le, Martial eagle. 800 le, Red bishop.
White-necked picathartes: No. 1738a, 50 le, eeding young. b, 100 le, On brown tree limb. c, 50 le, Two at nest. d, On gray limb, green leaves.
No. 1739, Greater flamingo, vert. No. 1740, /hite-necked picathartes up close, vert.

994, Aug. 10
734-1737 A227 Set of 4 8.50 8.50

Miniature Sheet of 9
738 A227 3 each, #a.-d. 6.00 6.00

Souvenir Sheets
739-1740 A227 1200 le each 4.75 4.75

World Wildlife Fund (#1738).

Orchids — A228

Designs: 50 le, Aerangis kotschyana. 100 le, rachycorythis kalbreyeri. 150 le, Diaphananthe ellucida. 200 le, Eulophia guineensis. 300 le, urychone rothschildana. 500 le, Tridactyle ridactylites. 750 le, Cyrtorchis arcuata. 900 le, ncistrochilus rothschildianus.
No. 1749, Plectrelminthus caudatus. No. 1750, olystachaya affinis.

994, Sept. 1
741-1748 A228 Set of 8 12.00 12.00

Souvenir Sheets
749-1750 A228 1500 le each 6.00 6.00

Christmas
A229 SIERRA LEONE Le50

Details or entire paintings: 50 le, The Birth of the Virgin, by Murillo. 100 le, Education of the Virgin, by Murillo. 150 le, Annunciation, by Filippino Lippi. 200 le, Marriage of the Virgin, by Bernard van Orley. 250 le, The Visitation, by Nicolas Vleughels. 300 le, Holy Infant from Castelfranco altarpiece, by Giorgione. 400 le, Adoration of the Magi, Workshop of Bartholome Zeitblom. 600 le, Presentation of Infant Jesus in the Temple, by Memling.
No. 1759, Nativity Altarpiece, by Lorenzo Monado. No. 1760, Allendale Nativity, by Giorgione.

1994, Dec. 1 Litho. *Perf. 13½x14*
1751-1758 A229 Set of 8 6.75 6.75

Souvenir Sheets
1759-1760 A229 1500 le each 5.00 5.00

Intl. Year of the Family
A230

1994, Dec. 20 Litho. *Perf. 14*
1761 A230 300 le Working in field 1.00 1.00
1762 A230 350 le At beach 1.10 1.10

Disney Christmas — A231

Designs: 50 le, Mickey's Christmas cat. 100 le, Goofy's Christmas tree, vert. 150 le, Daisy's Christmas gift. 200 le, Donald's Christmas surprise, vert. 250 le, Minnie's Christmas flight. 300 le, Goofy's Christmas snowball, vert. 400 le, Goofy's Christmas letters. 500 le, Christmas sled ride, vert. 600 le, Mickey's Christmas snowman. 800 le, Pluto's Christmas treat, vert.
No. 1773, Goofy hanging outdoor lights. No. 1774, Mickey asleep in chair, vert.

Perf. 14x13½, 13½x14
1995, Jan. 23 Litho.
1763-1772 A231 Set of 10 11.00 11.00

Souvenir Sheets
1773-1774 A231 1500 le each 5.00 5.00

Donald Duck's Gallery of Old Masters
A232

Name of painting, inspiration: 50 le, Madonna Duck, Leonardo da Vinci. 100 le, Portrait of a Venetian Duck, Tintoretto. 150 le, Duck with a Glove, Frans Hals. 200 le, Donald with a Pink, Quentin Massys. 250 le, Pinkie Daisy, Sir Thomas Lawrence. 300 le, Donald's Whistling Mother, Whistler. 400 le, El Quacko, El Greco. 500 le, The Noble Snob, Rembrandt. 600 le, The Blue Duck, by Gainsborough. 800 le, Modern Quack, Picasso.
No. 1785, Soup's On, Brueghel. No. 1786, Duck Dancers, Degas, horiz.

Perf. 13½x14, 14x13½
1995, Jan. 23
1775-1784 A232 Set of 10 11.00 11.00

Souvenir Sheets
1785-1786 A232 1500 le each 5.00 5.00

Miniature Sheets of 12

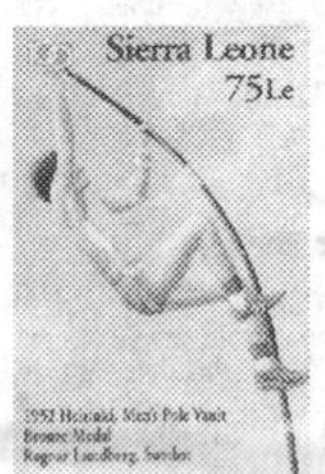

Olympic Medal Winners — A233

Summer Olympics: No. 1787a, Ragnar Lundberg, 1952 men's pole vault. b, Karin Janz, 1972 all-round gymnastics. c, Matthias Volz, 1936 gymnastics. d, Carl Lewis, 1988 long jump. e, Sara Simeoni, 1976 high jump. f, Daley Thompson, 1980 decathlon. g, Japan vs. Britain, 1964 soccer. h, Gabriella Dorio, 1984 1500-meters run. i, Daniela Hunger, 1988 200-meters individual medley swimming. j, Kyoko Iwasaki, 1992 200-meters breast stroke. k, Italian team member, 1960 water polo. l, David Wilkie, 1976 200-meters breast stroke.
1994 Winter Olympics, Lillehammer: No. 1788a, Katja Seizinger, downhill skiing. b, Hot air balloon (no medalist). c, Elvis Stojko, figure skating. d, Jens Weissflog, individual large hill ski jump. e, Bjorn Daehlie, 10k cross-country skiing. f, Germany, four-man bobsled. g, Markus Wasmeier, men's super giant slalom. h, Georg Hackl, luge. i, Trovill & Dean, ice dancing. j, Bonnie Blair, speed skating. k, Nancy Kerrigan, figure skating. l, Team Sweden, hockey.
No. 1789, torchbearer, horiz. No. 1790, Oksana Baiul, Nancy Kerrigan, Chen Lu, 1994 figure skating, horiz.

1995, Feb. 6 Litho. *Perf. 14*
1787 A233 75 le #a.-l. 3.00 3.00
1788 A233 200 le #a.-l. 8.00 8.00

Souvenir Sheets
1789-1790 A233 1000 le each 3.50 3.50

Miniature Sheets

Dinosaurs
A234

No. 1791: a, Ceratosaurus (d). b, Brachiosaurus. c, Pteranodon (b). d, Stegoceras. e, Saurolophus (h). f, Ornithomumus. g, Compsognathus (j). h, Deinonychus (i). i, Ornitholestes. j, Archaeopteryx. k, Heterodontosaurus (l). l, Lesothosaurus.
No. 1792: a, 100 le, Triceratops. b, 250 le, Protoceratops (c). c, 400 le, Monoclonius (b). d, 800 le, Styracosaurus (c).
No. 1793, Deinonychus. No. 1794, Rhamphorynchus.

1995, May 4 Litho. *Perf. 14*
1791 A234 200 le Sheet of 12, #a.-l. 8.00 8.00
1792 A234 Sheet of 4, #a.-d. 5.25 5.25

Souvenir Sheets
1793-1794 A234 2500 le each 8.25 8.25

Miniature Sheets of 9

Sierra Club, Cent.
A235

No. 1795, vert: a, L'Hoest's guenon. b, Black-footed cat. c, Colobus monkey up close. d, Colobus monkey in tree. e, Mandrill facing forward. f, Bonobo with young. g, Bonobo lying down. h, Mandrill facing right. i, Colobus monkey standing.
No. 1796: a, Black-faced impala facing forward. b, Herd of black-faced impala. c, Black-faced impala drinking. d, Bonobo. e, Black-footed cat. f, Black-footed cat up close. g, L'Hoest's guenon. h, L'Hoest's guenon, seated. i, Mandrills.

1995, May 10
1795-1796 A235 150 le #a.-i., each 4.50 4.50

New Year 1995 (Year of the Boar)
A236

Stylized boars: No. 1797a, red & multi, facing left. b, green & multi, facing right. c, green & multi, facing left. d, red & multi, facing right.
500 le, Two boars, vert.

1995, May 8 Litho. *Perf. 14*
1797 A236 100 le Block of 4, #a.-d. 1.25 1.25

Souvenir Sheet
1798 A236 500 le multicolored 1.65 1.65

Miniature Sheets of 9

Singapore '95
A237

Marine life: No. 1799a, Pufferfish. b, Coral grouper. c, Hawksbill turtle. d, Hogfish. e, Emperor angelfish. f, Butterflyfish. g, Lemon butterflyfish. h, Parrotfish. i, Moray eel.
Water birds, marine life: No. 1800a, Cape pigeons. b, Pelican. c, Puffin. d, Humpback whale. e, Greater shearwater. f, Bottlenose dolphin. g, Gurnard. h, Salmon. i, John dory.
#1801, Surgeonfish. #1802, Angelfish, vert.

1995
1799-1800 A237 300 le #a.-i., each 9.00 9.00

Souvenir Sheets
1801-1802 A237 1500 le each 5.00 5.00

Miniature Sheets of 6 or 8

A238

End of World War II, 50th Anniv.
A239

No. 1803: a, USS Idaho. b, HMS Ark Royal. c, Admiral Graf Spee. d, Destroyer. e, HMS Nelson. f, PT 109. g, USS Iowa. h, Bismark.
No. 1804: a, B-17. b, B-25. c, B-24 Liberator. d, USS Missouri. e, A-20 Boston. f, Pennsylvania, Colorado, Louisville, Portland, Columbia enter Lingayen Gulf.
No. 1805, HMS Indomitable launching aircraft. No. 1806, B-29 bomber.

1995, July 10
1803 A238 250 le #a.-h. + label 6.75 6.75
1804 A239 300 le #a.-f. + label 6.00 6.00

Souvenir Sheet
1805 A238 1500 le multicolored 5.00 5.00
1806 A239 1500 le multicolored 5.00 5.00

No. 1805 contains one 57x42mm stamp.

UN, 50th Anniv. — A240

No. 1807: a, 300 le, Dais, UN General Assembly. 400 le, Sec. Gen. U. Thant. 500 le, UN building, dove.
1500 le, Sec. Gen. Dag Hammarskjold.

1995, July 10 Litho. *Perf. 14*
1807 A240 Strip of 3, #a.-c. 4.00 4.00

Souvenir Sheet
1808 A240 1500 le multicolored 5.00 5.00

No. 1807 is a continuous design.

1995 Boy Scout Jamboree, Holland
A241

No. 1809: a, 400 le, Natl. flag. b, 500 le, Lord Baden-Powell. c, 600 le, Scout sign.
1500 le, Scout salute.

1995, July 10
1809 A241 Strip of 3, #a.-c. 5.00 5.00

Souvenir Sheet
1810 A241 1500 le multicolored 5.00 5.00

Queen Mother, 95th Birthday
A242

No. 1811: a, Drawing. b, Holding bouquet of flowers. c, Formal portrait. d, Without hat.
1500 le, Blue hat, dress.

1995, July 10 *Perf. 13½x14*
1811 A242 400 le Block or strip of 4, #a.-d. 5.25 5.25

Souvenir Sheet
1812 A242 1500 le multicolored 5.00 5.00

No. 1811 was issued in sheets of 8 stamps.

FAO, 50th Anniv. A243

No. 1813: a, 300 le, Man working with sack of food. b, 400 le, Boy carrying bundle of sticks on head. c, 500 le, Woman holding bowl of fruit. 1500 le, Woman holding baby, vert.

1995, July 10 *Perf. 14*
1813 A243 Strip of 3, #a.-c. 4.00 4.00

Souvenir Sheet
1814 A243 1500 le multicolored 5.00 5.00

Rotary Intl., 90th Anniv. A244

Designs: 500 le, Natl. flag, Rotary emblem. 1000 le, Paul Harris, Rotary emblem.

1995, July 10
1815 A244 500 le multicolored 1.75 1.75

Souvenir Sheet
1816 A244 1000 le multicolored 3.50 3.50

Miniature Sheets of 8

Singapore '95 — A245

Flora & fauna: No. 1817a, African tulip tree. b, Senegal bush locust. c, Killifish. d, Bird of paradise. e, Mandrill. f, Painted reed frog. g, Large spotted acraea. h, Carmine bee-eater.

No. 1818: a, Flame lily. b, Grants gazelle. c, Dogbane. d, Gold-banded forester. e, Horned chameleon. f, Malachite kingfisher. g, Leaf beetle. h, Acanthus.

No. 1819, Lion. No. 1820, African elephant.

1995, Sept. 5 **Litho.** *Perf. 14*
1817-1818 A245 300 le #a.-h., each 8.00 8.00

Souvenir Sheets
1819-1820 A245 1500 le each 5.00 5.00

Third UN Decade for Advancement of Women — A246

Designs: 300 le, Development. 500 le, Peace. 700 le, Equality.

1995 **Litho.** *Perf. 14*
1821-1823 A246 Set of 3 5.00 5.00

Sierra Leone Grammar School, 150th Anniv. A247

1995, Sept. 27 **Litho.** *Perf. 14*
1824 A247 300 le multicolored 1.00 1.00

Christmas A248

Details or entire paintings: 50 le, Holy Family, by Beccafumi. 100 le, Rest on Flight into Egypt, by Barocci. 150 le, La Vierge, by Bellini. 200 le, The Flight, by d'Arpino. 600 le, Adoration of the Magi, by Francken. 800 le, The Annunciation, by da Conegliano.

No. 1831, Virgin and child, by Cranach. No. 1832, Madonna and Child, by Berlinghiero.

1995, Dec. 1 **Litho.** *Perf. 13½x14*
1825-1830 A248 Set of 6 6.50 6.50

Souvenir Sheets
1831-1832 A248 1500 le each 5.00 5.00

Disney Christmas A249

Antique Disney toys: 5 le, Mickey Mouse doll. 10 le, Donald rag drum major. 15 le, Donald wind up. 20 le, Toothbrush holder. 25 le, Mickey telephone. 30 le, Walking wind-up. 800 le, Movie projector. 1000 le, Goofy tricycle.

No. 1841, Black Mickey Mouse. No. 1842, First Mickey book.

1995, Dec. 4 *Perf. 13½x14*
1833-1840 A249 Set of 8 6.50 6.50

Souvenir Sheets
1841-1842 A249 1500 le each 5.00 5.00

Miniature Sheets of 9

Nobel Prize Fund Established, Cent. — A250

Recipients: No. 1843a, Andrew Huxley, medicine, 1963. b, Nelson Mandela, peace, 1993. c, Gabriela Mistral, literature, 1945. d, Otto Diels, chemistry, 1950. e, Hannes Alfven, physics, 1970. f, Wole Soyinka, literature, 1986. g, Hans G. Dehmelt, physics, 1989. h, Desmond Tutu, peace, 1984. i, Leo Esaki, physics, 1973.

No. 1844: a, Maria Goeppert Mayer, physics, 1963. b, Irène Joliot-Curie, chemistry, 1935. c, Mother Teresa, peace, 1979. d, Selma Lagerlöf, literature, 1909. e, Rosalyn Yalow, medicine, 1977. f, Dorothy Hodgkin, chemistry, 1964. g, Rita Levi-Montalcini, medicine, 1986. h, Mairead Corrigan, peace, 1976. i, Betty Williams, peace, 1976.

No. 1845: a, Tobias Asser, peace, 1911. b, Andrei Sakharov, peace, 1975. c, Frederic Passy, peace, 1901. d, Dag Hammarskjöld, peace, 1961. e, Aung San Suu Kyi, peace, 1991. f, Ludwig Quidde, peace, 1927. g, Elie Wiesel, peace, 1986. h, Bertha von Suttner, peace, 1905. i, Dalai Lama, peace, 1989.

No. 1846: a, Richard Zsigmondy, chemistry, 1925. b, Robert Huber, chemistry, 1988. c, Wilhelm Ostwald, chemistry, 1909. d, Johann Deisenhofer, chemistry, 1988. e, Heinrich Wieland, chemistry, 1927. f, Gerhard Herzberg, chemistry, 1971. g, Hans von Euler-Chelpin, chemistry, 1929. h, Richard Willstätter, chemistry, 1915. i, Fritz Haber, chemistry, 1918.

No. 1847, Albert Einstein, physics, 1921. No. 1848, Wilhelm Röentgen, physics, 1901. No. 1849, Sin-Itiro Tomonaga, physics, 1965.

1995, Dec. 29 **Litho.** *Perf. 14*
1843-1846 A250 250 le #a.-i., each 7.50 7.50

Souvenir Sheets
1847-1849 A250 1500 le each 5.00 5.00

Miniature Sheets of 12

Railways of the World A251

No. 1850: a, Denver and Rio Grande Western. b, Central of Georgia. c, Seaboard Air Line. d, Missouri Pacific Lines. e, Atchison, Topeka and Santa Fe. f, Chicago, Milwaukee, St. Paul and Pacific. g, Texas and Pacific. h, Minneapolis, St. Paul & Sault Saint Marie. (Soo Line). i, Western Pacific. j, Great Northern. k, Baltimore & Ohio. l, Chicago, Rock Island and Pacific.

No. 1851: a, Southern Pacific 4-8-4 "Daylight" express, US. b, Belgian National 4-4-2 express. c, Indian Railways 4-6-2 "WP" express. d, South Australian 4-8-4 express. e, Union Pacific 4-8-8-4 "Big Boy," US. f, UK 4-6-2 "Royal Scot" streamlined. g, German Federal, class 052 2-10-0. h, Japanese National, 4-6-4 express. i, Pennsylvania, 4-4-4-4 streamlined, US. j, East African 4-8-2+2-8-4 Beyer-Garratt. k, Milwaukee Road 4-6-4 "Hiawatha" express, US. l, Paris-Orleans, 4-6-2 Pacific, France.

No. 1852: a, "Eurostar" express. b, ETR 401 Pendolino four-car tilting train, Italy. c, HST 125 inter-city high speed train, UK. d, "Virgin" B-B class high speed diesel-hydraulic express, Spain. e, French Natl. Railways TGV. f, Amtrak "Southwest Chief," US. g, TGV "Atlantique," France. h, "Peloponnese Express," Greece. i, "Shin-Kansen" high-speed electric train, Japan. j, Canadian Natl. turbo train. k, XPT high-speed diesel-electric train, Australia. l, SS1 Co-Co electric locomotive, China.

No. 1853: a, Canadian Natl. U1-F. b, Central Pacific No. 119 at Promontory, US. c, LNER "A4" class streamlined 4-6-2, UK. d, New York Central J32 "Empire State Express," US. e, Canadian Natl. 4-8-4. f, Class 38 Pacific 4-6-2 express, Australia. g, Canadian Pacific 4-6-2 express. h, Southern "West Country" class 4-6-2, UK.i, Norfolk & Western Class J 4-8-4, US. j, RM Class 4-6-0 Pacific, China. k, P-36 class 4-8-4 express, USSR. l, Great Western "King" class 4-6-0, UK.

No. 1853M, British Railways Jubilee class 4-6-0, No. 45627 named "Sierra Leone." No. 1853N, Denver & Rio Grande Western "California Zephyr," US. No. 1853O, 1st train to cross newly opened bridge over Yangtze River, 1968, China. No. 1853P, Beijing-Shanghai Express, China. No. 1853Q, China Railways, "QJ" class 2-10-2.

1995, May 23 **Litho.** *Perf. 14*
1850-1851 A251 200 le #a.-l., each 8.00 8.00
1852 A251 250 le #a.-l. 10.00 10.00
1853 A251 300 le #a.-l. 12.00 12.00

Souvenir Sheets
1853M-1853Q A251 1500 le each 5.00 5.00

Nos. 1853M-1853Q each contain one 56x43mm stamp. No. 1850 exists with two different top margin inscriptions, "THE COLOURFUL RAILROADS OF NORTH AMERICA" and "THE COLOURFUL RAILROADS OF THE WORLD."

New Year 1996 (Year of the Rat) A252

Different stylized rats: No. 1854a, Facing left, purple & multi. b, Facing right, blue green & multi. c, Facing left, blue green & multi. d, Facing right, blue & multi.

No. 1856, Rat, vert.

1996, Jan. 6
1854 A252 200 le Block of 4, #a.-d. 2.00 2.00

Miniature Sheet of 4
1855 A252 200 le #1854a-1854d 2.00 2.00

Souvenir Sheet
1856 A252 500 le multicolored 1.25 1.25

No. 1854 was issued in sheets of 16 stamps.

Disney Characters as Circus Performers A253

Designs: 100 le, Mickey, the magician. 200 le, Clarabelle Cow, the tightrope walker. 250 le, The clowns, Donald and Huey, Dewey and Louie. 300 le, Donald, the lion tamer. 800 le, Minnie, the bareback rider. 1000 le, Goofy and Minnie, the trapeze artists.

No. 1863, Mickey, horiz. No. 1864, Pluto, horiz.

1996, Jan. 29 **Litho.** *Perf. 14x13½*
1857-1862 A253 Set of 6 6.60 6.60

Souvenir Sheets
Perf. 13½x14½
1863-1864 A253 1500 le each 3.75 3.75

Miniature Sheets of 9

Motion Pictures, Cent. A254

No. 1865: a, Film projector. b, Pete. c, Silver. d, Rin-Tin-Tin. e, King Kong. f, Flipper. g, Jaws. h, Elsa. i, Moby Dick.

Directors or stars, scene from movie: No. 1866: a, Lumière Brothers. b, George Méliès. c, Toshiro Mifune d, Clark Gable, Vivian Leigh, David O. Selznick. e, Fritz Lang, Metropolis. f, Akira Kurosawa, Ran. g, Charlie Chaplin. h, Marlène Dietrich. i, Steven Spielberg, ET.

No. 1867, Lassie. No. 1868, Cecil B. de Mille.

1996, Feb. 26 **Litho.** *Perf. 14*
1865-1866 A254 250 le #a.-i., each 7.50 7.50

Souvenir Sheets
1867-1868 A254 1500 le each 3.75 3.75

Sheets of 8 + label

SIERRA LEONE Le200

Paintings from Metropolitan Museum of Art — A255

Entire paintings or details: No. 1869: a, Honfleur, by Jongkind. b, A Boat on the Shore, by Courbet. c, Barges at Pontoise, by Pissarro. d, The Dead Christ with Angels, by Manet. e, Salisbury Cathedral, by Constable. f, A Lady with a Setter Dog, by Eakins. g, Tahitian Women Bathing, by Gaugin. h, Majas on a Balcony, by Goya.

By Renoir: No. 1870: a, In the Meadow. b, By the Seashore. c, Still Life with Peaches and Grapes. d, Marguerite (Margot) Bérard. e, Young Girl in Pink and Black Hat. f, A Waitress at Duval's Restaurant. g, A Road in Louveciennes. h, Two Young Girls at the Piano.

No. 1871: a, Morning, an Overcast Day, Rouen, by Pissarro. b, The Horse Fair, by Bonheur. c, High

Tide: the Bathers, by Homer. d, The Dance Class, by Degas. e, The Brioche, by Manet. f, The Grand Canal, Venice, by Turner. g, St. Tecia Interceding for Plague-stricken Este, by Tiepolo. h, Bridge at Villeneuve, by Sisley.

No. 1872: a, Madame Charpentier, by Renoir. b, Head of Christ, by Rembrandt. c, The Standard-Bearer, by Rembrandt. d, Girl Asleep, by Vermeer. e, Lady with a Lute, by Vermeer. f, Portrait of a Woman, by Rembrandt. g, La Grenouillère, by Monet. h, Woman with Chrysanthemums, by Degas.

No. 1873, The Death of Socrates, by J.L. David. No. 1874, Battle of Constantine and Licinius, by Rubens. No. 1875, Samson and Delilah, by Rubens. No. 1876, The Emblem of Christ Appearing to Constantine, by Rubens.

1996 Litho. *Perf. 13½x14*
1869-1872 A255 200 le #a.-h., each 4.00 4.00

Souvenir Sheets
Perf. 14
1873-1876 A255 1500 le each 3.75 3.75

Nos. 1873-1876 each contain one 85x57mm.
Nos. 1874-1876 are not in the Metropolitan.

1996 Summer Olympic Games, Atlanta A256

100 le, 1932 Olympic Stadium, Los Angeles. 150 le, Archery. 500 le, Rings (gymnastics). 600 le, Pole vault.

No. 1881: a, Field hockey. b, Swimming. c, Equestrian. d, Boxing. e, Pommel horse. f, 100-meter dash.

1996, June 11 Litho. *Perf. 14*
1877-1880 A256 Set of 4 3.40 3.40
1881 A256 300 le Sheet of 6, #a.-f. 4.50 4.50

Souvenir Sheet
1882 A256 1500 le Runner 3.75 3.75

Queen Elizabeth II, 70th Birthday A257

Designs: a, Portrait. b, Receiving flowers. c, Holding flowers, wearing black hat, coat.
1500 le, Waving from balcony.

1996, July 15 Litho. *Perf. 13½x14*
1886 A257 600 le Strip of 3, #a.-c. 4.50 4.50

Souvenir Sheet
1887 A257 1500 le multicolored 3.75 3.75

No. 1886 was issued in sheets of 9 stamps.

UNICEF, 50th Anniv. A258

Designs: 300 le, Children reading. 400 le, Young man, woman reading. 500 le, Children in class.
1500 le, Children's faces.

1996, July 15 *Perf. 14*
1888-1890 A258 Set of 3 3.00 3.00

Souvenir Sheet
1891 A258 1500 le multicolored 3.75 3.75

Sheets of 12

Cats — A259

No. 1892: a, Abyssinian. b, British tabby. c, Norwegian forest. d, Maine coon. e, Bengal. f, Asian. g, American curl. h, Devon rex. i, Tonkinese. j, Egyptian mau. k, Burmese. l, Siamese.

No. 1893: a, British shorthair. b, Tiffany. c, Birman. d, Somali. e, Malayan. f, Japanese bobtail. g, Himalayan. h, Tortoiseshell. i, Oriental. j, Ocicat. k, Chartreux. l, Ragdoll.

No. 1894, Persian. No. 1895, Burmilla.

1996, June 17
1892-1893 A259 200 le #a.-l., each 6.00 6.00

Souvenir Sheets
1894-1895 A259 2000 le each 5.00 5.00

Mushrooms A260

50 le, Cinnabar-red chanterelle. 300 le, Larch suillus. 400 le, Yellow more. 500 le, Variable cort.

No. 1900: a, African driver ant, Indigo milky, Marshall's false monarch (e). b, Scally inky cap. c, Pyxie cup (b). d, Barometer earthstar (c), rainbow grasshopper (h). e, Felt-ringed agaricus, long-horned longhorn. f, Spotted mycena. g, Orange latex milky. h, Tawny grissett amanita fulva, lamellicorn larva.

No. 1901: a, Millar tiger, little nest polymore. b, Coral slime. c, Red-gilled cort. d, Parasitic volvamella, veined tiger. e, Onion-stalked lepiota. f, Blusher. g, Orange mock oyster. h, Lizard claw, red and yellow barbet.

No. 1903, Netted rhodotus. No. 1904, Parasitic psathyrella.

1996, June 17
1896-1899 A260 Set of 4 3.25 3.25

Sheets of 8
1900-1901 A260 250 le #a.-h., each 4.00 4.00

Souvenir Sheets
1902-1903 A260 1500 le each 3.75 3.75

Space Exploration — A261

Designs: a, Pioneer-Venus orbiter, 1986-92. b, Hubble space telescope. c, Voyager probe. d, Space Shuttle Challenger in orbit. e, Pioneer II. f, Mars-Viking 1 lander.
1500 le, Shuttle Challenger landing.

1996
1904 A261 300 le Sheet of 6, #a.-f. 4.50 4.50

Souvenir Sheet
1905 A261 1500 le multicolored 3.75 3.75

Butterflies — A262

Designs: 150 le, Charaxes pleione. 200 le, Eurema brigitta. 300 le, Charaxes ameliae. 500 le, Kallimoides rumia.

No. 1910: a, Precis orithya. b, Palla ussheri. c, Junonia orithya. d, Cymothoe sangaris. e, Cyrestis camillus. f, Precis rhadama. g, Precis cebrene. h, Hypolimnas misippus. i, Colotis danae.

No. 1911, Charaxes bohemani. No. 1912, Papilio antimachus.

1996, Aug. 15 Litho. *Perf. 14*
1906-1909 A262 Set of 4 2.90 2.90
1910 A262 250 le Sheet of 9, #a.-i. 5.60 5.60

Souvenir Sheets
1911-1912 A262 1500 le each 3.75 3.75

Flowers — A263

Designs: 150 le, Tulipa. 200 le, Helichrysum bracteatum. 400 le, Viola. 500 le, Phalaenopis.

No. 1917: a, Fountain. b, Begonia multiflora. c, Narcissus. d, Crocus speciosus. e, Chrysanthemum frutescens. Petunia. f, Cosmos pipinnatus. g, Anemone coronaria. h, Convolvulus minor.

No. 1918: a, Paphiopedilum. b, Cymbidium "Peach bloom." c, Sailboat. d, Miltonia. e, Parides gundalachianus. f, Laeliocatt leya. g, Lycaste aromatica. h, Brassolaeliocatt leya. i, Cymbidium "Southern Lace," Catastica teutila.

No. 1919, Helianthus annuus. No. 1920, Cymbidium "Lucifer."

1996, Aug. 19
1913-1916 A263 Set of 4 3.25 3.25
1917 A263 200 le Sheet of 9, #a.-i. 4.50 4.50
1918 A263 300 le Sheet of 9, #a.-i. 6.75 6.75

Souvenir Sheets
1919-1920 A263 1500 le each 3.75 3.75

Chinese Lunar Calendar A264

Year of the: a, Rat. b, Ox. c, Tiger. d, Hare. e, Dragon. f, Snake. g, Horse. h, Sheep. i, Monkey. j, Rooster. k, Dog. l, Pig.

1996, July 15 Litho. *Perf. 13½x14*
1921 A264 150 le Sheet of 12, #a.-l. 4.50 4.50

Ships A265

No. 1922: a, Clipper ship, "Cutty Sark," 19th cent. b, SS Great Britain, 1846. c, "Dreadnaught," 1906. d, RMS Queen Elizabeth, 1940-72. e, Ocean-going racing yacht, 1962. f, SS United States, 1952. g, Nuclear powered submarine, 1950's. h, Super tanker, 1960's. i, USS Enterprise, 1980s.

No. 1923: a, Greek war galley, 4th cent. BC. b, Roman war galley, 50AD. c, Viking ship, 9th cent. d, Flemish carrack, 15th cent. e, Merchant man, 16th cent. f, Tudor warship, 16th cent. g, Elizabethan galleon, 17th cent. h, Dutch Man of War, 17th cent. i, "Maestrale," Maltese galley, 18th cent.

No. 1924, Cruise ship "Legend of the Seas," 1996 Panama Canal. No. 1925, Egyptian ocean-going ship, 1480BC.

1996, Oct. 29 Litho. *Perf. 14*

Sheets of 9
1922-1923 A265 300 le #a.-i., each 6.75 6.75

Souvenir Sheets
1924-1925 A265 1500 le each 3.75 3.75

Nos. 1924-1925 each contain one 56x43mm stamp.

Christmas A266

Details or entire paintings, by Filippo Lippi: 200 le, Madonna of Humility. 250 le, Coronation of the Virgin. 400 le, 500 le, Annunciation. 600 le, Barbadori Altarpiece. 800 le, Coronation of the Virgin, diff.

Paintings by Rubens: No. 1932, Adoration of the Magi. No. 1933, Holy Family with St. Anne.

1996, Dec. 12 Litho. *Perf. 13½x14*
1926-1931 A266 Set of 6 6.75 6.75

Souvenir Sheets
1932-1933 A266 2000 le each 5.00 5.00

Souvenir Sheets

Fantasies of the Sea — A267

#1934, Sea Dragon's Daughter. #1935, Homo Aquaticus. #1936, Chinese Sea Fairy. #1937, Sea Totem. #1938, The Turtle, horiz. #1939, Mermaid, horiz. #1940, How the Whale Got its Throat, horiz. #1941, Killer Whale Crest. #1942, Aphrodite. #1943, Ship Figurehead. #1944, Lilith. #1945, Queen of the Orkney Islands. #1946, Haida Eagle. #1947, Captain Ahab. #1948, Waskos. #1949, Jonah. #1950, Odysseus. #1951, The Little Mermaid. #1952, Squamish Indians. #1953, Boy on a Dolphin. $1954, Airship to Atlantis. #1955, Sea Bishop. #1956, 20,000 Leagues Under the Sea. #1957, Whale Song. #1958, Arion. #1959, Dragonrider of Pern. #1960, Kelpie. #1961, Natsihlane. #1962, Merman. #1963, Albatross. #1964, City under polar ice melt. #1965, Tom Swift. #1966, The Flying Dutchman, horiz. #1967, Sea Centaur. #1968, Lang (dragon), horiz. #1969, Triton. #1970, Sea Serpent. #1971, Arthropod sea monster.

1996, Dec. 19 Litho. *Perf. 14*
1934-1971 A267 1500 le Each 3.75 3.75

Numbers have been reserved for additional listings to complete this set.

New Year 1997 (Year of the Ox) A268

Various stylized oxen, background color: Nos. 1975-1976: a, purple. b, green. c, blue. d, claret.
800 le, like #1975d, vert.

1997, Jan. 8 Litho. *Perf. 14*
1975 A268 150 le Block of 4, #a.-d. 1.50 1.50
1976 A268 250 le Sheet of 4, #a.-d. 2.50 2.50

Souvenir Sheet
1977 A268 800 le multicolored 2.00 2.00

No. 1975 was issued in sheets of 16 stamps.

Disney's Aladdin in Christmas Scenes — A269

Designs: 10 le, Aladdin, Jasmine. 15 le, Santa, Genie. 20 le, Aladdin, Jasmine on magic carpet. 25 le, Genie as Christmas tree. 30 le, Aladdin, Genie "Santa." 100 le, Jasmine, Aladdin, Genie. 800 le, Genie's letter to Santa. 1000 le, Genie's Christmas carol.

No. 1986, Aladdin, Abu. No. 1987, Jasmine, Aladdin, horiz.

1997, Jan. 27 ***Perf. 14x13½***

1978-1985 A269 Set of 8 5.00 5.00

Souvenir Sheets

Perf. 14x13½, 13½x14

1986-1987 A269 2000 le each 5.00 5.00

Hong Kong — A270

Panoramic view of Hong Kong: No. 1988, in daytime. No. 1989, at night.

1997, Feb. 12 **Litho.** ***Perf. 14***

Sheets of 4

1988-1989 A270 500 le #a.-d., each 5.30 5.30

UNESCO, 50th Anniv. A271

World Heritage Sites: 60 le, Town of Kizhi Pogost, Russia. 200 le, Durmitor Natl. Park, Yugoslavia. 250 le, City of Nessebar, Bulgaria. 400 le, City of Bukhara, Uzbekistan. 500 le, Monastery of Kiev-Pechersk, Ukraine. 700 le, Mountain Walks, Vlkolinec, Slovakia.

No. 1996: a, Town of Roros, Norway. b, City of Warsaw, Poland. c, Cathedral of Notre Dame, Luxembourg. d, City of Vilnius, Lithuania. e, Jelling, Denmark. f, Old Church of Petäjävesi, Finland. g, Sweden. h, Cathedral City of Bern, Switzerland.

No. 1997: a, Area surrounding Mt. Kilimanjaro, Tanzania. b, Monument, Fasil Ghebbi, Ethiopia. c, Natl. Park, Mt. Ruwenzori, Uganda. d, Abu Simbel, Egypt. e, Tsingy Bemaraha Strict Nature Reserve, Madagascar. f, House, Djenne, Mali. g, Traditional house construction, Ghana. h, Large house, Aromey.

Various views of Himeji-Jo, Japan, vert: No. 1998: a, b, c, d, e.

No. 1999, Natl. Bird Sanctuary, Djudj, Senegal, horiz. No. 2000, Acropolis, Athens, Greece, horiz.

1997, Mar. 24 **Litho.** ***Perf. 13½x14***

1990-1995 A271 Set of 6 5.50 5.50

Sheets of 8 + Label

1996-1997 A271 300 le #a.-h., each 6.00 6.00

Sheet of 5 + Label

1998 A271 500 le #a.-e. 6.25 6.25

Souvenir Sheets

1999-2000 A271 2000 le each 5.00 5.00

Sierra Leone Le400 Paintings by Hiroshige (1797-1858) A272

No. 2001: a, Hatsune Riding Grounds, Bakuro-cho. b, Mannen Bridge, Fukagawa. c, Ryogoku Bridge and the Great Riverbank. d, Asakusa River, Great Riverbank, Miyato River. e, Silk-goods Lane, Odenma-cho. f, Mokuboji Temple, Uchigawa Inlet, Gozensaihata.

No. 2002, Tsukudajima from Eitai Bridge. No. 2003, Nihonbashi Bridge and Edobashi Bridge.

1997 **Litho.** ***Perf. 13½x14***

2001 A272 400 le Sheet of 6, #a.-f. 6.50 6.50

Souvenir Sheets

2002-2003 A272 1500 le each 3.75 3.75

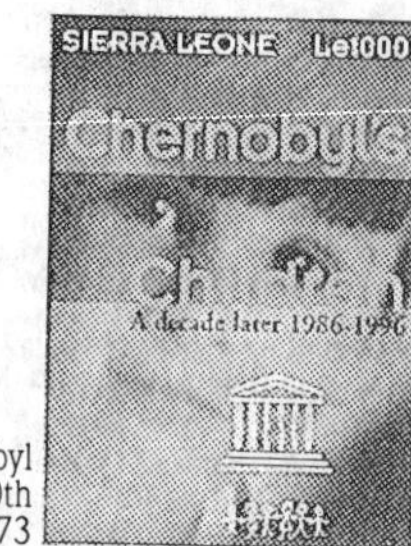

Chernobyl Disaster, 10th Anniv. — A273

Designs: 1000 le, UNESCO. 1500 le, Chabad's Children of Chernobyl.

1997, June 23

2004 A273 1000 le multicolored 2.75 2.75

2005 A273 1500 le multicolored 4.00 4.00

Queen Elizabeth II and Prince Philip, 50th Wedding Anniv. A274

No. 2006: a, Queen. b, Royal arms. c, Black & white photograph, Prince in dress uniform. d, Black & white photograph, Prince in tuxedo, bow tie. e, Palace of Holyroodhouse. f, Prince in hat guiding horses.

1500 le, Queen, Prince in colored photograph.

1997, June 23 ***Perf. 14***

2006 A274 400 le Sheet of 6, #a.-f. 6.50 6.50

Souvenir Sheet

2007 A274 1500 le multicolored 4.00 4.00

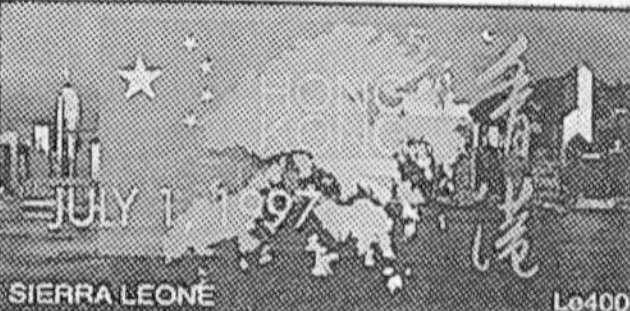

Return of Hong Kong to China — A275

Designs: 400 le, Flag of China, map of China, Hong Kong, Victoria at night. 500 le, 650 le, Flag of China, July 1, 1997, city scene inside letters spelling "Hong Kong." 550 le, 600 le, Flag of China, Victoria harbor inside letters spelling "Hong Kong '97." 800 le, Victoria harbor, Deng Xiaoping (1904-97).

Illustration reduced.

1997, June 23

2008-2013 A275 Set of 6 9.50 9.50

Nos. 2008-2013 were each issued in sheets of 3.

Souvenir Sheets

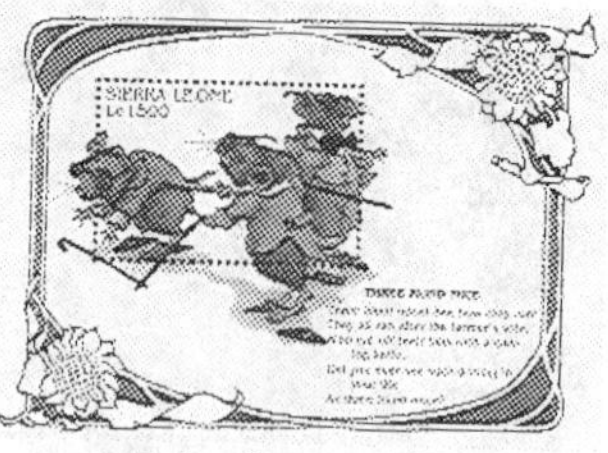

Mother Goose — A276

Designs: No. 2014, Three Blind Mice. No. 2015, Woman holding out full skirt as "Myself."

1997, June 23 **Litho.** ***Perf. 14***

2014-2015 A276 1500 le each 4.00 4.00

1998 Winter Olympic Games, Nagano A277

Designs: 250 le, Stadium, Calgary, 1988, American Indian. 300 le, Freestyle aerial skiing, vert. 500 le, Ice hockey, vert. 800 le, Dan Jansen, 1000-meter speed skater, vert.

No. 2022, vert: a, Peggy Fleming, figure skating. b, Japanese ski jumper, Nordic combined. c, 2-man luge, Germany. d, Frank-Peter Roetsch, biathlon, E. Germany.

No. 2023, Jamaican bobsled team, vert. No. 2024, Johann Olav Koss, Norway, vert.

1997, July 16 **Litho.** ***Perf. 14***

2018-2021 A277 Set of 4 4.90 4.90

2022 A276 300 le Strip of 4, #a.-d. 3.25 3.25

Souvenir Sheets

2023-2024 A277 1500 le each 4.00 4.00

No. 2022 was issued in sheets of 8 stamps.

1998 World Cup Soccer Championships, France — A278

Players: 100 le, Stabile, Uruguay. 150 le, Schiavio, Italy. 200 le, Kocsis, Hungary. 250 le, Nejedly, Czechoslovakia. 500 le, Leonidas, Brazil. 600 le, Ademir, Brazil.

No. 2031: a, Dwight Yorke, Trinidad & Tobago. b, Dennis Bergkamp, Holland. c, Steve McManaman, England. d, Ryan Giggs, Wales. e, Romario, Brazil, f, Faustino Asprilla, Colombia. g, Roy Keane, Ireland. h, Peter Schmeichel, Denmark.

No. 2032, Pele, Brazil, horiz. No. 2033, Lato, Poland, horiz.

Perf. 13½x14, 14x13½

1997, July 23

2025-2030 A278 Set of 6 4.75 4.75

Sheet of 8

2031 A278 300 le #a.-h. + 2 labels 6.50 6.50

Souvenir Sheets

2032-2033 A278 1500 le each 4.00 4.00

Classic Horror Movies A279

Lead character, movie: No. 2034: a, Lon Chaney, "Phantom of the Opera," 1934. b, Boris Karloff, "The Mummy," 1932. c, Fredric March, "Dr. Jekyll & Mr. Hyde, " 1932. d, Lon Chaney, Jr., "The Wolf Man," 1941. e, Charles Laughton, "Island of Lost Souls," 1933. f, Lionel Atwill, "Mystery of the Wax Museum, " 1933. g, Bela Lugosi, "Dracula," 1931. h, Vincent Price, "The Haunted Palace," 1963. i, Elsa Lanchester, "Bride of Frankenstein," 1935.

3000 le, Bela Lugosi, Boris Karloff, "Son of Frankenstein," 1939.

1997, Aug. 15 ***Perf. 14***

2034 A279 300 le Sheet of 9, #a.-i. 7.25 7.25

Souvenir Sheet

2035 A279 3000 le multicolored 8.00 8.00

Domestic Cats — A280

Designs: 150 le, American short hair tabby. 200 le, British short hair. 500 le, Turkish angora.

No. 2039: a, Chartreux. b, Abyssinian. c, Burmese. d, White angora. e, Japanese bobtail. f, Cymric.

1500 le, Egyptian mau.

1997, Aug. 29

2036-2038 A280 Set of 3 2.25 2.25

2039 A280 400 le Sheet of 6, #a.-f. 6.50 6.50

Souvenir Sheet

2040 A280 1500 le multicolored 4.00 4.00

No. 2040 contains one 64x32mm stamp.

Butterflies — A281 Orchids — A282

Designs: 150 le, Vindula erota. 200 le, Pereutel leucodrosime. 250 le, Dynstor napolean. 300 le, Thauria aliris. 600 le, Papilio aegeus. 800 le, Amblypodia anita. 1500 le, Kallimoides rumia. 2000 le, Papilio dardanas.

No. 2049: a, Lycaena dispar. b, Graphium sarpedon. c, Euploe core. d, Papilio cresphontes. e, Colotis danae. f, Battus philenor.

No. 2050: a, Mylothris chloris. b, Argynnis lathonia. c, Elymnias agondas. d, Palla ussheri. e, Papilio glaucus. f, Cercyonis pegala.

No. 2051, Hebomoia glaucippe, horiz. No. 2052, Colias eurytheme, horiz.

1997, Aug. 1 **Litho.** ***Perf. 14***

2041-2048 A281 Set of 8 15.00 15.00

Sheets of 6

2049 A281 500 le #a.-f. 8.00 8.00

2050 A281 600 le #a.-f. 9.75 9.75

Souvenir Sheets

2051-2052 A281 3000 le each 8.00 8.00

1997, Sept. 1

Designs: 150 le, Ansellia africana. 200 le, Maxillaria praestans. 250 le, Cymbidium mimi. 300 le, Dendrobium bigibbum. 500 le, Encyclia vitellina. 800 le, Epidendrum prismatocarpum.

No. 2059: a, Laelia anceps. b, Paphiopedilum fairrieanum. c, Restrepia lansbergii. d, Yamadara cattleya. e, Cleistes divaricata. f, Calypso bulbosa.

No. 2060, Odontoglossum schlieperianum. No. 2061, Paphiopedilum tonsum.

2053-2058 A282 Set of 6 6.00 6.00

2059 A282 400 le Sheet of 6, #a.-f. 3.25 3.25

Souvenir Sheets

2060-2061 A282 1500 le each 4.00 4.00

Motion Pictures Directed by Alfred Hitchcock A283

No. 2062: a, Ray Milland in "Dial M for Murder." b, James Stewart, Kim Novak in "Vertigo." c, Cary Grant, Ingrid Bergman in "Notorious." d, John Dall, James Stewart in "Rope." e, Cary Grant in "North by Northwest." f, Grace Kelly, James Stewart in "Rear Window." g, Joan Fontaine, Laurence Olivier in "Rebecca." h, Tippi Hedren in "The Birds." i, Janet Leigh in "Psycho."
1500 le, Alfred Hitchcock.

1997, Aug. 15 Litho. *Perf. 14*
2062 A283 350 le Sheet of 9, #a.-i. 8.50 8.50

Souvenir Sheet
2063 A283 1500 le multicolored 4.00 4.00

Dogs — A284

Designs: 100 le, Shetland sheep dog. 250 le, Alaskan husky. 600 le, Jack Russell terrier.
No. 2067: a, Basset hound. b, Irish setter. c, St. Bernard. d, German shepherd. e, Dalmatian. f, Cocker spaniel.
1500 le, Boxer.

1997, Aug. 29
2064-2066 A284 Set of 3 2.50 2.50
2067 A284 400 le Sheet of 6, #a.-f. 6.50 6.50

Souvenir Sheet
2068 A284 1500 le multicolored 4.00 4.00

No. 2068 contains one 31x63mm stamp.

Disney Christmas Stamps A285

Designs: 150 le, Huey, Dewey, & Louie. 200 le, Mickey's kids. 250 le, Daisy Duck. 300 le, Minnie. 400 le, Mickey. 500 le, Donald Duck. 600 le, Pluto. 800 le, Goofy.
No. 2077: a, like #2071. b, like #2069. c, like #2074. d, like #2072. e, like #2070. f, like #2073.
No. 2078, Mickey in sleigh. No. 2079, Mickey, Donald, Daisy in Santa suits, horiz.

1997, Oct. 1 *Perf. 13½x14, 14x13½*
2069-2076 A285 Set of 8 8.50 8.50
2077 A285 50 le Sheet of 6, #a.-f. 1.60 1.60

Souvenir Sheets
2078-2079 A285 2000 le multi 5.25 5.25

Civilian Airliners A286

No. 2080: a, SUD Caravelle 6. b, DeHavilland comet. c, Boeing 707. d, Airbus industrie A-300.
No. 2080E: f, Benoist Type XIV. g, Junkers JU52/3m. h, Douglas DC-3. i, Sikorsky S-42.
#2081, Concorde. #2081A, Lockheed L-1649A Starliner.

1997, Oct. 6 *Perf. 14*
2080 A286 600 le Sheet of 4, #a.-d. + label 6.50 6.50
2080E A286 600 le Sheet of 4, #f.-i. + label 6.50 6.50

Souvenir Sheets
2081-2081A A286 2000 le each 5.25 5.25

Nos. 2081-2081A contain one 91x34mm stamp.

Christmas A287

Entire paintings or details: 100 le, 150 le, The Annunciation, by Titian (diff. details). 200 le, Madonna of Foligno, by Raphael. 250 le, The Annunciation, by Michelino. 500 le, The Prophet Isaiah, by Michelangelo. 600 le, Three Angels, by Master of the Rhenish Housebook.
No. 2088, The Fall of the Rebel Angels, by Peter Bruegel the Elder, horiz. No. 2089, Unidentified painting of Angel pointing hand in air, man with book, horiz.

1997, Dec. 24
2082-2087 A287 Set of 6 4.75 4.75

Souvenir Sheets
2088-2089 A287 2000 le each 5.25 5.25

Diana, Princess of Wales (1961-97) — A288

Various portraits, color of sheet margin: No. 2090, Pale pink. No. 2091, Pale blue. No. 2092, Pale yellow.
No. 2093, Wearing wide-brimmed hat. No. 2094, With Prince Harry (in margin). No. 2095, Helping to feed needy.

1998, Jan. 12 Litho. *Perf. 14*

Sheets of 6
2090-2092 A288 400 le #a.-f., each 6.50 6.50

Souvenir Sheets
2093-2095 A288 1500 le each 4.00 4.00

New Year 1998 (Year of the Tiger) A289

Various stylized tigers in: No. 2096: a, purple. b, maroon. c, bright lilac rose. d, orange.
800 le, maroon, vert.

1998, Jan. 26 Litho. *Perf. 14*
2096 A289 250 le Sheet of 4, #a.-d. 2.75 2.75

Souvenir Sheet
2097 A289 800 le red org & multi 2.25 2.25

AIR POST STAMPS

Catalogue values for unused stamps in this section are for Never Hinged items.

Independence — Progress Issue

Nos. 197, 199, 204 and 206 Surcharged Like Nos. 242-247 plus "AIRMAIL" in Carmine, Red, Violet, Blue or Orange

Perf. 13, 13½

1963, Apr. 27 Wmk. 4 Engr.

Center in Black

C1 A27 7p on 1½p (C) .15 .15
C2 A27 1sh3p on 1½p (R) .18 .18
C3 A28 2sh6p brown org (V) .38 .38
C4 A28 3sh on 3p (Bl) .42 .42
C5 A28 6sh on 3p (O) .52 .52
C6 A27 11sh on 10sh (C) 1.65 1.65
C7 A27 11sh on £1 (C) 500.00 175.00
Nos. C1-C6 (6) 3.30 3.30

Nos. 221, 224, 213, 223 and 207 Surcharged or Overprinted in Brown, Red, Black, Violet, Ultramarine or Orange

1853–1859–1963
Oldest Postage Stamp
Newest G.P.O.
in West Africa
AIRMAIL 2/6

Perf. 13x13½, 13½x13, 13

1963, Nov. 4 Wmk. 4, 336
C8 A31 7p on 3p (Br) .20 .20
C9 A32 1sh3p blue & blk (R) .24 .24
C10 A30 2sh6p on 4p (Bk) .48 .48
C11 A31 3sh on 3p (V) .60 .60
C12 A32 6sh on 6p (U) 1.25 1.25
C13 A27 £1 orange & blk (O) 8.50 8.50
Nos. C8-C13 (6) 11.27 11.27

Overprint is in 6 lines on Nos. C8, C11 and C12. A number of surcharge varieties and errors exist.

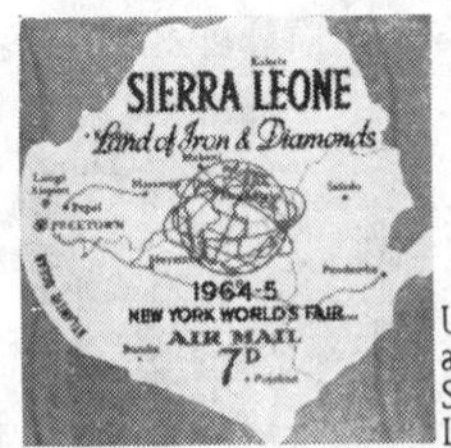

Unisphere and Map of Sierra Leone — AP1

Engraved and Lithographed

1964, Feb. 10 Unwmk. *Imperf.*

Self-adhesive
C14 AP1 7p multicolored .15 .15
C15 AP1 9p multicolored .15 .15
C16 AP1 1sh3p multicolored .18 .18
C17 AP1 2sh6p multicolored .35 .35
C18 AP1 3sh6p multicolored .50 .50
C19 AP1 6sh multicolored .90 .90
C20 AP1 11sh multicolored 1.40 1.40
Nos. C14-C20 (7) 3.63 3.63

New York World's Fair, 1964-65.
For surcharge see No. C33.

John F. Kennedy AP2

Self-adhesive

1964, May 11
C21 AP2 7p multicolored .15 .15
C22 AP2 9p multicolored .15 .15
C23 AP2 1sh3p multicolored .22 .22
C24 AP2 2sh6p multicolored .42 .42
C25 AP2 3sh6p multicolored .60 .60
C26 AP2 6sh multicolored 1.10 1.10
C27 AP2 11sh multicolored 1.75 1.75
Nos. C21-C27 (7) 4.39 4.39

For surcharges see Nos. C32, C34-C36.

Nos. 241, 213, 219 and 218 Surcharged in Dark Blue, Black, Red or Violet Blue

Perf. 11½x11, 13½x13, 13x13½

1964, Aug. 4 Engr. Wmk. 336
C28 A36 7c on 1sh3p (#241) (DB) .22 .22
C29 A30 20c on 4p (#213) .42 .42
C30 A29 30c on 10sh (#219) (R) .70 .70
C31 A29 40c on 5sh (#218) (VB) .85 .85
Nos. C28-C31 (4) 2.19 2.19

Map-shaped Issues of 1964 Surcharged in Red or Black

Engraved and Lithographed

1964-65 Unwmk. *Imperf.*
C32 AP2 7c on 7p (#C21) (R) .15 .15
C33 AP1 7c on 9p (#C15) .85 .85
C34 AP2 60c on 9p (#C22) 1.25 1.25
C35 AP2 1 le on 1sh3p (#C23) (R) 2.00 2.00
C36 AP2 2 le on 11sh (#C27) 4.25 4.25
Nos. C32-C36 (5) 8.50 8.50

Issue dates: Aug. 4, 1964, Nos. C35-C36. Jan. 20, 1965, Nos. C32, C34. April, 1965, No. C33.

Regular Issue of 1963 Surcharged like Nos. 300-305 with "AIRMAIL" added

Wmk. 336

1965, May 19 Photo. *Perf. 14*

Designs of Surcharge: No. C37, C39-C40, Sir Milton Margai and Sir Winston Churchill. No. C38, Margai. No. C41, Churchill.

C37 A35 7c on 2p (#230) .15 .15
C38 A34 15c on ½p (#227) .40 .40
C39 A35 30c on 6p (#233) .75 .75
C40 A35 1 le on £1 (#239) 2.75 2.75
C41 A34 2 le on 10sh (#238) 5.50 5.50
Nos. C37-C41 (5) 9.55 9.55

The portraits and inscription on No. C39 are white, the denomination and "AIRMAIL" are orange.
Ten more surcharges were issued Nov. 9, 1965: "2c" on Nos. C16, C23 and C25. "3c" on Nos. C14 and C22. "5c" on Nos. C17-C19, C24, and C26. Value $4 each.
One further surcharge was issued Jan. 28, 1966: "TWO/Leones" on No. C39. Value $10.

Type of Regular Issue and

Diamond Necklace — AP3

Litho.; Reversed Embossing

1965, Dec. 17 Unwmk. *Imperf.*

Self-adhesive
C53 AP3 7c black, grn, gold & bl .35 .35
C54 AP3 15c black, brnz, car & bl .75 .75

Engr. and Embossed on Paper
C55 A41 40c multi, *cream* 1.75 1.75
Nos. C53-C55 (3) 2.85 2.85

Various advertisements printed on peelable paper backing. Nos. C54-C55 have side tabs for handling and come packed in boxes of 100. No. C53 is without side tab and comes 25 stamps attached to one sheet.
For overprints and surcharges see Nos. C68-C69, C79-C83.

Nos. 248, 229, 232, 234 and 236 Surcharged and Overprinted: "AIRMAIL/FIVE YEARS/INDEPENDENCE/1961-1966"

1966, Apr. 27 Wmk. 336
C56 A37 7c on 3p pur & red .15 .15
C57 A34 15c on 1sh multi .35 .35
C58 A34 25c on 2sh6p multi .55 .55
C59 A34 50c on 1½p multi 1.10 1.10
C60 A34 1 le on 4p multi 2.50 2.50
Nos. C56-C60 (5) 4.65 4.65

The denomination on No. C60 is spelled out "One Leone."

Self-adhesive & Imperf.
Nos. C61-C131, C135-C142 are self-adhesive and imperforate.

Gold Coin Type of Regular Issue

Designs: 7c, 10c, ¼ Golde coin. 15c, 30c, ½ Golde coin. 50c, 2 le, 1 Golde coin. (7c, 15c, 50c, Map of Sierra Leone. 10c, 30c, 2 le, Lion's head.)
Diameter: 7c, 10c, 38mm; 15c, 30c, 54mm; 50c, 2 le, 82mm.

Lithographed; Embossed on Gilt Foil

1966, Nov. 12 Unwmk.
C61 A42 7c red & orange .15 .15
C62 A42 10c dull blue & red .15 .15
C63 A42 15c red & orange .20 .20
C64 A42 30c black & rose lilac .40 .40

C65	A42	50c rose lilac & emer	.75	.75
C66	A42	2 le green & black	3.75	3.75
		Nos. C61-C66 (6)	5.40	5.40

Advertising printed on paper backing.

Type of Regular Issue, 1965 and No. C55 Surcharged 11½

1967, Dec. 2 **Engr. & Embossed**

C67	A41	10c multi (red frame), *cream*	.50	.50
a.		Black frame	.50	.50
C68	A41	11½c on 40c multi, *cr*	.40	.40
C69	A41	25c on 40c multi, *cr*	1.00	1.00
		Nos. C67-C69 (3)	1.90	1.90

Eagle — AP4

Embossed Foil on Black Paper

1967, Dec. 2 **Unwmk.**

C70	AP4	9½c black, gold & red	.75	.75
C71	AP4	15c black, gold & grn	.90	.90

Various advertisements printed on peelable paper backing. See Nos. C98-C99, C118-C124.

Map Type of Regular Issue

Designs: Each denomination shows map of Africa with map of one of the following countries — Portuguese Guinea, South Africa, Mozambique, Rhodesia, South West Africa or Angola. Sheets of 30 (6x5) have 5 horizontal rows containing one stamp of each design.

1968, Sept. 25 **Litho.**

C72	A43	7½c multicolored	.30	.30
C73	A43	9½c multicolored	.45	.45
C74	A43	14½c multicolored	.65	.65
C75	A43	18½c multicolored	.75	.75
C76	A43	25c multicolored	1.25	1.25
C77	A43	1 le multicolored	7.50	7.50
C78	A43	2 le multicolored	17.50	17.50
		Nos. C72-C78 (7)	28.40	28.40
		7 Strips of 6, 1 of each design (42)	170.40	

No. C55 Overprinted and Surcharged in Red Similar to Nos. 364-368

Engraved and Embossed on Paper

1968, Nov. 30

C79	A41	6½c on 40c multi	.15	.15
C80	A41	17½c on 40c multi	.38	.38
C81	A41	22½c on 40c multi	.38	.38
C82	A41	28½c on 40c multi	.55	.55
C83	A41	40c multicolored	.85	.85
		Nos. C79-C83 (5)	2.31	2.31

Scroll Type of Regular Issue

Designs: 7½c, #C54. 9½c, #C70. 20c, #C16. 30c, #C26. 50c, #165. 2 le, #207 with "2nd Year of Independence" overprint. All are horiz.

1969, Mar. 1 **Litho.**

C84	A44	7½c multicolored	.24	.24
C85	A44	9½c multicolored	.28	.28
C86	A44	20c multicolored	.60	.60
C87	A44	30c multicolored	.90	.90
C88	A44	50c multicolored	2.25	2.25
C89	A44	2 le multicolored	15.00	15.00
		Nos. C84-C89 (6)	19.27	19.27

Various advertisements printed on peelable paper backing. No. C84 has side tab for handling and comes packed in boxes of 50. Nos. C85-C89 are without side tabs and come 20 stamps attached to one sheet.

For surcharges see Nos. C135-C136.

Pepel Port Types of Regular Issue

Designs: 7½c, 15c, Globe, tanker, flags of Sierra Leone and Japan. Anvil Shape with Flags of Sierra Leone and: 9½c, 2 le, Union Jack. 25c, Netherlands. 1 le, West Germany.

1969, July 10

C90	A45	7½c multicolored	.15	.15
C91	A46	9½c multicolored	.16	.16
C92	A45	15c multicolored	.26	.26
C93	A46	25c multicolored	.40	.40
C94	A46	1 le multicolored	1.65	1.65
C95	A46	2 le multicolored	3.25	3.25
		Nos. C90-C95 (6)	5.87	5.87

Various advertisements printed on peelable paper backing. No. C90 has side tab for handling and comes packed in boxes of 50. Nos. C91-C95 are without side tabs and come 20 stamps attached to one sheet.

Bank Type of Regular Issue

Lithographed; Gold Impressed

1969, Sept. 10

C96	A47	9½c yel grn, vio & gold	.90	.90

Advertising printed on peelable paper backing; 20 imperf. stamps to a sheet of backing, roulette 10.

Cola Nut Type of Regular Issue and Type of 1967

Typo.; Embossed on White Paper

1969, Sept. 10

C97	A40	7c yellow, maroon & car	.40	.40

Embossed Foil on Black Paper

C98	AP4	9½c black, gold & blue	.50	.50
C99	AP4	15c black, gold & red	.75	.75
		Nos. C97-C99 (3)	1.65	1.65

No. C97 has side tab for handling and comes packed in boxes of 100. Nos. C98-C99 have advertisements printed on peelable paper backing, side tabs and come packed in boxes of 50.

Boy Scout, Lord Baden-Powell and Scout Emblem — AP5

1969, Dec. 6 **Litho.**

C100	AP5	7½c multicolored	.48	.40
C101	AP5	9½c multicolored	.60	.48
C102	AP5	15c multicolored	1.25	.80
C103	AP5	22c multicolored	2.00	1.40
C104	AP5	55c multicolored	8.00	6.50
C105	AP5	3 le multicolored	100.00	72.50
		Nos. C100-C105 (6)	112.33	82.08

60th anniv. of the Sierra Leone Boy Scouts. Various advertising printed on peelable paper backing. No. C100 has side tab for handling and comes packed in boxes of 100. Nos. C101-C105 are without side tabs and come 20 stamps attached to one sheet.

No. 357 Surcharged "AIRMAIL" and New Denomination in Metallic Emerald, Lilac, Blue, Green, Bronze or Silver

1970, Mar 28

C106	A43	7½c on ½c (E)	.30	.30
C107	A43	9½c on ½c (L)	.40	.40
C108	A43	15c on ½c (Bl)	.50	.50
C109	A43	28c on ½c (G)	1.00	1.00
C110	A43	40c on ½c (Br)	1.75	1.75
C111	A43	2 le on ½c (S)	9.00	9.00
		Nos. C106-C111 (6)	12.95	12.95

See design paragraph over No. 357.

EXPO Type of Regular Issue

Maps of Sierra Leone and Japan.

1970, June 22 **Litho.**

C112	A49	7½c multicolored	.16	.16
C113	A49	9½c multicolored	.20	.20
C114	A49	15c multicolored	.35	.35
C115	A49	25c multicolored	.70	.70
C116	A49	50c multicolored	1.50	1.50
C117	A49	3 le multicolored	7.75	7.75
		Nos. C112-C117 (6)	10.66	10.66

Various advertising printed on peelable paper backing.

Eagle Type of 1967

1970, Oct. 3 **Embossed Foil**

C118	AP4	7½c crimson & gold	.45	.45
C119	AP4	9½c emerald & cop	.55	.50
C120	AP4	15½c grnsh bl & sil	.85	.65
C121	AP4	25c brt red lil & gold	1.40	1.10
C122	AP4	50c gold & emer	2.75	2.25
C123	AP4	1 le silver & dk bl	5.50	4.50
C124	AP4	2 le gold & brt bl	11.00	9.25
		Nos. C118-C124 (7)	22.50	18.70

Advertisements printed on peelable paper backing. Issued in sheets of 10.

"Treasure of Sierra Leone" Diamond — AP6

Lithographed and Embossed

1970, Dec. 30

C125	AP6	7½c multicolored	.25	.25
C126	AP6	9½c multicolored	.30	.30
C127	AP6	15c multicolored	.50	.50
C128	AP6	25c multicolored	.50	.50
C129	AP6	75c multicolored	5.00	4.00
C130	AP6	2 le multicolored	22.50	17.50
		Nos. C125-C130 (6)	29.05	23.05

Diamond industry. Advertisement printed on peelable paper backing. Sheets of 20.

Traffic Type of Regular Issue

1971, Mar. 1 **Litho.**

C131	A53	9½c vio blue & org	.75	.75

Advertisements printed on peelable paper backing.

Nos. 211, 215, 228 and C87 Surcharged in Dark Red, Dark Blue or Black

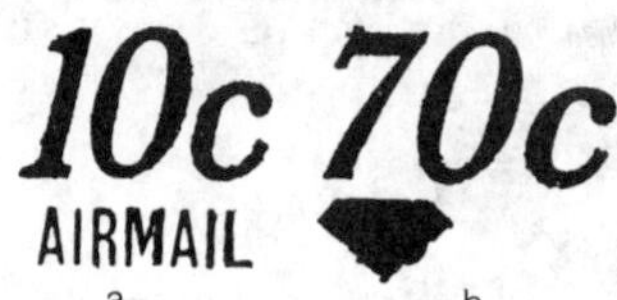

1971, Mar. 1 **Engr.** **Wmk. 336**

C132	A29(a)	10c on 2p (DR)	.35	.32
C133	A29(a)	20c on 1sh (DB)	.70	.65

Photo. ***Perf. 14***

C134	A35(a)	50c on 1p (Bk)	1.75	1.50

Unwmk.

Litho. ***Imperf.***

C135	A44(b)	70c on 30c (DB)	2.75	2.50
C136	A44(b)	1 le on 30c (Bk)	4.00	3.25
		Nos. C132-C136 (5)	9.55	8.22

Lion's Head and Bugles AP7

Lithographed and Embossed (Gold)

1971, Apr. 27

C137	AP7	7½c multicolored	.16	.16
C138	AP7	9½c multicolored	.18	.18
C139	AP7	15c multicolored	.26	.26
C140	AP7	25c multicolored	.45	.45
C141	AP7	75c multicolored	1.75	1.75
C142	AP7	2 le multicolored	6.00	6.00
		Nos. C137-C142 (6)	8.80	8.80

10th anniversary of independence. Advertisements printed on peelable paper backing. Stamps are in shape of Sierra Leone map and in flag colors.

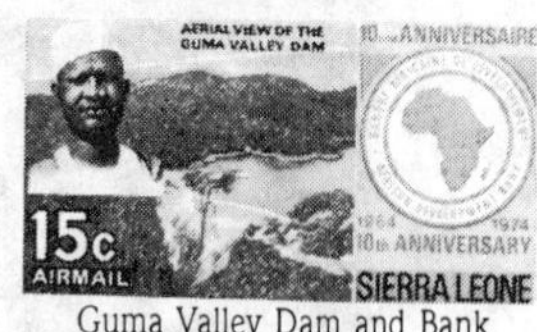

Guma Valley Dam and Bank Emblem — AP8

1975, Jan. 14 **Litho.** ***Perf. 13½***

C143	AP8	15c multicolored	1.00	1.00

African Development Bank, 10th anniv.

Congo River Type of 1975

1975, Aug. 24 **Litho.** ***Perf. 13x13½***

C144	A57	20c multicolored	.75	.75

Mano River Type of 1975

1975, Oct. 3 ***Perf. 13x13½***

C145	A58	15c multicolored	.60	.60

SINGAPORE

'siŋ-ə-ˌpȯr

LOCATION — An island just off the southern tip of the Malay Peninsula, south of Johore
GOVT. — Republic in British Commonwealth
AREA — 239 sq. mi.
POP. — 2,529,100 (est. 1984)
CAPITAL — Singapore

Singapore, Malacca and Penang were the British settlements which, together with the Federated Malay States, composed the former colony of Straits Settlements. On April 1, 1946, Singapore became a separate colony when the Straits Settlements colony was dissolved. Malacca and Penang joined the Malayan Union, which was renamed the Federation of Malaya in 1948. In 1959 Singapore became a state with internal self-government.

Singapore joined the Federation of Malaysia in 1963 and withdrew in 1965.

100 Cents = 1 Dollar

Catalogue values for all unused stamps in this country are for Never Hinged items.

Watermark

Wmk. 366- S multiple

King George VI — A1

1948 **Wmk. 4** **Typo.** ***Perf. 14***

1	A1	1c black	.15	.15
2	A1	2c orange	.15	.15
3	A1	3c green	.30	.15
4	A1	4c chocolate	.30	.15
6	A1	6c gray	.30	.15
7	A1	8c rose red	.40	.30
9	A1	10c plum	.35	.15
11	A1	15c ultra	2.75	.15
12	A1	20c dk green & blk	1.65	.40
14	A1	25c org & rose lilac	1.50	.15
16	A1	40c dk vio & rose red	7.25	10.00
17	A1	50c ultra & black	8.50	.25
18	A1	$1 vio brn & ultra	12.50	.40
19	A1	$2 rose red & emer	72.50	3.00
20	A1	$5 chocolate & emer	150.00	3.75
		Nos. 1-20 (15)	258.60	19.30
		Set, hinged	140.00	

1949-52 *Perf. 18*
1a A1 1c black ('52) .65 .15
2a A1 2c orange .65 .15
4a A1 4c chocolate .65 .15
5 A1 5c rose violet ('52) 3.25 .15
6a A1 6c gray ('52) 1.65 .15
8 A1 8c green ('52) 6.50 2.50
9a A1 10c plum ('50) 1.10 .15
10 A1 12c rose red ('52) 6.50 2.50
11a A1 15c ultra ('50) 7.50 .30
12a A1 20c dark green & black 6.50 1.25
13 A1 20c ultra ('52) 5.25 .75
14a A1 25c orange & rose lilac ('50) 3.25 .15
15 A1 35c dk vio & rose red ('52) 10.00 3.00
16a A1 40c dk vio & rose red ('51) 26.00 15.00
17a A1 50c ultra & black ('50) 10.00 .15
18a A1 $1 violet brown & ultra 19.00 .75
b. Wmk. 4a (error) *1,000.*
19a A1 $2 rose red & emer ('51) 150.00 3.00
b. Wmk. 4a (error) *1,000.*
20a A1 $5 choc & emerald ('51) 250.00 3.75
Nos. 1a-20a (18) 508.45 34.00
Set, hinged 260.00

Common Design Types pictured following the introduction.

Silver Wedding Issue
Common Design Types
Inscribed: "Singapore"

1948, Oct. 25 Photo. *Perf. 14x14½*
21 CD304 10c purple 1.00 .15

Engraved; Name Typographed
Perf. 11½x11
22 CD305 $5 light brown 125.00 27.50

UPU Issue
Common Design Types
Inscribed: "Malaya-Singapore"
Engr.; Name Typo. on 15c, 25c
Perf. 13½, 11x11½

1949, Oct. 10 Wmk. 4
23 CD306 10c rose violet 1.40 .25
24 CD307 15c indigo 2.75 .75
25 CD308 25c orange 4.50 1.25
26 CD309 50c slate 9.25 4.25
Nos. 23-26 (4) 17.90 6.50

Coronation Issue
Common Design Type

1953, June 2 Engr. *Perf. 13½x13*
27 CD312 10c magenta & black 1.75 .15

Chinese Sampans — A2

Sir Stamford Raffles Statue — A3

Singapore River — A4

Designs: 2c, Malay kolek. 4c, Twa-kow. 5c, Lombok sloop. 6c, Trengganu pinas. 8c, Palari. 10c, Timber tongkong. 12c, Hylam trader. 20c, Cocos-Keeling schooner. 25c, Argonaut plane. 30c, Oil tanker. 50c, Liner (M.S. Chusan). $5, Arms of Singapore.

Perf. 13½x14½

1955, Sept. 4 Photo. Wmk. 4
28 A2 1c sepia .15 .15
29 A2 2c orange yellow .15 .15
30 A2 4c orange brown .30 .15
31 A2 5c magenta .30 .15
32 A2 6c gray blue .30 .15
33 A2 8c aqua .95 .35
34 A2 10c dark purple .50 .15
35 A2 12c rose red 2.00 .65
36 A2 20c violet blue 2.00 .15
37 A2 25c orange & purple 1.10 .15
38 A2 30c purple & plum 1.65 .15
39 A2 50c bright blue 3.25 .15

Perf. 13½x14, 14x13½
Engr.
40 A3 $1 blue & purple 9.50 .20
41 A4 $2 blue green & red 32.50 .50

Engr.; Arms Typo.
42 A3 $5 multicolored 65.00 2.25
Nos. 28-42 (15) 119.65
Set value 4.50

For a later printing of the 10c and 50c, plates with finer screen (250) than normal (200) were used.

Singapore Lion and Administrative Center — A5

Perf. 11½x12

1959, June 1 Photo. Wmk. 314
Lion in Gold
43 A5 4c deep rose red .25 .15
44 A5 10c magenta .50 .15
45 A5 20c ultra 1.40 .50
46 A5 25c yellow green 1.75 .55
47 A5 30c bright violet 1.90 1.00
48 A5 50c bluish gray 4.25 2.00
Nos. 43-48 (6) 10.05 4.35

New Constitution of Singapore.

State Flag of Singapore — A6

1960, June 3 Litho. *Perf. 13½*
49 A6 4c blue, red & yellow .40 .15
50 A6 10c gray, red & yellow .85 .30

Issued for National Day, June 3, 1960.

Hands and Map of Singapore — A7

1961, June 3 Photo.
51 A7 4c brown, yellow & gray .50 .20
52 A7 10c green, yellow & gray .75 .25

Issued for National Day, June 3, 1961.

Sea Horse — A8

Malayan Fish: 4c, Tiger barb, horiz. 5c, Anemone fish, horiz. 6c, Archerfish. 10c, Harlequin fish, horiz. 20c, Butterflyfish. 25c, Two-spot gourami, horiz.

Perf. 14½x13½, 13½x14½

1962, Mar. 31 Wmk. 314
53 A8 2c lt green & red brown .15 .15
54 A8 4c red orange & blk .15 .15
a. Black omitted 110.00
55 A8 5c gray & red org .15 .15
a. Red orange omitted 110.00
b. Wmkd. sideways ('67) .20 .15
56 A8 6c yellow & blk .20 .15
57 A8 10c dk gray & red org .30 .15
a. Red orange omitted 85.00
b. Wmkd. sideways ('67) .40 .15
58 A8 20c blue & orange .80 .15
a. Orange omitted 125.00
59 A8 25c orange & black .80 .15
a. Black omitted 100.00
b. Wmkd. sideways ('67) .85 .25
Nos. 53-59 (7) 2.55
Set value .40

For surcharge see No. 370.

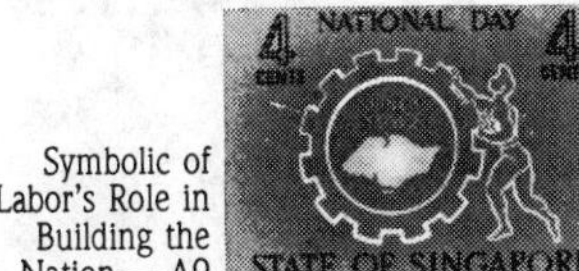

Symbolic of Labor's Role in Building the Nation — A9

1962, June 3 Unwmk. *Perf. 11½*
60 A9 4c brt rose, blk & yel .40 .15
61 A9 10c brt blue, blk & yel .65 .25

Issued for National Day, June 3, 1962.

Vanda Tan Chay Yan — A10

Yellow-Breasted Sunbird — A11

Designs: 1c, Arachnis Maggie Oei, horiz. 12c, Grammatophyllum speciosum. 30c, Vanda Miss Joaquim. 50c, Shama, horiz. $1, White-breasted kingfisher, horiz. $5, White-tailed sea eagle.

Perf. 12½, 13½x13 (50c, $1), 13x13½ ($2, $5)

1963, Mar. 10 Photo. Wmk. 314
Flowers and Birds in Natural Colors
Size: 37x26mm, 26x37mm
62 A10 1c brt pink & ultra .15 .15
a. Wmkd. sideways ('67) .15 .15
63 A10 8c lt blue & mag .55 .55
64 A10 12c salmon & brown 1.10 .30
65 A10 30c tan & ol green 1.65 .15
a. tan omitted 50.00

Size: 35½x25½mm, 25½x35½mm
66 A11 50c yel green & blk 1.90 .15
a. Wmkd. sideways ('66) 3.00 .85
67 A11 $1 yellow & blk 5.75 .20
a. Wmkd. sideways ('67) 6.25 3.25
68 A11 $2 dull blue & blk 11.00 1.10
69 A11 $5 pale blue & blk 32.50 2.75
Nos. 62-69 (8) 54.60 5.35

See No. 76.

Government Housing Project A12

1963, June 3 *Perf. 12½*
70 A12 4c multicolored .45 .15
71 A12 10c multicolored .65 .25

Issued for National Day, June 3, 1963.

Folk Dancers — A13

1963, Aug. 8 Photo. *Perf. 14x14½*
72 A13 5c multicolored .35 .15

Southeast Asia Cultural Festival.

Workers, Factory and Apartment House A14

Wmk. 314 (30c), Unwmd. (15, 20c)

1966, Aug. 9 Photo. *Perf. 12½x13*
73 A14 15c ultra & multi .45 .20
74 A14 20c red & multi .65 .45
75 A14 30c yellow & multi 1.10 .70
Nos. 73-75 (3) 2.20 1.35

First anniversary of the Republic.

Bird Type of 1963

Design: 15c, Black-naped tern (sterna).

1966, Nov. 9 Wmk. 314 *Perf. 12½*
Bird in Natural Colors
Size: 26x37mm
76 A11 15c blue & black .50 .15
a. Orange (eye) omitted 12.50

Marching Women, Chinese Inscription A15

15c, Malay inscription. 50c, Tamil inscription.

Perf. 14x14½

1967, Aug. 9 Photo. Unwmk.
77 A15 6c lt brown, gray & red .15 .15
78 A15 15c multicolored .40 .20
79 A15 50c multicolored 1.65 1.00
Nos. 77-79 (3) 2.20 1.35

"Build a Vigorous Singapore" campaign.

Buildings and Map of Africa and Southeast Asia — A16

1967, Oct. 7 *Perf. 14x13½*
Black Overprint
80 A16 10c multicolored .20 .15
81 A16 25c multicolored .60 .45
82 A16 50c multicolored 1.25 .90
Nos. 80-82 (3) 2.05 1.50

2nd Afro-Asian Housing Cong., Oct. 7-15. No. 80 exists without overprint.

Map of Singapore and Symbolic Worker — A17

Sword Dance — A18

Stamps are inscribed "Work for Prosperity" in English and: 6c, Chinese. 15c, Malay. 50c, Tamil.

Perf. 13½x14½

1968, Aug. 9 Photo. Unwmk.

83 A17 6c red, black & gold .20 .20
84 A17 15c brt yel grn, blk & gold .45 .35
85 A17 50c brt blue, blk & gold 1.40 1.25
Nos. 83-85 (3) 2.05 1.80

Issued for National Day, 1968.

Wmk. Rectangles (334)

1968 Photo. *Perf. 14*

Designs: 6c, Lion dance. 10c, Bharatha Natyam, Indian dance. 15c, Tari Payong, Sumatran dance. 20c, Kathak Kali, Indian dance mask. 25c, Lu Chih Shen and Lin Chung, Chinese opera masks. 30c, Dragon dance, horiz. 50c, Tari Lilin, Malayan candle dance. 75c, Tarian Kuda Kepang, Javanese dance. $1, Yao Chi, Chinese opera mask.

86 A18 5c yellow & multi .25 .15
87 A18 6c orange & multi .30 .15
88 A18 10c blue green & multi .45 .15
89 A18 15c lt brown & multi .60 .30
a. Booklet pane of 4 ('69) 2.50
90 A18 20c brown & multi .75 .30
91 A18 25c dp car & multi 1.25 .50
92 A18 30c pink & multi 1.50 .50
93 A18 50c brown org & multi 1.75 1.00
94 A18 75c brt rose & multi 3.00 1.50
95 A18 $1 olive grn & multi 4.00 2.00
Nos. 86-95 (10) 13.85 6.55

Issue dates: 6c, 20c, 30c, 50c, 75c, Dec. 1; 5c, 10c, 15c, 25c, $1, Dec. 29.

1973 *Perf. 13*

86a A18 5c yellow & multi .70 .45
88a A18 10c blue green & multi .95 .55
90a A18 20c brown & multi 1.65 .95
91a A18 25c deep carmine & multi 2.75 1.50
92a A18 30c pink & multi 3.75 1.90
93a A18 50c brown orange & multi 5.50 3.25
95a A18 $1 olive green & multi 13.00 6.50
Nos. 86a-95a (7) 28.30 15.10

Cogwheel and Emblem — A19

1969, Apr. 15 Unwmk. *Perf. 13*

96 A19 15c blue, black & silver .40 .25
97 A19 30c red, black & silver .80 .65
98 A19 75c violet, black & silver 2.00 1.50
Nos. 96-98 (3) 3.20 2.40

25th Plenary Session of the Economic Commission for Asia and the Far East (ECAFE), Singapore, Apr. 15-28.

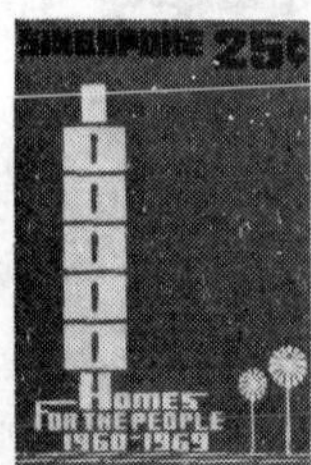

"Homes for the People" A20

Plane over Docks of Singapore A21

Perf. 13x13½

1969, July 20 Litho. Unwmk.

99 A20 25c emerald & black 1.00 .70
100 A20 50c dark blue & black 1.50 1.25

1960-69 building program of the Housing and Development Board.

1969, Aug. 9 *Perf. 14x14½*

Designs: 30c, UN emblem and map of Singapore. 75c, Flags and map of Malaya and Borneo. $1, Uplifted hands and Singapore flag. $5, Tail of Japanese plane and searchlights. $10, Statue of Sir Thomas Stamford Raffles.

101 A21 15c yellow, blk & org .30 .25
102 A21 30c brt blue & blk .70 .55
103 A21 75c orange & multi 2.25 1.40
104 A21 $1 red & black 5.00 2.50
105 A21 $5 gray, blk & red 32.50 19.00
106 A21 $10 emerald & blk 60.00 37.50
a. Souvenir sheet of 6, #101-106 500.00 425.00
Nos. 101-106 (6) 100.75 61.20

Sesquicent. of the founding of Singapore.

Mirudhangam, South Indian Drum — A22

Musical Instruments: 4c, Pi Pa, Chinese, 4 strings, vert. $2, Rebab, Malay violin, 3 strings, vert. $5, Vina, Indian, 7 strings. $10, Ta Ku, Chinese drum.

1969 Photo. Wmk. 366 *Perf. 13*

107 A22 1c multicolored .15 .15
108 A22 4c multicolored .15 .15
109 A22 $2 multicolored 6.00 3.75
110 A22 $5 multicolored 13.00 8.75
111 A22 $10 multicolored 35.00 20.00
Nos. 107-111 (5) 54.30 32.80

Issue dates: 1c, 4c, $2, $5, Nov. 10; $10, Dec. 6.

Sea Shells — A23

Designs: 30c, Tropical fish. 75c, Greater flamingo and helmeted hornbill. $1, Orchids.

Perf. 13½

1970, Mar. 15 Unwmk. Litho.

112 A23 15c pale violet & multi .65 .25
113 A23 30c lt blue & multi 2.25 .80
114 A23 75c yellow & multi 6.00 3.50
115 A23 $1 lt green & multi 7.00 4.00
a. Souvenir sheet of 4, #112-115 22.50 11.00
Nos. 112-115 (4) 15.90 8.55

EXPO '70 International Exposition, Osaka, Japan, Mar. 15-Sept. 13.

Child Playing (Kindergarten) — A24

50c, Sports activities. 75c, Cultural activities.

1970, July Unwmk. *Perf. 13½*

116 A24 15c deep orange & blk .75 .30
117 A24 50c orange, blk & vio bl 2.50 1.50
118 A24 75c black & dp lilac rose 3.75 2.50
Nos. 116-118 (3) 7.00 4.30

People's Association, 10th anniversary.

Soldier and Map of Singapore — A25

Designs: Map and soldiers in various positions.

1970, Aug. 9 Litho. Unwmk.

119 A25 15c emerald, blk & org .65 .25
120 A25 50c orange, blk & brt mag 3.25 1.90
121 A25 $1 brt mag, blk & emer 4.50 4.00
Nos. 119-121 (3) 8.40 6.15

National military service.

Runners A26

1970, Aug. 23 Photo. *Perf. 13*

122 A26 10c shown .60 .25
123 A26 15c Swimmers 1.00 .50
124 A26 25c Badminton 1.90 1.75
125 A26 50c Automobile race 3.25 3.00
a. Strip of 4, #122-125 7.25 7.25

1970 Festival of Sports.

Ship and Emblem of National Line (Neptune Oriental Lines) — A27

Designs: 30c, Ship in first container berth. 75c, Ship repairing and ship building.

1970, Nov. 1 Litho. *Perf. 12*

126 A27 15c vio blue, lemon & red 1.65 .35
127 A27 30c dp ultra & lemon 3.75 1.40
128 A27 75c red & lemon 9.50 4.00
Nos. 126-128 (3) 14.90 5.75

Singapore shipping industry.

Flags of Commonwealth Nations — A28

Designs: 15c, Circular arrangement of names of Commonwealth members. 30c, Flags arranged in circle. $1, Flags (different arrangement).

1971, Jan. 14 *Perf. 15x14½*

Size: 46½x31mm

129 A28 15c gold & multi .55 .25
130 A28 30c gold & multi 1.25 .80
131 A28 75c gold & multi 2.00 1.90

Size: 67x31mm

Perf. 14

132 A28 $1 gold & multi 5.00 3.00
Nos. 129-132 (4) 8.80 5.95

Commonwealth Heads of Government Meeting, Singapore, Jan. 12-14.

Cycle Rickshaws — A29

Houses of Worship in Singapore — A30

Perf. 11½

1971, Apr. 4 Unwmk. Litho.

133 A29 15c shown .60 .25
134 A29 20c Sampans .90 .50
135 A29 30c Market place 2.75 .85

Perf. 13x13½

136 A30 50c Waterfront 3.25 1.40
137 A30 75c shown 6.00 1.65
Nos. 133-137 (5) 13.50 4.65

Tourist publicity.

Chinese New Year — A31

Singapore Festivals: 30c, Hari Raya Puasa (Moslem). 50c, Deepavali (Hindu). 75c, Christmas.

1971, Aug. 9 Litho. *Perf. 14*

138 A31 15c multicolored .90 .30
139 A31 30c multicolored 2.00 1.00
140 A31 50c multicolored 3.50 1.90
141 A31 75c multicolored 5.50 2.75
a. Souvenir sheet of 4, #138-141 77.50 77.50
Nos. 138-141 (4) 11.90 5.95

Satellite Earth Station, Sentosa Island — A32

No. 143 as 15c, enlarged to cover 4 stamps.

1971, Oct. 23 Unwmk. *Perf. 13½*

142 A32 15c red & multi 5.00 1.50
143 A32 Block of 4 50.00 40.00
a. 30c (yellow numeral) 12.50 10.00
b. 30c (green numeral) 12.50 10.00
c. 30c (rose numeral) 12.50 10.00
d. 30c (orange numeral) 12.50 10.00

Establishment of Singapore's satellite earth station, Sentosa Island.

Singapore River and Fort Canning, 1843-1847 — A33

Views of Singapore, from 19th century art works: 15c, The Padang, 1851. 20c, Waterfront, 1848-1849. 35c, View from Fort Canning, 1846. 50c, View from Mount Wallich, 1857. $1, Waterfront with ships, from the sea, 1861.

1971, Dec. 5 Unwmk. *Perf. 13x12½*

Size: 52x45mm

144 A33 10c gold & multi 1.10 .50
145 A33 15c gold & multi 1.65 .75
146 A33 20c gold & multi 2.75 1.10
147 A33 35c gold & multi 6.25 3.25

Perf. 12½x13
Size: 68x47mm

148 A33 50c gold & multi 11.00 5.50
149 A33 $1 gold & multi 27.50 13.00
Nos. 144-149 (6) 50.25 24.10

George V 1c Copper Coin, 1920 — A34

Singapore Coins: 35c, Silver dollar, 1969. $1, Gold $150, 1969 commemorative coin for sesquicentennial of founding of Singapore.

1972, June 4 Litho. Perf. 13½

150 A34 15c dk grn, dp org & blk 1.10 .25
151 A34 35c red & black 2.75 .85
152 A34 $1 ultra, yellow & blk 4.00 4.00
Nos. 150-152 (3) 7.85 5.10

"Moon Festival," by Seah Kim Joo — A35

Paintings by Singapore Artists: 35c, "Complimentary Force," by Thomas Yeo. 50c, "Rhythm in Blue," by Yusman Aman. $1, "Gibbons," by Chen Wen Hsi.

1972, July 9 Litho. Perf. 12½
Size: 40x43½mm

153 A35 15c brown org & multi .60 .30

Size: 35½x53½mm

154 A35 35c blue green & multi 1.65 1.00
155 A35 50c dull violet & multi 2.25 1.40

Size: 40x43½mm

156 A35 $1 bister & multi 5.75 3.00
Nos. 153-156 (4) 10.25 5.70

Chinese New Year — A36

Festivals: 35c, Hari Raya Puasa (candles and ornament). 50c, Deepavali (incense and teapot). 75c, Christmas (candle and stained glass window).

1972, Aug. 9 Litho. Perf. 13x12½

157 A36 15c deep rose & multi .60 .30
158 A36 35c violet & multi 1.65 1.00
159 A36 50c green & multi 2.00 1.25
160 A36 75c blue & multi 3.25 1.90
Nos. 157-160 (4) 7.50 4.45

Technical and Scientific Training A37

Designs: 35c, Sport. $1, Art and culture.

1972, Oct. 1 Photo. Perf. 12

161 A37 15c orange & multi .65 .35
162 A37 35c blue & multi 1.65 1.25
163 A37 $1 orange & multi 4.50 3.50
Nos. 161-163 (3) 6.80 5.10

Youth of Singapore.

Neptune Ruby A38

1972, Dec. 17 Litho. Perf. 14x14½
Size: 42x28½mm

164 A38 15c shown .45 .40

Size: 29½x28½mm

165 A38 75c Maria Rickmers 3.50 3.50
166 A38 $1 Chinese junk 11.00 11.00
a. Souvenir sheet of 3, #164-166 35.00 15.00
Nos. 164-166 (3) 14.95 14.90

Singapore shipping industry.

Quality and Reliability Emblem — A39

Birds, Jurong Bird Park — A40

15c, Emblem & initials of participating organizations: Singapore Institute of Standards & Industrial Research, Singapore Manufacturers' Association, Natl. Trades Union Congress. 75c, Emblem & "Prosperity through Quality & Reliability" in multiple rows. $1, Quality & Reliability emblem.

1973, Feb. 25 Litho. Perf. 14½x14

167 A39 15c gold & multi .35 .30
168 A39 35c gold & multi .85 .70
169 A39 75c gold & multi 1.90 1.75
170 A39 $1 gold & multi 2.75 2.50
Nos. 167-170 (4) 5.85 5.25

Prosperity through Quality and Reliability campaign.

1973, Apr. 29 Perf. 12½

Landmarks: 35c, Dancers, National Theater. 50c, City Hall and ballplayers. $1, Singapore River with boats and buildings.

171 A40 15c vermilion & blk .50 .30
172 A40 35c dull green & blk 1.50 .90
173 A40 50c brown & blk 2.50 1.25
174 A40 $1 dark violet & blk 4.75 2.75
Nos. 171-174 (4) 9.25 5.20

Airline Emblems A41

35c, Emblem of Singapore Airlines and intl. destinations. 75c, SIA emblem on stylized tail of Boeing jet. $1, SIA emblems circling globe.

1973, June 24 Litho. Perf. 13½

175 A41 10c multicolored .40 .20
176 A41 35c multicolored 1.00 .90
177 A41 75c multicolored 2.50 1.75
178 A41 $1 multicolored 3.50 3.00
Nos. 175-178 (4) 7.40 5.85

Singapore Intl. Airport at Paya Lebar.

Entertainers — A42

Running, Judo, Boxing — A43

Composite of various forms of entertainment.

1973, Aug. 9 Litho. Perf. 13½x14

179 A42 10c black & orange red .55 .30
180 A42 35c black & orange red 1.50 1.25
181 A42 50c black & orange red 2.25 1.90
182 A42 75c black & orange red 4.00 3.25
a. Block of 4, #179-182 8.50 8.50

National Day 1973.

1973, Sept. 1 Photo. Perf. 14

Designs: 15c, Bicycling, weight lifting, pistol shoot, yachting. 25c, Various balls. 35c, Tennis racket, ball, hockey stick. 50c, Swimming. $1, Singapore National Stadium.

Size: 25x25mm

183 A43 10c gold, silver & ind .60 .30
184 A43 15c gold & dk brown .65 .35
185 A43 25c silver, gold & blk 1.10 .85
186 A43 35c gold, silver & dk pur 1.65 1.40

Perf. 13x14
Size: 40½x25mm

187 A43 50c gold & multi 2.00 1.75
188 A43 $1 silver, vio bl & emer 5.50 5.00
a. Souvenir sheet of 6, #183-188 27.50 6.50
Nos. 183-188 (6) 11.50 9.65

7th South East Asia (SEAP) Games, Singapore.

Agave A44

Mangosteen A45

Designs: Stylized flowers and fruit.

1973 Photo. Perf. 13

189 A44 1c shown .15 .15
190 A44 5c Coleus blumei .15 .15
a. Booklet pane of 10 (4 #190, 4 #191 + 2 #193) 2.25
191 A44 10c Madagascar periwinkle .20 .15
192 A44 15c Sunflower .25 .15
193 A44 20c Dwarf palm .40 .15
194 A44 25c Yellow daisy .45 .15
195 A44 35c Chrysanthemum .75 .40
196 A44 50c Costus 1.10 .50
197 A44 75c Transvaal daisy 1.50 .75
198 A45 $1 shown 2.00 1.25
199 A45 $2 Jackfruit 4.25 2.75
200 A45 $5 Coconuts 10.50 6.50
201 A45 $10 Pineapple 20.00 13.00
Nos. 189-201 (13) 41.70 26.05

Nos. 189-201 have fluorescent underprint "Singapore" in multiple rows.

Tiger and Orangutans — A46

Tropical Fish — A47

1973, Dec. 16 Litho. Perf. 13

202 A46 5c shown .55 .15
203 A46 10c Leopard and deer 1.10 .30
204 A46 35c Panther and stag 3.25 1.25
205 A46 75c White horse & lion 6.00 3.25
Nos. 202-205 (4) 10.90 4.95

Opening of Singapore Zoo.

1974, Apr. 21 Perf. 13½x14

Designs: Various poecilia reticulata fish.

206 A47 5c apple green & multi .40 .15
207 A47 10c pink & multi .65 .30
208 A47 35c brt blue & multi 1.65 1.40
209 A47 $1 brt green & multi 5.50 3.75
Nos. 206-209 (4) 8.20 5.60

Scout Conference Emblem — A48

1974, June 9 Perf. 13½x14½

210 A48 10c multicolored .45 .30
211 A48 75c multicolored 2.75 2.75

9th Asia-Pacific Boy Scout Conf., Singapore.

UPU Emblem, Circle and "Centenary" Multiple — A49

UPU, cent.: 35c, Circle and UN emblems, multiple. 75c, Circle and pigeons, multiple.

1974, July 7 Litho. Perf. 14½x13½

212 A49 10c orange brn & multi .25 .15
213 A49 35c blue & multi .80 .55
214 A49 75c emerald & multi 2.00 1.40
Nos. 212-214 (3) 3.05 2.10

Family — A50

1974, Aug. 9 Litho. Perf. 13x13½

215 A50 10c shown .25 .15
216 A50 35c Symbols for male & female .90 .70
217 A50 75c World map and WPY emblem 2.25 2.00
Nos. 215-217 (3) 3.40 2.85

Natl. Day and World Population Year 1974.

"Sun and Tree" — A51

Children's Drawings: 10c, "My Daddy and Mommy." 35c, "A Dump Truck." 50c, "My Aunt."

1974, Oct. 1 Photo. Perf. 14x13½

218 A51 5c multicolored .35 .15
219 A51 10c multicolored .75 .50
220 A51 35c multicolored 2.00 1.65
221 A51 50c multicolored 3.25 2.50
a. Souv. sheet of 4, #218-221, perf. 13 18.00 5.00
Nos. 218-221 (4) 6.35 4.80

Children's drawings for Children's Day (UNICEF).

Alfresco Dining A52

Tourist publicity: 20c, Singapore River. $1, "Kelong" fish traps.

1975, Jan. 26 Litho. Perf. 14

222 A52 15c multicolored .45 .30
223 A52 20c multicolored .55 .45
224 A52 $1 multicolored 5.00 3.25
Nos. 222-224 (3) 6.00 4.00

Prows of Barges and Wave Design — A53

25c, Cargo ships & ship's wheel. 50c, Tanker & signal flags. $1, Container ship & propellers.

1975, Mar. 10 Litho. Perf. 13½

225 A53 5c multicolored .20 .15
226 A53 25c multicolored .85 .75
227 A53 50c multicolored 1.65 1.50
228 A53 $1 multicolored 3.75 3.00
Nos. 225-228 (4) 6.45 5.40

9th Biennial Conf. of the Intl. Assoc. of Ports and Harbors, Singapore, Mar. 8-15.

Satellite Earth Stations, Sentosa Island — A54

Oil Refinery — A55

Science and Industry: 75c, Brain surgery, Medical Center, Jurong.

1975, June 29 Photo. *Perf. 13½*

No.	Type	Description	Unused	Used
229	A54	10c multicolored	.25	.15
230	A55	35c multicolored	.75	.55
231	A54	75c multicolored	2.50	1.50
		Nos. 229-231 (3)	3.50	2.20

"10" and "Homes and Gardens for the People" — A56

Crowned Cranes — A57

Tenth Natl. Day ("10" and): 35c, "Shipping and ship building." 75c, "Communications and technology." $1, "Trade, commerce and industry."

1975, Aug. 9 Litho. *Perf. 13½*

No.	Type	Description	Unused	Used
232	A56	10c multicolored	.30	.15
233	A56	35c multicolored	.90	.60
234	A56	75c multicolored	2.25	1.40
235	A56	$1 multicolored	2.75	1.65
		Nos. 232-235 (4)	6.20	3.80

1975, Oct. 5 Litho. *Perf. 14½x13½*

Birds: 10c, Great hornbill. 35c, White-breasted and white-collared kingfishers. $1, Sulphur-crested cockatoo and blue and yellow macaw.

No.	Type	Description	Unused	Used
236	A57	5c emerald & multi	.75	.20
237	A57	10c emerald & multi	1.10	.45
238	A57	35c emerald & multi	6.50	2.50
239	A57	$1 emerald & multi	15.00	8.00
		Nos. 236-239 (4)	23.35	11.15

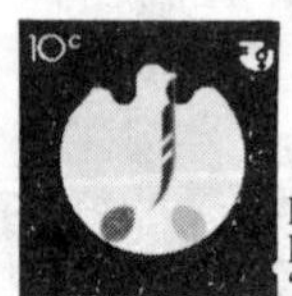

IWY Emblem, Peace Dove as "Equality" — A58

Designs (IWY Emblem): 35c, Peace dove with eggs in basket, symbolizing "Development." 75c, Peace dove and young, symbolizing "Peace."

1975, Dec. 7 Litho. *Perf. 13½*

No.	Type	Description	Unused	Used
240	A58	10c blk, blue & pink	.50	.25
241	A58	35c orange & multi	1.65	1.10
242	A58	75c dp violet & multi	3.25	2.25
a.		Souvenir sheet of 3, #240-242	14.00	14.00
		Nos. 240-242 (3)	5.40	3.60

International Women's Year 1975.

Yellow Flame — A59

Aranda Hybrid — A60

Wayside Trees: 35c, Cabbage tree. 50c, Rose of India. 75c, Variegated coral tree.

1976, Apr. 18 Litho. *Perf. 14*

No.	Type	Description	Unused	Used
243	A59	10c multicolored	.50	.25
244	A59	35c multicolored	1.50	1.25
245	A59	50c multicolored	2.25	1.65
246	A59	75c multicolored	4.25	2.50
		Nos. 243-246 (4)	8.50	5.65

1976, June 20 Litho. *Perf. 14*

Designs: Varieties of aranda orchids.

No.	Type	Description	Unused	Used
247	A60	10c black & multi	.50	.15
248	A60	35c black & multi	1.90	.95
249	A60	50c black & multi	3.75	1.50
250	A60	75c black & multi	5.50	2.25
		Nos. 247-250 (4)	11.65	4.85

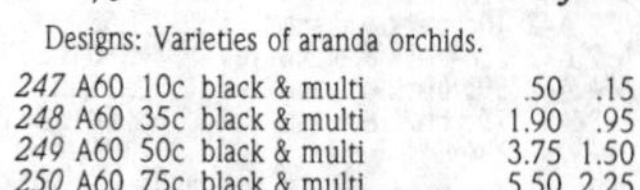

"10" and Children's Band — A61

35c, Running boys. 75c, Dancing children.

1976, Aug. 9 Litho. *Perf. 12½*

No.	Type	Description	Unused	Used
251	A61	10c multicolored	.30	.20
252	A61	35c multicolored	1.00	.70
253	A61	75c multicolored	3.00	1.65
		Nos. 251-253 (3)	4.30	2.55

Singapore Youth Festival, 10th anniversary.

Queen Elizabeth Walk — A62

Paintings of Old Singapore, c. 1905-10: 50c, The Padang. $1, Raffles Place.

1976, Nov. 14 Litho. *Perf. 14*

No.	Type	Description	Unused	Used
254	A62	10c multicolored	.50	.20
255	A62	50c multicolored	2.25	1.40
256	A62	$1 multicolored	4.75	2.75
a.		Souvenir sheet of 3, #254-256, perf. 13½	15.00	15.00
		Nos. 254-256 (3)	7.50	4.35

Chinese Bridal Costume — A63

Radar, Surface to Air Missile, Soldiers — A64

Designs: 35c, Indian bridal costume. 75c, Malay bridal costume.

1976, Dec. 19 Litho. *Perf. 14½*

No.	Type	Description	Unused	Used
257	A63	10c lt green & multi	.50	.15
258	A63	35c lilac & multi	1.75	.80
259	A63	75c yellow & multi	3.75	2.00
		Nos. 257-259 (3)	6.00	2.95

1977, Mar. 12 Litho. *Perf. 14½*

Designs: 50c, Infantry soldiers and tank. 75c, Jet fighter, pilot, telecommunications center.

No.	Type	Description	Unused	Used
260	A64	10c multicolored	.35	.20
261	A64	50c multicolored	1.65	1.00
262	A64	75c multicolored	3.00	1.65
		Nos. 260-262 (3)	5.00	2.85

National Service, 10th anniversary.

Lyrate Cockle A65

Spotted Hermit Crab A66

Sea Shells: 5c, Folded scallop. 10c, Marble cone. 15c, Scorpion conch. 20c, Amplustre bubble. 25c, Spiral Babylon. 35c, Regal thorny oyster. 50c, Winged frog shell. 75c, Troschel's murex.

Marine Life: $2, Stingray. $5, Cuttlefish. $10, Lionfish.

1977 *Perf. 13½*

No.	Type	Description	Unused	Used
263	A65	1c orange & multi	.15	.15
264	A65	5c orange & multi	.15	.15
a.		Bklt. pane, 4 #264, 8 #265	1.25	
265	A65	10c orange & multi	.15	.15
266	A65	15c orange & multi	.15	.15
267	A65	20c orange & multi	.30	.15
268	A65	25c orange & multi	.30	.25
269	A65	35c orange & multi	.45	.35
270	A65	50c orange & multi	.75	.60
271	A65	75c orange & multi	1.10	.90
		Perf. 14		
272	A66	$1 multicolored	1.40	1.10
273	A66	$2 multicolored	2.75	2.25
274	A66	$5 multicolored	7.00	5.25
275	A66	$10 multicolored	13.00	11.00
		Nos. 263-275 (13)	27.65	22.45

No. 264a has a large inscribed selvage, the size of 6 stamps.

Issue dates: #263-271, Apr. 9; others, June 4.

Singapore Harbor Improvements A67

Labor Day: 50c, Construction workers. 75c, Road workers.

1977, May 1 Litho. *Perf. 13x12½*

No.	Type	Description	Unused	Used
276	A67	10c multicolored	.20	.15
277	A67	50c multicolored	1.10	.65
278	A67	75c multicolored	1.90	1.25
		Nos. 276-278 (3)	3.20	2.05

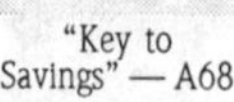

"Key to Savings" — A68

Grain and Cattle — A69

Designs: 35c, "On-line Banking Service." 75c, "GIRO Service."

1977, July 16 Litho. *Perf. 13*

No.	Type	Description	Unused	Used
279	A68	10c multicolored	.20	.15
280	A68	35c multicolored	.75	.45
281	A68	75c multicolored	2.25	1.40
		Nos. 279-281 (3)	3.20	2.00

Centenary of Post Office Savings Bank.

1977, Aug. 8 Litho. *Perf. 14*

Designs: 10c, Flags of founding members: Thailand, Indonesia, Singapore, Malaysia and Philippines. 75c, Steel, oil and chemical industries.

No.	Type	Description	Unused	Used
282	A69	10c multicolored	.25	.15
283	A69	35c multicolored	.70	.45
284	A69	75c multicolored	2.25	.95
		Nos. 282-284 (3)	3.20	1.55

Association of South East Asian Nations (ASEAN), 10th anniversary.

Bus Stop — A70

Children's Drawings: 10c, Chingay procession, vert. 75c, Playground.

1977, Oct. 1 *Perf. 12½*

No.	Type	Description	Unused	Used
285	A70	10c multicolored	.35	.15
286	A70	35c multicolored	1.00	.65
287	A70	75c multicolored	3.25	1.50
a.		Souvenir sheet of 3, #285-287	10.00	10.00
		Nos. 285-287 (3)	4.60	2.30

Symbols of Life Sciences — A71

Botanical Gardens — A72

Singapore Science Center: 35c, "Physical sciences." 75c, "Science and technology." $1, Science Center.

1977, Dec. 10 Litho. *Perf. 14½x14*

No.	Type	Description	Unused	Used
288	A71	10c multicolored	.15	.15
289	A71	35c multicolored	.50	.30
290	A71	75c multicolored	1.10	.70
291	A71	$1 multicolored	1.75	1.10
		Nos. 288-291 (4)	3.50	2.25

1978, Apr. 22 Litho. *Perf. 14½*

Singapore Parks and Gardens: 10c, Jurong Bird Park, horiz. 35c, East Coast Lagoon and Park.

No.	Type	Description	Unused	Used
292	A72	10c multicolored	.20	.15
293	A72	35c multicolored	.60	.45
294	A72	75c multicolored	1.65	1.10
		Nos. 292-294 (3)	2.45	1.70

Red-whiskered Bulbul — A73

Songbirds: 35c, White eyes. 50c, White-rumped shama. 75c, White-crested laughing thrush.

1978, July 1 Litho. *Perf. 13½*

No.	Type	Description	Unused	Used
295	A73	10c multicolored	.30	.15
296	A73	35c multicolored	.90	.45
297	A73	50c multicolored	1.65	.75
298	A73	75c multicolored	2.25	1.25
		Nos. 295-298 (4)	5.10	2.60

Thian Hock Keng Temple — A74

National Monuments: No. 303a, like No. 299. Nos. 300, 303b, Hajjah Fatimah Mosque. Nos. 301, 303c, Armenian Church. Nos. 302, 303d, Sri Mariamman Temple.

1978, Aug. 9

No.	Type	Description	Unused	Used
299	A74	10c tan & multi	.30	.15
300	A74	10c green & multi	.30	.15
301	A74	10c blue & multi	.30	.15
302	A74	10c lilac & multi	.30	.15
		Nos. 299-302 (4)	1.20	
		Set value		.40

Souvenir Sheet

No.	Type	Description	Unused	Used
303		Sheet of 4	4.50	4.50
a.	A74	35c tan & multi	.65	
b.	A74	35c green & multi	.65	
c.	A74	35c blue & multi	.65	
d.	A74	35c lilac & multi	.65	

Map of Proposed Cable Network — A75

1978, Oct. 30 Litho. *Perf. 14*

No.	Type	Description	Unused	Used
304	A75	10c multicolored	.15	.15
305	A75	35c multicolored	.55	.45
306	A75	50c multicolored	.80	.65
307	A75	75c multicolored	1.25	1.10
		Nos. 304-307 (4)	2.75	2.35

ASEAN Submarine Cable Network. Nos. 304-307 printed in sheets of 100. Stamps have perforations around design and around edges. See No. 429a.

Neptune Spinel — A76

Ships: 35c, Neptune Aries. 50c, Arno Temasek. 75c, Neptune Pearl.

1978, Nov. 18 Litho. *Perf. 13½x14*

308 A76 10c multicolored .20 .15
309 A76 35c multicolored .60 .60
310 A76 50c multicolored 1.00 1.00
311 A76 75c multicolored 1.65 1.65
Nos. 308-311 (4) 3.45 3.40

Neptune Oriental Shipping Lines, 10th anniv.

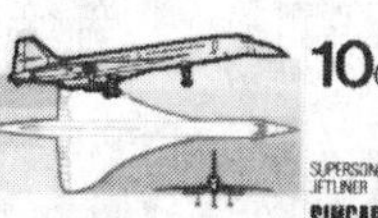

Concorde A77

Aviation Development: 35c, Vickers-Vimy, 1st aircraft to land in Singapore. 50c, Boeing 747B. 75c, Wright Brothers' Flyer I.

1978, Dec. 16 *Perf. 13½*

312 A77 10c yellow green & blk .25 .15
313 A77 35c blue & black .65 .65
314 A77 50c carmine & black 1.00 1.00
315 A77 75c brown & black 1.50 1.50
Nos. 312-315 (4) 3.40 3.30

75th anniversary of 1st powered flight.

Distance Marker in Kilometers A78

Vanda Orchids A79

Designs: 35c, Tape measure in centimeters. 75c, Scales in grams and kilograms.

1979, Jan. 24 Litho. *Perf. 13x13½*

316 A78 10c multicolored .15 .15
317 A78 35c multicolored .60 .40
318 A78 75c multicolored 1.25 .80
Nos. 316-318 (3) 2.00 1.35

Introduction of metric system.

Perf. 14½x14, 14x14½

1979, Apr. 14 Litho.

Varieties of vanda hybrids. 10c, 35c, horiz.

319 A79 10c multicolored .20 .15
320 A79 35c multicolored .55 .55
321 A79 50c multicolored .90 .90
322 A79 75c multicolored 1.25 1.25
Nos. 319-322 (4) 2.90 2.85

Envelope Addressed to Postmaster A80

50c, Envelope addressed to Philatelic Bureau.

1979, July 1 Litho. *Perf. 12½x13*

323 A80 10c orange & multi .25 .15
324 A80 50c dark blue & multi .95 .55

Singapore's postal code system.

Old Phone, Telephone Lines — A81

Designs: 35c, Dial, world map. 50c, Push-button phone, skyline. 75c, Line network.

1979, Oct. 5 Litho. *Perf. 13½*

325 A81 10c multicolored .20 .15
326 A81 35c multicolored .40 .35
327 A81 50c multicolored .65 .45
328 A81 75c multicolored .90 .65
Nos. 325-328 (4) 2.15 1.60

Telephone service centenary.

IYC Emblem, Lanterns Festival A82

IYC Emblem, Children's Drawings: 35c, Singapore Harbor. 50c, "Use Your Hands." 75c, Soccer.

1979, Nov. 10 Litho. *Perf. 13*

329 A82 10c multicolored .15 .15
330 A82 35c multicolored .45 .45
331 A82 50c multicolored .60 .60
332 A82 75c multicolored .90 .90
a. Souvenir sheet of 4, #329-332 3.00 3.00
Nos. 329-332 (4) 2.10 2.10

International Year of the Child.

Botanic Gardens, 120th Anniversary A83

1979, Dec. 15 *Perf. 13½*

333 A83 10c shown .20 .15
334 A83 50c Gazebo .85 .60
335 A83 $1 Greenhouse 1.75 1.25
Nos. 333-335 (3) 2.80 2.00

Hainan Junk — A84

1980 Litho. *Perf. 14*

336 A84 1c shown .15 .15
337 A84 5c Clipper .15 .15
338 A84 10c Fujian junk .15 .15
a. Booklet pane of 10 1.00
339 A84 15c Golekkan .15 .15
340 A84 20c Palari .15 .15
341 A84 25c East Indiaman .20 .20
342 A84 35c Galleon .30 .30
343 A84 50c Caravel .45 .45
344 A84 75c Jiangsu trader .65 .65

Size: 41½x24½mm

Perf. 13½

345 A84 $1 Coaster .90 .90
346 A84 $2 Oil tanker 1.75 1.75
347 A84 $5 Screw steamer 4.50 4.50
348 A84 $10 Paddle wheel steamer 9.00 9.00
Nos. 336-348 (13) 18.50 18.50

Issue dates: #336-344, Apr. 26; others, Apr. 5.

Straits Settlements No. 1, Old Singapore Map, London 1980 Emblem A85

London 1980 Emblem and: 35c, Straits Settlements No. 146, letter. $1, Singapore No. 19, map of Straits. $2, Singapore No. 106, letter, 1819.

1980, May 6 Litho. *Perf. 13*

349 A85 10c multicolored .15 .15
350 A85 35c multicolored .30 .30
351 A85 $1 multicolored .85 .85
352 A85 $2 multicolored 1.65 1.65
a. Souvenir sheet of 4, #349-352 4.00 4.00
Nos. 349-352 (4) 2.95 2.95

London 1980 Intl. Stamp Exhib., May 6-14.

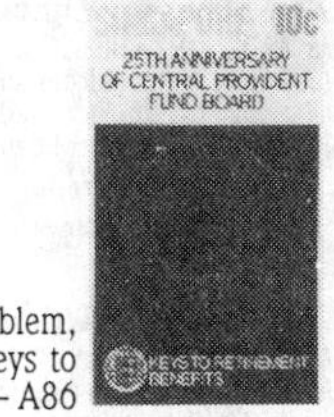

Fund Board Emblem, Keys to Retirement — A86

1980, July 1 Litho. *Perf. 13*

353 A86 10c shown .15 .15
354 A86 50c Home ownership savings .55 .55
355 A86 $1 Old age savings 1.10 1.10
Nos. 353-355 (3) 1.80 1.80

Central Provident Fund Board, 25th anniv.

Map Showing Singapore-Indonesia Cable Route — A87

1980, Aug. 8 Litho. *Perf. 14*

356 A87 10c multicolored .15 .15
357 A87 35c multicolored .50 .50
358 A87 50c multicolored .70 .70
359 A87 75c multicolored 1.10 1.10
Nos. 356-359 (4) 2.45 2.45

ASEAN Submarine Cable Network extension. Stamps perforated around design and around edges. See No. 429a.

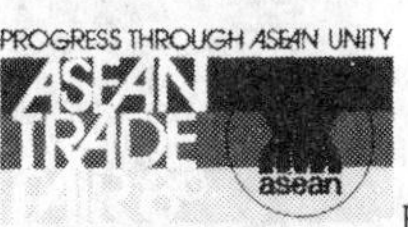

Fair Emblem A88

1980, Oct. 3 Litho. *Perf. 13*

360 A88 10c multicolored .15 .15
361 A88 35c multicolored .45 .45
362 A88 75c multicolored .95 .95
Nos. 360-362 (3) 1.55 1.55

Asean Trade Fair, Oct. 3-12.

A89 A90

1980, Nov. 2 Litho. *Perf. 13½*

363 A89 10c Flame of the wood .15 .15
364 A89 35c Golden trumpet .40 .40
365 A89 50c Sky vine .50 .50
366 A89 75c Bougainvillea .80 .80
Nos. 363-366 (4) 1.85 1.85

1981, Jan. 24 Litho. *Perf. 14x14½*

367 A90 10c multicolored .15 .15
368 A90 35c multicolored .35 .35
369 A90 75c multicolored .75 .75
Nos. 367-369 (3) 1.25 1.25

Monetary Authority of Singapore, 10th anniv.

No. 54 Surcharged

Perf. 13½x14½

1981, Mar. 5 Photo. Wmk. 314

370 A8 10c on 4c red org & blk .15 .15

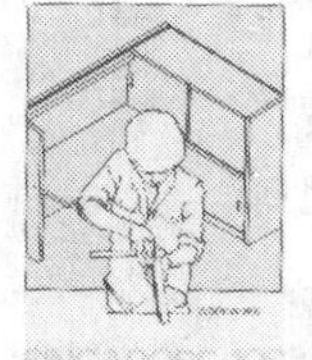

A91 A92

Unwmk.

1981, Apr. 11 Litho. *Perf. 13*

371 A91 10c Technical Training (Woodworking) .15 .15
372 A91 35c Building construction .30 .30
373 A91 50c Electronics .45 .45
374 A91 75c Precision machinery .65 .65
Nos. 371-374 (4) 1.55 1.55

1981, Aug. 25 Litho. *Perf. 14*

Sports For All: Various sports.

375 A92 10c multicolored .15 .15
376 A92 75c multicolored .85 .85
377 A92 $1 multicolored 1.25 1.25
Nos. 375-377 (3) 2.25 2.25

A93 A94

1981, Nov. 24 Litho. *Perf. 14½*

378 A93 10c Man in wheelchair .15 .15
379 A93 35c Group .50 .50
380 A93 50c Teacher, student .75 .75
381 A93 75c Blind communications worker 1.10 1.10
Nos. 378-381 (4) 2.50 2.50

Intl. Year of the Disabled.

1981, Dec. 29 Litho. *Perf. 14x13½*

382 A94 10c multicolored .15 .15
383 A94 35c multicolored .40 .40
384 A94 50c multicolored .50 .50
385 A94 75c multicolored .75 .75
386 A94 $1 multicolored 1.00 1.00
a. Souvenir sheet of 5, #382-386 3.50 3.50
Nos. 382-386 (5) 2.80 2.80

Changi airport opening.

A95

1982, Mar. 3 Litho. *Perf. 14x14½*

387 A95 10c Clipper .15 .15
388 A95 50c Blue grassy tiger .75 .75
389 A95 $1 Raja Brooke's birdwing 1.50 1.50
Nos. 387-389 (3) 2.40 2.40

A96 A97

1982, June 14 Litho. *Perf. 14*

390 A96 10c multicolored .15 .15
391 A96 35c multicolored .35 .35
392 A96 50c multicolored .50 .50
393 A96 75c multicolored .80 .80
Nos. 390-393 (4) 1.80 1.80

15th ASEAN Ministerial meeting.

1982, July 9 Litho. *Perf. 12*
394 A97 10c multicolored .15 .15
395 A97 75c multicolored .85 .85
396 A97 $1 multicolored 1.25 1.25
Nos. 394-396 (3) 2.25 2.25

1982 World Cup.

Sultan Shoal Lighthouse, 1896 — A98

1982, Aug. 7
397 A98 10c shown .15 .15
398 A98 75c Horsburgh, 1851 .70 .70
399 A98 $1 Raffles, 1855 1.00 1.00
a. Souvenir sheet of 3, #397-399 2.50 2.50
Nos. 397-399 (3) 1.85 1.85

10th Anniv. of PSA Container Terminal A99

1982, Sept. 15 Litho. *Perf. 13½*
400 A99 10c Yard gantry cranes .15 .15
401 A99 35c Computer .40 .40
402 A99 50c Freightlifter .55 .55
403 A99 75c Straddle carrier .80 .80
Nos. 400-403 (4) 1.90 1.90

A100

A101

1982, Oct. 15 Litho. *Perf. 14x13½*
404 A100 10c Color guard .20 .20
405 A100 35c Hiking .60 .60
406 A100 50c Building tower .80 .80
407 A100 75c Kayaking 1.25 1.25
Nos. 404-407 (4) 2.85 2.85

Scouting Year.

1982, Nov. 17 *Perf. 13½*
408 A101 10c Text .15 .15
409 A101 35c Housing .45 .45
410 A101 50c Quality control meeting .65 .65
411 A101 75c Participation 1.00 1.00
Nos. 408-411 (4) 2.25 2.25

Productivity movement.

A102

A103

1983, May 14 Litho. *Perf. 13½x13*
412 A102 10c multicolored .15 .15
413 A102 35c multicolored .40 .40
414 A102 75c multicolored .75 .75
415 A102 $1 multicolored 1.00 1.00
Nos. 412-415 (4) 2.30 2.30

Commonwealth Day.

1983, May 28 Litho. *Perf. 14x13½*
416 A103 10c Soccer .15 .15
417 A103 35c Racket games .35 .35
418 A103 75c Athletics .75 .75
419 A103 $1 Swimming 1.00 1.00
Nos. 416-419 (4) 2.25 2.25

12th Southeast Asia Games.

Neighborhood Watch Safety Campaign — A104

1983, June 24 Litho. *Perf. 14*
420 A104 10c Family .15 .15
421 A104 35c Children .55 .55
422 A104 75c Community 1.25 1.25
Nos. 420-422 (3) 1.95 1.95

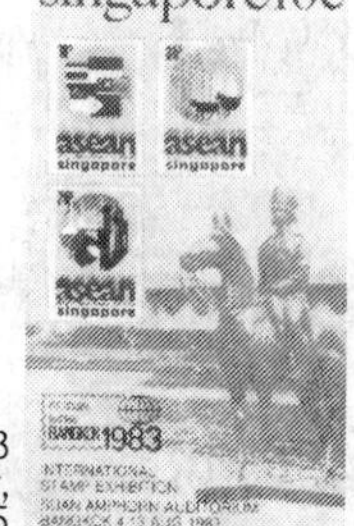

BANGKOK '83 Intl. Stamp Show, Aug. 4-13 — A105

10c, #282-284, statue of King Chulalongkorn (1868-1910). 35c, #304-307, map of southeast Asia. $1, #390-393, Declaration of ASEAN (Assoc. of South East Asian Nations) signatures, 1976.

1983, Aug. 4 Litho. *Perf. 14x14½*
423 A105 10c multicolored .15 .15
424 A105 35c multicolored .40 .40
425 A105 $1 multicolored 1.25 1.25
a. Souvenir sheet of 3, #423-425 2.75 2.75
Nos. 423-425 (3) 1.80 1.80

ASEAN Submarine Cable Network — A106

1983, Sept. 27 Litho. *Perf. 14*
426 A106 10c multicolored .15 .15
427 A106 35c multicolored .45 .45
428 A106 50c multicolored .65 .65
429 A106 75c multicolored .95 .95
a. Souv. sheet of 6, #304, 359, 426-429 3.00 3.00
Nos. 426-429 (4) 2.20 2.20

World Communications Year — A107

1983, Nov. 10 Litho. *Perf. 13*
430 A107 10c Telex service .15 .15
431 A107 35c Telephone numbering plan .35 .35
432 A107 75c Satellite transmission .75 .75
433 A107 $1 Sea communications 1.00 1.00
Nos. 430-433 (4) 2.25 2.25

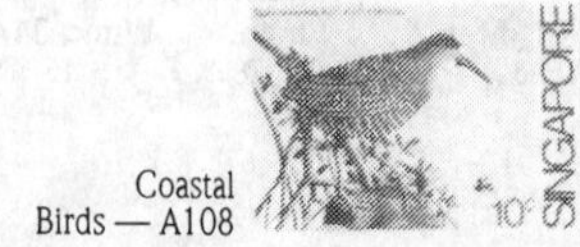

Coastal Birds — A108

Perf. 14½x13½
1984, Mar. 15 Litho.
434 A108 10c Slaty-breasted rail .20 .20
435 A108 35c Black bittern .80 .80
436 A108 50c Brahminy kite 1.25 1.25
437 A108 75c Common moorhens 1.75 1.75
Nos. 434-437 (4) 4.00 4.00

Natl. Monuments A109

Designs: 10c, House of Tan Yeok Nee (merchant), 1885. 35c, Thong Chai Building (former hospital), 1892. 50c, Telok Ayer Market, 1894. $1, Nagore Durgha Muslim Shrine, 1828.

1984, June 7 Litho. *Perf. 12*
438 A109 10c multicolored .15 .15
439 A109 35c multicolored .40 .40
440 A109 50c multicolored .60 .60
441 A109 $1 multicolored 1.25 1.25
Nos. 438-441 (4) 2.40 2.40

A110

A111

1984, Aug. 9 Litho. *Perf. 14*
442 A110 10c No. 121 .15 .15
443 A110 35c No. 377 .40 .40
444 A110 50c No. 99 .55 .55
445 A110 75c No. 243 .80 .80
446 A110 $1 No. 386 1.10 1.10
447 A110 $2 No. 367 2.25 2.25
a. Souvenir sheet of 6, #442-447 7.00 7.00
Nos. 442-447 (6) 5.25 5.25

25th anniv. of self-government.

1984, Oct. 26 Litho. *Perf. 12*

Total Defense: a, This is our country. b, We are one. c, We work together. d, We are prepared. e, We are ready.

448 Strip of 5 .70 .70
a.-e. A111 10c any single .15 .15

Bridges A112

1985, Mar. 15 Engr. *Perf. 14½x14*
449 A112 10c Coleman .15 .15
450 A112 35c Cavenagh .35 .35
451 A112 75c Elgin .85 .85
452 A112 $1 Benjamin Sheares 1.25 1.25
Nos. 449-452 (4) 2.60 2.60

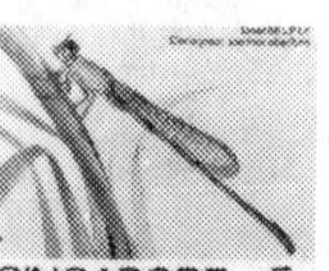

Insects — A113

1985 Litho. *Perf. 13x13½*
453 A113 5c Ceriagrion cerinorubellum .15 .15
454 A113 10c Apis javana .15 .15
455 A113 15c Delta arcuata .15 .15
456 A113 20c Xylocopa caerulea .15 .15
457 A113 25c Donacia javana .25 .25
458 A113 35c Heteroneda reticulata .35 .35
459 A113 50c Catacanthus nigripes .50 .50
460 A113 75c Chremistica pontianaka .75 .75

Litho. & Engr.
Size: 35x30mm

461 A113 $1 Homoeoxipha lycoides 1.00 1.00
462 A113 $2 Traulia azureipennis 2.00 2.00
463 A113 $5 Trithemis aurora 5.00 5.00
464 A113 $10 Scambophyllum sanguinolentum 10.00 10.00
Nos. 453-464 (12) 20.45 20.45

Issued: #453-460, Apr. 24; #461-464, June 5.

People's Assoc., 25th Anniv. — A114

Montage of public services.

1985, July 1 *Perf. 13½x14*
465 A114 10c multicolored .15 .15
466 A114 35c multicolored .40 .40
467 A114 50c multicolored .65 .65
468 A114 75c multicolored .90 .90
Nos. 465-468 (4) 2.10 2.10

Public Housing, 25th Anniv. — A115

Modern housing developments.

1985, Aug. 9
469 A115 10c multicolored .15 .15
470 A115 35c multicolored .40 .40
471 A115 50c multicolored .55 .55
472 A115 75c multicolored .90 .90
a. Souvenir sheet of 4, #469-472 2.50 2.50
Nos. 469-472 (4) 2.00 2.00

Girl Guides, 75th Anniv. — A116

Activities.

1985, Nov 6 *Perf. 14½x14*
473 A116 10c Brownies .15 .15
474 A116 35c Guides .40 .40
475 A116 50c Seniors .60 .60
476 A116 75c Guide leaders .95 .95
Nos. 473-476 (4) 2.10 2.10

Intl. Youth Year — A117

1985, Dec. 18 *Perf. 13*
477 A117 10c Youth assoc. emblems .15 .15
478 A117 75c Hand, sapling .85 .85
479 A117 $1 Dove, stick figures 1.10 1.10
Nos. 477-479 (3) 2.10 2.10

Indigenous Fruit — A118
Natl. Trade Unions Cong., 25th Anniv. — A119

1986, Feb. 26 Litho. *Perf. 14½x14*
480 A118 10c Psidium guajava .15 .15
481 A118 35c Eugenia aquea .45 .45
482 A118 50c Nephelium lappaceum .60 .60
483 A118 75c Manilkara zapota .90 .90
Nos. 480-483 (4) 2.10 2.10

1986, May 1 *Perf. 13½*

Progress: a, Science and technology. b, Communications. c, Industry. d, Education.

484 Strip of 4 1.00 1.00
a.-d. A119 10c any single .20 .20

Souvenir Sheet

485 Sheet of 4 2.00 2.00
a.-d. A119 35c any single .50 .50

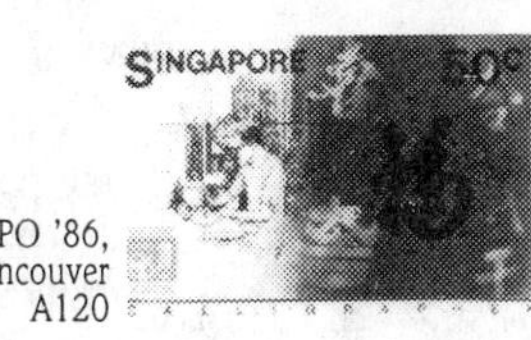

EXPO '86, Vancouver A120

1986, May 2 *Perf. 14½x14*

486 Strip of 3 2.50 2.50
a. A120 50c Calligraphy .55 .55
b. A120 75c Garland making .75 .75
c. A120 $1 Batik printing 1.10 1.10

Economic Development Board, 25th Anniv. — A121

1986, Aug. 1 *Perf. 15*

487 A121 10c Automation .15 .15
488 A121 35c Precision engineering .30 .30
489 A121 50c Electronics .45 .45
490 A121 75c Biotechnology .70 .70
Nos. 487-490 (4) 1.60 1.60

Submarine Cable — A122

1986, Sept. 8 *Perf. 13½*

491 A122 10c multicolored .15 .15
492 A122 35c multicolored .50 .50
493 A122 50c multicolored .70 .70
494 A122 75c multicolored 1.00 1.00
Nos. 491-494 (4) 2.35 2.35

Citizens' Consultative Committees, 21st Anniv. — A123

1986, Oct 15 *Perf. 12*

495 A123 Block of 4 2.50 2.50
a. 10c multicolored .15 .15
b. 35c multicolored .50 .50
c. 50c multicolored .75 .75
d. 75c multicolored 1.10 1.10

Intl. Peace Year — A124

1986, Dec. 17 **Litho.** *Perf. 14x13½*

496 A124 10c People .15 .15
497 A124 35c Southeast Asia map .45 .45
498 A124 $1 Globe 1.40 1.40
Nos. 496-498 (3) 2.00 2.00

Views of Singapore A125

1986, Feb. 25 *Perf. 12x12½*

499 A125 10c Orchard Road .15 .15
500 A125 50c Central business district .70 .70
501 A125 75c Marina Center, Raffles City .95 .95
Nos. 499-501 (3) 1.80 1.80

Assoc. of Southeast Asian Nations (ASEAN), 20th Anniv. — A126

National Service, 20th Anniv. — A127

1987, June 15 *Perf. 12*

502 A126 10c multicolored .15 .15
503 A126 35c multicolored .35 .35
504 A126 50c multicolored .55 .55
505 A126 75c multicolored .80 .80
Nos. 502-505 (4) 1.85 1.85

1987, July 1 *Perf. 15x14*

Designs: a, Army. b, Navy. c, Air Force. d, Pledge of Allegiance. e, Singapore Lion.

506 Strip of 4 1.00 1.00
a.-d. A127 10c any single .20 .20
507 Sheet of 5 2.00 2.00
a.-e. A127 35c any single .40 .40

River Life — A128

1987, Sept. 2 *Perf. 14*

508 A128 10c Singapore River .15 .15
509 A128 50c Kallang Basin .65 .65
510 A128 $1 Kranji Reservoir 1.40 1.40
Nos. 508-510 (3) 2.20 2.20

Natl. Museum Cent. A129

Views of the museum and artifacts: 10c, Majapahis gold bracelet, 14th-15th cent. 75c, Ming fluted kendi (water jar). $1, Seventeen-wave kris (sword with silver hilt, sheath), property of Sultan Abdul Jalil Sabat, 1699.

1987, Oct. 12 **Litho.** *Perf. 13½x14*

511 A129 10c multicolored .15 .15
512 A129 75c multicolored .75 .75
513 A129 $1 multicolored .95 .95
Nos. 511-513 (3) 1.85 1.85

Singapore Science Center, 10th Anniv. A130

Attractions.

1987, Dec. 10 *Perf. 14½*

514 A130 10c Omni Theater .15 .15
515 A130 35c Omni Planetarium .40 .40
516 A130 75c Cellular model .85 .85
517 A130 $1 Science exhibits 1.10 1.10
Nos. 514-517 (4) 2.50 2.50

Artillery, Cent. A131

Designs: 10c, 155-Gun Howitzer and Khatib Camp, headquarters of the Singapore Gunners. 35c, 25-Pound gun salute and Singapore City Hall. 50c, 4.5-inch Howitzer and Singapore Cricket Club, c. 1928. $1, Ft. Fullerton Drill Hall, c. 1893, and .405 Maxim gun.

1988, Feb. 22 **Litho.** *Perf. 13½x14*

518 A131 10c multicolored .15 .15
519 A131 35c multicolored .40 .40
520 A131 50c multicolored .65 .65
521 A131 $1 multicolored 1.25 1.25
Nos. 518-521 (4) 2.45 2.45

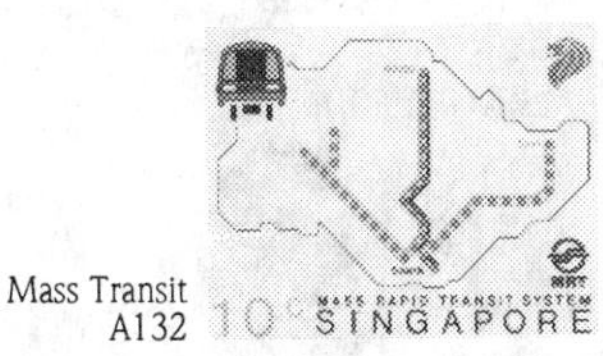

Mass Transit A132

1988, Mar. 12 *Perf. 14*

522 A132 10c Rail car, map .15 .15
523 A132 50c Elevated train .60 .60
524 A132 $1 Urban subway 1.25 1.25
Nos. 522-524 (3) 2.00 2.00

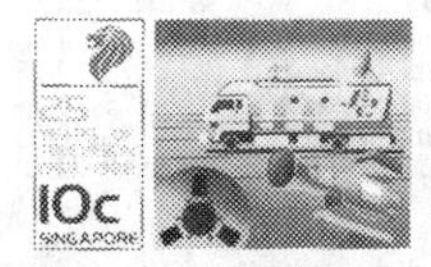

Natl. Television Broadcast System, 25th Anniv. A133

1988, Apr. 4 **Litho.** *Perf. 13½x14*

525 A133 10c shown .15 .15
526 A133 35c Studio .35 .35
527 A133 75c Television, transmission tower .75 .75
528 A133 $1 Screen, satellite dish 1.00 1.00
Nos. 525-528 (4) 2.25 2.25

Public Utilities Board, 25th Anniv. — A134

1988, May 4 **Litho.** *Perf. 13½*

529 A134 10c Water works .15 .15
530 A134 50c Electric company .60 .60
531 A134 $1 Fossil fuels 1.25 1.25
a. Souvenir sheet of 3, #529-531 2.25 2.25
Nos. 529-531 (3) 2.00 2.00

Courtesy Campaign, 10th Anniv. A135

Singa the lion (character trademark) and: 10c, Neighbors. 30c, Store service counter. $1, Helping the elderly.

1988, July 6 **Litho.** *Perf. 14½*

532 A135 10c multicolored .15 .15
533 A135 30c multicolored .30 .30
534 A135 $1 multicolored 1.00 1.00
Nos. 532-534 (3) 1.45 1.45

Fire Service, Cent. — A136

1988, Nov. 1 **Litho.** *Perf. 13½*

535 A136 10c Turntable ladder truck .15 .15
536 A136 $1 1890s Steam pump 2.25 2.25

Port Authority, 25th Anniv. — A137

Various facilities.

1989, Apr. 3 **Litho.** *Perf. 14x13½*

537 A137 10c multicolored .15 .15
538 A137 30c multi, diff. .40 .40
539 A137 75c multi, diff. 1.00 1.00
540 A137 $1 multi, diff. 1.40 1.40
Nos. 537-540 (4) 2.95 2.95

Old Chinatown A138

1989, May 17 **Litho.** *Perf. 14½*

541 A138 10c Sago St. .15 .15
542 A138 35c Pagoda St. .60 .60
543 A138 75c Trengganu St. 1.25 1.25
544 A138 $1 Temple St. 1.65 1.65
Nos. 541-544 (4) 3.65 3.65

Maps of Singapore — A139

Early 19th cent. map Singapore Showing Principal Residences and Places of Interest: No. 545a, Upper left. No. 545b, Upper right. No. 545c, Lower left. No. 545d, Lower right. (Illustration reduced).

1989, July 26 **Litho.** *Perf. 14½*

545 A139 Block of 4 .65 .65
a.-d. 15c any single .15 .15

Size: 33x31mm

Perf. 12½x13

546 A139 50c Singapore and Dependencies .55 .55
547 A139 $1 Plan of the British Settlement 1.10 1.10
Nos. 545-547 (3) 2.30 2.30

Fish — A140

1989, Sept. 6 *Perf. 14*

548 A140 15c Clown triggerfish .15 .15
549 A140 30c Majestic angelfish .30 .30
550 A140 75c Emperor angelfish .80 .80
551 A140 $1 Royal empress angelfish 1.10 1.10
Nos. 548-551 (4) 2.35 2.35

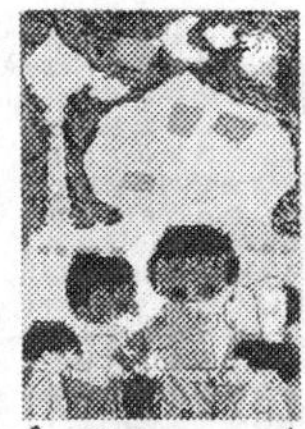

Festivals — A141

Children's drawings: 15c, *Hari Raya Puasa*, by Loke Yoke Yen. 35c, *Chinese New Year*, by Simon Koh. 75c, *Thaipusam*, by Henry Setiono. $1, *Christmas*, by Wendy Ang Lin.

1989, Oct. 25 Litho. *Perf. 14½*

552 A141 15c multicolored .15 .15
553 A141 35c multicolored .40 .40
554 A141 75c multicolored .80 .80
555 A141 $1 multicolored 1.10 1.10
a. Souv. sheet of 4, #552-555, perf. 14 2.50 2.50
Nos. 552-555 (4) 2.45 2.45

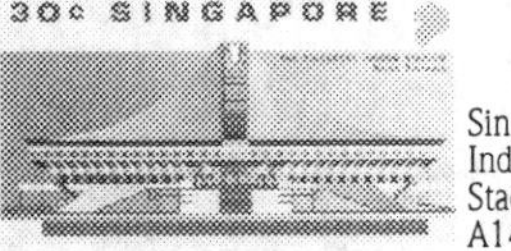

Singapore Indoor Stadium A142

1989, Dec. 27 Litho. *Perf. 14½*

556 A142 30c North entrance .35 .35
557 A142 75c Interior .80 .80
558 A142 $1 East entrance 1.10 1.10
a. Souvenir sheet of 3, #556-558 2.25 2.25
Nos. 556-558 (3) 2.25 2.25

Sports issue.

Lithographs of 19th Cent. Singapore A143

1990, Feb. 21 Litho. *Perf. 13*

559 A143 15c Singapore River, 1839 .15 .15
560 A143 30c Chinatown, 1837 .30 .30
561 A143 75c Waterfront, 1837 .80 .80
562 A143 $1 View from Ft. Canning, 1824 1.10 1.10
Nos. 559-562 (4) 2.35 2.35

First Postage Stamps, 150th Anniv. — A144

Maps and: 50c, Nos. 101-106. 75c, Cover to Scotland. $1, Cover to Ireland $2, Great Britain Nos. 1, 2.

1990, May 3 Litho. *Perf. 13½*

563 A144 50c multicolored .50 .50
564 A144 75c multicolored .75 .75
565 A144 $1 multicolored 1.00 1.00
566 A144 $2 multicolored 2.00 2.00
a. Souvenir sheet of 4, #563-566 4.75 4.75
Nos. 563-566 (4) 4.25 4.25

Tourism — A145

1990, July 4 *Perf. 14½*

567 A145 5c Zoo .15 .15
568 A145 15c Resort .15 .15
a. Booklet pane of 10 1.65
569 A145 20c City .25 .25
570 A145 25c Dragon boat race .30 .30
571 A145 30c Hotel .35 .35
572 A145 35c Caged birds .40 .40
573 A145 40c Park .45 .45
574 A145 50c Festival .55 .55
575 A145 75c Building, diff. .85 .85
Nos. 567-575 (9) 3.45 3.45

Independence, 25th Anniv. — A146

1990, Aug. 16 Litho. *Perf. 14x14½*

576 A146 15c shown .15 .15
a. Booklet pane of 10 1.65
577 A146 35c One Singapore .40 .40
578 A146 75c One hope .85 .85
579 A146 $1 One people 1.10 1.10
Nos. 576-579 (4) 2.50 2.50

Tourism A147

Designs: $1, Chinese opera singer, Siong Lim Temple. $2, Malay dancer, Sultan Mosque. $5, Indian dancer, Sri Mariamman Temple. $10, Ballet dancer, Victoria Memorial Hall.

Photo. & Engr.

1990, Oct. 10 *Perf. 15x14*

580 A147 $1 multicolored 1.40 1.40
581 A147 $2 multicolored 2.75 2.75
582 A147 $5 multicolored 6.75 6.75
583 A147 $10 multicolored 12.00 12.00
Nos. 580-583 (4) 22.90 22.90

Ferns — A148

1990, Nov. 14 Litho. *Perf. 14*

584 A148 15c Stag's horn .15 .15
585 A148 35c Maiden hair .40 .40
586 A148 75c Bird's nest .85 .85
587 A148 $1 Rabbit's foot 1.10 1.10
Nos. 584-587 (4) 2.50 2.50

A149

Houses of Worship A150

Designs: 20c, Hong San See Temple, 1912. 50c, Abdul Gattoor Mosque, 1910. 75c, Sri Perumal Temple, 1961. $1, St. Andrew's Cathedral, 1863.

1991, Jan. 23 Litho. *Perf. 14½*

588 A149 20c multicolored .25 .25
589 A150 20c multicolored .25 .25
a. Pair, #588-589 .45 .45
590 A149 50c multicolored .55 .55
591 A150 50c multicolored .55 .55
a. Pair, #590-591 1.10 1.10
592 A149 75c multicolored .85 .85
593 A150 75c multicolored .85 .85
a. Pair, #592-593 1.65 1.65
594 A149 $1 multicolored 1.10 1.10
595 A150 $1 multicolored 1.10 1.10
a. Pair, #594-595 2.25 2.25
Nos. 588-595 (8) 5.50 5.50

Vanda Miss Joaquim — A151

Design: No. 597, Dendrobium Anocha.

1991, Apr. 24 Litho. *Perf. 14*

596 A151 $2 multicolored 2.25 2.25
597 A151 $2 multicolored 2.25 2.25
a. Pair, #596-597 + label 4.50 4.50

Singapore '95 Intl. Philatelic Exhibition.
See Nos. 615-616, 664-665, 685-686, 716-717.

Civilian Airports — A152

Designs: 20c, Boeing 747, Changi Terminal II, 1991. 75c, Boeing 747, Changi Terminal I, 1981. $1, Concorde, Paya Lebar, 1955-1981. $2, DC-3, Kallang, 1937-1955.

Perf. 13½x14½

1991, July 1 Litho. & Engr.

598 A152 20c multicolored .25 .25
599 A152 75c multicolored .85 .85
600 A152 $1 multicolored 1.10 1.10
601 A152 $2 multicolored 2.25 2.25
Nos. 598-601 (4) 4.45 4.45

Arachnopsis Eric Holttum A153

Orchids: 30c, Cattleya Meadii. $1, Calanthe vestita.

1991, Aug. 8 Litho. *Perf. 14½x13½*

602 A153 20c multicolored .25 .25
603 A153 30c multicolored .35 .35
604 A153 $1 multicolored 1.10 1.10
Nos. 602-604 (3) 1.70 1.70

Birds — A154

Designs: 20c, Common tailorbird. 35c, Scarlet-backed flowerpecker. 75c, Black-naped oriole. $1, Common tora.

1991, Sept. 19 *Perf. 14*

605 A154 20c multicolored .20 .20
a. Booklet pane of 10 2.25 2.25
606 A154 35c multicolored .40 .40
607 A154 75c multicolored .85 .85
608 A154 $1 multicolored 1.10 1.10
Nos. 605-608 (4) 2.55 2.55

10 Years of Productivity — A155

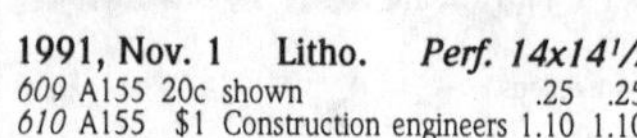

Phila Nippon '91 — A156

1991, Nov. 1 Litho. *Perf. 14x14½*

609 A155 20c shown .25 .25
610 A155 $1 Construction engineers 1.10 1.10

1991, Nov. 16 *Perf. 14½x14*

Flowers: 30c, Railway creeper. 75c, Asystasia. $1, Singapore rhododendron. $2, Coat buttons.

611 A156 30c multicolored .35 .35
612 A156 75c multicolored .85 .85
613 A156 $1 multicolored 1.10 1.10
614 A156 $2 multicolored 2.25 2.25
a. Souvenir sheet of 4, #611-614 4.75 4.75
Nos. 611-614 (4) 4.55 4.55

Flower Type of 1991

Designs: No. 615, Dendrobium Sharifah Fatimah. No. 616, Phalaenopsis Shim Beauty.

1992, Jan. 22 Litho. *Perf. 14*

615 A151 $2 multicolored 2.25 2.25
616 A151 $2 multicolored 2.25 2.25
a. Pair, #615-616 + label 4.75 4.75
b. Souvenir sheet of 2, #615-616 4.75 4.75

Singapore '95 Intl. Philatelic Exhibition.

Paintings — A157

1992, Mar. 11 Litho. *Perf. 14*

617 A157 20c Singapore Waterfront, 1958 .25 .25
618 A157 75c Kampung Hut, 1973 .85 .85
619 A157 $1 Bridge, 1983 1.10 1.10
620 A157 $2 Singapore River, 1984 2.25 2.25
Nos. 617-620 (4) 4.45 4.45

1992 Summer Olympics, Barcelona A158

1992, Apr. 24 *Perf. 14*

621 A158 20c Soccer .30 .30
622 A158 35c Relay races .50 .50
623 A158 50c Swimming .70 .70
624 A158 75c Basketball 1.00 1.00
625 A158 $1 Tennis 1.25 1.25
626 A158 $2 Sailing 2.75 2.75
a. Souvenir sheet of 6, #621-626 7.00 7.00
Nos. 621-626 (6) 6.50 6.50

Costumes, 1910 — A159

1992, Apr. 24 Litho. *Perf. 14½*

627 A159 20c Chinese family .25 .25
628 A159 35c Malay family .45 .45
629 A159 75c Indian family .90 .90
630 A159 $2 Straits Chinese family 2.50 2.50
Nos. 627-630 (4) 4.10 4.10

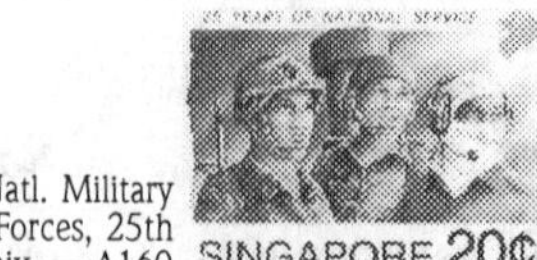

Natl. Military Forces, 25th Anniv. — A160

Designs: 35c, Frogman with gun, fighter plane, artillery. $1, Fighter, tank, ship.

1992, July 1

631 A160 20c multicolored .25 .25
632 A160 35c multicolored .45 .45
633 A160 $1 multicolored 1.25 1.25
Nos. 631-633 (3) 1.95 1.95

Visit ASEAN Year, 25th Anniv. A161

Designs: 20c, Mask, bird, sea life. 35c, Costumed women. $1, Outdoor scenery.

1992, Aug. 8

634 A161 20c multicolored .25 .25
635 A161 35c multicolored .45 .45
636 A161 $1 multicolored 1.25 1.25
Nos. 634-636 (3) 1.95 1.95

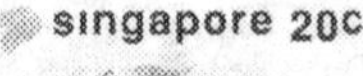

Crabs A162

Designs: 20c, Mosaic crab. 50c, Johnson's freshwater crab. 75c, Singapore freshwater crab. $1, Swamp forest crab.

1992, Aug. 21 *Perf. 14½x15*

637 A162 20c multicolored .25 .25
a. Booklet pane of 10 2.50
638 A162 50c multicolored .60 .60
639 A162 75c multicolored .90 .90
640 A162 $1 multicolored 1.25 1.25
Nos. 637-640 (4) 3.00 3.00

Currency, Notes and Coins A163

1992, Oct. 2 **Litho.** *Perf. 14½*

641 A163 20c Coins .25 .25
642 A163 75c Coin, flowers on note .90 .90
643 A163 $1 Boat on note, coins 1.25 1.25
644 A163 $2 Bird on note 2.50 2.50
a. Block of 4, #641-644 4.75 4.75

Wild Animals A164

1993, Jan. 13 **Litho.** *Perf. 14½x15*

645 A164 20c Sun bear .25 .25
646 A164 30c Orangutan .35 .35
647 A164 75c Slow loris .90 .90
648 A164 $2 Large mouse deer 2.50 2.50
Nos. 645-648 (4) 4.00 4.00

Greetings Stamps — A165

Designs: a, Thank you. b, Congratulations. c, Best wishes. d, Happy birthday. e, Get well soon.

Perf. 14½x14 on 3 Sides

1993, Feb. 10

Booklet Stamps

649 A165 20c Strip of 5, #a.-e. 1.25 1.25
f. Booklet pane of 2 #649 2.50 2.50

Preservation of Tanjong Pagar — A166

1993, Mar. 10 **Litho.** *Perf. 14*

650 A166 20c shown .25 .25
651 A166 30c Building facade, tower .35 .35
652 A166 $2 Aerial view 2.50 2.50
Nos. 650-652 (3) 3.10 3.10

A167

A168

1993, May 29 *Perf. 12x11½*

653 A167 $2 Cranes, by Chen Wen Hsi 2.50 2.50

Indopex '93.

1993, June 12 **Litho.** *Perf. 14*

654 A168 20c Soccer .25 .25
655 A168 35c Basketball .45 .45
656 A168 50c Badminton .60 .60
657 A168 75c Running .90 .90
658 A168 $1 Water polo 1.25 1.25
659 A168 $2 Yachting 2.50 2.50
Nos. 654-659 (6) 5.95 5.95

17th Sea Games, Singapore.

Butterflies — A169

Fruits — A170

1993, Aug. 21 **Litho.** *Perf. 14½*

660 A169 20c Plain tiger .25 .25
a. Booklet pane of 10 2.50
661 A169 50c Malay lacewing .60 .60
662 A169 75c Palm king .90 .90
663 A169 $1 Banded swallowtail 1.25 1.25
Nos. 660-663 (4) 3.00 3.00

Flower Type of 1991

1993, Aug. 13

Size: 26x34mm

664 A151 $2 Phalaenopsis amabilis 2.50 2.50
665 A151 $2 Vanda sumatrana 2.50 2.50
a. Pair, #664-665 + label 5.00 5.00
b. Souvenir sheet of 2, #664-665, perf. 15x14½ 5.00 5.00

Singapore '95 World Stamp Exhibition and Taipei '93, Asian Intl. Invitation Stamp Exhibition (#665b).

1993, Oct. 1 **Litho.** *Perf. 14½x14*

666 A170 20c Papaya .25 .25
667 A170 35c Pomegranate .45 .45
668 A170 75c Starfruit .95 .95
669 A170 $2 Durian 2.50 2.50
a. Souvenir sheet of 4, #666-669 4.50 4.50
Nos. 666-669 (4) 4.15 4.15

Bangkok '93 (#669a).

Chinese Egrets — A171

Designs: 20c, Two, one with bill in water. 25c, Two, one with fish in mouth. 30c, Two facing opposite directions. 35c, In flight.

1993, Nov. 10 **Litho.** *Perf. 13½x14*

670 A171 20c multicolored .40 .40
671 A171 25c multicolored .55 .55
672 A171 30c multicolored .65 .65
673 A171 35c multicolored .75 .75
a. Strip of 4, #670-673 2.50 2.50

World Wildlife Fund.

Palm Tree — A171a

1993, Nov. 24 **Photo.** *Die Cut*

Self-Adhesive

Booklet Stamp

673B A171a (20c) multicolored .25 .25
c. Booklet pane of 15 3.75

By its nature, No. 673c is a complete booklet. The peelable backing serves as a booklet cover.

Marine Life — A172

Type A Perforations

A. On two longer sides, groups of three and eighteen holes separated by an oval hole equal in width to three holes.

Perf. 13x13½, 13½x14 (675B)

1994 **Litho.**

674 A172 5c Tiger cowrie .15 .15
675 A172 20c Sea fan .25 .25
a. Booklet pane of 10 2.50
675B A172 (20c) Blue-spotted stingray .30 .30
676 A172 25c Tunicate .35 .35
677 A172 30c Clownfish .40 .40
678 A172 35c Nudibranch .45 .45
679 A172 40c Sea urchin .50 .50
680 A172 50c Soft coral .65 .65
681 A172 75c Pin cushion star .95 .95

Litho. & Embossed

Perf. 14 Syncopated Type A (2 Sides)

682 A172 $1 Knob coral 1.40 1.40
683 A172 $2 Mushroom coral 2.75 2.75
684 A172 $5 Bubble coral 7.00 7.00
684A A172 $10 Octopus coral 14.00 14.00
Nos. 674-684A (13) 29.15 29.15

Self-Adhesive

Die Cut Perf. 8½

684B A172 (20c) Blue-spotted stingray .30 .30
c. Booklet pane of 10 3.00

Nos. 675B, 684B inscribed "FOR LOCAL ADDRESSES ONLY." By its nature, No. 684c is a complete booklet. The peelable paper backing serves as a booklet cover.

Issued: 5c-75c, 1/12/94; $1-$10, 3/23/94; #675B, 684B, 11/16/94.

See Nos. 816-824.

Flower Type of 1991

Designs: No. 685, Paphiopedilum vicotriaregina. No. 686, Dendrobium smillieae.

1994, Feb. 18 **Litho.** *Perf. 14½*

Size: 26x35mm

685 A151 $2 multicolored 2.75 2.75
686 A151 $2 multicolored 2.75 2.75
a. Pair, #685-686 + label 5.50 5.50
b. Souvenir sheet of 2, #685-686 5.50 5.50

Singapore '95 and Hong Kong '94 (#686b).

Spring Festival — A173

1994, May 18 **Litho.** *Perf. 13½*

687 A173 20c Ballet .30 .30
688 A173 30c Mime, puppets .40 .40
689 A173 50c Musicians .70 .70
690 A173 $1 Crafts 1.40 1.40
Nos. 687-690 (4) 2.80 2.80

Operationally Ready Natl. Servicemen, 25th Anniv. — A174

Civilian-soldiers: 20c, Saluting flag, aiming anti-tank missile. 30c, With family, on jungle patrol with automatic rifle. 35c, Reading newspaper, aiming machine gun. 75c, Working with computer, and as commander, looking through binoculars.

1994, July 1 **Litho.** *Perf. 13½*

691 A174 20c multicolored .30 .30
692 A174 30c multicolored .45 .45
693 A174 35c multicolored .50 .50
694 A174 75c multicolored 1.10 1.10
Nos. 691-694 (4) 2.35 2.35

Herons — A175

1994, Aug. 16 **Litho.** *Perf. 14*

695 A175 20c Black-crowned night heron .30 .30
a. Booklet pane of 10 3.00
696 A175 50c Little heron .70 .70
697 A175 75c Purple heron 1.00 1.00
698 A175 $1 Gray heron 1.40 1.40
a. Block of 4, #695-698 3.50 3.50
Nos. 695-698 (4) 3.40 3.40

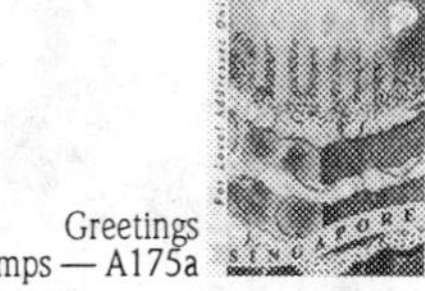
Greetings Stamps — A175a

Designs: No. 698B, Birthday cake. No. 698C, Bouquet of flowers. No. 698D, Gift-wrapped present. No. 698E, Fireworks. No. 698F, Balloons.

Die Cut Perf. 11½

1994, Sept. 14 **Litho.**

Self-Adhesive

Booklet Stamps

698B A175a (20c) multicolored .30 .30
698C A175a (20c) multicolored .30 .30
698D A175a (20c) multicolored .30 .30
698E A175a (20c) multicolored .30 .30
698F A175a (20c) multicolored .30 .30
g. Bklt. pane, 2 each #698B-698F 3.00
Nos. 698B-698F (5) 1.50 1.50

Nos. 698B-693F inscribed "For Local Addresses Only." By its nature, No. 698g is a complete booklet. The peelable paper backing serves as a booklet cover. The outside of the cover contains 10 peelable labels.

Modern Singapore, 175th Anniv. — A176

Early, modern scenes: 20c, Schoolchildren reading, graduating seniors. 50c, Horse-drawn carriages, high-speed train. 75c, Small boats, container ship dock. $1, Skyline.

1994, Sept. 30 *Perf. 13½x14*
699 A176 20c multicolored .30 .30
700 A176 50c multicolored .70 .70
701 A176 75c multicolored 1.00 1.00
702 A176 $1 multicolored 1.40 1.40
a. Souvenir sheet of 4, #699-702 3.40 3.40
Nos. 699-702 (4) 3.40 3.40

ICAO, 50th Anniv. — A177

Designs: 35c, Control tower, passenger jet. 75c, Terminal, Concord jet. $2, Control tower, communication satellite, passenger jet.

1994, Oct. 5 **Litho.** *Perf. 14*
703 A177 20c multicolored .30 .30
704 A177 35c multicolored .50 .50
705 A177 75c multicolored 1.10 1.10
706 A177 $2 multicolored 3.00 3.00
Nos. 703-706 (4) 4.90 4.90

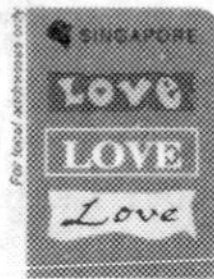

Love Stamps — A178

Designs: No. 707, "Love" in three different inscriptions. No. 708, Spiral of "Love." No. 709, "Love" on two lines. No. 710, "Love" in different languages. No. 711, Geometrical "Love."

Die Cut Perf. 11½
1995, Feb. 8 **Litho.**
Self-Adhesive
Booklet Stamps
707 A178 (20c) multicolored .30 .30
708 A178 (20c) multicolored .30 .30
709 A178 (20c) multicolored .30 .30
710 A178 (20c) multicolored .30 .30
711 A178 (20c) multicolored .30 .30
a. Booklet pane, 2 each #707-711 3.00
Nos. 707-711 (5) 1.50 1.50

Nos. 707-711 inscribed "FOR LOCAL ADDRESSES ONLY." By its nature, No. 711a is a complete booklet. The peelable paper backing serves as a booklet cover. The outside of the cover contains 10 peelable labels.

Meet in Singapore A179

Scenes in Suntec City: (20c), Intl. Convention & Exhibition Center. 75c, High rise buildings. $1, Temasek Boulevard. $2, Fountain Terrace.

1995, Jan. 11 *Perf. 13½x14*
712 A179 (20c) multicolored .30 .30
713 A179 75c multicolored 1.10 1.10
714 A179 $1 multicolored 1.50 1.50
715 A179 $2 multicolored 3.00 3.00
Nos. 712-715 (4) 5.90 5.90

Singapore '95. No. 712 inscribed "FOR LOCAL ADDRESSES ONLY."

Souvenir Sheets of 2, #712, 715 Inscribed:

715a FIP DAY 4.00 4.00
715b OLYMPIC DAY-YOUTH 4.00 4.00
715c FIAP DAY 4.00 4.00
715d LETTER WRITING DAY 4.00 4.00
715e STAMP COLLECTING DAY 4.00 4.00
715f SINGAPORE '95 DAY 4.00 4.00
715g PHILATELIC MUSEUM DAY 4.00 4.00
715h SINGAPORE POST DAY 4.00 4.00
715i AWARDSDAY 4.00 4.00
715j THEMATIC PHILATELY DAY 4.00 4.00

Flower Type of 1991

Designs: No. 716, Vanda Marlie Dolera, No. 717, Vanda limbata.

1995, Mar. 15 **Litho.** *Perf. 14*
716 A151 $2 multicolored 3.00 3.00
717 A151 $2 multicolored 3.00 3.00
a. Pair, #716-717 + label 6.00 6.00
b. Souvenir sheet, #716-717 6.00 6.00

Singapore '95 (#717a-717b).

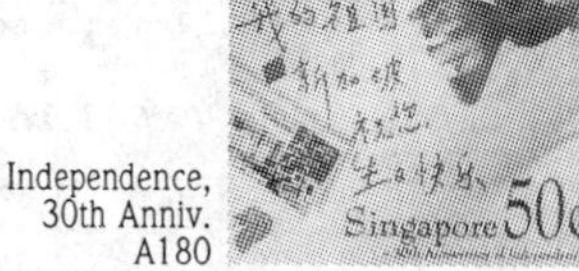

Independence, 30th Anniv. A180

"My Singapore, My Country, Happy Birthday" in various languages and: 20c, "30" formed in ribbon, vert. 50c, #471, flower. 75c, #598, Music sheet. $1, Natl. flag, #489, music sheets, vert.

Perf. 14x13½, 13½x14
1995, Apr. 19 **Litho.**
718 A180 (20c) multicolored .30 .30
719 A180 50c multicolored .70 .70
720 A180 75c multicolored 1.10 1.10
721 A180 $1 multicolored 1.40 1.40
a. Souvenir sheet of 4, #718-721 3.75 3.75
Nos. 718-721 (4) 3.50 3.50

No. 718 inscribed "For Local Addresses Only." No. 721a is a continuous design.

End of World War II, 50th Anniv. A181

Designs: (20c), Crowd celebrating, Straits Settlements #271, vert. 60c, Lord Mountbatten receiving Japanese surrender of Singapore, Straits Settlements #265, vert. 70c, Food kitchen. $2, Police road block.

Perf. 14x13½, 13½x14
1995, June 21 **Litho.**
723 A181 (20c) multicolored .30 .30
724 A181 60c multicolored .90 .90
725 A181 70c multicolored 1.00 1.00
726 A181 $2 multicolored 3.00 3.00
Nos. 723-726 (4) 5.20 5.20

No. 723 inscribed "For Local Addresses Only" and sold for 20c on day of issue.

New Six Digit Postal Code A182

1995, Sept. 1 **Litho.** *Perf. 14x14½*
727 A182 (20c) shown .30 .30
728 A182 $2 Six boxes, numbers 3.00 3.00

No. 728 inscribed "For Local Addresses Only."

Philatelic Museum, Singapore A183

Museum building, various stamps, featuring: 20c, #12. 50c, #157. 60c, #661. $2, Displays of stamps.

1995, Aug. 19 *Perf. 13x13½*
729 A183 (20c) multicolored .30 .30
730 A183 50c multicolored .75 .75
731 A183 60c multicolored .90 .90
732 A183 $2 multicolored 3.00 3.00
Nos. 729-732 (4) 4.95 4.95

No. 729 inscribed "For Local Addresses Only."

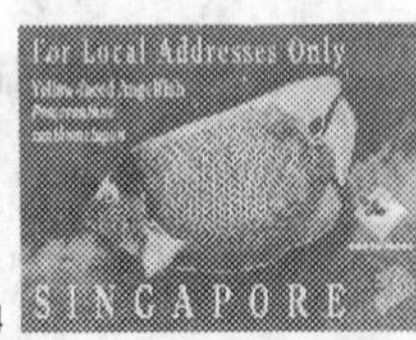

Fish — A184

1995, July 19 **Litho.** *Perf. 13½x14*
733 A184 (20c) Yellow-faced angelfish .30 .30
Complete booklet, 10 #733 3.00
734 A184 60c Harlequin sweetlips .90 .90
735 A184 70c Lionfish 1.00 1.00
736 A184 $1 Longfin bannerfish 1.50 1.50
Nos. 733-736 (4) 3.70 3.70

No. 733 inscribed "For Local Addresses Only."

Paintings in Singapore Art Museum A185

Designs: (20c), Tropical Fruits, by Georgette Chen. 30c, Bali Beach, by Cheong Soo Pieng. 70c, Gibbons, by Chen Wen Hsi. $2, Shi (Lion), by Pan Shou (calligraphy).

1995, Oct. 20 **Litho.** *Perf. 12½*
737 A185 (20c) multicolored .30 .30
738 A185 30c multicolored .45 .45
739 A185 70c multicolored 1.00 1.00

Perf. 13½x13
740 A185 $2 multicolored 3.00 3.00
Nos. 737-740 (4) 4.75 4.75

No. 737 inscribed "For Local Addresses Only." No. 740 is 22½x39mm.

New Year 1996 (Year of the Rat) — A186

1996, Feb. 9 **Litho.** *Perf. 12*
741 A186 (20c) shown .25 .25
742 A186 $2 Rat with orange 3.00 3.00
a. Souvenir sheet, #742, #742d 3.25 3.25
b. As "a," diff. sheet margin 3.25 3.25
c. As "a," diff. sheet margin 3.25 3.25
d. 22c like #741 .25 .25

No. 741 inscribed "For Local Addresses Only."
Sheet margins contain exhibition emblems for: #742: a, Indonesia '96; b, China '96; c, CAPEX '96.
Issued: #742a, 3/21; #742b, 5/18; #742c, 6/8.

Architectural Styles — A187

Designs: (20c), Bukit Pasoh, Chinatown. 35c, Jalan Sultan, Kampong Glam. 70c, Dalhousie Lane, Little India. $1, Supreme Court, Civic District.

1996, Jan. 17 *Perf. 13½x14*
743 A187 (20c) multicolored .30 .30
744 A187 35c multicolored .55 .55
745 A187 70c multicolored 1.00 1.00
746 A187 $1 multicolored 1.50 1.50
Nos. 743-746 (4) 3.35 3.35

No. 743 inscribed "For Local Addresses Only."

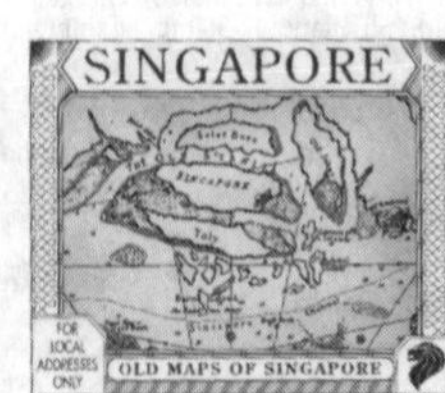

Old Maps of Singapore A188

Designs: (20c), Old Straits. 60c, Detail of town. $1, Part of Malay Penisula, Singapore. $2, Town and entrance.

1996, Mar. 13 **Litho.** *Perf. 12*
747 A188 (20c) multicolored .30 .30
748 A188 60c multicolored .90 .90
749 A188 $1 multicolored 1.50 1.50
750 A188 $2 multicolored 3.00 3.00
Nos. 747-750 (4) 5.70 5.70

No. 747 inscribed "For Local Addresses Only."

Greetings Stamps — A189

Children's drawings about courtesy: (22c), Child telling another to be quiet in library. 35c, Children helping elderly during outdoor activities. 50c, Giving seat at bus stop to expectant mother. 60c, Sharing umbrella. $1, Giving up seat on bus to senior citizen.

1996, July 10 **Litho.** *Die Cut Perf. 11*
Self-Adhesive
Booklet Stamps
751 A189 (22c) multicolored .30 .30
a. Booklet pane of 10 3.00
752 A189 35c multicolored .55 .55
753 A189 50c multicolored .75 .75
754 A189 60c multicolored .90 .90
755 A189 $1 multicolored 1.50 1.50
a. Booklet pane of 10, 5 #751, 2 #752, 1 each #753-755 5.75
b. Sheet of 5, #752-755, 755c 4.00 4.00
c. 22c like #751 .30 .30
Nos. 751-755 (5) 4.00 4.00

No. 751 inscribed "For Local Addresses Only." By their nature Nos. 751a and 755a are complete booklets. The peelable paper backing serves as a booklet cover. The outside of the cover contains 10 peelable labels.

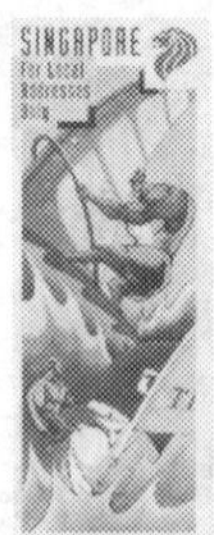

1996 Summer Olympic Games, Atlanta — A190

Designs: (22c), #759b, Board, dinghy sailing. 60c, Soccer, tennis. 70c, Pole vault, hurdles. $2, Diving, swimming.

1996, July 19 **Litho.** *Perf. 14½*
756 A190 (22c) multicolored .30 .30
757 A190 60c multicolored .90 .90
758 A190 70c multicolored 1.00 1.00
759 A190 $2 multicolored 3.00 3.00
a. Souvenir sheet of 4, #757-759, 759b 5.20 5.20
b. 22c multicolored .30 .30

No. 756 inscribed "For Local Addresses Only."

Asian Civilizations Museum A191

(22c), Calligraphy in Caoshu, Ming Dynasty 17th cent. 60c, Javanese Divination manuscript, Surkarta (Solo), Indonesia, 1842. 70c, Temple hanging, Tamilnadu. South India, 19th cent. $2, Calligraphic implements, Persia and Turkey, 17th-19th cent.

1996, June 5 **Litho.** *Perf. 13½x14*
760 A191 (22c) multicolored .30 .30
761 A191 60c multicolored .90 .90
762 A191 70c multicolored 1.00 1.00
763 A191 $2 multicolored 3.00 3.00
Nos. 760-763 (4) 5.20 5.20

No. 760 inscribed "For Local Addresses Only."

Care for Nature — A192

Native trees: (22c), Cinnamomum iners. 60c, Hibiscus tiliaceus. 70c, Parkia speciosa. $1, Terminalia catappa.

1996, Sept. 11 Litho. *Perf. 13½*
764 A192 (22c) multicolored .30 .30
a. Booklet pane of 10 3.00
Complete booklet, #764a 3.00
765 A192 60c multicolored .90 .90
766 A192 70c multicolored 1.00 1.00
767 A192 $1 multicolored 1.50 1.50
Nos. 764-767 (4) 3.70 3.70

No. 764 inscribed "For Local Addresses Only."

Panmen, Suzhou, China — A193

Design: 60c, Singapore waterfront.

1996, Oct. 9 Litho. *Perf. 13x13½*
768 A193 (22c) multicolored .30 .30
769 A193 60c multicolored .90 .90
a. Souvenir sheet, #769, 769b 1.20 1.20
b. 22c like #768 .30 .30
c. As "a," ovptd. in sheet margin 1.20 1.20

No. 768 inscribed "For Local Addresses Only."
No. 769c is ovptd. in sheet margin with violet on gold Singapore-China Stamp Exhibition emblem.
See People's Republic of China Nos. 2733-2734.

First World Trade Organization Ministerial Conference — A194

Illustration reduced.

1996, Nov. 20 Litho. *Perf. 14*
770 A194 (22c) pink, vio & multi .35 .35
771 A194 60c ver, grn & multi .90 .90
772 A194 $1 bl, yel org & multi 1.50 1.50
773 A194 $2 grn, car & multi 3.00 3.00
Nos. 770-773 (4) 5.75 5.75

No. 770 inscribed "For Local Addresses Only."

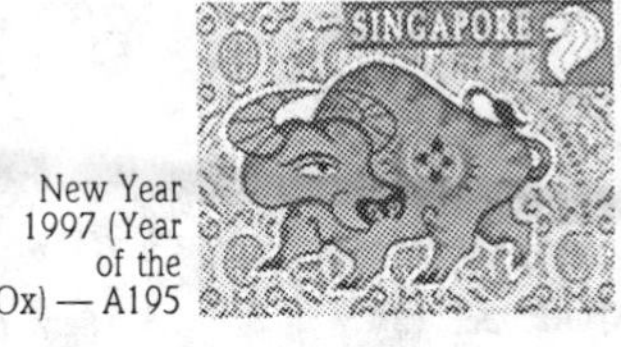

New Year 1997 (Year of the Ox) — A195

Nos. 774, 775, Different stylized oxen.

1997, Jan. 10 *Perf. 13½x14*
774 A195 (22c) multicolored .35 .35
775 A195 $2 multicolored 3.00 3.00
a. Sheet, 9 each #774-775 31.50
b. Souvenir sheet, #775, #775d 3.40 3.40
c. As "b," diff. sheet margin 3.40 3.40
d. 22c like #774 .35 .35
e. As "b," diff. sheet margin 3.40 3.40

No. 774 inscribed "For Local Addresses Only."
Sheet margin contains exhibition emblem: #775b Hong Kong '97; #775c Pacific '97; #775e Shanghai 1997.
Issued: #775b, 2/12/97; #775c, 5/29/97; #775e, 11/19/97.

Traditional Games A196

Ground Transportation A197

1997, Feb. 21 Litho. *Perf. 14½*
776 A196 (22c) Shuttlecock .35 .35
777 A196 35c Marbles .55 .55
778 A196 60c Tops .90 .90
779 A196 $1 Fivestones 1.50 1.50
a. Souvenir sheet of 4, #776-779 3.30 3.30
Nos. 776-779 (4) 3.30 3.30

No. 776 inscribed "For Local Addresses Only." Singpex '97 (#779a).

1997, Mar. 19 *Perf. 13½*
780 A197 5c Bullock cart .15 .15
781 A197 20c Bicycle .30 .30
782 A197 (22c) Rickshaw .35 .35
783 A197 30c Electric tram .45 .45
784 A197 35c Trolley bus .55 .55
785 A197 40c Trishaw .60 .60
786 A197 50c Vintage car .75 .75
787 A197 60c Horse-drawn carriage .90 .90
788 A197 70c Fire engine 1.00 1.00
a. Souvenir sheet, #780-781, 783-788, 788b 5.00 5.00
b. 22c like #782 .35 .35
Nos. 780-788 (9) 5.05 5.05

Self-Adhesive
Serpentine Die Cut Perf. 11½
Booklet Stamp

789 A197 (22c) like #782 .35 .35
a. Booklet pane of 10 3.50

Nos. 782, 789 are inscribed "For Local Addresses Only." Nos. 780, 783-784, 787-788 are horiz.
By its nature No. 789a is a complete booklet. The peelable paper backing serves as a booklet cover.

1997, Apr. 23 Litho. & Engr. *Perf. 13*

$1, Taxi. $2, Bus, horiz. $5, Mass rapid transit system. $10, Light rapid transit system, horiz.

Size: 28x35mm (#790, 792), 43x24mm (#791, 793)

790 A197 $1 multicolored 1.50 1.50
791 A197 $2 multicolored 3.00 3.00
792 A197 $5 multicolored 7.50 7.50
793 A197 $10 multicolored 15.00 15.00
a. Souvenir sheet, #790-793 27.00 27.00
Nos. 790-793 (4) 27.00 27.00

Greetings Stamps — A198

Word "Friends" used in making designs: #794, Man's head. #795, Sharing umbrella. #796, Penguins. #797, Butterflies, hand. #798, Coffee cup. #799, Flower. #800, Candle. #801, Tree. #802, Jar holding stars. #803, Two cans connected by string.

Serpentine Die Cut 14½
1997, May 14 Litho.
Self-Adhesive
Booklet Stamps

794 A198 (22c) multicolored .35 .35
795 A198 (22c) multicolored .35 .35
796 A198 (22c) multicolored .35 .35
797 A198 (22c) multicolored .35 .35
798 A198 (22c) multicolored .35 .35
a. Booklet pane, 2 each #794-798 3.50
Nos. 794-798 (5) 1.75 1.75
799 A198 (22c) multicolored .35 .35
800 A198 (22c) multicolored .35 .35
801 A198 (22c) multicolored .35 .35
802 A198 (22c) multicolored .35 .35
803 A198 (22c) multicolored .35 .35
a. Booklet pane, 2 each #799-803 3.50
Nos. 799-803 (5) 1.75 1.75

Nos. 794-803 are inscribed "For Local Addresses Only." By their nature Nos. 798a and 803a are complete booklets. The peelable paper backing serves as a booklet cover. The outside cover contains 10 peelable labels.

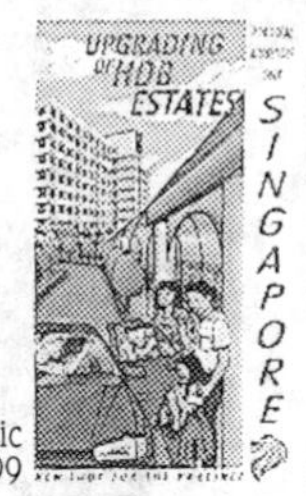

Upgrading of Public Housing — A199

Designs: (22c) New look for the precinct. 30c, Outdoor facilities. 70c, Landscaped gardens. $1, Additional space, balcony.

1997, July 16 Litho. *Perf. 14*
804 A199 (22c) multicolored .30 .30
805 A199 30c multicolored .40 .40
806 A199 70c multicolored .95 .95
807 A199 $1 multicolored 1.40 1.40
Nos. 804-807 (4) 3.05 3.05

No. 804 is inscribed "For Local Addresses Only."

ASEAN, 30th Anniv. A200

Designs: (22c), 30 years of "dates," globe, hands clasped, sky. 35c, Southeast Asian cultures. 60c, Satellite dish, circuit board, map of Southeast Asia, sky. $1, Tourist attractions in ASEAN countries.

1997, Aug. 8 Litho. *Perf. 14*
808 A200 (22c) multicolored .30 .30
809 A200 35c multicolored .50 .50
810 A200 60c multicolored .80 .80
811 A200 $1 multicolored 1.40 1.40
Nos. 808-811 (4) 3.00 3.00

No. 808 is inscribed "For Local Addresses Only." Value is for copy with surrounding selvage.

Protection of the Environment — A201

Designs: (22c), Clean Environment. 60c, Clean waters. 70c, Clean air. $1, Clean homes.

1997, Sept. 13 Litho. *Perf. 14x13½*
812 A201 (22c) multicolored .30 .30
a. Booklet pane of 10 3.00
Complete booklet, #812a 3.00
813 A201 60c multicolored .80 .80
814 A201 70c multicolored .90 .90
815 A201 $1 multicolored 1.30 1.30
Nos. 812-815 (4) 3.30 3.30

No. 812 is inscribed "For Local Addresses Only."

Marine Life Type of 1994

1997 Photo. *Perf. 13x13½*
816 A172 5c like #674 .15 .15
816A A172 (20c) like #675B .35 .35
817 A172 25c like #676 .30 .30
818 A172 30c like #677 .40 .40
819 A172 35c like #678 .45 .45
820 A172 40c like #679 .50 .50
821 A172 50c like #680 .65 .65
821A A172 75c like #681 1.25 1.25

Photo. & Embossed
Perf. 14 Syncopated Type A (2 Sides)

822 A172 $1 like #682 1.25 1.25
822A A172 $2 like #683 3.25 3.25
823 A172 $5 like #684 6.25 6.25
824 A172 $10 like #684A 12.50 12.50
Nos. 816-824 (12) 27.30 27.30

No. 816A is inscribed "For Local Addresses Only."
Nos. 822-824 have embossed logo in center of stamp and denomination and country are white. Nos. 682, 684, 684A have embossed lettering for country name and denomination.

Shells of Singapore and Thailand A202

Designs: (22c), Drupa morum. 35c, Nerita chamaeleon. 60c, Littoraria melanostoma. $!, Cryptospira elegans.

1997, Oct. 9 Litho. *Perf. 13x14*
825 A202 (22c) multicolored .30 .30
826 A202 35c multicolored .45 .45
827 A202 60c multicolored .75 .75
828 A202 $1 multicolored 1.25 1.25
a. Souvenir sheet, #826-828, #828b 2.75 2.75
b. 22c like #825 .30 .30
Nos. 825-828 (4) 2.75 2.75

No. 825 inscribed "For Local Addresses Only."
See Thailand Nos. 1771-1774.

New Year 1998 (Year of the Tiger) A203

Different stylized tigers.

1998, Jan. 9 Litho. *Perf. 13x14*
829 A203 (22c) multicolored .30 .30
830 A203 $2 multicolored 2.50 2.50
a. Horiz. or vert. pair, #829-830 2.80 2.80
b. Sheet of 9 each, #829-830 27.00 27.00

No. 829 inscribed "For Local Addresses Only."
Stamps in No. 830b are arranged in a checkerboard fashion.

Dinosaurs — A204

1998, Apr. 22 Photo. *Die Cut*
831 A204 (22c) Pentaceratops .30 .30
832 A204 (22c) Apatosaurus .30 .30
833 A204 (22c) Albertosaurus .30 .30
a. Pane, 5 each #831-833 4.50
Nos. 831-833 (3) .90 .90

Nos. 831-833 are inscribed "For Local Addresses Only."

POSTAGE DUE STAMPS

D1

D2

Wmk. 314

1968, Feb. 1 Litho. *Perf. 9*
J1 D1 1c emerald .25 .25
J2 D1 2c red org .35 .35
J3 D1 4c yel org .75 .75
J4 D1 8c brown .90 .90
J5 D1 10c rose mag 2.25 2.25
J6 D1 12c dl vio 1.25 1.25
J7 D1 20c brt bl 2.75 2.75
J8 D1 50c gray grn 6.50 6.50
Nos. J1-J8 (8) 15.00 15.00

1973-77 *Perf. 13x13½*
J1a D1 1c Unwmkd. ('77) *30.00 30.00*
J3a D1 4c Unwmkd. ('77) *35.00 35.00*
J5a D1 10c 1.00 1.00
b. Unwmkd. ('77) *35.00 35.00*
J7a D1 20c Unwmkd. ('77) *45.00 50.00*
J8a D1 50c *8.00 8.00*
b. Unwmkd. ('77) *55.00 55.00*

1981 Unwmk. *Perf. 12x11½*
J9 D2 1c emerald .15 .15
J10 D2 4c orange .15 .15
J11 D2 10c carmine .55 .55
J12 D2 20c light blue .60 .60
J13 D2 50c light yellow green .85 .85
Nos. J9-J13 (5) 2.30 2.30

1978, Sept. 25 *Perf. 13x13½*

J9a	D2	1c	.70	.70
J10a	D2	4c	.80	.80
J11a	D2	10c	.80	.80
J12a	D2	20c	1.00	1.00
J13a	D2	50c	1.75	1.75
		Nos. J9a-J13a (5)	5.05	5.05

D3

1989, July 12 Litho. *Perf. 13x13½*

J14	D3	5c	red lilac	.15	.15
J15	D3	10c	red	.15	.15
J16	D3	20c	light blue	.25	.25
J17	D3	50c	yellow green	.70	.70
			Set value	1.10	1.10

SLOVAKIA

slō-'vä-kē-ə

LOCATION — Central Europe
GOVT. — Republic
AREA — 18,932 sq. mi.
POP. — 5,296,768 (est. 1992)
CAPITAL — Bratislava

Formerly a province of Czechoslovakia, Slovakia declared its independence in Mar., 1939. A treaty was immediately concluded with Germany guaranteeing Slovakian independence but providing for German "protection" for 25 years.

In 1945 the republic ended and Slovakia again became a part of Czechoslovakia.

On January 1, 1993, Czechoslovakia split into the Czech Republic and Slovakia.

100 Halierov = 1 Koruna

Catalogue values for unused stamps in this country are for never hinged items, beginning with Scott 26 in the regular postage section, Scott B1 in the semi-postal section, Scott C1 in the airmail section, Scott EX1 in the personal delivery section, Scott J1 in the postage due section, and Scott P10 in the newspaper section.

Watermark

Wmk. 263- Double-Barred Cross Multiple

Stamps of Czechoslovakia, 1928-39, Overprinted in Red or Blue

Slovenský štát 1939

1939 *Perf. 10, 12½, 12x12½*

2	A29	5h	dk ultra	.50	.90
3	A29	10h	brown	.15	.15
4	A29	20h	red (Bl)	.15	.15
5	A29	25h	green	.95	*1.75*
6	A29	30h	red violet (Bl)	.15	.15
7	A61a	40h	dark blue	.15	.20
8	A73	50h	deep green	.15	.15
9	A63	50h	deep green	.15	.15
10	A63	60h	dull violet	.15	.15
11	A63	60h	dull blue	5.75	*8.75*
12	A60	1k	rose lake (Bl) (On No. 212)	.15	.15

Overprinted Diagonally

13	A64	1.20k	rose lilac (Bl)	.20	*.35*
14	A65	1.50k	carmine (Bl)	.20	*.35*
15	A79	1.60k	olive grn (Bl)	1.75	*2.50*
16	A66	2k	dk blue green	1.75	*2.50*
17	A67	2.50k	dark blue	.30	*.55*
18	A68	3k	brown	.40	*.65*
19	A69	3.50k	dk violet	17.50	*26.00*
20	A69	3.50k	dk violet (Bl)	20.00	*30.00*
21	A70	4k	dk violet	8.75	*12.50*

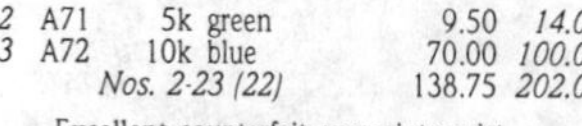

22	A71	5k	green	9.50	*14.00*
23	A72	10k	blue	70.00	*100.00*
			Nos. 2-23 (22)	138.75	*202.05*

Excellent counterfeit overprints exist.

Andrej Hlinka
A1 A2

Overprinted in Red or Blue

Perf. 12½

1939, Apr. Unwmk. Photo.

24	A1 50h dark green (R)		1.00	.75
a.	Perf. 10½		1.00	.95
b.	Perf. 10½x12½		2.75	3.00
25	A1 1k dk car rose (Bl)		.95	.75
a.	Perf. 10½		45.00	*72.50*
b.	Perf. 10½x12½		4.50	6.50

Catalogue values for unused stamps in this section, from this point to the end of the section, are for Never Hinged items.

1939 Unwmk. *Perf. 12½*

26	A2	5h	brt ultra	.50	*.55*
27	A2	10h	olive green	.80	*.85*
a.	Perf. 10½x12½			20.00	9.00
b.	Perf. 10½			17.00	14.00
28	A2	20h	orange red	.80	*.85*
a.	Imperf.			.85	*.80*
29	A2	30h	dp violet	.80	*.85*
a.	Imperf.			1.00	*1.25*
b.	Perf. 10½x12½			5.00	*6.25*
c.	Perf. 10½			7.50	*7.00*
30	A2	50h	dk green	.80	*.85*
31	A2	1k	dk carmine rose	1.00	*.85*
32	A2	2.50k	brt blue	1.00	.40
33	A2	3k	black brown	3.00	.40
			Nos. 26-33 (8)	8.70	*5.60*

On Nos. 32 and 33 a pearl frame surrounds the medallion. See Nos. 55-57, 69.

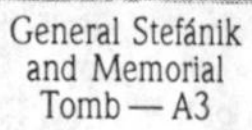
General Stefánik and Memorial Tomb — A3

Rev. Josef Murgas and Radio Towers — A4

1939, May *Perf. 12½*

Size: 25x20mm

34	A3	40h	dark blue	.90
35	A3	60h	slate green	.90
36	A3	1k	gray violet	.90

Size: 30x23¾mm

37	A3	2k	bl vio & sepia	.90
			Nos. 34-37 (4)	3.60

20th anniv. of the death of Gen. Milan Stefánik, but not issued.

1939 Unwmk.

38	A4	60h	purple	.25	.30
39	A4	1.20k	slate black	.50	.20

10th anniv. of the death of Rev. Josef Murgas. See No. 65.

Girl Embroidering — A5

Woodcutter — A6

Girl at Spring — A7

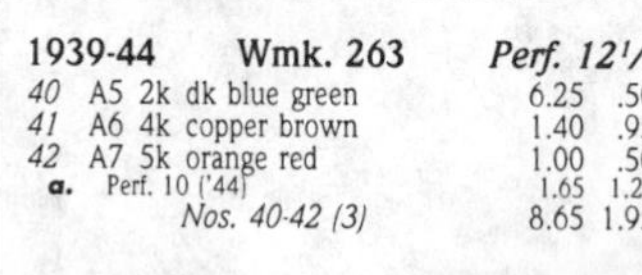

1939-44 Wmk. 263 *Perf. 12½*

40	A5	2k	dk blue green	6.25	.50
41	A6	4k	copper brown	1.40	.95
42	A7	5k	orange red	1.00	.50
a.	Perf. 10 ('44)			1.65	1.25
			Nos. 40-42 (3)	8.65	1.95

Dr. Josef Tiso — A8

Presidential Residence — A9

1939-44 Wmk. 263 *Perf. 12½*

43	A8	50h	slate green	.45	.30
43A	A8	70h	dk red brn ('42)	.30	.20
b.	Perf. 10½ ('44)			.50	.35

See No. 88.

1940, Mar. 14

44	A9	10k	deep blue	1.00	.75

Tatra Mountains — A10

Krivan Peak — A11

Edelweiss in the Tatra Mountains A12

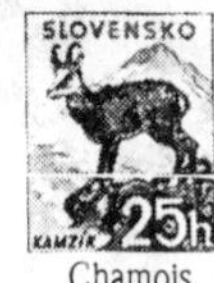
Chamois A13

Church at Javorina — A14

1940-43 Wmk. 263 *Perf. 12½*

Size: 17x21mm

45	A10	5h	dk olive grn	.20	.20
46	A11	10h	deep brown	.15	.15
47	A12	20h	blue black	.15	.15
48	A13	25h	olive brown	.75	.40
49	A14	30h	chestnut brown	.35	.35
a.	Perf. 10½ ('43)			2.50	1.00
			Nos. 45-49 (5)	1.60	1.25

See Nos. 84-87, 103-107.

Hlinka Type of 1939

1940-42 Wmk. 263 *Perf. 12½*

55	A2	1k	dk car rose	.80	.60
56	A2	2.50k	brt blue ('42)	1.00	.75
a.	Perf. 10½			.75	.75
57	A2	3k	black brn ('41)	2.00	1.00
a.	Perf. 10½			1.75	.90

On Nos. 56 and 57 a pearl frame surrounds the medallion.

Stiavnica A15

Lietava A16

Spissky Hrad — A17

Bojnice — A18

1941 *Perf. 12½*

58	A15	1.20k	rose lake	.25	.20
59	A16	1.50k	rose pink	.25	.20
60	A17	1.60k	royal blue	.25	.15
61	A18	2k	dk gray green	.25	.15
			Nos. 58-61 (4)	1.00	
			Set value		.60

Slovakian Castles.

S. M. Daxner and Stefan Moyses — A19

Andrej Hlinka — A20

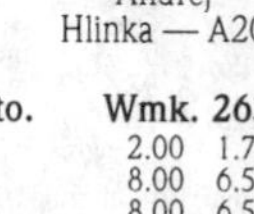

1941, May 26 Photo. Wmk. 263

62	A19	50h	olive green	2.00	1.75
63	A19	1k	slate blue	8.00	6.50
64	A19	2k	black	8.00	6.50
			Nos. 62-64 (3)	18.00	14.75

80th anniv. of the Memorandum of the Slovak Nation.

Murgas Type of 1939

1941 Wmk. 263

65	A4	60h	purple	.50	.25

1942

69	A20	1.30k	dark purple	.45	.20

Post Horn and Miniature Stamp — A21

Philatelist — A22

Philatelist — A23

1942, May 23

70	A21	30h	dark green	1.10	1.25
71	A22	70h	dk car rose	1.10	1.25
72	A23	80h	purple	1.10	1.25
73	A21	1.30k	dark brown	1.10	1.25
			Nos. 70-73 (4)	4.40	5.00

Natl. Philatelic Exhibition at Bratislava.

On No. 70 the miniature stamp bears the coat-of-arms of Bratislava; on No. 73 it shows the National arms of Slovakia.

St. Stephen's Cathedral, Vienna — A24

1942, Oct. 12 *Perf. 14*

74	A24	70h	blue green	.75	1.10
75	A24	1.30k	olive green	.75	1.10
76	A24	2k	sapphire	1.50	*3.00*
			Nos. 74-76 (3)	3.00	*5.20*

European Postal Congress held in Vienna.

Slovakian Educational Society — A25

1942, Dec. 14

77	A25	70h	black	.15	.20
78	A25	1k	rose red	.35	.35
79	A25	1.30k	sapphire	.15	*.25*
80	A25	2k	chestnut brown	.35	.35

81 A25 3k dark green .40 .60
82 A25 4k dull purple .40 .75
Nos. 77-82 (6) 1.80 2.50

Slovakian Educational Soc., 150th anniv.

Andrej Hlinka — A26

1943 **Wmk. 263**
83 A26 1.30k brt ultra .25 .20

See Nos. 93-94A.

Types of 1939-40

1943 **Unwmk.** *Perf. 12½*
84 A11 10h deep brown .25 .20
85 A12 20h blue black .70 .50
86 A13 25h olive brown .70 .50
87 A14 30h chestnut brown .45 .35
88 A8 70h dk red brown .85 .95
Nos. 84-88 (5) 2.95 2.50

Presov Church A27

Locomotive A28

Railway Tunnel — A29

Viaduct — A30

1943, Sept. 5 *Perf. 14*
89 A27 70h dk rose violet .45 .40
90 A28 80h sapphire .45 .40
91 A29 1.30k black .45 .40
92 A30 2k dk violet brn .60 *.70*
Nos. 89-92 (4) 1.95 1.90

Inauguration of the new railroad line between Presov and Strazske.

Hlinka Type of 1943 and

Ludovit Stur — A31

Martin Razus — A32

1944 **Unwmk.**
93 A31 80h slate green .15 .15
94 A32 1k brown red .15 .20
94A A26 1.30k brt ultra .70 .70
Nos. 93-94A (3) 1.00 1.05

Prince Pribina — A33

Designs: 70h, Prince Mojmir. 80h, Prince Ratislav. 1.30k, King Svatopluk. 2k, Prince Kocel. 3k, Prince Mojmir II. 5k, Prince Svatopluk II. 10k, Prince Braslav.

1944, Mar. 14
95 A33 50h dark green .15 .15
96 A33 70h lilac rose .15 .15
97 A33 80h red brown .15 .15
98 A33 1.30k brt ultra .15 .15
99 A33 2k Prus blue .15 .20
100 A33 3k dark brown .45 .30
101 A33 5k violet .95 .70
102 A33 10k black 2.50 2.00
Nos. 95-102 (8) 4.65 3.80

Scenic Types of 1940

1944, Apr. 1 *Perf. 14*

Size: 18x23mm

103 A11 10h bright carmine .15 *.30*
104 A12 20h bright blue .15 *.30*
105 A13 25h brown red .15 *.30*
106 A14 30h red violet .15 *.30*
107 A10 50h deep green .15 *.30*
Nos. 103-107 (5) .75 *1.50*

5th anniv. of Slovakia's independence.

Symbolic of National Protection — A41

President Josef Tiso — A42

1944, Oct. 6 **Wmk. 263**
108 A41 2k green .40 *.60*
109 A41 3.80k red violet .40 *.90*

1945 **Unwmk.**
110 A42 1k orange 1.10 .90
111 A42 1.50k brown .30 .20
112 A42 2k green .40 .20
113 A42 4k rose red 1.10 .90
114 A42 5k sapphire 1.10 .90

Wmk. 263

115 A42 10k red violet .75 .45
Nos. 110-115 (6) 4.75 3.55

6th anniv. of the Republic of Slovakia's declaration of independence, Mar. 14, 1939.

Natl. Arms — A50

1993 **Photo. & Engr.** *Perf. 11½*
150 A50 3k multicolored *.30*

Engr.

Perf. 12

Size: 30x44mm

151 A50 8k multicolored *1.25*

Issue dates: 3k, Jan. 2. 8k, Jan. 1. No. 151 does not have black frameline.

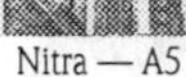

Nitra — A51

Banska Bystrica — A52

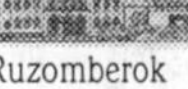

Ruzomberok A53

Kosice A54

Zvolen — A55

Bratislava — A56

#152-155 are churches, #156-157 castles.

Perf. 11½x12, 12x11½

1993-95 **Photo. & Engr.**
152 A51 2k multicolored *.15*
153 A52 3k multicolored *.25*
154 A53 5k multicolored *.40*
155 A54 10k multicolored *.80*
156 A55 30k multicolored *2.50*
157 A56 50k multicolored *6.50*
Nos. 152-157 (6) *10.60*

Issued: 5k, 10k, 1993; 30k, 9/12/93; 50k, 12/31/93; 3k, 11/15/94; 2k, 3/15/95.

St. John Nepomuk, 600th Death Anniv. A57

1993 **Photo. & Engr.** *Perf. 12x11½*
158 A57 8k multicolored *.75*

See Czech Republic #2880; Germany #1776.

A58

A59

President Michal Kovac

1993 **Engr.** *Perf. 12x11½*
159 A58 2k dark gray blue *.15*
159A A58 3k red brown & red *.25*

Issued: 2k, 3/2/93; 3k, 11/3/93.

Photo. & Engr.

1993, May 14 *Perf. 11½*

Trees.

160 A59 3k Quercus robur *.25*
161 A59 4k Carpinus betulus *.35*
162 A59 10k Pinus silvestris *.85*
Nos. 160-162 (3) *1.45*

A60

A61

Famous Men: 5k, Jan Levoslav Bella (1843-1936), composer. 8k, Alexander Dubcek (1921-92), politician. 20k, Jan Kollar (1793-1852), writer.

Photo. & Engr.

1993, May 20 *Perf. 12x11½*
163 A60 5k red brown & blue *.75*
164 A60 8k brown & lilac red *1.20*
165 A60 20k gray blue & orange *3.00*
Nos. 163-165 (3) *4.95*

1993, May 31 **Engr.** *Perf. 12*

Woman with Pitcher, by Marian Cunderlik.

166 A61 14k multicolored *1.50*

Europa.

Literary Slovak Language, 150th Anniv. A62

Design: 8k, Arrival of St. Cyril and St. Methodius, 1130th Anniv.

Photo. & Engr.

1993, June 22 *Perf. 12x11½*
167 A62 2k multicolored *.20*
168 A62 8k multicolored *.75*

See Czech Republic No. 2886.

A63

A64

Arms of Dubnica nad Vahom.

Photo. & Engr.

1993, July 8 *Perf. 12x11½*
169 A63 1k multicolored *.15*

Photo. & Engr.

1993, Sept. 2 *Perf. 11½*

The Big Pets, by Lane Smith.

170 A64 5k multicolored *.45*

Bratislava Biennial of Illustrators.

Gavcikovo Dam — A65

Photo. & Engr.

1993, Nov. 12 *Perf. 11½*
172 A65 10k multicolored *1.25*

No. 172 issued se-tenant with label.

Madonna and Child, by J. B. Klemens (1817-83) — A66

Photo. & Engr.

1993, Dec. 1 *Perf. 11½*
173 A66 2k multicolored *.30*

Christmas.

Souvenir Sheet

Monument to Gen. Milan Stefanik — A67

1993, Dec. 17 **Engr.** *Perf. 11½x12*
174 A67 16k multicolored *2.00*

Art from Bratislava Natl. Gallery A68

Sculpture: 9k, Plough of Springtime, by Josef Kostka.

1993, Dec. 31

175 A68 9k multicolored 1.00

See Nos. 199-200, 237-238, 255.

A69

A70

Photo. & Engr.

1994, Jan. 26 *Perf. 11x11½*

176 A69 2k multicolored .20

1994 Winter Olympics, Lillehammer.

Photo. & Engr.

1994, Apr. 29 *Perf. 11x11½*

177 A70 3k multicolored .25

Intl. Year of the Family.

Jan Andrej Segner (1704-77), Physicist — A71

Design: 9k, Antoine de Saint-Exupery (1900-44), aviator, author.

Photo. & Engr.

1994, May 25 *Perf. 11½x11*

178 A71 8k red brown & blue .80
179 A71 9k black, blue & pink .90

See Nos. 196-198.

Josef Murgas (1864-1929), Inventor of Radio Transmitters — A72

1994, May 27 Engr. *Perf. 11½*

180 A72 28k multicolored 2.25

Europa.

A73

A74

Photo. & Engr.

1994, May 31 *Perf. 11½x11*

181 A73 3k multicolored .25

Intl. Stop Smoking Day.

Photo. & Engr.

1994, June 10 *Perf. 11½*

182 A74 2k blue, black & green .15

1994 World Cup Soccer Championships, US.

Intl. Olympic Committee, Cent. A75

Photo. & Engr.

1994, June 23 *Perf. 12x11½*

183 A75 3k multicolored .40

No. 183 issued with se-tenant label.

Raptors — A76

Photo. & Engr.

1994, July 4 *Perf. 11½x12*

184 A76 4k Aquila chrysaetos .40
185 A76 5k Falco peregrinus .50
186 A76 7k Bubo bubo .70
Nos. 184-186 (3) 1.60

Prince Svatopluk of Moravia (870-894) — A77

1994, July 20 Engr. *Perf. 12*

187 A77 12k red brown, buff & black 1.25

UPU, 120th Anniv. — A78

Photo. & Engr.

1994, Aug. 1 *Perf. 11½x12*

188 A78 8k multicolored .55

Slovak Uprising, 50th Anniv. A79

Design: 6k, Gen. Rudolf Viest, Gen. Jan. Golian. 8k, French Volunteers' Memorial, Strecno hill.

Photo. & Engr.

1994, Aug. 27 *Perf. 12x11½*

189 A79 6k multicolored 1.40
190 A79 8k multicolored .75

Nos. 189-190 printed with se-tenant label.

Souvenir Sheet

Janko Matuska, Lyricist, 150th Death Anniv. A80

Design: 34k, Matuska, woman with pitcher, verse of "A Well She Dug."

Photo. & Engr.

1994, Sept. 1 *Perf. 12x11½*

191 A80 34k multicolored 3.25

Comenius University, 75th Anniv. — A81

Photo. & Engr.

1994, Oct. 18 *Perf. 11½x12*

192 A81 12k multicolored 1.25

Mojmirovce Horse Race, 180th Anniv. — A82

1994, Oct. 25 *Perf. 12x11½*

193 A82 2k multicolored .20

St. George's Church, Kostotany pod Tribecom A83

1994, Nov. 8 *Perf. 11*

194 A83 20k multicolored 1.90

Christmas — A84

1994, Nov. 29 *Perf. 11½*

195 A84 2k multicolored .20

Personalities Type of 1994

Designs: 5k, Chatam Sofer (1762-1839), rabbi. 6k, Wolfgang Kempelen (1734-1804), polytechnician. 10k, Stefan Banic (1870-1941), inventor of aviation parachute.

1994, Dec. 12 *Perf. 11½x11*

196 A71 5k multicolored .50
197 A71 6k multicolored .60
198 A71 10k multicolored 1.00
Nos. 196-198 (3) 2.10

Bratislava Art Type of 1993

Designs: 7k, Girls, by Janko Alexy, horiz. 14k, The Bulls, by Vincent Hloznik.

Perf. 12x11½, 11½x12

1994, Dec. 15 Engr.

199 A68 7k multicolored .70
200 A68 14k multicolored 1.40

Ships A85

Designs: 5k, Cargo ship, NL EMS. 8k, Cargo ship, Ryn. 10k, 400-passenger cruise ship.

Photo. & Engr.

1994, Dec. 30 *Perf. 12x11½*

201 A85 5k multicolored .50
202 A85 8k multicolored .75
203 A85 10k multicolored 1.00
Nos. 201-203 (3) 2.25

Samuel Jurkovic, Founder of of Landlords Assoc., 1845 — A86

Photo. & Engr.

1995, Feb. 8 *Perf. 11½*

204 A86 9k multicolored .65

European Nature Conservation Year — A87

Protected plants: 2k, Ciminalis clusii. 3k, Pulsatilla slavica. 8k, Onosma tornense.

1995, Feb. 28

205 A87 2k multicolored .15
Complete booklet, 10 #205 1.25
206 A87 3k multicolored .20
Complete booklet, 5 #206 1.00
207 A87 8k multicolored .55
Nos. 205-207 (3) .90

Slovak Natl. Theatre, 75th Anniv. A88

1995, Feb. 28 *Perf. 12x11½*

208 A88 10k multicolored .70

1995 Group B World Cup Ice Hockey Championships, Bratislava — A89

1995, Mar. 29 *Perf. 11½*

209 A89 5k blue & yellow .35

Bela Bartok (1881-1945), Composer — A90

Design: 6k, Jan Bahyl (1856-1916), inventor.

Photo. & Engr.

1995, Apr. 20 *Perf. 12x11½*

210 A90 3k multicolored .20
211 A90 6k multicolored .40

Slovakia stamps can be mounted in the Scott Czechoslovakia part 1 or Germany part 2 albums, or the annual Czech Republic and Slovakia supplement.

Souvenir Sheet

Ludovit Stur (1815-56), Writer — A91

1995, Apr. 20 *Perf. 11½*
212 A91 16k multicolored *1.10*

Europa A92

1995, May 5 **Engr.** *Perf. 12*
213 A92 8k multicolored .55

Liberation of the Concentration Camps, 50th Anniv. — A93

1995, May 5 **Photo. & Engr.** *Perf. 11*
214 A93 12k multicolored .80

Slovak Scouting A94

1995, May 18 *Perf. 11½x11*
215 A94 5k multicolored .35

Visit of Pope John Paul II — A95

1995, May 29 **Engr.**
216 A95 3k red .20
Complete booklet, 10 #216 2.00

Organized Philately in Slovakia, Cent. — A96

Photo. & Engr.

1995, June 1 *Perf. 11½x12*
217 A96 3k blue, black & gray .20
a. Souv. sheet of 2, perf 11½x11 .40

Dunafila '95.

Trinity Statue & Town Hall, Nova Bana — A100

Trencin Castle — A103

1995 **Photo. & Engr.** *Perf. 12x11½*
221 A100 4k black, green & blue .30
224 A103 8k black, blue & red .55

Issued: 4k, 6/15/95; 8k, 9/12/95. This is an expanding set. Numbers may change.

UNESCO World Heritage Sites A107

Perf. 11½x12, 12x11½

1995, July 19 **Photo. & Engr.**
228 A107 7k Banska Stiavnica, vert. .50
229 A107 10k Spissky Hrad .70
230 A107 15k Vlkolinec 1.00
Nos. 228-230 (3) 2.20

Volleyball, Cent. — A108

1995, Aug. 16 *Perf. 11½*
231 A108 9k multicolored .60

A109

A110

Bratislava Biennial of Illustrators: 2k, Clown, by Lorenzo Mattotti, Italy. 3k, Two characters, by Dusan Kallay, Slovakia.

Photo. & Engr.

1995, Sept. 5 *Perf. 11½*
232 A109 2k multicolored .15
Complete booklet, 10 #232 1.50
233 A109 3k multicolored .20
Complete booklet, 10 #233 2.00

1995, Sept. 14
234 A110 4k multicolored .30

St. Adalbert Assoc.

The Cleveland Agreement, 80th Anniv. — A111

Photo. & Engr.

1995, Oct. 20 *Perf. 12x11½*
235 A111 5k multicolored .40

UN, 50th Anniv. A112

1995, Oct. 24 **Engr.** *Perf. 11½x12*
235A A112 8k multicolored .60

Issued in sheets of 8 + 2 labels.

Christmas A113

Photo. & Engr.

1995, Oct. 27 *Perf. 11½*
236 A113 2k multicolored .15

Bratislava Art Type of 1993

Designs: 8k, The Hlohovec Nativity. 16k, Two Women, by Mikulás Galanda.

Photo. & Engr.

1995, Nov. 30 *Perf. 11½x12*
237 A68 8k multicolored .55
238 A68 16k multicolored 1.10

Issued in sheets of 4 + 2 labels.

Jozef Cíger-Hronsky (1896-1960) — A114

Olympic Games, Cent. — A115

Design: 4k, Jozef L'udovít Holuby (1836-1923).

Photo. & Engr.

1996, Feb. 15 *Perf. 11½*
239 A114 3k multicolored .20
240 A114 4k multicolored .25

See Nos. 293-295.

1996, Feb. 15
241 A115 9k multicolored .60

Folk Traditions — A116

Easter tradition of dousing women with water

Photo. & Engr.

1996, Mar. 15 *Perf. 11½*
242 A116 2k multicolored .15

Souvenir Sheet

Year for the Eradication of Poverty A117

1996, Apr. 15 **Engr.** *Perf. 12*
243 A117 7k multicolored .45

A118

A119

Europa: a, Holding thistle, carduus textorianus marg. b, Portrait, daphne cneorum.

1996, May 3 **Engr.** *Perf. 11½*
244 A118 8k Pair, #a.-b. 1.00

Izabela Textorisová (1866-1949), Slovakia's 1st female botanist. Issued in sheets of 4.

Souvenir Sheet

Motion Pictures, Cent.: Two frames from 1936 film, Jánosík.

1996, May 15 *Perf. 11½x12*
245 A119 16k multicolored 1.00

Printed se-tenant with label.

Round Slovakia Cycle Race — A120

1996, May 30 **Engr.** *Perf. 11½*
246 A120 3k multicolored .20
Complete booklet, 10 #246 2.00

Slovak Perspectives, 150th Anniv. — A121

1996, May 30
247 A121 18k multicolored 1.15

A122

A123

Photo. & Engr.

1996, June 14 *Perf. 12x11½*
248 A122 6k Coat of arms .40

Town of Senica.

Nature protection: No. 249, Ovis musimon. No. 250, Bison bonasus. No. 251, Rupicapra rupicapra.

1996, July 16 *Perf. 11½x12*
249 A123 4k multicolored .30
Complete booklet, 10 #249 3.00
250 A123 4k multicolored .30
Complete booklet, 10 #250 3.00
251 A123 4k multicolored .30
Complete booklet, 10 #251 3.00
Nos. 249-251 (3) .90

Splendors of Homeland — A124

Photo. & Engr.

1996, Sept. 25 *Perf. 11½x12*

252 A124 4k Popradské Lake .30
253 A124 8k Skalnaté Lake .60
254 A124 12k Strbské Lake .90
Nos. 252-254 (3) 1.80

Bratislava Art Type of 1993

The Baroque Chair, by Endre Nemes (1909-85).

1996, Oct. 5 Engr. *Perf. 11½x12*

255 A68 14k multicolored 1.00

See Czech Republic #2995, Sweden #2199. Issued in sheets of 4 + label.

Technological Advances A125

Designs: 4k, Bratislava-Trnava horse-drawn railway. 6k, Andrej Kvasz's (1883-1974) airplane.

Photo. & Engr.

1996, Oct. 15 *Perf. 11*

256 A125 4k multicolored .30
Complete booklet, 10 #256 3.00
257 A125 6k multicolored .45
Complete booklet, 10 #257 4.50

Queen Ntombi Twala, by Andy Warhol (1928-87) A126

Design: 10k, Suppressed Laughter, by Franz Xaver Messerschmidt (1736-83).

1996 Engr. *Perf. 11½*

258 A126 7k multicolored .45 .20
259 A126 10k multicolored .65 .30

Each issued in sheets of 4.
Issued: 7k, 11/13/96; 10k, 10/5/96.
See Nos. 284-286.

Christmas, Kysuce Village — A127

Photo. & Engr.

1996, Nov. 5 *Perf. 11½*

260 A127 2k multicolored .15 .15

Michael Martikén, Olympic Gold Medalist, Canoeing A128

Photo. & Engr.

1996, Dec. 18 *Perf. 12x11½*

261 A128 3k brown & yellow .20 .15

Stamp Day A129

Designs: Unexecuted 1938 stamp design of a woman with patriarchal cross, dove, Martin Benka, stamp designer.

1996, Dec. 18

262 A129 3k violet & buff .20 .15

No. 262 was printed se-tenant with label.

Bishop Stefan Moyses (1797-1869) — A130

Design: 4k, Svetozar Hurban Vajansky (1847-1916), politician.

Photo. & Engr.

1997, Jan. 16 *Perf. 11½*

263 A130 3k multicolored .25 .15
264 A130 4k multicolored .30 .15

A131 A132

Photo. & Engr.

1997, Jan. 31 *Perf. 11½*

265 A131 6k multicolored .35 .15

1997 World Biathlon Championships, Osrblie.

Photo. & Engr.

1997, Feb. 15 *Perf. 11½*

266 A132 3k multicolored .20 .15
Complete booklet, 10 #266 2.00

Folk Tradition of collecting dew.

Franciscan Church, Bratislava, 700th Anniv. — A133

Parochial Church, City Arms, Zilina — A134

Photo. & Engr.

1997, Mar. 25 *Perf. 11½x12*

267 A133 16k multicolored 1.00 .50

1997, Apr. 15 *Perf. 12x11½*

268 A134 9k multicolored .55 .30

See No. 275.

Radio, Cent. A135

1997, Apr. 15 *Perf. 12x11½*

269 A135 10k multicolored .60 .30

A136 A137

Europa (Stories and Legends): Miraculous rain near Hron.

1997, May 5 Engr. *Perf. 12x11½*

270 A136 9k multicolored .55 .30

1997, June 12 Engr. *Perf. 12x11½*

Limestone Formations: 6k, Domica Cavern, Silická. 8k, Aragonit Cavern, Ochtiná.

271 A137 6k multicolored .35 .15
272 A137 8k multicolored .50 .25

Souvenir Sheet

Folklore Festival, Vychodná — A138

1997, June 12 Photo. & Engr.

273 A138 11k multicolored .65 .35

Triennale of Naive Art, Bratislava A139

Photo. & Engr.

1996, June 26 *Perf. 12x11½*

274 A139 3k multicolored .20 .15
Complete booklet, 10 #274 2.00

Church Type of 1997

Church of St. Martin, Martin.

1997, July 17

275 A134 7k multicolored .40 .20

World Year of Slovaks — A140

Bratislava Biennale of Illustrators — A141

1997, July 17 *Perf. 11½*

276 A140 9k multicolored .50 .25

Photo. & Engr.

1997, Aug. 5 *Perf. 11½*

277 A141 3k multicolored .20 .15
Complete booklet, 10 #277 2.00

Water Mill, Jelka — A142

1997, Aug. 5

278 A142 4k multicolored .25 .15
Complete booklet, 10 #278 2.50

A143 A144

Photo. & Engr.

1997, Sept. 1 *Perf. 11½*

279 A143 4k multicolored .25 .15

Constitution, 5th anniv.

1997, Sept. 17

280 A144 9k multicolored .55 .30

6th Half Marathon World Championships, Kosice.

A145

Mushrooms: #281, Boletus aereus. #282, Morchella esculenta. #283, Catathelasma imperiale.

1997, Sept. 17 *Perf. 12*

281 A145 9k multicolored .55 .30
282 A145 9k multicolored .55 .30
283 A145 9k multicolored .55 .30
a. Souvenir sheet, #281-283 1.70 .90
Nos. 281-283 (3) 1.65 .90

Art Type of 1996

Designs: 9k, Self-portrait, by Ján Kupecky (1667-1740). 10k, Bojnice Altar, St. Peter and St. Lucia, by Nardo Di Cione, 14th cent., horiz. 12k, Towards the Goal (The Miners), by Koloman Sokol (b. 1902).

1997, Oct. 15 Engr. *Perf. 11½*

284 A126 9k multicolored .55 .30
285 A126 10k multicolored .60 .30
286 A126 12k multicolored .70 .35
Nos. 284-286 (3) 1.85 .95

A146 A147

Cernova 1907: Lamenting woman, church.

Photo. & Engr.

1997, Oct. 24 *Perf. 11½x12*

287 A146 4k deep green .30 .15

1997, Nov. 3 *Perf. 11½*

288 A147 3k Nativity .25 .15

Christmas.

A148

A149

1997, Nov. 3

289 A148 5k multicolored .35 .15

Ondrej Nepala, figure skater.

Photo. & Engr.

1997, Dec. 1 *Perf. 11½*

290 A149 4k Resurrection of Christ .25 .15
Complete booklet, 10 #290 2.50

Spiritual renewal.

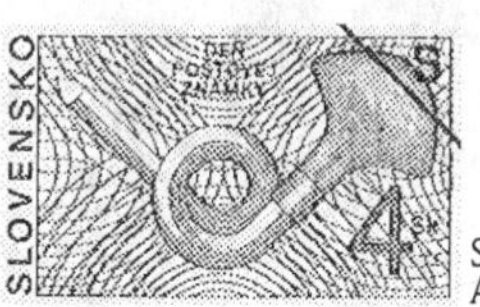

Stamp Day A150

1997, Dec. 18

291 A150 4k dark brown & blue .25 .15
Complete booklet, 9 #291 + 12 labels 2.25

No. 291 was printed se-tenant with label.

Slovak Republic, 5th Anniv. — A151

Photo. & Engr.

1998, Jan. 1 *Perf. 11½*

292 A151 4k multicolored .25 .15
Complete booklet, 10 #292 2.50

Personality Type of 1996

Writers: No. 293, Martin Rázus (1888-1937), politician. No. 294, Ján Smrek (1898-1982), poet. No. 295, Jozef Skultéty (1853-1948), linquist, editor.

1998, Jan. 19

293 A114 4k multicolored .25 .15
294 A114 4k multicolored .25 .15
295 A114 4k multicolored .25 .15
Nos. 293-295 (3) .75 .45

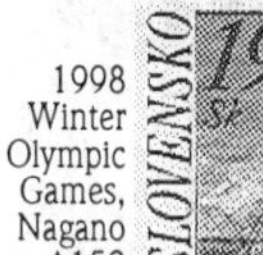
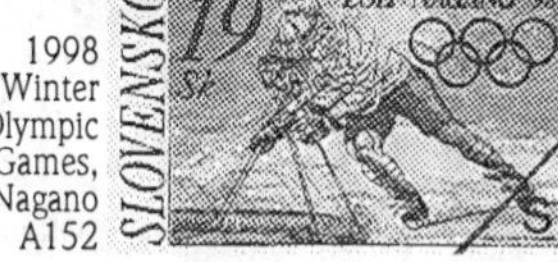

1998 Winter Olympic Games, Nagano A152

1998, Jan. 19 *Perf. 12x11½*

296 A152 19k Hockey player 1.10 .55

Folk Tradition, Banishing of Winter — A153

Photo. & Engr.

1998, Mar. 3 *Perf. 11½*

297 A153 3k multicolored .20 .15

Castles A154

1998, Mar. 3

298 A154 6k Budatin .35 .20
299 A154 11k Krásna Horka .65 .30

Souvenir Sheet

300 A154 18k Nitra 1.00 .50

SEMI-POSTAL STAMPS

Catalogue values for unused stamps in this section are for Never Hinged items.

Josef Tiso — SP1

Perf. 12½

1939, Nov. 6 Photo. Wmk. 263

B1 SP1 2.50k + 2.50k royal blue 3.25 *3.50*

The surtax was used for Child Welfare.

Medical Corpsman and Wounded Soldier — SP2

1941, Nov. 10

B2	SP2	50h + 50h dull green	.55	.60
B3	SP2	1k + 1k rose lake	.80	.80
B4	SP2	2k + 1k brt blue	2.00	2.00
		Nos. B2-B4 (3)	3.35	3.40

Mother and Child — SP3

Soldier and Hlinka Youth — SP4

1941, Dec. 10

B5	SP3	50h + 50h dull green	.95	.95
B6	SP3	1k + 1k brown	.95	.95
B7	SP3	2k + 1k violet	.95	.95
		Nos. B5-B7 (3)	2.85	2.85

Surtax for the benefit of child welfare.

1942, Mar. 14

B8	SP4	70h + 1k brown org	.50	.50
B9	SP4	1.30k + 1k brt blue	.70	.60
B10	SP4	2k + 1k rose red	1.40	1.40
		Nos. B8-B10 (3)	2.60	2.50

The surtax aided the Hlinka Youth Society "Hlinkova Mladez."

National Costumes
SP5 SP6 SP7

1943 *Perf. 14*

B11	SP5	50h + 50h dk slate grn	.30	.35
B12	SP6	70h + 1k dp carmine	.30	.35
B13	SP7	80h + 2k dark blue	.30	.35
		Nos. B11-B13 (3)	.90	1.05

The surtax was for the benefit of children, the Red Cross and winter relief of the Slovakian popular party.

Infantrymen — SP8

Aviator — SP9

Tank and Gun Crew SP10

1943, July 28

B14	SP8	70h + 2k rose brown	.90	.75
B15	SP9	1.30k + 2k sapphire	.90	.75
B16	SP10	2k + 2k olive green	1.00	.95
		Nos. B14-B16 (3)	2.80	2.45

The surtax was for soldiers' welfare.

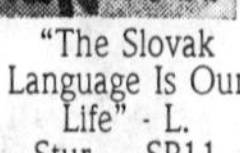

"The Slovak Language Is Our Life" - L. Stur — SP11

Slovakian National Museum — SP12

Slovakian Foundation — SP13

Slovakian Peasant — SP14

1943, Oct. 16

B17	SP11	30h + 1k brown red	.45	.35
B18	SP12	70h + 1k slate green	.60	.55
B19	SP13	80h + 2k slate blue	.45	.35
B20	SP14	1.30k + 2k dull brown	.45	.35
		Nos. B17-B20 (4)	1.95	1.60

The surtax was for the benefit of Slovakian cultural institutions.

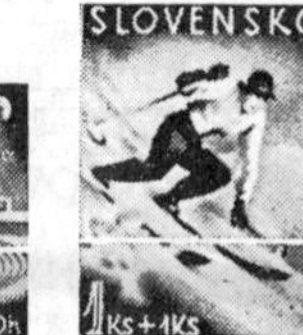

Soccer Player — SP15

Skier — SP16

Diver — SP17

Relay Race — SP18

1944, Apr. 30 Unwmk.

B21	SP15	70h + 70h slate grn	.60	*1.00*
B22	SP16	1k + 1k violet	.75	*1.25*
B23	SP17	1.30k + 1.30k Prus bl	.75	*1.25*
B24	SP18	2k + 2k chnt brn	.90	*1.65*
		Nos. B21-B24 (4)	3.00	*5.15*

Symbolic of National Protection SP19

Children SP20

1944, Oct. 6 Wmk. 263

B25	SP19	70h + 4h sapphire	1.10	*1.75*
B26	SP19	1.30k + 4k red brown	1.10	*1.75*

The surtax was for the benefit of social institutions.

1944, Dec. 18

B27 SP20 2k + 4k light blue 4.00 *4.25*
a. Sheet of 8 + Label 50.00 *62.50*

The surtax was to aid social work for Slovak youth.

Red Cross — SP21

Photo. & Engr.

1993, Nov. 15 *Perf. 11x11½*

B28 SP21 3k +1k red & gray blue *.30*

Souvenir Sheet

1996 Summer Olympics, Atlanta — SP22

Photo. & Engr.

1996, May 15 *Perf. 12x11½*

B29 SP22 12k +2k multi *.90*

Surcharge for Slovak Olympic Committee.

AIR POST STAMPS

Catalogue values for unused stamps in this section are for Never Hinged items.

Planes over Tatra Mountains
AP1 AP2

Perf. 12½

1939, Nov. 20 Photo. Unwmk.

C1	AP1	30h violet	.35	*.50*
C2	AP1	50h dark green	.35	*.50*
C3	AP1	1k vermilion	.40	*.50*
C4	AP2	2k grnsh black	.60	*.75*
C5	AP2	3k dark brown	1.00	*1.50*
C6	AP2	4k slate blue	2.00	*2.75*
		Nos. C1-C6 (6)	4.70	*6.50*

See No. C10.

Plane in Flight — AP3

1940, Nov. 30 Wmk. 263 *Perf. 12½*

C7 AP3 5k dk violet brn 1.10 *1.40*
C8 AP3 10k gray black 1.65 *1.65*
C9 AP3 20k myrtle green 1.75 *2.00*
Nos. C7-C9 (3) 4.50 *5.05*

Type of 1939

1944, Sept. 15 Wmk. 263

C10 AP1 1k vermilion 1.00 1.00

PERSONAL DELIVERY STAMPS

Catalogue values for unused stamps in this section are for Never Hinged items.

PD1

1940 Wmk. 263 Photo. *Imperf.*

EX1 PD1 50h indigo & blue .90 *1.90*
EX2 PD1 50h carmine & rose .90 *1.90*

POSTAGE DUE STAMPS

Catalogue values for unused stamps in this section are for Never Hinged items.

D1

Letter, Post Horn — D2

1939 Unwmk. Photo. *Perf. 12½*

J1 D1 5h bright blue .30 *.55*
J2 D1 10h bright blue .30 *.55*
J3 D1 20h bright blue .30 *.55*
J4 D1 30h bright blue 1.40 .95
J5 D1 40h bright blue .65 .75
J6 D1 50h bright blue 1.65 .80
J7 D1 60h bright blue 1.40 .80
J8 D1 1k dark carmine 14.00 8.25
J9 D1 2k dark carmine 14.00 2.50
J10 D1 5k dark carmine 4.50 2.50
J11 D1 10k dark carmine 37.50 7.50
J12 D1 20k dark carmine 15.00 9.25
Nos. J1-J12 (12) 91.00 34.95

1940-41 Wmk. 263

J13 D1 5h bright blue ('41) .75 .55
J14 D1 10h bright blue ('41) .30 .30
J15 D1 20h bright blue ('41) .50 .30
J16 D1 30h bright blue ('41) 6.00 4.50
J17 D1 40h bright blue ('41) .60 .55
J18 D1 50h bright blue ('41) .75 .95
J19 D1 60h bright blue .90 .95
J20 D1 1k dark carmine ('41) .90 1.10
J21 D1 2k dark carmine ('41) 9.00 7.50
J22 D1 5k dark carmine ('41) 2.50 2.75
J23 D1 10k dark carmine ('41) 3.00 3.25
Nos. J13-J23 (11) 25.20 22.70

1942 Unwmk. *Perf. 14*

J24 D2 10h deep brown .15 .15
J25 D2 20h deep brown .15 .20
J26 D2 40h deep brown .15 .20
J27 D2 50h deep brown 1.00 .60
J28 D2 60h deep brown .20 .20
J29 D2 80h deep brown .30 .20
J30 D2 1k rose red .35 .20
J31 D2 1.10k rose red .70 .60
J32 D2 1.30k rose red .40 .20
J33 D2 1.60k rose red .50 .20
J34 D2 2k rose red .70 .20
J35 D2 2.60k rose red 1.25 1.00
J36 D2 3.50k rose red 7.75 6.50
J37 D2 5k rose red 3.00 2.25
J38 D2 10k rose red 3.25 2.75
Nos. J24-J38 (15) 19.85 15.45

NEWSPAPER STAMPS

Newspaper Stamps of Czechoslovakia, 1937, Overprinted in Red or Blue

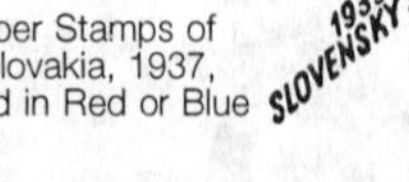

1939, Apr. Unwmk. *Imperf.*

P1 N2 2h bister brn (Bl) .30 *.40*
P2 N2 5h dull blue (R) .30 *.40*
P3 N2 7h red org (Bl) .30 *.40*
P4 N2 9h emerald (R) .30 *.40*
P5 N2 10h henna brn (Bl) .30 *.40*
P6 N2 12h ultra (R) .30 *.40*
P7 N2 20h dk green (R) .60 *.85*
P8 N2 50h dk brown (Bl) 2.00 *2.50*
P9 N2 1k grnsh gray (R) 6.75 *10.50*
Nos. P1-P9 (9) 11.15 *16.25*

Excellent counterfeits exist of Nos. P1-P9.

Catalogue values for unused stamps in this section, from this point to the end of the section, are for Never Hinged items.

Arms of Slovakia
N1

Type Block "N" (for "Noviny" - Newspaper)
N2

1939 Typo.

P10 N1 2h ocher .15 *.20*
P11 N1 5h ultra .25 *.40*
P12 N1 7h red orange .20 *.30*
P13 N1 9h emerald .20 *.30*
P14 N1 10h henna brown .95 1.10
P15 N1 12h dk ultra .20 *.35*
P16 N1 20h dark green .95 1.10
P17 N1 50h red brown 1.10 1.25
P18 N1 1k grnsh gray 1.10 1.10
Nos. P10-P18 (9) 5.10 6.10

1940-41 Wmk. 263

P20 N1 5h ultra .15 .15
P23 N1 10h henna brown .15 .15
P24 N1 15h brt purple ('41) .20 .15
P25 N1 20h dark green .35 .35
P26 N1 25h lt blue ('41) .35 .35
P27 N1 40h red org ('41) .35 .35
P28 N1 50h chocolate .60 .55
P29 N1 1k grnsh gray ('41) .60 .55
P30 N1 2k emerald ('41) 1.25 1.40
Nos. P20-P30 (9) 4.00 4.00

1943 Photo. Unwmk.

P31 N2 10h green .15 .20
P32 N2 15h dark brown .15 .20
P33 N2 20h ultra .25 .20
P34 N2 50h rose red .30 .35
P35 N2 1k slate green .65 .50
P36 N2 2k intense blue 1.10 1.00
Nos. P31-P36 (6) 2.60 2.45

SLOVENIA

slō-'vē-nē-ə

LOCATION — Southeastern Europe
GOVT. — Independent state
AREA — 7,819 sq. mi.
POP. — 1,725,088 (1971)
CAPITAL — Ljubljana

A constituent republic of Yugoslavia since 1945, Slovenia declared its independence on June 25, 1991.

100 Paras = 1 Dinar
100 Stotin = 1 Tolar

Catalogue values for unused stamps in this country are for Never Hinged items, beginning with Scott 100 in the regular postage section and Scott RA1 in the postal tax section.

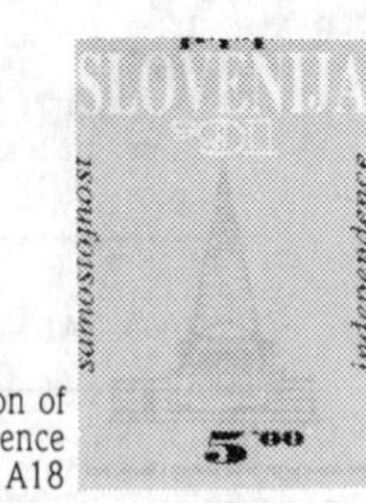

Declaration of Independence
A18

1991, June 26 Litho. *Perf. 10½*

100 A18 5d Parliament building .75

National Arms
A19 A20

1991-92 *Perf. 14*

Background Color

101 A19 1t brown .15
102 A20 1t brown .15
103 A20 2t lilac rose .15
105 A19 4t green .25
106 A20 4t green .25
107 A19 5t salmon .30
108 A20 5t salmon .30
109 A20 6t yellow .35
114 A19 11t orange .60
115 A20 11t orange .60
119 A20 15t blue .85
123 A20 20t purple 1.10
126 A20 50t dark green 2.75
131 A20 100t gray 5.50
Nos. 101-131 (14) 13.30

Issued: #108, 3/6/91; #101, 105, 107, 114, 12/26/91; #102, 6t, 20t, 50t, 100t, 2/12/92; 2t, 15t, #106, 115, 3/16/92.

This is an expanding set. Numbers may change.

1992 Winter Olympics, Albertville — A21

Designs: a, 30t, Ski jumper. b, 50t, Alpine skier.

1992, Feb. 8

134 A21 Pair, #a.-b., + 1 or 2 labels 4.25

Rhomboid stamps issued in sheets of 3 #134 plus 4 labels. See No. 143.

Ljubljana Opera House, Cent.
A22

1992, Mar. 31

135 A22 20t multicolored 1.00

Giuseppe Tartini (1692-1770), Italian Violinist and Composer — A23

1992, Apr. 8

136 A23 27t multicolored 1.40

Discovery of America, 500th Anniv.
A24

Designs: a, 27t, Map of northwestern Mexico and Gulf of California, Marko Anton Kappus preaching to natives. b, 47t, Map of parts of North and South America, sailing ship.

1992, Apr. 21

137 A24 Pair, #a.-b. 2.50

Issued in sheets containing 6 No. 137.

A. M. Slomsek (1800-1862), Bishop of Maribor — A26

Mountain Rescue Service, 80th Anniv. — A27

Intl. Conference of Interior Designers, Ljubljana
A25

1992, May 17

138 A25 41t multicolored 1.65

1992, May 29

139 A26 6t multicolored .25

1992, June 12

140 A27 41t multicolored 1.65

A28

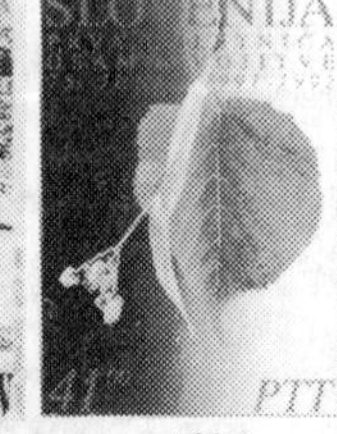

A29

1992, June 20

141 A28 6t multicolored .25

Ljubljana Boatmen's Competition, 900th anniv.

1992, June 25

142 A29 41t multicolored 1.65

Independence, 1st anniv.

Olympic Type of 1992

a, 40t, Leon Stukelj, triple medalist in 1924, 1928. b, 46t, Olympic rings, three heads of Apollo.

1992, July 25

143 A21 Pair, #a.-b. +1 or 2 labels 2.50

1992 Summer Olympics, Barcelona. Rhomboid stamps issued in sheets of 3 #143 plus 4 labels.

World Championship of Registered Dogs, Ljubljana — A30

1992, Sept. 4

144 A30 40t Slovenian sheep dog 1.00

Marij Kogoj (1892-1956), Composer — A31

Self-Portrait, by Matevz Langus (1792-1855), Painter — A32

1992, Sept. 30

145 A31 40t multicolored 1.00

1992, Oct. 30

146 A32 40t multicolored 1.00

Christmas A33

Designs: 6t, 7t, Nativity Scene, Ljubljana. 41t, Stained glass window of Madonna and Child, St. Mary's Church, Bovec, vert.

1992

147	A33	6t multicolored	.15
147A	A33	7t multicolored	.20
148	A33	41t multicolored	1.00
		Nos. 147-148 (3)	1.35

Issued: 6t, 41t, Nov. 20. 7t, Dec. 15.

Herman Potocnik, Theoretician of Geosynchronous Satellite Orbit, Birth Cent. — A34

1992, Nov. 27 Litho. *Perf. 14*

149 A34 46t multicolored 1.00

Prezihov Voranc (1893-1950), Writer — A35

1993, Jan. 22 Litho. *Perf. 14*

150 A35 7t multicolored .20

Rihard Jakopic (1869-1943), Painter — A36

1993, Jan. 22

151 A36 44t multicolored 1.00

Jozef Stefan (1835-93), Physicist A37

1993, Jan. 22

152 A37 51t multicolored 1.25

A38

Designs: 1t, Early cake. 2t, Pan pipes. 5t, Lonceni bajs. 6t, Early building. 7t, Zither. 8t, Water mill. 9t, Sled. 10t, Drum. 11t, Kraski kos. 12t, Statue of boy on horseback, Ribnica. 20t, Cross-section of house. 44t, Stone building. 50t, Wind-powered pump. 100t, Potica.

1993-94

153	A38	1t multicolored	.15
154	A38	2t multicolored	.15
155	A38	5t multicolored	.15
156	A38	6t multicolored	.15
157	A38	7t multicolored	.15
158	A38	8t multicolored	.20
159	A38	9t multicolored	.20
160	A38	10t multicolored	.20
160A	A38	11t multicolored	.20
160B	A38	12t multicolored	.25
161	A38	20t multicolored	.40
162	A38	44t multicolored	1.00
163	A38	50t multicolored	1.00
164	A38	100t multicolored	2.00
		Nos. 153-164 (14)	6.20

Issued: 1t, 6t, 7t, 44t, 2/18/93; 2t, 5t, 10t, 20t, 50t, 5/14/93; 8t, 9t, 8/25/93; 11t, 12t, 7/8/94. See Nos. 209-214.

Mountain Climbers A39

1993, Feb. 27

165	A39	7t shown	.15
166	A39	44t Route map, mountain	1.00

Slovenian Alpine Club, centennial (#165). Joza Cop (1893-1975), mountain climber (#166).

A40 A41

1993, Mar. 19

167 A40 7t multicolored .25

Slovenian Post Office, 75th anniv.

1993, Apr. 9 Litho. *Perf. 14*

Designs: 7t, Altarpiece, by Tintoretto. 44t, Coat of arms.

168	A41	7t multicolored	.15
169	A41	44t multicolored	1.00

Collegiate Church of Novo Mesto, 500th anniv.

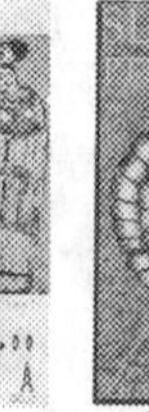

Contemporary Art — A42

Schwagerina Carniolica — A43

Europa: 44t, Round Table of Pompeii, by Marij Pregelj (1913-1967). 159t, Little Girl at Play, by Gabrijel Stupica (1913-1990).

1993, Apr. 29 Litho. *Perf. 14*

170	A42	44t multicolored	.95
171	A42	159t multicolored	3.25
a.		Pair, #170-171	4.25

1993, May 7

172 A43 44t multicolored .95

Admission of Slovenia to UN, 1st Anniv. A44

1993, May 21 Litho. *Perf. 14*

173 A44 62t multicolored 1.25

Mediterranean Youth Games, Agde, France — A45

1993, June 8

174 A45 36t multicolored .75

Battle of Sisak, 400th Anniv. — A46

1993, June 22 Litho. *Perf. 14*

175 A46 49t multicolored 1.00

Aphaenopidius Kamnikensis — A47

Designs: 7t, Monolistra spinosissima. 55t, Proteus anguinus. 65t, Zospeum spelaeum.

1993, July 12 Litho. *Perf. 14*

176	A47	7t multicolored	.15
177	A47	40t multicolored	.80
178	A47	55t multicolored	1.10
179	A47	65t multicolored	1.25
		Nos. 176-179 (4)	3.30

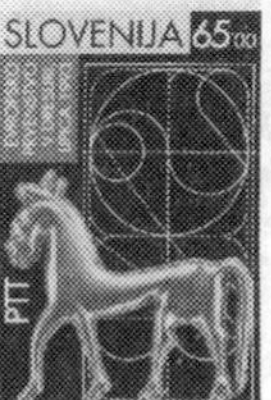

A48 A49

1993, July 30

180 A48 65t multicolored 1.25

World dressage competition.

1993, Oct. 29 Litho. *Perf. 14*

Coats of Arms: 9t, Janez Vajkard Valvasor. 65t, Citizen's Academy of Ljubljana.

181	A49	9t multicolored	*.20*
182	A49	65t multicolored	*1.25*

Christmas A50

Designs: 9t, Slovenian Family Viewing Nativity, by Maxim Gaspari (1883-1980). 65t, Archbishop Joze Pogacnik (1902-80), writer.

1993, Nov. 15

183	A50	9t multicolored	*.20*
184	A50	65t multicolored	*1.25*

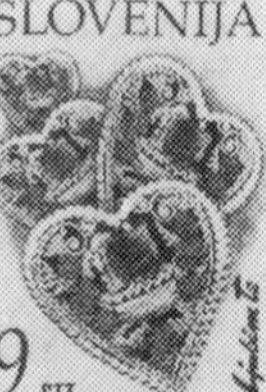

Famous People — A51

Love — A52

Works by: 8t, Josip Jurcic (1844-81), writer. 9t, Simon Gregorcic (1844-1906), poet. 55t, Stanislav Skrabec (1844-1918), linguist. 65t, Jernej Kopitar (1780-1844), linguist.

1994, Jan. 14 Litho. *Perf. 14*

185	A51	8t multicolored	*.15*
186	A51	9t multicolored	*.15*
187	A51	55t multicolored	*1.00*
188	A51	65t multicolored	*1.10*
		Nos. 185-188 (4)	*2.40*

1994, Jan. 25

189 A52 9t multicolored *.30*

1994 Winter Olympics, Lillehammer A53

1994, Feb. 4

190	A53	9t Cross-country skiing	*.15*
191	A53	65t Slalom skiing	*1.10*
a.		Pair, #190-191	*1.25*

World Ski Jumping Championships, Planica — A54

1994, Mar. 11 Litho. *Perf. 14*

192 A54 70t multicolored *1.25*

City of Ljubljana, 850th Anniv. A55

1994, Mar. 25 Litho. *Perf. 14*
193 A55 9t multicolored .20

Europa A56

70t, Janez Puhar, camera. 215t, Moon, Jurij Vega.

1994, Apr. 22
194 A56 70t multicolored 1.25
195 A56 215t multicolored 3.50
a. Pair, #194-195 4.75

Miniature Sheet

Flowers of Slovenia A57

Designs: a, 9t, Primula carniolica. b, 44t, Hladnikia pastinacifolia. c, 60t, Daphne blagayana. d, 70t, Campanula zoysii.

1994, May 20 Litho. *Perf. 14*
196 A57 Sheet of 4 + 2 labels 3.25

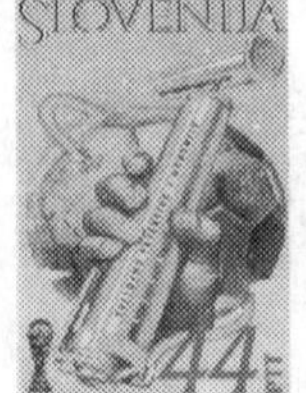

1994 World Cup Soccer Championships, US — A58

1994, June 10
197 A58 44t multicolored .80

Intl. Olympic Committee, Cent. — A59

1994, June 10
198 A59 100t multicolored 1.75

Mt. Ojstrica — A60

Max Pletersnik, Professors — A61

1994, July 1 Litho. *Perf. 14*
199 A60 12t multicolored .25

1994, July 22
200 A61 70t multicolored 1.25

First Slovenian-German dictionary published by Max Pletersnik (1840-1932), cent.

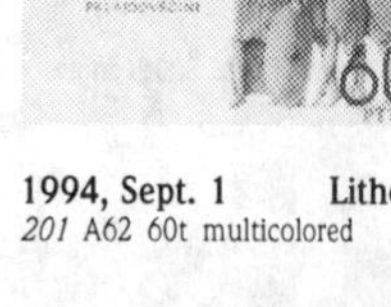

Battle of the Frigidus, 1600th Anniv. A62

1994, Sept. 1 Litho. *Perf. 14*
201 A62 60t multicolored 1.10

Maribor Post Office, Cent. — A63

1994, Sept. 23 Litho. *Perf. 14*
202 A63 70t multicolored 1.25

Ljubljana-Novo Mesto Railway, Cent. — A64

1994, Sept. 24 Litho. *Perf. 14*
203 A64 70t Locomotive 5722, 1893 1.25

See Nos. 233, 243, 291.

Philharmonic Assoc., Bicent. A65

Designs: 12t, Building, Ljubljana. 70t, Beethoven, Brahms, Dvorak, Haydn, Paganini.

1994, Oct. 20
204 A65 12t multicolored .20
205 A65 70t multicolored 1.25

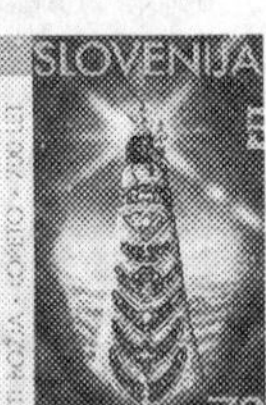

Black Madonna of Loreto, 700th Anniv. — A66

1994, Nov. 18
206 A66 70t multicolored 1.25

Christmas — A67

Intl. Year of the Family — A68

1994, Nov. 18
207 A67 12t multicolored .20

1994, Nov. 18
208 A68 70t multicolored 1.25

Type of 1993

13t, Wind rattle, Priekija. 14t, Sentjernej pottery cock. 55t, Easter eggs, Bela Krajina. 65t, Cobbler's lamp with glass spheres, Trzic. 70t, Snow skis. 75t, 1812 Iron window lattice, Srednja vas, Bohinj. 80t, Palm Sunday bundle. 90t, Beehive. 300t, Slamnati doznjek. 400t, Wine press.

1994-97 Litho. *Perf. 14*

208A	A38	13t multicolored	.15	.15
208B	A38	14t multicolored	.15	.15
209	A38	55t multicolored	.80	.40
209A	A38	65t multicolored	1.00	.50
210	A38	70t multicolored	1.25	.60
211	A38	75t multicolored	1.10	.55
211A	A38	80t multicolored	1.00	.50
211B	A38	90t multicolored	1.15	.60
212	A38	300t brown	4.50	2.25
214	A38	400t brown & lake	6.00	3.00
		Nos. 209-214 (8)	16.80	8.40

Issued: 300t, 400t, 11/7/94; 70t, 11/16/95; 55t, 65t, 75t, 3/22/96; 80t, 3/20/97; 13t, 14t, 8/8/97; 90t, 5/30/97. This is an expanding set. Numbers may change.

Ljubljana University, 75th Anniv. — A69

Design: 70t, Provincial palace buildings, founders, I. Hribar, M. Rostohar, D. Majaron.

1994, Dec. 3 Litho. *Perf. 14*
221 A69 70t multicolored 1.10

Postal Service Emblem — A70

1995, Jan. 27
222 A70 13t multicolored .25

Love — A71

Famous People — A72

1995, Feb. 7
223 A71 20t multicolored .35

1995, Feb. 7

Works by: 20t, Anton Tomaz Linhart (1756-95), playwrite, horiz. No. 225, Ivan Vurnik (1884-1971), architect. No. 226, Lili Novy (1885-1958), poet, horiz.

224 A72 20t multicolored .35
225 A72 70t multicolored 1.10
226 A72 70t multicolored 1.10
Nos. 224-226 (3) 2.55

A73

A74

1995, Mar. 29 Litho. *Perf. 14*
227 A73 13t multicolored .25

End of World War II, 50th anniv.

1995, Mar. 29
228 A74 70t Karavankina schellwieni 1.25

Liberation of the Concentration Camps, 50th Anniv. — A75

Europa: 60t, Skeleton of Death lying on bride. 70t, Nike going from dark to light.

1995, Mar. 29
229 A75 60t multicolored 1.10
230 A75 70t multicolored 1.25

Nos. 229-230 were issued in sheets of 4 each.

European Nature Conservation Year — A76

1995, Mar. 29
231 A76 70t Triglav Natl. Park 1.25

Town of Radovljica, 500th Anniv. A77

1995, June 8 Litho. *Perf. 14*
232 A77 44t multicolored .75

Railways Type of 1994

Design: 70t, Locomotive KRB 37, Podnart.

1995, June 8
233 A64 70t multicolored 1.25

Ljubljana-Jesenice Line, 125th anniv.

Aljaz Tower, Cent. — A78

1995, June 8 *Perf. 13½*
234 A78 100t multicolored 1.75

Portions of the design on No. 234 were applied by a thermogrphic process producing a shiny, raised effect.

Endangered Birds A79

Designs: a, 13t, Falco naumanni. b, 60t, Coracias garrulus. c, 70t, Lanius minor. d, 215t, Emberiza melanocephala.

1995, June 8 *Perf. 14*
235 A79 Block of 4, #a.-d. 6.25

Slovenian Boy Scouts — A80

1995, Sept. 26 **Litho.** ***Perf. 14***

236 A80 70t multicolored *1.25*

Comtemporary Art, by France Kralj — A81

1995, Sept. 26

237 A81 60t Smrt genija, 1921 *1.00*
238 A81 70t Konjska druzina, 1959 *1.25*
a. Pair, #237-238 *2.25*

A82

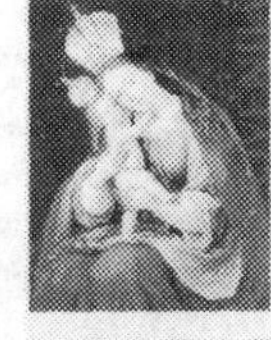

A83

UN, FAO, 50th Anniv.: No. 239, Stylized pictures of food products, faces of people from many nations. No. 240, Black & white figures touching hands, faces of people from many nations.

1995, Sept. 26

239 A82 70t multicolored *1.25*
240 A82 70t multicolored *1.25*
a. Pair, #239-240 *2.50*

Issued in miniature sheets of 4 stamps.

1995, Nov. 16

Christmas (Paintings): 13t, Winter, by Marlenka Stupica. 70t, St. Mary of Succour, Brezje, by Leopold Layer.

241 A83 13t multicolored *.20*
a. Booklet pane of 10 + 2 labels *2.00*
Complete booklet *2.00*
242 A83 70t multicolored *1.25*
a. Booklet pane of 10 + 2 labels *12.50*
Complete booklet *12.50*

Railways Type of 1994

Design: 70t, Locomotive "Aussee."

1996, Jan. 31 **Litho.** ***Perf. 14***

243 A64 70t multicolored *1.00*

The Graz-Celje Line, 150th anniv.

St. Gregory's Day A84

1996, Jan. 31 **Litho.** ***Perf. 14***

244 A84 13t multicolored *.20*

Carnival Costumes A85

1996, Jan. 31

245 A85 13t Ptujsko region *.20*
246 A85 70t Dravsko region *1.00*

See Nos. 281-282.

Emys Orbicularis A86

World Wildlife Fund: a, 13t, Peeking head out of water. b, 50t, Two young. c, 60t, Adult crawling though water. d, 70t, Laying eggs.

1996, Jan. 31

247 A86 Strip of 4, #a.-d. *3.00*

No. 247 printed in sheets of 4 vertical or horizontal strips, each having a different order.

Fran Saleski Finzgar (1871-1962), Writer, Priest — A87

1996, Apr. 18 **Litho.** ***Perf. 14***

248 A87 13t multicolored *.20*

UNICEF, 50th Anniv. — A88

1996, Apr. 18

249 A88 65t multicolored *1.00*

Ivana Kobilca (1861-1926), Painter — A89

Paintings: 65t, Children on Grass (detail). 75t, Bouquet of Dahlias.

1996, Apr. 18

250 A89 65t multicolored *1.00*
251 A89 75t multicolored *1.10*
a. Pair, Nos. 250-251 *2.10*

Issued in sheets of 8 stamps. Europa.

Ita Rina (1907-79), Film Actress A90

1996, Apr. 18

252 A90 100t multicolored *1.50*

Visit of Pope John Paul II, May 17-19 — A91

1996, Apr. 18

253 A91 75t multicolored *1.10*

Souvenir Sheet

254 A91 200t multicolored *3.00*

City of Zagorje ob Savi, 700th Anniv. A92

1996, June 6 **Litho.** ***Perf. 14***

255 A92 24t Gallenberg Castle *.35*

World Junior Cycling Championships, Novo Mesto — A93

1996, June 6

256 A93 55t multicolored *.80*

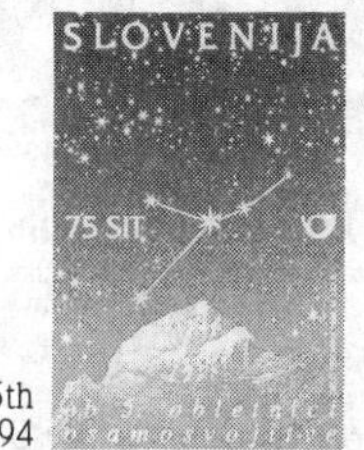

Independence, 5th Anniv. — A94

1996, June 6

257 A94 75t multicolored *1.10*

Mushrooms A95

Designs: a, 65t, Cantharellus cibarius. b, 75t, Boletus aestivalis.

1996, June 6

258 A95 Sheet of 2, #a.-b. *2.00*

Modern Olympic Games, Cent., 1996 Summer Olympics, Atlanta — A96

Designs: 75t, Iztok Cop, rower; Fredja Marsic, kayaker. 100t, Britta Bilac, high jumper; Brigita Bukovec, hurdler.

1996, June 6

259 A96 75t multicolored *1.10*
260 A96 100t multicolored *1.45*
a. Pair, #259-260+label *2.55*

No. 260a issued in sheets of 6 stamps + 3 labels.

Two versions of the sheet exist. One with white, red & blue flag, the other with white, blue & red flag.

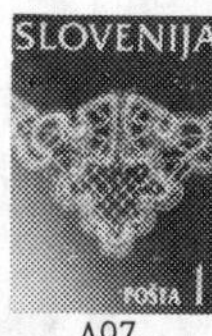

A97

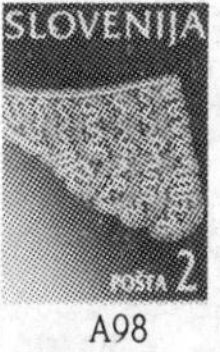

A98

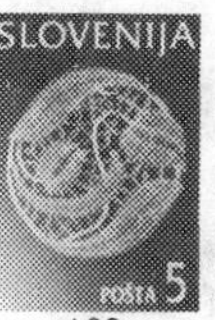

A99

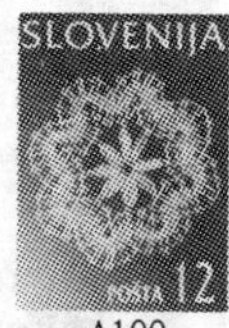

A100

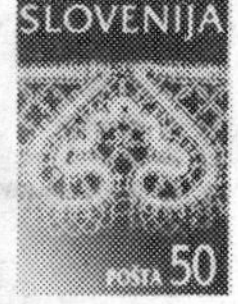

Idrijan Lace
A101 A102

1996, June 21 **Litho.** ***Perf. 14***

261 A97 1t shown *.15*
262 A97 1t olive gray, diff. *.15*
a. Pair, #261-262 *.15*
263 A98 2t shown *.15*
264 A98 2t carmine, diff. *.15*
a. Pair, #263-264 *.15*
265 A99 5t shown *.15*
266 A99 5t square *.15*
a. Pair, #265-266 *.15*
267 A100 12t shown *.20*
268 A100 12t diamond *.20*
a. Pair, #267-268 *.35*
269 A101 13t shown *.20*
270 A101 13t red, diff. *.20*
a. Pair, #269-270 *.40*
271 A102 50t shown *.75*
272 A102 50t lilac, diff. *.75*
a. Pair, #272-272 *1.50*
Set value *2.40*

The background of the designs on Nos. 261-272 contain "1996," posthorn, and security lettering that appear under UV light.

See Nos. 297-304.

Modern Cardiology, Cent. — A103

1996, Sept. 6 **Litho.** ***Perf. 14***

273 A103 12t multicolored *.20*

Grammar School, Novo Mesto, 250th Anniv. A104

1996, Sept. 6

274 A104 55t multicolored *.80*

Skocjan Caves, Karst Region, UNESCO World Heritage Site A105

1996, Sept. 6

275 A105 55t multicolored *.80*

Moscon Family Portrait, by Jozef Tominc (1790-1866) — A106

1996, Sept. 6

276 A106 65t multicolored *1.00*

Post Office, Ljubljana, Cent. — A107

1996, Oct. 18 Litho. *Perf. 14*

277 A107 100t multicolored 1.45 .70

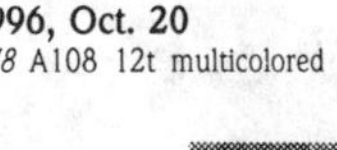

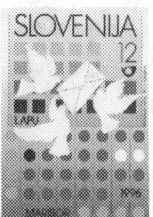

Introduction of Automatic Letter Sorting Machines, Maribor — A108

1996, Oct. 20

278 A108 12t multicolored .20 .15

A109

Christmas A110

1996, Nov. 20 Litho. *Perf. 14*

279 A109 12t Children sledding .20 .15
a. Booklet pane of 10 2.00
Complete booklet, #279a 2.00
280 A110 65t Nativity 1.00 .50
a. Booklet pane of 10 10.00
Complete booklet, #280a 10.00

Carnival Costumes Type of 1996

From Cerkno region: 20t, "Ta terjast." 80t, "Pust."

1997, Jan. 21 Litho. *Perf. 14*

281 A85 20t multicolored .30 .15
282 A85 80t multicolored 1.10 .55

Love A111

1997, Jan. 21 Litho. *Perf. 14*

283 A111 15t multicolored .20 .15

Sneznik Mountain A112

1997, Jan. 21

284 A112 20t multicolored .30 .15

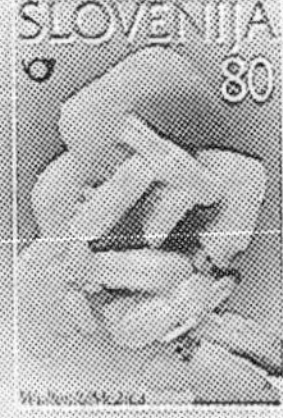
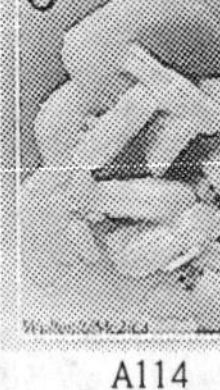

A113 A114

1997, Mar. 27 Litho. *Perf. 14*

285 A113 80t Legend of the Goldenhorn 1.00 .50

Europa.

1997, Mar. 27

286 A114 80t Wulfenite 1.00 .50

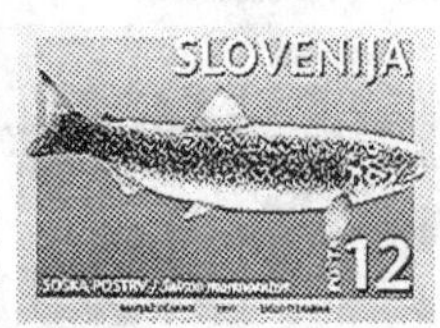

Endangered Fish A115

1997, Mar. 27

287 A115 12t Salmo marmoratus .15 .15
288 A115 13t Zingel streber .20 .15
289 A115 80t Vimba vimba 1.00 .50
290 A115 90t Umbra krameri 1.20 .60
a. Souvenir sheet, #287-290 2.55 1.30
Nos. 287-290 (4) 2.55 1.40

Railways Type of 1994

Design: 80t, Locomotive SZ 03-002, Ljubljana-Trieste Railway Line, 140th anniv.

1997, May 30 Litho. *Perf. 14*

291 A64 80t multicolored 1.00 .50

Volunteer Fire Fighting Brigades in Slovenia — A116

1997, May 30

292 A116 70t multicolored .90 .45

Famous People — A117

Designs: 13t, Matija Cop (1797-1835), literary expert. 24t, Sigismundus Zois (1747-1819), economist, natural scientist. 80t, Bishop Friderik Irenej Baraga (1797-1868), missionary, linguist.

1997, May 30

293 A117 13t multicolored .20 .15
294 A117 24t multicolored .30 .15
295 A117 80t multicolored 1.00 .50
Nos. 293-295 (3) 1.50 .80

Souvenir Sheet

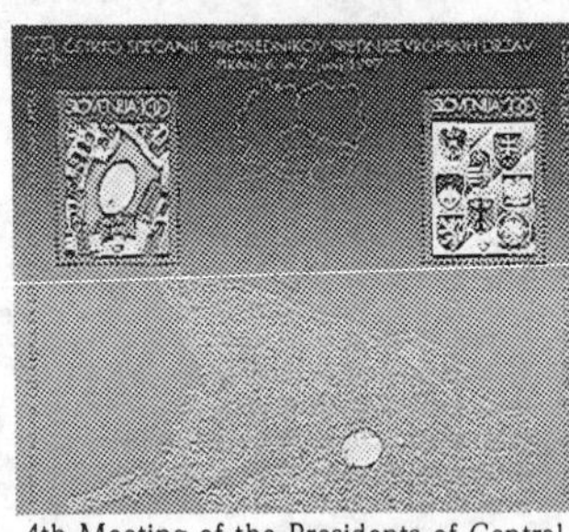

4th Meeting of the Presidents of Central European Countries, Piran — A118

Designs: a, 100t, Tartini Square. b, 200t, Coats of arms from eight countries.

1997, June 6

296 A118 Sheet of 2, #a.-b. 3.75 1.90

Idrijan Lace Type of 1996

Shape of lace: No. 297, Flower in center of oval. No. 298, Circular outside with swirl at bottom. No. 299, Butterfly. No. 300, Diamond. No. 301, Square. No. 302, Circle. No. 303, Leaves. No. 304, Tulip.

1997, June 20 Litho. *Perf. 14*

297 A97 10t magenta .15 .15
298 A97 10t magenta .15 .15
a. Pair, #297-298 .25 .15
299 A97 20t violet .25 .15
300 A97 20t violet .25 .15
a. Pair, #299-300 .50 .25
301 A97 44t bright blue .55 .25
302 A97 44t bright blue .55 .25
a. Pair, #301-302 1.10 .50
303 A97 100t gray brown 1.20 .60
304 A97 100t gray brown 1.20 .60
a. Pair, #303-304 2.40 1.20
Nos. 299-304 (6) 4.00 2.00

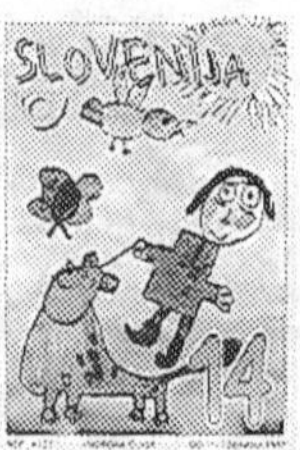

A119 A120

1997, Sept. 9

305 A119 14t multicolored .20 .15

Children's Week.

1997, Sept. 9

306 A120 50t multicolored .60 .30

Return of Primorska, 50th anniv.

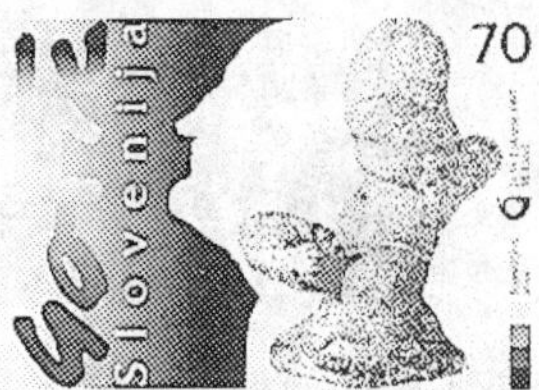

France Gorse (1897-1986), Sculptor — A121

1997, Sept. 9

307 A121 70t "Bashful Armor" .85 .45
308 A121 80t "Peasant Woman" .95 .50
a. Pair, #307-308 1.80 .95

A122 A123

1997, Sept. 9

309 A122 90t multicolored 1.10 .55

MEJP '97, European Youth Judo Championship.

1997, Nov. 18 Litho. *Perf. 14*

310 A123 90t multicolored 1.10 .55

Golden Fox World Cup Ski Competition for Women, 35th anniv.

Christmas & New Year — A124

Designs: 14t, Children watching birds and snow outside window. 90t, Sculptured Nativity scene, by Liza Hribar (1913-96).

1997, Nov. 18

311 A124 14t multicolored .20 .15
312 A124 90t multicolored 1.10 .55
a. Booklet pane of 8, 5 #311, 3 #312 4.40
Complete booklet, #312a 4.40

New Mail Center, Ljubljana — A125

1997, Nov. 28

313 A125 30t multicolored .35 .20

Borovo Gostüvanje (Pine Wedding) — A126

Designs: 20t, Participating "players," tree. 80t, Participants, "bride & groom," top of pine tree.

1998, Jan. 22 Litho. *Perf. 14*

314 A126 20t multicolored .25 .15
315 A126 80t multicolored .95 .50
a. Pair, #314-315 1.20 .60

1998 Winter Olympic Games, Nagano A127

1998, Jan. 22

316 A127 70t Woman skater .85 .45
317 A127 90t Biathlete 1.10 .55
a. Vert. pair, #316-317 + label 2.00 1.00

Issued in sheets of 6 stamps + 3 labels.

EUROCONTROL (European Organization for Safety of Air Navigation), 35th Anniv. — A128

1998, Jan. 22

318 A128 90t multicolored 1.10 .55

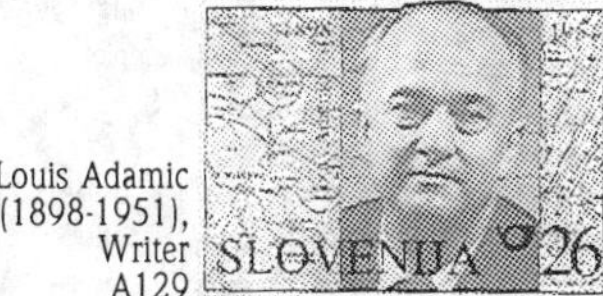

Louis Adamic (1898-1951), Writer A129

90t, Francesco Robba (1698-1757), sculptor.

1998, Mar. 25 Litho. *Perf. 14*

319 A129 26t multicolored .30 .15
320 A129 90t multicolored 1.10 .55

Jurjevanje (Green George's Festival) A130

1998, Mar. 25

321 A130 90t multicolored 1.10 .55

Europa.

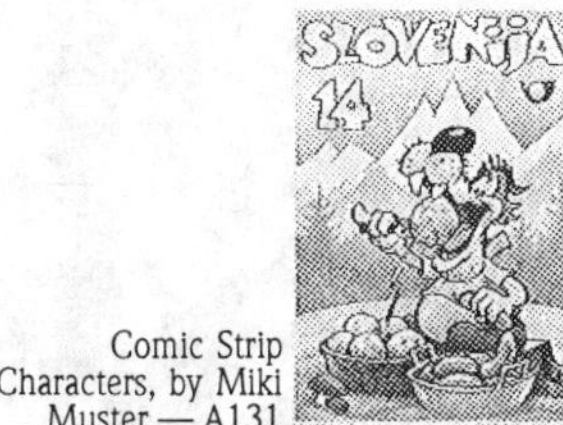

Comic Strip Characters, by Miki Muster — A131

1998, Mar. 25

322 A131 14t Fox .20 .15
323 A131 105t Turtle 1.25 .60
324 A131 118t Wolf 1.40 .70
a. Sheet of 2 each, #322-324 5.75 2.90
Nos. 322-324 (3) 2.85 1.45

POSTAL TAX STAMPS

Catalogue values for unused stamps in this section are for Never Hinged items.

Red Cross — PT1

1992, May 8 Litho. *Perf. 14*

RA1 PT1 3t blue, black & red .20

PT2

PT3

1992, June 2 *Perf. 14½x14*

RA2 PT2 3t multicolored .20

Red Cross, Solidarity.

1992, Sept. 14 Litho. *Perf. 14*

RA3 PT3 3t multicolored .15

Stop Smoking Week, Sept. 14-21.

Red Cross — PT4

Rescue Team — PT5

1993, May 8 Litho. *Perf. 14*

RA4 PT4 3.50t blue, black & red .15

1993, June 1

RA5 PT5 3.50t multicolored .15

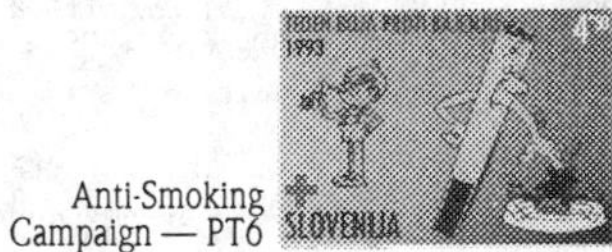

Anti-Smoking Campaign — PT6

1993, Sept. 14 Litho. *Perf. 14*

RA6 PT6 4.50t multicolored *.15*

PT7

1994, May 8 Litho. *Perf. 14*

RA7 PT7 4.50t multicolored *.15*

Obligatory on mail May 8-15.

Red Cross Worker, Child — PT8

1994, June 1

RA8 PT8 4.50t multicolored *.15*

Obligatory on mail June 1-7.

Red Cross, Solidarity
PT9 PT10

1995, May 8 Litho. *Perf. 14*

RA9 PT9 6.50t multicolored *.15*

Obligatory on mail May 8-15.

1995, June 1 Litho. *Perf. 14*

RA10 PT10 6.50t multicolored *.15*

Obligatory on mail June 1-7.

Red Cross, Solidarity — PT11

1996, May 8 Litho. *Perf. 14*

RA11 PT11 7t multicolored .15 .15

Obligatory on mail May 8-15.

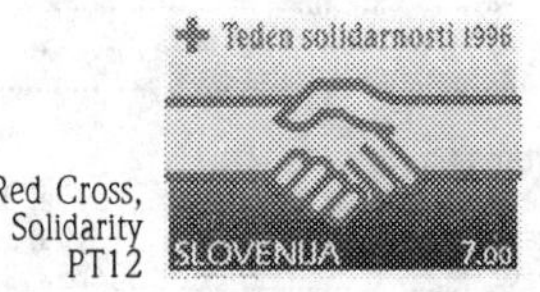

Red Cross, Solidarity PT12

1996, June 1 Litho. *Perf. 14*

RA12 PT12 7t multicolored *.15*

Obligatory on mail June 1-7.

Red Cross, Solidarity — PT13

1997, May 8 Litho. *Perf. 14*

RA13 PT13 7t multicolored *.15*

Obligatory on mail May 8-14.

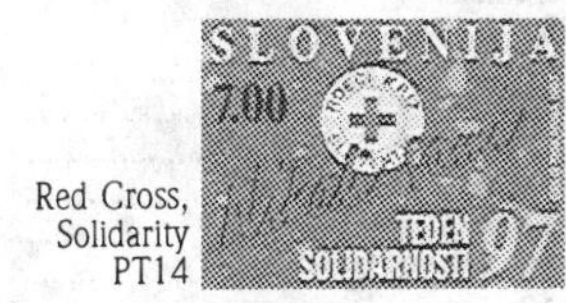

Red Cross, Solidarity PT14

1997, June 1

RA14 PT14 7t multicolored *.15*

Obligatory on mail June 1-7.

1999 Vol. 5 Catalogue Number Additions, Deletions & Changes

Number in 1998 Catalogue	Number in 1999 Catalogue
Pakistan	
25	25a
25a	25
38, 39, 40	38a, 39a, 40a
38a, 39a, 40a	38, 39, 40
43	43a
43a	43
Palau	
C22	C23
C23	C22
Panama	
new	583a
Paraguay	
new	C334, C338, C353, C400
Penrhyn Island	
181a	181a-181c
182a	182a-182c
183a	183a-183c
Philippines	
4	4a
4a	4
20	20a
20a	20
new	25b
new	437a
new	1715a, 1948a
2222-2222A	2221-2222
Portugal	
new	84a, 89d
Rhodesia	
79b	79a
79a	79b, 79c, 79d
104	104a
104a	104
117	117a
117a	117
Rhodesia (continued)	
120	120a
120a	120
122	122a
122a	122
124	124a
124a	124
132	132a
132a	132
Romania	
new	3315a, 3317a
new	3319a, 3321a
new	3475a, 3477a
new	3479a, 3481a
new	C51a, C52a
new	C182a
Russia	
new	35c
new	199b
new	2732
2732	2732a
2732a	2732d
2733	2732b
2733a	2732e
2734	2732c
2734a	2732f
2732b, 2733b, 2734b	deleted
new	5258a
St. Lucia	
35	35a
35a	35
110	110a
110a	110
114	114a
114a	114
119	119a
119a	119
121	121a
121a	121
774-781	774-777
St. Pierre & Miquelon	
643-644	640-641
645-649	642-646
640-641	647-648
650	649
642	650
J46	J46a
J46a	J46
St. Thomas & Prince Islands	
1048	1049
1049	1048
St. Vincent	
new	396a
new	448a, 450a, 452a
new	454a, 456a
new	603a
new	620a, 622a, 624a, 626a
new	634a
1875-1877	deleted
Bequia	
186-193	186-189
Salvador	
new	1100a, 1102a, 1104a, 1106a
new	1132a, 1134a, 1136a, 1138a
new	1140a, 1142a, 1144a, 1146a
new	1148a, 1150a, 1152a, 1154a
new	1166a
new	C530a, C532a, C534a
Samoa	
8	8a
8a	8
Saudi Arabia	
177	RA4B
J5	deleted
Senegal	
new	746a, 756a

Dies of British Colonial Stamps Referred to in the Catalogue

DIE A

DIE B

DIE A:
1. The lines in the groundwork vary in thickness and are not uniformly straight.
2. The seventh and eighth lines from the top, in the groundwork, converge where they meet the head.
3. There is a small dash in the upper part of the second jewel in the band of the crown.
4. The vertical color line in front of the throat stops at the sixth line of shading on the neck.

DIE B:
1. The lines in the groundwork are all thin and straight.
2. All the lines of the background are parallel.
3. There is no dash in the upper part of the second jewel in the band of the crown.
4. The vertical color line in front of the throat stops at the eighth line of shading on the neck.

DIE I

DIE II

DIE I:
1. The base of the crown is well below the level of the inner white line around the vignette.
2. The labels inscribed "POSTAGE" and "REVENUE" are cut square at the top.
3. There is a white "bud" on the outer side of the main stem of the curved ornaments in each lower corner.
4. The second (thick) line below the country name has the ends next to the crown cut diagonally.

DIE Ia.	DIE Ib.
1 as die II.	1 and 3 as die II.
2 and 3 as die I.	2 as die I.

DIE II:
1. The base of the crown is aligned with the underside of the white line around the vignette.
2. The labels curve inward at the top inner corners.
3. The "bud" has been removed from the outer curve of the ornaments in each corner.
4. The second line below the country name has the ends next to the crown cut vertically.

British Colonial and Crown Agents Watermarks

Wmk. 1
Crown and C C

Wmk. 2
Crown and C A

Wmk. 3
Multiple Crown and C A

Wmk. 4
Multiple Crown and Script C A

Wmk. 4a

Wmk. 314
St. Edward's Crown and C A Multiple

Wmk. 373

Wmk. 384

Watermarks 1 to 4, 314, 373, and 384, common to many British territories, are illustrated here to avoid duplication.

The letters "CC" of Wmk. 1 identify the paper as having been made for the use of the Crown Colonies, while the letters "CA" of the others stand for "Crown Agents." Both Wmks. 1 and 2 were used on stamps printed by De La Rue & Co.

Wmk. 3 was adopted in 1904; Wmk. 4 in 1921; Wmk. 314 in 1957; Wmk. 373 in 1974; and Wmk. 384 in 1985.

In Wmk. 4a, a non-matching crown of the general St. Edwards type (bulging on both sides at top) was substituted for one of the Wmk. 4 crowns which fell off the dandy roll. The non-matching crown occurs in 1950-52 printings in a horizontal row of crowns on certain regular stamps of Johore and Seychelles, and on various postage due stamps of Barbados, Basutoland, British Guiana, Gold Coast, Grenada, Northern Rhodesia, St. Lucia, Swaziland and Trinidad and Tobago. A variation of Wmk. 4a, with the non-matching crown in a horizontal row of crown-CA-crown, occurs on regular stamps of Bahamas, St. Kitts-Nevis and Singapore.

Wmk. 314 was intentionally used sideways, starting in 1966. When a stamp was issued with Wmk. 314 both upright and sideways, the sideways varieties usually are listed also – with minor numbers. In many of the later issues, Wmk. 314 is slightly visible.

Wmk. 373 is usually only faintly visible.

Illustrated Identifier

This section pictures stamps or parts of stamp designs that will help identify postage stamps that do not have English words on them.

Many of the symbols that identify stamps of countries are shown here as well as typical examples of their stamps.

See the Index and Identifier on the previous pages for stamps with inscriptions such as "sen," "posta," "Baja Porto," "Helvetia," "K.S.A.", etc.

Linn's Stamp Identifier is now available. The 144 pages include more 2,000 inscriptions and over 500 large stamp illustrations. Available from Linn's Stamp News, P.O. Box 29, Sidney, OH 45365-0029.

1. HEADS, PICTURES AND NUMERALS

GREAT BRITAIN

Great Britain stamps never show the country name, but, except for postage dues, show a picture of the reigning monarch.

Victoria

Edward VII George V Edward VIII

George VI

Elizabeth II

Some George VI and Elizabeth II stamps are surcharged in annas, new paisa or rupees. These are listed under Oman.

Silhouette (sometimes facing right, generally at the top of stamp)

The silhouette indicates this is a British stamp. It is not a U.S. stamp.

VICTORIA

Queen Victoria

INDIA

Other stamps of India show this portrait of Queen Victoria and the words "Service" and "Annas."

AUSTRIA

YUGOSLAVIA

(Also BOSNIA & HERZEGOVINA if imperf.)

BOSNIA & HERZEGOVINA

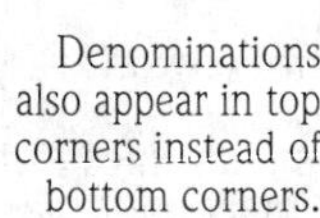

Denominations also appear in top corners instead of bottom corners.

HUNGARY

Another stamp has posthorn facing left

BRAZIL

AUSTRALIA

Kangaroo and Emu

GERMANY

Mecklenburg-Vorpommern

SWITZERLAND

2. ORIENTAL INSCRIPTIONS

CHINA

中 中

Any stamp with this one character is from China (Imperial, Republic or People's Republic). This character appears in a four-character overprint on stamps of Manchukuo. These stamps are local provisionals, which are unlisted. Other overprinted Manchukuo stamps show this character, but have more than four characters in the overprints. These are listed in People's Republic of China.

Some Chinese stamps show the Sun.

Most stamps of Republic of China show this series of characters.

Stamps with the China character and this character are from People's Republic of China. 人

Calligraphic form of People's Republic of China

Chinese stamps without China character

REPUBLIC OF CHINA

PEOPLE'S REPUBLIC OF CHINA

Mao Tse-tung

MANCHUKUO

Temple Emperor Pu-Yi

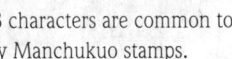

The first 3 characters are common to many Manchukuo stamps.

The last 3 characters are common to other Manchukuo stamps.

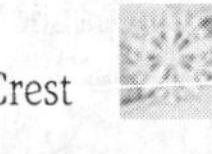

Orchid Crest

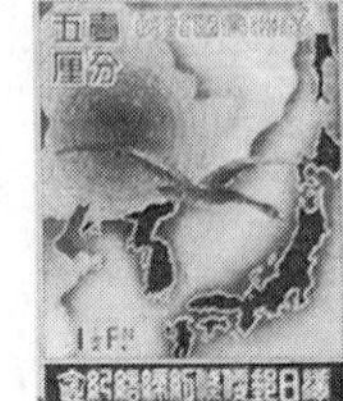

Manchukuo stamp without these elements

JAPAN

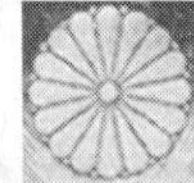

Chrysanthemum Crest Country Name

Japanese stamps without these elements

The number of characters in the center and the design of dragons on the sides will vary.

RYUKYU ISLANDS

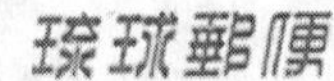

Country Name

PHILIPPINES (Japanese Occupation)

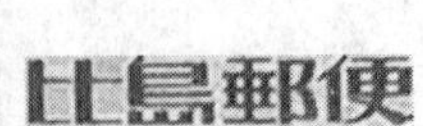

Country Name

NORTH BORNEO (Japanese Occupation)

Indicates Japanese Occupation Country Name

MALAYA (Japanese Occupation)

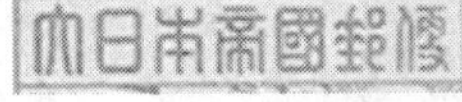
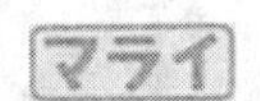

Indicates Japanese Occupation Country Name

BURMA (Japanese Occupation)

Indicates Japanese Occupation Country Name

Other Burma Japanese Occupation stamps without these elements

Burmese Script

KOREA

These two characters, in any order, are common to stamps from the Republic of Korea (South Korea) or the unlisted stamps of the People's Democratic Republic of Korea (North Korea).

This series of four characters can be found on the stamps of both Koreas.

Yin Yang appears on some stamps.

대한민국우표

대한민국우표

Indicates Republic of Korea (South Korea)

South Korean postage stamps issed after 1952 do not show currency expressed in Latin letters. Stamps wiith "HW," "HWAN," "WON," "WN," "W" or "W" with two lines through it, if not illustrated in listings of stamps before this date, are revenues. North Korean postage stamps do not have currency expressed in Latin letters.

THAILAND

Country Name

King Chulalongkorn

King Prajadhipok and Chao P'ya Chakri

3. CENTRAL AND EASTERN ASIAN INSCRIPTIONS

INDIA - FEUDATORY STATES

Alwar

Bhor

Bundi

Similar stamps come with different designs in corners and differently drawn daggers (at center of circle).

Dhar

Faridkot

Hyderabad

Similar stamps exist with straight line frame around stamp, and also with different central design which is inscribed "Postage" or "Post & Receipt."

Indore

Jhalawar

A similar stamp has the central figure in an oval.

Nandgaon

Nowanuggur

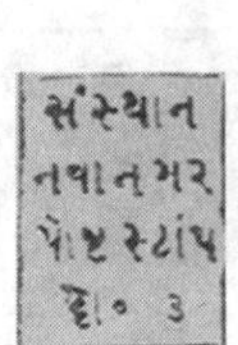

Poonch

Similar stamps exist in various sizes

Rajpeepla

Soruth

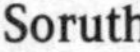

BANGLADESH

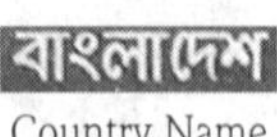

Country Name

NEPAL

Similar stamps are smaller, have squares in upper corners and have five or nine characters in central bottom panel.

TANNU TUVA

ISRAEL

GEORGIA

This inscription is found on other pictorial stamps.

Country Name

ARMENIA

The four characters are found somewhere on pictorial stamps. On some stamps only the middle two are found.

4. AFRICAN INSCRIPTIONS

ETHIOPIA

5. ARABIC INSCRIPTIONS

AFGHANISTAN

Many early Afghanistan stamps show Tiger's head, many of these have ornaments protruding from outer ring, others show inscriptions in black.

Arabic Script

Mosque Gate & Crossed Cannons
The four characters are found somewhere on pictorial stamps. On some stamps only the middle two are found.

BAHRAIN

EGYPT

Postage

INDIA - FEUDATORY STATES

Jammu & Kashmir

Text and thickness of ovals vary. Some stamps have flower devices in corners.

India-Hyderabad

IRAN

Country Name

Royal Crown

Lion with Sword

Symbol

IRAQ

JORDAN

LEBANON

Similar types have denominations at top and slightly different design.

LIBYA

Country Name in various styles

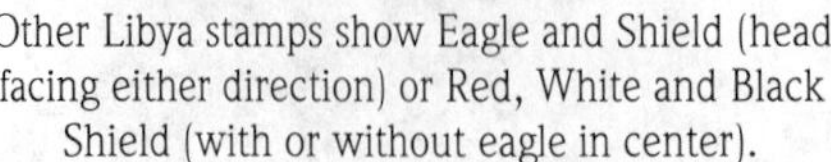

Other Libya stamps show Eagle and Shield (head facing either direction) or Red, White and Black Shield (with or without eagle in center).

SAUDI ARABIA

Tughra (Central design)

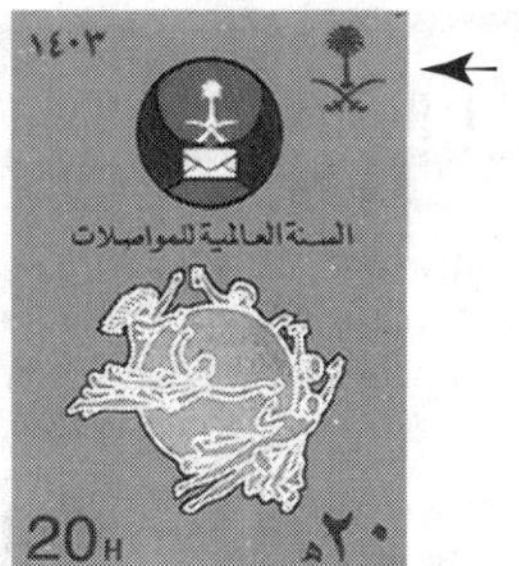

Palm Tree and Swords

SYRIA

THRACE

YEMEN

PAKISTAN

PAKISTAN - Bahawalpur

Country Name in top panel, star and crescent

TURKEY

Star & Crescent is a device found on many Turkish stamps, but is also found on stamps from other Arabic areas (see Pakistan-Bahawalpur)

Tughra (similar tughras can be found on stamps of Turkey in Asia, Afghanistan and Saudi Arabia)

Mohammed V

Mustafa Kemal

Plane, Star and Crescent

TURKEY IN ASIA

Other Turkey in Asia pictorials show star & crescent.
Other stamps show tughra shown under Turkey.

6. GREEK INSCRIPTIONS

GREECE

Country Name in various styles
(Some Crete stamps overprinted with the Greece country name are listed in Crete.)

Lepta

ΔΡΑΧΜΗ 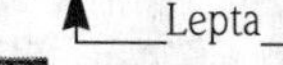 ΛΕΠΤΟΝ

Drachma Drachmas Lepton

Abbreviated Country Name ΕΛΛ

Other forms of Country Name

No country name

CRETE

Country Name

These words are on other stamps

Grosion

Crete stamps with a surcharge that have the year "1922" are listed under Greece.

EPIRUS

Country Name

IONIAN ISLANDS

7. CYRILLIC INSCRIPTIONS

RUSSIA

Postage Stamp

Imperial Eagle

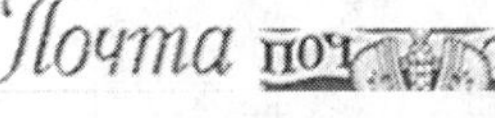

Postage in various styles

Abbreviation for Kopeck

Abbreviation for Ruble

Russia

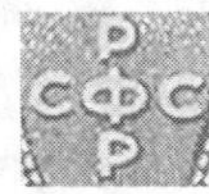

Abbreviation for Russian Soviet Federated Socialist Republic
RSFSR stamps were overprinted (see below)

Abbreviation for Union of Soviet Socialist Republics

This item is footnoted in Latvia

RUSSIA - Army of the North

"OKCA"

RUSSIA - Wenden

RUSSIAN OFFICES IN THE TURKISH EMPIRE

These letters appear on other stamps of the Russian offices.

The unoverprinted version of this stamp and a similar stamp were overprinted by various countries (see below).

ARMENIA

BELARUS

FAR EASTERN REPUBLIC

Country Name

SOUTH RUSSIA

Country Name

FINLAND

Circles and Dots on stamps similar to Imperial Russia issues

BATUM

Forms of Country Name

TRANSCAUCASIAN FEDERATED REPUBLICS

Abbreviation for Country Name

KAZAKHSTAN

Country Name

KYRGYZSTAN

КЫРГЫЗСТАН

КЫРГЫЗСТАН Counrty Name

ROMANIA

TADJIKISTAN

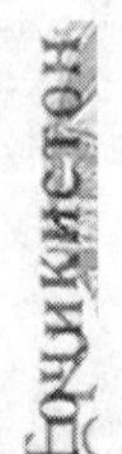

Тадж.

Counrty Name & Abbreviation

UKRAINE

Пошта України України

Україні

Country Name in various forms

УС РР

The trident appears on many stamps, usually as an overprint.

Abbreviation for Ukrainian Soviet Socialist Republic

WESTERN UKRAINE

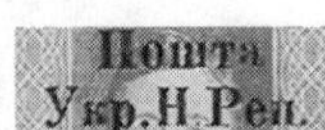

Abbreviation for Country Name

AZERBAIJAN

AZƏRBAYCAN

Country Name

А.С.С.Р. Abbreviation for Azerbaijan Soviet Socialist Republic

MONTENEGRO

ЦРНЕГОРЕ

ЦРНА ГОРА

Country Name in various forms

ЦР.ГОРЕ

Abbreviation for country name

No country name (A similar Montenegro stamp without country name has same vignette.)

SERBIA

СРПСКА СРБИЈА

Country Name in various forms

СРП К.С.

Abbreviation for country name

No country name

YUGOSLAVIA

ЈУГОСЛАВИЈА

Showing country name

No Country Name

MACEDONIA

МАКЕДОНИЈА

МАКЕДОНИЈА

Country Name

BULGARIA

Country Name

Postage

СТОТИНКА

Stotinka

STOTINKI

Stotinki (plural)

СТОТ.

Abbreviation for Stotinki

Country Name in various forms and styles

БЪЛГАРИЯ

Н Р България

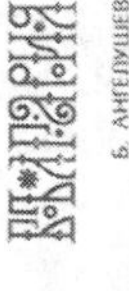

No country name

Abbreviation for Lev, leva

MONGOLIA

ШУУДАН
Country name in one word

ТӨГРӨГ
Tugrik in Cyrillic

МОНГОЛ ШУУДАН
Country name in two words

МӨНГӨ
Mung in Cyrillic

Mung in Mongolian

Tugrik in Mongolian

Arms

No Country Name

Index and Identifier

All page numbers shown are those in this Volume 5.

Postage stamps that do not have English words on them are shown in the Identifier which begins on page 846.

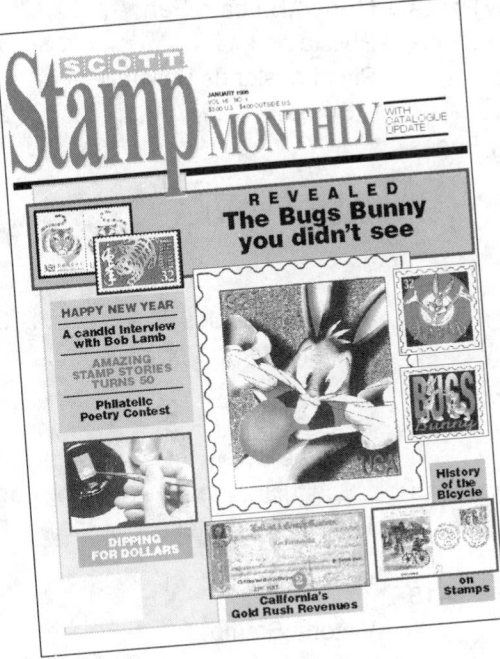

INDEX TO ADVERTISERS – 1999 VOLUME 5

1999 VOLUME 5 DEALER DIRECTORY YELLOW PAGE LISTINGS

This section of your Scott Catalogue contains advertisements to help you conveniently find what you need, when you need it...!

Accessories

BROOKLYN GALLERY COIN & STAMP
8725 4th Ave.
Brooklyn, NY 11209
718-745-5701
718-745-2775 Fax

Albums & Accessories

THE KEEPING ROOM
P.O. Box 257
Trumbull, CT 06611-0257
203-372-8436

Antarctic

ANTARCTIC PHILATELIC EXCHANGE
92015-1562 Danforth Ave.
Toronto, ON M4J 5C1
Canada
416-406-2760
http://www.south-pole.com
Email:jporter@interlog.com

Appraisals

UNIQUE ESTATE APPRAISALS
1937 NE Broadway
Portland, OR 97232
503-287-4200 or
800-646-1147
Email:uea@stampsandcoins.com
http:www.stampsandcoins.com

Approvals - Personalized Worldwide & U.S.

THE KEEPING ROOM
P.O. Box 257
Trumbull, CT 06611-0257
203-372-8436

Approvals Worldwide

ROSS WETREICH INC.
P.O. Box 1300
Valley Stream, NY 11582-1300
516-825-8974

Approvals Worldwide - Collections

S. R. L. STAMPS
P.O. Box 296
Huguenot, NY 12746
800-369-4617 pin 3429 Phone &Fax

Asia

MICHAEL ROGERS, INC.
199 E. Welbourne Ave.
Winter Park, FL 32789
407-644-2290
407-645-4434 Fax
http://www.michaelrogersinc.com

SOUTHEAST STAMPS
P.O. Box 6768
Shreveport, LA 71106

THE STAMP ACT
P.O. Box 1136
Belmont, CA 94002
650-592-3315
650-508-8104 Fax
http://www.Bchang@IX.netcom.com

Auction House

B TRADING CO.
114 Quail Street
Albany, NY 12206
518-465-3497 Telephone & Fax
Email:btradeco@wizvax.net

Auctions

CHARLES G. FIRBY AUCTIONS
6695 Highland Road Suite #107
Waterford, MI 48327-1967
248-666-5333
248-666-5020 Fax

DANIEL F. KELLEHER CO., INC.
24 Farnsworth St.
Ste. 605
Boston, MA 02210
617-443-0033
617-443-0789 Fax

LAKESIDE PHILATELIC AUCTIONS
3935 Lakeside Rd.
Penticton, BC V2A 8W1
Canada
250-493-5239
250-493-3324 Fax
http://vvv.com/~greek
Email:greek@tnet.net

JACQUES C. SCHIFF, JR., INC.
195 Main St.
Ridgefield Park, NJ 07660
201-641-5566 from NYC 662-2777
201-641-5705 Fax

JUAN N. SIMONA
Ventas Filatelicas
Casilla de Correo #40
7311 Chillar (Buenos Aires)
Argentina
54-281-97281or 54-281-97346
Phone & Fax
Email:simonafilatelia@
simoafilatelia.com.ar
http://www.simonafilatelia.com.ar

Auctions

Auctions

STAMP CENTER / DUTCH COUNTRY AUCTIONS
4115 Concord Pike
Wilmington, DE 19803
302-478-8740
302-478-8779 Fax
http://www.thestampcenter.com

THE STAMP & COIN SHOP/ AUCTIONS
725 Pike St. #6
Seattle, WA 98101
206-624-1400
206-621-8975 Fax
http://WWW.Stamp-Coin.com

Auctions - Public

ALAN BLAIR STAMPS / AUCTIONS
5520A Lakeside Avenue
Richmond, VA 23228
800-689-5602 Telephone & Fax

CONNEXUS
P.O. Box 130
Tryon, NC 28782
828-859-5882
828-859-2702 Fax
Email:Connexus1@worldnet.att.net

Austria

JOSEPH EDER
P.O. Box 5517
Hamden, CT 06518
203-281-0742
203-230-2410 Fax
Email:jeder@nai.net

Beanie Babies

M.A. STORK
651 Forest Ave.
Portland, ME 04101
800-734-7271

British Colonies

EMPIRE STAMP COMPANY
P.O. Box 19248
Encino, CA 91416
818-880-6764
818-880-6860 Fax
Email:EMPIRECOLL@AOL.COM

British Commonwealth

BRITISH COMMONWEALTH STAMP CO.
P.O. Box 10218
Wilmington, NC 28405
Email:bcstamp@stamp-mall.com
910-256-0971 Fax

DAUWALDERS OF SALISBURY
92-94 Fisherton St.
Wiltshire, SP27QY
United Kingdom
1-44-1722-412100
1-44-1722-410074 Fax
Email:DAUSTAMPS@AOL.COM

British Commonwealth

JAY'S STAMP COMPANY
Box 28484 Dept. S
Philadelphia, PA 19149
215-743-0207 Telephone & Fax
Email:JASC@Juno.com
http://jaysco.com

VICTORIA STAMP COMPANY
P.O. Box 745
Ridgewood, NJ 07451
201-652-7283
201-612-0024 Fax

British Commonwealth

British Commonwealth

British Pacific

OVPT PHILATELICS
P.O. Box 36217
Los Angeles, CA 90036
818-893-4603 Telephone & Fax
Email:ovptphmc@aol

Canada - Postal Bid Sales

BOW CITY PHILATELICS LTD.
P.O. Box 6444 Central P.O.
Suite 614 206 7th Ave. SW
Calgary, AB T2P 2E1
Canada
403-237-5828
403-264-5287 Fax
Email:bow.city@bbs.logicnet.com
http:www.logicnet.com/bow.city

Buying

Collections

China

MICHAEL ROGERS, INC.
199 E. Welbourne Ave.
Winter Park, FL 32789
407-644-2290
407-645-4434 Fax
http://www.michaelrogersinc.com

China - Peoples Republic

GUANLUN HONG
P.O. Box 12623
Toledo, OH 43606
419-382-6096
419-382-0203 Fax
Email:guanlun@usa.net

Collections

BOB & MARTHA FRIEDMAN STAMPS
624 Homestead Place
Joliet, IL 60434
815-725-6666
815-725-4134 Fax

DR. ROBERT FRIEDMAN & SONS
2029 West 75th St.
Woodridge, IL 60517
630-985-1515
630-985-1588 Fax

HENRY GITNER PHILATELISTS, INC.
P.O. Box 3077-S
Middletown, NY 10940
914-343-5151 or 800-947-8267
914-343-0068 Fax
Email:hgitner@hgitner.com
http://www.hgitner.com

Disney

BROOKMAN STAMP COMPANY
P.O. Box 90
Vancouver, WA 98666
360-695-1391 or 800-545-4871
360-695-1616 Fax
Email:brookman@stampdealers.com
http:www.brookmanstamps.com

Duck Stamps

MICHAEL JAFFE STAMPS, INC.
P.O. Box 61484
Vancouver, WA 98666
360-695-6161 or 800-782-6770
360-695-1616 Fax
Email:mjaffe@brookmanstamps.com
http://www.brookmanstamps.com

METROPOLITAN STAMP CO. of CHICAGO, INC.
P.O. Box 1133
Chicago, IL 60690-1133
815-439-0142
815-439-0143 Fax

TRENTON STAMP & COIN CO. - THOMAS DeLUCA
Forest Glen Plaza
1804 Route 33
Hamilton Square, NJ 08690
800-446-8664
609-587-8664 Fax

Errors, Freaks & Oddities

MILL CREEK LIMITED
P.O. Box 236
Bothell, WA 98041-0236
U.S.800-495-6868 outside of U.S.
425-487-2789
Email:MillCreek@StampDealers.com
http://www.stampdealers.com/millcreek/

Exchange

ROBERT'S STAMP EXCHANGE/Robert LeFrancois
444 Summit St.
Elgin, Il 60120
847-695-6568

Foreign Duck Stamps

METROPOLITAN STAMP CO. of CHICAGO, INC.
P.O. Box 1133
Chicago, IL 60690-1133
815-439-0142
815-439-0143 Fax

France

JOSEPH EDER
P.O. Box 5517
Hamden, CT 06518
203-281-0742
203-230-2410 Fax
Email:jeder@nai.net

German Areas

JOSEPH EDER
P.O. Box 5517
Hamden, CT 06518
203-281-0742
203-230-2410 Fax
Email:jeder@nai.net

German Colonies

COLONIAL STAMP COMPANY
5757 Wilshire Blvd. PH #8
Los Angeles, CA 90036
213-933-9435
213-939-9930 Fax

Great Britain

COLONIAL STAMP COMPANY
5757 Wilshire Blvd. PH #8
Los Angeles, CA 90036
213-933-9435
213-939-9930 Fax

NOVA PHILATELIC SALES
Box 161
Lakeside, N.S. B3T 1M6
Canada
902-826-2165
902-826-1049 Fax
Email:novafil@ns.sympatico.ca

Imperial China

TREASURE -HUNTERS LIMITED
G.P.O. Box 11446
Hong Kong
852-2507-3773 or 2507-5770
852-2519-6820 Fax

Insurance

COLLECTIBLES INSURANCE AGENCY, INC.
P.O. Box 1200 SSC
Westminster, MD 21158-0299
888-837-9537 or 410-876-8833
410-876-9233 Fax
Email:collectinsure@pipeline.com

Iran - Classics

DE MOTTE STAMPS INTERNATIONAL COMPANY
2555 W. Middlefield Rd.
Ste. 212
Mountainview, CA 94043
650-968-2636
650-938-1610 Fax

Israel - New Issues

ISRAEL PHILATELIC AGENCY
535 Fifth Ave.
Suite 300
New York, NY 10017
212-818-9160 or 800-607-2799
212-818-9012 Fax

Latin America

JUAN N. SIMONA
Ventas Filatelicas
Casilla de Correo #40
7311 Chillar (Buenos Aires)
Argentina
54-281-97281or 54-281-97346
Phone & Fax
Email:simonafilatelia@simonafilatelia.com.ar
http://www.simonafilatelia.com.ar

Literature

OVPT PHILATELICS
P.O. Box 36217
Los Angeles, CA 90036
818-893-4603 Telephone & Fax
Email:ovptphmc@aol

Lots & Collections

BOB & MARTHA FRIEDMAN STAMPS
624 Homestead Place
Joliet, IL 60434
815-725-6666
815-725-4134 Fax

DR. ROBERT FRIEDMAN & SONS
2029 West 75th St.
Woodridge, IL 60517
630-985-1515
630-985-1588 Fax

Mail Sales

New Issues

Mail Order

ALMAZ CO., DEPT. VY
P.O. Box 100-812
Vanderveer Station
Brooklyn, NY 11210
718-241-6360 Telephone & Fax

SHARI'S STAMPS
104-3 Old Highway 40 #130
O'Fallon, MO 63366
800-382-3597
314-980-1552 Fax

New Issues

DAVIDSON'S STAMP SERVICE
P.O. Box 36355
Indianapolis, IN 46236-0355
317-826-2620
Email:davidson@in.net

New Issues - Retail

BOMBAY PHILATELIC CO., INC.
P.O. Box 7719
Delray Beach, FL 33482-7719
561-499-7990
561-499-7553 Fax
Email:sales@bombaystamps.com
http:www.bombaystamps.com

STANLEY M. PILLER
3351 Grand Ave.
Oakland, CA 94610
510-465-8290
510-465-7121 Fax
Email:stmpdlr@aol.com

New Issues - Wholesale

BOMBAY PHILATELIC CO., INC.
P.O. Box 7719
Delray Beach, FL 33482-7719
561-499-7990
561-499-7553 Fax
Email:sales@bombaystamps.com
http:www.bombaystamps.com

Palau

FRANK GEIGER PHILATELISTS
Suite 2
242 West Saddle River Road
Saddle River, NJ 07458-2620
201-236-8122
201-236-8133 Fax
http://www.worldstamps.com

Papua New Guinea

COLONIAL STAMP COMPANY
5757 Wilshire Blvd. PH #8
Los Angeles, CA 90036
213-933-9435
213-939-9930 Fax

FRANK GEIGER PHILATELISTS
Suite 2
242 West Saddle River Road
Saddle River, NJ 07458-2620
201-236-8122
201-236-8133 Fax
http://www.worldstamps.com

OVPT PHILATELICS
P.O. Box 36217
Los Angeles, CA 90036
818-893-4603 Ph. & Fax
Email:ovptphmc@aol

Penrhyn Islands

OVPT PHILATELICS
P.O. Box 36217
Los Angeles, CA 90036
818-893-4603 Ph. & Fax
Email:ovptphmc@aol

Peru

VICTOR R. OSTOLAZA
Casilla #4338
Lima 100
Peru
511-476-2102 Ph. & Fax
Email:apalma@msn.com

Philippines

FRANK GEIGER PHILATELISTS
Suite 2
242 West Saddle River Road
Saddle River, NJ 07458-2620
201-236-8122
201-236-8133 Fax
http://www.worldstamps.com

Pitcairn Islands

FRANK GEIGER PHILATELISTS
Suite 2
242 West Saddle River Road
Saddle River, NJ 07458-2620
201-236-8122
201-236-8133 Fax
http://www.worldstamps.com

PITCAIRN ISLAND STUDY GROUP
contact: William S. Volk
2184 6th Ave.
Yuma, AZ 85364

Poland

FRANK GEIGER PHILATELISTS
Suite 2
242 West Saddle River Road
Saddle River, NJ 07458-2620
201-236-8122
201-236-8133 Fax
http://www.worldstamps.com

HUNGARIA STAMP EXCHANGE
P.O. Box 3024
Andover, MA 01810
508-682-0242
508-794-2567 Fax

Portugal

LEON FISCHER
P.O. Box 1338 Gracie Sta.
New York, NY 10028

FRANK GEIGER PHILATELISTS
Suite 2
242 West Saddle River Road
Saddle River, NJ 07458-2620
201-236-8122
201-236-8133 Fax
http://www.worldstamps.com

Portuguese Colonies

AMEEN STAMPS
8849 Long Point Rd.
Houston, TX 77055
713-468-0644
713-468-2420 Fax

Postal History

JUNO STAMPS
1765 Juno Ave.
St. Paul, MN 55116

Price Lists - Worldwide

HALL'S STAMPS
P.O. Box 8095
Spokane, WA 99203
509-838-4564
509-838-1903 Fax

Proofs & Essays

HENRY GITNER PHILATELISTS, INC.
P.O. Box 3077-S
Middletown, NY 10940
914-343-5151 or 800-947-8267
914-343-0068 Fax
Email:hgitner@hgitner.com
http://www.hgitner.com

Publications / Collector

AMERICAN PHILATELIST
Dept. TZ
P.O. Box 8000
State College, PA 16803
814-237-3803
814-237-6128 Fax
Email:flsente@stamps.org
http://www.west.net/~stamps1/aps.html

GLOBAL STAMP NEWS
P.O. Box 97
Sidney, OH 45365-0097
937-492-3183
937-492-6514 Fax
Email:global@bright.net

Rhodesia

COLONIAL STAMP COMPANY
5757 Wilshire Blvd. PH #8
Los Angeles, CA 90036
213-933-9435
213-939-9930 Fax

Romania

FRANK GEIGER PHILATELISTS
Suite 2
242 West Saddle River Road
Saddle River, NJ 07458-2620
201-236-8122
201-236-8133 Fax
http://www.worldstamps.com

HUNGARIA STAMP EXCHANGE
P.O. Box 3024
Andover, MA 01810
508-682-0242
508-794-2567 Fax

Russia

AMEEN STAMPS
8849 Long Point Rd.
Houston, TX 77055
713-468-0644
713-468-2420 Fax

FRANK GEIGER PHILATELISTS
Suite 2
242 West Saddle River Road
Saddle River, NJ 07458-2620
201-236-8122
201-236-8133 Fax
http://www.worldstamps.com

JR STAMPS
3110 Cannongate
Fort Wayne, IN 46808-4511
219-471-3746
Email:jrstamps@hotmail.com

Russia - New Issues

RUSSIA STAMP AGENCY IN NORTH AMERICA
One Unicover Center
Cheyenne, WY 82008-0012
800-443-4225
800-628-3132 Fax
http://www.unicover.com

St. Christopher

COLONIAL STAMP COMPANY
5757 Wilshire Blvd. PH #8
Los Angeles, CA 90036
213-933-9435
213-939-9930 Fax

St. Helena

COLONIAL STAMP COMPANY
5757 Wilshire Blvd. PH #8
Los Angeles, CA 90036
213-933-9435
213-939-9930 Fax

St. Kitts & Nevis

COLONIAL STAMP COMPANY
5757 Wilshire Blvd. PH #8
Los Angeles, CA 90036
213-933-9435
213-939-9930 Fax

St. Lucia

COLONIAL STAMP COMPANY
5757 Wilshire Blvd. PH #8
Los Angeles, CA 90036
213-933-9435
213-939-9930 Fax

St. Pierre & Miquelon

FRANK GEIGER PHILATELISTS
Suite 2
242 West Saddle River Road
Saddle River, NJ 07458-2620
201-236-8122
201-236-8133 Fax
http://www.worldstamps.com

E. JOSEPH MCCONNELL INC.
P.O. Box 683
Monroe, NY 10950
914-496-5916
914-782-0347 Fax

S. SEREBRAKIAN, INC.
P.O. Box 448
Monroe, NY 10950
914-783-9791
914-782-0347 Fax

St. Vincent

COLONIAL STAMP COMPANY
5757 Wilshire Blvd. PH #8
Los Angeles, CA 90036
213-933-9435
213-939-9930 Fax

Samoa

COLONIAL STAMP COMPANY
5757 Wilshire Blvd. PH #8
Los Angeles, CA 90036
213-933-9435
213-939-9930 Fax

San Marino

FRANK GEIGER PHILATELISTS
Suite 2
242 West Saddle River Road
Saddle River, NJ 07458-2620
201-236-8122
201-236-8133 Fax
http://www.worldstamps.com

Sarawak

COLONIAL STAMP COMPANY
5757 Wilshire Blvd. PH #8
Los Angeles, CA 90036
213-933-9435
213-939-9930 Fax

Scandinavia - New Issues

NORDICA
P.O. Box 284
Old Bethpage, NY 11804
516-931-3485 Telephone & Fax
Email:NordicaD@aol.com

Seychelles

COLONIAL STAMP COMPANY
5757 Wilshire Blvd. PH #8
Los Angeles, CA 90036
213-933-9435
213-939-9930 Fax

Sierra Leone

COLONIAL STAMP COMPANY
5757 Wilshire Blvd. PH #8
Los Angeles, CA 90036
213-933-9435
213-939-9930 Fax

Slovakia

SOCIETY FOR CZECHOSLOVAK PHILATELY, INC.
Tom Cossaboom, SCP Secretary
Box 25332
Scott Air Force Base, IL 62225
USA

FRANK GEIGER PHILATELISTS
Suite 2
242 West Saddle River Road
Saddle River, NJ 07458-2620
201-236-8122
201-236-8133 Fax
http://www.worldstamps.com

Slovenia

FRANK GEIGER PHILATELISTS
Suite 2
242 West Saddle River Road
Saddle River, NJ 07458-2620
201-236-8122
201-236-8133 Fax
http://www.worldstamps.com

Spain

STAMPTRACKS
P.O. Box 70
Holtsville, NY 11742
516-289-6359 Ph. & Fax

Stamp Shows

ATLANTIC COAST EXHIBITIONS
Divison of Beach Philatelics
42 Baltimore Lane
Palm Coast, FL 32137-8850
904-445-4550
904-447-0811 Fax
Email:mrstamp2@aol.com
http://members.tripod.com/~SmitX/BeachPhilatelics.htm

STAMP STORES

Arizona

B.J.'S STAMPS / BARBARA J. JOHNSON
6342 W. Bell Road
Glendale, AZ 85308
602-878-2080
602-412-3456 Fax

MOLNAR'S STAMP & COIN SHOP
7118 E. Sahuaro Dr.
Scottsdale, AZ 85254
602-948-9672
602-948-8425 Fax

AMERICAN STAMP & COIN CO.
7225 N. Oracle Rd.
Suite #102
Tucson, AZ 85704
520-297-3456
Email:stamps@azstarnet.com

California

ASHTREE STAMP & COIN
2410 N. Blackstone
Fresno, CA 93703
209-227-7167

BROSIUS STAMP & COIN
2105 Main Street
Santa Monica, CA 90405
310-396-7480
310-396-7455 Fax

COLONIAL STAMP COMPANY/ BRITISH EMPIRE SPECIALIST
5757 Wilshire Blvd. PH #8
(appt. only)
Los Angeles, CA 90036
213-933-9435
213-939-9930 Fax

FISCHER - WOLK PHILATELICS
24771 "G" Alicia Parkway
Laguna Hills, CA 92653
714-837-2932

NATICK STAMPS & HOBBIES
405 S. Myrtle Avenue
Monrovia, CA 91016
818-305-7333
818-305-7335 Fax
http://www.natickco.com

STANLEY M. PILLER
3351 Grand Ave.
Oakland, CA 94610
510-465-8290
510-465-7121 Fax
Email:stmpdlr@aol.com

THE STAMP GALLERY
1515 Locust Street
Walnut Creek, CA 94596
925-944-9111

STAMPCRAFT
P.O. Box 2425
Santa Clara, CA 95055
800-245-5389
408-241-4440 Fax

Colorado

ACKLEY'S ROCKS & STAMPS
3230 N. Stone Ave.
Colorado Springs, CO 80907
719-633-1153

SHOWCASE STAMPS
3865 Wadsworth Blvd.
Wheat Ridge, CO 80033
303-425-9252
303-425-7410 Fax

Connecticut

MILLER'S STAMP SHOP
41 New London Turnpike
Uncasville, CT 06382
860-848-0468 Telephone & Fax

SILVER CITY COIN & STAMP
41 Colony Street
Meriden, CT 06451
203-235-7634

Florida

CLARK'S CORNER
4223 Bee Ridge Rd.
Sarasota, FL 34233
941-377-6909 or 800-927-3351
941-377-6604 Fax

CORBIN STAMP & COIN
115-A East Brandon Blvd.
Brandon, FL 33511
813-651-3266

HAUSER'S COIN & STAMP
3425 S. Florida Ave.
Lakeland, FL 33803
941-647-2052
941-644-5738 Fax

INTERCONTINENTAL / RICARDO DEL CAMPO
7379 Coral Way
Miami, FL 33155-1402
305-264-4983
305-262-2919 Fax

ROBERT LEVINE STAMPS, INC.
2219 South University Dr.
Davie, FL 33324
954-473-1303
954-473-1305 Fax

NEW ENGLAND STAMP
4987 Tamiami Trail East
Village Falls Professional Ctr.
Naples, FL 34113
941-732-8000
941-732-7701 Fax
Email:STAMPS@SPRINTMAIL.COM

JERRY SIEGEL / STAMPS FOR COLLECTORS
1920 E. Hallandale Beach Blvd.
Suite 507
Hallandale, FL 33009
954-457-0422 Telephone & Fax

Florida

THE STAMP PLACE
576 First Avenue North
St. Petersburg, FL 33701
813-894-4082

WINTER PARK STAMP SHOP
199 E. Welbourne Ave.
Suite 201
Winter Park, FL 32789
800-845-1819
407-628-0091 Fax

Georgia

STAMPS UNLIMITED OF GEORGIA
133 Carnegie Way
Room 250
Atlanta, GA 30303
404-688-9161

Illinois

DON CLARK'S STAMPS
937 1/2 W. Galena Blvd.
Aurora, IL 60506
630-896-4606

DR. ROBERT FRIEDMAN & SONS
2029 West 75th St.
Woodridge, IL 60517
630-985-1515
630-985-1588 Fax

MARSHALL FIELD'S STAMP DEPT.
111 N. State Street
Chicago, IL 60602
312-781-4237

Indiana

J & J COINS & STAMPS
7019 Calumet Avenue or
6526 Indianapolis Blvd.
Hammond, IN 46324
219-932-5818
219-845-2003 Fax

KNIGHT STAMP & COIN COMPANY
237 Main Street
Hobart, IN 46342
219-942-7529 or
800-634-2646

Florida

Kentucky

COLLECTORS STAMPS LTD.
4012 DuPont Circle #313
Louisville, KY 40207
502-897-9045
Email:csl/aye.net

TREASURE ISLAND COINS & STAMPS
232 W. Broadway
Louisville, KY 40202
502-583-1222

Maryland

BALTIMORE COIN & STAMP EXCHANGE, INC.
10194 Baltimore National Pike
Unit 104
Ellicott City, MD 21042
410-418-8282
410-418-4813 Fax

BULLDOG STAMP CO.
4641 Montgomery Ave.
Bethesda, MD 20814
301-654-1138

STAMP & COIN WORLD
511-A Delaware Avenue
Towson, MD 21286
410-828-4465 or 800-452-4560
410-828-4560 Fax

Massachusetts

FALMOUTH STAMP & COIN
11 Town Hall Square
Falmouth, MA 02540
508-548-7075 or 800-341-3701

J & N FORTIER COIN STAMPS & ANTIQUES
484 Main St.
Worcester, MA 01608
508-757-3657
508-852-8329 Fax

KAPPY'S COINS & STAMPS
534 Washington St.
Norwood, MA 02062
781-762-5552
781-762-3292 Fax

Michigan

BIRMINGHAM COIN AND JEWELRY
33802 Woodward
Birmingham, MI 48009
248-642-1234
248-642-4207 Fax

THE MOUSE AND SUCH
696 N. Mill Street
Plymouth, MI 48170
313-454-1515

Minnesota

CROSSROADS STAMP SHOP
2211 West 54th Street
Minneapolis, MN 55419-1515
612-928-0119

Nebraska

TUVA ENTERPRISES
209 So. 72nd Street
Omaha, NE 68114
402-397-9937

STAMP STORES

New Jersey

AALLSTAMPS & COLLECTABLES
38 North Main Street
P.O. Box 249
Milltown, NJ 08850
732-247-1093
732-247-1094 Fax

A.D.A STAMP CO., INC.
910 Boyd Street
Toms River, NJ 08753 or
P.O. Drawer J
Island Heights, NJ 08732
732-240-1131
732-240-2620 Fax

BERGEN STAMPS & COLLECTABLES
717 American Legion Dr.
Teaneck, NJ 07666
201-836-8987

CHARLES STAMP SHOP
47 Old Post Road
Edison, NJ 08817
732-985-1071
732-819-0549 Fax

FAIRIDGE STAMP INC.
447 Broadway
Westwood, NJ 07675
201-666-8869

RON RITZER STAMPS & COLLECTIBLES
Millburn Mall
2933 Vauxhall Road
Vauxhall, NJ 07088
908-687-0007
908-687-0795 Fax

TRENTON STAMP & COIN CO. - THOMAS DeLUCA
Forest Glen Plaza
1804 Route 33
Hamilton Square, NJ 08690
800-446-8664
609-587-8664 Fax

New York

CHAMPION STAMP CO.
432 West 54th Street
New York, NY 10019
212-489-8130
212-581-8130 Fax

THE FIFTH AVENUE STAMP GALLERY
535 Fifth Ave.
Suite 300
New York, NY 10017
212-818-9160 or 800-607-2799
212-818-9012 Fax

JOHN'S COINS, CARDS & STAMPS INC.
36 West 34th Street
2nd Floor
New York, NY 10001
212-244-2646

LINCOLN COIN & STAMP
33 West Tupper Street
Buffalo, NY 14202
716-856-1884

Ohio

FEDERAL COIN INC. AND ARCADE STAMP & COIN
39 The Arcade
Cleveland, OH 44114
216-861-1160
216-861-5960 Fax

HILLTOP STAMP SERVICE
P.O. Box 626
Wooster, OH 44691
330-262-8907 Telephone & Fax or
330-262-5378
Email:hilltop@bright.net

J L F STAMP STORE
3041 E. Waterloo Road
Akron, OH 44312
330-628-8343

THE LINK STAMP CO.
3461 E. Livingston Ave.
Columbus, OH 43227
614-237-4125
or 800-546-5726

NEWARK STAMP COMPANY
49 North Fourth Street
Newark, OH 43055
740-349-7900

Oklahoma

GARY'S STAMP SHOP
120 E. Broadway
Box 6011
Enid, OK 73701
405-233-0007

Oregon

UNIQUE ESTATE APPRAISALS
1937 NE Broadway
Portland, OR 97232
503-287-4200
or 800-646-1147
Email:uea@stampsandcoins.com
http:www.stampsandcoins.com

Pennsylvania

DAVE ALLEGO
648 Merchant St.
Ambridge, PA 15003
724-266-4237

LARRY LEE STAMPS
322 S. Front Street
Greater Harrisburg Area
Wormleysburg, PA 17043
717-763-7605

PHILLY STAMP & COIN CO. INC.
1804 Chestnut Street
Philadelphia, PA 19103
215-563-7341
215-563-7382 Fax
Email:adelphia@uscom.com

TREASURE HUNT COLLECTABLE COINS & STAMPS
1687 Washington Road Suite 200
Pittsburgh, PA 15228
412-851-9991 or
800-259-4727

Rhode Island

PODRAT COIN EXCHANGE INC.
769 Hope Street
Providence, RI 02906
401-861-7640
401-272-3032 Fax

South Carolina

THE STAMP OUTLET
Oakbrook Center #9
4650 Ladson Road
Summerville, SC 29485
843-873-4655
843-871-6704 Fax

Tennessee

AMERICAN COIN & STAMP EXCHANGE
330 S. Gallatin Road
Madison, TN 37115
615-865-8791
615-865-4005 Fax

HERRON HILL, INC.
5007 Black Road
Suite 140
Memphis, TN 38117-4505
901-683-9644

Texas

ALAMO HEIGHTS STAMP SHOP
1201 Austin Hwy
Suite 128
San Antonio, TX 78209
800-214-9526

AUSTIN STAMP & COIN
13107 FM 969
Austin, TX 78724
512-276-7793

DALLAS STAMP GALLERY
1002 North Central Expressway
Suite 501
Richardson, TX 75080
972-669-4741
972-669-4742 Fax

Virginia

ALAN BLAIR STAMPS / AUCTIONS
5520A Lakeside Avenue
Richmond, VA 23228
800-689-5602 Telephone & Fax

KENNEDY'S STAMPS & COINS
7059 Brookfield Plaza
Springfield, VA 22150
703-569-7300
703-569-7644 Fax

LATHEROW & CO. INC.
5054 Lee Highway
Arlington, VA 22207
703-538-2727

PRINCE WILLIAM STAMP & COIN CO.
14011-H St. Germain Dr.
Centreville, VA 20121
703-830-4669

Washington

HIDDEN TREASURES INC.
328 Madison Ave.
Bainebridge Island, WA 98110
360-692-1999 or 800-322-1993
In Bainebrige 206-855-9007
206-855-9011 Fax
Email:ht@ix.netcom.com

THE STAMP & COIN PLACE
1310 Commercial
Bellingham, WA 98225
360-676-8720
360-647-6947 Fax

THE STAMP & COIN SHOP
725 Pike St. #6
Seattle, WA 98101
206-624-1400
206-621-8975 Fax
http://WWW.Stamp-Coin.com

TACOMA MALL BLVD. COIN & STAMP
5225 Tacoma Mall Blvd. E-101
Tacoma, WA 98409
253-472-9632
253-472-8948 Fax
Email:kfeldman01@sprynet.com

West Viriginia

DAVID HILL LTD.
6433 U.S. Route 60 E
Barboursville, WV 25504
304-736-4383

Wisconsin

JIM LUKES' STAMP & COIN
815 Jay Street
P.O. Box 1780
Manitowoc, WI 54221
414-682-2324

Supplies & Accessories

BEACH PHILATELICS
42 Baltimore Lane
Palm Coast, FL 32137-8850
904-445-4550
904-447-0811 Fax
Email:mrstamp2@aol.com
http://members.tripod.com/~SmitX/BeachPhilatelics.htm

Supplies - Mail Order

GOPHER SUPPLY CO.
1973 Sloan Place #20
Maplewood, MN 55117
612-771-8840 or 800-815-3868
612-771-8850 Fax
Email:gopher@pclink.com

STAMPCRAFT
P.O. Box 2425
Santa Clara, CA 95055
800-245-5389
408-241-4440 Fax

Supplies - Stamps & Coins

ECONOMICAL SUPPLY CO.
6 King Philip Road
Worcester, MA 01606
508-853-3127
508-852-8329 Fax

M.A. STORCK CO.
651 Forest Ave.
Portland, ME 04101
800-734-7271
207-774-7272 Fax

Topicals - Columbus

MR. COLUMBUS
Box 1492
Frankenmuth, MI 48734

Topicals - Miscellaneous

BOMBAY PHILATELIC CO., INC.
P.O. Box 7719
Delray Beach, FL 33482-7719
561-499-7990
561-499-7553 Fax
Email:sales@bombaystamps.com
http:www.bombaystamps.com

HENRY GITNER PHILATELISTS, INC.
P.O. Box 3077-S
Middletown, NY 10940
914-343-5151 or 800-947-8267
914-343-0068 Fax
Email:hgitner@hgitner.com
http://www.hgitner.com

MINI - ARTS
P.O. Box 457
Estherville, IA 51334
712-362-4710

Topicals - Railroad

HENRY GITNER PHILATELISTS, INC.
P.O. Box 3077-S
Middletown, NY 10940
914-343-5151 or 800-947-8267
914-343-0068 Fax
Email:hgitner@hgitner.com
http://www.hgitner.com

Ukraine

MR. VAL ZABIJAKA
P.O. Box 3711
Silver Spring, MD 20918
301-593-5316 Telephone & Fax
Email:BNM123@EROLS.COM

United Nations

BEACH PHILATELICS
42 Baltimore Lane
Palm Coast, FL 32137-8850
904-445-4550
904-447-0811 Fax
Email:mrstamp2@aol.com
http://members.tripod.com/~SmitX/BeachPhilatelics.htm

United States

BEACH PHILATELICS
42 Baltimore Lane
Palm Coast, FL 32137-8850
904-445-4550
904-447-0811 Fax
Email:mrstamp2@aol.com
http://members.tripod.com/~SmitX/BeachPhilatelics.htm

United States - Plate Blocks

BEACH PHILATELICS
42 Baltimore Lane
Palm Coast, FL 32137-8850
904-445-4550
904-447-0811 Fax
Email:mrstamp2@aol.com
http://members.tripod.com/~SmitX/BeachPhilatelics.htm

BOB & MARTHA FRIEDMAN STAMPS
624 Homestead Place
Joliet, IL 60434
815-725-6666
815-725-4134 Fax

DR. ROBERT FRIEDMAN & SONS
2029 West 75th St.
Woodridge, IL 60517
630-985-1515
630-985-1588 Fax

Topicals

United States - Price Lists

ROBERT E. BARKER
P.O. Box 888063
Dunwoody, GA 30356
770-395-1757
770-671-8918 Fax
Email:rebarker@rebarker.com

United States - Stamps

BOB & MARTHA FRIEDMAN STAMPS
624 Homestead Place
Joliet, IL 60434
815-725-6666
815-725-4134 Fax

DR. ROBERT FRIEDMAN & SONS
2029 West 75th St.
Woodridge, IL 60517
630-985-1515
630-985-1588 Fax

United States - Worldwide Mixtures

MIXTURE MART/STAMPS UNIQUE
907 Sandy Lane
Espanola, NM 87532
505-753-4078

Want Lists

BROOKMAN INTERNATIONAL
P.O. Box 450
Vancouver, WA 98666
360-695-4311 or Toll Free 888-695-4311
360-695-1616 Fax
Email:brookman@stampdealers.com

CHARLES P. SCHWARTZ
P.O. Box 165
Mora, MN 55051
320-679-4705

Want Lists - British Empire/1840-1935 German Col./Offices

COLONIAL STAMP COMPANY
5757 Wilshire Blvd. PH #8
Los Angeles, CA 90036
213-933-9435
213-939-9930 Fax

Western Europe

EDWARD J. MCKIM
1373 Isabelle
Memphis, TN 38122
901-327-8959

Wholesale

HENRY GITNER PHILATELISTS, INC.
P.O. Box 3077-S
Middletown, NY 10940
914-343-5151 or 800-947-8267
914-343-0068 Fax
Email:hgitrier@hgitner.com
http://www.hgitner.com

Wholesale Collections

A.D.A STAMP CO., INC.
910 Boyd Street
Toms River, NJ 08753 or
P.O. Drawer J
Island Heights, NJ 08732
732-240-1131
732-240-2620 Fax

Wholesale Philatelic & Numismatic Accessories

CHARLES R. HEISLER INC.
500 Oak Grove Drive
Lancaster, PA 17601
800-784-6886
717-299-2366 Fax

M.A. STORCK CO.
651 Forest Ave.
Portland, ME 04101
800-734-7271
207-774-7272 Fax

Wholesale Supplies

JOHN VAN ALSTYNE STAMPS & SUPPLIES
1787 Tribute Rd. Suite J
Sacramento, CA 95815
916-565-0600
916-565-0539 Fax
Email:sherjohn@softcom.net

Worldwide

ALLKOR STAMP COMPANY
Box 1346
Port Washington, NY 11050
516-883-3296 Telephone & Fax

Worldwide Collections

BOB & MARTHA FRIEDMAN STAMPS
624 Homestead Place
Joliet, IL 60434
815-725-6666
815-725-4134 Fax

DR. ROBERT FRIEDMAN & SONS
2029 West 75th St.
Woodridge, IL 60517
630-985-1515
630-985-1588 Fax

Worldwide - Romania

GEORGE ARGHIR, PHILATELISTS
Detunata Str. 17-27
P.O. Box 521
RO-3400 Cluj-Napoca 9
Romania
+40-64-414036 Telephone & Fax

Worldwide - Year Sets

BOMBAY PHILATELIC CO., INC.
P.O. Box 7719
Delray Beach, FL 33482-7719
561-499-7990
561-499-7553 Fax
Email:sales@bombaystamps.com
http:www.bombaystamps.com

WALLACE STAMPS
Box 82
Port Washington, NY 11050
516-883-5578

Cover & Mint Sheet Storage

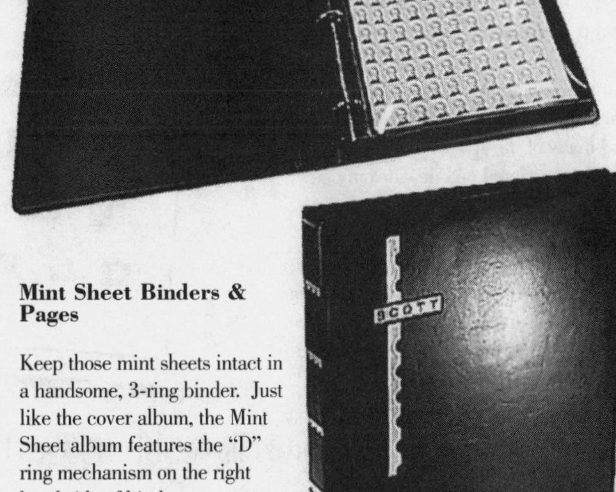

Cover Box
Keep your collection organized in a 7 ½" x 10 ½" x 4 ¼" cover box. Box will hold hundreds of covers. Available in classic marble styling .

Item		Retail
CVBOX	Marble Cover Box	$6.95

Cover Binders & Pages
Padded, durable, 3-ring binder will hold up to 100 covers. Features the "D" ring mechanism on the right hand side of album so you don't have to worry about creasing or wrinkling covers when
opening or closing binder.

Cover pages sold separately.

Item		Retail
CBRD	Cover Binder - Red	$7.95
CBBL	Cover Binder - Blue	$7.95
CBGY	Cover Binder - Gray	$7.95
CBBK	Cover Binder - Black	$7.95
T2	Cover Pages Black (25 per pack)	$4.95
T2C	Cover Pages Clear (25 per pack)	$4.95

Mint Sheet Binders & Pages

Keep those mint sheets intact in a handsome, 3-ring binder. Just like the cover album, the Mint Sheet album features the "D" ring mechanism on the right hand side of binder
so you don't have to worry about damagingyour stamps when turning the pages. Mint Sheet binder available in four colors.

Mint sheet pages sold separately.

Item		Retail
MBRD	Mint Sheet Binder - Red	$9.95
MBBL	Mint Sheet Binder - Blue	$9.95
MBGY	Mint Sheet Binder - Gray	$9.95
MBBK	Mint Sheet Binder - Black	$9.95
MS1	Mint Sheet Pages (25 per pack)	$5.95

Mint Sheet and Plate Block Storage

Item		Retail
191A000	Regular Plate Block File 24 pockets	$2.50
193A000	Mint Sheet File 24 pockets	$5.50

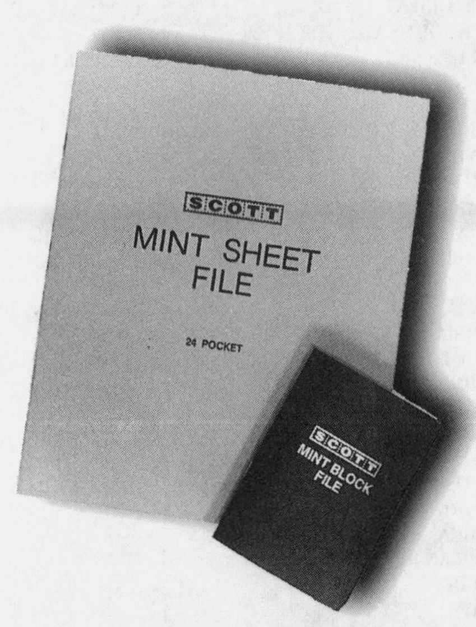

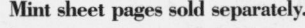

Available from your favorite stamp dealer direct from:

P.O. Box 828
Sidney OH 45365-0828
1-800-572-6885

Specialty Series

Scott produces album pages for more than 160 different countries. Scott Specialty pages are renowned for their quality and detail. There are spaces for every major variety of postage stamp within each country or specialty area. Each space is identified by Scott number and many of the spaces are illustrated. Pages are printed on one side only on chemically neutral paper that will not harm your stamps.

Below is complete list of the entire line of foriegn pages produced by Scott. Albums are updated annually. For page and price breakouts see your favorite dealer or call Scott Publishing Co. direct.

Scott Produces Album Pages for more than 160 countries.

ADEN
AFGHANISTAN
ALBANIA
ALGERIA
ANTIGUA
AUSTRALIA
AUSTRALIA DEPENDENCIES
AUSTRIA
BAHAMAS
BAHRAIN
BALTIC STATES
BANGLADESH
BARBADOS
BELGIUM
BELIZE
BERMUDA
BHUTAN
BOLIVIA
BOTSWANA
BRAZIL
BRITISH AFRICA
BRITISH ANTARCTIC TERRITORIES
BRITISH EUROPE
BRITISH HONDURAS
BRITISH ORIENT
BRITISH SOUTH ATLANTIC
BRUNEI
BULGARIA
BURKINA FASO
BURMA
BURUNDI
CANADA
CAYMAN ISLANDS
CENTRAL AFRICA
CHANNEL ISLANDS
CHILE
CHINA
COLOMBIA
COM. OF INDEPENDENT STATES
COMORO ISLANDS
CONGO
COSTA RICA
CROATIA
CZECHOSLOVAKIA
DENMARK
DOMINICA
DOMINICAN REPUBLIC
ECUADOR
EGYPT

EQUATORIAL GUINEA
ERITREA
ETHIOPIA
FALKLAND ISLANDS
FAROE ISLANDS
FIJI
FINLAND & ALAND ISLANDS
FRANCE
FRENCH OFFICES ABROAD
FRENCH POLYNESIA
FRENCH SOUTH. & ANTARCTIC TERRIT.
GABON
GAMBIA
GERMANY
EAST GERMANY
GHANA
GILBERT & ELLICE ISLANDS
GREAT BRITAIN
GREAT BRITAIN OFFICES ABROAD
GREECE
GREENLAND
GRENADA
GUATEMALA
GUINEA
GUINEA-BISSAU
HAITI
HONDURAS
HUNGARY
ICELAND
INDIA
INDONESIA
IRELAND
ISRAEL
ISRAEL TABS
ITALIAN COLONIES
ITALY
IVORY COAST
JAMAICA
JAPAN
JORDAN
KENYA
KIRIBATI
KOREA
KUWAIT
LAOS

LEBANON
LESOTHO
LIBERIA
LIECHTENSTEIN
LUXEMBOURG
MACEDONIA
MADAGASCAR
MALAWI
MALAYSIA
MALDIVE ISLANDS
MALI
MAURITIUS
MEXICO
MONACO & FRENCH ANDORRA
MONTSERRAT
MOROCCO
NAMIBIA
NAURU
NEPAL
NEW CALEDONIA
NEW HEBRIDES (BRITISH)
NEW HEBRIDES (FRENCH)
NEW ZEALAND
NEW ZEALAND DEPENDENCIES
NEVIS/ST KITTS
NICARAGUA
NIGER
NIGERIA
NORWAY
OMAN
PAKISTAN
PANAMA
PARAGUAY
PAKISTAN
PANAMA
PARAGUAY
PEOPLE'S REPUBLIC OF CHINA
PERU
PHILIPPINES
PITCAIRN ISLANDS
POLAND
PORTUGAL
PORTUGUESE COLONIES
QATAR
ROMANIA

RUSSIA
SALVADOR
SAMOA
SAN MARINO
SAUDI ARABIA
SENEGAL
SEYCHELLES
SIERRA LEONE
SLOVENIA
SOLOMON ISLANDS
SOUTH AFRICA
SPAIN & SPANISH ANDORRA
SRI LANKA
ST LUCIA
ST PIERRE & MIQUELON
ST THOMAS & PRINCE ISLANDS
ST VINCENT
SUDAN
SWAZILAND
SWEDEN
SWITZERLAND
SYRIA
TAIWAN
TANZANIA
THAILAND
TOGO
TONGA
TRINIDAD
TUNISIA
TURKEY
TURKS & CAICOS ISLANDS
TUVALU
UGANDA
UNITED ARAB EMIRATES
URUGUAY
VANUATU
VATICAN CITY
VENEZUELA
VIRGIN ISLANDS
WALLIS & FUTUNA
YEMEN
YUGOSLAVIA
ZAIRE
ZAMBIA
ZIMBABWE

SCOTT

1-800-572-6885

Specialty Binders & Accessories

NATIONAL AND SPECIALTY SERIES BINDERS

Binders are available for all pages in two sizes. They're covered with a tough green leatherette material that is washable and reinforced at stress points for long wear.

Large 3-Ring Binder

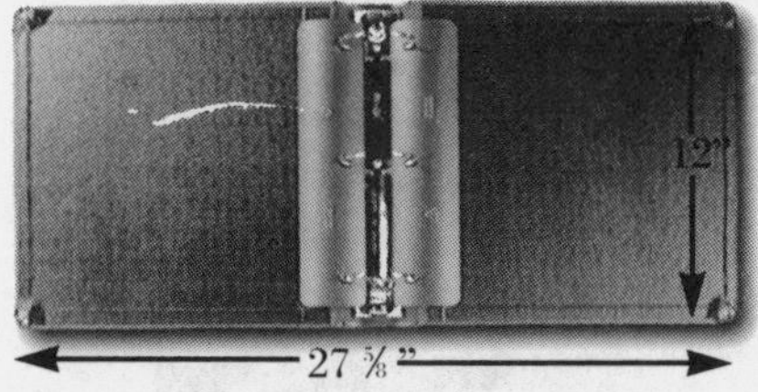

Item		Retail
ACBR01	Small 3-Ring Binder Holds up to 100 pages	**$25.00**
ACBR03	Large 3-Ring Binder Holds up to 250 pages	**$?5.00**

Large 2-Post Binder

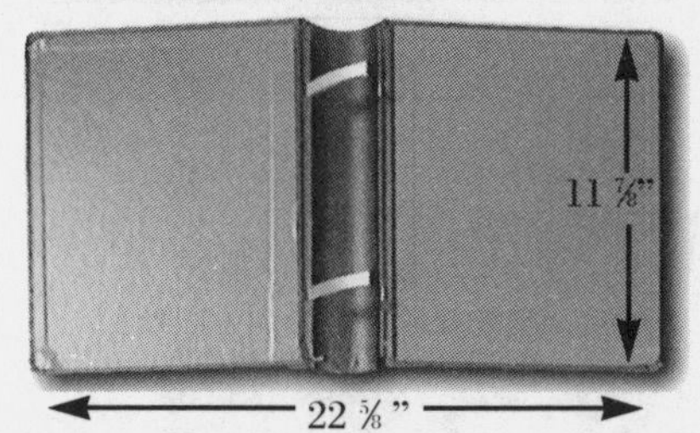

Item		Retail
ACBS0S	Small 2-Post Binder Holds up to 75 pages	**$45.00**
ACBS03	Large 2-Post Binder Holds up to 250 pages	**$45.00**

UNIVERSAL BINDER

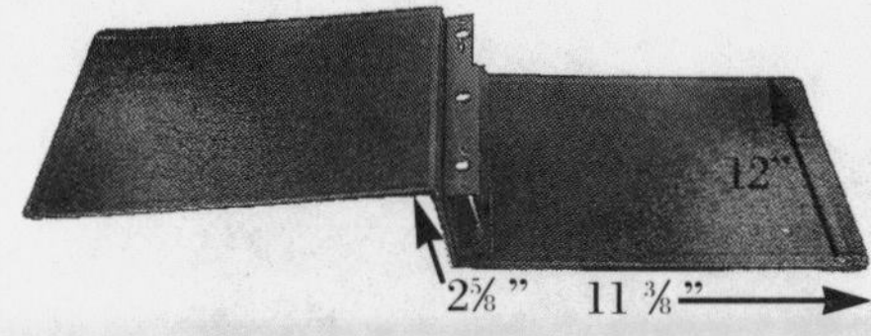

The binder features 3 adjustable screw posts to accomodate every album page sold by Scott, including the multi-ring Schaubek pages, and Platinum pages. Binder matches the traditional National/Specialty Series binder in every respect, including the handsome green leatherette covering. Use National and Specialty series labels to identify albums. Matching slipcase also available.

Item		Retail
ACBU	Universal Binder Holds up to 200 pages	**$25.00**
ACSU	Universal Slipcase	**$20.00**

SLIPCASES

Protect your binders and the album pages inside from the harmful effects of dust and dirt with slipcases. Cases available in two sizes.

Item		Retail
ACSR01	Small 3-Ring Slipcase	**$20.00**
ACSR03	Large 3-Ring Slipcase	**$20.00**
ACSS0S	Small 2-Post Slipcase	**$20.00**
ACSS03	Large 2-Post Slipcase	**$20.00**

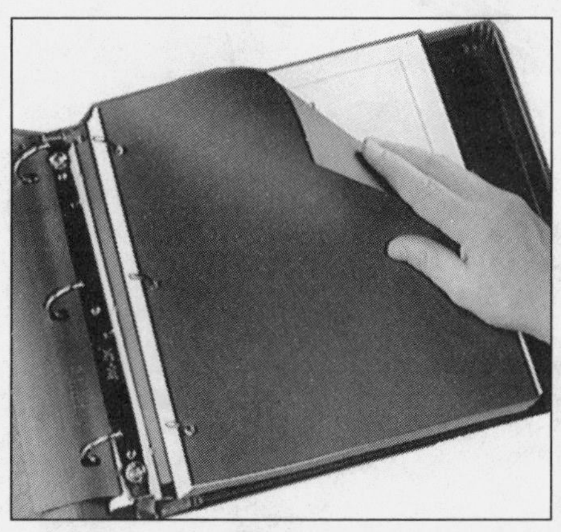

BINDER ACCESSORIES

Item		Retail
ACC101	Green Protector Fly Sheets For 2-post binders (2 per pack)	**$1.95**
ACC102	Black Protector Fly Sheets For 3-ring binders (2 per pack)	**$1.95**
ACC107	Glassine Interleaving (100 sheets per pack)	**$8.95**

SCOTT FILLER STRIPS

Use these strips every 15 to 20 pages in your 2 post albums to balance your overstuffed binders.

Item		Retail
ACC105	24 strips per package	**$3.95**

Specialty album accessories are available from your favorite dealer or direct from:
Scott Publishing Co.
P.O. Box 828
Sidney OH 45365-0828
1-800-572-6885

Pictured are the 3-ring slipcases.

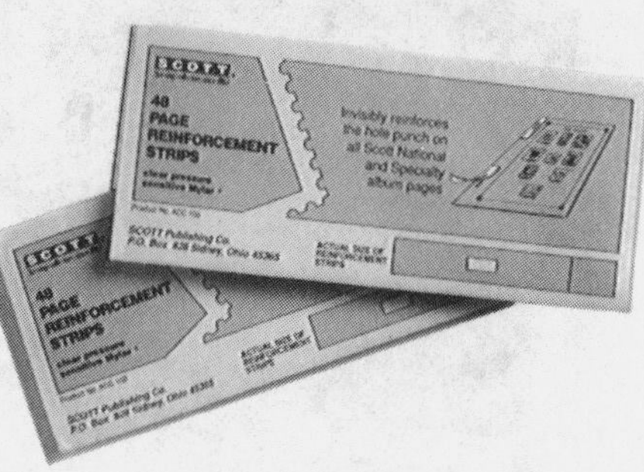

REINFORCEMENT STRIPS

Invisibly reinforce the 2-post or 3-ring holes on all album pages with clear pressure sensitive mylar.

Item		Retail
ACC100	48 Mylar strips For 2-post pages	**$3.95**
ACC103	200 Mylar rings For 3-ring pages	**$1.95**

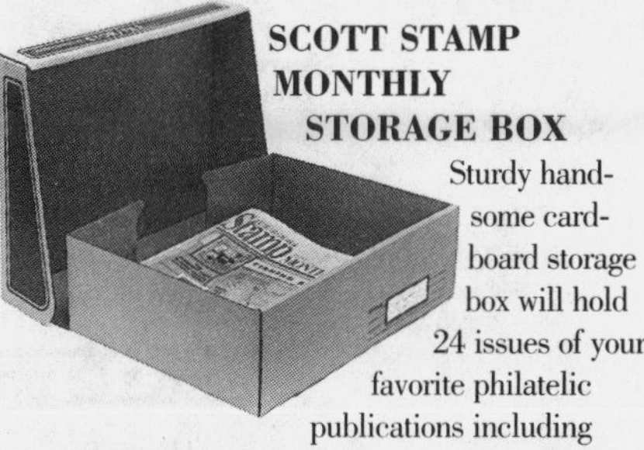

SCOTT STAMP MONTHLY STORAGE BOX

Sturdy handsome cardboard storage box will hold 24 issues of your favorite philatelic publications including Scott Stamp Monthly and Linn's. It's a great way to keep your information organized.

Item	Retail
SSMBOX	**$8.95**

Value Priced Stockbooks

Stockbooks are a classic and convenient storage alternative for many collectors. These German-made stockbooks feature heavyweight archival quality paper with 9 pockets on each page. The 8½" x 11⅝" pages are bound inside a handsome leatherette grain cover and include glassine interleaving between the pages for added protection. The Value Priced Stockbooks are available in two page styles, the white page stockbooks feature glassine pockets while the black page variety includes clear acetate pockets

BLACK PAGE STOCKBOOKS ACETATE POCKETS

Item	Color	Pages	Retail
ST16RD	Red	16 pages	$9.95
ST16GR	Green	16 pages	$9.95
ST16BL	Blue	16 pages	$9.95
ST16BK	Black	16 pages	$9.95
ST32RD	Red	32 pages	$14.95
ST32GR	Green	32 pages	$14.95
ST32BL	Blue	32 pages	$14.95
ST32BK	Black	32 pages	$14.95
ST64RD	Red	64 pages	$27.95
ST64GR	Green	64 pages	$27.95
ST64BL	Blue	64 pages	$27.95
ST64BK	Black	64 pages	$27.95

WHITE PAGE STOCKBOOKS GLASSINE POCKETS

Item	Description		Retail
SW16BL	Blue	16 pages	$5.95
SW16GR	Green	16 pages	$5.95
SW16RD	Red	16 pages	$5.95

The black page stockbook is available in three sizes:
16 pages
32 pages
64 pages.

Scott Value Priced Stockbooks are available from your favorite dealer or direct from:

SCOTT

P.O. Box 828
Sidney OH 45365-0828

1-800-572-6885

Scott Stamp Monthly

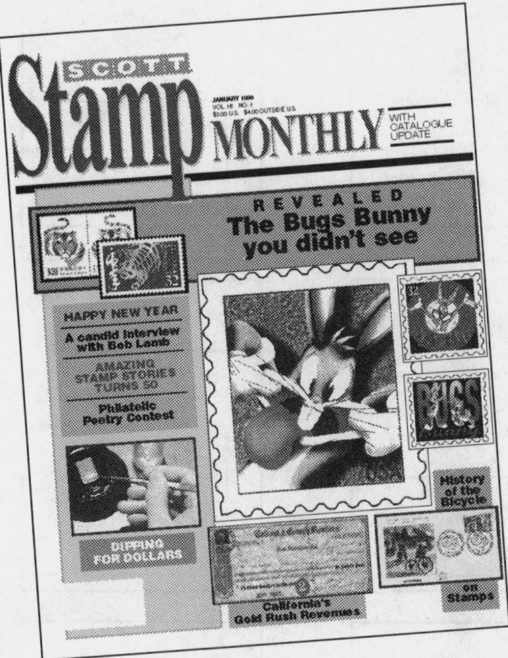

Stamp collecting's most entertaining read!

12 issues $17.95
24 issues $29.95

Every month you'll get an entertaining, informative look at the world of stamp collecting from some of the hobby's most talented writers. Enjoy a wide variety of articles and regular features on U.S., foreign stamps, covers and more. In-depth stories, time-saving hints, incredible stamp discoveries plus the very latest information on the new stamp issues from around the world, you'll find it all in Scott Stamp Monthly. As a subscriber not only do you save big on all the products offered by Scott, you also get what many people consider the most original and thought-provoking read in philately today.

You get all this and more every month!

Favorite Find - Stories about stamp discoveries in some of the mostunlikely places. Learn how you too can make finds.

Catalogue Update - The #1 source for new issue news. Each month you get Scott numbers and illustrations for hundreds of stamps. The By Topic column organizes stamps by subject matter.

Amazing Stamp Stories - A new stamp story every month done in the classic-illustrated style of *Ripley's Believe It Or Not*.

Hungry Mind - A just for fun trivia quiz that tests your stamp knowledge.

Spotlight - The column zeros-in and explores a different topic every month.

Free-For-All - It's your chance to get free stamps or related collectable simply by sending in stamped addressed envelope. It's fun, It's easy, but best of all it's FREE!

Stamp Traveler - Explore some of stampdom's most famous places and the chance stamp encounter that made the trip memorable.

Catalogue Column - A behind-the-scenes look at key Scott Catalogue editorial decisions.

To Err Is Divine - A lighthearted look at stamp designs goofs and gaffes.

Stars & Stripes and Judaica - are in-depth articles covering specific areas of interest in the stamp kingdom. Each columnis written by some of the hobby's best writers.

Tip Of The Hat - Tips and techniques for the busy collector.

For subscriptions in Canada, add $8 (U.S. funds) per year.

Outside the U.S. and Canada, add $23 (U.S. funds) per year for for foreign surface mail.

SCOTT

To subscribe call 1-800-572-6885

Advantage Stock Sheets

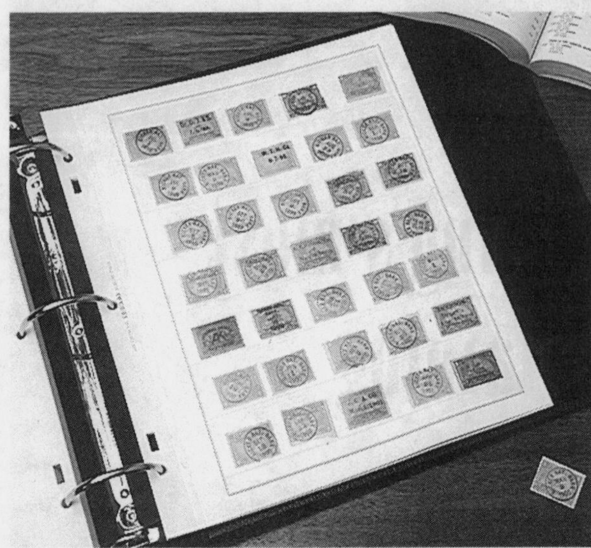

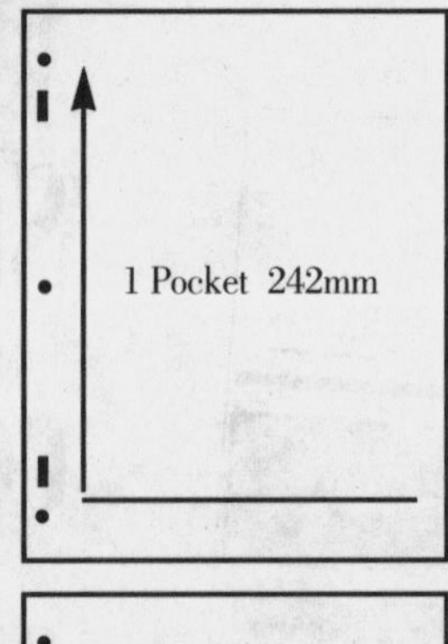

2 Pockets 119mm

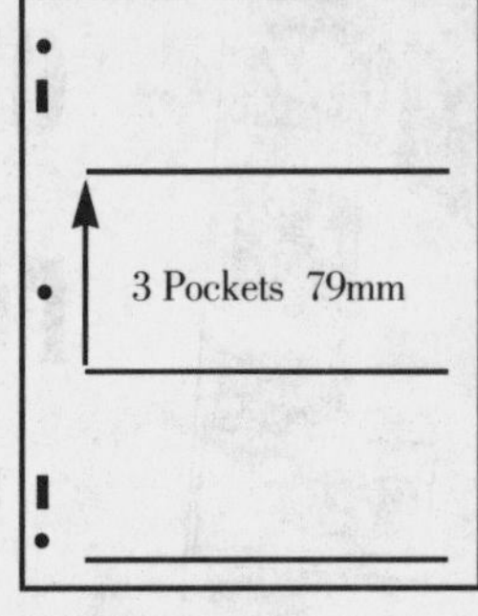

4 Pockets 58mm

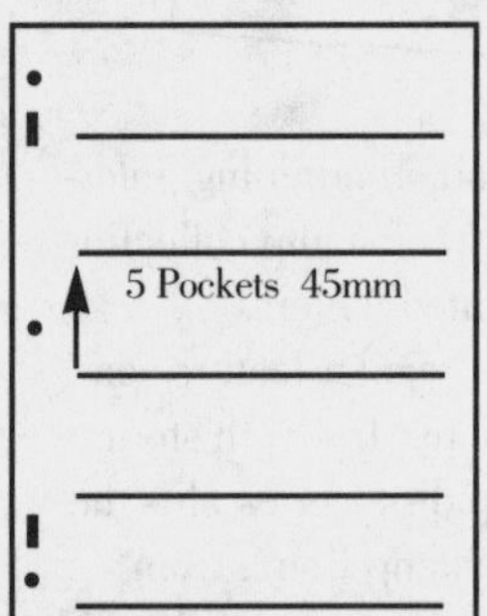

6 Pockets 45mm

7 Pockets 31mm

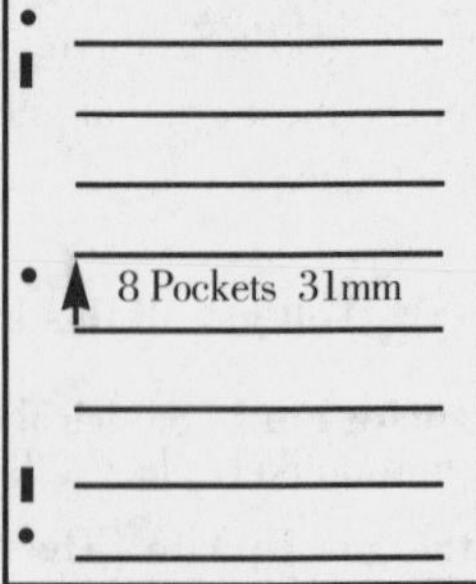

Designed with the collector in mind, Advantage stock sheets fit directly in your 2-post or 3-ring National or Specialty album. For unprecedented durability and flexibility choose Advantage Stocksheets. Choose from 1 to 8 pockets.

Sheets are sold in packages of 10

- Stock sheets match album pages in every respect, including border, size texture and color.
- Punched and drilled to fit perfectly in binder.
- Available with 1 to 8 pockets. Ideal for storing minor varieties and collateral material. A great place to keep new issues until the next supplement is available.
- Provides the protection and durability of crystal clear acetate pockets on heavyweight pages.

Item		Retail
AD111	1 Pocket National border	$12.95
AD112	2 Pockets National border	$12.95
AD113	3 Pockets National border	$12.95
AD114	4 Pockets National border	$12.95
AD115	5 Pockets National border	$12.95
AD116	6 Pockets National border	$12.95
AD117	7 Pockets National border	$12.95
AD118	8 Pockets National border	$12.95
AD121	1 Pocket Specialty border	$12.95
AD122	2 Pockets Specialty border	$12.95
AD123	3 Pockets Specialty border	$12.95
AD124	4 Pockets Specialty border	$12.95
AD125	5 Pockets Specialty border	$12.95
AD126	6 Pockets Specialty border	$12.95
AD127	7 Pockets Specialty border	$12.95
AD128	8 Pockets Specialty border	$12.95

Available from your favorite dealer or direct from
Scott Publishing Co. P.O. Box 828 Sidney OH 45365-0828
1-800-572-6885

SCOTT